IRONWEED

BROADCAST NEWS

DARK EYES

HOUSE OF GAMES

THE LAST EMPEROR

STREET SMART

HOPE AND GLORY

The Motion Picture Guide

★ ★ ★ ★ ★ ★ ★ ★ ★ ★ ★ ★ ★ ★

1988 Annual

THE MOTION PICTURE GUIDE

★ ★ ★ ★ ★ ★ ★ ★ ★ ★ ★ ★ ★ ★

1988 ANNUAL (THE FILMS OF 1987)

Jay Robert Nash
Stanley Ralph Ross

James J. Mulay
Daniel Curran
Jeffrey H. Wallenfeldt

CineBooks, Inc.
Evanston, Illinois, 1988

Publishers: Jay Robert Nash, Stanley Ralph Ross; **President:** Anita L. Werling; **Editorial Director:** William Leahy; **Senior Writers:** James J. Mulay, Daniel Curran; **Senior Editor:** Jeffrey H. Wallenfeldt; **Research Director:** William C. Clogston; **Production Assistant:** Jeannette Hori; **Associate Editor:** Michaela Tuohy; **Contributing Writers:** Michael Theobald, Arnie Bernstein, Chuck Krusling, Victoria Thor.

Business Manager: Jack Medor; **Assistant:** Bernie Gregoryk; **Advertising Manager:** Craig Carter.

ACKNOWLEDGEMENTS

The publishers which to thank the following individuals and organizations for their assistance in providing information on new releases in their countries: Czechoslovakia: Michael Malek (Ceskoslovensky Filmexport); Denmark: Helge Strunk (The Danish Film Institute); Finland: The Finnish Film Foundation; Greece: Greek Film Centre; Iceland: Anna Maria Hilmarsdottirl (The Icelandic Film Fund); Iran: Ali R. Shoja Noori (Farabi Cinema Foundation); Israel: Yoram Golan (Israel Film Centre); Japan: UniJapan Film; Kenya: L.D. Nguru (Kenya Film Corporation); Morocco: Abdallah Bayahia (Centre Cinematographique Maorcain); The Netherlands: Ministry of Welfare, Health and Cultural Affairs; New Zealand: Lindsay Shelton (New Zealand Film Commission); Norway: The Norwegian Film Institute; Poland: Film Polski; Portugal: The Portuguese Film Institute; Romania: Nicolae Cacovean (Centrala Romaniafilm); Spain: Ministerio de Cultura; Sweden: Bodil Ludvigsson (Svenska Filminstitutet); USSR: Sovexportfilm.

Editorial & Sales Offices
CINEBOOKS
990 Grove Street
Evanston, Illinois 60201

Library of Congress Catalog Number: 85-71145

ISBN: 0-933997-00-0 THE MOTION PICTURE GUIDE (10 Vols.)
ISBN: 0-933997-11-6 THE MOTION PICTURE GUIDE INDEX (2 Vols.)
ISBN: 0-933997-16-7 THE MOTION PICTURE GUIDE 1988 ANNUAL (THE FILMS OF 1987)

CINEBOOKS, INC. is a McPherson's Publishing Company

Printed in the United States
First Edition
1 2 3 4 5 6 7 8 9 10

Table of Contents

How to Use this Guide vii

1987 Film Reviews 1

People to Watch 343

Obituaries 353

Awards 391

Masterlist 401

Index 565

Films by Country 567

Name Index 574

Photo Credits 798

HOW TO USE THIS GUIDE

Titles

All entries are arranged alphabetically by title, with any articles (A, AN, THE) appearing after the main title.

Where necessary, alternate titles (AKA) and foreign titles are listed parenthetically after the color/black & white notation.

Foreign-language films reviewed in the country of origin before their US release often have English-language translations of their titles provided by distributors. Such translated titles are displayed parenthetically and designated as "Trans:".

Star Rating

Films which have been seen by our reviewers have been given star ratings from zero to five. The ratings indicate: *****—masterpiece; ****—excellent; ***—good; **—fair; *—poor; zero—without merit. Films not seen, and as a result not reviewed, by our staff, are indicated with a dagger (‡).

International Productions

When a film has been produced by a country other than the US, the country is noted within the parentheses containing the year of release. Countries are abbreviated as follows: Arg., Argentina; Aus., Australia; Aust., Austria; Bel., Belgium; Braz., Brazil; Brit., Great Britain; Can., Canada; Chi., China; Czech., Czechoslovakia; Den., Denmark; E. Ger., East Germany; Fin., Finland; Fr., France; Ger., Germany; Gr., Greece; Hung., Hungary; It., Italy; Jap., Japan; Mex., Mexico; Neth., Netherlands; Phil., Philippines; Pol., Poland; Rum., Rumania; Span., Spain; Swed., Sweden; Switz., Switzerland; Thai., Thailand; USSR, Union of Soviet Socialist Republics; Yugo., Yugoslavia. Where no country designation appears, the film is a US production.

Producing/Releasing Companies

The film's producing company or companies are listed first, with a slash (/) separating them from the releasing company or companies. The following abbreviations are used for major studios: BV—Buena Vista; COL—Columbia; DEG—DeLaurentiis Entertainment Group; EM—*Embassy Pictures; FOX—20th Century Fox; NW—New World; PAR—*Paramount; UA—United Artists; UNIV—Universal; WB—Warner Bros.

Production Credits

The credits for the creative and technical personnel of a film include: p (producer); d (director); w (screenwriter, followed by source); ph (cinematographer, followed by camera system and color process); m (composer of musical score); ed (film editor); md (music director); art d (art director); set d (set decoration); cos (costumes); spec eff (special effects); ch (choreography); m/l (music and lyrics); makeup; stunts, and other credits when merited. When the same person receives two or more credits in a single film the credits may be combined (p&d, Steven Spielberg) or the name repeated (p, Steven Spielberg, Kathleen Kennedy; d, Steven Spielberg).

GENRES/SUBJECT

Each film is categorized by up to three genres. The genres are: Action, Adventure, Animated, Biography, Children's, Comedy, Crime, Dance, Disaster, Docudrama, Drama, Fantasy, Historical, Horror, Martial Arts, Musical, Mystery, Prison, Religious, Romance, Science Fiction, Sports, Spy, Thriller, War, Western.

Parental Recommendations

The Parental Recommendation (PR) provides parents with an indication of the film's suitability for children. The PR ratings are as follow: AAA (must for children); AA (good for children); A (acceptable for children); C (cautionary, some objectionable scenes); O (objectionable for children).

FILM REVIEWS

A COR DO SEU DESTINO (SEE: COLOR OF DESTINY, 1987, Braz.)

A DANCA DOS BONECOS † (1987, Braz.) 90m Grupo Novo de Cinema e TV/Embrafilme c (Trans: Dance of the Dolls)

Wilson Grey *(Mr. Kapa)*, Kimura Schettino *(Geleia)*, Cinthia Vieira *(Ritinha)*), Ezequias Marques *(Jack Domina)*, Divana Brandao *(Iara)*, Rui Pollanah *(Destino)*, Claudia Gimenez *(Almerinda)*, Rogerio Fallabela *(Vitorino)*, Derly De'Cea *(Rua)*.

When they encounter a dollmaker whose business is failing, two traveling street performers attempt to swindle him by selling him what they purport to be "magic water." The liquid, however, proves to have magical power as it brings several of the dollmaker's creations to life. The transformations then lead to a flurry of criminal activity.

d, Helvecio Ratton; w, Helvecio Ratton, Tairone Feitosa, Angela Santoro; ph, Fernando Duarte (Eastmancolor); m, Nivaldo Ornelas; ed, Vera Freire; art d & cos, Paulo Henrique Pessoa, Juliana Junqueira, Anisio Medeiros.

Children's **(PR:NR MPAA:NR)**

A DOS AGUAS† (1987, Arg.) 74m Jorge Estrada Mora & Avica/Metropolis World Sales c (Trans: The Entire Life)

Miguel Angel Sola *(Rey)*, Barbara Mugica *(Isabel)*, Cipe Lincovsky *(Maria)*, Aldo Braga *(Patricio/Weintraub)*, Jorge Sassi *(Rey's Alter Ego)*, Osvaldo Tesser, Monica Lacoste, Mario Sanchez Rivera, Antonio Ugo.

A DOS AGUAS deals with characters returning to Argentina after leaving the country years before when it was under fascist control. Sola, who left Argentina to escape the rigid discipline of his father, has now returned for his father's funeral. Mugica fled the country following the disappearance of her lover, abandoning her husband and son. She has come back due to the illness of both. Sola and Mugica, who had been school friends, are reunited as Sola, who had wanted to be a filmmaker but became a lawyer to please his father, makes plans to shoot an autobiographical film

d, Carlos Olguin; w, Carlos Olguin, Martha Gavensky; ph, Rodolfo Denevi; m, Rodolfo Mederos; ed, Armando Blanco, Jorge Valencia; art d, Julio Lavallen.

Drama **(PR:NR MPAA:NR)**

A FIOR DI PELLE† (1987, It.) 85m Fiordifilm Milano c (Trans: Skin Deep)

Mariella Valentini, Claudio Bisio, John Murphy, Athina Cenci.

A man and woman try to help each other recover from failed love affairs.

d, Gianluca Fumagalli; w, Edoardo Erba, Roberto Traverso, Gianluca Fumagalli; ph, Fabio Cianchetti; m, Roberto Cacciapaglia; ed, Osvaldo Bargero.

Drama **(PR:NR MPAA:NR)**

A JAVOR† (1987, Hung.) 106m Hungarian Film Institute bw

Pal Javor, Iren Agay, Katalin Karady, Lili Murati, Klari Tolnay, Gyula Csortos, Gyula Kabos.

Using footage from 24 Hungarian features produced from 1933 to 1943, the filmmakers have created a movie which tells a story centering on Pal Javor, a Hungarian movie star of the 1930s. Over the course of the film, Javor falls in and out of love with a variety of women and succeeds and fails in business, all leading to a happy, song-filled conclusion.

[No credits available.]

Romance **(PR:NR MPAA:NR)**

A LOS CUATRO VIENTOS† (1987, Span.) Nueva Films c (Trans: To The Four Winds; AKA: LAUAXETA)

Xabier Elorriaga *(Maj. Esteban Urkiaga/"Lauaxeta")*, Anne Louise Lambert *(Georgina)*, Jean Claude Bouillaud *(Col. Baldie Monnier)*, Peter Leeper *(George Steer, London Times War Correspondent)*, Antonio Passy *(Guillaume)*, Ramon Barea *(Genaro)*, Ramon Aguirre *(President Jose Antonio Aguirre, Basque Province)*, Miguel Munarriz *(Beldarrain)*, Roberto Negro *(Hormaetxea)*, Rafael Enrique Uralde *(Patxi)*, Carlos Lucas *(Guinea Pig)*, Joan Llaneras *(Francoist Officer)*, Jose Manuel Gorospe *(Venancio)*, Jose Balbuena *(Tony)*, Sergio Sadaba *(Josu)*, Esther Velasco *(Martina)*, Peio Gutierrez *(Roadblock Militiaman)*, Roberto Larrion *(Navarran Requete)*, Eneko Olasagasti *(Basque Soldier)*, Alberto Martin Arinaga *(Pancracio)*, Lander Iglesias *(Manu)*, Patxo Telleria *(Manu's Companion)*, Begona Baena *(Dolores, Prostitute)*, Luis Angel Herran *(Militiaman at Granja Bar)*, Jose Luis Ramon *(Drunk)*, Aitor Mazo *(Fireman)*, Mentxu Blanco *(Mission Housekeeper)*, Antonio Ruperez *(Torrontegui Maitre d'Hotel)*, Agustin Arrazola *(Doctor)*, Conchita Leza *(Mother in Axpe Town Square)*, M. Carmen Pardo *(Woman in Axpe Town Square)*, Jose Ramon Zoroiz *(Sapper

Lieutenant)*, Josu Camara *(Sapper Captain)*, Felipe Loza *(Major of Musician Platoon)*, Luis Blazquez *(Anarchist)*, Javier Mezquiriz *(Sentry at Bon Martiartu Farm)*, Eloy Beato *(Cooper)*, Carlos Elejalde *(Guernica Soldier)*, Patxi Barco *(Cryptographer)*, Joseba Apaolaza, Luis Garcia *(Army Lieutenants)*, Juan Luis Mendiaraz *(Luis)*, Isidoro Fernandez *(Ander)*, Mikel Martinez *(Kepa)*, Ameli and his Orchestra *(Bar Orchestra)*.

Based on actual characters and incidents, A LOS CUATRO VIENTOS is set in 1937 during the Spanish Civil War. Elorriaga stars as a major in the civilian army, preparing to protect the village of Bilbao from an attack by Francoist troops. Over the course of the battle, the Francoists bomb the village of Guernica in an effort to break the spirit of the civilian army. It is history's first intentional and massive bombing of a civilian target, and though it horrifies the rest of the world, the Francoists are victorious and Elorriaga is captured and executed. The film is the second feature by Zorrilla, who won the New Directors Prize at the 1983 San Sebastian Film Festival for EL ARREGLO.

p, Angel Amigo; d, Jose A. Zorrilla; w, Jose A. Zorrilla, Arantxa Urretavizcaya, Xabier Elorriaga (based on an idea by Angel Amigo); ph, Jose Garcia Galisteo; m, Carmelo Bernaola; ed, Pablo Gonzalez Del Amo; prod d, Andres Santana; art d, Luis Valles; cos, Javier Artinano; spec eff, Isidro Ruano, Felix Cordon; makeup, Jose Quetglas.

Historical/War **(PR:NR MPAA:NR)**

A SANTA DERVIS† (1987, Hung.) 101m Mafilm-Tadjikfilm c

Gyula Benedek *(Armin Vambery)*, Ato Mukhamedjanov *(Mirzo)*, Sukhrat Irgachev *(Hamid)*, Abib Abdurazakov *(Caravanebachi)*.

A young academic becomes obsessed with the origins of the Magyars, the dominant people of Hungary. He spends the remainder of his life traveling through Europe and Asia in an effort to trace the ancestral roots of the people.

d, Jozsef Kis, Valeri Akhadov; w, Zsuzsa Szemes, Leonid Mahkamov (based on an idea by Szemes); ph, Laszlo Baranyai (Eastmancolor); m, Firus Bakhor.

Adventure **(PR:NR MPAA:NR)**

AAJ KA ROBIN HOOD† (1987, India) R.A. Jalan-Children's Film Society of India p, R.A. Jalan; d, Tapan Sinha.

Children's **(PR:NR MPAA:NR)**

ABBES† (1987, Morocco) 100m c

Malika El Oumari, Aziz Mouhoub, Salwa El Jouhari, Noureddine Bikr, Majda Badreddine, Ahmed El Basri.

ABBES is a social satire that explores some of the characters of the village of Sidi Khla. These include a teacher, a public letter-writer, a real estate agent, and a provincial deputy. Plots abound when the scion of landowners comes into the last remaining piece of property belonging to the family. This is complicated by the fact that his sister, a minor, is joint-inheritor.

p,d&w, Mohamed Tazi; ph, Ahmed Zanati; m, Mohamed Smires, Abdelouaheb Doukkali, Nass El Ghiwane, Rimsky-Korsakoff; ed, Lahcen El Khabbaz; set d, Mustapha Abou-Soufiane.

Drama **(PR:NR MPAA:NR)**

ACCROCHE-COEUR† (1987, Fr.) 90m Europimages/Extension c (Trans: Lovelock)

Patrick Bauchau *(Leo)*, Sandrine Dumas *(Sara)*, Laslo Szabo, Elisabeth Kaza.

After just going through a tough divorce, Bauchau decides to drive to the south of France for a holiday. The youthful Dumas has a crush on Bauchau and she persuades him to allow her to come along for the first part of the journey. The remainder of the film recounts how Bauchau, longing only for a little solitude, finds he is unable to get away from Dumas.

p, Lionel Bellina; d&w, Chantal Picault (based on *Les Platanes* by Monique Lange); ph, Gilberto Azevedo (Fujicolor); m, Luc Le Masne; ed, Frederic de Chateaubriant.

Comedy **(PR:NR MPAA:NR)**

ADELMO † (1987, It.) 103m Nuovo c

Rocco Mortelliti *(Adelmo)*, Francesca Topi *(Paola)*, Vincenzo De Angelis *(Mayor)*, Rina Franchetti *(Mother)*, Stefania Mortelliti, Giovanni Zaniboni, Marlo D'Orazio, Pietro Bontempo, Archimede Fala, Bernardo Zeppari.

Mortelliti wrote, directed and stars in this story of a young retarded man who lives in a village outside Rome with his mother, who is also retarded. The mayor of the town is cheating the mother out of government money to which she is entitled, and most of the townspeople treat Mortelliti with scorn. Topi, a doctor, arrives in town and takes an interest in Mortelliti, attention to which the unhappy man eagerly responds. Since Topi is quite a desirable woman, her relationship with Mortelliti arouses the jealousy of many and they escalate their cruel treatment of the man until he finally goes completely mad and begins assaulting anyone in sight. A mob gathers and begins chasing Mortelliti through the town. The film then cuts to a shot of the crew shooting the scene as Mortelliti the director rides off at the film's end.

d, Rocco Mortelliti; w, Rocco Mortelliti, Andreina Camilleri, Roberto Pagni; ph, Felice De Maria; ed, Marcello Malvestito.

Drama **(PR:NR MPAA:NR)**

ADULT EDUCATION (SEE: HIDING OUT, 1987)

ADVENTURE OF THE ACTION HUNTERS† (1987) 80m Bonner/Troma c

Ronald Hunter *(Walter)*, Sean Murphy *(Betty)*, Joseph Cimino *(1st Gangster)*, Art Donovan *(2nd Gangster)*, Steve Beauchamp *(Skipper)*, Peter Walker *(Oliver)*.

Filmed in 1982, this actioner found its way into a few theaters in 1987 through the efforts of exploitation experts Troma, Inc. Originally titled "Two For The Money," it stars Hunter and Murphy (who, according to the press release, are "the most exciting, adventurous couple . . . since Michael Douglas and Kathleen Turner in JEWEL OF THE NILE"), as a pair of adventurers who are attracted to each other and to the prospects of finding a $500,000 booty. When some gangsters accidentally blow-up a boat called the "Oliver Twist," they kill an old sailor who has the half-million dollar cache hidden away. Murphy and her boy friend hear his plea for help and try to find the missing money. The search leads them to Hunter's boat, tagged "Olive or Twist" as in "Would you like your martini with an . . . ?" Murphy and Hunter then get caught up in a succession of chases, explosions, shootouts and the like. All of this is set against a 1950s backdrop for some unknown reason. This shot-in-Baltimore production features former Baltimore Colts football player Art Donovan as a gangster.

p, Mary Holland; d, Lee Bonner; w, Lee Bonner, Leif Elsmo; ph, David Insley (Technicolor); m, John Pallumbo; ed, Lee Bonner; art d, Vincent Perranso.

Action/Comedy **(PR:NR MPAA:PG)**

ADVENTURES IN BABYSITTING½** (1987) 99m Hill-Obst-Touchstone-Silver Screen Partners III/BV c

Elisabeth Shue *(Chris Parker)*, Maia Brewton *(Sara Anderson)*, Keith Coogan *(Brad Anderson)*, Anthony Rapp *(Daryl Coopersmith)*, Calvin Levels *(Joe Gipp)*, Vincent Phillip D'Onofrio *(Dawson)*, Penelope Ann Miller *(Brenda)*, George Newburn *(Dan)*, John Ford Noonan *(John Pruitt)*, Bradley Whitford *(Mike Tedwell)*, John Chandler *(Gangster)*, Albert Collins *(Blues Club Performer)*.

ADVENTURES IN BABYSITTING could have been sub-titled "Every Parent's Nightmare." If local PTA members decide to view this feature, the present and future teenage baby-sitters of the world might have to seek new vocations. Even the most liberal parents will think twice about leaving their darlings in the care of an adolescent after seeing this. As the movie begins, Shue is preparing for a hot date, lip-syncing (a la Tom Cruise in RISKY BUSINESS) a tune, but her dreams of a good time are put on hold when the hunk of her fantasies calls and cancels. Left without a thing to do, Shue is coaxed by her parents to accept a baby-sitting job for the night. The intended family is wealthy and their young daughter, Maia Brewton, is a little brat who thinks comic book hero "Thor" is "just the neatest

guy" (she talks like that). Shue arrives at the large house and Brewton's brother, Coogan (grandson of Jackie Coogan and a very good actor), decides he wants to be sat as well. Coogan is a 15-year-old and someone that age hardly needs a sitter, but he is smitten with Shue (who does much better here than in her KARATE KID debut) so he plans to stay home that night and drool. Shue's kooky girl friend, Miller, tracks her down by phone. Miller was running away from her Chicago home and wicked stepmother, but when she arrived at the bus station, she became frightened at the flotsam and jetsam there and now wants Shue to rescue her. Shue packs up Brewton and Coogan, plus Coogan's best pal, Rapp, and they all get into the family station wagon for the trip downtown. A tire blows and Shue ruefully realizes she's left her purse at home and has no money to pay for repairs. Help comes in the person of a one-armed nut-case of a truck driver. He's been shadowing his wife, whom he suspects of infidelity. The next scene has them all getting into a car that is being hot-wired by professional auto thief Levels. This takes them to the national headquarters of a huge car-theft ring. The kids escape but not before wisecracker Rapp lifts a copy of *Playboy* in which vital information belonging to gangster Chandler is concealed. The reason Rapp has taken the magazine is that he thinks Shue looks like a prospective centerfold. A chase begins. Chandler is desperately trying to get his magazine back and the kids duck into a local blues club in a black neighborhood. Veteran bluesman Albert Collins is singing there and he won't allow them to leave until one of them shouts the blues. (This is an almost direct steal from Hitchcock's THE 39 STEPS when Robert Donat wanders onto a stage at a political rally while being chased by both police and villains.) Shue improvises a ditty that comes very close to being a racial slur. After she finishes the song, they all exit and try to make it to the train that will take them to their car. Urban transportation being what it can sometimes be, they meet up with a tough racially mixed gang, a fight ensues and Coogan has a stab wound in his foot, thereby forcing a trip to the local hospital. Once again, they encounter the jealous truck driver and he tells them how to get where they must go. On their way, the gangsters catch up with them and they find shelter at a fraternity party. Shue meets a handsome young man who offers to take her to her car and even takes up a collection so she can pay for the repairs. They arrive at the garage and the mechanic looks like "Thor" (D'Onofrio), which drives Brewton ga-ga. They are $5 short of payment for the car, but the handsome mechanic lets them have it anyhow. They still haven't picked up Miller at the bus station where she is being frightened by the various bag ladies and mendicants. Along the route, they drive past a chi-chi French restaurant where Shue spots the guy who stood her up earlier. Stopping for a moment to check out his story (he'd claimed his sister was ill), Shue discovers him nestling with another young woman. This initiates a minor fracas featuring flying food, pastry, and other assorted items before Shue and the others exit in a huff. As they depart the boite, the villains spot them and the chase commences once again. This time, it ends when they are cornered in the same high-rise North Shore building where Coogan's and Brewton's parents are attending a fancy party. Another ruckus begins and features a few hairy moments as Brewton hangs outside a window of the skyscraper. And while all of this is going on, the parents have no idea their children are in the vicinity, much less in all that trouble. The kids race back to the suburbs after nabbing Miller and arrive there with scant seconds to spare. As Shue is leaving the mansion, the preppy who helped her out at the frat beer bust arrives with an item Brewton had lost. With stars in her eyes, Shue leaves with her new love.

Twenty-eight-year-old director Columbus made his debut behind the camera with this film, after having written several successful movies including GREMLINS, THE GOONIES, and YOUNG SHERLOCK HOLMES. Not a bad start for one so young. The film is supposed to be taking place in Chicago, but was actually shot, for the most part, more than 430 miles northeast of The Windy City in Toronto. Producer Hill's career included all the HALLOWEEN films as well as CLUE, ESCAPE FROM NEW YORK, THE FOG, and some truly sleazy pictures like SATAN'S CHEERLEADERS and MAFIA ON THE BOUNTY. Co-producer Obst was a former executive at Casablanca Filmworks where she helped develop FLASHDANCE. ADVENTURES IN BABYSITTING did well enough at the box office but might have had even greater success with a different title. *(Profanity.)*

p, Debra Hill, Lynda Obst; d, Chris Columbus; w, David Simkins; ph, Ric Waite (DeLuxe Color); m, Michael Kamen; ed, Fredric Steinkamp, William Steinkamp; prod d, Todd Hallowell; art d, Gregory Keen; set d, Dan May.

Comedy **(PR:C MPAA:PG-13)**

AGENT TROUBLE† (1987, Fr.) 88m AFC-Koala-Canal Plus-FR3/Bac c

Catherine Deneuve *(Amanda Weber)*, Richard Bohringer *(Alex)*, Tom Novembre *(Victorien)*, Dominique Lavanant *(Karen)*, Pierre Arditi *(Stanislas)*, Sylvie Joly *(Edna)*, Kristin Scott Thomas *(Julie)*, Sophie Moyse *(Delphine)*, Herve Manson *(Tony)*, Helena Manson *(Museum Director)*, Jean-Pierre Mocky *(Government Man)*.

Bohringer is a hired killer on the trail of Deneuve. It seems that recently all the travelers on a tour bus were slain, including Deneuve's nephew, and she's out to find out why. Bohringer was in on the mass murder, and Deneuve learns he was working on orders from the government in an attempt to cover up a chemical waste accident.

p, Maurice Bernart; d&w, Jean-Pierre Mocky (based on *The Man who Liked Zoos* by Malcolm Bosse); ph, William Lubtchansky (Eastmancolor); m, Garbiel Yared; ed, Jean-Pierre Mocky.

Thriller **(PR:NR MPAA:NR)**

AKALLINEN MIES† (1987, Fin.) 116m M.Y. Kinosto/MTV c (Trans: The Farmer Has a Wife)

Martti Jarvinen, Elisabeth Haavisto, Kauko Helovirta, Raili Tiensuu, Esa Saario, Maija-Leena Soinee, Ahti Kuoppala, Kaija Sinisalo-Lahtinen, Ismo Kallio, Maija-Liisa Peuhu.

A sequel to Laine's AKATON MIES (1984), this film focuses on a family vacationing in the country during the summer.

d, Edvard Laine; w, Seppo Lappalainen; ph, Olavie Tuomi; m, Risto Hiltunen; ed, Eva Jaakontalo.

Comedy **(PR:NR MPAA:NR)**

AKTSIA† (1987, USSR) 91m Mosfilm/Sovexportfilm c (Trans: Action)

Boris Galkin, Georgy Yumatov, Oleg Strizhenov, Yekaterina Vasilyeva, Alexander Novikov, Artyom Kaminsky.

Soviet saboteurs deliver a crushing blow to the German war effort during WW II.

d, Vladimir Shamshurin; w, Anatoly Stepanov; ph, Alexei Naidenov; m, Viktor Babushkin; art d, Yevgeny Serganov.

War **(PR:NR MPAA:NR)**

A LA ITKE IINES† (1987, Fin.) 92m Osuuskunta RT-Media/Ryhmateatteri c (Trans: Gone with the Mind)

Eija Vilpas, Sari Mallinen, Kari Vaananen, Pirkka-Pekka Petelius, Vesa Vierikko, Pertti Sveholm, Sanna Fransman, Kari Heiskanen, Timo Torikka, Matti Laustela, Vesa-Matti Loiri.

Set in Helsinki, this comedy focuses on a variety of urban types, including a group of young people who have made their home on the roof of a building. Director Kuusi worked from his own story, but allowed his actors to improvise most of their dialog.

d&w, Janne Kuusi; ph, Tahvo Hirvonen; m, Kim Kuusi; ed, Anne Lakanen; set d, Pertti Hilkamo.

Comedy **(PR:NR MPAA:NR)**

ALADDIN zero (1987, It.) 97m Compania Generale R.T./Cannon c (SUPERFANTAGENIO)

Bud Spencer *(Genie)*, Luca Venantini *(Al Haddin)*, Janet Agren *(Mrs. Haddin)*, Fred Buck *(Sgt. O'Connor)*, Tony Adams *(Monty Siracusa)*, Carlo Carbucci *(Red)*, Cristiano Ciancio *(Harry)*, Giancarlo Bastianoni *(Randy)*, Sergio Smacchi *(Mark)*, Riccardo Rainieri *(Larry)*, Umberto Raho, Julian Voloshin, Daimy Spencer.

An idiotic Italian-produced kiddie film shot in Miami about a boy, Venantini, who works in a junk store. One day he is polishing an old oil lamp when Spencer appears, telling Venantini he is a genie who can grant any wish. Venantini wishes for: a Rolls-Royce that can fly over traffic jams; to be the victor in a waterski tournament; to be a basketball star; and to have a girl friend. The genie grants all the wishes, leading to rather predictable consequences. The police try to figure out where the Rolls-Royce came from, the CIA thinks Russian spies must be involved, and the local mob chief, for whom Venantini's mother works, thinks Spencer must be some kind of cop. The bad guys are defeated and Spencer asks that the boy dump the lamp into the deepest part of the ocean, but instead he makes one more wish and the end finds Venantini, his mother, and his grandfather the owners of a swank nightclub where Spencer plays the piano behind a row of showgirls. It's unlikely kids will be able to tolerate this tedious, blatantly manipulative film. Spencer is best known for his appearances in the TRINITY films of 20 years ago, and he is the best thing here, but that's not enough to recommend it. *(Comic violence.)*

p, Ugo Tucci; d, Bruno Corbucci; w, Mario Amendola, Marcello Fondato, Bruno Corbucci; ph, Silvano Ippoliti (Telecolor); m, Fabio Frizzi; ed, Daniele Alabiso; cos, Mario Russo.

Children's **Cas.** **(PR:A MPAA:PG)**

ALAPAAP† (1987, Phil.) 79m Roadshow c (Trans: Clouds)

[No cast or credits available.]

A film writer reads a newspaper account of the murder of a young woman and persuades two friends to accompany him to the village where the crime took place in order to learn more about it. The spirit of the dead girl arises and begins taking revenge on her killers and anyone else in the vicinity.

Horror **(PR:NR MPAA:NR)**

ALBURES MEXICANOS† (1987, Mex.) 90m Filmadora Dal/Peliculas Mexicanas (Trans: Mexican Double-Entendres) c

Alfonso Zayas *(Chief Jr.)*, Carmen Salinas *(Susana)*, Grace Renate *(Rita)*, Sergio Ramos *(Ruperto Colorado)*.

The title is a Mexican idiom which refers to a popular word-play game which is filled with sexual puns and innuendo. The story concerns a traveling carnival which illegally settles on Zayas' land. The film then cuts back and forth between the efforts to evict the carnival and the carnival members performing their acts.

p, David Agrasanchez; d, Alfredo B. Crevenna; ph, Antonio de Anda; m, Pedro Placenicia; ed, Jorge Rivera.

Comedy **(PR:NR MPAA:NR)**

ALIEN PREDATOR* (1987) 90m Continental/Trans World c (AKA: THE FALLING)

Dennis Christopher *(Damon)*, Martin Hewitt *(Michael)*, Lynn-Holly Johnson *(Samantha)*, Luis Prendes *(Prof. Tracer)*, J.O. Bosso *(Capt. Wells)*, Yousaf Bokhari *(Mr. Bodi)*, Yolanda Palomo *(Mrs. Bodi)*, Christina Augustin *(Baby Bodi)*, Christina San Juan *(Waitress)*, Pablo Garcia *(Man in Store)*, Carlos Ramirez *(Gas Station Attendant)*.

Filmed in Spain in 1984 and then put on the shelf when its distributor, Film Ventures International, folded, ALIEN PREDATOR was finally given a limited release in 1987 by video-firm-turned-theatrical-distributor TWE. As anyone could have predicted, this is one film that should have stayed on the shelf. Poorly scripted, directed, and acted, ALIEN PREDATOR is a tedious excuse for a science fiction film that even the most undiscriminating fans of the genre will find pointless. The film begins in 1979 when a chunk of Skylab lands in Spain. Five years later three obnoxious American youths, Christopher, Hewitt, and Johnson, are on holiday touring Spain in a huge recreational vehicle with dune-buggy in tow. They wander into a small village where, unknown to them, an alien microbe that had attached itself to the Skylab debris has spread among the residents and driven them mad. Meanwhile, a NASA scientist (Prendes) arrives at the space administration's secret station, which runs five floors beneath an old Spanish castle. There he meets Capt. Bosso, the only surviving member of a NASA team which was wiped out by the mutating microbes. Bosso shows Prendes the mutated corpse of one of his men, and while Prendes examines the body, contaminated blood splashes Bosso, infecting him. Prendes plans to make a serum using Bosso's contaminated blood, but Bosso panics and shoots himself instead of letting the microbe destroy him. Eventually Prendes enlists the aid of the young American tourists and makes himself the guinea pig. By this time the entire town has gone mad and blocked all the exits. Knowing he cannot let the microbe spread any further, Prendes orders an American napalm strike on the town. Just before the F-14s zoom overhead, Prendes inoculates the youths. Unfortunately, he is too late to cure himself and he runs off to his doom before becoming completely possessed by the aliens. The three Americans crash the flaming barriers and escape the town just as the napalm is dropped. At an outlying gas station however, a fully evolved alien monster bursts from the chest of the attendant and tries to climb up the windshield of the RV. Christopher simply turns on the windshield wipers and knocks the creature to the ground. He then squashes it beneath the tires of the huge RV. As the relieved Hewitt and Johnson celebrate in the back, Christopher's nose begins to bleed—a sure sign that he is infected.

The concept is a rip-off of ALIEN, the title is an amalgamation of the aforementioned film and Arnold Schwarzenegger's then yet-to-be released PREDA-

TOR, and the whole film comes disturbingly close to being a distasteful mockery of the disease AIDS (people catching the microbe by simply being splashed with contaminated blood). There is so little creative inspiration here that writer-director Sarafian pads the story with several lengthy and unexciting car chases. Most of the film is nothing but talk, punctuated by an occasional bloody special effects scene. Christopher (remember when he used to be a promising young actor after BREAKING AWAY?), Hewitt, and Johnson are simply awful, with much of the blame going to Sarafian's incredibly lame dialog. Prendes fares no better and the serious scientific mumbo-jumbo he is supposed to be obsessed with is simply laughable. Perhaps most disappointing is that when the alien is finally revealed after more than an hour, it is nothing more than a small spindly puppet covered with red slime that is dispatched in less than a minute. While the premise may be silly and the acting lousy, low-budget science fiction can be of some interest if it contains some unique thrills. Unfortunately, ALIEN PREDATOR violates this essential rule. *(Violence, gore effects, profanity.)*

p, Deran Sarafian, Carlos Aured, Michael Sourapas; d&w, Deran Sarafian (based on the screenplay "Massacre At R.V. Park" by Noah Blogh); ph, Tote Trenas; m, Chase/Rucker Productions; ed, Dennis Hill, Peter Teschner; art d, Gomer Andres; spec eff, John Balandin, James Cummins, Bill Sturgeon, Margaret Bessara, Mark Shoftrom; cos, Flavia Lovatelli.

Science Fiction Cas. (PR:O MPAA:R)

ALLAN QUATERMAIN AND THE LOST CITY OF GOLD* (1987) 99m Golan-Globus/Cannon c

Richard Chamberlain *(Allan Quatermain)*, Sharon Stone *(Jesse Huston)*, James Earl Jones *(Umslopogaas)*, Henry Silva *(Agon)*, Robert Donner *(Swarma)*, Doghmi Larbi *(Nasta)*, Aileen Marson *(Queen Nyleptha)*, Cassandra Peterson *(Sorais)*, Martin Rabbett *(Robeson Quatermain)*, Rory Kilalea *(Dumont)*, Alex Heyns *(Dutchman)*, Themsi Times *(Nurse)*, Philip Boucher *(Bartender)*, Stuart Goakes *(Trader)*, Fidelis Cheza *(Eshowe Warrior Chief)*, Nic Lesley *(Toothless Arab)*, George Chiota *(George)*.

Even if you loved the 1985 remake of KING SOLOMON'S MINES, you're not likely to enjoy this lame adventure tale which again pairs Chamberlain and Stone and employs a Zimbabwe backdrop. This time Chamberlain and Stone postpone their trip back to the United States and their marital vows in order to venture through the jungles in search of Chamberlain's brother, Rabbett, and the fabled Lost City of Gold. Accompanying them is Jones, a quiet and intimidating warrior who sports a gigantic battle axe; Donner, a bumbling, cowardly Hindu swami; and a few native bearers. Along the way they journey to the center of the Earth where they barely escape death, fend off a bloodthirsty tribe of warriors and barely escape death, and are attacked by slimy, vicious earthworms, barely escaping death. The only ones who don't escape death are the dispensable natives. About halfway through the film Chamberlain and his gang arrive at the lost city, which bears more than a passing resemblance to the white-walled Shangri-La of LOST HORIZON. Here he finds his brother living amongst an interracial tribe of people ruled by the evil Silva, a grumpy looking leader who wears a fright wig. At his side is his queen, Marson, and her nasty sister, Peterson (of television's "Elvira" fame). The only time Silva enjoys himself is when he is dipping natives in a pit of molten gold, producing gilded statues. Together Chamberlain and Jones banish Silva, promising the city's inhabitants the days of sacrifices are over. A lengthy battle ensues in which Silva tries to recapture his kingdom. Just when things start to look grim, Chamberlain opens a reservoir of molten gold which pours over the attackers, killing them and leaving their gilded carcasses behind. Everyone's happy and safe, while Chamberlain and Stone prepare to return to America and finally get married.

Shot at the same time as KING SOLOMON'S MINES (1985), this entry sat on Cannon's shelves for some time before Golan and Globus decided to release it. A heavy publicity campaign accompanied the film, but it still laid an egg at the box office. Chamberlain, more of a draw for a television mini-series than for a film, couldn't attract viewers to the theater, nor could the forgettable Stone. Cannon should have taken heed when KING SOLOMON'S MINES failed at the box office. The film is filled with fourth-rate RAIDERS OF THE LOST ARK rip-offs, which are supposed to be coupled with a sense of humor. Nothing is funny though. Director Nelson's direction is inept, the pacing is pathetic, the script is brainless, and Chamberlain and Stone don't have one iota of rapport. Even worse, the special effects are laughable, the matte work obvious, and the various reptiles and critters clearly fake. The costumes are so bad that one character wears a head dress decorated with a pair of antlers that are obviously made of rubber. Every time he moves they flop around uncontrollably, an (unintentionally comic) effect akin to the bumblebee antennas in the long-running "Saturday Night Live" skit. To top it all off, the film is decidedly racist. With the exception of Jones, every black in the film is treated without the least bit of respect. No one even speaks to the bearers and they are subsequently left to die while Chamberlain and Stone are saved countless times. The African extras stand around with wobbly knees and frightened looks, waiting to be killed off for sport. A meager effort on all fronts, this one won't even interest fans of old time serials. A night is better spent with RAIDERS or INDIANA JONES or ROMANCING THE STONE or even the worst entries in the TARZAN series. *(Comic violence, gore effects.)*

p, Menahem Golan, Yoram Globus; d, Gary Nelson, Newt Arnold; w, Gene Quintano, Lee Reynolds (based on the novel *Allan Quatermain* by H. Rider Haggard); ph, Alex Phillips, Frederick Elmes (J-D-C Widescreen, Rank Color); m, Michael Linn, Jerry Goldsmith; ed, Alain Jakubowicz, Gary Griffen, Dan Loewenthal; prod d, Trevor Williams, Leslie Dilley; set d, Patrick Willis, Portia Iversen; cos, Marianne Fassler; spec eff, Eric Allard, Colin Arthur; stunts, Solly Marx, Don Pike.

Adventure Cas. (PR:A-C MPAA:PG)

ALLARI KRISHNAYA† (1987, India)

Balakrishna, Banupriya.

p, S. Bhaskar, Ch. Satyanarayana; d, Nandamuri Ramesh.

(PR:NR MPAA:NR)

ALLNIGHTER, THE zero (1987) 108m UNIV c

Susanna Hoffs *(Molly)*, Dedee Pfeiffer *(Val)*, Joan Cusack *(Gina)*, John Terlesky *(C.J.)*, James Anthony Shanta *(Killer)*, Michael Ontkean *(Mickey Leroi)*, Pam Grier *(Sgt. MacLeish)*, Phil Brock *(Brad)*, Meshach Taylor *(Philip, House Detective)*, Will Seltzer *(Ted, House Detective)*, Denise Dummont *(Julie)*, Mary Petrie *(Anna)*, Kelly Lynn Pushkin *(Nancy)*, Todd Field *(Bellhop)*, Bradford Bancroft *(Joe, Bartender)*, Danyi Deats *(Junkie)*, Sarah Elgart *(Jail Attendant)*, Gordon Roos *(Arrest Cop)*, Josh Richman *(Raymond)*, Molly Cleator *(Rose)*, Robert Goldman *(Chad)*, Max Perlich *(Benny)*, Walter Brachlemanns M.D. *(President Edmunds)*, Ruth Zaharian *(Brunette in Bikini)*, Christine Lane *(Blonde in Bikini)*, Debi Lester *(Killer's Date)*, Steve Ferguson *(Piano Player)*, Reese Patterson, Davey Miller, Richard Vanderwyth *(Surfers)*, Larry Chapman, Michael Gurley, Louis Gutierrez, David Salimas *("Louis & Clark" Band)*.

At the ostensible climax of THE ALLNIGHTER, valedictorian Susanna Hoffs, the lead singer of The Bangles (in her movie debut), delivers a speech to the graduating class of a Southern California college. She informs them that " . . . experience is really your best teacher." Indeed, experience teaches us that most youth pictures are incredibly mindless exercises that revel in exploiting the nubile bodies of young women whilst portraying them and their male counterparts as total morons. What such experience has not yet prepared us for is that a girl's *own mother* would exploit her child's popularity in order to helm a rancid low-budget feature such as this. Part of the appeal of THE ALLNIGHTER is the viewer's curiosity as to just what sort of humiliation a mother might put her daughter through for the sake of her "art." However, the film is surprisingly chaste, tame, and subsequently downright boring. Set on the eve of a college graduation, the movie revolves around three roommates—Hoffs, Pfeiffer (sister of Michelle), and Cusack (sister of John)—who share a hip beach house. Pfeiffer, the blonde goddess of the trio, is engaged to a boorish yuppie type (Brock), Cusack is a slightly whacked-out video artist who is never without her camera, and Hoffs is the brains of the group. Next door live two cretinous surfers, Terlesky and Shanta, who refer to each other as "dude" and speak in a continual flow of pseudo-Spanish: "Let's fiesta, dude," or "Whoa . . . dude . . . cervezas!" or "Uno momento, dude." Terlesky, the less deficient of the pair, plans to go to law school and has the hots for Hoffs. Hoffs likes the guy, but thinks he is kind of shallow and wants to have a real romance before graduating. Just before the big graduation beach-bash (called the fiesta, naturally) she meets fading rock idol Ontkean, who has stopped by her house because he used to live there. They share a dance, and in an attempt to be friendly, he invites her to his hotel room. After watching her classmates pass out from drinking too many cervezas and margaritas, Hoffs dolls herself up (but first dances around in her underwear to Aretha Franklin's version of "Respect") and goes to the hotel. Unfortunately, Ontkean is expecting a romantic visit from a former flame (Hoffs' guidance counselor). He hides Hoffs on the terrace and forgets about her. Hoffs phones her roommates and begs them to come and rescue her, but at the hotel Pfieffer and Cusack get mixed up with some prostitutes and are arrested. Hoffs escapes, wakes Terlesky from his coma, and they go to the police station at dawn to bail out their friends. Of course, Pfieffer's fiance sees her leaving the police station and after a short argument she breaks the engagement. The trio goes home to put on their caps and gowns, but Hoffs has yet to have her big romance and she just stares drearily at the ocean. Finally she decides she might as well get it on with her surfer. Moments before graduation she has a meaningful coupling with the lunkhead and then dashes off to give her big speech.

Although there is nothing particularly offensive about THE ALLNIGHTER (little profanity, no drugs, no nudity—in fact, Hoffs is swaddled in a sheet during her big love scene), the film is so incredibly stupid as to warrant nothing but disdain. Tamar Simon Hoffs, who coproduced and cowrote the interesting STONY ISLAND (1978), is a terrible director who has absolutely no feel for such fundamentals as characterization, comedic timing, pacing, narrative structure, or composition. The humor here is so ill-conceived, narrow, and scattershot that the film plays like daily rushes from a home movie. Indeed, this is one of those films made by rich Californians for rich Californians and bears no resemblance to life east of Los Angeles. As for Susanna Hoffs, she displays a screen presence not unlike that in her rock videos: lots of coy glances from side to side and a pout. Not that the script gives her anything more challenging to do, but even what may be nominally considered a showcase scene fails miserably because of the elder Hoffs' wretched direction. Both Susanna's dance with Ontkean and her little striptease are shot from security-camera angles that make it appear as if her mother was embarrassed to get too close (mom's unease is matched by her daughter's, for Susanna looks extremely self-conscious and uncomfortable during both scenes). The love scene is all disembodied arms, legs, hands, and backs with a studied avoidance of any facial close-ups (presumably so Susanna does not have to feign ecstasy). The rest of the cast suffers as well. Pfeiffer's role is inane, Ontkean looks uncomfortable, Shanta watched Sean Penn in FAST TIMES AT RIDGEMONT HIGH too often, Terlesky should be on the cover of *GQ*, and the still-gorgeous Grier is totally wasted as a cop. Only Cusack manages to bring some life to her part via some spontaneous goofiness. THE ALLNIGHTER was justifiably savaged by critics and evaporated at the box office. Luckily, Susanna has another, much more successful, career to fall back on, but the elder Hoffs should definitely stick to home video.

Songs include: "In the Darkness" (Billy Steinberg, Tom Kelly, performed by Boomerang), "Dangerous" (Jeff Stephens, performed by Exploding White Mice; Ronnie Spector), "Take the Reins" (B.A. Robertson, Mike Rutherford, Chris Weil, performed by Mike and the Mechanics), "Boo Hoo" (Charles Bernstein, performed by Angie Jaree), "Love is You" (Robert Heckler, performed by Redd Kross), "Who's Gonna Dance with Me" (Sheila Burns, Ron Riddle, performed by The Burns Sisters), "No TV, No Phone" (Tommy Price, Kasim Sulton, performed by Price Sulton), "Shangri-La" (Charles Berstein, performed by Peter Hex), "Salsa Verde," "Take A Mile," "This Could Be a Slow Song" (Louis Gutierrez, M. Clark Gurley, performed by Louis and Clark), "Respect" (Otis Redding, performed by Aretha Franklin), "Piano Lounge Music" (Steve Ferguson), "The Girl in the Sweater" (The Hard Ons), "True Love" (Charles Bernstein, performed by Linda Harmon), "The Future's So Bright I Gotta Wear Shades" (Pat McDonald, performed by Timbuck 3), "All in My Mind" (Daniel Ash, Love and Rockets, performed by Love and Rockets), "I've Been the One" (Lowell George, performed by The Golden Palaminos), "Never Thought" (Dan Hill). *(Sexual situations, profanity.)*

p, Tamar Simon Hoffs, Nancy Israel; d&w, Tamar Simon Hoffs; ph, Joseph Urbanczyk (CFI Color); m, Charles Bernstein; ed, Dan M. Rich; prod d, Cynthia Sowder; set d, Debra Combs; cos, Isis Mussenden; m/l, Billy Steinberg, Tom Kelly, Jeff Stephens, B.A. Robertson, Mike Rutherford, Chris Neil, Charles Bernstein, Robert Heckler, Sheila Burns, Ron Riddle, Tommy Price, Kasim Sulton, Louis Gutierrez, M. Clark Gurley, Otis Redding, Steve Ferguson, The Hard Ons, Pat McDonald, Daniel Ash, Love and Rockets, Lowell George, Dan Hill; stunts, Christopher Doyle.

Comedy **Cas.** **(PR:C-O MPAA:PG-13)**

ALPINE FIRE† (1987, Switz.) 117m Bernard Lang/Vestron c

Thomas Nock *(The Boy)*, Johanna Lier *(Belli, His Sister)*, Dorothea Moritz *(The Mother)*, Rolf Illig *(The Father)*, Tilli Breidenbach *(The Grandmother)*, Joerg Odermatt *(The Grandfather)*.

Set high in the Swiss Alps, this 1985 first feature from documentarian Murer is part ethnographic study of the mountain people known as the "Irascibles" and part surreal family drama. The story centers on Nock, a mute teenage boy, simply called "Boy" whose sexual awakening wreaks havoc on his family. His parents, Illig and Moritz, have lived an isolated life on an ancient family farm and show no signs of letting their children leave for a more modern life in the city. Their daughter, a nubile young woman played by Lier, wants desperately to attend a city school, but she is forced to remain on the farm and educate her brother. Bursting with the sexual energy of puberty, Nock distances himself from his family and, after an explosive argument with his father, retreats to a secluded mountain hideout. Brother-sister incest, patricide, and the grieving death of the mother follow, leaving the siblings to carry on by themselves. The winner of the 1985 Locarno Film Festival and a Bronze Hugo winner at the 1985 Chicago Film Festival, ALPINE FIRE was released in New York and L.A. in 1987.

p, Bernard Lang; d&w, Fredi M. Murer (based on his novel); ph, Pio Corradi; m, Mario Beretta; ed, Helena Gerber; set d, Bernhard Sauter.

Drama **(PR:NR MPAA:R)**

ALS IN EEN ROES† (1987, Neth.) 85m Altamira Films c (Trans: Intoxicated)

Herbert Flack, Liz Snoyink, Thom Hoffman, Devika Strooker, Ellen Vogel.

During rehearsal for a play, a director and his lover, who has the lead in the play, engage in a disruptive battle of wills.

p, Lea Wongsoredjo, Ruud den Drijver; d&w, Pim de la Parra; ph, Frans Bromet; m, Lodewijk de Boer, Adriaan van Noord, Jose Le; ed, Sharon Brown; art d, Rebecca Geskus, Liesje Smolders.

Drama **(PR:NR MPAA:NR)**

ALSHAZHIA† (1987, Libya) 100m General Cinema Organization bw (Trans: Shrapnel)

Ali Aliresi, Altaher Alquabaili, Kariman Gabr.

This film is set in a section of the desert which is still filled with lethal mines planted during WW II. A nomad, whose wife has been killed in a mine explosion, encounters a criminal on the run from the law. The criminal steals the nomad's camel, but the two develop a close relationship as the nomad leads the way through the mine-infested desert.

d, Mohamed Ali Alfarjani; w, Mohamed Ali Alfarjani, Abdul Salam Almadani.

Drama **(PR:NR MPAA:NR)**

AL-TAUQ WAL-ISWIRA† (1987, Egypt) 116m El Alamia c (Trans: The Collar and the Bracelet)

Ezzat el-Alaili *(Behit el-Beshari/Mustapha)*, Sherihan *(Fahima/Farham)*, Fardos Abdel-Hamid *(Hazina)*, Ahmed Abdel-Azuz *(El-Haddad)*, Mohammed Mounir *(Mohamed Effendi)*, Ahmed Bedeir *(Mansour)*.

Set in a poor village between 1930 and 1950, this film focuses on the sexual problems of three generations of women from the same family.

p, Hussein Kalla; d, Khairy Beshara; w, Yehia Azmi, Khairy Beshara, Abdel-Rashman el-Abnoudir; ph, Tarek el-Telmessani; ed, Adel Mounir.

Drama **(PR:NR MPAA:NR)**

AMAR BANDHAN† (1987, India) Joy Tara

Tapas Paul, Satabdi Roy.

An athletic young villager falls in love with the daughter of a wealthy man. (In Begali.)

d, Tapan Saha; m, Manoranjan.

Romance **(PR:NR MPAA:NR)**

AMAR KANTAK† (1987, India)

Dipankar De, Moon Moon Sen, Sukhen Das, Soma Mukherjee.

A story of a debauched feudal landlord and his two daughters. (In Bengali.)

p, Parna Chitram; d, Sukhen Das; m, Ajay Das.

Drama **(PR:NR MPAA:NR)**

AMAR SANGI† (1987, India)

Vijayeta Pandit.

(In Bengali).

d, Sujit Guha.

Drama **(PR:NR MPAA:NR)**

AMAZING GRACE AND CHUCK** (1987) 115m Turnstar-Rastar-ML Delphi/Tri-Star c

Jamie Lee Curtis *(Lynn Taylor)*, Alex English *(Amazing Grace Smith)*, Gregory Peck *(President)*, William L. Petersen *(Russell Murdock)*, Joshua Zuehlke *(Chuck Murdock)*, Dennis Lipscomb *(Johnny B. Goode)*, Lee Richardson *(Jeffries)*, Frances Conroy *(Pamela Murdock)*, Dean Alexander *(Sports Broadcaster)*, Jim Allen *(Missile Soldier)*, Jim Antonio *(Strickland)*, Red Auerbach *(Himself)*, Alan Autry *(George)*, Michael Bond *(Aide)*, Steven Bothun *(Reporter)*, Michael Bowen *(Hot Dog)*, James Cotterell *(Third Baseman)*, Clarence Felder *(Dick Ferguson)*, Lynne Turner Fitzgerald *(Network Anchor)*, Brian R. Hager *(First Baseman)*, Robert Harper *(Bowman)*, James Lindley Hathaway *(Jerome)*, A.J. Kallan *(Man in Truck)*, Matt Kerns *(Shortstop)*, Cortney Kutner *(Carolyn)*, Harvey Martin *(Mad Dog)*, Johnny Most *(Himself)*, Natalie Oliver *(Boston Reporter)*, Kurt Olsson *(Tommy)*, Gwen Petersen *(Teacher)*, Maite Petersen *(School Girl)*, John Russell *(Stuart Shipley)*, Joe Sabatini *(Airplane Mechanic)*, Robert Schenkkan *(Pollack)*, Vasek C. Simek *(Soviet Premier)*, Harris Smithe, Robert Tilson

(Soldiers), Rudolf Svehla *(Russian Translator)*, Manfred Sypold *(Johann)*, James Tuomey *(Aide)*, Cara Wilder *(Laura)*.

Sports "widows" and anti-nuclear protestors will probably enjoy this noble attempt that didn't quite reach its goal. Produced by a consortium which included Rastar (The Ray Stark organization), Turnstar, and ML Delphi, it's a sweet tale of what happens when all professional sports games are halted in the United States until a nuclear disarmament is signed. And it's all due to the determination of a 12-year-old Little League pitcher. If it sounds fanciful and Capra-cornish, it is, but the idea behind the story has just enough credibility to make it a pleasant, if not enlightening, way to spend just short of two hours in a darkened theater.

Taken on a tour of the local missile facility in Montana, Zuehlke is traumatized by what he sees. He learns of the awesome killing power of nuclear weapons and the destruction possible if the fury of these atomic behemoths were to be unleashed. This is compounded by the fact that Zuehlke's father, Petersen, is an Air Force Reserve pilot who might eventually be called upon to kill millions. The boy is frightened that his father, who transports missiles from time to time, could

perish on a mission. When he learns that if his sister dropped a fork from the table at the same moment as a nuclear explosion, she would be vaporized before the fork hit the linoleum, he becomes determined to do what he can to end such madness. Zuehlke is a star hurler on his baseball team and at his next game, he announces that he is refusing to pitch unless an agreement is signed to eliminate nuclear weapons. The game is canceled and the media, having nothing better to do as it must have been a slow day for international news, picks up the story. It is transmitted across the country with the speed of light and English, a professional basketball star for the Boston Celtics, hears about it, as do millions of Americans. English is mourning the loss of his wife and child and decides that this 12-year-old has a real cause, so he flies to Montana to help the lad spread the word. Curtis, his manager, goes along for the ride but she hopes English will go back to lay-ups and jump shots as soon as possible. It isn't long before other sports luminaries follow. Football's Harvey Martin and Dennis Lipscomb, as well as Celtics president Red Auerbach (playing himself) join the protest. In a flash, the tiny Montana hamlet is transformed into a media commune. Shortly thereafter, all professional sporting events are canceled as one athlete after another joins in. When English is murdered, the children of the world unite in a vow of silence. U.S. President Peck and the chief Soviet, Simek, are so moved by what has swept the world they arrange a secret summit meeting and decide to rid the planet of nuclear weapons, a process which will take the next seven years. These political terms are not nearly fast enough for Zuehlke who holds out for and gets immediate and total nuclear disarmament. Once that's accomplished, he dons his Little League uniform once more and with Peck, Simek, and media mogul Ted Turner in attendance, he strides out to the mound again to pitch.

In the traditional sense, it's another "little guy beats the big guys" story. Although the situation could not happen in real life (in 1987, the National Football League players struck and had several defections—so much for sports solidarity), it's heartening to imagine that it could. English does well as the basketball player, perhaps because that is what he does when he's not emoting. The producers cast about for a tall black actor who could be convincing as a performer as well as on the hardwood. However, other than Lou Gossett (who is about 6 feet 4 but is pushing 50), they couldn't find any actors to fill the bill, so they went into the pro ranks to locate a player who could act, rather than an actor who could play. Although English toils for the Denver Nuggets and is always among the NBA's high scorers, it was decided that since the Celtics are so well-known, and have a reputation as being one of the classiest managements in all of sports, they should be the team. South Carolina graduate English lives up to his name, having obtained a degree in English and gone on to publish three poetry books. He is also a man devoted to causes and was instrumental in "Hands Across America" as well as being at the forefront of the Ethiopian Relief Fund, long before most of the country was aware of the terrible famine in that country. Auerbach, who used to coach the Celtics before moving upstairs, liked the script and when informed that English would be enacting the role of a Celtic said, "I only wish I could keep him." Finding Zuehlke proved even more difficult than casting English. Producer Field (a one-time Fox executive before turning his hand to scripting) and his aides looked at thousands of young men. Zuehlke is an excellent athlete and understood the sacrifice the character was making. Petersen, who had starred in TO LIVE AND DIE IN L.A. and MANHUNTER, was appearing in his third picture. In addition to William, the credits include Petersens named Gwen (a teacher), Maite (a student) and Susan (a wardrobe assistant). Was nepotism alive and well in this production? Peck had been in semi-retirement but was lured back to work by the promise of the script and commented: "If this could only happen, the world would be a wonderful place." Made, for the most part, in two Montana towns (Bozeman and Livingston), the picture also used venerable old Boston Garden, as well as veteran Celtics' voice Johnny Most. The NBA arranged to have an exhibition game between the Celtics and the 76ers filmed in early October, 1985. In the 2 minutes and 28 seconds in which English appeared as a Bostonian, he scored a goal from the floor, passed off for a pair of assists, and stole the ball once. The crowd loved it. There were many plugs for Ted Turner's Cable News Network and he was credited as a "consultant." It was around this time that Turner was involved with a U.S./Soviet sports project and so it's easy to understand his involvement. Englishman Newell, who directed DANCE WITH A STRANGER, was an odd choice for so American a movie, but someone must have thought he could look at the USA with "new eyes," in much the same way as Englishman Michael Apted did with COAL MINER'S DAUGHTER. It didn't work. Whereas a movie of this sort demands a light, airy, almost fairy-tale touch, the direction and the script are heavy, lacking in any whimsy and the sincerity is obscured by the handling. Ray Stark's long-time unit production manager Roger Rothstein holds down that job here as well as functioning as executive producer. English and Zuehlke are both "finds" and when Zuehlke hangs up his spikes and English hangs up his sneakers, they'll have acting to fall back upon. Some rough language is what gives this fable the MPG A-C rating. *(Profanity.)*

p, David Field; d, Mike Newell; w, David Field; ph, Robert Elswit (Metrocolor); m, Elmer Bernstein; ed, Peter Hollywood; prod d, Dena Roth; art d, John Myhre; set d, Dawn Snyder; cos, Jack Buehler; spec eff, Rick Kerrigan; stunts, Orwin Harvey; makeup, Kathy Estocin.

Drama **(PR:A-C MPAA:PG)**

AMAZON WOMEN ON THE MOON** (1987) 85m UNIV c/bw

Michelle Pfeiffer *(Brenda)*, Steve Forrest *(Capt. Nelson)*, Joey Travolta *(Butch)*, David Alan Grier *(Don Simmons)*, Rosanna Arquette *(Karen)*, Steve Guttenberg *(Jerry)*, Archie Hahn *(Harvey Pitnik)*, Ed Begley, Jr. *(Griffin)*, Matt Adler *(George)*, Ralph Bellamy *(Mr. Gower)*, Carrie Fisher *(Mary Brown)*, Peter Horton *(Brenda's Husband)*, Steve Allen, Sybil Danning, Griffin Dunne, Henny Youngman, Paul Bartel, Rip Taylor, Howard Hesseman, Russ Meyer, B.B. King, Lou Jacobi, Arsenio Hall, Donald Muhich, Monique Gabrielle, Erica Yahn, Joe Pantoliano, Stanley Brock, Robert Colbert, Lohman and Barkley, T.K. Carter, Belinda Balaski, William Marshall, John Ingle, Angel Tompkins, Terence McGovern, Marc McClure, Kelly Preston, Henry Silva, Charlie Callas.

Director Landis returns to the style of what many consider to be his funniest film, KENTUCKY FRIED MOVIE, presenting 20 different comedy sketches directed by himself and four others (Dante, Gottlieb, Horton, and Weiss). Basically a swipe at late-night TV programming (bad local commercials, old movies, etc.), AMAZON WOMEN ON THE MOON is from the hit-or-miss school and here it mostly misses. Among the skits that do work are a parody of the INVISIBLE MAN entitled "Son of the Invisible Man" starring Begley as a scientist who thinks he is invisible but is merely running around naked (segment directed by Gottlieb); "Hospital" sees crazed obstetrician Dunne misplace the newborn baby of couple Pfeiffer and Horton. To cover up his mistake he attempts to persuade them that they have given birth to a Mr. Potato Head (directed by Landis); another is a parody of a "Ripley's Believe It or Not"-type show which presents preposterous theories such as the supposition that the Loch Ness Monster and Jack the Ripper were one and the same (directed by Dante); and another parody of the Gene Siskel/Roger Ebert-type film critic show which sees the critics mercilessly savaging the miserable life of one of their viewers, one Harvey Pitnik, giving him a "thumbs down" which leads poor Harvey to a fatal heart-attack. Later his funeral turns into a roast with the likes of Henny Youngman, Rip Taylor, and Charlie Callas continuing the verbal abuse (directed by Dante); and the title sketch, a flawless, straight-faced parody of bad 1950s science fiction film starring Forrest as the space commander and Travolta as his sidekick (directed by Weiss). Others not-so-successful include a running gag commercial which features Grier as mundane black pop singer Don "No Soul" Simmons singing tunes like "Tie a Yellow Ribbon 'Round the Old Oak Tree," "Blame It On The Bossa Nova," and "The Ballad of the Green Berets"; a shy teenager (Adler) going to buy condoms; a spoof of REEFER MADNESS starring Fisher and Bartel; and commercials for things like "Silly Pate." All of this tumbles out, rapid-fire, in less than 90 minutes.

The basic problem with AMAZON WOMEN ON THE MOON is that most of the humor is based on things that are beyond parody. Bad television commercials and lame low-budget films are funny enough as they are and exaggerating their ridiculousness is really unnecessary. Ask any devotee of "Psychotronic" cinema (a term derived from Michael Weldon's excellent and entertaining encyclopedia of off-beat films *The Psychotronic Encyclopedia of Film*) whether they would rather watch a parody of a bad film or a bad film itself and they will invariably pick the real thing. What is successful about AMAZON WOMEN ON THE MOON is the painstakingly accurate recreation of everything from the commercials to the title skit. These talented filmmakers demonstrate that they can handle a multitude of directing chores, and although the scripting may lack imagination, the visuals are handled quite well. Always worthwhile is the work of Dante for a dose of his dark, caustic wit and cinematic verve. *(Nudity, adult situations, profanity.)*

p, Robert K. Weiss; d, Joe Dante, Carl Gottlieb, Peter Horton, John Landis, Robert K. Weiss; w, Michael Barrie, Jim Mulholland; ph, Daniel Pearl (Technicolor); ed, Bert Lovitt, Marshall Harvey, Malcolm Campbell; prod d, Ivo Cristante; art d, Alex Hajdu; set d, Julie Kaye Towery; cos, Taryn DeChellis.

Comedy **(PR:O MPAA:R)**

AMAZONS* (1987) 76m Concorde-Aries/MGM-UA Home Video c

Windsor Taylor Randolph *(Dyala)*, Penelope Reed *(Tashi)*, Joseph Whipp *(Kalungo)*, Danitza Kingsley *(Tashinge)*, Wolfram Hoechst *(Matlin)*, Jacques Arndt *(High Priest)*, Charles Finch *(Timar)*, Frank Cocza *(Baligur)*, Annie Larronde *(Emerald Queen)*, Armand Capo *(Hitron)*, Santiago Mallo *(Halfhead)*, Mary Fournery *(Vishiti)*, Noelle Balfour *(Lati)*, Esther Velazquez *(Azundati)*, Marc Woinsky *(Artan)*, Fabiana Smith *(Lioness/Akam)*, Albert Marty *(Male Noble)*, William Reta *(Guard)*, Lena Marie Johansson, Linda Guzman *(Female Nobles)*.

A hopeless sword-and-sorcery fantasy which contains some less-than-special special effects and numerous statuesque warrior queens baring their ample bosoms to the enemy. The convoluted plot has the Amazon city of Imbissi being terrorized by the evil, all-powerful lord Whipp and his sword-wielding followers known as the Pegash. Only the holder of the magical Sword of Azundati can defeat Whipp, so the Amazon Queen, Larronde, sends her two best warriors to find the sword. The chosen warriors—Taylor Randolph and Reed—come from feuding families, but eventually grow to like and respect one another. There are a few scrapes along the way, but the pair makes it safely to the sword's hiding place. Just as the sword is removed from its sacred place, the pair are confronted by Smith, a woman who has the ability to transform herself into a lion. Smith has been sent by Whipp to steal the sword and bring it back to the Pegash. A battle follows and only Taylor Randolph survives. With the help of a magical horse, she arrives back in her village just as Whipp is about to enslave all the Imbissi warriors. She beheads the evil warrior, saves her people, becomes a great hero, and returns the sword to its hiding place.

There are no surprises here—just the standard sword-and-sorcery ingredients. The characters babble on in the most serious of tones about ancient legends, omnipotent leaders, and conquering the world, but nothing makes much sense. The actresses do little more than show off their physical prowess and their agility in wrestling the enemy—all the while baring their bodies. Although the film is about a tribe of Amazon women who are stronger than their male counterparts, there is still a rather odious theme of male domination that runs through the film, manifesting itself in the form of beatings, attempted rape, and bloody sacrifices of women. AMAZONS is competently made (Roger Corman was associate producer) and there is one interesting sequence which takes place in a haunted forest and employs a visually impressive strobe-lighting technique, but overall the film is a waste of time. *(Violence, nudity, sexual situations.)*

p, Hector Olivera; d, Alex Sessa; w, Charles Saunders; ph, Leonard Solis; m, Oscar Camp; ed, Edward Lowe; art d, Julie Bertotto; cos, Betty Abraham; spec eff, Willy Smith; makeup, Laura Zelop.

Action/Fantasy **Cas.** **(PR:O MPAA:R)**

AMERICA ABBAI† (1987, India)

Rajasekhar, Aswini, Radhika.

Shot entirely in the US, this film deals with the problems Indians face in leaving their homeland. (In Telugu.)

p, D. Madhusudhana Rao; d, Singeetham Srinivas Rao.

Drama **(PR:NR MPAA:NR)**

AMERICAN DRIVE-IN† (1987) 97m Patel/Shah c

Emily Longstreth *(Bobbie-Ann)*, Pat Kirton *(Jack)*, Joel Bennett *(Sarge)*, Rhonda Snow, John Rice, Allison Heath, Mika, Kevin Miller.

An attempt at satirizing the phenomenon of the drive-in movie is the object of this low-budget exploitation film which saw only a brief release in Los Angeles. Directed by the Indian-born Shah, who also delivered the 1972 Joan Hackett-Robert Klein picture RIVALS and the failed Cicely Tyson-James Earl Jones-Lou Gossett 1975 film THE RIVER NIGER. The episodic plot revolves around a number of drive-in patrons—a young couple debating whether or not to marry before the bride-to-be gets kidnaped by a biker gang; a family of heavyweights nearly emptying the concession stand; a local politician's attempts to get his son to police the drive-in; and the wacky escapades of a drunken projectionist. The film-within-the-film that is playing on the drive-in screen is HARD ROCK ZOMBIES, Shah's 1985 picture.

p&d, Krishna Shah; w, Krishna Shah, David Ball; ph, Steve Posey; m, Paul Sabu; ed, Amit Bose; art d, Cynthia Sowder.

Comedy **(PR:NR MPAA:R)**

AMERICAN NINJA 2: THE CONFRONTATION½** (1987) 89m Golan-Globus/Cannon c

Michael Dudikoff *(Joe Armstrong)*, Steve James *(Curtis Jackson)*, Larry Poindexter *(Sgt. Charlie McDonald)*, Gary Conway *(Leo [The Lion] Burke)*, Jeff Weston *(Col. [Wild Bill] Woodward)*, Michelle Botes *(Alicia Sanborn)*, Michael Stone *(Tojo Ken)*, Len Sparrowhawk *(Pat McCarthy)*, Jonathan Pienaar *(Taylor)*.

You can tell by the title that this is a sequel but that's where the similarity ends. This one is superior in almost every respect to the first, with slam-bang action, many humorous moments, and an excellent performance by James in what should be his break-through role. Dudikoff and James are a duo of US Army Rangers who have been given an interesting assignment. There's a small British-controlled island in the Caribbean with a tiny corps of American soldiers stationed there to guard the US embassy. One by one, the Marines on the island have been disappearing and Dudikoff and James have to find out why and who is behind this. The island features balmy weather, beautiful vacationers in scanty swimsuits, and an underlying feeling of evil. Although the picture was made in South Africa, director Firstenberg and cinematographer Porath quickly convince the eyes that the action is taking place somewhere in the Western Hemisphere. The bottom line of the plot is the fact that local drug lord Conway (who also cowrote the script) has in his employ a genetic engineer. Conway is nabbing the tough Marines in order to clone their strong cells to build his own assassination force of Ninja killers who will then go out and murder everyone he points them toward. The head of Conway's laboratory is a kidnaped scientist with a comely daughter, Botes. Now, if this sounds vaguely familiar, try to recall DR. NO and see if some of the elements don't match up, such as the Ursula Andress character being the daughter of a captured scientist on a tropical isle. The local government chiefs are also in on the scam, as Conway has them on his huge payroll, which is financed by narcotics trafficking. The picture seems to be one fight after another with respites only for some very funny moments. James gets most of the good lines, such as the scene where he is dispensing with a horde of Ninjas and happily yells: "Come on, I love it, I love it. Bring on some more. Come on, you midgets!" In the end, after what seems like hundreds of Ninjas have been taken out of commission, Dudikoff and James save the day and the picture ends with nary a hair on the heroes' heads having been mussed.

Martial arts fans will love the well-staged fights by choreographer Michael Stone, but, as in so many of these movies, when the producers find a lead who is adept at kicks and such, he usually falls short in the emoting department. Such is the case with handsome Dudikoff, who knows his way around Karate weaponry but whose acting ability needs to be sharpened. Not so with James, who demonstrates that he can handle dialog as well as he can toss a nunchuck. Excellent editing by Duthie and a just-right score by Clinton. Anyone who takes this seriously has made a mistake because it is truly a send-up of the genre and must be viewed that way. *(Graphic violence, profanity.)*

p, Menahem Golan, Yoram Globus; d, Sam Firstenberg; w, Gary Conway, James Booth (based on a story by Gary Conway from characters created by Avi Kleinberger, Gideon Amir); ph, Gideon Porath (TVC Color); m, George S. Clinton; ed, Michael J. Duthie; prod d, Holger Gross; art d, Robert Jenkinson; cos, Audrey M. Bansmer; ch, Michael Stone; stunts, B.J. Davis.

Martial Arts **(PR:C-O MPAA:R)**

AMOR EN CAMPO MINADO† (1987, Cuba) 96m Icaic c (Trans: Love in a Minefield)

Daisy Granados, Adolfo Llaurado, Omar Valdes, Ana Lillian Renteria.

Set in 1964 following the overthrow of Brazil's president Goulart, the story focuses on a leftist journalist who goes into hiding to avoid arrest. While in hiding he faces a crisis in his marriage and comes to the realization that his political commitments were never has deeply held as he led others to believe.

p, Dario Larramendi; d, Pastor Vega; w, Pastor Vega (based on the play be Dias Gomes); m, Chico Buarque de Hollanda.

Drama **(PR:NR MPAA:NR)**

AMRITAMGAMAYA† (1987, India) Shirdisai Creations

Mohanlal, Geetha, Devan, Johny, Captain Raju, Pappu, Parvathy.

Responsible for the death of a fellow medical student, a doctor gets the chance to pay back his moral debt many years later. (In Malayalam.)

d, Hariharan.

(PR:NR MPAA:NR)

ANAYURT OTELI† (1987, Turk.) 110m Odak c (Trans: Motherland Hotel)

Macid Koper *(Zebercet)*, Sera Yilmaz, Orhan Cagman.

Koper plays a young man who inherits a large old hotel from his parents. He falls in love with an attractive female guest, and when she spurns him he begins a descent into madness which culminates in murder and suicide.

p, Cengiz Ergin; d&w, Omer Kavur; ph, Orhan Oguz; m, Atilla Ozdomiroglu; ed, Mevlud Kogak.

Horror **(PR:NR MPAA:NR)**

ANDJEO CUVAR† (1987, Yugo.) 88m Singidinum-Jugoart-Morava/ Jugoslavia Films c (Trans: Guardian Angel)

Ljubisa Samardzic *(Dragan)*, Neda Arneric *(Mila)*, Jakup Amzic *(Chayine)*, Saban Bajramovic *(Chayine's Father)*.

Based on actual incidents, this film features Samardzic as a newspaper reporter investigating the sale of Yugoslavian Gypsy children to criminal elements in Italy and other parts of Europe. The children suffer incredible abuse at the hands of their "owners" and are forced to be beggars and thieves. Though Samardzic gets some positive results in attempting to help some of these children, it all proves to be for naught and he is eventually murdered by Gypsy bosses who believe he has learned too much.

p,d&w, Goran Paskaljevic; ph, Milan Spasic; m, Zoran Simijanovic; ed, Olga Skrigin, Olga Obradov.

Crime **(PR:NR MPAA:NR)**

ANGEL HEART½** (1987) 113m Winkast-Union-Carolco Intl./Tri-Star c

Mickey Rourke *(Harry Angel)*, Robert De Niro *(Louis Cyphre)*, Lisa Bonet *(Epiphany Proudfoot)*, Charlotte Rampling *(Margaret Krusemark)*, Stocker Fontelieu *(Ethan Krusemark)*, Brownie McGhee *(Toots Sweet)*, Michael Higgins *(Dr. Fowler)*, Elizabeth Whitcraft *(Connie)*, Eliott Keener *(Sterne)*, Charles Gordone *(Spider Simpson)*, Dann Florek *(Winesap)*, Kathleen Wilhoite *(Nurse)*, George Buck *(Izzy)*, Judith Drake *(Izzy's Wife)*, Gerald L. Orange *(Pastor John)*, Peggy Severe *(Mammy Carter)*, Pruitt Taylor Vince *(Deimos)*, David Petitjean *(Baptism Preacher)*, Rick Washburn *(Cajun Heavy)*, Neil Newlon *(2nd Cajun Heavy)*, Oakley Dalton *(Big Jacket)*, Yvonne Bywaters *(Margaret's Maid)*, Loys T. Bergeron *(Mike)*, Joshua Frank *(Toothless)*, Karmen Harris *(Harlem Mourner)*, Nicole Burdette *(Ellie)*, Kendell Lupe, Percy Martin *(Oyster Cajuns)*, Viola Dunbar *(Concierge)*, Murray Bandel *(Bartender)*, Jarrett Narcisse *(Epiphany's Child)*, Ernest Watson *(Oyster Bar Saxophonist)*, Rickie Monie *(Oyster Bar Pianist)*, Roselyn Lionhart *(Voodoo Musician)*, Toots Sweet Band: Sugar Blue *(Harmonica)*, Pinetop Perkins *(Piano)*, Deacon Johnmoore *(Lead Guitar)*, Richard Payne *(Double Bass)*, W. Alonzo Stewart *(Drums)*, Lillian Boutte *(Vocalist)*, Joel Adam, Darrel Beasley, Stephen Beasley, Jerome Reddick *(Tap Dancers)*, Louis Freddie Kohlman, Stephen Kenyatta Simon, Curtis Pierre, Kufaru Aaron Mouton *(Voodoo Drums)*, Marilyn Banks, Lula Elzy, Francesca J. Ridge, Hope Clarke, Oscar Best, Sarita Allen, Noel Jones, Valerie Jackson, Greer Goff, Arlena Rolant, Karen Davis, Shirleta Jones, Mark Taylor *(Voodoo Dancers)*.

One of the goriest films ever made (ranking next to the hideous SCARFACE remake with Al Pacino), this thriller with the trick ending is soaked in symbolism, as well as blood. Despite its allusions to Satanism and Voodoo bloodbaths, one cannot deny ANGEL HEART is nevertheless stylish (at least with its traditional private eye beginning), captivating, and authentic in its 1955 posture. Rourke is a cheap private eye who specializes in divorce and insurance claims. He is asked to go to Harlem to meet wealthy, mysterious De Niro, by his lawyer, Florek. The intellectual, goateed De Niro pays Rourke to find a 1940s crooner named Johnny, who has reneged on a contract. Rourke goes to a New York sanitarium but finds that the singer, injured during the war and suffering from amnesia, has been transferred, according to hospital records. He breaks into the house of the doctor, Higgins, who had been treating the singer, and learns that Higgins had been paid $25,000 to falsify records to cover Johnny's disappearance. When Rourke returns to see Higgins, he finds the doctor has been killed, shot in the head. He follows leads that eventually take him to Coney Island, where he learns the singer had been seeing a black magic socialite from New Orleans, Rampling, and had dumped her for a "mambo priestess." In New Orleans, Rourke sees Rampling, a product of wealth and nightmarish superstition. After he asks that she read his palm and sketch his fortune, he begins to ask questions about the singer and she asks him to leave. He finds the daughter of the "mambo priestess," Bonet, who tells him little. When he tries to interview an old jazz guitar player, McGhee, who worked with the singer, Rourke is thrown out of the club. Later he follows McGhee to a voodoo ceremony in a remote area and sees Bonet do a ritualistic dance, half naked, smearing blood from chickens over her body, writhing, and clawing at the ground. He visits McGhee and grills him about the whereabouts of the singer. When the old man tell him nothing, Rourke leaves his name and hotel address on a piece of paper.

He is awakened by two New Orleans cops the next morning. They tell him that McGhee has been killed, his genitals cut off and stuffed down his throat. They found Rourke's name and address on a piece of paper clutched by the old man, they say. Rourke shrugs this off, saying the killing has nothing to do with him, that he is merely investigating the whereabouts of a missing person. When he refuses to give the name of his client, police check with Florek who confirms Rourke's assignment. When Rourke returns to see Rampling, he finds her spread out on a table in her ancient mansion, slaughtered, her heart cut out. He races away, later seeing Bonet at his cheap hotel room, where they make love. Bonet has already told him that the missing singer was her father and has admitted that her child was conceived by an unknown man in a voodoo ceremony. Rourke then confers with De Niro in a church. Rourke asks De Niro exactly who he is and when he gets evasive answers, he begins to curse. De Niro reminds him he's in a church, then asks: "Are you an atheist?" "Yes," snorts Rourke, "I'm from Brooklyn." Meanwhile, Cajun thugs have been chasing Rourke about the area, trying to kill him. He finally tracks down Fontelieu, Rampling's wealthy father, and learns from him that the singer, Johnny, was a Satanist who turned his daughter into a black magic practitioner, and that it was he, Fontelieu, who removed Johnny from the hospital in 1943 with a vague reference to the singer's having had plastic surgery on his face. He goes on to tell Rourke how Johnny earlier conjured up Satan before his eyes by picking a soldier out of a New York crowd, cutting out the young man's heart and eating it. This is too much for even the hardboiled Rourke, and he goes to a bathroom to vomit. Upon returning, he finds Fontelieu is also dead, his head stuffed into a vat of boiling gumbo. He dashes back to Rampling's mansion to look for the dogtags of the sacrificial soldier, which Fontelieu said his daughter sealed in a jar. He finds the jar, breaks it, and looks down to read "ANGEL, HAROLD," his own name, on the dogtags. Turning, he sees De Niro, who tells him that it is he, Rourke, suffering with amnesia, who is really the missing singer and Satanist, and that he took the name of the soldier he killed. Then, with his face changed, he slaughtered everyone he interviewed on the quest to find himself. The bloody bodies of Higgins, Rampling and McGhee, with himself standing over them, now reappear to Rourke, and he realizes that he is the murdering singer and that De Niro, using the name "Louis Cyphre," is really "Lucifer." De Niro admits that he is the Devil and that he has come to claim Rourke's now recognizable soul. Rourke flees back to his hotel room to find detectives standing next to the nude body of Bonet, his daughter, and he realizes that he has also murdered her. "You're going to burn for this," one detective says. "Yes," Rourke replies knowingly, "in hell." Bonet's mulatto child is carried out of a closet and he looks at Rourke with yellowing devilish eyes, pointing at him for a very creepy closing.

ANGEL HEART is very deceptive, beginning as a crime yarn and then exploding into a Satanistic orgy, veiled cleverly as the exploits of voodoo crackpots by director Parker, who wrote the eerie story. Of course, the red herring here is De Niro, who all will believe, until the end, is the singer being sought. But much more clouds the story and is never explained; the Cajun thugs and why they try to kill Rourke remains in the realm of the inexplicable. There are so many twists and turns, all accompanied with fearful cutaways by Parker, that the confused viewer will welcome the almost too pat ending without really wanting to try to piece this one together. This is definitely not a film one will want to see again to spot the

weaknesses and fallacies of the plot and to chronicle Rourke's gruesome odyssey. It's just too bloody and sickening to stand twice. Parker does drop hints along the way that Rourke is really seeking his maniacal self. He endures nightmares in which fans turn, nuns sit silent against bleak walls, chain doors slam shut, blood soaks Rourke's front and spouts from his fingers, and the rain leaking through the ancient ceiling of his hotel room turns to a torrent of blood while he makes love to Bonet, sinister slivers of memory seeping back into his own brain. But, in one film or another, this has been done before, Stanley Kubrick's experiment with mystical Satan and human gore, THE SHINING, being a primary influence. There are many other little pickups Parker employs, either consciously or subconsciously, such as his blatant symbolism of four-bladed fans turning slowly, graphically dovetailed with symbolic pendants worn by the murder victims. The fan symbols are almost identical in use to the "X" symbols used by Howard Hawks when he made SCARFACE in 1932 to indicate a gang murder (to illustrate the gangster term "X marks the spot"). At one point Parker pays oblique tribute to ON THE WATERFRONT by having Rourke use the term "Palookaville," a word synonymous with that Marlon Brando crime yarn. On another occasion Bonet tells Rourke that a person he is looking for "could be six feet under." Rourke retorts: "Then I'll have to buy a shovel." This exchange can be found almost word-for-word in the crime drama CALL NORTHSIDE 777 in a conversation between information-hunting reporter James Stewart and cop Richard Rober. His role is powerful here and he gives an electrifying profile that proves his deep talent. Everyone else, even the fantastic De Niro with his low-keyed characterization of the Devil, is a prop to Rourke and his journey to self. This devotion to a constant perspective, and unswerving if indiscernible point of view, is to Parker's credit. He has kept faithfully to his protagonist, exposing him to a plot that must be unidentified until the end. This is the most courageous and traditional manner of telling a story on film, and is accomplished with great vigor. Most directors today either refuse to or cannot deal with the single perspective, preferring fragmentary points of view, varying characterizations, and wandering plots. It's simply easier that way, even though such techniques burden the viewer mercilessly. Parker has kept to the marrow of his tale, and, harrowing as it is, the viewer will not veer from its carnage. There is a horrible fascination with this film, like others of the mixed genre, where the viewer will go away feeling guilty for participating in such a repulsive nightmarish story. (This one will leave no one but maniacs laughing.) And that is why the film fails to rise above its murky motives. Nothing is redeemed; no one is saved. Rourke's discovery of self-guilt is not enough, for hope has been tricked by Parker and desperate horror captured at the expense of the viewer. Under no circumstances should this blood-letting film be seen by youngsters, for it betrays human decency and respect for life itself, almost venerating the power of evil. *(Graphic violence, nudity, excessive profanity.)*

p, Alan Marshall, Elliott Kastner; d&w, Alan Parker (based on the novel *Falling Angel* by William Hjortsberg); ph, Michael Seresin (Technicolor); m, Trevor Jones; ed, Gerry Hambling; prod d, Brian Morris; art d, Kristi Zea, Armin Ganz; set d, Robert J. Franco, Leslie Pope; cos, Aude Bronson-Howard; spec eff, J.C. Brotherhood; ch, Louis Falco; m/l, Brownie McGhee, Clarence Williams, Eddie Green, Spencer Williams, Anthony Evans, Sunny Clapp, Arthur Freed, Gus Arnheim, Abe Lyman; stunts, Harry Madsen; makeup, David Forrest, Carla White, Robert Laden.

Mystery/Thriller **Cas.** **(PR:O MPAA:R)**

ANGELOS† (1987, Gr.) 118m George Katakouzinos-Greek Film Centre c

Michael Maniatis *(Angelos)*, Dionyssis Xanthos *(Michael)*, Katerina Helmi *(Angelos' Mother)*, Maria Alkeou *(Grandmother)*.

Maniatis plays a shy homosexual who leaves home after he falls in love with sailor Xanthos. Xanthos persuades his lover to engage in transvestite prostitution, and, in the process, Maniatis suffers a severe beating and his seamy life-style is exposed. The scandal causes Maniatis' father to commit suicide and then Maniatis realizes he is only being used by Xanthos.

d, George Katakouzinos; w, George Katakouzinos; ph, Tassos Alexakis; m, Stamatis Spanoudakis; ed, Aristide Karydis-Fuchs.

Drama **(PR:NR MPAA:NR)**

ANGELUS NOVUS† (1987, It.) 80m Libra/Insituto Luce c

Domenico Pesce *(The Poet)*, Tomaso Ricordy, Stefano Valoppi, Eliana Cifa, Ignazio Fenu.

With the late Pier Paolo Passolini as his subject, first-time director Misuraca makes an attempt to abstractly convey the spirit and the political leanings of the great filmmaker.

p, Francesca Noe; d&w, Pasquale Misuraca; ph, Bruno Di Virgillo; m, Vittorio Gelmetti; ed, Roberto Perpignani.

Biography **(PR:NR MPAA:NR)**

ANGUSTIA† (1987, Span.) 89m Samba P.C.-Luna/Lauren c (Trans: Anguish)

Zelda Rubinstein *(Alice, John's Mother)*, Michael Lerner *(John, Lab Technician)*, Talia Paul *(Patty, Student Moviegoer)*, Angel Jove *(Assassin)*, Clara Pastor *(Linda, Student Moviegoer)*, Isabel Garcia Lorca *(Caroline)*, Nat Baker *(Professor)*, Edward Ledden *(Doctor)*, Jose M. Chucarro *(Friend)*, Antonella Murgia *(Ticket Seller)*, Josephine Borchaca *(Laura)*, George Pinkley *(Don)*, Benito Pocino *(Somnambulist)*, Victor Guillen *(Projectionist)*, Evelyn Rosenka *(Washerwoman)*, Michael Chandler *(Taxi Driver)*.

The first half of this horror entry focuses on a lab technician who is fired and seeks revenge by slitting the throats and gouging out the eyes of a woman and her husband. It's then revealed that this is all part of movie being watched by a pair of teenage girls in a seedy Los Angeles theater. One of the girls goes to the lobby where she encounters a killer with a gun, and the rest of the film revolves around the interaction between the murderers on-screen and off. Filmed in Spain, New York, and California.

d&w, Bigas Luna; ph, Josep Maria Civit (Eastmancolor); m, J.M. Pagan; ed, Tom Sabin; prod d, Andreu Coromina; art d. Felipe de Paco; spec eff, Paco Teres; makeup, Matilde Fabregat.

Horror **(PR:NR MPAA:NR)**

ANITA—DANCES OF VICE*½** (1987, Ger.) 85m Road Movies-ZDF/ Exportfilm Bischoff bw/c (ANITA—TANZE DES LASTERS)

Lotti Huber *(Mrs. Kutowski/"Anita Berber")*, Ina Blum *(Young Anita Berber/ Nurse)*, Mikael Honesseau *(Sebastian Droste/Doctor)*.

Applying his eccentric, flamboyant style to the biography of one of 20th century Germany's most notorious counterculture heroes, Anita Berber, camp filmmaker Rosa von Praunheim has created another unusual, original, and beautiful film. Berber, a nude dancer in 1920s Germany, became famous for her decadent life-style—a life-style which changed with the Third Reich's emergence and the restoration of "moral" order. It would hardly be expected that a director like von Praunheim (A VIRUS HAS NO MORALS, RED LOVE) would approach such a subject in a straightforward manner. Instead, he juxtaposes fragments from the dancer's life with those of a modern-day figure, the 75-year-old Huber, a woman who claims to be Berber and who was placed in a mental hospital after baring her rear end on the streets of Berlin. (Berber actually died in 1928 at the age of 29 from tuberculosis.) The modern tale, which occurs mainly inside the mental hospital, is photographed in a harsh black and white, while the scenes of the young dancer, played by Blum and presumably the product of Huber's imagination, are in lush, vibrant color. These scenes are also without dialog, using title cards that recall the movies of the day. This gives these sequences an expressionistic feeling that is something of a cross between the baroque style of Visconti and the silent features of Clarence Brown.

There is virtually no semblance of a strict narrative form in relating the plights of these two women. The overweight, exceedingly obnoxious Huber is brought to a mental hospital where she does her best to make life miserable for the stuffy doctors and nurses, and bullies the other patients in her loud, crass manner. She is convinced that she is Berber, and wants to continue in the same decadent life-style as the dancer. When a nurse attempts to inject her with Thorazine to calm her down, she asks for cocaine. When another patient incessantly talks about politics, Huber responds by saying she is more concerned with having a go at it "between the sheets." By the film's end, Huber's temporal existence has come to an end. Her body lies on an operating table where an autopsy is performed. The doctors and nurses leave the body alone; Huber's spirit rises. There is a bewildered look on her face as she wonders where everyone has gone before she waddles off in search of more fun. The 1920s sequences concentrate more on visual effect than the camp comedy and social satire that are von Praunheim's trademark. A variety of scenes show Blum as she dances, seduces both men and women, and desperately searches for cocaine. She is often accompanied by her dance partner, Sebastian Droste (played by Honesseau, a man with a chiseled body and face), an ardent cocaine user with a sexual preference for boyish-looking young men. Some aspects of Berber's history are suggested: that her extreme behavior resulted partly from a strict, bureaucratic father who never showed her the love she needed; that Berber considered her dances an art form to be appreciated for its revelations about the human moral condition, while her audiences were mainly hedonistic men who wanted to see her naked; and that because of her many followers, she found it virtually impossible to find work, and was forced into poverty and an early death.

Von Praunheim uses the majority of his actors in roles in both periods. For instance, Blum and Honesseau, who play Berber and Droste in the 1920s, also play a nurse and doctor in the modern sequences. Blum looks exceedingly plain in the modern scenes, a stark contrast to her appearance as the exotic Berber. There are instances when Blum's profile is photographed as beautifully and enticingly as any ever done of Greta Garbo under Clarence Brown's direction. The other bit actors were chosen mainly for their eccentric, sometimes bizarre, facial qualities. The most interesting of all these characters is the elderly Huber, whose energetic presence (amazing for a woman of her age) never ceases to entertain. Though she may not possess the beauty of Anita Berber, she does have that same spirit that sparks the desire to live instinctively, despite society's criticism.

p&d, Rosa von Praunheim [Holger Mischwitzki]; w, Rosa von Praunheim, Hannelene Limpach; ph, Elfi Mikesch; m, Konrad Elfers, Rainer Rubbert, Alan Marks, Ed Lieber; ed, Mike Shephard; set d, Inge Stiborski; cos, Anne Jud; makeup, Uschi Menzel, Willi P. Konze, Oliver Ziem.

Biography/Drama **(PR: MPAA:NR)**

ANJAAM† (1987, India)

Hema Malini, Shashi Kapoor, Shafi Inamdar, Parjiat.

In order to protect the honor of her family, a wife must kill her malevolent husband. Kapoor, who has appeared in numerous British films, costars. (In Hindi.)

p, Ramesh Tiwari; d, Hariharan.

(PR:NR MPAA:NR)

ANJOS DA NOITE (SEE: NIGHT ANGELS, 1987, Braz.)

ANJOS DO ARRABALDE† (1987, Braz.) 104m A.P. Galante-Embrafilme c (Trans: Suburban Angels)

Betty Faria *(Dalia)*, Clarisse Abujamra *(Rosa)*, Irene Stefania *(Carmo)*, Vanessa Alves *(Aninha)*, Enio Goncalves *(Henrique)*, Emilio Di Biasi *(Carmona)*, Ricardo Blat *(Afonso)*, Carlos Koppa *(Gaucho)*, Chica Burza *(Holanda)*, Kiko Guerra *(Nivaldo)*, Silas Gregorio *(Joao)*, Elaine Marcondes *(Valeria)*, Josmar Martins *(Pai de Aninha)*, Jessica Canoletti *(Filha de Carmo)*, Lygia Reichenbach *(Dentista)*, Marcia Regina *(Sonia)*, Nicole Puzzi *(Fernanda)*, Jose De Abreu *(Soares)*.

A realistic look at the savagery in a Sao Paulo public school. The arrival of four women teachers brings the hope that the hostilities which exist can be overcome, but not without the teachers endangering their own lives.

p, Antonio Polo Galante; d&w, Carlos Reichenbach; ph, Conrado Sanchez (Eastmancolor); m, Manoel Paiva, Luis Chagas; ed, Eder Mazini; art d, Sebastiao de Souza.

Drama **(PR:NR MPAA:NR)**

ANJUMAN† (1987, India) 133m Collective c

Shabana Azmi *(Anjuman)*, Farouque Shaikh *(Sajjid)*, Rahini Hattangady *(Eye-Doctor)*, Shankat Kaifi *(Chidiya Khala)*, Mushtaq Khan *(Banke Nawab)*.

Azmi is the title character, a young woman and poet who works alongside the other women of Lucknow doing *chikan* embroidery. She attracts the attention of the villagers when she defiantly refuses (at the altar) to marry her wealthy suitor and leads the *chikan* workers in a strike for better wages. (In Hindi.)

p, Muzaffar Ali, Shabha Doctor; d, Muzaffar Ali; w, Rahi Masoom Reza; ph, Ishan Arya; m, Khayyam.

Drama **(PR:NR MPAA:NR)**

ANNA† (1987) 95m Magnus/Vestron c

Sally Kirkland *(Anna)*, Robert Fields *(Daniel)*, Paulina Porizkova *(Krystyna)*, Gibby Brand *(Director #1)*, John Robert Tillotson *(Director #2)*, Joe Aufiery *(Stage Manager)*, Charles Randall *(Agent)*, Mimi Wedell *(Agent's Secretary)*, Larry Pine *(Baskin)*, Lola Pashalinksi *(Producer)*, Stefan Schnabel *(Professor)*, Steven Gilborn *(Tonda)*, Julianne Gilliam, Ruth Maleczech.

Former Andy Warhol actress, 1960's underground figure, and experienced stage actress Kirkland co-stars with Czechoslovakian supermodel Porizkova in this reworking of ALL ABOUT EVE. Porizkova is a Czech waif dressed in rags who leaves her homeland without money or a command of the English language. She arrives in New York City with a picture of "Anna"—a superstar Czech actress exiled during the communist invasion of 1968. When Porizkova tracks down Anna, played by Kirkland, she finds her idol trying to scrape together work way off-Broadway. Kirkland isn't happy with her life, struggling to get her next part and married to an inattentive director of rock videos. Kirkland and Porizkova find strength in one another and before long the little Czech waif is a *tres chic* actress who speaks perfect English. A first feature from Bogayevicz, co-scripted with Agnieszka Holland (director of the 1986 German film ANGRY HARVEST), and budgeted at under $1 million, ANNA received a limited release in 1987, coupled with film festival showings in New York, Chicago, and San Francisco. Porizkova, whose fame as a model has been heightened by her *Sports Illustrated* swimsuit photos and frequent appearances on "Late Night With David Letterman," has received nothing but praise, likening her film debut to that of Audrey Hepburn. Kirkland's performance earned her a shared Best Actress award from the Los Angeles Film Critics, which also acknowledged Holly Hunter's work in BROADCAST NEWS.

p, Yurek Bogayevicz, Zanne Devine; d, Yurek Bogayevicz; w, Agnieszka Holland (based on a story by Yurek Bogayevicz, Agnieszka Holland); ph, Bobby Bukowski; m, Greg Hawkes; ed, Julie Sloane; prod d, Lester Cohen; art d, Danny Talpers; set d, John Tatlock; cos, Hali Breindel.

(PR:NR MPAA:PG-13)

APAN GHAREY† (1987, India)

Prasanjit, Moon Moon Sen, Subhendu Chatterjee, Devika Mitra.

A story about a young man and his undying devotion to his mother. (In Bengali.)

p&d, Pinaki Chowdhury; m, Mrinal Banerjee.

Drama **(PR:NR MPAA:NR)**

APOUSIES† (1987, Gr.) 110m Greek Film Centre c (Trans: Absences)

Themis Bazaka, Pemy Zouni, Nikitas Tsakiroglou, Caterina Sarri, Maria Konstadakou, Nikos Tzoias, Elena Nathanail.

Relationships among three sisters during WW I is examined in a film greatly inspired by two paintings from Norwegian Edvard Munch—"The Three Seasons of Woman" and "The Cry."

p, George Crezias, George Katakouzinos; d, George Katakouzinos; w, George Katakouzinos, Dimitris Nollas; ph, Tassos Alexakis; m, Stamatis Spanoudakis; ed, Aristides Karydis-Fuchs; art d, Marilena Aravadinou; cos, Giannis Karidis.

Drama **(PR:NR MPAA:NR)**

ARCHANGELOS TOU PATHOUS† (1987, Gr.) 105m Greek Film Centre c (aka: POTLATCH)

Antonis Kafetzopoulos, Isabel Otero, Patrick Bauchau, Olia Lazaridou, Fenya Papadodima, Lydia Ewande, Ilona Coulom.

A story of a young man's passion for a girl named Aphrodite, whom he falls in love with after seeing her photo in a newspaper. Years later he tracks the girl down in Paris and vows to kill himself if he cannot make her fall in love with him.

p,d&w, Nicos Vergitsis; ph, Andreas Bellis; m, Dimitris Papadimitriou; ed, Giannis Tsitsopoulos; art d, Lili Pezanou.

Drama **(PR:NR MPAA:NR)**

AREIAS ESCALADANTES† (1987, Braz.) 105m Naive Producoes Aristicas c (Trans: Burning Sands)

Regina Case, Christina Ache, Diogo Vilela.

Shown at the 1987 Berlin Film Festival this comedy, set in the near future, concerns a group of terrorists in a mythical country.

d, Francisco de Paula.

Comedy **(PR:NR MPAA:NR)**

ARIA† (1987, US/Brit.) 98m RVP-Virgin Vision c

Sequence 1, "Un Ballo in Maschera": Theresa Russell *(King Zog)*, Stephanie Lane *(Baroness)*, Roy Hyatt, George Ellis Jones *(Chauffeurs)*, Sevilla Delofski *(Maid)*, Ruth Halliday *(Companion)*, Arthur Cox *(Major)*, Dennis Holmes *(Colonel)*, Paul Brightwell, Frank Baker, Chris Hunter *(Assassins)*, Paul Collard *(Valet)*, Danny Fitzgerald *(Mercedes Man)*, Johnny Dolye *(Blind Balloon Man)*, David Ross *(Doorman)*, Lucy Oliver *(Woman)*, Gordon Winter *(Man)*, Derek Farmer *(Motorbike Man)*, Michelle Read *(Nanny)*, Maximillian Roeg *(Child)*, voices of: Leontyne Price, Carlo Bergonzi, Robert Merrill, Shirley Verrett, Reri Grist; Sequence 2, "La Forza del Destino": Nicola Swain *(Marie)*, Jack Kyle *(Travis)*, Marianne McLoughlin *(Kate)*, voices of: Leontyne Price, Giorgio Tozzi, Ezio Flagello; Sequence 3, "Armide": Marion Peterson, Valerie Allain *(Young Girls)*, Jacques Neuville, Luke Corre, Christian Cauchon, Philippe Pellant, Patrice Linguet, Lionel Sorin, Jean Coffinet, Alexandre Des Granges, Gerrard Vives, Frederick Brosse, Pascal Bermont, Bernard Gaudray, Dominique Mano, Patrice Tridian *(Bodybuilders)*, voices of: Rachel Yakar, Zeger Vandersteene, Daniele Borst; Sequence 4, "Rigoletto": Buck Henry *(Preston)*, Anita Morris *(Phoebe)*, Beverly D'Angelo *(Gilda)*, Gary Kasper *(Jake)*, John Hostetter *(Elvis Impersonator)*, Albie Selznick *(Bellboy)*, Stan Mazin, Dominic Salinero, Jeff Calhoun *(Dancers)*, voices of: Alfredo Kraus, Anna Moffo, Annadi Stasio; Sequence 5, "Die Tote Stadt": Elizabeth Hurley *(Marietta)*, Peter Birch *(Paul)*, voices of: Carol Neblett, Rene Kollo; Sequence 6, "Les Boreades": Julie Hagerty, Genevieve Page, Cris Campion, Sandrine Dumas, Anne Canovas, Jody Guelb, Philipine Leroy-Beaulieu, Delphine Rich, Louis-Marie Taillefer, voices of: Jennifer Smith, Anne-Marie Rodde, Philip Langridge, Sequence 7, "Tristan und Isolde": Bridget Fonda, James Mathers *(The Lovers)*, Angie Tetamontie, Ester Buchanan, Lorraine Cote, Renee Korn *(Las Vegas Ladies)*, Bertha Weiss *(Lady with Glove)*, Diane Thorne, Howie Maurer *(Bride and Groom)*, Derick Coleman, Quentin Brown *(Indian Boys)*, voice of: Leontyne Price; Sequence 8, "Turandot": Linzi Drew *(Girl)*, Andreas Wisniewski, Kwabena Manso, Bella Enahoro, Bunty Mathias, Angela Walker, voice of: Jussi Bjoerling; Sequence 9, "Louise": Tilda Swinton *(Young Girl)*, Spencer Leigh *(Young Man)*, Amy Johnson *(Old Lady)*, voice of: Leontyne Price; Sequence 10, "I Pagliacci": John Hurt *(Actor)*, Sophie Ward *(Young Girl)*, Fernand Dumont *(Baritone Voice)*, voice of: Enrico Caruso.

Without dialog or narration, ARIA is a compilation of ten short filmed operas from some of cinema's most heralded directors, ranging from the most innovative (Godard, Roeg, Altman, Temple, Russell, Jarman) to the mainstream (Roddam, Beresford) to the obscure (Sturridge, Bryden). Produced by Don Boyd with the cooperation of Virgin Vision and RCA Video, each director had total control over his episode and filming took place all over the world, from London to Las Vegas. Besides the appeal of the directors and the composers (Verdi, Puccini, Wagner and others), ARIA boasts an odd variety of actors—John Hurt, Buck Henry, Beverly D'Angelo, Theresa Russell, Julie Haggerty—and two of film's most exciting new cinematographers—Oliver Stapleton (ABSOLUTE BEGINNERS, MY BEAUTIFUL LAUNDRETTE) and Frederick Elmes (BLUE VELVET, RIVER'S EDGE). Other directors who were approached to participate were Federico Fellini (whose early involvement helped gain financing for the project), Woody Allen, Hal Ashby, Jean-Jacques Beineix, Peter Brook, Werner Herzog, and David Byrne (who began pre-production but withdrew after a dispute with RCA). Released this year at the Cannes Film Festival and scheduled for a US theatrical release in 1988.

p, Don Boyd; Sequence 1: d&w, Nicolas Roeg; ph, Harvey Harrison; ed, Tony Lawson; m, Giuseppe Verdi; prod d, Diana Johnstone; cos, Shuna Harwood; ch, Terry Gilbert; makeup, Jenny Shircore, Anni Buchanan; Sequence 2: d&w, Charles Sturridge; ph, Gale Tattersall; ed, Matthew Longfellow; m, Giuseppe Verdi; prod d, Andrew McAlpine; cos, Leslie Gilda; sepc eff, Tom Harris; makeup, Penny Delamar Shawyer; Sequence 3: d&w, Jean-Luc Godard; ph, Carolyn Champetier; ed, Jean-Luc Godard; m, Jean-Baptiste Lully; prod d, Stephen Altman; set d, Arnaud De Moleron; cos, Jay Hay; makeup, Dominique De Vorges, Philomene Sammartino; Sequence 4: d, Julien Temple; ph, Oliver Stapleton; ed, Neil Abrahamson; m, Giuseppe Verdi; Sequence 5: d, Bruce Beresford; ph, Dante Spinotti; ed, Marie-Therese Boiche; m, Erich Wolfgang Korngold; Sequence 6: d, Robert Altman; ph, Pierre Mignot; m, Jean-Philippe Rameau; ed, Jennifer Auge; prod d, Scott Bushnell, John Hay; Sequence 7: d, Franc Roddam; ph, Frederick Elmes; m, Richard Wagner; ed, Rick Elgood; prod d, Mathew Jacobs; makeup, Vilborg Aradottir, Rick Casboro; Sequence 8: d&w, Ken Russell; ph, Gabriel Beristain; m, Giacomo Puccini; ed, Michael Bradsell; prod d, Paul Dufficey; cos, Victoria Russell; spec eff, Tom Harris; makeup, Penny Delamar Shawyer, Glauca Rossi, Phylis Cohen, Glynn McKay; Sequence 9: d&w, Derek Jarman; ph, Mike Southon; m, Gustave Charpentier; ed, Peter Cartwright, Angus Cook; prod d, Christopher Hobbs; cos, Sandy Powell; makeup, Morag Ross; Sequence 10 and linking scenario: d, Bill Bryden; ph, Gabriel Beristain; m, Ruggero Leoncavallo; ed, Marie-Therese Boiche; cos, Alison Chitty; makeup, Penny Delamar Shawyer.

Opera **(PR:NR MPAA:NR)**

AROUND THE WORLD IN EIGHTY WAYS**** (1987, Aus.) 91m Palm Beach Ent.-Australian European Finance-Commonwealth Bank of Australia c

Philip Quast *(Wally Davis)*, Allan Penney *(Roly Davis)*, Gosia Dobrowolska *(Nurse Ophelia Cox)*, Diana Davidson *(Mavis Davis)*, Kelly Dingwall *(Eddie Davis)*, Rob Steele *(Alec Moffatt)*, Judith Fisher *(Lotte Boyle)*, Jane Markey *(Miserable Midge)*, John Howard *(Dr. Proctor)*, Frank Lloyd *(Mr. Tinkle)*, Cathren Michalak *(Mrs. Tinkle)*, Ric Carter *(Financier)*, Jack Allan *(Mailman)*, Nell Schofield *(Scottish Scrooge)*, Kaarin Fairfax *(Checkout Chick)*, Micki Gardner, Helen Simon, Elizabeth Burton *(Geisha Girls)*.

For some time the Australians have been known for exporting powerful dramas and wild action films, but of late they have found new success with comedy, mainly on the strength of CROCODILE DUNDEE, the most lucrative foreign film ever to play the US. While the world waits for Paul Hogan to get his sequel under way, however, this superb bizarre comedy has passed unnoticed by all but a few festival attenders. Penney is an old man who over the years has lost his business, his health, his eyesight, and his ability to walk. He also has watched his former partner (Steele) grow successful and disgusting as he constructs a residential monument to bad taste right next door. His wife (Davidson) is fed up with taking care of the old man and she finally resolves to put him into a nursing home and take the world tour of which she has always dreamed. Steele, however, has always dreamed of Davidson, and he books himself on the same tour, with seduction in mind. Meanwhile, Penney's gay son, Quast, a small-time banana plantation tour guide on Australia's north shore, is about to lose his business unless he can raise some money, so he heads home to see what he can milk out of the family. When his audio-expert younger brother (Dingwall) takes him to the deplorable old folk's home to visit Penney, they learn of a secret bank account that the old man wants to use to chase after his wife. The sons decide to take Penney home and stage the trip for him in Steele's house and backyard. They are joined in this performance by Dobrowolska, a nurse from the home with some unorthodox treatments she wants to try. The first stop on the imaginary tour is Hawaii, where Quast impersonates a hula girl, a hotel clerk, and more as he is floated around in the pool while Dingwall plays convincing sound effects. When Penney demands to see his wife, they tell him that she has already left for Las Vegas. They push him through a shopping mall, telling him it's the airport, and then aboard a bus they pass off as a plane, driving up a steep hill to simulate takeoff. For their mock Las Vegas they light up the whole place, with Quast playing a black chauffeur, Elvis Presley, a chorus girl, and others. By this time, however, Penney is starting to regain some of his old vigor and a little of his vision. They hustle him along to "Rome," but while the others sleep, he wakes up and tries to go for a walk. A familiar dog reveals to him where he is, and he decides to see how far they can take their game. He demands to see the Pope, who Quast duly impersonates; then he wants to go to Tokyo. Receiving a blow on the head, he recovers his vision completely, but he keeps this fact secret, demanding geisha girls. When he learns that Steele and his wife are returning—having barely escaped a tidal wave on what turned out to be a nightmarish trip—Penney decides to destroy the house, overturning the pool with a forklift just as the bus lets Steele and Davidson off out front. The happy ending has the entire family living "up north" (the tropics, from a down under perspective) and running a dance school.

A thoroughly enjoyable comedy with some loopy humor and a convoluted but easy-to-understand plot that never stops moving. The cast all seem to be having a good time, one of the best qualities any movie can have, with Quast and Dobrowolska particularly delightful. The film was obviously made under heavy budgetary constraints, but these only seem to enhance the story, in which the sons don't have much money for staging their illusions either. Director Maclean makes his feature debut here, and an auspicious one it is. American audiences will almost certainly be denied a wider opportunity to see this film (unless it surfaces on video), so we can only hope that Maclean will have more success in the future.

p, David Elfick, Steve Knapman; d, Stephen Maclean; w, Stephen Maclean, Paul Leadon; ph, Louis Irving (Colorfilm); m, Chris Neal; ed, Marc von Buuren; prod d, Lissa Coote; cos, Clarrissa Patterson.

Comedy **(PR:A-C MPAA:NR)**

ARPAN† (1987, India) BAM

Tapas Paul, Debasree Roy, Prasanjit.

A story revolving around the interconnecting love affairs of three people—an enlightened young woman, an aristocrat, and a philanthropist. (In Bengali.)

d, Srinivas Chakraborty; m, Ajay Das.

Romance **(PR:NR MPAA:NR)**

ARQUIESTA EMILIO VARELA† (1987, Mex.) 87m Cipsa/Peliculas Mexicanas (Trans: Emilio Varela's Band)

Mario Almada *(Emilio Varela)*, Silvia Manriquez *(Camelia)*, Jorge Russek, Jose Castro.

Almada is part of a counterfeiting operation who wants to quit the business. Manriquez, head of the operation, has Almada shot and his body dumped in the desert. He's found by a woman and her uncle who nurse him back to health so that he can take vengeance on Manriquez and her gang.

p, Miguel Angel Barragan; d, Ralph Portillo; w, Ralph Portillo, Jose Castro; ph, Adolfo Martinez Solares; m, Rafael Carrion; ed, Pedro Velasquez.

Crime **(PR:NR MPAA:NR)**

AS TIME GOES BY† (1987, Aus.) 97m Monroe Stahr/Valhalla c

Bruno Lawrence *(Ryder)*, Nique Needles *(Mike)*, Max Gillies *(Joe Bogart, The Alien)*, Ray Barrett *(J.L. Weston)*, Marcelle Schmitz *(Connie Stanton)*, Mitchell Faircloth *(James McCauley)*, Deborah Force *(Cheryl)*, Christine Keogh *(Margie)*, Don Bridges *(Ern)*, Ian Shrives *(Greaser)*, Jane Clifton *(Mechanic)*, Chris Kiely *(Connie's Father)*.

Needles plays a young surfer who travels to the Australian desert and gets involved with alien visitors. In this case the aliens have disguised their space craft as a 1940s diner, which is run by Gilles, an alien who speaks in phrases from old movies while doing impressions of such stars as Humphrey Bogart, James Cagney and even Greta Garbo.

Chris Kiely; d&w, Barry Peak; ph, John Ogden; m, Peter Sullivan; ed, Ralph Strasser; prod d, Paddy Reardon.

Science Fiction **(PR:NR MPAA:NR)**

ASI COMO HABIAN SIDO† (1987, Span.) 88m Multivideo ALPC c (Trans: The Way They Were)

Massimo Ghini *(Tomas, Concert Pianist)*, Juan Diego *(Alberto)*, Antonio Banderas *(Damian)*, Nina Van Pallandt *(Elena, Tomas' Wife)*, Ana Vasoni *(Carol)*.

Ghini is an acclaimed concert pianist who leaves the US to return to Spain and seek out two college friends who are also musicians and whom he hasn't seen in more than ten years. One friend is now a record company employee, while the other is living a life of solitude, an accident having rendered his left arm useless. As he meets his old friends and talks of the past, Ghini learns how important they have been to his success.

d, Andres Linares; w, Andres Linares, Joaquin Jorda; ph, Federico Ribes (Eastmancolor); ed, Guillermo S. Maldonado; set d, Fernando Verdugo; cos, Maria Jose Iglesias.

Drama **(PR:NR MPAA:NR)**

ASIGNATURA APROBADA† (1987, Span.) 95m Nickelodeon Dos/United c (Trans: Passing the Course)

Jesus Puente *(Jose Manuel Alcantara, Playwright)*, Victoria Vera *(Elena)*, Teresa Gimpera *(Lola/Dr. Perkins)*, Eduardo Hoyo *(Edi)*, Pastor Serrador *(Doctor)*, Manuel Lorenzo *(Manolo)*, Pablo Hoyo *(Pablo)*, Juan Cueto *(Juan)*, Santiago Amon *(Don Santiago)*, Pedro Lazaga *(Miguel)*.

Seemingly a sequel to his first film, 1977's ASIGNATURA PENDIENTE (Flunking Out), Garci's latest effort focuses on Puente, who bemoans the world's inhumanity and his own inability to find happiness. Garci, whose VOLVER A EMPEZAR won an Academy Award in 1982 as best foreign film, is Spain's only Oscar-winning director.

p&d, Jose Luis Garci; w, Jose Luis Garci, Horacio Valcarcel; ph, Manuel Rojas (Fujicolor); m, Jesus Gluck, Johann Strauss, Sr.; ed, Miguel Gonzalez Sinde; set d, Jesus Quiros, Luis Vazquez; cos, Maiki Marin; makeup, Romi Gonzalez.

Drama **(PR:NR MPAA:NR)**

ASSASSINATION½** (1987) 88m Golan-Globus/Cannon c

Charles Bronson *(Jay Killian)*, Jill Ireland *(Laramie Royce Craig)*, Stephen Elliott *(Fitzroy)*, Jan Gan Boyd *(Charlotte Chang)*, Randy Brooks *(Tyler Loudermilk)*, Erik Stern *(Reno Bracken)*, Michael Ansara *(Sen. Hector Bunsen)*, James Staley *(Briggs)*, Kathryn Leigh Scott *(Polly Sims)*, James Acheson *(Osborne Weems)*, Jim McMullan *("The Zipper")*, William Prince *(H.H. Royce)*, William Hayes *(Pritchard Young)*, Charles Howerton *(President Calvin Craig)*, Chris Alcaide *(Chief Justice)*, Jack Gill *(Kerry Fane)*, Mischa Hausserman *(Danzig)*, Robert Axelrod *(Finney)*, Peter Lupus *(TV Announcer)*, Lori Stephens *(Female TV Reporter)*, Beverly Thompson *(June Merkel)*, Natalie Alexander *(Claire Thompson)*, Linda Harwood *(Sally Moore)*, Mihoko Tokoro *(Reporter)*, Susan J. Thompson *(Journalist)*, Arthur Hansel *(Barstow)*, John Salvi *(Platt)*, Frank Zagarino *(Secret Service Driver)*, Tony Borgia *(Bomb Squad Man)*, Paul McCallum *(Sandy Ott)*, Robert Dowdell *(Capt. Ogilvy, "Cappy")*, Vivian Tyus *(Maid)*, Jason Scura *(Capt. Hammond)*, David L. Bilson *(Wally Maine)*, Larry Sellers *(Indian Joe)*, Elizabeth Lauren *(Moonbeam)*, Lucille Bliss *(Crone)*, John Hawker *(Porter)*, J. Michael Patterson *(Conductor)*, James Clark *(Locomotive Engineer)*, Ed Levitt, Michael Welden *(FBI Agents)*.

A harebrained thriller rolled off the Cannon assembly line, ASSASSINATION stars Ireland as the First Lady and Bronson as the Secret Service agent assigned to protect her. These are post-Ron and Nancy days and the new First Lady is a far cry from Mrs. Reagan (several references are made to her). She is a free-and-easy adventurer who is determined to live life to its fullest, regardless of the embarrassment this causes her husband. She especially doesn't like the Secret Service tailing her and ordering her around. Caught in the cross fire is Bronson, a consummate professional who is determined to keep a tight grip on the First Lady's reins. They get off to a bad start and Bronson is temporarily reassigned at the behest of Ansara, a senator with close ties to the President. After a few attempts are made on the First Lady's life, Ireland is finally convinced that she *is* in danger. When Bronson isn't saving Ireland's life, he is warding off the sexual advances of his partner, Boyd, a cute and perky nymphomaniac who is more than willing to become Bronson's wife. Eventually, the determined Ireland sneaks away from Washington. Bronson, however, is right behind her, and the two head across country in order to avoid her assassins. The truth about Ireland is slowly revealed. She entered into a marriage agreement because no one believed that a bachelor could get elected. It was then agreed that she would get a discreet divorce and continue living her life in the fast lane. The power-hungry Ansara, however, fears a scandal that will damage the President's chances of re-election and believes the commander in chief will have more luck with the voters as a widower than as a divorcee. A final confrontation between Bronson and Ansara ends with the latter's death. Ireland is left to deal with the problems of being the First Lady, and Bronson resigns from the force, having to contend with Boyd's recurring marriage request.

Far less violent than his DEATH WISH films, this Bronson vehicle is a slipshod production from start to finish. Although it has an interesting, albeit implausible, premise, ASSASSINATION must battle a pathetic script by Sale (he previously penned the Frank Sinatra vehicle SUDDENLY and John Ford's WHEN WILLIE COMES MARCHING HOME), unexciting direction by Hunt (whose career has gone downhill since his 1969 debut, ON HER MAJESTY'S SECRET SERVICE), and some less-than-inspired acting by both leads. The script tries to be witty and marginally humorous, but comedy has never been Bronson's forte and here the lines just don't come off. Oddly, while Bronson and Ireland are married in real life, there is very little chemistry between them on screen. The film only clicks when the adorable Boyd (A CHORUS LINE) appears. The plot has enough twists and turns to make it better suited for a comic book. Nothing is very plausible, but maybe that's the point. If the farce had been carried out, then maybe ASSASSINATION would have been enjoyable; instead it's just a bungled attempt. *(Sexual situations, violence.)*

p, Pancho Kohner; d, Peter Hunt; w, Richard Sale; ph, Hanania Baer (TVC Color); m, Robert O. Ragland, Valentine McCallum; ed, James Heckert; prod d, William Cruse; md, Paula Erickson; art d, Joshua S. Culp; set d, Patricia Hall; cos, Shelley Komarov; stunts, Jack Gill; makeup, Claudia Thompson.

Drama/Action **Cas.** **(PR:A-C MPAA:PG-13)**

ATTENTION BANDITS** (1987, Fr.) 108m Films 13-TFI/AAA c (Trans: Warning, Bandits)

Jean Yanne *(Simon Verini)*, Marie-Sophie L. [Lelouch] *(Marie-Sophie)*, Patrick Bruel *(Mozart)*, Charles Gerard *(Tonton)*, Corinne Marchand *(Manouchka)*, Christine Barbelivien *(Mme. Verini)*, Helene Surgere, Herve Favre.

In 1976, a sophisticated outlaw (Jean Yanne) enjoys a moment of serenity on his family estate as he teaches his small daughter (Marie-Sophie L.) and a close family friend (Patrick Bruel) the refined art of fishing. When they return to Yanne's mansion, a television newscaster is bemoaning the loss of actor Jean Gabin, whose death, he feels, will bring about the decline of the gangster film. The subsequent announcement of a robbery at Cartier's famed jewelry store is seemingly ignored by the family in the wake of the great actor's demise. Bruel, the leader of the gang responsible for the theft at Cartier's, brings the stolen loot to Yanne so that he may exchange it for them at a premium price. Yanne's wife is then kidnaped and held for ransom by two of the gang members in an effort to get the jewels back. After the merchandise is returned, she is murdered by one of the fleeing bandits. Yanne's only visible reaction is to send his daughter to a Swiss boarding school to prevent her from learning of her mother's death. He is then framed for the theft, apprehended, and sentenced to ten years in prison. From his cell, he carries on a correspondence with his daughter, who is unaware of his whereabouts. She is regaled with an unending assortment of manufactured tales of her father's adventures around the world and her mother's mysterious activities in South America. In her own letters, she tells stories of her emotional and physical growth, much to the delight of her father. Eventually she learns her father is in a prison cell and her mother is dead.

Moving forward to 1986, Marie-Sophie L., during her ten-year separation from her father, has created an image of her father based solely on his letters to her. After his release from prison occurs, he entertains her with his charmingly underhanded acts, and she concludes that they are extensions of his heroic character. She is invited to accompany her father to a festive dance where she happens upon Bruel, an outcast in the family since the death of her mother. While her father is busy uncovering the identities of the killers, she assesses Bruel and concludes that he did not murder her mother. Yanne suddenly packs up his daughter and her friend Bruel, and takes them to a small hotel where he guns down the pair of men who were responsible for the death of his wife. Marie-Sophie L. is appalled by her father's chilling act, and moves away with her new lover (Charles Gerard). Yanne, in the meantime, is transported back to prison when the body of his dead wife is excavated on his former estate. The moral dilemma quickly and effortlessly resolves itself for Marie-Sophie L., and she implores the shifty Bruel to help her father escape from jail. Through an utterly preposterous series of events, he does successfully obtain the older man's release. She reluctantly informs her present lover of the arrangement she has made—to marry Bruel if he successfully extricates her father from jail—and he accepts this as a fact of life. She broods about this new crisis at her father's hideout while she awaits the barge that will slip him out of the country. When she finds Bruel serenely fishing along the canal, she decides their relationship is one worth testing.

The TV announcer commenting on the death of Jean Gabin asserts that, without Gabin, gangster films are sunk. Director Lelouch has wisely avoided an attempt at resurrecting the genre and uses Gabin's death as a springboard for his portrayal of the gangster as venerable and ultimately impotent rather than as iconographic and truly dynamic. But his real fascination lies with the presentation of the gangster's daughter (not surprising since Marie-Sophie L. is the real-life Mrs. Lelouch), her discovery and assessment of a questionable family background, and her attempts to forge a separate identity for herself. Moreover, the film continually engages the audience by promoting a fundamental but often forgotten principle of motion picture entertainment—to transform the presentation of a real state into the experience of an illusory one. In a noteworthy scene where Lelouch's sleight of hand is put to masterful use, Marie-Sophie L. watches from behind a closed automobile window as her father makes his entry from the enclosure of the prison walls into an expanse of open space. His movements toward the vehicle, viewed by the audience as a reflection in his daughter's section of the car window, enable father and daughter to magically occupy the same visual and emotional planes, but not the same material one. When he steps out of the reflection and into the vehicle to join her, he crosses the barrier that will transform the illusion of his resurgence into the recognition of his irrelevance. Unfortunately, the emphasis of Lelouch's story is placed on the plotting without much regard for narrative logic or character motivation. Characters are plunged into a series of critical situations, given a brief set of insipid lines of dialog to exchange, then bounced along to endure another series of excruciating events. By the conclusion of the film a lifetime of human crises have been exposed without the slightest insight into the experiences. *(Adult situations.)*

p&d, Claude Lelouch; w, Claude Lelouch, Pierre Uytterhoeven; ph, Jean-Yves Le Mener (Fujicolor); m, Francis Lai; ed, Hugues Darmois; art d, Jacques Bufnoir.

Crime **(PR:C MPAA:NR)**

AU REVOIR, LES ENFANTS† (1987, Fr./Ger.) 104m Nouvelles Editions de Films-MK2-Stella-NEF/MK2 c (Trans: Goodbye, Children)

Gaspard Manesse *(Julien)*, Raphael Fejto *(Bonnet)*, Francine Racette *(Mme. Quentin)*, Stanislas Carre de Malberg *(Francois Quentin)*, Philippe Morier-Genoud *(Father Jean)*, Francois Berleand *(Father Michel)*, Francois Negret *(Joseph)*, Peter Fitz *(Muller)*, Pascal Rivet, Benoit Henriet, Richard Leboeuf, Xavier Legrand, Arnaud Henriet.

After more than a decade in the US, making such films as PRETTY BABY, ATLANTIC CITY, and MY DINNER WITH ANDRE, Louis Malle returned to his native France to make this semi-autobiographical film set in his homeland in

1944. The story is seen through the eyes of Manesse, an 11-year-old student in a Catholic boarding school. The school officials, in a quiet way, have taken a stand against the Nazis who occupy France, and the brutal anti-Semitism they purvey. Jewish students are enrolled in the school under false names in an effort to protect them from the clutches of the Gestapo. One of these students is Fejto, and Manesse befriends the boy, not knowing he is Jewish, but gradually becoming aware of his friend's "secret." Nazi defeats along the Eastern front lead the Gestapo to be more dutiful than ever in searching for Jews and Resistance members, and their scrutiny of the school intensifies. Finally, after being given information by Negret, a former employee of the school fired for black-market activities, the Nazis raid the school and arrest Morier-Genoud, the school's director, Fejto, and two other Jewish students.

Malle has stated that he has wanted to make this film since the beginning of his career, but the painful memories it depicts were difficult for him to face. Though it did not receive a US release in 1987, it did play several film festivals, including Telluride, and was shown in Los Angeles in December to qualify for the 1988 Oscars (it was selected as the official French entry in the Foreign Film Oscar competition). The film was named Best Foreign Film for 1987 by the Los Angeles Film Critics, and won the Golden Lion for best film at the 1987 Venice Film Festival.

p,d&w, Louis Malle; ph, Renato Berta; ed, Emmanuelle Castro; art d, Willy Holt.

Historical **(PR:NR MPAA:NR)**

AURELIA† (1987, It.) 86m Antea-Telecentauro/BIM c

Maddalena Crippa *(Guiditta)*, Fabio Sartor *(Tommaso)*, Nicola Pistoia *(Car Driver)*, Carlo Monni *(Truck Driver)*, Vittorio Crippa *(Bicyclist)*, Macha Musi, Gastone Moschin.

A talky and philosophical story about a man who meets a beautiful stranger while traveling the northern Italian road of the title on his way to his wedding. In the two days before the wedding, the man and woman carry on a passionate romance—the man's last fling before commiting himself to his wife.

d&w, Giorgio Molteni; ph, Raffaele Mertes (Technicolor); m, Paolo Conte; ed, Carlo Fontana.

Drama **(PR:NR MPAA:NR)**

AUTUMN'S TALE, AN† (1987, Hong Kong) 98m D&B c

Chow Yun Fat, Cheri Chung, Danny Chan, Gigi Wong, Wong Man, Brenda Lo, Joyce Houseknecht, Cindy Ou.

Chung leaves her home country to go to school in New York, where she is to study acting. Once there, she is reunited with Chan, her wealthy boy friend, only to find he has a new beau. Fat, a distant relative, helps over her trauma and advises her on how to adjust to life in the US. He falls in love with her, but is unable to convey his feelings for her, and the two part as merely friends at the film's end.

p, John Sham; d, Yuen Ting Chueng; w, Alex Law; m, Lowell Lo.

Romance **(PR:NR MPAA:NR)**

AVRIL BRISE† (1987, Fr.) 100m JM-Telema Smepa-La Franco American-La Sept-Icav./JM c (Trans: Broken April)

Jean-Claude Audelin *(Gjerg)*, Violeta Sanchez *(Diane Vorpsi)*, Alexandre Arbatt *(Bessian Vorpsi)*, Sadri Sheta, Hasan Zhubi, Xhemil Vraniqi, Hajredim Islamaj.

Set in a remote area of Albania in 1933, AVRIL BRISE concerns a government emissary's attempts to settle a long-running feud between two mountain families. The feud, which has claimed over 40 lives in the last century, is perpetuated when Audelin kills the man who murdered his brother. Arbatt, the emissary, tries to bring a Western sensibility to the senseless feud but cannot cut through the strictly obeyed Albanian customs. The script was penned by French film critic Assayas and Greek novelist Vassilikos, whose novel *Z* was brought to the screen by Costa-Gavras.

p, Frederic Mitterrand, Charles Gassot, Jacques Arnaud, Jacques Tronel, Denys Pleutot; d, Liria Begeja; w, Liria Begeja, Olivier Assayas, Vassilis Vassilikos (based on the novel by Ismail Kadare); ph, Patrick Blossier; m, Steve Beresford; ed, Luc Barnier; prod d, Michel Lagrange; cos, Judy Shewsbury.

Drama **(PR:NR MPAA:NR)**

AZ ERDO KAPITANYA† (1987, Hung.) 80m Pannonia c (Trans: The Captain of the Forest)

The evil cat-criminal Zero engages in kidnaping and fraud, all the while pursued by the Chief Inspector Captain.

d, Attila Dargay; w, Jozsef Nepp, Attila Dargay; ph, Iren Henrik, Arpad Lossonczy (Eastmancolor); m, Zsolt Petho; ed, Magda Hap; prod d, Atilla Dargay.

Animated/Children's **(PR:NR MPAA:NR)**

AZ UTOLSO KEZIRAT† (1987, Hung.) 109m Mafilm Dialog Studio/Hungarofilm c (Trans: The Last Manuscript)

Jozef Kroner *(Gyorgy Nyary, the Writer)*, Alexander Bardini *(Aurel Mark [Relli])*, Eszter Nagy-Kalozy *(Flora)*, Iren Psota *(Vica)*, Hedi Varadi *(Emilia)*, Bela Both *(Franz)*.

A dying writer's final days cause a great deal of heartache for those close to him who fear his rumoured final manuscript contains damaging information. Each person involved is convinced the manuscript contains something that will prove personally harmful. The writer's wife fears she will lose her social status; certain government officials fear they will be exposed; dissident intellectuals fear the same; and one close friend has been paid to use his friendship to uncover the missing manuscript. Director Makk, whose LILY IN LOVE received much critical acclaim, opens his film with a surreal scene of the writer's funeral in which the writer rises from his coffin and walks toward his grave. The film was shown in competition at this year's Cannes Film Festival.

d, Karoly Makk; w, Karoly Makk, Zoltan Kamondy (based on the novel *A Merry Funeral* by Tibor Dery); ph, Janos Toth (Eastmancolor); m, Laszlo Vidovszky; ed, Gyorgy Sivo; art d, Tamas Vayer; cos, Emoke Csengey.

Drama **(PR:NR MPAA:NR)**

B

BABETTE'S GASTEBUD† (1987, Den.) 102m Just Betzer-Panorama Film Int'l.-Nordisk-Danish Film Institute/Walter Manley c (Trans: Babette's Feast)

Stephane Audran *(Babette)*, Jean-Philippe Lafont *(Achille Papin)*, Gudmar Wivesson *(Lorenz Lowenhielm as a Young Man)*, Jarl Kulle *(Lorenz Lowenhielm as a Old Man)*, Bibi Andersson *(Swedish Court Lady-In-Waiting)*, Hanne Stensgaard *(Young Filippa)*, Bodil Kjer *(Old Filippa)*, Vibeke Hastrup *(Young Martine)*, Birgitte Federspiel *(Old Martine)*, Bendt Rothe *(Old Nielsen)*, Ebbe Rode *(Christopher)*, Lisbeth Movin *(The Widow)*, Prebe Lerdorff Rye *(The Captain)*, Pouel Kern *(The Vicar)*, Michel Bouquet *(Narrator's Voice)*, Tina Kiberg *(Filippa's Singing Voice)*, Axel Strobye *(Driver)*, Ebba With, Else Petersen, Therese Hojgaard, Asta Esper Andersen, Finn Nielsen, Holger Perfort, Erik Petersen, Lars Lohmann, Tine Miehe-Renard.

Based on a novella by famed Danish writer Isak Dinesen (the author and subject of OUT OF AFRICA), this film is packed with emotions as it explores the artist's role in society. Audran (the wife of director Claude Chabrol and the winner of a Cesar for her performance in VIOLETTE), plays the title character, a Frenchwoman who, in 1871, has fled the Paris Commune and seeks refuge in a fishing village on the rugged coast of Denmark's Jutland peninsula. She is taken in by Federspiel and Kjer, the daughters of the town's late minister, who still casts a huge shadow over the austere lives of his former flock. To earn her keep, Audran cooks for the sisters, preparing them the drab meals of cod and ale-and-bread soup called for by their spartan doctrines. Her single connection with her French past is the lottery ticket that a friend purchases for her yearly. After 14 years, Audran wins 10,000 Golden Francs in the lottery. Rather than return to France, she decides to use the money to prepare a sumptuous feast for the townspeople. It is revealed that she had been a renowned culinary artist in Paris, the *chef de cuisine* of the Cafe Anglais. However, the prospect of such a feast poses a moral dilemma for the spartan locals.

BABETTE'S GASTEBUD caused quite a stir in Denmark as a result of the handling of its domestic distribution. Nordisk showed the film in two of its own Copenhagen venues but offered only limited access to other exhibitors, and BABETTE'S producers accused the distributor of pursuing its self-interest to the ultimate detriment of the film's success. It was directed by Gabriel Axel, a Dane who was born in Paris and has worked in both Denmark and France. In addition to a number of notable actors from the Danish stage, the film features performances by Ingmar Bergman stalwarts Jarl Kulle and Bibi Andersson and French opera star Jean-Philippe Lafont.

p, Bo Christensen; d&w, Gabriel Axel (based on the novel by Karen Blixen); ph, Henning Kristiansen (Eastmancolor); m, Per Norgard; ed, Finn Henriksen; art d, Sven Wichman; cos, Annelise Hauberg, Pia Myrdal, Karl Lagerfeld; spec eff, Henning Bahs.

Drama **(PR:NR MPAA:NR)**

BABULA† (1987, India) C.F.S.

Sanghamitra, Swastik, Sarat Pujari, Anita Das, Debu Brahma, Gadi, Basant Samal, Nathuram.

The first children's film in the Oriya language.

d, Sadhu Meher; m, Bhubaneshwar Misra.

Children's **(PR:NR MPAA:NR)**

BABY BOOM*** (1987) 103m UA/MGM-UA c

Diane Keaton *(J.C. Wiatt, Management Consultant)*, Harold Ramis *(Steven Buchner, Investment Banker)*, Sam Wanamaker *(Fritz Curtis)*, Sam Shepard *(Dr. Jeff Cooper, Veterinarian)*, James Spader *(Ken Arrenberg)*, Pat Hingle *(Hughes Larrabee)*, Britt Leach *(Vern Boone)*, Kristina Kennedy, Michelle Kennedy *(Elizabeth Wiatt)*, Mary Gross *(Receptionist)*, Victoria Jackson *(Eve, the Nanny)*, Annie Shyer *(Young Girl at Dance)*, Jack Hall, Dorothy Hall *(Restaurant Guests)*, Linda Ellerbee *(Narrator)*, Kim Sebastian, Patricia Estrin, Elizabeth Bennett, Peter Elbing, Shera Danese.

Although it has roots in the Frank Capra, Preston Sturges, and Howard Hawks comedies of the 1930s, BABY BOOM is the type of film that could only exist in the 1980s. In what other decade could the audience be expected to believe that a woman has no concept of child rearing? It has always been assumed that women have had a natural ability (something biological even) that makes them adept at motherhood, but in BABY BOOM that is proven a misconception. As we are told through Linda Ellerbee's opening narration, Keaton is a high-powered business executive who lives for her job. She earns a six-figure salary, lives in a ritzy Manhattan high-rise, and has an equally over-achieving live-in lover, Ramis. Her life changes drastically, however, when she inherits a 14-month-old girl from two distant relatives who have just been killed. Keaton is determined not to take the child ("I can't have a baby. I have a 12:30 lunch meeting," she explains), but is railroaded into it. Naturally, Keaton's life is turned upside down. She has just been offered a partnership by her boss, Wanamaker, who has warned her that she cannot "have it all." She puts the child up for adoption but grows too attached to the girl to go through with the process. The demands of child rearing cause her to fall behind in her work, losing her chance at a partnership. She then loses her top account and is ultimately forced to resign. To make things even worse, Ramis moves out when the baby moves in. Having said goodbye to the Manhattan rat race, Keaton purchases a 62-acre farmhouse in rural Virginia and discovers the simple life. In just a few days time, her pipes freeze, her roof collapses under the weight of a blizzard, and her well dries up. She has all but packed for her return to New York when she meets Shepard, a calm, reassuring veterinarian who takes a liking to the sophisticated city girl. Keaton denies her attraction to Shepard but by the time spring rolls around she is in love with him. In the meantime, Keaton's entrepreneurial skills lead to a rapidly expanding gourmet baby food business. A business call from Wanamaker coaxes her back to New York for a proposed buy-out of her company. Instead of returning to the rat race, Keaton turns down a $3 million offer and heads back to her lover and child in Virginia.

The most amazing aspect of BABY BOOM's often trite and cliched script is that it takes a situation which begins as a yuppie nightmare (an unexpected child interfering with one's professional life) and turns it into the American Dream. Once Keaton's professional life is destroyed she turns right around, starts anew, pulls herself up by her bootstraps, and makes a name for herself—all the while preparing herself for a Norman Rockwell-like nuclear family. Since the script is just one notch above a TV sitcom, it is Keaton who must carry the film. While she often has trouble shedding her ANNIE HALL mannerisms, here they crop up only occasionally, working to her advantage when they do. (After all, her "Annie Hall" character must be partially credited with being an early prototype of the 1980s career woman.) Keaton is too spacey to be credible as a shrewd business-woman (her nickname is the "Tiger Lady") and she never really convinces as a mother, either. Somehow, she manages to survive the script's inanities and make her character real. Not since ANNIE HALL has Keaton's "gee-whiz" personality and excellent comic ability been so properly used. This is even more surprising, since her costar is an adorable baby—the kind which steals scenes from less accomplished performers. The baby is actually played by twin girls Kristina and Michelle Kennedy, thereby enabling the production to comply with child labor laws. As for the rest of the cast, Ramis is little more than a walk-on, Wanamaker is superb in his power position, Spader is again the cold-hearted young Republican on the move, and Shepard has all the down-home, earthy qualities one would expect from Gary Cooper (not coincidentally his character name is Cooper). Undermining the film are Conti's pathetically sappy score (with a theme song by Burt Bacharach and Carole Bayer Sager) and Fraker's cinematography which relies too heavily on the softness of diffusion filters and the TV commercial technique of atmospheric smoke. BABY BOOM is an enjoyable, though flawed, film which is chiefly interesting as an examination of the yuppie culture. In 1979's KRAMER VS. KRAMER it was the Dustin Hoffman businessman who discovered the joy of parenting. At that time women were striving to rise in the business world. As a result, motherhood took a back seat to professionalism, and maternity clothes were replaced by gray power suits and running shoes. Once again, however, cultural demographics point to a rise in the number of working women who want to become mothers. In that respect, BABY BOOM is most interesting in its redefinition of the term "having it all." *(Mild profanity.)*

p, Nancy Meyers; d, Charles Shyer; w, Nancy Meyers, Charles Shyer; ph, William A. Fraker; m, Bill Conti; ed, Lynzee Klingman; prod d, Jeffrey Howard; art d, Beala Neel; set d, Lisa Fischer; cos, Susan Becker; m/l, Burt Bacharach, Carole Bayer Sager, Bill Conti.

Comedy **(PR:A MPAA:PG)**

BACH AND BROCCOLI† (1987, Can.) 90m La Fete/Cinema Plus c (BACH ET BOTTINE)

Mahee Paiement *(Fanny)*, Raymond Legault *(Jonathan)*, Harry Marciano *(Sean)*, Andree Pelletier *(Bernice)*, France Arbour *(Grandmother)*, Jacqueline Barrette, Regent Gauvin, Jack Robitaille, Marie-France Carrier, Marie Michaud, Pierrette Robitaille, Marcel Leboeuf, Pierick Houdy, Murielle Dutil, Patrick St. Pierre, Louis-George Girard.

Paiment is an 11-year-old girl whose parents are killed in a car accident. She's sent to stay with Legault, her uncle, a bachelor set in his ways who does not welcome the intruder. He is obsessed with the composer Bach and spends most of his time getting ready to enter a Bach organ competition. She loves animals, especially her pet skunk, Broccoli. Slowly they become attached to one another, and when Paiment is to be sent to a foster home, Legault won't let her go.

p, Rock Demers; d, Andre Melancon; w, Bernadette Renaud, Andre Melancon; ph, Guy Dufaux; m, Pierick Houdy; art d, Violette Daneau; cos, Hugette Gagne; m/l, Michel Rivaud, Fabienne Thibault; makeup, Daine Simard.

Comedy/Drama **(PR:NR MPAA:NR)**

BACHELOR GIRL† (1987, Aus.) 83m Film Victoria-Australian Film Commission/Yarra Bank c

Lyn Pierse *(Dot Bloom)*, Kim Gyngell *(Karl Stanton)*, Jan Friedl *(Helen Carter)*, Bruce Spence *(Alistair Dredge Jr.)*, Doug Tremlett *(Charles)*, Ruth Yaffe *(Aunt Esther)*, Jack Perry *(Uncle Isaac)*, Monica Maughan *(Sybil)*, Tim Robertson *(Grant)*, Mark Minchinton *(Gazza)*, Denis Moore *(Bert)*, Gary Samolin *(Morris Glass)*, Sue Jones *(Audrey Amore)*.

Pierse is a single, 32-year-old woman with "82 potted plants to support." She earns a living writing scripts for a soap opera, and spends her free time considering marriage to a number of eligible males, none of whom suit her needs.

p, Ned Lander; d, Rivka Hartman; w, Rivka Hartman, Maggie Power, Keith Thompson; ph, John Whitteron; m, Burkhart Von Dallwitz; ed, Tony Stevens; prod d, Ro Cooke.

Comedy **(PR:NR MPAA:NR)**

BACK TO THE BEACH½** (1987) 92m PAR c

Annette Funicello *(Annette)*, Frankie Avalon *(The Big Kahuna)*, Connie Stevens *(Connie)*, Lori Loughlin *(Sandi)*, Tommy Hinkley *(Michael)*, Demian Slade *(Bobby)*, John Calvin *(Troy)*, Joe Holland *(Zed)*, David Bowe *(Mountain)*, Pee Wee Herman, Don Adams, Bob Denver, Alan Hale [, Jr.], Tony Dow, Jerry Mathers, Dick Dale, Stevie Ray Vaughan.

For anyone longing for a film which both satirizes and waxes nostalgic the mediocre beach party films of the 1960s, this is a must-see. For those who saw the original Avalon-Funicello beach movies and rightly found them witless, moronic and utterly empty of everything but sand and surfboards, BACK TO THE BEACH offers an unwelcome deja vu. It's 25 years and six beach movies later and we find clean-cut Funicello and Avalon living as married people and enjoying a secure middle class life in Ohio, far from the ocean, California beaches, and surfers. Avalon is a successful car salesman while mom Funicello putters about the house feeding her son Slade so many peanut butter sandwiches (a play on Funicello's long-standing TV advertisements) that he is driven half-mad as he chokes on them. (This joke goes on and on and on throughout the movie.) The couple and their offspring decide to take a trip West, and once in L.A. they stop to visit an older daughter, Loughlin, and are dismayed to find that she's living with an apprentice punk rocker/surfer, Hinkley, and that Hinkley hangs around with a snarling gang of plug uglies who are terrorizing the beach visitors. Funicello waltzes about in a 1960s hairdo and a swim suit (still one piece) of modest trim, decorated with polka dots and complete with matching headband. She is jolted by wisecracking Stevens, a bar owner who makes a giant play for Avalon, known here as "The Big Kahuna." The family unit is imperiled mightily with Funicello and Avalon headed for a breakup and the children drifting toward vagrancy and crime. But, as with all the previous beach movies, BACK TO THE BEACH ends predictably enough at the beach where the punk rocker/surfers are bested, Funicello and Avalon reunite, and the kids straighten up and fly right.

Much more could have been done to enliven this film if the script truly aimed at satirizing the simple-minded original films instead of parading the same inanities with a smirk this second (and hopefully last) time around. Funicello, now 45 and Avalon, 48, are pleasant enough people but there is something miserable and not a little embarrassing about their attempt to recapture a childish success two and a half decades later. Paramount hyped this film as a "culture-clashing" film, but the two groups bumping up against each other represent little from present mainstream society. An interesting notion of presenting many TV personalities from the 1960s in cameo appearances does not come off. Don Adams, Bob Denver, Tony Dow and others step forth to repeat lines that died in the 1960s and Pee-Wee Herman utters gibberish never born at all. It's harmless, this film, but it's also much in need of a transfusion.

p, Frank Mancuso, Jr.; d, Lyndall Hobbs; w, Peter Krikes, Steve Meerson, Christopher Thompson (based on a story by James Komack from characters created by Lou Rusoff); ph, Bruce Surtees; m, Steve Dorff; ed, David Finfer; prod d, Michael Helmy; cos, Marlene Steward.

Comedy **(PR:C MPAA:PG)**

BAD BLOOD**** (1987, Fr.) 128m Films Plain Chant-Soprofilms-FR3 Films-CNC-Sofima/AAA Classic c (MAUVAIS SANG; GB: THE NIGHT IS YOUNG)

Denis Lavant *(Alex)*, Juliette Binoche *(Anna)*, Michel Piccoli *(Marc)*, Hans Meyer *(Hans)*, Julie Delpy *(Lise)*, Carroll Brooks *(The American Woman)*, Hugo Pratt *(Boris)*, Serge Reggiani *(Charlie)*, Mireille Perrier *(The Young Mother)*, Jerome Zucca *(Thomas)*, Charles Schmitt *(Commissar)*, Philippe Fretun, Ralph Brown, Paul Handford, Francois Negret.

An exhilarating celebration of cinema by 26-year-old Frenchman Leos Carax whose previous film, BOY MEETS GIRL (1984), found a small but enthusiastic following. The plot, which takes a backseat to Carax's technique and invention, is drawn from pulp crime novels and concerns a fictional AIDS-like plague called STBO which one contracts by "making love without love." The majority of those infected are adolescents whose lovemaking had previously been without consequence. The only known serum is locked away at the top of a skyscraper. Lavant, the son of a recently murdered criminal, is relatively content—spending his time with the innocent-looking Delpy, his 16-year-old sweetheart. They take romantic walks through the woods, smoke cigarettes together, ride on Lavant's motorcycle, and always use condoms when they make love. Lavant, however, has spent some time in prison and feels the need to get out from under his father's criminal shadow. He leaves Delpy behind and takes refuge with two of his father's friends—Piccoli and Meyer. Piccoli, who is deeply in debt, has been approached by Brooks, an aging woman known only as "The American," who has given him two weeks to steal the STBO serum. Lavant gets drawn into their planned heist, but in the meantime, he falls in love with Binoche, Piccoli's beautiful young moll. Lavant spends all his time trying to win Binoche's love, but she is determined to remain faithful to Piccoli, who is many years her senior. The evening of the big heist finally arrives and Lavant escapes with the serum, but not before killing a cop. Later, Lavant is shot by "The American" and her thugs who steal what they believe to be the serum. Lavant, however, has hidden the serum elsewhere. Lavant, Binoche, Piccoli, and Meyer hop in their car and head for a nearby airfield to escape to Switzerland, pursued all the while by "The American's" car and, even further behind, by the motorcycle-riding Delpy. A shoot-out between Piccoli and "The American's" thugs follows, leaving all of the heavies dead. Before Lavant can get on the plane, he dies of his gunshot wound. Piccoli and Meyer do all they can to save him but it is too late. Delpy, who loved Lavant to the end, finally catches up to Lavant, who bids farewell to his "motorcycle angel." The film ends as Binoche runs down the airport runway—her arms outstretched as she tries to take off into the clouds.

It is not the *film noir*-style pulp plot that makes BAD BLOOD such a superb film but Carax's unflinchingly gutsy use of technique. As a director, the energetic Carax does *whatever* he wants *whenever* he wants. The opening credits, for example, are intercut with grainy, slow-motion shots of swans—shots which have no real bearing on the rest of the film. At one point, during a conversation between Lavant, Binoche, and Piccoli, Carax switches from modern color and lighting to a flickering black-and-white sequence which pays homage to silent film. Instead of satisfying narrative or commercial expectations, Carax follows his cinematic and poetic instincts. As a result BAD BLOOD is one of the most refreshing new films since the days of the French New Wave. The film is filled with energetic and challenging sequences. One scene has Lavant, Binoche, and Piccoli parachuting from an airplane—an especially harrowing feat for the apprehensive Binoche. She is the first to jump, but her cord gets caught, suspending the now-unconscious girl from the back of the plane. Lavant climbs down the cord and, after Piccoli cuts them loose, parachutes safely to the ground with Binoche in his arms. Visually, this scene of the lovers' leap leaves one breathless as the camera accompanies the pair in their descent, capturing angles above, beside, and in front of them. Another scene has Lavant spinning the radio dial randomly until he lands on a station. After one song finishes, David Bowie's "Modern Love" comes over the airwaves. Inspired, Lavant runs at breakneck pace, shadowboxing through the night-shrouded city streets. The combination of the song's powerful tempo, the continuous camera movement which quickly tracks along side Lavant, and Lavant's full-speed sprint complete with a cartwheel makes for one of the most invigorating scenes in film history. Carax is not without a sense of humor, including numerous gags—both visual and verbal. The most memorable is the succession of magic tricks Lavant uses to cheer up Binoche. Through the magic of editing, Lavant performs the "apple trick" for Binoche—making an apple appear to fall from above (out of frame) into his hand. He tries it again, this time throwing the apple into the air. The film cuts and a stalk of celery falls into Lavant's hand. The magic trick then takes on a surreal slapstick quality as Lavant tries the "pineapple trick"—throwing an apple in the air and attempting to make a pineapple appear in its place. Instead of a pineapple, however, a cornucopia of fruits and vegetables fall from above, pummeling the shocked Lavant on the head.

It is this sort of scene which typifies Carax love of cinematic magic and trickery. Like Jean Cocteau (whom Carax pays homage to in a very funny scene), Carax addresses romantic myths amd makes use of mirrors. He even makes a reference to the motorcycle angels of ORPHEUS. Like Jean-Luc Godard, the filmmaker to whom Carax is most often compared, he does not let the audience forget that they are experiencing a film. His intercutting between black-and-white and color, the sudden bursts of music, and his voice-over techniques constantly jar the audience back into the realization that they are watching a film. Carax's casting is excellent, resurrecting Lavant and his "Alex" character (Carax's real name is Alex Dupont) from BOY MEETS GIRL and bringing back both Brooks and Meyer from the same film. Carax has also found two more actresses with the same angelic quality that Mireille Perrier brought to BOY MEETS GIRL. With her short, dark hair, Binoche (previously seen opposite Lambert Wilson and Jean-Louis Trintignant in RENDEZVOUS, and in a supporting role in Godard's HAIL, MARY) has the appearance of a silent movie starlet—a look which is essential to Carax's atmosphere and one which helped her receive a Cesar nomination for Best Actress. Delpy, a long-haired blonde equivalent of the purity of Binoche, is also perfectly cast as Lavant's true love—a role which earned her a Cesar nomination as Most Promising Female Newcomer. Much of the film's success is due to cinematographer Escoffier (BOY MEETS GIRL, THREE MEN AND A CRADLE) whose camerawork adapts to Carax's needs—lush outdoor romanticism, shadowy *film noir* stylistics, and the black-and-white of silent film-making. Released in France in 1986. Included on the soundtrack are excerpts from Benjamin Britten's "Simple Symphony" and "Variations on a Theme of Franck Bridge," Serge Prokofiev's "Peter and the Wolf," "Romeo and Juliet" and "Erato," and Charles Chaplin's "Limelight." Also included is "J'ai pas de Regrets" (Boris Vian, J. Walter, performed by Serge Reggiani). (In French; English subtitles.) *(Sexual situations.)*

p, Philippe Diaz; d&w, Leos Carax; ph, Jean-Yves Escoffier (Fujicolor); m, Benjamin Britten, Serge Prokofiev, Charlie Chaplin; ed, Nelly Quettier; art d, Michel Vandestien, Thomas Peckre, Jack Dubus; m/l, David Bowie, Charles Aznavour, Boris Vian, J. Walter; cos, Robert Nardone, Dominique Gregogna, Martine Metert; makeup, Chantal Houdoy; ch, Christine Burgos; spec eff, Guy Trielli.

Crime/Romance (PR:A-C MPAA:NR)

BAIXO GAVEA† (1987, Braz.) 116m H.M. Barbosa Producoes Cinematograficos/Embrafilme-Empresa Brasileiro de Filmes-Rio de Janeiro c (Trans: Gavea Girls)

Lucelia Santos *(Dora)*, Louise Cardoso *(Ana)*, Carlos Gregorio, Jose Wilker.

Santos, the most popular Brazilian actress since Sonia Braga, stars as a theater director who devotes half of her days to a play about poet Fernando Pessoa and the other half to her troubled love life. Playing the lead role in the play is Santos' roommate Cardoso, a lesbian who loves Santos and awaits the day when they will be together. Although Cardoso's love is true, Santos denies her attraction to the lesbian and continues to search for a male partner. d&w, Haroldo Marinho Barbosa; ph, Antonio Penido; m, Sergio G. Saraceni; ed, Gilberto Santeiro; art d, Paulo Dubois; cos, Mila Achcar.

Romance (PR:NR MPAA:NR)

BALADA DA PRAIA DOS CAES† (1987, Port./Span.) 90m Animatografo-Andrea Film-Filmform c (Trans: The Ballad of Dogs' Beach)

Raul Solnado *(Inspector Elias)*, Assumpta Serna *(Mena)*, Patrick Bauchau *(Capt. Luis Dantas)*, Sergei Mateu, Henrique Viana, Mario Pardo, Pedro Efe.

It's 1960 in Portugal, the country under military dictatorship. When a jailed army captain, Bauchau, escapes and is found murdered on the beach, Solnado is called upon to investigate the crime. His investigation reveals Bauchau was having a torrid affair with Serna, a relationship which ultimately led to his demise.

d, Jose Fonseca e Costa; w, Jose Fonseca e Costa, Antonio Larreta, Pedro Bandiera Freire (based on a story by Jose Cardoso Pires); ph, Acacio de Almeida; m, Alberto Iglesias; ed, Pablo del Almo.

Crime (PR:NR MPAA:NR)

BANZAI RUNNER* (1987) 86m Montage c

Dean Stockwell *(Billy Baxter)*, John Shepherd *(Beck Baxter)*, Charles Dierkop *(Traven)*, Dawn Schneider *(Shelley)*, Ann Cooper *(Maysie)*, Barry Sattles *(Osborne)*, Billy Drago *(Syszek)*, Rick Fitts *(Winston)*, Marylou Kenworthy *(Dallas)*, John Wheeler *(Hawkins)*, Eric Mason *(Capt. Hernandez)*, Ron Sloan *(Greg)*, Steve Jamieson *(Dale)*, Kim Knode *(Moira)*, Bill Yeager *(Graham)*, Ted Warren *(Ron)*, Cindy Rome *(Sweet Young Thing)*, Riba Meryl *(Donna)*, Michael Tullin *(The Judge)*, David Workman *(Krause)*, Michael McCabe *(District Attorney)*, William Dearth *(Truck Driver)*.

One thing that makes chase movies so popular is the undeniable fact that fast cars are really sexy. There's a certain vicarious thrill in seeing men and machines going after each other, a factor well exploited in the "Mad Max" series and countless other films. However, BANZAI RUNNER misses that whole point and in doing so presents a lackluster action film overloaded with boring chase sequences. Stockwell is a California highway patrolman who zealously pursues what he calls "runners," those speed freaks who zip up and down the roads after the sun goes down. He wants his patrol car souped up so he can catch these fast-moving automobiles, but Stockwell's boss consistently tells him to go after a more dangerous menace, drunken drivers. Stockwell is divorced and lives with his brother's son, Shepherd, a good kid who annoys his uncle by smoking marijuana. The boy's parents were killed by a hit-and-run highway runner, and Stockwell is determined to chase runners until he finds his brother's killer. However, other problems divert him from this quest. His ex-wife is suing him for the house Stockwell inherited from his father. If he can raise enough money to pay off this harpy, Stockwell can keep his home. Meanwhile, his girl friend Cooper is increasingly angered by her lover's moody periods and threatens to break off the relationship. Stockwell goes to Dierkop, a mechanic friend who promises to surreptitiously soup up Stockwell's patrol car in return for a favor. Stockwell manages to get a judge to drop some old charges against Dierkop, but this leads to his dismissal from the force. Enter the Drug Enforcement Agency, which wants Stockwell's assistance in nabbing a group of fast-driving cocaine dealers. He agrees to help and takes Shepherd with him on the assignment. Sattles and the sneering Drago (THE UNTOUCHABLES) allow Stockwell to join their gang and the smooth-talking leader challenges him to a race. Stockwell, who has learned that Drago may be the man behind his brother's death, agrees, not realizing Sattles is on to him. After a high speed chase, there is a shoot-out, and then Stockwell pursues Drago one more time. Dierkop arrives at the last minute to help out, and Drago ultimately meets his maker in a fiery crash.

This is a fairly schizophrenic package. It begins as a chase film, then it turns into a family drama before becoming a portrait of a troubled romance. There's even some teen sex tossed in courtesy of an inconsequential subplot involving Shepherd and his girl friend Schneider. Mostly BANZAI RUNNER plays like 20 minutes of car chases padded with 60 minutes of filler. The plot is fairly ludicrous and it's really hard to care about any of the characters. There's no insight, no tension, just a group of actors going through the paces in a passable, uninvolving manner. Stockwell seems bored with his part, while the lesser names act as if they have been cast in a forgettable made-for-TV movie. The car chases, which clearly were designed as the film's highlight, are as unexciting as they come. Director Thomas has no visual flair or imagination when it comes to chase choreography. Despite the title, this has nothing to do with marital arts, suicide rituals, or anything remotely related to the Orient. Songs include: "Two Broken Hearts," "One More Time" (Randy Nicklaus, performed by Nicklaus), "Snake Eyes" (Burt McTeague, Jr., performed by McTeague, Jr.), "On the Line" (Roger Freeland, Joe Pizzulo, performed by Los Bad Jamming Gringos, featuring Roger Freeland), "Chill Factor" (Andy Zuckerman, performed by Zuckerman), "Someone'll Find You" (Jack Mierop, Phil Tarczon, performed by Jax), "Hammer Down," "It's Everything" (Joel Goldsmith, Kevin Dukes, Jerry Riopelle, performed by Riopelle). *(Violence, brief nudity.)*

p&d, John G. Thomas; w, Phillip L. Harnage; ph, Howard A. Wexler (United Color); m, Joel Goldsmith; ed, Drake Silliman; spec eff, Tom Callaway, Stephen Stanton; m/l, Randy Nicklaus, Bert McTeague, Jr., Roger Freeland, Joe Pizzulo, Andy Zuckerman, Jack Mierop, Phil Tarczon, Joel Goldsmith, Kevin Dukes, Jerry Riopelle; makeup, Martha Reisman.

Action/Drama Cas. (PR:C MPAA:NR)

BAR-CEL-ONA† (1987, Span.) 90m Center Promotor de la Image/ Cinematografia de la Generalitat de Catalunya c

Alfred Luchetti *(Manolo)*, Ovidi Montllor *(Ona)*.

Set in the spirited, independent Spanish provincial capital of Barcelona, the film centers on Montllor who plays a character named "Ona," as in Bar-cel-ONA. She too is spirited and independent—a symbol of Barcelona. When she meets Luchetti, a young musician who is preparing to leave on the next ship, she convinces him to stay and remain true to both her and their city.

d, Ferran Llagostera i Colli; w, Josep Albanelli; ph, Antonio Ono.

Romance (PR:NR MPAA:NR)

BARBARIANS, THE* (1987, US/It.) 88m Cannon c (AKA: THE BARBARIANS AND CO.)

David Paul *(Kutchek)*, Peter Paul *(Gore)*, Richard Lynch *(Kadar)*, Eva La Rue *(Ismena/Cara)*, Virginia Bryant *(Canary)*, Sheeba Alahani *(China)*, Michael Berryman *(Dirtmaster)*, Tiziana Di Gennaro *(Kara)*, Nanni Bernini, Angelo Ragusa, Lucio Rosato, Franco Pistoni, Raffaella Baracchi, Benito Stefanelli, Pasquale Bellazecca, Luigi Di Gennaro, Giovanni Cianfriglia, Renzo Pevarello, L. Carosi, Paolo Risi, Wilma Mazilli.

A dim-witted but oddly likable sword-and-sorcery tale, THE BARBARIANS stars the Paul brothers (David and Peter)—a muscular pair known to some as "The Bad Boys of Bodybuilding." Apparently in one of their weaker moments, Cannon bosses Menahem Golan and Yoram Globus must have thought these brawny brothers would become matinee idols. The film begins when the brothers are just young tykes traveling through barren wasteland with a nomadic tribe called the Ragnicks. These Ragnicks are a happy-go-lucky troupe of entertainers who can wander fearlessly through dangerous lands because they are protected by Bryant, a virgin queen who wears a magic ruby in her navel. Magical belly or no magical belly, the evil Lynch decides to overtake the caravan and capture the queen. After a lengthy chase, the Ragnicks become Lynch's prisoners. The junior he-men are tossed into a slave-labor dungeon called "The Pit," which is ruled by the sadistic Berryman. Ten years pass and the Paul brothers are determined to escape the clutches of Lynch. It turns out that the magical ruby is no longer in its navel home, but is now under the guard of a dragon with a nasty disposition. The Pauls spend their days and nights trying to get the ruby back. However, they also must get themselves a new virgin queen. The lucky girl is La Rue—some sort of prehistoric Valley girl who, coincidentally, was a young Ragnick many years ago. After some more swordplay, a battle with a dragon, some splashing around in a murky swamp, and an encounter with a bevy of aspiring virgin queens, the Paul brothers restore peace and tranquility to the Ragnick tribe—and the world is a better place as a result.

A US/Italian coproduction, THE BARBARIANS was the first of a three-picture deal between the Paul brothers and Cannon. Hailing from Connecticut, the 6-foot tall, 260-pound body builders were previously seen in the wretched Mr. T vehicle D.C. CAB and the Matt Dillon picture THE FLAMINGO KID. There's a certain camp value to THE BARBARIANS, mostly because the film refuses to take itself seriously. According to Peter, the elder Paul: "There's a lot of humor in it. The director let us ad-lib a lot because we'd come up with these one-liners that cracked everyone up." Don't be fooled, however, into thinking THE BARBARIANS is a laugh riot. It's not. In fact, it's pretty mind-numbing, but sometimes a mind-numbing sword-and-sorcery videocassette is the perfect ice-breaker at late-night parties. *(Graphic violence, excessive nudity.)*

p, John Thompson; d, Ruggero Deodato; w, James R. Silke; ph, Gianlorenzo Battaglia (Telecolor); m, Pino Donaggio; ed, Eugenio Alabiso; prod d, Giuseppe Mangano; cos, Francesca Panicali, Michela Gisotti; makeup, Francesco Paolocci, Gaetano Paolocci; stunts, Benito Stefanelli.

Fantasy/Adventure **(PR:O MPAA:R)**

BARFLY**** (1987) 100m Francis Ford Coppola-Golan-Globus/Cannon c

Mickey Rourke *(Henry Chinaski)*, Faye Dunaway *(Wanda Wilcox)*, Alice Krige *(Tully Sorenson)*, Jack Nance *(Detective)*, J.C. Quinn *(Jim)*, Frank Stallone *(Eddie)*, Gloria LeRoy *(Grandma Moses)*, Sandy Martin *(Janice)*, Roberta Bassin *(Lilly)*, Joe Unger *(Ben)*, Harry Cohn *(Rick)*, Pruitt Taylor Vince *(Joe)*, Joe Rice *(Old Man in Bar)*, Julie "Sunny" Pearson *(Hooker in Bar)*, Donald L. Norden *(Man in Alley)*, Wil Albert *(Carl)*, Hal Shafer *(Mike)*, Zeek Manners *(Roger)*, Pearl Shear *(Helen)*, Rik Colitti *(Jack)*, Michael Collins *("Elbow Inn" Bartender)*, Ron Joseph *(Liquor Store Clerk)*, Vance Colvig *(Alcoholic Man)*, Stacey Pickern *(Lady Manager)*, Leonard Termo *(Harry)*, Gary Cox *(Lenny)*, Fritz Feld *(Bum)*, Albert Henderson *(Louie)*, Sandy Rose *(Louie's Woman)*, Madalyn Carol *(Young Girl Hooker)*, George Marshall Ruge *(Lovebird Man)*, Debbie Lynn Ross *(Lovebird Woman)*, Damons Hines, Leonard J. Tate *(Black Kids)*, Carlos Cervantes, Peter Conti *(Cops)*.

In BARFLY, the world of Charles Bukowski is placed under a cinematic microscope, revealing to the curious the poetry of decadence. Bukowski is a poet/novelist whose gutter existence has made him something of a modern myth of survival. Although barely known in America, California resident Bukowski has a strong following in Europe where an insatiable interest in American life-styles has brought fame to the writer. Rourke plays the young Bukowski (here called Henry Chinaski; those who know Bukowski call him "Hank"), a hard-drinking, fistfighting barfly who fuels himself with liquor, and revels in his existence. He doesn't like people but, given a little money, he fills the stools around him with other drinkers. He doesn't like work, but takes it when he can find it, just to get the money for booze. Most of all, he hates wasting time thinking about the things he could be or do. Unlike the other bar regulars, he is a sometime writer whose simple, honest style reveals something about life's often unseen underbelly.

The film opens as the camera wanders into a dimly lit bar in a Los Angeles slum. The place is empty except for a bartender who reads the newspaper. All the regulars are out back where a completely soused Rourke is brawling with Stallone, the macho, well-built bartender. Although Rourke stumbles, he holds his own. For every punch he receives, he defiantly goads Stallone. After he is savagely beaten, Rourke lies bloody and still while everyone else returns to the bar. This is simply part of his daily routine, however, and by the next morning he is back on his feet. He lives in a dilapidated apartment building in a filthy, disorderly room where he drinks and writes. His clothes haven't seen soap in ages, he is unshaven, his hair is a stringy mess, and he is unable to function without a drink. After just a couple of hours at home, he heads back to the bar to begin again. When he sees a new face at the bar, Dunaway, a haggard but attractive drunk, he approaches her, ignoring a warning that she is crazy. They quickly hit it off, each impressed with the other's misanthropy. Rourke orders a couple of rounds and then announces that he is out of money, or "back to normal," as he puts it. Dunaway invites him back to her place, picking up some booze along the way. She warns him that she'll run off with the next guy who offers her a drink, but Rourke falls for her anyway. The next morning, Dunaway invites Rourke to move in with her. They exchange thoughts on what they love, hate, fear, and desire. Their relationship is tested when Dunaway spends the night with Stallone, which infuriates and hurts Rourke, who sees Stallone as the posturing, macho

embodiment of everything he loathes. Rourke's life takes a turn when Krige, a wealthy, pretty, and self-assured publisher, approaches Rourke and offers him a handsome sum for one of his stories. Having read a number of Rourke's submissions, Krige (who had to hire a detective to find him) has become dangerously infatuated with him. Attracted to his filthy, smelly world which is so different from her pristine life-style, she invites him to her luxurious hilltop home. They get drunk and sleep together. Krige hopes to reform Rourke and tries to convince him he'll adjust to her life-style, but Rourke knows better and returns to the bar and Dunaway. He quickly spends his money buying rounds for everyone in the bar, including Stallone. Krige then wanders in, forcing the jealous Dunaway into a brawl. Since Dunaway's world and Krige's world cannot coexist, one has to make way for the other. Krige takes a pounding from Dunaway and, realizing she won't win Rourke, leaves the bar. Rourke gets himself into another entanglement with Stallone and the pair head outside. The regulars follow and the camera wanders out of the bar back into the streets of L.A.

It is a rare film event to see a romantic comedy about two stumbling drunks who wallow in seedy bar-life. It is especially rare when these characters are portrayed in a sympathetic and even heroic light. The script, penned by Bukowski, is clearly written by a man who has been to hell and back, goading death every step of the way. Drawing on his own experiences in Philadelphia and Los Angeles bars, Bukowski creates an atmosphere of stench, crusted blood, stale beer, and old whores. His people are real and, despite their somewhat comic and almost Felliniesque portrayal, Bukowski loves them. He doesn't pass judgement or inject morality, he simply presents them as people. (The extras in the film are actual bar regulars.) These people, just like the WALL STREET traders, or the FATAL ATTRACTION lovers, or the SEPTEMBER neurotics, have emotions, feelings, and beliefs. It's as if Bukowski is making a plea for the rights of alcoholics, bums, and perverts—that element of society that people refuse to acknowledge. It's here that he finds truth in a Bukowskian sense—"like Dostoyevskian, but drunk," he has described it. Perhaps BARFLY will seem to some a glorification of alcoholism or a poor example to struggling young writers who think success can be achieved through drinking. Bukowski the Writer, who has survived life in the gutter and crawled out of it, doesn't seem concerned with the social effects of Bukowski the Role Model. Bukowski and director Schroeder tell a story of a drunk, and often pathetic, individual who doesn't care how he is perceived by others. Bukowski and his Harry Chinaski alter ego don't care about society's perception of them, otherwise they'd pull themselves out of the gutter and join the "respectable" working class. In Bukowski's writing and Schroeder's direction, BARFLY strives for the integrity of self-exposure. The result is a beautiful, sincere film which gives the viewer a chance to see how the proverbial "other half" lives. In BARFLY, Bukowski does as he has done in his novels and poetry for years; he bares himself completely as very few writers, much less people in general, have the courage or ability to do.

Perhaps the most amazing thing about BARFLY is that the film is entertaining, enjoyable, and funny. What could easily have been 100 minutes of drinking, vomiting, emotional torture, and violence instead becomes 100 minutes of brilliant filmmaking. Schroeder's direction is gutsy, light-handed, humorous, and tense—in all the right places. Rourke, who turns in the best performance of his shaky but courageous career, takes a character who could be seen as pathetic and despicable and makes him a likable hero. Sweaty, dirty, and unshaven, with greasy hair falling in his eyes, a hunched walk, and grimy boxer shorts, Rourke manages to make his character charming, and when not charming, fascinating. The viewer is not necessarily supposed to like Harry Chinaski, or even respect him, but Rourke's performance at least helps one to understand him. In addition to his interaction with the bottle, Rourke is seen interacting with Dunaway, the woman he loves. In BARFLY, Dunaway is no longer the glamorous star who exuded Hollywood bitchiness. Here she gives a gritty performance that contradicts and improves upon everything she has done since BONNIE AND CLYDE. Without the crutch of makeup or a flashy wardrobe, Dunaway is forced to stand on her acting abilities. Her exceptional performance is one of naked emotion and romantic vulnerability—a complete contrast to the cold-steel facade of her NETWORK performance. Despite Rourke's bravura portrayal, Dunaway is never eclipsed. The Rourke-Dunaway romance is one of the most touching love stories to reach the screen in some time. Theirs is more touching than most because there is no artifice. They don't love each other for looks, or money, or power, or sexual virility. They are two souls completely in tune with each other who are in love for the purest, most romantic of reasons. In contrast to Dunaway and Rourke is

Krige, the curious, wealthy, intellectual dilettante who finds herself inexplicably attracted to the drunken writer. In the BARFLY world of bars and booze where one can easily forget what a life of sobriety looks like, Krige is the one character who injects some reality. She is also the character with whom it is easiest to identify (since most barflies don't spend their time watching films about themselves). She represents the audience's perception of Bukowski and, like most of his fans, wishes, but is unable, to live Bukowski's life. The pretty, long-haired Krige, who is best remembered as the ghost in 1981's GHOST STORY and later played Bathsheba in the forgotten KING DAVID, is perfect in her role. While her character could have been a stereotypical opportunist, she is instead a complex woman who is torn between the security of her beauty, wealth, and intellect and her desire to face her base instincts (much like the Maria Schneider character in LAST TANGO IN PARIS who becomes attracted to the beastly Marlon Brando).

The making of BARFLY was nearly as extreme as anything in the film. In 1979, Schroeder, who has produced numerous Eric Rohmer and Jacques Rivette films and has directed documentaries on Gen. Idi Amin Dada and Koko the Gorilla, commissioned Bukowski to write a screenplay for $20,000. The 67-year-old Bukowski, whose first novel, *Post Office*, was not published until 1971, obliged even though he had nothing but contempt for most movies. After Schroeder searched six years for a producer, Fred Roos (Francis Coppola's producer) and Tom Luddy (the producer of MISHIMA) signed on, presenting the film through Coppola. Sean Penn read the script and expressed interest in playing the Bukowski character. Penn, however, wanted his friend Dennis Hopper to direct, which Bukowski objected to for two reasons—Schroeder had already worked many years on the project, and, reportedly, Hopper once told Schroeder he "couldn't direct traffic." (Hopper and Penn later hooked up for COLORS, a 1988 release about an L.A. cop.) Not quite willing to risk the $4 million budget on the relatively unknown Schroeder, Cannon, the film's eventual executive producer and distributor, remained hesitant. Schroeder proved his determination by entering the office of Cannon president Menahem Golan with a small electric handsaw. He proceeded to inject his pinky finger with novocain and then threatened to cut it off, with other body parts to follow, unless Cannon made the film. After initially refusing, Golan realized Schroeder's obsession with BARFLY and eventually gave the project the go ahead. Bukowski's writing had been adapted just once before in 1983 by Marco Ferrari in the Italian production TALES OF ORDINARY MADNESS, a misguided Ben Gazzara vehicle which was made without Bukowski's cooperation. Also released this year was LOVE IS A DOG FROM HELL, a Belgian picture based chiefly on the Bukowski story "The Copulating Mermaids of Venice, California." Includes the songs "Hip Hug-Her" (Steve Cropper, Booker T. Jones, Al Jackson, Jr., Donald Dunn, performed by Booker T. and the MGs); "Nine Below Zero" (Sonny Boy Williamson, performed by The Nighthawks); "The Sermon" (Jimmy Smith, performed by Smith); "Theme for Ernie" (Fred Lacey, performed by John Coltrane); "Silver Threads Among the Gold" (performed by Shot Jackson and Friends); "Hair Street" (John Lurie, performed by the Young Lizards); "Born Under a Bad Sign" (Booker T. Jones, William Bell, performed by Albert King). *(Violence, brief nudity, sexual situations, adult situations, excessive profanity, substance abuse.)*

p, Barbet Schroeder, Fred Roos, Tom Luddy; d, Barbet Schroeder; w, Charles Bukowski; ph, Robby Muller (TVC color); ed, Eva Gardos; prod d, Bob Ziembicki; set d, Lisa Dean; cos, Milena Canonero; m/l, Steve Cropper, Booker T. Jones, Al Jackson, Jr., Donald Dunn, Sonny Boy Williamson, Jimmy Smith, Fred Lacey, John Lurie, William Bell.

Comedy/Drama/Romance **(PR:O MPAA:R)**

BATTERIES NOT INCLUDED* (1987) 106m Amblin Ent./UNIV c

Hume Cronyn *(Frank Riley)*, Jessica Tandy *(Faye Riley)*, Frank McRae *(Harry Noble)*, Elizabeth Pena *(Marisa)*, Michael Carmine *(Carlos)*, Dennis Boutsikaris *(Mason)*, Tom Aldredge *(Sid)*, Jane Hoffman *(Muriel)*, John DiSanti *(Gus)*, John Pankow *(Kovacs)*, MacIntyre Dixon *(DeWitt)*, Michael Greene *(Lacey)*.

Steven Spielberg's Amblin Productions has come up with a film here that is the complete opposite of his far superior EMPIRE OF THE SUN. Unlike EMPIRE, BATTERIES NOT INCLUDED is a typical heartwarming fantasy which retreads the ground covered by E.T., COCOON, and SHORT CIRCUIT by including cute (and marketable) aliens who work miracles for a small group of oppressed people. Set in the slums of Manhattan's Lower East Side, BATTERIES NOT INCLUDED stars Tandy and Cronyn (COCOON) as an elderly couple who, along with a few other residents, resist the gentrification plans of a greedy real estate developer. When the developer's thugs, led by Carmine, pressure the tenants to move, most take the money and run. Cronyn, however, stands firm. He runs a diner on the first floor and has been doing so for much of his life. Tandy has become a burden to him, falling into senility and prancing around their apartment like a full-blown nut case. Unable to cope with the present, she retreats into her past and habitually mistakes Carmine for her long-dead son Bobby. Also residing in the building are Pena, a pregnant, unwed Latino woman whose boyfriend has left her; Boutsikaris, a yuppie painter who lives in the slums to surround himself with "reality"; and McRae, an oafish black janitor and ex-boxing champ who has dreams of restoring the building's tile floor and says only things he has heard on television commercials. After Carmine and his thugs destroy Cronyn's diner, things look grim for the remaining residents. Cronyn groans that they need a miracle. Before one can say "Close encounters of the third kind," two flying saucers the size of hubcaps enter through Tandy's bedroom window. These saucers—one male, one female—have eyes that blink, retractable hands and feet, and an electromagnetic power which enables them to fix broken objects. Their power source is electricity—which they find a great deal of in Cronyn's kitchen outlet. The following morning, the previously trashed diner is back in shape and the residents have received their miracle. This, of course, only makes Carmine angrier. He steps up the pressure, only to have the saucers fight back by hitting him in the head with a metal pot. Carmine runs scared but vows to get the residents out. In the meantime, the saucers have been subsisting on anything metal—nuts, bolts, frying pans, toasters, aluminum cans—and recharging themselves on electricity. The residents are then overwhelmed with joy at the "birth" of two baby saucers. A third baby is stillborn, prompting McRae to say, "Batteries not included." McRae takes the stillborn saucer into his workshop and revives it, saying, a la the General Electric advertising slogan, "We bring good things to life." The saucers help Cronyn run his diner by working in the kitchen and flipping burgers. In one comic mishap a mischievous baby saucer wanders onto the grill and gets a piece of cheese plopped on his head. He then ends up between two hamburger buns on the plate of a hungry customer. He manages to sneak away before he is devoured, landing next in a tureen of soup, before getting tossed in the dishwater by a giddy Tandy. Angered by Carmine's lack of results, the developer hires an arsonist to torch the building. Believing that the apartments are vacant, he prepares to burn the place down. Carmine then notices Tandy in her apartment window. With only minutes remaining, he rescues her. The building goes up in flames and it appears that all is lost. Later that evening, however, an entire army of flying saucers arrives on the scene and turns the smoking, smoldering rubble into a fully restored apartment building. The final shot of the film shows the little six-story apartment dwarfed by the glass and metal high rises of the real estate development.

Dripping with cutesy sentimentality, BATTERIES NOT INCLUDED provides an overdose of family entertainment in which "reality" consists of the stereotypes and caricatures that fit neatly into a tried-and-true formula. The setting is a homogenized All-American ghetto with old people, young people, white people, black people, Hispanic people, married people, unmarried people, nice people, and mean people. Like all the downtrodden masses, these people could use a miracle and without one they are doomed. As in so many similar films, this miracle comes from the skies. And, in keeping with the tradition of Amblin Entertainment and the rest of Hollywood, this miracle is Marketable. Like E.T., the aliens have big, innocent eyes; like CLOSE ENCOUNTERS, they zip around the skies and leave everyone with their mouths agape; like COCOON, they are able to revitalize peoples' spirits; and, like SHORT CIRCUIT, they are pieces of metal with human qualities. In other words, BATTERIES NOT INCLUDED is a mishmash of everything you've seen before tossed into a word processor and spit back out in another form. Although it is filled with elements of previous films, it still provides enough entertainment to hold the attention of the audience, especially if that audience is below the age of reason. The performances are passable, especially since the actors are often upstaged by the saucers. Tandy and Cronyn are talented enough to avoid looking foolish, though they are not given the same quality of material as in COCOON. In a feeble attempt to inject reality, the screenwriters have made Tandy's character senile and Pena's character an unwed mother-to-be. However, the result is Hollywood's unimaginative idea of reality.

BATTERIES NOT INCLUDED (an asterisk precedes the title in the advertisements and on the screen) began as a 30-minute episode of Spielberg's short-lived television series "Amazing Stories." Scripted for television by Spielberg, the episode never made it to production. Mike Garris, the story editor for "Amazing Stories," wrote the initial draft of the film script, which was then turned over to Robbins (the screenwriter of Spielberg's first theatrical feature, SUGARLAND EXPRESS) and Bird. The final script was the product of Maddock and Wilson, the screenwriters of SHORT CIRCUIT. It is given life by the talents of Industrial Light and Magic, the special effects shop begun by George Lucas. Employing various stop-motion techniques and hand-activated rod puppets, the special effects team has created some truly convincing sequences which give the saucers more personality than the human characters. Credit must also be given to modelmaker Greg Jein, who also constructed the spaceships for CLOSE ENCOUNTERS OF THE THIRD KIND. Originally scheduled as a summer release, BATTERIES NOT INCLUDED was pushed back to Christmas by Universal when they realized that there was a large gap in holiday family fare. In order to hype BATTERIES NOT INCLUDED (with its $20 million budget) and bypass a critical whipping, Universal scheduled free advance screenings across the country for families. The advertisements then boasted that 400,000 people already had seen and loved the film, and Universal hoped that good word-of-mouth would cancel out the negative reviews. The production of the film ran into some problems when residents of the run-down neighborhood (on East Eighth Street between Avenues C and D) objected to the amount of money being spent—none of which filtered down to them. Sentiments changed after Universal promised to put some money back into the neighborhood and provide residents with needed building materials. *(Profanity.)*

p, Ronald L. Schwary; d, Matthew Robbins; w, Matthew Robbins, Brad Bird, Brent Maddock, S.S. Wilson (based on a story by Mick Garris and an uncredited television script by Steven Spielberg); ph, John McPherson (Deluxe Color); m, James Horner; ed, Cynthia Scheider; prod d, Ted Haworth; art d, Angelo Graham; set d, George R. Nelson; cos, Aggie Guerard Rodgers; spec eff, Industrial Light & Magic.

Science Fiction/Fantasy (PR:AA MPAA:PG)

BEAKS† (1987, Mex.) 87m Ascot Entertainment-Productora Filmica Real/ International Video Entertainment c (AKA: BIRDS OF PREY)

Christopher Atkins *(Peter)*, Michelle Johnson *(Vanessa Cartwright)*, Sonia Infante *(Carmen)*, Salvador Pineda *(Joe)*, Carol Connery *(Susan)*, Aldo Sambrel *(Arthur Neilsen)*, Gabriele Tinti *(Rod)*, Carol James *(Nurse)*, May Heatherly *(Olivia)*.

Johnson, best known as the object of Michael Caine's desire in BLAME IT ON RIO, plays a European TV journalist assigned to cover stories involving birds. As in Alfred Hitchcock's THE BIRDS, feathered creatues in this film begin attacking humans throughout the world, while Johnson and others try to figure out why. Filmed on location in Spain, Rome, Puerto Rico, Morocco, Peru, and Mexico.

p, Francis Medina, Rene Cardona Jr.; d&w, Rene Cardona Jr.; ph, Leopoldo Villasenor; m, Stelvio Cipriani; ed, Jesus Paredes.

Horror Cas. (PR:NR MPAA:NR)

BEAT, THE*½ (1987) 98m Vestron c

John Savage *(Mr. Ellsworth, English Teacher)*, David Jacobson *(Rex Voorhaus Ormine)*, William McNamara *(Billy Kane)*, Kara Glover *(Kate Kane)*, Jeffrey Horowitz *(Dr. Waxman)*.

The only thing worse than a great stage play made into a lousy movie is a *bad* stage play made into a lousy movie. Originally conceived and presented as an Off-Broadway play by writer-director Mones, THE BEAT is a horribly pretentious and inept production that offers nothing but stock characters and sophomoric philosophy. Set in the ghettos of New York City, the film presents rival street gangs who must leave their hostilities outside when they enter the classroom of hip English teacher Savage. Young and dedicated, Savage runs his class in an informal manner in an attempt to get the kids to forget their posturing and open up. His efforts are relatively futile until a new kid, Jacobson, enters the classroom. Nerdy and sullen, Jacobson is at first looked upon as a "retard" by his fellow classmates. As the days go by, however, Jacobson reveals himself to be a strange bird who spouts torrents of bad beat-style poetry and seems to live in a world created in his imagination. McNamara and Glover, a brother and sister, warm to Jacobson and are willingly included in his imaginary world with the magic words "Lemme Lecke Solomon." He dubs Glover the Princess/Priestess and McNamara the Beggar, and the three of them wander his fictitious post-nuclear city ready to start a new civilization, all to the tune of their mantra, "The beat, the beat, dum, dum." Although at first their friends think they have all flipped out, Jacobson's imagination begins to fuel others and soon the rival gangs have patched up their differences and all are reciting beat poetry in class for the delighted Savage. Their enthusiasm leads them to take their act to the school talent show, calling themselves the Mutants of Sound. Just before the big day, the exasperated school psychiatrist decides that he's had enough of Jacobson's goofy antics and calls the men in the white coats. The kids help Jacobson escape and he hides in the park while the talent show goes up for grabs when a gang fight breaks out. To placate the mob, McNamara, Glover, and another friend perform their Mutants of Sound act without Jacobson. The combination of pretentious poetry and bongo drums wins the audience over and peace is restored. Hoping to share their triumph with Jacobson, they run to the park only to find that he has disappeared. They then rush to the shore of the river to find Jacobson gone, with only his jacket left as a memento. Muttering inane platitudes like "It's cool, he's free now" and the like, the kids turn and face the big, bad city skyline with renewed vigor and self-respect.

THE BEAT plays like a botched collage of RIVER'S EDGE and an episode of "The Lone Ranger" (Who was that weird kid? Gosh, and we forgot to thank him!). Filmed in a deadeningly dull manner by writer-director Mones, THE BEAT, which was shot in 24 days on a budget of $1 million, is about as uncinematic as they come. A standard TV visual style is employed here and the film is nothing but talk, talk, talk, with most of it in the form of bad poetry. Mones must be the only director in the history of film to have shot on location in NYC and then come away with an entire movie that looks as if it were filmed on a stage. The streets, the parks, the schoolyard—even the beach—look stiff and artificial. Cinematographer DiCillo's lighting scheme is straight from Broadway and makes no allowances for subtlety or naturalism. Mones' dialog is even worse. Straining hard to capture the rhythms of the street, the lines are peppered with a ludicrous amount of slang and profanity. What is supposed to sound like realistic dialog merely becomes a playwright's self-conscious striving for it. Despite all the talk, there is precious little characterization in this film and none of the characters ring even remotely true. From the kids to the teachers, everyone is a stereotype and the young cast struggles mightily to wrest some meaning from it all (Glover and McNamara are fairly impressive). Although Mones has called his film "a fable for our times," it is nothing more than a dull, trite, banal, and deliriously self-important drama filmed in a flat, unimaginative manner. With the exception of some fresh young actors, there is nothing to recommend this movie. Shown at film festivals in 1987 and picked up by Vestron for distribution, THE BEAT will likely pass up theatrical release and go straight to home video. *(Violence, substance abuse, excessive profanity.)*

p, Julia Phillips, Jon Klik, Nick Wechsler; d&w, Paul Mones; ph, Tom DiCillo; m, Carter Burwell; ed, Elizabeth Kling; prod d, George Stoll.

Drama (PR:C-O MPAA:NR)

BEAUTY AND THE BEAST† (1987) 93m Golan-Globus/Cannon c

Rebecca DeMornay *(Beauty)*, John Savage *(Beast/Prince)*, Yossi Graber *(Father)*, Michael Schneider *(Kuppel)*, Carmela Marner *(Bettina)*, Ruth Harlap *(Isabella)*, Joseph Bee *(Oliver)*.

Another of Cannon's children's films, this retells the classic fairy tale with Rebecca DeMornay as Beauty and John Savage as the Beast-turned-Prince. This timeless story was done in 1946 under Jean Cocteau's brilliant direction. The same fairy tale was the basis for a network television series in the fall of 1987. Besides acting, DeMornay and Savage also handle their own singing chores.

p, Menahem Golan, Yoram Globus; d, Eugene Marner; w, Carole Lucia Satrina (based on the story by Madame De Villeneuve); ph, Avi Karpick; m, Lori McKelvey; ed, Tova Ascher; prod d, Marek Dobrowolski; cos, Buki Shiff.

Children's (PR:NR MPAA:G)

BEDROOM WINDOW, THE*** (1987) 112m DEG c

Steve Guttenberg *(Terry Lambert)*, Elizabeth McGovern *(Denise)*, Isabelle Huppert *(Sylvia Wentworth)*, Paul Shenar *(Collin Wentworth)*, Frederick Coffin *(Detective Jessup)*, Carl Lumbly *(Detective Quirk)*, Wallace Shawn *(Defense Attorney)*, Brad Greenquist *(Henderson)*, Robert Shenkkan *(State's Attorney Peters)*, Maury Chaykin *(Pool Player)*, Sara Carlson *(Dancing Girl)*, Mark Margolis *(Man in Phone Booth)*, Kate McGregor-Stewart *(Blowsy Neighbor)*, Penelope Allen *(Judge)*, Myvanwy Jenn *(Maid)*, Francis V. Guinan, Jr. *(Bartender at Edgar's)*, Kevin O'Rourke, Richard McGough *(Policemen)*, Sydney Conrad *(First Victim)*, Wendy Womble *(Receptionist)*, Libra Marrian *(Secretary)*, Scott Colson *(Usher)*, Carl Whitney *(Man in Theater)*, Jodi Long *(Cocktail Waitress)*, Richard Olsen *(Late Night Shopper)*, Leon Rippy *(Seedy Bartender)*, John Patrick Maloney *(Pool Player's Friend)*, Kerry Lang *(Waitress at Edgar's)*, J. Michael Hunter *(Pool Player)*, Joyce Flick Wendl *(Henderson's Mother)*, Joyce Greer *(Police Receptionist)*, Winston Hemingway *(Bailiff)*, Michael Lynn Burgess *(Assistant State's Attorney)*, J. Richard Leonard *(Court Clerk)*, Craig Jahelka *(TV Newsman)*, Tobi Marsh *(TV Newswoman)*.

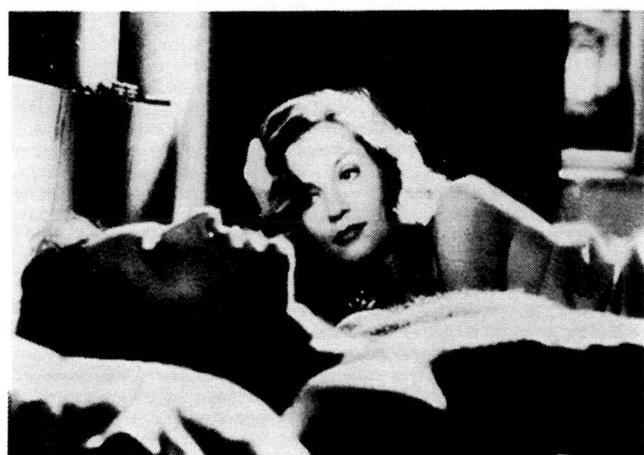

Though muddling moments dilute the potency of this above-average thriller, the assets of THE BEDROOM WINDOW are many. The girthsome shadow of Alfred Hitchcock falls over many a scene in Hanson's oblique tribute to the master, yet the film has its own unique if offbeat identity. Film hero Guttenberg, youthfully suave and much too self-assured as a well-paid and up-and-coming architect, is very much in the mold of the Hitchcock protagonist, basically a good, honest, and naively innocent victim of his own grandstanding. His confident posture is slowly bent in fear when he realizes that through a beau geste lie he has placed himself and others in high jeopardy. Guttenberg is shown greeting beautiful, selfish Huppert, the French-born wife of his boss, Shenar. (The boss is one of those slightly repugnant slicksters who spends most of his lucrative life reading the stock reports and collecting such curios as a nickel-plated automatic once owned by L.A. gangster Benjamin "Bugsy" Siegel, and proudly announcing: "Forty years and it's never been registered.") Guttenberg and Huppert have begun an affair right beneath Shenar's flaring nostrils. During their first tryst, while Guttenberg is in the bathroom, Huppert goes to the window in response to a girl's screams. She looks down to see a tall, red-haired man in a tan jacket trying to strangle a girl, McGovern. By the time Guttenberg answers Huppert's call, he can only see people crowding around the prone girl outside, the attacker having fled after hearing the noise of the window opened by Huppert and glancing up to see her standing in all her naked splendor. Later, Huppert and Guttenberg discuss the attack with the detached concern of upscale people talking about far away famines in India. The next day Guttenberg learns that another girl had been killed the previous night and soon realizes that the girl attacked outside his window could have been killed, and that the murderer of the other woman was probably the same attacker. Huppert comes to his room the next day and, after making love, they talk about what she has seen. "I'd like to do the right thing," she tells Guttenberg (not that this is a woman who does the right thing, but she talks about it to edify an ego that demands she appear noble, even to herself). Guttenberg encourages her, telling her that by informing police about the attacker she may help to catch a real murderer. Now, this is really going too far. It's one thing to talk about "doing the right thing"; it's a drastically different matter to do it. "Why should my life be turned upside down," Huppert prettily pouts, "just because I happened to look out the window? It's not fair." Then, of course, if she talked to the police, she would have to admit where she was when witnessing the attack, which would expose her affair with her husband's handsome employee. No, no, not a good idea at all. But Guttenberg is a lover craving to go to the rescue, and to impress his lady, tells her that *he* will do the right thing for her. To prove his own nobility, Guttenberg impulsively picks up the phone, calls the Baltimore police department and says that he saw the attacker—"tall, red-haired, tan jacket, jeans and tennis shoes," parroting Huppert's description of the man. Huppert is thrilled by his "romantic" gesture and begins to make passionate love to him as his reward. Guttenberg tells her to hurry up because detectives are coming to visit him shortly. Startled, Huppert races to dress and make a hasty exit. Reality, like the falling of iron horseshoes, begins to thud loudly into Guttenberg's comfortable life. Two detectives, Lumbly and Coffin, arrive and begin to ask hardnosed, detailed questions. Lumbly asks Guttenberg if he smokes and he says no, then notices the cigarettes left by Huppert and freezes momentarily at being compromised. He slides the cigarettes furtively into his pocket. To his "tan jacket" description, he is asked whether he means "windbreaker or sports jacket" He is tense now and guesses: "Windbreaker." Later, meeting Huppert, Guttenberg asks about the jacket and she tells him it was a windbreaker, which relieves Guttenberg. The pair then drive to the site where the second girl was raped and murdered and walk about, Guttenberg playing amateur sleuth and both of them discussing the killing like tourists casually strolling through Madame Tussaud's Wax Museum. Guttenberg reconstructs the killing from what he has learned from the papers and the police. It's a melancholy game, this conversation, and both Huppert and Guttenberg feel it has concluded with his statements to the police. But the detectives call Guttenberg and ask him to come to the station. While waiting to be seen, he sits next to McGovern, the girl who was attacked. The now worried Guttenberg, with McGovern, is asked to view a lineup of six men. As they stand behind a one-way glass, neither can make a positive identification, even though one of the men, the tall, red-haired Greenquist, has a background of such attacks. Guttenberg later walks McGovern to her car, learning that she is a cocktail waitress. She tells him that she has been on guard ever since the attack and is afraid to walk home from her job at night, driving instead. After McGovern leaves, Guttenberg follows Greenquist to a brownstone and later to his workplace, a construction site. He then brings Huppert to the site to see if she can identify Greenquist; Guttenberg has been caught up in his own nobility and wants to be sure, since this may be the same man who has murdered and may murder again. Huppert, from the safe distance of her car, looks over the construction worker but tells Guttenberg she cannot identify the man as the attacker. However, Guttenberg won't give up and begins to tail Greenquist, following him to a bar to observe his actions. He's not Sam Spade or Sherlock Holmes, but he's now obsessed with stopping the suspect from killing again. In the bar, Guttenberg watches as Greenquist squints coldly at a blonde who does a lascivious table-top dance. Guttenberg then loses his man, but later tracks him back to his townhouse. While driving home, Guttenberg sees a body being removed from a lot by police—the same blonde who had been dancing at the bar.

Guttenberg goes to the police and tells them that he can now identify Greenquist as the attacker. A slick state's attorney, Shenkkan, tells him that he will be helping to put away a murderer, and the police go to work in assembling circumstantial evidence. The evidence is too weak to support a murder charge, however, and Shenkkan decides to pursue the assault case, relying on Guttenberg's testimony. When Guttenberg explains all this to Huppert, she becomes upset, saying: "So far all you've done is grandstand, first for me, then for them [the police]. From the beginning you've wanted to play the hero. You can see where it's gotten us. And I am the one with everything to lose!" She walks away in a huff. McGovern sees Guttenberg and thanks him for identifying the attacker. "I want to get him," McGovern says. "I want to tell you how much it means to me to see someone like you who's not afraid to get involved." Huppert later says she is sorry for being selfish and will be in court to give him support: "When you testify, you'll be testifying for the both of us." In court Guttenberg identifies Greenquist as the attacker. Under a slow, detailed cross-examination by defense attorney Shawn, a conniving, clever, word-mincing attorney, Guttenberg's pat testimony goes to pieces. Shawn surprises the police and the district attorney by revealing that Guttenberg wears hard contact lenses to correct severe near-sightedness. Shawn then proves that without the contact lenses, which Guttenberg admits he was not wearing at the time of the attack, it would be nearly impossible for Guttenberg to identify anyone from the distance at which he claims to have witnessed the attack. Guttenberg's identification of Greenquist is shattered and the case is dismissed. Worse, during the course of his Guttenberg's testimony, Huppert has tried to coach him from her seat in the courtroom, and killer Greenquist recognized her as the woman he saw in the window when he attacked McGovern.

To add to the hero's woes, a neighbor tells police that she saw him coming into the building after the attack. Now *he* has become a suspect in the case. Moreover,

McGovern visits him and says she saw Huppert in the park with him, saw her coaching him in court, and easily deduced that Huppert was the one who witnessed the attack and that Guttenberg was shielding her. At the office, boss Shenar tells Guttenberg that the police have been inquiring about his employee's background and movements at the time of the attacks. Huppert and Guttenberg meet, and he tells her he believes the police are watching him and that they may have tapped his phone. Huppert realizes she is being drawn further and further into Guttenberg's mushrooming problems with the police and fears exposure. "I didn't get us into this," she snorts and walks away from him. Guttenberg goes to the bar where McGovern works and tells her that now he is a suspect and that Huppert has almost quit him. McGovern tells him that "you're either a romantic fool or an idiot, I don't know which is worse." She agrees to help him any way she can. Police call him in for questioning, telling him that a cocktail waitress remembered seeing him in the bar where the blonde girl had been just before she was murdered. Guttenberg tells police that he will seek legal counsel before answering more questions. That night he calls Huppert, who hangs up on him, and he later follows her to the ballet. He confronts Huppert and pleads with her to come forward and support the identification. She refuses, telling him that she has confessed her affair to Shenar and he has forgiven her, on the proviso that he will swear she was sleeping with him on the night of the attack so they will not be "dragged into this mess." Huppert then tells Guttenberg she's through with him. As Guttenberg leaves he sees Greenquist's truck outside the theater. He rushes back inside to find Huppert stabbed by Greenquist in a curtained aisle; the killer grins maniacally, then vanishes. Guttenberg grabs Huppert as she sinks, dying, into his arms just as Shenar comes forward, the lights go on, and Guttenberg appears to hundreds of horrified spectators as a cold-blooded murderer. Escaping, Guttenberg goes to McGovern and asks for her help. She harbors him, then works out a plan to entice Greenquist into exposing himself as a murderer. Wearing a wig and sexy attire, she follows Greenquist to a bar. Guttenberg has called police to ask them to go to McGovern's apartment building. Greenquist takes the bait, follows McGovern, and tries to kill her. Guttenberg interrupts and struggles with Greenquist. McGovern sprays mace into Greenquist's face, but he manages to climb into his truck, Guttenberg fighting with him. Police arrive and a wild chase ensues which ends with the truck smashing into a police car. Greenquist is captured, Guttenberg is exonerated, and both he and McGovern get a lecture from Coffin. Of course, the last image of Guttenberg and McGovern together more than suggests that he has, through peril of his life, found the girl who is right for him.

THE BEDROOM WINDOW is a taut film with plenty of thrills and twists for crime genre fans, and Hanson is to be credited with procuring a clever script and fast-action sequences that build solid suspense. He also, unlike the De Palma school that opts for gore instead of real substance, provides a sophisticated process for developing his characters. Huppert and, to a lesser degree, Shenar are the perfect social dilettantes who use other people as they please, then retreat into their own world of money and power to disassociate themselves from the unpleasant aftereffects of their actions. Guttenberg is transformed by his impulsive honesty from a slick clone of Shenar to an authentic human being willing to risk his career and even his life to correct a mistake he has made as well as help capture a killer—a somewhat self-serving resolve but nonetheless admirable, and in the end he receives grudging respect from the police for his reckless ways. Guttenberg is often too boyish for his increasingly forceful role here, but that aspect of his personality proves, on the other hand, to make his unjudicious actions believable. Huppert is a standout as the cool, extra-sensual European beauty, playing the epitome of the pampered woman who cannot be bothered by lovers who complicate her stylish life. Shenar is equally convincing as the unattractive, in-control husband and McGovern, although not really featured until the last part of the film, is solid as the clean-living, street-smart cocktail waitress whose heart is pure and courage constant. Hanson draws pleasingly upon Hitchcock masterpieces—the premise of REAR WINDOW and situations sliced from SABOTEUR and THE MAN WHO KNEW TOO MUCH. The stabbing scene at the ballet, leaving Guttenberg holding the dying Huppert before scores of people, is right out of NORTH BY NORTHWEST, almost duplicating the scene where Cary Grant appears to have stabbed a diplomat at the U.N. building before dozens of horrified witnesses. But the overall effect is still entertaining, and there are more than enough original scenes from Hanson to make this indelibly his own film. Shot entirely in Baltimore, the overall look of the film reflects the image of an Old World City almost Germanic-gothic in structure, which is not off the mark, since Baltimore is one of America's oldest communities. *(Violence, mild profanity, brief nudity.)*

p, Martha Schumacher; d&w, Curtis Hanson (based on the novel *The Witnesses* by Anne Holden); ph, Gil Taylor (CinemaScope, Technicolor); m, Michael Shrieve, Patrick Gleeson, Felix Mendlessohn; ed, Scott Conrad; prod d, Ron Foreman; art d, Rafael Caro; set d, Hilton Rosemarin; cos, Clifford Capone; ch, Michael Owens; m/l, Raun Butcher, Jon Butcher, Robert Palmer, Dennis Nelson, Tony Haynes, Rick James, Danny Wilde, Mildred J. Hill, Patty S. Hill, Mike Kendred, W.C. Clark, Brian Holland, Edward Holland, Lamont Dozier; stunts, Thomas Rosaies; makeup, Stefano Fava.

Thriller Cas. (PR:O MPAA:R)

BEIJO NA BOCA† (1987, Braz.) 91m Encontro-Sincrocine-Sagitarius-Embrafilme/Embrafilme-Empresa Brasileira de Filmes c (Trans: The French Kiss)

Mario Gomes *(Mario)*, Claudia Ohana *(Celeste)*, Joana Fomm, Milton Moraes, Denis Carvalho, Stepan Nercessian, Perfeito Fortuna, Claudia Celeste, Sandro Soviatti.

A Brazilian Bonnie and Clyde story about two lovers whose highly passionate romance leads to the erotic thrills of danger, guns, and drugs. They grow increasingly more deadly until their story makes it to the front page.

d, Paulo Sergio de Almeida; w, Euclydes Marinho; ph, Antonio Penido; m, Sergio Guilherme Saraceni; ed, Raphael Valverde.

Romance (PR:NR MPAA:NR)

BEJALAI† (1987, Malaysia) 95m Action Films c (Trans: To Go On A Journey)

Dickie Isaac *(Rentap)*, Saloma Kumpeing *(The Girl)*, Chiling Nyanggai *(The Old Man)*.

Believed to be the first feature film made in the Iban language, this film is set in a village in Sarawak, one of the states of the Federation of Malaysia. It tells the story of what happens to the villagers when they are forced to leave their homes because of a dam construction. (In Iban.)

p, Stephen Teo, Zarul Albakri; d&w, Stephen Teo; ph, Jim Shum; ed, Zhang Jiande, Shen Shengde.

Drama (PR:NR MPAA:NR)

BELIEVERS, THE zero (1987) 114m Orion c

Martin Sheen *(Dr. Cal Jamison)*, Helen Shaver *(Jessica Halliday)*, Harley Cross *(Chris Jamison)*, Robert Loggia *(Lt. Sean McTaggert)*, Elizabeth Wilson *(Kate Maslow)*, Harris Yulin *(Donald Calder)*, Lee Richardson *(Dennis Maslow)*, Richard Masur *(Marty Wertheimer)*, Carla Pinza *(Mrs. Ruiz)*, Jimmy Smits *(Tom Lopez)*, Raul Davila *(Sezine)*, Malick Bowens *(Palo)*, Janet-Laine Green *(Lisa)*, Larry Ramos *(Diner Counterman)*, Philip Corey, Jennifer Lee *(Calder's Assistants)*, Nonnie Griffin, Bob Clout *(Cigar Couple)*, Harvey Chao, Christine Pak *(Chinese Couple)*, Joan Kaye *(Woman in Park)*, Eddie Jones *(Police Patient)*, John Bendel *(Theater Detective)*, Joseph Pentangleo, Joseph Wilkens *(Theater Cops)*, Robert Clohessy *(Diner Detective)*, Dick Martinsen *(Diner Cop)*, Robert Connelly, Tony Desantis *(Precinct Detectives)*, Frank Rivers *(Park Cop)*, Ana Maria Quintana *(A.C.H.E. Secretary)*, Ray Paisley *(Customs Agent)*, Dick Callahan *(Bartender)*, Christopher Brown *(Carpenter)*, Gary Farmer, Ramsey Fadiman *(Movers)*, Juan Manuel Aguero *(News Vendor)*, Maria Magdaleno *(Woman at Newstand)*, Shirley Anthony *(Marty's Secretary)*, Elizabeth Hanna *(Doctor at Hospital)*, Micki Moore, Richard Spiegelman, Fernando Queija, Maria Lebb *(Believers)*, Khali Keyi *(African Shaman)*, Leroy Radcliffe *(Chief Dancer)*, Wilhelmina Taylor, Antwanette Abel, Vaune Blalock, Quentin Clark, Denise Hawthorne, Leona Heyward, Harry Kimbrough, Lindsey Floyd, Jewel Love, Thomas Reid, Diana Taylor *(Tribal Dancers)*, Raymond Graham *(Lead Drummer)*, James Cherry, Monique Martin, Willie White, Phillip Williamson *(Drummers)*.

This is another cultist, blood-splattering occult-mania film that brutalizes story, cast, and viewer indiscriminately, a tasteless and essentially offensive film which will appeal to no one but the crackpot crowd and those lured by the past strengths of actor Sheen and director Schlesinger. Voodoo and all its heinous practices of bloodletting and sacrifice, in this case the hedonistic blood sacrifice of a seven-year-old boy, is the root of this film's evil and its downfall. Psychologist Sheen lives with his wife and boy, Cross, in Minneapolis. Sheen's wife is electrocuted while standing in a puddle of milk in her kitchen. The widower and son move to New York and are soon threatened by voodoo practitioners of a cult called Santeria. Sheen works with the police and his first case involves an hysterical Latino cop (Smits) who has found a young boy murdered in such a way that he appears to be a sacrificial victim to the dreaded Santeria sect. The cop later commits suicide and an autopsy reveals he has a snake in his stomach (gruesome shades of ALIEN). Meanwhile, young Cross is learning Spanish and is wearing a strange amulet he picked up in a park next to a decapitated cat (yes, another example of the sect's reach-out program). Hard cop Loggia believes the recent rash of stabbings and brutal murders involving dissection are the work of a serial killer. Sheen, when not busy romancing Shaver, his sexy landlady, slowly learns the voodoo sect is behind the murders. The sect, it turns out, has been after his son Cross all along and somehow caused the accidental death of Sheen's wife in Minneapolis. But it will take Sheen's own hand to deliver the boy's life to Santeria. To what end? If a person desires all the world's success, according to the voodoo ritual here, he must kill his first born. Sheen inevitably moves toward

this unthinkable conclusion, his will power turned to jelly as the voodoo takes charge of his mind and heart. Cross remains in constant jeopardy and only an unrealistic twist ending prevents his demise, but then the whole film in unrealistic, unsavory and disgusting.

Sheen moves about like an automaton under the heavy-handed direction of Schlesinger, whose career has dipped to the dung heap since making such outstanding films as DAY OF THE LOCUST and MARATHON MAN. He lards his scenes heavily with symbolism and tricky camera angles, taking very long scenes and then cutting them to almost subliminal, red-herring images in his editing. It all looks professional but it is empty; this film should mark Schlesinger's swan song as a director of repute. He blatantly capitalizes upon the freakish, the bizarre, and the sadistic with no thought of the disservice he does his production or the audience. Another film dealing with a similar theme, ANGEL HEART, though equally repugnant in theme and bloodletting, is far superior from a production standpoint. Under no circumstances should any youngster be subjected to this sickening and insulting film. *(Graphic violence, gore effects, sexual situations.)*

p, John Schlesinger, Michael Childers, Beverly Camhe; d, John Schlesinger; w, Mark Frost (based on the novel *The Religion* by Nicholas Conde); ph, Robby Muller (DeLuxe Color); m, J. Peter Robinson; ed, Peter Honess; prod d, Simon Holland; art d, John Kasarda, Carol Spier; set d, Susan Bode, Elinor Rose Galbraith; ch, Wilhelmina Taylor; cos, Shay Cunliffe; spec eff, Ted Ross, Connie Brink; makeup, Kevin Hayney, Micky Scott; stunts, Dean Jeffries.

Horror (PR:O MPAA:R)

BELINDA† (1987, Aus.) 97m Fontana Films c

Deanne Jeffs *(Belinda)*, Mary Regan *(Crystal)*, Kaarin Fairfax *(Sandra)*, Nicos Lathouris *(Benny)*, Hazel Phillips *(Doreen)*, John Jarratt *(Graeme)*, Elizabeth Lord *(Mandy)*, Gerda Nicholsen *(Belinda's mother)*, Alan Cassell *(Belinda's father)*, Tim Burns *(Jamie)*, Caz Lederman *(Rhonda)*, John Haddon *(Jeremy Shaw)*, Joy Smithers *(Liz)*, Armando Hurley *(Billy James)*.

Jeffs is a 16-year-old aspiring ballerina who takes a job as a dancer in a seedy night club in Sydney. She meets a variety of characters, some shady and some sympathetic, before finally abandoning the club while continuing to pursue her dreams. Director/writer Gibbons is herself a former dancer, and much of the material is autobiographical. Her husband, McCullogh, served as cinematographer on the project.

p, Bedrich Kabriel; d&w, Pamela Gibbons; ph, Malcolm McCullogh; m, Les Gock; ed, David Hugget; prod d, Herbert Pinter; ch, Robyn Moase.

Drama (PR:NR MPAA:NR)

BELL DIAMOND*** (1987) 96m Light c

Marshall Gaddis *(Jeff Dolan)*, Sarah Wyss *(Cathy Dolan)*, Terrilyn Williams *(Hailey)*, Scott Andersen *(Scott)*, Pat O'Connor *(The Boss)*, Kristi Jean Hager *(Laura)*, Hal Waldrup *(Mick)*, Dan Cornell *(Danny)*, Ron Hanekan *(Ron)*, Alan Goddard *(Alan Goddard, Radio Announcer)*, Anne Kolesar *(Social Counsellor)*.

Directed by Jon Jost, America's least-known independent filmmaker, BELL DIAMOND is as interesting an examination of the filmmaking process as it is as a film. The story is a simple one which has been seen numerous times in many variations. Set in Butte, Montana, the film stars Gaddis as a Vietnam vet whose seven-year marriage to Wyss is coming to an end. She desperately wants to have a child, but his wartime exposure to Agent Orange has left him sterile. Gaddis has also become emotionally sterile, and spends endless hours sitting in front of the TV watching ball games and guzzling beer. Like many citizens of Butte, he is an unemployed mine worker and turns to alcohol for comfort. Wyss packs her bags and leaves despite Gaddis' inarticulate and surprisingly passionate objections. Emotionally paralyzed by her absence, Gaddis finds no comfort in his friends Waldrup and Cornell, two men in similarly downtrodden, though less extreme, positions. Sitting atop a tower with his two buddies, Gaddis breaks down in tears and appears on the verge of suicide. Waldrup notifies a local radio call-in show and Gaddis is brought down to safety without incident. After an unsuccessful stint with a social worker, Gaddis returns to his former ways—watching television and missing Wyss. Without warning, Wyss telephones Gaddis and arranges to meet him at the bus depot. When she arrives with suitcase in hand, Gaddis sees that she is pregnant. The film cuts to Gaddis' happy face and freezes on that moment—before he is able to question who the father is?, why she has returned?, and what they are going to do next?

Unlike such talented American independents as Spike Lee or Jim Jarmusch, Jon Jost has received no distribution deals, no critical raves from TV reviewers, and no studio deals to make slicker, bigger budget films. He began making feature films in 1974 with SPEAKING DIRECTLY on a budget of $2,000 (approximately the price of coffee and donuts on a Hollywood feature). After gaining the attention of some perceptive critics and the praise of director Jean-Luc Godard, Jost soon became the most highly respected independent filmmaker in America. Partly because Hollywood will have nothing to do with him and partly because he'll have nothing to do with Hollywood, the 44-year-old Jost has retained this status. Still, he is practically unknown in America and has a larger following in Europe. For BELL DIAMOND, Jost had a "big" budget of $25,000 (his second largest to date), which came from a National Endowment for the Arts grant. The idea for BELL DIAMOND came when the San Francisco-based Jost decided to travel to Butte, Montana, without a script, without an idea, without a cast, and with practically no cash or crew. He arrived in a local tavern and began asking people if they'd like to act in a film. Those who said yes were cast. Those who displayed the most enthusiasm were cast in lead roles. Disenchanted with the Hollywood's filmmaking, starmaking, and method acting, Jost believes that most people, given the proper encouragement, direction, and set of circumstances, can be just as effective as actors as can professionals. Developing BELL DIAMOND's "script" with his cast, he then filmed them as they improvised their dialog. With Jost operating the camera himself (using only available light) and his then girl friend, Alenka Pavlin, working the sound, his filmmaking process was unintimidating, primitive, and revolutionary (by today's standards). As a result, all of his "non-actors" turn in marvelously convincing performances, especially Wyss who is one of the most realistic characters ever seen in a fiction film. BELL DIAMOND is not without faults, but its imperfections make it even more exciting and revolutionary than most other films seen today. *(Adult situations, profanity.)*

p,d,w&ph, Jon Jost; m, Jon English, Jon Jost; ed, Jon Jost.

Drama **(PR:C MPAA:NR)**

BELLIFRESCHI† (1987, It.) International Dean/Medusa c (Trans: Lovely and Fresh)

Lino Banfi, Christian De Sica, Lionel Stander, Marina Viro, Monica Frassinelli, Rosanna Banfi, Lisa Lavendre, Giuseppina Gaspardis D'Eva.

Two frustrated Italian actors go to America where they break into Sylvester Stallone's mansion and fire a machinegun barrage at the actor. They have a series of adventures while on the run from the FBI and the CIA, before finding safety in Mexico.

d, Enrico Oldoini; w, Enrico Oldoini, Liliana Betti, Paolo Costella; ph, Giorgio di Battista; m, Manuel De Sica; ed, Raimondo Crociani.

Action/Adventure **(PR:NR MPAA:NR)**

BELLMAN & TRUE† (1987, Brit.) 122m Hand Made-Euston/Hand Made c

Bernard Hill *(Hiller, Computer Systems Engineer)*, Derek Newark *(Guv'nor, Cockney Gang Leader)*, Richard Hope *(Salto)*, Ken Bones *(Gort, Salto's Henchman)*, Frances Tomelty *(Anna)*, Kieran O'Brien *(Boy, Hiller's Stepson)*, John Kavanagh *(The Donkey)*, Arthur Whybrow *(The Peterman)*, Jim Dowdall *(The Wheelman)*, Peter Howell *(The Bellman)*, Kate McEnery *(Mo)*, Anne Carroll *(Pauline)*, Richard Strange *(Man with Walkman)*, Peter Jonfield *(Security Sergeant)*, Andrew Paul *(Young Security Guard)*, Richard Walsh *(Security Driver)*, Camilla Nash *(Anna's Lover)*, Badi Uzzaman *(Shopkeeper)*, William Sleigh *(Hotel Clerk)*, Chris Sanders *(Commuter)*, Greg Powell *(Coach Driver)*, Alisa Bosschaert *(Ticket Check-In Clerk)*, Michael Shaw *(Policeman)*, Alan Downer *(Immigration Officer)*, Michael Bertenshaw *(Steward)*, Stephen Churchett *(Commercial Traveller)*, Michael Watkins *(Man on Roof)*, Roger McKern *(Lorry Driver)*.

Originally intended as a two-part TV presentation, this caper film directed by Richard Loncraine (THE MISSIONARY) tells the story of a computer systems analyst (Hill) who finds himself in the middle of a big heist. An inveterate drunkard, Hill has been deserted by his wife, who leaves behind her son by a previous marriage, O'Brien. Hill's employer has conducted a security study for a banking concern. Hope, a shady operator, is aware of the study and Hill's drinking problem, believing it makes him vulnerable to bribery. For 1,000 pounds sterling, Hill consents to steal the tape that reveals the study's secrets, but before he gets a chance, he is fired. Hill takes O'Brien and flees to London, but Hope catches up with them and confines them in a run-down nightclub. Hill is forced to obtain a copy of the tape and to design a method to disarm the security system. (In this way Hill becomes a "bellman," the person responsible for neutralizing alarms during a hold-up.) Newark and a gang of toughs join the operation. The masterfully planned heist is undertaken but goes awry. The whole crew escapes to the seaside where a plane is to take them to safety. Hope becomes convinced that Newark has no intention of taking him or Hill along. Hill sets up an explosion that kills Newark and his toughs. In the end, with the booty in their possession, father and stepson prepare to leave the country. Songs include: "[D'Ye Ken] John Peel" (John Woodcock Graves, performed by Lonnie Donegan), "I Saw Mommy Kissing Santa Claus" (Thomas Conner, performed by Stephanie De-Sykes).

p, Michael Wearing, Christopher Neame; d, Richard Loncraine; w, Desmond Lowden, Richard Loncraine, Michael Wearing (based on the novel by Desmond Lowden); ph, Ken Westbury (Technicolor); m, Colin Towns; ed, Paul Green; prod d, Jon Bunker; md, Alan Wilson; art d, John Ralph; set d, Ann Mollo; cos, David Perry; m/l, John Woodcock Graves, Thomas Conner; spec eff, Ace Effects; makeup, Viven Placks; stunts, Terry Forrestal.

Crime **(PR:NR MPAA:NR)**

BELLY OF AN ARCHITECT, THE*** (1987, Brit./It.) 108m Callender/Hemdale c

Brian Dennehy *(Stourley Kracklite)*, Chloe Webb *(Louisa Kracklite)*, Lambert Wilson *(Caspasian Speckler)*, Vanni Corbellini *(Frederico)*, Sergio Fantoni *(Io Speckler)*, Stefania Casini *(Flavia Speckler)*, Alfredo Varelli *(Julio Ficcone)*, Geoffrey Copleston *(Caspetti)*, Francesco Carnelutti *(Pastarri)*, Marino Mase *(Trettorio)*, Marne Maitland *(Battistino)*, Claudio Spadaro *(Mori)*, Rate Furlan *(Violinist)*, Julian Jenkins *(Old Doctor)*, Enrica Maria Scrivano *(Mother)*, Riccardo Ussani *(Little Boy)*, Stefano Gragnani *(The Nose Man)*, Andrea Prodan *(Young Doctor)*, Fabio Sartor *(Policeman)*.

Capturing the glory of Roman architecture, this exquisitely shot film about obsession reaffirms director Peter Greenaway's reputation as one of the most visually stunning filmmakers working today. Dennehy, a corpulent Chicago architect of some renown, travels to Rome with his considerably younger wife Webb to oversee an exhibition commemorating a little-known 18th-century French architect, Etienne-Louis Boullee (an actual historical figure). It has long been Dennehy's dream to mount this tribute to his idol and the exhibition is to be done on a grand scale. A handsome young Italian architect, Wilson, is in charge of the project's finances, and he covets both Dennehy's control of the exhibition and Webb. Like the other Italians working with Dennehy, he has contempt for both the American and Boullee. Upon his arrival in Rome, Dennehy begins to experience terrible abdominal pains. As he notices the interest Wilson is taking in his wife and she in him, Dennehy begins to suspect that Webb is trying to poison him. He visits a doctor and is told he is suffering from dyspepsia and given some medication. As the months of arduous preparation wear on, Dennehy becomes totally immersed in the project and increasingly concerned with his stomach problems. Meanwhile, Wilson and Webb conduct a passionate affair that Dennehy is aware of but does nothing to stop. His obsession with his aching belly leads him to an almost fetishist interest in other stomachs, particularly those of the famous rendered in paintings and statues, of which he makes endless photocopies. But for all his interest in bellies, he fails to notice that Webb is pregnant. She assures him that it is his child and not Wilson's, but she makes no attempt to hide her affair. Throughout the film, Dennehy has written letters to the long-dead Boullee, and it is these missives that express the true state of his mind. All along Wilson has been skimming funds from the exhibition's budget to finance the restoration of a Mussolini-commissioned structure. As the funds grow tighter and as others become aware that Dennehy is a very sick man, the pressure grows to replace him with Wilson. Desperate to complete the project his way, Dennehy tells Webb that he wants to mortgage their Chicago home and change his will to come up with the necessary money. She refuses to allow this and tells him that she is leaving him for Wilson. In a short time, Dennehy also loses control of the exhibition to his young Italian rival. He undergoes a more thorough examination and is informed that he has pancreatic cancer and only a few months to live. Dennehy does not appear at the exhibition's opening ceremony, but instead watches from a balcony above, and when Webb cuts the ribbon, he leaps to his death through an open window.

THE BELLY OF AN ARCHITECT is without doubt Greenaway's most *well-rounded* film. Visually it is a tour de force. Collaborating with cinematographer Vierny, who has worked with Bunuel and Resnais and is known for his painstaking lighting and mastery of deep-focus photography, Greenaway presents one beautifully composed image after another. Each densely textured composition is like a painting in its own right. Employing mostly long and medium shots, Greenaway enhances this effect by framing his scenes within doorways and arches. As in his past films (THE DRAUGHTSMAN'S CONTRACT, A ZED & TWO NOUGHTS), Greenaway's arrangements of the elements within the shot are triumphs of symmetry, and, perhaps, even more than a cinematic painter, Greenaway can be seen as an architect of images. Though he is not formally trained as an architect, Greenaway has an erstwhile interest in architecture which has been evident in his earlier films but is in the forefront here in his subject

matter, his compositions, and his reverence for the great buildings of Rome. He sees parallels between the architect's role and the filmmaker's. In an interview in *Sight and Sound* (Summer 1987), he explained that both are accountable to those who have put up the money for a project, to the people who will see the finished product, and to the architect's/filmmaker's need for self-satisfaction and fulfillment of his idea of culture. In this way, THE BELLY OF AN ARCHITECT is somewhat autobiographical and Dennehy can be seen as kind of surrogate for Greenaway. Greenaway is also an admirer of the heretofore little-appreciated Boullee and, in effect, he mounts his own tribute to the Frenchman with his film. Yet another autobiographical component is the fact that both of Greenaway's parents died of stomach cancer, and he has said that in some way all of his films deal with loss.

The film's themes, like its symbolism, are difficult to interpret, though Greenaway provides a more traditional narrative structure and more well-rounded characters than in his other films. At the center of the film is Dennehy's extraordinary performance. Using his stomach almost like a character itself, he makes his fixation on it and his battle to stage the perfect tribute to Boullee seem like the center of the universe for 108 minutes. Then we realize with Dennehy, that like the Roman emperors before him, he will die but art endures. Both Dennehy's health and his marriage are secondary to staging the tribute to the architect who, like Dennehy, has left few buildings behind to speak for him. Dennehy magnificently conveys the architect's obsessive behavior, laying naked Stourley's ego as it waxes and wanes. As believable as his physical pain is his mental anguish as both his wife and his project slowly slip from his grasp. He is like a man running around in a dream he knows is a dream but from which he can't awaken. Webb (SID AND NANCY) is not entirely successful with her role. Her flightiness and boredom with her older husband are plausible prerequisites for her affair, but one is left wondering how she and Dennehy would have ever gotten together in the first place. Wilson is totally convincing as the architect of Dennehy's downfall. Handsome, suave, and completely unprincipled, he is every inch the swine and there is tremendous viewer satisfaction when Dennehy punches him in the nose. Though this is Greenaway's most accessible film it will probably still appeal only to a limited audience. *(Sexual situations, nudity, profanity, adult situations.).*

p, Colin Callender, Walter Donohue; d&w, Peter Greenaway; ph, Sacha Vierny (Technicolor); m, Wim Mertens, Glenn Branca; ed, John Wilson; art d, Luciana Vedovelli; set d, Giorgio Desideri; cos, Maurizio Millenotti; makeup, Franco Corridoni.

Drama **(PR:O MPAA:NR)**

BENJI THE HUNTED*½** (1987) 88m Mulberry Square-Embark/BV c

Benji *(Himself)*, Red Steagall *(Hunter)*, Nancy Francis *(Newscaster)*, Mike Francis *(TV Cameraman)*, Frank Inn *(Himself)*.

The lovable pooch homers again in his fourth feature after having struck out with a co-starring role opposite Chevy Chase in OH, HEAVENLY DOG. This time, Benji is separated from his trainer, Frank Inn (his trainer in real life as well), after a fishing accident in the Pacific Northwest. Benji bravely dogpaddles to shore in the wilds and finds himself the unwitting protector of a litter of orphaned cougar cubs. The remainder of this charming movie deals with the tribulations of life and death in the Great Out There as Benji frantically searches for food and shelter for himself and the cubs while Inn continues his desperate quest for his "best friend." Along the way, Benji encounters the usual hardships of the wilderness while avoiding various predators, including a jet black timber wolf who would like nothing better than to make Benji and the cubs his dinner. Since dogs are more intelligent than wolves (at least *this* dog is), Benji manages to outthink the villain and tricks him into jumping off the edge of a steep precipice. What remains is for Benji to locate a new mother for the cubs, while Inn continues his search via helicopter. Naturally, all ends well.

There are some interesting sidelights involved with the film's production. After FOR THE LOVE OF BENJI, Joe and Carolyn Camp, the husband-wife team responsible for the first two films, decided that making these movies was just too difficult. Then this story came up and Joe Camp thought it was too good to ignore, especially since it practically dispensed with the human actors in favor of the animals. Filmed in Oregon and Washington state, the picture has almost no dialog after the first 12-minute set-up. Still, once one gets into watching the animals perform, that opening dialog seems long. The picture was edited in the "Kuleshov style" which means that several shots of the animal's head are taken, then a shot of the action the dog is watching, then back to the animal. Even if the animal is not as good an emoter as Benji, adroit editing can make it seem that there is a legitimate and honest response to what has just been seen. In such a way, pictures tell the story and words seem superfluous. Disney fans know that if the animals are on their game, humans are seldom needed. Among Benji's compatriots, the cast includes a Kodiak bear, ferrets, raccoons, an eagle, rabbits, a skunk, and one very valiant frog who had the unenviable task of being a plaything for the cougars. More than 20 cougar cubs were used to portray the litter because they grew too quickly to keep their roles. This edition of Benji is female. She is the daughter of the late, lamented original Benji whose real name was Higgins and who appeared in the 1960s TV show "Petticoat Junction." (This should not come as a surprise to those who have always known that "Lassie" was, for the most part, played by a male animal.) The current Benji (nee Benjean) was 11 years of age at the time the movie was made and had been playing the part ever since she took over for her daddy in 1977's FOR THE LOVE OF BENJI. She comes from a show business family as it was her mother who chased the tiny horses in the Chuck Wagon Dog Food commercials. Several weeks before shooting began, Inn's associate Bryan Renfro began a rigorous training schedule for Benji which included swimming, running and a regimen of exercises that put the dog in superb condition. Those who read the Camp script thought it would be impossible for any animal to do all the tough tasks required but they didn't reckon on Benji's determination.

The picture cost almost $5 million to make but when one realizes that the original cost one tenth of that and grossed around $45 million, it was a fairly good risk. Produced by Camp's Mulberry Square Productions and his Embark distributing company, the movie was well-distributed by Disney's Buena Vista

company. Walt would have loved it. Sad to say, Benjean has been "fixed" and can bear no pups of her own so it will be nephews and nieces in the role if and when another film is made. At present, the star is living in happy semi-retirement, enjoying her life as a dog, making the odd personal appearance to promote the film and various other items and causes. She created quite a stir at the 1987 fair for "Actors and Others for Animals" in Los Angeles. Some of the biggest names in movies and television were all but snubbed when Benji arrived. Not a small feat to outshine such stellar stars but Benji did it with her customary panache. For the record, the original Benji (referred to as "The Old Man" in reverential tones by those who knew him) was a foundling at a San Fernando Valley Animal Shelter when Inn picked him up. Inn's credits in movies and TV include training "Arnold the Pig" for "Green Acres," as well as several other notable animals. With this picture, Benji takes a place in the Canine Hall of Fame along with Lassie, Rin-Tin-Tin, Asta (from THE THIN MAN series), Strongheart (a popular silent screen dog who rivaled Rinty for a while), Petey (from the OUR GANG comedies), and, of course, Daisy (from the BLONDIE series). Since the story of BENJI THE HUNTED took second place to the star's acting abilities, one could safely say that it was not a case of the tale wagging the dog.

p, Ben Vaughn; d&w, Joe Camp; ph, Don Reddy (CFI color); m, Euel Box, Betty Box; ed, Karen Thorndike; art d, Bob Riggs, Ray Brown.

Children's **(PR:AAA MPAA:G)**

BESAME MUCHO† (1987, Braz.) 95m H.B. Filmes/Embrafilme c (Trans: Kiss Me Much)

Antonio Fagundes *(Tuca)*, Christiane Torloni *(Dina)*, Jose Wilker *(Xico)*, Gloria Pires *(Olga)*, Isabel Ribeiro *(Soror Encarnacion)*, Paulo Betti *(Cesar)*, Giulia Gam, Sylvio Mazzucca, Jessie James, Marthus Mathias, Iara Janra, Vera Zimmermann, Linda Gay, Wilma de Aguiar.

Co-produced by Hector Babenco, the Brazilian director of PIXOTE and KISS OF THE SPIDER WOMAN, this picture looks at two married couples, all four of them friends, whose relationships stretch from the 1960s through the 1980s.

The film begins in the present as both couples are splitting apart and works its way back to the initial meeting between the then-young twosomes as the strains of the popular bolero "Besame Mucho" (Consuelo Velazquez) are heard. The film's structure is similar to 1983's BETRAYAL which was penned by Harold Pinter.

p, Hector Babenco, Francisco Ramalho, Jr.; d, Francisco Ramalho, Jr.; w, Mario Prata, Francisco Ramalho, Jr. (based on the play by Mario Prata); ph, Jose Tadeu Ribeiro (Eastmancolor); m, Wagner Tiso, Consuelo Velazquez; ed, Mauro Alice; art d, Marcos Weinstock; set d, Nordana Benetazzo; cos, Domingos Fischini.

Romance **(PR:NR MPAA:NR)**

BEST SELLER*½** (1987) 110m Hemdale/Orion c

James Woods *(Cleve)*, Brian Dennehy *(Detective Lieutenant Dennis Meechum)*, Victoria Tennant *(Roberta Gillian)*, Allison Balson *(Holly Meechum)*, Paul Shenar *(David Madlock)*, George Coe *(Graham, Madlock's Lawyer)*, Anne Pitoniak *(Mrs. Foster)*, Mary Carver *(Cleve's Mother)*, Sully Boyar *(Monks)*, Kathleen Lloyd *(Annie)*, Harold Tyner *(Cleve's Father)*, E. Brian Dean *(Taxi Driver)*, Jeffrey Josephson *(Pearlman)*, Edward Blackoff *(Thorn)*, Branscombe Richmond *(Longshoreman)*, J.P. Bumstead *(Rothman)*, William Bronder *(Foley)*, Jenny Gago *(Woman in Laundry)*, Michael Crabtree, Ted Markland *(Men in Bar)*, Clare Fields *(Bartender)*, Claudia Stenke *(Woman at Bar)*, David Byrd *(Quentin)*, Loyda Ramos *(Female Officer)*, Obaka Adedunyo *(Man in Car)*, Phil Hoover *(Roud)*, David Blackwood *(Senator)*, David Ursin *(Meechum's Lawyer)*, Jay Ingram *(Turner)*, Daniel Trent *(Jarvis)*, Gary Kirk *(Jason)*, Dean Abston *(Cabot)*, David Cass *(Cop in Depository)*, Bill Mitchell *(El Paso TV Anchor)*, John Howard Swain *(Man at Airport)*, Dennis Acree, Mark Venturini, Larry Holt, Jeff Ramsey *(Bodyguards)*, James Winburn *(Supervisor)*, Peter Stader *(Dock Worker)*, Brian Gaffikin *(Waiter)*, Michael White *(Young Cop)*, Martin West *(Mature Cop)*, Wally Burr *(Talk Show Host)*, Arlin Miller *(News Reporter)*, Sands Hall *(Teacher)*, Samuel V. Baldoni, Hank Woessner *(Men)*.

An intriguing crime thriller scripted by cult writer/director Larry Cohen (IT'S ALIVE, GOD TOLD ME TO, Q) and starring two of America's finest character actors, Woods and Dennehy. Dennehy plays a Joseph Wambaugh-type cop who writes best-selling crime novels on the side. Having recently lost his beloved wife to cancer and faced with raising his teenage daughter (Balson) alone, Dennehy finds himself in the throes of severe writer's block. Under extreme pressure to deliver a long-overdue book, he is desperate for some inspiration. Enter Woods, a fastidious, extremely well dressed hit man who gets Dennehy's attention by saving the cop's life during a shoot-out with diamond smugglers. Woods wants Dennehy to write his life story. Seething with contempt for the hired killer, Dennehy would just as soon arrest Woods, but the assassin spins a fascinating

tale that Dennehy cannot resist. Woods used to be on the payroll of ultra-rich and powerful industrialist Shenar—as an corporate assassin. Over the years Woods has murdered dozens of prominent politicians and business people who have had the misfortune of getting in the way of Shenar's ambition (most of the killings have looked like accidents). Having helped build Shenar's empire from the ground up, Woods expected status and power. Instead, the killer found himself dumped by the corporation. Now Woods seeks fame and revenge through a sensational book detailing the crimes he committed for the respectable Shenar (amazingly, Woods wants assurances from Dennehy that he [Woods] will come off "sympathetic"). Dennehy is decidedly dubious of Woods' allegations, so the sleazy assassin takes the author on a coast-to-coast tour of his crime sites, proving his involvement every step of the way. Trailing the duo are Shenar's goons, which lends even more credibility to Woods' story.

Eventually, Dennehy is convinced enough to write the book, although he is determined to portray Woods as the cold-blooded killer that he is. Obsessed with his portrayal in print, Woods breaks into the home of Dennehy's editor, Tennant, and demands to see the manuscript. Tennant reveals that there is only one copy—and Dennehy took it home with him. Woods then breaks into Dennehy's house, only to find one of Shenar's goons looking for the manuscript as well. Seeing that the goon is about to kill Dennehy's daughter, Woods dispatches him and then takes the girl back to Tennant's for safekeeping. Meanwhile, Shenar has invited Dennehy to attend a children's fund-raiser held at his mansion. There, Shenar attempts to buy off Dennehy by offering to make him a rich man with a cushy position in the corporation. Unbeknownst to Shenar, however, Woods has trailed Dennehy to the mansion and is intent on killing the industrialist to provide the perfect "ending" for the book. At the same time, both Woods and Dennehy are unaware that Shenar traced Dennehy's daughter to Tennant's home and has kidnaped the girl in case the author refuses to comply. As Shenar and Dennehy talk, Woods calmly kills several of the industrialist's bodyguards while dozens of children wearing party hats and carrying balloons play nearby. Finally, Woods kills the bodyguard holding Dennehy's daughter hostage and tells the girl to stay put while he goes downstairs to confront Shenar. When Woods appears, Shenar pulls a gun and shoots Dennehy. The writer's daughter runs to her father's aid, only to be grabbed by Shenar. Shielding himself with the girl, Shenar dares Woods to shoot. In an amazing display of compassion, Woods drops his gun, only to be shot by Shenar. As Woods lies dying at the foot of the stairs, Shenar releases the girl. Dennehy then swiftly grabs Woods' gun and aims it at Shenar, ready to pull the trigger. Dennehy's daughter begs him not to shoot and the cop/author lets the man live. Months later, Dennehy's book is a runaway best-seller.

Boasting two strong leads (Woods is downright superb) and a typically intelligent and outrageous script from Cohen, BEST SELLER could have been a superior thriller had it not been for Flynn's frequently lackluster direction. For a story as fraught with potential incongruities and plot holes as BEST SELLER is, the film has to move at a breathtaking pace that simply rolls over any nagging doubts the audience may have about plausibility. As a director, Cohen has pulled it off time and time again. He has gotten audiences to accept killer babies (the IT'S ALIVE films), giant flying serpents nesting in New York City's Chrysler Building (Q), and that a tasty new yogurtlike dessert could rule the world (THE STUFF). Unfortunately, Flynn does not possess Cohen's utterly unique sensibilities. Whereas Cohen creates his own movie universe where anything can happen, Flynn is much too literate a director and takes the material totally at face value (thus giving the audience way too much leeway to pick at the plot).

Luckily, Woods seems to understand Cohen's script better than Flynn does and plays it accordingly. His character is a jumble of contradictions that run the range from darkly humorous (his vanity) to deadly. His obsession with being portrayed sympathetically in Dennehy's book and his desperate desire to be accepted by the cop/writer becomes as endearing as it is revolting. Purportedly inspired by STRANGERS ON A TRAIN, BEST SELLER shares that film's underlying homoeroticism. The men's perverse fascination with each other and love-hate feelings are superbly conveyed in a scene where Dennehy lies in bed trying to sleep. Woods suddenly appears with his face very close to Dennehy's and produces a huge pistol that he cocks and holds to the author's head. Dennehy suddenly produces his own pistol and, in turn, holds it to Woods' head. Although in the narrative it is a scene detailing the men's distrust of each other, it plays on film like a love scene complete with romantic moonlight. In addition to Woods' insightful reading of his part, enough of Cohen's signature shines through to ensure that the film maintains a peculiar slant. The opening robbery of the film committed by three men wearing Richard Nixon masks, the uneasy reunion dinner between Woods and his God-fearing rural parents (with Dennehy as Woods' "date"), and the climactic gun-battle with scores of small children as witnesses (unfortunately, badly choreographed by Flynn) all are definite signs of Cohen's obsessions with the horrors of politics, capitalism, and the nuclear family. Considering that most modern American mainstream films are virtually devoid of any distinct personality, BEST SELLER, despite its flaws, is a satisfyingly offbeat adult thriller. *(Graphic violence, profanity, brief nudity, adult situations).*

p, Carter De Haven; d, John Flynn; w, Larry Cohen; ph, Fred Murphy (CFI color); m, Jay Ferguson; ed, David Rosenbloom; prod d, Gene Rudolf; md, Budd Carr; art d, Robert Howland; set d, Chris Butler, Susan Kaufman; spec eff, Ken Speed, Robert Olmstead, Peter Kunz; m/l, Lamont Dozier, Jean Paul Martini, Claude Debussy; stunts, Steve Lambert; makeup, Deborah Figuly, Susan Kaufman.

Thriller **(PR:O MPAA:R)**

BETTER TOMORROW, A*½** (1987, Hong Kong) 98m Cinema City/ Golden Princess c (YINGXIONG BENSE)

Ti Lung *(Ho)*, Leslie Cheung *(Kit)*, Chow Yuen Fat *(Mark)*, Lee Tse Ho *(Shing)*, Emily Chu *(Jackie)*, Young Pao I.

Once again the Hong Kong cinema proves that it has become better at producing enthralling Hollywood-style entertainments than Hollywood currently is. Set in modern-day Hong Kong, the film follows the story of two brothers who have gone their separate ways in life. The older brother, Ti Lung, has become the powerful second-in-command to the local underworld kingpin. Expert in the art of counterfeiting, Ti Lung is flanked by his loyal right- hand man, Chow Yuen Fat, and a new kid they're just breaking in, Lee Tse Ho. Ti Lung hides his true identity from his adoring younger brother, Leslie Cheung, a recent graduate from the police academy who looks forward to making his family proud by quickly moving up in the ranks and marrying his beautiful fiancee, Chu. After making a promise to their ailing father, Ti Lung decides to ease out of the underworld for his brother's sake. Unfortunately, during a final "business" trip to Taiwan, Ti Lung is set up by the ambitious Lee Tse Ho and forced to surrender to police. In a related incident, Ti Lung's father is killed when gangsters attempt to kidnap the old man in order to silence Ti Lung. Three years later Ti Lung is released from prison and is shocked to find that his best friend, Chow Yuen Fat, is partially crippled (his leg was shattered by several bullets while performing a "hit") and now relegated to the gangster car-pool. He also learns that Lee Tse Ho has become the gang's most powerful figure. Worst of all, however, he discovers that Cheung blames him for their father's death and has vowed to put him back in prison. Determined to go straight, Ti Lung gets a job as a taxi driver and does his best to convince his brother that his lawless days are behind him, but to no avail. He must even crush his best friends' hopes of recapturing their former glory by refusing to reenter the mob. Ti Lung is threatened by the ruthless Lee Tse Ho, who demands that he persuade his policeman brother to do business with the mob. Ti Lung and Chow Yuen Fat then decide to destroy the gang by themselves. Armed to the teeth, Chow Yuen Fat invades the mob headquarters and steals the priceless computer plate that enables the gang to counterfeit American currency. Ti Lung sends the plate to Cheung, but the gesture means nothing to the dedicated cop and he immediately sets out to arrest his brother. After a brief firefight on the waterfront between Ti Lung, Chow Yuen Fat, and dozens of gangsters, Ti Lung sends his loyal buddy away on a speedboat and orders him to escape while he settles his score with Lee Tse Ho. Chow Yuen Fat leaves reluctantly, but when he hears rapid gunfire and explosions, he turns the boat around and speeds back to the wharf. Meanwhile, Cheung has blundered into the midst of the gang war and is now fighting for his life alongside his brother, whom he is still determined to bring in. Fighting like men possessed and ignoring several bloody wounds, the trio manages to eliminate most of the gang. Seeing that Ti Lung is badly wounded, Chow Yuen Fat desperately tries to persuade Cheung to forgive his brother's past sins. Before he can end his impassioned speech, Chow Yuen Fat is shot in the head and dies. Together, Ti Lung and Cheung finally corner Lee Tse Ho, but Ti Lung is out of bullets and a small army of police has arrived. Gloating, Lee Tse Ho raises his arms and goes to surrender to police, secure in the knowledge that his influence will have him out of jail in a matter of days. Ti Lung, however, is facing a lengthy and harsh prison sentence. Violating every principle he has ever stood for, Cheung gives his brother his fully loaded pistol and Ti Lung kills Lee Tse Ho. Leaning on his younger brother for support, Ti Lung surrenders to the police.

With a plot that could have come from a classic Warner Brothers gangster film, A BETTER TOMORROW brings new energy to old cliches via the superior direction of John Woo. Woo imbues his movie with the kind of skill, panache, and insight found in the work of Sam Peckinpah and creates a set of vivid, well-delineated characters that command attention and sympathy. The complex emotional relationships between all the characters are effectively established with an economy of style little seen since the golden age of movies. The actors do a superb job of conveying the passage of time and change of character. Cheung and Chu exude a giddy youthful exuberance in their early scenes that later turns to bitterness and pain as Cheung's vendetta against his brother threatens to destroy his marriage and career. Ti Lung and Chow Yuen Fat are excellent as well. Arrogant, powerful, and supremely self-confident as gangsters, their conceits are destroyed by fate. Ti Lung's transition from gangster to cabbie is heartfelt, humble, and sincere, as he desperately seeks to atone for his criminal past; while Chow Yuen Fat becomes cynical and embittered at his loss of status within the underworld. Perhaps the most surprising character transition is that of Lee Tse Ho, who goes from naive underling to ruthless mob boss in the blink of an eye. Director Woo imbues his film with a strong sense of family, and it is Ti Lung's efforts to restore his shattered household that fuel the narrative. Director Woo proves himself to be a superior action director and he choreographs his scenes of bloody violence with imagination and dexterity. Although stunning, his action scenes are not mere set pieces designed to fulfill audience expectations. Woo skillfully integrates the shoot-outs into the narrative, advancing the character and plot development within the sequence instead of having his film grind to a halt for a display of pyrotechnics. This kind of storytelling skill used to be common in Hollywood, but alas, it is an ability that has escaped most current American directors. Woo has obviously studied the films of Peckinpah, for his climactic shoot-out is very reminiscent of THE WILD BUNCH. The complicated, emotional relationship between Ti Lung and Chow Yuen Fat is very similar to the William Holden-Ernest Borgnine pairing, right down to the half-desperate, half-joyous glances that are exchanged during a gun battle that most certainly will bring their deaths. This is not the work of a mindless industry hack, but of a man who understands the action genre and knows how to make it work as well as it can. Lest the reader assume too much, this is, after all, just a violent gangster movie; but it is one done with a vitality and mastery little seen on American screens these days. *(Graphic violence.)*

p, Tsui Hark; d, John Woo; w, John Woo, Chan Hing-kai, Leung Suk-wah; ph, Wong Wing-hang; m, Joseph Koo; ed, Kam Ma; art d, Bennie Liu.

Crime/Drama **(PR:O MPAA:NR)**

BEVERLY HILLS COP II* (1987) 102m PAR c

Eddie Murphy *(Axel Foley)*, Judge Reinhold *(Billy Rosewood)*, Jurgen Prochnow *(Maxwell Dent)*, Ronny Cox *(Andrew Bogomil)*, John Ashton *(John Taggart)*, Brigitte Nielsen *(Karla Fry)*, Allen Garfield *(Harold Lutz)*, Dean Stockwell *(Charles "Chip" Cain)*, Paul Reiser *(Jeffrey Friedman)*, Gil Hill *(Inspector Todd)*, Paul Guilfoyle *(Nikos Thomopolis)*, Robert Ridgley *(Mayor Egan)*, Brian O'Connor *(Biddle)*, Alice Adair *(Jan Bogomil)*, Eugene Butler *(May)*, Glenn Withrow *(Willie)*, Stephen Liska *(Chauffeur)*, Gilbert Gottfried *(Sidney Bernstein)*, Hugh Hefner *(Himself)*, Carrie Leigh *(Herself)*, Tom Bower *(Russ Fielding)*, Valerie Wildman *(Gun CLub Receptionist)*, Frank J. Pesce *(Carlotta)*, Vic Manni *(Rap Singing Guard)*, Sheri Levinsky *(Waitress)*, Ray Murphy, Sr. *(Uncle Ray)*, Todd Susman *(Foreman)*, Chris Rock *(Parking Valet)*, Susan Lentini *(Receptionist at Hef's)*, Anthony D'Andrea *(Granby)*, Robert Pastorelli *(Vinnie)*, Kopi Sotiropulos *(Barkeep)*, Richard Tienkin *(Mr. Anderson)*, Teal Roberts, Peggy Sands *(Strippers)*, Larry Carroll *(TV Reporter)*, Carlos Cervantes *(Mendoza)*, Michael DeMarlo *(Doorman at Adriano's)*, Dana Gladstone *(Francesco)*, Richmond Harrison *(Construction Worker)*, Darryl Henriques *(Maitre d' at 385)*, John Hostetter *(Stiles)*, Tom "Tiny" Lister, Jr. *(Orvis)*, Ed Pansullo *(Ailey)*, Rudy Ramos *(Ignacio)*, Ritch Shydner *(Guard at Hef's)*, John Lisbon Wood *(Bobby Morgan)*, Carl Bringas, Joe Duquette, Michael Hehr, Sam Sako *(Bodyguards)*, Michael F. Kelly *(Guard at Gate)*, William Lamar, Christopher R. Adams, Danny Nero, Devin Bartlett *(Thugs)*, Dayna O'Brien *(Girl at Club)*, Eugene Mounts *(Policeman)*, Everett Sherman, Jr. *(Man at Street Corner)*, Catrin Cole *(Vinnie's Girl)*, Ola Ray, Alana Soares, Venice Kong, Luann Lee, Rebecca Ferratti, Kymberly Paige, Kymberly Herrin *(Playboy Playmates)*, Leilani Soares, Anne Lammot, Pamela Santini, Sarah Quick, Marlenne Kingsland, Monet Swann, Natalie Smith, Kari Whitman *(Playboy Models)*.

The frenetic, loud, screaming and profane black cop who invaded the posh confines of Beverly Hills the first time around is back, though far less engaging this time around. The mania from the first film is heightened to absolute frenzy in this dismal sequel, filled with idiotic dialog and nonstop violence. As the film

opens, Beverly Hills is undergoing a siege of robberies, committed by leather-jacketed punks led by Stockwell and Nielsen. During their first robbery, jewelry store customers are mistreated, thrown to the floor, and the place looted. Before departing, the wacko thugs spray the entire place, blasting every piece of crystal to tiny fragments just to prove to the viewer that they are very nasty people. Murphy, the tough street-smart cop from Detroit, is called upon to return to set things right, aiding the dumb and helpless Beverly Hills detectives Reinhold and Ashton, and compromising the new and nasty police chief, Garfield, who is more dedicated to firing everyone on the force than solving the rash of violent robberies plaguing his coveted community. (It should be noted that Beverly Hills, in reality, has one of the most efficient and respected police departments in the country with more cops per citizen than most other towns and an excellent capture rate.) When Murphy disdainfully returns to Beverly Hills he finds that the naive Reinhold is just as stupid as in the original. He has put together a personal arsenal to rival the Krupp Works, but spends most of his time doting on the myriad exotic plants in his greenhouse. Murphy's job, of course, is to rid the rich town of the punk thieves and he runs about like a man who has made millions of dollars from the original film (which he did) and is frantically eager to finish this montage of endless shootouts, roadblocks, dragnets, and car chases so that he can do it all over again. He is obnoxious and insulting, discarding the personal humor he had injected into the original film, screaming and ranting at intimidated receptionists and secretaries and generally proving that he is, indeed, a boorish oaf whose street savvy consists of manic gibberish. Along the way, of course, and this was the appeal of the original film, Murphy has his usual confrontations with the Rodeo Drive residents, deflating their opulent egos in one putdown after another, cheap shots to curdle the blood of coupon clippers everywhere. The end of the film is, as had been the case throughout, a duplication of the original, with Murphy facing down the baddies in a broken-down shed and emerging victorious.

BEVERLY HILLS COP was an enormous blockbuster, gleaning more than $350 million in box office rentals and this sequel, which is really a plagiarism of the original, matched that success, topping the box office charts for 1987. Yet the film, with a budget of $30 million, simply isn't funny and even the villains are as overcooked as the script, the Amazonian crook Nielsen lurching about and attempting to be the sexy menace. Nielsen, Sylvester Stallone's ex-wife, was handpicked by Murphy for this role. In fact, Murphy actually controlled the destiny of this film and should bear the brunt of criticism for its slam-bang predictability. This one is an embarrassment for Murphy, although Paramount now envisions a whole string of films, a la the James Bond movies, to continue with the same mindless character. It's a strange phenomenon: How to show utter contempt for your viewing audience and still make millions. The film is jam-packed with songs which translates into a soundtrack album and even more money. Songs include "Shakedown" (Harold Faltermeyer, Keith Forsey, Bob Seger, performed by Seger), "In Deep" (Charlie Sexton, Scott Wilk, performed by Sexton), "Hold On" (James Wirrick, performed by Corey Hart, also performed by Ketta Bill), "Cross My Broken Heart" (Stephen Bray, Tony Pierce, performed by The Jets),

"Be There" (Allee Willis, Franne Golde, performed by The Pointer Sisters), "I Can't Stand It" (David Allen Jones, Harold Payne, performed by Sue Ann), "All Revved Up" (Giorgio Morodor, Tom Whitlock, performed by Jermaine Jackson), "Better Way" (Andre Cymone, performed by James Ingram), "I Want Your Sex" (George Michael, performed by Michael), "36 Lovers" (John Eaton, Melvin Riley, Jr., Gary Spaniola, performed by Ready For The World), "Love/Hate" (Andre Cymone, Julian Jackson, performed by Pebbles), "Spanish Flea" (Julius Wechter). *(Violence, excessive profanity.)*

p, Don Simpson, Jerry Bruckheimer; d, Tony Scott; w, Larry Ferguson, Warren Skaaren (based on a story by Eddie Murphy, Robert D. Wachs from characters created by Danilo Bach, Daniel Petrie, Jr.); ph, Jeffrey L. Kimball (Technicolor); m, Harold Faltermeyer; ed, Billy Weber, Chris Lebenzon, Michael Tronick; prod d, Ken Davis; art d, James J. Murakami; set d, John Anderson; cos, James W. Tyson, Bobbie Read; makeup, Steve Abrums; m/l, Harold Faltermeyer, Keith Forsey, Bob Seger, Charlie Sexton, Scott Wilk, James Wirrick, Stephen Bray, Tony Pierce, Allee Willis, Franne Golde, David Allen Jones, Harold Payne, Giorgio Morodor, Tom Whitlock, Andre Cymone, George Michael, John Eaton, Melvin Riley, Jr., Gary Spaniola, Julian Jackson, Julius Wechter; stunts, Gary McLarty, Alan Oliney.

Comedy **Cas.** **(PR:O MPAA:R)**

BEYOND THERAPY* (1987) 93m Sandcastle 5/NW c

Julie Hagerty *(Prudence)*, Jeff Goldblum *(Bruce)*, Glenda Jackson *(Charlotte, Bruce's Therapist)*, Tom Conti *(Dr. Stuart Framingham, Prudence's Therapist)*, Christopher Guest *(Bob)*, Genevieve Page *(Zizi, Bob's Mother)*, Cris Campion *(Andrew, Waiter)*, Sandrine Dumas *(Cindy)*, Bertrand Bonvoisin *(Le Gerant)*, Nicole Evans *(The Cashier)*, Louis-Marie Taillefer *(Le Chef)*, Matthew Lesniak *(Mr. Bean)*, Laure Killing *(Charlie)*, Gilbert Blin, Vincent Longuemare *(Waiters)*, Francoise Armel, Sylvie Lenoir, Annie Monnier, Jeanne Cellard, Helene Constantine, Yvette Prayer, Joan Tyrrell *(Zizi's Friends)*.

BEYOND THERAPY is the type of film which, a few years ago, would have been called a *disappointing* Robert Altman film, in light of the director's previous accomplishments. Now, however, after he has turned out numerous misguided efforts like this one, BEYOND THERAPY can be called a *typical* Altman film. Based on Christopher Durang's play, which starred John Lithgow and Dianne Wiest on Broadway, BEYOND THERAPY is a farce about the absurdity of psychotherapy. Goldblum stars as a bisexual, Francophile New Yorker who, tiring of his flamboyant lover, Guest, places an ad in a personal column. He meets the uptight Hagerty in an expensive French restaurant located in an unidentifiable part of New York. Brimming with neuroses, the couple open their rendezvous with an uneasy exchange: "You have lovely breasts." "Do you wear contact lenses?" "I like the timbre of your voice—it's soft." "I love the smell of the Brut you're wearing." They never really communicate and are soon at odds. Goldblum admits he is bisexual; Hagerty gets disgusted and nearly leaves. Goldblum persuades her to stay, sucks her toes, bursts out into tears, and eventually they throw water at each other. All the while, in a Bunuelian touch, they try to order dinner to no avail. Both then go off to their analysts—Goldblum to Jackson, and Hagerty to Conti. The analysts have offices directly next to each other and are as neurotic as their patients. Jackson has an aphasiac disorder (she says "dirigible" when she means "secretary"), and Conti has sex with his patients. Jackson and Conti also have a perfect (and more or less implied) sexual relationship which they carry on anonymously. She hates foreplay and has reduced sex to a purely physical act, and Conti has a problem with premature ejaculation. Goldblum and Hagerty decide to try the personal ads again, both changing their wording somewhat. Nevertheless, they meet again at the same French restaurant and, after hurdling a few obstacles, they become attracted to each other. Goldblum invites Hagerty to his apartment for dinner, but the intended romance of the evening is spoiled by the presence of Guest, Goldblum's lover. Hagerty and Guest initially despise each other, but soon grow civil. After exchanging a number of insults (including Goldblum calling Guest's overbearing mother a transvestite), the threesome heads for Goldblum's analyst hoping that she can help Guest. Eventually all the characters end up back at the French restaurant where, in a near-slapstick slow-motion scene, Guest wildly fires a starter pistol and scatters the patrons. By the end, the two analysts have gone off to make love; Guest sits down to dinner with his mother and agrees to meet later with waiter Campion; and Goldblum and Hagerty are free to begin their relationship anew without any interference.

A thoroughly irritating film, BEYOND THERAPY is meant to be a comedy on the order of the classic French farce, but instead is a haphazard collection of partly funny segments without the invention or focus to be of any interest. However, there are some fine performances. Goldblum and Hagerty have a splendid rapport, and much of the dialog between Conti and Hagerty is viciously funny. The camerawork is excellent, and Yared contributes a dreamy Parisian score. There is also Altman's creative use of multilayered sound, with dialog tracks overlapping and dropping into the background. One repeated motif is the sound of crashing cars, heard outside and in the distance, giving the viewer a subconscious sense of anxiety. Just the same, all of this adds up to nothing more than scatterbrained, neurotic characters jabbering with other scatterbrained, neurotic characters. In the background, struggling to come to the forefront, are numerous quirky characters, or more accurately extras, on whom Altman seems intent on concentrating his camera. Perhaps, Altman intended to make an annoying film about annoying people. If so, he has done it with phenomenal success. The intriguing, but weakly executed, final shot reveals that the entire film took place not in New York, but in Paris. Although initially confusing (American cars and taxis have been seen throughout the film), this becomes Altman's comment on Paris as a state of mind. The George and Ira Gershwin song "Someone To Watch Over Me" is heard in three musical interludes, sung first by Linda Ronstadt, then by Lena Horne, and over the final credits by Yves Montand. *(Nudity, adult situations, excessive profanity.)*

p, Steven M. Haft; d, Robert Altman; w, Christopher Durang, Robert Altman (based on the play by Christopher Durang); ph, Pierre Mignot; m, Gabriel Yared; ed, Steve Dunn, Jennifer Auge; prod d, Stephen Altman; art d, Annie Senechal; cos, John Hay; m/l, George Gershwin, Ira Gershwin; makeup, Ronaldo Ribeiro De Abreu, Dominique De Vorges.

Comedy **Cas.** **(PR:O MPAA:R)**

BHARGAVA RAMUDU† (1987, India)

Balakrishna, Vijayashanti, Mandakini, Bhanupriya.

When a young boy grows to manhood he is finally able to avenge the injustices done to his father. (In Telugu.)

p, Rao Gopalrao; d, A. Kodidandarami Reddy.

Drama **(PR:NR MPAA:NR)**

BIDROHI† (1987, India)

Ranjit Mullick, Santu Mukherjee, Alpana Goswami.

Angered by the wrongs committed against the poor, a slum dweller rises up and fights a governmental system of graft and corruption. (In Bengali.)

p, Bhabesh Kundu; d, Anjan Chowdhury; m, Samir Seal.

Drama **(PR:NR MPAA:NR)**

BIG BAD MAMA II† (1987) 83m Concorde c

Angie Dickinson *(Wilma McClatchie)*, Robert Culp *(Daryl Pearson)*, Danielle Brisebois *(Billie Jean McClatchie)*, Julie McCullogh *(Polly McClatchie)*, Bruce Glover *(Crawford)*, Jeff Yahger *(Jordan Crawford)*, Jacque Lynn Colton *(Alma)*, Ebbe Roe Smith, Charles Cyphers, Kelli Maroney, Linda Shayne.

This reportedly rancid sequel to Corman's 1974 cult favorite was given a lightening quick release in regional markets and closed in a week, before most critics—not to mention the public—had a chance to see it. Dickinson, the only cast member from the original film to return for the sequel, resumes her role as a tough-talking, machine gun-toting Texas gangster of the 1930s. The film begins as the villainous Glover has Dickinson's husband murdered, forcing the widow and her two daughters, Brisebois and McCullogh, out of their home. Dickinson is determined to get revenge and sets out to ruin Glover's campaign for governor. She kidnaps Glover's son, Yahger, and goes on a bank-robbing spree with Philadelphia reporter Culp in hot pursuit of a great scoop. Directed by Wynorski, a former Corman publicist and writer for the long-defunct-but-fondly-remembered magazine *Castle of Frankenstein*, BIG BAD MAMA II features a montage of action scenes from the first film and the bare breasts of Brisebois, the former child star of TV's "Archie's Place." Also on hand for the requisite dose of nudity are former *Playboy* centerfold McCullogh and Dickinson's usual body double. Likely to make an immediate debut on home video, which, no doubt, is what the producers intended all along.

p, Roger Corman; d, Jim Wynorski; w, R.J. Robertson, Jim Wynorski; ph, Robert C. New (Foto-Kem Color); m, Chuck Cirino; ed, Noah Blough, Nancy Nuttall; art d, Billie Greenbaum.

Crime **(PR:NR MPAA:R)**

BIG BANG, THE† (1987, Fr./Bel.) 77m Comedia-Zwanz-Ministere de la Culture-Ministere de la Communaute Francaise/FOX France c (LE BIG BANG)

Voices: David Lander *(Fred Hero)*, Carol Androfsky *(Liberty)*, Marshall Efron *(Comrade in Chief)*, Alice Playten *(Una)*, Marvin Silbersher *(First)*, Joanna Lehman *(Trixie)*, Jerry Bledsoe, Josh Daniel, Bob Kaliban, George Osterman, Ray Owens, Deborah Taylor, Ron Vernan, Roberta Wallach.

Working from a script by British humorist Hendra, Belgian Picha's third animated feature (SHAME OF THE JUNGLE, THE MISSING LINK) is filled with puns and sexual humor. Set after a nuclear war has left earth divided into two nations, one male and one female, the story concerns the efforts of a rather inept hero named Fred to prevent another war.

p, Boris Szulzinger; d, Jean-Marc Picha; w, Jean-Marc Picha, Tony Hendra; m, Roy Budd; ed, Nicole Garnier-Klippel; anim, Stout Studio; m/l, Delroy, Van Holmen, Brian Wilson.

Animation **(PR:NR MPAA:NR)**

BIG EASY, THE*** (1987) 108m Kings Road Ent./COL c

Dennis Quaid *(Remy McSwain)*, Ellen Barkin *(Anne Osborne)*, Ned Beatty *(Jack Kellom)*, Ebbe Roe Smith *(Detective Dodge)*, John Goodman *(Detective DeSoto)*, Lisa Jane Persky *(Detective McCabe)*, Charles Ludlam *(Lamar)*, Thomas O'Brien *(Bobby)*, Honorable James Garrison *(Judge Noland)*, Carole Sutton *(Judge Raskov)*, David Petitjean *(Uncle Sal)*, Nick Hagler *(Hugh Dowling)*, Marc Lawrence *("Cannon" Di Moti)*, Jim Chimento *(Freddy Angelo)*, Grace Zabriski *(Mama, Remy's Mother)*, Steve Broussard *(Dewey Piersall)*, Solomon Burke *(Daddy Mention)*, Eliott Keener *(George Joel)*, August Krinke, John Schluter, Zepherin Hymel *(I.A. Cops)*, Gailard Sartain *(Chef Paul)*, Arden M. Jones, Rickey Pierre *(Muggers)*, Margie O'Dair *(Mugged Woman)*, Robert Lessor *(Foster)*, Irma Thomas *(Marcelline)*, Edward St. Pe *(Patrolman)*, George Dureau *(Maitre d')*, Jack Harris *(Waiter)*, Robert Kearney *(Desk Sergeant)*, Patric Frederick, Lane Trippe *(Lawyers)*, Gary Sturgis, Byron Nora *(Car Vandals)*, Jeff Hollis *(Sgt. Duvivier)*, Joy N. Houck, Jr. *(Sgt. Guerra)*, Peter Gabb *(Proprietor)*, Dennis Curren *(Cousin Nick)*, Cary Alden, David Dahlgren *(Uniform Cops)*, Little Buddy Quaid *(Justin)*, Dewey Balfa *(Uncle Lafayette)*, Ricco Wheat *(Rodney)*.

Unless you have the eyes of a Black Skimmer (a southern US bird that flies close to the water seeking prey), the opening credits of THE BIG EASY are sure to leave the viewer myopic, cross-eyed, and certainly queasy. Behind the credits is fast-rolling aerial footage of the Louisiana water basin, vistas which diminish as the camera appears to descend, horizonless, and, without that visual point of reference, a dizzying (though seemingly unintentional) effect is created, until the scene settles upon a body floating face downward in an ornate pool a la SUNSET BOULEVARD. The corpse is quickly identified by slick police lieutenant of detectives Quaid who knows what every hoodlum and criminal in New Orleans looks like. Quaid affects a strange sometimes garbled delivery of a Cajun-Creole accent, and is later shown to be a Cajun who comes from a police dynasty, with many of his relatives still serving in the New Orleans Police Department. Quaid believes the dead man, a Mafia soldier in the ranks of boss Lawrence, has been killed as a warning to Lawrence. This view is shared by Beatty, who is not only Quaid's superior in the homicide division but is a close friend who is about to marry Quaid's mother. Into Quaid's cop life steps blonde Barkin, an assistant district attorney who has been assigned to look into possible police corruption. Quaid overcomes Barkin's businesslike objections to having dinner with him, then annoys her by parking illegally and almost accepting a free dinner. She leaves him to go shopping, telling him to go home, but when she stops a purse-snatcher she is confronted by a switchblade-wielding thug. Out of nowhere appears Quaid to knock the thug and his partner senseless, handcuffing both men to his car and walking an appreciative Barkin to her apartment. Barkin's idea of police work differs greatly from Quaid's; she is a stickler for protocol and he feels it's necessary to bend the rules a bit to survive in the streets. The next night Quaid picks up Barkin after work, delivering a report on the killing of the Mafioso, along with a pizza. They go to her apartment where Barkin cannot resist Quaid's suave advances. In the middle of their contortionist love scene (obligatory scene as producers call it), Quaid gets a call informing him that more murders have occurred and he rushes to a Storyville house to find three black hoodlums slaughtered, killed by shotgun blasts. A package of heroin is discovered and police conclude that a dope war has broken out between Italian and black gangsters. Men in Quaid's command, especially detectives Smith and Goodman, voice concern over the probing Barkin, fearing she might discover the

"Widows and Orphans Fund," the kickback money collected from businessmen which is split weekly by members of the force. Quaid tells them that Barkin has no idea about this supposedly harmless department corruption. But things get complicated when Quaid is persuaded by detectives in his department to see a bar owner who is complaining that he is being shaken down by so many cops he cannot afford the kickbacks. Quaid is set up in the bar where the owner shoves an envelope full of bills into his pocket. He grabs the man, shouting, "You wearin' a wire?" then dashes for a rear exit, tossing the bills in the air and swallowing the envelope before other plainclothes officers arrest him. He is charged with taking a bribe with Barkin set to prosecute. Released on a small bail, Quaid fakes a bank robbery, throwing a powerful magnet through the bank window. The magnet is impounded as evidence and Quaid then arranges with the police property man to have it placed next to a video tape which shows Quaid ostensibly taking the bribe in the bar. Naturally, by the time Barkin is about to show the tape in court her deciding piece of evidence has been erased by the magnet. The case is dismissed, Barkin is mad as a nest of disturbed hornets, and their brief love affair appears to have gone to ruin.

While jogging Barkin is picked up by an officer in a squad who turns out to be one of Quaid's relatives; he drives her to a Cajun barbecue and dance where Quaid, Beatty, and other Cajun cops are celebrating Quaid's triumph in court. Barkin reluctantly dances with Quaid but breaks away, rejecting him because of his transgressions. So upset about this rejection is Quaid that he takes himself off the pad, refusing to partake in the "Widows and Orphans Fund," or any other perk he has been used to receiving. In following up a lead that endorses the mob war theory, Quaid next interviews black mob leader Burke whose dope runners practice voodoo, which might explain why the latest Mafia victim had his heart torn out. Burke has no idea why the war has broken out, he tells Barkin whose interrogation is interrupted by the appearance of Quaid. Then a shoot-out occurs in which Burke is slain and Quaid tries to stop the killers. He tells Barkin that the slayers had to be cops driving in an unmarked police car and now believes that the black-Italian mob war has been a setup. The two study the reports on the recent killings, make love, and appear ready to face the world together instead of battling each other. Quaid's younger brother is then shot but survives, mistaken for Quaid while wearing his raincoat in a storm. Quaid discovers that Beatty has been breaking the small rules all along, as had Quaid's father, but that Beatty has also been killing mobsters and absconding with huge caches of heroin, aided by Smith and Goodman, the two corrupt detectives on Quaid's squad. Quaid confronts Beatty, slapping him. Beatty draws his pistol but then runs off. Quaid and Barkin later find him at the police boat dock, in the hold of a boat containing all the bags of heroin Beatty, Smith, and Goodman have been skimming in their phony slaughterhouse raids. Smith and Goodman shoot Beatty, then begin firing at Quaid and Barkin who dive into the water, Quaid emerging to climb onto another boat docked nearby, Barkin to climb back onto the police boat where Beatty is dying in the hold. She tries to help Beatty but is confronted by one of the killers and is about to be blasted when Beatty shoots and kills his henchman, then dies. The other killer then tries to murder Quaid but he is dispatched when Quaid shoves a burning flare into his stomach. (This last ploy has been used many times earlier to dispatch heavies at sea, including MARA MARU.) The final scene of this offbeat thriller has Quaid and Barkin entering their bridal chamber after just having been married, fading out as Quaid struggles to remove Barkin's wedding garter.

THE BIG EASY, supposedly a synonym for New Orleans, was originally scripted to take place in Chicago but director McBride chose New Orleans as the site of the movie, feeling that police corruption was more associated with that city, even though he later stated his intention was to show police corruption as "ambiguous." There is nothing ambiguous about the corruption shown in the New Orleans Police Department, so much so that it is doubtful that that department would ever again want to cooperate with any movie company shooting in the city. In another era, the city of New Orleans would certainly have sued the film company making any such unsubstantiated and blatant claims. Now, it's anything goes, apparently. The acting, especially on Quaid's part, seems genuine, particularly the street scenes, but this is understandable since Quaid spent considerable time making the rounds with New Orleans cops. Barkin spent some time with a local prosecutor, patterning her character after this legal lady and the locale shooting is impressive for its realism. The company spent 11 weeks shooting the entire film in New Orleans, McBride concentrating on the French Quarter with one building, the Germaine Wells mansion, serving as the site for Quaid's apartment interior and some other interiors and exteriors. Overall, there is a clamminess and closeness about the film which certainly reflects the muggy, unpredictable climate of the city where it rains every other second. Unnerving is Quaid's manufactured Cajun accent, thick with "de's," "dat's," and "do's," mingled with a hinting lisp and slurring sounds suggesting that a few molars are about to come loose. All of this affectatious vocal rendering makes it extremely difficult to understand Quaid and some others drawling in the same fashion. Quaid rambles about so loosely that it often appears as if he is disjointed and his oddball behavior is interesting for about 30 minutes, then predictable. Barkin is the prim and proper lady who falls for the easy-going cop and much of her role is stereotyped. Her mannerisms, crinkling of nose, twitching smile, are pure Meryl Streepisms and she often strikes the pose of the petulant girl instead of the mature woman she is supposed to be playing. Beatty offers solid support but he goes little beyond his huffing-puffing prototype as established in so many other movies.

There is a great deal of gore here with bodies fully depicted as being shot, burned, mutilated; not for the squeamish and certainly not for any children, including early teenagers. McBride's direction is inconsistently stylish, the flow of the tale interrupted too abruptly by slaughterhouse murders that seem to intrude on the Quaid-Barkin romance where McBride has concentrated his efforts. Is this a romance, a crime movie, what? McBride doesn't seem to want to make up his mind nor allow his actors to place emphasis in either genre. The hybrid film has reached the peak of its popularity in 1987 with curious mix movies like THE UNTOUCHABLES and ROBOCOP, half serious, half cartoon efforts, and THE BIG EASY is no exception, its purpose suffering, its conclusions too pat. There are some humorous, memorable moments, mostly early in the film, such as when Quaid subdues the two purse snatchers, threatening their lives if they injure his car to which he is handcuffing them, and then, for the benefit of law-and-order Barkin some distance away, loudly pretending to read them their "Miranda" rights. The excessive violence and McBride's penchant for lingering on scenes littered with bodies with torn flesh undoes the few empathetic feelings the viewer might have mustered for the hero. Of course the use of mangled bodies here is to assure the audience that this is realistic police work but it presumes that no one knows what a shotgun blast can do to a human face. Barkin vomiting into a toilet bowl as a reaction to these gruesome scenes is no less crude and offensive, and the snickering directorial topper of distaste is the next scene where she hastily brushes her teeth, then french kisses Quaid. Very hard to swallow. *(Profanity, sexual situations.)*

p, Stephen Friedman; d, Jim McBride; w, Daniel Petrie, Jr., Jack Baran; ph, Affonso Beato (DeLuxe Color); m, Brad Feidel; ed, Mia Goldman; prod d, Jeannine Claudia Oppewall; set d, Lisa Fischer; cos, Tracy Tynan; spec eff, Bill Purcell; stunts, Diamond Farnsworth; makeup, Julie Purcell.

Thriller/Crime **(PR:O MPAA:R)**

BIG PARADE, THE*** (1987, China) 102m Guangxi Film Studio/China Film c (DA YUE BING)

Huang Xueqi, Sun Chun, Lu Lei, Wu Ruofu.

Chinese director Chen Kaige's long-awaited second feature (his first was the critically acclaimed YELLOW EARTH) is a somewhat uneven effort because the cliched narrative fails to live up to the brilliance of the imagery. Set in modern-day China, the film follows a single airborne squadron as it undergoes a grueling training session in preparation for the prestigious parade in Beijing celebrating the 35th anniversary of the revolution. Led by a tough drill sergeant who is a veteran of a China-Vietnam conflict, the undisciplined young men are slowly whipped into shape until they become a flawless unit capable of marching in perfect synchronization. During the training we meet the usual collection of soldiers: the content, disgruntled, dedicated, naive, and near-hopeless. The drill sergeant subjects the men to everything from long marches to standing perfectly still—in full uniform—for hours in the hot sun. Despite his strict discipline, the sergeant is a compassionate man who refuses to eliminate some of his lesser men because he does not wish to rob them of the once-in-a-lifetime honor of marching in the parade. After weeks of training, soul-searching, and some painful decisions, the squadron is ready to become just one of many units that march in perfect step past the reviewing stand on the big day.

In THE BIG PARADE director Kaige strives for something more than what some critics have called the "Chinese FULL METAL JACKET," and instead illustrates the conflict between the group and the individual in today's China. This somewhat subversive theme may have been the reason Chinese officials prevented the film's release for two years (it was filmed in 1985). Unfortunately, to Western eyes weaned on countless war films, the exploration of this theme may be a bit too banal. Although the characters and situations are standard basic-training fare, Kaige visualizes his film in a frequently breathtaking manner. From the opening helicopter shot which shows miles and miles of troops training on the tarmac to the final slow-motion shots of the various units marching in perfect synchronization, Kaige continually comes up with beautiful and fascinating images of men in motion. Most remarkable, however, is the sequence where the men are *not* in motion—the arduous drill where the soldiers must stand still in the blazing sun. With the wide-screen image shimmering from the brutal heat and the soldiers standing at attention with sweat pouring from beneath their helmets, Kaige presents a brilliant, unforgettable image of individual human endurance, and at the same time, mass stupidity. *(Profanity in subtitles.)*

d, Chen Kaige; w, Gao Lili; ph, Zhang Yimou (Widescreen); m, Qu Xiaosong, Zhao Quiping; ed, Zhou Xinxia; prod d, He Qun.

Drama **(PR:A-C MPAA:NR)**

BIG SHOTS*** (1987) 90m Lorimar/FOX c

Rickie Busker *(Obie)*, Darius McCrary *(Jeremy "Scam" Henderson)*, Robert Joy *(Dickie)*, Robert Prosky *(Keegan, Pawnbroker)*, Jerzy Skolimowski *(Doc)*, Paul Winfield *(Johnnie Red)*, Brynn Thayer *(Obie's Mom)*, Bill Hudson *(Obie's Dad)*, Jim Antonio *(Uncle Harry)*, Andrea Bebel *(Alley)*, Hutton Cobb *(Bible Salesman)*, Joe Seneca *(Ferryman)*, Beah Richards *(Miss Hanks, Hotel Manager)*, Olivia Cole *(Mrs. Newton)*, Mitch Beasley *(Duane Henderson)*, Pauline Brailsford *(Science Teacher)*, Cedric Young *(Ghetto Bartender)*, Timothy Scott *(Smiley)*, Elise Langan *(The Waitress)*, Wilbert Bradley, Bernard Chestleigh *(Social Service Men)*, Ron Dean, Tim Halligan, Richard Caine, Sephus Booker *(Policemen)*, Jeffrey Harris, Antoine Roshell, Michael Stoyanov *(Teenagers)*, Shirley Spiegler Jacobs, Lorraine Matthews *(Social Service Women)*, Oscar Jordan *(One of the Guys)*, Michael Krawic *(Street Person)*, Maria McCrary *(Bank Teller)*, Sherry Narens *(Teacher)*, Jack R. Orend *(Asst. Bank Manager)*, Frank Rice *(Counselor)*, Dick Sollenberger *(Doctor)*, James Spinks *(Bank Guard)*, Ken White *(Sheriff)*, Dave Adams *(Deputy)*, Hank Underwood *(Bartender)*, Ellen Geer *(Bar Waitress)*, Janet MacLachlan *(Welfare Worker)*, David S. Dunard *(Louisiana Cop)*.

BIG SHOTS came and went with the speed of light and it's too bad because this pre-teen version of THE DEFIANT ONES had more fun in it than many of 1987's more successful releases. Hudson and Busker are father and son. They are out fishing one day and the 12-year-old boy asks his father about the facts of life in a very touching and funny scene. Hudson wears a heavy diver's watch that Busker longs for and his father gives it to him. In another scene, Busker learns that his young father has succumbed to a heart attack. He loves his dad so much (wonderfully established in the opening) that he is stunned and enraged such a good man should have been taken so early. Busker gets on his bike and rides as far as his short legs can carry him, tears blinding him. By the time he awakens to his surroundings, he is deep into a Chicago ghetto where he is set upon by a group of older teenage boys when he asks for directions to get home to the white, middle-class suburb where he lives with his mother, Thayer (making her film debut with a superb performance). The ruffians steal his watch and Busker soon meets McCrary, a black child about his own age. McCrary is a street-wise kid (although not as wise as he pretends to be) who lives in a dive hotel where he has convinced the management that his father will be along shortly to pay the back bills. McCrary is also dodging the social workers who would like to put him in an orphanage. He says he can help Busker find the watch that means so much to him and takes the boy to a local bar where they meet Winfield, a fence. Winfield says he knows nothing about the wristwatch, even though he usually gets first look at anything stolen in the neighborhood. The boys keep looking and finally locate the watch in the shop owned by Prosky, a sleazy and unscrupulous pawnbroker. Prosky demands a high sum for the watch and Busker goes to his bank and withdraws the money. When he gives the money to Prosky, the pawnbroker won't give them the watch and threatens to maim them if they try to get it. The two boys get a cap gun and rob the pawnshop, taking only the watch that has already been paid for. Meanwhile, the boys have stolen an expensive Mercedes owned by Skolimowski and Joy, a pair of hired killers who have murdered someone on a contract job. They will get their fee when they turn over the dead body to the person who paid for the kill and that body is in the trunk of the car. As all of this is going on, police are now after them and the bond between the boys deepens as they share the loss of their fathers. Beasley, McCrary's pop, is somewhere down south working. Little by little, Busker's naivete is disappearing as he learns how to drink, how to drive a car, and how to talk street language. Busker goes home to the suburbs, then learns that his good pal is no longer at the hotel but has been taken to the orphans' home. The Mercedes is hidden in a small garage and the killers are still looking for it and the boys. Busker realizes that his pal must be unhappy, so he enlists the aid of Winfield, who poses as McCrary's father and gets the boy out of the orphanage. Joy and Skolimowski catch the two boys, but Winfield saves their lives. The boys now get the Mercedes, and a long hegira from Chicago to the Deep South begins with Skolimowski and Joy on their tails. The killers have learned where the boys are going by posing as cops and talking to Thayer. On the road, the kids pick up a Bible salesman, Cobb, who turns out to be a scam artist and steals their car. They eventually get it back and continue on to meet McCrary's father after a moving sequence aboard a ferry with Seneca. A nice warm glow erupts when father and son are reunited and the picture ends after Skolimowski is killed and Joy is arrested.

Lots of action, a great deal of humor, and two terrific performances by McCrary and Busker, both of whom were rank amateurs when this picture was made. However, there are several false moments, times when one almost senses screenwriter Eszterhas (JAGGED EDGE) sitting at his typewriter saying "Here is where I think I'll put . . . " Director Mandel (INDEPENDENCE DAY, F/X) has a tendency to be speedy for speed's sake, but the warmth between the two boys and the solid performances by all involved tend to blur the faults. Both boys are better than any of the professionally precocious kids toiling on network TV today. In BUGSY MALONE, youngsters played adults. Here, the youngsters stay youngsters but are functioning in an adult world, and while some of the shenanigans are just fetched a bit too far to be believable, the results are genuinely fun. Busker, who lives in a suburb of Chicago and is very much like the lad he plays, had to learn to drive in order to make the movie and he also had to learn several words which are not usually spoken around the Busker household. McCrary is the son of respected gospel singer and composer Howard McCrary, so he's been on the fringes of one form of show business since birth. Skolimowski is the same man who directed MOONLIGHTING, THE LIGHTSHIP, and several European pictures in between acting chores (or is it the other way around?). Prosky, who made his debut as the vicious businessman in THIEF, won a Tony nomination for his work in "Glengarry Glen Ross" and is a veteran of TV's "Hill Street Blues." The executive producer, Ivan Reitman, had planned to direct but was sidetracked with the much lesser movie LEGAL EAGLES, so Mandel was hired. Unfortunately, the PG-13 rating will keep out the children who are the same age as the protagonists. The four-letter words weren't needed. *(Profanity, violence.)*

p, Joe Medjuck, Michael C. Gross; d, Robert Mandel; w, Joe Eszterhas; ph, Miroslav Ondricek (Panavision, Astral Film Labs color); m, Bruce Broughton; ed, Sheldon Kahn, William Anderson, Dennis Virkler; prod d, Bill Malley; set d, Gary Baugh, Bundy Trinz, Chuck Pierce; cos, Richard Bruno; makeup, Wally Schwartz, Frank Carrisosa; m/l, Richard Penniman, Joe Lubin, Dorothy La Bostrie, Steve Winwood, George Flemming, James Hooker, Ziggy Elman, Johnny Mercer, Billy Gale; spec eff, Bob Shelley, Bob Shelley, Jr., Andy Evans; stunts, Spike Silver.

Comedy/Drama **(PR:C MPAA:PG-13)**

BIG TOWN, THE** (1987) 109m COL c

Matt Dillon *(J.C. Cullen)*, Diane Lane *(Lorry Dane)*, Tommy Lee Jones *(George Cole)*, Bruce Dern *(Mr. Edwards)*, Lee Grant *(Ferguson Edwards)*, Tom Skerritt *(Phil Carpenter)*, Suzy Amis *(Aggie Donaldson)*, David Marshall Grant *(Sonny Binkley)*, Don Francks *(Carl Hooker)*, Del Close *(Deacon Daniels)*, Meg Hogarth *(Dorothy Cullen)*, Cherry Jones *(Ginger McDonald)*, Mark Danton *(Prager)*, David Elliott *(Cool Guy)*, Steve Yorke, Chris Owens *(Garage Boys)*, Sean McCann *(Roy McMullin)*, Kevin Fox *(Boss's Son)*, Marc Strange *(Madigan)*, Don Lake *(Patsy Fuqua)*, Angelo Rizacos *(Harold)*, Chris Benson *(Shooter)*, Gary Farmer *(Duke)*, Diego Matamoros *(Sid)*, Sarah Polley *(Christy Donaldson)*, Kirsten Bishop *(Adele)*, Ken McGregor *(Bartender)*, Viki Matthews, Cherie McGroarty, Sandy Czapiewski, Marie Siebert, Julie Conte *(Gem Club Dancers)*, Alar Aedma *(Doorman)*, Sam Malkin *(Bernstein)*, Robert Morelli *(Sideburns)*, Layne Coleman *(Murphy)*, Lolita David *(Black Lace Stripper)*, Bill Colgate, William Forrest MacDonald, Len Doncheff, Michael Caruana, Richard Comar, Lubomir Mykytiuk, Robert Ramsay Collins *(Gem Club Gamblers)*, Errol Slue *(Friendly Guy)*, Gerry Pearson *(Baptist Preacher)*, Hugo Dann *(Elmo)*, John Evans *(Marvin Brown)*, J. W. Carroll *(Detective)*, Diane Gordon *(Mrs. Rogers)*.

Although the plot line is contrived, wooden, and hopelessly cliched, THE BIG TOWN could at least have been an engaging celebration of old movie conventions. Instead, what we have is a strangely lifeless film, set in Chicago of the late 1950s, that fails to interest despite the efforts of its solid cast. Boasting some slick cinematography and a savvy selection of regional music from the period, THE BIG TOWN begins in the small town of Rockport, Indiana. Dillon, a upstanding young man who works in a auto repair shop by day, spends his nights shooting craps under the tutelage of his boss and mentor, Francks. Possessing an amazing amount of luck and a quick mind that instantly calculates the ever-changing odds, Dillon proves to be a devastating gambler. Francks, who has connections in Chicago, finally decides that Dillon is ready for the big time and sends the boy off to work as an "arm" for professional gamblers—Grant and her blind husband Dern. Dillon is hired to gamble with their money at tables they have approved. In exchange he receives room and board and a small percentage of his winnings. Dillon soon proves his worth by winning vast sums easily. One day, while shopping in a record store, Dillon meets Amis, a pretty unwed mother who wants to become a disc jockey. The pair hit it off well and become close friends. Meanwhile, bored with the tables he is supposed to work, Dillon enters a game in the back room of gambler Jones' strip club. The young Hoosier quickly comes close to breaking the bank, and Jones' only defense is to slip the kid some loaded dice and then accuse him of cheating. Although Dillon is hustled out of the club, he becomes infatuated with the star stripper, Lane, and pursues her. Dillon later learns that Lane is trapped in a miserable marriage to Jones, who used the girl to finance his club. Lane urges Dillon to return to the club and break the bank, thus putting her in a position to buy it back and freeze Jones out. Lane manipulates Dillon by appealing to his lust, and then promises him they will always be together. This, however, threatens to ruin his relationship with Amis, which has recently gone from platonic to passionate. Stuck between two women, Dillon finally decides to side with Lane and agrees to wipe Jones out. The trick works, but soon Dillon learns that Dern has contracted Jones to kill Skerritt, the man that blinded him many years before. Dillon has recently befriended Skerritt, and he runs off to warn him. Unfortunately, he is too late and arrives just as Jones guns down Skerritt. Jones is immediately caught by police and taken away. A distraught Dillon returns to Lane's apartment seeking solace, but finds the stripper in bed with the lawyer that has arranged for her to buy back the club. Feeling manipulated by everyone he meets, Dillon rejects Lane's protests of love and leaves her. Dillon returns to the loving arms of Amis and her child, and the trio moves back to Rockport to begin a new life.

Based on the novel *The Arm* by Clark Howard, THE BIG TOWN suffered a setback a mere five days into shooting when original director Harold Becker (THE ONION FIELD, VISION QUEST) had a falling out with producer Ransohoff and quit citing "artistic differences." Columbia chief David Puttnam (who has since resigned) called in Ben Bolt, son of award-winning screenwriter Robert Bolt (LAWRENCE OF ARABIA, DOCTOR ZHIVAGO, A MAN FOR ALL SEASONS, THE MISSION), to take over the directing chores. Having only directed short films and several television shows, Bolt made his feature debut with THE BIG TOWN. Unfortunately, Bolt's television roots show. The film is directed in a perfunctory manner with little attention paid to the internal rhythms of each scene. The unnecessarily complicated plot lurches from one subplot to the next acquiring new characters and then dismissing them unceremoniously (Dillon's friendship with fellow gambler David Marshall Grant is fully developed and then dropped suddenly, only to have Grant inexplicably reappear at the climax). Several important scenes take place offscreen, making one wonder if the film was trimmed severely before release. Bolt seems to hurry through the convoluted material, taking little time to actually *dramatize* the events. In THE COLOR OF MONEY, director Martin Scorsese proved that small objects rolling around on green felt can be quite exciting and cinematic; in THE BIG TOWN the crap games are simply dull. Bolt's apathetic direction doesn't end there, for Lane's big striptease is terribly tepid, Skerritt's murder is indifferently choreographed, and the first sex scene between Dillon and Lane is brutally unerotic. Despite all the trappings (props, costumes, music), the film conveys no feel for the city, the period, or the seedy gambling milieu. The production spent only five days in Chicago, shooting in the Wabash area under the elevated trains to establish the location. Then the company moved to Toronto where it is cheaper to film. For a movie which is supposed to take place on the mean streets of a big city, the film feels strangely studio bound and artificial.

The acting is spotty as well. Dillon seems uncomfortable or embarrassed by much of the cliche dialog he is forced to spout, and he does a fairly good job of mumbling the really bad lines hurriedly so that no one will pay much attention. Lane is simply miscast as the *femme fatale*—which is not to say that another actress could have done better with a role so absurdly transparent. Lee Grant and Bruce Dern sleepwalk through their dull roles, and always-interesting Skerritt is totally wasted. Only Jones and relative newcomer Amis score well here. Jones seems to delight in his vintage villainy and gets good mileage out of a sneer and a creepy glance. Amis is downright wonderful as the "good" girl, bringing natural beauty and grace to a role that could have been as mundane as the rest. It is an intelligent performance and one that is all the more impressive when one considers the basic blandness she is mired in. Songs include "Home of the Blues" (Johnny Cash, Glen Douglas, Lillie McAplin, performed by Cash), "Who Do You Love" (Ellis McDaniel, performed by Bo Diddley) "Big Town" (Ronnie Self, performed by Self), "Ruby Baby" (Jerry Leiber, Mike Stoller, performed by The Drifters), "C.C. Rider" (Chuck Willis, performed by Willis), "Shake, Rattle, and Roll" (Charles Calhoun, performed by Big Joe Turner), "Juke Joint Johnny" (Lattie Moore, performed by Red Sovine), "Lovesick Blues" (Irving Mills, Cliff Friend, performed by Cindy Fee), "Jim Dandy" (Lincoln Chase, performed by La Vern Baker), "Drown in My Own Tears" (Henry Glover, performed by Ray Charles), "Harlem Nocturne" (Earle Hagen), "Fever" (John Davenport, Eddie Cooley, performed by Little Willie John), "Moritat" (Kurt Weill, Bertolt Brecht), "Goodnight My Love (Pleasant Dreams)" (George Motola, John Marascalco, performed by Jesse Belvin), "Since I Met You Baby" (Ivory Joe Hunter, performed by Hunter). *(Violence, nudity, sexual situations, profanity.)*

p, Martin Ransohoff, Don Carmody; d, Ben Bolt; w, Robert Roy Pool (based on the novel *The Arm* by Clark Howard); ph, Ralf D. Bode (Medallion Film Labs); m, Michael Melvoin; ed, Stuart Pappe; prod d, Bill Kenney; art d, Dan Yarhi, Maher Ahmad; set d, Rose Marie McSherry, Mark Freeborn, Raymond Fleischman; cos, Wendy Partridge; ch, Kelly Robinson; makeup, Katherine Southern; m/l, Johnny Cash, Glen Douglas, Lillie McAlpin, Ellis McDaniel, Ronnie Self, Jerry Leiber, Mike Stoller, Chuck Willis, Charles Calhoun, Lattie Moore, Irving Mills, Cliff Friend, Lincoln Chase, Henry Glover, Earle Hagen, John Davenport, Eddie Cooley, Kurt Weill, Bertolt Brecht, George Motola, John Marascalco, Ivory Joe Hunter; spec eff, Neil Trifunovich; stunts, Stuntco Intl.

Drama **(PR:O MPAA:R)**

BIKINI SHOP, THE (SEE: MALIBU BIKINI SHOP, 1987)

BIRDS OF PREY* (1987, Can.) 90m Trapped Prods./Shapiro c

Jorge Montesi *(Carlos Solo)*, Joseph Patrick Finn *(Harry Card)*, Linda Elder *(The Woman)*, Maurice Brand *(Fence)*, Suzanne Tessier *(Cheryl)*, Jennifer Keene *(Thelma)*, Sam Mottrich *(Levre)*, Deryck Hazel *(Deryck)*, Mitchell Douglas *(Reilly)*, Peter Haynes *(Smarm)*, Ron Graham *(Andrews)*, Paul Wood *(Pimp)*, Mike Gazley *(Ed)*, Terry Keller *(Nose)*, Rollanda Lee *(Mother)*, Toby Lawrence *(Invisible Man)*, Brian Fustikan *(Bouvier)*, Bernie Bloom *(Bartender)*, Mark Olifson *(Carpenter)*, Chris Maginnis *(Haughty)*, Tom Crighton *(Pathology Technician)*, Ed Letain *(Forensics Technician)*, Roland De Yang *(Voice)*, David Kelly *(Frank)*, Don Marshall *(Knuckles)*, Jim Stanton *(Mayor)*, Wes Friesen *(Cop Who Dies)*, Guy Simon Gosselin *(Sid)*, Jeff Gruen *(Larry)*, Brent Baumann, Bill Keech, David Lanktree *(Detectives)*, Connie Edwards *(Smarm's Secretary)*, Wayne Crouse *(Staff Sergeant)*, Peter Campbell *(Nick the Pimp)*.

When a pimp is found crucified on a billboard and disemboweled, detective

Montesi is assigned to the case. Soon more men are dead and all the evidence points to Finn, a burglar and long-time friend of the cop. Montesi refuses to believe his old pal is guilty, and indeed, he is right—Finn has been framed and is now running for his life, with a beautiful but ruthless female hit person (Elder) on his trail. After eluding both the cops and the killer several times, he confronts the man who set him up, art dealer and fence Brand. Before he can kill the man though, Elder appears and does it for him. She then tosses her empty gun to Finn and disappears just as Montesi enters and shoots down his old friend. It takes at least half the film's running time before the story makes any sense and before the characters start to distinguish themselves from each other in the viewer's mind. Technically the film looks little better than amateur and most of the performances are even below that. No time is wasted on trivialities like character development as the film lurches from scene to scene. On the plus side, Elder makes a striking high fashion assassin, Montesi is nicely world-weary, and the film makes good use of locations in Windsor, Canada. *(Violence, nudity, adult situations.)*

p, Peter Haynes, Jorge Montesi; d, Jorge Montesi; w, Peter Haynes, Jorge Montesi; ph, Gary Armstrong; m, Paul Zsa Zsa; ed&art d, Jorge Montesi; cos, Jill Lakeman; makeup, Brent Baumann, Ernie Tomlinson.

Crime Cas. (PR:C-O MPAA:NR)

BIT PART, THE† (1987, Aus.) 87m Comedia Ltd. c

Chris Haywood *(Michael Thornton)*, Nicole Kidman *(Mary McAllister)*, Katrina Foster *(Helen Thornton)*, John Wood *(John Bainbridge)*, Maurie Fields *(Peter)*, Maureen Edwards *(Bev Howard)*, Deborra Lee-Furness *(Acting Teacher)*, Maggie Miller *(Molly)*, Wilbur Wilde *(Biker)*.

Thornton plays a man experiencing mid-life crisis who quits his job as an employment counselor to pursue a career in acting. He gets an agent and there follows a series of comic adventures as Thornton strives to make it in show business.

p, Stephen Vizard, John Gauchi, Peter Herbert; d, Brendan Maher, w, Stephen Vizard, Peter Herbert, Ian MacFadyen; ph, Ellery Ryan; m, Paul Grabowsky, Red Symons; ed, Scott McLennan; prod d, Carole Harvey.

Comedy (PR:NR MPAA:NR)

BLACK CANNON INCIDENT, THE† (1987, Chi.) 94m Xi'an Film Studio/ ICA Projects c (HEI PAO SHI JIAN)

Liu Zifeng *(Zhao Shuxin)*, Gerhard Olschewsky *(Hans Schmidt)*, Gao Ming *(Li Renzhong)*, Wang Yi *(Shou Yuzhen)*, Yang Yazhou *(Feng Liangcai)*, Ge Huai *(Wu Kegong)*.

Bureaucratic insensitivity is the theme of this drama which features Zifeng as a factory engineer who functions as interpreter for an East German who is a consultant to the factory. An inveterate player of a Chinese chess game, he loses a game piece (called "the black cannon") and sends a telegram to a friend, asking him to try to locate it. The message is intercepted by a government bureaucrat, who is unfamiliar with the chess game and who believes it is a coded message. The misunderstanding is compounded and Zifeng loses his job, only to be replaced by an incompetent who makes a shambles of his assignments.

d, Huang Jianxin; w, Li Wei, Huang Xang Xi; ph, Wang Xinsheng, Feng Wei; m, Zhu Shirui; prod d, Liu Yichuan.

Drama (PR:NR MPAA:NR)

BLACK DRAGON, THE† (1987, Hong Kong) 90m IFD-Intercontinental/ Joseph Lai-Terry Lai-Adda Audio Visual c

Dick Chan, Jimmy Lee, Tony Ferrer.

When their father is murdered, three brothers join forces with the police to find and take revenge on the killers.

d, Lo Gio.

Action (PR:NR MPAA:NR)

BLACK WIDOW**½ (1987) 103m Laurence Mark-Americent-American Entertainment Partners/FOX c

Debra Winger *(Alexandra Barnes)*, Theresa Russell *(Catharine)*, Sami Frey *(Paul Nuytten)*, Dennis Hopper *(Ben Dumers)*, Nicol Williamson *(William Macauley)*, Terry O'Quinn *(Bruce)*, James Hong *(Shin)*, Diane Ladd *(Etta)*, D.W. Moffett *(Michael)*, Lois Smith *(Sara)*, Leo Rossi *(Ricci)*, Danny Kamekona *(Detective)*, Rutanya Alda *(Irene)*, Mary Woronov *(Shelley)*, Wayne Heffley *(Etta's Husband)*, Raleigh Bond *(Martin)*, Donegan Smith *(Reporter)*, Christian Clemenson *(Artie)*, Arnsenio "Sonny" Trinidad *(Tran)*, Darrah Meeley *(Dawn)*, Kate Hall *(Young Girl)*, George Ricord *(Italian Man)*, Richard E. Arnold *(Doctor)*, Bea Kiyohara *(Clerk)*, Chris S. Ducey *(Poker Player)*, Tee Dennard *(Sid)*, David Mamet *(Herb)*, Johnny "Sugarbear" Willis *(James)*, Gene Callahan *(Mr. Foster)*, Thomas Hill *(Attorney)*, Juleen Murray *(Attendant)*, Ed Pang *(Waiter)*, Allen Nause *(Clerk)*, Denise Dennison *(Stewardess)*, Robert J. Peters *(Steward)*, David Kasparian *(Limo Driver)*, Mick Muldoon *(Doorman)*.

Director Rafelson is a man with a penchant for remaking other people's hits or near-hits, a habit which suggests he has a desperate need to improve upon others. He made a terrible copy of THE POSTMAN ALWAYS RINGS TWICE which deservedly bombed. The original POSTMAN, directed by Tay Garnett, was a deadly, lofty film, a classic *film noir* which Rafelson barely managed to acknowledge in his dreadful remake. In selecting BLACK WIDOW to remake, he chose a less imposing role model, one directed by Nunnally Johnson in 1954. But this BLACK WIDOW also falls considerably short of the original. The two dueling *femme fatales* here, Winger, as the righteous federal agent, and her nemesis, Russell, are in mortal combat in a cat and mouse, or more apt, a bug and spider game. Russell is the black widow, a subtle, cunning lady who marries millionaires, poisons them with undetectable fluids, and inherits their fortunes before slipping back into the void from which she creeps forth again and again, looking for new victims. Winger, a research agent for the Justice Department, begins to track the deaths of these millionaires, convinced that the widows in a number of suspicious deaths are all the same person. Her boss, O'Quinn, humors her, but refuses to accept her black widow killer as being real. Meanwhile Russell marries Dallas millionaire toy manufacturer Hopper and, after a few months, spikes a bottle of champagne with a lethal chemical dose. While she is out of town, Hopper drinks the champagne and dies. Russell always manages to be out of town when her victims perish. Again Winger charts the Hopper death, then learns that Russell has resurfaced on the West Coast, and goes to Seattle where she meets Russell's next victim, wealthy Williamson. She tries to learn about Russell's past from Williamson, passing herself off as a reporter, but Williamson gives her little information. When Williamson, who has already married Russell, tells his wife about the young woman inquiring about her, Russell tries to find Winger but she has already checked out of her hotel. Later Winger learns that Williamson has suddenly died, leaving his large estate to Russell. She regrets not having warned him that he might be married to a murderess.

Back at her job, Winger tells O'Quinn that she is quitting and is going to follow Russell to Hawaii, having gotten a tip that the black widow is heading that way. O'Quinn tries to talk Winger out of such a harebrained crusade. "If you want to catch her, " Winger tells him, "you have to think like she does." She sells her car and furniture and is off to Hawaii. Russell is already there, cultivating aesthetic millionaire hotel owner, Frey. She and Winger later meet at a scuba diving school and become friends, Winger having learned of Russell's whereabouts through Chinese detective Hong. Russell takes Winger to a party Frey gives and later tells Winger that Frey is fair game. Both women begin seeing him, but Russell wins out and marries the millionaire. Before this takes place the clever Russell goes to the same Chinese detective Winger hired and employs him to spy on Winger and Frey, and he takes photos of the two in compromising situations. After the marriage between Frey and Russell, black widow Russell goes back to Hong and tells him "you can die or you can die happy," pulling a gun on him and forcing him to overdose with mainline heroin. He is found after Frey has died of a strange poison while Russell is away in San Francisco. Winger is later arrested and charged not only with Frey's murder (the poison he has taken found in her apartment), but with Hong's death (the photos of Winger and Frey found by police). The whole thing has been deftly set up by Russell whose vanity insists that she visit Winger one last time in jail where Winger is being held. She tells Winger that the police believe she killed Frey out of jealousy because she lost him to Russell and implies Winger was in love with her as well. In her gloating over having outfoxed her pursuer, Russell gives herself away and turns, startled, to see Frey coming through the door. He did not die and the whole death was a set up. Winger stands up in her prison garb, triumphant. She later leaves the jail while reporters congratulate her for her brilliant trapping of Russell.

The mood here is as fuzzy as the lighting which is designed to heavily compliment both Winger and Russell, attempting to make them and the story more sophisticated than they or it really are. Russell is much less feminine in appearance than her role calls for and she speaks very softly, almost *sotto voce* in a voice that is neither mature nor correct in diction, and is more than reminiscent of the slangy Cathy Moriarity of RAGING BULL. For much of the film, Winger is dowdy in appearance, wearing Mother Hubbard dresses and skirts. However, Russell supervises a dramatic transformation in her appearance when the two are in Hawaii. In his direction of these two considerable talents, Rafelson manages to diminish their potency by having each actress try to underplay the other. The result is something like dialing down a radio drama until only the sound effects come through. The lower register sound score, the coy moves of the actresses, and an almost vacuous approach to camera settings, soften this crime yarn to Technicolor mush. There is no violence here, only the sinister suggestion of evil. Had the script offered sharper deductions and more believable moves on the part of the two actresses, this might have been a much better *film noir* entry. As it is BLACK WIDOW has no real bite. *(Mild language, adult situations.)*

p, Harold Schneider; d, Bob Rafelson; w, Ronald Bass; ph, Conrad L. Hall (DeLuxe Color); m, Michael Small; ed, John Bloom; prod d, Gene Callahan; set d, Jim Duffy, Buck Henshaw, Rick Simpson; cos, Patricia Norris; spec eff, Allen Hall, Jerry Williams; m/l, Peter Rafelson; makeup, Dorothy Pearl.

Mystery/Crime Cas. (PR:O MPAA:R)

BLIND CHANCE***½ (1987, Pol.) 122m Film Prod. Zespoly Filmowe, Unit TOR c (PRZYPADEK)

Boguslaw Linda *(Witek Dlugosz)*, Tadeusz Lomnicki *(Werner)*, Zbigniew Zapa Siewiez *(Adam)*, Boguslawa Pawelec *(Czuszka)*, Marzena Trybala *(Werka)*, Jacek Borowski *(Marek)*, Monika Godzdzik *(Olga)*, Zygmunt Hubner *(Faculty Dean)*, Zbigniew Zapasiewicz.

A young Polish medical student, Linda, experiences three different outcomes for his life, each commencing with a mad dash to catch a train, each ending at the airport, and taking the hero through different facets of the warped society that is modern Poland. After leaving behind his studies upon his father's death, Linda just makes the train where he meets an old Communist party member who instills in him some of his socialist fervor and sets him on his way through the Party hierarchy. Linda manages to quell a revolt of drug addicts at a government hospital, bringing him to the notice of his superiors, but he makes the mistake of falling in love with a young woman who is part of the samizdat underground press. At first his superiors tolerate his affair (they certainly know all about it), but later the woman is arrested along with the rest of her group and an enraged Linda attacks his mentor in his office. He is about to leave the country for a

meeting of Communist youths in Paris when an outbreak of deviationism calls him back from the airport. The next epsiode begins as he again runs to make the train, but this time he's not in time. Instead, he runs headlong into the station master, who has him arrested. Thrown onto a work gang for 30 days, he makes friends with a member of the samizdat and is soon working for them as a courier. Before long, though, the others in his group are arrested and he is suspected of being a traitor and thrown out. He joins the Church and is going to travel to Paris for a meeting of Catholic youths when he is denied a passport because he refuses to spy for the government while abroad. The third variation has him dashing to make the train, missing it, and instead meeting an old girl friend at the station. He returns to medical school, marries the girl, has a child, and is well on his way to domestic tranquility and comfortable mediocrity when the dean of the medical school (where he now works) asks to meet him at the bus station. He tells Linda about the arrest of his son and how this makes it impossible for him to attend a medical conference in Libya. He asks Linda to take his place and the young doctor readily agrees. He changes his plane reservation to a later date, however, in order to be with his wife on her birthday, and the new flight is routed through Paris. He boards the plane and is finally about to leave the country when it blows up just after takeoff.

Completed in 1982, the film was immediately banned under the recently imposed martial law regime of General Jaruzelski, and has only recently been released abroad. It was originally named as the official Polish entry at Cannes, but was dropped at the last minute in favor of a less controversial film. Linda gives a subdued performance as the main character who accepts and then rejects the Party, the Church, and the underground in his search for something on which to center his life. It is only when he stays away from controversy and politics that he achieves success and happiness, only to die in the airplane crash. The direction is surprisingly vigorous for a film which deals with ideas considered in half-light, but the three-part structure is confusing and it is possible to see the film both as a linear construction and as three alternative stories. Although widely praised, the film is unlikely to receive more than an odd art-house run. *(Full frontal nudity, profanity.)*

p,d&w, Krzysztof Kieslowski; ph, Krzysztof Pakulski; m, Wojciech Kilar; ed, Elzbieta Kurowska; prod d, Rafal Waltenberger.

Drama **(PR:O MPAA:NR)**

BLIND DATE** (1987) 93m Tri Star-Delphi V-ML Delphi Premier/Tri Star c

Kim Basinger *(Nadia Gates)*, Bruce Willis *(Walter Davis)*, John Larroquette *(David Bedford)*, William Daniels *(Judge Harold Bedford)*, George Coe *(Harry Gruen)*, Mark Blum *(Denny Gordon)*, Phil Hartman *(Ted Davis)*, Stephanie Faracy *(Susie Davis)*, Alice Hirson *(Muriel Bedford)*, Graham Stark *(Jordan the Bedford Butler)*, Joyce Van Patten *(Nadia's Mother)*, Jeannie Elias *(Walter's Secretary)*, Sacerdo Tanney *(Minister)*, Georgann Johnson *(Mrs. Gruen)*, Sab Shimono *(Mr. Yakamoto)*, Momo Yashima *(Mrs. Yakamoto)*, Armin Shimerman *(French Waiter)*, Brian George *(Maitre d')*, Ernest Harada *(Japanese Gardener)*, Emma Walton, Elaine Wilkes, Susan Lentini *(Muggers)*, Barry Sobel *(Gas Station Attendant)*, Arlene Lorre *(Court Stenographer)*, Timothy Stack *(Grant)*, Jack Gwillim *(Artist)*, Diana Bellamy *(Maid)*, Seth Isler *(Delivery Driver)*, Paul Carafotes *(Disco Dancer)*, Bob Ari *(Bailiff)*, Don Sparks, Bill Marcus *(Street Cops)*, Michael Genovese, Randall Bowers, John Demy *(Jail Officers)*, Jon Smet *(Car Lot Customer)*, Noele de Saint Gall *(Guest at Wedding)*, Julia Jennings *(Big Blonde)*, Dick Durock *(Bouncer)*, Stanley Jordan *(Himself)*, Billy Vera and the Beaters: Billy Vera, Peter Bunetta, Ricky Hirsch, Darrell Leonard, David Miner, Mike Murphy, Jerry Peterson, Lon Price, Ron Viola, Keith Robertson *(Nightclub Band)*.

Producer-director Edwards is a man who packages money pictures, the accent being on comedy of the bubbling, frothy, and generally forgettable sort. But there are a few exceptions, such as 10 and the Pink Panther series. In BLIND DATE, Edwards has taken a situation comedy sketch and blown it up to feature-film status, falling back on his usual pratfalls and slapstick. Yet he was smart enough to realize he could sell this vacuum tube by stuffing the widely popular TV actor Willis ("Moonlighting") in at one end, the silly-sinister Larroquette ("Night Court") at the other, and packing alluring Basinger (NO MERCY, NEVER SAY NEVER AGAIN, THE NATURAL, a curious string of "N" titles) somewhere in the middle. And sell, like the ever-blustering Barnum, is the name of this game, BLIND DATE gleaning more than $40 million at the box office only months after its release. The story is simple if not simpleminded, stemming from the prosaic life of Willis, who is, ironically, not punkish or smart-alecky at all, as has been the image that won the hearts of women in his "Moonlighting" wise-guy private-eye role. Those expecting to see the aggressive know-it-all from TV will be surprised when greeted with a down-to-earth paper-shuffler whose only ambition is to climb the corporate ladder.

As the film opens, Willis awakens from a desktop sleeping position. He quickly changes his shirt, gathers up his notes, and papers, and dashes to the office for a board meeting. Present at the meeting is a multimillionaire Japanese client, Shimono, a male chauvinist who insists his much-suppressed wife, Yashima, slavishly act like a half-baked geisha and who, it is stated at the board meeting, blithely keeps several concubines on the side. Willis is scheduled to attend an important dinner that night but is cautioned to find a proper suit and bring an acceptable date. His on-and-off girl friend is not available, so Willis desperately casts about for a replacement date, nervously accepting a strong suggestion from his sleazy, car-salesman brother, Hartman, to take Basinger, a southern girl who is new in town. With a great deal of apprehension (his brother has played him false on other blind dates), Willis picks up Basinger and is pleasantly surprised to find her to be beautiful, sensitive, and well-mannered. They stop by a recording studio where, Willis explains, he practiced to be a guitarist, but gave up that ambition to enter the business world. He then pours drinks from a bottle of champagne he has brought along as he and Basinger listen to a singer recording in a glass-encased soundstage. Oddly, Willis foists the champagne on his attractive date though his brother had warned him she gets wild when drinking. By the time the pair arrive at the posh supper club, Basinger is transformed into a hip-swinging, brash, loud-mouthed troublemaker. When Basinger slips while walking into the restaurant, she reaches out for support and tears away the breast pocket on Willis' new suit. Willis, embarrassed, escorts Basinger to a table, where she immediately causes an argument with a surly, haughty waiter. As Willis tries to mollify the waiter, Basinger jumps up and begins to create havoc at the main table, where Willis' boss is attempting to entertain the autocratic Japanese businessman, whose wife sits dutifully by his side, lighting his cigarettes and keeping her white-painted face downward in abject obedience. Basinger then begins ripping the breast pockets from the suits of Willis' fellow executives (including his boss), upsetting chairs, and sending waiters into a frenzy. In the turmoil, the Japanese wife loses her huge wig and races off to the W.C. in whimpering disgrace while the Japanese millionaire client fumes. Willis is summarily fired after Basinger reappears to announce that the much-abused Oriental lady wants to sue her husband for divorce. In the W.C. Basinger has informed the wife that community property laws in California will allow her to get half of her husband's great fortune. When Basinger announces the wife requires a lawyer to go after her husband's $100 million, attorneys spring to life from a half-dozen tables.

Willis leaves the restaurant with Basinger, his sanity intact, but quickly slipping away. He explains to the drunken lady that she has ruined his life. All he wants to do now is take her home. He is suddenly confronted by Basinger's former lover, Larroquette, an unbalanced lawyer who goes berserk any time he sees Basinger in the company of another man. Larroquette attacks Willis and follows him in a car chase that will last the entire night. Basinger, in a near stupor, has Willis drive her to a remote street in a bad neighborhood, insisting that this is where she will stay with friends. While they are knocking on the door of a dilapidated house, the house is suddenly whisked away from the front stoop, propelled by a huge house-moving apparatus, a startling sight gag that is too abrupt to work and never explained. Meanwhile, Willis' car is being stripped by car thieves and when he races after them, he is held up by a gang of female punk-rockers, who drop a

pistol in his car and take off when a police squad car appears. The officers make Willis go through a series of sobriety tests, which he passes. He then drives off with Basinger, who is perched on a wooden box in the vandalized sports car, now minus seats or doors. They go to a party Basinger had mentioned earlier and by now Willis has abandoned all sense of propriety, becoming a wild man, dancing crazily through a throng of well-dressed people in a sumptuous home, drinking madly, throwing food, washing his hands in the punch, causing the now sober Basinger to realize he is taking his revenge on her. When they leave the party it's Basinger's turn to be disgraced, but Willis is again attacked by the dogged Larroquette, who has driven into two storefronts and the wall of a flour plant while pursuing the pair through the Los Angeles streets. Willis is beside himself and, in his struggle with Larroquette discovers the discarded pistol in his car. He makes Larroquette dance by firing at the lawyer's quick-stepping feet. Police arrive and take Willis into custody, charging him with assault with a deadly weapon and other assorted offenses, which will certainly add up to a long prison term.

Basinger later goes to Larroquette and tells him that Willis, the man she really loves, is going to defend himself in court and she begs attorney Larroquette to represent him. He says he will, but only if she will marry him. After thinking it over, Basinger agrees to the ridiculous bargain, saying: "You mean we have to have sex?" Larroquette nods lasciviously and Basinger adds: "All right, but no kissing!" Larroquette appears for Willis in court and gets all charges dismissed, an easy enough task for him as the presiding judge, Daniels, happens to be his father. (Larroquette promises his father that he will never practice in his jurisdiction again in order to get Willis off.) Wedding plans are made and a huge fete is prepared, the nuptials to take place at the resplendent estate of Daniels. Willis by then realizes he loves Basinger and sneaks about the estate in a series of slapstick situations straight out of GETTING GERTIE'S GARTER and other better-made comedies. He spikes a box of candy with booze, knowing Basinger has a sweet tooth, and has it delivered to her on her wedding day. Of course, in the middle of the ceremonies having eaten all the candy, Basinger goes crazy again. She goes into a laughing jag just before saying "I do" and generally disrupts the elaborate services. (Awkward shades of the finale of IT HAPPENED ONE NIGHT.) Willis, hiding in a cabana on the other side of the pool, suddenly emerges and shouts Basinger's name. She pushes the preacher into the pool, brushes aside Larroquette, and races toward Willis; both dive into the pool and swim to each other, embracing under water and emerging in each other's arms—a blatant take off on THE GRADUATE. At the end, it's Willis and Basinger against the world with a guitar in his hands and a song on their lips.

The inane dialog, witless situations and forced physical comedy of BLIND DATE did not offer great grist for Willis in his first major motion picture. This debut and its huge financial returns is a curiosity success, one where millions (mostly women) flocked to view their popular TV anti-hero. But it's apparent that Willis is in a toss-away position in BLIND DATE, his TV popularity probably used up completely in what may be his last important box office release. The film is just this side of acceptable and so predictable is its plot, so blatant in its contrived physical guffaws, that adults will find little humor in the film after the first 30 minutes. A great deal of energy is expended by Larroquette in his unbelievable role, and a few nervous laughs will result from his frenetic behavior. Basinger is fetching in her naturally southern way (she is a native Georgian), but her conduct in and out of reason is too erratic. Her chemical imbalance is regulated not so much by booze as by a director, Edwards (this is his 45th film), hurrying along a plot that dare not be studied lest the viewer realize it is unappealing and boring. Some worthwhile moments in this pasted-together film are provided by the stuffy Daniels and the scheming brother, Hartman. A sure after-effect of BLIND DATE is the vexing thought that the viewer's time could have been better spent. One could easily envision Edwards saying to his cast: "Look, why bother upgrading the dialog, attempting wit and funny lines? Just keep falling down, insulting each other and throwing anything not nailed down into the faces of anything human. And, whatever you do, keep that car crashing into buildings. Forget about leaving the audience laughing. Moving pictures move and we must keep things moving." Especially audiences past that box office.

p, Tony Adams; d, Blake Edwards; w, Dale Launer; ph, Harry Stradling, Jr. (Panavision, Metrocolor); m, Henry Mancini; ed, Robert Pergament; prod d, Rodger Maus; md, Al Bunetta, Tom Bocci; art d, Peter Lansdown Smith; set d, Carl Biddiscombe; cos, Tracy Tynan; spec eff, Roy Downey; m/l, Henry Mancini, George Merrill, Shannon Rubicam, Stanley Jordan, L. Russell Brown, Billy Vera, Keith L'Neire, Larry Brown; stunts, Joe Dunne; makeup, Rick Sharp, Norman T. Leavitt.

Comedy **Cas.** **(PR:C MPAA:PG-13)**

BLOCK NOTES-DIE UN REGISTA-APPUNTI (SEE: INTERVISTA, 1987, It.)

BLOND DOLLY† (1987, Neth.) 105m Gijs Versluys-Riverside/Holland c

Hilde van Mieghem *(Dolly/Sylvia/Kitty)*, Peter Tuinman *(Eddy Cremer)*, Celia Nufaar, Fred Vaassen, Adrian Brine, Herbert Flack, Gilbert Gieske, Piet Kamerman, Astrid Seriese, Marieke van der Pol.

A mystery based on the 1959 murder of a prostitute who, it was later discovered, was a worldy and extremely wealthy divorcee with numerous connections in the business world.

p, Gijs Versluys; d, Gerrit van Elst; w, Hein Schutz, Alma Popeyus; ph, Theo Bierkens (Moviecam, Eastmancolor); m, Lucas Asselbergs; ed, Ton Ruys; art d, Jan Roelofs, Ben Van Os.

Crime **(PR:NR MPAA:NR)**

BLOOD DINER* (1987) 90m Lightning-PMS Filmworks/Vestron c

Rick Burks *(Michael Tutman)*, Carl Crew *(George Tutman)*, Roger Dauer *(Mark Shepard)*, LaNette La France *(Sheba Jackson)*, Lisa Guggenheim *(Connie Stanton)*, Max Morris *(Chief Miller)*, Roxanne Cybelle *(Little Michael)*.

This cartoonish, gory tribute to the films of Herschell Gordon Lewis details the attempts of two brothers to provide a body for an ancient goddess by using the hacked-up parts of dozens of scantily clad girls. The Tutman brothers (Burks and Crew) follow the practices taught them in childhood by their uncle, who later died in a hail of police bullets after going on a murderous rampage. Their first step in raising the goddess Sheetar is to dig up their uncle's moldering corpse and remove his brain, which they restore with incantations and place in a jar of liquid. The brain instructs them to prepare the Blood Banquet, which is to be made of teenager niblets, and to build the body for Sheetar out of the other human parts. The lads serve the leftovers in their health food restaurant, attracting a large and dedicated clientele. A competing restaurateur, upset over his own loss of business, breaks into their establishment during the night and steals the uncle's brain. With difficulty, the boys retrieve it in time for the Blood Banquet, which is held at a disco. They pass out hunger pills that cause the guests to dig into the stew of body parts. Burks and Crew also prepare to sacrifice a virgin at the precise moment that will give the stitched-up body life. The famished banqueters go crazy and begin devouring the feast and each other. In a full-blown tribute to George Romero, the police break and add to the carnage. Sheetar comes to life with big, nasty teeth and attacks anyone in range before disappearing. The brothers are killed, but Sheetar is last seen as a hooker on Sunset Boulevard. Although directed by a woman, BLOOD DINER demonstrates no more enlightened an attitude than those of I SPIT ON YOUR GRAVE or MANIAC. Kong watched most of H.G. Lewis' gore-fests before making this and admits that BLOOD FEAST was the primary source for the plot. Beyond this, Kong adds the sort of contempt for the original material that ruins most horror satires. There's nothing the least bit redeeming about BLOOD DINER. *(Gore effects, nudity, profanity.)*

p, Jimmy Maslon, Jackie Kong; d, Jackie Kong; w, Michael Sonye; ph, Jurg Walther; m, Don Preston; ed, Thomas Meshelski; prod d, Ron Petersen; art d, Keith Barrett; cos, Shiz Herrera; spec eff, Bruce Zahlava; m/l, Dino Lee, Jimmy Maslon, Denny Freeman, Dootsie Williams, H.B. Barnum, Don Julian, Stewart Crunk, Huey Roundtree; makeup, Loraina Drucker.

Horror **(PR:O MPAA:R)**

BLOOD HOOK† (1987) 95m Golden Chargers-Spider Lake/Troma c

Mark Jacobs *(Peter Van Clease)*, Don Cosgrove *(Roger Swain)*, Patrick Danz *(Rodney)*, Paul Drake *(Wayne Duerst)*, Dale Dunham *(Denny Dobyns)*, Donald Franke *(Grandfather)*, Ryan Franke *(Young Peter)*, John Galligan, Ron Kaiser *(Emcees)*, Sara Hauser *(Kiersten)*, Paul Heckman *(The Sheriff)*, Bonnie Lee *(Sheila Swain)*, Bill Lowrie *(Evelyn Duerst)*, Sandra Meuwissen *(Bev D.)*, Greg Nienas *(Irving Swain)*, Dana Remker *(Dickie)*, Lisa Todd *(Ann Colbert)*, Julie Vortanz *(Ruth-Ann Swain)*, Christopher Whiting *(Finner)*, Don Winters *(Leroy Leudke)*.

This continent's most peculiar film company, Troma, Inc., comes up with yet another intriguing exploitationer. Reminiscent of JAWS and PIRANHA, BLOOD HOOK centers on a series of killings in a Wisconsin fishing town. The bloodletting occurs during the "Muskie Madness" fishing contest and the town sheriff is wary of causing a panic which could have a negative effect on the tourist trade. A group of college-age kids—Jacobs, Todd, Danz, Hauser, and Whiting—head up to the long-abandoned farmhouse of Jacob's grandfather, who was mysteriously killed 17 years earlier. The demented killer is still wandering the woods it seems, reeling in his prey with a huge muskie lure. An equal amount of gore, comedy, music, and fishing make this as strange as anything Troma has ever done. Songs include "Fishing For Your Love" (Victoria Harper, performed by Harper, Thomas Naunas, D. Harris), "Things Aren't What They Seem" (Naunas, performed by Naunas, Brad Wray, Jeff Seitz, J. Whitehead, C. Deming), "Muskie Reggae" (Naunas, performed by Naunas, Wray, Seitz, Whitehead), "Red River Valley" (Naunas, performed by Naunas, Whitehead, Wray, Kevin Murphy), and "Rodney's Theme" (Naunas, Murphy, performed by

Naunas, Wray, Seitz, Whitehead, Murphy). *(Gore effects, violence, nudity, profanity.).*

p, David Herbert; d, James Mallon; w, Larry Edgerton, John Galligan (based on a story by Gail Anderson, David Herbert, James Mallon, Douglas Rand); ph, Marsha Kahm (Du Art Color); m, Thomas A. Naunas; ed, Marsha Kahm; cos, Patsy Herbert; m/l, Victoria Harper, Thomas A. Naunas, Kevin Murphy, Brad Wray, Jeff Seitz, J. Whitehead, C. Deming, D. Harris; makeup, Darcy Knight, James Suthers.

Horror/Comedy **(PR:NR MPAA:R)**

BLOOD SISTERS zero (1987) 86m Reeltime c

Amy Brentano *(Linda)*, Shannon McMahon *(Alice)*, Dan Erickson *(Russ)*, Maria Machart *(Marnie)*, Elizabeth Rose *(Bonnie)*, Cjerste Thor *(Cara)*, Patricia Finneran *(Diana)*, Gretchen Kingsley *(Ellen)*, Brigette Cossu *(Laurie)*, Randall Walden *(Jim)*, Brian Charlton Wrye *(John)*, John Fasano *(Larry)*, Pam La Testa *(The Madame)*, Mikhail Druhan *(Edna the Prostitute)*, Lynnea Benson, Ruth Collins *(Prostitutes)*, Michael Tilton *(The John)*, Derek Conte *(Sam)*, Seraphine Warrington *(Little Sally)*, Jesse D'Angelo *(Little Russ)*, Thomas Biscione, Robert P. Masci *(Policemen)*.

A poorly paced horror tale about a group of sorority pledges who are forced to spend an evening in an abandoned old house which was formerly a house of prostitution. Before the girls arrive, a couple of frat boys rig the house with rubber spiders, mannequins, and a variety of other things that go bump in the night. Of course all the girls are spooked, especially when they start falling victim to the frat boys' pranks. Sorority sister Brentano is in charge of the affair and orders the pledges to hunt through the dark house in search of a list of hidden items. As the girls wander around the twisting halls and empty rooms, they glimpse apparitions of prostitutes. Each time one of the pledges looks into a mirror, she enters a trancelike state and has a vision of the prostitutes who years ago occupied the room. As the night grows darker, the pledges disappear one by one, dying at the hands of an unseen attacker wearing a prostitute's negligee. The attacker is finally revealed to be Erickson, a young transvestite who has lived in the house all his life. The son of a prostitute, Erickson, as a young boy, killed all the hookers and their johns, and is eager to continue his killing spree.

A standard slasher entry, BLOOD SISTERS is only of interest because it was directed by Roberta Findlay, one of the more legendary names in exploitation films. Findlay, who worked throughout the 1960s and 1970s with her then-husband Michael, is perhaps best remembered for SNUFF, a movie in which the film's crew apparently murdered an actress before the cameras. It proved to be a grand hoax which sent many bloodthirsty viewers searching for *real* "snuff" films. (For the curious, none have ever been documented.) After working for some time as a porno director, Findlay delivered a 1986 entry called TENEMENT. Judging from this most recent effort, however, Findlay might as well go back to making porno films. BLOOD SISTERS is one of the most boring entries to come off the slasher conveyor belt. One would think the combination of seven perky young actresses and a sexually deranged killer would, at least, produce a scare or two. Not a chance. This film consists almost exclusively of frightened girls walking slowly (very slowly) throughout the house with their flashlights in hand. Nothing happens in BLOOD SISTERS until the last ten minutes. The audience is then treated to some unsuspenseful murders. The pacing is way off base, the photography (by Findlay) is unduly dark, the soundtrack is silly, and the acting is less than profound. Findlay shows restraint (probably motivated by a small budget) in showing gore, as there are only a couple of such shots. Although there are a few moments of gratuitous female nudity, it, too, is unusually restrained. Findlay has long been known for some inventive murders, and BLOOD SISTERS follows that tradition as one of the pledges gets strangled with a garter. That, however, is the best this anemic entry can offer. *(Profanity, nudity, sexual situations.)*

p, Walter E. Sear; d,w&ph, Roberta Findlay (Studio Film Color); m, Walter E. Sear, Michael Litovsky; ed, Walter E. Sear, Roberta Findlay; art d&cos, Jeffrey Wallach; makeup, Jean Carbolla.

Horror **Cas.** **(PR:O MPAA:R)**

BLOOD TRACKS† (1987, Swed.) 86m Smart Egg c

Jeff Harding *(John)*, Naomi Kaneda *(Suzie)*, Michael Fitzpatrick *(Bob)*, Brad Powell *(Soundman)*, Peter Merrill *(Nick)*, Harriet Robinson *(Carrie)*, Tina Shaw *(Sahra)*, Frances Kelly *(Louise)*, Karina Lee *(Mary)*, Helena Jacks *(Linda)*, Easy Action *(Solid Gold Group)*.

A rock group named Solid Gold (played by Swedish rockers Easy Action) visits Colorado to film a music video. Trapped in a snowbound cabin, the group members and their girl friends fall prey to a murderous family which lives in an abandoned factory nearby.

p, Tom Sjoberg; d, Mike Jackson [Mats Olsson]; w, Mike Jackson [Mats Olsson], Anna Wolf; ph, Hans von Dittmer (Fuji color); m, Dag Unenge; ed, David Gilbert; m/l, Easy Action; stunts, Tommy Ellgren; makeup, Dick Ljunggren.

Horror **(PR:NR MPAA:NR)**

BLOODSUCKERS FROM OUTER SPACE* (1987) 79m One-Of-Those-Prods./Reel Movies Intl. c

Thom Meyers *(Jeff Rhodes)*, Laura Ellis *(Julie)*, Dennis Letts *(Gen. Sanders)*, Chris Heldman *(Sam)*, Robert Bradeen *(Uncle Joe)*, Billie Keller *(Aunt Kate)*, John Webb *(Dr. Pace)*, Rick Garlington *(Maj. Hood)*, Kris Nicolau Sharpley *(Jeri Jett)*, Garl Latham *(B.J. Barton)*, Glen Coburn *(Ralph Rhodes)*, Samantha Walker *(Pam)*, Dan Gallion *(The Farmer)*, Charles Coburn *(Sheriff Don)*, Pat Paulsen *(The President)*, Richard Wainscott *(Richard)*, Jim Stafford *(Buford)*, Darrell Shelton *(Guard)*, Paul LaRocque *(Driver)*, Joyce Dixon *(Seductive Bloodsucker)*, Big John Brigham *(Norman)*, Jack Wilkinson *(The Coroner)*, John Duvall *(Dead Man)*, Franny Coppenbarger *(Dead Woman)*, Julie P. Oliver-Touchstone *(Screamer)*, Derel Chick *(Headless Farmer)*, David Cunningham, Jack Hammack, John Latham *(Soldiers)*, Christine Crowe *(President's Playmate)*, Roy Russell, Charlie Seybert *(Bloodsucking Codgers)*.

An airborne virus from outer space invades a lonely farming community in central Texas and turns the inhabitants into bloodsucking zombies. While scientists at the nearby top-secret laboratory installation known as "Research City" debate what to do about the virus, a crazed Army general, Letts, wants to drop the atomic bomb on the town. Meanwhile, a young newspaper photographer, Meyers, and his girl friend, Ellis, try to escape the increasingly zombified population. Eventually, general Letts gets permission from an annoyed President Paulsen to drop the bomb, but the blast hits 60 miles past its target, presumably killing thousands of innocent people. Having finally escaped, Meyers and Ellis leave a contented town of bloodsucking zombies behind and start a new life.

Played for laughs, this ultra-low budget production does contain a few funny moments, but it's strictly amateur night in the Lone Star state. With a cast and crew made up of siblings, friends, and neighbors, BLOODSUCKERS FROM OUTER SPACE exudes a certain rural charm as it struggles to generate some laughs from its underdeveloped screenplay. Part NIGHT OF THE LIVING DEAD and part DR. STRANGELOVE, the movie is a hodgepodge of bad one-liners, forced gags, comic gore, and film school self-consciousness (i.e., the director and actors constantly remind the audience that they're watching a movie by interrupting the narrative to comment on the action—"Wow, that incidental music sure is creepy," Meyers says at one point). Writer-director Coburn assaults rural small-mindedness at every opportunity, with the result that BLOODSUCKERS FROM OUTER SPACE is more an attack on the stifling boredom of farm life than an attempt at a horror/science-fiction film. The residents of this small Texas town are a racist, xenophobic, incestuous (figuratively) lot who are suspicious of anyone who would want to leave town. Their transformation into zombies is a logical extension of their clannishness taken to an absurd extreme. Meyers' photographer desperately wants to leave town for a better life, and the grotesque situation only heightens his feelings of alienation. While analysis such as this sounds pretentious when applied to a film like BLOODSUCKERS FROM OUTER SPACE, these classic science- fiction/horror themes are indeed there, however poorly presented. Beneath the half-baked jokes and amateur production there seems to be a raw creative sensibility struggling to develop. Although the film's distributor is listed as Reel Movies International, no evidence of a theatrical release has been found and the film received a general release via Karl-Lorimar Home Video. Songs include: "They're Out for Blood" (Ann Armstrong, Emilie Aronson, Steve Hughes), "Just a Mirage" (Emilie Aronson, Steve Hughes), "I Want You" (Ann Armstrong), "Step into the Night" (Steve Hughes), and "Bloodsucker Theme" (John England)—all songs performed by Ann Armstrong, Emilie Aronson. *(Violence, gore effects, profanity, brief nudity, sexual situations, substance abuse.)*

p, Garl Boyd Latham; d&w, Glen Coburn; ph, Chad D. Smith; ed, Karen D. Latham; art d, Rick Garlington; set d, Joan M. Kienlan; cos, Karen Pierce; spec eff, Tim McDowell, J.P. Joyce; m/l, Ann Armstrong, Emilie Aronson, Steve Hughes, John England; makeup, Tim McDowell, J.P. Joyce.

Science Fiction/Comedy **Cas.** **(PR:O MPAA:NR)**

BLOODY NEW YEAR† (1987, Brit.) 90m Lazer Entertainment-Cinema & Theater Seating/Smart Egg c (AKA: TIME WARP TERROR)

Suzy Aitchison *(Lesley)*, Nikki Brooks *(Janet)*, Colin Heywood *(Spud)*, Mark Powley *(Rick)*, Catherine Roman *(Carol)*, Julian Ronnie *(Tom)*.

An entry in the teen blood-letting field, this one has six teenagers stranded on an island and taking refuge in an old hotel. Much mayhem follows as they are haunted by murderous ghosts. Seems there was a New Year's party in the hotel in 1960 which ended rather badly for some of the guests, and they're still upset about it.

p, Hayden Pearce, Maxine Julius; d, Norman J. Warren; w, Frazer Pearce,

Norman J. Warren, Hayden Pearce; ph, John Shann (Fujicolor by Rank); m, Nick Magnus; ed, Carl Thomson; prod d, Hayden Pearce.

Horror **Cas.** **(PR:NR MPAA:NR)**

BLOODY WEDNESDAY† (1987) 96m Gilmark/Visto Intl. c

Raymond Elmendorf *(Harry)*, Pamela Baker *(Dr. Johnson)*, Navarre Perry *(Ben Curtis)*, Teresa Mae Allen *(Elaine Curtis)*, Jeff O'Haco *(Animal)*, John Landtroop *(Bellman)*.

Originally titled "The Great American Massacre," this exploitationer was filmed in 1984 and released this year on videocassette. Elmendorf stars as an auto mechanic who gradually loses touch with reality. He wanders naked into his local church, entertains sexual fantasies about his psychiatrist, has visions of a suicide that occurred years before, and eventually machine-guns (in slow-motion) a crowd of people in a local diner. Scripted and produced by the once-great Hollywood screenwriter Philip Yordan, who penned such Nick Ray classics as JOHNNY GUITAR, THE HARDER THEY FALL, KING OF KINGS, and 55 DAYS AT PEKING and Anthony Mann's THE LAST FRONTIER, EL CID, and THE MAN FROM LARAMIE. Post-production consultant Gene Ruggiero is a long-time Hollywood editor who cut NINOTCHKA, THE SHOP AROUND THE CORNER, THE TOAST OF NEW ORLEANS, AROUND THE WORLD IN 80 DAYS, and many others.

p, Philip Yordan, Mark G. Gilhuis, Robert Ryan, Susan Gilhuis; d, Mark G. Gilhuis; w, Philip Yordan; ph, Robert Ryan (United Color); m, Al Sendry; art d, Phil Adipietro.

Drama **Cas.** **(PR:NR MPAA:NR)**

BLUDNYY SYN† (1987, USSR) 89m Lithuanian Film Studio/Sovexportfilm c (Trans: The Prodigal Son)

Rimas Morkunas, Doloresa Kazragite, Uldis Vazdiks, Brone Braskite, Eva Paskene, Eduardas Kunavicus.

This story of redemption and roots details a prodigal son's return to his family and native village after his wife leaves him. Though his parents are in bad health, they accept their long-absent son with open arms, as does his brother, who has remained in the village. The prodigal son finds the old ways a little unfamiliar but comforting. After meeting a beautiful local woman, he decides that he is finally home, and home is where he will stay.

d, Marionas Gedris; w, Pranas Morkus; ph, Yonas Tomasiavicus; m, Yuosas Sirvinskas; art d, Algimantas Sugzda.

Drama **(PR:NR MPAA:NR)**

BLUE MONKEY† (1987) 98m Spectrafilm c (AKA: GREEN MONKEY)

Steve Railsback *(Detective Jim Bishop)*, Gwynyth Walsh *(Dr. Rachel Carson)*, Susan Anspach *(Dr. Judith Glass)*, John Vernon *(Roger Levering, Hospital Administrator)*, Joe Flaherty *(George Baker)*, Robin Duke *(Sandra Baker)*, Don Lake *(Elliot Jacobs, Entomologist)*, Sandy Webster *(Fred Adams, Repairman)*, Helen Hughes *(Marwella Harbison, Greenhouse Owner)*, Joy Coghill *(Dede Wilkens)*, Bill Lake *(Paramedic)*, Peter Van Wart *(Oscar Willets)*, Stuart Stone *(Joey)*, Marsha Moreau *(Marcy)*, Nathan Adamson *(Tyrone)*, Sarah Polley *(Ellen)*, Cynthia Belliveau *(Alice Bradley)*, Phillip Akin *(Anthony Rivers)*, Dan Lett *(Ted Andrews)*, Michael J. Reynolds *(Albert Hooper)*, Michael Caruana *(Technician)*, Gina Wilkinson *(Michelle Williams)*, David Clement *(Surgeon)*, Ursula Balzer *(O.R. Nurse)*, Les Rubie *(Rollo Jordan)*, Reg Dreger *(Policeman)*, Karen Scanlan *(I.S.O. Nurse)*, Ralph Small *(Security Guard)*, Harry Booker *(Bill Clemmins)*, Jo Anne Bates *(Lobby Nurse)*, Walker Boone *(Johnson)*, Allan Rosenthal *(Dr. Steinberg)*, Ken Quinn *(Patient)*, Don Ritchie, Robert Wilton *(Orderlies)*, Laurs Dickson, Jane Dingle *(Desk Nurses)*, Ivan E. Roth *(The Creature)*.

The only reason anyone paid any attention to this film during its brief theatrical release was due to its perplexing title, one that left many to wonder: What in the hell is a blue monkey? Well the blue monkey used to be a green monkey before the title was changed at the last minute because of calls from the media asking if the film was about the now-infamous African primates that are believed to be the originators of the AIDS virus. Strangest of all, the monster is not a monkey at all, but a giant hybrid of an insect with the head of wasp, the eyes of a dragonfly, the stomach of a scorpion, the back of "various" beetles, and the arms of a praying mantis. Then why use the word "monkey" in the title at all, no matter what color? Who knows? Who cares? Although there is a throwaway line stating that a group of children have given the creature the "Blue Monkey" nickname (these children apparently have had little or no instruction in the finer points of biology, zoology, or entomology).

The whole sordid mess begins when a hapless gardener cuts himself on a mysterious plant and collapses. Rushed to the emergency room of County Memorial Hospital, the gardener suddenly goes into convulsions and vomits up a squiggly larvae. Doctors Anspach and Walsh send the disgusting little item down to the lab where it is cut open to reveal a small insect. Before expert entomologists have a chance to identify the strange creature, a group of mischievous children feed the bug some liquid steroids and it immediately grows to huge proportions, killing a horny orderly and his candy-striped friend, and then sucking the calcium out of their bones. By now the hospital has been quarantined, leaving those inside trapped with the creature. To make matters worse, the insect has given birth to a mate which lays numerous eggs in every nook and cranny in the place. Led by brave police officer Railsback, the humans find the insect's mate and incinerate it along with the eggs. The "blue monkey" flies into a rage, but Railsback lures it into a trap where he is able to blind the monster with a laser. Can Railsback defeat the monster? Are there any eggs left undestroyed? Will there be an equally

ridiculous sequel that retains the pointless title? These and other questions can be answered by seeing the film on videotape for it was not in movie theaters long enough to be seen by our staff.

p, Martin Walters; d, William Fruet; w, George Goldsmith; ph, Brenton Spencer; m, Patrick Coleman, Paul Novotny; ed, Michael Fruet; art d, Reuben Freed; set d, Brendon Smith; cos, Gina Kiellerman; spec eff, Jill Compton, Sirius Effects, L. Michael Roberts; makeup, Cheree Van Dyk; stunts, Shane Cardwell.

Horror **(PR:NR MPAA:R)**

BLUES LAHOFESH HAGADOL (SEE: LATE SUMMER BLUES, 1987, Israel)

BOHATER ROKU† (1987, Pol.) 115m Zespoly Filmowe-Perspektywa Film Unit c (Trans: Hero of the Year)

Jerzy Stuhr *(Ludwik Danielak)*, Mieczyslaw Franaszek *(Zbigniew Tataj, Grocer)*, Katarzyna Kozak-Paszkowska *(Maja)*, Piotr Machalica, Marian Opania, Boguslaw Sobczuk, Michal Tarkowski.

Director Falk here presents a sequel to his 1978 film TOP DOG, with Stuhr reprising his character from the earlier film. Stuhr had been a television perfomer, but lost that job and now thinks only of returning to the small screen. He comes up with a concept for a show called "Hero of the Year" which will focus on common people who perform acts of heroism. The show gets on the air with Franaszek, who saved residents of an apartment building from a gas explosion, featured as the first "hero." The show tours Poland, as Franaszek grows disgusted with the speeches he is forced to read. He finally walks out, leaving Stuhr with another failure.

d&w, Feliks Falk; ph, Witold Adamek; m, Jan Kanty Pawluskiewicz; ed, Lucja Osko; prod d, Halina Dobrowolska.

Drama **(PR:NR MPAA:NR)**

BORAN—ZEIT ZUM ZIELEN† (1987, W. Ger./Bel.) 100m Daniel Zuta Filmproduktion-Alain Keytsman/Cine-Intl. c (Trans: Boran—Time To Aim)

Bernard Rud *(Philip Boran)*, Renee Soutendijk *(Linda Mars)*, Julien Schoenaerts *(Maconnet)*, Jean-Pierre Leaud *(His Deputy)*.

The first West German/Belgian coproduction and first feature for director Zuta, it tells the story of criminal who goes straight and becomes a movie star. Rud, who also cowrote the script, is the reformed crook who finds himself at odds with the law once more when his brother is killed by police during a bank robbery. Certain his brother was innocent, Rud sets out to entrap the cops who did the killing.

p, Daniel Zuta, Alain Keytsman; d, Daniel Zuta; w, Daniel Zuta, Bernard Rud; ph, Walther Van Den Ende; m, Okko Berger, Jan Kruger, Lonzo Westphal; ed, Uta Ajoub; prod d, Jurgen Schnell; spec eff, Gunther Schaidt.

Crime **(PR:NR MPAA:NR)**

BORDER RADIO† (1987) 84m Coyote Films bw

Chris D. *(Jeff)*, John Doe *(Dean)*, Luana Anders *(Lu)*, Chris Shearer *(Chris)*, Dave Alvin *(Dave)*, Iris Berry *(Scenester)*, Texacala Jones *(Babysitter)*, Devon Anders *(Devon)*, Chuck Shepard *(Expatriot)*, Craig Stark, Eddie Flowers, Sebastian Copeland *(Thugs)*, Green On Red *(Themselves)*.

Shown at the American Film Institute's Independent Festival, BORDER RADIO is a low-budget black-and-white film about three L.A. rockers who struggle as a band and with their personal lives while traveling from Los Angeles to Mexico and back. Doe, Alvin, and Chris D.—three real-life musicians—begin their journey south after they rob a club owner of the money that is owed them from an unpaid booking. Written and directed by three people, the film features a score by Dave Alvin, formerly of the L.A. rockabilly band The Blasters and more recently a member of Doe's band X.

p, Marcus De Leon; d&w, Allison Anders, Dean Lent, Kurt Voss; ph, Dean Lent; m, Dave Alvin, Steve Berlin, Bill Bateman, John Bazz, DJ Bonebrake, John Doe.

Musical/Drama **(PR:NR MPAA:NR)**

BORN IN EAST L.A.½** (1987) 84m Clear Type/UNIV c

Cheech Marin *(Rudy Robles)*, Paul Rodriguez *(Javier)*, Daniel Stern *(Jimmy)*, Kamala Lopez *(Dolores)*, Jan-Michael Vincent *(McCalister)*, Neith Hunter *(Marcie)*, Alma Martinez *(Gloria)*, Tony Plana *(Feo)*, Lupe Ontiveros *(Rudy's Mother)*, Urbanie Lucero *(Rudy's Sister)*.

These days many films spawn hit singles and rock videos, but BORN IN EAST L.A. is one of the few to come to the screen *after* both the song and video. (Some may remember GIRLS JUST WANT TO HAVE FUN, 1985's opportunistic rip-off of Cyndi Lauper's hit song, which was filmed without Lauper's participation or her version of the song.) The genesis of BORN IN EAST L.A. began when director Marin read about the 1985 case of a 14-year-old American citizen who was snatched up by Immigration and Naturalization workers and sent south of the border. He wrote a song parodying Bruce Springsteen's "Born in the U.S.A." entitled "Born in East L.A." and made a video to accompany it. Universal then approached Marin with the idea of writing, directing, and starring

in a picture budgeted at $5 million. Marin, on his own after the break-up of a 15-year partnership with Tommy Chong, set out, in BORN IN EAST L.A., to make a "social comedy" about the plight of illegal aliens in the US, specifically in California. Marin plays a third-generation Mexican-American who installs car radios at an auto shop in East L.A. His nightmarish odyssey begins when he stops by a toy factory to pick up a visiting cousin, Rodriguez. The factory, which employs a cheap labor force of "illegals," is raided by immigration officials. Having left his wallet at home and unable to call his mother or sister, who are vacationing in Fresno, Marin is carted off with a bunch of "illegals" and sent back across the border. Not only is Marin penniless and *peso*less, he is unable to *habla* anything but the most elementary Spanish (and a little bit of German). He soon hooks up with Stern, an American who operates a sleazy saloon/pool hall in Tijuana called El Dragon Rojo. Stern hires Marin to stand outside his establishment and lure visiting Americans inside. Hoping to earn enough money to buy safe passage into the US, Marin supplements his income by doing tattoo drawings, playing in a street-corner *mariachi* band, selling oranges, and peddling phony passports During his many adventures, Marin meets and falls in love with Lopez, a very pretty and intelligent girl from El Salvador who speaks no English. Like Marin, she is trying to raise enough money to enter the US. After desperately storming the border along with hundreds of other Hispanics (accompanied by Neil Diamond's song "America"), Marin finally finds his way back home. In the process he comes to appreciate both his own citizenship and the difficulties of life south of the border.

After years of comic vulgarity as half of "Cheech and Chong," Marin has left behind the drug-related humor of UP IN SMOKE and turned to a more accessible form of comedy. Citing Charles Chaplin's social comedies as an influence, Marin has found that it is possible to make a comedy with relevance, even in today's narrow-minded Hollywood. While Marin's humor was previously seen as socially and morally corrupt, he has found an entertaining way to make an audience pay attention to a serious issue. On the other hand, with LEONARD PART 6, the much-respected Bill Cosby turned out a comedy which is the antithesis of Marin's intentions—appealing to a lowest common denominator of stupidity, concerned with commercial hucksterism and not issues. While BORN IN EAST L.A. is not high art, it is entertaining, funny, and surprisingly touching. The audience, along with Marin, grows increasingly sympathetic to the cause of the South and Central Americans who want desperately to come to the US and experience for themselves this legendary "land of opportunities." Although the US government and the Department of Immigration and Naturalization are put through the grinder, there is still some unabashed patriotism throughout film. Marin has proven himself to be a capable director and writer, though large portions of the film fall into incredible logic gaps. Lopez makes a stunning appearance as Marin's non-English-speaking love interest. In the often-hilarious role of Marin's Mexican cousin is Rodriguez, whose finest moment comes when he hears voices coming from Marin's answering machine, which is hidden behind a painting of Jesus and leads Rodriguez to believe that Jesus is miraculously speaking. Like this year's LA BAMBA, BORN IN EAST L.A. attracted a large Hispanic audience, prompting the release of Spanish subtitled or dubbed prints. These prints accounted for some four percent of the film's first-week box-office take. It was, in fact, a Spanish subtitled print that took in the nation's highest per-screen average ($35,544 in Los Angeles's Orpheum Theatre) during BORN IN EAST L.A.'s opening weekend. *(Profanity, sexual situations.)*

p, Peter Macgregor-Scott; d&w, Richard (Cheech) Marin; ph, Alex Phillips (CFI Color); m, Lee Holdridge; ed, Don Brocha; art d, J. Rae Fox, Lynda Burbank, Hector Rodriguez; set d, Steven Karatzas, Enrique Estevez; cos, Isabella Van Soest.

Comedy **(PR:O MPAA:R)**

BORN OF FIRE zero (1987, Brit.) 84m Film Four Int'l./IFEX-Vidmark c

Peter Firth, Suzan Crowley, Stefan Kalipha, Nabil Shaban, Oh-Tee.

Although it features some arresting photography, this bombastic occult film may make you appreciate every other movie you've ever seen. Firth, an English flutist, begins to hear strange music in his head during a performance. Crowley, an astronomer, comes to him. She's heard it too. What's more, she's convinced it's tied in with solar disturbances on the sun and volcanic eruptions in Turkey. Firth's father, also a famous flutist, had years before ventured to Turkey to learn the breathing secrets of the "Master Musician" and died there. Firth goes to the mysterious village where his father died and meets a shaman who tells him of the Djinn, whom the Islamic God created from the fire of scorching winds and who can take a variety of forms—everything from a snake to a maiden. Joined by Crowley, Firth begins to have visions of the demise of his father and his Turkish wife, who gave birth to a deformed child and was killed by superstitious villagers when subsequent newborns died. Firth's father attacked the "Master Musician" and cut off his hand before perishing in fire. En route to these discoveries, Crowley, who has become Firth's lover and who bears a striking resemblance to the his Turkish "mother," comes under the spell of the "Master Musician" and conceives an evil force which splits open her stomach and kills her. This, we are to infer, is a microcosmic example of what the "Master Musician" is on about: he apparently intends to use music to lacerate the Earth's surface so that it will be consumed by fire. But not if Firth can help it. He assumes a safe spot in "the circle"—in the middle of one of a series of terraced alabaster pools—and out-pipes the "Master Musician," sending torrents of water to drown him in his cavernous subterranean home. The villagers, who have been mysteriously absent during most of the film, return to the mosque at the mouth of the Master's old digs. The film ends with titles which explain (or purport to) the origins of the Djinn.

If the makers of BORN OF FIRE were hoping to do with occult films what THE PRINCESS BRIDE did with swashbuckling movies (that is, send them up while, at the same time, presenting an involving story within the genre's conventions), then they have only failed on one level. They have created an often-hilarious film, but they have not managed to present a credible occult tale. The trouble is that BORN OF FIRE is presented in pompous, would-be philosophical earnestness and its humor is unintentional. If the filmmakers did not take themselves so seriously, this film wouldn't be such an offensive waste of time. Structurally it is an elliptical mess, jumping back and forth between reality and Firth's visions. Although one is left with a relatively clear understanding of the events surrounding the death of Firth's father, the role of his "mother" never comes into focus. Likewise, the "Master Musician" remains an enigma. There is never a clue as to how he has gone from the bald guy playing the wooden flute in the visions to the older, totally naked bald guy sending fire out of his eyes in his underground home. If there is a weighty symbolic message concerning the essence of music or the nature of the struggle between good and evil contained in the film, as its creators appear to believe there is, it is even more elusive than the

Djinn. It is difficult to say much about the performances. The actors are convincingly surprised and bewildered, though they may well be reacting to the ridiculous dialog and preposterous situations as much as to their fantastic experiences. To its credit, the film is slickly photographed and the Turkish locations are beautiful and intriguing. The village, carved into gumdrop hills, looks like surreal cliff dwellings designed by Gaudi. *(Nudity, sexual situations, violence.)*

p, Jamil Dehlavi, Therese Pickard; d, Jamil Dehlavi; w, Raficq Abdulla; ph, Bruce McGowan.

Horror **(PR:O MPAA:R)**

BOUBA† (1987, Israel) 87m Hetz 2 Ltd. c

Zeev Revah *(Bouba)*, Hanny Steinmetz-Nahmias *(Rachel)*, Eli Dankner *(Eli)*, Yossi Graber, Yona Elian, Asher Tzarfati, Shlomo Wishinsky, Shlomo Tarshish, Ezra Kafri, Ruth Segal.

Crippled as a result of a war wound, Revah seeks solitude, living in an abandoned bus and working in a gas station. Dankner, Revah's brother, is on the run after swindling his boss and hides out with Revah. At the same time, Steinmetz-Nahmias, a young girl on her way to a dance competition, is stranded at the gas station where Revah works and she also asks for shelter. Their night together proves to be emotionally charged and tragic. Long a popular comic in his homeland, director/writer/actor Revah is now devoting himself to more serious pursuits.

p, Jacob Koyzky; d, Zeev Revah; w, Hillel Mittelpunkt, Zeev Revah, Jacob Kotzky (based on a play by Hillel Mittelpunkt); ph, Ilan Rosenberg; m, Duby Zeltzer; ed, Zion Avrahamian; art d, Eitan Levy.

Drama **(PR:NR MPAA:NR)**

BOY RENTS GIRL (SEE: CAN'T BUY ME LOVE, 1987)

BOY SOLDIER*½** (1987, Wales) 100m Cine Cymru-S4C/The Other Cinema c (MILWR BYCHAN)

Richard Lynch *(Pvt. Wil Thomas)*, Dafydd Hywel *(Sgt. Crane)*, James Donnelly *(Lt. Col. Truscott-Jones)*, Bernard Hill *(Officer)*, Emer Gillespie *(Deirdre)*, Bernard Latham *(Cpl. Roberts)*, Robert Pugh *(RSM)*, Simon Coady *(Quinnell)*, Ian Saynor *(Captain)*, Timothy Scott *(Red Band)*, Roger Nott *(Captain, SIB)*, Terry Jackson *(Sergeant, SIB)*, Timothy Lyn *(Gary)*, Dylan Davies *(Joe)*, Russell Gomer *(Wright)*, Dani Grehan *(Dewi)*, Elfed Dafis *(Tom)*, Kevin Staples *(Hywel)*, Isaac Maynard, Ian Rowlands, Stephen Kelly *(Soldiers)*, David Wyn Roberts, Edward Thomas, Ian McLaren *(Prisoners)*, W.J. Phillips *(Kevin)*, Menna Trussler *(Wil's Mother)*, Eric Wyn *(Uncle Daniel)*, Mary Crofton *(Older Lady)*, Peter Dinnion *(Lorry Driver)*, Laurence Hynam *(Lorry Driver's Mate)*, Marion McLoughlen *(Abusive Woman)*, Patrick Waldron, Ciaren McIntyre *(Fishermen)*, Brian Nash *(Intruder)*, Stephen Lyons *(Hotel Manager)*, Jill Greenhalgh *(Woman in Flat)*, Eamonn Collinge *(Youngster)*, Nicola Redmond *(Woman at Daniel's House)*, Siobhan Hadden *(Girl)*, Dewi Savage *(Superintendent)*, Nigel Watson *(Doctor)*, Moira Mouse *(Singer)*.

Lynch is a 19-year-old "squaddie," a member of a British army unit stationed in Northern Ireland. Trying to quell a riot, he and another soldier are isolated and faced by an angry advancing mob. In self-defense, Lynch shoots and kills a man. He is whisked off and incarcerated in England, where the powers that be, seeking to defuse the attendant controversy, have determined to make an example of the young Welshman by trying him for murder. Lynch will have no part of it, and pleads innocent. The narrative jumps back and forth between Lynch's struggle for survival in the face of harassment by his guards and flashbacks to the events leading up to the shooting, including his love affair with Gillespie, a young Irish Catholic woman. She doesn't know he's a squaddie, and when she finds out, Gillespie breaks off the relationship. Later, Lynch discovers she has been tarred and feathered for her association with him. The instructions he and his comrades received upon arrival in Northern Ireland are also recounted. Hywel, the unit's Welsh sergeant, tells them to use "minimum force," explaining that for an old woman this means a swift kick, and for "Mick the gunman" it means blowing off his head. Back in the present, in the military prison, Lynch is denied proper medical treatment, refused his right to contact someone on the outside, poorly fed, beaten, and tortured. His main adversary is the brutal corporal Latham, whom Lynch taunts in a variety of ways—relentlessly ringing the bell that calls the guard to his cell. Higher up the chain of command, English lieutenant colonel Donnelly, along with Hill, a sinister representative of the government, are distressed by Lynch's steadfast refusal to cooperate. Calling upon a tremendous reservoir of inner strength, Lynch perseveres. Hywel sneaks him a manual that informs him of the rights he then demands, and later the sergeant gives Latham some of his own medicine when he catches him beating Lynch. In an attempt to reach a quick resolution to the problem, the charge is reduced to manslaughter, but Lynch still refuses to plead guilty. He is visited by Phillips (COMING UP ROSES), an old friend and a Salvation Army officer, who helps channel Lynch's moral resolve in a spiritual direction. Lynch aids a number of other prisoners in an escape (though he remains behind) and is rewarded with electro-shock treatments. Finally, the government reduces the charge to armed assault, and Lynch, thinking this appropriate, pleads guilty and is discharged and sentenced to two years imprisonment. Hywel leaves the army.

BOY SOLDIER does not attempt to address the complex situation in Northern Ireland as a whole; rather it concentrates on the precarious position of the British soldiers stationed there, showing them to be both peace keepers and imperialist bullies. In either case, they have been given an impossible task. Officially they are directed to use restraint; unofficially they are told to do what they have to do to protect themselves. When Lynch, backed into a corner, does just that, he is set up

as a scapegoat. However, he refuses to accept the blame that rightly belongs to history, society, and the British government. It is significant that Lynch is Welsh. Like the Irish, the Welsh have traditionally been subject to English domination (both in terms of language and politics). Both Northern Ireland and Wales are severely economically depressed, a fact that isn't lost on Lynch, who has joined the army because he is otherwise without prospects. He is aware of other similarities, too, but he is, above all, a good and dedicated soldier whose bucking of the system and subsequent discharge cause him to lose "the only real home" he's ever had. Even in winning, in holding out for the lesser charge, he loses. In Northern Ireland there are no winners, but, perhaps, the army is the bigger loser in that two good soldiers, Lynch and Hywel, leave the service.

Writer-director Francis presents the narrative in kaleidoscopic shifts between the present and memory. These transitions are not always easy to follow, but the result is like taking a roller-coaster ride through the young soldier's troubled conscience. Lynch gives a performance of considerable depth. His marathon pursuit of honorable treatment is characterized by mental toughness and physical courage, but also by bewilderment, doubt, anger, and fear. His tears are as believable as his clinch-jawed gutsiness. The psychological battle of attrition with Latham is the focus of Lynch's survival (prior to his spiritual transformation), and the actors work well together, giving the contest both its import and underlying humor. Hywel, who was so wonderful in another outstanding Welsh-language film, COMING UP ROSES, is very good here as the laconic soldier's soldier who refuses to see his countryman become the fall guy. BOY SOLDIER was produced for Welsh television and released in Britain in 1986. It was given a festival release in the US in 1987. (In English and Welsh; English subtitles.) *(Violence, profanity.)*

p, Karl Francis, Hayden Pierce; d&w, Karl Francis; ph, Roger Pugh Evans (Rank Color); m, Graham Williams; ed, Aled Evans; prod d, Hayden Pierce; cos, Katie Pegg, Sue Rawsthorne, Llinos Non Parry; spec eff, David Williams; makeup, Irene Ranger.

Drama **(PR:C-O MPAA:NR)**

BRAVE LITTLE TOASTER, THE† (1987) 80m Hyperion-Kushner-Lockec

Voices of: Jon Lovitz *(Radio)*, Tim Stack *(Lampy)*, Timothy E. Day *(Blanky)*, Thurl Ravencroft *(Kirby)*, Deanna Oliver *(Toaster)*, Phil Hartman *(Air Conditioner, Hanging Lamp)*, Jonathon Benair *(B&W TV)*, Joe Ranft *(Elmo St. Peters)*.

An animated tale of five household appliances—Radio (Lovitz), Lampy the Lamp (Stack), Blanky the Electric Blanket (Day), Kirby the Vacuum Cleaner (Ravencroft), and the brave Toaster of the title (Oliver)—and their search for "Rob" the head of the household and their former master. The journey begins in a quiet summer cottage and takes them into the wilds of the inner city. After braving rainstorms, repairmen, and an electromagnet, the appliances find happiness in an urban junkyard. Jon Lovitz, a member of NBC's Saturday Night Live, does the voice of Radio, broadcasting a variety of oldtime bits. Impressionist Hartman imitates Jack Nicholson, Peter Lorre and others in doing voices of some of the characters. The project, purchased by Disney in 1982, was co-produced by Thomas Wilhite, a former Disney executive who employed the talents of other former Disney employees on this picture. Rees directed the animated sequences of Disney's 1982 entry TRON. Shown briefly in 1987 in Los Angeles.

p, Donald Kushner, Thomas L. Wilhite; d, Jerry Rees; w, Jerry Rees, Joe Ranft (based on a story by Jerry Rees, Joe Ranft, Brian McEntee from the novella by Thomas M. Disch); m, David Newman; art d, Brian McEntee, A. Kendall O'Connor; m/l, Van Dyke Parks.

Children's/Animation **(PR:NR MPAA:NR)**

BROADCAST NEWS**** (1987) 131m FOX c

William Hurt *(Tom Grunick)*, Albert Brooks *(Aaron Altman)*, Holly Hunter *(Jane Craig)*, Robert Prosky *(Ernie Merriman)*, Lois Chiles *(Jennifer Mack)*,

Joan Cusack *(Blair Litton)*, Peter Hackes *(Paul Moore)*, Jack Nicholson *(Bill Rorich, News Anchor)*, Christina Clemenson *(Bobby)*, Robert Katims *(Martin Klein)*, Ed Wheeler *(George Weln)*, Stephen Mendillo *(Gerald Grunick)*, Kimber Shoop *(Young Tom)*, Dwayne Markee *(Young Aaron)*, Gennie James *(Young Jane)*, Leo Burmeister *(Jane's Dad)*, Amy Brooks *(Elli Merriman)*, Jane Welch *(Anne Merriman)*, Jonathan Benya *(Clifford Altman)*, Frank Doubleday *(Mercenary)*, Sally Knight *(Lila)*, Manny Alvarez *(Spanish Cameraman)*, Luis Valderrama *(Guerilla Leader)*, Francisco Garcia *(Guerilla Soldier)*, Richard Thomsen *(Gen. McGuire)*, Nathan Benchley *(Commander)*, Marita Geraghty *(Date-Rape Victim)*, Nicholas D. Blanchet *(Weekend News Producer)*, Maura Moynihan *(Makeup Woman)*, Chuck Lippman *(Floor Manager)*, Nanette Rickert *(Paul's Secretary)*, Tim White *(Edward Towne)*, Peggy Pridemore *(Tom's Soundwoman)*, Emily Crowley *(Emily)*, Gerald Ender *(Newsroom Worker)*, David Long *(Donny)*, Josh Billings *(Chyron Operator)*, Richard Pehle *(Control Room Director)*, James V. Franco *(Weekend News Director)*, Mike Skehan *(Technician)*, Franklyn L. Bullard *(Audio Visual Engineer)*, Alex Mathews *(Lecture Host)*, Steve Smith *(Aaron's Cameraman)*, Martha L. Smith *(Aaron's Soundwoman)*, Cynthia B. Hayes *(Mother in Hall)*, Susan Marie Feldman *(Ellen)*, Jean Bourne Carinci *(Tom's Female Colleague)*, M. Fekade-Salassie *(Cab Driver)*, Jerry Gough *(Uniformed Cop)*, Robert Rasch *(Defense Dept. Spokesman)*, Robert Walsh *(NATO Spokesman)*, John Cusack *(Angry Messenger)*, Rochelle Deering *(Woman at Speech)*, Albert Murphy, Sr. *(Man in Airport)*, Eleanore C. Kopecky *(Woman in Airport)*, Jeffrey Alan Thomas *(Airport Cabbie)*, Glenn Faigen, Robert Grevemberg, Jr. *(Technical Directors)*, Jimmy Mel Green, Raoul N. Rizik *(Assistant Directors)*, Glen Roven, Marc Shaiman *(News Theme Writers)*, Dean Nitz, Phil Ugel, Lance Wain *(Young Toughs)*, John Badila, Heather Ehlers, Arlene M. Dillon, Sam Samuels *(Guests at Ball)*.

After a virtual sweep of the Academy Awards with his unabashedly manipulative hit TERMS OF ENDEARMENT (1983), producer/director/writer James L. Brooks waited four years to deliver a second film which is more intelligent, mature, and assured than his first. Blessed with a superior script and three outstanding lead performances (which is not to slight the marvelous supporting cast), BROADCAST NEWS examines the ethics of modern-day electronic journalism and the often frazzled emotions of a tightly knit group of workaholics who find that their personal and professional lives have become one and the same. After a pat and unnecessary prolog which shows the three main characters as children, the film kicks into gear. Network news producer Hunter and her best pal, veteran correspondent Albert Brooks (both based in the all-important Washington, DC, bureau), are on assignment. The two work well together and share not only the same high ethical standards, but a warm and goofy sense of humor that serves to ease the tension that is a part of the job. Hunter is so manic that she sets aside a few minutes at the beginning of each day to have a good cry. Brooks, a bundle of nerves and insecurity, defends his weaknesses with caustic wit. Both tend to wrap themselves in a shroud of moral and intellectual superiority that sometimes annoys their coworkers. (Later in the film when Hunter's boss, Hackes, states sarcastically, "It must be nice to think you're the smartest person in the room," Hunter responds in all seriousness, "No, it's awful.") Although Hunter considers Brooks her best friend and they are as close as siblings, Brooks pines for a more romantic relationship with the feisty producer. Enter Hurt, a handsome, affable, but somewhat dim newscaster who meets Hunter at a journalism seminar. Despite the fact that his shallowness and ignorance represent everything she hates about television journalism, Hunter is attracted to Hurt physically and is charmed by his refreshing candor. Hurt freely admits he can't write and doesn't understand most of the news he is asked to read. When she hurts him with a smug remark, he leaves her room without making love to her, later phoning to inform her that her network has just hired him as a news correspondent. Back in Washington, the hustle of everyday deadline pressure hums along as Hurt stands around observing the operation. Brooks is pleased when a story he has taped gets the seal of approval from all-powerful New York anchorman Nicholson (a slight smile before going to a commercial is the sign). Soon after, Hurt contributes a story about "date rape" and is so moved by one victim's story he cries on camera. Brooks is outraged by the sappy tears, but Hunter is genuinely touched by the piece. After weeks of put-downs from Brooks, Hurt finally gets his chance to be on camera when Nicholson is on vacation during a crisis involving Libya. Miffed that Hackes didn't pick him to anchor, Brooks, who has been to Libya several times and is one of the few American journalists to have interviewed Muammar Quaddafi, sits in his apartment and gets drunk. Finally his professionalism takes over and he phones Hunter, providing her with crucial information that she in turn relays to Hurt via an earphone. The trick works with precision and Hurt conveys the vital information with such panache that a new network star is born. Afterwards an excited Hurt proclaims the experience of having Hunter "inside his head" was like "great sex." Their relationship grows closer and Brooks begins to feel pushed out of the picture. Told by bureau chief Prosky that the network is cutting the news budget and massive layoffs are imminent, Brooks tries to secure his position by getting a shot at weekend anchorman. He even humbles himself enough to allow Hurt to coach him in the fine art of reading on camera (sit on your jacket so your shoulders look smooth, tilt your good side toward the camera, emphasize a phrase in each sentence, and sell, sell, sell). Unfortunately, Brooks suffers a massive case of *flop sweat* during the broadcast ("That's more than Nixon ever sweated!" an amazed technician remarks) and winds up embarrassing both himself and the network. Making matters worse, Hunter has gone to a fancy party with Hurt and decides to sleep with him. Feeling guilty that she hasn't seen Brooks' broadcast, Hunter puts Hurt on hold and dashes off to see Brooks. When Brooks learns that she plans to go back and spend the night with Hurt, he explodes with a litany of vindictive accusations, ending in a desperate declaration of love for Hunter. When Brooks says "I'm in love with you," Hunter looks as if she has been smacked in the head with a brick. Brooks goes on to say that Hurt is the devil, a man who is handsome, nice, charming, helpful, but will slowly whittle away at our standards and values, and in the end " . . . get all the great women." Because Hunter has spent so much time with Brooks, Hurt postpones their tryst. Hunter goes home emotionally confused and alone. The next day the godlike Nicholson makes a rare appearance in the newsroom; it is the day of the layoffs and he is there to show superficial solidarity with the workers. When Hackes jokingly remarks that quite a few jobs could be saved if Nicholson would knock $1 million off his salary, he is met with a cold, intimidating stare from Nicholson that leaves no doubt where the anchorman's true sympathies lie. (Nicholson is onscreen for a matter of minutes, yet he is the embodiment of the smug, self-important New York anchorman, part Chet Huntley, part Dan Rather. It is a wonderfully powerful little performance that does not at all smack of "guest-star" posturing.) When the smoke clears, Prosky, Hunter's mentor, has been "retired" and Hunter has been given his prestigious job; Brooks, who was not laid off, quits; and Hurt is made London correspondent (which means that he is being groomed for Nicholson's job). In an effort to see what their relationship would be like away from the office, Hunter agrees to go on an island vacation with Hurt. Before he departs for a job at a TV station of Portland, the spurned Brooks tells Hunter to look at the unedited videotape of Hurt's "date rape" story. To her horror she sees that Hurt had faked the tearfulness that she assumed was spontaneous. Unable to ignore Hurt's blatant and unrepentant manipulation of the values she holds so dear, Hunter refuses to go away with him and breaks off the relationship. Seven years later, Hurt, Brooks, and Hunter meet again. Brooks is doing well in Portland and has a wife and child, Hurt has replaced the retired Nicholson and is engaged to a vapid society type, and Hunter is still a dynamo who is now dating a man from outside the news business.

Fascinating, touching, biting, and extremely funny, BROADCAST NEWS is a wholly entertaining film that boasts three of the finest performances to grace the screen in 1987. Hunter, who was so good in RAISING ARIZONA, is a revelation here. Cast at the last minute to replace the pregnant Debra Winger (for whom director Brooks had tailored the role), the diminutive Hunter charges into this complex role with incredible skill and verve. Blissfully aware that she was handed one of the best women's roles in years, Hunter not only lives up to the script's potential, but surpasses it. Hunter's Jane Craig is a highly intelligent, dedicated professional woman who really is superior to just about everyone at the station. But as so many successful career people discover, success at work can mean failure at home. There is a void in her life that part of her feels the need to fulfill, but in reality she probably could do without a man, home life, or even sex (Hurt's comment that their work was like "great sex" is particularly revealing). Hunter touches all the emotional and intellectual bases with this performance and she is a joy to watch. Hurt is superb as well. Never before has he allowed himself to play a role where he appeared to be so vague, superficial, and seemingly dim-witted. It is a tribute to his skills as an actor that he somehow transforms this somewhat ignoble character into a sympathetic human being. We are attracted to what Hunter's character finds so attractive about him—his charm and charisma. It is the most difficult role in the film and Hurt plays it magnificently without calling attention to his "technique." Albert Brooks, however, nearly walks off with the film. An undeniably brilliant comedian and a brave film director in his own right (REAL LIFE, MODERN ROMANCE, LOST IN AMERICA), Brooks contributes most of the big laughs in BROADCAST NEWS and also conveys a moving portrait of an insecure man clinging to an unrequited love. There has always been a tinge of real anger to the characters Brooks plays in his own films. The actor/director has courageously explored his dark side, and the petty, selfish, cruel, and desperate nature we all share has been a fertile ground for some unique and perceptive comedies. The Albert Brooks character is not a loveable neurotic like Woody Allen, but a genuinely complicated character driven by personal demons he is unable to control. Brooks finds no comfort in romantic illusions—he is not "cuddly." In BROADCAST NEWS he has taken this persona to new heights with a wonderfully tempered performance that is nearly flawless. Although insecure, manic, and neurotic, the Brooks character is not merely a pathetic victim whining his way to acceptance and love. When rejected he becomes brutally vindictive and cruel, a master of biting verbal abuse that is both funny and sad.

Brooks' Aaron Altman, Hurt's Tom Grunick, and Hunter's Jane Craig are fascinatingly complex characters. Rather than try to insinuate these characters with an overly complicated or visually manipulative film style that would detract from their complexity, director James Brooks—like Leo McCarey before him—had the good sense to select smart, conservative camera placements and let his script and his actors do their stuff unhindered by a heavy directorial hand (and Brooks' hand can get *quite heavy*—see TERMS OF ENDEARMENT). This is not to say the film is dead cinematically. The various set pieces—which include such dissimilar sequences as trying to get a taped segment on the air under the wire, the Libyan crisis, and the massive layoff—are shot and edited exceedingly well, skillfully combining visual and verbal humor with exciting and moving dramatics. Brooks' portrayal of people working closely together under great stress is impeccable and exhilarating. Unfortunately his television roots (he created "The Mary Tyler Moore Show," "Lou Grant," and "Taxi") show at times and he overplays his hand with a prolog which, while amusing, is totally unnecessary and immediately pigeonholes his characters, making them seem much simpler than they eventually prove to be. He also inserts a hastily conceived and poorly executed epilog (the color timing on a reaction shot of Hunter is horribly off) which ties up loose ends needlessly. The entire sequence is a concession to audience expectations that neither enlightens nor satisfies. Minor problems notwithstanding, the film was a smash with the critics and a hit with the public. It also prompted debate among the media that it criticizes (self-analysis is something the news media loves to do), but what is really important about BROADCAST NEWS is its wonderfully vivid characters and what they can teach us about ourselves. Includes the songs "L'Edition Speciale" (Francis Cabrel, performed by Cabrel) "Midnight Train to Georgia" (Jim Weatherly, performed by Gladys Knight and the Pips). *(Profanity, sexual situations, partial nudity, adult situations.)*

p, James L. Brooks, Penney Finkelman Cox; d&w, James L. Brooks; ph, Michael Ballhaus (Deluxe color); m, Bill Conti; ed, Richard Marks; prod d, Charles Rosen; art d, Kristi Zea; set d, Jane Bogart; m/l, Francis Cabrel, Jim Weatherly; cos, Molly Maginnis.

Comedy/Romance **(PR:C-O MPAA:R)**

BROTHERHOOD† (1987, Hong Kong) 98m D&B Production c

Danny Lee, Alex Man, Vincent Lam, Ho Chuen Hung, Lam Wai.

A mob chief finds his life threatened by three of his men, angry because they face lengthy prison terms. A loyal friend of the mob leader vows to kill all three men before they can carry out their plan.

p, Dickson Poon, Linda Kuk; d, Stephen Shin.

Crime/Drama **(PR:NR MPAA:NR)**

BUDAWANNY† (1987, Irish) 79m Cinegael-Irish Film Board-Arts Council-Channel 4 b&w/c

Donal McCann *(The Priest)*, Maggie Fegan *(The Woman)*, Tomas O'Flatharta *(The Sacristan)*, Peadar Lamb *(The Bishop)*, Freda Gillen *(The Garden Woman)*, Sean O'Colsdealbha *(The Publican)*.

While at sea off the coast of Ireland, an unhappy woman jumps overboard in an apparent suicide attempt. She's rescued and taken to an island where she finds shelter with a priest. The two become lovers, and the priest writes a book called *Budawanny* about his life, including his affair.

p,d&w, Bob Quinn; ph, Seamus Deasy; m, Roger Doyle; ed, Martin Duffy; prod d, Tom Conroy.

Drama **(PR:NR MPAA:NR)**

BUDDHA'S LOCK† (1987, Hong Kong/Chi.) 90m Highland-Shen Zhen c

John X. Heart, Zhang Lu-tong, Yan Bi De, Suen Fei Hu, Wei Zong Wan, Steve Horowitz.

Based on an actual incident in which an American Army officer was captured by a tribe in northern China in 1945 and kept as a slave for ten years, this film features Heart as the American prisoner. While in captivity, he falls in love with a widow, and when slavery is abolished in China and he is free to leave, he is torn between his love and his desire to return home.

d, Yim Ho; w, Kong Liang; ph, Lu Yue, Wang Ziao Lie; m, Zhao Ji Ping.

Biography **(PR:NR MPAA:NR)**

BUISSON ARDENT† (1987, Fr.) 84m Scopitone-Maison de la Culture of Le Havre-Films de l'Atalante-Sept/Films de l'Atalante c (Trans: Burning Bush)

Jessica Forde *(Julie)*, Jean-Claude Adelin *(Jean)*, Alice de Poncheville *(Caroline)*, Simon de la Brosse *(Henri)*, Anne Brochet *(Elizabeth)*, Anouk Ferjac *(Christine)*, Philippe Morier Genoud, Jacques Boudet, Serge Riaboukine.

Childhood sweethearts are separated when the boy moves away. He returns years later, disrupting the life of his former love, now engaged to another.

p, Jean-Luc Ormieres; d, Laurent Perrin; w, Benoit Jacquot, Guy Patrick Saindrichin, Laurent Perrin, Marguerite Arnaud; ph, Dominique Le Rigoleur (Eastmancolor); m, Jorge Arriagada; art d, Francois-Renaud Labarthe.

Drama **(PR:NR MPAA:NR)**

BULLETPROOF† (1987) 85m Cinetel c

Gary Busey *(Frank "Bulletproof" McBain)*, Darlanne Fluegel *(Lt. Devon Shepard)*, Rene Enriquez *(Gen. Brogado)*, Henry Silva *(Col Kartiff)*, Bill Smith *(Russian Major)*, Thalmus Rasulala, L.Q. Jones, R.G. Armstrong.

Director Carver, who is responsible for the Chuck Norris vehicles AN EYE FOR AN EYE and LONE WOLF MCQUADE, here casts Busey in the role of Rambo-esque tough guy Frank "Bulletproof" McBain. A former L.A. cop, Busey is lured out of retirement by the US government to lead a dangerous mission to recapture a secret weapon from a Soviet-Libyan-Cuban terrorist gang hiding in a Mexican border town. The weapon, known as "Thunderblast," was under the care of sexy femme lieutenant Fluegel when she was ambushed by the terrorist gang, led by Mexican general Enriquez and Libyan colonel Silva. Since Busey and Fluegel were once lovers, it is only natural that he should save the day. Busey finds the gang, is captured and nearly killed, but fights back with the strength of an army. Released in late 1987 in Britain.

p, Paul Hertzberg; d, Steve Carver; w, Steve Carver, T.L. Lankford (based on a story by T.L. Lankford, Fred Olen Ray); ph, Francis Grumman; ed, Jeff Freeman.

Action/Adventure **(PR:NR MPAA:NR)**

BURGLAR zero (1987) 102m Nelvana/WB c

Whoopi Goldberg *(Bernice Rhodenbarr)*, Bob Goldthwait *(Carl Hefler)*, G.W. Bailey *(Ray Kirschman)*, Lesley Ann Warren *(Dr. Cynthia Sheldrake)*, James Handy *(Carson Verrill)*, Anne DeSalvo *(Detective Todras)*, John Goodman *(Detective Nyswander)*, Elizabeth Ruscio *(Frankie)*, Vyto Ruginis *(Graybow)*, Larry Mintz *(Knobby)*, Thom Bray, Raye Birk.

The theme of the innocent person being involved in a murder and wrongly prosecuted has been knocked senseless in recent years, but in this film the premise is hammered to death, dissected and then discarded piece by piece, littering the screen with its unattractive debris. Goldberg is a habitual burglar recently released from prison. She works in a bookstore but she cannot resist looting the domiciles of the wealthy. At the beginning, she is seen made up as an elderly cleaning lady, delivered to suburbia by bus, shuffling into a large home whose occupant, she carefully notes, is out jogging. Goldberg promptly cops his money and gold watch, and professionally turns the tumblers of a small safe to open it and withdraw rare stamps. The homeowner and his chauffeur corner Goldberg just as she steps outside and she becomes hysterical, screaming that she has seen the burglars flee through a hedge. The two men race off after the mythical burglars while Goldberg escapes, vowing to quit her criminal pursuits—a promise often broken. Back in San Francisco, a crooked retired cop, Bailey, tells Goldberg that unless she pays him off with a fur coat and $20,000, he will put the police on her trail. A fence buys her latest stolen goods and she tells him she needs a lot of money. He sends Goldberg to a dentist, Warren, who confides that her jewels have been stolen by her estranged husband and wants Goldberg to steal them back. (Warren appears briefly in this film and is generally wasted as a neurotic, greedy female.) Goldberg goes to the man's apartment and puts the jewelry in a briefcase, but is interrupted when Warren's husband returns unexpectedly with a woman. Goldberg hides in a closet until she no longer hears wild lovemaking noises in the bedroom. When she emerges she finds the husband dead, a dental instrument plunged into his chest, and her briefcase gone. Warren is arrested and thrown into jail, where she hysterically tells her lawyer Handy to "get me out of here! I'm wearing cotton underwear!"

Goldberg is then suspected of killing the husband and police force their way into her apartment, overcoming a steel door and a piercing alarm that can only be cut off by chopping out a wall. The place is wrecked when Goldberg casually emerges from a small room hidden by a fake wall behind a closet. She realizes she must find the real killer or go to jail for murdering Warren's husband, or at least that's *her* reasoning. Her psychotic boy friend, Goldthwait, who speaks in high-pitched, hysterical outbursts where his words all run together, wants her to go straight and agrees to help in her investigation (which is not dissimilar to asking a helpless cretin to interpret the Lorentz Transformations). The two haunt San Francisco bars until Goldberg digs up Ruscio, who tells her Warren's husband hung around the Maytime bar and made some strange friends, including brutish artist Ruginis, bald-headed Mintz and another man known only as "Johnny." Goldberg barges into Ruginis' studio and is terrified by his Doberman and his manhandling, casing the place while being pushed around by the muscle-bound artist whom she disables by kicking in the groin. She later breaks into Mintz's place and finds $100,000 in counterfeit bills and then locates the plates for making these bills in Ruginis' digs. Both of these men are killed by unknown mobsters before she can learn more about their involvement with the murdered husband. Finally Warren is released from jail, but when she returns to her apartment with lawyer Handy, Goldberg is waiting. Goldberg has figured it all out and explains, while holding a gun on the pair, that Warren was the woman who returned to the apartment with her estranged husband. Warren nervously admits this but denies killing him. Later Goldberg calls Handy and tells him that she knows he killed the husband and tells the lawyer to meet her in some remote woods. Handy shows up carrying Goldberg's briefcase and admits, after Goldberg pressures him, that he killed the husband. (He is a latent homosexual and the reason for murdering his lover was his jealousy over the husband sleeping with Warren!) Ruscio then shows up and identifies Handy as "Johnny from the bar." He attacks both women, then runs, with Goldberg in pursuit. The two fight it out in a river where Goldberg is almost drowned, but being a boxing champion, knocks out the bulky Handy. Goldthwait and Bailey appear and aid Goldberg at the film's impossible finale.

Loaded with gratuitous violence, gutter language and sex, BURGLAR's few laughs are lost in a sea of bad taste. A crazy chase, with Goldberg driving a police motorcycle and scores of cop cars in hot pursuit, sailing over the hills of San Francisco, is a direct, unforgivable lift from BULLITT. Very little that Goldberg does and says is funny and she is not an empathetic character, but rather a relentless thief with no regard for the law and as good an example for youngsters to emulate as was Belle Starr. Viewers cannot lower their standards in seeing this

hodge-podge, since no standards exist whatsoever in BURGLAR. It's a stumble-through routine for performers with very little to say or do. Goldberg's guttural mumblings provide a few chuckles, but this technique, which seems to be her entire repertoire, soon wears thin, then vanishes altogether. The unimaginative script, the indifferent direction, and a pace that limps or lurches makes BURGLAR a lowball loser all the way. *(Excessive profanity.)*

p, Kevin McCormick, Michael Hirsh; d, Hugh Wilson; w, Joseph Loeb III, Matthew Weisman, Hugh Wilson (based on books by Lawrence Block); ph, William A. Fraker (Technicolor); m, Sylvester Levay; ed, Fredric Steinkamp, William Steinkamp; prod d, Todd Hallowell; art d, Michael Corenblith; set d, Daniel Loren May; cos, Susan Becker.

Comedy **Cas.** **(PR:O MPAA:R)**

BUS† (1987, Jap.) 80m Pia c

Hiroyasu Ito *(Micho/Bengal Tiger)*, Kyoichi Ando *(Rinzo)*, Hidehiko Komatsu *(Kosaku)*, O.W. Nicole *(Fool on the Hill)*, Tomoko Kuroiwa *(Kaori)*, Katsumi Yamanoi, Kaneo Osuga, Takehiko Suzuki.

In his debut feature, Japanese director Komatsu seeks to create an Orwellian nightmare world where Mama stands in for Big Brother. The setting for the tale is a village where enforced conformity is the rule and a shadowy figure who wields a huge telephone is the ruler. Ah, but dissent is in the air—however futile it may be.

p, Yutaka Suzuki; d&w, Takashi Komatsu; ph, Yoshihisa Fujii; m, Kiyoski Takeo; ed, Takashi Komatsu; prod d, Takeo Kasai; art d, Souki Murakoshi; set d, Atsushi Honda; cos, Morihiko Katsushima.

Drama **(PR:NR MPAA:NR)**

BUSHFIRE MOON† (1987, Aus.) 98m Entertainment Media-Disney Channel-Australian Children's Film and Television Foundation-Film Victoria/Disney Channel c

Dee Wallace Stone *(Elizabeth O'Day)*, John Waters *(Patrick O'Day)*, Bill Kerr *(Trevor Watson)*, Charles Tingwell *(Max Bell)*, Nadine Garner *(Sarah O'Day)*, Andrew Ferguson *(Ned O'Day)*, Grant Piro *(Angus Watson)*, Rosie Sturgess *(Miss Daly)*, Francis Bell *(Sharkey)*, Christopher Stevenson *(Jamie)*, Kim Gyngell *(Hungry Bill)*, David Ravenswood *(Mr. Gullett)*, Maggie Millar *(Mrs. Gullett)*, Francine Ormrod *(Penelope Gullett)*, Bruce Kilpatrick *(Adam McKimmie)*, Callie Gray *(Pip McKimmie)*, Christine Keogh *(Heather McKimmie)*, Martin Redpath *(Sgt. Gibbs)*.

Helmed by Australian George Miller, who directed THE MAN FROM SNOWY RIVER and is not to be confused with his same-named compatriot who directed the MAD MAX films, BUSHFIRE MOON is part A CHRISTMAS CAROL and part MIRACLE ON 34TH STREET. Set in the Outback at Christmas time in the early 1890s, it is the story of a family's struggle to keep their small sheep ranch from failing during a drought. Christmas doesn't promise to be a very merry one for 8-year-old Ferguson and his family: Stone, his mother; Waters, his father; and Garner, his sister. Mean-spirited neighbor Kerr has more than enough water to help them through this hard spell, but, Scrooge-like, he refuses to part with a drop. Tingwell, Kerr's former partner, appears wearing white whiskers that make him look suspiciously like a well-know character from a distinctly colder climate and events take a happy turn. Even crotchety old Kerr is imbued with the Christmas spirit.

p, Peter Beilby, Robert Le Tet; d, George Miller; w, Jeff Peck; ph, David Connell (Eastmancolor); m, Bruce Rowland; ed, Tim Wellburn; prod d, Otello Stolfo; art d, Bernadette Wynack; cos, Rose Chong; spec eff, Peter Stubbs; makeup, Amanda Rowbottom.

Drama **(PR:NR MPAA:NR)**

BUSINESS AS USUAL† (1987, Brit.) 89m London Cannon-Film Four, Moleworx/Cannon Group c

Glenda Jackson *(Babs Flynn)*, John Thaw *(Kieran Flynn)*, Cathy Tyson *(Josie Patterson)*, Mark McGann *(Stevie Flynn)*, Eamon Boland *(Peter Barry)*, James Hazeldine *(Mark)*, Buki Armstrong *(Paula Douglas)*, Stephen McGann *(Terry Flynn)*, Philip Foster *(Tim Flynn)*, Natalie Duffy *(Rosa)*, Jack Carr *(Brian Lewis)*, Mel Martin *(Joan Sankey)*, Michelle Byatt *(Jude)*, Robert Keegan *(Doug)*, Angela Elliot *(Flora)*, Craig Charles *(Eddie)*, Christine Moore *(Mrs. Rummage)*, Stephen Dillon *(Mr. Dunlop)*, Lucy Sheen *(Rowena Freeman)*, Eithne Browne *(Trisha Lane)*, Roland Oliver *(Solicitor)*, Graham Callan *(TV Producer)*, John Flanagan *(PC Whitcombe)*, Peter Christian *(Police Sergeant)*, Kathy Jamieson, Rachael Laurence *(Policewomen)*, Will Tracy *(Desk Sergeant)*, Barry Eaton, Mark Reader, Dean Williams *(Lads)*, Tom Pepper *(Tennants Hall Comedian)*, Sharon Power *(Young Punk)*, Ann Aris *(Elegant Woman)*, Lorraine Michaels *(Barmaid)*, Ian Puleston-Davies *(Young Workman)*, Lesley Diane, Margot Stanley, Cathy Williams *(Shoppers)*, Simon Barrett *(Aggressive Man)*.

Jackson works as the manager of a boutique while her husband, Thaw, unemployed since the factory where he was a shop steward closed, stays home. The store which employs Jackson is part of a chain, and plans are being made for the chain to introduce a new line of clothing. Boland, an executive with the chain, is sent to Jackson's store to advise on preparations for the new campaign and while there makes sexual advances toward Tyson, one of Jackson's employees. Tyson complains to Jackson who confronts Boland. He calls Tyson a liar, then later forces an argument with Jackson, after which he fires her. There then begins a series of struggles as Jackson, with the help of her family, the union, and media people, fights to get her job back.

p, Sara Geater; d&w, Lezli-An Barrett; ph, Ernie Vincze; m, Andrew Scott, Paul Weller; ed, Henry Richardson; prod d, Hildegard Betchler; cos, Monica Howe; m/l, Paul Weller; makeup, Sue Black.

Drama **(PR:NR MPAA:NR)**

BUTTERFLY REVOLUTION, THE (SEE: SUMMER CAMP NIGHTMARE, 1987)

C.K. DEZERTERZY† (1987, Pol./Hung.) 166m Film Polski-Zodiak Unit-Mafilm c (Trans: The Deserters)

Marek Kondrat *(Kania)*, Zoltan Bezeredy *(Benedek)*, Wiktor Zborowski *(Chudej)*, Jacek Sas-Uhrynowski *(Haber)*, Zbigniew Zapasiewicz *(Captain)*, Robert Koltai, Josef Abraham.

This Polish-Hungarian coproduction follows the misadventures of a unit of the Austro-Hungarian army stationed in a small town in Hungary during WW I. A kind of European variation of the melting-pot squads that populate American WW II films, this unit is made up of men from all over the Austro-Hungarian empire, including a Hungarian, a Czech, a Pole, an Italian, and an Austrian Jew. A hard-line German officer arrives on the scene, and the men, who are used to having a free rein that includes more than a little whoring in town, are suddenly confronted with a sadistic disciplinarian. When he pushes them too far, they find their own ways of humiliating the German and discrediting him with his superiors. The soldiers then desert to Budapest where they participate in further high jinks before being captured and remanded to the custody of their old nemesis.

d, Janusz Majewski; w, Janusz Majewski, Pavel Hajny (based on the novel by Kazimierz Sejda); ph, Witold Adamek; m, Gyorgy Selmeczy; ed, Elzbieta Kurkowska; prod d, Andrzej Halinski.

Comedy **(PR:NR MPAA:NR)**

CALE† (1987, Span.) 87m Procines c

Monica Randall *(Cris)*, Rosario Flores *(Estrella)*, Joan Miralles *(Luis)*, Antonio Llopis *(Victor)*, Antonio Flores *(Nono)*, Pedro Maria Sanchez *(Paco)*, Eduardo MacGregor *(Enrique)*, Felicidad Blanc *(Andrea)*, Carmen Balague *(Elena)*.

Randall, a leading stage actress and the divorced mother of one, is hired to play the title character in a production of "Pygmalian." Her life is then thrown into turmoil when she begins having an affair with Flores, a poor gypsy girl hired to help her get ready for her role.

p&d, Carlos Serrano; w, Joaquin Oristrell, Carlos Serrano; ph, Federico Ribes (Eastmancolor); m, Beltran Moner; ed, Gloria Carrion; prod d, Joaquin F. Igual; cos, Lola Salvador.

Drama **(PR:NR MPAA:NR)**

CAMPING DEL TERRORE† (1987, It.) Titanus-Racing Pictures c (Trans: Terror Camping Site)

Bruce Penhall, Mimsy, David Hess, Luisa Maneri, Andrew Lederer, Nicola Farron, Stefano Madia, John Steiner, Nancy Brilli, Elena Pompei, Charles Napier.

An innocent camping trip for a group of teens turns ugly when the man who murdered a boy and a girl on the same site 11 years previously reappears and picks up where he left off. One by one the horny teenagers are killed, while the bewildered sheriff tries to nail the killer. All the while, the key to the mystery rests with the camp site's owner.

d, Ruggero Deodato; w, Alesandro Capone; ph, Emilio Loffredo; m, Claudio Simonetti; ed, Eugenio Alabiso.

Horror **(PR:NR MPAA:NR)**

CAMPUS MAN½** (1987) 94m RKO/PAR c

John Dye *(Todd Barrett)*, Steve Lyon *(Brett Wilson)*, Kim Delaney *(Dayna Thomas)*, Kathleen Wilhoite *(Molly Gibson)*, Miles O'Keeffe *(Cactus Jack)*, Morgan Fairchild *(Katherine Van Buren)*, John Welsh *(Prof. Jarman)*, Josef Rainer *(Charles McCormick)*, Dick Alexander *(Mr. Bowersox)*, Steve Archer, Eden Brandy.

Unlike most teen sex comedies, CAMPUS MAN doesn't heavily emphasize nudity and sex. Instead, the film almost has a sense of naivete to it. Dye is a student at Arizona State University who can't cover his tuition costs. Then he hits on a novel idea: Using his hopelessly handsome roommate Lyon (a muscular, blond diving champ) as a model, Dye decides to print a calendar which he hopes to sell for big bucks. Dye turns to loan shark O'Keeffe for financial backing, then sets his scheme into motion. He persuades Wilhoite, who runs the campus newspaper, to let him use her staff to produce the calendar. Wilhoite agrees, but only if Dye promises to donate $1,000 to a charity drive she's running. His tuition gets paid in short order, but the calendar sales don't cover the price of O'Keeffe's loan. O'Keeffe ups his interest, so Dye must resort to new measures to get the money. He sends the calendar to a top New York fashion magazine run by Fairchild, and suddenly Lyon is a beefcake sensation. This gets him in trouble with the NCAA, threatening his status as an amateur diver, but Dye is able to work everything out.

This is fairly silly stuff, though it's played with good energy. Dye performs the expected machinations with a certain degree of charm, and O'Keeffe has some amusing moments in his supporting role. CAMPUS MAN's biggest problem is its vacuous plot. Pinup calendars can be found at nearly every major state university in the country, and they have long since lost their shock value. It's hard to believe Lyon's posing for a couple of pictures would upset the authorities to the extent depicted here. On the other hand, the film does have some factual basis. Todd Headlee, the film's associate producer, is a former Arizona State student who printed a similar calendar some years ago. This led to trouble for the enterprising young man, but the low-level controversy helped get him a foothold in the movie business. Songs include: "Point of No Return" (John Smith, Valerie Day, performed by Nu Shooz), "Some Become Strangers" (David William, Amy La Televison, Peter Rafelson, performed by The Williams Brothers), "Dancing with My Mirror" (performed by Corey Hart), "Tear It Down" (Rick Szelugia, Mike Whyle, performed by E-I-E-I-O), "False Accusations" (Robert Cray, Dennis Walker, Richard Cousins, performed by The Robert Cray Band), "Rock Until You Drop" (Michael Sembello, Danny Sembello, Dick Rudolph, performed by Michael Sembello), "Lookin' Up" (Michael Sembello, Alfred Rubalcava, Dick Rudolph, performed by Michael Semvello), "Midnight Rider" (Robert Payne, Greg Allman, performed by The Allman Brothers), "The Future's So Bright I Gotta Wear Shades" (Pat McDonald, performed by Timbuk 3). *(Profanity, brief nudity.)*

p, Peggy Fowler, Jon Landau; d, Ron Casden; w, Matt Dorff, Alex Horvat, Geoffrey Baere (based on a story by Matt Dorff, Alex Horvat); ph, Francis Kenny (Metrocolor); m, James Newton Howard; ed, Steven Polivka; prod d, David Gropman; art d, Karen Schulz; set d, J. Allen Highfill; m/l, John Smith, Valerie Day, David William, Amy La Televison, Peter Rafelson, Rick Szelugia, Mike Whyle, Robert Cray, Dennis Walker, Richard Cousins, Michael Sembello, Danny Sembello, Dick Rudolph, Alfred Rubalcava, Robert Payne, Greg Allman, Pat McDonald; cos, Elisabetta Rogiani.

Comedy **(PR:C MPAA:PG)**

CAN'T BUY ME LOVE** (1987) 94m Apollo-Mount/Touchstone-Silver Screen Partners III-BV c

Patrick Dempsey *(Ronald Miller)*, Amanda Peterson *(Cindy Mancini)*, Courtney Gains *(Kenneth Wurman)*, Tina Caspary *(Barbara)*, Seth Green *(Chuckie Miller)*, Sharon Farrell *(Mrs. Mancini)*, Darcy De Moss *(Patty)*, Dennis Dugan *(David Miller)*, Cloyce Morrow *(Judy Miller)*, Devin Devasquez *(Iris)*, Eric Bruskotter *(Big John)*, Gerardo Mejia *(Ricky)*, Cort McCown *(Quint)*, Ami Dolenz *(Fran)*, Max Perlich *(Lester)*, David Schermerhorn *(Albert)*, Steve Franken *(Moda Clerk)*, Phil Simms *(Rock)*, Tudor Sherrard *(Brent)*, George Gray, III *(Bobby Hilton)*, Jimmie Lee Mitchell *(Mr. Webbly)*, Jan Rooney *(Mrs. Hagmer)*, James Gooden *(Mr. Wurman)*, Erin O'Flaherty *(Jr. Wurman)*, Ty Gray *(Duane)*, Will Hannah *(Camera Salesman)*, Todd Walsh *(Stocky Jones)*, Wayne Chandler *(African Host)*, Meredith Wagelie, Jennifer Nelson *(Freshmen)*, Corissa Miller *(Transfer Girl)*, Lisa Givens *(Bambi La Brock)*.

Originally titled "Boy Rents Girl," this teen comedy from the John Hughes school is part love story, part morality play, and only partly successful. Dempsey plays a nerdish Tucson high schooler who longs for a memorable senior year. He and his "mutant" friends—including the freckled Gains—have spent their high school years watching football games from the visiting bleachers and passed Saturday nights drinking root beer and playing cards. A summer of mowing lawns has earned Dempsey $1,500, which he plans to use to purchase a telescope, though what he most longs for is Peterson, the unattainable blonde beauty who lives next door and also happens to be the queen of the "cool" kids. Peterson doesn't even know Dempsey exists until she ruins the suede outfit her mother had forbidden her to borrow. Dempsey is present at the mall when she tries unsuccessfully to exchange the ruined suit. Thinking quickly, he offers Peterson a deal—he'll give her $1,000—the price of the outfit—if she will be seen with him for one month. Reluctantly, Peterson agrees. On the first day of classes, she meets Dempsey and works a little fashion magic. With the sleeves ripped from his shirt, his glasses off, and his hair moussed, Dempsey is suddenly in fashion. Each day his confidence grows and his sartorial splendor increases. Before long, he is greeting jocks in the hallways with "high five" handshakes. In the meantime, Dempsey and Peterson have grown close. One night, Dempsey takes her to his special place, an airplane "graveyard," where the two do some telescopic moon watching from a helicopter. Peterson is falling in love with Dempsey, but, unaware of this, he is falling in love with being popular. The end of the month arrives and Dempsey and Peterson stage a dramatic breakup. Having dumped the campus queen, Dempsey is suddenly *The* heartbreaker, chased after by "cool" cuties. In the process, he not only ignores Gains and his old friends, but also Peterson. Hurt by him and disgusted, she begins dating a local college boy. Before going to a dance, Dempsey, a non-dancer, nervously tries to get down a few steps by watching "American Bandstand." Unknown to him, he has been

watching a PBS presentation on African culture, but his gyrations are an instant sensation at the dance. Dempsey accompanies jocks Bruskotter and Mejia on some Halloween mischief, finding the target is Gains' house. Gains waits for the inevitable assault, in which Dempsey reluctantly participates. Dempsey is then trapped in a net, but when Gains sees the assailant is his old friend, he lets him go. At a New Year's Eve party, Peterson stumbles onto Dempsey as he makes love to Devasquez while quoting lines from Peterson's poetry. Later that evening, a drunken Peterson reveals to all Dempsey's plot to gain popularity. Dempsey becomes an instant pariah, spurned by cool kids and nerds alike. One lunch hour, Gains sits at a table full of "cool" girls, helping one of them with her schoolwork. McCown, a jock, confronts him, telling him to leave, that he isn't going to pull another "Ronald Miller" (Dempsey). Dempsey, who has been sitting alone and has nothing to lose, comes to his defense, wielding a baseball bat and explaining that Gains is simply trying to make friends. He leaves, Gains and McCown shake hands, and the onlookers applaud. In the film's upbeat finale, Peterson, who is ready to accept the "real" Dempsey's testament of love, appears and rides off into the picturesque Arizona sunset with him on his lawn mower.

The basic premise of CAN'T BUY ME LOVE is engaging and its theme of self-acceptance in the capricious world of high school hits its mark, though it is driven home with hamfisted didacticism. Director Rash (THE BUDDY HOLLY STORY, UNDER THE RAINBOW) and first-time screenwriter Swerdlick are most successful with their lead characters. Dempsey and Gains are not merely cartoon nerds; the relationship between Dempsey and Peterson is filled with subtle touches; and all three turn in fine performances. Dempsey, whom some critics have likened to John Cusack, nicely balances his real, sensitive side with the over-the-top hipness of his Mr. Hyde. Gains, in a smaller role, turns in an effectively understated performance as the shunned best friend. Peterson (a 16-year-old high-school student who has been acting since age eight) is equally good. Though she is certainly stunning, Peterson looks and acts like a teenager, unlike the other "girls" in the film who look and talk like they've stepped from the pages of a *Playboy* "Girls of Fantasy High School" spread. Because he felt that he "had a story that worked well on a non-exploitation level," Rash has stated that he attempted to avoid certain of the genre's exploitive elements—"nudity, a lot of language, some scatological humor." However, a gratuitous locker-room scene remains in which the "girls," clad only in bras and panties, discuss Dempsey's sexual prowess. There is also recurring flatulent humor that quickly runs out of gas. But the problem with CAN'T BUY ME LOVE is that too often characters do and say things teenagers wouldn't. At times this is a funny, touching film, but more often it isn't. Made on a budget of approximately $5 million, the film was shot on location in Tucson, Arizona, and at Tucson High School. *(Sexual situations, profanity.)*

p, Thom Mount; d, Steve Rash; w, Michael Swerdlick; ph, Peter Lyons Collister (Foto-Kem Color); m, Robert Folk; ed, Jeff Gourson; md, Robert Folk; prod d, Donald L. Harris; set d, Christian W. Russhon, Andrew Bernard; cos, Gregory Poe; ch, Paula Abdul; makeup, Cher Slater.

Comedy **(PR:C MPAA:PG-13)**

CHAPETAN MEITANOS: I IKONA ENOS MYTHIKOU PROSSOPOU
(SEE: I KONA ENOS MYTHIKOU PROSOPOU, 1987, Gr.)

CAPRICCIO† (1987, It.) 100m San Francisco/Filmauro-DEG c (Trans: Letters from Capri)

Nicola Warren *(Jennifer)*, Andy J. Forest *(Fred)*, Francesca Dellera *(Rosalba)*, Luigi Laezza *(Ciro)*, Vittorio Caprioli *(Don Vincenzo)*, Isabella Biagini, Bea, Matteo, Lulu, Venantino Venantini, Osiride Pevarello, Eolo Capritti, Simona Tedeschi, Laila Peloso, Armando Marra, Jean-Rene Lemoine, Dodi Moscati.

In 1947, Warren and Forest, an American couple, return to Italy, where they met during WW II. Though they have a child, much of the passion has gone out of their marriage and they find themselves thinking about their former lovers. Forest contacts Dellera, the prostitute he *knew* once upon a time, and takes her with him when on a business trip. Warren writes to Laezza, who is now a pimp, and implores him to join her in Capri. However, Warren and Forrest find their old lovers to be far less satisfying than their memories. Directed by Tinto Brass, who helmed CALIGULA and THE KEY.

p, Giovanni Bertolucci; d&w, Giovanni Tinto Brass; ph, Silvano Ippoliti (Technicolor); m, Riz Ortolani; ed, Giovanni Tinto Brass; art d, Paolo Biagetti.

Romance **(PR:NR MPAA:NR)**

CAPTAIN KHORSHID† (1987, Iran) Pakhshiran-Peiman/Farabi Cinema Foundation

Ali Nassirian, Darioush Arjmand, Parvaneh Massoumi.

An Iranian adaptation of Ernest Hemingway's *To Have and Have Not* (filmed in 1944 by Howard Hawks), this version takes place in a port town on the Persian Gulf. A world-weary boat captain finds that in order to assure the survival of himself and his family he must aid in the escape of a group of criminals.

d&w, Nasser Taghvai; ph, Mehrdad Fakhimi; m, F. Naseri; ed, Nasser Taghvai.

Crime **(PR:NR MPAA:NR)**

CARA DE ACELGA† (1987, Span.) 101m Incine-Jet-Lince c (Trans: Spinach Face)

Jose Sacristan *(Antonio)*, Fernando Fernan Gomez *(Madariaga)*, Marisa Paredes *(Olga)*, Emilio Gutierrez Caba *(Eusebio)*, Amparo Baro *(Loles)*, Rafaela Aparicio *(Hospital Woman)*, Raul Sender *(Agustin)*, Luis Barberto *(Hospital Man)*, Maria Isbert.

Director/writer/star Sacristan plays a drifter hitching rides in the Spanish countryside. As he travels, he finds work as a waiter, a theater usher, and an art thief, all leading to comic adventures.

d&w, Jose Sacristan (based on a story by Carlos P. Merinero, Jose Sacristan); ph, Carlos Suarez (Eastmancolor); m, Ricardo Miralles; ed, Jose Luis Matesanz; set d, Felix Murcia; cos, Luis Valles.

Comedy **(PR:NR MPAA:NR)**

CARAMELLE DA UNO SCONOSCIUTO† (1987, It.) ReteItalia/Numero Uno Cinematografice S.r.l.-CIDIF c (Trans: Sweets from a Stranger)

Barbara De Rossi, Marina Suma, Athina Cenci, Mara Venier, Laura Betti, Annie Papa, Gerardo Amato, Sabrina Ferilli, Antonella Ponziani, Alessandra Bonarota, Ilaria Cecchi.

A mad man is killing prostitutes left and right, and it's getting hard for a working girl to make a living. The ladies of the night convene to try to put a stop to these disastrous occurrences, but their efforts are unsuccessful. However, the murder weapon is later discovered and a special police unit swings into action.

d, Franco Ferrini; w, Franco Ferrini, Andrea Giuseppini; ph, Giuseppe Berardini; m, Umberto Smaila; ed, Franco Fraticelli.

Crime **(PR:NR MPAA:NR)**

CARE BEARS ADVENTURE IN WONDERLAND, THE* (1987, Can.) 75m Nelvana/Cineplex Odeon Films c

Voices of: Bob Dermer *(Grumpy Bear)*, Eva Almos *(Swift Heart Rabbit)*, Dan Hennessey *(Brave Heart Lion/Dum)*, Jim Henshaw *(Tenderheart Bear)*, Marla Lukofsky *(Good Luck Bear)*, Luba Goy *(Lots-A-Heart Elephant)*, Keith Knight *(White Rabbit)*, Tracey Moore *(Alice)*, Colin Fox *(Wizard)*, John Stocker *(Dim/Cheshire Cat)*, Don McManus *(Caterpillar)*, Elizabeth Hanna *(Queen of Wonderland)*, Alan Fawcett *(Flamingo)*, Keith Hampshire *(Mad Hatter/Jabberwocky)*, Alyson Court *(Princess)*.

Strictly for the smallest tots, this animated feature will bore anyone over the age of puberty. It might also enrage anyone with a knowledge of movies as it poaches many other pictures in a forlorn attempt at originality. This is the third of the CARE BEARS features. These creatures began as toys and were quite successful. This led to the movies. Screenwriters De Klein and Snooks, working from a story by Sauder, have interposed the Bears with Lewis Carroll, stirred in a dollop of L. Frank Baum, and topped it with some George Bernard Shaw in order to concoct a treacly sweet souffle that is hard to digest.

Alice is the local Wonderland princess. When she is dragged through the looking glass by a nefarious and malevolent wizard who wants to rule, guess who is called in—like a furry cavalry? Right, the Care Bears. One group of bears goes after Alice while the other searches for an Alice *doppelganger* to impersonate the princess. They meet an amalgam of characters including a cat (Cheshire, of course) who does a John Sebastian "rap" tune, a Jabberwock, and the Mad Hatter, who sings "Mad About Hats" (Sebastian) as he changes chapeaux. Other Carroll characters in evidence are Tweedledee and Tweedledum (renamed Dim and Dum here), the White Rabbit, and the regular contingent of Care Bears with diabetic names like Tenderheart Bear, Good Luck Bear, et al. There's even an always-hungry Grumpy Bear who is almost exactly the character in SNOW WHITE AND THE SEVEN DWARFS. Matter of fact, the Wizard even looks like the Bad Queen from the aforementioned half-century-old classic. The animation is simple, almost crude. The colors have no subtlety and the movement is herky-jerk. Knowledgeable film fans will also note "borrowings" from TREASURE ISLAND, THE PRISONER OF ZENDA, and THE THREE MUSKETEERS. Plenty of nonviolent "action" (which is really movement) and a few other Sebastian tunes. Natalie Cole sings "Rise and Shine" (Maribeth Solomon) and composer Patricia Cullen plays her own score. Lots of children's level philosophy both in the script and the songs, one of which, Sebastian's "We Might Have to Look All Over the World for This Girl," is sung by the Bears as they search for Alice. The Care Bears began in 1981 and originated at a company named "Those Characters From Cleveland," which is owned by American Greetings. The TV series which springs from the toys (as most of them do these days) can be seen all over the US and England and the movies have grossed nearly $50 million. The underlying message in most of the Care Bears projects is that these creatures are the "Furry Defenders of Feelings." Phew! Perfect for the under-6 crowd, but these cheap animated features make one mourn Uncle Walt Disney even more than one did before.

p, Michael Hirsh, Patrick Loubert, Clive A. Smith; d, Raymond Jafelice; w, Susan Snooks, John De Klein (based on a story by Peter Sauder); m, Trish Cullen; ed, Rob Kirkpatrick; m/l, John Sebastian, Maribeth Solomon; anim, John Laurence Collins.

Children's/Animation **(PR:AAA MPAA:G)**

CARTOLINE ITALIANE† (1987, It.) 93m Italnoleggio-Mean Cinematografica/Instituto Luce-Italnoleggio-RAI TV c (Trans: Italian Postcards)

Genevieve Page *(Silvana)*, Lindsay Kemp *(Vinicio Secchi)*, Cristiana Borghi *(Lidia)*, David Brandon *(Vittorio)*, Stefano Davanzati, Antonello Fassari, Rosa Fumetto, Alessandro Genesi, Isabella Martelli, Rita Falcone, Tomoko Tanaka.

All the world's a stage or, at least, the boarding house run by a famous but reclusive former actress is. Brandon, a TV journalist, persuades his girl friend, Borghi, to become a lodger at the boarding house. She is wired for sound and the plan is for her to "interview" the grand dame. The joke is on Borghi when Page masquerades as the famous leading lady. Although calamity befalls her and her purpose is exposed, Borghi chooses not to leave this odd little world.

d, Meme Perlini; w, Meme Perlini, Gianni Romoli; ph, Carlo Carlini; m, Stefano Mainotti; ed, Carlo Fontana; art d&cos, Antonello Agliotti.

Drama **(PR:NR MPAA:NR)**

CARTUCHA CORTADA† (1987, Mex.) 89m Produciones Tollocan/ Peliculas Mexicanas c (Trans: Cocked Gun)

Fernando Almada *(Dr. Ceasar Fuentes)*, Mario Almada *(El Comandante)*, Marta Ortiz *(Ana Fuentes)*, Victor Junco *(Don Queaga)*, Humberto Herrera, Luis Elias, Villasenor Kuri, Pancho Muller, Lupita Bustamentes.

After appearing together in 1986's RAFAGA DE PLOMO, two of the Mexican cinema's favorite action performers, brothers Fernando and Mario Almada, are teamed again in this story of decent men pushed to the brink. Fernando plays a successful physician whose life is thrown into turmoil when his young son is abducted and held for ransom. The kingpin of a drug-running operation and Fernando's former gardener are the kidnapers, and the doctor decides to take the law into his own hands when they allow his boy to die. Turning the tables on them, he kidnaps the drug smuggler's son.

p, Guillermo Herrera; d, Rafael Villasenor Kuri; ph, Antonio Ruiz Juarez; m, Carlos Torres; ed, Max Sanchez.

Action/Crime **(PR:NR MPAA:NR)**

CASPAR DAVID FRIEDRICH† (1987, Ger.) 84m Allianz/Filmverlag der Autoren c

Helmut Griem *(Carl Gustav Carus)*, Sabine Sinjen *(Caroline Friedrich)*, Hans Peter Hallwachs *(V.A. Schukowski)*, Walter Schmidinger *(Ramdohr)*, Hans Quest *(Ernst Moritz)*, Lothar Blumhagen, Udo Samel, Friedrich Schonfelder.

Nominally a biography, this film has less to do with the life of the innovative 19th century German landscape artist Caspar David Friedrich than with the land that served as his inspiration. Filmed in the style of Friedrich's paintings, which emphasize the landscape over their human inhabitants, the picture concentrates on the natural settings that were his subjects. Sinjen plays the artist's wife and Griem acts the role of his devoted supporter, but the real stars here are Friedrich's paintings—many of which are shown—and the mountains, seas, and sunsets they capture.

p&d, Peter Schamoni; w, Peter Schamoni, Hans A. Neunzig; ph, Gerard Vandenberg (Eastmancolor), m, Hans Posegga, Franz Schubert; ed, Katja Dringenberg; cos, Christian Dorst

Biography **(PR:NR MPAA:NR)**

CASSANDRA† (1987, Aus.) 93m Parrallel c

Tessa Humphries *(Cassandra)*, Shane Briant *(Steven Roberts)*, Briony Behets *(Helen Roberts)*, Susan Barling *(Libby)*, Tim Burns *(Graham)*, Lee James, Jeff Trueman.

Australian thriller that stars Humphries as a woman whose recurring dream proves to be founded on her family's real-life deep, dark secret. In her nightmare she witnesses a young boy provoke a woman's suicide. Eventually Humphries learns that her mother isn't her mother but is, instead, her aunt—her father's sister. When her father's mistress is murdered, Humphries learns that the boy in her dream is her twin brother, and that he has been locked up in a mental institution ever since causing their mother's death when they were kids. Now he's loose again and on a rampage.

p, Trevor Lucas; d, Colin Eggleston; w, Colin Eggleston, John Ruane, Chris Fitchett; ph, Gary Wapshott (Agfa Color); m, Trevor Lucas, Ian Mason; ed, Josephine Cooke; prod d, Stewart Burnside.

Thriller **(PR:NR MPAA:NR)**

CAT CITY† (1987, Hung./Can./Ger.) 93m Pannonia Film/Sefel Pictures-Infafilm GmbH c (MACSKAFOGO)

A full-length animated feature from Budapest's leading animation studio, Pannonia, which spoofs gangster and spy pictures in an international game of cat-and-mouse, literally. It is the year 80 A.M.M. (After Mickey Mouse) and the civilized mice of the world are losing control to the mean and nasty cats. When Intermaus, an international mouse intelligence agency, learns of the development of a secret weapon they send out their best agent, a beefy rodent named Grabowski. Although the cats hire some rat mercenaries, Grabowski reaches his destination and finds the blueprints to the "cattrap." Peace is finally restored and the cats are put back into their subservient places. CAT CITY received a US release at the Los Angeles Animation Celebration.

d, Bela Ternovszky; w, Jozsef Nepp; ph, Maria Nemenyi, Csaba Nagy, Gyorgy Varga (Eastmancolor); m, Tamas Deak; ed, Magda Hap; anim, Jozsef Gemes, Zoltan Maros.

Animation **(PR:NR MPAA:NR)**

CATCH THE HEAT* (1987) 87m M'Amsel Tea-Negocios/Trans World c (AKA: FEEL THE HEAT)

David Dukes *(Waldo)*, Tiana Alexandra *(Checkers Goldberg)*, Rod Steiger *(Jason Hannibal)*, Brian Thompson *(Danny)*, Jorge Martinez *(Raul)*, John Hancock *(Ike)*, Brian Libby *(Brody)*, Jessica Schultz *(Maria)*, Prof. Toru Tanaka *(Dozu)*.

Trans World Entertainment is a new entity that seems to be filling the void for low-budget melodramas created when Cannon went up-market. There is a certain sadness about this picture because it has such good talents involved with it, yet is such a mediocre movie. The script was written by Stirling Silliphant, one of the best TV writers of the 1960s, a man who was responsible for memorable episodes of "Route 66" and "Naked City" as well as scripts for IN THE HEAT OF THE NIGHT, THE SLENDER THREAD, CHARLY, THE KILLER ELITE, and many more. Among director Silberg's credits is BREAKIN', a fast-moving 1984 picture that was a smash hit. Add to that such stellar actors as Rod Steiger and David Dukes and, on paper at least, this movie should have been a hit. But movies are made on film, not on paper, and all the best-laid plans went agley here.

Asian actress Alexandra (Silliphant's spouse in actuality) works for the US Narcotics Bureau. Her name in the film is "Checkers Goldberg" (wonder where she got that) and her boss is Dukes. He sends her on assignment to Buenos Aires to infiltrate the operations of Steiger, a drug smuggler. She is pretending to be a dancer and Steiger takes immediate notice of her form and face. In a trice, Alexandra is on to Steiger's means of smuggling. He has several dancers in his employ, women with small bosoms whom he has surgically altered. But instead of the doctor placing the usual filler into their breasts, the women's chests are stuffed with drugs. Once they get to the US, the narcotics will be replaced with silicone, or whatever it is they use. Alexandra is due for the implant operation, which will mean her doom. She's been wearing tight bindings to mask her copious mammaries and the minute she's stripped, Steiger will catch wise (or so the plot says). It goes without saying that truth and justice triumph and Alexandra manages to escape that fate.

Despite the nepotism of starring in a film written by her husband, Alexandra is not without charm, talent, and a magnificent figure. She is also well-schooled in the martial arts and uses her abilities as a female Chuck Norris to destroy the villains. Lots of action, chases, guns, and gore plus a cameo appearance by pro wrestler Tanaka. If she gets the right material, Alexandra could be another Sybil Danning, if that's what she wants. All the smaller roles were well chosen by casting director Caro Jones, who was responsible for the people in many better films, such as ROCKY. *(Nudity, sexual situations.)*

p, Don Van Atta; d, Joel Silberg; w, Stirling Silliphant; ph, Nissim Leon Nitcho, Frank Harris (Cinecolor); m, Thomas Chase, Steve Rucker; ed, Christopher Holmes, Darren Holmes; prod d, Jorge Marchegiani; stunts, Alan Amiel.

Action **(PR:C MPAA:R)**

CAUGHT† (1987) 113m World Wide Pictures c

John Shepherd *(Tim Devon)*, Amerjit Deu *(Rajam Prasad)*, Jill Ireland *(Janet Devon)*, Alex Tetteh-Lartey *(Abraham Abimue)*, Frederik DeGroot *(Jacques)*, Marnix Kappers *(Erik de Bie)*, Kimberly Simms *(Aimee Lynn)*, Hans Kenna *(Tourist Clerk)*, Pim Vosmaer *(Wouter)*, Erik J. Meijer *(Sprug)*, Bruni Heincke *(Mrs. de Bie)*, Rene Klijn *(Tibbe)*, Peter Blok *(Dude)*, Ethel Smyth, Kerry Cederberg, Deborah Smyth, Iris Misset, Martin Versluys, Annie de Jong, Bart Romer, Edward Kolderwijn, Elvira Wilson, Leontien de Rijiter, Billy Graham.

Produced by evangelist Billy Graham's film production company, World Wide Pictures, CAUGHT stars Deu as an Indian evangelist traveling to Amsterdam who happens to meet and befriend American junkie Shepherd. After a series of misadventures which sees Shepherd getting in and out of trouble, Deu succeeds in converting his troubled new friend to Christianity. Charles Bronson's wife, Jill Ireland, turns in a cameo appearance, as does the Reverend Graham. Only the 10th film produced by Graham in the last 22 years, CAUGHT received limited distribution during the fall of 1987 and may turn up on home video.

p, Jerry Ballew; d&w, James F. Collier; ph, Eddie Van Der Enden; m, Ted Neeley; prod d, J. Michael Hooser.

Drama **Cas.** **(PR:NR MPAA:PG-13)**

CEMIL† (1987, Ger.) 82m Johannes Schafer c

Vedat Uluocak *(Cemil Ersoy)*, Alexandra Kuntzel *(Nina Kuntzel)*, Sissy Elbir *(Hulya Ersoy)*, Halil Yucekaya *(Hassan Ersoy)*.

This ultra-low-budget West German film deals with the plight of the title teenager (Uluocak) whose parents have decided to leave Berlin to return to their native Turkey. Uluocak has grown up in Germany and has no desire to leave the country he knows as his home for a *foreign* land. When his family prepares to depart, Uluocak deserts them at the airport, choosing to remain behind with his German girl friend, Kuntzel. Their passion fades and Uluocak grows tired of living on handouts, so he contritely takes a train to rejoin his family in Turkey. Made for $5,000 and shot on Super 8.

p,d&w, Jo Schafer; ph, Robert Schneider; m, Fancy, Frank Flebig; ed, Robert Schneider, Jo Schafer.

Drama **(PR:NR MPAA:NR)**

CENA MEDU† (1987, Czech.) 76m Barrandov

Oldrich Vlach *(Dr. Vrba)*, Petr Pospichal *(Dr. Kavan)*, Jiri Vondracek, Marta Hrachovinova *(Petovi Rodice [Parents])*, Miroslav Zounar *(Dr. Malina)*, Hana Vavrova *(Monika)*, Daniela Srajerova *(Stanicni Sestra)*, Petr Lepsa, Zdenek David *(Prislusnici VB)*, Lubos Vesely *(Kaja)*, Jakub Zdenek *(Peta)*, Miroslav Streda *(Customs Officer Janda)*, Vaclav Sloup, Karel Kolousek, Vlastimil Hasek, Jan Kraus, Ladislav Trojan, Vaclav Helsus.

[No plot information available.]

d, Jaromir Borek; w, Pavel Hajny; ph, Martin Benoni; m, Milan Dvorak; ed, Ivana Kacirkova; art d, Ludvik Siroky; cos, Dimitrij Kadrnozka.

Drama **(PR:NR MPAA:NR)**

CENA ODVAHY† (1987, Czech.) 79m Slovenska Filmova

Maria Proboszova *(Lenka/Z. Studenkova)*, Andrej Hryc *(Peter Vanak)*, Michal Docolomansky *(Dano Zaruba)*, Julius Pantik *(Sojka)*, Adriana Tarabkova *(Erika/L. Mandzarova)*, Lucia Bernusova *(Bognarova)*, Igor Cillik *(Bognar)*, Ivo Gogal *(Andy)*, Frantisek Desset *(Kostal)*.

[No plot information available.]

d&w, Ludovit Filan; ph, Dodo Simoncic; m, Stepan Konicek; ed, Eduard Klenovsky; art d, Roman Rjachovsky; cos, Maria Silberska.

Drama **(PR:NR MPAA:NR)**

CERNITE LEBEDI† (1987, Bulg.) 104m Bulgarian Cinematography c (Trans: Black Swans)

Diana Raynova *(Violetta)*, Dorothea Tontcheva *(Mimi)*, Zornitsa Mladenova *(Young Violetta)*, Todor Kolev, Leda Tasseva, Yassen Vultchanov, Irina Stoyanova.

Made in 1984, this Bulgarian film enters Herbert Ross country in its telling of a young woman's struggle to become a prima ballerina. Raynova plays the ballerina who has chased a dancer's dream since she was a young girl, enduring years of demanding training and sacrifice. Along the way she has had many unsuccessful relationships, undergone an abortion, and chosen ballet over the love of a man who made her decide between him and her career.

d&w Ivan Nitchev (based on the novel by Bogumil Raynov); ph, Richard Lentchevski; m, Bojidar Petkov.

Dance/Drama **(PR:NR MPAA:NR)**

CHAMP D'HONNEUR† (1987, Fr.) 87m Baccara-Plamyre-Selena Audiovisuel-La SEPT/AAA c (Trans: Field of Honor)

Cris Campion, Pascale Rocard, Eric Wapler, Frederic Mayer, Andre Wilms, Vincent Martin, Marion Audier.

Set during the Franco-Prussian War, this is a story of the horrors of battle and the immensity of human compassion and friendship. Wapler, the son of a wealthy family, is conscripted into the army, but pays Campion, a poor farm boy, to take his place. On the fields of the Prussian-invaded Alsace, Campion experiences the brutality of war. Fleeing the carnage, he encounters Mayer, a young Alsacian boy, whom he befriends and escorts to the safety of the soldier's hometown.

p, Antoine Gannage, Eric Dussart; d, Jean-Pierre Denis; w, Jean-Pierre Denis, Hubert au Petit, Christian Faure, Francoise Dudognong; ph, Francois Catonne; m, Michel Portal; ed, Genevieve Winding; prod d, Marc Petitjean; cos, Anne Le Mol.

War **(PR:NR MPAA:NR)**

CHARLIE DINGO† (1987, Fr.) 100m Septembre/UGC c (Trans: Charlie Loco)

Guy Marchand *(Charlie Maladieu)*, Caroline Cellier *(Georgia)*, Laurent Malet *(Mathieu)*, Niels Arestrup *(William Wolski)*, Maurice Barrier *(Chinaski)*, Brigitte Rouan *(Marie)*, Jean-Claude Dauphin *(Jupin)*.

Sort of standing DOUBLE INDEMNITY on its head, director Behat (URGENCE, LES LONGS MANTEAUX) and screenwriter/novelist Vautrin present the story of a man (Marchand) who is thought to have died in an automobile accident but returns to his Normandy home after many years away. His wife, Cellier, has remarried Arestrup, an unscrupulous cop, and both anxiously await the payment of Marchand's two million-franc life insurance policy.

p, Jean Nainchrik; d&w, Gilles Behat; w, Jean Vautrin; ph, Pierre Lhomme; ed, Genevieve Vaury; m, Christian Chevalier; art d, Jacques Dugied.

Drama **(PR:NR MPAA:NR)**

CHECHECHELA—UNA CHICA DEL BARRIO† (1987, Arg.) 90m Instituto Nacional de Cinematografica c (Trans: Hey, Hey, Chela)

Ana Marie Picchio *(Celia, "Chechechela")*, Victor Laplace *(Julio/Titti/Alberto)*, Tina Serrana, Julio Lopez, Silvana Sileri, Noemi Morelli, Renee Roxana.

Satirizing the Argentine TV soap operas that have become popular throughout the Spanish-speaking Pan America, this comedy stars Picchio as a bride who, in flashback, reconsiders the three great loves of her life as she approaches the altar. Laplace, plays each of the lovers, adding a mustache for one, whiskers for another, and remaining clean-shaven for the third. As a lad from the provinces, a secret policeman, and a man whom Picchio encounters on the streets of Buenos Aires, Laplace vies with himself for the love of the woman who works in a clothing store and lives in a cacophonous slum. CHECHECHELA—UNA CHICA DEL BARRIO was a big hit in Argentina in 1986.

p, Rolando Gardelin; d&w, Bebe Kamin; w, Mirko Buchin; ph, Rodolfo Denevi; m, Jose Louis Castineiras de Dios; art d, Alfredo Iglesias.

Comedy **(PR:NR MPAA:NR)**

CHECKPOINT† (1987) 91m New Film Group-MTA c

Mary Apick *(Firouzeh)*, Houshang Touzie *(Kazem)*, Peter Spreague *(Mike)*, Mark Nichols *(Bob)*, Buck Kartalian *(Frank)*, Michael Zand *(Farhad)*, Mayeva Martin *(Kate)*, Ali Poutash *(Hatam)*, Ali F. Dean *(Ali)*, Masha Manesh *(Abe)*, Zohreh Ramsey *(Zari)*, Keyvan Nekoui *(Iraj)*, Parviz Sayyad *(Younesi)*.

Shown at the Locarno Film Festival and given a brief run in Los Angeles, CHECKPOINT, directed by Iranian filmmaker Sayyad, is apparently based on a factual incident that took place in 1980 at the height of the Iranian hostage crisis. A bus returning Michigan college students from a field trip to Ontario is stopped at the border by US officials who will not allow the eight Iranian students into the country until their visas are checked. The three US citizens aboard refuse to leave their comrades behind, so the travelers spend the cold night on the bus awaiting clearance. The situation leads to a discussion of the events taking place in Iran and the Iranian students split along ideological lines and argue the evils and virtues of the Khomeini revolution, while the Americans sit still and try to make sense of the debate. Director Sayyad and executive producer Apick play the most vehemently anti-Khomeini students.

p,d&w, Parviz Sayyad; ph, Michael Davis; m, Ahmad Pejman; ed, Parviz Sayyad.

Drama **(PR:NR MPAA:NR)**

CHEGEMSKIY DETEKTIV† (1987, USSR) 83m Mosfilm-Gruziafilm/ Sovexportfilm c (Trans: Cheghem Detective Story)

Kurbei Kamkia, Ruslan Mikaberidze, Baadur Begalishvili, Rolan Bykov.

Set in the village of Cheghem just after WW II, the story concerns the search for the thief who stole money from a farm collective.

d, Alexander Svetlov; w, Fasil Iskanderov; ph, Valentin Piganov; m, Iosif Bardanashvili; art d, Yevgeny Vinnitsky.

Comedy **(PR:NR MPAA:NR)**

CHELOVEK C AKKORDEONOM† (1987, USSR) 91m Mosfilm/ Sovexportfilm c (Trans: The Man with the Accordion)

Valery Zolotukhin, Irina Alferova, Arina Aleinikova, Vladimir Soshalsky, Mikhail Pugovkin, Yelena Pletneva.

After suffering a serious chest wound during WW II, a musician decides to pursue a career in finance. He continues to play the accordian, however, until he plays at a wedding and discovers the bride is the woman he had loved and searched for after the war. He puts his accordian away, but retrieves it for a veterans' gathering at the film's end.

d, Nikolai Dostal; w, Alexander Borodyansky; ph, Yuri Nevsky; m, Alexander Goldstein; art d, Alexander Boim, Alexander Makarov.

Drama **(PR:NR MPAA:NR)**

CHEREZ STO LET V MAE† (1987, USSR) 96m Tallinfilm/Sovexportfilm c (Trans: May, Hundred Years After)

Juri Krukov, Jaan Rekkor, Arvo Kukumiagi, Evald Hermakul, Maria Klenskaya.

The film depicts the last three days in the life of Viktor Kingisepp, a Russian hero who fought against the German army in Estonia in 1918.

d, Kalie Kiysk; w, Mati Unt; ph, Juri Sillart; m, Erkki-Sven Tuur; art d, Toomas Hyrak.

Historical **(PR:NR MPAA:NR)**

CHI C'E C'E† (1987, It.) 100m Azione Cinematografica c (Trans: Whoever Is Here, Is Here)

Piero Natoli, Luisa Maneri, Nicola Pistoia, Anita Zagaria, Paola Nazzaro, Flavio Andreini, Claudia Poggiani, Lorenzo Alessandri.

Directed by Piero Natoli, who also takes a lead role, this Italian film is a rumination on failed relationships and the attempts of the jilted and jealous to put their lives back together. Broken-hearted sagas are related and romantic meetings conducted by such personages as an actress and a would-be writer who feels trapped by his family and his job as an executive with a publishing firm.

d&w, Piero Natoli; w, Paola Pascolini; ph, Carlo Cerchio; ed, Domenico Varone; m, Lamberto Macchi.

Drama **(PR:NR MPAA:NR)**

CHINA GIRL½** (1987) 88m Street Lite/Great American-Vestron c

James Russo *(Alberto "Alby" Monte)*, Richard Panebianco *(Tony Monte)*, Sari Chang *(Tyan-Hwa)*, David Caruso *(Johnny Mercury)*, Russell Wong *(Yung-Gan)*, Joey Chin *(Tsu-Shin)*, Judith Malina *(Maria)*, James Hong *(Gung-Tu)*, Robert Miano *(Perito)*, Paul Hipp *(Nino)*, Doreen Chan, Randy Sabusawa.

A bit of a disappointment from the writer-director team of Ferrara and St. John, a collaboration that has produced three very interesting low-budget exploitation films since 1979: DRILLER KILLER, MS. 45, FEAR CITY. Set in modern-day Manhattan, CHINA GIRL is yet another update of "Romeo and Juliet" with a heavy dose of the equally derivative WEST SIDE STORY and Martin Scorsese's MEAN STREETS thrown into the mix. The film begins as a cappuccino shop in Little Italy is replaced by a Chinese restaurant that has been moved across the Canal Street border from Chinatown. This does not sit well with pizza parlor owner Russo and his Italian friends, all of whom blame the Chinese for the decline of their neighborhood. Meanwhile, Russo's teenage brother, Panebianco, ventures into a disco on neutral territory and is immediately attracted to a beautiful Chinese girl, Chang. The pair share a sizzling dance that is broken up when a gang of Chinese boys led by Chang's brother (Wong) chases Panebianco off. Panebianco leads the pursuing Chinese back to Little Italy where he is rescued by Russo and his gang. A brief rumble between the Italians and Chinese ensues, but the police break it up. Back at home Wong berates his sister for socializing with non-Chinese and tells her that if she cannot stay in Chinatown then she will not be allowed out of the apartment. Similarly, Russo dresses down Panebianco for the same infraction. It seems that Wong is being groomed by Hong, leader of the Chinatown mafia (known as the "Tongs"), for a powerful spot in the organization. He is warned by Hong that the Italians and Chinese must coexist peacefully, otherwise the lucrative tourist trade the colorful neighborhoods enjoy will vanish. Hong specifically cites Wong's headstrong and violent cousin Chin as a problem. Determined to collect protection money from the Chinese restaurant in Little Italy—despite the fact that it has been declared off-limits because it is no longer in Chinatown—Chin and his goons try to shake down the owner. When the owner refuses, Chin blows up the man's restaurant and the concussion from the blast shatters the windows of Russo's pizza parlor. This sends the Italian boys into a murderous frenzy and they attack the Chinese with guns. The escalating violence spurs both the Italian and Chinese mobs into action and they unite against the youths, sending one Italian hit man and one Chinese hit man out to dispatch the troublesome Chin and his gang. All of the Chinese youths are assassinated by the combined mobs, save Chin, who has gone into hiding. Meanwhile, Panebianco and Chang continue their romance in clandestine fashion, meeting in alleys and abandoned tenements. Pressed by Hong to locate Chin, Wong finds his cousin and talks him in to returning to Hong Kong before he is murdered. As the pair leave the hideout, they stumble across Panebianco and Chang who are necking in an alley. Just as the Chinese are about to pounce on the Italian boy, a pair of mounted policemen happen by and chase them off. That night, at the annual Italian fest, Chin impulsively kills Russo. Knowing that their days are numbered (they will face the wrath of both the Italian youths and the combined Chinese-Italian mafia), Wong tells Chang to pack her bags, for they and their cousin are going back to Hong Kong immediately. Chang refuses and runs off with Panebianco. The young lovers do not get far, however, for the crazed Chin fires a single bullet at them that passes through Chang's heart and enters Panebianco, killing them both. A crowd of angry old Chinese mobs Chin and kills him while the lovers lie dead in the street, hand-in-hand.

While director Ferrara does manage to combine a violent gangster story with a cliched romance, making a strong statement about senseless racism in the process, CHINA GIRL suffers from an over-abundance of hollow cinematic style and a weak performance from new-comer Chang. In his previous films Ferrara has proven himself an imaginative and innovative director when working on a shoestring budget. His visual composition, camera movements, and creative use of color separate his work from the mundane majority. Unfortunately, his forays into television with both Michael Mann's "Miami Vice" and "Crime Story" seem to have affected his judgement. Whereas a slick and superficial visual style can be used effectively to enhance the excitement of traditional small-screen fare, this style-for-style's sake look only seems gratuitous and silly on the big screen. Puddles of water reflecting colorful neon and garish lighting gels (pinks, purples, reds, greens, and blues) are ridiculously overused in CHINA GIRL and merely become a near-comic distraction. The film fails to convey a real sense of community from either neighborhood, thus leaving the audience to wonder just why it is that nobody wants to leave these violent streets for greener pastures only a few blocks away. Never afraid of blood, Ferrara employed buckets here, and seemingly instructed his cinematographer to search the frame for more. In at least two shots the hand-held camera seems to wander the frame looking to add either a bloody handprint on the wall or a puddle of blood on the floor to the composition. Although one expects explicit gore from Ferrara, this somehow seems infantile and gratuitous. In the past Ferrara has shown that he has few peers when it comes to directing scenes of violent action, and he continues to do so here (the gang warfare sequences are the best thing about this film), but when it comes to the delicate romance between the teenagers the film is unimaginative and listless. Making matters worse, Chang, a beautiful and photogenic young woman, seems uncomfortable on camera and uncertain in her actions. Her eyes wander, she looks lost, and during what is supposed to be her passionate love-making scene with Panebianco, she stares at the ceiling like an unsatisfied housewife. Ferrara seems uninterested in this aspect of his story and his direction of this inexperienced young actress betrays his apathy. On the plus side, Panebianco (whose family owns a clam house in Little Italy) is a real find, combining the swagger of Matt Dillon with his own earnest sensitivity. Also excellent are Russo, Wong, Chin, and Hong, but red-headed Caruso nearly steals the film with his zealously racist patter. He utters the film's one genuinely funny line after nearly getting into a fist-fight with Panebianco over some anti-Chinese remarks: "Take him home! Take Gandhi home!" he screams as some friends separate them. Still more interesting than the majority of low-budget genre efforts, CHINA GIRL must be considered a step back in Ferrara's development as a street artist. *(Graphic violence, sexual situations, excessive profanity.)*

p, Michael Nozik; d, Abel Ferrara; w, Nicholas St. John; ph, Bojan Bazelli (Du Art Color); m, Joe Delia; ed, Anthony Redman; prod d, Dan Leigh; set d, Leslie Rollins; cos, Richard Hornung.

Romance/Crime **(PR:O MPAA:R)**

CHINESE ARE COMING, THE† (1987, Ger.) 99m Journal-Maran/Delta c (DIE CHINESEN KOMMEN)

Jorg Hube *(Hansi Pfnurr)*, Hans Brenner *(Schorsch Schmierer)*, Martin Sperr *(Ralth)*, Monika Baumgartner *(Rosa)*, Rolf Zacher *(Junior)*, Hu Bo *(Li)*, Lu Chuhlian *(Wang)*.

The place where the Chinese are coming in this German comedy is a small Bavarian town. The town's all-important factory shut its doors two years earlier when the owner refused to continue to battle the aggressive union. Now a Chinese concern has purchased the factory and a delegation has been sent to collect its machinery and transport it to China. Hube, the former union representative who had caused the old management so much grief, is sad to see the equipment leave but lends his expertise as the Chinese prepare it for shipment. Meanwhile, Brenner—Hube's friend and the father of his girl friend, Baumgartner—sets about trying to pilfer the machine that he worked on for so many years, hoping he can use it to establish his own business. So preoccupied are Hube and Brenner that they don't notice Baumgartner has begun to look to the Chinese to provide the love she has been missing.

p, Klaus Volkenborn; d, Manfred Stelzer; w, Manfred Stelzer, Ulrich Enzensberger; ph, David Slama; ed, Thorsten Nater; m, Rio Reiser.

Comedy **(PR:NR MPAA:NR)**

CHINESE GHOST STORY, A† (1987, Hong Kong) 98m Golden Princess/Cinema City c

Leslie Cheung *(Ling Choi Sin)*, Wong Tsu Hsien *(Lit Siu Seen)*, Wo Ma *(Monk Yin Chek Hsia)*.

Based on classic tales from Chinese literature, this particular ghost story brings Cheung to the doorstep of an allegedly haunted temple. There he meets and falls in love with Wong, a beautiful woman who, unbeknownst to Cheung, tried to kill him as he slept after his arrival. She is possessed by an evil spirit that perpetuates its eternal life by feeding off the men who are murdered by his soul-less minions. Wo, the temple's monk, was responsible for preventing Wong's attempt on Cheung's life, and now he comes to Cheung's rescue as he battles the evil spirit.

p, Tsui Hark; p, Claudue Cheung; d, Ching Siu Tung.

Horror **(PR:NR MPAA:NR)**

CHINNATHAMBI PERIYATHAMBI† (1987, India) Chemba Creations

Sathyaraj, Nadia, Prabhu, Sudha Chandran.

(In Tamil.)

d, Manivarnan; m, Ganagai Amaran.

Drama **(PR:NR MPAA:NR)**

CHIPMUNK ADVENTURE, THE**½ (1987) 76m Bagdasarian/Samuel Goldwyn c

Voices of: Ross Bagdasarian [, Jr.], Janice Karman, Dody Goodman, Susan Tyrrell, Anthony DeLongis, Frank Welker, Nancy Cartwright, Ken Samsom, Charles Adler, Philip Clark, George Poulos, Pat Pinney.

Some 30 years ago, Ross Bagdasarian, Sr. came up with a multi-million-dollar idea when he speeded up the voices on a record and called the creatures "the Chipmunks." The disc was made for Liberty and two of the characters are named after the top executives at that company. "Simon" is the namesake of Si Waronker and "Alvin" is named after Al Bennett. Since then, many records have been pressed, there has been a TV series, movies, etc. Ross, Sr. passed away and his son, Ross, Jr., has taken over, carrying on the family tradition with this animated feature, and the results are very good.

Dave Seville is being sent abroad on a business venture and the chipmunks are rankled because he hasn't asked them along and they have to stay in the care of an old lady. The boys are rock musicians (as in their TV show), always short of acorns and barely scraping out of trouble. The Chipmunks meet the Chipettes, a trio of femmes, and the two groups hassle over a video game as they argue about which of the groups is better at playing it. A female smuggler of precious stones comes upon them and thinks that they are just dumb enough to be perfect patsies. Unable to get through the rigors of Customs, she uses the animals as her couriers by placing the illegal gems in toy dolls and challenging the trios to a round-the-globe race. The team that girdles the earth first will take home a huge prize of $100,000. Along the way, their assignment is to deposit these dolls to prove that they have been to all the places on their itinerary. In actuality, this is the only sure way to get the stones delivered. Thus begins the animated version of AROUND THE WORLD IN 76 MINUTES as the trios visit climes far and wide, including Greece, Africa, Mexico, the Alps, the South Seas, Egypt, Rio, Bermuda, several places in Europe one finds on postage stamps, and even the Antarctic, where they bring a baby penguin back to its mother. In the end, the villains are defeated and a good time has been had by all.

The animation is nothing special but the music is better than most children's pictures and the voices, which include Dody Goodman, the amazing Frank Welker, and director Karman (who is also the cowriter with her husband), are excellent. The slick score includes: "Witch Doctor" (written by Ross Bagdasarian, Sr., who had another career as a songwriter and penned a number of tunes for the Chipmunks under his "nom de musique," David Seville), "Come On-a My House" (cowritten by Bagdasarian, Sr. with his cousin William Sarayan), "Diamond Dolls," (Elysee Alexander, Donna Wriss), "The Girls of Rock and Roll," (Terry Shaddick, Jay Levy), "Wooly Bully" (Domingo Samudio), and several others by composers Edelman, Randy Goldrum, Wriss, and Shaddick. Oddly, the tunes are, by and large, not aimed at children and the lyrics will be lost on the very audience to which they are appealing. Unfortunately, most of the drawings are herky-jerk, with none of the smoothness of Disney or even Don Bluth's THE SECRET OF NIMH. However, children of today, who have been brought up on the mediocrity of Saturday morning animation, won't notice the difference. It's a combination of adventure, comedy, music, and a fairly good geography lesson for children with a couple of sentimental moments tossed in to cloud the eyes. After almost three decades, nearly 40 million records sold, many awards and millions of fans, the Chipmunks show no signs of age and will probably be around long enough to have Ross Bagdasarian III to lead them.

p, Ross Bagdasarian [, Jr.]; d, Janice Karman; w, Janice Karman, Ross Bagdasarian [, Jr.]; m, Randy Edelman; prod d, Carol Holman Grosvenor; anim, Skip Jones, Don Spencer, Andrew Gaskill, Mitch Rochon, Becky Bristow.

Children's/Animation **(PR:AAA MPAA:G)**

CHKATULKA IZ KREPOSTI† (1987, USSR) 75m Azerbaidjanfilm/Sovexportfilm c (Trans: A Jewel Box from a Castle)

Kyamran Shakhmerdanov, Mikahil Kerimov, Ibragim Aliyev, Gasan Turabov.

In the village of Baku, school boys playing in some ruins find a valuable artifact. The treasure is stolen by a criminal and the boys help police track the man down.

d, Gulbeniz Azimzade; w, Svetlana Kazimova, Semyon Listov; ph, Alekper Muradov, Valery Kerimov; m, Rafik Aliyev; art d, Arif Abdurakhmanov.

Drama **(PR:NR MPAA:NR)**

CHOBOTNICE Z II. PATRA† (1987, Czech.) 92m Barrandov c

Dagmar Veskrnova *(Andrea)*, Pavel Zednicek *(Honza)*, Zaneta Fuchsova *(Eva)*, Milan Simacek *(Honzik)*, Miroslav Machacek *(George)*, Josef Blaha *(Porucik)*, Premsyl Koci *(Mefisto)*, Jaroslav Moucka *(Nekvasil)*, Vlastimil Brodsky *(Grandfather Holan)*, Ondrej Havelka *(Boda)*, Jaroslava Kretschmerova *(Jirina)*, Otto Simanek, Jirina Bohdalova, Frantisek Filipovsky.

[No plot information available.]

d, Jindrich Polak; w, Ota Hoffman, Jindrich Polak; ph, Emil Sirotek; m, Angelo Michajlov, Charles-Francois Gounod; ed, Dalibor Lipsky; art d, Jindrich Goetz; cos, Sarka Hejnova; anim, J. Vojta, Seishi Katto.

Children's **(PR:NR MPAA:NR)**

CHOCOLATE INSPECTOR† (1987, Hong Kong) 98m Michael Hui-Golden Harvest c

Michael Hui, Anita Miu, Ricky Hui, Michael Chow.

Popular actor-director Michael Hui follows HAPPY DIN DON, his 1986 variation on SOME LIKE IT HOT, with a slapstick comedy about a sweet-toothed policeman who is investigating the kidnaping of the child of a TV star. Hui plays the inspector whose longing for chocolate candy is never satisfied, and Anita Miu, actress and singer, plays Anita Miu, actress and singer. CHOCOLATE INSPECTOR was a box-office hit in its native Hong Kong.

p, Michael Hui; p, Raymond Chow; d, Philip Chan; art d, David Chan.

Comedy **(PR:NR MPAA:NR)**

CHORROS† (1987, Arg.) 82m Magia/Sentimientos c (Trans: Crooks)

Victor Laplace *(Pablo)*, Norberto Diaz *(Kaplan)*, Hugo Arana *(Traverso)*, Javier Portales *(Piaggio)*.

The second outing this year for the directorial team of Jorge Cosica and Saura, this comedy is a departure from their earlier collaboration, SENTIMIENTOS: MIRTA DE LINIERS A ESTANBUL, a political film about oppression and exile. Though based on the reality of Argentina's wildly fluctuating economy and the sort of creative but wholly illegal responses some banks have made to the crisis, CHORROS takes a light-hearted approach to the situation. When the higher-ups of a bank decide to stage a phony bankruptcy, some of the rank and file organize a heist. If the money doesn't exist, as the bank owners assert, then how can it be reported as stolen?

p, Guillermo Saura; d&w, Guillermo Saura, Jorge Coscia; w,Julio Fernandez Baraibar; ph, Salvador Melita; ed, Dario Tedesco, Liliana Nadal; m, Leo Sujatovich; cos, Monica Mendoza.

Comedy **(PR:NR MPAA:NR)**

CHOZE AHAVA† (1987, Israel) 90m The Lonely Spy Ltd c (Trans: The Love Contract)

Ika Zohar, Anat Atzmon, Shmuel Atzmon, Ravit Zohar.

Dan Wolman (NANA, THE DREAMER) directs this Israeli feature about the love that blossoms between a resort's pool maintenance and the daughter of the hotel's owner. This romance, however, is something of an artificial flower, as the maintenance man realizes when he learns the hotel owner has planned the whole thing.

p, Dan Wolman, Ehud Blieberg; d, Dan Wolman; w, Dan Wolman, Ehud Blieberg, Reuven Heker, Yair Harel; ph, Yossi Wein; ed, Shoshi Wolman.

Drama **(PR:NR MPAA:NR)**

CHRONICLE OF A DEATH FORETOLD† (1987, It./Fr.) 109m Italmedia-Soprofilms-Les Films Ariane-FR 3-RAI 2/Istituto Luce-Italnoleggio Cinematografico c (CRONACA DI UNA MORTE ANNUNCIATA)

Rupert Everett *(Bayardo San Roman)*, Ornella Muti *(Angela Vicario)*, Gian Maria Volonte *(Dr. Cristo Bedoya)*, Irene Papas *(Angela's Mother)*, Lucia Bose *(Placida Linero, Santiago's Mother)*, Anthony Delon *(Santiago Nasar)*, Alain Cuny *(Widower)*, Sergi Mateu *(Young Cristo Bedoya)*, Carolina Rosi *(Flora Miguel)*, Caroline Lang *(Margot)*, Carlos Miranda, Rogerio Miranda *(Pablo and Pedro Vicario, Twin Brothers)*, Silverio Blasi, Leonor Gonzales, Vicky Hernandez, Edgardo Roman, Lucy Martinez, Mariela Rivas, Yolande Garcia, Matilde Suescun, Gabriel Pazos, Isabel De Leon, Denis Julio, Carlos Varela, Pablo Soler, Maritza De Avila, Nelson Pineres, Dora Izquierdo, Lina Botero, Divo Cavicchioli, Cesar Fernandez, Arquimedes Erazo, Bienvenida Chamorro, Carmencita De Rizo, Bill Moore, Antonio De La Vega, Regulo Ahumada, Maria Elena Castro.

As he did in SALVATORE GIULIANO, director Franco Rossi reconstructs the events which combined to bring about a murder in this Italian-French coproduction based on a novel by Nobel Prize winner Gabriel Garcia Marquez. Set in a provincial Colombian river town, the story begins in the present as Volonte (THE DEATH OF MARIO RICCI, EBOLI), a doctor in his fifties, returns to his home after nearly 20 years to investigate a murder that occurred just before he left. In flashback, Everett (DANCE WITH A STRANGER, ANOTHER COUNTRY, DUET FOR ONE), the son of a wealthy general, visits the town in search of a bride and falls in love with the beautiful Muti. They wed, but soon after the ceremony, Everett discovers that Muti is not a virgin and returns his bride to her shamed family. Muti's father beats her until she names the man who deflowered her, Delon, a brazen young womanizer, who may or may not have actually compromised Muti. Her twin brothers, Carlos and Rogerio Miranda, are then honor-bound to make Delon pay for his indiscretion. The whole town knows what is about to happen, but no one warns Delon. Since Delon makes no attempt to escape the twins reluctantly kill him. Back in the present, Everett suddenly reappears and encounters Muti, bringing with him all of the unopened letters she has written to him since their separation those many years ago.

p, Yves Gasser, Francis Von Buren; d, Francesco Rosi; w, Francesco Rosi, Tonino Guerra (based on a novel by Gabriel Garcia Marquez); ph, Pasqualino de Santis (Panavision, Eastmancolor); m, Piero Piccioni; ed, Ruggero Mastroianni; md, Enrico De Melis; art d, Andrea Crisanti; set d, Mauro Passi; cos, Enrico

Sabbatini; makeup, Giuliano Laurenti, Maurizio Silvi, Federico Laurenti, Walter Cossu.

Drama **(PR:NR MPAA:NR)**

CHUZHIE ZDES NE KHODYAT† (1987, USSR) 76m Lenfilm/Sovexportfilm c (Trans: Aliens Are Forbidden)

Vladimir Basov, Yury Belyayev, Sergei Kozyrev.

A young and resourceful militia lieutenant tracks the clever thief who stole a large amount of money from a fishing collective.

d, Anatoly Vokhotko, Roman Yershov; w, Vladimir Valutsky, Pavel Finn; ph, Alexander Chechulin; m, Yefrem Podheiz; art d, Vladimir Kostin.

Crime **(PR:NR MPAA:NR)**

CHYORNAYA STRELA† (1987, USSR) Mosfilm/Sovexportfilm c (Trans: The Black Arrow)

Igor Shavlak, Galina Belyaeva, Leonid Kulagin, Algimantas Masyulis, Boris Khimichev.

[No plot information available.]

d&w, Sergei Tarasov (based on the novel by Robert Louis Stevenson); ph, Mikhail Ardabyevsky; m, Igor Kantyukov; art d, Alexander Kuznetsov.

Adventure **(PR:NR MPAA:NR)**

CIDADE OCULTA† (1987, Braz.) 74m Orion Cinema e Video/Embrafilme-Empresa Brasileiro de Filmes (Trans: Hidden City)

Carla Camurati *(Shirley Sombra)*, Arrigo Barnabe *(Anjo)*, Claudio Mamberti *(Ratao)*, Celso Saiki *(Japa)*.

A short feature which is set, like so many Brazilian crime films, on the streets of Sao Paulo against a backdrop of rape, murder, and drugs. This one tells the tale of prostitute Camurati and her ex-con lover Barnabe as they fight police chief Mamberti, a corrupt heroin addict. Heavy on car chases and gun play.

p, Wagner Carvalho; d, Chico Botelho; w, Chico Botelho, Arrigo Barnabe, Walter Rogerio; ph, Jose Roberto Eliezar; m, Arrigo Barnabe; ed, Danilo Tadeu; art d&cos, Ana Maria Abreu.

Crime **(PR:NR MPAA:NR)**

CINCO NACOS ASALTAN A LAS VEGAS† (1987, Mex.) 87m Victor Films/Peliculas Mexicanas c (Trans: Five Nerds Take Las Vegas)

Edwardo de la Pena *(Pelonchas)*, Sergio Ramos *(Chaquetas)*, Luis de Alba *(Babas)*, Sergio Corona *(Perrote)*, Guillermo Rivas *(Borras)*, Al Alvarez *(Peter McCabe)*.

OCEAN'S ELEVEN meets REVENGE OF THE NERDS in this south-of-the-border comedy in which five impoverished Mexican nerds stand in for the Rat Pack. Tired of their marriages and anxious to put some money where their wives mouths are, the *nacos* make an illegal crossing into the US and venture to the bright lights of Las Vegas to pull off a big heist. Lead by de la Pena (who also wrote the screenplay), they manage to rip off the Dunes Hotel, where the location shooting for the film took place. Several *naco* sequels are planned.

p, Victor Herrera, Salvador Barrajas; d, Alfredo B. Crevenna; w, Eduardo de la Pena; w, J.A. Rodriguez; ph, Juan Herrera, Pedro Ramirez; ed, Roberto Benet Portillo; m, Luis Alcaraz.

Comedy **(PR:NR MPAA:NR)**

CITY AND THE DOGS, THE*½** (1987, Peru) 144m Cinevista c (LA CIUDAD Y LOS PERROS)

Pablo Serra *(Poet)*, Gustavo Bueno *(Lt. Gamboa)*, Juan Manuel Ochoa *(Jaguar)*, Luis Alvarez *(Colonel)*, Eduardo Adrianzen *(Slave)*, Liliana Navarro *(Teresa)*, Miguel Iza *(Arrospide)*.

This often engrossing tale of shifting loyalties and revenge is set in the volatile world of a boys' military academy. The social castes within this rigidly structured society are seemingly unbreakable, and the boys look to Ochoa as their leader. Ochoa is a pockmarked, sneering individual who goes by the nickname "The Jaguar." With three other boys he forms "The Circle," a powerful unit which provides students with liquor, cigarettes, pornography, and test answers. Serra, not a member of The Circle, has found his niche by writing love letters and erotic stories for his classmates. For his creativity Serra has earned the nickname "The Poet." Finally there is Adrianzen, a weak and cowardly young man whom The Circle members refer to as "The Slave." Adrianzen is out of place within this closed society, with only Serra as his confidante. But Serra is not the loyal friend Adrianzen would like to believe. When Adrianzen cannot make a date with Navarro, a local girl he has spoken with once, he sends Serra to take his place. Serra begins seeing Navarro himself, but doesn't tell the love-struck Adrianzen. Ochoa has one of his flunkies steal some important test answers. When the crime is uncovered, Adrianzen becomes the scapegoat. After being confined to his quarters for five successive weekends, the boy finally cracks and fingers The Circle. Later, while the group is on maneuvers in a nearby mountainous region, Adrianzen is mysteriously shot in the back of the head. Serra, consumed with guilt over how he had treated the unhappy boy, is convinced Ochoa killed Adrianzen for being a snitch. Serra goes to Bueno, the brutal army official who oversees the boys' activities, and tells his commander what he knows. Bueno is at first disbelieving, but he puts Serra into protective custody before reopening the investigation into Adrianzen's death. Officials at the school, trying to avoid further scandal, attempt to squelch Bueno's new inquiry, though Ochoa is held for questioning. A surprise inspection on the barracks turns up the illegal items Ochoa had helped procure for the boys, and his friends are convinced Ochoa has snitched on them. Ochoa continues to deny he killed Adrianzen, while the pressure mounts on Bueno to turn up evidence or call off his investigation. Eventually it's decided that Ochoa is innocent, and Bueno is to be transferred to a new military post. Serra is called before the general in charge of the academy, where he is asked about his pornographic stories. Any of the boy's fleeting hopes of convicting Ochoa are dashed. The general tells Serra he should be expelled, though the boy will be given a chance to redeem himself. Serra is moved into Ochoa's cell, where the two engage in a violent struggle. When they return to the barracks Ochoa finds himself an outcast. Though he knows Serra informed authorities about student contraband, Ochoa refuses to dishonor himself by snitching. As Bueno walks through the gates leading out of the academy, he is confronted by Ochoa. Ochoa confesses to the murder, handing his former commander a written statement. Furious, Bueno tears this up, saying the investigation is over. Ochoa joins Serra a few yards away, and the two hardened students watch Bueno leave.

The portrayal of day-to-day military discipline is as unflinching as anything in the boot camp scenes of Stanley Kubrick's FULL METAL JACKET. Yet unlike Kubrick, director Lombardi does not make this a cold and sterile world. His opening sequence is a surrealistic nightmare, as students undergo their initiation into the academy's social structure. New cadets, dubbed "dogs" by senior students, are forced to wear canine-like paint on their faces while goaded into humiliating behavior by their seasoned peers. In the midst of this madness, one student sits in a circle of fire while another is hung upside down and beaten. Ochoa separates himself from the others by using his belt as a whip, defying anyone to touch him. It's a glimpse into an inferno, as Lombardi uses a few strokes to set his story. The ensemble is first rate, allowing an array of strong personalities to emerge without any one performance overshadowing another. Serra, Ochoa, and Bueno are particular standouts, each handling their difficult roles with an assured sense of self.

Though many ideas are explored in THE CITY AND THE DOGS, the film's most prominent theme deals with the multifaceted nature of honor. Each group or relationship is permeated by a strict code of behavior which condemns even the smallest violation. Lombardi contrasts the neo-fascism of The Circle with the more socially acceptable system of military authority. When Bueno defies his superiors he must be removed. The Circle, an equally unforgiving group, turns on their own leader when they suspect him of duplicity. On a more personal level, Serra's overwhelming guilt does not stop him from seeing Navarro or lying about this relationship to Adrianzen. As long as he can maintain a good cover, Serra chooses to internalize the problem rather than let the truth surface. By allowing these troubles to develop, Lombardi succeeds in giving a strong sense of underlying tension to his already emotionally charged events. The film was first released in Peru in 1985. *(Violence.)*

p&d, Francisco J. Lombardi; w, Jose Watanabe (based on the novel by Mario Vargas Llosa); ph, Pili Flores Guerra.

Drama **(PR:O MPAA:NR)**

CITY ON FIRE† (1987, Hong Kong) 98m Cinema City/Golden Princess c

Chow Yun Fat *(Ko Chow)*, Sun Yueh *(Inspector Lau)*, Lee Sau Yin *(Ah Foo)*.

Not unlike 1987's Charlie Sheen-D.B. Sweeney starrer NO MAN'S LAND, this film from Hong Kong tells the story of the tenuous, less-than-honest friendship that grows between Chow Yun Fat (A BETTER TOMORROW, DREAM LOVERS), an undercover cop, and Lee Sau Yin, one of the mob toughs he is investigating. Chow is given the assignment by Sun Yeuh when the undercover agent previously handling the task is murdered. Posing as an arms dealer, Chow infiltrates the mob's jewel theft operation, but not before he is checked out by Lee, whose trust and comradeship he wins.

p&d, Ringo Lam; w, Tommy Sham; ed, Sone Ming Lam; ph, Andrew Lam; m, Teddy Robin; art d, Luk Tze Fung.

Crime **(PR:NR MPAA:NR)**

CIZIM VSTUP POVOLEN† (1987, Czech./USSR) 72m Filmove Studio Gottwaldov-M. Gorkeho

Jana Palenickova *(Jana)*, Anton Samulejev *(Dimka)*, Vadim Chryckin *(Saska)*, Natalija Durovova *(Manager)*, Lubomir Lipsky *(Strycek Karel)*, Raisa Rjazanovova *(Polipovna)*, Oleg Popov *(Himself)*, Eva Jakoubkova, Miroslav Mejzlik *(Koudelkovi)*, Natalija Varlejova, Jevgenij Gerasimov *(Koroljovovi)*, Milena Marcilisova, Eva Matalova, Marcela Chlupova.

[No plot information available.]

d, Josef Pinkava; w, Valerij Karen, Milan Simek (based on a story by Valerij Karen); ph, Juraj Fandli; m, Zdenek John; ed, Ivan Matous; art d, Nikolaj Terechov, Petr Smola; cos, Nadezda Fadejevova.

Drama **(PR:NR MPAA:NR)**

CLIMB, THE† (1987, Can.) 90m Wacko/Cinetel-Cineplex Odeon c

Bruce Greenwood *(Herman Buhl)*, James Hurdle *(Dr. Karl Herrligkoffer)*, Kenneth Walsh *(Walter Frauenberger)*, Ken Pogue *(Peter Aschenbrenner)*.

Scripted and directed by Don Shebib, this Canadian adventure chronicles the 1953 attempt by a team of German and Austrian climbers to conquer Nanga Parbat, a 26,000-foot Himalayan titan. The expedition was lead by Dr. Karl

Herrligkoffer (Hurdle), whose half-brother was killed in a 1932 assault on the peak, and also included Herman Buhl (Greenwood), another renowned mountain climber. Tension builds throughout the film as a result of the constant clash of wills between Hurdle and Greenwood, each of whom is certain that only he knows the right way to approach the awesome ascent.

p, Wendy Wacko; d&w, Don Shebib; ed, Ron Wisman; ph, Richard Letterman; m, Peter Jermyn.

Adventure **(PR:NR MPAA:NR)**

CLUB DE RENCONTRES† (1987, Fr.) 98m T.Films-Films A2/AMLF c (Trans: Lonelyhearts Club)

Francis Perrin *(Nicolas)*, Jean-Paul Comart *(Bernard)*, Valerie Allain *(Cricri)*, Isabelle Mergault *(Bunny)*, Herma Vos, Blanche Ravalec, Caroline Jacquin, Leon Spiegelman, Katia Tchenko, Henri Guybet, Mike Marshall, Annie Jouzier.

French writer/director Michel Lang (THE GIFT, A NOUS LES GARCONS) serves up another of his patented sex comedies with this film focusing on the operator of a lonely hearts club. Francis Perrin (BILLY ZE KICK, CA N'ARRIVE QU'A MOI) plays the club operator, a ladies man who works his operation to his own advantage, satisfying himself with a shifting array of concubines while living a no-strings-attached existence. Eventually, however, he learns that, in the greater scheme of things, you can't love 'em and leave 'em.

p, Alain Terzian; d, Michel Lang; w, Michel Lang, Guy Lionel; ph, Daniel Gaudry; m, Michel Legrand; ed, Helene Plemiannikov; art d, Jean-Pierre Bazerolle.

Comedy **(PR:NR MPAA:NR)**

CLUB LIFE** (1987) 92m Tiger Prods.-Cineworld Ent./Troma Team c

Tom Parsekian *(Cal)*, Michael Parks *(Tank)*, Jamie Barrett *(Sissy)*, Tony Curtis *(Hector)*, Dee Wallace [Stone] *(Tilly Francesca)*, Ron Kuhlman *(The Doctor)*, Pat Ast *(Butch)*, Bruce Reed *(Punk)*, Kristine Debell *(Fern)*, Sal Landi *(Sonny)*, Robert Miano *(Ferd)*, Ron Gilbert *(Mace)*, Bleu McKenzie *(Button Man)*, Michael Aaron *(Ray the Bartender)*, Herb Abrams *(Chief Parking Attendant)*, Domenick Allen *(Disc Jockey)*, Gene Scott Casey *(Leather Friend)*, Ross Fenton *(Jewel Studded Kid)*, Kate Finlayson *(Brunette Fighter)*, Whip Hubley *(Herb, Parking Valet)*, Jay Arlen Jones *(Black Punk)*, Elizabeth Lamers *(Singer at Funeral)*, Barbara Powers *(Blonde Fighter)*, Yayonne Smith, Valerie Shaldene *(Girls at Racetrack)*, John Vidor *(Timmy)*, Charles Prior *(Waiter)*, Yana Nirvana, Lisa LeCover, Kimberlee Carlson *(The Butchettes)*, Michael Rooney, Nell Alano, Richard Sullivant *(Dancers)*.

After making a name for himself as a motocross racer in New Jersey, Parsekian decides to leave his racing career behind and hit the big time as an actor in Hollywood. It comes as no surprise that this young tough ends up in the seediest part of town, fending off leather-clad punks and drug dealers. He soon gets hired as a bouncer at a high-tech, neon-lit dance club run by Curtis, a former bouncer who has spent his whole life at the club. Learning the ropes from middle-aged head bouncer Parks, Parsekian fits right in at the club. He becomes like a son to Curtis and also gains the affections of Wallace, Curtis' likable but pathetic girl friend. Everybody warns Parsekian that "club life" can suck the life out of anyone who spends all his nights drinking and dancing. Things get rough at the club when Curtis is made an offer he can't refuse by a gang of drug-peddling mafiosos. Curtis refuses to sell, an act of defiance that gets Parks killed as a warning. In the meantime, Parsekian's former girl friend, Barrett, arrives on the scene and their romance is rekindled. Parsekian then learns that Barrett is involved with Kuhlman, one of the thugs who organized Parks' murder. Parsekian tries to leave the club, but is too devoted to Curtis. Later, when Curtis is gunned down by the same group of thugs, Parsekian realizes that there is no way out of club life. With Barrett on the back of his motorcycle, Parsekian heads out of Hollywood to find a better life.

Far from a realistic portrayal of life on the edge, CLUB LIFE does take an interesting approach to the subject. Rather than show how wonderful life can be in nightclubs, producer-writer-director Vane has painted a rather bleak portrait. There is no way out of the destructive, parasitic life-style Vane puts up on the screen—a fact that Parsekian has enough sense to realize. While much of the dialog is clumsy, the performances are compelling enough to hold the picture together. Parsekian plays his tough kid role as if he went to the James Caan School of Intimidation. As his mentor, Curtis does a fine job and makes the whole film worthwhile. Unfortunately his gutsy performance will go unseen by many, as CLUB LIFE came and went in barely the blink of an eye. Also notable is some glitzy art direction and an ingenious love scene between Parsekian and Barrett which is photographed through a clear goldfish-filled waterbed. The film drags considerably, however, due to an excess of carefully choreographed dance routines highlighted by some standard rock tunes. Songs include: "Inspiration" (Jack Conrad, Frank Musker, performed by Elizabeth Lamers), "Don't Close Your Eyes" (Richard Kerr, Musker, performed by Lamers), "My Opinion," "Nightshift" (Kim Tyler, performed by Urok), "First Class Male" (Andy Hill, Musker, performed by Lamers), "Club Life" (Trevor Lawrence, Musker, Lamers, performed by Dee Wallace), "Living on the Outside" (Michael Sembello, Musker, performed by Musker), "I Want to Stay in Love with You" (Jon Close, Musker, performed by Close), "I Can Hear Your Heartbeat" (Craig Bartack, performed by Bartack, Harlan Lansky), "Tough Guys" (Bartack, Lansky, performed by Bartack, Lansky), "Too Much Energy" (Dominic Bugatti, performed by Bugatti, Kara Noble), "Action" (David Harvey, Cynthia Manley, performed by Manley), "Only the Strong Survive" (Jack Conrad, Jay Levy, performed by Rainey), "Savage Streets" (Levy, Terry Shaddick, performed by Rainey). *(Nudity, sexual situations, excessive profanity, violence.)*

p,d&w, Norman Thaddeus Vane (based on a story by Norman Thaddeus Vane and Bleu McKenzie); ph, Joel King (CFI Color); m, Jack Conrad; ed, David Kern; md, Philip Moores; art d, Cynthia Sowder, Philip Duffin; set d, Sherry Dreizen, Michelle Hormel, Katherine Vallin; cos, Elisabeth Scott; ch, Denmon Rawles; m/l, Frank Musker, Elizabeth Lamers, Trevor Lawrence, Jack Conrad, Richard Kerr, Kim Tyler, Andy Hill, Michael Sembello, Jon Close, Craig Bartack, Dominic Bugatti, David Harvey, Cynthia Manley, Jay Levy, Terry Shaddick; makeup, Sher Flowers.

Crime/Drama **Cas.** **(PR:O MPAA:R)**

COBRA THUNDERBOLT† (1987, Thailand) Davian-Sunny-Saha Mongol c

Sorapong Chatri, Rapeepan Kornsakul.

The daughter of a brilliant military colonel takes on the Laotian army as she tries to rescue her kidnaped father—the inventor of the titled fighting machine.

p, Somsak Techaratanaprsert; d, Tanong Srichua.

Action **(PR:NR MPAA:NR)**

COBRA VERDE† (1987, Ger.) 110m ZDF-Ghana Film Industry/UGC-DEG c (Trans: Green Cobra; AKA: SLAVE COAST)

Klaus Kinski *(Francisco Manoel da Silva)*, King Ampaw *(Taparica)*, Jose Lewgoy *(Don Octavio Coutinho)*, Salvatore Basile *(Capt. Fraternidade)*, His Royal Highness Nana Agyefi Kwame II de Nsein *(Bossa Ahadee)*.

Civilization and primitivism clash once again in Werner Herzog's latest film. Kinski plays a poor 19th century Brazilian who is sent to the African coast to start up a slave trade. He is befriended by a volatile local king, amasses a great fortune, and fathers a brood of children, yet he still hopes to return to his native Brazil. When Kinski breaks with the king, he joins a revolutionary force begun by the king's brother, only to learn that he's been double-crossed. Released in Europe in 1987 and scheduled for a 1988 De Laurentiis (DEG) release in the US as THE SLAVE COAST.

p, Lucki Stipetic; d&w, Werner Herzog (based on *The Viceroy of Ouidah* by Bruce Chatwin); ph, Viktor Ruzicka, Thomas Mauch; m, Popol Vuh; ed, Maximiliane Mainka; prod d, Fabrizio Carola; cos, Gisela Stoch; makeup, Berthold Sack.

Adventure **(PR:NR MPAA:NR)**

CODA† (1987, Aus) 99m Genesis/Premiere Film Marketing c

Penny Cook *(Kate Martin)*, Arna-Maria Winchester *(Dr. Steiner)*, Liddy Clark *(Sally Reid)*, Olivia Hamnett *(Det.-Sgt. Turner)*, Patrick Frost *(Mike Martin)*, Vivienne Graves *(Anna)*.

Set on a college campus, this Australian nail-biter features a zoned-out professor (Winchester) who takes a page from Norman Bates' book, dressing as the brother she long ago killed. Her first on-campus victim is one of her students, but the prime suspect is the husband of Cook, one of the girl's friends. Before long, Hamnett, the investigating officer, is a dead woman. Cook and friend Clark are terrified they will be next, and are constantly on the lookout for the *man* behind these murders. After a brief theatrical release this one was made VCR compatible.

p, Terry Jennings; d, Craig Lahiff; w, Terry Jennings, Craig Lahiff; ph, David Foreman; ed, Catherine Murphy; m, Frank Strangio.

Thriller **Cas.** **(PR:NR MPAA:NR)**

CODE NAME ZEBRA† (1987) 94m Pac-West Cineman/Trans World c

Jim Mitchum *(Frank Barnes)*, Mike Lane *(Carmine Longo)*, Timmy Brown *(Cougar)*, Joe Donte *(Voce)*, Chuck Morrell *(Lt. Dietrich)*, Deanna Jurgens *(Julie)*, Lindsey Crosby *(Police Sergeant)*, Chris Costello *(Mrs. Noble)*, Frank Sinatra, Jr. *(Koslo)*, Charles Dierkop *(Crazy)*, George "Buck" Flower *(Bundy)*.

Another direct-to-video action film featuring the sons of Robert Mitchum, Frank Sinatra, and Jim Brown. The Zebra Force is an elite group of Vietnam veterans led by Brown who now combat crime throughout the world. When imprisoned mafia hitman Lane is released, he vows vengenance. The head of the mob, Donte, tries to dissuade Lane from his vendetta, but discovers that he cannot control the crazed hitman. The action climaxes in a bloody shootout involving the mob, the police, and the Zebra Force.

p, Joseph Lucchese; d, Joe Tornatore; w, Robert Leone; ph, Bill Dickson, Tom Denove; m, Louis Febre, Peter Rotter; ed, Ed Hanson.

Action **Cas.** **(PR:NR MPAA:NR)**

COERS CROISES† (1987, Fr.) 87m Incite-SEPT/Forum Distribution c

Caroline Loeb *(Paulette)*, Roger Mirmont *(Ferdinand)*, Julie Jezequel *(Tina)*, Laure Tran *(Marylou)*, Bernard Farcy *(Fano)*, Cecile Corre *(Lucie)*, Hammou Graia *(Hads)*, Anton Nicoglou *(Thomas)*, Tonie Marshall, Eric Do.

Written and directed by Stephanie de Mareuil, a French journalist trying her hand at filmmaking, COEURS CROISES is a loaf's worth of slices of life from an apartment house in Paris' red light district. French pop singer Caroline Loeb is featured.

p, Joel Santoni, Daniel Messere; d&w, Stephanie de Mareuil; ph, Helene Louvart; ed, Anne-Marie Hardouin; m, Vladimir Cosma.

Drama **(PR:NR MPAA:NR)**

COLD STEEL† (1987) 90m Cinetel c

Brad Davis *(Johnny Modine)*, Sharon Stone *(Kathy Connors)*, Jonathan Banks *(Iceman)*, Jay Acovone *(Cookie Manero, Johnny's Partner)*, Adam Ant *(Mick)*, Eddie Egan *(Lt. Hill)*, Sy Richardson *(Rashid)*, Anne Haney *(Anna Modine)*, Ron Karabatsos *(Fishman)*.

Dorothy Puzo, daughter of Godfather author Mario Puzo, made her feature film directorial debut with this cop thriller starring Brad (MIDNIGHT EXPRESS) Davis as a cop obsessed with finding the killer of his aged father. The killer, Banks, is a hideously scarred man who must speak through a voice-box in his throat. Aided by associates Ant and Richardson (one of director Alex Cox's regular players), Banks seeks revenge on Davis for an incident that occurred when both men were youths. It seems that Davis, Banks, and a friend were attacked by a vicious gang back when the cops were just cadets. The friend was killed and Banks suffered severe stab wounds in the face and throat, while Davis emerging unscathed. After many car chases, double-crosses, and shootings, Davis finally tracks down Banks and a showdown ensues. Released briefly in Los Angeles late in 1987, COLD STEEL will no doubt find new life on home video.

p, Lisa M. Hansen; d, Dorothy Ann Puzo; w, Michael Sonye, Moe Quigley (based on stories by Michael Sonye, Dorothy Ann Puzo, Lisa M. Hansen); ph, Tom Denove (Foto-Kem Color); m, David A. Jackson; ed, David Bartlett; art d, Maxine Shepard; set d, Scott Ambrose.

Crime **(PR:NR MPAA:R)**

COLOR OF DESTINY, THE*½** (1987, Braz.) 104m Nativa/Embrafilme c (A COR DO SEU DESTINO)

Guilherme Fontes *(Paulo)*, Norma Bengel *(Laura)*, Franklin Caicedo *(Victor)*, Julia Lemmertz *(Patricia)*, Andrea Beltrao *(Helena)*, Chico Diaz, Antonio Grassi, Anderson Schereiber, Antonio Ameijeiras, Marcos Palmeira, Paulinho Mosca, Anderson Muller, Duda Monteiro.

With THE COLOR OF DESTINY, Brazilian director Jorge Duran has created a sensitive portrayal of adolescent angst. Fontes is a teenager living in Rio de Janeiro with his parents, Bengel and Caicedo, the family having fled Chile for political reasons. Though faithful to his girl friend Beltrao, he is brokenhearted when he finally recognizes she has been engaged in an ongoing affair with their high-school art teacher. Fontes retreats to the privacy of his bedroom, where he creates experimental works of art. Fontes is burdened by the memory of an older brother who was tortured and killed for political activity in Chile. Fontes often confronts his late brother in dream sequences, while his parents worry that he will follow in their dead son's footsteps. Word comes from Santiago that Lemmertz, Fontes' 18-year-old cousin who was arrested by Chilean authorities during a demonstration, has been freed from prison. She is sent to her relatives in Brazil to recuperate from her experience, and is welcomed with open arms by her aunt and uncle. However, Fontes and Lemmertz develop a more antagonistic relationship. Still, Fontes can't help but admire his cousin for what she has undergone and slowly finds himself falling for her. Fontes finally realizes he must follow his brother's example by becoming involved in Chile's political turmoil. He asks his parents for permission to fly to Santiago, a request they repeatedly deny. Determined to take action, Fontes and Lemmertz plot an expression of their outrage toward the Pinochet government. Joined at the last minute by Beltrao, the teenagers go to Chile's Brazilian embassy under the pretense of obtaining information for a school assignment. Once inside, they make their way into an official's office and splash it with symbolic red paint. Fontes feels vindicated, and as an eight-year-old in a closing dream sequence, he finally is able to say goodbye to his older brother.

What makes this film work so well are the naturalistic performances by its teenaged leads. We feel Fontes' pain and frustration as he undergoes enormous psychological changes. Fontes creates a complex character who experiences myriad emotional difficulties. Fontes' guilt over his brother's death constantly bubbles beneath the surface before finally surfacing after Lemmertz's arrival. Fontes allows his feelings to slowly seep through, a fine achievement for an actor of his age. Lemmertz is another find, and Duran's casting of her must have been based as much on her physical appearance as her talent. Thin and baby-faced, she looks more like a 12-year-old than an 18-year-old, and when her features harden while Fontes questions her about the Chilean tortures, we know her innocent countenance hides a dark interior. That such a childlike woman should have suffered at the hands of her captors makes Lemmertz's ordeal all the more horrifying. Duran directs with great heart. He is sympathetic to these adolescents and never afraid to show his political leanings. The dream sequences are nicely integrated into the story, quietly revealing some of the terrible things plaguing Fontes. The last scene, in which Fontes finally is able to reconcile past and present, is a lovely moment that ties the film's themes together without forced sentiment. The parallel Duran creates between Fontes' emotional state and his artistic development is another good touch which speaks volumes in its simplistic presentation. This is Duran's debut feature as a director (following an apprenticeship as a screenwriter in the Brazilian film industry), and his ability to deal with multi-layered issues points towards a strong career behind the camera.

p&d, Jorge Duran; w, Nelson Natotti, Jorge Duran, Jose Joffily (based on a story by Jorge Duran); ph, Jose Tadeu Ribeiro (Eastmancolor); m, David Tygel; ed, Dominique Paris; set d, Clovis Bueno.

Drama **(PR:C-O MPAA:NR)**

COMEDY!*** (1987, Fr.) 82m Sara/Sara-CDF c (COMEDIE!)

Jane Birkin *(She)*, Alain Souchon *(He)*.

The third film pairing of director Doillon and his wife Birkin, COMEDY! is an intensely emotional story about relationships which delivers its serious subject matter in a somewhat comic tone. French pop star Souchon and Birkin star as lovers who go on holiday to Souchon's summer home in the south of France. Birkin, who has never been to Souchon's home, instantly becomes consumed by jealousy as she imagines all the women he previously entertained there. She has had only a few lovers, but has fantasized about many others. As their visit continues, the atmosphere grows more tense. They play out fantasy roles—a milkman, a prostitute, a busboy—to overcome their destructive jealousies. While Birkin holds contempt for Souchon's numerous past lovers, Souchon attacks Birkin's equally numerous fantasy lovers. Birkin and Souchon eventually come to terms and exorcise their past "ghosts" from the house as they profess their love for each other.

Like most of Doillon's pictures, the plot of COMEDY! is a slim one. Instead he concerns himself with the characterizations and emotional level of the performers. He is perhaps closest in style to John Cassavetes, with a touch of Eric Rohmer, which explains, unfortunately, why his films go unreleased in America. While the films of Cassavetes and Rohmer are the result of exhaustive improvisation, Doillon's are rigidly scripted. His scripts are so compelling, his characters so complex, and his direction so unpredictable that his films are able to exist with as little as two characters. At a time when most French directors are still imitating the high-tech visuals of Jean-Jacques Beineix's DIVA, the multi-textured script and emotionally charged performances of Doillon's films come as an inspired departure. Souchon is excellent as the perplexed recipient of Birkin's neurotic jealousy, but it is the magnificent Birkin (who never watches her own performances) who carries the weight of the film. She began her working relationship with Doillon (whom she later married) in 1981 in the controversial LA FILLE PRODIGUE (The Prodigal Daughter), in which she was cast as Michel Piccoli's mentally unstable daughter. The film outraged many in its exploration of a father-daughter relationship which revolves around jealousy, manipulation, and eventually incest. In 1984's LA PIRATE, Birkin played a distressed wife who finds that she is no longer attractive to her husband, but who tries to leave his control when a beautiful young woman (Marushka Detmers) falls in love with her.

In COMEDY! Doillon and Birkin, continue to explore the emotional limits of cinema. It is this sort of exploration which tends to alienate the audience. Since the performances often become uncomfortably intense, one is forced to withdraw from the film and create some distance from the characters on the screen. Doillon simultaneously repels and attracts, holding helpless viewers in his grip until they can tolerate no more. In COMEDY! this response would be impossible without Birkin, whose contribution to this film is more valuable than in the two previous pictures. Her character (simply called "She") is largely based on herself and was largely written by her. The film is undeniably autobiographical, and is even set in Birkin and Doillon's summer home. While Doillon's directing style appears loose and improvisatory, it is, in fact, just the opposite. In order to capture the sense of immediacy—the single moment of real life—that he discovers so miraculously on film, Doillon often goes through numerous takes. Doillon and his actors push the performance so far that the wall of artificiality breaks down and a rush of emotional intensity charges through. One such moment in COMEDY!—Souchon conversing with Birkin as she stands topless and covered in shampoo—took 91 takes and two days to shoot. As a result Birkin's skin turned raw and peeled, but a brilliant performance was put on the screen. Originally, COMEDY! was intended to be a more obvious comedy with a variety of characters entering and leaving Souchon's home. Instead Doillon ingeniously decided to let Birkin and Souchon play the other roles; however, they never play them so convincingly that the audience forgets they are playacting. Beautifully photographed by Lubtchansky and featuring an end-credits song sung by Souchon and Birkin, COMEDY! did little business in France, though it was shown in competition at the Venice Film Festival. Shown in the US as part of this country's first, and much deserved, Jacques Doillon retrospective. (In French; English subtitles.) *(Profanity, nudity, sexual situations.)*

p, Alain Sarde; d, Jacques Doillon; w, Jacques Doillon, Jean-Francois Goyet, Denis Ferraris; ph, William Lubtchansky (Eastmancolor); m, Philippe Sarde; ed, Catherine Quesemand; m/l, Alain Souchon (performed by Souchon, Jane Birkin).

Comedy/Drama **(PR:C-O MPAA:NR)**

COMMANDER LAMIN† (1987, Thailand) Davian-Sunny c

Dante Varona, Bonafe Estrella, Danny Rojo.

A war hero returns to his village and family to find violence and corruption. When the corrupt mayor tries to kill him, he fights back with the help of a group of guerrilla rebels.

p, Naty A. Almanza; d, Eddie Nicart.

Action **(PR:NR MPAA:NR)**

COMMANDO SQUAD** (1987) 89m Trans World c

Kathy Shower *(Kat Withers)*, Brian Thompson *(Clint Jensen)*, William Smith *(Morgan Denny)*, Robert Quarry *(Milo)*, Sid Haig *(Iggy)*, Mel Welles *(Quintano)*, Marie Windsor *(Casey)*, Benita Martinez *(Anita)*, Toni Nero *(Putita)*, Dawn Wildsmith *(Consuela)*, Ross Hagen *(Cowboy)*, Russ Tamblyn *(Anchor)*, Tang McClure *(Sunny)*, John Dresden *(Pilot)*, Dan Sanders *(Drug Runner)*, Jeff Hutchinson *(Red Neck)*.

When one drug agent after another disappears while investigating a cocaine factory in Mexico, there's nobody left to send but the toughest drug agent of them all, Shower. She doesn't want to take the job at first, but when she learns that her old boy friend is the latest missing agent, she skips her long-awaited vacation to head south. There she finds her arrival has been expected by the drug runners, led by Smith, a former colleague gone bad. She manages to elude them time and again, and retrieving a cache of arms and explosives sent down for her use, she locates the drug camp, rescues Thompson (who has had some of his teeth pulled out with a pair of pliers as torture), and blows up the whole operation. Smith gets his in a brutal fight in which he gets a special "vengeance knife" with a break-off handle filled with sulphuric acid shoved in his ribs. He falls down screaming with smoke coming out of his nose and mouth. After a nicely constructed and lit beginning in which Shower, dressed in leather and looking like a streetwalker, chases some drug dealers through a factory and nails them one by one, the film slows to a crawl until the final shootout, which is indistinguishable from a hundred scenes in a hundred movies just like it. Shower was a *Playboy* Playmate of the Year and acts like it, with most of her lines voiceover narration. After the first scene she takes off her black wig to reveal flowing blonde hair underneath, but when she goes to Mexico she apparently wears the wig all the time. Uncomfortable to say the least. Thompson shows even less talent and looks more like a lifeguard than a top drug agent. What the film does have going for it is a gang of B-movie stalwarts who are always welcome in trash like this. Smith, who got his start in biker movies, is one of the best villains in the business, and his sidekick Haig has a distinguished exploitation career going back to such memorable films as SPIDER BABY and BLACK MAMA, WHITE MAMA. Mel Welles, fondly remembered as Mushnik in Roger Corman's LITTLE SHOP OF HORRORS is on-hand as the corrupt and slovenly mayor of the Mexican village. Marie Windsor appears as the proprietor of a movie memorabilia shop who does a business in gunrunning on the side. Robert Quarry, best known as COUNT YORGA, is Shower's boss, and even Russ Tamblyn, of WEST SIDE STORY fame makes an appearance. Nothing especially redeeming about this explosion-filled actioner, but, if your taste runs to this sort of thing, nothing particularly damning, either. *(Violence, mild profanity.)*

p, Alan Amiel, Fred Olen Ray; d, Fred Olen Ray; w, David A. Jackson, James Saad, Tom Riparetti, Steve Le Gassick; ph, Gary Graver (Foto-Kem Color); ed, Kathie Weaver; art d, Corey Kaplan; spec eff, Kevin McCarthy, Sandy McCarthy.

Action **Cas.** **(PR:C MPAA:R)**

COMRADES*** (1987, Brit.) 180m Skreba-National Film Finance-Film Four Intl./Curzon c

Robin Soans *(George Loveless)*, William Gaminara *(James Loveless)*, Philip Davis *(Young Stanfield)*, Stephen Bateman *(Old Tom Stanfield)*, Keith Allen *(James Hammett)*, Patrick Field *(John Hammett)*, Jeremy Flynn *(Brine)*, Robert Stephens *(Frampton)*, Michael Hordern *(Mr. Pitt)*, Freddie Jones *(Vicar)*, Barbara Windsor *(Mrs. Wetham)*, Murray Melvin *(Clerk)*, Imelda Staunton *(Betsy Loveless)*, Amber Wilkinson *(Hetty Loveless)*, Katy Behean *(Sarah Loveless)*, Sandra Voe *(Diana Stanfield)*, Valerie Whittington *(Elvi Stanfield)*, Harriet Doyle *(Charity Stanfield)*, Heather Page *(Bridget Hammett)*, Patricia Healey *(Mrs. Brine)*, Shane Down *(Joseph Brine)*, Joanna David *(Mrs. Frampton)*, Trevor Ainsley, Malcolm Terris *(Gentlemen Farmers)*, Dave Atkins *(Mr. Frampton's Foreman)*, Collette Barker *(Frampton's Servant Girl)*, Michael Clark *(Sailor)*, Alex McCrindle *(Jailor)*, Jack Chissick *(Policeman)*, Sarah Reed *(Blonde Girl)*, Nicola Hayward *(Dark Girl)*, Mark Brown *(Legg)*, Sophie Randall, Emma Tuck *(Legg's Children)*, John Holman, Jan Holman *(Gypsy Band)*, Bevan James *(Escapologist)*, John Lee *(Juggler)*, Vanessa Redgrave *(Mrs. Carlyle)*, James Fox *(Norfolk)*, Arthur Dignam *(Fop)*, John Hargreaves *(Convict)*, Simon Parsonage *(Charlie)*, Lynette Curran *(Prostitute)*, Alex Norton *(Lanternist/Sgt. Bell/Diorama Showman/Laughing Cavalier/Mr. Wetham/Wollaston/Ranger/Tramp/Sea Captain/McCallumm/Silhouettist/Mad Photographer/Usher/Witch)*.

A meticulously detailed film set in the 1830s, COMRADES tells the story of the "Tolpuddle Martyrs," a group of English farm laborers who formed a union in the hope of winning higher wages and paid a high price for their victory. Soans is the spiritual leader of a Methodist congregation in the small rural community of southwestern England where the laborers are exploited by land owner Stephens and his overseer Melvin. Because of their meager wages Soans and his fellow workers are unable to sufficiently provide for their families. After visiting Hordern in Dorchester, Soans returns to Tolpuddle and founds a secret Society of Friends (in effect, a union). A meeting takes place between the workers and Stephens in which they are promised better pay, but when the time comes to collect it, their wages are even less. Led by Soans they begin a strike (to the strains of the traditional song "Eight Shillings a Week"). Before long, the six of them—Soans, Gaminara, Davis, Bateman, Allen, and Flynn—are charged with what amounts to sedition. Trade unionism is on the rise in Britain, but the landed gentry in Dorset still hold enough sway to see to it that "Tolpuddle Martyrs," as they come to be known, are sent to Australia for seven years. Down under, they are separated, with each enduring his own trials and travails. Soans is forced to make a 300-mile trek on foot to his job; Gaminara is luckier, working in the service of kindly sheep rancher Redgrave. Least fortunate is Allen, who is only in Australia because he has been mistaken for his brother. He has the misfortune of being caught after causing a accident that injures his master, and is sent to a penal colony. In Britain, the London-Dorchester Committee, spearheaded by the efforts of Hordern, has rallied tradesmen behind the Martyrs, and when the voice of the people becomes loud enough, they are repatriated. At a London rally celebrating their return, the names of the trades whose support has brought the Martyrs home are proudly called out in a show of working-class solidarity.

Director Douglas presents his story in painstaking detail. The work, domestic deprivation, and social and spiritual lives of the people of Tolpuddle are intricately captured. Before the *action* shifts to Australia, Douglas allows his scenes to unfold with extraordinary slowness. The camera patiently contemplates his carefully composed shots, providing a wealth of visual information about his characters and their lives. Much of the early dialog, too, seems designed to familiarize the viewer with the way these people interact. At 180 minutes, the film can feel as if it is progressing at soporific pace, but in many ways the slower first section, which allows the patient viewer to thoroughly immerse himself in the world of the Tolpuddle Martyrs, is more satisfying than the faster-paced, more dramatic occurrences in Australia. Nonetheless, this wealth of detail can become overwhelming and events within the narrative are not always clear. The historically faithful story, a cornerstone of the lore of British trade unionism, is compelling in itself, and it takes on even greater significance when considered in light of recent British history and the union bashing that has occurred under Thatcherism.

COMRADES also takes a different kind of historical approach. In offering a lanternist, one of the filmmaker's earliest ancestors, as the film's quasi-narrator, and including dioramas and other early entertainments accomplished in darkened rooms, Douglas invites the viewer to consider both history of the cinema and to ponder how the cinema treats history. The performances in COMRADES are strong, and though they are accomplished with an ensemble approach, Soans and Gaminara both deserve to be singled out. Fox is memorable in a small role, as is Redgrave, who, as the hardy sheep rancher with flyaway auburn hair, is as lovely as ever. COMRADES is not for everyone and the impatient need not apply, but those who are prepared to concentrate for 180 minutes (or least for most of that time) will come away from the film enriched. Filmed on location in Dorset and Australia, COMRADES was released in Britain in 1986 and received festival showings in the US in 1987. *(Violence.)*

p, Simon Relph; d&w, Bill Douglas; ph, Gale Tattersall (Technicolor); m, Hans Werner Henze, David Graham; ed, Michael Audsley; prod d, Michael Pickwoad; md, Hans Werner Henze; art d, Henry Harris, Derrick Chetwyn; cos, Doreen Watkinson, Bruce Finlayson; m/l, George Deacon; stunts, Peter Armstrong; makeup, Elaine Carew.

Historical **(PR:C MPAA:NR)**

CONCRETE ANGELS*½ (1987, Can.) 97m Brightstar-Leader Media Film/Shapiro-Academy Ent. c

Joseph Dimambro *(Bello Vecchio)*, Luke McKeehan *(Sean)*, Omie Craden *(Ira)*, Dean Bosacki *(Jessie)*, Derrick Jones *(Bullet)*, Rosemary Varnese *(Carla)*, Simon Craig *(Mick)*, Dion Farentino *(Gigi, Bello's Cousin)*, Joe Speciale *(Bozo)*, Andrea Swartz *(Sean's Sister)*, T.J. Criscione, Eric Herbert *(Boys)*, Tony Nardi *(Sal, Bello's Uncle)*, Monica de Santis *(Norma)*, Tom Maccarone *(Mr. Vecchio)*, Anna Migliarisi *(Mrs. Vecchio)*, Clare Barclay *(Miss Hutchins)*, Michael Lebovic *(Mr. Levinson)*, Cayle Chernin *(Mrs. Levinson)*, Terry Steele *(CHUK D.J.)*, Stephen Rusnak *(Ralphie)*, John Stocker *(Mr. Stock)*, Thomas Rickert, Ian Large *(Judges)*, Martin Donlevy *(Franklin)*, Greg Spottiswood *(Hospital Youth)*, George Hevenor *(Howie)*, Warren Van Evera *(Derelict)*, John Kemp, Pareg Chakravarti, Mike Cramer, Ron Kunhegyi, Mike Taylor *(Jimmy Duke & the Royals)*, Katya Ladan *(Mrs. Bielski)*, Vincent Dale *(Eddie)*, Sarah Chapple *(Girl in Pool Hall)*, Mark Benson, Greg George, Gary Grimes, Bob Miller *(Beatles' Voices)*, Ingrid Bower, Desmond Ellis *(Sean's Parents' Voices)*, Josie di Blasi, Rina di Blasi *(Twins)*, Michael Emmett *(Banana)*.

CONCRETE ANGELS, another entry in the well-worn "Troubled Teens Find Themselves Through Music" genre, tries really hard to approach something resembling significance. However its meandering plot, coupled with weak acting, makes this minor feature less than notable. It is summer, 1964, and teenagers all over Toronto are excited about the upcoming Labor Day concert The Beatles are giving at the Maple Leaf Gardens. To add to the anticipation, one local radio station is sponsoring a "Battle of the Bands" contest for local youth, with the winning group being allowed to open the show. Dimambro, a 14-year-old Italian kid from the proverbial wrong side of the tracks, desperately wants the chance to prove himself by opening for The Beatles, so he begins working with his friends on forming a band. Eventually he recruits McKeehan and Bosacki, then reluctantly takes in Craden as drummer. Craden is a nerdy Jewish kid, whom the others clearly dislike, though he does offer the back room of his father's hair salon as a rehearsal space. While the group rehearses, Dimambro tries to deal with the difficulties surrounding his everyday life. His father Maccarone, an immigrant farmer, doesn't understand Dimambro's yearnings, and dreams of his son getting an education. Meanwhile Dimambro continues to hang out at a pool hall run by his seedy uncle Nardi. Farentino, an older cousin, gets Dimambro a janitorial job at the hospital where she works, and introduces him to her pretty friend Varnese. Dimambro makes tentative courtship gestures towards Varnese, and continues rehearsing with his band. The boys make the semi-finals, but lose to a veteran older doo-wop group. The losers are given tickets for the concert as consolation, but Dimambro sells them. He and his friends join Jones, a local hood, the night The Beatles perform. Figuring the Toronto police will be concentrating on the concert, the boys burglarize the hospital where Dimambro works. The operation is nearly bungled, but the group manages to escape and return to Nardi's pool hall. After the others depart, Dimambro and McKeehan, sit and talk, then realize the new school year is to begin the next day.

Liconti accurately captures the look of the era, and keeps the story moving with his direction, but CONCRETE ANGELS never amounts to much. It begins as Dimambro and his pals fence stolen good to Nardi, then switches to a teacher castigating her class of slow learners, before finally settling down to its "Battle of the Bands" plot line. The opening vignettes hold some potential, but when the focus switches to the development of the band, CONCRETE ANGELS turns stale. Nardi, by far the film's best actor and most interesting character, is really wasted. He is the quintessential sleaze, using his teen-aged admirers for running illegal operations, as well as an occasional sexual encounter. He is thoroughly distasteful, yet fascinating, a credit to Nardi's acting skills. The youthful ensemble is another story. Dimambro and McKeehan strut about with moody demeanor, performing like wooden James Dean imitators. Craden is lifeless, while Varnese is a barely adequate love interest. Many of these kids, cast from Toronto high schools, were non-professional actors which becomes painfully obvious as the film goes on. They toss out their respective lines as if reading from cue cards.

For all its faults, CONCRETE ANGELS does have a terrific soundtrack featuring top songs from the early 1960s. Sound-alike groups provided cover versions of the original Beatles songs, and amazingly these reproductions sound like the genuine item. Songs include: "Not Fade Away" (C. Holley, N. Petty, performed by Blushing Brides), "Money (That's What I Want)" (Berry Gordy, J. Bradford, performed by 1964), "She Loves You," "From Me to You" (John Lennon, Paul McCartney, performed by Quasi Hands), "Love Me Do," "Misery," "P.S. I Love You," "A Hard Day's Night," "I Saw Her Standing There" (John Lennon, Paul McCartney, performed by 1964), "Johnny B. Goode" (Chuck Berry, by Berry), "(The) Loco Motion" (Gerry Goffin, Carole King, performed by Little Eva), "Will You Still Love Me Tomorrow?" (Gerry Goffin, Carole King, performed by The Shirelles), "Runaround Sue" (E. Maresca, D. DiMucci, performed by Dion), "One Fine Day" (Gerry Goffin, Carole King, performed by The Chiffons), "Mr. Bass Man" (John Cymbal, performed by Quasi Hands), "Twist and Shout" (P. Medley, B. Russel, performed by 1964), "Big Town Boy" (Rambeau Rehak, performed by Shirley Matthews).

p, Anthony Kramreither, Carlo Liconti; d, Carlo Liconti; w, Jim Purdy; ph, Karol Ike; ed, John Harding; art d, Tom Doherty; m/l, C. Holley, N. Petty, Berry Gordy, J. Bradford, John Lennon, Paul McCartney, Chuck Berry, Gerry Goffin, Carole King, E. Maresca, D. DiMucci, John Cymbal, P. Medley, B. Russel, Rambeau Rehak; makeup, Janine Fleet.

Drama **Cas.** **(PR:C-O MPAA:R)**

CONSEIL DE FAMILLE (SEE: FAMILY BUSINESS, 1987)

CORRUPCION† (1987, Mex.) 87m Peliculas Mexicanas c (Trans: Corruption)

Eduardo Loys *(Dr. Antonio Arenas)*, Abril Campillo *(Virginia Arenas)*, Carmen Salinas *(Jesusa)*, Pedro Infante Jr. *(Valentin Bravo)* Alberto Rojas [Caballo] *(Uncle Rene)*, Rafeal Inclan, Rosita Bonchot, Charito Granados, Lucy Gallardo, Ana Luisa Peluffo, Gustavo Rojo.

Life in the big city is the great corruptor in this film about a widowed physician who leaves his quiet rural existence to accept a position at a hospital in Mexico City. Accompanying the doctor (Loys) is his daughter, Campillo, for whom the big move proves to be disastrous. She deserts her true-blue fiance (Infante) and falls into a relationship that results in pregnancy and an abortion. Meanwhile, Loys accepts a bribe and gives his seal of approval to an unproven drug, the same drug that eventually kills his daughter.

d, Ismeal Rodriguez; w, Ismeal Rodriguez, Ricardo Gariby; ph, Fernando Colin; m, Ernesto Cortazar.

Drama **(PR:NR MPAA:NR)**

CRAZY BOYS½** (1987, Ger.) 89m Horizont Film/Export Film Bischoff & Co. c

Barbara Fenner *(Sigrid)*, Albert Heins *(Theo)*, Udo Schenk *(Hans)*, Zacharias Preen *(Erich)*, Mehmed Yandirer *(Abdull)*, Axel Tudsen *(Willy)*, Marianne Sagebrecht *(Frl. Hermann)*, Isolde Barth *(Frau Leinen)*, Angie Stardust *(Elvira)*, Domenica Creco *(Countess)*, Karina Fallenstein *(Her Daughter)*, Pierre Wendt *(Alfons)*, Rita Werner *(Frl. Blei)*, Marcel Bijou *(Gigi)*, Sugar *(Dodo)*, Margit Symo, Hannelore Wust *(Ladies)*, Uwe Strumpel *(Registrar)*, Detlef Theune *(Photographer)*.

This film has an offbeat premise but CRAZY BOYS never quite fulfills its eccentric intentions. Owners of a bar in Hamburg, hoping to increase cash flow, decide to change their property from a transvestite bar to a male strip-tease joint

for a female clientele. Fenner, the bar's manager, enlists her sophisticated friends Barth and Werner to help select from the applicants auditioning for the four spots. Also chosen as a judge is Sagebrecht (the star of SUGARBABY), a heavy-set and lonely pet shop employee with a good heart. They select Preen, a handsome blond student; Heins, a muscular deaf-mute; Yandirer, a dark young Turk; and Schenk, Fenner's roguish boy friend. The bar, renamed "The Crazy Boys" after the dancing quartet's moniker, is soon doing big business. Eager women gladly stuff money into the strippers' jockstraps, and, for the right price, a customer can do more than just watch. For 100 marks, a customer can see her choice of the four in a back room; for 150 marks he's hers to take home. Preen is bought by a wealthy, middle-aged countess (Creco) and taken to her posh estate on the outskirts of Hamburg. Preen struts about, thinking he's about to be seduced, but Creco has bought the boy for her daughter, Fallenstein, a pretty teenager who has become catatonic as the result of an accident. Creco brings Preen to her home time and time again, hoping to bring Fallenstein back to normal. Sagebrecht becomes a steady buyer as well. She turns her affections to Yandirer, who comes to love his purchaser as well. However when Yandirer decides to get married so he can remain in Germany, he weds a crass young woman who is only going through the ceremony for the money. Sagebrecht is crushed, and tries to kill herself. Yandirer finds her unconscious, revives her and begs for forgiveness. Another figure in the club is Stardust, an aging black cabaret artist who acts as a sort of sluttish mother-figure for everyone around. She must deal with her own failed ambitions, while she watches the young boys rising to a glory she has never known. Meanwhile Fenner grows jealous as Schenk quickly becomes well versed in his new craft. His popularity with The Crazy Boys' clients proves to be too much for Fenner, and she begins spiking his drinks with a chemical that decreases his ability to maintain erections. Schenk eventually realizes what's going on and accuses Fenner of being involved with Tudsen, the club's owner. He decks Tudsen, then walks out of the door and Fenner's life. In the final sequence, The Crazy Boys have taken on a new color. Heins, Preen and Yandirer are still dancing away, but they're joined in the review by newcomers Tudsen and Fenner.

This is a film loaded with potential, yet director Kern never explores his material below the surface. Characters are introduced, then shunted off as the film goes merrily onto the next episode. This is more than a little frustrating, for CRAZY BOYS is chock full of energy and good feelings. The story of Yandirer and Sagebrecht is by far the most interesting, but Kern never quite makes it clear why the Turk chooses to marry a hired bride rather than the woman he loves. Still, Yandirer and especially Sagebrecht are enormously appealing, and their chemistry overcomes the story weaknesses. The relationship between Preen and Fallenstein is another under-developed situation. Preen gradually brings the girl out of her shell, but just how this is accomplished is never made clear. Many of the scenes between the pair are cut off before coming to a natural conclusion. CRAZY BOYS is at its best when it focuses on these people. His ending is much too abrupt, leaving several plot strings unresolved.

Kern, who has appeared in such German films as OUR HITLER and FRANCESCA, based his story on some of his real-life encounters in Hamburg. The film was shot at its namesake bar, which is a haven for tourists, transvestites, and night creatures looking for a wild time. Made for only $200,000, Kern shot the production in a rapid 16 days. Though CRAZY BOYS' slick look belies the budget and schedule, Kern's speed undoubtedly led to the superficial treatment he gave his subject.

p, Heinz Diego Leers; d&w, Peter Kern; ph, Eberhard Geick; m, Franz Plasa; ed, Ina Rasche; art d, Detlef Theune; ch, Angie Stardust.

Comedy **(PR:O MPAA:NR)**

CRAZY LOVE (SEE: LOVE IS A DOG FROM HELL, 1987, Bel.)

CREEPOZOIDS† (1987) 71m Titan/Urban Classics c

Linnea Quigley *(Bianca)*, Ken Abraham *(Butch)*, Michael Aranda *(Jesse)*, *Richard Hawkins (Jake)*, Kim McKamy *(Kate)*, Joi Wilson *(Scientist)*.

Another ALIEN-inspired monster movie, this time set in 1998 after a nuclear holocaust. Seeking to avoid the acid rain which is falling throughout the land, five US Army deserters take shelter in a science lab. Unfortunately, a giant monster lurks in the shadows and feasts on the hapless defectors. As it turns out, the monster is a female scientist who has mutated into something resembling a giant beetle and at the climax she/it gives birth to a baby monster. CREEPOZOIDS received a quick theatrical release before going to videocassette earlier in 1988.

p, David DeCouteau, John Showalter; d, David DeCouteau; w, Buford Hauser, David DeCouteau; ph, Thomas Calloway; ed, Miriam Preissel; m, Guy Moon.

Horror **Cas.** **(PR:NR MPAA:R)**

CREEPSHOW 2* (1987) 89m Laurel/NW c

Lois Chiles *(Annie Lansing)*, George Kennedy *(Ray Spruce)*, Dorothy Lamour *(Martha Spruce)*, Tom Savini *(The Creep)*, Domenick John *(Boy Billy)*, Frank S. Salsedo *(Ben Whitemoon)*, Holt McCallany *(Sam Whitemoon)*, David Holbrook *(Fatso Gribbens)*, Don Harvey *(Andy Cavenaugh)*, Paul Satterfield *(Deke)*, Jeremy Green *(Laverne)*, Daniel Beer *(Randy)*, Page Hannah *(Rachel)*, David Beecroft *(Annie's Lover)*, Tom Wright *(The Hitchhiker)*, Richard Parks *(George Lansing)*, Stephen King *(Truck Driver)*, Joe Silver *(Voice of the Creep)*, Dan Kamin *(Indian)*, Philip Dore *(Curly)*, Maltby Napoleon, Tyrone Tonto *(Indians)*, Deane Smith *(Mr. Cavenaugh)*, Shirley Sonderegger *(Mrs. Cavenaugh)*, Chere Bryson *(Woman At Accident)*, Gordon Connell, Marc Stephan Delgatto, Jason Late, P.J. Morrison, Brian Noodt, Clark Utterback *(Animation Voices)*.

Reviewed variously at 89 minutes, 90 minutes, and 92 minutes, one realizes the running time matters naught if the picture has any quality. This is a very long hour and a half and is one more feeble attempt to turn Stephen King's stories into films. Only a few have made it to the screen with any style and the memory of CARRIE, SALEM'S LOT, and THE SHINING triumphs over such duds as this, THE SILVER BULLET (directed by King), CUJO, CHRISTINE, and FIRESTARTER. In this film, based on one published story by King and two others that remained deservedly unpublished, very little of merit can be found.

The first tale, "Old Chief Wood'nhead," is about a cigar store Indian that comes to life. The Indian, played by mime Dan Kamin, awakens in order to avenge the murders of Kennedy and Lamour, who are a sweet Southwestern couple running a general store in a small, desiccated town. He does this by removing one killer's scalp, among other things. Lamour, who hadn't made a feature film in almost two decades and whose last TV appearance was more than 10 years ago in a TV film, dies almost before we can see what she looks like. It is a particularly gory death scene, using special "blood tubes" placed strategically under her dress. According to Lamour, it required several takes and when she got home, she couldn't remove her underthings because they were stuck to her body with all the goo. She had to shower several times in her lingerie in order to peel off the bra and pantyhose.

Story number two, "The Raft," is the only one that saw print. Hannah, Satterfield, Beer, and Green are a quartet of pot-smoking teenagers who attend college. They swim to a raft in the middle of a lake and are attacked by a large black glob of goop. It's an oil slick with a mind of its own. Two survive the rigors of the night and when dawn breaks, the remaining boy is overcome with terminal hots and begins to caress the girl just as the carnivorous black creature emerges to wreak the final havoc.

The last story, "The Hitchhiker," has Lois Chiles as a cheating wife who pays her lover for her pleasure. She is returning from a tryst and hits a black hitchhiker, Wright, who then survives and keeps popping up again, causing her to have to kill him several times. In the end, she dies of carbon monoxide poisoning in her own garage.

The segments were filmed in Arizona (first and second) and Maine. Years ago, E.C. Magazines published a comic called "Creepshow" and the first of the movies borrowing the title did fair business (about $11 million in the US alone), thus spawning this sequel. It was a far better film with suspense, some violence, and several laughs. King and Romero (famous for NIGHT OF THE LIVING DEAD) would seem to be a perfect blend of talents for this genre but it may have been a case of "too many cooks." That plus the fact that Gornick was making his directorial debut after a career as a cinematographer which included the first CREEPSHOW. Appearing as the Creep again is Savini, with a superb makeup job. Both pictures utilized weak animation to tie things together and the cartooning here isn't any better than it was the first time around. (Credit Rick Catizone for that . . . or discredit him.) King does a cameo in the final sequence as a truck driver. Segment one was made in the town of Humboldt, segment two at Great Basin Lake near Prescott, and the animation was drawn in Pittsburgh, Romero's longtime base. The picture cost about $4 million all told, most of it wasted. The movie did about $4 million in business the first week but word of mouth dropped it to $2 million the second week and that means it will have to sell a lot of videos to break even. When interviewed recently, King was asked how he compared his work with that of equally prolific Joyce Carol Oates. King remarked that it was impossible to compare the two. She wrote good stuff. "I write salami," added King. "There are all different kinds of salami, good and bad. I happen to write good salami, but it's still salami." Unfortunately, CREEPSHOW 2 is baloney. *(Gore effects, profanity, sexual situations.)*

p, David Ball; d, Michael Gornick; w, George A. Romero (based on stories by Stephen King); ph, Dick Hart, Tom Hurwitz (Technicolor); m, Les Reed, Rick Wakeman; ed, Peter Weatherly; prod d, Bruce Miller; cos, Eileen Sieff; stunts, Taso N. Stavrakis; anim, Rick Catizone; makeup, Howard Berger, Ed French.

Horror **(PR:C-O MPAA:R)**

CRIME OF HONOR* (1987, Ger.) 95m Channel 4/Academy Home Ent. c

David Suchet *(Stephen Dyer)*, Maria Schneider *(Madeline Dyer)*, Anne-Marie Blanc *(Meman)*, Reinhard Glemnitz *(Weipel)*, Georges Claisse *(Dulourd)*, Deitmar Schonherr *(Junger)*, Robert Freitag *(Meser)*, Michael Gempart *(Ehrill)*, Jurgen Brugger *(Dr. Bauer)*, Giovanni Vettorazzo *(Sencini)*, Manfred Reddemann *(Henze)*, Inigo Gallo *(Captain)*, Ernst Schroder *(Herr Directer)*, Brigitta Furgler, Frank Lehart, Sebastian C. Schroder, Rudolf Ruf, Siegfried Kernen, Fritz Hamner, Laura Jansen, Vincent Jensen.

This tale of corporate espionage, originally shown in England in 1985, opens with Suchet (best known as Sean Penn's Russian contact in THE FALCON AND THE SNOWMAN) as a high-ranking official for an international pharmaceutical company. Having seen gross ethical violations by his employers while stationed in South America, Suchet decides he can no longer work for such a corrupt organization. He begins supplying authorities with information which implicates the company in illegal business practices. This coincides with Suchet's pending retirement from the company, as he now plans to raise pigs on a farm in Italy. His wife, Schneider, breaks down at a farewell party when she realizes she is going to be the wife of a pig farmer, but eventually she comes to accept Suchet's choice. While returning from Italy for the Christmas holidays, Suchet is detained by a border guard. He is informed that he's wanted for questioning, though Schneider and their children are free to go. Like Joseph K. in Franz Kafka's *The Trial*, Suchet is held without ever being charged and denied the opportunity to call an attorney. Gradually it's learned that his former employer is using its political connections to take revenge on Suchet. Schneider is told she won't see her husband for 20 years, and the woman kills herself. Suchet is not allowed to attend Schneider's funeral, but eventually he is released through the efforts of an attorney who had been contacted by Schneider before her death. But Suchet's former employer is not finished. Flashing forward to his post-trial life, Suchet holds a press conference explaining his side of the story. He has lost everything: his job, his farm, and his wife, and is heavily in debt. Though morally on the side of justice, Suchet has paid a hard price for following his conscience.

The story unfolds very slowly which results in a deadly boring film. It doesn't take much to figure out what's going on long before it's revealed. One keeps waiting for the story to catch up with the audience, but CRIME OF HONOR just never comes together. It's a suspense film lacking any real tension, a problem Goldschmidt never attempts to alleviate in his stagnant direction. Although Suchet is good in the lead, the majority of the ensemble is cold and bloodless, giving machine-like performances. Schneider has come a long way from LAST TANGO IN PARIS and THE PASSENGER. Though she still has an intriguing face, Schneider simply spends the majority of her scenes looking sad and confused. Her rapport with Suchet is nonexistent, thus giving little credibility to her desperate actions. *(Nudity, adult situations.)*

d, John Goldschmidt; w, Peter Prince; ph, Wolfgang Treu; m, Carl Davis; ed, Richard Key; md, Carl Davis; art d, Ingo Togel, Max Stubenrauch, Mathias Matthies; cos, Regina Batz; makeup, Gerlinde Kunz.

Drama **Cas.** **(PR:O MPAA:NR)**

CRITICAL CONDITION*½ (1987) 99m Par c

Richard Pryor *(Eddie)*, Rachel Ticotin *(Rachel)*, Ruben Blades *(Louis)*, Joe Mantegna *(Chambers)*, Bob Dishy *(Dr. Foster)*, Sylvia Miles *(Maggie)*, Joe Dallesandro *(Stucky)*, Randall "Tex" Cobb *(Box)*, Bob Saget *(Dr. Joffe)*, Garrett Morris *(Helicopter Junkie)*.

The vital signs are fluctuating, the prognosis is poor. CRITICAL CONDITION is far more than critical, it's verging on being fatal, unless the viewer happens to be a diehard Richard Pryor fan and thinks the actor can do no wrong. After JOJO DANCER, YOUR LIFE IS CALLING, BREWSTER'S MILLIONS, and THE TOY, Pryor's own critical capabilities could have been questioned when it came to choosing material. Then he signed on to do this and if there are such things as "movie malpractice" lawyers, they should have been called in. Pryor is an eccentric businessman with grandiose ideas. When he needs a loan for the construction of a cineplex, he can't secure the money in the normal fashion and thus must consult a loan shark. He might know better than to do business with the bent-nose boys. Suddenly, he is smack-dab in the middle of a police "sting" operation, is arrested and tossed into prison, which is a fate that might seem better than having to deal with the mob. When he sees that he might spend some long period of time inside the walls of the Graybar Hotel, Pryor decides to fake insanity and he is so convincing that he is taken to a New York hospital for the insane. Once there, he makes friends with all the loonies in the psycho ward. Then fate (or script contrivance) takes a hand and there is a total blackout which allows Pryor to escape. Another quirk of fate has him meeting Ticotin (you might recall her from FORT APACHE, THE BRONX), a hospital administrator. She thinks Pryor is an emergency room physician and presses him into service. Pryor goes along with her mistaken impression. During the blackout, the nuts have taken the hospital chief as a hostage. After the man escapes from their clutches, he blows the whistle on Pryor and wants him arrested. But by this time, Pryor has ingratiated himself with everyone else in the hospital, including macho, hip orderly Blades, drug addict Morris, and behemoth psychotic Cobb (the former heavyweight boxer). Pryor covers himself with glory when he captures escaped killer Dallesandro, the long-time Andy Warhol leading man. In the end, Pryor is forgiven by the administrator who destroys the official records and the hero is free to leave.

The picture is predictable and the fault lies in the hands of the brothers Hamill, who teamed to write the script. The jokes are feeble and tasteless, such as the moment when Pryor is given a pair of rubber gloves and told his assignment is to "unclog" a heavy-set dowager's constipated condition. Since Pryor has become a star, a new person, Eddie Murphy, came on the horizon to eclipse him, and Pryor takes a subtle shot at Murphy in this film by singing a bit of a Murphy tune "Party All the Time." Blades, who holds a Harvard degree in international law, shows that he is just as good an actor as he is an attorney and Mantegna turns in a fine performance, but the scene stealer is Dishy, who is hilarious as a medical man with a mania for malpractice. Englishman Apted (COAL MINER'S DAUGHTER) does not show much comedy pacing and many of the jokes lay there like an athlete in traction. Miles is the head nurse, as nuts in her own way as the patients, and any hospital with a boss like Miles is in trouble from the start. And so was this movie. The Hamills previous screen credit was on TURK-182, an equally sappy story that attempted (as did this) to update the Capra "little guy triumphs" theme. The advertising called this "A Comedy Of Epidemic Proportions." It's an epidemic you may want to avoid. *(Language).*

p, Ted Field, Robert Cort; d, Michael Apted; w, Denis Hamill, John Hamill (based on a story by Denis Hamill, John Hamill, Alan Swyer); ph, Ralf D. Bode (Technicolor); m, Alan Silvestri; ed, Robert K. Lambert; prod d, John Lloyd; set d, George Robert Nelson; cos, Coleen Atwood.

Comedy **Cas.** **(PR:C MPAA:R)**

CRONACA DI UNA MORTE ANNUNCIATA (SEE: CHRONICLE OF A DEATH FORETOLD, 1987, It./Fr.)

CROSS† (1987, Fr.) 85m Cinemas-Cinema 5/AAA c

Michel Sardou *(Thomas "Cross" Crosky)*, Roland Giraud *(Eli Cantor)*, Patrick Bauchau *(Simon Lenhardt)*, Marie-Anne Chazel *(Catherine Crosky)*, Stephane Jobert *(Jacques Kester)*, Maxime Leroux *(Sandro)*.

When his daughter and former wife are abducted, a vengeful cop does more than take the law into his own hands: he puts it into the hands of a professional hit man. French singer Michel Sardou makes his film debut as the cop in this first-time directorial effort by screenwriter Philippe Setbon.

p, Andre Djaoui; d&w, Philippe Setbon; ph, Jacques Steyn; m, Michel Goglat; ed, Nicole Lubtchansky.

Crime **(PR:NR MPAA:NR)**

CROSS MY HEART**½ (1987) 96m UNIV c

Martin Short *(David)*, Annette O'Toole *(Kathy)*, Paul Reiser *(Bruce)*, Joanna Kerns *(Nancy)*, Jessica Puscas *(Jessica)*, Lee Arenberg *(Parking Attendant)*, Corinne Bohrer *(Susan)*, Jason Stuart *(Waiter)*, Shelley Taylor Morgan *(Woman in Restaurant)*, Michael D. Simms *(Stud)*, Eric Poppick *(Maitre d')*, Lori Hall *(Woman Outside Restaurant)*, Mary Gillis *(Cashier)*, Patty Regan *(Waitress)*, Marti Muller *(Girl in Car)*, David Nail *(Convenience Store Clerk)*.

Short is a sunglasses salesman who has just been fired. O'Toole is a single mother who has been "around the track" a few times. CROSS MY HEART opens as both prepare themselves for the all-important third date—a date which will determine whether their relationship will become serious. Unfortunately, their relationship has been founded on a series of lies and deceptions which threaten to catch up with both of them. O'Toole is hiding the fact that she smokes and that she has a 7-year-old daughter. Short, who has been bragging about an imminent promotion, has just been fired. Rather than call off the date, Short borrows his friend Reiser's new car and swanky apartment and intends to pass them off as his own. At dinner, however, the car is stolen. Although she is not yet ready to commit to a sexual relationship with Short, O'Toole agrees to go back to his place out of sympathy over the stolen car. After some strenuous attempts at seduction (and lots of hasty explanations as to why he seems a bit disoriented in his own apartment), Short finally persuades the wary O'Toole to go to bed with him. After much nervousness, self-consciousness, and a brief safe-sex lecture

(this must be the first film where a man actually uses a condom), Short and O'Toole indulge in a bit of carnal knowledge. Although fireworks do not go off for either of them, they both agree that it was pleasant enough and look forward to better sex together. But their post-coital bliss is shattered when the phone rings and Reiser's voice comes from the answering machine. Before Short can figure out how to shut off the machine, the caller leaves a message for Reiser bemoaning the fact that Short has lost his job. The truth revealed, Short makes a partial confession regarding his career, but still maintains the illusion that the apartment and car are his. O'Toole feels sorry for Short and decides to stay the night and comfort him. She goes to another phone and calls her sister (who is baby-sitting) to inform her that she won't be coming home. Short eavesdrops and confronts O'Toole about her daughter. While they argue about the various deceptions that have been revealed over the course of the date, Reiser walks in. Short and Reiser clumsily try to act as if Reiser has the wrong apartment, but O'Toole is wise to them and storms out. Short follows her and tries to patch things up while she calls a cab from a pay phone in a nearby restaurant. To their amazement, Reiser's stolen car pulls up to a convenience store and the thief goes in to buy a six-pack. Quaking with fear, Short confronts the man and, to his amazement, gets the keys back. Impressed by his bravado, O'Toole allows Short to drive her home. With the truth about each other now out in the open, they agree to forget about their disastrous evening and start the date over again on another night—this time telling the truth.

Bearing remarkable similarity to the low-budget independent comedy THE PERFECT MATCH (which was shown at festivals in the US in 1987 and may not get a release until 1988), CROSS MY HEART is a hopelessly contrived comedy that is almost saved by the engaging performances of Short and O'Toole. Both films base their comedy on singles who spin elaborate lies during a date to impress each other. Both then chronicle the subsequent revelations and recriminations which, inevitably, bring the characters closer together. While there may be isolated moments of humor here, this is strictly situation comedy that must be supported by numerous contrivances and implausibilities to keep the narrative moving. In films like this the characters become secondary to the plot machinations, leaving little room for spontaneity, insight, or relevance. Luckily, CROSS MY HEART boasts two talented leads who manage to bring more to the film than was written into the screenplay, especially O'Toole. Whereas Short does his best to insert some lively surprises with some obvious improvisation, O'Toole brings a depth of understanding to her character and conveys it with intelligence and subtlety. Her character is a jumble of contradictions. Although she is physically attracted to Short and really enjoys sex (perhaps too much, she worries), she tries hard to repress her desires because she has fallen into too many bad relationships too quickly. The deep hurt she feels when she learns that Short has lied to her (she initially perceives it as yet another cynical betrayal of her sexuality) is tempered somewhat by the guilt she feels for having kept the truth about herself from him. With the film on the verge of exploring some interesting emotional complexities, screenwriters Bernstein and Parent suddenly veer off the path and reintroduce the ridiculous plot device of the stolen car, once again warping the film so that plot dictates the narrative rather than character. CROSS MY HEART does contain a lengthy and refreshingly realistic lovemaking scene, however, where more time is spent on getting to know a stranger intimately (nervousness, fumbling, lights on or off, shyness about nudity, trying to get comfortable, accidental poking and pulling hair, etc.) than actual lovemaking. The aforementioned condom discussion could have come off as just another superficial stab at social responsibility by Hollywood, but it actually is integrated fairly naturally into the scene and does not seem gratuitous. *(Nudity, sexual situations, adult situations, profanity.)*

p, Lawrence Kasdan; d, Armyan Bernstein; w, Armyan Bernstein, Gail Parent; ph, Thomas Del Ruth (Deluxe Color); m, Bruce Broughton; ed, Mia Goldman; prod d, Lawrence G. Paull; art d, Bill Elliot; set d, Nick Navarro; cos, Marilyn Vance-Straker; spec eff, George Zamora; m/l, Steve Legassick, Brian Ray, Narada Michael Walden, Preston Glass, Jeffrey Cohen, David Byrne, Chris Frantz, Mick Hucknall, Neil Moss, William Jackson, George Williams, Roy Straigis; makeup, Tom Case.

Comedy **(PR:O MPAA:R)**

CRY FREEDOM½** (1987, Brit.) 154m UNIV c

Denzel Washington *(Stephen Biko)*, Kevin Kline *(Donald Woods)*, Penelope Wilton *(Wendy Woods)*, Kate Hardie *(Jane Woods)*, Josette Simon *(Dr. Ramphele)*, John Thaw *(Kruger)*, Zakes Mokae *(Father Kani)*, Sophie Mgcina *(Evalina)*, Joseph Marcell *(Moses)*, John Hargreaves *(Bruce)*, Alec McCowen *(Acting High Commissioner)*, Kevin McNally *(Ken)*, Ian Richardson *(State Prosecutor)*, Timothy West *(Capt. de Wet)*, Miles Anderson *(Lemick)*, Tommy Buson *(Tami)*, Jim Findley *(Peter Jones)*, Julian Glover *(John Card)*, Alton Kumalo *(Speaker)*, Louis Mahoney *(Lesotho Government Official)*, Mawa Makondo *(Jason)*, John Matshikiza *(Mapetla)*, John Paul *(Wendy's Stepfather)*, Wabei Siyolwe *(Tenjy)*, Gwen Watford *(Wendy's Mother)*, Juanita Waterman *(Ntsiki Biko)*, Graeme Taylor *(Dillon Woods)*, Adam Stuart Walker *(Duncan Woods)*, Hamish Stuart Walker *(Gavin Woods)*, Spring Stuart Walker *(Mary Woods)*, James Coine *(Young Boy)*, Albert Ndinda *(Alec)*, Andrew Whaley *(Sub-Editor)*, Shelley Borkum *(Woods's Receptionist)*, Patricia Gumede *(Shebeen Queen)*, Angela Gavaza *(Shebeen Queen's Niece)*, Nocebo Mlambo *(Aunt)*, Walter Matemavi *(Nephew)*, Clement Muchachi *(Father)*, Ruth Chinamando *(Mother)*, Basil Chidyamathamba *(Brother-in-law)*, Marcy Mushore *(Niece)*, Lawrence Simbrashe *(Informer)*, Tichatonga Mazhindu *(Dilima)*, Neil McPherson *(Lemick's Assistant)*, Hepburn Graham *(Soga)*, Munyaradzi Kanaventi *(Samora Biko)*, George Lovell *(Nkosinathi Biko)*, Andrew McCulloch *(Policeman Nel)*, Graham Fletcher Cook *(Nel's Partner)*, Karen Drury *(Young Secretary)*, Gerald Sim *(Police Doctor)*, Peter Cartwright *(Senior Police Officer)*, Gary Whelan *(Police Sergeant)*, Dudley Dickin *(Nationalist Party Delegate)*, David Trevena *(Mortician)*, Badi Uzzaman *(Mortician's Assistant)*, Robert Phillips *(Speaker at Funeral)*, Fishoo Tembo *(Biko's Brother)*, Peggy Marsh *("Helen Suzman")*, Gwyneth Strong *(Girl at Funeral)*, Philip Bretherton *(Maj. Boshoff)*, Paul Herzberg *(Beukes)*, Kimpton Mativenga *(Black Security Policeman)*, David Henry *(Afrikaner Farmer)*, Michael Turner *(Judge Boshoff)*, Kalie Hanekom *(Magistrate Prins)*, Paul Jerricho *(Sgt. Louw)*, Peter Cary *(White Frontier Policeman)*, Dominic Kanaventi *(Black Frontier Policeman)*, Sam Mathambo *(Lesotho Passport Officer)*, Walter Muparutsa *(Lesotho Businessman)*, Judy Cornwall *(Receptionist)*, Simon Shumba *(Young Lesotho Official)*, Garrick Hagon *(McElrea)*, Nick Tate *(Richie)*, Marilyn Poole *(Acting High Commissioner's Wife)*, William Marlowe *(Police Captain at Soweto)*, Evelyn Sithole, Xoliswa Sithole *(Nurses at Clinic)*, Carl Chase, Morgan Sheppard *(Policemen)*, Claude Maredza, Carlton Chance *(Rugby Players)*, Glen Murphy, Russell Keith Grant *(Security Guards)*, Niven Boyd, Tony Vogel, Christopher Hurst *(Roadblock Policemen)*, Robert McNamara, Hans Sittig *(Security Policemen)*, Star Ncube, David Guwaza *(Prisoners)*, Hilary Minister, James Aubrey, Michael Graham Cox, John Hartley *(Passport Control Officers)*.

Richard Attenborough, the producer-director of GANDHI, returns with another film of profound political significance. CRY FREEDOM is the story of the friendship between Stephen Biko, leader of the Black Consciousness movement in South Africa in the 1970s, and Donald Woods, the white journalist who, with his family, fled his homeland to publish a book telling the world of Biko's brutal murder at the hands of South African authorities in 1977. Woods (Kline) is the liberal, anti-apartheid editor of the *Daily Dispatch* in the provincial South African city of East London. He is convinced that Biko (Washington) is a racist, but Simon, a black physician, brings the two men together. Washington has been "banned" by the government: prohibited from publishing anything, not permitted to meet with more than one person at a time, forbidden to leave his district. Just the same, Washington endeavors to acquaint Kline with the reality of black life under apartheid, talking to him at length, taking him to visit a desperate township. They continue their risky meetings and Woods becomes Washington's friend and takes an increasingly stronger stance against apartheid in his newspaper. When a church-cum-community center that Biko has established is destroyed by security forces, Kline travels to visit Thaw, the government minister in charge of the police, and reports the action. Thaw pays lip service to righting this wrong, but soon the security police begin to harass Kline and his family. Against all advisement, Washington attempts to attend a rally and is arrested. While in prison, he dies after being horribly beaten by his captors, who announce that his death is the result of a self-imposed hunger strike. Kline knows better, and he, Washington's wife, and a photographer go to the morgue and see Washington's battered corpse. Bringing the photographic proof with him, Kline tries to leave the country. He is stopped by the police, and after the pictures are discovered, he, too, becomes a banned person, under constant surveillance. Kline writes a book telling Washington's story and is determined to escape to England to publish it. Wilton, his wife, has also been Washington's friend and an enemy of apartheid, but she is reluctant to leave their friends, family, and comfortable life. After the harassment is directed at their five children, she is also ready to leave. With the help of an Australian journalist and Mokae, a black priest, Kline undertakes a dangerous escape. Posing as a priest he hitchhikes cross-country to Lesotho, the independent nation surrounded by South Africa. After his safe arrival he contacts

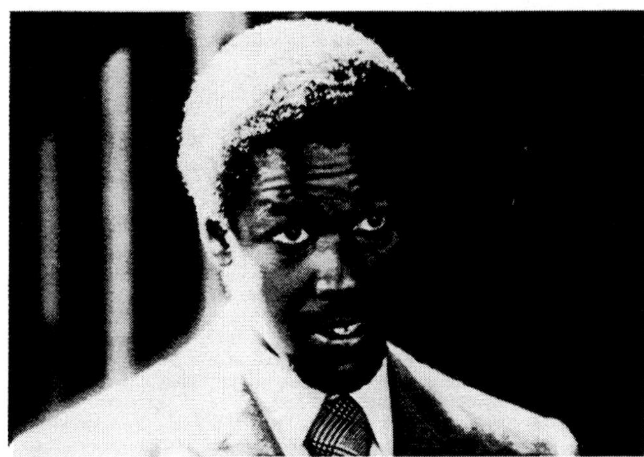

Wilton, and, that same night, she and the children rush to make a rain-swept, tension-filled crossing of the bridge at the Lesotho border. Kline and family climb into a small private plane and fly over South Africa to safety in Botswana. Intercut throughout the last half of the film are Kline's memories of Washington. The action also flashes back to a historically compacted re-creation of the 1976 Soweto riots in which 700 children were killed by South African security forces as they demonstrated. They had refused to learn Afrikaans in school, an action inspired by Biko's Black Consciousness movement.

While many critics praised the political intent of CRY FREEDOM, they also found much fault with it. The most frequent complaint was that the film is less about Biko than it is about Woods. Most pointed out that Washington dies little more than an hour into the film. Some contended that Attenborough, with an eye on the box office, was afraid to cast a black in the lead. Others felt the horror of apartheid is shown in the reactions of the central white characters and not in the on-screen lives of the black characters. While the first hour of the movie does provides a strong sense of the courage, intelligence, and humanity of Biko, Attenborough's film is not really about Biko. It is more about the radicalization of a white liberal. However, beyond all else, Attenborough has tried to make a film about South Africa's nightmare. In attempting to raise the consciousness of a broad audience, Attenborough may, indeed, have purposefully shifted the focus of the film from Washington to Kline. In trying to awaken predominantly pink-skinned Westerners to the abomination of apartheid, Attenborough has taken the proven route—what might be called THE KILLING FIELDS formula. In a better world he might not have felt the need to focus on a white person's change in the hope of moving other white people to action, but a better world wouldn't tolerate apartheid.

As humanist agitprop it is difficult to dispute the effectiveness of CRY FREEDOM, but as art and entertainment it definitely has some problems. Kline and his family's thrilling escape may make the film more intriguing for some viewers (and draw some to the theater who wouldn't otherwise come); however, its race-against-the-clock structure is familiar and predictable. Surprisingly, these episodes are the creation of screenwriter Briley (who also wrote GANDHI) only in that he had to temper their factual equivalents, which apparently were more Hollywoodesque than Attenborough thought the film could stand. Attenborough also *tells* rather than *shows* much of his story. CRY FREEDOM is talky and much of what is said is didactic, but it is never really preachy. Though the audience is the ultimate target of these lessons, they also make dramatic sense, as Washington, an extremely articulate man, uses language to communicate his vision to Kline, a man who makes his living with words. (Their visit to the township also expresses much in its visuals alone and there are other arresting images in the film, most notably the Soweto riots.) The relationship between Washington and Kline at the heart of the picture is believable and compelling. It is of no small significance that Kline becomes not only Washington's friend but his follower. Washington (TV's "St. Elsewhere") brings tremendous intelligence, dignity, and charisma to his Biko. Although the script tends to canonize him and Attenborough even chooses to present him with a back-lit halo in his initial appearance, it is the human touches that Washington brings to the part that make his Biko endearing. In GANDHI, Ben Kingsley captured the man behind the myth, and in his best moments Washington does the same for Biko. Kline (THE BIG CHILL) is also very good as the Mercedes-driving editor who goes from talking a good liberal game to living it, giving up virtually everything so that he can make the truth known about Washington. Both American actors handle their South African accents deftly. Attenborough had hoped to cast a South African as Biko, but after much auditioning, he remembered Washington from his work in A SOLDIER'S STORY. Wilton delivers a fine performance as the woman who abhors apartheid but finds it difficult to leave her home. Mokae, erstwhile collaborator with South African playwright Athol Fugard, also turns in an excellent supporting performance as the priest who helps Kline escape. Attenborough began considering screenplays about apartheid 20 years ago, but it was his introduction to the two books by Woods on which the film is based—*Biko* and *Asking for Trouble*—and a visit to South Africa in 1984 that gave him the impetus to make CRY FREEDOM. The film was shot in Zimbabwe. *(Violence.)*

p, Sir Richard Attenborough, Norman Spencer, John Briley; d, Sir Richard Attenborough; w, John Briley (based on the books *Biko* and *Asking for Trouble* by Donald Woods); ph, Ronnie Taylor (Panavision; m, George Fenton, Jonas Gwangwa; ed, Lesley Walker; prod d, Stuart Craig; md, George Fenton; art d,

Norman Dorme, George Richardson, John King; set d, Michael Seirton; cos, John Mollo; spec eff, David Harris; makeup, Wally Schneiderman; stunts, Peter Brace; tech adv, Donald Woods, Wendy Woods.

Biography/Drama **(PR:C MPAA:PG)**

CRY WILDERNESS zero (1987) 95m Visto Intl. c

Eric Foster *(Paul Cooper)*, Maurice Grandmaison *(Will Cooper)*, Griffin Casey *(Morgan)*, John Tallman *(Jim)*, Faith Clift *(Dr. Helen Foster)*.

Bigfoot lives, at least as an actor garbed with a cheap gorilla suit, in this inane and poorly made feature. Foster is a young man who goes to school in Los Angeles. The previous summer he had stayed in northern California with his father Grandmaison, who works in the rough mountain woods as a forest ranger. While living in this remote area Foster met the notorious Bigfoot and became friendly with the beast. One night a vision of the beast makes an appearance, telling Foster that his father is in danger. Foster thumbs his way up the coast where he finds Grandmaison, in the company of an Indian and a *Soldier of Fortune* devotee, tramping through the forest, trying to gun down Bigfoot. Amazingly, this gun happy trio is convinced they are tracking down an escaped circus tiger. Foster does what he can to help his furry pal, and the results are just about what you'd expect in such tripe. The acting is awful, but that's only in keeping with the film's other production values. There's even a bit of gratuitous cheesecake sex for those willing to slog through this non-adventure. Cleaning your fingernails is a far better alternative to watching CRY WILDERNESS and probably a much more creative enterprise as well. *(Profanity.)*

p, Philip Yordan, Jay Schlossberg-Cohen; d, Jay Schlossberg Cohen; w, Philip Yordan; ph, Joseph D. Urbanczyk; m, Fritz Heede; md, Ralph Ives.

Action/Drama **(PR:C MPAA:PG)**

CRYSTAL HEART** (1987) 103m NW c

Lee Curreri *(Christopher Newley)*, Tawny Kitaen *(Alley Daniels)*, Lloyd Bochner *(Frank Newley)*, May Heatherly *(Diana Newley)*, Simon Andreu *(Jean-Claude, Alley's Manager)*, Marina Saura *(Justine)*, LaGena Lookabill *(Jasper)*, Cal Gibson *(Delivery Man)*, Emiliano Redondo *(Dr. Navarro)*, Jack Taylor *(Journalist)*, Marcea D. Lane *(Marcea)*, Richard Blade *(Himself)*, Gil Bettman *(Commercial Asst.)*, Traci Couveau, Lydia Patino, Lara Belmonte, Mary Adams, Debbie Palmer *(Pool Party Girls)*, Carlos Blanco *(Magazine Photographer)*.

Though it looks good and the acting is better than passable, CRYSTAL HEART is done in by too much sentiment. Curreri (of the television show "Fame") is a young man confined to a sterilized environment due to a genetic inability to produce natural immunities. Fortunately, Curreri's parents, Bochner and Heatherly, are fabulously wealthy, so his surroundings are equipped with a variety of electronic gizmos. In his solitude Curreri develops some musical talent and writes fan letters to Kitaen, a rising young pop queen. Kitaen is charmed by Curreri—who is nationally known because of his circumstances—but balks when her sleazy manager Andreu suggests she meet her admirer. Eventually Kitaen acquiesces and even takes a liking to Curreri. Heatherly, ever the protective mother, distrusts the girl but begrudgingly allows her to continue her visits. Not surprisingly, Curreri and Kitaen fall in love, though Curreri's enclosure precludes physical contact. Still, the lovers don't let this impede their hormonal urges, and get it on through the glass pane. Curreri proposes to Kitaen, who is hesitant but realizes how deeply she loves him. She is also concerned with her career, and is desperately trying to get a European booking. She does get her desired big booking, and goes out to celebrate with Andreu, who attempts to seduce her when they return to her home. Later, when Curreri calls, Andreu answers the phone and says Kitaen is engaged in other physical activities. Kitaen is furious and runs out to explain things to Curreri. In the meantime, Curreri has decided that enough is enough. He smashes a glass panel and escapes from his room, heading out to find his beloved. Eventually the two connect and have an idyllic interlude, though we all know this won't last long. Sure enough, Curreri's deficient immune system catches up with him and he develops a deadly cough. In his romantically beautiful death, Curreri explains that he's finally done all the things he's ever dreamed of doing. Kitaen goes on to perform a meaningful dance number written (as if you had to guess) by that special guy who touched her life.

If it were just mawkish, CRYSTAL HEART might have been entertaining in a campy sort of way. The story is wholly ridiculous, but the performers are good looking and earnest. Kitaen, a stunning redhead, appears to have some acting ability, as does Curreri, who easily could win the junior division of a Judd Hirsh look-alike Contest. However, their scenes together are pure soap opera. The through-the-glass lovemaking session is a wonderful exercise in unintended hilarity, and is perhaps the ultimate solution for filmmakers who are skittish about showing sex to AIDS-conscious audiences. CRYSTAL HEART simply isn't much of a story, and plenty of padding is added in the form of numerous rock videos, none of which is particularly original. Ultimately, the film bores more than it entertains. The premise was handled in a much better manner in "The Boy in the Plastic Bubble," a 1976 made-for-television movie that featured John Travolta and was directed by Randal Kleiser. The songs include: "Don't Touch the Heart" (Jeff Neiman, performed by Andrea Robinson), "Night Rockin'" (Jamie James, performed by James), "Give It Up" (Joel Goldsmith, Jerry Ropelle, performed by Ropelle), "Two Girls Dancing," "Desperate Days" (John St. James, performed by Formula One), "Crossing Out" (Janis Liebhart, David Sepack, performed by Dennis Churchill), "Can't Run Away" (Randy Jackson, Liz Jackson, performed by Room With a View), "Desire" (Joel Goldsmith, performed by Andrea Robinson), "Brave New World," "Let Me Believe in You" (Jay Ferguson, performed by Ferguson), "Hearts Beat On" (Kevin Dukes, Roger Freeland, performed by Andrea Robinson), "Castles in the Sand" (Jeff Neiman, performed by Dennis Churchill), "The Model" (John St. James, performed by SSO), "Actions Speak Louder" (Baxter Robertson, performed by Robertson).

p, Carlos Vasallo; d, Gil Bettman; w, Linda Shayne (based on a story by Alberto Vazquez-Figueroa); ph, Alexander [Alejandro] Ulloa (Technicolor); m, Joel Goldsmith; ed, Nicholas Wentworth; prod d, Jose Maria Alarcon; cos, Ella Leff; spec eff, Antonio Molina; ch, Marcea D. Lane; m/l, Jeff Neiman, Jamie James, Joel Goldsmith, Jerry Ropelle, John St. James, Janis Liebhart, David Sepack, Randy Jackson, Liz Jackson, Jay Ferguson, Kevin Dukes, Roger Freeland, Baxter Robertson; makeup, Manuel Martin, Lisa Ann Pedrianna.

Drama **Cas.** **(PR:C-O MPAA:R)**

CSOK, ANYU† (1987, Hung.) 102m Objektiv-Mafilm c (Trans: Love, Mother)

Dorottya Udvaros *(Juli Kalmar)*, Robert Koltai *(Geza Kalmar)*, Kati Lajtai *(Mari Kalmar)*, Simon G. Gevai *(Peti Kalmar)*, Ildiko Bansagi *(Schoolmistress)*, Erika Bodnar *(Neighbor)*, Zsuzsa Toreky *(Geza's Mistress)*, Peter Andorai *(Comrade Csezmiczey)*.

A busy working couple finds little time to spend with their children, creating an empty family life. The death of the children's grandmother causes the couple to examine their priorities, but their familial concerns are short lived as they quickly return to their self-centered life-styles. This sometimes humorous account of modern-day family life won the top prize at the Hungarian Film Week.

d, Janos Rozsa; w, Miklos Vamos; ph, Elemer Ragalyi (Eastmancolor); m, Janos Brody; ed, Zsuzsa Csakany; prod d, Jozsef Romvari; cos, Fanni Kemenes.

Drama **(PR:NR MPAA:NR)**

CUDZOZIEMKA† (1987, Pol.) 115m Zespoly Fimowe-Film Unit OKO c (Trans: The Stranger)

Ewa Wisniewska *(Roza, Violinist)*, Joanna Szczepkowska *(Marta, Roza's Daughter)*, Jerzy Kamas *(Alan, Roza's Husband)*, Andrzej Precigs, Katarzyna Chrzanowska, Malgotzata Lorentowicz.

Frustrated because she was thwarted in her attempt to become a concert violinist, a bitter woman makes life miserable for those around her.

d, Ryszard Ber; w, Maria Kuncewiczowa (based on her novel); ph, Jerzy Stowicki; m, Anna Izykowska-Mironowicz; art d, Andrzej Borecki.

Drama **(PR:NR MPAA:NR)**

CUDOWNE DZIECKO (SEE: LE JEUNE MAGICIEN, 1987, Can./Pol.)

CUO WEI† (1987, China) 88m Xi'an/China c (Trans: The Stand-In)

Liu Zifeng *(Zhao Shuxin)*, Mou Hong, Yang Kun, Sun Kihu.

This Chinese variation on MAKING MR. RIGHT (1987) features Liu Zifeng in the John Malkovich roles as both creator and creation. Trained as an engineer, Liu has risen to the top of his company, but swallowed up by his administrative duties, he no longer has the opportunity to do any hands-on work. To free himself of this burden, he invents a look-alike robot to perform those tasks he has no interest in, but the plan backfires when his creation takes on a life of its own. Before the situation gets completely out of hand, Liu wakes from this nightmare.

d, Huang Jianxin; w, Huang Xin, Zhang Min; ph, Wang Xinsheng, m, Han Yong.

Comedy **(PR:NR MPAA:NR)**

CURSE, THE*½ (1987) 90m Trans World c (AKA: THE FARM)

Wil Wheaton *(Zachary Hayes)*, Claude Akins *(Nathan Hayes)*, Malcolm Danare *(Cyrus)*, Cooper Huckabee *(Dr. Alan Forbes)*, John Schneider *(Carl Willis)*, Amy Wheaton *(Alice Hayes)*, Steve Carlisle *(Charley Davidson)*, Kathleen Jordan Gregory *(Frances Hayes)*, Hope North *(Esther Forbes)*, Steve Davis *(Mike)*.

The directing debut of actor David Keith (AN OFFICER AND A GENTLE-

MAN, THE LORDS OF DISCIPLINE, FIRESTARTER) is a nauseating little horror film shot on the actor/director's own property in Tennessee (interiors were filmed in Rome). Set on a lonely farm, the film stars young Wheaton (STAND BY ME) as an unhappy boy who does not get along with his Bible-quoting stepfather Akins. Wheaton and his little sister (Amy Wheaton, the actor's real-life sister) try to make the best of the situation, despite the fact that Akins' obese and cruel son, Danare, goes out of his way to make their lives miserable. Also unhappy is Wheaton's mother, Gregory. Having married Akins out of necessity, she has grown frustrated with his religious fanaticism and ultraconservative views toward family relationships. Sex-starved, she sneaks into the barn one night and seduces Davis, the lunkheaded handyman who has dug Akins a new well. During their lovemaking, a strange meteorite zooms out of the sky and crashes in Akins' field. As the family members rush outside to see what has happened, Akins discovers his wife's infidelity, but is content to let God handle her punishment.

Although local authorities realize that the strange object from outer space is abnormal, they placate Akins by telling him that the large, cold object is merely sewage jettisoned by a passing airliner that has frozen and fallen to earth (it melts into the ground the very next day). Real estate tycoon Carlisle and town doctor Huckabee lie to Akins because they don't want to spoil their get-rich-quick scheme (they hope to buy Akins' failing farm and then sell it to Tennessee Valley Authority official Schneider, who is looking to build a new dam in the area). Unfortunately, the object from space melts into Akins' well water and contaminates the crops, the animals (they become infested with wriggling maggots), and then the family itself. The first to succumb is Gregory. She begins sprouting horrible sores on her face and becomes homicidal. Akins accepts this as God's punishment and locks his wife in the fruit cellar. Wheaton, who has been suspicious of the meteor all along, refuses to drink the water or eat the food and keeps his sister from doing the same. Soon Akins and son Danare become pus-oozing monsters, leaving Wheaton to defend himself and his sister from their murderous rage (Huckabee and Carlisle also fall victim to the maniacs). During the climactic battle between children and step-family, the house begins to self-destruct. Just as things look hopeless for the little Wheatons, TVA agent Schneider comes out of nowhere to rescue the tots. As they run to safety, the house implodes on Akins and Danare, and is sucked into the ground. The shell-shocked kids whimper as Schneider drives them away. Thanks to a pre-credits scene at the beginning of the film, we have learned that the space-ooze has contaminated other water supplies and, in six months, more citizens will become homicidal monsters.

Employing the now-standard examination of the corruption of the nuclear family, Keith and screenwriter Chaskin (NIGHTMARE ON ELM STREET II) manage to create a suitably claustrophobic horror film that is much more effective in the early going than it is once the meteor hits. Akins and his loutish son Danare are horrible enough monsters *before* the alien contamination, thus making their physical transformation into overtly homicidal maniacs rather redundant. Tying the arrival of the meteor to the frustrated farm wife's infidelity smacks of biblical prophecy and must have looked effective on paper, but as visualized by Keith, it is almost comic (also, the handyman character literally vanishes from the film at this point). Keith does get some mileage out of Wheaton's mother slowly becoming a monster—thus adding to the boy's dilemma by removing the one adult in the family he can trust—but the lapses of logic in the script eat away at the emotional effectiveness. Overall, the performances are serviceable, with Akins evoking R.G. Armstrong's similar role in Sam Peckinpah's western RIDE THE HIGH COUNTRY and Danare (HEAVEN HELP US) disarmingly grotesque. Wheaton does a fine job of looking helpless and frustrated, but the role is a step backwards from STAND BY ME, and his sister does little more than yelp like a scared cat and whimper a lot. The best performance in the film is that of Gregory, who manages to run the gamut from concerned parent to horny housewife to raving lunatic quite effectively. The film becomes almost totally incoherent in the last 15 minutes and seems as if it was slapped together hastily. Gore effects by Italian Franco Ruffini are predictably disgusting. In THE CURSE, director Keith attempted to make some sort of comment on the seedy underbelly of the American family farm, but instead succeeded in making a gross, silly, and ultimately forgettable little horror film. Note: This film was titled THE FARM right until an eleventh-hour switch to THE CURSE before general release. *(Graphic violence, gore effects, sexual situations, profanity.)*

p, Ovidio G. Assonitis; d, David Keith; w, David Chaskin; ph, Robert D. Forges (Widescreen, Technicolor); m, Franco Micalizzi; ed, Claudio M. Cutry; prod, d, Frank Vanorio; spec eff, Kevin Erham, Mark Moller; makeup, Frank Russell.

Horror **(PR:O MPAA:R)**

CUSTODY† (1987, Aus.) 92m Film Australia c

Peter Carroll *(Narrator)*, Judith Stratford *(Christine Byrne)*, Peter Browne *(Andrew Byrne)*, Michael Cudlin *(Justin Byrne)*, Sheridan Murphy *(Cathy Byrne)*, Stuart Fowler *(Christine's Solicitor)*, June Musgrave *(Andrew's Solicitor)*, Lillian Thompson-Austen *(Magistrate)*, Justice Eric Baker *(Judge)*, Ann Charlton *(Legal Aid)*, Rosemary Michelin, Norman Goodsell *(Court Counsellors)*, Robert Lethbridge, Robert Harding *(Barristers)*.

Using a mixture of experienced actors and real-life legal professionals, this Australian docu-drama re-creates a child custody case involving the break-up of a 12-year marriage. Stratford's infidelity to husband Browne precipitates their divorce and subsequent battle for their two children. Following the events both inside and out of the courtroom, the film traces the tragic dissolution of a family.

p, Tristram Miall; d, Ian Munro; w, (based on a story by Ann Charlton, Anna Grieve); ph, Joel Peterson; m, Peter Best; ed, Denise Haslem.

Docu-drama **(PR:NR MPAA:NR)**

CYCLONE** (1987) 83m Cinetel Films c

Heather Thomas *(Teri Marshall)*, Jeffrey Combs *(Rick Davenport)*, Ashley Ferrare *(Carla Hastings)*, Dar Robinson *(Rolf)*, Martine Beswicke *(Waters)*, Robert Quarry *(Knowles)*, Martin Landau *(Bosarian)*, Huntz Hall *(Long John)*, Troy Donahue *(Bob Jenkins)*, Michael Reagan *(McCardy)*, Tim Conway, Jr. *(Barrell)*, Dawn Wildsmith *(Henna)*, Bruce Fairbairn *(Lt. Cutter)*, Sam Hiona *(Buyer)*, John Stewart, Paul Short, Bob Bragg *(Scruffies)*, Lauren Hertzberg, Jordan Hertzberg *(Children with Groceries)*, Billy Joe Brown, David Jackson, Tony Brewster, Gary Bettmann, Grant Waldman *(Policemen)*, Paul Stuart, Neil Lundell *(Paramedics)*, Jesse Long *(Photographer)*, Jack Davidson *(Lava Club Manager)*, Michael Sonye, Tom Cush, Joe Ramirez, Kingsley Candler *(Haunted Garage)*, Russ Tamblyn.

Thomas is the girl friend of Combs, a scientist and motorcycle builder. He has designed a super motorcycle equipped with the firepower of an F-16 and a "transformer," a device that converts oxygen into energy, providing the ultimate inexhaustible free energy source. Of course, there are powers who are too fond of Combs' deveopments. While at a nightclub, Combs meets his end when an ice pick is driven into the base of his skull. Thomas barely escapes with her life and when she returns home she finds a video message from Combs. Anticipating his death, Thomas has left instructions on how to operate the motorcycle and where to deliver it. Thomas arranges to deliver the motorcyle to the contact identified by Combs, but he is shot down by assassins Robinson and Wildsmith. Thomas flees to her gym instructor's home, who, it turns out, is in league with the killers. Thomas is captured and tortured, but refuses to reveal the whereabouts of the transformer. Eventually government agent Beswicke breaks in and helps her escape, leading to the inevitable chase. All the bad guys die, Thomas beats up her gym instructor, and throws the transformer away, declaring it "trouble." Thomas is a likable enough heroine, though the script makes no real demands of her. The real source of interest is the cast of B-movie veterans director Ray habitually collects for his films. This time we're treated to Bowery Boy Huntz Hall (not looking so good), Martin Landau, Robert Quarry (Count Yorga), Troy Donahue, Martine Beswicke, the President's son Michael Reagan, and others. The film is dedicated to the memory of Dar Robinson, a stuntman who was beginning to make the transition to actor when he was killed during the production of MILLION DOLLAR MYSTERY. *(Violence, brief nudity.)*

p, Paul Hertzberg; d, Fred Olen Ray; w, Paul Garson, T.L. Lankford (based on a story by Fred Olen Ray); ph, Paul Elliot; m, David A. Jackson, James Saad; art d, Maxine Shepard; cos, Dorothy Amos; spec eff, Kevin McCarthy, Tracy Design, Inc.; stunts, John Stewart; makeup, Kathy Shorkey.

Action **(PR:C MPAA:R)**

CZAS NADZIEI† (1987, Pol.) 103m Zespoly Filmowe-Film Unit Profil c (Trans: Time Of Hope)

Jerzy A. Braszka *(Szostak)*, Halina Kossobudzka *(His Wife)*, Edward Sosna *(Waldek Rzewinski, His Son-in-Law)*.

Braszka, reprising his character from Wionczek's 1985 film GODNOSC (Dignity), must deal with unemployment and family problems against the backdrop of martial law in Poland in 1981. He eventually returns to work at the factory where he had been a strike breaker, but finds little satisfaction and still must contend with the fact that his family is falling apart.

d, Roman Wionczek; w, Jerzy Grzymkowski; ph, Wladyslaw Nagy; set d, Joanna Wionczek-Lozinska.

Drama **(PR:NR MPAA:NR)**

D'ANNUNZIO† (1987, It.) 109m Selvaggia c

Robert Powell *(Gabriele D'Annunzio)*, Stefania Sandrelli *(Elvira/Barbara Leoni)*, Sonia Petrovna *(Maria Gravina)*, Teresa Ann Savoy *(lst Wife)*, Florence Guerin, Paolo Bonacelli, Laurent Terzieff, Stefano Torossi, Carmen Onorati, Benny Cardoso, Rita Rubirosa, Veronica Wells, Giovanna Mainardi, Bruna Martelli, Giuseppe Magdalone, Giampaolo Poddighe, Annabella Schiavone, Achille Brunini, Cesare Barbetti, Fiorenza Marchegiani, Eva Grimaldi, Roberto Alpi.

This film focuses on five years in the life of Italian author Gabriele D'Annunzio (1863-1938). Around the turn of the century, D'Annunzio was moving from a career in journalism to that of a novelist, writing *Pleasure* and *The Innocent*. Powell, starring as the author, goes through two marriages and a torrid affair with Sandrelli over the course of the film.

p, Franco Casati, Sergio Martinelli; d, Sergio Nasca; w, Piero Chiara, Fabio D'Agostini, Sergio Nasca; ph, Romano Albani; m, Sergio Sandrelli; ed, Nino Baragli; art d, Giorgio Luppi.

Biography **(PR:NR MPAA:NR)**

DA YUE BING (SEE: BIG PARADE, THE, 1987, Chin.)

DACAIT† (1987, India)

Sunny Deol *(Arjun Singh)*, Raakee *(Arjun's Mother)*, Raj Nanvag *(Makkan Mallah)*, Meenakshi Seshadri *(Chawli, Arjun's Wife)*, Raza Murad *(Thakur Bhawar Singh)*, Shafi Inamdar *(SP)*, Suresh Oberoi.

After completing his education, a young man returns to his village to find one of his best friends has become a *dacoit*, an outlaw. He cannot understand his friend's behavior, but when he realizes how corrupt and unjust the local government and police are, he too becomes a *dacoit*. (In Hindi.)

p&d, Rahul Rawail; w, Javed Akhtar; ph, Rajan Kothari; m, R.D. Burman.

Action **(PR:NR MPAA:NR)**

DADAGIRI† (1987, India)

Dharmendra, Padmini Kolhapure, Govinda, Amrish Puri.

A young girl sheds her shyness to get the best of her clever uncle. (In Hindi.)

p&d, Deepak Shivdasani; m, Annu Malik.

Drama **(PR:NR MPAA:NR)**

DAKU HASINA† (1987, India)

Zeenat Aman, Rajnikant, Raakesh Roshan.

A young woman becomes an outlaw in order to get revenge on the four men who raped her. (In Hindi.)

p, B.K. Adarsh; d, Ashok Roy; m, Usha Khanna.

Crime **(PR:NR MPAA:NR)**

DAMORTIS† (1987, Phil.) 93m c

Madeleine Nicolas *(Anna)*, Lito Carating *(Miguel)*, Roberto Villanueva *(Lando)*.

Shown at the Asian American International Film Festival in New York, this Filipino film dating from 1984 stars Carating as a faith healer whose methods are so successful that he takes on a student healer who soon becomes even more successful than his teacher.

p, Maria Branca; d, Briccio Santos; w, Briccio Santos, Jorge Arago; ph, Ricky Ligon; m, Winston.

Drama **(PR:NR MPAA:NR)**

DANCERS** (1987) 99m Golan-Globus/Cannon c

Mikhail Baryshnikov *(Anton "Tony" Sergoyev)*, Alessandra Ferri *(Francesca)*, Leslie Browne *(Nadine)*, Thomas Rall *(Patrick)*, Lynn Seymour *(Muriel)*, Victor Barbee *(Wade)*, Julie Kent *(Lisa)*, Mariangela Melato *(Contessa)*, Leandro Amato *(Paolo)*, Gianmarco Tognazzi *(Guido)*, Desmond Kelly *(Duke of Courland)*, Ghrisa Keramidas *(Bathilde)*, Amy Werba *(Interviewer)*, Jack Brodsky *(Jack)*, Robert Argand *(Impresario)*, Amanda McKerrow *(Moyna)*, Bonnie Moore *(Zulma)*, American Ballet Theater Dancers.

Herbert Ross' 20th film in as many years is a return to the territory of THE TURNING POINT, his 1977 dance drama which garnered 11 Oscar nominations and won none. Baryshnikov, who made his film debut in THE TURNING POINT, stars here (not surprisingly) as the world's top ballet dancer. In southern Italy for a film production of "Giselle," Baryshnikov is auditioning dancers and beginning rehearsals. Something of a Don Juan (again no surprise), Baryshnikov is engaged to jet-setter Melato and has been involved with a number of his troupe's dancers, including Ferri, who is dancing the lead in "Giselle," and Browne (his costar from THE TURNING POINT), who has a vehement hatred for men. When Baryshnikov spots 17-year-old ingenue Kent, an innocent American auditioning for a place in the company, sitting in a restaurant, he sends her an ice cream cake which immediately melts her heart. An impressionable teenager, Kent is completely infatuated with Baryshnikov. Her head begins to swim with the attention he pays her, especially when he gives her a part in his production without so much as an audition. Watching Baryshnikov in caddish action angers Browne. Years ago she was the ingenue whose heart he broke, and now she tries to warn Kent. Eventually, Kent learns of Baryshnikov's callousness, and while watching him perform from the wings, she runs from the theater. Her coat is later found floating in a nearby river, and Baryshnikov blames himself for her death. When it is finally discovered that Kent is not dead, Baryshnikov is redeemed. He finds that he is again in touch with his feelings and his dance performance is imbued with a missing vitality.

Although the script is a weak one, DANCERS is not dependent on its story. It would have helped if the story had the necessary dramatics and narrative drive, but DANCERS exists for Baryshnikov's brilliance and for the talents of his American Ballet Theater dancers. Heavily cliched and downright silly at times, DANCERS drags for its first half as its back story and a truncated telling of "Giselle" weigh down the proceedings. By the last half, the dancers become the stars. Ross, who began his career as a choreographer, knows better than most how to photograph dance scenes with the full benefit of the camera. While directors often fall into the trap of moving the camera with the dancers (which renders them visually motionless in relation to their background), Ross rarely moves his camera during the dance scenes. Other directors often over-cut their dance scenes, but Ross realizes that the uninterrupted flow of motion is essential for a successful scene. Though it began as a straight filming of "Giselle" a la Franco Zeffirelli, DANCERS eventually evolved into a telling of a behind-the-scenes story of a ballet company which is interwoven with the story of "Giselle." For ballet enthusiasts, the greatest enjoyment (besides watching Baryshnikov) will come in putting together the "Giselle" vs. DANCERS puzzle, connecting the movie characters with their ballet counterparts. Baryshnikov is a modern-day Count Albrecht, the chauvinist who exercises his feudal rights over various village women but wins the heart of a peasant girl by disguising himself as a villager. Kent plays Giselle, the wide-eyed peasant whose love for Albrecht/Baryshnikov knows no bounds. Among the other parallels between life and art are the ballet company assistant Amato as woodcutter Hilarion; Baryshnikov's jet-setter fiancee Milato as Albrecht's princess fiancee Bathilde; and man-hater Browne as the Queen of the Wilis.

Budgeted at $7 million and shot in a speedy six weeks, the film features the American Ballet Theater (which Baryshnikov has directed since 1980) and the music of "Giselle" played by the London Symphony Orchestra conducted by Michael Tilson Thomas. Baryshnikov, in his third film role (he appeared in WHITE NIGHTS between his two Ross projects), is a fine actor but an even better dancer. He is also credited with staging the ballet sequences, which, judging from the length of these scenes, is tantamount to a codirection credit. The supporting cast is equally impressive, from Kent, in her film debut, to Browne, who received a Best Supporting Actress nomination for THE TURNING POINT, to Ferri, who is known to non-dance fans as the Dewar's Scotch girl. The film is dedicated to the late Nora Kaye, Ross's wife and frequent collaborator, who found fame as a ballerina in the 1940s and 1950s. She died in February 1987 just before the completion of DANCERS, on which she served as co-executive producer. Although DANCERS has some exceptional dancing and a creative parallel to the original ballet, it pales in comparison to the much more passionate Carlos Saura-Antonio Gades collaborations BLOOD WEDDING, CARMEN, and EL AMOR BRUJO. *(Sexual situations.)*

p, Menahem Golan, Yoram Globus; d, Herbert Ross; w, Sarah Kernochan; ph, Ennio Guarnieri (Cinecitta Color); m, Adolphe Adam, Pino Donaggio; ed, William Reynolds; prod d, Gianni Quaranta; md, Michael Tilson Thomas; art d, Luigi Marchione; set d, Ello Altamura; cos, Adriana Spadaro, Anna Anni, Enrico Serafini; ch, Mikhail Baryshnikov.

Drama (PR:A MPAA:PG)

DANGER ZONE, THE* (1987) 89m Danger Zone/Skouras c

Robert Canada *(Reaper)*, Jason Williams *(Wade)*, Kris Braxton *(Judy)*, G. Cervi *(Simon)*, Dana Dowell *(Kim)*, Mickey Elders *(Reptile)*, Jamie Ferreira *(Jamie)*, Daniel Friedman *(Needles)*, Cynthia Gray *(Linda)*, R.A. Mihailoff *(Munch)*, Rick Nightingale *(Jake)*, Juanita Ranney *(Skin)*, Axel Roberts *(Ronnie)*, Joe Sabatino *(P.J.)*, Suzanne Tara *(Heather)*, Theresa Trousdale *(Summer)*, Michael Wayne *(Nose)*, Mike Wiles *(Curtis)*.

Just as BACK TO THE BEACH time warped its way onto today's screens to recall the vacuous vagaries of the beach films of the 1960s, this low-budget production attempts to revive the interest of those weirdo audiences thriving on the Hell's Angels biker movies. A dirty, ruthless, sadistic band of bikers finds a group of girls stranded in their broken-down car while heading toward Las Vegas and a chance to appear on a talent show. Canada and other drug-smuggling bikers hold the girls hostage and terrorize them, having nothing better to do in the arid desert locale. Their tortures and tribulations are finally called to a halt by Williams, a member of the biker gang who is also an undercover narcotics agent, with the not inconsiderable help of prospector Nightingale. It's all been done and seen before and it's not any better than the original junk movies that tried to read significance into instantly forgettable and inhuman characters. A waste of time and, because of the extreme violence and sadism displayed, not for youngsters. *(Graphic violence, harsh language.)*

p, Jason Williams, Tom Friedman; d, Henry Vernon; w, Jason Williams, Tom Friedman, Karen Levitt; ph, Daniel Yarussi (United Color); m, Robert Etoll; ed, Louis George, Susan Medaglia; art d, Marty Cusack.

Crime Cas. (PR:O MPAA:R)

DANN IST NICHTS MEHR WIE VORHER† (1987, Ger.) 87m Olga-Bayerischen Rundfunk-Berliner Filmforderung-Bayern Filmfoderung c (Trans: Then Nothing Was the Same Anymore)

Zacharias Preen *(Norbert Kalka)*, Barbara Rudnik *(Gabriele Matern)*, Karin Baal *(Hilde Kalka)*, Heinz Honig, Shaun Lawton.

Preen plays a Berliner who loves the cinema but finds that he cannot relate to any of the people in his life. Searching to fill that void, he wanders the frozen streets of his city and eventually meets Rudnik, an older, similarly lost woman with whom he carries on a hotel room affair.

d, Gerd Roman Forsch; w, Edeltraud Rabitzer, Gerd Roman Forsch; ph, Jurgen Jurges; m, Lutz Kohler.

Drama (PR:NR MPAA:NR)

DAO MA DAN (SEE: PEKING OPERA BLUES, 1987, Hong Kong)

DAO MAZEI† (1987, Chi.) 86m Xi'an Film/China Film c (Trans: Horse Thief)

Cexiang Rigzin, Dan Zhiji, Daiba.

Made in 1985, this Chinese production is a wide-screen tale set in the mountains of Tibet in 1923. Rigzin is a poor shepherd who is forced to turn to thievery to provide for his wife and son. He is later caught stealing from officials of the local temple and driven out of the village. His son dies in the process and he and his wife must start a new family. Released in a very limited noncommercial run in 1987 as THE HORSE THIEF, it earned the highest of praise from those few who saw it. (In Tibetan; English subtitles.)

d, Tian Zhuang-zhuang; w, Zhang Rui; ph, Hou Yong, Zhao Fei (CinemaScope).

Drama (PR:NR MPAA:NR)

DARK EYES*½** (1987, It.) 118m Excelsior Film-TV-RAI 1/Island c (OCI CIORNIE)

Marcello Mastroianni *(Romano)*, Silvana Mangano *(Elisa, Romano's Wife)*, Marthe Keller *(Tina, Romano's Mistress)*, Elena Sofonova *(Anna Sergeyevna, Governor's Wife)*, Vsevolod Larionov *(Pavel, Russian Ship Passenger)*, Innokenti Smoktunovsky *(Governor of Sisoiev)*, Pina Cei *(Elisa's Mother)*, Roberto Herlitzka *(Lawyer)*, Dimitri Zolothukin *(Konstantin)*, Paolo Baroni, Oleg Tabakov, Yuri Bogatiriov, Carola Stagnaro.

It is a special occurrence in film when an actor can capture an audience the way Mastroianni has in DARK EYES, a film of such warmth, melancholy, tragedy, and beauty that one does not want it to end. Directed by Russian Mikhalkov (his first film outside the USSR), the film represents a union between Soviet and Italian cast and crew, and brings a new cross-cultural interpretation to the Chekhov stories on which the film is based—chiefly "The Lady with the Little Dog," "Anna Around the Neck," "The Name-Day Party," and "My Wife." Set at the turn of the century, the film stars Mastroianni as a paunchy, alcoholic waiter who works in the dining room of a cruise ship. While voyaging from Greece to Italy, Mastroianni meets a jovial Russian, Larionov, who is celebrating his honeymoon with his much younger Russian wife. Mastroianni begins to reminisce to Larionov while staring at a photo of his wife. As a young architecture student, Mastroianni fell in love with Mangano, a wealthy heiress, despite the objections of her high-society family. Always the devoted but philandering husband, Mastroianni stood by his wife, and she, in turn, always defended his childish and charming ways to her respectable relatives. During a birthday party at the family's lavish country estate, Mastroianni learns that his wife's finances have gone dry. Forced to sell everything she has, Mangano verbally attacks Mastroianni and cruelly accuses him of marrying her only for her money. Hurt by what she has said and unwilling to put up with any more accusations, Mastroianni leaves "to take the waters" at a lavish health spa. As if he were a resident of heaven, Mastroianni lives a relaxed life at the spa. He finds willing young ladies to sleep with, pulls an occasional

practical joke, watches old women racing through the marble-columned grounds in their wheelchairs, wanders through the beautifully manicured lawns, and eats extravagant meals. It is here that he meets Sofonova, a timid, lovely, easily embarrassed young Russian woman with dark eyes and a lapdog. Mesmerized by her very presence and the magical sparkle of her hat pin, Mastroianni becomes obsessed. In a comical and touching courtship scene, Sofonova mistakenly assumes that Mastroianni has a debilitating leg disease and supports him as they walk through the grounds. Playing along with her misconception, Mastroianni explains that his disease dates back to his "Vesuvian" relatives, and that his grandfather was miraculously cured when a Russian woman whispered in his ear. As a test, Sofonova whispers a Russian word in Mastroianni's ear—*Sabatchka*, the word for little dog. As if a cleansing spirit had just entered his body, Mastroianni stands upright, feels his legs, and leaps around the grounds, sending the frightened Sofonova running away in a fit of screams. Mastroianni follows but trips and falls, actually hurting his leg this time. Once their romance is consummated, she returns to Russia, leaving him nothing but a scented note. Determined to see her again, he heads for Sisoiev, a small village outside of St. Petersburg whose inhabitants have never met a foreigner. Pretending that he is planning to open a glass-manufacturing plant, Mastroianni visits with the village's top officials, who lay out the red carpet, shower him with gifts and flowers, and treat him to a musical greeting by a band of local gypsies. All the while he is looking for Sofonova and her *Sabatchka*. He has his longest visit with Smoktunovsky, the egotistical, half-wit governor of Sisoiev who, Mastroianni soon learns, is married to Sofonova. Mastroianni and Sofonova secretly meet and promise each other that they will leave their spouses. Mastroianni must first return to Italy to tell his wife, then he will then come back for Sofonova. Upon his arrival in Italy, he finds Mangano showing her now-empty estate to a potential buyer. She has nothing left in the world but Mastroianni. It is just as Mastroianni had always wished—they now possess nothing but their love for each other. When Mangano confronts him about the scented letter, he denies that he has a Russian lover and remains with his wife. He never returns to Russia, and later, when Mangano recoups her fortune, he leaves her to become a waiter. The story picks up again in the ship's dining room as Larionov is carefully listening to Mastroianni. It is here that Mastroianni has the revelation that he has almost no memories—just his mother's voice, his wife's face "the first time," and the Russian mist. As Mastroianni rushes off to prepare for the lunch crowd, Larionov heads up to the deck to wake his wife. When she awakens and turns her head, we see that it is Sofonova.

As superb as Mastroianni is (he won the Best Actor prize at this year's Cannes Film Festival for his work here), it is not his performance alone which makes DARK EYES so enjoyable; Mikhalkov's richly textured and meticulously detailed direction is equally responsible. Instead of bombarding his audience with large statements about memories and lost youth, Mikhalkov films the small details that cause the audience to reminisce. This careful scripting and Mastroianni's hauntingly expressive face add up to an endearing film. DARK EYES is one of those rare films that stirs the full range of emotions in its audience—from uproarious comedy to quiet sadness. One such scene has Mastroianni and Sofonova sitting in a gazebo on a rainy afternoon as two children play with a wheelchair. The children, full of innocence, push each other around gleefully until the mother drags them away. With a certain sadness in his eyes, Mastroianni appreciates their childishness and heads for the wheelchair. Overcome by youthful exuberance, he stands on his head in the wheelchair and propels himself across the courtyard while the charmed Sofonova watches. In another scene, which is destined to become a Mastroianni classic, he and Sofonova are sitting at the spa beside a therapeutic bath when her very elegant hat is blown off by a sudden gust of wind and lands in the middle of the bath. As the attendants look around dumfounded, Mastroianni, dressed from head to toe in a fine white suit, rises from his chair and in a gentlemanly strut walks into the therapeutic waters. While everyone watches in amazement, Mastroianni proceeds as if nothing is unusual. Waist high in the waters, he fetches the hat, walks out of the bath with his pants terribly soiled, and presents Sofonova with her "chapeau."

Besides Mastroianni, upon whom too much praise cannot be bestowed, the rest of the cast is exceptional: Mangano as the elegant and often cruel heiress; Keller as Mastroianni's flighty but longtime friend and mistress; Larionov as the captivated Russian ship passenger; Smoktunovsky as the egomaniacal Russian governor; and Zolothukin as the Russian radical who begs Mastroianni not to build his factory in the village because such progress will mean the end of the beautiful forests and rivers. The film's greatest discovery, however, is the lovely Sofonova, a 31-year-old Soviet actress with previous experience in some 20 films but no exposure outside of her native country. Like Audrey Hepburn in ROMAN HOLIDAY, Sofonova has a fragile romantic quality that is the opposite of what Mastroianni's character usually falls for. Mangano is powerful, Keller is forward, the others are playthings, but Sofonova is a mystery and remains so. Underneath her elegant hat and behind her lace veil are the dark eyes that Mastroianni followed all the way to Russia—the same eyes which saw him as the vulnerable lover no other woman had seen. Mikhalkov doesn't merely tell his audience that Sofonova is Mastroianni's love, he makes her the love of the audience as well. A marvelously acted, expertly photographed, and thoughtfully directed film which is a complete joy to experience. *(Brief nudity.)*

p, Silvia D'Amico Bendico, Carlo Cucchi; d, Nikita Mikhalkov; w, Alexander Adabachian, Nikita Mikhalkov, Suso Cecchi D'Amico (based on material from the Anton Chekhov stories "The Lady With the Little Dog," "The Name-Day Party," "Anna Around the Neck," "My Wife"); ph, Franco di Giacomo (Eastmancolor); m, Francis Lai; ed, Enzo Meniconi; art d, Mario Garbuglia, Alexander Adabachian; set d, Carlo Gervasci; cos, Carlo Diappi.

Romance/Comedy **(PR:A-C MPAA:NR)**

DAS SCHWEIGEN DES DISHTERS (SEE: POET'S SILENCE, THE, 1987, Ger.)

DAS TREIBHAUS (1987, Ger.) 98m WDR, NDR, BR, HR and SWF TV Cult Film TV Filmproduktion bw/c (Trans: The Hothouse)

Christian Doermer, Jorg Hube, Hanns Zischler, O.A. Buck, Leila-Florentine Freer.

Coproduced by numerous German television stations and shown at the Berlin Film Festival, this entry is based on a 1953 Wolfgang Koeppen novel entitled *Das Treibhaus*. This 16mm film includes a dramatization of the novel as well as interview footage of the author discussing his work.

d&w, Peter Goedel (based on the novel by Wolfgang Koeppen); ph, David Slama; ed, Christiane Jahn, Peter Goedel; art d, Bohdan Wozniak.

Drama **(PR:NR MPAA:NR)**

DATE WITH AN ANGEL*** (1987) 105m DEG c

Michael E. Knight *(Jim Sanders)*, Phoebe Cates *(Patty Winston)*, Emmanuelle Beart *(Angel)*, David Dukes *(Ed Winston)*, Phil Brock *(George)*, Albert Macklin *(Don)*, Pete Kowanko *(Rex)*, Vinny Argiro *(Ben Sanders)*, Bibi Besch *(Grace Sanders)*, Cheryl A. Pollak *(Rhonda/Cashier in Market)*, Steven Banks *(Aldridge)*, Charles Lane *(Father O'Shea)*, J. Don Ferguson *(Harlan Rafferty)*, Bert Hogue, O'Clair Alexander *(Police Officers)*, Tony Reitano *(Love Bug Delivery Boy)*, Eve Brent, Muriel "Dolly" Sherman *(Matrons)*, Karen Durda *(Italian Lady)*, Leslie Norris *(Receptionist)*, Thomas L. McIntyre, Nancy McLoughlin, Bonnie Cook *(Executives)*, Albert Ash *(Wimpy Executive)*, D. Anthony Pender *(Wertheimer)*, Anna Maria Poon, David Fitzsimmons, Joe Herold, Mi Mi Green *(Reporters)*, Jerry Campbell *(Gas Station Attendant)*, Tom McLoughlin *(Owlish Man in Church)*.

A simple and rather charming movie that consciously goes after the feel of old Frank Capra films, DATE WITH AN ANGEL opens in a heaven filled with moving lights as Beart, a heavenly messenger, is sent to claim "with love" a young man suffering from a brain tumor (or some such ailment). Swooping across the cosmos toward Earth, she collides with a communications satellite and plummets uncontrollably into the swimming pool of Knight, the young man she seeks. He is engaged to Cates, the daughter of a cosmetics tycoon, and is recovering on the floor from his blowout bachelor party when he is awakened by the splash of the angel landing in his pool and gallons of water rushing in under his back door. He finds Beart floating face down and pulls her out, reviving her with mouth-to-mouth resuscitation. She tries to envelope him in her wings, but one of

them is broken, and Knight takes her inside and fixes it up in a splint. His three best buddies come over to help him clean up the party debris and Knight tries to keep them out, but they force their way in and see Beart, wings and all. They immediately conceive of a dozen or more ways to exploit this incredible find, ranging from T-shirts to concert tours. Knight manages to get rid of them, but is immediately concerned with dealing with his fiancee, who is furious about his departure from a swank affair her parents had thrown the previous night. Cates also sees Beart and immediately assumes that Knight has spent the night with her. She leaves in a huff. Knight makes repeated efforts to convince Cates that he still wants to marry her and that nothing is going on between him and Beart, but she is unswayed, and slowly turns angry as she tries to drown her sorrow in gin. Meanwhile, Knight's buddies are undeterred by his protests and hatch a plan to kidnap Beart and put her on display. Just in the nick of time, Knight finds them and rescues Beart before her wings can be shown to a mob of reporters. He flees with her into the forest where there is an old tree house from his childhood. There the two of them live in something like bliss and he realizes that he loves her as his headaches become worse and her wing gets better. Eventually all the other characters—Knight's father, his three chums, Cates (with a shotgun in tow) and her parents—as well as the cops, figure out where the pair is hiding. Beart disappears just as they show up and helps invisibly in the fight that ensues, dousing Cates and her daddy in miniature rainstorms and zapping others with lightning. Knight slumps to the ground unconscious and is taken to the hospital. There doctors declare he has only a short time to live. Beart appears in Knight's room and takes him into her wings in an embrace of death. Later his friends come into the room to apologize. They think he is dead for a moment, but a nurse comes in and tells them that she knows he will be all right. They look and see that it is Beart, now human. She explains to Knight that this is the answer to an angel's prayer.

This could have been botched in a hundred ways, falling into cheap sentiment or becoming a worthless chase movie or something similar, but, thanks almost entirely to Beart, it all works. This French actress, who won a Cesar (the French Oscar) for her role in Claude Berri's MANON DES SOURCES, was chosen after

the producers auditioned over 6,000 others. They couldn't have made a better choice. Beart is truly ethereal. Bathed in white light, she exerts the same kind of goodwill over the audience that she does over the characters in the film, all without speaking a word. Knight is most familiar as Tad Martin on the TV soap opera "All My Children." Director McLoughlin's only previous credit is FRIDAY THE 13TH PART VI: JASON LIVES, but he certainly shows he is capable of more, deftly keeping his story on track. The old cliche runs that they don't make them like that anymore, and it's true, but this is close, and it will do for now, until they run HERE COMES MR. JORDAN on the late show again. *(Profanity, comic violence.)*

p, Martha Schumacher; d&w, Tom McLoughlin; ph, Alex Thomson (Technicolor); m, Randy Kerber; ed, Marshall Harvey; prod d, Craig Stearns; art d, Jeffrey S. Ginn; set d, Randy Moore; cos, Donna O'Neal; spec eff, Richard Edlund; m/l, Carole King, Gerry Goffin, "Ric" Ocasek, Men Without Hats, Richard Penniman, Dorothy LaBostrie, Joe Lubin, Francis Lai, Fred Steiner, Albert Hammond, Randy Kerber, Steve Winwood, Will Jennings, Robert Ian McNabb, Natalie Pace, No Prisoners, Rose Hamlin; stunts, Thomas Rosales, Jr.; makeup, Rose Marie Zurlo.

Fantasy/Comedy **(PR:A-C MPAA:PG)**

DAUGHTERS OF EVE† (1987, Phil.) Roadshow c

Isabel Lopez *(Tonya)*, Mark Joseph *(Simon Kalabaw)*, Sarsi Emmanuelle *(Selda)*, Myra Manibog *(Mona)*, Daren Craig Johnson.

A virginal village schoolteacher surrenders herself to a local gigolo only to be jilted when he falls for the charms of another. He is made an enemy of the people, and, when accused of murder, is lynched by the local schoolchildren.

[No credits available.]

Drama **(PR:NR MPAA:NR)**

DAY THEY ROBBED AMERICA, THE† (1987, Phil.) Sunny-Vanguard/Davian c

James Acheson, Rudy Fernandez.

Sent off for some rest and recuperation, a Vietnam war hero is confronted with gun runners and bank robbers. When the robbers take his girl friend hostage, he reverts to his Vietnam training, hunting down and killing each member of the gang.

d, Manuel Cinco.

Action **(PR:NR MPAA:NR)**

DE FLYGANDE DJAVLARNA† (1987, Swed.) 100m Crone-Swedish Film Institute-Svensk Filmindustri c (Trans: The Flying Devils)

Mario David, Erland Josephson, Senta Berger, Peter Lee Wilson, Karmen Atias.

Erland Josephson of Andrei Tarkovsky's THE SACRIFICE and numerous Ingmar Bergman pictures costars with Senta Berger in this drama about a group of trapeze artists.

d, Anders Refn.

Drama **(PR:NR MPAA:NR)**

DE MUJER A MUJER† (1987, Venezuela/Colombia) 109m E.M.-Cinematograficas Uno/Pel-Mex c (Trans: Woman to Woman)

Humberto Zurita *(Sergio)*, Elba Escobar *(Elsa)*, Daniel Alvarado *(Eloy)*, Amparo Grisales *(Miranda)*.

The friendship between two women—Escobar and Grisales—is destroyed when they become involved with the same man, Zurita, an animalistic brute with a sexual hold over both women. After Escobar is jilted by Zurita, who comes to favor Grisales, Escobar sets her sights on Alvarado, Grisales' former lover. This uncontrolled sexual energy ultimately ends in the death of all involved. Shown in New York.

p, Luis Felipe Betancourt, Bella Ventura; d, Mauricio Walerstein; ph, Jose Alcalde; m, Alejandro Blanco Uribe.

Drama **(PR:NR MPAA:NR)**

DE ORIONNEVEL† (1987, Neth.) 81m Horizon/Cor Koppies c (Trans: Orion Nebula)

Bert Kuizenga *(Gerdo)*, Han Kerckhoffs *(Bril)*, Michiel Romeyn *(Baard)*.

The story of a tender friendship between three men in their early thirties, all of whom drift through their lives without any direction or purpose. Filmed in Super 16mm, this is the feature debut from Rood, who also contributed to the score.

p, Frans Rasker; d&w, Jurrien Rood, ph, Goert Giltay (Kodacolor); m, Jurrien Rood; Arjen Hogendorp; ed, Hans von Dongen; art d, Gert Brinkers.

Comedy **(PR:NR MPAA:NR)**

DE RATELRAT† (1987, Neth.) 88m Spiegel Filmproductiemaatschappi-Avro TV/Concorde c (Trans: The Rattlerat)

Rijk de Gooijer *(Capt. Grijpstra)*, Peter Faber *(Lt. De Gier)*, Bernard Droog, Hidde Maas, Femke Boersma, Annemieke Verdoorn.

Two Dutch police detectives do battle with crooked cops and Chinese drug dealers.

p, Frans Rasker; d, Wim Verstappen; w, Wim Verstappen, Jan Willem van de Wetering, Rogier Proper (based on the novel by Jan Willem van de Wetering); ph, Frans Bromet (Agfa Color); m, Ruud Bos; ed, Rob van Steensel; art d, Dorus van der Linden.

Crime **(PR:NR MPAA:NR)**

DE TAL PEDRO, TAL ASTILLA† (1987, Cuba) 90m ICAIC c (Trans: Like Father, Like Daughter)

Reynaldo Miravilles, Gilberto Reyes, Thais Valdes, Nestor Rivero, Hilario Pena, Tania Perez James, Orlando Casin.

A Cuban musical comedy about two rival cattle ranchers whose children become romantically linked, leading to all the usual complications.

p, Ricardo Avila; d&w, Luis Felipe Bernaza; ph, Jorge Haydu; m, Tony Tano, Aneiro Tano; ed, Mirita Lores.

Musical/Comedy **(PR:NR MPAA:NR)**

DEAD, THE***** (1987) 83m Liffey/Vestron-Zenith c

Anjelica Huston *(Gretta Conroy)*, Donal McCann *(Gabriel Conroy, Her Husband)*, Rachael Dowling *(Lily)*, Cathleen Delany *(Aunt Julia Morkan)*, Helena Carroll *(Aunt Kate Morkan)*, Ingrid Craigie *(Mary Jane)*, Dan O'Herlihy *(Mr. Browne)*, Frank Patterson *(Bartell D'Arcy)*, Donal Donnelly *(Freddy Malins)*, Marie Kean *(Mrs. Malins)*, Maria McDernottroe *(Molly Ivors)*, Sean McClory *(Mr. Grace)*, Kate O'Toole *(Miss Furlong)*, Maria Hayden *(Miss O'Callaghan)*, Bairbre Dowling *(Miss Higgins)*, Lyda Anderson *(Miss Daly)*, Dara Clarke *(Miss Power)*, Colm Meany *(Mr. Bergin)*, Cormac O'Herlihy *(Mr. Kerrigan)*, Paul Grant *(Mr. Duffy)*, Patrick Gallagher *(Mr. Egan)*, Amanda Baird *(Young Lady)*, Paul Carroll *(Young Gentleman)*, Redmond M. Gleason *(Nightporter)*, Brendon Dillon *(Cabman)*.

This sublime adaptation of the last story in James Joyce's *Dubliners* became John Huston's final film, and it is as beautiful, delicate, and moving an epitaph as any filmmaker could ever desire. Set in Dublin on the chilly night of January 6, 1904, the day of the Epiphany, THE DEAD takes place at the home of spinster aunts Carroll and Delany and their niece Craigie. Every year their post-holidays party is an event to be cherished. Music, dancing, and good food are shared by relatives and friends alike. The spinsters' favorite guest is their sophisticated nephew, McCann, and his beautiful wife, Anjelica Huston. Always bothersome are the alcoholic Donnelly and his friend O'Herlihy, both of whom drink too much and cause Donnelly's aged mother, Kean, grief and upset. During dinner many topics are discussed, including opera, politics, and religion. Aunts Carroll and Delany become wistful about the departed singers they admire. McCann breaks the momentarily gloomy mood with his annual toast, praising the hospitality and generosity of his aunts. Both women are moved to tears during McCann's eloquent declaration. Following dinner, after most of the guests have left, Huston is struck by the haunting rendition of "The Lass of Aughrim" sung by one of the guests, Patterson. McCann watches his wife as she stands still on the stairs, listening intently to the song. On the cab ride back to their hotel, Huston is distant, lost in her thoughts. McCann tries to cajole his brooding wife with a feeble joke, but she barely acknowledges his effort. In their room, a tearful Huston confesses to McCann that the song has stirred long-suppressed memories of a brief and tragic romance from her youth. The boy's name was Michael Furey, a delicate lad with big dark eyes whom she used to go walking with in Galway. He sang that song. McCann experiences a flash of jealousy and asks if she is in love with this Michael Furey. "He is dead," she replies. "He died when he was only 17. Isn't it a terrible thing to die so young as that?" When asked the cause of Michael Furey's death, Huston replies, "I think he died for me." Trying to stave off another burst of tears, Huston tells her husband that the boy was suffering from consumption, and when it came time for her to leave Galway to go to the convent in Dublin, a badly ill Michael Furey braved the rainy winter weather to come to her window and tell her that he no longer cared to live. She told him to go home, and he did, but one week later word arrived that he had died. After relating this, Huston breaks down and cries herself to sleep. McCann stands at the window, watching the snow fall. Feeling lost, depressed, and jealous, McCann marvels at the power that the dead hold over the living. He thinks that soon he will be attending the wake of his Aunt Delany and of how useless his words of comfort will be. He thinks of his wife and the terrible love that she has had locked in her heart for so many years. He contemplates the boy who would rather die than lose her: "I had never felt like that myself toward any woman, but I know that such a feeling must be love." With tears in his eyes, McCann imagines snow falling all over Ireland that night—over the central plain and the treeless hills. As Joyce puts it: "It was falling, too, upon every part of the lonely churchyard on the hill where Michael Furey lay buried. It lay thickly drifted on the crooked crosses and headstones, on the spears of the little gate, on the barren thorns. His soul swooned slowly as he heard the snow falling faintly through the universe and faintly falling, like the descent of their last end, upon all the living and the dead."

THE DEAD is a breathtakingly beautiful movie that is the mature work of a master filmmaker. Assured, delicate, and subtle, this flawlessly realized film is the antithesis of current trends in Hollywood filmmaking and should be all the more cherished because of it. John Huston had wanted to make a film adaptation of "The Dead" since the 1950s when it was suggested to him during the filming of MOBY DICK. The subject came up again in the 1980s when producer Schulz-Keil and Huston were discussing literary examinations of marriage during the filming of UNDER THE VOLCANO. Huston, a lifelong admirer of Joyce ("Joyce was and remains the most influential writer in my life," he said during the filming of THE DEAD) who remembered his mother smuggling a forbidden copy of *Ulysses* into the US back in 1928 when the book was banned, put the idea of filming the story on the back burner because of its uncommercial nature. But Schulz-Keil decided that the time was right and hired Huston's eldest son, Tony, to write the screenplay, which is scrupulously faithful to Joyce. Schulz-Keil managed to raise $5.5 million to make the film (a mere pittance these days) by persuading fledgling distributor Vestron and four foreign companies to put up the money. Although John wanted to shoot the film in his beloved Ireland, his health didn't permit it and the lush indoor set was built in an abandoned warehouse in Valencia, California (second unit photography was done in Dublin where the house Joyce describes is still standing). John insisted that every detail be perfect, from the all-Irish cast (including his daughter Angelica, who was raised in Galway, Ireland—the same place from which her character hails) to the antique props.

The casting is superb and Huston allows all his performers equal screen time until the end when Anjelica Huston and Donal McCann become the focus of the piece. The party scene is a flurry of detailed movement, immaculately choreographed to give the viewer the impression that he is one of the guests at this annual affair. Huston concentrates on the interaction of the characters—the conversations, the movements, the rituals—and glories in the nuances of human behavior. The film's most powerful sequence, however, is the scene between husband and wife. Anjelica Huston is superb as she tearfully relates the story of Michael Furey. Striking the perfect balance of emotions, Anjelica deftly plays the scene for all its sad and tragic impact without ever resorting to histrionics. It is a performance of grace and eloquence. Equally excellent is McCann, who somehow manages to convey with a minimum of visible *acting* the dawning self-awareness described by Joyce. His reading of Joyce's closing words is supremely moving. John Huston must have known that THE DEAD was to be his final film, for one cannot imagine a more glorious coda to such a fruitful career. THE DEAD was made by a man who had a deep appreciation for all the arts and how they enrich the human experience, and his intelligence and passion is evident in every exquisite moment. Rarely has language, performance, and cinematography been so skillfully intertwined to produce such a poignant display of emotion, acumen, and beauty. THE DEAD is a film for the ages, one that stands outside of time and fashion.

p, Wieland Schulz-Keil, Chris Sievernich; d, John Huston; w, Tony Huston (based on the short story from *The Dubliners* by James Joyce); ph, Fred Murphy (Foto-Kem Color); m, Alex North; ed, Roberto Silvi; prod d, Stephen Grimes, Dennis Washington; set d, Josie McAvin; cos, Dorothy Jeakins.

Drama **(PR:A MPAA:PG)**

DEAD OF WINTER½** (1987) 100m MGM/MGM-UA c

Mary Steenburgen *(Katie McGovern)*, Roddy McDowall *(Mr. Murray)*, Jan Rubes *(Dr. Joseph Lewis)*, William Russ *(Rob Sweeney)*, Mark Malone *(Roland McGovern)*, Ken Pogue, Wayne Robson, Michael Copeman, Sam Malkin.

This one is a chestnut roasted over many times, the damsel in so much distress through the machinations of maniac blackmailers that her awful plight is absurdly laughable in a macabre sort of way. Steenburgen, with her gangling frame and tremulous voice, is a struggling New York actress who is offered a part, or the chance for a part in a film, by weirdo McDowall, playing the role of an agent, or pretending to be a talent agent. He takes one look at Steenburgen and hires her. McDowall tells her that she must undergo some testing in upstate New York at the home of a film producer and offers her $3,000. If she has a successful videotape test she will be paid another $9,000 to play the role which was slated for an actress who has disappeared. Steenburgen goes along with McDowall with the blessings of her husband, Malone, who is disabled with a broken leg. Once in a remote area, Steenburgen is transformed to look like the actress who vanished and does her video test before wheelchair-bound Rubes, pretending to be the producer. Then Steenburgen tries to make a call but finds the phone is out of order; the storm has brought the lines down, she is told. Later she looks into the burning fireplace to see in amazement her own driver's license afire. Upstairs in her room, she finds that all her identification, has been removed from her purse. She confronts McDowall and Rubes but they tell her she is imagining things and she is given a sedative, told to go to sleep and lock the door if she mistrusts her hosts. She bolts the door to her bedroom and awakens the next day to find the ring finger on her left hand has been cut off, a bandage covering the wound, bloodstains on the sheets and pillow case of her bed. Of course, there is no film being made. The video tape made by Steenburgen was part of a blackmailing scheme on the part of Rubes and McDowall. They explain to the terrified Steenburgen that the woman she is impersonating was murdered by a hired killer in the employ of the dead woman's sister whom McDowall and Rubes continue to blackmail. The hired killer had cut off his victim's finger as proof of completing his assignment, but the dead woman's body was later recovered by McDowall and the corpse is hidden in the attic of Rubes' mansion. She had been their companion in blackmail, having evidence that her sister had murdered her way to wealth. With her dead, they needed a replacement and found Steenburgen, the perfect doppelganger. They made the videotape to prove to the sister that her sibling was still alive and then they cut her finger off so that the mutilated hand would match that of the wound inflicted on the murdered sister. (It gets even more involved but these are the principal twists of this maze-like thriller.) Steenburgen manages to get to an attic room through the mirror-door in her room. Here she finds a phone and calls her husband in New York, blurting near-incoherent directions to the remote mansion. He tells her that he'll find her and orders her to call the police. She does call police but McDowall finds her and drags her downstairs. Police arrive later and Rubes informs them that Steenburgen is his patient, a mentally disturbed woman who has cut off her own finger. She tells them hysterically that there's a dead woman in the attic but they find nothing and leave, even though she tells them that McDowall and Rubes are going to kill her. Again she is drugged and revives to see her own mirror image once more; the sister being blackmailed has arrived to verify that the blackmailing sister is still alive and has the evidence to convict her of murder. She negotiates with Rubes while McDowall again takes Steenburgen upstairs, holding her until the sister pays Rubes the blackmail money. Then the two men plan to turn Steenburgen over to the sister so she can be murdered. Through a ruse, Steenburgen escapes, and while McDowall and Rubes look for her she confronts the sister who tries to kill her. When the two men return, she pretends to be the sister, having killed the murderess and hidden her body in a window seat. She later kills McDowall and is about to escape when Rubes guesses that she is not the murdering sister but the struggling actress and he begins to chase her, an amazingly agile cripple who could not earlier leave his wheelchair. He lurches through the house, up the stairs, cornering Steenburgen in the attic where, through another ruse, Steenburgen buries a knife in the mad doctor's back. Still he comes at her like a cat with nine lives, she striking him with objects. He is about to strangle her when he steps into a bear trap and falls back on the knife in his back, dead. Steenburgen cowers in a corner when to her horror, she sees Rubes bolt upright into a sitting position, but it's her husband, Malone, come to rescue her, throwing up the attic trap door upon which the zany doctor had fallen. The actress is removed from the mad house worse the wear by a finger and undoubtedly cautious about future auditions.

Penn uses every trick in the old horror book to pull this one off and nothing really works, including his accent on scary noises, from car horns to clicking camera shutters, from creaking stairs and doors to howling winter winds. Everything is forced, contrived, and not too neatly lifted from other classic doppelganger films such as DEAD RINGER and THE DARK MIRROR. Early on, when Steenburgen first arrives at the old mansion, Rubes points out that there are mousetraps everywhere (no doubt a nod by Penn to Agatha Christie's forever running London play, THE MOUSETRAP). And hiding the dead body of the blackmailing sister in the window seat is, of course, straight out of ARSENIC AND OLD LACE. Then there's the mansion itself, which could pass for a double of THE OLD DARK HOUSE. McDowall and Rubes delight in their roles so much that no one, not even the most naive actress blinded with hopes for a starring role, could accept them as anything other than a couple of lunatics up to no good. Steenburgen gets to play herself three times over, as the actress, the murdering sister, and the corpse of the blackmailing sister, stuffed away in an attic with a mouse running across her pale face. She's not convincing in any of these roles and, as the struggling actress, is as helpless as a paraplegic. Her escape scene in the woods during a snow storm is pathetic. She is outside no more than a few minutes when she falls to the ground and begins clawing her way forward, the camera at ground level, closing on her fluttering eyes, a blatant, shameful lift from scenes in D.W. Griffith's WAY DOWN EAST, a silent film where Lillian Gish claws her way across an iceflow. Penn, who staged on Broadway a similar situation thriller, WAIT UNTIL DARK, fails miserably with the archaic premise of this film and employs poverty techniques that question his authentic abilities as a director of distinction (BONNIE AND CLYDE). As a previous Penn failure (TARGET) proved, suspense is not his metier and DEAD OF WINTER seals the verdict. *(Graphic violence.)*

p, John Bloomgarden, Marc Shmuger; d, Arthur Penn; w, Marc Shmuger, Mark Malone; ph, Jan Weincke (Metrocolor); m, Richard Einhorn; ed, Rich Shaine; prod d, Bill Brodie; set d, Mark S. Freeborn; cos, Arthur Roswell.

Suspense/Thriller Cas. **(PR:O MPAA:R)**

DEADLINE** (1987, Brit./Ger./Israel) 99m Creative-Caro-Norddeutcher Rundfunk GPMS Intl./Skouras c

Christopher Walken *(Don Stevens)*, Marita Marschall *(Linda Larson)*, Hywel Bennett *(Mike Jessop)*, Arnon Zadok *(Hamdi Abu-Yussuf)*, Amos Lavie *(Yessin Abu-Riadd)*, Ette Ankri *(Samira)*, Martin Umbach *(Bernard)*, Moshe Ivgi *(Abdul)*, Sason Gabay *(Bassam)*, Shahar Cohen *(Habib)*, Sholomo Bar-Aba *(Micha)*, Gaby Shoshan *(Salim)*, Igal Naor *(Antoine)*, Jerry Weinstock *(Snyder)*, Reuven Dayan *(Karim)*, Nader Masraawi *(Daoud)*, David Menachem *(Phalangist)*, Shlomo Tarshish *(Yoram)*, Moni Mushonov *(Danny)*.

Yet another "enlightening" political drama that chooses one of the world's hot spots and throws a detached American journalist into the abyss so that he can undergo a change of character and sort out the complicated mess for the moviegoing public. Like Volker Schlondorff's CIRCLE OF DECEIT (1982), DEADLINE is set in war-torn Beirut where the PLO and the Christian Phalangists battle while the Israeli army acts as referee (at least that's director Gutman and writer Peled's view of Israeli participation in the tragedy). Enter lazy, cynical American correspondent Walken. Fresh from covering a fashion show in Paris, he has been sent to Beirut by his fictional network, ABS, to act as a temporary replacement for the regular reporter who has fallen ill. Content to stay far away from the action and piece together his reports from outtakes filmed by other correspondents, Walken spends his time by the hotel pool getting drunk. Things change a bit when he is given a shot at an exclusive interview with a disgruntled PLO leader. The leader tells Walken that he feels it is time to abandon terrorism and look for a negotiated settlement with the Israelis. This news sends shock waves around the world and draws immediate denials from the PLO, who claim that the man was an impostor. As it turns out, the man Walken interviewed was a charlatan, and the American becomes determined to get to the bottom of the mystery. Eventually he is led to the real PLO leader, Lavie, who shares the views espoused by the impostor and agrees to say as much on camera. Just as the interview begins, terrorists burst into the room and murder Lavie. Walken takes the PLO leader and his young son to the hospital, but it is too late. There he meets a European nurse, Marschall, who is Lavie's estranged lover. Walken later learns that Marschall was an agent for the Israeli Mossad, but that she left its ranks after falling in love with Lavie. She tells Walken that the PLO plans to bomb the Phalange headquarters. Hoping to save lives, Walken goes to the Israeli military and warns them of the bombings. Before the Israelis have a chance to investigate, the Phalange headquarters is destroyed and many die. Knowing that the Phalange will retaliate by slaughtering innocent Palestinian refugees, Walken once again tries to get the Israeli army to do something, but is shrugged off by them. Walken goes to the Palestinian encampment himself and urges the people to flee, but the PLO demands that they stay and face the Phalangists rather than allow themselves to be run off their settlements again. Walken is imprisoned by the PLO and that night he listens in horror as hundreds of men, women, and children are slaughtered by the Phalangists. With nothing left to do but report the tragedy, Walken walks among the corpses with his video camera taking footage of the carnage. Because the rest of the press is prevented from entering the settlement by the Israelis, Walken leaves with a world exclusive.

DEADLINE is set in one of the world's most violent and chaotic places, yet somehow it manages to be deadeningly dull and hopelessly middle-of-the-road. Although the filmmakers pretend to approach the material with a level head and to present the confusing complexities with an even hand, they merely turn all the players into meaningless one-dimensional caricatures. The Phalangists are a bunch of psychotic murderers, the PLO a band of vicious-but-misunderstood killers, and the Israeli army an overworked police force. Not that a filmmaker can sort out the turbulent problems of the Middle East in less than two hours, but this approach tells viewers nothing. The cliche use of a detached journalist as the audience identification character is as unimaginative as it is misguided. The notion that a journalist would suddenly become so involved that he calls the

various leaders by their first names and acts as a liaison between them in an effort to directly influence world events is as troubling as it is fanciful. This trick has been used in a rash of films in the 1980s, among them UNDER FIRE, THE YEAR OF LIVING DANGEROUSLY, SALVADOR, and THE KILLING FIELDS. Unfortunately, Walken's drab performance makes the action all the more unbelievable. He plays his character as a guy who looks like he has trouble getting out of bed in the morning, and even when he is passionately involved, he affects a strange air of boredom and detachment. Gutman's direction is just as lazy, and he lets the realistic locations (shot mostly in Israel) do the work for him. Gutman tries desperately to portray events in a balanced manner, but in doing so he invariably leans toward the official Israeli version of events and renders the whole project pointless. *(Graphic violence, profanity.)*

p, Elisabeth Wolters-Alfs; d, Nathaniel Gutman; w, Hanan Peled; ph, Amnon Salomon, Thomas Mauch (Geyer-Werhe Color); m, Jacques Zwart, Hans Jansen; ed, Peter Przygodda; art d, Yoram Barzily; spec eff, Yoram Polack.

Drama **(PR:O MPAA:R)**

DEADLY ILLUSION† (1987) 87m Pound Ridge/Cinetel c

Billy Dee Williams *(Hamberger)*, Vanity *(Rina)*, Morgan Fairchild *(Jane/Sharon)*, Joe Cortese *(Detective Lefferts)*, Dennis Hallahan *(Fake Burton)*, Jenny Cornuelle *(Gloria Reid)*, Michael Wilding, Jr. *(Costillion)*, Allison Woodward *(Nancy Costillion)*, Joe Spinell *(Man with Gun)*, Michael Emil *(Medical Examiner)*.

Prolific independent filmmaker Larry Cohen squeaks yet another film into distribution. Unfortunately, this latest effort had a brief run in New York City in early November and did not find a release in the rest of the country. Cohen continues his reexamination of crime film genres begun with BLACK CAESAR (1973) adding a touch of grim humor. Billy Dee Williams stars as a charming rogue of a detective who has a reputation for leaving a trail of corpses behind during his investigations. Willing to do just about anything for money, Williams accepts $25,000 from Hallahan, a client who wants his wife murdered. Pocketing the retainer, Williams then goes to warn the wife, played by Fairchild (her famous blonde locks disguised by a black wig). Williams and Fairchild pause for a sexual liaison and then she disappears. Moments later Williams discovers Hallahan's real wife has been murdered and that his client was an impostor. Staying one step ahead of Cortese, a cop determined to nail him, Williams' investigation takes him into the high-fashion modeling world where he uncovers a drug-smuggling ring headed by Fairchild (sans wig). Ultra low-budget and filmed in the hit-and-run style that Cohen is expert at, the producers of DEADLY ILLUSION fired Cohen sometime during the production and hired FLASHPOINT (1984) director William Tannen to finish.

p, Irwin Meyer; d, William Tannen, Larry Cohen; w, Larry Cohen; ph, Daniel Pearl (Deluxe Color); m, Patrick Gleason; ed, Steve Mirkovich, Ronald Spang; art d, Marina Zurkow, Ruth Lounsbury.

Crime **(PR:NR MPAA:R)**

DEADLY PREY† (1987) 88m Action Intl. c

Cameron Mitchell *(Jaimy's Dad)*, Troy Donahue *(Don Michaelson)*, Ted Prior *(Michael Danton)*, Fritz Matthews *(Lt. Thornton)*, David Campbell *(Col. Hogan)*, Dawn Abraham *(Sybil)*, William Zipp *(Cooper)*, Suzzane Tara *(Jaimy)*.

From the director and cast of KILL ZONE, a wretched 1985 RAMBO ripoff, comes DEADLY PREY. Relying on THE MOST DANGEROUS GAME for inspiration, this survivalist adventure film stars Prior as a human target for a demented mercenary, Campbell. As in the original 1932 film, the target fends off his attackers while scurrying through a jungle setting. After killing off Campbell's guards one-by-one, the prey finally comes face-to-face with his hunter. Donahue and Mitchell are little more than walk-ons. Released straight to video.

p, Peter Yuval; d&w, David A. Prior; ph, Stephen A. Blake (United Color); m, Steve McClintock, Tim James, Tim Heintz; ed, Brian Evans; stunts, Fritz Matthews.

Action Cas. **(PR:NR MPAA:NR)**

DEADLY STING (SEE: EVIL SPAWN, 1987)

DEADTIME STORIES zero (1987) 81m Scary Stuff Prods./Bedford Ent. c

Michael Mesmer *(Uncle Mike)*, Brian DePersia *(Little Brian)*, Scott Valentine *(Peter)*, Phyllis Craig *(Hanagohl)*, Anne Redfern *(Florinda)*, Kathy Fleg *(Miranda)*, Casper Roos *(Vicar)*, Barbara Seldon, Leigh Kirlton *(Seductresses)*, Lesley Sank *(Reviving Magoga)*, Lisa Cain *(Living Magoga)*, Jeff Delman *(Strangling Man)*, Nicole Picard *(Rachel)*, Matt Mitler *(Willie)*, Michael Berlinger *(Greg)*, Fran Lopate *(Grandma)*, John Bachelder *(Drugstore Clerk)*, Caroline Carrigan *(Nurse)*, Oded Carmi *(Groundskeeper)*, Heather L. Bailey *(Girl in Store)*, Thea *(Dog)*, Cathryn DePrume *(Goldi Lox)*, Melissa Leo *(Melissa "Mama" Baer)*, Kevin Hannon *(Beresford "Papa" Baer)*, Timothy Rule *(Wilmont "Baby" Baer)*, Robert Trimboli *(Lt. Jack B. Nimble)*, Harvey Pierce *(Capt. Jack B. Quick)*, Rondell Sheridan *(Looney Bin Guard)*, Beth Felty *(Reporter)*, Pat McCord *(Anchorman)*, Michele Mars *(Waitress)*, Ron Bush *(Bank Guard)*, Oded Carmi *(Postman)*, Bryant Tausek *(Man at Car)*, Suzanna Vaucher *(Weather Girl)*, Leif Wennerstrom, Jim Nocell *(Dead Bodies)*.

A lame anthology of three skewed fairy tales bridged by a framing story in which DePersia, a little boy who can't sleep and who keeps seeing monsters in his dark bedroom, is told the stories by his slightly vengeful uncle, Mesmer, who is upset about missing the Nude Miss World contest on cable TV. In the first story, "Peter and the Witches," a sturdy young lad who was sold into slavery as a child is the lackey of a pair of hideous witches. He lures a lecherous preacher to their lair where the witches drug him, then burn off his hand. A few incantations turn the hand into a talisman that helps the two hags locate the moldering bones of their sister. Carting the bones back to their home, they next send the boy out to attract a sacrificial young virgin. When he returns, the lad kills the two witches, but their sister has already come back to life and fled. Running through the woods, the boy and girl encounter the witch and survive only when he tears out her heart. Back in the framing story, DePersia is unsatisfied with this ending and so Mesmer tells him that the witch suddenly came back to life and killed the youngsters, a resolution that suits DePersia better. The next story, "Little Red Runninghood," is about a nubile high-school girl who stops by the pharmacy to pick up a prescription for Granny. Unfortunately, the package is mixed up with one for a young man who needs powerful sleeping pills to prevent him from becoming a werewolf during the full moon. He proceeds to Granny's house to rectify matters, but Granny refuses to let him in, saying, "I have a meat cleaver and I know how to use it." Come moonrise, he turns into a wolf and mauls her. Just then the heroine arrives after spending the last few hours losing her virginity in a toolshed. The werewolf attacks and she barely manages to survive by driving a silver cake knife into his neck. Granny survives but falls victim to lycanthropy herself. "What big teeth you have," Red tells her as the story fades out. In "Goldi Lox and the Three Baers," Beresford "Papa" Baer and his idiot son Wilmont "Baby" Baer break out of the loony bin and head to their old house, now occupied by Goldi Lox, a fellow escaped lunatic with telekinetic powers. It's a match made in heaven and they all escape together just as police, led by Lt. Jack B. Nimble and Capt. Jack B. Quick, charge in to the empty house, guns blazing.

Miserable production values plague this film shot over the course of four years in upstate New York and Connecticut. Director Delman makes his debut, although the press kit notes that his grandfather's cousin was legendary movie music composer Bernard Herrmann, suggesting that talent is not hereditary. The film does have some wacky humor going for it, but comedy is not what horror film fans are after. They look for jolts, special effects, and edge-of-the-seat tension, none of which are in evidence here. *(Nudity, gore effects, sexual situations.)*

p, Bill Paul; d, Jeffrey Delman; w, Jeffrey Delman, Charles F. Shelton (based on a story by Jeffrey Delman); ph, Daniel B. Canton; m, Taj; ed, William Szarka; art d, Joan Lopate, Mark Pruess, Jorge Toro; set d, Joan Lopate; cos, Angela Pruess, Regina Schuster; spec eff, Bryant Tausek, Edward French; m/l, Larry Juris, Jeffrey Delman; makeup, Laurie Aiello Williams, Ephraim Hunte, Lorraine Altamura, Matiki Anaff.

Horror **Cas.** **(PR:O MPAA:R)**

DEAR CARDHOLDER† (1987, Aus.) 90m Mermaid Beach-Multifilms c

Robin Ramsay *(Hec Harris)*, Jennifer Cluff *(Aggie Smith)*, Marion Chirgwin *(Jo Harris)*, Russell Newman *(Alfred Block)*, John Ewart *(Hart, Landlord)*, Patrick Cook *(Ardent)*, Bob Ellis *(Terence)*, Arianthe Galani *(Antoinette)*.

A comedy from the director of the ultraserious BACKLASH (1986), starring Ramsay as a widower who works as a lowly tax clerk. Ramsay has a scheme to become rich—he will devise a computer program that will make it easy for consumers to fill out their tax forms. Unfortunately, he doesn't own a computer and can't afford one because he has always paid cash for his purchases and has no credit rating. To obtain credit he borrows $500 from a bank and immediately returns it. He then applies for a credit card and racks up $10,000 worth of purchases. To pay off the debt he applies for more credit cards and soon finds himself in a spiral of massive deficit spending. To make matters worse, he loses his job and his 12-year-old daughter is taken from him and put in a welfare home. Just as things appear to be at their worst, Ramsay miraculously lands a job with Apple Computers and is able to pay his debts.

p,d&w, Bill Bennett; ph, Tony Wilson; m, Michael Atkinson; ed, Denise Hunter.

Comedy **(PR:NR MPAA:NR)**

DEATH BEFORE DISHONOR½** (1987) 95m Lawrence Kubik-M.P.I.-Bima/NW-Balcor c

Fred Dryer *(Sgt. Jack Burns)*, Joey Gian *(Ramirez)*, Sasha Mitchell *(Ruggieri)*, Peter Parros *(James)*, Brian Keith *(Col. Halloran)*, Paul Winfield *(Ambassador)*, Joanna Pacula *(Elli)*, Kasey Walker *(Maude)*, Rockne Tarkington *(Jihad)*, Dan Chodos *(Amin)*, Muhamad Bakri *(Gavril)*, Haim Geraffi *(Zabib)*, Jullianno Merr *(Said)*, Tuvia Tavi *(Elias)*, Yossi Ashdot *(Hamed)*, Yossi Virzansky *(Attache)*, Rinat Raz *(Wife)*, Guri Weinberg *(Son)*, Katya Bishoff *(Daughter)*, Rassan Tanus *(Arab Boy)*.

The title comes from the tattoo that so many Marines have stenciled on their upper arms. Dryer, the ex-Los Angeles Ram, has turned actor in a big way. His TV series "Hunter" was a fair hit and this feature proves that he, like former teammate Merlin Olsen, has a career ahead of him in the thespian profession. Here he plays a tough-as-nails Marine who has been sent to the mythical Middle Eastern country of "Jamal" (Lebanon by another name). Dryer is reminiscent of Lou Gossett in AN OFFICER AND A GENTLEMAN in that he has a short fuse, has no time for by-the-book officers, and he has put the nose of many a superior out of joint. His old pal Keith is a colonel and sends Dryer off to run the security at the US embassy. Dryer stews as Arabs burn the US flag in front of the embassy but he is hamstrung by his orders. Although technically a security person, his real job is as an observer and helper to the local military forces, who are always being besieged by the terrorists that seem to pop up in these countries with grave regularity. After almost starting a full-scale battle when some US equipment bound for the local army is hijacked, Dryer is held back. Then Keith is kidnaped by a cadre led by Walker and Bakri. Dryer wants to go after them right away, as he fears for his buddy's life, but US ambassador Winfield insists on "playing this by the book." Now them's fightin' words to Dryer. His best friend has been kidnaped, an Israeli diplomat and his family have been killed, the flag has been burned. It's enough to give a guy a migraine. Dryer knows that photographer Pacula (GORKY PARK) has an in with the terrorists, who believe that there is nothing as effective as good pictures of themselves and their captives. Through her, he manages to find the location. It's only then that Dryer learns that Pacula is working undercover for another group that wants to wipe out the terrorists (who *they* are is muddy). In the end, Dryer becomes a taller, fairer RAMBO, kills every Arab in sight, removes a small flag patch he'd taken from a dead comrade, attaches it to his Jeep antenna, and drives off into the distance as Gen. Ulysses S. Grant whirls in his grave while the familiar strains of "The Battle Hymn of the Republic" begin to rise in the background and Dryer's eyes fill with tears.

War cliches, bullets, and bombs abound. There is a brutal scene where an electric drill is used on Keith's hand to force him to sign a bogus confession and a refugee camp massacre. However, there are a few funny moments, such as the time when Winfield states unequivocally, "The United States does not, nor will not, negotiate with terrorists" (although this is inadvertent humor). Director Leonard spent most of his career helming second units and handling stunts. This is his first time out in the director's chair. He knows his way around grenades but needs a few more turns at bat with actors. The script spends too much time with unnecessary scenes of the terrorists, who seem to be the state of the art in gloating. Israeli locations are substituted for the thinly veiled Lebanon, with much of the action taking place at Nebbi Mussa, a Moslem fort built near Jordan in the 12th Century. The film company asked for and received permission to shoot at the holy place where thousands of Moslems pray annually. There is plenty of action, but it all seemed right for the plot and not nearly as gratuitous as many of Stallone's blood-and-guts pictures. With some judicious editing, this should be a good TV movie. *(Violence, profanity.).*

p, Lawrence Kubik; d, Terry J. Leonard; w, John Gatliff, Lawrence Kubik (based on a story by John Gatliff, Lawrence Kubik); ph, Don Burgess (DeLuxe Color); m, Brian May; ed, Steve Mirkovich; prod d, Kuli Sandor; md, Brian May; art d, Ladislav Wilheim; set d, Doron Efrat; cos, Rochelle Zaltzman; spec eff, Gary Monak, Eugene Crum; stunts, Kerry Rossall; makeup, Don Angier.

Action **(PR:C MPAA:R)**

DEATH OF A BEAUTIFUL DREAM† (1987, Czech.) Barrandov Film

Karel Hermanek, Marta Vancururova, Marek Valter, Jiri Stach, Jan Jiranek.

In Czechoslovakia on the eve of WW II, a father comes to terms with his Jewishness just as the Nazis arrive in his town. This film was passed over for selection for the Berlin Film Festival in favor of Vera Chytilova's ridiculous science-fiction allegory WOLF'S HOLE, but it was subsequently entered in the Moscow Film Festival.

d&w, Karel Kachyna; ph, Vladimir Smutny; m, Lubos Fiser; art d, Karel Lier.

Drama **(PR:NR MPAA:NR)**

DEATH SHADOWS† (1987, Jap.) 116m Shochiku c (JITTEMAI)

Mariko Ishihara *(Ocho, the Flower Storm)*, Masanori Sera *(Shipping Agent)*, Mari Natsuki *(Oren)*, Takuzo Kawatani, Takeo Chii, Naoto Takenaka, Eitaro Ozawa.

Samurai film from that genre's best director, Hideo Gosha, starring Ishihara as a female member of the Shadows, a secret police force employed by the Shogunate. Ishihara, who is skilled with a silken whip, is assigned the task of proving that a respected nobleman is smuggling goods for vicious crime boss Natsuki.

d, Hideo Gosha; w, Motomu Furuta (based on a story by Hideo Gosha, Kotaro Mori); ph, Fujiro Morita; m, Masaru Sato; art d, Yoshinobu Nishioka.

Action **(PR:NR MPAA:NR)**

DEATH STONE† (1987, Ger.) 95m NRF-Tarprobane-CCC c

Albert Fortell *(Kumar)*, Birte Berg *(Jane Lindstrom)*, Ravindra *(Wrickremapala)*, Brad Harris *(Brian)*, Siegfried Rauch *(Hemingway)*, Heather Thomas *(Merryl Davis)*, Elke Sommer *(Kris Patterson)*, Tony Kendall *(Miguel Gomez)*, Serge Falck *(Frank)*.

This German-produced action film shot in Sri Lanka and performed in English is a good candidate for a straight-to-video release in the US. Fortell stars as an architect whose fiancee, Berg, finds a trinket on the beach known as the "Death Stone." Local superstition has it that whosoever possesses the stone will die. Shortly thereafter, Berg falls prey to a gang of ruthless drug dealers. Predictably, Fortell declares a private war on the criminals and much pyrotechnics follow. Elke Sommer and Heather Thomas make cameo appearances to enhance US audience appeal.

p, Theo M. Werner, Chandran Rutnam; d, Franz Josef Gottlieb; w, H.W. John, John Ferguson; m, Luigi Ceccarelli.

Action **(PR:NR MPAA:NR)**

DEATH WISH 4: THE CRACKDOWN* (1987) 99m Golan-Globus/Cannon c

Charles Bronson *(Paul Kersey)*, Kay Lenz *(Karen Sheldon)*, John P. Ryan *(Nathan White)*, Perry Lopez *(Ed Zacharias)*, George Dickerson *(Detective Reiner)*, Soon-Teck Oh *(Detective Nozaki)*, Dana Barron *(Erica Sheldon)*, Jesse Dabson *(Randy Viscovich)*.

Citizen avenger Paul Kersey undertakes another violent crusade against lawlessness in the fourth installment of the phenomenally successful DEATH WISH series. The film opens with Bronson, not getting any younger, growing close to divorcee Lenz and her teenage daughter, Barron. When Barron goes off on a date, Bronson sees her smoke a joint with her boy friend and he expresses some concern about the boy to Lenz. Next thing we know, a fatal dose of crack finishes Barron. Bronson tracks down the seller and kills him. Some time later he is summoned to the mansion of millionaire Ryan, who tells Bronson about the death of his daughter due to drugs and makes the rather Draconian pronouncement, "Anyone connected with drugs deserves to die." He offers to finance Bronson on a crusade against the two biggest drug gangs in southern California, giving him dossiers on the organizations and their leaders. Bronson is soon on the job against the gangs, and a pair of detectives (Oh and Dickerson) is assigned to the case. Oh turns out to work for one of the drug dealers and he tries to buy off then kill Bronson, but Bronson is faster on the draw than the detective. Bronson provokes a gang war, leading to a furious gun battle with few survivors. Suddenly, though, an attempt is made on Bronson's life by a pair of policemen and Bronson storms up to Ryan's house. It's not Ryan's house after all, as Bronson learns when he meets the real owner. Bronson cleverly concludes that Ryan is a drug kingpin who used him to wipe out the competition, and boy is he mad. Ryan realizes his predicament and makes several unsuccessful attempts on Bronson's life. The climax comes at a skating rink where Ryan puts a gun against Lenz's head and heads for a back door. Bronson lets him go, but Ryan spitefully (and foolishly) shoots Lenz in the back and Bronson blows him away.

No one was exactly clamoring for this one and Bronson has vowed it will be the last DEATH WISH, so now it is possible to look at the series in its entirety. The first movie, set in New York, in 1974 had Bronson a respectable family man who driven to violence after his wife is murdered and his daughter gang-raped. It was more than eight years before the next installment emerged, and this time Bronson's catatonic daughter is attacked and killed, leaving Bronson to take vengeance against the scum of Los Angeles. The third reached the nadir, with Bronson protecting the inhabitants of a tenement building from marauding punk thugs whom Bronson destroyed with laughably heavy-handed weaponry. Now, we find him the dupe of a criminal himself, so ready to kill for justice that he simply accepts Ryan's word and starts shooting. The most thankless roles in these films are those of the family and friends of Bronson, subjected to heartwarming or romantic vignettes with Bronson, then dying horribly to push him into what the real point of the film is, righteous anger and bloody retribution. *(Violence, brief nudity, excessive profanity, substance abuse.)*

p, Pancho Kohner; d, J. Lee-Thompson; w, Gail Morgan Hickman (based on characters created by Brian Garfield); ph, Gideon Porath (TVC Color); m, Paul McCallum, Valentine McCallum, John Bisharat; ed, Peter Lee-Thompson; art d, Whitney Brooke Wheeler; set d, Mark Andrew; stunts, Ernie Orsatti.

Crime **(PR:O MPAA:R)**

DEATHROW GAMESHOW zero (1987) 83m Pirromount/Crown Intl. c

John McCafferty *(Chuck Toedan)*, Robin Blythe *(Gloria Sternvirgin)*, Beano *(Luigi Pappalardo)*, Mark Lasky *(Momma)*, Darwyn Carson *(Trudy)*, Debra Lamb *(Shanna Shallow)*, Paul Farbman *(Dinko)*.

An idiotic ripoff of THE RUNNING MAN, featuring McCafferty as the host of the wildly controversial gameshow "Live or Die" in which death row inmate contestants perform silly and dangerous tasks for reprieves or prizes for their families. The audiences applaud furiously when contestants are guillotined on the air, then examined to determine if a face up roll of the head qualifies his family for a set of major kitchen appliances. McCafferty is the frequent target of death threats and hate mail, and one afternoon, while on a television talk show, he meets Blythe, head of Women Against Anything Men Are For. She and McCafferty trade insults on the air and in the parking lot, where several gunmen make an attempt on his life. McCafferty explains that Mafia killers are after him since the execution of a gang chief on the show. Beano, the chief killer, calls McCafferty and agrees to talk to him about ceasing these attacks, providing the host can get Beano's aged mother on another gameshow. Beano persuades Blythe to have lunch with him and ends up planning marriage with the unwilling woman. In the meantime, Beano's mother shows up for her game show appearance, accidentally wanders into the wrong line and ends up on "Live or Die," going up in flames. McCafferty and Blythe manage to subdue the enraged Beano and enter him as a "Live or Die" contestant, where he is smothered in an airtight box while trying to spell "I want to live" out of blocks. He isn't dead after all, as it turns out, and he comes back to toss McCafferty and Blythe in the box. They are saved when a deranged fan who wants to get on the show kills Beano and lets them out. McCafferty has learned his lesson and ends his sadistic program, but the closing credits show a series of commercials using the cadavers of the show's victims in testimonials for lawnmowers, wristwatches, and other products.

Aggressively, annoyingly stupid, the film looks like something out of another time, the days of THE GROOVE TUBE, KENTUCKY FRIED MOVIE and the like. The film is packed with gags that aren't funny and monotonous dialog. The style is cartoonish, the acting broad (but not entirely bad), and the production values below criticism. Still, there are some undeniably funny moments, in a sick way. *(Nudity, cartoon violence, profanity.)*

p, Brian J. Smith; d, Mark Pirro; w, Mark Pirro, Alan Gries; ph, Craig Bassuk; m, Gregg Gross; ed, Tim Shoemaker; prod d, Mark Simon; stunts, Eric Megison.

Horror **(PR:O MPAA:R)**

DEGIRMEN† (1987, Turkey) 100m OJak c (Trans: The Mill)

Sener Sen *(Halil Hilmi, District Officer)*, Serap Aksoy *(Naciye, Belly Dancer)*, Levent Yilmaz.

Set in a small town near Istanbul in 1914, this comedy from prolific Turkish director Atif Yilmaz makes light of civil service bureaucrats. After a mild earthquake shakes his poverty-stricken town, new district officer Sen is assigned the task of convincing national officials that the practically undamaged hamlet has suffered a major catastrophe. Because many buildings in the town were in various stages of collapse *before* the earthquake, Sen simply draws attention to the impoverished conditions that his people live under on a daily basis and claims that the earthquake caused the damage.

p, Cengiz Ergun; d, Atif Yilmaz; w, Baris Pirhasan; ph, Orhan Oguz; m, Arif Erkin.

Comedy **(PR:NR MPAA:NR)**

DELINCUENTE† (1987, Mex.) 96m Cinematografica Tabasco/Peliculas Mexicanas c (Trans: Delinquent)

Pedrito Fernandez *(Alejandro)*, Lucerito *(Cecilia)*, Jose Elias Moreno *(Gonzalo)*, Carlos Riquelme, Julio Urreta, Jaime Santos, Martin Rangel.

Child singer-actor Fernandez, now an adolescent, stars as a street urchin who is taken in by three college students. Washed and fed, Fernandez is now able to mingle among the middle class. He meets Lucerito, the daughter of a wealthy businessman, and falls in love. Eager to impress, Fernandez has his college buddies teach him how to speak proper Spanish and lands a job at the local grocery. In addition, Fernandez tries to pass himself off as the cousin of one of the students. Unfortunately, the courtship is abruptly ended after Lucerito's father learns the truth about the boy. Fernandez returns to the streets, bitter at having been allowed to dream of a better life.

p, Daniel Galindo; d, Sergio Vejar; w, Kiki Galindo; ph, Luis Medina; m, Jonathan Zarzosa; ed, Jose Liho.

Drama **(PR:NR MPAA:NR)**

DELIRIA† (1987, It.) Filmirage/D.M.V.

David Brandon, Barbara Cupisti, Robert Gligorov, Martin Philip, Loredana Parrella, Giovanni Lombardi Radice, Ulrike Schwerk, Mary Sellers.

A troupe of singers and dancers is rehearsing in an abandoned warehouse for a production entitled "Horror Music." The show is based on crimes committed by a real-life maniac, and when the deranged killer escapes from his captors, he begins murdering troupe members.

d, Michele Soavi; w, Luigi Montefiori; ph, Renato Tafuri; m, Simon Boswell; ed, Rosanna Landi.

Horror **(PR:NR MPAA:NR)**

DELIRIUM (SEE: LE FOTO DI GIOIA, 1987, It.)

DELITTI† (1987, It.) Cooperativa Mezzogiorno Nuovo D'Italia (Trans: Crimes)

Saverio Vallone, Michela Miti, Giovanna Lenzi, Alessandra Izzo, Linda Christian, Giorgio Ardisson, Gianni Dei, Lara Orfei, Emi Valentini, Gianfranco Gallo.

Italian police attempt to track down a clever murderer who has claimed seven victims.

d, Giovanna Lenzi; w, George Vidor; m, Maurizio De Angelis, Guido De Angelis.

Mystery **(PR:NR MPAA:NR)**

DELIZIA† (1987, It.) Filmirage-I.I.F. c (Trans: Delight)

Tini Cansino, Luca Giordana, Giorgio Pietrangeli, Valerio Castellano, Maurizio Marchisio, Stefania Miniucci, Donatella Clarizio, Gina Poli, Adriana Russo.

A group of young Italians is fascinated by the beautiful American woman on the cover of a magazine. She turns out to be the cousin of one of the group members, and the pair have an affair when she visits Italy.

d, Aristide Massaccesi; w, Riccardo Ghione, Elena Dreoni; ph, Aristide Massaccesi; m, Stefano Mainetti, Elena Dreoni; ed, Aristide Massaccesi.

Romance **(PR:NR MPAA:NR)**

DELOS ADVENTURE, THE* (1987) 99m Delos Ltd./American Cinema c

Roger Kern *(Bard Clemens)*, Jenny Neumann *(Deni Trion)*, Kurtwood Smith *(Arthur McNeil)*, E.J. Castillo *(Luis Vasquez)*, Kevin Brophy *(Greg Bachman)*, Al Mancini *(Koutsavaki)*, Charles Lanyer *(Dr. James DeKalb)*, James Higgins *(Karl Darrensbourg)*, Kathryn Noble *(Stacy)*, Sands Hall *(Tana)*, David Vallalpando *(Alfonso)*, Steve Frohardt *(Commando)*.

A team of scientists sets out for a remote island off the coast of Chile in order to plant seismic sensors on the bottom of the ocean to monitor earthquake activity. The next day, however, their camp and boat are attacked by frogmen with rocket launchers, and the leader of the party is killed. The four survivors flee in different directions, but eventually find each other. They are scientist Kern, pretty Neumann, daughter of an environmentalist who safeguards the island (although he is sick on the mainland), and the boat's Greek skipper and his first mate (Mancini and Castillo, respectively). They manage to get a message out over the satellite link before their terminal goes dead, but back in the US a security lid has been clamped over the whole thing. Eventually they figure out that the sensors they planted were not to detect earthquakes, but to track Russian submarines. They also learn there is a Russian underwater platform just offshore that is the base for the frogmen. Kern dons scuba gear conveniently left behind by one of the frogmen and swims for the base, where he opens a plug on the top and destroys the platform. A thoroughly dull action drama with endless padding consisting of birds flying overhead, waves crashing, crabs crabbing, and actors explaining every little detail of the tracking device to each other, but failing to recognize the guns the Russians carry as AK-47s (in this age when they are carried by most terrorists and much of the third world, as well as the entire Communist bloc). The story doesn't get moving until halfway through the film and none of the characters are more than slightly likable. By far the most interesting thing about the film is the appearance of Kurtwood Smith, who made a memorable villain in this year's ROBOCOP. Not surprisingly, this 1985 production languished on the shelf for two years before going straight to video. *(Nudity, violence.)*

p&d, Joseph Purcell; w, Joseph Purcell, Roger Kern; ph, William Meurer (United Color); m, Richard DeLabio, Kenny Kotwitz; art d, Tony Stabley; spec eff, Paul Staples; stunts, Steve Frohardt.

Action **Cas.** **(PR:C-O MPAA:R)**

DEMONS½** (1987, Swed.) 125m Viking-Swedish Film Institute/Swedish Film Institute c (DEMONER)

Ewa Froling *(Katarina)*, Lars Green *(Frank)*, Bjorn Granath *(Thomas)*, Pia Oscarsson *(Jenna)*.

Released in Sweden in 1986 and based on a play by Lars Noren, this portrait of marital turmoil makes WHO'S AFRAID OF VIRGINIA WOOLF? look like "The Honeymooners." Green and Froling have been married for ten years, though from the outset it's clear that anger and resentment dominate their life together. On the eve of his mother's funeral, Green returns to their flat with her cremated ashes. He has been phoning all day, but there has been no answer, and he suspects the sultry Froling of infidelity. They begin the barbed insults that grow more brutal and rancorous as the long evening wears on. Green's brother and sister-in-law are due to arrive, but they cancel the engagement. Dreading the thought of spending the evening alone with Froling, Green invites Granath and Oscarsson, a couple from their building, to come up for drinks. Before the young couple arrives, Green and Froling make violent love. Granath is bespectacled and rather straight-laced; Oscarsson complains about the constraints of motherhood. One drink follows another and the tension builds as the vitriol between Green and Froling increases to dangerous levels. Soon, Granath and Oscarsson are behaving badly towards each other. Oscarsson is worried about their infant son and anxious to go home, but Granath, titillated by Froling, wants to remain. Green, the cold, distant instigator of most of this ugliness, eventually pushes Froling so far that she launches herself through a glass door. Her psychological attack then becomes as cutting as her husbands'. With the women out of the room, Green homosexually propositions Granath as the two play an aggressive game of catch with a valuable glass vase. At first, it appears he is only trying to make Granath uncomfortable, then it seems his desire is genuine. Disgusted, Granath knocks Green around the room. Froling announces that her husband is impotent, saying that only bizarre fantasies like watching her make love with other men excite him. She says that on a trip to North Africa he exhorted her to bring young boys back to the room with her. Granath makes love with Froling, though he is racked with guilt almost immediately. Oscarsson mothers Green. As dawn breaks, Green and Froling are left alone in the living room, which Oscarsson has festooned with hundreds of small candles. Producing a hammer and nails, Froling crucifies Green on the floor amidst the flickering candles.

As in Edward Albee's play, the soul-crushing psychological warfare being waged here is born of desperation. Froling is desperate for some show of emotion from Green, who is unflagging in his stoic refusal. He tells Froling he loves her but he does not like her, and when she fears he will hit her, he promises he will do it only when she is certain he will never do it again. Yet Green admits there are times when he wakes up in bed next to her and can only think of how helpless she is and how she must be protected. Green, too, craves tenderness but does not know how to ask for it. Whether or not he is gay is less important than his inability to admit how much he needs to feel loved. He is deeply hurt when Froling says all he has ever been was a way of passing the time after the devastation of her break-up with her only real love. Ironically, nothing could be further from the truth, and she will do anything to keep Green. Froling may or may not actually nail Green to the floor, but the symbolic intent of this action would seem to have something to do with a desperate attempt to "save" the relationship. Granath's and Oscarsson's cruelty to each other is less severe, and though their children may serve as a bond missing in the other couple's relationship, it seems implicit that they, too, may be headed for the same battles. There are several instances in which glass is broken and it is the film's dominant symbol, suggesting that a marriage, like glass, is a fragile thing, which when shattered, is capable of inflicting tremendous hurt.

There is a self-contained quality to DEMONS which belies its theatrical origins (it was originally directed by Brandt at the Stockholm Municipal Theatre in 1984), but this is a story which demands a claustrophobic treatment. Brandt introduces the film with a slow-moving camera that ponders the details of the apartment before we ever see the actors and he departs the scene the same way. The film is generally well-paced, though a bit overlong if only because of the magnitude of the emotional sparring we witness. (There is one notable instance of comic relief as Green, after being belted by Granath, carries on with a hanky spouting like a carnation from one of his nostrils.) The performances are strong, particularly the ravishing Froling; however, it is difficult to like any of these people, save, perhaps, Oscarsson, who is slower than the others but more in touch with her ability to show compassion. It is a problem that we are never given a chance to see a more sympathetic side to these characters, because it is hard to feel much empathy for their suffering. However, this works both ways, for if we cared more for them it might be even more difficult to endure the deluge of pain they heap upon each other. This may have been playwright Noren and screenwriter-director Brandt's intention, but though they have certainly succeeded in laying out a naked lunch of anger, frustration, and suffering, not everyone will leave the table satisfied. *(Nudity, violence, profanity, sexual situations, adult situations.)*

p, Bo Jonsson; d&w, Carsten Brandt (based on the play "Demons" by Lars Noren); ph, Goran Nilsson (Fujicolor); m, Federico Mompou, Giuseppe Verdi, Giacomo Puccini, Gianna Nannini; ed, Kasper Schyberg, Lars Hagstrom; prod d, Mona Theresia Forsen; cos, Mona Theresia Forsen, Elisabeth Hamfeldt; makeup, Suzanne Bergmark; stunts, Jan Kreigsman.

Drama **(PR:O MPAA:NR)**

DER BARENHAUTER† (1987, E. Ger.) 81m DEFA c (Trans: Bear-Skinned Man)

Jen-Uwe Bogadtke *(Christoffel)*, Janina Hartwig *(Katarina)*, Manfred Heine *(Satan)*.

Based on a Brothers Grimm fairy tale, this film stars Bogadtke as a handsome young lad who makes a pact with the Devil not to bathe or cut his hair for seven years in return for a magic coat with pockets full of gold. A few years later Bogadtke finds that his hairy visage is loathsome to everyone, save beautiful young maiden Hartwig. She, of course, sees through his repulsive veneer and encourages him to hang in there and collect the prize. When the seven years are up, the Devil (Heine) admits defeat and sends in soap and a straight razor to clean up Bogadtke. In the end, Bogadtke makes off with both the magic coat and the beautiful damsel.

p, Siegfried Kabitzke; d&w, Walter Beck (based on a fairy tale by the Brothers Grimm); ph, Gunter Heimann; m, Gunther Fischer; ed, Ilse Peters; art d, Paul Lehmann; anim, Erich Gunther, Heiko Ebert, Tony Loeser, Frank Wittstock, Wolfgang Chevallier.

Children's **(PR:NR MPAA:NR)**

DER FLIEGER (SEE: FLYER, THE, 1987, Ger.)

DER HIMMEL UBER BERLIN† (1987, Ger./Fr.) 130m Road Movies-Argos-WDR bw/c (Trans: The Sky Over Berlin; AKA: WINGS OF DESIRE)

Bruno Ganz *(Daniel)*, Solveig Dommartin *(Marion)*, Otto Sander *(Cassiel)*, Curt Bois *(Homer)*, Peter Falk *(Himself)*.

Wim Wenders' first fiction feature since 1984's PARIS, TEXAS, DER HIMMEL UBER BERLIN won Wenders the Best Director prize at this year's Cannes Film Festival. Bruno Ganz (THE AMERICAN FRIEND) and Otto Sander star as a pair of angels who keep a close watch on the lives of various Berliners—Bois, an old man who shares remembrances of his past; Dommartin, a trapeze artist with whom Ganz falls in love; and Falk, an American actor preparing for a picture about Nazi Germany. As Ganz falls deeper in love with Dommartin, he becomes mortal, discovering that Falk was once an angel himself. Wenders is again collaborating with the same family that has worked on many of his previous German films—Handke has coscripted, Knieper has scored, and Przygodda has edited. Only cameraman Robby Muller is missing, replaced here by Henri Alekan, who, in 1948, photographed Jean Cocteau's BEAUTY AND THE BEAST. Wenders dedicated this film to "all the former angels—Yasujiro Ozu, Andrei Tarkovsky, and Francois Truffaut." Released in Germany, with a US release as WINGS OF DESIRE scheduled for early 1988.

p, Wim Wenders, Anatole Dauman; d, Wim Wenders; w, Wim Wenders, Peter Handke; ph, Henri Alekan; m, Jurgen Knieper; ed, Peter Przygodda; prod d, Heidi Ludi; cos, Monika Jacobs.

Drama/Fantasy **(PR:NR MPAA:NR)**

DER JUNGE MIT DEM GROSSEN SCHWARZEN HUND† (1987, E. Ger.) 78m DEFA c (Trans: The Boy with the Big Black Dog)

Niels Anschutz *(Ulf Kahleberg)*, Dagmar Manzel *(Mother Kahleberg)*, Hort Hiemer *(Father Kahleberg)*, Kurt Bowe *(Oscar)*, Miriam Knabe *(Sabine Schonerstedt)*.

A young boy brings home a stray dog, but his parents do not allow him to keep it. Instead of getting rid of the animal, he takes it to a retired carnival showman, who keeps the dog for him. Lectured by the carny about responsibility, the boy earns money to pay for the dog's care.

d, Hannelore Unterberg; w, Margot Bleicher (based on the book by Hildegard Schumacher, Siegfried Schumacher); ph, Michael Gothe, Norbert Kuhrober (Orwocolor); m, Gerhard Schone, Dieter Beckert; ed, Elsa Krause; set d, Joachim Keller; cos, Isolde Warcyzek; makeup, Karin Menzel.

Children's **(PR:NR MPAA:NR)**

DER KLEINE STATSAN WALT (SEE: LITTLE PROSECUTOR, THE 1987, Ger.)

DER NACHBAR† (1987, Switz./Ger.) 96m Boa Filmproduktion-ZDF/Rex Film Zollikon c (Trans: The Neighbor)

Rolf Hoppe *(Georg Walz)*, Eva Scheurer *(Rita Romani)*, Larbi Tahiri *(Ali)*, Marco Morelli *(Renato)*, Vera Schweiger *(Barmaid)*, Erika Eberhard *(Eva)*, David Honer *(Hassan/Peter)*, Eva Scheurer *(Susanne)*, Ales Urbanczik *(Taxi Driver)*, Erwin Parker *(Old Man)*.

Swiss-German coproduction tells the story of an ex-policeman who looks for revenge and redemption after permanently injuring a bystander while pursuing a suspect. Becoming obsessed with a young woman who looks like the woman he accidentally shot, the former cop becomes dangerously entangled in her love life.

d, Markus Fischer; w, Markus Fischer, Alex Gfeller; ph, Jorg Schmidt-Reitwein; m, Pi-Rats; ed, Markus Fischer; art d, Hans Gloor; cos, Ann Poppel.

Drama **(PR:NR MPAA:NR)**

DER TOD DES EMPEDOKLES† (1987, Fr./Ger.) 132m Janus-Les Films du Losange-Hessian TV-Dopa-French Center National de la Cinematographie/Dopa-Hamburger c (Trans: The Death of Empedocles)

Andreas von Rauch *(Empedocles)*, Howard Vernon *(Hermocrates)*, Vladimir Baratta *(Pausanias)*, Martina Baratta *(Panthea)*, Ute Cremer *(Delia)*, Federico Hecker, Peter Boom, Giorgio Baratta, Manfred Esser, Achille Brunini, Peter Kammerer.

Based on German poet Friedrich Holderlin's verse play, this philosophical film deals with the life and death of Greek philosopher-statesman Empedocles (von Rauch), who lived in the 5th century B.C. and, according to legend, died by throwing himself into the crater of Mt. Etna to prove that he was a god.

p, Klaus Hellwig, Rosy Gockel; d&w, Jean-Marie Straub, Daniele Huillet (based on the verse play by Friedrich Holderlin); ph, Renato Berta, Jean-Paul Toraille, Giovanni Canfarelli (Eastmancolor); ed, Jean-Marie Straub, Daniele Huillet; cos, Daniele Huillet.

Drama **(PR:NR MPAA:NR)**

DER TRAUM VOM ELCH† (1987, E. Ger.) 88m DEFA-Studio fur Spielfilme c (Trans: I Dreamed of My Elk)

Katrin Satz *(Anna)*, Detlef Heintze *(Stefan)*, Christian Steyer *(Ludwig)*, Marie Gruber *(Anette)*.

A complex love story from East Germany that focuses on a woman who loves a man she almost never sees. The woman, Satz, then becomes involved with the lover of a friend who eventually kills herself.

d, Siegfried Kuhn; w, Christa Muller, Hasso Hartmann (based on a novel by Herbert Otto); ph, Peter Brand; m, Hans Jurgen Wenzel; ed, Brigitte Krex.

Drama/Romance **(PR:NR MPAA:NR)**

DER UNSICHTBARE† (1987, Ger.) 90m Luna-Solaris-Neue Constantin c (Trans: The Invisible Man)

Klaus Wennemann *(Peter Benjamin)*, Barbara Rudnik *(Helene, His Wife)*, Nena *(Jo Schnell)*, Benedict Freitag *(Eduard)*, Camilla Horn *(Mother)*.

In this German entry, a cap with extraordinary powers bestows upon TV personality Wennemann (DAS BOOT, OUT OF ORDER) the *invis-ability* that Claude Rains' scientist stumbled upon through experimentation in Universal's THE INVISIBLE MAN (1933). While invisible, however, Wennemann learns of wife Rudnik's infidelity. German rocker Nena appears in a supporting role.

p, Sabine Eichinger, Peter Zenk; d, Ulf Miehe; w, Ulf Miehe, Klaus Richter; ph, Franz Rath; m, Boris Jojic; ed Barbara von Weitershausen; art d, Hans Gailling, Renate Ereth; spec eff, Stephan Schultze-Jena.

Comedy/Fantasy **(PR:NR MPAA:NR)**

DERANGED† (1987) 81m Platinum Pictures c

Jane Hamilton [Veronica Hart] *(Joyce)*, Paul Siederman *(Frank)*, Jennifer Delora *(Mary Ann)*, Jill Cumer *(Mother)*, James Gillis [Jamie Gillis] *(Father)*, Gary Goldman *(Nick)*, John Brett *(Darren)*, Loretta Palma, Jessica Rose.

Another film from the former porno team of Chuck Vincent and Veronica Hart (billed here under her real name, Jane Hamilton), who continue in their attempt to gain a foothold in mainstream films. A cross between Roman Polanski's REPULSION and various Alfred Hitchcock films (chiefly ROPE and DIAL M FOR MURDER), DERANGED features Hamilton as a woman on the verge of a breakdown. After seeing her uncaring husband off at the airport (he's headed for London), Hamilton visits her selfish mother (Cumer) and her antagonistic sister (Delora). Upset by the visit, Hamilton returns to her apartment alone and finds an intruder. She manages to kill the man with a pair of scissors, the incident pushing her over the edge. In her dementia she declines to call the police and wanders about the apartment imagining visits from her incestuous father who had recently committed suicide, her mother, and her former therapist. She even imagines the intruder has come back to life. This seemingly ambitious low-budget effort received a brief release in Times Square theaters and will likely find a general release on home video and cable.

p&d, Chuck Vincent; w, Craig Horrall; ph, Larry Revene; m, Bill Heller; ed, James Davalos; art d, Marc Ubell; spec eff, Vincent Guastini.

Thriller **(PR:NR MPAA:R)**

DET STORA LOFTET† (1987, Swed.) 94m SVT 2-Swedish Film Institute-Svensk Filmindustri-Mariedamfilm c (Trans: Promises)

Eva Carlsson, Marketta Fansila, My Friberg, Eva Remaeus, Erik Kiviniemi.

All work and no play ruins the family life of an industrialist whose wife and son dream of a more meaningful relationship with the indefatigable bread winner.

d, Bengt Danneborn.

Drama **(PR:NR MPAA:NR)**

DEVIL IN THE FLESH½** (1986, It./Fr.) 110m Instituto Luce-Italnoleggio-Film Sextile-L.P. Film/Orion Classics c (IL DIAVOLO IN CORPO)

Maruschka Detmers *(Giulia Dozza)*, Federico Pitzalis *(Andrea Raimondi)*, Anita Laurenzi *(Mrs. Pulcini)*, Riccardo De Torrebruna *(Giacomo Pulcini)*, Anna Orso *(Mrs. Dozza)*, Alberto Di Stasio *(Prof. Raimondi)*, Catherine Diamant *(Mrs. Raimondi)*, Claudio Botosso *(Don Pisacane)*, Lidia Broccolino, Stefano Abbati *(Terrorists)*.

In 1921, at the age of 18, a French writer named Raymond Radiguet wrote his masterpiece, *Le Diable Au Corps*. Two years later typhoid claimed his life. In 1947, the novel was brought to the screen in France by Claude Autant-Lara, resulting in a monumental scandal. It has taken nearly 40 years for the story to resurface, and again controversy has followed. Released in 1986 in Italy, this Bellocchio-directed entry shocked audiences with a short but graphic oral sex scene. Hoping to latch onto the same fervor that surrounded Bernardo Bertolucci's X-rated 1973 film, LAST TANGO IN PARIS, Orion Classics decided to release the picture to U.S. art houses with an MPAA rating of X.

The story, which bears only a minor resemblance to the novel, centers on the romance between the gorgeous Detmers and her teenage admirer Pitzalis. The film opens as a suicidal woman dressed only in a negligee stands on a roof and threatens to jump into the courtyard below. Nearby, a classroom full of *lycee* students watches. Across the courtyard, Detmers looks on. Having just awakened, Detmers is scantily clad in a negligee (not unlike the one worn by the woman on the rooftop) and attracts the attention of student Pitzalis. Detmers begins to sob as she watches the woman, identifying with her impassioned madness. Not long afterwards, Pitzalis notices Detmers leaving her apartment and getting into a limousine. He sneaks out of class, hops on his motorcycle, and follows her. Her path leads to a courtroom where her lover, De Torrebruna, is standing trial for a terrorist attack on Detmers' father. Detmers and the terrorist's mother, Laurenzi, hope that the court will have mercy on De Torrebruna and release him in exchange for information he has supplied. Although it is planned that Detmers and De Torrebruna shall live a quiet middle-class life of mediocrity, Detmers wants more. She is soon trying to seduce Pitzalis. Pitzalis, like any young man, is attracted to Detmers' sexual openness. She freely displays her body, is wildly passionate, wholly unpredictable, has a voracious sexual appetite, and seems to thoroughly enjoy laughing. Underneath her desirable flesh, however, is a frightening and clearly demented being who is permanently perched on the razor's edge between madness and sanity. When Di Stasio, Pitzalis' psychiatrist father, learns of his son's new romance, he tries to persuade the boy to stay away from her. He admits to his son that Detmers is a former patient of his and that she is a complete lunatic. Soon nothing matters to the lovers except themselves. De Torrebruna is finally released from prison and the wedding plans go into effect. Detmers, however, leaves her groom standing alone at the altar, choosing instead to attend Pitzalis' oral exam, allying herself with her young unrepressed lover instead of with the bourgeois values of mediocrity with which middle-class mothers-in-law and reformed terrorists are content.

Bellocchio, who began his career in 1966 with the critically hailed FIST IN HIS POCKET and followed with the equally impressive CHINA IS NEAR, has become, in recent years, bogged down by the heavy Leftist perspective that has permeated much of his work. As a result his pictures rarely make it to American screens. With DEVIL IN THE FLESH, however, Bellocchio has found his ticket. While Orion Classics must be credited with releasing an X-rated non-pornographic picture, one can't help but be a bit suspicious. DEVIL IN THE FLESH is not much of a film. It's not that it is bad, it's just too average to warrant its publicity. It's all too clear that this film won a U.S. release because it contains a few seconds of fairly explicit oral sex. (For the curious, this scene was staged with only Detmers and Pitzalis in a room with a running camera. Not even Bellocchio was present.) The film is attractively photographed, Dutch actress Detmers (whose voice had to be dubbed into Italian) has a superb aura (first seen in Jean-Luc Godard's FIRST NAME: CARMEN, released in the U.S. in 1984), and the non-professional Pitzalis is excellent. Unfortunately, much of the film is philosophically empty—wonderful to look at, but empty. A much better telling of this tale—a simple man entranced by a half-crazed sexual predator—is told in Jean-Jacques Beineix's 1986 film, BETTY BLUE, which is truly revolutionary in its views, instead of just pretending to be. (In Italian; with English subtitles.) *(Explicit nudity, sexual situations.)*

p, Leo Pescarolo; d, Marco Bellocchio; w, Marco Bellocchio, Ennio De Concini (based on the novel *Le Diable au Corps* by Raymond Radiguet); ph, Giuseppe Lanci; m, Carlo Crivelli; ed, Mirco Garrone; art d, Andrea Crisanti; cos, Lina Nerli Taviani.

Drama **(PR:O MPAA:X)**

DEVIL'S ODDS (SEE: WILD PAIR, THE 1987)

DEVILS PARADISE, THE† (1987, Ger.) 91m Atossa/Overview c

Jurgen Prochnow *(Escher)*, Sam Waterston *(Mr. Jones)*, Suzanna Hamilton *(Julie)*, Mario Adorf *(Schomberg)*, Dominique Pilon *(Gato)*, Ingrid Caven *(Madame)*, Wong Chun-man *(Wong)*, Vadim Glowna *(Capt. Davidson)*, Tony Doyle *(Quinn)*.

Based on Joseph Conrad's novel *Victory*, this English-language West German production sets the action in the 1930s in Indonesia (though it was shot in Thailand). Prochnow plays a man who has long wandered the world and finally found a home of sorts on a small island where he and partner Doyle operate a coal mine. When Doyle is killed Prochnow ventures to the main island where he runs afoul of Waterston (THE KILLING FIELDS, SEPTEMBER), a slimy troublemaker. After rescuing Hamilton, a member of an all-girl band who is about to become a white slave, Prochnow returns with her to his island. However, Waterston and some thugs later follow them. This is the third cinematic treatment of Conrad's novel. It was preceded by one silent, VICTORY (1919), and two sound films, DANGEROUS PARADISE (1930) and VICTORY (1940).

p, Vera Tschechowa, Vadim Glowna; d, Vadim Glowna; w, Leonard Tuck, Vadim Glowna, Joe Hembus, Chris Doherty; ph, Martin Schafer (Agfacolor); m, Jurgen Knieper; ed, Heidi Handof; prod d, Nicos Perakis; cos, Regine Batz.

Drama **(PR:NR MPAA:NR)**

DIARY FOR MY LOVED ONES† (1987, Hung.) 135m Mafilm-Budapest Studio c/bw (NAPLO SZERELMEIMNEK)

Zsuzsa Zczinkoczi *(Juli)*, Anna Polony *(Magda)*, Jan Nowicki *(Janos)*, Pal Zolnay *(Grandfather)*, Mari Szemes *(Grandmother)*, Irina Kouberskaya *(Anna Pavlova)*, Adel Kovats *(Natacha)*, Erzsebet Kutvolgyi *(Erzsi)*.

DIARY FOR MY CHILDREN, filmed in 1982 but not shown in Hungary until 1984, told the story of a young girl growing up in the Soviet Union and returning to her native Hungary after WW II. This film is a sequel, covering the years 1950-56 as the girl (Zczinkoczi), now 18 and an aspiring film director, moves out of her foster mother's house and attempts to make a life of her own. She gets a scholarship to a film school in Moscow and makes a documentary about peasant life in Hungary, a film which is too realistic to suit government officials. The film concludes with the uprising in Budapest in 1956, with Zczinkoczi unable to return to her homeland because of the unrest. The film was shown at the New York Film Festival in 1987, and is the second in a trilogy planned by Meszaros.

d, Marta Meszaros; w, Marta Meszaros, Eva Pataki; ph, Miklos Jancso, Jr. (Eastmancolor); m, Zsolt Dome; ed, Eva Karmento; prod d, Eva Martin; cos, Fanni Kemenes.

Drama/Biography **(PR:NR MPAA:NR)**

DIARY OF A MAD OLD MAN† (1987, Neth./Bel./Fr.) 89m Fons Rademakers Productie-Iblis-Dedalus/Cannon c (DAGBOEK VAN EEN OUDE DWAAS)

Ralph Michael *(Marcel Hamelinck)*, Beatie Edney *(Simone)*, Suzanne Flon *(Denise Hamelinck)*, Derek de Lint *(Philippe)*, Dora van der Groen *(Sister Alma)*, Ina van der Molen *(Karin)*.

Michael stars as the title character, a man who lives with his family in Belgium and who falls in love with his daughter-in-law, a love that quickly becomes an obsession. This is the second feature by Rademakers (MINUET, 1982), whose husband Fons won the 1986 Best Foreign-Language Film Academy Award with THE ASSAULT. (In English.)

p, Henry Lange, Pierre Drouot, Fons Rademakers; d, Lili Rademakers; w, Hugo Claus, Claudine Bouvier (based on the novel by Junichiro Tanizaki); ph, Paul van den Bos (Fujicolor); m, Egisto Macchi; ed, Ton de Graaff; prod d, Philippe Graff.

Drama **(PR:NR MPAA:NR)**

DIE DRECKSCHLEUDER† (1987, Aust.) 60m Teamfilm/Austrian Film Commission c (Trans: The Muckrakers)

Andreas Vitasek *(Mario Ubermorgen)*, Christian Schmidt *(Assistant)*.

Austrian writer-director Niki List follows his 1986 genre hybrid MULLER'S BURO with this comedy featuring the stars of his earlier film, Andreas Vitasek and Christian Schmidt. Here they are involved with a small-town variety show.

d&w, Niki List; ph, Hans Selikovsky; m, Ernie Seuberth; ed, Ingrid Koller, Brigitte Tauchner; art d, Rudolf Czettel.

Comedy **(PR:NR MPAA:NR)**

DIE KAMELIENDAME (SEE: LADY OF THE CAMELLIAS, 1987, Ger.)

DIE VERLIEBTEN† (1987, Ger./Yugo.) 95m Art Film 80-Zeta Film Budva/Metropolis c (Trans: Days to Remember)

Barbara Sukowa *(Katharina)*, Horst-Gunter Marx *(Peter)*, Bata Zivojinovic *(Uncle Savo)*, Rade Serbedzija *(Dusan)*, Ljiljana Kontic *(Mother)*, Milan Erak *(Motorbike Driver)*, Veljko Mandic *(Old Ivo)*.

Sukowa plays a native of Yugoslavia who has grown up in Germany and now works as a reporter for a German TV station. While on assignment in Yugoslavia, she meets Marx, a German whose father was stationed in Yugoslavia during WW II. He's interested in his father's past and she becomes interested in him. Their romance is short-lived however, as Marx perishes in an explosion after he sets out to explore an area which had been planted with land mines during the war. In addition to this film, Sukowa also appeared in 1987's THE SICILIAN.

p, Joachim von Vietinghoff, Aleksandar Stojanovic; d&w, Jeanine Meerapfel; ph, Predrag Popovic; m, Jurgen Knieper; ed, Ursula West; prod d, Rainer Schaper; art d, Veljko Despotovic.

Drama/Romance **(PR:NR MPAA:NR)**

DIKIY KHMEL† (1987, USSR) 85m Mosfilm/Sovexportfilm c (Trans: Wild Hop)

Svetlana Ryabova, Alexander Martynov, Viktor Pavlov, Yelena Fadeyeva.

A young woman, a worker in a shoe factory, falls in love with a journalist and the two marry. The marriage is threatened as the wife rises through ranks at the factory to become a shift superintendent, while the husband experiences nothing but dissatisfaction with his work.

Oleg Bondarev; w, Yury Avdeyenko; ph, Igor Melnikov; m, Alexander Belyayev; art d, Leonid Platov, Pyotr Kazorezenko.

Drama **(PR:NR MPAA:NR)**

DILAN† (1987, Turk./Switz./Ger.) 92m Hakan-Limbo-ZDF/Metropolis c

Derya Arbas *(Dilan)*, Hakan Balamir *(Kerim)*, Yilmaz Zafer *(Paso Bey)*, Mehmet Erikci *(Mirkan)*, Guler Okten *(Dilan's Mother)*, Dilaver Yuanik *(Dilan's Father)*, Keriman Ulusoy *(Paso's Mother)*, Ebru, Handan, Yusuf *(Children)*.

Arbas stars as a young woman in a village in eastern Turkey who is loved by both a poor shepherd and the son of a wealthy land owner. Arbas was born in Los Angeles and still lives there, but has been making films in Turkey since 1985.

p, Luciano Gloor, Hakan Balamir; d, Erden Kiral; w, Omer Polat, Erden Kiral (based on the novel by Omer Polat); ph, Martin Gressmann (Agfacolor); m, Nizamettin; ed, Roswitha Henze.

Romance **(PR:NR MPAA:NR)**

DIRTY DANCING*½** (1987) 97m Vestron c

Jennifer Grey *(Frances "Baby" Houseman)*, Patrick Swayze *(Johnny Castle)*, Jerry Orbach *(Dr. Jake Houseman)*, Cynthia Rhodes *(Penny Johnson)*, Jack Weston *(Max Kellerman)*, Jane Brucker *(Lisa Houseman)*, Kelly Bishop *(Marjorie Houseman)*, Lonny Price *(Neil Kellerman)*, Max Cantor *(Robbie Gould)*, Charles Honi Coles *(Tito Suarez)*, Neal Jones *(Billy Kostecki)*, "Cousin Brucie" Morrow *(Magician)*, Wayne Knight *(Stan)*, Paula Trueman *(Mrs. Schumacher)*, Alvin Myerovich *(Mr. Schumacher)*, Miranda Garrison *(Vivian Pressman)*, Garry Goodrow *(Moe Pressman)*, Antone Pagan *(Staff Kid)*, Tom Cannold *(Bus Boy)*, M.R. Fletcher, Jesus Fuentes, Heather Lea Gerdes, Karen Getz, Andrew Charles Koch, D.A. Pauley, Dorian Sanchez, Jennifer Stahl *(Dirty Dancers)*, Jonathan Barnes, Dwyght Bryan, Tom Drake, John Gotz, Dwayne Malphus, Dr. Clifford Watkins *(Tito's Band)*.

A deceptively charming movie that may be appreciated far more by anyone who lived through the 1960s as a teenager, DIRTY DANCING suffers from a title which is inappropriate for the subject matter but didn't seem to hurt the brisk box-office business, once word-of-mouth took over. It's the summer of 1963, Kennedy still leads the country, rock 'n' roll is king, and all's right with the world. Orbach is a New York doctor married to Bishop. They have two daughters, Grey and Brucker, who are about as much alike as Molly and Whoopi Goldberg. The family arrives at the resort hotel owned by Weston and run by him and his twerp son, Price. Grey is a 60s activist, even though she's only in her teens. A middle-class Jewish girl, her father's favorite, Grey is planning to attend college in the fall and take courses about economics in The Third World as part of her preparation for entering the Peace Corps. This is her last summer as a "Baby" (which is her nickname), before she presumably becomes an adult. The hotel is supposed to be a Catskill Mountains resort (much larger and far more successful than the Lorraine Hotel in SWEET LORRAINE) but the film was actually shot at Mountain Lake, Virginia, because, by the time they got to shooting, the summer green was already turning to fall orange and gold in upstate New York. Grey meets the hotel's resident swain, Swayze. He teaches mambo and cha cha and all the other trendy dances as well as overseeing the hotel's shows. His partner is Rhodes, and although they steam up the stage when they trip the light fantastic, they are close friends, not lovers. Rhodes runs the "Simple Simon" exercises and functions as Swayze's assistant. While the patrons of the hotel are overeating, playing cards, seeing shows, and dancing to the sedate music of their youth, the hotel's employees are engaging in "dirty dancing" in their quarters. This refers to the pulsating music where bodies rub and undulate around each other. Grey is soon bored by what's happening on the guests' side of the hotel and goes to the off-limits employee's area, mainly to escape the smarmy clutches of Price. When she sees Swayze and Rhodes dance, she naturally assumes that they are lovers and is surprised to learn that they are not. Matter of fact, Rhodes is pregnant by Grey's waiter, Cantor, a handsome Ivy League snob who is planning to go to medical school and doesn't much care who he impregnates. Grey becomes part of the employee coterie as she falls in love with Swayze. At first, she is not welcomed by the others who work at the hotel, as they feel she is from another world, but she soon convinces them that she can be one of the boys . . . and girls. When she learns of Rhodes' problem and the fact that nobody has enough money for an abortion, Grey borrows the cash from her father. Orbach mistakenly thinks that Swayze is the father of the unborn child and is shocked when he learns that his daughter is spending time with the rogue. By this time, Grey and Swayze have been making love regularly, and although they come from two different worlds, he is anything but a rakehell and there is a possibility that this is more than just a "Will I see you in September?" romance. Swayze's second "job" is to keep some of the more sensuous patrons of the hotel in sexual bliss. When he throws over a 50ish woman in favor of Grey, the matron decides to take revenge. In another subplot, Brucker (who is also a virgin at the start of the film) falls for waiter Cantor and is planning to give herself to him. Grey tries to talk her out of it because she knows what a cad Cantor is, but Brucker is determined to finally "do it" with Cantor until she surprises the waiter in his room with the same woman Swayze had tossed aside. Meanwhile, Rhodes has the abortion and is in danger of losing her life through infection caused by the inept abortionist. Orbach is called upon to help and does. Rhodes and Swayze had been booked to dance at another hotel and now that she is not available who can fill in? One guess is all you need. Swayze drills Grey in the primaries of dancing in a long montage and she is finally ready. (It's sort of a terpsichorean version of Henry Higgins teaching Eliza Dolittle how to speak without dropping an *h*.) There is an old couple from Weston's hotel at the other resort when Swayze and Grey perform, and the dancers are frightened that the aged duo will recognize Grey and spill the beans to Orbach and Bishop. But that doesn't happen and Swayze and Gray are a great success. Back at Weston's hotel, the matron's husband has had his wallet stolen and she points the finger at Swayze (a plot contrivance and totally unnecessary) and he is told to leave. But he won't go until he stages the final show of the season in which several of the hotel's guests will appear, including Brucker in a hysterical hula number where she proves that only one of the sisters has any talent. Weston wants the standard closing number, but Swayze, who figures he's lost his job anyway, gets Grey on stage and they do a "dirty dance." Then the hotel's nubile staff joins in and the conclusion has everyone, including the graying patrons, dancing and having a good time. The plot wraps up when Orbach learns that Cantor was responsible for Rhodes' pregnancy and that the old couple are purse and wallet thieves.

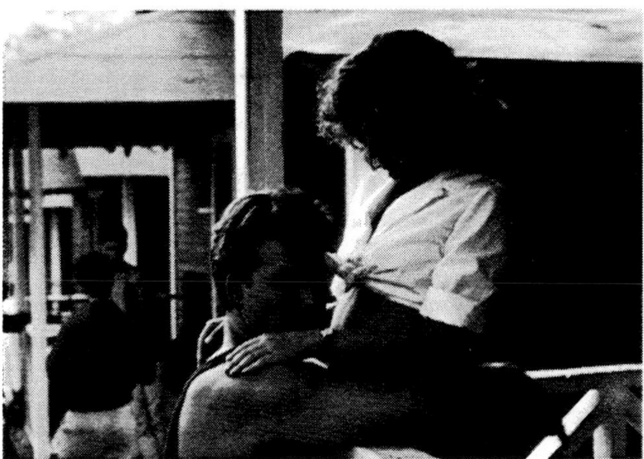

There will be an inevitable comparison between this and SATURDAY NIGHT FEVER and/or FLASHDANCE because of all the musical numbers. This one is as good as the former and far better than the latter. This was the first time documentary maker Ardolino was behind the camera for a fiction feature and he bears watching. (He has already won an Oscar for "He Makes Me Feel Like Dancin'," a live short film.) The fact that Ardolino and choreographer Ortega have made certain that every single one of the kids who works at the hotel is a superb dancer is a little fib, but they must have applied for and received poetic license to do that. By delving deeper into the psyches of the principals, Bergstein's screenplay avoided most of the cliches that usually accompany teen coming-of-age stories. There haven't been all that many movies made abut the Catskills. There was, of course, MARJORIE MORNINGSTAR, HAVING WONDERFUL TIME, THE GIG, and 1987's SWEET LORRAINE. All of them had something different to say about the Catskill experience and most of what they had to say was valid. There is one big lie in DIRTY DANCING and that is the nature of the staff at the hotel. We are led to believe that they are all handsome young men and women. The truth is that the entire dining room staff, bell staff, and maintenance crew are always male. The few females who work in these hotels are ususally the children's counselors or the chambermaids, and then almost always older, mothers, and generally from another country.

Grey, who is the daughter of Joel Grey and granddaughter of the late Yiddish comic Mickey Katz, is excellent and can look beautiful or very plain, depending on what is required. Her previous film appearances include small roles in RED DAWN, THE COTTON CLUB, AMERICAN FLYERS, RECKLESS, and FERRIS BUELLER'S DAY OFF. Swayze is a real find, a macho dancer who can act. He'd been a principal with Eliot Feld's ballet company before hurting his knee and turning to acting in RED DAWN and GRANDVIEW U.S.A. He is a far better dancer than Travolta, as well as a better actor. Of particular interest is the appearance and performance of Cynthia Rhodes. When she is on the screen, all eyes are riveted to her. Her part isn't large but she is absolutely believable as an actress and spectacular as a dancer. Her prior movies include STAYIN' ALIVE and FLASHDANCE but she went unnoticed in them. Not any more. This $6 million production was the first out of the chute for Vestron, previously a home video distributor. They will do very well. A cameo by Charles Honi Coles, the renowned tap dancer, is wasted. DIRTY DANCING produced a top-selling soundtrack album and the hit single "(I've Had) The Time Of My Life" (Frank Previte, Donald Markowitz, John DeNicola, performed by Bill Medley & Jennifer Warrens), which is completely out of context with the 1960s and Latin tunes from the film. Other songs include: "Big Girls Don't Cry" (B. Gaudio, B. Crewe, performed by Franki Valli and The Four Seasons), "Love Man," "These Arms Of Mine" (Otis Redding, performed by Redding), "Do You Love Me?"

(Berry Gordy, performed by The Contours), "Be My Baby" (Jeff Barry, Ellie Greenwich, Phil Spector, performed by The Ronettes), "Stay" (Maurice Williams, performed by Maurice Williams and The Zodiacs), "Wipe Out" (The Surfaris, performed by The Surfaris), "Hungry Eyes" (Frank Previte, John DeNicola, performed by Eric Carmen), "Some Kind Of Wonderful" (C. King, Gerry Goffin, performed by The Drifters), "Cry To Me" (B. Russell, performed by Solomon Burke), "Will You Love Me Tomorrow" (Carole King, Gerry Goffin, performed by The Shirelles), "Love Is Strange" (E. Smith, M. Baker, S. Robinson, performed by Mickey & Sylvia), "You Don't Own Me" (D. White, J. Madera, performed by The Blow Monkeys), "Yes" (Terry Fryer, Neal Cavanaugh, Tom Graf, performed by Merry Clayton), "In The Still Of The Night" (F. Parris, performed by The Five Satins), "She's Like The Wind" (Patrick Swayze, Stacy Widelitz, performed by Swayze and featuring Wendy Fraser), "Fox Trot," "Waltz" (Michael Lloyd, John D'Andrea), "Merengue" "Johnny's Mambo" (Lloyd, D'Andrea, Erich Bulling), "Where Are You Tonight" (Mark Scola, performed by Tom Johnston), "Overload" (Alfie Zappacosta, Marko Luciani, performed by Zappacosta), "Hey Baby" (Bruce Channel, M. Cobb, performed by Channel), "De Todo Un Poco" (Lou Perez, performed by Melon). *(Sexual situations, excessive profanity.)*

p, Linda Gottlieb, Eleanor Bergstein; d, Emile Ardolino; w, Eleanor Bergstein; ph, Jeff Jur; m, John Morris; ed, Peter C. Frank; prod d, David Chapman; art d, Mark Haack, Stephen Lineweaver; set d, Clay Griffith; cos, Hilary Rosenfeld; ch, Kenny Ortega, makeup, Gilbert La Chapelle, David Forrest; m/l, Jeff Barry, Ellie Greenwich, Phil Spector, B. Gaudio, B. Crewe, Erich Bulling, John D'Andrea, Michael Lloyd, Mark Scola, Berry Gordy, Otis Redding, Maurice Williams, The Surfaris, Frankie Previte, John DeNicola, Alfie Zappacosta, Marko Luciani, Bruce Channel, M. Cobb, Lou Perez, Carole King, Gerry Goffin, B. Russell, E. Smith, M. Baker, S. Robinson, D. White, J. Madara, Terry Fryer, Neal Cavanaugh, Tom Graf, F. Parris, Patrick Swayze, Stacy Widelitz, Don Markowitz.

Drama/Dance **(PR:C MPAA:PG-13)**

DIRTY LAUNDRY zero (1987) 79m Westwind 480-DeYoung/Skouras c

Leigh McCloskey *(Jay)*, Jeanne O'Brien *(Trish)*, Frankie Valli *(Macho Marty Benedictine)*, Sonny Bono *(Maurice)*, Nicholas Worth *(Vito)*, Robbie Rist *(Oscar)*, Johnny B. Frank *(Ricky Savoy)*, Herta Ware *(Grandmother Verne)*, Theodocia Goodrich *(Grandmother Heidi)*, Eric Fleeks *(Black Man at Laundromat)*, Angela Gibbs *(Black Woman at Laundromat)*, Ben Mittleman *(Arrogant Cop)*, David Dunaro *(Other Cop)*, Greg Louganis *(Larry)*, Hope North *(Bimbo Corrine)*, Jill Terashita *(Bimbo Lulu)*, John Moschitta, Jr. *(Fast Talking Lawyer)*, Joe Levitt *(Rowdy)*, Deanna Booher *(Big Lady with Whip)*, Donald May *(Inspector Fred Zimbalist)*, Harry Woolf, Rupert Harris *(Cops)*, Carl Lewis, Sean Coulter *(Miami Cops)*, Christina Cocek *(Cat Lady)*, Joe Morgan *(Newspaper Editor)*, Kurt Anderson *(Veronica)*, Paul Short *(Betty)*, Harry Singh *(Indian Man)*, Ernest Harada *(Sensei)*, Judith Goldstein *(Swimming Pool Lady)*, Edy Williams *(Poodle Lady)*, John Hawker *(Watts Man)*, Danette Rae *(Maid)*, Marshall Virden, Anthony Terrell *(Guards)*, Cindy Hedden *(Blonde in Convertible)*, Ken Segall *(Taxi Driver)*, Jeff Smolek *(Helicopter Pilot)*.

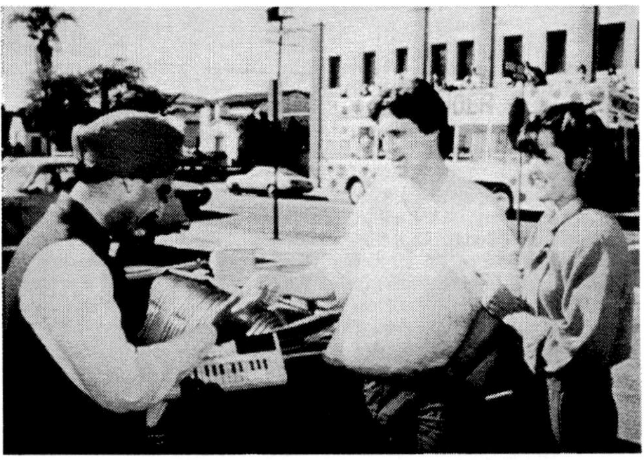

A torturous "comedy" which is about as insipid as they come. The inane premise has the hip McCloskey washing his clothes at the neighborhood laundromat when he inadvertently mixes his bag of laundry with a drug dealer's drop and wanders off with a $1 million. Without checking his bag, McCloskey tosses it in the trunk of his car, and then wonders why he is being terrorized by Worth, a bald, guntoting lug. Worth works for Valli, an infamous drug dealer who heads the FBI's Most Wanted list. Valli is also responsible for the meteoric rise of famous rock 'n' roller Frank. Coincidentally, McCloskey is the soundman for Frank's band. Worth puts pressure on Frank's manager, the satin-jacketed Bono, to get the money back, or else. McCloskey and O'Brien, a pretty but flighty cub reporter, are determined to expose Valli's drug ring and eventually do so after some stock car-chases and gunplay.

An embarrassment from start to finish, DIRTY LAUNDRY isn't worth the film stock it's photographed on. The direction is absent, the screenwriting better left undiscussed, and the acting uninspired. In fairness to the actors, not even a cast consisting of Marlon Brando, Jack Nicholson, and Laurence Olivier could breathe life into this mess. Surprisingly, it is Valli (as in Frankie Valli and the Four Seasons) that shows the greatest acting ability. Unfortunately, his character is so intense that it is out of place in comparison with his fluffy, stereotypical costars. Making screen debuts are Olympic stars Greg Louganis (diving) and Carl Lewis (track), who follow in the footsteps of previous recent Olympians who've found themselves in the movies—Mitch Gaylord (AMERICAN ANTHEM), Bart Conner (RAD) and Kurt Thomas (GYMKATA). The fast-talking John Moschitta, Jr. (of Federal Express TV commercials fame) also appears. Two moderately humorous bits recall popular TV shows—a tough federal agent named Inspector Zimbalist (a nod to "The FBI") and a pair of well-dressed Miami police detectives (a spoof of "Miami Vice"). Overlong at 79 minutes, DIRTY LAUNDRY bypassed theatrical release and went straight to video via the newly formed Sony Video Software Company. *(Brief sexual situations, mild profanity.)*

p, William Webb, Monica Webb; d, William Webb; w, Brad Munson (based on a story by William Webb); ph, John Huneck; m, Sam Winans, Elliot Solomon; ed, Richard Casey; art d, John Javonillo; cos, Scilla Scandiuzzi; m/l, Sam Winans, Jim Bond, Robbie Rist, Jenni Rosen, Robert Michaels; stunts, Jeff Smolek; makeup, Laya Saul.

Comedy **Cas.** **(PR:A-C MPAA:PG-13)**

DIRTY REBEL† (1987, Yugo./US) Film Danas-Noble/Noble

Roy McNeil, Burt Starger, Jean Winston.

Two soldiers, both participants in the Serbian nationalist movement's assassination of Austrian Archduke Franz Ferdinand, return after WW I to find their homeland at the mercy of swindlers and corrupt politicians. One of them becomes a Robin Hood-like outlaw, while the other, who accepts a position as a police captain, is compelled to hunt down his former comrade-in-arms. This US-Yugoslavian coproduction was directed by Alex Petko, who helmed 1986's THE WILD WIND.

p, Ika Panajotovic; d&w, Alex Petko [Alexander Petkovic]; ph, Tom Pinter; m, Robert Ragland, Voy Kostic; ed, Keith Stafford.

Action **(PR:NR MPAA:NR)**

DISCOPRIBEH† (1987, Czech.) 82m Barrandov

Rudolf Hrusinsky *(Jirka)*, Ladislav Potmesil *(Father)*, Mariana Slovakova *(Eva)*, Jaroslava Bobkova *(Jitka)*, Roman Piki *(Roman)*, Andrej Kraus *(Cafa)*, Radek Pospisil *(Sendvic)*, Tomas Maka *(Bedula)*, Antonin Kriz *(Doda)*, Karel Vochoc *(Mr. Jonak)*, Jana Krausova *(Mother)*, Pavel Novy *(Otcuv Partak)*, Bohumil Vavra *(Barber)*, Jirina Jelenska, Jaroslav Choc, Milan Pekny, Milan Vlachovsky, Tatiana Kuliskova.

d, Jaroslav Soukup; w, Boris Janicek, Jaroslav Soukup (based on a story by Boris Janicek); ph, Vladimir Smutny; ed, Jiri Brozek; art d, Jiri Matolin; ch, Jiri Rebec; cos, Hana Havelkova.

Musical **(PR:NR MPAA:NR)**

DISORDERLIES** (1987) 96m WB c

Damon Wimbley *(Kool Rock)*, Darren Robinson *(Buffy)*, Mark Morales *(Markie)*, Ralph Bellamy *(Albert Dennison)*, Tony Plana *(Miguel)*, Anthony Geary *(Winslow Lowry)*, Marco Rodriguez *(Luis Montana)*, Troy Beyer *(Carla)*.

A curious comedy which is simultaneously an embarrassment and throwback to the days of Three Stooges-style slapstick, DISORDERLIES is worth seeing simply for the novelty of 83-year-old Hollywood great Ralph Bellamy sharing the screen with three obese black rap singers called "The Fat Boys." Bellamy stars as a wheelchair-bound millionaire who teeters on the edge of death but just won't die. His slimy nephew Geary is aching to inherit Bellamy's fortune and is willing to do anything to kill off the old man. He travels to Brooklyn and pays a visit to "the worst nursing home in America," and whom does he find but The Fat Boys. These three beefy orderlies—Darren "The Human Beat Box" Robinson, Damon "Kool Rock-Ski" Wimbley, and Mark "Prince Markie Dee" Morales—have just been fired for eating 16 chocolate cakes and Geary instantly knows that their incompetence is just what Bellamy needs. Geary hopes that the inept trio will accidentally kill Bellamy and the fortune will legally pass into his possession. Well, as luck would have it, The Fat Boys' energy rejuvenates Bellamy. They bring him along to a roller disco which is populated by a number of young ladies who get Bellamy's blood flowing like it hasn't in years. In no time at all, Bellamy is a picture of physical fitness. The frustrated Geary takes Bellamy's life into his own hands, but The Fat Boys save the day and secure Bellamy's lasting friendship in the process.

There's not much to DISORDERLIES—just a lot of slapstick pratfalls: one Fat Boy kicking the other Fat Boy in his ample behind, Fat Boys falling down, Fat Boys struggling to get up. It's the sort of sophomoric humor that only becomes funny because it's so sophomoric. There is something inherently funny about three bungling Fat Boys bumping into each other as the soundtrack colorfully adds an assortment of "boi-oi-oi-ngs." Unfortunately, director Schultz tries to make The Fat Boys act—something which they just can't do very well. For some inexplicable reason they are only allowed to sing one song—a cover version of The Beatles' "Baby You're a Rich Man." Schultz, who previously directed The Fat Boys in KRUSH GROOVE, should have had sense enough to realize that The Fat Boys are meant to rap, not act. DISORDERLIES is harmless enough but will probably disappoint those who expect to hear The Fat Boys brand of rap music. *(Brief nudity, comic violence, mild profanity.)*

p, Michael Schultz, George Jackson, Michael Jaffe; d, Michael Schultz; w, Mark Feldberg, Mitchell Klebanoff; ph, Rolf Kesterman; ed, Ned Humphreys; art d, George Costello; cos, Susie De Santo.

Comedy **(PR:A-C MPAA:PG)**

DISTANT LIGHTS† (1987, It.) 89m Intersound-Reteitalia c

Tomas Milian *(Bernardo)*, Laura Morante *(Renata)*, William Berger, Giacomo Piperno.

Visitors from outer space invade a cemetery and turn its inhabitants into the living dead in this dubbed-in-English Italian science-fiction film. Using the stiffs as vehicles for their spirits, the aliens create an upheaval in the little town before willingly departing the corpses and the planet.

p, Claudio Argento; d, Aurelio Chiesa; w, Aurelio Chiesa, Roberto Lerici, Roberto Leoni; ph, Renato Tafuri; m, Angelo Branduardi; ed, Anna Napoli.

Science Fiction **(PR:NR MPAA:NR)**

DIVINAS PALABRAS† (1987, Span.) 105m Ion Producciones c (Trans: Divine Words)

Ana Belen *(Mari Gaila)*, Francisco Rabal *(Pedro Gailo, Mari's Husband)*, Imanol Arias *(Septimo Miau)*, Esperanza Roy *(Rosa "La Tatula")*, Aurora Bautista *(Marica Del Reino)*, Juan Echanove *(Miguelin "El Padrones")*.

An old beggar woman does extremely well at her trade primarily because of the sympathy generated by her deformed son, whom she pulls around in a hand-drawn cart. When the woman dies, her relatives battle for custody of the child in order to continue plying the old woman's trade. Belen wins the battle, and reaps the benefits by taking the child to country fairs. Her success is short-lived, however, as she leaves the boy unattended in a tavern and he dies from alcohol poisoning.

p, Victor Manuel San Jose Sanchez; d, Jose Luis Garcia Sanchez; w, Enrique Llovet, Diego Santillan, Jose Luis Garcia Sanchez (based on the play by Ramon del Valle-Inclan); ph, Fernando Arribas (CinemaScope); m, Milladoiro; ed, Pablo G. Del Amo; art d & cos, Gerardo Vera.

Drama **(PR:NR MPAA:NR)**

DIXIA QING† (1987, Hong Kong) 97m Pearl City/D&B c (Trans: Love Unto Waste)

Irene Wan *(Billie Yuen, the Model)*, Tsai Chin *(Chao Shu-Ling/Jane the Singer)*, Elaine Jin *(Liu Yuk-Ping/Jade Screen the Actress)*, Tony Leung *(Tony Cheung)*, Chow Yun-fat *(Inspector Lan)*, Yip Kuen-Chi *(Tony's Father)*, Mei Fang *(Shu Ling's Mother)*, Angie Chen *(Kwan, Film Director)*.

A dissolute young man makes the acquaintance of three friends, a model, a singer, and an aspiring actress. He becomes the lover of Wan, the model, despite the fact that he has a steady girl friend. Through Wan, an intimacy with the other girls develops. The plot evolves into a thriller when one night they discover that Chin, the singer has been murdered. Yun Fat, playing Inspector Lan, takes over the case, insinuating himself into the young people's lives.

p, Dickson Poon; d, Stanley Kwan; w, Lai Kit, Chiu Tai-An-Ping (based on a story by Lai Kit); ph, Johnny Koo; m, Violet Lam; ed, Chow Cheung-Kan; art d, William Chang.

Drama **(PR:NR MPAA:NR)**

DIXIELAND DAIMYO† (1987) 85m Daiei c

Ikko Furuya *(Uminogo)*, Ai Kanzaki *(Fumikohime)*, Mami Okamoto *(Matsuehime)*, Shinji Tonoyama *(Gensai)*, Ron Nelson *(Joe)*, Pharez Whitted *(Louis)*, Lenny Marsh *(Sam)*, George Sparky Smith *(Uncle Bob)*, Juro Kara *(Masumitsu)*, Ichiro Zaitsu *(Kurozaemon)*, Hirotaro Honda *(Monnosuke)*.

No doubt the first melding of jazz and Japanese feudal wars, this film begins shortly after the Civil War in the US when four black Dixieland jazz musicians decide to sail to Africa. Their ability to play Dixieland jazz decades before its development would seem to qualify them as musical geniuses, but they're not equally adept at booking travel arrangements, winding up in Japan instead of Africa. Japan is a country divided at the time and the musicians, now only three in number since their clarinet player died during the voyage, find themselves in a domain situated between two warring factions. The lord of the land is himself a musician, and when he hears the Americans play he just can't resist the beat and immediately becomes a proficient clarinet player. Soon the whole domain gets into the act, leading to the world's first all-night jam session. Evidently jazz was all the country needed to set itself straight as the next morning Japan's feudal period has ended and the country has become a new nation. The 36th film directed by Okamoto, DIXIELAND DAIMYO was screened at the Montreal Film Festival in 1987.

p, Yo Yamamoto, Masao Kobayashi; d, Kihachi Okamoto; w, Toshiro Ishido, Kihachi Okamoto (based on a story by Yasutaka Tsutsui); ph, Yudai Kato (VistaVision); m, Yasutaka Tsutsui, Yosuke Yamashita; ed, Yoshitami Kuroiwa; art d, Kazuo Takenaka.

Comedy/Musical **(PR:NR MPAA:NR)**

DJADDE HAYE SARD† (1987, Iran) 93m Farabi Cinema Foundation c (Trans: Frosty Roads)

Majid Nasiri *(Esmaeil)*, Ali Nassirian *(Moosavi)*, Hamid Jebeli *(Rahman)*, Esmaeil Mohammadi *(Darvish Gorgali)*, Frazaneh Neshat Akhavan *(Moosavi's Wife)*.

A disabled teacher, the village idiot, and a boy whose father is very ill travel the frosty roads of the translated title in this Iranian feature. Their destination is a town where they can get the medicine the boy's father needs. The journey is a perilous one, but their mission of mercy is a success. (In Farsi; English subtitles.)

p, Syamak Taghi Poor; d, Massoud Jafari Jozani; w, Symak Taghi Poor (based on the story "If Daddy Dies" by Reza Sarshar); ph, Toraj Mansoori; m, Kambiz Roshan Ravan; ed, Davood Yooseffian; prod d, Vahij Ollah Fariborzi.

Drama **(PR:NR MPAA:NR)**

DR. SUN YATSEN† (1987, Chi.) 109m Pearl River c

Liu Wenzhi *(Dr. Sun Yatsen)*.

Presented on an epic scale, this biographical film tells the story of Dr. Sun Yatsen, the father of modern China. Liu Wenzhi plays the great revolutionary leader, and the film shows him both in triumph—his instrumental role in the formation of the Chinese republic in 1912 and brief term as president—and in defeat—his flight to Japan in 1913 after leading an unsuccessful revolt to regain control of the government after he had peacefully ceded it to Yuan Shih-k'ai.

d, Sing Yinnan; w, He Mengfan, Zhang Lei; ph, Wang Hengli, Hou Young.

Biography **(PR:NR MPAA:NR)**

DOGS IN SPACE† (1987, Aus.) 108m Central Park Films/Skouras c

Michael Hutchence *(Sam)*, Saskia Post *(Anna)*, Nique Needles *(Tim)*, Deanna Bond *(The Girl)*, Tony Helou *(Luchio)*, Chris Haywood *(Chainsaw Man)*, Peter Walsh *(Anthony)*, Laura Swanson *(Clare)*, Adam Briscomb *(Grant)*, Sharon Jessop *(Leanne)*, Edward Clayton-Jones *(Nick)*, Martii Coles *(Mark)*, Chuck Meo *(Charles)*, Caroline Lee *(Jenny)*, Fiona Latham *(Barbara)*, Stephanie Johnson *(Erica)*, Gary Foley *(Barry)*, Glenys Osborne *(Lisa)*, Allanah Hill, Robyn McLellan *(Anna's Girlfriends)*, Troy Davies *(Skinhead)*, John Murphy, Troy Davies, Owen Robertson *(Leanne's Brothers)*, Helen Phillips *(Stacey)*, Kelly Hoare *(Chainsaw Woman)*, Robyn Lowenstein *(Chainsaw Baby)*, Robert Ratti *(Dealer)*, Barbara Jungwirth *(Sam's Mother)*, Beamish Elliot *(Hardcore Hippie)*, Noel Pennington, Ted Fahrner *(Policemen)*, Michelle Bennett, Lian Lunson *(Grant's Girls)*, George Maleckas *(Crazy George)*, Hugo Race *(Pierre)*, Joe Camilleri *(Terry Towelling Man)*, Liz Meyers, Tim McLaughlan *(Sales People)*, Lillian Wilson *(Mount Waverly Mum)*, Emma De Clario, Sybil Gibb *(Champion Girls)*, Helen Gianevsky *(TV Interviewer)*, Jean Osborne *(Anna's Mum)*, Gavin Wood *(Countdown Announcer)*, Bohdan *(3RRR D.J.)*, Edward Clayton-Jones, Michael Hutchence, Chuck Meo, Nique Needles, Glenys Osborne *(Dogs In Space)*, Marcus Bergner, Marie Hoy, John Murphy, James Rogers, Ollie Olsen *(Too Fat To Fit Through The Door)*, Terry Dooley, Denise Grant, Stuart Grant, David Light *(Primitive Calculators)*, Arnie Hanna, David Hoy, John Murphy, Ollie Olsen *(Whirlywirld)*, Marie Hoy, Denise Grant, Danila Stirpe, Jules Taylor *(Thrush and the C . . . S)*, Marie Hoy, Loki, Tim Millikan, John Murphy, Ollie Olsen *(Marie Hoy And Friends)*, Martha Butler, Kate Doherty, Harriet Freeman, Kelly Gallagher, Angela Howard, Tim Millikan, Marie Hoy, John Murphy, Sarah Newsome, Ollie Olsen, Miriam Smith, Miles Standish, Noah Taylor.

Employing a cinema verite approach and Robert Altman-influenced overlapping dialog, this Australian film—which was given only a scant US release—presents a look at a post-punk communal household in Melbourne, circa 1978. Hutchence, the lead singer of the popular Australian rock band INXS, plays the singer in a considerably less successful band. He is also the owner of a run-down, garbage-strewn house that serves as home for a shifting array of punks and hippies. Drug use is rampant, free love reigns, and music-making is the order of the day. In the midst of this anarchy, Helou, an engineering student, tries desperately to study for important tests, but the return of a former flame further complicates his efforts. Post, a part-time nurse, is Hutchence's girl friend; however, he sleeps with other of the house's female occupants, and even considers making it with 16-year-old runaway Bond. Although Post lives elsewhere, her obsessive love of Hutchence gets the better of her and her involvement in the freewheeling scene at the house eventually leads to her drug-overdose death. That event shakes up Hutchence and the household.

Set during the year when space debris from Skylab was landing in Australia, DOGS IN SPACE takes its title from the band which Hutchence fronts and from the canine cosmonaut that also played an important part in this year's MY LIFE AS A DOG. Here footage of the Soviet space-dog is intercut with the goings-on at the house. The film has a strong autobiographical element, as director-writer Richard Lowenstein lived for a time in an environment like the one depicted in his film. The lead characters have real-life counterparts and several of the actors who appear in film are veterans of similar scenes and literally play themselves. The director of STRIKEBOUND (1984), Lowenstein is perhaps better known for the music videos he has directed, including several for INXS and Pete Townshend's 50-minute "White City." Music plays a big part in DOGS IN SPACE. In its numerous live performances, the film seeks to recreate the "little band" phenomena which was a part of the Australian music scene in the late 1970s. These little bands were impromptu collections of "musicians" who came together to perform short, improvised sets (often covers), and Lowenstein decided to give his version of these bands a more polished sound than the originals had. The soundtrack features incidental songs from several Australian bands, including Nick Cave's iconoclastic Birthday Party, and seminal punk rocker Iggy Pop. The film is particularly significant for its use of four-channel Dolby sound, which it employed not only to record the music and special audio effects but also the often-overlapping dialog. DOGS IN SPACE came into being in 1984 over a breakfast Lowenstein and Hutchence shared in the south of France (INXS was in Nice to play a gig and the director had accompanied STRIKEBOUND to the Cannes Film Festival). Songs include: "Dog Food," "Endless Sea" (performed by Iggy Pop), "Dogs in Space" (Sam Sejavka, Mike Lewis), "Win/Lose," "Window to the World" (Ollie Olsen, performed by Whirlywirld), "True Love" (performed by the Marching Girls), "Sky Saw" (Brian Eno), "Skullbrains" (Marcus Bergner, Marie Hoy), "Shivers" (Roland S. Howard, performed by Boys Next Door), "Diseases" (Thrush and the C . . . s), "Pumping Ugly Muscle" (The Primitive Calculators), "Happy Birthday," "Mr. Clarinet" (The Birthday Party, performed by The Birthday Party), "Anthrax" (Gang of Four), "Tequila" (Chuck Rio), "Rooms for the Memory" (Olsen).

p, Glenys Rowe; d&w, Richard Lowenstein; ph, Andrew De Groot; ed, Jill Bilcock; md, Ollie Olsen; art d, Jody Borland; spec eff, Visual Effect P/L, Peter Stubbs, Jeff Little; m/l, Sam Sejavka, Mike Lewis, Ollie Olsen, Brian Eno, Marcus Bergner, Marie Hoy, Roland S. Howard, Thrush and the C . . . s, The Primitive Calculators, The Birthday Party, Gang of Four, Chuck Rio, Iggy Pop; stunts, Glenn Boswell; makeup, Carolyn Nott, Troy Davies.

Drama **(PR:NR MPAA:NR)**

DOKTOR MINORKA VIDOR NAGY NAPJA† (1987, Hung.) 77m Mafilm-Objektiv Studio c (Trans: Professor Vidor Minorka's Great Day)

Borbala Boldoghy *(Dorka)*, Agi Margittai *(Aunt Terez)*, Eszter Csakanyi *(Emilia)*, Denes Ujlaky *(Mr. Gravy)*, Nora Tabori *(Ida Bulb)*.

When a woman in a marketplace waves a magical feather duster over her head, the marketplace is suddenly changed into a battle zone. The butchers and the fish mongers wage all out war on each other and the feather duster is lost in the fray. Just as total distruction seems certain, the feather duster is located, waved in the air, and peace is restored.

d, Andras Solyom; w, Pal Bekes; ph, Lorand Mertz (Eastmancolor); m, Istvan Martha; ed, Hajnal Sello; set d, Andras Gyurki; cos, Erzsebet Mialkovszky.

Children's/Fantasy **(PR:NR MPAA:NR)**

DOLCE ASSENZA† (1987, It.) Raitre/Cidif (Trans: Sweet Absence)

Jo Champa, Fabienne Babe, Sergio Castellito, Pierluigi Crespi, Stavros Tornes, Franca Marchesi, Alessandro Balducci, Antonio Catania, Giuliana Rivera, Alessandro Wagner, Angela Finocchiaro, Giorgio Melazzi, Alessandro Marchetti, Desire Terenghi, Sergio Terenghi.

Set in Milan, the story concerns two young women who share an apartment. One is a glamorous model the other a shy wallflower who disappears one day. The model begins an intensive search for her roommate. She's aided by the missing girl's boy friend, and as they search, they fall in love with each other.

d, Claudio Sestieri; w, Sandro Petraglia, Claudio Sestieri; ph, Charles Rose; m, Mauro Pagani; ed, Gennaro Oliveti.

Drama **(PR:NR MPAA:NR)**

DOLCE PELLE DI ANGELA† (1987, It.) Cineglobo (Trans: Angela's Sweet Skin)

Michela Miti, Carlo Mucari, Piero Gerlini, Maria Pia Parisi, Svetlana Starcova, Guerrino Crivello, Roberto Pipino, Anita Ekberg.

A naive country girl moves to Rome where she becomes a prostitute. She has an affair with a criminal, but that ends when he is sent to jail. She meets and marries an aristocrat who soon dies, leaving her his fortune. She marries her former lover after he is released from jail.

d&w, Andrea Bianchi; ph, Pasqualino Fanetti; m, Ubaldo Continiello; ed, Cesare Bianchini.

Drama/Romance **(PR:NR MPAA:NR)**

DOLGHYIE PROVOD† (1987, USSR) 95m Odessa bw (Trans: The Long Goodbye)

Zenaida Sharko *(Mother)*, Oleg Vladimirski *(Son)*.

Shot in 1971 but blacklisted for 16 years, this film focuses on the relationship between a teenage boy and his mother. Mother and son battle each other while the boy dreams of leaving their home in Odessa to be with his father in Novosibirsk.

d&w, Kira Muratova; ph, Ghenadi Kariuk; m, O. Karabanchiuk; ed, V. Oleinik; art d, E. Rodrigues.

Drama **(PR:NR MPAA:NR)**

DOLLS*½ (1987) 77m Taryn/Empire c

Ian Patrick Williams *(David Bower)*, Carolyn Purdy-Gordon *(Rosemary Bower)*, Carrie Lorraine *(Judy Bower)*, Guy Rolfe *(Gabriel Hartwicke)*, Hilary Mason *(Hilary Hartwicke)*, Bunty Bailey *(Isabel Prange)*, Cassie Stuart *(Enid Tilley)*, Stephen Lee *(Ralph Morris)*.

Empire Pictures' most promising director, Stuart Gordon (RE-ANIMATOR, FROM BEYOND), must have had an off day when he helmed this uninspired mishmash of THE OLD DARK HOUSE and leftovers from "The Twilight Zone." Written by TROLLS screenwriter Naha (who has also penned such genre-film reference works as *Horrors from Screen to Scream* and *The Science Fictionary*), DOLLS begins on the proverbial dark and stormy night. The story centers on Lorraine, an unhappy little girl who does not get along with her new stepmother, Purdy-Gordon. Her father, Williams, is rather weak-willed and totally dominated by his venomous new wife. While vacationing in England, the miserable trio find themselves stranded in the midst of a storm. They are forced to seek shelter in the spooky mansion of a kindly old couple, Rolfe and Mason. Minutes later, more unexpected guests arrive in the form of kid-at-heart American businessman Lee, and Bailey and Stuart, two local punk girls he picked up on the road. The elderly couple take an immediate liking to Lorraine and the childlike Lee and show them their massive collection of dolls, most of which were made by Rolfe. They even present Lorraine with a Punch doll. Later, when everyone is tucked away for the night, the punkers decide to steal some of the elderly couple's antiques and make a hasty getaway. Bailey wanders off on her own and finds a room full of priceless jeweled boxes. Unfortunately, before she can make her escape, the dozens of dolls in the room suddenly come to life and attack her. Armed with little knives and tools, the dolls make quick work of the girl and drag her off, leaving a trail of blood. Little Lorraine witnesses the aftermath of the horrible event and tries to convince her father that the dolls have come to murderous life. Of course, Williams ignores the child. In desperation, Lorraine turns to Lee, and though disbelieving, he relates to the child and tries to humor her by investigating. To his horror he finds Bailey in the attic, her face transformed into that of a doll (she can even remove her glass eyes). With angry dolls snapping at his ankles, Lee flees the attic. Lee and Lorraine try to warn the rest of the household, and again they are ignored. During the course of the night, however, Purdy-Gordon and Stuart are murdered by the homicidal dolls. When an angry Williams finally confronts his daughter, her Punch doll comes to life and defends her. After a struggle, Williams manages to destroy the doll, only to be chastised by the horrified old dollmaker. Rolfe casts a spell on Williams and turns him into a tiny Punch doll. When morning finally comes, the elderly couple cast a spell on Lorraine and Lee which removes the night's events from their memories and then allow them to leave.

Filmed on a $1.2 million budget in six weeks, DOLLS was made by Gordon *before* his 1986 release, FROM BEYOND, but it was released *after* the Lovecraft film. Seeking to capitalize on RE-ANIMATOR's controversy and acclaim, Empire hustled FROM BEYOND into release ahead of DOLLS. While FROM

BEYOND possessed the same uniquely perverse vision as RE-ANIMATOR, DOLLS seems merely a dull interlude between the two Lovecraft films. Directed and scripted in a surprisingly perfunctory manner, DOLLS is incredibly tedious—even at the brief 77-minute running time. Gordon drags out every "Old Dark House" cliche in the book, and fails to add anything new. While young Lorraine turns in a credible performance, most of the rest of the cast appear to be going through the motions—with the exception of Gordon's wife, Purdy-Gordon, whose performance goes through the roof (she makes Margaret Hamilton's wicked witch in THE WIZARD OF OZ look restrained). Although the concept of small dolls coming to bloodthirsty life *sounds* scary, it just isn't enough to sustain fear after the initial shock. Occasionally it works, as in the final chapter of the made-for-TV film "Trilogy of Terror," but that pitted one crazed doll against one lone woman. In Gordon's film there are hundreds of dolls going after half a dozen humans. In this case more is not better, it's merely sillier. Gordon and his effects team do manage to evoke some chills, however, especially when the dolls whisper among themselves to decide the fate of their hostages right in front of the helpless victims. Unfortunately, these nightmarish moments are few and far between, and the viewer must suffer through innumerable speeches by Rolfe and Mason extolling the virtues of childlike innocence and parental responsibility—as if such pontification justifies the ensuing carnage! For a director who has so quickly pushed his way to the forefront of the horror genre with an intelligent, no-holds-barred approach, Gordon's DOLLS is surprisingly tame and wholly disappointing. *(Violence, gore effects, profanity.)*

p, Brian Yuzna; d, Stuart Gordon; w, Ed Naha; ph, Mac Ahlberg; m, Fuzzbee Morse; ed, Lee Percy; set d, Becky Block-Cummins; cos, Angee Beckett; makeup, Giancarlo Del Brocco; spec eff, John Brunner, Vivian Brunner, Giancarlo Del Brocco, John Carl Buechler, David Allen; stunts, Aldo Dell'Acqua.

Horror **(PR:O MPAA:R)**

DONGODUCHHADU† (1987, India)

Krishna, Radha.

(In Telugu.)

d, Kodi Ramakrishna.

Drama **(PR:NR MPAA:NR)**

DOT GOES TO HOLLYWOOD† (1987, Aus.) 75m Yoram Gross Film Studios

Voices of: Robyn Moore, Keith Scott.

Dot journeys from her native Australia to Hollywood to enter a talent contest in hopes of winning money to help her sick friend Gumley. She wins the contest and meets a host of America's biggest movie stars. This is the ninth in a series of part

animated/part live action films based on a popular Australian cartoon character. Director Gross is a native of Poland who moved to Australia in 1969 and founded his own studio.

p&d, Yoram Gross; w, John Palmer (based on the character created by Ethel Pedley); ph, Joseph Cabatuan, Graham Sharpe, Ngoc Minh Nguyen; m, Bob Young, Guy Gross; ed, Rod Hay; anim d, Athol Henry.

Children's/Animation **(PR:NR MPAA:NR)**

DOWN TWISTED† (1987) 97m Golan-Globus/Cannon c

Carey Lowell *(Maxine)*, Charles Rocket *(Reno)*, Trudi Dochtermann *(Michelle)*, Thom Mathews *(Damalas)*, Norbert Weisser *(Deltoid)*, Linda Kerridge *(Soames)*, Nicholas Guest *(Brady)*, Gaylyn Gorg *(Blake)*.

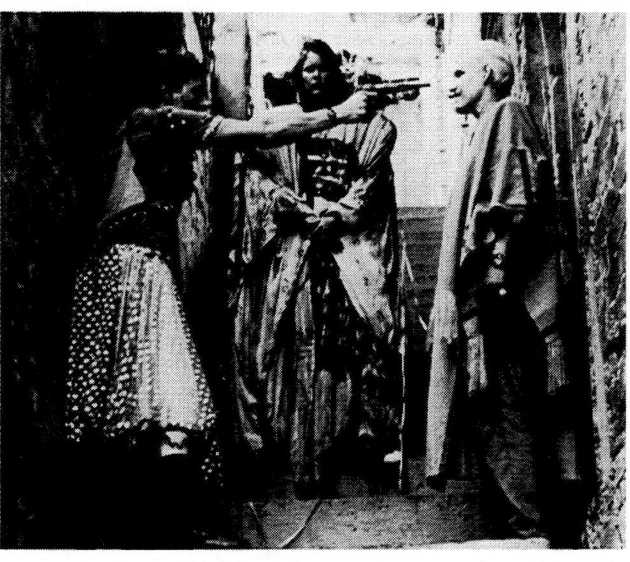

A hopelessly convoluted caper film set in a banana republic somewhere along the US/Mexican border. The plot is set into motion when a wealthy industrialist, Weisser, hires a small gang of international jewel thieves—Rocket, Dochtermann, Mathews, Guest, and Kerridge—to steal a gold religious relic. Along the way

Rocket falls for Dochtermann's naive roommate, Lowell, and they get dragged into various subplots involving terrorism, murder, double-crossing, explosions, military attacks, political eruptions, and the usual number of car chases. Directed by Pyun with a nod to the pulp novels of Raymond Chandler and Dashiell Hammett (not unlike his 1986 futuristic thriller RADIOACTIVE DREAMS) and the caper films of John Huston—THE MALTESE FALCON, THE BIG SLEEP, and BEAT THE DEVIL. Some viewers may remember lead Charles Rocket as a short-time member of the cast of "NBC's Saturday Night Live."

p, Menahem Golan, Yoram Globus; d, Albert Pyun; w, Gene O'Neill, Noreen Tobin (based on a story by Albert Pyun); ph, Walt Lloyd (TVC Color); m, Berlin Game; ed, Dennis O'Connor; prod d, Chester Kaczenski; art d, Richard Hummell, Douglas H. Leonard; cos, Renee Johnston.

Thriller **(PR:NR MPAA:R)**

DOXOBUS† (1987, Gr.) 105m Greek Film Centre c

Tassos Palaitzidis, Stelio Capatos, Barbara Mavromati, Panos Theodoridis, Alexis Migas, Stefanos Kyriakidis, Vassilis Gopis, Nicos Vrettos, Costas Santas, Lazaros Andreou, Costas Zacharakis, Stelios Goutis, Tassos Ifantis.

This film is set in the 14th century in the Greek fishing village of Doxobus. Rebels are battling the emperor, who is heavily taxing the public to pay for his defense. The abbot of the monastery in Doxobus is secretly supplying financial support to the rebels. An 11-year-old boy, whose father has died, is sent to the monastery where he stays for seven years, then leaves at the abbot's urging to make a life for himself. He joins the rebels, becomes one of their leaders and, when they defeat the emperor's forces, he is given "custody" of Doxobus.

d, Fotos Lambrinos; w, Fotos Lambrinos, Panos Theodoridis; ph, Giorgos Arvanitis; m, Costas Vomvolos; ed, Aristidis Karydis-Fuchs; art d, Mikes Karapiperis; cos, Ioanna Papantoniou.

Historical **(PR:NR MPAA:NR)**

DRACHENFUPTER (SEE: DRAGON'S FOOD, 1987, Ger./Switz.)

DRAGNET**½** (1987) 106m Applied Action/UNIV c

Dan Aykroyd *(Sgt. Joe Friday)*, Tom Hanks *(Pep Streebek)*, Christopher Plummer *(Rev. Whirley)*, Harry Morgan *(Capt. Bill Gannon)*, Alexandra Paul *(Connie Swail)*, Jack O'Halloran *(Emil Muzz)*, Elizabeth Ashley *(Police Commissioner Jane Kirkpatrick)*, Dabney Coleman *(Jerry Caesar)*, Kathleen Freeman, Bruce Gray, Lenka Peterson, Julia Jennings.

James Cagney, Humphrey Bogart, and Kirk Douglas, with their distinctive personalities and mannerisms, were for years the most mimicked Hollywood stars, and so, too, was the monosyllabic, taciturn Jack Webb, of "Dragnet" fame. The Webb character is once more parodied in this less-than-skillful satire, one which is really just another TV skit ballooned into a feature film. Here Aykroyd plays the nephew of the legendary Joe Friday, a repressive sort who minds the rules to the point of idiocy, driving his car at the precise speed of 48 mph down Los Angeles freeways to save gas for the police department. His rigid way of life is upset slightly by his more free-and-easy partner, Hanks, who rides a motorcycle and handily punctures Aykroyd's stuffy personality. But after the first 20 minutes of staccato interchanges between this pair, the parody evaporates into Hollywood steam and only the situation scenes involving Plummer, a devilish evangelist, and Coleman, a porn publisher (the two collaborating to control the corrupt destinies of L.A.), offer comic relief. There are some touching minor scenes involving Aykroyd and pretty girl Paul as the by-the-book cop attempts to convey his affection for the girl but, again, the love fumbling is overplayed. The conspiracy into which Aykroyd and Hanks stumble involves Ashley, a chic police chief, suave Plummer, and Coleman, who parades about in a bathrobe clutching a baby and spouting his Constitutional rights to publish his pornographic publications.

This is basically an uninspired limited action spoof of the Webb TV show where Webb's stylized monotone delivery and deadpan wit is hammered flat by Aykroyd. Made for $20 million, the shallow production was helmed by Mankiewicz, whose father Joseph created ALL ABOUT EVE, and whose uncle, Herman, wrote the magnificent script for CITIZEN KANE, with help from Orson Welles. Such stellar ancestry has no influence over this script. Mankiewicz, known as a script fixer in Hollywood, and writer of SUPERMAN II and many TV shows, brings little innovation and no surprises to DRAGNET. His direction is flat and without invention; he seems to be remaking a "Batman" skit, with the accent on droll. It simply doesn't come off and the viewer will be left with an empty feeling, a vacuous notion that somehow the laugh scenes slipped by unnoticed. They were never really there. *(Mild profanity, violence.)* p, David Permut, Robert K. Weiss; d, Tom Mankiewicz; w, Dan Aykroyd, Alan Zweibel, Tom Mankiewicz; ph, Matthew F. Leonetti (DeLuxe Color); m, Ira Newborn; ed, Richard Halsey, William D. Gordean; prod d, Robert F. Boyle; art d, Frank Richwood; set d, Arthur Jeph Parker; cos, Taryn DeChellis.

Comedy **(PR:C MPAA:PG-13)**

DRAGON'S FOOD*½** (1987, Ger./Switz.) 75m Novoskop-Probst-Bern-Kuratorium Junger Deutscher-Hamburger Filmburo Filmforderung bw (DRACHENFUTTER)

Bhasker *(Shezad)*, Ric Young *(Xiao)*, Buddy Uzzaman *(Rashid)*, Ulrich Wildgruber *(Cook)*, Wolf-Dieter Sprenger *(Herder)*, Frank Oladeinde *(Dale)*, Louis Blaise *(Louis)*, Su Zeng Hua *(Wang)*, Young Me Song *(Herder's Wife)*.

A young Pakistani immigrant (Bhasker) who is seeking political asylum in Hamburg is tossed out of a Chinese restaurant by a waiter (Young) when he attempts to sell roses to the customers. Crestfallen, he trudges back through the dreary, wintry landscape to his room in a state-operated dormitory, where he learns that his friend and fellow countryman (Uzzaman) has been denied political asylum and is soon to be deported. Uzzaman instead opts for an illegal and complicated oceanic crossing that will eventually land him in the US. His friend gone, Bhasker finds illegal work in the kitchen of the Chinese restaurant from which he was evicted and is befriended by the Chinese waiter, Young. They decide to form a partnership in a restaurant and organize a contest for Bhasker's dormitory mates to decide whether Pakistani or Chinese food will be the featured cuisine. After Bhasker ingeniously manages to secure the necessary capital, construction begins on a Pakistani restaurant. A letter from the immigration authorities arrives for Bhasker, but he places it unopened inside a cabinet drawer. The restaurant opens to a full house and a receptive clientele, but the authorities arrive, forcibly remove Bhasker from the premises and, subsequently, from the country. An unknown immigrant later enters the establishment with a bundle of roses for sale, but leaves when he finds Young staring disconsolately at a photo of Bhasker.

Jan Schutte's first feature film is a powerful and insightful look at the plight of Third World immigrants as they attempt to survive in the West. Presented in an understated manner, while using an approach that director Schutte describes as reductive, the film eliminates stylistic embellishments and narrative irrelevancies, providing, instead, the opportunity for the characters to tell their own stories. It is this directorial restraint that ultimately gives the film its remarkable strength, allowing the humanistic concern that Schutte feels for his characters to filter through without either elevating them to the status of victimized heroes or overtly attacking the society that seems to ignore them. Schutte developed this idea while filming an earlier documentary about an immigrant rose peddler. The main actor in the earlier film and several of his friends shared numerous stories about their immigrant experiences, inspiring Schutte to make DRAGON'S FOOD.

A primary focal point of the film is the feeling of alienation the numerous immigrants feel when confronted by the dominant German culture, a feeling underscored as Schutte only translates one of the 12 languages (German) heard in the film. The German authorities continually take refuge in official decrees as their guidelines for handling the problems of the refugees. They are civil and sometimes even pleasant, but they are unable to provide any real help. Whenever faced with an emotional display, they react by reciting a statement of the designated policy that pertains to the individual case. Ultimately the struggles of the neglected immigrants bind them into a collective alien culture that gives them the will to survive. It is this resilience of human nature that DRAGON'S FOOD truly celebrates. *(Adult situations.)*

d, Jan Schutte; w, Jan Schutte, Thomas Strittmatter; ph, Lutz Konermann; m, Claus Bantzer; ed, Renate Merck; art d, Katharina Mayer-Woppermann.

Drama **(PR:C MPAA:NR)**

DREAMANIAC zero (1987) 82m Taryn/Wizard Video-Infinity c

Thomas Bern *(Adam)*, Kim McKamy *(Pat)*, Sylvia Summers *(Lily)*, Lauren Peterson *(Jodi)*, Bob Pelham *(Jamie)*, Cynthia Crass *(Frances)*, Brad Laughlin *(Brad)*, Linda Watts *(Jan)*, Matthew Phelps *(Foster)*, Lisa Emery *(Rosie)*, Michael Warren *(Ace)*, Brent Black *(Doctor)*.

A young writer of heavy metal tunes conjures up a succubus who sets out on a spree of seduction, murder, and mutilation at a sorority party. Eventually the songwriter, too, comes under her spell and does some carving himself. Things look bad for the two surviving sorority sisters, but a guy in a white coat shows up and drags the demon back to the funny farm. Seems she wasn't a demon after all. Then it turns out that none of this was real. It was only a story made up by a writer, who looks just like the heavy metal kid. The doorbell rings, and when the writer opens it, the demonic woman kills him, blood splattering all over. Got that? Does it sound like fun? Well, DREAMANIAC is anything but fun. Instead, it is a relentlessly stupid exploitation gore film with nothing to recommend it. All the victims are catatonic or stupid and it's hard to care if any of them live. The ridiculous twist ending, in which the girl who has shown all these supernatural powers is revealed to be just an ordinary nut case, is the kind of thing that makes one want to fling a billiard ball through the TV screen. The film is a straight-to-video item that is marketed as "Too Terrifying for the Silver Screen," and while there is no shortage of blood and breasts, there is little to shock here. *(Gore effects, nudity, sexual situations, substance abuse, excessive profanity.)*

p&d, David DeCoteau; w, Helen Robinson; ph, Howard Wexler (Fotokem Color); ed, Peter Teschner; prod d, Rozanne Taucher; md, Tom Milano, Don Great; makeup, Tom Schwartz, Linda Nottestad; stunts, Jake Ryan.

Horror **Cas.** **(PR:O MPAA:NR)**

DREAMERS† (1987, Israel/Neth.) 110m Belbo/Hemdale c (AKA: ONCE WE WERE DREAMERS)

Kelly McGillis *(Anda)*, John Shea *(Marcus)*, Christine Boisson *(Sima)*, Arnon Zadok, Chad Schahar, Robert Pollak, Sinai Peter, Yaskov Amall, Zareh Vertanian.

Helmed by Uri Barbash, who directed BEYOND THE WALLS—the excellent 1984 Israeli feature which was nominated for an Academy Award as Best Foreign Film—this Israeli-Dutch coproduction features American actors Kelly McGillis (WITNESS, TOP GUN) and John Shea (MISSING, WINDY CITY). They are part of a small group of European Jews who venture to Galilee at the end of WW I in search of a better life. Shea, a violinist, and McGillis, a doctor, fall in love against the backdrop of their little community's utopian striving. The film was show at the Tokyo International Film Festival under the title ONCE WE WERE DREAMERS.

p, Ben Elkerbout, Ludi Boeken, Katrial Schory; d, Uri Barbash; w, Benny Barbash; ph, Amnon Salomon (United Color); m, Misha Segal; ed, Tova Asher; prod d, Eilon Levy.

Drama **(PR:NR MPAA:NR)**

DU MICH AUCH (SEE: SAME TO YOU, 1987, Ger.)

DUBLYOR NACHINAET DEYSTVOVAT† (1987, USSR) 87m Lenfilm/Sovexportfilm c (Trans: The Standby Moves In)

Boris Plotnikov, Natalya Danilova, Mikhail Gluzsky, Rimma Korostilyova, Ivan Krasko.

As an experiment, all the top managers at a factory take a one-month leave while junior staff members run the operation. The film then depicts the setbacks and victories the young engineers experience while managing the factory.

d, Ernest Yasan; w, Valentin Chernykh, Pyotr Karyakin, Ernest Yasan; ph, Vladimir Burykin; m, Vadim Bibergan; art d, Elena Fomina.

Drama **(PR:NR MPAA:NR)**

DUDES½** (1987) 89m Vista/New Century-Vista c

Jon Cryer *(Grant)*, Daniel Roebuck *(Biscuit)*, Flea [Michael Balzary] *(Milo)*, Lee Ving *(Missoula, Thief Gang Leader)*, Catherine Mary Stewart *(Jessie, Gas Station Owner)*, Billy Ray Sharkey, Glenn Withrow, Michael Melvin, Axxel G. Reese, Marc Rude, Calvin Bartlett, Pete Willcox, Vance Colvig, Pamela Gidley.

First Alex Cox's STRAIGHT TO HELL and now this, the second punk western to hit the screen this year. DUDES begins as three New York City punkers, Cryer, Roebuck (sporting a massive bleach-blond mohawk), and Flea, decide that they are fed up with the Big Apple and are ready to give sunny Los Angeles a try. The trio set out in Cryer's old Volkswagen bug and somewhere in the Southwest they encounter Willcox, an Elvis impersonator/rodeo clown/stunt driver, etc. whose huge Airstream trailer (with "Daredelvis" painted on the side) is stuck in a ditch. The boys give Willcox a hand and earn his undying gratitude. One night while camping out among the bluffs and buttes in John Ford's beloved Monument Valley, the punkers are attacked by a band of vicious biker types led by Ving. After being robbed and tormented, the boys try to escape the marauders only to have Flea caught and brutally murdered by Ving. Cryer and Roebuck return with the unsympathetic sheriff who finds no evidence of murder (the body is gone) and tells the strange-looking youths to get out of town. Seething with anger and plagued by visions of a mythic cowboy on horseback, Cryer vows to take the law into his own hands and kill Ving, while Roebuck just wants to forget the whole thing and continue on to L.A. But Cryer picks up the Ving's trail and pursues his vendetta. On the road they meet Stewart, a tough, independent, and pretty female auto mechanic, and she teaches Cryer how to shoot and ride.

Meanwhile, Roebuck, too, is visited by a vision where he sees himself as an Indian brave whose village is slaughtered by a cavalry unit led by Ving. Now both possessed with the spirit of the Old West, Cryer and Roebuck dress like a gunslinger and an Indian and prepare to do battle with Ving. With help from Elvis impersonator Willcox, they track Ving to a tiny town and corner him in a movie theater. As Henry King's classic western JESSE JAMES reaches its climactic Northfield shoot-out sequence, Cryer and Roebuck open fire on Ving and one of his cronies. The shooting spills out into the street and develops into a chase in which Cryer kills one man and then corners Ving in an abandoned factory. After a brief struggle, Cryer manages to gun down Ving. His mission complete, Cryer watches as the ghostly cowboy and Indians, accompanied by the spirit of Flea, bid farewell and disappear in a cloud of dust.

Penelope Spheeris *almost* pulls this off. Presented in a goofy what-the-hell manner, DUDES is a lot of fun at first and then bogs down in a screenplay that relies on too many outrageous coincidences to keep the limited amount of action flowing. Utah is a big state and these boys continually stumble across Ving, Willcox, and Stewart as if everyone in the film has been traveling in circles. Even with the massive suspension of disbelief required in this film, implausiblities abound and annoy. When Cryer, dressed like Jack Palance in SHANE, finally catches up to the killers and confronts them in a bar, neither of them recognizes him despite the fact that they had held a gun to his head just a few days before *and* that he had peppered their truck with bullets shortly thereafter. There are other problems as well. Spheeris pushes the spirit-of-the-West thing to the limit and wastes a lot of screen time on the phantom cowboys and Indians routine. Also the action scenes themselves are fairly uninspired. After it leaves the movie theater, the climactic shoot-out is a big disappointment and is padded with gratuitous after-the-fact optically-printed slow motion. The cast, however, does a pretty good job making this silliness palatable. Ving, former leader of the now-defunct L.A. punk band Fear (which was featured in Spheeris's first film, the documentary THE DECLINE OF WESTERN CIVILIZATION), makes a supremely evil villain. Stewart does what she can with a badly underdeveloped role, Flea is memorable as the doomed punker, Willcox is hilarious as the Elvis impersonator, and Roebuck (the hulking killer in RIVER'S EDGE) steals the film with all the best lines and lots of funny business. Cryer, unfortunately, isn't very convincing as the punker suddenly possessed by the "a man's gotta do what a man's gotta do" spirit and seems a bit lost. Nineteen eighty-seven was a banner year for genre hybrids with STRAIGHT TO HELL on the low end of the spectrum and Kathryn Bigelow's NEAR DARK on the high end. DUDES, however, falls somewhere in the middle. *(Graphic violence, profanity.)*

p, Herb Jaffe, Miguel Tejada-Flores; d, Penelope Spheeris; w, J. Randal Johnson; ph, Robert Richardson; m, Charles Bernstein; ed, Andy Horvitch; prod d, Robert Ziembicki.

Western **(PR:O MPAA:R)**

DUMA VEZ POR TODAS† (1987, Portugal) 105m Rosi Burgeute Prods. c (Trans: Play . . . Boy)

Pedro Ayres Magalhaes, Vicky, Filipe Ferrer, Jasmin de Matos, Julian Maynard, Vitor Norte, Henrique Viana, Natalina Jose.

Feature film debut of director Leitao stars Magalhaes as a hotel desk clerk who becomes obsessed with his beautiful neighbor, Vicky, after indulging in a little voyeurism. As it turns out, Vicky is a call girl and Magalhaes is slowly drawn into a violent world of drug dealing and murder.

d&w, Joaquim Leitao; ph, Daniel Del Negro; m, Antonio Emiliano; ed, Leonor Guterres; art d, Nuno Carinhas.

Action **(PR:NR MPAA:NR)**

DVADTSTAT DNEI BEZ† (1987, USSR) 100m Lenfilm/The Other Cinema c (Trans: Twenty Days Without War)

Konstantin Simonov *(Narrator)*, Yuri Nikulin *(Maj. Lopatin)*, Liudmila Gurchenko *(Nina Nikolayevna)*, R. Sadykov *(Party Secretary)*, A. Petrenko *(Pilot)*, E. Vasilyeva *(Mrs. Rubtsov)*, N. Grinko *(Vyachesla)*, P. Ovchinnikova *(Kseniya)*.

After the battle of Stalingrad during WW II, Nikulin, a major in the Russian army, visits his home where a film is being shot, based on his writings about the war. He meets with the filmmakers and grows frustrated as they show little interest in the reality he feels he writing conveys. He visits his ex-wife, who has left him for another man, then decides to cut his visit short. Before leaving, he spends the night with Gurchenko, a woman who was abandoned by her husband before the war.

d, Alexei Gherman; w, Konstantin Simonov; ph, Valery Fedosov; m, V. Lavrov; ed, E. Makhankovoi; prod d, Yevgeny Gukov; art d, M. Krakovsky; cos, N. Torgeyevoi; makeup, B. Solovyeva.

War **(PR:NR MPAA:NR)**

DUTCH TREAT** (1987) 84m Golan-Globus/Cannon c

David Landsberg *(Jerry)*, Lorin Dreyfuss *(Norm)*, The Dolly Dots *(Themselves)*, Terry Camilleri, Linda Lutz, Robbie Sella.

This brisk comedy vanished without a trace and didn't deserve such a swift demise. It's lighter than helium and the plot can be outlined in a sentence, but along the way there are jokes galore and the stars/writers (in their second movie) make a fine team. If the stars would hire other writers, they just might find themselves successful. Dreyfuss (brother of Richard) and Landsberg (a TV commercial actor who also appeared in the Don Rickles TV show "CPO Sharkey" in 1977) are employees on a cruise ship. Every ship on the waters has at least one duo who either juggle or toss knives. They do the latter. Through a series of misadventures, two of the ship's officers are discovered with knife punctures in them and the logical (or illogical) thought is that they have been done in by Dreyfuss and Landsberg, although there is no real reason for thinking that. The ship docks and the boys are tossed into a Dutch prison. When reason prevails, Dreyfuss and Landsberg are allowed to exit the jail on bail. It is then that they encounter a very popular singing group known as "The Dolly Dots." They convince the DDs that they are big-time music mavens and manage to get back to the USA in that guise. The picture ends happily, if not satisfactorily.

Lots of sight gags, some old, some new, a breakneck pace and you'll forget it the moment it's over. But while it's on, you'll have a few good chuckles. Not for children as they do reach down deep into smut for some of the jokes. Dreyfuss and Landsberg's first movie, a Roman candle of a comedy known as DUMB DICKS, must have convinced the powers-that-be at Cannon that this was a new team to don the foolscaps of such duos as Laurel and Hardy or Abbott and Costello. Not yet. Like so many performers, Dreyfuss and Landsberg feel that only they can write for themselves. Even the Marx Brothers knew enough to hire such screenwriters as Arthur Sheekman, George S. Kaufman, Morrie Ryskind, Al Boasberg, Harry Ruby, Bert Kalmar, George Seaton, Robert Pirosh, George Oppenheimer, S.J. Perelman, Ray Golden, Sid Kuller, Hal Fimberg, and Nat Perrin. *(Profanity.)*

p, Menahem Golan, Yoram Globus; d, Boaz Davidson; w, Lorin Dreyfuss, David Landsberg; m, Steve Bates; ed, Bruria Davidson; art d, Phil Dagort.

Comedy **(PR:C-O MPAA:R)**

DVOE POD ODNIM ZONTOM (1987, USSR) 92m Odessa/Sovexportfilm c (Trans: Two Under One Umbrella)

Ivar Kalnyn, Innokenti Smoktounovski, Helena Safonova, Natalia Andreitchenko.

Love in the circus world is the focus of this film. A juggler believes he has it made until he falls in love with another performer and finds true happiness.

d, Georgy Yungwald-Khilkevich; w, Sergei Abramov; ph, Albert Osipov; m, Isaak Shwarz; art d, Igor Bryl, Marc Konik.

Romance **(PR:NR MPAA:NR)**

E

ESD† (1987, Pol.) 99m Zespoly Filmowe-Kadr Film Unit c

Elzbieta Helman *(Ida Borejko)*, Alicja Wojtkowiak *(Gabriela Borejko)*, Justyna Zaremba *(Natalia)*, Dorota Woronowicz *(Patricia)*.

ESD stands for "Experimental Signal of Do-Good," a program started by a group of high school students who believe "good begets good." Over the course of the film, their theory proves to be correct.

d, Anna Sokolowska; w, Malgorzata Musierowicz, Anna Sokolowska; ph, Jacek Korcelli; m, Piotr Marczewski; ed, Teresa Miziolek; set d, Marek Morawski.

Children's **(PR:NR MPAA:NR)**

EASTERN CONDORS† (1987, Hong Kong) 96m Golden Harvest c

Samo Hung, Yuen Biao, Joyce Mina Godenzi, Lam Ching, Ying, Kiki Cheung, Y. Karata, Dr. Haing S. Ngor.

Producer/director/writer/actor Samo Hung (THE MILLIONAIRE'S EXPRESS), helms and stars in this film from Hong Kong about a group of jailbirds who are enlisted to pull off a mission in Vietnam for the American government. Note the presence of Dr. Haing S. Ngor, who won a Best Supporting Actor Oscar for his performance in THE KILLING FIELDS (1984). Shot in the Philippines. (In Cantonese; English subtitles.)

p, Leonard Ho; d, Samo Hung; ph, Wong Yau Tai; art d, Lee King Man.

Action/War **(PR:NR MPAA:NR)**

EAT THE PEACH*** (1987, Brit.) 95m Strongbow/Skouras c

Stephen Brennan *(Vinnie)*, Eamon Morrissey *(Arthur)*, Catherine Byrne *(Nora, Vinnie's Wife)*, Niall Toibin *(Boots)*, Joe Lynch *(Boss Murtagh)*, Tony Doyle *(Sean Murtagh)*, Takashi Kawahara *(Bunzo)*, Victoria Armstrong *(Vicky, Vinnie's Daughter)*, Barbara Adair *(Mrs. Fleck)*, Bernadette O'Neill *(Nuala)*, Paul Raynor *(O'Hagen)*, Martin Dempsey *(Quiz Master)*, Maeliosa Stafford *(Priest)*, Jill Doyle *(Aileen)*, Don Foley *(Journalist)*, Brian J. Hogg *(Danny)*, Pat Kenny *(TV Reporter)*, Barry Kelly *(TV Cameraman)*, Edmund Lynch *(TV Soundman)*, Jack Lynch *(Man at Petrol Station)*, Liam Sweeney *(Cattle Drover)*, Ronan Wilmot *(Cahill)*, Robert Byrne *(Lookout at Border Bar)*, Mark Shelley *(Patrol Leader)*, Dick Keating, Jim Reid, Frank Quinlan *(Nashville Three)*, John Gallagher, Finian McKeown, David Nolan *(Murtagh's Heavies)*, Akiko Hoashi, Kobayashi *(Japanese)*, Patricia Jeffares *(Hospital Sister)*, David Carey, Chris Dunne, Peter Gowan, Tim McDonnell, Frank Melia, Noel O'Donovan, Stephan Ryan *(Locals)*, Charles Winter *(Wall of Death Rider)*.

Based on real-life occurrences and set in an Irish border town, this restrained comedy opens as Brennan and brother-in-law Morrissey lose their factory jobs when the Japanese company they work for shuts down its local operation. While watching Elvis Presley's ROUSTABOUT on a VCR, Brennan is captivated by its thrilling motorcycle stunts. They are performed on the cylindrical "Wall of Death," around which the rider speeds parallel to the ground with the aid of centrifugal force. Brennan and Morrissey, both of whom are motorcycle riders, decide to build their own Wall of Death in Brennan's backyard. Byrne, Brennan's long-suffering, pregnant wife becomes fed up with their tilting at windmills and she and Armstrong, her young daughter, move back in with her mother. Slowly the huge wooden cylinder begins to take shape, but supplies are expensive and Brennan and Morrissey begin smuggling goods into Northern Ireland for the operation run by Lynch. Wearing a cowboy hat and boots, Toibin, who works as the ramrod for Lynch's "commodity relocation" truckers, affects the pose of a shrewd American impresario. He is enthralled with Brennan's wall and becomes the project's public relations man, promising TV coverage. Before long, Byrne and Armstrong have returned, the wall has been completed, and Brennan has mastered horizontal riding. On the minus side, Brennan and Morrissey have had something of a run-in with the British army, prompting Lynch to fire them, and Brennan's house has been devastated by an explosion caused by carelessness. Nonetheless they begin making plans for a gala demonstration of the wall and dream about fame and fortune. On the big day, Toibin is summoned by Lynch, who has learned that his foreman has been watering down the boss' booze cargo. Lynch sees to it that Toibin ends up in the hospital and not at the opening ceremonies. The gallery at the top of the wall is packed as Brennan begins the show; however, the rickety structure shakes and sways as he zooms around it, and the frightened spectators disappear. After everyone is gone, a TV crew shows up and shoots Brennan on the wall. During the broadcast that night, a phone number is given for anyone who would like to support Brennan's efforts to take the show on the road. He waits by a phone booth all night but no one calls. Thoroughly dejected, be burns the wall to the ground. Time passes. Byrne gives birth, the house is rebuilt, Brennan and Morrissey have jobs again, and Toibin is well enough to visit. However, Brennan and Morrissey aren't finished dreaming, and as the film ends, they unveil their latest work in progress, a helicopter.

Taking its title from the famous question posed in T.S. Eliot's "The Love Song of J. Alfred Prufrock" ("Do I dare to eat a peach?"), this is the story of people who dare to dream even though dreaming has apparently become redundant in their economically depressed environment. Although its plot is a little thin and develops slowly, EAT THE PEACH presents charming, believable characters who create an engaging portrait of the indomitable human spirit. The building of the wall may seem like useless folly, but it is the pursuit and realization of the dream and not its nature which is important here. The film doesn't end triumphantly, but it does end hopefully. EAT THE PEACH is based on real-life occurrences and the filmmakers' decision to stick relatively close to the facts may have limited the scope of the narrative, but ultimately the film's uplifting message is all the more encouraging considering that these events really did occur. While working for Irish television, director/cowriter Peter Ormrod filed a report on Connie Kiernan, an Irishman who had, indeed, been inspired by ROUSTABOUT to build his own Wall of Death with the help of his brother-in-law. As in the film, no one called Kiernan after his number was given during the broadcast. When Ormrod visited him 18 months later, he found that Kiernan had destroyed his creation, but as he was leaving, Ormrod spotted the helicopter Kiernan had begun to build. (Kiernan acted as adviser for the construction of the film's Wall of Death and also served as a stunt rider.)

Brennan, Morrissey, and Byrne, all veterans of the Irish stage, turn in nicely understated performances. Toibin is also excellent as the man who has never been to the US, but who fashions his identity—his accent, his dress, his whole manner—out of movie and myth inspired ideas of what it is to be an American hustler. In addition to these first-rate lead performances, the film is full of nicely drawn secondary characters. The camerawork is also outstanding. Director of photography Wooster served as the director of cameramen on the action sequences for a number of James Bond films, so his adept handling of the wall of death action isn't surprising, but he also makes particularly good use of the landscape. This is not the Ireland of rolling green hills usually seen in films because EAT THE PEACH was primarily shot in County Kildare, in the middle of the Bog of Allen, and Wooster and director Ormrod use the setting to ground their story in reality. Made for $2 million, the film received some financing from Film Four International and the Irish Film Board, but most of its funding came from individual investors. Some of these people gave as little as $750 and a number of them appear in the film in the gallery during Brennan's public demonstration of his Wall-of-Death riding. EAT THE PEACH was presented in the US by director Jonathan Demme (SOMETHING WILD, MELVIN AND HOWARD). *(Profanity, sexual situations.)*

p, John Kelleher; d, Peter Ormrod; w, Peter Ormrod, John Kelleher; ph, Arthur Wooster; m, Donal Lunny; ed, J. Patrick Duffner; prod d, David Wilson; set d, Josie McAvin; m/l, Paul Brady, Donal Lunny; makeup, Toni Delany.

Drama **(PR:A-C MPAA:NR)**

EAT THE RICH† (1987, Brit.) 88m Comic Strip Film-British Screen-Film Four Intl.-Recorded Releasing-Smart Egg/New Line Cinema c

Ronald Allen *(Commander Fortune)*, Sandra Dorne *(Sandra, Home Secretary's Wife)*, Jimmy Fagg *(Jimmy, Farmer)*, Lemmy *(Spider, Arms Dealer)*, Lanah Pellay *(Alex, Waiter)*, Nosher Powell *(Nosher, Home Secretary)*, Fiona Richmond *(Fiona, Call Girl)*, Ron Tarr *(Ron)*, Robbie Coltrane *(Jeremy)*, David Beard *(Gen. Karpov)*, Angie Bowie *(Henry's Wife)*, Kevin Allen, Lez Bubb, Robert Davis, Adrian Funnell, John Wilson, Simon Drake *(Waiters)*, Rowena Bently *(Indecisive Girlfriend)*, Simon Brint *(Dickie the Pianist)*, Rene Bruchet *(Janet)*, Kathy Burke *(Kathy)*, Katrin Cartlidge *(Katrin)*, Sean Chapman *(Mark)*, Miles Copeland *(Derek)*, Hugh Cornwell *(Edgeley)*, Neil Cunningham *(TV Reporter)*, Robert Davis *(Waiter)*, Neil Dickson *(Gerry)*, Adrian Edmondson *(Charles)*, Norman Fisher *(Footman/Equerry)*, Bob Flagg *(Indecisive Customer)*, Peter Fontaine *(Banquet Man)*, Dawn French *(Debbie Draws)*, Fran Fullenwider *(Queen)*, Joanne Good *(Jaqualine)*, Cathryn Harrison *(Joanne)*, Jools Holland, Roland Rivron *("Sun" Reporters)*, Debbie Lindon *(Layla)*, Christopher Malcolm *(Steinbeck)*, Rik Mayall *(Micky)*, Frank Murray, Shane McGowan, Terence Wood *(Terrorists)*, Derren Nesbitt *(Manager)*, Nigel Planer *(DHSS Manager)*, Avril Rankin *(Avril)*, Miranda Richardson *(DHSS Blond)*, Marika Rivera *(Marika)*, Tricia Ronane *(Tricia)*, Jennifer Saunders *(Lady Caroline)*, Sandy Shaw *(Edgeley's Girlfriend)*, Koo Stark *(Hazel)*, Jonathan Stratt *(Policeman)*, Rupert Vansittart *(Rupert)*, Steve Walsh *(Record Executive)*, Ruby Wax *(Bibi de Coutts)*, Bill Wyman *(Toilet Victim)*, Salim Haider *(General)*, Sue Lloyd *(Val)*, Daniel Peacock *(Terence)*, Andrew Rankin *(Reporter)*, Peter Rosengard *(Israeli Ambassador)*, Barney Sharp *(Barney)*, Colin Thomas *(Bishop)*, Eddie Yeoh *(Mr. Chow)*, Paul McCartney *(Himself)*, Peter Stacey *(Band Member)*, Cayenne *(Latin American Band)*.

Set in England in the near future, EAT THE RICH chronicles the battle between a group of revolutionaries, led by the unemployed Pellay, against Powell, the fascist home secretary, who refers to the poor as "lazy bastards" during television speeches. Pellay and his group take over a restaurant called "Bastards," where the idle rich like to relax and taunt the less fortunate, and rename it "Eat the Rich," where they intend to literally feed off the wealthy.

p, Tim Van Rellim; d, Peter Richardson; w, Peter Richardson, Peter Richens; ph, Witold Stok; m, Simon Brint, Roland Rivron; ed, Chris Ridsdale; art d, Caroline Amies; cos, Frances Haggett; spec eff, Tom Harris, Any Effects, Ace Effects; m/l, Ian Kilmister, Michael Burston, Peter Gill, Phillip Campbell, Michael Burston, Jimmy Fagg; stunts, Mark McBride, Dinny Powell, Eddie Stacey, Chris Webb; makeup, Gordon Kay; stunts, Rocky Taylor, Roy Alon, Terry Walsh.

Comedy **(PR:NR MPAA:NR)**

EDGE OF HELL (SEE: ROCK 'N' ROLL NIGHTMARE, 1987, Can.)

EEN MAAND LATER† (1987, Neth.) 98m Sigma Filmproductions/WB c (Trans: One Month Later)

Monique van de Ven *(Monika)*, Renee Soutendijk *(Liesbeth van de Bergh)*, Edwin de Vries *(Constant van de Bergh)*, Sunny Bergman *(Judith)*, Tijmen Bergman *(Jonas)*, Jeroen Oostenbrink *(Jobje)*, Bas Voets *(Steffie)*, Jean Yves Berteloot *(Hugo)*, Marjo van der Meulen *(Ingrid)*, Coot van Doesburgh *(Astrid)*, Kietje Sewrattan *(Jessica)*, Marion Bloem *(Tinelou)*, Femke van Hoven *(Betty)*, Pauline Daniels *(Susan)*, Yvonne Ristie, Marjolein Sligter, Els Weenink *(Applicants)*, A Case Of Tomatoes *(Pop Group)*, Michael Sanders *(Arthur)*, Sigrid Adrienne *(Arthur's Mother)*, Jan Jaap Hoekstra *(Maurits)*, Allard Bekker *(Jogger)*, Joost Boer *(Jeroen)*, Sep van Kampen *(Dorus)*, Maarten Wansdronk *(Neighbour)*, Remco Daalder *(Construction Worker)*, Mr. van der Zee *(Greengrocer)*, Mrs. Boon *(Woman at Market)*, Mr. van Eimeren *(Man at Market)*.

A social comedy about a housewife, Soutendijk, who feels she is missing something in her life. A devoted mother to her three children and faithful wife to psychiatrist de Vries, she places an ad in a local newspaper offering to exchange her life with someone else's. Van de Ven, a free-spirited journalist, responds out of curiosity and thirst for a good story. Initially both women have difficulty in adjusting to their new roles, but they soon learn to like what they previously have been missing. Soutendijk becomes more liberated as she carries on with van de Ven's many lovers, and van de Ven grows attached to the children and to her "husband"—teaching both women something about themselves. Produced in English and Dutch versions, EEN MAAND LATER is the first Netherlands film to be picked up in production by a major U.S. distributor. The idea for the film came from a actual ad which screenwriter Donkers saw in a 1985 issue of *The Village Voice*.

p, Matthijs van Heijningen; d, Nouchka van Brakel; w, Nouchka van Brakel, Ate de Jong, Jan Donkers (based on the play by Jan Donkers); ph, Peter de Bont (Agfacolor); m, Rob van Donselaar; ed, Edgar Burcksen; art d, Hadassah Kann; cos, Linda Bogers; m/l, Rob van Donselaar, Victor Heeremans, Roy Kushel; makeup, Nancy Badoux.

Comedy **(PR:NR MPAA:NR)**

EIGA JOYU† (1987, Jap.) 130m Toho/Toho Eiga c (Trans: Actress)

Sayuri Yoshinaga *(Kinuyo Tanaka)*, Mitsuko Mori *(Mother)*, Bunta Sugawara *(Kenji Mizoguchi)*, Koji Ishizaka *(Shiro Kido)*, Yasuko Sawaguchi *(Seiko)*.

The latest film from veteran Japanese director Kon Ichikawa is another examination of the early years of Japanese filmmaking, a subject explored by Yoji Yamada in 1987's FINAL TAKE: THE GOLDEN AGE OF MOVIES (KINEMA NO TENCHI). Scripted by Ichikawa, fellow director Kaneto Shindo, and Shinya Hidaka, EIGA JOYU follows the career of famed actress Kinuyo Tanaka (played by look-alike Sayuri Yoshinaga) from her days in silent movies, beginning in 1922, to her superb performance in Kenji Mizoguchi's masterpiece THE LIFE OF OHARU in 1952. A sweeping history of the development of the Japanese cinema, as well as a film biography, EIGA JOYU provides dozens of historical tidbits culled from the director's more than 50 years of experience in the business.

p, Tomoyuki Tanaka, Kon Ichikawa; d, Kon Ichikawa; w, Kaneto Shindo, Shinya Hidaka, Kon Ichikawa; ph, Yukio Isohata; m, Kensaku Tanigawa; ed, Chizuko Osada; prod d, Shinobu Muraki.

Biography **(PR:NR MPAA:NR)**

EIN BLICK-UND DIE LIEBE BRICHT AUS*** (1987, Ger.) 85m Von Vietinghoff Filmproduktion/Metropolis Film c (TRANS: One Look and Love Begins) (AKA: ONE LOOK AND LOVE BEGINS)

Elida Araoz, Rosario Blefari, Regina Lamm, Margarita Munoz, Maria Elena Rivera, Norberto Serra, Daniela Trajanovsky.

Jutta Bruckner is one of Germany's leading women directors and in ONE LOOK-AND LOVE BEGINS she expounds on the subject of relations between men and women with a masterful sense for her medium. Unfortunately her ideas are simplistic variations on old issues. Consequently, the film is a beautiful work with a hollow center. There is no straightforward story, rather seven loosely strung vignettes developed in a surrealistic manner. The heroines of the stories range from a young bride to a client of a back-alley abortionist. Bruckner sets much of the action within the confines of an abandoned warehouse as characters perform scenes amidst strewn garbage, neon, and a variety of mirrors. The film develops like a symphony with repeating visual motifs employed as a composer would use repeating refrains. A marching line of gaily costumed women is one such example, counterbalanced by white garbed schoolgirls carrying candles through an empty cathedral. Bruckner's *mise-en-scene* is carefully arranged, suggesting the director has the eye of a surrealist painter. She colors the screen with hues of red and blue neon lighting, creating images of striking beauty. Mirrors break up the frame, causing players to be multiplied and distorted within the context of the "real" picture. The influence of theatrical traditions and performance art is also exhibited. Shot partially in Buenos Aires (though no locations are employed), Bruckner cast members of an Argentine dance troupe in many of the roles. Their stylized movement adds to the musicality of her film, again repeating motifs like components of a symphony. The film's soundtrack is equally important. Electronic tango music, poetry, distorted sound, and deadly silence accompany visual conceptions, and the effect is aesthetically striking.

Bruckner's subject, the exploitation of women by men, is an important one but she never really explores the topic. Throughout the film the audience is subjected to repeated images of women being brutalized by macho, unfeeling males. The sex act is reduced to rape of quasi-masturbation, with women submitting themselves openly time and again. The female characters are dispassionate with their lovers, rapists, and abortionists. What's missing is the sense of rage at these violent attacks. Bruckner continually shows women in subservient positions when men are in the frame, allowing her protagonists freedom only when alone or with other women. The point is obvious and a discredit to Bruckner's genius for visual and acoustical composition. Bruckner has created an artistically stunning achievement tinged by thematic flaws. Better thought out, this could have been an unqualified masterpiece. Released in Germany in 1986.

p, Joachim von Vietinghoff; d&w, Jutta Bruckner; ph, Marcelo Camorino; m, Brynmore Jones; ed, Ursula Hof, Jutta Bruckner; art d, Guillermo Kuitka; cos, Marion Vollmer, Britta Vollmer.

Drama **(PR:O MPAA:NR)**

84 CHARING CROSS ROAD*** (1987) 97m Brooksfilms/COL c

Anne Bancroft *(Helene Hanff)*, Anthony Hopkins *(Frank Doel)*, Judi Dench *(Nora Doel)*, Jean De Baer *(Maxine Bellamy)*, Maurice Denham *(George Martin)*, Eleanor David *(Cecily Farr)*, Mercedes Ruehl *(Kay)*, Daniel Gerroll *(Brian)*, Wendy Morgan *(Megan Wells)*, Ian McNeice *(Bill Humphries)*, J. Smith-Cameron *(Ginny)*, Tom Isbell *(Ed)*, Anne Dyson *(Mrs. Boulton)*, Connie Booth *(Lady from Delaware)*, Ronn Carroll *(Businessman on Plane)*, Sam Stoneburner *(New York Bookseller)*, Charles Lewsen *(Print Buyer)*, Bernie Passeltiner *(Willie, Deli Owner)*, Michael John McGann *(Maxine's Stage Manager)*, Gwen Nelson *(Bill's Great Aunt)*, Roger Ostime *(Stately Home Butler)*, John Bardon *(Labour Party Canvasser)*, Betty Low *(Maxine's Mom)*, James Eckhouse *(Joey the Dentist)*, David Davenport, Max Harvey, Rupert Holliday-Evans, Freda Rogers *(Coronation Party Friends)*, Marty Glickman *(Baseball Commentator)*, Tony Todd *(Demolition Workman)*, Kevin McClarnon *(Cop at Columbia)*, Janet Dale *(Joan*

Todd), Zoe Hodges *(Mary Doel at Age 4)*, Kate Napier Brown *(Mary Doel at Age 21)*, Rebecca Bradley *(Sheila Doel at Age 12)*, Barbara Thorn *(Sheila Doel at Age 29)*, Danielle Burns, Lee Burns *(Cecily Farr's Children)*.

This might have been better titled "Pen Pals," but since it was based on a book, a TV show, and then a play of the same name, executive producer Mel Brooks decided to keep the title when he gave this project to his wife, Anne Bancroft, for what was allegedly a wedding anniversary gift. It's understated (except for Bancroft, who goes over the top more often than John Wayne in a war movie), charming, and should have jerked more tears than it did, yet it remains an intelligent, often witty, and perceptive love story between two people who never meet. Bancroft is a struggling New York writer in 1949. She pounds her typewriter, smokes one cigarette after another, and has made friends with her gin bottle. She loves good editions of her favorite books and pooh-poohs the Modern Library versions, preferring good leather-bound used books to new ones. After reading an ad in *The Saturday Review of Literature*, from an antiquarian bookshop at 84 Charing Cross Road in London, she writes a funny letter regarding her wants, and the missive is answered by Hopkins, a dry, reserved man who runs the overseas department of Marks & Company. The book she requests is sent forthwith and thus begins a 20-year letter-writing relationship between Bancroft, the assertive and sometimes acerbic spinster, and Hopkins, a married man with two children, a plain wife, and a sparse home—one of those men who live in quiet desperation. The start of this correspondence takes place while England is still reeling from the shortages of the war and Bancroft sends a bundle to Britain with items impossible to find there. She arranges this by ordering the food from a company in Denmark. The employees at Marks & Co. are thrilled at her thoughtfulness. As the story unfolds, the picture cuts back and forth between their lives. Time passes, the age of the autos changes, styles alter, but the affection between the writers increases by dint of their ability to pour out their emotion on paper. In 1952, Bancroft plans a trip to London to meet Hopkins, but she has an emergency in her mouth and the travel money goes right to her dentist. In her apartment, prominently displayed, is a photo of a naval man, but we never find out who he is. That kind of red herring is disturbing because we seldom go beneath the surfaces of the protagonists and thus don't get to know their "back stories" as well as we might like to. Hopkins is far less emotional than Bancroft, which is as it should be. Even the photography alters between New York and London, with the U.S. getting brighter, flashier colors, while London seems to be shot through a dulling lens. This was a definite choice by director Jones, a longtime Royal Shakespeare Company director, and cinematographer West. Hopkins and Bancroft both have huge holes in their emotional lives and rely upon each other's letters to help fill them. Meanwhile, Hopkins' wife, Dench, is becoming genuinely jealous over his literary love affair. Two decades roll by and Bancroft, who is now writing for TV shows like "Ellery Queen" and "The Hallmark Hall of Fame," is finally able to afford the trip to London. When she gets there, she is stunned to learn that Hopkins has died unexpectedly and that the bookstore is about to be torn down. She turns to the camera (she's been addressing it throughout the movie, a throwback to the stage play) and poignantly shrugs, saying, "Well, I finally got here," as the film ends.

84 CHARING CROSS ROAD is one of the more literate scripts to be shot in recent years. It is also uncompromisingly "stagy" and there seemed to be no way to overcome that. Upon learning that a movie is based on a series of letters and that the lovers never even have a brief encounter, it might appear to be boring. It is not. Scripter Hugh Whitemore (STEVIE) used Hanff's book and the stage adaptation by James Roose-Evans and has crafted an excellent and occasionally moving love story. But *crafted* is exactly what it is. True emotion seems to be as sparse as the furnishings and what might have been a four-hankie movie just gets a few pieces of Kleenex. Director Jones might have toned Bancroft down a bit, as her histrionics are more suited for a large stage than a screen. One comes away wondering what would have happened if they met. Would it be love at first sight or is the fantasy better than the reality? There were more than 25 locations in New York, which made it far more difficult than the London work, which was shot at Shepperton for the most part. The book is based upon Ms. Hanff's memoirs and letters from her friend. It was a TV play in 1975, then staged in London successfully in 1981. The New York production closed in 1982, falling just short of 100 performances. *(Mild profanity.)*

p, Geoffrey Helman; d, David Jones; w, Hugh Whitemore (based on the book by Helene Hanff); ph, Brian West (Rank/TVC Color); m, George Fenton; ed, Chris Wimble; prod d, Eileen Diss, Edward Pisoni; cos, Jane Greenwood, Lindy Hemming.

Drama **Cas.** **(PR:A-C MPAA:PG)**

EL ANO DE LAS LUCES (SEE: YEAR OF AWAKENING, THE, Span.)

EL AMOR ES UNA MUJER GORDA† (1987, Arg.) 80m Movimiento Falso-Allart's bw (Trans: Love Is a Fat Woman)

Elio Marchi *(Jose)*, Sergio Poves Campos *(Caferata)*, Carlos Roffe, Humberto Tito Haas, Enrique Morales, Harry Havilio, Sergio Lerer.

Marchi stars as a part-time journalist and full-time angry young man who seeks to find his way in an Argentina still reeling from the aftereffects of tyrannical military rule. Behind his sense of outrage is his deep pain over the loss of his lover who disappeared during the dark days before democracy was won.

d&w, Alejandro Agresti; ph, Nestor Sanz; m, Paul Michael Van Brugge; ed, Rene Wiegmans.

Drama **(PR:NR MPAA:NR)**

EL BOSQUE ANIMADO† (1987, Span.) 109m Classic c (Trans: The Enchanted Forest)

Alfredo Landa *(Malvis)*, Fernando Valverde *(Geraldo)*, Alejandra Grepi *(Hermelinda)*, Encarna Paso, Miguel Rellan, Maria Isbert, Luma Gomez, Fernando Rey.

In the 1920s, a group of villagers encounter a variety of humorous characters as they attempt to cross through a forest.

p, Eduardo Ducay; d, Jose Luis Cuerda; w, Rafael Azcona (based on the novel by Wenceslao Fernandez Florez); ph, Xavier Aguirresarobe; m, Pepe Nieto; ed, Juan Ignacio San Mateo; set d, Felix Murcia.

Comedy **(PR:NR MPAA:NR)**

EL DIABLO, EL SANTO Y EL TONTO† (1987, Mex.) 92m Cumbres/Peliculas Mexicanas c (Trans: The Devil, the Saint and the Fool)

Vicente Fernandez *(Refugio Romero/Carmelo Romero/Mariano Romero)*, Sasha Montenegro *(Liane)*, Pedro Weber [Chatanooga] *(Don Abor)*, Carmelita Gonzalez *(Rafaela Vega)*, Martha Ortiz, Felipe Arriaga, Patsy, Frank Tostado.

The devil, saint, and fool of the title are the sons of a Mexican rancher who sewed his share of wild oats as a young man. All three roles are played by actor/*ranchero* singer Fernandez. As he is dying, the rancher tells his goofy but legitimate son about his illegitimate brothers and sends him to find them so that they may benefit from his will. Unfortunately, through a mix-up, each son is bequeathed a property that is better suited to the personality of one of his brothers. Fernandez sings at least one song as each of the brothers, including "Cielito Lindo" (traditional, Carlo Fernandez).

d, Rafael Villasenor Kuri; w, Adolfo Torres Portillo; ph, Agustin Lara; m, Heriberto Aceves; ed, Max Sanchez; m/l, Carlo Fernandez.

Comedy **(PR:NR MPAA:NR)**

EL DUENO DEL SOL† (1987, Arg.) 101m Luz Comunicaciones c (Trans: The Owner of the Sun)

Alfredo Alcon *(Father)*, Luis Luque *(Juan)*, Noemi Frenkel *(Ana)*, Gustavo Belatti *(Martin)*.

Heavy with political symbolism, this Argentine entry tells the story of a wealthy family ripped apart by sibling rivalry when the death of its patriarch is imminent. The old man, "the owner of the sun" of the title (a mythical evil character), finds a strange satisfaction in turning his sons and daughters against each other. The directorial debut for Mortola.

d&w, Rodolfo Mortola; ph, Anibal Di Salvor; m, Mario Ferre; ed, Jorge Pappalardo; art d, Anibal Di Salvor; set d, Miguel Angel Lumaldo, Enrique Bordolin.

Drama **(PR:NR MPAA:NR)**

EL ANO DEL CONEJO† (1987, Arg.) 103m Aries Cinematografica Argentina c (Trans: The Year of the Rabbit)

Federico Luppi *(Pepe)*, Luisina Brando *(Norma)*, Juan Carlos Dual *(Sergio)*, Katja Alemann *(Karina)*, Ulises Dumont *(Milo)*, Gerardo Romano *(Marcelo)*, Andrea Barbieri, Daniel Galarza.

Hector Olivera produced and Fernando Ayala directed the excellent Argentine black comedy A FUNNY, DIRTY LITTLE WAR (1985). Here they switch roles for this mixture of the serious and the humorous. Luppi stars as a middle-aged banker who decides to try to make the best of Argentina's inflationary economy by becoming a part owner, along with Romano, of an investment firm. In doing so, he changes his life completely, quitting his job, leaving his wife (Brando), and selling his home.

p, Hector Olivera; d, Fernando Ayala; w, Oscar Viale (based on an idea by Hector Olivera); ph, Leonardo Rodriguez Solis; m, Leo Sujatovich; ed, Eduardo Lopez; set d, Emilio Basaldua; cos, Patricia Pernia.

Comedy/Drama **(PR:NR MPAA:NR)**

EL AMOR DE AHORA† (1987, Span.) 90m Independent Basque/Sendeja c (Trans: Love Today)

Klara Badiola *(Arantza)*, Antonio Valero *(Luis)*, Patxi Bisquert *(Pello)*, Walter Vidarte *(Lombardi, TV Writer)*, Miguel Angeliglesias *(Miguel)*, Javier Loyola *(Arantza's Father)*, Concha Leza *(Arantza's Mother)*, Esteban Astarloa *(Pello's Father)*, Alex Angulo *(Inaki)*, Asuncion Balaguer *(Elvira)*.

After years of living in exile in France, two Spanish terrorists decide to return to their homeland.

p, Luis Eguiraun; d, Ernesto Del Rio; w, Luis Eguiraun, Santiago Gonzalez, Ernesto Del Rio; ph, Carlos Gusi; m, Angel Munoz-Alonso; ed, Juan San Mateo; art d, Mikel Aranburuzabala

Drama **(PR:NR MPAA:NR)**

EL GRAN SERAFIN† (1987, Span.) Mare Nostrum c (Trans: The Great Seraph)

Ana Obregon *(Hilda, Waitress)*, Laura del Sol *(Blanchette)*, Fernando Guillen *(Campolongo)*, Mercedes Sombra *(Senora Medor, Blanchette's Mother)*, Ramon Madaula *(Martin, Young Pianist)*, Fernando Fernan Gomez *(Cura)*, Noel Samsom *(Lynch)*, John Grey *(Doberman)*, Xavier Sala.

Set in a seaside hotel, this film focuses on how the guests and staff react when they hear on a newscast that the world is about to end.

d, Jose Maria Ulloque; w, Jose Maria Ulloque, Pere Vila (based on the book by Adolfo Bioy Casares); ph, Hans Burmann (Eastmancolor); ed, Emilio Ortiz; art d, Arturo Olmo; spec eff, Carlo de Marchis; makeup, Toni Nieto.

Drama **(PR:NR MPAA:NR)**

EL HIJO DE PEDRO NAVAJAS† (1987, Mex.) 91m Cineproducciones Intl./Peliculas Mexicanas c (Trans: The Son of Pedro Navajas)

Guillermo Capetillo *(Pedro Navajas, Jr.)*, Sasha Montenegro *(Tismany)*, Adalberto Martinez [Resortes] *(Mickey)*, Gabriela Goldsmied *(Sandra)*, Jorge Luke *(Burth)*, Rodolfo de Anda *(Filos)*, Ana Luisa Peluffo *(Roja)*, Diana Ferreti *(Susana)*, Pepe Romey, Socorro Bonilla, Isaura Espinoza, Carmelina Encinas, Griselda Mejia, Mari Carmen Resendes, Paco Sanudo.

This Mexican entry is a sequel to PEDRO NAVAJAS, which was based on a song by Ruben Blades (CROSSOVER DREAMS) and, like this film, was directed by Alfonso Rosas Priego R. The son (Capetillo), very different from his pimp father, has been raised in the US, but ventures south of the border after his mother's murder. There he develops into just as tough an hombre as his father was.

p&d, Alfonso Rosas Priego R.; w, Ramon Obon, Alfonso Rosas Priego R. (based on the song "Pedro Navajas" by Ruben Blades); ph, Antonio de Anda; m, Arturo Castro.

Drama **(PR:NR MPAA:NR)**

EL ANSIA DE MATAR† (1987, Mex.) 82m Cinematografica de Sol/ Peliculas Mexicanas c (Trans: The Urge to Kill)

Mario Almada *(Roberto Robles)*, Gilberto Trujillo *(Quillo)*, Jorge Luke *(Guerrilla Captain)*, Diana Golden *(Lorena)*, Tere Velazquez *(Magda)*, Gabriela Ruffo *(Maria)*, Raul Trujillo *(Deaf Guerrilla)*, Valentin Trujillo *(Major)*, Jorge Munoz, Alfonso Davila, Xorge Noble, Agustin Bernal, Luis Guevara, Alberto Arvizu, Arturo Martinez, Jr., Gilberto de Anda.

In 1983, Guatemalans seeking political asylum in southern Mexico were massacred by a squadron of guerillas from their homeland. This film uses that incident as its basis, and introduces elements of kidnaping and revenge as Almada goes after the guerillas who have captured his family.

p,d&w, Gilberto de Anda; ph, Antonio de Anda; m, Diego Herrera; ed, Sergio Soto.

Action **(PR:NR MPAA:NR)**

EL HOMBRE DE LA DEUDA EXTERNA† (1987, Arg.) 95m Kane/Irondel c (Trans: The Man of the Foreign Debt)

Hector Alterio *(Pedro)*, Luisina Brando *(Alicia)*, Jorge Mayorano *(Marcelo)*, Adriana Gardiazabal *(Ines)*, Carlos Caceres, Carola Reyna, Palmer, Rosa Rosen, Perla Santalla.

Yet another film from Argentina that uses that debt-ridden nation's troubled economy as a jumping off point. Alterio (THE OFFICIAL STORY, CONTAR HASTA TEN) plays a man whose life is dramatically changed for the better when he becomes an overnight billionaire. Altruistically, he puts his beloved country first and uses the windfall to square Argentina with its creditors. He is rewarded by being killed, but (who would have believed it?) it was all a dream.

d, Pablo Olivo; w, Pablo Olivo, Carlos Brandi; ph, Juan Carlos Lenardi; m, Carlos Fradkin, Daniel Berardi; ed, Sergio Zotola; prod d, Jorge Marchegiani.

Comedy **(PR:NR MPAA:NR)**

EL HOMBRE DESNUDO† (1987, Mex.) 89m Uranio/Peliculas Mexicanas c (Trans: The Naked Man)

Barry Coe *(Moe)*, Jose Alonso *(Nameless Drifter)*, Irma Lozano *(Lisa Hastings)*, Celene La Freniere *(Virginia)*, Terry Kelly, Barney O'Sullivan, Dan Logan, John Scott, Ivor Harries, Wanda Wallenson.

This Mexican production, shot in Canada with a passel of Anglo actors, follows gunfighter Alonso as he searches for the man who killed his parents. At the same time, it tells the tale of the attempts by some townsfolk to fend off a bunch of land-hungry varmints. In a strange twist, Alonso continually forces desperadoes to drop their pants in his never-ending quest for the scarred rear end that belongs to his parents' killer.

p, Jose Lorenzo Zakani; d, Rogelio A. Gonzalez, Jr.; w, Myriam S. Price, Rogelio A. Gonzalez, Jr.; ph, Francisco Colin; m, Javier Castro, Francisco Rodriguez; ed, Carlos Savage; spec eff, Dan Logan, Jim Nielson.

Western **(PR:NR MPAA:NR)**

EL IMPERIO DE LA FORTUNA (SEE: REALM OF FORTUNE, THE, 1987, Mex.)

EL LUTE—CAMINA O REVIENTA† (1987, Span.) 120m M.G.C.-Multivideo c (Trans: El Lute—Forge on or Die)

Imanol Arias *(Eleuterio "El Lute" Sanchez)*, Victoria Abril *(Consuelo Sanchez, His Wife)*, Antonio Valero *(Medrano)*, Carlos Tristancho *(Agudo)*, Diana Penalver *(Esperanza)*, Margarita Calahorra *(Mother Consuelo)*, Manuel De Blas *(Smiling Policeman)*, Jose Cerro *(Father-in-Law & Godfather)*, Jose Manuel Cervino *(Rufino)*, Luis Marin, Manolo Zarzo *(Policemen)*, Raul Fraire, Rafael Hernandez *(Civil Guards)*.

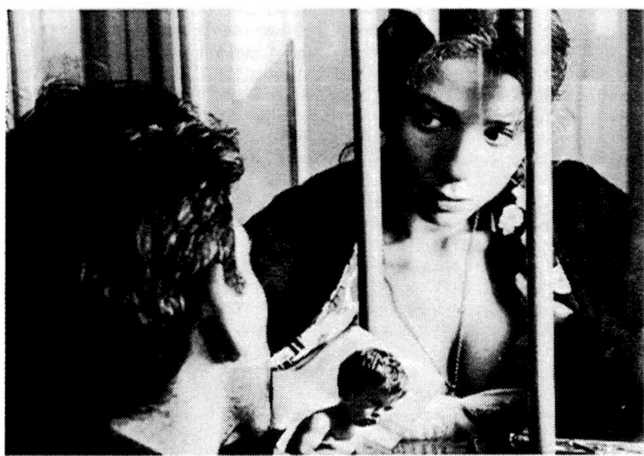

Based on fact, this film tells the story of the early years of "El Lute," a well-known Spanish criminal and escape artist. The movie follows El Lute from his beginning as a minor thief to his incarceration and escape following a jewelry store robbery in which a murder was committed. El Lute's later years were to be chronicled in a sequel.

p, Isabel Mula, Jose Maria Cunilles; d, Vicente Aranda; w, Joaquin Jorda, Vicente Aranda, Eleuterio Sanchez (based on the autobiography by Eleuterio Sanchez); ph, Jose Luis Alcaine (Fuji Color); m, Jose Nieto; ed, Teresa Font; set d, Josep Rosell; makeup, Juan Pedro Hernandez.

Biography **(PR:NR MPAA:NR)**

EL MOFLES Y LOS MECANICOS† (1987, Mex.) 85m Tijuana/Peliculas Mexicanas c (Trans: Muffler and the Mechanics)

Rafael Inclan *(Luis/El Mofles)*, Maribel Fernandez [Pelongocha] *(Lupita)*, Pedro Weber [Chatanooga] *(Pepe/El Jefe)*, Manuel [Flaco] Ibanez *(Abrelatas)*, Susana Cabrera *(Dona Chole)*, Victor Manuel Castro *(Don Gaston)*, Polo Ortin *(Chocorro)*, Rasalba Brambila, Alfredo Solares.

Popular Mexican comedian Inclan stars as a poor auto mechanic named "Muffler" (Mofles) who lives with his fellow grease monkeys in a tenament building near the garage where they all work. Although impoverished, the mechanics know how to have a good time and throw a raucous birthday party for one of their friends. The plot thickens when Inclan becomes entangled with a gang of thieves who have just robbed a nearby bottling plant.

p, Juan Abusaid, Pedro Martinez Garrido; d, Victor Manuel Castro; w, Jorge Patino, Marco E. Contreras; ph, Jose Antonio Ruiz; m, Gustavo Pimentel; ed, Sergio Soto.

Comedy **(PR:NR MPAA:NR)**

EL MUERTO DEL PALOMO† (1987, Mex.) 82m Intl. Films-Cinematografica Sol/Peliculas Mexicanas c (Trans: The Death of Palomo)

Valentin Trujillo *(Valente Trevino)*, Mario Almada *(Don Julio)*, Carmen Montejo *(Julia)*, Pedro Infante, Jr. *(Roberto Robles)*, Humberto Elizondo *(Gilberto Dominguez)*, Lourdes Munguia *(Nana)*, Carlos Agosti *(Luis Robles)*, Carlos y Jose.

Trujillo stars as a jockey who loses everything, including his girl friend, after being defeated in a race. Even worse, the jockey discovers he has been framed for the murder of his best friend and is sent to prison. After serving several years of his sentence, Trujillo is released, determined to clear his name.

p, Jesus Galindo; d, Pedro Galindo III; w, Ramon Obon, Adolfo Torres Portillo; ph, Luis Medina; m, Ricardo Carrion.

Drama **(PR:NR MPAA:NR)**

EL PLACER DE LA VENGANZA† (1987, Mex.) 89m Esme-Alianza Cinematografica Mexicana/Peliculas Mexicanas c (Trans: The Pleasure of Vengeance)

Susana Dosamantes *(Cristina Ruiz)*, Hugo Stiglitz *(Adrian Parra)*, Pedro Armendariz *(Commandante Gallardo)*, Eleazar Garcia, Jr. *(Julius)*, Ricardo Carrion, Raul Araiza, Jr.

A revenge tale starring Dosamantes as a successful psychiatrist who is shocked to learn that her husband and children have been murdered by a vicious gang of robbers after they stumbled upon the scene of an armored car holdup. Incredibly, one of the killers (Garcia, Jr.) suffers guilt feelings and unknowingly comes to Dosamantes for psychological counseling. Dosamantes uses the information she extracts from the murderer to hunt down and kill those who slaughtered her family.

p, Carlos Vasallo; d, Hernando Name; w, Carlos Valdemar, Roberto Schlosser; ph, Xavier Cruz; m, Carlos Torres Marin; ed, Rogelio Zuniga.

Thriller **(PR:NR MPAA:NR)**

EL SOCIO DE DIOS† (1987, Cuba/Peru) 102m Kuntar-ICAIC c (Trans: God's Partner)

Adolfo Llaurado, Ricardo Tosco, Rene de la Cruz, Delicia Zalazar, Eslinda Nunez.

A Cuban-Peruvian coproduction based on the saga of real-life rubber baron Julio Cesar Arana, an Amazon adventurer who exploited the Indians to build a rubber empire at the turn of the century. Always lurking in the background are representatives of the United States and British governments, merely biding their time until they can seize Arana's riches for their respective countries. Eventually liberal forces compel the brutalized Indians to rebel, while US and British concerns siphon off Arana's European markets, thus causing his empire to collapse. This gives the Brits and Yanks the opportunity to pick up where Arana left off, exploiting the Indians and the land. Interestingly, the subject of German director Werner Herzog's FITZCARRALDO, Irish adventurer Brian Sweeney Fitzgerald, makes an appearance here as one of Arana's competitors.

d. Federico Garcia; ph, Rodolfo Lopez; m, Juan Marquez, ed, Roberto Bravo.

Biography **(PR:NR MPAA:NR)**

ELISE† (1987, Den.) 107m Danish Film Institute c

Ann-Mari Max Hansen, Ole Ernst, Frits Helmuth, Henning Jensen.

Based on a 19th century short story by Danish author Blicher, this film stars Hansen as the wife of a small-town doctor (Ernst) who falls into an affair with a handsome captain of the dragoons. The tryst throws the lives of her loved ones into a turmoil, but she remains relatively unscathed. Released in Denmark in 1985, ELISE received its American premiere at the Fourth American Film Institute European Community Film Festival. (Subtitled.)

d, Claus Ploug; w, Mogens Rukow (based on the short story "Belated Awakening" by Steen Steensen Blicher).

Drama **(PR:NR MPAA:NR)**

ELE, O BOTO† (1987, Braz.) 100m Lorentzen Empreendimentos-Embrafilme-Cine de Tempo-Transvideo/Embrafilme c (Trans: He, the Dolphin)

Carlos Alberto Riccelli *(The Dolphin)*, Cassia Kiss *(Tereza)*, Ney Latorraca *(Rufino)*, Dira Paes *(Corina)*, Paulo Vinicius *(Luciano)*, Ruy Polanah *(Ze Amaro)*, Maria Silvia *(Aunt)*, Sandro Solviati *(Fishermen)*, Rolando Boldrin.

A cinematic examination of old Brazilian legends that tell of dolphins who can transform themselves into handsome men—invisible to ordinary men—and come ashore to breed with the wives of fishermen. The women find these creatures irresistible and the offspring they produce are half-man, half-dolphin. Similar material was explored in the American-produced WHERE THE RIVER RUNS BLACK (1986).

p, L.C. Barreto; d, Walter Lima, Jr.; w, Walter Lima, Jr., Tirone Feitosa (based on a writing by Lima Barreto, from an idea of Vanja Orico); ph, Pedro Farkas (Eastmancolor); m, Wagner Tiso; ed, Mair Tavares; art d, Paulo Flaksman; set d, Ana Schlee; cos, Sergio Silveira; spec eff, Sergio Farjallo, Marco Antonio Franca, Persio Freire.

Drama/Fantasy **(PR:NR MPAA:NR)**

ELVIS-KISSAN JALJILLA† (1987, Fin.) 83m Kinotuotanto c (Trans: On the Trail of Elvis the Cat)

Claes Olsson *(Tom)*, Satu Silvo *(Sirpa, Pirjo, Vaimo)*, Markus Weckstrom *(Taxi Driver)*, Marita Siirtola *(Marilyn Monroe)*, Eboni *(Striptease Dancer)*, Heidi Siljander, Sisko Ramsay, Heikki T. Partanen, Vera Olsson.

Olsson, the writer-director-producer of this Finnish effort, stars as a film producer in his late thirties who seeks to escape his increasingly complicated life by retracing his youth. The impetus for this journey into the past is Olsson's viewing of old home movies (actual 8mm footage of Olsson and the real-life friends he lived with on a commune from 1969-1973). In them he sees his cat Elvis, who no longer lives with him. Determined to retrieve *her*, he begins looking up old friends (the same folks from the home movies) and eventually discovers Elvis dead in the apartment of his old girl friend, who has been carted off to a mental hospital. Olsson searches for a place to bury his erstwhile feline friend and ends up deciding on his own backyard. After giving Elvis a suitable funeral, Olsson gets back to the business of life. This is the first feature film for Olsson, an award-winning maker of shorts, animated films, and documentaries.

p,d&w, Claes Olsson; ph, Sakari Rimminen; m, Yari; ed, Alvaro Pardo; cos, Johanna Hanninen, Sirkku Katila; makeup, Helena Lindberg.

Comedy/Fantasy **(PR:NR MPAA:NR)**

EMANON* (1987) 94m Paul Ent. c

Stuart Paul *(Emanon)*, Cheryl M. Lynn *(Molly Ballentine)*, Patrick Wright *(Max)*, Jeremy Miller *(Jason Ballentine)*, Tallie Cochrane *(Laura Lowe)*, William F. Collard *(Masora)*, Robert Hackman *(Barnie)*, Shawn Campbell *(Nickie)*, B.J. Garrett *(Bruce)*, Bonnie Paul *(Jean Pierson)*, Jack Marston *(Policeman)*, Ellen Gersten *(Lynn)*, Terry Jenkins *(Ted Kraft)*, Aaron Binder *(Tony Hawks)*, Hilda Allen *(Florence)*, Janis Jamison *(Idee)*, Stacy Strauss *(Rosa)*, Al Bordighi *(Preacher)*, John Miranda *(Angry Man)*, Jay Scorpio *(Single Wing)*, Joanne Jackson *(Ernestine)*, Billie James *(Crabby Man)*, Mark Stuart Lane *(Santa Claus)*, Robert Huerta *(Husband)*, Denise Conti *(Pregnant Woman)*, Don Daniel *(Waiter)*, George O'Mara *(Body Builder)*, Steve Price *(Fat Husband)*, Barbara Fisk *(Fat Wife)*, Robin McKee *(Mr. Lindsay)*, Deanna McKinstry *(Reporter)*, Rana Ford, Lori Garland *(Models)*, Steven Paul *(TV Director)*, Eric Simon *(TV Assistant Director)*, Ron Ross *(Store Owner)*, Jason Stuart *(Newstand Man)*, Marty Davis *(Rabbi)*, Gene Collins, James C. Wright *(Priests)*, George Jammal *(Moslem)*, Tim Colceri *(Construction Worker)*, Natalle Carlino *(Camera Operator)*, Jon Greene, Abe Koster, Tim Wise *(Policemen)*, Art Paxton *(Minister)*, Todd Hoffman *(Crew Member)*, Ralph Gerowitz *(Old Drunk)*.

A religious message film which is built on the question, What if Christ were to come back to Earth as a skid row alcoholic? Set in New York City (but filmed mostly in Los Angeles), EMANON begins as the sappy, heart-tugging story of a crippled little rich kid, Miller, and his pretty young mother, Lynn. Although they are disgustingly wealthy, Lynn and Miller have fallen on hard times since the unexpected death of Lynn's husband, a top fashion designer and president of the Ballentine Corporation. Put in charge of her husband's company, the brainless Lynn pours her heart out to Miller: "It all happened so fast . . . Your father died and then I was a widow with a little boy and a multimillion dollar company I knew nothing about." Since Lynn doesn't know a sewing machine from a can opener, a rival fashion designer tries to sabotage the Ballentine Corporation. While Lynn spends her days in board meetings giving weepy speeches about integrity, little Miller gets chauffeured around town by the jovial Wright. Miller's idea of a good time is driving through skid row and looking at the winos—a pastime he likes better than television. Eventually he meets a kind, thoughtful alcoholic, Paul, who is always lending a hand to the downtrodden. Paul has no name so Miller gives him one—"Emanon," or "no name" spelled backwards. To make things clear to Miller (and the audience), the pious Paul is illuminated by holy light and, in one scene, the shadows of a cross and the Star of David fall across him. Once Miller realizes who Paul is, he contemplates pairing his mother with him. Paul and Lynn finally meet and take a romantic walk through the seedy back-alley world of winos and junkies. She even wears wino clothes—multilayered bundles of rags—just like Paul and his friends. The following morning, when Lynn arrives at work in her rags, everyone in the office thinks it is a new fashion. The rag look becomes all the rage in New York City and everyone on the street is dressed like Emanon. Newspaper vendors hawk a morning edition with the headline "God's prophet here in N.Y.C.—selling clothes, no less!" The Ballentine Corporation rises back to the top of the fashion world and, having done his small miracle, Paul leaves Lynn and Miller. Wanting to show their gratitude, they search the streets of N.Y.C. for him. They locate him in Central Park where he is speaking to a group of believers. An argument erupts when a Catholic, a Jew, and a Moslem debate whether Paul is Jesus Christ, the Messiah, or Mohammed. Fighting breaks out and Paul is denounced as a heretic, hauled off to a nearby tree, and crucified by the angry mob (using ropes to tie him there). Lynn and Miller, who by this time has thrown down his crutches, run to Paul's aid. After Paul tells them that he must move on and continue his work, he walks off into the misty forest.

Unlike most of today's films, EMANON takes a moral stand, one with which some disagree, but a stand nonetheless. The film raises interesting issues about religious divisions (each group's claim that they are the "chosen people") and the nature of miracles (seen here as internal strength instead of as external action), but good intentions simply can't carry this project. The scripting is too mindless to be believed, the acting less than convincing, the music incredibly saccharine, and the direction nearly nonexistent. The film's whole concept is treated with the depth of a television sitcom, especially in the filmmakers' use of the crippled boy cliche, the sterile, artificial locations and skid row bums, and the fashion subplot. There is also something morally objectionable about a little rich kid being chauffeured through skid row to watch the winos as an entertainment substitute for TV. EMANON is basically a right-wing film which preaches to the converted, who will, in all probability, take offense at the film's unconventional religious message. EMANON is a family affair from Paul Entertainment. Writer-director Stuart Paul also takes the lead role (playing Emanon something like a bearded Steve Guttenberg), his brother Steven (the director of the Jerry Lewis/Kurt Vonnegut debacle SLAPSTICK OF ANOTHER KIND) serves as executive producer, parents Hank and Dorothy are the film's producers, and sister Bonnie costars. She also sings two songs cowritten by Dorothy, "Emanon" and "Eyes of

Love" (Dorothy Paul, Lennie Niehaus, performed by Bonnie Paul). *(Profanity, substance abuse.)*

p, Hank Paul, Dorothy Koster-Paul; d&w, Stuart Paul; ph, John Lambert (Deluxe Color); m, Lennie Niehaus; ed, Richard Meyer, Janet Riley; art d, Donna Stamps; set d, Christina Volz; spec eff, John Carter; m/l, Lennie Niehaus, Dorothy Paul; makeup, Sheri Short.

Drama **Cas.** **(PR:A-C MPAA:PG)**

EMPEROR'S NEW CLOTHES, THE† (1987) 80m Golan-Globus/Cannon c

Robert Morse *(Henry)*, Jason Carter *(Nicholas)*, Lysette Anthony *(Gilda)*, Clive Revill *(Prime Minister)*, Julian Joy-Chagrin *(Duke)*, Eli Gorenstein *(Sergeant)*, Israel Gurion *(Wenceslas)*, Susan Berlin-Irving *(Christine)*, Sid Caesar *(Emperor)*.

The classic children's story about the vainglorious ruler who couldn't tell a fine suit of clothes from a familiar birthday suit is given the Cannon *costume* treatment here. Legendary TV funnyman Sid Caesar tries on the role of the emperor and uses the opportunity to demonstrate once more his fluency in nonsense foreign languages—one of his most enduring bits of shtick. Also prominent is the cast is Robert "How to Succeed in Business Without Really Trying" Morse. What's more this is a musical version of the tale, featuring a number of original songs.

p, Menahem Golan, Yoram Globus; d, David Irving; w, Anna Mathias, Len Talan, David Irving (based on the story by Hans Christian Andersen); ph, David Gurfinkel; m, David Krivoshei; ed, Tova Neeman; prod d, Marek Dobrowlski; art d, Avi Avivi; cos, Buki Shieff.

Children's **(PR:NR MPAA:NR)**

EMMANUELLE 5* (1987, Fr.) 78m AS/AAA c

Monique Gabrielle *(Emmanuelle)*, Dana Burns Westberg *(Charles Foster)*, Crofton Hardester *(Eric)*, Yaseen Khan *(Rajid)*.

There have been four James Bonds and no one has balked; now there have been three Emmanuelles and it's time for balking. This is a real ho-hummer from start to finish. What can be said about EMMANUELLE 5 that hasn't been said about the first four? It's the same softcore porn, the same boring moans and groans (which sound as though they were added in post-production), the same dull script. All that has changed are the players. Sylvia Kristel held down the fort the first three times around, followed by Mia Nygren and now Monique Gabrielle. In this latest saga, Gabrielle (born in France but raised in California) is a sex kitten who is starring in a new steamy movie being shown at the Cannes Film Festival. Her appearance creates a minor sensation and something of a scandal and she is soon languishing in the arms of an industrialist with oodles of money and a strong libido. From there, it's into the bed of Khan, an Arabian king who would like nothing better than to make her the No. 1 lady in his harem. That's about it for the story. Just the average trials and tribulations of a working girl who is on her feet and dying to get back on her back again. If there's nothing else to watch on late night cable TV, you'll find this a pleasant way to fall asleep. Directed by a man who should know better and whose credits include the far superior BLANCH AND THE BEAST. With all the sequels around these days, it won't be long before RAMBO VIII is cavorting with EMMANUELLE VII in STAR TREK VI as they are both rescued by SUPERMAN V. *(Nudity, sexual situations.)*

p, Alain Siritzky; d, Walerian Borowczyk; w, Walerian Borowczyk, Alex Cunningham (based on an idea by Emmanuelle Arsan); ph, Max Montheillet; m, Pierre Bachelet; ed, Franck Mathieu; art d, Alain Faure.

Romance **(PR:O MPAA:NR)**

EMPIRE OF THE SUN**** (1987) 152m Amblin Ent./WB c

Christian Bale *(Jim Graham)*, John Malkovich *(Basie)*, Miranda Richardson *(Mrs. Victor)*, Nigel Havers *(Dr. Rawlins)*, Joe Pantoliano *(Frank Demerest)*, Leslie Phillips *(Maxton)*, Masato Ibu *(Sgt. Nagata)*, Emily Richard *(Jim's Mother)*, Rupert Frazer *(Jim's Father)*, Peter Gale *(Mr. Victor)*, Takatoro Kataoka *(Kamikaze Boy Pilot)*, Ben Stiller *(Dainty)*, David Neidorf *(Tiptree)*, Ralph Seymour *(Cohen)*, Robert Stephens *(Mr. Lockwood)*, Zhai Nai She *(Yang)*, Guts Ishimatsu *(Sgt. Uchida)*, Emma Piper *(Amy Matthews)*, James Walker *(Mr. Radik)*, Jack Dearlove *(Singing Prisoner)*, Anna Turner *(Mrs. Gilmour)*, Ann Castle *(Mrs. Phillips)*, Yvonne Gilan *(Mrs. Lockwood)*, Ralph Michael *(Mr. Partridge)*, Sybil Maas *(Mrs. Hug)*, Eric Flynn, James Greene, Simon Harrison, Barrie Houghton, Paula Hamilton, Thea Ranft, Tony Boncza, Nigel Leach, Sheridan Forbes, Peter Copley, Barbara Bolton, Francesca Longrigg, Samantha Warden *(British Prisoners)*, Kieron Jecchinis, Michael Crossman, Gary Parker, Ray Charleson *(American Prisoners)*, Burt Kwouk *(Mr. Chen)*, Tom Danaher *(Col. Marshall)*, Kong-Guo-Jun *(Chinese Youth)*, Takao Yamada *(Japanese Truck Driver)*, Hiro Arai *(Japanese Sergeant/Airfield)*, Paul McGann *(Lt. Price)*, Marc De Jonge *(Frenchman)*, Susan Leong *(Amah)*, Nicholas Dastor *(Paul)*, Edith Platten *(Paul's Sister)*, Shirley Chantrell *(Chinese Cook at Detention Center)*, John Moore *(Mr. Pym)*, Ann Queensberry *(Mrs. Pym)*, Sylvia Marriott *(Mrs. Partridge)*, Frank Duncan *(Mrs. Hug's Father)*, Ronald Eng *(Mr. Chen's Aide)*, Za Chuan Ce, Shi Rui Qing *(Shopkeepers)*, Lu Ye, Guo Xue Liang, Ge Yan Zhao *(Merchants)*, J.G. Ballard *(Guest at Costume Party)*.

Continuing on the transitional path toward a cinema that is simultaneously literary and visual, Steven Spielberg has delivered the most emotionally complex film of his career in EMPIRE OF THE SUN. Based on the 1984 quasi-autobiographical novel by J.G. Ballard, the film explores WW II through the eyes of an adolescent boy, and does so almost entirely on the level of visual storytelling—more akin to silent filmmaking than anything modern. Spielberg's vision is no longer one of innocent wonderment. Contrarily, he has made a film about the end of innocence—a young boy thrown into adulthood and an entire generation thrown into an atomic age. The film takes place during Spielberg's most beloved decade, the 1940s, just before the Japanese attack on Pearl Harbor. Bale is a 9-year-old spoiled English brat who has lived his entire life in Shanghai with his aristocratic parents—Frazer and Richard. Although he is adventurous—he likes to ride his bicycle wildly, or pretend to fly above the city in the cockpit of a Japanese Zero—he is wholly dependent on his parents and servants. He lives a perfectly sheltered life in a lovely mansion with carefully manicured grounds. During his visits to downtown Shanghai, he is kept safely in the back of his chauffeured Packard. He gazes curiously, though not thoughtlessly, at the Chinese peasants as they beg for change or pick pieces of rice off the ground. His heroes, however, are the Japanese occupying forces whose bravery and individualism is a complete contrast to the faceless masses of the Chinese people. Bale dreams about flying and, during a costume ball given by a family friend, escapes to a nearby field which is home to a downed Japanese plane. With his balsa wood flyer in hand, he sits in the cockpit of the weather-beaten, bullet-riddled plane. He loses himself in his imagined flight, as the camera soars around him. He flings his balsa wood plane into the air, watching it land out of sight on the other side of a small hill. When he tries to retrieve it, he finds himself face-to-face with a division of Japanese soldiers in a trench. Though it's potentially a volatile situation, Bale luckily retreats unharmed. Later, while lying in bed playing with his toy Zero, Bale hears the sounds of a battleship outside his window. Moments later a blinding explosion rocks Shanghai as the Japanese conquer the city. At the same time in the US, Pearl Harbor is attacked and the war intensifies. Bale and his parents, along with thousands of other panicked people, pour into the city streets in an attempt to flee. The hysterical masses push with the force of a bursting dike, knocking over any person or thing that gets in the way. In a fatefully symbolic move, Bale tries to retrieve the toy Zero he has just dropped. Pulled in one direction by his mother, Bale grabs the plane but is pulled the other way by the crowd. Standing atop a nearby car, Bale screams for his "mum," but the mass hysteria is too great. He takes refuge at his parent's desolate mansion and, after surviving on his own for some time, drifts back into Shanghai's war-torn streets. When he meets up with Malkovich, an opportunistic merchant seaman who is Shanghai's version of the legendary Fagin of *Oliver Twist*, Bale's life takes a different turn. Malkovich, somewhat reluctantly, takes him under his wing and teaches him the most Darwinian methods of survival. Shortly thereafter, Malkovich and Bale are hauled off to a prison camp. Although the camp is filled with human suffering, Bale sees in it a world of unexplored adventure. Liberated from his parents and the limitations of childhood, Bale discovers a new world opening up for him. From Malkovich, he learns how to scavenge, to steal, to charm, to exploit, and to make deals. He sees his British counterparts as complacent and unheroic, idolizing instead the tough Americans and the fearless Japanese kamikazes. By 1945, Bale has turned 13 and has grown from a bratty aristocrat into a tough, leather-jacketed young man who can no longer even remember his mother's face. He has been exposed to brutal violence, death, sex, and the horrors of war. When a sickly woman dies beside Bale, a bright white light flashes in the sky. Bale believes the light is her soul ascending to heaven. Only later does he learn it was the light from the atomic bomb in Hiroshima. With the war's end, Bale, along with numerous other youngsters, is taken to a center where children can be reunited with their parents. Standing in crowds, the children face the adults as everyone's eyes search the room for their loved ones. Nearly catatonic, Bale stares straight ahead, not knowing for whom he is looking, as his parents cautiously approach the young man who used to be their little boy.

More than any other American filmmaker working today, Steven Spielberg with EMPIRE OF THE SUN displays an almost frightening control over the language of cinema. Like the greatest of directors (from Orson Welles to Francois Truffaut to Andrei Tarkovsky), he films with a spiritual passion that is evident in every frame. "I started to realize," Spielberg stated in an interview with Myra Forsberg, "that maybe I should please a part of me that I haven't pleased before . . . a side that doesn't necessarily think of the audience with every thought and breath, but thinks about what I need to be satisfied." Stripped of the marketing, manipulation, and drippy sentimentality that has permeated every Spielberg film since JAWS (in increasingly disheartening proportions), EMPIRE OF THE SUN is Spielberg's first truly "personal" film. It is personal in the sense that it comes from his heart and not from the patterns supplied by his previous blockbusters. Taking a risk comparable to Woody Allen's SEPTEMBER, Spielberg has made the film he wanted to make instead of the one everyone expected. (In terms of a career risk, EMPIRE OF THE SUN was a gutsier move for Spielberg than this year's other filmed-in-China epic THE LAST EMPEROR was for Bernardo Bertolucci, a director whose career has been built on far riskier projects.) EMPIRE OF THE SUN, with its $35 million budget, is not a traditional Hollywood blockbuster. It does, in fact, break most of Hollywood's rules. It has an unknown lead, a barely known supporting cast, and almost no plot at all. To even further stack the odds against himself, Spielberg has adapted a novel which few have read, set it in far-off Shanghai, and made his lead character a Britisher who idolizes the Japanese. It should come as no surprise then, that after a month at the box office EMPIRE OF THE SUN grossed only $14 million—a small sum in relation to the usual box-office tallies for Spielberg-directed films. Originally EMPIRE OF THE SUN was not even going to be directed by Spielberg. It was conceived as a project for the master of the epic genre, David Lean, with Spielberg serving as producer.

In addition to Spielberg's sincere and enthusiastic direction, EMPIRE OF THE SUN can boast one of the most honest child performances ever seen on the screen. Present in almost every shot of this 152-minute film, newcomer Bale (who bears a resemblance to another of film's great young performers, Jean-Pierre Leaud of THE FOUR HUNDRED BLOWS, which is perhaps a subconscious casting decision in light of Spielberg's admiration for Francois Truffaut) has such a commanding screen presence that he can take this epic story and make it intimate and personal. While Spielberg has in the past been praised for his direction of children, never before were they expected to carry a film as has Bale. Chosen from 4,000 hopefuls, Bale did television commercials and some stage work in England before landing a role in the American television film "Anastasia" as the son of lead Amy Irving, Spielberg's real-life wife. (Bale's press material fails to mention a 1987 Soviet/Swedish/Norwegian coproduction called MIO, MOY MIO.) Also turning in an excellent performance is Malkovich, who plays his character with equal parts of compassion and opportunism. He's callous, nasty, and far from heroic, but he's all Bale's got. The rest of the cast is serviceable in parts which are dwarfed by the attention paid Bale. It is this unfaltering attention to Bale that is the film's lifeblood. Constructed in episodes that revolve around Bale, instead of in a more typical linear fashion, the film has many memorable moments. On a couple of occasions, a hungry Bale is turned into a "wild child" as he forages for food, at one point shoveling chocolate liqueur candies into his mouth. Another great scene takes place during an American bombing raid on the runways inside the camp. Bale stands atop a tower and cheers the Americans. He leaps and yells "P-51, Cadillac of the Sky" as he imagines a low-flying bomber pilot waving at him. This moment is the most surreal scene of any Spielberg film—turning a spectacularly explosive bombing raid into a private moment which occurs in the imagination of the now-emotionally-twisted Bale. Later, after the dropping of the atomic bomb, Bale's emotional state hits the breaking point. Returning to the camp after being marched (along with all the other prisoners) to an intended death in the desert, Bale sees a young Japanese kamikaze, Kataoka, hysterically trying to start his plane. The boy, who throughout the picture has been Bale's counterpart—a youngster equally in love with flying—is an emotional mess, dishonoring his country by failing to give his life for it. He and Bale greet each other. There is no longer a fence between them, and their differing languages pose no barrier. Amidst the American/Japanese hatred and the wartime massacres, these two boys share a piece of fruit while sitting on the wing of Kataoka's plane. They are approached by Malkovich and his band of marauders who misread the situation and gun down Kataoka. As the dead Japanese flyer splashes into a pool of muddy water, Bale tries to revive him while shouting, "I can bring him back, I can bring everyone back." It is a frightening moment of mortality which symbolizes the emotions of an entire population of wartime survivors. It also marks a new beginning for Spielberg, who a few years ago would have given this kamikaze E.T. a glowing heart light and a fairy-tale second chance at life.

Curiously, at the 1986 Academy Awards ceremony, Spielberg made an acceptance speech upon being awarded the Irving G. Thalberg Award. He declared, "I think it's time to renew our romance with words. Only a generation of readers will spawn a generation of writers." What makes this statement odd is the fact the EMPIRE OF THE SUN, while based on a beautifully written novel, is a story told almost exclusively through visuals. Somewhere in the credits is the name of playwright Tom Stoppard, but his words are not in the movie, nor are Ballard's. Spielberg relies on the purely visual and as a result EMPIRE OF THE SUN is a brilliant adaptation. It remains true to the spirit of the novel and, where Ballard told his story perfectly with words, Spielberg does so with visuals. In each case the storyteller makes the fullest use of his medium. All of the film's finest moments exist on a visual level which approaches the religious. Whether it is Bale mesmerized by the glowing welder sparks of a Japanese airplane, or his angelic singing of a Welsh hymn ("Suo Gan," the film's recurring theme) during a kamikaze ceremony, EMPIRE OF THE SUN is a celebration of the spirit and an affirmation of Spielberg's passion for filmmaking—a passion all too rare in cinema today. Besides John Williams' score (which is only occasionally bombastic), the songs include the Welsh hymn "Suo Gan" (performed by The Ambrosian Junior Choir, soloist James Rainbird), "A Nightingale Sang in Berkeley Square" (Manning Sherwin, Eric Maschwitz, performed by Elizabeth Welch), "These Foolish Things (Remind Me Of You)" (Jack Strachey, Harry Link, Holt Marvell [Eric Maschwitz], performed by Welch), "South of the Border" (Jimmy Kennedy, Michael Carr, performed by Al Bowly, The Mayfair Orchestra, and Ronnie Munro), and "Swing Is in the Air" (performed by Jack Hylton). *(Violence, adult situations.)*

p, Steven Spielberg, Kathleen Kennedy, Frank Marshall; d, Steven Spielberg; w, Tom Stoppard, Menno Meyjes (uncredited) (based on the novel by J.G. Ballard); ph, Allen Daviau (Technicolor); m, John Williams; ed, Michael Kahn; prod d, Norman Reynolds; art d, Charles Bishop, Frederick Hole, Maurice Fowler, Huang Qia Gui, Norman Dorme; set d, Harry Cordwell, Michael D. Ford; spec eff, Kit West, David Watkins, Ye Mao Gen, Antonio Parra, Industrial Light and Magic; m/l, Manning Sherwin, Eric Maschwitz, Jack Strachey, Harry Link, Holt Marvell [Eric Maschwitz], Jimmy Kennedy, Michael Carr; stunts, Vic Armstrong; makeup, Paul Engelen.

Action/War/Drama **(PR:A MPAA:PG)**

EMPIRE STATE† (1987, Brit.) 104m Team/Virgin-Miracle c

Ray McAnally *(Frank)*, Cathryn Harrison *(Marion)*, Martin Landau *(Chuck)*, Emily Bolton *(Susan)*, Lee Drysdale *(Johnny, Rent-Boy)*, Elizabeth Hickling *(Cheryl)*, Lorcan Cranitch *(Richard)*, Jamie Foreman *(Danny)*, Jason Hoganson *(Pete)*, Ian Sears *(Paul)*, Jay Simpson *(Jeff)*, Roger Ashton Griffiths *(Punter in Cafe)*, David Lyon *(Mr. Cavendish)*, Tristram Wymark *(Tom)*, Tim Brierley *(Wellington Horne-Ryder)*, Ian McCurrach *("Metropolis" Editor)*, Jenny Bolt *(Tricia)*, Alan Talbot *(Billy Senior)*, Eric Gold *(2nd Man)*, Perry Fenwick *(Darren)*, Jimmy Flint *(Billy)*, Ron Berry *(Trainer)*, Josephine Melville *(Secretary)*, Glen Murphy *(Vince)*, Debbie Killingback *(Gaynor)*, Stuart Turton *(Roy)*, David Rhule *(Ken)*, Sadie Frost *(Tracy)*, John Levitt *(Harry)*, Gary Webster *(Paul's Man)*, Clare McIntyre *(Businesswoman)*, Steve Ausden *(Bouncer)*, Stanford Calaman *(Hollywood Barman)*, James Simmons, Michael Mueller, Ronan Vibert *(Businessmen)*, Melita Clark *(Receptionist)*, Doreen Taylor *(Cloak Lady)*, Harry Walker *(George the Book)*, Terry Plummer *(Big Red)*, David Foreman *(Stevie Kwon)*.

British *film noir* set in the Docklands area of London, which is undergoing an urban renaissance fueled by international investment. The action revolves around a swank nightclub called the "Empire State," owned by local bigwig McAnally. A power struggle develops between McAnally and Sears, a former male prostitute who has become a gangster. Sears has cooked up a lucrative real estate scheme that would allow him to buy up massive amounts of riverfront property and take over the Empire State. Unfortunately, his scheme depends on the heavy financial participation of American businessman Landau, who toys with Sears before finally pulling out of the deal at the last minute. The film climaxes with a bloody shoot-out at the Empire State. Songs include: "Murder" (New Order, performed by New Order), "Summerland," "Empire State" (Steve Parsons, performed by Sarah Jane Morris), "Heaven's Above" (Jimmy Somerville, Richard Coles, performed by The Communards), "Vicious Games" (Boris Blank, Dieter Meier, performed by Yello), "Grey Skies Turning Blue" (Somerville, performed by Somerville), "Ship of Fools" (A Bigger Splash, performed by A Bigger Splash), "Money" (performed by Steve Parsons).

p, Norma Heyman; d, Ron Peck; w, Ron Peck, Mark Ayres; ph, Tony Imi (Eastmancolor); ed, Christopher Kelly; prod d, Adrian Smith; art d, Val Wolstenholme; cos, William Peirce; m/l, New Order, Steve Parsons, Jimmy Somerville, Richard Coles, Boris Blank, Dieter Meier, A Bigger Splash; makeup, Ann Spiers; stunts, Marc Boyle.

Crime **(PR:NR MPAA:NR)**

EN EL NOMBRE DEL HIJO† (1987, Arg.) 90m Jorge Estrada Mora c (Trans: In the Name of the Son)

Ariel Bonomi *(Bobby)*, Margotita Moreyra *(Mother)*, Fernando Madanes, Jorge Sabate, Maria Sanguinetti.

Offbeat Argentine filmmaker Polaco's second feature examines traditional notions of beauty in art. It stars elderly actress Moreyra as a mother who enjoys an incestuous relationship with her 40-year-old son Bonomi. The two bathe together, dance a tango in their underwear, and play dress-up in a dusty apartment that has not been opened since the death of Bonomi's father ten years before. Although his work has been critically acclaimed, director Polaco has yet to find wide international distribution for his intensely personal films.

d&w, Jorge Polaco; ph, Esteban Coutalon; m, Pepe Motta; ed, Marcela Saenz; set d&cos, Norma Romano.

Drama **(PR:NR MPAA:NR)**

EN RETIRADA† (1987, Arg.) 87m Arte Diez/Instituto Nacional de Cinematografia Argentina c (Trans: In Retirement)

Rodolfo Ranni *(Ricardo, "Oso")*, Julio de Grazia *(Julio)*, Osvaldo Terranova, Lidia Lamaison, Villanueva Cosse, Edda Bustamante, Osvaldo Tesser, Jorge Sassi, Maria Vaner, Gerardo Sofovich.

Filmed in 1984, not long after the "dirty war" conducted by the Argentine military from 1976 to 1983, EN RETIRADA stars Ranni as one of the brutal torturers who dispatched many Argentine citizens to the ranks of the "disappeared." Suddenly powerless following governmental reforms, Ranni finds himself being followed by the father of one of his victims. Seeking to escape, he goes to the country to visit his mother only to find that there is no longer a place for him at home. Upon his return to Buenos Aires Ranni discovers that his organization has abandoned him and gone underground. Outraged at this betrayal, Ranni seeks vengeance against his military compadres and in the process becomes a problem to both the current government and the former junta.

d&w, Juan Carlos de Sanzo (based on a story by Juan Carlos de Sanzo, Feinmann, Oves); ph, Juan Carlos Lenardi; m, Baby Lopez Furst; ed, Sergio Zottla; art d, Pablo Olivo.

Drama **(PR:NR MPAA:NR)**

ENEMY TERRITORY† (1987) 90m Millennial/Empire c

Gary Frank *(Barry)*, Ray Parker, Jr. *(Jackson)*, Jan-Michael Vincent *(Parker)*, Frances Foster *(Elva Briggs)*, Tony Todd *(The Count)*, Stacey Dash *(Toni Briggs)*, Deon Richmond *(Chet)*, Tiger Haynes *(Barton)*, Charles Randall *(Mr. Beckhorne)*, Peter Wise *(Haj)*, Robert Lee Rush *(Psycho)*.

Given a scant release in New York City before winding up on home video, ENEMY TERRITORY stars Frank as a wimpy white insurance man who is sent by his boss to collect some money from a resident of a ghetto high rise. Frank agrees to the after-hours assignment because he needs the money. While there, he inadvertently insults a black youth who turns out to be the wrong kid to mess with. The young man is a member of the building's street gang, known as The Vampires, a group led by Todd, who goes by the moniker "The Count." The Vampires begin chasing the hapless Frank around the complex, killing a security guard in the process. Parker (the singer of the GHOSTBUSTERS theme song, here in his acting debut) is a black telephone repairman who happens to be on the scene at the same time. He hooks up with Frank, and attempts to help the man escape The Vampire's clutches. Also helping is Vincent, a disabled Vietnam veteran, who lives in one of the building's apartments. Vincent's place is a steel-lined bunker, stocked with a small arsenal. The chase goes on through the night, with Frank making narrow and lucky escape after narrow and lucky escape. Somehow, he survives The Vampire's maddened frenzy, and listens with relief to the sound of approaching police sirens.

One cannot help but wonder if co-screenwriter Kaminsky, a professor and head of the film division of the department of radio, television, and film at Northwestern University—author of several fiction and non-fiction books—named his villains after the criminal gang found in French director Louis Feuillade's classic silent serial LES VAMPIRES (1915).

p, Cynthia DePaula, Tim Kincaid; d, Peter Manoogian; w, Stuart M. Kaminsky, Bobby Liddell (based on a story by Stuart M. Kaminsky); ph, Ernest Dickerson (Precision Color); m, Sam Winans, Richard Koz Kosinaki; ed, Peter Teschner; prod d, Medusa Studios, Marina Zurkow; art d, Joanne Besinger; spec eff, Matt Vogel; makeup, John Bisson; stunts, Dave Copeland.

Action **Cas.** **(PR:NR MPAA:R)**

ENNEMIS INTIMES† (1987, Fr.) 95m Films Ariane-FR3-Slav 1/AAA c (Trans: Intimate Enemies)

Michel Serrault *(Baudin)*, Wadeck Stanczak *(Tayar)*, Ingrid Held *(Mona)*, Anne Gautier *(Billie)*, Thierry Rey *(Schlitz)*, Roch Leibovici *(El Loco)*, Yannick Soulier *(Tendinite)*, Sylvie Coffin *(Feeling)*.

A hit at the French box office, this action film was nonetheless disavowed prior to its release by its star, Michel Serrault, who claimed that director Amar ignored essential plot and character details. In the film Serrault and Stanczak take refuge from a band of marauding teens in a remote movie theater located on the edge of a cliff. Although rivals for the love of a mysterious young woman, the two team up to fend off the homicidal delinquents using karate skills and samurai-style swordplay.

d, Denia Amar; w, Bruno Tardon, Denis Amar; ph, Gerard de Battista (Eastmancolor); m, Philippe Sarde; ed, Jacques Witta; prod d, Jean-Pierre Kohut-Svelko; stunts, Daniel Verite.

Action **(PR:NR MPAA:NR)**

ENTRE FICHERAS ANDA EL DIABLO† (1987, Mex.) 100m Filmadora Exito/Peliculas Mexicanas c (Trans: The Devil Lurks Among Bar-Girls)

Jorge Rivero *(Gerardo)*, Sasha Montenegro *(Gerardo's Wife)*, Carmen Salinas *(Cochola)*, Rafael Inclan *(Rafael)*, Alfonso Zayas *(Satan)*, Manuel [Loco] Valdez *(Don Cacama)*, Luis de Alba *(The Devil)*, Ana Luisa Peluffo *(Donanita)*, Angelica Chain *(Perla)*, Lalo [El Mimo] *(Butler)*, Hector Suarez *(Dr. Judo)*, Jaime Moreno *(Dr. Barrientos)*, Cristina Molina, Raul Padilla, Cesar Escalero, Mary Montiel, Leandro Espinoza.

Featuring a cast of popular Mexican actors, this comedy is comprised of three loosely connected vignettes. In the first, Montenegro, a painter, uses her well-built husband Rivero as the model for Atlas. Rivero is called away on business, and Montenegro finishes the painting in his absence. However, upon his return, Rivero is suspicious of his wife's extracurricular activities when the nude is a perfect likeness for Rivero except for one prominent part of its anatomy. In the second story, Suarez plays a veterinarian who loses his head over chorus cutie Chain. The last sketch features Zayas as a Hades dweller who decides to have a helluva good time on earth for awhile.

p, Guillermo Calderon Stell; d, Miguel M. Delgado; w, Francisco Cavazos, Victor Manuel [Guero] Castro; ph, Fernando Colin; m, Gustavo C. Carrion; ed, Jorge Bustos; set d&ch, Juan Alonso, Enrique Sanchez.

Comedy **(PR:NR MPAA:NR)**

EPIDEMIC† (1987, Den.) 106m Element Film-Danish Film Institute/Obel Film bw/c

Lars von Trier *(The Film Director/The Epidemologist)*, Niels Vorsel *(The Screenwriter)*, Udo Kier *(Udo Kier)*, Susanne Ottesen *(Writer's Wife)*, Claes Kastholm Hansen *(Film Institute Producer)*, Svend Ali Hamann *(Hypnotist)*, Gitte Lind *(His Medium)*, Jorgen Christian Kruff *(Oenologist)*, Jan Kornum Larsen *(Customs' Officer)*, Caecilia Holbek *(Nurse)*, Olaf Ussing *(Pathologist)*, Ib Hansen *(Neurologist)*, Ole Ernst *(Orthopedist)*, Michael Simpson *(Priest)*, Michael Gelting *(Librarian)*, Allan de Waal, Gert Holbek, Leif Magnusson, Gunner Ottesen, Lennart Pasborg, Tony Shine.

The second part of a trilogy which began with 1984's THE ELEMENT OF CRIME, EPIDEMIC is an experiment in narrative from Denmark's most daring filmmaker, Lars von Trier. Starring in the film as a film director, von Trier struggles with his screenwriter Vorsel over an idea for a horror film. Intercut with these scenes are imagined scenes from the horror film itself in which von Trier plays an epidemologist who is trying to prevent the outbreak of a plague. Filmed in 16mm black-and-white for the real-life scenes and 35mm color stock for the horror scenes (the latter by Henning Bendtsen, the cinematographer for Carl Dreyer's ORDET and GERTRUD), EPIDEMIC was shown as part of the "Un Certain Regard" section at the 1987 Cannes Film Festival.

p, Jacob Eriksen; d, Lars von Trier; w, Lars von Trier, Niels Vorsel; ph, Kristoffer Nyholm, Henning Bendtsen (Eastmancolor); m, Peter Bach, Richard Wagner, J.S. Bach; ed, Lars von Trier, Thomas Krag; spec eff, Soren Gam Henriksen.

Drama/Horror **(PR:NR MPAA:NR)**

EQUALIZER 2000* (1987) 79m Concorde c

Richard Norton *(Slade)*, Corinne Wahl *(Karen)*, William Steis *(Lawton)*, Robert Patrick *(Deke)*, Frederick Bailey *(Hayward)*, Rex Cutter *(Dixon)*, Warren McLean *(Fletcher)*, Peter Shilton *(MacLaine)*, Dan Gordon *(Gossage)*, Ramon D'Salva *(Firewall)*, Vic Diaz *(Bone)*, Bobbie Greenwood *(Dinan)*, Henry Strzalkowski *(Alamo)*, Bill Kipp *(Tailfin)*, Steve Cook *(Skidplate)*, Willie Schorber *(Lube Job)*, Daniel De Long *(Boze)*.

Like their Italian counterparts, Filipino science-fiction action-adventures almost defy criticism. Both shamelessly imitate superior American, British, or Australian films, reworking stock plots that were old when sound came to the movies, but adding more sex and violence and car crashes. This MAD MAX rip-off is set in Alaska "after the Nuclear Winter," which means that the 49th state has become a desert. Oil, the most prized commodity, is lorded over by The Ownership, a kind of mini-military-industrial complex. Naturally there's a rebel movement, not to mention an Indian-like group—the mountain people. Norton is an officer for the Ownership who deserts when his father is betrayed during a rebel ambush. He is captured by the rebels, but escapes, and soon meets Wahl, a voluptuous babe who is being chased by a gang of white-trash lowlifes. After a series of car crashes, she takes him back to her home. There he converts his rifle into a super machine-gun-rocket-and-grenade-launcher that becomes the terror of the north slope, easily overwhelming the puny revolvers that everyone carries in this particular post-Apocalyptic milieu. Eventually Norton joins an attack on the Ownership by the combined forces of the rebels and mountain people, and a bloody battle ensues in which everyone but Norton dies. Apart from car chases, there's little here of interest. The film was apparently largely filmed within a quarry, and audiences will begin to feel as if they've seen certain streches of rock-wall background before. Norton doesn't do much beyond flexing his pectorals and looking rugged, while Wahl, a former *Penthouse* magazine pet of the year and wife of actor Ken Wahl, looks nice but has a silly voice. There is little to distinguish this straight-to-video release from a host of nearly identical films. *(Violence, profanity, adult situations.)*

p, Leonard Hermes; d, Cirio H. Santiago; w, Frederick Bailey (based on a story by Frederick Bailey, Joe Mari Avellana); ph, Johnny Araojo; ed, Pacifico Sanchez, Jr.; prod d, Joe Mari Avellana; md, Edward Achacoso; art d, Ronnie Cruz; set d, Boyet Camaya; cos, Ramon Alonzo; spec eff, Jess St. Domingo; makeup, Teresa Merceder.

Action/Adventure **Cas.** **(PR:O MPAA:R)**

ERNEST GOES TO CAMP* (1987) 93m Touchstone/BV c

Jim Varney *(Ernest P. Worrell)*, Victoria Racimo *(Nurse St. Cloud)*, John Vernon *(Sherman Krader)*, Iron Eyes Cody *(Old Indian Chief)*, Lyle Alzado *(Bronk Stinson [Foreman])*, Gailard Sartain *(Jake)*, Daniel Butler *(Eddy)*, Patrick Day *(Bobby Wayne)*, Scott Menville *(Crutchfield)*, Jacob Vargas *(Bubba Vargas)*, Danny Capri *(Danny)*, Hakeem Abdul-Samad *(Moustafa Hakeem-Jones)*, Todd Loyd *(Chip Ozgood)*, Andy Woodworth *(Pennington)*, Richard Speight, Jr. *(Brooks)*, Buck Ford *(Attorney Elliott Blatz)*, Larry Black *(Mr. Tipton)*, Eddy Schumacher *(Counselor Stennis)*, Hugh Sinclair *(Counselor Sparks)*, Johnson West *(Counselor Puckett)*, Jean Wilson *(State Supervisor)*, Mac Bennett, John Brown *(Technicians)*, Robert G. Benson III, Adam Ruff, Michael Chappelear, Lance Bridgesmith *(Campers)*, Paulo Deleon *(Young Indian Brave)*, Harvey Godwin, Jr. *(Brave's Father)*, Jeff Standing Bear *(Medicine Man)*, Ivan Green *(Mr. Stewart)*, Christian Haas *(Molly Stewart)*, Brenda Haynes *(Mrs. Stewart)*.

Watching Mrs. Olson sell coffee for 93 minutes would be a chore. Ditto for Ed McMahon and Budweiser. The Touchstone division of Disney must have thought that a commercial actor's popularity might carry over into the world of feature films when they accepted this movie. And with such stellar executive producers as Elmo Williams (an Oscar-winning editor for HIGH NOON as well as the man in charge of such features as PATTON, THE FRENCH CONNECTION, BUTCH CASSIDY AND THE SUNDANCE KID) and Martin Erlichman (longtime manager for Barbra Streisand and producer of FOR PETE'S SAKE, COMA, and the remake of BREATHLESS), they felt they would be getting a "class" production. Wrong. Jim Varney is the commercial spokesman for scores of companies. A brainchild of ad agency exec John R. Cherry III (who directed the movie as well as the commercials), Varney's character of "Ernest" is well-known in most states and even has his own fan club so it seemed like a good idea to make a movie starring the know-it-all handyman.

The plot is as simpleminded as the character. Varney wants to become a counselor at Camp Kikakee. Instead, he is handed the janitorial position, mostly for the reason that it allows the writers to fashion some sight gags, many of which came right from the silent movie days. When one of the other counselors has an accident, Varney is assigned the task of overseeing some young misfits who have just arrived. These juvenile delinquents abuse Varney for awhile then the villain, Vernon, enters. He tries to use Varney to persuade Cody, the camp's owner, to sign away all rights to the land and close the place. This is because Vernon is one of those evil-doers known as a "strip miner" who will rape the land and leave great gaping holes in it. This would be a tragic event as the camp has religious and historical significance for Cody's rapidly diminishing tribe. United by this threat, the rotten kids team with Varney to help defeat the villains in a 10-minute battle scene using everything from smoke bombs and Coleman lanterns to burning arrows. The camp is saved and Varney is proclaimed a hero.

The dialog is dumb, the acting is dull, the attempts at physical humor are, for the most part, as predictable as a stomach rumble after Mexican food. Varney wears his traditional baseball cap, says his traditional commercial lines, and shows that the jump from small screen to big screen might not always work out. Indian Cody, playing an Indian, does his best with what he has. Former footballer Lyle Alzado is properly menacing and a couple of small roles stand out, such as Sartain and Abdul-Samad. Special kudos to an unnamed turtle who attaches himself to Varney's nose and stays there. Varney's fan club members number between 17,000 and 20,000, not enough to make a $3.5 million picture a hit. Kentucky-born Varney began his commercials career in the 1970s, appearing as "Sergeant Glory" for a dairy. The spots ran for almost five years then Cherry, co-owner of the ad agency, concentrated on his business as Varney went West and did several TV shows, including "Operation Petticoat," "Fernwood Tonight," and the memorable "Pink Lady and Jeff". Cherry brought Varney back for "Ernest" and it began an incredibly successful run as they syndicated the character so he could appear in spots advertising automobiles, TV stations, food products (both fast and slow), and many more. To date, he has made more than 2,000 commericals. ERNEST GOES TO CAMP was a lame attempt to capitalize on Varney's popularity in a MEATBALLS setting. They are now talking about a sequel. Ugh. *(Profanity.)*

p, Stacy Williams; d, John R. Cherry III; w, John R. Cherry III, Coke Sams; ph, Harry Mathias, Jim May (DeLuxe color); m, Shane Keister; ed, Marshall Harvey; art d,& set d, Kathy Emily Cherry; cos, Bianca Dorso; makeup, Norma Gerson, Karen Duncan; spec eff, Jaime Bird; stunts, Keith Teller.

Comedy/Adventure **(PR:A-C MPAA:PG)**

ESCAPES zero (1987, Brit.) 72m Visual Perceptions/Prism Ent. c

Hall Of Faces: Vincent Price *(Mailman)*, Todd Fulton *(Matt Wilson)*; A Little Fishy: Jerry Grishaw *(Fisherman)*; Coffee Break: Michael Patton-Hall *(Delivery Driver)*, John Mitchum *(Mr. Olson)*, Lee Cranfield, Roelle Mitchell *(Young Couple)*, Nick Martin, P.K. Kearns, Vera Briggs, Arleta Johnson, Delbert Johnson, Jim Sundown, Julie Ann Daly, Bob Pittinger, Wesley Widerholt, Audrey Heyser, Albert H. Harris *(People in Cafe)*; Who's There: Ken Thorley *(Jogger)*, Jeff Boudov *(Scientist)*, Mark Steensland, Shawn Hannon *(Large Creatures)*, Matthew Mattingly, Caleb Mattingly *(Small Creatures)*; Jonah's Dream: Shirley O'Key *(Mary Tucker)*, Robert Elson *(Young Jonah)*, Bill Sibley *(Storekeeper)*; Think Twice: Gil Reade *(Bum)*, Rocky Capella *(Mugger)*, Bob Peeler *(Man in Car)*, David Newham *(Policeman)*, Neal Hahn *(Wino)*, Mike Martinez *(Driver)*.

Vincent Price narrates this limp horror anthology, telling audiences at the beginning that they will see 10 tales. Actually there are only half that many, but audiences are unlikely to quibble about this point, being more relieved to finally see the thing come to an end. In the first story a man out fishing picks up an apple on the shore. Taking a bite, he finds a hook in his mouth. A line leading under the water starts to pull and he is reeled under. In the next tale, a young messenger finds himself lost in the mountains. He disregards an old man's instructions to slow down and have a cup of coffee, and instead finds himself going around in circles until he is trapped in the local diner, somehow forced to spend eternity slowly sipping at a cup of java. Next we are presented with a fat jogger who is chased through the woods by horrible beasts until he falls down and one of them runs up to him, touches him, and says, "Tag, you're it." The fourth story concerns an old woman who has tried to make a living from the meager gleanings of gold on her mountain. One night a flying saucer crashes into her barn. She goes out and clears the debris from it, and the machine takes off, leaving the ground where it crashed gltttering with gold, apparently having exposed the mother lode in its crash. The last story concerns a thief who steals a magic crystal from a bum who uses it to make food appear. The robber is promptly run over by a car, but the bum recovers the stone, heals the robber, and brings a police car to arrest him, having put a purse and knife in his hands magically. Not a single one of the stories is at all worthwhile, with only the second showing a little style. Most of them are relentlessly padded to make the thin stories fill the time. It was all shot in northern California and the cast seems amateur. Vincent Price must only do these for the money.

p, David Steensland, Angela Sanders; d&w, David Steensland; ph, Gary Tomsic; m, Todd Popple; ed, Dane Westvic, Kiplan Hall; m/l, Not So Not So, Mick Mantin; makeup, Charles Blackman, Robert Friedin.

Horror **Cas.** **(PR:A MPAA:NR)**

ESTA NOCHE CENA PANCHO (DESPEDIDA DE SOLTERO)† (1987, Mex.) 86m Film Exito/Peliculas Mexicanas c (Trans: Tonight Pancho Dines Out—Bachelor Party)

Alfonso Zayas *(Pancho Medrano)*, Carmen Salinas *(Senora Medrana)*, Armando Silvestre *(Marcelo Granadas)*, Alberto [Caballo] Rojas *(Sergio)*, Alfredo [Pelon] Solares *(Oscar)*, Rebeca Silva, Rosalba Brambile, Leandro Espinosa, Patricia Castro, Morris Grey, Chico Che y La Crisis.

Low-budget Mexican sex comedy starring Zayas as an unhappily married lawyer who throws a raunchy bachelor party for Silvestre, a friend who is about to elope with the daughter of a prominent businessman. Popular salsa combo Chico Che and La Crisis make a token appearance.

p, Guillermo Calderon; d, Victor Manuel [Guero] Castro; w, Francisco Cavazos, Alfonso Anuya, Victor Manuel [Guero] Castro; ph, Raul Dominguez; m, Marcos Lifshitz; ed, Jose Liho.

Comedy **(PR:NR MPAA:NR)**

ETTER RUBICON† (1987, Norway) 96m Filmeffekt-Norsk-Credit Service Group-Viking/VCM c (AKA: RUBICON; Trans: After Rubicon)

Sverre Anker Ousdal *(Jon Hoff)*, Ewa Carlsson *(Mona Axen)*, Ellen Horn *(Maria Hamaroy)*, Toralv Maurstad *(Carl Berntsen)*, Jack Fjeldstad *(Thorvald Hoff)*, Alf Malland, Jan Harstad, Stein Erik Skattum, John Ausland.

When a freighter is found drifting without a crew off the coast of northern Norway, the region's chief medical officer unravels a plot that includes political coverups, nuclear radiation, and a conspiracy engineered by NATO and the Norwegian Armed Forces. Filmed in both English and Norwegian, ETTER RUBICON was produced by the same man (Filmeffekt's Dag Alveberg) who was behind ORION'S BELT, the top-grossing Norwegian film of the last decade.

p, Dag Alveberg; d, Leidulv Risan; w, Leifulv Risan, Arthur Johansen; ph, Harald Paalgard (Eastmancolor, Fuji Color); m, Geir Bohren, Bent Aserud; ed, Russell Lloyd, Yngve Refseth; prod d, Frode Krogh; cos, Wenche Petersen, Anne Siri Bryhni; spec eff, Petter Borgli.

Thriller **(PR:NR MPAA:NR)**

EU† (1987, Braz.) 120m Embrafilme-Cinearte c (Trans: I)

Tarcisio Meira [Marcelo Rondi], Bia Seidl, Monique Lafond, Christiane Torloni, Walter Forster.

Softcore erotica from Brazil starring Meira as a middle-aged businessman whose pursuit of beautiful young women merely disguises his incestuous lust for his own daughter.

p, Anibal Massaini Neto; d&w, Walter Hugo Khouri; ph, Antonio Meliande; m, Juilio Medaglia; ed, Luiz Elias; prod d, Jose Duarte de Aguiar; cos, Marineida M.C. Massaini.

Drama **(PR:NR MPAA:NR)**

EULALIA† (1987, Costa Rica) 90m Cinematografica del Istmo c

Maureen Jimenez *(Eulalia)*, Alfredo [Pato] Catania *(Don Jose)*, Miguel Calacci *(Rafael)*, Ruben Pagura *(Gustavo)*, Rosita Zuniga *(Yami)*, Bernal Garcia, Olga Marta Barranto, Luis Herrera, Jorge de Castillo, Train Latino.

Latin sex comedy starring Jimenez as a beautiful farmer's daughter who has moved to the big city to become a maid. Predictably, Jimenez spends much of her time fending off the amorous advances of her employer and his son. When the woman of the house discovers this, Jimenez is dismissed and takes a job at a Pizza Hut. There she meets and falls for a handsome young man, but she is abandoned by him after becoming pregnant. She then enters into a marriage of convenience with an impotent elderly man. Much to her chagrin, the old man's hormones undergo a renaissance and she must contend with his lusty attentions.

p&d, Oscar Castillo; w, Samuel Rovinski; ph, Victor Vega; m, Alvaro Esquivel; ed, Sigfrido Bacyne.

Comedy **(PR:NR MPAA:NR)**

EVA: GUERRILLERA† (1987, Can.) 83m Soleil/Les Films du Crepescule c

Angelo Roa *(Eva)*, Carmen Ferland *(Journalist)*.

Roa stars as a middle-class doctor in El Salvador who willingly abandons her life of comfort to join the leftist guerrilla army in 1978. The battles with government forces and death squads are difficult and bloody, leaving many of her comrades dead. Eventually caught and tortured, Roa manages to escape and flees to Montreal where journalists and leftist groups are eager to hear her speak of the battle for El Salvador. Tired of the publicity mill and anxious to continue the fight, Roa returns to her homeland and is killed while fighting in the mountains. Shot on 16mm in Central America by Seattle-born filmmaker Levitin.

p, Jacqueline Levitin, Chantal Lapaire; d&w, Jacqueline Levitin; ph, Jean-Charles Tremblay; m, Barry Goold; ed, Herve Kerlaan; art d, Karine Lepp.

Drama **(PR:NR MPAA:NR)**

EVIL DEAD 2: DEAD BY DAWN*** (1987) 85m Renaissance/Rosebud c

Bruce Campbell *(Ash)*, Sarah Berry *(Annie)*, Dan Hicks *(Jake)*, Kassie Wesley *(Bobby Joe)*, Theodore Raimi *(Possessed Henrietta)*, Denise Bixler *(Linda)*, Richard Domeier *(Ed)*, John Peaks *(Prof. Raymond Knowby)*, Lou Hancock *(Henrietta)*.

Director Sam Raimi strikes again with this manic, and very funny, sequel to his stunningly inventive 1983 low-budget fever dream, THE EVIL DEAD. As in the first film, Raimi lets out all the stops and plays every cinematic trick in the book. Instead of "Dead by Dawn," the subtitle of this film should be "Help! There's a Camera Chasing Me!" More a remake than a sequel, the film opens as the lone survivor from the first film, Campbell (who also served as co-producer), ventures out to a lonely cabin for a romantic weekend with his girl friend, Bixler. In the cabin Campbell discovers a tape recorder left behind by the former owner, an

archeologist. When Campbell plays the tape, he learns that the archeologist had discovered the ancient Egyptian "Book of the Dead" and had begun to translate it. When the archeologist reads aloud from the book, a vicious evil force awakens in the woods and rushes into the house, attacking Bixler. Possessed, Bixler tries to kill Campbell. The confused boy friend is forced to decapitate the crazed girl, but the unseen evil force rushes back to the house and literally grabs Campbell and hurtles him through the woods. Now, he, too, is possessed, but the sunrise brings him back to normal. Campbell then tries to escape the cabin, but finds that the bridge—the only exit—has been destroyed. From this point on the evil force tortures poor Campbell relentlessly by doing such nightmarish things as bringing his decapitated girl friend back to life and turning his own hand against him. Nearly hysterical, Campbell is forced to dismember his hand, only to discover that the thing has taken on a life of its own (scurrying around the cabin like a mouse). Enter Berry, the daughter of the archeologist; her associate Domeier; and two locals, Hicks and Wesley. Thinking Campbell insane, they lock him in the cellar. Unfortunately, they soon learn that Berry's possessed mother has turned into an ugly monster and is living down there. After tormenting the new guests, the evil force makes quick work of Domeier, Wesley, and Hicks, leaving the tenacious Campbell and the resourceful Berry to do battle with the evil by themselves. With help from her father's ghost, Berry discovers that she can defeat the evil by reciting an incantation found in the book. While all hell breaks loose around them, the dying Berry utters the magic words and a huge vortex appears and begins to engulf the property. Campbell (who has attached a chainsaw to his handless wrist and armed himself with a shotgun) is also sucked into the void, only to find himself plopped into the middle of a 14th Century battle. When the knights are attacked by a flying demon, Campbell blasts the beast with his shotgun and is hailed as a god.

A purely cinematic experience for those with a taste for *Grand Guignol*, the impact of EVIL DEAD 2 cannot be described. Grotesque, gory, silly, and at times, quite funny, Raimi's creation is a relentlessly energetic nightmare world where anything can (and does) happen. By taking everything to an absurd extreme, the film frequently leaves the realm of horror and becomes a cartoon gone mad. Campbell's ultraserious performance is almost Keatonesque as he gamely tries to handle everything Raimi throws at him, and Raimi has a lot of ammo. The 26-year-old director employs a myriad of cinematic tricks and visual styles, including: stop-motion animation, undercranking the camera, point-of-view shots, crane shots, hand-held shots, Dutch angles, special makeup, turning sets on their sides, rear-screen projection, anamorphic lenses, radio-controlled mechanics, mattes, miniatures, sound effects, and good-old-fashioned dramatic lighting. The film is a breathless celebration of the possibilities of the medium and should be viewed as such. Obviously, dramatic narrative holds little interest for Raimi. The setting and story are merely functional, and most of the dialog is perfunctory—sometimes hilariously so. This is by no means a psychological horror film; nor one that seeks to examine the repressed underbelly of American society. Pure visceral impact is what this film is all about and it succeeds brilliantly.

Raimi launched this project to make some money for those private investors who saw little return on the first film. Seeking studio funding, he first tried to strike a deal with Embassy Home Entertainment. But while Embassy dragged its feet, Dino De Laurentiis called Raimi personally and offered to fund the film 24 hours after reading the screenplay. Raimi severed his ties with Embassy and gladly accepted DEG's $3.75 million budget. De Laurentiis' one stipulation was that Raimi had to deliver an "R" rated film (the original film went unrated to avoid the dreaded "X"—which meant limited distribution). Raimi subsequently toned down the sadism and instead went for a cartoonish extreme from which sprang much black humor. DEG officials took one look at the finished product and didn't even bother submitting the film to the MPAA. Instead of forcing Raimi to make drastic cuts to receive an "R," DEG turned the distribution rights over to an independent distributor, Rosebud Releasing, while retaining all other rights to the picture. Regardless of the film's rating or distribution, Raimi once again has delivered his distinctly bizarre and unique brand of filmmaking to horror fans starved for something more than the plague of formula slasher films that has polluted the genre since HALLOWEEN. *(Graphic violence, gore effects, profanity.)*

p, Robert G. Tapert; d, Sam Raimi; w, Sam Raimi, Scott Spiegel; ph, Peter Deming, Eugene Shlugleit (Technicolor); m, Joseph Lo Duca; ed, Kaye Davis; art d, Philip Duffin, Randy Bennett; set d, Elizabeth Moore; ch, Susan Labatt, Andrea Brown, Tam G. Warner; makeup, Wendy Bell, Mark Shostrom; spec eff, Vern Hyde, Doug Beswick Productions, Tom Sullivan, Rick Catizone.

Horror **Cas.** **(PR:O MPAA:NR)**

EVIL SPAWN† (1987) 73m Camp Motion Pictures-American Independent Prods. c (AKA: DEADLY STING; ALIVE BY NIGHT)

Bobbie Bresee *(Lynn Roman)*, Drew Godderis *(Ross Anderson)*, John Terrence *(Brent Price)*, Donna Shock [Dawn Wildsmith] *(Evelyn)*, Jerry Fox *(Harry Fox)*, Pamela Gilbert *(Elaine Talbot)*, John Carradine *(Dr. Zeitman)*, Mark Anthony *(Mark Randall)*, Leslie Eve *(Tracy)*, Chris Kobin *(Will)*, Sue Mashaw *(Betty)*, Gary J. Levinson *(Dr. Leibowitz)*, Michael S. Deak *(Symanski)*, Roger McCoin *(Bordona)*, Forrest J. Ackerman *(Pool Man)*.

Rip-off of Roger Corman's cult classic THE WASP WOMAN (1959) features Bresee as an aging starlet who is eager to undergo an experimental treatment that will make her look younger. Administered by evil woman scientist Shock (aka: Wildsmith), the treatment works at first, but a nasty side-affect sees Bresee turn into a hideous insect-monster with a taste for human blood. A straight-to-home-video release. Forrest Ackerman, the former editor-in-chief of the now-defunct horror film magazine *Famous Monsters of Filmland* adds another cameo appearance to his resume with this entry.

p, Anthony Brewster, Frank Bresee; d&w, Kenneth J. Hall; ph, Christopher Condon; m, Paul Natzke; ed, William Shaffer; art d, Roger McCoin; spec eff, Dan Bordona, Christopher Ray; makeup, Cleve Hall, Thom Floutz; creature design, Ralph Miller, III.

Horror **Cas.** **(PR:NR MPAA:NR)**

EVIL TOWN† (1987) 82m Mars/Trans World Ent. c

James Keach *(Dr. Chris Fuller)*, Michele Marsh *(Julie)*, Doria Cook *(Linda)*, Robert Walker *(Mike)*, Dean Jagger *(Dr. Schaeffer)*, Keith Hefner, Greg Finley, E.J. Andre, Dabbs Greer, Scott Hunter, Lynda Wiesmeier, Christie Houser, Noelle Harling, Paul McCauley, Jillian Kesner, Lurene Tuttle, Regis Toomey.

Featuring several familiar faces, this horror film tells the story of a loony research scientist whose study of the relationship between the pituitary gland and the aging process requires *considerable* sacrifice by his human subjects. The scientist, Jagger, needs human organ donors, and his Smalltown neighbors are only too happy to oblige, though not with their own vitals. Instead, they abduct unsuspecting travelers and donate them to Jagger's research efforts. Physician Keach, his girl friend, and another couple come to the area to commune with nature and end up as unwilling guests at Jagger's clinic. Jagger is anxious for Keach to become his assistant, but the young doctor has escape on his mind, which he and his girl friend eventually manage to do. The other inmate guinea pigs then revolt and kill Jagger. EVIL TOWN, which went into production in 1984, went through no less than four directors. In addition to Hollywood veterans Regis Toomey, Dabbs Greer, and Lurene Tuttle, it features former Playmate Lynda Wiesmeier, or at least her bare breasts.

p, Peter S. Traynor, William D. Sklar; d, Edward Collins, Peter S. Traynor, Larry Spiegel, Mardi Rustam; w, Larry Spiegel, Richard Benson (based on a story by Royce Applegate); ph, Bill Mann, Bob Ioniccio (United Color); m, Michael Linn; ed, Jess Mancilla, David G. Blangsted, Peter Parasheles; art d, Richard Gillis.

Horror **Cas.** **(PR:NR MPAA:NR)**

EXTREME PREJUDICE*** (1987) 104m Carolco/Tri-Star c

Nick Nolte *(Jack Benteen, Texas Ranger)*, Powers Boothe *(Cash Bailey)*, Michael Ironside *(Maj. Paul Hackett)*, Maria Conchita Alonso *(Sarita Cisneros)*, Rip Torn *(Sheriff Hank Pearson)*, Clancy Brown *(Sgt. Larry McRose)*, William Forsythe *(Sgt. Buck Atwater)*, Matt Mulhern *(Sgt. Declan Patrick Coker)*, Larry B. Scott *(Sgt. Charles Biddle)*, Dan Tullis, Jr. *(Sgt. Luther Fry)*, John Dennis Johnston *(Merv, Cash's Accountant)*, Luis Contreras *(Lupo)*, Carlos Cervantes *(Hector)*, Tom "Tiny" Lister, Jr. *(Monday)*, Marco Rodriguez *(Deputy Cortez)*, James Lashly *(Deputy Purvis)*, Tony Frank *(Clarence King)*, Mickey Jones *(Chub*

Luke), Kent Lipham *(T.C. Luke)*, Sam Gauny *(Pearly Grips)*, Gil Reyes *(Rincon Norte Bartender)*, Rick Garcia *(Arturo)*, Richard Duran *(Man with Chub)*, Larry Duran *(Jesus)*, Christina Garcia *(Biddle's Girl)*, Charles Lewis *(Chicken Champ Kid)*, Humberto De La Torre *(Andy)*, Fred Eisenlohr, Anthony Galvan III *(Deputies)*, Erin Bowden *(Donna Lee)*, Frank Lugo *(Jalisco Bartender)*, Jimmy Ortega *(Young Mexican Man)*, Lin Shaye *(Employment Office Clerk)*, Anthony Lattanzio *(Man in Employment Office)*, Ken Medlock *(Redneck in Bank)*, Michelle Lynn Rosen *(Woman in Airport)*.

Nolte is undoubtedly one of the best actors on screen today, versatile and resilient, one whose forceful personality compels viewership. When this riveting character is coupled with a good film, the end product is something worthy of watching. Such is the case with EXTREME PREJUDICE, despite its abundance of violence. Nolte is an old-fashioned Texas Ranger working out of El Paso; across the border in a small Mexican village resides his one-time childhood friend Boothe who has clawed his way up the illegal ladder to become the district's drug-running king and he lords it over the peons with an army of lethal gunmen. The two men have another link in swarthy, sensual Alonso, one-time mistress to Boothe, now Nolte's lover. Both men are cast in traditional hero and villain molds, particularly Boothe who is reminiscent of the evil excesses practiced by Richard Boone in HOMBRE. In Boothe's first scene we see him dressed in immaculate white suit and hat, fondling a scorpion and then squeezing the life out of the creature. Now we *know* this guy is bad through and through. Boothe flits about the Texas and Mexican border in private helicopters with his roving eye on the sexy Alonso. She is growing weary of her mediocre existence with the hardworking Nolte, a man who returns home to her each night so exhausted after battling dope runners all day that all he can do is fall into a stupor. Boothe takes Alonso away from him, holding her as a sort of willing, vexing hostage. Both men run up against a CIA-backed paramilitary group headed by Ironside, a cold and calculating army major. Ironside and his men plan to rob a bank where Boothe's cash resides in an effort to get evidence to bring Boothe to justice. Since the bank is located in Nolte's town, the operatives have to contend with him to reach their goal. The robbery turns into a debacle and Nolte captures two of the group members. To free his men, Ironside reveals all to Nolte, then allows him to join on an excursion to Mexico where they plan to terminate Boothe with "extreme prejudice." In the meantime, Ironside informs his men that the lawman knows too much and has to be killed. Objections are raised, but squelched when Ironside tells them it's a direct order. Nolte first enters Boothe's heavily guarded bastion alone. Events soon reveal that Ironside is actually in league with Boothe and is conspiring to get everyone killed so that he can escape with a fortune in drug money. Aware of the deception, Ironside's men kill him during a violent confrontation between the CIA men and the Boothe bandits, as both sides utterly destroy each other in a wild bloodbath. All the operatives are killed, leaving Nolte and Boothe to face each other in an old-fashioned western duel. Nolte triumphs and Alonso decides that the better part of sexual valor is to go off with a live winner.

The plot isn't much but director Hill's stylized approach to his subject lifts this one out of the mire of mediocrity and Nolte's direct and powerful performance as a man of the law is worth the film itself. Boothe and Alonso are good, and Torn, as a broken-down sheriff with ancient ideas about honor and nobility, is exceptional. But killing him off early in the film, thus giving Nolte a personal reason for eliminating his boyhood friend Boothe, leaves the viewer wanting more from this talented and surprising veteran actor. Production values are very high but the violence tends to distract from the mannered tone of the film. *(Graphic violence, profanity.)*

p, Buzz Feitshans; d, Walter Hill; w, Deric Washburn, Harry Kleiner (based on a story by John Milius, Fred Rexer); ph, Matthew F. Leonetti (Technicolor); m, Jerry Goldsmith; ed, Freeman Davies; prod d, Albert Heschong; art d, Joseph C. Nemec, III; set d, Beverli Eagan; cos, Dan Moore; spec eff, Tom Fisher; m/l, Tomas Ponce Reyes, Filiberto Benavides, Manuel Esperon, Ernesto Cortazar, Jose Alfredo Jimenez, Lydia Mendosa, Jose Lopez Espinoza, Jesus Monge, Gilberto Parro, Hermanos Martinez Gil, Narciso Serradell; stunts, Bennie Dobbins; makeup, Michael Germain.

Action **(PR:O MPAA:R)**

EYE OF THE EAGLE† (1987, Phil.) 82m Concorde c

Brett Clark *(Sgt. Rick Stratton)*, Robert Patrick *(Johnny Ransom)*, Ed Crick *(Sgt. Rattner)*, William Steis *(Capt. Carter)*, Cec Verrell *(Chris Chandler)*, Rey Malonzo *(Capt. Willy Leung)*, Mike Monty *(Col. Stark)*, Vic Diaz *(Col. Trang)*, Henry Strzalkowski *(Col. Watkins)*, David Light *(Sgt. Maddox)*.

Another straight-to-home-video release from Cirio H. Santiago, the director of such Filipino classics as THE BLOOD DRINKERS (1966) and THE VAMPIRE HOOKERS (1979). This film concerns itself with a group of American soldiers listed as either MIA's or POW's in Vietnam who are, in reality, very much alive and have formed a renegade "lost command." Led by Crick, they continue to wage war on the Vietnamese communists. Female news reporter Verrell gets wind of the lost command and goes into the jungle to investigate. She later hooks up with US Army commando Clark, who has been sent to eliminate the renegade group. As it turns out Clark's brother was murdered by Crick years earlier and the two soldiers eventually face off man-to-man.

p&d, Cirio H. Santiago; w, Joseph Zucchero, Nigel Hogge (based on a story by Catherine Santiago); ph, Ricardo Remias; ed, Gervacio Santos; prod d, Joe Mari Avellana; md, Marita Manuel; stunts, Fred Espiana.

Action **Cas.** **(PR:NR MPAA:R)**

F . . . ING FERNAND† (1987, Fr./Ger.) 84m Stephen-UGC-Films A2-ICE-Richard Clause-Delta/UGC c

Thierry Lhermitte *(Fernand Le Batard)*, Jean Yanne *(Binet)*, Marie Laforet *(Lotte)*, Charlotte Valandrey *(Lily)*, Martin Lamotte *(La Fouine)*, Hark Bohm *(Von Schaltz)*, Patrice Valota *(Vigneault)*.

Lhermitte plays a 30-year-old blind man who has been institutionalized by his family. He's still a virgin and anxious to do something about it. When the Germans invade France during WW II, the asylum in which Lhermitte is incarcerated is destroyed and he escapes. He meets up with Yanne, a murderer on the run from the law, and they head south, ending up in a bordello where Lhermitte's longings are satisfied.

p, Vera Belmont; d, Gerard Mordillat; w, Jean Aurenche, Vera Belmont, Gerard Mordillat (based on a novel by Walter Lewino); ph, Jean Monsigny; m, Jean-Claude Petit; ed, Nicole Saunier; art d, Jacques Bufnoir; cos, Ulrike Schutte.

Comedy/Drama **(PR:NR MPAA:NR)**

FACES OF WOMEN† (1987, Ivory Coast) 105m New Yorker c

Eugenie Cisse Roland *(Bernadette)*, Sidiki Bakaba *(Kouassi)*, Albertine N'Guessan *(N'Guessan)*, Kouadio Brou *(Brou)*, Mahile Veronique *(Affoue)*.

The woman in African society is the focus of this film from the Ivory Coast that tells two stories, shot in 1973 and 1983. The first deals with a woman who, unhappy with her married life, has an affair with her husband's brother. In the second, a woman who operates her own business finds that her husband and other family members have been skimming profits. Ecare, the film's writer/director/producer, studied film in Paris before returning to his native land in 1973, working a variety of jobs while trying to complete this film.

p,d&w, Desire Ecare; ph, Francois Migeat, Dominique Gentil; ed, Giselle Miski, Mme Dje-dje, Nicholas Barrachin.

Drama **(PR:NR MPAA:NR)**

FADERN, SONEN OCH DEN HELIGE ANDE† (1987, Swed.) HB Hinden c (Trans: The Father, the Son and the Holy Ghost)

Ernst-Hugo Jaregard, Olof Buckard, Dag Cramer, Charlotte Gyllenhammer, Rolf Skoglund, Heinz Hopf, Jonas Bergstrom, Kaj Nuora, Johannes Brost, Ake Pallarp.

[No plot information available.]

d&w, Marie-Louise De Geer Bergenstrahle.

Drama **(PR:NR MPAA:NR)**

FAKELOS POLK STON AERA† (1987, Gr.) Greek Film Center-Cinegroup c (Trans: The Polk File on the Air)

Agape Manoura, Michalis Kosmidis, Vangelis Kazan, Katerina Karayanni, Pavlos Kontoyannidis, Alkis Panayotidis, Tassos Polychronopoulos, Dimitris Poulikakos, Constantinos Tzoumas, Christos Tsangas, Panos Hadzikoutselis, Costas Hadzoudis *(Grigoris Staktopoulos in 1948)*, Nikos Hitas *(George Polk)*.

In 1948 in Thessaloniki, American journalist George Polk was the first foreign correspondent to be killed during the post-war period. The case is still unsolved and director Grigoratos recreates events and re-examines evidence with the help of two main characters—a freelance sound recordist who studies and collects the criminal information and an actress who relives the emotions and relationships of the people involved. All of this is done within the context of a radio program of which both characters are a part.

d&w, Dionyssis Grigoratos; ph, Prokopis Dafnos; m, Costas Mylonas; art d, Dora Lelouda; cos, Dora Lelouda.

Docu-drama **(PR:NR MPAA:NR)**

FALSCH† (1987, Bel./Fr.) 82m Derives-RTBF-Arcanal-Theatre de la Place-Belgian Ministry for the French Community c

Bruno Cremer *(Joe)*, Jacqueline Bollen *(Lilli)*, Nicole Colchat *(Mina)*, Christian Crahay *(Gustav)*, Millie Dardenne *(Bela)*, Berangere Dautun *(Rachel)*, John Dobrynine *(Georg)*, Andre Lenaerts *(Ruben)*, Christian Maillet *(Jacob)*, Jean Mallamaci *(Benjamin)*, Gisele Oudart *(Natalia)*, Marie-Rose Roland *(Daniella)*, Francois Sikivie *(Oscar)*.

The Dardenne brothers are well known in Europe for their documentaries, and this is their first venture into feature filmmaking. It tells the story of a German Jewish family which has a reunion—after all the members are dead.

d&w, Jean-Pierre Dardenne, Luc Dardenne (based on the play by Rene Kalisky); ph, Walther Vanden Ende (Eastmancolor); m, Jean-Marie Billy, Jan Franssen; ed, Denise Vindevogel; art d, Wim Vermeylen.

Drama **(PR:NR MPAA:NR)**

FAMILY, THE*½** (1987, It./Fr.) 127m Maasfilm-Cinecitta-RAI TV Channel 1-Les Films Ariane Cinemax/Vestron c (LA FAMIGLIA)

Vittorio Gassman *(Carlo)*, Fanny Ardant *(Adriana)*, Stefania Sandrelli *(Beatrice)*, Andrea Occhipinti *(Young Carlo)*, Jo Champa *(Young Adriana)*, Alberto Gimignani, Massimo Dapporto, Carlo Dapporto, Cecilia Dazzi, Ottavia Piccolo, Athina Cenci, Alessandra Panelli, Monica Scattini, Ricky Tognazzi, Renzo Palmer, Philippe Noiret, Meme Perlini, Sergio Castellitto, Dagmar Lassander.

After venturing off into pedestrian comedy as he did with his last film, MACARONI, director Scola returns to the single set limitations of his LE BAL (1984) for this pleasant drama which covers 80 years in the life of one Italian family. The film opens in 1906 as a family gathers in a large Roman apartment for a group photograph. The narration begins as Gassman points himself out in the picture—an infant who has just been baptized. Gassman narrates the entire picture and time passes, never showing the characters outside of the apartment. In addition to Gassman, the family includes his brother, his parents, a maid, and three matronly aunts. By 1926, Gassman (played as a young man by Occhipinti) has become a teacher, giving private lessons at home to the younger Sandrelli. She has a crush on her instructor, but he is more interested in her older sister, the more worldly Champa (played later by Ardant). Eventually, Gassman weds Sandrelli and Ardant starts a new life in Paris. Two wars pass and Gassman and Sandrelli have become parents and then grandparents many times over. As Gassman approaches his later years, his love for Ardant is finally consummated in a one-night affair. Although Sandrelli knows, she never lets on, preferring to keep the love of her husband and the companionship of her sister. When Sandrelli dies, Gassman and Ardant, both growing gray and feeble, treasure the friendship and romance which has survived for so many years. The film ends as it begins—with a family photograph—only this time Gassman is the patriarch.

Like so many of the films of Ingmar Bergman and Woody Allen, THE FAMILY goes to great lengths to recreate a family portrait album. Since THE FAMILY spans 80 years there is little room for a plot, concerning itself instead with characters. Scola gives his audience a collection of characters, each with qualities and idiosyncrasies which change and develop over the course of time. As a stylistic unifying thread, Scola uses a recurring dolly shot through the apartment's empty hall which symbolizes the time that passes. Filled with humor, sadness, and anger, THE FAMILY includes a number of memorable vignettes. As young boys, Occhipinti and his brother steal money from a relative who later goes to jail when he boards a bus without having the money to pay the fare; the young Occhipinti meeting the young Ardant for the first time and watching her do a risque dance at a family gathering; the three aunts continually bickering until one by one they die; the aging Gassman telling his wife that she deserved so much more than him; and a feisty, playful exchange between the octogenarian Gassman and the sharp-tongued Ardant. Though THE FAMILY encompasses nearly all the political and social events of 20th century Italy, it manages to retain a feeling of intimacy because of the single set. Gassman carries the film in a brilliant performance and receives excellent support from everyone involved, especially Sandrelli and the increasingly more visible Ardant. (In Italian; English subtitles.)

p, Franco Committeri; d, Ettore Scola; w, Ruggero Maccari, Furio Scarpelli, Ettore Scola; ph, Ricardo Aronovich (Cinecitta color); m, Armando Trovajoli; ed, Ettore Scola; art d, Luciano Ricceri.

Comedy **(PR:A MPAA:NR)**

FAMILY BUSINESS** (1987, Fr.) 98m European Classics c (CONSEIL DE FAMILLE)

Johnny Hallyday *(The Father)*, Fanny Ardant *(The Mother)*, Guy Marchand *(Faucon)*, Laurent Romor *(Francois as a Teen)*, Remi Martin *(Francois as an Adult)*, Juliette Rennes *(Martine as a Child)*, Caroline Pochon *(Martine as a Teen)*, Anne Gisel Glass, Fabrice Luchini, Patrick Bauchau, Francoise Bette, Francoise Michaud, Laurent Peters, Rosine Cadoret, Vincent Martin, Julien Bertheau, Philippe de Brugada, Robert Deslandes, Michel Cremades, Anne Macina, Gerard Dubois, Charly Chemouny, Mouss, Alexandra Vidal, Stephanie Vidal, Emmanuelle Collomb, Florence Collomb, Anne Loisel, Emmanuelle Loisel.

Costa-Gavras, the director of such fine political thrillers as MISSING and Z, tries his hand at comedy this time around and is less than successful. The family business of the title is safecracking, and as the film opens, a young boy, Romor, is teased by his friends because his father is in prison—but not for long. Papa Hallyday and his longtime partner and friend Marchand are soon out of the joint and back to their old tricks. However, they are not your average thieves. The preparations for each of their "projects" are painstakingly detailed, as if they were mounting an invasion, or, more to the point, launching a new business. Hallyday and Marchand are very modern criminals indeed, and their training includes mind-and-body preoccupations like vitamins and meditation. When zero hour arrives, Hallyday's wife, Ardant, waits anxiously at home, trying to calm her nerves by playing the cello. Eventually the day arrives when Romor demands to get in on the act. Hallyday is reluctant at first, but eventually takes him along on a disastrous night-time heist. Sent to get a glass of water for his perspiring father, Romor starts a chain of events that culminates with a water pipe loosing a jet stream that sends the thieves rushing off. As years go by, the boy (now played by Martin) becomes an asset to the operation. Because Martin is something of an electronics genius, the thieves can take on more challenging projects, aided by increasingly sophisticated tools of the trade. Before long, they shift their targets from jewels to *objets d'art* and the quality of their lives skyrockets. When they achieve international fame, Hallyday and Marchand venture to New York to conduct merger negotiations with the Mafia. Upon their return they learn that Martin wants out so he can be apprenticed to a furniture maker. Hallyday will not hear of it since it is Martin's talents that the syndicate wants to acquire. He keeps his son under house arrest until Martin agrees to go along with the program. However, Martin turns the tables when he calls the police and informs on his father and Marchand, who are hauled away.

Possessed of an odd tone that vacillates between melancholy and mirth, FAMILY BUSINESS is never really "ha-ha" funny. The humor comes primarily from the incongruity of its situations. Romor is read the riot act when he steals a bicycle because the last thing the family business needs is that kind of publicity. Likewise, little sister Rennes shows a precocious proclivity for theft, and though she is discouraged, she is aware of the nature of the trade the family plies at a tender age. Then, of course, there is the "white collar," holistic approach to crime that Marchand and Hallyday take, and the new twist they add to their odd criminal personas with the goofy, Mafia-inspired attire they sport on the return from the States. At the same time, the film's underlying melancholy is also the result of the odd nature of their business. Although the family (including Marchand) holds meetings to make decisions, dissent is out of the question, and the relationships of the family members are characterized by missed communication and increasingly divergent goals. By the film's end Hallyday has so lost touch with his wife, daughter, and son that the only way for them to continue as a family is to see him behind bars. FAMILY BUSINESS is never very funny nor is it particularly dramatically satisfying, and the performances are serviceable but little more. It is not that the film is offensive in any way, or even that it is particularly boring; rather, it would seem that Costa-Gavras, an inspired film-maker when working at his metier, has merely overstepped himself.

p, Michele Ray-Gavras; d&w, Constantin Costa-Gavras (based on the novel by Francis Ryck); ph, Robert Alazraki (Eastmancolor); m. Georges Delerue; ed, Marie-Sophie Dubus; art d, Eric Simon.

Crime/Comedy **(PR:C MPAA:NR)**

FAMILY VIEWING† (1987, Can.) 86m Ego Film Arts-Ontario Film Development-Canada Council-Ontario Arts Council/Cinephile c

David Hemblen *(Stan)*, Aidan Tierney *(Van)*, Gabrielle Rose *(Sandra)*, Arsinee Khanjian *(Aline)*, Selma Keklikian *(Armen)*, Jeanne Sabourin *(Aline's Mother)*, Rose Sarkisyan *(Van's Mother)*, Vasag Baghboudarian *(Young Van)*, David Mackay, Hrant Alianak, John Shafer, Garfield Andrews, Edwin Stephenson, Aino Pirskanen, Souren Chekijian, Johnnie Eisen, John Pellatt.

Recent college graduate Tierney lives with his oversexed father, Hemblen, and Dad's mistress, Rose. Mom has abandoned the family and the nasty Hemblen has stuck his mother-in-law (Armen) in a nursing home, much to Tierney's chagrin. While visiting Armen, Tierney strikes up an acquaintance with call girl Khanjian, whose mother shares a room with Armen, and the two of them conspire to free Armen from the home.

d&w, Atom Egoyan; ph, Robert Macdonald, Peter Mettler; m, Michael Danna; ed, Atom Egoyan, Bruce Macdonald; art d, Linda Del Rosario.

Drama **(PR:NR MPAA:NR)**

FAREWELL† (1987, USSR) 128m Mosfilm/Sovexportfilm c (PROSHCHANIE)

Stefaniya Staniuta, Lev Durov, Alexei Petrenko, Vadim Yakovenko, Maya Bulgakova.

Construction of a dam in Siberia forces the relocation of a number of inhabitants, including those of the village of Maytora. The story focuses on an elderly woman who has lived in Maytora all her life and her son who helps her survive the trauma of moving.

d, Elem Klimov; w, Larisa Shepitko, Rudolf Turin, German Klimov (based on the novel *Farewell to Matyora* by Valentin Rasputin); ph, Alexei Rodionov, Yuri Shhirtladze, Sergei Tataskin.

Drama **(PR:NR MPAA:NR)**

FARM, THE (SEE: CURSE, THE, 1987)

FATAL ATTRACTION**½ (1987) 119m PAR c

Michael Douglas *(Dan Gallagher)*, Glenn Close *(Alex Forrest)*, Anne Archer *(Beth Gallagher)*, Ellen Hamilton Latzen *(Ellen Gallagher)*, Stuart Pankin *(Jimmy)*, Ellen Foley *(Hildy)*, Fred Gwynne *(Arthur)*, Meg Mundy *(Joan Rogerson)*, Tom Brennan *(Howard Rogerson)*, Lois Smith *(Martha)*, Mike Nussbaum *(Bob Drimmer)*, J.J. Johnston.

Taking in more than $123 million, FATAL ATTRACTION was more than a box-office smash; it was a cultural phenomenon, prompting countless discussions and magazine articles, including a *Time* cover story. Directed by Adrian Lyne, who put the flash in FLASHDANCE and the flesh in 9 1/2 WEEKS, this story of an extramarital fling that turns into a nightmare is an excellent psychological thriller until psychology takes a back seat to thrills in its final minutes. Douglas plays a Manhattan lawyer with a gorgeous wife (Archer) and a cute-as-a-button 6-year-old daughter (Latzen). When he meets Close, an attractive associate editor, at a publishing party, he is intrigued, but unavailable; he is, after all, a happily married man. A weekend approaches and Archer and Latzen are off to visit relatives. A rainstorm, a faulty umbrella, and a chance meeting combine to bring Close and Douglas together over dinner. Talk turns to the topic of consenting adults, and, almost before the captivated Douglas knows it, he and Close have turned the kitchen of her loft apartment into Cupid's gym, doused by the sink faucet as they wrestle. A trip to a dance club follows and, returning from it, their passion unabated, they make wild love in the elevator of her building. The next morning, Douglas is gone, leaving a note behind, but Close coaxes him into spending the day with her. When Douglas tries to say his final goodbye that evening, Close presents him with her slashed wrists. He sees her through the night, and when she seems more rational in the morning, Douglas departs, anxious to see his returning family. Close, however, is anything but rational. Obsessed with Douglas and unwilling to accept the transience of their two-night stand, she visits him at his office, calls him endlessly at work and at home, and eventually informs him that she is pregnant. Refusing an abortion, she demands that Douglas "meet his responsibility." The more Douglas tries to get her out of his life, the harder Close tries to become a part of it. Haunted by the threat of exposure, Douglas is himself walking the edge. When he moves his family to exurbia, Close's methods become more extreme—and violent. Returning home on one occasion, Latzen finds her rabbit's cage empty and Archer discovers the hare boiling on the stove. (In this well-orchestrated sequence, Lyne cuts rapidly between Latzen anxiously running to the hutch and Archer curiously approaching the pot, with Douglas literally caught between the screams of his loved ones.) At this point, Douglas confesses his infidelity. Stung and outraged, Archer throws him out, but before he goes, they call Close to put a stop to her intimidation. Close reacts by picking up Latzen after school and taking her on a roller coaster while Archer frantically searches for her and has a car accident that sends her to the hospital. Close returns the child, but Douglas races to Close's apartment, where their across-the-floor struggle is eerily reminiscent of their earlier sexual escapades. Douglas stops short of killing Close, leaving her with a knife that seems destined for her wrists. Back at the house, a scarred and bruised Archer prepares a bath while downstairs Douglas boils water for tea and locks the doors. Archer wipes steam from the mirror; Close glares back at her from it, wielding a knife. The tub overflows and water seeps through the ceiling, but only the dog notices. Archer's screams, drowned out by the whistling teapot, are finally heard by Douglas, who rushes upstairs and struggles with Close, submerging her in the bath water. It's over . . . or is it? With a look of demonic bliss, Close rises out of the tub with the knife, but Archer blasts her with the family pistol.

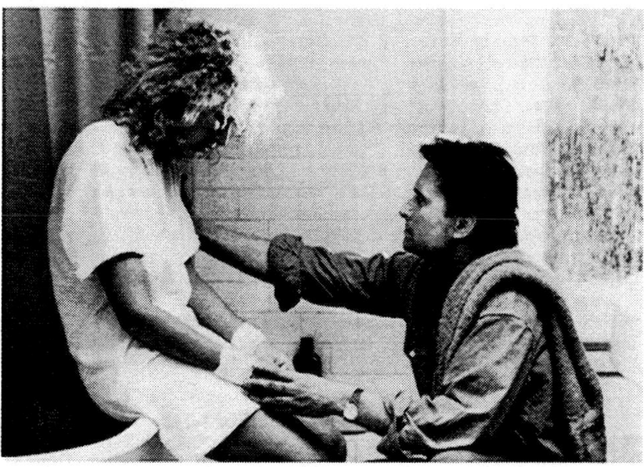

With his first two films, director Lyne proved himself a capable stylist, imbuing his glossy images with palpable sexuality, but his was style without much substance. In FATAL ATTRACTION his glitzy form finds a function. Here he demonstrates an ability to present well-developed characters and explore interesting themes. Much of the credit for this, however, should go to screenwriter James Dearden, who has created a set of believable characters, placed them in a familiar situation, and then drastically upped the stakes. The motivations for the characters' actions are, for the most part, carefully provided; their psychologies plausibly worked out. It is suggested, for example, that Close is somewhat unbalanced even before her encounter with Douglas—the result of having witnessed the death of her father while a young child. Moreover, there is the ring of truth in the pain of a woman who finds a "great" man and can't have him because he's already taken. Douglas also reacts as one might expect a man in his position to. He has a wonderful wife and child, but is caught up in the passion of the moment, overcome by the charms of an extraordinarily seductive woman. Understandably, he is reluctant to continue the affair. Unfortunately, psychological concerns are thrown out the window in the final reel when the film degenerates into an exercise in genre pyrotechnics. To be sure audiences are brought to the edges of their seats, but in the process a very good film is compromised. The blame for this doesn't rest entirely with Lyne or Dearden, in that the producers tested the filmmakers' original ending and preview audiences found it less than satisfying. The thrill-a-minute conclusion was then shot and substituted. (In the original ending, Close commits suicide—accompanied by "Madame Butterfly"—after setting up Douglas to take the fall by leaving his fingerprints on the knife. Reportedly the producers considered retaining that ending for the Japanese release of the picture.) The producers decided to risk disapproval by the critics in hopes of box-office success, and (aided, no doubt, by the film's outstanding trailer) were vindicated not only at the box office but also by a number of critics. For other critics, Close's prompt return from her near-death experience was nothing less than preposterous. The entire final sequence is extremely manipulative and, because it relies on genre shortcuts, predictable. When Douglas goes around locking the doors, it's clear that he's already too late; when the kettle is put on to boil, it is certain its whistle will signal some catastrophe. All of this is to be expected in a genre picture, but until the last reel, FINAL ATTRACTION aspires to be and is much more.

Notwithstanding the ending, the performances are excellent. Playing against type, Close (THE BIG CHILL, MAXIE, THE NATURAL) is overtly sexy, while at the same time, making her obsession and her slide into madness both convincing and pathetic. The scene in which she sits alone in her apartment flipping the lights on and off with "Madame Butterfly" playing mournfully on the stereo invests her desperate actions with a profound emotional reality. To prepare for the role, Close consulted three psychiatrists to be convinced that her character's extreme behavior was possible. She then analyzed the "emotional flow" of her role in terms of musical movements, marking her script with different colored tabs so that she knew exactly where Alex was emotionally at any given moment. After doing this, she decided not to look at the script again unless it was absolutely necessary and chose not to learn her lines until the day she was to say them so she could deliver them intuitively. Douglas, who also gives a performance of considerable depth, was equally committed to his part. Having read *Virgin Kisses*, a book about a man whose life is destroyed by lust, he approached producer Stanley Jaffe with the idea of making a movie about "impossible attraction for someone," only to discover Jaffe was developing a similar project. Jaffe and coproducer Sherry Lansing then proceeded on the project with Douglas in mind. Archer (of TV's "Falcon Crest") also does a nice turn as Douglas' steady but alluring wife. She is particularly believable in her devastated, angry reaction to Douglas' admission of infidelity. If only the ending were a little different. *(Violence, nudity, excessive profanity.)*

p, Stanley R. Jaffe, Sherry Lansing; d, Adrian Lyne; w, James Dearden; ph, Howard Atherton (Technicolor); m, Maurice Jarre; ed, Michael Kahn, Peter E. Berger; prod d, Mel Bourne; art d, Jack Blackman; set d, George DeTitta; cos, Ellen Mirojnick.

Thriller/Romance **(PR:O MPAA:R)**

FATAL BEAUTY*½ (1987) 103m MGM-CST Communications/MGM-UA c

Whoopi Goldberg *(Det. Rita Rizzoli)*, Sam Elliott *(Mike Marshak)*, Ruben Blades *(Carl Jimenez, Rita's Partner)*, Harris Yulin *(Conrad Kroll)*, John P. Ryan *(Lt. Kellerman)*, Jennifer Warren *(Cecile Jaeger)*, Brad Dourif *(Leo Nova)*, Mike Jolly *(Earl Skinner)*, Charles Hallahan *(Deputy Getz)*, David Harris *(Raphael)*, James Le Gros *(Zack Jaeger)*, Neill Barry *(Denny Miflin)*, Mark Pellegrino *(Frankenstein)*, Clayton Landey *(Jimmy Silver)*, Fred Asparagus *(Delgadillo)*, Catherine Blore *(Charlene)*, Michael Champion *(Buzz)*, Steve Akahoshi *(Shigeta)*, Richard Milholland *(Charlie)*, David Dunard *(Cowboy Hat)*, Cheech Marin *(Bartender)*, James Smith *(Ritchie)*, Larry Hankin *(Jerry Murphy)*, Michael DeLorenzo *(Falco)*, Rick Telles *(Epifanio)*, Carlos Cervantes *(Basqual)*, Emilia Ayarza *(Candy)*, Ebbe Roe Smith *(Marty)*, Walter Robles *(Clay)*, M.C. Gainey *(Barndollar)*, Bernie Hern *(Mike Weinstein)*, Prince Hughes *(Big Bubba)*, Jim Bentley *(Paramedic)*, Lucia Lexington *(Stripper)*, Jane Chung *(Chinese Lady)*, Ellarye *(Chinese Daughter)*, Phil Chong *(Chinese Father)*, Joycelyne Lew *(Chinese Mother)*, Jonathan Wong *(Chinese Son)*, Tom Spiroff *(Cop in Kitchen)*, William Martin Brennan *(1st Assistant Chef)*, Read Morgan *(Fletch)*, Cliff Murdock *(Len)*, Belinda Mayne *(Traci)*, Celeste Yarnall *(Laura)*, Sandra Bogan *(Teri)*, Parker Whitman *(Coroner's Attendant)*, Dower Phillips, Josh Pickard *(Teenagers)*.

Here's a picture that should have been called "Fatal Turkey." With the success of FATAL ATTRACTION, one might think that this title was hastily tacked on to take advantage of the fame of that box-office smash, but that's not the case because the title here is very much a part of the movie. This marks the third dud in a row for Whoopi Goldberg, with the promise of more to come unless she and her representatives stop trying to make her into an Eddie Murphy with curves. Goldberg is a police detective by the name of Rizzoli, though how she came to get that most Italian name is never mentioned. She has a personal vendetta against drug dealers and keeps a list of all the people she knew who have died due to narcotics. In the course of her investigations, she dresses up as a streetwalker and, just as she's about to arrest a peddler, she spies a real hooker being beaten. She tries to intervene but winds up having to shoot the man after he attacks her. This tips the dealer off and he escapes. There's a drug-mixing room manned by several Asians and one of them is the best customer for the stuff. He's higher than a satellite and has been packaging glassine envelopes with pure powder. His hand is so unsteady that when he marks the envelope with the name "Fatal Beauty," it is somewhat awry, so these lethal packets can be spotted easily by anyone who knows what's happened. Two hoodlums come into the heavily guarded room and machine-gun everyone there. Goldberg makes a connection between the now-dead dealer and narcotics kingpin Yulin, who lives in guarded, gated splendor on a huge estate. She manages to elude the security forces, chieftained by Elliott, and confronts Yulin. He has such good connections with the city politicians that he is able to have her called off. Then, in a logic hole large enough to fly Howard Hughes' "Spruce Goose" through, Yulin assigns Elliott to "keep an eye on her." This, of course, forces the two to be close and Elliott starts to realize that his boss is a criminal. Not that he didn't know it before; he just turned the other way. Yulin's cover is that he is a legitimate businessman and land developer, but anyone with Elliott's presumed intelligence should fathom that Yulin is as Kosher as Porky Pig. Goldberg and her partner, Blades, continue their peregrinations through a Los Angeles that exists only in director Holland's imagination. There is a huge (and wholly fictitious) street downtown where drugs are bought and sold with the ease of ice cream cones and Goldberg, with Elliott following her, goes there to find out more because, by this time, "Fatal Beauty" has hit the streets and people are dying in droves. A huge shoot-out follows and Goldberg and Elliott manage to work together to escape the hail of bullets that rains down upon them. Dourif is a killer with Jolly as his aide, and they use their machine guns to cut down anyone in their way. It's not too long before Goldberg and Elliott have to face them in a shoot-out at a shopping mall with hundreds of people ducking the bullets. The picture ends with Elliott having been shot, but it is presumed he will recover and see Goldberg again after he serves a short term in jail for bad judgement, something the makers of this film should also be forced to do.

There is one standout scene between Goldberg and Elliott as she explains why she has this vendetta against anyone who traffics in drugs. This solitary sequence shows that Goldberg is able to touch the heart. A few good cameos dot the film's landscape, most notably by Cheech Marin (of Cheech and Chong). There is also a corking good performance by Catherine Blore—one of the busiest voice-over actresses in Los Angeles—as a prostitute who dies as a result of an overdose. Ryan is wasted in the standard police lieutenant part that we've seen on TV for the last 30 years. If the screenplay had paid more attention to punctuating the carnage with a few contrapuntal quiet times, such as the aforementioned confession from Goldberg that her own daughter died of drugs, there might have been enough contrast to make the action make sense. Director Holland handles action well and obviously feels more comfortable with guns and crashing vehicles than human revelation. Among the locations used for the film were Los Angeles' trendy Melrose Avenue and a Pasedena mansion that hit the newspapers in 1987 as one of the properties reputedly owned by Ferdinand Marcos. After her Broadway debut under the guidance of Mike Nichols and her Oscar-nominated performance in THE COLOR PURPLE, Goldberg has appeared in JUMPING JACK FLASH, BURGLAR, and now this. Her next picture is TELEPHONE and there is already a great deal of controversy surrounding it, with the director suing the film company because of certain edits. FATAL BEAUTY had been given an "X" rating until some cuts were made in the film's violence. If one wonders why Goldberg accepted this job after it was turned down by Cher, one need only know that she was paid $2.25 million for her work, and that was after the failure of her previous two movies. So there *is* such a thing as failing upward in the movie business. Songs include: "Sin City" (Harold Faltermeyer, Scott Wilk, Linda Never; performed by War), "On the Edge of Love" (Cynthia Weil, Scott Cutler; performed by Miki Howard), "Criminal" (Sylvester Levay, Tom Whitlock; performed by Shannon), "Make It My Night" (Danny Sembello, Tony Haynes; performed by Donna Allen), "Casanova" (Reggie Calloway; performed by Levert), "Didn't I Blow Your Mind" (Mic Murphy, David Frank; performed by the System), "Red Hot" (Debbie Gibson; performed by Gibson), "Just That Type of Girl" (Bernadette Cooper, Cornelius Mimms, John Bokowski; performed by Madame X). *(Substance abuse, violence, profanity.)*

p, Leonard Kroll; d, Tom Holland; w, Hilary Henkin, Dean Riesner (based on a story by Bill Svanoe); ph, David M. Walsh (Metrocolor); m, Harold Faltermeyer; ed, Don Zimmerman; prod d, James William Newport; set d, E.C. Chen; cos, Aggie Guerard Rodgers; m/l, Harold Faltermeyer, Scott Wilk, Linda Never, Cynthia Weil, Scott Cutler, Sylvester Levay, Tom Whitlock, Danny Sembello, Tony Haynes, Reggie Calloway, Mic Murphy, David Frank, Debbie Gibson, Bernadette Cooper, Cornelius Mimms, John Bokowski; makeup, Mike Germain, Joe McKinney; spec eff, Kenneth D. Pepiot; stunts, Walter Scott.

Action/Drama **(PR:O MPAA:R)**

FEDERICO FELLINO'S INTERVISTA (SEE: INTERVISTA, 1987, It.)

FEEL THE HEAT (SEE: CATCH THE HEAT, 1987)

FELDMANN CASE, THE*½** (1987, Norway) 94m Marcus-Norsk-Esselte Video-Sunnmorsbanken-Kodak Norge/Norsk Film A/S c (OVER GRENSEN)

Bjorn Sundquist *(Arnfinn Madsen)*, Sverre Anker Ousdal *(Mikkel Arness)*, Inger Lise Rypdal *(Holly)*, Ingerid Vardund *(Rakel Feldmann)*, Finn Kvalem *(Jacob Feldmann)*, Oivind Berven *(Harald Sagstuen)*, Trond Braerne *(Paul Plassen)*, Terje Dahl *(Ole Sagstuen)*, Henrik Scheele.

Producer-turned-director Bente Erichsen's first feature is a detective story based on the true case of Rakel and Jacob Feldmann. The Feldmanns were executed by resistance members who were guiding the couple to the border as they were fleeing occupied Norway in 1942. The film focuses on the postwar investigation and the trial of the resistance members. Sundquist, playing a young journalist, is skeptical of the killers' claim that the execution was necessary because the Feldmanns were too old and feeble to make the journey, and their condition jeopardized the entire operation. He uncovers evidence that the wealthy Feldmanns were carrying large amounts of cash with them. He speculates the killers were motivated by greed and possibly anti-Semitism. He is joined by police detective Ousdal on a trip to the small village on the Norwegian border where the incident occurred. For Ousdal, a former resistance member, the investigation brings back many memories, and rekindles an affair with Rypdal, who has important information relating to the case. The villagers are united in their refusal to cooperate with the investigation, but eventually the killers are brought to trial. Though Rypdal offers testimony that indicates the killings were not necessary, the evidence is inconclusive and the men are acquitted.

The film is not so much concerned with uncovering evil as it is with the liberating power of truth. As the investigation unfolds, long-buried guilt is exposed and must be confronted. Though ostensibly a mystery, the film breaks with the conventions of the genre to such a degree that it becomes more of a psychological drama. The film is expertly crafted with strong performances by Sundquist and Ousdal. The movie was shown at the 1987 Chicago Film Festival. *(Adult situations.)*

p, Jeanette Sundby, Bente Erichsen; d&w, Bente Erichsen (based on a novel by Sigurd Senje); ph, Rolv Haan (Eastmancolor); m, Nissa Nyberget; ed, Bjorn Breigutu; cos, Alain Touzinaud.

Historical/Biographical **(PR:O MPAA:NR)**

FIERAS EN BRAMA† (1987, Mex.) 97m Cinematografica Intercontinental-Cinematografica Jalisco/Peliculas Mexicanas c (Trans: Savage Creatures in Heat)

Valentin Trujillo *(Pedro)*, Sasha Montenegro *(Elisa)*, Eric del Castillo *(Don Rodrigo)*, Monica Sanchez Navarro *(Maria)*, Don Raul de Anda *(Don Porfirio)*, Gilberto de Anda *(Juan)*, Gilberto Trujillo, Ada Carrasco, Edgardo Gazcon.

On the eve of taking his vows, a novice returns to his village to find himself tempted by the local vixen. He is tested not only in the ways of the flesh but by a gang of thugs who taunt him into physical violence. The film stars Trujillo, one of Mexico's more popular action stars.

p, Edgardo Gazcon, Raul de Anda; d, Gilberto de Anda; w, T. Serranda (with adaptation by Dean St. Gilbert); ph, Antonio de Anda; m, Ernesto Cortazar; ed, Francisco Chiu.

Action **(PR:NR MPAA:NR)**

FINAL TAKE: THE GOLDEN AGE OF MOVIES*** (1987, Jap.) 118m Shochiku c (KINEMA NO TENCHI)

Narimi Arimori *(Koharu Tanaka)*, Kiyoshi Atsumi *(Kihachi, Her Father)*, Kiichi Nakai *(Kenjiro Shimada)*, Chieko Baisho *(Yuki)*, Koshiro Matsumoto *(Kida, Studio Head)*, Keiko Matsuzaka *(Sumie Kawahima)*, Kei Suma *(Ogura)*, Ittoku Kishibe *(Ogata, Film Director)*, Chishu Ryu *(Tomo, Studio Janitor)*.

An often fascinating look at the early days of film production in Japan that is, unfortunately, hampered by some cliche plotting and a very diffuse narrative. Set in 1933, the film stars Narimi Arimori as a beautiful and naive young girl who sells candy at the local movie theater. Spotted by Kishibe, a famous film director patterned after the great Yasujiro Ozu, Arimori is offered a chance to become a movie actress. Stuck playing bit parts, Arimori becomes frustrated at her lack of acting ability and downright embarrassed when uttering a single line requires more than a dozen takes. Although disappointed, Kishibe has faith in the girl and allows her to get more experience from other directors working at Shochiku's Ofuna Studios. Eventually Arimori gets her big break when the studio's leading actress elopes and causes a scandal just as a prestigious production of the oft-filmed classic "Floating Weeds" is about to begin shooting under Kishibe's direction. Under protest from studio chief Matsumoto, the desperate Kishibe gives the inexperienced Arimori the lead. All goes well until the climactic scene which requires an intensity of emotion that Arimori is unable to muster. After a full day of wasted takes, an angry Kishibe closes down the set and vows to continue trying the next morning. Upset and frustrated, Arimori tells her ailing father, Atsumi, of her desire to quit acting. Sensing her despair, Atsumi, an unsuccessful stage actor in his youth, tells his daughter of her late mother's tragic life and deep dark secret—that Arimori was conceived out of wedlock and abandoned by her real father. Atsumi married Arimori's mother and gave her child his name. Shocked and ashamed that the man she assumed was her father is, in fact, her stepfather, Arimori runs off to her room sobbing. However, the next day at the studio, Arimori is able to call up these emotions and use them in her big scene—which she performs flawlessly on the first take. The film turns out to be a hit and Arimori suddenly becomes the most popular movie actress in Japan.

A loving tribute to the golden age of Japanese film production, FINAL TAKE offers a wonderful behind-the-cameras glimpse of the industry's infancy. The hustle and bustle of studio life is vividly conveyed as the actors and technicians rush to punch in on time, while the writers and directors slouch in their offices brainstorming ideas for new films. In one of the film's highlights, a young assistant director pours his heart and soul into an ultraserious screenplay entitled "Caged Bird," only to see that another director has taken it and made it into a ribald slapstick comedy. While the pure-joy-of-moviemaking aspects of this film are quite interesting and entertaining, director Yamada gets bogged down with innumerable subplots that merely serve to confuse the narrative. One such subplot concerns the young assistant director's relationship with his best friend, a young Communist wanted by the police. In yet another, a very popular and vain actor comes to grips with his stagnant career. While these scenes broaden the film's scope, they are also poorly developed and simply digress from the main thrust of the film. There is also an unfortunate amount of melodrama that rarely rises above the cliche. Both Arimori and the assistant director are made to suffer before being able to blossom as artists; the terminally ill Atsumi dies quietly in his seat while watching the premiere of his daughter's first starring role (the scene is so touching that Yamada actually pulls it off); there is a wise old janitor (played by Ozu favorite Ryu) who knows a rising star when he sees one; etc. Luckily the rest of the film rises above such banalities, leaving behind a heartfelt and nostalgic celebration of the early days of motion pictures.

p, Yoshitaro Nomura, Shigemi Sugisaki, Nobutoshi Masmuoto, Kiyoshi Shimazu; d, Yoji Yamada; w, Hisashi Inoue, Taichi Yamada, Yoshitaka Asama, Yoji Yamada; ph, Tetsuo Takaba; m, Naozumi Yamamoto; art d, Mitsuo Dekawa.

Drama **(PR:A MPAA:NR)**

FINAL TEST, THE† (1987, Hong Kong) 98m Bo Ho-Golden Harvest Group c/b&w

Wai Tin Chi *(Ben)*, Chin Siu Ho *(Plant Foreman)*, Debra Sim *(Plant Doctor)*.

Set in the 21st Century with a plot borrowed from OUTLAND (1981), THE FINAL TEST deals with a factory security chief (Wai Tin Chi) who learns that a foreman is secretly injecting employees with an addictive drug in an effort to make them completely dependent upon the company. Company executives hire a bunch of bad guys to kill Wai Tin Chi before he can reveal the secret, but the good guy beats them all. (In Cantonese; English subtitles.)

p, Leonard Ho; d&w, Lo Kin.

Science Fiction **(PR:NR MPAA:NR)**

FIRE AND ICE** (1987) 95m Concorde c/bw

John Eaves *(John)*, Suzy Chaffee *(Suzy)*, John Denver *(Narrator)*, John Cooper *(John's Voice)*, Tom Sims, Steve Link, Kelby Anno, Matt Schweitzer, Mike Waltze, Philippe Bernard, Jan Bucher, Kevin Wright, Richard Pinheiro.

Ski aficionados will find FIRE AND ICE to be something of a minor masterpiece. Although there's a sliver of plot, the film is largely comprised of action-packed ski footage, staged in numerous and often imaginative ways. Eaves plays a French-Canadian skier who is determined to catch up with Chaffee, a fellow skier whom he meets by accident and falls in love with immediately. He hitchhikes from New York to Aspen, fantasizing about skiing and Chaffee all the way. So much for the minuscule story line. The real raison d'etre of the production is to show scene after scene of the skiers engaged in various activities, not all of which take place on the slopes. There's a bicycle chase through Manhattan, glacial skiing, windsurfing, ice boating, hang gliding, snow boarding, fireworks, airborne somersaults, new-wave-fashion skiing, and even a little break dancing tossed in for good measure. FIRE AND ICE comes off like a second unit director's fantasy film, completely forgoing story for filler material. It should come as no surprise then that the film's director, Willy Bogner, was the guiding force behind the action sequences for several James Bond pictures, including ON HER MAJESTY'S SECRET SERVICE and A VIEW TO A KILL. His casting is appropriate, to say the least. Canadian John Eaves is skiing's freestyle world champion, while Suzy Chaffee (aka: Suzy Chapstick) was a member of the US Olympic ski team. Unfortunately, their collective acting ability doesn't exactly set the screen on fire. The film isn't helped much by the dubbing, an amateurish job that doesn't always follow the actors' lip movements. Eaves' screen voice was provided by John Cooper, whose French-Canadian accent has an uncanny resemblance to Pepe Lepew's. In many ways Eaves' relentless pursuit of Ms. Chaffee is not unlike the amorous adventures of the Looney Toons' *skunk de peu*, though the old Warner Brothers' cartoons hold far more entertainment. The thin story is held together by narrator John Denver, whose down-home earnestness grows a little tiresome after the first 10 minutes. But overall, none of this really matters. Eaves' and Chaffee's downhill abilities, coupled with Bogner's often exciting camerawork, are the real stars here. Bogner captures the speed and excitement of skiing, following his stars with long, deep focus takes. The camera zooms down a bobsled run, zips through skiers's legs, and nimbly runs under a truck, among other feats. This film was also reviewed in an 80 minute version. *(Adult situations, sexual situations.)*

p,d,w&ph, Willy Bogner; m, Harold Faltermeyer, Gary Wright, Panarama, Alan Parsons, John Denver; ed, Petra Von Oelffen, Claudia Travnecek; spec eff, Richard Richtsfeld.

Romance **Cas.** **(PR:A MPAA:PG)**

FIREHOUSE zero (1987) 91m Too Hot/Academy Home Ent. c

Gianna Rains *(Barrett Hopkins)*, Martha Peterson *(Shannon Murphy)*, Renee Raiford *(Violet Brown)*, Gideon Fountain *(John Anderson)*, Peter MacKenzie *(Dickson Willoughby III)*, Joe Viviani *(Lt. Wally)*, Jonathan Mandel *(Timmy Ryan)*, Henry David Keller *(Warren Frump)*, Parnes Cartwright *(Darnell Fibbs)*, Peter Onorati *(Ron J. Sleek)*, Andy Ryan *(Sid Finegold)*, Dog Thomas *(The Extinguisher)*, Dick Biel *(Ward Hopkins)*, Joanne Fox *(June Hopkins)*, Kevin Delaney *(Poindexter)*, Maurice J. DeGennaro *(Murray)*, Ralph Douglas *(Pops)*, Butch Ford *(Jerome)*, Kenny Edwards *(Zone)*, Kristin Roudebush *(Estee)*, Susan Van Deven *(Bunny)*, Elizabeth Richardson *(Lizzy)*, Donna Davidge *(Donna)*, Jamie Lesser *(A.D.)*, Ruth Collins *(Bubbles)*, Jennifer Stahl *(Mindy)*, Charles Tighe, Sr. *(Watchman)*, Charles Tighe, Jr. *(Pumper Driver)*, Mike Polding *(Ladder Driver)*, Ken Lieberman *(Hood)*, Sasha *(Sparky the Dog)*.

A moronic and technically inept sex "comedy" about a trio of sexy young women who become fire fighters and continuously turn the heads of their under-sexed coworkers. Released straight to video for reasons that become obvious after only a couple of minutes, FIREHOUSE is set at Hose Company No. 1, a fire company that has come under attack for being insensitive to the neighborhood's needs. These firemen are a brain-dead bunch of rowdies who drink large quantities of beer, hang out in strip joints, and know nothing at all about putting out a fire. Shortly after the three female recruits—Rains, Peterson, and Raiford—are hired, they uncover a plan engineered by a real estate developer named Frump. The developer has paid arsonists to torch a number of buildings in the neighborhood, which he then buys out. After some supposedly zany mishaps, the girls triumph and the developer is put behind bars.

Aspiring to do for firemen what POLICE ACADEMY did for police recruits, FIREHOUSE doesn't even come close. In comparison with FIREHOUSE, POLICE ACADEMY is intellectually stimulating. This smoldering entry has all the usual stereotypes and such hilarious antics as a bearded fireman running around dressed as a nun and a fire chief berating the girls with his thick Irish accent. And who can forget all the jokes about fire hoses? Ha-ha-ha—sounds real funny doesn't it? There are also the obligatory topless girls and the sophomoric sexual comments which accompany such scenes. Films buffs will groan when one worldly fire fighter shows his faulty knowledge of the cinema by referring to the "French neorealists, especially Alain Robbe-Grillet." One truly hopes the director is joking, since the neorealists are Italian and Robbe-Grillet is neither Italian nor a neorealist. *(Excessive nudity, sexual situations, profanity.)*

p, J. Christian Ingvordsen, Steven Kaman; d, J. Christian Ingvordsen; w, J. Christian Ingvordsen, Steven Kaman (based on a story by Rick Marx, J. Christian Ingvordsen, Steven Kaman); ph, Steven Kaman; m, Michael Montes, David Biglin; ed, Steven Kaman; prod d, Debbie Devilla; art d, Beth Rubino; m/l, Dan McCafferty, Bill Barnes, Steve Johnson, Butch Ford, Jimmy Giardi; spec eff, Scott Gagnon.

Comedy **Cas.** **(PR:O MPAA:R)**

FLICKS* (1987) 78m Flicks/United c (AKA: HOLLYWEIRD; LOOSE JOINTS)

Pamela Sue Martin *(Liz)*, Joan Hackett *(Capt. Grace)*, Martin Mull *(Arthur/Tang)*, Betty Kennedy *(Beth Lyle)*, Richard Belzer, Barry Pearl, Lincoln Kilpatrick, Paula Victor, Danny Dayton, George [Buck] Flower, Voices of: Harry Shearer, Sandra Kearns, Gregory Mark Lewis.

Originally shot in 1981, FLICKS is a painfully unfunny movie spoof that was never given a theatrical release and for good reason. Despite some of the people involved (including such talented comedians as Martin Mull, Richard Belzer, and Harry Shearer), this is a moronic mess, which only saw light of day because of video distribution. Essentially the film is a series of blackout sketches poking fun at such things as newsreels, cartoons, and coming attractions. There are also a couple of extended film parodies. "Night of the Living Corpse" is a mini-horror film featuring Mull and Betty Kennedy in an all-stops-pulled affair which heaps on cliche after cliche without eliciting much laughter. "Philip Alien, Space Detective" goes after *film noir* and stars Shearer and Sandra Kearns (actually, they provide the voices for actors wearing giant moth suits). They play giant intergalactic moth detectives who arrive on Earth to investigate a crime. Nonetheless, FLICKS may gain some rentals because of the cast's name value.

p, Bert Kamerman, David Axelrod; d, Peter Winograd; w, Larry Arnstein, David Hurwitz, Lane Sarasohn, Peter Winograd; ph, Scott Miller (Movielab Color); m, John Morgan; ed, Barbara Pokras; prod d, Jack McAnelly; art d, Philip Thomas; set d, Linda Burbank; cos, Pat Tonnema; spec eff, Anthony Doublin; stunts, David Cass; animation, Kirk Henderson. *(Profanity, nudity.)*

Comedy **Cas.** **(PR:O MPAA:R)**

FLOWERS IN THE ATTIC*½ (1987) 95m NW-Fries Ent. c

Louise Fletcher *(Grandmother)*, Victoria Tennant *(Corinne)*, Kristy Swanson *(Cathy)*, Jeb Stuart Adams *(Chris)*, Ben Ganger *(Cory)*, Lindsay Parker *(Carrie)*, Marshall Colt *(Father)*, Nathan Davis *(Grandfather)*, Alex Koba *(John Hall)*.

A stilted film adaptation of the bizarre V.C. Andrews' novel which was a massive hit with adolescent teenage girls in 1979 and spawned two equally popular sequels. The film opens on a textbook perfect domestic scene where teenagers Swanson and Adams and their younger siblings, twins Ganger and Parker, all greet their hard-working businessman father (Colt) at the door when he comes home from a trip. Mother Tennant is in the kitchen cooking a sumptuous dinner and all is well in the world. Or is it? There are some vague suggestions of an unnaturally close relationship between dad and his oldest daughter, but before this angle proceeds any further, Colt is killed in a car wreck. With no insurance, no education, no previous job experience, and no money, Tennant is forced to sell the family home and go begging at her rich parents' mansion door. Disinherited because her parents did not approve of her marriage (the children are later told that their mother and father were actually niece and uncle and that they are the product of an unholy incestuous bond), Tennant is now determined to win back her invalid father's love and reap big financial rewards upon his imminent demise. Unfortunately for the children, there is just one catch: Tennant's father (Davis) has never learned of the children's existence, and therefore they must be kept locked in one small room while Tennant works to regain his love. Watched over by their pinched-faced, Bible-toting grandmother (Fletcher), the children are not allowed to make noise and are visited briefly once every day by Tennant. The children's only source of amusement is the huge attic which they have access to from their closet. As the weeks drag on the children create a world of their own among the dusty old things in the attic and wait patiently for their mother to complete her mission. More time passes and Tennant's visits become infrequent and eventually end. Growing suspicious, Swanson and Adams venture out of their room and secretly witness a party where Tennant dances with a handsome man. Soon after, one of the twins, Ganger, grows very ill and is taken away. The remaining children are later told that the boy has died. Adams discovers that their food is being poisoned, and upon further investigation, they realize that their grandfather has long-since died and that their mother is trying to kill them to gain the inheritence (she won't get a dime if she has kids). To make matters worse, Tennant plans to wed her handsome lawyer (the man with whom she was dancing). On the wedding day, the kids conk Fletcher on the head and escape the room. Just as the wedding vows are being exchanged, the three emaciated children confront their mother in front of hundreds of guests. Horrified, Tennant runs out onto the terrace and accidentally falls, hanging herself on her veil. Having triumphed over evil, the three children leave the mansion never to return.

Considering that incest, murder, sadomasochism, repression, and warped religious zeal are the main themes here, the film version of Andrews' novel is incredibly tame and downright boring. Screenwriter/director Bloom has produced a bad script (Wes Craven had written an earlier draft) and his direction of young actors is even worse. The dialog seems to be taken directly from the novel and is recited by the cast in a laughably stiff and deliberate manner that bears no resemblance to the natural cadence of human speech. Teen actors Swanson and Adams struggle in vain with the awkward dialog and try hard to be convincing. Their younger costars, Ganger (who looks like Basil Rathbone's curly haired son in SON OF FRANKENSTEIN) and Parker, are hopelessly lost, given little direction, and allowed to become annoyingly precocious. Tennant turns in a one-note performance that conveys no sympathy for, or even simple understanding of, her character. She is distant and aloof from her first scene to her last, although doubtless the shallow script did not help her cause. Only Fletcher manages to wring some ambiguity from her role, and she handles the wretched dialog admirably. (Author Andrews makes a cameo appearance as a maid that was filmed shortly before her death.) As to Bloom's seeming avoidance of the more sensationalistic aspects of the novel (the teenage siblings engage in some incestuous behavior during their captivity), the director's original cut of the film faced these issues head on. A preview audience stocked with rabid fans of the novel became uncomfortable and disturbed when the "naughty" passages that they had thrilled to in the novel were enacted before their eyes. Because of adverse audience reaction, Bloom was forced to eliminate the incest angle and cut most of a scene where Tennant strips before her invalid father and is whipped by her mother. The ending was also altered significantly from the one in the book, a move which required extensive reshooting by another director. Nothing very explicit survives in the final cut, leaving Andrews' grim ruminations on the horrors of a perverted family life obtuse and undeveloped. Despite the troubled production and the fact that the film was dumped on the market by New World just before the holiday season, the $4 million FLOWERS IN THE ATTIC will easily turn a profit, if only from the patronage of the 24 million readers of V.C. Andrews' novels. *(Adult situations, violence.)*

p, Sy Levin, Thomas Fries; d&w, Jeffrey Bloom (based on the novel by V.C. Andrews); ph, Frank Byers, Gil Hubbs (CFI Color); m, Christopher Young; ed, Gregory F. Plotts; prod d, John Muto; set d, Michele Starbuck; cos, Ann Somers Major; spec eff, Dick Albain.

Thriller **(PR:C-O MPAA:PG-13)**

FLYER, THE½** (1987, Ger.) 102m (DER FLIEGER)

Martin May, Ulrike Kriener, Birgit Franz, Norbert Mahler.

In the provincial town of Coburg, in southeastern Germany, 20-year-old May, the son of a furrier, spends nine-to-five working for a large insurance company. When his time is his own, he likes to hang glide and dream of traveling to Bolivia to set a world record by gliding from the peak of Mount Palomani—19,000 feet high in the Andes—to Ixiamas on the other side of the jungle. He has even built a detailed model of the route such a flight would take. His other favorite activities are rock 'n' roll dancing with his teenage girl friend and insurance fraud—helping policy holders collect benefits that technicalities would have prevented them from receiving. He meets a journalist who has moved to the Coburg from Berlin and he and this older woman begin an affair. She takes interest in his Bolivian dream and writes an article about it for the local newspaper. May finds himself something of a celebrity, and then the journalist begins lining up sponsors for the adventure, promising their names will be emblazoned on the hang glider's wings. The management of his insurance company pledges a sizeable amount of money and grants him a leave of absence to train. The trip and flight will cost more than 30,000 Deutsche marks, but as the fund-raising campaign nears its goal, May begins to have second thoughts, having learned how difficult a flight it will be and how wild and remote the jungle is should he come down too soon. He

increases the required budget in hopes of prolonging (permanently) his departure. Meanwhile, the insurance company learns of his Robin Hood-like bilking of their coffers, and, knowing that firing him would result in too much bad press, they give him the rest of the money he needs, hoping he won't survive the flight. Having run out of excuses, May and his journalist lover venture to Bolivia, and, accompanied by an American reporter and photographer, they make the taxing climb to Mt. Palomani's peak. Almost delirious from the combination of fear, exhaustion, the effects of the altitude, and anticipation, May takes off, gliding over the beautiful but imposing Andes as the film ends ambiguously.

Though slow-paced and occasionally woodenly acted, this debut feature from director Keusch features more than a little wry humor and is generally engaging. May is an unlikely looking but amiable protagonist to whom one warms as his self-doubts come to the surface and his predicament becomes more threatening. At the heart of the film is a reflection on the effects of celebrity on the newly famous, and a consideration of what is lost. Keusch and screenwriter Timm also ponder the nature of dreams that become reality, suggesting that the dreaming, wishing, and waiting, in some ways, may be more fulfilling—and in May's case much less frightening—than the realization of a dream. However, the film's final image of the exhilarated May implies though it may be terrifying, it is better to take your best shot rather than to be lost in unexamined anticipation. Keusch's depiction of provincial German life is very nearly as intriguing as May's story. It is unlikely that THE FLYER will receive US distribution beyond the festival release it was given in 1987. *(Sexual situations, nudity, profanity in subtitles.)*

p, Michel Bergmann; d, Erwin Keusch; w, Uwe Timm; ph, Jurgen Jurges.

Drama **(PR:O MPAA:NR)**

FONTE DA SAUDADE† (1987, Braz.) 80m Diadema/Embrafilme-Empresa Brasiliero c (Trans: Deep Illusion)

Lucelia Santos *(Barbara/Guida/Alba)*, Norma Bengell, Claudio Marzo, Jose Wilker, Paulo Betti, Xuxa Lopes, Thales Pan Chacon, Chico Diaz.

Set in Ipanema, the film stars Santos as three different women, all of whom live in the same town square. Although their lives and personalities are very different, they all have one thing in common—they lost their father when they were young. Each, therefore, is emotionally maladjusted and has difficulty in romantic relationships.

d, Marcos Altberg; w, Julia Altberg; ph, Pedro Farkas; m, Antonio Carlos Jobim; ed, Carlos Brajsblat; art d, Carlos Prieto.

Drama **(PR:NR MPAA:NR)**

FORAJIDOS EN LA MIRA† (1987, Mex.) 106m Producciones Latinas Americanas-Producciones P.L.A.C. II/Peliculas Mexicanas c (Trans: Outlaws in the Viewfinder)

Sergio Goyri *(Julian Morieta)*, Silvia Manriquez *(Rosa)*, Fernando Casanova *(Marshal)*, Eric del Castillo *(Lucio Alvarez)*, Juan Gallardo *(Pistola Taylor)*, Alejandro Camacho *(Flaco)*, Carlos Rotzinga, Priscila, Antonio Raxel, Ramon Menendez, Benjamin Islas, Regino Herrera, Jose Luis Avendano, Jaime Pizano, Ines Murillo, Rafael Fernandez, Raymundo Gomez, Alejandro de la Pena, Jose Luis Salgado, Manuel Anaya, Fidel Abrego.

A Mexican western with familiar themes of vengeance and justice, starring heart throb Goyri. After avenging the murder of his parents, Goyri becomes a feared gunslinger and marshal. He sends a lawless gang to prison and assumes a quiet family life, but when the gang members are released they come after Goyri for the climactic showdown. Released in the US to New York's Hispanic audiences.

p, Orlando R. Mendoza; d&w, Alberto Mariscal (based on a story by Orlando R. Mendoza, Gilberto de Anda; ph, Manuel Tejeda Monreal; m, Gustavo Cesar Carrion; ed, Angel Camacho Leppe.

Western **(PR:NR MPAA:NR)**

FOREVER, LULU† (1987) 85m Lulu/Tri-Star c

Hanna Schygulla *(Elaine Hines)*, Deborah Harry *(Lulu)*, Alec Baldwin *(Buck)*, Annie Golden *(Diana)*, Paul Gleason *(Robert)*, Dr. Ruth Westheimer *(Herself)*, Raymond Serra *(Alphonse)*, George Kyle *(Pepe)*, Harold Guskin *(Archie)*, Bill Corsair *(Blackmailer)*, Jonathan Freeman *(Don)*, Amos Kollek *(Larry, Publisher)*, Charles Ludlam *(Harvey)*, Cathy Gati *(Lisa)*, Beatrice Pons *(Fortune Teller)*, Sally Jane Heit *(Martha)*, Helen Lloyd Breed *(Landlady)*, Justine Johnson *(Judith Cabot)*, Susan Blommaert *(Jackie Coles)*, Kenny Marino *(Detective Calhoun)*, Joanne Carlo *(Donna)*, Wayne Knight *(Stevie)*, Jennifer Leigh Warren *(Hooker)*, Yvette Edelhart *(Dolores)*, Antonia Rey *(Clara)*, Charles Prior *(Blind Man)*, Andrew Craig *(Crazy Cabbie)*, Everett Quinton *(Waiter)*, Christine Jensen *(Political Activist)*, Anthony Powers *(Bebino)*, Dennis Green *(Kelly)*, Patti Astor *(Mary Anne Zlutnik)*, Judith Cohen *(Charley)*, Earnest Abuba, Sydney D. Sheriff, Jr. *(Muggers)*, Michael Steinhardt *(Ticket Taker)*, Felix Mintz, Lazar Mintz *(Goons)*, Adriane Lenox *(Girl in Strip Club)*, R.L. Ryan *(Fat Man)*, Mike Hodge *(Police Commissioner)*, Clifford Arashi *(Hiroshi)*, Ron Ryan *(Barman)*, Sassy Gearhardt, Bill Masters *(Reporters)*, James Langrall *(Newscaster)*, Joe Lissi *(Cop)*, Bernie Friedman *(Benny)*, Martina Ferenczy, Samantha Louca *(Bar Patrons)*, Julia Robinson *(Street Walker)*.

In and out of the theaters in the blink of an eye, FOREVER, LULU is Amos Kollek's follow-up film to his 1985 debut, GOODBYE, NEW YORK. An independent production picked up for release by Tri-Star Pictures, FOREVER, LULU was savaged by critics before it ever made it to a wide release. Similar to DESPERATELY SEEKING SUSAN, the film stars Schygulla as a German immigrant living in New York's seedy Lower East Side struggling to become a novelist. To make ends meet she writes pornography and works for a toilet-seat manufacturer. Her life quickly goes downhill. Her marriage fails, her sex life is nonexistent, she loses her job, and gets evicted. Driven to the brink of suicide, Schygulla wanders down the street in the rain, brandishing a handgun. A frightened couple hands over a white fur coat, and from there Schygulla's odyssey begins. In the coat she finds a package belonging to the mob, entangling her in an underworld whirlwind involving the police and the mob. She also finds a photo signed "Forever, Lulu." She places ads in the newspaper looking for clues to Lulu's whereabouts. Lulu, played by Harry (the former singer for the seminal New York punk/new wave band Blondie), is an elusive one who pops up every now and again, but isn't united with Schygulla until the picture's end. Along the way, Schygulla gets deeper and deeper into the dark side of New York life, surviving the flurry of death and destruction that goes on around her. Her unpublished novel attracts the attention of a publisher, played by Kollek. The events surrounding her have now made Schygulla into a national celebrity, the book is a great success, and she even lands a spot on Dr. Ruth Westheimer's talk show.

FOREVER, LULU was the first American starring role for Hanna Schygulla, one of the finest actresses in the world and best known for her collaboration with Germany's most prolific director, the late Rainer Werner Fassbinder. Starring in such internationally heralded pictures as Fassbinder's THE BITTER TEARS OF PETRA VON KANT, THE MARRIAGE OF MARIA BRAUN, and LILI MARLEEN; Jean-Luc Godard's PASSION; Margarethe Von Trotta's SHEER MADNESS; and Andrzej Wajda's A LOVE IN GERMANY, Schygulla inexplicably made her first US appearance in the 1986 Chuck Norris actioner THE DELTA FORCE. She then appeared in NBC's 8-hour mini-series "Peter the Great." Her performance in FOREVER, LULU marks the continuation of her questionable choice of films and adds fuel to the theory that there are two Hanna Schygullas working in film today. The film's editing consultant was Ralph Rosenblum, who is best known for his work with Woody Allen.

p,d&w, Amos Kollek; ph, Lisa Rinzler; ed, Jay Freund; prod d, Stephen McCabe; set d, Victor Zolfo; cos, Candace Clements, Barbara Weiss; spec eff, Willie Caban; stunts, Erik Koniger; makeup, Joanna Robinson.

Comedy/Adventure **(PR:NR MPAA:R)**

FORTY DAYS OF MUSA DAGH† (1987) 94m High Investments c

Kabir Bedi *(Gabriel Bagradian)*, Ronnie Carol *(Juliette Bagradian)*, Guy Stockwell *(Simon Tomassian)*, Peter Haskell *(Maris Durand, Reporter)*, David Opatoshu *(Henry Morgenthau, Sr.)*, Michael Constantine *(Talaat Pasha)*, Manuel Kichian *(Kilikian)*, Maurice Sherbanee *(Civil Governor)*, Victoria Woodbeck *(Karoon)*, David Mauro, Sid Haig, John Hoyt, Gilbert Green, Sydney Lassick, Paul King, Robert Wood.

Featuring an international cast, this straight-to-video release deals with one chapter in the long struggle for Armenian independence. In the aftermath of the Russo-Turkish War of 1877-78, a revolutionary nationalist movement was born and a series of uprisings and retaliatory massacres followed as the Armenians sought freedom from the domination of Ottoman Turks. By 1896 as many as 200,000 Armenians had been killed. FORTY DAYS OF MUSA DAGH deals with one of the local rebellions that occurred during 1915, at the height of WW I. Bedi is a businessman and officer in the Turkish army, but, more important, he is Armenian. After he learns that Armenians are being slaughtered in the Syrian desert, Bedi sets about organizing resistance to this bloody oppression. Fearing for the safety of his French wife, Carol, and his son, he tries to send them abroad, but fails. Inspired by Bedi, many of his Armenian compatriots go with him to Mt. Musa Dagh, where they put up a brave defense against the Turks. In the 1930s MGM considered making a film about the events at Mt. Musa Dagh, but the project never got off the ground. This version of the story was filmed in California, though it carries a Turkish copyright.

p, John Kurkjian; d, Sarky Mouradian; w, Alex Hakobian (based on the novel *The Forty Days Of Musa Dagh* by Franz Werfel); ph, Gregory Sandor; m, Jaime Mendoza-Nava; ed, Tony De Zarraga; art d, Randy Ser; cos, Patrick Norris; makeup, Donn Markel.

Historical **Cas.** **(PR:NR MPAA:NR)**

FOURTH PROTOCOL, THE** (1987, Brit.) 119m Fourth Protocol/Lorimar c

Michael Caine *(John Preston)*, Pierce Brosnan *(Maj. Valeri Petrofsky)*, Joanna Cassidy *(Col. Irina Vassilieva)*, Ned Beatty *(Gen. Borisov)*, Betsy Brantley *(Eileen MacWhirter)*, Peter Cartwright *(Jan Marais)*, Sean Chapman *(Capt. Lyndhurst)*, Rosy Clayton *(Susie Adrian)*, David Conville *(Burnham)*, Matt Frewer *(Tom MacWhirter)*, Julian Glover *(Brian Harcourt-Smith)*, Michael Gough *(Sir Bernard Hemmings)*, Jerry Harte *(Prof. Krilov)*, John Horsley *(Sir Anthony Plumb)*, Michael J. Jackson *(Maj. Pavlov)*, Philip Jackson *(Harry Burkinshaw)*, Ray McAnally *(Gen. Karpov)*, Matthew Marsh *(Barry Banks)*, Alan North *(Gen. Govorshin)*, James Older *(Timmy Preston)*, Ronald Pickup *(Dr. Wynne-Evans)*, George Phillips *(Jerry Adrian)*, Ian Richardson *(Sir Nigel Irvine)*, Anton Rodgers *(George Berenson)*, Jiri Stanislav *(Ivan Timoshenko/Winkler)*, Aaron Swartz *(Gregoriev)*, Octavia Verdin *(Jill Dunkley)*, Johnny Allan *(Night Porter)*, Roy Alon *(Russian Seaman)*, Michael Bilton *(Kim Philby)*, Sarah Bullen *(Dorothy)*, Rebecca Burrill *(Nurse)*, Rosy Clayton *(Mrs. Adrian)*, David Conville *(Burnham)*, Cyril Conway *(Military Figure)*, Nancy Crane *(Natasha, Karpov's Secretary)*, Joanna Dickens *(Woman Shopper)*, Sam Douglas *(Russian Soldier)*, Mick Ford *(Sgt. Bilbow)*, Ronnie Golden *(Busker)*, Steve Halliwell *(Plastercast Courier)*, Gordon Honeycombe *(TV Announcer)*, Boris Isarov *(Dresser)*, Julian Jacobson *(Conductor)*, Alexei Jawdokimov *(Aeroflot Pilot)*, Clare Kelly *(Landlady)*, Sally Kinghorn *(Girlfriend)*, Ronnie Laughlin *(Driver at Scene)*, Renos Liondaris, George Zenios *(Greek Cafe Owners)*, Peter Manning *(Violinist)*, Kenneth Midwood *(Chaplain)*, John Murtagh *(Scottish Policeman)*, William Parker *(Cruiser)*, Stephen Persaud *(Black Kid)*, Neville Phillips *(Man in Overcoat)*, Richard Ridings, Christopher Walker *(Skinheads)*, Mark Rolston *(Russian Decoder)*, Michael Seezen *(Joey)*, Patsy Smart *(Preston's Housekeeper)*, Phil Smeeton *(Boyfriend)*, Juanita Waterman *(Black Girl on Underground Train)*, Tariq Yunus *(Immigration Officer)*, Caroline Blakiston *(Angela Berenson)*, Joseph Brady *(Carmichael)*.

THE FOURTH PROTOCOL might just be the fastest cutting-room-to-airplane movie in history, in that it was released aboard British Airtours flights before it got to theaters in Los Angeles. Frederick Forsyth's three previous novels to be made into movies were THE DAY OF THE JACKAL (superb), THE ODESSA FILE (good), and THE DOGS OF WAR (ho-hum, mostly due to Chris Walken's sleepwalking performance). This time, Forsyth took a much more active role, writing the screenplay and functioning as the executive producer. It didn't help much. Based somewhat in reality, this spy thriller concerns the 1968 agreement between the Soviet Union, Britain, and the United States stipulating that none of them would attempt to smuggle a nuclear weapon into the other's country. To do so would mean that there would be no time for an alert, a counter strike, or even to learn who did it. When some maverick Russian and British spies decide to get rid of NATO by arranging just such an operation, Caine is called in to stop the proposed devastation. North is the head honcho at the KGB, a man who will stop at nothing to get his way. To that end, he engages Brosnan, his top agent, and sends him off to England. Brosnan speaks with no accent so he is a perfect choice to put the plan into effect. He checks into a small room in a tiny town that sits next to an air base which is filled with US planes. The whole idea is to make it look as though a nuclear accident has been caused by the Americans. At that same time, Caine is in the process of catching Rodgers, a Russian mole who has been passing secrets to Moscow for years. Rodgers faces the rest of his life in Wormwood Scrubs (or some other equally colorful prison) so he agrees to stay in the employ of Moscow, but to be manipulated by the British forces. By having a double agent unknown to the original spy masters, Britain will have an edge on Moscow and be able to feed whatever information it cares to. Richardson is the chief of British intelligence and keeps a tight rein on the now-turned Rodgers, making certain to hand-feed him only the information they want the Russians to have. Brosnan ensconces himself in the Suffolk town and, one by one, couriers bring him the various elements which make an atomic bomb. A spy in the guise of a merchant seaman is questioned. His cool is cracked, he races away, and is hit and killed by a truck. Caine is the man assigned to this seemingly unimportant case, and when he finds a polonium disc in the dead "sailor's" effects, he puts

two and two together. Lithium and polonium are necessary to make a nuclear detonator, and since it takes less than 10 components to build the bomb, Caine reckons that is what's happening. He quickly tells his boss, Glover, what he's discovered, but Glover thinks that Caine may be paranoid and seeing plots around every corner. After all, there is such a thing as The Fourth Protocol (the secret stipulation of the 1968 treaty) and it's certain that neither the US or the USSR would break it. Richardson, however, thinks Caine may be on to something and tells him to keep going until he runs out of clues.

Meanwhile, there are a few Russians who are also in the dark, as this is a personal operation rather than one through official channels. McAnally is a high-ranking KGB general. He discusses the situation with his pal Beatty and they wonder why Brosnan has been sent on a top secret mission of which they have no knowledge. They correctly reckon that North is the brains behind this but wonder why. McAnally uses his power to get the answer and is now aware of the plot. He marvels at the Machiavellian nuances of North, but he feels the man has gone too far, and that if the truth ever came out, a full-scale war might begin. He tells Beatty and is convinced that they can get North out of his position once they secure the proof. Beatty, who is semi-retired, chickens out. He fears North and the man's tentacles and says that he doesn't want to get involved. Now alone with the realization that he may be the only man who can stop this, McAnally can do nothing more than cogitate on his next move. Richardson and McAnally are old-time rivals, through several changes of administrations. Each thinks he knows the other's weaknesses and strengths, and Richardson doesn't believe that this could have been a McAnally ploy but he's not sure. He sends turncoat Rodgers off to tell McAnally that the jig may soon be up. Meanwhile, Caine is vainly trying to track down everyone who has come into England from an Eastern Bloc country. He is alerted to the fact that an "Austrian" has just arrived with a passport that might have been made in a third-grade forgery class. It's in the possession of Stanislav. Caine does a thorough check on the man and learns he is a Czech agent with close KGB ties. He follows him to a seaside village where Brosnan's short wave radio has been hidden in a place owned by a pair of Greek Communists. Caine stakes out the location but Brosnan doesn't show. He now has everything he needs for the bomb, except the person to assemble it. That's taken care of when Cassidy arrives. She's a nuclear expert and the two of them put the thing together. What Brosnan doesn't know is that she has arranged the timer in such a fashion that he will never be able to get away from Ground Zero in time to live. What she doesn't know is that, once they have made love, he will kill her. Brosnan arrives on his motorcycle at the Greek cafe. He radios his boss that the plan is going according to schedule, then leaves, with Caine on his tail. Brosnan sheds the motorcycle and gets into a car, losing Caine for a while, until a crash on the highway causes Caine to catch up with him again. In a scene not unlike the final one in DAY OF THE JACKAL, Caine catches up with Brosnan just as the Russian is about to turn the bomb on, still not knowing that it will detonate immediately. There's a coda concerning Richardson and his opposite number, McAnally, but it's not needed.

Very heavily plotted, there is hardly a moment in the picture for any characterization. We never learn much about Caine or Brosnan, and the Russian and British spy masters are shown to be either dolts or traitors, which is probably what they are in real life. Richard Burridge added some "additional material" to Forsyth's screenplay, but since that is not the usual credit given out by the Writer's Guild in the US, we can only surmise what that material was. Mackenzie, who also directed Caine in BEYOND THE LIMIT, keeps things moving at a fast pace, aided greatly by Schifrin's score. Forsyth's novel sold almost 8 million copies, but it is doubtful that many people will see this movie. Finland was used to simulate Russia for the Soviet scenes, with the movie company putting up stakes at Rovaniemi, on the edge of the Arctic Circle. The British scenes were shot in Milton Keynes, a town which has only been around for less than two decades. Interiors were done at Elstree. Forsyth's foreign correspondent background has stood him in good stead and made him a millionaire many times over as he has used his experience as fodder for his literary cannons. *(Violence, sexual situations.)*

p, Timothy Burrill; d, John Mackenzie; w, Frederick Forsyth, Richard Burridge (based on the novel by Frederick Forsyth); ph, Phil Meheux (Rank Color); m, Lalo Schifrin, Francis Shaw; ed, Graham Walker; prod d, Allan Cameron; md, Lalo Schifrin; art d, Tim Hutchinson; set d, Peter Howitt; cos, Tiny Nicholls; spec eff, Peter Hutchinson; stunts, Eddie Stacey; makeup, Peter Robb King.

Spy/Thriller **(PR:C MPAA:R)**

FRANCESCA*½** (1987, Ger.) 93m Heide Breitel Film/German Export Union c

Eva Lissa *(Countess)*, Dorothea Neff *(Cook)*, Bernhard Wosien *(Grujinski)*, Dolly Worzbach *(Dolly)*, Olga von Togni *(Olga)*, Karl Donch *(Matisti)*, Ruth Drexel *(Anita Meyer)*, Pietro Tordi *(Giacomo)*, Gina Rovere *(Elena)*, Tito Le Duc *(Transvestite)*, Barbara Herrera *(Mamma Lupa)*, Alessandra Vazzoler *(Silent Film Star)*, Arnaldo Colombaioni *(Clown)*, Fulvio Di Stafano *(Accordion Player)*, Big Vanity Sisters, Marianne Hoppe, Bernhard Minetti, Sisters of St. Mary's Convent in Niederviehbach, Bavaria, Mother Superior Roswitha Schneider.

This charming pseudodocumentary recounts the life of "Francesca Aramonte," a German actress raised in a convent who became a star for Federico Fellini. We never see Francesca (a wholly fictional character), though her life and influence are recounted by friends, enemies, and colleagues. Lissa, an unhappy widowed countess, recalls how she found Francesca as a baby. Her husband, a cruel, self-centered man, refused to let her keep the foundling so Francesca was given to convent nuns. While some of the sisters loved the girl and were convinced the child had seen angels, others thought Francesca to be unscrupulous. Francesca is then remembered by her cohorts in the theater. Did she have many men in her life? Was she a lesbian? Both are hinted at but never quite answered. Like the nuns, some of the thespians see Francesca as a gifted actress, while others are convinced she was a schemer. The last group portrayed is composed of extras who worked under Fellini. They celebrate what would have been Francesca's 80th birthday, argue, and reminisce about days gone by.

Though a little slow to get going, FRANCESCA becomes enormous fun once the film's premise is firmly established. Rudolph, making her directorial debut, shows a wonderful sense for satire. She pokes fun at religion, theatrical and film legends, and the little occurrences of every day life. Using a cinema verite style, she makes her fiction seem real, creating an altogether engaging work. Rudolph's casting of her actors is a masterstroke. We believe in Francesca because the people on screen so fervently praise and damn the fictional woman. Many of the ensemble are nonprofessionals, and an order of nuns play themselves. The best moments come when Rudolph examines the Fellini extras. This eccentric band is comprised of real-life Fellini actors, all of whom had minor roles in some of the Italian director's work, including AMACORD and 8 ½. They discuss their real experiences while talking about "Frances Degli Angeli," the starring role Francesca played for the director in 1950. Rudolph merely gave the group an outline, then let them improvise while she filmed the results. Consequently these sequences very much resemble a Fellini film, while the cast members clearly enjoy themselves. Filmed in Germany in 1986, FRANCESCA was screened at world film festivals in 1987.

p, Elke Peters; d&w, Verena Rudolph; ph, Eberhard Geick; m, Fulvio Di Stafano, Leopoldo Sanfelice; ed, Susann Lahaye; art d, Mario-Angela Capuano, Hans Thiemann; set d, Nazzareno Scolacchia.

Comedy **(PR:O MPAA:NR)**

FRENCHMAN'S FARM† (1987, Aus.) 102m Mavis Bramston/Goldfarb c

Tracey Tainsh *(Jackie Grenville)*, David Reyne *(Barry Norden)*, Ray Barrett *(Harry Benson)*, Norman Kaye *(Rev. Aldershot)*, John Meillon *(Sgt. Bill Dolan)*, Andrew Blackman *(Det. John Mainsbridge)*, Phil Brock *(John Hatcher)*, Kym Lynch *(George Slater)*, Andrew Johnston *(William Morris)*, Lynne Schofield *(Mme. Cheveraux)*, Tui Bow *(Miss Morton, Little Old Lady at Harrisville Museum)*, Jennifer Flowers *(Mrs. Grenville)*, Mark Albiston *(Joshua Reynolds, Jr.)*, Maurice Hughes *(Harrisville Policeman)*, Alexandra Black *(Archives Clerk)*, Ian Leigh-Cooper *(Library Clerk)*, Robert Eastgate *(Second Detective)*, Billy Watson *(Harrisville Farmer)*, Laurence Hodge *(Passer-by)*, Errol O'Neill, Penny Jones *(Computer Programmers)*.

Supernatural story which sees university student Tainsh drive through a time warp in Queensland and witness the decapitation of a soldier on Frenchman's Farm in 1944. Back in modern times Tainsh and her boy friend Reyne set out to investigate the strange phenomena and their sleuthing uncovers the existence of a treasure in gold buried somewhere on the farm. Unfortunately, while they search, the killer from the past continues his murderous ways.

p, James Fishburn; d, Ron Way; w, Ron Way, James Fishburn, Matt White (based on a screenplay by William Russell); ph, Malcolm McCulloch (Eastmancolor); m, Tommy Tycho; ed, Pippa Anderson; art d, Richard Rooker.

Horror **(PR:NR MPAA:NR)**

FRIDA† (1987, Mex.) 108m Clasa Films Mundiales c

Ofelia Medina *(Frida Kahlo)*, Juan Jose Gurrola *(Diego Rivera)*, Salvador Sanchez *(David Siqueros)*, Max Kerlow *(Leon Trotsky)*, Claudio Brook *(Frida's Father)*, Cecilia Toussaint *(Frida's Sister)*, Valentina Leduc *(Young Frida)*.

The extraordinary life of Mexican painter Frida Kahlo (1907-54) is the subject of this biopic, which opens with the artist on her deathbed. The film chronicles her bout with polio at age six; her involvement in a traffic accident at age 18 which left her partially paralyzed and led to more than 30 operations; her marriage to painter Diego Rivera; and her affair with Leon Trotsky. Kahlo's art and the landscapes which inspired her also occupy a vital position in the film.

p, Manuel Barbachanco Ponce, Paul Leduc; d, Paul Leduc; w, Jose Joaquin Blanco, Paul Leduc; ph, Angel Goded; ed, Rafael Castanedo.

Biography **(PR:NR MPAA:NR)**

FRIENDS FOREVER (SEE: VENNER FOR ALTIO, 1987, Den.)

FRIENDSHIP'S DEATH† (1987, Brit.) 78m BFI-Channel 4/BFI-Modelmark c

Bill Paterson *(Sullivan)*, Tilda Swinton *(Friendship)*, Patrick Bauchau *(Kubler)*, Ruby Baker *(Catherine)*, Joumana Gill *(Palestinian)*.

Film theoretician and author of *Signs and Meanings in the Cinema*, Peter Wollen has here combined his personal experiences as a journalist in Amman, Jordan in 1970 with his passion for science fiction films. Set during "Black September," a bloody period when the Jordanians ousted the PLO from its inner-city stronghold, the film stars Paterson as a journalist with ties to the PLO. When Swinton is detained by the PLO for traveling without her papers, Paterson pretends to know her and brings her back to his hotel to find out who she is. He initially believes her to be a spy, but soon discovers she is an extraterrestrial named Friendship from the planet Procryon. She was on a mission headed for Massachusetts Institute of Technology, but accidentally landed in the midst of "Black September." Although she looks like a woman, she is, in fact, a robot designed specifically to gather information on Earth. By the time Paterson arranges for her safe passage out of Jordan, she no longer wants to leave, having become sympathetic to the cause of the homeless PLO. Made on a low budget with the help of the British Film Institute and Britain's Channel Four, FRIENDSHIP'S DEATH has established that Wollen is as compelling a filmmaker as he is a writer. Wollen is also known as one of the co-writers of Michelangelo Antonioni's THE PASSENGER, another film revolving around a journalist's involvement in third world politics. In an interview with Simon Field of the *Monthly Film Bulletin*, Wollen said of FRIENDSHIP'S DEATH, "In a way, I saw it as a sequel to THE PASSENGER, with the obvious difference that THE PASSENGER is a road movie whereas this one is about being trapped, not being able to get out, rather than constantly moving on."

p, Rebecca O'Brien; d&w, Peter Wollen (based on his own short story); ph, Witold Stok (Technicolor); m, Barrington Pheloung; ed, Robert Hargreaves; prod d, Gemma Jackson; set d, Denise Rubens; cos, Cathy Cook; makeup, Morag Ross.

Science Fiction/War **(PR:NR MPAA:NR)**

FROM A WHISPER TO A SCREAM (SEE: OFFSPRING, THE, 1987)

FROM THE HIP* (1987) 111m Indian Neck/DEG c

Judd Nelson *(Robin Weathers)*, Elizabeth Perkins *(Jo Ann)*, John Hurt *(Douglas Benoit)*, Darren McGavin *(Craig Duncan)*, Dan Monahan *(Larry)*, David Alan Grier *(Steve Hadley)*, Nancy Marchand *(Roberta Winnaker)*, Allan Arbus *(Phil Amos)*, Edward Winter *(Raymond Torkenson)*, Richard Zobel *(Matt Cowens)*, Ray Walston *(lst Judge)*, Robert Irvin Elliott *(Scott Murray)*, Beatrice Winde *(2nd Judge)*, Art Hindle *(Lt. Matt Sosha)*, Priscilla Pointer *(Mrs. Martha Williams)*, Meshach Taylor.

The title can be taken two ways. It might mean that the hero, Nelson, is the kind of legal hotshot who shoots from the hip. Or it might mean that the picture was supposedly made by a group of hip people. Neither interpretation is accurate. Nelson is just out of law school and has taken a job with one of those prestigious law firms usually headed by John Houseman or someone of his ilk. In this case, the company is run by McGavin, Marchand, and Arbus. Nelson is the typical yuppie, eager to get ahead at all costs, despite some early protestations regarding his desires to remain ethical. He worms his way into representing Winter in a case (this is the earliest case of the suspension of disbelief on record) where the man has admitted hitting another person and is quite willing to cop a plea and pay the fine. Nelson uses all sorts of shoddy, shyster tactics to get the client off, shenanigans reminiscent of 1930s films about silly lawyers. In a twinkling, Nelson has achieved publicity and all the other clients of the law firm are clamoring for his services. So he is made a junior partner about 12 minutes later (another stretch of credulity). The three seniors decide to give Nelson his comeuppance and hand him a case which they feel can't be won. Hurt, an egocentric professor, has been accused of molesting and then murdering a young woman. He was found with the weapon in his possession and it looks bleak. Nelson thinks he can get his client off on a technicality. Hurt is totally smug and refuses to help his lawyer. At the trial, Nelson reaches back into his trick bag and uses every possible outlandish and unbelievable ploy to get Hurt acquitted. As he continues his representation of Hurt, Nelson begins to believe that maybe Hurt is guilty. Suddenly stricken with a conscience, he brings Hurt to the stand and tricks the man into admitting his guilt. Nelson's activities land him in contempt of court (at last!) but he emerges a better man for his efforts.

Half the movie is mildly funny while the second half turns deadly serious. Perry Mason he isn't and Nelson's entire role seems to be little more than a vanity production to show off his limited abilities. When in scenes with superior actors, such as Hurt, it's like watching Pee Wee Herman trying to outperform Laurence Olivier. The script bears little resemblance to actual legal practice and this is surprising since the writer is, in fact, an attorney who later wound up with the NBC show "L.A. Law." Some much better actors than Nelson are wasted here. Walston does well as a judge, so does the uncredited Meshach Taylor playing a screaming black queen named "Hollywood." Not so fortunate is Perkins (so good in ABOUT LAST NIGHT) whose role was barely touched by the writers. Director Clark has to be given credit for trying different things. This is the same man who helmed TURK 182, PORKY'S, and the sensitive A CHRISTMAS STORY (also with Darren McGavin). But in that last script, he had material from Jean Shepherd and therein lies the difference. Anyone even vaguely considering a career in the legal profession should not see this because they'll be as turned off to the study of law as most people were to the study of this movie. The shame of it all was that the picture could have been wonderful. *(Profanity.)*

p, Rene Dupont, Bob Clark; d, Bob Clark; w, David E. Kelley, Bob Clark (based on a story by David E. Kelley); ph, Dante Spinotti (J-D-C Widescreen, Technicolor); m, Paul Zaza; ed, Stan Cole; prod d, Michael Stringer; art d, Dennis Bradford; set d, Edward [Tantar] LeViseur; cos, Clifford Capone.

Comedy **Cas.** **(PR:C MPAA:PG)**

FUEGOS† (1987, Fr.) 93m Oliane-Films A2-CNC/UGC c

Vittorio Mezzogiorno *(El Gringo)*, Angela Molina *(Adela)*, Catherine Rouvel *(Clara)*, Valentina Vargas *(Margarita)*, Marilu Marini *(La Polaca)*, Christine Camaya *(Mecha)*, Didier Guedj *(Nacho)*, Gabriel Monnet *(Don Braulio)*.

Gerard Brach, Roman Polanski's longtime co-screenwriter, and Raoul Coutard and Agnes Guillemot, the cinematographer and editor for both Francois Truffaut and Jean-Luc Godard, combine their talents under the first-time direction of Arias, a Paris-based Argentine stage director. Mezzogiorno stars as a decadent, patriarchal landowner who treats the women in his life—wife Rouvel, sister-in-law/mistress Molina, prostitute Marini, and servant Vargas—with such contempt that one of his children eventually tries to poison him. Set in South America, but shot in the Camarague region of France.

p, Marie-Laure Reyre; d, Alfredo Arias; w, Gerard Brach (based on a story by Alfredo Arias, Kado Kostzer); ph, Raoul Coutard (Fujicolor); m, Jean-Marie Senia; ed, Agnes Guillemot; art d, Roberto Plate; cos, Claudine Lachaud.

Drama **(PR:NR MPAA:NR)**

FULL METAL JACKET**** (1987) 116m Natant/WB c

Matthew Modine *(Pvt. Joker)*, Adam Baldwin *(Animal Mother)*, Vincent D'Onofrio *(Leonard Lawrence, Pvt. Gomer Pyle)*, Lee Ermey *(Gunnery Sgt. Hartman)*, Dorian Harewood *(Eightball)*, Arliss Howard *(Pvt. Cowboy)*, Kevyn Major Howard *(Rafterman)*, Ed O'Ross *(Walter J. Schinoski, Lt. Touchdown)*, John Stafford *(Doc Jay)*, John Terry *(Lt. Lockhart)*, Kirk Taylor *(Payback)*, Ian Tyler *(Lt. Cleves)*, Papillon Soo Soo *(Da Nang Hooker)*, Tan Hung Francione *(ARVN Pimp)*, Costas Dino Chimona *(Chili)*, Peter Merrill *(TV Journalist)*, Keirson Jecchinis *(Crazy Earl)*, Gary Landon Mills *(Donlon)*, Ngoc Le *(Vietcong Sniper)*, Leanna Hong *(Motorbike Hooker)*, Gil Kopel *(Stork)*, Herbert Norville *(Daytona Dave)*, Bruce Boa *(Poge Colonel)*, Tim Colceri *(Doorgunner)*, Sal Lopez *(T.H.E. Rock)*, Peter Edmund *(Snowball)*, Marcus D'Amico *(Handjob)*, Keith Hodiak *(Daddy Da)*, Nguyen Hue Phong *(Camera Thief)*, Du Hu Ta *(Dead NVA)*, Martin Adams, Kevin Aldridge, Del Anderson, Philip Bailey, Louis Barlotti, John Beddows, Patrick Benn, Steve Boucher, Adrian Bush, Tony Garey, Gary Cheeseman, Wayne Clark, Chris Cornibert, Danny Cornibert, John Curtis, John Davis, Harry Davies, Kevin Day, Gordon Duncan, Phil Elmer, Colin Elvis, Hadrian Follett, Sean Frank, David George, Laurie Gomes, Brian Goodwin, Nigel Goulding, Tony Hague, Steve Hands, Chris Harris, Bob Hart, Derek Hart, Barry Hayes, Tony Hayes, Robin Hedgeland, Duncan Henry, Kenneth Head, Liam Hogan, Trevor Hogan, Luke Hogdal, Steve Hudson, Tony Howard, Sean Lamming, Dan Landin, Tony Leete, Nigel Lough, Terry Lowe, Frank McCardle, Gary Meyer, Brett Middleton, David Milner, Sean Minmagh, Tony Minmagh, John Morrison, Russell Mott, John Ness, Robert Nichols, David Perry, Peter Rommely, Pat Sands, Jim Sarup, Chris Schmidt-Maybach, Al Simpron, Russell Slater, Gary Smith, Roger Smith, Tony Smith, Anthony Styliano, Bill Thompson, Mike Turjansky, Dan Weldon, Dennis Wells, Michael Williams, John Wilson, John Wonderling. *(Parris Island Recruits/Vietnam Platoon)*.

Director Stanley Kubrick is saddled with the image of having made too many good films (THE KILLING, PATHS OF GLORY, 2001) and is often compelled to strive too mightily to create one critical success after another. He doesn't

always manage—no one can—but here, in this cold, cynical, and devastatingly realistic war film, Kubrick's cinema vision is in sharp focus. "Moving pictures move," a movie mogul once mouthed enthusiastically and Kubrick proves it here with a vengeance, his cameras so fluid, his shots so inventive, his actors so mobile that the action overwhelms the viewer. This is as it should be given the prosaic story which really requires no character development. These are Marines, the visual tale tells us bluntly through the film, America's shock troops. They actually volunteered to fight Viet Cong and North Vietnamese troops during the Vietnam conflict. No one dragged these characters kicking and screaming into boot camp. And it is in boot camp where Kubrick pops open his camera lens. He shows a vitriolic, shouting, precisely correct Ermey, marching down the aisle of a recruit barracks while his men, youths with shaved heads, stand like stone statues during his tirade. Ermey is a near-sadistic D.I. whose mouth streams obscenities and who never speaks when shouting will do. For the first 45 minutes the viewer is subjected to the merciless, hard-nosed training these recruits undergo, routines that exhaust the viewer; the most disturbing scenes deal with Ermey's maniacal behavior with his impressionistic youth, the most emotionally unstable being D'Onofrio, an overweight recruit who becomes the butt of Ermey's reviling remarks. The D.I. nicknames his men according to their dialect, posture, and attitude; his appellation for the smiling D'Onofrio is Gomer Pyle after the inept TV soldier. Modine, incurring Ermey's wrath by making a joke during one of the D.I.'s tirades, earns the nickname Joker; Texan Arliss Howard inevitably becomes Cowboy. Later in the film, Kubrick introduces other soldiers known only by nicknames, including Harewood (Eightball) and, Baldwin (Animal Mother). Kubrick does not echo the myriad war films of the past by establishing his characters as instant generic stereotypes but instead emphasizes those stereotypes as the inevitable identities of young men without real histories or pasts or personalities that would set them apart from their fellow volunteers. Kubrick's lengthy concentration on the training period of these young men is to accentuate their loss of identity and their formation into a group culture of killers (and here Kubrick is as fascinated with group violence as he was in A CLOCKWORK ORANGE). The fear of the group expressed toward the ranting and raving Ermey is chinked when Modine nerves up his courage to talk back to the profane sergeant which instantly makes him the hero of the group but also isolates him from it by elevating him to leadership he does not covet. Worse, Modine is spitefully put in charge of shaping up the bumbling, hopeless D'Onofrio by the vicious Ermey. (There is no human side to Ermey; Kubrick narrowly shows him as a vessel-popping tyrant without compassion, understanding or a basic psychological perception of the recruits. Ermey is simply a machine turning embryo humans into machines designed to survive warfare and kill the enemy.) Painstakingly, Modine attempts to mold the cumbersome, heavyset D'Onofrio into a Marine, spending time with him in rifle drills and urging him through the horrendous obstacle courses, but the clumsy, flabby D'Onofrio fails at every attempt to stay up with his gung-ho peers. He is miserable, and Modine, who has become his unwilling protector, cannot stand the responsibility. And there is the constant threat from the deranged Ermey. This psychotic at one point praises two former Marines who later became killers, mass-slayer Charles Whitman and President Kennedy's assassin, Lee Harvey Oswald, by bellowing: "Outstanding! These individuals showed what one Marine and a rifle can do!" (This is, of course, a disgustingly gratuitous remark which stereotypes Ermey as a nut and subsequently all D.I.s as lunatics. This Kubrick ploy, much beneath him, indicts the Marine Corps as a whole through the vile images of two murderers who in reality disgraced its colors.) Ermey's persecution of D'Onofrio intensifies and when the D.I. finds a doughnut in the fat recruit's locker the entire platoon is punished. In retaliation, the recruits that night, bathed in the bluish light created by cinemagraphic wizard Milsome, wrap soap bars in towels and assault the hapless, pathetic D'Onofrio, pelting him furiously in the rolls of his stomach. Modine, D'Onofrio's apprentice mentor, resists punishing the recruit but, acceding to the group mentality or the lack of it, finally joins in, hitting D'Onofrio harder and longer than the rest, vindicating his station as leader and preventing himself from joining D'Onofrio in pariahland. The beating has its desired and stereotyped effect. D'Onofrio not only shapes up but, amazingly, becomes the sharpest quickest rifleman in the squad, one who drills with his rifle as would an automaton. In this transformation D'Onofrio's humanity and memories of anything gentle are gone forever. D'Onofrio becomes the extension of his M-14 rifle which has been Ermey's only ambition for his charges. But there is no heart left in D'Onofrio. His scrambled brain now only radiates thoughts of madness, seen clearly on his face through a twisted smile and a hooded blank stare (the head downward, the eyes looking up so that they are nearly cut in half by heavy brows, a look that was practiced frighteningly by Jack Nicholson in Kubrick's nightmare film, THE SHINING, a look that Kubrick himself is said to register in times of directorial strife and stress). The flabby, vulnerable D'Onofrio has been dehumanized completely and is now ready to kill the enemy with alacrity, but he will never step beyond the shores of America to do so. During the recruits' last night on Parris Island, Modine, who has drawn fire watch, finds D'Onofrio in the bathroom, maniacally loading live rounds into his rifle. He then loudly begins to recite the ode to his weapon which has been relentlessly drilled into his head. The commotion awakens Ermey, who enters the bathroom and is told by Modine that D'Onofrio's rifle is loaded. In a shocking confrontation, D'Onofrio uses his rifle to blast his sergeant into eternity and then turns the weapon upon himself, blowing his head in a gruesome splatter of brains and blood against the pristine white wall of the barracks.

Enough, Kubrick says, and fades to black, reopening the film in Vietnam, where Modine is now a reporter for *Stars and Stripes*, teamed with photographer Kevyn Major Howard. Still living up to his "Joker" nickname, Modine has scrawled "Born to Kill" on his helmet, yet wears a peace symbol on his jacket. His sarcasm again puts him at odds with his commanding officer, and earns him assignment on the front lines, where he is reunited with Arliss Howard in a battle-hardened platoon that includes Baldwin and Harewood. There is a total lack of humanity in all these men, with the possible exception of Modine (who of course is being saved for the last by Kubrick to fall into the black well of disinterest for human life). The Marines through one blazing firefight after another treat the enemy as if they were wild beasts on an African savannah, posing next to the dead bodies of Vietnamese troopers like prize wildebeests shot for sport, as does Kierson Jecchinis, who has his picture taken and snaps not too wittily: "After we rotate back to the world, we're gonna miss not havin' anybody around worth shootin'." The streets are also peopled by Vietnamese whores in tight satin dresses, slit up the thigh, wobbling over rubble in high heels to be auctioned off to the highest Marine bidder, refusing to have sex with black soldiers in a weird reversal of racism. The Marine unit is given orders to mop up a section of Hue and as it goes forth, it is enveloped by an enemy barrage. This is a point where Kubrick portrays battle as only he can show it (of course, taking a great leaf from the fluid battle scenes vividly portrayed by director Lewis Milestone, who pioneered incredible mobility of camera viewpoints in his classic WW I film, ALL QUIET ON THE WESTERN FRONT, and his equally superb WW II film A WALK IN THE SUN, aka, SALERNO BEACHHEAD). In FULL METAL JACKET, Kubrick follows the Marine platoon into battle, keeping pace with them, then lagging behind at low angle. He shows their forward thrust, then a creeping artillery barrage from the distance, with shells exploding in the platoon's ranks, killing platoon leader O'Ross. The effect is startling, brutally realistic, and visually awesome. The platoon goes out too far and is apparently cut off, a sniper forcing its members to take cover and doubt begins to vex Arliss Howard, then a nervous platoon leader. Unsure of their position, he sends Harewood out to reconnoiter some bombed out buildings. Satisfied that the area is safe, Harewood begins to signal for the rest of the men to advance when he is cut down by a sniper's bullet. Howard, who has radioed for tank support, refuses to allow any more men to risk themselves in going to Harewood's aid. (Shades of scenes from SANDS OF IWO JIMA where stout-hearted but regulation-bound sergeant John Wayne will not allow his men to go to the aid of a wounded buddy who cries his name.) Stafford ignores the order and runs to Harewood, but he is also shot attempting to drag the wounded man to safety. Howard is certain the platoon is being set up for an ambush, but Baldwin disagrees. Saying there's just one sniper, Baldwin charges off to the building cluster. As he watches, the sniper finishes off Harewood and Stafford, after Stafford points out the approximate position of the sniper. At Baldwin's urging, the rest of the platoon advances. Before they can search for the sniper, Howard again tries to radio for help, but takes a bullet in the back in the process, dying shortly thereafter in Modine's arms. "Now let's get some payback," Baldwin says, and the platoon begins searching for the sniper. The men move through deserted buildings, or the gutted shells of buildings, cautiously, like specters searching for their own lost graves. (Again, Kubrick logically goes back to his own past and here shows, through eerie tracking shots, the men entering one building, then going room by room, the fourth wall being the camera, chronicling their increased tension as they get nearer to the dreaded sniper, a technique Kubrick used effectively in THE KILLING where he showed a gang of criminals moving through an apartment, going from room to room while the camera tracked them with an open or fourth wall from the perspective of the camera.) Modine locates the sniper, a teenage girl, but his rifle jams as he tries to shoot her. She then fires a barrage in his direction, and begins to advance toward him, but is cut down by a burst of fire from Kevyn Major Howard. The mortally wounded girl writhes at the feet of the Marines, begging them to shoot her and put her out of her agony. (Here again Kubrick goes to the WW II film well and does a variation of a scene shown in OBJECTIVE BURMA!, one where Errol Flynn discovers the half-alive body of his friend, William Prince, a victim of Japanese torture, with Prince begging the agonizing Flynn to shoot him.) None of the hardened young Marines can bring themselves to shoot the girl and it is Modine who finally squeezes the trigger, the camera lingering on his face to show the last sensibilities of his being literally vanish from his half-redeemable character, like a soul departing a body. In the end, the survivors of the Hue battle stoically march through the ruined city at night, bursting into song, not the Marine Hymn as might be expected but, and this is the final Kubrick irony, the theme song from the Mickey Mouse tv show. As they march, grotesquely silhouetted by exploding flares and bombs and burning buildings, Modine says in narration as the film ends, "I am in a world of s---. But I am alive and I am not afraid."

Technically, FULL METAL JACKET (the title being a reference to the type of cartridge used in the M-14 rifle) is a work of cinemagraphic genius, perfect in its craft and design. This film has been wrongly compared with other Vietnam war films, APOCALYPSE NOW and PLATOON, but such exercises are specious in that this film makes no attempt to study character development and reaction to the horrors of warfare. It is a profile of a *group* of men, Marines, shock troops, volunteers who are met in the first frame, all having the resolve to go to Vietnam and destroy a foreign enemy ("inside of every gook is an American trying to get out," seems to be the philosophy, as stated by an officer in Vietnam). The camera does dwell on D'Onofrio at the beginning, but he is only meant to be an element of the group, a weak link grown strong but warped, eliminated as defective in the end (taking with him his tormentor and creator, the D.I. sergeant Ermey as a sort of an oblique apology from Kubrick for savaging the Corps). Modine emerges as a stronger character, but only briefly, for his life is really dedicated to the group. And war is seen here as a realistic wonder where events occur so rapidly that there is little or no time to analyze them, or evaluate the human reaction to them. (Anyone who has ever been under fire will relate, at least visually, to FULL METAL JACKET.) There are outright stupidities created by Kubrick, if they are not cynical nods to past war films, such as one soldier moronically picking up a stuffed animal bear in the middle of a battlefield and being blown up by the booby trap attached to it. Training at Parris Island includes strict indoctrination in apparent booby traps. But this is a quibble with a film that is both accurate in its visual portrayal of the Vietnam war as well as precise in its depiction of troops under fire and their common, impulsive actions, albeit the training period of the movie takes the old perception of Marine training as seen in such films as THE D.I., with Jack Webb, beyond the reef of reason. All in all, FULL METAL JACKET is a devastating and excellent film that focuses upon a real fighting element of American forces in Vietnam and, as such, may be the most honest film made about that sorry conflict, discarding the homefront revisionist empathies mouthed by PLATOON and the awful intellectual indulgences created in APOCALYPSE NOW and even the extravagantly exotic (and near unbelievable) adventures of THE DEER HUNTER. The men of this raw war film kill and are killed, receptive to a fate learned on Parris Island. They are Americans, yes, but they are not the boys next door. These are hard cases molded into a group weapon, the answer to the fanatical elements of any enemy forces, the very kind of people we praised in the past for performance at the Marne during WW I when the 2nd Marines broke the back of the German armies forever by its suicidal charges, ironically led by a sergeant who jumped from a trench where the Marines momentarily hesitated and shouted: "Come on, you s.o.b.'s, do you want to live forever?" There was no less resignation to inflicting and accepting death in battle by those Marines who stormed ashore in WW II at Tarawa, Iwo Jima, and hundreds of other Pacific islands. Historically it is the job of the Marine Corps to do what others cannot or will not do. This is what Kubrick sought to portray in his clinical, no-reservations style, and he has succeeded with spellbinding effectiveness, remaining loyal not to heroic myth but to the practical reality of just why the Marine Corps exists and who are these Marines anyway? Were they really dehumanized by their experiences here or were the crusts of their true natures unchanged, only baked harder by experience in training and battle? Ermey might be the prime example. He was originally hired by Kubrick as a technical adviser, having been a D.I. in the early 1960s, but he was so demonstrative in his advice and use of epithets that Kubrick put him before the cameras where he strutted his Marine stuff. Ermey was patiently guided by Kubrick, who loves to use nameless people in his films, working with the director on diction, lines, and mannerisms. Kubrick shot Ermey's opening scene 25 times and still wasn't satisfied with it. He put the scene on hold and Ermey, meanwhile, got into a car accident. When he returned he did the scene again, this time portraying the sadistic character to Kubrick's satisfaction. In this $30 million production, filmed entirely in England, Kubrick's penchant for perfection was demonstrated in his constant retaking of scenes. Dozens of scenes lasting as long as eight to ten minutes, including the expensive panoramic battle scenes, had as many as 30 takes to the scene. Such demands certainly produce exhaustion on the part of the cast and crew but Kubrick undoubtedly meant to have his actors exhausted and have them appear as such, bone-weary of battle, worn out by war, his war. What shows is exactly what Kubrick wanted. His meticulousness knows no bounds in FULL METAL JACKET. It was Kubrick

who scouted the locations and chose a military barracks outside of London which doubles for the Parris Island segment of the film. He located a vast deserted gas works in London's East End, a plant area that had been bombed to ruination during WW II, and he further destroyed the area to great effectiveness. The starkness of this film is achieved in many ways, particularly through contrasting lighting and the use of white walls, white lime poured on bodies, white powder covering faces and clothes, a chalky ghostlike appearance permeating the film to suggest that the living dead are being portrayed. The director ordered special color film used here, a type with a grainy visual effect which aided Kubrick's successful attempt to give FULL METAL JACKET a documentary "feel" and look. This is also the reason, no doubt, Kubrick insisted the sound be monophonic instead of using the Dolby stereo approach, again harkening to the documentary approach of the past. The director spent more than a year preparing this film and the production took six months of actual shooting with 20 weeks of downtime attributed to injuries among cast and crew members harrowing through Kubrick's personal vision of war. His vision proves deadly accurate, emotionally and intellectually wrenching, but one so full of impact that FULL METAL JACKET will be the film about the Vietnam conflict that will prove most memorable. Kubrick's refreshing, but peculiar choice of music includes "Hello Vietnam" (Tom T. Hall, performed by Johnny Wright), "These Boots Are Made for Walking" (Lee Hazlewood, performed by Nancy Sinatra), "Chapel of Love" (Jeff Barry, Ellie Greenwich, Phil Spector, performed by The Dixie Cups), "Wooly Bully" (Domingo Samudio, performed by Sam the Sham and The Pharaohs), "Paint It Black" (Mick Jagger, Keith Richards, performed by The Rolling Stones), "Surfin' Bird" (A. Frazier, C. White, T. Wilson, Jr., J. Harris, performed by The Trashmen), "The Marines Hymn" (performed by The Goldman Band). *(Excessive profanity, graphic violence, sexual situations.)*

p&d, Stanley Kubrick; w, Stanley Kubrick, Michael Herr, Gustav Hasford (based on the novel *The Short-Timers* by Gustav Hasford); ph, Douglas Milsome (Rank Color); m, Abigail Mead; ed, Martin Hunter; prod d, Anton Furst; art d, Rod Stratford, Les Tomkins, Keith Pain; set d, Stephen Simmonds; cos, Keith Denny; makeup, Jennifer Boost, Christine Allsop; spec eff, John Evans; tech adv, Lee Ermey; m/l, Mick Jagger, Keith Richards, Tom T. Hall, Lee Hazlewood, Jeff Barry, Ellie Greenwich, Phil Spector, Domingo Samudio, A. Frazier, C. White, T. Wilson, Jr., J. Harris.

War **Cas.** **(PR:O MPAA:R)**

G

GABY—A TRUE STORY† (1987) 114m Tri-Star c

Liv Ullmann *(Sari Brimmer)*, Norma Aleandro *(Florencia Morales, Gaby's Nurse)*, Robert Loggia *(Michel Brimmer)*, Rachel Levin *(Gabriela "Gaby" Brimmer)*, Lawrence Monoson *(Fernando)*, Robert Beltran *(Luis)*, Beatriz Sheridan *(Fernando's Mother)*, Tony Goldwyn *(David)*, Danny De La Paz *(Carlos)*, Paulina Gomez *(Gaby at the Age of 3)*, Enrique Lucero *(Minister of Education)*, Eduardo Lopez Rojas *(Hector Bulle Goyri)*, Ana Ofelia Murguia *(Nurse at Brimmer House)*, Hugh Harleston *(University Professor)*, Carolyn Valero *(Teacher at Rehabilitation Center)*, Eduardo Noriega *(Bureaucrat)*, Alejandra Flores *(Neighbor Maid)*, Zaide Silva *(Hospital Nurse)*, Nailea Norvind *(Terry)*, Cecilia Tijerina *(Lupe)*, Carlos Romano *(High School Teacher)*, Susana Alexander *(Betty)*, George Belanger *(Otto)*, Miguel Andrade *(Roberto)*, Dr. Juan Mandoki *(Therapy Doctor)*, Enrique Kahan *(Professor at Exam)*, Ramon Barragan *(Professor's Assistant)*, Anais De Melo *(Secretary to Newspaper Publisher)*, Arturo Fernandez *(Hospital Admitting Orderly)*, Manuel Kaminer *(Rabbi at Funeral)*, Jesus Romero Chiapa, Fernando Moreno *(Guys Drinking Beer)*.

Biography of Gabriela Brimmer, who was stricken with severe cerebral palsy from birth but overcame the odds and became one of Mexico's most popular and celebrated authors. Born in 1938 to Jewish parents (Ullmann and Loggia) who had emigrated from Austria to Mexico in order to escape the Nazi persecutions of the Jews, Gabriela's (Levin) affliction left her nearly immobile (she can move her left leg) and mute. Levin's nanny, Aleandro, devotes her life to the girl and teaches her to communicate via chalk board and typewriter. Levin is unimpaired mentally, and Aleandro encourages her intellectual development. While attending a school for the handicapped, Levin meets and falls in love with a similarly afflicted boy (Monoson) and the pair explore their sexuality together. Their relationship collapses, however, when Levin becomes determined to attend "normal" schools and encourages Monoson to do the same. Monoson's parents refuse to consider the notion. Levin eventually graduates from college and fulfills her ambition by becoming a successful author.

Mexican director Mandoki spent seven years trying to get this uplifting saga to the screen and he received full cooperation from the real-life Gabriela Brimmer. Incredibly, new-comer Rachel Levin had recently recovered from a bout with the crippling Guillian-Barre syndrome, a neurological ailment that had left her totally paralyzed. After 80 days in the hospital and two years of rehabilitation, Levin regained 98 percent of her mobility and continued her career as a stage actress. Although she brought unusual insight to her role, her affliction and that of Brimmer, are very different and Levin had to educate herself on the effects of cerebral palsy. GABY—A TRUE STORY was released in New York and Los Angeles late in 1987 to qualify for Academy Award nominations and will likely receive wide theatrical release in 1988. Musical selections include: "Toccata and Fugue, D. Minor" (Johann Sebastian Bach), "Beethoven Piano Concerto #4" (performed by Ivan Moravec), "I Think I Love You" (Tony Romeo; performed by the Partridge Family), "Ay Te Dejo En San Antonio" (Santiago Jimenez; performed by Los Lobos), "La Negra Petronia" (Policarpop Calle; performed by "Jumbos").

p, Pinchas Perry, Luis Mandoki; d, Luis Mandoki; w, Martin Salinas, Michael James Love (based on the story developed by Luis Mandoki from events narrated to him by Gabriela Brimmer); ph, Lajos Koltai (Technicolor); m, Maurice Jarre; ed, Garth Craven; art d, Alejandro Luna; set d, Olivia Bond; cos, Tolita Figueroa, Lucile Donay; makeup, Barbara Guedel, Lucrecia Munoz; m/l, Johann Sebastian Bach, Ludwig van Beethoven, Tony Romeo, Santiago Jimenez, Policarpop Calle; stunts, Margot Shaw.

Biography **(PR:NR MPAA:R)**

GADBAD GHOTALA† (1987, India)

Ashok Saraf, Savita Prabhune, Laxmikant Berde, Sharad Talwalkar.

A marital misundertanding leads to several comedic situations. (In Marathi.)

p, Ahluwalia; d, Raja Bargir; w, Datta Keshav; m, Vinod Kumar.

Comedy **(PR:NR MPAA:NR)**

GANDAHAR† (1987, Fr.) 83m Colimason-Films A2-Revcom Television c

An animated science-fiction feature from Rene Laloux whose 1973 film FANTASTIC PLANET achieved cult status. The story concerns a handsome young hero, Syl, who, with his band of mutant warriors, defends his planet Gandahar from the attacking hordes of Man-Machines. Like FANTASTIC PLANET, GANDAHAR features some creative animation but the film is weighed down by a leaden script. Set to be released in the US as LIGHT YEARS with a new script by Isaac Asimov.

d, Rene Laloux; w, Rene Laloux, Raphael Cluzel (based on the novel by Jean-Pierre Andrevon); m, Gabriel Yared; anim, Philippe Caza.

Animated/Science Fiction **(PR:NR MPAA:NR)**

GARBAGE PAIL KIDS MOVIE, THE zero (1987) 100m Topps Chewing Gum/Atlantic Entertainment Group c

Anthony Newley *(Capt. Manzini)*, Mackenzie Astin *(Dodger)*, Katie Barberi *(Tangerine)*, Ron MacLachlan *(Juice)*, Kevin Thompson *(Ali Gator)*, Phil Fondacaro *(Greaser Greg)*, Robert Bell *(Foul Phil)*, Larry Green *(Nat Nerd)*, Arturo Gil *(Windy Winston)*, Sue Rossitto *(Messy Tessie)*, Debbie Lee Carrington *(Valerie Vomit)*, J.P. Amateau *(Wally)*, Marjory Graue *(Blythe)*, John Cade *(Bartender)*, Lynn Cartwright *(Authoritative Voice)*, Chester Grimes *(Sandalfoot Biker)*, Patty Lloyd *(Foster Mother)*, Lindy Huddleson *(Girl with Mask/Blonde Boy)*, John Herman Shaner *(Police Officer)*, Joan L. Burton *(Woman in Theater)*, Leo V. Gordon, Gavin Moloney *(Guards)*, Kristine McKeon, Debbie Lytton *(Girls)*; Voices: Kevin Thompson *(Ali Gator)*, Debbie Lee Carrington *(Valerie Vomit)*, Arturo Gil *(Windy Winston)*, Jim Cummings *(Greaser Greg/Nat Nerd)*, Chloe Amateau *(Foul Phil)*, Teri Benaron *(Messy Tessie)*.

A stunningly inept and totally reprehensible film, THE GARBAGE PAIL KIDS MOVIE must surely be the only movie ever to be based on bubble-gum cards (the cards in question are a gross-out parody of the popular Cabbage Patch dolls). From the opening credit, which announces that the film is a "Topps Chewing Gum Production," the viewer knows that he's in store for something a little different. A garbage can from space lands on Earth and winds up in the possession of kindly antique store owner Newley (his first film in 12 years). A retired magician who knows a bad omen when he sees one, Newley forbids his young helper Astin (actress Patty Duke's son) to open the garbage can. Unfortunately, Astin has problems of his own, for he is constantly being harassed by teenager MacLachlan and his sadistic gang of goons. To make matters worse, Astin has a crush on MacLachlan's skinny girl friend, Barberi, who, believe it or not, is a amateur fashion designer. One day Astin is attacked by the gang while on duty in Newley's shop. During the struggle, the forbidden garbage can is opened and from it emerge several small, ugly creatures (midgets in costumes), each with its own disgusting habit. Messy Tessie has a nasty case of nasal drip; Windy Winston is given to frequent bouts of flatulence; Nat Nerd has trouble controlling his bladder; Foul Phil has terminally bad breath; Greaser Greg carries a switchblade, Ali Gator likes to eat human toes; and Valerie Vomit is, unfortunately, self-explanatory. The Garbage Pail Kids make quick work of the villains, leaving Astin to hit on the much older Barberi. Newley is dismayed to discover that the vile creatures have been let out and he assigns Astin the task of keeping them under control while he sits at a piano and tries to figure out a way to coax the kids back into the can by using music. From here the movie is a series of barely cogent vignettes designed to give the loathsome title characters ample opportunity to demonstrate their disgusting habits. Seeking revenge, MacLachlan informs the "State Home for the Ugly" that Newley is harboring some escapees. The kids are rounded up and imprisoned, but Newley and Astin rescue them. Before Newley can get them back in the garbage can, however, the kids ruin Barberi's first professional fashion show by once again graphically living up to their reputations. Eventually the kids return to the can, leaving young Astin behind to ponder the lessons he has learned (never trust a woman, it's okay to be gross and impolite if you're doing it for a good cause, etc.).

If Atlantic Entertainment can market this as a children's film, what's next? "The Zombie Babies" or "Friday The 13th: The Childhood Years?" Not only is THE GARBAGE PAIL KIDS MOVIE crude, obnoxious, and disgusting (it reminds one of the kid in grade school who used to squirt a whole bottle of Elmer's Glue into his mouth and then swallow it), but it is totally inept. Haphazard scripting and editing give the movie a jumbled, confused feel. There is no narrative cohesion whatsoever, as various scenes are played out with little relation to others. Newley continually floats in and out of the film, turning up to utter a pointless line of dialog, and then vanishing for another 10 minutes (he tries hard to lend some credibility to the affair, but he should have stayed home). The Garbage Pail Kids' costumes are basically stiff rubber and seem terribly uncomfortable, forcing the poor actors to stumble through the film as if drunk. At one point Thompson (Ali Gator) raises his arm so high that his costume no longer covers the fact that his green arms are merely rubber gloves that run only halfway down his forearm (the actor's pink flesh is clearly visible for several seconds). The entire film was shot on what is very obviously a back lot, and the climactic fashion show looks as if it was filmed in somebody's basement. Obviously those in charge didn't have a lot of confidence in this project.

Gross-out bubble gum cards have long had a special appeal for children be-

cause they celebrate things that make adults uncomfortable (ugliness, bad habits and behavior). Unfortunately, what may be devilishly silly and relatively inoffensive on a card looks downright repulsive when put on the screen. Watching an acne-faced, bloated kid wearing glasses and a super-hero costume (Nat Nerd) urinate on the floor every five minutes is not even remotely funny, nor is a pig-tailed girl spewing vomit in someone's face (thankfully, this only occurs once). Apparently the public concurred, for outraged parents forced the distributor to pull television commercials for THE GARBAGE PAIL KIDS MOVIE off the air and the film died an incredibly quick death at the box office. Also, backlash from the film may have contributed to the decision by CBS executives to cancel the already-filmed "Garbage Pail Kids" animated Saturday morning cartoon show, just four days before it was to air. *(Comic violence, graphic gross-out effects.)*

p&d, Rod Amateau; w, Melinda Palmer, Rod Amateau; ph, Harvey Genkins (Image Transform, United Color); m, Michael Lloyd; ed, Leon Carrere; prod d, Robert I. Jillson; set d, Hub Braden; cos, Judie Champion; makeup, Gail Brubaker; spec eff, John Buechler, Mechanical Make-up Imageries, Inc.

Children's **(PR:C MPAA:PG)**

GARDENS OF STONE** (1987) 111m Tri-Star-ML Delphi Premier/Tri-Star c

James Caan *(Sgt. Clell Hazard)*, Anjelica Huston *(Samantha Davis)*, James Earl Jones *(Sgt.-Major "Goody" Nelson)*, D.B. Sweeney *(Pvt. Jackie Willow)*, Dean Stockwell *(Capt. Homer Thomas)*, Mary Stuart Masterson *(Rachel Feld)*, Dick Anthony Williams *(First Sgt. "Slasher" Williams)*, Lonette McKee *(Betty Rae)*, Sam Bottoms *(Lt. Webber)*, Elias Koteas *(Pete Deveber, Company Clerk)*, Larry Fishburne *(Cpl. Flanagan)*, Casey Siemaszko *(Pvt. Albert Wildman)*, Peter Masterson *(Col. Feld)*, Carlin Glynn *(Mrs. Feld)*, Erik Holland *(Col. Godwin)*, Bill Graham *(Don Brubaker)*, Terrence Currier *(Editor)*, Terry Hinz *(Navy Captain)*, Lisa-Marie Felter *(Daughter)*, William Williamson *(Lt. Colonel)*, Joseph A. Ross, Jr. *(General)*, Matthew Litchfield *(Lt. Atkins)*, Nick Mathwick *(Lt. Horton)*, Robert Frerichs *(Private)*, Grant Lee Douglass *(Blue Lieutenant)*, Mark Frazer, Terry Foster, Marshall Sizemore, Steve Barcanic *(Soldiers)*, Hajna O. Moss *(Wedding Friend)*, Arthur V. Gorman, Jr. *(Chaplain)*, Louis Rangel *(ANC Driver)*.

A tragic pallor hung over the shooting of GARDENS OF STONE because director Coppola's son Gian Carlo was killed in a boating accident at the start. The accident must have taken a great toll on the sensibility of the movie because it is a low-water mark for almost everyone concerned. Caan is an Army man through and through, a hard-bitten veteran who hates the Vietnam War and loves the service. He presides over "The Gardens of Stone," the many graves that dominate the landscape of Arlington National Cemetery. Caan has fought in two wars he thought were right, but now, in 1968, he feels that Vietnam is an unwinnable conflict and is opposed to it. His job at present is to oversee the men assigned to The Old Guard, that elite corps of soldiers who stand watch over The Tomb of the Unknown Soldier, escort the many bodies to their final resting places, and engage in various drill exercises as a public relations function for the government. Sweeney is assigned to Caan's unit. He is a gung ho soldier, the son of a slain veteran who had been Caan's pal, and a young man who feels constrained by having to do his duty at Fort Myer, Virginia, when he wants to be at the front. With no father, Sweeney becomes a surrogate son to both Caan and Jones, another grizzled veteran attached to the unit. Both men attempt to talk him out of his desires, but their words fall on deaf ears. Caan meets newspaper reporter Huston, a woman who is devoted to bringing the war to an end. Simultaneously, Sweeney reunites with former girl friend Masterson and before long the two wed. Caan and Jones are thrilled, as they think that, perhaps, the addition of a wife may bring Sweeney to his senses, but it doesn't change the lad one bit. Soon enough, Sweeney is happy to be transferred to where the action is and he is killed almost immediately. The picture ends as Sweeney's body is shipped back to the very "Gardens of Stone" he once guarded.

Since the picture commenced with Sweeney's funeral and ends with it, there is virtually no suspense engendered. Further, Sweeney is so single-minded throughout the movie that there is little time for any characterization other than that of a man bound and determined to die for his country. He does have a few nice moments, such as the scene in which he meets Masterson's parents (played by her real-life parents, Carlin Glynn and Peter Masterson) and the ice fairly freezes on their faces. The relationship between antiwar activist Huston and pro-Army Caan is tricky, but they pull it off when they realize that they both decry the stupidity of Vietnam conflict. The novel on which the film is based was written by a man who actually served in The Old Guard and also as a correspondent in Vietnam, so he knows of what he writes. Coppola told the war story in APOCALYPSE NOW and this is its flip side, but it will not be remembered as well as the earlier film. As usual, Coppola's camera is fluid. The real problem here is that there are several incidents and no real thrust to the plot. The US Army approved the script and helped greatly by providing many extras, a military band, hundreds of well-drilled soldiers as well as technical advice, uniforms, and equipment. Anyone who has visited Arlington will be struck with awe, something this movie doesn't inspire.

There is a nice cameo by Lonette McKee (THE COTTON CLUB, ROUND MIDNIGHT) as Jones' girl friend and a surprise acting chore for San Francisco music guru Bill Graham, who plays an attorney given to wearing the Nehru jackets of the era. Similarities between this picture and a few others are annoying. Caan reminds one of a shorter, balding Clint Eastwood from HEARTBREAK RIDGE, and because he is a soldier with no war to fight, he falls right into the mold established by Lewis John Carlino when he wrote and directed THE GREAT SANTINI, starring Robert Duvall. Caan, who was returning to films after a five-year hiatus due to personal problems, holds his acting in check and is moving at times. Not so with Jones, who overacts mightily and, with all the weight he's gained, resembles a deep-throated Buddha. The movie is dedicated to the Third US Infantry, the men of The Old Guard of the Army stationed at Fort Myer. *(Violence, excessive profanity.)*

p, Michael I. Levy, Francis Coppola; d, Francis Coppola; w, Ronald Bass (based on the novel by Nicholas Proffitt); ph, Jordan Cronenweth (DeLuxe Color); m, Carmine Coppola; ed, Barry Malkin; prod d, Dean Tavoularis; art d, Alex Tavoularis; set d, Gary Fettis; cos, Willa Kim, Judianna Makovsky; makeup, Monty Westmore, Bernadette Mazur, Brad Wilder; spec eff, John Frazier, Robin Hauser; stunts, Buddy Joe Hooker.

Drama **Cas.** **(PR:O MPAA:R)**

GATE, THE½** (1987, Can.) 92m Alliance/New Century-Vista c

Stephen Dorff *(Glen)*, Christa Denton *(Alexandra "Al", Glen's Sister)*, Louis Tripp *(Terry)*, Kelly Rowan *(Lori Lee)*, Jennifer Irwin *(Linda Lee, Lori's Sister)*, Deborah Grover *(Mom)*, Scot Denton *(Dad)*, Ingrid Veninger *(Paula)*, Sean Fagan *(Eric)*, Linda Goranson *(Terry's Mom)*, Carl Kraines *(Workman)*, Andrew Gunn *(Brad)*.

A surprisingly effective low-budget horror film that plays on universal childhood fears while managing to be scary without resorting to sadism or graphic bloodlet-

ting. Instead, the film relies on its likable cast of young actors and some truly imaginative special effects. Set in a Spielbergian suburb, the film centers on a young boy, Dorff, and his older sister, Denton, who, for the first time, have been left in charge of the house while their parents go away for the weekend. After his sister goes off to the mall with a friend, the bored Dorff and his bespectacled buddy Tripp investigate a hole in the backyard that was left behind when workmen uprooted an old tree. Inside the hole the boys find a geode. Tripp takes the geode home and when he splits it open a strange gas emerges. The boy then notices that bizarre markings have appeared on a nearby slate and he recognizes them as the same marks that appear on a heavy-metal band's album cover. By reading the liner notes of the record, Tripp learns that the hole in the backyard is really a gate to hell and that if a sacrifice is made, demons will burst through and attempt to take over the upper world. The gate can be sealed before the sacrifice if the record is played backwards. Unfortunately, before Tripp can convince anyone to listen to him, several bizarre things happen, including the death of Dorff's dog. Too distraught to take the dog's corpse to the pound, Denton asks a boy friend to do it. When the boy finds the pound closed, he decides to dump the dog's body in the mysterious hole. This "sacrifice" causes an eruption in the hole which literally opens the gate to hell. That night, a dozen one-foot-tall mischievous minions from hell emerge from the hole and wreak havoc on the house in preparation for the coming of the Demon Lord. The minions eventually kidnap both Denton and Tripp, leaving Dorff alone to face the giant four-eyed, four-limbed Demon Lord. Remembering that the demon can be defeated only through "energy derived from love and light," Dorff grabs the toy rocket his sister had given him for his birthday and shoots it into the monster. The demon is destroyed, thus freeing Tripp, Denton, and the family dog to escape from hell.

Despite all its dealings with the denizens of hell and the occult, THE GATE is a remarkably amiable horror movie. The message here is that love is stronger than hate, and in the end no one really dies. While hard-core horror addicts may consider THE GATE rather wimpy, it is a refreshing change from the rash of ultra-bleak, cynical, humorless, and irredeemably sadistic films that have been polluting the screens of late. Director Takacs spends plenty of time developing his characters, showing them as likable human beings who elicit viewer sympathy and support (as opposed to most horror films where the characters are merely fodder for the gore effects). The performances Takacs gets from his young cast are solid, with all three leads (Dorff, Denton, and Tripp) reacting as real kids would and not like the precocious, ultra-hip children found in Spielberg films. Even more impressive than the performances is the grab-bag of superior special effects that were created quickly on a relatively small budget ($6 million). Although the matte work and stop-motion animation are superior, the most impressive effect is the flawless use of forced perspective in the scenes involving the minions. Instead of constructing a dozen tiny articulated armatures and then having to stop-motion animate them (a time-consuming and expensive procedure used only on the Demon Lord), special effects coordinator Randall Cook opted to use short actors dressed in costumes and then made them appear to be one-foot tall via forced perspective. By placing the actor (Tripp) and the camera 15 feet above the soundstage floor, constructing a huge leg and gym shoe to be placed below them, and then having the costumed actors 15 feet below tugging on the phony leg, it appears that Tripp is struggling with the tiny creatures. With the sets, props, actors, and camera all properly crafted and positioned (via precise mathematical calculations), the trick should work in the camera with no additional optical printing or enhancements involved, and it does. The forced perspectives in THE GATE work beautifully, allowing for fluid interaction between the actors and the "one-foot tall" minions. Not since Disney's DARBY O'GILL AND THE LITTLE PEOPLE has forced perspective been used on such a scale. Apparently the combination of clever effects work and imaginative storytelling caught the public's imagination, for THE GATE was a surprise early-summer hit at the box office. *(Violence.)*

p, John Kemeny, Andras Hamori; d, Tibor Takacs; w, Michael Nankin; ph, Thomas Vamos (Medallion Film Labs color); m, Michael Hoenig, J. Peter Robinson; ed, Rit Wallis; prod d, William Beeton; set d, Jeff Cutler, Marlene Graham; m/l, Eva Everything, Vince Carlucci, Sandy MacFayden, Carl Tafel, Julia Bourque; cos, Trysha Bakker; makeup, Linda Preston; Craig Reardon; spec eff, Frank Carere, Randall William Cook.

Horror **Cas.** **(PR:C MPAA:PG-13)**

GAUGIN: WOLF AT THE DOOR (SEE: WOLF AT THE DOOR, 1987, Den./Fr.)

GEROY YEYO ROMANA† (1987, USSR) 77m Mosfilm/Sovexportfilm c (Trans: The Hero of Her Dreams)

Vladimir Schevelkov, Galina Belyaeva, Mikhail Kozakov, Victor Pavlov, Anatoly Romashin.

A musical comedy set in a provincial town in the 1920s starring Belyaeva as a young girl who falls in love with a defense department worker who also happens to play the French horn. Their relationship takes a number of twists and turns but ultimately they realize they are meant for each other.

d, Yuri Gorkovenko; w, Vyacheslav Verbin, Yuri Gorkovenko; ph, Henry Abramyan; m, Victor Lebedev; art d, Valentina Vyrvich.

Comedy/Musical **(PR:NR MPAA:NR)**

GET THE TERRORISTS† (1987, Phil.) Puzon c

Craig Alan, George Nicholas, Robert Marius, Frank Dux, Judy Green, Nick Nicholson, Mel Davidson, Ronnie Paterson, Jeff Griffith.

Filipino actioner about the son of a corrupt tire manufacturer who goes to Cuba and learns the fine art of terrorism. When he returns from his training he goes to the tiny US satellite of Costa Verde and forms a terrorist group known as People for Freedom. After he terrorizes the locals and tourists with a series of attacks, the Costa Verde government decides to fight back by hiring an American mercenary. A Vietnam vet is hired and he recruits a German mercenary and a bank robber. Later, the beautiful blonde daughter of an informant joins the troupe. When assigned to protect a visiting US senator the stubborn mercenaries cannot agree on tactics and the German and the bank robber quit. The Vietnam vet goes it alone, only to be killed when the terrorists kidnap the senator. The remaining mercenaries reunite and avenge their comrade's death by rescuing the senator and wiping out the terrorists. Songs include "We're Gonna Get You" (Marita A. Manuel, performed by Ruth Vergara), "Let's Move It" (Manuel, performed by Jane Crawford).

p, Conrad C. Puzon, Pierre C. Lee; d, Dominic Elmo Smith; w, Dominic Elmo Smith, David Brass; ph, Jun Perreira; m, Marita A. Manuel; ed, Amang Sanchez, Marc Tarnate; prod d, Robert Lee; md, Marita A. Manuel; art d, Jun Sancha; set d, Cornelio Ramirez; cos, Danika Myen; spec eff, Guy Noelgas; m/l, Marita A. Manuel; stunts, Roland Falcis, Jolly Joqueta; makeup, Malou Talplacido.

Action **(PR:NR MPAA:NR)**

GHOST FEVER zero (1987) 86m Infinite/Miramax-Charter c

Sherman Hemsley *(Buford/Jethro)*, Luis Avalos *(Benny)*, Jennifer Rhodes *(Mme. St. Espirt)*, Deborah Benson *(Linda)*, Diana Brookes *(Lisa)*, Pepper Martin *(Beauregard Lee/Sheriff Clay)*, Myron Healey *(Andrew Lee)*, Joe Frazier *(Terrible Tucker)*, Kenneth Johnston *(Terrible Tucker's Manager)*, Roger Cudney *(TV Announcer)*, Patrick Welch *(Ring Announcer)*, Steve Stone *(Reporter)*, Ramon Beramen *(Referee)*, George Palmiero *(Terrible Tucker's Trainer)*.

In the silent era through the 1940s, black characters such as Stepin Fetchit, Mantan Moreland, and Sleep 'n' Eat [Willie Best] dotted screen comedies as buffoons. Playing on racial stereotypes, these men usually played lazy, slow-witted servants whose childish behavior was considered a constant source for amusement. While GHOST FEVER upgrades it's black protagonist's social status and pays some sort of homage to racial equality, the film is merely a reworking of the old stereotypes for modern audiences.

The story opens in the 1860s. Martin, a Southern plantation owner, has just passed away and is met on the other side by Hemsley, one of his late father's former slaves. Hemsley is now a guide through the spiritual world for the newly dead. Martin is allowed to remain on his father's old estate, content with the knowledge he'll be able to haunt the place forever. One hundred and twenty years later, a local sheriff (also played by Martin) assigns two detectives to evict the current residents of the estate. The old homestead stands in the way of a planned freeway. The lawful duo, Hemsley (in a dual role) and Avalos (best known for his ensemble work on the educational television show "The Electric Company"), head out to the mansion, though Hemsley expresses some fears about the assignment. Upon arriving, Hemsley's worst fears come true as an invisible ghost begins playing havoc with the two policemen. Gradually it's learned that ghostly Martin's father was a notorious racist and is furious that a black and a Latino are going to destroy his beloved estate. Benson and Brookes are sibling Southern belles, the great-great-granddaughters of ghostly Martin, who now inhabit the place. It turns out they are ghosts as well, and can only exist within the confines of his home. With the help of Rhodes, a crazed French medium, the girls plot to deceive Hemsley and Avalos in order to save the estate. Each girl begins pitching woo with one man while ghostly Martin's angered father continues his assault. Ghostly Martin appeals for help from ghostly Hemsley, but the latter must be off on another mission. He promises to return at midnight though, and help settle the increasingly messy affair. Eventually Hemsley and Avalos have a change of heart and realize they cannot evict the girls. Benson and Brookes have turned as well, for the sisters have both fallen for their would-be victims. They explain their situation, and just like CITY LIGHTS (in the most rudimentary fashion, anyway), Avalos agrees to enter a boxing exhibition against a touring champ (played by real-life former heavyweight champ Joe Frazier) in hopes of winning the prize money. This way Benson and Brookes will be able to pay off their debts, thus allowing them to keep their mansion. With some ethereal assistance, Avalos wins the match but it's still not a happy ending. Knowing they won't be able to join their new girl friends in their present physical state, Hemsley and Avalos leave the mansion with heavy hearts. But two quick deaths later, the cops are transformed into ghosts and consequently rejoin Benson and Brookes for all eternity.

Even if it didn't rely on racism to carry the humor, this would still be an undeniably bad film. There's little logic within the fantasy elements, and most of the action is poorly staged, with a choppy continuity. Direction is credited to "Alan Smithee," an old Hollywood pseudonym used when a director takes his name off a project. In this case, the anonymous Mr. Smithee has obviously taken the only out he could; not even the most talentless hack would want something like this on a resume. Sherman Hemsley leads the way in reliving those inglorious racist days of yesteryear, attempting in his own way to become a sort of "Mantan Moreland for the eighties." Though his performance consists of largely bored detachment, Hemsley does manage to work in nearly every element used by his cinematic forebears. His cowardice in dealing with ghosts is fairly noxious in and of itself, but Hemsley really pushes things to a limit when he actually challenges a ghost's honor by tap dancing! The only thing that's missing is Hemsley's eyes popping out of his head while he screams "Ooo-weee!" The miscegenation element plays like a feeble attempt to cover GHOST FEVER's racist qualities, but there's no real stance taken on the issue. Rather, Hemsley occasionally spouts something about a bigoted ghost and that's as far as it goes. Considering the ghost is supposed to be a former slave owner who despises blacks, the invisible spirit is surprisingly versatile. At one point, in response to Hemsley's tap dance, the ghost dons mummy-like wrapping, then launches into a lively breakdance number. GHOST FEVER is a fantasy all right, and one that should shame anyone associated with the project. Songs include: "Swanee" (Ross Vannelli, performed by Sherman Hemsley), "Don't Count Me Out" (Vannelli, performed by Ross Vannelli), "Foot of the Pony" (Randall Rumage, James Hart, Sandy Sherman, performed by James Carnelli), "Ghost Fever" (Hart, Carnelli, Sherman, performed by Hemsley). *(Profanity.)*

p, Edward Coe, Ron Rich; d, Alan Smithee [Lee Madden]; w, Oscar Brodney, Ron Rich, Richard Egan; ph, Zavier Cruz Ruvalcaba; m, James Hart; ed, James Ruxin; prod d, Dora Corona; cos, Susan Chevalier, Leslie Levin; spec eff, Miguel Vasquez; ch, Carleton Johnson; makeup, Tony Ramirez.

Comedy/Fantasy Cas. (PR:C MPAA:PG)

GHULAMI KI ZANJEER† (1987, India)

Chander Sharma, Sona, Kader Khan.

A patriotic crime thriller. (In Hindi.)

p&d, Chander Sharma; m, Ravindra Jain.

Crime (PR:NR MPAA:NR)

GIRL, THE*½ (1987, Brit.) 104m Lux Film Prods./Shapiro Ent. c

Franco Nero *(John Berg)*, Bernice Stegers *(Eva Berg)*, Clare Powney *(Pat Carlsson, the Girl)*, Frank Brennan *(Bill Lindberg, Reporter)*, Mark Robinson *(Hans, Cab Driver)*, Clifford Rose *(Gen. Carlsson)*, Rosie Jauckens *(Mrs. Carlsson)*, Derek Benfield *(Janitor)*, Mark Dowling *(Zilenski)*, Lenore Zann *(Vivecka)*, Christopher Lee *(Peter Storm)*, Sam Cook *(Antonio)*, Heinz Hopf *(David)*, Pontus Platin *(Sandberg)*, Olle Bjorling *(The Host)*, Hanna Brogren *(Housekeeper)*, Gunnar Ernblad, Tim Earle *(Editors)*, Christer Banck *(Locksmith)*, Damir Majovsek *(Grandenz, Berg's Client)*, Sara Key *(Adriana)*, Ragnar Ulfung.

Although it's billed as "an erotic thriller" THE GIRL is hardly either—smothering any of its eroticism in a mundane and tedious story and relegating its "thriller" elements to an obscure subplot which is nearly forgotten. The premise is familiar, seen in LOLITA and countless soft-core "art" films—a young girl's sexual hold over an older man causing his destruction. In THE GIRL, a British film with a Swedish director and Italian locations, the girl is a 14-year-old played by Powney, an actress who hasn't seen 14 in at least a decade. A cross between Brigitte Bardot and Pippi Longstocking, Powney, with her pigtail hairdo, is a schoolgirl who offers herself to Nero for a mere 300 crowns—an offer he cautiously accepts. When they arrive at his apartment, he gives her the 300 crowns, but instead of making love to her he offers her lunch (it is, after all, her school lunchbreak), complete with a big glass of milk. Later Nero, a respected lawyer, is approached by cub journalist Brennan, who is breaking a story about a client of Nero's who is trying to smuggle currency out of the country. In the process, Brennan discovers the scandal-in-the-making between Nero and Powney, who also happens to be the daughter of a rich and powerful general. The following day, Powney shows up at Nero's and seduces him. For Nero, it's love. Suddenly Nero is planning a long "business" trip—a trip his wife, Stegers, welcomes because she is carrying on with a sleazy young taxi driver. Nero and Powney run off to an island retreat which can be reached only by boat. Their life of erotic bliss begins. They make love day and night, indoors and outdoors. Before long Brennan has arrived, hoping to blackmail Nero into revealing his client's whereabouts by threatening to expose his relationship with and "kidnaping" of Powney. Nero and Powney turn the tables on Brennan by sabotaging the only boat on the island, thereby cutting off his contact with the mainland. He is made their prisoner. On one sunny afternoon, Powney heads for the beach, takes a swim, removes her wet bathing suit, and entices Brennan to make love to her. She then coldly plunges two knives into his back. When Nero discovers what she has done, he sets the corpse ablaze, and gets rid of any trace of Brennan. Nero eventually returns to his job and he and Powney reunite in his second apartment. There the devilish Powney awakens early one day, turns on the gas stove, and kills Nero. The murder is then pinned on the taxi driver lover of Nero's wife, who coldly refuses to provide an alibi for her lover.

One of the dumbest movies to be exported to American screens in some time, THE GIRL tries desperately to be a complex thriller with interwoven stories and subplots. It is so superficial and simple-minded that it exists only as artsy soft-core pornography which is padded out to an insufferable 104 minutes. There are three films going on in THE GIRL—the Nero-Powney erotic romance; Brennan's journalistic pursuits; and the totally ridiculous affair between Stegers and her degrading lover Robinson, the taxi driver. This subplot is an attempt to parallel a wife's behavior with a husband's, but it seems like it's been pulled from another movie and inserted just to stretch out the running time. Although Powney and Nero have chemistry (they at least seem comfortable together), their story is too one-dimensional to sustain much interest. The nudity (no full frontal nudity is ever shown) is not as exploitative as one would expect, treated with more subtlety and matter-of-factness than usual. Released briefly in New York. The video release has Christopher Lee second-billed, though Lee fans will be heartily disappointed to see that he is on screen for no more than two minutes. *(Excessive nudity, violence, profanity, sexual situations.)*

p&d, Arne Mattson; w, Ernest Hotch; ph, Tomislav Pinter; m, Alfi Kabiljo, Ilan

Kabiljo; ed, Derek Trigg; prod d, Anders Barreus; art d, Zeljko Senecic, Anders Barreus; cos, Mago; makeup, Eva Helene Wiktorson, Jan Kindahl.

Thriller **Cas.** **(PR:O MPAA:NR)**

GLASS MENAGERIE, THE*½** (1987) 135m Cineplex Odeon c

Joanne Woodward *(Amanda)*, John Malkovich *(Tom)*, Karen Allen *(Laura)*, James Naughton *(Gentleman Caller)*.

Directed by Paul Newman, this third filmed version of the Tennessee Williams classic is painstakingly faithful to the play and features extraordinary performances from all four actors. Malkovich is the story's narrator, a merchant seaman who has returned to the vacant St. Louis apartment that he lived in with his mother and sister in the 1930s. He explains that the viewer is about to witness a "memory play," and introduces the characters: Malkovich himself is a poet who works in a warehouse to support his family but who longs for escape. Woodward (Newman's wife) is his mother, a southern belle who forsook her genteel background to marry "a telephone man who fell in love with long distances" and eventually "skipped the light fantastic out of town," leaving his family with only a photograph of himself (Malkovich with a mustache). Allen is his sister, the victim of a childhood disease that left one of her legs shorter than the other, though she is even more crippled by shyness. Finally, Naughton plays the gentleman caller, Malkovich's coworker at the warehouse. The apartment becomes as it was in the 1930s. Woodward discovers that Allen has not been going to the typing classes her mother has worked so hard to pay for. Then Woodward, who is wont to go on about the multitude of gentleman callers she entertained as a young woman, wants to know when her daughter expects a male visitor. Allen doesn't expect any callers, nor has she ever had any. She is most often engrossed in the world of the fragile glass figurines that she collects, or listening to old phonograph records. Woodward badgers Malkovich, wanting to know why he isn't more ambitious, asking him why he spends so much time at the movies. He tells her that the movies provide him with adventure. (Drinking provides him with an equally immediate escape.) They battle but later Woodward tells Malkovich she knows he wants to go away. She asks only that he help find a husband for Allen first. One evening, Malkovich announces he will bring a gentleman caller home

for dinner. Woodward works overtime preparing for the visit, but, when the big night arrives, Allen is paralyzed with fear, particularly when she learns the caller is Naughton, whom she had a crush on in high school. While Woodward charms Naughton, Allen lies on the sofa. After the meal, Woodward and Malkovich retire to do the dishes. Naughton talks with Allen, not recognizing her until she reminds him of the nickname he used to call her, "Blue Roses." In the dim light, she flatters him with her memories of his singing voice and high-school accomplishments. Naughton talks optimistically about his night school courses and the future. He tells her that he hardly noticed her disability in high school and that she is selling herself short. She shows him her glass menagerie. They dance. The glass unicorn, her favorite figure, is broken. Naughton kisses Allen tenderly, then realizes he is getting in over his head. He explains that he already has a fiancee, and, shortly thereafter, leaves. Woodward blames Malkovich, who is as surprised as his mother to learn about Naughton's engagement. Malkovich leaves for the movies as Woodward calls after him: "Go to the moon—you selfish dreamer!" The action returns to Malkovich in the empty apartment. He explains that he left St. Louis but that guilt followed him everywhere and that at any time he might turn around and see his sister's eyes.

It is often said pejoratively that certain movies are little more than filmed stage plays. The conventional cinematic alternative is to open up the play, to move the action outside and to new locales. Irving Rapper's 1950 version of the GLASS MENAGERIE did just that, including a visit to a dance hall by Kirk Douglas' gentleman caller and Jane Wyman's Laura. However, Paul Newman has said that he approached THE GLASS MENAGERIE less as a filmmaker than as an archivist, and his version is, in essence, a filmed stage play. Other than the exterior shot of Malkovich making his way to the empty apartment, the action of the film is confined entirely to the apartment and the fire escape. For the most part, Newman has even foregone the fancy camera work that would have announced his intent to treat the material *cinematically*. (The most notable exception, the shot that circles the panicked Allen when she learns the identity of the gentleman caller, is both appropriate and effective.) It is something of a cliche to give a filmed play a claustrophobic feel, but THE GLASS MENAGERIE and its

trapped characters cry out for such a treatment and Newman has effectively evoked it. Newman, cinematographer Ballhaus, and production designer Walton have also bathed the film in rich amber light and in so doing captured the ambience of the "memory play" Williams intended "The Glass Menagerie" to be. Beyond these important atmospheric undertakings, Newman lets the actors and Williams' poetic language do the work.

Ultimately the most cinematic element of THE GLASS MENAGERIE is the acting. Although all of the actors have done their roles on the stage (the film is an outgrowth of the stage production that was mounted in Massachusetts in summer 1985 and in Connecticut in spring 1986, and which starred Woodward, Naughton, and Allen), none of their performances has stage-bound qualities. Their actions, expressions, and readings have the minutely nuanced quality that the requirements of the stage prohibit. All of the performances are superb. Woodward's delightful Amanda is full of contradictions. She is both earthy and refined, a romantic dreamer living in the past and an aggressive pragmatist, a doting mother and a nag. Malkovich reportedly wanted to play Williams' autobiographical narrator more selfishly and with stronger homosexual overtones. For good or ill, Newman dissuaded him, and the result is a brilliant performance from Malkovich. His Tom is a product of frustration, romantic dreams, and guilt, but Malkovich also finds much humor in the role. Naughton brings a heartfelt sensitivity to his self-absorbed go-getter that makes his scenes with Allen extremely touching. Allen is perhaps the biggest surprise, as her previous film roles have asked so little of her. Here she plumbs emotions of considerable depth. Her Laura is so achingly shy that her strange retreat into her glass menagerie is plausible and profoundly affecting. Yet there is an innocent openness in her portrayal that not only invites Naughton in but that leaves room for her to delight in his attention. Because Allen is both capable of opening up like a flower and as fragile as a glass figurine, Malkovich's guilt is all the more piercing. After a two-week rehearsal period, THE GLASS MENAGERIE was shot in 30 days at the Kaufman Astoria Studio on Long Island. It was made on a budget of $3.5 million. In addition to the 1955 Rapper film, Anthony Harvey did a TV version of the play in 1973 with Katharine Hepburn and Michael Moriarity. *(Adult situations.)*

p, Burtt Harris; d, Paul Newman; w, Tennessee Williams (based on his play); ph, Michael Ballhaus (Du Art Color); m, Henry Mancini; ed, David Ray; prod d, Tony Walton; art d, John Kasarda; set d, Susan Bode; cos, Tony Walton.

Drama **(PR:C MPAA:PG)**

GLI OCCHIALI D'ORO† (1987, It./Fr./Yugo.) 110m L.P.-Reteltelia-Paradis-Avala Profilm/D.M.V. c (Trans: The Gold Spectacles)

Philippe Noiret *(Dr. Fadigati)*, Rupert Everett *(Davide Lattes)*, Valeria Golino *(Nora Treves)*, Nicola Farron *(Eraldo)*, Stefania Sandrelli *(Mrs. Lavezzoli)*, Ivana Despotovic *(Carlotta)*, Rade Markovic *(Bruno Lattes)*, Roberto Herlitzka, Luca Zingaretti, Esmeralda Ruspoli, Arianna Felloni.

Set in pre-WW II fascist Italy, this drama of persecution stars Noiret as a doctor ostracized by his friends when they learn of his homosexuality. When his young lover leaves him, Noiret becomes friends with Everett, a persecuted young Jew whose girl friend, Golino, has left him for a fascist official. Their friendship grows until Noiret commits suicide and Everett resigns himself to his fate. Shown in competition at the Venice Film Festival.

p, Leo Pescarolo; d, Giuliano Montaldo; w, Nicola Badalucco, Antonella Grassi, Giuliano Montaldo (based on the novel by Giorgio Bassani); ph, Armando Nannuzzi (Agfa-Gevaert color); m, Ennio Morricone; ed, Alfredo Muschietti; art d, Luciano Ricceri; cos, Nana Cecchi.

Drama **(PR:NR MPAA:NR)**

GONDOLA† (1987, Jap.) 112m OM c-bw

Keiko Uemura *(Kagari)*, Kenta Kai *(Ryo)*, Midori Kiuchi, Sumie Sasaki, Hideo Satoh, Hide Demon.

Sadasue's debut feature is set in Tokyo and deals with the friendship between a preteen girl and a lonely window washer. The girl, Uemura, lives in a Tokyo highrise and receives little affection from her mother. The building's window washer is Kai, who hails from a small fishing village and has no family or friends in Tokyo. Together they build a friendship which provides the support both of them desperately need. Filmed with some highly stylized camera work in both color and black-and-white.

p, Mayato Sadasue; d, Chisho Itoh; w, Chisho Itoh, Yashi Natsume; ph, Toshihiko Uriu; m, Satoru Yoshida; ed, Shuichi Kakesu.

Drama **(PR:NR MPAA:NR)**

GONDOVISELES† (1987, Hung.) 97m Mafilm-Hungarian TV/Hungarofilm c (Trans: Tolerance)

Denes Dobrei *(Andras)*, Erika Ozsda *(Eva)*.

The third film from director Erdoss to star Erika Ozsda (following THE PRINCESS and COUNTDOWN) in an examination of Hungarian social problems is Erdoss' first color film. After serving a two-and-a-half year prison sentence for selling items stolen from his work place, Dobrei finds his daughters have been placed in separate foster homes. Together with his wife Ozsda (who has served time for assaulting a man who tried to rape her), Dobrei sets out to retrieve his daughters. After bribes, threats, and an actual assault on one set of recalcitrant foster parents, the children are returned to Dobrei and Ozsda. Unfortunately, the idyllic family life they had imagined does not materialize. Ozsda is haunted by her rape and prison experiences, while the frustrated Dobrei begins a disastrous affair that tears the family apart.

d, Pal Erdoss; w, Istvan Kardos; ph, Ferenc Pap, Tamas Sas (Eastmancolor); m, Ferenc Balazs; ed, Klara Majoros; set d, Ferenc Jely; cos, Flora Torok.

Drama **(PR:NR MPAA:NR)**

GOOD MORNING BABYLON**½ (1987, It./Fr./USA) 116m Filmtre-MK2-Pressman-RA-1-Films A2/Vestron c (GOOD MORNING BABILONIA)

Vincent Spano *(Nicola Bonnano)*, Joaquim de Almeida *(Andrea Bonnano)*, Greta Scacchi *(Edna)*, Desiree Becker *(Mabel)*, Omero Antonutti *(Bonnano, Nicola & Andrea's Father)*, Charles Dance *(D.W. Griffith)*, Berangere Bonvoisin *(Mrs. Moglie Griffith)*, David Brandon *(Grass)*, Brian Freilino *(Thompson)*, Margarita Lozano *(The Venetian)*, Massimo Venturiello *(Duccio)*, Andrea Prodan *(Irish Cameraman)*, Dorotea Ausenda, Ugo Bencini, Daniel Bosch, Renzo Cantini, Marco Cavicchioli, Fiorenza d'Alessandro, Lionello Pio Di Savoia, Maurizio Fardo, Domenico Fiore, Mirio Guidelli, John Francis Lane, Ubaldo Lo Presti, Luciano Macherelli, Sandro Mellegni, Elio Marconato, Michele Melega, Mauro Monni, Lamberto Petrecca, Diego Ribon, Antonio Russo, Giuseppe Scarcella, Leontine Snel, Egidio Termine, Francesco Tola, Pinon Toska.

The dawn of Hollywood is brought to the screen in this fable about two Italian brothers—Spano and de Almeida—who apply their craftsmanship to D.W. Griffith's 1916 masterpiece INTOLERANCE. The film begins in Tuscany in 1913 as Antonutti, a master facade restorer, and his seven sons put the finishing touches on an exquisite old basilica. Afterwards, at a family dinner, Antonutti announces that he is selling his unprofitable company. His two favorite sons, Spano and de Almeida, who inherited his "hands of gold," vow to make a fortune in America and then return to buy back the family business. Antonutti's only advice to his sons is to remain equal and avoid fighting each other. After a transatlantic voyage which consciously recalls the Charles Chaplin short THE IMMIGRANT (the rough journey is illustrated by a bowl of soup which slides from one end of the table to the other), the brothers arrive in New York with wide-eyed awe. Their dreams of being discovered as great artisans are far from realized, however. They travel across the country taking such menial jobs as pig caretakers. When they meet a train-car full of singing Italian artisans en route to California for the 1915 Exposition, the brothers join them. Once in California, they help their countrymen construct the magnificent Italian Pavilion which attracts the attention of everyone, including film director D.W. Griffith (played as with supreme southern gentility by Dance). Dance is once again impressed by the craftsmanship of the Italians, having already been awed by the Hollywood premiere of Giovanni Pastrone's 1914 epic CABIRIA. Dance is so inspired by that film that he cancels production of his current picture and takes up work on a long-standing project, INTOLERANCE. "Are you thinking of your old idea, INTOLERANCE," Mrs. Griffith (Bonvoisin) coyly inquires. "I can always tell when it crops up in your head."

Dance tries to hire the foremen of the crew that built the Italian Pavilion, but he is too late—they have just embarked on their return voyage to Italy. Attempting to capitalize on the opportunity, Spano and de Almeida try to pass themselves off as the foremen—a ruse which is quickly discovered. The brothers manage to find a small job on the set as caretakers of the thousands of birds which are to be used in INTOLERANCE. During an argument with Brandon, the film's production manager, the brothers raise their fists defiantly. "We are the sons of the sons of the sons of Michelangelo and Leonardo," they loudly declare, "Whose sons are you?" In the meantime, the brothers fall in love with two pretty extras—Scacchi and Becker—who, although they are attracted to the poor Spano and de Almeida, have made a vow to only accept dates from producers or directors. The brothers try to woo the girls by offering them hundreds of short poems which they deliver in bird cages. The girls are impressed but the ultraromantic poetic sense of the Italians becomes the target of many jokes. When the brothers learn that Dance is not pleased with any of the designs for the gigantic elephant statues for INTOLERANCE's "Babylon" set, they begin work on their own. Their elephant, constructed in a nearby forest from papier-mache, is a brilliant work of art—the giant creature is seated upright with its front legs and trunk raised high into the skies as if praying to the gods. The elephant is filmed by a friend, an action which proves invaluable after the brother's creation is destroyed by the jealous Brandon and his coworkers. Upon seeing the film of the elephant, Dance recognizes the brothers' genius and hires them. Soon afterwards, the brothers marry (Spano weds Scacchi, de Almeida marries Becker) and Dance honors them at a wedding dinner which takes place outdoors in front of the Babylon set. Attending the dinner is Antonutti, who arrives from Italy for the event. Antonutti, however, is displeased with his sons' decision to stay in America and work on films. Dance respectfully defends the brothers and explains to Antonutti that, like the many generations of Italian craftsmen before them, Spano and de Almeida are artisans, though their medium has changed from marble and stone to celluloid. With the premiere of INTOLERANCE comes artistic respect for the brothers whose future as Hollywood craftsmen now looks bright. Coinciding with the premiere is the news that America has entered WW I. The brothers' idyllic and equal lives are thrown off balance when Scacchi dies in childbirth. Spano's son survives, but he refuses to raise him and instead returns to Italy to fight in the war. De Almeida also enlists, but in the American Army. While fighting on Italian soil, in front of the old basilica they earlier renovated, the brothers are reunited. Having both been seriously wounded, they use a newsreel camera to record their final moments for their sons.

Paolo and Vittorio Taviani (whose previous efforts ALLONSANFAN, PADRE PADRONE, NIGHT OF THE SHOOTING STARS, and KAOS found great critical acclaim) have made clear their attempt to create a fable, and, unfortunately, GOOD MORNING BABYLON succeeds on that one level only. In what must be one of the most disappointing major releases in recent years, GOOD MORNING BABYLON promises to capture the dawn of cinema and, more specifically, Hollywood as the birthplace of a new, collaborative community of artisans not unlike those great craftsmen who spent years creating Italian cathedrals. GOOD MORNING BABYLON is not about D.W. Griffith or the making of INTOLERANCE, nor is it about two real-life Italian artisan brothers. (There were reportedly three Italians from the San Francisco Exposition who were hired by Griffith, but the similarities end there.) What the Tavianis have successfully done is to revive a mythical world called Hollywood, which is re-created on obvious sets in Italy (outside Pisa and at Cinecitta studios) in much the same manner that Griffith re-created Babylon in Hollywood. While Griffith dealt with man's intolerance towards his fellow man throughout history, the Taviani's have dealt with man's intolerance towards the Immigrant (hence the Chaplin bow) in America. In the same way that Hollywood distorted reality through cinematic re-creation, so have the Tavianis distorted the real Hollywood. The brothers' first glimpse of America is an artificial New York skyline; the supposedly awe-inspiring Italian Pavilion is obviously a small-scale model; and the Babylon set is infinitely less impressive than in Griffith's 1915 film. This is not because the Tavianis are incompetent or saddled with budgetary restrictions (the $6.5 million budget is hefty for a foreign production), but because the artificiality of the Cinecitta/Fellini-style sets is important to the Hollywood myth. GOOD MORNING BABYLON is about the craftsmen and artisans whose work is captured on celluloid instead of preserved in stone. If the film looked "real" this aspect of their craft would be lost.

What GOOD MORNING BABYLON lacks, however, is a script. Not only does it fail to re-create the epic quality of a Griffith film, but its characters fall as flat as the facades they create. Spano and de Almeida are both accomplished actors who adeptly handle the transition from Italian to Italian-American, but they are given very little substance. One wants to believe that their one-dimensional characters were intentionally created by the Tavianis as a comment on the Hollywood myth, but that would have been dramatically foolish. Even less real are Scacchi and Becker, who are no more human than the papier-mache elephant that the brothers create. This lack of well-rounded characters only causes a sense of frustration, as if the Tavianis had cared more for the artificiality of the craft than for the humanity of the craftsman. While Dance performs admirably as Griffith (the role was first offered to Sam Shepherd and then to James Woods), employing the legendary director's theatricality and southern manner, it is Antonutti who turns in the most effective performance. Having previously starred in PADRE PADRONE and THE NIGHT OF THE SHOOTING STARS, Antonutti is a commanding presence who seems to be more comfortable with his character (and the directors' techniques) than any of his costars. A coproduction between Italy, France, and American producer Edward Pressman, GOOD MORNING BABYLON is the first English-language production for the Tavianis. (In English and Italian; English subtitles.) *(Brief nudity.)*

p, Giuliani G. De Negri; d, Paolo Taviani, Vittorio Taviani; w, Paolo Taviani, Vittorio Taviani, Tonino Guerra (based on an idea by Lloyd Fonvielle); ph, Giuseppe Lanci (Eastmancolor); m, Nicola Piovani; ed, Roberto Perpignani; art d, Gianni Sbarra; cos, Lina Nerli Taviani; ch, Gino Landi; makeup, Gianfranco Mecacci.

Historical/Drama **(PR:C-O MPAA:PG-13)**

GOOD MORNING, VIETNAM***½ (1987) 119m Touchstone-Silver Partners III/Buena Vista c

Robin Williams *(Adrian Cronauer)*, Forest Whitaker *(Edward Garlick)*, Tung Thanh Tran *(Tuan)*, Chintara Sukapatana *(Trinh)*, Bruno Kirby *(Lt. Steven Hauk)*, Robert Wuhl *(Marty Lee Dreiwitz)*, J.T. Walsh *(Sgt. Major Dickerson)*, Noble Willingham *(Gen. Taylor)*, Richard Edson *(Pvt. Abersold)*, Juney Smith *(Phil McPherson, Radio Engineer)*, Richard Portnow *(Dan "The Man" Levitan)*, Floyd Vivino *(Eddie Kirk)*, Cu Ba Nguyen *(Jimmy Wah, Saloon Owner)*, Dan R. Stanton, Don E. Stanton *(Censors)*, Danny Aiello III, J.J. *(MP's)*, James McIntire, Peter Mackenzie *(Sergeants at Jimmy Wah's)*, No Tran, Hoa Nguyen, Uikey Kuay, Suvit Abakaz, Panas Wiwatpanachat, Lerdcharn Namkiri, Hanh Hi Nguyen, Tuan Lai, Boonchai Jakraworawut, Joe B. Veokeki, Wichien Chaopramong, Kien Chufak, Prasert Tangpantarat *(Vietnamese Students)*, Tim O'Hare, John Goyer, Louis Hood, Christopher Mangan, Kenneth Pitochelli, Jonathan MacLeod, Gregg T. Knight *(Convoy Soldiers)*, Ralph Tabakin *(Chaplain Noel)*, Sangad Sangkao, Vanlap Sangkao *(Viet Cong Leaders in Jungle)*.

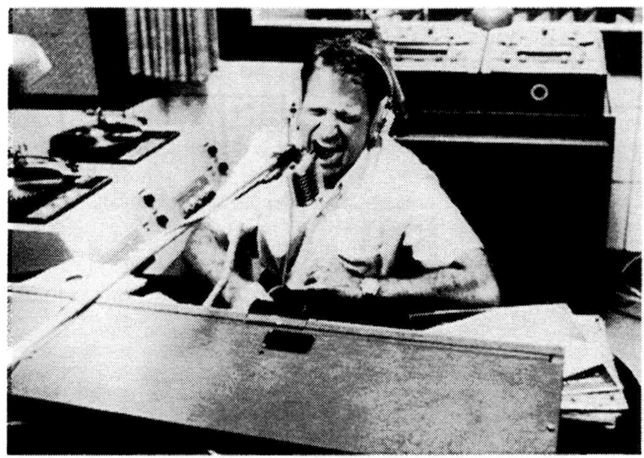

After suffering through a series of unsuccessful films that forced his unique talents into an uncomfortably conventional direction, Robin Williams has finally been given a showcase for his rapid-fire improvisational wit in this, the first comedy set in Vietnam. Based very loosely on the experiences of real-life Armed Forces Radio (AFR) disc jockey Adrian Cronauer, GOOD MORNING, VIETNAM begins in 1965 as Cronauer (Williams) steps off a plane in Saigon. Previously stationed in Crete, Williams has been imported by general Willingham because his comedic broadcasts have proven to be a huge moral-booster. Williams arrives at the Army's Saigon radio station facing stiff opposition from his uptight superiors, sergeant major Walsh and lieutenant Kirby. Current AFR programming features zombie-like disc jockeys, health and safety tips, Army-censored news, and a playlist derived from such geriatric favorites as Lawrence Welk, Mantovanni, and Percy Faith. In his first broadcast, Williams literally knocks the troops out of their stupor with his howling salutation, "Gooooood morning, Vietnammmmm!" and then plays a forbidden Martha and the Vandellas song, "Nowhere to Hide." During his twice daily broadcasts, Williams launches into a torrent of comedic improvisation: he pokes fun at President Lyndon Johnson and his daughters ("President Johnson today signed a highway beautification bill. Basically, the bill said that his daughters could not drive in a convertible on public highways"), he compares Ho Chi Minh and Colonel Sanders ("Are they the same person? The lines are open"), has a an imaginary conversation with a military fashion designer who hates camouflage ("If you go into battle you should clash!"), sees the soldiers as Dorothy in THE WIZARD OF OZ (with the Viet Cong as munchkins singing, "Follow the Ho Chi Minh Trail"), and plays such banned artists as James Brown and the Beach Boys. Kirby, who is the type of guy who sends "Humor in Uniform" anecdotes to *Reader's Digest*, is outraged by Williams' behavior and doesn't think his brand of humor funny. Luckily for Williams he has the full support of Willingham and is the first d.j. in AFR history to receive fan mail from the troops. Outside the station, Williams becomes infatuated with a beautiful young Vietnamese girl, Sukapatana, and begins teaching an English class that she is enrolled in just to be near her. He befriends the girl's brother (Tung Thanh Tran) and the boy acts as a go-between, arranging for them to have a date. Unfortunately, the 12 members of Sukapatana's family come along as chaperons and his desire to bed her never materializes. Although in 1965 the war seems unreal and distant, it soon comes home to Saigon when Williams is nearly caught in a terrorist bomb-blast that destroys the local G.I. hangout, Jimmy Wah's, killing two soldiers and wounding three others. Williams is determined to go on the air with the news, but his superiors forbid it. He broadcasts the news anyway, and gets cut off in mid-sentence and suspended. Kirby, determined to prove Williams unfunny, takes his place with what he considers "wacky" scripted material and an arm-load of polka records. The replacement program is a dismal failure and Williams is soon reinstated ("In my heart I know that I'm funny," Kirby protests). Williams, however, is tired of censorship and refuses to go back on the air. Desperate to get Williams back on the air, his loyal aide-de-camp, Whitaker, identifies him before several truckloads of troops being sent to the front. Personal contact with the men to whom he's broadcasting motivates Williams to return to the microphone. Walsh, however, hopes to get rid of Williams once and for all by sending him out to visit the troops by way of a trail held by the enemy. With Whitaker at the wheel, they drive there, but their jeep hits a mine and both men are stranded in enemy territory. Tung Thanh Tran hears of this and rushes off to rescue the soldiers, easily slipping in and out of enemy-held territory. When the men return to the station, Williams is told that military intelligence has learned that Tung Thanh Tran is a V.C. terrorist and will be executed if caught. Because of his fraternizing with the enemy, Williams is discharged from the Army. Before leaving Saigon, Williams confronts Tung Thanh Tran and learns that the boy harbors deep resentment toward the American military presence and will die if necessary in the battle to free his country from foreign invaders. Sobered by the reality of the American intervention and his role in it, Williams leaves Vietnam just as the US military commitment increases dramatically. Meanwhile, back at the radio station, Whitaker carries on Williams' legacy at the microphone.

Fueled by a superb performance from Robin Williams, GOOD MORNING, VIETNAM works better than it has any right to. Screenwriter Markowitz's script stumbles whenever Williams is not at the microphone, placing him in melodramatic or hackneyed situations that become increasingly predictable and preposterous (Walsh's clandestine effort to have Williams killed is a bit hard to swallow). A film structured around a star whose strong suit is runaway improvisation poses considerable problems for a director. One can either concentrate exclusively on the performer for the duration of the monolog (such as director Jonathan Demme did with Spaulding Grey in the performance documentary SWIMMING TO CAMBODIA), or fall back on reaction shots of the audience to break up the visual tedium. Unfortunately, Levinson opts for the later, cutting to seemingly endless shots of soldiers laughing and grooving to Williams' antics on portable radios. While this approach is at first used to establish Williams' listening audience and the effect he has on them, it quickly becomes dull and repetitive, detracting from the performance instead of enhancing it. To his credit, however, the director does manage to sneak in several *Levinsonesque* touches, such as the fey Jimmy Wah's obsession with obtaining naked photos of Walter Brennan, the Army censors who are obese identical twins, and the interaction of the soldiers at the radio station—all recall some of the most inspired moments of DINER and TIN MEN. Levinson also manages to be one of the few filmmakers working in the Vietnam genre who has put a face on the Vietnamese themselves. The film spends a considerable amount of time with the locals and we watch as Williams makes a futile effort to assimilate into their culture. We see Vietnamese farms, businesses, schools, and shanty towns and the people who inhabit them. For once the Vietnamese are treated as complex people with a strong culture, and not as helpless victims or the faceless enemy. The fact that this aspect of the story line collapses into some hard-to-take melodramatics is more the fault of the screenplay than of the director or actors. And the actors are marvelous. Williams, of course, is the dynamic center of the film and he gives the screen performance of his career. One simply sits in awe of his motor-mouth improvisations, which veer into all sorts of unexpected and hilarious directions. However, in his enthusiasm Williams occasionally steps into territory that doesn't belong in a film set in 1965. In the scene where he entertains the troops about to be shipped to the front, Williams manages to combine the best of his wit with his talents as a serious actor and comes away with what may be the most affecting part of the film. Whitaker does wonders with a thankless part, Willingham is delightful as the sympathetic general, Thai actress Sukapatana is impressive, and Wuhl, Walsh, Edson, Smith, and Portnow are terrific as the radio station gang. Kirby, also seen in Levinson's TIN MEN, comes as close as any actor can to walking off with a film dominated by Robin Williams at his best. His portrayal of the totally ineffectual lieutenant with aspirations of being a comedian is wonderfully funny and insightful, bringing new dimension to the cliched role of the nerdy, frustrated bureaucrat. Despite some disappointing problems, GOOD MORNING, VIETNAM is a wholly entertaining movie that manages to work some freshness into what is rapidly becoming an overworked genre—the Vietnam film. *(Violence, profanity.)*

p, Mark Johnson, Larry Brezner, Ben Moses, Harry Benn; d, Barry Levinson; w, Mitch Markowitz; ph, Peter Sova (Deluxe Color); m, Alex North; ed, Stu Linder; prod d, Roy Walker; art d, Steve Spence; set d, Tessa Davies; cos, Keith Denny; spec eff, Fred Cramer; stunts, Clive Curtis; makeup, Eric Allwright.

Comedy/Drama **(PR:O MPAA:R)**

GOOD WIFE, THE** (1987, Aus.) 97m Laughing Kookaburra/Atlantic c (AKA: THE UMBRELLA WOMAN)

Rachel Ward *(Marge Hills)*, Bryan Brown *(Sonny Hills)*, Steven Vidler *(Sugar Hills)*, Sam Neill *(Neville Gifford)*, Jennifer Claire *(Daisy)*, Bruce Barry *(Archie)*, Peter Cummins *(Ned Hooper)*, Carole Skinner *(Mrs. Gibson)*, Clarissa Kaye-Mason *(Mrs. Jackson)*, Barry Hill *(Mr. Fielding)*, Susan Lyons *(Mrs Fielding)*, Helen Jones *(Rosie Gibbs)*, Lisa Hensley *(Sylvia)*, May Howlett *(Mrs. Carmichael)*, Maureen Green *(Sal Day)*, Garry Cook *(Gerry Day)*, Harold Kissin *(Davis, the Station Master)*, Oliver Hall *(Mick Jones)*, Sue Ingleton *(Rita)*, Robert Barrett *(Heckler at Bar)*, Maurice Hughes *(Sgt. Larkin)*, Margarita Haynes *(Greta)*, Bill Bader *(Train Guard)*, Dick May *(Waiter)*, Trevor Thomas *(Chemist)*, Philip Wilton *(Train Porter)*, Craig Fuller *(Charlie)*, Peter Ford *(Drunk in Bar)*.

Another ponderous Australian production that squanders its resources on an obsession with period detail while leaving the plot and characters bereft of anything resembling personality or motivation. Set in the small town of Corrimandel in 1939, THE GOOD WIFE stars Ward as the title character, the dutiful spouse of rugged lumberjack Brown. While her husband is off at work, Ward busies herself with helping out those in need, including duty as the local midwife. Although her marriage is a happy one and Brown is a good provider, he is a dud in bed. Living with Brown and Ward is Brown's younger brother, Vidler. After accidentally spying husband and wife making love, Vidler's hormones go into overdrive and he innocently asks Ward if she could do with him what she does with Sonny. Without missing a beat the sexually frustrated Ward merely replies, "Why don't you ask Sonny?" Inexplicably, Brown agrees to let his brother sleep with his wife. Unfortunately for Ward, Vidler is even worse in bed than Brown and the tryst is over in a matter of seconds. Later, in town, Ward spots a handsome stranger, Neill, and begins to become obsessed with him. Fancying himself a Don Juan, Neill takes note of Ward's appreciative stare and immediately tries to have his way with her against a wall. Shocked, Ward resists his advances. Leaving her with a cryptic "You'll only get one chance with me, sweetheart," Neill goes off to his new job as bartender at the local pub and subsequently beds every woman in town but Ward. At the same time a frustrated and jealous Vidler lets it slip in public that he and Ward have slept together. The ensuing gossip, combined with Ward's increasingly irrational obsession with the handsome bartender, drives her to go into town, get drunk, and harass Neill in public. After this outburst, Ward packs her bags and leaves the confused-but-ever-patient Brown. She moves into a boarding house across the street from Neill's hotel and spends her days watching his room. Neill's last sexual conquest is the wife of a prominent local businessman and he arranges to meet her at his hotel. The jealous Vidler (who has befriended Neill) blows the whistle on the tryst and Neill is caught with the businessman's wife in his room. Forced to leave

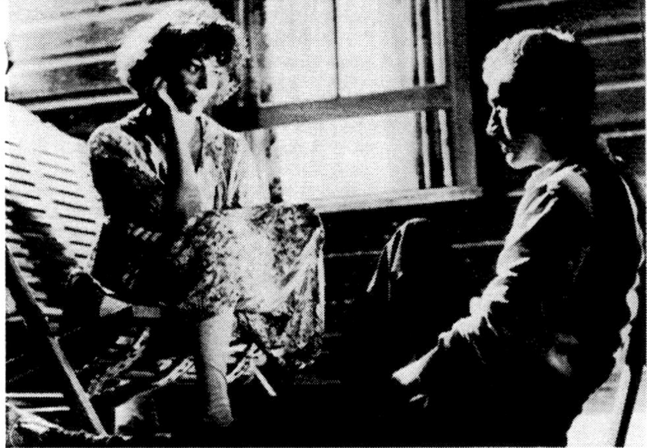

town, Neill boards the next train only to find the manic Ward there, begging to be his loyal concubine. Bored with this little game, Neill unceremoniously tosses Ward from the moving train and bids her adieu. Some townsfolk find the unconscious Ward and bring her home to the ever-understanding Brown, who nurses her back to health. The object of her desire gone, Ward resumes her dull marriage to Brown, but keeps an eye on the passing trains.

Made somewhat palatable by a strong performance from Ward, THE GOOD WIFE is much like this year's American film SUMMER HEAT—both movies try so hard to ooze a moody sense of sexual tension that they squeeze the life out of the material. All of the ludicrous action in THE GOOD WIFE occurs with such nonchalance that the viewer is left wondering if these people are really zombies from a nearby horror film. Screenwriter Kenna ignores anything that could have been remotely interesting in the material and instead tosses in some textbook "psychological" motivations for Ward's neuroses, placing most of the blame on Ward's wanton, alcoholic mother. Perhaps most annoying is the relationship between Brown and Vidler. Every scene they have together turns into a Three Stooges-type routine with Brown smacking his dim sibling in the head. Vidler's character is so stupid it's a wonder he can tie his shoes by himself. As for Neill, he practically repeats his role from MY BRILLIANT CAREER and is given no help from the underwritten script and lackluster direction. Director Cameron has no grasp of character and his film is so scrupulously decent that it takes no stance and, therefore, is without passion—a fatal flaw in a film about obsession and lust. If one expects nothing more from movies than pretty pictures and vintage clothing, then by all means see THE GOOD WIFE; for those looking for something more, it's like watching FATAL ATTRACTION without the sex and violence. *(Sexual situations, profanity.)*

p, Jan Sharp; d, Ken Cameron; w, Peter Kenna; ph, James Bartle (Eastmancolor); m, Cameron Allan; ed, John Scott; prod d, Sally Campbell; cos, Jennie Tate; makeup, Sally Gordon; stunts, Chris Anderson.

Drama **(PR:C-O MPAA:R)**

GOOFBALLS* (1987) 87m Filmcap/Shapiro c

Ben Gordon, Ron James, John Kozak, Wayne Robson, Cynthia Belliveau, Laura Robinson, Ilana Linden, Wayne Flemming, John Hemphill.

A perfect title because it describes the producers who thought this film had any merit. There have been a number of movies in the last year or so with the same setting, including CLUB PARADISE. None of them was very good and this one is the worst to date. Set in a golf resort in the Bahamas where Gordon is the effervescent *tummler* (all-around entertainment director), the confusing story has to do with gangsters, Arabs, and pretty women in bathing suits, leading to a general ho-hum feeling of "we've seen this all before, done better." Years before, Gordon had been a wheelman on a robbery and a pal of his took the fall and went to the pen. That pal calls Gordon now and says there will be a small contingent of dark, swarthy men who have broken noses and wear very thin gold watches coming to the resort. Gordon is asked to give them proper consideration and make their stay pleasant. Meanwhile, some Arabian types are stashing ill-gotten gold under a boulder in the resort's botanical area and they think Gordon has purloined some valuables from them. At the same time, the mucky-mucks of a group like the PGA are surveying the area's course with the idea of holding a large tournament there. Gordon is ordered to stage a golf match and promises a host of celebrities. When none of the celebs show up, Gordon has to put on a show with untalented relatives and friends. The gangsters, always on the lookout for a fast buck, prevail on Gordon to "fix" the golf tournament. Of course, it all winds up with every dog having his day and every crook getting his due.

The dialog is pedestrian and the most annoying bits of it are spoken by Gordon's smart-alec parrot whose voice, typically dubbed by a human, sounds like a bad imitation of Mel Blanc. An attempt at the kind of gang comedy that made Bill Murray and John Candy stars, but that will do absolutely nothing for anyone in this project. *(Profanity.)*

p, Dale Falconer; d, Brad Turner; w, Skip West; m, Robert Rettberg.

Comedy **(PR:C MPAA:NR)**

GOSPODA AVANTYURISTY† (1987, USSR) 88m Gruziafilm/Sovexportfilm c (Trans: Gentlemen Adventurers)

Mamuka Kikaleishvili, Tristan Saralidze, Kakha Kavsadze, Guram Pirtskhalava.

A spoof of spy films which takes place in Soviet Georgia as two agents try to track down the heir of a wealthy, deceased businessman. The agents pose as tourists in order to track down the heir, hoping to kill him and anyone else who might be in line for the fortune.

d, Bidzina Chkheidze; w, Amiran Chichinadze; ph, Georgy Chelidze, Nugzar Erkomanishvili; m, Yakov Bobokhidze.

Comedy **(PR:NR MPAA:NR)**

GOTHIC*½ (1987, Brit.) 90m Virgin Vision/Virgin Films c

Gabriel Byrne *(Lord Byron)*, Julian Sands *(Percy Bysshe Shelley)*, Natasha Richardson *(Mary Godwin)*, Myriam Cyr *(Claire Clairmont)*, Timothy Spall *(Dr. John Polidori)*, Andreas Wisniewski *(Fletcher)*, Alec Mango *(Murray)*, Dexter Fletcher *(Rushton)*, Pascal King *(Justice)*, Tom Hickey *(Tour Guide)*, Linda Coggin *(Turkish Mechanical Doll)*, Kristine Landon-Smith *(Mechanical Woman)*, Chris Chappell *(Man in Armour)*, Mark Pickard *(Young William)*, Kiran Shah *(Fuseli Monster)*, Christine Newby, Kim Tillesley *(Shelley Fans)*.

On the night of June 16, 1816, at the Swiss villa of Lord Byron, Percy Bysshe Shelley, his 19-year-old mistress, Mary Wollstonecraft Godwin (soon to be Shelley), her half-sister, Claire Clairmont, and Byron's personal physician, Dr. John Polidori, gathered to invent their own ghost stories. That evening, two classics of gothic horror literature were born: Mary Shelley's *Frankenstein* and Dr. Polidori's *The Vampyre*, an influential precursor to Bram Stoker's *Dracula*. This historic occasion, which was portrayed so succinctly in the opening five minutes of James Whale's masterpiece THE BRIDE OF FRANKENSTEIN, is now transformed into an deranged sex-and-blood orgy of cinematic excess by the Bacchus of filmmaking himself, Ken Russell, in GOTHIC. Since the true tortured personal lives of those involved (bisexuality, homosexuality, incest, miscarriages, suicide) could not even have been suggested by Whale back in 1935, the subject matter does seem ripe for a reinterpretation. Unfortunately, Russell takes screenwriter Stephen Volk's interesting premise and creates a film that plays more like a

drug-trip romp from the 1960s than a gothic horror story. The plot, such as it is, begins with the aforementioned gathering. After the guests drink plenty of laudanum (liquid opium and alcohol) and watch Byron (Byrne) torment his toadish lover Polidori (Spall), they indulge in an orgy in which Shelley (Sands) is paired with Godwin (Richardson), Byrne is paired with Clairmont (Cyr), and Spall stands in the corner watching. A sudden bolt of lightning inspires them to attempt a seance to summon the demons of their deepest fears. They clasp hands around the skull of a monk who sold his soul to the devil, and their incantations result in Cyr collapsing into a fit. She is put to bed while the others begin hallucinating everything from horrible little dwarfs to mysterious dark figures. Meanwhile, Byrne seeks to satisfy his libido by having sex with his maid (whom he calls "Augusta" after his beloved sister), then with the prone Cyr (while wretched Spall sits sobbing in the next room and repeatedly impales his hand on a nail that once held a crucifix), and finally by attempting seductions of both Richardson and Sands. After much screaming, running, billowing curtains, cobwebs, lightning, and bombastic music cues from Thomas Dolby, Richardson hallucinates the deaths of Sands (drowning), Byrne (a bad case of bleeding by leeches), and Spall (suicide by poisoning), and then tries to hurl herself off a balcony, only to be saved by Sands at the last second. Believe it or not, the whole thing turns out to be merely a dream, and the next morning Richardson relates her idea for *Frankenstein*.

GOTHIC is a frustrating film, for the premise is so full of compelling potential that Russell's subsequent mindless pretensions and wanton decadence serve only to annoy and anger when one thinks of what might have been. As is his wont when dealing with the lives of historical figures, Russell gleefully jumps upon the more sordid details and builds his film around them. To be sure the bizarre lives of those involved make for some perversely fascinating dramatics, but Russell presents them as if they were escapees from the local asylum. The people in this film don't seem to be able to tear themselves away from their various obsessions long enough to jot down a few notes, let alone write a poem or novel. The cast, especially Richardson (daughter of Vanessa Redgrave and Tony Richardson), try hard to lend some credibility to this exercise, but Russell gives them so many theatrically extreme things to do and say that they merely appear ridiculous (Sands wanders around bug-eyed muttering, "Decay! Decay!"; Spall spends the latter half of the film crawling on the floor with a shaved head and no pants; Cyr slithers around naked, covered with a thin film of mud, clutching a dead rat in her mouth; etc.). To his credit, Russell does manage to present some memorable horrific images, but they seem far too self-conscious and isolated, more the product of an "artsy" film director than a drug-induced 19th-Century nightmare. Despite the fact that Russell keeps the parade of vulgar images coming at a furious pace, GOTHIC becomes boring, excessive, and repetitive, leaving the viewer hoping that Mary Shelley will wake up and write a lot sooner than she finally does. *(Violence, gore effects, nudity, sexual situations, substance abuse.)*

p, Penny Corke; d, Ken Russell; w, Stephen Volk; ph, Mike Southon (Eastmancolor); m, Thomas Dolby; ed, Michael Bradsell; prod d, Christopher Hobbs; art d, Michael Buchanan; cos, Victoria Russell, Kay Gallwey; spec eff, Ace Effects; stunts, Roy Street; makeup, Pat Hay.

Horror/Biography Cas. **(PR:O MPAA:R)**

GOVORIT MOSKVA† (1987, USSR) 98m M. Gorky/Sovexportfilm c (Trans: This Is Radio Moscow)

Lyudmila Zaitseva *(Lyubov)*, Boris Nevzorov *(Orlov)*.

A romance between the president of the district executive committee, Zaitseva, and a young tank commander, Nevzorov, is strained by long years of war and the resulting traumas. As the main characters deepen their commitment to each other, they also become stronger in their opposition to fascism.

d, Renita Grigoryeva, Yury Grigoryeva; w, Renita Grigoryeva; ph, Nikolai Puchkov; m, Pavel Chekalov; art d, Galina Anfilova.

War/Romance **(PR:NR MPAA:NR)**

GOZARESH-E YEK GHATL† (1987, Iran) 87m Hedayat/Farabi c (Trans: Report on a Murder)

Akbar Zanjanpour, Homa Rousta, Nasser Hashemi, Mahnaz Afzali, Ghotoboddin Sadeghi, Ali Asghar Garmsiry.

A young Iranian communist is imprisoned in 1953 during a CIA-engineered military coup, spending 20 years behind bars. He takes a job in a steel factory and later kills the man he holds responsible for his imprisonment. A lawyer is assigned to track him down and, after searching countless files and documents, manages to locate him.

d, Mohammed Ali Nadjafi; w, Mohammed Ali Nadjafi, Ali Reza Rayesian (based on an idea by H. Hedayat); ph, Mohammed Aladpoush; m, Farhad Fakhreldini; ed, Samad Tavazoie; prod d, Ebrahim Haghighi; cos, A. Radgabi; makeup, Mahein Navedi, Saeed Jallali.

Crime/Drama **(PR:NR MPAA:NR)**

GRAND GUIGNOL† (1987, Fr.) 87m Films du Chantier-Monthyon-UGC-Top 1-Films Aramis/UGC c

Guy Marchand *(Baptiste)*, Caroline Cellier *(Sarah)*, Jean-Claude Brialy *(Mr. Albert)*, Michel Galabru *(Charlie)*, Marie Dubois *(Germaine)*, Olivia Brunaux *(Coco)*, Denis Manuel *(The Proprietor)*, Jacques Chailleux *(Paolo)*, Claire Nadeau *(Adelaide)*, Catherine d'At *(The Creature)*, Serge Marquand, Violetta Ferrer *(Clients)*.

A drama with comic undertones, this entry draws parallels between the offstage relationships of a theater troupe and the Grand Guignol stage show they are producing. The phony blood of the stage show becomes real when novelty shop owner Galabru is hacked to death by his axe-wielding wife Dubois. Director Marboeuf explored the connections between stage and reality in his 1985 film, VAUDEVILLE.

p,d,&w, Jean Marboeuf; ph, Gerard Simon (Eastmancolor); ed, Anne-France Lebrun; art d, Jerome Clement; cos & makeup, Danielle Vuarin, Pascale Bouquiere.

Comedy/Drama **(PR:NR MPAA:NR)**

GRAVEYARD SHIFT*½ (1987) 88m Cinema Ventures-Lightshow/Shapiro c

Silvio Oliviero *(Stephen Tsepes)*, Helen Papas *(Michelle)*, Cliff Stoker *(Eric Hayden)*, Dorin Ferber *(Gilda)*, Dan Rose, Don Jones.

Made in late 1985 in Toronto, Canada, GRAVEYARD SHIFT is another of the low-budget shockers put out by the aggressive salespeople at Shapiro Entertainment, a company not known for making movies that alter or illuminate our time. The expression "graveyard shift" comes from those hours between midnight and eight a.m. when factory workers, toiling on the third of three shifts, get their jobs done. Oliviero is a 350-year-old vampire who drives a cab in what is supposed to be New York. Papas is a television director who is estranged from husband Stoker and she looks just like Oliviero's 300-years-dead girl friend, which is enough for him to bare his teeth. He is not the Lugosi or Lee or Cushing type. Rather, Oliviero is so good-looking that he is even more scary because it's difficult to believe he would do the things he does. In the past, we'd been led to believe that vampires prey only on sweet young things (virgins preferred), but the scarcity of virgins being what it is in New York, Oliviero goes after everyone, mostly people who fear death or are close to it. By sinking his teeth into their necks, he gives them eternal life, if only at night. In order for vampires to live, they must get fresh blood all the time so what happens is like an epidemic. Oliviero bites Papas and the two are now a pair. This doesn't delight Stoker who seeks out and employs a vampire-killer to knock off Oliviero. (Where does one find a vampire-killer these days? In the Yellow Pages?) At the conclusion, Papas gets behind the wheel of the taxi and will carry on the tradition. There is more style than content in this picture and when director/writer Ciccoritti is able to raise some decent money for a movie, he will step forward to become one of the better genre directors, if that's his aim. He might also think of hiring someone else to write his scripts as he is better behind the camera than behind the typewriter. *(Gore effects, nudity.)*

p, Michael Bockner; d&w, Gerard Ciccoritti; ph, Robert Bergman; m, Nicholas Pike; ed, Robert Bergman, Norman Smith; prod d, Lester Berman.

Horror **(PR:C-O MPAA:R)**

GREAT LAND OF SMALL, THE† (1987, Can.) 94m Les Prods.-La Fete/NW-Cinema Plus c

Karen Elkin *(Jenny)*, Michael Blouin *(David)*, Michael J. Anderson *(Fritz)*, Ken Roberts *(Flannigan)*, Lorraine Desmarais *(Mother)*, Francoise Graton *(Grandma)*, Michelle Elaine Turmel *(Sarah)*.

Two young city children—Elkin and Blouin—visit their grandparents in the country and find themselves swept into a secret world of magic, mysticism, and mystery known as the Great Land of Small. Leading them into this land is a small creature named Fritz (played by Anderson) who enlists the children's aid in his quest to recover a lost pouch of magic gold dust. They get involved in a series of adventures involving a malevolent innkeeper and a friendly hunchback, culminating at the peak of a magical mountain. One of five family films by Canadian producer Demers.

p, Rock Demers; d, Vojtech Jasny; w, David Sigmund; ph, Michel Brault; m,

Guy Trepanier; ed, Helene Girard; art d, Violette Daneau; cos, Michele Hamel; spec eff, Louis Craig, Les Productions, Pascal Blais.

Children's/Fantasy **Cas.** **(PR:AAA MPAA:G)**

GREEN MONKEY, THE (SEE: BLUE MONKEY, THE, 1987)

GROUND ZERO† (1987, Aus.) 109m Michael Pattinson-Burrowes Film Group-BDB/Hoyts c

Colin Friels *(Harvey Denton)*, Jack Thompson *(Trebilcock)*, Donald Pleasence *(Prosper Gaffney)*, Natalie Bate *(Pat Denton)*, Simon Chilvers *(Commission President)*, Neil Fitzpatrick *(Hooking)*, Bob Maza *(Wallemare)*, Peter Cummins *(Ballantyne)*, Stuart Faichney *(ASIO Agent)*.

A critically-acclaimed thriller which stars Friels as a director of television commercials who is informed that his father, whom Friels believed drowned 30 years earlier, was, in fact, murdered. His father, he is told, was a cameraman who took films of a British nuclear test sight in Australia. These films provide evidence that the British lied about the extent of the fallout effects on the Aboriginal population. With the help of a British ex-patriot-turned-hermit, Pleasence, Friels gathers the evidence that will prove the British involvement and subsequent cover-up. This controversial film, based partially on fact, earned nine nominations in the 1987 Australian Film Awards, winning for Best Cinematography, Best Editing, Best Production Design, and Best Sound.

p, Michael Pattinson; d, Michael Pattinson, Bruce Myles; w, Jan Sardi, Mac Gudgeon; ph, Steve Dobson (Eastmancolor); m, Chris Neal; ed, David Pulbrook; prod d, Brian Thompson; art d, Robert Dein.

Thriller **(PR:NR MPAA:NR)**

GRUBAYA POSADKA† (1987, USSR) 75m Uzbekfilm/Sovexportfilm c (Trans: Rough Landing)

Bakhram Matchanov, Anatoly Romashin, Anatoly Vassilyev, Irina Alferova, Olga Bityukova.

When a distraught colonel crashes his plane into the ocean and dies, his friend and protege comes to his defense and takes the blame for the accident. Only after an inquiry is it revealed that the colonel was the one at fault.

d, Mukhtar Aga-Mirzayev; w, Tevgeny Mesyatsev; ph, Leonid Travitsky; m, Anatoly Kalovarsky; art d, Anatoly Shibayev.

Drama **(PR:NR MPAA:NR)**

GRUZ BEZ MARKIROVKI† (1987, USSR) 92m A. Dovzhenko Kiev Film/ Sovexportfilm c (Trans: Unmarked Cargo)

Aleksei Gorbunov *(Stenjko)*, Tiinu Kark, Yury Grigoriev.

A drug-smuggling adventure set in a Soviet port begins when the crew of a foreign cargo ship in the process of refueling is suspected of transporting drugs. The ship's captain attempts to conceal the illegal goods, but customs officers eventually ferret them out. Dating from 1985, GRUZ BEZ MARKIROVKI was released in 1987. (In Ukranian; English subtitles.)

d, Vladimir Popkov; w, Vladimir Mazur; ph, Valery Anisimov; m, Oleg Kiva; art d, Vyacheslav Ershov.

Action/Adventure **(PR:NR MPAA:NR)**

GUNPOWDER** (1987, Brit.) 85m Lazer c

David Gilliam *(Gunn)*, Martin Potter *(Powder)*, Gordon Jackson *(Sir Anthony Phelps)*, Anthony Schaeffer *(Lovell)*, David Miller *(Dr. Vache)*, Debra Burton *(Coffee Carradine)*, Susan Rutherford *(Penny Keynes)*, Rachel Laurence *(Miss Belt)*.

This mundane James Bond imitation opens with the Western economic system being destroyed by large volume sales of gold. Jackson, a top British official, realizes that only two men can save the day. He calls in the team of Gunn (Gilliam), a rugged secret agent, and Powder (Potter), his slightly effeminate sidekick. The duo stumbles onto Miller, a mad scientist from the Goldfinger school who tries to destroy the world economy by keeping gold in a liquid state, which he is able to do with an invention of his. Miller has Rutherford, a pretty British scientist, in his clutches, but eventually Gilliam and Potter save the day for capitalists everywhere, to say nothing of pretty British scientists. GUNPOWDER doesn't really have much to recommend it, other than a few laughs and a somewhat comical performance by Potter. The action sequences are adequate, but, like the low-grade plot, reflect the production's obvious budget and talent limitations.

p, Maxine Julius; d, Norman J. Warren; w, Rory H. MacLean; ph, Alistair Cameron (Rank Color); m, Jeffrey Wood; ed, Maxine Julius; prod d, Hayden Pearce; spec eff, Ben Trumble.

Action **Cas.** **(PR:C MPAA:NR)**

HA' INSTALATOR† (1987, Israel) 100m Rosenfilm/Trinity c (Trans: The Plumber)

Tuvia Tzafir *(Pinkhas)*, Clara Ron *(Mimi)*, Assi Hanegbi *(Striker)*, Rami Baruch, Avner Hizkiahu, Avi Kushnir, Avraham Asseo, Ophelia Strahl.

Popular Israeli television entertainer Tuvia Tzafir stars as a lowly plumber who is mistaken for a Swiss financial genius when he arrives at the Ministry of Finance to fix the pipes. Tzafir soon finds himself swept into politics and before he knows it he has been appointed the new Minister of Finance. In direct contrast to the corrupt government bureaucrats around him, Tzafir makes a sincere effort to excel at his new position while maintaining his job as a plumber in his spare time. The debut feature of director Behagan who had previously made several short films, commercials, and music videos.

p, Mel Rosen, Rafi Reibenbach; d, Miki Behagan; w, Hanan Peled; ph, Gad Danzig; m, Miki Gabrielov; ed, Nissim Moussek; art d, Yosi Ohrbach, Sergio Aronshon; cos, Obbie Ossi.

Comedy **(PR:NR MPAA:NR)**

HAMARI JUNG† (1987, India)

Shiva, Arup, Sanchita.

Four friends team up against a dangerous band of hoodlums known as the "Cobra Gang." (In Hindi.)

p, Sultan Hussain; d, Rajesh Bahaduri; m, Sonik Omi.

Drama **(PR:NR MPAA:NR)**

HAMBURGER HILL*½** (1987) 110m RKO/PAR c

Anthony Barrile *(Languilli)*, Michael Patrick Boatman *(Motown)*, Don Cheadle *(Washburn)*, Michael Dolan *(Murphy)*, Don James *(McDaniel)*, Dylan McDermott *(Sgt. Frantz)*, M.A. Nickles *(Galvin)*, Harry O'Reilly *(Duffy)*, Daniel O'Shea *(Gaigin)*, Tim Quill *(Beletsky)*, Tommy Swerdlow *(Bienstock)*, Courtney Vance *(Doc Johnson)*, Steven Weber *(Sgt. Worcester)*, Tegan West *(Lt. Eden)*, Kieu Chinh *(Mama San)*, Doug Goodman *(Lagunas)*, J.C. Palmore *(Healy)*, J.D. Van Sickle *(Newsman)*.

Instead of trying to match the hallucinatory bombast of APOCALYPSE NOW, the surreal metaphysics of PLATOON, or the studied idiosyncrasy of FULL METAL JACKET, director Irvin reaches back to such classic combat films as THE SANDS OF IWO JIMA and PORK CHOP HILL for his inspiration. So straightforward as to be old-fashioned, HAMBURGER HILL becomes unique by virtue of its unwillingness to participate in the current cycle of war-as-philosophical-metaphor Vietnam films and instead going for a more conventional approach. Almost realistic to a fault, Irvin's film is an account of the 3rd squad, 1st platoon, Bravo Company of the 101st Airborne Division and its battle to secure Hill 937 in the Ashau Valley, Vietnam, 1969. Led by sergeants McDermott and Weber, the interracial platoon must contend with little support from the homefront, a contentious news media, racial tensions, personality conflicts, questionable tactics, and friendly fire, all while facing a well-entrenched army of North Vietnamese regulars who refuse to give up. After 11 assaults during 10 days of stifling heat and intense rain, after struggling through rivers of mud and suffering a 70 percent casualty rate, the surviving soldiers take the hill. In a title card at the conclusion of the film, we are informed that one month later the US deserted the hill and it was soon reclaimed by the North Vietnamese.

While the above synopsis may seem scant, there is very little else in the way of a linear plot in HAMBURGER HILL. The film is made up of isolated moments that merge to form a whole. Letters from home, chats, arguments, visits to a brothel, and of course, intense combat are what constitute a "plot" here. All of this is performed with vigor by an almost faceless ensemble of unknown actors spouting an incomprehensible stream of G.I. lingo that only a veteran could keep up with. And, in fact, a veteran wrote the script. Jim Carabatsos, who had previously penned HEROES, HEARTBREAK RIDGE, and NO MERCY, served in Vietnam with the 1st Air Cavalry Division in 1968-69. His script certainly seems to capture the day-to-day reality of men at war, but it falters when he attempts to expand the concept into something larger. The combat scenes are broken up by poorly integrated speeches that run the gamut from outrage over the antiwar movement to racial strife between the soldiers. While the actors do a commendable job of making these lectures palatable, the speeches seem clumsy and gratuitous—as if a concession to the current trend that requires instant analysis of the entire conflict within a single film. Luckily, director Irvin and cinematographer MacDonald's exquisite imagery easily overpowers the more worrisome shortcomings of Carabarsos' script. Shot in an unfussy, realistic manner with emphasis on wide angles and deep focus, HAMBURGER HILL bombards the senses without resorting to the kind of hallucinatory imagery found in several popular films on Vietnam (Irvin was in Vietnam in 1969 filming a documentary, thus he has a legitimate claim at first-hand experience). The battle for the hill is exhausting to watch as the soldiers struggle upwards in the mud, clinging to exposed roots, tree stumps, and each other in a desperate effort to advance. This is conveyed visually in a fundamentally simple manner—Irvin positions his frame so that actors are struggling on a diagonal plane that runs from the bottom of screen left to the top of screen right. By framing in this manner, the sense of climbing *uphill* is relentless, for the viewer watches as actors

struggle to reach the *top of the frame*. Irvin rarely allows a glimpse of the top of the hill (the goal), further keeping the viewer from thinking ahead and instead forcing him to concentrate on climbing the few feet visible before him. Only when the few surviving soldiers reach the top of the hill does the film take on a slightly surreal air. As the harsh sunlight cuts through the dense smoke, three exhausted soldiers sit next to a gnarled tree stump, mere silhouettes at the summit of a hill littered with bodies. This final image is an eloquent and moving homage to the brave and determined men who gave their all for naught.

Oddly, composer Philip Glass was commissioned to provide a score for HAMBURGER HILL, but with the exception of the opening credits and a badly cued burst of music during the final charge, there is no other incidental music. Pop songs from the period fill out the rest of the film, including "When a Man Loves a Woman" (Calvin Lewis, Andrew Wright, performed by Percy Sledge), "Ruby, Don't Take Your Love to Town" (Mel Tillis, performed by Waylon Jennings), "(Sittin' On) The Dock of the Bay" (Otis Redding, Steve Cropper, performed by Redding), "I-Feel-Like-I'm-Fixin'-to-Die-Rag" (Joe McDonald, performed by Country Joe and the Fish), "I Wish It Would Rain" (Barrett Strong, Norman Whitfield, Rodger Penzabene, Sr., Helga Penzabene, Carl Penzabene, Rodger Penzabene, Jr., performed by The Temptations), "Gimme Some Lovin' " (Steve Winwood, Muff Winwood, Spencer Davis, performed by The Spencer Davis Group), "We Gotta Get Out of This Place" (Barry Mann, Cynthia Weil, performed by The Animals), "I Second That Emotion" (Alfred Cleveland, William Robinson, Jr.), "Subterranean Homesick Blues" (Bob Dylan). *(Graphic violence, nudity, sexual situations, extreme profanity.)*

p, Marcia Nasatir, JIm Carabatsos; d, John Irvin; w, Jim Carabatsos; ph, Peter MacDonald (Rank Color); m, Philip Glass; ed, Peter Tanner; prod d, Austen Spriggs; art d, Toto Castillo; makeup, Cecille Baun, Neville Smallwood; m/l, Calvin Lewis, Andrew Wright, Mel Tillis, Otis Redding, Steve Cropper, Joe McDonald, Barrett Strong, Norman Whitfield, Rodger Penzabene, Sr., Helga Penzabene, Carl Penzabene, Rodger Penzabene, Jr., Steve Winwood, Muff Winwood, Spencer Davis, Barry Mann, Cynthia Weil, Alfred Cleveland, William Robinson, Jr., Bob Dylan; spec eff, Joe Lombardi; stunts, Tip Tipping.

War **(PR:O MPAA:R)**

HAMLET† (1987, Fin.) 80m Villealfa Filmproductions Oy-Aki Kaurismaki c

Pirkka-Pekka Petelius, Kari Vaananen, Kati Outinen, Matti Pellonpaa.

Farcical film adaptation of the Shakespeare classic set in the Finnish wood-refining industry. Part of a tongue-in-cheek Shakespeare trilogy, produced by the Film Total group, which put a contemporary spin on "King Lear" and "Macbeth" as well.

d&w, Aki Kaurismaki; ph, Timo Salminen.

Drama **(PR:NR MPAA:NR)**

HANOI HILTON, THE½** (1987) 123m Golan-Globus/Cannon c

Michael Moriarty *(Lt. Comdr. Williamson)*, Jeffrey Jones *(Maj. Fischer)*, Paul Le Mat *(Hubman)*, Stephen Davies *(Capt. Robert Miles)*, Lawrence Pressman *(Col. Cathcart)*, Aki Aleong *(Maj. Ngo "Cat" Doc)*, Gloria Carlin *(Paula)*, John Diehl *(Murphy)*, Rick Fitts *(Capt. Turner)*, David Soul *(Maj. Oldham)*, David Anthony Smith *(Gregory)*, Ken Wright *(Kennedy)*, Doug Savant *(Ashby)*, John Vargas *(Oliviera)*, Michael Russo *(Fidel the Cuban)*.

For liberals and conservatives alike, the Vietnam war will undoubtedly remain a political *cause celebre* for many years to come. THE HANOI HILTON will add fuel to those political fires. Where PLATOON indicted American involvement in Vietnam (and FULL METAL JACKET gave that war an apolitical but devastating landscaping), this film, a crusade really by its director-writer Chetwynd, attempts to vindicate the American presence in Vietnam, or, at least, bring another perspective to that conflict. Thanks to its visual and script limitations, THE HANOI HILTON neither fails nor succeeds, but falls somewhere in the middle, leaving the viewer to ponder its doctrine. This is not a war-action film but one that deals with American POWs behind the walls of the dreaded Hoa Lo Prison in Hanoi, better known as The Hanoi Hilton.

The film opens with an American plane being shot down and its pilot captured and taken to the prison which houses mostly American officer pilots, a tough and

resolute bunch headed by ranking officer Pressman. He is a by-the-book colonel who insists that military order and protocol be maintained despite the humiliation and torture inflicted upon his men. The prison commandant, Aleong, who enacts his role with the stereotyped vindictiveness of ancient Hollywood villains of WW II—Philip Ahn, Richard Loo—resolves to break the colonel and puts him through excruciating torture. When Pressman dies the mantle of leadership falls to Navy flier Moriarty (whose natural acting methods make him appear a jittery flake at best) and he continues to maintain Pressman's rigid code of honor, resisting every effort by Aleong to break him and make him confess to war crimes he did not commit. Others such as the easy going Le Mat, are more vulnerable and they begin to confess to what they consider to be harmless acts of war, giving information they believe will be useless to the North Vietnamese. The torture and brutalities inflicted upon the prisoners is almost non-stop and occurs over many years so that the prisoners age mercilessly. The torture ceases briefly due to the appearance of an ultra-liberal political activist actress, Carlin, who, as an American of some status, comes to Hanoi convinced the Communists are correct in their aggressive war and tries to get American prisoners to cooperate with them. She is a vainglorious and thoroughly repulsive person who is so naive that she doesn't know she is being manipulated by the North Vietnamese, even though some American prisoners shout at her: "You're being used! Used!" This character, of course, is based on political activist-actress Jane Fonda, a characterization which stirred up more controversy about the film than its basic premise. Unflattering though this portrait is, it is largely based on facts concerning the actress' activities during the Vietnam war. (Scores of Vietnam veterans, interviewed by the production company later stated on camera their abiding dislike of Fonda for her pro-North Vietnamese actions during that sad time.)

Aside from the erratic Moriarty, who is a study in and of himself, there is little character development among the prisoners who are typecast in roles that have been identified many times over in scores of other POW films, from THE PURPLE HEART to STALAG 17, but with much less verve and impact. And there is no relief, until the surviving prisoners are finally packed aboard a plane at war's end and sent back home. Much of THE HANOI HILTON is filmed in tiny rooms without much light and the claustrophobia spills over into the story. Visually, the film relentlessly assaults the viewer with its message, which is that American POWs were betrayed by senseless idiots from Hollywood and liberal leftists. There is no doubt that Americans underwent unspeakable tortures at the hands of the enemy. Further, the innermost motives of US fighting men were pure and reasonably associated with concepts of liberty and freedom is a premise most wish to embrace. And all of this is brought into play by the well-intentioned Chetwynd but it is shown with less than top-flight production credits and a wandering script. Chetwynd tried for almost a decade to get this film made, ever since this Canadian worked for Columbia Pictures in Europe. He failed to interest Columbia in making the film and struck out with ABC-TV, HBO, and Paramount Pictures, finally convincing Golan-Globus to do the film. His labor of love is to be respected as such but a labor of high art it is not. *(Harsh language, violence.)*

p, Menahem Golan, Yoram Globus; d&w, Lionel Chetwynd; ph, Mark Irwin (TVC Color); m, Jimmy Webb; ed, Penelope Shaw; prod d, R. Clifford Searcy; art d, Carol Bosselman; set d, Ian Cramer; cos, Richard LaMotte.

War/Drama **Cas.** **(PR:O MPAA:R)**

HANSEL AND GRETEL† (1987) 86m Golan-Globus/Cannon c

Hugh Pollard *(Hansel)*, Nicola Stapleton *(Gretel)*, Emily Richard *(Mother)*, David Warner *(Father)*, Cloris Leachman *(Witch)*, Eugene Kline, Warren M. Feigin, Lutuf Nouasser, Beatrice Shimshoni.

The Brothers Grimm classic "Hansel and Gretel" gets the Cannon treatment as part of its children's fairy tale series. The title characters—Pollard and Stapleton—are two curious children who end up imprisoned by witch Leachman. When it looks as if the wicked witch will make a feast of the youngsters, events take a turn for the better and the fairy tale ends happily. The score is from the 19th Century opera by Engelbert Humperdinck.

p, Menahem Golan, Yoram Globus; d, Len Talan; w, Nancy Weems, Len Talan (based on the fairy tale by the brothers Grimm); ph, Ilan Rosenberg; m, Michael Cohen (based on score by Engelbert Humperdinck); ed, Irit Raz; prod d, Marek Dobrowolski; cos, Meira Steinmatz; m/l, Michael Cohen, Enid Futterman.

Children's **(PR:NR MPAA:NR)**

HAPPY BIGAMIST† (1987, Hong Kong) 98m Bo Ho/Golden Harvest c

Chan Friend, Kenny Bee, Anita Miu, Patricia Ha.

Chinese bedroom farce directed by and starring Chan Friend as a man happily married to his second wife (Anita Miu) when his first wife (Patricia Ha) arrives and decides to stay with them. Jealousy rages between the two women until the determined Miu matches Ha with family friend Kenny Bee, thus ridding herself of the troublesome interloper. Much to Miu's chagrin, however, her husband is annoyed that his ex-wife has hooked up with Bee and the action climaxes with a public confrontation at the local opera house. A huge hit at the Hong Kong box office.

d, Chan Friend; ph, Cheung Shing-tung; art d, Szeto Wai-hong.

Comedy **(PR:NR MPAA:NR)**

HAPPY HOUR zero (1987) 88m Four Square/The Movie Store c

Richard Gilliland *(Blake Teagarden)*, Jamie Farr *(Crummy Fred)*, Tawny Kitaen *(Misty Roberts)*, Ty Henderson *(Bill)*, Rich Little *(Mr. X/Roger Fudmunger/ "Scooter" Johnson)*, Eddie Deezen *(Hancock)*, Kathi Diamant *(Cathy Teagarden)*, Debbie Gates *(Meredith Casey)*, Jim Parrott *(Barbarian Leader)*, Jim Newell *(Jack Marshall)*, Herb Kronsberg *(Jenkins)*, Arnie Miller *(Trainer)*, Mary Egan *(Old Woman)*, D.J. Sullivan *(Fred's Neighbor)*, Steve Andrich *(Himself)*, Steve Peace *(Spencer Markham)*, Chad Burlingame *(Billy Teagarden)*, Amber Bohan *(Mary Teagarden)*, Spike Sorrentino *(Security Officer)*, Frank Davis *("Killer" the Guard)*, Susan Shepard *(Mrs. Baker)*, Paul Engman *(Anchorman)*, John De Bello *(Charles White)*, Steve Welch *(Young Man)*, David Paynter *(Older Man)*, Gordon Benson *(Congressman Billings)*, Kary Lynn Vail *(Waitress)*, Newell Tarrant *(Don Adiger)*, Nigel Barber *(Marshall Beer)*, Kelly Kreger *(Office Worker)*, Ryk Williams *(Gas Station Attendant)*, Beverly Todd *(Laura)*, Monty Jordan *(P.J. Yarbourough)*, Roxanne Masterson *(Lakeside Guide)*, John Ara Martin, Linda Lutz *(Lakeside Security Guards)*, Costa Dillon *(Driver at Mexican Border)*, Jack Regan *(Denver D.J. Voiceover)*, Skip Conover *(Beer Commercial Voiceover)*, Eric Christmas *("Harry" the Guard)*, Debi Fares.

HAPPY HOUR'S title is a complete misnomer. Its not so much a happy hour as it is a dismal eight-eight minutes. The plot has all the linear quality of a yarn ball after being attacked by a playful kitten. See, there's this beer company in Denver which accidentally stumbles onto a secret ingredient which makes the public gaga over the firm's product. Somehow the formula's been lost, so there are only two tiny vials left of this magic potion. This stuff has enormous power though, and a single drop will enhance several million cans of beer. It seems a rival beer company has managed to steal one of the vials. Each brewery hires a mercenary (the dapper Rich Little and the slimy Jamie Farr) to steal the vial their respective rival has. But wait! It seems two high-ranking employees from each side were activists together in college. Now they feel guilty about selling oodles and oodles of beer under false pretenses, so they decide to take action. Been able to follow so far? Good, because there's more. Seems the secret formula has made beer so popular that the national drinking age has been lowered to six, and everyone is stumbling about in various states of inebriation. Meanwhile Farr and his two assistants end up in Mexico where they fight off dope smugglers, then sneak across the border. Little convinces security guards he's Cary Grant (the film was made in 1985, before Grant's death). Lots of shooting and explosions later, the vials are destroyed, making America safe for beer drinkers everywhere and a pretty blonde woman informs the audience that we're not smart enough to understand the film.

Yeah, right. It doesn't exactly take a Rhodes scholar to figure out this movie's problem. It tosses characters and plot around willy-nilly, interspersing the confusion with tasteless humor and noxious performances. In his 1978 opus ATTACK OF THE KILLER TOMATOES, director John De Bello made a bad film that attempted to satirize bad films. Here he's simply dropped the satire, but maintained the quality level. Though there's a certain flair for frenzied pacing in his work, De Bello goes for the obvious every time. Crashes, explosions, four letter words, and sexual humor are the building blocks this story uses. Acting style consists of screaming and arm waving for nearly everyone, though Little walks through his role with a certain bored detachment. The alcohol jokes are particularly unfunny, unless your idea of humor is watching drunken tots guzzle booze while watching TV. The film deservedly sat around for a couple of years before finally sneaking out in a near-anonymous release. One song, written and performed by the pop group Devo, "I Wouldn't Do That to You." *(Profanity, violence, substance abuse.)*

p, J. Stephen Peace, John De Bello; d, John De Bello; w, John De Bello; Constantine Dillon, J. Stephen Peace; ph, Kevin Morrisey (CFI Color); m, Rick Patterson, Neal Fox; ed, John De Bello; prod d, Constantine Dillon; set d, Charly Kohlmeyer; m/l, Devo; spec eff, A & A Special Effects; makeup, Debra Enders, Marce Hannig; stunts, Monty Jordan.

Comedy **Cas.** **(PR:O MPAA:R)**

HAPPY NEW YEAR½** (1987) 85m COL-Delphi IV/COL c

Peter Falk *(Nick)*, Charles Durning *(Charlie)*, Wendy Hughes *(Carolyn Benedict, Antique Dealer)*, Tom Courtenay *(Edward Sanders, Jewelry Store Manager)*, Joan Copeland *(Sunny)*, Tracy Brooks Swope *(Nina)*, Daniel Gerroll *(Curator)*, Bruce Malmuth *(Police Lieutenant)*, Claude Lelouch *(Man on Train)*, Peter Sellars, Anthony Heald, The Temptations.

Dumped on the market with little fanfare after sitting on the shelf for nearly two years, this remake of Claude Lelouch's LA BONNE ANNEE (1973) is a charming romance/caper film with a particulary winning performance by Peter Falk. He and Durning are longtime associates in crime, polished professionals who've done time and have no interest in repeating the experience. Durning's opening narration sets the stage for their trip to Palm Beach, where these aging thieves think they might find the pickings a little easier than in New York. Falk sets about planning the "psychological" robbery of a Harry Winston jewelry store, beginning an intricate con game that sets up the theft. Donning rubber masks and makeup, Falk establishes two identities: a romantic octogenarian whose wife is deathly ill and his equally ancient sister. In these guises he visits the jewelry store, gradually winning the trust of its manager, Courtenay, whose calm, solicitous demeanor hides the aggressive, slightly unprincipled salesman within. Meanwhile, Falk has been smitten by Hughes, a beautiful high-brow who runs a nearby antique store, and has undertaken a little scam to win her heart. He purchases a piece of furniture from a restaurant that he knows Hughes wants but has been unable to obtain. A series of encounters follows in which Falk and Hughes try to get the best of each other in striking a deal for the antique. All the while, Falk and Hughes are falling for each other. The night of the heist arrives. Falk, in disguise, returns after closing hours to the jewelry store where Courtenay has been waiting alone to sell the old man a very expensive final present for his dying wife. With the elaborate alarm system momentarily shut off, Falk sets about robbing the place, and Durning, who has played the role of the chauffeur, arrives to collect the loot and then makes his carefully orchestrated escape. The scheme backfires, however, when Falk is trapped inside by the time-lock door. His capture is witnessed by Hughes, who makes plain her love for him anyway, and Falk is convicted and imprisoned. Durning escapes with the booty and lays low; Hughes moves to Falk's New York apartment to wait for his eventual release. When he gets out, Falk is tailed by the authorities, anxious to recover the stolen jewels. He discovers that Hughes has had a lover while he's been incarcerated, but under the advisement of Durning, whom he carefully contacts, Falk forgives her. In the finale, Durning, Hughes, and a disguised Falk wing their way to Brazil with the spoils.

Frequently funny, particularly during Falk's masquerades, HAPPY NEW YEAR is relatively faithful to Lelouch's original, though the emphasis here is on comedy while the love story was at the heart of the French film. Director Avildsen (ROCKY, THE KARATE KID) moves his film along at a nice pace and coaxes fine performances from Hughes, Courtenay, and the always reliable Durning, who establishes an excellent rapport with Falk. Their mutual admiration is deftly presented and the film's "buddy" element works because Falk and Durning seem like the kind of guys who could easily remain partners through thick and thin. But when all is said and done, this is Falk's picture. He is outstanding in the role that Lino Ventura essayed in the original. His Nick is a clever, exacting planner, but he is also an old-fashioned romantic with simple tastes. Falk doesn't opt for easy laughs by playing his masquerades broadly. Sure, half the fun is in knowing that it's cock-eyed, gravel-voiced Falk underneath the masks, wigs, and dresses, but he mines more humor from the plausible little touches he brings to these characters than from the comedy inherent in the situation. At the same time that he is pulling the wool over Courtenay's eyes with his elderly characters, he creates a warm portrait of lasting love, both between the old man and his unseen wife, and between the aging sister and brother. His portrayal of the old woman is particularly effective, much more in the vein of Dustin Hoffman's TOOTSIE than Jack Lemmon's and Tony Curtis' drag work in SOME LIKE IT HOT. The old woman was not in Lelouch's film, and Falk created and wrote the role, modeling it after his mother.

HAPPY NEW YEAR was shot in May, 1985, but because of contract obligations, Avildsen was unable to edit it until after he directed THE KARATE KID. Not long thereafter, there was a shift in the upper echelons of Columbia, and the new honchos showed little interest in the film. When it was released in 1987, it was virtually unaccompanied by promotion and given only limited distribution. *(Profanity.)*

p, Jerry Weintraub; d, John G. Avildsen; w, Warren Lane [Nancy Dowd] (based on the film LA BONNE ANNEE by Claude Lelouch); ph, James Crabe (Continental Color); m, Bill Conti; ed, Jane Kurson; prod d, William J. Cassidy; art d, William F. Matthews; set d, Don Ivey; makeup, Robert Laden.

Comedy Cas. (PR:C MPAA:PG)

HARD TICKET TO HAWAII† (1987) 96m Malibu Bay c

Ronn Moss *(Rowdy Abilene)*, Dona Speir *(Donna)*, Hope Marie Carlton *(Taryn)*, Harold Diamond *(Jade)*, Rodrigo Obregon *(Seth Romero)*, Cynthia Brimhall *(Edy)*, Patty Duffek *(Pattycakes)*, Wolf Larson *(Jimmy-John Jackson)*, Lory Green *(Rosie)*, Rustam Branaman *(Kimo)*, David DeShay *(Ashley)*, Michael Andrews *(Michelle/Michael)*, Andy Sidaris *(Whitey)*, Russell Howell *(Skateboard Rider)*, Kwan Hi Lim, Joseph Hieu, Peter Bromilow, Joey Meran, Shawne Zarubica.

Taking a hiatus from his thrill-of-victory/agony-of-defeat work for ABC-TV sports, Andy Sidaris directs this actioner featuring pneumatic former *Playboy* models Dona Speir and Hope Marie Carlton. The operators of a Hawaiian air freight company, they become involved with diamond smugglers. Moss and partner Diamond, a chop-socky expert, are called on to help the girls battle the smugglers and the cancer-carrying snake that slithers through the film. When the snake surprises Speir in a bathroom, the bazooka-wielding Moss makes a well-timed appearance and blows it to kingdom come, just as he has done earlier to Howell, a skateboard-riding villain. There is also some intrigue involving drug running, but the plot here is secondary to the *exposure* that Speir and Carlton receive—soaking t-shirts and bare skin being the order of the day. HARD TICKET TO HAWAII was given a limited regional release but should see new life as a videocassette.

p, Arlene Sidaris; d&w, Andy Sidaris; ph, Howard Wexler (United Color); m, Gary Stockdale; ed, Michael Haight; prod d, Sal Grasso, Peter Munneke; cos, Fionn; martial arts ch, Harold Diamond; skateboard stunts, Russell Howell.

Action (PR:NR MPAA:R)

HARRY AND THE HENDERSONS** (1987) 110m UNIV-Amblin Entertainment/UNIV c

John Lithgow *(George Henderson)*, Melinda Dillon *(Nancy Henderson)*, Margaret Langrick *(Sarah Henderson)*, Joshua Rudoy *(Ernie Henderson)*, Kevin Peter Hall *(Harry)*, David Suchet *(Jacques Lafleur)*, Lainie Kazan *(Irene Moffitt)*, Don Ameche *(Dr. Wallace Wrightwood)*, M. Emmet Walsh *(George Henderson, Sr.)*, Bill Ontiverous *(Sgt. Mancini)*, David Richardt *(Dirty Harry Officer)*.

In the early 1980s, comedian Brad Garrett (who stands about 6 foot 9 inches) tried to peddle a TV idea whereby he would play a Sasquatch/Yeti/Abominable Snowman who was adopted by a Jewish family when he was found by the 12-year-old son about to be Bar Mitzvahed. Garrett's story had the creature domesticated and participating in a dual rite of passage with the young lad. It was intended to be a half-hour comedy and that's what HARRY AND THE HENDERSONS should have been. Garrett, who was unknown at the time, couldn't sell his idea, but Steven Spielberg, whose company produced this film, is so important in the movie business that studios would line up to film his version of *Roget's Thesaurus* or *The Kama Sutra*. And so it was that this essentially 30-minute sitcom came to be an overblown movie. Despite the mistakes in emphasis and the fact that the movie peaks far too early, there are some nice moments and it won't offend undiscerning audiences.

Lithgow and Dillon are the Wonder Bread parents of Rudoy and Langrick. They are returning home from a family vacation in the family station wagon when Lithgow drives a bit too fast and hits a huge "thing" that has attempted to make it across the road. The creature, which they first think is a mutant grizzly bear, appears to be dead, so it is then strapped to the top of the car. However, it is only stunned, wakes up and causes Lithgow to step on the brakes. The creature slides off the wagon and is hit again. They bring it back home and realize that it is the legendary "Big Foot" that has been spotted every so often in this Northwest area near Mount Rainier. Back at the typical Spielberg house, the family decides, like the boy in E.T., to keep him. They dub him "Harry" and he is soon part of the family, kept under cover while they plan their next moves. Surely, the existence of such a seven-footer would be mammoth news around the world, but they don't want the beast to be taken to a zoo and put on display. Lithgow is a hunter who works in his father's gun store. Daddy, played by Walsh, is a tough cookie who believes in shooting animals, and the walls of Lithgow's home are festooned with the heads of dead beasts he has shot. Harry (we'll call him that even though he is played by former George Washington University basketball star Kevin Peter Hall) makes short work of the animal heads and gives them a proper burial in the yard. Next door neighbor Kazan, who is the area's rumor monger, has to be kept away because if she learns about the presence of Harry, the news will be spread around town with the speed of summer lightning. At the same time, the subplot has to do with avowed "Big Foot" hunter Suchet, who is determined to be the first man to find and kill one of these creatures. Ameche is a local anthropologist who runs a "Big Foot" museum and has very little to do. In the course of events, there is a mixture of comedy (most of which has to do with Harry's size—he keeps banging into doorways and going through furniture—and Harry's smell, which is not easy to demonstrate on screen unless the theater is equipped with Smell-o-Rama) and pathos, such as the moment when Harry shows that he's not such a dumb animal and manages to save evil Suchet's life. The picture fades when Lithgow's family, Suchet, and Ameche watch as Harry walks back into the forest whence he came and is soon joined by *his* family of creatures. Naturally, it is meant to tug the heart in much the same way that E.T.'s departure to his home planet did. It doesn't.

This is a flat-out formula movie but the ingredients in the mixture are not quite right. The Lithgow family is too cutesy and too perfect, almost a foursome out of the 1950s stable of Columbia/Screen Gems sitcoms. Even though this takes place in Seattle, the house in which they live looks like one of the homes on the same street where E.T. and POLTERGEIST and any number of other Spielberg movies took place. It's unbearably predictable, down to the fact that the creature's makeup, designed by Rick Baker, seems to have somewhat of a resemblance to Lithgow's face, thus making a not-too-subtle point about hunting down oneself. The character of Harry is also too darn sweet, too smart, and too human to inspire any dread or even respect. He seems to be an overgrown stuffed animal who is a cross between Yogi Bear, King Kong, Chewbacca, and your favorite uncle. Seattle is a pretty town and the outlying areas are gorgeous, especially as seen through the lens of cinematographer Daviau (who also did E.T.). It has recently become an area filmmakers are discovering—as with the shooting done there for BLACK WIDOW and HOUSE OF GAMES. Hall's previous experience was on TV's "Misfits of Science" as well as PROPHECY, WITHOUT WARNING, and ONE DARK NIGHT. At 7 feet 2 inches, he is limited in his roles in much the same way as Richard Kiel ("Jaws" in the James Bond pictures), but he acquits himself well. One funny line stands out. Lithgow is an amateur artist who sketches a picture of Harry and shows it to his father, who is happy because the many sightings of the beast have caused a run on rifles at the gun shop. Walsh, the menace in BLOOD SIMPLE, sneers at the drawing and says, "I wanted King Kong and you brought me a giant gerbil." Lithgow, thrice Oscar-nominated, is not given enough to chew on here and so becomes a typical Disney-type hero of the Dean Jones era. The only other vaguely humorous moments come when Harry begins to eat money. It's green and looks like something that grows on trees to him. Director Dear, making his second film after having previously done TIMERIDER, impressed Spielberg with a segment of TV's "Amazing Stories." *(Profanity.)*

p, Richard Vane, William Dear; d, William Dear; w, William Dear, William E. Martin, Ezra D. Rappaport; ph, Allen Daviau (DeLuxe Color); m, Bruce Broughton; ed, Donn Cambern; prod d, James Bissell; art d, Don Woodruff; set d, William James Teegarden; spec eff, Rick Baker.

Comedy **Cas.** **(PR:A-C MPAA:PG)**

HAUNTING OF HAMILTON HIGH, THE (SEE: HELLO MARY LOU: PROM NIGHT II, 1987)

HAVINCK† (1987, Neth.) 99m Riverside/Holland c

Willem Nijholt *(Havinck)*, Anne Martien Lousberg *(Eva)*, Will van Kralingen *(Lydia)*, Carolien van den Berg *(Maud)*, Coen Flink *(Bork)*, Dora van der Groen, Kenneth Herdigein.

The latest film from acclaimed Dutch director Weisz swept the annual Dutch Filmdays awards winning the critics' prize for Best Film and two Golden Calves: best actor (Nijholt) and best supporting actress (van Kralingen), even before it was officially released. Nijolt stars as a cold, insensitive lawyer who treats his wife, his teenage daughter, and his mistress as if they were merely items on his daily schedule that must be dealt with. Unable to take any more neglect the wife, van Kralingen, commits suicide by crashing her car head-on into another, not only killing herself, but the driver of the other vehicle as well. Shocked by his wife's action, Nijolt makes a half-hearted attempt at patching things up with his estranged daughter and this effort forces him to re-examine the choices he has made in life. Finally, feelings of guilt and regret invade his cold, business-like psyche. Shot by the marvelously talented Italian cinematographer Giuseppe Lanci (Tarkovsky's NOSTALGHIA, the Taviani brothers' KAOS, Bellocchio's HENRY IV, and Wertmuller's CAMMORA are among his most notable accomplishments).

p, Gys Versluys; d, Franz Weisz; w, Ger Thijs (based on the novel by Marja Brouwers); ph, Giuseppe Lanci (Eastmancolor); m, Egisto Macchi; ed, Ton Ruys; art d, Jan Roelfs, Ben van Os.

Drama **(PR:NR MPAA:NR)**

HAY QUE DESHACER LA CASA† (1987, Span.) 93m Lince-Jet-Incine c (Trans: We Must Undo The House)

Amparo Rivelles *(Ana)*, Amparo Soler Leal *(Laura, Ana's Sister)*, Joaquin Kremel *(Frutos)*, Jose Maria Pou *(Ramon)*, Jose Luis Lopez Vazquez *(Pepe Luis)*, Agustin Gonzalez *(Huete)*, Luis Merlo, Luis Ciges, Felix Rotaeta, Guillermo Montesinos, Antonio Gamero.

Two sisters come to better know each other as they meet and delve into their pasts following the death of their father.

p, Luis Sanz; d, Jose Luis Garcia Sanchez; w, Jose Luis Garcia Sanchez, Rafael Azcona; ph, Jose Luis Alcaine (Eastmancolor); m, Miguel Morales; ed, Pablo G. del Amo; set d, Gerardo Vera.

Drama **(PR:NR MPAA:NR)**

HEART† (1987) 90m NW c

Brad Davis *(Eddie Brennan)*, Francis Fisher *(Jeannie)*, Steve Buscemi *(Nicky, Eddie's Manager)*, Robinson Frank Adu *(Buddy, Eddie's Trainer)*, Jesse Doran *(Diddy)*, Sam Gray *(Leo)*, Bill Costello *(Fighter)*.

A low-budget effort which stars Brad Davis (MIDNIGHT EXPRESS, QUERELLE) as a not-too-bright former boxer who attempts a comeback even though he is long past his prime. Making a living in a produce market, Davis is enticed back into the ring by his sleazy manager Buscemi. Over the objections of girl friend Fisher, Davis takes a matchup against Costello, a younger and better fighter who is the odds-on favorite. Unknown to Davis, Buscemi has fixed the fight in advance. Like all boxing dramas, HEART leads up to the final showdown of fists in the ring. Barely released in late 1987.

p, Randy Jurgensen; d, James Lemmo; w, James Lemmo, Randy Jurgensen; ph, Jacek Laskus (TVC Color); m, Geoff Levin, Chris Many; ed, Lorenzo Marinelli; prod d, Vicki Paul; art d, Susan Raney; cos, Ticia Blackburn.

Sports **(PR:NR MPAA:R)**

HEARTBEAT 100† (1987, Hong Kong) 98m Cinema City/Golden Princess c

Lui Fong, Maggie Cheung, Bonnie Law, Mark Cheng.

Cheung, a female mystery writer, takes a trip into the countryside with her sister (Law) and a friend (Lui Fong) in search of a plot for her new novel. At an old village the trio uncovers a series of murders and Cheung's relentless digging results in a face-to-face confrontation with the culprit.

p, Raymond Wong; d, Kent Cheng, Lo Kin; w, Raymond Wong, Philip Chong, Ng Man Fai; ph, James Chan; m, David Wu; art d, Andy Li.

Thriller **(PR:NR MPAA:NR)**

HEARTS OF FIRE† (1987) 95m Phoenix Ent./Lorimar c

Bob Dylan *(Billy Parker)*, Rupert Everett *(James Colt)*, Fiona [Flanagan] *(Molly McGuire)*, Julian Glover *(Alfred)*, Suzanne Bertish *(Anne Ashton)*, Ian Dury *(Bones)*, Richie Havens *(Pepper Ward)*, Larry Lamb *(Jack Rosner)*, Tim Capello *(Nico)*, Susannah Hoffmann *(Blind Woman)*, Maury Chaykin *(Charlie Kelso)*, Tony Rosato *(Woody)*, Stella Duncan-Petley *(Eliza)*, Lesleh Donaldson *(Penny)*, Bill Block *(Donnie)*, David Blacker *(Dave)*, Kevin Fox *(Tee)*, Jeremy Ratchford *(Jimbo)*, Richard Comar *(Mr. Daniels)*, Steve Bolton *(Spyder)*, Mark Rylance *(Fizz)*, Barbara Barnes-Hopkins, Myra Fied, Arlene Duncan *(Tollbooth Cashiers)*, Robert Lannon *(Bus Driver)*, Raymond Mason *(Bellboy)*, Zoe Nathenson, Honey Hazel *(Fans at Funfair)*, Norman Gregory, Allan Corduner *(Music Executives)*, Peter Sugden, Tony Aitken, Robin Brunskill, Julian Firth *(Reporters)*, Sidney Livingstone *(Cabbie)*, Reb Beach, Fred Fairbrass, Chris Botti, Philip Poppa, Tony Carlucci, Michael Skinner, Taborah Johnson, Cree Summer Francks *(Colt's Band)*.

What became of the final film of director Richard Marquand (who died of a massive heart attack in 1987) has been rumored to be an embarrassment for all concerned and has become a sad coda to a frequently interesting career (EYE OF THE NEEDLE, RETURN OF THE JEDI, JAGGED EDGE). Released only in Great Britain—where it was critically reviled—there are no plans for distribution in the US as of yet. Look for this one to quietly appear on home video. Heralded in pre-production press conferences as singer-songwriter Bob Dylan's return to the big screen (he previously appeared in Sam Peckinpah's PAT GARRETT AND BILLY THE KID, D.A. Pennebaker's documentary DON'T LOOK BACK, and the four-hour RENALDO AND CLARA which he himself directed), HEARTS OF FIRE begins in Pittsburgh as aspiring rock singer Flanagan (an obscure rocker in real life) gigs with her band at a local watering hole. There she is surprised to meet Dylan, an aging rock idol now retired and living in seclusion on his chicken farm. Impressed with Flanagan's talents (musically and physically), Dylan offers her a chance to play guitar for him at a "golden oldies" concert he is to play in England. She accepts, but once in England finds Dylan's cynical disregard for his image and his music contemptible. Disillusioned, she soon insinuates herself with currently celebrated British synth-pop star Rupert (DANCE WITH A STRANGER) Everett. Everett is also impressed with Flanagan's talents and offers to produce her first album. Under Everett's tutelage Flanagan becomes a star in her own right. The jealous Dylan departs England warning Flanagan that Everett is just as jaded as he is. Shortly thereafter, Everett and Flanagan (who are now sleeping together) come to America on a concert tour. Frightened into hiding by a blind fan who attempts to kill him and then kills herself, Everett abandons the tour. Distraught, Flanagan turns to Dylan for help and he agrees to appear on stage with her. Much to everyone's surprise, Everett reappears and the three perform together for an enthusiastic crowd. In the end, Flanagan abandons both men in pursuit of her own stardom. Although HEARTS OF FIRE was not released in the US, the soundtrack album was. Songs include "Tainted Love" (Edward C. Cobb), "Feel My Love" (Wang Chung), "In My Heart" (Bruce Woolley, Simon Darlow), "The Other Side" (Steve Jolley, Tony Swain, Steve Warwick, performed by Rupert Everett), "Proud Mary" (John C. Fogerty), "Cinnamon Girl" (Neil Young), "Hair of the Dog (That Bit You)" (Sam Bryant), "I'm in It for Love" (Andy Goldmark, Patrick Henderson), "Carry On" (John Mark, Mark Rice, Brad Hornbacher), "The Nights We Spent on Earth" (Sue Sheridan, Steve Diamond), "Hearts of Fire" (Fiona Flanagan, Beau Hill), "Let the Good Times Roll" (John Dexter, Paul Hackman, performed by Fiona Flanagan), "The Usual" (John Hiatt), "When the Night Comes Falling from the Sky," "Night After Night" (Bob Dylan), "Couple More Years" (Shel Silverstein, Dennis Locorriere, performed by Bob Dylan), "Bus Stop Blues" (James Harpham, performed by Rory McLeod), "Fear, Hate, Envy, Jealousy"

(Art Neville, Cyril Neville, performed by Richie Havens), "Had a Dream About You Baby" (Bob Dylan, performed by Dylan and Fiona Flanagan).

p, Richard Marquand, Jennifer Miller, Jennifer Alward, Iain Smith; d, Richard Marquand; w, Scott Richardson, Joe Eszterhas; ph, Alan Hume (Technicolor); m, John Barry; ed, Sean Barton; prod d, Roger Murray-Leach; art d, Kit Surrey, Barbara Dunphy; md, Beau Hill; cos, Pip Newbery, Antony Price; m/l, Edward C. Cobb, Wang Chung, Bruce Woolley, Simon Darlow, Steve Jolley, Tony Swain, Steve Warwick, John C. Fogerty, Neil Young, Sam Bryant, Andy Goldmark, Patrick Henderson, John Mark, Mark [Spark] Rice, Brad Hornbacher, Sue Sheridan Steve Diamond, Fiona Flanagan, Beau Hill, John Dexter, Paul Hackman, John Hiatt, Bob Dylan, Shel Silverstein, Dennis Locorriere, James Harpham, Art Neville, Cyril Neville; stunts, Gareth Milne, T.J. Scott; makeup, Pat Hay.

Drama **(PR:NR MPAA:R)**

HEAT** (1987) 101m Cassian Elwes-Escalante Prods./New Century-Vista c

Burt Reynolds *(Nick "Mex" Escalante)*, Karen Young *(Holly)*, Peter MacNicol *(Cyrus Kinnick)*, Howard Hesseman *(Pinchus Zion)*, Neill Barry *(Danny DeMarco)*, Diana Scarwid *(Cassie)*, Joe Mascolo *(Baby)*, Alfie Wise *(Felix)*, Deborah Rush, Wendell Burton.

Following his masterful role in DELIVERANCE, Reynolds vowed he would never again work as hard as he did in that film. He has continued to keep that promise in HEAT, a greased-pig film in which Reynolds acts his way through a potboiler script with the unconcerned, almost annoyed attitude of a star being imposed upon to appear before the camera. He is a self-assured, all-knowing Las Vegas bodyguard—"chaperon" he calls himself. He shares an office with lawyer Hesseman (TV sitcom flake) and whiles away his considerable time by doing favors for friends. At film's opening, he allows a short, bald-headed pal to beat him up to impress his date, a chore which earns him $300. Meanwhile, hooker Young is thrown out of a car, her face bloody and torn. The following day she calls Reynolds at his office and asks to see him. Before Reynolds leaves for her house, MacNicol, a clean-cut computer wizard who has recently made $7 million by inventing a new microchip, arrives to hire Reynolds as his chaperon as he makes the rounds of the casinos. Reynolds later finds Young recovering from her beating; she tells him that she wants to sue the sadistic young man who brutalized her, along with his bodyguards. Reynolds finds out that the sadist is Barry, son of a Mafia don, a spoiled, arrogant psychopath. Then Young says she doesn't really want to sue Barry, she wants to savage his privates in revenge for scarring her lovely face. Reynolds, who has known this prostitute since she "had pimples on her face . . . and wore braces," agrees to help her. Dressed in a garish outfit that would delight the most unsophisticated pimp, Reynolds brazenly enters Barry's duplex suite where he demolishes the towering body-building bodyguards and slaps Barry into submission. With all three tied up, Reynolds ushers Young into the suite and she takes her revenge on Barry by nipping his privates with a scissors and taking $20,000 in cash from a desk drawer. Reynolds escorts her to her car, telling her that she had better leave town, that the Mafia will now be looking for both of them. As she drives away, Young stops a stranger and has him deliver the $20,000 to Reynolds. After briefly taking care of MacNicol at a casino where the youth dithers and twitches over making $25 bets, Reynolds brushes off his client and sits down with his friend and blackjack dealer, Scarwid, using the $20,000 to run up his fortune to more than $100,000. He runs into MacNicol who urges him to take the money and go to the land of his dreams, Venice, Italy. Reynolds decides he needs more money and loses everything. MacNicol then hires him to teach him how to be brave and how to defend himself.

Meanwhile, the insidious Barry has gone to the local Mafia chief, Mascolo, who arbitrates the feud, deciding in Reynolds' favor. Reynolds learns just how insane Barry really is when Barry describes how Reynolds shot and killed his two bodyguards while they were tied up; obviously, Barry killed his own men to make his case against Reynolds even stronger. When the reigning mob boss fails to punish Reynolds, Barry hires his own crew of thugs and goes hunting for Reynolds, finding him and MacNicol in Reynolds' office late at night. MacNicol, having taken some preliminary martial arts lessons from Reynolds, thinks to save his idol by slugging one of Barry's hoods and jumping in front of Reynolds as Barry and the other hoods open fire. MacNicol's chest is shredded but Reynolds escapes, the hoods in hot pursuit. Without a gun, Reynolds manages to eliminate the thugs one by one at a huge construction complex, crushing one killer under a pile of concrete blocks, spearing another with an iron rod, setting another on fire, until only Barry is left. When the now terrified Barry returns to his casino duplex he finds the lights not working. He hears Reynolds taunting him in the darkness and fires wildly, almost emptying his automatic. Reynolds, who has been wounded by one of the random shots, tells Barry from his hiding place that he has one more shot and that he, Reynolds, will still manage to "tear your face off . . . the face you love so much." Rather than die disfigured, Barry uses his last bullet to commit suicide. Reynolds is seen the next day walking along a hospital corridor after having been treated for a minor flesh wound and learning that his friend MacNicol has survived. (This is the most astounding aspect of this wholly unbelievable film, as we had clearly seen a bevy of bullets stitch into MacNicol's frail chest.) Before departing, Reynolds stops to see MacNicol, who tells him that they will both go to Venice where Reynolds will teach him the manly arts of courage, karate, and death-defying bravado he has so rashly displayed throughout this impossible saga. As the credits roll up, Reynolds is shown lounging inside a luxurious gondola as it is being poled down a lovely canal in Venice.

This stroll-through role for Reynolds does nothing to aid a sagging career, and, although he considers HEAT a "serious" film, its baggy beginning is eventually crushed by a pants presser ending, all full of steam and hisses. Young as the hooker and Scarwid as the sympathetic dealer are merely types hovering about Reynolds' macho aura. MacNicol is slightly engaging as the naive electronics

wizard who looks up to his mercenary hero. Barry, as the boyish psychopath, is unconvincing. Hesseman has a toss-away role as the sidekick lawyer. There's not much going on here except an endless string of dull cliches about gambling addicts trying to salvage their lives, noble-hearted whores, and a lowlife society that does little to improve Las Vegas' image as a plastic playground for the middle class. Oddly, we see mostly people who work in Las Vegas and very few patrons. The largest group of tourist gamblers before the camera is assembled in one scene only to cheer Reynolds on to his $100,000 score. Reynolds' posture here is that of a man who sees through the "glitter and glitz" of night-time Las Vegas and whose past puts him leagues beyond those who peddle the city's get-rich-quick promises. But we never really know what that past is, except for MacNicol's references to stories about Reynolds in such sterling publications as *Soldier of Fortune*, and Mascolo's remark about how Reynolds never uses a gun (this puts him up on the hoodlums who do) and that he is feared as lethal, a man who uses only "cutting edge" weaponry. We know this for certain because earlier we had seen Reynolds employ credit cards to slash the faces of brutish bodyguards. Once again Reynolds holds himself up as a generous but tough character who is to be envied for an inner character too noble to emerge in the society of other human beings. Reynolds did prove he was tough on the set of HEAT, at least, by knocking director Richards unconscious over a directorial point. (Richards later sued the actor for $25 million.) Three more directors dipped their hands into HEAT's tepid stew, including Jerry Jameson, but Richards, in a gritty Director's Guild arbitration, was given the lion's share of the credit. Not that he should have fought for such recognition from the looks of the product, which, at best, gives Reynolds back to his fans once again but without a single car chase in a frame. *(Profanity, graphic violence.)*

p, Keith Rotman, George Pappas; d, R.M. [Dick] Richards; w, William Goldman (based on his novel); ph, James Contner (Technicolor); m, Michael Gibbs; ed, Jeffrey Wolf; art d, Jerry Wunderlich; cos, Norman Salling.

Crime **Cas.** **(PR:O MPAA:R)**

HEATED FISTS† (1987, Phil.) Cinex/F. Puzon c

[No cast available.]

A group of martial arts experts take on the mob.

[No credits available.]

Action **(PR:NR MPAA:NR)**

HECTOR† (1987, Belg./Neth.) 95m Multimedia-Linden

Urbanus, Frank Aendenboom, Sylvia Millecam, Marc van Eeghem.

Flemish stand-up comedian Urbanus co-wrote, co-financed, and stars as a 33-year-old orphan in this, his feature film debut. For the first time in his life, the dim-witted Urbanus is allowed to spend his vacation outside the orphanage. Taken in by his uncle, Urbanus is made to work in the family bakery so that his cousin can dedicate more time to his career as a racing cyclist. At first Urbanus doesn't mind the work because he has a crush on his beautiful aunt, but he eventually learns that she is in love with the local insurance salesman whose son is her son's chief rival at the upcoming bicycle race.

p, Erwin Provoost, Jos van der Linden; d, Stijn Coninx; w, Urbanus, Stijn Coninx, Walter van den Broeck; ph, Willy Stassen; m, Jan de Wilde; ed, Kees Linthorst.

Comedy **(PR:NR MPAA:NR)**

HEI PAO SHI JIAN (SEE: BLACK CANNON INCIDENT, THE, 1987, Chi.)

HELLO AGAIN* (1987) 100m Touchstone-Silver Screen Partners III/BV c

Shelley Long *(Lucy Chadman)*, Judith Ivey *(Zelda, Lucy's Sister)*, Gabriel Byrne *(Dr. Kevin Scanlon)*, Corbin Bernsen *(Dr. Jason Chadman)*, Sela Ward *(Kim Lacey)*, Austin Pendleton *(Junior Lacey)*, Carrie Nye *(Regina Holt)*, Robert Lewis *(Phineas Devereux)*, Madeleine Potter *(Felicity)*, Thor Fields *(Danny Chadman)*, John Cunningham *(Bruce Holt)*, I.M. Hobson *(Butler)*, Mary Fogarty *(Maid)*, Elkan Abramowitz *(Burns)*, Shirley Rich *(Miss Tammy)*, Kaiulani

Lee *(Miss Lee)*, John Rothman *(Bearded Man)*, John Tillinger *(T.V. Moderator)*, Debra D. Stewart *(E.R. Nurse)*, Patricia Gage *(Bejewelled Woman)*, Mary Armstrong *(Financial Newscaster)*, Colin R. Fox *(Clergyman)*, Rose Indri *(Plastic Surgery Patient)*, Elyzebeth Chrystea *(Lady at Party)*, Suzanne Barnes *(Jason's Nurse)*, Karen Shallo *(Wig-Pulling Woman)*, Paul Royce *(Hospital Bystander)*, Illeana Douglas *(Woman in Park)*, Kate McGregor-Stewart, Lynne Thigpen, Royce Rich, Chip Zien, Anna Marie Wieder, Robert Lempert *(Reporters)*, Susan Isaacs, Marcell Rosenblatt, Catherine Tambini, Everett Quinton *(Occultists)*, Esther Gordon, John J. Healey, Jo Jones *(International News Reporters)*.

The premise of a dead spouse coming back to life to haunt her living partner is not a new one. A recent example of the bearded plot was KISS ME GOODBYE, the 1982 remake of DONA FLOR AND HER TWO HUSBANDS. The best of the lot was, of course, BLITHE SPIRIT. Screenwriter/novelist Susan Isaacs (COMPROMISING POSITIONS) must have thought she had stumbled on a new idea when she wrote the 50-page outline that turned into the script under director Perry's watchful eye. The two had worked together before on COMPROMISING POSITIONS and Isaacs' ear for dialog and penchant for plot twists was realized in her previous novels *Close Relations* and *Almost Paradise*. It would seem, then, that the creative forces behind the scenes would mesh well with the comedic talents they'd chosen to play the roles. Such was not the case and HELLO AGAIN turns out to be one of the rare duds put out by the Touchstone subsidiary of Disney Studios. Long is a nice Long Island *hausfrau* married to Bernsen, a plastic surgeon. Their lives are going along well enough until she takes a huge bite of a Korean chicken hors d'oeuvre and chokes to death. All the while they were married, Bernsen yearned for the Manhattan glitz and glamor, while Long preferred the more sedate existence east of the city. Long's sister, Ivey, is an occultist and, with the help of her pals, she manages to bring her sister back after about a year. Much has changed since Long's departure. Bernsen has remarried Long's good friend Ward, who was lusting after the handsome Bernsen for years. The remainder of the picture is as predictable as the sun rising as it attempts to add some new twists to an old plot but comes up very short. Director Perry's last two pictures were MOMMIE DEAREST and MONSIGNOR, which were, unfortunately, funnier than HELLO AGAIN, although they didn't mean to be. Long is hard to believe as the state-of-the-art klutz who falls down more in the first reel than a punch-drunk fighter. The one saving grace is the performance of Ivey, who was also in COMPROMISING POSITIONS. She always seems to triumph over her material. The picture was shot in New York City and on Long Island. The hospital that is seen is Mount Sinai (here known as "Knickerbocker Hospital") and some of the other locations include the Society of America's building and the Ukrainian Institute. Nye appears in a brief bit as a snooty upper-crust type. She is the wife of comedian Dick Cavett, who should have rewritten the script. The same editor who worked on COMPROMISING POSITIONS, Frank, proves the point here that no matter how good an editor is, he (or she) can't edit what isn't there. What isn't here is a comedy. Director Perry has made 14 movies, including LAST SUMMER, THE SWIMMER, PLAY IT AS IT LAYS, and DAVID AND LISA, with the closest to comedy being RANCHO DELUXE and DIARY OF A MAD HOUSEWIFE. He should stick with what he knows and leave the light work to people whose hands aren't made of lead.

p, Frank Perry, G. Mac Brown, Martin Mickelson, Susan Isaacs, Thomas Folino; d, Frank Perry; w, Susan Isaacs; ph, Jan Weincke; m, William Goldstein; ed, Peter C. Frank, Trudy Ship; prod d, Edward Pisoni; art d, William Barclay; set d, Robert J. Franco; cos, Ruth Morley, Sandra Culotta; makeup, Kathryn Bihr, Mickey Scott.

Comedy **(PR:A-C MPAA:PG)**

HELLO MARY LOU, PROM NIGHT II* (1987, Can.) 96m Simcom/Norstar c (AKA: HAUNTING OF HAMILTON HIGH, THE)

Lisa Schrage *(Mary Lou Maloney)*, Wendy Lyon *(Vicki Carpenter)*, Michael Ironside *(Principal Bill, Sr.)*, Justin Louis *(Bill, Jr.)*, Richard Monette *(Father)*.

Hail to thee, our alma mater. Hamilton High's hallowed halls are chockablock with revenge, death, horror, and the usual ennui shown by high school students during their terms of learning. A sequel to PROM NIGHT (1980) in name only (although Simpson repeats his chores as producer), this one begins with a prolog set in 1957 where we see prom queen Schrage accidentally burned to death by her jilted boy friend just as she is about to receive her tiara. Thirty years later the culprit, now played by Ironside, is the principal of the school. Evidently his mild indiscretion of 30 years before didn't deter the educational system of Edmonton, Alberta (where this was shot), because he is now the man in charge. It's just a few days prior to this year's prom and wholesome teen Lyon is a nominee for queen. Unfortunately the vengeful spirit of Schrage possesses Lyon and we're off to a gore-a-thon. A girl friend is strangled by a cape with a life of its own, the local cleric (and former boy friend of Schrage) is busily praying at the shrine of his former flame (pardon the pun) when he is impaled by a crucifix, a youth is zapped by his computer, and a few other bodies are strewn about for bad measure. It all comes to a close when Ironside repeats what he did years ago by shooting Lyon just as she is about to assume the throne. Then, the charred corpse of Schrage comes out of Lyon's body and swiftly transforms back to her beautiful self. Schrage continues her rampage until Ironside grabs the 30-year-old tiara and finally crowns the angry prom queen. This seems to placate Schrage and she disappears, although we are led to believe that her spirit now lives in Ironside's body, which must mean that yet another sequel is in store.

This film was shown at Cannes as THE HAUNTING OF HAMILTON HIGH and was later retitled HELLO MARY LOU, PROM NIGHT II before its general release just before Halloween. To enhance the new title, plenty of old songs containing the name Mary Lou in the lyrics are prominently featured on the soundtrack. Director Pittman, who was Oscar-nominated for his 1984 short, "The Painted Door," shows promise and, with better material, he may do well. He does manage to squeeze some suspense and surprise out of a few scenes, especially in a confrontation between the possessed Lyon and one of her girl friends in the school locker room. First-screenplay author Oliver studied the works of others to write this, or so it seems, because there is more than a little influence from several better films. The obsession with Catholicism from ALICE SWEET ALICE, and nearly the entire concept of CARRIE are the most obvious borrowings. Good special effects from Jim Doyle, who worked on NIGHTMARE ON ELM STREET and used his budget well to achieve some fine, eerie moments, including a hobby horse that comes to life and a blackboard that suddenly turns into a swirling black pool. This is not a bargain basement movie. There was some serious money spent here and it shows. What doesn't show is any wit, and precious little originality in the conception. And yet, there is enough good about this movie to make it worth renting (not buying) on videotape. *(Graphic violence, gore effects, full frontal nudity, sexual situations, profanity.)*

p, Peter Simpson; d, Bruce Pittman; w, Ron Oliver; ph, John Herzog; m, Paul Zaza; ed, Nick Rotundo; prod d, Sandy Kybartas; spec eff, Jim Doyle.

Horror **(PR:O MPAA:R)**

HELLRAISER½** (1987, Brit.) 90m Cinemarque-Film Futures/NW c

Andrew Robinson *(Larry Cotton)*, Clare Higgins *(Julia Cotton)*, Ashley Laurence *(Kirsty Swanson)*, Sean Chapman *(Frank Cotton)*, Oliver Smith *(Frank the Monster)*, Robert Hines *(Steve)*, Antony Allen *(1st Victim)*, Leon Davis *(2nd Victim)*, Michael Cassidy *(3rd Victim)*, Frank Baker *(Derelict)*, Kenneth Nelson *(Bill)*, Gay Barnes *(Evelyn)*, Niall Buggy *(Dinner Guest)*, Dave Atkins, Oliver Parker *(Moving Men)*, Pamela Sholto *(Complaining Customer)*, Doug Bradley *(Lead Cenobite)*, Nicholas Vince *(Chattering Cenobite)*, Simon Bamford *("Butterball" Cenobite)*, Grace Kirby *(Female Cenobite)*, Sharon Bower *(Nurse)*, Raul Newney *(Doctor)*.

A somewhat disappointing directorial debut from the "future of horror fiction" (according to Stephen King), Clive Barker, based on his own novella *The Hell-Bound Heart*. The film begins as Chapman, a sexual adventurer in search of new carnal pleasures, purchases a mysterious Chinese puzzle box while visiting an unnamed Third World country. Back home in England, Chapman opens the box only to discover that he has unlocked the door to hell. He is pulled into another dimension where the inhabitants, known as Cenobites, push him over the fine line between pleasure and pain by ripping him apart with tiny fish hooks. Years later, Chapman's doting brother Robinson moves his family into the house. Through a flashback, we learn that Robinson's bored and frigid wife, Higgins, had an affair with Chapman mere days before her wedding, and that the woman is still sexually obsessed with her husband's missing brother. During the move, Robinson cuts his hand and blood from the wound drips onto the floor of the room from which Chapman disappeared. Shockingly, the wooden floor absorbs the blood, and, later in the day, the near-skeletal form of Chapman reappears—alive. Higgins discovers the animated corpse and is amazed to recognize it as Chapman. He begs Higgins to help him regenerate by seducing men into the room and then killing them so that he can suck the life out of their bodies and continue his regeneration. He stresses that there is a time factor involved, for the Cenobites will soon discover that he's escaped his eternal suffering and come looking for him. With promises of carnal pleasures to come, Higgins agrees to help Chapman, and with each victim, more muscle, nerves, and skin begin to form on his skeletal frame. Meanwhile, Robinson's daughter from a previous marriage, Laurence, begins to suspect her hated stepmother of having an affair. To her horror she discovers her "Uncle Frank" in mid-regeneration. Chapman is attracted to his nubile young niece, and in the ensuing struggle, the girl manages to escape with the puzzle box. When she opens it, the Cenobites appear to take her away, but she strikes a deal with the demons: If she can lead them to escapee Chapman, they will let her go. Back at the house, Chapman finally persuades Higgins to sacrifice Robinson so that the regeneration can be complete. She does so, and Chapman takes on Robinson's features. When Laurence returns, Chapman kills Higgins in favor of the younger woman. Though momentarily fooled by Chapman's appearance as Robinson, Laurence realizes the truth just as the Cenobites arrive to claim her. The Cenobites recapture Chapman, and to his eternal horror, they again rip his flesh apart with tiny hooks.

Barker's excellent horror fiction preys on universal fears—mostly very adult—

and exaggerates them to horrific extremes. Obsession with, and fear of, sexuality plays an important part in Barker's writing. This, his superb sense of characterization, and a unique eye for atypical subject matter, are combined with a literate, relatively restrained prose style that separates him from the pack of sophomoric writers who wallow in gore-for-gore's sake. Unfortunately, in his first feature film, Barker seems to have trouble striking this subtle balance in a visual medium. Undoubtedly head-and-shoulders above average horror fare thematically, HELLRAISER is, however, extremely graphic, badly paced, and, with few exceptions, poorly acted. As a director, Barker does possess a striking visual sensibility (he performs miracles on a $2.5 million budget). The film literally drips with horrific ambience. The old house is suitably creepy and Barker does well playing on the audiences' fear of what may lie upstairs in the dark. Also intriguing is the hellish dimension inhabited by the bizarre-looking Cenobites. While the author's cinematic sense is a pleasant surprise, his narrative is shockingly haphazard. The film lurches from one set piece to the next with little dramatic rhythm. Some scenes are so poorly integrated that they feel more like rehearsals than actual scenes. Seemingly significant characters appear and then suddenly disappear without further explanation. Although Barker does a respectable job developing the characters of Higgins and Chapman and the lustful ties that bind them, the writer/director is clearly less interested in his victims, Robinson and Laurence. The film never gets a handle on these characters and Barker never bothers to provide enough characterization so that the viewer cares about their fate—a marked contrast to his fiction. He is not helped at all by the performances. Robinson, who was so gripping as Scorpio, the psycho-killer in DIRTY HARRY, wanders through the film as if looking for direction, and Laurence (in her film debut), is simply inadequate to any task other than screaming. Higgins, on the other hand, turns in a fascinatingly perverse performance as the sexually obsessed housewife. Despite its considerable flaws, there is enough promise evidenced in HELLRAISER to make one hopeful that Barker may be able to transfer his "future of horror" mantle to the cinema. *(Graphic violence, gore effects, sexual situations, adult situations, profanity.)*

p, Christopher Figg; d&w, Clive Barker (based on his novella "The Hellbound Heart"); ph, Robin Vidgeon (Technicolor); m, Christopher Young; ed, Richard Marden; prod d, Mike Buchanan; md, Paul Francis Witt; art d, Jocelyn James; cos, Joanna Johnston; makeup, Sally Sutton; spec eff, Bob Keen; stunts, Jim Dowdall.

Horror **(PR:O MPAA:R)**

HELSINKI NAPOLI—ALL NIGHT LONG† (1987, Fin.) 85m Villealfa Filmproductions Oy c

Kari Vaananen, Roberta Manfredi, Renate Rossner, Remo Remotti.

A Finnish taxi driver thinks his financial woes are over when he finds a briefcase full of money on the back seat of his cab. Unfortunately, the case sits between two dead men and someone dangerous is sure to be looking for it.

d, Mika Kaurismaki; w, Mika Kaurismaki, Richard Reitinger; ph, Helge Weindler; set d, Albrecht Conrad.

Drama **(PR:NR MPAA:NR)**

HERENCIA DE VALIENTES† (1987, Mex.) 85m Producciones Hermanos Tamez/Peliculas Mexicanas c (Trans: Legacy of the Brave)

Sergio Goyri *(Marcos)*, Edgardo Gazcon *(Sosteras)*, Patsy *(Daniela)*, Roberto Canedo *(Don Imperio)*, Fernando Almada, Gregorio Casal, Antonio Zubiaga, Carlos Cardan, Jorge Victoria, Guillermo Lagunes, Clarissa Ahuet, Jorge Noble, Sergio Sanchez, Nena Delgado, Chelelo, Isaura Espinoza.

A sequel to TODOS ERAN VALIENTES which sees Patsy, the daughter of an influential politician, caught up in a robbery and taken hostage. Goyri and Gazcon arrive on the scene and ignore the efforts of the police while working to rescue her. Scenes from the first film featuring Fernando Almada and Gregorio Casal are shown in slow motion and black and white during the credits sequence.

p, Orlando Tamez, Guadalupe Viuda de Tamez; d, Fernando Duran; w, Carlos Valdemar (based on an idea by Arnulfo Benavides); ph, Agustin Lara; m, Diego Herrera; ed, Enrique Murillo.

Action **(PR:NR MPAA:NR)**

HEROIC PIONEERS† (1987, Taiwan) 110m Taiwan Film Studio c

Ko-Chin-hsiung, Chen Li Li, Ma Jafung, Chiu Su-yi, Chang Yuan-ting.

Strange-sounding amalgam of modern musical numbers, kung-fu, and historical pageantry set in Taiwan during the 1700s. The film follows a group of brave Chinese adventurers who decide to pull up stakes and move to Kawnlan, an undeveloped area perfect for farming. Before they go barging into the virgin territory, the settlers attempt to make peace with the local chieftain. Although the chief is easy to please, his independent-minded daughter resists his efforts to marry her off to one of the interlopers. Eventually all the natives are won over when the settlers use their modern medicines to cure an epidemic that sweeps through the native population.

p, Li Chi-tse; d, Lee Shing; w, Chung Lai; ph, Chow Yuan-Xing.

Historical **(PR:NR MPAA:NR)**

HE'S MY GIRL* (1987) 104m Scotti Bros. c

T.K. Carter *(Reggie/Regina)*, David Hallyday *(Bryan Peters)*, Misha McK *(Tasha)*, Jennifer Tilly *(Lisa)*, Warwick Sims *(Simon Sledge)*, David Clennon *(Mason Morgan)*, Monica Parker *(Sally)*.

A confoundedly unfunny comedy about love, rock 'n' roll, and transvestism which places its one-dimensional characters in the urban void of Los Angeles. Hallyday is a blonde singer-songwriter from Missouri who dreams of becoming a rock star. After entering a contest sponsored by an L.A. video channel called Video-LaLa, he wins a trip to Los Angeles and the chance to meet rock megastar Sims. There's one catch—he must bring along a girl friend, which means he must leave his best friend and personal manager, Carter, behind in Missouri. Carter, a quick-witted black man named Reggie hits on an idea—he dons a wig, dresses in a sleek gown complete with falsies, and, voila, he becomes Regina. Upon their arrival in Los Angeles, Clennon, the obnoxious head of Video-LaLa, greets the pair with a movie crew, and is a bit shocked to find an interracial couple. Not long afterwards, both Hallyday and Carter fall in love with the first girls they set their eyes on. Hallyday is enamored with Tilly, a ditzy waitress/conceptual sculptress with a shrill voice and a fast motorcycle. Carter is swept away by the pretty McK, an employee of Video-LaLa who, of course, doesn't realize Regina is a male. Carter spends much of his time switching back and forth between Reggie and Regina, and McK is never the wiser. To add to the confusion, McK confides her feelings for Reggie to Regina. A subplot has Clennon trying to get the nearly catatonic Sims to write a song and do a new video. Clennon gets a copy of Hallyday's latest song, gives it to Sims, and—surprise!—it's a big hit. Sims, in an act of honest nobility, has Hallyday perform the song on stage to a crowd of screaming fans. Meanwhile, everything ends happily ever after for the two couples.

If HE'S MY GIRL were a half-way decent film then it could be seen as some sort of modern hybrid of SOME LIKE IT HOT and SPINAL TAP, but that would be giving credit where credit isn't due. It's more like an overlong, insufferable television sitcom with some toilet humor and an occasional topless girl tossed in. Hallyday (the son of French pop stars Johnny Hallyday and Sylvie Vartan) has the vapid teenager act down perfect, Tilly (sister of AGNES OF GOD's Meg) is the type of character who exists only in a screenwriter's mind, and the same can be said for the entire supporting cast. Only McK and Carter escape this mess unscathed. The beautiful McK has a certain sweetness, while Carter's enthusiasm is phenomenal, considering the insipid role he's been forced to play. Carter seems to be truly enjoying himself, while the rest of the cast (McK excepted) couldn't look more foolish. There are problems too numerous to mention, but the only one that matters is a very simple one—HE'S MY GIRL is not funny. *(Profanity, brief nudity.)*

p, Lawrence Taylor Mortorff, Angela Schapiro; d, Gabrielle Beaumont; w, Taylor Ames, Charles F. Bohl; ph, Peter Lyons Collister (Guffanti Labs Color); ed, Roy Watts; art d, Cyntha Kay Charette; set d, Gary D. Randall; cos, Patricia Field.

Comedy/Romance **(PR:C MPAA:PG-13)**

HEY BABU RIBA*** (1987, Yugo.) 112m Avala-Inex/Smart Egg c (BAL NA VODI; Trans: Dancing on Water)

Gala Videnovic *(Miriana/Esther)*, Milan Strljic *(Ristic)*, Dragan Bjelogrlic *(Young Sasha)*, Goran Radakovic *(Young Pop)*, Relja Basic *(Glen)*, Nebojsa Bakocevic *(Young Glen)*, Marko Todorovic *(Sacha)*, Milos Zutic *(Kicha)*, Srdjan Todorovic *(Young Kicha)*, Djordge Nenadovic *(Pop)*.

A nostalgic and universally appealing look at adolescence in 1950s Yugoslavia, HEY BABU RIBA is a bittersweet tale of four teenage boys, "the foursome," as they call themselves, who grow up loving the same girl, hating the same political system, and dancing to the same American music. The film begins as four middle-aged men who live in different cities—New York, London, Paris, and Milan—plan a trip to Belgrade for the funeral of Esther, a girl whom they all loved in their youth. They gather, along with one other person, at her grave site and approach the dead woman's daughter. She knows that one of the men is her father, but too much time has passed for her to care. The foursome agree to have a drink with the fifth person, a former Communist who *is* the young woman's father. They reflect on their youth and remember the times they spent with Esther. In flashback, the foursome—Bakocevic, Bjelogrlic, Todorovic, and Radakovic—are members of a rowing team and their coxswain is Videnovic, a pretty teenage girl whose real name is Miriana, but who calls herself Esther after Esther Williams. Like many teenagers throughout the world, the foursome are obsessed with American culture. They love Glenn Miller, Levis, Marlboros, and American films, especially the 1944 Esther Williams picture BATHING BEAUTY. Although the political climate under Marshal Tito makes everyone's life difficult, the foursome survive on the strength of their friendship. Their bond is threatened, however, as each boy declares his love for Videnovic, who is determined to keep her relationship with them platonic. Each of the lads is feeling the pressures of puberty and ready to cross the bridge from boy to man. Each finds an older woman who will take him into her bed—either a local black marketeer, a prostitute, or an Italian schoolteacher. The day following each boy's ascent to manhood, he symbolically changes—wearing blue jeans and smoking cigarettes. The naive Videnovic makes no connection between their smoking and their loss of virginity. She is still more concerned with friendship than sexual relations. Things begin to change for her when she is courted by Strljic, a Communist who is a few years her senior and has pictures of Stalin and Lenin tattooed on his wrists. She falls in love with Strljic, and after watching a soft-core Swedish art film (ONE SUMMER OF HAPPINESS, mistitled "She Only Danced One Summer"), she makes love to him. The next morning, like her male friends, she is seen smoking a cigarette. Videnovic's life is not as worry-free as her friends' lives. Her father is a political prisoner in Italy and her mother suffers from an illness that eventually kills her. Videnovic then learns that she is pregnant by Strljic. Desperate to reunite with her father, she unsuccessfully attempts to obtain a passport. The foursome finally get her out of the country by rowing her across the Adriatic into Italian waters. They are taken ashore and Videnovic and her father are reunited. Her father then confronts the foursome and demands to know which boy has impregnated Videnovic. When no one speaks up, he informs them that they will never be allowed to see his daughter again. Shifting back to the present, the foursome gather around a piano, drinking and raising an old song they used to sing with their Esther.

A semi-autobiographical account of life in Yugoslavia, HEY BABU RIBA is the work of three lifelong friends who, like the characters in the film, have all gone on to highly successful careers outside of their native country. The second feature from director Jovan Acin (his first, THE CONCRETE ROSE, made in 1975, angered the authorities and led to his leaving the country), HEY BABU RIBA originated during a yearly reunion between Acin and the film's two producers—George Zecevic and Petar Jankovic. Nostalgically looking back on their youth, they decided to go back to Yugoslavia and film a romantic drama with political overtones. Benefitting from a foothold in the film business (Zecevic's Smart Egg Pictures coproduced the NIGHTMARE ON ELM STREET films and Dusan Makavejev's MONTENEGRO) and financial independence (the budget of under $1 million came from their own pockets), the production of HEY BABU RIBA was very much one of close friendship. As a result, the film was immensely popular in Yugoslavia and has received a wide art house run in the US under the Orion Classics banner. Similar in some ways to AMERICAN GRAFFITI (its tender nostalgia), DINER, FOUR FRIENDS (the male bonding), and MACARTHUR'S CHILDREN (the characters' hunger for anything American), HEY BABU RIBA is a success because, despite the larger political and social implications of the subject, it remains a small, intimate film about friendship. Finding a delicate balance between politics and daily life, director Acin has made a film which is universal in its appeal. The performances all capture a certain adolescent honesty, with the stunning 16-year-old Videnovic photographing beautifully. One only wishes that her underdeveloped character had the depth and complexity to match her lovely face. The film was released in Yugoslavia in 1986 under the title BAL NA VODI, which translates as "Dancing on Water"—the Yugoslavian title of BATHING BEAUTY. The US release title, HEY BABU RIBA, comes from "Hey! Ba-Ba-Re-Bop," the Lionel Hampton-Curley Hamner song popularized by The Tex Beneke-Glenn Miller Orchestra in 1946. (In Serbo-Croatian; English subtitles.) *(Sexual situations, brief nudity.)*

p, George Zecevic, Dragoljub Popovic, Nikola Popovic; d&w, Jovan Acin (based on memories of Petar Jankovic, George Zecevic, Jovan Acin); ph, Tomislav Pinter; m, Zoran Simjanovic; ed, Shezana Ivanovic; art d, Sava Acin.

Drama **(PR:C MPAA:NR)**

HI-FI† (1987, Yugo.) 106m Vardar c

Danco Cevrevski *(Matthew)*, Fabijan Sovagovic *(Boris)*, Elizabeta Dorevska, Meto Jovanovski, Vukosava Doneva, Aco Jovanovski, Dusko Kostovski.

A play adaptation starring Sovagovic as a disagreeable old man who has just been released from prison after serving a five-year term. Determined to have his son type his mundane prison memoirs, Sovagovic returns home to discover that his boy, Cevrevski, has become a long-haired hippie who shares his home with a girl friend (Dorevska) and an American drifter. Together the trio has turned the house into a crude recording studio where they cut rock 'n' roll records. Horrified, Sovagovic sets out to restore order in his house, an operation which includes handcuffing Cevrevski to the typewriter so that the boy is forced to transcribe the all-important memoirs. This is the first feature of director Blazevski who was awarded Best Director at the Pula Film Festival.

d, Vladimir Blazevski; w, Goran Stefanovski (based on his play); ph, Miso Samoilovski; m, Ljupco Konstantinov; ed, Petar Markovic; art d, Nikola Lazarevski.

Drama **(PR:NR MPAA:NR)**

HIDDEN, THE*½** (1987) 96m New Line Cinema-Heron Communications c

Michael Nouri *(Tom Beck)*, Kyle MacLachlan *(Lloyd Gallagher)*, Ed O'Ross *(Cliff Willis)*, Clu Gulager *(Ed Flynn)*, Claudia Christian *(Brenda Lee)*, Clarence Felder *(John Masterson)*, William Boyett, Richard Brooks, Catherine Cannon, Larry Cedar, John McCann, Chris Mulkey.

A thrilling mix of science fiction, cop thriller, and buddy film, THE HIDDEN joins Kathryn Bigelow's NEAR DARK as one of the most exciting and unique genre hybrids of the year. The movie opens with a slam-bang action sequence that sees DeVries, a well-groomed young stock broker with a strange glint in his eye, rob a bank, steal a Ferarri, and drive non-stop through several police blockades while blissfully listening to pounding rock music on the stereo. Finally a small army of police force the car into a fiery crash that sends DeVries to the hospital with a plethora of fatal bullet wounds and severe burns. Later that day a mysterious young FBI officer, MacLachlan, arrives at LAPD headquarters to enlist the aid of veteran detective Nouri. MacLachlan produces a picture of DeVries and states that he is a wanted fugitive. When informed that the man is about to die, MacLachlan storms out of the police station and makes a mad dash for the hospital. In the meantime, however, DeVries has died but his body gets up and out of its mouth crawls a slimy alien creature that then slithers into the mouth of middle-aged heart patient Boyett. Now possessed by this creature, Boyett gets up, leaves the hospital, steals some rock 'n' roll cassette tapes, a ghetto blaster, and another Ferarri, killing several people in the process. After assessing the situation MacLachlan informs Nouri that he is now chasing Boyett. Nouri's persistent questioning gets MacLachlan to reveal that Boyett and DeVries are part of the same gang and that they killed his partner, wife, and child. Nouri is a bit incredulous for both men were upstanding citizens and family men until just a few days previous. Before MacLachlan and Nouri can catch up to Boyett, the alien has discovered the body has a bum ticker and slithers its way into the body of a beautiful stripper. From the stripper, the alien moves on to a dog, and then to Nouri's superior officer with MacLachlan following every step of the way. Fed up with MacLachlan's vague explanations of the bizarre events, Nouri has him arrested, confiscates a strange-looking weapon, and discovers that he is not an FBI agent at all, but a man who has taken the identity of a dead agent. MacLachlan privately informs Nouri that he is a police officer from another planet who has been tracking an alien criminal across the universe. Both aliens have the ability to inhabit human bodies and control them (it can only be killed by his special ray gun while outside a human body, the gun having no effect on human flesh). Nouri simply rolls his eyes, and sarcastically retorts, "Are we talkin' spacemen here?" He throws MacLachlan in a cell insisting that he come up with a better story. The next day, however, the alien—as Nouri's boss—arms itself to the teeth and blasts his way through the police station looking for MacLachlan. Now convinced MacLachlan is telling the truth, Nouri lets his prisoner out and gives him the ray-gun. By the time the shooting stops, the alien has vacated the chief and entered the body of Nouri's partner, O'Ross. O'Ross is in charge of security for a speech to be given by a senator running for president and the alien decides to inhabit the politician's body. Since the Secret Service doesn't let a local policeman get too close to the senator, there is a massive shootout which sees Nouri mortally wounded and MacLachlan failing to get to the alien before he transfers to the politician. Faced with the prospect of an evil alien winning the presidency of the United States, MacLachlan invades a political rally and makes a last desperate attempt at getting his man. He barrels his way through a hail of Secret Service gunfire and blasts the senator with a flame thrower. The flames force the alien out of the body, and as hundreds of horrified spectators look on, MacLachlan zaps the creature with his ray gun and finally destroys it. Back at the hospital, Nouri dies from his wounds. But before the doctors notice, MacLachlan sneaks into the room and transfers his life force into Nouri's body and takes up residence.

Bob Hunt's screenplay and John Sholder's direction combine to create an action picture replete with exciting chases, well-staged shootouts, and some ex-

tremely funny black humor. Most impressive, however, is that the characters are finely delineated and therefore, sympathetic and interesting throughout. There is a relaxed naturalness to the interaction and Sholder captures the rhythms of the police station as well as any episode of "Hill Street Blues." Perhaps Sholder's biggest coup is his ability to suspend our disbelief. Nouri's reaction to MacLachlan's extraterrestrial revelations seems totally realistic as the incredulous cop throws the apparent nut in the slammer instead of accepting the ludicrous explanation. Only when outrageous events around confirm MacLachlan's story does Nouri finally force himself to believe the outlandish tale. This adds an extra dimension of believability to the proceedings for Nouri acts as anyone in the audience would. Nouri and MacLachlan turn in superior performances here (as does the rest of the large cast), for it is their relationship that forms the core of the film. MacLachlan is downright endearing as the alien who seems to be having a bit of trouble adjusting to life inside a new body. His eyes are a bit vacant, his gait is a slightly awkward, and after two sips of beer the whole thing breaks down in a comic dinner scene at Nouri's house. MacLachlan does a nice job conveying the alien's loneliness and heartbreak at having lost his wife, child, and partner, and the viewer finds themselves rooting for this odd character. Nouri is excellent as well, as his character moves from annoyance to compassion to disgust, shock, and finally compassion again as he learns the true identity of his new partner. This is the best buddy team since Nick Nolte and Eddie Murphy in 48 HRS. Sholder does wonders on a $4.5 million budget, staging complicated chase scenes and several shootouts with dozens of actors. This is intelligent and effective low-budget filmmaking at its best. *(Graphic violence, profanity.)*

p, Robert Shaye, Gerald T. Olson, Michael Meltzer; d, Jack Sholder; w, Bob Hunt; ph, Jacques Haitkin; m, Michael Convertino; ed, Michael Knue; prod d, C.J. Strawn, Mick Strawn.

Science Fiction/Thriller **(PR:O MPAA:R)**

HIDDEN CITY† (1987, Brit.) 107m Hidden City c

Charles Dance *(James Richards)*, Cassie Stuart *(Sharon Newton)*, Bill Paterson *(Anthony)*, Richard E. Grant *(Brewster)*, Alex Horton *(Hillcombe)*, Tusse Silberg *(Barbara)*, Laura Welch *(Jodie)*.

Dance plays a London statistician whose life is one of uninterrupted order. His world is turned upside down, though, when he meets Stuart, a woman who's hooked on a government conspiracy theory. She is determined to find some mysterious microfilm the British authorities have hidden and persuades Dance to help her. They discover secret underground tunnels beneath London, and the trail grows more dangerous when the police begin trailing the pair. Written and directed by playwright Stephen Poliakoff.

p, Irving Teitelbaum; d&w, Stephen Poliakoff; ph, Witold Stok; m, Michael Storey; ed, Peter Coulson; prod d, Martin Johnson; art d, Alastair Paton; cos, Daphne Dare.

Drama **(PR:NR MPAA:NR)**

HIDING OUT*** (1987) 98m Evenmore-Locomotion/DEG c

Jon Cryer *(Andrew Morenski/"Maxwell Hauser")*, Keith Coogan *(Patrick Morenski)*, Annabeth Gish *(Ryan Campbell)*, Oliver Cotton *(Killer)*, Claude Brooks *(Clinton)*, Tim Quill *(Kevin O'Roarke)*, Alexandra Auder *(Melissa)*, Tony Soper *(Ahern, Stockbroker)*, Ned Eisenberg *(Rodriguez, Stockbroker)*, Marita Geraghty *(Janie Rooney)*, Steven Small *(Driver)*, John Walker *(Pratt)*, John Spencer *(Bakey, FBI Agent)*, Gretchen Cryer *(Aunt Lucy)*, Anne Pitoniak *(Grandma Jennie Morenski)*, Lou Walker *(Ezzard, School Custodian)*, Beth Ehlers *(Chloe)*, Nancy Fish *(Mrs. Billings, Civics Teacher)*, Richard Portnow *(Mr. Lessig, Driving Instructor)*, Gerry Bamman *(Mr. Stevens)*, Jack Gilpin *(Dr. Gusick)*, Lee Anthony Brisbon, David L. Robinson, Daryl Smith *(Clinton's Rappers)*, Gloria Crist *(Spanish Teacher)*, Tom Morgan *(Vice Principal)*, Joy Behar *(Gertrude)*, Dolly Sherman *(Registrar)*, Lorri Lindberg *(Waitress in Diner)*, Rick Warner *(Bob Campbell)*, Lou Criscuolo *(Transient Bum)*, Nicky Hammerhead *(Garage Attendant)*, Dick Olsen *(Morrill)*, Warren Keith *(Breech)*, Tom McGovern *(Bailiff)*, Paul Sparer *(Judge)*, Phillip Suarez *(Kapados)*, Lamon Spainhour *(Shawn)*, John Ward *(Ethan)*, Jeffrey Manning, Joshua Schouten *(Kids in Office)*, Tim Caudle *(Gym Teacher)*, Joe Foley *(Parking Attendant)*, Andrew S. Herzog, Mike Schutte *(Punkers)*, Mary B. Erne, Herbert Erne, Jr. *(Mini Mart Clerks)*, Elizabeth A. Bache, Dereck Fulton, David Higgins, George Whitley *(Students)*, Joe Fagen *(Drop)*.

Cryer is a hotshot New York stockbroker in his middle-20s who, as the result of involvement in some shady dealings, finds himself hunted by a professional killer out to erase all traces of the transaction. After one of his colleagues is murdered, Cryer is placed under FBI protection, but while in a restaurant, is recognized by the assassin, who opens fire, killing one agent and wounding another. Cryer dives through a window and is chased until he manages to catch a train just pulling out of the station. He makes his way to Delaware, where his older sister lives along with her high school-age son, Coogan. He shaves his beard and dyes his hair and then goes to meet his sister at the school where she works. He is amazed by how readily he is accepted as a student and hits upon an idea. He proceeds to the registration office and enrolls as a 17-year-old named Maxwell Hauser (the name taken off a coffee can in the office). He reveals himself to his cousin, who takes him under his wing and shows him the long-forgotten ropes of high school. "Think repression," he tells him. In a contemporary history class he argues with a teacher who rants about how Nixon was framed and soon he is known to every student in the school. He is approached about running for senior class president by a delegation of students who don't want to see the jock who is the only candidate win. Cryer is reluctant, but the campaign gears up anyway. Coogan sets him up with keys to the school building, where he takes up residence, roller skating through the halls and making announcements over the loudspeaker at night. Meanwhile, he is finding love in the person of Gish, whose paper he defended against the fascist teacher. He tries to stay uninvolved but he finds himself genuinely in love and when she demands to know a little more about the past, he reveals his true identity. The killer manages to track him to the town through a birthday card he sent to his grandmother, and eventually figures out Cryer's cover, drawing his old beard and glasses on one of his campaign posters. At the school assembly to announce the winner, he is relieved to hear he has lost, but his rival knows the results were fixed and immediately demands a vocal recount. The students vote overwhelmingly for Cryer, but while he is at the podium making his speech, the assassin is taking aim at him from the balcony. A friendly ex-boxer janitor manages to spoil his aim and Cryer leads a howling mob of students after the killer, who flees onto the catwalks. Cryer goes after him and, taunting him, causes him to fall to his death. The end finds Cryer testifying in court, then taking on a new identity with government help. He goes to Iowa where Gish is studying and finds her again for the happy ending.

For as bad as the premise initially sounds, the film is actually a pleasant surprise. Cryer does an admirable job of pulling off both ages, and Coogan is even better just playing one, a hapless young man caught in all the worst aspects of high school education. Director Giraldi, known for Michael Jackson videos and beer commercials, gives it all a good deal of energy, especially in the first part, shot in a gray and ominous New York that takes on new menace under Giraldi's slick visual style. Cryer is just 22 now, and this is the film he hopes will take him out of the teenage John Hughes-style roles he has been playing and place him in the public's mind as an adult. His performance here may not do that, but it certainly does his reputation no harm. *(Profanity, violence.)*

p, Jeff Rothberg; d, Bob Giraldi; w, Joe Menosky, Jeff Rothberg; ph, Daniel Pearl (Technicolor); m, Anne Dudley; ed, Edward Warschilka; prod d, Dan Leigh; art d, Carol Wood; set d, Leslie Rollins, C.J. Simpson; cos, Susan Gammie; spec eff, Matt Vogel; m/l, Allee Willis, Danny Sembello, Peter Loov, Niklas Hellberg, Patrik Willard, Allan Dias, Lu Edmonds, John Lydon, John McGeoch, Bruce Smith, Michael Jones, David Sanchez, Rene Campos, Ron Elliston, Kevin Elliston, Roderick Hart, William D. Strowman, Mick A'Court, Benkt Svensson, Stan Booberg, Mick Blood, Gregory Kane, Patrick Kane, Jade Starling, Whey Cooler, Roy Orbison, Joe Melson, Larry Williams, Robin Hild, Charles Zimmerman, Felix Cavaliere, Michael Mugrage; stunts, Bill Couch; makeup, Sharon Ilsen Reed.

Action/Comedy **(PR:C MPAA:PG-13)**

HIGH SEASON† (1987, Brit.) 92m British Screen-Hemdale-Film Four-Curzon-Michael White/Hemdale c

Jacqueline Bisset *(Katherine)*, James Fox *(Patrick, Katherine's Husband)*, Irene Papas *(Penelope)*, Sebastian Shaw *(Basil Sharp, Art Historian)*, Kenneth Branagh *(Rick Lamb)*, Lesley Manville *(Carol Lamb)*, Robert Stephens *(Konstantinis, Art Dealer)*, Geoffrey Rose *(Thompson, Rick's Boss)*, Paris Tselios *(Yanni, Penelope's Son & Shopowner)*, Ruby Baker *(Chloe, Katherine's Daughter)*, Mark Williams *(Benny)*, Shelly Laurenti *(June)*, George Diakoyorgio *(Mayor)*, Father Bassili *(Pappas)*, Capt. Stelios *(Fisherman)*.

A satire on the effects of the tourist trade, HIGH SEASON stars Bisset as a photographer living on a Greek island with her daughter, Baker, and her estranged sculptor husband Fox. Unable to make ends meet, Bisset plans to sell a rare Grecian urn through the services of art historian Shaw, who is later revealed to be a spy. Posing as tourists are two other spies—Branagh and Manville—both of whom are shadowing Shaw. To further complicate matters Manville becomes involved with Tselios, a local shopkeeper who intends on turning his tavern into a tourist shop—an idea which his mother Papas opposes. The subplots twist uncontrollably—the urn is accidentally broken by Manville; Bisset unintentionally gets involved with Branagh whom she mistakes for Fox; Fox is commissioned to erect a statue to the "Unknown Tourist"; and Papas, during the unveiling of the statue, decapitates it with a spray of gunfire. The photography is by Chris Menges, the Oscar-winning cinematographer of THE MISSION. Co-scripter Mark Peploe (the brother of director Clare) previously co-wrote Michelangelo Antonioni's THE PASSENGER and this year co-wrote THE LAST EMPEROR, directed by Clare's husband, Bernardo Bertolucci. Filmed on location on the Greek islands of Lindos and Lahania.

p, Clare Downs; d, Clare Peploe; w, Mark Peploe, Clare Peploe; ph, Chris Menges; m, Jason Osborn; ed, Gabriella Cristiani, Peter Dansie; md, Jason Osborn; prod d, Andrew McAlpine; art d, Caroline Haninia, Petros Kapouralis; cos, Louise Stjernsward; makeup, Nick Forder.

Comedy **(PR:NR MPAA:NR)**

HIGH STAKES† (1987, Can.) 82m Simcom/Norstar bw/c

David Foley *(Bo Baker)*, Roberta Weiss *(Terri Carson)*, Winston Rekert *(Dorian Kruger)*, Jackson Davies *(Bill)*, Jack Webster *(Eric Roberts)*, Alex Diakun *(Frank Valenta)*, Anthony Holland *(Nicholas Von Reich)*.

Foley stars as a nerdy cub reporter who works at his uncle's television station and spends much of his time daydreaming in black and white. In his fantasies, Foley sees himself as a Humphrey Bogart-type character involved with a beautiful blonde moll (Weiss). Unfortunately, her boy friend is a half-Chinese, half-Italian gangster who owns a casino frequented by infamous Nazi war criminal Holland. The Nazi is looking to recover a lost cache of riches and the goods wind up with Foley, who finds that everyone he meets is after the treasure. Produced by a consortium of independent Canadian television stations but shown theatrically, HIGH STAKES may see a home video release in the US.

p, Peter Simpson; d, Larry Kent; w, Bryan McCann, John Sheppard; ph, Doug McKay; m, Paul Zaza; ed, Frank Irvine.

Comedy **(PR:NR MPAA:NR)**

HIGH TIDE½** (1987, Aus.) 103m Hemdale c

Judy Davis *(Lilli)*, Jan Adele *(Bet)*, Claudia Karvan *(Ally)*, Colin Friels *(Mick, Fisherman/Artist)*, John Clayton *(Col)*, Frankie J. Holden *(Lester)*, Monica Trapaga *(Tracey)*, Mark Hembrow *(Mechanic)*.

This Australian story of mother and child reunion reteams the star (Judy Davis) and director (Gillian Armstrong) of the outstanding MY BRILLIANT CAREER. Davis, a back-up singer for an Elvis impersonator, is given the sack at the end of a tour of provincial Australian towns. Unable to pay for the repair of her broken-down car, she is stuck in Eden, a tiny fishing village. She rents a tiny house trailer near the beach and tries to come up with the $300 she needs. Fate has brought her to the very same trailer park where her mother-in-law, Adele, lives with Karvan, the daughter Davis abandoned years before when her young husband died. At first, she doesn't recognize the quiet teenage surfer as her daughter, but when she runs into Adele, Davis makes the connection. Adele, who unjustly blames Davis for her son's death, wants her daughter-in-law to leave immediately and demands that she not tell Karvan that she is her mother. However, Davis is drawn to the girl and Karvan to her. Worldly wise and hardened by years on the road without any ties, Davis is forced to confront long-submerged feelings of love and loss. Friels, a local fisherman and would-be artist, falls in love with Davis. Meanwhile, Davis endeavors to leave Eden, accepting a one-night gig as a stripper at the local nightclub where Adele sings in amateur contests. Davis and Friels go away for the weekend and she tells him that Karvan is her daughter. Overwhelmed with the need to see her, Davis rushes back, taking Karvan out to lunch and giving her a book on surfing. Friels stumbles upon Karvan when he returns, and, discovering that Davis has said nothing, he tells the girl that Davis is the mother who Adele has said was dead. A highly emotional scene follows in which Karvan confronts Davis, telling her that she loves her and wanting to know if she is loved. Racked with guilt, Davis tries to explain why she left her. In the process, it becomes clear that the wound opened by her husband's death has never healed. Adele, who has acted as the girl's mother for so many years, is furious when she finds out that Karvan knows the truth and more determined than ever to see that Davis leaves. After one more night of public disrobing, Davis has enough money to pay for her car (the mechanic, operating on good faith, has already allowed her to use it). Before she leaves, Davis asks Karvan if she wants to come with her. With little hesitation, Karvan accepts, but, once they are on the road, she asks if she can go back and say good-bye to Adele. They return and there is a tearful farewell. Back on the road Davis and Karvan stop at a restaurant. Karvan goes inside and waits at a table; Davis contemplates abandoning her yet again. Davis goes to her daughter and the film ends.

HIGH TIDE takes its title from the swelling emotions that engulf Davis. Into the void that has characterized her emotional life after the death of the husband she loved so much comes a deluge of memories and heartache. In abandoning her daughter, Davis fled responsibility and commitment, but, more important, she has been a refugee from love. From her experience, love only brings inescapable sorrow. She must first allow herself to feel again and then she has to find the courage to take the first shaky steps toward permitting herself to care for someone again. Only after she makes the decision to go into the restaurant is it clear she has found that courage. Davis is excellent as the tough cookie who reawakens to feeling. Underplaying and maintaining a hard edge, she prevents her character from becoming the recipient of too-easy sympathy. Karvan captures well the innocence and confused delight of the quiet teenager who, in embracing one mother, must say goodbye to another. Adele also turns in a strong performance as the "mother" who, believing that she has lost one child to Davis, doesn't want to let go of another. Friels, a most capable actor when given the opportunity, is adequate in a role that is little more than a plot device. Somebody has to tell Karvan that Davis is her mother, and it might as well be Friels. However, his character wouldn't be so problematic if he didn't just disappear from the film after he gives the news to Karvan.

Though each step of Davis' struggle toward self-awareness is painstakingly conveyed, stages in the emotional development of other characters are missing. Most notably, Adele's acceptance of Karvan's departure is too easy. There has been no indication that she has had any change of heart toward Davis. In the absence of any demonstrations of self-realization from Adele, it is difficult to believe that she would permit Karvan to go without a fight. The problem here would seem to be in the script, which, despite flaws like these, is generally engaging. Both screenwriter Jones and director Armstrong are women and there is an appropriately gentle and feminine sensibility to HIGH TIDE. Armstrong has never been more in control of the camera than in this movie. In past films she has demonstrated the ability to capture arresting images, but in HIGH TIDE it is her camera movement that is particularly assured, creative without being obtrusive. Though flawed and not the equal of the earlier Armstrong-Davis collaboration, this film allowed US festival audiences in 1987 to witness two of the Australian cinema's finest talents continuing to progress as artists.

p, Sandra Levy; d, Gillian Armstrong; w, Laura Jones; ph, Russell Boyd; m, Mark Moffiatt, Ricky Fataar; ed, Nicholas Beauman; prod d, Sally Campbell.

Drama **(PR:A-C MPAA:NR)**

HIGHER EDUCATION† (1987, Can.) 92m Simcom/Norstar c

Kevin Hicks *(Andy Cooper)*, Isabelle Mejias *(Carrie Hansen)*, Lori Hallier *(Nicole Hubert)*, Stephen Black *(Dean Roberts)*, Maury Chaykin *(Guido)*, Richard Monette *(Robert Bley)*.

Teen sex comedy starring Canadian pop-singer Hicks as a small-town boy who enrolls in a big-city university to study art. He soon learns that his roommate is the son of a Mafia don and must contend with the boy's over-zealous bodyguard (Chaykin). Hicks meets perky co-ed Mejias and she coaches him in the ways of culture, art, society, and of course sex. He is also pursued by his hot-to-trot art teacher, Hallier, and when Mejias leaves the campus for a spell, he winds up in bed with the horny instructor. Upon her return, Mejias learns of the fling and dumps Hicks, only to be won back by him later. Look for this one to turn up on home video in the US.

p, Peter Simpson, Ilana Frank, Ray Sager; d, John Sheppard; w, John Sheppard, Dan Nathanson; ph, Brenton Spencer; m, Paul Zaza; ed, Stephan Fanfara; art d, Andrew Deskin.

Comedy **(PR:NR MPAA:NR)**

HIKARU ANNA† (1987, Jap.) 110m Toho c (Trans: Luminous Woman)

Keiji Mutoh *(Sensaku Matsunami)*, Narumi Nasuda *(Kuriko Sakura)*, Michiru Akiyoshi *(Yoshino Koyama)*, Suma Kei *(Cabaret Owner)*.

Promising young director Shinji Somai's first feature since winning $750,000 in the Tokyo Film Festival's "Young Cinema" competition in 1985 for his film TYPHOON CLUB. His new film stars Keiji Mutoh (a professional wrestler in his movie debut) as a loutish country boy who ventures into Tokyo in search of his sweetheart, Narumi Nasuda, who has disappeared somewhere in the red light district. She has fallen in with vile cabaret owner Sumi Kei and Mutoh must try to bring her back to Hokkaido, their northern island homeland.

d, Shinji Somai; w, Yozo Tanaka (based on a novel by Hiroshi Koshiyama); ph, Mutsuo Naganuma (Agfa color); m, Shigeaki Saegusa.

Drama **(PR:NR MPAA:NR)**

HILL 171† (1987, Phil.) Sunny/Davian c

Yusuf Salim, Robert Miller.

A terrorist sets up a huge marijuana plantation in the jungle in order to trade pot for guns with the local munitions supplier. Then, with all the kids hooked on dope and ready to obey his bidding, the terrorist plans to stage a revolution against the current government and seize power. The government recruits a retired soldier and his five army buddies to find the secret plantation and destroy it. Employing a variety of disguises, the soldiers manage to infiltrate the area and uncover the location of the terrorist operation. Facing impossible odds, the six soldiers launch an attack against the heavily armed terrorist forces.

d, Romeo Montaya.

Action **(PR:NR MPAA:NR)**

HIMMO MELECH YERUSHALAIM† (1987, Israel) 84m Udi-Belleville/Gelfand c (Trans: Himmo, King of Jerusalem)

Alona Kimchi *(Hamutal)*, Amiram Gavriel *(Frangi)*, Dov Navon *(Assa)*, Amos Lavi *(Marco)*, Yossi Graber *(Doctor)*, Aliza Rosen *(Nun)*.

Set in a monastery-turned-hospital in Jerusalem, the story concerns a nurse who is traumatized by the patients with whom she must work, particularly one who is blind and limbless, communicating only in screams. Guttman's third feature, it's based on a popular and critically acclaimed novel.

p, Enrique Rottenberg, Ehud Bleiberg; d, Amos Guttman; w, Edna Mazia (based on the novel by Yoram Kaniuk); ph, Jorge Gurevitz; m, Ilan Virtzberg; ed, Ziva Postek; art d, Ron Kedmi, cos, Suzy Barda.

Drama/War **(PR:NR MPAA:NR)**

HIP, HIP, HURRA!† (1987, Swed./Den./Nor.) 110m Swedish Film Institute-Sandrew Film 86KB-Danish Film Institute-Palle Foghtdal-Norsk Film/Sandrews-Karne-KF c (Trans: Hip, Hip, Hurrah!; AKA: Hip, Hip, Hooray!)

Stellan Skarsgard *(Soren Kroyer)*, Lene Brondum *(Lille)*, Pia Wieth *(Marie Kroyer)*, Helge Jordal *(Christian Krogh)*, Morten Grunwald *(Michael Ancher)*, Karen Lise Mynster *(Martha Johansen)*, Jesper Christensen *(Viggo Johansen)*, Lene Tiemroth *(Elsie)*, Stefan Sauk *(Hugo Alfen)*, Ove Sprogoe *(Bonatzie)*, Ghita Norby, Preben Lerdorff Rye, Benny Poulsen, Tove Maes, Henning Jensen, Tor Stokke, Linn Stokke, Jens Arentzen, Bjorn Kjellmann, Johan Hison Kjellgren, Percy Brandt, Erik Paaske.

The life of famed 19th century Danish painter P.S. Kroyer, one of the members of the Skaw (Skagen) Colony of painters, is explored in this film biography hailed in Europe for its lush visuals. Skarsgard stars as the artist who disguised his dark, troubled personal life with bright, beautiful paintings and a happy-go-lucky attitude. HIP, HIP, HURRA! won the Special Jury and Best Cinematography awards at the Venice Film Festival in 1987.

p, Katinka Farago; d&w, Kjell Grede; ph, Sten Holmberg (Eastmancolor); m, Fuzzy, Johannes Brahms, Gustav Mahler; ed, Sigurd Hallman; prod d, Peter Hoimark; cos, Jette Termann, Kerstin Lokrantz.

Biography **(PR:NR MPAA:NR)**

HOL VOLT, HOL NEM VOLT† (1987, Hung.) 97m Mafilm-Objektiv/Hungarofilm c/bw (Trans: A Hungarian Fairy Tale)

Arpad Vermes *(Andris)*, Maria Varga *(Maria, his Mother)*, Frantisek Husak *(Antal Orban)*, Eszter Csakanyi *(Young Woman)*, Szilvia Toth *(Tunde)*, Judit Pogany *(Tunde's Mother)*, Geza Balkay *(Tunde's Stepfather)*, Gabor Reviczky *(Tunde's Father)*.

Inspired by Vittorio de Sica's classic MIRACLE IN MILAN, HOL VOLT, HOL NEM VOLT chronicles a young boy's efforts to find his father after the accidental death of his mother. Unknown to the boy is a law that stipulates if an unwed mother has not given her child a surname upon its third birthday, one must be invented so that the records will be complete. The boy's mother had used the family name of the clerk who processed the birth certificate, and now, years later, the boy is searching for his fictitious father. Meanwhile, the clerk in a fit of bureaucratic frustration, has gone mad and stolen all the records he had ever processed and burned them. The boy and the clerk then meet a nurse who has experienced the same disappointment with the bureaucracy and the three of them are chased by the authorities to a national monument. They climb atop a giant eagle in the monument and the bird suddenly comes to life, taking the three to a magic land where their troubles will be over.

d, Gyula Gazdag; w, Gyula Gazdag, Miklos Gyorffy; ph, Elemer Ragalyi (Eastmancolor); m, Mozart; ed, Julia Sivo; set d, Jozsef Romvari; cos, Andrea Flesch.

Drama/Fantasy **(PR:NR MPAA:NR)**

HOLLYWOOD SHUFFLE½** (1987) 82m Conquering Unicorn/Samuel Goldwyn c

Robert Townsend *(Bobby Taylor)*, Anne-Marie Johnson *(Lydia)*, Starletta Dupois *(Bobby's Mother)*, Helen Martin *(Bobby's Grandmother)*, Craigus R. Johnson *(Stevie, Bobby's Brother)*, Paul Mooney *(NAACP President)*, Lisa Mende *(Casting Director)*, Robert Shafer *(Commercial Director)*, John Witherspoon *(Mr. Jones)*, Ludie Washington *(Tiny)*, Keenen Ivory Wayans *(Donald/Jerry Curl)*, Marc Figueroa *(Sitcom Father)*, Sarah Katie Coughlin *(Sitcom Girl Friend)*, Brad Sanders *(Batty Boy)*, David McKnight *(Uncle Ray)*, Don Reed *(Maurice)*, Kim Wayans *(Customer in Chair)*, Gregory "Popeye" Alexander *(Pimp)*, Conni Marie Brazelton, Lorrie Marlow *(Hookers)*, Sena Ayn Black *(Receptionist)*, Dom Jack Irrera *(Writer)*, Eugene R. Glazer *(Director)*, Roy Fegan *(Jesse Wilson)*, Jesse Aragon, Bobby Mardis, Verda Bridges, Bobby McGee, Rusty Cundieff, Richard "Romeo" McGregor, Carl Craig, E.J. Murray, Jr., Nancy Cheryll Davis, Angela Teek, Tony Edwards, Grand Bush, Richard Cummings, Jr., Michael T. Smith, Michael Conn, Jimmy Woodward, Franklyn Ajaye, Damon Wayans, Michael K. Colyar, Donald Douglas, Christopher Jackson, Kim Genelle, Larry Cortinas, Shirley Ann Jenkins, Nick Stewart, Jesse Kitten, Steve W. James, Le Tari, Greg Nave Hartwell, Jake Blackschmidt, Howard Allen, Steven Fertig, Michael LaViolette, Beverly Brown, Tamra Naggar, Peter Krug, Brad Laven, Lorrie Marlow, Myra J., Wren T. Brown, Tony Livingston, Kathleen Clark, Tammy Kaitz, Lydia Nichole, Mark Westover, Robert Shafer, Nancy Schier, Stephen Adrianson.

Through dedication, sacrifice, perseverance, and in spite of Hollywood, two promising black directorial talents have burst onto the scene in the last two years. Last year it was Spike Lee with SHE'S GOTTA HAVE IT. This year it was Robert Townsend with his satire on Hollywood's attitudes toward blacks, HOLLYWOOD SHUFFLE. Although haphazardly paced and scattershot in approach, when it works, HOLLYWOOD SHUFFLE is downright hilarious. Townsend (who also cowrote, produced, and directed) stars as a struggling young actor trying to land a big role in a "blaxploitation" film entitled "Jivetime Jimmy's Revenge." The movie opens with Townsend standing in front of the bathroom mirror practicing "Jivetime's" insipid "street" dialog while his little brother, Johnson, coaches him. Contorting his body like a junkie going through withdrawal, Townsend puts a whiny jive spin on lines like "You done messed wif da wrong dude, ba-by" and "Why you be gotta pull a knife on me? I ain't be got no weapon!" His grandmother, Martin, does not approve of the role he is after and worries that young Johnson, who adores Townsend, will grow up thinking that blacks can aspire to be nothing more than pimps, thieves, street hoods, murderers, rapists, and slaves—all images from television. In fact, Johnson's favorite TV show is an absurd sit-com entitled "There's a Bat in My House" which stars black actor Sanders as "Batty Boy." The show asks the burning question "Can a black bat from Detroit find happiness with a white suburban family?" "He's half-bat, half-soul-brother, but together he adds up to big laughs!" Lines like "Wings don't fail me now!" are the order of the day here. Taking yet another day off from "Winky Dinky Dog," the hot dog stand he works at part-time (the employees must wear caps with hot-dog halves sticking out of them like horns), Townsend goes to the audition. In one of the film's most successful scenes, a series of black actors audition for a white woman producer, a white male director, and the white male screenwriter. Willing to do anything to get the role, the actors tolerate these whites telling them to act "more black." In the sequence's most hilarious segment, a black graduate of London's Royal Academy of Dramatic Art stumbles over the line "You be messin' wif da wrong dude, bro!" because he's reading it as if it were written by Shakespeare. Eventually Townsend lands the coveted role, but he feels ambivalent about taking it. His grandmother dismisses the notion that actors must act and that this is, after all, work by stating, "There's *work* at the post office." While Townsend struggles with this moral dilemma, we are treated to various scenarios from the actor's fertile imagination. One is a commercial for the world's first "black acting school" where pompous white instructors teach blacks jive-talk, how to act like Stepin Fetchit, and the finer points of walking "black." Another is a hysterical parody of the Gene Siskel/Roger Ebert movie review show called "Sneakin' into the Movies" which features Townsend and Woodward as two street youths reviewing films. The pair analyze clips from such films as "Amadeus Meets Salieri" ("The title's too hard to pronounce!"), "Dirty Larry" ("Make my day! Do 50 bullets in yo' ass make yo' day!"), and "Attack of the Zombie Street Pimps" ("That was a good movie. You know that sh____ could really happen"). They also rate them via the Siskel/Ebert thumbs up/thumbs down method, although they add the "finger" and the "serious high-five" to the mix. As the first day of rehearsal for "Jivetime Jimmy's Revenge" approaches, Townsend imagines the NAACP picketing his house and a spokesman declaring that blacks, "Won't play Rambos until we stop playing Sambos." Townsend then imagines himself as the star of "Rambro: First Youngblood." Finally, when the big day of rehearsal comes and Townsend finds himself fitted with a ridiculously huge Afro wig and a yellow pimp-suit, his pride takes over and he quits the film, urging the other blacks and the Latino actors to do the same. Heeding his grandmother's advice, Townsend finds work at the post office, playing a mailman in a postal commercial.

Rarely has a film so ineptly directed produced so much intentional laughter. The film's limitations are not entirely due to its minuscule budget, but Townsend freely admits that he had never studied filmmaking technique and that HOLLYWOOD SHUFFLE was a learning experience for him from start to finish. It is heartening to know that an actor with no behind-the-camera experience could scrape together $100,000 and produce a film that—although imperfect—had such great impact. Using $60,000 saved from his acting roles and an additional $40,000 from credit cards, Townsend shot his film on weekends over a three-year period. (For more about the production and the director see Townsend's entry in the People to Watch section.) What separates THE HOLLYWOOD SHUFFLE from the myriad of low-budget comedies is that here is a film with something important to say. Disgusted with the stereotypical roles offered black actors, Townsend decided to attack the Hollywood system head-on. Townsend is foremost a comedian, and because of this he tempers his accusations with humor—a method which, although it can be an imperfect vehicle when raising important social issues, appeals to a wide audience. Most of what Townsend has to say is right on target and he presents it in a manner that is not judgmental. He sees white writers and producers as ignorant not because of inherent racism, but because limited personal experience with blacks leaves them to rely on what they know of blacks from television. Because Townsend is a comedian striving for the kind of mainstream acceptance pioneered by Bill Cosby, he is loathe to alienate his white audience by dealing with the harsh reality that inherent racism is pervasive in this country and is not merely a symptom of misguided media stereotypes. A less cynical approach may be to recognize Townsend as an optimist who prefers to see the good in all people. Either way there are some disturbing lapses in his logic. While the film makes valid points about Hollywood's treatment of blacks, Townsend himself is guilty of some thoughtless gay-bashing, Jewish stereotypes, and male chauvinism in HOLLYWOOD SHUFFLE. In interviews he has been defensive about such accusations and dismisses them by saying that he has known mincing gays, pushy Jews, and complacent women like the characters in his film, and hey, it was just for laughs. Unfortunately he seems to be missing the point that his film sets out to make: Until Hollywood stops feeding the public such stereotypes—for laughs or otherwise—no progress toward ending them will be made. What does make THE HOLLYWOOD SHUFFLE successful is that it at least *raises the issue*. However, Townsend is not yet skilled enough as a writer or director to successfully integrate all his ideas and get big laughs to boot without compromising his message. Because the film was a hit at the box office and because Townsend is a tireless self-promoter, he has bought himself enough time to hone his craft. Townsend followed HOLLYWOOD SHUFFLE with the hit Eddie Murphy concert documentary RAW and a comedy special on HBO which featured many of the talented cast members of HOLLYWOOD SHUFFLE. Songs include: "Not Just One in a Million (Bobby's Theme)" (Patrice Rushen, Sheree Brown, performed by Rushen), "Closer to You" (Rushen, Brown, performed by Rushen, Howard Smith), "There's a Bat in My House (Batty Boy's Theme)" (Robert Townsend, performed by Townsend), "Rags to Riches" (Gregory Alexander, James Hopkins, performed by Alexander), "Rebels of the Night" (Bruce Cecil, Morris O'Connor, Townsend, performed by R. McGregor, A. Teek, R. Fegan, D. Irrera). *(Adult situations, profanity.)*

p&d, Robert Townsend; w, Robert Townsend, Keenen Ivory Wayans; ph, Peter Deming; m, Patrice Rushen, Udi Harpaz; ed, W.O. Garrett; art d, Melba Katzman Farquhar; ch, Donald Douglass; m/l, Patrice Rushen, Sheree Brown, Robert Townsend, Gregory "Popeye" Alexander, James Hopkins, Bruce Cecil, Morris O'Connor; stunts, Steve W. James.

Comedy **Cas.** **(PR:O MPAA:R)**

HOME IS WHERE THE HART IS zero (1987, Can.) 94m Atlantic c

Valri Bromfield *(Belle Haimes)*, Stephen E. Miller *(Rex Haimes)*, Deanne Henry *(Selma Dodge)*, Martin Mull *(Carson Boundy, Lawyer)*, Eric Christmas *(Martin Hart)*, Ted Stidder *(Art Hart)*, Leslie Nielsen *(Sheriff Nashville Schwartz)*, Joe Austin *(Slim "Pappy" Hart)*, Enid Saunders *(Minnie Hart)*, Leslie Jones *(Night Nurse)*, Dana Still *(Blind Man)*, Jeni LeGon *(Wanda Fuch)*, Jackson Davies *(Minister at Funeral)*, Hagan Beggs *(Gravedigger)*, Marc Bourrel *(Chester Nimms)*, Joe Sala *(Nun)*, Mark Acheson *(Cafe Customer)*, Adrien Dorval *(Deputy Worse)*, Jeanette Lewis *(Millie)*, Ian Tracey *(Punk Kid)*, Simon Webb *(Justice of the Peace)*, Janet Wright *(J.P.'s Wife)*.

Although the genre listing says Comedy, HOME IS WHERE THE HART IS might as well be described as a Northwoods Adventure/Musical since that designation comes closer to categorizing the film than the first one does. The weak premise has two 73-year-old British twin brothers, Christmas and Stidder, coming home to visit "Pappy" (Austin), their 103-year-old cowboyish, senile father. After overcoming a few obstacles—their rented car is stolen by a hitchhiking nun who turns out to be a criminal in disguise—the twins arrive home to find that Austin, his convalescent newlywed bride, and most of their possessions are missing from their huge estate. They eventually learn that Austin has been kidnaped by Bromfield, a roller-derby queen-turned-nurse who has killed Austin's bride and is plotting to marry the 104-year-old codger to get his fortune. The rest of the lamebrained plot has the twins enlisting the help of town sheriff Nielsen in tracking down "Pappy." Directed by Rex Bromfield and starring his sister Valri (who had an extremely short television career as a cast member of the "Saturday Night Live" spinoff "The New Show"), HOME IS WHERE THE HART IS fails on every level. Its attempts at black comedy fall flat since Bromfield displays no sense of comedic pacing; the performances are nearly nonexistent; the photography murky and underlit; and the writing sophomoric. Martin Mull has a role as a seedy lawyer, but his character could have been played by a cardboard stand-up to more effect. Had HOME IS WHERE THE HART IS been played for its full potential as a black comedy (something a director like Paul Bartel could have better handled) then maybe, just maybe, it would have worked. The only point of interest is the casting of the 73-year-old twins—Christmas and Stidder—who are not related but look remarkably similar onscreen. HOME IS WHERE THE HART IS was filmed outside Vancouver in an area that could pass for any nameless American town, which was exactly the filmmaker's intention. *(Profanity, adult situations.)*

p, John M. Eckert; d&w, Rex Bromfield; ph, Robert Ennis; m, Eric N. Robertson; ed, Michael Todd; art d, Jill Scott; set d, Lesley Beale; cos, Jane Still; m/l, Long John Baldry; makeup, Connie Parker.

Comedy **(PR:C MPAA:PG-13)**

HOPE AND GLORY***** (1987, Brit.) 113m COL c

Sebastian Rice-Edwards *(Bill Rohan)*, Geraldine Muir *(Sue Rohan, Bill's 5-year-old Sister)*, Sarah Miles *(Grace Rohan, Bill's Mother)*, David Hayman *(Clive Rohan, Bill's Father)*, Sammi Davis *(Dawn Rohan, Bill's 15-year-old Sister)*, Derrick O'Connor *(Mac, the Rohan's Neighbor)*, Susan Wooldridge *(Molly, Mac's Wife)*, Jean-Marc Barr *(Cpl. Bruce Carey, Canadian Soldier)*, Ian Bannen *(George, Bill's Grandfather)*, Annie Leon *(Bill's Grandmother)*, Jill Baker *(Faith)*, Amelda Brown *(Hope)*, Katrine Boorman *(Charity)*, Colin Higgins *(Clive's Friend)*, Shelagh Fraser *(WVS Woman)*, Gerald James *(Headmaster)*, Barbara Pierson *(Teacher)*, Nicky Taylor *(Roger)*, Sara Langton *(Pauline)*, Imogen Cawrse *(Jennifer)*, Susan Brown *(Mrs. Evans)*, Charley Boorman *(Luftwaffe Pilot)*, Peter Hughes *(Policeman)*, Christine Crowshaw *(Pianist)*, William Armstrong *(Canadian Sergeant)*, Arthur Cox *(Fireman)*, Ann Thornton, Andrew Bicknell *(Honeymoon Couple)*, Jodie Andrews, Nicholas Askew, Jamie Bowman, Colin Dale, David Parkin, Carlton Taylor *(Roger's Gang)*, John Boorman *(Narrator)*.

The vast majority of mainstream films are bland connect-the-dots products—the direct result of the bottom-line accountant mentality so pervasive in today's Hollywood. Men and women who know nothing about cinema consult marketing surveys and consider fads, trends, and fashion before making a committee decisions regarding the sort of films they choose to produce. The endless number of pointless sequels released in a single year is a lamentable testament to the contempt Hollywood conglomerates hold for personal inspiration and artistic creativity. Therefore, it is a rare and wonderful thing indeed when a film that is among the year's most intelligent, heartfelt, and personal also happens to be one of the most marvelously entertaining of the decade. HOPE AND GLORY is a semi-autobiographical film from maverick British director John Boorman and concerns life during wartime. Boorman was a young boy when Great Britain declared war on Hitler's Germany in September of 1939, and he lived with his parents in a brand-new suburban London housing development known as "Bhin-Tal." His film begins on the Saturday morning that war was declared as Boorman's cinematic alter ego, 9-year-old Rice-Edwards, plays with his tin knights in the family garden. Suddenly, the cacophony of lawn mowers that is a normal part of any Saturday, stops. Sensing that something is wrong, Rice-Edwards rushes into the house in time to hear the voice of Prime Minister Chamberlain declare war on Germany. The very next day Rice-Edwards' ineffectual-but-kindly father (Hayman) enlists, hoping that this war will take him back to the excitement he felt while soldiering during WW I (to his chagrin he is assigned typing-pool duties in England). Before leaving, Hayman teaches his son the "googly," a wrist-spun, off-break bowl used in the game of cricket to baffle batsmen. This is done with great solemnity, as if discussing the secrets of the birds and bees. Worried that her children may be harmed in the war, Rice-Edwards' mother (Miles) decides to send her son and his little sister (Muir) to live with a relative in Australia for the duration. Rice-Edwards balks at the notion vociferously, moaning that he'll " . . . miss the war!" As hundreds of children are led off like cattle at the train station, Miles has a sudden change of heart and tearfully snatches her little ones from the crowd. Incredibly, Rice-Edwards angrily denounces his mother for changing her mind, complaining that he has been embarrassed in front of his mates. Soon after, the Blitz begins and Miles immediately regrets having selfishly kept her children from fleeing to safety. Huddled under the stairs with Rice-Edwards, Muir, and her teenage daughter, Davis, Miles tries to keep a stiff upper lip as Nazi bombs explode about the neighborhood. Unwilling to sit there waiting to die, the rebellious Davis leaves the shelter and dances into the yard daring the bombs to hit her. During the day, Rice-Edwards runs with a gang of boys who search the rubble of destroyed tract houses for precious pieces of enemy shrapnel. The boys take this golden opportunity to wantonly "smash things" and spend much of their time breaking windows and abandoned furniture and household items that have somehow survived the Nazi bombs. Despite the war, school is still a bore and the air raids that seem to interrupt studies on a daily basis are looked upon by the children as a welcome liberation from the dull routine. Meanwhile, Davis has fallen in love with a handsome young Canadian soldier (Barr) who is waiting to be shipped out. Her nocturnal wanderings with Barr lead to a vicious argument between mother and daughter in which Davis defiantly declares her sexual intentions. Miles takes the news with a resigned "Well, we might all be dead tomorrow," and concludes with "Just don't fall in love with him." "Who said anything about love?" Davis sneers. By Christmas time, however, Davis is pregnant and in love. Although she informs her parents, Davis refuses to tell Barr, who has just received his orders to go overseas. Miles, in the meantime, has come to look upon the war as a liberating force. She shocks her friends by stating that she has come to prefer sleeping by herself and really gets along quite nicely without Hayman, or, indeed, any man. She does, however, still hold a place in her heart for former flame and family friend O'Connor, but is mature enough to simply enjoy his companionship. After returning home from a day at the beach, Miles is horrified to see her house on fire. Ironically, the destruction was not the result of the Blitz, but merely a common household accident. Miles and her brood move in with her cantankerous father (Bannen) and her doting mother (Leon), who live on the Thames far from London. Their riverside cottage is a magical place for Rice-Edwards. The brick streets of his home are replaced by green grass, lush trees, boating, fishing, and games of cricket where he confounds his grandfather with the "googly." Eventually Barr learns of Davis' pregnancy and deserts his unit to marry her. While relatives try to take photos of the happy couple following the ceremony, Barr is dragged off by the MPs. Shortly thereafter, Davis goes into labor. While his little sister and aunts excitedly witness the birth, Rice-Edwards passes out. When summer ends, Rice-Edwards must return to

school. He is driven there by Bannen, who complains endlessly that school merely ruins young minds by confusing them with useless facts. Sadly, Rice-Edwards bids good-bye to the sympathetic old man and walks to the school-yard only to discover that it has been hit by a Nazi bomb and destroyed. Hundreds of kids hold a celebration amid the smoldering rubble ("Thank you, Adolf!" one boy cries) while the exacerbated schoolmaster tries to retain order. The delighted grandfather picks the boy up and returns him to his beloved Thames. Director Boorman concludes his film with narration spoken in his own voice: "In all my life, nothing ever quite matched the perfect joy of that moment. My school lay in ruins; the river beckoned with the promise of stolen days."

HOPE AND GLORY is John Boorman's most personal film and certainly his most accessible. While Americans may find it a bit disconcerting to accept the fact that the horrors of the Blitz could be the setting for a nostalgic comedy, the truth is that for a young boy the war was a particularly exciting and vivid time, and a joyous feeling permeates the film. The total upheaval of the staid family order, the lack of normal restrictions and discipline, and the wholly liberating effect the war had on women are all brilliantly conveyed by Boorman because he views the war through a child's perspective. Of course there was pain, destruction, and death, but a child does not fully grasp the implications of such tragedy—especially when it is experienced by others. Children accept, adapt, and move on. Told in a series of vignettes, HOPE AND GLORY unfolds in a surprisingly nonchalant manner, tossing out its vividly realized observations at every turn. Boorman skillfully combines nuggets of truth with moments of mirth and is always prepared to surprise and amuse without sentimentalizing. From the family's guilt and suspicion over eating a can of German jam which has washed ashore to the delightful escape of an huge barrage balloon that clumsily floats over the neighborhood like a flying whale until the forces of order come and shoot it down, HOPE AND GLORY offers rare gems in every scene. Although quintessentially British, the film is remarkably universal, especially for those who have lived through wartime (director Milos Forman, a Czech who grew up in Prague during the war, congratulated Boorman on the remarkable accuracy of his vision). Boorman had the suburban street where he grew up re-created on a 40-acre outdoor set built on an abandoned airfield in Surrey. The set, which cost an estimated $1 million, was the largest constructed in England since WW II. Every brick, prop, and item of clothing smacks of fond personal recollection.

Boorman's casting is superb as well. Young Rice-Edwards is a real find, able to convey a wide range of thought and emotion without ever falling back on the kinds of cheap tricks child actors can get away with. Miles, who was blessed with her best role in years, rises to the occasion and turns in a performance of skill and grace. The strong supporting cast is flawless, with both Davis and Bannen nearly stealing the film. Most interesting to cineastes, however, is the rare personal glimpse into the creative mind of John Boorman. HOPE AND GLORY holds a valuable key to understanding Boorman's other work. Rarely has a filmmaker opened the door to the origin of his obsessions with such honesty and good nature. The alienation of man from nature, the magical properties of running water, the liberating effect of violence, his love of the Arthurian legend, and his passion for the cinema begin to bud for Boorman in HOPE AND GLORY. What is most remarkable about this film, however, is the discovery of a more gentle, playful side to Boorman's personality—an aspect that has been hidden by his previous macho and violent films. His adoration and respect for women is a true revelation, as is his delightful sense of humor. But even those who are not Boorman fans will enjoy the film immensely. Rich in insight, humor, and a keen sense of observation that illuminates both the artist and the human condition, HOPE AND GLORY is a delight to behold. *(Sexual situations, profanity.)*

p, John Boorman, Michael Dryhurst; d&w, John Boorman; ph, Philippe Rousselot, John Harris (Eastmancolor); m, Peter Martin; ed, Ian Crafford; prod d, Anthony Pratt; md, Peter Martin; art d, Don Dossett; set d, Joan Woollard; cos, Shirley Russell; ch, Anthony Van Laast; spec eff, Rodney Fuller, Michael Collins, Phil Stokes; makeup, Anna Dryhurst.

Comedy/Drama **(PR:C MPAA:PG-13)**

HOSTAGE*½ (1987) 95m Blue Flower-Alpine/Noble Ent. c

Wings Hauser *(Sam Striker)*, Karen Black *(Laura Lawrence)*, Kevin McCarthy *(Col. Tim Shaw)*, Nancy Locke *(Nicole)*, Robert Whitehead *(Harry, Laura's Agent)*, Billy Second *(Rona)*, Ian Steadman *(Yamani)*, Robert K. Brown *(Himself)*, John Donovan *(Himself)*, Michael Brunner *(John)*, Pamela Perry *(Edna)*, At Botha *(Raoul)*, Marcel van Heerden *(Hussein)*, Gerhard Hametner *(Tommy, Nicole's Son)*, Limpie Basson *(Zennin Kushu)*, Tulio Moneta *(Terrorist Leader)*, Robert Haber *(Ambassador)*, Johann Kruger *(Hans)*, Tom Mphatsee *(Army Captain)*, Molly Seftel *(Zabo's Wife)*, Kurt Eggelhoff *(Zabo's Son)*, Sanette Smith *(Zabo's Daughter)*, Claire Marshall *(Sister Eugenia)*, Iain Winter.

Since the 1976 Israeli rescue of a planeload of hostages held by terrorists at an airport in Uganda, that brilliant strike has held a fascination in the minds of filmmakers and politicians alike. An entire Entebbe genre has grown, with at least three films on the actual event, and scores of others with similar operations integral to the plots. A durable formula it is, too. Establish sympathetic characters all en route somewhere, toss in a desperate group of hardcore terrorists (including one particularly sadistic woman, usually in tight jeans and highheel boots and toting an Uzi) to imperil them, then intercut between the interminable waiting of the hostages and terrorists and the preparation of the army, or mercenary force, or freedom fighters or whatever, to swoop in for a final battle that ends with lots of dead terrorists and some tearful reunions. All of these are in evidence in HOSTAGE, as dismal an effort as has come down the pike in a while. Kevin McCarthy is a retired American officer living in Africa with some sort of reputation that makes people say "THE Colonel Shaw?" whenever they hear his name. His daughter, Locke, and his grandson, Hametner, live with him. Locke is the fiancee of Hauser, a soldier of no small reputation himself. Hametner suddenly needs a kidney transplant in New York, so he and Locke are put on the next DC-3 out, which also happens to carry an important pacifist Moslem holy man and several terrorists. The terrorists force the plane down outside Nairobi and demand the release of their imprisoned leader and $25 million. McCarthy calls in Hauser and two soldier-of-fortune types (Donovan and Brown, playing themselves, whoever they are), and they prepare for an assault on the plane. Hauser swoops in on a hang glider and cuts a hole in the airplane to sneak aboard while the main force surrounds the area. The battle finally erupts, the terrorists are killed, and after a final fist fight with the last terrorist while Hametner sinks in quicksand, the tearful reunions take place as the credits roll. South African films are always sort of interesting for the way you can see the affects of apartheid even in films where it's never mentioned. Blacks are all seen as corrupt or lazy, while the whites rule over them benevolently. As a whole, the film isn't bad, though the terrorists, supposedly Arabs, are all played unconvincingly by South Africans, and McCarthy seems to have totally lost whatever talent he showed in decades past. Karen Black is on display too, as a soft-core sex queen at the end of her tether. Once an actress with a serious reputation made in such films as FIVE EASY PIECES, EASY RIDER, DAY OF THE LOCUST and others, she has lately been seen primarily in a series of foreign-made action/adventures in which she usually overacts to the point of hysteria. Filmed under the title of "Colt—Flight 802," HOSTAGE was released to video after a short theatrical release in the US. *(Violence, profanity, adult situations.)*

p, Thys Heyns, Paul Raleigh; d, Hanro Mohr; w, Norman Winski, Michael Leighton; ph, Johan van der Vyver; ed, Simon Grimley; art d, Geoff Hill; set d, Caron Hill; stunts, Reo Ruiters; makeup, Ann Schofield.

Action **Cas.** **(PR:C-O MPAA:R)**

HOSTAGE SYNDROME† (1987, Phil.) F. Puzon Film Ent.

Brad Zutaut, Karen Lundeen, Caroline Hudson, Costa Theodosopoulos, Robert Marius, David Brass, Cory Paul Sperry.

A California Highway Patrol officer who was drummed out of the corps for enacting personal revenge on the killers of his father is hired by the FBI. He is needed to help combat a Soviet super-criminal who plans to perfect a steroid formula that will turn regular soldiers into ultra-strong monsters. Teamed with a tough female FBI agent, the former cop defeats the villain and puts an end to the mad scheme.

d, Dominic Elmo Smith; w, Daniel Benton (based on a story by Dominic Elmo Smith, David Brass); ph, Arnold Alvaro; ed, Amang Sanchez, Marc Tarnate; prod d, Robert Lee; md, Marita Manuel; art d, Jun Sancha; cos, Daphne Aisa; spec eff, Guy Naelgas; stunts, Roland Falcis, Jolly Jogueta; makeup, Ed Cruz.

Action **(PR:NR MPAA:NR)**

HOT CHILD IN THE CITY* (1987) 85m Mediacom-Fairfield-MVA-1/Prism c

Leah Ayres Hendrix *(Rachel Wagner)*, Shari Shattuck *(Abby Wagner)*, Geof Prysirr *(Detective Ray Osborne)*, Antony Alda *(Charon)*, Will Bledsoe *(Tim Bradford)*, Ronn Moss *(Tony)*, Sally Kay Brown *(Finelli)*, Susann Altbach *(Receptionist)*, Danny Natan *(Bartender)*.

Yet another mundane crime story set on the flashy, neon-lit streets of Hollywood in which pretty young women are paraded around in skimpy outfits and men are self-centered brutes who take advantage of the supposedly weaker sex. Hendrix is one of the aforementioned pretty young women who comes to Los Angeles to visit her successful record executive sister, Shattuck. Hendrix is awestruck by Shattuck's life-style—a fancy house, a pool, a closet full of glitzy clothes—but is still a Kansas girl at heart. She's not in her sister's house for more than a couple minutes when she overhears a threatening message on the answering machine from a former lover who demands that a pricey bracelet be returned to him. Shattuck refuses to talk about it, however. After spending time swimming, drinking marguerítas, and trying on clothes, the sisters step out for the evening, dragging along the freakish Alda, an androgynous former rock star who is hoping for a comeback. Disgusted with the meat-market atmosphere of her sister's favorite nightclub, Hendrix heads home. In the meantime, Shattuck argues with both her former boy friend, Bledsoe, and with Alda. Shattuck is then found murdered, her body tossed in a dumpster in the alley behind the nightclub. Enter police detective Prysirr, a Harrison Ford type who immediately assumes that Alda is the killer. In the meantime, Hendrix begins to assume her sister's personality, dressing in her clothes and promiscuously parading around the nightclub. She attracts the attention of Bledsoe, who, after a night of lovemaking, reveals himself as Shattuck's killer. After a struggle, Hendrix kills the murderer. A short while later, Prysirr is invited over by Hendrix, who has now completely assumed her sister's personality. There's nothing even remotely original about HOT CHILD IN THE CITY and, in fact, it might as well have come off an assembly line. It contains all the usual ingredients—a rock'n'roll soundtrack, numerous trendy nightclubs scenes, unspectacular travelog shots of Hollywood Boulevard at night, and girls traipsing around in lingerie. The performances are generally wooden, with only Hendrix and sometimes Alda showing any sort of range. This is the first of a promised series of straight-to-video releases which are titled after once-popular rock songs. Those to follow are HOUSE OF THE RISING SON, BLUE SUEDE SHOES, and NIGHTS IN WHITE SATIN (which premiered on HBO even before its video release). Songs include: "Hot Child in the City" (Nick Gilder, James McCulloch, performed by Gilder), "Flesh for Fantasy," "Eyes Without a Face" (Billy Idol, Steve Stevens, performed by Idol), "Walk on the Wild Side" (Lou Reed, performed by Reed), "Our Lips Are Sealed" (Terry Hall, Jane Weidlin, performed by Fun Boy Three), "We Close Our Eyes" (P. Cox, R. Drummie, performed by Go West), "Traces of You" (performed by Lauren), "Tender Is the Night (This Side of Paradise)" (Andd More, performed by Andd More), "Reputation" (Jimmi James, Ira Ingber, performed by Jimmi James and the Flames), "Move" (Antony Alda, performed by Alda). *(Brief nudity, violence, substance abuse, profanity.)*

p, Giovanna Nigro-Chacon; d, John Florea; w, George Goldsmith; ph, Richard C. Glouner (Foto-Kem color); m, W. Michael Lewis; ed, Marcy Hamilton; prod d, Anthony Sabatino, William H. Harris; set d, George Peterson; m/l, Gilder-McCulloch, P. Cox, R. Drummie, Billy Idol, Steve Stevens, Andd More, Terry Hall, Jane Weidlin, Jimmi James, Ira Ingber, Lou Reed, Antony Alda; makeup, Nina Kent.

Crime/Drama **(PR:O MPAA:NR)**

HOT PURSUIT** (1987) 93m RKO/PAR c

John Cusack *(Dan Bartlett)*, Wendy Gazelle *(Lori Cronenberg)*, Robert Loggia *(Mac MacLaren)*, Jerry Stiller *(Victor Honeywell)*, Monte Markham *(Bill Cronenberg)*, Shelley Fabares *(Buffy Cronenberg)*, Dah-Ve Chodan *(Ginger Cronenberg)*, Ben Stiller *(Chris Honeywell)*, Terrence Cooper *(Capt. Andrew)*, Andaluz Russell *(Carmelina)*, Ursaline Bryant *(Roxanne)*, Keith David *(Alphonso)*, Paul Bates *(Cleon)*, Ted White, Andrew Cochrane.

John Cusack has the talent of making any film he appears in worthwhile. Best remembered for the Rob Reiner film THE SURE THING, Cusack has appeared in a number of other comedies but none of them has brought him the stardom he seems to deserve. Apparently unable to differentiate between a comedy script and a string of gags, Cusack appears in yet another forgettable picture that quickly disappeared from the theaters. Cast as a prep school student, Cusack is an overachiever who studies so hard that he fights a losing battle with exhaustion and flunks a chemistry test. As a result Cusack must take a makeup test during Easter vacation—a time he is supposed to spend sailing with his cheerleader girl friend, Gazelle, and her family. Luckily for Cusack, his chemistry teacher has a change of heart and excuses him from the exam. Cusack hurries to the airport, but, darn the luck, the plane has just taken off. Determined to catch Gazelle, Cusack boards the next plane to the Caribbean. Numerable mishaps follow, always leaving Cusack just one step behind the family. A trio of ganja-smoking Jamaicans offer assistance, but he misconstrues their intent and continues his pursuit alone. Eventually he meets up with Loggia, a weathered sea captain who, coincidentally, is looking for the yacht that Gazelle and her family are sailing on. Cusack has his doubts about accepting Loggia's help, but when the sea captain shanghais him, their adventure begins. After battling a some fierce high-sea storms, the pair discovers that the yacht has been hijacked by a gang of pirates. After a bit of gunplay, the pirates are beaten down and Cusack is reunited with Gazelle.

Limping along on a scant plot, HOT PURSUIT succeeds only because of Cusack's handling of his character. Rather than play it as a stereotype, he injects life by making the character an average person. Although there are no pretensions of making the *situations* real, his *character* somehow seems real. Aided by a fine sense of comic timing and the ability to underplay certain humorous scenes, Cusack carries the film. Loggia is always a pleasure to watch, even when his part is as mindless as it is here. Gazelle, as Cusack's love interest, is a pretty face, but she isn't given anything to do except an occasional acrobatic tumble. Director Lisberger's previous film was the visually innovative film TRON, which employed interesting computer graphics but was hampered by a barely average script. This time around Lisberger doesn't have computer graphics to support his direction and the result is rather unflattering. For a more entertaining version of this story turn to THAT MAN FROM RIO, a 1964 French comedy from Philippe de Broca which stars Jean-Paul Belmondo as a diehard romantic who pursues his kidnaped girl friend, Francoise Dorleac, all across South America. One of Lisberger's inside jokes is to name Gazelle's family "Cronenberg"—a name that horror film fans should recognize as shared by director David Cronenberg. The use of that name here is not just a coincidence, as Canadian producer Pierre

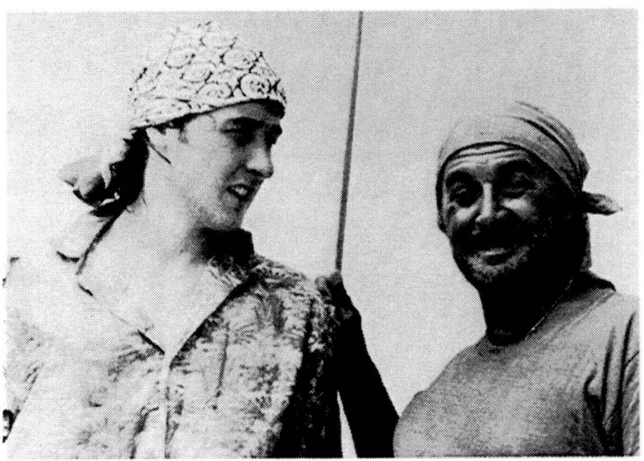

David previously produced Cronenberg's films THE BROOD, SCANNERS, and VIDEODROME. *(Comic violence, substance abuse.)*

p, Pierre David, Theodore R. Parvin; d, Steven Lisberger; w, Steven Lisberger, Steven Carabatsos (based on a story by Steven Lisberger); ph, Frank Tidy (Metrocolor); m, Rareview; ed, Mitchell Sinoway; prod d, William J. Creber; art d, Fernando Ramirez, Chris Dorrington; cos, Taryn "Teri" De Chellis.

Comedy **(PR:C-O MPAA:PG-13)**

HOTARUGAWA† (1987, Jap.) 114m Kinema Tokyo-Nichiei/Shochiku c (Trans: River Of Fireflies)

Takayuki Sakazume *(Tatsuo)*, Rentaro Mikune *(Shigetatsu)*, Yukiyo Toake *(Chiyo)*, Tamae Sawada *(Eiko)*, Tomoko Naraoka *(Harue)*, Taiji Tonoyama *(Ginzo)*.

Set in a small town in 1962 this film follows a few months in the life of 14-year-old Takayuki Sakazume as he pursues the affections of pretty classmate Tamae Sawada. At the same time the boy's father, Rentaro Mikune, is embroiled in personal and financial problems of his own. He regrets having left his first wife when his mistress—the mother of Sakazume—became pregnant. After having an honest talk with his boy, Mikune suffers a heart attack and dies. His death brings the boy and his mother closer to Mikune's first wife. The death of his father forces Sakazume to grow up fast and he assumes responsibility for his destitute mother's welfare. The film ends on a note of change and optimism as one of Mikune's old friends guides Sakazume, his mother, and Sawada to a secret place where fireflies gather to mate. Japanese legend tells that those who witness the event will eventually marry.

p, Kiyoshi Fujimoto; d, Eizo Sugawa; w, Eizo Sugawa, Kyohei Nakaoka (based on a novel by Teru Miyamoto); ph, Masahisa Himeda; m, Masatsugu Shinozaki; ed, Jun Nabeshima; prod d, Iwao Akune; cos, Satoyoshi Kubo, Tomio Okubo; spec eff, Koichi Kitakawa.

Drama **(PR:NR MPAA:NR)**

HOTEL COLONIAL* (1987, US/It.) 104m Yarno Cinematogafica-Legeis Theatrical-Hemdale/Orion c

John Savage *(Marco Venieri)*, Robert Duvall *(Carrasco)*, Rachel Ward *(Irene Costa)*, Massimo Troisi *(Werner)*, Claudio Baez *(Mario Anderson)*, Anna Galiena.

An incredibly bad Italian-American coproduction from 30-year-old Italian director Torrini which wastes the talents of Duvall, Savage, Ward, and cinematographer Rotunno (THE LEOPARD) on a totally lifeless, pointless, cliched, and hopelessly dull story. Savage plays an Italian (without a hint of an accent) living in New York City who receives a call from his distraught sister-in-law informing him that his brother—a former Red Brigade terrorist—has committed suicide in Colombia. Savage goes to Bogota to collect his remains and there he meets Ward, the beautiful assistant to the Italian ambassador (she *does* have an Italian accent). After viewing the badly decomposed body and looking over the crime scene, Savage concludes that the dead man was murdered, and, in fact, is not his brother (something the viewer has known since the opening scene). Following a tedious investigation, Savage traces his brother to the Colombia/Peru border where he is reputed to have become a partner in a powerful drug ring. Savage checks into the swanky (i.e., a swimming pool and no bugs) Hotel Colonial, which is owned by the man rumored to be his brother's partner. During his search, Savage befriends an Italian boat owner named "Werner" (played by Italian comic Troisi) who, well, he . . . he . . . he . . . stroogle to speaka da Eengleesh. (Why Troisi, who is an Italian, and Savage, who is an Italian, don't speak their native language to each other instead of struggling with English is merely one of many great mysteries to be found in this film.) Frustrated and about to give up, Savage finally meets the owner of the Hotel Colonial, a blond-wigged Duvall. This is where the film really gets dumb. At the beginning of the film the viewer is treated to a very grainy, high-contrast black-and-white flashback where Savage's brother—obviously played by Duvall—is seen speaking in the shadows. Throughout the film, Savage flashes a passport picture of his brother to countless locals. When Savage finally comes face to face with his brother, he fails to recognize him because of the blond hair and Colombian accent! This holds true for most of the rest of the film as several scenes between the two are played out with Savage failing to realize that Duvall is his own brother.

Duvall, who represents totally amoral evil incarnate (drug runner, poacher, white-slaver), takes his sibling on a hunting trip which includes the shotgun slaughter of a dozen cute Amazonian monkeys. A disgusted Savage returns to his hotel room and downs a gallon jug of vodka. As Savage lies in a drunken stupor, Duvall enters the room and reveals himself—sans blond wig and Colombian accent—to his brother. Slurring his speech and squinting, Savage points his finger at Duvall and blurts, "I knew it was you!" No kidding. To make matters even more ludicrous, there is a cut to a close-up of Duvall, and the line "You had plastic surgery," spoken by Savage, is dubbed in. In any case, Duvall tells Savage that he has a new life now and prefers to remain dead, etc. etc. Confused and sickened, Savage decides to leave Colombia, but before he goes he attempts to return the pistol that Duvall had loaned him on their hunting trip. While searching for a place to stash the gun on Duvall's yacht, Savage discovers the scalps of several young Indian girls, one belonging to a girl he had befriended earlier (he identifies it by an elastic band he had given her so she could make a ponytail). The monkey slaughter was bad enough, but this little atrocity really makes Savage mad. Seething with outrage, he goes back to the hotel and shoots Duvall three times. Sob, sob, fade to black.

HOTEL COLONIAL is a disaster. Faced with having to please the American investors who helped provide the $6 million needed to make the film, director Torrini found herself having to compromise the screenplay and "Americanize" the distinctly Italian narrative. Both Torrini and actor Duvall felt the changes damaged the integrity of the film and they engaged in heated quarrels with American producer Siegel, but their protests fell on deaf ears. Production problems notwithstanding, there is very little on-screen to indicate that the project was ever salvageable. The film is insufferably slow moving, with director Torrini desperately attempting to evoke mood and provide a seedy atmosphere for her "Heart of Darkness" tale. Consequently, the movie indulges in virtually every South American cliche in the book. Savage is exposed to cockfights, poaching, drug deals, street urchins, child pornography, corruption, bad food, rancid water, filthy hotel rooms, a tooth-jarring bus ride, sadistic cops, drunken rabble, and even a spell in a fabled South American prison; and he faces every one of these repugnant ordeals with the same blank expression. His utterly dull performance makes the first hour of this film torture. Finally, Troisi arrives on the scene and provides a badly needed blast of comic relief (he's the only sympathetic character in the entire film). Unfortunately, Troisi is never given much to do and becomes annoyingly repetitive. After what seems like an eternity, Duvall finally appears. One of the greatest living screen actors, even Duvall fails to inject any life into this film. Decked out in a ridiculous blond wig and wearing a series of bizarre outfits, he is more a quirky distraction than the embodiment of venality. (Duvall contributes one truly goofy moment when he stands in place and sort of does a cha-cha-cha dance by himself during a party scene—a brief moment which *almost* convinces one that suffering through this film was worthwhile.) By the time Savage realizes Duvall is his brother, it doesn't really matter because the whole quest—and the movie—proves to be completely pointless. By the way, the first title that appears after the fade-to-black informs the viewer that no live animals were hurt during the making of the film and that the cockfight and monkey slaughter were achieved via special makeup effects. Unfortunately, the producers make the ridiculous assumption that there will still be patrons left in the theater to read their reassuring message. *(Graphic violence, gore effects, nudity, sexual situations, profanity, adult situations.)*

p, Mauro Berardi, William M. Siegel; d, Cinzia Th Torrini; w, Enzo Monteleone, Cinzia Th Torrini, Robert Katz, Ira R. Barmak (based on a story by Enzo Monteleone); ph, Giuseppe Rotunno (Technicolor); m, Pino Donaggio; ed, Nino Baragli; art d, Giantito Burchilliaro.

Drama **(PR:O MPAA:NR)**

HOTEL DE FRANCE† (1987, Fr.) 98m Renn-Camera One Nanterre-Amandiers-Canal Plus-PTT/Les Film du Volcan c

Laurent Grevil *(Michel)*, Valeria Bruni-Tedeschi *(Sonia)*, Vincent Perez *(Serge)*, Laura Benson *(Anna)*, Thibault de Montalembert *(Nicolas)*, Marc Citti *(Philppe Galtier)*, Bernard Nisille *(Richard Veninger)*, Marianne Cuau *(Catherine)*, Isabelle Renaud *(Marie)*, Thierry Ravel *(Manu)*, Helene Saint-Pere, Jean-Louis Richard, Ivan Desny.

Second feature from director Chereau (L'HOMME BLESSE) is based on the Chekhov story "Platanov Chronicles" and takes place at the title hotel restaurant. The film follows a gathering of ten young friends who have not seen one another in nearly a decade. During the course of an afternoon and evening they recount what has happened in their lives since they last met, and a pair of former lovers, Grevil and Bruni-Tedeschi, reunite only to find they cannot recapture what they once had. Strangely, this film was shown on pay-tv in France three days before its theatrical release.

d, Patrice Chereau; w, Patrice Chereau, Jean-Francois Goyet (based on the story "Platanov Chronicles" by Anton Chekhov); ph, Pascal Marti (Agfacolor); ed, Albert Jurgenson; prod d, Sylvain Chauvelot; cos, Caroline de Vivaise.

Drama **(PR:NR MPAA:NR)**

HOTEL DU PARADIS† (1987, Brit.) 112m Umbrella-Portman c

Fernando Rey, Fabrice Luchini, Berengere Bonvoisin.

GRAND HOTEL-style drama where the plot focuses on the lives of the occupants of the title hotel. A woman tries to break free of a possessive lover, a young man spends much of his time on the phone trying to land a job as a filmmaker, and an aging European actor tries to revive his stalled career after spending several uneventful years in Hollywood features.

d&w, Jana Bokova; ph, Gerard de Battista; m, Rodolfo Mederos.

Drama **(PR:NR MPAA:NR)**

HOTREAL† (1987, Hung.) 80m Mafilm-Hunnia c (Trans: Damn Real)

Ildiko Czako *(Lili Ambrus)*, Geza Vincze *(Gyuri the Brother)*, Sandor Zsoter *(Adam)*, Attila Berencsi *(David)*.

Czako stars as a 20-year-old Budapest girl who works as a dressmaker and lives alone in a two-room flat while her trouble-making brother (Vincze) serves out a prison term. Eventually Vincze is released and the flat is soon shared by Czako, her friend Berencsi, Vincze, and his former cellmate Zsoter. Czako struggles to maintain some balance in her life, devoting attention to all her friends and relatives while desperately trying to retain her independence. After Vincze lands himself in more trouble, the remaining three fake a passport for him so that he can leave the country.

d&w, Ildiko Szabo; ph, Zoltan David; m, Janos Masik; ed, Zsuzsa Posan; set d, Pal Lovas; cos, Emoke Csengey.

Drama **(PR:NR MPAA:NR)**

HOT SHOT* (1987) 101m Intl. Film Marketing-Arista c

Jim Youngs *(Jimmy Kristidis)*, Pele *(Santos)*, Billy Warlock *(Vinnie Fortino)*, Leon Russom *(Coach)*, David Groh *(Jerry Norton)*, Rutanya Alda *(Georgia Kristidis)*, Peter Henry Schroeder *(Nick Kristidis)*, Weyman Thompson, Mario Van Peebles.

Youngs is a wealthy New York brat whose parents want him to undertake a career appropriate to their social standing. Instead, the egocentric young man decides to follow his own dreams and wins a place on the New York Rockers, a professional soccer team. He and teammate Warlock become good friends, though their coach, Russom, strongly dislikes the brash Youngs. Russom grows tired of Youngs' hotdog playing style and eventually confines him to the sidelines. When Warlock is paralyzed by a game injury, Youngs lets his tongue fly. Angered by this outburst, Russom responds by handing Youngs a two-month suspension. Frustrated by this series of events, Youngs decides to head down to Brazil, where he meets his hero, a retired soccer star, played by real-life retired soccer star Pele. Youngs beseeches Pele to help him improve his playing style, but seemingly to no avail. Pele is tired of the limelight and now lives a life of anonymous tranquility. Youngs' persistence finally causes Pele to change his mind, and the enthusiastic American becomes the Brazilian star's protege. Under his guidance, Youngs gradually refines both his playing style and overbearing personality. Upon returning to New York, he learns the team's business manager is about to forsake the crippled Warlock. Youngs fights back, helping out his pal and ultimately leading his team to victory in the Big Game. Had this been a run-of-the-mill retread of the ROCKY/KARATE KID formulas, HOTSHOT might have been tolerable on a visceral level. However, director King aims right for the heartstrings with every frame, and his mawkish sensibilities are matched by his shortcomings as a storyteller. There's not a single honest moment in the film, and when the going gets tough, the heart-tugging music swells. HOTSHOT's cast is another problem, and the acting is mostly wooden and unbelievable. There is also the obligatory slow-motion sports footage, but it fails to save this lost cause.

p, Steve Pappas; d, Rick King; w, Joe Sauter, Rick King, Ray Errol Fox, Bill Guttentag; ph, Greg Andracke, Edgar Moura (Deluxe Color); m, William Orbit; ed, Stan Salfas; prod d, Ruth Ammon, Berta Segall; set d, Betsy Klompus; cos, Karen Perry.

Drama **(PR:A MPAA:PG)**

HOUR OF THE ASSASSIN** (1987) 93m Concorde c

Erik Estrada *(Martin Fierro)*, Robert Vaughn *(Sam Merrick, CIA Agent)*, Alfred [Alfredo Alvarez] Calderon *(Ortiz)*, Roland [Orlando] Sacha *(Folco)*, Reynaldo Arenas *(Paladoro)*, Laura Burton [Lourdes Berninzon] *(Adriana)*, Ramon Garcia *(Navarro)*, Oswaldo Fernandez *(Casals, Head of Leftists)*, Francisco Giraldo *(Roberto Villaverde)*, Ramon Garcia Ribeyro *(Andujar)*, Gustavo McLennan *(Doc)*, Alberto Montalva *(Cost)*, German Gonzales *(Francisco)*, Estela Paredes *(Paladoro's Wife)*, Javier Solis *(Marcelo)*, Baldomero Caceres *(Tough Kid Castilla)*, Maria Teresa Gagodorca *(Luisa)*.

In one of those fictitious South American countries, a new moderate leader is about to be inaugurated, much to the dismay of the generals. When one assassination attempt fails, they try a new tack. They go to the US, where Estrada, a former Green Beret, lives. His father, a leftist newspaper editor, was murdered by the old regime, of which the new president was a member. The agent of the generals tells Estrada that the president was the man responsible. Further, he tells him that he represents the country's Left and that they want Estrada to assassinate the president. Estrada flies down and begins preparing for the job while the local CIA man, Vaughn, gets wind of the attempt and begins trying to foil it. Numerous car chases, train-top fistfights, and gun battles ensue, while everyone that Estrada talks to is soon thereafter visited by the police and murdered. Vaughn acts like a one man army, freeing leftists from jail, stealing cars, and leaving dead soldiers everywhere. Eventually Estrada learns the truth behind his mission, and on the day of the inauguration, he takes his place on the rooftop. However, it is not the president that he kills but the chief general. Vaughn helps Estrada escape, then lets him walk away. There is plenty of potential in this film, which was beautifully shot, skillfully cut, and intelligently written. Vaughn gives a sincere, if somewhat outlandish, performance, and the chase scenes are some of the best ever. In its best moments, it is almost reminiscent of Z and DAY OF THE JACKAL, two of the best political action dramas ever made. Unfortunately, this film is dragged down to mediocrity by Estrada, as wooden and untalented an actor as they come. Still, the opening unsuccessful assassination attempt alone makes this one worth your video rental dollars. *(Violence, brief nudity, adult situations, profanity.)*

p, Luis Llosa, Mary Ann Fisher; d, Luis Llosa; w, Matt Leipzig; ph, Cusi Barrio; m, Fred Myrow, Richard Emmett; ed, William Flicker; art d, Martha Mendez; set d, Esteban Mejia; cos, Julia Antolin, Martha Mayer; spec eff, Fernando Vasquez de Velasco; makeup, Narga Aguinaga; stunts, Patrick Statham.

Spy/Drama **Cas.** **(PR:O MPAA:R)**

HOUSE† (1987, Thai.) 110m Phol Siam c

[No cast available.]

An impoverished farm family leaves the country and moves to Bangkok where they find life just as difficult. The father, mother, and two young children all take menial jobs and try to save money for a house. Shortly thereafter, the grandfather arrives, having lost the family farm. He, too, pitches in and contributes a meager income gained from sharpening knives and scissors. Eventually the family is able to purchase a dilapidated shack, but the father loses his job and must try his luck on a fishing boat. One day the grandfather is mugged and the attack cripples him for life, leaving him to care for the two children. It all proves to be too much and the family collapses. The tiny house stands empty. Winner of the Best Screenplay prize at the Thaiwanese equivalent of the Academy Awards.

p, Manae Limpipholpiboon; d&w, Chart Kopjitti (based on his novel *Deadend*); ph, Boonyong Monkonmung.

Drama **(PR:NR MPAA:NR)**

HOUSE II: THE SECOND STORY* (1987) 85m NW c

Arye Gross *(Jesse McLaughlin)*, Jonathan Stark *(Charlie)*, Royal Dano *(Gramps)*, Bill Maher *(John)*, John Ratzenberger *(Bill Towner)*, Lar Park Lincoln *(Kate)*, Amy Yasbeck *(Lana)*, Gregory Walcott *(Sheriff)*, Dwier Brown *(Clarence)*, Lenora May *(Judith)*, Devin Devasquez *(Virgin)*, Jayne Modean *(Rochelle)*, Ronn Carroll *(Deputy)*, Dean Cleverdon *("Slim" Reezer)*, Doug MacHugh *(High Priest)*, Mitzi Kapture *(Cowgirl)*, David Arnott *(Banana)*, Kane Hodder *(Gorilla)*, Susan Isaac *(Cat)*, Gus Rethwisch *(Arnold the Barbarian)*, Gil Birmingham *(Featured Warrior)*.

Sequels are a hit-and-miss affair. If a company follows a great movie with a less-than-great sequel, they'll still manage to do some business based on the original. In the case of this picture, the original wasn't very much and this is far worse. Director/writer Wiley makes an inauspicious debut behind the camera after having co-authored the first HOUSE. He'd been a puppeteer on GREMLINS and someone must have thought his next career move should be directing. They were wrong. It's the old "haunted house" theme again with blood and guts substituting for intelligence and suspense. Gross and girl friend Lincoln move into a large old house once owned by Gross' great-great-grandpa, Dano, who was a well-known outlaw in the Old West and supposedly died many years before. Gross' parents had been murdered in that house more than 20 years ago so if anyone is wondering why he would want to go into such a place, that question is answered early: greed. It seems there is supposed to be a treasure trove of precious stones buried somewhere in the house, in the skull of one of his forebears. Gross and best pal Stark find a coffin, open it and there's a crystal skull, plus the mummy of Dano, who promptly sits up and plants a kiss on his great-great-grandson.

Dano (who looks like Abe Lincoln and has played him often when he isn't in such thick makeup) explains that he has been kept alive by this skull and its magical properties. The skull can make ancient people youthful and bring dead people to life. Since Dano seems like an all right old codger, Gross takes a liking to him. The kids toss a large costume party and someone steals the skull, prompting a search of the house. The search reveals that all of the rooms in the house have a different motif, sort of a horror fan's idea of a theme park. In one room, there's an Aztec sacrifice going on. Other rooms feature a Western setting with gunslingers who are either ghouls or zombies, and a jungle with all sorts of pre-historic creatures.

Since Wiley had worked on GREMLINS, he must have thought he could do well if he invented some cute critters so we are treated to several of them, including a baby pterodactyl named "Bippy." There's also a weird caterpillar/dog which attaches itself to Stark's leg and won't let go (Wiley's version of a pit bull). Special effects were by Chris Walas (THE FLY) who also supervised the makeup. The first film had George Wendt from TV's "Cheers." This time around, they tapped the same TV show for John Ratzenberger. It was shot at the-then Laird Studios in Culver City, where David O. Selznick used to headquarter in the grand days of movies. If he knew they were doing films like this on his beloved lot, he'd probably come back and haunt them. Other than the makeup and special effects, this HOUSE should have been razed before it was built. Producer Cunningham (FRIDAY THE 13TH) should know by now what it takes to make one of these work. There were a few attempts at humor but they were merely attempts. To their credit, the horror is not nearly as bloody as most of these films are, though gore may be what fans of these films want to see. *(Profanity, violence, brief nudity.)*

p, Sean S. Cunningham; d&w, Ethan Wiley; ph, Mac Ahlberg (Metrocolor); m, Henry Manfredini; ed, Marty Nicholson; prod d, Gregg Fonseca; art d, Larry Fulton, Don Diers; set d, Dorree Cooper; cos, Heidi Kaczenski, Heidi F. Gilles; spec eff, Jim Isaac, Chris Walas; stunts, Kane Hodder; makeup, Daniel Marc.

Horror **(PR:C-O MPAA:PG-13)**

HOUSE OF GAMES**** (1987) 102m Filmhaus/Orion c

Lindsay Crouse *(Dr. Margaret Ford, Psychologist)*, Joe Mantegna *(Mike)*, Mike Nussbaum *(Joey)*, Lilia Skala *(Dr. Littauer)*, J.T. Walsh *(Businessman)*, Willo Hausman *(Girl With Book)*, Karen Kohlhaas *(Prison Ward Patient)*, Steve Goldstein *(Billy Hahn)*, Jack Wallace *(Bartender, "House of Games")*, Ben Blakeman *(Bartender, "Charlie's Tavern")*, *Ricky Jay (George/Vegas Man)*, Scott Zigler *(Western Union Clerk)*, W.H. Macy *(Sgt. Moran)*, John Pritchett *(Hotel Desk Clerk)*, Meshach Taylor *(Mr. Dean)*, Sugarbear Willis *(Hotel Doorman)*, Josh Conescu *(Garage Attendant)*, Julie Mendenhall *(Late Student)*, Rachel Cline *(Student)*, Patricia Wolff *(Patient, Dr. Ford's Office)*, Paul Walsh *(Man in Restaurant)*, Roberta Maguire *(Restaurant Hostess)*, Jaqueline de la Chaume *(Woman with Lighter)*, G. Roy Levin, Bob Lumbra, Andy Potok, Allen Soule *(Poker Players)*.

Seldom has a playwright/director made the transition from stage to screen as deftly as David Mamet (GLENGARRY GLEN ROSS, AMERICAN BUFFALO) does in this *film noir*ish psychological caper. Crouse is a psychologist and the best-selling author of *Driven*, a study of obsessive and compulsive behavior. As driven as her patients, she is virtually without a personal life, and Skala, her mentor and friend, tells her to slow down and enjoy her success. One of Crouse's patients, Goldstein, a compulsive gambler, produces a gun and tells her that his life is in danger because he can't pay a huge gambling debt. Crouse goes to The House of Games and confronts Mantegna, who tells her that Goldstein only owes him $800, but that he will wipe out the debt if she helps him win a big hand in a high-stakes poker game taking place in the back room. As astute a student of human nature as the therapist, Mantegna explains that a "tell" is a mannerism that tips one off to the true feelings someone is trying to hide. He explains that Jay, who has been winning big all night, has a tell—he twists his ring when he is bluffing—but Jay knows that Mantegna knows and won't show it now. Mantegna tells Crouse to watch for the tell when he leaves the room. The big hand arrives, Mantegna goes to the bathroom, Jay twists his ring, Crouse tells Mantegna, and he wagers a bundle, only to lose big. Mantegna can't cover his losses, and, tension mounting, Jay pulls a gun. To bail out Mantegna, Crouse writes a check for $6,000, then abruptly stops. She notices water dripping from the weapon and recognizes it to be a squirt gun. The curtain comes down, so to speak; the whole affair has been an elaborate confidence game designed to snag Crouse. Instead of being angry, Crouse is captivated by Mantegna's charm and sexually intrigued. With vague thoughts about another book, she returns the next evening and asks Mantegna to teach her about confidence games. Noting that it's the victim who wins the con man's trust and not the other way around, Mantegna works a game on a Marine at a Western Union office. Then he and Crouse *borrow* a fancy hotel room and make love there. Leaving the hotel, Mantegna tells Crouse that she has to leave because a con is to take place in front of the hotel at that moment. She insists on being part of it. Nussbaum appears with Walsh, a conventioneer, and the scam involves a briefcase full of money seemingly left by a man rushing off in a taxi. The four go to a hotel room to decide how to split the money, but Crouse overhears Walsh in the bathroom talking on a radio. He's a cop. It's a set-up. When he prepares to make the bust, she tries to force her way out of the door and in the struggle his gun goes off and kills him. They flee the hotel in a stolen car, but Nussbaum has forgotten the money, which was borrowed from the mob for one night for the scam. Terrified, Crouse agrees to give them the money to cover the loan. Mantegna says that he and Nussbaum are leaving town and the distraught Crouse returns to her office to destroy any evidence connecting her with The House of Games. She is visited by Goldstein, whom she sends away, but as he leaves, she notices that the car he is driving is the same one that she "stole" from the hotel parking lot. That night she sneaks into the back of the tavern frequented by Mantegna. There, while hidden, she sees Mantegna, Nussbaum, Jay, Goldstein, and a born-again Walsh. The whole affair has been a confidence game and she's the victim. She hears Mantegna say that he is going to the airport that evening and runs into him there "by chance." She tries to con him but tips her hand, and he confronts her with her failure. Pushed, she plays the trump card, shooting and killing him. After a vacation, she lunches with Skala, whose advice she has taken and forgiven herself the unforgivable. "It's not as if you've killed someone," Skala had said when Crouse tried to tell her unsuccessfully about the "dead cop."

The dialog is vintage Mamet—to the point, funny, ironic, profane—and the

characters are from his unmistakable universe—sardonic hustlers following "the American Way," looking out for No. 1 and manipulating P.T. Barnum's plentiful suckers—yet while HOUSE OF GAMES occasionally has the feel of a play acted on life's stage, it is distinctly cinematic. Though Mamet is no stranger to screenplays (having written THE VERDICT, THE UNTOUCHABLES, Bob Rafelson's THE POSTMAN ALWAYS RINGS TWICE), this is his first try behind the camera. In the tradition of Alfred Hitchcock, he worked from his own storyboards which meticulously detailed how he wanted each shot to look. With cinematographer Juan Ruiz Anchia, he has created a neon-lit world of glistening streets, smoky, dark rooms, and occasional glaring daylight. Shadows lurk behind characters or cloak their faces and their intentions. This is not a world of half truths, but a wooden nickel world of deceit where lies are as intricately staged as a play. Mantegna and his cronies are like a troupe of performers mounting a command performance, but their objective isn't dramatic truth or Crouse's applause, it is her fortune. Through her contact with them, she comes to question her own usefulness to her patients, wondering if she isn't just running a game on them, giving her own performances for $75 an hour. The elaborate twists and turns of the plot are reminiscent of THE STING, yet the psychological element of HOUSE OF GAMES sets it apart, and there is something of PERSONA in Crouse's attraction to and identification with Mantegna.

Mamet's screenplay is airtight, as laden with traps for the viewer as it is for Crouse. The dialog often departs from a wholly naturalistic approach, but Mamet is not asking to be judged *realistically*, he is after deeper psychological truths, matters that are rationally insolvable. In this respect he has brought his theatrical approach to the screen, but despite his contention in *Writing in Restaurants* that "fantastic cinematography has been the death of the American film" he has brilliantly exploited the visual potential of the medium to tell his story and reach for his truths. The cast, made up mostly of actors who have worked with Mamet in the theater, deliver outstanding performances. Mantegna (SUSPECT) is suave, savvy, and, in an odd way, plainspoken as the con man who is as much a streetwise philosopher as a hustler, predatory without being malicious. Crouse (SLAPSHOT, PLACES IN THE HEART, ICEMAN), Mamet's wife, plays her therapist as a study in directed composure and sexual repression who, captivated by Mantegna and his exciting, shadowy world, falls prey to the very obsession and compulsion she has clinically chronicled. Shifting from her world to his, Crouse believes (and the audience with her) that she is savvy enough to survive, and because of this her anguish over her catastrophic failure is even more affecting. Nussbaum, Walsh, Skala, and Jay (the author of *Cards as Weapons*) give nicely understated performances in supporting roles. Some of the card players in the back-room game are Mamet's real-life poker-playing buddies in Vermont. HOUSE OF GAMES was originally set in Chicago but was filmed in Seattle because of lower production costs and brought in on budget of between $5 and $6 million. *(Excessive profanity, violence, sexual situations.)*

p, Michael Hausman; d&w, David Mamet; (based on a story by David Mamet, Jonathan Katz); ph, Juan Ruiz Anchia; m, Alaric Jans; ed, Trudy Ship; prod d, Michael Merritt; set d, Derek Hill; cos, Nan Cibula; spec eff, Robert Willard.

Crime/Drama **(PR:O MPAA:R)**

HOUSEKEEPER, THE* (1987, Can.) 106m Rawifilm-Schulz/Castlehill-Kodiak c (AKA: A JUDGEMENT IN STONE)

Rita Tushingham *(Eunice Parchman)*, Ross Petty *(George Coverdale)*, Shelley Peterson *(Jackie Coverdale)*, Jonathan Crombie *(Bobby Coverdale)*, Jessica Steen *(Melinda Coverdale)*, Jackie Burroughs *(Joan Smith)*, Tom Kneebone *(Norman Smith)*, Peter MacNeill *(William)*, Donald Ewer *(Mr. Parchman)*, Joyce Gordon *(Aunt)*, Aisha Tushingham *(Young Eunice)*, Gary Krawford *(Larry)*, Wanda Cannon *(Bernice)*, Layne Coleman *(Pastor)*, Betty Harris *(Teacher)*, Sean Collins, Julian Coutts *(Young Eunice's Schoolmates)*, Eileen Williams, Diane Fabian, Sandra Scott *(Church Members)*, Jamie Rainey, Jeffrey Neal *(Children in Shop)*, Andy Knott *(Patient)*, Gordon Kilner *(Vision)*.

A ridiculous and unintentionally comic thriller about a homely, illiterate Englishwoman, Tushingham, who unflinchingly murders those who cross her. The film opens with a schoolgirl being tormented by her teacher and classmates when she cannot read an in-class assignment. Cut to a time many years later when the young girl has grown into Tushingham. Still illiterate, she is berated by her father. She responds by suffocating him with a pillow. Having nowhere to turn, Tushingham moves to the US as a housekeeper. She is hired by Petty and Peterson, a wealthy New England couple who live in their large, handsome home with Steen and Crombie, their adolescent children from previous marriages. Initially, Tushingham performs quite well. She keeps to herself and asks that the family offer her the same respect. When Steen makes an effort to get acquainted with Tushingham, the housekeeper threatens to tell her parents about her budding romance with her half-brother Crombie. Tushingham's orderly life begins to crumble because she can't read notes left for her—grocery lists, Petty's suit-cleaning instructions, and, worst of all, instructions on how to water Petty's precious orchids. After the family returns from a vacation, Petty is devastated to discover she has neglected his plants and threatens to fire her. Tushingham becomes more deranged and is pushed over the edge by Burroughs, a religious zealot who is convinced she is a "messenger of God" and is determined to make Tushingham one of her followers. Burroughs is certain Petty and Peterson are sinners and convinces Tushingham of the same. The pair gets nuttier as the Christmas holidays near, eventually leading to Tushingham's dismissal by Petty. After a New Year's Eve party thrown by Petty and Peterson, Tushingham and Burroughs sneak into their home, make a mess of things, and murder all four family members with a double-barreled shotgun. In the process, Burroughs is also killed. The police arrive, the bloody bodies are removed, and Tushingham lets on that Burroughs was the killer. Burroughs' husband doesn't think so, however. Tushingham finds a new job with an elderly couple. But her problems are not over—Burroughs' husband sits outside their window waiting for Tushingham to make a mistake.

Directed by Tushingham's husband Rawi, a Canadian television commercial cameraman, THE HOUSEKEEPER is an excruciatingly ineffective thriller adapted from a terse novel by the prolific and popular British writer Ruth Rendell. What reads as a chilling account of the fears of being illiterate in today's society plays on the screen without suspense, depth, or interest. Although it is made clear that Tushingham was tormented as a child, there is never any attempt to explain her murderous side. Her father notes at the start that there are a half-million illiterate Englanders, but why then, if illiteracy is the cause of Tushingham's problems, aren't they all a bunch of bloodthirsty lunatics? Tushingham, a talented actress, simply has nothing to do but look disturbed, quiver her lips, and bulge her eyes. Perhaps she and the director understand her motives, but it would have been nice if they included them in the film. Instead, the script opts for irresponsible thrill effects rather than psychological depth. The rest of the cast is just lost, as if they are just trying to make it through their interminably trite dialog. One specific exchange has Petty and Peterson bickering with each other about the days before Tushingham's arrival: "This used to be a happy home"—"A messy home"—"I'd rather be happy than messy"—"If it were messy again then I'd be unhappy." While most of the performances are forgettable, Burroughs' cannot be erased from memory. Overplaying her religious zealot role to the extreme, she wanders around spouting biblical passages in an unbelievable hick accent while wearing the most obnoxious wardrobe in the whole of New England. To top it off, she is a survivalist who thinks she can fend off Armageddon with an arsenal of weapons. When Burroughs and Tushingham get together and slip deep into lunacy, it's as if Carol Burnett and Vicki Lawrence were doing Hitchcock. The photography is slick, despite a gross overuse of low-angle shots. The only thing more obvious are the music cues, which swell at all the cliched times. Released in Canada last year as A JUDGEMENT IN STONE before finding a very brief theatrical release in the US. *(Graphic Violence, Profanity.)*

p, Harve Sherman; d, Ousama Rawi; w, Elaine Waisglass (based on the novel by Ruth Rendell); ph, David Herrington; m, Patrick Coleman, Robert Murphy; ed, Stan Cole; art d, Reuben Freed; set d, Jaro Dick; cos, Linda Matheson; makeup, Suzanne Benoit; spec eff, Martin Malivoire, Mark Molin.

Thriller **Cas.** **(PR:C MPAA:R)**

HOUSEKEEPING*½** (1987) 116m COL c

Christine Lahti *(Sylvie)*, Sara Walker *(Ruth)*, Andrea Burchill *(Lucille)*, Anne Pitoniak *(Lily)*, Barbara Reese *(Nona)*, Bill Smillie *(Sheriff)*, Wayne Robson *(Mr. French)*, Margot Pinvidic *(Helen)*.

Set in the 1950s and based on a Marilynne Robinson novel that is passionately championed by its fans, this is the first American film from Scottish director Bill Forsyth (GREGORY'S GIRL, LOCAL HERO). After the suicide of their mother (Pinvidic), two young girls are brought up by their grandmother in the little lakeside town of Finger Bone, nestled in the mountains of Idaho. When she dies, a pair of elderly great-aunts (Pitoniak and Reese) come to take over, but they don't much like Finger Bone and write to try to persuade Pinvidic's itinerant sister to look after Walker and Burchill, who are now approaching adolescence. The sister, Lahti, arrives with her pockets stuffed with odds and ends and her mind seemingly elsewhere. The girls talk her into staying, the great-aunts depart, and Lahti and her nieces cheerfully endure a flood. Lahti, who has spent most of her life riding the rails and sleeping on benches, sets up housekeeping in her own fashion, crowding the house with mountains of tin cans and newspapers. Walker and Burchill become truants, expecting that Lahti will catch them and make them go to school. She doesn't. Burchill, more petite and more concerned with appearances than her gangly, bookish sister, begins to be embarrassed by Lahti's refusal to abide by society's conventions. When the girls go back to school, Burchill tries to fit in while Walker sticks to her flannel shirts and painful shyness. They begin to drift apart, and Burchill moves in with her home economics teacher's family. After her departure, Walker and Lahti grow closer. They make a special trip in a "borrowed" rowboat. (In a very funny scene, the boat's owner chases them. "Don't worry about him. That's what he always does," Lahti says ingenuously.) Lahti takes Walker to a dilapidated homesteaders' cabin in a clearing the sun never completely warms, a place where Lahti says children wait in the woods, and for whom she puts out marshmallows. On the way home, they hop a freight and then spend the night on the lake in the rowboat—because they want to. When Burchill learns of her sister's adventure, she tells her teacher, and, before long, Lahti and Walker are "visited," first by the sheriff and then by a deputation of concerned ladies. Lahti does her best to appear responsible, but the ladies don't buy it. Told there will be a custody hearing, Lahti bends over backwards to prove she is fit to look after Walker, cleaning the house and making sure Walker looks proper for school. Late one night, the sheriff arrives to check on Walker, but Lahti can't tell him where she is because Walker is hiding in the woods, part of a game of hide and seek. Even after the girl appears, the sheriff says he will be back the next day, the implication being that he will take Walker away. After he leaves, Lahti and Walker set fire to the house and scamper along the long bridge across the lake into the darkness.

Although featuring many funny moments, HOUSEKEEPING is more or less a reversal of the formula that has brought director Forsyth so much success. Instead of weaving dramatic moments into capricious comedy, he leavens this heartwarming drama with laughter. Forsyth is a master of character development and storytelling and he proves here that he is just as capable when working with more serious subject matter. Beyond all else, HOUSEKEEPING, like all of Forsyth's films, is characterized by his gentle reverence for human nature. While his comedies recall Frank Capra, the bittersweet sensibility of HOUSEKEEPING is more reminiscent of William Saroyan. The potential always exists for Forsyth's films to become too wonderful, but his gift is knowing when to pull back, and he stops short of the point where his characters or situations would become precious. Lahti is neither a typical lovable loon nor a run-of-the-mill free spirit. She is too unbalanced, too fragile to be either. Playing against type and avoiding what could have been a paint-by-numbers portrayal, Lahti plays Sylvie as loving and ingenuous, but beneath her surface bemusement is a half-glimpsed sense of tragedy and disappointment. She isn't just an eccentric acting "crazy," she is a little bit crazy. Like so many street people, her grasp of reality is tenuous and fleeting. However, she is not so *out there*, that she can't pull it almost together when need be. She loves Walker, and when it appears she may lose her, Lahti tries to plant her feet firmly on the ground. When that fails, she has the presence of mind to know that the only way they can stay together is to flee.

Walker and Burchill also turn in fine performances, capturing the special bond that exists between siblings so close in age, a bond that is strengthened by their situation. Burchill's clipped movements, impatience, and fastidiousness are just right for the sister who opts for conformity. Wonderfully conveying her shyness and self-consciousness, Walker is equally adept as the sister who opens herself up to Lahti's world of simple, innocent wonderment. When Lahti leaves her in the clearing near the old homestead, Walker almost sees the nonexistent children in the wood, and feels that they (like Lahti) are used to the cold and like it that way. Lahti has offered her not just a kind of freedom but an alternative reality. Because Walker's hindsight narration, which punctuates the film, is the equivalent of the novelist's address to her reader, we can assume Walker hasn't exactly gone the way of Lahti, but has learned from her the power of imagination and the ability to open up to experience. In telling his story, Forsyth presents many poetic images: moonlight dancing on the lake as the rowboat bobs, Lahti poised spread-eagle on the bridge's edge, the picturesque mountain backdrop, Lahti and Walker's flight across the long bridge into darkness. Some critics have suggested that in striving for arresting photography, Forsyth has either subordinated his story to mood or presented it dispassionately. However, given the deep appreciation for the humanness of HOUSEKEEPING and its characters with which one leaves the theater, it is difficult to see Forsyth's treatment as dispassionate. Moreover, an equally strong case can be made that the visual beauty of the film and the atmosphere it creates draws us closer to the characters and their touching story. Though set in the US, the film was shot in Nelson, British Columbia.

p, Robert L. Colesberry; d&w, Bill Forsyth (based on the novel by Marilynne Robinson); ph, Michael Coulter (Rank Color); m, Michael Gibbs; ed, Michael Ellis; prod d, Adrienne Atkinson; cos, Mary-Jane Reyner.

Drama **(PR:A-C MPAA:PG)**

HOWLING III, THE*½ (1987, Aus.) 94m Bacannia Ent./Square Pictures c (AKA: THE MARSUPIALS: THE HOWLING III)

Barry Otto *(Prof. Harry Beckmeyer)*, Imogen Annesley *(Jerboa)*, Dasha Blahova *(Olga Gorki, Ballerina)*, Max Fairchild *(Thylo, Werewolf Leader)*, Ralph Cotterill *(Prof. Sharp)*, Leigh Biolos *(Donny Martin, Assistant Director)*, Frank Thring *(Jack Citron, Film Director)*, Michael Pate *(U.S. President)*, Barry Humphries *(Dame Edna Everage)*, Carole Skinner *(Yara)*, Brian Adams *(Gen. Miller)*, Bill Collins *(Doctor)*, Christopher Pate *(Security Agent)*, Jenny Vuletic *(Goolah)*, Burnham Burnham *(Kendi)*, Alan Penney *(Spud)*.

The plight of the Australian marsupial lycanthrope (a cross between a werewolf and a koala) is given a comic treatment in this the second Philippe Mora sequel to Joe Dante's 1981 picture THE HOWLING. Mora's last sequel, 1985's THE HOWLING II . . . YOUR SISTER IS A WEREWOLF, boasted Christopher Lee and Sybil Danning. No such luck with THE HOWLING III. Although it sacrifices casting and is equally as inept on the technical side, THE HOWLING III makes up for its inefficiencies with a silly sense of humor—sort of like that classmate who is thoroughly obnoxious but every now and again succeeds in making the entire class burst out in laughter. The ridiculous plot involves a scientist, Otto (the lead from BLISS), whose goal in life is to study Australia's tribe of marsupial werewolves. The main difference between the Australian species and their European counterparts is a pouch in which their young are reared. Otto, with sidekick Cotterill, eventually makes contact with Fairchild, the tribal leader. He (It?) is married to Blahova, a Russian pouchless werewolf who is employed as a ballerina with an Australian dance company. Life gets tough for Blahova when she unexpectedly transforms into a werewolf—right there on stage at the Sydney Opera House in mid-pirouette. Some dissent within the tribe causes the pouched Annesley to pack her things and head for the big city, finding work as an extra on a horror film called "Shape Shifters, Part 8." During production she falls in love with assistant director Biolos who takes her on a date to another horror film entitled "It Came From Uranus." Since Annesley's family life is a real-life horror film none of the movie frights seem to faze her. Various subplots abound, including the stereotypical bad guys who try to kill off the tribe, and Annesley's big move to Los Angeles as a professional actress. It's all done in good, not-so-clean fun with a tongue-in-cheek (or "tongue-in-pouch," according to Mora) sense of humor. All technical aspects are pretty weak and Annesley's giving birth scene is full of ooze and gore, but nonetheless somewhat fascinating. THE HOWLING III is best saved for true-blue horror fans who'll appreciate the genre stereotypes that Mora is ridiculing. *(Violence, sexual situations, gore effects.)*

p, Charles Waterstreet, Philippe Mora; d&w, Philippe Mora (based on the book *Howling III* by Gary Brander); ph, Louis Irving; m, Allan Zavod; ed, Lee Smith; prod d, Ross Major; cos, Ross Major; spec eff, Bob McCarron.

Horror/Comedy **(PR:C-O MPAA:PG-13)**

HUNK*½ (1987) 102m Crown International c

John Allen Nelson *(Hunk Golden)*, Steve Levitt *(Bradley Brinkman)*, Deborah Shelton *(O'Brien)*, Rebeccah Bush *(Sunny)*, James Coco *(Dr. D.)*, Robert Morse *(Garrison Gaylord)*, Avery Schreiber *(Constantine Constapopolis)*, Cynthia Szigeti, Melanie Vicz, Doug Shanklin, Page Moseley, Hilary Shepard.

It would be easy to dismiss HUNK and say it's junk. That is not really the case. In THE BAND WAGON (1953 MGM musical), one of the characters (Jack Buchanan) states, "The Faust legend always works." HUNK is yet another reworking of the Faust legend, in the tradition of DAMN YANKEES, ALIAS NICK BEAL, THE DEVIL AND DANIEL WEBSTER and countless others. Fans of the old Charles Atlas ads which appeared on the back pages of comic books for so many years will enjoy this because it is the tale of the 98-pound weakling who is turned into an Adonis, not by "Dynamic Tension" (the Charles Atlas method), but by striking a deal with Old Nick himself. Levitt is a computer nerd who is harangued by his tough boss, Schreiber, into coming up with a selling idea. He stays up all night and whips out a book that becomes a huge success. Schreiber is so happy that in a burst of Greek gift-giving, he sends Levitt off to a seaside resort to think about his next project. Once in Lotus-Land (it was actually shot at Paradise Cove but identified as Sea Spray), Levitt finds that his face and his form are hardly fitting in with the bronzed, tall types surrounding him. Then Levitt meets gorgeous Shelton (of "Dallas" fame), who is the agent for Coco, the Devil. (It was Coco's last appearance before his death.) They make him a deal he can't refuse: a 30-day trial offer of a new face and form in return for his soul. If he likes being in that body, the deal will be permanent. If not, he'll turn back into the wimp he was on Labor Day. Levitt thinks it's worth a shot, if only for the month. He figures that he can get the old body back at the end of the time period and will have lots of memories to warm him over the next decades. Well, anyone who saw any of the aforementioned movies knows that dealing with the Devil is not like the satisfaction guaranteed promise one gets with Sears. The Devil rarely issues an escape clause. Levitt turns into Nelson, a muscular macho male who spends the next few reels making love to various women. This flaxen-haired actor has all the accouterments: height, strength, flashing teeth and eyes, a deep tan and a dull personality. After a while, Nelson begins to have second thoughts about the agreement and goes to see gorgeous analyst Bush who tells him that it's not the exterior that counts in a person, it is what he really is inside. With that in mind, Nelson escapes the clutches of Coco (as everyone knew he would from the very first moment) and the picture ends happily, if not predictably.

Coco has the chance to ham it up as he dons several costumes including those of Hitler, a pirate, a caveman, Attila the Hun and a few others. The problem is that there is not one speck of evil in Coco, something the audience realizes immediately so they know the hero is never in real danger. Shelton is a very attractive young woman but doesn't demonstrate the depth needed to be the equivalent of "Lola" to Coco's Devil. Schreiber chimes in with an excellent job as Levitt's hot-tempered boss and Morse does a neat parody of Robin Leach as he plays the role of a TV narrator with a show called "Filthy Rich." It could have been much funnier if the script were sharper and the lead characters had an edge

to them. But with golden boy Nelson in the lead role, it was truly a case of the blonde leading the bland. *(Sexual situations.)*

p, Marilyn J. Tenser; d&w, Lawrence Bassoff; ph, Bryan England (Fotokem color); m, David Kurtz; ed, Richard E. Westover; art d, Catherine Hardwicke; cos, Bernadette O'Brien.

Comedy **Cas.** **(PR:C MPAA:PG)**

HUNTED, THE† (1987, Phil.) Roadshow Films Int. c

Charito Solis, Alan Martell, Fred Galang, Mario Monte.

Criminals kidnap a village beauty, but she escapes and, after surviving the terrors of the jungle, takes revenge on the men who abducted her.

[No credits available.]

Action **(PR:NR MPAA:NR)**

HUNTER'S BLOOD½** (1987) 102m Cineventure/Concorde c

Sam Bottoms *(David Rand)*, Kim Delaney *(Melanie Rand)*, Clu Gulager *(Mason Rand)*, Ken Swofford *(Al Coleman)*, Joey Travolta *(Marty Adler)*, Mayf Nutter *(Ralph Coleman)*, Lee DeBroux *(Red Beard)*, Bruce Glover *(One Eye)*, Billy Drago *(Snake)*, Mickey Jones *(Wash Pot)*, Charles Cyphers *(Woody)*, Bryan Rasmussen *(Purty Boy)*, Joe Verroca *(Ants)*, David DeShay *(Tull)*, Michael Muscat *(Bubba)*, Connie Danese *(Tracy)*, Gene Glazer *(Harris)*, Ray Young *(Brinkley)*, Burr Middleton, Billy Million *(BBQ Men)*, Allen Lerner *(Redneck in Truck)*, Ron LaPere *(Tobe)*, Billy Bob Thornton *(Billy Bob)*, Beverly E. Schwartz *(Ol' Man)*, Nan J. Seitz *(Poacher Girl)*, Jerry Ratay, Dennis Dorantes, Daniel McFeeley *(Poachers)*.

Five men set out from the city to do some deer hunting in the remote wilds of Arkansas. Bottoms is a medical intern, Gulager his father, and both are experienced trackers and woodsmen. Their companions are Swofford, a good-ol'-boy deputy sheriff, Nutter, his drunkard lawyer brother, and Travolta, Nutter's loutish friend from the big city, who pretends to be an experienced hunter but who has never killed anything in his life. Stopping at a seedy tavern along a back road for beer, Travolta snaps pictures of the locals and talks excitedly about going to "a real redneck beer joint." Inside, they run afoul of the clientele, and are forced to hightail it out of there with the hicks in pursuit. They reach the tract of land Swofford has bought—sight unseen and despite dark rumors—and pitch camp while Gulager and Bottoms scout around for tracks. They encounter two extremely nervous game wardens on horseback who warn them about poachers in the area and hunters who have disappeared in the past. On the way back to camp they spot footprints around the perimeter. That night, the camp is invaded by several dirty, dangerous-looking hillbillies, who are about to rob, rape, and kill the men when Gulager and Bottoms, who woke up and slipped out of camp just before the poachers came in, enter with shotguns levelled and chase them away. The hunters discuss leaving, but decide against it. Hunting the next day, they stumble across the poachers' camp and watch as the game wardens show up, arrest the whole bunch and lead them away in chains. The wardens don't get far, though. They are killed and the hunters find their eviscerated bodies later, immediately realizing they are in real trouble. They head for a highway some miles distant, but in a gun battle Nutter is killed and Gulager wounded. Night falls and Bottoms sends Swofford and Travolta toward the highway carrying his father on a stretcher while he stays behind to try to divert the attackers. He manages to kill several during the night and the next day before he is captured. Meanwhile, Bottoms' wife, Delaney, has come down to visit, and encountering the same rednecks at the bar, finds herself tied up and delivered to the poachers as a sex slave (the last one "wore out"). Bottoms manages to free himself and her, killing the biggest bad guy of all, and the two of them make it to a railway, where they are pulled aboard a boxcar by Swofford and Travolta. They all sigh and think it's over. It isn't, but the movie is.

DELIVERANCE, THE HILLS HAVE EYES, and TEXAS CHAINSAW MASSACRE were the prime inspirations for this bloody adventure, in which all-American types are pitted against their opposites, a clan of bloodthirsty savages who are just as all-American. The acting is all surprisingly good, especially from Swofford and Nutter, whose character is akin to Jack Nicholson's alcoholic attorney from EASY RIDER. The evil clan is also effectively portrayed, not as frightening as the natives seen in the early scenes in DELIVERANCE, but more intimidating. Gulager is a little too stiff for his role, but he spends most of the film moaning on a stretcher, so he isn't too annoying. While not nearly so interesting as any of its predecessors, the film should do its job, making profits for the producers and keeping city folks far away from the woods. *(Graphic violence, gore effects, brief nudity, adult situations, substance abuse, excessive profanity.)*

p, Myrl A. Schriebman; d, Robert C. Hughes; w, Emmett Alston (based on a novel by Jere Cunningham); ph, Tom DeNobe (Deluxe Color); m, John D'Andrea; ed, Barry Zetlin; art d, Douglas Forsmith; set d, Catherine Wilshire; cos, Jacqueline Johnson; stunts, Rawn Hutchinson; makeup, Mike Spatola, Douglas J. White, John R. Fifer, Allan A. Apone.

Action **Cas.** **(PR:O MPAA:R)**

I

I KEKARMENI† (1987, Gr.) 107m D.M. c (Trans: Shaved Heads)

Spiros Ioannou *(Lakidis)*, K. Markopoulos *(The M.P.)*, Dora Chatzijanni *(Mary)*, M. Donadoni *(Tall Soldier)*, Cristina Gentile *(Young Girl)*, Christos Zarkadas *(Cook)*, Kali Feri *(Vaia)*, N. Tsakiridis *(Camp Commandant)*, T. Tessarin *(Sergeant)*.

Using an approach similar to that of Akira Kurosawa's RASHOMON, Greek director Makris tells his story of army life in 1953 from the perspective of several characters, looking at the same events through different eyes.

p&d, Dimitris Makris; w, Dimitris Makris, N. Kasdaglis (based on a novel by N. Kasdaglis); ph, Christos Triandafilou (Eastmancolor); m, N. Mavroudis; ed, K. Iordanidis; prod d, D. Moretti.

Drama **(PR:NR MPAA:NR)**

I LOVE N.Y.* (1987) 110m Manhattan/Manley c

Scott Baio *(Mario Cotone)*, Christopher Plummer *(John R. Yeats)*, Kelly Van Der Velden *(Nicole Yeats)*, Jennifer O'Neill *(Irene)*, Jerry Orbach *(Leo)*, Virna Lisi *(Anna Cotone)*.

Presented by Manhattan Films, I LOVE N.Y. is a semi-autobiographical story written, directed, and co-produced by the one-time king of the celebrity photographers, Gianni Bozzacchi. Prior to venturing into behind-the-movie camera production, he had been the personal "F Stop Fitzgerald" for Burton and Taylor, and we're not talking about Wendell Burton and Robert Taylor. He'd worked on more than 100 movies as the "still man" then produced the 1978 turkey CHINA 9, LIBERTY 7, directed by Monte Hellman with Sam Peckinpah doing a role as an actor. After a few other attempts, he sat down to write this script. Two years later, he completed it and then spent the next four years trying to get it financed. Since it cost nearly $9 million, that wasn't too easy. It was much ado about very little because the picture came and went with the speed of a three-card monte shark plying his trade on Broadway to unsuspecting tourists. Baio, playing an Italian-American photographer from the poor side of Manhattan, falls in love with Van Der Velden, the debutante daughter of Plummer, a well-known, respected and cantankerous stage personality. Naturally, the lovers are determined to show everyone that their affection transcends monetary and cultural differences. So, despite the expected harangues from Plummer and others about the impossibility of this kind of love, the two succeed and we fade out on a happy ending.

Not enough happens in the 110 minutes to warrant any excitement. In order to save money, the exteriors were done in New York but the interiors were shot at the Cinecitta studio, in Rome. Naturally, everyone who flew to Italy had a good time because shooting in the Eternal City is always a party, despite the almost-daily strikes. A name cast didn't help any as the basic saga was simply too mild to interest anyone beyond Bozzacchi who was directing a tale close to his own heart. It was an attempt to capture the romance of young love and the whole shebang could have been squeezed into a half hour. *(Profanity, sexual situations.)*

p, Andrew Garroni, Gianni Bozzacchi; d&w, Gianni Bozzacchi; ph, Armando Nannuzzi; m, Bill Conti.

Romance **(PR:C MPAA:NR)**

I MIEI PRIMI QUARANT'ANNI† (1987, It.) 106m C.G. Silver-Reteitalia/COL c (Trans: My First Forty Years)

Carol Alt *(Marina)*, Elliott Gould *(Editor)*, Jean Rochefort *(Duke)*, Pierre Cosso *(Count)*, Isabel Russinova, Capucine, Paola Quattrini, Teo Teocoli, Sebastiano Somma.

The film begins in postwar Italy and focuses on Alt, following her for the next 40 years, through her affairs, marriages, and other adventures, and tracing Italian history in the process.

p, Mario Cecchi Gori, Vittorio Cecchi Gori; d, Carlo Vanzina; w, Enrico Vanzina, Carlo Vanzina (based on the book by Marina Ripa di Meana); ph, Luigi Kuveiller (Eastmancolor); m, Umberto Smaila; ed, Ruggero Mastroianni; art d, Mario Chiari.

Comedy **(PR:NR MPAA:NR)**

I NIKTO NA SVETE† (1987, USSR) 81m Kiev/Sovexportfilm c (Trans: No One in the World)

Andrei Boltnev, Vladimir Volkov, Valery Yurchenko.

Set during WW II, this documentary-like Soviet film deals with the heroic defense of a bridge near a Ukrainian village by a small force awaiting reinforcements. Joining the Soviet ranks is a German whose father had opposed the Nazis. Though his loyalty is questioned at first, he proves his mettle in battle.

d, Vladimir Dovgan; w, Vladimir Oslyak, Vladimir Dovgan, Sergei Beloshnikov; ph, Vadim Vereschak; m, Vyacheslav Nazarov; art d, Vladimir Agranov.

Drama/War **(PR:NR MPAA:NR)**

I PHOTOGRAPHIA (SEE: PHOTOGRAPH, THE, 1987, Gr.)

I PICARI† (1987, It./Span.) 125m Clemi Cinematograficia-Dia/WB c (Trans: The Picaros)

Enrico Montesano *(Lazarillo)*, Giancarlo Giannini *(Guzman)*, Vittorio Gassman *(Baron)*, Nino Manfredi *(Beggar)*, Giuliana De Sio *(Whore)*, Bernard Blier, Vittorio Caprioli.

Blessed with another formidable cast, Italian director Mario Monicelli (BIG DEAL ON MADONNA STREET) follows his award-winning 1986 film, LET'S HOPE IT'S A GIRL, with this episodic adventure set in 17th Century Spain. Giannini and Montesano, the film's roguish heroes, are born from the criminal class and spend their lives getting in and out of mostly humorous jams, separately and together.

p, Giovanni Di Clemente; d, Mario Monicelli; w, Suso Cecchi D'Amico, Leo Benvenuti, Piero De Bernardi, Mario Monicelli; ph, Tonino Nardi; m, Lucio Dalla, Claudio Malavasi; ed, Ruggero Mastroianni; art d, Enrico Fiorentini.

Adventure/Comedy **(PR:NR MPAA:NR)**

I WAS A TEENAGE T.V. TERRORIST zeró (1987) 85m Amateur Hour/Troma c

Adam Nathan *(Paul Pierce)*, Julie Hanlon *(Donna Rose)*, John Mackay *(John Reid)*, Walt Willey *(Bill Johnson)*, Saul Alpiner *(Frank Romance)*, Mikhail Druhan *(Miss Murphy)*, Michael Griffith *(Marcel Pederewsky)*, Guillermo Gonzalez *(Rico)*, Natalie O'Connell *(Woman on Audition Line)*, Warren Shapiro *(Officer Mitchell)*, Marilyn Kray *(Paul's Mother)*, Tony Kruk *(Donna's Father)*, Howard Korder *(Drama Teacher)*, Edmund Loughlin *(Varick Vandam)*, Joel von Orsteiner *(Asparagus Director)*, George Ratchford *(Jim James)*, Russ Pennington *(Clint Richardson)*, Dawn Brezezinski *(Interviewer)*, Cheryl Josephson *(Becky Sue Stone)*, Voss Finn *(Officer O'Toole)*, Tracey Jibara *(Numbers Girl)*, Kevin McDonough *(Policeman)*, Mike Atkin *(Bodyguard)*, Suzanne Rees, Jami Simon, Mindy Morgenstern *(Asparagus)*, Amy McLellan, Kate Green, James Sheenan *(Reporters)*.

Another dreadfully dull Troma release that bypassed theatrical distribution and went straight to home video, this ambitious comedy with pretensions of social relevance boasts two of the most lethargic young stars every to grace the screen, Nathan and Hanlon. The movie opens as sullen teenager Nathan is kicked out by his shrewish mother and sent to live in the "big city" with his father, Mackay, an executive at a cable station in Jersey City. Since she, too, is having trouble at home, Nathan's girl friend, Hanlon, accompanies him on the move. They are greeted coolly by Mackay, who is the kind of businessman who uses military euphemisms when addressing his employees. He sets the couple up in a dilapidated apartment in a soon-to-be-leveled neighborhood and gives them both low-paying jobs in the TV station's dingy supply room. Nathan and Hanlon's supervisor, Druhan, is a demanding, brutish woman who works them like dogs. Hanlon, who dreams of being a great actress and lives by the word of famed acting coach Griffith, goes on casting calls in her spare time and is disappointed to discover that the only role she can land is as a frozen asparagus in a commercial—and she is fired from that job for blowing her lines. Meanwhile, Nathan decides to make ends meet by pilfering electronic equipment from the storeroom and selling it on the black market. Druhan discovers Nathan's scheme and demands 70 percent of the profits or she'll call the police. After a few days of living under this arrangement, Nathan balks and calls Druhan's bluff. Not surprisingly, he finds himself in jail and his father refuses to bail him out. When Nathan is eventually released, he decides to get even with his father and the station by staging a mock terrorist strike. He and Hanlon plant a phony bomb in Druhan's office, and when police search the office for clues, MacKay discovers documents showing that Druhan had been stealing from the company and subsequently fires her. The young couple plant more fake bombs and soon the station's newshounds are in a full-blown "crisis" mode. One ambitious reporter, Willey, discovers that Nathan and Hanlon are the culprits and blackmails them into staging a kidnaping of station owner Alpiner so that he can get exclusive coverage. On the day of the kidnaping, Nathan and Hanlon turn the tables on Willey and drag the reporter and Alpiner before the television cameras to reveal the insidious dealings perpetrated in the name of "news." With famed acting teacher Griffith present (the terrorists have interrupted a talk show), Nathan lectures the home viewers on the dangers of irresponsible, cynical, and exploitative television and condemns Alpiner and those of his ilk. Before the police arrive, Nathan's father shows up on the set to congratulate his son for producing the best show the station has ever aired and declares it a hit that is guaranteed to boost the ratings. The police cart off father and son while Hanlon leaves with her beloved acting instructor.

Shot on 16mm in 1985 and screened for critics under the title AMATEUR HOUR, this hopelessly dull and terribly unfunny comedy draws only one laugh—from the new title: I WAS A TEENAGE T.V. TERRORIST. Nathan, a young actor who had supporting roles in last year's PARTING GLANCES and STREETS OF GOLD, is just plain awful here. He mumbles his lines and stares at the floor as if trying to emulate both Marlon Brando and James Dean. Most of his dialog comes in the form of smart-ass remarks made under his breath, leaving other characters to respond, "What did you say?" Hanlon isn't much better. Her slim figure and delicate features make her photogenic, but her acting ability is . . . well . . . limited. Director Singer, who cowrote the pretentious script, has absolutely no idea how to direct a comedy or his actors and his film just drags on and on without any sense of pacing or dramatics. While there is nothing particularly offensive about I WAS A TEENAGE T.V. TERRORIST, there is nothing particularly interesting either. *(Profanity.)*

p, Susan Kaufman; d, Stanford Singer; w, Stanford Singer, Kevin McDonough; ph, Lisa Rinzler; m, Cengiz Yaltkaya; ed, Richard King; art d, Ann Williams, set d, Susan Goulder; cos, Jeanne Button Eaton, Muriel Stockdale; makeup, Jocelyn Beaudoin.

Comedy **Cas.** **(PR:C MPAA:NR)**

I WAS A TEENAGE ZOMBIE*½ (1987) 92m Periclean/Horizon c

Michael Rubin *(Dan Wake)*, George Seminara *(Gordy)*, Steve McCoy *(Mussolini)*, Peter Bush *(Rosencrantz)*, Cassie Madden *(Cindy Faithful)*, Cindy Keiter *(Miss Lugae)*, Gwyn Drischell *(Margo)*, Allen L. Rickman *(Lieberman)*, Lynnea Benson *(Hilda)*, Ray Stough *(Lenny)*, Robert C. Sabin *(Chuckie)*, Kevin Nagle *(The Byrd)*, Ted Polites *(Moon)*, Steve Reidy *(Policeman)*, Caren Pane *(Poetry Teacher)*, Sal Lumetta, Tom Caldoro *(Gangsters)*, Ken Baggett *(Kevin Kramer)*, Jim Martin *(Park Druggie)*, Brian Doyle *(Shish-Ka-Bobber)*, Denise Texeira, Joan Bostwick *(Girls at Lake)*, Gail Lucas *(Teacher at Dance/Cindy's Friend)*, Frank Devlin *(Radio Announcer's Voice)*.

This ultra-low-budget 16mm horror comedy has become something of a minor cult hit on the midnight show circuit in New York City and is now available on home video. Basically a take-off on the "I Was A Teenage . . . " movies of the 1950s, the film begins as five high school friends (Rubin, Seminara, Nagle, Bush, and Rickman) look to score some marijuana for the night of the spring dance. Seminara is elected to collect the money and buy the pot, but since the supply is low he is forced to score from seedy dealer McCoy. The unscrupulous McCoy sells Seminara some contaminated weed and the boys become ill from the bad pot. Pressured by greaser-type Nagle to get their money back, Seminara demands a refund from McCoy, but receives a pummeling instead. Seeking revenge, the five friends grab baseball bats and go after McCoy. Before the teens have a chance to do anything, McCoy slips on a banana peel and knocks himself out. Thinking the drug dealer dead, the boys decide to toss his body in a nearby river. Much to their surprise, McCoy awakens and tries to fight them off. Rubin, the baseball player of the group, smacks McCoy over the head with a bat, killing him. The boys then dump the body in the river. Unbeknownst to them, however, the river has been contaminated with radioactive waste dumped by a nearby nuclear power plant. The toxic chemicals revive McCoy, making him a green zombie. Seeking revenge, the zombie McCoy goes after the boys with the intention of killing them off one by one. Unfortunately, McCoy catches up with Rubin and kills him. The remaining friends steal Rubin's body from the funeral home and dump it in the river, thus creating a "good-guy" zombie to fight the "bad-guy" zombie. Rubin is a bit miffed at being revived ("Look at me . . . I'm a teenage zombie!") and the boys hide him in the basement of the local malt shop where they feed him glasses of toxic water so the radiation doesn't wear off. On the night of the big dance, McCoy shows up to terrorize the teens. Rubin arrives to do battle with the zombie drug dealer, but his girl friend (Madden) is killed by McCoy during the struggle. Eventually Rubin manages to decapitate McCoy. Saddened by the death of his girl friend, the teenage zombie carries her body to the toxic river where they will be able to spend some time together before the water is cleaned up and the "zombiefication" wears off.

Although cheap and juvenile, I WAS A TEENAGE ZOMBIE is amusing enough for those who enjoy the kinds of goofy films that turn up at midnight shows. Much of the film is intentionally funny and its amateurish production only adds to the overall effect. The film gets off to a slow start as director Michalakias takes time to establish his characters—but at least there are characters to establish—a marked difference from most teenage horror films where the actors are around only long enough to show some skin and then be murdered in a gory manner. There is the requisite gore in I WAS A TEENAGE ZOMBIE, but it is relatively sparse and more cartoonish than forensic. Michalakias and screenwriter Martin do a fairly good job mocking the conventions of 1950s horror films, but perhaps a better cast could have delivered the dialog with a bit more parodic panache. The soundtrack (which is available) is brimming with songs and they include "I Was A Teenage Zombie" (Peter Zaremba, performed by The Fleshtones), "Good Feeling" (Gordon Gano, performed by The Violent Femmes), "Have You Forgotten" (Dan Zanes, performed by The Del Fuegos), "Why Do You Do" (Cesar Rosas, performed by Los Lobos), "Halloween" (Karl Precoda, performed by The Dream Syndicate), "Stuff" (Alex Chilton, Rene Coman, performed by Alex Chilton), "Time and Time Again" (Pat DiNizio, performed by The Smithereens), "Neverland" (Peter Holsapple, performed by The db's), "I Know What Boys Like" (Chris Butler, performed by The Waitresses), "Vibrato in the Grotto" (Ben Vaughn, performed by The Ben Vaughn Combo), "Nobody Knows Where Love Goes" (Bob Pfeifer, Fred Brockman, performed by Bob Pfeifer), "Slimey" (A.J. Hirsh, Brian Stahl, performed by A.J., J.S., B.H., J.C., B.S.), "Looking For Something" (The Skunks, performed by The Skunks), "Why Must I Be a Teenage Zombie" (Brian Stanley, George Seminara, performed by Brian Stanley). *(Graphic violence, gore effects, sexual situations, substance abuse, profanity.)*

p, Richard Hirsh, John Elias Michalakias; d, John Elias Michalakias; w, James Martin, George Seminara, Steve McCoy; ph, Peter Lewnes; m, Jonathan Roberts, Craig Seeman; ed, John Elias Michalakias; art d, Tom Stampa, Dora Katsoulogiannakis; cos, Dora Katsoulogiannakis; spec eff, Carl Sorenson, Mike Lacky; makeup, Dora Katsoulogiannakis.

Comedy/Horror **Cas.** **(PR:O MPAA:NR)**

IBUNDA† (1987, Indonesia) 103m PT Satrya Perkasa Esthetika-PT Suptan c (Trans: Mother)

Tuti Indra Malaon, Alex Komang, Ria Irawan, Galeb Husin.

An Indonesian family is thrown into turmoil by the impetuous actions of a son and daughter, while widowed matriarch Malaon struggles to keep events under control. The son, an actor, falls for an actress and leaves his wife and child; the daughter becomes romantically involved with a young man from a different ethnic group, upsetting her Javanese relatives. Director Karya, Indonesia's most popular filmmaker, also helmed SECANGKIR KOPI PAHIT and DOEA TANDA MATA (both 1986).

p, Sudwakitmono, R. Soenarso; d&w, Teguh Karya; ph, George Kamarullah; m, Idris Sardi; ed, B. Benny.

Drama **(PR:NR MPAA:NR)**

IF LOOKS COULD KILL† (1987) 89m Platinum-Distant Horizons c

Kim Lambert [Sheri St. Claire] *(Laura Williamson)*, Tim Gail *(George Ringer)*, Alan Fisler *(Bob Crown)*, Jamie Gillis *(Jack Devonoff)*, Jeanne Marie *(Jeannie Burns)*, James Davies *(Carson)*, Jane Hamilton *(Mary Beth)*.

Another effort by former porno king Vincent to break into the mainstream (see: DERANGED), this time with a thriller inspired by Hitchcock's REAR WINDOW. Gail stars as a freelance video photographer who is hired by crooked lawyer Gillis to set up surveillance on the apartment of Lambert (aka: veteran porno star Sheri St. Claire), a woman suspected of embezzlement. Much to his surprise, Gail finds himself recording the sordid details of Lambert's rather unorthodox sex life. Gail becomes obsessed with Lambert and is drawn deeper and deeper into the case until he learns that he has been set up by Gillis to take the fall in an embezzlement and murder scheme. IF LOOKS COULD KILL bypassed a theatrical release and went straight to home video.

p&d, Chuck Vincent; w, Chuck Vincent, Craig Horrall; ph, Larry Revene; m, Susan Jopson, Jonathan Hannah; ed, James Davalos, Marc Ubell [Chuck Vincent]; art d, D. Gary Phelps.

Thriller **Cas.** **(PR:NR MPAA:R)**

IGOROTA† (1987, Phil.) 125m Roadshow Films Int.

Charito Solis, Ric Rodrigo, Mario Monte, Fred Galang, Eddie Garcia, Ben Perez, Lanie Gentica.

A multiple-award winner in its native Philippines, this bloody adventure film follows the plight of a young princess from the Igorot tribe as she returns to her mountain people after studying at an American university. She falls in love with a man from the lowlands and despite the objections of her chieftain father and family, they marry. After their spectacular wedding ceremony, a spurned suitor challenges her husband to a duel, but the chief forbids it. The newlyweds make their home in the lowlands, where life for the princess is nothing but trouble. After the senseless death of her daughter at the hands of prejudiced lowlanders, the princess returns to the mountains and embraces a savage existence. Her husband follows her, but is forced to fight and kill her brother. He, in turn, is murdered by warriors led by the princess' old suitor. The princess stabs the suitor then takes her own life. (In English.)

p,w&d, Luis Nepomuceno.

Adventure **(PR:NR MPAA:NR)**

IKONA ENOS MYTHIKOU PROSOPOU† (1987, Gr.) 120m Greek Film Center c (Trans: Image of a Mythical Personage)

Giorgos Michalakopoulos, Julio Brogi, Eleni Maniati, Alexandros Veronis, Panayotis Kaldis, Panos Botinis.

Divided into three parts—reality, fiction, and history—this Greek film deals first with a former diplomat who visits country monasteries to research a novel he is writing about Captain Meitanos, a 17th century soldier/chieftain. At one monastery he encounters an icon that seems germane to his story; however, the central image has been removed from the triptych. The second section follows his novel's protagonist. It also introduces Vaios, the iconographer who is responsible for the painting that the novelist has discovered, and explains the icon's origin. The third part presents the historical Vaios and Meitanos, whose real name was Francesco Morozini. He was, in fact, an opportunist who fought the Turks when that was in his best interest, but who later became a collaborator. As the film comes to a close, it returns to reality and the novelist. While traveling through the winter landscape, he comes upon a cave. Inside is the missing part of the icon that he has sought. However, he is ill, and the icon may be nothing more than a mirage born of deliriousness.

p,d&w, Dimos Theos; ph, Yannis Varvarigos; ed, Dimos Theos; cos, Dimitris Kakridas, Georgia Fakiola.

Drama **(PR:NR MPAA:NR)**

IL BURBERO† (1987, It.) 113m C.G. Silver/C.D.I. c (Trans: The Grouch)

Adriano Celentano *(Tito Torrisi)*, Debra Feuer *(Mary Cimino Macchiavelli)*, Jean Sorel *(Giulio Macchiavelli)*, Mattia Sbragia, Peppe Lanzetta, Percy Hogan.

Italian comedy stars popular actor Adriano Celentano as "the Grouch," an ill-tempered lawyer who helps American beauty Feuer track down her missing husband. Sorel, the object of their search, was mixed up in a bank heist, and the circuitous trail to him leads from Florence to Siena.

p, Mario Cecchi Gori, Vittorio Cecchi Gori; d&w, Castellano, Pipolo; ph, Alfio Contini (Cinecitta Color); m, Detto Mariano; ed, Antonio Siciliano; art d, Massimo Corevi.

Comedy/Mystery **(PR:NR MPAA:NR)**

IL CASO MORO (SEE: MORO AFFAIR, THE, 1987, It.)

IL CORAGGIO DI PARLARE† (1987, It.) Istituto Luce Italnoleggio Cinematografico-Centro Culturale Salesiano/Istituto Luce Italnoleggio Cinematografico (Trans: The Courage to Speak)

Gianluca Schiavoni, Riccardo Cucciolla, Giuliana Calandra, Leopoldo Trieste, Enzo Cannavale.

In southern Italy, Mafia members force minors to peddle drugs, aware that they will not be prosecuted because of their youth. The hero risks his life as he refuses to aid in the criminal activity.

d, Leandro Castellani; w, Vittorio Schiraldi (based on the novel *Il Coraggio Di Parlare* by Gina Basso); ph, Elio Bisignani; m, Paolo Zavallone.

Drama **(PR:NR MPAA:NR)**

IL EST GENIAL PAPY!† (1987, Fr.) 92m Clea-TF 1-Port Royal-Films de la Tour/Gaumont c (Trans: Gramps Is a Great Guy!)

Guy Bedos *(Sebastien)*, Marie Laforet *(Louise)*, Fabien Chombart, Isabelle Mergault, Elisabeth Vitali.

Bedos, the great-guy grandfather of the title, is a down-on-his luck violinist who sits in the first chair at a burlesque house. A little excitement is introduced into his drab life with the appearance of the young grandson whom he knows nothing of and who has come to live with him. Gene Wilder considered making his French debut as Gramps in this comedy but was unable to take the role.

p, Adolphe Viezzi; d, Michel Drach; w, Michel Drach, Jean-Claude Islert, Michel Lengline (based on the play "Grandpere" by Remo Forlani [uncredited]); ph, Daniel Vogel (Eastmancolor); m, Francois Chouchan, Johannes Brahms; ed, Jean-Francois Naudon, Catherine Bernard; art d, Jean-Pierre Bazerolle.

Comedy **(PR:NR MPAA:NR)**

IL FASCINO SOTTILE DEL PECCATO† (1987, It.) P.A.G. (Trans: The Subtle Fascination of Sin)

Claudia Cavalcanti, Saverio Vallone, Alessandra Delli Colli, Vito Fornari, Alfredo Gallo, Danila Trebbi.

After the death of a wealthy industrialist, members of his family are caught up in increasingly bizarre sexual affairs, leading to blackmail and the disintegration of the family.

d&w, Nini Grassia; ph, Luigi Ciccarese; m, Banio Amivi; ed, Tamburelli-Corvinino-Grassia.

Drama **(PR:NR MPAA:NR)**

IL GIORNO PRIMA† (1987, It./Can.) Cristaldifilm-Roma Alliance Ent.-Toronto C.G. Silver Film-Rai Cinecitta/Columbia Pictures Italia (Trans: The Day Before)

Zeudi Araya, Ben Gazzara, Erland Josephson, Kate Nelligan, Burt Lancaster, Flavio Bucci, Andrea Occhipinti, Cyrielle Claire, Andrea Ferreol, Jean Benguigui, William Berger, Alfredo Pea, Kate Reid, Ingrid Thulin.

A star-studded co-production set in Germany as 15 volunteers are chosen to partake in an experiment to test survival chances during a nuclear attack. The experiment is to last three weeks, but after a short while relationships among the participants, who are confined to their refuge, grow strained.

d, Giuliano Montaldo; w, Piero Angela, Giuliano Montaldo, Brian Moore, Jeremy Hole, Leo Benvenuti; ph, Armando Nannuzzi; m, Ennio Morricone; ed, Ruggero Mastroianni.

Drama **(PR:NR MPAA:NR)**

IL GRANDE BLEK† (1987, It.) 105m Vertigo c

Roberto DeFrancesco *(Yuri)*, Sergio Rubini *(Razzo)*, Federica Mastroianni *(Claudia)*, Dario Parisini *(Antonio)*, Riccardo De Torrebruna *(Marco)*.

Taking its title from a comic-book character, this political coming-of-age story set in Italy in the turbulent 1970s features Sergio Rubini, who played Federico Fellini's alter ego in 1987's INTERVISTA. After a flashback to the 1960s which shows what being an Italian teenager was like in that decade, the story shifts to the early 1970s. Political confrontation is in the air, and DeFrancesco jeopardizes his friendship with good-time buddy Rubini when he falls under the influence of Parisini and embraces Marxism. DeFrancesco's sister, Mastroianni (Marcello's niece), also becomes involved with Parisini, but her interest in him goes much deeper than his politics. When a big confrontation occurs, Rubini, who has joined the radical right, comes to DeFrancesco's defense. However, sticking up for his old friend leaves Rubini in a political no-man's land and leads to his suicide.

d, Giuseppe Piccioni; w, Maura Nuccetelli, Giuseppe Piccioni; ph, Alessio Gelsini; ed, Angelo Nicolini.

Drama **(PR:NR MPAA:NR)**

IL LUPO DI MARE† (1987, It.) Loop Cinematografica (Trans: The Sea Dog)

Andrea Roncato, Pierluigi Sammarchi, Dodo Gagliarde, Kerry Hubbard, Milly D'Abbraccio, Hegle Van Stuen, Serena Bennato, Anne-May Montanen, Kathryn Jake Davies, Francesca Viscardi, Roberta Marcucci, Francesca De Filippo, Valentina Visconti, Franco Diogene.

A seafaring Casanova is in a state of heavenly bliss when he finds himself on the same ship as a number of gorgeous models. He sets his sights on the most elusive of the ladies and nearly succeeds in seducing her when he instead becomes charmed by her lovely friend.

d, Maurizio Lucidi; w, Massimo Franciosa, Luisa Montagnana; ph, Claudio Cirillo; ed, Allesandro Lucidi.

Romance/Comedy **(PR:NR MPAA:NR)**

IL RAGAZZO DI EBALUS† (1987, It.) Ebalus/Ciak (Trans: The Boy from Ebalus)

Riccardo Cucciolla, Saverio Marconi, Teresa Ann Savoy, Alida Sessa, Paolo Amoruso, Chris Chiapperini, Giovanni Pinto.

A young terrorist fleeing from the police is befriended by a pretty teacher and an old man who offers refuge. The bond between the three grows strong, but is abruptly severed when the terrorist is gunned down.

d&w, Giuseppe Schito; ph, Paolo D'Ottavi; m, Marcella Pasquali; ed, Otello Colangeli.

Drama **(PR:NR MPAA:NR)**

ILLUMINAZIONI† (1987, It.) Cinema e Societa/Indipendenti Regionali (Trans: Illuminations)

Mario Castaldi, Alessandro Garofani, Annamaria Lancellotti, Lea Mattarella, Giuseppe Miele, Antonio Sacco.

A 10-year-old boy relives his deceased grandfather's life through the poetic power of his grandmother's careful recollections and the memories of the old man's best friend.

d&w, Roberto Petrocchi; ph, Riccardo De Luca; m, Marco Melia, Marco Schiavoni; ed, Riccardo De Luca.

Drama **(PR:NR MPAA:NR)**

IN DER WUSTE† (1987, Ger.) 74m Deutsche Film Fernsehakademie c (Trans: In the Wilderness)

Claudio Caceres Molina, Mustafa Saygili, Adriana Altaras, Meric Temucin.

The wilderness of the title is Berlin, an urban jungle which is roamed by two unemployed *guest* workers—one from Turkey and the other from Chile. Sharing a run-down apartment, they literally give their life's blood just to survive, but manage to find moments of happiness anyway. Shot on 16mm with a nearly nonexistent budget.

p, Hans Willy Muller; d, Rafael Fuster Pardo; w, Horst Stasiak (based on a story by Antonio Skarmeta); ph, Rafael Fuster Pardo; m, Inti-Illimani, Joycelyn Bernadette Smith & Band; ed, Rafael Fuster Pardo.

Drama **(PR:NR MPAA:NR)**

IN THE MOOD*** (1987) 98m Lorimar-Kings Road/Lorimar c

Patrick Dempsey *(Ellsworth "Sonny" Wisecarver)*, Talia Balsam *(Judy Cusimano)*, Beverly D'Angelo *(Francine Glatt)*, Michael Constantine *(Mr. Wisecarver)*, Betty Jinnette *(Mrs. Wisecarver)*, Kathleen Freeman *(Mrs. Marver, the Landlady)*, Peter Hobbs *(The Judge)*, Tony Longo *(Carlo, Judy's Husband)*, Douglas Rowe *(Uncle Clete)*, Ernie Brown *(Chief "Papa Bear" Kelsey)*, Kim Myers *(Wendy, the Usherette)*, Brian McNamara *(George)*, Dana Short *(Alberta)*, Josh Cadman *(Tony)*, Nan Woods *(Madeline)*, Tom Breznahan *(Gary)*, Gillian Grant *(Karen)*, Lisanne Falk *(Jamie)*, Barbara Wint *(School Nurse)*, Burr Middleton *(FBI Agent Harrow)*, Jared Chandler *(Western Union Messenger)*, Edith Fellows *(Mrs. Long, Judy's Mother)*, Neil Elliot *(Arresting Cop)*, Harvey J. Goldenberg *(Marriage License Clerk)*, Tom Maier *(Judge)*, Putter Smith *(Minister)*, Lenore Woodward *(Justice of the Peace)*, Armin Shimerman *(Priest)*, Lee Garlington *("Schlitz" Waitress)*, Charles Stevenson *(Telegraph Clerk)*, Carl Parker *(Bus Ticket Agent)*, Wayne Grace *(Bus Driver)*, Jeffrey Alan Chandler *(Hotel Clerk)*, Robert Gould *(Detective Glore)*, Jordan Myers *(Desk Sergeant)*, Walter G. Zeri *(Sonny's Cellmate, Denver)*, Valerie Reynolds *(Policewoman)*, Rocky Giordani *(Tough Inmate, Los Angeles)*, Darwin Swalve *(Huge Inmate, Los Angeles)*, W.T. Zacha *(Jail Guard)*, Kitty Swink *(Sponge Bath Nurse)*, Sarah Partridge *(Winking Nurse)*, Steve Whittaker *(Three-Fingered Surgeon)*, Thomas Albert Clay *(Five-Fingered Surgeon)*, Tony Monaco *(LA District Attorney)*, Terry Camilleri *(Judy's Lawyer)*, Mike Darrell *(Bailiff)*, Cletus Young *(Sonny's Guard)*, Bert Conway *(Newspaper Editor)*, Joycee Katz *(Rosie the Riveter)*, Ana Helena Berenguer *(Maria, the Tuna Lady)*, Jay Varela *(Her Husband, the Tuna Foreman)*, Michael Bandoni *(Rooming House Boarder)*, Sheila Rogers *(Mrs. "Mama Bear" Kelsey)*, S.A. Griffin *(Cpl. Howard Glatt, USMC)*, Tom Patten *(Marine with "Stars and Stripes" Newspaper)*, Ellsworth "Sonny" Wisecarver *(Mailman in Newsreel)*, Randy Peters *(Serviceman)*, Marilyn Cohen *(Yenta)*, Niles Brewster *(High School Principal)*, Bess Meyer *(Teenage Girl [Slapper])*, Max Perlich *(Teenage Boy [Slapee])*, Andrew Roperto *(Switchblade Kid)*, Tom Ashworth *(Man on Train)*, Rocky Parker *(Woman on Train)*, Crane Jackson, Tom Tarpey *(Front Yard Reporters, Willowbrook)*, Mae Williams, Janet Rotblatt *(Angry Neighbors, Willowbrook)*, Rick Salassi, Thomas Ryan *(News Photographers, Denver)*, Nitche Vo Miller, Laura Bastianelli *(Judy's Cellmates, Denver)*, Ted Noose, Charlie Holliday, Heath Jobes *(Denver Reporters)*, Guy Christopher, Paul Keith, Neal Jano *(LA Reporters)*, David Schermerhorn, John Zarchen *(LA Courtroom Hecklers)*, Kazan *(Sonny's Dog)*, Steve the Rabbit *(Himself)*.

Timing is everything. In 1987, the true story of Ellsworth Wisecarver might have merited a few lines on page 3 of the tabloids or possibly a stint on the Phil

Donahue or Geraldo Rivera TV shows. But in 1944, when it happened, the saga of "Sonny" was sensational news, pushing important war stories off the front pages. IN THE MOOD attempts to re-create the 1940s and accurately tell the story of what happened when an amorous teenager met two lonely women. The picture is presented with Dempsey giving voice-over fill-ins to the action. In so doing, he is close to Woody Allen in RADIO DAYS or the various narrators Neil Simon has provided in his personal memories of Brighton Beach. In real life, the action took place over an 18-month period while the "Woo Woo Kid" (which is what the newspapers dubbed him) went from age 14 to 16. In the movie, they've made Dempsey a generic 15 years of age for dramatic purposes. Other than that, there's been very little trifling with the truth, which makes the picture all the more bizarre.

Dempsey lives with his parents in Willowbrook, California, a suburb south of Los Angeles. Constantine and Jinnette don't pay their son much attention, except to criticize him. In voice-over Dempsey explains that this is a *true* story and he'd like to set the record straight, especially after all that's been written on the subject. Dempsey is sort of like Ferris Bueller in that he's always looking for some way to ditch the school he attends. He pals with some older boys who've already either quit school or graduated, boys who are waiting to be drafted. Normally, these three—Cadman, McNamara and Breznahan—would have nothing to do with a kid that much younger than they are (between three and four years), but Dempsey has a relative who works at a gas station and can thus bypass the necessary ration stamps and purchase gasoline, so they let him tag along. Across the street from Dempsey's house is the home of Longo and Balsam, an unmarried couple posing as husband and wife. Balsam is about 21 and Longo, a tough metal worker, is in his middle thirties and the father of Balsam's two very young daughters. While Longo, a boorish, belching beer-swiller, works, Balsam fills her days by throwing afternoon dance parties at her house. The older boys are usually there and Dempsey, now part of the group, also attends. When Balsam and Dempsey meet, she is taken by his sweet naivete, his shyness, and his sincerity. Dempsey learns that Longo had meant to marry Balsam when they eloped to Nevada. However, Longo became too drunk and she figured it didn't make all that much difference and that nobody would know but them, so they are still actually *un*married, though it's a common-law situation. (The two daughters are seldom seen and one wonders where they are during all the dancing and drinking at the Longo/Balsam house.) Days pass and Dempsey, without really making an obvious move, is gaga about Balsam, and she thinks it's wonderful. Since Longo treats her with disdain most of the time, it does her frail ego good to have a wide-eyed lad mooning over her. Longo is a brutish, inarticulate man and he beats Balsam. Dempsey, upon seeing her bruises, wants to take her away from all of this. His pal, McNamara, is leaving for Yuma with his fiancee, Short, and Dempsey has arranged the needed fuel for the convertible. Dempsey suggests that he and Balsam go along for the ride to Arizona; at which point Balsam says she doesn't think it would be wise for her to marry a 14-year-old boy. Dempsey has not said a word about marriage, but, upon reflection, why not? She's not legally married to that lousy Longo and he does love her, so . . . they journey to Yuma. The local marriage license clerk and all the rest of the people in the wedding industry of Yuma (it was the closest place to Los Angeles where passionate young couples could elope) must have been terribly myopic or quite greedy because Dempsey (like the real Wisecarver) looks underage. The couple spend a blissful honeymoon night in a local dive hotel, and the following day, Balsam sends a telegram to her mother, Fellows, asking for some money. They want to go to Denver to start a new life. They also want to put some distance between themselves and McNamara and Short, who think that they may be a latter-day Bonnie and Clyde as they plan to heist a service station to get enough gas to return home. The telegram arrives in California and Longo snatches it out of Fellows' hand before she can read it. In a trice, the cops in Denver pick up the couple and headlines across America scream: "Mother of Two Faces Charge of Stealing Neighbor's Son, 14." When interviewed by the press, Balsam, quoting a real line from the real woman (Elaine Monfredi), says: "You take Sinatra and have yourself a swoon. I'll take Sonny." Flashbulbs pop and the country is deluged by pictures of the manacled lovers as they kiss. Balsam is indicted for felony child stealing and Dempsey becomes a media dream. The country is still worrying about D-Day, large losses in the Pacific theater, rationing, and so forth. When the Dempsey/Balsam saga hits the papers, it's a welcome respite from the grim battles. Radio comedians like Bob Hope, Fred Allen, and Jack Benny pick up the story and their writers have a field day. But the best is yet to come.

Dempsey, who formerly had been only tolerated by his older pals, is now considered to be a full-fledged adult by everyone in town. He is suddenly very desirable to all the coeds at his high school, girls who'd previously spurned him as a goof. A trial takes place and Dempsey is lacerated by the judge who calls him an "oversexed punk." But since there is no law against that, per se, there is nothing with which Dempsey can be charged. Balsam gets 36 months probation and has to attend the church of her choice at least once a month. The marriage is annulled and they must stay apart or face contempt charges from the court, which would mean an actual jail sentence. Constantine and Jinnette, embarrassed by their son's behavior, ship him a few miles away to stay with his uncle, Rowe, a man who makes his living raising rabbits, wringing their necks, and selling their meat and fur. The thought of this sends Dempsey fleeing almost immediately. He takes a job at a nearby tuna cannery and rents a room at a local boarding house run by harridan Freeman, who has a roster of stringent rules about what her roomers can and cannot do. It isn't long before he meets D'Angelo, the wife of a soldier stationed in Japan. She is a streetwise woman of about 25 and is obviously missing the regular sex her husband provided her with during their brief time together. D'Angelo is attracted to the young man and the two of them decide to go out for burgers and malts instead of Freeman's dinner fare. They never come back. Instead, they travel up to the mountains and once the word gets out that the two of them have fled, the headlines begin again. Dempsey sees the newspapers and turns himself in to the local small-town police chief, Brown, who promptly handcuffs him. Dempsey is trying to protect the "good name" of D'Angelo, but it doesn't help and both are taken into custody. Back in Willowbrook, a court date is set for Dempsey, but Constantine neglects to tell his son. When the date comes and goes, a warrant is issued for Dempsey's arrest. There is a court sequence (right out of the transcripts) where Jinnette makes mention of the fact that Dempsey is "big for his age" when the court wants to know what makes him so incredibly attractive to older women. What she means is his height. The judge takes it another way and orders Dempsey to have his genitalia calibrated by a bailiff who then dutifully reports that the boy is "just normal." Dempsey is sentenced to several years at the California Youth Authority but manages to escape the minimum security prison after only a day. He flees to Utah and hides in a rectory. However, he must depart quickly when one of the priests, Shimerman, recognizes him. Dempsey thumbs a ride but somehow gets fouled up and lands back in California. Trying to keep out of the public eye (everyone in the US knows his face by now), he goes to a movie and stays until the theater closes, when his slumber is terminated by Myers, an usherette of 17. They have a late snack, learn that they have much in common, and are married three weeks later, with parental consent. As the picture ends, the narration explains that they had a child and that he never saw his first two loves again.

Dempsey is a find, as is Balsam, the daughter of actors Martin Balsam and Joyce Van Patten. D'Angelo does her usual competent job and adds enough spice to the picture to titillate. Wisecarver himself does a cameo as a postman who is interviewed and states, "I think he's a pervert and quite possibly a Communist, too." Wisecarver's marriage to the usherette lasted until he was almost 40. Then he married another woman half his age. That union ended in 1981 and he currently lives with his sister in Redlands, California, where he owns a phone installation company and occasionally drives a tour bus to Nevada. The picture was made for less than $5 million and the feeling is totally authentic. The homes used were built in the era and the neighborhood in San Pedro is fairly close to where it all happened. Robinson, working from a story by himself, David Simon, and Hollywood *wunderkind* Bob Kosberg, stayed as close as he could to the actual facts. He is to be lauded for that, but if he'd departed somewhat, more fun might have been had. Aiding and abetting the feeling that we've been plunged back into the 1940s are the sensational arrangements and original music by Ralph Burns. IN THE MOOD will be appreciated more by anyone old enough to recall the fervor that swept America while Sonny got blue. To anyone else, it's a curious period piece with barely enough humor to qualify it as a full-fledged comedy. Still, it is pleasant and far more enjoyable than many other pictures which did far better at the box office. A nice try for all, but no cigar . . . and no multimillion-dollar grosses. Songs include: "In the Mood" (Andy Razaf, Joseph Garland, additional lyrics by Bette Midler, Barry Manilow, performed by Jennifer Holliday), "Caldonia" (Fleecie Moore, performed by Woody Herman and His First Herd), "Solitude" (Eddie DeLange, Duke Ellington, Irving Mills, performed by Billie Holliday), "Stompin' at the Savoy" (Edgar Sampson, Benny Goodman, Chick Webb, Razaf), "I'll Never Smile Again" (Ruth Lowe), "Dream" (Johnny

Mercer), "Don't Be That Way" (Benny Goodman, Edgar Sampson, Mitchell Parish), "Memories of You" (Eubie Blake, Andy Razaf), "Take the A Train" (Billy Strayhorn), "Baby Blues [Sonny's Theme]" (Ralph Burns, Phil Alden Robinson, performed by Sally Stevens). *(Sexual situations.)*

p, Gary Adelson, Karen Mack; d&w, Phil Alden Robinson (based on a story by Bob Kosberg, David Simon, Phil Alden Robinson); ph, John Lindley (CFI Color); m, Ralph Burns; ed, Patrick Kennedy; prod d, Dennis Gassner; md, Ralph Burns; art d, Dins Danielson; set d, Richard Hoover; ch, Miguel Delgado; cos, Linda Bass; makeup, Richard Arrington; spec eff, Robby Knott; m/l, Andy Razaf, Joseph Garland, Bette Midler, Barry Manilow, Fleecie Moore, Eddie DeLange, Duke Ellington, Irving Mills, Edgar Sampson, Benny Goodman, Chick Webb, Ruth Lowe, Johnny Mercer, Mitchell Parish, Eubie Blake, Billy Strayhorn, Ralph Burns, Phil Alden Robinson.

Biography/Comedy **(PR:C MPAA:PG-13)**

INAAM DUS HAZAAR† (1987, India)

Sanjay Dutt, Meenakshi Seshadri, Amrish Puri.

When an innocent man is accused of being a murderer he must fight to clear his name. (In Hindi.)

p&d, Jyotin Goel; m, R.D. Burman.

Drama **(PR:NR MPAA:NR)**

INDIAN SUMMER† (1987, Brit.) 95m Bevanfield/Metro c

Peter Chelsom *(Oliver Sutherland)*, Shelagh McLeod *(Caroline Sutherland)*, Michelle Evans *(Marie)*, Trevor Baxter *(Patrick)*, Derek Waring *(Spencer)*, Rosalind Bailey *(Fiona)*, Bridget McConnell *(Victoria)*, Farida *(Maharanee)*, Asha *(Housekeeper)*, Charu Hassan *(Ray)*, Roshan Ara *(Meera)*.

Shot in India, this British film about a British film that is being shot in India tells the story of the torrid affair that may or may not be taking place between director Chelsom and his French star, Evans. Chelsom's wife, McLeod, has accompanied her husband to India, and, with too much time on her hands, she imagines, in sensuous detail, a fiery romance between Chelsom and Evans.

p, Laurie Hardie-Brown, Mary Swindale; d&w, Timothy Forder; ph, Walter Lassally (Metrocolor); m, Barrie Guard, Ilaya Raja; ed, Mike Murray; prod d, Manzoor Amrohi; cos, Christine Staszewska.

Romance **(PR:NR MPAA:NR)**

INITIATION† (1987, Aus.) 100m Filmbar/Goldfarb c

Bruno Lawrence *(Nat Molloy)*, Rodney Harvey *(Danny Molloy)*, Arna-Maria Winchester *(Sal)*, Miranda Otto *(Stevie)*, Bobby Smith *(Kulu)*, Tony Barry.

Mixing family drama with Aboriginal mysticism, INITIATION is an Australian rites-of-passage adventure with a young American lead. When his mother dies, 16-year-old Brooklynite Harvey travels to the Outback looking for the father he hasn't seen in ten years, Lawrence (UTU, THE QUIET EARTH). A Vietnam vet who is fighting a losing battle to keep his crop-dusting business in the black, Lawrence now lives with Winchester and her teenage daughter, Otto. He is not overjoyed at his son's arrival and their relationship is a rocky one. To salvage his business, Lawrence agrees to transport a load of marijuana in his plane, and Harvey, who has fallen for Otto, accompanies him. When the plane crashes, the two try to make their way back to civilization, but Lawrence is too badly hurt to continue. Harvey has to go on alone. Ever-mindful of the wisdom imparted to him by Aboriginal medicine man Smith, city kid Harvey survives his initiation into the ways of the Outback, finds help, and returns to rescue Lawrence.

p, Jane Ballantyne; d, Michael Pearce; w, James Barton; ph, Geoffrey Simpson (Eastmancolor); ed, Denise Haratzis; prod d, Jon Dowding.

Adventure **(PR:NR MPAA:NR)**

INNA WYSPA† (1987, Pol.) Zespoly Filmowe-OKO c (Trans: Another Island)

Jadwiga Jankowska-Cieslak, Edward Lubaszenko, Miroslawa Marcheluk, Daria Trafankowska, Teresa Sawicka, Barbara Ludwizanka.

A husband-and-wife architect team faces a crisis when the wife falls ill with a disease that prevents her from working.

d&w, Grazyna Kedzielawska; ph, Krzysztof Ptak; m, Gustav Mahler; ed, Marek Denys; set d, Tadeusz Kosarewicz.

Drama **(PR:NR MPAA:NR)**

INNERSPACE*** (1987) 120m Amblin-Guber-Peters/WB c

Dennis Quaid *(Lt. Tuck Pendelton)*, Martin Short *(Jack Putter)*, Meg Ryan *(Lydia Maxwell)*, Kevin McCarthy *(Victor Scrimshaw)*, Fiona Lewis *(Dr. Margaret Canker)*, Vernon Wells *(Mr. Igoe)*, Robert Picardo *(The Cowboy)*, Wendy Schaal *(Wendy)*, Harold Sylvester *(Pete Blanchard)*, William Schallert *(Dr. Greenbush)*, Henry Gibson *(Mr. Wormwood)*, John Hora *(Ozzie Wexler)*, Mark L. Taylor *(Dr. Niles)*, Orson Bean *(Lydia's Editor)*, Kevin Hooks *(Duane)*, Kathleen Freeman *(Dream Lady)*, Archie Hahn *(Messenger)*, Dick Miller *(Cab Driver)*, Kenneth Tobey *(Man in Restroom)*.

Blatantly borrowing its plot from FANTASTIC VOYAGE and ALL OF ME, this film still isn't a half-bad comedy, providing more than the expected laughs. Quaid is a bold American pilot ready for any adventure, which is just what he gets. He is miniaturized and slated to be inserted into the body of a rabbit as a vital government experiment. But evil business conglomerate forces, eager to obtain the miniaturization formula, interfere with the experiment and the syringe containing the microscopic Quaid and his small ship is seized. Quaid and his ship are accidentally injected into Short, a weak-willed nonentity. Quaid's ship works its way through Short's system while Quaid communicates with his host through a special microradio which causes Short to believe that he is either going crazy or that demons have taken over his being. At one hectic moment Short pathetically cries out: "Help me, help me, I'm possessed." Of course, he is, but he soon learns that Quaid means him no harm and before long he is taking lessons in rugged individualism from his tiny in-body mentor so that Short's mild-mannered personality undergoes a funny metamorphosis. But things get complicated when Short meets Quaid's lover, Ryan, and begins to fall for her and she for him. This frustrates Quaid no end and leads to some cute, comic situations. Quaid's problems increase when an assassin is injected into Short's body and an intestinal chase ensues; the villain is after the one element of the secret miniaturization formula that only Quaid possesses. While Quaid's fortunes seem to fade, Short's uneventful life fills with adventure. He begins to take on not only Quaid's personality but his lifestyle as well, zipping about San Francisco in Quaid's red sports car, becoming romantically involved with the seductive Ryan, and asserting himself to the edification of his long dormant macho ego. Moreover, Short, following instructions relayed by tiny Quaid, must accomplish a series of challenging feats to best the bad guys before Quaid's oxygen supply runs out. The challenges include stealing an important microchip from a Silicon Valley business and undergoing harrowing plastic surgery to his face. In addition, Short has to battle Lewis and McCarthy, who have been partially reduced to gremlin proportions through incomplete usage of the formula, and are working on the part of the evil business conglomerate. In the meantime, Quaid continues to fight an "internal" struggle with the assassin. The two of them tussle over what appears to be a volcanic pit bubbling lethal juices (this is really Short's stomach). During the course of this ridiculous but entertaining saga there are unexpected bursts of hilarity. At one point, Quaid turns on his radio, sending Sam Cooke's "Twistin' the Night Away" blasting into Short's ears. This sends Short into manic boogie gyrations, a dance that must go down in filmic annals as one of the wildest on record. In the end, the timid Short is transformed into the hero, taking on Quaid's personality and Quaid himself emerges a powerful mentor to a milquetoast. If anything detracts from this nonstop action comedy it's the furious intercutting between the lifesize dilemma and the dangers facing Quaid, leaving the viewer a bit bewildered if not exhausted by the frantic plot maneuvers. Dante's overall direction is above average and the script sparkles with inventiveness. Chalk up a winner for executive producer Spielberg who here proves that

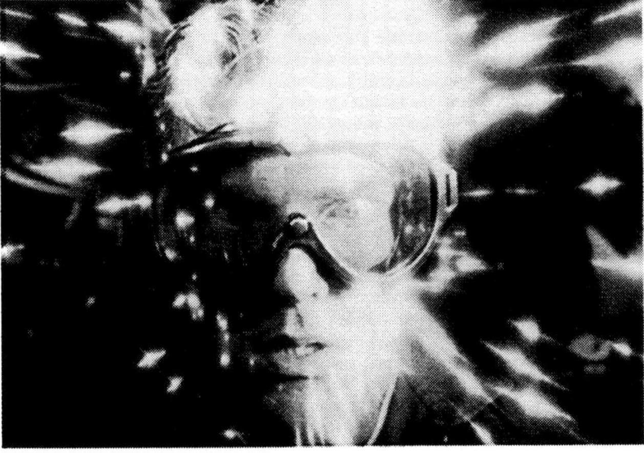

one can remake an old film by adding a new concept and injecting just the right blend of wacky humor and real hazard. *(Adult situations.)*

p, Michael Finnell, Chip Proser; d, Joe Dante; w, Jeffrey Boam, Chip Proser (based on a story by Chip Proser); ph, Andrew Laszlo (Technicolor); m, Jerry Goldsmith; ed, Kent Beyda; prod d, James H. Spencer; art d, William Matthews; set d, Judy Cammer, Gene Nollman; cos, Rosanna Norton; spec eff, Dennis Muren, Rob Bottin.

Comedy/Fantasy **(PR:C MPAA:PG)**

INSANIYAT KE DUSHMAN† (1987, India)

Dharmendra, Shatrughan Sinha, Raj Babbar, Dimple Kapadia, Anita Raaj.

A story of violence and revenge which pits the lawless against the lawmen. (In Hindi.)

p&d, Raj Kumar Kohli; m, Annu Malik.

Drama **(PR:NR MPAA:NR)**

INTERVENTSIA† (1987, USSR) 94m Lenfilm c (Trans: Intervention)

Vladimir Vysotsky *(Michel Voronov)*, Y. Bouriguine.

Made in 1968 but given a *glasnost* release only this year, this offbeat tribute to the Russian Revolution presents the events of October 1917 with an irreverence heretofore unseen. Vysotsky, the film's Communist hero, sews the seeds of revolt in an Odessa populated with capitalists who are literally clowns. Strange costumes and comic carrying on abound in this film which was to have celebrated the 50th anniversary of the Soviet state but stayed on the shelves for 20 years because it was deemed too controversial.

d, Gennady Poloka; w, Lev Slavine; ph, Vladimir Bourykine; m/l, Vladimir Vysotsky.

Fantasy/Musical **(PR:NR MPAA:NR)**

INTERVISTA**** (1987, It.) 105m Aljosha-RAI-TV-Cinecitta-Fernlyn c (AKA: FEDERICO FELLINI'S INTERVISTA; Trans: The Interview)

Federico Fellini *(Himself)*, Marcello Mastroianni *(Himself)*, Anita Ekberg *(Herself)*, Sergio Rubini *(Reporter)*, Maurizio Mein *(Himself)*, Lara Wendel *(Bride)*, Paola Liguori *(Star)*, Nadia Ottaviani *(Vestal Virgin)*, Antonella Ponziani *(Young Girl)*, Tonino Delli Colli *(Himself)*, Danilo Donati *(Himself)*, Leopoldo Trieste, Dagmar Lassander.

The most adventurous and structurally daring film by a major director since Alain Resnais' 1980 picture, MON ONCLE D'AMERIQUE, Federico Fellini's INTERVISTA is a brilliant autobiography which is obsessively personal in its approach. At times it is a documentary-style interview of one of the world's foremost directors, at other times it is a reminiscence of his days as a young reporter at the great Italian film studio Cinecitta, and at yet other times it becomes a celebration of Cinecitta's 50th anniversary and of filmmaking itself. Rather than tell a story in a linear narrative manner, Fellini (who appears as himself, the director of a new project—an adaptation of Franz Kafka's *Amerika*) scatters anecdotes and sketches throughout the film. The one thread that binds the film together as a whole is a Japanese TV documentary crew who question the director about specific facets of his career. They follow him through various scenes, each of which digresses to different memories in Fellini's mind. He remembers his days as a young reporter assigned his first interview at Cinecitta—with a glamorous, aging movie star (Liguori) who steps from her steamy shower to answer his questions. The young pimpled reporter (Rubini) is not specifically Fellini, but a young actor whom Fellini (the filmmaker within the film) chooses to play himself. In one of INTERVISTA's earliest scenes, Fellini reconstructs his youthful trolley ride from Rome to Cinecitta Studios, located just outside of the city. He fills the trolley with the faces that he remembers from his youth, including a pretty blonde starlet who is on her way to her first screen test. Outside their windows they see Rome's city streets, gorgeous waterfalls, a herd of elephants, and even a tribe of Indians—fantasy recollections of Fellini's which were fabricated within Cinecitta's walls. When the trolley arrives, the starlet runs off with her fiance and Fellini comments that he never saw her again. Once inside the studio, Fellini wanders through various soundstages—a mammoth series of sets, some containing elaborate decors like those used in the American production of BEN HUR, others filled with realistically painted wooden elephants which double for the real thing. One set, in the process of being born, is dark and quiet but for two men on scaffolds who insult each other while they paint a beautiful blue sky backdrop. On an outdoor stage, Rubini nearly ruins a long take of a wedding scene by accidentally walking past while the cameras are rolling.

As INTERVISTA continues, Fellini talks with the Japanese crew, with Rubini, and with various members of his real-life film crew: assistant director Maurizio Mein, cinematographer Tonino Delli Colli, and art director Danilo Donati. They discuss Fellini's upcoming adaptation of *Amerika* (a project which is actually being prepared by Fellini and INTERVISTA producer Moussa). On a casting assignment, Mein interviews numerous applicants for small roles—all of which require actors with the "Fellini face." He rides the subway, snapping photographs and offering people parts in the film. Later, during a bomb scare at Cinecitta's art department, Mastroianni appears outside the office window, dressed like Mandrake the Magician and waving a magical wand. He is at the studio to film a TV commercial, but decides instead to run off with Fellini to visit Anita Ekberg, Mastroianni's costar in Fellini's 1960 film, LA DOLCE VITA (released in the US in 1961). Fellini and his entourage—Mastroianni, Rubini, and the Japanese crew—arrive outside the security gates of Ekberg's country estate. After safely passing Ekberg's giant guard dogs (which Fellini jokingly refers to as lions), the crew is greeted by a bathrobed Ekberg who invites them all inside. To entertain his friends, Mastroianni waves his wand and, from a magical puff of smoke, a scene from LA DOLCE VITA appears. The soft, dreamy strains of Nino Rota's score are heard as we see Mastroianni and Ekberg, both looking fresher and thinner than today, dance romantically and then embrace in the classic Trevi Fountain scene. Together, the same pair, now 27 years older, watch themselves as part of the cast of INTERVISTA with Ekberg shedding a nostalgic tear. The curious finale has the entire cast and crew preparing to film a scene on a Cinecitta backlot (which duplicates the ending of Fellini's 8½), but a downpour halts production. Everyone scurries under a hastily rigged canopy to ride out the storm. Night soon falls but the rain continues. By dawn, the rain has stopped, but the entire crew is attacked by the tribe of Indians seen during the film's opening trolley ride. The Indians circle the film "troops" and are finally dispersed by gun-toting crew members. The production "wraps" and Fellini, now alone in a spotlit soundstage, decides to end his film. He blesses his INTERVISTA with "a ray of sunshine" and the film's title appears (seen for the first time) and credits role.

Fellini's finest film in many years, INTERVISTA makes clear that the 67-year-old director is not about to fall back on old methods. While the film is about Fellini's youth and early filmmaking career, it is not a sappy trip down memory lane, nor is it a fact-heavy documentary. Instead it is a filmed record of his dreamy memory of the past. The images and characters which are included may have existed or may just be distortions of his memory. As the Cinecitta trolley—complete with its views of waterfalls, elephants and Indians—arrives at the studio, Fellini admits that the ride wasn't quite like that. More than filming his past or even his memory of the past, Fellini is commenting on his own distorted nostalgia. Making the structure of INTERVISTA even more radical is the inclusion of the Japanese TV crew that "interviews" Fellini. Although they asks questions (which never really get answered), they are not really interviewing Fellini. The crew members are just characters in Fellini's film; in other words, Fellini is interviewing himself. If all this self-reflexivity isn't enough, there is also Rubini's character—the young Fellini-modeled journalist who is sent on his first interview (that word again) at Cinecitta. Paralleling Fellini's (as well as Mastroianni's and Ekberg's) rediscovery of the past is Rubini's discovery of the mysteries of Cinecitta and Karl Rossman's (Kafka's protagonist in *Amerika*) discovery of America. As complex as much of INTERVISTA is, it manages to play as an enjoyable, lightweight entertainment. It is filled with the usual Felliniesque characters, faces, and situations. It also shifts from being extremely funny to brilliantly moving (the LA DOLCE VITA scene). Rather than deliver everything in a straightforward manner, Fellini gives a scattered portrayal of his life and thoughts which weaves in and out between fiction and reality—a structure which is perhaps closest to the way one's (at least Fellini's) memory works. Fellini here defies the belief that a film must have a logical story, delivering instead a Proustian remembrance of filmmaking past. As Fellini has done before in 8½ (and as other great directors have also done—Jean-Luc Godard in CONTEMPT and PASSION, Francois Truffaut in DAY FOR NIGHT, Wim Wenders in THE STATE OF THINGS, and Luchino Visconti in BELLISSIMA, the latter set in Cinecitta), INTERVISTA spends much time on the process of filmmaking. As something of a tribute to all those who have helped him over the years, he includes his coworkers and friends in the film. Originally conceived as a film for Italian television, the film grew in proportion and became better suited as a theatrical release. First called "A Director's Block Notes," it was then retitled APPUNTI DI FEDERICO FELLINI (translated "Federico Fellini's Notebooks" or "Fellini's Scrapbook"). At one point, Fellini had wanted to title it with the Japanese word for *interview.* "I imagined the Japanese for *interview,*" Fellini explained, "would be some suave, cabalistic sequence of sounds—something like RASHOMON. So I made inquiries. Alas, the Japanese word for *interview* is . . . *interview*" (In Italian; English subtitles.) *(Profanity.)*

p, Ibrahim Moussa; d, Federico Fellini; w, Federico Fellini, Gianfranco Angelucci; ph, Tonino Delli Colli (Eastmancolor); m, Nicola Piovani; ed, Nino Baragli; art d, Danilo Donati, Paul Mazursky, Leon Capetanos.

Biography **(PR:C MPAA:NR)**

INUKSUK† (1987, Fin.) 90m Gironfilmi Oy c

Per-Olof Grape, Rasmus Thygesen, Eva Janikowa, Liisi Tandefelt.

The daily existence of a dedicated biologist who has established a research facility in the Arctic is the subject of this Finnish drama.

d, Markku Lehmuskallio; w, Niilo Hyttinen, Markku Lehmuskallio; ph, Pekka Martevo; m, Norrlatar, Sverige; set d, Matti Taponen.

Drama **(PR:NR MPAA:NR)**

IO E MIA SORELLA† (1987, It.) 89m C.G. Silver-RAI-TV/COL Italia c (Trans: Me and My Sister)

Carlo Verdone *(Carlo)*, Ornella Muti *(Silvia)*, Elena Sofia Ricci *(Serena)*, Sebastiano Balaw.

Popular Italian comedy director Verdone explores the bonds between a brother and a sister in this audience-pleaser released in Rome at the end of 1987. Verdone (who receives a co-writer credit) lives with his wife, Ricci, in Spoleto, both of them working as orchestra musicians. When Verdone's unpredictable sister, Muti, arrives on the scene, Verdone is torn between his devotion to her and to his wife. Muti tells her brother that she has borne a child in Hungary, thereby making Verdone an uncle. He travels to Budapest to retrieve the child, and upon his return finds that Muti has left town with an English rock star. Verdone tracks her down in Brighton and brings her back to Spoleto, only to find that his wife has left home. A box-office smash in Italy.

p, Mario Cecchi Gori, Vittorio Cecchi Gori; d, Carlo Verdone; w, Leo Benvenuti, Piero De Bernardi, Carlo Verdone; ph, Danilo Desideri; m, Fabio Liberatore; ed, Antonio Siciliano.

Comedy **(PR:NR MPAA:NR)**

IGRY DLJA DETEJ SKO'NOGO VOZRASTA† (1987, USSR) 88m Tallinfilm/Sovexportfilm c (Trans: Games for Schoolchildren)

Monika Jarv *(Marie)*, Hendrik Toompere *(Robby)*, Tauri Tellermaa *(Tauri)*, Kerttu Aaving *(Kerttu)*, Edit-Hellen Kuusk *(Melita)*, Sijri Sisask *(Sijri)*, Jaanika Kalleus *(Anne)*, Helle Kuningas *(Erzieherin)*, Evald Hermanjuns *(Marie's Father)*, Eduard Tinn *(Tauri's Father)*.

A grim adolescent drama which centers on a 16-year-old girl who lives in a Soviet foster care facility. She is a tender soul and her life is a rough one. She enjoys the attention paid to her by two very different boys. Things grow dim, however, when she is forced to inform on the boy she likes best, causing his transference to another facility.

d, Lejda Lajus, Arvo Icho; w, Marija Septunova (based on the novel *The Adoptive Mother* by S. Rannamaa); ph, Arvo Icho; m, Lepo Sumera; set d, Tynu Virve.

Drama **(PR:NR MPAA:NR)**

IRIS† (1987, Neth.) 90m Iris/Concorde c

Monique van de Ven *(Iris)*, John Kraaykamp *(Versteeg)*, Roger van Hool, Titus

Tiel Groenestege, Elsje Scherjon, Marja Habraken.

Upon turning 18, a girl leaves home and moves in with an architect. She then goes to school and becomes a veterinarian, setting up a practice in a poor village. Remainder of the film depicts her efforts to win the respect of the locals.

p, Frans Rasker; d, Mady Saks; w, Felix Thijssen (based on an idea by Mady Saks); ph, Frans Bromet (Agfa Color); m, Loek Dikker; ed, Jutta M. Brandstaedter; art d, Dorus van der Linden; set d, Wilem de Leeus.

Drama (PR:NR MPAA:NR)

IRON WARRIOR† (1987, It.) 82m Trans World Ent. c

Miles O'Keeffe *(Ator)*, Savina Gersak *(Janna)*, Iris Peynado *(Deeva)*, Elisabeth Kaza *(Phoedra)*, Tim Lane *(King)*, Frank Daddi.

Yet another cheapo sword-and-sorcery epic featuring the muscle-bound O'Keeffe as Ator, barbarian *extraordinaire*. This time out we learn that O'Keeffe was born a twin and that his brother was kidnaped by evil sorceress Kaza and turned into a zombie-like killing machine with an iron skull-mask. For this little indiscretion, Kaza's sister Peynado, a good sorceress, strips her of her powers and banishes Kaza into the netherworld. When O'Keeffe turns 18, Peynado assigns him to act as beautiful young princess Gersak's bodyguard. Unbeknownst to her, however, evil sister Kaza has regained her magic and has escaped the Netherworld to wreak havoc with ol' iron-skull leading her diabolic army. This, of course, leads to much swordplay between O'Keeffe and his evil twin. IRON WARRIOR was given a scant release in a few markets and wound up on home video where it probably belongs. Filmed on location in Malta and Gozo.

p, Sam Sill [Ovidio G. Assonitis]; d, Al Bradley [Alfonso Brescia]; w, Steven Luotto, Al Bradley [Alfonso Brescia]; ph, Wally Gentleman (Technicolor); m, Charles Scott; ed, Tom Kezner; cos, Dana Kwitney; spec eff, Mario Cassar.

Adventure/Fantasy Cas. (PR:NR MPAA:PG-13)

IRONWEED*½ (1987) 144m Taft Ent.-Keith Barish Prod./Tri-Star c

Jack Nicholson *(Francis Phelan)*, Meryl Streep *(Helen Archer)*, Carroll Baker *(Annie Phelan)*, Michael O'Keefe *(Billy Phelan)*, Diane Venora *(Peg Phelan)*, Fred Gwynne *(Oscar Reo, Singing Bartender)*, Margaret Whitton *(Katrina)*, Tom Waits *(Rudy)*, Jake Dengel *(Pee Wee)*, Nathan Lane *(Harold Allen)*, James Gammon *(Rev. Chester)*, Will Zahrn *(Rowdy Dick)*, Laura Esterman *(Nora)*, Joe Grifasi *(Jack)*, Hy Anzell *(Rosskam, Junk Dealer)*, Bethel Leslie *(Librarian)*, Richard Hamilton *(Donovan)*, Black-Eyed Susan *(Clara)*, Louise Phillips *(Flower Girl)*, Marjorie Slocum *(Elderly Woman)*, Lena Spencer *(Slatternly Woman)*, Lola Pashalinski *(Fat Woman with Turkey)*, Paul A. DiCocco, Jr. *(Bus Driver)*, Priscilla Smith *(Sandra)*, James Dukas *(Finny)*, Jared Swartout *(Guard Captain)*, Ted Levine *(Pocono Pete)*, Martin Patterson *(Foxy Phil Tooker)*, Terry O'Reilly *(Aldo Campione)*, Michael O'Gorman *(Strike Leader)*, Frank Whaley *(Young Francis)*, Jordan Valdina *(Youth at Strike)*, Louis St. Louis *(Piano Man)*, John Wright, Robin Wood-Chappelle, Nicole Weden, Peter Pryor, Duane Scholz, Matt McGrath *(Goblins)*, Lois Barden Stilley *(Mrs. Dillon)*, Cori Irwin *(Young Girl)*, Pamela Payton-Wright *(Mother)*, Boris McGiver *(Clerk)*, Phyllis Gottung *(Old Woman)*, James Yoham *(Bald Man)*, Ean Egas *(Danny)*, Nebraska Brace *(Andy)*, Jeff Morris *(Michigan Mac)*, William Duell *(Moose)*, George Rafferty, Robert Manion *(Raiders)*, Pat Devane *(Nurse)*.

IRONWEED is dim, grim, and relentlessly depressing. Set in Albany, New York, in 1938, it also flashes back to 1916 and 1901 as it seeks to establish Nicholson's character, an ex-Washington Senator infielder. He deserted his family 22 years before when, slightly tipsy on four beers, he dropped his infant son, cracking the child's head and killing him. This is given away in the first few minutes of the film as Nicholson and cohort Waits are at work digging graves to earn some money for a jug of wine and a place to flop. Waits is dying of cancer, a fact he announces happily to Nicholson: "My doc says I got cancer. Hah, I ain't never got *nothin'* before." Waits and Nicholson shovel some dirt, then go off to the local mission where they'll be fed soup and bread if they're willing to listen to Gammon, the local minister, harangue them. Nicholson is looking for Streep, his girl friend of the past nine years, who wandered off a few days earlier. He slept in the street the previous night and has no idea where she has gone. Streep, looking tired and using a voice that comes from somewhere deep below her stomach, ambles into the mission. Then Nicholson, Streep, and Waits walk the streets with Dengel, the man who dishes out the soup and beds for reverend Gammon. They try to help drunken Eskimo ex-whore Black-Eyed Susan (that's her real name, honest), who eventually dies in the street and is chewed on by a pack of wild dogs. The quartet continues to a local tavern where the bartender is Gwynne, a former radio singer who lost it all to the bottle and is now a teetotaler. Gwynne is singing "When You Were Sweet Sixteen" as the group enters. Half of the bar is filled with bums, the other half with swells. Streep admits that she used to sing and play the piano for a living, so she is prevailed upon to render a tune and does "He's Me Pal." Now the picture begins to play some tricks. Earlier, Nicholson had an argument with a "dead" man on a bus. At the age of 16, he was present at a strike of the local trolley company. Hundreds of people blocked the street and the young Nicholson (played by Frank Whaley) tossed a rock at a scab trolley driver, killing him. That man appears in Nicholson's mind as he and Waits ride the bus past streets where Nicholson had lived and worked. In the bar sequence, it appears that Streep is a terrific singer as she earns a standing ovation. But it's a sham. The camera cuts to Streep singing the end of the song and reveals that she's been imagining the response. They all leave the bar and now must find a place to sleep. Streep's bag has been stolen and Nicholson has spent his grave-digging earnings on drinks for everyone at the bar and a flower for Streep. They go to the home of Grifasi and Esterman, where Streep spent the previous night, but are asked to leave when they get drunk. It's pretty well indicated that Streep is willing to give sexual favors to anyone who will give her a place to sleep or a drink. However, as she insists to a plaster saint at a church where she has gone to get out of the cold, she's not a professional. When she finishes her confession to the saint, Streep miraculously finds $10 on the church floor. She then rents a room that she and Nicholson once shared and takes their suitcases out of the landlord's "safe-keeping" (they owed $6 back rent). While this is going on, Nicholson gets a day job as a rag picker's assistant with Anzell, a behemoth of a man who drives around in a two-horse wagon. This sends Nicholson's memory back again as he passes a house where he once had a turn-of-the-century relationship with a crazy, sexy woman played by Whitton. After working for most of the day with Anzell, Nicholson settles for partial payment of his day's wages because he wants to get off early. He buys a 12-pound turkey and returns to the home he left 22 years before. Wife Baker recognizes him and invites him in. His son, O'Keefe, is fairly friendly, but he is rebuffed by daughter Venora. Baker tries everything to make Nicholson comfortable. He meets his grandson, regales the youth with some baseball stories, takes a much-needed bath, and shaves. After dinner, there is a reconciliation with Venora, but Nicholson admits that he can't stay. He goes back into the streets and meets with Waits and a few of the other guys at a hobo jungle. Then they are attacked by business-suited, baseball bat-wielding "raiders" who are determined to get the bums out of the area. Waits is hit on the head. Nicholson practically carries him to the hospital, but Waits dies. Nicholson finds the furnished room where Streep is, but when he arrives, proffering a bottle of booze through the open door, he finds her dead on the carpet. He lies down next to Streep and promises that he will buy her the headstone she'd always wanted. Now, with his two best friends gone, Nicholson climbs aboard a freight train headed out of Albany. He has a bottle in his hand and the vision of Baker appears. She offers to pour him some tea and it looks very inviting. Nicholson angrily tosses his bottle away and one wonders if the train won't lurch and send him into the night through the wide-open door. The final scene is done with a point-of-view shot of his grandson's light, airy, and large room. We hear Baker telling Nicholson that he might like to stay there, that they could put a cot in, etc. Fade out. Phew.

In 144 minutes, Streep and Nicholson aren't together more than about 32 minutes, and if one were to count the time they actually spend talking to each other, it's far less. The picture is a Depression-era version of THE LOST WEEKEND with a bit of 1987's BARFLY added. Matter of fact, Faye Dunaway and Mickey Rourke could have switched roles with Nicholson and Streep and nobody would have noticed the difference. The novel the film is based on won a Pulitzer Prize and novelist William Kennedy did his own adaptation. There is no question that the book was beautifully written, but movies are a medium of revelation, whereby the characters reveal themselves by what they do and description has to take a back seat to what's on the screen. And what's up there in this film is deadly dull. For a few flickering moments, we care a bit about the people but then it's gone. Streep had been a pianist and singer who was evidently bilked out of her inheritance by an unseen attorney brother. Nicholson cracked up when he dropped his infant son and has been drinking ever since. The fact that he was not spotted by anyone he knew in Albany upon his return is hard to buy. There's no plot, other than the incidents mentioned, and the picture is far too long and fraught with allegory.

Director Babenco, coming off the success of KISS OF THE SPIDER WOMAN, which earned him an Oscar nomination in 1985, will have to find another script fast to make up for this. Babenco's sense of style is evident, but a sharper editing eye would have helped. This picture must have cost a great deal of money. The stars alone command enormous sums and the period sets and costumes were also expensive. But despite the presence of the high-powered cast, it's unlikely that IRONWEED will earn any serious money. Baker looks very different from her sultry, sexy roles in BABY DOLL and HARLOW, but her acting hasn't suffered. Fred Gwynne, who will always be recalled for his roles on "Car 54, Where Are You?" and "The Munsters," has enjoyed an enormous career resurgence. He has appeared in several recent movies and particularly distinguished himself as Bob Hoskins' sidekick in THE COTTON CLUB. The acting is universally good in IRONWEED with a special nod to Waits (who was also in COTTON CLUB), a man with a definite future in film. Two of Nicholson's buddies, Jeff Morris and William Duell, also perform here, as they did in a few of Nicholson's earlier films, including THE BORDER, GOIN' SOUTH, and ONE FLEW OVER THE CUCKOO'S NEST. The picture was dedicated to the memory of master set painter Jon O'Connell. There are a few musical moments but they hardly lighten the heavy proceedings. Tunes include: "When You Were Sweet Sixteen" (James Thornton, performed by Fred Gwynne), "He's Me Pal" (Gus Edwards, Vincent Bryan, performed by Streep), "Pappa Treetop Tall" (Hoagy Carmichael, Stanley Adams), "Poor Little Lamb" (Tom Waits, William Kennedy), "Margie" (Benny Davis, Con Conrad, J.R. Robinson), "Blessed Be the Name of the Lord," (traditional, arranged by Gary Leib, Toby Fitch), and "The Ninth Symphony." *(Profanity, adult situations.)*

p, Keith Barish, Marcia Nasatir, Gene Kirkwood, C.O. Erickson; d, Hector Babenco; w, William Kennedy (based on his novel); ph, Lauro Escorel (Technicolor); m, John Morris; ed, Anne Goursaud; prod d, Jeannine C. Oppewall; art d, Robert Guerra; set d, Leslie Pope; spec eff, Steve Kirshoff; m/l, James Thornton, Ludwig van Beethoven, Hoagy Carmichael, Stanley Adams, Con Conrad, J. Russel Robinson, Benny Davis, Vincent Bryan, Gus Edwards, Tom Waits, William Kennedy; stunts, Alan Gibbs; makeup, David Craig Forrest.

Drama (PR:C-O MPAA:R)

ISHTAR*** (1987) 107m COL-Delphi V/COL c

Warren Beatty *(Lyle Rogers)*, Dustin Hoffman *(Chuck Clarke)*, Isabelle Adjani *(Shirra Assel)*, Charles Grodin *(Jim Harrison, CIA Agent)*, Jack Weston *(Marty Freed, Talent Agent)*, Tess Harper *(Willa)*, Carol Kane *(Carol)*, Aharon Ipale *(Emir Yousef)*, Fijad Hageb *(Abdul)*, David Margulies *(Mr. Clarke)*, Rose Arrick *(Mrs. Clarke)*, Julie Garfield *(Dorothy)*, Christine Rose *(Siri Darma)*, Bob Girolami *(Bartender)*, Abe Kroll *(Mrs. Thomopoulos)*, Hannah Kroll *(Mrs. Thomopoulos)*, Herb Gardner *(Rabbi Pierce)*, Bill Moor *(U.S. Consulate)*, Edgar Smith *(Professor Barnes)*, J.C. Cutler *(Omar)*, Bill Bailey *(Gen. Westlake)*, Ian Gray *(Manager of Chez Casablanca)*, Maati Zaari *(Porter)*, Bouhaddane Larbi *(Taxi Driver)*, Fred Malamed *(Caid of Assari)*, Phillip Schopper *(Waiter)*, Aziz Ben Driss *(Waiter at Chez Casablanca)*, Kamarr *(Maitre 'D at Chez Casablanca)*, Warren Clarke *(English Gunrunner)*, Arthur Brauss *(German Gunrunner)*, Sumar Khan *(Ishtari Gunrunner)*, Jon Paul Morgan *(Djellabah Seller)*, Nadim Sawalha *(Rag Shop Owner/Camel Seller)*, Haluk Belginer *(Guerilla Leader)*, Ron Berglass, Neil Zevnick, Matt Brewer, Alex Hyde-White *(CIA Agents)*, Stefan Gryff, Alexei Jawdocimov *(KGB Agents)*, Eddy Nedari, Adam Hussein, George Masri *(Mohamed, The Camel Sellers)*, Mark Ryan, Stuart Abramson, John Freudenheim, Bruce Gordon *(Screamin' Honkers)*, Paul Standig, Joseph Omerek, John Trumpbour *(The Swing)*, Marie Jean Charles, Patrice Jean Charles, Danielle Jean Charles *(Teacher's Daughters)*.

ISHTAR is the type of entertainment that only Hollywood can provide—mainly because it's the type of entertainment that only Hollywood can afford. It's inevitable that when a film costs upwards of $40 million (some say as high as $57 million), stars two of the biggest names in Hollywood (Hoffman and Beatty), and is directed by a person (May) notorious for her wasteful shooting methods, the result will be savaged by industry insiders and film critics even before it is released. A victim of bad advance word of mouth, ISHTAR is not nearly as awful as has been described, nor is it the masterpiece that some believed May, often generously labeled a "comic genius," would produce. Taking its cue from the Bob Hope-Bing Crosby road movies of the 1940s (most notably ROAD TO MOROCCO), ISHTAR is, underneath its gargantuan budget and salaries, a small comedy about two common people who find themselves caught in a whirlwind that involves the fate of the free world. The film opens as struggling songwriters Hoffman and Beatty are banging out the music and lyrics to one of their pathetic, but honestly expressive songs, "Dangerous Business," which warns that "Telling the truth can be dangerous business/Honest and popular don't go hand in hand/If you admit you can play the accordion/No one'll hire you in a rock and roll band/ . . . but we can sing our hearts out . . . " Although they have only known each other for a few months, the bond between them, as friends and songwriters, has grown strong. Before they met, they led "lives of quiet desperation"—Beatty, an ice cream truck driver who spent his evenings writing songs and ignoring his sweetheart Harper, and Hoffman a performer in a Greek restaurant who neglected his devoted girl friend Kane. Their meeting, however, alters their directionless lives, much to the chagrin of Harper and Kane, both of whom pack their bags. Having formed a writing partnership, Hoffman and Beatty spend endless nights at the piano, hashing out melodies and lyrics to such songs as "Wardrobe of Love" ("She said 'Come look, there's a wardrobe of love in my eyes/Take your time, look around, and see if there's something your size' ") and "That A Lawnmower Can Do That" ("Saturday morning/The sound of a lawnmower touches my heart"). Convinced they are every bit as talented as Simon and Garfunkel, Warren and Hoffman call entertainment agent Weston and invite him to an "open mike" night at a local club. Although the audience sits dazed and slackjawed at their folk/punk rendition of "Dangerous Business," Weston offers them a booking . . . in Morocco. The scene shifts to an archeological dig in the mythical Ishtar, a North African country on the brink of civil war which is located somewhere near the Moroccan border. It is here that a secret map is unearthed which could lead to a Holy War in the Mid-East. The map, which predicts the arrival of two messengers of God, is hidden by the archeologist who discovered it, and moments later he is murdered. When Hoffman and Beatty stopover in Ishtar, Hoffman is approached in the airport by

Adjani, a member of the underground and sister of the murdered archaeologist. Her face and head covered in a black burnoose, Adjani is initially mistaken as a young homosexual by the nervous Hoffman. After she bares her breast to prove otherwise she asks him to save her life by giving her his passport and smuggling out her luggage. He obliges, but promises not to tell Beatty. Later, at their hotel, Hoffman is approached by CIA operative Grodin, who befriends Hoffman with the intention of uncovering Hoffman's connection to Adjani. Beatty, in the meantime, is surprised by an intruder who tries to steal Hoffman's luggage (which is really Adjani's, and contains the map which is hidden amongst her brother's belongings). The intruder turns out to be Adjani, who is again mistaken for a young homosexual—a discovery which doesn't stop Beatty from giving the intruder a passionate kiss. Adjani pleads with Beatty to help their cause and to be sympathetic to their attempts to overthrow the country's tyrannical ruler. She then tries to convince Beatty that Hoffman is a CIA agent and sets up a meeting for the following day at a nearby marketplace. Beatty remains silent about his contact with Adjani because he thinks Hoffman is a CIA agent, and Hoffman keeps his meetings with Grodin secret because he believes Beatty is a communist. At the marketplace, Beatty and Hoffman are followed by countless agents from many countries, all after the map. After a few attempts are made on their lives, they escape with the help of Hageb, their young native guide. In the meantime, Beatty and Hoffman have headed into the desert on a blind camel, while the CIA, Ishstar's leaders, and Adjani's friends all plot to kill the pair. Before long Hoffman and Beatty realize they are in trouble, as they begin to run out of water and a terrible windstorm kicks up. When morning comes they cross paths with a group of gunrunners. Hoffman masquerades as a translator and leads the auction of arms to buyers from various Ishtari tribes. With help from Beatty, who is hidden among the group of buyers and disguised in a burnoose, Hoffman is able to pull off the ruse. A helicopter, bearing a CIA assassin dispatched to kill Beatty and Hoffman, arrives on the scene, breaking up the auction and leaving Beatty and Hoffman alone with the remaining guns. In short order, Hoffman discovers the missing map sewn into the lining of his jacket, the pair are joined by Hageb and Adjani, who arrive on the scene by jeep, and the weapons left behind by the gunrunners provide the firepower needed to drive off the CIA assassins. Having beaten the CIA, Beatty and Hoffman send the secret map to Weston, who in turn blackmails the government on two counts—bringing about social reforms in Ishtar as dictated by Adjani, and promoting a live album and world concert tour for Hoffman and Beatty. They become the next big thing, selling out concert halls and getting the album on the charts with such unforgettable lyrics as "I can see her standing in the backyard of my mind/She cracks her knuckles and the scab that's on her knee won't go away." Just like before the crowd sits dazed and slackjawed, but this time people are urged to applaud by army MPs. In the audience sits Adjani, now dressed in civilian clothes. Even though everyone else thinks Beatty and Hoffman are awful, Adjani sees their sincerity and, through her tears of happiness, comments, "I think they're wonderful."

Because of the controversy and hype which surrounded the production and release of ISHTAR, it is nearly impossible to separate the discussion of the film's bloated budget from the film itself. If ISHTAR had been cast with two unknown actors and directed by an unknown, then perhaps criticism of the film would have been different. Instead, however, Beatty pulled in $5.5 million for his performance and another $1/2 million for producing, while Hoffman raked in $5.5 million. Another $1.5 million went to director/writer May, whose previous films MIKEY AND NICKY and A NEW LEAF have been highly praised but who has been duly criticized for her idiosyncratic and expensive directing technique. (She shoots long and numerous takes, which results in excessive shooting ratios—for MIKEY AND NICKY she shot 1.4 million feet of film and used only 10,000 in the finished product; in ISHTAR she restricted herself to a mere 1/2 million feet, again using only about 10,000.) The average Hollywood film costs about $17 million, yet ISHTAR'S costs for Beatty, Hoffman, and May were $13 million, and that's before film even started rolling. While it's not unusual for a film to cost $30-40 million, it *is* unusual for a small comedy. What is most distressing about the size of the budget is that the money is not on the screen. Somehow, May managed to spend $40 million on two guys singing, a bunch of robed extras, a blind camel, and some sand dunes. When such infinitely superior-looking films as Akira Kurosawa's RAN and Bernardo Bertolucci's THE LAST EMPEROR can cost only $11 million and $25 million, respectively, it's hard to fathom how $40 million can be spent on ISHTAR. Originally scheduled for a late November 1986 release, post-production delays (numerous editors working long hours to wade through the footage) set the release date back to late May 1987. In order to recoup the initial investment, ISHTAR must gross about $100 million. ISHTAR made $4.3 million and was the top-grossing film the week it opened, but those numbers fell rapidly as the film was savaged by critics and public alike. (In contrast, the number two grosser of the week, THE GATE, grossed $4.2 million, but only cost $4 million to make.)

For all the bad press ISHTAR received the film is actually a funny and oddly charming story of two common people whose emotional honesty and naive self-expression pulls them out of their "lives of quiet desperation" and carries them into an adventurous and exciting state of mind called "Ishtar." ("Hello Ishtar/ You're more than a country, you're a state of mind," sing Beatty and Hoffman in "Hello Ishtar.") Cast against type, Beatty and Hoffman both play a couple of down-on-their-luck goofs. Hollywood sex symbol and superstar Beatty plays a half-witted Texan who wears a hunting cap pulled over his ears and a less-than-fashionable parka. He drives an ice cream truck, he can barely sing, he cries when his girl friend leaves him, and he has no flair with the ladies. (The real Beatty, however, has been romantically linked with co-star Adjani.) Hoffman, who emerges by default as the leader of the pair, is an emotional and pained man who can't commit to his girl friend, has lived with his mother until age 32, and is nearly driven to suicide after reflecting on his seemingly pathetic life. As in the great "buddy" movies of the past, these characters are completely dependent upon each other, support each other, and genuinely love each other. (ISHTAR is not without some homosexual undertones—both mistake Adjani for a young boy and neither displays any romantic interest in her—but these feelings come across more as naively affectionate than deliberate.) Both turn in exceptional performances which are far more subtle than what one has come to expect from either actor. Adjani, the beautiful European actress whose appearances in Roman Polanski's THE TENANT, Francois Truffaut's THE STORY OF ADELE H., and Werner Herzog's NOSFERATU have made her a most sought after actress, is unfortunately given very little to do in ISHTAR. For most of the film, her face peaks out from behind her tribal black burnoose. Only in the final scene, as she watches Beatty and Hoffman on stage, does she give a sampling of her talent. ISHTAR also bears the photographic stamp of Vittorio Storaro (THE CONFORMIST, LAST TANGO IN PARIS, THE LAST EMPEROR and Beatty's REDS) whose romantic gold lighting fits the Moroccan setting but is somewhat peculiar for a comedy. (Federico Fellini's cameraman Giuseppe Rotunno was the original cinematographer, but scheduling delays forced him to drop out.) The biggest problem with ISHTAR is that the subtleness of the performances gets swallowed up by May's attempt to turn the film into an epic adventure story. Beatty and Hoffman have created complex characters, but CIA operatives, secret maps, messengers of God, gunrunners, and tyrannical rulers keep getting in their way. The film is filled with embarrassingly bad but still charming songs, with music written by Paul Williams and lyrics written by May, Hoffman, and Beatty. Plans for a soundtrack album were scuttled by the film's dismal box office showing. Beatty and Hoffman did their own singing and playing on the following songs: "Dangerous Business," "Carol," "That A Lawnmower Can Do That," "Wardrobe Of Love," "Hello Ishtar" (Paul Williams); "Portable Picnic," "Love In My Will," "Software," "The Echo Song," "I Look To Mecca," "How Big Am I?" (Williams, Elaine May); "Sitting On The Edge Of My Life," "Harem Girl" (Dustin Hoffman); "Half-Hour Song" (Hoffman, Warren Beatty); "My Lips On Fire," "Have Not Blues" (May, Beatty); "Bridge Over Troubled Water" (Paul Simon); "Strangers In The Night" (Charles Singleton, Eddie Snyder, Bert Kaempfert); "There's No Business Like Show Business" (Irving Berlin); "That's Amore" (Jack Brooks, Harry Warren) and "Little Darlin' " (Maurice Williams). Also included are "One For My Baby (And One More For The Road)" (Johnny Mercer, Harold Arlen, performed by Frank Sinatra); "What's Wrong With That" (Bruce Gordon, performed by The Screamin' Honkers); "You Took My Love" (Elaine May, performed by The Swing); "I'm Quitting High School" (May, John Strauss, performed by Teacher's Daughters); "Tomorrow" (Martin Charnin, Charles Strouse). *(Profanity, brief nudity.)*

p, Warren Beatty; d&w, Elaine May; ph, Vittorio Storaro (Technicolor); m, Bahjawa; ed, Stephen A. Rotter, William Reynolds, Richard Cirincione; prod d, Paul Sylbert; art d, Bill Groom, Vicki Paul, Peter Childs, Tony Reading; set d, Steve Jordan, Alan Hicks; cos, Anthony Powell; m/l, Paul Williams, Elaine May, Bruce Gordon, The Swing, John Strauss, Maurice Williams, Johnny Mercer, Harold Arlen, Jack Brooks, Harry Warren, Warren Beatty, Dustin Hoffman, Martin Charnin, Charles Strouse, Paul Simon, Charles Singleton, Eddie Snyder, Burt Kaempfert, Irving Berlin; makeup, Bob Jiras, Alan Boyle.

Comedy **Cas.** **(PR:A-C MPAA:PG-13)**

ISKRENNE VASH . . . † (1987, USSR) 91m Mosfilm/Sovexportfilm c (Trans: Yours Sincerely)

Vitaly Solomin, Vera Glagoleva, Viktor Ilyichev, Rolan Bykov, Armen Djigarkhanyan.

Ironically titled "Yours Sincerely," this Soviet film delves into the anguished soul that lurks beneath the happy exterior of a successful young man who is anything but sincere. Willing to do anything to get to the top, he lies, deceives his mother, and cheats on his wife with a friend's lover. Worst of all, the only person he isn't fooling is himself. Finally he admits to a friend that ten years before he compromised all he believed in and gave up his career as an astronomer to try to get ahead.

d, Alla Surikova; w, Valentin Azernikov; ph, Vsevolod Simakov; m, Viktor Lebedev; art d, Irina Shreter.

Drama **(PR:NR MPAA:NR)**

IS-SLOTTET† (1987, Nor.) Norsk c (Trans: The Ice Palace)

Line Storesund, Hilde Nyeggen Martinsen, Merete Moen, Sigrid Huun.

Based on a novel by Tarjei Vesaas and set in a small town in the Norwegian countryside, this is the story of two young girls who are overwhelmed by their nascent feelings of intimacy and sexuality. After the death of her mother, one of the 11-year-olds has moved to the community to live with her aunt. One night, she and her newfound friend find themselves alone, but the intensity of their feelings for each other terrifies them. This trauma sends one of them trudging off to the "Ice Palace," a frozen waterfall, and she is never seen again.

d&w, Per Blom (based on the novel by Tarjei Vesaas); ph, Halvor Naess.

Drama **(PR:NR MPAA:NR)**

ISTEN VELETEK, BARATAIM† (1987, Hung.) 106m Mafilm-Hunnia-Hungarian TV c (Trans: Farewell to You)

Cecilia Esztergalyos *(Actress)*, Laszlo Sinko *(Baron)*, Kornel Gelley *(Teacher)*, Sandor Zsoter *(Egon)*, Vera Pap *(Young Woman)*, Sandor Gaspar *(Upholsterer)*, Gyorgyi Kari *(Maid)*.

Set against a war-torn Budapest, this film spans six years (1938-1944) in the lives of the inhabitants of one tenement house. As the war starts their lives are only peripherally affected by the fighting. By 1942 the bombing has come closer and a cloud of fear settles around the house. By 1944 their lives are as devastated as their country. The film ends as the tenement is bombed, killing all but the lucky neighborhood "fool."

d, Sandor Simo; w, Zsuzsa Biro, Sandor Simo (based on the novel *The Story Of A Barrow* by Jozsi Jeno Tersanszky); ph, Tamas Andor (Eastmancolor); m, Zdenko Tamassy; ed, Maria Rigo; set d, Gyorgy Csik; cos, Fanni Kemenes.

Drama **(PR:NR MPAA:NR)**

ISKUSHENIE DON ZHUANA† (1987, USSR) 91m Odessa/Sovexportfilm c (Trans: The Temptation of Don Juan)

Ivar Kalnyns, Yelena Finogeyeva, Stanislav Sadalsky, Yelena Tonunts.

Lesya Ukrainka's play "The Stone Master" provided the basis for this Soviet variation on the legend of Don Juan. In this version the famous ladies man returns from exile to Spain and attempts to seduce the friend of his fiancee. This prompts a duel with her betrothed, the commander of the guard, whose job Don Juan assumes when he runs him through. But the commander gets lasting revenge when the arm of a granite statue of him falls on Don Juan and kills him during a defense of the castle.

d, Vasily Levin, Grigory Koltunov; w, Grigory Koltunov (based on the play "The Stone Master" by Lesya Ukrainka); ph, Mikhail Mednikov; m, M. Glinka, De Falla, G. Bizet; art d, Alexander Tokarev.

Historical/Romance **(PR:NR MPAA:NR)**

ITALIANI A RIO† (1987, It.) Devon-Dania-Intl. Dean/Medusa c (Trans: Italians in Rio)

Silvio Spaccesi, Mauro De Francesco, Gianni Ciardo, Milton Goncalves, Clelia Rondinella.

When three Italian bankers are sent to Rio de Janeiro as a bonus, they find themselves involved in a series of comic misadventures.

d, Michele Massimo Tarantini; w, Michele Massimo Tarantini, Roberto Leoni, Tonino Cervi; ph, Mario Lommi (Telecolor); m, Franco Campannio; ed, Fulvio Alabisio.

Comedy **(PR:NR MPAA:NR)**

ITAZU† (1987, Jap.) 117m Kobushi/Toei c (Trans: Forest of Little Bear)

Takahiro Tamura *(Ginzo)*, Hiroshi Miyata *(Ippei)*, Junko Sakurada *(Kimi)*, Nijiko Kiyokawa *(Grandmother)*, Toru Yuri *(Heisaku)*, B-Sako Sato *(Tashiro)*, Ryutaro Tatsumi *(Takahara)*.

A wilderness family film set in 1928 and centering on the relationship between an old man and his grandson. The grandfather, distraught over the loss of his son in the Siberian war, takes his grandson under his wing and teaches him how to live off the land. While in the forest one day, the grandfather kills an attacking grizzly bear, only to find out it was a mother bear. The old man and his grandson then adopt the mother bear's orphaned cub.

p, Hisashi Yabe; d, Toshio Goto; w, Ryunosuke Ono (based on a story by Toshio Goto); ph, Takaya Yamazaki; m, Masaru Sato; ed, Atsushi Nabeshima; prod, Akira Haruki; cos, Kyoto Isho.

Children's **(PR:A MPAA:NR)**

I'VE HEARD THE MERMAIDS SINGING† (1987, Can.) 81m Vos/ Miramax c/bw

Sheila McCarthy *(Polly Vandersma)*, Paule Baillargeon *(Gabrielle St. Peres)*, Ann Marie McDonald *(Mary Joseph)*, John Evans *(Warren)*, Brenda Kamino *(Japanese Waitress)*, Richard Monette *(Critic)*.

A first feature from 29-year-old Canadian director Rozema which stormed onto the international film scene by winning the Cannes Film Festival's *Prix de la Jeunesse*, or Youth Prize. Filmed on 16mm for under $300,000, the film employs both color and black-and-white photography as well as video. The story revolves around McCarthy, a 31-year-old amateur photographer who is too "organizationally impaired" to find steady work as a secretary. She gets hired at an upscale art gallery as an assistant to curator Baillargeon and the two hold a mutual curiosity/admiration for one another. McCarthy looks up to Baillargeon, but is shocked to discover that she is carrying on a lesbian affair with McDonald. When McCarthy displays one of Baillargeon's secret paintings for some critics, the curator is hailed as a brilliant new find. McCarthy then submits, under a pseudonym, some of her own photographs to Baillargeon, only to have them ridiculed. After a few more twists and turns of plot and a fantasy coda, McCarthy comes to terms with her position as an artist. The film's title, which is drawn from a line in T.S. Eliot's "The Love Song of J. Alfred Prufrock," relates to McCarthy's fantasies of flying through the air and walking on water while the song of the mermaids is heard. In addition to its Cannes showing, the film opened in New York and Los Angeles where much praise was heaped on both Rozema's direction and McCarthy's performance.

p, Patricia Rozema, Alexandra Raffe; d&w, Patricia Rozema; ph, Douglas Koch; m, Mark Korven; ed, Patricia Rozema; set d, Valanne Ridgeway.

Comedy/Drama **(PR:NR MPAA:NR)**

IZ ZHIZNI NACHALNIKA UGOLOVNOGO ROZYSKA† (1987, USSR) 89m Gorky/Sovexportfilm c (Trans: C.I.D. Chief's Experience)

Kirill Lavrov, Leonid Filatov, Elena Proklova, Leonid Kharitonov.

When a former thief, now a family man with a good job, realizes that he lives in the same apartment building as the official who put him in prison, his memories of the past are stirred. Although thoughts of revenge cross the thief's mind, his character is tested when he must come to the official's aid.

d, Stepan Puchinyan; w, Olga Lavrov, Alexander Lavrov; ph, Gassant Tutunov, Alexander Kovalchuk; m, Andrei Gevorgyan; art d, Alexander Vagichev.

Drama **(PR:NR MPAA:NR)**

IZ ZHIZNI POTAPOVA† (1987, USSR) 97m Mosfilm/Sovexportfilm c (Trans: Potapov's Life)

Alexander Filippenko *(Alexander Potapov)*, Tatiana Doghileva, Mikhail Gluzsky, Nikolai Penkov, Tamara Akulova.

A powerful and efficient official, Filippenko, is torn between his unfaltering devotion to his work and the traumas of his personal life. Although his relations with his wife, family, and friends threaten to distract him from his work, he eventually balances both without compromise.

d, Nikolai Skuybin; w, Sergei Ivanov, Nikolai Skuybin; ph, Vadim Alisov; m, Roman Ledenev; art d, Alexander Borisov.

Drama **(PR:NR MPAA:NR)**

IZVINITE POZHALUYSTA† (1987, USSR) 96m Lithuania Film Studio/ Sovexportfilm c (Trans: I Beg Your Pardon)

Alexander Kaydanovsky *(Pranas)*, Elena Solovey *(Inga)*, Regimantas Adomaytis, Niyole Ozhelite, Evgeniya Shulgayte.

A famous composer goes back to the Lithuanian village of his birth and struggles with the problem of returning to his roots. He is befriended by two other villagers who are trying to cope with the same dilemma, and together they face their future in the village.

d&w, Vitautas Zhalakyavichus; ph, Donatas Pechura; m, Vitautas Kyarnagis; art d, Vitautas Kalinauskas.

Drama **(PR:NR MPAA:NR)**

JAAHYVAISET PRESIDENTILLE† (1987, Fin.) 90m Skandia/Finnkino c (Trans: Farewell to the President)

Hanny Lauri *(Asko Mertanen)*, Laila Raikka *(Eeva-Maria Kilpinen)*, Antti Litja *(Hanhivaara)*, Esa Saario *(Chief Detective Kairamo)*, Tarmo Manni *(President)*, Markku Huhtamo, Markko Nieminen, Aake Kalliala, Olavi Ahonen, Tarja Simes, Pentti Jarventie.

The president of Finland visits the city of Tampere for the unveiling of a statue. Waiting for his arrival is a skilled rifleman who plans to assasinate the leader. Police are on the would-be killer's trail and successfully foil the assassination attempt.

p, Kaj Holmberg; d, Matti Kassila; w, Matti Kassila, Taavi Kassila (based on a novel by Pentti Kirstilan); ph, Kari Sohlberg (Eastmancolor); m, Heikki Sarmanto; ed, Irma Taina; set d, Erkki Saarainen; cos, Marjatta Nissinen.

Thriller **(PR:NR MPAA:NR)**

JAAN KAANTOPIIRI† (1987, Fin.) 120m Skandia Filmi Oy c (Trans: Tropic of Ice)

Tor Planting, Johanna Raunio, William Carson, Vladimir von Witte.

A Finnish businessman, successfully trading in both eastern and western countries, finds his business ruined as international relations become strained.

d, Lauri Torhonen; w, Juha Vakkuri, Lauri Torhonen (based on a novel by Juha Vakkuri); ph, Esa Vuorinen; m, Hector; ed, Tuula Mehtonen; cos, Airi Iso-Lotila.

Drama **(PR:NR MPAA:NR)**

JAG ELSKER DIG† (1987, Den.) 84m Danish Film Institute-DR TV/Metronome c (Trans: I Love You)

Peter Hesse Overgaard *(Jens)*, Pernille Hansen *(Janne)*, Ulla Henningsen *(Marriage Counselor)*, Sonja Oppenhage, Egon Stoldt, Jorgen Bing, Sissel Brandi-Hansen, Malene Krogh, Rolf Munkholm-Jensen.

A young married couple visits a marriage counselor who helps them to get in touch with their feelings and animosities. They manage to work things out once they realize that their parents are the cause of their problems. Based on actual cases studied by Danish psychologist Larsen, who is credited as dialog consultant. The cinematographer, Judy Irola, photographed WORKING GIRLS, the 1986 Lizzy Borden film about prostitutes and their clientele.

p, Ebbe Preisler, Finn Clausen; d, Li Vilstrup; w, Li Vilstrup, Hanne Hostrup Larsen; ph, Judy Irola (Eastmancolor); m, Claus Agmussen, Svend Agmussen; ed, Camilla Skousen; prod d, Per Flink Basse; cos, Mariann Preisler.

Docu-Drama **(PR:NR MPAA:NR)**

JAIDEV† (1987, India)

Uttam Mohanty *(Jaidev)*, Chakrapani, Tandra Ray, Jaya Swami, Byomkesh, Jayi, Pira Mishra.

An account of the life of noted Indian author Jaidev. (In Oriya.)

p, Sachi Routray; d, Shyamal Mukherjee; m, Balakrishna Das, Guru Keluchuran Mahapatra.

Biography **(PR:NR MPAA:NR)**

JALWA† (1987, India)

Naseeruddin Shah, Archana Puran Singh, Saeed Jaffrey, Tejeshwar Singh.

Vengeance motivates a police officer to go after the drug dealers who murdered his friend. (In Hindi.)

p, Gul Anand; d, Punkaj Parashar; m, Anand Milind.

Crime **(PR:NR MPAA:NR)**

JANE AND THE LOST CITY† (1987, Brit.) 93m Marcel-Robertson, Glen Films c

Sam Jones *(Jungle Jack Buck)*, Maude Adams *(Lola Pagola)*, Kirsten Hughes *(Jane)*, Jasper Carrott *(Heinrich)*, Robin Bailey *(The Colonel)*, Ian Roberts *(Carl)*, Elsa O'Toole *(Leopard Queen)*, Graham Stark, John Rapley.

During WW II a group of Brits is racing against time and the Nazis to find a hidden city in the jungles of Africa. There the plucky band hopes to uncover a cache of diamonds before the Germans can get their nefarious fingers on the jewels. This feature is based on a comic strip that had enormous popularity in England during the WW II era. The strip served as the inspiration for a previous cinematic tale, THE ADVENTURES OF JANE, in 1949.

p, Harry Robertson; d, Terry Marcel; w, Mervyn Haisman (based on the comic strip by Norman Pett); ph, Paul Beeson (Rank color); m, Harry Robertson; ed, Alan Jones; prod d, Mick Pickwoad.

Action/Adventure **(PR:NR MPAA:NR)**

JANUARY ORORMA† (1987, India) Tharangini

Mohanlal, Karthika, Suresh, Soman, Jayabharathi, Karamana, Lalu Alex, Jagathi, Rohini.

A lonely tour guide seeks someone to love. (In Hindi.)

d, Joshi; m, Ousappachan.

Romance **(PR:NR MPAA:NR)**

JAWAB HUM DENGE† (1987, India)

Shatrughan Sinha, Sridevi, Jackie Shroff.

An innocent union leader is aided by two police officers after he is framed for a crime. (In Hindi.)

p, K.C. Bokadia; d, Vijay Reddy; m, Laxmikant Pyarelal.

Crime **(PR:NR MPAA:NR)**

JAWS: THE REVENGE* (1987) 89m UNIV c

Lorraine Gary *(Ellen Brody)*, Lance Guest *(Michael Brody)*, Mario Van Peebles *(Jake)*, Karen Young *(Carla Brody)*, Michael Caine *(Hoagie)*, Judith Barsi *(Thea Brody)*, Lynn Whitfield *(Louisa)*, Mitchell Anderson *(Sean Brody)*, Jay Mello *(Young Sean)*, Cedric Scott *(Clarence)*, Charles Bowleg *(William)*, Melvin Van Peebles *(Mr. Witherspoon)*, Mary Smith *(Tiffany)*, Edna Billotto *(Polly)*, Fritzi Jane Courtney *(Mrs. Taft)*, Cyprian R. Dube *(Mayor)*, Lee Fierro *(Mrs. Kinter)*, John Griffin *(Man in Boat)*, Diane Hetfield *(Mrs. Ferguson)*, Daniel J. Manning *(Jesus)*, William E. Marks *(Lenny)*, James Martin *(Minister)*, David Wilson *(Tarkanian)*, Romeo Farrington *(Romeo)*, Anthony Delaney *(Charles Townsend)*, Heather Thompson *(Shirley)*, Levant Carey *(Houseman)*, Darlene Davis *(Irma)*.

As the toothy fish series plays out its string, the plots of the JAWS movies become more and more ludicrous, embarrassingly so with this, the fourth and most dismal of the group. Roy Scheider, who wisely opted to escape this endless fish story, has been eliminated from the New England town of Amity; his wife, the long-suffering Gary, has taken over the lead. One of her sons, Anderson, has become the police chief who is vexed by a terrorizing shark during the Christmas period and suddenly is killed by it. Gary, to escape the horror of her family's shark-infested history, travels to the Bahamas to visit her surviving son Guest, a marine biologist who spends most of his waking moments looking for rare sea snails with partner Van Peebles. Sure enough, the very shark that attacked Anderson, has followed Gary to the Bahamas and is out to kill her second son, all in the name of vengeance for the killing of its supposed relatives in prior JAWS films. Now here's a mammal with a memory! Gary, who has fallen in love with easy-living Caine, suddenly concludes that the shark will not give up attacking her second son unless she brings a halt to the vendetta by sacrificing herself. With true motherly love, Gary goes out to sea to offer herself to the flesh-loving shark. Caine, realizing what she is about to do, jumps into his plane and races after her, crashing his plane next to her boat just as the shark attacks. The shark smashes into the plane while underwater and tries to eat the sophisticated Caine who escapes with his dignity, and, oddly, though he has been underwater, emerges with dry pants and shirt in Gary's boat. The shark, acting more like a marlin, stands on its tail and wiggles menacingly toward the boat as Caine and Gary ram it to death.

The whole thing is an insult to any viewer. Even the special effects are lame in this one, offering a latex shark that is about as realistic as a fake goldfish. Poorly directed by Sargent who relies heavily on fast editing and cutting to create some tension, for there certainly isn't any written into the script. Of course there is a lot of blood mixing with ocean water, but even the gore is unrealistic, as if showing someone's recently deposited garbage from a Thanksgiving Day dinner. The script is such a throwaway that the European release of JAWS—THE REVENGE has a more upbeat ending which allows for the survival of a number of characters who were killed off in the U.S. version. Gary, 50, plays out her weak part valiantly, trying to overcome its inherent absurdities, this as a favor to her husband, Sidney J. Sheinberg, president of MCA, parent of Universal, a nepotistic deal reminiscent of the Herbert J. Yates productions which featured his wife

Vera Hruba Ralston three decades ago, and those films weren't worth watching either. It is hoped this disgraceful production, made for about 20 million wasted dollars, will mark the end of what was a fairly good horror notion years ago when people were convinced that sharks were possessed of deductive reasoning. Caine, who will appear in any film for money, as he has stated, could not accept an Academy Award for HANNAH AND HER SISTERS because he was making this film—which says a lot about the decline of moviemaking these days. Songs include "Nail It To The Wall" (Arnie Roman, Stephen Broughton Lunt, performed by Stacy Lattisaw), "You Got It All" (Rupert Holmes, performed by The Jets). *(Violence, gore effects.)*

p&d, Joseph Sargent; w, Michael de Guzman (based on characters created by Peter Benchley); ph, John McPherson; m, Michael Small, John Williams; prod d, John J. Lloyd; art d, Don Woodruff; set d, Steve Schwartz, Hal Gausman, John Dwyer; cos, Marla Denise Schlom, Hugo Pena; makeup, Dan Striepeke, Tony Lloyd; spec eff, Henry Millar.

Thriller **Cas.** **(PR:O MPAA:PG-13)**

JEAN DE FLORETTE*½** (1987, Fr.) 122m Renn-Films A2-RAI-D.D./ Orion Classics c

Yves Montand *(Cesar Soubeyran/"Le Papet")*, Gerard Depardieu *(Jean de Florette [Cadoret])*, Daniel Auteuil *(Ugolin Soubeyran/"Galignette")*, Elisabeth Depardieu *(Aimee Cadoret)*, Ernestine Mazurowna *(Manon Cadoret)*, Marcel Champel *(Pique-Bouffigue)*, Armand Meffre *(Philoxene)*, Andre Dupon *(Pamphile)*, Pierre Nougaro *(Casimir)*, Marc Betton *(Martial)*, Jean Maurel *(Anglade)*, Roger Souza *(Ange)*, Bertino Benedetto *(Giuseppe)*, Margarita Lozano *(Baptistine)*, Pierre Jean Rippert *(Pascal)*, Didier Pain *(Eliacin)*, Fransined *(Florist)*, Christian Tamisier *(Doctor)*, Marcel Berbert *(Notary)*, Jo Doumerg *(Muledriver)*, Chantal Liennel *(Amandine, Papet's Servant)*.

Released last year in France to a tremendous box-office showing, JEAN DE FLORETTE has come stateside for a wide U.S. release. The most talked-about French production of the year, this picture and its sequel, MANON OF THE SPRING (MANON DES SOURCES), were completed at a combined record-breaking budget of $17 million (about eight times the cost of the average French picture). Shot back-to-back with MANON OF THE SPRING over a nine-month stretch, JEAN DE FLORETTE takes place in a French farming village tucked into a rocky but picturesque hillside. As the film begins, Montand, a coarse local with a reputation as a swindler, welcomes the return to the village of his nephew, Auteuil. A grimy, idiotic misfit, Auteuil has dreams of growing carnations for resale at the local marketplace. Carnations, however, need a great deal of water—a sparse commodity in the village. When Montand realizes that Auteuil's idea is a profitable one, he offers to buy a neighbor's farm, knowing that it contains an untapped natural spring. The neighbor refuses, and a fight ensues, ending with Montand accidentally killing him. The farm is eventually passed to a relative of the deceased, Depardieu, a hunchbacked tax collector who bids farewell to city life in favor of a return to nature. Montand and Auteuil, however, refuse to let the farm slip through their fingers. They dig up the spring and cover the opening with cement. Arriving at the farmhouse with his wife and daughter, Depardieu is convinced that he has found heaven on Earth. Bathed in sunlight and covered by trees and grass, their new home has everything one could hope for. From the distance, Auteuil watches, aware that the family will have rough times ahead of it without a source of water. Convinced that Depardieu is a weak-willed city boy who will soon give up, Montand and Auteuil befriend their new neighbor, with the hope that he will sell his land to them. Auteuil is the perfect neighbor. He offers water from his own well on a daily basis, donates extra tiles for roof repairs, and even helps with the family garden. Depardieu's will surprises everyone. Although a hunchback, he is remarkably strong, both physically and mentally. Armed with a collection of how-to manuals and an accountant's knowledge of statistics, charts, and numbers, Depardieu plans his modern farm. He outlines a revolutionary method of breeding rabbits, plants tropical vines, and charts the amount of water necessary to grow a variety of vegetables. Montand, a veteran farmer, laughs at Depardieu's inexperience and becomes convinced that failure is just around the corner. When Auteuil's water supply proves insufficient, Depardieu takes his family and his mule and treks down the steep hillside to borrow from a gypsy couple who live nearby. With his manuals and city sensibility, Depardieu miraculously realizes all of his plans. His rabbits roam freely, his vegetables are the best in the village, and his future as a farmer looks secure. There is still the problem of water, however. Auteuil and Montand offer their friendship and advice but keep the nearby spring a secret. While other villagers are aware of the scam, no one bothers to talk, choosing instead to mind their own business. A summer drought slowly eats away at Depardieu's crops. As the water runs out, the rabbits die, the corn wilts, and the vegetables rot. At the same time, Depardieu's finances run dry. Desperate to succeed, Depardieu resorts to a divining rod and digs a well in the chosen spot. While dynamiting some rock, he gets injured and, soon afterwards, dies. In an apparent act of generosity, Montand purchases the farm from Depardieu's widow, allowing her and her daughter to return to the city. Before leaving, however, the young daughter sees Montand and Auteuil celebrating as they dig up the hidden well. In her young eyes, one can see that she will one day return to seek vengeance on the men who caused her father's death.

The first of two parts, JEAN DE FLORETTE was followed three months later by MANON OF THE SPRING, which spans a 10-year period to mark the return to the village of Depardieu's daughter. Directed by Claude Berri, the film is a throwback to the pre-Nouvelle Vague days of French cinema in the 1930s and 1940s when the Tradition of Quality was the norm. Based on the two-part novel *L'Eau des Collines* (The Water of the Hills), penned by Marcel Pagnol (which, in turn, was based on an unsuccessful 1952 film that he directed), the film offers the same sort of complex characterizations, careful scripting, beautiful country images, and heightened realism that were present in films such as Pagnol's early Marseilles trilogy—MARIUS (1931), FANNY (1932), and CESAR (1934). Berri has set up a number of forces, all of which are pointed against each other—Depardieu's will versus nature's persistence, Depardieu's knowledge against nature's unpredictability, Depardieu's will against Montand's greed, and Auteuil's aspirations versus his own conscience. With each of the three characters, it is in their hypocrisy that they are most interesting. One of Depardieu's strongest scenes occurs when, driven half-mad from exhaustion, he runs into the field and begs God for rain. It is at this moment (shot from a high angle looking down on Depardieu) that Depardieu is at his most vulnerable—having been stripped of dependency on statistics and how-to manuals, he must admit that his methods have failed and appeal to a higher power for help. Auteuil's character is also caught in an impasse. He is too ignorant to realize the consequences of his actions and, therefore, too innocent to be held responsible. He merely wants to grow carnations, but is manipulated by the greedy Montand. Although his character is underdeveloped in terms of his relationship with the other villagers, Montand is clearly an evil old man who has made his profits by stepping on others. He grabs at Depardieu's land, not because he needs it, but because he is motivated solely by greed. While there is much to be said in favor of JEAN DE FLORETTE—the exceptional photography, the powerful acting, the crisp sound (though sometimes too much so), the authentic production design—there are also some disheartening faults. There is very little of the pastoral realism that strengthened the French pictures of the 1930s (notably Jean Renoir's and the aforementioned Pagnol scripts). Berri shows us the villagers, but they exist merely as background pieces, none of them ever coming to life in the forefront. Also, Montand's character is originally painted as a thief, murderer, and swindler, but he is hardly treated as such by his neighbors. It is difficult to discern the village opinion of him, which is surprising considering that, when taken together, JEAN DE FLORETTE and MANON OF THE SPRING last four hours—certainly enough time for the characters to be fully fleshed out. Technically, the film is superbly crafted, but it is *so* perfect it sometimes disturbs. The background sounds—birds, footsteps, horses, cracking corn—are heightened to the point of ridiculousness. The music, which is drawn from a piece by Giuseppe Verdi, manages to swell at the most peculiar moments, as if Berri is poking fun at and exaggerating the film's already existing melodrama. Most disappointing is the film's ending, although it's not *what* happens at the end, but *how* it happens. Clearly setting the stage for the sequel, Berri has his previously patient characters—Montand and Auteuil—digging up the blocked spring before Depardieu's widow is out of sight. Naturally, the daughter witnesses the pair's celebration and runs off to her sequel. Unlike the separate GODFATHER films, neither JEAN DE FLORETTE nor MANON OF THE SPRING can stand on its own. Berri's characters, at the end of Part One, are in a state of transition. After watching the film for two hours, there is no feeling of satisfaction (MANON OF THE SPRING, on the other hand, does reach a resolution). Had Berri chosen to bring the film to a dramatic, climactic height (through his use of music, editing, and composition), then it would not feel as if the picture ended in midstep. Instead of functioning as a film on its own, JEAN DE FLORETTE ends as a manipulative cliff-hanger. The top-grossing French film of the year in France, JEAN DE FLORETTE ranked second at the box office behind OUT OF AFRICA, the U.S. entry in the Tradition of Quality category. Both parts of JEAN DE FLORETTE were showered with eight Cesar nominations: Best Film, Best Actor (Auteuil), Best Actress (Emmanuelle Beart, of Part Two), Best Director (Berri), Best Screenplay (Berri, Gerard Brach), Best Score (Petit), Best Cinematography (Nuytten), and Best Sound (Pierre Gamet, Dominique Hennequin).

p, Pierre Grunstein; d, Claude Berri; w, Claude Berri, Gerard Brach (based on the novel by Marcel Pagnol); ph, Bruno Nuytten (Technovision, Eastmancolor); m, Jean-Claude Petit; ed, Arlette Langmann, Herve de Luze, Noelle Boisson; md, Jean-Claude Petit; prod d, Bernard Vezat; set d, Marcel Laude; cos, Sylvie Gautrelet; makeup, Michele Deruelle, Jean-Pierre Eychenne.

Drama **(PR:A MPAA:PG)**

JENATSCH*** (1987, Switz./Fr.) 97m Limbo-Bleu-Beat Curti-Societe de Banque Suisse-Fernsehen DRS-ZDF/Metropolis c

Michel Voita *(Cristophe)*, Christine Boisson *(Nina)*, Vittorio Mezzogiorno *(Jorg Jenatsch)*, Jean Bouise *(Tobler)*, Laura Betti *(Miss von Planta)*, Carole Bouquet

(Lucrezia), Raul Gimenez *(Taxi Driver)*, Lucrezia Giovannini *(Old Servant)*, Fredi M. Murer *(Film Archivist)*, Peter Bonke *(Peter Hertig)*, Ursina Hartmann *(Esther Hertig)*, Teco Celio *(Cavelti)*, Yvonne Kupper *(Waitress at Thusis)* Beatrice Stoll *(Customer at Bar)*, Claudia Knapp *(Bar Girl)*, Frnaci Camus *(Waitress at Coire)*, Cecile Kung *(Librarian)*, Jean-Marc Henchoz *(Pompejus von Planta)*, Gian-Reto Schmidt *(Steward)*, Daniel Rohner *(Priest on Train)*, Andrea Zogg, Gian-Battista von Tscharner *(Jenatsch's Companions)*, Otto Biert *(Soldier)*, Bethli Obrist *(Neighbor)*, Wolfram Frank *(High Priest)*, Walter Lietha *(Watchman)*, Escarla Rijo-Vicente *(Dancer at Bar)*, Franz Camastral *(Venetian Envoy)*, Rolf Lyssy *(Security Man)*, Roland Bertin, Jean-Paul Muel, Georg Janett.

A predictable but nevertheless compelling picture which blurs the line between fantasy and reality as it explores the legend of 16th-Century folk figure Jorg Jenatsch. The film begins with a black-and white documentary of the excavation of Jenatsch's coffin, which is discovered underneath a church pew. A young journalist, Voita, is assigned a feature story on Bouise, the archeologist who discovered Jenatsch's remains. Bouise explains, in great deal, how Jenatsch, a powerful and vile murderer, had his head caved in by an unknown assailant during carnival time in his village. The only clue to the murderer's identity is a tarnished round bell which Jenatsch snatched from his killer in a last dying grasp. Voita, leaves the archeologist, only to later find the bell in his own pocket. Given some other leads, Voita heads deep into the mountains to visit the village and to speak with Betti, a descendant of the woman who supposedly engineered Jenatsch's murder. During his visit, Voita begins hallucinating—seeing images of 16th-Century villagers battered by plague and fearing the evil Jenatsch. When he witnesses (and plays an active part as an informant in) the brutal axe murder of Betti's ancestor, Voita becomes obsessed with finding Jenatsch's killer. Voita also becomes obsessed with Bouquet, the beautiful daughter of the murdered ancestor who also witnessed the murder. When he returns to his city apartment, Voita's girl friend Boisson does all she can to help him battle the hallucinations. She is instructed by a therapist to take Voita back to all the places he visited so he can face, and overcome, what possesses him. She even throws the old bell into a river, permanently disposing of it. After spending some time in the mountain village, things seem to improve for Voita. Then the hallucinations take hold again and he finds himself in the middle of carnival as crowds of masked villagers celebrate in the torch-lit streets. Through the crowd he finds Betti's ancestor, Bouquet, and is led into an inn where Jenatsch, played by Mezzogiorno, is drinking with a host of friends. Voita picks up an axe which rests nearby, lifts it high over his head and strikes Jenatsch at the temple. Before Jenatsch collapses to the ground, he grasps at Voita and yanks a round bell from his jacket. Later, living an apparently happy life with Boisson, Voita receives a package at his door which contains the bell.

Essentially an elaborate "Twilight Zone" episode, JENATSCH rises above the mundane by raising some interesting metaphysical questions about time and space. Schmid argues, through Betti's character, that the only thing that separates the *real* from the *unreal* is time. One must therefore share his space with all the others who have previously occupied it. Given this philosophy (which also serves as a plot convenience), director Schmid can freely travel between the historical past and the inquisitive present. Originally conceived as a period piece, Schmid created the journalist character as a way of uniting the past with the present while still filming a historical biography of Jorg Jenatsch. (Coincidentally, this is similar to the technique employed by Stephen Frears in this year's PRICK UP YOUR EARS, which uses the John Lahr character as a link to playwright Joe Orton.) Cinematographer Berta (who previously shot for Jean-Luc Godard, EVERY MAN FOR HIMSELF, and Eric Rohmer, FULL MOON IN PARIS) and art director Gimenez do a fine job of creating different visual styles for the past and present while using some trickery to draw on certain similarities between the two periods. Only Voita and Boisson, who have a pleasant chemistry, are given a chance to develop their characters, as the others are merely one-dimensional pawns in Schmid's story. A moody and often haunting score by Donaggio helps to heighten the atmosphere. (In French; English subtitles.) *(Violence.)*

p, Theres Scherer, Luciano Gloor; d, Daniel Schmid; w, Martin Suter, Daniel Schmid; ph, Renato Berta (Kodak Color); m, Pino Donaggio; ed, Daniela Roderer; art d, Raul Gimenez; cos, Marianne Milani, Habiba Lahiani; makeup, Guerino Todero, Thomas Nellen.

Drama **(PR:C MPAA:NR)**

JESUS: DER FILM† (1987, E. Ger./W. Ger.) 125m (Trans: Jesus: The Film) c

Michael Brynntrup *(The Lord)*.

While young American filmmakers make movies economically with their video cameras, young German filmmakers use Super-8—a format which, in the US, was once that of "home movies" and is now used only in some of the trendier television commercials. In Germany, however, the popularity of Super-8 has been steadily on the rise for some years. JESUS: DER FILM is one of the few German Super-8 films to be shown on an American screen. It is an extremely low-budget compilation of 35 episodes in the life of Christ, directed by 23 people from both East and West Germany. Based loosely on the New Testament, the stories takes great liberties with the original texts, ranging from the blasphemous to the humorous to the reverent. Compiled by Brynntrup, who directed nearly one-third of the episodes, including one in which the Three Wise Men find *two* Jesuses in the manger—one an infant, the other an adult played by Brynnstrup. Shown at the Film Center of the Art Institute of Chicago.

pd&w, Michael Brynntrup, 22 other filmmakers.

Historical **(PR:NR MPAA:NR)**

JESTER, THE*½** (1987, Portugal) 127m Animatografo c (O BOBO)

Fernando Heitor *(Francisco Bernardes/The Jester)*, Paula Guedes *(Rita Portugal/Dulce)*, Luis Lucas, Luisa Marques, Victor Ramos, Glicinia Quartim, Isabel Ruth, Joao Guedes, Maria Amelia Motta, Luis Miguel Cintra, Raul Solnado.

The top prize winner at the 1987 Locarno Film Festival, THE JESTER is a visually breathtaking debut feature from the 43-year-old Morais, with a puzzling style that falls somewhere between Raul Ruiz and Alain Resnais. The film begins as Heitor and Guedes, two former lovers, meet in a restaurant to discuss the recent murder of a mutual friend. The friend had been producing a film adaptation of "O Bobo," a 19th century Alexandre Herculano play about the foundation of a 12th century Portuguese monarchy. With the restaurant meeting framing the film, flashbacks are used to advance several stories, including the deterioration of the relationship between Heitor and Guedes; the theatrical group's attempt to film "O Bobo" on elaborate sets in an abandoned soundstage at Lisboa Films; the extremely theatrical adaptation itself; and the murder of the producer who has, throughout the film, been attempting to sell some weapons to a criminal gang. Multiplying the intricacy of the narrative is the fact that the restaurant conversation between Heitor and Guedes continues on the soundtrack throughout the film, even commenting on the "flashback" scenes of their own break-up. This, coupled with the technique of using Heitor and Guedes as characters in the film-within-the-film, makes for some fascinating, though puzzling, scenes. Surprisingly, however, the film never seems haphazard. Filmed in 16mm and completed over the course of six years, THE JESTER is a marvelous example of total filmmaking—from visual conception to script writing to editing (by Jose Nascimento, the director of 1986's REPORTER X). The music is brilliantly conceived, employing three Portuguese composers, numerous segments of classical pieces, and one brilliantly funny use of counterpoint in which "We're in the Money" comments on the producer's scheme to sell arms—a scene in which the former left-wing revolutionary's compromise of ideals is made frighteningly obvious. THE JESTER is not an easy film to follow, especially if one is not well-versed in Portuguese history, but what is clear is that it was directed by a visionary talent who will surely become a force in Portuguese cinema. Shown briefly in the US. (In Portuguese; English subtitles.) *(Violence, nudity.)*.

p, Henrique Espirito Santo; d, Jose Alvaro Morais; w, Jose Alvaro Morais, Rafael Godinho (based on a play by Alexandre Herculano); ph, Mario de Carvalho; m, Carlos Azevedo, Carlos Zingaro, Pedro Caldeira Cabral; ed, Jose Nascimento; art d, Jasmin.

Historical **(PR:O MPAA:NR)**

JEUX D'ARTIFICES† (1987, Fr.) Forum-Virgin France-Ministry of Culture-Investimage-Sofinergie/Forum c (Trans: Games of Artifice)

Myriam David *(Elisa)*, Gael Seguin *(Eric)*, Ludovic Henry *(Jacques)*, Dominic Gould *(Stan)*, Friquette Thevenet, Andree Putman, Eva Ionesco, Arielle Dombasle, Claude Chabrol, Etienne Daho, Philippe Collin, Marc Prince.

An updating of Jean Cocteau's poetic tale of incest, "Les Enfants Terribles," which stars David and Seguin as a sibling pair who turn their apartment into a photo studio. Passing before their camera lens is a parade of interesting street characters, one of whom attracts David's attention. Their sibling jealousy finally explodes when Sequin runs off with the object of David's desires. Director Claude Chabrol appears in a supporting role.

p, Claude-Eric Poiroux; d&w, Virginie Thevenet (loosely based on "Les Enfants Terrible" by Jean Cocteau); ph, Pascal Marti; m, Andre Demay; ed, Jacqueline Mariani; art d, David Rochline; cos, Friquette Thevenet; makeup, Genevieve Peyrelade.

Drama **(PR:NR MPAA:NR)**

JHANJHAAR† (1987, India)

Padmini Kolhapure, Sushant Ray, Ranjana.

Three youthful heroes lead villagers in overthrowing their oppressors. (In Hindi.)

p&d, V. Shantaram; m, Kalyanji-Anandji.

Drama **(PR:NR MPAA:NR)**

JHOOTHI† (1987, India)

Rekha, Raj Babbar, Amol Palekar.

A liar gets what he deserves. (In Hindi.)

p, Debesh Ghosh; d, Hrishikesh Mukherjee; m, Bappi Lahiri.

Comedy **(PR:NR MPAA:NR)**

JILTED† (1987, Aus.) 89m Mermaid Beach c

Richard Moir *(Al)*, Jennifer Cluff *(Harry)*, Steve Jacobs *(Bob)*, Tina Bursill *(Paula)*, Helen Mutkins *(Cindy)*, Ken Radley *(Doug)*.

Director Bennett's second film of the year (the first, DEAR CARDHOLDER, was shown at Cannes) stars his wife Cluff as a tough, independent, sensual woman who also happens to have almost no hair. She, like everyone else in the film, has jilted or been jilted by a lover. She arrives at an Australian resort, Fraser Island, and quickly throws the lives of the employees into disarray. She carries on an intense love affair with Moir, the hotel's cook, which in turn makes the manager, Jacobs, jealous. It also infuriates the hotel's accountant and a waitress—Bursill and Mutkins—both of whom have laid claims to Moir. The situation grows increasingly tense until the characters' emotional and sexual frustrations explode.

p, Bill Bennett, Jenny Day; d&w, Bill Bennett; ph, Geoff Simpson; m, Michael Atkinson ed, Denise Hunter.

Comedy/Drama **(PR:O MPAA:NR)**

JIM OCH PIRATERNA BLOM† (1987, Swed.) 91m Svensk Filmindustri-Stugan/Svensk Filmindustri c (Trans: Jim and the Pirates)

Johan Akerblom *(Jim)*, Ewa Froling *(His Mother)*, Stellan Skarsgard *(His Late Father)*, Jan Malmsjo *(Mother's Suitor)*, Hans Alfredson *(Mr. Kick-the-Bucket)*, Stig Olin *(Potato Al)*, Carl Billquist *(The Teacher)*, Lena T. Hansson *(Inez)*, Kenneth Milldorf *(Bruno)*, Jesper Danielsson/Sten Hellstrom *(Eskil Blom)*, Christina Schultzberg/Rolf Adolfsson *(Adam Blom)*, My Skarsgard, Sam Skarsgard, Borje Norrman, Mats Bergman, Vanja Rodefeldt, Jim Hughes.

When a little boy's father dies, he uses his very vivid imagination to create an adventurous fantasy world. The movie, screened at the Berlin Children's Film Festival in 1987, takes its name from "Terry and the Pirates" an American comic strip of the 1940s and 1950s (the strip was titled "Jim and the Pirates" in Europe).

p, Waldemar Bergendal; d, Hans Alfredson; w, Hans Alfredson, Stellan Skarsgard; ph, Ralph Evers, Bertil Rosengren (Eastmancolor); m, Stefan Nilsson; ed, Jan Persson; prod d, Stig Boquist; cos, Cecilia Lagergren, Gunilla Alfredson.

Children's **(PR:NR MPAA:NR)**

JINGCHA GUSHI (SEE: POLICE STORY, 1987, Hong Kong)

JITTEMAI (SEE: DEATH SHADOWS, 1987, Jap.)

JOCKS zero (1987) 90m Mt. Olympus/Crown c (AKA: ROAD TRIP)

Scott Strader *(The Kid)*, Perry Lang *(Jeff)*, Mariska Hargitay *(Nicole)*, Richard Roundtree *(Chip Williams)*, R.G. Armstrong *(Coach Beetlebom)*, Christopher Lee *(President White)*, Stoney Jackson *(Andy)*, Adam Mills *(Tex)*, Trinidad Silva *(Chito)*, Don Gibb *(Ripper)*, Katherine Kelly Lang *(Julie)*, Tom Shadyac *(Chris)*, Christopher Murphy *(Tony)*.

A pathetic and insufferable "comedy" about a college tennis team from Los Angeles which must win the championship or be cut out of the school's athletic program. College president Lee pressures athletic director Armstrong (who sports a silly toupee) to produce a championship team, or else. Armstrong, who thinks tennis is a "pansy sport," would prefer to cut the tennis program completely and spend the extra money on football. After tennis coach Roundtree pleads with him, Armstrong gives the team one last chance. The star of the team is Strader, a delinquent stud whose habitual partying has landed him on probation from the team. He's reinstated, however, and the team heads to Las Vegas for the regional finals. Besides Strader, the team of misfits includes Lang, a puritanical rich kid who's afraid of the ball; Silva, a Mexican who jumps around, babbles in Spanish, and prays; Jackson, an effeminate black; and Gibb, a bearded animal who is better suited to be a football linebacker. Instead of practicing for upcoming matches, this motley crew drinks to excess, dances till dawn, and dreams about easy sex. Taking a special interest in Strader is the pretty Hargitay (daughter of Jayne Mansfield and Mickey Hargitay), who refuses to help Strader's opponents conspire against him. Despite the team's lack of sleep and practice, they still manage to emerge victorious by the film's predictable end.

A full-blown time-waster, JOCKS has almost nothing going for it. The script is mindless and the acting is about as bad as can be imagined (even the veterans can't save it, nor can Roundtree's noble attempt). The thoroughly sophomoric plot is just too much to be believed. In fact, there's hardly any plot at all—just a bunch of college kids (half of whom are played by actors who are well into their thirties) who hang out in Vegas. The director tosses in a lot of sex jokes, a few topless girls, numerous references to Corona Beer, and two unbearably lengthy tennis matches. On top of it all, a substandard rock 'n' roll score runs throughout the picture. The songs include: "Foxy Lady," "Dirty with You" (David McHugh, performed by John Finley), "Tonight," "Got Some Lovin' for You" (McHugh, performed by Pamela Neal), "Road Trip" (Phillip Kennard, Tim Bryson, Bob Irving, performed by Kennard), "Misbehavin' " (Kennard, performed by Phillip Kennard and The Pups), "How Many Times" (Linda "Peaches" Green, performed by Green), "Power Play" (Green, Stephen Tavani, Rhet Lawrence, performed by Jimmy Osmond), "Body Bruiser" (Green, Tavani, Clay Mitchell, performed by Tavani), "Gettin' Hot in Here" (Tavani, Renee Ruff, Barry Ruff, performed by Green), "Sugar and Spice" (Linda McCrary, John Black, R. Ruff, B. Ruff, performed by Green), "Willie Willie" (David Backstrom, performed by Backstrom, Don Evans, Terry Wilson), "In Trouble Again" (Backstrom, Wilson, performed by Backstrom, Wilson). *(Nudity, excessive profanity, substance abuse, sexual situations.)*

p, Ahmet Yasa; d, Steve Carver; w, Michael Lanahan, David Oas; ph, Adam Greenberg (DeLuxe Color); m, David McHugh; ed, Richard Halsey, Tom Siiter; art d, Randy Ser; set d, Gregory Melton; m/l, David McHugh, Phillip Kennard, Tim Bryson, Bob Irving, Linda "Peaches" Green, Stephen Tavani, Rhet Lawrence, Clay Mitchell, Renee Ruff, Barry Ruff, Linda McCrary, John Black, David Backstrom, Terry Wilson; makeup, Ali Greene.

Comedy **Cas.** **(PR:O MPAA:R)**

JOHN AND THE MISSUS† (1987, Can.) 90m Cinema Group Ent.-CBC-Telefilm Canada-Ontario Film Development Corp. c

Gordon Pinsent *(John Munn)*, Jackie Burroughs *(Missus, John's Wife)*, Randy Follett *(Matt)*, Jessica Steen *(Faith)*, Roland Hewgill *(Fred Budgell)*, Timothy Webber *(Denny Boland)*, Neil Munro *(Tom Noble)*, Michael Wade *(Sid Pedigrew)*, Jerry Doyle *(Alf Sheppard)*, Jane Dingle, Frank Holden, Barry Greene, Ricky Raymond, Austin Davis, Judy Furlong, Brian Downey, Kevin Noble, Lulu Keating, Doug Seymour, Rick Hollett, Paul Steffler, Mack Furlong.

It's 1962 and a copper mine in Newfoundland has been closed, spelling economic doom for a nearby town. Government officials begin resettling the locals elsewhere, but one man refuses to go along with the plan, and struggles to save the place which has been his family's home for generations. Canadian actor Pinsent made his directorial debut here, adapting a novel he wrote in 1973. The film was screened at the US Film Festival in Park City, Utah.

p, Peter O'Brian, John Hunter; d&w, Gordon Pinsent (based on his novel); ph, Frank Tidy (Medallion color); m, Michael Conway Baker; ed, Bruce Nyznik; art d, Earl Preston; set d, Jeanie M. Staple; cos, Olga Dimitrov; makeup, Suzanne Benoit.

Drama **(PR:NR MPAA:PG)**

JOHNNY MONROE† (1987, Fr.) 80m ATC 3000-FR3 c

Jean-Luc Orofino *(Johnny Monroe)*, Philippe Caroit *(Ben)*, Jean-Pierre Aumont, Marisa Pavan, Gerard Guillaumat, Patrick Depeyrat, Jacqueline Danno, Clementine Celarie, Brigitte Lahaie.

A *film noir*-influenced buddy film which stars Orofino as a young midget who idolizes Marilyn Monroe (hence his name) and Caroit as a handsome, mute who befriends him. Orofino has criminal connections and introduces Caroit into the underworld, exposing him to prostitution, thievery, and high-living. A debut feature from Saint-Pierre, whose background is in television documentaries.

p, Benjamin Simon, Jacques Portet; d, Renaud Saint-Pierre; w, Louis Bellanti, Virginie Kirsch; ph, Serge Marcheux; m, Jean Musy; ed, Alain Caron.

Drama **(PR:NR MPAA:NR)**

JOR† (1987, Nor.) A.S. Mefistofilm c

Amanda Francisca Oms, Oyvin Berven, John Ege.

When a naive boy from the Norwegian countryside travels to Oslo in the hope of finding a girl friend, he hooks up with a prostitute/heroin addict who is already involved with someone else. Together they search for love and redemption, challenging the limitations of their relationships.

p&d, Svend Wam, Petter Vennerod; w, Svend Wam, Petter Vennerod, John Ege (based on a novel by Erland Kiosterud); ph, Philip Ogaard.

Drama **(PR:NR MPAA:NR)**

JUANA LA CANTINERA† (1987, Mex.) 91m Producciones Filmicas Rolo/Peliculas Mexicanas c (Trans: Juana the Saloon Keeper)

Rossy Mendoza *(Juana)*, Alvaro Zermeno *(Pancho)*, Ana Luisa Peluffo, Federico Villa, Ivonne Govea, Pedro Rodriguez, Yolanda Ciani, Jaime Reyes, Fernando Loza, Ireida Marquez, Cari Conesa.

A collection of a half-dozen different stories which examine the depravity that exists in today's society. The stories range from a man who demands that his infertile wife become pregnant in order to prove his verility, thereby forcing her into an adulterous affair, to a rape victim's revenge on her attackers. Shown in a New York neighborhood theater.

p,d&w, Pepe Loza; ph, Antonio Ruiz; m, Javier del Rio; ed, Enrique Murillo.

Drama **(PR:O MPAA:NR)**

JULIA'S GEHEIM† (1987, Neth.) 105m Topaz/Cinemien c (Trans: Juliet's Secret)

Funda Mujde *(Arzu)*, Nahit Guvendi *(Ibrahim)*.

Mujde is a young Turkish girl living in the Netherlands with her dressmaker father Guvendi. Mujde wants desperately to appear in her school theater group's presentation of "Romeo and Juliet," but her father will not allow it. She is chosen to play Juliet and must lie to her father in order to attend rehearsals. He eventually learns the truth, but is swayed by his daughter and school officials to let her appear on stage. In Dutch and Turkish, the film addresses the plight of the large Turkish population in the Netherlands.

p, Tom Burghard; d&w, Hans Hylkema; ph, Fred Mckenkamp (Eastmancolor); ed, Hetty Konink; art d, Anne Marie van Beverwijk.

Drama **(PR:NR MPAA:NR)**

JUNTOS† (1987, Mex.) 91m Producciones Rosales Duran/Peliculas Mexicanas c (Trans: Together)

Oscar Athie *(Himself)*, Laura Flores *(Laura)*, Hector Kiev [Tacho] *(Martin, Athie's Manager)*, Elvira Lodi *(Diana)*, Rafael Amador *(Rafael)*, Eduardo Noriega, Jorge Fegan, Carla Rodriguez, Bruno Rey, Pedro Vaquier, Ernesto Juarez, Jorge Abaunza, Gerardo Flores.

Loosely based on the life of Athie, a popular singer/actor in Mexico, the film chronicles his rise from poverty in Mexico City to become one of his country's biggest stars.

p, Robert Rosales Duran, Enrique Rosales Duran; d, Rafael Rosales Duran; w, Rafael Rosales Duran, Reynaldo Diaz; ph, Manuel Tejada (Eastmancolor); m, Marcos Flores; ed, Enrique Murillo.

Biography **(PR:NR MPAA:NR)**

KAK STAT SCHASTLIVYM† (1987, USSR) 89m Mosfilm/Sovexportfilm c (Trans: How to Be Happy)

Nikolai Karachentzev, Marina Diuzheva, Lev Durov, Vsevolod Shilovsky.

A young man in Moscow harbors dreams of being a famous novelist, but despite several years of fruitless effort he still refuses to admit that he lacks the skills necessary to succeed as a writer. One day the inventor of a machine that determines professional aptitude arrives in Moscow and sets about testing the local youth. Although many doubt the accuracy of the inventor's device, ten years later his predictions prove true—those who entered into fields of endeavour that the machine suggested begin to excell. The frustrated writer finally realizes the truth and abandons his dream in favor of a career more suited to his talents.

d, Yury Chuliukin; w, Georgy Kushnirenko, Yury Chuliukin; ph, Evgeny Guslinsky; m, Vladimir Dashkevitch.

Comedy **(PR:NR MPAA:NR)**

KALYANA THAMBULAM† (1987, India)

Sobhan Babu, Shanti.

(In Tamil.)

d, Bapu.

Drama **(PR:NR MPAA:NR)**

KAMPEN OM DEN RODE KO† (1987, Den.) 82m Regner Grasten-Obber Bov I/S-Special Assignment I/S c (Trans: The Fight for the Red Cow)

Jarl Friis Mikkelsen *(Svend Aage)*, Ole Stephensen *(Niels Peder)*, Axel Strobye *(Lawyer)*, Mari-Anne Jespersen *(Nicolette)*, Poul Bundgaard *(The Count)*, Anne Cathrine Herdorff *(Irma)*, Morten Eisner *(Morten)*, Preben Kristensen, Jacob Haugaard, Hanne Borchsenius, Thomas Eje, Jens Okking, Claus Nissen, Ulf Pilgaard, Lisbeth Dhal, Claus Ryskjar, Ellen Winther-Lembourn.

Popular television comedy duo Friis Mikkelsen and Stephensen add directing to their chores in this, their third feature film. Friis Mikkelsen is a vagabond and Stephensen a farmer who become involved with a beautiful young maiden and a financially-strapped count who is about to lose his estate. Because the count bet his fortune on an upcoming horse race, the duo must steal a local cow which has been known to predict the winner of such races with an authoritative moo. An unscrupulous lawyer out to get the count's land is also after the magic cow and soon the forces of good and evil are battling over possession of the psychic bovine. The comedy team's first two films were huge hits in Denmark.

d&w, Jarl Friis Mikkelsen, Ole Stephensen; ph, Peter Klitgaard (Agfacolor); m, Jan Glasel, Jarl Friis Mikkelsen; ed, May Soya.

Comedy **(PR:NR MPAA:NR)**

KAMILLA OG TYVEN† (1987, Nor.) Penelopefilm c (Trans: Kamilla and the Thief)

Veronica Flat, Dennis Storhoi, Agnete G. Haaland, Helge Nygaard.

Set in 1913, this film follows a young orphan girl, Kamilla, as she goes to live with her older sister. On the way she is attacked by a gang of children, but rescued by an older boy named Sebastian. Once safe at her sister's house and enrolled in school, Kamilla makes a bet with her friends that she can enter the local "haunted house" at midnight and stay for several minutes without coming to harm. The bet is made and Karmilla enters the house to discover her rescuer, Sebastian, hiding from the police. He admits to her that he is thief and Karmilla is left to decide whether to turn her friend in or help him escape. Filmed both in Norwegian and English.

p, Odd Hynnekleiv; d&w, Grete Salomonsen; ph, Tom McDougall.

Children's **(PR:NR MPAA:NR)**

KAPITAN "PILIGRIMA"† (1987, USSR) 118m Kiev Film Studio/ Sovexportfilm c (Trans: A Captain of "The Pilgrim")

Vyacheslav Khodchenko, Albert Filozov, Nodar Mgaloblishvili, Vergilio Echmendia, Lev Durov, Tatiana Parkina.

Based on the Jules Verne novel *The Fifteen-Year-Old Captain*, this film follows the adventures of a young ship's boy who is forced to assume command after his captain has been killed by the evil Negoro. The villain puts the ship off course and the survivors land in Africa instead of their original destination, Bolivia. The travelers are kidnapped by slave traders and it is up to the heroic boy to make good their escape.

d, Andrei Prachenko; w, Alexander Guselnikov (based on the novel *The Fifteen-Year-Old Captain* by Jules Verne); ph, Vasily Trushkovsky, Alexei Zolotaryov.

Children's/Drama **(PR:NR MPAA:NR)**

KAPKAN DLYA SHAKALOV† (1987, USSR) 81m Tajikfilm/Sovexportfilm c (Trans: Jackal Trap)

Alla Renzyayeva, Nurillo Abdullayev, Andrei Podoshyan, Yunus Yusupov, Vadim Mikheyenko.

Soviet-produced murder mystery set in the Turkestan region of central Asia which is divided among the Soviets, Chinese, and Afghans. Inspectors from the Ministry for Home Affairs are assigned to uncover a series of murders in the region. Their chief suspect, however, sets out to uncover the culprit himself and only gets in the way of the offical investigation. The answer to the mystery lies with a stolen cache of treasure which was almost spirited abroad during the first few years of Soviet rule in Turkestan.

d, Mukadas Mahmudov; w, Vladimir Akimov; ph, Okil Khamidov, Avraam Abramov; m, Tolib Shakhidi; art d, Abdulsalom Abdullayev.

Crime **(PR:NR MPAA:NR)**

KARUSEL NA BAZARNOY PLOSHCHADI† (1987, USSR) 88m Mosfilm/ Sovexportfilm c (Trans: Merry-Go-Round in a Market Square)

Regimantas Adomaitis, Sergei Garmash, Yelena Bondarchuk, Galina Dyomina, Nadezhda Butyrtseva.

As the end of WW II approaches a war hero who was blinded in battle takes a job playing accordian and running a merry-go-round for the local children. There he meets a military plant truck driver who was badly injured in a crash that killed an innocent woman. Guilt-ridden over the tragedy, the driver vowed to provide for the dead woman's three daughter and their grandmother. Unfortunately, the country is in the midst of a famine and the driver cannot feed his charges. The merry-go-round man offers to accompany the driver into the country to exchange clothes for food, but the men are ambushed in the forest and the blind man is killed. The blind man's widow takes her husband's place on the accordian and the driver runs the merry-go-round.

d, Nikolai Stambula; w, Albert Likhanov; ph, Boris Bondarenko; m, Oleg Yanchenko; art d, Nikolai Saushkin, Rais Nagayev.

Drama **(PR:NR MPAA:NR)**

KATAKU NO HITO† (1987, Jap.) 132m c (Trans: House on Fire)

Ken Ogata *(Kazuo Katsura)*, Ayumi Ishida *(Yoriko Katsura)*, Mieko Harada *(Keiko Yajima)*, Keiko Matsuzaka *(Yoko)*.

Based on the autobiographical novel by Kazuo Dan, this film recounts the tumultuous life of a writer trying to fulfill his roles as artist, husband, father, and lover. His immoderate lifestyle causes the key women in his life—his long-suffering wife and his mistress—to abandon him. Left alone with his six children, one of whom is terminally ill, he compulsively chronicles his troubled life for an adoring public.

p, Tan Takawa, Masao Sato; d, Kinji Fukasaku; w, Fumo Konami, Kinji Fukasaku (based on the novel by Kazuo Dan); ph, Daisaku Kimura; m, Takayuki Inoue.

Biography **(PR:NR MPAA:NR)**

KATHAKKU PINNIL† (1987, India) Merrit Enterprises

Mammooty, Nedumudi Venu, Thilakan, Ganesh, M.G. Soman, Jagathy, Surya, Devilalitha, Vijayalakshmi.

A playwright finds inspiration in the suffering of a young woman who has been taken advantage of by her cheating beau. Eventually, even art fails to make her pain palatable and she resorts to murder.

d, K.G. George; m, Ouseppachan.

Crime **(PR:NR MPAA:NR)**

KAUN KITNEY PAANI MEIN† (1987, India)

Mahendra Sandhu, Anuradha Patel, Anupam Kher, Danny, Amjad Khan.

The good cop at the center of this Indian film finds himself fighting an uphill battle. The criminals he is trying to bring to justice have the support of the crooked chief of police. (In Hindi.)

p, Mahendra Sandhu; m, Rax Laxman.

Crime **(PR:NR MPAA:NR)**

KAZHDYY OKHOTNIK ZHELAET ZNAT† (1987, USSR) 75m Kiev/Sovexportfilm c (Trans: Every Hunter Wants to Know)

Yegor Goloborodko, Rimma Markova, Sasha Bovtun, Yevgeny Pashin.

A young boy becomes attached to a stray dog and is thrilled when a local movie studio picks the hound to star in its latest production: a film about a dog that saves a fighter pilot. When the true owner of the dog arrives to reclaim her pet, the boy lies about the dog's whereabouts, but his grandmother forces the boy to return the dog and teaches her grandson a lesson about lying.

d&w, Michail Ilyenko; ph, Bogdan Verzhbitsky; m, Eduard Artemyev; art d, Alexander Sheremet.

Children's **(PR:NR MPAA:NR)**

KE DYO AVGA TOURKIAS† (1987, Gr.) 98m c (Trans: And Two Eggs from Turkey)

Dimitris Piatas *(Mustafa)*, Antonis Kafetzopoulos *(Yannis)*, Timos Perlengas *(Uncle)*, Athena Papa *(German Girl)*, Dimitris Poulicacos *(Gasoline Salesman)*, Dora Colanaki *(Grandmother)*.

This unlikely comedy is set against the backdrop of the longtime conflict between the Greeks and the Turks. Piatas, a Turk, is sent to the Greek border to deliver a package containing what he later learns to be drugs. Kafetzopoulos, a young Greek, meets him at the border and receives the shipment. Piatas then persuades his contact to allow him accompany him back to Athens, where he hopes to meet his grandmother, who he has been told is Greek. Kafetzopoulos is not particularly thrilled about bringing the Turk along, but he does so and is rewarded for his efforts when Piatas gets him out of jam. Eventually both learn the real nature of their delivery work. More surprisingly, they discover that they are related: Piatas' sought-after grandmother just happens to be Kafetzopoulos' grandmother, too.

p, Sakis Maniatis; d&w, Aris Foriadis; ph, Sakis Maniatis; m, Nicos Portocaloglou; ed, Elvira Varella.

Comedy **(PR:NR MPAA:NR)**

KEEPING TRACK† (1987, Can.) 102m Telescene [Keeping Track]-Telefilm Canada c

Michael Sarrazin *(Daniel Hawkins, TV Anchorman)*, Margot Kidder *(Claire Tremayne, Banking Analyst)*, Alan Scarfe *(Royle Wishert)*, Ken Pogue *(Capt. McCullough)*, John Boylan *(Double Agent)*, Vlasta Vrana *(Chuck)*, Donald Pilon *(Covington)*, James D. Morris *(Shanks)*, Shawn Lawrence, Pierre Zimmer, Louis Negin, Terry Haig, Patricia Phillips, Renee Girard, Leo Ilial, Jon Granik, Bob Pot, Michel Pasquier, Joy Boushel, Danette McKay, Linda Smith, Marc Dnis, Phil Pretten, Brian Dooley, Roland Nincheri, James Rae, Catherine Colvey, Mark Burns, Pier Kohl, Thomas Donohue, Claudia Cardianl, Danielle Lepage, Roger Clown, John Casuccio, Dave Rigby, Robert Parsons, John Walsh, Bill Haugland, Mark Walker, Rob Roy, Gary Plaxton, Raymond Belisle, Ken Ernhoffer, Jacques Des Baillets.

Directed by Robin Spry (PROLOGUE, ONE MAN), one of the brighter lights of the Canadian cinema during the 1960s, this Hitchcock-style thriller also features two Canadians who "went Hollywood" early in their careers, Michael Sarrazin and Margot Kidder. Sarrazin is a TV newsman in Montreal; Kidder is a banking analyst and computer whiz. On a train to New York City, they witness a murder and their attempts to get to the bottom of it involve them in political intrigue. Before long they are dodging the KGB and only a step or two ahead of the Mounties and CIA. It seems the Russians have gotten hold of a US-developed computer chip that is the key element in creating an extraordinary cyborg. Not surprisingly, the Yanks want it back, and Sarrazin and Kidder get caught in the middle. Much of the action is played out against the backdrop of Montreal.

p, Robin Spry, Jamie Brown; d, Robin Spry; w, Jamie Brown (based on a story by Robin Spry, Jamie Brown); ph, Ron Stannett (Sonolab color); m, Ben Low; ed, Diann Ilnicki; prod d, Michel Proulx; cos, Ginette Magny; makeup, Tom Booth; spec eff, Jacques Godbout; stunts, Dave Rigby.

Thriller **(PR:NR MPAA:R)**

KET VALASZTAS MAGYARORSZAGONKET VALASZTAS MAGYARORSZAGON† (1987, Hung.) 94m Mafilm-DIALOG c (Trans: Rear-Guard)

Peter Blasko *(Bodnar)fl, Imre Csiszar (Veres)*, Mari Szemes *(Mrs. Gera)*, Anna Kubik *(Agnes, her daughter)*, Istvan Fonyo *(Harmati)*, Gabor Madi Szabo *(Gruber)*, Andras Fekete *(Jakab)*.

Set during the election reforms of the mid-1980s this film follows the legal-but-unethical political maneuvering of the established leaders of a small town after they discover that the people prefer to elect a newcomer: the progressive director of the rural research institute. The conflict begins when the newcomer advises against a plan for a new quarry because it will destroy the environment. His honesty endears him to the townsfolk, but those already in power detest the interloper and try to freeze him out of the new municipal election which now decrees that there must be more than one candidate. After many dirty tricks, democracy triumphs and the people's choice is elected.

d&w, Andras Kovacs; ph, Ferenc Szecsenyi (Eastmancolor); ed, Maria Szecsenyi; set d, Peter Benedek.

Drama **(PR:NR MPAA:NR)**

KFAFOT† (1987, Israel) Emil Prods. (Trans: Gloves)

Ika Zohar, Ezra Kafri, Sharon Hacohen, Danny Muggia.

Set in Palestine circa WW II, a young Polish immigrant tries to make a name for himself as a boxer.

p, Ami Amir; d, Rafi Adar; w, Judith Sola-Adar, Rafi Adar; ph, Yossi Wein; m, Shalom Hanoch; ed, David Tour; art d, Yoram Sheir.

Drama **(PR:NR MPAA:NR)**

KID BROTHER, THE† (1987, Can./Jap./US) 95m Kinema Amerika-Yoshimura-Gagnon Toho c

Kenny Easterday *(Kenny)*, Caitlin Clarke *(Sharon)*, Liane Curtis *(Sharon Kay)*, Zack Grenier *(Jesse)*, Jesse Easterday, Jr. *(Eddy)*, Tom Reddy *(Billy)*, Alain St.-Alix *(Philippe)*, John Carpenter *(Grandfather)*.

Produced with Japanese money and made by a Canadian, this film is a fictionalized biography of its star, Easterday, a Pennsylvania youth who was born without legs or a lower torso. Easterday gets around by walking on his incredibly strong arms and has developed a remarkable agility. The film follows family conflicts that arise from Easterday's condition and concentrates on the boy's relationship with his teenage sister (played by actress Curtis). Jealous and alienated because she feels Easterday manipulates the family to his advantage, Curtis rebels and runs away to Pittsburgh. Determined to reconcile himself with his sister, Easterday fills a backpack and sets out on his own to find her. Eventually he locates Curtis and in an emotional confrontation brother and sister reveal their true feelings. Screened at the World Film Festival in Montreal, THE KID BROTHER will no doubt find a wide release sometime in 1988.

p, Kiyoshi Fujimoto; d&w, Claude Gagnon, ph, Yudai Kato (Fujicolor); m, Francois Dompierre; ed, Andre Corriveau; prod d, Bill Bilowit; cos, Maureen Hogan.

Drama **(PR:NR MPAA:NR)**

KILL CITY† (1987, Fin.) 73m PetFilms Oy bw

Petteri Salminen, Cal-Kristian Rundman, Tuula Amberla, Ville Nisonen, Anne-Maria Ylitapio, Jaska Ojala, Bjorn Teir, Shadowplay.

Allegorical drama about a group of alienated teens who set up their own society in an abandoned industrial building they dub "Kill City." The youths set up a resistance movement against the establishment and develop a computer system that enables them to break into the memory banks of financial institutions and transfer funds illegally. A ruthless detective representing the status quo is assigned the task of quashing the youthful rebellion and destroying Kill City.

d&w, Peter Lindholm; ph, Timo Telsavaara; ed, Jaska Ojala.

Drama **(PR:NR MPAA:NR)**

KILLER WORKOUT zero (1987) 86m Maverick/Winters Group c (AKA: AEROBICIDE)

Marcia Karr *(Rhonda Johnson/Valerie Johnson)*, David James Campbell *(Lt. Morgan)*, Fritz Matthews *(Jimmy Hallick)*, Ted Prior *(Chuck Dawson)*, Teresa Vander Woude *(Jaimy)*, Richard Bravo *(Tom)*, Dianne Copeland *(Debbie)*, Laurel Mock *(Diane Matthews)*, Lynn Meighan *(Cathy)*, Teresa Truesdale *(Rachael)*, Denise Martell *(Martha)*, Michael Beck *(Curtis)*, Deborah Norris *(Office Girl)*, Larry Reynolds *(Officer Peterson)*, Sharon Young, Irene Korman, Carol Maxwell *(Locker Room Girls)*, Charles Venniro, Pat Statham *(Paramedics)*, John Robb, Joel Hoffman, Wes Montgomery, Joseph Chandler, James Steele, Ronald Dais *(Weightlifters)*, Kellyann Sabatasso, Elizabeth Keeme, Veronica Davis, Sheila Howard, Kris Hagerty, Andrea Drever, Monica Karlson, Kathi Miller, Lorain Joyner, Lori E. Forsberg, Kima Lindquist, Eddie Swilling, Richard Turner, Krysia Javid *(Aerobics Dancers)*, Marilyn Pitzer, Tracy Rowe, Tamara, Vikki Lynn Vander Woude, Ellen Cole, Gina Varela, John Villani, Renessa Wasserman *(Gym Extras)*, Elke Muller *(Rhonda's Body Double)*.

An uneventful whodunit with enough bloody murders to classify as a slasher film, KILLER WORKOUT is set almost entirely in a Hollywood health club. The picture opens with a faceless young woman disrobing and getting into a tanning bed. An electrical fire starts and turns the curvaceous tanner into a screaming piece of toast. The scene shifts to "Rhonda's Workout," a spa run by the pretty Karr. The top aerobics instructor is Vander Woude who, like everyone else, prances about in revealing, skin-tight leotards. Physical fitness has its price, however, especially for one unlucky girl who is caught after hours in the shower by a safety-pin-wielding attacker who pokes her jugular. (This isn't your average safety pin, mind you, but a jumbo-sized one, although it sure pales in comparison to the standard butcher knife.) The hard-as-nails detective assigned to the case is Campbell, who overplays his tough guy image with an excess of intensity. A number of other murders follow, most performed with that goshdarned safety pin. Campbell digs into Karr's past, and learns that five years earlier she was headed for the top of the modeling world . . . before getting into the combustible tanning bed seen at the film's start. Resentful of all the perfectly contoured bodies that have passed daily through her club, she has decided to take revenge. But wait . . . the police have picked up Matthews, a local lunatic who is obsessed with Karr and has been identified as the killer. Time passes and the apparently innocent Karr is left to run her club. Campbell knows better, however, and lures

Karr out into the woods. Distraught because the legal system has failed, he prepares to execute Karr himself. In a surprise twist, Karr kills the little fascist and returns to her club ready to continue her killing spree.

A technically shabby production, KILLER WORKOUT is filled with plot holes and characters that act with absolutely no motivation. The basic premise—that a once-beautiful model (who incidentally is still beautiful) would go on a killing spree and use a safety pin as a weapon—is silly enough without having to subject the viewer to the uninspired acting and dim-witted scripting. Thankfully, the film is tame in comparison to most slasher films, allowing most of the bloodletting to take place offscreen and subjecting the viewer only to the bloody aftermath (a consideration which is more budgetary than it is humanitarian). What the film does have is an excess of aerobics dancers and a camera that dwells on all the possible anatomical angles. It should come as no surprise that KILLER WORKOUT never saw a theatrical release, seeing only the inside of a video store. The beat-heavy soundtrack includes a number of songs to which the viewer can perform his own aerobics routine. This way maybe some pounds can be shed while one watches. Songs include: "Woman on Fire" (Chip Halstead, John Melton, performed by Jill Colucci), "Only You Tonite" (Todd Hayen, David Cohen, Janice Cohen, performed by Donna De Lory), "Some Things Never Change," "Dust It Off" (Frank Hawkins, performed by The Lost Playboy Club), "Love Is a Four Letter Word" (Halstead, Bob McGilpin, John Hoke, Michael Thompson, performed by Didi Nelson), "Knockout" (Robert Michaels, performed by Michaels, Lisa Duran), "Animal Workout" (Michael Blum, performed by Pebbles Phillips), "Rock N'Roll" (Sunny Hilden, Joe Steinman, performed by Hilden), "Something to Feel" (Steve McClintock, Tim James, Tim Hientz, performed by Gina Harlan), "Aerobi-cide" (Dan Radlayer, performed by Mary Hylan). *(Nudity, sexual situations, excessive profanity, violence).*

p, Peter Yuval, David A. Prior; d&w, David A. Prior; ph, Peter Bonilla, Stephen Ashley-Blake (United color); m, Todd Hayen; ed, David A. Prior; ch, Sheila Howard, Dianne Copeland; m/l, Chip Halstead, John Melton, Todd Hayen, David Cohen, Janice Cohen, Frank Hawkins, Bob McGilpin, John Hoke, Michael Thompson, Robert Michaels, Michael Blum, Sunny Hilden, Joe Steinman, Steve McClintock, Tim James, Tim Hientz, Dan Radlayer; makeup, Robin Beauchesne, Suzana Rupe.

Horror **Cas.** **(PR:O MPAA:R)**

KILLER'S NOCTURNE† (1987, Hong Kong) 98m Bo Ho/Golden Harvest c

Alex Man, Chin Siu-ho, Patricia Ha, Tsen Yin.

Set in the fabled Shanghai of the 1930s, Chin Siu-Ho stars as the son of a wealthy man who was disgraced and then murdered by the evil gangster Alex Man. Chin Siu-Ho is given the chance to win back his family's honor in a game of mahjong. The film follows his training for the big game and includes several wild martial-arts battles. (In Cantonese with English subtitles).

d, Nam Lai-Choi; w, Man Chun (based on a story by Wong Ching); ph, Nam Nai Choi.

Action **(PR:NR MPAA:NR)**

KILLING TIME, THE† (1987) 95m New World c

Beau Bridges *(Sheriff Sam Wayburn)*, Kiefer Sutherland *(Brian Mars, Deputy)*, Wayne Rogers *(Jake Winslow)*, Joe Don Baker *(Sheriff Carl Cunningham)*, Camelia Kath *(Laura Winslow)*, Janet Carroll *(Lila Dagget)*, Michael Madsen *(Stu)*.

This low-budget crime thriller cast in the mold of James M. Cain and Jim Thompson features Sutherland as a mysterious drifter who murders a deputy sheriff and then assumes the dead man's identity. He then drifts into the sleepy seaside town of Santa Alba where he is hired as the new deputy by retiring sheriff Baker. Meanwhile, Baker's heir apparent, Bridges, has become entangled in a torrid romance with former flame Kath, who is now married to slimy real estate developer Rogers. The profit-hungry Rogers wants to construct a housing development in Santa Alba, but the locals worry that his project will destroy the town's quaintness. Eventually Bridges and Kath decide to murder Rogers and frame new-guy-in-town Sutherland for the crime. Unfortunately, the mysterious Sutherland is more than they have bargained for. THE KILLING TIME received a quick play-off in a limited number of markets and will no doubt find life on the video rental shelves.

p, Peter Abrams, Robert L. Levy; d, Rick King; w, Don Bohlinger, James Nathan, Bruce Franklin Singer; ph, Paul H. Goldsmith (Foto-Kem Color); m, Paul Chihara; ed, Lorenzo de Stefano; prod d, Bernt Amadeus Capra; set d, Byrnadette Di Santo; cos, Jean-Pierre Dorleac.

Crime **(PR:NR MPAA:R)**

KIN-DZA-DZA† (1987, USSR) 134m Mosfilm/Sovexportfilm c

Stanislav Lyubshin, Yevgeny Leonov, Yury Yakovlev, Levan Gabriadze.

This Soviet science-fiction comedy-with-a-point follows the exploits of a student and an engineer who suddenly find themselves transported to a desertlike planet. Friendly inhabitants inform the Earthlings this wasteland was once a nice place to live but because its environment was abused, desert sands have buried its towns and vegetation, and left its inhabitants amoral shells of the civilized creatures they once were.

d, Georgy Danelia; w, Revaz Gabriadze, Georgy Danelia; ph, Pavel Lebeshev; m, Gia Kancheli; art d, Alexander Samulekin, Teodor Tezhik.

Comedy **(PR:NR MPAA:NR)**

KINDRED, THE*½ (1987) 91m Norkat/F-M Entertainment c

David Allen Brooks *(John Hollins)*, Rod Steiger *(Dr. Phillip Lloyd)*, Amanda Pays *(Melissa Leftridge)*, Talia Balsam *(Sharon Raymond)*, Kim Hunter *(Amanda Hollins)*, Timothy Gibbs *(Hart Phillips)*, Peter Frechette *(Brad Baxter)*, Julia Montgomery *(Cindy Russell)*, Bunki Z *(Nell Valentine)*, Charles Grueber *(Harry)*, Bennet Guillory *(Dr. Stone)*, Edgar Small *(Dr. Larson)*, James Boeke *(Jackson)*, Randy Harrington *(Paramedic)*, Ben Perry *(Porsche Driver)*, Betty Freeman *(Nurse)*, John Farmer *(Minister)*, Steve Conte *(Orderly)*, Michael Shawn McCracken *(Full-Sized Anthony)*.

For what begins as a fairly promising low-budget ($2.5 million) science-fiction effort, THE KINDRED suddenly goes awry in its last half and collapses into a mess of mini-climaxes and disappointing special effects. Brooks stars as a young scientist whose dying mother, Hunter, also a scientist, begs him to destroy his "brother" Anthony upon her death. Brooks, however, is a bit puzzled by Hunter's last request because—to his knowledge—he has no brother. Gathering up his scientist girl friend, Balsam, and an odd assortment of young assistants, Brooks decides to spend a long weekend at his mother's home/laboratory to organize her legacy of genetic research. At Hunter's funeral, Brooks meets a beautiful young Oxford graduate, Pays, whose career has been inspired by Hunter. The woman volunteers to help Brooks and his team with Hunter's papers. Brooks accepts the offer—much to the dismay of Balsam—and invites her to join them. Soon after their arrival, Brooks' dog falls victim to a hideous tentacled creature that lives beneath the floorboards. Meanwhile, Steiger, a crazed genetic scientist who once worked with Hunter, knows that Anthony is a hybrid creature that Hunter had cloned from a cell sample of Brooks (hence, his "brother"). Steiger becomes determined to retrieve the creature alive and take credit for Hunter's research (he has a basement full of grotesque failed genetic experiments). Predictably, Anthony begins growing and attacks several young scientists. Pays turns out to be Steiger's agent, sent to protect Anthony, but after she reveals that her sympathies now lie with Brooks (with whom she has fallen in love), an angry Steiger withholds her "medicine." Before she can warn Brooks, Pays collapses and turns into a huge fish (Steiger had created her by crossing human genes with those of a fish). Brooks soon learns the truth about his "brother," but decides to destroy him nonetheless. Eventually Steiger decides to intervene personally and arrives at the house to take Anthony back with him. Unfortunately for Steiger, Anthony has grown huge and recalcitrant, and, failing to sympathize with Steiger, kills him. The surviving young scientists burn down the house, and Anthony—who has suddenly spawned dozens of little Anthonys—goes up in flames.

With five screenwriters (PSYCHO's Joseph Stefano among them!) and two directors, you'd think they could have come up with something better than this (to be fair, the directors also number among the writers). While THE KINDRED does boast some decent performances and fairly interesting character interaction, the plot is overly complicated and unengaging. The special effects by Michael McCracken, Sr. are wildly uneven. On the low end of the spectrum is Anthony, a poorly articulated rubber puppet covered with slime that is not particularly effective. McCracken did a better job with the special makeup done on Steiger's "reject" experiments and Pays' transformation into a fish. Although seen only briefly, these horrible creations are grotesque and memorable. The performances from the young cast members are solid, especially those of Balsam (daughter of Martin) and Brooks. Faring less well are veterans Hunter and Steiger. Hunter plays her entire role on her back in a hospital bed and manages to drag out every death-scene cliche in the book. She punctuates her brief appearance with gasping, coughing, wincing, and finally a big sigh as she dies. Steiger is even worse. Sporting a toupee that looks as if it should be living in the basement with his other genetic rejects, this once great actor shamelessly gnaws on the scenery while spouting volumes of scientific mumbo jumbo. Depending on one's viewpoint, Steiger is either wonderfully hammy or pathetically incompetent. The unintentionally funny climax of the film sees Steiger wearing a silly wide-brimmed hat that keeps the 10 gallons of icky slime spewed on his head from dripping in his face. Directors Obrow and Carpenter seem more concerned with impressing big-time producers with their lush production design and impressive cinematography than with telling a good horror story—as if the film is merely a resume. For all its slick trappings, THE KINDRED fails where it matters most—it simply doesn't scare. *(Gore effects, profanity.)*

p, Jeffrey Obrow; d, Jeffrey Obrow, Stephen Carpenter; w, Jeffrey Obrow, Stephen Carpenter, John Penney, Earl Ghaffari, Joseph Stefano; ph, Stephen Carpenter (Technicolor); m, David Newman; ed, John Penney, Earl Ghaffari; prod d, Chris Hopkins; art d, Becky Block; set d, Susan Emshwiller; cos, Lynne A. Holmes; spec eff, Michael John McCracken, Sr.; makeup, Matthew Mungle.

Science Fiction **Cas.** **(PR:O MPAA:R)**

KINEMA NO TENCHI (SEE: FINAL TAKE: THE GOLDEN DAYS OF MOVIES, 1987, Jap.)

KISS DADDY GOOD NIGHT† (1987) 80m Beast of Eden c

Uma Thurman *(Laura)*, Paul Dillon *(Sid)*, Paul Richards *(William B. Tilden)*, Steve Buscemi *(Johnny)*, Annabelle Gurwitch *(Sue)*, David Brisbin *(Nelson Blitz)*.

Thurman (a 16-year-old fashion model) stars as a beautiful-but-crazed blonde who dons a variety of wigs and sexy outfits in order to pick up unsuspecting men and bring them back to her apartment where she injects them with a drug and steals their valuables. Her neighbor, Richards, is a strange old man who becomes obsessed with Thurman's resemblance to his daughter and slowly works his way into her confidence. The feature film debut of Viennese director Huemer, KISS DADDY GOOD NIGHT was shot in New York City on 16mm film stock and received a screening at the American Film Institute Independent Film Festival. Major distribution failed to materialize in 1987, but the film may go the home video route.

p, Maureen O'Brien, William Ripka; d, Peter Ily Huemer; w, Peter Ily Huemer, Michael Gabrieli (based on a story by Peter Ily Huemer); ph, Bobby Bukowski; m, Don King, Duncan Lindsay; ed, Ila von Hasperg.

Crime **(PR:NR MPAA:NR)**

KITCHEN TOTO, THE† (1987, Brit.) 95m British Screen-Film Four-Skreba/Cannon c

Bob Peck *(John Graham)*, Phyllis Logan *(Janet Graham)*, Edwin Mahinda *(Mwangi)*, Kirsten Hughes *(Mary)*, Robert Urquhart *(D.C. McKinnon)*, Nicholas Chase *(Mugo, the Houseboy)*, Job Seda *(Kamau)*, Leo Wringer *(Sgt. Stephen)*, Edward Judd *(Dick Luis)*, Nathan Dambuza Mdledle *(Mwangi's Father)*, Ann Wanjugu *(Mwangi's Mother)*, Ronald Pirie *(Edward Graham)*.

It is 1950, and in Kenya conflicts are brewing between natives and British colonialists. Local Mau Maus have been making periodic raids on the white community, but one black clergyman urges his congregation not to follow in the terrorists' footsteps. After making these controversial statements, the priest is found murdered, and his 12-year-old son Mahinda is left orphaned. Peck, the local British police chief, is persuaded by his wife (Logan) to take in the boy as their "kitchen toto," a colloquialism the whites use to describe their native servants. Mahinda takes the position, but gradually he develops mixed feelings about his station. On one hand, he likes working for Peck and Logan despite their unintentional racism. However, Mahinda feels a yearning for the world he left behind and struggles to resolve this inner conflict. Meanwhile, tensions have further increased between the whites and the Mau Maus. One day, while Peck is sleeping with his mistress (Hughes), the natives attack. Logan is accidentally killed when her son tries to rescue her, and Mahinda is forced to make his inevitably tragic decision about where he stands. Twenty-seven-year-old Hooks, a graduate of England's National Film and Television school, makes his directorial debut with THE KITCHEN TOTO.

p, Ann Skinner; d&w, Harry Hook; ph, Roger Deakins; m, John Keane; ed, Tom Priestley; prod d, Jamie Leonard; cos, Barbara Kidd.

Drama **(PR:NR MPAA:NR)**

KLIOS† (1987, Gr.) 120m Greek Film Center-Profit, Ltd. c (Trans: The Noose)

Giorgos Michalakopoulos, Anna Fonsou, Giorgos Moschidis, Timos Perlegas, Antonis Katsaris, Christos Kalavrouzos, Dinos Lyras, Socrates Alafouzos, Aias Manthopoulos, Dimitris Karabetsis, Yerassimos Skiadaressis, Stelios Pavlou, Vladimiros Kyriakidis.

Set in civil war-torn Greece in 1948, this is the story of six young men who feel the noose of government repression tightening around their necks. Friends and teachers disappear without a word, yet the sham of quotidian existence continues as if there were no war. It all becomes too much for them and they plot to escape, which they accomplish by hijacking a plane to Yugoslavia. Even after they succeed, the noose isn't entirely taken from their necks. The Yugoslav authorities begin to act as if they will turn over the lads to the Greek government. Then they are spirited out of the country, back to Greece, but instead of being given over to the government, they find themselves in the mountains with the rebels, participants in the battle for freedom.

d, Costas Coutsomitis; w, Vangelis Goufas, Costas Coutsomitis, Giorgos Bramos; ph, Nikos Smaragdis; m, Argyris Kounadis; ed; Panos Papakyriakopoulos; cos, Rena Georgiadou.

Drama **(PR:NR MPAA:NR)**

KOL AHAVOTAI† (1987, Israel) 85m YNYL c (Trans: All My Loving)

Alon Aboutboul *(Daniel)*, Ree Rosenfeld *(Sigal)*, Dov Navon *(Oren)*, Dorit Adi, Dalia Malka, Ran Apfelberg.

Told mostly in flashback, this Israeli reminiscence of lost love is conjured up by Aboutboul, a young man who tries to sort out his painful romantic past by writing about it. Most of his reverie centers on Rosenfeld, who was his lover but to whom Aboutboul no longer sends all his loving.

p, Dov Keren; d&w, Yohanan [Jorge] Weller; ph, Gad Danzig; ed, Era Lapid; art d, Yaakov Stein.

Romance **(PR:NR MPAA:NR)**

KOLORMASK† (1987, Kenya) Kenya Film

Greg Adambo *(Dr. John Litodo)*, Caroline Berman *(Eliza Litodo)*, John Okite *(Toby Litodo)*, Constance Mwangemi *(Susan Litodo)*, Ester Njiru *(Auntie Maria)*, Jacqueline C. Davis *(Jacinta Macdonald)*, Jonathan Kariara *(Wilson Macdonald)*, Raymond B. Hamisi *(Joe Macdonald)*, Winnie Kandidah *(Rose Nambi)*, Shuma Ginny Shuma *(Loisy Brown)*, John T. Ngugi *(Mzee Toko)*, Wallace R. Morell *(Tom Johnson)*, Moniccah Adhiambo *(Dorothy Atieno)*, Donna Rey Klumpp *(Agnes Korir)*, Wallace Kairu *(Mzee Akili)*, Joseph Olita *(Uncle Tobosa)*, Anne Kimwele *(Gladys)*, Francis Imbuga *(Hon. Sekone)*, Ka Vundla *(Willo)*.

Examining the clash of European and African cultures, KOLORMASK—the first All-Kenyan film production—stars Adambo as a Kenyan doctor educated in London and Berman as his white English wife. After many years abroad, the couple and their two children return to Nairobi. Initially their life is without conflict, but as time passes the cultural differences emerge.

p,d&w, Sao Gamba; ph, Njuguna Gitau; ed, Tony Muscat; art d&cos, Winnie Oludhe; m/l, Mburak Achieng, Judy Kairo.

Drama **(PR:NR MPAA:NR)**

KOMEDIANCI Z WCZORAJSZEJ ULICY† (1987, Pol.) 105m Zespoly Filmowe-Iluzjon bw-c (Trans: Pretenders from Yesterday's Street)

Jerzy Cnota *(Ujek)*, Joanna Bartel *(Adela)*, Danuta Owczarek *(Krysta)*, Andrzej Chlapek *(Zeflik)*.

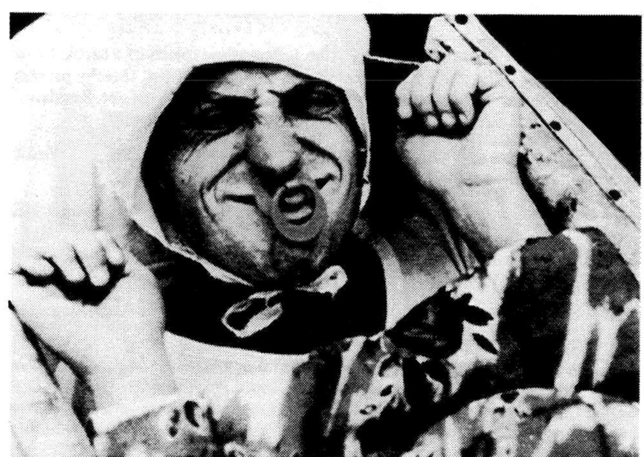

Two policeman on patrol discover a pair of robbers who have broken into a TV shop. Surprisingly, the thieves have delayed robbing the store to watch a film being broadcast that night (director Kidawa's previous effort, THE SINFUL LIFE OF FRANCISZEK BULA). The cops, too, are captivated by the movie and their blundering allows the criminals to escape. Fired from the force, the cops decide to form a street-performance troupe, just like the one they saw in the movie. Unfortunately, they run into a bureaucratic maze of forms, tests, and permits and find that the public is not interested in their act.

d&w, Janusz Kidawa (based on a story by Stanislaw Ligon); ph, Henryk Janas; m, Jaroslaw Kukulski; ed, Agnieszka Bojanowska; set d, Wojciech Majda.

Drama **(PR:NR MPAA:NR)**

KOMEDIANTKA† (1987, Pol.) 118m Zespoly Filmowe-Rondo c (Trans: The Pretender)

Malgorzata Pieczynska *(Janka)*, Beata Tyszkiewicz *(Cabinska)*, Marzena Trybala *(Majkowska)*, Krzysztof Kowalewski *(Cabinski)*.

Based on a novel by Nobel Prize-winning author Wladyslaw Stanislaw Reymont, this film, set early in the 20th century, follows the fortunes of a small-town girl who wants to be a famous actress. Her father, however, does not share her dream and forces her into an arranged marriage. The girl runs away to Warsaw, but the only job she can get is at a dance hall. She meets a handsome actor and they become lovers, but when she loses a big role in a play to a conniving friend, she finds herself alone, pregnant, and depressed enough to consider suicide.

d, Jerzy Sztwiertnia; w, (based on the novel by Wladyslaw Stanislaw Reymont); ph, Andrzej Ramlau; m, Adam Slawinski; ed, Anna Wilska; set d, Bogdan Solle.

Drama **(PR:NR MPAA:NR)**

KOMISSAR† (1987, USSR) 110m Gorky bw (Trans: Commissar)

Nonna Mordukova *(Klavdia Vavilova)*, Rolan Bykov *(Yefim Magazanik)*, Raisa Niedashkovskaya *(Mariya Magazanik)*, Vasili Shukshin *(Commander)*.

Banned in 1967 and unveiled at this year's Moscow Film Festival, where it was hailed by many as a masterpiece of Soviet cinema, KOMISSAR stars Mordukova as a tough, ruthless, woman commissar leading the Red Army in battle in the 1920s. She has an unfaltering devotion to her country and its cause, but her life changes when she becomes pregnant. She says farewell to the army and is quartered by a Jewish family. A strong mutual bond grows between the family and Mordukova as she finds new meaning in her life—a respect for life that comes with her child's birth and a reevaluation of the consequences of war. By the end, however, she returns to the front, leaving her Russian child to be reared by Jews. Clearly a statement against anti-Semitism, the film was immediately shelved by the censors at Gorky Studio in 1967 who called it that studio's "greatest political and aesthetic failure." Askoldov, who has directed only this film, was quickly dismissed by the studio for his "professional inadequacy." Like so many other banned Soviet films, KOMISSAR saw a release this year in light of Mikhail Gorbachev's policy of *glasnost*. KOMISSAR, however, was nearly kept on the shelf. During a press conference at the Moscow Film Festival, a reporter asked Elem Klimov (the first secretary of the Union of Soviet Filmmakers) if all bans had been lifted. Director Askoldov, who was in the audience, then announced that his picture had not yet been cleared for screening. KOMISSAR was then shown as part of the festival, out of competition, in the presence of numerous Soviet officials.

d&w, Alexander Askoldov (based on "The City Of Berdish" by Vasily Grossman); ph, Valeri Ginzberg; m, Alfred Schnitke; ed, Alexander Askoldov.

Drama/War **(PR:NR MPAA:NR)**

KONBU FINZE (SEE: TERRORIZERS, THE, 1987, Taiwan)

KONETS OPERATSII "REZIDENT"† (1987, USSR) M. Gorky/Sovexportfilm c (Trans: The End of Operation "Resident")

Georgy Zhzhenov, Pyotr Velyaminov, Leonid Bronevoi, Leonid Yarmolnik, Irina Azer.

The last entry in a four-film series, this film follows the exploits of a heroic Soviet agent who uncovers a plot to kidnap a powerful rocket scientist, thereby preventing an anti-Soviet act of terrorism. Preceded by "The Error of the Resident," "The Destiny of the Resident," and "The Return of the Resident."

d, Veniamin Dorman; w, Oleg Shmelev, Vladimir Vostokov; ph, Vadim Kornilyev; m, Michael Tariverdiyev; art d, Mark Gorelik.

Adventure **(PR:NR MPAA:NR)**

KONTRUDAR† (1987, USSR) 82m Kiev/Sovexportfilm c (Trans: Counter-Strike)

Victor Pavlov, Gennady Korolkov, Harry Liepinsh, Elena Shilkina.

The "Counter-strike" in question is the Soviet advance on the Germans in November and December of 1943 after the Red Army had won back Kiev. Led by Gen. Nikolai Vatutin, the Soviet forces have pushed across the Dnieper, but in so doing have stretched their supply lines and left themselves without a bridge over which to return. A military chess game ensues between the German commander, Field Marshal Manstein, and Vatutin, who wins and becomes one of the Soviet Union's great WW II heroes.

d, Vladimir Shevchenko; w, Igor Malishevsky; ph, Mikhail Chyorny, Aleksandr Chyorny; m, Evgeny Stankovich; art d, Victor Migulko.

War **(PR:NR MPAA:NR)**

KONZERT FUR DIE RECHTE HAND† (1987, Ger.) 79m Igelfilm c (Trans: Concerto for the Right Hand)

Miklos Koniger *(Sanitation Worker)*, Henry Akina *(Boutique Owner)*, Sushila Day *(The Hand/Waitress)*, Ivo Kviring *(Accordionist)*, Kio *("Lady" in Shop)*, Calvin Mackerron *(Pastor/Bartender)*.

Directed by Michael Bartlett, an American who earns his living as a classical musician in Germany, this film playfully examines gender distinctions as it tells its fantastic story. Koniger, a garbage collector, finds a mannequin in a park and takes it home to become his dream lover. En route, its arm falls off and is found by Akina, a slightly swishy gent who happens to be missing his right arm. In short order the feminine arm magically becomes a part of Akina's body. Before the film is over, Akina has replaced that arm with one of Koniger's, and, finally a whole man, he weds the mannequin of Koniger's dreams.

p, Albrecht Gmelin, Heinz Deddens; d&w, Michael Bartlett; ph, Gerhard Friedrich, Peter Kramm, Klaus Krieger; m, Lothar Mankewitz, Fernando Lafferriere; ed, Gaby Bartels, Michael Bartlett; md, Jens Holzkamp.

Drama/Fantasy **(PR:NR MPAA:NR)**

KOORDINATY SMERTI† (1987, USSR/Vietnam) 79m Gorky/Vietnamese Studio c (Trans: Coordinates of Death)

Alexander Galibin, Viet Bao, Tatyana Lebedeva, Le Van, Yury Nazarov.

Those who still insist on calling Jane Fonda "Hanoi Jane" shouldn't have much trouble figuring out who it is the makers of this Soviet feature used as their inspiration. The concerns an American actress' visit to worn-torn North Vietnam. At the height of the Vietnam War, actress "Kate Francis" travels the Ho Chi Min Trail and witnesses first hand the destruction heaped upon the Vietnamese people by the American forces. Before returning to the US, she organizes a press conference to relate all that she has seen and to literally sing the praises of the Vietnamese.

d, Samvel Gasparov, Nguen Shang Tyan; w, Alexander Lapshin, Hoang Tik Ti; ph, Sergei Filippov, Dan Thu; m, Yevgeny Krylatov; art d, Pyotr Pashkevich, Dao Dyk.

War **(PR:NR MPAA:NR)**

KORABL PRISHELTSEV† (1987, USSR) 92m Gorky/Sovexportfilm c (Trans: The Ship of Aliens)

Oleg Tabakov, Yekaterina Voronina, Sergei Nikonenko, Raivo Trass, Valery Gatayev.

Sort of a Soviet version of THE RIGHT STUFF with the emphasis on behind-the-scenes technicians, this deals with the efforts by officials of the Soviet space program to track down the craft that carried a dog into space in December 1960 but made an errant return to Earth. Once the spaceship is located, experts are able to determine what went wrong, thus paving the way for the world's first manned trip into space.

d, Sergei Nikonenko; w, Vladimir Gubarev; ph, Andrei Kirillov; m, Eduard Artemyev; art d, Viktor Safronov.

Drama **(PR:NR MPAA:NR)**

KOROTKIE VSTRECHI† (1987, USSR) 95m Odessa bw (Trans: Brief Encounters)

Nina Ruslanova *(Nidia)*, Vladimir Visotski *(Maxim)*, Kira Muratova *(Valentina Ivanovna)*, L. Bazilskaia, O. Vikland, A. Glazyrin, V. Isakov, T. Midnaia, K. Marinchenko.

Shelved since 1967, KOROTKIE VSTRECHI stars Muratova (who also directed and scripted) as an official of Odessa's city council who hires a housekeeper, Ruslanova, only to learn that she was once her husband's lover. Starring as the husband is Vladimir Visotski, a popular folk singer who was ostracized by the Communist party, but returned to favor after his death. Shown on the festival circuit in the US as BRIEF ENCOUNTERS. (In Russian, with English subtitles).

d, Kira Muratova; w, Kira Muratova, Leonid Zhukovitski; ph, Gennadi Kariuk; m, Oleg Karavaichuk, Vladimir Visotski; ed, Olga Charkova; art d, Alexandra Kanardova, Oleg Perederi.

Romance **(PR:NR MPAA:NR)**

KRALJEVA ZAVRSNICA† (1987, Yugo.) 98m Marjan-Centar c (Trans: King of Endings)

Irfan Mensur *(Branko Krajl)*, Ena Begovic *(Visnja)*, Vladica Milosavljevic *(Irene)*, Milan Strljic.

Mensur plays a lawyer whose love of chess playing and his affair with Milosavljevic leaves little time for his wife, Begovic. On a train trip to visit their son, Begovic is raped while Mensur is off watching a chess match. He returns to their compartment just as Begovic leaps to her death from the speeding train. Mensur then devotes his energy to avenging his wife's death.

d, Zivorad Tomic; w, Zivorad Tomic, Nebojsa Pajkic; ph, Boris Turkovic; m, Vuk Kulenovic; ed, Zoltan Wagner; art d, Mario Ivezic.

Drama **(PR:NR MPAA:NR)**

KRASNAYA STRELA† (1987, USSR) 88m Lenfilm/Sovexportfilm c (Trans: The Red Arrow)

Kirill Lavrov, Yelena Smirnova, Andrey Smirnov, Vladimir Yeremin, Artem Karapetyan.

A high-ranking office manager ignores the rights and wishes of his employees by adopting a dictatorial stance—a stance which carries over to his personal relationships. Soon both his workers and his wife lose respect for him, forcing him to change his ways.

d, Iskander Khamrayev, Igor Sheshukov; w, Edgar Dubrovsky, Alexander Ozhegov; ph, Vladimir Burykin; m, Vadim Bibergan; art d, Yevgeny Gukov.

Drama **(PR:NR MPAA:NR)**

KREUTZEROVA SONATA† (1987, USSR) 158m Mosfilm/Cannon c (Trans: The Kreutzer Sonata)

Oleg Yankovsky *(Vasili Pozdynshev)*, Irina Selezneva *(Lisa)*, Alexander Trofimov, Alla Demidova, Alexander Kalyagin.

An adaptation of Tolstoy's novel starring Yankovsky as a train passenger who confesses to a fellow passenger that he is guilty of murdering his wife. A lavish production running over 2 ½ hours and set for a release by Cannon.

d, Mikhail Schweitzer, Sofia Milkina; w, Mikhail Schweitzer (based on the novel by Leo Tolstoy); ph, Mikhail Agranovich; m, Sofia Gubaidulina; art d, Igor Lemeshev, Vladimir Farbikov.

Drama **(PR:NR MPAA:NR)**

KRUGOVOROT† (1987, USSR) 99m Gruziafilm/Sovexportfilm c (Trans: Turnover)

Leila Abashidze *(Manana)*, Liya Eliava, Guram Pirtskhalava, Otar Megvinetukhutsesi, Ninel Chankvetadze, Salome Alexi-Meskhishvili.

A chance meeting brings together two old, troubled friends who support one another in their time of desperation. One woman is a former actress who lives with her past glories and longs to again be admired for her talent and beauty. The other is an unhappily married scientist whose affair with a married man has left her an outsider. Filmed in the Georgian town of Tbilisi.

d, Lana Gogoberidze; w, Zaira Arsenishvili, Lana Gogoberidze; ph, Nugzar Erkomaishvili; m, Giya Kancheli; art d, Georgy Mikeladze.

Drama **(PR:NR MPAA:NR)**

KUNINGAS LEAR† (1987, Fin.) 80m Reppufilmi Oy c (Trans: King Lear)

Kalevi Kahra, Matti Pellonpaa.

A reworking of Shakespeare's "King Lear," set in the modern high-powered business world. Instead of having royal blood, this version's King Lear is a retiring board chairman who turns his company over to his four daughters.

d&w, Anssi Manttari (based on the play by William Shakespeare); ph, Heikki Katajisto.

Drama **(PR:NR MPAA:NR)**

KURIER† (1987, USSR) 89m Mosfilm/Sovexportfilm c (Trans: Messenger Boy)

Fyodor Dunayevsky *(Ivan Miroshnikov)*, Anastasia Nemolyayeva *(Katya Kuzhetsov)*, Inna Churikova *(Ivan's Mother)*, Oleg Basilashvili *(Professor Kuzhetsov)*, Svetlana Kryuchkova, Vladimir Menchov.

The recipient of the Silver Prize at the 1987 Moscow Film Festival, KURIER tells the story of a teenager, Dunayevsky, who rebels against his divorced parents, his university, and society in general. He takes a job as a messenger for a publishing company, delivering a package to a professor and attracting the attention of his pretty daughter, Nemolyayeva. Although the professor initially disapproves of the boy, he accepts him when the youngster takes a more serious look at his life.

d, Karen Shakhnazarov; w, Alexander Borodyansky (based on the short story by Karen Shakhnazarov); ph, Nikolai Nemolyayev; m, Eduard Artemyev; art d, Konstantin Forostenko.

Comedy/Drama **(PR:NR MPAA:NR)**

KYEOUL NAGUNE† (1987, S. Korea) 116m Don-A Exports c (Trans: The Winter Wayfarers)

Ahn Sung-ki, Kang Suk-woo, Lee Mee-sook, Lee Heh-young, Kim Chung-chul, Lee Hee-sung, Cho Roo-mee.

A melodrama from first-time director Chi-gyoon about a pair of young lovers who split when the young man gets involved with criminals. The girl searches for her lover with help of a male friend and, eventually, the searchers fall in love. When the lover-turned-criminal realizes his mistake, he tries to win his girl back, but his involvement in crime is far too deep.

p, Lee Woo-suk; d, Kwak Chi-gyoon; w, Choi In-ho; ph, Chung Kwang-suk; m, Kim Nam-yoon; ed, Kim Hee-su.

Romance **(PR:NR MPAA:NR)**

L

LA BAMBA**** (1987) 108m New Visions/COL c

Lou Diamond Phillips *(Ritchie Valens)*, Esai Morales *(Bob Morales)*, Rosana De Soto *(Connie Valenzuela)*, Elizabeth Pena *(Rosie Morales)*, Danielle von Zerneck *(Donna Ludwig)*, Joe Pantoliano *(Bob Keene)*, Rick Dees *(Ted Quillin)*, Marshall Crenshaw *(Buddy Holly)*, Howard Huntsberry *(Jackie Wilson)*, Brian Setzer *(Eddie Cochran)*, Daniel Valdez *(Lelo)*, Connie Alvarez, Irma Valcorta, *(Farm Workers)*, Mrs. Connie Valenzuela, Bob Morales.

In the late and innocent 1950s, when rock 'n' roll was young, novice composer-singers such as Buddy Holly registered high on the musical Richter scale with their then revolutionary music. Among these pleasant innovators was the subject of this film, a young Mexican-American, Ricardo Valenzuela, better known as Ritchie Valens. The film, though small in scope, is large in story and expertly handled by cast and crew alike. Phillips, playing the modest but dedicated teenager, is shown living in barrio poverty in the San Fernando Valley. Everywhere he goes he takes his guitar with him and that includes his daily attendance at high school. There he meets sweet and naive blonde von Zerneck who is later to be the role model for his smash song, "Donna." Phillips is supported by his waitress mother De Soto who slavishly devotes herself to her son's career while his half-brother, Morales, encourages Phillips, yet resents his talent. Morales is nothing but trouble, disappearing on his motorcycle, running dope from Mexico, drinking and carrying on like *both* Cheech and Chong, an illiterate, ignorant garbageman who mistreats his common-law wife Pena but, when sober, is remorseful for his brutal, unthinking acts. De Soto doesn't help matters by always putting Phillips and his music before her other son Morales, whom she jokingly says will be Phillips' "flunky" when the teenager hits it big with his songs. Phillips joins a small band and his aggressive ways and natural talent soon cause him to become the band's leader. Meanwhile, he continues to see high school heart throb von Zerneck, although her middle-class father frowns on her associating with a Mexican youth. De Soto finally manages to persuade the owner of a cowboy hangout to let Phillips debut there and he proves a success, with his brother Morales backing him up on the drums. Next De Soto organizes the neighborhood and Morales scoots about with his motorcycle gang plastering poles with advertisements about Phillips' upcoming appearance with his band in an American Legion hall. This event, too, draws an enormous and adoring crowd, but is marred when Morales, openly jealous of his brother's talent, arrives drunk with his gang and begins a brawl. The performance is not a total loss, however, since a start-up record producer spots Phillips and later has him make a recording. This leads to his hit songs "Donna" and "La Bamba" going to the top of the charts and pouring money into the teenager's threadbare pockets. But nothing goes to the head of this clean-cut kid, so clean-cut that when his brother Morales takes him to Tijuana dives and whorehouses he is only interested in playing with a local band banging out "La Bamba." Morales cannot bear the attention and success suddenly heaped upon his younger brother and, while emptying garbage at a local film studio, comes across a thrown-away artwork dealing with cartoon characters. He decides that, he, too, will become a performing artist, mostly to win approval from his mother, and enters a contest, winning a drawing board. Morales' attempt to become a cartoonist fails miserably while brother Phillips goes on to appear as an overnight sensation at an Alan Freed stage show in Brooklyn. Phillips, the ever-generous son, shares his wealth with his family, buying his mother a new house and himself a convertible with fins. He appears at his old school, wowing von Zerneck, his only love, and their teenage friends, giving autographs and telling von Zerneck that he is through with school, which she frowns upon. At a surprise birthday party Phillips gets into a fight with his brother, telling Morales that he no longer looks up to him because of his drinking, carousing, irresponsibility toward his wife and child, and the violent trauma he brings into the household as a result of his jealousy. Phillips goes off to appear on the road with Buddy Holly, played by Crenshaw. Before flying in a small chartered plane to the next gig, Phillips calls his home in California and talks with Morales, patching up their differences and making plans to meet in Chicago. The next day Morales, De Soto and the rest of the family in California hear a radio news report that Phillips has been killed in a plane crash. Throughout the film there are scenes of a plane crashing to earth into a school yard where little boys are killed, this being a recurrent dream haunting Phillips. He explains that when he was a child, a plane crashed in the playground of his school, killing several of his classmates. Ironically, he was attending his father's funeral that day, otherwise he would have been on the playground that day. He has always been troubled with guilt over the incident, feeling that he should have been there among his dead classmates. His dread of flying is ever present and heralds his premature death, but this does not ruin the film in that most viewers realize that Valens was killed in an airplane crash. (This was on February 3, 1959, during a blinding snowstorm, the plane en route to Fargo, North Dakota, crashed in an Iowa cornfield, killing Valens, Holly, The Big Bopper—J.P. Richardson—and the pilot, a tragic event later called "the day the music died.") The end of the film sees Morales going to a deserted field where he and his brother once raced up hills. There Morales, in anguish, cries out his brother's name.

LA BAMBA is not an ambitious, overblown production, but one that tells a simple, straightforward story that is poignant and rich with the period, directed and acted with earnest vigor. Director Valdez (ZOOT SUIT) accomplishes much with his $6 million budget, small by comparative standards. The principal characters are well developed and the conflict between Morales (BAD BOYS) and other members of his family is incisively shown while Phillips, affable and dedicated, is superb as Valens (born Ricardo Valenzuela in Los Angeles in 1941). It is really an

amazing, true-to-life rags-to-riches story in that Valens and his family were living as migrant workers in a tent only months before his first big hit "Donna" entered the top ten on the pop charts in 1958. "La Bamba" was equally successful in early 1959 just before Valens' death at age 17. All the cast members are realistic and unpretentious, living the lives of survivors who hope and plan in a land where they believe anything is possible and for this small, struggling and troubled family the American Dream, or a slice of it, was momentarily theirs before tragedy ended it all. This is really not a rock 'n' roll movie, although the music is there and it is performed well, accurately echoing an era which now seems soft and pleasing compared to rock's hardening and present day acidity. There are those playing today who are mightily influenced by the Valens specter, and these include Santana, Los Lobos and the Ramones. The Lobos group does an excellent job in recreating Valens' tunes and Santana offers a top-notch background score. This was one of the great sleepers of the year, a film that suddenly began breaking box office records and deservedly so, even though it was thought that rock 'n' roll of the long ago, tinged with the Hispanic background and Spanish lyrics, would not appeal to today's audiences. In fact, Phillips is told by his manager that "La Bamba" is not for mainstream teenage audiences and points out that he, Phillips-Valens, cannot even speak Spanish. Phillips, as did Valens, argues that if Nat King Cole can sing Spanish lyrics then so can he. He was never more right. Columbia released this film in three versions, in English, Spanish, and English with Spanish subtitles. *(Brief nudity, profanity.)*

p, Taylor Hackford, Bill Borden; d&w, Luis Valdez; ph, Adam Greenberg (DeLuxe Color); m, Carlos Santana, Miles Goodman; ed, Sheldon Kahn, Don Bruchu; prod d, Vince Cresciman; set d, Rosemary Brandenburg; cos, Sylvia Vega-Vasquez; m/l, Ritchie Valens, Buddy Holly.

Biography **Cas.** **(PR:C MPAA:PG-13)**

LA BRUTE† (1987, Fr.) 103m du Daunou-Artistique Caumartin-Capricorne-Gilmi/du Daunou c (Trans: The Brute)

Xavier Deluc *(Jacques Vauthier)*, Assumpta Serna *(Solange Vauthier)*, Jean Carmet *(Defense Attorney Deliot)*, Rosette *(Danielle Geny)*, Paul Crauchet *(Yves Rodallec)*, Magali Llorca *(Phylis)*, Alexandre Sousa *(John Bell)*.

When a lounge performer is murdered on a transatlantic cruise, the plot seems to be clear—a jealous husband kills the unfaithful wife who has been carrying on with the performer. The husband, however, turns out to be the deaf, dumb, and blind Deluc. It all leads to a courtroom drama in which defense attorney Carmet solves the mystery.

d&w, Claude Guillemot (based on the novel by Guy des Cars); ph, Denys Clerval (Fujicolor); m, Jean-Marie Senia, Magali Llorca; ed, Agnes Guillemot; art d, Frederic Astich-Barre.

Crime/Mystery **(PR:NR MPAA:NR)**

LA BUSQUEDA† (1987, Arg.) 91m Grupci-Cine-Intl./Cine-Intl. c (Trans: The Search)

Marta Gonzalez *(Patricia)*, Luisina Brando *(Monica)*, Rodolfo Ranni, Emilio Disi, Andrea Tenuta.

Violent revenge film in the DEATH WISH mold is an obvious bid for the American market by the Argentine film industry. Set in California, but starring Argentine actors dubbed into English, the film opens as a middle-class family of four sits down to breakfast. The meal is interrupted by a gang of brutes who terrorize the household, rape the women, and murder the father. In the aftermath Mom kills herself and the brother becomes a catatonic who must be institutionalized. This leaves Sis, Gonzalez, vowing revenge on those who destroyed her family. She takes a job at a seedy massage parlor, hoping to bait the gang. The trick works and she lures the savages to the house where they committed their crimes and kills them off one by one. Released in Germany and, incredibly, screened *in competition* at the India Film Festival.

d, John C. [Juan Carlos] Desanzo; w, Lito Espinosa; ph, John C. Lenardi; m, Baby Lopez Furts; ed, Sergio Zottola.

Action **(PR:NR MPAA:NR)**

LA CASA DE BERNARDA ALBA† (1987, Span.) 99m Paraiso c (Trans: The House of Bernarda Alba)

Irene Gutierrez Caba *(Bernarda Alba)*, Ana Belen *(Adela Alba)*, Florinda Chico *(Poncia, the Alba Family Maid)*, Enriqueta Carballeira *(Angustias Alba)*, Vicky Pena *(Martirio Alba)*, Aurora Pastor *(Magdalena Alba)*, Pilar Puchol *(Maid)*, Rosario Garcia-Ortega *(Maria Josefa, Bernarda's Mother)*, Ana Maria Ventura *(Prudencia)*, Paula Borrell *(Young Girl)*, Alvaro Quiroga *(Pepe El Romano, Angustias' Fiance)*.

Adaptation of a play by acclaimed Spanish poet and playwright Garcia Lorca which was finished only two months before its author was murdered during the Spanish Civil War in 1936. A political allegory set in the 1920s, it takes place almost entirely inside the house of Caba, who, upon her husband's death, forces her five daughters—all of marrying age—into a strict eight-year period of mourning. The daughters' repressed sexuality bubbles to the surface after Caba betroths one of them, Carballeira, to the handsome Quiroga. While Quiroga and Carballeira carry on a traditional courtship, another sister, Belen, begins a passionate and clandestine affair with her sister's fiance. When Caba discovers Quiroga in Belen's room, the old woman shoots at the fleeing Romeo, who vaults out an open window. Caba claims she has killed Quiroga, and the distraught Belen runs to her room, locks the door, and hangs herself. Shown at the Cannes Film Festival.

d, Mario Camus; w, Mario Camus, Antonio Larreta (based on the play by Federico Garcia Lorca); ph, Fernando Arribas (Eastmancolor); ed, Jose Maria Biurrun; set d, Rafael Palmero; cos, Jose Rubio; spec eff, Pedro Balandin; makeup, Juan P. Hernandez.

Drama **(PR:NR MPAA:NR)**

LA CODA DEL DIAVOLO† (1987, It.) Cinema e Cinema/Instituto Luce Italnoleggio Cinematografico (Trans: The Devil's Tail)

Robin Renucci, Isabelle Pasco, Piera Degli Esposti, Paolo Rossi, Gianfranco Barra, Maurizio Donadoni, Valeria Magli, Elena Magoia, Donal O'Brian, Franco Citti. Erland Josephson, Serge Spira, Andrzej Seweryn, Gerard Hardy.

An allegorical tale set in a leper colony. The inmates of this aslyum run the gamut from violent criminal to docile innocent. One of the patients, a prostitute, attracts the attention of the hospital director. He becomes so obsessed with curing her that his unorthodox methods threaten his very existence.

d, Giorgio Treves; w, Vincenzo Cerami, Giorgio Treves (based on a story by Vincenzo Cerami); ph, Giuseppe Ruzzolini; m, Egisto Macchi; ed, Giancarlo Simoncelli.

Drama **(PR:NR MPAA:NR)**

LA COMPROMISSION† (1987, Morocco) 93m Cinetelema S.A. c

Souad Amidou, Mehdi El Glaoui.

The story of a love affair between Mehdi El Glaoui, a young architect who is a deeply committed socialist, and Amidou, a naive social worker. As their relationship develops, Mehdi El Glaoui begins to moderate his views while Amidou becomes increasingly radicalized.

d, Latif Lahlou; w, Rachid Boujedria, Latif Lahlou; ph, Mohamed Abderrahmane Tazi; ed, Allal Sahbi.

Drama **(PR:NR MPAA:NR)**

LA COULEUR ENCERCLEE† (1987, Can.) 90m Les Production Quatre Vingts Neuf/Les Films du Crepuscule c (Trans: The Encircling of Color)

Jacques Rainville, Frederique Collin, Jean-Pierre Cartier.

French-Canadian experimental film which celebrates the work of Vincent Van Gogh while condemning the oppressive society in which artists are trapped. Virtually plotless and heavily dependent on the surreal repetition of live action and computer animation images, the film features a painter ("freedom") struggling against a powerful businessman ("oppression") who has the authority to decide whether or not his work will be exhibited.

d&w, Jean Gagne, Serge Gagne; ph, Martin Leclerc; m, Andre Duchesne; ed, Jean Dumieuz.

Drama **(PR:NR MPAA:NR)**

LA CROCE DALLE SETTE PIETRE† (1987, It.) G.C. Pictures/ Compagnia Distribuzione Internazionale P.R. (Trans: The Cross With The Seven Stones)

Eddy Andolfi, Annie Belle, Gordon Mitchell, Paolo Fiorino, Zaira Zaccheddu, Gino Serra, Piero Vivaldi, Stefano Mure.

Fantastic powers for good and evil reside in a child who is the result of intercourse with the devil. The secret of this child's force comes from a cross he wears and when it is stolen, authorities worldwide have cause for alarm. The story deals with the quest for the cross and the effects of its loss on the child, now a young man.

d&w, Marco Antonio Andolfi; ph, Carlo Poletti; m, Paolo Rustichelli; ed, Marco Antonio Andolfi.

Thriller **(PR:NR MPAA:NR)**

LA DONNA DEL TRAGHETTO† (1987, It.) Daedalus/Airone Cinematografica (Trans: The Ferry Woman)

Alessandro Haber, Terese Ann Savoy, Philippe Leroy, Paco Fabrini, Nicola Dipinto, Paolo Rossi, Gabriella Saitta, Giovanni Vettorazzo, Eugenio Masciari.

A lonely, guileless man who makes his living as a puppeteer befriends a woman who operates a ferry. This relationship agitates him to such a degree that his hold on reality becomes tenuous; he is afflicted with bouts of fantasy and memory loss. A baby, conceived on a night with this woman, miraculously restores him.

d, Amedeo Fago; w, Amedeo Fago, Stefano Ruli (based on a story by Amedeo Fago, Lia Morandini); ph, Aldo di Marcantonio; m, Franco Piersanti; ed, Alfredo Muschietti.

Drama **(PR:NR MPAA:NR)**

LA ESTACION DEL REGRESO† (1987, Chile) 86m Filmocentro c (Trans: The Season of Our Return)

Maria Erica Ramos *(Paula)*, Alejandro Cohen *(Gerardo)*, Carmen Pelissier *(Isabel)*, Luis Alarcon, Javier Maldonado, Gloria Laso, Jose Soza, Mauricio Pesutic, Hugo Medina, Ruben Sotoconil, Roberto Poblete.

Told mainly in flashback, this film follows kindergarten teacher Ramos as she searches for her husband who was dragged off by the authorities without an explanation. Her inquiries ignored by the government, Ramos is forced to continue her life alone. She moves in with an emotionally disturbed girl friend and has a loveless affair with an old boy friend who is now a stand-up comic at a lowly strip joint. Eventually Ramos receives word that her husband is being held in a prison camp in northern Chile. She makes the arduous journey alone, only to find the camp empty. A tentative attempt to protest conditions under the fascist dictatorship of General Augusto Pinochet Ugarte, this is the feature debut of television commercial director Kocking, who financed this film with $175,000 of his own company's money.

d, Leonardo Kocking; w, Jose Roman, Leonardo Kocking; ph, Beltran Garcia; ed, Pedro Chaskel.

Drama **(PR:NR MPAA:NR)**

LA ESTANQUERA DE VALLECAS† (1987, Span.) 104m EGA-TVE-CIA Iberoamericana/Nuevo Mundo c

Emma Penella *(Estanquera)*, Jose Luis Gomez *(Leandro)*, Jose Luis Manzano *(Tocho)*, Maribel Verdu *(Angeles)*, Fernando Guillen *(Police Doctor)*, Jesus Puente *(Inspector)*, Antonio Gamero *(Sergeant)*, Antonio Iranzo *(Pharmacist)*, Nieva Parola *(Lieutenant)*, Tina Sainz *(Thin Woman)*, Chari Moreno *(Fat Woman)*, Mabel Ordonez, Juana Ginzo *(Women Journalists)*, Coral Pellicer *(Balcony Neighbor)*, Jose Luis "Pirri" Fernandez *(Emaciated Child)*, Tony Valento *(Affected Man)*, Miguel De Grandy *(Radio Announcer)*, Victor Melero *(Fernandez, Policeman)*, Eduardo Sanchez *(Butcher)*, Jesus Cisneros *(Mechanic)*, Rafael Vallecillo *(Reporter)*, Pedro De Frutos *(TV Announcer)*, Azucena Hernandez *(RNE Announcer)*, Simon Andreu *(Governor)*, Raquel Daina, Elvira Diez, Consuelo Pascual *(Women Neighbors)*, Agustin Guevera, Jose Luis Lemos, Ricardo Gonzalez, Jose Antonio Diaz *(Men Neighbors)*, Juan Moreno.

[No plot information available.]

p, Angel Huete; d, Eloy de la Iglesia; w, Gonzalo Goicoechea, Eloy de la Iglesia; ph, Manuel Rojas (Panorama, Eastmancolor); m, Patxi Andion; ed, Julio Pena; art d, Julio Esteban; spec eff, Reyes Abades.

Crime **(PR:NR MPAA:NR)**

LA FAMIGLIA (SEE: FAMILY, THE, 1987, It./Fr.)

LA FUGA DE CARRASCO† (1987, Mex.) 80m Filmadora Dal/Peliculas Mexicanas c (Trans: Carrasco's Escape)

Jose Alonso *(Juan Carrasco)*, Blanca Guerra *(Leticia)*, Wolf Ruvinskis *(Danielo Rojas)*, Cristina Molina *(Rosalia)*, Guillermo Herrera, Hector Saez, Narciso Busquet, Milton Rodriguez, Ricardo Carrion.

Revenge is the motive here. A gun runner learns the whereabouts of the man who betrayed his father 20 years earlier. He enlists the aid of a smuggler and with savage violence pursues his goal.

p, David Agrasanchez; d, Alfredo B. Crevenna; w, Ramon Obon; ph, Jose Antonio Ruiz; m, Chilo Moran; ed, Jorge Rivera.

Crime **(PR:NR MPAA:NR)**

LA GRAN FIESTA† (1987, Puerto Rico) 101m Zaga c

Daniel Lugo *(Jose Manuel Gonzalez)*, Miguelangel Suarez *(District Attorney Vazquez)*, Luis Prendes *(Don Manolo Gonzalez)*, Cordelia Gonzalez *(Raquel)*, Laura Delano *(Rita de la Torre)*, Raul Carbonell, Jr. *(M.C.)*, Carlos Augusto Cestero *(Angel Luis)*, Raul Davila *(Don Miguel de la Torre)*, Raul Julia *(Poet)*, E.G. Marshall *(Judge Cropper)*, Julian Pastor *(Don Antonio Jimenez)*, Ivonne Coll *(Society Matron)*.

The first feature film to be produced by the fledgling Puerto Rican film industry, LA GRAN FIESTA was praised at film festivals and supported at home where it grossed more than ALIENS. Set in 1942, a crucial period in relations between Puerto Rico and the US, the film revolves around the last grand ball to be held at San Juan's opulent Casino de Puerto Rico before it is turned over to the American military to be used as a nightspot for troops. Political, social, and sexual intrigue play out among the Puerto Rican bourgeoisie as dancers move to the Latin rhythms. Actors Raul Julia and E.G. Marshall make cameo appearances.

p, Roberto Gandara, Marcos Zurinaga; d, Marcos Zurinaga; w, Ana Lydia Vega, Marcos Zurinaga; ph, Marcos Zurinaga; m, Angel "Cucco" Pena; ed, Roberto Gandara; set d. Maria Teresa Pecanins; cos, Gloria Saez, Federico Castillo.

Drama **(PR:NR MPAA:NR)**

LA GUERRA DE LOS LOCOS† (1987, Span.) 98m Xaloc c (Trans: The War of the Madmen)

Alvaro de Luna *(El Rubio)*, Jose Manuel Cervino *(Angelito)*, Juan Luis Galiardo *(Don Salvador)*, Pep Munne *(Andre)*, Pedro Diez del Corral *(Rufino)*, Luis Marin *(Roque)*, Emilio Lain *(Serafin)*, Joan Potau *(Rafael)*, Patxi Catala *(Emilio)*, Francisco Algora *(Domi)*, Alberto Alonso *(Bartolo)*, Jose Vivo (Dr. Frutos), Antonio Drove *(Mario)*, Cesareo Estebanez *(Paulino)*, Alicia Sanchez *(Felisa)*, Maite Blasco *(Hermana Matilde)*, Emilio Gutierrez Caba *(Commandante)*, Paco Algora, Achero Manas, Manuela Camacho.

Set at the dawn of the Spanish Civil War, this entry examines the insanity that accompanies war. It opens in a lunatic asylum as the Franco forces are approaching. The asylum staff flees, the lunatics escape, and Nationalist troops take control of the building. The lunatics steal a truck and head down the road, meeting both Nationalists and Republicans along the way but never taking sides. Shown in the US during New York's Spanish Film Week.

d&w, Manolo Matji; ph, Federico Ribes; ed, Nieves Martin; cos, Gumersindo Andres; makeup, Angel Luis de Diego.

War/Drama **(PR:NR MPAA:NR)**

LA LEI DEL DESEO (SEE: LAW OF DESIRE, THE, 1987, Sp.)

LA MONACA DI MONZA† (1987, It.) Clemi Cinematografica S.r.l.-Reteitalia S.p.A.-CDI c (Trans: The Nun of Monza)

Myriem Roussel, Alessandro Gassman, Renato De Carmine, Alina De Simone, Augusto Zucchi, Acquaroli Francesco, Berata Dominguez, Flaminia Lizzani, John Francis Lane, Stefania Bifano, Laura Devoti, Marcia Ferri, Eugenia Zanelli.

After causing a furor with her performance as the Virgin Mary in Jean-Luc Godard's HAIL MARY (1985), actress Myriem Roussel is at it again, this time playing a nun in feudal Italy who falls into a passionate affair with a local noble. The scandalous tryst reaches the ears of the Cardinal and Roussel's lover commits several crimes to cover up her sins, but she breaks down and confesses. Roussel is imprisoned by the church and her lover becomes a fugitive, only to be caught and stabbed to death by bounty hunters. Thirteen years later Roussel emerges from her prison prematurely aged and broken, but having truly repented.

d, Luciano Odorisio; w, Gino Capone, Carlo Lizzani, Luciano Odorisio, Piero Chiara; ph, Romano Albani; m, Pino Donaggio; ed, Mauro Bonanni.

Drama **(PR:NR MPAA:NR)**

LA MOINE ET LA SORCIERE† (1987, Fr./US) 90m Lara Classics-Bleu-La Cecilia-Selena Audiovisual-Sofinergie/European Classics c (Trans: The Monk and the Sorceress; AKA: SORCERESS)

Tcheky Karyo *(Etienne de Bourbon)*, Christine Boisson *(Elda)*, Jean Carmet *(The Cure)*, Raoul Billery *(Simeon)*, Catherine Frot *(Cecile)*, Feodor Atkine *(The Count)*, Maria de Medeiros.

Directed by Francois Truffaut's longtime screenplay collaborator, Suzanne Schiffman, LA MOINE ET LA SORCIERE is set in a 13th century French village and stars Karyo as Etienne de Bourbon, a real-life monk working for the Inquisition. Searching for heretics, Karyo travels to a walled village to investigate local faith healer Boisson. He discovers the villagers, at Karyo's urging, praying to Saint Guinefort, a dog which was sainted by a lord whose child's life was saved by the animal. Based in fact, the film was put into motion by Pamela Berger, a Boston College art history professor. While researching a book on pagan deities of the Middle Ages, she stumbled across the story of Etienne de Bourbon and Saint Guinefort. Having never written a script before, she completed a first-draft and applied to the National Endowment for the Humanities (NEH), netting an initial $88,000 for project development. Berger then telephoned the French Cultural Service in New York which put her in touch with Schiffman. Not only did Schiffman want to co-script, she also wanted to direct. Because of the NEH's involvement (they funded nearly half the $2,500,000 budget), the film had to have an English-language version in addition to the French-language version. It was shown theatrically in France and at the 1987 Boston Film Festival as SORCERESS.

p, Pamela Berger, Annie Leibovici, George Reinhart; d, Suzanne Schiffman; w, Pamela Berger, Suzanne Schiffman; ph, Patrick Blossier; m, Michel Portal; ed, Martine Barraque; art d, Bernard Vezat; cos, Mouchi Houblinne, Francoise Autran.

Drama/Historical **(PR:NR MPAA:NR)**

LA OVEJA NEGRA† (1987, Venezuela) 90m Gente de Cine c (Trans: The Black Sheep)

Eva Blanco *(La Nigua)*, Arturo Calderon *(Esoterico)*, Zamira Segura *(Sagrario)*, Javier Zapata *(Evelio)*, Carlos Montilla, Jose Manuel Ascensao, Freddy Pereira, Armando Gota, Bertha Moncayo, Gonzalo J. Camacho, Orangel Delfin, Conchita Obach.

Allegorical drama which sees a society of rogues and thieves living in an abandoned movie theater. When the disgruntled wife of a policeman takes up with one of the thieves and moves her belongings into the theater, her husband vows to destroy the troupe at any cost. He learns of an upcoming bank robbery planned by the gang and prepares a response. On the day of the robbery the cops are waiting for the thieves and there is a bloody shootout in front of the bank. All the thieves are killed and the police then turn their attentions to the theater, dissolving the rogue society.

p, Miguelangel Landa; d, Roman Chalbaud; w, Roman Chalbaud, David Suarez; ph, Javier Aguirresarobe; m, Federico Ruiz; ed, Sergio Curiel; set d, Rafael Reyeros.

Drama **(PR:NR MPAA:NR)**

LA PASSION BEATRICE† (1987, Fr./It.) 131m Clea-Little Bear-TF 1-Les Films de la Tour-AMLF-Scena/Goldwyn c (Trans: The Passion of Beatrice)

Bernard-Pierre Donnadieu *(Francois de Cortemart)*, Julie Delpy *(Beatrice)*, Nils Tavernier *(Arnaud)*, Monique Chaumette *(Francois' Mother)*, Robert Dhery *(Raoul)*, Maxime Leroux *(Richard)*, Jean-Claude Adelin *(Bertrand Lemartin)*, Claude Duneton *(The Priest)*, Albane Guilhe *(Recluse)*.

After the international success of the life-affirming ROUND MIDNIGHT, director Bertrand Tavernier returns to the screen with a bleak father-daughter relationship film set in 14th century France. Delpy, the Beatrice of the title, stars as the devoted daughter of a vicious feudal lord who corrupts her in an act of religious defiance. His life is one of blasphemy, anger, incest, and emotional abuse which finally ends in his murder. Tavernier has once again assembled his usual crew, which includes ex-wife Colo as screenwriter, and the brilliant de Keyzer (ROUND MIDNIGHT, A SUNDAY IN THE COUNTRY) behind the camera. Tavernier's own son, Nils, stars as the lord's effeminate son. Bernard-Pierre Donnadieu was previously seen in THE RETURN OF MARTIN GUERRE (as the *real* Martin Guerre) and Delpy made a lasting impression in Leos Carax's most recent film BAD BLOOD. Scheduled for release in 1988 by the Samuel Goldwyn Company.

d, Bertrand Tavernier; w, Colo Tavernier O'Hagan; ph, Bruno de Keyzer

(Eastmancolor); m, Ron Carter, Lili Boulanger; ed, Armand Psenny; prod d, Guy-Claude Francois; cos, Jacqueline Moreau; makeup, Paul Le Marinel.

Drama/Historical **(PR:NR MPAA:NR)**

LA PLAYA DE LOS PERROS† (1987, Span.) Andrea Film-Animatografo/ Nueva Films (Trans: Dogs' Beach)

Assumpta Serna *(Mena)*, Raul Solnado *(Inspector Elias Santana)*, Patrick Bauchau *(Capt. Luis Dantas)*, Sergi Mateu *(Fontenova)*, Carmen Dolores *(Otilia)*, Pedro Efe *(Cpl. Barroca)*, Henrique Viana *(Otero)*, Mario Pardo *(Roque)*, Cucha Carvalheiro *(Widow)*, Melim Teixeira *(Chauffeur)*, Luis Santos *(Majordomo)*, Francisco Pestana *(Official)*, Teresa Monica *(Maid)*.

[No plot information available.]

d, Jose Fonseca E Costa; w, Jose Fonseca E Costa, Antonio Larretta (based on the novel *Balada de la Playa de los Perros* by Jose Cardoso E Pires); ph, Acaccio D'Almeida; m, Alberto Iglesias; ed, Pablo Glez. Del Amo; set d, Nene Paraiso; spec eff, Reyes Abades; makeup, Miguel Sese.

Drama **(PR:NR MPAA:NR)**

LA RAZA NUNCA PIERDE—HUELE A GAS† (1987, Mex.) 100m Cinematografica Calderon/Peliculas Mexicanas c (Trans: The Race Never Loses—It Smells Like Gas)

Miguel Angel Rodriguez *(Jorge Torres, El Campion)*, Sasha Montenegro *(Magda del Rio)*, Rafael Inclan *(El Chilo)*, Roberto [Flaco] Guzman *(Flaco)*, Carmen Salinas *(Cocholata)*, Maria Cardinal *(Lorena)*, Elsa Montes *(Teresa)*, Christopher Lago *(Jorgito)*, Griselda Mejia, Humberto Elizondo, Guero Castro, Alma Thelma, Alfredo [Pelon] Solares, Pancho Muller, Serapio, Xorge Noble, Paty Castro, Gloria Alicia Inclan, Rafael de Quevedo, Pedrin, Carlos Bravo, Carlos Suarez, Ana Berumen, Carlhillos.

Mexican sex comedy/consumer awareness film set in the natural gas industry which combines ribald humor with helpful safety tips about the potential dangers of heating and cooking with gas. Rodriguez stars as a welterweight boxer who is forcibly retired because of health problems. Shortly thereafter he has a falling out with his movie-star wife, Montenegro, and leaves her and his young son behind. With the money he has left from boxing, he purchases a gas truck and hires two men (Inclan and Guzman) to be his delivery men. As the gas men go from house to house making eyes at maids and lonely housewives they demonstrate the aforementioned safety tips for the benefit of their customers (and the audience). As happens often in Mexican sex comedies, the filmmakers find a way to work in a musical guest appearance for the popular salsa band Chico Che and La Crisis.

p, Guillermo Calderon Stell; d, Victor Manuel [Guero] Castro; w, Victor Manuel [Guero] Castro, Francisco Cavazos; ph, Raul Dominguez; m, Marcos Lifshitz; ed, Jose Lino.

Comedy **(PR:NR MPAA:NR)**

LA RUBIA DEL BAR† (1987, Span.) 94m Els Films de la Rambia-Lauren-Ministerio de Cultura-Departamento de Cultura de la Generalitat de Catalunya c (Trans: The Blond at the Bar)

Enric Majo *(Mario, Novelist)*, Ramoncin *(Ortega, Marta's Pimp)*, Nuria Hosta *(Marta)*, Pepe Martin, Carme Sansa.

Melodrama set in the seedy nightspots of Barcelona starring Majo as an unhappily married would-be novelist who falls in love with prostitute Hosta. Eventually Majo leaves his wife to live in poverty with his love, but she soon finds fame as a porno star and deserts him. He uses his heartbreak as the basis for a novel and the cathartic act of writing allows him to forgive Hosta and make peace with himself.

d, Ventura Pons; w, Ventura Pons, Raul Nunez; ph, Tomas Pladevall; m, Gato Perez; ed, Amat Carreras; art d, Isabel Torras.

Drama **(PR:NR MPAA:NR)**

LA RULETERA† (1987, Mex.) 87m Prods. Tijuana/Peliculas Mexicanas c (Trans: The Female Cabbie)

Rafael Inclan *(Officer Ramon)*, Maribel Fernandez [La Pelangocha] *(Perla)*, Raul "Chato" Padilla *(Sergeant)*, Manuel "Flaco" Ibanez *(Lieutenant)*, Polo Ortin *(Client)*, Ricardo de Loera *(Commandante)*, Don Miguel Manzano, Joaquin Garcia [Boralas], Jackeline Castro, Griselda Mejia, Pancho Muller, Humberto Dupeyron, Jose Magana, Orietta Aguilar, Alfredo "Pelon" Solares, Sonia Pina, Maria Bardhal, Leo Villanueva, Veronica Hortensia Martinez, Juliana Aguilar F, Los Tremendos Sepultureros.

One of director Castro's many low-budget Mexican comedies, this one concerns a half-wit female cab driver and her escapades with an equally brainless traffic cop. Received a New York neighborhood release.

p, Juan Abusaid Rios, Pedro Martinez Garrido; d&w, Victor Manuel [Guero] Castro; ph, Antonio Ruiz; m, Gustavo Pimentel; ed, Sergio Soto.

Comedy **(PR:NR MPAA:NR)**

LA RUMBA† (1987, Fr.) 92m Progrefi-TF 1-Hachette Premiere/UIP-Hachette Premiere c

Roger Hanin *(Beppo Manzoni)*, Michel Piccoli *(Malleville)*, Niels Arestrup *(Xavier Detaix)*, Guy Marchand *(Ma Pomme)*, Patachou *(Mme. Meyrals)*, Corinne Touzet *(Regina)*, Sophie Michaud *(Valentine)*, Stephane Jobert *(Puppie Ziegler)*, Karim Allaoui *(Gino Motta)*, Vivian Reed *(Josephine Baker)*, Lino Ventura *(Nono Gozlan)*.

The criminal underworld of Paris in the 1930s is the setting of this gangster entry starring director Hanin as a powerful cabaret owner who is known for his illegal activities. Despite the efforts of right-wing police superintendent Arestrup, Hanin keeps close contact with the underworld, aids refugees from fascist Italy, and even organizes terrorist attacks against the fascists, led by Piccoli. Lino Ventura, who died in late 1987, guest stars as the head of the underworld. Music includes "Mes Deux Amours," performed by Vivian Reed, who stars as the legendary Josephine Baker, and the piano work of Claude Bolling.

d, Roger Hanin; w, Roger Hanin, Jean Curtelin; ph, Jean Penzer; m, Claude Bolling; ed, Youcef Tobni; prod d, Bernard Evein; cos, Laurence Brignon; makeup, Monique Huylebroeck.

Crime **(PR:NR MPAA:NR)**

LA RUSA† (1987, Span.) 125m Pedro Maso, P.C./Lauren c (Trans: Code Name: The Russian)

Angeli Van Os *(Begona, Professor of Political Law)*, Didier Flamand *(Juan Altamirano, Spanish Government Advisor)*, Muntsa Alcaniz *(Eva)*, Eusebio Lazaro *(Minister)*, Fernando Guillen *(Pedro)*, Luis Hostalot *(Jon)*, Juan Gea *(Ricardo)*, Jose Pedro Carrion *(Julian G. Hurtado)*, Jacques Francois *(Hernando)*.

Political thriller starring Flamand as a high-ranking government official who meets the beautiful blonde Os, 20 years his junior, at a peace conference and begins an affair. Although she claims to be a professor of political law, the Spanish secret service informs Flamand that she is a Russian spy. Flamand ignores the warning and tells her about his secret negotiations with ETA, the Basque separatist organization. Shortly thereafter, the ETA representative Flamand has communicated with is assassinated at the site of a secret meeting, and Flamand is faced with the reality that his lover could indeed be a Soviet spy. Directed by Mario Camus, who garnered many awards with his acclaimed 1984 film THE HOLY INNOCENTS.

d, Mario Camus; w, Juan Luis Cebrian, Mario Camus; ph, Hans Burmann; m, Anton Garcia Abril; ed, Jose Maria Biurrun; art d, Rafael Palmero; makeup, Cristobal Criado.

Thriller **(PR:NR MPAA:NR)**

LA SENYORA† (1987, Span.) 96m Virginia Films/Sharp Features c (Trans: The Lady)

Silvia Tortosa, Hermann Bonnin, Luis Merlo, Fernando Guillen Cuervo, Jeannine Mestre, Alfred Luchetti, Alfonso Guirao.

Erotic melodrama set at the turn of the century and starring Tortosa as a beautiful 23-year-old who finds herself betrothed to a 50-year-old man in a marriage arranged by her parents. Resigned to her fate Tortosa looks forward to the wedding night only to discover her husband disdains matters of the flesh. To conceive an heir the husband gives Tortosa a thimble-full of his "essence" and expects her to artificially inseminate herself. The disgusted Tortosa merely tosses the fluid down the drain, and continues to do so for years. As her husband ages he finds it increasingly difficult to produce the all-important thimbles by himself, so he must resort to having Tortosa undress before him and participate in a bit of titillation. Eventually the man dies without an heir, leaving his rich widow to finally indulge in some sexual peccadillos of her own. Director Cadena manages to avoid explict nudity or sex and instead relies on the cinematic power of suggestion.

d, Jordi Cadena; w, Jordi Cadena, Silvia Tortosa (based on the novel by Antoni Mus); ph, Jose G. Galisteo; ed, Amat Carreras; prod d, Jonni Bassiner; set d, J.M. Espada; cos, Andres Urdiciain.

Drama **(PR:NR MPAA:NR)**

LA TRASGRESSIONE† (1987, It.) Freeway-Italia/Film International (Trans: The Transgression)

Pierfrancesco Campanella, Milly D'Abbraccio, Claudia Cavalcanti, Rosanna Banfi, Giorgio Ardisson, Paolo Gozlino, Didi Perego.

An Italian university student becomes involved with a wealthy, psychologically twisted girl who draws him into a perverse relationship. Their love is accompanied by violence and after a series of murders, the pair begin to doubt themselves.

d, Fabrizio Rampelli; w, Pierfrancesco Campanella; ph, Carlo Poletti; m, Gianni Marchetti; ed, Luigi Gorini.

Drama **(PR:NR MPAA:NR)**

LA VALLEE FANTOME† (1987, Fr./Switz.) 102m Filmograph-MK2-Westdeutscher Rundfunk-TV Suisse Romande-La Sept-CAB/MK2 c (Trans: The Ghost Valley)

Jean-Louis Trintignant *(Paul)*, Jacob Berger *(Jean)*, Laura Morante *(Dara)*, Caroline Cartier *(Madeleine)*, Ray Serra *(Dara's Father)*, Jane Holzer *(Jane)*, Francoise Michaud *(Casting Director)*.

The always-interesting Swiss director, Alain Tanner, returns with another film in which the protagonist is a struggling filmmaker. Unable to decide on an actress for his next film, the director, played by Trintignant, hires an assistant, Berger, and sends him to Italy in search of Morante, an actress-turned-waitress. Morante has no intentions of appearing before the camera, but Berger strikes a deal. He will bring her to Brooklyn to reunite her with her father (the owner of a diner), if she will appear in the film. Along the way, of course, the pair fall in love. LA VALEE FANTOME received its premiere in competition at the Venice Film Festival.

p, Jean-Louis Porchet; d&w, Alain Tanner; ph, Patrick Blossier (Eastmancolor); m, Arie Dzierlatka; ed, Laurent Uhler.

Drama **(PR:NR MPAA:NR)**

LA VENGEANCE DU PROTECTEUR† (1987, Morocco) 100m c

Said Ali Souda, Paul Smith, Hamidou, Laura Stanley.

By the end of the 18th century, many of the great artworks of the Arab world had been stolen by invaders from the west. A secret society was formed to protect and keep these antiquities. This film is set in the present day when a man is recruited to track down objects taken from the very heart of the organization, and the trail takes him from Morocco to the east coast of the United States.

p&d, Said Ali Souda; w, Neal Adams; ph, John Fauer, Jean Fatori; prod d, Richard Megruve.

Drama **(PR:NR MPAA:NR)**

LA VIDA ALEGRE† (1987, Span.) 98m El Catelejo-Spanish Television-TVE/Nuevo Mundo c (Trans: A Life of Pleasure; AKA: GOOD LIFE)

Veronica Forque *(Ana)*, Antonio Resines *(Antonio, Ana's Husband)*, Ana Obregon *(Carolina)*, Massiel *(Rosi, Prostitute)*, Miguel A. Rellan *(Eduardo, Minister of Health)*, Guillermo Montesinos *(Manolo)*, Gloria Munoz *(Elvira)*, Jose A. Navarro *(Javi)*, Itziar Alvarez *(Cata)*, Alicia Sanchez *(Marta)*, El Gran Wyoming *(Federico)*, Javier Gurruchaga *(Ildefonso)*, Paloma Catalan *(Carmen)*, Maria Elena Flores *(Senora Tabaco)*, Paco Catala *(Customer)*, Josu Ormaeche *(Escort)*, Joaquin Notario *(Cachas)*, J. Luis Novoa *(Jose)*, Ursula Sanchez *(Olga)*, Maria Jose Del Valle *(Isabel)*, Maria Angeles Acevedo *(Secretary)*, Teresa Carrillo *(Agata)*, Jose De Castrillon *(Child in Shop)*, Juana Andueza *(Prostitute)*, Pedro Marzo *(Parish Priest)*, Rafaela Aparicio, Chus Lampreave *(Neighbors)*.

A box-office hit in Spain, this comedy stars Resines as a politically ambitious adviser to the minister of health who is horrified to discover that his wife, Forque, has started a campaign to stamp out venereal disease among prostitutes and their johns. Forque takes her crusade to the notorious red-light districts of Madrid, invading brothels and gay bars in her war on V.D. The humiliated Resines, eager to smooth the ruffled feathers of his powerful boss, agrees to take the man's beautiful mistress, Obregon, as his secretary despite her incompetence. To make matters worse, Resines falls into a brief affair with Obregon and tries desperately to hide his indiscretion from both his boss and his wife. Forque, however, becomes infected by her husband and winds up dragging all the major characters to her clinic for a healthy dose of penicillin.

d&w, Fernando Colomo; ph, Javier G. Salmones; m, Suburbano; ed, Miguel A. Santamaria; prod d, Manuel Jaen; cos, Lala Huete; makeup, Ana Puigcerver.

Comedy **(PR:NR MPAA:NR)**

LA VIE DISSOLUE DE GERARD FLOQUE† (1987, Fr.) 78m Cathala-Gaumont-Films 21-TFI/Gaumont c (Trans: The Debauched Life of Gerard Floque)

Roland Giraud *(Gerard Floque)*, Marie-Anne Chazel *(Martine)*, Clementine Celarie *(Cecile)*, Jacqueline Maillan *(Mammy)*, Gerard Rinaldi *(Francis)*, Mathilda May *(Pauline)*, Michel Galabru *(Nasal)*, Christian Clavier, Jacques Francois, Mireille Darc, Catherine Lachens, Laurent Gendron, Maaike Jansen, Dominique Besnehard, Richard Taxi.

A lightweight French comedy from veteran director Lautner who, by now, can probably direct these in his sleep. Giraud stars as the title character whose life takes a downward spiral when he is fired from his job at an advertising agency. Heading home, he finds his wife is having an affair and his daughter is a drug dealer. With nowhere else to turn, he takes up with his secretary and her lesbian lover, discovering a far wilder lifestyle.

d, Georges Lautner; w, Georges Lautner, Christian Clavier, Martin Lamotte (based on a story by Jean-Jacques Tarbes, Christian Watton); ph, Yves Rodallec (Fujicolor); m, Daily News; ed, Michele David; art d, Alain Gaudry; cos, Maika Guezel; makeup, Maryse Felix.

Comedy **(PR:NR MPAA:NR)**

LA VIE EST BELLE† (1987, Fr./Belg./Zaire) 85m Lamy-Stephan-Sol'oeil/Lamy c (Trans: Life Is Rosy)

Papa Wemba *(Kourou)*, Krubwa Bibi *(Kabibi)*, Landu Nzunzimbu *(Mamou)*, Kanku Kasongo *(Nvouandou)*, Lokinda Mengi Feza *(Nzazi)*, Kalimazi [Riva] Lombume *(Mongali)*, Mazaza Mukoko *(Mama Dingari)*, Mujinga Mbuji Inabanza *(Cherie Bondowe)*, Bwanando Ngimbi *(Nganga, the Lawyer)*, Tumba [Emoro] Ayila *(Emoro, the Dwarf)*, Pepe Kalle *(Grandpa Kalle)*, Alamba Engongo *(Nvouandou's Chauffeur)*, Maitre Nono.

Filmed in Zaire and co-directed by a Zairian and a Belgian, LA VIE EST BELLE stars local singing sensation Papa Wemba as a musician with high hopes of finding fame and fortune in the capital city of Kinshasa. Along this rocky road, he meets the beautiful Bibi, a waif whose mother tries to marry her off to Kasongo, a wealthy businessman whose other wife hasn't borne him children. When Kasongo visits a fortune teller, he is told to postpone the consummation of the marriage for a month, thereby giving the young lovers enough time to work out their dilemma. Shown in New York in late 1987. (In French; English subtitles.)

d, Benoit Lamy, Ngangura Mweze; w, Ngangura Mweze, Maryse Leon, Benoit Lamy; ph, Michel Baudour (Fujicolor); m, Papa Wemba, Klody, Zaiko Langa Langa, Tshala Muana; ed, Martine Giordano; art d, Mutoke Wa Mputu, Barly Baruti.

Comedy/Musical **(PR:NR MPAA:NR)**

LA VIE PLATINEE† (1987, Fr./Ivory Coast) 86m M.F.-Republique de Cote d'Ivorie-TF1 c (Trans: The Platinum Life; AKA: TREICHVILLE STORY)

L'Ensemble Koteba d'Abidjan, Nadia Do Sacremento, Souleymane Koly, Yves Zogbo Junior.

Shot in the picturesque Ivory Coast capital of Abidjan, this upbeat musical tale is about a dance troupe's efforts to raise money to take their act to Paris. A subplot involves the disappearance of the attractive lead singer whose modernized family disapproves of her traditional ways.

d, Claude Cadiou; w, Patrick Du Corail, Souleymane Koly; ph, Manuel Teran; m, Francois Breant; ed, Marie-Therese Boiche; prod d, Alma Kanate.

Musical **(PR:NR MPAA:NR)**

LADIES OF THE LOTUS zero (1987, Can.) 88m North American Pictures-Columbia Western Management c

Richard Dale *(Phillip)*, Angela Read *(Dominique)*, Patrick Bermel *(Sean)*, Darcia Carnie *(Tara)*, Martin Evans, Nathan Andrews, Lisanne Burk, April Alkins, Nikki Murdock Marloe, Marney McGiver, Hay Hay Jotie.

The title sounds like a pornographic novel some pre-teen might keep secreted beneath his mattress, but this is really a cheaply made gangster picture that goes heavy on the cheesecake. The confusing storyline, which really isn't all that important to begin with, involves Vancouver mobsters in the midst of a gang war. Lotus Inc., a modeling studio which fronts for a drug and prostitution business, is caught between the battling factions. Dale, one of Lotus' male employees, has installed a camera in the establishment's dressing room, thus giving the audience ample opportunity to view young women as they prance about in lingerie. Dale also takes to killing the girls, but ends up helping out fellow employee Carnie when she takes on the gangsters.

Director Simandl, to no great surprise, shows little cinematic talent other than the ability to point a camera at naked female flesh. He resorts to shootouts and poorly staged rock videos to carry his story, while his cast members run through the motions without much aplomb. *(Nudity, profanity, sexual situations.)*

p, John A. Curtis, Lloyd A. Simandl; d, Lloyd A. Simandl, Douglas C. Nicolle; w, Jane Mengering Hausen; ph, Victor Nicolle (Alpha Cine Color); m, Greg Ray; ed, Lloyd A. Simandl, Douglas C. Nicolle; prod d, Lyne J. Grantham; art d, George Pantages; cos, Christopher Knox, Gwen Bottomley; m/l, Collin Weinmaster, Michael Rheault, Greg Ray.

Drama **Cas.** **(PR:O MPAA:NR)**

LADY BEWARE† (1987) 108m Intl. Video Ent. c

Diane Lane *(Katya Yarno)*, Michael Woods *(Jack Price)*, Cotter Smith *(Mac Odell)*, Peter Nevargic *(Lionel)*, Edward Penn *(Thayer)*, Tyra Ferrell *(Nan)*.

An independently produced psychological thriller directed by Karen Arthur (THE MAFU CAGE) which was dumped unceremoniously onto the market for a one-week run in a small number of theaters prior to release on home video. Lane stars as a much-touted department store window dresser known for her rather kinky arrangements of mannequins. She lands a job with a big Pittsburgh store and her displays catch the attention of a demented X-ray technician, Woods, who decides that the woman responsible for such designs must be sexually repressed. A husband and a father, Woods begins a campaign of psychological rape that includes leaving lewd messages on Lane's answering machine, pilfering her mail, indulging in some Peeping Tomism, breaking into her apartment, playing with her lingerie, and leaving messages written in blood on her bathroom mirror. At first Lane is frightened by the intrusions, but once she figures out who the culprit is, she gets back at him by employing the same tactics he used on her. Director Arthur, who struggled for eight years to get this film funded, claimed that her right to final cut was revoked by the producers and that they trashed her version and released what she describes as a more exploitative cut.

p, Tony Scotti, Lawrence Taylor Mortorff; d, Karen Arthur; w, Susan Miller, Charles Zev Cohen; ph, Tom Neuwirth (United Color); m, Craig Safan; ed, Roy Watts; set d, Tom Wells; cos, Patricia Fields.

Thriller **Cas.** **(PR:NR MPAA:R)**

LADY OF THE CAMELIAS*** (1987, Ger.) 125m Polyphon Film-Fernseh GmbH c (DIE KAMELIENDAME)

Marcia Haydee *(Marguerite Gautier)*, Ivan Liska *(Armand Duval)*, Francois Klaus *(Mons. Duval)*, Colleen Scott *(Prudence Duvernoy)*, Vladimir Klos *(Gaston Rieux)*, Lynne Charles *(Manon Lescaut)*, Jeffrey Kirk *(Des Grieux)*, Gigi Hyatt *(Olympia)*, Beatrice Cordua *(Nanina)*, Victor Hughes *(Der Herzog)*, William Parton *(Graf N.)*, Richard Hoynes *(Pianist)*, Christina Fritschi, Anders Hellstrom *(Ehepaar)*, Edouardo Bertini, Ralf Dornen, Hocine Layada *(Manon's Admirers)*, Markus Annacker, Oliver Chanut, Fabrice Herrault *(Marguerite's Admirers)*, Stefanie Arndt, Bettina Beckmann, Marilyn Berlanger, Mette Bottcher, Stephan Bossyvine, Anne Brossier, Vladimir Bukovec, Judith Carlson, Jean-Jacques Defago, Indrani Delmaine, Ralf Dornen, Denis Feuillette, Jessica Funt, Vivienne Gilligan, Anna Grabka, Gabrielle Gunthard, Aurea Hammerli, Sonja Herrmann, Roger Hode, Susanne Klement, Johannes Kritzinger, Jean Laban, Mats Lindstrom, Franck Logeais, Carolina Lohfert, Gabriel Manferdini, Caroline Maylin, Janusz Mazon, Eric Miot, William Parton, Nathalie Perriraz, Tania Philip, Stephen Pier, Rena Robinson, Jeffrey Ross, Nicoletta Santoro, Karen Stephenson, Robin White.

LADY OF THE CAMELIAS is a silent choreographic evocation of the novel by Alexandre Dumas interwoven with a tale by Abbe Prevost entitled *Manon Lescaut*. An older woman (Marcia Haydee), outfitted in black, enters a room which is being emptied of its contents, then stares at a portrait of herself from an earlier era. The room quickly fills up with silent mourners, who have come as much to revive their memories as they have to pay their respects to the catatonic woman in black. A young blond man (Ivan Liska) is so overwhelmed by memories rekindled by the portrait that he passes out. He is then transported in time to relive his agonizing relationship with this woman. His liaisons with her are as passionate as they are ephemeral, and afterwards leave him immobilized with a sense of despair so severe, that he does not recover until his next meeting with her. She constantly demands the center of attention, and consequently has little control over her own activities and freedom. Her rendezvous with Liska are so brief that their moments together take on an almost illusory quality, and her subsequent fantasies are gripped by a predominant mood of helplessness. His yearnings, on the other hand, present themselves in more hopeful and carefully constructed fantasies. Eventually fate sweeps her out of his reach and into a rival's arms, before returning her to her designated spot as the center of attention. This endless succession of failures fuels the frustration he feels about her inattentiveness, and he sends her a letter of rejection. She becomes utterly disconsolate, her sorrow so boundless that it leads to her death. It is only while reading her diary after she has passed away that Liska discovers the depths of her love for him.

LADY OF THE CAMELIAS is a hauntingly beautiful rendition by American-born director and choreographer, John Neumeier, of his own magical ballet. The lead performance by Marcia Haydee is truly remarkable, not only for her gracefulness of dance, but for her presence before the camera. She possesses a range of gestures and emotions that conveys both an enormous sense of pride as well as an acute awareness of loss. The thinness of her face, the sadness of her eyes, and the inversion of her mouth, collectively underscore the presence of an extraordinary sensuality. Her vertically constructed face brings about an eruption of energy that transforms her private experience of pain into a tangible manifestation of it. Her partner, Ivan Liska, meets with more limited success, because his part calls primarily for the expression of two emotions, despair and joy. While he conveys a depth of feeling, his range is too limited to sustain interest in his part for such a lengthy silent film.

Neumeier's settings are strikingly rich in their vibrancy and simplicity of colors. Each set is dominated by a singularly vivid color, laced with a multiplicity of tonal gradations, then accented by a striking focal image that appears in a distinguished and contrasting hue. As the ballet shifts between the illusory and the real, the imagined and the experienced, the unblinking eye of the camera captures the magical transformation of colors and costumes, as well as the whirling motion and uninterrupted flow of the dance. In fact, the camera rarely wavers from its distant position, as it monitors the fatalism that overwhelms the characters. Yet, except for diehard ballet fans, two hours and five minutes of choreography without dialog are difficult to take. And unless one is already familiar with the ballet by Neumeier or the stories by Dumas and Prevost, it can be quite a challenge to follow the narrative. *(Adult situations.)*

d, John Neumeier; w, based on *The Lady of the Camelias* by Alexandre Dumas *fils* and *Manon Lescaut* by Abbe Prevost; ph, Ingo Hamer; m, Frederic Chopin; ch, John Neumeier.

Dance **(PR:C MPAA:NR)**

LAIN ULKOPUOLELLA† (1987, Fin.) 100m Filminor Oy c (Trans: Outside the Law)

Taneli Makela, Kari Heiskanen.

A drama about a frustrated man who is driven to take the law into his own hands.

d, Ville Makela; w, Olli-Pekka Parviainen; ph, Olli Varja.

Drama **(PR:NR MPAA:NR)**

LALAN FAKIR† (1987, India) Nag

Ashim Kumar, Sandhya Roy, Mahua Roy Chowdhury.

Set in the 1800s, this entry tells the story of a wandering minstrel whose music brings happiness to a troubled community. (In Bengali.)

d, Shakti Chatterjee; m, Hemanga Biswas.

Drama **(PR:NR MPAA:NR)**

L'AMI DE MON AMIE† (1987, Fr.) 102m Films du Losange/Orion Classics c (Trans: My Girlfriend's Boyfriend)

Emmanuelle Chaulet *(Blanche)*, Sophie Renoir *(Lea)*, Eric Veillard *(Fabien)*, Francois-Eric Gendron *(Alexandre)*, Anne-Laure Meury *(Adrienne)*.

Eric Rohmer's second film of 1987 and the sixth entry in his "Comedies and Proverbs" series (of which his previous film QUATRE AVENTURES DE REINETTE ET MIRABELLE is not a part) tells the tale of two couples who trade partners. The film opens with the meeting of two young women—Renoir and Chaulet—who fast become friends. Renoir is unfulfilled in her relationship with Veillard, while Chaulet has her sights set on Gendron. Renoir takes a solo vacation and Chaulet becomes involved with Veillard. When Renoir returns to town, she sees that Chaulet still has not paired up with Gendron and tries to arrange a meeting. In the process, however, Renoir falls for Gendron. Both girls, of course, keep their affairs secret and feel guilty about doing so. In the end, they part with their new mates and with their friendship intact. Scheduled for an early 1988 release in the US by Orion Classics. Shown as part of the 1987 New York Film Festival.

p, Margaret Menegoz; d&w, Eric Rohmer; ph, Bernard Lutic; m, Jean-Louis Valero; ed, Maria Luisa Garcia.

Romance **(PR:NR MPAA:NR)**

LAMP, THE (SEE: OUTING, THE, 1987)

LANDSLIDES† (1987, Aus.) 75m Red Heart-Film Australia/Australian Film Institute c

Experimental film from frequent collaborators Gibson and Lambert which explores the concept of "the body" by juxtaposing shots of babies, children, naked women, surgical operations, and NASA footage of heavenly bodies with a soundtrack comprised of discussions on such topics as aging, life on other planets, and bodily functions. The topics discussed do not accompany their logical visual counterpart—rather, the life-on-other-planets discussion occurs while watching the surgical footage and so on. Received a commerical release in Australia and played to enthusiastic crowds.

p,d&w, Sarah Gibson, Susan Lambert; ph, Michael Ewers, Jack Lambert, Mick Bornemann; m, Cameron Allan; ed, Ray Thomas; animation, Pam Lofts.

Experimental **(PR:NR MPAA:NR)**

L'ANNEE DES MEDUSES zero (1987, Fr.) 110m T.Films-FR3-Parafrance/European Classics c (Trans: The Year of the Jellyfish)

Valerie Kaprisky *(Chris)*, Bernard Giraudeau *(Romain)*, Caroline Celier *(Claude)*, Jacques Perrin *(Vic)*, Beatrice Agenin *(Marianne)*, Philippe Lemaire *(Lamotte)*, Pierre Vaneck *(Pierre)*, Barbara Nielsen *(Barbara)*, Charlotte Kadi, Betty Assenza, Jean-Paul Dubarry, Serge Gaubardy, Jean-Claude Pancrazi, Hedwige Thibuis.

A worthless exploitation picture released in France in 1984 which masqueraded in the US in 1987 as a "French art film." The attractive Kaprisky, who received her "Warholian" moment of fame in 1983's BREATHLESS, stars as an 18-year-old *femme fatale* who spends her summers on the beach at St. Tropez with her 38-year-old mother, Celier. Both mother and daughter are icons of sexual passion, which breeds something of a rivalry between them. Kaprisky, like everyone else in St. Tropez, disrobes more times than a runway model on amphetamines, proudly parading her bronze body before the camera. She attracts the attention of Perrin, a family man who leaves his wife after just one week with Kaprisky. He gets her pregnant, she gets an abortion, and naturally gives him the big brush-off. With his life completely ruined, she moves on to her next victim—Giraudeau, a local pimp who conducts business from his yacht. To complicate matters, Celier is attracted to Giraudeau but tries to keep their meetings secret from the disapproving Kaprisky. Sensing her dangerous side, Giraudeau avoids Kaprisky like the plague. When Giraudeau reveals his Achilles' heel—a deadly reaction to wasp and jellyfish stings—Kaprisky has the upper hand. She talks him into taking her for an evening cruise on his yacht. After dancing naked in front of him (he calls her "Salome," which seems to baffle everyone, especially Kaprisky), Kaprisky pushes Giraudeau overbaord into a school of feisty jellyfish. No one in St. Tropez can figure out that Kaprisky is the guilty one, and she gets off without even a raised eyebrow.

L'ANNEE DES MEDUSES exists for one reason only—for the exploitative purpose of filming countless half-nude women on the beaches of St. Tropez. When this is a film's sole *raison d'etre*, not much can be said about the art of the filmmaking. In contrast, Eric Rohmer has made a career out of filming beautiful young women who vacation on the beaches and yet has never resorted to the sort of banalities Christopher Frank uses. Kaprisky (whether dressed or undressed) is a beautiful woman whose sensuality can burn a hole in the celluloid, but bodacious ta-ta's do not a movie make. Frank tries to cloak the film's emptiness in some silly metaphors equating the deadly sting of a jellyfish with the treachery of Kaprisky's love, but it's a weak attempt. European Classics released the film in the US to an art-house crowd, but subtitles aren't enough to disguise this as an art film. Punk opera singer Nina Hagen contributes four songs to the soundtrack: "Lorelei," "Zarah," "African Reggae," and "Antiworld." Other songs include "Waiting For You" (Alain Wisniak, performed by Olivier Constantin); "Mrs. Hyde" (Wisniak, Carol Bowley et les Bowlettes); "Long Distance Flight" (Wisniak, Fitoussi, performed by F.R. David). (In French; English subtitles.) *(Excessive nudity, sexual situations, adult situations, profanity).*

p, Alain Terzian; d&w, Christopher Frank; ph, Renato Berta; m, Alain Wisniak; ed, Nathalie Lafaurie; art d, Jean-Jacques Caziot; cos, Yvette Frank; m/l, Nina Hagen, Alain Wisniak.

Drama Cas. (PR:O MPAA:NR)

LAONIANG GOU SAO† (1987, Hong Kong) 94m Moleson-Tomson-Maverick c (Trans: Soul)

Deanie Ip, Elaine Jin, Jacky Cheng, Hou Hsiao Hsien, Ko I-Chen, Sandy Lamb, Dennis Chan.

Intriguing combination of realistic and comic violence which begins with the suicide of a police inspector. The dead man's widow soon learns that her husband had a secret life which included a Tawainese mistress with whom he fathered a son. Shortly thereafter things turn murderous when an attempt is made on the wife's life. The clumsy villains wind up killing the mistress by mistake, leaving the wife to take care of her husband's four-year-old bastard son.

p, Sally Wu, Hsu Feng, John Sham; d, Shu Kei; w, Shu Kei, Manfred Wong; ph, Cristopher Doyle; m, Danny Chung; ed, Fong Po Wah; art d, Tony Au.

Drama (PR:NR MPAA:NR)

LAPUTA: THE CASTLE IN THE SKY† (1987, Jap.) 124m Tokuma Shoten c (TENKU NO SHIRO LAPUTA)

Animated adventure film inspired by portions of Jonathan Swift's *Gulliver's Travels* which follows a young girl and her pirate friends as she battles an evil military to reclaim her birthright as the lost princess of the legendary floating city of Laputa.

p, Tatsumi Yamashita, Hideo Ogata, Isao Takahata; d&w, Hayao Miyazaki; ph, Hirokata Takahashi; m, Jo Hisaishi; ed, Hayao Miyazaki; prod d, Toshiro Nozaki, Nizo Yamamoto; animation, Yoshinori Kanada.

Animation/Children's (PR:NR MPAA:NR)

LAS MOVIDAS DEL MOFLES† (1987, Mex.) 89m Tijuana/Peliculas Mexicanas c (Trans: Mofles' Escapades)

Rafael Inclan *(Mofles)*, Manuel [Flaco] Ibanez *(Abrelatas)*, Joaquin Garcia [Borolas] *(Chopo)*, Charly Valentino *(Don Gaston)*, Merle Uribe *(Rebeca del Mar)*, Myrra Saaveda, Maria Cardenal, Alejandro Ciangherotti, Victor Junco, Raul [Chato] Padilla, Yirah Aparicio, Leo Villanueva, Oscar Fentanes, Sonia Pina, Polo Ortin, Estrella Fuentes, Alfredo [Pelon] Solares, Arturo Cobo, Ginal Leal.

A quick sequel to EL MOFLES Y LOS MECHANICOS, once again featuring popular comedian Inclan as a bumbling mechanic nicknamed "Muffler." He gets involved in a series of ribald escapades with his drunken compadres at the garage. Popular bands Generacion 2000 and Los Infieles make musical guest appearances. Both films were shown in Spanish-language theaters in New York City this year.

p, Juan Abusaid Rios, Pedro Martin Gurrido; d, Javier Duran; w, Francisco [Pancho] Sanchez, Marco Eduardo Contreras; ph, Antonio Ruiz; m, Gustavo Pimentel; ed, Sergio Soto.

Comedy (PR:NR MPAA:NR)

LAS DOS ORILLAS† (1987, Span.) Caligari-Productura Andaluza De Programas c (Trans: The Two Banks)

Jose Luis Gomez *(Simon, TV Producer)*, Felipe Bollain *(Felipe, Simon's Son)*, Iciar Bollain *(Iciar)*, Marina Bollain *(Marina, Iciar's Twin Sister)*, Emilio Gutierrez Caba *(Atienza)*, Amparo Munoz *(Woman at Fiesta)*, Roberto Quintana *(Emilio)*, Pedro Alvarez-Osorio *(Commissioner)*, Antonio Andres Lapena *(Civil Servant)*, Antonio Dechent *(Tomas)*, Pepe Quero *(Goyo)*, Idilio Cardoso.

Gomez, a Spanish television producer who has made a name for himself in America, returns to Seville with his 11-year-old son. The two live on a houseboat on the Rio Guadalquivir and Gomez sets up a broadcasting station on the boat. One day, while testing the equipment, Gomez inadvertently videotapes something he shouldn't have and those implicated kidnap his son.

d, Juan Sebastian Bollain; w, Juan Sebastian Bollain, Alfonso Del Vando; ph, Vitor Estevao; m, Victor Young, Jesus Bola; ed, Juan Luis Berlanga; art d, Luis Manuel Carmona.

Drama (PR:NR MPAA:NR)

LAS TRAIGO . . . MUERTAS† (1987, Mex.) 85m Cinematografica Filmex/Peliculas Mexicanas c (Trans: I Do 'Em In)

Otto Sirgo *(Francisco [Paco] Gavilan)*, Sasha Montenegro *(Angelica Vidal de Cienfuegos)*, Maribel Guardia *(Marsha)*, Lalo [El Mimo], Polo Ortin, Cesar Bono, Oscar Fentanes.

Slapstick comedy starring Sirgo as a hapless gambler deep in debt. Pursued by everyone from bill collectors to mob loan sharks, Sirgo desperately searches for some way to pay his creditors. Inspired by a young widow who is living off a lucrative life insurance policy taken out on her husband, Sirgo decides to become a modern-day "Bluebeard." He plans to marry, insure, and then murder a series of wives and collect the money. Predictably, Sirgo is just as inept a murderer as he is a gambler and his scheme soon backfires.

p, J. Fernando Perez Gabilan; d, Rafael Baledon; w, Fernando Galindo; ph, Alberto Arellanos Bustamantes; m, Gustavo C. Carreon; ed, Francisco Chiu.

Comedy (PR:NR MPAA:NR)

L'ASSOCIATION DES MALFAITEURS† (1987, Fr.) 108m Films 7-FR3/AMLF c (Trans: Association of Wrongdoers)

Christophe Malavoy *(Gerard)*, Francois Cluzet *(Thierry)*, Gerard Lecaillon *(Francis)*, Jean-Claude Leguay *(Daniel)*, Claire Nebout *(Claire)*, Jean-Pierre Bisson *(Bernard Hassler)*, Hubert Deschamps *(Tonton Gadin)*, Veronique Genest *(Monique)*.

Malavoy and Cluzet costar as a pair of hip young businessmen who become fugitives from the law when a practical joke involving a safecracking backfires on them. Directed by Claude Zidi who made a big splash in 1984 with MY NEW PARTNER—another comic buddy film with a criminal backdrop.

p&d, Claude Zidi; w, Claude Zidi, Simon Mickael, Michel Fabre, Didier Kaminka; ph, Jean-Jacques Tarbes (Eastmancolor); m, Francis Lai; ed, Nicole Saunier; art d, Francoise Deleu; cos, Olga Pelletier.

Comedy/Crime/Drama (PR:NR MPAA:NR)

LAST EMPEROR, THE**** (1987) 160m COL c

John Lone *(Aisin-Gioro "Henry" Pu Yi as an Adult)*, Joan Chen *(Wan Jung, "Elizabeth")*, Peter O'Toole *(Reginald Johnston, "R.J.")*, Ying Ruocheng *(The Governor)*, Victor Wong *(Chen Pao Shen)*, Dennis Dun *(Big Li)*, Ryuichi Sakamoto *(Masahiko Amakasu)*, Maggie Han *(Eastern Jewel)*, Ric Young *(Interrogator)*, Wu Jun Mei *(Wen Hsiu)*, Cary Hiroyuki Tagawa *(Chang)*, Jade Go *(Ar Mo)*, Fumihiko Ikeda *(Yoshioka)*, Richard Vuu *(Pu Yi, Age 3)*, Tijger Tsou *(Pu Yi, Age 8)*, Wu Tao *(Pu Yi, Age 15)*, Fan Guang *(Pu Chieh)*, Henry Kyi *(Pu Chieh, Age 7)*, Alvin Riley III *(Pu Chieh, Age 14)*, Lisa Lu *(Tzu Hsui, The Empress Dowager)*, Hideo Takamatsu *(Gen. Ishikari)*, Hajime Tachibana *(Japanese Translator)*, Basil Pao *(Prince Chun)*, Jian Xireng *(Lord Chamberlain)*, Chen Kai Ge *(Captain of Imperial Guard)*, Zhang Liangbin *(Big Foot)*, Huang Wenjie *(Hunchback)*, Liang Dong *(Lady Aisin-Gioro)*, Dong Zhendong *(Old Doctor)*, Dong Jiechen *(Doctor)*, Constantine Gregory *(Oculist)*, Soong Huaikuei *(Lung Yu)*, Shao Ruzhen *(First High Consort)*, Li Yu *(Second High Consort)*, Li Guangli *(Third High Consort)*, Xu Chunqing *(Grey Eyes)*, Zhang Tianmin *(Old Tutor)*, Luo Hongnian *(Sleeping Old Tutor)*, Yang Baozong *(Gen. Yuan Shikai)*, Cai Hongxiang *(Scarface)*, Yu Shihong *(Hsiao Hsiu)*, Wu Jun *(Wen Hsiu, Age 12)*, Lucia Hwong *(Lady of the Book)*, Cui Jingping *(Lady of the Pen)*, Wu Hai *(Republican Officer)*, Gu Junguo *(Tang)*, Xu Tongrui *(Captain of Feng's Army)*, Li Fusheng *(Minister of Trade)*, Chen Shu *(Chang Chinghui)*, Cheng Shuyan *(Lady Hiro Saga)*, Zhang Lingmu *(Emperor Hirohito)*, Luo Shigang *(Chang Ching Hui's Secretary)*, Zhang Daxing *(Tough Warder)*, Zu Ruigang *(Second Warder)*, Jin Yuan *(Party Boss)*, Akira Ikuta *(Japanese Doctor)*, Ma Guang, Cui Xinmin *(Japanese Bodyguards)*, Li Zhenduo *(Dignitary)*, Yang Hongchang *(Scribe)*, Wang Biao *(Prisoner)*, Michael Vermaaten *(American)*, Matthew Spender, Martin Reynolds *(Englishmen)*.

Italian director Bernardo Bertolucci returns to the screen after a six-year absence, with the grand and powerful biography of China's last emperor, Aisin-Gioro "Henry" Pu Yi. As with turn-of-the-century czarist Russia, China at the dawn of the 1900s was one of the few civilized countries still under monarchial rule. With the start of this century, the Ching Dynasty which had ruled half the world's population since 1644, began to lose its power. In 1908, desperate to strengthen the dynasty, the dowager Empress Tzu-Hsui (played with chilling grotesqueness by Lisa Lu) chose as the new emperor the three-year-old Pu Yi. Told in an intricate flashback/flashforward narrative which uses Pu Yi's communist "remolding" period as its fulcrum, the film opens in 1950 at a train station where hundreds of Chinese prisoners, accused of treason and war crimes, are being returned to their now-communist homeland. Among them is Lone, who plays the adult Pu Yi, captured by Soviet Communist troops while fleeing Manchuria, or Manchukuo, during an invasion of that country. As Lone sits silently against the stone wall of the dank, gray building, he is approached by a group of Chinese who recognize him and begin to *kowtow* before him. Lone disappears into a small room nearby, locks the door behind him, and slits his wrists in a suicide attempt. As a guard bangs on the door, the scene shifts to China, 1908. Snatched from his simple home by the dowager Empress' warriors, the youngster (played by Richard Vuu) is separated from his mother and, with his wet nurse Ar Mo (Jade Go), is to be imprisoned as emperor in the Forbidden City. The only "man" within the walls of the Forbidden City (itself covering 250 acres and boasting 9,999 rooms—only heaven has 10,000 according to legend), the young emperor is surrounded by hundreds of eunuchs—a devoted but grossly corrupt group of emasculated servants. He is immediately brought to the bedchamber of the dowager Empress. From her gilded deathbed, Lu explains to the playful and curious youngster that

she is about to die, naming him as the "Lord of 10,000 Years" and the "Son of Heaven"—the next descendent of the Ching Dynasty. Later, Pu Yi is placed on the Dragon Throne in a massive ceremony during which he is officially named ruler of all China. Nevertheless, the emperor is still a playful young boy. Dressed in his imperial robes, he stands on the seat of the Dragon Throne and begins flapping the overlong arms of his robe. To calm the boy, a servant prophetically assures him, "It will soon be over," receiving an angry leer from an elder. The young emperor sneaks off his throne and heads for the Forbidden City's grounds, pushing aside the billowing drapery of imperial yellow to find himself standing outside before the kowtowing, geometrically arranged masses of his thousands of warriors, all dressed in colorful robes and helmets. During his reign as emperor he is catered to endlessly by his entourage of eunuchs who follow him wherever he goes, carry him, wash him, examine his excrement for dietary changes, entertain him, and are punished by him. While being bathed he becomes aware of his power—splashing and kicking water into the faces of his laughing servants as he defiantly chants, "I am the Son of Heaven."

By 1912, the emperor (now played by Tijger Tsou) is only a figurehead in China as the Ching Dynasty is forced to abdicate after the country has been declared a republic. Imprisoned in the Forbidden City, the emperor is unable to pass the gates that lead to the bustling and dangerous Peking, which is still in the throes of civil war. He is visited by his younger brother, Kyi, who comes to live with him, and his mother, Dong, who sees him only briefly before returning to her family. Thrilled at meeting another child, the emperor makes a companion of his brother. The emperor, who has almost no concept of the world outside the Forbidden City, soon learns that China has become a republic. As Pu Yi becomes an adolescent (played superbly by Wu Tao), he yearns to become more worldly and learn of the changes occurring in Peking—"the city of sounds." The arrival of a Scottish tutor, O'Toole, changes the young emperor's life. He is immediately curious about O'Toole and life in the West. He is fascinated by the lives of other rulers and emperors and dreams of one day studying at Oxford. As O'Toole's influence grows increasingly stronger, the emperor makes plans to escape the Forbidden City, though O'Toole convinces him that marriage is perhaps a more practical means of escape. O'Toole tests his power in the Forbidden City by insisting the emperor get spectacles. The High Consorts (wives of the previous emperor) gasp at such a radical thought. Only when O'Toole warns that the Emperor will go blind and, as a result, thousands of servants will lose their jobs, is the he allowed to have spectacles. Wearing his spectacles for the first time and deciding that he looks like Harold Lloyd, the emperor chooses his empress from a number of photos. The one he picks is the 17-year-old Chen, a Manchu descendent who, like the emperor, has been tutored and exposed to Western influence. Most of all, the emperor is pleased with his empress because she promises to teach him the "quick-step." In addition to the empress, he has a second wife, the concubine Wen Hsui (played by Wu Jun Mei). In a symbolic break with tradition, the emperor, now played by Lone, cuts off his *queue* (a long braid at the back of his head) and orders a reform of the Forbidden City. In an effort to assess the scale of the eunuchs' corruption he orders an inventory to be taken of the imperial storeroom. The eunuchs, however, set it ablaze rather than reveal the extent of their graft. In retaliation, the emperor dismisses his eunuchs from the Forbidden City.

By 1924, the Dynasty completely collapses as Feng Yu-Hsiang, an invading warlord, captures Peking and expels everyone from the Forbidden City. On only one hour's notice, they depart for the safety of Peking's Japanese Legation and from there they travel to the cosmopolitan city of Tientsin, where they are whisked away to the Japanese Concession and given safe quarter. Here, the emperor begins to live like a playboy, attending extravagant balls, dancing with the empress, and entertaining his guests by singing such popular tunes as "Am I Blue." When, in 1931, life in Tientsin becomes too dangerous for Lone—now the emperor of nothing—he escapes to Manchuria with the help of the Japanese and under the watchful eye of Japanese secret serviceman Masahiko Amakasu (played by Sakamoto, who also contributed to the film's score). It is in his decision to accept Japanese assistance in Manchuria that Lone makes his biggest mistake—one which will later bring him to trial for war crimes. Feeling a sense of loyalty to Manchuria—the land of his ancestors—Lone unknowingly becomes a pawn in Japan's attempt to gain international acceptance for their involvement in Manchuria. Desperate to regain the title of emperor and eventually return to China to rebuild the Ching Dynasty, Lone accepts Japan's offer to become emperor of Manchukuo, Japan's puppet government in Manchuria. Once again Lone is the emperor and Chen is the empress. By now, however, the situation has irreparably deteriorated. Lone's concubine has divorced him, the empress has become an opium addict and an embarrassment to the throne, and O'Toole is no longer present to offer advice. Arriving on the scene is Eastern Jewel (played in brilliant Mata Hari fashion by Maggie Han), a Japanese spy/aviatrix/bi-sexual/jetsetter who agrees to fill the void left by the emperor's departed concubine. Unbeknownst to the Emperor, Han is also carrying on with Sakamoto, who has now become head of the Manchurian film industry. As Japan's efforts to conquer the world change, so too does the Emperor's feelings towards the Japanese. After years in Manchukuo, he comes to realize that he is once again a prisoner/emperor. He is unable to leave the grounds or speak with his own ministers, his private guard of some 200 men is disarmed, and he is forced to sign numerous papers which endorse Japan's illegal war actions. Although he tries to stand up to Japanese pressure by refusing to sign papers which would name a corrupt official as Manchukuo's prime minister, the emperor eventually succumbs after the empress is revealed to be pregnant by their chauffeur. A hopeless opium addict, the empress is taken away to a sanitarium.

In 1945 the tables are turned on Japan and the emperor is whisked away to a nearby airport for an escape. Before they can take-off, however, parachuting Russian troops invade and take the Emperor prisoner. After spending five years in Russian prisons, the Emperor and thousands of other Chinese prisoners are returned to China for "remolding," the process of re-education by Mao Tse-Tung's Communist party. Again a prisoner, Lone struggles with his day-to-day existence. Having always been served and waited on, he is unable even to tie his own shoelaces or brush his teeth without someone's help. For the next nine years, the governor of the prison (Ying Ruocheng) coerces Lone into giving a written confession (like all the other prisoners) of his war crimes. Serving as a model prisoner, Lone is released in 1959 as the ultimate example of communist reeducation—remolded from emperor to citizen. Upon his release, Lone finds work doing gardening chores at Peking's Botanical Gardens. In 1967 during the height of the Cultural Revolution, Lone, now an ordinary citizen, finds himself witness to a demonstration of youthful Red Guard revolutionaries. Having seen China change throughout the century—from Ching Dynasty to Mao's communism—Lone pays a final visit to the Forbidden City, this time as a tourist. The film's coda shot is set in modern day as throngs of tourists descend upon the throne room as a guide explains that Pu Yi, the Last Emperor of China, died in 1967.

Combining the command of the historical epic he displayed in 1900 with the political intrigue and melodrama of THE CONFORMIST, Bertolucci has, in THE LAST EMPEROR, constructed a beautiful film about the transformation of one man and one country from monarchy to communism during the full-expanse of the 20th century. Admitting that he is a storyteller, not a historian, Bertolucci tells not one, but two stories in THE LAST EMPEROR—that of China's change, told through a selective sampling of events; and that of Pu Yi's change, told with an emphasis on myth rather than on fact. Spending two years in China researching the film, Bertolucci, with writing collaborators Enzo Ungari (who died before completion) and screenwriter Peploe (Bertolucci's brother-in-law), discovered in Pu Yi a fascinating character who became a tragic victim of circumstances and a pawn in a far-reaching game of world domination. Although Pu Yi began his life as the emperor of half the world's population, he is a relatively minor figure in the history of this century. (He usually rates only a small entry or a passing reference in most encyclopedias.) Essentially a puppet for his entire life, Pu Yi was placed on the throne at age three, too young to actually rule. By age six he was forced to abdicate the throne, retaining power only within the walls of the Forbidden City. By 29, he had been made the puppet emperor of Manchukuo to legitimize Japan's actions. By the end of his life, Pu Yi had become a puppet of Mao's government, free to live as a regular citizen but employed as a promotional tool in the communist re-education process. It is this lifelong imprisonment that is at the heart of THE LAST EMPEROR's narrative structure. Not actually told in a standard flashback form, the film hops from era to era at will. The first part of the film deals with Pu Yi's reeducation (1949-1959) and with the many events that came before (from the Forbidden City to Manchukuo). The latter part of the film also deals with the re-education period and with Pu Yi's life as a citizen. In each case, Pu Yi is a prisoner. Not only was Pu Yi manipulated in his later years, he was also, in one sense, returned to his rank as emperor since Chairman Mao had declared his intent to multiply this model citizen by a billion and thereby make China a country of "emperors."

In THE LAST EMPEROR, all the elements of filmmaking are working together perfectly. Bertolucci's direction is both epic (when inside the Forbidden City) and melodramatic (when watching Pu Yi's career, life, and marriage collapse in Manchukuo). Storaro's carefully constructed lighting schemes and moving camera are unmatched by any cinematographer working today. Lone, previously seen in ICEMAN and YEAR OF THE DRAGON, is wholly credible as he ages throughout the film. Wu Tao, as the adolescent Pu Yi, is every bit Lone's equal. Both actors convey the emperor's innocence, ignorance, and veiled sadistic streak. Chen shows her skill by playing both radiant teen bride and a rotting opium-addict. O'Toole shows more restraint than usual and simply *becomes* his character, as if he, like Reginald Johnston, would have made an excellent tutor for the emperor. Also worthy of note is the film's score which combines lush romanticism with traditional Chinese melodies and was written chiefly by Ryuichi Sakamoto (who also scored MERRY CHRISTMAS, MR. LAWRENCE) and David Byrne (of Talking Heads fame). The film's faults are two-fold—its condensation of history in the latter half and its refusal to paint Pu Yi in the darker light (his sadism and bisexuality go unexplored).

After the box-office and critical failure of 1979's LUNA and 1981's THE TRAGEDY OF A RIDICULOUS MAN (a title which could well serve as an alternate title for THE LAST EMPEROR, as could BEFORE THE REVOLUTION, THE CONFORMIST, or 1900), Bertolucci, once the poet-prodigy of Italian cinema, searched for a project which could, in effect, restore him to the throne he once sat upon. Efforts to film Dashiell Hammett's *Red Harvest* and

Alberto Moravia's *1934* ended in failure. Looking for change, Bertolucci left Italy for China with two proposals. His first choice was an adaptation of Andre Malraux's *Man's Fate*, the powerful novel of the 1927 Shanghai uprising, which the Chinese government found too controversial. The second choice was THE LAST EMPEROR, based on Pu Yi's 1964 autobiography *From Emperor To Citizen* (which was actually ghostwritten by party-appointed Li Wenda). Budgeted at $23 million, the film looks like it cost much more and, in fact, would have been many times that amount had the Chinese government not lent its full support. (The fact that Bertolucci is a member of the Italian Communist Party, albeit a non-active one, made contract talks easier.) After two years of negotiating (with the considerable efforts of producer Jeremy Thomas), China and Bertolucci became filmmaking partners. The Chinese were given approval of the script (only minor historical changes were made) and local distribution rights. In return, Bertolucci obtained permission to shoot anywhere within the walls of the Forbidden City—a privilege granted to no other Western filmmaker. Collaborating once again with his brilliant cameraman Vittorio Storaro, Bertolucci has captured the days of China's Dynasty with an indescribable visual splendor. The staggering production used 19,000 extras, many of them soldiers in the People's Liberation Army; an international cast and crew from Italy, China, the US, Britain, Hong Kong, and Japan; 9,000 costumes ranging from Kuomingtang uniforms to imperial robes to the elaborate coxcomb headdresses of Tibetan lamas; a collection of vintage cars from various decades and countries; and 2,000 kilos of pasta for the Italian crew. The camera rolled in August of 1986 and 15 weeks (a short time considering the magnitude and the running time) later principal photography was completed. By October of 1987, the finished film was given its premiere at the Tokyo International Film Festival. In addition to the 166-minute version, a 4-hour television version has also been prepared. The film's US release, although greeted with unanimously favorable reviews, failed to bring in the expected box-office receipts. Distributed by Columbia Pictures, THE LAST EMPEROR (like HOPE AND GLORY) fell victim to the changing of the guards when David Puttnam was replaced as studio head. Because THE LAST EMPEROR was a Puttnam project its release was sabotaged by the new regime, which preferred to promote films of its own making. As a result THE LAST EMPEROR never received a wide release, playing in less than 100 theaters across the country. (In English). *(Brief nudity, sexual situations, violence.)*

p, Jeremy Thomas; d, Bernardo Bertolucci; w, Mark Peploe, Bernardo Bertolucci, Enzo Ungari; ph, Vittorio Storaro (Technovision, Technicolor); m, Ryuichi Sakamoto, David Byrne, Cong Su; ed, Gabriella Cristiani; prod d, Ferdinando Scarfiotti; md, Ray Williams; art d, Gianni Giovagnoni, Gianni Silvestri, Maria Teresa Barbasso; cos, James Acheson; spec eff, Gino De Rossi, Fabrizio Martinelli; makeup, Fabrizio Sforza.

Historical/Biography **(PR:C MPAA:PG-13)**

LAST EMPRESS, THE† (1987, Chi.) 120m Changchun Studio c

Pan Hong, Jian Wen, Fu Yiwei.

Riding the coattails of Bernardo Bertolucci's epic THE LAST EMPEROR, this Chinese production concerns itself with the role of women in the life of Emperor Pu Yi. With a narrower scope, the film opens as Pu Yi weds his first wife Wan Jung, or "Elizabeth" (the Joan Chen character). Like the Bertolucci film, the emperor's life in Manchukuo is also depicted, but in a far darker vein. Pu Yi is shown as a cruel opportunist who willfully collaborated with the Japanese and who beat his wife, driving her into opium addiction. According to Pu Yi's biographers, the emperor's life-style was far more decadent than is portrayed in Bertolucci's film. THE LAST EMPRESS seemingly makes an effort to expose this dark side.

d, Chen Jialin, Sun Qingguo; w, Zhang Xiaotian; ph, An Zhiguo.

Biography/Historical **(PR:NR MPAA:NR)**

LAST OF ENGLAND, THE† (1987, Brit.) 91m Anglo Intl.-British Screen-Channel 4-ZDF/Tartan b&w/c

Spring, Gerrard McCarthur, John Phillips, Gay Gaynor, Matthew Hawkins, Tilda Swinton, Spencer Leigh, Voice of: Nigel Terry.

British avant-garde filmmaker Derek Jarman follows his most accessible film, CARAVAGGIO, with another experimental feature that combines home movies shot by his father and grandfather (from the late 1920s to the early 1950s) with documentary footage and sequences from an "imagined feature film" to create Jarman's personal ruminations on the decay of British society. Jarman regulars Tilda Swinton, Spencer Leigh, and Paul Reynolds are featured in the narrative sections. Jarman also contributed a segment to ARIA in 1987. Musical score includes: "Pomp and Circumstance" (Edward Elgar, performed by The Scottish National Orchestra), "Refugee Theme" (Barry Adamson, performed by Adamson, Martin Micarrick), "Terrorists" (Andy Gill, performed by Gill, Dean Garcia), "Disco Death" (Mayo Thompson, Albert Oehlen), "The Skye Boat Song" (performed by Marianne Faithfull), "La Treizieme Revient (The Thirteenth Returns)," "Deliver Me" (Diamanda Galas, performed by Brian Gulland, El Tito, Simon Turner).

p, James Mackey, Don Boyd; d, Derek Jarman; ph, Derek Jarman, Christopher Hughes, Cerith Wyn Evans, Richard Heslop, Tim Burk; m, Simon Turner, Edward Elgar; ed, Peter Cartwright, Angus Cook, John Maybury, Sally Yeadon; prod d, Christopher Hobbs; cos, Sandy Powell; spec eff, Tony Neale; m/l, Barry Adamson, Andy Gill, Mayo Thompson, Albert Oehlen, Diamanda Galas; makeup, Thelma Mathews, Wendy Selway.

Drama **(PR:NR MPAA:NR)**

LAST SONG, THE† (1987, Thai.) 90m c

A young farmboy arrives in Bangkok with dreams of becoming a singer. He soon finds his ambitions derailed when he enters an extravagant nightclub frequented by gays and transvestites. (Subtitled.)

d, Pisarn Akarasainee.

Drama **(PR:NR MPAA:NR)**

LAST STRAW, THE*** (1987, Can.) 98m National Film Board of Canada/Cinema Intl. Canada c

Salverio [Sam] Grana *(Alex)*, Fernanda Tavares *(Laura)*, Maurice Podbrey *(Dr. Cameron)*, Beverley Murray *(Nurse Thompson)*, Stefan Wodoslawsky *(Blue)*, Christine Pak *(Hyang-Sook)*, Wally Martin *(Manager)*, Gwynne Dyer *(National Security Advisor)*.

The third and final chapter of the Wilson/Walker trilogy produced by the National Film Board of Canada (the first two were THE MASCULINE MYSTIQUE and 90 DAYS) picks up where the last film left off as Grana begins his career as a sperm donor and Wodoslawsky settles into his marriage to Korean mail-order-bride Pak. Much to the clinic's surprise, Grana's sperm has an amazing motility rate of 99.5, making him The Most Potent Man in the World. Unfortunately, his physical appearance is so unremarkable that most women looking to be artificially inseminated skim past his picture in the photo album of sperm donors used by the clinic. Frustrated by his lack of popularity, Grana gets himself a seedy manager (Martin) and makes an appearance on a radio call-in show to tout his potency. The next morning there are women lined up all the way out the door of the clinic for a shot of Grana's sperm. Soon word of Grana's potency spreads to the television news and print media and he is heralded as a national treasure. A proud Canadian, Grana spurns lucrative offers for his services from competing countries, prefering to help bolster Canada's sagging birth rate. Meanwhile, Wodoslawsky and Pak discover that their inability to have children is caused by Wodoslawsky's low sperm count. After a number of ridiculous methods and contraptions designed to solve the problem fail miserably, they decide to visit the clinic. However, much to Grana's and the clinic's dismay, he has suddenly developed an impotency problem and cannot deliver the goods (so to speak). To make matters worse, a bevy of commandos from Australia posing as rugby players kidnap Grana, cure him of his impotency, and plan to take him back to the land of the koalas where his sperm can revitalize the disastrously low Aussie birth rate. To combat this covert act of war, the Canadian prime minister and his top aides meet for a briefing from the national security advisor (played by military expert and historian Gwynne Dyer in a hilarious cameo) who informs them that the declining birth rate in the Western world is directly attributable to the spread of feminism—an obvious Communist plot to destroy male confidence and provoke widespread impotency. Luckily, the Aussie's evil plan is stopped in the nick of time and Grana is freed to continue sharing his potency with the women of the Great White North.

Produced for $600,000 and more or less improvised by the cast (Wilson and Walker's usual working method), THE LAST STRAW is as about as tasteful as any comedy about artificial insemination can be. Director Walker stays away from the ribald gross-out inherent in this material, but still manages to make this film devilishly funny in spots. Because the characters are dealt with sensitively, the situation retains some dignity, thus enabling Walker to explore its absurdity without becoming vulgar. The deadpan Grana is terrific as the loyal Canuck who finds himself something of a national hero. Also excellent are Wodoslawsky and Pak as the young married couple trying desperately to sire children, only to find out that the best man at their wedding is now The Most Potent Man in the World and that a straw of his sperm will cost them $5,000. Canadian character actors Martin and Murray are used to great effect as well. Martin is riotous as the chain-smoking, plaid-suited manager, and Murray is unforgettable as the uptight, repressed nurse who won't go near the potent Grana without wearing rubber gloves. Despite all its strengths, however, THE LAST STRAW suffers from some haphazard pacing and a poorly developed climactic action—the film sort of stumbles to a halt. These problems are no doubt due to the improvised nature of the production, but that is simply no excuse for a flabby, unsatisfying ending. Although uneven, THE LAST STRAW's vision of the near future may well prove to be incredibly prophetic, and its good humor deserves to be enjoyed by those who will not be put off by the subject matter. *(Adult situations, sexual situations, profanity.)*

p, David Wilson, Giles Walker; d, Giles Walker; w, Giles Walker, David Wilson; ph, Andrew Kitzanuk; m, Robert Lauzon, Fernand Martel; ed, David Wilson; cos, Janet Campbell.

Comedy **(PR:O MPAA:NR)**

LATE SUMMER BLUES*** (1987, Israel) 101m Blues Ltd./Nachshon c (BLUES LA-CHOFESH HA-GODOL)

Dor Zweigenbom *(Arale)*, Yoav Zafir *(Mossi)*, Noa Goldberg *(Naomi)*, Vered Cohen *(Shosh)*, Sahar Segal *(Margo)*, Sharon Bar-Ziv *(Kobi)*, Ada Ben Nahum, Edna Fliedel, Miki Kam, Moshe Havatzeleth, Amith Gazith.

Four members of a graduating Tel Aviv high school class enjoy their final weeks of freedom prior to their induction into the Israeli army and subsequent service at the front during the Suez War in 1970. Each is exposed to the realities of the war. The opening segment focuses on Vered Cohen, who is drafted just ten days after his final class. He will miss his graduation ceremonies which are postponed because a graduate from the previous year's class has died at the front. During his last night before induction, he attends a farewell party, and he notes in his diary that he is proud, as the first draftee, to have a song written about him. He laments, however, that he will be a soldier before he has had the opportunity to either get a driver's license or go to bed with a girl. His classmates, in an effort to maintain the ephemeral closeness, try to ignore the war, which, as they realize, will soon control their lives. One member of the group, Sahar Segal, a budding filmmaker who likens himself to Fellini, roams through the crowd with his camera constantly poised to capture the moments of this last evening with his friends. The second part begins during the graduation ceremonies and concentrates on Dor Zweigenbom, the most radical of the graduating class. As the principal is to take the stage, she receives a phone message in her office that Cohen has been killed during his army training program, a conversation overheard by Zweigenbom and his group of friends. Zweigenbom confronts her during the ceremonies when she refuses to announce Cohen's death to the student body, and she breaks down. When Cohen's coffin is returned from the front, Segal records his funeral on film, and combines it with the earlier footage of his departure as a salute to his departed friend. Soon Zweigenbom, whose anti-war activities are incomprehensible to the majority of his classmates, is accused of cowardice because of his pacifist sentiments. Zweigenbom retreats into solitude in an effort to come to terms with the accusations. The third part features Yoav Zafir, a musician who is advised by an army officer to lower his draft rating to escape enlistment so that he may serve in the military band. During the graduation ceremonies, Zweigenbom quickly becomes suspicious that the songfest, arranged and conducted by Zafir, is being orchestrated to promote his musical talents and to enable him to escape army induction. Zafir, while asserting that he did what he thought was right, nevertheless joins the inductees when they depart for training camp. During the fourth part, the epilog, even Zweigenbom has enlisted due, as he says, to a moment of weakness. Only Segal, whose bout with diabetes has prevented him from serving in the army, remains in Tel Aviv. Segal moves to Paris and embarks upon a filmmaking career.

Renen Schorr's feature-film debut is a strong indictment of the compulsory draft that forces Israeli adolescents to surrender three prime years to the army. The fact that Israelis have been reluctant to critize the army because it is such a protective force in their lives makes the production of this film noteworthy. Even more noteworthy is the fact that the film was partially subsidized by the government. Schorr's choice of the more distant events of 1970 perhaps has made the film seem less threatening. While the film is critical of the prevailing attitudes, it presents a restrained and thoughtful look at its subject. Perhaps the strength of Schorr's film is in its recreation of the world of 1970. The use of the film within the film structure serves to enhance this sense of objectivity. Ultimately we watch as the four main characters, all of whom protest, with varying degrees of intensity, against the draft, give in to stronger forces and climb aboard the recruitment bus. Schorr's most intriguing character is the amateur filmmaker, a member of the group, but one who cannot experience the intensity of the emotional issues because he does not truly partake of them. In fact, he uses his camera to completely escape the emotional experiences. *(Adult situations.)*

p, Ilan De-Renen Schorr, Doron Nesher; d, Renen Schorr; w, Doron Nesher; ph, Eitan Harris; m, Rafi Kadishzon; ed, Shlomo Hazan; art d, Zmira Hershkowitz.

Drama **(PR:C MPAA:NR)**

LAURA† (1987, Hung.) 98m Mafilm-Objektiv/Hungarofilm c

Juli Basti *(Laura Boldog)*, Gabor Reviczky *(Ferenc Boldog, Her Husband)*, Hedy Temessy *(Berta Boldog, Her Mother-In-Law)*, Gyorgy Dorner *(Giraffe, Musician)*, Tamas Puskas *(Matyus, Young Man)*, Zbigniew Zapasiewicz *(Dr. Varga)*.

Basti is the title character, an unhappy young woman who is married to the son of a deceased national hero. Because her mother-in-law is influential, Basti is given a new job in a hospital as the head of the personnel department. She is far from content, however—her husband is lazy and inattentive, her job monotonous, and her mother-in-law overbearing. Into her life comes a former lover-turned-musician who tries to persuade Basti to join his group and be in his new rock video. She is also pursued by another man who becomes obsessed with her, following her incessantly. Her contact with these men and a physician who is being forced into retirement helps Basti to recognize the problems in her life. She finally finds the courage to sue for divorce and start life anew with her young daughter.

d&w, Geza Boszormenyi; ph, Ferenc Pap (Eastmancolor); m, Gyorgy Selmeczi, Ferenc Balazs; ed, Eva Karmento; set d, Jozsef Romvari; cos, Maria Benedek.

Drama **(PR:NR MPAA:NR)**

LAW OF DESIRE½** (1987, Span.) 100m El Deseo-Laurenfilm/Cinevista c (LA LEY DEL DESEO)

Eusebio Poncela *(Pablo Quintero)*, Carmen Maura *(Tina Quintero)*, Antonio Banderas *(Antonio Benitez)*, Miguel Molina *(Juan Bermudez)*, Manuela Velasco *(Ada, Child)*, Bibi Andersen *(Ada, Mother)*, Fernando Guillen *(Inspector)*, Nacho Martinez *(Dr. Martin)*, Helga Line *(Antonio's Mother)*, Fernando G. Cuervo *(Policeman, Child)*, German Cobos *(Priest)*, Maruchi Leon *(Maruchi)*, Marta Fernandez Muro *(Groupie)*, Marta Fernandez Muro *(Sergeant)*, Tinin Almodovar *(Lawyer)*, Lupe Barrado *(Nurse)*, Roxy Von Donna *(Woman on Telephone)*, Jose Manuel Bello *(Young Guard)*, Angie Gray *(Girl on Terrace)*, Jose Ramon Fernandez *(Pimp)*, Jose A. Granja *(Impossible Model)*, Pepe Patatin *(Clerk)*, Hector Saurit *(Reporter)*.

Pedro Almodovar, Spain's acclaimed comedy director, has stated he wants to reach audiences through their hearts, their minds, and their genitals. In LAW OF DESIRE he concentrates specifically on the latter for story appeal, resulting in an occasionally fun romp that never amounts to much. Poncela is a highly regarded filmmaker, whose exotic homosexual comedies are very popular. He is currently involved with Molina, a young working class male, who does not exclusively sleep with men. Confused about his identity, Molina decides to head for the seaside where he plans to think things over. While Molina is away, Poncela wants to be assured he receives only tender letters from his lover. It's agreed that Poncela will write these letters and send them to Molina who only has to sign and return them. After Molina departs, Poncela meets Banderas, the son of a public official, at a discotheque. The two begin an affair and Banderas becomes highly possessive of the director. In a subplot Poncela is developing his latest project, basing his new script on the life of his "sister" Maura. Maura began life as a male, then had a sex change operation. She is happy with her life, as is Maura's pubescent daughter. This child was born to Maura when, as a man, he impregnated a lesbian with whom he had a long affair. When Maura learns Poncela's new project has been inspired by her unusual history, she becomes livid, though eventually all is forgiven. Meanwhile Banderas, in a fit of jealousy, goes to Molina's seaside retreat. He demands Molina stop seeing Poncela, and the two men begin a struggle. Molina is thrown from the top of a cliff, and Banderas flees the scene. When Poncela arrives the next day he is shocked by his lover's death. Police suspect Poncela is the killer, and begin tailing him. Poncela confronts Banderas, who denies everything. Fatigued, Poncela accidentally drives his car into a tree and is rushed to a hospital. He has lost his memory, but eventually recovers it with Maura's help. He learns Maura has been sleeping with Banderas, though his sister has no idea of her new lover's relationship with Poncela. Meanwhile, Banderas goes crazy and takes Maura hostage at Poncela's apartment. The police surround the building and Banderas offers to let her go in exchange for one hour with Poncela. Poncela agrees and ends up making love with this madman. Afterwards Banderas leaves the room and shoots himself. The apartment is accidentally set ablaze, while Poncela is reunited with his sister and niece.

The problem with LAW OF DESIRE is that it tries too hard to be eccentric. Much of the humor is forced, and so overplayed that the satirical elements are lost. Furthermore, the majority of the humor is based on sexual situations. Though Almodovar certainly directs with energetic pacing, he is more interested in showing sexual orientation as character development than in taking any real chances with the material. After Molina's murder the film drags for an uncomfortable stretch until the final moments. Without sex, the film really has nothing to say. Poncela is handsome, with classic good looks and carries himself well. His tongue-in-cheek acting style makes the character enjoyable, nicely filling in the deficiencies of Almodovar's script. However, the real driving force to LAW OF DESIRE is the wonderfully zany Maura. She is a true free spirit, driven by her own passions and unafraid of what life has to offer. In one marvelous scene, she returns to the church of her childhood and begins singing an old hymn. When the pastor says Maura's voice reminds him of an old choir boy, Maura's face shines like a gleeful child as she explains who she is. Had Almodovar concentrated on Maura instead of a series of liaisons, he really would have had something unique. Songs include "Lo Dudo" (Los Panchos), "Ne Me Quitte Pas" (Maisa Matarazzo), "Guarda Que Luna" (Fred Bongusto), "Susan Get Down," "Satanasa" (Almodovar, McNamara), "La Despedida" (Bernardo Bonezzi), "Dejame Recordar" (Bola De Nieve). *(Nudity, sexual situations.)*

p, Miguel A. Perez Campos; d&w, Pedro Almodovar; ph, Angel Luis Fernandez (Eastmancolor); m, Igor Stravinsky, Dmitri Shostakovich; ed, Jose Salcedo; set d, Javier Fernandez; cos, Jose M. Cossio; m/l, Maisa Matarazzo, Fred Bongusto, Bernardo Bonezzi, Bola de Nieve, Los Panchos.

Comedy **(PR:O MPAA:NR)**

LAWYER SUHASINI† (1987, India)

Bhanuchander, Suhasini.

A woman defies tradition and defends her own case in a court of law. (In Tamil.)

p, Vamsi, D.S. Prasad; d, Vamsi.

Drama **(PR:NR MPAA:NR)**

LE BEAUF† (1987, Fr.) 105m G.P.F.I.-TFI c

Gerard Jugnot *(Gilbert)*, Marianne Basler *(Gisele)*, Gerard Darmon *(Serge)*, Zabou *(Maryline)*, Nicolas Wostrikoff *(Nicolas)*, Didier Sauvegrain *(Marc)*, Boris Bergman *(Rocky)*, Jean-Pol Dubois *(Bank Supervisor)*.

Comedian Jugnot takes a serious role as a complacent family man who has long ago surrendered his ideals in exchange for security. He meets up with a former friend, Darmon, and the pair share memories of their past as members of a local rock band. When Darmon learns what Jugnot does for a living—burning old bank notes in the incinerator at the Banque de France—his greedy mind goes to work. They plan a heist, but Jugnot sours when he discovers that his wife, Basler, is sleeping with Darmon. Jugnot plots to murder Darmon, but by the end things work themselves out.

p, Charlotte Fraisse; d, Yves Amoureux; w, Yves Amoureux, Guy Beaumont, Boris Bergman; ph, Thierry Arbogast (Eastmancolor); m, Alain Bashung; ed, Catherine Renault; art d, Jean Bauer.

Thriller **(PR:NR MPAA:NR)**

LE CRI DU HIBOU† (1987, Fr./It.) 102m Italfrance-Ci.Vi.Te.Ca.Sa./UIP c (Trans: The Cry of the Owl)

Christophe Malavoy *(Robert)*, Mathilda May *(Juliette)*, Virginie Thevenet *(Veronique)*, Jacques Penot *(Patrick)*, Jean-Pierre Kalfon *(Commissioner)*, Patrice Kerbrat *(Marcello)*.

Claude Chabrol is the only major French director associated with the New Wave of the 1950s who has fallen almost completely from critical grace. While others such as Godard, Resnais, Rohmer, Rivette, Malle, and Varda continue to garner critical acclaim, Chabrol has steadily delivered commercial psychological thrillers to Parisian audiences, including his two films this year, LE CRI DU HIBOU and MASQUES. LE CRI DU HIBOU, based on a novel by Patricia Highsmith (STRANGERS ON A TRAIN, THE AMERICAN FRIEND), stars Malavoy as a psychologically unstable Parisian. He leaves his wife and begins a relationship with a country woman, May, who is engaged to Penot. Caught in a web of deceit, Malavoy is soon being questioned for the murder of both May and Penot. He must convince police that May committed suicide and that Penot is still alive and intent on taking revenge.

p, Antonio Passalia; d, Claude Chabrol; w, Claude Chabrol, Odile Barski (based on a novel by Patricia Highsmith); ph, Jean Rabier; m, Mathieu Chabrol; ed, Monique Fardoulis; art d, Jacques Leguillon.

Drama **(PR:NR MPAA:NR)**

LE FOTO DI GIOIA† (1987, It.) Medusa-Dania-Devon-Films Int'l.-National Cinematografica-Rete Italia/Medusa Distribuzione c (Trans: Gioia's Photograph)

Serena Grandi, Daria Nicolodi, Vanni Corbellini, David Brando, Karl Zinny, Katrine Michelsen, Lino Salemme, Sabrina Salerno, Capucine, George Eastman.

A slasher film from DEMONS director Bava (son of Mario) which sees a female model for men's magazines terrorized by a mysterious killer who, in the end, appears to be her own brother. But as she lay recuperating in the hospital it is hinted that her rescuer, a crippled neighbor, may be the actual murderer.

d, Lamberto Bava; w, Gianfranco Clerici, Danilo Stroppa (based on a story by Luciano Martino); ph, Gianlorenzo Battaglia (Telecolor); m, Simon Boswell; ed, Mauro Bonanni.

Horror **(PR:NR MPAA:NR)**

LE GRAND CHEMIN† (1987, Fr.) 107m Flach-Selena Audiovisuel-TF1/AAA c (Trans: The Big Road)

Anemone *(Marcelle)*, Richard Bohringer *(Pello)*, Antoine Hubert *(Louis)*, Vanessa Guedj *(Martine)*, Christine Pascal *(Claire)*, Raoul Billery *(Priest)*, Pascale Roberts *(Yvonne)*, Marie Matheron *(Solange)*, Daniel Rialet *(Simon)*.

Echoing Rene Clement's FORBIDDEN GAMES, LE GRAND CHEMIN centers on two children—11-year-old Guedj and 9-year-old Hubert—who explore life, death, and sex while wandering around the country. The Parisian Hubert is sent by his pregnant mother Pascal to the country home of Anemone and Bohringer, who still have not overcome the grief they feel over the death years before of their child. The young Hubert is the son of director Jean-Loup.

p, Pascal Hommais, Jean-Francois Lepetit; d&w, Jean-Loup Hubert; ph, Claude Lecomte (Eastmancolor); m, Georges Granier; ed, Raymonde Guyot; art d, Thierry Flamand.

Drama **(PR:NR MPAA:NR)**

LE JEUNE MAGICIEN† (1987, Can./Pol.) 106m Les Productions La Fete-Film Tor Unit c (CUDOWNE DZIECKO; Trans: The Young Magician)

Rusty Jedwab *(Peter)*, Edward Garson *(Alexander)*, Daria Trafankowska *(Mother)*, Mariusz Benoit *(Father)*, Natasza Maraszek, Tomasz Klimasiewicz.

The fourth film in the Canadian children's series known as "Tales For All" (following THE DOG WHO STOPPED THE WAR, THE PEANUT BUTTER SOLUTION, and BACH AND BROCCOLI) is the first official Canada-Poland co-production. Jedwab stars as a 12-year-old boy who feels ostracized by his classmates because of his lack of interest in athletics. Jedwab finally discovers his calling when his parents take him to see a magic show. Picked by the magician to serve as his assistant during a trick, Jedwab becomes excited by the world of magic and immediately sets out to learn as much as he can. Not only does Jedwab

become proficient at prestidigitation, he discovers he possesses telekinetic powers. Unfortunately, his telekinesis only serves to further isolate him from his peers, for their parents fear his power. Things change for Jedwab when a national emergency arises and the government asks him to help. When Jedwab's efforts prove successful, he becomes a national hero and is accepted by all.

p, Rock Demers, Krzysztof Zanussi; d&w, Waldemar Dziki; ph, Wit Dabal; m, Krzesimir Debski; ed, Andre Corriveau.

Drama/Children's **(PR:NR MPAA:NR)**

LE JOURNAL D'UN FOU† (1987, Fr.) 90m Lydie Media-Films A2/Lydie Media c (Trans: The Diary of a Madman)

Roger Coggio *(Auxence Popritchin)*, Fanny Cottencon *(Sophie)*, Jean-Pierre Darras *(Sophie's Father)*, Charles Charras.

An adaptation of Nicolai Gogol's absurd tale of a sexually and socially repressed government clerk whose thoughts drive him to insanity. Coggio, who produced, directed, wrote, and stars, filmed this story once before in 1963.

p&d, Roger Coggio; w, Roger Coggio, Bernard G. Landry (based on the story by Nicolai Gogol); ph, Claude Lecomte (Eastmancolor); m, Jean Musy; ed, Helene Plemmianikoff; prod d, Guy-Claude Francois; cos, Francoise Tournafond.

Comedy/Drama **(PR:NR MPAA:NR)**

LE JUPON ROUGE (SEE: MANUELA'S LOVES, 1981, Fr.)

LE MIRACULE† (1987, Fr.) 85m Initial Groupe-Koala-FR3/Cannon c (Trans: The Miracle Healing)

Jean Poiret *(Papu)*, Michel Serrault *(Ronald Rox Terrier)*, Jeanne Moreau *(Sabine)*, Sophie Moyse *(Angelica)*, Jean Rougerie *(Monseigneur)*, Sylvie Joly *(Mme. Fox Terrier)*, Roland Blanche *(Plombie)*, Marc Maury *(Abbe Humus)*.

Veteran director Mocky reunites with actors Poiret and Serrault in this Bunuelian satire about two people on their way to Lourdes. Poiret is an opportunistic man who has made a false insurance claim and is being taken in a wheelchair to his destination by Moreau. Following along is Serrault, a mute insurance agent who suspects Poiret's scam. When they finally immerse themselves in the healing waters, Poiret actually becomes crippled, while Serrault regains the use of his voice.

d, Jean-Pierre Mocky; w, Jean-Pierre Mocky, Jean-Claude Romer, Patrick Granier; ph, Marcel Combes (Fujicolor); m, Jorge Arriagada; ed, Jean-Pierre Mocky; art d, Patrice Renault, Jean-Claude Sevenet, Etienne Mery.

Comedy **(PR:NR MPAA:NR)**

LE MOUSTACHU† (1987, Fr.) 86m CAPAC-Agepro Cinema-Selena Audiovisuel-TF1/AAA c (Trans: The Field Agent)

Jean Rochefort *(Duroc)*, Grace de Capitani *(The Girl)*, Jean-Claude Brialy *(Leroy)*, Jean-Louis Trintignant *(The General)*, Jean-Claude Leguay *(Young Motorist)*, Maxime Leroux *(Staub)*, Jacques Mathou *(Sully)*.

Rochefort stars in this parody of spy films as an operative who is transporting a specially rigged car to a gang of terrorists. Rochefort, however, gets caught between the politics of his superiors—Trintignant and Brialy—and the terrorist gang members who are waiting to ambush him. Credited as artistic adviser is the 81-year-old French art director Alexandre Trauner, famous for his work on such films as QUAI DES BRUMES (1938), LE JOUR SE LEVE (1939), LES VISITEURS DU SOIR (1942), and CHILDREN OF PARADISE (1944).

p, Marie-Christine de Montbrial, Paul Claudon; d&w, Dominique Chaussois; ph, Claude Agostini (Eastmancolor); m, Vladimir Cosma; ed, Georges Klotz; art d, Didier Naert, Alexandre Trauner (credited as artistic advisor).

Comedy/Spy **(PR:NR MPAA:NR)**

LE SOLITAIRE† (1987, Fr.) 94m Sara-Cerito/AMLF-Cerito c (Trans: The Loner)

Jean-Paul Belmondo *(Commissioner Stan Jalard)*, Jean-Pierre Malo *(Charly*

Schneider), Michel Creton *(Simon)*, Pierre Vernier, Michel Beaune, Patricia Malvoisin, Catherine Rouvel, Francois Dunoyer.

LE SOLITAIRE marks the return to the screen of Jean-Paul Belmondo, France's biggest box-office draw. Last seen in the 1985 picture HOLD-UP, Belmondo reunites in this picture with Deray, the director of Belmondo's super-successful LE MARGINAL (1983). LE SOLITAIRE is another *policier* in which Belmondo is a tough cop who hunts down the scum who killed his partner. Along the way, Belmondo shows compassion toward his partner's son by offering to raise the youngster.

p, Alain Belmondo; d, Jacques Deray; w, Jacques Deray, Alphonse Boudard, Simon Michael, Daniel Saint-Hamont; ph, Jean-Francois Robin (Fujicolor); ed, Henri Lanoe; art d, Jean-Claude Galloin; m/l, Andy Caine; stunts, Remy Julienne.

Crime **(PR:NR MPAA:NR)**

LE SOURD DANS LA VILLE† (1987, Can.) 97m Maison des Quartes Arts-Telefilm Canada-Societe du Cinema du Quebec-SuperEcran-Radio Quebec c (Trans: Deaf to the City)

Beatrice Picard *(Florence)*, Guillaume Lemay-Thivierge *(Mike)*, Angele Coutu *(Gloria)*, Pierre Theriaut *(Tim)*, Han Masson *(Judith)*, Claude Renart *(Charlie)*, Sophie Leger *(Lucia)*.

A grim drama which takes place mostly in a dilapidated hotel run by the vivacious Coutu, a stripper who resists succumbing to the sense of hopeless depression experienced by her guests. Devoted to her two daughters and a son with a brain tumor, Coutu dreams of taking a trip to San Francisco with the ailing boy. The hotel becomes the final stop for the desperate and among the guests are Coutu's lover who is a drunken ex-con (Renart), an old alcoholic (Theriaut) whose best friend is a dog, and a woman (Picard) who contemplates suicide because she was abandoned by her rich husband. The ranks of the despondent are visited by a cheery school teacher (Masson) who thinks she can help them all, but is unable to rouse them from their insulated misery.

d, Mireille Dansereau; w, Mireille Dansereau, Michele Mailhot, Jean-Joseph Tremblay (based on a story by Therese Berube from a novel by Marie-Claire Blaise); ph, Michel Caron; m, Ginette Bellavance; ed, Louise Cote; art d, Gaudeline Sauriol; set d, Pierre Gelinas; cos, Denis Sperdouklis.

Drama **(PR:NR MPAA:NR)**

LE VIE DEL SIGNORE SONO FINITE† (1987, It.) 103m Esterno Mediterraneo/COL c (Trans: The Ways of the Lord Are Finite)

Massimo Troisi *(Camillo)*, Jo Champa *(Vittoria)*, Marco Messeri *(Brother)*, Massimo Bonetti *(Orlando)*, Enzo Cannavale, Clelia Rondinella.

The fourth film directed by Italian comedian Troisi, who was seen this year by American audiences when he provided some badly needed comic relief in the dreadful South American thriller HOTEL COLONIAL. Set in Italy during the 1920s when the Fascists were on the rise, Troisi plays a provincial barber engaged to a beautiful French girl, Champa. Without warning, Champa breaks off the engagement and the distraught Troisi is stricken with a case of psychosomatic paralysis that confines him to a wheelchair. Cared for by his brother Messeri, Troisi strikes up a friendship with similarly handicapped poet Bonetti who has been paralyzed since birth. The sympathetic Troisi introduces the shy Bonetti to a girl friend of his ex-fiancee but both are disgusted to learn that the girl is a devoted Fascist. Troisi, meanwhile, has suddenly regained the use of his legs during a brief reconciliation with Champa, but is again paralyzed when he learns that his fickle fiancee has fallen for Bonetti. Soon after, Troisi is arrested by the Fascists and imprisoned for two years. Eventually he is released, but only through the good graces of Bonetti who has now become a powerful Fascist leader.

p, Mauro Berardi; d, Massimo Troisi; w, Massimo Troisi, Anna Pavagnano; ph, Camillo Bazzoni; m, Pino Daniele; ed, Nino Baragli; art d, Francesco Frigeri.

Comedy **(PR:NR MPAA:NR)**

LEADING EDGE, THE† (1987, N. Zealand) 78m Southern Light/Everard c

Mathurin Molgat, Bruce Grant, Evan Bloomfield, Mark Whetu, Christine Grant, Melanie Forbes, Billy T. James.

After a pair of dramas (HEART OF THE STAG and SYLVIA), director Firth returns to the subject matter that earned him an Oscar nomination for Best Documentary with OFF THE EDGE—skiing. THE LEADING EDGE follows Telluride ski-patroller Molgat as he travels from Colorado to New Zealand in search of bigger and better athletic thrills. There he meets a group of skiers known as the "Kiwi Cowboys," a crazy bunch of athletes who show Molgat how to ski glaciers and active volcanos. Eventually Molgat gains enough confidence to join in the annual Iron Man competition where he will have to mountain climb, ski, kayak, and foot race.

p, Barrie Everard; d, Mike Firth; w, Mike Firth, Grant Morris; ph, Stuart Dryburgh, Mike Firth; m, Mike Farrell; ed, Pat Monaghan; art d, Greg Taylor.

Adventure **(PR:NR MPAA:NR)**

LEGACY OF RAGE† (1987, Hong Kong) 95m D&B c

Brandon Lee, Michael Wong, Regina Kent, Chan Wai-man, Mang Hoi.

The unanticipated film debut of the immortal Bruce Lee's son, Brandon Lee, sees the 21-year-old Amerasian hunk framed for a crime he didn't commit. The evildoer is Lee's best friend, Wong, the son of a Chinese crime lord. While Lee languishes in prison, his girl runs off to Brazil. This nasty turn of events only serves to make young Lee mad and he prepares himself for the inevitable martial-arts orgy that will accompany his quest for vengeance. Now kung-fu devotees can stop settling for the plethora of pretenders to Bruce Lee's throne and root for their hero's own flesh-and-blood.

d, Ronnie Yu.

Action **(PR:NR MPAA:NR)**

LEGEND OF WISELY, THE† (1987, Hong Kong) 98m Cinema City/Golden Princess c

Sam Hui *(Wisely)*, Teddy Robin *(Prof. Kwan)*, Ti Lung, Bruce Baron, Wong Joe-Yin.

Big-budget science fiction adventure based on the popular novels of I Kwan starring executive producer Hui as an Indiana Jones-type who ventures to Nepal in search of his mentor Prof. Kwan (Robin). Robin had scoured the Himalayas in search of a fabled lost tribe, but had gotten himself in a predicament that only Hui could get him out of. Hui rescues the professor, but doesn't realize that the old bird had swiped a holy icon from the five-year-old "golden child" of the Himalayan monks. Later, Robin is killed in a plane crash and Hui returns to Katmandu to assist the young monk—who possesses magical powers—in the retrieval of the icon. Although the plot has similarities to both RAIDERS OF THE LOST ARK and THE GOLDEN CHILD, the novels upon which this film was based were published many years before either American effort was scripted.

d, Teddy Robin; w, (based on the science fiction novels of I Kwan); ph, Peter Bao; art d, Kenneth Yee Chung Man; cos, Shirley Chan Ku Fang.

Science Fiction **(PR:NR MPAA:NR)**

LEGENDA SEREBRYANOGO OZERA† (1987, USSR) 94m Azerbaidjanfilm/Sovexportfilm c (Trans: The Legend of Silver Lake)

Eldanis Rasulov, Yelena Seropova, Shukufa Yusupova.

Blessed with an interesting career, financial stability, respect from his peers, and a lovely fiancee, a young art scholar finds his life in turmoil after he falls in love with a woman he met during a trip to a small village while researching his latest project.

d, Eldar Kuliev; w, Eldar Kuliev, Issi Melikadze; ph, Rafik Kambarov; m, Muslim Magomaev; art d, Mais Agabekov.

Drama **(PR:NR MPAA:NR)**

LEIF† (1987, Swed.) 103m SF-Kulturtuben/Svensk Filmindustri c

Anders Eriksson *(Gunnar Volt)*, Kerstin Granlund *(Doris Volt, others)*, Claes Eriksson *(Max Koger, Councilman Hylen)*, Knut Agnred *("Rambo" Larsson, others)*, Per Fritzell *(Niklas Kortnoj, others)*, Peter Rangmar *(Inspector Mard, others)*, Jan Rippe *(Lars E.I. Fred, others)*, Per Westman, Laila Westersund, Bengt Hernvall, Pierre Jonsson, Kimmo Rajala.

A political satire featuring the "Mackan" (The Gas Station), a popular television comedy troupe making its movie debut. The target here is the dangerous relationship between munitions manufacturers and the government—an affiliation that often leads to arms being sold to anyone who has the money, even enemies.

p, Waldemar Bergendahl; d&w, Claes Eriksson; ph, Dan Myhrman (Eastmancolor); m, Claes Eriksson, Charles Falk; ed, Jan Persson; prod d, Rolf Allan Hakansson; cos, Gunilla Henkler; stunts, Johan Toren, Svenska Stuntgruppen.

Comedy **(PR:NR MPAA:NR)**

LEILA DINIZ† (1987, Braz.) 95m Ponto/Embrafilme c

Louise Cardoso *(Leila Diniz)*, Diogo Vilela *(Luiz Carlos Lacerda)*, Carlos Alberto Riccelli *(Domingos)*, Tony Ramos *(Leila's Father)*, Marieta Severo *(Leila's Mother)*, Stenio Garcia, Antonio Fagundes, Jose Wilker, Paulo Cesar Grande, Jayme Periard, Romulo Arantes, Yara Amaral, Otavio Augusto, Denis Carvalho, Hugo Carvana, Oswaldo Loureiro, Mariana de Moraes.

Biography of famous Brazilian actress Leila Diniz whose outrageous public behavior in the late 1960s paved the way for greater women's independence during a time when an oppressive dictatorship ruled the country. Written and directed by the actress' close friend Lacerda, the film stars Cardoso as Diniz and explores her movie career, love life, eventual transformation into a symbol for youth, and tragic death at the age of 27 in a plane crash in India. The characters are not fictionalized and many figures in Diniz's life play themselves.

d&w, Luiz Carlos Lacerda; ph, Nonato Estrela (Eastmancolor); m, David Tygel; ed, Ana Maria Diniz; art d, Yurika Yamasaki; cos, Mara Santos.

Biography/Musical Comedy **(PR:NR MPAA:NR)**

LENZ† (1987, Hung.) 99m Bela Balazs Studio/Hungarofilm c

Andras Szirtes *(Lenz)*.

An experimental film set to the music of Mahler (Symphony No. 1) which sees a nuclear physicist given an accidental overdose of radiation. Going to the mountains to recuperate, the physicist discovers the radiation has warped his perceptions so that he sees the very fabric of nature. Time, shape, color, clouds, and living things all take on new meaning. The physicist soon comes out of his trance and tries to build a device that will analyze his visions, but fails. Instead he decides to build a bomb that will destroy the world, but when his innocent young son wanders in at the last moment, the physicist abandons his plan.

d, Andras Szirtes; w, Andras Szirtes, Matyas Buki, Tamas Pap (based on the short story of Georg Buchner); ph, Andras David, Barna Mihok (Eastmancolor); m, Gustav Mahler; ed, Eszter Kovacs; set d&cos, Lujza Gecser, Laszlo Rajk.

Drama **(PR:NR MPAA:NR)**

LEONARD PART 6 zero (1987) 85m Sah Ent./COL c

Bill Cosby *(Leonard)*, Tom Courtenay *(Frayn, Leonard's Butler)*, Joe Don Baker *(Snyderburn)*, Moses Gunn *(Giorgio)*, Pat Colbert *(Allison)*, Gloria Foster *(Medusa)*, Victoria Rowell *(Joan)*, Anna Levine *(Nurse Carvalho)*, David Maier *(Man Ray)*, Grace Zabriskie *(Jefferson)*, Hal Bokar *(Andy)*, George Maguire *(Madison)*, John Hostetter *(Adams)*, William Hall *(Monroe)*, George Kirby *(Duchamp)*, Jane Fonda *(Herself)*.

Tom Courtenay, who both plays Bill Cosby's manservant and acts as LEONARD PART 6's narrator, explains at the beginning of the film that the first five of Leonard's adventures couldn't be revealed in the interest of national security. The movie-going public would have been better served had Leonard's most recent adventure also been kept under lock and key. Reportedly Cosby, who was extremely disappointed in the final product, attempted to do just that, offering to buy the film from Columbia to take it out of distribution. In this Bond spoof that is almost totally devoid of laughs, Cosby plays a retired CIA agent-cum-restaurateur who wants for nothing. However, the former super spy's opulent life is less than perfect. Seven years previously, his wife, Colbert, caught him in the tub with a 19-year-old, and now Colbert lives next door to his fabulous mansion but will have nothing to do with him. In addition, Cosby's dilettante actress daughter Rowell intends to marry her ancient director, Gunn. As if this is not enough, Foster is plotting to take over the world by using a special formula and a magical sphere to control the behavior of the long-oppressed animal kingdom. CIA chief Baker knows that Cosby is the only man for the job. Eventually Cosby consents to saving the world and visits mystic Levine, who speaks no English but looks into her crystal ball and provides Cosby with an odd collection of items that come in handy later. When Cosby assaults Foster's International Tuna fortress, he finds his weapons are of no use, but he uses the ballet slippers provided by Levine to dance himself out of danger. Cosby escapes with the sphere, but Colbert is kidnaped by Foster's cohorts and Cosby discovers Baker has gone power mad now that he is in possession of the sphere. Recapturing it, Cosby takes it to Foster to exchange for Colbert, but before he does, he substitutes dish-washing liquid for its secret fluids. To his surprise, the soap is all that has been in there all along and a secret word—*kwellish*—must be used to activate the animal mayhem. While Foster and her minions prepare to loose an animal attack on the Bay Area, the bound Cosby and Colbert are about to become the victims of an army of advancing lobsters. Using the melted butter Levine has given him, Cosby gets the best of the seafood and then fends off Foster's behemoth vegetarian henchman with raw hamburger patties provided by (you guessed it) Levine. In the end, Cosby saves the world, escapes the conflagration on the back of an ostrich, and patches things up with Colbert.

It is not difficult to see why Cosby would have wanted to keep this 85-minute snooze from his adoring public. However, it is surprising that, as the film's producer, he didn't have a better idea of just how bad it was going to be. Cosby also provided the story that was the basis for the screenplay, and while the film's concept may have looked very promising in outline form, as executed by director Paul Weiland from Jonathan Reynolds' script the result is neither funny nor interesting. The film's would-be tongue-in-cheek attitude lacks focus and instead of being self-consciously silly LEONARD PART 6 is simply insipid. At the film's center, Cosby is given plenty to do, but most of what he is called upon to execute is without humor or significance. Even his patented mugging falls flat. Long ago, on TV's "I Spy," Cosby proved that he is a capable actor. Here his work has less in common with that role or his immensely successful TV portrayal of Dr. Clifford Huxtable than it does with his capacity as the small screen's most famous pitchman. Almost as disheartening as the soporific narrative is LEONARD's blatant product placement (read advertising). A refrigerator in Cosby's restaurant is full of Coca-Cola (which also happens to be Columbia's parent company), Cosby intrusively drinks a bottle of "the real thing" in one scene, a mountain of Lava soap is inexplicably piled on top of a backstage table, and Palmolive dish liquid and Alka Seltzer become more important props than Cosby's attack Porsche. The recent Bond films have been similarly littered with well-placed products, but though this may be the only successful element of parody in LEONARD, parody hardly appears to have been the intent. Keeping this is mind, it is interesting to note that Weiland brought to the film a background as a director of British commercials. He was given this opportunity to direct his first feature film by David Puttnam, who resigned as the head of Columbia Pictures in 1987 amidst much controversy. That controversy apparently included the production of LEONARD PART 6. Reportedly Weiland and Cosby feuded, and the film's star, a Coca-Cola stockholder and spokesman, also felt that Puttnam wasn't giving LEONARD the personal attention Cosby felt it deserved. Foster, Gunn, and Baker are forgettable in throwaway parts, but Courtenay momentarily enlivens the proceedings with his brief recitations from Shakespeare as he attempts to inspire Cosby. The other flicker of humor is provided by Anna Levine as the mystic. Speaking fluent gibberish, she uses her expressive face to convey more comic subtext in her few minutes on the screen then the rest of the best-forgotten, big-budget fiasco manages to do. *(Brief nudity, comic violence.)*

p, Bill Cosby; d, Paul Weiland; w, Jonathan Reynolds (based on a story by Bill Cosby); ph, Jan DeBont (Monaco Color); m, Elmer Bernstein; ed, Gerry Hambling, Peter Boita; prod d, Geoffrey Kirkland; art d, Blake Russell; set d, Bill Beck, Paul Kraus; cos, Aggie Guerard Rodgers; spec eff, Richard Edlun ch, Louis Falco.

Comedy **(PR:A-C MPAA:P**

LERMONTOV† (1987, USSR) 99m Mosfilm/Sovexportfilm

Nikolai Burlyayev, Natalia Bondarchuk, Vanya Burlyayev, Boris Plotniko Galina Belyayeva, Inna Makarova, Maris Liepa.

A biography of famed Russian poet and novelist Mikhail Yuryevich Lermont (1814-1841) which begins during the author's childhood, then follows hi through the furor caused by his controversial works and his various exiles, endi with his death in a duel.

d&w, Nikolai Burlyayev; ph, Oleg Martynov; art d, Boris Petrov.

Biography **(PR:NR MPAA:N**

LES DEUX CROCODILES† (1987, Fr.) 88m Sara-Canal Plus/Sara-CDF (Trans: Two Crocodile

Jean-Pierre Marielle *(Rene Boutancard)*, Jean Carmet *(Emile Rivereau)*, Juli Guiomar *(Julien Derouineau)*, Catherine Lachens *(Greta)*, Dora Doll *(Felicite*

Carmet is an unassuming shopkeeper whose quiet life in the provinces takes comic turn when Marielle tries to swindle him. In the process, however, the m become friends and, eventually, lovers. A gangster subplot involving the kidna ing of Carmet's senile mother is thrown in for good measure.

p, Alain Sarde; d&w, Joel Seria; ph, Jean-Yves Le Mener; m, Philippe Sarde; e Claudine Bouche; art d, Annie Senechel.

Comedy **(PR:NR MPAA:N**

LES EXPLOITS D'UN JEUNE DON JUAN† (1987, Fr./It.) 95m Orph Arts-Selena Audiovisual-Films Ariane-Lagonda-Antea/AAA c (Trans: T Exploits of a Young Don Jua

Claudine Auger *(The Mother)*, Serena Grandi *(Ursule)*, Marina Vlady *(Mm Muller)*, Fabrice Josso *(Roger)*, Francois Perrot *(The Father)*, Berange Bonvoisin *(Aunt Marguerite)*, Rufus *(The Monk)*, Laurent Spielvogel *(M Frank)*, Rosette *(Helene)*, Alexandra Vandernoot *(Elisa)*, Marion Peters *(Kate)*, Virginie Ledoyen *(Berthe)*, Yves Lambrecht *(Roland)*, Aurelien Recoi *(Adolphe)*.

Based on one of French poet Guillaume Apollinaire's two pornographic novel this French-Italian co-production opens in 1914 and stars Josso as a teenag whose sexual desires pass the point of decadence. Tempted by the fruits of all t women around him, he carries on with the family maid, his aunt, and even h own sister, impregnating each of them. Then to legitimize his actions, he conce trates on marrying each of them off.

p, Claire Duval; d, Gianfranco Mingozzi; w, Jean-Claude Carriere, Peter Fleisc mann (based on the novel by Guillaume Apollinaire); ph, Luigi Verga (Agf Gevaert Color); m, Nicola Piovani; ed, Alfredo Muschietto; art d, Jacqu Saulnier; cos, Yvonne Sassinot de Nesle; makeup, Marc Blanchard.

Drama **(PR:O MPAA:N**

LES FOUS DE BASSAN† (1987, Can./Fr.) 107m Vivafilms Intl. c (AK IN THE SHADOW OF THE WIN

Steve Banner *(Stevens Brown)*, Charlotte Valandrey *(Olivia Atkins)*, Laure Ma sac *(Nora Atkins)*, Bernard-Pierre Donnadieu *(Pastor Jones)*, Lothaire Blute *(Perceval Brown)*, Marie Tifo *(Irene Jones)*, Jean-Louis Millette *(Stevens Brow as an old man)*, Angele Coutu *(Maureen)*, Paul Hebert, Roland Chenil, G Thauvette, Denise Gagnon, Pierre Powers, Henry Classe, Jocelyn Berube.

In 1986, 25-year-old Canadian Yves Simoneau directed a memorable, superb crafted film called INTIMATE POWER (released theatrically in New York th year) which marked him as an important force in Canadian cinema. Althou INTIMATE POWER received much less attention than this year's highly prais Quebecois thriller NIGHT ZOO from director Jean-Claude Lauzon, it is cle that Simoneau and not Lauzon is the director to watch. LES FOUS DE BA SAN, the official Canadian entry in the Berlin Film Festival, is set in the 1930s a sexually repressive Quebec seaside town governed by a Protestant moral cod The return to town of Banner sets the town's loins ablaze. He becomes involv with sister Marsac and Valandrey (the lovely star of 1986's RED KISS), a before long everyone is bedding everyone else. The whole tale is related Millette, who plays Banner in the present day as he sits in his study surrounded pictures of the characters in the film. Adapted from the prize-winning novel Anne Hebert.

p, Justine Heroux; d, Yves Simoneau; w, Sheldon Chad (adapted by Y Simoneau, Marcel Beaulieu, based on the novel by Anne Hebert); ph, Ala Dostie; m, Richard Gregoire; ed, Joelle Van Effenterre; art d, Michel Proul cos, Nicole Pelletier.

Drama **(PR:O MPAA:N**

LES MENDIANTS† (1987, Fr./Switz.) 95m Marion's-J.M.H.-La Televisi Suisse Romande-La Sept/Marion's Films c (Trans: The Beggar

Dominique Sanda *(Helene)*, Jean-Philippe Ecoffey *(Fred)*, Anne Roussel *(Ann belle)*, Assane Fall *(Gregoire)*, Pierre Forget *(Grandfather)*, Steve Baes *(T Catalan)*, Judith Godreche *(Catherine)*, Camille Clavel, Renaud Bernadet, P lippe Levy, Francois Nelias, Yann Marquand.

Flashy director Benoit Jacquot (CORPS ET BIENS) examines behavioral patterns among children, lovers, and criminals and finds that each group plays manipulating games of possession/power and betrayal/reprisal. Based on a popular novel by critic Louis-Rene Des Forets.

p, Jean-Marc Henchoz, Sylvette Frydman; d, Benoit Jacquot; w, Benoit Jacquot, Pascal Bonitzer (based on the novel by Louis-Rene Des Forets); ph, Acacio de Almeida, Jose Antonio Loureiro, Karim Youkana, Denis Jutzeler; m, Jorge Arriagada; ed, Dominique Auvray, Isabelle Lorente, Marielle Babinet; cos, Renee Renard.

Drama **(PR:NR MPAA:NR)**

LES MOIS D'AVRIL SONT MEURTRIERS† (1987, Fr.) 88m Sara-Canal Plus-Little Bear/Sara-CDF c (Trans: April Is a Deadly Month)

Jean-Pierre Marielle *(Fred)*, Jean-Pierre Bisson *(Gravier)*, Francois Berleand *(Baumann)*, Brigitte Rouan *(Clara)*, Guylaine Pean *(Christine)*.

Adaptation of American Robin Cook's thriller *The Devil's Home on Leave*, starring Bisson as a hired assassin who has recently committed a particularly heinous gangland hit. Pursued by clever police inspector Marielle, the film becomes a battle of wits between the hunter and the hunted. Co-scripter Bertrand Tavernier, director of A SUNDAY IN THE COUNTRY and ROUND MIDNIGHT, had originally planned to direct this feature himself, but turned the duties over to his collaborator Heynemann.

p, Louis Grau; d, Laurent Heynemann; w, Laurent Heynemann, Bertrand Tavernier, Philippe Boucher (based on the novel *The Devil's Home on Leave* by Robin Cook); ph, Jean-Francis Gondre (Fuji Color); m, Philippe Sarde; ed, Armand Psenny; art d, Valerie Grall; cos, Olga Berluti.

Thriller **(PR:NR MPAA:NR)**

LES NOCES BARBARES† (1987, Bel./Fr.) 99m Man's Film-Flach-RF 1-RTL TV1 c (Trans: The Barbarous Wedding; AKA: THE CRUEL EMBRACE)

Marianne Basler *(Nicole)*, Yves Cotton *(Ludovic as a Child)*, Thierry Fremont *(Ludovic as a Teenager)*, Andre Penvern *(Micho)*, Marie-Ange Dutheil *(Mlle. Rakoff)*, Frederic Sorel *(Tatav)*.

The third film from Belgian director Marian Hansel (her 1985 film DUST, starring Jane Birkin and Trevor Howard, won the Silver Prize at the Venice Film Festival) stars Basler as a woman whose first marriage resulted in a rape and an unwanted child. The child, Cotton, was raised by his grandmother who locked the youngster away in the attic. With Basler's second marriage, the child (now played by Fremont), is taken from the attic and integrated into the family. He is unable to cope, however, and is sent off to a mental institution. He later escapes and, driven by a psychotic passion, sets out to kill his mother. Adapted from the 1985 Goncourt Prize-winning novel by Yann Queffelec. Released in England as THE CRUEL EMBRACE. (In French, with English subtitles.)

p,d&w, Marion Hansel (based on the novel by Yann Queffelec); ph, Walther van den Ende (Agfa-Gevaert Color); m, Frederic Devrees; ed, Susana Rossberg; art d, Veronique Melery.

Drama **(PR:NR MPAA:NR)**

LES OREILLES ENTRE LES DENTS† (1987, Fr.) 98m Madeleine-Hachette Premiere/UGC c (Trans: Ears Between the Teeth)

Jean-Luc Bideau *(Jean-Paul Blido)*, Fabrice Luchini *(Luc Fabri)*, Laurent Gamelon *(Max)*, Jeanne Marine *(Lea Stagnari)*, Feodor Atkine *(Dancourt)*, Guy Montagne *(Gayat)*, Philippe Khorsand *(Korg)*, Gerard Manzetti *(Boris)*, Devin Burgos *(Atilla)*, Jeanne Herviale, Alain Boismery, Gabriel Cattand, Claude Melki, Christophe Salengro, Michele Brousse, Rosette.

Murder victims are being found with their ears cut off and stuffed into their mouths, and psychologist Bideau is called in to develop a mental portrait of the murderer. This is director Schulmann's followup to his 1985 hit P.R.O.F.S., but this film did not approach the box-office success of that comedy.

p, Gilbert de Goldschmidt; d, Patrick Schulmann; w, Patrick Schulmann, Didier Dolna, Michel Zemer; ph, Jacques Assuerus (Fujicolor); m, Patrick Schulmann; ed, Aline Asseo; art d, Michel Modai; cos, Olga Pelletier.

Mystery/Comedy **(PR:NR MPAA:NR)**

LES PATTERSON SAVES THE WORLD† (1987, Aus.) 95m Humpstead/Hoyts c

Barry Humphries *(Sir Les Patterson/Dame Edna Everage)*, Pamela Stephenson *(Veronique Crudite)*, Thaao Penghlis *(Col. Richard Godowni)*, Andrew Clarke *(Neville Thonge)*, Henri Szeps *(Dr. Herpes/Desiree)*, Hugh Keays-Byrne *(Inspector Farouk)*, Elizabeth Melvor *(Nancy Borovansky)*, Garth Meade *(Mustafa Toul)*, Arthur Sherman *(Gen. Evans)*, Josef Drewniak *(Mossolov)*, Joan Rivers *(US President)*, Esben Storm *(Russian Scientist)*, Joy Westmore *(Lady Gwen Patterson)*, Connie Hobbs *(Madge Allsop)*, Paul Jennings *(Australian Prime Minister)*, Graham Kennedy *(Brian Lannigan)*, John Clarke *(Mike Rooke)*, David Whitney *(Barry Mollison)*, Sally Tayler *(Rhonda)*, Peter Collingwood *(Jeremy Williams)*.

Comeback film for popular Aussie comedian Barry Humphries in which he stars as a drunken Australian diplomat exiled to Abu Niveah for embarrassing himself and his nation during a speech at the United Nations (combine extreme flatulence with a lit lighter and you get a flaming Arab oil sheik on the floor of the U.N.). In Abu Niveah Humphries discovers Arab colonel (Penghlis) plotting to export toilet seats contaminated with a deadly sexual disease known as HELP to Western nations. The Arab then plans to market a cure discovered by a meek French scientist and make billions. Humphries also appears in drag as his character Dame Edna Everage who is conducting a tour of Abu Niveah for a gaggle of Aussie women. Directed by the "other" George Miller (MAN FROM SNOW RIVER) for producers who thought they had made a film with the international crossover potential of CROCODILE DUNDEE. What they failed to realize, however, is that the blantantly rascist, sexist, gay-bashing, toilet humor that Humphries is known for isn't as appealing in the US as a relatively inoffensive romantic comedy from Paul Hogan. Consequently, there are no plans to release LES PATTERSON SAVES THE WORLD in the US, as of yet.

p, Sue Milliken; d, George Miller; w, Barry Humphries, Diane Millstead; ph, David Connell (Eastmancolor); m, Tim Finn; ed, Tim Wellburn; prod d, Graham [Grace] Walker; cos, Anna Senior; spec eff, Brian Cox, Bob McCarron.

Comedy **(PR:NR MPAA:NR)**

L'ESCOT† (1987, Span.) Opal c

Laura Conti *(Marta)*, Abel Folk *(Jaume)*, Jaume Valls *(Toni)*, Ferran Rane *(Luis)*.

Conti stars as the 23-year-old host of a late-night erotic radio program, broadcast from Ibiza, who relates her steamy sexual adventures to her eager listeners. This is the feature debut of director Verdaguer.

p, Josep Anton Perez Giner; d, Antoni Verdaguer; w, Vincenc Villatoro, Antoni Verdaguer (based on the novel by Maria Jaen; ph, Magi Torruella; m, Ramon Muntaner; ed, Amat Carreras; art d, Ramon B. Ivars; makeup, Joaquin Navarro.

Romance **(PR:NR MPAA:NR)**

LESS THAN ZERO*½ (1987) 96m FOX c

Andrew McCarthy *(Clay Easton)*, Jami Gertz *(Blair)*, Robert Downey, Jr. *(Julian Wells)*, James Spader *(Rip)*, Tony Bill *(Bradford Easton)*, Nicholas Pryor *(Benjamin Wells)*, Donna Mitchell *(Elaine Easton)*, Michael Bowen *(Hop)*, Sarah Buxton *(Markie)*, Lisanne Falk *(Patti)*, Michael Greene *(Robert Wells)*.

Loosely based on the novel by Bret Easton Ellis, LESS THAN ZERO refuses to take the risks necessary to capture the keen social observation of the widely read book. It's Christmas time in Los Angeles, and McCarthy, a freshman at an Eastern college, returns home for the holidays, mostly because Gertz (THE LOST BOYS), his old girl friend, has asked him to do so. McCarthy, Gertz, and Downey—rich kids and former high-school buddies—had been inseparable just four months before, but when McCarthy returned at Thanksgiving, he learned that Gertz and Downey had become an item. Now Gertz wants McCarthy to save Downey from the downward spiral of his drug abuse. Like Gertz, who is a model, Downey chose not to go to college. His father (Pryor) provided him with enough money to start a record company, but things failed to fall in place and the company went up in the smoke of Downey's crack habit. Pryor kicked him out of the house and now Downey is harassed by Spader, the drug dealer whom he owes $50,000. Downey hopes to borrow enough money from his uncle to start up a nightclub and get back on his feet. However, his uncle won't come through, and Downey is forced to literally prostitute himself for Spader, who sends him off to satisfy a homosexual clientele. McCarthy glides through most of the film in an emotionally neutral state, but it's clear that he is still in love with Gertz. Traveling in his vintage 'Vette from ultrahip, high-tech parties to ultrahip, high-tech clubs, McCarthy tries to straighten out Downey, and in the meantime, he and Gertz rekindle their passion. Eventually Downey hits rock bottom. After being seen through one particularly rough night by the love of McCarthy and Gertz, Downey resolves to turn his life around. He goes to Pryor, who is busy working on his tennis forehand, and finally convinces him that he is willing to try to stay clean. Then Downey travels to Palm Springs to tell Spader that he will give him his money but that he is through with drugs. Spader laughs this off, and after he and his henchman get Downey high, they send him off to drop his pants for a client. McCarthy bursts into the motel where all of this is taking place and liberates Downey. They return to the party where Gertz is waiting, only to encounter Spader and his thug. McCarthy and Gertz fight their way out and jump into the Corvette with the out-of-it Downey and drive through the desert back to L.A. En route Downey dies. The film closes with a post-funeral scene of Gertz and McCarthy, who laments that he did everything could to save Downey but that it wasn't enough.

Ellis's depressing novel is a sharply observed portrait of all-pervasive anomie among the rich sons and daughters of the beautiful people who inhabit the palm and pool paradise of wealthy L.A. However, the makers of LESS THAN ZERO chose only to use "characters and concepts" for their film and the result plays like a 96-minute "Say No to Drugs" spot. There were many reasons Hollywood felt that America wasn't ready for a faithful rendition of Ellis's story. To begin with it is relentlessly downbeat. Ellis's print protagonist, a frequent cocaine user himself, has little in common with McCarthy's drug-free Shane-like hero who arrives from the East to not quite save the day. While McCarthy is moonstruck with love for Gertz, Ellis's Clay is promiscuously bisexual—hardly the sort of thing AIDS-era Hollywood is interested in portraying. Screenwriter Peyton's moralistic script builds up the Downey role and heaps the tragedy that is global and unresolved in the novel upon his shoulders. The filmmakers apparently felt that there were no sympathetic characters in the novel, but in sanitizing and simplifying the story, in transforming it into a relatively conventional love story and a didactic tragedy, they have diluted the disturbing social reality of the novel. Ellis's flashback meditations on the dissolution of his family are also entirely left out, and the film suffers greatly for this. Scott Rubin, president of motion picture production at 20th-Century Fox, told the *New York Times* that the filmmakers felt that if they could "put a story in that would be more compelling and emotional than the story in the book" they would have the chance to make a picture like THE GRADUATE, "one of those pictures that seem to define a generation." However, by purposely toning down the downer ethos that is at the heart of Ellis's novel and also apparent in films like RIVER'S EDGE, LESS THAN ZERO misses its opportunity to say something important about a generation.

English director Kanievska (ANOTHER COUNTRY) has given the film a high-gloss, MTV look that for once is appropriate for the subject matter. However, by constantly highlighting the surreal nature of the environment, he further distances the story from its potential as social observation. The saving grace of LESS THAN ZERO is Downey (THE PICK-UP ARTIST). If the film was to succeed at all, given the changes in the story line, Downey had to give a truly inspired performance. He does. He is wholly believable as the rich kid whose winning ways have always been all he needed to survive a pedal-to-the-floor life-style but who comes to realize that his life is out of control and that he isn't fooling anyone anymore—not even himself. He makes his character a convincing lost cause but one that the audience wishes to see saved. Gertz's performance is uneven. At some moments she seems to epitomize shallow but sensitive beauty, at others she seems merely to be reading lines. Vacillating from blank looks to bug-eyed consternation, McCarthy (MANNEQUIN), usually a much better actor, brings little to his role. Spader is good as the malevolent, priggish dealer but this is the sort of role that he must be able to do in his sleep by now. Producer-director Tony Bill is perfectly cast as McCarthy's father, who appears for a Christmas family scene that includes both his ex-wife and his girl friend. *(Brief nudity, sexual situations, substance abuse, adult situations, violence.)*

p, Jon Avnet, Jordan Kerner, Marvin Worth; d, Marek Kanievska; w, Harley Peyton (based on the novel by Bret Easton Ellis); ph, Edward Lachman (Deluxe Color); m, Thomas Newman, Rick Rubin; ed, Peter E. Berger, Michael Tronick; prod d, Barbara Ling; art d, Stephen Rice; set d, Nancy Nye; cos, Richard Hornung.

Drama (PR:O MPAA:R)

L'ESTATE STA FINENDO† (1987, It.) Clesi Cinematografica-Italian Intl.-Raiuno/I.I.F. (Trans: The Summer Is Nearly Over)

Fiorenza Tessari, Leonardo Ferrantini, Sven Kruger, Fabrizio Vidale, Daysuke Kurihara, Barbara Gimmelli, Daniela Gimmelli, Giorgio Vignali, Ornella Marcucci, Angelo Infanti, Valeria Ciangottini, Anna Galiena, Renato Scarpa, Cinzia De Ponti, Antonella Fassari, Renato Cecchetto, Ennio Drovandi, Stefano Gragnani, Egidio Termine.

The teenage daughter of wealthy-but-divorced parents runs off on holiday with the caretaker's son without permission. They tour Italy and sleep outdoors while the girl's father scours the country looking for them.

d, Bruno Cortini; w, Francesca Archibugi, Gloria Malatesta, Claudia Sbarigia; ph, Blasco Giurato; m, Carmelo La Bionda, Michelangelo La Bionda; ed, Gino Bartolini.

Romance (PR:NR MPAA:NR)

L'ETE DERNIER A TANGER† (1987, Fr.) 123m Ariane-Alexandre-Films A2/AAA c (Trans: Last Summer In Tangiers)

Valeria Golino *(Carla/Claudia)*, Thierry Lhermitte *(Corrigan)*, Roger Hanin *(Barres)*, Vincent Lindon *(Roland Barres)*, Jean Bouise *(Max Pasquier)*, Julien Guiomar *(Gomez)*, Jacques Villeret *(Marcus)*, Anna Karina *(Myrrha)*, Said Amadis *(Karim)*.

French adaptation of the American crime novel *The Devil His Due* by William O'Farrell, with the action transplanted to Tangiers circa 1956 when that port city was being annexed by Morocco. The plot finds Golino enacting an elaborate and methodical vengeance on local gangster Hanin in retribution for the murder of her father several years before.

p&d, Alexandre Arcady; w, Alexandre Arcady, Alain Le Henry, Tito Topin (based on the novel *The Devil His Due* by William O'Farrell); ph, Robert Alazraki (Agfa-Gevaert Color); m, Philippe Sarde; ed, Luce Grunenvaldt; art d, Jean-Louis Poveda; cos, Mic Cheminal.

Drama (PR:NR MPAA:NR)

L'ETE EN PENTE DOUCE† (1987, Fr.) 98m Solus-Flach-Selena-Films A2/AAA c (Trans: Summer on a Soft Slope)

Jean-Pierre Bacri *(Fane)*, Pauline Lafont *(Lilas)*, Jacques Villeret *(Mo)*, Guy Marchand *(Andre Voke)*, Jean Bouise *(Olivier Voke)*, Jean-Paul Lilienfeld *(Shawenhick)*, Jacques Mathou *(Jeannot)*, Dominique Besnehard *(Mr. Leval)*, Claude Chabrol *(Priest)*.

Set in the south of France, this entry from Krawczyk (JE HAIS ACTEURS) follows three eccentric young characters—aspiring novelist Bacri, his moronic brother Villeret, and the seductive but daft Lafont—as they try to settle into a small, bigoted community. Their greatest opposition comes from Marchand, who pits the locals against the threesome, in order to force them off their property so he can buy it and expand his business. Director Claude Chabrol makes another of his numerous cameos.

p, Jean-Marie Duprez, Pascal Hommais, Jean-Francois Lepetit; d, Gerard Krawczyk; w, Gerard Krawczyk, Jean-Paul Lilienfeld (based on the novel by Pierre Pelot); ph, Michel Cenek; m, Roland Vincent; ed, Marie-Josephe Yoyotte; art d, Jacques Dugied.

Drama (PR:NR MPAA:NR)

LETHAL WEAPON½** (1987) 110m WB c

Mel Gibson *(Martin Riggs)*, Danny Glover *(Roger Murtaugh)*, Gary Busey *(Joshua)*, Mitchell Ryan *(The General)*, Tom Atkins *(Michael Hunsaker)*, Darlene Love *(Trish Murtaugh)*, Traci Wolfe *(Rianne Murtaugh)*, Jackie Swanson *(Amanda Hunsaker)*, Damon Hines *(Nick Murtaugh)*, Ebonie Smith *(Carrie Murtaugh)*, Lycia Naff *(Dixie)*, Selma Archerd *(Policewoman)*, Patrick Cameron, Don Gordon *(Police Detectives)*, Richard B. Whitaker *(Police Officer)*, Mary Ellen Trainor *(Psychologist)*, Steve Kahan *(Capt. Ed Murphy)*, Jack Thibeau *(McCaskey)*, Grand Bush *(Boyette)*, Ed O'Ross *(Mendez)*, Gustav Vintas *(Gustaf)*, Al Leong *(Endo)*, Michael Shaner *(McCleary)*, Natalie Zimmerman, Lenny Juliano *(Patrol Cops)*, Deborah Dismukes *(Blonde on Bike)*, Donald Gooden *(Alfred)*, Henry Brown *(Plainclothes Cop)*, Teresa Kadotani *(Hooker)*, John O'Neill *(Police Officer in Car #1)*, Tom Noga *(Police Officer in Car #2)*, Bill Kalmenson, Frank Reinhard *(Beat Cops)*, Jimmie F. Skaggs, Jason Ronard, Blackie Dammett *(Drug Dealers)*, Robert Fol, Gail Bowman *(Cops)*, Cheryl Baker, Terri Lynn Doss, Sharon K. Brecke *(Girls in Shower)*, Alphonse Philippe Mouzon, Shaun Hunter, Everitt Wayne Collins, Jr. *(Alfred's Friends)*, Paul Tuerpe, Chad Hayes, Chris D. Jardins, Sven Thorsen, Peter DuPont, Gilles Kholer, Cedric Adams, James Poslof *(Mercenaries)*, Burbank the Cat, Sam the Dog.

It's drugs again, this time in southern California with cop partners Gibson and Glover chasing sleazy dope runners in a nonstop crime actioner. There's a threat to life and limb in almost every frame but there's no room for characterization or any frills in a hard-nosed plot that has been seen many times before. Glover, who

is the only solid character in the film, is about to turn 50 and his gray hairs and scarred experiences cause him to exercise the kind of life-preserving caution that Gibson has recently discarded. Gibson's wife has just been killed in an accident and he doesn't care whether he lives or dies, just so long as he can take all the bad guys with him, an attitude that—at least it's expressed as such—gives him a decided edge on the villains. Gibson, newly teamed with Glover in the homicide division, is brought into Glover's warm family. Glover's wife, Love, and teenage daughter, Wolfe, try to make the miserable Gibson feel at home. Gibson seems to be caught in a time warp that speaks only to him of the 1960s and the horrors of the Vietnam War in which he served. Glover is also a veteran of the same war but he possesses the sensitivity and sanity of a man of modern times. Other Vietnam veterans include Ryan, who now heads a very successful drug dealing operation, and Busey, Ryan's cold-blooded top henchman, a white-haired killer who becomes the insidious enemy Gibson never conquered in Vietnam. Glover has a hard time surviving with such a self-destructive partner, watching in astonishment at Gibson's unerring knack for winding up in violent confrontations. Typical of his aberrant behavior is Gibson's confrontation with a man about to jump from a rooftop. He handcuffs the man to himself and then jumps, the two of them ending up on a safety device erected by firemen below. In one of their first cases, the partners investigate the death of Swanson, daughter of Atkins, an old friend of Glover's. Atkins reveals that he is part of an extensive drug smuggling operation run by Ryan, and then is killed for his candor. Ryan has assembled a group of men who were under his command in the Army, and has molded them into an extremely well organized and extremely dangerous drug smuggling unit. Glover and Gibson begin to investigate Ryan and his men which leads to kidnaping, captures, escapes, gun battles and more, all giving Gibson, who is classified a "lethal weapon" by the Los Angeles Police Department because of his martial arts skills, the chance to exhibit his physical skills. The last 30 minutes of the film is taut with hair-raising action of THE ROAD WARRIOR caliber and it provides a massive, bloody shootout between the cops and the drug dealers. Gibson and Busey square off for their long-awaited confrontation and, as Glover and half the L.A.P.D. look on, Gibson is the winner by a knockout.

The acceleration of this film, which has a brisk pace at the start, is dizzying at the finale and is accomplished mostly through fantastic editing cuts. It's an effective if not obvious ploy to blind the viewer to the fact that there is not much plot or character development in the predictable script which lards its dialog with unimaginative and cliched lines. Gibson is truly frightening as the cop about to go into orbit and Glover is a standout as the down-to-earth lawman with very much to lose. Busey is chilling as the emotionless Joshua, ready to maim or kill or to be maimed or killed at the request of his commanding officer. Donner, whose previous efforts include the first SUPERMAN and LADYHAWKE, had another hit with LETHAL WEAPON, which grossed more than $60 million at the box office within three months after its release. Naturally, such success makes a sequel inevitable and one is already in the works. Black, author of the original and a 1984 graduate of UCLA, has been retained to write a screenplay which will continue the saga of Riggs and Murtaugh. Songs include: "Jingle Bell Rock" (Joe Beal, Jim Boothe, performed by Bobby Helms), "A Christmas Carol," "College Football Game." *(Graphic violence, profanity, brief nudity.)*

p, Richard Donner, Joel Silver; d, Richard Donner; w, Shane Black; ph, Stephen Goldblatt (Technicolor); m, Michael Kamen, Eric Clapton; ed, Stuart Baird; prod d, J. Michael Riva; set d, Marvin March; cos, Mary Malin; makeup, Scott Eddo; spec eff, Chuck Gaspar; tech adv, Art Fransen, Rod Bernsen, Richard Whitaker; stunts, Bobby Bass, Dar Robinson.

Crime **Cas.** **(PR:O MPAA:R)**

LET'S GET HARRY** (1987) 107m Tri-Star-Delphi IV&V/Tri-Star c

Michael Schoeffling *(Corey Burke)*, Tom Wilson *(Pachowski)*, Glenn Frey *(Spence)*, Gary Busey *(Jack "Smilin' Jack" Abernathy)*, Robert Duvall *(Norman Shrike)*, Rick Rossovich *(Curt)*, Ben Johnson *(Harry Burke, Sr.)*, Matt Clark *(Walt Clayton)*, Gregory Sierra *(Alphonso)*, Elpidia Carrillo *(Veronica)*, Mark Harmon *(Harry Burke, Jr.)*, Bruce Gray *(Ambassador Douglas)*, Guillermo Rios *(Carlos Ochobar)*, Jere Burns *(Washington Aide)*, Cecile Callan *(Theresa)*, Rodolfo de Alexandre *(Pablo)*, Javier Estrada *(Dwarf)*, Salvador Godinez *(Boat Man)*, Jerry Hardin *(Dean Reilly)*, James Keane *(Al King)*, Pierrino Mascarino *(Pinilla)*, Diane Petersen *(Jack's Girl Friend)*, Robert Singer *(Bartender)*, Cesar Sobrevals *(Pinilla's Man)*, Jon Van Ness *(Mickey)*, Jorge Zepeda *(MP Captain)*, Fidel Abrego, Guillermo Lagunes, Jonathan Kano, Alfredo Ramirez *(Hoods)*, Terry Camilleri, David Hess, J.W. Smith *(Mercenaries)*.

Having received only a scant regional release late in 1986, LET'S GET HARRY finally saw general release via videocassette in 1987. Boasting a superb cast of supporting players (Duvall, Busey, Johnson, Clark, Harmon, and Sierra), this routine action film is crippled by a lackluster script and a weak set of young leads. The film opens in Colombia as Harmon, a young American sent to oversee the construction of a massive new pumping station (he describes himself as a "glorified plumber"), greets the American ambassador (Gray) who has come to participate in the opening ceremonies. Without warning, both Harmon and Gray are kidnaped by Colombian terrorists. The terrorists are not Communist insurgents, however, but are the agents of Rios, a ruthless Colombian drug dealer who wants the U.S. to release his imprisoned men in exchange for Gray and Harmon. Unfortunately for the hostages, the Reagan administration refuses to negotiate with terrorists (the film was obviously shot before the Iran-Contra scandal) and will neither heed their demands nor dispatch a rescue team. Back in Harmon's hometown of Aurora, Illinois, his friends and family wait helplessly. Frustrated by the Washington bureaucracy, Harmon's brother, Schoeffling, and three of his buddies (Wilson, Frey, and Rossovich) vow to hire a mercenary and "get Harry" themselves. After interviewing a number of goofballs claiming to be experienced mercenaries, the youths finally hook up with Duvall (sporting a shaved head and goatee), a Congressional Medal of Honor winner skilled in the art of war. To finance their mission, the boys turn to Busey, a local car dealer with a taste for adventure. Busey agrees to bankroll the trip—but only if he goes along. Once in Colombia, Duvall guides the inexperienced troop through a delicate maze of death squads, corrupt local officials, and arms merchants. Eventually, Duvall is given a lead on the location of the drug dealer's hideout, but the troop is ambushed by Rios' gang and Duvall is killed. Busey takes control of the situation and holds one of the terrorists, Carrillo, a woman, captive. He attempts to torture her into revealing the location of the hideout, but when Schoeffling catches him in the act, he clobbers Busey and lets the woman go. For some unexplained reason, Carrillo suddenly offers to help the Americans and she leads them to Rios' jungle compound. Like seasoned professionals, the boys invade the camp, blow up buildings, kill a lot of Colombians, and rescue Harmon and Gray. During the battle Busey is killed, but the others survive and return to the U.S. in triumph.

LET'S GET HARRY was originally conceived by veteran director Sam Fuller (PICKUP ON SOUTH STREET, THE BIG RED ONE), who had planned to direct the project in 1981. When that never materialized, the story was later turned into a screenplay by Carner and eventually assigned to COOL HAND LUKE director Stuart Rosenberg. Filmed in Mexico and Aurora, Illinois, in 1985, the project ran into great difficulty during postproduction and director Rosenberg walked off, demanding his name be removed from the credits. Although Rosenberg directed the entire film, the name "Alan Smithee" (a pseudonym used by many filmmakers unhappy with the final product—Don Siegel used it on DEATH OF A GUNFIGHTER, and Michael Ritchie used it on STUDENT BODIES) appears beneath the directing credit. While LET'S GET HARRY is a competent action film, it lacks the spark of creativity that would set it apart from other routine actioners. Only the performances of Duvall and Busey breathe life into this film, but their screen time is much too brief. Both actors do wonders with what little they are given, managing to create a pair of vivid and memorable characters with economy and style. Unfortunately, when Duvall and Busey are offscreen, the film becomes sluggish and uninvolving. The four young leads (Schoeffling, Wilson, Rossovich, and Frey) are not very magnetic and Carner's script affords them precious few opportunities to distinguish themselves. Frey (a former member of the California rock band The Eagles and author of hits "The Heat is On" and "You Belong to the City") makes his feature film debut here after a pair of effective TV performances in "Miami Vice." Despite some proven acting ability, Frey fails to separate himself from the blandness of his comrades and his Southern California accent creeps in on occasion, reminding viewers that he is not a pipe fitter from Aurora, Illinois. Reportedly, Frey wrote some music for the film, including a "blue-collar rock 'n' roll song," but his compositions never made it into the final cut. *(Violence, profanity.)*

p, Daniel H. Blatt, Robert Singer; d, Alan Smithee [Stuart Rosenberg]; w, Charles Robert Carner (based on a story by Mark Feldberg, Samuel Fuller); ph, James A. Contner (Metrocolor); m, Brad Fiedel; ed, Ralph E. Winters, Rick R. Sparr; art d, Mort Rabinowicz, Agustin Ituarte; set d, Mark Fabus, Enrique Estevez; makeup, Wes Dawn, Jefferson Dawn; cos, Gilda Texter; stunts, Bobby Bass; m/l, Timothy B. Schmit, Ed Sanford.

Action/Adventure **Cas.** **(PR:O MPAA:R)**

LEVSHA† (1987, USSR) 89m Lenfilm Studio c (Trans: Left-Hander)

Nikolai Stotsky *(Lefty)*, Vladimir Gostyukhin, Leonid Kuravlyov, Yury Yakovlev.

Adaptation of a Russian fairy tale which tells of an emperor who, while traveling Europe, purchases a microscopic steel flea which performs a dance when wound up. The flea was constructed by brilliant British craftsmen and the emperor paid one million pounds for the toy. Upon the emperor's death, his heir takes the flea to a group of impoverished Russian craftsmen and assigns them the task of improving on the design. After many hours of diligent work the youngest of the crew, known as "Lefty" presents the emperor with the improved flea. Upon peering into the microscope the emperor is amazed to find that the Russian craftsman have put shoes on the tiny flea, each inscribed with the names of those who worked on the project. The happy emperor declares that Russian craftsman have finally outdone the British.

d&w, Sergei Ovcharov (based on the story by N.S. Leskov); ph, Valery Fedosov; m, Igor Matsiyevsky; art d, Natalia Vasilyeva.

Children's **(PR:NR MPAA:NR)**

LEVY ET GOLIATH† (1987, Fr.) 97m Gaumont c

Richard Anconina *(Moses Levy)*, Michel Boujenah *(Albert Levy)*, Jean-Claude Brialy *(Bijou)*, Saouad Amidou *(Malika)*, Maxime Leroux *(Goliath)*, Sophie Barjac *(Brigitte Levy)*, Robert Hossein *(Drug Mogul)*.

Anconina is a Hasidic Jew whose life is turned upside down when a drug smuggler trying to avoid customs stashes some cocaine in Anconina's bags. Since Anconina is importing diamond powder to an auto manufacturing plant, the caches naturally get confused. Pursued through Paris by the smuggler's gang, Anconina must turn for help to Boujenah, his estanged brother. Veteran actor Brialy is cast as a detective working undercover as a transvestite.

p, Alain Poire; d, Gerard Oury; w, Gerard Oury, Daniele Thompson; ph, Wladimir Ivanov (Eastmancolor); m, Vladimir Cosma; ed, Albert Jurgenson; art d, Theo Meurisse.

Comedy/Crime **(PR:NR MPAA:NR)**

L'HOMME VOILE† (1987, Fr./Lebanon) 93m Intage-Paris Classics-Hachette Premiere-UGC-Les Films de la Saga/UGC c (Trans: The Veiled Man)

Bernard Giraudeau *(Pierre)*, Michel Piccoli *(Kassar)*, Laure Marsac *(Claire)*, Michal Albertini *(Kamal)*, Sandrine Dumas *(Julie)*, Fouad Naim, Sonia Ichti, Jonathan Layna, Kamal Kassar.

After spending several years in Lebanon, Giraudeau returns to his 16-year-old daughter (Marsac) in Paris. Marsac knows nothing about her father's more violent activities and assumes he was merely administering to the sick and wounded. In reality, Giraudeau's homecoming is tied to his pursuit of two heinous terrorists who have fled to Paris from Lebanon and he intends to assassinate them both. When Marsac learns the truth about her father's activites in Lebanon, she rebels by taking up with one of the terrorists (Albertini). This angers the terrorist's spurned wife, and she sets into action the violent climax.

p, Humbert Balsan; d, Maroun Bagdadi; w, Maroun Bagdadi, Didier Decoin; ph, Patric Blossier (Kodacolor); m, Gabriel Yared; ed, Luc Barnier; art d, Richard Peduzzi.

Drama **(PR:NR MPAA:NR)**

LICHNOE DELO SUDYI IVANOVOY† (1987, USSR) 86m Gorky Film/Sovexportfilm c (Trans: The Case of a Judge)

Oxana Datskaya, Natalia Gundareva, Sergei Shakurov, Lilia Gritsenko, Marina Zudina.

An experienced woman divorce-court judge is shocked to learn that her husband is having an affair with their 14-year-old daughter's music teacher. To shelter the child, the three adults live dual lives and pretend that nothing has changed, though their relationship is collapsing. The girl eventually senses the truth and, in the process, learns much about the adult world.

d, Ilya Frez; w, Galina Scherbakova; ph, Ilya Frez, Jr.; m, Mark Minkov; art d, Olga Kravchenya.

Drama **(PR:NR MPAA:NR)**

LIEN LIEN FUNG CHEN† (1987, Taiwan) 109m Central Motion Picture c (Trans: Dust in The Wind)

Sin Shu-Fen, Wang Tsin-Wen, Lee Tien-Mu, Mei Fang.

Popular Taiwanese director Hou Hsiao Hsien moves from his usual explorations of childhood into young adulthood in his latest film. It follows a young man as he moves from his provincial village to the big city. Hoping to land a good job so he can send money home to his family and fiancee, the young man discovers that his stay in the city will change his life forever.

p, Ling Deng Fei; d, Hou Hsiao Hsien; w, Wu Nien Jen, Chu Tien Wen; ph, Lee Ping Bin; ed, Liao Ching Sung; art d, Liu Ji Hwa.

Drama **(PR:NR MPAA:NR)**

LIFE CLASSES† (1987, Can.) 117m Picture Plant/Cinephile c

Jacinta Cormier *(Mary Cameron)*, Leon Dubinsky *(Earl)*, Evelyn Garbary *(Nanny)*, Mary Izzard *(Mrs. Miller)*, Francis Knickle *(Gloria)*, Jill Chatt *(Marie)*, Leo Jessome *(Mr. Cameron)*, Caitlyn Colquhoun *(Mrs. Sitwell)*.

Set in Nova Scotia, this film follows the life of a small-town woman (Cormier) whose hobby is painting. When she learns that she is pregnant by her dreary boy friend (Dubinsky), she decides to move to Halifax to have the baby rather than jump into a loveless marriage. After her daughter is born she lands a job in a department store and makes friends with a college student who encourages her to do some nude modeling for her life drawing class. Cormier learns much from the class and begins to sketch her child and herself, evetually becoming known for her work. In the end, she returns to her home town, determined to remain independent.

p, Stephen Reynolds; d&w, William D. MacGillivray; ph, Lionel Simmons; m, Alexandra Tilley; ed, William D. MacGillivray; art d, Mary Steckle.

Drama **(PR:NR MPAA:NR)**

LIGHT OF DAY** (1987) 107m Taft/Tri Star c

Michael J. Fox *(Joe Rasnick)*, Gena Rowlands *(Jeanette Rasnick)*, Joan Jett *(Patti Rasnick)* Michael McKean *(Bu Montgomery)*, Thomas G. Waites *(Smittie)*, Cherry Jones *(Cindy Montgomery)*, Michael Dolan *(Gene Bodine)*, Paul J. Harkins *(Billy Tettore)*, Billy Sullivan *(Benji Rasnick)*, Jason Miller *(Benjamin Rasnick)*.

Despite a few good moments here and there and a stunning mini-performance by Rowlands, LIGHT OF DAY is an anemic drama with little to say, a family set piece whose natural limitations best suit TV exposure. The film does not pack the gear of a theatrically released film. Much of the fault lies with director-writer Schrader, one-time *enfant terrible* of moviedom who has pulled in his horns of horror, schlock-shock and obsession with the degenerative, to opt for the simple life. Moreover, the film is too burdensome for likable but lightweight TV comedian Fox who carries the whole story on his frail shoulders and obviously staggers under the weight. He and his sister, Jett, are soft-rock musicians in Cleveland, playing in a family bar, Fox working in a manufacturing plant during the day, Jett minding her small boy. To Fox the band is an extension of his family, to Jett it's a crusade to prove that rock 'n' roll is a lifestyle unto itself. Visits to their parents are stressful for Jett since her mother, Rowlands, cannot forgive her for having her son, Sullivan, out of wedlock. Fox and Jett live together with the little boy, pooling their meager income to make ends meet, but they are always struggling to buy instruments for the band and when their synthesizer breaks down, Jett steals the tools to fix it. The band loses its gig, Fox is laid off, and he and Jett go on the road with the band. They are nickel-and-dimed out of a livable income by sleazy, marble-mouthed bar owners and music promoters. Jett takes to stealing from food stores and Fox rebels against such tactics, taking his nephew home to Cleveland. Jett by then is fanatically committed to ignoring her family and living only for her rock music, later joining a heavy metal rock band of freaks who play to the leather-whip-and-chain set. The crowds that flock to see her and the band (aptly named The Hunzz, after Attila, etc.) seem more interested in noise than music. When Rowlands falls ill, Fox goes to see Jett, who is playing out of town, telling her that their mother is gravely ill with cancer. All Jett can do is mouth inanities about her dedication to rock: "It's not heaven, it's not hell, it's the moments, the moments!" She finally relents, overcomes her animosity toward her mother, and sees Rowlands before she dies. The deathbed scene in the hospital proves Rowlands an actress of extraordinary depth, a magnificent portrayal of a mother, struggling to overcome memory loss and to set things right before she leaves the family she loves so much. At the end, Jett gives up her wandering lifestyle and rejoins Fox on the stage as their old band plays for the local Clevelanders.

Schrader's story is visually static for the most part, the beginning and middle of the film dragging on witlessly, without substantive conflict to create interest. His directorial talents are almost nil as he piles one flat scene upon another, sluggishly moves his cameras about and, when in doubt (which is often) opts for a closeup to heighten his crumbling drama, but provides nothing of significance in that closeup, no revelations, admissions or pivotal character surprises to warrant the use of the technique. Repeating these unimaginative techniques over and over sinks LIGHT OF DAY into a morass of commonplace events, thus stripping the essential ingredients from the drama. The commonplace all filmgoers understand; each seat in the theater is occupied by a viewer bringing that certain point of identification to any film, but it is essential to present the uncommon occurrence within the pedestrian setting to create the necessary drama and conflict that rises above the commonplace. Any story on film striving to present itself on screen in this manner usually deserves the attention of investments, superior talents in front of and behind the camera, and audience understanding. What Schrader has done here is to toss up upon the screen a poorly thought out family opus in hopes that it would stick. It does not. He concentrates upon the sagging and passe argument of rock 'n' roll's dubious distinction of being attached to the younger generation. It becomes a *cause celebre* for Jett and her reason for existence. *Her* cross is that she bore a child by the local minister, kept it secret, and learned to hate her religious mother who conveniently represented all that was hypocritical, a pat excuse for living like a bum. Schrader does provide in Jett a wholly obnoxious, near cretinous creature who hates herself enough to insist that she actually has talent to excuse her anti-family sentiments. LIGHT OF DAY is a depressing piece which ignores even average intelligence. Schrader's script, which must have been written in all of a week, provides nothing memorable, save Rowlands' death scene, and all the more readily points out the sorry state of film writing today. By comparison to other family film dramas, such as COME BACK LITTLE SHEBA and THE DARK AT THE TOP OF THE STAIRS, this is a mean-minded, empty-headed, niggardly portrait which is rather contemptuous of the public dollar Schrader insists be spent to see it. Also unforgivable is Schrader's use of Miller, a superb actor, who is given almost nothing to say and do in the film as the ineffectual father. *(Profanity, adult situations.)*

p, Rob Cohen, Keith Barish; d&w, Paul Schrader; ph, John Bailey (Astro Color); m, Thomas Newman; ed, Jacqueline Cambas; prod d, Jeannine Claudia Oppewall; set d, Lisa Fischer; cos, Jodie Tillen; m/l, Bruce Springsteen.

Drama **Cas.** **(PR:C MPAA:PG-13)**

LIGHTHORSEMEN, THE† (1987, Aus.) 128m Picture Show/Cinecom c

Jon Blake *(Scotty)*, Peter Phelps *(Dave Mitchell)*, Tony Bonner *(Lt. Col "Swagman Bill" Bourchier)*, Bill Kerr *(Lt. Gen. Sir Harry Chauvel)*, John Walton *(Tas)*, Gary Sweet *(Frank)*, Tim McKenzie *(Chiller)*, Sigrid Thornton *(Anne)*, Anthony Andrews *(Maj. Meinertzhagen)*, Anthony Hawkins *(Gen. Sir Edmund Allenby)*, Gerard Kennedy *(Ismet Bey)*, Shane Briant *(Reichert)*, Serge Lazareff *(Rankin)*, Ralph Cotterill *(Von Kressenstein)*, John Heywood *(Mr. Mitchell)*, Di O'Connor *(Mrs. Mitchell)*, Grant Piro *(Charlie)*, Patrick Frost *(Sgt. Ted Scager)*, Adrian Wright *(Lawson)*, Anne Scott-Pendlebury *(Nursing Sister)*, Brenton Whittle *(Padre)*, Jon Sidney *(Grant)*, Graham Dow *(Hodgson)*, James Wright *(Fitzgerald)*, Gary Stalker *(Nobby)*, Scott Bradley *(Lt. Burton)*, Peter Merrill *(Young German Officer)*, Peter Browne *(Arch)*.

An epic war film (produced on a $10 million budget—an unheard of sum in Australian movie making) set in 1917 during the British campaign in Palestine. The film follows a four-man section of the Australian Light Horse Regiment (Sweet, Walton, McKenzie, and Blake), all veterans of Gallipoli. When Sweet is wounded during a Bedouin ambush, he is replaced by Phelps, an inexperienced young recruit who has a reputation as a superior horseman. Despite his obvious skills, the other men worry over his ability to be a soldier and their fears are confirmed when Phelps cannot bring himself to kill a fleeing Turkish soldier. Phelps will soon have a chance to prove his mettle, for the success of the entire campaign rests on a sunset attack by the Lighthorsemen on the water-rich wells of

Beersheba—a battle that would become the last great cavalry charge in history. Star Jon Blake was seriously injured in an automobile accident that occured while he was driving home after the last day of shooting.

p, Ian Jones, Simon Wincer; d, Simon Wincer; w, Ian Jones; ph, Dean Semler (Panavision, Eastmancolor); m, Mario Millo; ed, Adrian Carr; prod d, Bernard Hides; cos, David Rowe; spec eff, Steve Courtley; stunts, Grant Page.

War/Drama **(PR:NR MPAA:NR)**

LIIAN ISO KEIKKA† (1987, Fin.) 106m Funny-Films Oy c (Trans: Too Big Gig)

Vesa-Matti Loiri, Ritva Valkama, Pentti Siimes, Hannele Lauri, Ville-Veikko Salminen, Aake Kalliala.

A crime comedy about a group of bumbling crooks who form a company known as Crime Services, Inc. in order to raise funding for a big bank heist. They soon find many clients willing to pay for petty burglaries, safe-cracking, fraud schemes, etc. Hot on their trail, however, is a dedicated police inspector and his loyal assistant, and their pursuit threatens to ruin the upcoming bank heist.

d&w, Ere Kokkonen; ph, Juha Jalasti; m, Aarno Raninen; ed, Eva Jaakontalo; set d, Tapio Rantanen.

Comedy **(PR:NR MPAA:NR)**

LIKE FATHER, LIKE SON** (1987) 98m Imagine Enter./Tri-Star c

Dudley Moore *(Dr. Jack Hammond)*, Kirk Cameron *(Chris Hammond)*, Margaret Colin *(Ginnie Armbruster)*, Catherine Hicks *(Dr. Amy Larkin)*, Patrick O'Neal *(Dr. Armbruster)*, Sean Astin *(Trigger)*, Cami Cooper *(Lori Beaumont)*, Micah Grant *(Rick Anderson)*, Bill Morrison *(Uncle Earl)*, Skeeter Vaughan *(Medicine Man)*, Larry Sellers *(Navajo Helper)*, Tami David *(Navajo Girl)*, Maxine Stuart *(Phyllis)*, David Wohl *(Dr. Roger Hartwood)*, Michael Horton *(Dr. Mike O'Donald)*, Randolph Dreyfuss *(Dr. Spellner)*, Art Frankel *(Mr. Racine)*, Christine Healy *(Hospital Administrator)*, Mary Jane Courier *(Operating Nurse)*, Chera Holland *(Nurse in Corridor)*, Debbie Zipp *(Nurse with Dying Patient)*, Teresa Bowman *(Nurse with Heart Patient)*, Brian Peck *(Intern with Heart Patient)*, Carol Swarbrick *(Norma)*, Kedric Wolfe *(Sidney, Board Member)*, Robert Balderson *(Hal Gilden, Board Member)*, Dakin Matthews *(Old Man Morrison)*, Les Lannom *(Coach Ellis)*, Lorna Hill *(Mrs. Davis)*, John Stinson *(Math Teacher)*, Bill Stevenson *(Biology Student)*, Alexandra Kenworthy *(Janice Stenfield)*, Todd Selby *(Rick's Friend)*, Lloyd Nelson *(Teacher in Hall)*, John Tokatlian, Mark McCannon, Jan Duncan *(Students)*, Armin Shimerman *(Trigger's Dad)*, Kitty Swink *(Trigger's Mom)*, Lisa Robins *(Bartender)*, Richard Gilberts *(Paper Boy)*, James Lashly *(Freemont)*, Corki Grazer *(Corky)*, Nancy Lenehan *(Waitress in Desert Diner)*, Edwin Brecht, Johnathan Brecht *(Newborns at Desert Diner)*, Steve Plunkett, Randy Rand, Steve Lynch, Keni E. Richards, Steven Isham *(Rock Concert Band, Autograph)*, James Deeth *(Helicopter Pilot)*.

The most amazing fact about this film is that it did such good business. The success at the box office far outstripped the potential of the material, which was, at best, a half-hour episode of "The Twilight Zone" or something one might see on a cable TV comedy anthology. What makes it work better than it should is the chemistry of Moore and Cameron. The idea of transference has been done before. Disney made FREAKY FRIDAY wherein mother Barbara Harris and daughter Jodie Foster changed personalities, and way back in 1940, Carole Landis and John Hubbard switched bodies in TURNABOUT. Since those who don't study history are condemned to repeat it, the people who made this picture either conveniently forgot that it had already been done, or they conveniently remembered and decided that they could do it better, which they came close to doing. The movie begins as Morrison is seen struggling across a bleak expanse of desert, barely able to crawl over the burning sands because his leg has been injured. He is found by some local Indians and taken to a place where he can rest. However, his condition is so weak that he may not be able to survive the next hours, so he is given a mind-switching drug by medicine man Vaughan. As he stares at young Navajo helper Sellers, the two men's minds switch into each others' bodies and now Morrison is strong enough to withstand the rigors of the next few hours when the crisis will come. After Morrison recovers, the personalities are switched back and Morrison, an archaeologist, is given some of the serum to take with him. Now if you don't swallow the above premise, read no further because your disbelief must be suspended in spades to take the rest of this movie tale. Morrison is the uncle to Astin (son of John), neighbor of Moore and his son Cameron. Astin finds the mysterious potion in his house and decides to let his pal Cameron in on his discovery. They try the stuff on Astin's dog and cat and the predictable happens—the cat barks and the dog runs away. They hide the potion in an old jar that resembles a Tabasco brand sauce container. Moore returns home from the hospital where he is a respected, if somewhat stuffy, cardiac surgeon, and tosses some of the potion into his nightly Bloody Mary. When he and Cameron look into each others' eyes, their brains and personalities are suddenly switched. Until now, Moore has been the somewhat conservative widowed father who is in line for the job of chief of staff at the hospital run by O'Neal, a fussbudget who is married to hot, steamy Colin. At the hospital, the rebellious Hicks tries to enlist Moore into one of her plans to improve matters, but Moore is not a boat-rocker and refuses. Cameron has been faring poorly in school, especially in science, and is in danger of raising Moore's wrath.

That being the setup, once the minds switch (the bodies remain the same), the comic possibilities are enormous, though hardly plumbed by the screenwriter and director. Cameron, given Moore's mind, is now able to lecture the class in biology and astound both students and teachers alike. Further, he is able to stand up to bully Grant who had been dating nubile Cooper until Cameron came along. Cameron, a speedy track star, has been chosen for the last leg of the important

relay race, beating out Grant. With Moore's brain in Cameron's body, naturally that all gets fouled up. Meanwhile, with Cameron's brain in Moore's body, there are some funny moments as the adult teenager tries to fake being a doctor while on rounds. At a staff meeting, Moore tosses his gum around and acts silly. Colin has always had the warmies for Moore, who has stayed away from her because she is the wife of the boss. Cameron doesn't have the same morals so he goes for it. Naturally, since this *is* a PG-13 film, that doesn't work out. The middle of the movie is mainly concerned with these sorts of switch gags. It's idiotic at times, cute at other times. Some of the lines are sharp, such as the moment when Cameron is watching Cooper at her school locker and his eyes glaze with teenage lust as he says to Astin: "She's so beautiful. How can she keep from feeling herself up all the time?"—or words to that effect. Why it takes them so long to attempt to switch back is never explained. Apparently, the drug wears off by itself because we never see the cat barking at the meowing dog. Astin enlists the aid of his uncle and they go out into the desert to find the antidote for the darn liquid that started all the trouble in the first place. Naturally, they find the root, brew it up like male versions of the three witches from "Macbeth," and all ends well. Moore realizes that his relationship with Cameron is worth far more than the job O'Neal hung out as a carrot and then jerked away when Moore (with Cameron's brain) was behaving in an odd fashion.

There is a bit of an attraction between Hicks and Moore that gets started and then seems to fade away, as though the editor decided that it wasn't going anywhere. Several extraneous scenes and some MTV-type slow-motion sequences are wasted, but, without them, the movie might have come in too short. Three basic interiors were used in the film: the house, the high school, and the new naval hospital in San Diego. Cameron has a great future in front of him. He has charm, an easy way with a comedy line, and the ability to look as though he's not acting. Moore, after having made WHOLLY MOSES, SIX WEEKS, LOVESICK, ROMANTIC COMEDY, UNFAITHFULLY YOURS, and SANTA CLAUS, may have a great future behind him. Fault Moore or his agents, but he has had more turkeys in the past few years than most families' Thanksgivings. If he keeps this up, everyone may soon forget the brilliance of the actor who made ARTHUR, 10, and FOUL PLAY into more than what they might have been. In a small role as the Navajo helper, note improvisational comedian Larry Sellers. Look for Colin to star in some upcoming movies. She pops off the screen with heavy sensuality. Lots of music to make up for the dull stretches. Tunes include: "All in the Name," "Wild Side" (performed by Motley Crue), "Dude" (performed by Aerosmith), "Somebody Put Something in My Drink" (performed by The Ramones), "Everybody Have Fun Tonight" (performed by Wang Chung), "I Ching" (performed by Mark Jordan), "It Comes to Me Naturally" (performed by The Fabulous Thunderbirds), "Hard Times in the Land of Plenty" (performed by Omar and The Howlers), "Dance All Night," "She Never Looked That Good to Me" (performed by Autograph). About 10 good laughs in the movie, or about 9.7 minutes worth. Director Daniel has been this way before, having helmed Michael J. Fox in TEEN WOLF and there are some similarities in the high-school sequences. A pleasant way to spend 98 minutes, provided you haven't anything better to see, like HOUSE OF GAMES or LA BAMBA or FULL METAL JACKET or any of many stronger 1987 pictures. *(Profanity, adult situations.)*

p, Brian Grazer, David Valdes; d, Rod Daniel; w, Lorne Cameron, Steven L. Bloom (based on a story by Lorne Cameron); ph, Jack N. Green (Technicolor); m, Miles Goodman; ed, Lois Freeman-Fox; prod d, Dennis Gassner; set d, John T. Walker; cos, Robert Turturice; makeup, Monty Westmore, Brogan Lane; spec eff, John Frazier.

Comedy **Cas.** **(PR:C MPAA:PG-13)**

LIONHEART† (1987) 104m Taliafilm II/Orion c

Eric Stoltz *(Robert Nerra)*, Gabriel Byrne *(The Black Prince)*, Nicola Cowper *(Blanche)*, Dexter Fletcher *(Michael)*, Deborah Barrymore *(Mathilda)*, Nicholas Clay *(Charles de Montfort)*, Bruce Purchase *(Simon Nerra)*, Neil Dickson *(King Richard)*, Chris Pitt *(Odo)*.

Despite the big names involved in this production (co-produced by actress Talia Shire, with her brother Francis Coppola serving as executive producer), the latest film from director Franklin J. Schaffner—a medieval epic—was released only in Canada to scathing reviews and seems doomed to the home video shelves in the

US. Filmed on location in Hungary and Portugal, the movie is set in the Middle Ages and features Stolz as a young knight who joins King Richard's crusade. En route to Paris, the place where he is to connect with the crusaders, Stotlz picks up a group of hangers-on, including brother and sister circus performers (Cowper and Fletcher), a thief, a young con artist, and King Richard's very own falconer. Along the way the gang must do battle with the evil Byrne, who is determined to seduce the young travelers and then sell them into slavery. A big-budget affair, the director made use of several castles and recruited hundreds of Slavic children to work as extras. Just exactly why the film has not been released in the US is anybody's guess, but universally negative reviews may have been enough to scare Orion into dumping the film in overseas markets and making a quick sale to pay-TV and video domestically.

p, Stanley O'Toole, Talia Shire; d, Franklin J. Schaffner; w, Menno Meyjes, Richard Outten (based on a story by Menno Meyjes); ph, Alec Mills; m, Jerry Goldsmith; ed, David Bretherton, Richard Haines; prod d, Gil Parrondo; cos, Nana Cecchi.

Adventure/Children's **(PR:NR MPAA:PG)**

LITTLE DORRIT† (1987, Brit.) Part I: Nobody's Fault 177m, Part II: Little Dorrit's Story 183m Sands Films-Cannon Screen Ent. c

Alec Guinness *(William Dorrit)*, Derek Jacobi *(Arthur Clennam)*, Cyril Cusack *(Frederick Dorrit)*, Sarah Pickering *(Little Dorrit)*, Joan Greenwood *(Mrs. Clennam)*, Max Wall *(Flintwinch)*, Amelda Brown *(Fanny Dorrit)*, Daniel Chatto *(Tip Dorrit)*, Miriam Margolyes *(Flora Finching)*, Bill Fraser *(Mr. Casby)*, Roshan Seth *(Mr. Pancks)*, Roger Hammond *(Mr. Megles)*, Sophie Ward *(Minnie Meagles)*, John Savident *(Tite Barnacle)*, Edward Burnham *(Daniel Doyce)*, Eleanor Bron *(Mrs. Merdle)*, Michael Elphick *(Mr. Merdle)*, Robert Morley *(Lord Decimus Barnacle)*, Alan Bennett *(The Bishop)*.

An ambitious adaptation of the Dickens novel. Set in the 1840s, the film plays in two parts running three hours each. Part I: "Nobody's Fault" is told from Jacobi's perspective. Upon returning to England from a business trip to China, Jacobi is taken with the sad story of Guinness, a man who has been locked in the dreaded Marshalsea debtor's prison for the last 25 years. His beautiful younger daughter, Pickering, was born there and has never known true freedom. Jacobi becomes determined to help the family and, with the assistance of debt collector Seth, he discovers a hidden inheritance owed to Guinness. Free at last, the family goes on a trip to Europe only to find their champion's own personal fortunes have taken a bad turn and he is now imprisoned at Marshalsea. Part II: "Little Dorrit's Story" covers the same ground as Part I, but this time the story is seen through Pickering's eyes. The details of her family's predicament are more vivid and we watch as Pickering slowly falls in love with the noble Jacobi. Once free and in Europe, Pickering watches as her father goes mad. Upon discovering Jacobi in prison, Pickering raises the money to secure his release and there is a happy, romantic ending in Clennam.

Shot by master cinematographer Bruno de Keyzer (A SUNDAY IN THE COUNTRY, ROUND MIDNIGHT) entirely in Sands Film Studios in Rotherhithe, London, LITTLE DORRITT was in pre-production for two years, post-production for nine months, with 135 days of shooting in between. Boasting 211 cast members, this six-hour epic was released in one theater in London late in 1987 and, remarkably, has played to enthusiastic crowds despite its very lengthy running time.

p, Richard Goodwin, John Brabourne; d&w, Christine Edzard (based on the novel *Little Dorrit* by Charles Dickens); ph, Bruno de Keyzer (Technicolor); m, Giuseppe Verdi; ed, Olivier Stockman, Fraser Maclean; md, Michel Sanvoisin; cos, Sands Films.

Drama **(PR:NR MPAA:NR)**

LITTLE PROSECUTOR, THE† (1987, Ger.) 91m Hamburg Kino-Kompanie Hark Bohm/Filmverlag der Autoren-NDR TV c (DER KLEINE STAATSAN WALT)

Hark Bohm *(Konig)*, Martin Luttge *(Kaiser)*, Corinna Harfouch *(Frau Meffert)*, Michael Gwisdek *(Wuttke)*, Alexander Radszun *(Siegmann)*, Ute Christensen *(Frau Keile)*, Ulrich von Dobschutz *(Dr. Kleinsteuber)*, Klaus Pohl *(Scepanek)*, Tilo Pruckner *(von Knorringen)*, Rainer Hunold *(Rademacher)*, Marquard Bohm *(Trumpeter)*.

Hark Bohm, the bespectacled character actor who has appeared in many Rainer Werner Fassbinder films—THE MARRIAGE OF MARIA BRAUN, LILI MARLEEN, EFFI BRIEST, DESPAIR, LOLA—makes his feature directorial debut from his own script, which satirizes the German bureaucracy. He plays a meek, small-time prosecuting attorney who takes on the bankruptcy case of a construction firm with the help of his aggressive female assistant, Harfouch. As they begin examining the case, they uncover a web of graft and corruption which entangles a number of high-ranking officials. In the process, however, their zeal clouds their judgement and an innocent executive, Luttge, is framed in what turns out to be a bankruptcy scam. Shown as part of the Chicago International Film Festival. (In German; English subtitles.)

p, Jurgen Bottcher; d&w, Hark Bohm; ph, Klaus Brix; m, Toots Thielemans, Herb Geller; ed, Inge Bohmann; art d, Jochen Krumpeter.

Drama **(PR:NR MPAA:NR)**

LIVING DAYLIGHTS, THE*½** (1987) 130m Eon-UA/MGM-UA c

Timothy Dalton *(James Bond)*, Maryam d'Abo *(Kara Malovy)*, Jeroen Krabbe *(Gen. Georgi Koskov)*, Joe Don Baker *(Brad Whitaker)*, John Rhys-Davies *(Gen. Leonid Pushkin)*, Art Malik *(Kamran Shah)*, Andreas Wisniewski *(Necros)*, Thomas Wheatley *(Saunders)*, Desmond Llewelyn *(Q)*, Robert Brown *(M)*, Geoffrey Keen *(Minister of Defence)*, Walter Gotell *(Gen. Anatol Gogol)*, Caroline Bliss *(Miss Moneypenny)*, John Terry *(Felix Leiter)*, John Bowe, Julie T. Wallace, Kell Tyler, Catherine Rabett, Dulice Liecier, Nadim Sawalha, Alan Talbot, Carl Rigg, Tony Cyrus, Atik Mohamed.

Where Nick Charles, Sam Spade, Sherlock Holmes, and Philip Marlowe are super sleuths whose *film noir* presences give permanent joy to viewers, the eternal espionage agent is certainly James Bond, suave, worldly (without being world-weary), deadly, a man for all hazards, risk-taker, woman-winner, idol of millions. Bond has worn many faces—Sean Connery, who made the role his own as the original super British agent; the experimental George Lazenby; and the sophisticated Roger Moore. Now, a new, more serious Bond emerges in the form of Dalton, a dark-eyed 007 whose constant battle against world forces of evil is approached with considerable dedication and little flippancy. This, as producer Broccoli insists, is the James Bond intended by author Ian Fleming. The accent on realism is evident in the first frames of THE LIVING DAYLIGHTS when Dalton drops with two other British agents from a spy plane high above Gibraltar in an experiment to test that British bastion's defense systems. The three agents free-fall through space pulling rip cords at the last second, their parachutes becoming mini-hang-gliders, allowing them to land on jutting precipices. Two of the men are killed by KGB agents while trying to scale the Gibraltar heights but Dalton survives, hurling himself onto the top of a truck speeding precariously down the narrow roadways. He slashes through the canvas top of the truck to dive inside and struggle with the driver as the truck sails over a railing and begins falling toward the sea. Dalton pulls the rip-cord of yet another parachute and is yanked out of the truck just before it and the opposing agent explode into tiny fragments. Dalton sails blissfully downward to land on a yacht where a beautiful playgirl is just at that moment seeking relief from the great ennui. All this before the opening credits promises and delivers a rousing action-jammed film with often more credibility of plot and villains than seen in earlier Bond films.

Dalton next receives an assignment to aid in the defection of a KGB general, Krabbe, traveling to Bratislava, Czechoslovakia. There Dalton meets with another British agent, Wheatley and is told he must kill a sniper who is assigned to murder Krabbe should the KGB general make a break for the West. Positioned outside a huge opera building where a symphony is in progress, Dalton arms himself with a high-powered rifle with infra-red sights. When Krabbe makes his break, Dalton spots the sniper perched high in a window of the opera building—beautiful, blonde d'Abo, a cellist in the symphony orchestra. Instead of sending a bullet crashing into her pretty head, Dalton fires a round that blasts d'Abo's rifle from her hands. Krabbe is then spirited by Dalton to the trans-Siberian natural gas pipeline where he inserts the general into a specially designed vehicle (not unlike the containers used in sending money and messages through vacuum systems in department stores decades ago) which whisks him to Austria. Later, Dalton returns to find that d'Abo was merely a victim of KGB intrigue and escapes with her to the West by first racing along the Czechoslovakian roadways, slick with snow, in his gimmicky Aston Martin sports car. (There were three actual cars used by special effects wizard Richardson, along with many dummy cars, the latter, when sailing through the air were actually sent through space by being fired from a huge cannon.) After eluding half the KGB and Red Army in Czechoslovakia, Dalton and d'Abo escape down a mountain pass by using her cello case as a sled, gliding into Austria and safety while d'Abo holds her priceless cello aloft. Meanwhile, Krabbe is abducted, or appears to be abducted, by KGB agents from a British Intelligence retreat in England after he has informed Western spymasters that the KGB intends to begin a worldwide series of high-level assassinations, a plan concocted by another KGB general, Rhys-Davies, and dove-tailing with the lethal events seen earlier at Gibraltar. Krabbe has not, however, been abducted by the KGB; he has pretended to be a captive of imitation KGB agents who are actually in the employ of a psychopathic American arms dealer, Baker, hiding out in Baker's remote villa in Tangier in a scheme to defraud the Russians of millions of dollars. In Vienna, Dalton begins to fall in love with d'Abo, while believing that the Krabbe defection and abduction are ruses. He is in contact with Wheatley, trying to learn more of Krabbe's whereabouts and that of Rhys-Davies. He is scheduled to meet with Wheatley at an amusement park and goes there with d'Abo, riding on the huge ferris wheel which offers enclosed boxes. (This scene smacks of a similar scene from THE THIRD

MAN and not by coincidence in that the director of THE LIVING DAYLIGHTS, Glen, worked on THE THIRD MAN with master director Carol Reed.) Just after vital information is passed onto Dalton by Wheatley, the British agent is crushed by an electronic door which has been fixed by Baker's top agent. This killing puts Dalton on the trail of the killer which leads him and d'Abo to Tangier, then to Afghanistan where the Krabbe plot becomes even more involved. Baker and Krabbe are trading diamonds purchased by Baker with $50 million he received from the Russians to buy arms for their mercenary armies. Instead Baker and Krabbe hope to double their profits by exchanging the diamonds for opium which will bring hundreds of millions in the illegal marketplace. Also, Dalton finds time to ostensibly assassinate Rhys-Davies at a public gathering, but the killing is faked so that Rhys-Davies can continue to operate against the Baker-Krabbe organization. In Afghanistan Dalton and d'Abo are captured by Krabbe's people and imprisoned at a Russian air base but they escape, freeing another prisoner, Malik, who turns out to be a leader of the Afghan revolt against the Russian invaders. He later aids Dalton in a spectacular raid on the air base—Afghan horsemen going up against Russian armor and doing well—while Dalton and d'Abo climb aboard a huge cargo plane, and take off with the bundled opium on board. Baker's top assassin, however, manages to climb aboard just before takeoff and he and Dalton battle in the cargo hold and then, fighting furiously, are accidentally sent out the cargo door by d'Abo at the controls, where they cling to a large net bag containing the opium, flapping in the open air. (This is one of the most harrowing fight scenes in any Bond opus or any recent adventure-action film for that matter, one that will make anyone with a fear of heights slightly dizzy.) Dalton manages to cut the assassin loose by slicing the laces of one of his own boots to which the assassin clings for life, sending the killer downward to a screaming death. Dalton climbs back into the plane and nonchalantly takes over the controls just as the plane is about to smack into a mountain. He jumps into a jeep with d'Abo which is inside the plane, releasing a parachute attached to the jeep just before the plane crashes. The jeep lands squarely on the ground and Dalton drives down a road toward civilization.

In Tangier, Dalton squares off against arms nut Baker, battling him inside Baker's war museum, exchanging gunfire over diaramas of ancient battles until a bust of Wellington (England's greatest general) crashes in historic retribution down upon Baker to kill him. Krabbe is finally nabbed by Rhys-Davies, who is very much alive, and sent back to Russia. Rhys-Davies allows defector d'Abo to go with Dalton to England where she is later shown performing a brilliant cello solo at a symphony performance, attended by Malik and other Afghan partisans. Her great love, Dalton, however, is not present to offer his kudos, or, at least d'Abo thinks he has ignored her triumph until entering her dressing room where she sees two champagne glasses bubbling and Dalton joins her for a final embrace.

This is certainly a new James Bond, played seriously and straight by newcomer Dalton, with only a bit of frivolity curling about his incredible exploits. Gone is the wry, tongue-in-cheek Connery and the droll Moore. Dalton is rugged and more physical than his predecessors and decidedly monogamous, now a one-woman man who expresses genuine love for the much harassed d'Abo, an oblique nod to the AIDS problem, no doubt. And he is also a gentleman here, spending very little time in bed. His conquests are on the traditional fields of honor, not in the boudoir. There is more action in this film than any other Bond film and the $30 million spent on LIVING DAYLIGHTS certainly shows. It's a visual, polished feast for the eyes. The KGB plot is certainly more credible than the absurd power-mad organizations Bond faced in other films. D'Abo is alluring, cool in the Grace Kelly tradition, and Rhys-Davies is believable as the KGB general. Krabbe, too, is the epitome of the double-dealing spymaster, but Baker merely hams his role to death as the arms crackpot, spreading his lines like molasses over a sticky character. He becomes a comic heavy close to the Batman series mold, and for a millionaire adventurer one could expect his self-styled uniforms to fit better; his large frame seems to be about to burst through the seams of his military jacket. The British players are all good, Bliss as the ever proper but winking Miss Moneypenny, Brown as the authoritative M, and Llewelyn as the reliable and ever-inventive Q, dreaming up wonderful new defense and attack gadgets to safeguard Bond's precarious life. Q's gimmicks in this film include a key that will open 90 percent of the world's locks, a gadget that emits stunning gas when "Rule Britannia" is whistled, and, of course, the multi-faceted Aston Martin. Director Glen is an old hand at James Bond films, having worked on three other 007 movies. He knows this popular spy well and does him great service in this well-paced film. This is the 15th of the series and celebrates the 25th anniversary of Bond on film, a series that has proved a constant bonanza for producer Broccoli, gleaning an estimated $750,000,000 from world box offices. THE LIVING DAYLIGHTS is one of the best of the series, if not *the* best. There are few laughs here, but there simply is not time for them. Dalton is moving too fast, only three or four steps ahead of himself in a non-stop series of wild adventures, although his confidence level is high enough to survive any threat. In light of the glut of gloomy, morose, and very contrived spy and crime films in 1987, this one stands tall on the entertainment level. Songs include: "The Living Daylights" (Pal Waaktaar, John Barry; performed by a-ha), "Where Has Every Body Gone," "If There Was A Man" (John Barry, Chrissie Hynde; performed by The Pretenders), and the James Bond theme (Monty Norman). *(Brief nudity, violence.)*

p, Albert R. Broccoli, Michael G. Wilson; d, John Glen; w, Richard Maibaum, Michael G. Wilson (based on a story by Ian Fleming); ph, Alec Mills (Panavision, Technicolor); m, John Barry; ed, John Grover, Peter Davies; prod d, Peter Lamont; art d, Terry Ackland-Snow; set d, Michael Ford; cos, Emma Porteous; spec eff, John Richardson; m/l, Pal Waaktaar, John Barry, Chrissie Hynde, Monty Norman; stunts, Paul Weston, Remy Julienne, B.J. Worth.

Action/Adventure **(PR:C MPAA:PG)**

LIVING ON TOKYO TIME** (1987) 83m Farallon/Skouras c

Minako Ohashi *(Kyoko)*, Ken Nakagawa *(Ken)*, Mitzie Abe *(Mimi)*, Bill Bonham *(Carl)*, Brenda Aoki *(Michelle)*, Kate Connell *(Lana)*, John McCormick *(Richie)*, Sue Matthews *(Nina)*, Jim Cranna *(Jimbo)*, Alex Herschlag *(Warren)*, Keith Choy *(Lambert)*, Judi Nihei *(Sheri)*, Lane Nishikawa *(Lane)*.

Ohashi, a 19-year-old Japanese girl from Tokyo whose whole life—including marriage—has been arranged by her parents from birth, leaves her homeland to come to America upon discovering that her fiance has been having an affair. Although she speaks little English and her family is against the move, Ohashi is determined to make it on her own. She takes up residence in San Francisco, studies English from a tape recorder, and finds a job as a dishwasher in a Japanese restaurant. There she is befriended by a waitress, Connell, a well-meaning white woman who is quick to give sage advice. Ohashi also meets a variety of Japanese-Americans whose outspoken and boisterous behavior is in direct contrast to her traditionally refined, quiet, and shy Japanese demeanor. When Ohashi's visa expires she worries that she will have to return to Japan. Connell's solution is to arrange a temporary marriage between Ohashi and her friend Nakagawa, a morose young Japanese-American janitor who wants to be a rock 'n' roll star. Ohashi moves into Nakagawa's shabby two-room apartment and he sleeps on a cot while she takes the bed. Because of Ohashi's limited grasp of English and Nakagawa's sullen inarticulateness (he can't speak a word of Japanese either), the two have trouble communicating. This suits Ohashi just fine, for she looks upon the arrangement as a business transaction and has every intention of divorcing Nakagawa after she gets her green card from Immigration (although she does weaken and makes love with him once). Nakagawa, however, becomes less self-absorbed and more communicative because of Ohashi and he enjoys showing off his pretty wife to friends—although both he and Ohashi keep the marriage from their families. After two months of marriage, the couple is interviewed by an Immigration official who separates them and then asks each specific questions about the other ("What kind of toothpaste does your husband use?, What color shirt did he wear yesterday?, What is your wife's favorite kind of food?") in an attempt to establish whether the marriage is legitimate and that they do indeed live together. Because they basically live separate lives while living under the same roof, they fail the test. The Immigration official schedules another visit before passing final judgement. Nakagawa is indignant and feels insulted, but Ohashi, who has become increasingly homesick, sees it as a sign that she should return to Japan before Nakagawa becomes too attached to the arrangement. One day Nakagawa comes home to find a letter from Ohashi biding him farewell and thanking him for his help. Back in Japan, Ohashi looks back on her American experience with great fondness, but she's glad to be home.

A low-budget independent film produced with assistance from the American Film Institute, LIVING ON TOKYO TIME is an interesting, well-intentioned film that suffers from some haphazard scripting and amateur acting. Shot on 16mm and then blown-up to 35mm for theatrical distribution, the film was directed and cowritten by Bay-Area filmmaker Okazaki, whose 1985 documentary, UNFINISHED BUSINESS, was nominated for an Academy Award. LIVING ON TOKYO TIME is reminiscent of Chinese-American independent filmmaker Wayne Wang's DIM SUM, which detailed the conflict between a traditional Chinese mother and her modern American daughter. Whereas Wang's film explored the depths of the family relationship with humor and insight (and several superior actors), LIVING ON TOKYO TIME is unfocused and lackluster. Okazaki and cowriter McCormick's script relies heavily on narration (Oshashi's letters home) to express emotions that the actors seem incapable of conveying. Much of the dialog is clumsy, the humor is flat, and there are several scenes devoted to discussions of rock music that seem gratuitous and arbitrary (the fact that cowriter McCormick plays the leader of Nakagawa's rock band probably accounts for such scenes). The clash between Ohashi and Nakagawa is a result of an uncommunicativeness that has more to do with their mopey personalities than with their cultural differences. While Ohashi's quiet demeanor can be beguiling, Nakagawa's gloomy musician is so dull, inarticulate, and boring that he creates a black hole in the screen that sucks all the life out of the film. The rest of the performances run the range from inferior to the merely competent. Although heartfelt and ambitious, LIVING ON TOKYO TIME rarely attains its noble aspirations. *(Adult situations.)*

p, Lynn O'Donnell, Dennis Hayashi; d, Steven Okazaki; w, John McCormick, Steven Okazaki; ph, Steven Okazaki, Zand Gee (Monaco color); ed, Steven Okazaki.

Drama **Cas.** **(PR:C MPAA:NR)**

LO DEL CESAR† (1987, Mex.) 105m Casablanca-Television Espanola c (Trans: What Is Caesar's)

Humberto Zurita *(Claudio O'Riley)*, Assumpta Serna *(Cecilia)*, Angelica Aragon *(Leonor)*, Manuel Ojeda *(Quijano)*, Jose Carlos Ruiz, Alejandro Aragon, Alfredo Sevilla.

Mexican update of the "Caesar" theme which sees a ruthless fishing magnate oppressing the local fishermen's co-op while behaving decadently by zooming around in his sports car and bedding the local women.

p, Carlos Resendi; d, Felipe Cazals; w, Tomas Perez Turrent; ph, Angel Goded; m, Amparo Rubin; ed, Sigfrido Garcia.

Drama **(PR:NR MPAA:NR)**

LO NEGRO DEL NEGRO† (1987, Mex.) 109m Cinematografica Escamilla-Gonzalez/Peliculas Mexicanas c (Trans: The Black Side of Blackie)

Rodolfo de Anda *(Flaco)*, Ricardo Deloera *(Negro)*, Ivon Govea *(Elvia)*, Rafael Buendia *(El General)*, Eric del Castillo *(Zenon)*, Juan Pelaez, Arturo Martinez, Jr., Bruno Rey, Fabian, Rubi Re, Cesar Sobrevals, Sergio Bustamante, Norma Lee, Roberto Canedo, Don Arturo Martinez, Consuelo Veronica, Ramon Blanco, Marta Elena Cervantes, Jorge Fegan.

Film adaptation of a sensationalistic book detailing corruption under Mexico City Police Chief Arturo "Negro" (Blackie) Durazo Moreno from 1976-82. Written by Moreno's bodyguard Jose Gonzalez Gonzalez, the film chronicles Moreno's various crimes (he was still on trial when the film was released in Mexico) and portrays Gonzalez as the only hard-working innocent in Moreno's administration.

d, Angel Rodriguez Vazquez, Benjamin Escamilla Espinosa; w, Angel Rodriguez (based on the book by Jose Gonzalez Gonzalez); ph, Fernando Alvarez Colin; m, Carlos Torres Marin; ed, Francisco Chiu.

Drama **(PR:NR MPAA:NR)**

LO SAM ZAYIN† (1987, Israel) 102m Roll/Gelfand c (Trans: Don't Give a Damn)

Ikka Zohar *(Rafi)*, Anath Waxman *(Nira)*, Liora Grossman *(Maya)*, Shmuel Vilojni *(Eli)*, Shlomo Tarshish *(Amnon)*, Dudu Ben Ze'ev, Idith Tzur, Shmuel Shilo, Motz Matalon, Dr. Avraham Ori.

Adapted from a best-selling Israeli novel, this film stars Zohar as a teenager who submits to the draft, is wounded in battle, and comes home paralyzed from the waist down. His struggle to adjust physically, psychologically, socially, and sexually comprises the majority of the action. A big hit at the Israeli box office.

p, Yair Pradelsky, Israel Ringel; d, Shmuel Imberman; w, Hanan Peled (based on a novel by Dan Ben Amotz); ph, Nissim [Nitcho] Leon; m, Benny Nagari; ed, Atara Horenstein.

Drama **(PR:NR MPAA:NR)**

LODGERS† (1987, Iran) 130m Farabi c

Ezatolah Entezami, Hamideh Kheir-Abadi, Hossein Sarshar, Akbar Abdi,

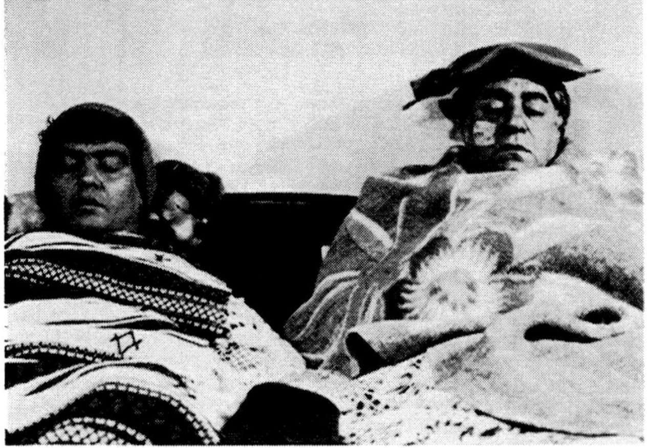

Ferdos Kaviani, Akbar Hassan-Rad, Hassan Tahmoors.

After the landlord flees the country, the greedy garden-apartment tenant tries to illegally take possession of the crumbling four-story building and kick the other tenants out.

d&w, Darioush Mehrjui; ph, Hassan Gholizadeh; m, Nasser Cheshm-Azar; ed, Hassan Hassan-Doost; makeup, Mehran Rohani-Moghadam.

Drama **(PR:NR MPAA:NR)**

L'OEIL AU BEURRE NOIR† (1987, Fr.) 92m Films Ariane-Lira/AAA c (Trans: A Black Eye)

Julie Jezequel *(Virginie)*, Smain *(Rachid)*, Pascal Legitimus *(Denis)*, Martin Lamotte *(Mr. Perroni)*, Dominique Lavanant *(Mrs. Perroni)*, Patrick Braoude *(Georges)*, Jean-Paul Lilienfeld *(Junior)*, Mahmoud Zemmouri *(Rachid's Father)*, Michel Berto *(Mr. Picard)*.

Popular Parisian nightclub comedians Smaim and Legitimus star in this gentle comedic attack on racism. Smaim is an Arab rogue who spends much of his time loitering with his buddies Braoude and Lilienfeld (who also happen to be the screenwriters) trying to pick up white girls. Legitimus is a black West Indian artist down on his luck. The men meet when both become interested in the same girl, Jezequel. She informs them that her parents are looking to rent out a swanky apartment and the two spend much energy trying to persuade the somewhat racist landlords that they would make perfect tenants.

p, Jean Nachbaur, Raymond Danon; d, Serge Meynard; w, Patrick Braoude, Jean-Paul Lilienfeld; ph, Jean-Jacques Tarbes; m, Francois Bernheim; ed, Georges Klotz; art d, Catherine Lavergne.

Comedy

LOHA† (1987, India)

Dharmendra, Shatrughan Sinha, Karan Kapoor, Madhavi, Mandakini, Kader Khan, Amrish Puri.

An infamous outlaw who is holding several hostages does battle with the three courageous heroes who have come to the rescue. (In Hindi.)

p, Salim; d, Raj Sippy; m, Laxmikant Pyarelal.

Action **(PR:NR MPAA:NR)**

LONELY PASSION OF JUDITH HEARNE, THE† (1987, Brit.) 110m Handmade/Island c

Maggie Smith *(Judith Hearne)*, Bob Hoskins *(James Madden)*, Wendy Hiller *(Aunt D'Arcy)*, Marie Kean *(Mrs. Rice)*, Ian McNiece *(Bernard)*, Alan Devlin *(Father Quigley)*, Rudi Davies *(Mary)*, Prunella Scales *(Moira O'Neill)*, Aine Ni Mhuri *(Edie Marinan)*, Sheila Reid *(Miss Friel)*.

Adaptation of the highly-praised novel by Brian Moore which is set in 1950s Ireland and stars Smith as a middle-aged spinster living in a dreary Dublin boarding house owned by the elderly Kean and her obese son McNeice. Smith, a meek piano-teacher who enters a room by saying, "It's only me," becomes intrigued with Hopkins, a new guest in the boarding house. The brother of Kean, Hopkins has just returned to Ireland after spending 30 years in America as a hotel entrepreneur. An ambitious man looking for investors in a new hotel scheme, Hopkins is receptive to Smith's attentions because he assumes she has money. Smith, unfortunately, assumes that Hopkins' interest in her is romantic and she falls in love with the burly American-sounding man. When Hopkins realizes the extent of Smith's delusions and learns that she has little money, he shatters her dreams by telling her the truth. This sends the lonely Smith into a tailspin of alcoholism and the devout woman experiences a crisis of faith. Her drinking lands her in a hospital and she slowly recovers, ready to begin life anew with a fresh perspective. Screened in New York and Los Angeles late in 1987 to qualify for Academy Award nominations, THE LONELY PASSION OF JUDITH HEARNE will receive a wide release in 1988.

p, Peter Nelson, Richard Johnson; d, Jack Clayton; w, Peter Nelson (based on the novel by Brian Moore); ph, Peter Hannan; m, Georges Delerue; ed, Terry Rawlings; prod d, Michael Pickwoad; art d, Henry Harris; set d, Josie MacAvin; cos, Elizabeth Waller.

Drama **(PR:NR MPAA:R)**

LONG STRIDER† (1987, Span.) 109m Berango c (PASOS LARGOS: EL ULTIMO BANDIDO ANDALUZ)

Tony Isbert *(Juan Mingolia Gallardo/"Pasos Largos")*, Marina Saura *(Maria)*, Eusebio Lazaro *(Lieutenant)*, Felipe Velez *(Juan)*, Covadonqa Guijar *(Juan's Wife)*, Raul Fraire *(Father)*, Francisco Guijar *(Don Esteban)*.

Fanciful film biography of the last Andalusian bandit, Juan Mingolla Gallardo (Isbert), whose activities were not brought to an end until shortly before the Spanish Civil War. At first a poacher, Isbert becomes a bandit to wreak havoc on brutal local militias and mask his own sexual impotence. Operating out of the mountains, Isbert sets about myth-making and turns himself into a folk hero. This film by director Alba has been compared to the best of Sam Peckinpah's work. Shown at the Berlin Film Festival. (In Spanish; English subtitles.)

d&w, Rafael Moreno Alba; ph, Jose Garcia Galisteo; m, Emilio de Diego; ed, Pedro del Rey; prod d, Javier Artinano, Eduardo Hidalgo.

Biography **(PR:NR MPAA:NR)**

LOOKING FOR EILEEN**½** (1987, Neth.) 98m Eerste Amsterdamse c (ZOEKEN NAAR EILEEN)

Thom Hoffman *(Philip)*, Lysette Anthony *(Marjan/Eileen/Karnen)*, Kenneth Herdigein, Hans Kemna, John van Dreelen.

A highly-polished romantic thriller—with shades of VERTIGO—set in Amsterdam and starring Hoffman and Anthony as a happily married and financially successful couple. When Anthony is killed in an automobile accident while on her way to London, Hoffman is plunged into a deep state of depression. After a year his love for his wife is reborn when he meets a woman named "Eileen," who looks exactly like his dead wife. With the help of Eileen's husband, Hoffman tries to track down this ghostly image from his past. She, however, has taken refuge with her lover and is fleeing her husband. Hoffman's pursuit drags him into the seedy Amsterdam underground, but he is unable to find Eileen. Two years pass and he meets her again, this time she calls herself "Karen" and works as a nanny in a mansion which is being restored by his architectural firm. She clues him in on her mysterious life. Determined to recapture his past, Hoffman is once again separated from his beloved, only to be reunited with her at the slow-motion finale.

A peculiar, somewhat illogical tale of love which begins on a stunning note but gradually sinks into confusion. The direction is dynamic, the cinematography gorgeous, the soundtrack pulsating, and the emotions powerful. The film's fault, however, is its tendency to sink to the ridiculous. Had the script and characterization been better developed, LOOKING FOR EILEEN could have been a superb tale of romantic obsession. Instead it is a half-intriguing, half-empty-headed film that stretches belief to the breaking point. LOOKING FOR EILEEN is similar to van den Berg's previous film BASTILLE. Both are based on novels by Leon de Winter and concern life's ambiguities, obsession and memory, and physical resemblances. *(Sexual situations, adult situations.)*

p, Leon de Winter, Eddy Wijngaarde; d, Rudolph van den Berg; w, Rudolph van den Berg, Leon de Winter (based on the novel by Leon de Winter); ph, Theo van de Sande; m, Boudewijn Tarenskeen, Pim Kops; ed, Win Louwrier.

Romance/Thriller (PR:O MPAA:NR)

LOS DUENOS DEL SILENCIO† (1987, Arg./Swed.) 95m GC-Crescendo/Sono c (Trans: The Owners of Silence)

Bibi Andersson *(Swedish Ambassador)*, Thomas Helberg *(Swedish Journalist)*, Peder Falk *(Argentine Captain)*, Oscar Martinez *(Argentine Lieutenant)*, Arturo Bonin *(Kidnapee's Father)*, Per Myrberg, Grynet Molveig, Sara Kay, Soledad Silveyra, Maria Valenzuela, Selva Aleman, Victor Laplace, Gabriel Rovito, Julio de Grazia, Maria Vaner.

Argentine director Lemos, who has lived and worked in Sweden since the late 1960s, returned to Buenos Aires to make a slightly fictionalized movie about the true-life kidnaping and presumed murder of Dagmar Hagelin. The girl, of dual Swedish-Argentine nationality, was snatched by the Argentine military during the "dirty war" that the army waged against suspected liberals in the 1970s.

p, Guillermo Calligari, Goran Lindstrom; d&w, Carlos Lemos; ph, Juan Carlos Lenardi; m, Luis de Matteo; ed, Luis Mutti; set d, Miguel Angel Lumaldo; cos, Angelica Fuentes.

Historical/Thriller (PR:NR MPAA:NR)

LOS INVITADOS† (1987, Span.) Impala/Warner Espanola c (Trans: The Invited)

Amparo Munoz *(La Catalana)*, Pablo Carbonell *(Tony Mackenzie)*, Raul Fraire *(El Capataz)*, Pedro Reyes *(El Canijo)*, Sonia Martinez *(Beatriz)*, Idilio Cardoso *(Pedro)*, Antonio Somoza *(Ferreira)*, Maria Luisa Borruel *(Maria)*, Lola Flores *(La Capataza)*.

[No plot information available.]

p,d&w, Victor Barrera (based on the novel by Alfonso Grosso); ph, Jose G. Galisteo; m, Raul Alcover; ed, Maria Luisa Soriano; cos, Gumersindo Andres; makeup, Cristobal Criado.

Action (PR:NR MPAA:NR)

LOST BOYS, THE**½** (1987) 97m WB c

Jason Patric *(Michael)*, Corey Haim *(Sam)*, Dianne Wiest *(Lucy)*, Barnard Hughes *(Grandpa)*, Ed [Edward] Herrmann *(Max)*, Kiefer Sutherland *(David)*, Jami Gertz *(Star)*, Corey Feldman *(Edgar Frog)*, Jamison Newlander *(Alan Frog)*, Brooke McCarter *(Paul)*, Billy Wirth *(Dwayne)*, Alexander Winter *(Marko)*, Chance Michael Corbitt *(Laddie)*.

Part horror, part comedy, THE LOST BOYS is a vampire thriller that brings some interesting twists to the genre, but is nearly defeated by director Schumacher's heavy-handed efforts to bring a hip, glitzy, MTV-like sensibility to the traditionally gothic material. The recently divorced Wiest packs up her belongings and, along with teenaged sons Patric and Haim, moves in with her eccentric father, Hughes, who lives in the Northern California town of Santa Cruz. Rumored to be the "Murder Capital of the World," the town is dominated by an old amusement park which serves as a beacon for the bored teenagers who gravitate toward it like moths to flame. Patric, the older of Wiest's boys, spies the beautiful Gertz and follows her throughout the park. Just as he is about to make his move, the girl mounts the motorcycle of her boy friend, Sutherland, the leader of a creepy gang of bikers. Sensing Patric's interest in Gertz, Sutherland invites him to join them on their nightly roaming. Eager to fit in, Patric agrees and is subjected to a dangerous initiation rite (a motorcycle race reminiscent of the fatal drag race in REBEL WITHOUT A CAUSE) before being allowed to enter the gang's hangout—an abandoned old hotel that fell into the fault during the 1906 earthquake. At the hangout, Sutherland dares Patric to drink from a bottle of "wine." Succumbing to peer pressure and his desire for Gertz, Patric drinks from the bottle, only later discovering that it contained human blood. He is now on his way to becoming a vampire—just like Sutherland and his gang. Meanwhile, the bored Haim (Wiest has taken a job at the local video store and has begun dating its somewhat nerdy owner, Herrmann) befriends Feldman and Newlander, two goofy brothers who run a comic-book store and fancy themselves experts on vampires (Feldman affects a deep Rambo-style voice in an attempt to sound menacing). They give the new kid a pair of vampire comic books and tell him to study them carefully—"They could save your life." His head filled with tales of vampires, Haim notices that his brother is showing all the symptoms: out all night, sleeping all day, wearing dark glasses, his reflection barely visible in the mirror. Although Patric tries his best to stay away from his brother, Haim is terrified and tells him, "You wait till Mom finds out!" Soon Sutherland and his gang take Patric out for his final initiation—a kill which will make him a full-fledged vampire. Urging Patric on with promises of "You'll never get old," Sutherland and his vampire buddies suddenly sprout fangs and nasty visages and descend on some unsuspecting teenagers, slaughtering them for blood. Patric cannot bring himself to do it, and with the help of the youthful vampire killers, Feldman and Newlander, he decides to defeat Sutherland and free himself, Gertz, and child-vampire Corbitt from the curse. After a slam-bang action/gore-effects finale that sees Sutherland impaled on a pair of antlers and Herrmann revealed as the king of the vampires (in an unsatisfying twist), good triumphs over evil and everyone returns to normal.

THE LOST BOYS adds some intriguing dimension to the traditional vampire legend by exploring the material through teenagers. Instead of the tragic Bela Lugosi-type vampire who is hopelessly cursed by his undead state, screenwriters Fischer, Jeremias, and Boam present vampires who seem to *want to be* hellish creatures. The script utilizes the age-old teenage themes of alienation, anger, and rebellion, the "I won't grow up" appeal of Peter Pan (hence the title), and the fervent desire to be "cool," and takes them to a fantastic extreme by creating the ultimate teenage clique. The vampires recruit new members by employing the traditional vampiric sexual seduction (by Gertz) combined with a heavy dose of peer pressure (this section of the film almost plays like a "Say No to Drugs" public service announcement). Also brought into play are themes commonly found in "divorce" dramas where children have trouble accepting the new romantic rovings of their mothers. In the film, Wiest invites new beau Herrmann over for dinner so he can meet Haim. Haim, Feldman, and Newlander are convinced that Herrmann is a vampire and try to prove it during dinner by making him eat garlic, splashing him with holy water, and getting him in front of a mirror. When all hell breaks loose at the table, Wiest believes it is because Haim cannot accept a new man in her life and is letting his aggression out on Herrmann (none of these tricks work on vampire Herrmann because he was *invited* into the house—thus making humans powerless against him). In addition, Wiest mistakes her older son's vampirism for dangerous youthful carousing and drug abuse. While most of this is played for laughs by director Schumacher, the underlying seriousness of these themes adds weight to a film otherwise concerned with a superficial excess of "style." The problem with THE LOST BOYS lies in the frustrating disposal of most of the thematics in favor of glitzy visuals and a slam-bang climax highly derivative of both FRIGHT NIGHT and the made-for-TV SALEM'S LOT. Schumacher's pacing is horrible (the film only runs 97 minutes but seems much longer) and he revels in the kind of stylistic excess commonly found in rock videos—including a nonstop rock 'n' roll soundtrack. Chapman's cinematography is superb (he shot RAGING BULL), but again the entire film panders to an audience used to getting cinematic virtuosity from MTV and any subtlety is buried under an avalanche of hip production design. The performances, however, are uniformly excellent, with Sutherland taking top honors as a truly creepy and dynamic vampire (speaking volumes with just a sly smile), and Haim quite convincing as the worried little brother (fans of 1986's LUCAS might not even recognize him—he's grown up). Despite its flaws, THE LOST BOYS is an interesting addition to vampire cinema. *(Violence, gore effects, one sexual situation, profanity.)*

p, Harvey Bernhard; d, Joel Schumacher; w, Janice Fischer, James Jeremias, Jeffrey Boam (based on a story by Janice Fischer, James Jeremias); ph, Michael Chapman (Panavision, Technicolor); m, Thomas Newman; ed, Robert Brown; prod d, Bo Welch; art d, Tom Duffield; set d, John Warnke; cos, Susan Becker; spec eff, Greg Cannom.

Horror (PR:O MPAA:R)

LOVECHILD, THE† (1987, Brit.) 102m Frontroom Film-British Film Institute-Channel 4-VPRO/British Film Institute c

Sheila Hancock *(Edith)*, Peter Capaldi *(Dillon)*, Percy Herbert *(Maurice)*, Lesley Sharp *(Bernadette)*, Alexei Sayle *(The Voices)*, Arthur Hewlett *(Stan)*, Cleo Sylvestre *(Celia)*, Stephen Lind *(Colin)*, Ajay Kumar *(Majid)*, Andrew Seear *(Tony)*, Kevin Allen *(Cliff)*, Robert Blythe *(Elvis)*, Cathy Murphy *(Linda)*, Stephen Frost *(Tough Policeman)*, Steven O'Donnell *(Young Policeman)*, Eric Kent *(Sergeant)*, Jon Raymond *(Litter Lout)*, Leon Berton *(Seventh Day Adventist)*, Christopher McHallem *(Barman)*, Lee Cornes *(Man in Supermarket)*, Evie Garratt *(Anxious Woman)*, Valerie Buchanan *(Supervisor)*, Kerryann White *(Cashier)*, Ray Kingsley *(Housing Officer)*, Marsha Millar *(Beverley)*, Nicola Lawrence *(Melanie)*, Geoff Ward *(Gerbil Punk)*, Andy Sutton *(Tall Punk)*, Gaylie Runciman *(Agent's Secretary)*, Christopher Whittingham *(Waiter in Restaurant)*, Irene Marot, Jack Fortune *(Young Couple)*, Isaac Grand *(Taxi Driver)*.

Capaldi (best known to American audiences for his part in LOCAL HERO) plays an orphaned young man who lives in the Brixton section of London with his unmarried grandmother Hancock. His parents, who were killed in an automobile acccident shortly after Capaldi was born, were unmarried as well. His father had been a popular rock 'n' roll singer, and Capaldi takes pride when he learns people still remember his music. Capaldi is inexperienced when it comes to women, but this soon changes when he meets Sharp (RITA, SUE AND BOB TOO), an unconventional artist who lives in an abandoned building. In the meantime, Hancock is surprised when Herbert arrives unexpectedly from Australia. Herbert had been Hancock's lover some 40 years previously, and left her after she became pregnant. Capaldi loses his job, but with help from the women in his life, he grows more assured of his place in the world.

p, Angela Topping; d, Robert Smith; w, Gordon Hann; ph, Thaddeus O'Sullivan; m, Colin Gibson, Kenny Craddock, Erik Satie; ed, John Davies; prod d, Caroline Hanania; cos, Katharine Naylor.

Comedy **(PR:NR MPAA:NR)**

LOVE IS A DOG FROM HELL† (1987, Belg.) 90m Multimedia c

Josse De Pauw *(Harry Voss)*, Geert Hunaerts *(Harry Voss, age 12)*, Michael Pas *(Stan)*, Gene Bervoerts *(Jeff)*, Amid Chakir *(Bill)*, Florence Beliard *(The Corpse)*, Karen Vanparys *(Harry's Mother)*, Carmela Locantore, An Van Essche, Doriane Moretus.

Unveiled at the Berlin Film Festival, this Belgian feature is the second film of 1987 to be based on the writings of Charles Bukowski. Where BARFLY was filmed from an original script of Bukowski's, LOVE IS A DOG FROM HELL (originally titled CRAZY LOVE) adapts some of his most base ideas about physical and romantic love, lust, and passion. The film is divided into three segments of the main character's life—early childhood at age 12; adolescence at age 19; and maturity at age 29. In the first story, the young Harry Voss (played by De Pauw) has filled his head with romantic notions of love, believing in the purest forms of romance—the type that exists between fairy tale prince and princess, or between lovers on the movie screen. He idealistically believes that his father eloped with his mother during a night of passion. He later finds out his mother was kidnaped and forced to marry his father. An older friend of De Pauw's then introduces him to the more realistic notion of physical love, revealing the secrets of voyeurism and masturbation. By age 19, Harry Voss (now played by Hunaerts) is attending his high school prom. He is a victim of the worst possible case of acne, covered with blistering boils. He wants desperately to dance with the most beautiful girl, who consents only after he wraps his hideous face in toilet paper. Contemplating the concept of beauty and ugliness, Hunaerts still believes in pure, romantic passion and turns to alcohol for comfort. By age 29, Hunaerts is a street bum who meets with an old friend and fellow bum, Chakir. After a bout with the bottle, they steal the corpse of a beautiful young woman (played by Beliard, the actress who embodied romantic love in the first segment). They engage in necrophilia and both agree the corpse was the greatest love they ever had. Although LOVE IS A DOG FROM HELL can be misunderstood as perverse and lustful, it is, like all of Bukowski's writings (and BARFLY), concerned with beauty, passion, desperation, dark secrets, frightening truths, and the aesthetic of love. Released in the US in California, Bukowski's home territory. (In Flemish; English subtitles.)

p, Erwin Provoost, Alain Keytsman; d, Dominique Deruddere; w, Marc Didden, Dominique Deruddere (based on "The Copulating Mermaids Of Venice, California" and other stories by Charles Bukowski); ph, Willy Stassen (Eastmancolor); m, Raymond Van Het Groenewoud; ed, Ludo Troch, Guido Henderickx; art d, Hubert Pouille, Erik Van Belleghem.

Drama **(PR:NR MPAA:NR)**

LOVE LETTER† (1987, Jap.) 85m Gentosha/Nikkatsu c

Keiko Sekine *(Yuko Kano)*, Katsuo Nakamura *(Toshiharu Oda)*, Mariko Kaga *(Toyo)*, Noboru Nakaya *(Murai)*.

Keiko Sekine stars as a schoolgirl who is seduced by a married poet, Katsuo Nakamura, who sets her up as his mistress and provides her with her own apartment with all the amenities. The apartment becomes her prison, however, for she is expected to sit and wait until he can find the time to visit her. The poet forbids her to have friends, though he indulges in a brief affair with her next-door neighbor. When she becomes pregnant, she looks forward to having the baby, but the poet forces her into an abortion. On the verge of suicide, Keiko is finally freed from her prison when the poet dies.

p, Katsuhiro Maeda; d, Yoichi Higashi; w, Yozoo Tanaka (based on the book by Mitsuharu Kanekoi); ph, Koichi Kawakami (CinemaScope); m, Michi Tanaka; ed, Keiko Ichihara; prod d, Toshiro Ayabe.

Drama **(PR:NR MPAA:NR)**

LUCKY RAVI† (1987, Fr.) 84m Out-One/Films du Volca c

Michel Didym *(Lucky Ravi)*, Assumpta Serna *(Miss Cote d'Azur)*, Rudiger Vogler *(Gino)*, Jean-Pierre Bisson *(Hotel Manager)*, Alain Cuny *(Plantation Owner)*.

A nasty plantation owner pays some drifters to set fire to a new hotel which he feels has destroyed the region's rustic flavor. The hotel is run by mobsters and one of their number, Didym, is a handsome lunkhead who falls into an affair with the beautiful-but-alcoholic lodger Serna. She has taken up with Didym on the rebound from another affair, and during the disasterous arson fire Didym accidentally shoots Serna's former lover. Serna rewards Didym by abruptly breaking off their relationship. This is the feature film debut of director Lombard.

d, Vincent Lombard; w, Vincent Lombard, Richard Matas; ph, Pascal Lebegue; m, Laurent Grangier; ed, Jean-Francois Naudon.

Drama **(PR:NR MPAA:NR)**

LUMIKUNINGATAR (SEE: SNOW QUEEN, 1987, Fin.)

LUNGA VITA ALLA SIGNORA!† (1987, It.) 115m RAI 1-Cinemaundici-Instituto Luce/Sacis Intl. c (Trans: Long Live the Lady!)

Marco Esposito *(Libenzio)*, Simona Brandalise *(Corinna)*, Simone Dalla Rosa *(Mao)*, Stefania Busarello *(Anna)*, Lorenzo Paolini *(Ciccio)*, Tarcisio Tosi *(Pigi)*, Marisa Abbate *(The Signorina)*.

Six teenagers enrolled in a hotel services school are sent to help serve an elaborate dinner party at an ancient castle which has been converted into a luxury hotel. Thrown by an elderly yet powerful society matron, the guests include Italy's most famous and influential personalities. During the course of the evening the star-struck and naive teens have their first sobering glimpse at the lives of the rich and famous. Director Olmi's first film after a four-year hiatus due to illness.

d&w, Ermanno Olmi; ph, Ermanno Olmi, Maurizio Zaccaro (Eastman Kodak); m, Georg Philip Teleman; ed, Ermanno Olmi, Giulia Ciniselli; cos, Francesca Sartori.

Drama **(PR:NR MPAA:NR)**

LUTRA† (1987, Hung.) 84m c

Zsolt Zagoni *(Miklos, Young Hunter)*, Csilla Herczeg *(Eszter, Miller's Daughter)*, Matyas Usztics *(Jancsi)*, Anna Nagy *(Eszter's Mother)*, Imre Suranyi *(Eszter's Father)*.

A clever otter known as Lutra becomes the bane of young hunter Zagoni's existence, for he is unable to kill the animal. Mocked by his friends and family for his failure, Zagoni is relieved to discover the otter has been driven out of his nest and must wander the countryside during the harsh winter trying to survive. Eventually Lutra makes his way to the sea where he can begin a new life far away from humans.

d, Mihaly Hars; w, Mihaly Hars, Domokos Varga (based on a novel by Istvan Fekete); ph, Janos Borbely; m, Gabor Oroszlan, Gyorgy Oroszlan; ed, Mihaly Hars.

Children's/Adventure **(PR:NR MPAA:NR)**

LYUBOVYU ZA LYUBOV† (1987, USSR) 84m Mosfilm/Sovexportfilm c (Trans: Lover for Love)

Larissa Udovichenko, Leonid Yarmolnik, Sergey Martynov, Aristarkh Livanov.

Film adaptation of the popular Bolshoy Theater opera "Lover for Love" which was based on Shakespeare's farce "Much Ado About Nothing."

d, Tatyana Berezantseva; w, Tatyana Berezantseva, Elena Lobachevskaya (based on the opera by Tikon Khrennikov); ph, Igor Gelein, Vladimir Stepanov; m, Tikhon Khrennikov; art d, Evgeny Chernyayev, Vladimir Fabrikov.

Musical Drama **(PR:NR MPAA:NR)**

MACBETH† (1987, Fr.) 135m Dedalus c

Leo Nucci *(Macbeth)*, Shirley Verrett *(Lady Macbeth)*, Johan Leysen *(Banquo)*, Philippe Volter *(Macduff)*, Voices: Samuel Ramey *(Banquo)*, Veriano Lucchetti *(Macduff)*.

Director d'Anna chose an actual castle in Belgium as the location for his filming of Verdi's operatic version of the Shakespeare tragedy.

d, Claude d'Anna; w, Francesco Maria Piave (based on the play by William Shakespeare); ph, Pierre Dupouey; m, Giuseppe Verdi; ed, Reine Wekstein; prod d, Eric Simon.

Opera **(PR:NR MPAA:NR)**

MAD KILLER† (1987, Phil.) Roadshow c

Anthony Alonzo *(Sgt. Ernest Valentin, Jr., "Junior")*.

More revenge, Filipino-style, as Vietnam vet Alonzo goes after the scum who raped his sister. He kills the villain, which angers the villain's brothers, who kill Alonzo's mother and sister. Now Alonzo is really upset. He kills the murderous brothers, then gives himself up to the police.

[No production credits available.]

Crime **(PR:NR MPAA:NR)**

MADE IN ARGENTINA† (1987, Arg.) 86m Progress Communications c

Luis Brandoni *(Osvaldo)*, Marta Bianchi *(Mabel)*, Leonor Manso *(Yoli)*, Patricio Contreras *(Negro)*, Alberto Busaid, Hugo Arana, Mario Luciani, Gabriela Flores, Alejo Garcia Pintos, Debbie Better, Frank Vincent.

Brandoni and Bianchi, who have lived in New York for ten years after leaving their native Argentina ten years earlier for political reasons, decide to return to their homeland for a visit. Bianchi is still bitter because many of their friends had disassociated themselves from the couple when they ran into political trouble, but Brandoni prefers to put those memories behind him. Shown in 1987 at film festivals in Montreal and Moscow.

d, Juan Jose Jusid; w, Nelly Fernandez Tiscornia (based on her play "Made In Lanus" from her TV play "Pals"); ph, Hugo Colace; m, Emilio Kauderer; ed, Juan Carlos Macia; art d, Luis Pedreira; cos, Pepe Uria.

Drama **(PR:NR MPAA:NR)**

MADE IN HEAVEN*** (1987) 102m Lorimar c

Timothy Hutton *(Mike Shea/Elmo Barnett)*, Kelly McGillis *(Annie Packert/Ally Chandler)*, Maureen Stapleton *(Mike's Aunt Lisa)*, Ann Wedgeworth *(Annette Shea, Mike's Mother)*, Himself [Debra Winger-Uncredited] *(Emmett Humbird)*, James Gammon *(Steve Shea, Mike's Father)*, Mare Winningham *(Brenda Carlucci)*, Don Murray *(Ben Chandler)*, Marj Dusay *(Mrs. Packert)*, Ray Gideon *(Mr. Packert)*, Zack Finch *(Billy Packert)*, Timothy Daly *(Tom Donnelly)*, Amanda Plummer *(Wiley Foxx)*, Ellen Barkin *(Lucille)*, Neil Young *(Truck Driver)*, Tom Petty *(Stanky, Mechanic)*, Ric Ocasek *(Shark)*, Tom Robbins *(Mario the Toymaker)*, John Considine *(Angel with Tophat)*, Gary Larson, James Tolkan, Vyto Ruginis, Gailard Sartain, Leon Martell, Matraca Berg, Rob Kneeper, Robert Gould, Debra Dusay, Willard Pugh, David Rasche.

Coming off the cult success of and generally favorable critical response to his past two low-budget films, CHOOSE ME and TROUBLE IN MIND, director Alan Rudolph here delivers a studio-backed picture from a script by the STAND BY ME writing team of Gideon and Evans. While CHOOSE ME and TROUBLE IN MIND (both of which Rudolph scripted) combined Rudolph's romantic themes with an ultrastylish, hyperrealistic urban backdrop, MADE IN HEAVEN is a wholly romantic fantasy with almost no contact with realism. Essentially, MADE IN HEAVEN is a genre picture on the order of HERE COMES MR. JORDAN, HEAVEN CAN WAIT (both the Alexander Hall and the Warren Beatty-Buck Henry versions), or ANGEL ON MY SHOULDER in which characters move freely from Heaven to Earth, falling into a seemingly impossible love with another soul. Because of the number of relationships that were torn apart during WW II, this genre became a popular one, providing the audience of the day with the hope that they would someday be reunited with their loved ones. Today, however, there isn't much of an audience for such a film, especially one which is as nontraditional as this one. A deeply poetic fantasy masquerading as a Hollywood film, MADE IN HEAVEN stars Hutton and McGillis as two souls who fall in love in Heaven, are separated, and eventually reunite on Earth. The film begins in black and white with a shot from Alfred Hitchcock's most romantic picture, NOTORIOUS. We are in a small-town theater in the 1940s and Hutton is in the audience with his parents, Gammon and Wedgeworth. Unable to find a job, Hutton packs his bags and heads for California. About 100 miles outside of town he arrives at the scene of an auto accident—a car has just plunged off a bridge and is sinking into the river below. Hutton jumps in and saves two children and their mother, only to then drown himself. The scene shifts to Heaven (in color) as Hutton is standing naked and alone in a sterile waiting room. He is greeted by a dead aunt, Stapleton, who breaks the news to him that he, too, is dead. It takes a while but Hutton gets used to the ways of Heaven—everything that exists on Earth also exists up above; souls move from place to place simply by imagining

their destination; souls meet one another by concentrating on the other person; and everyone has the ability to communicate through thoughts. Before long Hutton meets McGillis, a very pretty virginal soul who, like many others, was born in Heaven. Not only has she never been to Earth, but she has never been in love. Hutton and McGillis fall for each other, find themselves a quiet country home, and prepare for a heavenly future together. The only catch is that McGillis' time is up and she must leave Heaven to be born on Earth. Having just been separated from his family and friends, Hutton refuses to lose McGillis. After McGillis "dies," Hutton hunts down the administrative head of Heaven—an androgynous being named Emmett (played by an unbilled and unrecognizable Debra Winger)—and strikes a deal. Hutton is allowed to return to Earth and has until his 30th birthday to find McGillis. Back on Earth in the 1950s, McGillis is born to a recently widowed military man-turned-toy manufacturer, and Hutton is born to a hillbillyish woman who doesn't even know the identity of the boy's father. It seems unlikely that the pair will ever connect. McGillis goes to college and meets a New Wave-inspired film student, while Hutton leaves home and becomes a wanderer. McGillis marries and eventually heads her father's toy company, while Hutton still wanders. After hitchhiking a ride from Gammon and Wedgeworth (Hutton has no recollection of his previous life), Hutton discovers that he has musical talent. Having found a direction, he pursues his career. Meanwhile, McGillis has divorced and becomes involved with another man. On Hutton's 30th birthday, both he and McGillis stroll down a crowded city street and are inexplicably drawn to each other. Having met just under the wire of their 30-year deadline, Hutton and McGillis fall magically in love. Aside from Rudolph's stylistic invention and the illusory Gideon-Evans screenplay, the most interesting thing about MADE IN HEAVEN is that it was made in Hollywood. Looking more like an Americanized homage to the spirit of Jean Cocteau or the French New Wave, MADE IN HEAVEN is both technically playful and poetically romantic. A visionary working in a land of business deals and power lunches, Rudolph has accepted certain limitations and still managed to come up with a wholly personal film. Like the great Hollywood studio directors, Rudolph has taken someone else's script and a studio's backing and made it his own. Originally given a budget of $18-20 million, Rudolph talked the studio into reducing the special effects and cutting the budget in half ("I don't do movies like that, I don't believe in them," said Rudolph). Instead, he concentrates on the characters and his own imagination. Displaying a surreal visual quality which is even more exaggerated than in his previous two films, Rudolph has a field day with his conception of Heaven. Using the over-saturated colors of a Michael Powell film, Rudolph portrays Heaven as a dreamy version of Earth—mist and clouds roll by, background characters float past, people dissolve in and out of frame, the settings outside one's window change according to whim, and everyone speaks with an echo. In sharp contrast is the high-contrast black-and-white of the film's 1940s opening. By the time we get to the 1960s, the colors have become more earthy, gradually becoming more realistic and modern by the time we get to the present. Structured in a nontraditional manner and broken into tableaux that span 50 years, MADE IN HEAVEN is held together by the wonderful performances of Hutton and McGillis. Hutton does his best work since ORDINARY PEOPLE, McGillis fulfills the promise of WITNESS (jeopardized by TOP GUN), and together they become a pure, heavenly couple looking as if they were destined to be together forever. Both leads are chameleon-like in appearance. Hutton transforms from the simple Jimmy Stewart type in the 1940s to a Neil Young-fashioned Woodstock refugee in the 1960s, while McGillis changes from scene to scene—alternately angelic, sexy, bohemian, and yuppie. Standing out among the supporting cast are Gammon and Wedgeworth as Hutton's parents in the 1940s and as the older couple who give the reincarnated Hutton a lift to California 20 years later. The scene between them in which Wedgeworth remembers their dead son (Hutton) and then confesses that she is terminally ill is one of the most touching ever committed to film. Among the rest of the cast are a number of familiar names: rock stars Tom Petty, Ric Ocasek, and Neil Young, novelist Tom Robbins, coscreenwriter Raynold Gideon, Amanda Plummer, and Maureen Stapleton. One familiar face goes uncredited—Ellen Barkin as evil incarnate; and one unfamiliar face also goes uncredited—Debra Winger as Heaven's chief administrator, Emmett. Hiding behind an extensive makeup job, Winger (Hutton's real-life wife) looks like a cross between a Hollywood tough guy and Sigourney Weaver, and sounds like a raspy-voiced street kid. As inventive as MADE IN HEAVEN is, it occasionally falters and never completely comes together. The scenes with the Barkin temptress slow things down, and the subplot of Hutton rising to fame as a songwriter comes off as uninspired. Most disappointing is the absence of any real philosophical or religious stance. Includes the song "I Am a Child" (Neil Young, performed by Young) and the film's theme "We Never Danced" (Martha Davis, performed by Davis). *(Brief nudity, sexual situations.)*

p, Raynold Gideon, Bruce A. Evans, David Blocker; d, Alan Rudolph; w, Bruce A. Evans, Raynold Gideon; ph, Jan Kiesser; m, Mark Isham; ed, Tom Walls; prod d, Paul Peters; art d, Steve Legler; set d, Paul Peters; cos, April Ferry; m/l, Neil Young; spec eff, Max W. Anderson.

Romance/Fantasy **(PR:A MPAA:PG)**

MADRID† (1987, Span.) 98m Linterna Magica-RTV c

Rudiger Vogler *(Hans)*, Veronica Forque *(Lucia)*, Ricardo Contalapiedra *(Pancho)*, Jose Prat, Ana Duato, Maria Luisa Ponte, Felix Defauce.

A German TV director is sent to Madrid to do a documentary on the Civil War, but spends his time dawdling, philosophizing, and watching old news footage. Much of the picture is familiar documentary footage as Patino travels ground he covered with CAUDILLO and CANCOINES.

p, Luis Gutierrez, Jose Luis Garcia Sanchez; d&w, Basilio Martin Patino; ph, Augusto G. Fernandez Balbuena; m, Carmelo Bernaola; ed, Pablo Martin Pascual; set d, Polo I Bombin.

Drama **(PR:NR MPAA:NR)**

MAGDALENA VIRAGA† (1987) 90m Menkes c

Trinka Menkes *(Ida)*, Claire Aguilar *(Claire)*, Victor Flores, Paul Shuler, Nora Bendich.

An independent feature produced, directed, written, photographed and edited by California State University film instructor Menkes. Shown at the Toronto Festival of Festivals in 1987, the film tells the story of a despondent prostitute whose hopelessly ritualistic life leads her to murder one of her customers. The dialog is largely comprised of the writings of poets Gertrude Stein, Ann Sexton, and Mary Daly.

p,d,ph & ed, Nina Menkes; w, Nina Menkes (based on poetry by Gerturde Stein, Ann Sexton, Mary Daly); m, Grupo Travieso.

Drama **(PR:NR MPAA:NR)**

MAGIA CHYORNAYA I BELAYA† (1987, USSR) 77m Lenfilm/Sovexportfilm c (Trans: Black and White Magic)

Pavel Plisov, Anton Granat, Margarita Ivanova, Alexander Lenkov.

The mutually dependent relationship of a pair of grade-school boys is put out of kilter by the arrival of a new classmate, a pretty little girl from Lithuania. No longer able to help each other with the subjects that each is weak in, they watch their grades plummet and distract themselves with hobbies until they realize the importance of their friendship.

d, Naum Birman; w, Valery Priemykhov; ph, Genrikh Marandjan; m, Alexander Zhurbin; art d, Vsevolod Ulitko.

Children's **(PR:NR MPAA:NR)**

MAGIC STICKS† (1987, Ger./Aust.) 91m Wolfgang Odentahl Filmproduktion-Tale Film c

George Kranz *(Felix)*, Kelly Curtis *(Shirley)*, Joe Silver *(Pawnbroker)*, Chico Hamilton, Ted Lambert, Reginald Vel Johnson, Jack McGee, David Margulies, Mike Hodge.

A young musician (Kranz) sends New Yorkers into paroxysms of wild dancing when he pounds out a magical beat with the mysterious drumsticks that have come into his possession. His rhythmic conjuring gets him into some hot water with some toughs who have their own plans for his magic *wands*, but it also wins him the affection of Curtis. This English-language German-Austrian coproduction was shot on location in New York.

p, Wolfgang Odenthal; d, Peter Keglevic; w, Peter Keglevic, Chris Ragazzo, George Kranz; ph, Edward Klosinski; m, George Kranz; ed, Darren Kloomok; prod d, Stephen McCabe, Sid Bartholomew; cos, Ulrike Schutte.

Fantasy **(PR:NR MPAA:NR)**

MAGIC SNOWMAN, THE† (1987, US/Yugo.) 84m Pavlina Ltd.-Film i Ton/Miramax c (AKA: A WINTER TALE)

Justin Fried *(Jamie)*, Dragana Marjanovic *(Mandy)*, Jack Aronson, Christian James, Kyle Morris, Roger Moore *(Voice of Lumi Ukko, the Snowman)*.

Featuring a magic snowman that sounds like James Bond, this US-Yugoslavian children's film brings "Lumi Ukko"—a Finnish Frosty whose voice is provided by Roger Moore—into the life of Fried, a Yugoslavian lad who has his heart set on winning a big ice-skating race. Fried also wants to help out his father, who earns his living as a fisherman, and, with information provided by the snowman and his friend the Wind, he is able to do so. Problems arise, however, when Fried tries to cut a deal with the unscrupulous captain of a trawler. Moore apparently joined the production when he learned that some of the film's proceeds were earmarked for Unicef.

p, Pavlina Proevska, Jovan Markovic; d, C. Stanner; w, Dennis Maitland, Lyle Morris (based on a story by Dennis Maitland, adapted by Jovan Markovic); ph, Karpo Godina (CFS Color); m, John Berenzy.

Children's **(PR:NR MPAA:NR)**

MAGINO—MURA MONOGATARI† (1987, Jap.) 222m c (Trans: Tales from the Magino Village)

Tatsumi Hijikata, Junko Miyashita, Masao Kikuchi, Cho Kimura, Takahiro Tamura, Choichiro Kawarazaki, Renji Ishibashi, Shogo Shimada, Kichiemon Inoue, Masaki Kimura, Masuo Igarashi, Toshiro Takahashi, Toshio Takemura, Hideaki Yoshida.

This extraordinarily detailed exploration of the relationship between the realities and myths of village life in rural Japan was written and directed by Shinsuke Ogawa, best known as a documentarian with a deep interest in the socio-cultural heritage of his country. In attempting to delineate the myths, he first presents the villagers talking about them, then he gives some educators their say, and finally the myths are dramatized. Reportedly, Ogawa spent more than a dozen years researching the village that is the focus of his film.

p, Hiro Fuseya; d&w, Shinsuke Ogawa; ph, Masaki Tamura; m, Masahiko Togashi; ed, Shinsuke Ogawa, Toshio Iizuka, Yoko Shirashi; set d, Shiro Tatsumi, Sadatoshi Mikado.

Drama **(PR:NR MPAA:NR)**

MAGNAT† (1987, Pol.) Zespoly Filmowe-TOR/Film Polski c (Trans: The Magnate)

Jan Nowicki, Olgierd Lukaszewicz, Jan Englert, Boguslaw Linda, Grazyna Szapolowska, Maria Gladkowska.

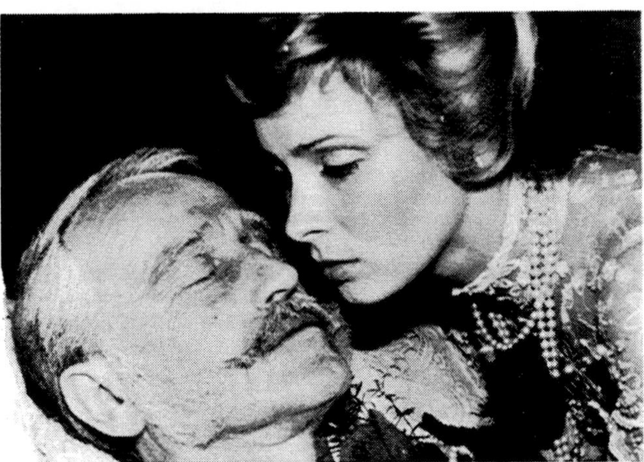

The harrowing saga of an aristocratic Polish family that begins at the turn of the century and ends just after WW II. As a young man, the patriarch prince befriends the German kaiser, then the ruler of Poland, but when Polish nationalism becomes the order of the day, the prince readily adapts to satisfy his countrymen. The advent of National Socialism in Germany rips the family apart when the prince's eldest son funds the local Nazi party. His middle son fights to keep the family fortune out of the hands of the Nazis, but, as a result, the youngest son is imprisoned and forced to become a guinea pig for dangerous experiments that eventually lead to his death. All of this wears away at the aging prince whose greatest concern is for his family and his estate.

d&w, Filip Bajon; ph, Piotr Sobocinski; m, Jerzy Satanowski; ed, Wanda Zeman; set d, Andrzej Kowalczyk.

Drama **(PR:NR MPAA:NR)**

MAGNIFICENT WARRIORS† (1987, Hong Kong) 95m D&B c

Richard Ng, Michelle Khan, Matsui Tetsuya, Yee Tung Shing, Lowell Lo.

Set in the Himalayan nation of Bhutan in the 1930s, this actioner from Hong Kong revolves around the attempts by five brave people to prevent Japanese forces from building a facility to be used to test gas chambers. Michelle Khan, a former beauty pageant winner, plays one of the magnificent warriors. (In Cantonese; English subtitles; also dubbed-in-English version.)

p, John Sham, Linda Kuk; d, David Chung; w, Tsang Kan Cheong; ph, Ma Chun Wah, Lam Wan Shing; m, Chan Wing Leong; ed, Chiang Kowk Kuon; art d, Oliver Wong.

Action/Drama **(PR:NR MPAA:NR)**

MAID TO ORDER½** (1987) 96m Vista/New Century-Vista c

Ally Sheedy *(Jessie Montgomery)*, Beverly D'Angelo *(Stella)*, Michael Ontkean *(Nick McGuire)*, Valerie Perrine *(Georgette Starkey)*, Dick Shawn *(Stan Starkey)*, Tom Skerritt *(Charles Montgomery)*, Merry Clayton *(Audrey James)*, Begona Plaza *(Maria)*, Rainbow Phoenix *(Brie Starkey)*, Leland Crooke *(Dude)*.

A modern fairy tale with some funny twists, MAID TO ORDER has Sheedy as a spoiled rich girl who has had everything in life and still wants more. Her father,

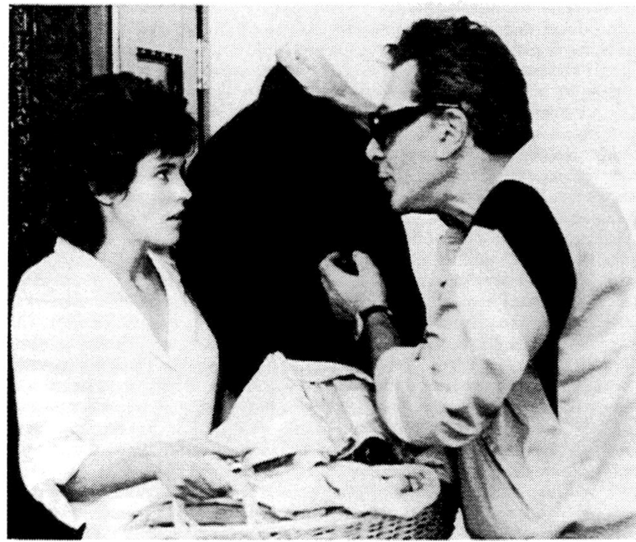

Skerritt, a millionaire philanthropist, is sick and tired of his daughter's excesses but he can't find it in his heart to deny her. Sheedy finally goes one step too far, picked up for reckless driving with cocaine in her purse. She is thrown into jail and Skerritt murmurs a black wish that she had never been born. Just as James Stewart in IT'S A WONDERFUL LIFE wished away his own life, fairy godmother D'Angelo is present to wave her wand and send Sheedy into the land of the nameless. Sheedy is suddenly without family, friends, money, or identity, becoming a lush living on the street, a derelict who now not only sees but experiences the way the other half lives. From Beverly Hills brat to destitute waif, the downcast Sheedy, finally lands a job as a maid for selfish Shawn and Perrine, who have a Malibu mansion and no taste at all. Perrine hires Sheedy since she is desperate for a white maid. Joining the household, Sheedy proves inept at the simplest chores but she is aided by her new-found friends, Plaza, the other maid, Clayton, the cook who had once been a blues singer, and chauffeur Ontkean, a decent guy who composes music on the side. Romance is sparked between Sheedy and Ontkean, but their lives are made hectic and often miserable by the demanding Perrine and the manic Shawn (this was Shawn's last film). She is the ultimate useless housewife who has money and spends it on the gorgeous and gaudy trinkets Rodeo Drive has to offer, a mindless housefrau who is always overdressed and underdeveloped in the intelligence department. Shawn is a greedy, conniving wheeler-dealer who will promote any kind of event to make money, from rock 'n' roll dropouts to questionable charity organizations. It is Shawn who has the funniest lines in the film. At one point, he watches his wife dress for a party with squinty-eyed concern, noting her metallic turban and black leotards under a gold lame skirt. Perrine is about to add even more jewelry to her already gem-bedecked body when Shawn quips: "It's only a wiener roast. Don't gild the lily. Less is more." Sheedy's plight is not as bad as one might expect, for she learns true friendship and affection in her new environment, along with concepts of responsibility decidedly lacking in her former life of luxury. Sadly, her own father, Skerritt, doesn't even recognize her when he passes her on a street, but he later comes back into her life when attending a Shawn party as Shawn tries to talk Skerritt into backing a charity show. It is at the party that the story all comes together and even allows fairy godmother D'Angelo to get into the real world act by coupling with Skerritt. The lightweight fare is not offensive in MAID TO ORDER, but neither is it absorbing, the script and direction meandering along with Sheedy as she awkwardly attempts to adjust to her new lifestyle. Although the Perrine-Shawn stereotypes of *nouveau riche* no-tasters is at first funny, their roles are predictable and interest in them dissipates halfway through the film. The sexy, vampy D'Angelo is really a standout here but limited in her scenes at playing the strange fairy godmother, unreal at the beginning, very real at the end when moving in on Skerritt. All in all a pleasant comedy with no pomp and little romp. *(Profanity.)*

p, Herb Jaffe, Mort Engelberg; d, Amy Jones; w, Amy Jones, Perry Howze, Randy Howze; ph, Shelly Johnson (Deluxe Color); m, Georges Delerue; ed, Sidney Wolinsky; prod d, Jeffrey Townsend; cos, Lisa Jensen.

Comedy **(PR:C MPAA:PG)**

MAJNU† (1987, India)

Nagarjuna, Rajini.

(In Telugu.)

p, Dasari Padma; d, Dasari Narayana Rao.

(PR:NR MPAA:NR)

MAKING MR. RIGHT* (1987) 95m Barry & Enright/Orion c

John Malkovich *(Dr. Jeff Peters/Ulysses)*, Ann Magnuson *(Frankie Stone)*, Glenne Headly *(Trish)*, Ben Masters *(Congressman Steve Marcus)*, Laurie Metcalf *(Sandy)*, Polly Bergen *(Estelle Stone)*, Harsh Nayyar *(Dr. Ravi Ramdas)*, Susan Berman *(Ivy Stone)*, Polly Draper *(Suzy Duncan)*, Hart Bochner *(Don)*, Robert Trebor *(Tux Salesman)*, Christian Clemenson *(Bruce Cohn)*, Merwin Goldsmith *(Moe Glickstein)*, Sid Raymond *(Manny)*, Sidney Armus *(Jeweler)*, John Hambrick *(TV Anchorman)*, Susan Lichtman, Steve Rondinaro *(Newscasters)*, Sherry Diamont *(Receptionist)*, Ruthe Geier *(Chemtec Receptionist)*, Mike Hanly *(Skippy)*, Donna Rosae *(Kitchen Maid)*, P.B. Floyd *(Station Wagon Driver)*, Trip Hamiton *(Photo Double)*, Jill Mallorie, Eve Mash *(Teenage Girls)*, Ronnie Rosado *(Hector)*, Roy Datz *(Hector's Uncle)*, Frank Sangineto *(Lupe Rodriguez)*, Stephen McFarland, Tom Schwartz, Ruth Mullen, Michael Seidelman *(Reporters)*, James F. Murtaugh *(Voice of Mission Control)*, Ralph Gunderman *(Mechanical Guard)*, Bob Cruz *(Marcus Promo Announcer)*, Harry Chase *(NASA Film Announcer)*, Ken Ceresne *(Wedding Photographer)*, Janice Frank *(Estelle's Friend)*, Stanley Kirk *(Angry Driver)*, Garitt Kono, Kevin Williams *(Valet Parkers)*, Clayton Ludovitch *(Mall Shopper)*, Alan B. Minor, Guy Trusty *(Themselves)*, Jose Ramirez *(Ramon Hernandez)*, Luisa Rodriguez *(Essie Hernandez)*, Gerald Owens *(Ulysses Photographer)*, Mr. Mike *(Robot)*, Penny *("Snowball")*.

For those who thrill to feminist sermonizing and relish a male android slavishly worshipping at a heroine's feet, then this movie is a must. For mainstream audiences, however, MAKING MR. RIGHT is all wrong as an entertainment vehicle, a misfire from director Seidelman, who created the worthy DESPERATELY SEEKING SUSAN. There is a touch of the "good-and-evil twin" theme here, but it's lost somewhere in the witless dialog and harangues from Magnuson, a supposedly liberated lady of the 1980s, a high-powered publicist who is trying (but not too hard) to have a relationship with Malkovich, a scientist who has created an affable android in his own image. Magnuson begins by moving in with Malkovich to teach his android (also played by Malkovich) the proper social and intellectual graces. The android is eventually to be launched into space, so one guesses he is being taught manners under the assumption he might meet someone he'll want to impress out there. The inventor is a cold and clinical sort who displays no human compassion at all, despite Magnuson's probings. Conversely, the android, instead of learning grammar and graces, starts to develop human emotions, becoming gentle, loving, and sensitive, in essence, just the man Magnuson is seeking. She falls for the android and the forced relationship is so contrived as to embarrass beach party movie enthusiasts. Magnuson attempts to display the inner dilemma of a modern feminist at odds with the traditional image of womanhood, but this only produces a lot of gobbledegook aimed at scientist Malkovich. Malkovich plays the android like a cretin, a smiling robot, a windup toy, or even one of those obscene rubber replicants to be blown up and cuddled by the ultra-lonely. The direction is dreary, plodding along without invention or creativity. The whole film should have been launched into space instead of being released. *(Profanity, sexual situations.)*

p, Mike Wise, Joel Tuber; d, Susan Seidelman; w, Floyd Byars, Laurie Frank; ph, Edward Lachman (Deluxe Color); m, Chaz Jankel; ed, Andrew Mondshein; prod d, Barbara Ling; art d, Jack Blackman; set d, Scott Jacobson, Jimmy Robinson II; cos, Rudy Dillon, Adelle Lutz; spec eff, Bran Ferren; makeup, Janet Flora; stunts, Jeff Moldovan, Paul Nuckles.

Comedy **(PR:C-O MPAA:PG-13)**

MALACCA† (1987, Swed.) 115m FilmStallet-Swedish Film Institute-SVT2 c

Gunilla Olsson, Charlotta Larsson, Carl Gustaf Lindstedt, Marc Klein-Essink.

Swedish thriller that follows young Westerners as they broaden their horizons with Asian adventures. The real, and very deadly, thrills enter the picture with the mysterious man who preys upon these backpack-wearing travelers.

p&d, Vilgot Sjoman.

Thriller **(PR:NR MPAA:NR)**

MALADIE D'AMOUR† (1987, Fr.) 116m Oliane-FR3-Sofica Investimage-Images Investissement-CNC/AMLF c (Trans: Malady of Love)

Nastassja Kinski *(Juliette)*, Jean-Hugues Anglade *(Clement)*, Michel Piccoli *(Raoul Bergeron)*, Jean-Claude Brialy, Souad Amidou, Jean-Paul Roussillon, Sophie D'Aulan, Jean-Luc Porraz.

Kinski is the mistress of Parisian doctor Piccoli whose younger assistant Anglade risks his career by falling in love with Kinski. Fearing Piccoli's wrath, the lovers take refuge in a provincial town where Anglade sets up a small practice. Kinski senses that he strives for greater heights and returns to Piccoli. Much later, after Anglade has risen to the top of his profession, he and Kinski meet again. Kinski learns that she is terminally ill and, instead of receiving medical treatment, heals herself with Anglade's love. Director Deray, a veteran of thrillers, is the third director connected with this project, taking the reins after the departure of Andrzej Zulawski and Andre Techine (RENDEZVOUS).

p, Marie-Laure Reyre; d, Jacques Deray; w, Daniele Thompson (based on an story by Andrzej Zulawski); ph, Jean-Francois Robin (Eastmancolor); m, Romano Musumarra; ed, Henri Lanoe; art d, Jean-Claude Gallouin.

Romance **(PR:NR MPAA:NR)**

MALARPIRATER† (1987, Swed.) 85m Sandrew-Swedish Film Institute-SVT1-Film Teknik/Sandrew c (Trans: Pirates of the Lake; AKA: PIRATES OF LAKE MALAREN)

Gustav Ljungberg *(Georg)*, Kristian Almgren *(Fabian)*, Jonas Eriksson *(Erik)*, Bjorn Gustafson *(The Count)*, Peter Stormare *(Beekeeper)*, Inga-Lil Rydberg *(Vilhelmina)*, Anita Ekstrom *(Mother)*, Bjorn Granath *(Father)*, Anita Wall, Allan Edwall, Mathias Henrikson, Lars-Erik Berenett, Ewa Munther, Carl Olof Alm.

Swedish actor-turned-director Allan Edwall (THE VIRGIN SPRING, FANNY AND ALEXANDER) helmed this tale about the summertime adventures of three young boys who set sail on a lake one day but are a long time in returning home. Based on a classic Swedish novel by Sigfrid Siwertz that owes much to Mark Twain's *Adventures of Huckleberry Finn* and *Tom Sawyer*, it follows the boys—Ljungberg, Almgren, and Eriksson—as they learn about survival in a not very accommodating world.

d&w, Allan Edwall (based on a novel by Sigfrid Siwertz); ph, Rune Ericson (Eastmancolor); m, Thomas Lindahl; ed, Thomas Holewa; prod d, Goran Wassberg; cos, Gertie Lindgren.

Adventure/Children's **(PR:NR MPAA:NR)**

MALCHIK ES PALCHIK (SEE: POHADKA O MALICKOVI, 1987, Czech./USSR)

MALDENIYE SIMION† (1987, Sri Lanka) 135m c (Trans: Simion of Maldeniye)

Joe Abeywicrema *(Simion)*, Anoja Weerasinghe *(Jane/Soma)*, Swarna Mallawarachchi *(Karuan)*, Ravindra Randeniya *(Dayaratne)*, Vincent Wass *(Village Headman)*, Dayaratne Jayawardene *(Police Chief)*.

Set in the 1930s in rural Sri Lanka, this film follows the fortunes of Abeywicrema, a gambler who operates a still but is unwilling to make graft payments to police. He is a man of questionable convictions who compels Weerasinghe to become his wife and then drives her into the arms of another man. Left with three children to care for but still deeply in love with Weerasinghe, he is then arrested and sentenced to 20 years in prison. After his release, he returns to his now-grown children, but due to his son's impassioned actions, Abeywicrema finds himself in the local slammer. Weerasinghe, now playing his daughter, sleeps with the police chief to secure her father's release and continues sacrificing for him right up to the bitter end. Weerasinghe won the Best Actress award at the Indian Film Festival for her dual role.

p, Vijaya Ramanayake; d,w&ph, D.B. Nihalsinghа; m, Premasiri Kemadasa; ed, Chandradasa Rubasinghe.

Drama **(PR:NR MPAA:NR)**

MALIBU BIKINI SHOP, THE* (1987) 99m Wescom-Romax/Intl. Film Marketing c

Michael David Wright *(Alan)*, Bruce Greenwood *(Todd)*, Barbra Horan *(Ronnie)*, Debra Blee *(Jane)*, Jay Robinson *(Ben)*, Galyn Gorg *(Cindy)*, Ami Julius *(Kathy)*, Frank Nelson *(Richard J. Remington)*, Kathleen Freeman *(Loraine Bender)*, Jon Rashad Kamal *(Eric Greene)*, Beverly Sanders *(Berta Hilgard)*, Harvey J. Goldenberg *(Julius Bender)*, Barbara Minkus *(Sylvia Rutledge)*, Rita Jenrette *(Aunt Ida)*, Jim Boelsen, Joel Kenney *(Delivery Men)*, Karen Anders *(Woman at Party)*, Teri Argula *(Policewoman)*, Jamie Baker, Michael Callahan *(Religious Zealots)*, James Boyce *(Burly Student)*, David Boyles *(Teen Boy at Party)*, Charles Brill *(Sol Felderman)*, Bara Byrnes *(Fran Finston)*, Lou Cutell *(Speaker)*, Marcia Christie *(Teen Girl at Party)*, Todd Del Pesco *(Drunken Young Man)*, Brad English, Hugh B. Holub *(Marshals)*, Michael Fox *(Uncle Dave)*, Norm Goodwins, Heidi Holicker, Christy Webb *(Customers)*, Melissa Gordon *(Party Guest)*, Hannah *(Confused Shopper)*, Elias Jacob *(Lou Finston)*, Christie Jakowpck *(Sheri Andrews)*, Dwight Larick *(Carpenter)*, Jeanna Loring *(Margie Hill)*, Larry Margo *(Waiter)*, Romy Mehlman *(Little Girl Shopper)*, Stephanie McLean *(Teenager)*, Gretchen Palmer *(Woman)*, Bobbi Pavis *(Stunning Girl)*, Allene Simmons *(Milinda Riley)*, Trudy Stolz *(Girlfriend)*, David Yanez *(Juan)*, Gerald York *(Cop)*, Roger Seward *(Radio D.J.)*.

Wright is a college business grad who is preparing to enter his father-in-law's business following his planned wedding to the spoiled and obnoxious Blee. When his aunt (a cameo role, camp fans will note, by Rita Jenrette) drowns, Wright heads to California to settle her business affairs. He moves into her home, a posh beachside estate, and discovers he is now co-owner of Jenrette's boutique, a bikini shop. His partner is Wright's sibling Greenwood, a beach bum who's as cool as Wright is square. Greenwood's idea of fun is to install one-way mirrors inside of dressing rooms so he can watch lovely young lasses disrobe, but Wright is determined to sell the place. He begins showing the shop to various clients sent to him by his late aunt's attorney. Horan, Gorg, and Julius are the trio of pretty young things who work in the shop. Horan, who is "The Smart One," dreams of becoming a fashion designer, and gradually develops some interest in Wright. Greenwood invites the three girls to move into their beach house, so naturally it's time in the plot for Blee to show up. She's outraged by the setup and demands Wright move into a hotel room. Eager to dump the shop, Wright makes a deal with Kamal, who turns out to be a cult leader. Kamal plans to use the site for his strange religion, and Wright tries to back out of the deal. Kamal agrees to sell back the place but at a higher price. Now Wright must raise the extra cash within two weeks. Greenwood manages to get hold of some hospital gowns, and with Horan's designing skills the plucky group creates a new line of bikinis. Since they are stuck with scads of green material, Horan goes for the obvious "Rambo-militaristic" look, and the bikinis are a hit. The shop is saved, and Wright ends up in Horan's embrace, but the new swimwear falls apart when it hits the water. Seems the thread used on the suits was surgical sutures designed to dissolve in water, thus exposing plenty of breasts to Greenwood's wide-grinned delight. This is typical fare for bad beach movies as far as the plot goes, but after the standard situations have been played out, there's nothing much left to do. Consequently, there's an excessive amount of padding, including a couple of poorly staged rock videos; outdoor party scenes which lead to expected inhibitions; and extraneous characters in witless situations. To the film's credit its leads are attractive, with Horan and Wright actually showing some semblance of talent. Blee, whose name suits her character nicely, exhibits some potential and might be able to rise above such film fare. Just for the record, the title establishment has nothing to do with its stated location. There's no mistaking this section of California, it's Venice pure and simple. The film, shot in 1984, saw limited screenings in 1986 under the title THE BIKINI SHOP. Perhaps between then and its wider release, the filmmakers forgot exactly where their story was set. Songs include: "Lookin' " (performed by Naomi Delgado), "Silly Boy" (Performed by Tami Holbrook), "If the Love Fits" (performed by Jacie Berry), "Give Me Your Love to Dream On" (performed by Steve Eaton), "Girls of Rock 'n' Roll" (performed by Carter Robinson, Tami Holbrook, Jacie Berry, Penny Summers), "Party Night" (performed by Light), "One Thing Leads to Another" (performed by Chris Farren), "Just Remember" (performed by Executive), "You Make Me Nervous" (performed by Diana DeWitt), "We Found Love" (performed by Chris Farren, Carter Robinson), "Into Something Good" (performed by Skip Adams, Light), "Don't Let the Moment Go" (performed by Jaunice Charmaine), "Running with a Stranger" (performed by Chris Farren). *(Profanity, brief nudity, sexual situations.)*

p, Gary Mehlman, J. Kenneth Rotcop, Leo Leichter; d&w, David Wechter; ph, Tom Richmond (CFI Color); ed, Jean-Marc Vasseur; md, Don Perry; art d, Dian Perryman; set d, Kayla Koeber; cos, Rita Riggs; spec eff, Tassilo Baur; ch, Doraine Grusman, Gentry Gorg; m/l, Sue Shifrin, Franne Golde, Susan Pomerantz, Steve Eaton, Gloria Skelrou, Lenny Malcaluso, Jan Levy, Terry Shaddick, Bob Summers, Penny Summers, Sam Kunin, Ernest Straughter, David Straughter, Louis Russell, Robert Russell, Julius Carey, Robert Mockler, Robbie Nevil, Mark Holding, Duncan Pain, Skip Adams, Jaunice Charmaine, Irene Koster, Chris Farren; makeup, Margaret Elliott.

Comedy **Cas.** **(PR:O MPAA:R)**

MALOM A POKOLBAN† (1987, Hung.) 101m Mafilm-Hunnia c (Trans: Mills of Hell)

Frigyes Funtek *(Janos Flandera)*, Dezso Garas *(Altschuler, Prosecuting Attorney)*, Anna Rackevei *(Nadezhda Altschuler)*, Edit Vlahovics *(Erzsi Bona)*, Marianna Moor *(Ildiko Demjen, Reporter)*.

Set in Budapest in 1950, this film tells of a talented but rebellious university student, Funtek, whose romantic interlude with an older woman prevents him from being sent to the Soviet Union on an academic scholarship. Instead he is sentenced to serve a year in a labor camp. He meets a young woman with whom he falls in love and later impregnates. After convincing her to get an abortion he moves on. He then falls in love with Rackevei, the polio-stricken daughter of a high-ranking official. When the girl's father learns of their romance, he tries to get Funtek called up for military service but is forced to reverse his stand when his daughter threatens suicide. Two years pass, Funtek and Rackevei marry, and Funtek has reentered the university. Tragedy follows, however, when Funtek has a chance meeting with his previous young lover and discovers that she gave birth to his son instead of going ahead with the abortion.

d, Gyula Maar; w, Gyorgy Moldova, Gyula Maar (based on a novel by Gyorgy Moldova); ph, Ivan Mark (Eastmancolor); ed, Julia Sivo; prod d, Tamas Banovich; cos, Judit Schaffer.

Drama **(PR:NR MPAA:NR)**

MALONE½** (1987) 93m Orion c

Burt Reynolds *(Richard Malone)*, Cliff Robertson *(Charles Delaney)*, Kenneth McMillan *(Sheriff Hawkins)*, Cynthia Gibb *(Jo Barlow)*, Scott Wilson (Paul Barlow), Lauren Hutton *(Jamie)*, Philip Anglim *(Harvey)*, Tracey Walter *(Calvin Bollard)*, Dennis Burkley *(Dan Bollard)*, Alex Diakun *(Madrid)*, Brooks Gardner *(Patterson)*, Mike Kirton *(Frank)*, Duncan Fraser *(Malone's Target)*, Janne Mortil *(Helen)*, Campbell Lane *(Tom Riggs)*, Tom McBeath *(Stringbean)*, Don Mackay *(Dr. Florian)*, Tom Herton *(Eli)*, Blu Mankuma *(Rev. Danby)*, Walter Marsh *(Congressman)*, Graydon Gould *(Lawyer)*, Bill Buck *(Banker)*, Don Davis *(Buddy)*, Frank C. Turner *(Andy)*, Mavor Moore *(Hausmann)*, Stephen E. Miller *(Clinton)*, Donna White *(Nurse)*, Dwight McFee *(Harry)*, Christianne Hirt *(Girl in Wagon)*.

Burt Reynolds turns in his best performance since SHARKEY'S MACHINE

(1981) in this updated version of the classic western SHANE. A CIA assassin who has grown tired of the business, Reynolds bids *adieu* to sexy female agent Hutton and drives off in his beloved 1969 Mustang. In Oregon (actually British Columbia) his transmission breaks and he pushes the car to a tiny gas station owned by Wilson and his pert teenage daughter Gibb. Wilson and Reynolds hit it off famously and since he is in no hurry, the ex-CIA agent agrees to bunk in Wilson's spare room for the three days it will take to repair the car. This news delights Gibb, who has developed quite a crush on the handsome stranger although his car is older than she is. During his stay Reynolds learns that a rich and powerful industrialist, Robertson, has bought up most of the property in town and is trying to push everyone out. Unbeknownst to the townsfolk, Robertson is the leader of a fanatical right-wing group that plans to set up military strongholds throughout the country in preparation for their "patriotic" revolution. As the days go by Reynolds becomes quite fond of Wilson and his daughter, but tries hard to stay out of the local conflict. Unfortunately, goons force his hand when they sexually harass Gibb and Reynolds dispatches one huge redneck with a flurry of karate chops. Seizing the opportunity to get rid of the troublesome stranger, one of Robertson's henchmen encourages the redneck's brother, Walter, to shoot Reynolds. Walter, however, is the one who gets shot. Thrown in jail by corrupt sheriff McMillan, Reynolds is interrogated by Robertson himself. Impressed with Reynolds' confident demeanor and obvious skill in the art of violence, Robertson tries to recruit him but fails. This of course prompts Robertson to hire two New York City assassins to get rid of Reynolds. Meanwhile, the CIA has gotten wind of the trouble and sends Hutton to terminate the recalcitrant Reynolds (nobody retires from the agency). Reynolds manages to kill both assassins sent by Robertson, and Hutton cannot bring herself to do him in either. Later, she is killed by Robertson's men and this finally pushes Reynolds over the edge. Working alone, he takes on Robertson's uzi-wielding army and kills them all, saving the crazed Robertson for last. Although the film disintegrates into the typical (albeit not particularly well-staged) gunplay and pyrotechnics display commonly found in movies of this ilk, the first half of MALONE is restrained, quiet, and beautifully acted by Reynolds, Gibb, and Wilson. At this point in his checkered career Reynolds has finally summoned up a mature world-weariness for this role and exposes a side of himself that has not been seen on the screen. This new persona is effective and interesting—a welcome relief from the insipid good ol' boy roles of the last ten years. The man has long claimed he is a better actor than the roles he gets, and here he proves it. His scenes with Gibb (a very impressive young actress) are charming, touching, and natural as this man who has just turned 50, gently and respectfully deflects the awe-struck teenager's delicate attempts to seduce him. His relationship with both Gibb and her father unfolds in spare, subtle passages with little significant dialog and adds great texture to what is otherwise a standard action film. Sadly, the Reynolds-Gibb-Wilson storyline is thrown to the wind as soon as the shooting starts. Hutton's character is badly integrated into the narrative, as is Robertson's hazy plan for world domination, and the film collapses into a hum-drum shootout that ends in an abrupt and unsatisfying manner. After enjoying the best 40 minutes of acting Reynolds has displayed in years, what follows is an unfortunate disappointment. *(Graphic violence, profanity.)*

p, Leo L. Fuchs; d, Harley Cokliss; w, Christopher Frank (based on the novel *Shotgun* by William Wingate); ph, Gerald Hirschfeld (Deluxe Color); m, David Newman; ed, Todd Ramsay; prod d, Graeme Murray; set d, Barry Brolly; cos, Norman Salling; spec eff, Dennis Dion, Dean Lockwood; makeup, Phyllis Newman, Tom Ellingwood; stunts, Bud Davis.

Action/Drama Cas. (PR:O MPAA:R)

MAN IN LOVE, A*½** (1987, Fr.) 108m Camera One-Alexandre-JMS/Cinecom c (UN HOMME AMOUREUX)

Greta Scacchi *(Jane Steiner)*, Peter Coyote *(Steve Elliott)*, Peter Riegert *(Michael Pozner)*, Claudia Cardinale *(Julia Steiner)*, John Berry *(Harry Steiner)*, Vincent Lindon *(Bruno Schlosser)*, Jamie Lee Curtis *(Susan Elliott)*, Jean Pigozzi *(Dante Pizani)*, Elia Katz *(Sam)*, Constantin Alexandrov *(De Vitta)*, Michele Melega *(Paolo)*, Jean-Claude de Goros *(Dr. Sandro)*.

The fourth film in ten years from the director of 1983's Oscar-nominated ENTRE NOUS, A MAN IN LOVE is a semi-autobiographical romantic melodrama which has been created on a grand, international scale. The picture takes place mostly in Italy's Cinecitta film studio, which also serves as the backdrop for much of the action. Coyote, a temperamental American actor, has been chosen as the lead in an Italian biography of Cesare Pavese (to whom Coyote bears a remarkable physical resemblance), a Communist intellectual and author who committed suicide in 1950 at the age of 41. Equally temperamental is the film's director, Pigozzi, who is the stereotypical obsessive filmmaker. Pigozzi casts, in a minor role, Scacchi, a relatively unknown English-speaking actress (though reared in Europe), to play one of the many women with whom Pavese falls in love during his lifetime. After learning the good news, Scacchi heads for Rome, leaving her mother, Cardinale, behind in Lyon, and her boy friend, Lindon, behind in Paris. With her journalist father, Berry, an amiable alcoholic, traveling beside her, Scacchi arrives at Cinecitta. Her first visit to the set, however, is explosive—a hint of things to come. Standing in the shadows, Scacchi watches as her father is thrown out after stubbornly and loudly demanding to interview Coyote. Disgusted at Coyote's selfish "star" behavior, Scacchi tells him off and storms off the set. Naturally, the situation is patched up and the Coyote-Scacchi relationship begins, both on and off the screen. Theirs is an unpredictable, sexually charged romance which soon takes its toll on Coyote's ability to assume Pavese's character on the set. His acting suffers and he becomes increasing irascible. While Coyote is on the set, Scacchi (whose part is soon finished) waits for him at his rented home, restlessly passing the days and eagerly awaiting the nights. Coyote's situation gets worse when his wife, Curtis, arrives from New York with their two children. He keeps his romance with Scacchi hidden, but the pressure grows. During a surprise visit, Curtis nearly catches Scacchi in the shower. A confrontation is avoided, however, when Coyote's longtime personal assistant, Riegert, helps Scacchi sneak out the back door. Problems continue to arise because of Coyote's and Scacchi's attraction for each other. Filming in interrupted when Coyote runs off; a tense Curtis explodes at the film's producers; Lindon tries to win back Scacchi's love; and Cardinale's poor health leads Scacchi to return home. Although Coyote has proven his love to Scacchi, their relationship is on a dead end since Coyote is convinced that people can love more than one person at a time, casting doubt on his ever leaving Curtis. When Scacchi returns home she is inspired by Cardinale's brave acceptance of her approaching death. Instead of leaving with Coyote, she stays home to write. Sitting alone in front of an old manual typewriter, she bangs out the oddly reflexive and autobiographical title—"A Man in Love." Although it was the official French entry at this year's Cannes Film Festival, A MAN IN LOVE is decidedly not French, nor is it Italian, or American. It is Kurys' first film in English (though parts are in French and Italian) and it transcends continental borders with its international atmosphere. Kurys displays remarkable directorial adroitness as she interweaves the film's various languages and locales (besides Cinecitta, filming takes place in Paris and the French countryside). One gets the feeling that every character in the movie can comfortably speak at least three languages. What makes this international quality even more praiseworthy is the complexity of the plot. Kurys and coscript-writer Schatzky have concocted a story which is essentially a melodrama. Although the film is peopled with eight strong characters, the plot effortlessly shifts from person to person in a manner worthy of the seamless style of Jean Renoir. The entire web of events begins with a seemingly minor decision that builds and builds, spinning around the two main characters and entangling all those around them. The events begin as Pigozzi and Coyote share a limousine ride. For the role of Cesare Pavese's last lover, the director narrows his choices to four actresses. Coyote looks at the photos and chooses one—a German actress who Pigozzi decides against. The second choice is Scacchi. At this moment Coyote doesn't realize the importance of his decision, but eventually it unravels before his eyes. This simple act of choosing a supporting actress nearly brings the entire picture to a halt, upsets two relationships, and has numerous other consequences. Everyone around Coyote is affected by his choice—from his wife to Scacchi's boy friend to the film's producers. As Francois Truffaut did in DAY FOR NIGHT, Kurys paints her characters as a unique group of people whose careers are enmeshed in a life of fiction which tends to confuse their real-life decisions and actions. Where Kurys' film differs is its lack of concentration on the filmmaking *process*—an area Truffaut reverently explored. (Kurys only occasionally attempts to blur the line between reality and fiction, and this she does in an obvious manner.) Coyote, who previously played a manipulative film director in 1984's STRANGERS KISS, here shines as a self-important actor who is pathetically full of himself, but who is simultaneously charming and sensitive. Scacchi, who made such an impact in 1985's THE COCA-COLA KID, is excellent as the young actress who gets caught in the whirlpool of filmmaking. Riegert, the young businessman from LOCAL HERO, is funny and sympathetic as Coyote's occasionally abused assistant (or "slave" as he calls himself) who seems to love Scacchi from a distance. As Scacchi's parents, both the beautiful Cardinale and the disheveled Berry (an American actor/director living in France) turn in fine performances. Also worthy of mention is the droopy-eyed Lindon (the singing policeman in 1985's BETTY BLUE) as Scacchi's complacent Parisian boy friend who is unable to compete with Coyote's allure. Technically, A MAN IN LOVE is thoroughly picturesque with cinematographer Zitzermann and art director Tavoularis meeting the challenge of filming both on Cinecitta's stages and in the natural surroundings of the French countryside. The prolific Georges Delerue provides yet another pleasant score which adds lushly romantic comments to the film's already beautiful images. A MAN IN LOVE establishes, even more firmly than ENTRE NOUS, that Kurys is one of the most compelling filmmakers to emerge from France in recent years. Released at the Cannes Film Festival with a running time of 117 minutes. *(Nudity, sexual situations, profanity.)*

p, Marjorie Israel, Armand Barbault, Roberto Guissani; d, Diane Kurys; w, Diane Kurys, Olivier Schatzky, Israel Horovitz; ph, Bernard Zitzermann (Eastmancolor); m, Georges Delerue; ed, Joele Van Effenterre; art d, Dean Tavoularis; cos, Brigitte Nierhaus; makeup, Joel Lavau.

Drama/Romance **(PR:O MPAA:R)**

MAN ON FIRE** (1987, It./Fr.) 93m 7 Films Cinema-Cima Produzioni-FR3/Tri-Star c

Scott Glenn *(Creasy)*, Jade Malle *(Samantha "Sam" Balletto)*, Joe Pesci *(David)*, Brooke Adams *(Jane Balletto)*, Jonathan Pryce *(Michael)*, Paul Shenar *(Ettore Balletto)*, Danny Aiello *(Conti)*, Laura Morante *(Julia, David's Wife)*, Giancarlo Prati *(Satta)*, Inigo Lezzi *(Bellu)*, Allesandro Haber *(Sandri)*, Franco Trevisi *(Rabbia)*, Lou Castel *(Violente)*, Lorenzo Piani *(Bruno)*, Giuseppe Cederna *(Snake)*, Giovani Mauriello *(Elio)*, Frederica Tatulli *(Elio's Wife)*, Anita Zagaria *(Conti's Wife)*, Enrica Rosso *(Maria)*, Anna Guerrieri *(Nurse)*, Angela Finocchiaro *(Foot Race Pro)*, Giovanni Visentin *(Marco)*, James Bradell *(School Guard)*, Enrico Papa *(Claudio)*, Luigi Mezza Notte, Piero Vida *(Kidnapers)*, Antoine Reb *(Man in Porno Theater)*, Alexandre Lopez, Allesandro Spadorcia *(Men in Street)*, Henri-Charles Alexandre *(Young Killer)*, Lucas Orlandini *(Boy at Party)*, Martine Malle, Marie Sellers *(Prostitutes)*, Antonio Petrocelli, Fabio Bussotti, Manfredi Aliquo, Leonardo Petrillo *(Policemen)*.

This European coproduction featuring an international cast (mostly American) disappeared quickly at the American box office and will likely find new life on cable television and home video. The film begins in a hospital as doctors and nurses scurry about in slow motion. We see Glenn, apparently dead, being zipped into a body bag. Suddenly Glenn's voice is heard saying, "So that's how I ended. A stiff in a body bag." From there the entire film is flashback. We learn that Glenn was a burned-out CIA operative who had been psychologically traumatized by his most recent assignment in Beirut where he witnessed a group of innocent children killed in a terrorist bombing. Haunted by nightmares of the incident, Glenn quits the CIA and goes to Northern Italy to visit his friend Pesci, an innkeeper. Advising Glenn to keep busy, Pesci suggests he take a job as bodyguard for wealthy Italian industrialist Shenar. With the recent wave of kidnapings, Shenar is worried that terrorists will snatch his 12-year-old daughter, Malle. Glenn takes the job and soon learns that Malle's home life is not a happy one. Her American mother, Adams, is bored and has had a series of love affairs. Shenar is too busy to pay much attention to his daughter, so the young girl turns to the morose Glenn for companionship. Too cynical and wounded from his experiences to warm up to anyone, Glenn resists the girl's efforts at friendship and tries to resign. When his resignation is refused, Glenn reluctantly returns to his post and soon finds himself coming out of his self-imposed emotional prison. Malle eventually succeeds in making friends with Glenn and soon a father-daughter relationship is established, with Glenn training the girl for an upcoming school track-and-field meet. Malle loses, but she finds comfort in Glenn's spirited and encouraging words. Predictably, just as Glenn has learned to live again, Malle is abducted by gang leader Aiello and Glenn is badly wounded. Determined to save the girl, Glenn leaves his hospital bed, cuts his shaggy hair, shaves his beard, and goes after the kidnapers using every nasty CIA trick in the book. The kidnapers are an amazingly dim-witted bunch, and Glenn manages to rescue the girl and kill a half a dozen people in the process. It appears that Glenn is fatally wounded during the rescue, but at the end we learn that the doctors have patched him up and that the CIA has faked his death so that he can adopt a new identity and live in peace. Although the film begins promisingly enough with an opening lifted from SUNSET BOULEVARD and maintains interest with the developing relationship between Glenn and Malle, MAN ON FIRE collapses in its last half as the bullets begin to spray and confusion reigns. We spend half the film with a man who is struggling to retrieve his humanity and eventually succeeds, only to have him chuck it all and go back to the ruthless procedures that traumatized him in the first place. There are annoying lapses of logic in the action scenes that further serve to erode the film's credibility. Why didn't the kidnapers slaughter Glenn like every other unfortunate bodyguard who has been caught up in terrorist attacks on European notables? Director Chouraqui wastes a pretty good cast, with Adams, Pesci, Aiello, and Pryce (who plays Adams' latest fling) given badly integrated cameos that seem to indicate that most of their footage wound up on the cutting room floor. The dependable Glenn tries hard to squeeze something viable from his underwritten role and succeeds at times. The real standout is young Malle, who, although she does not have as much screen time as she should, manages to make the best of some trite dialog and adds some zest to a film that everyone feels they've seen before. *(Graphic violence, profanity.)*

p, Arnon Milchan; d, Elie Chouraqui; w, Elie Chouraqui, Sergio Donati (based on the novel by A.J. Quinnell); ph, Gerry Fisher (Eastmancolor); m, John Scott; ed, Noelle Boisson; md, John Scott; art d, Giantito Burchiellaro; set d, Bruno Amalfitano; cos, Alberte Barsacq; makeup, Manlio Rocchetti; spec eff, Giovanni Corridori, Renato Agostini.

Thriller **(PR:O MPAA:R)**

MAN OUTSIDE† (1987) 109m Stouffer Enterprise Film Partners/Virgin Vision c

Robert Logan *(Jack Avery)*, Kathleen Quinlan *(Grace Freemont)*, Bradford Dillman *(Frank Simmons)*, Levon Helm *(Sheriff Leland Laughlin)*.

Originally titled "The Tuscaloosan: A Solitary Man," this modestly budgeted effort ($3.5 million) stars Logan as a man who has given up his lucrative law practice to live an isolated existence in backwater Arkansas. He blames himself for his wife's death in a fire and has more or less given up on humanity. Quinlan, a teacher, tries to get through to him, and he accepts her help when he becomes the prime suspect in a kidnaping. She helps him escape the jail cell sheriff Helm has put him, and the two of them nab the real kidnaper, Dillman. MAN OUTSIDE is director Stouffer's first feature film. Helm, the onetime drummer for The Band, played Laura Dern's father in SMOOTH TALK (1985) and returns both to acting and his native Arkansas with this role.

p, Mark Stouffer, Robert E. Yoss; d&w, Mark Stouffer; ph, William Wages; m, John McEuen; ed, Tony Lombardo.

Drama **(PR:NR MPAA:PG-13)**

MAN WITH THREE COFFINS, THE† (1987, S. Korea) 105m c

Myung-kon Kim *(Soon-suk Yang)*, Bo-hee Lee *(Yang's Wife/Nurse/Prostitute)*.

Bo-he Lee plays three roles in this South Korean film about a man (Myung-kon Kim) who journeys to the region his late wife came from so he can return her ashes to the land where she grew up. In his search for a better understanding of her past he meets Bo-hee Lee in her three roles—as a nurse, a hooker, and the ghost of his wife. Adapted by screenwriter Jacha Lee from his novella.

p, Myung-won Lee; d, Chang-ho Lee; w, Jacha Lee (based on his novella *The Wanderer Never Rests Even on the Road*); ph, Seung bae Park; m, Jong-gu Lee.

Drama **(PR:NR MPAA:NR)**

MANDALADHEESUDU† (1987, India) D.V.N. Raju

Kota Srinivasa Rao, P. Bhanumathi, Krishna.

A political attack on the Chief Minister of State, MANDALADHEESUDU is an attempt to ridicule the system of *mandals* (a group of villages under one control) and to bring about governmental change through the use of film. Released just before local elections, the film found an interested audience among the politically minded. (In Telugu.)

p, D.V.N. Raju; d, Prabhakara Reddy.

Drama **(PR:NR MPAA:NR)**

MANILA, OPEN CITY† (1987, Phil) Roadshow Films Intl.

Ric Rodrigo, Mario Monte, Charito Solis.

With the end of WW II imminent, Manila is declared an open city; however, the commander of the Japanese forces is unwilling to honor the decree. This Filipino film shows the Japanese refusal to give ground and how they used the innocent citizens of Manila as human shields against the advancing US Army, resulting in the ruin of the Philippine capital.

[No credits available.]

War **(PR:NR MPAA:NR)**

MANKILLERS zero (1987) 90m Action Int. c

Edd Byrnes *(Jack Marra)*, Gail Fisher *(Joan Hanson)*, Edy Williams *(Sgt. Roberts)*, Lynda Aldon *(Rachael McKenna)*, William Zipp *(John Mickland)*, Christine Lunde *(Maria Rosetti)*, Susanne Tegman *(Terry Davis)*, Marilyn Stafford *(Roxanne Taylor)*, Paul Bruno *(Bruno)*, Byron Clark *(Williams)*, Lizzie Borden *(Female Drug Runners Leader)*, Thyais Walsh *(Vicki Thompson)*, Bainbridge Scott *(Christine Rollins)*, Cyndi Domino *(Trish Daniels)*, Brian O'Conner *(Special CIA Agent)*, John Taylor *(Mannetti)*, Sheila Best *(Margaret Skinner)*, Naomi Delgado *(Vannesa Shaw)*, Arlene Julian *(Lisa Leonardo)*, Veronica Carothers *(Shannon Smith)*, Julie Smith, Christine Crowell *(High School Girls)*, Chet Hood, John Kelly *(CIA Agents)*, Cameron Rico *(Charlie)*, Craig Alan, Ed Garcia, Joe Ayala *(Drug Runners)*, Amber Star *(K.C. Grimes)*, Robert Beatheala *(Prison Guard)*, Wendy Gardner, Diane Copeland, Brooke Sette, Lisa Leonardi, Judea Brittan *(Captive Girls)*, Robert Cervi, Robert Magnusson, Roland Harrell, Art Camacho, Muneer Mansour, Richard Duarte, Al Fletcher, Robert Schmaltz, Ted Rexhepi, Michael James, Jeff Augenstein, David Macias, Jr., Henry Vega, Kevin Best, Leonard Flint, Chris Bunser, Julien Michaels, Tony Lima, Henry Gonzales, John Aragon, Lewis Strong, Gary Cooper, Tom Van Hoof, Gabriel Frimmel, Mike Pabsy, Daniel Brockman, Ron Reynaldi, Mauricio Si, Mark Love, Ron Rameriez, Jim Pickrell, Mike Masi *(Mickland's Men)*, Trish Furlow, Perla Christian, Diana Frank, Jennifer Marshal, Siobhan Samples, Christine Mummey, Darlene Manroe, Helen Augenstein, Holly Huddleston, Heather Kennedy, Candice Stacy *(Prison Girls)*.

When psychotic cocaine dealer Zipp bumps off some feds, a special government agency decides there's only one person who can stop this madman. They call on Aldon, a former agent Zipp thinks he killed long ago. Aldon agrees to take on her old foe if she can handpick her team of assistants. She does her recruiting at a prison, choosing 12 of the toughest and prettiest cutthroats imaginable. The girls begin rigorous training with the promise that they will be granted full pardons if they can successfully complete this dangerous mission. Lunde is the group's renegade, constantly disobeying Aldon's orders, though she changes her tune when Aldon saves the spirited redhead from being killed by a grenade. Meanwhile, Zipp tortures a government spy who has infiltrated his camp and learns of Aldon's mission. He prepares his men for battle, while the girls are ordered to head out before their training is completed. Several gun battles later, Aldon has become Zipp's prisoner. Lunde realizes she must lead the others to rescue their leader, though she is wounded in the operation. Aldon gets her girls out of the battle zone, then returns for a final confrontation. Zipp seemingly will not die, until Aldon blasts him with a bazooka. MANKILLERS is laughably awful in every respect. The silly dialog is poorly dubbed throughout the film, the special effects are cheap, and so are the onscreen deaths during the poorly staged action sequences. Considering that the squad is supposed to be undergoing grueling training, these Rambimbos are surprisingly able to find time to keep their makeup fresh and hair constantly permed. Zipp also finds some time for personal hygiene, going through no less than three different hairstyles in the course of the film. Songs include: "Freedom" (Tim James, Steve McClintock, performed by McClintock) and "Stand Tuff" (Jimmy Hammer). *(Violence, profanity, sexual situations.)*

p, Peter Yuval; d&w, David A. Prior; ph, Keith Holland; m, Tim James, Steve McClintock, Tim Heintz; ed, Alan Carrier; spec eff, Phoenix; m/l, Tim James, Steve McClintock, Jimmy Hammer; stunts, Fritz Matthews, Sean Holton; makeup, Angela Levine.

Action **Cas.** **(PR:O MPAA:NR)**

MANNEN FRAN MALLORCA† (1987, Swed.) 105m (Trans: The Man from Majorca)Drakfilm-Svensk Filmindustri-Swedish Film Institute-SVT2-Filmhuset-Crone/Cannon

Sven Wollter, Thomas Von Bromssen, Hakan Serner, Ernst Gunther.

Wollter and Von Bromssen are a pair of vice squad detectives who become involved in a robbery case where the clues lead all the way to the corrupt Justice Department.

p, Goran Lindstrom; d&w, Bo Widerberg; ph, Tomas Wahlberg; m, Bjorn Lindh; ed, Bo Widerberg; prod d, Jan Oquist.

Crime **(PR:NR MPAA:NR)**

MANNEQUIN* (1987) 89m Gladden/FOX c

Andrew McCarthy *(Jonathan Switcher)*, Kim Cattrall *(Emmy, Mannequin)*, Estelle Getty *(Clare Timkin)*, James Spader *(Richards)*, G.W. Bailey *(Felix, Nightwatchman)*, Carole Davis *(Roxie)*, Stephen Vinovich *(B.J. Wert)*, Christopher Maher *(Armand)*, Meshach Taylor *(Hollywood Montrose)*, Phyllis Newman *(Emmy's Mother, Egypt, 25 BC)*, Phil Rubenstein *(Mannequin Factory Boss)*, Jeffrey Lampert *(Factory Worker)*, Kenneth Lloyd *(Superdad)*, Jake Jundeff *(Superkid)*, Harvey Levine *(Balloon Boss)*, Thomas J. McCarthy *(Head Gardener)*, R.L. Ryan *(Pizzeria Manager)*, Glenn Davish *(Effete Executive)*, Steve Lippe *(Male Sales Clerk)*, Lee Golden *(Wino)*, Vernon R. DeVinney *(Older Man in Boardroom)*, Olivia Frances Williams *(Woman in Boardroom)*, Charles N. Lord *(Man in Boardroom)*, Ben Hammer *(Hans, Maitre d')*, Jane Moore *(Tina)*, Jane Carol Simms *(Lupe)*, Judi Goldhand *(Mrs. Thomas)*, Lara Harris *(Mannequin in Photo Window)*, Dan Lounsberry, Kitty Minehart *(Senior Citizens)*, Katherine Conklin *(Wert's Secretary)*, Andrew Hill Newman *(Compactor Room Janitor)*, Bill Greene *(Police Officer)*.

A lifeless and sophomoric attempt at romantic comedy which draws on the fantasy films of old Hollywood (most notably 1948's ONE TOUCH OF VENUS) but fails miserably. The picture opens in ancient Egypt with a title card that reads: "Edfu, Egypt: a really long time ago, right before lunch." After that sidesplitting opening, we see Cattrall as a young Egyptian woman who refuses to be married off to a camel-dung dealer. Rather than give in to her mother's wishes, she beckons the gods to take her away. The scene then switches to modern-day Philadelphia where McCarthy is working as a mannequin sculptor. He gets fired from that job, and then loses a string of others. Unable to hold the interest of his snotty girl friend Davis, McCarthy wanders around penniless and loveless. Then, in a store window display, he sees the last mannequin he created. The following morning, after saving the life of department store president Getty, McCarthy is given a job in the stockroom. Getty's department store is being driven into bankruptcy by Spader, a sleazy young vice-president, and Vinovich, the owner of a rival store. One evening, McCarthy's mannequin magically comes to life in the form of Cattrall. She can only be seen by him, however, suddenly reverting into a mannequin if anyone enters the room. Cattrall gives McCarthy the artistic confidence he needs to become a top window dresser. Practically overnight, the store is bustling with new business because of the innovative window displays. McCarthy is rewarded with more power and a better-paying position, while Spader and Vinovich devise new schemes to sabotage the store. They employ Davis to lure McCarthy into their company. When that fails they hire Bailey, a bungling security guard with a watchdog named Rambo (later replaced by a dog named Terminator), to take incriminating photos of McCarthy and his mannequin lover. Even though everyone thinks that McCarthy is frightfully perverted, no one can prove that he carries on with a mannequin. The only people who stand by him are Getty and the store's previous window dresser, Taylor, a flamboyant black with a penchant for strange eyeglasses. In a final act of sabotage, Spader and Bailey (after they've both been fired) break into the department store and steal all the female mannequins. They toss them all in a trash compactor, but McCarthy arrives in the nick of time to save Cattrall, who turns into a real person as she is rescued from obliteration. Cattrall and McCarthy, having apparently passed some test placed before them by the gods, can now lead normal lives without having to worry about Cattrall reverting to dummy form. All the bad guys are rounded up and arrested, while Cattrall and McCarthy are married in a ceremony that takes place in a department store window. MANNEQUIN is one of those films that puts the entire Hollywood system back into perspective. Just when you thought the public had begun to care about intelligent films again (look at last year's Oscar nominations for Best Picture), this moronic entry comes along and grosses $24 million in a month. It's not that MANNEQUIN is particularly offensive (it's about as tame as a Saturday morning cartoon with a little risque language tossed in), it's just lifeless. There's nothing to it, save for a couple of sweet moments between McCarthy and Cattrall. The fantasy plot takes up only a small portion of the film (Cattrall doesn't enter McCarthy's life until about one-third of the way into the film) with the remainder devoted to stupid caricatures and lamebrained plot contrivances. A first-time directorial effort from Gottlieb, a director of TV commercials, MANNEQUIN probably would have played better as a 30-second spot than as a 90-minute feature. It has no more depth of character than one would expect from a television commercial and is about as engaging. Perhaps if the screenplay (which Gottlieb cowrote) had concentrated more on the relationship (a la SPLASH) than on the incidental characters, MANNEQUIN would have approached the Hollywood fantasy genre it aimed at. Instead, MANNEQUIN is an empty-headed effort which wastes the considerable talents of both McCarthy (who did much better work in PRETTY IN PINK) and Cattrall. Songs include: "Nothing's Gonna Stop Us Now" (Albert Hammond, Diane Warren, performed by Starship), "Do You Dream About Me" (Warren, performed by Alisha), "In My Wildest Dreams" (Bob Crewe, Jerry Corbetta, Charlotte Caffey, performed by Belinda Carlisle), "My Girl" (William Robinson, Ronald White, performed by The Temptations). *(Mild profanity.)*

p, Art Levinson; d, Michael Gottlieb; w, Edward Rugoff, Michael Gottlieb; ph, Tim Suhrstedt (DuArt Color); m, Sylvester Levay; ed, Richard Halsey, Frank Jimenez; prod d, Josan Russo; art d, Richard Amend; set d, Elise "Cricket" Rowland; ch, Vincent Paterson; cos, Lisa Jensen; m/l, Albert Hammond, Diane Warren, Bob Crewe, Jerry Corbetta, Charlotte Caffey, William Robinson, Ronald White, makeup, Richard Arrington; stunts, Bobby Bass.

Comedy/Romance **Cas.** **(PR:A-C MPAA:PG)**

MANON** (1987, Venezuela) 112m Gente de Cine c

Mayra Alejandra *(Manon)*, Victor Mallarino *(Roberto)*, Miguelangel Landa *(Lescaut)*, Eva Moreno *(Obsidiana)*, Gonzalo J. Camacho *(Diaz Lopez)*.

Abbe Prevost's novel *Manon Lescaut* has been adapted by several filmmakers, including silent versions made in 1914 (US) and 1916 (Germany) as well as 1950 and 1968 French renditions. This contemporary Venezuelan version emphasizes the story's soap opera elements, but provides none of the passion inherent in the events. Mallarino is a seminary student who meets the beautiful Alejandra along the road and is instantly attracted to her. He learns that she is on her way to a convent where she is being sent by her parents as punishment for a past affair. These plans are quickly altered when Mallarino slips her a note imploring her to run off with him. Using the cash his wealthy father has provided for his studies, Mallarino and his love hole up in a posh hotel suite. They live an extravagant life until their funds begin to run out. Mallarino writes a letter to his father explaining where he is and that he loves Alejandra, but he cannot bring himself to mail it. Alejandra, who is growing bored with Mallarino, furtively posts the letter and the seminarian's relatives kidnap him from the hotel. Alejandra then takes up with Camacho, a wealthy oilman. He showers her with jewels, while Mallarino is sent back to the seminary. Eventually Alejandra has a change of heart. She finds Mallarino, and again they run off, this time to a seaside house owned by Alejandra's aunt. Alejandra's roguish brother Landa arrives and attempts to introduce the pair to prostitution. When Camacho reenters the picture, Alejandra claims to still love him. She and Landa run off with him, but Mallarino finds them at Camacho's posh digs. Masquerading as Alejandra's brother, Mallarino is allowed to stay as well. The trio soon take flight again, deciding to head north to Miami. They take refuge in a brothel run by Landa's old girl friend Moreno, then hit the road once more. But Camacho has put his thugs on the group's trail, and

Alejandra is kidnaped. Mallarino is sent back to the seminary once again, though he ultimately breaks loose to search for Alejandra. After rejoining Landa, he finds Alejandra being held captive in an insane asylum. She is spirited out, but Camacho's men are soon back on the chase. There is a shoot-out, and Landa is killed. Mallarino and Alejandra manage to escape, though the girl is badly wounded. The two find a secluded area, where the doomed girl dies in her lover's arms.

Though MANON occasionally resembles SOMETHING WILD with its twisted road plot, the film never really amounts to much. Mallarino and Alejandra are good-looking leads with little acting ability. They run through their parts without much energy, never generating the spark this turbulent romance demands. This is MANON's greatest flaw. It's hard to believe in the central romance when the two lovers barely show any motivation for their often rash actions. Landa and Moreno are better, giving some life to their bawdy characters. Chalbaud directs in a fairly straightforward manner. A former television director, he shows an occasional flair for visuals but doesn't provide his material with any strength. MANON was popular in its native land, however, where *telenovela* romances of similar nature are regularly broadcast. That Chalbaud and Alejandra are both veterans of that medium undoubtedly added to MANON's Venezuelan success. Released in Venezuela in 1986.

p, Miguelangel Landa; d, Roman Chalbaud; w, Emilio Carballido, Roman Chalbaud (based on the novel *Manon Lescaut* by Abbe Prevost); ph, Javier Aguirresarobe; m, Federico Ruiz; ed, Jose Alcalde.

Drama/Romance **(PR:O MPAA:NR)**

MANON OF THE SPRING*½** (1987, Fr.) 113m Renn-Films A2-RAI 2-DD/Orion Classics c (MANON DES SOURCES; AKA: JEAN DE FLORETTE 2)

Yves Montand *(Cesar "Le Papet" Soubeyran)*, Daniel Auteuil *(Ugolin Soubeyran)*, Emmanuelle Beart *(Manon Cadoret)*, Hippolyte Girardot *(Bernard Olivier)*, Elisabeth Depardieu *(Aimee Cadoret)*, Gabriel Bacquier *(Victor)*, Armand Meffre *(Philoxene)*, Andre Dupon *(Pamphile)*, Pierre Nougaro *(Casimir)*, Jean Maurel *(Anglade)*, Roger Souza *(Ange)*, Didier Pain *(Eliacin)*, Pierre-Jean Rippert *(Cabridan)*, Marc Betton *(Martial)*, Yvonne Gamy *(Delphine)*, Chantal Liennel *(Amandine)*, Lucien Damiani *(Belloiseau)*, Fransined *(Florist)*, Jean Bouchard *(Priest)*, Tiki Olgado *(Specialist)*, Francoise Trompette *(Village Woman)*.

Six months after the mid-1987 US release of JEAN DE FLORETTE (nearly a full year after its Paris opening), MANON OF THE SPRING resumes the story and brings its characters to their tragic ends. Ten years have now passed and newcomer Beart plays Manon, the daughter of the hunchbacked farmer Jean (played by Gerard Depardieu in part one). She has grown into a beautiful young shepherdess who tends her flock deep in the hills of Provence. In the years since Depardieu's death, Montand and nephew Auteuil have worked his land into a profitable carnation farm by unplugging the underground spring that they kept secret from the hard-working farmer. Auteuil's vibrant red carnations now blossom in full glory, enabling him to save a small fortune. Montand, now old and withered, pushes his nephew toward marriage. Unless Auteuil takes a wife and begins a family, the name of Soubeyran (once the most-powerful family in the region) will cease to exist. Auteuil, however, has no desire to marry. He prefers to grow his carnations and wander lazily through the gorgeous countryside. One day he spots Beart bathing in a small spring and falls instantly in love, admiring her only from afar, however. His daily routine changes as thoughts of Beart fill his heart. Even though he knows that he and Montand are responsible for her father's death, he cannot stop thinking of her. Instead of speaking to her, he follows her around, hiding behind bushes and rocks. He kills birds and rabbits and places them in the traps she has set. When she accidentally leaves a red hair ribbon behind, Auteuil keeps it as a treasure. In an extreme act of devotion, he sews the ribbon to his chest to keep it near his heart. Montand, who has been watching the ecstatic Auteuil glow with his newfound love, finally asks his nephew the name of the lucky girl. Auteuil is reluctant at first, but because of his happiness he cannot keep her name a secret any longer. Montand, rather than exploding with rage, accepts the news with reserve. Montand treks into the hills to get a look at Beart and later comments to Auteuil that she looks exactly like her grandmother—a deceased relative of Depardieu's and the woman who many years before owned Depardieu's farm. Montand gives his blessing and advises Auteuil to do all he can to impress Beart. When he finally expresses his love to the shepherdess, she turns her back on him and runs off. He gives chase, all the time shouting declarations of love, but is unable to persuade her to reciprocate. Emotionally beaten, Auteuil returns to the village with no prospects for marriage and no chance of carrying on the Soubeyran name.

Later, upon overhearing two villagers' conversation, Beart learns that Auteuil and Montand were the ones that blocked her father's spring years ago. She takes vengeance by stopping the subterranean spring which supplies not only Auteuil's carnations but the entire village. The locals panic and the mayor is forced to call in an engineer to solve their problem. The engineer resorts to incomprehensible scientific jargon, while the villagers grow increasing irate. It's not long before people start bringing up Montand and Auteuil's past meddling with Depardieu's spring. Everyone in town knows of their past "sin," and at a special church service, the priest gives accusatory looks to the pair. Afterwards, Beart publicly accuses Montand and Auteuil of blocking her father's spring. Montand is indignant in his denial, but when another villager speaks out against him, the truth is made clear. Before Montand and Auteuil can return to their farm, however, Auteuil makes one final attempt to win Beart's love. She is repulsed by Auteuil and runs to the safety of Girardot, the handsome young village schoolteacher who loves her. Later, Montand finds Auteuil's lifeless body hanging from a tree, unable to go on living without Beart. Before taking his life, Auteuil had willed his savings to Beart. In the meantime, Beart and Girardot wed in a magnificent ceremony which is attended by her mother, a famed opera singer (Elisabeth Depardieu) from Paris. By now, Girardot has persuaded Beart to unplug the spring. Girardot believes that Depardieu, had he lived, would have wanted to gain the villagers' friendship instead of taking revenge. During a religious ceremony in the village square, the water pipes begin to breathe and water once again flows freely, causing most villagers to believe in miracles. Later, Montand learns some secrets of his past from a blind old woman who was a lifelong friend of Florette, Beart's grandmother. It is revealed that Montand had loved Florette when both of them were young. Shortly after he went off to war, she sent him a letter stating that she was pregnant and would, if he wished, wait for him to return. Montand, however, never received the letter, learning of its existence only now from the old villager. Florette, however, took his silence as a rejection and married a blacksmith from another village. She then gave birth to a child that was really Montand's. Montand then learns that the child was born a hunchback. He is hit with the tragic realization that he is responsible for the death of his own son (Depardieu) and that the name of Soubeyran would have been carried on. Instead of being a sad old man with endless regrets, he would have been a happy grandfather with a prosperous farmer as a son and a beautiful young granddaughter in Beart. Unable to live with his guilt any longer, the defeated Montand wills his entire estate to Beart. He then surrenders himself to death, lying on his bed with his rosary in hand.

Like JEAN DE FLORETTE, MANON OF THE SPRING is filled with marvelous photography, gorgeous rolling landscapes, and spectacular performances. While part one of this story favored Depardieu and his struggles against both man and nature, part two concentrates on the tragic end of Montand and his final reconciliation with the higher forces of fate. Montand, who is always brilliant, turns in a performance which surely ranks with his best work. Aging 10 years from one film to the next, the 66-year-old Montand wonderfully captures his character's transition, remorse, and self-reflection. It is not until the final days of his life that he realizes the mistakes he has made. He is exposed by the villagers who previously minded their own business. He is left alone by his nephew's suicide and must accept the fact that he and the Soubeyran name are not immortal. Finally, and most mercilessly, he has been duped by the gods of romance who intercepted the letter which was meant for him. As a result he has lived his entire life without the woman he loved, been unable to raise a family, and caused the death of the son he never knew he had. It is Greek tragedy at its finest—the likes of which are rarely seen anymore in modern cinema. While much of the film is unbearably traditional, it is still an admirable piece of entertainment. Written by Claude Berri (who also directed) and Gerard Brach, both films combine the literary aspect of the original (Marcel Pagnol's 1953 film, which was, in turn, the basis for a two-part novel) with a beautiful cinematic technique that harks backs to the French Realism of the 1930s and 1940s. Where MANON surpasses JEAN DE FLORETTE is in its portrayal of the villagers—a necessary aspect which was virtually absent from part one.

Both films boast the excellent performance of Auteuil as the manipulated young fool who is caught between Depardieu, Montand, and Beart. Beart, while lovely to look at is given very little to do besides play the object of Auteuil's desire—a nature-loving, harmonica-playing nymph. Instead of playing a real person, Beart is cast as the catalyst who brings about the downfall of Auteuil and Montand. MANON OF THE SPRING was the No. 4 box-office hit in France in 1986, after OUT OF AFRICA, JEAN DE FLORETTE, and ROCKY IV. Taken as a whole, JEAN DE FLORETTE and MANON OF THE SPRING earned a total of eight Cesars: Best Film, Best Director, Best Actor (Auteuil), Best Actress (Beart), Best Screenplay (Berri, Brach), Best Score (Petit), Best Cinematography (Nuytten), and Best Sound (Pierre Gamet, Dominique Hennequin). (In French; English subtitles.) *(Nudity, adult situations.)* (SEE: JEAN DE FLORETTE, 1987, Fr.)

p, Pierre Grunstein; d, Claude Berri; w, Claude Berri, Gerard Brach (based on the novel by Marcel Pagnol); ph, Bruno Nuytten (Technovision, Eastmancolor); m, Jean-Claude Petit, Giuseppe Verdi; ed, Genevieve Louveau, Herve de Luze; prod d, Bernard Vezat; cos, Sylvie Gautrelet; makeup, Michele Deruelle, Jean-Pierre Eychenne.

Drama **(PR:C MPAA:R)**

MANUELA'S LOVES** (1987, Fr.) 90m Antares-Selena Audiovisual AAA-Bullock Prods./AAA Classic c (LE JUPON ROUGE)

Marie-Christine Barrault *(Manuela)*, Alida Valli *(Bacha)*, Guillemette Grobon *(Claude)*.

A meditative and quiet picture which examines the relationship between three European women of different generations—Valli, a 60ish survivor of Nazi concentration camps turned author; Barrault, an independent 40-year-old who works as Valli's assistant; and Grobon, a pretty 27-year-old acquaintance of Valli who becomes Barrault's lover. Barrault, the title character, is a successful theatrical costume designer who has agreed to help Valli research a new book. A respected author and lecturer, Valli is a human rights activist who fights Apartheid and the sanctioned torture that occurs in many Third World countries. Physically and emotionally scarred by Nazi experiments which were performed on her leg, Valli's very existence is a struggle. Although admired throughout Europe, Valli's only true friend is Barrault. Barrault, however, finds a friend in Grobon and spends much of her free time with her, ignoring her commitment to Valli's book. As a result, her relationship with Valli suffers. Barrault's friendship with Grobon soon evolves into a lesbian love affair, which makes Valli uncomfortable. Her health failing and her mind deteriorating, Valli locks herself in her apartment and refuses to speak to Barrault, or anyone else, for days. Without informing anyone of her whereabouts, Valli disappears to a Belgian hospital. When Barrault learns where Valli is, she breaks off her relationship with Grobon and drives to Brussels.

Barrault and Valli resolve their differences and return to Paris, their friendship surviving the ordeal.

MANUELA'S LOVES can be most accurately described as a "women's film," as it makes every attempt to define its conflicts and emotions from a woman's viewpoint. Every scene and situation in the film in included for the purpose of addressing the relationships that exist between women. Although it often slips into pointless feminist propaganda ("With women, everything is possible," claims one character), the film is generally a realistic portrayal of friendship, love, and jealousy—emotions that need not be reserved "for women only." Valli (who has appeared in some of cinema's finest films from THE THIRD MAN to SENSO) is exceptional as the fiercely independent defender of human rights who refuses to share Barrault with anyone else or to accept her new lover. One of the finest scenes in the film is Valli's confrontation with Grobon as she learns that Barrault has begun a lesbian romance. Without explanation she slaps Grobon, who previously admired Valli. The slap is a devastating and revealing twist for Valli's character since she had previously been so vocal in her defense of people's rights. It is at that very instant that the deterioration of her mind is evident. While Barrault is the central character, it is Valli, in all her contradictions, who is the most complex—she preaches peace, nonviolence, and the tolerance of those who are different, but when she disapproves of Barrault's life-style, she lashes out with irrational violence. What makes her even more complex is the implication that she, too, is in love with Barrault and driven to her extreme actions by jealousy. Grobon, the dark and beautiful woman who innocently becomes the wedge between Barrault and Valli's friendship, is pleasantly surprising in an energetic and sexually vulnerable role. As superb as Valli is, she cannot carry the entire weight of the film on her own. Barrault and Grobon are fine actors, but the scripting of their relationship is trite and predictable. The lesbian lovemaking is handled gently but in a conventionally serious tone which includes a stereotypical exchange of longing glances and tender touches. One of the film's weakest points technically is director Lefebvre's fondness for playing out numerous scenes in telephone conversation—an expository device which is painfully tedious and uncinematic. The US release title, MANUELA'S LOVES, is a more exploitative and commercial title than LE JUPON ROUGE (The Red Skirt) but brings little to the film. The unprovocative French title comes from a picture that Barrault sketches of Grobon in which the latter wears only a long red skirt. The film includes a scene from the 1985 Susan Munoz documentary LAS MADRES DE PLAZA DE MAYO. *(Brief nudity, sexual situations, profanity.)*

p, Michele Dimitri; d, Genevieve Lefebvre; w, Genevieve Lefebvre, Nicole Berckmans; ph, Ramon Suarez; m, Joanna Bruzdowicz; ed, Josie Miljevic; art d, Danka Semenowicz; cos, Christina Olhson; makeup, Chantal Houdoy; tech adv, Claude Luquet.

Drama **(PR:C-O MPAA:NR)**

MANUSCRIPTS† (1987, Iran) 130m Farabi c

Jalil Farjad, Amir Vatanzad, Behnam Shafi'ie, Shapoor Bakhshai, Al R. Shoja Noori.

A young terrorist given the assignment of assassinating an officer of the revolutionary committee tells his victim of the plot. This alliance allows the revolutionary guards to obtain precise information about the terrorist organization. A confrontation follows in which the terrorist is killed by his own people, who are subsequently exposed and annihilated.

d, Mehrzad Minoui; w, Behrouz Afkhami; ph, Al Akbar Mazinani; m, Mohammad Mirzamani; ed, Mehrzad Minoui; makeup, Asghar Hemat.

Drama **(PR:NR MPAA:NR)**

MARSUPIALS: THE HOWLING III (SEE: HOWLING III, THE, 1987, Aus.)

MARUSA NI ONNA (SEE: TAXING WOMAN, A, 1987, Jap.)

MAS ALLA DEL SILENCIO† (1987, Venezuela) 119m Cinearte c (Trans: Beyond Silence)

Jean Carlos Simancas, Javier Vidal, Julie Restifo, Doris Wells, Luis Rivas, Jose Gregorio Lavado, Maria Isabel Calderon.

A strange crime film about a deaf-mute boy who falls in with a gang of thieves. They are pursued by a brutal cop who is determined to capture them. Meanwhile, the boy enrolls in a school for the deaf and learns sign language from an instructor whose wife has just left him. In a bizarre sub-plot, the instructor gets revenge on his unfaithful wife by playing audio tapes he has made of their connubial lovemaking over the phone to the woman's new lover. If that isn't enough, the instructor fends off the amourous advances of his gorgeous young female assistant because he has recently become attracted to a transvestite and suspects that the sleeping homoerotic giant within him has awakened. At the same time, the deaf-mute thief has fallen for a similarly afflicted girl, but the dogged copper is hot on his trail and threatens to ruin their happiness.

p&d, Cesar Bolivar; w, Cesar Bolivar, Jose Ignacio Cabrujas; ph, Jose Vincente Scheuren; m, Vinicio Ludovic; ed, Cesar Bolivar.

Crime **(PR:NR MPAA:NR)**

MAS BUENAS QUE EL PAN† (1987, Mex.) 91m Productores Tollocan/Peliculas Mexicanas c (Trans: Better Than Bread)

Lalo el Mimo [Eduardo de la Pena] *(Felemon)*, Lilia Prado *(Jovita, Moyer's Wife)*, Pedro Weber [Chatanuga] *(Moyer)*, Arlette Pacheco, Jacquelin Castro *(Felemon's Daughters)*, Alfonso Davila, Fernando Ciangherotti, Lupe Pallas, Charlie Valentino, Jaime Reyes, Paco Muller, Felipe Arriaga.

A Mexican sex comedy about two friends, Lalo el Mimo and Weber, who live for sex and soccer. Lalo el Mimo covets Weber's wife, Weber lusts after his friend's young daughters, and both hope to hit it big with soccer bets.

p, Guillermo Herrera; d, Alfredo B. Crevenna; w, Ramon Obon; ph, Juan Manuel Herrera; m, Gustavo Pimentel.

Comedy **(PR:NR MPAA:NR)**

MAS VALE PAJARO EN MANO . . . † (1987, Mex.) 86m Cinematografica Filmex/Peliculas Mexicanas c (Trans: A Bird In The Hand Is Worth . . .)

Lalo el Mimo [Eduardo de la Pena] *(Rafael Lara [Rafa])*, Sergio Ramos [El Comanche] *(Tropico)*, Julio Alvarado *(Kaliman)*, Guillermo Rivas *(El Borras)*, Leticia Perdigon *(Lucero)*, Oscar Fentanes *(Mecanico)*, Maricarmen Resendez *(Eva)*, Merle Uribe *(Anabel)*, Jacqueline Castro *(Nancy)*, Humberto Elizondo *(Lawyer)*, Pancho Muller, Jose Zambrano, Ariadne Welter, Cesar Bono.

Another Lalo el Mimo comedy which has the comedian chasing skirts (four of them this time) while running a number of auto repair shops. Eventually his wheeling and dealing gets him sent to prison where everyone envies his exciting life.

p, J. Fernando Perez Gavilan; d, Jesus Fragoso Montoya; w, Jesus Fragoso Montoya, Eduardo de la Pena; ph, Alberto Arellanos Bustamante; m, Gustavo C. Carrion; ed, Rogelio Zuniga.

Comedy **(PR:NR MPAA:NR)**

MASCARA*½** (1987, US/Belg./Neth./Fr.) 98m Iblis-Praxino-Dedalus Atlantic Consolidated/Cannon c

Charlotte Rampling *(Gaby Hart, Widow)*, Michael Sarrazin *(Bert Sanders, Police Superintendent)*, Derek De Lint *(Chris Brine, Costume Designer)*, Jappe Claes *(Col. March)*, Herbert Flack *(David Hyde)*, Harry Cleven *(PC)*, Serge-Henri Valcke *(Harry Wellman)*, Romy Haag *(Lana)*, Eva Robbins *(Pepper)*, John Van Dreelen *(Minister Weinberger)*, Norma Christine Deumner *(Salome)*, Pascale Jean-Louis *(Divine)*, Alexandra Van Der Noot *(Euridice)*, Mark Verstraete *(Police Officer)*, Hugo Van Den Berghe, Lou De Prijck *(Policemen)*, Charlotte Berden *(Gaby's Daughter)*, Marie-Luce Bonfanti *(Norma)*, Carmela Locantore *(Orfeo)*, Lois Chacon *(Shanghai Lili)*, Michel Laborde *(Tcha Tcha Thai)*, Alain Zerar *(Tina Turner)*, Lida Lobo *(Golden Woman)*, Natalie Fritz *(Dead Body)*, Serge "Lydie" Lambert *(Gambler)*, Katja Delvos *(Divine's Shadow)*, Terry Fischer *(Opera Manager)*, Dimitri Anastasiades, Patrick Boets, Didier Bouillon, Katia, Patrick De Breuck, Hilt De Vos, Dorine Esser, Alberto Garcia, Jean Haster, Vincent Jongen, Rio Menegazzi, Michel Minuzzi, Michel Olemans, Carine Peeters, Roger Sabo, Sabrina, Yvan David, Patrice Septier, Jean-Paul Souille, Boas Toorgeman, Annick Van Avermaet, Marc Van Crombrugge, Frank Van Malder, Hillary Wagenar *(Creatures at Mister Butterfly)*, Firmin Allary, Jo Bertrand, Henri De Blaere, Josef De Busschere, Thean Decco, Marnix De Kuyper, Julien Demey, Charles De Wael, Joris Ghekire, Peter Grunenwald, Mark Janssens, Piet Labian, Alfons Maes, Louis Parez, Dirk Pierloot, Sebastien Radovitch, Tony Roels, Francis Rolot, Jean-Claude Soetens, Jan Vanderborght, Robert Van Cleemput, Johan Vandermeulen, Mike Vanderstraete, Gaston Van Laere, Christ Vermandere, Willy Wouters, Marco Wyn *(Members at Mister Butterfly)*.

While attending the festive premiere of the opera "Orfeo ed Euridice," police superintendent Sarrazin is called away to investigate an apparent suicide. He leaves behind his widowed sister (Rampling), who is quickly befriended by the show's costume designer (De Lint). In his office the following day, Sarrazin is given information, from a known transvestite (Haag), which indicates that the death he is investigating is a murder, a notion he rejects contemptuously. Sarrazin then unexpectedly requests Euridice's costume from De Lint for a friend to wear at a surprise birthday party. De Lint agrees, but only after he has convinced

himself that the costume will be worn by Rampling, with whom he has become infatuated. De Lint guardedly accompanies Sarrazin and the costume to Mister Butterfly, an underground nightclub along the coast. After De Lint is locked in a subterranean dressing room, Sarrazin presents the dress to Deumner, a youthful transvestite with whom he has carried on a lengthy platonic relationship. In Deumner's dressing room after the performance, Sarrazin works himself into a frenzy as he describes the happiest memory of his adolescence—a public display of affection that he received from his sister following her confirmation. Deumner mistakes this as a declaration of love and comes on to the policeman, prompting a maniacal eruption from Sarrazin that results in Deumner's death. This emotional rage turns into insane jealousy when Sarrazin learns that De Lint's friendship with Rampling has blossomed into an affair. When Haag becomes suspicious of the detective following the disappearance of Deumner, Sarrazin borrows the costume again and entices Haag into wearing it during her next performance at the club. Duplicating the method he used to eliminate Deumner, Sarrazin murders Haag and tries to frame De Lint, who, in the meantime, has been telling Rampling about Sarrazin's unusual behavior. The now deranged Sarrazin invites De Lint to again accompany him to the nightclub, where he himself dons the gown and performs the opera on stage. Still wearing the gown after the show, Sarrazin provokes De Lint with his sexual advances, then beats him in the labyrinthine corridors, before knocking him through a railing and into the raging sea below. When Rampling arrives, Sarrazin declares his love for her before toppling from the pier. After De Lint is pulled from the water unharmed, the pair unite in a desperate embrace.

In "MASCARA," director Patrick Conrad has provided a humorous and intriguing chronicle of a character's absurd descent into madness. He unleashes his characters in the exotic worlds of opera and transvestism—both of which prominently feature the use of masks—to explore the secret malevolence that underlies their behavior. Sarrazin's love for his sister has been as impossible to control as it has been to express. From the idealized memory of his adolescence, where he recognizes but cannot articulate his love for his sister, to the unfulfilled experiences of his adulthood, where he is truly reviled by the sexual displays of women, he has been uncontrollably drawn by feminine beauty, and takes refuge in the hidden world of the transvestite. His sister, Rampling, knows of his obsessions, but she fears confronting them, and as a result has become a veritable prisoner in his maddening world. Moreover, it is implied that Sarrazin may be responsible for Rampling's widowhood. De Lint tries to extricate Rampling from the madness of the world she occupies. The film continually focuses on impenetrable surfaces and enigmatic dialog. Rampling and Sarrazin are both terrified of darkened or enclosed spaces, but they never seem to find their way into the more open and less unsettling ones. Surface reality is frequently meant to deceive, and the characters are often confused. Outside the window of De Lint's flat, Rampling watches the separate planes of sea and land blur together. The impenetrable blueness of the water suddenly becomes indistinguishable from the glistening blondness of the sand. It is this presentation of a world that walks the fine line between the real and the unreal, and frequently blurs the distinctions between them, that gives the film its strength. *(Sexual situations, adult situations, violence.)*

p, Pierre Drouot, Rene Solleveld, Henry Lange; d, Patrick Conrad; w, Hugo Claus, Patrick Conrad, Pierre Drouot (based on an idea by Patrick Conrad); ph, Gilberto Azevedo; m, Egisto Macchi, Richard Strauss, Vincenzo Bellini, Christoph Willibald von Gluck, Franz Peter Schubert; ed, Susana Rossberg; art d, Dirk Debou, Misjel Vermeiren; set d, Veronique Mellery; cos, Yan Tax; m/l, Woody Herman, Joe Bishop, Lou Singer, Boris Bergman, J.P. Hawks, S. Van Holme, Danny Klein, R. Haag, P. Conrad, Lou De Prijck, Kris Kristofferson; makeup, Claudine Thryion; stunts, Thierry Hallard.

Thriller **(PR:O MPAA:NR)**

MASCHENKA† (1987, Brit./Ger.) 103m Clasart/Goldcrest c

Cary Elwes *(Ganin)*, Irina Brook *(Maschenka)*, Sunnyi Melles *(Lilli)*, Jonathan Coy *(Alfyrov)*, Freddie Jones *(Podtyagin)*, Michael Gough *(Vater)*, Jean-Claude Brialy *(Kolin)*, Lena Stolze *(Klara)*.

An adaptation of Vladimir Nabokov's novel *Mary* which stars the stunning Brook as the title character—a Russian woman loved by Elwes when they both lived in pre-revolutionary Russia. They've since separated and emigrated to Berlin, but Brook has married another in the process. When they reunite in 1924 Berlin, their romance is rekindled. Director Goldschmidt's previous outing was SHE'LL BE WEARING PINK PAJAMAS.

p, Herbert G. Kloiber, Fritz Buddenstedt; d, John Goldschmidt; w, John Mortimer (based on the novel *Mary* by Vladimir Nabokov); ph, Wolgang Treu (Geyer Berlin Color); m, Nick Glowna; ed, Tanja Schmidbauer; prod d, Jan Schlubach; art d, Albrect Conrad; cos, Barbara Baum.

Historical/Romance **(PR:NR MPAA:NR)**

MASKARADA† (1987, Pol.) Karol Irzykowski Film Studio-DOM c (Trans: The Masquerade)

Boguslaw Linda, Zbigniew Zapasiewicz, Teresa Budzisz-Krzyzanowska, Jadwiga Jankowska-Cieslak, Piotr Fronczewski, Andrzej Zaorski.

An acclaimed actor leaves the profession and moves to the solitude of a desolate ranch where he contemplates the limits of his art. At the same time, a rising young actor finds himself inundated with more work than he can handle. Although successful, he tires of being considered "number two" and determines to engage the retired veteran in a performance duel to prove his superiority.

d&w, Janusz Kijowski (partly based on the writings of Stanislaw Ignacy Witkiewicz [Witkacy]); ph, Przemyslaw Skwirczynski; m, Janusz Stoklosa, Mariusz Bogdanowicz; ed, Halina Prugar-Ketling; art d, Halina Dobrowolska.

Drama **(PR:NR MPAA:NR)**

MASQUES† (1987, Fr.) 100m MK2-Films A2/Cannon Classics c

Philippe Noiret *(Christian Legagneur)*, Robin Renucci *(Roland Wolf)*, Bernadette Lafont *(Patricia Marquet)*, Monique Chaumette *(Colette)*, Anne Brochet *(Catherine)*, Roger Dumas *(Manuel Marquet)*, Pierre-Francois Dumeniaud *(Max)*, Pierre Nougaro *(Gustave)*, Renee Dennsy *(Emilie)*, Yvonne Decade *(Antoinette)*, Blanche Ariel *(Rosette)*, Rene Marjac *(Maurice)*, Paul Vally *(Henry)*, Denise Pezzani *(Madame Lemonier)*, Pierre Risch *(Monsieur Loury)*, Michel Dupuy *(Assistant)*, Henri Attal *(Supervisor at Aida)*, Dominique Zardi *(Totor)*, Francois Lafont *(Man in Overalls)*.

Claude Chabrol once again juggles Hitchcockian themes and situations in his latest suspenser MASQUES, his first of two films this year (LE CRI DI HIBOU is the second). Noiret stars as the celebrity host of a television dating game show for the elderly. He is approached by young journalist Renucci, who is eager to write an autobiography of the celebrity. Renucci is invited to Noiret's country estate and they begin the memoirs. In reality, however, Renucci is not a reporter but the older brother of "Madeleine"—a friend of Noiret's goddaughter Brochet. "Madeleine" has disappeared and Noiret is suspected of killing her. Upon further investigation Renucci discovers proof that Noiret is keeping Brochet is a drug-induced stupor and stealing her sizable inheritance. Renucci and Brochet fall in love and plan to start a new life in Paris when Noiret catches on to their scheme. He and his co-conspirators—secretary Chaumette and chauffeur/cook Dumeniaud—shoot up Brochet with drugs, toss her body in a car, and take it to a wrecking company where it will be demolished. Renucci saves his love just in time and they confront Noiret at his television studio where he breaks down. Shown in competition at the Berlin Film Festival and released in England by Cannon. (In French; English subtitles.)

p, Marin Karmitz; d, Claude Chabrol; w, Claude Chabrol, Odile Barski; ph, Jean Rabier (Agfa Color); m, Matthieu Chabrol; ed, Monique Fardoulis; art d, Francoise Benoit-Frecso; md, Michel Ganot; cos, Magali Fustier; makeup, Jackie Reynal, Josee de Luca.

Drama **(PR:NR MPAA:NR)**

MASSACRE IN DINOSAUR VALLEY† (1987, It.) 82m Doral c

Michael Sopkiw *(Kevin)*, Susane Carvall [Suzanne Carvalho] *(Ellie)*, Milton Morris, Martha Anderson, Joffrey Soares, Gloria Cristal, Susie Hahn, Marie Reis, Andy Silas, Leonid Bayer, Carlos Imperial, Samuca, Ney Pen, Albert Silva, Jonas Dalbecchi, Paul Sky, Indio Xin, Robert Roney.

Straight-to-home-video exploitation film in which no dinosaurs are seen, only normal-sized leeches. A light plane crashes in a swamp stranding its passengers. One passenger, an archeologist played by Sopkiw (star of last year's MONSTER SHARK) must save the two female passengers from snakes, quicksand, hostile natives, and the aforementioned leeches before discovering dinosaur footprints. Just then a vicious mining boss kidnaps the trio and puts them to work among the slave labor at his digs. Once again Sopkiw must engineer a daring escape. Filmed in Brazil in 1985.

d, Michael E. Lemick [Michele Tarantini]; w, Michael E. Lemick [Michele Tarantini]; ph, Edison Batista (Luciano Vittori Color); ed, Michael E. Lemick [Michele Tarantini]; art d, Mauro Monteiro.

Adventure **Cas.** **(PR:NR MPAA:NR)**

MASTERBLASTER* (1987) 84m Radiance-First American Entertainment/Artist Entertainment Group c

Jeff Moldovan *(Jeremy Hawk)*, Donna Rosae *(Samantha)*, Joe Hess *(DeAngelo)*, Peter Lundblad *(Lewis)*, Robert Goodman *(Mike)*, Richard St. George, George Gill, Earleen Carey, Jim Reynolds, Julian Byrd, Ron Burgs, Tracy Hutchinson, Bill Whorman, Ray Forchion, Lou Ann Carroll, Kari Whitman.

One of those pictures where the credits read like a laundry list, MASTERBLASTER was made by Radiance Films International and/or First Entertainment and was released by Artists Entertainment domestically and by Overseas Filmgroup everywhere else. No matter. In MAD MAX BEYOND THUNDERDOME, there was a character called "Masterblaster" who was actually a combination of two people. "Master" was the dwarf Angelo Rossitto (who has been around since 1927) and "Blaster" was the behemoth Paul Larsson. This movie, unfortunately, took nothing but the title from the exciting Mel Gibson/Tina Turner starrer. It's a rehash of survival game pictures like TAG, THE ZERO BOYS, and GOTCHA, all superior to this. Co-author Moldavan is part of a tournament. The idea is that someone will survive the assassination game and win a prize. Former Vietnam soldier Moldavan is all for the tournament which features guns with paint instead of bullets. Do we need to tell you that someone is running around shooting real bullets? There are a few attempts at leading the audience astray with false clues and, for a while, we are gifted with more red herrings than a Moscow fish store. Many of the "dead" characters seem to mysteriously come back to life and there is no explanation for some of the occurrences. Little money was spent on this Florida-based picture and it shows. Several stunt people worked behind and in front of the camera, including director Wilder, who began as a stunt driver in THE LOVE BUG and did similar chores on such films as SHAMUS, ROUSTABOUT, MARCH OR DIE, and WHITE LIGHTNING. *(Violence.)*

p, Randy Grinter; d, Glenn R. Wilder; w, Randy Grinter, Glenn R. Wilder, Jeff Moldovan (based on a story by Randy Grinter); ph, Frank Pershing Flynn; m, Alain Salvati; ed, Angelo Ross; stunts, Scott Wilder.

Action **Cas.** **(PR:C-O MPAA:R)**

MASTERS OF THE UNIVERSE½** (1987) 106m Golan, Globus-Edward R. Pressman/Cannon c

Dolph Lundgren *(He-Man)*, Frank Langella *(Skeletor)*, Meg Foster *(Evil-Lyn)*, Billy Barty *(Gwildor)*, Courteney Cox *(Julie Winston)*, James Tolkan *(Detective Lubic)*, Christina Pickles *(Sorceress of Castle Greyskull)*, Robert Duncan McNeill *(Kevin)*, Jon Cypher *(Man-at-Arms)*, Chelsea Field *(Teela)*.

Cashing in on the toy line begun in the early 1980s and the Saturday morning TV cartoon show, *He-Man*, this overblown but technically interesting action film is a child's vision of space violence. MASTERS OF THE UNIVERSE is eventually disappointing and boasts no end of violence, the bane of every concerned parent. Lundgren is a terse and taciturn He-Man who is guided by furball dwarf Barty, creator of a magic key that gives unlimited power to its owner, one that opens the secrets of the universe. When the key is lost, Lundgren must search for it, along with the abducted good sorceress, Pickles, who is held captive by Langella, playing the dreaded Skeletor. All of this occurs on the distant planet of Eternia but the key somehow makes its way to earth and winds up in the possession of teenager Cox who is having trouble with boy friend McNeill. Lundgren and Barty, along with nemesis Langella, appear on earth and begin battling in their frantic search for the key. The film is ablaze with laser beams blasting opponents and walls to pieces and Langella parades about making speeches to feed his gigantic Skeletor ego, even gliding down the streets of Whittier, California on a surf-board like spacecraft as a sort of king of the roses parade. Lundgren and the evil Langella finally get locked into a wild battle and Lundgren winds up victorious (what else?), obtaining the key, with Cox's help. He, in turn, rewards the teenager with a trip through space.

This film is an obvious takeoff on STAR WARS and the grunting CONAN films with the bad guys strutting about in Darth Vader costumes and Barty doing a Yoda impression which isn't half bad. Langella intones endless stentorian lines such as: "I must possess all or I possess nothing," and "The Alpha and Omega: Death and Rebirth." Lundgren, who played the machine-like Russian boxer (he is six foot six inches) in ROCKY IV, merely flexes his muscles through this action film. There are many touches that will interest space fanatics, such as Barty changing an ancient fin-tipped American car into a spaceship and various other

special effects gimmicks that show some inventiveness. But this Golan-Globus production, budgeted at a little more than $15 million, the first feature-length film to spin off from a toy series, is definitely from the wrong side of the space tracks. *(Violence.)*

p, Menahem Golan, Yoram Globus; d, Gary Goddard; w, David Odell; ph, Hanania Baer (Metrocolor); m, Bill Conti; ed, Anne V. Coates; prod d, William Stout; art d, Robert Howland; set d, Daniel Gluck, Michael Johnson; cos, Julie Weiss; spec eff, Richard Edlund; makeup, Michael Westmore; stunts, Walter Scott.

Fantasy **(PR:C-O MPAA:PG)**

MATAR O MORIR† (1987, Mex.) 99m Cumbre/Peliculas Mexicanas c (Trans: Kill Or Die)

Vicente Fernandez *(Arturo Mendoza)*, Pedro Armendariz, [Jr.] *(Lt. Anthony Collins)*, Humberto Herrera *(Vicente Mendoza)*, Gabriela Leon *(Daniela)*, Maria Montano, Julieta Rosen, Lena Jimenez, Alma Thelma, Tito Guillen, Raul Guerrero, Manolo Cardenas.

Popular Mexican ranchero singer Fernandez stars in this comedy-murder mystery as a robust old rodeo rider who carouses with his equally vigorous son, Herrera, with both competing for the same women. One day Fernandez learns that his son has stolen from him to pay off gambling debts. Outraged, the old man disowns Herrera, only to be informed months later that the boy has been shot to death north of the border. Fernandez goes to the US to be near the investigation and finds that he must contend with a Mexican-hating cop, Armendariz.

p, Luis Berkis; d, Rafael Villasenor Kuri; w, Fernando Galiana; ph, Javier Cruz; m, Carlos Torres; ed, Max Sanchez.

Comedy/Mystery **(PR:NR MPAA:NR)**

MATEWAN**** (1987) 132m Red Dog/Cinecom c

Chris Cooper *(Joe Kenehan)*, Will Oldham *(Danny Radnor)*, Jace Alexander *(Hillard)*, Ken Jenkins *(Sephus Purcell)*, Bob Gunton *(C.E. Lively)*, Gary McCleery *(Ludie)*, Kevin Tighe *(Hickey)*, Gordon Clapp *(Griggs)*, Mary McDonnell *(Elma Radnor)*, James Earl Jones *("Few Clothes" Johnson)*, James Kizer *(Tolbert)*, Michael Preston *(Ellix)*, Jo Henderson *(Mrs. Elkins)*, Nancy Mette *(Bridey Mae)*, Joe Grifasi *(Fausto)*, Ronnie Stapleton *(Stennis)*, David Strathairn *(Police Chief Sid Hatfield)*, Ida Williams *(Mrs. Knightes)*, Maggie Renzi *(Rosaria)*, Thomas A. Carlin *(Turley)*, Tom Wright *(Tom)*, Josh Mostel *(Mayor Cabell Testerman)*, Davide Ferrario *(Gianni)*, Frank Payne, Jr. *(Old Miner)*, Stephen C. Hall *(Redneck Miner)*, Bill Morris *(Bass)*, Michael A. Mantel *(Doolin)*, Charles Haywood *(Sheb)*, Neale Clark *(Issac)*, Fred Decker *(James)*, Michael Frasher *(Lee Felts)*, John Sayles *(Hardshell Preacher)*, Jenni Cline *(Luann)*, Delmas Lawhorn *(Conductor)*, Hazel Dickens *(MT Singer)*, Thomas Poore *(Injured Black Man)*, Hazel Pearl *(Missus)*, Hal Phillips *(Boxcar Guard)*, Mitch Scott *(Mister)*, Percy Fruit *(Black Miner)*, Gerald Milnes *(Fiddler)*, William Dean, P. Michael Munsey *(Brokers)*, Mason Daring *(Picker)*, Tara Williams *(Woman)*.

Made for $4 million but looking as if it cost three times that amount, this is the finest film so far from America's best-known independent filmmaker, John Sayles. As the film opens, Oldham, a 15-year-old coal miner, scurries around in a mine carrying the news that the Stone Mountain Coal Company of Matewan, West Virginia, has decided to lower the tonnage rate paid the miners—again. A strike is called. A fuse sizzles away and the screen explodes into white. In voice-over, Oldham, as an old man, is heard: "Hit were 1920 in the southwest field and things was tough. The miners was trying to bring in the union to West Virginia and the coal operators and their gun thugs was set on keepin' 'em out." Cooper, a pacifist and former Wobbly, is sent by the United Mine Workers to coordinate the strike and to keep it from becoming violent, which would play into the hands of the owners, anxious to loose their mercenaries on the strikers. The striking miners are slow to accept Cooper; moreover, a group of Italian immigrants continues to work, as do the black miners whom the company has brought from Alabama. Cooper tries to bring all the miners together, but events come to a head when the company tries to sneak the "scabs" in for a night shift. The strikers confront the non-union miners and the company's armed guards at the mine

entrance. A gun battle seems inevitable, but Jones, the majestic black leader, tosses down his shovel and joins the strike, followed by the others. Tighe and Clapp, heavies for the Baldwin-Felts Detective Agency, are dispatched to deal with the strike and its "red" instigator. When they attempt to carry out evictions from company housing, they are stopped by poker-faced, gun-toting police chief Strathairn and mayor Mostel, who refuse to be bought. Later, at the camp the miners and their families have set up outside of town, Tighe and Clapp try to repossess company goods. This time a hunting party of hillfolk comes to the rescue.

Slowly, the three factions of the miners grow into a community. After a late-night attack on the camp, the native West Virginian miners retaliate. Keeping Cooper in the dark, they dynamite a mine shaft and wait in ambush for the company gunmen. It is the miners, however, who are ambushed, betrayed by Gunton, a company spy in their midst. Gunton tries to frame Cooper as the turncoat, telling Mette, a widow who has fallen for Cooper, that he has ridiculed her love letter and called her a whore. Coached by Gunton, she claims that Cooper raped her, and produces a letter implicating him as the spy. Jones draws the assignment of assassinating Cooper. At his mother's boarding house, Oldham is caught eavesdropping on Tighe and Clapp's discussion of Gunton's plan and threatened with the death of his mother (McDonnell) if he tells anyone. However, the boy is also a preacher, and that night, as Tighe and Clapp reel drunkenly in a back pew, Oldham twists the parable of Joseph and Potiphar beyond recognition, making clear to the assembled miners that Cooper has been wrongly accused. Saved from execution, Cooper can do no wrong in the miners' eyes. The strike spreads like wildfire, from holler to holler, with the Matewan miners its missionaries. Alexander, a teenage miner, is murdered by Clapp when he refuses to name names. At the same time, a new contingent of Baldwin-Felts thugs arrives and issues an ultimatum to Strathairn and Mostel. A showdown seems certain for the next day. In the early morning mist, the police chief and the mayor approach the mercenaries along the railroad tracks that are main-street Matewan. Cooper, sensing trouble, runs to town, too late. Bullets fly from everywhere; the miners appear from windows and around corners, blasting away. In the bloody, helter-skelter gun battle, most of the Baldwin-Felts agents are killed, but so is Mostel—and so is Cooper. The film ends with the image of Oldham back in the mine, his voice, as old as the hills, providing the epilog.

Many critics found MATEWAN a too well-intentioned and flawed film, citing melodramatic elements and political naivety, calling it overly romanticized. In addressing these criticisms, it is useful to consider Vincent Canby's contention that the union struggle depicted in MATEWAN is not viewed in a vacuum but with the knowledge of more than 60 years of labor triumphs and failures, including widespread corruption and leadership's loss of touch with the rank and file. MATEWAN is about the *promise* of unions and of people coming together. In it Sayles has captured the feel of a 1930s "people united" film, but grounded it in the complex reality of a world that refuses to present easy choices or idealized solutions. At its heart is Cooper's attempt to bring in the union without violence. The battle of Matewan may have temporarily put the company on the run, but the huge death toll of the coal wars of 1920-21 bears out Cooper's promise that violence would beget slaughter. Ironically, pacifist Cooper is among the first victims of that violence. Moreover, in the end, after the unity, after the struggle, after the deaths, there is no workers' utopia. Oldham returns to the mines, a union man—though still at risk of cave-ins and black lung—part of a community, enduring.

MATEWAN has the earmarks of Ford and Steinbeck, yet as reminiscent as it is of THE GRAPES OF WRATH, Sayles' film has even more in common with the great Ford westerns, borrowing their genre structure and sharing Ford's concern for community. In the manner of Ford, Sayles uses music as a celebration of community. Though perhaps a little heavy-handedly, he presents the music of three different cultures and then unites them in one hopeful song—the Italian mandolin player joined by the Appalachian fiddler and guitarist, and finally by the black harmonica player. MATEWAN, too, has its laconic good man with a gun, Strathairn, facing the money-grubbing forces of evil, but it also has the pacifist Cooper. Sayles tells the story from the point of view of both Oldham, a insider, and Cooper, an outsider. His decision to have a "red" hero was a daring one, though as a former Wobbly, Joe Kenehan would have been concerned with the workers' lot back when the czar still ruled in St. Petersburg.

After beginning his career as a screenwriter, Sayles has generally been praised for his dialog and characters, but critics have often noted the uncinematic quality of his films. In MATEWAN, with the help of Oscar-winning cinematographer Wexler, he shows a firm grasp of the grammar of the cinema. MATEWAN is beautifully shot, capturing the shifting light of the hills, the moody indoor lighting of tents and bars, the ominous cold and damp of the mine. Yet, as Sayles notes in his book *Thinking in Pictures: The Making of the Movie Matewan* (a step-by-step how-to on low-budget independent filmmaking), they have purposely eschewed a self-conscious, authorial camera, letting the action and the characters lead the viewer, drawing the audience into the story. Trying to evoke a period feel without using filters or tinting film stock, they manipulated the color and texture before the camera, and much credit is due production designer Chavooshian and costume designer Flynt, working on budgets of $96,000 and $25,000 respectively. The film was shot entirely in West Virginia, with the town of Thurmond standing for the too-modern Matewan and the Beckley Exhibition Coal Mine providing the below-ground scenes

There is not a weak performance in the film. Jones is a tower of dignity as the legendary "Few Clothes," to whom Louis Untermeyer dedicated his poem "Black Caliban of the Coal Mines." With the muscles of his face moving as if each were a character, he is forceful without upstaging anyone. Cooper is the epitome of quiet strength, sincerity, and conviction, cut from the mold of Henry Fonda or Gary Cooper. Oldham, a young performer and playwright from the Actors Theater in Louisville, glows with the passion of a zealot, first for God, then for the union. Tighe (TV's "Emergency") is a wonderful villain, every bit the hideous creep. A host of Sayles regulars also turn in stellar performances (Strathairn, Henderson, Clapp, and Renzi—the coproducer and Sayles' significant other), and as is his wont, Sayles appears as a red-bashing preacher and is hilarious. Sayles' script for the film was almost eight years old. He had hitchhiked through West Virginia in the 1960s and heard tales of the coal wars and the Matewan Massacre. Some of what he heard went into his second novel, *Union Dues*; the rest inspired MATEWAN, with its mix of historical and fictional characters. Prior to MATEWAN, only one film had dealt with the topic, "Smilin' Sid," a silent short whose only print was destroyed. The financing of the film took several years, and fell through two and a half times. Between attempts, Sayles made THE BROTHER FROM ANOTHER PLANET. Cinecom had a great deal of success as that picture's distributor and decided to finance MATEWAN. Sayles' film has the look and feel of a classic, and it is surprising that many critics—so often longing for the movies of the past—found fault with it for just that reason. *(Graphic violence, profanity.)*

p, Peggy Rajski, Maggie Renzi; d&w, John Sayles; ph, Haskell Wexler (DuArt Color); m, Mason Daring; ed, Sonya Polonsky; prod d, Nora Chavooshian; art d, Dan Bishop; set d, Anamarie Michnevich, Leslie Pope; cos, Cynthia Flynt; makeup, James Sarzotti.

Drama **(PR:C MPAA:PG-13)**

MATKA KROLOW† (1987, Pol.) 127m Zespoly Filmowe-"X"-Rondo/Filmpolski bw (Trans: The Mother of Kings)

Magda Teresa Wojcik *(Lucja Krol)*, Boguslaw Linda *(Klemens Krol)*, Zbigniew Zapasiewicz *(Dr. Wiktor Lewen)*, Franciszek Pieczka *(Cyga)*, Michael Juszczakiewicz *(Stasio Krol)*, Adam Ferency *(Zenon)*, Krzysztof Zaleski *(Roman)*.

This stark black-and-white drama is the story of a brave Mother Courage, Wojcik, who cleans and washes for others with only one dream—to bring up her children to be good people. When a Communist intellectual neighbor, Zapasiewicz, befriends the poverty stricken family, she hides him in her flat and allows him to hold Communist meetings. When he is arrested, she takes him parcels and patiently waits for him since it is her duty. After the war, her whole family is together again, until the arrest and torture of her Communist son Linda, accused by the new regime of being a collaborator. She then writes to the party chief, asking permission to keep her large apartment because she's waiting for her sons to return, unaware that Linda has died in prison. Wojcik won Best Actress laurels for her part and the film won the Gold Lion of Gdansk Award.

d&w, Janusz Zaorski (based on the novel by Kazimierz Brandys); ph, Edward Klosinski, Witold Adamek; m, Przemyslaw Gintrowski; ed, Jozef Bartczak; set d, Teresa Barska.

Drama **(PR:NR MPAA:NR)**

MAURICE**½ (1987, Brit.) 140m Cinecom-Merchant Ivory-Film Four Intl./Cinecom c

James Wilby *(Maurice Hall)*, Hugh Grant *(Clive Durham)*, Rupert Graves *(Alec Scudder)*, Denholm Elliott *(Dr. Barry)*, Simon Callow *(Mr. Ducie)*, Billie Whitelaw *(Mrs. Hall)*, Ben Kingsley *(Lasker-Jones)*, Judy Parfitt *(Mrs. Durham)*, Phoebe Nicholls *(Anne Durham)*, Mark Tandy *(Risley)*, Helena Mitchell *(Ada Hall)*, Kitty Aldridge *(Kitty Hall)*, Patrick Godfrey *(Simcox)*, Michael Jenn *(Archie)*, Barry Foster *(Dean Cornwalis)*, Peter Eyre *(Mr. Borenius)*, Catherine Rabett *(Pippa Durham)*, Orlando Wells *(Young Maurice)*, Helena Bonham Carter *(Young Lady at Cricket Match)*, Mark Payton *(Chapman)*, Maria Britneva *(Mrs. Sheepshanks)*, John Elmes *(Hill)*, Alan Foss *(Old Man at Train)*, Philip Fox *(Dr. Jowitt)*, Olwen Griffiths *(Mrs. Scudder)*, Chris Hunter *(Fred Scudder)*, Breffni McKenna *(Guardsman)*, Phillada Sewell *(Matron)*, Mathew Sim *(Fetherstonhaugh)*, Harriet Thorpe *(Barmaid)*, Julian Wadham *(Hull)*, Richard Warner *(Judge)*, Alan Whybrow *(Mr. Scudder)*, Miles Richardson, Andrew St. Clair, Gerald McArthur *(Undergraduates)*.

Following the enormous success of A ROOM WITH A VIEW, the producer director team of Ismail Merchant and James Ivory undertook yet another E.M. Forster adaptation, MAURICE (pronounced like the finicky cat). Based on the novel that Forster began in 1914 and periodically revised for the rest of his life, this story of a young man's homosexual awakening couldn't be published in an England where homosexuality was still unlawful, and didn't reach print until 1971, the year after the author's death.

Wilby plays the title character, a slightly wide-eyed underclassman at Cambridge in 1910. His middle-class Christian worldview is challenged by his elder and better classmates who espouse the glories of classical civilization, particularly the Platonic ideal of love between men. Wilby and Grant, an aristocratic music student, grow increasingly closer, until one day Grant tells Wilby that he loves him. Confused, Wilby initially rebuffs Grant and then confesses his love, too, and attempts to consummate it physically. This time Grant is reticent, convincing Wilby that to undertake "the unspeakable" would sully the purity of their relationship. They remain in love but do not become lovers (save for an occasional kiss). Even after Wilby is expelled from Cambridge, their relationship endures, with Wilby a frequent guest at Grant's ancestral country manor house. Living at home with his widowed mother Whitelaw and sisters Mitchell and Aldridge, Wilby follows in his father's footsteps to become a stockbroker and Grant becomes a barrister. Together they conduct an elegant London social life until Tandy, a Cambridge classmate, has his career ruined when he is convicted of making a homosexual proposition. Afraid to testify on behalf of his old friend and terrified at the thought of his own exposure, Grant takes ill and convalesces with a trip to Greece. When he returns, Grant renounces their relationship to the grief-stricken Wilby, declaring his intention to begin a "normal" life. Soon thereafter, he marries Nicholls, a charming lightweight, and undertakes a political career. Wilby also attempts to put his desires behind him. He consults family physician Elliott, but is told that there is nothing wrong with him, that his desires are rubbish. Wilby also visits Kingsley, an American hypnotist, but his attempts to channel Wilby's interest toward women fail and he advises the young man to move to France or Italy where there is tolerance for such proclivities. While a house guest, Wilby arouses Graves, Grant's rustic gamekeeper. One night, without warning, Graves comes to Wilby's bedroom and ravishes him. Wilby's longing for physical love is finally satisfied, but he is terrified that this unwashed prole will try to blackmail him. Graves, who is set to emigrate to Argentina, seeks out Wilby in London. After a clumsy attempt at extortion, he admits his love for Wilby and his disappointment that the gentleman hasn't accepted his invitation to meet him at the boathouse. They spend the night together at a hotel, but Wilby is unable to persuade the gamekeeper to remain in England. Wilby goes to the Southampton docks to see him off, but Graves misses his boat. Hoping that this is no accident, Wilby travels to Grant's country estate, confesses his love for the gamekeeper to Grant, and goes to the boathouse where Graves is waiting for him.

In the Merchant-Ivory tradition, MAURICE is beautifully mounted and shot, capturing the look and spirit of Edwardian England in exquisite detail. The interiors are subtly lit and combined with the evocative production design of Ackland-Snow and the excellent costumes of Academy Award winners Beavan and Bright recall John Singer Sargent paintings. Cinematographer Lhomme's country landscapes and cloudy seaside scenes are equally artistic, drenched in cool greens and grays. As with other Merchant-Ivory productions, the film is highly literary, sticking close to the letter of the Forster novel. The major invention by Ivory and coscreenwriter Hesketh-Harvey is the trial and conviction of Risley (Tandy), which serve to heighten the risks undertaken by Grant and Wilby and prompt Grant's emotional crisis. (Risley is based on Lytton Strachey, the famed biographer and Bloomsbury Group friend of Forster to whom the author first showed *Maurice*). The film covers approximately four years and Ivory presents it episodically, allowing it to unfold slowly. While A ROOM WITH A VIEW was buoyant and whimsical, MAURICE is stolid, full of repressed emotions and unexpressed passion. Yet this tenuously controlled dispassion is precisely the effect Ivory seeks. The sexual claustrophobia that afflicts Wilby may seem a bit dated, but Forster and Ivory are dealing with a time when homosexuals were treated as criminals. Given that context, the improbable coupling of two men who seem to have nothing in common beyond their mutual attraction and willingness to express it is understandable if a little hard to accept. Forster himself

needed to have a happy ending even if it stretched credibility and Ivory has preserved that intent.

At its best, MAURICE is moving and thought provoking, but at other moments it is unintentionally silly. It is not the story but the telling of it that is the problem. At 140 minutes, MAURICE simply goes on too long, belaboring plot points, presenting scenes that do little to advance the narrative or enhance the characters, lingering overlong on emotional moments until they seem contrived. Nonetheless, the performances are generally convincing. Of the principal players, Wilby and Graves (ROOM WITH A VIEW) are adequate, but Grant seems to go beyond what is required of him. He is cool and seemingly content in his "normal life," but the young idealist who strove for perfection in love can occasionally be glimpsed and he is the film's real tragic figure. Callow (A ROOM WITH A VIEW, THE GOOD FATHER), playing the schoolteacher who informs a young Maurice about the physical desires he will soon experiencing, and Elliott do nice turns but are only seen briefly. The most intriguing performance is by Kingsley, who plays his convincing hypnotist as an American. Ivory worked without his usual screenwriter, Ruth Prawer Jhabvala, who was deep in the final draft of her novel *The Three Continents* and felt that *Maurice* was a flawed book. Her replacement, Hesketh-Harvey, was chosen at least partly because he is a Cambridge graduate and familiar with the story's milieux. A ROOM WITH A VIEW costar Julian Sands had been slated to perform the title role but pulled out because his personal life was in upheaval. Surprisingly, Forster's Kings College, Cambridge, literary executors tried to dissuade Ivory from making the film, not because the novel was controversial but because they felt it was a minor Forster work and not as deserving as many others. MAURICE was made for approximately $2.65 million. *(Sexual situations, nudity.)*

p, Ismail Merchant; d, James Ivory; w, Kit Hesketh-Harvey, James Ivory (based on the novel by E.M. Forster); ph, Pierre Lhomme (Technicolor); m, Richard Robbins; ed, Katherine Wenning; prod d, Brian Ackland-Snow; art d, Peter James; cos, Jenny Beavan, John Bright; makeup, Mary Hillman.

Drama **(PR:O MPAA:NR)**

MAUVAIS SANG (SEE: BAD BLOOD, 1987, Fr.)

MEATBALLS III*½ (1987) 88m Dalco/The Movie Store c

Sally Kellerman *(Roxy Du Jour)*, Patrick Dempsey *(Rudy)*, Al Waxman *(Saint Peter)*, Isabelle Mejias *(Wendy)*, Shannon Tweed *(The Love Goddess)*, Jan Taylor *(Rita)*, George Buza *(Mean Gene)*, Ronnie Hawkins.

Although Bill Murray and Chris Makepeace of the 1979 original are still nowhere in sight, this second sequel manages to be moderately entertaining for what it is—a shameless T&A sex comedy. Dempsey is a nerdy 14-year-old virgin who works at a riverside hangout called "Mean Gene's," a place populated by the unlikely combination of a speedboat/biker gang and preppy college kids. Dempsey wants desperately to lose his virginity, preferably to "The Love Goddess" (ex-Playmate Tweed), an object of desire who just happens to belong to the nasty gang leader, Buza. Anyone who even looks at Tweed, who is only seen at her bedroom window, has to answer to Buza's wrath. Although Dempsey is surrounded by bikini-clad bimbos and has caught the eye of Mejias, a nice girl his own age, Dempsey isn't content. He's the butt of everyone's cruel pranks and grows more sexually frustrated. Enter Kellerman, a porn star named Roxanne Du Jour who has recently died on the set of her latest film. (Her last words, as a newsman reports them, were "Oh God, Oh my, Oh yes, Oh yes, yes, Oh my God, yes, yes, Oh, Oh, Oh, Oh, YES!") Before she can pass through the pearly gates of Heaven (depicted as a giant movie studio) she must return to Earth and do a good deed. She is designated to help Dempsey lose his virginity. This job becomes more complicated when Kellerman, now a ghost, realizes she can't be the one he loses it to. A few local girls look to be likely candidates, and "The Love Goddess" nearly becomes the one, but in the end Dempsey goes off with the sweet Mejias. Having done right by Heaven's standards, Kellerman is granted admission.

Amidst all of MEATBALLS III's standard sex comedy routines, there is a rather noble story about true love. Although much of the film is typical trash (close-ups on jiggling breasts, a wet t-shirt contest, unbearably dumb sexual innuendos), the Kellerman-Dempsey story is somewhat touching. As Kellerman coaches and advises Dempsey (she is unseen by all but the young virgin), she grows fond of him in a maternal way. She steers him away from an eager older

woman, prevents him from deflowering a likable girl whom he has only just met, and brings him together with Mejias. When her good deed is done, Kellerman is saddened by having to leave him. It is Kellerman who steals the film. Playing more of a Hollywood starlet (a la Harlow, Lombard, and Monroe) than a porn queen, Kellerman creates a thoroughly engaging and respectable character who can't be nearly as bad as the guard at Heaven's gate made her out to be. Mejias also turns in a pleasant performance, nicely blending innocence and sexuality. Some excellent support comes from Buza as the neanderthal "Mean Gene" and from Tweed who, surprisingly, is not Buza's sex-toy but his visiting PhD candidate sister. To avoid unduly overpraising MEATBALLS III, most of the film is uninspired tedium that was, deservedly, shelved for nearly three years. Even the morality of the film is pretty confused. On one hand Kellerman is keeping a watchful eye on Dempsey, but at the same time she's telling him that if a girl says "No" then she really means "Yes"—a reprehensible philosophy which is practically an invitation to rape. MEATBALLS III is dumb entertainment, but lurking around at its core is a sense of morality, even if it is warped. Songs include "Hot Girls in Love," "The Kid Is Hot Tonight" (performed by Loverboy). *(Nudity, excessive profanity, sexual situations.)*

p, Don Carmody, John Dunning; d, George Mendeluk; w, Michael Paseornek, Bradley Kesden (based on a story by Chuck Workman); ph, Peter Benison; m, Paul Zaza; ed, Debra Karen; prod d, Charles Dunlop.

Comedy **Cas.** **(PR:O MPAA:R)**

MEFISTO FUNK† (1987, It.) Metamorphosi/CIDIF c

Flavio Bonacci, Alessandro Ferrara, Sebastiano Filocamo, Luis Molteni, Silvia Cohen.

A variation on the Faust legend in which a man makes a pact with the devil in order to become more adept with technology—an aspect of modern life with which he cannot come to terms.

d&w, Marco Poma (based on the play "Faust" by Johann Wolfgang von Goethe); ph, Roberto Mezzabotta; m, Maurizio Marisco; ed, Lia Bottanelli.

Drama **(PR:NR MPAA:NR)**

MEIER*** (1987, Ger.) 98m Pro-ject Film im Filmverlag der Autoren c

Rainer Grenkowitz *(Meier)*, Nadja Engelbrecht *(Lore)*, Alexander Hauff *(Kalle)*, Thomas Bestvater *(Erwin)*, Rene Grams *(Klausi)*, Joachim Kemmer *(Escape Organizer)*, Dieter Hildebrandt *(Waiter)*, Jurgen Klauss.

Peter Timm, an East German who was expelled from that country for his political activities, makes a fine directorial debut with this clever tongue-in-cheek satire. Grenkowitz is an East German who heads a crew of wallpaper hangers. When he learns a small inheritance awaits him in West Berlin, Grenkowitz is allowed to cross the border. With the money, Grenkowitz takes a sojourn around the world before returning to his East Berlin home. In doing so, Grenkowitz manages to secure a new passport, thus giving him legal papers for both East and West Germany. Upon his return, Grenkowitz tells friends he had only visited Bulgaria (a common vacation for East Germans), and goes back to his paper hanging job. His customers are tired of the tacky floral patterns Grenkowitz's company offers, so the wily man decides to capitalize on his dual passports. Grenkowitz begins smuggling plain woodgrain paper across the border, telling his superiors that he makes the stuff himself. The wallpaper proves to be such a hit that Grenkowitz and his crew dramatically increase their productivity. But now Grenkowitz must keep up with the orders, so his travels across the border must increase. Since he can't tell his girl friend Engelbrecht why he is absent, the angered woman begins to suspect Grenkowitz of infidelity. East German officials, impressed by Grenkowitz's output, declare him to be an excellent example for the country's workers. He's given an award, which is followed by a lavish celebration. The party, however, causes Grenkowitz to be a few minutes late for his nightly border crossing. In his haste, Grenkowitz inadvertently shows the wrong passport and is taken into custody. Though his actions would normally merit a 15-year sentence, authorities realize it wouldn't do to toss a recently decorated citizen into prison. Thus Grenkowitz is allowed to go free, though his actions are to be monitored by two government agents. He is reunited with Engelbrecht, and the couple is surprised to see a large picture of Grenkowitz and his crew emblazoned on a public wall.

While a serious political theme lurks below MEIER's surface, Timm handles his material in a light, energetic manner. In doing so, he throws a humorous but decidedly sharp jab at the Berlin Wall's overwhelming symbolic nature. Grenkowitz has a nice roguish air to him that furthers Timm's intentions. Though given ample opportunity to defect, Grenkowitz remains in East Germany because this is where his life is rooted. His success in the East compensates for the freedom the West offers, and Grenkowitz is a genuinely happy man. MEIER was a big hit with West German audiences as a good amount of its humor is dependent on the native political situation. Consequently, while the basic satire is unmarred, many of the jokes will be lost to those unfamiliar with the day-to-day world of East and West Berlin. Released in Germany in 1986.

p, Herbert Rimbach; d&w, Peter Timm; ph, Klaus Eichhammer; ed, Corinna Dietz; art d, Martin Dostal; cos, Petra Kranz.

Comedy **(PR:O MPAA:NR)**

MELO***** (1987, Fr.) 110m MK2-Films A2-CNC/MK2-European Classics c

Sabine Azema *(Romaine Belcroix)*, Pierre Arditi *(Pierre Belcroix)*, Andre Dussollier *(Marcel Blanc)*, Fanny Ardant *(Christiane Levesque)*, Jacques Dacqmine *(Dr. Remy)*, Hubert Gignoux *(Priest)*, Catherine Arditi *(Yvonne)*.

Since appearing on the international film scene in 1959 with his brilliant HIROSHIMA, MON AMOUR, Alain Resnais has become recognized as a great innovator whose experiments with nonlinear structure and the relationship between the past and one's memory of the past have placed him among the ranks of the greatest directors working today. From the bewildering narrative puzzles of LAST YEAR AT MARIENBAD to the intricate narrative complexities of MON ONCLE D'AMERIQUE, Resnais has consistently surprised audiences and critics alike with his predictably unpredictable deconstruction of film form. It is because of his previous accomplishments that MELO is such a shock. MELO is a traditionally constructed linear narrative adapted from a 1929 Parisian melodrama written for the stage by Henry Bernstein, a long-forgotten and once-popular playwright. Deceptively simple in appearance, MELO is the story of two musicians—Dussollier and Arditi—whose friendship dates back to their days at the conservatory. Dussollier has gone on to international fame as a soloist while Arditi has settled down in a Parisian suburb to lead a simple life with his wife Azema. After a quiet evening of drink and reminiscence, Dussollier is fascinated by Azema and she with him. The following day she visits him at his apartment in Paris and the two begin a passionate affair. Rather than confess the affair to the unsuspecting and good-natured Arditi, Azema plots to gradually poison her husband. When a doctor nearly discovers her plot, Azema jumps to her death in the Seine. Her suicide note for Arditi makes no mention of Dussollier, instead declaring her love for her husband. Three years later, Arditi (now a father and married to Azema's cousin Ardant) calls on Dussollier, whom he has not seen since Azema's funeral, and accuses him of having had an affair with Azema. Rather than lose Arditi's friendship and destroy the image Arditi has created of Azema, Dussollier insists that no secret romance ever existed. The film ends as Dussollier agrees to accompany Arditi in playing Brahms' Sonata for Violin and Piano—a piece of music both men had previously played in duet with Azema.

Masterfully directed, MELO contains all of Resnais' usual themes and places them not in a complex structure but in a popular form of entertainment—the melodrama. The result is a pure work of art which can be enjoyed on one level as an entertaining romantic melodrama and on a second, more complex, level as an extension of Resnais' ideas about memory and imagination, reality and fiction. As he did in HIROSHIMA MON AMOUR, Resnais gives us characters who are haunted by their memories—so haunted that their past continues to live on into the present, thereby blurring the line between the two. From the opening scene of MELO the characters become lost in reminiscence. While visiting with Arditi and Azema, Dussollier recounts the story of a love affair that has since ended. In one long, unbroken shot Dussollier describes "Helene" and how she became attracted to another man during one of Dussollier's concerts. He is not, however, merely *telling* Arditi and Azema a story, but *reliving* it. Although the camera shows only a close-up of his face, it is as if the entire scene is played out before our eyes. Like Dussollier, Arditi is given to reminiscing—recalling days when both men were music students at the conservatory. However, Azema, the spontaneous and unpredictable woman of the present, can take no part in their reminiscing. It is this superb and lengthy (lasting some 20 minutes) opening that sets the stage for the rest of MELO. By the end of the film both Dussollier and Arditi are filled with the memory of Azema. Arditi refuses to let his dead wife's memory fade away and asks Dussollier to accompany him as they play Brahms—the piece of music which Arditi and Azema would always play together and the same piece that Dussollier played with Azema. It is during the finale, when Azema's two lovers play Brahms together, that Azema ceases to be a thing of the past.

One of the most interesting aspects of MELO is Resnais' paradoxical interplay between theatricality and reality. The film begins with its opening credits printed on the turning pages of a playbill. A stage curtain then dissolves into the patio scene—an obvious set which comes complete with a painted moon and stars. (With the exception of Azema's suicide, the entire film is shot on sets.) Resnais' use of long takes, however, adds a contrasting dimension. Long argued by French film theorist Andre Bazin as a technique of realism, the long take in MELO simultaneously gives a sense of reality and of theatricality. This paradox is achieved through Resnais' ability to combine theatrical techniques with realism. Although the theatricality of the melodrama is evident in every frame, the viewer never forgets he is watching a film. As always in a Resnais film, one can sense that the director is in perfect control of the frame—the camera movement, the production design, the sound, and the actors themselves. In MELO, unlike other

Resnais films, the concentration is purely on the actors instead of on film technique. Like his 1984 picture, L'AMOUR A MORT (unreleased in the US), MELO stars Ardant, Arditi, Azema, and Dussollier—all of whom perform beautifully in roles which combine melodramatic and silent film acting techniques with modern mannerisms and emotions. Only rarely is a film this simple *and* this complex. Such filmmakers as Carl Dreyer, Ernst Lubitsch, Jean Renoir, and Charles Chaplin have consistently reached such a level and now, with MELO, so, too, has Resnais. MELO was showered with Cesar nominations, winning two awards—Azema for Best Actress and Arditi for Best Supporting Actor. Other nominations were for Best Picture/Best Director, Best Actor (Dussollier), Best Cinematography, Best Production Design, and Best Costumes.

Bernstein's play was filmed previously on five occasions—in 1932, in French, as MELO starring Gaby Morlay and Pierre Blanchar; the same year, in German, as DER TRAUMENDE MUND and starring Elisabeth Bergner; in 1937, in English, as DREAMING LIPS and again starring Bergner; in 1938, in French, as MELO; and then in 1953 as DER TRAUMENDE MUND (released in the US in 1958 as DREAMING LIPS) starring Maria Schell. The first version was to star Charles Boyer in his first talkie. He had appeared in the stage version with Morlay and Blanchar and was a protege of Bernstein, but he was instead lured to Hollywood. The play opened in Paris at the Gymnase on March 11, 1929, and had a successful run of over a year. Bernstein, largely forgotten today, has an ardent admirer in Resnais, who has, as a result of MELO, renewed interest in the playwright. Bernstein, who died in 1953, wrote nearly 30 plays in his career, 14 of which were produced on Broadway. Throughout the 1920s, one could always find a Henry Bernstein play being staged somewhere in Paris; and at one point, 80 performances of his plays were being staged throughout Europe. (In French; English subtitles.)

p, Marin Karmitz; d&w, Alain Resnais (based on the play "Melo" by Henry Bernstein); ph, Charlie Van Damme (Agfa-Gevaert Color); m, Johannes Brahms, Johann Sebastian Bach, Philippe Gerard; ed, Albert Jurgenson; prod d, Jacques Saulnier; cos, Catherine Leterrier; makeup, Dominique De Vorges.

Drama/Romance **(PR:A MPAA:NR)**

MEMOIRE DES APPARENCES: LA VIE EST UN SONGE† (1987, Fr.) 105m INA-Maison de la Culture du Havre-La Sept-Ministere des Affaires Etrangeres-CNC-Ministere des PTT c (Trans: Memory of Appearences: Life Is a Dream)

Sylvain Thirolle, Roch Leibovici, Benedicte Sire, Laurence Cortadellas, Jean-Bernard Guillard, Alain Halle-Halle, Jean-Francoise Lapalus, Alain Rimoux.

The world's most prolific director, Raul Ruiz, sets this picture inside a movie theater attended by a Chilean revolutionary who is trying to remember passages from the play "Life is a Dream" by Calderon de la Barca.

p, Jean-Luc Larguier; d&w, Raul Ruiz (based on the play by Pedro Calderon de la Barca); ph, Jacques Bouquin; m, Jorge Arriagada; ed, Martine Bouquin, Rodolpho Wedeles; prod d, Christian Olivares; cos, Pierre Albert.

Fantasy **(PR:NR MPAA:NR)**

MERA LAHOO† (1987, India)

Govinda, Kimi Katkar, Raj Kiran, Gulshan Grover.

A village boy adopts the life of an outlaw in order to avenge the murder of his brother. (In Hindi.)

p, Ravindra Dhanoa, Bhargav Bhatt; d, Virendra; m, Annu Malik.

Drama **(PR:NR MPAA:NR)**

MESSENGER, THE† (1987, US/It.) 92m Realta Cinematografica-Po' Boy/Snizzlefritz c

Fred Williamson *(Jake Sebastian Turner)*, Sandy Cummings *(Sabrina)*, Val Avery *(Clark)*, Michael Dante *(Emerson)*, Chris Connelly *(FBI Agent Parker)*, Cameron Mitchell *(Police Capt. Carter)*, Peter Turner *(Harris)*, Joe Spinell *(Rico)*.

Williamson, the "blaxploitation" star of the 1970s, stars in this US-Italian coproduction as a musical prodigy from Chicago who, after spending time in an Italian prison on theft charges, gets mixed up with the Mafia. His wife, Cummings, has become involved in international drug trade and, as a result, is killed by mob thugs. Williamson goes on a rampage, hunting down and killing the men responsible for her demise. His avenging takes him throughout Italy and eventually into Chicago and Las Vegas where he evens up the score.

p, Fred Williamson, Pier Luigi Ciriaci; d, Fred Williamson; w, Brian Johnson, Conchita Lee, Anthony Wisdom (based on a story by Fred Williamson); ph, Giancarlo Ferrando, Craig Greene (Fujicolor); m, William Stuckey; ed, Meuller.

Action **(PR:NR MPAA:R)**

MI GENERAL (SEE: MY GENERAL, 1987, Span.)

MI NOMBRE ES GATILLO† (1987, Mex.) 89m Galmex Films-Telefilms/Peliculas Mexicanas c (Trans: My Name Is Gatillo)

Alvaro Zermeno *(Pablo Moncada [Gatillo])*, Ana Luisa Peluffo *(Andrea Orsina)*, Eleazar Garcia, Jr. *(Lucio Contreras [Ruso])*, Julio Ahuet *(Chato)*, Juan Gallardo *(Capt. Nichols)*, Roxanna Chavez *(Rebeca)*, Javier Garcia, Christopher Lago, Reynaldo Martinez [El Gallero], Manuel Benitez, Carlos Gonzalez, Manuel Rodero, Jr., Jorge Guerra, Armando Galvan, Martin Quintana, Antonio Lopez, Baltazar Guzman.

A Mexican crime actioner which stars Zermeno as a crime-fighting US narcotics agent whose nickname is "Gatillo," or "Trigger." Together with his partner Ahuet, Zermeno tracks a gang of smugglers to a Nazi-styled Texas hideout for a dose of gunplay and justice. Shown briefly in New York City.

p, Pedro Galindo, Jr.; d, Pedro Galindo III; w, Pedro Galindo, Jr., Carlos Valdemar, Pedro Galindo, III; ph, Miguel Arana; m, Manuel Esperon; ed, Carlos Savage; spec eff, Pepe Parra; stunts, Alberto Vazquez.

Action **(PR:NR MPAA:NR)**

MIDNIGHT† (1987, Hong Kong) 98m Make Hero/Lui Ming c

Chan Pui Kee, Ngan Lai Yu, Yu Chi Wei, Lee Wan Kwong, Charles—Tao, Chan Yuen Lai, Chan Shuk Yee.

Tao stars as an evil pimp who forces a young woman to work for him to pay back a debt. The woman's sister gallantly takes her place and dooms herself to a life of servitutde and degradation. (In Cantonese; English subtitles.)

d, Yeung Ka On; w, Yeung Ka On; ph, Ma Kam Cheung; art d, Hua Wing Choi.

Drama **(PR:NR MPAA:NR)**

MIEDZY USTAMI A BRZEGIEM PUCHARU† (1987, Pol.) 125m Zespoly Filmowe-PROFIL c (Trans: Between the Cup and the Lip)

Jacek Chmielnik *(Count Wentzel Croy-Dulmen)*, Katarzyna Gniewkowska *(Jadwiga Chrzastkowska)*, Henryk Bista *(Wentzel's Servant)*.

A wealthy German count is smitten by a beautiful stranger at the opera and follows her to her home in Poland, which was also his birthplace and still home to his grandmother. He is spurned by the lady and his grandmother as he does not speak Polish and knows nothing of the culture and history of the country. Undaunted, he returns to Berlin and undertakes the study of Polish and the Poles. Upon his return to the little Polish town, he is challenged to a duel by the fiance of the woman he loves, and is badly wounded. The young lady breaks off her engagement and together with the count's grandmother, nurses him back to health.

d, Zbigniew Kuzminski; w, Kazimierz Radowicz (based on the novel by Maria Rodziewiczowna); ph, Tomasz Tarasin; m, Piotr Marczewski; ed, Maria Lebiedzik; set d, Jaroslaw Switoniak.

Romance **(PR:NR MPAA:NR)**

MIENTRAS HAYA LUZ† (1987, Span.) 102m Vienna b&w (Trans: While There Is Light)

Rafael Diaz *(Jaime)*, Jorge de Juap *(Jorge)*, Teresa Madruga *(Teresa)*, Marisa Paredes *(Marisa)*, Joaquin Hinojosa, Iciar Bollain, Jose Segura Garcia.

A convoluted plot concerns an anthropologist on the run, trailed by two gunmen. He is sought by his friend who has returned to Spain from the US with his black girl friend.

d&w, Felipe Vega; ph, Jose Luis Lopez Linares; m, Bernardo Bonezzi; ed, Miguel A. Santamaria, Ivan Aledo.

Crime **(PR:NR MPAA:NR)**

MILLION DOLLAR MYSTERY* (1987) 95m DEG c

Eddie Deezen *(Rollie)*, Wendy Sherman *(Lollie)*, Rick Overton *(Stuart Briggs)*, Mona Lyden *(Barbara Briggs)*, Douglas Emerson *(Howie Briggs)*, Royce D. Applegate *(Tugger)*, Pam Matteson *(Dotty)*, Daniel McDonald *(Crush)*, Penny Baker *(Charity)*, Tawny Fere *(Faith)*, LaGena Hart *(Hope)*, Tom Bosley *(Sidney Preston)*, Mack Dryden *(Fred, FBI Man)*, Jamie Alcroft *(Bob, FBI Man)*, Rich Hall *(Slaughter)*, Gail Neely *(Officer Gretchen)*, Kevin Pollak *(Officer Quinn)*, H.B. Haggerty *(Awful Abdul)*, Bob Schott *(Bad Boris)*, Peter Pitofsky *(Toxic Werewolf)*, Greg Travis *(Toxic Man)*, Tommy Sledge *(Private Eye)*, Christopher Cary *(Chuck)*, Rudy De Luca *(Money Counter)*, Mark Regan *(Newscaster)*, John Gilgreen *(Motel Manager)*, Katie La Bourdette *(Private Eye's Secretary)*, Pat McGroarty, Clark Coleman *(Gas Station Attendants)*, Paul Stader *(Old Man in Car)*, Rosemary Johnston *(Old Woman in Car)*, David Trim *(Scout Leader)*,

Susann Benn *(Stewardess)*, John Hammil *(Pilot)*, Gary Kelson *(Co-Pilot)*, Sal Lopez *(Hijacker)*, Augustine Lam *(Tour Guide)*, Jack Carpenter *(Biker Window)*, Andy Epper *(Biker)*.

It might have been called MILLION DOLLAR MISERY because whoever wants to solve the promotional gimmick and win the million-dollar prize will have to sit through this several times. Dino De Laurentiis, through his DEG company, has come up with yet another in a seemingly endless string of dud firecrackers. This borrows heavily from the failed SCAVENGER HUNT and IT'S A MAD, MAD, MAD, MAD WORLD. Bosley is a government official who has been involved in a scam whereby he took the Libyans for $4 million. He's stashed his loot in four places, with a million in each spot. Bosley stops at the Apache Acres Motel and Diner and the spicy chili causes him to have a massive heart attack. At the moment, the diner is occupied by a standard group of people. Bosley goes through a lengthy and simply awful death scene wherein he recounts the history of the robbery and the fact that the money is out there. Before he gives up the ghost he utters the first clue, "Start at the city of the bridge." Now, what does that mean? A bridge could be in someone's mouth, could span a river, could be a card game, might be across someone's nose, etc. The other patrons of the Apache Acres hear this confession and thus begins a crazed scramble as they practically trample each other to get out of the restaurant and on the trail of the money. A

number of characters are in the diner, including owners Applegate and Matteson. The others, seemingly chosen from a list of racial and ethnic stereotypes, are feisty couple Lyden and Overton, their bratty son Emerson; singer McDonald and his all-girl trio of backup singers, Baker, Hart and Fere. As the search goes on, inept FBI men Dryden and Alcroft plus Hall, playing a macho Vietnam veteran, join in. They, in turn, are joined by cops Neely and Pollak. Neely is a heavyset female cop and impressionist Pollak gets his chance to show his stuff in an aping of Peter Falk's "Colombo," as well as Woody Allen. Rounding out the treasure hunters are Haggerty and Schott, a pair of pseudo-Sumo types. The chase features the heists of cars, an airplane, motorcycles, and a fire truck. By the fade out, the audience has been given clues as to where a million dollars is stashed. Not all the clues are legitimate and it is up to the audience to decide which are real. The winner was to be named in January, 1988, but the picture took in so little money it's questionable if they'll be able to cover the prize. Information on the whereabouts of the money was handed out in the movie houses as well as in Glad Bags packages so it's no wonder that Bosley was chosen to play the role he did, as he is the Glad Bags man on the TV spots. In the story, $3 million is found and the remaining money is somewhere out there for you, the audience, to locate. Glad Bags pulled off a coup as there are clues to be found in their product, but one could also write to the company and receive an official entry form with no purchase needed. The money was to be found inside a handle-tie Glad Bag. Where else would one stash that kind of money? It's the first place an intelligent person would look.

Veteran director Fleischer, 70, who made some of the best genre pictures ever (FANTASTIC VOYAGE, SOYLENT GREEN, TORA! TORA! TORA!), shows his comedic sense is as heavy-handed as the man who rings J. Arthur Rank's gong. The movie is dedicated to the memory of Dar Robinson, who died tragically doing what appeared to be a simple stunt. Robinson had been known as the highest paid stuntman in the business, receiving $100,000 for his free-fall from the CN Tower in Toronto for the movie HIGH POINT. Several stand-up comics were given their chance at cinema stardom with this movie and it's unfortunate so few people had the opportunity to see their work. Sledge's act is that of a Raymond Chandler-type detective and he never fails to please. Overton and Hall (who wrote the best seller "Sniglets" based on his TV appearances on many shows) show they have acting careers ahead of them. Mack Dryden and Jamie Alcroft had a TV show for a few months in 1986 called "Comedy Break." It's too bad that they had to be teamed in such an unfunny script. Oscar winner Jack Cardiff (cinematographer of such films as BLACK NARCISSUS, THE RED SHOES, THE AFRICAN QUEEN and others, as well as the director of many movies) can't do much with the Arizona desertscape. Songs include "Million Dollar Mystery," "All the Money in the World," "Maybe Tonight" (Barry Mann, John Lewis Parker), "E-Z Money" (Parker), All the aforementioned were done by New Money. Other tunes were: "Love Is Not Like This" (Ashley Hall, Stephanie Tyrell, performed by Hall), "If It's Love You Want" (Parker, performed by Parker), "Surfin' On the Bridge to Liberty" (Mann, performed by Shelby Daniel, Donna DeLory), "Don't Burn that Bridge" (Steve Stone, performed by Jerry Fuller), "Rich, Young and Pretty" (Paul Sabu, Tim Riely, E.J. Curcio, Mark Hawkins, performed by Silent Rage), "Shopping for Boys" (Jo Wells, Floyd Hyman, Rich Barden, performed by Third Language). None of them helped. *(Violence, profanity.)*

p, Stephen F. Kesten; d, Richard Fleischer; w, Tim Metcalfe, Miguel Tejada-Flores, Rudy De Luca; ph, Jack Cardiff (Technicolor); m, Al Gorgoni; ed, John W. Wheeler; prod d, Jack G. Taylor, Jr.; art d, Dawn Snyder; set d, Stephen Potter, Richard Boris, Ron Green, Bob Trow, Bruce Ayres; cos, Clifford Capone; spec eff, John Stirber; m/l, Barry Mann, John Lewis Parker, Stephanie Tyrell, Ashley Hall, Steve Stone, Jo Wells, Rich Barden, Floyd Hyman, E.J. Curcio, Tim Riely, Mark Hawkins, Paul Sabu; stunts, George Fisher, Dar Robinson; makeup, Michelle Ross, Patty Androff.

Comedy/Mystery **(PR:A-C MPAA:PG)**

MILLION V BRACHNOY KORZINE† (1987, USSR) 94m Odessa Film/Sovexportfilm c (Trans: A Million in the Wedding Basket)

Alexander Shirvindt, Sofico Chiaureli, Galina Sokolova, Larisa Udovichenko, Olga Kabo.

A bittersweet comedy featuring an unemployed man who provides for his family by being a "professional" guest at parties, weddings, funerals, and society functions. After giving his usual speech, the man pockets bottles of cognac and other saleable items, later exchanging them for food for his destitute family.

d&w, Vsevolod Shilovsky (based on the play "Society Signor Is My Profession" by D. Scarnacci and R. Tarabusi); ph, Vadim Avloshenko, Nikolai Ivanov; m, Ilya Katayev; art d, Natalia Iyevleva.

Comedy/Drama **(PR:NR MPAA:NR)**

MILWR BYCHAN (SEE: BOY SOLDIERS, 1987, Wales)

MIND KILLER† (1987) 86m Prism Ent.-Flash Features c

Joe McDonald *(Warren)*, Christopher Wade *(Larry)*, Shirley Ross *(Sandy)*, Kevin Hart *(Brad)*, Tom Henry *(Vivac Chandra)*, Diana Calhoun *(Mrs. Chandra)*, George Flynn *(Townsend)*.

Ultra low-budget horror film from Denver that went straight to home video. It features McDonald as an oafish library employee who can't get a date until his equally inept pal (Wade) finds a book on mind control and puts it to good use. Using the secrets foretold in the book, both boys become self-confident Don Juans able to seduce beautiful women via mind-power. Unfortunately these new-found mind skills mutate McDonald into a monster.

p, Sarah H. Liles; d, Michael Krueger; w, Michael Krueger, Dave Sipos, Curtis Hannum (based on a story by Michael Krueger, Doug Olson); ph, Jim Kelley; m, Jeffrey Wood; ed, Jonathan Moser; spec eff, Ted A. Bohus, Vincent J. Guastini.

Horror **Cas.** **(PR:NR MPAA:NR)**

MIO, MOY MIO† (1987, USSR/Swed./Norway) 100m Gorki-Nordisk Tonefilm International-Sovenfilm-Swedish Film Institute-Norwegian Assoc. of Film Development/Sovexportfilm c (Trans: Mio, My Mio)

Nicholas Pickard *(Mio)*, Christian Bale *(Jum-Jum)*, Timothy Bottoms *(The King)*, Susannah York *(The Weaver Woman)*, Christopher Lee *(The Wicked Knight)*, Sverre Anker Ousdal *(The Sword Maker)*, Linne Stokke, Stig Egstrom, Geoffrey Staines, Igor Yasulovich.

Bale (who also appears in EMPIRE OF THE SUN) is an unhappy little boy from Stockholm, who runs away to search for his father, and finds him, with the help of a wizard, ruling a faraway fairy country. Happy now with his new friend Yum-Yum, the boys travel through the beautiful country until their adventures take them to the border of a foreign land where an evil sorcerer turns children into birds.

d, Vladimir Grammatikov; w, William Aldridge (based on a story by Astrid Lindgren); ph, Alexander Antipenko; m, Benny Anderson, Anders Elias; prod d, Konstantin Zagorsky.

Children's **(PR:NR MPAA:NR)**

MIRACLES**½ (1987) 87m HBO-Cannon/Orion c

Tom Conti *(Dr. Roger Briggs)*, Teri Garr *(Jean Briggs)*, Paul Rodriguez *(Juan)*, Christopher Lloyd *(Harry)*, Adalberto Martinez "Resortes" *(Witch Doctor)*, Jorge Russek *(Judge)*, Jorge Reynoso *(K'In)*, Charles Rocket *(Michael)*, Barbara Whinnery *(Hooker)*, Ken Hixon *(Missionary)*, Zaide Silvia Gutierrez *(K'In's Wife)*, Erika Faraon *(K'In's Daughter)*, Paco Moranta *(Sgt. Gomez)*, Alvaro Carcano *(Lt. Arnez)*, Ken Lerner *(Stuart)*, Shelby Leverington *(Mother in Hospital)*, Mae E. Campbell, Susan Wheeler Duff *(Nurses)*, John Macchia *(Martin)*, Squire Fridell *(Yates)*, Rene Pereura *(Tito)*, Guillermo Rios *(Pete)*, Tina Romero *(Juanita)*, Margarita Sanz *(Carol)*, Roger Cudney *(Captain)*, Joseph Whip, Chris Hendrie, Leopoldo Frances *(L.A. Cops)*, Bob Nelson *(Sgt. Levit)*, C. Victor Alcoper Gomez *(Bartender)*, Eduardo Lugo *(Old Bum)*, Alejandro Bracho, Carlos Vendrell *(Bank Robbers)*, Douglas Sandoval *(Donkeyman)*, Regino Herrera *(Sea Captain)*, Jose Chavez Trowe *(Mexican Policeman)*, Dr. Francisco Funes *(Hospital Doctor)*, Marie Butler *(Interpreter)*, Paco Pharrez *(Priest)*, Miguel Angel Fuentes, Carlos Gonzales *(Village Men)*, Roberto Sosa *(Little Boy)*, Andaluz Russel *(Peasant Woman)*, Gerardo Moreno *(Peasant Man)*, Mario Arevalo *(Man Hit by Rock)*, Rodolfo De Alexandre *(Peasant Translator)*.

Though by no means a great screwball comedy, MIRACLES recalls those films from the 1930s where zany plots and characters ruled the day. It pays little heed to such an outrageous notion as logic, and at times is great fun. The story opens deep in a remote Mexican jungle. Reynoso is a tribal chieftain whose daughter (Faraon) is stricken with an unknown illness. Martinez, the local medicine man, is unable to cure the girl and is consequently staked to the ground as punishment. Hoping to end his suffering, Martinez prays to the Almighty, begging for some sort of divine intervention. Meanwhile, in Los Angeles, bumbling robbers Rodriguez and Lloyd accidentally blow up a jewelry store, which forces the pair to take quick flight. Lloyd gets on a motorcycle, but Rodriguez is stuck because his car has a flat. While all *this* is going on, in another part of town Garr is leaving a party. She has been celebrating the end of her ten-year marriage to Conti, a surgeon, and now just wants to get home. At a city hospital Conti has just finished an operation. Wearing a tuxedo under his medical greens, he too has a celebration to attend. But neither he nor Garr end up where they want to be, for the two are accidentally reunited when Garr nearly runs down Rodriguez in her car, and subsequently forces Conti's auto off the road. Rodriguez takes the two hostage, then realizes he's got more than he bargained for when the couple begin fighting. Rodriguez takes the pair to his hideout, then ties up Conti and Garr before locking them in a closet. Conti laments that his worst nightmare has come true: he's trapped in a room with his ex-wife! A SWAT team surrounds Rodriguez's place and he again takes flight with Conti and Garr as hostages. They manage to get to an airfield, where Lloyd is waiting in a rickety airplane. Rodriguez is wounded in a shootout, but they manage to get the plane airborne. Lloyd and Rodriguez secretly parachute out of the getaway plane, leaving the bickering couple to find instructions, simply labeled "How to Land," scrawled on the back of a beer carton. In the film's funniest scene, Conti and Garr argue over the worst moment of their marriage, then fall into a fit of giggles, all the while trying to bring the craft down safely. Eventually they land in the Mexican desert, and are quickly picked up by police.

Garr and Conti, thought to be drug smugglers, are taken to court. No one believes their wild story, and the pair are tossed into a dingy jail cell. But Rodriguez, who coincidentally has landed in the same town, overhears people talking about the incarcerated *gringos*. He and Lloyd use dynamite to rescue Conti and Garr, and the four run from the law. Conti and Garr are put on a boat, with the promise that they will be sent to California. The police arrive and another shoot out begins. The couple is knocked unconscious in the ensuing melee, and their leaky boat accidentally drifts out to sea. Conti and Garr awake during a terrible storm, convinced that they are about to meet their maker. But Conti decides to be brave and attempts to steer the boat to shore. He's knocked unconscious again, and wakes up on a beach. Unable to find Garr, he follows a set of footprints and ends up being captured by the jungle natives. Garr, in the meantime, has washed up further along the coast and prepares to return to Los Angeles. Though worried about Conti, she is told there is nothing she can do. Conti is brought to Faraon's bedside, where he quickly realizes the girl has a ruptured appendix. He manages to convince the natives to get Faraon to a hospital, but the only facility available is a nearby mission. Not too coincidentally, this was the same place where Garr had been rescued. Conti, using somewhat primitive methods, performs a successful appendectomy, then heads to Mexico City. He tries to persuade embassy officials to help him find Garr, but the authorities insist she is probably dead. Lloyd and Rodriguez are also in town, once again trying to pull off a robbery. They set off an explosion which causes cars to collide, leading to Conti's second accidental reunion with his ex-wife. Realizing that they love one another, Conti and Garr decide to remarry.

Conti and Garr make an amusing team. Their constant quarreling in the midst of incredible circumstances is well played. The two simply ignore their surroundings and go at it. In doing so, they make the already unusual situation deliciously absurd. Garr, wearing a pink formal gown throughout most of the picture, has a wonderful sense of timing, firing off her lines with dexterity. She easily steals scenes from Conti with her delightful performance. Rodriguez and Lloyd fill out the subplot nicely. Their slapstick sequences are a good counterpart to the wittier exchanges between Garr and Conti. With MIRACLES writer-director Kouf delivers a decidedly schizophrenic package. When he sticks to the screwball aspects, MIRACLES is something of a minor gem. Kouf shows a real talent for frenzied pacing, and makes effective use of throwaway gags. His dialog often crackles with wit, providing many funny exchanges for his leads. This is a real surprise considering Kouf's past work. His previous outings (all as screenwriter) include such forgettable comedies as UTILITIES, UP THE CREEK, and the particularly obnoxious SECRET ADMIRER.

When Kouf humanizes the story, MIRACLES turns more than a little dull. Conti's mission of mercy changes the film's tone considerably, and it's an uneasy shift. Had Kouf stuck with his goofier inclinations he would have been better off. Surprisingly, despite the name value of Garr and Conti, MIRACLES never saw much of a release. Shot in Mexico in 1984, the finished product sat on studio shelves awhile until a brief, unnoticed release in the summer of 1986. The film finally reached a wider market with a videocassette release in 1987, but it's unlikely to recoup its reported $10 million budget. Songs include: "Getaway" (performed by Jim Stowell), "You're My Prisoner" (performed by Mark Terry), "I Need a Woman" (performed by Peter Hix), "Jazz Minn" (performed by Elizabeth Kubotz). ***(Profanity, sexual situations.)***

p, Steve Roth, Bernard Williams; d&w, Jim Kouf; ph, John Alcott (Super Techniscope, Technicolor); m, Peter Bernstein; ed, Susan E. Morse, Dennis Virkler; prod d, Terence Marsh; art d, Fernando Ramirez "El Polo," George Richardson, Craig Edgar; set d, Michael Seirton; cos, Cynthia Bales; spec eff, John Stears; m/l, Jim Stowell, Alan Kirk, Mark Terry, Ron Gertz, Pearl Batella, Dan Slider; stunts, Bud Davis; makeup, Giancarlo Del Brocco.

Comedy **Cas.** **(PR:C MPAA:PG)**

MIRAGE† (1987, China/Hong Kong) 95m Golden Principal-China Film c

Yu Yung Kang *(Tant Ting Xuan)*, Siu-Ming Tsui *(Fatty)*, Pasha Romani *(Gazanova)*, Connie Khan *(Nice Girl)*, Fang Dong Yu, Wang Hwa.

A wide-screen martial arts spectacular set in 1930s China starring Yu Yung Kang as a photographer who spots a mirage of a beautiful woman (Romani) riding a white horse while traveling with a trade caravan on the Silk Route. The photographer falls in love with the mirage and goes off in search of his vision. After many battles he finds her and discovers that she is a fiesty bandit queen. Although she despises him at first and considers him an enemy, she eventually falls in love with the photographer, but now it is his turn to reject her. A Peking-Hong Kong coproduction from the same team that successfully exported SHAOLIN TEMPLE to Europe.

d&w, Siu-Ming Tsui; ph, Li Wan Jie; m, Joseph Koo; stunts, Siu-Ming Tsui.

Martial Arts **(PR:NR MPAA:NR)**

MIRAZHI LYUBRI† (1987, USSR/Syria) 98m Kirghizfilm-Tadzhikfilm-Ganem-film/Sovexportfilm c (Trans: Mirages of Love)

Fakhridin Makhamatdinov, Asel Eshimbayeva, Farhad Mirzoyev.

Filmed on locations in Bukhara, Samarkand, Kirghizia, Damascus, Basra, and Palmira, this film follows the career of a talented young artist who, when forced to leave his homeland, traveled throughout the Orient and became a master of painting and architecture. Although in love with a beautiful woman, the artist sacrifices romance in favor of his work.

d, Tolomush Okeyev; w, Timur Zulfikarov, Tolomush Okeyev; ph, Nurtai Borbiyev; m, Rumil Vildanov; art d, Rustam Odinayev, Sergey Romankulov.

Drama **(PR:NR MPAA:NR)**

MIRCH MASALA† (1987, India) 125m National Film Development c (Trans: A Touch of Spice)

Naseeruddin Shah *(Sudebar)*, Smita Patil *(Sonbai)*, Suresh Oberoi *(Mukhi)*, Deepti Naval *(Mukhi's Wife)*, Om Puri *(Guard)*.

Set in the pre-independence 1940's MIRCH MASALA tells the story of a young woman, Patil, who resists the lecherous advances of tax collector Shah. Rather than give in to Shah, Patil takes refuge in a local spice factory where the female workers eventually come to her defense. Shown in competition at the Moscow Film Festival. (In Hindi.)

d, Ketan Mehta; w, Hriday Lani, Trijawani Sharma; ph, Jahangir Choudhury; m, Rajat Dholakia; ed, Sanjiv Shah.

Drama **(PR:NR MPAA:NR)**

MISS MARY** (1987, Arg.) 100m GEA/NW c

Julie Christie *(Miss Mary Mulligan)*, Sofia Viruboff *(Carolina)*, Donald McIntire *(Johnny)*, Barbara Bunge *(Teresa as a Child)*, Nacha Guevara *(Mecha [Mother])*, Eduardo [Tato] Pavlovsky *(Alfredo [Father])*, Guillermo Battaglia *(Uncle Ernesto)*, Iris Marga *(Aunt)*, Luisina Brando *(Perla)*, Nora Zinsky *(Teresa as an Adult)*, Gerardo Romano *(Ernesto)*, Regina Lam, Anne Henry, Sandra Ballesteros, Anita Larronde, Alfredo Quesada, Osvaldo Flores, Tessie Gilligan, Carlos Usay, Oscar Lopez, Susana Veron, Alberto Marty, Beatriz Thibaudin, Laura Feal, Lidia Cortinez, Juan Palomina, Facundo Zuviria, Lila Di Palma, Mercedes Van Gelderen, Paula Maria Muschietti, Julio Cesar Srur.

The follow-up to director Bemberg's Oscar-nominated CAMILA (1985), MISS MARY stars Christie in the title role as a spinsterish but attractive Englishwoman who travels to an opulent estate in Argentina in 1938 to act as the governess for three children. Told episodically with flashbacks, it opens with a pre-credit scene that introduces both Christie's female charges and establishes the film's political and cultural context. In 1930, two little girls are put to bed by their British governess (Christie's predecessor); their parents prepare to attend a party celebrating the military coup that has replaced the democratically elected government with a right-wing faction that will oppressively rule the country for the next 15 years. The Argentine upper class, which is so influenced by British culture that many of them chose to speak English rather than their native tongue, has "wholeheartedly supported this break of constitutional rule." In 1945, this era of right-wing domination is about to end, and Christie, after noticing the announcement of the marriage of one of the girls she had looked after, reflects on her arrival at the estate of the archconservative and machismo patriarch Pavlovsky and his delicate wife Guevara. Christie is to be the governess for their daughters, Viruboff and Bunge, and 14-year-old son McIntire. Also on the estate are Guevara's brother, Battaglia, a handsome fascist; a grandmother and grandfather; and just about anything one could desire. Pavlovsky tells Christie he wants his children reared with a strong sense of Catholicism, thereby keeping the girls out of trouble in a country where men apparently can't be trusted. Guevara shares her husband's protective attitude and, from the beginning, has the girls checking under their beds at night for men. Christie is herself sexually repressed and provides a perfect example of chastity for teenager Viruboff and little sister Bunge. McIntire, however, sees Christie with different eyes, smitten by her almost from her arrival.

The film jumps back and forth between past events on the estate and the present (1945) in Buenos Aires, where Christie attends grown-up Bunge's wedding, veiled and unnoticed by the family except for McIntire, to whom she hands a note. Back in the past, Christie resolutely but warmly oversees the children's playful passage through puberty: Viruboff, vivacious and sensitive; Bunge, the precocious baby of the family; McIntire, handsome and moody; all of them

coming to love her in their own way. When the virile, philandering Pavlovsky romances a sexy widow, prompting Guevara to take a shot at him, Christie is a calming influence on the children. After that incident, Guevara, who sits for hours at the piano, retreats even further into her melancholy, seeking refuge in her "little crying room" (a storage closet). As a present for McIntire's 15th birthday, Battaglia takes him to a prostitute. But the experience leaves McIntire with an empty feeling and he rushes through a rainstorm back to Christie. Her understanding embrace is transformed by McIntire's passion and they make love. Guevara sees McIntire leaving Christie's room, clothes in hand, and dismisses the governess the following day. She leaves the estate while the children, who have been locked into a room, scream her name. Returning to the present, all of this hangs heavily in the air as Christie has tea in her flat with McIntire, now married and an officer in the military. She explains that with the war over she will be returning to England. He tells her (and we see in flashback) how Bunge has been forced to marry after being caught in the act of premarital sex, and how this has pushed the sensitive Viruboff over the edge. Finally, McIntire reminds Christie of that rainy night, but she tells him that it is not raining now. The next day, with General Juan Peron ready to assume power and a new era dawning in Argentina, Christie boards the boat that will take her back to England.

Christie skillfully essays this Englishwoman abroad whose calm exterior belies the confusion and discontent festering within. However, the details of her past are so sketchy—a photograph of a dead soldier (her former lover), rose-colored letters home to her mother—that she remains too elusive. One cares about her, but only so much. The nuances of the stultifying aristocratic environment in which she finds herself are carefully conveyed (as she did in CAMILA, Bemberg has focused her attention on a specific and important period in Argentine history and adroitly captured it), yet the trials and travails of this patrician family are never very compelling. This was something of an autobiographical film for director and co-screenwriter Bemberg, who is herself the product of a wealthy family and a restrictive religious upbringing by foreign governesses. She has said she has been a feminist since childhood and one of the things she hoped to accomplish with the film was to "get even " for the indignity her mother suffered at the hands of her macho, authoritarian husband. But while MISS MARY is full of female victims—the sullen Guevara, the mad Viruboff, Bunge, who is forced to marry a man she doesn't love, and Christie—the conditions and events that have led these women to their unhappy states are never communicated with enough force or complexity. All which is not to say Bemberg hasn't succeeded in pointing a well-deserved finger at the macho code, but only that, in the process, she has not created a very involving drama. Songs and music include: "Carolina" (Luis Maria Serra), "Gnossienes" (Erik Satie), "Ain't She Sweet" (Milton Ager, Jack Yellen, performed by Picadilly Revels Band), "Don't Get Around Much Anymore" (Duke Ellington, Bob Russell, performed by Santa Maria Jazz Band), "Stars Fell on Alabama" (Frank Perkins, Mitchell Parish, performed by Santa Maria Jazz Band), "Moten Swing" (Bennie Moten, Buster Moten, performed by Santa Maria Jazz Band), "I Can't Give You Anything But Love Baby" (Jimmy McHugh, Dorothy Fields, performed by Benny Goodman), "It's Been So Long" (Walter Donaldson, Harold Adamson, performed by Benny Goodman), "Elmer's Tune" (Elmer Albrecht, Sammy Gallup, Dick Jurgens, performed by Glenn Miller). Filmed in Argentina in both an English-language version and a Spanish-language version, MISS MARY received a foreign and festival release in 1986. *(Sexual situations.)*

p, Lita Stantic; d, Maria Luisa Bemberg; w, Jorge Goldenberg, Maria Luisa Bemberg (based on a story by Maria Luisa Bemberg, Beda Docampo Feijoo, Juan Batista Stagnaro); ph, Miguel Rodriguez (Eastmancolor); m, Luis Maria Serra, Erik Satie; ed, Luis Cesar D'Angiolillo; art d, Esmeralda Almonacid; cos, Graciela Galan; m/l, Milton Ager, Jack Yellen, Duke Ellington, Bob Russell, Frank Perkins, Mitchell Parish, Bennie Moten, Buster Moten, Jimmy McHugh, Dorothy Fields, Elmer Albrecht, Sammy Gallup, Dick Jurgens, Harold Adamson, Walter Donaldson; makeup, Selva Chomnalez.

Drama **Cas.** **(PR:O MPAA:R)**

MISS MONA*1/2** (1987, Fr.) 98m KG/AKG-AAA-World Marketing Film c

Jean Carmet *(Miss Mona)*, Ben Smail *(Samir)*, Albert Delpy *(Jean, Subway Conductor)*, Daniel Schad *(Manu)*, Francis Frappat *(Club Organizer)*, Andre Chaumeau *(Gilbert)*, Albert Klein *(Father)*, Philippe de Brugada, Yvette Petit, Michel Peyleron, Maximilien Decroux, Kader Boukhanef, Remi Martin.

In the slums of Paris, Smail, a 30-year-old Arab drifter, is picked up by Carmet, an aging transvestite. Carmet, who lives in a trailer with Klein, a senile old man who also cross dresses, tells fortunes for a living by day and turns tricks in Parisian streets by night. He is getting too old for the prostitution business, so he intends to make Smail his protege. Smail, who is living in France illegally, protests, but his desperate situation forces him to accept Carmet's offer. Smail's first customer is Delpy, a closet homosexual, who has an anonymous tryst with Smail in a restaurant bathroom. At first Smail is filled with revulsion, but he eventually moves into Carmet's tiny trailer. Smail becomes more involved with Paris' homosexual underworld, led by his eager mentor's guiding hand. Carmet explains to Smail that he is unhappy as a man, and dreams of going to Sweden for a sex-change operation. Years before, while living with another transvestite, Carmet had diligently saved his money for the operation. These plans had gone sour when Carmet's roommate stole his money and went to Sweden for his/her own operation. Now she runs a Paris cafe with her husband, unaware that her former roommate knows of her whereabouts. Smail becomes involved with a young homosexual stripper whom Carmet instantly dislikes. Carmet's worst fears come true when this boy steals his money. The boy, who works in a sleazy strip joint, kills himself on stage soon afterwards. In order to raise money for Carmet's operation and illegal residence papers for Smail, the unlikely duo take to theft. At first they are successful, but tragedy strikes when Smail and Carmet attempt to rob Carmet's former roommate. The two surprise the woman and Smail knocks her unconscious before taking her money. Carmet is afraid he has been recognized so Smail goes back to kill the woman. He plans to meet Carmet later that night, but before the rendezvous Smail is stopped in the subway by two policemen. He attempts to escape but the lawmen tell the conductor to stop the train and Smail is arrested. Ironically, the conductor is Smail's first customer, Delpy.

MISS MONA is a bleak, yet not unsympathetic view of society's down and outers. Both Smail and Carmet are schemers, obviously using one another's talents for personal gain, yet their offbeat friendship brims with affection. Their love/hate relationship and business dealings within the seamy world of male prostitution plays like a latter-day Joe Buck and Ratso Rizzo of MIDNIGHT COWBOY, a film MISS MONA occasionally resembles. Writer/director Charef dealt with similar themes of friendship amidst slum life and prostitution in his previous film TEA AT THE HAREM OF ARCHIMEDES. He expands on those ideas with this uncompromising look at unhappy people desperately trying to better themselves.

Carmet gives a fine performance in the title role. He relies on subtle mannerisms to create the character, and always carries himself with a sense of dignity. Carmet also infuses this troubled man/woman with good humor, a person able to see the comedy within a desperate situation. In one marvelous scene, Carmet strolls down a boulevard wearing a white dress patterned after the one Marilyn Monroe wore in THE SEVEN YEAR ITCH. When he passes over a subway grate in the sidewalk, the temptation is irresistible as he allows the rush of air to billow his skirt just like Monroe's. Smail makes a good counterpart to Carmet. Dark, with bushy hair and beard, Smail spends much of the film garbed in black clothing, further emphasizing his alienation. He rarely speaks, instead conveying his feelings through brooding eyes. He is troubled by the world he has been swept into, yet realizes it's a way out of a hopeless situation. Like Charef's previous film, MISS MONA was produced by Michele Ray-Gavras, the wife of noted director Constantin Costa-Gavras.

p, Michele Ray-Gavras; d&w, Mehdi Charef; ph, Patrick Blossier (Eastmancolor); m, Bernard Lubat; ed, Kenout Peltier; cos, Edith Vesperini, Maika Guezel.

Drama **(PR:O MPAA:NR)**

MISSING IN ACTION† (1987, Phil.) Roadshow c

Charito Solis, Lauro Delgado, Nova Villa, Lani Gentica.

A pair of surgeons volunteer to serve in Vietnam and are sent to the front lines where one is wounded and the other is listed as MIA. The survivor returns home and becomes engaged to the widow of the missing man, but just before the wedding the hideously disfigured husband returns.

[No credits available.]

War **(PR:NR MPAA:NR)**

MISSION KILL** (1987) 97m Media Home Ent./Goldfarb Dist. c

Robert Ginty *(Cooper)*, Cameron Mitchell *(Harry)*, Merete Van Kamp *(Sydney)*, Olivia D'Abo *(Rebel Girl)*, Henry Darrow *(Borghini)*, Sandy Baron *(Bingo)*, Clement St. George *(Kennedy)*, Eduardo Lopez Rojas *(Ariban)*, Jorge Reynoso *(Carlos)*, Juan Ignacio Aranda *(Miguel)*, Jorge Eepeda *(Juan)*, Luke Walter *(Scar)*, Luis Contreras *(Officer)*, Walter Mathews *(Foreman)*, Lisa Coppenolle *(Hooker)*, Jonathon Cripple, Sonny Shields *(Mercenaries)*, Alessandro Tasca *(Priest)*, Miguel Angel Fuentes *(Platoon Leader)*, Magdalena Doria *(Teacher)*, Alvaro Carlano *(Interrogator)*, Laly Roffiel *(Drunk Woman)*, Rene Barrera *(Guard)*, Paco Mauri, Bruce Rothchild *(Soldiers)*, Alfredo Ramirez, Rigoberto Carmona, Antonio Rangel *(Men)*, Raul Santa Maria *(Butler)*, Sebastian Ligardi *(Secretary)*, Carlos Romano *(Newscaster)*, Jess Fontana, Arminus Arzatz *(Guards)*, Isela Diaz Garcia *(Little Girl)*, Louis Waldon, Katie Barry *(Tourists at Border)*, Brooke Bundy *(Katie)*, David Kaufman *(Glenn)*.

A competent actioner featuring Ginty as a demolitions expert who accompanies old Marine buddy Mitchell to a fictitious Central American country while the latter delivers a shipment of guns to rebel fighters trying to overthrow bloody dictator Rojas. Unfortunately, Mitchell is killed by a band of mercenaries employed by Rojas' second-in-command, Darrow, and the weapons are confiscated. Seeking revenge, Ginty slaughters the mercenaries and takes their leader's identity. Soon after, Ginty is captured by government forces and thrown into a prison cell with the soon-to-be-executed revolutionary leader. Luckily, the rebels blow a hole in the prison wall and rescue their leader. Ginty is brought along for the ride and the rebel leader decides to let him live, although pretty young revolutionary D'Abo would rather see him dead. When Ginty witnesses government troops execute civilians, he decides to aid the rebels by helping them blow up bridges, power stations, and ship yards. Free-lance journalist Baron dubs Ginty "Robin Hood" in the press and turns him into a folk hero. Eventually the rebels decide to enact an all-out assault on the dictator and his forces during the dictator's anniversary celebration. While Ginty goes to blow up a huge bridge nearby, D'Abo poses as a peasant girl sent to satisfy the dictator. Unfortunately, one of the rebels is a spy for Darrow and he has informed the ambitious toady of the plan. Just as D'Abo is about to stab the rotund Rojas, Darrow walks in and shoots her. He then shoots Rojas and claims that D'Abo is the killer. Meanwhile, hundreds of government troops come out of hiding and a massive battle with the rebels ensues. When the smoke clears, most of the rebels are dead and Ginty is presumed to be among the casualties. Days later, Darrow is flown to his coronation by helicopter. Much to the new dictator's surprise, his pilot is none other than Ginty. Darrow desperately offers Ginty a $500,000 bribe and Ginty appears to accept, but when the helicopter approaches the grandstand, Ginty shoves Darrow out of the helicopter and the would-be dictator falls to his death hundreds of feet below. Ginty flies back to the US with the $500,000.

Another straight-to-home-video feature for low-budget action hero Ginty, who turns in his usual stoic portrayal. While the script is nothing but the usual batch of overused action-film cliches, director Winters stages the action (filmed mostly in Mexico) with flair and the actors do an efficient job with cartoonish roles. But D'Abo, who uses a Spanish accent and dyed her blonde hair black for the role, is more than a little ridiculous as the fiery female rebel. Her accent is laughable as she utters such lines as "I vant to keel de peeg!" with a menacing scowl on her face. Also quite overblown is Mexican actor Rojas as the dictator. In his big scene with Darrow he pounds his fist on his desk, swaggers around, and shouts at the top of his lungs whenever he mentions the rebels. Yet no one rents a Robert Ginty movie expecting Oscar-winning performances and MISSION KILL is a fairly inoffensive time-waster for the undiscriminating. Songs include "Leave Me Alone" (Jesse Frederick, performed by Jill Colbucci), "Stand" (Jesse Frederick, performed by Frederick). *(Graphic violence.)*

p&d, David Winters; w, Maria Dante; ph, Tom Denove; m, Jesse Frederick, Jeff Koz; ed, Ned Humphreys; art d, Francisco Magallon, Richard McGuire; set d, Eva Gibra; cos, Lennie Baron; spec eff, Wayne Beauchamp; stunts, Sonny Shields, Tom Moraga; m/l, Jesse Frederick; makeup, June Brickman, Pam Pieteman, Alan Apone.

Action **Cas.** **(PR:C-O MPAA:NR)**

MISSIONE EROICA† (1987, It.) C.G. Silver-Maura Intl./Columbia Pictures Italia (Trans: Heroic Mission)

Paolo Villaggio, Lino Banfi, Massimo Boldi, Christian De Sica, Teo Teocoli, Franca Gonella, Luc Merenda, Corrado Olmi, Clarita Gatto.

A light comedy of the misadventures of an Italian Fireman's Corps whose blunders result in the hospitalization of their commander and place them under the tutelege of a visiting American instructor. They are then sent on a mission to pick up a large charge of TNT thinking it is only an exercise and the TNT is not real. Predictable chaos results.

d, Giorgio Capitani; w, Laura Toscano, Franco Marotta; ph, Sandro D'Eva; m, Bruno Zambrini; ed, Sergio Montanari.

Comedy **(PR:NR MPAA:NR)**

MISTER INDIA† (1987, India) 180m Narsimha Ent.

Anil Kapoor *(Arun Verma)*, Sridevi *(Seema)*, Amrish Puri *(Mogambo)*, Ashok Kumar.

Three-hour long fantasy film from India which sounds like an amalgamation of SUPERMAN and the 1939 Bela Lugosi serial THE PHANTOM CREEPS. Kindly orphange-owner Kapoor has trouble keeping the kids fed. Evil gun-runner Puri sends some goons over to make an offer on the orphange with plans to set up a smuggling operation on the premises. Kapoor resists and is joined by lady reporter Sridevi in his struggle against the power-hungry gangster. In the basement of the orphange, Kapoor discovers a device worn on the wrist which enables him to become invisible. Determined to rid the world of the ruthless Puri, Kapoor becomes an invisible superhero known as "Mr. India." The Indian producers plan to shorten the film, dub it into English, and release it in the West.

p, Boney Kapoor; d, Shekhar Kapur; w, Salim Javed; ph, Baba Azmi; m, Laxmikant, Pyarelal; ed, Waman, Guru; spec eff, Peter Pereira; ch, Saroj Khan; m/l, Javed Akhtar.

Fantasy **(PR:NR MPAA:NR)**

MITT HJARTA HAR TVA TUNGOR† (1987, Swed.) 90m FilmStallet-Swedish Film Institute-SVT1-Manvargen c (Trans: My Heart Has Two Voices)

Maud Nycander *(Mona)*.

A young photographer takes many risks in her search for feminine identity.

d, Mikael Wistrom.

Drama **(PR:NR MPAA:NR)**

MON BEL AMOUR, MA DECHIRURE† (1987, Fr.) 107m Odessa-Canal Plus-Generale d'Images/Bac c (Trans: My True Love, My Wound)

Stephane Ferrara *(Patrick)*, Catherine Wilkening *(Catherine)*, Vera Gregh *(The Director)*, Veronique Barrault *(Clementine)*, Jacques Castaldo *(Jean-Ba)*, Philippe Manesse *(Julien)*, Jacky Sigaux *(Jacky)*, Mouss *(Mouss)*.

Similar in theme to the award-winning RENDEZVOUS (1985), this film features former French middleweight boxer Ferrara (featured in Godard's DETECTIVE) as a street hood who wanders into a small cafe theater to collect a debt from the acting troupe's manager. There he spies a beautiful young actress, Wilkening, and decides he must have her. He waits for her after the show and rapes her in an alley, but much to his (and her) surprise, she enjoys the experience and begins an animalistic affair with the brute. Once she lands the lead in a major production, however, her sexual passions cool and she devotes more time to rehearsals than to Ferrara. When she finally breaks off the relationship, the angry hood kidnaps the actress and holds her in his car while he drives them both into a spectacular accident. He is killed, but Wilkening somehow survives the wreck and goes on to become a hit on the stage. This film has a chance at release stateside, but it may receive an "X" rating (a la DEVIL IN THE FLESH) because of its male and female full frontal nudity and graphically brutal sex sequences.

p, Yannick Bernard; d, Jose Pinheiro; w, Louis Calaferte, Sotha, Jose Pinheiro; ph, Richard Andry; m, Romano Musumarra; ed, Claire Pinheiro-L'Itevevder; art d, Theo Meurisse; cos, Delphine Bernard, Karlien Nel, Frederique Menichetti; spec eff, Reiko Kruk, Dominique Colladant; m/l, Romano Musumarra; makeup, Rieko Kruk, Dominique Colladant.

Drama **(PR:NR MPAA:NR)**

MONSTER IN THE CLOSET** (1987) 87m Closet/Troma c

Donald Grant *(Richard Clark)*, Denise DuBarry *(Diane Bennett)*, Henry Gibson *(Dr. Pennyworth)*, Howard Duff *(Father Finnegan)*, Donald Moffat *(Gen. Turnbull)*, Claude Akins *(Sheriff Ketchum)*, Paul Walker *(The Professor)*, Frank Ashmore *(Scoop Johnson)*, John Carradine *(Old Joe)*, Paul Dooley *(Roy Crane)*, Stella Stevens *(Margo Crane)*, Jesse White *(Ben Bernstein)*, Kevin Peter Hall *(The Monster)*, Stacy Ferguson *(Lucy)*, Ritchie Montgomery *(Deputy Spiro)*, Arthur Berggren *(Jimmy's Father)*, Daryle Ann Lindley *(Jimmy's Mother)*, Gordon Metcalfe *(Turnbull's Aide)*, David Anthony *(Paperboy)*, Annie Glynn *(Newsstand Woman)*, Arlee Reed *(Passerby)*, James Arone, Andrew Cofrin *(Soldiers)*, Benny Baker *(Mr. McGinty)*, Doc Duhame *(Deputy Connor)*, Jonna Lee *(Sorority Girl)*, Arthur Taxier, Archie Lang, Claire Nono, John Walsh *(TV Newscasters)*, Wycliffe Young, Paul Latchaw *(Globe Reporters)*, David McCharen, Patricia Richarde, Carole Kean, Jack Tate, Sheldon Feldner, Terrence Beasor, Katherine Lyons, Jack Shearer *(Reporters)*, Richie Egan *(Charlie)*, Jonathan Aluzas *(Chip)*, Brad Kester *(Rex)*, Evan Arnold *(Beaver)*, Corky Pigeon *(Danny)*, Stephanie White *(Maggie, Scoop's Girl)*.

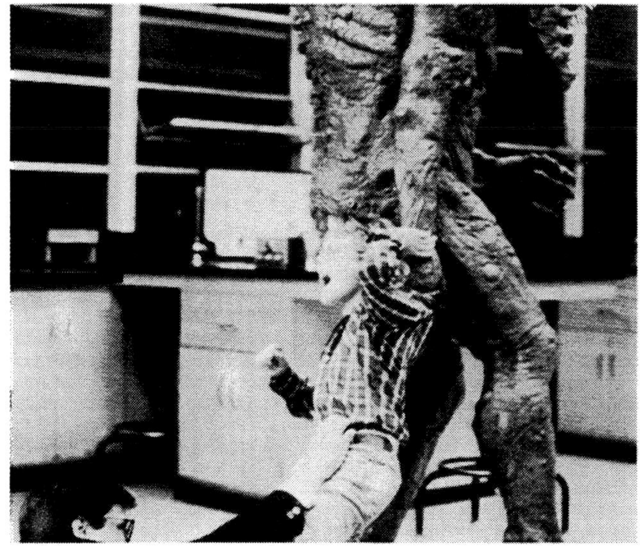

Funnier than it has any right to be, MONSTER IN THE CLOSET is an affectionate parody of the low-budget science-fiction and horror films of the 1950s, with several jabs at Hitchcock, Spielberg, and even KING KONG thrown in for good measure. Set in San Francisco, the film begins with a pre-credits sequence in which a college coed, an old blind man (Carradine), and a small child are yanked into their closets, never to return (no blood or gore here, just clothes spewing out of the closets). Hapless obit reporter Grant is assigned to cover the strange disappearances. During his investigation, Grant meets sexy biology professor DuBarry and her precocious young son known as "The Professor" (Walker). DuBarry is all business and shows no interest in Grant until the reporter removes his glasses. Sans eyewear, Grant has a strange power over DuBarry and she instantly falls in love with him (of course, the bumbling Grant is completely ignorant of this phenomenon). Several celebrity guest-star murders later, the monster finally reveals itself to be a tall, ugly creature with a huge, gaping mouth. The Army, led by the blustering Moffat, blasts away at the creature, but the shells have no effect and the creature wanders over to the nearest closet. Enter scientist Gibson (who plays his role straight—just like those ultraserious 1950s sci-fi movie scientists), who attempts to coax the monster out of hiding by playing musical notes (a la CLOSE ENCOUNTERS OF THE THIRD KIND) on a child's xylophone. When this fails, the only thing left to do is to alert the public to "Destroy All Closets!" Seeking to entice the monster into a trap, DuBarry leaves her closets intact. When the monster arrives she and Grant try to electrocute the creature (in a scene straight out of the 1951 version of THE THING) but the plan goes awry. During the struggle, Grant's glasses are knocked off and the monster is suddenly dumbstruck with love. Like King Kong in love with Fay Wray, the monster sweeps Grant into its arms and wanders the streets of San Francisco looking for a closet to call home. Finally, exhausted from the fruitless search (and tired from carrying Grant), the monster collapses in a heap, leaving witnesses to utter, "Twas not a closet, but beauty killed the beast!"

Scattershot and sophomoric in approach, MONSTER IN THE CLOSET somehow manages to generate enough chuckles to sustain viewer interest (although the going gets a little dull in the middle). Director Dahlin, a Chicago native who won a student Academy Award while at Northwestern with his sophisticated parody of Hitchcock films entitled SUSPENSION, obviously knows and loves the genres he parodies. Normally the casting of this many down-on-their luck stars spells trouble, but Dahlin uses Akins, Stevens, Dooley, Carradine, Duff, White, Moffat, and especially Gibson to great effect. Gibson nearly walks off with the film, turning in a very funny deadpan performance. The monster is played by none other than Kevin Peter Hall, who played the monsters in HARRY AND THE HENDERSONS and PREDATOR this year. Luckily for director Dahlin, his distributor, Troma, long known for its truly disgusting little forays into the sex-and-gore brand of filmmaking, allowed him to produce a surprisingly tame picture. Any gore or nudity would have taken this film out of the realm of goofy innocence and driven it right into the arena of tasteless exploitation. *(Comic violence.)*

p, David Levy, Peter L. Bergquist; d&w, Bob Dahlin (based on a story by Bob Dahlin, Peter L. Bergquist); ph, Ronald W. McLeish; m, Barrie Guard; ed, Raja Gosnell, Stephanie Palewski; prod d, Lynda Cohen; set d, Patricia Hall; cos, Kathleen Brodbeck; spec eff, Martin Becker; stunts, Doc Duhame; makeup, Penelope Stanley.

Science Fiction/Comedy Cas. (PR:A-C MPAA:PG)

MONSTER SQUAD, THE** (1987) 82m Taft Entertainment-Keith Barish-Home Box Office/Tri-Star c

Andre Gower *(Sean)*, Robby Kiger *(Patrick)*, Stephen Macht *(Del, Sean's Father)*, Duncan Regehr *(Count Dracula)*, Tom Noonan *(Frankenstein)*, Brent Chalem *(Horace)*, Ryan Lambert *(Rudy)*, Ashley Bank *(Phoebe, Sean's Sister)*, Michael Faustino *(Eugene)*, Mary Ellen Trainor *(Emily)*, Leonardo Cimino *(Scary German Guy)*, Jonathan Gries *(Desperate Man)*, Stan Shaw *(Detective Sapir)*, Lisa Fuller *(Patrick's Sister)*, Jason Hervey *(E.J.)*, Adam Carl *(Derek)*, Carl Thibault *(Wolfman)*, Tom Woodruff, Jr. *(Gill-Man)*, Michael MacKay *(Mummy)*, Jack Gwillim *(Van Helsing)*, David Proval *(Pilot)*, Daryl Anderson *(Co-Pilot)*, Robert Lesser *(Eugene's Dad)*, Gwill Richards *(Mr. Metzger)*, Ernie Brown *(Night Watchman)*, Sonia Curtis *(Peasant Girl)*, Brian Kestner *(Rookie Cop)*, Denver Mattson *(Beefy Cop)*, Diana Lewis *(TV Anchorwoman)*, Gary Rebstock *(TV Anchorman)*, David Wendel *(Army General)*, Charly Morgan *(Vampire Bride with Possom)*, Phil Culotta *(Driver of Coroner Van)*, Marianne De Camp *(Mrs. Carlsen/Cat Head)*, Mary Albee, Joan-Carroll Baron *(Pantry Girls/Vampires)*, Paul Barringer, Julius Le Flore, Jim Stephen *(Squad Room Cops)*.

In an era when most American films are patched together from parts of last year's hits, THE MONSTER SQUAD sports a fairly innovative combination; namely, the 1986 hit STAND BY ME and a potpourri of the 1940s Universal horror epics (HOUSE OF FRANKENSTEIN, HOUSE OF DRACULA, ABBOTT AND COSTELLO MEET FRANKENSTEIN). THE MONSTER SQUAD begins as Dracula (Regehr) and Frankenstein's Monster (Noonan) hook up with their pals the Mummy (MacKay), the Wolfman (Thibault), and the Gill-Man (Woodruff, Jr.) in a suburb which could have been borrowed from a Steven Spielberg film. Led by Dracula, the monsters are searching for an ancient amulet that will help them rule the world. Meanwhile, a group of grade-school friends devoted to the lore of Hollywood monsters (Gower, Kiger, Chalem, Faustino, Lambert, and Bank) meet in their treehouse and quiz one another on the finer aspects of movie-monsterdom. When the kids learn that several strange events have occurred around town (the Mummy getting up and walking out of the museum, a werewolf terrorizing the area, etc.), they know exactly what to do. With the help of a lonely old man known to the neighborhood children only as "Scary German Guy" (Cimino), the kids learn of the secret amulet and Dracula's plans to steal it. They then arm themselves with wooden stakes, silver bullets, crosses and the like and race off on their bicycles to defeat the monsters. Surprisingly, the kids pick up an unexpected ally: the Frankenstein Monster. Tired of being bossed around by Dracula, the monster wanders off on his own and befriends Bank, Gower's five-year-old sister. The monster aids the kids during the climactic showdown, but it takes a mystic incantation read by a virgin (Kiger's teenage sister proves to be no help here, so little Bank must read the magic words) to dispatch the creatures of the night. Try as she might to save the kindly Frankenstein Monster, Bank watches helplessly as he, too, is sucked into the vortex created by the incantation.

This second feature film from young director Dekker (NIGHT OF THE CREEPS) is a poorly paced and haphazardly scripted (by LETHAL WEAPON writer Black—yes, together they are Black & Dekker) horror/comedy that is neither scary nor particularly funny. The attempt to create a STAND BY ME type of childhood ambience is strained to the breaking point by a cast of amazingly precocious youngsters who, in fine Spielberg fashion, are much more capable and intelligent than their parents. The adults in this film come off as likable dolts (Gower's father) or impatient shrews (Gower's mother). Only Cimino escapes this fate, but he is given special dispensation because the tattoo on his wrist marks him as a victim of the Holocaust. (The line that goes something like, "Yes, children, I know a lot about monsters," is inappropriate and in bad taste—especially since the kids never know what he is referring to.) Also in questionable taste is the film's obsession with virginity. The search for a female virgin to read the mystic incantation leads younger brother Kiger to quiz his older sister about her sex life. To make the joke work, the girl is portrayed as a complete bubblehead who doesn't realize that she has lost her virginity (claiming later that she thought sex with her boy friend "didn't count"). Not only is this sequence unsuitable for children, but it also manages to be completely insulting to women. As far as the monsters are concerned, they are a tepid lot, and the special makeup is terribly plastic. Regehr's Dracula is about as menacing as last month's *GQ* coverboy, the Gill-Man spends the entire film jumping out of sewers, the Mummy—never a particularly intimidating monster—is easily unraveled, and the Wolfman is doubled over by a kick to the groin. Only Noonan (last seen as the villain in MANHUNTER) scores as the Frankenstein Monster. Dekker, Black, and Noonan understand that children have always sympathized with the Frankenstein Monster because they see him as a misunderstood victim—not as a monster. Like KING KONG (whom kids also adore), the Frankenstein Monster has never sought the wrath of humans; he just has trouble communicating, and his frustration leads to outbursts of rage. Children readily identify with such a dilemma and they always root for the monster. Thus, when the children make him an honorary member of their club, it is perfectly logical, if not downright sentimental. Unfortunately, Dekker's schizophrenic direction combines movie nostalgia with Spielbergian excess and creates a half-baked film that leaves a bad aftertaste. *(Graphic violence, mild profanity, sexual innuendo.)*

p, Jonathan A. Zimbert, Neil A. Machlis; d, Fred Dekker; w, Shane Black, Fred Dekker; ph, Bradford May (Panavision, Metrocolor); m, Bruce Broughton; ed. James Mitchell; prod d, Albert Brenner; art d, David M. Haber; set d, Roland Hill, Harold Fuhrman; cos, Michael Hoffman, Aggie Lyon; spec eff, Phil Cory, Richard Edlund, Stan Winston; makeup, Zoltan, Katalin Elek; stunts, John Moio.

Horror/Comedy (PR:A-C MPAA:PG-13)

MONTECARLO GRAN CASINO† (1987, It.) 97m Filmauro c

Christian De Sica *(Furio)*, Massimo Boldi *(Gino)*, Florence Guerin *(Silvia)*, Ezio Greggio *(Oscar)*, Lisa Stothard *(Patrizia)*, Paolo Rossi, Philippe Leroy, Lucia Stara, Guido Nicheli.

Montecarlo is the backdrop for three separate stories about Italians who come to the famous Riviera gambling spot with different agendas. In one story, De Sica wins big but then is swindled out of his loot. Left with a huge hotel bill that he can't pay, he is unable to leave his room. To free himself from this private debtor's prison, he agrees to minister to the sexual needs of an heiress whose wallet is nearly as fat as she is. In the end, though, he has a change of heart and pushes his benefactor into the swimming pool. In the second story, Boldi and his brother come to Monaco to buy an apartment. Before they make the purchase, Boldi falls for a beautiful woman who also happens to be an insatiable gambler (Guerin), and their money disappears quickly in the casino. To try to recoup their loses, Guerin, Boldi, and his brother pull off a jewel heist, but they remain losers because the diamond necklace they nab isn't real. In the final installment, Greggio, a professional gambler, is cheated by a ruthless Frenchman, and, with the help of a younger gambler, he gets his revenge.

p, Luigi De Laurentiis, Aurelio De Laurentiis; d, Carlo Vanzina; w, Carlo Vanzina, Enrico Vanzina; ph, Luigi Kuveiller (Technicolor); m, Manuel De Sica; ed, Ruggero Mastroianni.

Comedy/Drama (PR:NR MPAA:NR)

MONTH IN THE COUNTRY, A† (1987, Brit.) 96m Euston/Orion Classics c

Colin Firth *(Birkin)*, Kenneth Branagh *(Moon)*, Natasha Richardson *(Mrs. Keach)*, Patrick Malahide *(Rev. Keach)*, Tony Haygarth *(Douthwaite)*, Jim Carter *(Ellerback)*, Richard Vernon *(Col. Hebron)*, Vicky Arundale *(Kathy)*.

The director of 1984's CAL, Pat O'Connor returns to the screen with an adaptation of J.L. Carr's novel about two disturbed WW I veterans whose paths cross. Firth is a twitching, stammering vet who is hired to uncover a medieval wall painting at a local church. Working nearby is Branagh, a fellow vet who is excavating a grave just outside the churchyard. The men become friends and share their memories of war. In the meantime, Firth becomes enamored with Richardson, the sensual wife of the church vicar. By the summer's end, the men bid farewell to each other and the Yorkshire village of Oxgodby. Shown at the 1987 New York Film Festival.

p, Kenith Trodd; d, Pat O'Connor; w, Simon Gray (based on the novel by J.L. Carr); ph, Kenneth Macmillan; m, Howard Blake; ed, John Victor Smith; prod d, Leo Austin; art d, Richard Elton; cos, Judy Moorcroft.

Drama **(PR:NR MPAA:PG)**

MOON IN SCORPIO* (1987) 90m Trans World c

Britt Ekland *(Linda)*, John Phillip Law *(Allen)*, William Smith *(Burt)*, Louis Van Bergen *(Mark)*, April Wayne *(Isabel)*, Robert Quarry *(Dr. Khokda)*, Jillian Kesner *(Claire)*, Bruno Marcotulli *(The Driver)*, Ken Smolka *(Police Officer)*, Thomas Bloom *(Soldier)*, James Booth *(Dr. Torrance)*, Donna Kei Benz *(Nurse Mitchell)*, Don Scribner *(Richard Vargas)*.

A yacht adrift off the coast of California is boarded by policemen, who find only one person aboard, Ekland. She is hysterical and stabs the first policeman who touches her. In a doctor's office, she begins to tell her story. Seems she had just married Law, and they were going to spend their honeymoon yachting to Acapulco with two of Law's Vietnam buddies and their girl friends. Law is plagued by dreams of Vietnam and a fear of water after a nasty experience in a pond with a decaying corpse. Out at sea, they start dying one by one, killed with a razor-edged grappling hook. First to die is the drunken, sluttish Kesner, then Van Bergen, Smith, and Law. Finally Ekland is left alone with pretty but weird Wayne, who is apparently possessed by some Vietnamese ghost. Ekland manages to kill her in a fight, but after the doctor congratulates her on surviving her encounter with the escaped psychopath, we see that Ekland is now confined in a padded room herself. There are a few interesting elements to recommend this film to the slightly discriminating. William Smith, one of the best "B" bad guys ever, plays a sympathetic part here, as the fellow who can't control his woman. Wayne is effectively spooky, and Law is effectively spooked, but anyone who's paying attention will be able to figure out the killer's identity. Do we need to add that this went straight to video? Songs include: "Prisoner," "Don't Wake Me Till It's Over" (Robert O. Ragland), "Lay That Body Down" (Robert O. Ragland, Marcia Woods). *(Profanity, brief nudity, graphic violence.)*

p, Alan Amiel; d, Gary Graver; w, Robert S. Aiken; ph, Gary Graver; m, Robert O. Ragland; ed, Omer Tal; cos, Lisa Cacavas; m/l, Robert O. Ragland, Marcia Woods; makeup, Nina Kraft.

Mystery **Cas.** **(PR:O MPAA:NR)**

MOONSTRUCK*½** (1987) 102m MGM/UA c

Cher *(Loretta Castorini)*, Nicolas Cage *(Ronny Cammareri)*, Vincent Gardenia *(Cosmo Castorini)*, Olympia Dukakis *(Rose Castorini)*, Danny Aiello *(Mr. Johnny Cammareri)*, Julie Bovasso *(Rita Cappomaggi)*, John Mahoney *(Perry)*, Louis Guss *(Raymond Cappomaggi)*, Feodor Chaliapin [, Jr.] *(Old Man, Loretta's Grandfather)*, Anita Gillette *(Mona)*, Nada Despotovich *(Chrissy)*.

This delightful romantic comedy directed by Norman Jewison and deftly scripted by John Patrick Shanley features excellent ensemble performances and an acting tour de force from Cher. The 38-year-old widow of a man who was run over by a bus, Cher works as a bookkeeper and lives in Brooklyn with her very Italian-American family: her father, Gardenia, a prosperous plumber; her mother, Dukakis; and her grandfather, Chaliapin. At a quaint Italian restaurant, Aiello, her longtime boy friend, proposes to her. She is anything but passionately in love with him, but after he drops to his knees—at her prompting—she accepts. However, before the wedding can take place, Aiello must travel to his mother's death bed in Sicily. Meanwhile, Cher is to contact Aiello's brother, Cage, to whom he hasn't spoken in five years. Cher calls to invite Cage to the ceremony, but he hangs up on her. She visits the bakery Cage operates and when she tries to learn the reason for Cage's hostility, he bursts into an emotional torrent. It seems he was to have been married himself, but while working with a slicer one day, he was distracted by Aiello and cut off one of his hands. As a result his marriage was called off and his hand was replaced by a wooden one. Cage has refused to forgive Aiello and is still consumed by anger and self-pity. Cher goes with Cage to his apartment atop the bakery, and over a bottle they discover they understand each other. Overcome with passion, they sleep together. The next day, full of guilt and remorse, Cher tells Cage their affair must end. He says he loves her, but that he will be satisfied if she will go to the opera with him that night so he might indulge in the two things he loves most. Cher prepares for her date with Cage by transforming her dowdy appearance: getting her gray-streaked hair colored and styled, buying a sleek dress and new shoes. Cage greets her in a tuxedo. They see Puccini's "La Boheme" at the Met, and Cher is tremendously moved by it. In the lobby afterwards, an astonished Cher runs into Gardenia, who is there with his mistress, Gillette. Meanwhile, Dukakis dines alone at the Italian restaurant. Mahoney, a college professor, is at another table with an attractive young woman who throws water in his face and storms out. He joins Dukakis and she asks him why men fool around. He tells her that it is because they are afraid of death. As he walks Dukakis home, Mahoney comes on to her, but she remains faithful to Gardenia. En route Chaliapin sees them together. Later that night, Aiello returns from abroad and comes to the house, but Cher has not returned home; she is spending the night with Cage. The next morning, Cher returns, followed by Cage, who is determined to marry her. At a breakfast table gathering, Dukakis gives Gardenia an ultimatum and he promises to remain faithful. Aiello arrives, and Cher and Cage prepare to tell him they want to marry. Before they can, Aiello announces that the wedding is off because a miracle has saved his mother and there is no reason for him to get married now. Cher then says she and Cage will be married and they use the same pinky ring Aiello had used as an ersatz engagement ring.

From its credit sequence set to Dean Martin's rendition of "That's Amore" (Jack Brooks, Harry Warren) to its kitchen-table climax, MOONSTRUCK brilliantly captures its Italian-American milieu. Director Jewison (AGNES OF GOD, A SOLDIER'S STORY, IN THE HEAT OF THE NIGHT) and screenwriter Shanley have fashioned a charming, funny tale of infidelity and transcendent love whose cultural setting provides both content and context. Shanley, "the Bard from the Bronx," is best known as a playwright ("Danny and the Deep Blue Sea"), but in 1987 he wrote the screenplays for both this and Tony Bill's FIVE CORNERS. Though he is of Irish extraction, Shanley grew up surrounded by Italian-Americans, and his dialog and characters are suffused with authenticity. MOONSTRUCK's storyline is as simple as the film's emotions are complex. Having married for love once and been the victim of exceedingly bad luck, Cher has decided to marry sensibly. Both she and Cage have resigned themselves to the idea that they will never know true love again, and when they find it, all rules of morality are called into question. Guss, Dukakis' brother, remembers that when Gardenia was courting his sister, he was awakened one night by a particularly bright full moon. Going to the window, he saw Gardenia (Cosmo) standing outside the house. "Cosmo's moon," as Guss calls it, is back in the sky, pale and luminous, glowing magically over the Manhattan skyline as the events in the film transpire. A symbol of the undeniable power and unpredictability of passionate love, the moon is there not only for Cher and Cage, but also for Gardenia and Dukakis.

Essentially a bedroom farce, the film finds much of its humor in the confrontations between the moonstruck lovers who, because of previous commitments, have no business being with each other. However, as much, if not more, of the film's humor comes in the realization of the characters. Cher, in particular, turns in an outstanding performance. Less emotional, though no less expressive, than her extraordinary work in MASK, her performance here is technically precise but sincere. Her excellent Brooklyn accent is just one aspect of a finely shaded portrayal in which this actress of Armenian, French, and Cherokee extraction *becomes* an Italian-American New Yorker. Cage's performance is more problematic—highly praised in many quarters, but faulted in others. Perhaps cowed by the criticism he received for his vocal mannerisms in PEGGY SUE GOT MARRIED, Cage makes no attempt whatever at "Brooklynese," and his performance suffers for it. In attempting to create a character that is full of contradictions, he is only partly successful. Shanley's original title for his screenplay was "The Bride and the Wolf," and though Cage occasionally slides into a kind of open-mouthed indolence, he effectively conveys Ronny's wolfish qualities—his emotional explosiveness, his sullen vindictiveness, his macho passion. Ronny is largely inarticulate, but he is a devotee of one of the most tragic and touching art forms, opera. He is also allowed moments of sweeping philosophical insight, and Cage is considerably less successful at integrating these aspects of Ronny's personality into his portrayal. The supporting performances are all superb and wonderfully nuanced. However, special praise is due stage veteran Dukakis, who is marvelous as the patient mature beauty who is the calm at the center of the romantic tempest stirred up by Cosmo's moon. That moon and the whole of the film are beautifully photographed by Oscar winner David Watkin (OUT OF AFRICA). The evocative score is augmented by Vicki Carr's rendition of "It

Must Be Him" (Gilbert Becaud, Mack David), which Gardenia listens to endlessly. Simply stated, it is difficult not to be swept up by this charming picture. *(Sexual situations, adult situations, profanity.)*

p, Patrick Palmer, Norman Jewison; d, Norman Jewison; w, John Patrick Shanley; ph, David Watkin; m, Dick Hyman; ed, Lou Lombardo; prod d, Philip Rosenberg; ch, Lofti Travolta.

Romance/Comedy **(PR:C MPAA:PG)**

MORE ABOUT THE CHILDREN OF BULLERBY VILLAGE† (1987, Swed.) 86m SF c (MER OM OSS BARN I BULLERBY)

Linda Bergstrom *(Lisa)*, Crispin Dickson Wendenius *(Lasse)*, Henrik Larsson *(Bosse)*, Ellen Demerus *(Britta)*, Anna Sahlin *(Anna)*, Harald Lonnbro *(Olle)*, Tove Edfeldt *(Kerstin)*, Olof Sjogren *(Shoemaker)*, Soren Pettersson, Ann-Sofie Knape, Bill Jonsson, Catti Edfeldt, Louise Raeder, Ewa Carlsoon.

A sequel to director Hallstrom's THE CHILDREN OF BULLERBY VILLAGE, based on Astrid Lindgren's tiny tots Bullerby novels and her own screenplay. This time the tots are back in school, cavorting happily in their own little world seen through a golden haze, beautifully recorded by Jens Fischer's camera.

p, Waldemar Bergendahl; d, Lasse Hallstrom; w, Astrid Lindgren (based on her novels); ph, Jens Fischer (Eastmancolor); m, George Riedel; w, Susanne Linnman; prod d, Lasse Westfelt; cos, Inger Pehrsson, Susanne Falck.

Children's **(PR:NR MPAA:NR)**

MORE BAD NEWS† (1987, Brit.) 53m Comic Strip Ltd./Palace Pictures c

Adrian Edmondson *(Vim Fuego)*, Rik Mayall *(Colin)*, Nigel Planer *(Den)*, Peter Richardson *(Spider)*, Jennifer Saunders *(Sally)*, Dawn French *(Rachel)*, Judy Jawkins *(Spider's Wife)*, Tommy Vance *(Concert Crony)*, Steve Walsh *(Concert Organiser)*, Anne Cunningham *(Colin's Mother)*, Gerard Kelly *(Promo Director)*, Anthony Head *(Recording Studio Engineer)*, Jonathan Stratt *(Heavy)*, Yusuf Kyhan *(Waiter)*, Jonathan Caplan *(Virgin Megastore Shop Assistant)*, Gordan Kane *(Assistant in Chart Shop)*, Susy Anne Watkins *(Sexy Girl in Promo)*.

The sequel to a British TV offering called "Bad News," MORE BAD NEWS might have been titled "More 'This Is Spinal Tap'." Like Rob Reiner's hilarious film, this is a spoof rockumentary that chronicles the reunion of Bad News, a heavy metal band whose members haven't played together for four years. In the interim the band members—Edmondson, Mayall, Planer, and Richardson—have occupied themselves with more mundane occupations. With interviewer Saunders along for the ride, they perform again at the pub where they first made their name, cut a new single ("Warrior of Genghis Khan"), shoot a music-video, and make a disastrous appearance at an outdoor festival.

p, Simon Wright, Peter Richardson; d&w, Adrian Edmondson; ph, John Metcalfe; ed, Rob Wright; art d, Denise Ruben; cos, Frances Haggett; spec eff, Dave Barton; makeup, Sally Sutton.

Comedy **(PR:NR MPAA:NR)**

MORGAN STEWART'S COMING HOME** (1987) 96m Kings Road/New Century-Vista c (AKA: HOME FRONT)

Jon Cryer *(Morgan Stewart)*, Lynn Redgrave *(Nancy Stewart)*, Nicholas Pryor *(Senator Tom Stewart)*, Viveka Davis *(Emily)*, Paul Gleason *(Jay Springsteen, Political Campaign Manager)*, Andrew Duncan *(Gen. Fenton)*, Savely Kramorov *(Ivan)*, John David Cullum *(Garrett)*, Robert Sedgwick *(Creighton)*, Waweru Njenga *(Ahmed)*, Sudhir Rad *(Mahatma)*, Alan Beck *(Frank)*, Brendan O'Meara *(Thompson)*, Letza Vinnichenko *(Anna)*, Glenn Wilder *(Chauffeur)*, Gary Wheeler *(Reporter)*, William Edwards *(Cocktail Party Guest)*, Avril Gentiles *(Socialite)*, Tammy Amerson *(Heather Whitewood)*, Bill Cohn *(Mr. Whitewood)*, Andrew Lassman *(Headless Ghoul)*, Roger Bowen *(Dr. Cabot)*, Horace Boykin *(Delivery Boy)*, Chip Dell *(Boy)*, Joseph Bova *(Emily's Father)*, Barbara C. Lewis *(Emily's Mother)*, Nina Hansen *(Emily's Grandmother)*, Ronald C. Byram, Dale R. Blosser, Stu Kerr, Prentiss Rowe *(Police Officers)*, Jude Ciccolella *(Workman)*, Charles Bennett *(Bank Manager)*, Alison Davies *(Bank Teller)*, Perk Bennett *(Santa Claus)*, Melvin Crickenberger, Jim Yates *(Mansion Party Guests)*, Bruce Morrow *(Delivery Man)*.

Yet another film directed by the inimitable Alan Smithee. Who is Alan Smithee? you may ask. Well, Mr. Smithee has directed such paragons of the cinema as FADE-IN (1968), DEATH OF A GUNFIGHTER (1969), STUDENT BODIES (1981), and LET'S GET HARRY and GHOST FEVER (both 1987). If you haven't guessed by now, Alan Smithee is a pseudonym used by directors who are ashamed of the final product and demand their names be removed from the credits. In the case of MORGAN STEWART'S COMING HOME, Alan Smithee is actually two directors: Briton Terry Winsor began filming and was replaced by Paul Aaron. What is odd about the entire affair is that this film is not that awful. Granted, at times it is incredibly stupid and somewhat inept, but certainly no worse than the dozens of other teenage comedies that a myriad of directors have been proud to put their names on.

Shot in 1985 and shelved until New Century/Vista dusted it off for a quick release to capitalize on the sudden popularity of Jon Cryer in PRETTY IN PINK, the film begins as lonely boarding school student Cryer learns that his parents will not have time to celebrate the holidays with him once again. The son of wimpy Republican senator Pryor and ambitious socialite Redgrave, Cryer was put in boarding school at the age of 10, and now, seven years later, he has been kicked out of eight schools. When not striving for attention, Cryer immerses himself in horror films and his dorm room is plastered with posters, masks, and other gory memorabilia. A few days after Cryer gets the news from his parents, he is

shocked to learn that they have had a sudden change of heart and have sent for him to come home—permanently. Overjoyed at the chance to establish a real family life, Cryer makes a supreme effort to be a model son. Unfortunately his efforts are for naught, as his homecoming is merely a political ploy designed by his father's campaign manager (Gleason) to give the senator a more family-oriented image that will appeal to voters. One day the miserable Cryer sneaks off to a mall to get the autograph of horror movie director George Romero, who is signing copies of *The Zombies That Ate Pittsburgh*, a book about his life and films. In line Cryer meets the spunky Davis, a female horror fanatic. She invites him home for dinner and he is delighted to find that she is a member of a "real," ethnic (Italian) family that eats dinner together and shares a few good laughs. But Cryer's joy is cut short when he is grounded by his parents for sneaking out (he borrowed the car without permission), and Redgrave has surveillance cameras installed in the house so that she can watch his every move. Things get worse for Cryer when Davis comes to visit him and the two wind up in the shower together (in their underwear). Caught by his horrified mother, Cryer, still in his underwear, runs after the fleeing Davis and finds himself standing in front of his father, Gleason, and an important Washington, D.C., couple. This final outrage proves too much and Redgrave decides to send Cryer to a sadistic military school posthaste. Cryer runs away with Davis and stops at the bank to withdraw his silver dollar collection from his safety deposit box. What he finds is a quarter of a million dollars in skimmed campaign contributions and evidence that Gleason (who has been working for Pryor's rival all along) is about to blackmail his father into dropping out of the race. Loyal son that he is, Cryer returns home with the evidence. In a prolonged and unfunny slapstick chase involving jeeps, a motorbike, and a platoon of military school cadets, Cryer manages to save his dad's campaign. Shown the error of their ways, Pryor and Redgrave vow to become caring parents and pay more attention to Cryer.

Saddled with a dim-witted script that is strictly sit-com, MORGAN STEWART'S COMING HOME is nearly saved by the energetic Cryer. A smart young actor who knows when he is trapped in a turkey, Cryer does his best to subvert the picture by letting the audience know how stupid he thinks it is. He constantly shoots disgusted glances at the camera and puts a defiant spin on bad dialog in order to get a self-conscious laugh out of a hopelessly unfunny scene. Cryer does not out-and-out mug, but is a bit more subtle, inserting little throwaways that those paying attention will catch. Also effective is Davis, who is believable and extremely likable as the female horror film aficionado. She and Cryer make a good pair and engage in a goofy grinning contest on her doorstep that further subverts the stupidity of the film. Given the little he is asked to do, Pryor is also fine, managing to inject a small dose of complexity and compassion into his role. Redgrave, however, is a dragon lady from her first scene, and her emotional turnaround at the end of the film is a bit tough to accept. The filmmakers seem to be taking a vague shot at Ron and Nancy Reagan with the characters of Pryor and Redgrave, but the political satire is lost in the shuffle. *(Mild profanity.)*

p, Stephen Friedman; d, Alan Smithee [Terry Winsor; Paul Aaron]; w, Ken Hixon, David Titcher; ph, Richard Brooks (Deluxe Color); m, Peter Bernstein; ed, Bob Letterman; prod d, Charles Bennett; set d, Victor Kempster; m/l, The Silencers, The Surfaris, John Manikoff, Timothy Duckworth, Bernard Herrmann, Chris Isaak.

Comedy **Cas.** **(PR:A-C MPAA:PG-13)**

MORNING MAN, THE† (1987, Can.) 97m SDA-3 Themes-Telefilm Canada-Societe Generale du Cinema du Quebec-CBC c

Bruno Doyon *(Paul Nadeau)*, Kerrie Keane *(Dr. Kate Johnson)*, Alan Fawcett *(Roger)*, Marc Strange *(Detective Mailer)*, Rob Roy *(Gerry)*, Linda Smith *(Estelle)*, Marc Blutman, Walter Massey, Vlasta Vrana, Damir Andrei, Yvette Brind'Amour, Doris Petrie, Ralph Millman, Dorian Joe Clark, Anick Faris, Stephanie Morgenstern, Danette Mackay, Sandy Stahlbrand, Luis de Cespedes, Ruth Dahan, Sam Lemarquand, John Novak, Dean Hagopean, Joan Heney, Robert Heney, Robert Lavalle-Menard, Guy Belanger, Jaqueline Blais, Hamish McEwan, Anthony Sherwood, Peter Colvey, Griffith Brewer, Roch Lafortune, Ken Roberts, Robert Parson, Pier Kohl Paquette, Gayle Garfinkle, Donald Lamoureux, Darry Edward Blake, Andrew Johnston, Babs Gadbois, Arthur Corber, Vincent Glorioso, John St.-Denis, Ian McDonald, Brigitte Boucher, Anthony Ulc, Michel Therrien, Joe Singerman, Cassandre Fournier.

Based on a true story, a young criminal convicted on 22 charges of armed robbery, escapes from jail. He goes to live in a swank apartment with an attractive woman doctor who tends his wounds. Later, he manages to foil a robbery planned by his old buddies, then becomes a successful morning man for a radio station in Quebec, and on the first anniversary of his escape, turns himself in. Truth is better than fiction.

p, Gaston Cousineau, Daniele J. Suissa; d, Daniele J. Suissa; w, Clarke Wallace; ph, Rene Verzier; m, Diane Juster; ed, Yves Langlois, Jean Lepage; art d, Charles Dunlop, Francois Seguin; set d, Jean-Baptiste Tard, Gilles Aird, cos, Nicoletta Massone; spec eff, Ryal Cosgrove, John Walsh; makeup, Marie-Angele Breitner-Protat.

Crime/Biography **(PR:NR MPAA:NR)**

MORO AFFAIR, THE*½** (1986, It.) 110m Yarno Cinematografica/Columbia c (IL CASO MORO)

Gian Maria Volonte *(Aldo Moro)*, Margarita Lozano *(Eleanora Moro)*, Sergio Rubini, Daniela De Silva, Emanuela Taschini, Ginella Vocca *(Moro Family)*, Mattia Sbragia, Bruno Zanin, Consuelo Ferrara, Enrica Maria Modugno, Enrica Rosso, Maurizio Donadoni, Stefano Abbati, Danilo Mattei, Massimo Tedde, Francesco Capitano *(Red Brigades)*, Daniele Dublino, Piero Vida, Bruno Corazzari, Gabriele Villa, Francesco Carnelutti, Paolo M. Scalondro, Dante Biagioni *(Politicians)*, Umberto Raho, Luciano Bartoli, Silverio Blasi, Franco Trevisi, Pino Ferrara, Nicola Di Pinto *(Secret Service)*, Augusto Zucchi, M. Ferrara Santamaria *(The Vatican)*.

This documentary-like film of the tragic kidnaping and subsequent execution of Italian Christian Democrat president Aldo Moro in 1978 caused a firestorm of controversy among Italian politicos and played to packed movie houses throughout Italy. The faithful reconstruction of the complicated events which unfolded over 54 days from March to May, 1978, is presented in a concise and straightforward manner by director Ferrara. Based on the Pulitzer Prize-nominated book *Days of Wrath* by American reporter Robert Katz (who contributed to the screenplay), the film begins as Moro (Volante), the first man in 40 years to have unified all the political parties of Italy—including the Communist party—is waylaid en route to church by a band of Red Brigade terrorists. His five bodyguards brutally slaughtered, the soon-to-be president of Italy is whisked away to a secret "people's prison" where he is interrogated by the terrorists and ordered to reveal information that could damage the new coalition. Meanwhile, Moro's own party, the Christian Democrats, and the newly empowered Communist party vow to take a hard line on the situation and refuse to recognize or negotiate with the Red Brigades. A massive manhunt is launched in an effort to find Moro, but the search is conducted in a haphazard and perfunctory manner (twice police knocked on the door of the apartment where Moro was being held, and twice they left without further investigation). Moro, who before his kidnaping had advocated a "soft line" when dealing with terrorists, is allowed to send letters to his government suggesting an exchange of prisoners to be negotiated by the Vatican. As the government continues to drag its feet, Moro's letters become increasingly critical of his own party. In an effort to sway public opinion away from Moro, his party and the press begin to portray him as a desperate, drug-addled madman who has succumbed to torture, and even the validity of his letters is called into question. Although the Vatican also subscribes to the "hard line," Pope Paul VI makes a personal plea to the Red Brigades for the unconditional release of Moro. At the same time the Socialist party, and Moro's family, also break with the "hard line" and begin to push for an exchange of prisoners. Knowing that he has been totally abandoned by the very government he created, Moro makes a last-ditch attempt to save himself by sending a flurry of letters urging a grass-roots rebellion against his party. Frustrated at the lack of progress, the Red Brigades announce that the "People's Tribunal" has sentenced Moro to death. There is much internal dissension among the Red Brigade membership over whether or not to execute Moro, but it is finally decided that he must die lest the terrorists lose their credibility. The Socialists make some headway in the negotiations and get the Red Brigades to agree to exchange Moro for one terminally ill imprisoned *brigatista*. At first outgoing chief of state Giovanni Leone agrees to grant the pardon, but he then begins stalling tactics and ultimately refuses after pressure from the Christian Democrat leadership. During a private meeting between Socialist and Christian Democrat leaders, news is received that Moro's bullet-riddled body has been found stuffed in the hatch of a red Renault parked between the headquarters of the Christian Democrats and the Communists. As a black-and-white still of Moro's body recedes into the frame, Moro's funeral wishes are heard: " . . . I do not want the men of power around me. I want near me those who truly loved me and will continue to love me and pray for me."

Fueled by a superb performance from Gian Maria Volante, who was given the Best Actor award at the Venice Film Festival, THE MORO AFFAIR is a gripping, vexing, and ultimately sad cinematic version of tragic historical events that continue to be controversial. Upon its release in Italy the Christian Democrats condemned the picture, mostly because it once again raised some nagging questions about the whole affair that they would prefer forgotten: What happened to Moro's briefcase full of sensitive documents that the Red Brigades failed to notice during the kidnaping? Why was the investigation that was conducted by Italian antiterrorist police so incompetent? Were they actually responsible for acts blamed on the Red Brigades (acts undertaken as a way of keeping the official Communist party off balance and in line)? Who was the author of the phony Red Brigade communique stating that Moro had committed suicide and was buried at the bottom of a frozen lake which could only be reached by helicopter?

Director Ferrara moves quickly through the chronology of events and never seems unfair or terribly biased. He merely presents the documented facts and lets the audience decide, however uncomfortable that might be for the Italian government and press. Politics aside, the film is also a moving examination of a man who maintains his values, dignity, and honor during a crisis that sorely tested his love of country and eventually claimed his life. Volante's sensitive performance is all the more impressive when one recalls that the actor had turned in a mocking portrayal of Moro in Elio Petri's devasting indictment of the Christian Democrats, TODO MODO (1976). Petri's film was made in the days when the Left saw Moro as a decadent establishment buffoon, just before his true political character had fully emerged. The fact that Volante, a staunch Leftist, could completely forsake his earlier view of Moro and convey the truly heroic and noble aspects of this complicated man is very moving in and of itself. Ferrara elicits memorable performances from his entire cast as well, especially Lozano as Moro's dedicated and strong-willed wife. Although shown at film festivals in the US this year, American audiences may not fully fathom the complicated Italian political system and the scrupulously detailed account of the events that have been a source of controversy ever since. Nonetheless, THE MORO AFFAIR is certainly worth the effort for those even marginally interested in the destruction of Aldo Moro. *(Graphic violence, profanity in subtitles.)*

p, Mauro Berardi; d, Giuseppe Ferrara; w, Robert Katz, Armenia Balducci, Giuseppe Ferrara (based on the book *Days Of Wrath* by Robert Katz); ph, Camillo Bazzoni; m, Pino Donaggio; ed, Roberto Perpignani; md, Natale Massara; art d, Francesco Frigeri; cos, Laura Vaccari.

Historical/Drama **(PR:C-O MPAA:NR)**

MOROS Y CRISTIANOS† (1987, Span.) 120m Estela c (Trans: Moors and Christians)

Fernando Fernan Gomez *(Fernando)*, Andres Pajares *(Marcial)*, Rosa Maria Sarda *(Cuqui)*, Jose Luis Lopez Vazquez *(Lopez)*, Agustin Gonzalez *(Agustin)*, Pedro Ruiz *(Pepe)*, Maria Luisa Ponte *(Marcella)*, Veronica Forque *(Monique)*, Antonio Resines, Chus Lampreave, Luis Escobar, Luis Ciges, Jose Luis Coll.

A family of candy makers from the small town of Alicante, known for a pageant which re-enacts the historical struggles between Moors and Christians in medieval Spain, decides to travel to Madrid in an attempt to promote their product, a popular treat at Christmastime. Dressed in the costumes of Moors and Christians, the bumbling family enthusiastically tries to fit in with big city ways. Good acting and dialog from Berlanga and Azcona who have a good ear and eye for the absurdities of modern life.

p, Felix Tusell; d, Luis Garcia Berlanga; w, Luis Garcia Berlanga, Rafael Azcona; ph, Domingo Solano (Agfacolor); ed, Jose Luis Matesanz; set d, Veronica Toledo, Victor Alarcon.

Comedy **(PR:NR MPAA:NR)**

MOSCA ADDIO† (1987, It.) 102m Roseo-RAI TV/Istituto Luce-Italnoleggio c (Trans: Moscow Farewell)

Liv Ullmann *(Ida Nudel)*, Daniel Olbrychski *(Yuli)*, Aurore Clement *(Elena, Ida's Sister)*, Carmen Scarpitta, Nino Fuscagni, Saverio Vallone.

A chilling story, based on the unhappy life of Ida Nudel, a Jewish dissident still living in the USSR. Because of her involvement in demonstrations against anti-Semitism she is denied a visa and banished to Siberia where she is assigned to an all-male camp. Upon her release, she joyfully returns to Moscow only to find another family living in her apartment, the man she loves married to someone else, and that she has been banished from the city. A powerful and moving condemnation of anti-Semitism, Soviet immigration policy, and the labor camps.

d, Mauro Bolognini; w, Enrico Roseo, Marcello Andrei; ph, Ennio Guarnieri (Cinecitta Color); m, Ennio Morricone; ed, Nino Baragli.

Drama/Biography **(PR:NR MPAA:NR)**

MOVING TARGETS*** (1987, Aus.) 95m South Australian/Academy c

Carmen Duncan *(Eve)*, Michael Aitkens *(Riley)*, Shane Briant *(Terrier)*, Redmond Symons *(Pitt)*, Nicholas Eadie *(Toe)*, Annie Jones *(Chrissie)*, David Clencie *(Paul)*, Peter Stratford *(Meyerdahl)*, Simone Buchanan *(Cathy)*, Sarah de Teliga *(Sue)*, Roger L. Howell *(Frank)*, Allen Lyne *(Pilot)*, Edward Caddick *(Clough)*, Conor McDermotroe *(Collins)*, Heather Steen *(Landlady)*, Tony Gordon *(Reporter)*, Keith Hind *(Bank Security)*, John Hamblin *(Cathy's Father)*, Emma Salter *(Principal)*, Joanna Moore *(Cricket Coach)*, Dominic Bianca *(Sydney Tough)*, Faith Kleinig, Phyllis Burford *(Gossips)*, Glen Boswell, Hans Van Gyen, Johnny Hallyday *(Toe's Mates)*.

An Australian action drama starring Duncan as a Sydney mother with a 15-year-old daughter (Jones) and a secret past as a German terrorist, not to mention piles of old robbery loot in her bank account. Into her life comes Aitkens, her ex-lover and an IRA killer. He is trying to avoid his former colleagues after having killed one while refusing to blow up an intended target's innocent family. Aitkens has tracked down Duncan and wants part of the ill-gotten money in order to run away with her and Jones. Instead, she manages to get the money and ditch him, fleeing cross-country with Jones. Aitkens pursues, but already on his trail is Briant, a professional killer. Duncan and Jones run afoul of a local punk gang, but Duncan faces them down with her shotgun. Eventually she tries to hide out in the Australian wine country, but Briant and his two associates—one of them the punk gang leader—locate her and hold both women hostage. They then wait for Aitkens to arrive. Duncan manages to warn Aitkens, and also tells him that Jones is his daughter. He hatches a plan whereby he will pretend to kidnap Jones for the money, luring Briant into an ambush. It doesn't go as smoothly as that, though, and a wild shoot-out follows. Briant's colleagues are eliminated and he is thoroughly thrashed by Aitkens, who gives him a ring to convince the IRA that he is dead. Duncan, Aitkens, and Jones all escape to live happily ever after. This is actually not a bad little drama. Aitkens looks like Rutger Hauer and Duncan looks like Sybil Danning, and both give quality performances. It is techincally superb in the manner of the British spy dramas and the whole thing is surprisingly tense. Songs include: "Enemy of Man" (Tony Murray, performed by Wendy Matthews), "Somebody's Forgetting Somebody" (Paul Kelly, performed by Kelly), "Take Out the Lead" (The Blockheads, performed by The Blockheads), "Stuck on Love" (Stephen Cummings, Ian Stepheen, performed by Cummings), "Let's Get Rich Together" (Tony Murray, performed by Spare Change). *(Violence, adult situations.)*

p, Harley Manners; d, Chris Langman; w, Graham Hartley (based on the novel *When We Ran* by Keith Leopold); ph, Ernest Clark; m, Robert Kretschmer; ed, Andrew Prouse; prod d, Alistair Livingstone; art d, Herbert Pinter; cos, Catherine Cantlon; m/l, Tony Murray, Paul Kelly, The Blockheads, Stephen Cummings, Ian Stepheen; spec eff, Brian Pearce, Jamie Thompson; makeup, Helen Evans.

Action Cas. (PR:C MPAA:NR)

MOY LYUBIMYY KLOUN† (1987, USSR) 86m Mosfilm/Sovexportfilm c (Trans: My Beloved Clown)

Oleg Menshikov, Vladimir Ilyin, Oleg Strizhenov, Natalia Saiko, Tatyana Dogileva.

A circus clown has second thoughts about raising an orphan he and his wife have adopted after the wife changes her mind and leaves the country. But the boy falls in love with the circus and the clown finds a new and rewarding "profession" as a father.

d, Yury Kushnerov; w, Alexander Adabashyan, Nikita Mikhalkov (based on the story by Vasily Livanov); ph, Igor Bek; m, Olga Petrova; art d, Viktor Zenkov.

Drama (PR:NR MPAA:NR)

MOYA MALENKAYA ZHENA† (1987, USSR) 80m Lithuanian Film Studio/Sovexportfilm c (Trans: My Little Wife)

Eleonora Korpunaite, Saulus Balandis.

Student Balandis meets a pretty girl in a cafe who is a drop-out, but she lies to him saying her father is a professor at the school Balandis attends. When the truth finally surfaces, it makes no difference—love has conquered all.

d, Raimundas Banionis; w, Rimantes Savalis; ph, Algimantas Mikutenas; m, Faustas Latenas; art d, Galgos Klicus.

Drama (PR:NR MPAA:NR)

MUJERES DE LA FRONTERA† (1987, Cuba/Nicaragua) 60m Instituto Cubano del Arte-Industria Cinematografica/Empresa Nicaraguense de Distribucion y Exhibicion Cinematografica c (Trans: Women of the Frontier)

Chana Rivera, Luisa Jimenez.

Alex Cox's WALKER wasn't the only film made in Nicaragua to be released in 1987. Following in the footsteps of the underrated ALSINO AND THE CONDOR (1983), MUJERES DE LA FRONTERA is a Nicaraguan/Cuban coproduction that relates wartime difficulties for the people of a Nicaraguan village near the Honduran border. Set between 1982 and 1983 and narrated in diary form by Rivera, who plays a strong-willed village woman, it shows the *Nicas'* faith in the post-revolutionary dream of a better society and their determination to bring it about. With the men at the front lines, the women leave places of safety to return to their homes and to work the fields.

p, Carlos Alvarez; d, Ivan Arguello; w, Ivan Arguello, Ramiro Lacayo, Gioconda Belli, Antonio Conte; ph, Rafael Ruiz, Luis Garcia Mesa; m, Cedrick d'lla Torre; ed, Eduardo Guandamuz, Justo Vega.

Drama (PR:NR MPAA:NR)

MUJERES SALVAJES† (1987, Mex.) Cooperativa Rio Mixcoac/Peliculas Mexicanas c (Trans: Savage Women)

Tina Romero *(Gaviota)*, Jorge Santoyo *(Pablo)*, Abel Woolrich *(Arturo)*, Patricia Mayers *(Lucha)*, Vicky Vazquez, Gonzalo Lora, Isabel Quintanar, Tomas Leal, Alejandro Tamayo.

Director Retes who received national critical attention for his socially realistic films CHIN CHIN EL TEPOROCHO, NUEVO MUNDO, and BANDERA ROTA, follows up with this story of six women who escape from prison with information on the whereabouts of a buried treasure. They flee to a deserted beach where they immediately take off their clothes and start looking for the treasure. Of course, there are six men camping on the beach and Retes concentrates on the contrast between the two groups—cold, selfish men vs. gentle, affectionate women. When the women learn two of the men are homosexual, they demand their execution, while at the same time forgiving a man who brutally rapes one of the women. From then on it is survival of the fittest, as their numbers diminish in a sea of nudity, male and female homosexuality, masturbation, and other excesses photographed amid the white sand and palm trees.

p,d&w, Gabriel Retes; ph, Genaro Hurtado; m, Juan Jose Calayud; ed, Edgardo Pavan.

Drama (PR:NR MPAA:NR)

MUNCHIES zero (1987) 85m Concorde/MGM-UA c

Harvey Korman *(Cecil/Simon)*, Charles Stratton *(Paul)*, Nadine Van Der Velde *(Cindy)*, Alix Elias *(Melvis)*, Charlie Phillips *(Eddie)*, Hardy Rawls *(Big Ed)*, Jon Stafford *(Dude)*, Robert Picardo *(Bob Marvelle)*, Wendy Schaal *(Marge Marvelle)*, Scott Sherk *(Buddy Holly)*, Lori Birdsong *(Terry)*, Traci Huber Sheridan *(Amy)*, Paul Bartel *(Dr. Crowder)*, Ellen Albertini Dow *(Little Old Lady)*, Jerado De Cordovier *(Old Indian)*, Chip Heller *(Burgerland Manager)*, Roberto A. Jimenez *(Ramon)*, Michael Lee Gogin, Larry Nicholas, Kevin Thompson *(Burgerland Employees)*, Justin Dreyfuss *(Dwight)*, Jan Kuljis *(Biker Chick)*, Steven Bernstein *(Dean)*, Paul Short *(Head Biker)*, Frank Welker *(Munchie Voices)*, Fred Newman.

GREMLINS, the Steven Spielberg-Joe Dante film of 1984, was an indisputably violent picture chronicling the mayhem wreaked on a community by a group of strange little creatures. For all its problems, at least the film got a reaction from its audience. This bland horror comedy, an unashamed GREMLINS ripoff, doesn't even do that. The story opens in a South American cave where Korman, an anthropologist, is looking for a space alien he hopes will bring him professional recognition. Accompanying him is Korman's teenaged son Stratton, who takes a decidedly dim view of his father's activities. But, lo and behold, what should they stumble upon but a small creature secreted behind some old Aztec ruins. They capture it, dub it a "Munchie," and bring it home where Stratton is reunited with his girl friend Van Der Velde. Also greeting them is a sleazy but powerful businessman who is Korman's twin brother and absolute nemesis. This polyester-clad sibling is played by Korman as well, a dual role that requires no stretch of acting ability. When good Korman goes off to a local research facility, he allows Stratton to keep an eye on the Munchie. Stratton and Van Der Velde, who call the little guy Arnold Ziffel after the famed pig on television's "Green Acres," repair to the bedroom while bad Korman schemes to get his hands on the creature. Bad Korman wants good Korman's land, and he decides to hold Arnold Ziffel hostage to get the desired acreage. Bad Korman's burnt-out stepson Stafford is enlisted to capture the Munchie, but Arnold goes on the defensive and Stafford responds by chopping his foe into little bits. This proves to be a rather foolish move, for when the creature is divided it ends up multiplying. Four new munchies rise from the mess, and they're out to cause trouble. Stafford is quickly done in, and the creatures run off with his car. Stratton and Van Der Velde quickly get on their trail, joined by Elias, a nerdy police officer. Meanwhile bad Korman and his ditzy wife go off searching for the Munchies themselves. Bad Korman is convinced the creatures will find his underground storage cave where he secretly has been storing toxic wastes. The chase gets pretty hot and heavy as the Munchies attack some girls at a swimming hole, torment a group of bikers, then destroy a miniature golf course. Along the way Stratton accidentally discovers the creatures turn to stone if hit by an electrical charge. Eventually they end up at—you guessed it—bad Korman's underground storage site where Stratton ultimately defeats the Munchies. He exposes bad Korman's secret, then Stratton and Van Der Velde return with a stone Munchie to good Korman's house. He's been oblivious to the destruction that's gone on and is now accompanied by Bartel, a scientist from a local university. Bartel believes the hardened Munchie to be a rare Aztec statue and offers a fantastic sum for it, thus assuring good Korman's place in the scientific world.

What can be said about a film where the best performances are given by puppets? The Munchies, which are simplistic creations at best, are the liveliest thespians in the cast, blowing away their human counterparts with ease. The ensemble is uniformly wooden. Even Bartel, who's given many a funny cameo performance, is a dullard. Hirsch's direction is straightforward stuff, filming the action at a steady pace without giving it any additional energy. No one seems to care what's going on, save the Munchies, and they're not even real. There's a few off-handed movie jokes referring to this film's inspiration and E.T., but these gags aren't exactly brimming with wit. Songs include "Get Even," performed by Bruce Goldstein, Joel Raney. *(Violence, profanity.)*

p, Roger Corman, Ginny Nugent; d, Bettina Hirsch; w, Lance Smith; ph, Jonathan West; art d, John Ballowe; set d, Naomi Shohan; cos, Katie Sparks; makeup, Devorah Fischa, Lynne Eagan; m/l, Bruce Goldstein, Joel Raney, Steve Gideon; spec eff, Roger George.

Comedy/Horror Cas. (PR:C MPAA:PG)

MURDER LUST† (1987) 90m Easy Street Filmworks c

Eli Rich *(Steve)*, Rochelle Taylor *(Cheryl)*, Dennis Gannon *(Neil)*, Bonnie Schneider *(Marene)*, Lisa Nichols *(Debbie)*, H. Burton Leary *(Joe)*, Bill Walsh *(Lyman)*, George J. Engelson, Dayna Quinn, Linda Tucker-Smith, James Lane.

Filmed in 1985 but not released until this year when it debuted on home video, MURDER LUST stars Rich as an outwardly normal security guard who, in reality, is a homicidal killer. Sexually impotent, the ashamed Rich satisfies his lust by picking up prostitutes and then strangling them. Fired from his job for harassing a customer, Rich fakes several college degrees so that he can get work in an adolescent crisis center run by Taylor. Rich lands the job and finds a veritable stable of troubled young women he can murder. Unfortunately, Taylor delays the crisis center's funding until the infamous serial killer is caught because she worries that the center would be the perfect place for the killer to find new victims. Faced with a dilemma (no funding = no new victims), Rich's mind finally snaps completely. Director Jones co-directed a similar project in the black comedy THE LOVE BUTCHER which was shot in 1975 but not released until 1982.

p, James Lane; d, Donald Jones; w, James Lane; ph, James Mattison; m, James Lane; ed, Donald Jones; stunts, William J. Kulzer.

Thriller Cas. (PR:NR MPAA:NR)

MURIERON A MITAD DEL RIO† (1987, Mex.) 91m Cineasta Realiciones Cinematograficas-Prods. Esme-Alianza Cinematografica-Soltar/Peliculas Mexicanas c (Trans: They Died in the Middle of the River)

Hector Suarez *(Jose Pavan)*, Tony Bravo *(Lupe Flores)*, Jorge Luke *(Luis Alvarez)*, Rodrigo Puebla, Arturo Alegro, Max Kerlowe, Paola Morelli.

Episodic story narrates the travails of four illegal aliens who swim across the Rio Grande in search of the riches to be found on the other side of the border. The first is abandoned mid-river, the second is killed, the third deported, and only one is left to deliver a message meant as an appeal to his countrymen not to abandon Mexico during this time of crisis.

p, Carlos Vasallo; d&w, Jose Nieto Ramirez (based on the novel by Luis Spota); ph, Leoncio (Cuco) Villarias; m, Joel Goldsmith; ed, Nieto Ramirez.

Drama **(PR:NR MPAA:NR)**

MUTANT HUNT zero (1987) 77m Entertainment Concepts/Wizard Video-Infinity c (AKA: MATT RIKER; MUTANT HUNT)

Rick Gianasi *(Matt Riker)*, Mary Fahey *(Darla Haynes)*, Ron Reynaldi *(Johhny Felix)*, Taunie Vrenon *(Elaine Eliot)*, Bill Peterson *(Z)*, Mark Umile *(Dr. Paul Haynes)*, Stormy Spill *(Domina)*, Doug De Vos *(Hydro)*, Warren Ulaner *(Alpha Cyborg)*, Mark Legan *(Beta Cyborg)*, Asie Kid *(Duc Toy)*, Leeanne Baker *(Pleasure Droid)*, Nancy Arons *(Window Lady)*, Adriane Lee *(Amber Dawn)*, Ed Mallia *(Boy Friend)*, Eliza Little *(Tawney Lynn)*, Owen Flynn, Joel Van Orsteiner, Lemy Tobi *(Cyborg Fighters)*, Christina Sisinini, Manuel Siverio *(Latin Lovers)*, Chris McNamee, Michael "Spike" Iozzino, Damian *(Gang Fighters)*, Pedro Rosa, Leon Woods, Hector Morales, Michael Cummings, Manuel Cordero, Max Mollison, Ron Hill, Elijah Goodman, Ralph Crawford, William Higgs, Henry Oliver *(Worker Cyborgs)*.

The third and (with any luck) final installment of a distribution deal between New York based low-budget science fiction producers Tycin Entertainment and West Coast schlock kings Empire Pictures (all three films—the others being BREEDERS and ROBOT HOLOCAUST—went straight to Empire's video subsidiary, Wizard Video, bypassing theatrical distribution). MUTANT HUNT is the worst of the lot. New York City sometime in the near future: Peterson, the evil chairman of the Inteltrax Corporation, has taken a small army of cyborgs designed to perform hazardous tasks and altered them with the sexual narcotic Euphoron so they go mad and kill humans for pleasure. The inventor of the cyborgs, Umile, is held captive by Peterson. Umile's sister, Fahey, goes to her brother's old friend Gianasi for help. Gianasi is some sort of secret agent expert in high-tech weaponry and martial arts, as are his fellow operatives, Reynaldi and Vrenon. Just as Gianasi agrees to help, two cyborgs burst in and he is forced to dispatch them in a tortuously long and poorly choreographed fight scene. Another obstacle in our hero's way is Spill, an equally evil rival of Peterson who has created her own super-cyborg and plans to defeat her sworn enemy and capture his supply of Euphoron. After a half-dozen fight sequences as laughably bad as the first, the film stumbles to its climax: a showdown between all the principal's (including a half-destroyed cyborg who has suddenly become a good-guy) at Peterson's Euphoron warehouse. In the end, all the evildoers and their cyborgs are destroyed, Umile and his sister are reunited, and the heros walk off in formation.

MUTANT HUNT is incredibly silly. From the truly wretched acting to the badly staged action scenes, almost nothing in this film is successful. The comic-book script is overly complicated, and at the same time woefully underdeveloped. Some of the dialog, however, is priceless. During one fight scene the heroic Gianasi very seriously intones: "Don't get me steamed, Cyborg." In another scene the evil Spill has captured Gianasi and implanted an explosive device in his head. After babbling about her plans to conquer the world (or some such evil scheme), Gianasi retorts: "What the hell does that have to do with putting a bomb in my head?" The special effects by Ed French are spotty, running the range from a well-articulated puppet of the half-destroyed cyborg (the effect is quite good), to the downright laughable attempt at having the cyborg's arms stretch like taffy (the actors appear to have cardboard mailing tubes attached to their wrists). One surprise is the nearly total lack of gratuitous nudity in MUTANT HUNT. After BREEDERS, where women were disrobing every 30 seconds or so, MUTANT HUNT seems chaste by mainly relying on short skirts and cleavage. *(Brief nudity, sexual situations, gore effects, some profanity.)*

p, Cynthia DePaula; d&w, Tim Kincaid; ph, Thomas Murphy (Precision color); ed, Barry Zetlin; md, Tom Milano; prod d, Ruth Lounsbury; set d, Marina Zurkow; cos, Jeffrey Wallach; makeup, Ed French; spec eff, Matt Vogel, Tom Lauten; ch, Ron Reynaldi.

Science Fiction **Cas.** **(PR:O MPAA:NR)**

MY DARK LADY½** (1987) 104m Frederick King Keller/Film Gallery c

Fred A. Keller *(Sam Booth)*, Lorna Hill *(Lorna Dahomey)*, Raymond Holder *(Malcolm Dahomey)*, John Buscaglia *(Jonathan Park, Headmaster)*, Evan Perry *(Samuel T. MacMillan)*, Barbara Cady *(Sarah Teasdale, Drama Coach)*, Stuart Roth *(Horace Babinski)*, Tess Spangler *(Minnie O'Hara)*, Steven Cooper *(Terry Terranova)*.

Take the music out of Lerner and Lowe's well-loved show "My Fair Lady," and most people would come up with George Bernard Shaw's classic play "Pygmalion". While MY DARK LADY certainly doesn't match up to either of those works, this rendition of the "Pygmalion" theme has a few moments which might amuse some audiences. Keller (who is the real-life father of the film's director Frederick King Keller) plays a failed Shakespearean actor who goes on the run after being caught shoplifting while dressed as Santa Claus. He holes up in a boarding house run by Hill, a black woman, and becomes friendly with her son Holder. The boy has some acting talent himself, and Keller begins tutoring him. Keller then sets out to help Hill increase her income, and soon her boarding house is a thriving little business. With the sudden wealth, Hill can afford to send her son to an elite boarding school. But trouble arises when headmaster Buscaglia learns of Holder's unimpressive background and he moves to have the boy kicked out of the institution. Keller and Hill unite to save the boy's future, and the film concludes on a happy note.

Though the racial angle is a little hard to swallow in a more enlightened age, MY DARK LADY is basically a well-meaning comedy that benefits from good performances by the ensemble. Holder is a real standout, a child actor whose screen presence doesn't smack of forced charm. Frederick Keller directs with a light touch, keeping the story moving at a good pace without compromising any of the plot's simple events.

p, Carole Terranova, Stratton Rawson; d, Frederick King Keller; w, Fred A. Keller, Gene Brook, Frederick King Keller (based on an original story by Fred A. Keller); ph, Thom Marini; m, Ken Kaufman; ed, Darren Kloomok; prod d, Stratton Rawson; set d, Gary Matwijkow; cos, Elizabeth Haas Keller.

Comedy **(PR:A MPAA:NR)**

MY DEMON LOVER*½ (1987) 86m New Line Cinema c

Scott Valentine *(Kaz)*, Michelle Little *(Denny)*, Arnold Johnson *(Fixer)*, Robert Trebor *(Charles)*, Alan Fudge *(Capt. Phil Janus)*, Gina Gallego *(Sonia)*, Calvert DeForest *(Man in Healthfood Store)*.

The phrase, "you bring out the beast in me," has not been portrayed more accurately than in this film. Valentine is a street derelict who is the subject of an old Rumanian curse. It seems that whenever he becomes sexually aroused, he turns into any one of several beasts. Once his male hormones begin tingling, get out of the way because he sprouts horns, a tail, and all the other accouterments which go with old Rumanian curses. He's a talented man but down on his luck in many ways. Meanwhile, Little is a loser at love with a talent for picking the wrong men. She comes home early on her birthday to find her apartment being robbed by her latest boy friend. She is depressed and winds up dining at an outdoor cafe on New York's West Side where she sees a bundle of rags that turns out to be Valentine. He begs her for some food and she tries to ignore him but he attaches himself to her and follows her back to her apartment. Little allows the lug to come in since he seems harmless enough. When the thief returns, Valentine has already begun to have his beastly transformation. The guy exits like a racehorse upon seeing Valentine's fangs and body hair and Little keels over in a dead faint. When she come to, Little thinks it was all a dream and Valentine doesn't tell her the truth. She invites Valentine to stay at her place and he agrees with the proviso that they be roommates, not lovers. Valentine seeks out Johnson (known as "The Fixer") because Johnson (who is straight out of "The Twilight Zone") is a man who knows his way around potions and spells. Johnson makes use of a doorknob (he can't afford a crystal ball) and discovers that Valentine was cursed

because he tried to take an old Rumanian woman's daughter to bed. At the same time, New York is being frightened by a character known as "The Mangler," and Valentine, who doesn't recall anything from those moments when he is into one of his forms, thinks that he might be the malfeasant. Johnson says he has solved the problem. Rumanian curses can only be expunged if the cursee does something special, a deed that is so noble that Nobel would have given the person an award. If that should occur, the curse will depart the body and be immediately transferred to the closest person. Valentine is desperate because he fears he might attack Little. (In the course of the movie, Valentine becomes a skinhead letch, a wimp, a character known as Mr. Sardonicus, and a shrewish old woman.) Little talks to her best pal, Gallego, who is also a psychic. Gallego is going around with a New York police captain, Fudge. Gallego's sister had been one of the victims of "The Mangler" and she is determined to bring the attacker to justice. Little and Valentine are at her apartment and she wonders why he is so standoffish. Every other man she's ever been with has wanted to make love to her, yet he is adhering to their deal that they remain friends only. This is beginning to gnaw at Little. Valentine confesses his problem, but Little doesn't believe him until he lets his eyes wander over her glorious figure and the arousal turns him into a demon. Little wants to exit, but she loves Valentine and understands that he needs her help in order to free himself. Gallego has by now psychically learned Valentine's secret and she manages to con Little out of her apartment so she can go after Valentine with a sword. Little is on the street and is attacked by the real "Mangler," who drags her to an area in Central Park that has a bogus castle erected there. The final sequence involves a chase around the Park. Gallego realizes that Valentine is not the "Mangler" because she sees what happens to him when he is aroused. Valentine captures the "Mangler" and saves Little. It is when Johnson is standing near him that the curse leaves Valentine's body and attaches itself to Johnson.

Author Ray is a sometime actress and does a cameo as the "leggy redhead." She claims that the script was based on her own relationships with men in New York. Perhaps she should consider a professional matchmaker. Loventhal was also making his feature film debut with MY DEMON LOVER and acquitted himself well enough. The real stars were the special effects people who created some dandy masks and body prosthetics and needed every moment of the four-month preproduction schedule to get ready. A nice gritty feel to the East Village settings makes it seem almost authentic, if one believes in such things. Valentine is a regular on TV's "Family Ties," Gallego is the former costar of "Santa Barbara," Little was on "Falcon Crest," and Johnson recurred on "Hill Street Blues," so if anyone is wondering where the new movie stars are going to come from, the answer is television. *(Sexual situations.)*

p, Robert Shaye; d, Charles Loventhal; w, Leslie Ray; ph, Jacques Haitkin; m, David Newman; ed, Ronald Roose; prod d, Brent Swift; md, Kevin Benson; art d, Douglas Dick; cos, Tom McKinley; spec eff, Carl Fullerton, John Caglione, Jr., Neal Martz, Doug Drexler.

Horror/Comedy **(PR:C MPAA:PG-13)**

MY GENERAL† (1987, Span.) 107m Figaro c (MI GENERAL)

Fernando Rey *(Adm. Comesana)*, Fernando Fernan-Gomez *(Gen. Del Pozo)*, Hector Alterio *(Gen. Mendizabal)*, Jose Luis Lopez Vazquez *(Gen. Torres)*, Monica Randall *(Beatriz Palomares)*, Rafael Alonso *(Gen. Izquierdo)*, Joaquin Kremel *(Capt. Sarabia)*, Alvaro de Luna *(Commandant Barbadillo)*, Juanjo Puigcorbe *(Capt. Pujol)*, Manuel Torremocha *(Gen. Serrano)*, Alfred Luchetti *(Gen. Marques)*, Joan Borras *(Father Pazos)*, Jose M. Moratalla *(Sarrasqueta)*.

A group of Spanish generals is sent back to school for a special training course in modern warfare, taught by five young and extremely competent captains. The aging military men carry on like school children, causing friction in and out of the classroom. Their self-important bumblings are foiled when the junior officers show them their ignorance from spelling to nuclear missiles. The film is peppered with virtually every well-known male actor in Spain, all of them playing generals.

d, Jaime de Arminan; w, Jaime de Arminan, Fernando Fernan-Gomez, Manuel Pilares; ph, Teo Escamilla (Agfa Color); m, Vainica Doble; ed, Jose Luis Matesanz; set d, Felix Murcia; makeup, Ramon de Diego.

Comedy **(PR:NR MPAA:NR)**

MY LIFE AS A DOG*** (1987, Swed.) 101m Svensk Filmindustri-AB Filmteknik/Svensk Filmindustri c (MITT LIV SOM HUND)

Anton Glanzelius *(Ingemar Johansson)*, Anki Liden *(His Mother)*, Tomas von Bromssen *(Uncle Gunnar)*, Manfred Serner *(Erik, His Brother)*, Melinda Kinnaman *(Saga)*, Ing-Marie Carlsson *(Berit)*, Kicki Rundgren *(Aunt Ulla)*, Lennart Hjulstrom *(Konstnaren, the Sculptor)*, Leif Ericsson *(Farbor Sandberg)*, Christina Carlwind *(Fru Sandberg)*, Ralph Carlsson *(Harry)*, Didrik Gustavsson *(Mr. Arvidsson)*, Vivi Johansson *(Mrs. Arvidsson)*, Jan-Philip Hollstrom *(Manne)*, Arnold Alfredsson *(Manne's Grandfather)*, Fritz Elofsson *(Glassworks Master)*, Per Ottosson *(Tommy)*, Johanna Udehn *(Lilla Grodan)*, Susanna Wetterholm *(Karin)*, Viveca Dahlen *(Woman in Laundry)*, Magnus Rask *(Fransson)*, Tony Rix, Klimpen.

Released in Sweden in 1985, where it was named Best Picture and earned its 12-year-old star Glanzelius a best actor award, MY LIFE AS A DOG is a sensitive portrayal of adolescence which is simultaneously tragic and comic. Set in 1959, the film centers on Glanzelius, a remarkable young actor with an upturned mouth and a pug nose, who lives with his abusive brother Serner and his terminally ill mother Liden. His father is long gone and the prospect of any sort of normal family life is dim. Bedridden, Liden seems to genuinely love her children but no longer has the energy for their mischief and rambunctious behavior. Glanzelius does all he can for her. He tells her stories and tries his best to make her laugh, but she prefers to absorb herself in books. He is not discouraged, however, because at age 12 he already has his own philosophy about life. "You have to compare things all the time," says Glanzelius, "to get a distance on things." Sure, he has it bad, but not as bad as Laika, the Soviet spacedog that was sent spinning into space in the name of science. Tested and observed and analyzed, Laika served his researchers well. They, however, failed to provide him with enough food and he starved to death while in orbit. Glanzelius can't get Laika out of his mind, even getting down on all fours and barking when the situation calls for it. There are others that Glanzelius compares himself to—the man who was killed by a thrown javelin as he walked across the stadium grounds, or the person who received a "successful" liver transplant only to die shortly afterwards. On the brink of sexual awareness, Glanzelius' life has begun to spin out of control and, like Laika, there is little to be done to prevent it. When a doctor advises Liden to get some peace and quiet to help her recovery, Glanzelius is sent away for the summer. It is decided over Glanzelius' objections, that Sickan (his dog) will temporarily live in a kennel. Glanzelius is taken in by his amiable uncle von Bromssen and aunt Rundgren, whose modest village is home to the Boda glassworks. A likable couple in their thirties, von Bromssen and Rundgren treat their new boarder more like a friend than a child. Working with von Bromssen at the glass-blowing plant, Glanzelius meets a number of village eccentrics who take

kindly to him. He also joins a soccer team whose best player is Kinnaman, a tomboyish girl who disguises herself as a boy by tightly bandaging her budding breasts in order to secure her position on the team. Eventually Glanzelius and Kinnaman become friends and, to satisfy Kinnaman's love of boxing, sparring partners as well. Although he becomes adept at handling any punch she throws, Glanzelius is caught off guard by her sexual advances. When she shows him her breasts, he does not know how to react. When she attempts to undress him, he runs off. Although only 12 years old, Glanzelius is surrounded by sexuality. von Bromssen is obsessed with mammaries and constantly plays a Swedish version of "I've Got A Lovely Bunch Of Coconuts" (English version, Fred Heatherton) on his battered record player; Gustavsson, an elderly bedridden man who lives upstairs, always asks Glanzelius to read to him from the pages of a lingerie catalog; and most overtly sexual is Ing-Marie Carlsson, a buxom Bardot-style blonde who poses nude for a sculptor and captures the curiosity of Glanzelius. Eventually, both his mother and his dog die, and all Glanzelius can do is hold on to the happier times he had. In a hazy shot repeated throughout the film, Glanzelius is on the beach with his mother, regaling her with his silly acts. With these memories and his ability to "get a distance on things" Glanzelius returns to the village with an inner strength that will enable him to survive from one day to the next.

The misconception among American filmgoers that all Swedish films are from the Ingmar Bergman school of gloom is proven wrong in MY LIFE AS A DOG, Hallstrom's fifth film since 1974. (He had previously directed ABBA—THE MOVIE and has since directed two other pictures, THE CHILDREN OF BALLERBY VILLAGE and MORE ABOUT THE CHILDREN OF BALLERBY VILLAGE, both based on characters created by "Pippi Longstocking" author Astrid Lindgren.) Like most films that look at childhood, MY LIFE AS A DOG is an episodic tale which takes a central character, Glanzelius, and places him in a variety of revealing situations. His emotions are universally felt—the humor and the tragedy touching almost everybody in the audience. Fortunately, Hallstrom is skilled enough as a director to avoid a sappy, nostalgic look at childhood. He does not paint Glanzelius' character as the perfect child victimized by nasty grown-ups. Rather, Glanzelius is a troubled youngster on whom Hallstrom refuses to pass judgement.

As in the Jiri Menzel's Czech comedy of 1986, MY SWEET LITTLE VILLAGE, Hallstrom has given us a glimpse of village life—the inhabitants, the morals, the tradition, and the eccentricities that make this specific village unique. It is the villagers themselves that make Smaland (shot in Aforf) worthy of filming. One character whose presence is felt throughout the entire picture is an old man who is always on his roof, hammering away at any loose tiles. When he isn't seen, he's heard—the thud of his hammer echoing throughout the village. ("He has the best roof in town," admits von Bromssen.) The film is filled with such characters, and they help to define the village's personality. Glanzelius, originally an outsider in Smaland, is as eccentric as the rest of the villagers. He gets down on all fours and barks, he stares at the stars in sympathy with a Russian spacedog, and he has an embarrassing nervous habit of splashing milk in his face. It is only natural that this odd youngster will grow up in this odd village.

Although it's assumed that MY LIFE AS A DOG is an autobiographical account of the director's childhood (as, for example, THE 400 BLOWS was drawn from Francois Truffaut's life), it is actually based on the 1983 autobiography of Reidar Jonsson. "The attitude of the boy is very much mine," says Hallstrom, "trying to keep away from disasters and tough emotions by comparing with other people's disasters. So I can relate to that really. But it's not my childhood, it's the writer's entirely." What Hallstrom brings to the film are a number of brilliant directorial touches which are soft enough to create a sense of warmth and honesty. The mother's death scene, which could have been terribly maudlin, is handled off-screen. Glanzelius learns of her death when a relative asks to speak to him . . . alone. It is clear what the boy is about to be told, and the scene ends before another word is spoken. Another wonderful touch is Glanzelius' visit to the sanatarium to visit his mother. In the waiting room, he refuses to remove his jacket, preferring to keep it zipped to his chin. After speaking to his dying mother, the boy feels a certain freedom that compels him to joyously unzip his jacket. MY LIFE AS A DOG is not just another charming film about growing up. It is an expertly directed tale which takes a small, simple subject and colors it with invention and inspiration. (In Swedish; English subtitles.) *(Nudity, adult situations, sexual situations.)*

p, Waldemar Bergendahl; d, Lasse Hallstrom; w, Lasse Hallstrom, Reidar Jonsson, Brasse Brannstrom, Per Berglund (based on the novel by Reidar Jonsson); ph, Jorgen Persson, Rolf Lindstrom (Fujicolor); m, Bjorn Isfalt; ed, Christer Furubrand, Susanne Linnman; art d, Lasse Westfelt; cos, Inger Pehrsson, Susanne Falck; m/l, Povel Ramel; makeup, Helena Olofsson-Carmback, Agneta Jalemo.

Comedy/Drama **(PR:C MPAA:PG-13)**

MY LITTLE GIRL† (1987) 119m Black Swan-Merchant Ivory/Hemdale c

Mary Stuart Masterson *(Franny Bettinger)*, James Earl Jones *(Ike Bailey, Children's Center Director)*, Geraldine Page *(Grandmother Molly)*, Pamela Payton-Wright *(Mrs. Bettinger)*, Peter Michael Goetz *(Mr. Bettinger)*, Traci Lin *(Alice)*, Erika Alexander *(Joan)*, Anne Meara *(Mrs. Chopper)*, Peter Gallagher *(Kai, Alice's Boyfriend)*, Naeemah Wilmore *(Camille, Joan's Sister)*, Jordan Charney, Page Hannah, Jennifer Lopez, George Newberth, Bill O'Connell.

Filmed in 1985 and unveiled at the Montreal World Film Festival in 1986, MY LITTLE GIRL turned up in a brief theatrical run in 1987 after being picked up by Hemdale Releasing. The film stars Masterson (the exceptionally talented actress who appeared this year in GARDENS OF STONE and SOME KIND OF WONDERFUL) as the rich kid daughter of two unperceptive parents. She decides to take a job at a home for wayward girls, run by Jones (who also appeared in GARDENS OF STONE). Jones suspects of her of assuming a dilettante social worker pose and assigns her to three difficult charges—Wilmore, a silent, black 10-year-old; Alexander, her 24-year-old sister; and Lin, a 17-year-old hooker. Gradually, Masterson wins the respect, not only of her charges, but of Jones as well. Appearing in her final film is Geraldine Page, who died on June 13, 1987. Made on a budget of around $2 million, MY LITTLE GIRL marks the feature debut for the 41-year-old Kaiserman who previously acted as associate producer on five Merchant Ivory productions (of ROOM WITH A VIEW fame), including HEAT AND DUST and THE BOSTONIANS.

p&d, Connie Kaiserman; w, Connie Kaiserman, Nan Mason; ph, Pierre Lhomme; m, Richard Robbins; ed, Katherine Wenning; prod d, Dan Leigh; cos, Susan Gammie.

Drama **(PR:NR MPAA:R)**

MY OBVINYAEM† (1987, USSR) 130m Dovzhenko/Sovexportfilm c (Trans: We Accuse)

Sergei Yakovlev, Remigius Sabulis, Stepan Olexenko, Mirdza Martinsone.

The Francis Gary Powers U-2 spy incident of 1960 is told from the Russian point of view as USSR General Prosecutor Roman Rudenko brings the pilot to trial.

d, Timofei Levchuk; w, Ivan Mendzheritsky, Boris Antonov; ph, Eduard Pluchik; art d, Vladimir Arganov.

Docu-drama **(PR:NR MPAA:NR)**

MY WILL, I WILL† (1987, Hong Kong) 98m Molesworth c

Chow Yun Fat, Do Do Cheng.

A light-hearted romantic comedy in which a woman tries to get pregnant in order to produce a legal heir for her fortune in the US.

d&w, Luk Kim Ming.

Comedy/Romance **(PR:NR MPAA:NR)**

NA PUTA ZA KATANGU† (1987, Yugo.) 107m Film Danas-Baker Film c (Trans: On the Road to Katanga)

Svetozar Cvetkovic *(Palve Bezuha)*, Mirjana Karanovic *(Zhana)*, Rados Bajic.

Translated as "On the Road to Katanga," this Yugoslav film has absolutely nothing in common with the similarly titled Bob Hope-Bing Crosby-Dorothy Lamour musical comedies of the 1940s. It is, instead, the story of a man's search for his place in the world. Booted out of France by the authorities, Cvetkovic, a Yugoslav expatriate and the embodiment of rugged individualism, returns to his homeland to oversee the sale of his late father's house. When that is taken care of, he is determined to seek his fortune in Katanga, the diamond-mining region in southeastern Zaire. First, he has to deal with old friends and new ones in his hometown, which is also dominated by the mining industry. Catastrophe strikes an old friend, Cvetkovic ends up a loser with two women, and he decides the best thing to do is head for Africa, but before he gets very far, Cvetkovic finally realizes where his home is.

d, Zivojin Pavlovic; w, Rados Bajic; ph, Radoslav Vladic; m, Baronijan Vartkes; art d, Miodrag Miric.

Adventure/Drama **(PR:NR MPAA:NR)**

NABAT NA RASSVETE† (1987, USSR) 100m Mosfilm/Sovexportfilm c (Trans: The Tocsin)

Georgy Taratorkin, Irina Pechernikova, Nikolai Rachinsky, Leonid Kayurov, Maria Levtova.

Famed Russian academic Vladimir Vernadsky provided the inspiration for this tale about a patriotic scientist and explorer whose 60 years are filled with triumph and adventure as well as with hardship and disappointment. As a young man he battles a cholera epidemic; later he is part of an expedition that searches for uranium in Central Asia. Above all, he is determined to make the most of Russia's natural resources, but only after the October Revolution are his plans taken seriously by those in power.

d, Arkady Kordon; w, Oleg Stukalov-Pogodin, Arkady Filatov, Arkady Kordon, Alexander Bykhovsky; ph, Roman Veseler; m, Yury Butsko; art d, Dmitry Bogorodsky.

Drama **(PR:NR MPAA:NR)**

NAD NIEMNEM† (1987, Pol.) 176m Zespoly Filmowe-PROFIL/Film Polski c (Trans: On the Neman River)

Iwona Pawlak, Adam Marjanski, Marta Lipinska, Janusz Zakrzenski, Bozena Rogalska, Michal Pawlicki, Zbigniew Bogdanski, Jacek Chmielnik.

Set against the backdrop of the 1863 Polish revolt against Russian rule, this is the story of love that crosses class lines. While Poles fight to retain control of their own land, the young man and woman from vastly different social stations struggle to overcome the obstacles that society has placed in cupid's path. Based on a time-honored novel by Polish writer Eliza Orzeszkowa.

d, Zbigniew Kuzminski; w, Kazimierz Radowicz (based on the novel by Eliza Orzeszkowa); ph, Tomasz Tarasin; m, Andrzej Kurylewicz; ed, Maria Kuzminska-Lebiedzik; art d, Zenon Rozewicz.

(PR:NR MPAA:NR)

NADINE** (1987) 83m Tri-Star-ML Delphi Premier/Tri-Star c

Jeff Bridges *(Vernon Hightower)*, Kim Basinger *(Nadine Hightower)*, Rip Torn *(Buford Pope)*, Gwen Verdon *(Vera)*, Glenne Headly *(Renee Lomax)*, Jerry Stiller *(Raymond Escobar)*, Jay Patterson *(Dwight Estes)*, William Youmans

(Boyd), Mickey Jones *(Floyd)*, Gary Grubbs *(Cecil)*, Blue Deckert *(Mountain)*, Harlan Jordan *(Sheriff Rusk)*, Norman Bennett *(Reverend)*, James Harrell *(Deacon)*, John Galt *(Officer Lloyd)*, Joe Berryman *(Reporter)*, Linwood P. Walker III *(Janitor)*, Ray Walker *(TV Announcer)*, Shelby Brammer *(Michelle)*, Loyd Catlett *(Charley Draper)*, Sidney Brammer *(Estes' Girl Friend)*.

Robert Benton's great success with KRAMER VS. KRAMER was unusual in that the plot could have come right from a TV movie and would have been exactly that with someone like Robert Reed or Judd Hirsch playing the role instead of Dustin Hoffman. Much the same can be said for this original screenplay set in Benton's boyhood home of Texas. Of late, there have been several films with titles taken from songs of the 50s and 60s—movies like WALK LIKE A MAN, STAND BY ME, PEGGY SUE GOT MARRIED, and now this, which has the same name as the famed Chuck Berry tune. The plot could have come right from a "Mod Squad" episode and wouldn't have even made a good TV movie were it not for the talents of Basinger, Torn, and Bridges, all of whom filled out the thin material given them by Benton. Basinger is the estranged wife of Bridges. She's pregnant but she won't tell her soon-to-be-ex the news and she wants him to come across with a new car before she agrees to sign the divorce papers. The movie takes place in Austin, Texas, circa 1954 and the art direction is stunning because we really feel we are there (except for a brief mention of 7-11, which was not around at the time). It seems that Basinger made the mistake of posing for some "art studies" at the second floor studio of sleazy photographer Stiller. Now, she wants them back, despite Stiller's insistence that he knows Hugh Hefner, a pal who has just started a new magazine called *Playboy*. When Stiller won't return the pictures, Basinger is miffed. Someone else comes to the studio and Basinger is asked to wait in another room. She hears some noise, walks into the reception area, and sees Stiller dead with a knife in his back. This gives her the opportunity to steal the photos. She reaches into the file, takes out an envelope marked "Nadine," and thinks she has the pictures. Meanwhile, Bridges is happily involved with "Pecan Queen" Headly, a bimbo who works at the brewery that Bridges owes a great deal of money to. Bridges owns a downbeat bar where nobody ever goes, but he has "big plans" for the Bluebonnet Lounge, and if he has to come across with the car to secure Basinger's name on the divorce papers, he won't be able to expand. Basinger is a manicurist at the salon run by Verdon and she returns there after the murder, hardly shaken up at all (a false note in the film, unless she happens to see men stabbed to death on a daily basis). The nude photos aren't in the envelope. Instead, there are some plans for a new highway. Whoever knows about this will make a killing in Texas real estate. When Bridges learns about the plans, he contacts lawyer Patterson, a distant relative, and says that they can both get rich. Patterson, who has been stung in the past by Bridges' schemes, notifies the local real estate czar and resident slime-ball villain, Torn. Torn wants the plans back. Bridges doesn't want to give them back. The cops are after Basinger and Bridges, Torn is also after them and that recalls the Hitchcock format: "Innocent person is accused of crime, must get from point A to point B in order to clear him or herself. Along the way, hero meets reluctant heroine and the two are tossed together and eventually triumph." With Torn and his hoods after them, Bridges and Basinger are forced to spend a great deal of time together and this reawakens their love for each other. At the conclusion, by some enormous stroke of luck, a police officer tells them they are cleared and that the knife in Stiller's back has been traced to Torn. Why the cops didn't figure this one out earlier is a mystery. But the picture isn't. There is hardly one moment of suspense that is not telegraphed.

Basinger keeps getting better. She is this generation's Carole Lombard, and when she is handed the right script, her star will shine brightly. Bridges turns in the same kind of job he usually does, competent but hardly inspired. In this fashion, he is becoming America's Michael Caine in that he has the ability to be involved with a stinker and come out smelling like a rose. Texan Torn is type-cast in the same kind of mean-spirited role he's played so often and he does it well, even subtly. Benton meant to make a 1950s screwball comedy, but the screws came loose and what happened was not very funny, hardly gripping, and somewhat dissatisfying, especially since it came from the same man who mined the Texas territory so well with PLACES IN THE HEART and whose underrated THE LATE SHOW was such a delight. Almendros did well with his camera, a job he has performed before for Benton. In the past, two of Alemndros' best jobs were supposedly Texas-based, but DAYS OF HEAVEN was actually done in Canada and GOIN' SOUTH was made in Mexico. This time, they really were in

Texas and shot everything on location in Austin with a side trip to San Antonio. Many of the locations were "impractical" and not sets. Most notable was Bridges' bar, which smacked of authenticity. The picture began shooting at the end of September, 1986 and looks a lot better than it is. The executive producer for this most American of stories was German-born Wolfgang Glattes who worked in various capacities on such films as STAR 80, ALL THAT JAZZ, and CABARET (all with Bob Fosse). Songs include: "If You've Got the Money, I've Got the Time" (performed by Lefty Frizzell), the Gershwin's "Love Is Here to Stay" (performed by Jackie Gleason and His Orchestra), "La Chivita" (performed by Trio San Antonio), "Seven Nights to Rock" (performed by Moon Mullican), and "I Can't Resist," "Since I Found You," and "Midnight Girl/Sunset Town" (performed by Sweethearts of the Rodeo). The most one can say for this misfire is that it gave America another chance to see how good Basinger has become and that it also handed us the opportunity to watch Headly, whose comedic timing is superb. *(Violence, profanity.)*

p, Arlene Donovan; d&w, Robert Benton; ph, Nestor Almendros (Metrocolor); m, Howard Shore; ed, Sam O'Steen; prod d, Paul Sylbert; art d, Peter Lansdown Smith, Cary White; set d, Lee Poll; cos, Albert Wolsky; spec eff, Roy Downey, Mark Sullivan, Jack Monroe; makeup, Robert Mills; stunts, Diamond Farnsworth.

Comedy **(PR:C MPAA:PG)**

NAE-SHI† (1987, S. Korea) 108m Doo Sung Cinema-Seoul/Action Bros. c (Trans: Eunuchs)

Ahn Song-ki, Lee Mee-sok, Nam Koong-won, Kim Jin-ah, Kil Yong-woo, Tae Hyon-sil, Tae Il, Pyon Hee-bong.

Set in 16th Century Korea, this dark tale of ill-fated love between the daughter of an ambitious member of the king's retinue and the son of a minor functionary is full of sadistic punishments for the young would-be lovers. For starters, the title translates as "Eunuchs," a group the young man joins when he fouls up the girl's father's plans to have his daughter marry the king.

p&d, Lee Doo-yong; w, Kwak Il-lo (based on an idea by Yoon Sam-Yook); ph, Sohn Hyon-chae; m, Chong Yon-joo; ed, Lee Kyong-ja; set d, Park Hyo-jin; cos, Lee Hye-yoon.

Drama **(PR:NR MPAA:NR)**

NAGRA SOMMARKVALLAR PA JORDEN† (1987, Swed.) 104m Spice Film-SFI-Swedish Television-SVT-2/Swedish Film Institute c (Trans: Summer Nights)

Sif Ruud *(Karna)*, Margaretha Bystrom *(Ulrika)*, Per Mattsson *(Tomas)*, Harriet Andersson *(Magda)*, Leif Ahrle *(Bror)*, Mona Malm *(Gertrud)*, Ulf Johanson *(Fredrik)*, Inga-Lill Andersson *(Tanja)*.

The third film to be helmed by Swedish actress-director Gunnel Lindblom, who appeared in such Bergman classics as WILD STRAWBERRIES, THE VIRGIN SPRING, and THE SEVENTH SEAL, this family drama is based on a play by Agneta Pleijel that Lindblom directed for the Royal Dramatic, Sweden's national theater. The story revolves around a family reunion that takes place at a summer home on one of the tiny islands in the Stockholm archipelago. Three sisters return to the place where so many pleasant summers had passed when they were younger. Their mother, happy to be in that role again, welcomes her grown daughters but finds that they have changed. "Summer Nights" was made with the same cast that appeared in the stage version and was shot in 30 days while the play was still in production.

p, Peter Hald; d&w, Gunnel Lindblom (based on a play by Agneta Pleijel); ph, Lasse Bjorne (Eastmancolor); m, Goran Klintberg, Thirteen Moons; ed, Helene Berlin; prod d, Kaj Larsen.

Drama **(PR:NR MPAA:NR)**

NAIL GUN MASSACRE† (1987) 84m Futuristic Films/Reel Movies Intl. c

Rocky Patterson *(Doc)*, Michelle Meyer *(Linda)*, Ron Queen *(Sheriff)*, Beau Leland *(Bubba)*, Sebrina Lawless, Monica Lawless, Mike Coady, Staci Gordon, Randy Hayes, Joanne Hazelbarth, Roger Payne, Kit Mitchell.

Ultra low-budget gore from Texas which opens with the rape of a girl by a gang of construction workers. Some time later a killer dressed in army fatigues and a black motorcycle helmet goes around killing construction workers with a nail gun. Although it seems obvious that the heavily disguised killer is the rape victim seeking revenge, in reality the nail gun is wielded by the girl's brother. Not surprisingly this film never received a theatrical release and went straight to home video.

p, Terry Lofton; d, Terry Lofton, Bill Leslie; w, Terry Lofton; ph, Bill Leslie (Ultracolor); m, Whitey Thomas; ed, Lynn Leneau Calmes; spec eff, Terry Lofton.

Horror **Cas.** **(PR:NR MPAA:NR)**

NAKEMIIN, HYVASTI† (1987, Fin.) 99m Reppufilmi/Finnkino c (Trans: Farewell, Goodbye)

Aino Seppo *(Tuula)*, Elisa Partanen *(Ellu)*, Juuso Hirvikangas *(Jorma)*, Eero Saarinen *(Mononen)*, Harri Nikkonen *(Juho)*, Ritva Arvelo *(Elisa)*, Lasse Poysti *(Dr. Lauri Valve, Tuula's Father)*, Tiina Nystrom, Mikko Hanninen, Liisa Halonen, Alina.

A comedy about a father and daughter who have reached important points in their lives. The father (Poysti) is a respected cancer surgeon who feels like a failure both professionally and personally. Fed up with the hospital bureaucracy and his stagnant marriage, he suddenly decides to pull up stakes and join the Red Cross in Africa. His daughter (Seppo) is recently divorced with a small child and has moved to a cramped apartment in the suburbs. She meets a new man whom she likes, but her ex-husband, who has since remarried, refuses to give up on their relationship and only adds to her emotional confusion.

p, Petra Tarjanne; d&w, Anssi Manttari; ph, Heikki Katajisto (Eastmancolor); ed, Marjo Valve; set d, Erkki Lehtinen.

Comedy **(PR:NR MPAA:NR)**

NAPLO SZERELMEIMNER (SEE: DIARY FOR MY LOVED ONES, 1987, Hung.)

NARCO TERROR† (1987, Mex.) 86m Galubi-Torrente Dinamic/Peliculas Mexicanas c (Trans: Narcotics Terror)

Eduardo Yanez *(Roca Duran)*, Alfredo Leal *(Arturo Duran)*, Juan Gallardo *(Bernardo Trevino)*, Felicia Mercado *(Maura Trevino)*, Juan Verduzco *(Morris Serur)*, Raul Meraz, Claudio Baez, Leo Villanueva, Gabriela Goldshmied, Alfredo Gutierrez, Roberto Montiel, Fabian Aranza, Vicky Conti, Carlos Gonzalez.

Popular Mexican action star Yanez again teams up with director Galindo to play yet another man driven by circumstance to seek vengeance. On the day of his wedding Yanez learns his father, a banker with mob connections, is to be assassinated by the Mafia after refusing to participate in a drug-dealing scheme. Ignoring the impending nuptials, Yanez takes his father into hiding and tries to stay one step ahead of the mob. Eventually the gangsters catch up to them and Yanez's father is killed in a shootout. The wounded Yanez survives and returns to take on an army of gangsters by himself.

p, Ruben Galindo Ubierna; d, Ruben Galindo; w, Ruben Galindo, Carlos Valdemar; ph, Antonio de Anda; m, Jesus [Chucho] Zarzosa; ed, Carlos Savage.

Action/Crime **(PR:NR MPAA:NR)**

NAZRANA† (1987, India)

Rajesh Khanna, Smita Patil, Sridevi, Preeti Sapru.

Learning that her employer is in trouble, a loyal servant girl makes a supreme sacrifice to solve the problem. (In Hindi.)

p, C.V.K. Sastry; d, Ravi Tandon; m, Laxmikant Pyarelal.

Drama **(PR:NR MPAA:NR)**

NEAR DARK*½** (1987) 95m F-M Entertainment/DEG c

Adrian Pasdar *(Caleb)*, Jenny Wright *(Mae)*, Lance Henriksen *(Jesse)*, Bill Paxton *(Severen)*, Jenette Goldstein *(Diamondback)*, Tim Thomerson *(Loy)*, Joshua Miller *(Homer)*, Marcie Leeds *(Sarah)*, Kenny Call *(Deputy Sheriff)*, Ed Corbett *(Ticket Seller)*, Troy Evans *(Plainclothes Officer)*, Bill Cross *(Sheriff Eakers)*, Roger Aaron Brown *(Cajun Truck Driver)*, Thomas Wagner *(Bartender)*, Robert Winley *(Patron in Bar)*, James LeGros *(Teenage Cowboy)*, Jan King *(Waitress)*, Danny Kopel *(Biker in Bar)*, Billy Beck *(Motel Manager)*, S.A. Griffin *(Police Officer at Motel)*, Don Pugsley *(Second Truck Driver)*, Neith Hunter, Theresa Randle *(Ladies in Car)*, Tony Pierce, Gordon Haight *(Highway Youths)*, Leo Geter, Gary Wayne Cunningham *(Caleb's Friends)*, Bob Terhune, William T. Lane, Gary Littlejohn, Paul Michael Lane, Eddie Mulder *(State Troopers)*.

An auspicious solo directing debut from Kathryn Bigelow (she codirected THE LOVELESS in 1982) which combines such diverse genres as horror, western, crime, and romance into what may be the first vampire road movie. Set in the American Southwest, the film begins as a bored farm boy, Pasdar, spots the beguiling Wright at his usual Friday night hangout. A stranger in town, Wright asks Pasdar for a ride home and the lonely farm boy is more than eager to oblige. The pair cavorts through the sleepy towns until the break of dawn, when Wright becomes extremely edgy, demanding that Pasdar hurry up and get her home. Pasdar refuses to budge until she gives him a kiss, and she capitulates, only to bite him on the neck and run off. Unable to restart his truck, Pasdar walks across his father's field toward home. As daylight breaks, Pasdar begins to suffer severe cramps and his flesh begins to smoke. The boy's father (Thomerson) and grade school-aged sister (Leeds) see him stumbling across the field. Suddenly, a Winnebago—its windows covered with tinfoil—roars into view. The door of the vehicle swings open and the leather-clad Paxton yanks Pasdar into the speeding trailer home. The confused Pasdar finds himself faced with Wright and her bizarre "family"—a rag-tag group of vampires led by Henriksen, a man who has been undead since before the Civil War. Also in the van are the buxom Goldstein (Henriksen's woman), biker-type Paxton, and the creepy Miller, a sexually frustrated vampire whose body stopped growing when he was "turned" at the age of 14, but whose adult mind harbors lust for Wright. To his horror, Pasdar learns that he has been "nipped" (i.e., he is almost a full-fledged vampire). To graduate he must kill and drink blood. Sensing that Wright is in love with the boy, Henriksen gives Pasdar a week to perform his first kill. Unfortunately, Pasdar is unable to bring himself to murder, so Wright does the killing for him and then lets the farm boy drink from her wrist. Henriksen soon learns of the deception and gives Pasdar one last chance. The entire troupe invades a lonely honky-tonk patronized by a biker and a few good ol' boys and makes quick work of everyone inside, leaving Pasdar to kill the final victim. The terrified man escapes through a window and Pasdar gives chase, but when he finally catches up, he can't bring himself to kill. Incensed at yet another failure, Henriksen is about to kill Pasdar, but the sunrise postpones the execution and forces the vampires to make a dash for the nearest motel where they hole up until nightfall.

While they sleep, the survivor from the bar slaughter goes to the cops, and the vampires are awakened by a hail of bullets hitting their motel room. Although bullets are harmless to the undead, beams of golden sunlight (caused by bullet holes) flood the room, hitting the vampires and causing their flesh to singe and burn. The well-armed vampires engage the cops in a massive shoot-out, while Pasdar bravely volunteers to risk exposure to the sunlight to get the van. Spattered with bullets and using only a blanket as a shield, Pasdar runs to the van while his flesh bursts into flames. Badly burned, the boy crashes the van into the motel room, picks up his comrades, and drives off. This successful bit of bravery buys Pasdar one more chance to make his own kill. Meanwhile, Pasdar's father and sister have been combing the area searching for him. By coincidence, the vampires and Pasdar's family are staying at the very same motel. Miller encounters little Leeds and invites her into his room to watch TV. Henriksen immediately dispatches Paxton to fetch the girl's father. Just as the vampires are about to kill his family, Pasdar enters the room and tries to stop them. In the ensuing struggle, Pasdar manages to escape with his father and sister. Through a blood transfusion, Pasdar returns to normal and tries to pick up where he left off with his life. One night, Wright shows up and tells Pasdar how lonely she is without him. Still in love, Pasdar embraces the vampire girl, only to discover that she has been used as bait so that Miller could sneak into the house and kidnap Leeds (the 14-year-old vampire is determined to find a mate). Finding his tires slashed, Pasdar mounts his horse and rides off to rescue his little sister. Facing the vampires alone, the farm boy manages to kill Paxton in a fiery explosion and then frees his sister. With the sun rising, Pasdar throws his coat over Wright and tries to escape with her and Leeds. Desperate for companionship, Miller ignores the sunlight and runs after Leeds, only to burst into flames and then explode. Caught without proper protection in the sunlight, Henriksen and Goldstein make one last attempt to run down Pasdar with a car, but the sun proves too much for them and they burst into flames. Pasdar brings Wright home, and after a transfusion, she, too, returns to normal and is eager to begin a new life with the farm boy.

Although several movie genres are represented here, NEAR DARK is most obviously based on director Nicholas Ray's 1949 feature debut, THEY LIVE BY NIGHT (Bigelow's characters literally *must* "live by night"). Both films focus on a young couple desperately in love but trapped into a life-style they detest by their surrogate families (bank robbers and vampires respectively). But NEAR DARK is much more than a mere homage to Nicholas Ray. Director Bigelow and coscreenwriter Red (THE HITCHER) demonstrate a keen understanding and appreciation of the history of American cinema and create a unique film which explores the conventions of the vampire movie while moving it from dank European castles to modern-day Southwestern America. Bigelow sees the vampire (a word never used in the film) as a nomadic outlaw, much like the fabled gunslingers of the Old West or the roving bands of bank robbers that dotted the landscape during the Depression. Although monsters, the vampires are shown to be fiercely loyal to each other. This loyalty is born of loneliness and it is the fear of being alone that binds them together as a family. This, of course, is really nothing new for vampire movies (1987's other vampire film, THE LOST BOYS, presents vampirism as a youth gang recruiting members via peer pressure), but NEAR DARK does jettison certain conventions. Religious iconography, garlic, mirrors, and stakes are never shown and would probably prove to be merely minor annoyances that these vampires would encounter only rarely. Sunlight, however, is the eternal enemy. Director Bigelow puts the viewer in sympathy with the vampires by portraying the night as lush, exciting, and evocative, while the day is seen as harsh, bright, and arid. The humans who must deal with the choking dust and stifling heat seem worse off than the vampires. Bigelow infuses her film with an eerie mood that perfectly captures her characters and their milieu (her first feature, THE LOVELESS, a strange biker film set in the 1950s, is virtually plotless—a study of ambience and atmosphere). She also knows how to build and sustain a superb action sequence. The honky-tonk slaughter and the ensuing shoot-out with police are among the best-directed scenes of visceral terror and excitement seen on the screen in years. The casting of NEAR DARK is flawless. Pasdar and Wright are perfect as the troubled lovers, Miller is even more frightening than he was in RIVER'S EDGE, and Henriksen, Goldstein, and Paxton (reunited from the cast of ALIENS) are all effectively creepy, with Henriksen taking top honors. Only the weak climax and subsequent happy ending damage this otherwise fine film (THEY LIVE BY NIGHT has a much bleaker ending). Bigelow is clearly not interested in the demise of her vampires, and the uninspired scripting and direction betray this lack of interest. Although disappointing, the weak ending should not deter anyone from witnessing the development of a talent who may prove to be one of the most exciting and valuable new American filmmakers of the next decade: Kathryn Bigelow. Songs include: "Naughty, Naughty" (John Parr, performed by Parr), "Morse Code" (D. Woody, P. Simmons, performed by Jools Holland), "Fever" (John Davenport, Eddie Cooley, performed by The Cramps), "The Cowboy Rides Away" (Sonny Throckmorten, Casey Kelly, performed by George Strait). *(Graphic violence, profanity.)*

p, Steven-Charles Jaffe, Eric Red; d, Kathryn Bigelow; w, Eric Red, Kathryn Bigelow; ph, Adam Greenberg (CFI Color); m, Tangerine Dream; ed, Howard Smith; prod d, Stephen Altman; art d, Dian Perryman; m/l, John Parr, D. Woody, P. Simmons, John Davenport, Eddie Cooley, Sonny Throckmorten, Casey Kelly; cos, Joseph Porro; makeup, Davida Simon, Gordon Smith; spec eff, Steve Galich, Dale Martin; stunts, Everett Creach.

Horror **(PR:O MPAA:R)**

NECROPOLIS zero (1987) 76m Tycin Ent./Empire c

LeeAnne Baker *(Eva)*, Jacquie Fitz *(Dawn)*, Michael Conte *(Billy)*, William K. Reed *(Rev. Henry James)*, Paul Ruben *(Benny)*, Andrew Bausili *(Tony/ Preacher)*, Gy Mirano *(Rosa)*, Letnam Yekim *(Rudy)*, George Anthony-Bayza *(Philly)*, Anthony Gioia *(Steady Eddie)*, Jett Julian *(Snake)*, Jennifer Stahl *(Cat)*, Nadine Hartstein *(Candy)*, Jacqueline Pearson, Vicki Bell *(Hookers)*, Adriane Lee, Joel Von Ornsteiner, Christina Sisinni, Norris Culf, Michael Zezima *(Cult Members)*, Aloyius R. Burke *(Truck Driver)*, Jeff Meyer, David Benson *(Paramedics)*, John Abbato, Aledia E. Casanas, Mary Felix, Sandy Green, Andrew Howarth, Eddie Mallia, Ronald Wertheim *(New Amsterdam Townspeople)*, Mark Pagano, Jerry Emigholz, Colleen Feeney, Robert Santorelli, John Dardia, Matt Mallard, Dana Balacek, Tracy Gallagher, Peter Quinn, Margie Schoff, Nora Hart, Timothy McAlinden, Thomas McAlinden, Mark O'Neill *(Street Kids)*.

As if BREEDERS, MUTANT HUNT, and ROBOT HOLOCAUST weren't enough, New York City-based Tycin Entertainment has come up with yet another tedious and revolting low-budget genre effort that fails miserably on all counts. Formerly a Tycin bit-player, Baker (BREEDERS) has the dubious task of carrying this entire film. She is cast as a 300-year-old witch who is out to complete a ceremonial virgin sacrifice that was interrupted back in 1685. When consummated, the satanic rite will give Baker and her sextet of zombies eternal life. Tooling around Manhattan on a red motorcycle, dressed in a short black leather skirt and lacy black nylons with garters, Baker sets about sucking the "lifeforce" out of hapless New Yorkers while searching for the reincarnated souls of those who foiled her virgin sacrifice 300 years before. Those very souls happen to be Fitz, a National Public Radio reporter with a British accent; Conte, a veteran N.Y.C. police detective; and Reed, a black priest who runs a drug rehab center. After much killing and lapping of gooey substances by Baker, there is a showdown between all the principals. In it Reed disposes of the villains with an armload of wooden crosses and a can of gasoline. Not so easily defeated, Baker's charred, severed hand (alive because it wears a magic ring) wriggles its way to Fitz's apartment and possesses her. Fitz kills Conte and assumes Baker's mission, decked out in her own kinky leather outfit.

After suffering through the aforementioned Tycin efforts, what is left to say about them? Cheaply made, badly scripted, and atrociously acted, the Tycin films occasionally boast some fairly creative low- budget effects (usually by Ed French), but even they look the same from film to film. This is formula filmmaking at its most insipid. These films fail to prompt the suspension of disbelief, have no internal logic, and unfold at a snail's pace. The unintentionally funny highlights of NECROPOLIS include Baker's sudden display of three sets of breasts which allow her sextet of zombies to suckle the all important "lifeforce." There are also several impromptu dance numbers wherein Baker writhes about by herself to the beat of lame rock songs. Good for a few additional snickers is that old Tycin standby: actors in their early twenties playing characters twice their age. Oh yes, the obligatory limp-wristed bitchy bureaucrat—this time a coroner—is around for a bit of good-old-fashioned gay-bashing. Stay away. *(Graphic violence, gore effects, sexual situations, nudity, excessive profanity.)*

p, Cynthia DePaula, Tim Kincaid; d&w, Bruce Hickey; ph, Arthur D. Marks (Precision Color); m, Don Great, Tom Milano; ed, Barry Zetlin, Tom Mesherski; art d, Ruth Lounsbury, Marina Zurkow; set d, David Morong; spec eff, Ed French; ch, Taunie Vrenon; m/l, M. Bernard, P. Silva, S. Hilden, J. Steinman.

Horror **Cas.** **(PR:O MPAA:R)**

NEGERKYS & LABRE LARVER† (1987, Den.) 68m Metronome Film-Danish Film Institute/Metronome c (Trans: Creampuffs & Lollipops)

Kathrina Dauscha *(Nana)*, Lise S. Steffensen *(Conny)*, Thomas Hansen *(Anders)*, Mark Jackman *(Michael Jackson Lookalike)*, Peter Hesse Overgaard *(Teacher)*, Teresia Madeleine Ronne, Puk Schaufus, Ulla Henningsen, Helle Ryslinge, Sabine Lindeberg.

Sort of a grammar-school version of THE SECRET LIFE OF WALTER MITTY, this Danish children's film revolves around the fantasy lives of young girls. In their reverie they experience fame, motherhood, and romantic encounters with celebrities—not necessarily in that order.

p, Tivi Magnusson; d, Li Vilstrup; w, Li Vilstrup, Dortea Birkedal Andersen; ph, Bodil Trier (Eastmancolor); m, Sanne Bruel; ed, Camilla Skousen; cos, Lotte Dandanell, Manon Rasmussen.

Children's **(PR:NR MPAA:NR)**

NEYLONOVAYA YOLKA† (1987, USSR) 79m Gruziafilm Studio/Sovexportfilm c (Trans: A Nylon Christmas Tree)

Ruslan Mikaberidze, Guram Petriashvili, Zurab Kipshidze, Edisher Magalashvili, Irina Kalinovskaya.

Taking place mostly on a bus, this Soviet picture surveys the vagaries of the human condition as embodied in the odd assortment of passengers who are trying to make their way to New Year's Eve parties.

d, Rezo Esadze; w, Rezo Esadze, Amiran Dolidze; ph, Levan Paatashvili; m, Bidzin Kvernadze; art d, Temur Ardjevanidze.

Drama **(PR:NR MPAA:NR)**

NGATI*** (1987, New Zealand) 88m Pacific Films c

Tuta Ngarimu Tamati *(Uncle Eru)*, Ngawai Harrison *(Hine)*, Wi Kuki Kaa *(Iwi, Ropata's Father)*, Oliver Jones *(Ropata)*, Ross Girven *(Greg Shaw)*, Johnny Coleman *(Drover)*, Judy McIntosh *(Jenny Bennett)*, Barry Allen *(Headmaster)*, Connie Pewhairangi *(Sally)*, Alice Fraser *(Sam Bennett)*, Norman Fletcher *(Dr. Paul Bennett)*, Michael Tibble *(Tione)*, Erica Hovell, Priscilla Hovell *(Tione's Sisters)*, Iranui Haig *(Nanny Huia)*, Kiri McCorkindale *(Sue)*, Luckie Renata *(Dike)*, Paki Cherrington *(Mac)*.

A young Australian just out of medical school is sent on a world tour by his father, on the condition that he first visit the tiny New Zealand village where he was born and where his mother died. There he quickly grows to like the mostly Maori population, who immediately take to him as one of their own. He soon learns that he is one of their own, his late mother having been a Maori. Meanwhile, the local meat-freezing plant is going to be shut down and a young boy is dying of leukemia, beyond the help of either Western or Maori medicine. The boy dies, the villagers come together to take over the freezing plant themselves, and the young doctor decides to make the tiny village his home. A simple film that is more concerned with detailing the ways in which Maori society works than with thrilling its audience, it still manages to become a rather effective work. This is the first film directed and written by Maoris, and it became a surprise success at Cannes and other festivals. The producers trained a group of Maoris in the filmmaking crafts. They became the core crew for the film and enlisted the aid of an entire community in the production. The evocation of the slow-paced life in a small coastal village in the late 1940s is beautiful, and the Maori life it shows, full of close family ties and frequent feasts, is the best ever seen in a feature (see UTU for a Western perspective on the Maoris). The performances vary wildly in their quality—evidence of the largely amateur cast—but the film has some undeniable moments of power and more than a few laughs. NGATI is yet another example of why the developing New Zealand film industry in one of the most fascinating in the world today.

p, John O'Shea; d, Barry Barclay; w, Tama Poata; ph, Rory O'Shea; m, Dalvanius; ed, Dell King; art d, Matthew Murphy.

Drama **(PR:A MPAA:NR)**

NI DE AQUI, NI DE ALLA† (1987, Mex.) 94m Produciones Vlady/Peliculas Mexicanas c (Trans: From Neither Here Nor There)

Maria Elena Velasco [La India Maria] *(Maria Nicolasa)*, Don Rafael Banquells *(Tata)*, Cruz Infante *(Cook)*, Bruno Schwebel *(Mr. Taylor)*, Sergio Kleiner, Memo de Alvarado [Condorito], Poly Marichal, Pepe Romay, Blackaman, Martin Ayllet, Leon Escobar, Ana Arjonce, Raymond Kettles, Silvestre Mendez.

Set in Los Angeles, this Mexican comedy follows the fortunes of an illegal alien who has the misfortune to be present when a political leader is killed. Thoroughly confused, she dodges both the FBI and the assassin. Velasco, who Mexican audiences have come to know and love as La India Maria, plays the unlucky immigrant, trotting out her well-known rural bumpkin character.

p, Ivan Lipkies; d, Maria Elena Velasco [La India Maria]; w, Ivette Lipkies (based on an idea by Maria Elena Velasco); ph, Alberto Arellanos; m, Chucho Zarzosa; ed, Jorge Rivera.

Comedy **(PR:NR MPAA:NR)**

NICE GIRLS DON'T EXPLODE½** (1987) 92m Nice Girls/NW c

Barbara Harris *(Mom)*, Michelle Meyrink *(April)*, William O'Leary *(Andy)*, Wallace Shawn *(Ellen)*, James Nardini *(Ken)*, Margot Gray *(Little April)*, Jonas Baugham *(Little Andy)*, William Kuhlke *(Dr. Stewart)*, Belinda Wells, Irwin Keyes.

So dumb that it's smart, this quirky low-budget comedy from first-time director Martinez spoofs the likes of CARRIE and FIRESTARTER while presenting the tale of a divorced mother who refuses to let her daughter grow up. From the opening credits—done as a scrapbook/photo album—it's clear that mom Harris has long doted upon her daughter. In a sequence set 13 years prior to the main action of the film, a young boy (Baugham) comes to play with Harris' little girl (Gray), who, at that moment, is at the end of a retractable leash in the backyard. Harris tells the boy that Gray doesn't want to see him, but he knows better and, switching the collar from Gray to Fluffy the cat, the two go off to play. However, when the force of leash turns the cat into a projectile, Harris realizes that something is up besides Fluffy. Thirteen years later, her little girl has grown up into Meyrink, a slightly overweight teenager with a big problem—every time she gets in the least bit intimate with a boy, sparks literally fly, and everything from plants to automobiles burst into flames. This incendiary proclivity is Meyrink's telekinetic curse, or so says Harris. Meyrink, who brings a travel-size fire extinguisher on dates, does her best to keep cool, but neither will power nor ice-cold baths seem to help, and for good reason—the real firestarter is Harris. Constantly lurking in the background, she uses a remote controlled detonator to set off the flammable surprises she deploys to make sure things get hot whenever Meyrink's dates get heavy.

Things look up for Meyrink when O'Leary, her childhood playmate, moves back to town. A world-class ping pong player but otherwise ineffectual, O'Leary falls for Meyrink and refuses to buy Harris' story, even when his car goes up in flames. More than once Harris barges in on him at home, bringing cookies with her but refusing to let him put his clothes on as she attempts to discourage his pursuit of her daughter. When O'Leary takes Meyrink to consult a psychiatrist, she meets Shawn, a lonely arsonist named Ellen. ("Not Helen. Ellen!" Shawn says at one point. "Helen would be an absurd name for a man.") Learning that Meyrink also starts fires, Shawn thinks they are meant for each other. O'Leary decides to turn the tables on Harris, and, catching her clad only in a towel, he tells her that he knows her secret. All the while, he has a tape recorder hidden to capture her confession. However, it is O'Leary who ends up getting caught with his pants down and carted off to jail, where he shares a cell with Shawn. Mistaken for Shawn, whose release has been secured by his lawyer, O'Leary rushes off to reveal Harris' hoax. Dousing himself with gasoline and placing Meyrink on top of a garbage can, he dares Harris to start a fire. When an onlooker tosses a sparkler in O'Leary's direction, Harris pushes him to safety. In the process, Meyrink discovers Harris' remote control device and ignites all the little fires hidden on the premises. On the defensive, Harris claims that many years before a nut had put "mini-flam" in vanilla extract bottles and that she had used one of these bottles for baking cookies for her little girl, which, according to Harris, means that if Meyrink gets too agitated she will explode. O'Leary and Meyrink don't believe her and go to his place to commence a whole lotta shakin'. Outside the window, in the pouring rain, Harris emotionally confesses to everything, explaining that the only thing more difficult than being a mother is not being a mother. Having deceived Harris, O'Leary and Meyrink return to the Harris place, where they encounter Shawn, who has come looking for Meyrink and found her with his "buddy" O'Leary. Meyrink and O'Leary make love and there is a tremendous explosion, but the blast is the result of a bomb Shawn has hidden in a bouquet of flowers and not the couple's experiment. In the end, the reconciled, big, happy family even journeys to China so O'Leary can do his ping pong thing.

For the most part, the self-conscious silliness of NICE GIRLS DON'T EXPLODE works, challenging the viewer to be hip enough to accept its arch goofiness. The film's premise is innovative, offbeat, and funny, but by repeatedly trading on the same gags and concepts it eventually becomes wearisome. Made for only $1.3 million, this is anything but a seamless film; nonetheless, there are some wonderful performances and clever, capable cinematic touches. Harris is excellent as the slightly deranged mother, going over the top with her apple-pie momness but conveying the very real fear of being left alone that leads to her bizarre manipulations. O'Leary is often endearing as he fecklessly perseveres and Meyrink (VALLEY GIRL, REAL GENIUS) is oddly sensual as the imprudently naive object of his desires; however, it is Shawn who provides the film's funniest moments. Without his quirky indignation and presence, the Helen-Ellen business would fall flat; with it, these are very laughable moments indeed. Shawn's initial appearance is one of the film's best scenes. Wearing horribly mismatched clothing and a stupid smile, he tentatively approaches an attractive woman sitting on a park bench, then disappears out of the left side of the frame, reappears, disappears again, and finally sits next to her. Offering an awful come-on line—"I'm sorry; I didn't get your name"—he ends up with a bag of popcorn dumped on his head. The problem with the film isn't a lack of wit or style, but that the filmmakers arrive at clever concepts and then overwork them. Costume designer Wells and production designer Rotstein both deserve credit for their excellent work. From Harris' ever-present flower-print aprons to O'Leary's radical geekware, the costumes are perfect, and Harris' house, overflowing with photos and childhood memorabilia, is like a museum dedicated to Meyrink's arrested development. Originally intended as an independently financed production, the film caught the interest of New World Pictures which footed the bulk of the bill for the project, shot on location in Lawrence, Kansas. *(Sexual situations.)*

p, Doug Curtis, John Wells; d, Chuck Martinez; w, Paul Harris; ph, Steven Katz; m, Brian Banks, Anthony Marinelli; ed, Wende Phifer Mate; prod d, Sarina Rotstein; cos, Belinda Wells; makeup, Margaret Sunshine.

Comedy **(PR:C MPAA:PG)**

NIGHT ANGELS*** (1987, Braz.) 98m Superfilmes/Embrafilme c (ANJOS DA NOITE)

Zeze Motta *(Malu)*, Antonio Fagundes *(Jorge)*, Marilia Pera *(Marta)*, Marco Nanini *(Guto)*, Chiquinho Brandao *(Mauro)*, Aldo Bueno *(Bimbo)*, Claudio Mamberti *(Fofo)*, Ana Ramalho *(Maria Clara)*, Guilherme Leme *(Teddy)*, Aida Lerner *(Milene)*, Be Valerio *(Cissa)*.

Director Barros, in his first feature film, makes use of distancing, nonlinear narrative techniques to blur the line between illusion and reality in this highly stylized film about street life in Sao Paulo. Interconnecting several characters and their stories, the film opens with a transvestite and his murder victim. The camera pulls back, however, to reveal them as actors at a play rehearsal. This is followed by a shot of a man driving in a convertible. He is gunned down. A woman screams. She is an actress, and this action is part of a film that is being shot. Eventually the theater director and the film actress meet and their stories connect with those of a wealthy socialite, a homosexual prostitute, a transvestite, a performance artist, an aging starlet, and a sociology student who is drawn to watching videotapes of the gay prostitute. While giving equal time to a variety of visual media—film, theater, television, performance art—Barros explores the various aspects of Sao Paulo nightlife—the sex, violence, drugs, and hopelessness. When taken as separate scenes, the film is rich and intriguing, and shows Barros to be a truly talented visual stylist. The disjointed narrative, however, seems less a structural decision than merely the reflection of a lack of cohesiveness. As a result, NIGHT ANGELS is more successful as a series of set pieces than as a whole. Impeccably photographed and carefully cast, NIGHT ANGELS is one of many recent Brazilian films that burrow into the dark underworld of Sao Paulo in a style that exists somewhere between gritty realism and flashy stylization. It received film festival showings in 1987. (In Portuguese; English subtitles.) *(Sexual situations, nudity, violence, drug abuse.)*.

d&w, Wilson Barros; ph, Jose Roberto Eliezer; m, Servulo Augusto; ed, Renato Neiva Moreira; art d, Cristiano Amaral, Francisco de Andrade; cos, Marisa Guimaraes.

Drama **(PR:O MPAA:NR)**

NIGHT IS YOUNG, THE (SEE: BAD BLOOD, 1987, Fr.)

NIGHT STALKER, THE* (1987) 89m Chrystie-Striker/Almi c

Charles Napier *(Sgt. J.J. Striker)*, Michelle Reese *(Rene)*, Katherine Kelly Lang *(Denise)*, Robert Viharo *(Charlie Garrett)*, Joey Gian *(Buddy Brown)*, Robert Zdar *(Sommers)*, Leila Carlin *(Terry)*, Gary Crosby *(Vic Gallegher)*, James Louis Watkins *(Julius)*, John Goff *(Captain)*, Diane Sommerfield *(Lannie)*, Tally Chanel *(Brenda)*, Ola Ray *(Sable Fox)*, Joan Chen *(Mai Wing)*, Roy Jenson *(Cook)*, Buck Flower *(Tramp)*.

Any similarity between this and the interesting TV series starring Darren McGavin is unintentional, and ends with the title. In Los Angeles, a few years ago, there was a killer named Richard Ramirez who was terrorizing the city and dubbed "The Night Stalker" by the media. Someone dreamed up the idea of doing a movie that loosely paralleled the Ramirez case and the defense attorneys for the accused rightly questioned their client's ability to receive a fair trial in light of the fact that both Ramirez and the character in the movie preyed mainly on women and were prone to Satanic symbols. (In a 1986 court appearance, Ramirez shouted "Hail, Satan!") Zdar is the killer, a muscular giant who seems to be able to repel bullets as he strangles various streetwalkers. He's pursued by Napier, a tired cop who spends more time with Jack Daniels than he does at his desk. Zdar's *modus operandi* is to choke the living daylights out of the women, then decorate their bodies with Chinese writing. Napier and partner Viharo, who goes over the acting top, keep after the killer. Napier has a vested interest in capturing the wacko because he's frightened that his girl friend, Reese, a prostitute, may be next. Napier and Reese show a tender side with their mother-henning of Lang, a sweet young thing who, like Brooke Shields in PRETTY BABY, has been brought up among the "working women." As in many movies of this sort, the killer is captured and then a coda is added when a psychoanalyst explains the man's motivation for all the letting of blood.

Napier will be recalled as the macho man in MOONFIRE, THE SEVEN MINUTES, CITIZENS BAND, and THUNDER AND LIGHTNING before graduating to MELVIN AND HOWARD, with some time out for the oversized BLUES BROTHERS. Good-looking women abound (Ray, Chen, Chanel) and Gary Crosby, who is an overlooked character actor, does well with an unsympathetic role as a cop who must have a liaison with a hooker who turns out to be a guy in doll's clothing. Co-author/producer Edmonds will remembered for his directorial chores on TENDER LOVING CARE, SOUTHERN DOUBLE CROSS, and BARE KNUCKLES. Prior to those films, he'd been an actor in GIDGET GOES HAWAIIAN, THE INTERNS, BEACH BALL, and others. Director Kleven made his mark by being one of the best second-unit action men around. The problem with THE NIGHT STALKER is that he didn't hold a firm enough grip on the actors and the result is a loss of reality. Look for better work from him in the future as he has a sharp eye and a knack for action. *(Violence.)*

p, Don Edmonds; d, Max Kleven; w, John Goff, Don Edmonds; ph, Don Burgess (Alpha Cine Color); m, David Kitay; ed, Stanford C. Allen; prod d, Allen Terry; md, Steve Tyrell; spec eff, Paul Stapley; stunts, James Winburn.

Crime/Mystery **(PR:O MPAA:R)**

NIGHT ZOO** (1987, Can.) 115m Cinema Plus-Les Productions Oz c (UN ZOO, LA NUIT)

Roger Le Bel *(Albert)*, Gilles Maheu *(Marcel)*, Lynne Adams *(Julie)*, Lorne Brass *(Georges)*, Germain Houde *(Charlie)*, Jerry Snell.

A much-heralded Canadian picture from first-time director Lauzon which sets a father-son relationship against the glossy backdrop of Quebec's criminal underworld. Maheu, a former drug dealer for a corrupt cop Houde, emerges from prison after a two-year stint. The night before his release, however, a homosexual prisoner rapes Maheu on orders from Houde. The rape is a warning to Maheu, who, before beginning his term, skimmed $200,000 and a cache of cocaine from Houde. The money is safely hidden away in Maheu's uncle's restaurant, but when Maheu goes to retrieve it, he finds it missing. The money is later returned to Maheu by his father, Le Bel, an old man with a heart condition who has kept the loot out of Houde's reach. Le Bel, whose wife has just left him, wants nothing more than to be reunited with his son. He dreams of going fishing and hunting like a father and his son should. Maheu thinks his father is a bit crazy and prefers to return to Quebec's fast lane. Houde, who is now partnered with the sadistic homosexual Brass, keeps a close watch on Maheu, threatening to harm his father and his former girl friend, Adams, if the missing cash doesn't surface. Maheu then pays a visit to Adams, a leather-clad punk, whom he violently makes love to on a rooftop before riding off into the night on his motorcycle. In an effort to renew his relationship with his father, Maheu takes him on a fishing trip. Drifting on a placid, fog-shrouded lake, father and son strengthen their bond—fishing, making moose calls, and sharing laughs. For Le Bel's birthday, Maheu buys a hunting rifle and promises to take his father moose hunting. In the meantime, Maheu has been pressured by Houde and Brass into paying back the money after the pair nearly kill Adams in the peep show booth where she works. Maheu, however, outsmarts the cops and guns down both of them in a seedy sex motel. In the meantime, Le Bel has a heart attack and is hospitalized. Rather than forget about the hunting trip, Maheu arrives at his father's bedside with a movie projector. He blows some cocaine up his father's nose and together they watch a super-8 wilderness film of a moose. If that isn't enough excitement for one night, Maheu puts his father in a wheelchair, arms him with his hunting rifle, and takes him to the nearest zoo. Since this zoo doesn't have a moose, the ecologically minded father and son decide to bag an elephant. Later, Le Bel's condition worsens, leaving Maheu to care for him. Le Bel then dies happily, having regained the devotion of his son.

Carried by its highly polished visual style, NIGHT ZOO is a brutal, misanthropic, sleazy crime film which is only made worthwhile by the heartfelt and somewhat sappy father-son relationship that offsets the violence. NIGHT ZOO attempts to show the contradictions of a nasty character who survives in a dangerous world, yet has very human and gentle feelings towards his father. Unfortunately, the film doesn't reach the level of complexity that one hopes it would, failing to capture the more profound ambiguity of Coppola's GODFATHER films. The seedy underbelly of Quebec that is exposed is no different from that captured in countless other flashy crime films of late, from DIVA to SUBWAY to last year's dazzling Canadian entry POUVOIR INTIME—sadistic, perverse, and essentially one-dimensional. In NIGHT ZOO's criminal universe all the men are super macho, wearing tight blue jeans and leather jackets, flashing their big guns and riding down the street on their even bigger motorcycles. Along with all this macho posing comes a built-in misogyny that is directed at Adams, the only woman in the film. Apparently her only purpose in life is to be physically, verbally, sexually, and emotionally abused by every man she meets. What separates NIGHT ZOO from other films in this league is the parallel father-son story. Although director Lauzon seems content to fill his criminal world with cliches, he treats the father-son relationship with some heart. Le Bel's character is a truly sympathetic one who will do anything to impress his son. He is a beaten man who has been deserted by his wife, ignored by his relatives, and victimized by his ailing heart. However, just when Lauzon gains audience sympathy (in the hospital scene), he resorts to the pathetic (but supposedly funny) scene in which Maheu blows cocaine into his father's nose, nearly choking the already weak-hearted man. The two then become thoroughly reprehensible when they proceed to the zoo and kill an elephant. While these scenes could have meant something had they explored the pathetic qualities of the two characters, they instead are played for laughs. Along with I'VE HEARD THE MERMAIDS SINGING, NIGHT ZOO has attracted a great deal of attention for Canada at international festivals this year—continuing to arouse an interest in Canadian cinema which reached a high point last year with Denys Arcand's THE DECLINE OF THE AMERICAN EMPIRE, Anne Wheeler's LOYALTIES, and Leon Marr's DANCING IN THE DARK. (In French and English; English subtitles). *(Violence, sexual situations, substance abuse.)*

p, Roger Frappier, Pierre Gendron; d&w, Jean-Claude Lauzon; ph, Guy Dufaux; m, Jean Corriveau; ed, Michel Arcand; art d, Jean-Baptists Tard; set d, Michele Forest; cos, Andree Morin.

Crime/Drama **(PR:O MPAA:NR)**

NIGHTFLYERS† (1987) 89m Vista/Vista-New Century c

Catherine Mary Stewart *(Miranda)*, Michael Praed *(Royd)*, John Standing *(D'Branin)*, Lisa Blount *(Audrey)*, Glenn Withrow *(Keelor)*, James Avery *(Darryl)*, Helene Udy *(Lilly)*, Annabel Brooks *(Eliza)*, Michael Des Barres *(Jon Winderman)*.

This adaptation of science-fiction author George R.R. Martin's popular novella was given a scant theatrical play-off at Halloween and will probably find a wider audience on cable and home video. Set in the 21st Century, NIGHTFLYERS concerns an old space ship which is haunted by an evil force. The somewhat decrepit ship is leased by a team of scientists who are launching a search for evidence of a fabled race of aliens known as the *Voleryn*. The ship's captain, Praed, is only seen as a computer generated hologram. Stewart, the team coordinator, falls in love with Praed's ghostly image and he with her. Other members of the team are cryptologist Blount, sighting specialist Avery, computer whiz Udy, biologist Withrow, and Des Barres, a troubled telepath who, predictably, winds up being the channel for the evil spirit that goes after the scientists and kills them one by one. NIGHTFLYERS had a fairly troubled production history, including the departure of the original director, Fritz Kiersch, who quit and was replaced by Robert Collector. Although Collector saw the project through shooting, he left when the producers became unhappy with his cut of the film. He insisted that his name be taken off the credits, and consequently the pseudonym "T.C. Blake" appears under the director credit. Producer/screenwriter Jaffe (DEMON SEED) took over editing chores and many effects scenes were reshot in order to patch up rough gaps in the narrative.

p, Robert Jaffe; d, "T.C. Blake" [Robert Collector]; w, Robert Jaffe (based on the novella by George R.R. Martin); ph, Shelly Johnson (Foto-Kem Color); m, Doug Timm; ed, Tom Siiter; prod d, John Muto; art d, Mike Bingham; set d, Anne Huntley-Ahrens; cos, Brad R. Loman; spec eff, Robert Short, Gene Warren, Jr.

Science Fiction **(PR:NR MPAA:R)**

NIGHTFORCE* (1987) 82m Star Cinema/Vestron c

Linda Blair *(Carla)*, James Van Patten *(Steve Worthington)*, Richard Lynch *(Bishop)*, Chad McQueen *(Henry)*, Dean R. Miller *(Eddie)*, James Marcel *(Mack)*, Claudia Udy *(Christy Hanson)*, Bruce Fisher *(Estoban)*, Cameron Mitchell *(Senator Hanson)*, Cork Hubbert *(Raoul)*, Jeanne Baird *(Mrs. Hanson)*, Casey King *(Bob Worthington)*, Mitchell Edmonds *(Detective Buchanan)*, Bob McCracken *(Mike Collins)*, T.J. Acosta *(Fat Man)*, Barry Lynch *(Bob's Law Partner)*, David S. Holt *(Diego)*, Michael Martin, Al Cutillo, Al Sanchez *(Kidnapping Terrorists)*, Raymond Soto *(Mexican Tough)*, Wendy Harrison *(TV Newscaster)*, Judith Schwartz, Francine Witkin *(Socialites)*, Jill Kaufman, Karen LaCava *(Prostitutes)*, Kathleen Kinmont *(Cindy)*, Dushan Naumovsia *(Spanish Priest)*, Gary McLarty *(Ralph)*, Ben Moore *(Al)*, Peter Griffin, Donald Tornatore, Jim Halty, David LeBell *(Stadium Workers)*, Billy Lucas *(Stadium Guard)*, Bobby Cummings, Jim Ortega, Matt Johnson, Tim Davidson, Tommy Huff *(Stadium Terrorists)*, Todd Mason Covert *(Stable Boy)*, Mark Dias, Mark Baliani, Rene Alexander, Rick Diaz, Phillip Navarro, John Wellamette, Rudy Sigalla, David Macias, Ralph A. Rodriguez, Mike Martin *(Terrorists at Copter)*.

When Udy, the daughter of a prominent US senator, is kidnaped by Central American Communist insurgents, her friends find the government unable to help. They decide to go after her themselves, so four guys (Van Patten, McQueen, Miller, and Marcel) and one tough girl (Blair) load up a jeep with a bunch of guns and drive to Central America. They don't get far before they run into trouble, from which they are extricated by Lynch, a former CIA man who never went home after Vietnam. He takes them under his wing and leads them to the guerilla camp, which they proceed to shoot up in a prolonged firefight. Three of the boys are killed before the others, including Udy, manage to make their way to a helicopter and fly out. There are literally dozens of similarly plotted films that go direct to video every year, and one can only wonder at them. They all seem to be filmed in the same area (just outside L.A., no doubt), all concern a bunch of Americans shooting up swarms of lesser nationalities, and all feature some babe with a submachine gun on the cassette box art. They can hardly be called art, but they can be entertainment. Unfortunately, NIGHTFORCE doesn't succeed on either count. The action scenes are flat, the story is badly paced, and the acting is indifferent. There are great dollops of nudity from Udy, whose only plot function is to be raped several times and to cower. There's nothing here to interest anyone, but that probably won't stop this from turning up in every video store across the country. *(Nudity, sexual situations, violence.)*

p, Victoria Paige Meyerink, Lawrence D. Foldes, Russell W. Colgin, William S. Weiner; d, Lawrence D. Foldes; w, Lawrence D. Foldes, Russell W. Colgin, Michael Engel, Don O'Melveny (based on a story by Lawrence D. Foldes); ph, Roy H. Wagner, Billy Dickson (Fotokem Color); m, Nigel Harrison, Bob Rose; ed, Ed Hansen; prod d, Curtis A. Schnell; art d, Colin Irwin, Mike Gulbin; set d, Phoebe Schmidt, Doug Mowat; cos, Jacqueline Johnson; spec eff, Paul Staples; m/l, Bob Rose, Nigel Harrison, Steven Kay; stunts, Terrance James, Eddy Donino; makeup, N. Kristine Chadwick.

Action/Adventure **Cas.** **(PR:O MPAA:R)**

NIGHTMARE AT SHADOW WOODS† (1987) 84m FCG c

Louise Lasser *(Maddy)*, Mark Soper *(Todd/Terry)*, Marianne Kanter *(Dr. Berman)*, Julie Gordon *(Karen)*, Jayne Bentzen *(Julie)*, William Fuller *(Brad)*.

Typical slasher movie set in Jacksonville, Florida, and featuring Soper in a dual role as a teenager and his evil twin brother. One night while attending a drive-in movie with their mother, Lasser (just what she's doing in this film is anybody's guess), the boys sneak off and wander the lot. The evil Soper slits a patron's throat and then splashes blood on his incredulous brother while handing him the knife. The cops drag off the good Soper and toss him into a prison for the criminally insane, while the evil Soper bides his time playing the role of the perfect son. Ten years later, on Thanksgiving day, Lasser announces that she and her boy friend are going to be married. Just as the news leaves her lips, Lasser receives a phone call informing her that her son has escaped from prison. This delights the evil Soper, for now he has an excuse to go out and slaughter more people and pin the blame on his brother the escaped homicidal maniac. The evil Soper grabs a machete and hacks his way through mom's fiance, some friends at school, the neighbors, his girl friend, and eventually Lasser. Filmed in 1984, the film received a short release in Detroit and will no doubt wind up on home video.

p, Marianne Kanter; d, John W. Grissmer; w, Richard Lamden; ph, Richard E. Brooks (CFI Color); m, Richard Einhorn; ed, Michael R. Miller; prod d, Jim Rule; spec eff, Ed French.

Horror **(PR:NR MPAA:R)**

NIGHTMARE ON ELM STREET 3: DREAM WARRIORS, A**½ (1987) 96m New Line-Heron-Smart Egg/New Line c

Heather Langenkamp *(Nancy Thompson)*, Patricia Arquette *(Kristen Parker)*, Larry Fishburne *(Max)*, Priscilla Pointer *(Dr. Elizabeth Simms)*, Craig Wasson *(Dr. Neil Goldman)*, Brooke Bundy *(Elaine Parker)*, Rodney Eastman *(Joey)*, Bradley Gregg *(Phillip)*, Ira Heiden *(Will)*, Ken Sagoes *(Kincaid)*, Penelope Sudrow *(Jennifer)*, Jennifer Rubin *(Taryn)*, Clayton Landey *(Lorenzo, Orderly)*, Nan Martin *(Nun)*, Stacey Alden *(Marcie)*, Kristin Clayton *(Little Girl)*, Sally Piper, Rozlyn Sorrell *(Nurses)*, James Carroll *(Neurosurgeon)*, Jack Shea *(Priest at Funeral)*, Michael Rougas *(Priest in Church)*, Robert Englund *(Freddy Krueger)*, John Saxon *(Lt. John Thompson)*, Dick Cavett, Zsa Zsa Gabor *(Themselves)*.

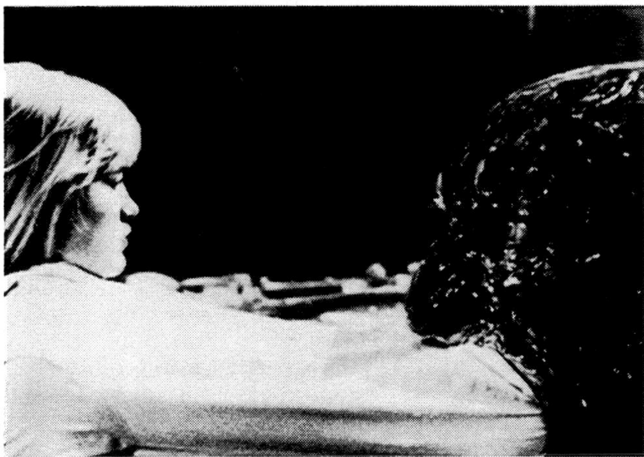

The third chapter of the phenomenally successful horror series based on director Wes Craven's superior original. Although Craven had nothing to do with PART II, he returned to cowrite and to serve as associate producer on PART III, and his influence is quite apparent. The film takes place in a small town which is experiencing a rash of teenage suicides. Arquette (younger sister of Rosanna), a teenager plagued by horrible nightmares, tries to slash her wrists and is subsequently admitted to a psychiatric hospital where she is put under the care of Wasson, a young doctor who specializes in teenage problems. Wasson is faced with teens (Eastman, Gregg, Heiden, Sagoes, Sudrow, and Rubin) who refuse to sleep at night for fear of their nightmares. What is odd is that the teens insist that the same nightmarish figure appears in all their dreams, a horribly scarred man dressed in a ratty red and black striped sweater. Wasson doesn't know what to make of these symptoms until Langenkamp arrives on the scene. A young doctor who specializes in dream disorders, Langenkamp knows exactly what the teens are going through because she has met and done battle with the very same creature in her dreams—and his name is Freddy Krueger (Englund). Langenkamp soon learns that all the teens once lived on Elm Street, on the block where Englund once committed heinous crimes against children and where he was eventually caught and killed by angry parents. The teenagers are the sons and daughters of the parents who murdered Englund, and now his spirit is taking its revenge in the dreams of their children. Englund can be defeated in the dream world, but it is difficult to do on one's own. Langenkamp fights Englund off by taking an experimental drug that allows her to repress her dreams while sleeping. She demands the teens be allowed to go on the medication, but hospital officials deny the request. Without the drug, the teens soon lose the battle against their dreams and several are killed in a variety of horrible ways by Englund, who preys on their deepest fears. Langenkamp discovers that Arquette possesses a special psychic ability which allows several people to share her dream, so she attempts to pull the remaining teenagers into a single nightmare so that they can do battle against Englund as a team. Meanwhile, Wasson learns from a mysterious nun that Englund was the son of a woman who had been held captive in a lunatic asylum and was raped repeatedly by the inmates, hence the "bastard son of a hundred maniacs." She also informs Wasson that after Englund's murder the parents buried the bones on unconsecrated ground and that is why his spirit is restless. Wasson enlists the aid of Saxon, Langenkamp's father, who is the only surviving member of the parents who knows where the bones are buried. Saxon takes Wasson to a junkyard and they proceed to dig up the remains. In dreamland, however, Langenkamp and the teens are losing the battle against Englund. Several of their number are killed by the clever murderer before Wasson and Saxon find the bones. To their horror, the bones come to life and Englund's skeleton impales Saxon on the fin of an old Cadillac. At the same time, in dreamland, Englund tricks Langenkamp and kills her. Soon after, Wasson is able to destroy the skeleton and bury the bones on hallowed ground, thus destroying Englund's nightmarish spirit and saving the lives of the remaining teens. Although deeply saddened by Langenkamp's death, Wasson learns that he can visit with her in his dreams.

Produced on a mere $4.5 million budget, A NIGHTMARE ON ELM STREET PART III: DREAM WARRIORS grossed $8.8 million on its opening weekend, thus making it one of the most successful openings in independent distribution history. The film went on to take in more than $40 million, making New Line Cinema one of the most successful independent production companies in Hollywood. Part of this success is no doubt due to the cult status attained by the character of Freddy Krueger. Whereas Jason of the FRIDAY THE 13TH movies proved popular, he is merely a lunk in a hockey mask with no personality. Freddy, however, is an energetic, clever killer with a warped sense of humor who seems to really enjoy tormenting teenagers. As played by classically trained actor Englund, Freddy is a vital killer who brings a sense of creepy fun to his demented work—moviegoers actually *like* the guy. The nightmares themselves are another reason for the series' success. Seldom have films explored the nightmare world with such effect, style, and panache. In PART III, special effects wizards Yagher, Shostrum, Biggs, and Cannom created a variety of bizarre images including: a teen who is literally tongue-tied to his bed, a television that turns into Freddy, Freddy's transformation into a marionette and growth into a giant, and a huge Freddy head that tries to swallow Arquette whole. Unfortunately, these scenes have become the set pieces of the series, with increasingly less attention paid to the scenes that precede and follow them. While the script for PART III is a bit more interesting than the one for PART II, there are nagging inconsistencies when it comes to the "rules" that govern Freddy's existence, and the characterizations are becoming less important. What separated Craven's original film from the pack was his eye for character and his ability to infuse his teens with an intelligence and passion previously unknown in "dead teenager movies." These kids weren't content to be victims, they fought back. The same still holds true in PART III, but the teens are more amorphous and much less interesting. The performances are weak as well. Wasson turns in another earnest-yet-forgettable portrayal, Arquette screams well but isn't given a chance to do much more, Langenkamp—who was excellent in Part I—is downright lame here and fails in her attempt to play a character several years older than herself. The other teens are unremarkable, and Saxon simply looks embarrassed. Only Englund continues to score, but that is because he has the best part. The NIGHTMARE movies are by no means bad horror films; in fact, they are better than most of the competition. But undoubtedly there will be a Part IV to the series, and one can only hope that some fresh ideas will emerge. *(Graphic violence, gore effects, nudity, profanity.)*

p, Robert Shaye, Sara Risher; d, Chuck Russell; w, Wes Craven, Bruce Wagner, Chuck Russell, Frank Darabont (based on a story by Wes Craven, Bruce Wagner and characters created by Wes Craven); ph, Roy Wagner (Deluxe Color); m, Angelo Badalamenti; ed, Terry Stokes, Chuck Weiss; art d, Mick Strawn, C.J. Strawn; set d, James Barrows; makeup, Kevin Yagher, Mark Shostrum, Chris Biggs, Greg Cannom, Mathew Mungel; m/l, Ken Harrison, Don Dokken; spec eff, Hoyt Yeatman, Peter Chesney; stunts, Rich Barker.

Horror **Cas.** **(PR:O MPAA:R)**

NIGHTSTICK† (1987, Can.) 94m Production Distribution Co. c (AKA: CALHOUN)

Bruce Fairbairn *(Jack Calhoun)*, Kerrie Keane *(Robin Malone)*, Robert Vaughn *(Ray Melton)*, John Vernon *(Adam Beardsley)*, Leslie Nielsen *(Evans)*, Walker Boone *(Roger Bantam)*, Tony De Santis *(Jerry Bantam)*, David Mucci *(Pat Bantam)*.

Filmed in Canada but set in New York City, NIGHTSTICK features "Knot's Landing" actor Fairbairn as a renegade cop assigned by boss Nielsen to foil a group of terrorists who have been raiding chemical companies and stealing the ingredients needed to make nitroglycerin. As it turns out the "terrorists" (De Santis, Boone, and Mucci) are merely bank robbers trying to intimidate bank president Vernon into paying a $5 million ransom. If the money is not paid, the gang will blow up all of Vernon's Manhattan banks. Fairbairn, however, is hot on their trail and ready to make his move. Before the super-cop can act, however, the gangsters kidnap Fairbairn's girl friend (Keane) and hold her hostage, forcing a showdown in an abandoned warehouse while the time-bombs tick away. NIGHTSTICK was given a brief release in Boston before going the home video route.

p, Martin Walters; d, Joseph L. Scanlan; w, James J. Docherty; ph, Robert Fresco; m, Robert O. Ragland; ed, Richard Wells, Daniel Radford; art d, Reuben Freed; set d, Tony Duggan-Smith; cos, Eva Gord; spec eff, Carere Special Effects.

Action/Crime **Cas.** **(PR:NR MPAA:R)**

NILAKURINHI POOTHAPPOL† (1987, India)

Girish Karnad, Karthika, Nedumudi Venu, Srinivasan, Innocent, Lalitha.

The scandalous love affair between a middle-aged army officer and the teenage daugher of his best friend is explored. (In Malayalam.)

p, Sam Philadelphia; d, Bharathan; m, Jerry Amaldev.

Romance **(PR:NR MPAA:NR)**

NINJA THUNDERBOLT† (1987, Hong Kong) 90m IFD Films and Arts Ltd. c

Richard Harrison, Wang Tao, Randy To, Kulada Yasuaki, Barbara Yuen, Anna Lewis, Sidney Pang, Tracey Yeh, John Ladalski, Mohammad Abel, Richard Cheng, Steve Kwan, Jackie Chan.

A ninja is hired by a corrupt industrialist and his evil daughter to steal a jade statue from them so that they can collect the lucrative insurance money. The ninja fulfills his obligation only to find that his employers intend to murder him. Hunted by the police, the insurance investigator, and the murderous minions of the industrialist, the ninja must fight them all to retain his honor.

p, Joseph Lai, Betty Chan, Chiang Hsien Chang; d&w, Godfrey Ho (based on a story by AAV Creative Unit); ph, Raymond Cheung (CinemaScope, Eastmancolor); ed, Leung Wing Chan; prod d, Stephen So; art d, Eagle Leung; set d, Sam Lee; spec eff, Martin Ho; stunts, Tom Li; makeup, Jenny Choi.

Martial Arts **(PR:NR MPAA:NR)**

NIONDE KOMPANIET† (1987, Swed.) 105m Svensk Filmindustri c (Trans: Company Nine)

Thomas Hanzon *(Bertil Rosencrantz)*, Tomas Fryk *(Gunnar Jonsson)*, Harald Hamrell *(Mogren)*, Jan Mybrand *(Persson)*, Birger Oesterberg *(Kling)*, Dan Eriksson *(Andersson)*, Patrik Bergner *(Hoden)*, Krister Henriksson *(The Vicar)*, Margreth Weivers *(His Mother)*, Hans Straat *(Arvid Jonsson)*, Gunilla Nyrood *(Alva Jonsson)*, Lennart Hjulstrom, Sara Forsberg, Robert Sjoblom, Sten Johan Hedman, Marika Lindstrom, Jerry Williams.

With his first feature film, director Colin Nutley—a Briton who works in Sweden—presents a grim comedy about group of soldiers who sell army property for personal profit. When higher-ups discover the scam, they take a piece of the action rather than initiating disciplinary action.

p, Jan Marnell; d, Colin Nutley; w, Colin Nutley, Sven-Gosta Holm; ph, Jens Fischer (Eastmancolor); ed, Perry Schaffer; prod d, Lasse Westfelt; cos, Katja Watkins; stunts, Johan Toren.

Drama/Comedy **(PR:NR MPAA:NR)**

NITWITS† (1987, Neth.) 112m Preston Prods./Holland Film Releasing c

Ramses Shaffy *(Joel Palsma)*, Monique Rosier *(Danielle Kooiman)*, Leen Jongewaard *(Receptionist)*, Martin Oversteegen *(Eddie)*, Muriel Chaal-Gohier *(Magda)*.

The linchpin of this Dutch series of vignettes is Shaffy, who plays an actor who has more roles than he can handle. He rushes from one acting gig to another and from his wife and child to a number of mistresses.

p, Chris Houtman; d&w, Nikolai van der Heyde; ph, Peter de Bont (Kodak, Haghe Film); m, Vladimir Cosma; ed, Ton de Graaff; art d, Freek Biessiot; set d, Pieter Brull.

Drama **(PR:NR MPAA:NR)**

NO BLOOD NO SURRENDER† (1987, Phil.) Roadshow Films Intl. c

Palito Panchito, Max Alvarado, Michelle Aquino, Ernie Ortega, Ruben Ramos, Eddie Llanita, Janice Jurado, Brandy Ayala, Sheella Mari.

d, Rudy Dominguez; w, Ernie Ortega; ph, Rudy Quijano; m, Caloy Rodriguez.

Action **(PR:NR MPAA:NR)**

NO DEAD HEROES zero (1987) 86m Cineventures-Maharaj-Miller c

Max Thayer *(Ric Sanders)*, John Dresden *(Harry Cotter)*, Toni Nero *(Barbara Perez)*, Nick Nicholson *(Ivan Dimanovitch)*, Mike Monty *(Frank Baylor)*, Dave Anderson *(Gen. Craig)*, Dan Oliver, Rex Smith *(Montagnards)*, John Carr *(Camp Commanding Officer)*, Danny Bell *(Vietnamese Officer)*, Steve Rogers, Ronny Patterson, Warren McLean, Eric Hahn, Geraldo Tosco, Joseph Collins, Harry Lausman *(Green Berets)*.

MISSING IN ACTION meets THE MANCHURIAN CANDIDATE in this poorly conceived and abysmally executed war-espionage drama. The movie opens during the Vietnam War, as Lt. Thayer and Capt. Dresden are sent on a secret mission to extract a captured CIA agent from a North Vietnamese POW camp. The camp is supervised by a sadistic Russian advisor (Nicholson) whose sophisticated interrogation technique consists of punching Americans in the face a few times, asking them a question, then shooting them when they don't talk. The rescue goes badly, and all the prisoners and most of the commando team wind up dead on the way back to the spot where helicopters are to pick them up. Only Dresden and Thayer remain and Dresden is wounded and left behind after placing a wounded Thayer aboard. A title announces the passing of ten years, and we see Dresden in Moscow, where a tiny microchip is being implanted in his brain that will turn him into a programmed killer at the push of a button. Since strong emotions can overwhelm the programming, his first mission is to wipe out his own family, along with Thayer's, who are there for a birthday party. Thayer is approached by the CIA to help track down and kill Dresden and he accepts, going through a rigorous training program. Meanwhile, in Kampuchea, Dresden too is undergoing training for a mission to assassinate the pope during a Central American visit. Thayer and a team of commandoes wipe out the training base, but Nicholson and Dresden escape. Proceeding to El Salvador, Thayer is contacted by a beautiful double agent, Nero, who leads him to the rebel camp. he is captured and tortured and Nero raped, but she escapes to free him and lead an attack on the base. Thayer and Dresden fight hand to hand until a blow to the head loosens Dresden's connections and he starts yelling at Thayer to get in the chopper. Nicholson arrives to shoot him dead, along with Nero, and Thayer is left to plug Nicholson between the eyes and walk out alone, apparently the sole survivor. There may have been some potential in the story, but the strictly amateur hour production values undermine whatever serious content someone might have intended with such florid dialog as " We are the watchdogs of the world, if we go to sleep, the Communists will steal our freedoms like thieves in the night." All of the sound is badly synchronized and the scenes unimaginatively shot. People don't even fall down dead interestingly here, tipping over like logs. No one gives any semblance of a performance, and the only thing impressive is the size of the sets they blow up. Needless to say, this never saw anything like a theatrical release. *(Violence, adult situations, profanity, brief nudity.)*

p&d, J.C. Miller; w, J.C. Miller, Arthur N. Gelfield; ph, Freddie C. Grant; m, Marita M. Wellman; ed, Edgar Vine; art d, Donnie Gonzalez, Ramon Nicdao; set d, Arthur Gelfield; spec eff, Jun Rambell; stunts, Val Morris; makeup, Cecile Bann.

War **Cas.** **(PR:O MPAA:NR)**

NO MAN'S LAND** (1987) 107m Orion c

D.B. Sweeney *(Benjy Taylor)*, Charlie Sheen *(Ted Varrick)*, Lara Harris *(Ann Varrick)*, Randy Quaid *(Lt. Vincent Bracey)*, Bill Duke *(Malcolm)*, R.D. Call *(Frank Martin)*, Arlen Dean Snyder *(Lt. Loos)*, M. Emmet Walsh *(Capt. Haun)*.

Sweeney is a young cop, new to the sheriff's department in Los Angeles. His background is working class but he has a passion for Porsches and is in the process of restoring an old, beat-up one. Lieutenant Quaid needs someone to go undercover at a Porsche dealership where another cop was murdered while trying to get the low-down on a stolen car ring and Sweeney fits the bill. Quaid is convinced that Sheen, the flashy rich-kid owner of the dealership, is the murderer. Sweeney gets a job as a mechanic at the shop, and one night, Sweeney is sent to repair Sheen's stalled car. He makes a few adjustments, and then, with Sweeney behind the wheel, the two go on a hair-raising test drive, darting in and out of traffic, flying around curves. The two become fast friends, and Sheen introduces Sweeney to the "lives of the rich and aimless" at chic L.A. night spots and Harris, his pretty sister who has no idea about Sheen's illegal thrill-seeking. Sheen is not only behind the stolen car ring, but he is also its most prolific thief. However, the police aren't the only ones with Sheen's number; a rival gang of car thieves headed by Call is no less unhappy about Sheen's success. Before long, Sheen personally trains Sweeney in the fine art of Porsche theft. Meanwhile, Quaid is beginning to worry that Sweeney is going "native," having a little too good a time in the fast lane. Sweeney is convinced that his buddy couldn't possibly be a killer, and he and Harris are also falling for each other. When Duke, who runs the shop for Sheen, is murdered, Sheen goes after Call and shoots him on a disco dance floor. During the investigation of Duke's murder, Sweeney is called in for questioning and blows his cover in front of crooked cop Snyder, who, as it turns out, actually killed the cop that Quaid believes was Sheen's victim. However, Snyder performed the murder at Sheen's behest. He calls the rich kid to demand $20,000 to keep him from copping a plea and blowing the whistle and for the information that Sweeney is a cop. By chance, Harris learns Sweeney's identity, too, and wants nothing more to do with him. Sheen and Sweeney go to meet Snyder. Sweeney gives Snyder the $20,000 and when the crooked cop prepares to kill him, Sheen runs him over in a car. Sweeney goes to Quaid's home to tell him what has happened, but after Sweeney departs, the lieutenant is murdered. Sheen and Sweeney meet at a mall and go to the rooftop of the parking lot, ostensibly to steal a car, both wishing there were some way out of the situation but aware that there isn't, both feeling betrayed. They draw on each other and Sheen is killed.

Sweeney's seduction by the good life and the friendship that develops between these two young men from opposite sides of the tracks and on opposite sides of the law has the makings of an intriguing story. However, director Werner ("Moonlighting") and scripter Wolf ("Hill Street Blues"), both TV veterans, treat their story conventionally and there are few surprises in NO MAN'S LAND. The final showdown, despite its interesting acknowledgement of mutual betrayal, is predictable and dramatically unsatisfying. A complex relationship such as the one between Sheen and Sweeney cries out for a less pat resolution. The film's car chases are well handled but hardly innovative; the airborne auto slicing through a semi-trailer notwithstanding, they could have come from any number of cop films or TV shows. To Wolf's credit there is some clever dialog. The film's pace, however, is a bit choppy, particularly in the early going where scenes are never given a chance to develop. NO MAN'S LAND's saving grace are the performances by Sheen (PLATOON, WALL STREET) and Sweeney. Sheen's cynical equanimity, conveyed with deft touches, is perfect for the capable rich kid who has everything and nothing. Sheen's Ted isn't inherently bad, just bored. Instead of having nothing to lose, he has nothing to gain except a little excitement and challenge and so he acts according to different rules. Sweeney (GARDENS OF STONE) plays his undercover cop like a man in limbo. He still isn't quite sure how to be a cop, and though he isn't sure how to be a criminal either, he is enthralled with both life in the fast lane and Harris. His exhilaration, his confusion, and his sense of guilt and betrayal all have the ring of truth. Harris, who at moments looks like both Rosanna Arquette and Isabella Rossellini, is adequate in a skin-deep role that might easily have been played by someone wearing a sign reading "Love Interest" or "Plot Complication." Quaid, who has been better elsewhere, is awful here, maintaining the same perturbed expression throughout the film. *(Violence, profanity, sexual situations.)*

p, Joseph Stern, Dick Wolf; d, Peter Werner; w, Dick Wolf, Jack Behr, Sandy Kroopf; ph, Hiro Narita; m, Basil Poledouris; ed, Steve Cohen; prod d, Paul Peters.

Crime **(PR:O MPAA:R)**

NO WAY OUT*½ (1987) 114m Neufeld, Ziskin, Garland/Orion c

Kevin Costner *(Lt. Cmdr. Tom Farrell)*, Gene Hackman *(David Brice, Secretary of Defense)*, Sean Young *(Susan Atwell)*, Will Patton *(Scott Pritchard, General Counsel to the Secretary of Defense)*, Howard Duff *(Sen. Willy Duvall, Intelligence Committee Chairman)*, George Dzundza *(Dr. Sam Hesselman, Computer Dept. Head)*, Jason Bernard *(Maj. Donovan)*, Iman *(Nina Beka)*, Fred Dalton Thompson *(Marshall, CIA Director)*, Leon Russom *(Kevin O'Brien, CIA Official)*, Dennis Burkley *(Mate)*, Marshall Bell, Chris D *(Contras)*, Michael Shillo *(Schiller)*, Nicholas Worth *(Cup Breaker)*, Leo Geter *(Ensign Fox)*, Matthew Barry *(Bellboy)*, John DiAquino *(Lt. John Chadway)*, Peter Bell *(Seaman Dufor)*, Tony Webster *(Helmsman)*, Matthew Evans *(J.O.D.)*, Gregory Le Noel *(Quartermaster)*, Joan McMurtrey *(Programmer)*, Edith Fields *(Lorraine, Secretary to the Secretary of Defense)*, Frederick Allen *(Enlisted Man)*, Scott Freeman *(M.P.)*, Noel Manchan *(Computer Clerk)*, June Chandler *(Margaret Brice)*, Lee Shael *(Band Singer)*, Jeffrey Sudzin *(Man with Lighter)*, Gordon Needham *(Limo Driver)*, Austin Kelly *(Cab Driver)*, Charles Middleton *(Airport Cop)*, Stephen R. Asinas *(Filipino Urchin)*, Terrance Cooper *(N.Z. Ambassador)*, Dorothy Parke *(TV Reporter)*, Jay Arlen Jones, Rob Sullivan *(Marine Guards)*, Gregory Avellone, Jeremy Glenn, David Paymer, Charles Walker *(Technicians)*, Bob Courts, Bruce Dobus, Eugene Robert Glazer, Darryl Henriques, John Hostetter, Michael Hungerford, Robert Kerman *(C.I.D. Men)*, Jill Clark, Cindy Keung, Steve Keung, Lorna Martyn, Arona McDonald *(Maori Dancers)*.

No matter the talents involved, those undertaking the remake of superior films are climbing the same mountain and invariably take an alternate path that brings them far short of the once-conquered summit. The inherent and usually self-defeating problem is that those behind the remakes attempt to go over the same successful ground but update (a synonym for change to suit presumed modern tastes) the material so that it loses the flavor, ingenuity, and excitement of the original. Such a fate has befallen NO WAY OUT, a remake of the *film noir* classic THE BIG CLOCK (1948) which starred Ray Milland, Charles Laughton, and George Macready, and was directed impeccably by John Farrow. The plot, as it was with the original, depicts Costner as being an innocent victim having to hunt himself in a murder case. The problem is that in the remake the plot becomes even more complex and baffling than the original. Costner is a Naval officer who meets and falls in love with sexy call girl Young at a Washington party. Their first love scene is definitely on the steamy side, one where he undresses her to garter belt and nylons in the back seat of a limousine and goes at it while the car cruises past national monuments. Duty calls and Costner sees service on board a warship, saving a sailor during a typhoon and earning a medal. He is sent back to the US, requested by Hackman, who is the Secretary of Defense, to act as his top military aide. Costner takes up once more with Young who admits that she is kept in high style by the married Hackman. As his mistress, she is to be available whenever he seeks special company and attend parties where Hackman can see her. On these occasions Hackman takes his wife to the parties but gets his sick kicks from viewing his concubine from across the room. Costner becomes resentful of Hackman and later enraged when Hackman arrives unexpectedly at Young's lavish duplex and he must sneak out a side door. Hackman sees him in the dark street outside but cannot identify him before he meets with Young. In a jealous outburst, Hackman and Young get into a fierce argument which leads Hackman to lash out at her. She falls backward over a railing and crashes downward to the floor below, smashing into a huge glass table

and dying upon impact. Hackman returns to his offices in the Pentagon and there seeks the help of another aide, Patton, a ruthlessly ambitious homosexual. Patton, upon hearing of his boss' folly, goes to the Young duplex, wiping away fingerprints and removing all traces of Hackman. Next, to throw off investigators, he introduces a theory that a KGB mole long thought to be in Washington, is the real killer of Young for reasons that remain inexplicable. Costner is then put into the ironic position of having to ferret out the KGB mole and sets off on a nervous hunt, not believing for a minute that the mole ever existed. He must act furtively since several witnesses saw Costner with Young shortly before she was killed. Found in Young's duplex is an undeveloped negative from a Polaroid camera, a picture of Costner which is next to impossible to develop, this being a photo hastily taken of Costner by Young in a moment of caprice. The negative is given to computer wizard Dzundza, a wheelchair-bound friend of Costner's, who works night and day in the communications nerve center of the Pentagon. Dzundza puts in motion a computer reconstruction of the negative which he believes will give a clear impression of the person in the photo. In the meantime, Costner must avoid the witnesses brought into the Pentagon, one of them recognizing him at a distance with security people dragging the witnesses room by room through the enormous Pentagon complex. Costner desperately attempts to put a case together against the real killer, Hackman, but is followed everywhere by two goons working for Patton. He seeks help from Dzundza, revealing that he was having an affair with Young and is the man in the photo. He also tells Dzundza that Hackman is Young's killer. Dzundza tries to help by slowing down the computer photo reconstruction, then, believing that Costner is under too much stress, meets secretly with Patton and tells him of Costner's affair with Young and his contention that Hackman is the killer. Patton thanks him for the information, then shoots him to death. Meanwhile, the witnesses are closing in on Costner and his photo is becoming more clear. He barges in on Hackman and Patton and confronts Hackman with what he knows about Young's death. Patton then tells Hackman about Costner's affair with Young, and adds that it was Costner who saw Hackman entering her apartment the night of the murder. Thinking quickly, Hackman puts it all on to the obnoxious Patton, saying that he, not Hackman, killed Young. The homosexual Patton, who has longed for a relationship with Hackman, draws a pistol and shoots himself. Hackman thus presents Patton's convenient corpse to investigators as that of the killer and the mythical KGB mole, with Costner off the hook. But wait . . . in the film's final scene, a haggard Costner is being interrogated by two men in a hotel room. A man emerges from behind a two-way mirror and speaks in Russian to Costner, who, in an off-the-wall conclusion, turns out to be the KGB mole after all.

The beginning of NO WAY OUT is promising and it pulsates with high energy, but after Young plunges to her death the movie crashes downward with her. The troubles are many in that the plot becomes so involved that it serves to confuse rather than telescope answers. Hackman has little to do but sit in his office and fret while Costner runs about like a madman, creating little or no suspense. There is no humor whatsoever in this film and none of the sophisticated performances that marked THE BIG CLOCK as a terrific production are repeated. Instead of intellectual sleuthing as was the case in the original, NO WAY OUT relies wholly upon the mechanical world of computers, electronic gadgetry, and systems analysts to create tension. The result is boredom. Except for one chase scene, Donaldson's direction is static, uninteresting and, in the second half of the film, lethargic to the point of creating a strong desire on the part of the viewer for the film to end. Costner doesn't help, affecting such a low profile of non-emotional stances that he appears to be more like a bank clerk worried that the examiner is going to find an error in his addition. Costner is typical of the anti-hero in films today, weak-chinned, unremarkable features, gangling body, some producer's idea of the universal man who is at best ubiquitous. There is something stationary about Costner's personality that is disturbing, as if he were a stand-in for a real star who never arrives on the set. He is not a star who acts, but reacts, like Gary Cooper, but without Cooper's strong presence and stalwart personality. Costner's leaden, noncommittal character was even more in evidence in the violent gangster film THE UNTOUCHABLES also released in 1987. On the whole, NO WAY OUT is an overblown chiller that will send no thrills or chills up and down anyone's spine, mostly because the film is itself spineless, poorly constructed, and written as if for a sophomore play production. Songs include: "No Way Out" (Paul Anka, Michael McDonald; performed by Julia Migenes, Paul Anka), "Say It" (Paul Anka, Richard Marx; performed by Paul Anka). *(Brief nudity, sexual situations, mild language.)*

p, Laura Ziskin, Robert Garland; d, Roger Donaldson; w, Robert Garland (based on the novel *The Big Clock* by Kenneth Fearing); ph, John Alcott (Metrocolor); m, Maurice Jarre; ed, Neil Travis; prod d, Dennis Washington, Kai Hawkins; art d. Anthony Brockliss; set d, Bruce Gibeson; m/l, Paul Anka, Michael McDonald, Richard Marx; spec eff, Jack Monroe, Terry Frazee, Ken Durey; makeup, Michael A. Hancock; stunts, Richard Diamond Farnsworth, Peter Bell.

Crime/Thriller **(PR:O MPAA:R)**

NOCE EN GALILEE† (1987, Bel./Fr.) 113m Marisa Films-LPA-French Ministry of Culture-French Community Ministry-ZDF/Lasa Films c (Trans: A Wedding In Galilee)

Ali Mohammed Akili *(The Moktar)*, Nazih Akly *(The Groom)*, Mabram Khouri *(Military Governor)*, Anna Achdian *(Bride)*, Sonia Amar *(Young Sister)*, Emtiaz Diab, Georges Khleifi, Hassan Diab, Abkas Himas.

In light of the violent measures taken by the Israeli army to deal with Arab demonstrations in West Bank villages at the end of 1987, this French-Belgian coproduction directed by Palestinian Michel Khleifi is strikingly topical. Akili, a revered Arab villager, is determined to see that his son has a big, joyous wedding; however, because of recent demonstrations, a curfew has been imposed that will make this nearly impossible. Akili appeals to the local Israeli military administrator and is told that the ceremony can take place as the old man wishes provided that the administrator be there to oversee the goings-on. The Arab's acceptance of this condition infuriates many of the less conciliatory villagers and the possibilty of a terrorist reprisal looms.

p, Michel Khleifi, Bernard Lorain; d&w, Michel Khleifi; ph, Walther van den Ende; m, Jean-Marie Senia; ed, Marie Castro Vasquez; art d, Yves Brover.

Drama **(PR:NR MPAA:NR)**

NOCTURNO AMOR QUE TE VAS† (1987, Mex.) 101m Universidad Nacional Autonoma de Mexico-Direccion de Actividades Cinematograficas/ Peliculas Mexicanas c (Trans: Nocturnal Love That Goes Away)

Patricia Reyes Spindola *(Carmen Perez)*, Sergio Ramos [Camanche] *(Trompetas)*, Leonor Llansas *(Alcoholic Mother)*, Uriel Chavez *(Chuy)*, Dunia Saldivar, Ivone Chavez, Yair de Rubi.

Punctuated with surreal symbolism, this Marcela Fernandez Violante-directed feature begins with the happy union of divorcee Reyes Spindola and cab driver Chavez but takes a nightmarish turn when he disappears one night after picking up a mysterious fare. He did the same thing the night after their wedding and returned after a long drive with lots of cash; however, this time the only thing that turns up is his bloody cab. Produced by the film department of Mexico's National University.

p, Patricia Weingartshofer; d, Marcela Fernandez Violante; w, Jorge Perez Grovas (adapted by Jorge Perez Grovas and Marcela Fernandez Violante); ph, Arturo de la Rosa; ed, Ramon Aupart.

Drama **(PR:NR MPAA:NR)**

NOI UOMINI DURI† (1987, It.) 90m C.G. Silver Film/CDI c (Trans: Us Real Men)

Renato Pozzetto *(Silvio)*, Enrico Montesano *(Mario)*, Isabel Russinova, Antonella Vitale, Alessandra Mussolini, Maria Angela Giordano, Ovidio Martucci, Novello Novelli, Maria Pia Casilio, Francesco Brandinelli, Marco D'Aquili, Igor Zalewski, Carlo Solin, Albano Bufalini, Jean Emile Luis, Valerio Andrei, Maurizio Fardo, Gianluigi Ghione.

Pozzetto is a sexually impotent man who is advised by his psychiatrist to become more aware of his body. Montesano is a bank clerk who feels insecure after his wife has left him. Both men enroll in a grueling course that teaches how to survive in the Amazon forest after one's supplies have been washed away by a flash flood. Together with 16 other equally incompetent strangers, Pozzetto and Montesano undergo the brutal ordeal and by the time they complete the course they have become fast friends. A big hit at the Italian box office in 1987.

p, Mario Cecchi Gori, Vittorio Cecchi Gori; d, Maurizio Ponzi; w, Leo Benvenuti, Piero De Bernardi, Maurizio Ponzi; ph, Alessandro D'Eva (Eastmancolor); m, Beppe Cantarelli; ed, Sergio Montanari.

Comedy **(PR:NR MPAA:NR)**

NORTH SHORE** (1987) 96m UNIV c

Matt Adler *(Rick)*, Gregory Harrison *(Chandler)*, Nia Peeples *(Kiani)*, John Philbin *(Turtle)*, Gerry Lopez *(Vince)*, Laird Hamilton *(Lance Burkhart)*, Robbie Page *(Alex Rogers)*, Mark Occhilupo *(Occy)*, John Parragon *(Professor)*, Cristina Raines *(Rick's Mother)*, Lord James Blears *(Contest Director)*.

Adolescents will appreciate this film, sort of a travelogue-fantasy of the awesome, legendary surfing waves of Hawaii. Adler, who does well in his first screen role, is a naive, good-natured youth from Arizona who has won a prize by surfing in a synthetic wave tank and has now come to touch the real thing. But the real world quickly intrudes upon Adler's youthful dreams. During his first attempt at surfing in the ocean, his bag and money are stolen at the beach and he collides with another surfer, injuring his back and breaking his priceless board. Another

surfer, Philbin, takes pity on Adler and befriends him, introducing him to old surfer pro, Harrison, who is religiously devoted to surfing, having an almost mythical perception of the ocean. He makes Adler his protege and teaches him all the tricks in his surfing bag so that Adler can triumph against the waves and some underhanded competition. En route to this embryonic enlightenment, Adler meets and falls in love with Hawaiian girl Peeples, later winning her hand.

NORTH SHORE is an innocuous little film, heavily laced with rock music. The performances by Adler and Harrison are straightforward and somewhat rewarding while the surfing action is captured in splendid action photography, some being stock footage. Harrison, a star of the "Trapper John, MD" tv series, is a real-life surfer and is credited with supervising the shooting of much of the surfing footage. John Milius attempted to make much more out of surfing in his BIG WEDNESDAY, with little success. This film, with fewer pretentions, is honest, modest, and pleasant.

p, William Finnegan; d, William Phelps; w, Tim McCanlies, William Phelps (based on a story by William Phelps, Randal Kleiser); ph, Peter Smokler (Duart color); m, Richard Stone; ed, Robert Gordon; prod d, Mark Balet; set d, Wally White; cos, Kathe James.

Action **(PR:C MPAA:PG)**

NOS REIMOS DE LA MIGRA† (1987, Mex.) 98m Filmadora Exito/ Peliculas Mexicanas c (Trans: Poking Fun at the Border Patrol)

Isela Vega *(Monica)*, Rafael Inclan *(Meto)*, Roberto [Flaco] Guzman *(Ruben)*, Carmen Salinas *(Cocholata)*, Polo Ortin *(Nacho)*, Joaquin Garcia [Borolas] *(Chapatin)*, Rebeca Silva *(Lola)*, Maria Cardinal, Carmen del Valle, Griselda Mejia, Luis Manuel Pelayo, Claudio Tate, Angelica Ruiz, Lilly Soto, Rocio Rilke, Edith Olivia Anorve, Ana Berumen, Xorge Noble, Guero Castro, Sonora Santanera.

Inclan, Ortin, and Guzman are the ones poking fun at the Border Patrol in this Mexican comedy that adds a twist to the usual Rio Grande-crossing funny business. This time our heroes are trying to get into Mexico not out of it. Vega, the girl friend of one of these three amigos and the niece of a Texas Mafia don, is held against her will by her uncle after she learns more about his operations than she should have. Inclan, Ortin, Guzman and their girl friends get into the US easily enough, and even manage to liberate Vega, but, no matter how hard they try, they can't seem to get south of the border.

p, Guillermo Calderon Stell; d, Victor Manuel [Guero] Castro; w, Francisco Cavazos, Victor Manuel Castro; ph, Raul Dominguez; m, Marcos Lifshitz, Sonora Santanera; ed, Jose Liho.

Comedy **(PR:NR MPAA:NR)**

NOTTE ITALIANA† (1987, It.) 92m Sacher Film-RAI-TV Channel 1-So. Fin. A./Titanus c (Trans: Italian Night)

Marco Messeri *(Otello)*, Giulia Boschi *(Daria)*, Mario Adorf *(Tornova)*, Meme Perlini *(Cecco)*, Tino Carraro *(Melandri)*, Ruggeri Brothers *(Surveyors)*, Antonio Petrocelli, Remo Remotti *(Italo)*, Silvana De Santis *(Innkeeper)*.

The directorial debut of Mazzacurati, NOTTE ITALIAN is set in the Po Delta in northern Italy, where Messeri, a lawyer, comes to conduct a study of the area to determine if it should be protected as a park. Intrigue and danger enter the story when he learns that last man given his task was murdered. This is the first film produced by Sacher, the independent production company formed by Angelo Barbagallo and Nanni Moretti, the director-star of the excellent THE MASS IS ENDED, which won the Special Jury Prize at the Berlin Film Festival.

p, Nanni Moretti, Angelo Barbagallo; d, Carlo Mazzacurati; w, Carlo Mazzacurati, Franco Bernini; ph, Agostino Castiglioni; m, Fiorenzo Carpi; ed, Mirco Garrone; art d, Giancarlo Basili, Leonardo Scarpa.

Drama/Thriller **(PR:NR MPAA:NR)**

NOVYE SKAZKI SHAKHEREZADY† (1987, USSR/Syria) 133m Tadjikfilm-Ganem-Film-Sovinfilm/Sovexportfilm c (Trans: New Fairy Tales Of Sheherezade)

Ulugbek Muzaffarov, Tamara Yandiyeva, Gennady Chetverikov, Yelena Tonunts, Burkhon Radjabov.

Borrowing from the fairy-tale classic *A Thousand and One Nights*, this Soviet-Syrian coproduction details the adventures of a shoemaker who flees his shrewish wife and encounters all manner of good and bad fortune in his travels.

d, Takhir Sabirov; w, Valery Karen, Takhir Sabirov (based on the fairy tales from "1001 Nights"); ph, Rustam Mukhamedjanov; m, Gennady Alexandrov; art d, Leonid Shponko, Konstantin Avakov.

Children's **(PR:NR MPAA:NR)**

NOWHERE TO HIDE** (1987, Can.) 90m Alliance Entertainment-John Kemeny/New Century Entertainment-Vista c

Amy Madigan *(Barbara Cutter)*, Daniel Hugh Kelly *(Rob Cutter)*, Robin MacEachern *(Johnny Cutter)*, Michael Ironside *(Ben)*, John Colicos *(Gen. Howard)*, Maury Chaykin.

Madigan, nominated for an Oscar for her performance in TWICE IN A LIFETIME, helps solidify the notion of female action heroes with her inspired performance in this uninspiring Canadian film. She plays the wife of Kelly, the revered leader of a Marine helicopter squadron who is infuriated when two of his crews go down in crashes in newly delivered whirlybirds. Suspecting a design fault, he works around the clock testing parts and discovers the C-ring the manufacturers had contracted to make out of titanium is, in fact, made of a weaker, less expensive alloy. Before Kelly can take his discovery "right to the top," he is assassinated in his own home, while his 6-year-old son, MacEachern, watches. Madigan, who has been working on a metal sculpture in the garage, defends herself with a blow torch and sends the gunmen running. However, they've left behind confidential Marine documents that cast suspicion on Kelly and Madigan. The thugs work for a not-so-complex military-industrial cabal consisting of Marine general Colicos and the helicopters' manufacturers who will go to any extent to cover up their cost-cutting scam. The sergeant who helped Kelly with the testing is killed and Madigan is on-hand when the henchmen do in an unrelenting investigative reporter. They try to add her to their tally, but haven't reckoned with the fact that this pretty mom is also a most capable ex-Marine. Shotgun shells fly as she leads them on a harrowing car chase, eventually escaping to a motel. There, with her voice fraught with emotion, Madigan tries to explain Kelly's death to the traumatized MacEachern, who refuses to part with the robot toy to which he has innocently attached the incriminating C-ring. Following the homing device they've hidden on Madigan's car, the gunmen arrive at the motel. She spots one of them placing explosives under her car's chassis and moves the charge to their vehicle, permanently ending their pursuit. Madigan takes MacEachern to the nearby mountains, leaving the car behind but not the flashing homing device, which MacEachern, without his mother's knowledge, brings with him. They search the mountains for Ironside, an emotionally scared Vietnam vet whose sole contact with civilization since the death of his lover and son had been Kelly. They find him, and he takes them to his secluded cabin. Later, Madigan discovers the missing piece in the puzzle—the C-ring; however, the homing signal goes undetected, and the next morning, the cabin is attacked in force. In the ensuing bloody battle, Ironside loses his life protecting MacEachern, who is spirited away by the one surviving attacker. Madigan goes directly to the bar frequented by Kelly's old squadron and confronts the pilots with the C-ring. She then goes looking for Colicos and is taken to a warehouse where she trades the C-ring for MacEachern's freedom. When Colicos says he'll never allow them to leave alive, Madigan reveals a hidden microphone that has captured Colicos' admission of guilt as Marine helicopters come into view. Colicos speeds away in a car, pursued by Madigan at the controls of a helicopter. With machine-gun fire, she forces his car over a cliff and for good measure blasts it with a rocket.

With political intrigue at its center, NOWHERE TO HIDE is reminiscent of THREE DAYS OF THE CONDOR and NO WAY OUT, but, for the most part, it is a predictable, unexceptional action-adventure film that relies too much on coincidence and plot contrivances. What is significant about it is that the person who performs its Rambo-like heroics is a woman. Like Sigourney Weaver in ALIENS, Madigan thinks on her feet and can take punishment and dish it out with the best of them. The notion of a female action hero is not unprecedented, however. Angie Dickinson, TV's "Policewoman," and the various Mrs. Peels of "The Avengers" comported themselves well with firearms and well-placed kicks, but their male partners were usually not too far away, and, except for the battle at the cabin, Madigan works alone. Her character is also notable because, despite her dexterity at the rough stuff, she retains her femininity. A caring, gentle mother, she doesn't throw up her hands and shriek when faced with danger, but though she copes, she also trembles and screams and cries. This fallible, fearful side lends her character a credibility missing in most male action heroes, and Madigan's earnest performance rises far above the material. Ironside and Colicos, who wears corrupt villainy like a second skin, also turn in noteworthy performances. While it is commendable that NOWHERE TO HIDE presents a strong and capable female lead, it is, nevertheless, of no more intrinsic value that a woman passes 90 minutes littering the screen with bodies than it is when Sylvester Stallone or Chuck Norris does. NOWHERE TO HIDE has more than its share of gratuitous bloodletting, and whether it is lapsing into melodrama or sending rockets into Colicos' car as he already plunges to certain death, the film suffers from overkill. The first feature film for Canadian TV director Azzopardi, it was shot on location in Quebec. *(Graphic violence, brief nudity.)*

p, Andras Hamori; d, Mario Azzopardi; w, Alex Rebar, George Goldsmith (based on a story by Alex Rebar); ph, Vic Sarin; m, Brad Fiedel; ed, Rit Wallis.

Action/Adventure **(PR:O MPAA:R)**

NOYADE INTERDITE† (1987, Fr./It.) 101m Paradis Films-FR3 Films-Compagnie Generale d'Images-LP Films/Bac Film c (Trans: No Drowning Allowed; AKA: WIDOW'S WALK)

Philippe Noiret *(Molinat)*, Guy Marchand *(Leroyer)*, Elizabeth Bourgine *(Elizabeth)*, Anne Roussel *(Marie)*, Gabrielle Lazure *(Jeanne)*, Marie Trintignant *(Isabelle)*, Suzanne Flon *(Hazelle)*, Stefania Sandrelli *(Winny)*, Andrea Ferreol *(Cora)*, Laura Betti *(Keli)*.

Based on Andrew Coburn's novel *Widow's Walk*, this *policier* features Noiret as a cop who is trying to get to the bottom of a series of murders in French coastal resort town. Marchand, his longtime rival, is also assigned to the case, and the two cops spend almost as much time trying to outsmart each other as they do working on the case. In the end Noiret solves the murders and gets his revenge.

p, Eric Heumann, Stephane Sorlat; d, Pierre Granier-Deferre; w, Pierre Granier-Deferre, Dominique Roulet (based on the novel *Widow's Walk* by Andrew Coburn); ph, Charles Van Damme (Eastmancolor); m, Philippe Sarde; ed, Jean Ravel; art d, Dominique Andre.

Mystery/Drama **(PR:NR MPAA:NR)**

NUIT DOCILE† (1987, Fr.) 90m Tracol Film/Sinfonia c/bw (Trans: Docile Night)

Patrick Jouane *(Jean)*, Claire Nebout *(Stella)*, Pascal Kelaf *(Jeannot)*, Francoise Arnoul *(Madeleine)*.

A painter wanders Paris trying to resolve the question Jack Kerouac posed in *The Subterraneans*: Is it possible to both create art and love someone completely? Jouane is the artist who deserts his lover but can't leave behind his constant concern with why he has done it. Mixing black-and-white and color footage, this French feature jumps back and forth between the past and the present.

d&w, Guy Gilles; ph, Jacques Boumendil (Eastmancolor); m, Vincent Marie; ed, Marie-Helene Quinton.

Drama **(PR:NR MPAA:NR)**

NUMBER ONE WITH A BULLET* (1987) 101m Golan-Globus/Cannon c

Robert Carradine *(Nicholas "Nick" Berzak)*, Billy Dee Williams *(Frank Hazeltine)*, Valerie Bertinelli *(Teresa Berzak)*, Peter Graves *(Capt. P. Ferris)*, Doris Roberts *(Mrs. Berzak)*, Bobby Di Cicco *(Malcolm)*, Ray Girardin *(Lt. Larry Kaminski)*, Barry Sattels *(Harry Da Costa)*, Mykel T. Williamson *(Casey)*.

The title comes from an old record company expression that used to designate where a disc was on the charts. If a song was No. 10 but had a "bullet" next to it in the trade magazines, that meant it was shooting upwards and might even make it to the top. Some years ago, a novel about the record business appeared with the same title but has no connection with this film. Jack Smight is a stylish director who can be superior when he has the right script, as in HARPER, KALEIDOSCOPE, and NO WAY TO TREAT A LADY. But since no director can triumph over a bad scenario (some old-timer once said, "If it ain't on the page, it ain't on the stage"), he has also come a cropper too often with movies like THE SECRET WAR OF HARRY FRIGG, DAMNATION ALLEY, LOVING COUPLES, and many more. This time around, Smight tries his best to get a movie out of the thin script (cowritten by James Belushi, among others) but fails. It's another cops-and-dopers movie not unlike so many these days. Carradine and Williams are the cops who will go to any lengths to make a bust, using the same against-the-rules tactics that can be seen weekly on reruns of "Mod Squad" or "Starsky and Hutch." Sattels is the villain of the piece, an upstanding and seemingly solid member of the town's hierarchy who just happens to be the kingpin of the drug trade. Carradine is apart from wife Bertinelli and jealous of her whereabouts, so he employs a youngster to watch her comings-and-goings. Williams is a state-of-the-art womanizer. He loves 'em, leaves 'em, but they never seem to get angry. Lots of action, mostly predictable but well shot by Smight and his cinematographer, Phillips. NUMBER ONE WITH A BULLET is one of those movies that goes directly from five days in the theaters to five years on cable TV. Graves and the excellent Doris Roberts are not onscreen enough to register (however, in the best scene of the film, Roberts using her best officious "Remington Steele" manner, diverts a police property clerk's attention while Carradine takes some drug evidence from the police vault for a scam to catch some dealers). It looks like a TV movie with foul language thrown in to make it work for the drive-ins. Some good and funny moments between Carradine and Williams which may (or may not) have been inserted by Belushi. When there are four writers on a screenplay credit, it usually means that there have been many rewrites at the behest of producers who can't make up their minds. A quartet of scribes in one room can only mean one of two things: an argument or a poker game, never a decent script. *(Profanity.)*

p, Menahem Golan, Yoram Globus; d, Jack Smight; w, Gail Morgan Hickman, Andrew Kurtzman, Rob Riley, James Belushi (based on a story by Gail Morgan Hickman); ph, Alex Phillips; m, Alf Clausen; ed, Michael J. Duthie; prod d, Norm Baron; set d, Linda Allen; stunts, Fred Lerner.

Crime **Cas.** **(PR:C-O MPAA:R)**

NUTS*** (1987) 116m Barwood/WB c

Barbra Streisand *(Claudia Draper)*, Richard Dreyfuss *(Aaron Levinsky)*, Maureen Stapleton *(Rose Kirk, Claudia's Mother)*, Karl Malden *(Arthur Kirk)*, Eli Wallach *(Dr. Herbert A. Morrison, Psychiatrist)*, Robert Webber *(Francis MacMillan, Prosecuting Attorney)*, James Whitmore *(Judge Stanley Murdoch)*, Leslie Nielsen *(Allen Green)*, William Prince *(Clarence Middleton)*, Dakin Matthews, Paul Benjamin.

The fact that Barbra Streisand produced NUTS and also wrote the music for it will have some people wondering if this isn't another one of her grandstand plays to garner an Oscar. The truth is she showed remarkable restraint. Whereas in YENTL she sang every song and completely overpowered everyone else around her, in NUTS, producer Streisand has wisely opted to surround star Streisand with a terrific complement of actors. These other actors get an opportunity for their own "star turns" as was the case in Tom Topor's original play, which opened on Broadway in late April 1980. The picture is almost entirely shot inside, which severely limits any feeling of motion and so it has to be deemed talky, an acknowledgement of the stagebound beginnings of the story.

Streisand is a high-priced ($500 per hour) prostitute. She has been arrested for killing one of her johns (Nielsen) and her erratic behavior and frequent outbursts would lead one to believe she is crazy. Her parents, mother Stapleton and stepfather Malden, have conspired with their $250-per-hour attorney, Prince, to have Streisand committed to a mental institution rather than have her go on trial for manslaughter. Streisand knows that if she is committed, she may never get out of her hospital gown. There is a law in New York which states that a patient can be kept inside for an indeterminate time, until "they" decide he or she is fit to stand trial for a felony. Streisand wants a sanity hearing and wishes to stand trial. She feels she can prove the killing was in self-defense. At her first hearing, Prince is trying to make a deal with Webber, the prosecuting attorney, to clap her away in a loony bin. Streisand is restrained and not allowed to approach the bench. When Prince attempts to explain to Streisand what's being done, she reacts by punching him in the face and breaking his nose. He immediately asks to be taken off the case and a hapless public defender, Dreyfuss, is given the task of dealing with the wild woman. He attempts to squirm out of the assignment but the harried judge says he must take the job or fall out of favor in that court. (The heavy case load and the deals made between public defenders and prosecutors are quickly sketched and Dreyfuss has no choice.) Dreyfuss visits Streisand in jail and she is seen to be a shrew, subject to 180-degree mood swings, the kind of client no lawyer wants. She doesn't trust Dreyfuss or anyone else for that matter. She explains that her entire mental examination consisted of 15 minutes with a non-English-speaking psychiatrist and about 55 minutes with Wallach, the man in charge of the mental department of the institution. Both men have recommended she be remanded to a mental facility rather than face trial because they can't believe she understands the charges against her. Dreyfuss has to make her understand that he cares and wants to do as she wishes. Stapleton and Malden are all for putting Streisand away. He is a successful businessman and this sort of scandal is embarrassing. Nevertheless, Dreyfuss manages to have the sanity hearing brought into the court of grizzled judge Whitmore. From this moment on, the picture stays almost exclusively in the courtroom with a few flashbacks to establish that the deck has been stacked against Streisand. She comes from an upper-class home, the only child of Stapleton, whose husband departed when the girl was small. Malden married Stapleton and became a father to the girl. He claims, while being cross-examined, that he ran the house like a business—if the child cleaned her room, she received a dollar, etc. He is always smiling and apparently the perfect stepfather. Stapleton testifies that she just can't understand what happened. When her daughter turned 16, she became promiscuous, used marijuana, and changed from a sweet young girl into an angry, wild person. Wallach testifies that in his opinion Streisand is a danger to herself and anyone else around her and Dreyfuss can't seem to shake his words. The judge would like to have an independent psychiatrist take a couple of weeks to examine Streisand, but she vetoes that, as is her privilege. It is while Malden is on the stand that he lets slip a phrase which Dreyfuss jumps upon. Malden had said that he helped the youngster with her homework, dressed her, bathed her . . . and now we learn that Malden had in fact bathed his stepdaughter until she was 16! Further, through the use of flashbacks, we see Malden slip a $20 bill under the bathroom door so he will be allowed in. Stapleton swears she knows nothing of this. Streisand goes on the stand to be examined by Webber and, in one of the most effective scenes, she explains what she does for a living and talks to Webber as though he were a john, carefully detailing everything she does to a man with her hands, her body, her mouth. Streisand is dressed in hospital clothes at this point and fighting to overcome tranquilizers she'd been fed by Wallach the night before. Webber's uncomfortable squirming as Streisand minces no words provides one of the few humorous moments in the picture. Streisand then does her

"star turn" as she sums up her case. Whitmore takes a few minutes to consider his verdict and repairs to his chambers. Streisand and Stapleton embrace (Malden is nowhere to be seen) and bury the hatchet. Whitmore emerges to say that he believes the defendant is capable of understanding the charges and orders her to trial. For the time being, however, she is to be released on her own recognizance. Streisand walks out of the court and onto the street, still in her hospital garb, and enters the crowds, noting a real nut-cast talking to himself as he walks past her. She steals a scarf off a passing rack, tosses it around her neck, and strolls along with a smile on her face. The picture ends, and none too soon.

There are holes galore in the script, most notably Whitmore's allowing a manslaughter defendant (which Streisand now is) to be released over the objection of the prosecutor, who asks for bail. As a story, it's thin. As cinema, it's static. There is enough in all the performances to make it a diversion, but little more. The flashbacks indicate that Streisand was truly acting in self-defense when Nielsen attempted to get her into a bubble bath and take her for the second time (they'd already been together once and she had another appointment). Whether or not the bath had anything to do with Malden intruding upon the teenager's bathing after slipping money under the door is not totally explained. Dreyfuss is portrayed as a tired, hard-working defender of the public with an unseen wife and three unseen children in Brooklyn. For a fleeting moment, there is just a scintilla of attraction between Dreyfuss and Streisand but that's tossed aside in favor of the bare-bones plot. Although he is costarred, Dreyfuss has fashioned more of a Best Supporting Actor performance and was happy to stand outside the glow of Streisand's histrionics. Although she doesn't sing (there's not even a place for her to hum), Streisand's speaking voice probably reaches as many octaves in her role as when she does sing. Despite all of her emoting, the picture seldom catches fire. At first, it's hard to like the character of the once-divorced hooker. As the picture continues, she softens enough for the audience to want her to get her way, even though that might mean a prison sentence. Streisand wants to have a definite answer from the courts, not the vague promise of eventual release, and the only way to get that is to be tried for the crime. Streisand looks smashing, even without makeup. However, the most difficult part to believe is that any man, no matter how sexually desirous, would be willing to fork over that kind of money to a woman her age. There are lots of close-ups of Streisand and it seems that every time she does something in the court there is a series of quick cuts to everyone else in the room, so there's no mistaking how they feel about what's taken place. The language is very rough and almost all of it comes from Streisand in what appears to be an attempt to smash her squeaky-clean image and show she can get down and dirty.

All of the secondary roles are well cast. Stapleton is particularly good as the doting mother and has her moment on the stand. Malden is telegraphed as a villain because it's impossible that any stepfather could be as warm and wonderful as he masquerades as being. Wallach is rapidly established as a psychiatrist who can't make it on Park or Fifth Avenue and has been relegated to a job with the state, a job where he wields the kind of power he loves, the power over weaker human beings. With the least lines in the script, Whitmore gets the most mileage and accomplishes more with a raised eyebrow or a grin than other actors might with 10 pages of monolog. What is never dealt with is the fact that the Streisand character might well be really insane. Surely anyone watching that kind of behavior might be inclined to feel that way. Ritt's direction is as good as it can be, considering the script's limitations. Topor's play script has been reworked to fit the movies by Darryl Ponicsan (novelist and screenwriter with credits that include CINDERELLA LIBERTY and TAPS) and Alvin Sargent (who wrote PAPER MOON and ORDINARY PEOPLE). Neither man was accustomed to working with anyone else, but director Mark Rydell, who was supposed to helm the picture, evidently asked both writers to do the rewrite. Rydell was eventually replaced after having incurred the enmity of many. Ponicsan and Sargent finally did work together (there had been other attempts at rewrites by Carol Sobieski, Rydell, and someone named Andy Lewis) after many conferences with producer Streisand, who didn't think the script was right for star Streisand. The picture plays like a fine TV movie in the tried-and-true mold of women-in-trouble, but with the added fillip of filthy language. One interesting note was the casting of Webber, Stapleton, and Malden, who sport three of the biggest schnozzes in the business. Did Streisand cast this trio to make her own nose look smaller? Like the nightclub owner who hires midget waiters to make the drinks look bigger? *(Profanity.)*

p, Barbra Streisand; d, Martin Ritt; w, Tom Topor, Darryl Ponicsan, Alvin Sargent (based on the play by Tom Topor); ph, Andrzej Bartkowiak (Technicolor); m, Barbra Streisand; ed, Sidney Levin; prod d, Joel Schiller; art d, Eric Orbom; set d, Anne McCulley; cos, Joe Tomkins.

Drama **(PR:C-O MPAA:R)**

O.C. AND STIGGS* (1987) 109m MGM-UA c

Daniel H. Jenkins *(Oliver Cromwell "O.C." Ogilvie)*, Neill Barry *(Mark Stiggs)*, Paul Dooley *(Randall Schwab)*, Jane Curtin *(Elinore Schwab)*, Jon Cryer *(Randall Schwab, Jr.)*, Ray Walston *(Gramps)*, Louis Nye *(Garth Sloan)*, Tina Louise *(Florence Beaugereaux)*, Martin Mull *(Pat Coletti)*, Dennis Hopper *(Sponson)*, Melvin Van Peebles *(Wino Bob)*, Donald May *(Jack Stiggs)*, Carla Borelli *(Stella Stiggs)*, Cynthia Nixon *(Michelle)*, Laura Urstein *(Lenore Schwab)*, Victor Ho *(Frankie Tang)*, Stephanie Elfrink *(Missie Stiggs)*, James Gilsenan *(Barney Beaugereaux)*, Greg Mangler *(Jefferson Washington)*, Alan Autry *(Goon)*, Dan Ziskie *(Rusty Calloway)*, Tiffany Helm *(Charlotte)*, Dana Andersen *(Robin)*, Bob Vecker *(Himself)*, Margery Bond *(Mrs. Bunny)*, Jeannine Ann Cole *(Nancy Pearson)*, Nina Van Pallandt *(Claire Dejavve)*, Thomas Hal Phillips *(Hal Phillip Walker)*, Danny Darst *(Schwab Commercial Singer)*, Caroline Aaron *(Janine)*, Tom Flagg *(Policeman)*, Maurice Orozco *(Bandito)*, Louis Enriques *(Promoter)*, Frank Sprague *(Actor in Play)*, Robert Fortier *(Wino Jim)*, Allan Berne, Bob Reilly, Roy Gunsberg, Wayne Wallace, Robert Ledford, D.C. Warren, Lobo, Florence White *(Winos)*, Fred Newman *(Bongo Voice)*, King Sunny Ade and his African Beats.

Of the six films director Robert Altman has made in the last five years, O.C. AND STIGGS is the only one that was not adapted from a stage play. Instead he turned to that bastion of sophomoric humor *National Lampoon* for inspiration and based this alleged comedy on a short story entitled "The Utterly Monstrous, Mind-Roasting Summer of O.C. and Stiggs." While that story had some merit as adolescent humor, Altman's film version is a terribly overlong bore featuring a parade of pointless celebrity cameos. MGM executives decided the film was so bad that they let it languish in storage for nearly three years before dusting it off for a limited theatrical run prior to release on home video. While no better or worse than the myriad of stupid teenage comedies that are distributed on a regular basis, one shouldn't forget that O.C. AND STIGGS was directed by the man who gave us M*A*S*H, THE LONG GOODBYE, and NASHVILLE.

Starring Jenkins and Barry—two young unknown actors who have had the good sense to remain unknown since this debacle—the film, set in Arizona, follows the exploits of two mischievous high-school dorks who have made it their life's mission to harass boorish insurance salesman Dooley and his family. It seems Dooley cancelled Jenkins' grandfather's (Walston) old age insurance and the boys are out for revenge. Dooley and his family are a middle-class suburban mess. He is a paranoid right-winger with a huge bomb shelter beneath his home; his wife, Curtin, is a hopeless alcoholic; his daughter, Urstein, is a whining brat about to marry his Chinese caddy; and his son, Cryer, is a nerd from the Jerry Lewis school. Harassing these people is like flogging a dead horse, but flog away they do—for nearly two interminable hours. Jenkins and Barry do everything from breaking up Urstein's wedding reception with an Uzi machine gun to stocking Dooley's house with a dozen winos and calling it a charity ball. Eventually Dooley corners the boys in his bomb shelter, but they are rescued by Hopper (in an unfunny parody of his APOCALYPSE NOW character) and his pal Autry, a pair of wacked out Vietnam vets with their own helicopter.

Despite a few brief chuckles, O.C. AND STIGGS is a complete failure. The film lurches from scene to scene with little sense of pacing or structure, and the lighting and camerawork are alarmingly sloppy. The performances . . . well, at least no one embarrasses himself too badly, despite Altman's best attempts to humiliate both men and women and every social class, creed, color, and sexual orientation. One of the highlights of the film is also one of its most poorly integrated sequences: a musical number by African Ju-Ju musician King Sunny Ade and his band the African Beats. Barry's character is obsessed with African culture and his musical hero is King Sunny Ade. The boys chatter endlessly about the band and then guess what? They happen to get the chance to meet the King himself! There hasn't been a musical guest star appearance this gratuitous since those beach-party movies where popular bands suddenly turned up to give impromptu concerts. What was Altman aiming for here? He tries so hard to build up some sort of cultish myth around his characters that even Leo the MGM Lion is forced to growl "O.C., Stiggs" before the opening credits. The movie fails as genre revisionism and as a social statement on middle-class values. Worst of all, there is nary a laugh to be had. *(Brief nudity, adult situations, profanity.)*

p, Robert Altman, Peter Newman; d, Robert Altman; w, Donald Cantrell, Ted Mann (based on a story by Tod Carroll, Ted Mann from a story in "Natonal Lampoon" magazine); ph, Pierre Mignot (Metrocolor); m, King Sunny Ade and his African Beats; ed, Elizabeth Kling; prod d, Scott Bushnell; art d, David Gropman; set d, John Hay; spec eff, Allan Hall; stunts, Randy Fife; makeup, David Craig Forrest.

Comedy **Cas.** **(PR:O MPAA:R)**

O BOBO (SEE: JESTER, THE, 1987, Port.)

O DESEJADO—LES MONTAGNES DE LA LUNE† (1987, Port./Fr.) 120m Arion-Suma-La Sept-Centre National de la Cinematographie-Institut Portugais du Cinema-Canal Plus-Sofica Investimages-RTP Lisbonne-Fondation Gulbenkian c (Trans: Mountains of the Moon)

Luis Miguel Cintra *(Joao)*, Caroline Chaniolleau *(Antonia)*, Jacques Bonnaffe *(Tiago)*, Manuela de Freitas *(Isabel)*, Yves Afonso, Isabel Ruth, Isabel Castro, Duarte de Almeida, Ines de Medeiros.

No one can resist the charisma of Cintra, a rapidly rising Portuguese politician who delights in the effect he has on others. He meets his match, however, when he travels to Italy to bring back Chaniolleau, a gorgeous relative who has become the family's black sheep because she has taken up with a terrorist. For the first time, Cintra is faced with a woman who doesn't want him as much as he wants her. Adding insult to injury, she becomes involved with his illegitimate son. The Japanese tale on which the film is based—Murasaki Shikibu's "Genji Monogatari"—has been updated and given an Iberian flavor.

p, Patrick Sandrin, Paulo Rocha; d, Paulo Rocha; w, Paulo Rocha, Jorge Silva Melo (based on "Genji Monogatari" by Murasaki Shikibu); ph, Kozo Okazaki; m, Philippe Hersant; ed, Christiane Lack; art d, Luis Montero, Jose Matos.

Drama **(PR:NR MPAA:NR)**

O PARADISSOS ANIGI ME ANTIKLIDI† (1987, Gr.) 93m Greek Film Center-Ann c (Trans: Red Ants)

Ian Dury, Cassandra Voyiatzi, Stefanos Eliot, Nikos Milas, Lydia Lenossi, Manolis Destounis, Giorgos Partsalakis, Michalis Bogiaridis, Thanos Grammenos, Theodoros Syriotis, Christos Afthinos.

Starring English rocker Ian Dury (who also appeared in ROCINANTE, 1986), this Greek film focuses on three children who fend for themselves in a less-than-accommodating city in 1950. They live in a broken-down old bus and share the friendship of a crippled acrobat whose girl friend floats high above in a balloon. When adults start making their lives even tougher, the trio decide to nab some horses and head for the hills. On the eve of their departure, the young girl of the trio is arrested for trying to steal some shoes. The acrobat, who has been deserted by his girl friend, comes to their assistance. Using a toy gun that has gotten them out of some tough scrapes in the past, they free the girl and escape via tunnels, horses, and, finally, in the acrobat's balloon.

d&w, Vassilis Buduris; ph, Stavros Hassapis; m, Michalis Grigoriou; ed, Andreas Tsilifonis, Despina Zervou; art d&cos, Miltiadis Makris.

Children's **(PR:NR MPAA:NR)**

O ROZVRASHCHENII ZABYT† (1987, USSR) 80m Moldova-film/Sovexportfilm c (Trans: Without Return)

Alexander Filippenko, Vladas Bagdonas, Sergey Balabanov.

Based on a real episode toward the end of the WW II, the Nazis use a new submarine with a crew trained under the direct supervision of Hitler. The cream of the German Reich is then engaged in a battle of wits with a Soviet submarine, which blows them out of the water.

d, Vasily Brescanu; w, Alexander Moldavsky; ph, Ivan Pozdnyakov; m, Valery Loginov; art d, Vladlen Ivanov.

War/Drama **(PR:NR MPAA:NR)**

OBESHCHAYU BYT† (1987, USSR) 76m Gorky/Sovexportfilm c (Trans: I Promise)

Vladimir Nosik, Maria Vinogradova, Victor Proskurin.

When a new sports instructor wins the respect of the children in a pioneer camp, he locks horns with his superior who disapproves of his kindly manner, feeling the children should be treated more strictly. In spite of the supervisor's opposition, the instructor takes the children on a three-day hike where they learn valuable lessons about endurance, friendship, and cooperation.

d&w, Vyacheslav Maksakov; ph, Konstantin Arutyunov; m, Vladimir Komarov, art d, Arseny Klopotovsky.

Drama **(PR:NR MPAA:NR)**

OBOROTEN TOM† (1987, USSR) 88m Riga/Sovexportfilm c (Trans: Werewolf Tom)

Gunnar Tsylinsky, Uldis Vazdiks, Helmuts Kalnynsh, Olga Drage.

In this story based on folklore, three brothers, after brutal treatment from their landlord, escape to the forest and start a struggle against their oppressors. They begin by taming a pack of wolves, which strikes terror in the hearts of the local barons whose superstitious fear of werewolves does them in.

d&w, Eric Latsis; ph, Davis Simanis; m, Pauls Dambis; art d, Andris Merkmanis.

Adventure **(PR:NR MPAA:NR)**

OBRYV† (1987, USSR) 143m Lenfilm/Sovexportfilm c (Trans: The Precipice)

Georgy Antonov, Elena Finogenova, Nikolay Kochegarov, Rimma Markova, Elena Solovey.

An adaptation of a 19th century novel about a man who returns from St. Petersburg to his family estate and rekindles his zest for life and love.

d&w, Vladimir Vengerov (based on the novel by Ivan Goncharov); ph, Anatoly Zabolotsky; m, Isaak Shvarts; art d, Marina Azyzyan.

Drama **(PR:NR MPAA:NR)**

OBVINYAETSYA SVADBA† (1987, USSR) 78m Kiev/Sovexportfilm c (Trans: A Wedding Party Is Accused)

Tauras Cizas, Yelena Shilkina, Alexei Serebryakov, Alexander Adabashyan, Olga Mateshko.

The members of a wedding party are accused of the murder of the bridal couple in this morality play. An investigation proves the crime could have been avoided.

d, Alexander Itygilov; w, Konstantin Yershov, Ramiz Fataliyev; ph, Alexander Yanovsky; m, Vladimir Bystryakov, art d, Eduard Sheykin.

Drama **(PR:NR MPAA:NR)**

OCHNAYA STAVKA† (1987, USSR) 89m Mosfilm/Sovexportfilm c (Trans: Confrontation)

Yelena Safonova, Nikolai Karachentsov, Lyudmila Polyakova, Yelena Popova.

A young boy loses his powers of speech after surviving a home fire and he is unable to help authorities find the cause of the fire. Matches were found at the scene though the boy was alone and asleep when the fire broke out. After a series of investigations, the boy's mother realizes it was she who set the room on fire when drunk.

d, Valery Kremnev; w, Alexei Leontyev, Valery Kremnev; ph, Vladimir Nakhabtsev; m, Yury Saulsky; art d, Leonid Plakhov.

Mystery/Drama **(PR:NR MPAA:NR)**

OCI CIORNIE (SEE: DARK EYES, 1987, It.)

ODINOKAYA ORESHINA† (1987, USSR) 145m Armenfilm/Sovexportfilm c (Trans: The Lone Hazel)

Frunze Dovlatyan, Armen Djigarkhanyan, Aneta Arutyunyan.

Lernasar, a small village in Armenia that has been in existence for over a thousand years, is faced with a declining population, vacant buildings, and unused resources. Worried that Lernasar is about to become a ghost town, the local schoolteacher decides to celebrate the millennium of the village by inviting back all the former villagers who have gone on to fame and fortune in the hope they will use their influence to save the town. Unfortunately, most of those invited merely send postcards of congratulations, leaving the future of Lernasar in the hands of the secretary of the district party committee.

d, Frunze Dovlatyan; w, Arnold Agababov, Frunze Dovlatyan; ph, Albert Yavuryan; m, Martin Vartazaryan, art d, Rafael Babayan.

Drama **(PR:NR MPAA:NR)**

ODINOKAYA ZHENCHINA ZHELAET POZNAKOMITAYA† (1987, USSR) 90m Kiev/Sovexportfilm c (Trans: A Lonely Woman Is Looking for a Life Companion)

Irina Kupchenko *(Klavdia)*, Alexander Zbruyev *(Valentin)*, Yelena Solovey *(Neighbor)*, Marianna Vertinskaya.

Kupchenko, an attractive 43-year-old spinster with a dull-but-stable job, impulsively posts a note reading, "A lonely woman is looking for a life companion . . . " Just as she decides that it was a bad idea, dozens of men come calling for her. While her robust neighbor, Solovey, is glad to take a look at the rejects, Kupchenko finds that she is stuck with one persistent caller, Zbruyev. Although he is a broken-down alcoholic, Kupchenko sees a glimmer of intelligence in the man and begins to fall for him. Eventually she learns that he was once a famed circus performer who was injured in an accident and forced to retire. The ensuing bout of self-pity has led to his heavy drinking. Kupchenko and Zbruyev try to make a go of it but their relationship is a revolving door of break-ups and make-ups. A surprise hit at the Moscow Film Festival.

d, Vyacheslav Krishtofovich; w, Viktor Merezhko; ph, Vasily Trutkovsky; m, Vadim Khrapachev; art d, Alexei Levchenko.

Drama **(PR:NR MPAA:NR)**

ODINOKIJ GOLOS CELOVEKA† (1987, USSR) 90m Lenfilm/Sovexportfilm bw/c (Trans: Man's Solitary Voice)

Andrei Gradov, Tatiana Goriatcheva.

Shot in 1978 but unreleased until *glasnost* freed it from the vaults, this film follows the uneasy relationship between a dedicated revolutionary and the daughter of a deposed bourgeois family at the beginning of the Russian revolution. Director Sokourov was a protege of the late Andrei Tarkovsky and the film is dedicated to Tarkovsky. Shown in competition at the Locarno Film Festival.

d, Aleksandr Sokourov; w, Joury Arabov (based on stories by Andrei Platonov); ph, Sergei Yourizditzky; art d, Vladimir Lebedev.

Drama **(PR:NR MPAA:NR)**

ODYSSEE D'AMOUR† (1987, Neth.) 107m Altamira/Concorde c (Trans: Love Odyssey)

Herbert Flack *(Paul Henkes)*, Sarah Brackett *(Elizabeth)*, Patty Brard *(Valerie)*, Liz Snoyink *(Zippy)*, Eddy Marchena *(Ramon)*, Ramon Todd Dandare *(Nicholas)*, Devika Strooker *(Ramona)*, John van Dreelen *(Alexander de Winter)*.

Flack stars as an engineer living in the Dutch Antilles with sculptress Brackett. When his son dies unexpectedly, Flack slides into a state of shock, from which he is eventually stirred by the arrival of his half-sister Zippy (Snoyinck). Flack and Snoyinck rekindle a long-standing incestuous relationship which naturally leads to sexual tension and emotional explosions. Padded with many mythological references, a dose of soft-core sex, and artfully photographed nudity.

p, Lea Wongsoredjo, Ruud den Drijver; d, Pim de la Parra; w, Pim de la Parra, Rudi F. Kross, Dorna van Rouveroy; ph, Frans Bromet (Fujicolor); m, Adriaan van Noord, Eddy Bennett; ed, Kees Linthorst; prod d, Rebecca Geskus.

Romance/Drama **(PR:NR MPAA:NR)**

OFICIR S RUZOM† (1987, Yugo.) 106m Jadran-Centar c (Trans: Officer with a Rose)

Ksenija Pajic *(Matilda)*, Zarko Lausevic *(Petar Horvat)*, Dragana Mrkic *(Ljiljana)*, Vicko Ruic, Boris Buzancic, Vida Jermank, Zvonko Torijanac.

Pajic is a beautiful young war widow who lives a bourgeois existence in postwar Zagreb. Into her apartment building moves Mrkic, a militant Communist who is about to marry party lieutenant Lausevic. The manly, aggressive Mrkic becomes attracted to the delicate Pajic, as does Lausevic. Eventually Pajic becomes pregnant and Lausevic is forced to choose between the woman he loves and the country he serves.

p, Suleymane Kapic, Djordje Milojevic; d&w, Dejan Sorak; ph, Goran Trbuljak (Eastmancolor); ed, Vesna Lazeta; art d, Stanko Dobrina.

Romance/Drama **(PR:NR MPAA:NR)**

OFELAS† (1987, Norway) 90m Filmkammeraterne/Mayco c (Trans: Pathfinder)

Mikkel Gaup *(Aigin)*, Nils Utsi *(Raste)*, Svein Scharffenberg *(Tchude Chief)*, Helgi Skulason *(Tchude With Scar)*, Sverre Porsanger *(Sierge)*, Svein Birger Olsen *(Diemis)*, Ailu Gaup *(Orbes)*, Sara Marit Gaup *(Sahve)*, Anne-Marja Blind *(Varia)*, Henrik H. Buljo, Ingvald Guttorm, Knut Walle, Ellen Anne Buljo, Inger Utsi.

Based on a Lapp legend from the 12th century, this 70mm/Dolby stereo film stars Mikkel Gaup as a young man taken prisoner by the Tchudes, an enemy tribe from the east. He is forced to act as their pathfinder through the treacherous mountainous Arctic North. Gaup, however, outsmarts his captors and leads them over a cliff where they perish under an avalanche. His brave actions free his Lapp tribe from the threat of the Tchudes, thereby enabling them to live a peaceful undisturbed existence as nomadic hunters. The first picture ever to be filmed in the Lapp language.

p, John M. Jacobsen; d&w, Nils Gaup; ph, Erling Thurmann-Andersen (Panavision 70, Eastmancolor); m, Nils-Aslak Valkeapaa, Marlus Muller, Kjetil Bjerkestrand; ed, Niels Pagh Andersen; cos, Eva Scholberg, Marit Sofie Holmestrand; stunts, Martin Grace.

Drama/Adventure **(PR:NR MPAA:NR)**

OFF THE MARK† (1987) 90m Fries Ent. c (AKA: CRAZY LEGS)

Mark Neely, Terry Farrell, Clarence Gilyard, Jr., Norman Alden, Virginia Capers, Jon Cypher, Barry Corbin, Billy Barty.

Neely stars as a college athlete training for an upcoming triathlon (marathon, swimming, cycling) where he will compete against an ambitious woman (Farrell) and a Russian exchange student. Unfortunately Neely is afflicted with a strange disorder which sometimes makes his legs go into convulsions and act as if they have a will of their own. This weird phenomena was engendered by Neely in a childhood fall and he has spent the rest of his life trying to overcome it. Shown for one week only in three small Kansas City theaters, OFF THE MARK seems a likely candidate to go the home video route.

p, Temple Matthews, Ira Trattner; d, Bill Berry; w, Temple Matthews, Bill Berry; ph, Arledge Armenaki; m, David Frank.

Comedy **(PR:NR MPAA:R)**

OFFSPRING, THE** (1987) 96m Conquest Entertainment/TMS c (AKA: FROM A WHISPER TO A SCREAM)

Vincent Price *(Julian White)*, Clu Gulager *(Stanley Burnside)*, Terry Kiser *(Jesse Hardwicke)*, Harry Caesar *(Felder Evans)*, Rosalind Cash *(The Snake Woman, Sideshow Owner)*, Cameron Mitchell *(Sgt. Gallen)*, Susan Tyrrell *(Bess Chandler)*, Martine Beswicke *(Katherine White)*, Angelo Rossitto *(Carny Barker)*, Lawrence Tierney *(Official at Execution)*, Ron Brooke *(Stephen Arden)*, Didi Lanier *(Amaryllis)*.

An effective low-budget horror anthology featuring an ensemble cast of familiar faces that manages to capture the look and feel of the classic E.C. horror comics of the 1950s without resorting to the kind of overly dramatic "comic-book" lighting used by George Romero in CREEPSHOW. The film opens as Beswicke is given a lethal injection after committing a series of murders. After witnessing the execution, a reporter, Tyrrell, travels to the small town of Oldfield, Tennessee, to visit Price, the woman's uncle and curator of the local library. Price tells Tyrrell that Beswicke was doomed from the start, for the town itself is evil. To demonstrate his point, Price spins four hideous tales for the reporter.

The first concerns Gulager, a bespectacled middle-aged nerd whose glasses are so thick his eyes look five times larger than they are. Desperately lonely and more than a little warped, Gulager lives with his demanding sister, an invalid who requires nightly ice baths to lower her body temperature. One evening he works up enough nerve to ask a beautiful young coworker out on a date. The woman reluctantly agrees, but when she resists his romantic advances, he strangles her and dumps the body on the road. The night before her funeral, the crazed

Gulager breaks into the funeral home and has his way with the body. Nine months later, a monster baby digs its way out of the grave and comes home to daddy.

The second story sees small-time hood Kiser suffering from a gunshot wound and seeking refuge in the swamps. He is rescued by an eccentric old black man, Caesar, who lives by himself in a cabin. One day while Caesar is gone, Kiser rummages around the cabin looking for something to steal and finds a scrapbook indicating that Caesar is at least 200 years old. Kiser tries to force Caesar to tell him the secret of eternal life, and when the old man refuses, Kiser hits him over the head and dumps the body in the swamp. Much to his surprise, Caesar returns and attacks him. Once he has Kiser subdued, Caesar reveals that he had already given Kiser enough of the magic potion so that he would live another 70 years—a period during which he *cannot* die. Disgusted by the greedy crook, Caesar decides to make Kiser's remaining 70 years as miserable as possible and cuts off the man's arms and legs. He then sets Kiser on fire, forcing him to spend the rest of his long life as a charred oddity.

The third story takes place in a obscure carny and features a handsome young man—the glass eater in the freak show—who is in love with a local girl. Although forbidden to court the girl by carnival owner Cash, the man runs off with her anyway. Unfortunately, Cash is a voodoo priestess and to get revenge she makes everything the boy has ever eaten (glass, razor blades, etc.) explode from his body, and then forces his girl friend to replace him in the freak show as a human pin cushion.

The fourth story takes place at the end of the Civil War and stars Mitchell as a mean and surly Union sergeant who is captured along with three comrades by a band of children whose parents were killed in the war. Although the war has just ended, the children will not rest until all adults are made to pay for starting the fighting. Despite his best efforts to escape, Mitchell is forced to watch as his comrades are tortured and killed (the children play a ghoulish version of pin-the-tail-on-the-donkey with one soldier's dismembered body parts). Eventually, Mitchell, too, is killed and consumed by the children, who vow to continue their fight against thoughtless adults. The coda of the film sees a crazed Tyrrell, who reveals herself to be a friend of Beswicke, killing Price for having poisoned Beswicke's mind with such tales of horror.

Although these loathsome little tales run the gamut from necrophilia to cannibalism, first-time director Burr presents them in a slight tongue-in-cheek manner that captures the ghoulish spirit of horror comic books. He imbues each sequence with a different feel and juggles his obvious low-budget with considerable skill. Burr self-consciously echoes Tod Browning's classic FREAKS in the carny episode, and the mood is enhanced by the cameo appearance of veteran midget actor Angelo Rossitto, who was featured in the Browning film. Burr also manages to evoke a good sense of the historical period in the Civil War episode and creates an impressive, albeit brief, battle sequence seen in a flashback. The veteran cast members are impressive as well. Gulager has a field day with his hammy performance as the pathetic little man who looks like Ernie Kovacs' "Percy Dovetonsils" character and brings an air of uneasy comedy to his segment. Caesar is appropriately mysterious and underplayed, while Kiser is malicious and somewhat manic in the swamp story. Cash is delightfully evil as the dreadlock-maned voodoo priestess, with Rossitto lending his solid support as the senior midget of the freak show in the carny episode. In the Civil War tale, Mitchell once again proves himself to be one of the kings of "B" pictures with yet another solid performance as the hostile and amoral soldier. Most disappointing, however, are the Price sequences, which are weak and perfunctory. Price seems out of place in a film with so much hard-core gore, and the resolution of his tale seems gratuitous (does anybody really want to see such a great old actor with a knife in his throat?). Despite the emphasis on gore and some pretty vile subject matter, Burr has a definite appreciation for history of the horror genre and presents more here than just your average slasher film. *(Graphic violence, gore effects, nudity, sexual situations, adult situations, profanity.)*

p, Darin Scott, William Burr; d, Jeff Burr; w, Courtney Joyner, Darin Scott, Jeff Burr; ph, Craig Greene (United Color); m, Jim Manzie, Pat Regan; ed, W.O. Garrett; spec makeup eff, Rob Burman.

Horror **(PR:O MPAA:R)**

OH, BABYLON† (1987, Gr.) 90m Greek Film Center-Andromeda II c

Alkis Panayotidis, Sotiria Leonardou, Giorgos Moschidis, Constantinos Paliatsaras, Maxi Priest.

A metaphorical film that reflects director Ferris' belief that civilization is in the process of shifting into a new phase. The film presents 36 hours in the life of a man who must come to grips with the sudden resurgence of his long-repressed desires.

d&w, Costas Ferris; ph, Takis Zervoulakos; m, Thessia Panayotou; ed, Babis Alepis; art d, Tassos Zografos; cos, Pavlos Kyriakidis.

Fantasy **(PR:NR MPAA:NR)**

OGNI† (1987, USSR) 88m Lenfilm/Sovexportfilm c (Trans: Lights)

Evgeny Leonov-Gladyshev, Tatyana Dogileva, Vladislav Strzhelchik.

Adapted from stories by Anton Chekhov, this film follows a young railway contruction engineer as he returns to the small town he had left ten years before. The opening of a new railway line has brought him back, and while there he meets his former love, now unhappily married. At first the young man feels his love for the woman has returned and he plans to run off with her, but upon reflection he realizes they will not be happy. She too knows this, and encourages him to leave the town and fulfill his bright future without her.

d, Solomon Shuster; w, Aleksandr Chervinsky (based on stories by Anton Chekhov); ph, Dmitry Dolinin; m, Boris Tishenko; art d, Georgy Kropachyov.

Drama **(PR:NR MPAA:NR)**

OKTOBERFEST† (1987, Yugo.) 120m Inex c

Svetislav Goncic *(Luka Benjamin)*, Zeljka Cvijetan, Zoran Cvijanovic, Tatjana Pujin, Zarko Lausevic, Vesna Trivalic, Vladica Milosavljevic, Velimir-Bata Zivojinovic.

Based on a best-selling novel, this film deals with the hopeless conditions college-educated youths face when trying to find white-collar employment in times of economic crisis. Goncic stars as an unemployed college graduate who spends all his time hanging out with his similarly troubled friends. Arriving home after a brief trip abroad, Goncic gets in trouble with the police over a small amount of drugs and has his passport confiscated. This cancels his planned trip to Munich during Oktoberfest and Goncic daydreams about the wonderful, liberating time he would have. There are several violent run-ins with both a gang of punkers and the police and one by one his buddies must admit defeat and take menial blue-collar jobs. Finally, Goncic's mother is able to secure his passport, but he declines to go to Oktoberfest, prefering to dream about it. Shot in Belgrade and Munich, OKTOBERFEST is the third feature film by critically acclaimed director Dragan Kresoja. Shown in competition at the Moscow Film Festival.

d, Dragan Kresoja; w, Goran Radovanovic, Dragan Kresoja; ph, Predrag Popovic; m, Vranesevic Brothers; ed, Andrija Zafranovic; art d, Vladislav Lasic.

Drama **(PR:NR MPAA:NR)**

OKHOTA NA DRAKONA† (1987, USSR/Nicaragua) 98m Uzbekfilm-INCINE-V/O Sovinfilm/Sovexportfilm c (Trans: Hunting the Dragon)

Alisher Pirmukhamedov, Mirdza Martinsone, Albert Filozov, Bokhodyr Yurdashev, Boris Zaidenberg.

A Soviet-Nicaraguan co-production which sees a team of Russian scientists, local authorities, and American journalists trying to uncover the source of a series of devastating water-spouts that have been wreaking havoc on a fictitious Central American country. During a hurricane the leading Soviet scientist investigating the phenomena disappears along with his notes. Eventually it is learned that the spouts, which are caused by meteorological rockets launched from the US, are a CIA plot designed to de-stabilize the country.

d, Latif Faiziyev; w, Nikolai Ivanov; ph, Leonid Travitsky; m, Mikhail Ziv, art d, Sadritdin Ziyamukhamedov.

Mystery/Drama **(PR:NR MPAA:NR)**

OLD WELL† (1987, Chi.) 140m Xi'an (LAO JING) c

Zhang Yimou *(Sun Wangquan)*, Liang Yujin *(Zhao Qiaoying)*, Lu Liping *(Duan Zifeng)*, Wu Tianming *(Communist Party Secretary)*.

Entered in the Tokyo International Film Festival, OLD WELL surprisingly won the Grand Prize for Best Picture, the Governor's Award, the Best Actor's Prize, and the FIPRESCI Special Recognition. The film is set in China's remote Taihang mountain region in a dusty, barren village which is without water. For years the inhabitants have been digging for water. In honor of those who have dug for water and lost their lives, a memorial has been erected listing the 127 names of the dead. Into the village comes Yimou, a villager who went to the city to study "hydro-geology." He returns with a knowledge of applicable science and organizes the others in an attempt to dig another well, despite the fact that his father was killed in a dig years before. Yimou's dig ends in disaster, killing his brother and trapping him underground with the girl he loves, Yujin. They are eventually rescued, but Yimou does not surrender. He and the villagers raise the money to purchase excavation equipment that will make the dig possible and bring them into the modern world. Zhang Yimou, who was the recipient of the Best Actor prize, is also credited as co-cinematographer. Director Tianming is the head of Xi'an Film Studios, which has delivered such internationally acclaimed films as IN THE WILD MOUNTAINS, THE BIG PARADE, HORSE THIEF, and THE BLACK CANNON INCIDENT, becoming a major force in the new wave of Chinese cinema. Shown in the US at the Hawaii International Film Festival.

d, Wu Tianming; w, Zheng Yi; ph, Chen Wancai, Zhang Yimou; m, Xu Youfu; ed, Chen Dali; art d, Yang Gang.

Drama **(PR:NR MPAA:NR)**

OLOR A MUERTE† (1987, Mex.) 84m Rodriguez-Cinematografica-Sol/Peliculas Mexicanas c (Trans: Scent of Death)

Gilberto Trujillo *(Dr. Salvador Guizar)*, Alma Delfina *(Piedad)*, Raul Trujillo *(Victor)*, Arturo Vazquez *(Roger)*, Carmen Salinas *(Carmelita)*, Miguel Manzano, Jose Carlos Ruiz, Pepe Romay, Gerardo Cepeda, Maria Jose-Garrido, Victor Lozoya, Valentin Trujillo.

The problem of teenage delinquency, gang warfare, and drug use is explored in this social drama about three youngsters—Raul Trujillo, Delfina, and Vazquez—who fall victim to the streets. Their tale is told in flashback by doctor Gilberto Trujillo who lays the blame for their death on society. Released in neighborhood theaters in New York.

p, Tonatihu Rodriguez; d&w, Ismael Rodriguez, Jr.; ph, Francisco Colon; m, Ernesto Cortazar; ed, Angel Camacho.

Drama **(PR:O MPAA:NR)**

OM KARLEK† (1987, Swed.) 97m Omega-Swedish Television-SVT 1-The Swedish Film Institute/Sandrews c (Trans: About Love)

Sven Wollter *(Peter)*, Linn Stokke *(Helene)*, Sverre Anker Ousdal *(Christian)*, Pia Green *(Eva)*, Kalle Wollter, Maria Koblanck, Emma Samuelson, Ruth Stevens.

At a school graduation, Wollter, the divorced father of two, meets Stokke, the newly married stepmother of one, and sparks fly. Soon afterwards both families holiday on Majorca. Wollter and Stokke run into each other and love blossoms in the Spanish sun. When the adulterous lovers rendezvous in Sweden, things don't go well and it looks as if their affair is doomed. Wrong.

p, Peter Kropenin; d, Mats Arehn; w, Mats Arehn, Thomas Samuelson, Anette Kullenberg; ph, Mischa Gavrjusjov (Fujicolor); m, Ulf Wahlberg, Wlodek Gulgowski; ed, Thomas Samuelson; prod d, Cian Bornebusch.

Romance **(PR:NR MPAA:NR)**

OMEGA SYNDROME** (1987) 88m Prey-Smart Egg/NW c

Ken Wahl *(Jack Corbett)*, George DiCenzo *(Philadelphia "Phil" Horton)*, Nicole Eggert *(Jessie Corbett)*, Doug McClure *(Detective Milnor)*, Patti Tipo *(Sally)*, Robert Kim *(Detective Lo)*, Perla Walter *(Spanish Lady)*, John Lisbon Wood *(Terry Lemson)*, Dick Butler *(Dr. Moor)*, George Fisher *(Ralph Dunlap)*, Len Glascow, Janet Brady *(Couple Killed on Street)*, Christopher Doyle *(Leonard Waxman)*, Doc Duhame *(Frank)*, Dick Warlock, Ed Ulrich, Spiro Razatos *(Marshalls)*, Thomas Rosales *(Fredo)*, Xander R. Berkeley, Ron Kuhlman, Bill Morey, Robert Gray, Colm Meaney, Bob Tzudiker, Al White.

Wahl is a down-on-his-luck journalist whose daughter is kidnaped by white supremacist fanatics. The kidnapers are trying to force the girl's doctor grandfather to kill an informer who is being kept under guard in the security wing of the hospital. Wahl, however, is not a man to be trifled with. He begins his own investigation with the help of an old buddy from Vietnam, DiCenzo. They receive little help from the police, in the person of McClure, but a reporter gives them a list of Nazi loonies and they manage to force one of them to reveal where the girl is being held. A routine shoot-em-up in the empty warehouse ensues, climaxed when the leader of the group chases the girl onto the rooftop with Wahl close behind. They struggle with a knife until Wahl manages to fling the heavy off the building. While the action of this film is indistinguishable from a hundred others, at least this one has its heart in the right place. Rather than blowing up Third World nationalists, our heroes take on fascist creeps. Wahl does as good a job as can be expected with the material, while DiCenzo's wisecracking sidekick performance is even better. Mostly, though, the film is a bore, all talk and feeble action and never once does the audience care about Wahl or his daughter. There were actually a few scattered engagements for this effort in the early part of 1987 before it was consigned to obscurity in the video racks.

p, Luigi G. Cingolani; d, Joseph Manduke; w, John Sharkey; ph, Harvey Genkins (United Color); m, Nicholas Carras, Jack Cookerly; ed, Stephen A. Isaacs; art d, Nancy Arnold; set d, T. Edward Cliff; cos, Judy Babcock; stunts, Spiro Razatos; makeup, Nancy J. Hvasta.

Action **Cas.** **(PR:O MPAA:R)**

ON THE EDGE OF HELL† (1987, Phil.) Roadshow c

Dante Varona *(Vergel)*.

Varona stars as a villager who is separated from his sweetheart when his parents decide he must become a priest. Varona is separated from his girl friend when she is kidnaped by his family. He retreats into the mountains and, after becoming the leader of a band of natives, he locates her and together they renew their love.

[No Credits Available].

Adventure/Romance **(PR:NR MPAA:NR)**

120 DECIBELS† (1987, Gr.) 90m Greek Film Center-Sigma c

Haris Sozos, Rubini Vassilakopoulou, Aneza Papadopoulou, Kariofilia Karabeti, Tassos Ifantis, Alkis Panayotidis, Athena Tsilyra, Nellie Angelidou, Dora Volanaki, Athinodoros Proussalis, Costas Voutsas.

Told primarily in flashback, 120 DECIBELS is a story of love, jealousy, and friendship. A young man lies in a coma in a hospital bed after an automobile accident and is visited by friends and lovers—past and present—who reflect on moments spent with him. Many of the characters' relationships overlap. The present girl friend of the injured man is the former girl friend of his ex-best friend, etc. The title comes from the protagonist's hobby, tape recording sounds—any sounds.

d&w, Vassilis Vafeas; ph&ed, Dinos Katsouridis; art d, Damianos Zarifis.

Drama **(PR:NR MPAA:NR)**

ONIRO ARISTERIS NICHTAS† (1987, Gr.) Greek Film Center-Kinotek c (Trans: A Leftist Night's Dream)

Nikos Kaloyeropoulos *(Polychronis)*, Vassilis Tsibidis, Tavyeti Basouri, Dimitris Katsimanis, Christina Avlianou, Costas Dalianis, Melina Botelli, Giorgos Kendros, Dimitra Zeza, Andreas Varouchas, Dimitris Yannakopoulos, Yannis Firios, Rika Vayani.

The struggle for survival of a disillusioned political radical is at the heart of this film. Faced with the failure of the Left, he tries to find a way to keep his spirit from sinking. All around him, former comrades have sold out in one way or another. Pushed to the brink of insanity, he contemplates suicide, but finds the will to carry on. To make sense of the past, he begins work on a book; to make something of the rest of his life, he begins working on the present. Co-written, co-directed, photographed, and edited by noted Greek cinematographer Dinos Katsouridis.

d&w, Dinos Katsouridis, N. Kaloyeropoulos; ph&ed, Dinos Katsouridis; set d&cos, Yannis Lekkos.

Drama **(PR:NR MPAA:NR)**

OPEN HOUSE* (1987) 95m Intercontinental c

Joseph Bottoms *(Dr. David Kelley)*, Adrienne Barbeau *(Lisa Grant)*, Rudy Ramos *(Rudy Estevez)*, Mary Stavin *(Katie Thatcher)*, Scott Thompson Baker *(Joe Pearcy)*, Darwyn Swalve *(Harry)*, Robert Miano *(Shapiro)*, Page Moseley *(Toby)*, Johnny Haymer *(Paul Bernal)*, Leonard Lightfoot *(T.J.)*, Barry Hope *(Barney Resnick)*, Stacey Adams *(Tracy)*, Roxanne Baird *(Allison)*, Tiffany Bolling *(Judy Roberts)*, Dena Drotar *(The Fan)*, Christina Gallegos *(Pilar)*, Cathryn Hartt *(Melody)*, Lee Moore *(Donald Spectre)*, Stephen Nemeth *(Tommy)*, Joanne Norman *(Agent #1)*, Richard Parnes *(Lenny)*, Sheila Ryan *(Ellen)*, A. Gerald Singer *(Capt. Blake)*, Bryan Utman *(Policeman)*, Susan Widem *(Policewoman)*, Eddie Wong *(Mr. Yoshida)*.

This low-budget, independently made slasher film which bypassed theatrical distribution and debuted in the US on home video stars Bottoms as a pop psychologist who hosts a popular Los Angeles radio call-in show. Making headlines is a string of murders of beautiful female real estate agents. One day Bottoms gets a mysterious call from a disturbed man who calls himself "Harry." The caller makes some brutal statements and ends by saying that those who were killed "deserved it." Bottoms worries about Harry, and the serial killer, because his girl friend, Barbeau, is a successful real estate agent. As the killings continue (in a variety of perversely imaginative—and graphic—ways) the calls from Harry become more frequent. Bottoms agrees to let police detective Miano tap the station's phone lines in an attempt to trace Harry's calls. Meanwhile, Barbeau begins to suspect a rival real estate agent, Hope, of the murders. An obese slob who sees women as mere sex objects, Hope makes no apologies for his behavior and freely admits to attempting to destroy Barbeau's business. Of course, Hope is only a red herring, for he is decapitated by the real killer in the last half hour. In the film's climax Barbeau and Bottoms are at the radio station awaiting the call from Harry. Finally the killer phones and the police trace the call back to the radio station. By this time, however, the killer has kidnaped Barbeau and whisked her away to one of the houses she represents. With a clue from Barbeau, Bottoms figures out where she is being held and dashes off to rescue her. The killer, Swalve, is a hulking homeless man who blames real estate agents for the inflated cost of housing. Predictably, the cops burst in and shoot Swalve before he can harm Barbeau. In a ridiculous coda, the apparently dead Swalve suddenly rises up—leaving half his brains splattered on the floor—and attacks Miano. The detective throws a few punches, sidesteps the oncoming killer, and watches as Swalve takes the stunt-dive off the balcony in slow motion.

Overlong and lacking in suspense, OPEN HOUSE is a pretty dull affair. Padded out with endless scenes of Bottoms talking to wacko callers on the radio and Playmate-calendar types showing houses, the film merely grinds its gears until the next bloody killing. The gore effects are poorly done and the camera lingers on the nasty goo far too long. Not only does director Mundhra fail when it comes to evoking suspense, shock, or horror, but his sense of humor is limited to some particularly offensive gay stereotyping (Bottoms' producer is a mincing gay who blows kisses). As usual, Bottoms turns in his typical performance—professional and unremarkable—while Barbeau surprises, not only because she is in a bargain basement slasher film (not that we expect to see her doing Shakespeare), but because she performs a brief and very gratuitous topless scene after having avoided doing so for many years. The rest of the cast is serviceable and includes some very attractive women as the usual murder victims. Hope and Swalve are memorable as two particularly despicable representatives of the male gender. All in all, OPEN HOUSE is just another poorly made, gory, misogynistic slasher film with no redeeming value whatsoever. *(Graphic violence, gore effects, nudity, sexual situations, profanity.)*

p, Sandy Cobe; d, Jag Mundhra; w, David Mickey Evans (from a story by Jag Mundhra); ph, Robert Hayes, Gary Louzon; m, Jim Studer; ed, Dan Selakovich; prod d, Naomi Shohan; art d, Zachary Spoon, Susan Mordfin; cos, Leslie Peters Ballard; makeup, John A. Naulin, Didier Offredo; stunts, John Stewart.

Horror Cas. (PR:O MPAA:R)

OPERA† (1987, It.) 90m Group Tiger Cinematografica-ADC-RAI-TV/COL Italia c

Cristina Marsillach *(Betty)*, Urbano Barberini *(Commissioner)*, Daria Nicolodi *(Mira)*, Ian Charleson, Antonella Vitale, William McNamara, Coralina Cataldi Tassoni, Barbara Cupisti, Gyorgy Gyoriwanyi, Francesca Cassola.

Another Dario Argento slasher film, this one centering on a performance of Verdi's "Macbeth." When the star breaks her leg, her understudy, Marsillach, must take the stage. A rash of murders follows. The killer then kidnaps Marsillach, props her eyes open (ala CLOCKWORK ORANGE), and forces her to watch as he dismembers her lover, and various other theater employees. Equally as charming as Argento's previous films, which inexplicably do great at the Italian box office. Marsillach is a Spanish actress who was picked by Argento after she was cast by Martin Scorsese for an Armani television commercial.

p, Mario Cecchi Gori, Vittorio Cecchi Gori; d, Dario Argento; w, Dario Argento, Franco Ferrini; ph, Ronald Charles Taylor; m, The Rolling Stones, Giuseppe Verdi, Giacomo Puccini; ed, Franco Fraticelli; art d, Davide Bassan.

Horror (PR:O MPAA:NR)

OPERACION MARIJUANA† (1987, Mex.) 98m Cinematografica Rodriguez/Peliculas Mexicanas c (Trans: Operation Marijuana)

Mario Almada *(Macario)*, Victor Loza *(Benito)*, Narciso Busquets *(Bruno Sanchez)*, Jose Carlos Ruiz *(Foreman)*, Ernesto Gomez Cruz *(Muchi)*, Raul Vale *(Pedro, the Reporter)*, Jorge Victoria, Juan Pelaez.

A docu-drama based on the 1984 discovery in Mexico of a marijuana slave plantation in Chihuahua manned by thousands of laborers. Almada stars as a deported Mexican who returns to his family to find that his young brother has taken work on the marijuana plantation. Almada sets out after him and discovers the giant plantation system, reporting what he finds to government authorities. OPERACION MARIJUANA, which played New York neighborhood theaters, is the second film on this subject in 1987, following YERBA SANGRIENTE directed by producer Robert Rodriquez's brother, Ismael.

p, Robert Rodriguez; d, Jose Luis Urquieta; w, Jorge Patino (based on an idea by Robert Rodriguez); ph, Armando Arellanos Bustamante; m, Susy Rodriguez; ed, Rogelio Zuniga.

Docu-drama (PR:NR MPAA:NR)

OPERATION: GET VICTOR CORPUS THE REBEL SOLDIER† (1987, Phil.) Vanguard/Sunny-Davian c

Rudy Fernandez, Jay Ilagan, Sandy Andolong.

Based on fact, this distinctly post-Marcos-era Filipino film tells the story of Victor Corpus, a graduate of the Philippine Military Academy, who deserted the Army in 1970 to join the New People's Army (NPA), the military wing of the Filipino Communist Party. Even in his cadet days, Corpus is shown to be sympathetic to the anti-imperialist movement. While leading a squad into action at a rally, Corpus spots and falls in love with activist Mely Tanglao. Later they marry. Thoroughly fed up with the government's abuse of power and the military's role in it, Corpus joins the rebels in 1970. He helps train the guerilla forces and leads an NPA contingent to a rendezvous with *MV Karagatan*, a cargo ship laden with weapons for the rebels. The operation becomes a disaster when government jets appear and Corpus and his group are forced into a long retreat. As the years goes by, Corpus becomes skeptical of the methods and objectives of the NPA. When the Aquino government takes power, Corpus comes down from the hills and surrenders.

d, Pablo Santiago.

Action/Historical (PR:NR MPAA:NR)

OPPOSING FORCE½** (1987) 97m Glaser & Berk-Eros Intl./Orion c

Tom Skerritt *(Maj. Logan)*, Lisa Eichhorn *(Lt. Casey)*, Anthony Zerbe *(Becker)*, Richard Roundtree *(Sgt. Stafford)*, Robert Wightman *(Gen. McGowan)*, John Considine *(Gen. MacDonald)*, George Kee Cheung *(Tuan)*, Paul Joynt *(Ripkin)*, Jay Louden *(Stevenson)*, Ken Wright *(Conway)*, Dan Hamilton *(Ross)*, Michael James *(Webb)*, Warren MacLean *(Dunn)*, John Melchier *(Jarrell)*, Scott Sanders *(De Carlo)*, Jerald Williams *(Fisher)*, Steven Rogers *(Brady)*, David Light, Victor Ordonez, Ding Navasero, James Gaines, Roy Batiwala, Rafael Shulz, Renato Morado, Bent Pederson, Berto Spoor, Steve Cook, Bill Kipp, Boy Ybanez, Tony Williams, Jeff Moldava *(Guards)*.

Eichhorn is a US Air Force officer who volunteers for the toughest training available, the escape and evasion school for reconnaissance pilots. She is paired with another student and they are dropped onto a tropical island and instructed to avoid capture by mock enemy forces while making their way to a safe location. Things go wrong almost immediately, though, as Eichhorn's assigned partner ditches her. She teams up with Skerritt, who injured his leg in the jump. They make a good run of it, actually reaching the safe house, but the game is not being played as they were told. They are brutally beaten and thrown into a stockade along with all the other trainees and forced to endure a series of humiliations. The captors force the men (and woman) to strip, then give them bright orange ponchos to wear. They are put to hard labor, cajoled, threatened, set against each other. Zerbe is the commander of the place and Roundtree is the top sergeant. Roundtree is just a soldier doing a job he doesn't especially like, but Zerbe is at a dead end in his career and, exiled to this island, he has clearly gone over the edge. His most faithful follower is a mean-looking former South Vietnamese army officer. Zerbe is now faced with trying to break down the first woman with whom he has ever had to deal. First he separates her from the others to make them think she is getting special treatment and later, rationalizing that it would happen to her in a real situation, he rapes her. Skerritt learns of this and tries to call off the whole exercise, but Zerbe just maintains that Skerritt has cracked under the stress. Skerritt manages to escape, killing the Vietnamese sent to murder him. Then he goes back to free Eichhorn and the other men while most of the guards are out looking for him. He captures Roundtree and convinces him that Zerbe is insane. They flee after tying Roundtree to a chair, but when Zerbe returns he realizes that Roundtree is lying and shoots him, telling the men that Skerritt did it. A chase through the jungle follows, with Skerritt, Eichhorn, and another soldier fighting a running battle to the top of a mountain where they hold off Zerbe's men with rifles and grenades. Skerritt and the other man are killed and it is left to Eichhorn to finish off Zerbe. The film immediately freeze-frames and Eichhorn gives a sappy closing narration. This interesting action drama came and went with only the slightest of regional releases before being consigned to the video racks. It is a surprisingly effective, intelligent, and well-acted movie that raises a number of issues about realism in military training and the use of psychological torture. Zerbe (always an underrated actor) is terrific in his role as he calmly discusses with Eichhorn the fact that he is raping her for her own good. "After a few times," he tells her, "you'll be the one in control." Skerritt is also good, playing a character very similar to the one he portrayed in TOP GUN. Eichhorn is thoroughly deglamorized and believable in her role, as well. It used to be that films would come and go and never be seen again, but thanks to the video boom, OPPOSING FORCE can still be sought out by viewers looking for something better than THUNDER WARRIOR TWO. *(Violence, excessive profanity, nudity, adult situations.)*

p, Daniel Jay Berk, Tamar E. Glaser; d, Eric Karson; w, Gil Cowan; ph, Michael A. Jones (DeLuxe Color); m, Marc Donohue; ed, Mark Conte; prod d, Art Dicdao; art d, Janice Flating; stunts, Ray Lykins, Ricou Browning.

Action Cas. (PR:O MPAA:R)

ORACLE, THE† (1987) 94m Laurel/Reeltime c

Caroline Capers Powers *(Jennifer)*, Roger Neil *(Ray, Jennifer's Husband)*, Pam LaTesta *(Farkas, Dorothy's Servant)*, Victoria Dryden *(Dorothy Graham)*, Chris Maria DeKoron *(Pappas)*, Dan Lutzky *(Tom Varney)*, Stacey Graves *(Cindy)*, G. Gordon Cronce *(Ben)*.

Filmed in 1984, given scant release in 1986, and finally distributed nationally via home video in 1987, THE ORACLE is a low budget gore film starring Powers as a young woman who finds an ancient Ouija board in an old crate. At a Christmas party Powers, her husband Neil, and another couple play with the mysterious board and conjure up a spirit message. Only Powers believes in the ghost and in subsequent seances she learns that the spirit is that of a murdered businessman. Although the police reported his death as a suicide, the ghost reveals that his evil wife, Dryden, killed him and covered up her crime. Plagued by visions of the murder, Powers decides to investigate on her own and confronts Dryden. Of course Dryden denies any knowledge of the claim and dismisses it as ridiculous, but when Powers leaves, Dryden dispatches her hulking woman servant LaTesta to kill the curious Powers. Another horror film with a Ouija board prominent in the plot, WITCHBOARD, featuring the vivacious Tawny Kitaen, also was released in 1987.

p, Walter E. Sear; d, Roberta Findlay; w, R. Allen Leider; ph, Roberta Findlay (Cineffects Color); m, Walter E. Sear, Michael Litovsky; ed, Roberta Findlay; set d, Cecilla Holzman; spec eff, Horrorefx; stunts, Webster Whinery; makeup, Jean Carballo.

Horror Cas. (PR:NR MPAA:R)

ORMENS VAG PA HALLEBERGET (SEE: SERPENT'S WAY, 1987, Swed.)

ORPHANS**** (1987) 115m Lorimar c

Albert Finney *(Harold)*, Matthew Modine *(Treat)*, Kevin Anderson *(Phillip)*, John Kellogg *(Barney)*, Anthony Heald *(Man in Park)*, Novella Nelson *(Mattie)*, Elizabeth Parrish *(Rich Woman)*, B. Constance Barry *(Lady in Crosswalk)*, Frank Ferrara *(Cab Driver)*, Clifford Fearl *(Doorman)*.

After the dismal failure of 1986's DREAM LOVER, director Alan J. Pakula has returned to top form with the screen version of the popular 1985 Lyle Kessler play, "Orphans." Basically a three-man show, ORPHANS stars Modine and Anderson as a pair of orphaned brothers who live in a dilapidated old house in a seedy part of Newark, New Jersey. Modine, a potentially dangerous petty thief with a closely cropped haircut, is the dominant sibling. Fearing that he will lose his brother just as he lost his parents, Modine keeps Anderson, a long-haired, socially maladjusted "wild child," imprisoned in his own home. He fills Anderson's head with the notion that the outside air will kill him should he breathe it. While Modine preys on wealthy New Yorkers, Anderson sits at home and secretly buries himself in the books that his brother has strictly forbidden him to read. While on the prowl, Modine takes notice of Finney, a well-dressed drunkard who is careful to keep a watchful eye on his briefcase. Modine, too, eyes the briefcase

and invites the soused Finney back to his house. When Finney passes out on the brothers' couch, Modine opens the briefcase to find it brimming with stocks, bonds, and securities. Modine hits on a plan to kidnap Finney and, with Anderson's help, ties the sleeping Finney to a chair and stuffs a gag in his mouth. The following morning, Modine leaves Anderson in charge of Finney while he tries to locate someone to pay the ransom. Meanwhile, Anderson grows curious about their prisoner, but has been strictly warned not to go near or touch him. Even though he is bound and gagged, Finney begins to take control of the situation. When Anderson isn't paying attention, Finney pulls himself and his chair into an adjoining room. Anderson is understandably surprised to find that Finney has moved. Before long, Finney has removed his gag and loosened the ropes enough to get one arm free, while Anderson cowers in the corner and fears the wrath of his brother. Finney gradually gains the sheepish Anderson's trust, and when he learns that Anderson cannot tie his own shoelaces, he promises to buy him a pair of loafers in his favorite color—pale yellow. Aware that Anderson has never been shown any love, Finney extends his arm and offers a little "encouragement." Anderson slowly approaches Finney, crouches down beside him, and allows Finney to wrap his free arm around his shoulder in an embrace of fatherly encouragement. When Modine arrives home, he finds a freshly shaven Finney emerging from the bathroom. Modine is furious that he has lost control and fears he now has no chance of collecting a ransom. Finney, who reveals himself as a Chicago gangster on the lam, has a better idea—he offers to pay Modine a handsome salary to work as his bodyguard. Using some persuasion, Finney hires Modine and Anderson at a package rate. Soon Modine is dressing in tailored pinstripes, while a clean-cut Anderson finally has his pair of pale yellow loafers. Together Anderson and Finney turn the run-down house into a picture-perfect living space, complete with new paint, curtains, furniture, VCR and everything else that one finds in a typical household. While Anderson and Finney redecorate, Modine makes daily trips to the local post office to await an expected package for Finney. It is during this time that Anderson comes out of the shadow of his brother. Finney dispels Anderson's belief that the outside air will hurt him, guiding the anxious boy out the front door and letting him run freely through a grassy lot nearby. Finney also gives Anderson a map of Newark to provide him the security of knowing his geographic relationship to the rest of the world. Modine gradually realizes that Anderson is no longer dependent on him and fears that his brother will leave him just as his parents did. When the package (which is filled with money) finally arrives at the post office, Finney is able to leave town. He sneaks away without telling Anderson or Modine. The building resentment between the brothers finally explodes—Modine taking out his anger over Anderson's newfound independence, and Anderson lashing out at Modine's attempts to keep him imprisoned. In the midst of their fighting, Finney returns unexpectedly, blood soaking through his shirt where a bullet entered his stomach. Knowing he is about to die, Finney tries to make contact with Modine. He extends his arm and offers to give him some "encouragement." Modine, however, cannot surrender his feelings as easily as Anderson did earlier and he remains on the other side of the room as Finney dies. Anderson rushes to Finney's side and buries himself under Finney's arm for a last bit of encouragement. Only then does Modine realize how much he needed Finney and his encouragement, breaking down into a violent crying fit with his face buried in his arms.

It's not often that a play can survive the transition from stage to screen without suffering some loss. The temptation is to "open up" the play and move the action to an exterior location, as if exteriors are inherently more cinematic than interiors. ORPHANS, however, resists this temptation. Because the play "Orphans" had only one location (presented in two acts, before and after the renovation of the house) and just three characters, it is natural to think that a screen version would necessitate "opening up." Fortunately, Kessler (who wrote both the stage play and the screenplay) worked his claustrophobic, prisonlike setting to the film's advantage. Because Anderson's character cannot emotionally leave the house that imprisons him, it is logical that the camera and characters remain inside as well. To the credit of Kessler and Pakula, the film opens with a wonderfully constructed pre-credit sequence in which Modine is in the process of mugging a yuppie New Yorker in the middle of Central Park. Modine lays on the charm to win his victim's confidence, then resorts to a switchblade in order to get the victim's watch. Modine's spree continues when he outsmarts a cabbie and steals his taxi. He then drives the cab up to a swanky New York hotel, puts his "passenger's" bags in the trunk, and speeds off before his fare can get in. After this energetic opening one quickly forgets that this is an adapted play. When the audience is finally taken into the house, it seems like the natural order of events. Instead of feeling like the play is "opening up," the reverse effect is felt, as if the film is "closing down" into the orphan world of Modine and Anderson. While ORPHANS is surely not the first film to succeed as both a play *and* film, it is unique in the way it uses its film location to its advantage.

More important to the success of ORPHANS than Pakula's and Kessler's techniques of adaptation is the brilliant acting by all three leads. Finney, whose appearances of late have been few (UNDER THE VOLCANO, 1984, and THE DRESSER, 1983, were his two most recent), turns in a spectacular performance. Modine, who earlier in the year played the calm "Pvt. Joker" in FULL METAL JACKET, here displays the opposite end of his acting spectrum as the violent, emotionally confused Treat. Keeping pace with (and often surpassing) his costars is the largely unseen Anderson whose "wild child" image changes as his character becomes readied for the outside world. Anderson (who previously starred in PINK NIGHTS, an independent comedy which received a 1985 Chicago Film Festival showing, and had a bit part in RISKY BUSINESS) makes his character come alive through a combination of odd and often humorous dialog and a heavy dependence on physical acting—leaping across the living room furniture and bouncing off the walls. In other scenes he cowers in the corner like a frightened animal hiding behind his filthy mane of hair.

The play itself has a short but impressive history, beginning with its opening run at the Matrix, a small Los Angeles theater, during which Kessler did a great deal of rewriting. The end, for example, originally had Finney's character living—a happier but less successful notion. Then, in 1985, Chicago's Steppenwolf Theater mounted a production that starred Anderson, Gary Sinise (who also directed), and John Mahoney. An Off-Broadway run followed where it was seen by Finney, who was impressed enough to bring the play to London. Anderson remained on board, Finney took Mahoney's role, and Sinise (who left the cast to direct a film) was replaced by a British actor. Upon seeing the New York performance, Pakula pursued the prospect of bringing the play to the screen—a possibility which improved with Finney's participation. With Anderson and Finney cast, the search began for someone to play Treat, as Sinise was deemed too old (he's in his thirties). Modine, who came to this picture fresh from Stanley Kubrick's year-long shoot of FULL METAL JACKET, rounded out the cast. It is perhaps because of its deceptively simple emotions and themes that ORPHANS (both the play and the film) has been such a wide-spread success. Part fairy tale and part heightened reality, it manages to strike an emotional chord with almost everyone who sees it. Finney, who is the type of character everyone should meet at least once, is not so much a real person as a representation of encouragement and strength. He is the ultimate father who is always there when you need him, and his words and actions remain long after his death. Finney comes suddenly into the orphans' lives and then leaves just as suddenly. He is a dream-come-true fairy-tale prince who encourages both the characters in the film and the audience. Songs include "The Charge of the Light Brigade" (Max Steiner), "Chicago" (Fred Fisher), "Is It True What They Say About Dixie" (Irving Caesar, Samuel Lerner, Gerald Marks), "The Prisoner's Song" (Guy Massey). *(Mild profanity, adult situations.)*

p, Alan J. Pakula, Susan Solt; d, Alan J. Pakula; w, Lyle Kessler (based on his play); ph, Donald McAlpine (Technicolor); m, Michael Small; ed, Evan Lottman; prod d, George Jenkins; art d, John Jay Moore; set d, Carol Joffe; cos, John Boxer; ch, Lynnette Barkley; m/l, Max Steiner, Fred Fisher, Irving Caesar, Samuel Lerner, Gerald Marks, Guy Massey; makeup, Allen Weisinger; stunts, Vic Magnotta, Frank Ferrara.

Drama **(PR:A-C MPAA:R)**

OTOKOWA TSURAIYO SHIAWASE NO AOI TORI (SEE: TORA-SAN'S BUEBIRD FANTASY, 1987, Jap.)

OTTO—DER NEUE FILM† (1987, Ger.) 90m Rialto Filmproduktion/Tobis c (Trans: Otto—The New Film)

Otto Waalkes *(Otto)*, Anja Jaenicke *(Anna)*, Ute Sander *(Gaby)*, Joachim Kemmer, Friedrich Schoenfelder.

The record-breaking success in Germany of 1985's OTTO—DER FILM is followed by OTTO—DER NEUE FILM, which stars the country's top comedian Otto Waalkes. Waalkes stars as a country bumpkin who cannot cope with life in the city. He can't go back home, however, until he pays his back rent. He's evicted, given a place to stay in the apartment basement, and forced to take menial jobs. Working as a bungling handyman, he meets the sexy Sander, causing his former sweetheart Jaenicke to become jealous. Eventually Waalkes gets jilted by Sander, who has fallen in love with an Arnold Schwarzenegger doppelganger, and returns to his true love Jaenicke.

p, Horst Wendlandt; d, Xaver Schwarzenberger, Otto Waalkes; w, Otto Waalkes, Bernd Eilert, Robert Gernhardt, Peter Knorr; ph, Xaver Schwarzenberger; m, Thomas Kukuck, Christoph Leis Hendorff; ed, Jutta Hering; prod d, Ulrich Schroder, Albrecht Konrad.

Comedy **(PR:NR MPAA:NR)**

OUT OF ORDER† (1987, Brit.) Birmingham Film & Video Workshop-BFI-Channel 4

Gary Webster, Sharon Fryer, Cheryl Maiker, Natasha Williams, Sandra Lawrence, Samantha Lawrence, Pete Lee-Wilson, George Baker, David Yip, Stephen Lewis, Glynn Edwards, Sue Hanson, Roland Gift.

A shot-on-videotape feature from the youth-oriented Birmingham Film and Video Workshop which stars Webster as a neighborhood kid who surprises everyone, especially his girl friend, when he joins the police force. Made for

$600,000, with the backing of the British Film Institute and Channel 4, the script for OUT OF ORDER was written by a collective of young people known as the Dead Honest Soul Searchers. (Howard Schuman, the writer of "Rock Follies," was brought in as script consultant.) Appearing in a cameo is Roland Gift of the rock group Fine Young Cannibals, who also appeared this year in SAMMY AND ROSIE GET LAID.

p, Roger Shannon, Lucy Hooberman; d, Jonnie Turpie; w, The Dead Honest Soul Searchers, Graham Peet, Jonnie Turpie; ph, Terry Flaxton; m, Working Week, Wee Papa Girl Rappers; ed, Phil Woodward; prod d, Jock Scott; cos, Ruth Willis; makeup, Sula Loizou.

Comedy/Drama/Musical (PR:NR MPAA:NR)

OUT OF ROSENHEIM† (1987, Ger.) 108m Pelemele Film-Project Filmproduktion-BR-HR/Futura-Filmverlag der Autoren c

Marianne Sagebrecht *(Jasmin)*, CCH Pounder *(Brenda)*, Jack Palance *(Rudy Cox)*, Christine Kaufmann *(Debbie)*, Monica Calhoun *(Phyllis)*, Darron Flagg *(Sal Jr.)*, George Aquilar *(Caguenga)*, Aspesanshkwat *(Sheriff)*, Alan S. Craig *(Eric)*.

Percy Adlon and Marianne Sagebrecht, the director and star of SUGARBABY, the refreshing hit German film from 1985, return in OUT OF ROSENHEIM. Filmed in the US and in English, this comedy stars the hefty Sagebrecht as a traditional German businesswoman who is stranded in the middle of the desert when her husband leaves her while en route to Las Vegas. Sagebrecht makes her way to a diner in Bagdad, California called Brenda's Palace and run by an unkempt black woman, Pounder. Naturally, Sagebrecht is treated like the alien she is, but eventually she charms the locals and turns Brenda's Palace into a favorite eatery, winning the friendship of Pounder and artist Palance. Winner of the Golden Toucan award for Best Film at the Rio de Janeiro International Film Festival.

p, Percy Adlon, Eleonore Adlon; d, Percy Adlon; w, Percy Adlon, Eleonore Adlon, Christopher Doherty (based on a story by Percy Adlon); ph, Bernd Heinl; m, Bob Telson; ed, Norbert Herzner; art d, Bernt Amadeus Capra, Byrnadette di Santo; cos, Elizabeth Warner, Regine Baetz; makeup, Lizbeth Williamson.

Comedy (PR:NR MPAA:NR)

OUTING, THE*½ (1987) 85m Warren Chaney-HIT/TMS c (AKA: THE LAMP)

Deborah Winters *(Eve Farrell)*, James Huston *(Dr. Al Wallace)*, Andra St. Ivanyi *(Alex Wallace)*, Scott Bankston *(Ted Pinson)*, Mark Mitchell *(Mike Daley)*, Andre Chimene *(Tony Greco)*, Damon Merrill *(Babe)*, Barry Coffing *(Ross)*, Tracye Walker *(Gwen)*, Raan Lewis *(Terry)*, Hank Amigo *(Harley)*, Brian Floores *(Max)*, Michelle Watkins *(Faylene)*, Danny D. Daniels.

Although the advertising this film received in its brief theatrical run made it look like just another slasher-in-the-woods splatter film, THE OUTING is actually about a monstrous genie in a lamp and most of the action takes place in a natural history museum. The film opens as a depraved gang of thieves breaks into the house of an old woman. Searching for money stashed in a hidden safe, they murder the confused woman and then smash into a bedroom wall only to find an Aladdin-type lamp hidden there. Before you can say "Alakazam" someone rubs the lamp and bolts of green lightning kill the intruders in a variety of hideous ways. The lamp then turns up at curator Huston's museum. While her father runs some tests on the lamp, Huston's teenage daughter, St. Ivanyi, rummages through some of the old woman's other artifacts, finds a bracelet, and puts it on. Unfortunately, she can't get it off and hides it from her father. The next day, during a school field trip to her father's museum (her teacher, Winters, is Huston's lover), the genie escapes and possesses St. Ivanyi (she who wears the bracelet is the keeper of the lamp, etc.). St. Ivanyi, her boy friend, and two other teenage couples decide to hide in the museum after closing and spend the night. Little do they know that St. Ivanyi's jealous former boy friend and his creepy pal plan to do the same. After the possessed St. Ivanyi sneaks her friends past the security guards, the genie temporarily releases his hold on the teenager and goes off to dismember the guards. One by one the genie kills off the teenagers by ripping them in half, sending deadly cobras up their pant legs, bringing a mummy back to life to strangle them, and the like. Eventually, Huston and Winters figure out something is wrong at the museum and they arrive to find St. Ivanyi the sole survivor. The genie finally reveals himself to be a 20-foot-tall monster and chases the trio around the museum for a while until Huston sacrifices his life so that St. Ivanyi has time to destroy the lamp, thus defeating the genie.

Produced independently by Houston-based HIT films (THE BUDDY HOLLY STORY), THE OUTING brings some badly needed variety to the splatter genre by using an ancient genie to dispatch its cast of nubile young teenagers instead of employing the usual knife-wielding psycho. The film also earns some bonus points for setting the action inside a dark natural history museum, and director Daley makes fairly good use of the creepy location. Producer/scriptwriter Chaney boasts a bizarre life history, including a stint as a professional magician and ventriloquist, which somehow segued into a professorship of behavioral science. Naturally, it was just a hop, skip, and jump from there to being the writer/producer of low-budget exploitation films. Reportedly, at one point the film had a lengthy prolog set in the 1800s which showed how the lamp traveled from its native Iraq to Houston, but no such scenes exist in the final cut. The special effects in THE OUTING are unremarkable, with the 20-foot-tall genie (actually only eight feet tall) looking very inanimate as it is rolled around the set while a cloud of liquid nitrogen gas rising from below hides the crew operating it. THE OUTING (which cost $3 million) received a perfunctory theatrical release and will no doubt do most of its business on home video. *(Graphic violence, gore effects, nudity, sexual situations, profanity.)*

p, Warren Chaney; d, Tom Daley; w, Warren Chaney; ph, Herbert Raditschnig; m, Joel Rosenbaum; ed, Claudio Cutry; prod d, Robert Burns; spec eff, Frank Inez, Martin Becker, Reel EFX, Inc.

Horror (PR:O MPAA:R)

OUTRAGEOUS FORTUNE** (1987) 100m Interscope-Touchstone/BV c

Shelley Long *(Lauren Ames)*, Bette Midler *(Sandy Brozinsky)*, Peter Coyote *(Michael)*, Robert Prosky *(Stanislov Korzenowski)*, John Schuck *(Atkins)*, George Carlin *(Frank)*, Anthony Heald *(Weldon)*, Ji-Tu Cumbuka *(Cab Driver)*, Florence Stanley *(Ticket Agent)*, Jerry Zaks *(Tobacco Clerk)*, John Di Santi *(Police Lieutenant)*, Diana Bellamy *(Madam)*, Gary Morgan *(Panansky)*, Chris McDonald *(George)*, Tony Epper *(Russell)*, Bill Hart *(Boyd)*, Sally R. Brown *(Actress)*, Carol Ann Susi *(Receptionist)*, R.G. Clayton *(Coroner)*, Donald Ambabo *(Helicopter Pilot)*, Paul Brooks *(Airport Attendant)*, Barbara De Kins *(Airport Woman)*, Thomas Dillon *(Security Officer Brown)*, Sandra Eng *(Newswoman)*, Roger Engstrom *(Airport Husband)*, Neil Hunt *(Fencing Teacher)*, Coral Kassel *(Meter Maid)*, Tom Lillard *(Vasily)*, James McIntire *(Bartender)*, Joan McMurtrey *(Fencer #2)*, Greg Mace *(Policeman)*, Bill Marcus *(Dispatcher)*, Phil Mead *(Airport Security Guard)*, J. Clell Miller *(Oil Rig Driver)*, Lonna Montrose *(Airport Patron)*, Bob O'Connell *(Gate Attendant)*, Steven Rotblatt *(Eddie)*, Johnny Sanchez *(Puerto Rican Kid)*, Pat Santino *(Secuity Guard)*, Ade Small *(Ballet Teacher)*, Bunny Summers *(Costume Lady)*, Anna Marie Wieder *(Ruby, Hooker)*, Eyan Williams *(Black Girl Dancer)*, J.W. Smith, Robert Pastorelli *(Dealers)*, Jose G. Garcia, Barney Garcia, James Espinoza *(Pick-Up Truck Riders)*, Mike Henry, Ebbe Roe Smith *(Russians)*, Debra A. Deliso *(Ballet Double for Lauren)*, Tammy Manville *(Ballet Dancer for Lauren)*.

The plot here has been played out hundreds of times in other films and often better. For the record, it concerns two women in love with the same man and their increasing perils as they attempt to best each other in capturing the male. Midler and Long are both acting students in love with the perfect teacher, Coyote. They vie with each other for his sideways attentions, employing all the catty and petty devices that are supposed to pass for comedy. Midler plays off her image of manic schlock artist, bragging about her film appearances in such stellar productions as NINJA VIXENS and Long, really doing a reprise of her role in the TV series "Cheers," is a Yale graduate with intellectual pretensions. Coyote is their ideal male, considerate, understanding, endowed with intelligence and wit. But the battle for his attentions evaporates when the ladies learn their dreamboat has simply vanished and they embark upon a quest to find him. They travel from New York to New Mexico where they become involved in a complicated KGB plot to destroy spy Coyote and are menaced by Russian agents. The usual car chases and near misses abound and the climax sees Long leaping from one precarious butte to another in a wild chase.

The film is mostly one long cliche borrowed from comedy spy plots and Long is wholly ineffective while Midler provides most of the laughs, but these come in bits and pieces. The comedic bits are forced such as the airport scene where the girls try to bluff their way onto an airplane for which they have no reservations. Hiller's pedestrian direction doesn't help much as he jumps from one set-piece scene to another without bothering to cover the gaping holes in a threadbare script. The car chases even seem canned or appear as stock footage borrowed from a bevy of B films. Carlin, essaying a befuddled hippie leftover from the last generation, wandering about the New Mexico desert in search of a guru, gets some genuine laughs, but even this small role wears thin quickly. The story and direction look like a corporate group effort where producers marked off a checklist of formula scenes and let it go at that. Midler tries hard to live up to her raucous reputation in scenes such as one where she offers oral sex in exchange for information, but the effort only comes off as embarrassingly tawdry and gauche. OUTRAGEOUS FORTUNE is an effort on the part of Disney to prove it can distribute adult films but it only proves that it has no real perception of what adult films are all about. *(Profanity, sexual situations.)*

p, Ted Field, Robert W. Cort, Peter V. Herald, Scott Kroopf, Martin Mickelson; d, Arthur Hiller; w, Leslie Dixon; ph, David M. Walsh (Deluxe Color); m, Alan Silvestri; ed, Tom Rolf; prod d, James D. Vance; art d, Sandy Veneziano; set d,

Daniel Maltese, Rick T. Gentz, George DeTitta; cos, Gloris Gresham; spec eff, Dennis Dion; makeup, Del Armstrong, Bob Mills, Tom Lucas; stunts, Glenn R. Wilder.

Comedy **Cas.** **(PR:O MPAA:R)**

OUTSIDERS, THE*** (1987, Taiwan) 90m Dragon's Group/Oriental Films c

Suen Yueh, Su Ming Ming, Sheo Hsin, Lee Tai Ling, Kuang-Kuang, Chau Jan, Chiang Ho-jen, Tien Wei-wei.

An adolescent boy named Ah-Ching is savagely beaten and expelled from his home when his father finds him in bed with another man. The distraught youth takes refuge in a section of a downtown park, commonly known as "the Office," which serves as the gathering place for other abandoned gay men. As Ah-Ching bemoans his fate, he is befriended by an older photographer who invites him to his home, a makeshift photography studio, where he is given food and shelter for the evening. When the boy tries to sleep, he is subjected to an assortment of nightmarish recollections of his family life. In the dream, he witnesses the seductive relationship between his mother and his younger brother, while he is placed in the position of an enslaved outsider, forced to perform the household chores. He then watches his father pummel his mother after she flirts with a young man. His mother then disappears, and Ah-Ching is uncertain whether she has chosen to abandon the family or has been driven away by his father. When he awakens, his host invites him to turn his temporary refuge into a permanent home. Ah-Ching accepts, thankful for the kindness shown by the photographer and his landlady. Ah-Ching then becomes romantically involved with the legendary Dragon, who disappeared some years earlier after reputedly killing his lover during the heat of passion. As this romance develops, his nightmares intensify and he is forced to watch as his father guns down his mother when she has an affair with her younger son. Later, Ah-Ching finds his aged mother performing in a burlesque show and making preparations for her own death. When Ah-Ching reveals that his brother died in his arms of pneumonia many years earlier, she hysterically accuses him of killing her beloved son and attempts to strangle him in an emotional rage. After spending a memorable evening with Dragon, Ah-Ching learns that his mother has died. He is given an urn filled with her ashes and instructions to return them to his father's house, as she wants to be buried next to her son. His father is enraged by the request and shatters the urn on the living room floor. Ah-Ching's father later attempts to visit him at his present home, but leaves in disgust. When Ah-Ching's surrogate mother, the landlady, unexpectedly passes away, he decides to return home and attempt a reconciliation with his father.

Taiwanese director Yu K'an-p'ing's layered adaptation of the novel by the best-selling gay author Pai Hsien-jung (Kenneth Pai) is the story of a homosexual outsider who exists on the periphery of love. Yu presents his tale from the perspective of an adolescent who recalls unhappy events from his childhood and attempts to understand the deterioration of his family. Throughout his childhood, Ah-Ching has been an observer, watching as the members of his family experience the joys and the pains of familial belonging. He assumes the futile responsibility of keeping his self-destructive family together, as no one else has either the strength or the inclination to do so. But this does not earn him the acceptance he craves, and the members of the family begin to disappear despite his attempts to hold them together. The expulsion by his father is the final act in an endless series of family debacles that convinces him he is a failure. As the film progresses, it becomes apparent that love is an ephemeral state that brings only temporary solace from loneliness. When Ah-Ching finally leaves the safety of the photographer's home, he takes his first step toward controlling his own life. *(Nudity, sexual situations, adult situations.)*

p, Hu Chi-chung, Wu Gon, Lin Lang; d, Yu K'an-p'ing; w, Suen Jeung Gwo (based on the novel by Kenneth Pai [Pai Hsien-jung]); ph, Heh Yong Jeng; ed, Laiw Ching Song.

Drama **(PR:O MPAA:NR)**

OUTTAKES† (1987) 71m Sell Pictures/Marketechnics c

Forrest Tucker, Bobbi Wexler, Joleen Lutz, Curt Colbert, Marilyn Abrams, Warren Davis, Coleen Downey, Jack M. Sell.

An X-rated film starring Forrest Tucker is almost too much to fathom, which is perhaps why OUTTAKES surrendered its MPAA "X" rating and was released, instead, as "unrated." Citing THE GROOVE TUBE and KENTUCKY FRIED MOVIE as its influences, OUTTAKES is a collection of comic skits, hosted by Tucker. The film is "guaranteed to offend everyone" and starts by poking fun at television news anchors, Phil Donahue, and Santa Claus. Producer Jack M. Sell manages to appear on-screen in a few skits—somehow finding time to show up in front of the camera in between his multiple duties as director/writer/cameraman/editor/singer/songwriter. Tucker's scenes were shot in 1983, the film was finished in 1985, and Marketechnics gave the film a brief theatrical release in 1987.

p, Jack M. Sell, Adrianne Richmond; d, Jack M. Sell; w, Jack M. Sell, Adrianne Richmond, Jim Fay; ph, Ron Bell, Jack M. Sell; m, Jack M. Sell, Rich Daniels, Chris Lay; ed, Jack M. Sell; art d, Marianne Heidecke.

Comedy **Cas.** **(PR:NR MPAA:X)**

OVER GRENSEN (SEE: FELDMANN CASE, THE, 1987, Nor.)

OVER THE TOP* (1987) 93m Cannon Group-Golan-Globus/WB c

Sylvester Stallone *(Lincoln Hawk)*, Robert Loggia *(Jason Cutler)*, Susan Blakely *(Christina Hawk)*, Rick Zumwalt *(Bob "Bull" Hurley)*, David Mendenhall *(Michael Cutler)*, Chris McCarty *(Tim Salanger)*, Terry Funk *(Ruker)*, Bob Beattie *(Announcer)*, Alan Graf *(Collins)*, Magic Schwarz *(Smasher)*, Bruce Way *(Grizzly)*, Jimmy Keegan *("Big Boy"/Richie)*, John Braden *(Col. Davis)*, Tony Munafo *(Tony)*, Randy Raney *(Mad Dog Madison)*, Paul Sullivan *(Carl Adams)*, Jack Wright *(Big Bill Larson)*, Sam Scarber *(Bosco)*, Richie Giachetti *(Landis)*, Michael Fox *(Jim Olson)*, Ross St. Phillip *(McBroom)*, Seth Mitchell *(First Policeman)*, Dale Benson *(Salesman)*, Joe Kiel *(Taxi Driver)*, Dean Abston *(Turnkey)*, Flo Gerrish *(Martha the Waitress)*, David Van Gorder *(Second Boy)*, Reggie Bennett *(Female Arm Wrestler)*, Joshua Lee Patton *(Arm Wrestler)*, James Mendenhall *(Minister)*, Danny Capri *(Third Boy)*, Gregory Braendel *(Limo Driver)*, Sly Ali Smith *(Red Cap)*, Rose Dursey *(Hospital Clerk)*, Marion Mickens II *(Officer of the Day)*, Dave Patton *(Trainer)*, Alexa Lambert *(Cocktail Waitress)*, Ronnie Rondell, Jr. *(Guard)*, James H. Shana *(Officer)*, Terry Burns, William Nichols Buck *(Doctors)*, Bob Eazor, Ed Levitt, Andrew Rhodes, Bob Rogers *(Referees)*, Norman Howell, Rex Pierson *(Men)*.

Stallone is a grunting truck driver who picks up his young son, Mendenhall, at a military academy where he is a snobby cadet. Mendenhall's mother, Blakely, has allowed the school to release her son to Stallone so that the boy can get to know his father on the three-day trip to California where she is about to undergo serious surgery. This infuriates wealthy Loggia, the boy's grandfather, who hates Stallone and who orders his flunkies to find the boy on the road. Meanwhile, Stallone stops with Mendenhall to have lunch in a murky bar and he is immediately challenged by a towering plug-ugly to an arm wrestling match for $1,000, shouting and goading Stallone, who appears reluctant, to match his strength against his own. Stallone accepts and beats the braggart, wins the $1,000, and is challenged by bull-necked, bald-headed Zumwalt, but tells the behemoth he will have to wait for the scheduled matches in Las Vegas. While heading west Stallone and Mendenhall exercise and train for the upcoming matches. Stallone actually does weight pull-ups in his truck while driving, yanking on a pulley rigged in his cab with one hand while controlling the wheel with the other. Mendenhall suggests that Stallone is an intellectual pygmy and Stallone shows how wrong the boy is by insisting that the boy drive the big truck. Mendenhall struggles at the wheel and manages to move the semi down the road, realizing the intellectual joy of barreling a truck along the highway. What exactly Stallone proves here and in subsequent tests, pitting his son against other boys in arm-wrestling matches, is that unless you have the strength to beat others you don't count for much. Stallone gives Mendenhall a lot of mumbo-jumbo like "you beat yourself" and "the world meets nobody half way." He tells his son to go back to a bigger boy who has just beaten him and take him. He does, reporting by phone to his mother that he drove the truck, and beat the other boy in an arm-wrestling match. Blakely tells Stallone on the phone that "whatever happens, I want you to stay with him," adding that Loggia, who has spoiled the boy, is too set in his ways to change. At that moment Loggia's goons arrive and kidnap Mendenhall, but Stallone overcomes two of the men and then follows in his truck overtaking and crashing into a fast-moving pickup to regain his uninjured boy. When Stallone and Mendenhall get to California they find that Blakely has died. Loggia moves to take custody of the boy but Stallone, intent on enforcing Blakely's last wishes, intends to keep him and raise him like a Stallone. Loggia takes the boy and Stallone goes to Loggia's estate where strong-arm goons tell him to get his truck off the property. He drives his truck through the gates, smashing priceless fountains, statuary, and Cadillacs, plowing through the front door of Loggia's mansion, where he demands that Loggia turn Mendenhall over to him. Police arrive and drag Stallone away while his son sobs. Later Mendenhall visits Stallone and tells him he has a home with his grandfather and that he can't go with him. Charges are dropped against Stallone and he leaves, working the weight-pulley in his cab as he drives to Las Vegas for the big match with the bald-headed Zumwalt. He sells his truck for $7,000, but removes the silver figure of the hawk (that's his name) from the hood to keep. Meanwhile, Mendenhall rifles through his grandfather's closet and finds all of Stallone's touching letters, which Loggia kept from the boy over the years. He decides to join his father. In Las Vegas, Stallone learns that the odds against him are 20 to 1 and he bets the $7,000 on himself, naturally. Mendenhall takes off in the family pickup truck, while his father bests one muscle-bound challenger after another in the championship arm-wrestling contests. Loggia by then is in pursuit, flying to Vegas in his private jet. Loggia offers Stallone the best truck ever built and a check for $500,000 to get out of his and his grandson's life. Stallone refuses, vowing to get his son back. Mendenhall arrives in Vegas to see Stallone win several matches and goes to him backstage to tell him he wants to be with him, encouraging him to win the big one against Zumwalt. In a grunting, screeching, sweating seesaw battle, Stallone finally brings down the arm of the giant, beating Zumwalt and becoming the world champion. He lifts up Mendenhall who holds the world championship cup and Loggia looks on, realizing that Mendenhall belongs with his father. Father and son take to the road in a brand new truck, forming a company, "Hawk & Son."

This sorry, tear-jerking mess is a rip-off of Stallone's own "Rocky" films, substituting the arm-wrestling table for the boxing ring. It's a disgrace to motherless children, truck drivers and arm-wrestlers around the world. The whole sorry plot is predictable within the first ten minutes of the film and Stallone, who received $12 million for this terrible project, offers little in the way of drama. Mendenhall is engaging and Loggia tries hard to be a distasteful heavy, but his heart's not in it. There are blatant ads for every product from Alka Seltzer to Valvoline in this film, emblazoned on shirts worn by the contestants in the Las Vegas meets. This is just another miserable outing from Cannon which specializes in cheap action films that are poorly directed and scripted. Useless. Songs include these Giorgio Moroder, Tom Whitlock numbers "In This Country" (performed by Eddie Money), "Gypsy Soul" (performed by Asia), "All I Need is You," "I Will Be Strong" (performed by Big Trouble), "Meet Me Half Way" (performed by Kenny Loggins), "Mind Over Matter," "Take It Higher" (performed by Larry Greene), "Winner Takes All" (performed by Sammy Hagar) and "Bad Night" (Frank Stallone, Peter H. Schless, performed by Frank Stallone), "The Fight" (Giorgio Moroder, performed by Moroder). *(Harsh language, violence.)*

p, Menahem Golan, Yoram Globus; d, Menahem Golan; w, Stirling Silliphant, Sylvester Stallone (based on a story by Gary Conway, David C. Engelbach); ph, David Gurfinkel (Panavision, Metrocolor); m, Giorgio Moroder; ed, Don Zimmerman, James Symons; prod d, James Schoppe; md, Paula Erickson; art d, William Skinner; set d, Roland E. Hill, Jr., Ross Gallichotte; m/l, Giorgio Moroder, Tom Whitlock, Frank Stallone, Peter H. Schless; spec eff, Dennis Peterson; cos, Tom Bronson; makeup, Robert J. Mills, Christina Smith; stunts, Gary McLarty; arm wrestling tech adv, Marvin Cohen.

Drama/Action Cas. (PR:C MPAA:PG)

OVERBOARD** (1987) 112m MGM/MGM-UA c

Goldie Hawn *(Joanna Stayton/"Annie Proffitt")*, Kurt Russell *(Dean Proffitt, Carpenter)*, Edward Herrmann *(Grant Stayton III)*, Katherine Helmond *(Edith Mintz, Joanna's Mother)*, Michael Hagerty *(Billy Pratt)*, Roddy McDowall *(Andrew, Butler)*, Jared Rushton *(Charlie Proffitt)*, Jeffrey Wiseman *(Joey Proffitt)*, Brian Price *(Travis Proffitt)*, Jamie Wild *(Greg Proffitt, Charlie's Twin Brother)*, Frank Campanella *(Capt. Karl)*, Harvey Alan Miller *(Dr. Norman Korman)*, Frank Buxton *(Wilbur Budd, TV Broadcaster)*, Carol Williard *(Rose Budd)*, Hector Elizondo *(LeHondro Tunatti, Garbage Scow Captain)*, Doris Hess *(Adele Burbridge)*, Ed Cree *(Thud Gittman)*, Mona Lyden *(Gertie)*, Lucinda Crosby *(Tess)*, Bing Russell *(Sheriff Earl)*, Richard Stahl *(Hospital Psychiatrist)*, Ray Combs *(Cop at Hospital)*, Marvin Braverman *(Doctor at Hospital)*, Israel Juarbe *(Engine Room Crewman)*, Paul Fonteyn *(Chef Paul)*, Antonio Martinez Garcia *(Chef Antonio)*, Robert Goldman *(Crew Helmsman)*, Keith Syphers, Robert Meadows *(Crew)*, Lisa Hunter, Erin Grant, Lisa Beth Ross, Liz Stewart, Laura Fabian, Julie Paris *(Grant's Girlfriends)*, Paul Tinder *(Coast Guard Captain)*, Scott Marshall *(Coast Guard Spotter Lucas)*, Bill Applebaum *(Coast Guard Friend)*, Don Thompson *(Coast Guard Guy)*, The Wright Brothers Band: Tim Wright, Tom Wright, John McDowell, Steven Walker.

Offscreen companions Goldie Hawn and Kurt Russell are paired in this screwball comedy by the director of NOTHING IN COMMON, Garry Marshall. Hawn is the pampered, ever-demanding wife of upper-crust twit Herrmann. The luxurious yacht they call home docks for repairs in Elk Cove, Oregon, and Hawn summons local carpenter Russell to rebuild her closet. She is revolted by his earthiness; he finds her regal disdain unbearable. When Russell builds the closet of oak rather than cedar, Hawn not only refuses to pay, but pushes the carpenter overboard. That night, back at sea, Hawn falls overboard herself, and is rescued by a garbage scow and returned to Elk Cove. However, she remembers nothing of her privileged past. Herrmann spots her photo on TV, but refuses to claim her at the hospital. Russell, bent on revenge, goes to the hospital and identifies Hawn as his wife (Russell's real spouse has been dead for several years). He takes her to the rundown house he shares with his four undisciplined sons—Rushton, Wiseman, Price, and Wild. The boys willingly go along with the deception. Still curious and confused about her past, Hawn becomes a virtual slave, cooking, cleaning, and caring for the kids. At first her ineptitude, inexperience, and the boys work against her, but eventually she masters the art of domestic engineering. She also wins the love of *her sons*, who come to think of her as their mother and refuse to acknowledge her as anything but that when Russell tries to tell her the truth. Russell and buddy Hagerty have their hearts set on securing the financing for a miniature golf course, and Hawn both provides them with a catchy theme—"Wonders of the World"—and helps design the course. Just as Russell and Hawn are falling for each other and the future looks bright, Herrmann returns to retrieve Hawn, and his presence jogs her memory. She is aghast at Russell's deception and rejoins Herrmann on the yacht, though she is a changed person, respectful and apologetic to the help she has abused for so many years. When she learns that Herrmann could have rescued her from the hospital and didn't, Hawn demands that the yacht head back to Elk Cove. From the other direction, Russell and the boys speed in pursuit of her on a Coast Guard cutter. The vessels are about to meet when an urgent call diverts the Coast Guard craft. Like the star-crossed lovers of local lore, Russell and Hawn leap into the water and swim to each other. What's more, the money has been Hawn's and not Herrmann's all along.

OVERBOARD aspires to be a wacky, heart-warming screwball comedy, but it

is neither memorable nor particularly funny. The amnesia that serves as the cornerstone of the plot long ago became a staple of TV soap operas and the idea of a rich person being given a lesson in humanity as result of a downward mobility is also old hat. There is nothing wrong with using proven formulas, but for them to work they need inspired treatment. OVERBOARD holds no real surprises. Hawn and Russell have both shown themselves capable of bringing this kind of light comedy to life in the past, but even their likable screen presences aren't enough to enliven this one. Much of the film's humor is derived from Hawn's awkward attempts at domesticity. The vacuum cleaner, chain saw, and washing machine all take on lives of their own, and though Hawn is appropriately harried, these bits have been done before—and better. In the absence of witty repartee—the bread and butter of the 1930s screwball comedies—screenwriter Leslie Dixon (OUTRAGEOUS FORTUNE) serves up one-liners and their visual equivalents with the regularity of a tennis trainer. Some of them connect, most of them don't, many are simply stupid. In marked contrast with director Marshall's last two films—NOTHING IN COMMON and THE FLAMINGO KID—the characters in OVERBOARD are broadly drawn. Those films were built on closely observed moments and subtle shadings of character. OVERBOARD is much more obvious. The film is also a love story not just between Russell and Hawn, but between Hawn and the boys. As such it is well-intentioned testimony to the importance of the family. Although more successful in this realm it still comes on too strong. If Marshall's intention was to literally go overboard, he has succeeded but that doesn't make the film funny or touching.

Neither Russell nor Hawn, working together for the second time (both were in SWINGSHIFT), give memorable performances. Both create amiable characters, but fail to bring the necessary depth to the portrayals. Hawn reputedly saw this role as a transition between the goofy but lovable types she's played in the past and more serious parts. She might have done better waiting for another script. Some of the film's best laughs are provided by the smallest roles. Buxton is funny as the newsman at KRAB-TV, the family station run by his family, and Hector Elizondo flashes humorously across the screen as the garbage scow captain. With the exception of Hagerty, who does a nice job as Russell's dependable buddy, the other supporting performances are unexceptional. Herrmann plays his ineffectual blue blood as a cartoon character, and Helmond, as Hawn's mother, and McDowell, who plays a manservant (as well as acting as the film's executive producer) are given next to nothing to do. OVERBOARD was shot along the Mendocino Coast of Northern California. *(Sexual situations, profanity.)*

p, Alexandra Rose, Anthea Sylbert; d, Garry Marshall; w, Leslie Dixon; ph, John A. Alonzo (Technicolor); m, Alan Silvestri; ed, Dov Hoenig, Sonny Baskin; art d, James Shanahan, Jim Dultz; set d, Judy Cammer, Ron Yates, William James Teegarden; cos, Wayne Finkelman; spec eff, Alan E. Lorimer; m/l, Harvey Miller; stunts, Hal Burton; makeup, Robert J. Mills, E. Thomas Case.

Comedy (PR:C MPAA:PG)

OVERKILL zero (1987) 81m United Independent/Movie Factory-Manson c

Steve Rally *(Mickey Delano)*, John Nishio *(Akashi)*, Laura Burkett *(Jamie)*, Allen Wisch *(Collins)*, Antonio Caprio *(Chief of Police)*, Roy Summersett *(Steiner)*, Shiro Tomita *(Nagumo, Sr.)*, Chris Tashima *(Nagumo, Jr.)*, Bruce Yamone *(Toguchi)*, Bill Ghent *(Osaki)*, Pylah Chan *(Tomoko Osaki)*, Craig Watanabe *(Tanaki)*, Tony Livingstone *(Michelle)*, Diana Tanaki *(Hayaki's Mother)*, Yong Bhang *(Hayaki's Father)*, Michelle Bauer *(Neighbor)*, Noam Bon *(Customer)*, Ben Misagawa *(Doctor)*, Tish Shiroto *(Priest)*, Ginsey Moss *(Girl)*, Sebastian Moore *(Guy)*, Judy Molona *(Girl Killer)*, James Ogawa *(Yakuza Boss)*, Ken Shimizu, Chris Peredes, Andy Wong, Raven Hurt, Steve Reid, Frank Disario, Leo Lee, Tran Ngoc *(Yakuza Hitmen)*, Morikan Kaikure, Marie Koksui, Kathleena Marie, Joyce Lew, Peggy Lang, Sunny Lee *(Yakuza Women)*, Robert Harden, Randy Banks, Jim Colandrelli, Harvey Scott, Sam Hammer, Sid Stern, Mac Kearney, Ben Kasaki, Frank Kennedy, Willie Burton, Don Shannon *(Detectives)*, Galen Yung, Sam Hsu, Joe Wang, Wah Toe Kim, Paul Avaki, Glen Ichikawa *(Yakuza Members)*, Ellwood Glassber, Jim Bodanza *(Customs Officers)*, Ken Nagayama *(Japanese Sword Fighter)*.

Right below the title on the artwork that accompanies this straight-to-video release, it says: " . . . the body count is overwhelming." While OVERKILL is bloody, the body count is not overwhelming and neither is the film. It tells the story of a Los Angeles policeman, Rally, who is convinced that Japanese gangsters, the *Yakuza*, are moving into the area. He is constantly stymied by his superiors and his partner is killed. Rally questions the son of a restaurant owner murdered for refusing to pay protection money. In the process he meets the boy's uncle, Nishio, a Tokyo policeman who knows how to deal with the *Yakuza* (by carving up their foreheads or slicing off their ears, for example). Rally and Nishio team up and soon the *Yakuza* are very concerned. The pair witness a meeting between the *Yakuza* and the crooked police commissioner, but when they try to arrest the participants, a shoot-out ensues in which Nishio is killed. Rally kills the police commissioner, then quits the force to take care of Nishio's paralyzed nephew and to become a sushi chef. The *Yakuzas* make a few more attempts on his life before offering to call it quits. The film ends with Rally taking the paralyzed boy horseback riding. A miserable, boring, badly made exploitation effort by one-time Fassbinder protege Ulli Lommel. There is nothing of interest here for anyone. The action scenes are flat, and the acting flatter. The wise will stay away. Needless to say, this film went straight to video. *(Violence.)*

p&d, Ulli Lommel; w, Ulli Lommel, David Scott Kroes; ph, James Takashi; m, Bill Roebuck; ed, Ron Norman; md, Bill Roebuck; prod d, Manuel Riva; set d, Bob McElvin; cos, Vickie Wolker; stunts, Frank Disanto.

Crime **Cas.** **(PR:O MPAA:NR)**

PQ

P.I. PRIVATE INVESTIGATIONS† (1987) 91m MGM-Polygram/MGM-UA c

Clayton Rohner *(Joey Bradley, Architect)*, Ray Sharkey *(Ryan)*, Paul LeMat *(Detective Wexler)*, Talia Balsam *(Jenny Fox)*, Phil Morris *(Eddie Gordon)*, Martin Balsam *(Cliff Dowling)*, Anthony Zerbe *(Charles Bradley, Joey's Father and Newspaper Editor)*, Robert Ito *(Kim)*, Vernon Wells *(Detective North)*, Anthony Geary *(Larry)*, Justin Lord *(Howard White)*, Richard Cummings, Jr. *(Hollister)*, Desiree Boschetti *(Denise)*, Andy Romano *(Mr. Watson)*, Sydney Walsh *(Janet)*, Jon St. Elwood *(Gil)*, Rex Ryon *(Lou)*, Richard Herkert *(Kim's Driver)*, Frank Gargani *(Wire Tapper)*, Big Yank *(Clay)*, Nigel Dick *(Photographer)*, Dennis Phung *(Cafe Owner)*, Sharonlee McLean *(Cafe Waitress)*, Michelle Seipp *(Woman in Restaurant), Stan Yale (Bum)*, Hugh Slate *(Himself)*, Robert Torti, Jean Glaude *(Burglars)*, Del Zamora, Luis Manuel *("Car Thieves")*.

With a California setting, a hard-driving rock-and-roll soundtrack, and slick camerawork, P.I. PRIVATE INVESTIGATIONS tells the usual tale of police corruption, underworld criminals, a crusading newspaper editor, and an innocent victim who gets entangled in this web of vice. Rohner is an architect in his mid-twenties who gets drawn into the Los Angeles underworld when his father, newspaper man Zerbe, prepares to go public with an all-revealing story on the connection between the police and drug dealing. A detective, Sharkey, is hired to keep a watchful eye over Rohner, but instead the private eye tries to kill the architect. Rohner is forced to go on the run, hiding out in L.A. and, by chance, meeting the pretty Talia Balsam, who offers Rohner a place to stay. Balsam and Rohner inevitably become lovers and together learn that Zerbe and his informant Ito have been discovered by the underworld. A shootout at an abandoned western movie set leaves Sharkey dead, Zerbe's investigations proving effective, and Balsam and Rohner as two lovers determined to stay together. The first feature outing for British writer/director Dick, who attracted some attention by directing the video for Band Aid's Ethiopian relief song "Do They Know It's Christmas Time?" The soundtrack includes the songs "Wanted Dead or Alive" (Bon Jovi, R. Sambora, performed by Bon Jovi); "Something About You" (M. Lindup, P. Gould, M. King, R. Gould, W. Badarou, performed by Level 42); "Hold the Heart" (S. Adamson, performed by Big Country); "Layla" (Eric Clapton, J. Gordon, performed by Derek and the Dominoes); "River of People" (J. Grant, performed by Love and Money); "City of Shadows" (D.W. Charles, P. Glenister, performed by Lone Prey); "Walk the Dinosaur" (Don Was, David Was, performed by Was (Not Was)); "The Loving of a Stranger" (Paul Brady, performed by Brady); "True Confessions" (Jolley, Swain, Fahey, Woodward, Dallin; performed by Bananarama); "Long White Car" (McElbone, Skinner, Travers, performed by Hipsway); "Ghost Town" (Murray Munro, performed by Munro); "Mother's Talk" (R. Orzabal, Stanley, performed by Tears For Fears).

p, Steven Golin, Sigurjon Sighvatsson; d, Nigel Dick; w, John Dahl, David Warfield (based on a story by Nigel Dick); ph, David Bridges, Bryan Duggan; m, Murray Munro; ed, Scott Chestnut; prod d, Piers Plowden; art d, Nick Rafter; set d, Deborah Evans; cos, Charmin Espinoza; m/l, M. Lindup, P. Gould, M. King, R. Gould, W. Badarou, S. Adamson, Bon Jovi, R. Sambora, Eric Clapton, J. Gordon, J. Grant, D.W. Charles, P. Glenister, A. Murray, Nigel Dick, Ron Was, David Was, Paul Brady, Jolley, Swain, Fahey, Woodward, Dallin, McElbone, Skinner, Travers, Murray Munro, R. Orzabal, Stanley; spec eff, John Eggett; makeup, Vilborg Aradottir; stunts, Alan Oliney.

Action/Crime **(PR:NR MPAA:R)**

P.K. & THE KID½** (1987) 90m Sunn Classics/Lorimar Home Video c

Paul LeMat *(William "Kid" Kane)*, Molly Ringwald *(Paula Kathleen "P.K" Bayette)*, Alex Rocco *(Les)*, Charles Hallahan *(Bazooka)*, John Disanti *(Benny)*, Fionnula Flanagan *(Flo)*, Bert Remsen *(Al)*, Leigh Hamilton *(Louise)*, John Madden, John Matuszak *(Themselves)*, Esther Rolle *(Mim)*, Charlene *(Dolly)*, Benny Marino *(City Market Rabble Rouser)*, Robert Wentz *(Billy)*, George Fisher *(Scratch)*, Gene Le Bell *(Big Mac)*, Mike Adams *(Ernie)*, Jimmy Payne *(Announcer)*, Jim Lefebvre *(Ritter)*, Joe Bellman *(Registrar)*, Ray Goman *(Doctor)*, Anne H. Bradley *(Cafe Waitress)*, Bud Smith *(Gas Station Attendant)*, Jerry Gatlin *(Andy)*, Fred Lerner *(Hal)*, Bob Eggenweiler *(Paymaster)*, Kenneth R. Mills *(Forklift Driver)*, Cheryl Watts *(Cocktail Waitress)*, Mimi Wickliff *(Gas Station Customer)*, John Favalor *(Fish Cutter)*, Gina Lombardo *(Calamari Salesgirl)*, Lynn Lombardo *(Bookkeeper)*, Bill Ackridge, Gary Pettinger, Denny Delk *(Deputies)*, Sally Train, Sue Murphy *(Waitresses)*, Bob Howell, Rudy Ortega, Joseph L. Brandt, Mark Payne *(Referees)*, J. Zachariah Rainbow *(Mime)*, Jeanette Blake *(P.A. Operator)*, Jim Bradley *(Ambulance Attendant)*, Ned Dowd *(Bartender)*, Jim Zewe *(Watermelon Thrower)*, Dick Bright *(Watermelon Commentator)*, Nancy Cone, Perry Huseman, John Perryman, Tracey Steele, Denis Stewart *(Watermelon Contestants)*, Kelly Kosik, James Payne, Mark Payne, Rhondell Rasmus, Albert Scott, Terry E. Silva, Brett William Stine, Maureen M. Thornburg, Robert N. Thornburg *(Wrist Wrestlers)*.

Before Molly Ringwald made a name for herself in 1984's teen hit SIXTEEN CANDLES, she had a few lesser-known roles. She debuted in Paul Mazursky's 1982 picture, THE TEMPEST, next appeared in a television film entitled "Packin It In," and, in 1983, had a part in the 3D sci-fi film SPACEHUNTER: ADVENTURES IN THE FORBIDDEN ZONE. She also starred opposite Paul LeMat in P.K. & THE KID, a 1982 film which was shelved until surfacing this year on videocassette. Starring as the "P.K." of the title, Ringwald is a likable

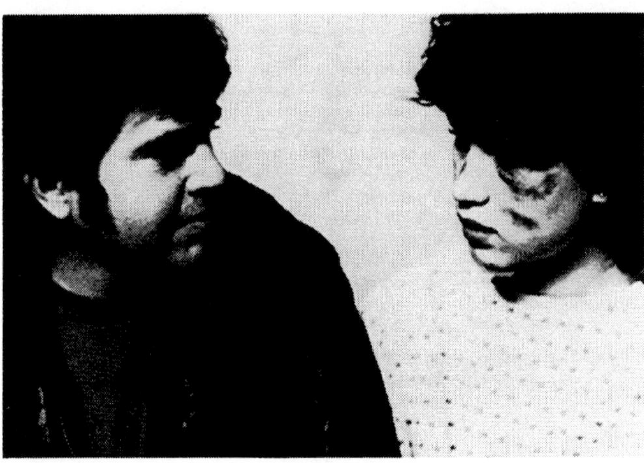

15-year-old from Boulder, Colorado, who runs away from home because her stepfather, Rocco, is a cruel, sadistic man who is constantly pawing her. She meets up with LeMat (the other half of the title), a pickup-driving nobody who dreams of winning a national arm-wrestling contest and finally becoming a somebody. The two travel together, meeting a variety of characters along the way, including Disanti, LeMat's best friend, and Rolle, the black woman who cared for him as a young boy. Before long LeMat has a run-in with Hallahan, the reigning arm-wrestling champion, who tries to intimidate LeMat by sending his thugs after Disanti. The greatest obstacle that the pair must face is Rocco, who is determined to get Ringwald back home. He is always one step behind them and, on the day of the championship, he gets his stepdaughter back by having LeMat hauled off to jail for contributing to the delinquency of a minor. Rocco then drags Ringwald back to his car, stuffs her into the trunk, and drives her down a deserted back road intent on raping her. Ringwald fights back, escapes, enlists the aid of Rolle, and secures LeMat's release. At the championship, LeMat faces rival Hallahan and, after an arduous match, wins the trophy. Rocco, who is still lurking about, later drags Ringwald off to a deserted storehouse. He savagely beats her, but is stopped by LeMat. After a short hospital stay, Ringwald thanks LeMat for his friendship and decides to return to her mother, now that Rocco is behind bars.

P.K. & THE KID offers a fairly standard plot, stereotypical characters, and a colorful arm-wrestling background—all of which add up to average entertainment. What makes the film watchable is the chemistry between LeMat and Ringwald. While neither of their performances is earth-shattering, they both come across as average, everyday people. LeMat, who is bearded through much of the early going, falls somewhere between tough and awkward, and is visibly intimidated by the 15-year-old at his side. Ringwald, here displaying early signs of the star presence later honed by director John Hughes, is thoroughly believable as a young runaway who learns a thing or two about trust and friendship. While the script is clumsy at times, the film is well-intentioned enough to overcome this handicap. A special mention has to go to Rocco (best remembered as Las Vegas kingpin Moe Green in THE GODFATHER), who is especially creepy as Ringwald's vile stepfather. Although there is some rough language and some very brief nudity, P.K. & THE KID is still probably a good choice for young viewers because, unlike so many films today, it takes a positive moral stance. Includes the songs "So Afraid to Cry," "Reel Me In" (Michael Manning, performed by The Randolph Scott Band), "Listen to the Lights," "In the Rain" (Clyde Jorgensen, Mark Espy, performed by The Ralph 'N Clyde Band), and "Roughneck Blues" (Jorgensen, Espy, Ronnie Reed, performed by The Ralph 'N Clyde Band). *(Brief nudity, profanity.)*

p, Joe Roth; d, Lou Lombardo; w, Neal Barbera; ph, Ed Koons (CFI color); m, James Horner; ed, Tony Lombardo; prod d, Chet Allen; art d, Bill Cornford; set d, Dian Perryman; makeup, Rocky Frier; cos, Sandy Bates; m/l, Michael Manning, Clyde Jorgensen, Mark Espy, Ronnie Reed.

Drama **Cas.** **(PR:A MPAA:PG-13)**

PA STIGENDE KURS† (1987, Nor.) 96m Floifilm-Norsk Film/KF c (Trans: Rising Stock)

Dab Froland *(Roger)*, Anders Hatlo *(Treasury Agent)*, Mari Maurstad *(Roger's Wife)*, Wenche Foss *(His Mother-in-Law)*, Kjersti Holmen *(His Miami Flirt)*, Arve Opsahl *(Police Chief)*, Kristian Guldbrandsen, Christine Larsen, Sven Wickstrom, Knut M. Hansson, Karl Sundby, Rolf Soder.

This Norwegian satire, based on the novel by Kare Prytz, is the story of a beleaguered nine-to-fiver who suddenly finds himself wealthy beyond his wildest dreams. Froland slaves for an unappreciative boss and is beset with a shrewish wife and a pair of demanding kids. Trying to keep the government from getting its hands on some of his money, Froland buys a few shares of stock in SAS. Suddenly the airline stock skyrockets and he finds himself a rich man. Froland takes some of his newfound wealth and heads for the Caribbean with his mistress. However, misfortune accompanies fortune and bankruptcy looms on the horizon.

p, Stein Roger Bull; d, Bo Hermansson; w, Andreas Markusson, Bo Hermansson (based on a novel by Kare Prytz); ph, Svein Krovel (Eastmancolor); m, Egil

Monn-Iversen; ed, Bo Hermansson; prod d, Sven Wickman; cos, Anne Hamre, Runa Fonne.

Comedy **(PR:NR MPAA:NR)**

PADUREANCA† (1987, Rum.) 125m Film Company 4-Rumaniafilm c (Trans: The Maiden of the Woods)

Victor Rebengiuc, Adrian Pintea, Serban Ionescu, Manuela Harabor, Melania Ursu, Dorel Visan, Nicolae Toma, Mihai Constantin.

Set in Transylvania but vampireless, this romance Romanian-style centers on the 19th Century competition that takes place between the son of a landowner and the son of a servant for the hand of a beautiful young woman, the maiden of the woods of the title. Based on a short story by Ioan Slavici, it unfolds against the backdrop of a cholera epidemic that has forced the landowner's son to leave the city and return home.

d, Nicolae Margineanu; w, Agustin Buzura, Nicolae Margineanu (based on a short story by Ioan Slavici); ph, Doru Mitran; m, Cornel Taranu; ed, Nita Chivulescu; prod d, Magdalena Marasescu; cos, Mioara Trandafira.

Romance **(PR:NR MPAA:NR)**

PAN SAMOCHODZIK I NIESAMOWITY DWOR† (1987, Pol.) Zespoly Filmowe-PROFIL/Film Polski c (Trans: Mister Fancy Car and the Eerie Manor)

Piotr Krukowski, Ludwik Benoit, Slawomira Lozinska, Wieslaw Wojcik.

Kids are responsible for most of the unexplained events in this Polish ghost story. An art expert whose flashy wheels earn him the nickname "Mister Fancy Car" and two of his assistants travel to an ancient manor house to help transform it

into a museum. They are told by one of the locals that the eerie old place is haunted, and, following advice, they hold a seance. But instead of conjuring up any spirits, they are locked up in a room. The art expert escapes through a window and, hopping into his fancy car, trails the car that is carrying the people behind the seance hoax. He learns that the leader of the bunch is an old friend who is now in the antique business and is convinced that he and his cohorts are after the manor house's valuable antiques. Meanwhile back at the house, more mysterious occurrences are taking place, most notably the continual disappearance and reappearance of one of the art expert's assistants. After several more surprises the would-be robbers are foiled and the ghostly goings-on are explained; the only ghosts to be found are local kids in white sheets and the assistant's disappearances were the result of a revolving wall.

d, Janusz Kidawa; w, Zbigniew Nowicki-Nienacki (based on the novels by Zbigniew Nienacki); ph, Henryk Janas; m, Jaroslaw Kukulski; ed, Jaroslaw Ostanowko; art d, Tadeusz Cielewicz.

Children's/Horror **(PR:NR MPAA:NR)**

PANCHAGNI† (1987, India) 140m c (Trans: Five Fires)

Geeta *(Indira)*, Mohanlal *(Rashid)*, Nadia Moidu *(Savitri)*, Tilakan *(Ramettan)*.

Set during the extremist movement in Kerala during the 1960s and '70s, PANCHAGNI follows a young revolutionary, Geeta, as she assassinates an evil landowner and is sentenced to a life term (14 years in India). Released after serving eight years, Geeta arrives home just before the death of her mother. Shunned by her neighbors, Geeta is comforted by Mohanlal, a journalist, and the two grow close. Their romance is shattered, however, when Geeta once again murders one of the villainous gentry and is thrown back in prison to serve another life sentence.

p, G.P. Vijay Kumar, M.G. Gopinath; d, Hariharan; w, M.T. Vasudevan Nair; ph, Shaji; m, Ravi; ed, M.S. Mani; art d, S. Vonnanadu.

Drama **(PR:NR MPAA:NR)**

PANCHVATI† (1987, India/Nepal) 148m Time & Space-Royal Nepal c

Suresh Oberoi, Dipti Naval, Jatin, Anuradha Tarafdar, Nabendu Ghosh.

Indian-Nepalese coproduction that deals with the failure of a cross-caste romance between a wealthy Indian and a Nepalese artist. Already disgusted by her husband's philistine worldview, the artist leaves him when he beats her. She is escorted back to Nepal by her brother-in-law, who instigated the marriage as a result of his own attraction to her, but who is already married. Nonetheless, at a hotel on the way, they make love, resulting in her pregnancy, though he returns to his family.

p, Shobha Doctor, Basu Bhattacharya; d, Basu Bhattacharya; w, Basu Bhattacharya, Kusum Ansal; ph, Rajsh Joshi; m, Sarang Dev; ed, Om Prahash; prod d, Bhaswati Bhattacharya.

Romance **(PR:NR MPAA:NR)**

PANDAVAPURAM† (1987, India) 90m c

Jamila *(Devi)*, Appu *(Jaran)*, James *(Unni)*, Master Deepak *(Son)*.

Abandoned by her husband, school teacher Jamila ventures to the train station every day and waits for his return. The people of her small village are saddened by her odd ritual, until one day a man (Appu) gets off the train claiming to be her lover. Jamila denies his claims, despite the fact that he insists they met in Pandavapuram. Appu persists in following Jamila home and though she is properly chaperoned, the villagers begin vicious gossip about the pair. Eventually the village elder threatens Appu, and after having a nightmare, he decides to leave. But now Jamila magically compels him to stay and forces him to make love to her. The next morning Appu is gone and the neighbors don't remember ever having seen the man. Jamila goes back to the train station and resumes her wait.

p&d, G.S. Panicker; w, Sethu, G.S. Panicker (based on the novel by Sethu); ph, Divakara Menon; m, Mohan; ed, Suresh Babu.

Romance **(PR:NR MPAA:NR)**

PARTY CAMP* (1987) 96m Lightning c

Andrew Ross *(Jerry Riviera)*, Kerry Brennan *(Heather)*, Billy Jacoby *(D.A.)*, Jewel Shepard *(Dyanne)*, Peter Jason *(Sarge)*, Kirk Cribb *(Tad)*, Dean R. Miller *(Cody)*, Corky Pigeon *(Winslow)*, Stacy Baptist *(Kelly)*, Paula Irvine *(Devi)*, Betsy Chasse *(Lisa)*, Jon Pine *(Ned-Man)*, April Wayne *(Nurse Brenda)*, Cherie Franklin *(Mrs. Beadle)*, Troy Shire *(Les)*, Erik Smith *(Paul)*, Kevin Telles *(Ferris)*, Rashad Barzaghi *(Camper)*, Marsha McClelland *(Miss Hollywood)*.

Ross is an idle young man who takes a job as a summer camp counselor after spotting the girl of his dreams in a brochure for the place. Arriving by bus, the laid-back Ross instantly runs afoul of the athletic Cribb and his cabin of "Falcons," the elite of the camp. Ross finds himself leader of the "Squirrels," the lowest cabin on the totem pole. Humiliated repeatedly by the Falcons and the camp administration, Ross instills in the Squirrels a sense of confidence, leading them in a series of retaliatory strikes against the Falcons. Meanwhile Ross has located Brennan, the lifeguard he spotted in the brochure, but is having some difficulty in earning her respect or affection because of what she perceives as his childish behavior. All of this meanders along with no particular place to go until it reaches an arbitrary climax in a big race on skateboards, dirt bikes, four-wheel ATVs, and mountain bicycles in which only the Falcons and Squirrels, and none of the other campers, participate. Of course anybody can figure out who wins, and while Cribb is beside himself with rage, Brennan practically leaps into Ross' arms. At the big dance that night, the rest of the Squirrels get girls too. Idiot fare at its worse, aimed at a sniggering pubescent audience that shouldn't even be able to see it, given the R rating. Ross is an unsympathetic lead whose constant excuse for his mischief is that he just wants to have fun. Everyone else is simply dumb. *(Brief nudity, adult situations, mild profanity.)*

p, Mark Borde; d, Gary Graver; w, Paul L. Brown; ph, Gary Graver (United Color); m, Dennis Dreith; ed, Michael B. Hoggan, Joyce L. Hoggan; set d, Terril Foutz; stunts, Denny Arnold; makeup, Michael Stein.

Comedy **Cas.** **(PR:O MPAA:R)**

PASOS LARGOS (SEE: LONG STRIDER, 1987, Span.)

PEDDLER, THE† (1987, Iran) 95m Farabi c

Zohreh Saramadi, Esmail Sarmadian, Behzad Behzadpour, Faridkashan Fallah, Morteza Zarrabi.

Divided into three sections, this Iranian film probes the lives of those on the lower end of Iran's social spectrum in search of socio-political and philosophical insights. In one episode, a peddler's life is threatened when he gets involved with a bunch of smugglers who come to believe that he has double-crossed them.

d&w, Mohsen Makhmal Baf (based on a story by Alberto Morya); ph, Homayun Payvar, Mehrdad Fakhimi, Ali R. Zarindast; m, Madjid Entezami; ed, Mohsen Makhmal Baf.

Drama **(PR:NR MPAA:NR)**

PEKING OPERA BLUES*½** (1986, Hong Kong) 104m Cinema City/Golden Princess-Gordon c (DAO MA DAN)

Lin Ching Hsia, Sally Yeh, Cherie Chung, Mark Cheng, Ling Pak Hoi.

A delightfully frenetic comedy/adventure which serves as a terrific introduction to the energetic popular cinema of Hong Kong. Set in China circa 1913, the fast-paced and complicated story centers on three young women from different social classes who become embroiled in a revolutionary plot to overthrow the military government. Surprisingly, one of the key players in the revolution is the beautiful Lin Ching Hsia, the daughter of China's most powerful general. She and a male accomplice are ordered to steal some secret documents from her father's safe. Through a series of slapstick circumstances, a winsome but dim-witted street performer (Cherie Chung), a disaffected soldier, and the attractive daughter of the local opera house owner (Sally Yeh) become involved in the plot and wind up comrades of the revolutionaries. Together the five do battle with the army, the generals, and the secret police, with most of the zany action revolving around the colorful opera house. After a series of nonstop seductions, disguises, gunfights, kung-fu skirmishes, gymnastics, chases, double crosses, separations and reunions, the heroes succeed in getting the valued documents to the revolutionary leaders. The film ends with the five on horseback vowing to meet again someday before going their separate ways.

In an era where most American films are either lifeless bores or cynical exercises in mass marketing (or both), PEKING OPERA BLUES is a welcome burst of manic energy that never fails to please. The skillful combination of breathtaking action and slapstick comedy in this film is nearly indescribable. Martial arts coordinator Ching Sui Tung's innovative choreography of the film's numerous action scenes is superb and he continually manages to thrill and surprise. The cast, boasting three of Hong Kong's most popular actresses, is marvelous as well. Lin Ching Hsia, Cherie Chung, and Sally Yeh are all vivacious, beautiful, and charming. They make a splendidly entertaining team and their comedic timing together is flawless. Tsui Hark directs with a verve and style little seen on American screens, and while he always entertains, he also slips in some genuinely touching scenes and loads of relevant social observations. Although the film was a massive box-office hit in Hong Kong last year and has proved popular with film festival audiences in Europe and North America, US distribution would seem unlikely. The only American film to even approach the kind of energy and comedy found in PEKING OPERA BLUES was last year's BIG TROUBLE IN LITTLE CHINA, directed by John Carpenter. A loving *hommage* to the wild and rambunctious popular films of Hong Kong, Carpenter's movie never found an audience and sunk like a stone. Unfortunately, the same fate will probably be in store for PEKING OPERA BLUES: it's too "common" for the art-house crowd and the regular folks will think it just another silly kung-fu epic, and that is a shame, for this is about as much fun as one can have at the movies. *(Violence.)*

p, Tsui Hark [Hsu K'e, Xu Ke], Claudie Chung; d, Tsui Hark; w, To Kwok Wai; ph, Poon Hung Seng; m, James Wong; ed, David Wu; art d, Vicent Wai, Ho Kim Sing, Leung Chi Hing; cos, Ng Po Ling; ch, Ching Sui Tung; m/l, James Wong; spec eff, Cinefex Workshop.

Action/Comedy **(PR:C MPAA:NR)**

PEKKA PUUPAA POLIISINA† (1987, Fin.) 112m Filmituotanto c (Trans: Pekka As a Policeman)

Esko Roine, Kristiina Elstela, Jaakko Kallio.

"Pekka Puupaa" is one of the most familiar characters in the history of the Finnish cinema; here, the perpetually ineffectual goof-up takes an assignment as a temporary policeman. Predictably, he and his equally goofy partner, "Numbskull Emptybrook," make a shambles of their police work, but their good intentions eventually triumph over their ineptitude.

d, Visa Makinen; w, Antero Viljanen; ph, Keijo Makinen; m, Bogart Co, Matti Tuominen.

Comedy **(PR:NR MPAA:NR)**

PELLE EROVRAREN† (1987, Swed./Den.) 160m Svensk Filmindustri-Danish Film Institute-Swedish Film Institute-DR TV-SID/Kaerne c (Trans: Pelle the Conqueror)

Max von Sydow *(Pappa Lasse)*, Pelle Hvenegaard *(Pelle, His Son)*, Erik Paaske *(Farm Foreman)*, Bjorn Granath *(Farmhand Erik)*, Axel Strobye *(Kongstrup)*, Astrid Villaume *(Mrs. Kongstrup)*, Troels Asmussen *(Rud)*, John Wittig *(Schoolteacher)*, Anne Lise Hirsch Bjerrum *(Karna)*, Sofie Grabol *(Miss Sine)*, Lena Pia Bernhardsson *(The Sow)*, Kristina Tornquist *(Little Anna)*, Buster Larsen, Henrik Bodker, Lars Simonsen, Thure Lindhardt, Benjamin Holck Henricksen, Nis Bank-Mikkelsen.

Bille August, the director of TWIST AND SHOUT (1986), the most commercially successful Danish film ever, follows that teen drama with this Swedish-Danish coproduction set in the 1890s and starring Max von Sydow as an impoverished Swedish widower who moves to Bornholm, a Danish island in the Baltic, hoping to improve his lot in life. He takes his 7-year-old son, Hvenegaard, with him, but instead of finding a better life, they are reduced to virtual slavery. Von Sydow works endlessly for terrible food and worse wages and the threat of violence is ever present. A grim story of deprived and depraved humanity unfolds, focusing on both the oppressed and the oppressors. One worker tries to revolt and is rewarded with a beating that leaves him a near-catatonic shadow of himself. Young Hvenegaard resolves to escape this awful existence and eventually does, fleeing to become the master of his own destiny. Based on the first volume of the "Pelle the Conqueror" trilogy written by Danish proletarian novelist Martin Anderson Nexo.

p, Per Holst; d&w, Bille August (based on volume one of a novel by Martin Andersen Nexo); ph, Jorgen Persson (Fujicolor); m, Stefan Nilsson; ed, Janus Billeskov Jansen; prod d, Anna Asp; cos, Kicki Ilander, Gitte Kolvig, Birthe Qualmann.

Drama **(PR:NR MPAA:NR)**

PENG! DU BIST TOT!† (1987, Ger.) 96m WDR-Delta c (Trans: Bang! You're Dead!)

Ingolf Luck *(Kai Westerburg)*, Rebecca Pauly *(Andrea Flanagan)*, Hermann Lause *(Peters)*, Volker Spengler *(Soviet Agent)*, Rolf Zacher *(Major)*, Pascale Jean-Louis *(Luna)*, Ulrich Wilduruber *(Vagrant)*.

Pauly plays an American schoolteacher who travels to Frankfurt for a convention of teachers of German. On her flight she meets Lause a zoned-out and vaguely diabolical computer genius who plans to use his expertise to generally foul up the world. Once in Germany, Pauly crosses paths with Luck, Lause's well-intentioned assistant, and the two of them work together to try and put a stop to Lause's scheming.

p, Richard Claus, Alexander Wesemann; d, Adolf Winkelmann; w, Walter Kempley, Mathias Seelig; ph, David Slama; m, Piet Klocke; ed, Margot Lohlein; set d, Klaus von Schilling.

Comedy **(PR:NR MPAA:NR)**

PENITENTIARY III½** (1987) 91m Cannon c

Leon Isaac Kennedy *(Too Sweet)*, Anthony Geary *(Serenghetti)*, Steve Antin *(Roscoe)*, Ric Mancini *(Warden)*, Kessler Raymond *(Midnight Thud Jessup)*, Jim Bailey *(Cleopatra)*, Magic Schwarz *(Hugo)*, Windsor Taylor Randolph *(Sugar)*, Rick Zumwalt, Janet Rotblatt, Madison Campudoni, Bert Williams, Mark Kemble, Jack Rader.

Leon Isaac Kennedy joins with director Jamaa Fanaka for the third installment of the saga of Too Sweet, a young man whose boxing skills come in handy in prison. The first film was a surprisingly effective black exploitation effort, full of grim insights about prison and the ways, sexual and otherwise, that the inmates prey on each other. The sequel, PEN II, was set outside prison for the most part, and fell flat. This time, though, Fanaka wastes little time on the outside. Kennedy is boxing against a good friend when his manager slips a drug into his water bottle turning Kennedy into a raging monster who beats the other man to death in the ring. Next thing we know Kennedy is on the prison bus headed up the river on a three-year manslaughter rap. A fellow prisoner describes the set-up inside. There are two sides in the joint, the warden's, and convicted mobster Geary's, and the two contest each other in boxing tournaments. Kennedy is first approached by the warden's men, but he refuses to consider going into the ring again after the death of his friend. Next he is taken to Geary, who lives in a plush cell with his transvestite lover, and is told that he will fight for him. Kennedy refuses, which naturally makes the mobster angry. That night, while Kennedy sleeps, guards in Geary's employ bring up The Midnight Thud, a lunatic black dwarf who attacks and rapes whomever he's tossed in with. There is a terrific battle as the semi-magical dwarf flies about the darkened cell and Kennedy, in his underwear, fights him off, eventually knocking him out. Kennedy is next taken to the dungeon below the prison where he is tortured with electric shocks. He is found by Randolph, a boxer for the warden, who nurses Kennedy back to health then has him train him for the big fight. When it comes, Kennedy is set up with a pretty female prisoner then locked in a room while Randolph gets the stuffing beat out of him by one of Geary's men. Kennedy has now been pushed too far, and he challenges any of Geary's men to a fight. The challenge is accepted by the massive Schwarz, and Kennedy returns to the dungeon for some serious training. There he is surprised when The Midnight Thud speaks for the first time, offering to help. He turns out to be a Jamaican mystic who tells Kennedy about his energy being located two inches below his navel. The big fight finally comes, with all of Geary's money riding on the outcome. It goes back and forth and things frequently look bad for Kennedy, but he triumphs and pummels the larger man to a quivering hulk. The warden regains control of his prison and Kennedy returns to his cell to await his release.

This is certainly a long way from art, but thanks to the occasionally crude but vigorous direction of Fanaka and some bizarre humor, it is a thoroughly entertaining exploitation effort. Some sort of height in surrealism must have been reached in the fight between Kennedy and the Thud, and when Thud turns out to be a comic hero with mystic powers, the silliness is sublime. Where else does a homosexual rapist get so many funny lines? Geary, remembered as Luke on the TV soap GENERAL HOSPITAL, is also a pleasure to watch with white hair, different colored eyes, and a French chef who comes to his cell three times a day pushing a trolley. At one point, the warden tells Geary, "You know your problem? You've seen too many bad prison movies." To which Geary looks off into space and says, "Yes, I think you're right." No treatise on penal reform, PENITENTIARY III is a welcome addition to the canon of bad prison movies. *(Violence, brief nudity, sexual situations, excessive profanity, substance abuse.)*

p, Jamaa Fanaka, Leon Isaac Kennedy; d&w, Jamaa Fanaka; ph, Marty Ollstein; m, Garry Schyman; ed, Ed Harker; prod d, Marshall Toomey; art d, Craig Freitag; cos, Maria Burrell Fanaka; stunts, John Sherrod.

Prison **(PR:O MPAA:R)**

PERFECT MATCH, THE** (1987) 93m Airtight c

Marc McClure *(Tim Wainwright)*, Jennifer Edwards *(Nancy Bryant)*, Diane Stilwell *(Vicki)*, Rob Paulsen *(John Wainwright)*.

A likable but lamentably average low-budget romantic comedy starring McClure as an insecure loner rapidly approaching the age of 30 who takes out a personal ad in the *L.A. Reader* in a desperate attempt to meet a nice girl (his last date stole his car). McClure lies about his athletic prowess and cultural interests in the ad (he's a junk-food-eating couch potato), and receives dozens of calls from bizarre-sounding women that are more scary than intriguing. Just as he is about to give up, he hears from someone who sounds nice, Edwards, a shy professional college student also on the verge of turning 30. On their first date, both put on airs for the other and lie about their backgrounds. McClure borrows his successful brother's BMW and acts as if he has his own defense-contracting business. Edwards tells him that she is a college professor. At a chic restaurant, McClure learns that Edwards is a strict vegetarian and cannot stand the sight of meat. Back at Edwards' apartment, McClure clumsily tries to seduce her and only succeeds in making her angry. He apologizes and leaves, but as the days pass they both find themselves thinking about each other. They arrange a second date, and this time Edwards picks a health food restaurant. McClure forces himself to eat the "Soy Bean Surprise" and their night out goes much smoother than before. After a few more dates they decide to try a long recreational weekend together in the mountains (separate rooms) complete with skiing, tennis, hiking, and camping. The trip turns out to be a disaster as both fail miserably at the various physical tasks that they have claimed to be expert at. After much bickering, they return home vowing never to speak to each other again. But, of course, by now they have fallen in love and reuinte to confess their various lies and make a fresh start.

Despite some bright moments provided by McClure (Jimmy Olsen of the SUPERMAN movies) and Edwards (daugher of director Blake Edwards), THE PERFECT MATCH never rises above the level of an average made-for-TV movie. Director Deimel, in his film debut, shows he has a nice flair for casting and light comedy, but his film is superficial, only mildly entertaining, and instantly forgettable. Missing is the energetic bite found in any Albert Brooks film, or the cleverness and insight of Woody Allen's work. Although obviously constrained by a minuscule budget, Deimel demonstrates little interest in cinematic visuals and instead opts for the unimaginative "talking heads" method that has become a numbing television mainstay. A better director with the same amount of money to spend would have come up with something more interesting visually, and frankly this suggests that Deimel's talents may be more suited to sitcoms than cinema. Shown at film festivals in the US in 1987. *(Adult situations, mild profanity.)*

p, Mark Deimel, Bob Torrance; d, Mark Deimel; w, Nick Duretta, David Burr, Mark Deimel; ph, Bob Torrance; m, Tim Torrance; ed, Craig Colton; prod d, Maxine Shepard.

Comedy **(PR:C MPAA:NR)**

PERLYOTNIYE PTIT† (1987, Afghanistan) 103m Afghan c (Trans: Migrating Birds)

Nasser Aziz *(Nawob)*, Asadullah Aram *(Noor Goul)*, Odella Adim *(Girl)*.

Presenting a more or less one-sided view of the conflict in Afghanistan, PERLYOTNIYE PTIT, which translates as "Migrating Birds," deals with the plight of a young Afghan bride whose husband is killed during their wedding by a jealous former boy friend. According to tradition, the bride-cum-widow, Adim, is to marry the brother of the deceased; however, the brother happens to be the leader of a group of rebels opposing the Soviet-sponsored government. Adim's father-in-law leads an excursion to Pakistan, which Adim and the rebels use as their base of operations. Reluctantly, Aram accedes to tradition, but the effectiveness of his leadership is compromised in the process. Ultimately the film shows the rebels to be divided and dispirited.

d, Latif Abdul Latif; w, Latif Abdul Latif, Sarwar Anwari; ph, Kader Tahiri; m, Mohamed Shah Hakparast.

Drama **(PR:NR MPAA:NR)**

PERSONAGGI & INTERPRETI† (1987, Switz.) 90m SA-RTSI c

Teco Celio, Sara Donzelli, Richard Gordon, Dino Saluzzi, Giovanni Del Giudice, Francesco Spano, Silvio Orlando, Rita Silva, Giorgio Rossi, Raffaella Giordano, Roberto Castello.

[No plot information available.]

p, Al Castello; d, Heinz Butler; w, Angelo Gregorio, Heinz Butler; ph, Hansueli Schenkel; m, Dino Saluzzi; ed, Paoloa Gebhard.

Comedy **(PR:NR MPAA:NR)**

PERSONAL FOUL½** (1987) 92m Personal Foul Ltd. c

Adam Arkin *(Jeremy)*, David Morse *(Ben)*, Susan Wheeler Duff *(Lisa)*, F. William Parker *(Principal)*.

An independent production shot in the Midwest, PERSONAL FOUL stars Adam Arkin (son of Alan) as a grade school teacher who loves to nurture students, but abhors the bureaucratic activity that accompanies his job. He's a loner who keeps his distance from his fellow teachers and the school's principal. To pass the time, Arkin heads to the basketball court and shoots hoops by himself. He does, however, notice a new arrival from Texas, Duff, a pretty, personable young woman to whom he is attracted. The third main character is Morse, an introverted drifter who lives in a van and sells handmade paper flowers. Arkin befriends Morse by drawing him into a game of basketball, and later having him teach the students how to make paper flowers. While Duff is attracted to Arkin, she cannot cope with his emotional instability. In frustration, she turns her attentions to Morse, who is no more emotionally fit than Arkin to handle a relationship. Just when their friendship has reached the breaking point, the three confront their fears of commitment and involvement. A reconciliation follows and Arkin discovers in himself the strength to continue his friendship with Morse and pursue a relationship with Duff.

Producer-director-writer Lichtenheld describes PERSONAL FOUL, his first feature, as a "film of cautious people who get involved despite their caution." While Lichtenheld takes a warm and honest look at three fragile people, the direction is unfortunately too "cautious" to reach the level of emotional intensity and involvement dictated by the subject matter. Instead of assuming that the audience has seen this type of story before (which they no doubt have), Lichtenheld proceeds at a pace that is just too slow and methodical. As a result, emotional complexity gives way to predictability. Lichtenheld, however, must be commended for his restraint in creating a peaceful atmosphere. All of this is helped along by three engaging performances and a soundtrack full of folk music. Shown this year at festivals in Montreal and Chicago. *(Profanity, adult situations.)*

p, Ted Lichtenheld, Kathleen Long; d&w, Ted Lichtenheld; ph, J. Leblanc; m, Greg Brown; ed, Steve Mullenix; prod d, Bill Jones; cos, Elizabeth Palmer.

Drama **(PR:A-C MPAA:NR)**

PERSONAL SERVICES*** (1987, Brit.) 105m Zenith/UIP-Vestron c

Julie Walters *(Christine Painter)*, Alec McCowen *(Wing Cmdr. Morton)*, Shirley Stelfox *(Shirley)*, Danny Schiller *(Dolly)*, Victoria Hardcastle *(Rose)*, Tim Woodward *(Timms)*, Dave Atkins *(Sydney)*, Leon Lissek *(Mr. Popozogolou)*, Benjamin Whitrow *(Mr. Marsden)*, Peter Cellier *(Mr. Marples)*, Stephen Lewis *(Mr. Dunkley)*, Andrew MacLachlan *(Mr. McClellan)*, Anthony Collin *(Mr. Webb)*, Ewan Hooper *(Edward)*, Beverly Foster *(Elizabeth)*, Alan Bowyer *(David Painter)*, Nigel Le Vaillant *(The Man)*, Antony Carrick *(Edgar)*, Michelle Collins *(June)*, Arthur Whybrow *(Mac)*, Ron Pember *(Ron)*, Pamela Duncan *(Jackie)*, Sheila Gill *(Mrs. Winter)*, Toni Palmer *(Aunt Winnie)*, Lorraine Brunning *(Angela)*, Rupert Holliday Evans *(Terry)*, Claire Waugh *(Girl in Film)*, Wayne Morris *(Man in Film)*, Renny Lister *(Pat)*, Shulie Bannister *(The Woman)*, Jagdish Kumar *(Mr. Shah)*, Jason Smart *(PC Hart)*, Jeffrey Daunton *(PC Williams)*, Arnold Brown *(Vicar)*, Janie Booth *(Court Usher)*, Nick Stringer *(PC Baker)*, Paul Imbusch *(Solicitor)*, Bernard Brown *(John)*, Andreas Markos *(Mr. Grivas)*, Peter Wight *(Detective Gibson)*, John Bailey *(Mr. Gardner)*, Helen Gemmell *(Jenny)*, Clare Clifford *(Fay)*, John Shrapnel *(Lionel)*, Michael Packer *(Ralph)*, Stanley Lebor *(Jones)*, Suzette Llewellyn *(Helen)*, Carolyn Allen *(Carol)*, Arthur Hewlett *(Mr. Francis)*, Joanna Dickens *(Gloria)*, Ivor Roberts *(Glossop)*, Arthur Cox *(Lennox)*, Lorena Lee *(The Angel)*, Badi Uzzaman *(Mr. Pater)*, Ian McNeice *(Harry)*, Michael Irving *(Lawson)*, Allan Stirland *(Phil)*, Charlotte Seely *(Diane)*, Mark Hardy *(Nicole)*, David Leland *(Mr. Pilkington/Danielle)*.

A disclaimer at the opening indicates that this is not the story of Cynthia Payne, London's famed proprietress of the "House of Cyn," yet it becomes quite clear that the movie is a blow-by-blow description of the life and times of the famed madam. The credits go on to state that it was loosely "suggested" by Payne's life. Perhaps the producers decided to add that to take any onus off the many men who patronized her and whose names might have been mentioned in the lurid press accounts of the business she ran. Julie (EDUCATING RITA) Walters is appropriately flamboyant as the brothelkeeper with a heart of gold plate. She begins as a waitress, perpetually out of money, raising a young son and trying to keep ends meeting. In order to supplement her meager wages and tips, she lets out her flat during the day to various streetwalkers who are willing to pay an hourly fee. At one point, she is very close to being evicted because she's not been able to collect from her subletters, so she uses sex to convince the landlord that he should allow her some leeway. Walters is not really a sexual person, but she knows that she is sitting on a valuable asset and can put it to good use. She enlists the aid of Stelfox—a seasoned veteran of "the life" and a woman who has a list of sado-masochistic clients—and the backing of McCowen, a former RAF wing commander given to wearing bras and panties. McCowen freely admits that he flew many of his more than 200 missions attired in that fashion. Then Schiller, a transvestite, joins the team as the maid, and the house becomes a home to a burgeoning roster of clients, mostly middle-aged professional men who are into kinkiness. Walters finds that dealing with older men who are keen for a bit of naughtiness is much easier than dealing with young bucks. Much of the movie consists of poking fun at the priggish exterior of British sexual behavior, then delving beneath it to see just how weird it is. Satire, rather than vulgarity, is the order of the day, but there are moments when it does go over the invisible line, such as the sequence where Walters has both her teenage son and her widowed father enjoy the personal services of one of her employees. In a moment right out of Mack Sennett, the establishment is raided by the cops and everyone is taken in. At the trial, Walter's defense is that the party at the house was a private gathering of some old friends who just happened to have sex. It was all quite legal, as there is no law against private orgies and the only problem arises when money changes hands. There have been several plainclothes police officers at her parties and they talk about the whips and leather knickers that seem to have been present. Then a host of her clients testify that the parties were innocent get-togethers. Walters is released and the picture concludes with the suggestion that these parties will go on just the way they have.

This is not a porno movie and not even close to the smarminess of THE HAPPY HOOKER or films of that ilk. The movie is well made, funny, sometimes touching, and boasts the gifted Walters, who shows that her screeching Cockney accent in EDUCATING RITA was just an act. With this performance, plus her role as Joe Orton's mother in PRICK UP YOUR EARS, Walters establishes herself as an actress with immense depth and a wide scope of histrionic talent. The author, Leland, seems fascinated by the life of "working girls," as he was the co-author of the excellent MONA LISA. Director Jones was making his first movie without his "Monty Python" pals and shows that there is life after Cleese and Chapman and Palin and Gilliam and Idle. Jones' two prior "Python" films, THE MEANING OF LIFE and LIFE OF BRIAN, were banned in Ireland, as was this. Cynthia Payne was a "consultant" on the film and should be very pleased with the superb casting and the excellent results. Her place of business was raided in 1978, which means it took nine years for this tale to come to the

screen. It was worth the wait. Like many of the "Monty Python" sketches, it descends into silliness and twittery at times and there will be those who are offended at much of the pomposity puncturing, but it's a good-natured arrow that's been fired, dipped in affection rather than curare. *(Nudity, sexual situations, profanity.)*

p, Tim Bevan; d, Terry Jones; w, David Leland; ph, Roger Deakins (Eastmancolor); m, John Duprez; ed, George Akers; prod d, Hugo Luczyc-Wyhowski; md, David Snell; art d, Jane Coleman; cos, Shuna Harwood; m/l, Jester Hairston, May Brahe, Helen Taylor; stunts, Jim Dowdall, Alan Stuart; makeup, Jenny Shircore, Sancia Simpson.

Comedy **(PR:O MPAA:R)**

PIERRE ET DJEMILA† (1987, Fr.) 86m Films Plain Chant-Prods. du Cercle Bleu-Selena Audiovisual-AAA-A2-Xanadu/AAA Classic c

Jean-Pierre Andre *(Pierre)*, Nadja Reski *(Djemila)*, Abdelkader *(Djaffar)*, Salah Teskouk *(Djemila's Father)*, Fathia Cheriguene *(Djemila's Mother)*, Lakhdar Kasri *(Lakhdar)*, Djedjigue Ait-Hamouda *(Alicha)*, Jacques Brunet *(Pierre's Father)*, Francine Debaisieux *(Pierre's Mother)*.

Abel Ferrara's CHINA GIRL (1987) updated "Romeo and Juliet" and set it in New York's Little Italy and Chinatown; this French film, with nonprofessional actors in the leads, sets the story in modern-day Roubiax, an industrial town in the north of France. Andre, a 16-year-old French boy, and Reski, a 14-year-old second generation Algerian immigrant, live in the same working-class area. Despite an overwhelming climate of racial intolerance, they fall in love. Brunet, Andre's father, a veteran of the Algerian War, is dead set against integration, but he tries to understand his son's love for Reski. Her brother is much less sympathetic and kills Andre to put an end to the affair so that his sister will proceed with her traditionally arranged marriage. The distraught Reski, however, reacts by taking her own life. Director Blain began his career as an actor in French New Wave films.

p, Philippe Diaz; d, Gerard Blain; w, Gerard Blain, Michel Marmin, Mohamed Bouchibi; ph, Emmanuel Machuel; m, Olivier Kowalski, Gabor Kristof; ed, Catherine Deiller; art d, Michel Vandestien, Pierre Gattoni; m/l, Olivier Kowalski, Gabor Kristof, Maurice Rollot.

Romance **(PR:NR MPAA:NR)**

PESN PROSHEDSHIKH DNEY† (1987, USSR) 89m Armenfilm/ Sovexportfilm c (Trans: Song of Bygone Days)

Frunze Mkrtchyan, Shaum Kazaryan, Verchaluis Miridjanyan, Guzh Manukyan, Narine Bagdasaryan.

Dealing with the tremendous human cost of WW II for the Soviet Union and, in particular, Armenia, this begins in 1941 as an amateur theater group mounts a production of "Brave Nazar." On opening night, the play's prompter suddenly announces that war has begun. Nearly three years later, all but five of the people associated with the production are dead, and three of them have returned from the front disabled. In an attempt to regain hope, the villagers begin to rehearse a new production of the play. Finally they are ready, and on the night of the premiere, a man bursts into the theater and joyously declares that the war is over.

d&w, Albert Mkrtchyan; ph, Rudolf Vatinyan; m, Tigran Mansuryan; art d, Raphael Babayan.

War **(PR:NR MPAA:NR)**

PETER VON SCHOLTEN† (1987, Den.) 110m Crone Film-Metronome-Danish Film Institute/Warner-Metronome c

Ole Ernst *(Peter von Scholten)*, Karen Lise Mynster *(Anna von Scholten)*, Jesper Langberg *(Frederik von Scholten)*, Etta Cameron *(Anna Heegaard)*, Dale Smith *(Buddhoe)*, Preben Kristensen *(Edvard Heilbuth)*, Soren Pilmark *(Lt. Irminger)*, Torben Jensen *(Kunzen)*, Arne Hansen *(Petersen)*, Preben Neergaard *(Frederik Oxholm)*, Henning Jensen *(Falbe)*, Helge Schuer *(Andreson)*, Henning Moritzen *(King Christian VIII)*, Olaf Ussing *(Organist Pram)*, Bodil Udsen *(Mrs. Holten)*, Leonard Malone *(Katka)*, Lars Lunoe, Raymond Adjavon, Bodil Lassen, Guido Paevatalu, Dick Kaysoe, Torben Jetsmark, Anna Adair, Hans Henrik Krause, Edwin Donoghue, Birgit Conradi, Hans Christian Aegidius, Fritze Hedemann, John Larsen.

Historical saga about Peter von Scholten (Ernst), the last Danish governor-general of the Virgin Islands circa 1848. The film details von Scholten's quest to grant a dignified freedom to the black slaves of the West Indies by preparing them for their new status via education. Arrested, tried, and convicted of treason by the Danish government for his unauthorized actions, von Scholten was eventually acquitted by a higher court, but died a broken man shortly thereafter.

p, Jorgen Hinsch, Nico, Jane Graun, Tivi Magnusson; d, Palle Kjarulff-Schmidt; w, Sven Holm; ph, Mikael Salomon (Eastmancolor); m, Bent Fabricius-Bjerre; ed, Kasper Schyberg, Merete Brusendorff; art d, Soren Krag Sorensen; cos, Lotte Dandanell, Marcella Kjeltoft, Else Drangsgaard; makeup, Birthe Lyngsoe.

Biography **(PR:NR MPAA:NR)**

PHERA† (1987, India)

Subrata Nandy *(Sasanka)*, Alakananda Roy-Dutta *(Saruju, Widow)*, Aniket Sengupta *(Kanu, Saruju's Son)*, Sunil Mukherjee *(Pashu)*, Chhanda Dutt *(Kalyani, Pashu's Wife)*, Kamu Mukherjee *(Businessman)*, Biplab Chatterjee.

Helmed by Buddhadeb Dasgupta, PHERA examines both the artist's place in society and the inability of people to truly communicate with one another. Nandy writes and performs in plays done in the style of the traditional folk theater of Bengal, *jatra*. He lives in a decrepit mansion which is the last vestige of the great wealth his family once possessed. Now, not only have audiences become thin, but his jatra company has been taken over by a businessman who is more interested in box-office receipts than artistic integrity. Though Nandy's wife has left him, her recently widowed sister Roy-Dutta appears. With nowhere else to turn, she allows Nandy to have his way with her sexually in return for shelter for herself and her son, Sengupta. The boy breaks through Nandy's cruel facade and the two develop a special closeness as Sengupta picks up the jatra torch.

p,d&w, Buddhadeb Dasgupta (based on a story by Narendranath Mitra); ph, Dhrubajyoti Bose; m, Jyothishka Dasgupta.

Drama **(PR:NR MPAA:NR)**

PHOTOGRAPH, THE*** (1987, Gr.) 102m Ikones EPE-Greek Film Center/Greek Film Center c (I PHOTOGRAPHIA)

Aris Retsos *(Ilias Apostolou)*, Christos Tsangas *(Giorgios Tzivas)*, Zozo Zarpa, Despina Tomazani, Christos Valavanidis.

A superbly-acted allegory which has both national and social implications relating to the political climate in Greece from 1971 to July, 1974 when government was returned to the people. The film begins in 1971 in Kastoria as Retsos, the persecuted son of a Communist, decides to leave his homeland for a better life in Paris. He hopes to stay with Tsangas, an illiterate distant cousin twice his age, who lives and works as a furrier in a rundown French suburb. Before Retsos leaves, he discovers that Tsangas is being cheated by a corrupt Greek official who is slowly draining Tsangas' parents' bank account. What Tsangas does not know is that his parents have been dead for two years. As Retsos prepares to depart he finds a photograph of a singer named "Joy" which he treasures as a good luck charm. When Retsos arrives at Tsangas' house with the death certificates, his cousin angrily throws him out the door. In the process, Retsos loses the picture of Joy in the house. Tsangas later realizes Retsos' intentions are good and allows him to enter the house. Together they mourn the death of Tsangas' parents. When Tsangas asks about the picture of Joy, Retsos lies and says she is his 23-year-old unmarried sister. Tsangas becomes obsessed with thoughts of Joy and asks Retsos to send her a proposal of marriage. Meanwhile, Retsos is trying to find work in the fur trade, but is turned down everywhere since the corrupt Kastorian official has sent out a warning that he was a political radical. As he loses hope and grows more indebted to Tsangas, Retsos agrees to write a letter of proposal to Joy—even though no such person exists. With help from his reluctant mother, Retsos sends self-addressed letters to Kastoria, which she mails back to him as if they were from Joy. After a few letters, each one more convincing than the last, Joy agrees to marry Tsangas, but only if he decorates and furnishes the house to her liking. Seeing this as an opportunity to live in a modern, well-furnished home, Retsos places great demands on the love-smitten Tsangas. In order to finance the redecorating Tsangas must work longer hours. He builds a workshop, equips it with new tools, and works his pelts late into the evening. Retsos, who has now backed himself into an impossible situation, tries to deter Tsangas from marrying Joy, but the groom-to-be only becomes more determined. Instead of waiting for her arrival, Tsangas makes plans to marry her in Kastoria. Together Retsos and Tsangas begin the long drive to Greece, which by now (July, 1974) has seen the end of military rule. Tsangas' spirits are high, but Retsos is nearly out of options—his ruse will soon be found out. He tries to discourage Tsangas by leading him in the wrong direction through the twisting, narrow mountain roads. As Tsangas grows more frustrated and Retsos grows more impatient, they drive faster, nearly getting run off the road. When their tire blows, the car swerves and stops only inches from the edge of a steep cliff. Rather than disappoint Tsangas with the truth that there is no Joy, he caves his head in with a heavy rock, letting him die with his dream of marriage.

Voted Best Picture by the Panhellenic Union of Film Critics and chosen as Best Screenplay at the 1986 Thessaloniki Film Festival (an award which producer-director-writer Papatakis refused), THE PHOTOGRAPH paints a remarkable picture of the Greek state of affairs during a politically explosive period. The film starts in 1971 during the rule of Col. George Papadopoulos and his right-wing junta. During this time martial law was enacted and numerous young Greeks, not unlike the Retsos character, looked to other countries for personal and political freedom. By the time the characters return to Greece (in their quest for the aptly named fictional character "Joy"), the political climate has changed—Papadopoulos has been ousted by a military coup, and Gen. Phaidon Gizikis has announced that the government will return to the hands of the citizens. A very talky picture (the film's major fault), THE PHOTOGRAPH is blessed with two excellent lead performances and a powerful script which holds nothing back. Though the photography is merely adequate, the film does succeed in conveying its Greek culture even though most of the film takes place in France—an atmospheric achievement for which Papatakis and his cinematographer Stavrou must be commended. The excellent score by Chalaris is also a strong contribution. (In Greek; English subtitles.)

d&w, Nikos Papatakis; ph, Aris Stavrou, Arnaud Desplechin; m, Christodoulos Chalaris; ed, Delphine Desfons; set d&cos, Nikos Meletopoulos.

Drama **(PR:C MPAA:NR)**

PICK-UP ARTIST, THE** (1987) 81m Amercent-American Entertainment Partners-FOX/FOX c

Molly Ringwald *(Randy Jensen)*, Robert Downey *(Jack Jericho)*, Dennis Hopper *(Flash Jensen)*, Danny Aiello *(Phil)*, Mildred Dunnock *(Nellie, Jack's Grandmother)*, Harvey Keitel *(Alonzo)*, Brian Hamill *(Mike)*, Tamara Bruno *(Karen)*, Vanessa Williams *(Rae)*, Angie Kempf *(Jack's Student)*, Polly Draper *(Pat)*, Frederick Koehler *(Richie)*, Robert Towne *(Stan)*, Victoria Jackson *(Lulu)*, Lorraine Bracco *(Carla)*, Bob Gunton *(Portacarrero)*, Clemenze Caserta *(Clem)*, Christine Baranski *(Harriet)*, Joe Spinell *(Eddie)*, Tony Conforti *(Tony)*, Jilly Rizzo *(Floor Manager)*, Tom Signorelli *(Marty)*, Reni Santoni.

As a writer (THE GAMBLER) and director (FINGERS, LOVE AND MONEY, EXPOSED), James Toback's obsessions have dealt with the seductive qualities of both money and women. While his previous films have had a intense, passionate destructiveness to them, THE PICK-UP ARTIST presents this theme in a sanitized, watered-down manner which is acceptable for family audiences. The "pick-up artist" of the title is Downey, a self-confident womanizer who practices pick-up lines while standing before his bathroom mirror. "Hi, my name is Jack Jericho" is how his speech begins, followed shortly thereafter by "Did anyone ever tell you that you have the face of a Botticelli and the body of a Degas?" He walks down the streets of New York gambling on every beautiful woman who crosses his path—some walk away, others are flattered, a few give him their phone numbers. Not surprisingly, Downey has a phenomenal collection of phone numbers. His interest, however, is not in finding the perfect love but merely in testing his pick-up technique—a technique which he is constantly polishing. One day, he tries out his Botticelli line on Ringwald who, as fate would have it, is carrying a book on the artist. Ringwald is Downey's perfect match—she has a comeback for every line and is even more aggressive than he. When he tells her he would like to seduce her, she nonchalantly complies. In the ultimate payoff, Downey makes love to Ringwald in his car. The incident goes down as the high-point in Downey's history of pick-ups. Ringwald, however, isn't one to get emotionally attached, fearing that dependency on a man will lead to heartache. She leaves his car without even giving out her phone number or last name. The ever-persistent Downey snoops around and learns that she works as a museum tour guide and lives with her father Hopper, a broken down alcoholic gambler who owes the mobster Keitel $25,418. Hopper has until noon the following day to pay up, but neither he nor Ringwald has the money. Keitel does offer the pair a way out—if Ringwald allows herself to be seduced by a wealthy Colombian who is obsessed by her red hair the debt will be erased. Downey gets in deep with Ringwald and tries to raise the money himself, turning to his friend Aiello for aid. In the meantime, Ringwald runs off to Atlantic City with a few hundred dollars and increases it to $13,000 at the blackjack table. With one turn of the card, however, she loses it all. Downey, now completely under Ringwald's spell, sells his car and heads for the roulette wheel. He and Ringwald put money on their lucky numbers, the wheel spins, and their gamble pays off. Downey confronts Keitel, but during all the commotion, Ringwald slips away. When Downey catches up to her, he finds she wants to end the relationship. Certain they are both obsessive gamblers (with love and money), she fears they will destroy each other before long. Downey argues more convincingly that their love is not a gamble but a pre-ordained fact, and the they walk off together arm in arm.

A classic example of a great idea soured by poor execution, THE PICK-UP ARTIST suffers on almost all counts. While there are some effective moments, the film often becomes downright embarrassing. When Toback concentrates on the Downey character the film comes alive, but when the weight shifts to the gambling-underworld connection it falls into cliche-ridden parody. Keitel, as the supposedly threatening thug, turns in the sort of performance he could now probably do in his sleep—it's well-done but familiar. Ditto for Hopper who is to drunkards what Keitel is to crime figures. The film is carried by Downey, appearing in his first starring role. He was previously seen in BACK TO SCHOOL and during the 1985 season on "Saturday Night Live." He has a self-assured romantic charm that recalls Francois Truffaut's "Antoine Doinel" character had Doinel been a young American in the 1980's. Ringwald, while performing her chores well, just doesn't seem right for the role. (Others were considered, including the excellent Mary Stuart Masterson of SOME KIND OF WONDERFUL and GARDENS OF STONE, and Mia Sara of FERRIS BUELLER'S DAY OFF.) Her character is supposed to be a sexually explosive, intelligent, impulsive, risk-taker, yet she comes across as the same pouty redhead we've become accustomed to. It's as if she fell out of the pages of a John Hughes script and into those of Toback's. Ringwald's character is written as an alluring femme fatale who could ruin Downey but Ringwald plays her as a well-dressed virginal teenager. In THE PICK-UP ARTIST Toback has devised an interesting premise which draws parallels between risking one's heart and one's wallet, but the picture never gels. The Hopper-Keitel plot keeps getting in the way of Downey and Ringwald. Perhaps, in an attempt to capture the commerciality which eluded his previous pictures, Toback tried to funnel his obsessions into a marketable film. The film lacks the passionate spark that ignited his previous works, lumbering along (though running only 81 minutes) to its longed for finale. One can't help but feel that part of this film ended up on the cutting room floor. The running time is shorter than usual, the MPAA re-rated it from "R" to "PG-13" (meaning more of Ringwald's young fans can see the film), and the profanity has been tempered down. If one watches the character's lips closely this dubbing becomes obvious. What's left on the screen is an emasculated, kiddie version of a what once seemed aggressive and mature. *(Profanity, sexual situations.)*

p, David L. McLeod [Warren Beatty], d&w, James Toback; ph, Gordon Willis (Deluxe Color); m, Georges Delerue; ed, David Bretherton, Angelo Corrao; prod d, Paul Sylbert; art d, Bill Groom; set d, John Alan Hicks; cos, Colleen Atwood.

Romance/Crime **(PR:A-C MPAA:PG-13)**

PIERSCIEN I ROZA† (1987, Pol.) 92m Zespoly Filmowe-KADR c (Trans: The Rose and the Ring)

Katarzyna Figura *(Rose)*, Stefan Kazuro *(Prince Lulejko)*, Katarzyna Cygan *(Princess Angelica)*, Zbigniew Zamachowski *(Prince Bulbo)*.

This Polish adaptation of William Makepeace Thackeray's tongue-in-cheek fairy tale *The Rose and the Ring*, tells the story of two rightful rulers whose places on the thrones of their respective principalities are filled by others. The crown that should be Kazuro's is worn by his cousin, Cygan, a princess whom everyone finds to be both beautiful and adorable, provided that she is wearing the magic ring that lends her these qualities. Similarly, Figura should be a princess, but Zamachowski rules in her place. The Black Fairy, however, watches over the fortunes of both Kazuro and Figura, and, with her help, they not only regain their rightful stations in life, but also fall in love with each other.

d&w, Jerzy Gruza (based on the novel by William Makepeace Thackeray); ph, Jacek Korcelli; m, Andrzej Korzynski; ed, Jozef Bartczak; set d, Marek Lewandowski.

Children's **(PR:NR MPAA:NR)**

PIKKUPOJAT† (1987, Fin.) 84m Spede-Team c (Trans: Little Boys)

Spede Pasanen, Vesa-Matti Loiri, Simo Salminen.

In "Little Boys" three popular Finnish TV comedians—Spede Pasanen, Vesa-Matti Loiri, and Simo Salminen—set aside the reputations they've made in the "Numbskull Emptybrook" film comedies and take on new roles (two each, to be exact). Salminen essays the roles of both a 4-year-old lad and an inventor, Pasanen plays a 5-year-old boy and his father, and Loiri plays a vacationing army officer and a 6-year-old.

d, Ere Kokkonen; w, Spede Pasanen; ph, Jussi Jalasti, Eero Jaakkola, Timo Jalasti; m, Olli Ahvenlahti.

Comedy **(PR:NR MPAA:NR)**

PINOCCHIO AND THE EMPEROR OF THE NIGHT*** (1987) 88m Filmation/NW c

Voices of: Edward Asner *(Scalawag)*, Tom Bosley *(Geppetto)*, Lana Beeson *(Twinkle)*, James Earl Jones *(Emperor of the Night)*, Rickie Lee Jones *(Fairy Godmother)*, Don Knotts *(Gee Willikers)*, Scott Grimes *(Pinocchio)*, Linda Gary *(Bee-atrice)*, Jonathan Harris *(Lt. Grumblebee)*, William Windom *(Puppetino)*, Frank Welker *(Igor)*.

What's the difference between an unofficial sequel and a complete rip-off? *Zilch* in the case of PINOCCHIO AND THE EMPEROR OF THE NIGHT. Though this animated feature has some impressive sequences, coupled by an extremely varied voice cast, it is void of originality. The film opens as a mysterious carnival, which travels by ship, settles down in a quiet meadow, disturbing the tranquility of the veddy British winged insect, Grumblebee (voiced by Jonathan Harris). From this ominous beginning, we switch to the oh-so-happy life of Geppetto (voiced by Tom Bosley) and his son, the former puppet and now real live boy, Pinocchio (voiced by Scott Grimes). It is Pinocchio's birthday and to celebrate, his old pal the Blue Fairy (voiced by singer Rickie Lee Jones) shows up to sing a song. She tells Pinocchio the greatest gift of all is free will, thus setting up the possibility this could turn into a philosophical kiddie picture. Instead, Pinocchio annoys Geppetto until the kindly old woodcarver allows his son to deliver an important jewel box to the mayor. To Pinocchio's surprise, his toy glowbug has come to life thanks to The Blue Fairy's magic. The bug is dubbed "Gee Willikers" (voiced by Don Knotts), and he beseeches Pinocchio not to get sidetracked from his mission. There wouldn't be much of a story if Pinocchio didn't get into trouble, so the wide-eyed lad hooks up with Scalawag (voiced by Ed Asner), a shyster raccoon, accompanied by a monkey assistant, Igor (voiced by Frank Welker). After the two con Pinocchio out of the jewel box, the shamed lad decides his only recourse is to join the traveling carnival. There he catches the eye of Puppetino (voiced by William Windom), an evil puppet master whose star attraction is the beautiful marionette Twinkle (voiced by Lana Beeson). Pinocchio is tricked, and turned back into a wooden puppet. Later, The Blue Fairy arrives and turns him back into a real live boy. Pinocchio is now determined to find the missing jewel box. Willikers, seeking some help for his master, meets Grumblebee while kindly old Geppetto goes out looking for Pinocchio. Pinocchio is tricked by Scalawag once more, but the two form a quick bond when the ominous carnival ship swallows them up. Once inside, Pinocchio is seduced into "The Land Where Dreams Come True," a seeming paradise for happy young boys. But this turns out to be a trick, and Pinocchio is once more turned into a puppet. He discovers that the evil Emperor of the Night (voiced by James Earl Jones) has captured Geppetto, making the old man teeny-weeny. Risking all, Pinocchio contests the Emperor's power, then leads his friends to safety. They wake up on a beach, with Geppetto restored to normal size, while both Pinocchio and Twinkle are real live children.

If the folks behind this wanted to remake Walt Disney's classic PINOCCHIO, then why did they even bother to come up with a supposedly brand new adventure? PINOCCHIO AND THE EMPEROR OF THE NIGHT employs nearly every major character and scene from the 1940 film, thinly disguising the original material with supposedly new personalities and adventures. But PINOCCHIO isn't the only source for this film. The mysterious carnival setting is similar to Ray Bradbury's "Something Wicked This Way Comes," a story also filmed by the Disney Studios. The real kicker comes via the casting of James Earl Jones. Among his other accomplishments, Jones is well known as the voice of Darth Vader, a character whose evil nature and methods are closely mirrored by this film's Emperor of the Night. Just as Vader told Luke Skywalker to join up with him, the Emperor makes a similar overture to Pinocchio. And when the two finally duke it out, the only thing missing is the light sabers.

Of course we all know what happens when Pinoccio lies, but PINOCCHIO AND THE EMPEROR OF THE NIGHT uses this device in a rather dubious manner. When running from the Emperor, Pinocchio and friends are horrified when they see a door latch just out of their reach. Thinking fast, Pinocchio tells oodles of falsehoods, thus making his proboscis long enough to undo the latch. It may help move things plotwise, but by using Pinocchio's often satirized nasal capabilities in such a manner, the filmmakers have effectively told their intended young audience its okay to lie if it gets you out of trouble.

To their credit, director Hal Sutherland and his crew at Filmation have done a fine job with the animation. The sequences aboard the Emperor's ship have a nice surreal look, while the characters are far more lively than those in most children's animated features. This is a real surprise, considering Sutherland's previous credits include a number of forgettable Saturday morning television cartoons.

p, Lou Scheimer; d, Hal Sutherland; w, Robby London, Barry O'Brien, Dennis O'Flaherty (based on a story by Dennis O'Flaherty from *The Adventures of Pinocchio* by Carlo Collodi); ph, Ervin L. Kaplan (CFI Color); m, Anthony Marinelli, Brian Banks; ed, Jeffrey Patrick Gehr; md, Erika Scheimer; art d, John Grusd; ch, Alfredo Desio; m/l, Will Jennings, Barry Mann, Steve Tyrell, Anthony Marinelli; animation, John Celestri, Chuck Harvey, Kamoon Song.

Animation/Children's (PR:AAA MPAA:G)

PISMA MYORTVOVO CHELOVYEKA (SEE: LETTERS FROM A DEAD MAN, 1987, USSR)

PLANES, TRAINS AND AUTOMOBILES*** (1987) 93m PAR c

Steve Martin *(Neal Page)*, John Candy *(Del Griffith)*, Laila Robins *(Susan Page)*, Michael McKean *(State Trooper)*, Kevin Bacon *(Taxi Racer)*, Dylan Baker *(Owen)*, Carol Bruce *(Joy Page)*, Olivia Burnette *(Marti)*, Diana Douglas *(Peg)*, William Windom *(Boss)*, Martin Ferrero *(Motel Clerk)*, Larry Hankin *(Doobie)*, Richard Herd *(Walt)*, Susan Kellerman *(Waitress)*, Matthew Lawrence *(Little Neal Page)*, Edie McClurg *(Car Rental Agent)*, George O. Petrie *(Martin Page)*, Gary Riley *(Motel Thief)*, Charles Tyner *(Gus)*, Lyman Ward *(John Dole)*, Nicholas Wyman, Ben Stein, John Randolph Jones.

The guru of teenager movies, John Hughes, enters the world of adults (more or less) with this seasonal comedy based on the horrors of transportation in America. The film opens two days before Thanksgiving in New York City as yuppie marketing consultant Martin finds himself with barely enough time to make it to the airport to catch his flight home to Chicago. Although hailing a cab at the height of Manhattan's rush hour turns into a nightmare, Martin gets to the airport in the nick of time and races to the terminal only to find that his flight has been delayed. Hours later, he boards the airplane and learns that he has been bumped from first class and must sit in coach next to John Candy, a huge slob wearing a polyester suit. Candy is a shower-curtain-ring salesman who is obnoxious, overbearing, and ceaselessly talkative. With Chicago's O'Hare Airport closed by a blizzard, the flight is detoured to Wichita for the night. With all the airport hotels full, Martin finds himself tagging along with Candy, who has booked a room at a seedy motel on the other side of town. ("I know the owner and he owes me a favor. I sold him all his shower-curtain rings," Candy explains.) Unfortunately, there is only one bed and the men are forced to sleep together. After Candy goes through his annoying nightly rituals—including everything from using up all the bathroom towels to clearing his sinus—a tired, crowded Martin is unable to sleep and finally explodes. He bombards Candy with a litany of insults, complaining about his bad habits, endless chatter, and pointless stories. Hurt by Martin's ridicule but retaining his dignity, Candy bitterly fires back. He reminds Martin of his generosity and states that he is perfectly aware that he is a blabbermouth, but that at least he's compassionate and takes the time to listen to other people. "I like me. My wife likes me. My customers like me," Candy says before going back to bed. Feeling chastised and guilty, Martin climbs into the bed. The next morning Martin awakes to find Candy's arms around him; then he gets a little kiss on the check from the sleepy salesman who mistakes Martin for his wife. Once fully awake, both horrified men leap from the bed and immediately try to reassert their manhood by mumbling comments like "How about that Bears game?" With O'Hare still snowed in and flights backed up for days, Candy arranges for them to get to Chicago by train. Martin ditches Candy on the train, but after the trip is halted in the middle of a cornfield due to engine problems, he finds himself sitting next to Candy once again on a bus. In St. Louis, Martin and Candy again part ways, and Martin rents a car. Dropped off in the middle of a huge parking lot by a shuttle bus, Martin goes to find his rental car and discovers that it is not there. Forced to walk several miles back to the rental agency and crazed with frustration, Martin looses a stream of profanity on rental agent McClurg, only to find that there are no more cars available. Candy, however, has gotten a rental car and Martin once again is stuck with the chatty salesman. On the trip from St. Louis to Chicago, Candy virtually destroys the car by setting it on fire with a carelessly disposed of cigarette, and the men are forced to drive in the freezing cold without a roof. The next morning they are pulled over by a state trooper who impounds their car because it is unfit to drive. Candy manages to hitch a ride for them in a refrigerator truck, but they are forced to sit in the freezer. Finally, on Thanksgiving day, Martin and Candy make it to Chicago. The men say farewell on the "El" platform and while Martin rides toward home he reflects on the outrageous trip and his growing fondness for Candy. Suddenly Martin realizes that Candy has been lying about having a wife (there have been clues all along) and will spend Thanksgiving alone. He goes back to find Candy and invites him to dinner. When Martin confronts him, Candy shyly admits that his wife passed away years ago. Dismissing the salesman's protests, Martin forces Candy to come home with him for turkey dinner and introduces his "friend" to the family.

With a concept as thin as this, PLANES, TRAINS AND AUTOMOBILES could have easily become a repetitious bore. Instead, Hughes infuses his film with an appealing sense of sentiment and humanity that overrides the rather limited narrative. Granted the situations are repetitive and Hughes is forced to rely on coincidence and exaggeration to keep the film going, but most of the events are not too far removed from the truth—anyone who has flown, taken a bus, or rented a car can attest to this. What saves the film from being merely clever is the interaction of the urbane, patronizing Martin with the earthy, chatty, lower-class Candy. Hughes makes Candy out to be everyone's nightmare traveling companion and encourages the audience to laugh at his obnoxious behavior. By letting the audience feel smug and superior along with Martin, Hughes sets us up to be hit in the face with our own petty cruelness when Martin hurts the big lug's feelings. In Candy's finest moment, the lonely salesman holds back tears during Martin's insensitive tirade. But instead of getting easy sympathy by having his character cry, Hughes has Candy regain his composure and bitterly fight back, asserting his dignity and humanity, effectively making Martin, and the audience, feel guilty for their superior attitude. As the trip continues Candy is no less obnoxious, but because our feelings toward him have changed, we, and Martin, are able to tolerate him as we would a family member. By the end of the film, when Martin realizes that Candy's behavior stems from loneliness and insecurity—from the need to be accepted—all that has gone before is forgivable. This is not to say that Hughes paints Candy's character as a pathetic wretch. Candy is more self-sufficient and savvy in the ways of mass transportation than Martin. Without him, Martin never would have made it home in time for Thanksgiving dinner.

After years of being handed disappointing vehicles in which to display his considerable talent, Candy finally has a bravura role. Able to elicit hearty laughs or sentimental sniffles without ever resorting to cheap tricks, Candy proves himself not only to be a superb comedian, but also a fine actor. He doesn't play Del Griffith as a happy-go-lucky bumpkin, but as a man who is proud, smart, optimistic, practical, fun-loving, and kind—a human being and not a stereotype. Martin, in the less flamboyant of the two roles, is excellent as well. He humanizes his self-absorbed character during the course of the film and, by the end, convinces the audience that Neal Page *would* turn back to retrieve his new friend. Both actors are skilled physical comedians and execute their sometimes complicated shtick with verve. Unfortunately, Hughes' direction does not quite live up to the excellence of his performers. The middle of the film drags a bit, and the comedy suffers from some uninspired repetition. More annoying is Hughes' insistence on cramming the film with a glut of pop songs that in most cases do nothing to complement the action—he should save them for the teenagers. Despite its flaws, PLANES, TRAINS AND AUTOMOBILES did well at the box office because of the superb performances of Candy and Martin. *(Excessive profanity.)*

p,d&w, John Hughes; ph, Don Peterman (Technicolor); m, Ira Newborn; ed, Paul Hirsch; prod d, John W. Corso; art d, Harold Michelson; set d, Louis Mann; cos, April Ferry.

Comedy **(PR:O MPAA:R)**

PLASTPOSEN† (1987, Norway) 90m Filminvest-Norsk/Norsk c (Trans: The Plastic Bag; AKA: ANDERSEN'S RUN)

Jon Skolmen *(Andersen)*, Hilde Grythe *(Patrolwoman Eva)*, Sverre Anker Ousdal *(Bank Robber)*, Ingar Helge Gimle *(Patrolman Osvald)*, Elsa Lysted *(Kiosk Lady)*, Per Schaanning, Reidar Sorensen, Anne-Marie Ottersen, Ragnhild Nygaard, Marianne Ustvedt, Mette Tank, Jan Harstadt.

Popular Norwegian comedian Jon Skolmen, who is best known throughout Scandinavia for his roles as Lasse Aberg's sidekick in that Swedish writer-director's "Charter Trip" films, stars here as a man who simply wants to get rid of a bag full of garbage that won't fit down the chute in his apartment building. This, however, doesn't prove to be as easy as it first appears, and in the course of his garbage detail, Skolmen becomes a suspect in a bank robbery. Having thrown caution and his garbage to the wind, Skolmen is thought to be an accomplice in the crooks' getaway because some of his trash ends up in the face of a pursuing policewoman and allows the robbers to make good their getaway.

p, Wenche Solum; d, Hans Otto Nicolayssen; w, Kerry Crabbe (based on an idea by Jon Skolmen); ph, Halvor Nass (Eastmancolor); m, Geir Bohren, Bent Aserud; ed, Margit Nordquist; prod d, Frode Krogh.

Comedy **(PR:NR MPAA:NR)**

PLIUMBUM, ILI OPASNAIA IGIA† (1987, USSR) 96m Mosfilm c (Trans: Plumbum, or a Dangerous Game)

Anton Androsov *(Ruslan Chutro)*, Elena Dmitrieva *(Sonia)*, Elena Yakovleva *(Maria)*, Alexander Foklistov *(Grey)*, Alexander Pashutin *(Father)*, Vladimir Sieklov *(Lopatov)*, Soia Lirova *(Mother)*, Alexeit Saitsev *(Kolia-Oleg)*.

A strange morality tale that could not have been made before *glasnost* stars Androsov as a 15-year-old boy who lives a double life: devoted son and high-school student by day, vigilante informer at night. The boy spies on and informs the state of black marketeers, gamblers, and street peddlers with a religious fervor, delighting in the power he holds over the lives of strangers. No one is exempt from his fanaticism, not even his father who was caught fishing out of season. In the end, Androsov meets with a bad fate because he failed to temper his zealousness with understanding, proportion, or compassion. Shown in competition at the Venice Film Festival.

d, Vadim Abdrashitov; w, Alexander Mindadze; ph, George Rerberg; m, Vladimir Dashkevich; art d, Alexander Tolkachev.

Drama **(PR:NR MPAA:NR)**

PLOSHCHAD VOSSTANIA† (1987, USSR) 81m Mosfilm/Sovexportfilm c (Trans: Insurrection Square)

Lyudmilla Gladunko, Vladimir Simonov, Sergei Shakurov, Boris Khimichev, Shavkat Gaziyev, Pavel Alexeyev.

A Russian historian traces the background of a messenger (known as "The Violinst") of a special branch of government in Moscow and his importance in the revolution of 1905.

d, Boris Tokarev; w, Yury Yakovlev, Boris Tokarev; ph, Nikolai Nemolyayev; m, Isaak Schwarz; art d, Lyudmila Kusakova.

Drama **(PR:NR MPAA:NR)**

PO GLAVNOY ULITSE S ORKESTROM† (1987, USSR) 93m Mosfilm/Sovexportfilm c (Trans: Downtown with a Band)

Oleg Borisov, Lidia Fedoseyeva-Shukshina, Marina Zudina, Valentin Gaft, Igor Kostolevsky.

A musical comedy about the experiences of a family man going through mid-life crisis. Bored with his humdrum existance, he leaves his job and family to start a new life, but the separation convinces him he has made a mistake and he returns to his wife and daughter with new resolve.

d, Pyotr Todorovsky; w, Alexander Buravsky, Pyotr Todorovsky; ph, Valery Shuvalov; m, Igor Kantyukov; art d, Valentin Konovalov.

Musical Comedy **(PR:NR MPAA:NR)**

PO ZAKONU VOENNOGO VREMENI† (1987, USSR) 79m Mosfilm/Sovexportfilm c (Trans: Under War-Time Law)

Olga Ageyeva, Igor Yasulovich, Boris Smorchkov, Vladimir Shirokov.

Four young Soviet soldiers miss the train that is to take them to the front during the early years of WW II. Knowing that they can be charged with a criminal offense by the military for missing their transport, the four decide to get to the front by themselves instead of reporting to their commandant's office. After several harrowing adventures, the four soldiers arrive at the rendezvous point before their comrades on the train. Taking refuge in an abandoned church, the four Soviets notice Nazi soldiers preparing to blow up the railway bridge. Heroically, the hopelessly out-numbered Soviet soldiers give their lives to stop the Nazis and save their comrades from certain death.

d, Igor Slabnevich; w, Nikolai Arsenyev, Evgeny Vinokurov, Igor Slabnevich; ph, Alexei Temerin; m, Valery Zubkov; art d, Vassily Golikov.

War **(PR:NR MPAA:NR)**

POCIAG DO HOLLYWOOD† (1987, Pol.) 97m Zespoly Filmowe, Rondo Unit c (Trans: Train to Hollywood)

Katarzyna Figura *("Marilyn")*, Piotr Siwkiewicz *(Piotrus)*, Rafal Wegrzyniak *(Rafal)*, Grazyna Kruk *(Sandra)*, Jerzy Stuhr *(The Director)*, Eugeniusz Priwiezncew, Krystyna Feldman.

A Polish comedy featuring Figura as a young woman who was bitten by the acting bug as a little girl after having seen Marilyn Monroe in Billy Wilder's classic SOME LIKE IT HOT. Figura patterns herself after MM and upon graduating high school she goes to the Film Academy to take a screen test. Rejected because of her crooked teeth, Figura takes a job selling beer on a passenger train and begins a letter-writing campaign to Billy Wilder in an effort to get him to cast her in his next movie. At the train station she meets Siwkiewicz, a would-be cinematographer save for one small affliction—he's color-blind. The two become fast friends, sharing their dreams of going to Hollywood. One day Figura finds a goldfish trapped in a beer bottle. She sets the fish free and makes three wishes—not for herself, but for her friends. To her surprise all of her wishes come true, including Siwkiewicz being cured of his color-blindness. As a reward, Figura finally receives the long-awaited call from Billy Wilder. Director Piwowarski won the main prize at the Festival of Polish Films in Gdansk and the Film Critics prize for best Polish film of 1986 for his previous feature MY MOTHER'S LOVERS.

d&w, Radislaw Piwowarski; ph, Witold Adamek; m, Jerzy Matula; ed, Irena Chorynska; prod d, Tadeusz Kosarewicz.

Comedy **(PR:NR MPAA:NR)**

PODSUDIMYY† (1987, USSR) 89m Lenfilm/Sovexportfilm c (Trans: The Accused)

Mikhail Zhigalov, Tatiana Shestakova, Rolan Bykov, Yury Kuznetsov.

A middle-aged war veteran shoots and kills a young man who invaded his orchard, and accepting his guilt does nothing to defend himself at his trial. But his lawyer feels there was provocation and sets out to prove it. The evidence he gathers assures a new trial for the veteran, but causes a heart attack and death for the lawyer.

d, Iosif Heifits; w, Boris Vasilyev, Iosif Heifits; ph, Valery Blinov; m, Sergei Rachmaninoff; art d, Yelena Fomina.

Crime **(PR:NR MPAA:NR)**

POET'S SILENCE, THE*** (1987, Ger.) 98m Westdeutscher Rundfunk/Filmverlag der Autoren c (DAS SCHWEIGEN DES DICHTERS)

Jacov Lind *(Jacob)*, Len Ramras *(Gideon)*, Daniel Kedem *(Gideon as a Child)*,

Towje Kleiner *(Fayermann)*, Vladimir Weigl *(Avi)*, Barbara Lass *(Janina)*, Gudrun Weichenhanh *(Naomi)*, Jacob Ben-Sira *(Schiffrin)*, Peter Freistadt *(Dr. Marx)*, Mischa Natan *(Mandel)*, Jehuda Cohen *(School Maintenance Man)*, Anat Mesner *(Secretary)*, Roberto Polac.

Peter Lilienthal has been one of Germany's most prominent and consistent directors, with several major awards to his credit (including the 1979 Berlin Festival's Golden Bear for DAVID). Despite this his films have remained virtually unseen outside of Western Europe. THE POET'S SILENCE was shown briefly in the States on the festival circuit, and will more than likely remain shelved until some retrospective of Lilienthal's work is mounted. Like many of his previous films, THE POET'S SILENCE is concerned with the artist's—particularly the writer's—ability to work in an environment that is often hostile to the creative process. Lind plays a once successful Israeli poet who, for some unknown reason, cannot find the inspiration to continue writing. Several possibilities are suggested as the cause of Lind's "silence," including the Yom Kippur War that left his brother blind and the long sickness and death of his wife, who became virtually bedridden after giving birth to a half-wit son late in life. Lind's excuse for not writing is that he must take care of his son. While Lind claims his son is only mildly retarded, others believe the boy should be sent to a home. For the most part, THE POET'S SILENCE concentrates on the relationship between the boy (played by Kedem as a young child) and his father. As the film opens, Kedem is shown as an unruly child who tries the patience of other adults. He continually creates havoc and only his father sees the boy as special. He insists that his son remain at home with him, despite the trouble he causes. Even Lind's adult daughter begs her father to put Kedem in an institution where he can be looked after properly. Lind's wife dies, and the film jumps several years into the future. Kedem grows into the 17-year-old Ramras and is beset with the same problem he had as a child—the inability to effectively express himself. In spite of this, Ramras possesses a carefree yet tranquil aura which makes it almost impossible to dislike him. The youth's main task becomes the care of his father. He cooks and cleans while Lind spends his days as a newspaper editor. This peaceful existence is strained when Ramras learns that his father was once a successful poet. Ramras blames himself for the demise of Lind's writing, and immediately does all he can to persuade his father to take up the pen again. Ramras copies down line after line of Lind's old poems on large pieces of paper, posting them throughout the house in the hope that Lind will be inspired. He even goes so far as to bring his father's work to a vanity press in a feeble attempt to have it published. When Ramras is convinced that he is thwarting his father's creative process—a feeling that is intensified after Lind has an affair with a woman whom Ramras doesn't like—the teenager does his best to stay out of the house. He looks for odd jobs and carouses with friends. However, Lind seems determined never to write again, and makes plans to spend his remaining days traveling alone. Just as Lind prepares to undertake his sojourn, the boat he is to leave on is forced to remain in dock. As the film ends, the poet returns to his work by renting a small hotel room with a window overlooking the sea. Lind once again allows his pen to describe the images that have long laid dormant in the back of his mind. THE POET'S SILENCE was released in Germany in 1986.

p, Edgar Reitz; d&w, Peter Lilienthal (based on a story by Abraham B. Yohoshua); ph, Justus Pankau; m, Claus Bantzer; ed, Siegrun Jager; art d, Charlie Leon, Franz Bauer; cos, Rina Doron.

Drama **(PR:C MPAA:NR)**

POEZD VNE RASPISANIA† (1987, USSR) 80m Odessa/Sovexportfilm c (Trans: Unscheduled Train)

Vladimir Shevelkov, Igor Shavlak, Natalia Vavilova, Olga Kuznetsova.

A young man who has a romantic crush on an unsuspecting girl is given a chance to prove his heroism when the train in which they are riding becomes a runaway due to an accidental fire.

d, Alexander Grishin; w, Alexei Leontyev, Anatoly Tsarenko, Alexander Grishin; ph, Vladimir Pankov, Viktor Kabachenko; m, Grigory Gladkov; art d, Mikhail Katz.

Drama **(PR:NR MPAA:NR)**

POEZDKI NA STAROM AVTOMOBILE† (1987, USSR) 86m Mosfilm/ Sovexportfilm c (Trans: Rides on an Old Car)

Lyudmila Maxakova, Andrei Boltnev.

A musical comedy about a middle-aged stage manager at an amateur theater who is dismayed to find that her son is getting a divorce and her daughter-in-law will not allow her to see her grandson. The woman later meets and falls for a middle-aged referee but is shocked to discover that he is the father of her former daughter-in-law's new husband.

d, Pyotr Fomenko; w, Emil Braginsky; ph, Vsevolod Simakov; m, Sergei Nikitin; art d, Irina Shreter.

Musical Comedy **(PR:NR MPAA:NR)**

POHADKA O MALICKOVI† (1987, Czech./USSR) 80m RIGA Film Studios-Barrandov c (USSR: MALCHIK S PALCHIK)

Roland Nejland *(Malicek/J. Klima)*, Dace Gasjunova *(Lienite/J. Palenickova)*, Dzintra Kletniecova *(Stepmother/H. Pastejrikova)*, Elvira Baldinova *(Grandmother/L. Roubikova)*, Zdenek Rehor *(King)*, Miroslava Souckova *(Princess)*, Miroslav Horacek *(Devil/M. Pavlata)*, Antra Liedskalnynova *(Witch)*, Juris Strenga *(Miser)*, Anda Zajcova *(Servant)*, Alfreds Videnieks *(Starec)*, Astrida Kajrisova *(Mother Vetru)*, Mirdza Martinsonova *(Mother Lesu)*, Miroslav Moravec *(Giant)*, Egon Majsaks *(Herold)*, Elza Radzinova *(Court Lady)*, Jan Skopecek, Vlasta Zehrova, Milena Steinmasslova, Jana Viscakova.

d&w, Gunar Piesis (based on the fairy tale by Anna Brigadere); ph, Martins Klejns; m, Imant Kalnyns; ed, Lienite Balinova; art d, Ivar Majlitis, Milos Cervinka; cos, Ieva Kundzinova; ch, Frantisek Pokorny.

Children's **(PR:NR MPAA:NR)**

POISONS† (1987, Switz./Fr.) 105m Light Night-Maison de la Culture du Havre-Television Suisse Romande/Light Night c

Maurice Garrel *(Northrup)*, Mimsy Farmer *(Ann)*, Pierre Dubillard *(Loiseau)*, Francois Berthet *(Marc)*, Rufus *(Lewis)*.

Allegorical tale about a famous painter, Garrel, who is held captive in a remote villa by a trio of brothers who try to force him to work so that they can live off his earnings. Although he maintains a pacifistic stance with his captors, the artist refuses to paint, thus frustrating their plans. Complications arise when a woman admirer of Garrel's work arrives on the scene. Shown in competition at the Locarno Film Festival.

d&w, Pierre Maillard; ph, Patrice Cologne; m, Jacques Robellaz; ed, Rodolfo Wedeles; art d&cos, Laurence Bruley.

Drama **(PR:NR MPAA:NR)**

POKAYANIYE (SEE: REPENTANCE, 1987, USSR)

POKLONIS DO ZEMLI† (1987, USSR) 78m Kiev/Sovexportfilm c (Trans: Bow Your Head)

Stefania Stanyuta, Pavel Kormunin, Nina Tobilevich, Les Serdyuk.

A peasant woman loses her will to live when her husband and children are killed in the war. But when she finds a baby near the body of its dead mother her life takes on new meaning. She adopts three babies, naming them after her dead children, and lives to see her grandchildren.

d, Leonid Osyka; w, Valentin Yezhov, Vladimir Lyubomudrov, Leonid Osyka; ph, Valery Kvas; m, Vladimir Guba; art d, Pyotr Slabinsky.

Drama **(PR:NR MPAA:NR)**

POLEVAYA GVARDIA MOZZHUKHINA† (1987, USSR) 100m Mosfilm/ Sovexportfilm c (Trans: Mozjukhin's Field Guard)

Vasily Bochkarev, Andrei Tashkov, Eduard Bocharov, Titiana Aksyuta.

A successful engineer returns to the village of his birth after many years of work at different construction projects. He enlists the support of an old friend and his son in a new, progressive plan for the workers which draws criticism as well as support from the villagers. His only reservation is the immaturity of his friend's son, but when misfortune sends the engineer to the hospital, the boy shows his true mettle.

d, Valery Lonskoy; w, Budimir Metalnikov; ph, Yury Nevsky; m, Isaak Schwarz; art d, Eleonora Nemechek.

Drama **(PR:NR MPAA:NR)**

POLICE ACADEMY 4: CITIZENS ON PATROL* (1987) 87m WB c

Steve Guttenberg *(Mahoney)*, Bubba Smith *(Hightower)*, Michael Winslow *(Jones)*, David Graf *(Tackleberry)*, Tim Kazurinsky *(Sweetchuck)*, Sharon Stone *(Claire Mattson)*, Leslie Easterbrook *(Callahan)*, Marion Ramsey *(Hooks)*, Lance Kinsey *(Proctor)*, G.W. Bailey *(Capt. Harris)*, Bobcat Goldthwait *(Zed)*, George Gaynes *(Commandant Lassard)*, Derek McGrath *(Butterworth)*, Scott Thomson *(Copeland)*, Billie Bird *(Mrs. Feldman)*, George R. Robertson *(Commissioner Hurst)*, Brian Tochi *(Nogata)*, Brian Backer *(Arnie)*, David Spade *(Kyle)*, Tab Thacker *(House)*, Corinne Bohrer *(Laura)*, Randall "Tex" Cobb *(Zack)*, Michael McManus *(Todd)*, Colleen Camp *(Mrs. Kirkland-Tackleberry)*, Andrew Paris *(Bud Kirkland)*, Arthur Batanides *(Mr. Kirkland)*, Jackie Joseph *(Mrs. Kirkland)*; Police Officials: Arnie Hardt *(German)*, Frank Canino *(Italian)*, Bob Lem *(Chinese)*, Francois Klanfer *(French)*; Their Translators: Denis de Laviolette *(German)*, Joey Pomanti *(Italian)*, Harvey Chao *(Chinese)*, Michele Duquet *(French)*; Jack Creley *(Judge)*, Ted Simonett *(Copeland's Partner)*, Kay Hartrey *(Poetess)*, Sid Gould *(Man with Harmonica)*, Megan Smith, Don Ritchie *(Couple at Elevator)*, Rummy Bishop *(Party Man)*, Carolyn Scott *(Nurse)*, Marc Leger *(Headquarters Cop)*, Larry Schwartz *(Warehouse Cop)*, James Carroll *(Warehouse Supplier)*, Michael Rhoades *(Hood in Balloon)*, Brent Myers *(Bank Robber)*, Diane Fabian *(Purse Snatching Victim)*, Glenn Preston *(Blue Oyster Patron)*.

With this, the fourth in the series, receipts should top the $400 million mark, which is more than the budget for several Third World countries. For some strange reason the series has been very popular overseas as well as domestically. After viewing the first three, it was difficult to imagine that there might be anything original to show in this one but the boys in blue are back in an even sillier film. To make this palatable to a larger audience, much of the sleaze has been deleted and the tasteless jokes run to gags about bird droppings, genitalia, stomach disorders, and the like. Gaynes is again the dippy Academy chief. He's on the verge of retirement and has decided to put a master plan into action. He thinks that by engaging the services of the public, new neighborhood watch programs might be able to supplement his hard-working charges. To that end, he asks for the average citizen to step forward and be trained by his staff, led again by Guttenberg, who is top-billed but doesn't really have all that much to do in this ensemble piece. The cops train the civilians, but while Gaynes is off at a

convention of police chiefs, his rival, Bailey, comes in to wreak havoc and show that there is no place for untrained amateurs. When a cadre of kung-fu toughs and motorcycle riders flee prison, they are captured by the real cops and the volunteers after a chase that includes hot air balloons and some vintage planes. The jokes come thick and fast and if you don't like one, wait a few seconds and another will be right along. With a huge cast that is almost lost in the action, POLICE ACADEMY 4 features so many old sight gags that anyone who grew up on Charles Chaplin, Harold Lloyd, and Harry Langdon will be insulted. But if you haven't seen the originals and don't know whence the gags sprung, there are some funny, albeit reminiscent, moments. Screenwriter Kazurinsky (ABOUT LAST NIGHT) is back wearing his actor's hat, but doesn't have enough time on screen. He should have had a say in the script because Quintano's work is sadly lacking any wit and any motivation. The whole idea of the air show at the conclusion seems thoroughly contrived, as if it were just there to give the film an interesting visual conclusion. Many of the jokes are the same ones seen in earlier POLICE ACADEMY movies. It's as though the producers think the audience has the collective memory of a flea.

Everything moves so quickly under director Drake's hand that one hardly has time to realize just how stale all of this is. Easterbrook repeats her role and does well. Brian Tochi, so good in REVENGE OF THE NERDS, is not put to any good use. Veteran Jackie Joseph, who starred as "Audrey" in the original cult classic LITTLE SHOP OF HORRORS, appears briefly. In a cute role, note old-timer Billie Bird in a part Molly Picon usually plays. Bubba Smith, the former Colt and Raider lineman, looks small compared to Thacker, a behemoth who weighs in at close to 400 pounds. Lots of songs to take your mind off the stupidity on screen. They include: "It Doesn't Have to Be This Way" (Dr. Robert, performed by The Blow Monkeys), "Shoot for the Moon" (Harry Maslin, Kurt Howell, performed by Southern Pacific), "Winning Streak" (Garry Glenn, performed by Glenn), "Rock the House" (Claude Ganem, performed by Jean-Marc Dompierre and His orchestra), "Citizens on Patrol" (Arthur Funaro, Mike Stuart, performed by Michael Winslow and the L.A. Dream Team), "Dancin' Up a Storm" (Sandy Sherman, Janice Liebhart, performed by Stacy Lattisaw), "I Like My Body" (Gary Taylor, performed by Chico De Barge), "It's Time to Move" (Dan Navarro, Eric Lowen, Rick Boston, performed by S.O.S. Band), "Rescue Me" (Victor Brooks, Rudy Pardee, Michael Person, performed by Family Dream), and "Lets Go to Heaven in My Car" (Brian Wilson, Gary Usher, Eugene E. Landy, performed by Wilson). Fans of the films will be delighted to know that yet another sequel is in the works. *(Profanity, sexual situations.)*

p, Paul Maslansky; d, Jim Drake; w, Gene Quintano (based on characters created by Neal Israel, Pat Proft); ph, Robert Saad (Medallion Color); m, Robert Folk; ed, David Rawlins; prod d, Trevor Williams; art d, Rhiley Fuller; set d, Steve Shewchuk; cos, Aleida MacDonald; m/l, Mike Stuart, Arthur Funaro, Darryl Duncan, Gary Taylor, Rick Boston, Eric Lowen, Dan Navarro, Garry Glenn, Rudy Pardee, Michael Person, Victor Brooks, Sandy Sherman, Janice Liebhart, Brian Wilson, Eugene E. Landy, Gary Usher, Kurt Howell, Harry Maslin, Claude Ganem, Dr. Robert; spec eff, Gene Grigg; stunts, Michael DeLuna; makeup, Ken Brooke.

Comedy Cas. **(PR:C MPAA:PG)**

POLICIA† (1987, Span.) A.S.H.-Impala/Warner Espanola c

Emilio Aragon *(Gumer)*, Agustin Gonzalez *(Cpl. Lopez)*, Ana Obregon *(Luisa)*, Juan Luis Galiardo *(Maxi)*, Jose Guardiola *(Don Ramon)*, Pilar Alcon *(Pepa)*, Jack Taylor *(Inspector Ferrara)*, Adriano Dominguez *(Comisario Jefe)*, Viky Lagos *(Manoli)*, Bruno Vella *(Tomas)*, Fernando Sancho *(Comandante Castillejo)*, Alberto Fernandez *(Sgt. Ortiz)*.

[No plot information available.]

d&w, Alvaro Saenz de Heredia; ph, Jose M. Civit; m, Emilio Aragon; ed, Antonio Ramirez; set d, Jose Luis Galicia; cos, Kia Nelke; makeup, Tony Nieto.

Action **(PR:NR MPAA:NR)**

POLICIAS DE NARCOTICOS† (1987, Mex.) 87m Cinematografica Sol/ Peliculas Mexicanas c (Trans: Narcotics Police)

Valentin Trujillo *(Julian Carrera)*, Sergio Goyri *(Roberto Rojas)*, Rodolfo de Anda *(Antonio Farkas)*, Angelica Chain *(Albina)*, Julio Aleman *(El Licenciado)*, Bruno Rey, Isaura Espinoza, Arturo Alegro, Edgardo Gazcon, Edna Bolkan.

In 1986, Valentin Trujillo directed and starred in UN HOMBRE VIOLENTE, the story of a violent family feud. In POLICIAS DE NARCOTICOS, the sequel to that film, Trujillo is still the star but the directorial chores have been assumed by Gilberto de Anda, the producer and writer of the earlier film. After having exacted his honor-bound vengeance in the first film, Trujillo now looks for justice in more general terms as a policeman. He and partner Goyri do their best to bust Rodolfo de Anda (who also served as the film's producer) and Chain, partners in dope smuggling who are willing to go to any bloody extreme to protect their operation.

p, Rodolfo de Anda; d, Gilberto de Anda; w, X. Randa; ph, Antonio de Anda; m, Gustavo Pimental; ed, Sergio Soto.

Crime **(PR:NR MPAA:NR)**

POOVIZHI VASALILE† (1987, India)

Sathyaraj, Karthika, Raghuvaran, Sujatha.

[No plot information available.] (In Tamil.)

d, Fazil; m, Ilayaraja.

(PR:NR MPAA:NR)

POR LOS CAMINOS VERDES† (1987, Venezuela) 93m c (Trans: On the Green Path)

Jorge Canelon, Joel Escala, Alberto Acevedo, Yulay Sanchez, Pablo Masabet, Ricardo Salazar, Carlos J. Gonzalez, Carlos Julio Ramirez, Lucila d'Avanzo.

A group of refugees from Colombia illegally enters Venezuela in the hopes of establishing a better life. The film details the refugees efforts at assimilating into their new culture and follows them as they find jobs, romance, and even death when one becomes involved with drug dealers. The feature debut of woman director Vera, a British-born South American. Ruben Blades, the popular Panamanian salsa musician and star of the film CROSSOVER DREAMS, composed the music for this film.

p&d, Marilda Vera; w, Milagros Rodriquez, Marilda Vera; ph, Carlos Tovar, Miquel Curiel; m, Ruben Blades; ed, Armando Valero; set d, Maria Adelina Vera.

Drama **(PR:NR MPAA:NR)**

POSLEDNYAYA DOROGA† (1987, USSR) 101m Lenfilm/Sovexportfilm c (Trans: The Last Road)

Alexander Kalyagin, Vadim Medvedev, Irina Kupchenko, Yelena Karadjova, Anna Kamenkova, Innokenty Smoktunovsky.

In a film dedicated to the memory of the great Russian poet Alexander Sergeyevich Puschkin, the events of the last days of his life are portrayed through his relatives, friends, enemies, and the people on the street. Discovering his wife's unfaithfulness with the son of the Dutch ambassador, the gauntlet is thrown down and retrieved by the errant lover, resulting in the duel which cost Puschkin his life.

d, Leonid Menaker; w, Yakov Gordon, Leonid Menaker; ph, Vladimir Kovzel; m, Andrei Petrov; art d, Marksen Gaukhman-Sverdlov.

Biography **(PR:NR MPAA:NR)**

POULE ET FRITES† (1987, Fr.) 87m Intl. Prods.-Planetes et Compagnie-C.K. Music-Sofinergie Stone/Gaumont c (Trans: Chicken and Fries)

Luis Rego *(Roger)*, Anemone *(Bebe)*, Michel Galabru *(Martinez)*, Claire Nadeau *(Minou)*, Carole Jacquinot *(Vera)*, Claude Gensac *(Francoise)*, Laurent Romor *(Jimmy)*, Eva Darlan, Marc Jolivet.

Rego stars as a philanderer who runs an illicit concession stand on the Riviera. Although he has maintained a successful relationship with both his wife and his mistress for years, he bites off more than he can chew when he starts an affair with a sadomasochistic cabaret singer. The directorial debut of popular French comedian Rego.

p, Pierre Sayag; d, Luis Rego; w, Luis Rego, Michel Ehlers, Jackie Berroyer; ph, Gerard de Battista; m, Luis Rego, Scott Allen, Vincent Palmer; Miguel Castagnos; ed, Catherine Kelber; art d, Olivier Paultre.

Comedy **(PR:NR MPAA:NR)**

POUSSIERE D'ANGE† (1987, Fr.) 94m President-UGC Top 1-Films de la Saga-FR3-La Sofica/UGC c (Trans: Angel Dust)

Bernard Giraudeau *(Simon Blount)*, Fanny Bastien *(Violetta Reverdy)*, Fanny Cottencon *(Martine Blount)*, Jean-Pierre Sentier *(Landry)*, Michel Aumont *(Florimont)*, Gerard Blain *(Broz)*, Luc Lavandier *(Gabriel)*, Veronique Silver, Daniel Laloux, Yveline Aihaud, Patrick Bonnel, Bertie Cortez, Henri Marteau, Daniel Russo.

Stylish French *film noir* starring Giraudeau as an alcoholic detective who loses the will to live after his wife leaves him for another man. He is saved from the abyss by Bastien, a beautiful *femme fatale* who seduces him into her web of intrigue and murder. Seeking vengence for the killing of her mother—a prostitute—Bastien cold-bloodedly arranges the deaths of those she holds responsible for the deed. Director Niermans creates a hybrid urban enviornment for his film, shooting on locations in Paris, Lyons, and Marseille, and making them one strange-but-familiar city.

d, Edouard Niermans; w, Edouard Niermans; Jacques Audiard, Alain Le Henry; ph, Bernard Lutic (Eastmancolor); m, Leon Senza, Vincent-Marie Bouvot; ed, Yves Deschamps, Jacques Witta; art d, Dominique Maleret.

Drama **(PR:NR MPAA:NR)**

PRATELE BERMUDSKEHO TROJUHELNIKU† (1987, Czech.) 101m Filmove Studio Barrandov

Frantisek Husak *(Arnost)*, Martin Dejdar *(Burglar)*, Lubomir Kostelka *(Grandfather)*, Jiri Helekal *(Singer)*, Jan Zachar *(Karel Jindrisek/M. Pavlata)*, Vlasta Spicnerova *(Helena)*, Zdenek Dusek *(Dvorak)*, Vaclav Mares *(Chairman)*, Karol Calik *(Tonda)*, Milan Gargula *(Milan)*, Marek Brodsky *(Student)*, Magda Reifova *(His Girl)*, Dagmar Vesknrova *(Marketa)*, Ondrej Vetchy *(Savko)*, Karel Augusta *(Actor)*, Jaroslav Cmiral *(Ucitel)*, Leos Sucharipa *(Deputy)*, Martin Rusek *(Professor)*, Josef Langmiler *(Chief)*, Ladislav Trojan *(Captain)*, Robert Vrchota, Vera Tichankova *(Savko's Parents)*, Vladimir Hrabanek, Milan Steindler, Pavel Novy, Jaroslav Cmiral.

d, Vaclav Kristek, Jan Prokop, Petr Sicha; w, Frantisek R. Cech, Petr Novotny, Jiri Just; ph, Antonin Holub; m, Daniel Fikejz, Nahral D. Fikejz; ed, Petr Sitar; art d, Boris Halmi; cos, Kristyna Novotna.

Comedy **(PR:NR MPAA:NR)**

PRATIGHAAT† (1987, India) Ushakiron/Rajshri (Trans: Counter-Attack)

Sujata Mehta, Arvind Kumar, Charanraj, Rohini Hattangady, Ashok Saraf, Mohan Bhandari, K. Sriniwas Rao, A. Ramarao, Gyan Shivpuri, Nana Patekar, Aashish Kuki, Anil Rajput, Rahul Choudhary, Anuradha Sawant, Subbiraj, Ravi Patwardhan, Suhas Palshikar, Nandlal Sharma, Bhimraj, Prem Rishi, Balwant Bansal, Dilip Joshi, Khalid Shah, Deo Malhotra, Vijay Pimprikar, Ashok Raj, Alfred Maan, Anand Bijnori, Alok Sharad, Mahesh Kumar, Ashok Chavan, Aizaz, Tom Tom, Lallan, Raj Bharati, Rajesh Bombaywalla, Suresh, Ranjana Sachdev, Usha Nadkarni, Sanjivani, Savita Balaj, Prabha Misra, Baby Mini Tabassum, Baby Pooja Thakar.

A vicious killer holds a small town in his evil grip through intimidation and corruption of the local officals. A woman lecturer at the college becomes outraged when she discovers that the evildoer's influence reaches the school as well. Finding the situation intolerable, the determined woman persuades a brave police inspector to arrest the criminal. When the inspector is gunned down in broad daylight, the woman decides to run as a rival candidate against the villain in the next election. Dispatching his minions to intimidate the voters, the villain wins easily. At the victory celebration, the woman seizes the silver axe that serves as the symbol of the villain's election campaign and assassinates him, martyring herself to save the oppressed citizens.

p, Ramoji Rao; d, N. Chandra; w, T. Krishna, N. Chandra; ph, H. Laxmi Narayan; art d, Bijon Dasgupta; cos, Tulsi Pawar; ch, Subal Sarkar; makeup, S. Jayanta.

Drama **(PR:NR MPAA:NR)**

PRAYER FOR THE DYING, A** (1987) 104m Goldwyn c

Mickey Rourke *(Martin Fallon)*, Alan Bates *(Jack Meehan)*, Bob Hoskins *(Father Da Costa)*, Sammi Davis *(Anna)*, Christopher Fulford *(Billy)*, Liam Neeson *(Liam Docherty)*, Alison Doody *(Siobhan Donovan)*, Camille Coduri *(Jenny)*, Ian Bartholomew, Mark Lambert, Cliff Burnett, Anthony Head, David Lumsden, Lenny Termo.

Pared down to its basics, A PRAYER FOR THE DYING is a film about moral self-examination which addresses the dilemma "to kill or not to kill." It's an honest attempt to understand the morality of murder which instead sinks, however unintentionally, into silly campiness and treacly melodrama. The film opens in Northern Ireland as Rourke and two fellow IRA terrorists accidentally blow up a school bus instead of a British military transport. Rourke's pals escape in a waiting car, but Rourke, who is mentally torn apart by the incident, turns his back on the Cause and escapes to London, where he hopes to find safe passage to the U.S. With the IRA *and* the British police on his trail, Rourke turns to Bates, a vile gangster who fronts as a mortician. In exchange for a passport, Rourke is assigned the task of murdering Bates' strongest rival. Rourke, however, is slowly losing touch with reality. He has nearly lost his desire to live, and with it his desire to kill. Desiring freedom more than anything, he agrees to be a gun for hire. Finding his target praying in a cemetery, Rourke coldly fires a single shot into the man's back. The murder is witnessed by Hoskins, the parish priest, but Rourke is not so ruthless as to kill him also. Later, Rourke divulges his secret to Hoskins in the sanctity of the confessional. Bound by his theological responsibility, Hoskins is unable to give the police the killer's identity. Bates, however, wants no witnesses and orders Hoskins killed. Rourke refuses and offers Hoskins protection from the gangster and his thugs, especially Bates' demented brother (Fulford).

While keeping an eye on Hoskins, Rourke meets Davis, Hoskins' blind niece, who is also the church organist. Through her, Rourke finds in himself the feelings and emotions that have since vanished from his life, while she is able to "see" the goodness in Rourke that all the others have overlooked. Tensions escalate between Rourke and Bates, with Hoskins getting caught in the middle. Bates pays a street gang to desecrate Hoskins' church, and Hoskins retaliates by beating senseless three of Bates' thugs (Hoskins, it is revealed, saw combat in the British army . . . and liked it). Davis is the next target of Bates' wrath when Fulford terrorizes the seemingly helpless blind girl. She manages to kill him just before Rourke arrives. (In one of the film's best moments, Davis asks if she killed her attacker. Rourke, sheltering her from the conscience-wrenching truth, tells her that the attacker ran off.) Determined to put an end to his problems, Bates sets up Rourke to be killed and then plants a bomb in Hoskins' church. Rourke manages to rescue Hoskins and Davis from the church bell tower and confronts Bates. He is held prisoner by Rourke atop the church as they wait for the impending explosion—Bates, terribly afraid of dying, and Rourke realizing that he's been dead for quite a while. The comically maudlin finale has Rourke falling from the tower just moments before the bomb explodes. Crushed under the weight of a crumbled crucifix, Rourke begs for forgiveness as Hoskins administers last rights.

Based on a novel by Jack Higgins (*The Eagle Has Landed*), A PRAYER FOR THE DYING had troubles in preproduction, during production, and in its release. Difficulties arose from the start when the film's original director, Franc Roddam (QUADROPHENIA, THE LORDS OF DISCIPLINE), left the project, citing irreparable script problems. With just a few weeks remaining before the cameras were set to roll, Mike Hodges stepped aboard. Hodges, who directed two fine Michael Caine pictures early in his career (GET CARTER, 1971, and PULP, 1972), hadn't had much of a chance to duplicate that success, instead turning out such mediocrities as FLASH GORDON and 1985's MORONS FROM OUTER SPACE. Not long into the $6 million project, things began to go awry. The top-billed Rourke found himself more and more interested in his character's Belfast background and the IRA's influence on his desire to kill. "I didn't want to make this character some kind of romantic hero who coasts through the movie killing people," explained Rourke. "I wanted to make a film where we didn't Mickey Mouse around but one that gets to the point of what makes this guy pick up a gun, why he can't live peacefully." When the film left Hodges' hands and was sent to the studio's editing room, it came out quite unlike what he and Rourke had imagined it would. Hodges complained that the film had "lost all its tension," singling out a re-edit and the Bill Conti score as destroying the subtlety. He then publicly disowned the film and demanded that his name be removed from the credits. Rourke's outrage was voiced during a Cannes Film Festival press conference in which he fired a personal attack at studio head Samuel Goldwyn, Jr. "I was making a small movie that I hoped would make things clearer about what's going on in [Northern Ireland]," said Rourke. "He wanted to turn it into a big commercial extravaganza-type thing."

The result is neither a small movie about Northern Ireland (a subject that was well covered in 1984's excellent CAL) nor an exploitative shoot-'em-up. The fault is not in Conti's score (which has a lovely melody but is often bombastic and horribly cued) nor in the less-than-subtle editing, but in the often ridiculous script. With equal helpings of criminal pulp, preachy soul-searching, religious iconography, and sappy romance (the use of the perceptive blind girl, even though Davis plays the part well, is just *too* silly), A PRAYER FOR THE DYING sinks under its own weight. While it starts out as a captivating introspection, it soon becomes an exercise in pomposity and overstatement. The only reason to see A PRAYER FOR THE DYING is for Rourke's chameleonic performance. Hiding behind flaming red hair, eyeglasses, and an effective upper-register brogue, Rourke is barely recognizable. A la Brando, Rourke undergoes a physical alteration in his role and walks the razor's edge between a brilliant performance and a campy one. Unfortunately, one has the feeling that Rourke's interpretation of the character is pulling his performance one way, while the script is pulling it another way. The remarkable Hoskins does what he can with his underdeveloped role, never getting the chance to reach his peak. Bates, on the other hand, could have used a little restraint. As if Hodges was out to lunch during the filming of his scenes, Bates carries on like a leering lunatic in a grade-Z horror picture. He's supposed to be sick and sadistic (for example, he thrills in embalming pretty girls and is angered when anyone interrupts his perverse fetish), but also has a place in his heart for kind old women that remind him of his dear mum. Like Rourke, Bates takes on a wholly different appearance for this film (compared to last year's DUET FOR ONE); dressed in a stiff suit amd sporting a plastered-down hairdo, he minces about like Dirk Bogarde. The film's only other plus is the pleasing photography by newcomer Mike Garfath (LAMB, CAR TROUBLE) that combines modern color and style with classical religious compositions. *(Violence, profanity.)*

p, Peter Snell; d, Mike Hodges; w, Edmund Ward, Martin Lynch; ph, Mike Garfath (Kay/Metrocolor); m, Bill Conti; ed, Peter Boyle; prod d, Evan Hercules; cos, Evangeline Harrison; spec eff, Ian Scoones; stunts, Colin Skeaping.

Crime/Drama **(PR:C-O MPAA:R)**

PREDATOR** (1987) 107m Gordon-Silver-Davis-American-American Entertainment Partners/FOX c

Arnold Schwarzenegger *(Maj. Alan "Dutch" Schaefer)*, Carl Weathers *(Dillon)*, Elpidia Carrillo *(Anna)*, Bill Duke *(Mac)*, Jesse Ventura *(Sgt. Blain)*, Sonny Landham *(Billy)*, Richard Chaves *(Pancho)*, R.G. Armstrong *(Gen. Phillips)*, Shane Black *(Hawkins)*, Kevin Peter Hall *(Predator)*.

Never look to Schwarzenegger for any kind of film that doesn't muscle its way through impossible odds, absurd characters, and pygmy-brained scripts, as was the case with his ultra-violent THE TERMINATOR. This film, however, has a great deal of suspense and is technically above average, although its premise is just as ludicrous as Schwarzenegger's earlier films. The menace, an other-world creature, is established early on in PREDATOR, but the muscle-flexing Schwarzenegger and his fellow soldiers-of-fortune, including Weathers, have to learn the hard way in dense Central American jungles, that they are not up against the usual human enemies. These fly-by-night military men undertake to rescue some captured American soldiers and follow some wily guerrillas into the jungles. Weathers probably has more lines to utter than the body-building star, but they are inconsequential generalities. Schwarzenegger responds to Weathers' questions re the Libya operations as to why he didn't take part in the raid there by stating firmly: "We're a rescue team, not assassins!" Schwarzenegger and company finally cut their way through to a site where they destroy the guerrillas in a firefight but they come away with no Americans. These they later find dead, skinned, and hanging like sides of beef from the jungle trees. Then the predator, an alien from outer space, begins to prey on the soldiers-of-fortune, so that they are compelled to retreat in a wild escape through the almost impenetrable jungle. One by one, in terrible and bloody death scenes, the rescue team members are killed until only Schwarzenegger is left to battle the alien. Coated with blood and mud (accidentally discovering that his mud covering prevents the predator's X-ray vision from seeing him), he dispatches his relentless antagonist with a pedestrian bow and arrow. Technically, this film is well done and the special effects in creating the alien are top-notch. But the improbability of such a creature living in a jungle just to kill humans (the film offers no explanation for its presence) undermines the project. The pace and direction of PREDATOR are handled well by McTiernan. *(Violence, gore effects.)*

p, Lawrence Gordon, Joel Silver, John Davis; d, John McTiernan; w, Jim Thomas, John Thomas; ph, Donald McAlpine (Deluxe Color); m, Alan Silvestri; ed, John F. Link, Mark Helfrich; prod d, John Vallone; art d, Frank Richwood, Jorge Saenz, John K. Reinhart, Jr.; set d, Enrique Estevez; spec eff, R/Greenberg, Joel Hynek, Stuart Robertson, Dream Quest Images, Al Di Sarro, Laurencio "Choby" Cordero, Stan Winston; stunts, Craig Baxley.

Thriller **(PR:O MPAA:R)**

PRETTY SMART zero (1987) 84m Balcor Film Investors-Chroma III-First American Film Capital/NW c

Tricia Leigh Fisher *(Daphne "Zigs" Ziegler)*, Lisa Lorient *(Jennifer Ziegler)*, Dennis Cole *(Richard Crawley, Headmaster)*, Patricia Arquette *(Zero)*, Paris Vaughan *(Torch)*, Kimberly B. Delfin *(Yuko)*, Brad Zutaut *(Alexis)*, Kim Waltrip *(Sara Gernhy)*, Kimberly B. Delfin *(Yuko)*, Joely Fisher, Beckish, Kierstin Viebrock *(Subs)*, Julie Kirstin Smith *(Samantha)*, Holly Nelson *(Jessica)*, Syndle Kirkland *(Angelica)*, Elizabeth Davis *(Diane)*, Charlot-Michele Grenzier *(Michelle)*, Andrea Kokonos, Terri Patterson, Joanie Berglund *(Preems)*, Nana, Cecilia Deloriae, Anita Lanzen, Pia Algelear *(Ingrid Swenson)*, Michael Karman *(Trip)*, Robert Schlief *(Gordy)*, Richard Syare *(Mr. Abercrenerchie)*, Konstantinos Tzoumas *(Mr. Trull)*, Michelle Valley *(Ms. LaCroch)*, Maria De Vial *(Miss Dunlop)*, George Kotandis *(Prof. Raj)*, Nicholas Gelozzi *(Tennis Pro)*, Brad Zutant *(Alexis)*, Ken Solomon *(Count Hawke)*, Tamara Hyler *(Tour Guide)*, Mindy Miller *(Mrs. Ziegler)*, Michael Piller *(Mr. Ziegler)*, Debra Cunningham *(Beth)*, Michael Yannatos *(The Turk)*, Vassili Karis *(The Motion)*, Joseph Meduwar *(The Lebanese)*, Paul Mathus *(The Columbian)*,Thanos Calliris, Vassilis Pertilis, Michael Kapaulos, Manos Dimitriox, Georgia Hill.

PRETTY SMART is one of those B-pictures in which several cast members are related to famous personalities. The lead, Tricia Leigh Fisher, is the daughter of Connie Stevens and Eddie Fisher. One of her cohorts is essayed by singer Sarah Vaughan's daughter Paris, while another is played by Rosanna Arquette's younger sister Patricia. Patricia Arquette's acting occasionally recalls Rosanna's delightful style of dimwittedness, though there is a distinct difference. Rosanna's also blessed with comic talent. But then again, Patricia's lackluster performance is only in keeping with the spirit of PRETTY SMART, a misnomer film title if ever one existed.

Fisher is a rebellious teenager who, with her sister Lorient, is sent off to a finishing school in Greece. This school is one of those institutions where girls split into groups on the basis of social class and hair color. Lorient, being blonde and refined, goes off with the snobby "Preems" (short for "Supremes"), while the dark-haired Fisher joins up with Vaughan and Arquette in the low-life "Subs" (short for "Subculture"). The school, a former castle which still attracts tourist groups, is run by Cole, a man whose slimy personality is matched only by his disgusting exploitation of the girls. Knowing that girls' finishing schools are hotbeds of sexual activity (or at least in low-budget movies they are), Cole keeps video cameras secreted in strategic locations around the institution and its dormitories. With this technology, Cole creates a wide array of home-made pornography which he sells to high-paying clients. Cole also uses the unknowing students as drug runners by planting illegal substances on good students when they are "rewarded" with trips to exotic European cities. Cole's plan is to maintain the friction between the Preems and Subs, thus insuring his work can continue unimpeded. Meanwhile, Fisher has grown bored with the institution, and leads her fellow Subs in various rebellious acts. Waltrip is a sympathetic literature teacher, who had been a student at the school years before. She sees past Fisher's tough exterior and gradually helps her deal with her anger. When Cole catches Waltrip in a nude sunbathing session with her students, he angrily fires her. Next, he tries to divide the Subs by breaking up Fisher's surprise birthday party. Lorient, risking her social status, comes to her sister's defense. When the Subs run a night mission to recover a confiscated radio, they discover Cole's secret video operation. Working with the Preems, they foil Cole at his own game, driving him from the academy they have all come to love. Waltrip is brought in to run the place, while the Subs and Preems celebrate their new-found friendship.

There's nothing in PRETTY SMART's plotting which makes it different from any number of similar students-versus-authority films. Easily identifiable stereotypes abound, while predictable situations and some nice Greek scenery help pass the time. What makes this film particularly loathsome though is its reliance on teenage sexuality. There's all too many scenes of girls in their lingerie, showering together, or sneaking in boy friends from a nearby prep school. In one rather repugnant sequence, the Subs sit around watching a pornographic videotape and comment on the physical techniques involved in the action. There's no insight or wit, merely a group of teens mouthing stock responses to graphic sex. The academy's depraved sex education teacher occasionally gives lectures on such topics as "Fornication: A Thing of Beauty or Kafkaesque Nightmare?" Had the humor stuck along these lines, PRETTY SMART might have been mildly amusing. Instead the film is sex for its own sake, and the results are merely repulsive. Songs: "Pretty Smart" (performed by Tricia Leigh Fisher), "Breakdown" (performed by Jay Levy), "Good Love Turn to Bad," "Foreign Relations," "Keep On Following Your Heart" (performed by Jay Levy, Eddie Arkin, Dale Morgan), "Born to Rock" (performed by Dale Morgan). *(Nudity, profanity, sexual situations.)*

p, Ken Solomon, Jeff Begun, Melanie J. Alschuler; d, Dimitri Logothetis; w, Dan Hoskins (based on an original story by Jeff Begun, Melanie J. Alschuler); ph, Dimitri Papacostantis; m, Jay Levy, Eddie Arkin; ed, Daniel Gross; prod d, Beau Peterson; set d, Tajos Diskomonous; cos, Gaelle Allen; makeup, Theresa Baca; m/l, Jay Levy, Eddie Arkin, Terry Shaddick.

Comedy **Cas.** **(PR:O MPAA:R)**

PRETTYKILL* (1987) 95m Dax Avant/Spectrafilm c

David Birney *(Sgt. Larry Turner)*, Season Hubley *(Heather Todd)*, Susannah York *(Toni)*, Yaphet Kotto *(Lt. Harris)*, Suzanne Snyder *(Francie/Stella/Paul)*, Germaine Houde *(Jacques Mercier)*, Lenore Zann *(Carrie)*, Vito Rezza *(Bartender)*, Marsha Moreau *(Stephie)*, Sarah Polley *(Karla)*, Peter Colvey *(Assistant)*, Tim Burd *(Cab Driver)*, Anna Louise Richardson *(Courtney)*, O.L. Duke *(Eddie K.)*, Heather Smith *(Eve)*, Erik King *(Sullivan)*, Richard Fitzpatrick *(Policeman)*, Ron White *(Rickert)*, Gary Majchrizak *(Lightnin' Boy)*, Louis Turenne *(Olaf Nilsson, Swedish Ambassador)*, J. Winston Carroll *(Smiley)*, Catherine Gallant *(Detective Green)*, Philip Akin *(Joey)*, Al Bernardo *(Vendor)*, Belinda Metz *(Escort)*, Garrick Hagon *(Chambers)*, Paul Haddad *(Lover)*, Allan Royal *(Conley Reid)*.

Birney is a detective whose longtime lover is high-class call girl Hubley. He's investigating the murder of a narcotics agent, and the case is drawing perilously close to Hubley because she is harboring Snyder, who is wanted for questioning. Hubley is teaching Snyder the ropes of her profession, unaware that the seemingly innocent southern belle is actually a dangerous schizoid. In the past, Snyder has taken on the voice and personality of her incestuous father, killed her associates in a vengeful rage, and even raped herself. Birney loses his job when Kotto, his superior, cruelly arrests madam York in front of her kids and Birney punches him. Inevitably, Snyder flips her wig and goes after Hubley with a pair of scissors but falls through a stair railing. Hubley quits the profession and she and Birney prepare to leave town together. PRETTYKILL is a thoroughly dull crime drama with nothing to recommmend it except its snicker potential. Hubley is hilarious as the Grace Kelly-look-alike hooker who says things like, "I don't like to keep the ambassador waiting," and is so aloof that sex with her is about as appealing as sleeping with a mannequin. Birney doesn't have much to do, and Kotto is asked only to be stupid as the heavy. Snyder's over-the-top split personality bit gives the movie its most hilarious moments. She chews up the scenery with three different personalities that alternately attack Hubley and beg her forgiveness. What little sex and nudity the film has is all in one scene that includes none of the principals and was shot with a separately credited crew. None of this should recommend PRETTYKILL, but the ad art, featuring a negligee-clad Snyder on a bed with a knife, may guarantee long-term returns for video rentals. *(Nudity, adult situations, sexual situations, excessive profanity, violence.)*

p, John R. Bowey, Martin Walters; d, George Kaczender; w, Sandra K. Bailey; ph, Joao Fernandes; m, Robert O. Ragland; ed, Tom Merchant; art d, Andris Hausmanis, Jimmy Williams; set d, Jeff Cutler; cos, Trish Bakker; stunts, Dan Bradley, Shane Cardwell; weapons specialist, Frank Carere; makeup, Marysue Heron, Ronnie Spector.

Crime Cas. **(PR:O MPAA:R)**

PRICK UP YOUR EARS*½** (1987, Brit.) 111m Civilhand Zenith/Goldwyn c

Gary Oldman *(Joe Orton)*, Alfred Molina *(Kenneth Halliwell)*, Vanessa Redgrave *(Peggy Ramsay)*, Wallace Shawn *(John Lahr)*, Lindsay Duncan *(Anthea Lahr)*, Julie Walters *(Elsie Orton)*, James Grant *(William Orton)*, Janet Dale *(Mrs. Sugden)*, Dave Atkins *(Mr. Sugden)*, Margaret Tyzack *(Mme. Lambert)*, Eric Richard *(Education Officer)*, Charlotte Wodehouse *(Janet)*, Linda Spurrier *(RADA Instructor)*, Charles McKowen *(Mr. Cunliffe)*, Selina Cadell *(Miss Datersby)*, Liam Staic *(Brickie)*, Bert Parnaby *(Magistrate)*, Frances Barber *(Leonie Orton)*, Stephen Bill *(George Barnett)*, Max Stafford-Clark *(Awards Chairman)*, William Job *(RADA Chairman)*, Rosalind Knight, Angus Mackay *(RADA Judges)*, Helena Michell, Sean Pertwee *(Orton's Friends)*, Antony Carrick *(Counsel)*, Neil Dudgeon *(Policeman)*, Richard Wilson *(Psychiatrist)*, Christopher Guinee *(Publisher)*, Stevan Rimkus *(Kenneth)*, Michael Mueller, Anthony Douse *(BBC Actors)*, John Kane *(Director)*, Steven Mackintosh *(Simon Ward)*, Garry Cooper, Roger Lloyd Pack *(Actors)*, Joanne Connelly *(Stage Manager)*, John Moffatt *(Wigmaker)*, Philippa Davies *(Peggy Ramsay's Secretary)*, David Cardy *(Brian Epstein)*, Julie Legrand *(Gallery Owner)*, Noel Davis *(Philip)*, Jane Blackburn, Stella Richman *(Women in Gallery)*, Neville Phillips *(Man in Gallery)*, Jonathan Phillips *(Youth Outside Lavatory)*, Richard Ireson *(Man Outside Lavatory)*, Ahmed El Jheur, Moktar Dagmouni *(Moroccan Boys)*, Sian Thomas *(Marilyn Orton)*, Karl Johnson *(Douglas Orton)*, David Bradley *(Undertaker)*, Simon Adams *(Undertaker's Boy)*, James Duggan *(Labourer)*, Mark Brignal *(Beatles' Chauffeur)*, Joan Sanderson *(Anthea's Mother)*, Neville Smith *(Police Inspector)*, Spencer Leigh *(Constable)*, John Salthouse *(Chauffeur)*, Robin Hooper *(Mortuary Attendant)*.

The subject matter may be offensive to some people, but there is no question that this is a well-made picture and what appears to be an accurate biography of the homosexual writer who dazzled the stage with his words and was murdered by his lover at the apex of his career. Joe Orton (born John Orton in Leicester, England) died at the age of 34 when his longtime lover hammered in his head with a half-dozen blows before downing two handfuls of Nembutal and taking his own life. The movie begins with the murder and suicide and if it can be said that a murder/suicide was handled with restraint, it was done so here. Oldman, who was so believable in another biographical role, that of Sid Vicious in SID AND NANCY, seems to have shed all of his viciousness and actually becomes Orton. At 17, Oldman arrives in London to attend the Royal Academy of Dramatic Art (RADA) where he meets the hulking Molina, who is several years older and has an independent income. Both men are homosexual and they soon move in together in a squalid bed-sitter in North London. (This was to be their home for the next 16 years, despite all of the financial success Orton would reap.) Molina has writing aspirations and the two men attempt a few novels with no success. Molina soon settles in to being the long-suffering wife half of the relationship while Oldman spends a good deal of time haunting various public bathrooms in search of new sexual experiences. When their novels are summarily rejected, Oldman and Molina wreak revenge by defacing books in a local library and writing profanity on the pages and flyleaves. They are caught and incarcerated separately. Alone for the first time in many years, Oldman uses his six-month term to write a radio play. When he is sprung, the play, "The Ruffian on the Stair" (which was based upon an unpublished novel that the two men had written in the early 50s), gives the author an entree into the literary world and he is soon snapped up by one of London's leading agents, Redgrave, in a superb performance. She guides his professional career but not his personal life. As Oldman's star rises, Molina becomes increasingly bitter and feels left out. Oldman wins a prestigious award and elects to take Redgrave to the ceremony instead of his longtime lover and Molina is crushed. Molina's hair has been falling out and Oldman buys him a rotten-looking wig, thereby making him a subject of derision. Meanwhile, Oldman is still hanging around public washrooms and getting into near-scrapes. He seems to be thrilled as much by the fact that homosexual liaisons are illegal and thus subject to jail sentences as he is by the acts themselves. Molina begins making collages and has an exhibition, hoping that he can now step out of Oldman's shadow. It doesn't work out. The men go off to Tangier on a vacation and engage in sexual orgies with any number of teenage boys, but Molina continues to be depressed. Oldman goes home to Leicester for his mother's funeral while Molina tries unsuccessfully to get help from a psychiatrist. Upon returning to London, Oldman says that he thinks their relationship is at an end. Molina responds by bashing in Oldman's head, killing himself, and leaving a note that says that Orton's diaries should explain everything. When the ashes of both are mixed at the funeral, Barber (Oldman's sister) is worried that the mixture may not be quite equal and Redgrave humorously remarks, "It's a gesture, not a recipe."

The picture is told in flashback as Shawn, playing the role of John Lahr, Orton's biographer, seeks to learn all he can about his subject. Functioning in much the same way William Alland did in CITIZEN KANE as he interviewed the people Kane touched, Shawn spends most of his time triggering the flashbacks and playing out a small subplot in which he is disdainful of his wife's suggestions—a relationship that parallels Halliwell and Orton's. The film might have been better done as a straight biography, with none of the flashbacks and surely no character played by Shawn, who seems to be an industrial strength twit. This is director Frears' second theatrical release with a homosexual theme, the first being MY BEAUTIFUL LAUNDRETTE. He attempted to delve deeply into the gay relationship between the men, something that the people of the time never understood since Orton was a pixie whom everyone adored and Halliwell, an apparent millstone. Molina's casting may have been a mistake because one wonders what Oldman sees in him. In real life, Halliwell was not the bearish brute that Molina's physical presence indicates and those who knew him said that he had a certain charm of his own, as well as a Svengali influence over Orton. Many of the titles for Orton's works (including the title of this movie) were Halliwell's and a great deal of Halliwell's editing and suggestions were admittedly folded into every Orton script. Feeling abandoned and unappreciated, Halliwell decided that if they couldn't be together in life, then they would be united in death. Orton's career was brief and ended when he was 34 years old. "Entertaining Mr. Sloane" opened in May, 1964, "Loot" followed in February, 1965, there were a few radio and TV plays, and then, two years after his death, Orton's play "What the Butler Saw" opened in London.

There are some very funny and bizarre moments in the film. When his mother dies of a wasp sting, Oldman takes the false teeth of which she was so proud and hands them to an actor about to make an entrance in "Loot" on opening night. Anyone who has seen the play will be struck by that inside joke. The playwright was also to pen a script for the Beatles and that incident is hilariously recorded in a brief scene with Cardy, playing the Fab Four's manager, Brian Epstein. Lahr, who is the son of the late Bert Lahr (the Cowardly Lion in WIZARD OF OZ, among other roles), was not only the author of the Orton biography but also the editor of Orton's own explicit posthumously published diaries when they were published, and Bennett, who wrote the screenplay, added to that research and wrote a corking good script for this low-budget picture. Some of the more quotable lines are from Walters. She introduces her mate, Grant, by saying, "This is my husband. Ignore him." She also tells Oldman, "Dirk Bogarde never distempered his mother's bedspread." Walters, best recalled for the role of "Rita" in EDUCATING RITA, is virtually unrecognizable here and shows that she can do just about anything. Other than the miscasting of Molina (who is an excellent actor and proved that before when he played the Russian sailor in LETTER TO BREZHNEV) and Shawn, everyone else is right on the money. Oldman is the key and holds it all together with a performance that indicates he may be the next Albert Finney. *(Profanity, sexual situations.)*

p, Andrew Brown; d, Stephen Frears; w, Alan Bennett (based on the biography by John Lahr); ph, Oliver Stapleton (Eastmancolor); m, Stanley Myers; ed, Mick Audsley; prod d, Hugo Luczyc-Wyhowski; md, John Harle; art d, Philip Elton; cos, Bob Ringwood; m/l, Stanley Myers, Richard Myhill, Harry Carroll, Harold Atteridge, John Lennon, Paul McCartney; makeup, Elaine Carew.

Biography **(PR:O MPAA:R)**

PRIKLYUCHENIA NA MALENKIKH OSTROVEKH† (1987, USSR) 76m Turkmenfilm/Sovexportfilm c (Trans: Adventures on Little Islands)

At Dovletov, Serdar Durdyev, Maya Nuryagdyeva.

A seven-year-old boy goes to live with his grandfather who works as a meteorologist on a small island in the Caspian Sea. The boy develops a deep affection for a colony of seagulls that comes to the island to lay their eggs and he becomes their protector, fending off poachers, geologists, and other intruders. During his stay on the island the boy learns of the delicate balance between nature and civilization.

d&w, Usman Saparov; ph, Yakub Muratnazarov; m, Alexander Koblyakov; art d, Viktoria Atayeva.

Children's **(PR:NR MPAA:NR)**

PRINCE OF DARKNESS*** (1987) 101m Alive/UNIV c

Donald Pleasence *(Priest)*, Jameson Parker *(Brian)*, Victor Wong *(Professor Birack)*, Lisa Blount *(Catherine)*, Dennis Dun *(Walter)*, Susan Blanchard *(Kelly)*, Anne Howard *(Susan)*, Ann Yen *(Lisa, Language Expert)*, Alice Cooper *(Street-People Leader)*, Ken Wright, Dirk Blocker, Jessie Lawrence Ferguson, Peter Jason.

After a short flirtation with big-budget filmmaking, director John Carpenter returns to his low-budget horror film roots and presents a strange tale of religion, science, and pure evil. Veteran Carpenter performer Pleasence stars as a priest who discovers the existence of a strange canister full of swirling green liquid that was hidden in the basement of an old church in Los Angeles many years before. Near the container is an old book that seems to be an alternate *Bible* and that is nearly indecipherable. Afraid of the energy he feels emanating from the canister, Pleasence turns to his old friend and associate Wong, a brilliant physics professor, and asks for his help. Wong mobilizes a bevy of his graduate students and truckloads of state-of-the-art analytical equipment to study the canister. An expert in ancient languages, Yen, deciphers the book and, to everyone's horror, learns that the canister contains the energy of Satan's son. It seems that several thousand years ago Satan (who was an alien) was exiled to the "dark side," a mirror world of our own. Before leaving, Satan locked his son in a container in preparation for his return. When the conditions are right, the son will unlatch the

container from the inside and fetch his father back from his exile. Therefore, Pure Evil is a tangible entity that exists—not within each man's heart, as the church would like us to believe—but in that container. Jesus Christ (who was also an alien) knew about the container and tried to warn the world, but was crucified for his efforts. His apostles, however, created a brotherhood that would care for the container to ensure that it would never fall into the wrong hands. Now, fueled by the light of a supernova that exploded seven million years before, the container is about to open. (Parts of the above explanation may be incorrect, for the information comes at a furious pace, shrouded in so much scientific and religious mumbo-jumbo, that it is difficult to keep up with it.) These revelations have badly shaken Pleasence's faith and he is dismayed to discover that the church has known the truth all along and has fabricated the concept of original sin to convert the heathens. Already the container has the power to mobilize lower forms of life (ants, worms, etc.) and has managed to control a small army of zombielike street people led by Cooper. As the young scientists go about their work, the liquid begins to seep out of the container and possesses some of the female members of the troupe. They in turn convert most of the men into zombies who pave the way for the return of Satan. The survivors (Pleasence, Wong, Dun, Parker, and Blount) have holed up in a small room to escape their possessed comrades. One woman, Blanchard, is chosen to be the host for the evil liquid's human form. After a short gestation period, Blanchard emerges as the embodiment of Satan's son and goes to a full-length mirror to fetch his father. Blanchard reaches her hand into the mirror and on the other side we see a huge, demonic-looking hand stretched out in anticipation. Making the ultimate sacrifice, Blount throws herself at Blanchard, knocking both of them into the mirror world. At the same time, Pleasence manages to toss an ax at the mirror and shatter it, thus sealing Satan, his son, and Blount forever in the dark side.

Written by Carpenter under the pseudonym "Martin Quatermass" (a tribute to British sci-fi writer Nigel Kneale, who created the excellent series of films featuring the character Prof. Bernard Quatermass), PRINCE OF DARKNESS evokes themes strongly reminiscent of Larry Cohen's superior GOD TOLD ME TO. Not only does Carpenter create a terrifying tale that works on the visceral level of a horror film, but he also explores the fundamental conflict between religion, science, and the unknown, adding an intellectual dimension sorely lacking in most current films of this genre. Provocative plot aside, Carpenter once again proves his mastery of the visual aspects of the medium with his excellent use of the wide-screen format and a bag of simple cinematic tricks that seem to have been forgotten in these days of high-priced, state-of-the-art effects crews. Although Carpenter names his church St. Godard's in tribute to director Jean-Luc Godard, his film bears a much greater resemblance to the masterful work of Jean Cocteau, especially ORPHEUS. Tilted sets, forced perspectives, filming in reverse, and, most of all, the ability to reach into a mirror and discover an alternate reality are all borrowed from ORPHEUS and used to great effect in PRINCE OF DARKNESS. Carpenter has long honored film history by naming his characters after great directors or memorable characters from classic movies, but this is the first time that he has evoked their influence in such a grand visual tour de force. Carpenter isn't stealing by doing this, but merely reaffirming that cinematic tricks discovered at the dawn of the medium by people like Georges Melies are as valid and useful now as they were 90 years ago. While Carpenter's impressive knowledge and successful integration of several levels of film history into a mainstream horror movie is exciting to sophisticated film aficionados, PRINCE OF DARKNESS works well enough for those unconcerned with such matters. Unfortunately, the film does begin to unravel when he makes concessions to current genre expectations. The zombie aspect of the film is tiresome, as is the characters-getting-knocked-off-one-by-one syndrome that he himself elevated to new heights in HALLOWEEN. There is reason to be optimistic, however, for Carpenter has struck a five-picture deal with progressive Alive Films that ensures his low-budget pictures turn a profit *before* a frame is shot (through advance sales), thus enabling him to have total creative freedom without having to worry about making a box-office hit. For a director as smart and creative as John Carpenter is, this is good news indeed. *(Graphic violence, limited gore effects, sexual situations, profanity.)*

p, Larry Franco; d, John Carpenter; w, Martin Quatermass [John Carpenter]; ph, Gary B. Kibbe (Panavision); m, John Carpenter, Alan Howarth; ed, Steve Mirkovich; prod d, Daniel Lomino

Horror **(PR:O MPAA:R)**

PRINCESS ACADEMY, THE zero (1987, US/Yugo./Fr.) 90m Cloverleaf-Jadran-Sofracima/Empire c

Eva Gabor *(Countess)*, Lar Park Lincoln *(Cindy)*, Lu Leonard *(Fraulein Stickenschmidt)*, Richard Paul *(Drago)*, Carole Davis *(Sonia)*, Badar Howar *(Sarah)*, Barbara Rovsek *(Izzie)*, Yolande Palfrey *(Pamela)*, Britt Helfer *(Lulu)*.

Every good reason *not* to send one's daughter to boarding school is depicted in this movie, one of the most inept features to come along in modern times. The advertising read: "Today's Lesson, the three *R*'s . . . *R*ich Men, *R*omance, and *R*ock Stars." It should have been amended to stand for *r*otten acting, *r*evolting script, and *r*uinous direction. Actually, in the hands of better writers, a better director, and better actors, it might have worked as a concept, but since execution, not the idea, is what matters, this falls flatter than the Kansas landscape. The story takes place at the Von Pupsin Academy (supposedly in Switzerland, actually shot in Yugoslavia) where Gabor, a princess, holds forth as the headmistress of an educational institution where the rich and/or famous send their daughters to further their intellects and social graces. Lincoln, the newest student at the school is there on a scholarship, as she is a poor and naive orphan. The curriculum is mainly devoted to how to catch a rich husband, with side trips to: how to fake an orgasm, how to shop, etc. Lincoln is immediately despised by the snobs at the school as well as by Leonard, who plays the same semi-lesbian Nazi role she usually does. Leonard thinks that Lincoln may be spying for Gabor so she sides with the snooty girls to make Lincoln's life miserable and cause her to leave. A few of the nicer students take Lincoln in as one of their own, so the story gets down to the good girls versus the bad ones. With this as the premise, the author has made room for any number of hostile pranks, all meant to be funny, none of which are—wacky gags like putting itching powder into one of the snob's tampons, always a lot of laughs. Lincoln becomes a victim when some pranks get out of hand at a local brothel. Two lovesick virgins from different academies (one boy, one girl) are to meet at the brothel to get their first taste of physical love. Before that can happen, Leonard arrives and shatters their fantasies. Then the girls use blackmail to quiet Leonard, as it seems she has been having a fling with Paul, the school's wimpish administrator. Action-adventure fans will enjoy the thrilling scene in which Lincoln slides down a hill trapped in an outhouse and slams into a tree. At the conclusion, which comes about 88 minutes too late, Lincoln and some of her compatriots wind up jammed into a tank, firing its cannon. Despite all of this, Lincoln manages to realize the dream of every one of the princesses in training; she is proposed to by an English nerd.

Hard to believe this picture was written by a woman (the author/producer is also the executive producer's daughter). It is sexist, angry, and, worst of all, not well made. The editing is jagged, the songs are as hummable as a Gregorian chant, and most of the technical credits look like your nephew's home movies. Fred Weintraub, who made a few interesting pictures like ENTER THE DRAGON and OUTLAW BLUES, embarrassed himself with this one. The fact that his offspring wrote and produced the movie makes one wonder about a father's duty to protect his children from harm. Oddly enough, there is virtually no nudity. They foreswore the ubiquitous shower scene that seems to be the crux of every flesh and teenager movie and, instead, concentrated on what they thought would be a social satire. It was not social or satirical. They might have been better served to use some nudity. It could have taken the audience's mind off the rest of the movie. *(Sexual situations.)*

p, Sandra Weintraub; d, Bruce Block; w, Sandra Weintraub (based on an idea by Fred Weintraub); ph, Kent Wakeford; m, Roger Bellon; ed, Martin Cohen; cos, Nolan Miller.

Comedy **(PR:C-O MPAA:R)**

PRINCESS BRIDE, THE*½** (1987) 98m Act III Communications/FOX c

Cary Elwes *(Westley)*, Mandy Patinkin *(Inigo Montoya)*, Chris Sarandon *(Prince Humperdinck)*, Christopher Guest *(Count Rugen)*, Wallace Shawn *(Vizzini)*, Andre the Giant *(Fezzik)*, Fred Savage *(The Grandson)*, Robin Wright *(Buttercup the Princess Bride)*, Peter Falk *(The Grandfather)*, Peter Cook *(The Impressive Clergyman)*, Billy Crystal *(Miracle Max the Wizard)*, Carol Kane *(Valerie, the Wizard's Wife)*, Mel Smith *(The Albino)*, Willoughby Gray, Malcolm Storry.

A charming, hilarious mixture of Errol Flynn swashbuckler and Monty Python send-up, THE PRINCESS BRIDE works as a love story, as an adventure, and as a satire. In the framing story, Falk comes to the sick bed of Savage (THE BOY WHO COULD FLY), his 10-year-old grandson, who would rather play video games than endure the "kissing" story his grandfather has brought to read. "Back in my day, television was called books," Falk tells him, launching into *The Princess Bride*. In the medieval make-believe land of Florin, a flaxen-haired beauty, Buttercup (Wright), and her handsome farm-boy servant, Westley (Elwes), fall in love. Because he is poor, he crosses the sea to seek his fortune so they may marry. "I will always come back to you," he promises her, "because this is true love." Word soon arrives that he has been killed by the Dread Pirate Roberts, and after five years of grieving, Wright is betrothed to Florin's ruling prince, Sarandon. While horseback riding, she is kidnaped by crafty Sicilian Shawn and his hirelings, Patinkin, a talented Spanish swordsman who has spent the last 20 years trying to find the six-fingered man who murdered his father, and Andre the Giant (the professional wrestler), who plays, well . . . a giant. The plan is to sail to the kingdom of Guilder and murder Wright, thereby pushing the people of Florin into war. However, their ship is followed. At the Treacherous Cliffs of Insanity, a mysterious man in black chases them up the rope which Andre climbs with the others clinging to him. Reaching the top even after the rope has been cut, the pursuer locks steel with Patinkin and defeats him after a see-saw battle. ("There's something you don't know—I'm not left-handed," Patinkin says switching hands. "There's something you don't know," the masked man replies moments later, "I'm not left-handed either.") Next, he bests

Andre in hand-to-hand combat. Each of them he disposes of without permanent injury. Shawn is not so lucky when the masked man catches up with him and Wright and tricks the Sicilian into drinking a glass of poisoned wine. Soon after, it is revealed that Elwes is behind the mask, that he wasn't killed by the Dread Pirate Roberts but instead became his apprentice and took over the pirate's name and life's work when he retired. Happily reunited, the young couple discover that Prince Sarandon, his six-fingered right-hand man Guest, and a troupe of soldiers are on their tail. They escape into the Dreaded Fireswamp, where they triumph over flamespurts, lightning sand, and ROUS's (Rodents of Unusual Size), only to be apprehended as they exit. Sarandon promises Wright that Elwes will be returned to his ship, but he is actually transported to a subterranean torture chamber, where Guest, a lifelong student of pain, sucks the life out of him with "the machine." The Royal wedding is scheduled to proceed. When the Thieves' Forest is cleared of its rabble prior to the ceremony, Patinkin and Andre are reunited. Discovering that Guest is the man he has sought all these years, Patinkin is anxious to storm the castle, but it is now guarded by 60 men, put there to fend off a rumored attempt to snatch Wright. In fact, Sarandon plans to murder her himself to bring about the war Shawn was unable to instigate. Patinkin and Andre are afraid to proceed without someone to plan their attack, and they go in search of Elwes, finding him dead on the torture table. They take him to Crystal, a wizened, acerbic Jewish miracle maker, who declares Elwes to be only "mostly dead." Goaded by his ancient wife, Kane, who is touched by Elwes pursuit of true love, Crystal produces a pill that brings him back to life, albeit limply. Under Elwes' direction, the trio storms the castle. Meanwhile, minister Cook performs a truncated marriage ceremony. Once inside, Patinkin corners Guest, who sends a knife flying into the Spaniard's chest. Summoning 20 years of vengeful strength, Patinkin staggers toward him. "My name is Inigo Montoya. You killed my father. Prepare to die," he says repeatedly before running the villain through. In her chamber, Wright, who refuses to be Sarandon's wife, prepares to commit suicide. Ah, but who should be lying in her bed but Elwes. Before the couple are finally reunited, Elwes outwits Sarandon, whom he scares into submission with a promise to fight "to the pain." Andre appears with four white stallions and he, Elwes, Wright, and Patinkin ride away. To the delight of the converted Savage, the story ends with the most passionate kiss in recorded history.

Viewers of all ages will find something to delight them in THE PRINCESS BRIDE. Director Reiner (THIS IS SPINAL TAP, THE SURE THING, STAND BY ME) and scripter Goldman have created a dazzling adventure for younger viewers while at the same time hilariously sending up the very same genre, though never to the detriment of the underlying tale. Their tongues in cheek and their hearts on their sleeves, Goldman and Reiner have woven a warm love story that is as much about the grandfather and grandson experiencing the book together as it is about the maiden and her farm boy. Falk wants Savage to understand that the world isn't always just, that people who love each other don't always end up together, but, at the same time, he is tickled to be able to relate this happiest of endings. Reiner's visuals are unspectacular but appropriate and the pace never lags. The laughs are seldom far apart, and when the story begins to become a little too saccharine or melancholy, you can bet that Savage will interrupt the proceedings to be gently guided back into the story by Falk. The humor is often Pythonesque, specializing in absurdity, anachronism, non-sequiturs, and reversals of expectations. Elwes is given an assortment of wry one-liners reminiscent of Sean Connery's James Bond.

The performances are excellent, save for Shawn, who goes way over the top with his pint-sized tyrant. Elwes (LADY JANE) and Wright (who was chosen from hundreds of would-be princesses) are beautiful, fresh-faced, and a little too perfect—in other words, just right for the story. Sarandon is evil without being distant, Guest (SPINAL TAP) is poker-faced perfect as the man "writing the definitive work" on torture, and the casting of Andre the Giant was a brilliant stroke (granted, there aren't many people who call themselves giants, but there are plenty of big actors who could have been cast). Savage is restrained and believable as the kid who practically demands a big-kiss finale, and Falk is wonderful as the slightly surly but loving grandfather. As with Elwes, it is clear that when Falk says "As you wish," it means "I love you." Crystal, with fine support from Kane, provides the film's funniest scene, taking over the screen as if it were "Saturday Night Live," and this his greatest hit. The film's finest performance, though, is Patinkin's. More than anyone else, he embodies the film's dual approach and appeal. Employing a comically caricatured Spanish accent, a set of subtle Latin mannerisms, and an Iberian sense of irony and tragedy, he is both funny and heartwarming. When he finally avenges his father's death, both laughter and tears are appropriate.

Oscar-winning screenwriter Goldman (BUTCH CASSIDY AND THE SUNDANCE KID, ALL THE PRESIDENT'S MEN) adapted THE PRINCESS BRIDE from his own 1973 novel, which he, in turn, *abridged* from the children's book written by "S. Morgenstern" that his grandfather read to him. For nearly 14 years, Goldman's screenplay made the rounds. At one time or another, 20th Century-Fox, Norman Jewison, Richard Lester, John Boorman, and Francois Truffaut all showed interest in the film only to beg off. Goldman finally bought back the rights to it himself. Reiner, a longtime Goldman fan, convinced the author, who so loves the story that he wants *The Princess Bride* on his tombstone, that he would do it justice. Reiner secured the backing of mentor Norman Lear's Act III Productions and set about making the film on a budget of $17 million, with Fox picking up the distribution rights. Shot on location in England, Ireland, and at Shepperton Studios, the film's backdrop is a combination of beautiful real-life scenery and slightly fantastic sets that combine to provide just the air of unreality that the story demands. And what a story! *(Violence.)*

p, Arnold Scheinman, Rob Reiner; d, Rob Reiner; w, William Goldman (based on his novel); ph, Adrian Biddle (Deluxe Color); m, Mark Knopfler; ed, Robert Leighton; prod d, Norman Garwood; art d, Keith Pain, Richard Holland; set d, Maggie Gray; cos, Phyllis Dalton; spec eff, Nick Adler.

Children's/Comedy **(PR:A-C MPAA:PG)**

PRINCESS FROM THE MOON† (1987, Jap.) 120m Toho-Fuji Television/Toho Intl. c (TAKETORI MONOGATARI)

Toshiro Mifune *(Taketori-no-Miyatsuko)*, Ayako Wakao *(Tayoshime, his Wife)*, Yasuko Sawaguchi *(Kaya, Princess Kaguya)*, Koji Ishizaka *(Mikado)*, Kiichi Nakai *(Otomo-no-Dainagon, Minister of the Military)*, Koasa Shumputei *(Kuramochi-no-Miko, Minister of Culture)*, Takatoshi Takeda *(Abe-no-Udaijin, Minister of Finance)*, Megumi Odaka *(Akeno)*, Katsuo Nakamura, Shiro Itoh, Fujio Tokita, Takeshi Kato, Kyoto Kishida, Hirokazu Yamaguchi, Jun Hamamura, Gen Idemitsu, Michiyo Yokoyama, Hirokazu Inoue, Miho Nakano.

The latest film from director Kon Ichikawa (THE BURMESE HARP, FIRES ON THE PLAIN) is an elaborate adaptation of a 9th century Japanese legend which tells of an extraterrestrial woman from the moon who is temporarily stranded on Earth. Mifune stars as a bamboo cutter who finds a strange golden capsule containing a beautiful baby holding a crystal ball. The infant immediately grows into a five-year-old before Mifune's astonished eyes. He brings the child home to his wife, Wakao, and because they are mourning the recent death of their only child, the couple decide to adopt the mysterious baby. The child soon becomes a beguiling adult (Sawaguchi) whose glowing blue eyes prove irresistible to all men. Mifune sells the golden capsule that he found the baby in and uses the money to build an opulent house in the country, far away from curious eyes. Despite his efforts, three nobleman fall in love with the beautiful girl and she assigns them each an impossible task to fulfill. He who completes the task will receive her hand in marriage. One night when the moon is full, however, Sawaguchi's crystal ball emits an eerie sound informing her that she must return home. PRINCESS FROM THE MOON received its world premiere at New York's Museum of Modern Art as part of a celebration of a gift of more than 50 Japanese films to the museum's film archive from Toho International Studios. Director Kon Ichikawa, actors Toshiro Mifune and Yasuko Sawaguchi, and Oscar-winning costume designer Emi Wada (RAN) all attended the festivities. PRINCESS FROM THE MOON was also shown out of competition on the opening night of the Tokyo International Film Festival and will no doubt receive an international release some time in 1988-89.

p, Masaru Kakutani, Hiroaki Fujii, Junichi Shinsaka; d, Kon Ichikawa; w, Ryuzou Kikushima, Mitsutoshi Ishigami, Shinya Hidaka, Kon Ichikawa; ph, Setsuo Kobayashi; ed, Chizuko Osada; md, Kensaku Tanigawa; set d, Shinobu Muraki; cos, Emi Wada; spec eff, Shokei Nakano.

Fantasy **(PR:NR MPAA:NR)**

PRINCIPAL, THE*½ (1987) 109m Tri-Star-ML Delphi Premier-Doric/Tri-Star c

James Belushi *(Rick Latimer)*, Louis Gossett, Jr. *(Jake Phillips)*, Rae Dawn Chong *(Hilary Orozco)*, Michael Wright *(Victor Duncan)*, J.J. Cohen *("White Zac")*, Esai Morales *(Raymi Rojas)*, Troy Winbush *("Baby" Emile)*, Jacob Vargas *(Arturo Diego)*, Thomas Ryan *(Robert Darcy)*, Reggie Johnson *(Jojo)*, Kelly Minter *(Treena Lester)*, Ruth Beckford *(Mrs. Jenkins)*, Julian Brooks *(Kevin)*, Joan Valderrama *(Secretary)*, Rick Hamilton *(Mr. Harkley)*, Martin Pistone *(Security Guard)*, Joe Flood *(Terhune)*, Ann Armour *(Mrs. Ripton)*, Tony Haney *(Police Officer)*, Sharon Thomas *(Kimberly)*, Daniel Royal *(Will)*, Delores Mitchell *(Mrs. Coswell)*, Zoltan Gray *(P.E. Teacher)*, John Allen Vick *(Frank Valdis)*, Sean Allen Barnes *(Rolf)*, Yuri Lane *(Lance Woodbury)*, Steve W. Birger *(Stevie B.)*, Gus Dimas *(Gus)*, Leo Downey *(George Pierce)*, Tom Winston *(Principal O'Connor)*, Kathryn Knotts *(Jan Buchanan)*, Marshall Jones *(Gang Member)*, Josh Wood *(Charles Lester)*, Mark Anger *(Desk Officer)*, Frank Deese *(Mr. Petersen)*, J.J. Johnson *(Will)*, Doug White *(Eric)*, Wat Takeshita *(Maintenance Man)*, Elliott S. Valderrama *(Drug Dealer)*, Joel Valentin *(Kid)*, Tom Bryant *(Shocked Teacher)*, Danny Kovacs *(Substitute Teacher)*, Charmaine Anderson *(Hilary's Student)*, Melanie G. Muters *(Alley Girl)*, Linda Trowbridge *(Nurse)*, Danny Williams *(Dangerous Danny)*, Bill Yarbrough *(Randall)*, Richard Duppell, Peter Fitzsimmons *(Buddies)*, Jessica Wilson, Kaprice Wilson, Bridgette Rodriguez *(Girls)*, Terry Coleman, Melissa Lee Holloman, Luis Zuno, Nemon Wade, Eural Wills *(Students)*, James Edward Griffin, David Williams *(Gang Students)*.

Providing James Belushi with his first staring role as the title character, this lackluster tale of redemption invests THE BLACKBOARD JUNGLE school of drama with violence aplenty and an undercurrent of humor. Belushi is a screw-up teacher at a white bread high school whose life is falling apart. In a bar one night, he spots his ex-wife with the lawyer who handled their divorce, and he flies off the handle, demolishing the windows of the lawyer's sports car. His police record doesn't sit well with the school board who present him with an ultimatum. The district's most troublesome high school, Brandel High, the last refuge for students expelled from other schools, needs a principal. Either Belushi can accept the position or find a new employer. He finds himself at the helm of an inner-city school decorated with graffiti and boarded-up windows and populated by violent gangs, drug dealers, and other delinquents. The teachers appear to be going through the motions and the only rules seem to be those established by Wright and his vicious gang. Convinced that he has nowhere else to go, Belushi is determined to reclaim the school from Wright. He institutes the "No More" policy (no more drugs, arson, extortion, etc.) and is assisted by chief of security Gossett, a Brandel graduate whose pro football career was cut short by a knee injury. Putting his physical well-being on the line again and again, Belushi earns the respect of Gossett, Chong—a dedicated teacher—and even some of the students. He is threatened, badly beaten, and his prized motorcycle is destroyed, but

he keeps coming back for more. When Chong is raped in her classroom after school, "El Principal" charges to the rescue on his rebuilt Honda (the handiwork of the won-over Latinos in the auto shop), flying down halls and up stairs to pound her assailant, Cohen, the leader of the school's white gang. Later, Winbush, a likable fat kid who quits Wright's gang, is dropped through a skylight. Belushi has already taken on Wright directly but this is the last straw. They face off with mutual threats and Wright declares that if the principal returns the next day, he's dead. The final confrontation occurs after school. Gossett is locked in a closet and Belushi confronts Wright and two of his punks in the maze-like stalls of the girls locker room. Gossett escapes and takes care of one, as well as Cohen, who has broken bail to join the festivities. After cornering Belushi, Wright commands his henchman to kill his nemesis, but he refuses and Wright shoots him. "My turn," Belushi says, and proceeds to pound the hell out of Wright, literally throwing him out of school, where the student body awaits the outcome.

Belushi does his best with a part that is frequently hard to buy. Looking fitter than he has in any other film, he more than pulls off his tough-guy stance and is convincing as a guy who not only tries to prove he isn't a loser but wants to see some young minds opened along the way. His often humorous outlook comes across naturally as a believable facet of his character, as do his moments of fear and self-doubt, but too often he is called upon to perform actions that stretch credulity (the perfectly timed motorcycle rescue, for example). As a result his performance is generally winning but uneven. In support, Gossett is rock solid in a role that seems to call for nothing more, though he, too, injects some lighter moments with knowing looks. Chong does an adequate job with what she is given, considering there is no real justification for her presence except as the beneficiary of Belushi's motorcycle heroics and as an unfocused love interest. The "students" are generally believable, but sadly, Morales (who was so good in LA BAMBA) is wasted. Winbush, on the other hand, a 17-year-old making his film debut, is particularly good as the conscience-stricken kid who is won over by Belushi. It is Wright (STREAMERS), however, who leaves the most lasting impression. He is truly menacing, making it seem plausible that he could dominate a hellhole like Brandel. One genuinely fears Belushi's inevitable confrontation with him.

Because Wright is so believable and threatening, the tension and release at the film's core works well. This escalating tension is director Cain's (THE STONE BOY; THAT WAS THEN, THIS IS NOW) major success. Some critics found his handling of the characters and the camerawork of Albert to be well executed, but the shots of Belushi on his motorcycle, accompanied by the pounding soundtrack, quickly become tedious and much of the direction is unexceptional. The script by first-time screenwriter Deese is full of cliches drawn from the likes of BLACKBOARD JUNGLE, TO SIR WITH LOVE, and UP THE DOWN STAIRCASE but played out considerably more violently here. THE PRINCIPAL was primarily shot on the campus of Merritt College in Oakland, California, and many area youths were brought in to help convert the old structure into a usable set. Several local kids also appear in the film, including the "38th Avenue Locos," a Chicano gang whose members are recognizable by their khaki threads and dark sunglasses. The film crew included several out-of-the ordinary production assistants, members of the Oakland chapter of the Hell's Angels who helped recruit and control the student extras. Songs include: "Livin' in the Line of Fire" (Jay Gruska, Bruce Roberts, Andy Goldmark), "Straight into the Fire" (Gruska, Jon Lind), "Our Own Eyes" (Gruska, Paul Gordon), "Morning Light" (Gruska), "Gotta Get Air" (performed by Surf M.C's), "Jingo" (performed by Jellybean), "Woman's Touch" (performed by John Waite), "Hello Heaven" (performed by Rob Jungklas), "Set It Off" (performed by Strafe). *(Violence, excessive profanity.)*

p, Thomas H. Brodek; d, Christopher Cain; w, Frank Deese; ph, Arthur Albert (Monaco Labs color); m, Jay Gruska; ed, Jack Hofstra; md, Jellybean Benitez; art d, Mark Billerman; set d, Rick Brown; cos, Marianna Astrom-DeFina; spec eff, David Pier; m/l, Jay Gruska, Bruce Roberts, Andy Goldmark, Jon Lind, Paul Gordon; makeup, Balazs, Steve E. Anderson; stunts, Everett Creach.

Drama **(PR:O MPAA:R)**

PRINSEN FRA FOGO† (1987, Nor.) Regional Film c (Trans: The Prince of Fogo)

Carlos Alberto Alves De Veiga Da Pina.

An eight-year-old boy living off the coast of Senegal on the poverty-stricken Cape Verde islands must adjust to life without his mother for she has gone to another country in search of work.

d, Inge Tenvik; w, Inge Tenvik, Trond G. Lockertsen; ph, Svein Krovel.

Children's **(PR:NR MPAA:NR)**

PRISON ON FIRE† (1987, Hong Kong) 98m Cinema City/Golden Princess c

Chow Yun Fat, Leung Ka Fai, Roy Cheung.

Leung Ka Fai stars as a promising young designer for an advertising agency whose life is shattered when he is sent to prison for the accidental murder of a thief. Frightened and intimidated by the brutality of prison life, Leung Ka Fai is given some hope when he befriends older inmate Chow Yun Fat, a gambler who had murdered his wife. The men become as close as brothers, but when Chow Yun Fat becomes deeply involved with Triad gang warfare he ensures himself a longer sentence. Eventually Leung Ka Fai is released and he leaves the prison with his friend advising him never to give up hope. Matinee idol Chow Yun Fat was also featured in director John Woo's excellent crime drama A BETTER TOMORROW (1987), a film which became a surprise hit on the festival circuit.

p, Catherine Chang; d, Ringo Lam; w, Nam Yim; m, Lowell Lo; ed, Cinema City; art d, Luk Tze Fung.

Prison **(PR:NR MPAA:NR)**

PRIVATE INVESTIGATIONS (SEE: P.I. PRIVATE INVESTIGATIONS)

PRIZEMYAVANE† (1987, Bulgaria) 113m Bulgariafilm c (Trans: Return to Earth)

Plamena Getova *(Christina Daneva)*, Vassil Mihailov, Detelina Lazarova, Georgi Kishkilov, Yuri Yakovlev, Bogdana Voulpe, Zhana Karaivanova, Georgi Mamalev.

This aptly named film concerns a crisis in the life of a liberated Bulgarian woman. Getova is a successful radio executive and a prize-winning writer of children's books, whose professional life does not allow enough time for her husband, son, and lover. When her son is involved in the death of a playmate, she is shattered by his pain. She re-examines her life, analyzes her responsibilities, and begins to withdraw from her hectic schedule.

d, Roumyana Petrova; w, Nevelina Popova; ph, Svetla Ganeea; m, Raicho Lyubenov; art d, Yuliana Bozhkova.

Drama **(PR:NR MPAA:NR)**

PROC?† (1987, Czech.) 86m Filmove Studio Barrandov

Jiri Langmajer *(Jirka)*, Martin Sobotka *(Michal)*, Pavel Zvaric *(Petr)*, Pavlina Mourkova *(Marie)*, Jan Potmesil *(Milan)*, Daniel Vetrovsky *(Vlasta)*, Daniel Landa *(Pavel)*, Marketa Zmozkova *(Anca)*, Martin Dejdar *(Sury)*, Emilia

Zimkova *(Conductor)*, Emma Cerna *(Mother Mariina)*, Gabriela Wilhemova *(Mother Monicina)*, Katerina Fejlkova *(Hanka)*, Zdenek Pechacek *(Student)*, Leos Sucharipa *(Psychologist)*, Zdenek Dusek *(Farmer)*, Jan Vlasak *(Father Milanuv)*, Adolf Kohuth, Eva Lecchiova *(Stupkovi)*, Karel Pospisil, Vladislava Machackova, Alena Streblova, Ladislav Jakim, Radek John, Karel Smyczek.

[No plot available.]

d, Karel Smyczek; w, Radek John, Karel Smyczek; ph, Jaroslav Brabec; m, Michal Pavlicek; ed, Jan Svoboda; art d, Boris Halmi; cos, Petr Kolinsky.

(PR:NR MPAA:NR)

PRODELKI V STARINNOM DUKHE† (1987, USSR) 74m Mosfilm/Sovexportfilm c (Trans: Pranks, Old Days Style)

Darya Mikhailova, Vladimir Samoilov, Nikolai Trofimov, Mikhail Kononov, Alexei Nesterenko.

This comedy, based on some early stories by Alexei Tolstoy takes place on the eve of Napoleon's invasion, in the spring of 1812. The high-spirited daughter of an officer is courted by a brave soldier newly returned from the Turkish campaign. Unsure of his sincerity, the strong-willed girl resists his offer of marriage until he proves his love.

d, Alexander Pankratov; w, Andrei Strekov, Alexander Pankratov; ph, Grigory Belenky (Sovscope); m, Mark Minkov; art d, Nikolai Saushin, Rais Nagayev.

Comedy **(PR:NR MPAA:NR)**

PROFUMO† (1987, It.) Metrofilm S.r.1/Faso (Trans: Perfume)

Florence Guerin, Luciano Bartoli, Robert Egon Spechtenhauser, Giuliano Sestili, Vasco Santoni, Erminia Garofano.

A young wife is persecuted by her engineer husband's increasingly threatening sexual fantasies, which he compels her to act out. When she can't stand it anymore, she flees, taking a house in a coastal town. There she falls in love with a gentle young man, but the specter of her husband's perversity haunts her. Soon, her young lover seems to be picking up these bad vibes and taking on the twisted desires of her husband. Looking for a solution, she murders her husband, but the young man seeks his own escape in the US.

d, Giuliana Gamba; w, Massimo Nota Cerasi, Giuliana Gamba (based on a story by Giuliana Gamba); ph, Giorgio Di Battista; m, Franco Piersanti; ed, Sergio Montanari.

Drama/Romance **(PR:NR MPAA:NR)**

PROGRAMMED TO KILL† (1987) 91m Retaliator Prod./Trans World Ent. c (AKA: RETALIATOR)

Robert Ginty *(Eric Mathews)*, Sandahl Bergman *(Samira)*, James Booth *(Broxk)*, Alex Courtney *(Blake)*, Paul W. Walker *(Jason)*, Louise Caire Clark *(Sharon)*, Peter Bromilow *(Donovan)*, George Fisher *(Mike)*, Jim Turner *(Chris)*, Arnon Tzador *(Hassim)*.

A TERMINATOR rip-off starring the beautiful dancer Sandahl Bergman (remember the "Taking Off" dance sequence in ALL THAT JAZZ? She was the one on the platform.) She plays a dedicated member of a PLO "splinter group" sowing terrorism throughout the Middle East. With her boy friend Tzador and some underlings, she travels to Crete where they slaughter a group of American tourists doing some shopping. Two small children are kidnaped and the helpless CIA must call in weary mercenary Ginty (who should put a patent on this part) to come in and ferret out the terrorists. Ginty and his goons assault the terrorist hideout and Bergman is mortally wounded while Tzador escapes (by hiding under a bed!). Inexplicably, Bergman's body is flown to the US and operated on by a team of surgeons who implant computer chips into the brain-dead terrorist, turning her into a killing machine that obeys orders. The CIA then sends the Bergman/cyborg back to the Middle East with orders to seek out and destroy Tzador and his comrades. Dressed in a rather flattering black leather mini-skirt, Bergman goes to Beruit and kills Tzador and his gang. Shortly thereafter, however, Bergman experiences a short-circuit and her memory returns. Remembering that Ginty was the one who killed her, Bergman returns to the US determined to avenge her death and subsequent robotization. After littering the landscape with bodies, the big showdown takes place on a military airfield with Ginty mounting a bulldozer to combat the unstoppable Bergman. Given a short play in Los Angeles, PROGRAMMED TO KILL is now available on home video.

p, Don Stern; d, Allan Holzman, Robert Short; w, Robert Short; ph, Nitcho Lion Nissim, Ernest Holzman; m, Jerry Immel, Craig Huxley; ed, Michael Kelly; set d, Michael Parker, Pola Schreiber; cos, Vicki Graff, Lennie Barin; spec eff, Vern Hyde, John Carter; makeup, Maria Haro.

Action/Science Fiction **Cas.** **(PR:NR MPAA:R)**

PROINI PERIPOLOS† (1987, Gr.) 108m Greek Film Center c (Trans: Morning Patrol)

Michelle Valley (The Woman), Takis Spyridakis *(The Man)*.

In a desolate world, a young woman wanders alone searching for another human being. Buildings are still intact, machines continue to operate, and famous faces stare out from movie and TV screens, but not a soul is in sight. Finally, she encounters a man. Like her, his memory is scorched by the awful occurrences that have so changed their world. They cling each other, try to piece together their strange reality, and consider the almost imponderable past and future.

d&w, Nikos Nikolaidis; ph, Dinos Katsouridis; m, Giorgios Hadzinassios; ed, Andreas Andreadakis; art d&cos, Marie Louise Bartholomew.

Drama **(PR:NR MPAA:NR)**

PROJECT A—PART II† (1987, Hong Kong) 98m Golden Harvest-Golden Ways c

Jackie Chan, Maggie Cheung, Rosamund Kwan, Carina Lau.

The sequel to martial arts star Jackie Chan's phenomenally successful (in Hong Kong) 1985 film PROJECT A, proved to be just as potent at the box office as the original. Chan again stars as a turn-of-the-century do-gooder who this time is inducted into the Hong Kong police force to help battle a group of Sun Yat Sen revolutionaries. Wild martial arts action combined with Keystone Cops-style slapstick has proven a successful formula for Chan who has thrilled US audiences in the action films THE BIG BRAWL (1980) and THE PROTECTOR (1985). An English-language version of PROJECT A—PART II is being prepared for release in international markets.

p, Leonard Ho; d, Jackie Chan.

Martial Arts **(PR:NR MPAA:NR)**

PROJECT X*** (1987) 108m Parkes-Lasker-Amercent-American Entertainment Partners/FOX c

Matthew Broderick *(Jimmy Garrett)*, Helen Hunt *(Teresa "Teri" McDonald, Psychologist)*, Bill Sadler *(Dr. Lynnard Carroll)*, Johnny Ray McGhee *(Isaac Robertson)*, Jonathan Stark *(Sgt. "Kreig" Kreiger)*, Robin Gammell *(Col. Niles)*, Stephen Lang *(Watts)*, Jean Smart *(Dr. Criswell)*, Chuck Bennett *(Gen. Claybourne)*, Daniel Roebuck *(Hadfield)*, Mark Harden *(Airman Lewis)*, Duncan Wilmore *(Maj. Duncan)*, Marvin J. McIntyre *(Jimmy's Cellmate)*, Swede Johnson *(Senator)*, Harry E. Northrup *(Congressman)*, Michael Eric Kramer *(Lt. Voeks)*, Reed R. McCants *(Lt. Frohman)*, Ward Costello *(Price)*, Jackson Sleet *(Tavel)*, Lance August *(Cochran)*, Stan Foster *(Daniels)*, Gil Mandelik *(Perks)*, Shelly Desai *(Mr. Verrous)*, Dick Miller *(Max King, Freight Clerk)*, Michael Milgroom *(Melvin)*, Catherine Paolone *(Miss Decker)*, John Chilton *(Dr. Hutchins)*, David Raynr *(Airman Curtis)*, Lynn Eastman *(Sgt. Huntley)*, Julian Sylvester *(Airman)*, Kim Robillard *(Lt. Rainey)*, David Stenstrom *(Lt. Durschlag)*, Richard Cummings, Jr. *(Lt. Hayes)*, Randal Patrick *(Mackler)*, Sonny Davis *(Sgt. Ridley)*, Robert Covarrubias *(M.P. Rodriguez)*, Dino Shorte *(M.P. Jones)*, Ken Lerner *(Finley)*, Travis Swords *(Fanara)*, William Snider *(Warden)*, Philip A. Roberson *(Reeves)*, Bob Minor, Raymond Elmendorf *(Air Policemen)*, Michael McGrady *(Wilson)*, Rob Fitzgerald *(Dryer)*, Pamela Ludwig *(Lenore)*, Deborah Offner *(Carol Lee)*, Lance Nichols *(Hamer)*, Tee Rodgers *(Brig M.P.)*, Jackie Kinner *(United Way Volunteer)*, Mady Kaplan *(TV Announcer)*, Chevis Cooper *(Customer)*, Kenneth Sagoes *(Patrolman)*, Louis A. Peretz *(Bellhop)*, Sam Laws *(Bartender)*, Chimps: Willie *(Virgil)*, Okko *(Goofy)*, Karanja *(Goliath)*, Luke *(Bluebeard)*, Harry *(Ginger)*, Clatu *(Spike)*, Lucy *(Razzberry)*, Lulu *(Ethel)*, Mousie *(New Recruit)*.

A perfect example of expertly crafted but mindless entertainment, PROJECT X offers a bare minimum of plot, drapes it in a meaningful cause (animal rights), and pulls on the heartstrings so carefully that one just can't help but get suckered into the film. Opening with a title crawl that legitimizes the otherwise preposterous plot by stating that it is based in fact, the story begins in a university research lab as graduate student Hunt is teaching sign language to a chimpanzee named Virgil. After having worked for three years on her research, she is informed that the university is cutting her funding. Hunt is devastated at the prospect of losing her nearly human companion, but is reassured by university officials that the animal will be well cared for in a Houston zoo. The scene then shifts to a Florida Air Force base at which a top-secret experimental research project (dubbed "Project X") is being staged. New to the project is Broderick, a hot-shot pilot who has just been reassigned because of his carefree antics. Besides being grounded, Broderick is given duty as an animal trainer. Along with his fellow trainers, Broderick teaches chimps how to work a flight simulator. What he later learns is that the chimpanzees, while in the simulator cockpit, are subjected to high levels of radiation. The results of this project will supposedly give the Air Force an idea of how long pilots can continue to fly after being exposed to a nuclear blast. Naturally, Broderick meets up with Virgil (who obviously has not been sent to a zoo) and the animal's attempts to communicate prompt the young pilot to learn sign language. Broderick grows fond of Virgil, as well as many of the other chimps, each of which is given a unique personality and a moniker to match. When Broderick realizes that the chimps are being senselessly destroyed, he voices his objection to his commanding officers. After rifling some files, Broderick learns that Hunt is the person who trained Virgil. He contacts her but, fearing court martial, refuses to reveal anything about Project X. Although he morally objects to the testing, Broderick is forced to continue in the program. With a senator and some high military brass in attendance, Broderick points out a fault in a experiment in which Virgil is to be killed and temporarily saves the chimps' life. In the process, however, he loses his job and is ordered to leave the base. The night before he is to leave, Broderick connects with Hunt and the pair break into the base to save the chimps. After the mischievous chimps nearly cause a nuclear meltdown, Broderick and Hunt load the animals into a small Air Force plane and attempt to fly away to safety. Before they can do so, they are apprehended by a pair of military policemen. The MP's fail, however, to round up the chimps. Employing the skills he learned on the flight simulator, Virgil sits in the pilot's seat, starts the engine, heads down the runway, and takes off into the sky. Later, the plane is found after crash-landing in an Everglades swamp, its chimpanzee crew having found freedom at last.

Directed by one-time Roger Corman protege Kaplan, PROJECT X echoes that familiar "saving-the-alien" plot structure that Steven Spielberg perfected in E.T. All the elements are present: an intelligent, lovable creature (be it extraterrestrial or primate) communicates with and is saved from the evil establishment by a caring group of individuals who then help the poor creature find its way home. This time around the creature has more fur and likes apples instead of Reeses Pieces. There's practically nothing wrong with PROJECT X; it hits all the marks with a craftsmanlike perfection. Besides having its "can't lose" E.T. styled script blueprint, PROJECT X has a number of cute and cuddly chimpanzees that have facial expressions even a poacher could love. Broderick is superb as always and proves that he is a commanding screen presence even in the company of a cute chimp. Hunt, looking vaguely like Jodie Foster, also turns in a fine performance. Surprisingly, even the film's bad guy, research head Sadler, has some redeeming qualities, preventing the script from becoming patently simpleminded. Other than some basic filmmaking ingredients, however, there isn't much to PROJECT X. It's well-crafted entertainment—nothing more, nothing less—and there's nothing wrong with that.

Underneath the entertainment there is something of a statement against the medical and scientific abuse of animals. With the growing strength of such antivivisectionist movements as Animal Liberation and the Society Against Vivisection, much has been reported in the media about the tortures that research animals (usually rhesus monkeys) undergo in laboratories. Although PROJECT X takes an obvious vivisectionist stand, the Society Against Vivisection and animal rights advocate/TV game-show host Bob Barker still objected to the picture. A paid advertisement in the May 8 *Daily Variety* offered a $5,000 reward for anyone who would testify that animals were abused on the set of PROJECT X. Some crew members testified that the chimps were beaten and punched by trainers. However, The American Humane Association, which was on the set for all of the 81 shooting days, reported that no such abuses took place. Whatever did take place, the film itself does not resort to visualizing such inhumane treatment on the screen, making the picture safe for impressionable youngsters. Songs include: "Shock the Monkey" (Peter Gabriel, performed by Gabriel), "You Baby You" (Chris McCarty, Gary Mallaber, performed by Billy Burnette). *(Profanity.)*

p, Walter F. Parkes, Lawrence Lasker; d, Jonathan Kaplan; w, Stanley Weiser (from a story by Stanley Weiser, Lawrence Lasker); ph, Dean Cundey (Deluxe Color); m, James Horner; ed, O. Nicholas Brown; prod d, Lawrence G. Paull; set d, Joseph Pacelli, Lynn Christopher; cos, Mary Vogt; m/l, Peter Gabriel, Chris McCarty, Gary Mallaber; spec eff, Michael Fink.

Comedy **Cas.** **(PR:A MPAA:PG)**

PROMISED LAND*** (1987) 85m Vestron-Great American-Wildwood-Oxford/Vestron c

Jason Gedrick *(Davey Hancock)*, Kiefer Sutherland *(Danny Rivers)*, Meg Ryan *(Bev)*, Tracy Pollan *(Mary)*, Googy Gress *(Baines)*, Deborah Richter *(Pammie)*, Oscar Rowland *(Mr. Rivers)*, Sondra Seacat *(Mrs. Rivers)*, Jay Underwood *(Circle K Clerk)*, Herta Ware *(Mrs. Higgins)*.

Following the fortunes of four young adults, this third picture from the producer-director team of Rick Stevenson and Michael Hoffman seeks to examine the unfulfilled promises of the American Dream. The film opens in 1984, with a high-school basketball district championship game that is won by the last-minute heroics of Gedrick (IRON EAGLE) and witnessed by his cheerleader girl friend Pollan and by Sutherland, nicknamed "Senator" because of his father's oft-stated belief that with enough hard work any American can be one. Gedrick is bound for college on a basketball scholarship, and Pollan wonders if things will change between them. Sutherland, who sees himself as a loser, drops out of school and leaves the little town of Ashville, Utah. Two years later, Christmas draws near. Gedrick is now an Ashville policeman, having failed to make the grade in college ball. Pollan is home from college for the holidays. Gedrick tries desperately to keep their romance going, but, with her horizons broadened and a boy friend back at school, Pollan wants out. Meanwhile, in Nevada, Sutherland marries Ryan, an impetuous hellraiser with pink hair, whom he has known for only three days. The film then cuts back and forth between Gedrick's attempts to hold on to Pollan and Sutherland and Ryan's journey through the mountainous expanse of Nevada and Utah to meet his parents. En route it becomes clear that Ryan's outrageous behavior—running a road block, shoplifting, excessive drinking—is more than just a wild streak. Drugs and a tough-luck background have made her frenetic and fearless, yet she is touched by the attention paid her by the mild-mannered, sensitive Sutherland and anxious to make a good impression on his family. Back in Ashville, Pollan is confused by the feelings she still has for Gedrick, but realizes they inhabit different worlds now. Sutherland and Ryan arrive but things don't go well. Sutherland tries to talk with his sickly father Rowland, but nothing of consequence is said. Sutherland explains to Ryan that if he and his father *really* talked, Rowland would have to admit that Sutherland wasn't the son he hoped for, and Sutherland would have to tell him that he wasn't the father he wanted. Sutherland wants to leave town, but they are out of money. He and Ryan go to a convenience store, and, to his shock, she pulls a gun. Gedrick and Pollan, who have been arguing, pull up in a car. In the confused moments that follow, Gedrick, acting the policeman, shoots and kills Sutherland. The next day, Gedrick goes to console Rowland, and later turns in his badge.

PROMISED LAND is a well-intentioned film, but despite strong performances, an engaging plot, and some arresting photography, its ambitious reach exceeds its grasp. In attempting to show that the American Dream is a pipe dream for many, writer-director Hoffman has taken a stance that flies in the face of Reagan-era optimism. Rather than making his characters *poor people*, Hoffman has chosen to place the action in a small town and, with the significant exception of Pollan (whose background gives her choices unavailable to the others), to focus on the lives of working-class Americans. The locale is also important, particularly Sutherland and Ryan's pilgrimage (the car is a Plymouth, its prominent hood ornament an angel) through wide open spaces and majestic mountains of Utah and Nevada. Long the symbol of unbounded opportunity, the West has provided little for either Sutherland or Ryan. Reno's neon-lit casinos are also a poignant symbolic reminder of the gamble and promise of the big pot at the heart of capitalism. What is disappointing about PROMISED LAND is that these symbolic elements seem to exist on a different plane. Instead of being shown as the stuff of which American Dreams are made, the film's symbolism has a grafted-on quality. The presidential portrait that hangs in Rowland's shabby living room makes Hoffman's point too heavy handedly. Similarly, Rowland himself is a caricature of lumpen enervation.

That said, Hoffman still delivers an intriguing, well-paced story that draws the viewer in as it builds to its tragic climax. His characters come across as real people both because they have been well-written and because of the convincing performances of the four leads. All-American pretty, Pollan (formerly of TV's "Family Ties") makes the inner struggle of the young woman with a future believable. Gedrick's portrayal of the frustrated one-time basketball star is affecting because he knows exactly why Pollan is drifting away from him. The best performances, though, are by Sutherland and Ryan, playing emotional polar opposites. Sutherland underplays his quiet, sensitive loner (a departure from his recent tough-guy roles in STAND BY ME and THE LOST BOYS) without allowing him to disappear or become too pathetic. Drugged, drunken, and psychotic, Ryan (TOP GUN, INNERSPACE) is a jittery ball of unfocused energy, a bad-news comet that catches Sutherland in her tail and hurtles him towards disaster.

The photography of the mountains, plains, and huge Western skies is gorgeous and Hoffman's use of the camera is occasionally dazzling. There are many memorable images in PROMISED LAND, but the most unforgettable is a shot of the Plymouth and the distant mountains reflected on the shimmering salt flats. Hoffman is himself from a small town in Idaho where a shooting similar to the one in the film occurred. He knew both of the former high-school friends who were involved and has dedicated his film to them. Developed at the Sundance Institute, PROMISED LAND was shot on location in Utah and Reno, Nevada. Robert Redford served as an executive producer and all the actors worked for scale. This is the third collaboration (following PRIVILEGED and RESTLESS NATIVES) for Hoffman and producer Stevenson, Americans who met while studying at Oxford and who will bear watching in the future. *(Profanity, nudity, sexual situations, violence.)*

p, Rick Stevenson; d&w, Michael Hoffman; ph, Ueli Steiger, Alexander Gruszynski; m, James Newton Howard; ed, David Spiers; prod d, Eugenio Zanetti; cos, Victoria Holloway.

Drama **(PR:O MPAA:NR)**

PRORYV† (1987, USSR) 98m Lenfilm/Sovexportfilm c (Trans: Breakthrough)

Oleg Borisov, Andrei Rostotsky, Yury Demich, Alexander Susnin, Yury Kuznetsov.

A local construction accident creates a ripple in the earth which in turn causes major destruction and the evacuation of many buildings. The workers and managers join with the city authorities in averting further danger.

d, Dimitry Svetozarov; w, Albina Shulgina; ph, Sergey Astakhov; m, Andrei Makarevich; art d, Mikhail Suzdalev.

Drama **(PR:NR MPAA:NR)**

PROSHAL ZELEN LETA† (1987, USSR) 92m Uzbekfilmstudio/Sovexportfilm bw/c (Trans: Farewell Green Summer)

Fakhretdin Manafarov *(Timur)*, Larisa Belogurova *(Ulphat)*, Rustam Sagdullaev, Borislav Brondukov.

This bittersweet tale of star-crossed love is gradually reduced to an indictment of corruption in its native Uzbekistan. Two lovers are thwarted in their attempt to marry by the girl's father and brothers, who whisk her away and pummel her sweetheart half to death. Years later they meet briefly on a train, but she is married, and he has turned down the road to corruption. Enriched by the memory of his one, true love, the boy reassesses his life, tries to right the wrongs he has committed and is, of course, killed for his efforts.

d, Elyor Ishmukhamedov; w, Dzhasur Iskhakov, Elyor Ishmukhamedov; ph, Yury Liubshin; m, Eduard Artemyev; art d, Igor Gulenko.

Romance **(PR:NR MPAA:NR)**

PROSHANIE (SEE: FAREWELL, 1987, USSR)

PROSTI† (1987, USSR) 82m Lenfilm/Sovexportfilm c (Trans: Forgive Me)

Natalia Andreichenko *(Masha)*, Igor Kostolevsky *(Kiril)*, Viktor Merezhko *(Vladimir)*, Alexandra Yakovleva *(Natasha)*, Alisa Freindlich *(Elisaveta Andreevna)*, Vladimir Menshov, Alexi Zarkov, Tatiana Mikhailova.

Andreichenko is a modern woman with a good job, a nice apartment, a loving husband and a daughter she neglects. When she discovers her husband has a mistress she is shattered and throws him out of the house. She then embarks upon a round of parties with her friends, in order to meet men. Hurrying home one night to the daughter she has left alone, she is attacked by a gang of toughs. Humiliated, she stumbles home to find her husband has left his mistress and returned to her.

d, Ernest Jassan; w, Viktor Merezhko; ph, Ivan Bagayev; m, Vadim Bibergan; art d, Stanislav Romanovsky.

Comedy **(PR:NR MPAA:NR)**

PRYWATNE SLEDZTWO† (1987, Pol.) 99m Zespoly Filmowe-Zodiak/Film Polski c (Trans: Private Investigation)

Roman Wilhelmi *(Rafal Skonecki)*, Jan Peszek *(Marek, Rafal's Friend)*, Janusz Bukowski *(Major)*, Piotr Dejmek, Jan Jankowski *(Detectives)*, Miroslawa Marcheluk *(Drunk)*, Andrzej Pieczynski, Jerzy Trela.

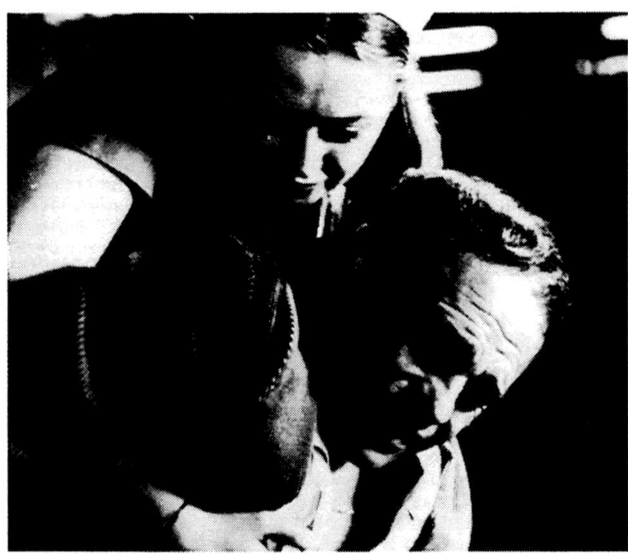

After his wife and children are killed in an accident caused by a drunken truck driver, a distraught Wilhelmi vows revenge. Disatisfied with the indifference of the police, he mounts his motorbike and covers Poland from one end to the other in his search for the hit and run driver. A series of brutal slayings of reckless truck drivers casts suspicion on Wilhelmi, but in the end he catches his family's killer, and the murderer of the truck drivers is apprehended.

d&w, Wojciech Wojcik; ph, Jacek Mieroslawski; m, Zbigniew Gorny; ed, Marek Denys; art d, Malgorzata Wloch.

Action **(PR:NR MPAA:NR)**

PRZYJACIEL WESOLEGO DIABLA† (1987, Pol.) 88m Se-Ma-For c (Trans: The Friend of a Jolly Devil)

Waldemar Kalisz *(Janek)*, Piotr Dziamarski *(Piszczalka, Monster)*, Franciszek Pieczka *(Witalis, Woodsman)*, Zbigniew Grabski, Janusz Sterninski, Marcin Zdenicki, Krystyna Lech-Maczka.

Based on a novel by Kornel Makuszynski, this Polish children's film is packed with adventure and fantastic characters. Pieczka, a woodsman, finds an abandoned child in the forest one day and raises him as his son. The babe grows into Kalisz, and when he has reached the age of 10, Pieczka suddenly goes blind. Kaliz is determined to help his "father" and answers a mysterious call that lets him know that he must seek out the Spirit of Darkness and defeat him if Pieczka is to see again. While searching for the Spirit, Kalisz encounters Dziamarski, a friendly monster who joins the boy in his quest. The road to the Spirit of Darkness is fraught with danger, but the boy and his monster friend survive every test, including the final confrontation with their sought-after foe, and Kalisz returns to Pieczka, who is able to see again.

d&w, Jerzy Lukaszewicz (based on the novel by Kornel Makuszynski); ph, Jerzy Lukaszewicz; m, Marek Bilinski; ed, Miroslawa Garlicka; art d, Piotr Dumala.

Children **(PR:NR MPAA:NR)**

PRZYPADEK (SEE: BLIND CHANCE, 1987, Pol.)

PSYCHO GIRLS† (1987, Can.) 92m Lightshow/Cannon c

John Haslett Cuff *(Richard Foster)*, Darlene Mignacco *(Sarah)*, Agi Gallus *(Victoria)*, Rose Graham, Silvio Oliviero, Pier Giorgio Dicicco, Michael Hoole, Dan Rose, Kim Cayer, Dorin Ferber, Frank Procopio, Fernn Kane, Michael Bockner, Maria Cortese, Nikki Pezaro, Gerard Ciccoritti.

Low-budget Canadian horror filmed late in 1984 and released straight-to-home-video by Cannon. Narrated by a corpse a la SUNSET BOULEVARD, the film begins in 1966 as crazy young Mignacco is hauled off to an asylum for poisoning her parents on their anniversary. Fifteen years later Mignacco escapes and seeks revenge on her sister (Gallus), who, of course, is the real culprit. As it turns out Gallus is working as a cook for detective-novel writer Cuff (the narrator). Mignacco kills her sister, takes her place, and prepares a "special" meal for the writer's wedding-anniversary celebration. The crazed Mignacco and two accomplices kill the guests off one by one until it is revealed that the narrator is speaking to the viewer from beyond the grave.

p, Michael Bockner; d, Gerard Ciccoritti; w, Michael Bockner, Gerard Ciccoritti; ph, Robert Bergman (Film House Color); m, Joel Rosenbaum; ed, Robert Bergman; art d, Craig Richards.

Horror **Cas.** **(PR:NR MPAA:R)**

PSYCHOS IN LOVE*½ (1987) 87m Generic/Wizard Home Video-ICN Bleecker-Infinity c

Carmine Capobianco *(Joe)*, Debi Thibeault *(Kate)*, Frank Stewart *(Herman)*, Cecilia Wilde *(Nikki)*, Donna Davidge *(Heather)*, Patti Chambers *(Girl in Bed)*, Carla Bragoli *(Girl in Woods)*, Carrie Gordon *(Girl in Toilet)*, Angela Nicholas *(Dianne)*, Peach Gribauskas *(Bar Waitress)*, Ed Powers *(Man)*, Frank Christopher *(Man at Picnic)*, Professor Morono *(Joey the Creep)*, Shawn Light *(Girl in Sauna)*, Scott Sears *(Frightened Man)*, Lee Ann Baker *(Heavy Metal Girl)*, Linda Strouth *(Cathy)*, Eric Lutes *(Mechanic)*, Mike Brady *(Redneck)*, Ruth Collins *(Susan)*, Jerry Rakow *(Henry)*, Irma St. Paule *(Sara)*, Tressa Zannino *(Hooker)*, "Big" Marty *(Bopper's D.J.)*, Michael Citriniti *(Weather Man)*, Kate McCamy *(Woman)*, Loren Freeman *(Video Store Clerk)*, Jan Redder *(Blood Pumper)*, Matt Brooks *(Assistant Blood Pumper)*, Kathy Milani *(Photographer)*, Shaun Cashman *(Soundman)*, Joe Murphy *(Waiter)*, Barry Clark *(Man in Restaurant)*, Robert Suttile, Lum Pang Chang, Danny Noyes, Herb Klinger, Wally Gribauskas *(Bar Patrons)*.

An ambitious low-budget horror parody that actually contains a few redeeming moments of social satire and is fairly interesting stylistically. A balding, overweight bar owner, Capobianco, is a self-confessed psycho who despises grapes (" . . . all kinds of grapes! Purple grapes! Green grapes! Peeled grapes and non-peeled grapes! Grapes with seeds! Grapes without seeds! Grapes in bunches or in small clumps of twos and threes!") and has problems sustaining a relationship. He picks up attractive women, and when the dates goes badly, he kills them. His life changes, however, when he meets a girl (Thibeault) who shares his hatred of grapes. She also happens to be a female psycho killer who goes out with men and then kills them after they utter bad pickup lines. Crazy in love, the happy couple move in together and vow to have an open relationship which allows them to continue their peculiar dating habits. After several additional murders, however, they discover that the thrill of killing is gone. Capobianco and Thibeault decide to get married, retire from killing, and live vicariously through slasher-movie videocassettes. Their marital bliss is interrupted by Stewart, a plumber who comes to unclog their kitchen sink. When Stewart finds human body parts have stopped-up the drain, he reveals that he is a cannibal and tries to blackmail Capobianco and Thibeault into coming out of retirement to provide him with fresh meat. The couple does decide to come out of retirement—but only long enough to dispose of Stewart. The film then collapses into a bout of film school self-consciousness where the sound man, still photographer, and special-effects crew are seen pumping stage blood into the scene. Capobianco and Thibeault then adjourn to a restaurant where they argue over whether a raisin is indeed a dried grape.

Sophomoric, gross, warped, and more than a bit depraved, PSYCHOS IN LOVE succeeds at being a low-budget satire of American dating rituals, modern relationships, suburbia, and slasher movies. Although at times the pacing is sluggish and only about half the jokes are funny, the film does have a zany originality. Structured like a Woody Allen film (with heavy overtones of Paul Bartel's EATING RAOUL), the movie is narrated by both Capobianco and Thibeault, who are seen separately in close-ups—shot on grainy black-and-white stock—where they comment on the action and each other (a situation similar to Spike Lee's SHE'S GOTTA HAVE IT). The two leads are actually likable young actors, with Capobianco possessing a goofy sense of humor that seems to actually set Thibeault giggling. Not only is the climax of the film self-reflexive, but during the entire film the viewer is reminded that it's all "just a movie." Actors make asides to the camera, Capobianco puts his hand over the lens a few times, and at one point the mike-boom comes into frame and Thibeault slaps it away. Both actors performed several offscreen roles for the low-budget production. Capobianco wrote and performed the music (including a rather funny love duet sung by him and Thibeault), served as second assistant director, and helped out with the gore effects. Thibeault also served as the costumer and as assistant editor. Shot on 16mm, PSYCHOS IN LOVE had a strange distribution pattern. It was released on videotape *first*, and then released to theaters on the East Coast several months later in a truncated version (seven minutes were cut). While certainly not for the squeamish, PSYCHOS IN LOVE does have a certain grotesque charm and it may achieve a minor sort of cult status among fans of the bizarre. *(Violence, gore effects, nudity, sexual situations, profanity.)*

p&d, Gorman Bechard; w, Carmine Capobianco, Gorman Bechard; ph, Gorman Bechard (Precision color); m, Carmine Capobianco, Gorman Bechard; ed, Gorman Bechard; cos, Debi Thibeault; spec eff, H. Shep Pamplin, Matt Brooks, Jan Radder, Jan Pedis, Nina Port, Carmine Capobianco, Jennifer Aspinall, Tom Molinelli; makeup, Frank Stewart.

Horror/Comedy **Cas.** **(PR:O MPAA:NR)**

PUDHCHE PAOL† (1987, India)

Yashwant Dutt, Ashalata Wabgaonkar, Sagar, Prashant, Manasi.

A won't-be bride causes an uproar when she balks at her arranged marriage. She learns that her future husband's previous two wives committed suicide, and, not wishing to follow in their footsteps, she will have no part of the union. (In Marath.)

p, Vinay Newalkar; d, Raj Dutt; w, Jaywant Dalvi; m, Sudhir Phadke.

Comedy **(PR:NR MPAA:NR)**

PURSUIT OF HAPPINESS, THE† (1987, Aus.) 85m Jequerity c

Laura Black *(Anna)*, Peter Hardy *(John)*, Anna Gare *(Mandy)*, Jack Coleman *(Stan)*, Dennis Schultz, Senator Jo Vallentine, Alec Smith, Don Allison, Mayor John Catalini.

Part family drama, part political message film, THE PURSUIT OF HAPPINESS is an exploration of an Australian teenager's opposition to nuclear proliferation and her mother's growing sympathy with the her daughter's beliefs. Gare, a 15-year-old, lives in Fremantle, Western Australia, where US nuclear vessels dock. She plays in a rock band and works with an anti-nuclear group that is trying to put a halt to visits by the US ships and submarines. Black, her mother, has recently undertaken a career as journalist and her daughter's concerns have led her to ponder the "big question." Studying interviews with Russian and American spokesmen, and watching and rewatching a videocassette of ON THE BEACH (1959)—the film adaptation of Nevil Shute's classic anti-*bomb* novel—she begins to share he daughter's fears. Her superiors at the newspaper are less open-minded, and Hardy, Black's husband, is outraged by his wife's and daughter's stance on the issue. Ultimately, mother, daughter, and even Hardy's father, Coleman, come together to demonstrate against the visit of US nuclear vessels to Fremantle.

p&d, Martha Ansara; w, Martha Ansara, Alex Glasgow, Laura Black; ph, Michael Edols; ed, Kit Guyatt.

Drama **(PR:NR MPAA:NR)**

PYAR KARKE DEKHO† (1987, India)

Govinda, Mandakini, Kader Khan.

A man pretends he is married in order to get a house and later is shocked when his "wife" shows up at his door. (In Hindi.)

p, Kishan Paul; d, D. Rajendra Babu; m, Bappi Lahiri.

Comedy **(PR:NR MPAA:NR)**

PYAT NEVEST DO LYUBIMOY† (1987, USSR) 83m Gruziafilm/Sovexportfilm c (Trans: Five Brides, Then a Sweetheart)

Badri Kakavaze, Mikhail Samsonadze, Rusudan Bolkvadze, Iya Ninidze.

Soviet comedy that centers around the attempts by a group of friends to fix up one of their buddies with an appropriately charming, lovely, and intelligent woman. While his friends are busy sending him off on one date after another, the would-be groom longs for his less impressive girl friend. Finally the guys stop trying to force schoolteachers, reporters, and musicians on their put-upon pal and let true love take its course.

d&w, Leila Gordeladze; ph, Yury Kikabidze; m, Vakhtang Kukhiaindze; art d, Nodar Badurashvili.

Comedy **(PR:NR MPAA:NR)**

QUARTIERE** (1987, It.) 124m Marzo Cinematografica/Istituto Luce-Italnoleggio c (ANOTHER DAY)

Vittoria Zinny *(Mother)*, Alessandra Corsale, Paola Agosti *(Two Sisters)*, Lorenzo Negri *(Rich Boy)*, Ivano Errera *(His Friend)*, Sergio Bini *(Nino)*, Nino Manzone *(Old Bum)*, Giorgetta Ranucci *(Doorkeeper)*, Dario Ghirardi, Valeria Sable, Lino Salemme, Francesca Trevisannelo, Elisabetta Pellgrini, Elena Donnici, Benedetto Simonelli.

This film contains four vignettes which explore heartaches that come with relationships. The first involves two sisters (Corsale and Agosti) going out for a New Year's Eve celebration. They are picked up by a carload of boys, who subsequently rape one of the girls. Despite the horror of this act, the victim comes to fall in love with one of her attackers. In the second tale, two young men (Negri and Errera) spend a weekend at a country estate owned by Negri's wealthy father. The duo have been good friends for a long time, and finally consummate their relationship. Despite this foray into homosexuality, Errera insists he still intends to wed his fiancee. Negri is left alone, watching from a distance as Errera is reunited with his female love. He returns to his now-hollow estate, wandering the empty rooms while listening to "Tosca" on the stereo. In the next vignette, a woman leaves her lover, and he grows despondent. He glimpses the image of a Bengal tiger on television and quickly becomes fascinated with the jungle cat. He takes to watching the animal at a local zoo, and refuses to see his former love when she decides to return. In the final episode Manzone plays a derelict who lives in an abandoned automobile. He dispenses sage philosophy to anyone who listens, and is one day visited by Ranucci. She is the doorkeeper for the building Manzone's "home" is parked near, and finds herself inexplicably attracted to this vagrant. She sleeps with him in the car, and Manzone confesses it is his first sexual encounter. The film closes with a title explaining that all these stories are based on true incidents.

Filmed over the course of three years, director Agosti has stated he is more interested in the visual elements of cinema rather than telling a story. But in concentrating exclusively on this aspect, his work is merely a series of wonderfully arranged shots which ultimately say nothing. The rape sequence, shot in tight close-ups and moody lighting, looks more exotic than horrifying. The second story develops in a more realistic manner while maintaining the well-stylized visual design and consequently is the film's most interesting vignette. The man and tiger story is nearly impossible to figure out, merely a series of carefully created pictures linked together on the most meager of premises. The final sequence, like the first, is dependent on tight close-ups and a darkly lit frame. When Manzone makes his confession to Ranucci it's hard to sympathize with him. It's admirable for a director to return to cinema's roots, allowing picture to dominate, but by sacrificing the story Agosti has created an empty two hours. We are distanced from the characters for they exist only in a world of cinematic tricks. This is the sort of film that would have played art houses in the 1960s to great acclaim, hiding its empty shell under the all-protective flag of aesthetics.

p,d&w, Silvano Agosti; ph, Silvano Agosti (Luciano Vittori color); m, Ennio Morricone; ed, Silvano Agosti.

Drama **(PR:O MPAA:NR)**

QUATRE AVENTURES DE REINETTE ET MIRABELLE† (1987, Fr.) 97m Losange c (Trans: Four Adventures of Reinette and Mirabelle)

Jessica Forde *(Mirabelle)*, Joelle Miquel *(Reinette)*, Philippe Laudenbach *(Waiter)*, Fabrice Luchini *(Gallery Owner)*, Marie Riviere *(The Cheat)*, Francois-Marie Banier, Jean-Claude Brisseau, Beatrice Romand, Yasmine Haury, Gerard Courant, David Rocksavage, Jacques Auffray, Haydee Caillot, Marie Bouteloup, Francois Valier, The Housseau Family.

Eric Rohmer's intermission from his ongoing "Comedies and Proverbs" series, QUATRE AVENTURES (Rohmer's first of two films this year) follows the friendship of two young French women—Parisian Forde and country girl Miquel. Divided into four episodes, the film begins with "L'Heure Bleu," in which Forde and Miquel wait for the pre-dawn moment called the "Blue Hour" when nature is quiet. Adventure number two, "Le Garcon de Cafe," has Forde inviting Miquel to Paris during which time Miquel is confronted by an obstinate cafe waiter, Laudenbach. The third episode, "Le Mendiant, la cleptomane, l'arnaqueuse," is a parallel tale in which Miquel stops a train station cheat, Riviere (SUMMER), while Forde protects a shoplifter. The final adventure has Miquel, having taken a 24-hour vow of silence, trying to sell a painting to art dealer Luchini (FULL MOON IN PARIS). Rohmer followed this film with another in the "Comedy and Proverbs" series, L'AMI DE MON AMI. Filmed in 16mm.

d&w, Eric Rohmer; ph, Sophie Maintigneux; m, Ronan Girre, Jean-Louis Valero; ed, Maria-Luisa Garcia.

Drama **(PR:NR MPAA:NR)**

QUATRE MAINS† (1987, Ger./Neth.) 90m Added-Die Nieuwe Unie-Provobis c (Trans: Four Hands)

Peter Ritz *(Alexander)*, Renee Fokker *(Marte)*, Reinhard von Bauer *(German Friend)*, Thore Seeberg.

Fitz stars as a 60-year-old concentration camp survivor unable to reconcile himself with his past. A concert pianist, the moody Fitz cannot properly express himself verbally and instead relies on the piano to communicate his feelings. He tries to reach out to his rebellious niece, Fokker, but the two are only harmonious when playing quatre mains (four-hand piano pieces) together. Fokker begins an affair with German combat photographer von Bauer and she accompanies him to Hamburg. Fitz follows the couple, for Hamburg is the place where he was born and he has not been back since 1938. He visits the house where he was born and the line between past and present begins to blur. He sees von Bauer as a Nazi and tries to kill the photographer by running him over with a car. Fitz then takes Fokker to the coast where he breaks into a beach house and is finally able to explain himself. He tells his niece that he has been dead for the last 40 years and that time has stood still for him since leaving the concentration camp. He now realizes that his behavior has suffocated her. As an act of reconciliation they sit down at the pianos and play Schubert's "Der Leiermann." This is the feature film debut of director Hans Fels, whose previous films were documentaries dealing with the effect WW II had on people's lives.

p, Dirk Schreiner, Rolf Orthel, Jurgen Haase; d, Hans Fels; ph, Tony Kuhn; m, Paul Prenen; ed, Hans Dunnewijk; art d, Dick Schillemans.

Drama **(PR:NR MPAA:NR)**

QUEL RAGAZZO DELLA CURVA "B"† (1987, It.) Gloria Cinematografica/Titanus (Trans: That Boy from the "B" End)

Nino D'Angelo, Laurentina Giudotti, Benito Artesi, Aldo Tarantino, Antonella Patti, Tommaso Bianco, Antonio Allocca, Gennaro Palummella, Giuseppe Bruscolotti, Bruno Giordano, Francesco Romano, Andrea Carnevale, Pietro Punzone, Bruno Pesaola, Bibi e Coco.

That boy from the "B" end is a Neapolitan mechanic who lives for Sundays and the opportunity to cheer his favorite soccer team. The leader of a group of fans who always sit in the same section, he takes it upon himself to sort out the riffraff who are giving the die-hard supporters a bad name. However, the rowdies—some of whom are involved in drug dealing—aren't anxious to be reformed and make life extremely difficult for the No. 1 fan and his girl friend. Everything works out fine in the end, though, and Sundays are still special in the "B" end.

p, Nino Masiello; d, Romano Scandariato; w, Nino Masiello, Piero Regnoli; ph, Silvio Fraschetti; m, Franco Chiaravalle; ed, Carlo Broglio.

Crime **(PR:NR MPAA:NR)**

RADIO DAYS*1/2** (1987) 85m Orion c

Woody Allen *(Narrator)*, Seth Green *(Little Joe)*, Julie Kavner *(Mother)*, Michael Tucker *(Father)*, Dianne Wiest *(Aunt Bea)*, Josh Mostel *(Uncle Abe)*, Renee Lippin *(Aunt Ceil)*, William Magerman *(Grandpa)*, Leah Carrey *(Grandma)*, Joy Newman *(Ruthie)*, Mia Farrow *(Sally White)*, Julie Kurnitz *(Irene)*, David Warrilow *(Roger)*, Wallace Shawn *(Masked Avenger)*, Kenneth Mars *(Rabbi Baumel)*, Jeff Daniels *(Biff Baxter)*, Danny Aiello *(Rocco)*, Gina DeAngelis *(Rocco's Mother)*, Tony Roberts *("Silver Dollar" Emcee)*, Diane Keaton *(New Year's Singer)*, Guy LeBow *(Bill Kern)*, Marc Colner *(Whiz Kid)*, Richard Portnow *(Sy)*, Roger Hammer *(Richard)*, Mike Starr, Paul Herman *(Burglars)*, Don Pardo *("Guess That Tune" Host)*, Martin Rosenblatt *(Mr. Needleman)*, Helen Miller *(Mrs. Needleman)*, Danielle Ferland *(Child Star)*, Michael Murray *(Avenger Crook)*, William Flanagan *(Avenger Announcer)*, Hy Anzell *(Mr. Waldbaum)*, Judith Malina *(Mrs. Waldbaum)*, Fletcher Farrow Previn *(Andrew)*, Oliver Block *(Nick)*, Maurice Toueg *(Dave)*, Sal Tuminello *(Burt)*, Rebecca Nickels *(Evelyn Goorwitz)*, Mindy Morgenstern *("Show and Tell" Teacher)*, David Mosberg *(Arnold)*, Ross Morgenstern *(Ross)*, Andrew Clark *(Sidney Manulis)*, Lee Erwin *(Roller Rink Organist)*, Terry Lee Swarts, Margaret Thomson *(Night Club Customers)*, Tito Puente *(Latin Band Leader)*, Denise Dumont *(Latin Singer)*, Dimitri Vassilopoulos *(Porfirio)*, Larry David *(Communist Neighbor)*, Rebecca Schaeffer *(Communist's Daughter)*, Belle Berger *(Mrs. Silberman)*, Brian Mannain *(Kirby Kyle)*, Stan Burns *(Ventriloquist)*, Todd Field *(Crooner)*, Peter Lombard *(Abercrombie Host)*, Martin Sherman *(Mr. Abercrombie)*, Crystal Field, Maurice Shrog *(Abercrombie Couple)*, Roberta Bennett *(Teacher with Carrot)*, Joel Eidelsberg *(Mr. Zipsky)*, Peter Castellotti *(Mr. Davis)*, Shelley Delaney *(Chekhov Actress)*, Dwight Weist *(Pearl Harbor Announcer)*, Ken Levinsky, Ray Marchica *(USO Musicians)*, J.R. Horne *(Biff Announcer)*, Kuno Sponholz *(German)*, Henry Yuk *(Japanese)*, Sydney A. Blake *(Miss Gordon)*, Kitty Carlisle Hart *(Radio Singer)*, Robert Joy *(Fred)*, Henry Cowen *(Principal)*, Philip Shultz *(Whistler)*, Greg Gerard *(Songwriter)*, David Cale *(Director)*, Ira Wheeler *(Sponsor)*, Hannah Rabinowitz *(Sponsor's Wife)*, Edward S. Kotkin *(Diction Teacher)*, Ruby Payne, Jackie Safra *(Diction Students)*, Paul Berman *("Gay White Way" Announcer)*, Ivan Kronenfeld *(On-the-spot Newsman)*, Frank O'Brien *(Fireman)*, Yolanda Childress *(Polly's Mother)*, Artie Butler *(New Year's Bandleader)*, Mercedes Ruehl, Bruce Jarchow *(Ad Men)*, Barbara Gallo, Jane Jarvis, Liz Vochecowizc *(Dance Palace Musicians)*, Gregg Almquist, Jackson Beck, Wendell Craig, W.H. Macy, Ken Roberts, Norman Rose, Kenneth Welsh *(Radio Voices)*.

In October, 1987, people in the United States and the rest of the world held their breath to see if 18-month-old Jessica McClure would be rescued from the well into which she had fallen in Midland, Texas. The ending to that story was a happy one. Not so in the case of Kathy Fiscus, a three-year-old in Los Angeles who perished in a similar accident in the 1940s. Changing the location to Pennsylvania and the girl's name to Polly Phelps, that story is one of the many real-life moments Woody Allen has adapted for this exercise in nostalgia for an era when radio was the theater of the mind. Allen cross-cuts between the Brooklyn of his youth (in this case it was the Rockaway area although Allen himself was from another neighborhood and attended school in mid-Brooklyn) and the uptown life being led by radio personalities. Allen has always been fascinated with the beach front section (witness the Coney Island sequence in ANNIE HALL) and gives us a typical yet intriguing family. Green is the youthful protagonist, a short lad, son of Kavner and Tucker. Also in the extended household are grandparents Magerman and Carrey, maiden aunt Wiest, uncle Mostel (son of Zero), his wife Lippin, and their daughter Newman. In narration, Allen (who doesn't appear in the film) relates stories about members of the household. Green is obsessed with "The Masked Avenger" and conspires to get the money to buy a secret decoder ring promoted by his hero. (This sets up one of the film's funniest scenes as Green, who has stolen money collected for the Jewish Homeland Fund, is knocked around by mother, father, and rabbi (Mars) as the adults argue about who should discipline the child.) Kavner and Tucker bicker often, but without rancor. While Tucker is continually dreaming up new ways to make a fortune. Wiest is always looking for Mr. Right but she doesn't even come close with a succession of losers. In one instance, she's out with a man who looks like he might be *the* guy. The two of them are parked at foggy Breezy Point and listening to the radio. Suddenly, Orson Welles' famed "War of the Worlds' broadcast is heard and the man races out of the car because he thinks that the Martians have landed in New Jersey. Mostel has a friend in the Sheepshead Bay fish business and is always bringing fish home for his wife to prepare, telling her, when she complains to "take the gas pipe." Lippin spends most of her time listening to the neighbors on the party line and doing Carmen Miranda impressions. Other neighborhood stories related by Allen include: the time Mostel visited the leftist neighbors on the Jewish High Holidays to chastise them for their boisterousness, only to return a convert to the Marxist-Leninist cause; how aged neighbor Berger has a fatal heart attack when she sees a black man plant a huge kiss on a white woman's lips; the time a local kindly old man went berserk and ran through the neighborhood in his underwear, waving a meat cleaver at all he encountered.

While all of this is happening in Brooklyn, Allen intercuts stories about radio and its personalities. Many of the stories focus on Farrow, a cigarette girl with a dreadful "Noo Yawk" accent who dreams of radio stardom. On her way to the top, she has a rooftop tryst with Warrilow (who is married to Kurnitz and is one-half of a radio show not unlike "Breakfast With Dorothy and Dick" was); almost winds up a stiff after witnessing hitman Aiello kill a night club owner; and becomes the leading gossip monger of the airwaves after finally learning to speak

correctly. In another instance, two crooks are robbing a house when the phone rings. It's a quiz show hosted by Don Pardo. The crooks answer the question correctly, winning a truckload of merchandise, then leave the house. The homeowners are then pleasingly puzzled the next day when the prizes are delivered to their door. Tony Roberts appears as a quiz show host when Wiest is a contestant. She is asked to identify various kinds of fish and, since Mostel has been bringing fish around the house for years, the questions are a snap and she wins $50. The funniest single segment is a satire of sportscaster Bill Stern and one of his questionable "true stories." In a tale similar to the Monty Stratton story (the White Sox pitcher who lost a leg in a hunting accident and came back to pitch; James Stewart teamed with June Allyson in the movie), the pitcher loses a great deal more than a leg. It's worth the price of admission for that vignette.

If the above sounds disjointed, it is exactly that. There is no real story, just a succession of funny and nostalgic interludes featuring many actors who have appeared for Allen in other films. The film ends as the Manhattan merry-gorounders stand atop a tall building (in a magnificent set) and wonder aloud if they will ever be remembered and what the future will bring. Simultaneously, as the radio folks are sipping champagne, the Rockawayfarers are swilling Hoffman's soda and wondering the same things, sort of. The humorous moments are punctuated by sadness, such as the realization that the little girl in the well has died, which causes Tucker to stop hitting Green and to embrace the boy, glad that he is alive. This picture is choppy and that is both an asset and a liability. By cutting so quickly, Allen has been able to present a host of anecdotes and remembrances of things past. In the case of BRIGHTON BEACH MEMOIRS, a movie which also took place in a seaside area at roughly the same time this century, the story was more confined but ultimately not as satisfying. Pathos, sentimentality, and tears are as evident as the comedy. Allen uses many of the real folks who made radio what it was. People like Kitty Carlisle Hart (widow of Moss Hart), announcer Dwight Weist (who handles the Pearl Harbor chores), Don Pardo (who can still be seen and heard on NBC), plus the voices of many of radio's best announcers, such as Jackson Beck, Wendell Craig, and Ken Roberts, father of Tony. Don't expect a full sit-down meal for the eyes with RADIO DAYS. It's a sumptuous buffet, with everything you might want, but one wishes it could have been slightly more cohesive. Anyone who thinks radio is just a place to find music or news is probably too young to understand how important radio was in those days and will surely have difficulty appreciating this motion picture. Excellent editing from Susan Morse and fine cinematography from Di Palma, a switch from Allen's usual camera person, Gordon Willis. One of the joys in this picture, as it was in 1987's IN THE MOOD, is the use of songs to indicate the period. There are 43 tunes en toto and they are a rainbow of memory for anyone who lived in those radio days. The musical numbers include: "The Flight of the Bumblebee" (N.A. Rimsky-Korsakoff, performed by Harry James), "September Song" (Maxwell Anderson, Kurt Weill), "Dancing in the Dark" (Arthur Schwartz, Howard Deitz), "Body and Soul" (John W. Green, Edward Heyman, Robert Sour, Frank Eyton, performed by Benny Goodman), "Chinatown, My Chinatown" (William Jerome, Jean Schwartz), "In the Mood" (Joe Garland, performed by Glenn Miller), "Let's All Sing Like the Birdies Sing" (Robert Hargreaves, Stanley J. Damerell, Tolchard Evans), "I Double Dare You" (Jimmy Eaton, Terry Shand, performed by Larry Clinton), "Carioca" (Vincent Youmans, Gus Kahn, Edward Eliscu), "You're Getting to be a Habit with Me" (Harry Warren, Al Dubin), "Tico Tico" (Zequinha Abreu, Aloysio Oliveira, Ervin Drake), "La Cumparsita" (Matos Rodriguez, performed by The Castilians), "Opus One" (Sy Oliver, performed by Tommy Dorsey), "Frenesi" (A. Dominguez, performed by Artie Shaw), "You and I" (Meredith Willson), "All or Nothing at All" (Jack Lawrence, Arthur Altman), "Paper Doll" (Johnny S. Black, performed by The Mills Brothers), "The Donkey Serenade" (Herbert Stothart, Rudolph Friml, Bob Wright, Chet Forrest, performed by Allan Jones), "Pistol Packin' Mama" (Al Dexter, performed by Bing Crosby and The Andrews Sisters), "South American Way" (Al Dubin, Jimmy McHugh, performed by Carmen Miranda), "If I Didn't Care" (Jack Lawrence, performed by The Ink Spots), "Mairzy Doats" (Milton Drake, Al Hoffman, Jerry Livingston, performed by The Merry Macs), "Schloff mein Kind" (performed by Emil Decameron), "I Don't Want to Walk Without

You" (Jule Styne, Frank Loesser), "If You are but a Dream" (Moe Jaffe, Jack Fulton, Nat Bonx, performed by Frank Sinatra), "Remember Pearl Harbor" (Sammy Kaye, Don Reid, performed by Kaye), "Babalu" (Margarita Lecuona, S.K. Russell, performed by Xavier Cugat), "(There'll Be Blue Birds Over) The White Cliffs of Dover" (Walter Kent, Nat Burton, performed by Glenn Miller), "They're Either Too Young or Too Old" (Arthur Schwartz, Frank Loesser), "Goodbye" (Gordon Jenkins, performed by Benny Goodman), "That Old Feeling" (Lew Brown, Sammy Fain, performed by Guy Lombardo), "I'm Gettin' Sentimental Over You" (Ned Washington, George Bassman, performed by Tommy Dorsey), "Re-Lax Jingle" (Dick Hyman), "Lullaby of Broadway" (Al Dubin, Harry Warren, performed by Richard Himber), "You'll Never Know" (Harry Warren, Mack Gordon), "One, Two, Three, Kick" (Xavier Cugat, Al Stillman, performed by Cugat), "American Patrol" (F.W. Meacham, performed by Glenn Miller), "Take the 'A' Train" (Billy Strayhorn, performed by Duke Ellington), "Begin the Beguine," "Just One of Those Things," "You'd Be So Nice to Come Home To," "Night and Day" (Cole Porter). *(Mild profanity.)*

p, Robert Greenhut; d&w, Woody Allen; ph, Carlo Di Palma (Duart Color); ed, Susan E. Morse; md, Dick Hyman; prod d, Santo Loquasto; art d, Speed Hopkins; set d, Carol Joffe, Les Bloom; cos, Jeffrey Kurland; m/l, N.A. Rimsky-Korsakoff, Maxwell Anderson, Kurt Weill, Arthur Schwartz, Howard Deitz, John W. Green, Edward Heyman, Robert Sour, Frank Eyton, William Jerome, Jean Schwartz, Joe Garland, Robert Hargreaves, Stanley J. Damerell, Tolchard Evans, Jimmy Eaton, Terry Shand, Larry Clinton, Vincent Youmans, Gus Kahn, Edward Eliscu, Harry Warren, Al Dubin, Zequinha Abreu, Aloysio Oliveira, Ervin Drake, Matos Rodriguez, Cole Porter, Sy Oliver, A. Dominguez, Meredith Willson, Jack Lawrence, Arthur Altman, Johnny S. Black, Herbert Stothart, Rudolph Friml, Bob Wright, Chet Forrest, Al Dexter, Jimmy McHugh, Milton Drake, Al Hoffman, Jerry Livingston, Jule Styne, Frank Loesser, Moe Jaffe, Jack Fulton, Nat Bonx, Sammy Kaye, Don Reid, Margarita Lecuona, S.K. Russell, Walter Kent, Nat Burton, Arthur Schwartz, Gordon Jenkins, Lew Brown, Sammy Fain, Ned Washington, George Bassman, Dick Hyman, Mack Gordon, Xavier Cugat, Al Stillman, F.W. Meacham, Billy Strayhorn, makeup, Fern Buchner

Comedy **Cas.** **(PR:A-C MPAA:PG)**

RAGE OF HONOR** (1987) 91m Rage/Trans World c

Sho Kosugi *(Shiro Tanaka)*, Lewis Van Bergen *(Drug Lord)*, Robin Evans *(Jennifer)*, Richard Wiley *(Ray Jones)*, Armando Caro *(Juan)*, Marlee Jepson *(Girl in Convertible)*, Eric Seward *(Desk Clerk)*, Ned Kovas *(Havlock's Guard)*, Lilian Rinar *(Havlock's Girlfriend)*, Hugo Halbritch, Alejo Apsega, Ezequiel Ezkenazi *(Killers)*, Martin Coria *(Jorge)*, Masfumi Sakanashi, Kiyatsu Shimoyama *(Prison Ninjas)*, Ulises Dumont, Ted McNabney, Gerry Gibson, Chip Lucia, Carlos Estrada, Alan Amiel.

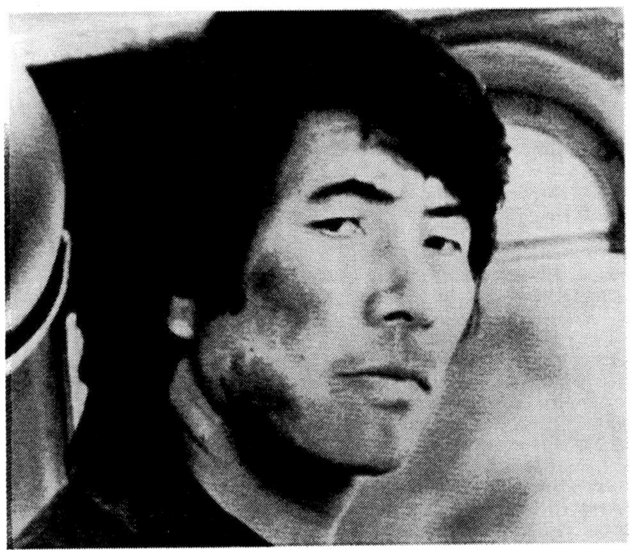

Martial arts star Kosugi follows up his highly entertaining PRAY FOR DEATH with a less successful entry which resorts to dramatic cliches and overextended fight sequences. This time around Kosugi is a narcotics agent based in Phoenix who, with his partner Wiley, makes life difficult for drug runners. When Wiley is set up by someone within the force and murdered by drug kingpin Van Bergen, Kosugi's rage begins. Pretending to take a vacation in Buenos Aires with his pretty blonde girl friend Evans, Kosugi continues his search for Van Bergen. Along the way, the drug runners get their hands on a secret government computer disk which contains the names of dealers and their contacts. When Evans is nearly thrown from the balcony of her hotel, Kosugi arranges to have her sent back to Phoenix on the next flight. The plane gets hijacked, however, and she is taken to a remote region where the drug runners have set up their operation. Kosugi is airlifted deep into the jungle where he must battle a tribe of vicious indians before locating Evans. After annihilating countless well-armed guards, Kosugi comes face to face with Van Bergen and the pair engage in a brutal hand-to-hand fight. Kosugi emerges victorious, saves Evans, and awaits his rescue by US narcotics agents. He quickly finds out, however, that the narcotics officials are part of a plot engineered by the US government to share in the profits of South American drug running. They attempt to kill Kosugi, but that proves to be impossible, even with such heavy artillery as machine guns, explosives, and hand-held rocket launchers. After saving Evans once again and killing off all the government bad guys, Kosugi faces one final battle with Van Bergen, who apparently did not die after the last whipping he received. Although things look bad for Kosugi, he outsmarts and kills his opponent.

While RAGE OF HONOR is technically impressive and generally well acted, it lacks the believability and script strength necessary to provide compelling entertainment. With PRAY FOR DEATH, Kosugi and director Hessler created a strong story which had a Ninja/martial arts backdrop. This time, the film relies almost completely on the choreographed violence. The drug-running plot is simply mumbo-jumbo to get from one fight sequence to the next. While it is these fight sequences that most martial arts devotees pay their money to see, in RAGE OF HONOR they are less than spectacular. For the most part, Kosugi is fighting a bunch of uncoordinated, overweight thugs who couldn't scare a defenseless old woman much less an unstoppable killing machine like our hero. Some of Kosugi's James Bond-style gadgetry is fun and the jungle locations of the film's later half are interesting (though better employed in GYMKATA), but this one is a step down from Kosugi's previous effort. There is a considerable amount of violence, but it relies more on nonrealistic choreographed body movement than on graphic bloodletting. *(Violence.)*

p, Don Van Atta; d, Gordon Hessler; w, Robert Short, Wallace Bennett (from a story by Robert Short); ph, Julio Bragado (Technicolor/Cinecolor); m, Stelvio Cipriani; ed, Robert Gordon; prod d, Adrian Gorton; art d, Kirk Demusiak, Abel Facello; set d, Laurie Scott; cos, Ed Fincher, Jean Aikens, Ana Tasaki; ch, Sho Kosugi; spec eff, Paul Staples, Tom Cundom, Hugo Diaz; makeup, Ann Mayo, Alice Adamson, Bob Smith.

Martial Arts/Crime **Cas.** **(PR:O MPAA:NR)**

RAISING ARIZONA*** (1987) 94m Circle/FOX c

Nicolas Cage *(H.I. McDonnough)*, Holly Hunter *(Edwina)*, Trey Wilson *(Nathan Arizona, Sr.)*, John Goodman *(Gale)*, William Forsythe *(Evelle)*, Sam McMurray *(Glen)*, Frances McDormand *(Dot)*, Randall "Tex" Cobb *(Leonard Smalls)*, T.J. Kuhn *(Nathan Arizona, Jr.)*, Lynne Dumin Kitei *(Florence Arizona)*, Peter Benedek *(Prison Counsellor)*, Charles "Lew" Smith *(Nice Old Grocery Man)*, Warren Keith *(Younger FBI Agent)*, Sidney Dawson *(Ear-Bending Cellmate)*, Richard Blake *(Parole Board Chairman)*, Troy Nabors, Mary Seibel *(Parole Board Members)*, John O'Donnal *(Hayseed in Pick-Up)*, Keith Jandacek *(Whitey)*, Warren Forsythe *(Minister)*, Ruben Young *("Trapped" Convict)*, Dennis Sullivan, Dick Alexander *(Policemen in Arizona House)*, Rusty Lee *(Feisty Hayseed)*, James Yeater *(Fingerprint Technician)*, Bill Andres, Carver Barnes *(Reporters)*, Margaret H. McCormack *(Unpainted Secretary)*, Bill Rocz *(Newscaster)*, Mary F. Glenn *(Payroll Cashier)*, Jeremy Babendure *(Scamp with Squirt Gun)*, Bill Dobbins *(Adoption Agent)*, Ralph Norton *(Gynecologist)*, Henry Tank *(Mopping Convict)*, Frank Outlaw *(Supermarket Manager)*, Todd Michael Rogers *(Varsity Nathan, Jr.)*, M. Emmet Walsh *(Machine Shop Earbender)*, Robert Gray, Katie Thrasher, Derek Russell, Nicole Russell, Zachary Sanders, Noell Sanders *(Glen and Dot's Kids)*, Cody Ranger, Jeremy Arendt, Ashley Hammon, Crystal Hiller, Olivia Hughes, Emily Malin, Melanie Malin, Craig McLaughlin, Adam Savageau, Benjamin Savageau, David Schneider, Michael Stewart *(Arizona Quints)*.

The promise of talent that was evident in the Coen brothers' 1984 debut, BLOOD SIMPLE, is fulfilled in this entertaining, energetic, and stylish comedy about a loving, simplistic couple who long to be parents. In a lengthy and superbly constructed precredit sequence, the stage is set. Cage, playing a character whose initials spell "Hi," is a sloppily dressed, sleepy-looking petty crook who can't pass a convenience store without holding it up. Because he never uses a loaded gun, he manages to avoid an armed robbery rap. Habitually breaking parole, Cage is repeatedly sent back to prison, going through the same routine every time he's convicted. Each time he has his mug shot taken by a stern but pretty booking officer, Hunter, who orders him, in a military tone of voice, to "turn to the right!" so she can snap his profile. He is then carted off to the Munroe County Maximum Security Correctional Facility for Men in Tempe, Arizona, where the same threatening inmate is always seen mopping the floors. Then comes the parole hearing, which always ends in his release. Tired of this routine, he asks Hunter to marry him, and they settle down in a airstream trailer in the middle of an Arizona desert. All of this is filmed in short, cartoonish scenes with Cage's folksy, quasi-eloquent narration carrying the story. Cage has now turned away from his life of crime and hopes to have a normal 1980s family life with Hunter. But, as Cage puts it, "Biology and the prejudices of others conspired to keep us childless." Longing to be parents of a little "critter," they descend upon adoption agencies, only to be denied because of Cage's criminal history.

Their luck changes, however, when they see a news story about Nathan Arizona (played by Wilson), the Unfinished Furniture King of the Southwest, whose wife has just given birth to quintuplets—Harry, Barry, Larry, Garry, and Nathan, Jr. Assuming that five is more than any one couple can handle, Cage and Hunter decide to steal one for themselves. Sneaking in the bedroom window, Cage survives a comic fiasco involving the five gurgling, crawling, uncontrollable babies. He eventually decides that Nathan, Jr. is the one he wants. Back home, he and Hunter are thrilled to be parents, but are unable to decide on a name for the baby, alternately calling him "Ed, Jr." (after Hunter) and "Hi, Jr." (after Cage). Their familial bliss doesn't last long, changing with the arrival of two recently escaped former prison mates of Cage's—Goodman and Forsythe. A demented, slobbish, beer-guzzling pair, they mean for their stay to be a short one, but it drags on long enough to try Cage's and Hunter's patience. Goodman and

Forsythe try to recruit Cage for a bank robbery, but he resists. Meanwhile, Cage has a nightmarish vision of the "Lone Biker of the Apocalypse," a scuzzy, bearded madman (Cobb) who roars down the desert highway on his Harley-Davidson, blowing up jackrabbits with hand grenades and shooting lizards to pieces.

Reports of the Arizona kidnaping fill newscasts, arousing the suspicions of Cage's boss and friend McMurray, who tries to blackmail Cage into giving him the child. It turns out that Cobb is not merely a madman, but a bounty hunter who tries to strike a deal with Wilson. Cobb arrives at Cage's trailer to claim the baby, but is too late; Goodman and Forsythe have already taken the baby in the hope of collecting the posted reward. A series of chases follows, with the baby, while still in his car seat, being left atop the roof of Goodman and Forsythe's car and tumbling off into the middle of the highway. The baby changes hands a few times until the climactic showdown between Cage and Cobb. Although Cage is beaten to a pulp, he outsmarts Cobb by blowing him apart with one of his own grenades. After returning Nathan, Jr. to the crib he previously shared with his fellow quints, Cage and Hunter nearly split up but realize that their love is stronger than before. The picture ends with Cage describing a dream of his in which he saw himself and Hunter as old people at a family gathering with their children and grandchildren. "And it seemed real," Cage explains. "It seemed like us. And it seemed like . . . our home. If not Arizona, then a land not too far away, where all the parents are strong and wise and capable, and all the children are happy and beloved . . . Maybe it was Utah."

With the conservative outlook of the 1980s, the Coens have fashioned a comedy which takes a stance, albeit a lighthearted and twisted one, in the favor of the nuclear family. The lead characters in the film—Cage and Hunter—are a misguided pair trying desperately to get on the road to a healthy, happy home life. Although he has a background as a criminal, Cage is an upstanding husband and father. He defends his wife when his boss suggests wife-swapping, and steals a package of Huggies diapers for his new son when he robs a convenience store. Part of his reason for stealing Nathan, Jr. is, in his mind, humanitarian—he wants to ease the responsibility of the Arizona family, who are being taxed by the thought of raising quints. Perhaps unintentionally, Joel and Ethan Coen (who are 32 and 29 years old respectively, and childless) have come across as proponents of family life. Most important, they have made this conservative appeal with the most radical visual styles seen in some time. With their debut film, BLOOD SIMPLE (a stylish but empty endeavour), the Coens proved that they knew how to use a camera. Although much of their camerawork (breakneck tracking shots, excessive wide angles, startling point-of-view shots) crosses the line between effective and self-indulgent, there is still enough invention in their films to be worthy of praise.

As with BLOOD SIMPLE, the Coens have populated this film with excellent performances. Cage, perhaps best remembered for his 1983 role in VALLEY GIRL, creates a homey and thoroughly likable character who earns the respect of the audience, but Hunter is the real surprise of the film. Appearing in her first starring role, she displays so much energy that she forces the audience to watch her instead of focusing on the often overbearing camerawork. (Originally she was to star in BLOOD SIMPLE, but chose instead to act on Broadway in her third Beth "Crimes of the Heart" Henley play.) The supporting cast is equally impressive. Goodman and Forsythe (seen in a similar role in THE LIGHTSHIP) are wonderful as the goofy escaped cons, Cobb is nasty enough to intimidate most of the people in ROAD WARRIOR, Wilson's salesman's pitch is perfect for his role as the Unfinished Furniture King, and McMurray and McDormand (the lead in BLOOD SIMPLE) do fine as Cage and Hunter's obnoxious friends.

Even with its lightning-fast pace, however, RAISING ARIZONA makes its 94 minutes feel like two hours. While there are some excellent moments in the film, much of it drags. The chase scenes go on and on only to show off the elaborate camerawork, and the scene with McMurray and McDormand's children wrecking Cage's trailer lasts forever. Worst of all is the final showdown between Cobb and Cage. The Coens' style is dependent on the distance they create between their characters and the audience by means of the self-conscious camerawork. The presence of the director is felt in every frame. That distance, however, is deadening in the showdown scene. What should be emotional and gripping ends up being just another exercise in tricks and techniques, thereby rendering the scene ineffective. There seems little doubt that the Coens will eventually hit on a successful combination of style and substance, perhaps even resulting in a masterpiece of modern American filmmaking. RAISING ARIZONA is a leap in the right direction and seems to be a promise of better things to come. *(Violence.)*

p, Ethan Coen, Mark Silverman; d, Joel Coen; w, Ethan Coen, Joel Coen; ph, Barry Sonnenfeld (Duart color); m, Carter Burwell; ed, Michael R. Miller; prod d, Jane Musky; art d, Harold Thrasher; set d, Robert Kracik; cos, Richard Hornung; makeup, Katherine James-Cosburn; m/l, Charlie Monroe, Pete Seeger; stunts, Jery Hewitt.

Comedy **(PR:C MPAA:PG-13)**

RATAS DE LA CIUDAD† (1987, Mex.) 93m Cinematografica Sol-Cinematografica Jalisco/Peliculas Mexicanas c (Trans: City Rats)

Valentin Trujillo *(Pedro Macias)*, Rodolfo de Anda *(Zuniga)*, Angelica Chain *(Rita Gonzalez)*, Enrique "Flaco" Guzman *(Pachuco)*, Humberto Elizondo *(El Flaco)*, Isaura Espinoza, Joaquin Cordero, Munguia, Los Caminantes.

Valentin Trujillo, an actor rapidly becoming the Mexican equivalent of action *auteur* Slyvester Stallone, co-wrote, directed, and starred in this revenge tale about an unemployed physical therapist whose son is injured in a car accident. Trujillo takes the boy to the hospital and then goes to the police to make a complaint. There he sees the driver of the car, Elizondo, and learns that the man is a member of the secret police. Realizing the culprit will go free, Trujillo flies into a rage and gets himself jailed. When his son is released from the hospital, he assumes that his father has abandoned him. The boy joins a group of vicious street urchins who roam the slums attacking those weaker than they. Trujillo teams up with a female social worker, Chain, to find his son and wreak vengeance on Elizondo. Trujillo, who performed similar chores in last year's UN HOMBRE VIOLENTE, won best director and four other Diosa de Plata (Silver Goddess) awards from the cinema writers' group for RATAS DE LA CIUDAD.

p, Rodolfo de Anda; d, Valentin Trujillo; w, Valentin Trujillo, Gilberto de Anda; ph, Antonio de Anda; m, Marco Flores; ed, Sergio Soto; m/l, Los Caminantes.

Drama **(PR:NR MPAA:NR)**

RAWHEAD REX* (1987, Brit.) 89m Alpine-Paradise-Green Man/Empire c

David Dukes *(Howard Hallenbeck)*, Kelly Piper *(Elaine Hallenbeck)*, Hugh O'Conor *(Robbie Hallenbeck)*, Cora Lunny *(Minty Hallenbeck)*, Ronan Wilmot *(Declan O'Brien)*, Niall Toibin *(Rev. Coot)*, Niall O'Brien *(Det. Insp. Isaac Gissing)*, Heinrich Von Schellendorf *(Rawhead Rex)*, Donal McCann *(Tom Garron)*, Eleanor Feely *(Jenny Nicholson)*, Gladys Sheehan *(Ena Benedict)*, Madelyn Erskine *(Alice Gibson)*, Gerry Walsh *(Dennis McHugh)*, Noel O'Donovan *(Mitch Harney)*, John Olohan *(Dennis Nicholson)*, Peter Donovan *(Liam Blanchfield)*, Bob Carlile *(Garda Conroy)*, Patrick Dawson *(Det. Larkin)*, Barry Lynch *(Andy Johnson)*, Maeve Germaine *(Katrina)*, Simon Kelly *(Neil Johnson)*, Derry Power *(Sean Power)*, Sheila Flitton *(Nancy Power)*, Derek Halligan *(Caravaner)*, Bairbee Ni Chaoimh *(Laurie)*, Tom Lawlor *(1st Man Possessed)*, Dave Carey *(Caravaner Gunman)*, Vincent Smith, Mary Ryan *(Survivors)*, Michael Ford *(Gissing's Driver)*, Frank Melia *(Journalist)*, Lana McDonald *(Screaming Woman)*, Robert Byrne *(Photographer)*, Bob Coyle *(Larkin's Driver)*, David Nolan *(Police Marksman)*, Mary Ryan *(Survivor)*, Julie Hamilton *(Hooded Villager)*, Liv Clausen *(Hooded Priestess)*.

There are two good reasons why British horror author Clive Barker decided to direct his own stories beginning with HELLRAISER: one of them is UNDERWORLD (1985) and the other is RAWHEAD REX, both produced and directed by the same inept team. Although Barker wrote both screenplays and director Pavlou is a friend, neither film captures the essence of the stories from which they were derived. Set in Ireland, RAWHEAD REX begins promisingly enough as a farmer tries to dig up an ancient stone that has been standing in his field for centuries. Suddenly, something grabs the spade and pulls it into the ground. The farmer strains to pull the shovel back and winds up unearthing a huge, snarling, mythical monster that was an ancient god in the days before Christianity—Rawhead Rex (played by seven-foot-tall German actor Von Schellendorf). The monster kills the man and goes on a rampage, taking big fatal bites out of several locals, including the young son of American university professor Dukes, who is visiting Ireland with his family. An expert in history and anthropology, Dukes has been studying the local churches and cemeteries with a special interest in pre-Christian artifacts. Through his investigation Dukes uncovers the history of Rawhead Rex and figures out how to destroy him. Locked in the altar of the church is a small stone figure that will subdue the beast. Unfortunately, the altar is guarded by the slavishly loyal Wilmot, a church employee who has been possessed by the monster. Dukes finally manages to circumvent Wilmot and retrieve the statue, only to find that it has no effect on Rawhead Rex. Knocked about like a rag doll by the unholy beast, Dukes loses the statue. Piper, Dukes' wife, recovers the statue and holds it over her head. This time blue lazers shoot out of the statue and surround the monster, sapping his energy and driving him back into the grave (a woman is needed to wield the ancient weapon—something to do with a Druid priestess and whatnot).

For starters, the monster suit concocted by special effects wiz Litten is downright laughable. The beast is supposed to have been buried beneath the earth for hundreds of years (Barker's description of this in the story is *very* vivid), but this Rawhead Rex is a squeaky clean latex rubber man fresh out of the mold. With a minimum of facial movement and gobs of runny red goo dripping out of its mouth, the monster looks more like a drooling college football mascot than an evil ancient god. Also, from the way poor Von Schellendorf lumbers around crashing into things, it must have been impossible to see out of the suit. Worse than the costume is the acting. Dukes, once the toast of Broadway, storms through this film spewing a litany of threats and foulness as he demands that the authorities do something about the beast. Piper's performance is just plain schizophrenic, alternating between curt bitchiness and nymphomania, only interrupted by an all-too-brief bout of catatonia after the death of her son. Worst of all, however, is Irish actor Wilmot, who literally froths at the mouth, whines, shrieks, and cackles like Dwight Frye in fast motion. Wilmot's performance is embarrassingly cartoonish and unintentionally hilarious. The gore effects are relatively sparse and not too gory, although there is a laughable bit of ultra-gratuitous nudity when the dress is ripped off a female victim for no apparent reason and she is thrashed around naked for a few moments before old Rawhead puts the kibosh on her. Director Pavlou moves his film at a snail's pace, demonstrating little flair for suspense or even simple shock. The last word on Pavlou's directorial cleverness is that he is not beyond intercutting shots of gory violence with a housewife cutting up some meat for a stew. Gosh, what an ingenious juxtaposition. Ugh. *(Graphic violence, gore effects, nudity, excessive profanity.)*

p, Kevin Attew, Don Hawkins; d, George Pavlou; w, Clive Barker (based on his short story); ph, John Metcalfe (Rank color); m, Collin Towns; ed, Andy Horvitch; art d, Len Huntingford; cos, Consolata Boyle; creature eff, Peter Litten; spec eff, Gerry Johnston; stunts, Peter Brayham.

Horror **Cas.** **(PR:O MPAA:R)**

RAZMAKH KRYLIEV† (1987, USSR) 94m Odessa/Sovexportfilm c (Trans: Wingspan)

Yevgeny Karelskikh, Vladimir Zamansky, Sergei Sazontyev, Vyacheslav Baranov, Vitaly Doroshenko, Anna Gulyarenko.

A Soviet disaster film—the equivalent of the American AIRPORT movies—which details the bravery of the pilots and passengers on a commerical airliner en route from Irkutsk to Sverdlovsk. The plane loses both engines over the Siberian swamps and it is three hours to the nearest airport. While the crew does what it can to get the plane to the airport, ground personnel scramble their emergency units and prepare for a crash landing.

d, Gennady Glagolev; w, Boris Rakhamamin; ph, Valery Sevastyanov; m, Ivar Vigner, Alexander Griva; art d, Vladimir Shinkevich, Oleg Ivanov.

Drama (PR:NR MPAA:NR)

REAL MEN† (1987) 96m MGM/UA c

James Belushi *(Nick Pirandello)*, John Ritter *(Bob Wilson)*, Barbara Barrie *(Mom)*, Bill Morey *(Cunard)*, Iva Andersen *(Dolly)*, Gail Berle *(Sherry)*, Mark Herrier *(Bradshaw)*, Matthew Brooks *(Bob, Jr.)*.

The unappealing coming attraction for this film—Belushi and Ritter talking to the camera for three minutes while the theme from "Peter Gunn" blares in the background—played off and on throughout 1987. As it turns out the release was held up for months due to rumored editing problems, and REAL MEN finally debuted late in the year in Kansas City and St. Louis where it died a quick death at the box office. With a plot that combines intrigue with a gaggle of aliens from outer space, wide release seems unlikely. Belushi is a tough-as-nails CIA agent who is assigned to keep an eye on wimpy family man Ritter, who was drafted by the "Company" to transport a secret map from California to Washington, D.C. Benevolent aliens from outer space are introduced into the story and, with their help, an economic disaster is averted. Predictably the entire experience serves to make Ritter more of a man, and when his mission is completed, he has the confidence to go home and beat up the neighborhood bullies. REAL MEN seems a likely candidate for cable TV and home video.

p, Martin Bregman; d&w, Dennis Feldman; ph, John A. Alonzo (Metrocolor); art d, William J. Cassidy, James Allen; set d, Tom Pedigo; set d, Dan Maltese; cos, Jodie Tillen.

Comedy (PR:NR MPAA:PG-13)

REALM OF FORTUNE, THE*** (1986, Mex.) 132m Imcine-Conacine/Azteca c (EL IMPERIO DE LA FORTUNA)

Ernesto Gomez Cruz *(Dionisio Pinzon)*, Blanca Guerra *(Bernarda Cutino/La Caponera)*, Alejandro Parodi *(Lorenzo Benavides)*, Zaide Silvia Gutierrez *(La Pinzona)*, Margarita Sanz *(Cara de Canario/"Canary Face")*, Ernesto Yanez *(Patilludo)*.

A humble peasant (Cruz) who works as the town crier is hired to be the announcer at a cockfight. When the victorious but badly injured bird is about to be killed, he persuades the owner to give it to him. At home, Cruz nurses the bird back to health, oblivious to the fact that his mother is lying dead on the floor. He enters the rooster in the fights and wins several bouts, leading gambler Parodi to try to buy the bird. Shunned by Cruz, the angry gambler predicts the bird will lose its next fight, which it does. Later Parodi and his girl friend (Guerra) tell Cruz the fight was fixed, revealing that the bird's ribs were cracked before the bout. The gambler then takes Cruz to his huge, dusty house and teaches him how to be a gamesman. Cruz soon takes to the road himself and is joined by Guerra, who has left Parodi. She proves to be his lucky charm, and he never seems to lose while she is in the room. Years later, the two have a daughter and they go to visit Parodi. The mentor and his pupil play an all-night card game, with Cruz winning everything, including Parodi's estate. More years pass and Guerra grows unhappy as her husband's human talisman, while their daughter commits adultery. One night, while Cruz is playing cards, his luck turns against him. Eventually he loses the house himself, and then discovers that Guerra is dead. He excuses himself for a moment, goes into another room, and shoots himself.

A fascinating film with Bunuelian overtones (director Ripstein was once Luis Bunuel's assistant), this work swept the Mexican film awards in 1986, later playing to good reviews in the US. Cruz gives a spotty performance, but Guerra is terrific as the carnival singer who is forced to be nothing but a good luck charm for her husband. Filled with odd details and blackly humorous subplots, this is easily one of the best film to emerge from Mexico is recent years. *(Nudity, sexual situations.)*

d, Arturo Ripstein; w, Paz Alicia Garciadiego (based on a story by Juan Rulfo); ph, Angel Goded; m, Lucia Alvarez; ed, Carlos Savage; art d, Anna Sanchez.

Drama (PR:O MPAA:NR)

RED DESERT PENITENTIARY† (1987, Neth./US) 94m MGS Film Amsterdam-Sweetwater Little Theater/Cupido c

James Michael Taylor *(Dan McMan)*, Cathryn Bissell *(Myrna Grenbaum)*, Bill Rose *(James Gagan)*, Jim Wortham *(Chet Kofman)*, Giovanni Korporaal *(Mickey Slavasky)*, Trudy Wortham *(Rosalie)*.

During the filming of a B western, the sexually experienced star seduces his naive female lead, hoping this will enhance their on-screen romance. Gradually their affair takes on dangerous consequences as reality begins to become a blur.

p,d&w, George Sluizer (based on a short story by Tim Krabbe); ph, Toni Kuhn; m, James Michael Taylor; ed, Julie Sloane, George Sluizer.

Western/Drama Cas. (PR:NR MPAA:NR)

RED HEADED STRANGER** (1987) 105m Alive c

Willie Nelson *(Rev. Julian Shay)*, Morgan Fairchild *(Raysha Shay)*, Katharine Ross *(Laurie)*, Royal Dano *(Larn Claver)*, R.G. Armstrong *(Sheriff)*.

The American cinema would be well served by the resurrection of its richest genre—the western. Unfortunately, RED HEADED STRANGER just drives another nail into the coffin. Based on Willie Nelson's best-selling album of the same title, it stars the singer as a Philadelphia preacher who moves his new bride (Fairchild) to the wilds of Montana where he plans to take over a ministry. Fairchild is against the move, and we learn (via some less-than-subtle glances on her wedding day) that she's really in love with another man. Upon their arrival, Nelson and his wife discover that the townsfolk are less than devout. The town suffers under the thumb of evil rancher Dano and his cruel brood of sons. Dano has controlled the local water supply ever since the town well dried-up, and has totally intimidated the burly sheriff, Armstrong. Nelson fails in his initial attempt to unite the townsfolk, so he rolls up his sleeves and sets about fixing the dried up well himself. Eventually Armstrong joins the cause and soon the townsfolk begin to see an end to Dano's vicious reign. Meanwhile, the bored Fairchild—who does not share her husband's enthusiasm for Montana—has been carrying on a secret correspondence with her beau in Philly. Just as the town's hopes for a better future peak, Fairchild runs off with her lover and Nelson's mind snaps. He abandons the townsfolk and rides off seeking revenge. He catches up with the adulterous pair in the next town and kills them. Having broken several of the Ten Commandments, Nelson is unable to return to the way of the cloth and instead becomes an infamous gunslinger, killing anyone who looks at him cross-eyed. Meanwhile, back at the ranch, Dano uses Nelson's absence to reestablish his grip on the town. He and his brood practically cripple the rebellious Armstrong, destroy the new well, and terrorize the townsfolk. Armstrong blames Nelson for the trouble and makes it his life's mission to find the crazed preacher and kill him. Nelson drifts to the farm of pretty widow Ross and takes on work as a farmhand. Contact with the good woman and her young son brings Nelson back to reality and he decides to let go of his bitterness and embrace a new life. At this point, however, Armstrong catches up with Nelson and tries to kill him. The attempt fails, Nelson and Armstrong patch up their differences, and the former preacher agrees to return to the town he abandoned to make amends. Together Nelson and Armstrong take on Dano and his boys, and with some surprise help from the usually reluctant townsfolk, the good guys win.

RED HEADED STRANGER boasts outstanding production values, nice cinematography, and a good cast. Unfortunately, the film is poorly scripted, haphazardly directed, and badly paced. Nelson's transformation from kindly preacher to homicidal lunatic is so abrupt as to be laughable. Fairchild is portrayed as a conniving harlot from her first close-up, Nelson as an insensitive chauvinist, and director Wittliff spends no time developing any kind of loving relationship between them. From what is seen on the screen, Nelson's reaction to Fairchild's adultery should be a disinterested shrug. Only after Nelson is a lonely gunslinger do we see flashbacks of a heretofore unseen loving marriage, accompanied by the singer's haunting "Blue Eyes Crying in the Rain." If Wittliff had shown these scenes *before* the betrayal, perhaps the viewer would have developed some compassion for these people. Instead, Wittliff wastes the scenes on a meaningless montage that is actually a thinly disguised music video. In fact, much of Nelson's music seems arbitrarily inserted, as if Willie's singing might somehow save the movie. Director Wittliff (who wrote and produced Nelson's superior western BARBAROSA) clearly knows the western genre and quotes liberally from Hawks' RIO BRAVO, Ford's MY DARLING CLEMENTINE, Anthony Mann's MAN OF THE WEST, and Sam Peckinpah's THE WILD BUNCH and PAT GARRETT & BILLY THE KID. Indeed, his casting reflects a love and appreciation of the genre's past. Dano, who had played one of Lee J. Cobb's psychotic sons in MAN OF THE WEST, now inherits the mantle of the patriarch of an evil family that is a virtual duplicate of the one in the Mann film. Armstrong, a Peckinpah regular, is fine as the wary sheriff who regains his self-respect thanks to Nelson. He and Dano were given the best roles they have had in years and they showed their thanks by more than rising to the occasion—the film is almost worth seeing for them alone. Regrettably, the same cannot be said for Nelson. He has proved himself a capable actor several times, but in RED HEADED STRANGER his mind seems to be elsewhere. Perhaps he was troubled by a script that did not provide proper motivation for his character. Perhaps he saw the project that he had tried so hard to realize for so many years slipping through his fingers. In any case, Nelson turns in a weak, distracted performance. To her credit, Fairchild tries hard in a role that was cursed from the time it was typed, and Ross does a nice job looking earthy. A film like RED HEADED STRANGER is doubly doomed: firstly, because it is a western, and secondly, because it is a *bad* western. After being screened at several film festivals in 1986, the film was given an indifferent theatrical release in the South before it wound up on videocassette. *(Graphic violence.)*

p, Willie Nelson, William Wittliff; d&w, William Wittliff; ph, Neil Roach.

Western/Drama Cas. (PR:C-O MPAA:R)

RED RIDING HOOD† (1987) 80m Golan-Globus/Cannon c

Craig T. Nelson *(Godfrey/Percival)*, Isabella Rossellini *(Lady Jeanne, Percival's Wife)*, Amelia Shankley *(Red Riding Hood)*, Rocco Sisto *(Dagger, Godfrey's Henchman/The Wolf)*, Linda Kaye *(Badger Kate)*, Helen Glazary *(Nanny Bess, Red Riding Hood's Grandmother)*, Julian Joy-Chagrin *(Allen Owen)*.

Another in the series of Cannon fairy-tale films that received a very limited distribution before securing a place in the home video market. Padded with a new plot line and several songs, the film stars Nelson as an evil prince who has taken over the throne after the wartime disappearance of his nice twin brother (also played by Nelson). Obsessed with obtaining his brother's beautiful wife (Rossellini), the evil Nelson casts a magic spell that enables Sisto, his bumbling toady, to turn into a wolf and then back again so that he can spy more successfully. Sisto encounters Red Riding Hood (Shankley), a girl who possesses a magical red coat which protects her from harm. Shankley was given the coat by her kindly grandmother (Glazary), but the clever wolf figures out a way to get around the magical garment and dine on little Red Riding Hood. In the end good triumphs over evil, but not before a few scares.

p, Menahem Golan, Yoram Globus; d, Adam Brooks; w, Carole Lucia Satrina (based on the fairytale by the Brothers Grimm); ph, Danny Shnegur, Ye'ehi Neyman (Rank Color); m, Stephen Lawrence; ed, David Tour; cos, Mirra Steinmatz; m/l, Stephen Lawrence, Michael Korie.

Children's **(PR:NR MPAA:NR)**

REDONDELA† (1987, Span.) 113m Pedro Costa c

Patrick Newell *(Jose Maria Gil Ramos, Lawyer)*, Carlos Velat *(Padin)*, Fernando Guillen *(Jose Luis Pena)*, Carlos Larranaga *(Arturo Mendez)*, Marina Saura *(Celia Villar)*, Agustin Gonzalez *(Fernando G. Prat)*, Ricardo Lucia *(Angel G. Prat)*, Blanca Sendino *(Matilde G. Prat)*, Francisco Merino *(Noceda)*, Conrado San Martin *(Ferrer)*, Manuel de Blas *(Antonio Valldares)*, Francisca Gabaldon *(Yuyi)*.

Set in 1972 near the end Francisco Franco's long reign, this Spanish story of political intrigue tries to tie together some of the still loose ends surrounding the mysterious theft of more than 4,000 tons of oil that year. English actor Newell plays a lawyer (generally acknowledged to be based on political activist Gil Robles) who defends a bureaucrat who has been set up to take the fall for the oil heist to protect Franco's cronies and the *Generalissimo's* brother, who, it is implied, were actually responsible for the disappearance of the black gold. The title is taken from the Galician town that serves as one of the film's settings.

p&d, Pedro Costa Muste; w, Manuel Marinero, Pedro Costa Muste; ph, Juan Amoros (Fujicolor); m, Jesus Gluck; ed, Pablo G. Del Amo; set d, Eduardo Hidalgo, Julio Esteban.

Mystery **(PR:NR MPAA:NR)**

REGINA† (1987, It.) 83m Falco/Instituto Luce-Italnoleggio bw

Ida Di Benedetto *(Regina)*, Fabrizio Bentivoglio *(Lorenzo)*, Giuliana Calandra *(Lalla)*, Mariano Regillo, Claudia Gianotti, Anita Laurenzi, Marika Ferri, Paolo Hermanin.

The disturbing story of a sadomasochistic relationship between the title character, a famous 40-year-old actress (Di Benedetto), and an aspiring 25-year-old actor who makes ends meet by posing for pornographic magazines (Bentivoglio). They meet at a party and Bentivoglio falls hard for Di Benedetto; however, she is more interested in getting her masochistic kicks. At one point, Di Benedetto even forces her young lover to make it with Calandra, her shrewish agent, while the actress looks on. Finally, Di Benedetto loses interest and tells Bentivoglio that she doesn't want to see him anymore. Calandra brings them together again but the result is fatal. Director-writer Piscicelli and producer-writer Apuzzo also worked together on BLUES METROPOLITANO and IMMACOLATA AND CONCETTA.

p, Carla Apuzzo; d, Salvatore Piscicelli; w, Carla Apuzzo, Salvatore Piscicelli; ph, Tonino Nardi; m, Helmut Laberer; ed, Salvatore Piscicelli, Domenico Varone; art d, Luciano Vedonilli-Levi.

Drama **(PR:NR MPAA:NR)**

REIGN OF THE RASCALS, THE† (1987, Phil.) Roadshow c

Lito Lapid *(Isaac)*.

Lito Lapid stars as a Filipino who was orphaned at a young age and raised in near seclusion by a mountain man. Leaving the high country, he dedicates himself to a life of fighting oppression and freeing the "little man" from the yoke of tyrannical rule. Arriving at a small village that is under the thumb of a vicious landowner, Lapid is presented with the opportunity to do good in a big way. He takes on the tyrant and his thugs, and after being tortured by them, returns to the villagers and organizes them in a successful defense of their property. One tyrant down and many to go, Lapid moves on.

[No Credits Available].

Adventure **(PR:NR MPAA:NR)**

RELACAO FIEL E VERDADEIRA† (1987, Portugal) 85m Margarida Gil-Instituto Portugues de Cinema Rado-tevisao Portuguesa c (Trans: A True and Accurate Story)

Catarina Alves Costa, Antonio Manuel Sequeira, Jorge Rola, Laura Soveral, Cremilde Gil, Sonia Guimaraes, Aurora Gaia, Adelaide Teixeira, Philip Snipelli, Luis Cunha.

Tracing the events that lead a young woman from a bad marriage to the convent, this Portuguese feature is a modern-day updating of the story told in the autobiography of Antonia Margarida, a 17th Century nun. At her mother's behest, a young woman marries a gambler who has the right last name but no money to go along with it. He is constantly jealous, though his young wife gives him no reason to be. Finally, when their child dies, the woman decides that she can no longer live with her husband and gives herself to the service of God. Shot on 16mm, this is the debut feature for director Gil.

d, Margarida Gil; w, Margarida Gil, Joao Cesar Monteiro (based on the autobiography of Antonia Margarida de Castelo Branco); ph, Manuel Costa e Silva; m, Jose Alberto Gil; ed, Leonor Guterres; art d, Juan Sotullo.

Biography **(PR:NR MPAA:NR)**

REMEMBERING MEL† (1987, Can.) 78m Taurus 7 c

Robert Kolomeir, Arthur Holden, Jim Connolly, Guy Laprade, Natalie Timoschuk, Allan Lallouz, Steven Light, Ariel Grumberg, Isadore Lapin, Estelle Cooney, Bob Brenhouse, Anna Harris, Roger Racine, Evelyn Kussner, Zander Ary, Stuart Simmonds, Tom Gormley, Julie Allen, Essar Raskin, Sharon Woloshen, Dan Prevost, Jacob Greenbaum, Chris Thurnheer, Roland Silva, Bill Conabree, Neil Asbil, Sailor White, Simona Thurnheer, Leslie Tochinsky, Keith Brown.

Employing the movie-within-a-movie format, this film about recent Canadian film school graduates trying to make a movie was made by recent Canadian film school graduates—director-writer Harris and cowriter Raskin. Their film within the film might be called a mockumentary; that is, a self-satirizing documentary after the fashion of THIS IS SPINAL TAP. The focus of the documentary is one Mel, the epitome of ineffectual ineptitude, and he is remembered by old teachers, friends, etc. Made in Montreal, REMEMBERING MEL came into being when, in December 1984, Harris, then an employee of Taurus 7, learned the company had some investment money that had to be spent by the end of the year but no project in which to invest it. Harris and Raskin then banged out a screenplay in three days and before the year was over they had finished most of the shooting. However, it took them nearly another year to complete the editing. Songs include: "The Camera Never Lies" (performed by T. No), "Holiday," "King's Service" (performed by Images in Vogue), "Promised Land" (performed by Tchukon), "Sexual Outlaw" (performed by Carole Pope and Rough Trade), "Soldiers in the Night" (performed by Walter Rossi), "Must I Always Remember," "With all this Cash" (performed by The Box), "Dancing with a Mystery," "I'd Rather Be Dancing" (performed by Foreign Affairs), "Talk, Talk" (performed by The Arrows).

p, Claude Castravelli, Peter Serapilia; d, Doug Harris; w, Doug Harris, Larry Raskin; ph, Steve Campanelli, Nicolas Marion, David Franco; m, Les Leroux; ed, Doug Harris, Larry Raskin, Don Rennick.

Comedy **(PR:NR MPAA:NR)**

RENEGADE, UN OSSO TROPPO DURO† (1987, It.) Paloma Films-Cinecitta/C.D.I. c (Trans: Renegade: A Very Tough Guy)

Terence Hill [Mario Girotti], Robert Vaughn, Ross Hill, Norman Bowler, Beatrice Palme, Donald Hodson, Cyros Elias, Sandy, Valeria Sabel, Luisa Maneri, Gigi Bonos.

A new spaghetti western from veteran genre director Clucher [Barboni], who began as a cinematographer before breaking into directing by starring Terence Hill [Girotti] and Bud Spencer [Carlo Pedersoli] in the successful series of slapstick westerns beginning with THEY CALL ME TRINITY in 1970. Seventeen years later Hill stars as a new character, "Renegade," a drifter with a clever horse called Jo Brown. On the trail Hill is joined by the 14-year-old son of an imprisoned friend and together they head for the boy's home, Green Heaven. After an arduous journey the duo finally make it to the homestead which more than lives up to its name. Unfortunately, Vaughn, the local tycoon, is trying to buy up all the land in the area and it is he who is responsible for the imprisonment of the boy's father. Like Shane before him, Hill takes a stand and saves the homestead, but then mounts his trusty horse and rides off into the sunset. This attempt to revive the spaghetti western may turn up in the US on home video.

d, E.B. Clucher [Enzo Barboni]; w, Marco Tullio Barboni, Terence Hill [Mario Girotti], Sergio Donati; ph, Alfio Contini; ed, Eugenio Alabiso.

Western **(PR:NR MPAA:NR)**

REQUIEM† (1987, USSR) 91m Tallinfilm/Sovexportfilm c

Aarne Yukskyula, Reghina Rasuma, Andrus Varik, Sulev Luik, Ivo Linn, Sven Grunberg.

Set during WW II this film details the revelation of conscience of a complacent Estonian musician who cares nothing about the war as long as he is left alone on his farm so that he can stay in his workshop and play the organ. The musician is forced to face the war when two Soviet pilots—one Russian, one Estonian—are shot down nearby and seek refuge in his barn. He reluctantly hides the wounded pilots and in doing so, opens his eyes to the Nazi horrors all around him.

d, Olav Neuland; w, Teet Kallas, Olav Neuland; ph, Yury Sillart; m, Sven Grunberg; art d, Tomas Khrac.

War **(PR:NR MPAA:NR)**

REPENTANCE† (1987, USSR) 145m Gruziya Film/Cannon c (POKAYANIYE; AKA: CONFESSION)

Avtandil Makharadze *(Varlam Aravidze, Father/Abel Aravidze, Son)*, Ija Ninidze *(Guliko, Varlam's Daughter-in-Law)*, Merab Ninidze *(Tornike, Varlam's Grandson)*, Zejnab Botsvadze *(Ketevan Barateli, Sandro's Daughter)*, Ketevan Abuladze *(Nino Barateli, Sandro's Wife)*, Edisher Giorgobiani *(Sandro Barateli, Painter)*, Kahki Kavsadze *(Mikhail Korisheli)*, Nino Zakariadze *(Elena Korisheli)*, Nato Otijigava *(Ketevan as a Child)*, Dato Kemkhadze *(Abel as a Child)*.

Liberated from the obscurity of state censorship by Soviet Prime Minister Mikhail Gorbachev's policy of *glasnost*, REPENTANCE is a 1984 film which finally emerged this year. Reviewed by the Union of Cinematographers headed by Elem Klimov (COME AND SEE), REPENTANCE was given a Soviet release, despite the fact that it paints Josef Stalin as a murderous dictator and indicts the generation which emerged after Stalin's demise as guilty of the sins of silence. At 145 minutes, the film stars Makharadze in two roles—as Varlam Aravidze, a recently deceased Georgian mayor, and as Abel Aravidze, the mayor's son. Varlam, the mayor, is a composite dictator. A Georgian like Stalin, he has a similar haircut. Like Mussolini, he cloaks his intimidating physique in a black shirt. He sports a mustache like Hitler's and wears the *pince-nez* of Stalin's chief of secret police, Lavrenti Beria, who carried out the purges that killed many millions. The film is told through the eyes of Botsvadze, a troubled woman whose life was torn apart by the horrors caused by Varlam and his supporters. As the film opens, Varlam's body is being laid to rest at an elaborate funeral ceremony. His son and grandson are among the mourners. The body is interred, but the following morning the corpse reappears. It is interred again, but continuously reappears after each interment. An investigation is ordered and it is discovered that Botsvadze is responsible. She tells the court that Varlam's crimes cannot be buried away and forgotten. "As long as I live, Varlam Aravidze will not be in the grave," she warns. The court cannot, with good conscience, sentence her for her actions. Varlam's son, Abel is determined not to let her win, and tries to get her committed to an asylum. He is content with forgetting about the past and covering up the sins of his father. But Abel himself has a son who refuses to forget history and eventually commits suicide. It takes this loss to move Abel, who then takes his father's corpse and throws it into a precipice. Praised for its visionary direction and courageous political stance, REPENTANCE has garnered stupendous international success and has found its way onto a few selected US screens in 1987. It took the Special Jury Prize at 1987's Cannes Film Festival and was submitted to the Academy Awards as the official Soviet entry in the Foreign Film category. REPENTANCE made its American bow at the Telluride (Colorado) Film Festival; was awarded the Gold Hugo (for Best Picture) and Silver Hugo (for Best Actor) at the 1987 Chicago International Film Festival; and was picked up for US release by Cannon Films.

d, Tenghiz Abuladze; w, Nana Djanelidze, Tenghiz Abuladze, Rezo Kveselava; ph, Mikhail Agranovich (Orwo Color); m, Nana Djanelidze; prod d, Georgy Mikeladze.

Political Allegory **(PR:NR MPAA:NR)**

RES ALDRIG PA ENKEL BILJETT† (1987, Swed.) Alexandersson & De Geer Bildproduktion c (Trans: Never Travel on a One-Way Ticket)

Mikael Samuelson, Ylva Tornlund.

Futuristic crime drama set in a desperate and impoverished world about a hard-boiled detective hired by a mysterious woman to investigate a mass murder.

d, Hakan Alexandersson.

Crime/Science Fiction **(PR:NR MPAA:NR)**

RESAN TILL MELONIA† (1987, Nor./Swed.) 100m Pennfilm-Swedish Film Institute-Sandrew Film & Theater AB-Svenska Ord-Swedish TV-SVT-2-Norsk Film A/S-Jar c (Trans: Voyage to Melonia)

Animated adaptation of Shakespeare's "The Tempest" which follows two rogues from the dark island of Plutonia as they travel to the idyllic island of Melonia (named after the active melon-shaped volcano located there) to steal a magic elixir concocted by the benevolent ruler of Melonia.

d, Per Ahlin; w, Per Ahlin, Karl Rasmusson (based on William Shakespeare's play "The Tempest").

Animation/Children's **(PR:NR MPAA:NR)**

RETALIATOR (SEE: PROGRAMMED TO KILL, 1987)

RETO A LA VIDA† (1987, Mex.) 91m Cinematografica Filmex/Peliculas Mexicanas c (Trans: Challenge to Life)

Julio Alvarado *(Carlos Munoz)*, Helena Rojo *(Elena Sandoval)*, Olivia Collins *(Yolanda "Yolis" Sanchez)*, Jorge Luke *(Inspector)*, Manuel Ojeda *(Tijuana)*, Jose Carlos Ruis *(Doctor)*, Jaime Garza *(Don Jose)*, Luis Manuel Pelayo, Oscar Fernandez, Ademar Arau I., Jorge Gonzalez H., Ruben Conoray, Queta Carrasco, Pablo Marquez, Efren Martinez G., Eduardo Munoz, Raul Antonio Palacio, Monica Munoz, Alfonso Duran, Grupo Eslabon, Jose Zambrano, Los Galleros.

A hodgepodge of genres, this Mexican effort is part social problem film (drug abuse and dealing), part actioner, part romance, and part musical. Alvarado returns home after serving four years in prison for pushing only to discover that his younger brother has taken the same sinful path. Alvarado decides to continue paying his debt to society on the outside. After opening an electronics repair business, he begins mending the lives of the kids who call the streets home. The film's musical element is also provided by Alvarado, who warbles no less than five songs.

p, J. Fernando Gavilan; d, Rafael Baledon; w, Fernando Galiana; ph, Alberto Arellanos Bustamente; m, Armando Manzanero; ed, Francisco Chiu; md, Rogelio Vergara; art d, Ana Maria Martinez.

Drama **(PR:NR MPAA:NR)**

RETURN OF JOSEY WALES, THE*½ (1987) 90m Multi-Tacar/Reel Movies Int'l. c

Michael Parks *(Josey Wales)*, Raphael Campos *(Chato)*, Charlie McCoy *(Charlie)*, Everett Sifuentes *(Capt. Jesus Escobedo)*, Suzie Humphreys *(Rose, Bar Maid)*, John Galt *(Kelly, Bartender)*, Joe Kurtzo *(Nacole)*, Paco Vela *(Paco)*, Bob Magruder *(Tenspot)*, Benita Faulkner *(Enloe)*, Charles Escamillia *(Lt. Valdez)*, Arturo R. Tamez *(Pancho Marino)*, Manuel Valdez *(Manny)*, Paul Flores *(Sargent)*, Valentino *(Mexican Guitarist)*, Chenco Lopez *(Mexican Singer)*, Mary Ellen Averett *(Josey's Wife)*, Ron Bledsoe *(Billy)*, Mike Bledsoe *(Mike)*, Doug Bledsoe *(Seth)*, Happy Shahan *(Grandpa)*, Larry Melton *(Larry)*, John Burkhead *(John)*, Buddy Harper *(Jim Taylor)*, Russ Taylor *(Jess the Boy)*, Donny Fountain *(Morgan)*, Ron Taylor *(Travis)*, Ron Bradley, Tom Rayhall *(Gringo Gunfighters)*, Gaye Pyritz, June Holland *(Mexican Women)*, Joe De Hoyas, Jose Morante, Joe Liserio *(Mexican Singer Musicians)*.

One of Clint Eastwood's finest directorial efforts was THE OUTLAW JOSEY WALES (1976), in which he played a Missouri farmer who became a Confederate raider after the slaughter of his family by Yankee marauders. At war's end he trekked south, leaving a trail of dead bounty hunters behind him. This unlikely sequel, directed by and starring Michael Parks, picks up Josey's story a short time later, with Parks trying to live in peace in southern Texas. When two of his friends are murdered and another taken off by Mexican *Rurales* (rural police), Parks heads down to Mexico with a couple of his amigos to get back his friend and take vengeance. The *Rurale* captain, Sifuentes, learns of his approach and offers a local bandit chief free run of a town if he will kill Parks first. However, Parks is faster on the draw than the bandit, who dies in the dust. Campos, one of Parks' men, is sent to Sifuentes posing as a bandit. He tells the captain that Parks is dead, and Sifuentes shoots him in the back. That night Parks takes out some of the guards and frees his friend, along with two Apache prisoners, including a woman. They flee north, with Sifuentes and his men in pursuit. A shoot-out ends with all the *Rurales* dead, Sifuentes buried up to his neck, and Parks riding back across the Rio Grande. No one makes movies like this anymore, basic westerns with the stock characters and stock plots that once spoke so directly to the concerns of a growing America. Parks is not uncomfortable in his role, and while he is no Clint Eastwood, he just might be Johnny Mack Brown. There are severe technical problems: murky photography, unintelligible dialog, and similar problems that often typify low-budget filmmaking. Not exactly worthy of its predecessor, but interesting nonetheless. *(Violence, adult situations.)*

p, Mickey Grant; d, Michael Parks, R.O. Taylor; w, Forrest Carter, R.O. Taylor (based on the novel *Vengeance Trail of Josey Wales* by Forrest Carter); ph, Brant A. Hughes (CFI Color); m, Rusty Thornhill; ed, Ivan L. Bigley; art d, Larry Melton; cos, Karen Essex; spec eff, Randy Fite, Tex Hill; stunts, Mike Bledsoe, Joe Kurtzo; makeup, Susan Posnick.

Western **Cas.** **(PR:C MPAA:R)**

RETURN TO HORROR HIGH*½ (1987) 95m NW/Balcor c

Lori Lethin *(Callie Cassidy/Sarah/Susan)*, Brendan Hughes *(Steven Blake)*, Alex Rocco *(Harry Sleerik)*, Scott Jacoby *(Josh Forbes)*, Andy Romano *(Principal Kastleman)*, Richard Brestoff *(Arthur Lyman [Kastleman])*, Al Fann *(Amos)*, Pepper Martin *(Chief Deyner)*, Maureen McCormick *(Officer Tyler)*, Vince Edwards *(Richard Birnbaum)*, Philip McKeon *(Richard Farley)*, Panchito Gomez *(Choo Choo)*, Michael Eric Kramer *(Donny Porter)*, Marvin McIntyre *(Robbie Rice)*, George Clooney *(Oliver)*, Remy O'Neill *(Esther Molvania)*, Darcy DeMoss *(Sheri Haines)*, Cliff Emmich *(Dillon)*, Will Etra *(Mangled Face/Hatchet Face)*, George Fisher *(Masked Figure)*, Dexter Hamlett *(Freddie)*, Joy Heston *(Becky)*, Frank Kniest *(Camera Assistant)*, John Mueller *(Jimmy)*, Alison Noble *(Jeanine)*, Kristi Somers *(Ginny McCall)*, Larry Spinak *(Peter)*.

This is one of those horror films that tries way too hard to be something different and merely winds up as a confused mess. Combining gore with comedy and presenting it in a movie-within-a-movie-within-a-dream-within-a-movie format, RETURN TO HORROR HIGH opens as local police arrive at a high school brimming with the bloody bodies of a film crew who were shooting a horror movie there. The chief, Martin, is informed by pretty officer McCormick (remember Marsha from "The Brady Bunch"?) that the only survivor is Brestoff, the screenwriter. Brestoff explains what happened and in a flashback we see a hapless low-budget film crew shooting at a high school where a real-life unsolved mass-murder took place several years before. The producer of the film, Rocco (one of the few performers who actually elicits as many laughs as he aims for), is an incredibly sleazy Hollywood type who wanders the set with his mobile phone screaming "More blood!" while trying to bed as many nubile young local gals as he can. The idealistic young director, Jacoby, is attempting to elevate his gory little slasher film into the realm of "art," but is constantly frustrated by his low budget and Rocco's insistence on more blood. When his lead actor walks, Jacoby hires local cop Hughes—the real-life counterpart of the main character—to play himself. He is paired with Lethin, a tough young actress who has to play three different roles because the budget is so small. Also in the cast are the school's real principal, Romano, and a biology teacher, Edwards, who play themselves. Not unexpectedly, as shooting progresses, cast and crew members begin to be murdered off one by one until Lethin and Hughes uncover that the killer is Romano. Meanwhile, back in the present, when the police aren't looking, all the dead bodies get up and drive off. The cast and crew were made-up by the horror movie makeup specialist (who menacingly mutters "Next time for real" under his breath) to appear dead and dismembered. It seems that the whole thing was cooked up by producer Rocco to garner free publicity for the movie, and there will be a sequel, for screenwriter Brestoff is in reality the crazed son of killer Romano.

Although RETURN TO HORROR HIGH attempts to be something more than

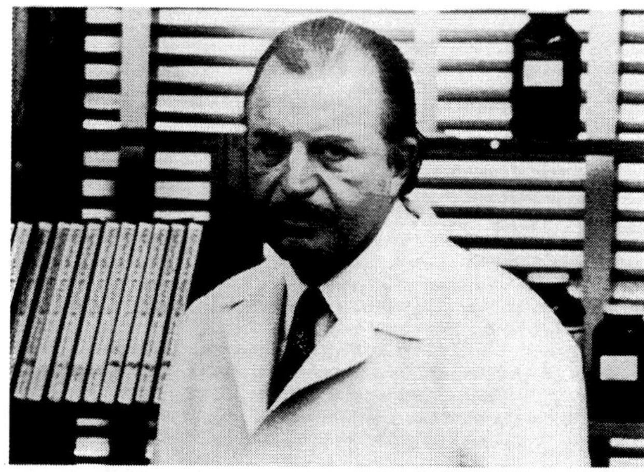

the average slasher film, it fails because it is too eager to be different. The innumerable twists and turns of the plot, combined with several shifts in time and perspective, wind up being more confusing than intriguing. (In fact, the above synopsis may be wrong—only because it is hard to tell just exactly what is going on in this film—especially regarding the killer and his motives.) Most of the humor is purely sophomoric, but some of the "in" jokes about the industry in general and horror films in particular are good for a few laughs (when an actor playing a corpse complains about a lack of motivation, the frustrated director screams, "Dead people have no motivation!"). The performances are standard horror film fare, with Rocco and Edwards the campy standouts. Fans of "The Brady Bunch" will be particularly shocked—or delighted, depending upon one's perspective—by McCormick's over-the-top performance. Blood seems to turn her on, and at one point she excitedly clutches her breast, smearing her uniform with blood. Froehlich (director/cowriter) and Lisson (producer/cowriter) are experienced TV writer-producers and RETURN TO HORROR HIGH is their first feature. Unfortunately, their television experience shows in the visuals, for the film is shot in an unimaginative manner with emphasis on master shots, close-ups, and standard cutting. Songs include "Greet the Teacher," "Scary Movies" (Larry Weir, performed by Pleasant Company), and "Man For Me" (Stacy Widelitz, Wendy Fraser, performed by Fraser). *(Violence, gore effects, brief nudity, sexual situations, profanity.)*

p, Mark Lisson; d, Bill Froehlich; w, Bill Froehlich, Mark Lisson, Dana Escalante, Greg H. Sims; ph, Roy Wagner; m, Stacy Widelitz; ed, Nancy Forner; prod d, Greta Grigorian; cos, Marcy Grace Froehlich; makeup, Mike Spatola; m/l, Larry Weir, Stacy Widelitz, Wendy Fraser; spec eff, James Wayne Beauchamp; stunts, George Fisher.

Comedy/Horror Cas. (PR:O MPAA:R)

REVENGE OF THE NERDS II: NERDS IN PARADISE* (1987) 92m Interscope Comm./FOX c

Robert Carradine *(Lewis Skolnick)*, Curtis Armstrong *(Dudley "Booger" Dawson)*, Larry B. Scott *(Lamar Latrelle)*, Timothy Busfield *(Arnold Poindexter)*, Courtney Thorne-Smith *(Sunny Carstairs, Hotel Desk Clerk)*, Andrew Cassese *(Harold Wormser)*, Donald Gibb *(Ogre)*, Bradley Whitford *(Roger)*, Ed Lauter *(Buzz)*, Barry Sobel *(Stewart Lipsey)*, Patricia Lopez *(Aldonza)*, Anthony Edwards *(Hotel Bell Captain)*, James Hong, James Cromwell, Tom Hodges, Jason Julien, Richard Joseph Paul, Rhonda Waymire, Donna Rosae, Susan Vanech.

In 1984, REVENGE OF THE NERDS was a surprise hit. Perhaps they waited too long to make this sequel because much of the steam is gone and all of the intelligence. Many in the original cast have returned: Carradine, Busfield, Armstrong, Scott and Cassese. When last we left the nerds, their college frat (Tri-Lambda) had just defeated the Alpha Beta blockheads and thus had become kings of the campus, with all the comely sorority girls hanging on their every sentence. This one begins as the plastic pocket protector (worn by nerds as a badge of honor) comes floating through space in a STAR WARS or 2001 parody. We then learn that the nerds are on their way to Fort Lauderdale for a conference of national fraternities. With new nerd Sobel in tow, they travel south to a land where bikinis and bottoms and busts are as rampant as mosquitoes on the sand. Once there, the geek Greeks at Alpha Beta arrange to have the Tri-Lambda boys ousted from their posh hotel and forced to take refuge in a rundown Cuban place run by a cliche Latina (Lopez). Their accommodations are dubbed the "Ricky Riccardo Suite" to give you an idea of the level of humor. A few funny moments such as the scene where Armstrong (he plays a character named "Booger" and the reason for that is too disgusting to print here) has a belching contest with Asian James Hong. The romantic interest is adorable Thorne-Smith and Carradine uses a special technique to get her to come across. The rest of the movie is lower than lowbrow.

Most of the jokes are either ethnic slurs, homosexual japes, or unfunny gags with not a shred of wit. Anthony Edwards, who was so good in the first, was busy making TOP GUN so he could only stop by to do a cameo as a hotel employee. The girls are around but the jokes are flat and "babes and brewskis" are just not enough to carry an entire picture. They had intended to shoot this in the seaside resort (actually bayside) of Puerto Vallarta, Mexico, but the price of bringing in equipment and an English-speaking crew would have been prohibitive. The only difference between this and WHERE THE BOYS ARE or SPRING BREAK or any number of other "college kids in a resort" movies is that those all look like CITIZEN KANE by comparison. Blame the dumb screenplay by Marshall and Guntzelman for most of the problem. *(Profanity, sexual situations.)*

p, Ted Field, Robert Cort, Peter Bart; d, Joe Roth; w, Dan Guntzelman, Steve Marshall (based on characters created by Tim Metcalfe, Miguel Tejada-Flores, Steve Zacharias, Jeff Buhai); ph, Charles Correll (Deluxe Color); m, Mark Mothersbaugh, Gerald V. Casale; ed, Richard Chew; prod d, Trevor Williams; cos, Jeffrey Kurland.

Comedy (PR:C MPAA:PG-13)

RICH AND FAMOUS† (1987, Hong Kong) 98m c

Chow Yun Fat, Alex Man, Man Chi Leung, Andy Lau, Alan Tam, Carina Liu, Li Sau Yin.

Violent Hong Kong actioner starring the ever-popular Chow Yun Fat (A BETTER TOMORROW, PRISON ON FIRE) as a mob boss betrayed by one of his men, Man Chi Leung, who goes to work for a rival gang. Man Chi Leung has betrayed his parents, brother, and wife to make this ambitious move and in the end he learns that dishonor does not pay.

p, Johnny Mak; d, Wong Tai Lo.

Crime (PR:NR MPAA:NR)

RIGHT HAND MAN, THE† (1987) 101m Yarraman/NW c

Rupert Everett *(Harry Ironminster)*, Hugo Weaving *(Ned Devine)*, Arthur Dignam *(Dr. Redbridge)*, Jennifer Claire *(Lady Ironminster)*, Catherine McClements *(Sarah Redbridge)*, Ralph Cotterill *(Sam)*, Adam Cockburn *(Violet Head)*, Tim Eliott *(Lord Ironminster)*.

Australian import which played briefly in New York and Los Angeles after receiving favorable notices at the Monterey Film Festival in early 1987. Set in 1860, the film stars Everett as the only male heir to the prestigious Ironminster estate—a wealthy family devoted to the art of horse breeding and racing. Unfortunately, Everett is a diabetic—a fatal affliction in 1860—prone to fainting spells and weakness. Everett is cared for by doctor Dignam with his daughter, McClements, acting as nurse. A romance develops between patient and nurse, and there is talk of marriage. Despite his illness, Everett is a passionate horseman and expert rider. Tragedy strikes the family during a buggy race when Everett passes out while driving and his father is killed in the wreck. Everett himself is severely injured and doctors are forced to amputate his arm. Everett's domineering mother, Claire, bitterly blames her son for the death of her husband. Unable to ride, Everett becomes deeply depressed and not even McClements can shake him out of his doldrums. Not willing to give up, Everett hires experienced horseman Weaving to be his right-hand man—to supervise the breeding and do the riding and racing. The men become fast friends, so close in fact that Everett, who hesitates to marry McClements because he does not want his offspring to inherit his diabetes (which is hereditary), asks Weaving to be the surrogate father of his children. Surprisingly both Weaving and McClements agree to the unusual arrangement, although boundaries of class and family threaten to destroy the trio's relationship. THE RIGHT HAND MAN is the directorial debut of woman director Di Drew.

p, Steven Grives, Tom Oliver, Basil Appleby; d, Di Drew; w, Helen Hodgman (based on the novel by Kathleen Peyton); ph, Peter James (Eastmancolor); m, Allan Zavod; ed, Don Saunders; prod d, Neil Angwin; cos, Graham Purcell.

Drama (PR:NR MPAA:R)

RIMINI RIMINI† (1987, It.) 116m Scena/Medusa c

Paolo Villaggio *(Gildo)*, Serena Grandi *(Lola)*, Eleonora Brigliadori *(Liliana)*, Laura Antonelli *(Rich Woman)*, Jerry Cala *(Gianni)*, Gigi and Andrea, Paolo Bonacelli, Maurizio Micheli, Sylva Koscina, Elvire Audray.

Set in Rimini, the heavily touristed resort town on Italy's Adriatic coast, this Italian sex comedy presents a myriad of usual couplings, strange bedfellows, and compromising positions. Among the Not-Ready-for-Their-Libidos players are Villaggio, a straight-laced chief of police who dresses in drag to win the heart of a porno queen; Antonelli, a wealthy woman whose supposedly drowned husband reappears and provides her with the kind of serious consolation her concerned brothers wouldn't have dared suggest; and Brigliadori, a recently separated woman beds down with a 10-year-old.

p, Augusto Caminito; d, Sergio Corbucci; w, Bernandino Zapponi, Sergio Corbucci, Bruno Corbucci, Mario Amendola, Marco Risi, Gianni Romoli, Massimo Franciosa; ph, Danilo Desideri (Eastmancolor); ed, Tatiana Casini Morigi; art d, Marco Dentici.

Comedy (PR:NR MPAA:NR)

RITA, SUE AND BOB TOO!*** (1987, Brit.) 95m Film Four Intl-Umbrella-British Screen/Orion Classics c

Michelle Holmes *(Sue)*, Siobhan Finneran *(Rita)*, George Costigan *(Bob)*, Lesley Sharp *(Michelle, Bob's Wife)*, Willie Ross *(Sue's Father)*, Patti Nicholls *(Sue's Mother)*, Kulvinder Ghir *(Aslam)*, Paul Oldham *(Lee)*, Bryan Heeley *(Michael)*.

Based on two stage plays but not stagy, a sex comedy virtually without sex, RITA, SUE AND BOB TOO! is as defiant of expectations as are its heroines. Holmes and Finneran are hefty teenage girls who live in a deteriorating council estate (read project) in Bradford, in the economically depressed north of England. As the film opens, they trek across town to baby-sit for Costigan and

Sharp, a thirtyish middle-class couple whose somewhat garish suburban house is full of goodies the girls envy. Instead of driving the baby-sitters home at the end of the evening, Costigan takes them out on the darkened moors, where he produces a condom for their inspection and then proposes to put it to use. After a bit of glib demurring, they accept. Holmes, the cheekier—and bustier—of the two, is the first into the reclining passenger seat. Finneran waits while Costigan's naked "bum" bounces in the moonlight and Holmes repeatedly kicks the horn. Finneran then summarily replaces her mate, though her time in the hot seat is briefer. All three are more or less delighted by the experience and repeat it frequently: after baby-sitting or escaping from school, in a model home or back on the moors. Their cozy arrangement is threatened, however, when Sharp discovers an empty condom package in her husband's coat. Though he admits his infidelity, blaming his wife's sexual inactivity, he denies the girls are involved. Later, one of Sharp's friends spots the threesome bumping and grinding at a nightclub. The next day, Sharp charges to the housing estate, roughly collects Finneran, and makes a beeline for Holmes' place. Costigan arrives just as his wife does, and in front of the building, they encounter not only Holmes but Ross, her obstreperous, drunken father, and Nicholls, her mother. While the neighbors, who have nothing better to do, cheer from their windows and porches, a tremendous rhubarb ensues from which Finneran is rescued cavalry-style by her brood of biker brothers. The upshot is that Sharp and the children leave Costigan, and shortly thereafter, Finneran, who is pregnant, moves in with Costigan. Though he has told Holmes that things can continue as they were, she's not having it, and eventually takes up with Ghir, a sweet but violently possessive Bradford-born Pakistani. When Finneran miscarries, Holmes visits her, and is later dropped off by Costigan. Ghir assumes they've had another romp and flies into a rage that sends Holmes running to Finneran and the safety of Costigan's home. When Costigan returns he finds the girls united again in friendship. Resignedly he trudges up the stairs, expecting to be the odd man out, but when he opens the bedroom door, Holmes and Finneran are waiting on either side of the big bed covered with a Union Jack bedspread. "What took you so long?" they ask just before his freeze-frame leap back into their unconventional relationship.

Eight years of Thatcherism have produced not only a politically and economically polarized Britain, but also, of late, an outpouring of bleak comedies (emphasis on *bleak*) whose primarily working-class protagonists confront declining expectations with nonconformist pluck. Unlike the "angry young men" of an earlier generation, these filmmakers do not present characters who rail against the oppressiveness of the class system; instead, their characters stage personal revolutions, fighting their battles on the psychological front. Armed with dry senses of humor and acerbic wit, they flaunt the mores of a postwar Britain that sought societal transformation but has sunk even deeper into class division. RITA, SUE AND BOB TOO! joins a list of offbeat British films that includes WISH YOU WERE HERE!, SHADEY, and WITHNAIL AND I in 1987, and NO SURRENDER, LETTER TO BREZHNEV, and MY BEAUTIFUL LAUNDRETTE in 1986.

Based on two plays by Andrea Dunbar, who grew up in the Buttershaw Estates where the film is set, this is a sex comedy in which the on-screen sex (for the most part, limited to the initial escapade in the car, and including no nudity beyond Costigan's nether regions) is far less important than the idea of that sex. The *menage a trois* at the film's center and the longed-for joyous "jumps" become a *raison d'etre* for the girls. They are capable of bringing some excitement to their lives even if the surrounding world—the massive unemployment of post-industrial Yorkshire, the decaying estate—wallows in hopeless inertia. From the opening moments, Holmes and Finneran are almost constantly in motion, striding quickly across the screen to Costigan's house, the tracking camera in pursuit. Even when director Clarke (SCUM) takes the action indoors, his hand-held camera seems a step behind the girls, battling to keep up. These interior shots at the estate have a documentary quality, and, tightly framed, reinforce the claustrophobic, stagnant life the girls are trying to escape. At the same time, the suburbs aren't much of an alternative. Despite its more comfortable surroundings, Costigan's life is equally without meaning, though his lusting after thrills seems more sordid than existential.

Bug-eyed with anticipation or smugly self-satisfied with his conquests, Costigan makes his crotch-driven fool both smarmy and charming. The supporting roles are well played, particularly Ross, the malevolent drunk who, unable to get a job, is consequently incapable of walking a straight line. Without the buoyant, energetic performances of Holmes and Finneran, however, the efforts of the others would have been wasted. Baby-fat sexy in tight sweaters and skirts, they are both optimistic innocents (appropriate for their age) and cynical smart alecks (right for their environment), and their premature world-weariness provides the film's funniest lines and moments. With Costigan along for the ride, they don't exactly triumph over the narrow possibilities of their lives, but they do fight to an irreverent standoff. They are down but not out. Although there are some slow sections, RITA, SUE AND BOB TOO! provides a number of good laughs and also more than a few empathetic winces. Bleak comedies indeed. *(Brief nudity, sexual situations, profanity.)*

p, Sandy Lieberson, Patsy Pollock; d, Alan Clarke; w, Andrea Dunbar (based on her plays "The Arbor," "Rita, Sue And Bob Too"); ph, Ivan Strasburg (Eastmancolor); m, Michael Kamen; ed, Stephen Singleton; art d, Len Huntingford; cos, Catherine Cooke.

Comedy **(PR:O MPAA:R)**

RIVER'S EDGE***½

(1987) 99m Hemdale/Island c

Crispin Glover *(Layne)*, Keanu Reeves *(Matt)*, Ione Skye Leitch *(Clarissa)*, Daniel Roebuck *(Samson "John" Tollette)*, Dennis Hopper *(Feck)*, Joshua Miller *(Tim, Matt's Brother)*, Roxana Zal *(Maggie)*, Josh Richman *(Tony)*, Phil Brock *(Mike)*, Tom Bower *(Bennett)*, Constance Forslund *(Madeleine, Matt's Mother)*, Leo Rossi *(Jim)*, Jim Metzler *(Burkewaite, Teacher)*, Tammy Smith *(Kim, Matt's Sister)*, Danyi Deats *(Jamie)*, Yuzo Nishihara *(Moko)*, Taylor Negron *(Checker)*, Chris Peters *(Tom)*, Richard Richcreek *(Kevin)*, Maeve Odum *(Student)*, Frances De L'Etanche Du Bois *(Aunto)*, Mike Hungerford *(Tony's Father)*, James Terry *(Cop)*.

One of the most haunting films of this or any other decade, RIVER'S EDGE takes a look at a 1980s post-punk generation of children who have no causes, no morals, no feelings, and, worst of all, no future. This controversial film, based on a notorious 1981 murder case, opens with two characters—Miller, an androgynous 12-year-old, and Roebuck, a hulking teenager—who are in the process of killing. Miller throws his little sister's rag doll off a bridge and into a river, while nearby Roebuck has just strangled his girl friend. As he sits by her naked body, Roebuck delivers a primitive yell of exhilaration. Miller, who has seen Roebuck with the corpse, befriends the killer at a local convenience store by stealing some beer for him. Together they search for some dope, ending up at the dilapidated home of Hopper, a burned-out, one-legged former biker from the 1960s who, after killing his beloved girl friend, has given his heart to a blow-up sex doll named "Ellie." Miller later arrives at his hell-hole of a home. His little sister is crying hysterically because he *killed* her doll; his young mother is yelling; his stepfather is complaining about the noise; and his older brother, Reeves, knocks

Miller around, telling him that "it's stupid enough to pull a stunt like [*killing* the doll], but then to go and brag about it . . . " Onto the scene arrives Glover, a speed-freak friend of Reeves who drives a modified Volkswagen bug. Glover and Reeves drive off to visit Hopper, their hard-driving rock 'n' roll drowning out Miller's plea to join them. Miller tries unsuccessfully to bribe them into taking him with them by promising to show them a dead body. Later, at the schoolyard, they meet up with the rest of their friends—Leitch, the girl both Glover and Reeves *like*; Richman, who wants to live the life of an "Easy Rider," and Zal, who, like the others, is chiefly concerned with "getting stoned." When beer-guzzling Roebuck arrives, he matter-of-factly tells his friends that he has killed "Jamie"—one of their crowd and Leitch's best friend. Everyone laughs it off and assumes Roebuck is just being "strange." Roebuck drags Glover and Reeves to the river's edge to see Jamie (played by Danyi Deats, in the ultimate thankless role). Glover is convinced that it is a joke, but after poking the corpse with a stick, he knows otherwise. When asked why he did it, the unemotional Roebuck responds, "She was talking some s______." Reeves displays some moral conscience by walking away from the body, but Glover sees the situation as something out of a movie—an exciting chance for the gang to stick together and "test their loyalty" to Roebuck. In Glover's eyes, Jamie was a friend, but now she's dead; Roebuck is also their friend, but he is still alive and needs their help. In contrast to the frightfully detached kids is Metzler, the high-school history teacher who basks in the glory days of the 1960s when he and his friends "stopped" the war in Vietnam, brought about change in the government, and "made a difference" in America. After class, Glover organizes another expedition to the river's edge to show other friends the body. All the while, Reeves is disturbed by the situation, as if he's thinking about what he told his brother—that "it's stupid enough to pull a stunt like that, but then to go and brag about it . . . " After the others see the body, Glover tries unsuccessfully to enlist their help in burying it. Since not even Roebuck will help, they leave, and the naked Jamie turns progressively bluer as she lies in the rain.

Leitch is the first one to consider calling the police. She and Zal dial the telephone together, but hang up without saying anything. Reeves sits in his living room, watching television, holding the telephone in his hand, contemplating a call. Meanwhile, Roebuck showing no remorse, stays at home with his senile aunt (his mother is dead), fixing her dinner and promising to read her a Dr. Seuss children's book. Later that evening, without help from his friends, Glover pushes Jamie's corpse into the river. Wrestling with his conscience, Reeves calls the police and leads them to the body, which has washed ashore. When the police arrive at Roebuck's house, he and Glover have taken refuge with Hopper. Although Roebuck and Hopper have met before, this is the first time they've met as killers. When Glover tells Hopper that Jamie's murder was accidental, Hopper responds unemotionally: "I killed a girl once; it was no accident. Put the gun right to the back of her head, blew her brains right out the front. I was in love." Eager to tell his story, Roebuck says, "I strangled mine." Hopper asks, "Did you love her?" Roebuck heartlessly answers, "She was okay." Meanwhile, Miller, who all along has been alienated from the gang but has sided with Glover and

Roebuck, tells Reeves that he knows he informed and that he's "going to die for it." Then, with the help of a friend, Miller plots his revenge. In the middle of the night, Glover picks up Reeves and Leitch to help in Roebuck's escape. Glover, however, becomes annoyed at his friends' lack of loyalty and leaves them. Rather than go home, Reeves and Leitch take two sleeping bags to the park, where Reeves confesses that he told the police. They talk about Jamie, and how much she meant to them. Leitch reveals that she couldn't cry for Jamie even though she "cried when that guy in 'Brian's Song' died." Afterwards they make love. Meanwhile, having run out of beer, Roebuck talks Hopper into a "beer run." After picking up some beer, they go to the river's edge where, after a few drinks, Roebuck and Hopper talk about the murders. As Roebuck explains how he felt when he killed Jamie, the murder is intercut with Leitch and Reeves' lovemaking. "I had total control of her . . . It all felt so real . . . She was dead there in front of me and I felt so f—-ing alive," he says. As Hopper comes to the realization that there is no hope for Roebuck, he promises to be the boy's friend. Hopper then puts the gun to Roebuck's head and kills him. The following morning, when Hopper returns home, Miller ambushes him and steals his gun. As the police apprehend Hopper, the kids go back to the river's edge where they find Roebuck's body. At the sight of his dead friend, Glover breaks down, unable to cope with the fact that his movie-influenced ideas of friendship and loyalty are unrealistic. Also arriving on the scene is the gun-toting Miller, who prepares to kill his brother but cannot. In a hospital room interview with reporters, Hopper explains his reasons for killing Roebuck. Then he asks them to leave: "I'm very tired and sort of depressed . . . I lost a good friend today, you know." While the bluesy "I'm Gonna Miss You" plays on the soundtrack, the kids are seen at Jamie's funeral, dressed in their Sunday best and looking at the dead girl's body—in much the same way they did when she lay at the river's edge.

Not since Luis Bunuel's 1950 portrait of youth in Mexico City's slums, LOS OLVIDADOS, has a film so perfectly captured a generation's lack of hope and direction. Although the characters, settings, styles, and stories of the two films are very different, the dismal pictures of youth they paint are similar. Coming in an era when Hollywood's idea of empty youth is the saccharine LESS THAN ZERO, RIVER'S EDGE strikes a blow against films that are *manufactured* and readily marketable. Made on a budget of $1.7 million, it involved virtually no risk on the part of the producers (Midge Sanford and Sarah Pillsbury) or the distributor (Hemdale), despite its controversial nature. Directed by Tim Hunter, who coscripted the somewhat similar youth film OVER THE EDGE and directed TEX and SYLVESTER, RIVER'S EDGE is successful because of Neal Jimenez's excellent script. Written in 1981 while Jimenez was still a graduate student at UCLA, "The River," as it was then called, honestly captures the fundamental malaise of today's youth. The RIVER'S EDGE generation's post-punk worldview is rooted in nihilism, detachment, fear of nuclear annihilation, and the belief that there is no future. As a result, the concepts of life and death become blurred and irrelevant, since nothing matters except friends, rock 'n' roll, and getting "stoned." The scariest thing about RIVER'S EDGE is that it isn't fiction. It is based (though not explicitly—neither the town nor the real names are used or even implied) on an actual murder which occurred in Milpitas, California, in 1981. (Interestingly, a 1987 screening of RIVER'S EDGE in Milpitas was canceled by townspeople who preferred to believe that the incident never happened.) Where the film hits its mark is in its screenplay. Twenty-seven-year-old Jimenez's understanding of the characters goes beyond the usual societal and parental stereotypes, digs beneath the facades which teenagers hide behind, and comes up with some honest and complex portraits.

RIVER'S EDGE features the best cast of unknowns since Francis Ford Coppola's THE OUTSIDERS (which included nearly all of today's young stars—Tom Cruise, Patrick Swayze, Emilio Estevez, Ralph Macchio, Diane Lane and others). Reeves and Leitch (who has since dropped her last name) are superb as the moral centers of the film—the two kids who, despite having the odds stacked against them, will probably turn out okay. Roebuck is also great as the killer, a monster born of cold, unfeeling surroundings. Equally impressive are the supporting characters, especially the creepy Miller (son of playwright and EXORCIST star Jason Miller) as the little brother torn between his admiration for the amoral Roebuck and the moral Reeves. (See: People to Watch.) Better known than the rest of the young stars is Glover, who appeared last year as Michael J. Fox's 1950's father in BACK TO THE FUTURE. Glover was accused of overacting in RIVER'S EDGE, and his performance is a peculiar caricature which doesn't fit comfortably with the rest of the film's performances. It is one of such intensity, however, that it cannot be forgotten. Glover does more than act, he reveals his vulnerability in front of the camera and, as a result, risks, and often receives, critical lambasting. Cast as a symbol of the 1960s is Hopper, whose freewheeling, pot-smoking EASY RIDER character is the role model for the RIVER'S EDGE kids. Because of the inclusion of the Hopper character, the film becomes more than a look at a modern killer. It is a comparison between two different types of killers—the one who kills for love, or for a cause, or for a belief and the one who is simply a monster. Roebuck is hopeless because he killed to make himself feel alive; Hopper, on the other hand, killed because he loved someone more than he could handle. In a lecture to his students, Metzler nostalgically looks back to the 1960s when hippies, however misguided, "wasted pigs" in an effort to save America. Hopper states it most simply in his hospital bed interview: "I don't like killing people, but sometimes it's necessary." Hopper, who has appeared in a slew of recent films, is excellent as "Feck," playing his part somewhere between lunacy and honesty. Perhaps not coincidentally, Hopper has appeared in some of the most important and controversial films of the last four decades—REBEL WITHOUT A CAUSE (1955), EASY RIDER (1969), APOCALYPSE NOW (1979), and BLUE VELVET (1986)—a testament to his qualities as a risk-taker and survivor.

Technically the film is remarkable, especially for its thin budget. The cinematography by Elmes (BLUE VELVET) is outstanding, and the score by Knieper (THE AMERICAN FRIEND and THE STATE OF THINGS) is downright eerie. The least inspired aspect of the film, unfortunately, is Hunter's direction. Everything is presented in a generally straightforward manner with static, master-shot compositions which show little visual imagination. This sort of unobtrusive style would suit a less complex script, but RIVER'S EDGE is brimming with moments of black comedy and surrealism that go unrecognized by the direction. The circumstances and characters in RIVER'S EDGE, especially Glover, beg for a more poetic visual style that would do justice to the frightening morality, or lack thereof, that the characters display. The disturbing characters that Roebuck and Hopper play are the kind of anti-heroes that deserve more than Hunter's plain direction. The mind reels at the thought of what RIVER'S EDGE might have been had Bunuel or David Lynch or even Martin Scorsese directed. One example of a missed opportunity for surrealism is the frequent cutting back to the corpse. While in the film it grows increasingly blue and stiff (more dead looking), the original script had it becoming increasingly beautiful. The soundtrack is filled with heavy metal and hard-core punk music, including "Kyrie Eleison" (Jim Matheos, John Arch, performed by Fates Warning), "Captor of Sin," "Evil Has No Boundaries" (Jeff Hannemann, Kerry King, performed by Slayer), "Tormentor," "Die by the Sword" (Hannemann, performed by Slayer), "Lethal Tendencies" (Stacy Anderson, performed by Hallow's Eve), "Let Me Know" (Greg Sage, performed by Vipers), "Fire in the Rain" (Mike Palm, performed by Agent Orange), "Happy Day" (Winston Rooney, performed by Burning Spear), "Let's Go, Let's Go, Let's Go" and "I'm Gonna Miss You" (Hank Ballard, performed by Ballard). While RIVER'S EDGE is emotionally disturbing—it contains numerous scenes of drinking, pill-popping, and driving combined; is filled with profanity; and often cuts back to a young girl's naked, lifeless body—it deals with issues of profound importance to parents and teenagers alike. *(Violence, excessive profanity, nudity, sexual situations, substance abuse.)*

p, Sarah Pillsbury, Midge Sanford, David Streit; d, Tim Hunter; w, Neal Jimenez; ph, Frederick Elmes (Metrocolor); m, Jurgen Knieper; ed, Howard Smith, Sonya Sones; prod d, John Muto; art d, Mick Muhlfriedel; set d, Anne Huntley; cos, Claudia Brown; makeup, Gabor Kernyaiszky, Ken Myers.

Drama **(PR:O MPAA:R)**

ROBA DA RICCHI† (1987, It.) 105m Scena-Reteitalia/Medusa c (Trans: For the Rich; AKA: MONTECARLO, MONTECARLO)

Lino Banfi *(Aldo)*, Laura Antonelli *(Mapi)*, Renato Pozzetto *(Priest)*, Francesca Dellera *(Princess)*, Paolo Villaggio *(Insurance Agent)*, Serena Grandi *(Dora)*, Milena Vukotic *(Doctor)*, Vittorio Caprioli *(Monsignor)*, Maurizio Micheli.

A virtual remake of his own RIMINI RIMINI, prolific Italian director Corbucci takes the same cast and submits this comedy trilogy which mocks the peccadillos of the rich on holiday at Montecarlo. The first episode features Pozzetto as a hapless Italian priest pursued by the Princess of Montecarlo (Dellera) who has become erotically obssessed with him. The second episode stars the ever-beautiful Laura Antonelli as a woman who pretends to fall in love with a scruffy bum in a plot to turn the tables on her philandering husband, Banfi. The final story is a parody of DOUBLE INDEMNITY starring Villaggio as a bumbling insurance agent hired by *femme fatale* Grandi to murder her husband. As is typical of Italian productions, the screenplay was written by a small army of contributors, including the director and his brother, veteran Cinecitta screenwriter Bruno Corbucci. Director Corbucci, who is also known under the anglo pseudonyms "Stanley Corbett" and "Gordon Wilson, Jr.," is probably best known for his work in spaghetti westerns, most notably DJANGO (1966).

p, Augusto Caminito; d, Sergio Corbucci; w, Mario Amendola, Bruno Corbucci, Sergio Corbucci, Massimo Franciosa, Giovanni Romali, Bernardino Zapponi; ph, Sergio D'Offizi (Telecolor); m, Carmelo La Bionda, Michelangelo La Bionda; ed, Ruggero Mastroianni; art d, Giovanni Licheri.

Comedy **(PR:NR MPAA:NR)**

ROBACHICOS† (1987, Mex.) 101m Instituto Mexicano de Cinematografia-Conacine/Peliculas Mexicanas c (Trans: Childstealers)

Gerado Vigil *(Juanito Aguilar)*, Jose Carlos Ruiz *(Julian)*, Alma Muriel *(Victoria)*, Narciso Busquets *(El Commandante)*, Maria Rojo, Elsa Maya, Sergio Bustamante, Noe Murayama.

An expose on Mexico's efforts to control the illegal trafficking of children. Vigil plays a private detective who searches the city streets for trafficking kingpin Ruiz, witnessing all forms of child abuse in the process.

d&w, Alberto Bojorquez; ph, Guadalupe Garcia; m, Leonardo Valazquez; ed, Reynaldo Portillo; art d, Enrique Dominquez.

Crime **(PR:O MPAA:NR)**

ROBINSON NO NIWA† (1987, Jap.) 123m Lay Line/Daiei c (Trans: Robinson's Garden)

Kumiko Ohta *(Kumi)*, Machizo Machida *(Kii)*, Yuko Ueno *(Yu)*, Cheebo *(Maki)*, Oto *(Oto)*, Mitsuwa Sakamoto *(Erika)*, Mariko Chiku *(Saki)*, Ryoji Nomura *(Nomu)*, Izaba *(Pon)*, Sakevi Yokoyama *(Yo)*, Kinji Okumura *(Ryo)*, Yo Mizoguchi *(Shun)*, Johann Messelli *(Jim)*, Norihiko Hirabayashi *(Ossan)*, Mitsugu Kanazawa *(Grandfather)*, Nami Miyahara *(Children Kumi)*.

Acclaimed by critics at the Berlin Film Festival, ROBINSON NO NIWA is the second feature of promising young Japanese director Masashi Yamamoto who came to international prominence after a screening of his 16mm feature CARNIVAL OF THE NIGHT at the Berlin fest in 1982. Borrowing American independent filmmaker Jim Jarmusch's (STRANGER THAN PARADISE, DOWN BY LAW) cinematographer, Tom Dicillo, and lighting designer, Jim Heyman, director Yamamoto creates a strikingly beautiful film set in modern-day Tokyo. It follows the discovery of self-awarness by a bored, jaded, middle-class youth (Kumiko Ohta) who supports herself with an occasional drug deal. One day while walking through a back alley she discovers an abandoned building with a lush, overgrown green garden nearby. Ohta immediately moves her belongings into the building and, like Robinson Crusoe, sets up her own little world. She spray-paints the walls, hangs neon lights, and plants cabbages in the wild garden. She befriends a mischievous little girl who wanders in to take advantage of the unlimited freedom the hide-away offers. Ohta makes the mistake of inviting some of her friends over for a party, and the rowdies nearly destroy her new home. The months go by and Ohta continues to tend her garden. Inexplicably she falls ill and begins to hallucinate about her deceased grandfather. Try as she might to stave the encroaching foliage, the garden creeps in and begins taking over the fragile residence, forcing Ohta to abandon her island. The little girl returns and digs through the rubble until she finds a mechanical bird. She winds it up, sets it free, and it flies in circles, chirping away. The exotic musical score—a combination of Japanese, Arab, and Indian sounds—is provided by Japanese composer Yoichirou Yoshikawa, the five-man group Jagatara, and Sudanese composer Hamza Bl Din.

p, Aya Shinohara; d&w, Masashi Yamamoto; ph, Tom Dicillo; m, Jagatara, Hamza Bl Din, Yoichirou Yoshikawa; art d, Minoru Osawa, Yuji Hayashida, Akira Ishige; makeup, Mako Kato.

Drama **(PR:NR MPAA:NR)**

ROBOCOP*½** (1987) 103m Orion c

Peter Weller *(Alex J. Murphy/Robocop)*, Nancy Allen *(Anne Lewis)*, Ronny Cox *(Richard "Dick" Jones)*, Kurtwood Smith *(Clarence J. Boddicker)*, Miguel Ferrer *(Robert Morton)*, Robert DoQui *(Sgt. Reed)*, Daniel [Dan] O'Herlihy *(The Old Man)*, Ray Wise *(Leon Nash)*, Felton Perry *(Johnson)*, Mario Machado, *(Casey Wong, TV Newsman)*, Leeza Gibbons *(Jesse Perkins, TV Newsman)*, Paul McCrane *(Emil Antonowsky)*, Lee De Broux *(Sal, Drug Dealer)*, Ken Page *(Kinney, OCP Marketing Executive)*, Jesse Goins, Del Zamora, Calvin Jung.

Where the historical perspective was popular with Hollywood decades ago, the obsession with the future, especially in the crime genre, seems to offer vent to moviemaking's greatest box office asset, special effects. The decline of the durable actor with individual and distinctive style and appearance has been aided by the emotionless, expressionless and wholly dehumanizing cyborg (half human, half machine) who accomplishes the superhuman feat without having to make moral decisions. ROBOCOP is probably the epitome of this kind of modern film hero, a futuristic comic book protagonist programmed to ferret out and destroy human evil doers without compassion, conscience, or legal concern. A first-rate production of non-stop action and inventive special effects makes this one a spellbinder, despite the human gore that spills into almost every frame. It is 1991 in crime-ridden Detroit which claims the dubious honor of being the murder capital of the U.S. A corporate conglomerate has taken over the responsibility of running the city and its primary concern is to stop crime in the streets. So far the big brother company has had little success in besting the bestial gangs that prowl the city streets; killers have claimed the lives of 31 police officers since the corporation has taken over and corporate director O'Herlihy is displeased. One of his top men, Cox, an insidious inveigler of corporate intrigue, has created a huge, awkward metal android to combat rampant street crime and this cannon-fisted creation is presented to corporate executives in their towering conference suite. A simple and dreadful demonstration has a junior executive hold a gun on the spasmodic droid which has been programmed to order evildoers to put down their weapons at a count of five. The executive complies but the machine drones out a count of five and then fires a burst of bullets into the startled executive, killing him. This vicious scene sets the tone for the bloodbath that is to follow. The only sensibilities jarred by this ugly killing are registered by corporate executives upset that the droid has too many "glitches" in it to be presently marketed for millions. Yuppie corporate climber Ferrer, who has barely escaped being a victim in the lethal droid demonstration, sees an opportunity to better his company position by building a better cop machine, leapfrogging over Cox's corporate position. Just what kind of machine he will create is uncertain but the embryo of this creation is at the time patrolling the streets of Detroit in the form of Weller, a cop working with female counterpart Allen. The two cops corner a gang of sadistic hoodlums, led by sinister Smith. Allen is knocked out and Weller trapped. Lining up in front of him, gang members shoot him repeatedly while laughing like maniacs and asking Weller as he bleeds from a dozen wounds: "Does it hurt?" Smith tires of the game and finally fires a shot into Weller's brain, killing him. Or has he? His body is recovered and rushed to an emergency room where his pulse goes to nothing and the screen goes blank for some seconds to indicate the nothingness of death (if the filmmaker's presumption of a lack of afterlife is correct). The screen flickers to life as technicians reconstruct Weller's body, piecing it together with steel and microchips, giving the viewer a brief perspective of a cyborg coming to life. The new creation, dubbed Robocop, is the pet project of Ferrer. The reconstructed Weller, the front of his face intact, the rest of his body mechanized, soon goes into action against street criminals and proves more than effective, dispatching whole gangs of robbers, rapists, burglars, and assorted malefactors. The new machine elevates Ferrer to top corporate management, which vexes the scheming Cox no end. To undo the effectiveness of the fast-moving cyborg, Cox makes a pact with super villain Smith to destroy Robocop. Meanwhile, Weller is recognized by his former partner Allen and she teams up with him to capture Smith and his ugly band of vicious thugs. Midway through the film Weller's human side begins to slip into his mechanical makeup. He has recurrent dreams and nightmares, particularly those dealing with his wife and child who have left their home after his official death. He relives his human past, uncovering the realities of his former existence and these scenes are especially poignant. Weaving in and out of the cyborg's mechanical elimination of bad guys is Smith's plot to get rid of the remade Weller and, in the final bloody shootout between Weller, assisted by Allen, Smith and his plug-uglies are sent to flesh-ripping perdition. Weller must face one last obstacle, however, and that is Cox's own gigantic killing machine. The cyborg and the Cox machine face off in a slam-bang battle which culminates with the destruction of the evil machine when it is unable to pursue Weller down stairs. Cox himself is dispatched at a board meeting by Weller after O'Herlihy fires Cox so that Weller can arrest him, having been programmed never to molest any corporate member of the firm. With a "well done, officer Murphy," from O'Herlihy, Weller exits triumphant and slightly more human than he was when reconstructed, a finale which begs for a sequel which is sure to come, given the enormous success of this comic book action film.

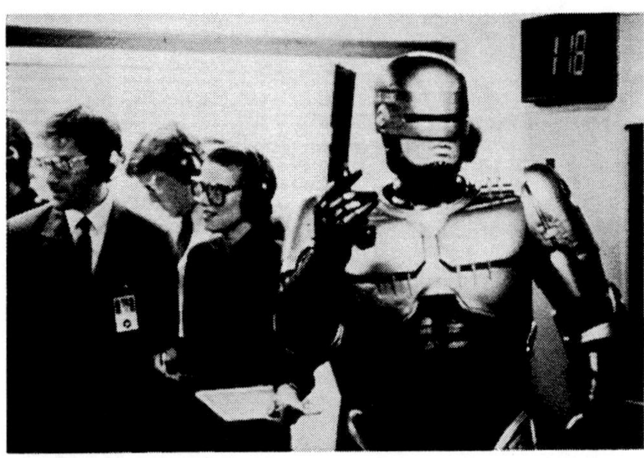

ROBOCOP was made for slightly more than $13 million and has returned many times that amount at this writing. This futuristic crime film is not replete with great acting because acting is not necessary. Weller (THE ADVENTURES OF BUCKAROO BANZAI, JUST TELL ME WHAT YOU WANT, SHOOT THE MOON) is not really required to act, only to speak in a rather monotone voice, slightly altered to give it a robot-like drone of authority that cannot be questioned. His actions are for the common good and therefore cheers are in order, but he is as relentless as an electric can-opener. Once he has started on a mission the outcome will certainly not affect human vulnerability which is somehow strangely comforting. The bad guys are blown to pieces as would be other robots, except that this is human flesh, albeit corrupted flesh, and the viewer is therefore expected to accept their grisly demise as proper revenge and retribution. Big brotherhood abounds in this designer film which is wholly dependent upon dazzling special effects, except that the Cox machine moves with seemingly sinister gestures (we know from the beginning that this is a mechanical monster gone wrong, much like H.A.L. in 2001) which are emotionally disturbing. It has an otherworld eeriness similar to the erratically moving monsters of such fantasies as JASON AND THE ARGONAUTS. The human satire is that of the corporate executive which this film certainly intends to malign and maim, with no one in that board room, with the possible exception of fatherly O'Herlihy, being empathetic enough to earn viewer sympathy or concern. Oddly, when the executive is shot by Cox's machine at the beginning, the whole thing is treated as a messy business error and no alarm at the loss of a human life is expressed. The true villains, Cox and the ruthless Smith, are humans and when they are destroyed by the mechanical inventions of man, they are considered necessary and worthwhile deaths. And this is the most disturbing aspect of ROBOCOP, along with the incredible violence and bloodletting shown on an almost nonstop basis. The comic book approach of the script is actually the film's excuse for such drastic abuses of humanity, a tactic which earned this film an "X" rating from the MPAA when it was initially reviewed. After several appeals, the film was given a hard "R" rating and even that was more consideration for a film that shows little or no consideration for human sensibilities. This is one of the most violent films ever made and, as such, is certainly not for youngsters. The only morality offered in ROBOCOP is projected by the cyborg, a machine reflecting the directives of its creative masters. To believe that, once programmed, such cyborgs will continue to uphold the public good is to place eternal belief in our vacuum cleaners, that they should arbitrate divorce, abortion, drug use, suicide, murder, etc. Just turn on the switch and fear no evil is the overriding message.

Yet ROBOCOP is a study in itself for the mature moviegoer who will easily dismiss the comic book characters and plot and concentrate on the premise that the absurd has become reality. So much wonderful style, even in the goriest scenes, is evident here from director Verhoeven, a Dutch helmsman (THE FOURTH MAN, SOLDIER OF ORANGE) that every scene seems to sparkle with tilted dimensions, oddball twists, and special effects wonders. Throughout there are the expressionistic attitudes of a Fritz Lang, offering jarring scenes of devastation. There, too, is a cynicism rampant throughout the film, one that seems to say that humanity is not much good and that only *certain* machines can be trusted to do the right thing. Well, yes, the flesh is weak, and here we get an exercise on how it can be severed, blown up, slashed, cut, exploded, and reduced to fragments of flying bodies. Weller's piecemeal memory and human emotions that somehow ridiculously survive oddly offer a sliver of redemption at film's end. Then none of this can be taken too seriously since its executive producer, Davison, knew full well the commercial ploys to be worked to achieve a box office bonanza, he being the moving force behind such absurdities as AIR-

PLANE! But thanks to Verhoeven, a mathematical genius whose interests have always run to the mystical, we have a film offering a combination of reality and fantasy in a hardboiled world of robots and people who act like them. Much of the credit for the potent visual style of the film must go to Vacano who was the cinematographer of DAS BOOT and the same kind of urgency and wild desperation appearing in that claustrophobic but powerful film can be felt in ROBOCOP. Of course special effects wizards Bottin, Davies, Kuran, Ronzani, Martin, and Blalack take top honors for their startling robot creations. *(Graphic violence, profanity, substance abuse.)*

p, Arne Schmidt; d, Paul Verhoeven; w, Edward Neumeier, Michael Miner; ph, Jost Vacano (DuArt Color); m, Basil Poledouris; ed, Frank J. Urioste; prod d, William Sandell; art d, Gayle Simon; set d, Robert Gould, James Tocci; cos, Erica Edell Phillips; spec eff, Dale Martin, Rob Bottin, Craig Davies, Peter Ronzani.

Science Fiction/Crime (PR:O MPAA:R)

ROBOT HOLOCAUST zero (1987) 79m Tycin Entertainment/Wizard Video-Infinity c

Norris Culf *(Neo)*, Nadine Hart *(Deeja)*, Joel Von Ornsteiner *(Klyton)*, Jennifer Delora *(Myta)*, Andrew Howarth *(Kai)*, Angelika Jager *(Valaria)*, Rick Gianasi *(Torque)*, Michael Dowend *(Jorn)*, George Gray *(Bray)*, Nicholas Reiner *(Haim)*, Michael Azzolina *(Roan)*, John Blaylock *(Koria)*, Amy Brentano *(Irradiated Female)*, Michael Zezima, Edward Mallia *(Airslave Fighters)*, Dave Martin, Keith Schwabinger *(Guardbots)*.

The second installment of New York City-based Tycin Entertainment's three-picture deal with Empire Pictures—released via Empire's subsidiary Wizard Video—is even worse than the first (last year's BREEDERS). Set in the future, the "Robot Holocaust" of the title takes place off screen before the film begins. Through bland narration we learn that society was nearly destroyed when the millions of robots enslaved by man revolted and took revenge upon their masters. Humans are now either slaves controlled by the Dark One or nomads. The Dark One (who is just a disembodied voice through most of the movie) keeps the humans in check by controlling the atmosphere—making it poisonous when humans get out of line—from a place known as the Power Station. (Much of the film was actually shot at the abandoned Brooklyn Navy Yard power station.) When the Dark One discovers that scientist Dowend has invented a device which enables humans to breathe the poisoned air, he dispatches his robot enforcer Gianasi to kidnap the human. Dowend is brought to the Power Station and tortured by the Dark One's beautiful assistant Jager (who speaks like a Teutonic Barbara Walters). The scientist's daughter, Hart, enlists the aid of a band of nomads who can somehow breathe the poisoned air (Hart and her father possess the only two breathing devices) and they embark on a quest to defeat the Dark One. After encountering a number of ridiculous obstacles (mutants, wormlike hand puppets, one badly constructed giant spider leg, etc.), the heroes finally invade the Power Station. The Dark One punishes Jager for her failure to eliminate the intruders by blasting away her flesh to reveal that she's a robot (surprise, surprise). After some badly choreographed fight scenes, the good guys succeed in disconnecting the Power Station, but are horrified to learn that the Dark One (who seems to be an organic being) has turned Hart's father into something resembling a human eggplant. Regretfully, our heroes must kill Dowend in order to destroy the Dark One and make the post-holocaust world a better place.

ROBOT HOLOCAUST combines the worst elements of post-apocalyptic science fiction and sword-and-sorcery epics. With the good guys dressed in loin cloths and armed with swords fighting flashily outfitted villains with ray-guns, the whole film plays like outtakes from a "Flash Gordon" serial of the 1930s. Writer-director Kincaid not only borrows from "Flash Gordon," but from STAR WARS as well. The heroes are accompanied by a friendly, wisecracking robot which moans and complains throughout the movie—a blatant rip-off of the C3PO robot in STAR WARS. The lack of originality in ROBOT HOLOCAUST is exacerbated by the failure of Kincaid to extract any excitement from his paper-thin plot. The movie is just plain boring. The quest goes on and on, punctuated only by poorly executed action scenes and pathetically lame attempts at humor. Kincaid gets no help from his actors, however, for they are uniformly wooden. Perhaps the fatal flaw in all three Tycin efforts is Kincaid's choice to play this material straight. Hampered by a low budget and amateur actors, it may have been advisable to go for a lighter, tongue-in-cheek approach, rather than the somber, deadly serious presentation Kincaid opted for. With a campy approach the budget limitations could have been played for intentional laughs, thus short-circuiting the unintentional laughs that the film now garners. *(Violence, nudity.)*

p, Cynthia DePaula; d&w, Tim Kincaid; ph, Arthur D. Marks (Precision Color); ed, Barry Zetlin; prod d, Medusa; art d, Marina Zurkow, Ruth Lounsbury; cos, Celeste Hines; makeup, Tom Lauten; spec eff, Jeremie Frank, Ralph Cordero, Valarie McNeill, Ed French.

Science Fiction Cas. (PR:O MPAA:NR)

ROCK 'N' ROLL NIGHTMARE zero (1987, Can.) 83m Thunder/Shapiro c (AKA: THE EDGE OF HELL)

Jon-Mikl Thor *(John Triton)*, Jillian Peri *(Lou Anne)*, Frank Dietz *(Roger Eburt)*, Dave Lane *(Max)*, Teresa Simpson *(Randy)*, Clara Pater *(Mother)*, Jesse D'Angelo *(Little Boy)*, Chris Finkel *(Father)*, Liane Abel *(Mary Eburt)*, Denise Dicandia *(Dee Dee)*, Jim Cirile *(Stig)*, David Lane *(Max)*, Gene Kroth *(Karl)*, Rusty Hamilton *(Seductress)*, Carrie Schiffler *(Cindy Connelly)*, Tralle O'Farrell, Layra Daans, Nancy Bush *(Groupies)*.

Even the most hardened veteran of bad cinema will sit slack-jawed as this incredibly amateurish vanity production boasting cheap thrills and even cheaper rock 'n' roll unfolds. In a remote Canadian farmhouse, an unseen evil force slaughters an entire family. Years later, a heavy-metal rock band has converted the barn into a recording studio and plans to spend five weeks there rehearsing new songs for their upcoming album and tour. The leader of the band, the muscle-bound Thor (who also sports long blond locks), is a committed musician who has little tolerance for the tomfoolery of other band members—most of whom spend the weekend cavorting with their girl friends. Unbeknownst to the band, however, several poorly crafted puppet creatures are crawling around the set possessing hapless cast members. Just what effect these monsters have on the humans is never clearly defined. The girl friend of one band member is turned into an ugly monster who bites the shoulder of the group's manager (who subsequently becomes a zombie), while another musician becomes a sexual dynamo whose chest later bursts to reveal the scaly arm of a demon. Other cast members simply disappear without explanation. Eventually, only Thor and his girl friend are left, and when she reveals herself to be Satan (a badly articulated puppet obviously made from rubber and plastic), the heavy-metal rocker is unfazed. Thor calmly explains to Satan (whom he refers to as "Bub") that he (Thor) is the archangel Triton and that all the other characters in the film were merely illusions created to lure Satan and his demons out into the open. Satan retaliates by throwing several small, one-eyed rubber starfish at Thor. Thor grimaces in pain as he struggles to remove the nasty creatures (he actually holds them to his chest pretending that they are attached to his flesh). After defeating the starfish creatures, Thor physically attacks Satan and throttles the demon into submission. Satan mutters a weak "You win this time" and disappears in a burst of flames (actually a roman candle held just out of frame beneath the puppet). Thor visits the graves of the family murdered in the first scene and mutters that they have been "avenged."

An unbelievably silly ego-trip for obscure heavy-metal rocker Thor, who wrote, produced, and starred in this overlong rock video which features several of his insipid songs. Director Fasano's only contributions are several Sam Raimi/EVIL DEAD-inspired camera moves where the camera races throughout the farmhouse taking the point-of-view of the evil force. The acting is uniformly awful, with one band member slipping in and out of a pathetic British accent and most female cast members slipping in and out of their clothes. No one, however, shows as much flesh as Thor himself. Dressed in nothing but a studded loin cloth for the climactic battle scene with Satan, Thor flexes his overworked muscles in an unintentionally hilarious parody of Sly Stallone or Arnold Schwarzenegger. The special effects are even worse. Most of the creatures are the rubber-hand-puppet-covered-with-slime variety found in films like GHOULIES; others are simply actors wearing stiff Halloween masks and rubber gloves. The entire production is strictly amateurish and unfolds like a home movie wherein heavy-metalers try to align themselves with Christians *against* the very Satan that they've been accused of worshiping.

ROCK 'N' ROLL NIGHTMARE does boast one technical first—it is believed to be the first full-length feature shot on 35mm and edited entirely on digital videotape (the film rushes were transferred to video). Because video editing is much simpler than film editing, a normal two-month edit can be accomplished in a mere two weeks and the soundtrack is kept one generation cleaner (thus making the sound quality of Thor's songs that much better—if such a thing is possible, or even desirable). Fans of bad cinema need not fret, for Thor's production company, Thunder Films, has signed a six-picture deal with Shapiro Entertainment. Songs include: "We Live to Rock" (Jon-Mikl Thor, Steve Price), "Energy" (Peppi Marchello), "Edge of Hell (Wildlife)," "Danger," "The Challenge" (Steven Scott), "Live It Up" (Rok Manonoff), "Steal Your Thunder" (Steven Scott, David Aplin), "Heads Will Turn" (Elliot Solomon), "Touch Me Feel Me" (Frank Boehm, Steven Scott, John Tonin), "Maybe It's Love" (Thomas Dicandia). *(Violence, gore effects, nudity, sexual situations, profanity.)*

p, Jon-Mikl Thor; d, John Fasano; w, Jon-Mikl Thor; ph, Mark MacKay (Medallion color); ed, Robert Williams; art d, Wolfgang Siebert; m/l, Jon-Mikl Thor, Steve Price, Peppi Marchello, Steven Scott, Rok Manonoff, David Aplin, Elliot Solomon, Frank Boehm, John Tonin, Thomas Dicandia; spec eff, Arnold Gargiulo II, John Fasano, John Gibson, Jim Cirile, Anthony Bua, Frank Dietz, Vincent Modica.

Horror Cas. (PR:O MPAA:R)

RODNIK DLIA ZHAZHDUSHCHIKH† (1987, USSR) 70m Dovzhenko bw (Trans: A Fountain for the Thirsty)

Miliutenko, Alisova, Kadochnikova, Majouga, Erchov.

Filmed in 1965 and shelved until 1987, this Soviet film revolves around an old well situated in an otherwise barren landscape and tended to by an old man and his family. Passersby drink from the well, each of them affecting the landscape around them. Filmed in black-and-white, the film employs a visual language instead of dialog, which is used sparingly.

d, Yuri Ilienko; w, Dratch; ph, Yuri Ilienko.

Drama (PR:NR MPAA:NR)

ROMANCA FINAL† (1987, Span.) 130m Orfeo-Euskal Telebista-TV3 Televisio de Catalunya c (Trans: Last Romance)

Jose Carreras *(Julian Gayarre, Opera Tenor)*, Sydne Rome *(Alicia)*, Montserrat Caballe *(The Diva)*.

The life of populist opera star Julian Gayarre is told with equal importance placed on his career and his secret romance. The son of a peasant and himself a blacksmith, Gayarre (played by Carreras) is discovered while singing by a passing priest who contacts various patrons of the art. The tenor works his way up through the ranks, finding fame in Spain before dying in 1890 at the age of 45. In his quest for fame and success, however, he neglects his love affair with Rome, the wife of a Spanish aristocrat. Sydne Rome is perhaps best known to American and European audiences as the star of Roman Polanski's forgotten film QUE?, released on videotape in the US as DIARY OF FORBIDDEN DREAMS.

p&d, Jose Maria Forque; w, Jose Maria Forque, Hermongenes Sainz; ph, Alejandro Ulloa; m, Wolfgang Amadeus Mozart, Giuseppe Verdi, Richard Wagner; ed, Mercedes Alonso; md, Anton Garcia Abril; set d, Wolfgang Burman; cos, Juan Antonio Cidron.

Biography/Opera/Romance **(PR:NR MPAA:NR)**

ROMANCE OF BOOK AND SWORD, THE† (1987, Hong Kong/Chi.) 180m Yeung Tse Kong Movie Ent.-SIL Metropole-Tianjin c

Zhang Duo Fu, Da Shi Chang, Ai Nuo, Liu Jia.

From Ann Hui, the director of the critically acclaimed 1983 film BOAT PEOPLE, comes a historical epic which has been 3½ years in the making. Set in the 1600s, during the overthrow of the Ming Dynasty by the Ching tribe, THE ROMANCE OF BOOK AND SWORD follows the lives of two brothers who are fighting on different sides. Based on one of the most famous novels from Jin Yung, considered the master of kung fu literature, this is the eighth adaptation of the book. Running at 180 minutes, this makes an interesting companion to Bertolucci's THE LAST EMPEROR, which is about the end of the Ching Dynasty nearly 300 years later.

d&w, Ann Hui (based on the novel by Jin Yung); ed, Chow Muk-leung.

Historical/Martial Arts **(PR:NR MPAA:NR)**

ROSA DE LA FRONTERA† (1987, Mex.) 89m Esme-Alianza Cinematografica Mexicana/Peliculas Mexicanas c (Trans: Rose of the Border)

Susana Dosamantes *(Rose Guerra)*, Humberto Herrera *(Tomas)*, Eleazar Garcia *(Gabion)*, Hugo Stiglitz *(Sheriff)*, Jorge Vargas *(Emilio Guerra)*, Eric del Castillo, Diana Ferreti, Carlos East, Paulino Vargas.

Dosamentes stars in this actioner as a tough Mexican woman who gets entangled in a murder and flees to the US, only to find that life north of the border is just as dangerous. Shown in New York neighrborhood theaters.

p, Carlos Vasallo; d, Hernando Name; w, Hernando Name, Roberto Schlosser; ph, Xavier Cruz; m, Ricardo Carrion; ed, Sigfredo Garcia, Enrique Murillo.

Action **(PR:NR MPAA:NR)**

ROSARY MURDERS, THE** (1987) 105m First Take/New Line c

Donald Sutherland *(Father Bob Koesler)*, Charles Durning *(Father Ted Nabors)*, Josef Sommer *(Lt. Walt Koznicki)*, Belinda Bauer *(Pat Lennon, Reporter)*, James Murtaugh *(Javison)*, John Danelle *(Detective Harris)*, Addison Powell *(Father Killeen)*, Kathleen Tolan *(Sister Ann Vania)*, Tom Mardirosian *(Detective Fallon)*, Anita Barone *(Irene Jimenez)*.

Despite the best efforts of actors Sutherland and Durning and coscreenwriter Elmore Leonard, THE ROSARY MURDERS is a dreadfully dull murder mystery that will intrigue no one. Set during the winter in a cold, blustery Detroit, the film stars Sutherland as a kindly liberal priest who is not beyond baptizing illegitimate children against pastor Durning's orders. The daily routine of the Detroit archdiocese is violently interrupted when it finds itself in the grip of a serial killer who murders priests and nuns every Friday. His calling card: a string of rosary beads left in the hand of every victim. Sutherland, who knew the first two victims, is quizzed first by police detective Sommer and then by beautiful *Detroit Free Press* reporter Bauer. Sutherland, who is the editor of the local Catholic newspaper, finds himself drawn to Bauer and they frequently go for walks to discuss the case. One day while hearing confessions, Sutherland is shocked to find the killer whispering his deeds. Restricted by his vows from relating what he has heard in the confessional, Sutherland nonetheless has been provided with enough clues to investigate the identity of the murderer. Told by the killer that the murders are revenge against the church for the death of his teenage daughter three years earlier, Sutherland checks the church records and finds the name of a student who had committed suicide. The priest works up enough nerve to confront the killer at his home, but when he rings the bell, no one answers and the door is locked. Spying an open window, Sutherland enters the house through the dead girl's bedroom and finds that it is a shrine. He is horrified to see that everything has been left intact, including the rope with which the girl hanged herself. When Sutherland opens the bedroom door, he is shocked to find the killer on the other side. The priest's reflexes take hold and he slams the door shut. Seconds later he opens it again, only to find that the killer has disappeared. Sutherland leaves the house and decides to talk with a nun who was the girl's teacher. Unfortunately, the nun has taken a vow of silence since the girl's suicide and Sutherland is forced to get special permission from the bishop allowing the woman to break her vow for the interview. The nun informs Sutherland that the girl had sought help because her father was forcing her into incestuous relations. Tearfully the nun tells Sutherland that she had called the girl a liar and forbidden her to speak of it again. A few weeks later the girl killed herself and the shamed nun took a vow of silence. The priest now has all the facts, but he is still unable to tell the police what he knows. Luckily, he stumbles upon a clue that enables him to predict whom the killer will strike next—Durning. Because he has deduced this himself, Sutherland tells the police, and Durning is put under their protection. Unfortunately, the killer (Murtaugh) slips into the rectory on the pretense of arranging a funeral. Sutherland knows that Murtaugh is the killer, but he cannot break his vows and identify him. Luckily, just as Murtaugh is about to shoot Durning, police sharpshooters, who have been keeping an eye on things from across the street, fire through the window and kill him. Sutherland's faith is shaken badly by the entire affair, and his future in the church remains in doubt.

Other than a nicely subdued performance from Sutherland, there is nothing particularly engrossing in THE ROSARY MURDERS and it is unlikely to shake anyone's faith—other than their belief in Hollywood. Although the film is based on a best-selling novel by ex-priest William X. Kienzle, its central moral dilemma is a cliche that has been seen in films ranging from Hitchcock's I CONFESS, which was based on a 1902 stage play and released in 1953, to this year's A PRAYER FOR THE DYING. The body count in this film is high and precious few victims are given any personality—thus the audience will undoubtedly have difficulty mustering any concern for Sutherland's quest. For some strange reason the face of the killer is hidden throughout the film, even though the viewer already knows his motives and identity. The clumsy scripting also fails to develop Bauer's character into anything other than an obvious sexual temptation for Sutherland. She disappears halfway through the film (after confessing to Sutherland that she sometimes has slept with more than one man at the same time), only to turn up again in the last shot to stare lustily at Sutherland while the cops are cleaning up the bloody mess they have made. Other performances are serviceable, with Durning turning in an adequate portrayal of a vulgar pastor who is less than pious when away from the altar. Director Walton does a fine job evoking some eerie moods, and cinematographer Golia captures the gloomy, somewhat spooky interiors of old Catholic churches. Unfortunately, Walton indulges in several shamelessly clunky Hitchcock *hommages*, including one where a priest walks up behind an old woman in a rocking chair and softly calls, "Mrs. Gates?" (lifted directly from the "Mrs. Bates?" scene in PSYCHO). *(Graphic violence, adult situations, profanity.)*

p, Robert G. Laurel; d, Fred Walton; w, Elmore Leonard, Fred Walton (based on the novel by William X. Kienzle); ph, David Golia; m, Bobby Laurel, Don Sebesky; ed, Sam Vitale.

Mystery **(PR:O MPAA:R)**

ROWDY POLICE† (1987, India)

Bhanuchander, Radhika.

[No plot information available.]

p, G.V. Raju; d, Mouli.

(PR:NR MPAA:NR)

ROXANNE*½** (1987) 107m COL c

Steve Martin *(Charlie "C.D." Bales)*, Daryl Hannah *(Roxanne Kowalski)*, Rick Rossovich *(Chris McDonell)*, Shelley Duvall *(Dixie)*, John Kapelos *(Chuck)*, Fred Willard *(Mayor Deebs)*, Max Alexander *(Dean)*, Michael J. Pollard *(Andy)*, Shandra Beri *(Sandy, Barmaid)*, Brian George *(Dr. David Schepisi, Cosmetic Surgeon)*, Steve Mittleman *(Ralston)*, Damon Wayans *(Jerry)*, Matt Lattanzi *(Trent)*, Blanche Rubin *(Sophie)*, Jane Campbell *(Dottie)*, Jean Sincere *(Nina)*, Claire Caplan *(Lydia)*, Thom Curley *(Jim)*, Ritch Shydner, Kevin Nealon *(Drunks)*, Maureen Murphy *(Cosmetics Clerk)*, Jeffrey Joseph *(Stationery Clerk)*, Make Glavas *(Peter Quinn)*, Merrilyn Gann *(Mrs. Quinn)*, Bernadette Sabath *(Berni)*, Caroline Barclay *(Girl in Street)*, Heidi Sorensen *(Trudy)*.

Unlike many of his comedic contemporaries, Steve Martin likes to take risks. His history of failed and successful films proves that he is forever searching to expand himself. With movies like THE JERK, ALL OF ME, PENNIES FROM HEAVEN, DEAD MEN DON'T WEAR PLAID and even his brief but brilliant cameo in LITTLE SHOP OF HORRORS, Martin continues to stretch, which is more than one can say for colleagues such as Chevy Chase, Dan Ackroyd, and Eddie Murphy. Martin served as executive producer and wrote the screenplay for this modernization of Edmond Rostand's *Cyrano de Bergerac*, a task that began years before as the script went through almost 30 variations. Taking on a classic can be treacherous. Jose Ferrer won an Oscar for his 1950 portrayal of the famed swordsman/poet and anything short of that would have been a danger. Martin wisely decided to go all the way in the comedy department, but retained the winsome, touching love story.

Martin is the fire chief in a small Northwestern town (supposedly in the state of Washington, but the film was shot in British Columbia). The town is a ski resort not unlike Aspen, Colorado, where Martin lived for many years. It's the summer off-season and Martin quickly establishes himself as a much beloved, witty, and not-easily intimidated man, despite the huge proboscis which precedes him by a few seconds. When a pair of ruffians make some comments about his schnozz, Martin dispenses with them with ease, using his tennis racket instead of Cyrano's rapier. Martin heads a comical corps of volunteer firemen, none of whom has a modicum of ability. He knows he needs a professional to help out and so he has arranged to hire Rossovich, a handsome dimwit who knows his way around hoses, but not around women. Rossovich is the equivalent of "Christian" in the original. Hannah is an astronomer who has rented a local house for the summer as she searches for a comet she just *knows* is up there. When Hannah is locked out of her house wearing not a stitch, she meets Martin, who is able to deftly climb into the house and let her in without Hannah losing a shred of her modesty. It's scant moments before we see that Martin is mad about Hannah, something he confides to pal Duvall, who runs the local coffee shop. When Duvall tells Martin that all he need do is declare himself, Martin's verbal abilities fail him. Hannah gets a look at Rossovich and falls for him. Rossovich, who hasn't much of a brain in his head, asks Martin for help in wooing Hannah and Martin agrees, albeit reluctantly. If he can't have her in the flesh, at least he can do it intellectually. Martin writes several letters to Hannah in Rossovich's name and when an actual date is to take place, Martin arranges to cue Rossovich through a short wave radio, the receiver hidden in a hat sported by Rossovich.

In the meantime, the town's mayor, Willard, is attempting to bring some business to the sleepy summer season by arranging an *Oktoberfest* for July. At a local bar, in a scene reminiscent of the famous moment when Cyrano dueled with a chevalier at the theatre, Martin listens to a man insult his nose, then proceeds to come up with two score more insults, some of which are very funny, but most of which fall short of the originals as translated by Brian Hooker for the 1950 film. In the end, Martin doesn't "thrust home," but does knock the boor unconscious. Martin continues to aid and abet Rossovich in his quest for Hannah, and even succeeds in getting the hunk into Hannah's bed. Rossovich, however, finds he has more in common with local barmaid Shandra Beri and the two of them go off together. With an assist from Duvall, Hannah learns that Martin has truly been putting words into Rossovich's mouth all along. Of course, she realizes she really loves the author of the captivating prose, and with Martin she finds the happiness and true love which eluded Cyrano and Roxane (that's right, she had just one "n" in her name) in the original story.

Many wonderful jokes which come right out of character (the best kind) dot the picture but it is, in essence, a love story and most satisfying in that respect. By making his character so downright amiable and lovable, Martin forces the audience to look past his nose and deeper into his heart. The reason he won't have his nose done is dealt with by a convenience as Martin explains that he is allergic to the anesthesia he would need for the operation. It might have been better if Martin's attitude was that he is who he is, nose and all, and there is no reason to alter what God put there. A bright, literate screenplay that sometimes descends into slapstick, the story stays close enough to the original that it pays homage, rather than rips it off. Rostand might have liked it. Director Schepisi, who made THE CHANT OF JIMMY BLACKSMITH and PLENTY, shows he is tentative in staging comedy. His work is weak, but it can't defeat the excellence of the script. Hannah's last few pictures have been abysmal performances in less-than-satisfying roles. The Chicago-born actress began with a brief bit in De Palma's THE FURY and went on to make BLADE RUNNER and several others where she played strange roles. In this movie, she is not a dumb blonde and shows a fire she hasn't demonstrated in other efforts. Nice to see Michael J. Pollard again, if only in a small role as one of the firemen. His unique face and his range of expressions add to what is an underwritten character. Special kudos to Michael Westmore (of the famed makeup family) for his excellent nose in the $14 million project. Duvall, who has been making her mark as a producer of children's tales for TV, is believable, as is Willard in a wacky role. In an era when romance seems to have taken second place to blatant sex, it's heartwarming to see a film like ROXANNE bring back the loveliness of love. *(Profanity, sexual situations.)*

p, Michael Rachmil, Daniel Melnick; d, Fred Schepisi; w, Steve Martin (based on the play "Cyrano de Bergerac" by Edmond Rostand); ph, Ian Baker (Deluxe Color); m, Bruce Smeaton; ed, John Scott; prod d, Jack DeGovia; art d, David Fischer; set d, Kimberly Richardson; cos, Richard Bruno, Tish Monaghan; spec eff, Bill Orr; m/l, Bruce Smeaton, Peter R. Melnick, Joe Curiale, Terry Cox, Jeff Kent, Paul Pesco, Jeff "Skunk" Baxter, Rick Boston; makeup, Michael Westmore; stunts, Joe Dunne, V. John Wardlow; tech adv, Bruce Meldrum.

Comedy **(PR:A-C MPAA:PG)**

RUDRABEENA† (1987, India)

Anil Chatterjee, Ranji Mullick, Tapas Paul, Madhabi Chakraborty.

After trying to change the world through education, a burned-out teacher moves to Varanasi in northern India in hopes of finding a more peaceful life. (In Bengali.)

p, Shilpi Sansad; d, Pinaki Mukherjee; m, V. Balsara.

Drama **(PR:NR MPAA:NR)**

RUMPELSTILTSKIN**½ (1987) 92m Cannon c

Amy Irving *(Katie)*, Clive Revill *(King Mezzer)*, Billy Barty *(Rumpelstiltskin)*, Priscilla Pointer *(Queen Grizelda)*, Robert Symonds *(Victor, Katie's Father)*, John Moulder-Brown *(The Prince)*, Yehuda Efroni, Johnny Phillips, Jack Messenger, Michael Schneider, Yael Uziely

Golan and Globus, who are not known for producing "soft" movies, backed this fine adaptation of the classic fairy tale. It's a family affair with Amy Irving in the lead, her brother David writing and directing, her mother, Pointer, as the queen, and her stepfather, Symonds, as the miller. The only person missing was Amy's son (by director Steven Spielberg), and he was, for a while, considered for the role of an infant. At the last minute, they decided against it.

Symonds is the local miller, a bit of a fool. He has nothing in life beyond the love of his daughter, Irving, and the many falsehoods he tells his village friends to impress them. He lies by saying Irving has the ability to turn straw into gold, and when word of that gets across the country, the avaricious king, Revill, wants to meet her. Irving is taken to the Revill's residence. Her task is to produce gold by morning. If she doesn't, Symonds will be shown to be a liar and suffer the consequences. Revill's wife, Pointer, is angered when she learns her son, Moulder-Brown, has fallen in love with Irving, who is pretty but just a common miller's daughter and thus no sutable for the prince. Irving is tossed into a dark room packed with straw, and soon Barty, an elf, appears mysteriously. He says he can help Irving with her assignment, but there is a price to pay which Irving agrees upon. The following day, the dungeon room is filled with gold. This inflames Revill's lust for the metal and further piques Pointer. Now, Irving is told she must produce the gold for three consecutive nights. Each evening, Barty appears and exacts tribute. On the final night, Irving has nothing more to offer

the devilish imp so he says she can repay him in full if he can have her firstborn. With nowhere else to turn, Irving nods a solemn yes. Having withstood the test, Irving and Moulder-Brown marry, and in a flash, she has given birth to a darling son. Barty returns to collect on the IOU, but Irving pleads with him to give her one slim chance to keep her baby. Barty considers it for a moment and allows that she can keep the child if she can guess his name. She has three days in which to discover it. In adapting the story, a few changes had to be made and the most major was the manner in which Barty's name is revealed. A young dumb girl hears the name from a raven and forces herself to speak. The filmmakers had intended the girl to play a more vocal role, but while the production was shooting in the Holy Land, they tried unsuccessfully to find a girl to play the part. Since the movie was shot on a shoestring, they thought it might be too expensive to bring someone from the States, and since none of the local girls of that age spoke English, they opted for this twist and thereby avoided having to dub the entire scene.

Producer Golan ran a children's theater in Israel at one time and always loved the genre so Cannon has produced several other fairy tales, including HANSEL AND GRETEL with Cloris Leachman, BEAUTY AND THE BEAST with Rebecca De Mornay, LITTLE RED RIDING HOOD with Isabella Rossellini as Red Riding Hood's mother, and SNOW WHITE with Diana Rigg. Billy Barty, who has been in movies for almost 50 years, is wonderfully sly, cunning, and grumpy in his role. In order to make the movie within its mini-budget, many corners were cut, but not in the sets, which were lovely. They were built near Jaffa and included a castle, a cottage, and what seemed to be an entire village. David Irving was making his debut and an auspicious one it is. There is a good tune from Max Roberts, although the picture doesn't quite qualify as being a full-fledged musical. This was Amy Irving's second time around with the elf. When she was but nine months old, she appeared on the stage in the San Francisco production of the story that was written, directed, and starred her late father, Jules Irving, who had cofounded the San Francisco Actor's Workshop (with Herbert Blau) before becoming the director of Lincoln Center's rep group in New York. A fine picture for children.

p, Menahem Golan, Yoram Globus; d&w, David Irving; ph, David Gurfinkel; m, Max Robert; ed, Tova Neeman; prod d, Marek Dobrowolski; cos, Debbie Leon.

Children's/Fantasy **Cas.** **(PR:AAA MPAA:G)**

RUNNING FROM THE GUNS† (1987, Aus.) 87m Burrowes/Hoyts c

Jon Blake *(Dave Williams)*, Mark Hembrow *(Peter)*, Nikki Coghill *(Jill)*, Terence Donovan *(Bangles)*, Bill Kerr *(Gilman)*, Peter Whitford *(Terence)*, Warwick Sims *(Martin)*, Gerard Kennedy *(Big Jim)*, Toni Lamond *(Dave's Mum)*, Greg Ross *(Mallard)*, Gus Mercurio *(Chazza)*, Ken Snodgrass *(Ocker)*, Barry Hill *(Sir Julian)*, Patrick Ward *(Mulcahy)*, Delilah *(Marathon Mandy)*, Nick Waters *(Raeburn)*, David Bickerstaff *(Cranston)*, Ray Rivamonte *(Muppet)*, James Wright *(The Chairman)*, Susie Masterton *(The Madame)*, Ben Michael *(The Apprentice)*.

A big screen good guys/bad guys picture with roots in television cops shows from first time director Dixon. Blake and Hembrow are two friends who accidentally get involved in a corrupt big business scheme when they arrive at a Melbourne dock warehouse to pick up a shipment of toys, but instead get a package meant for crime boss Kerr. Mob henchmen set out after Blake and Hembrow without realizing that the whole switcheroo was part of a master money-making plan engineered by the even more corrupt Donovan. This one includes a little bit of everything in its lean 87 minutes: comedy, car chases, romance, gangsters, sadistic murder, Vietnam vets, striking dock workers, and a barrage of rock-and-roll tunes on the soundtrack.

p, Geoff Burrowes; d&w, John Dixon; ph, Keith Wagstaff; m, Bruce Rowland; ed, Ray Daley; prod d, Leslie Binns; spec eff, Brian Pearce; stunts, Chris Anderson.

Comedy/Thriller **(PR:O MPAA:NR)**

RUNNING MAN, THE** (1987) 100m Taft-Keith Barish/Tri-Star c

Arnold Schwarzenegger *(Ben "Butcher of Bakersfield" Richards)*, Maria Conchita Alonso *(Amber Mendez, ICS Jingle Writer)*, Yaphet Kotto *(Laughlin)*, Jim Brown *(Fireball, Stalker)*, Jesse Ventura *(Captain Freedom, "Running Man" Color Commentator)*, Erland Van Lidth *(Dynamo, Stalker)*, Marvin J. McIntyre *(Weiss)*, Gus Rethwisch *(Buzzsaw, Stalker)*, Professor Toru Tanaka *(Subzero, Stalker)*, Mick Fleetwood *(Mic, Underground Resistance Leader)*, Dweezil Zappa *(Stevie, Mic's Son)*, Richard Dawson *(Damon Killian, "Running Man" Game-Show Host)*, Karen Leigh Hopkins *(Brenda, Damon's Assistant)*, Sven Thorsen *(Sven)*, Eddie Bunker *(Lenny)*, Bryan Kestner *(Med Tech)*, Anthony Penya *(Valdez)*, Kurt Fuller *(Tony)*, Kenneth Lerner *(Agent)*, Dey Young *(Amy)*, Roger Bumpass *(Don Pardo)*, Dona Hardy *(Mrs. McArdle)*, Lynne Stewart *(Edith Wiggins)*, Bill Margolin *(Leon)*, George P. Wilbur *(Lt. Saunders)*, Tom Rosales, Jr. *(Chico)*, Sondra Holt *(Suzie Checkpoint)*, Sidney Chankin *(Custodian)*, Kim Pawlik *(Newscaster)*, Roger Kern *(Travel Pass Guard)*, Barbara Lux *(Elderly Lady)*, Lin Shaye *(Propaganda Officer)*, Boyd R. Kestner *(Yuppie Yeller)*, Charlie Phillips *(Teen-Age Punk)*, Greg Lewis *(Locker Room Manager)*, John William James *(Barrio Bettor)*, Jon Cutler *(Underground Tech)*, Anthony Brubaker, Joel Kramer, Billy Lucas *(Soldiers)*, Daniel Celario, Mario Celario *(Barrio Foremen)*, Wayne Grace, Franco Columbu *(911 Security Officers)*, Kerry Brennan, Paula Brown, Megan Gallivan, Suzie Hardy, Debby Harris, Melissa Hurley, Marlene Lange, Morgan Lawley, Cindy Millican, Andrea Moen, Mary Ann Oedy, Karen Owens, Sharon Owens, Pamela Rossi, Mia Togo *(Dancers)*, Joe Leahy *(Narrator)*.

Los Angeles in the year 2017. The world has suffered total economic collapse and the US has become a police state. Television is controlled by the government and the impoverished masses are placated with violent shows like "The Hate Boat" and "Pain American Style." Most popular of all, however, is a gladiatorial game show called "The Running Man." The contestants are convicts who are made to run through a four-phase course that pits them against a variety of outlandish killers known as "Stalkers." If a contestant somehow manages to survive, his prizes are amnesty for his crimes and a condo in Hawaii. Presiding over the spectacle is Dawson, a supremely slimy game show host who is the evil genius behind the entire affair. Working closely with the Justice Department's "Entertainment Division," Dawson selects the contestants personally and is always on the lookout for someone who could boost the ratings. Schwarzenegger is just such a contestant. A former government officer who was imprisoned for refusing to slaughter unarmed rioters, Schwarzenegger has been turned into a villain by the network via reedited video tape of the incident which made it appear that he actually did kill dozens of innocent women and children, earning him the nickname "The Butcher of Bakersfield." With the help of fellow inmates Kotto and McIntyre (both members of a fledgling underground resistance), Schwarzenegger stages a daring escape from prison. Although Schwarzenegger and his comrades are soon recaptured, Dawson spots video footage of the escape on the network news and vows that the "Butcher of Bakersfield" and his friends will be his next contestants. (Kotto and McIntyre are eventually killed, but Dawson throws traitorous network employee Alonso in for romantic interest.) Unfortunately for Dawson, Schwarzenegger is more than he bargained for. This contestant makes quick work of such beloved Stalkers as "Subzero" (professional wrestler Tanaka, wielding a razor-sharp hockey stick), "Buzzsaw" (champion weightlifter Rethwisch, armed with a chainsaw), "Dynamo" (Van Lidth, lit up like a Christmas tree and shooting lightning bolts), and "Fireball" (football legend Brown with a flamethrower). Dawson is left with no choice but to call ex-Stalker-turned-color commentator Ventura out of retirement to fake an ending where Schwarzenegger loses. But even that cannot stop Schwarzenegger, who, with help from the Fleetwood and Zappa-led resistance, jams the airwaves and shows the nation the truth about the network, Dawson, and his fixed gameshow. Schwarzenegger finally corners the now-powerless Dawson and makes him play an abridged version of "The Running Man."

Based on an early novel by Stephen King (published under his "Richard Bachman" pseudonym) which borrows liberally from THE MOST DANGEROUS GAME, ROLLERBALL, THE TENTH VICTIM, and parts of Ray Bradbury's *Fahrenheit 451*, THE RUNNING MAN had a troubled production history. In 1985 the film was originally conceived as a $10 million project to star Christopher Reeve with RAMBO director George Cosmatos at the helm. When Cosmatos tried to boost the budget to more than $18 million, the producers fired him. Reeve soon moved on to other things and Schwarzenegger came aboard. Three more directors appeared and disappeared: Carl Schenkel (OUT OF ORDER), Ferdinand Fairfax (NATE AND HAYES), and Andrew Davis (CODE OF SILENCE), with Davis actually shooting for nine days before being replaced by actor-turned-director Glaser. With a bevy of television shows and one flop feature under his belt (BAND OF THE HAND), Glaser launched into production with only two days of preparation. By the time the smoke cleared, the budget had

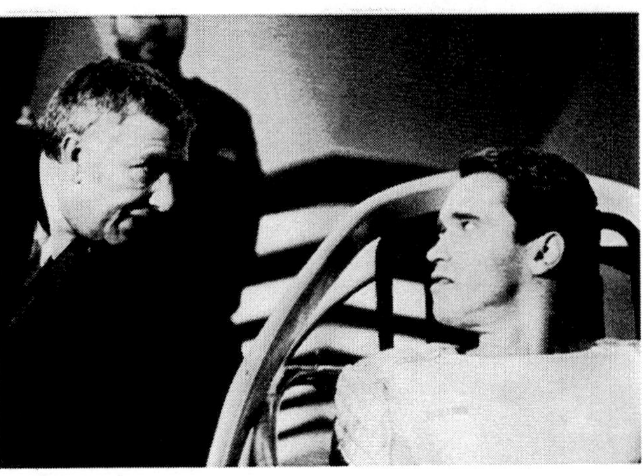

ballooned to more than $27 millon and the resulting film seems hardly worth the trouble. With a wholly derivative concept, confused scripting, and incredibly sloppy direction, THE RUNNING MAN is a frustrating experience. Where the money went is anybody's guess because it is certainly not on the screen. The sets are fairly simple, the effects are kept to a minimum, the crowd scenes are laughably sparse, the action scenes are repetitive and wholly unimaginative, and Glaser simply lets his actors flounder. Schwarzenegger can be an effective screen presence when held in check by a strong director like James Cameron in THE TERMINATOR. But when left to his own devices, Schwarzenegger's views on violence and humor can become distinctly unfunny. After every killing in THE RUNNING MAN Schwarzenegger spouts bad puns and lines cribbed from his other movies: "Can I give you a lift?" he asks as he throws a man off a catwalk; "He had to split," he says refering to a man he has just cut in half with a chainsaw; "How 'bout a light?" he queries as he blows up a man, and so on. Once or twice to break the tension is one thing, but here half his dialog is bad jokes and it can get mighty tiresome, not to mention increasingly tasteless. Kotto, Alonso, McIntyre, Brown, and Ventura's proven talents are wasted by Glaser's laziness, and Fleetwood and Zappa make terribly inauspicious movie debuts (the former is virtually unrecognizable under a ton of old-age makeup). Only Richard Dawson—brilliantly cast—redeems this mess with a superior performance. Not only does he play on the obvious identification factor from years as host of the "Family Feud" game show, but he brings a biting edge to the role that can only come from a man who has seen television's cynical manipulation of the audience first hand. Dawson contributes an intelligence and depth here not provided by the screenplay or the director and makes this film his exclusive property. His scenes have a fascinating life of their own as he alternates between smarmy game show host in front of the audience and coldly calculating, chainsmoking, abusive, show-biz brute backstage—Jerry Lewis is the only other actor who could have played this role so convincingly. Unfortunately, Dawson is the only one involved in the film who seems to really understand what it's all about. Glaser's attempts to provide a nightmarish vision of future television (one of the major strengths of ROBOCOP) lack insight and technical finesse (scenes from the beginning of the movie are regurgitated later and used shot-for-shot as "news footage," rather than fresh videotape of the same scenes shot from a different angle—a lazy cost-cutting measure that should not be seen in a $28 million movie). Technical sloppiness aside, perhaps the most basic problem with THE RUNNING MAN is that it is difficult to swallow the film's condemnation of gladiatorial violence peddled as entertainment when such violence is exactly what the filmmakers are exploiting. *(Graphic violence, profanity.)*

p, Tim Zinnemann, George Linder; d, Paul Michael Glaser; w, Steven E. de Souza (based on the novel by Richard Bachman [Stephen King]); ph, Thomas Del Ruth, Reynaldo Villalobos (Technicolor); m, Harold Faltermeyer; ed, Mark Roy Warner, Edward A. Warschilka, John Wright; prod d, Jack T. Collis; set d, Nancy Patton, Nick Navarro, Richard G. Berger, Jim Duffy; cos, Robert Blackman; ch, Paula Abdul; makeup, Jefferson Dawn, The Burman Studio; spec eff, Larry Cavanaugh, Bruce Steinheimer, Chris Casady; stunts, Bennie Dobbins.

Science Fiction **(PR:O MPAA:R)**

RUS IZNACHALNA† (1987, USSR) 142m Gorky/Sovexportfilm c (Trans: Ancient Russia)

Vladimir Antonik, Boris Nevzorov, Innokenty Smoktunovsky, Yelena Kondulainen, Lyudmila Chursina, Margarita Terekhova.

A history lesson in ancient Russia which takes place in the 6th Century as the Byzantine Empire is toppled by Slavic tribes which had united in order to defeat their enemies. A two-part film in 70mm.

d, Gennady Vasilyev; w, Gennady Vasilyev, Mikhail Vorfolomeyev; ph, Alexander Garibyan; m, Alexei Rybnikov; art d, Alfred Talantsev.

Historical **(PR:NR MPAA:NR)**

RUSSKIES* (1987) 98m New Century-Vista c

Whip Hubley *(Mischa, Russian Sailor)*, Leaf Phoenix, Peter Billingsley, Stefan DeSalle, Carole King.

Good intentions do not a good film make. Designed to counter the plethora of jingoistic Stallone, Norris, and Schwarzenegger epics that have polluted the screen in recent years, RUSSKIES presents a tale of peace, love, and understanding. Unfortunately, director Rosenthal presides over a numbingly inept film that is not only terminally contrived and stupid, but downright boring as well. Set in Key West, Florida, on the Fourth of July, the story follows three friends, two young Army brats (Phoenix and DeSalle) and the son of a conscientious-objector-turned-yuppie (Billingsley), who have been "Ramboized" by the rash of military films, toys, comics, and clothes that have become so popular in the Reagan era. On a visit to their secret hideout, the trio is shocked to discover Hubley, a shipwrecked Russian sailor. Hubley and two comrades were sent to meet an American traitor who was to sell them top-secret computer parts stolen from the local Army base, but rough weather capsized their raft and Hubley found himself alone. The distrustful boys manage to get the drop on Hubley and subdue him, leaving Billingsley to stand guard while the other two go home to tell their parents. The adults, of course, don't believe the kids, and by the time Phoenix and DeSalle return, Billingsley has made friends with the amiable Russian. Although Phoenix continues to be very wary of Hubley's "typical Commie tricks," the other boys decide to help the Russian get back to his ship. Meanwhile, Hubley's comrades also turn up onshore and decide to complete their mission. After much Americanizing of Hubley (a trip to McDonalds, preppie clothes, a romantic liaison with Billingsley's teenage sister, etc.), the boys plan to sail the homesick Russian to Cuba. Unfortunately, Hubley's comrades arrive and force him to help them steal back the computer parts. When they blunder, the Army discovers their presence and soon an all-out manhunt for the Russians is launched by an overzealous young Rambo-type officer. Much to Hubley's dismay, his comrades panic and hold the boys hostage until a Soviet submarine (which looks like it was constructed from chicken wire and paper mache) arrives to take them home. In an ending very reminiscent of THE RUSSIANS ARE COMING, THE RUSSIANS ARE COMING, young Phoenix is about to drown when Hubley, ignoring all the guns pointed at him—both American and Russian—jumps into the drink to save the boy. This act of compassion melts everyone's heart and the smiling Americans allow the smiling Russians to get in their sub and go home.

This film should have been called "Stand By Mischa." Wholly derivative of every youth film from E.T. to STAND BY ME, RUSSKIES is a mess of unabashed and unskilled audience manipulation. Screenwriter Glueckman and director Rosenthal heap on the cliches and contrivances so thickly that after a certain point the whole thing becomes comical. It's the Fourth of July; Phoenix's father was driven out of Hungary by the Commies when he was just a youngster; Billingsley's father is a liberal wimp; DeSalle's father is a tough-but-compassionate drill sergeant type; we see a copy of Tolstoy's *War and Peace*; Hubley teaches the boys to drink vodka; the boys teach him to shop; Billingsley's sister falls in love with the sailor, and he with her; the boys fend off some mean rednecks by using karate; and most of the Russian and American military are buffoons. Worst of all, Phoenix learns that his favorite superhero (on hand for the Independence Day festivities) is a pathetic alcoholic and then borrows his jet-powered backpack to zoom to Hubley's rescue. *Trust* and the world's lack thereof is a theme repeated ad nauseum. With a concept as thin as this, Rosenthal continually needs to pad his film with tedious montages of the boys showing Hubley the "good life" (basically shopping and eating) while instantly forgettable rock songs drone away on the soundtrack. There isn't even a smidgen of plausibility in any of this, but logic be damned when world peace is at stake. All the characters are cardboard and the actors fail to bring anything extra to their roles. Phoenix (brother of River) spends the entire film with a scowl on his face, Hubley looks about as Russian as your average California surfer, and singer-songwriter Carole King makes an embarrassing film debut as Phoenix's dippy mother. Simply put, this is just a bad film. Although its basic message is much easier to take than that of RED DAWN, it's not nearly as fun to watch.

p, Mark Levinson, Scott Rosenfelt; d, Rick Rosenthal; w, Allan Jay Glueckman, Sheldon Lettich, Michael Nankin; ph, Reed Smoot; spec eff, Tom Anderson, Karl Herrmann.

Drama **(PR:A MPAA:PG)**

RYKOWISKO† (1987, Pol.) 81m Zespoly Filmowe-Rondo c (Trans: The Rutting Ground)

Roman Wilhelmi *(Victor Szalaj)*, Franciszek Pieczka *(The Old Man)*, Slawomira Lozinska *(Barbara)*, Zbigniew Buczkowski *(Commando, Forest Inspector)*.

Wilhelmi is a former forest inspector who is fired and imprisoned when he is found to be operating a distillery. Wilhelmi is released to find the new inspector, Buczkowski, misusing his power by rounding up the animals and placing them in cages. The arrival of an American politician, Wilhelmi's old friend and hunting buddy, gives Wilhelmi an idea. He holds the American hostage in the old distillery and demands that the forest be governed correctly.

d, Grzegorz Skurski; w, Andrzej Mularczyk; ph, Przemyslaw Skwirczynski; m, Andrzej Kurylewicz; ed, Irena Chorynska; set d, Roman Wolyniec.

Drama **(PR:NR MPAA:NR)**

RYOMA O KITTA OTOKO† (1987, Jap.) 109m Shochiku-Fuji c (Trans: The Man Who Assassinated Ryoma)

Kenichi Hagiwara *(Tedasaburo Sasaki)*, Jinpachi Nezu *(Ryoma Sakamoto)*, Miwako Fujitani *(Yae)*, Reiko Nakamura *(Nei)*.

A battle rages between two opposing Japanese factions—the Shogun Kyoto Guard, led by master swordsman Hagiwara, and the restorationists, led by the Western-influenced intellectual Nezu. Driven into a severe state of self-criticism and remorse, Hagiwara, assassinates the opposition leader in the name of the Kyoto Guard. Hagiwara and Nezu both co-starred in Akira Kurosawa'a 1980 warrior epic KAGEMUSHA.

p, Yoshinobu Nishioka, Kinuko Kon; d, Kosaku Yamashita; w, Tsutomu Nakamura (based on the novel by Mitsugu Saotome); ph, Fujio Morita; m, Shuichi Chino; prod d, Yoshinobu Nishioka.

Action/Historical **(PR:NR MPAA:NR)**

SAKURA KILLERS† (1987, US/Taiwan) 87m Bonaire c

Chuck Connors *(The Colonel)*, Mike Kelly *(Sonny)*, George Nichols *(Dennis)*, Cara Casey *(Karen)*, Manji Otsuki *(Manji)*, John Ladalski, Brian Wong, Thomas Lung.

Essentially two films, each shot by a different director, this amalgamated martial arts adventure begins in the US and then shifts to Taiwan. In the first half, written and directed by Nelson, a top secret videotape with information about genetic engineering research is stolen from American scientists. The valuable information has been nabbed by Ninjas who are working in the service of the Sakura family, an arm of the Japanese mob, and Connors dispatches Nichols and Kelly to Taiwan to recover the videotape. In the Ward-directed Taiwanese portion of the film, Kelly and Nichols come under the tutelage of a martial arts master and, well-prepared, get the best of the "Sakura killers," preventing them from selling the videotape to the Soviets.

p, K.L. Lim, Roy McAree; d, Richard Ward, Dusty Nelson; w, David Marks, Dusty Nelson; ph, Alan Brennecke (United Color); m, William Scott.

Martial Arts **Cas.** **(PR:NR MPAA:NR)**

SALE DESTIN!† (1987, Fr.) 95m Solus-Flach-Selena-Films A2/AAA c (Trans: Rotten Fate!)

Victor Lanoux *(Francois Marboni)*, Pauline Lafont *(Rache)*, Marie Laforet *(Marthe Marboni)*, Jacques Penot *(Alexandre Ragueneau)*, Michel Aumont *(Inspector Marchandon)*, Martin Lamotte *(Denis)*, Jean-Francois Stevenin *(Djebel Zanera)*, Aurelle Doazan *(Estelle Marboni)*, Jean-Paul Lillienfeld, Claude Chabrol, Charlotte de Turckheim.

Bleak French comedy features Lanoux as a butcher in a bind. The affair he has been carrying on with a hooker, LaFont, is in danger of being revealed to his wife, Laforet, if he doesn't satisfy the demands of blackmailers. Rather than capitulate, Lanoux takes the offensive and hires a professional killer (Stevenin) to rid him of his nemeses. His problem has only escalated, however, because the killer decides to add extortionist to his criminal resume. Directed by Sylvain Madigan, who is best known for his short films.

p, Jean-Marie Duprez, Pascal Hommais, Jean-Francois Lepetit; d, Sylvain Madigan; w, Sylvain Madigan, Michel Wichegrod, Jean-Paul Lillienfeld; ph, Patrick Blossier (Eastmancolor); m, Pascal Arroyo; ed, Dominique B. Martin; art d, Robert Nardone.

Comedy **(PR:NR MPAA:NR)**

SALVATION!½** (1987) 80m B Movies/Circle c (AKA: SALVATION! HAVE YOU SAID YOUR PRAYERS TODAY?)

Stephen McHattie *(Rev. Edward Randall)*, Dominique Davalos *(Lenore Finley)*, Exene Cervenka *(Rhonda Stample)*, Viggo Mortensen *(Jerome Stample)*, Rockets Redglare *(Oliver)*, Billy Bastiani *(Stanley)*.

In 1987, television evangelism suffered a scandalous fall from grace, and when so-called holy wars blanketed the media, this black comedy by idiosyncratic independent filmmaker Beth B. was waiting with a prescient look at the world of C.O.D. salvation. In the headlines, Jim and Tammy Faye Bakker, the first family of the PTL Christian television network, were forced to hand over the reins of their multimillion-dollar ministry/enterprise to fellow small-screen evangelist Jerry Falwell when it was revealed that the bible-college sweethearts had strayed far from the path of righteousness. Rev. Bakker had frolicked with one of his flock, and his wife had a drug problem (and the misfortune to have posed as a scantily clad dance-hall girl for a photograph that found its way into print).

SALVATION! paints its picture of sordid duplicity on a broader canvas, beginning with a domestic scene that Norman Rockwell would have fled in disgust. Looking as if he has crawled from beneath a rock, sleazy, beer-swilling Mortensen plays more than footsie with his slatternly sister-in-law Davalos. Oblivious to this carrying on, his wife, Cervenka (poet and vocalist for seminal L.A. hardcore rock band X), is blissfully transfixed by the TV preaching of McHattie. With bug-eyed, southern-fried charisma, the reverend makes fire-and-brimstone pronouncements, including a discourse on New York City's immoral majority of non-Christian heathens (atheists, Jews, and Catholics). Cervenka clearly buys into his program (and has done so literally, like the tens of thousands of others who support his ministry with their contributions). Davalos and Mortensen are unconvinced but not unaffected. Mortensen leaves for his factory job, where he is told that he has been fired. Later, in his super-secure, well-appointed manse, McHattie prepares for his next sermon by watching pornographic slides. Outside, Davalos, wearing a blonde wig and as alluring as ever, knocks desperately on his door. She tells McHattie that she has car trouble and he reluctantly lets her in. Once inside, she sets about seducing him. He is both repulsed and overcome with lust, and after a wild struggle, they end up upstairs. They are interrupted by Redglare and Bastiani, who have arrived at the front door because they have heard a "party" is taking place. Davalos' cries filter downstairs, but McHattie is able to dismiss the odd duo. He then savagely forces himself upon Davalos—though it appears she is not entirely unwilling—losing himself in a reverie of wild sexual fantasy filled with skewed religious imagery.

The holy rolling complete, Davalos crumples into unconsciousness. Is she dead? Before McHattie can find out, he is set upon by Mortensen, who has broken in, caught the reverend red-handed, and pummels him, eventually dragging him to the beach. Revived, Davalos seemingly prevents the drowning of McHattie. Redglare and Bastiani are back on the scene; McHattie has been setup. A prisoner in his own home, he attempts to escape by climbing down the huge neon cross in front of his house, but is recaptured. Blackmail is Mortensen's game and he won't be satisfied until McHattie makes Cervenka co-pastor of his "living room" parish and Mortensen the beneficiary of half of the donations. After ostensibly agreeing, McHattie makes another attempt to free himself, trying the neon cross again, but crashing to the ground when it gives way. Scampering to his feet, he makes it to the road, where Cervenka picks him in her car. Some time later, Cervenka has become Tammy Faye to McHattie's Jim, but with a twist. In an attempt to redeem youthful sinners, Cervenka employs the devil's music for God's work. She is a big hit and the coffers overflow. McHattie increasingly gives in to temptation, though he never reaches the level of dissipation achieved by Mortensen and his cronies, whom McHattie and Cervenka finally see given the heave-ho. In the final scene, the pneumatic, sexily clad Cervenka delivers the ultimate "Destroy All Evil" sermon as a heavy metal rave-up.

This is Beth B.'s first 35mm film, after a career of 16mm and super-8 avant-garde filmmaking. Made on a budget of $800,000—her biggest to date—it has the stylized look of a rock video. (In fact, SALVATION! includes a music video B. made earlier for Davalos' "Dominatrix Sleeps Tonight.") B.'s camera is often in motion, but it seldom calls attention to itself. Hers is not style for style's sake, though arguably the film is occasionally a little short on content. The characters are not as well developed as they might have been and as a result the tongue-in-cheek insights B. provides into the phenomenon of television evangelism are limited. This, however, is a trap in which those working in satire are often caught, and SALVATION! is frequently a very funny movie. Nonetheless, B. suggests that there is repressed sexuality and violence co-existing with greed beneath the surface piety of the evangelist that threatens to burst forth in a variety of bizarre ways. Judging by the headlines of 1987, this is hardly implausible.

The performances are generally good, with special kudos for McHattie, who is more than suitably tortured and tempted. Cervenka is less successful. Although her initial zombielike obsession with McHattie's tele-sermons is convincing, her range is limited, and she is best after her transformation into the rock priestess. It should be pointed out, however, that she *is* acting in those scenes, conveying a character distinct from her front-person role with X. The film is hampered by an overly compact plot and some choppy transitions, apparently the result of a flawed screenplay rather than the editing. Songs include: "Sputnik," "Skullcrusher," "Let's Go," "Salvation! Theme," "Touched by the Hand of God" (New Order, performed by New Order), "Nightmare" (written and performed by Arthur Baker and The Hood), "Cooler Than Thou" (The Hood, Mosimann, performed by The Hood), "Play the Beat" (Nicki Camp, Dominique Davalos, performed by Dominique), "Jesus Saves" (Cabaret Voltaire, performed by Cabaret Voltaire), "Salvation! Have You Said Your Prayers Today?" (The Hood, performed by The Hood), "Come On" (Baker, Angelo), "Unanswered Prayer" (Baker, Stu Kimball, Charlie Ferran, performed by Baker), "You Can't Blackmail Jesus" (Baker, Kimball, performed by Jumpin' Jesus), "Sermon Score" (Richard Scher, performed by Scher), "Land of the Free" (Baker, Andy B.), "Destroy All Evil" (Nicki Camp, Beth B., performed by Dominique, Pamela Roman). *(Profanity, brief nudity, violence.)*

p, Beth B., Michael H. Shamberg; d, Beth B.; w, Beth B., Tom Robinson; ph, Francis Kenny; ed, Elizabeth Kling; prod d, Lester Cohen; art d, Jessica Lanier; set d, Sermin Kardestuncer; cos, Tanya Seeman, Pamela Goldman, Karen Von Oppen; spec eff, David Dumont; m/l, New Order, Arthur Baker, The Hood, Mosimann, Nicki Camp, Dominique Davalos, Cabaret Voltaire, Angelo, Stu Kimball, Charlie Ferran, Richard Scher, Andy B., Beth B.; makeup, Debra Reece, Karen Ragozzine, Chris Bingham; stunts, Jeffrey Lee Gibson.

Comedy **(PR:O MPAA:NR)**

SAMAYA OBAYATELNAYA I PRIVLEKATELNAYA† (1987, USSR) 85m Mosfilm/Sovexportfilm c (Trans: The Most Charming and Attractive)

Irina Muravyova, Tatyana Vasilyeva, Alexandr Abdulov, Leonid Kuravlyov.

A sociologist decides to use her training to systematically come up with a husband for a friend in this Soviet comedy. The social engineer is determined that the rather plain woman hook up with only the finest of the species and gives her a crash course in self-hypnosis to convince her that she is the "most charming and attractive" woman available. Once the hunt for the perfect man is complete, they set about bagging him.

d, Gerald Bezhanov; w, Anatoly Eiramdzhan, Gerald Bezhanov; ph, Valentin Piganov; m, Vladimir Rubashevsky; art d, Evgeny Vinnitzky.

Comedy **(PR:NR MPAA:NR)**

SAME TO YOU** (1987, Ger./Switz) 90m Kanguruh-Filmkollektiv/Metropolis b&w (DU MICH AUCH; AKA: SO WHAT?)

Anja Franke *(Julia)*, Dani Levy *(Romeo)*, Jens Naumann *(Gigolo)*, Mathias Gnadinger *(Romeo's Father)*, Regine Lutz *(Romeo's Mother)*, Helma Fehrmann *(Madame)*, Karleen Rutherford *(Sunshine)*, Michael Kesting *(Small Bodyguard)*, Hans-Eckart Eckhardt *(Big Bodyguard)*, Ruth Fahlke *(Woman in Bath)*.

A modest independent that gained fairly widespread attention on the festival circuit, SAME TO YOU concerns a pair of musicians, Franke and Levy, whose romance has lost its sparkle and who are looking for a way to end it without too much pain. Levy storms out of the apartment one day and goes to a brothel, where his attempt at sex with a black prostitute is unsuccessful. Later he gets a

message from Franke to join her for a gig at a 50th wedding anniversary. There they play dance tunes, tell jokes, and do scenes while Franke is given the eye by a handsome American in a white dinner jacket. They argue in the bathroom and a woman who has been hidden in the tub drinking champagne gives them the address of a couple she knows who are still in love after decades of marriage. Back out in the party, the two are about to do the balcony scene from "Romeo and Juliet" when suddenly the lights go out. There is a scream, the lights go back up, and the hostess is lying at Levy's feet with a knife in her. Levy bends over to pick up the knife and immediately the whole crowd is after them. Levy and Franke manage to escape the American, who turns out to be a killer, and make their way back home. There, however, they see the police waiting outside, so they are forced to sleep on the streets that night. They go looking for the old couple the woman in the tub told them about, but with no luck. They do, however, meet a man who is locked in his apartment, having thrown the key out the window while planning suicide but then thinking better of the idea. They go to Levy's parents' apartment, where they celebrate his birthday with a huge meal. In her saxophone, Franke finds the reason for the murder, a roll of Super-8 film showing a prominent politician with the same prostitute Levy had visited. Back at their apartment, they are just waking up when the American and his colleagues arrive to search the place. Levy manages to escape out the window, but Franke is taken back to the brothel where she is left under the guard of the prostitute. Levy steals a car to follow them and finds a pistol in the glove compartment. After Franke is rescued with little difficulty, they return to their apartment to get a few things before lighting out to sunny Italy. They get to horsing around on the bed, though, and pretty soon the killer comes in and shoots them both dead.

Shot in grainy, jerky, black-and-white and obviously largely improvised (the two leads get screenplay credit, along with the director), the film certainly possesses some charm. Franke and Levy are a pleasant enough couple as their romance is recharged despite (or because of) the danger, but if ever the category Too-Stupid-To-Live applied to anyone, these are the people. They are relentlessly careless, and the inevitable final murder seems more like a mercy killing to put these fools out of their misery. *(Sexual situations, violence.)*

d&w, Helmut Berger, Anja Franke, Dani Levy; ph, Carl Friedrich Koschnick; m, Nicki Reiser; prod d, Marion Strohschein.

Comedy/Drama **(PR:O MPAA:NR)**

SAMMY AND ROSIE GET LAID*½** (1987, Brit.) 100m Cinecom Intl.-Film Four/Cinecom c

Shashi Kapoor *(Rafi Rahman)*, Claire Bloom *(Alice)*, Ayub Khan Din *(Sammy)*, Frances Barber *(Rosie Hobbs)*, Roland Gift *(Danny/Victoria)*, Wendy Gazelle *(Anna)*, Suzette Llewellyn *(Vivia)*, Meera Syal *(Rani)*, Badi Uzzaman *(Ghost)*.

Director Frears and screenwriter Kureishi team again to follow the international success of MY BEAUTIFUL LAUNDRETTE with another scathing indictment of Prime Minister Thatcher's Britain. Their vision of London is a surrealistic nightmare of riots, bombed-out buildings, burning cars, interracial relationships, and rampant sexuality. Definitely not the merry England of old, it is a cynical, apocalyptic look at life under Thatcher's rule. The film opens with portions of Thatcher's speech after her third election victory, and while she calls for renewed efforts to end unemployment and urban blight on the soundtrack, the visuals ironically show her failed attempts. In the midst of this Beirut-styled battle zone live Samir, or Sammy (Din), and Rosie (Barber), a married couple in their late twenties who lead a yuppie existence but find it fashionable to live in a ghetto. Din is an accountant who snorts cocaine and listens to Shostakovich, Barber is a social worker who is writing a book entitled *The Intelligent Woman's Guide to Kissing in History*, and together they thrive on the "affirmation of the human spirit" that their oppressed neighbors express in their class struggle. They are a liberal young couple whose socio-political beliefs are reflected in their marriage—for theirs is a relationship based on "freedom plus commitment." In practice, that means that they sleep with whomever they want whenever they want, but they are still deeply in love with each other. Din's favorite extramarital lover is Gazelle, a free-spirited photojournalist from New York who is working on an exhibition called "Images of a Decaying Europe," while Barber's lover is Gift, a quiet black squatter who lives in a trailer painted over with poetry. Into this amoral world comes Din's father, Kapoor, whom he has not seen in years. Forced out of Pakistan by his political allies, Kapoor returns to an England he has not seen in years and one which does not live up to his memories. Having made a fortune in his political dealings, Kapoor has returned to transfer his wealth into his son's account. His only condition is that Din and Barber buy a house in a civilized part of England that "isn't twinned with Beirut" and that they supply him with a grandson. His other reason for returning to England is to rekindle a romance with Bloom, an "extremely white" (his description) woman whom he loved as a young man but later deserted. Syal, a lesbian Pakistani friend of Barber's, digs into Kapoor's past and learns that he was a corrupt, fascist official who murdered and tortured anyone who opposed him. Although he may have been a monster in his homeland, Kapoor comes across as genteel and charming to his son and daughter-in-law. Din, whose liberal political beliefs apparently pertain only to his neighbors, is complacent about father's wicked past. In fact, he begins to see his father as a means of escaping his present life-style. He envisions a different life for himself—a house in a civilized part of town, children, and an end to the sanctioned adultery of his marriage. Barber, however, enjoys the "spark" of her other lovers. During a party, Barber runs off with Gift, and Din grows increasingly jealous. ("Jealousy is wickeder than adultery," preaches Barber.) After the party ends, Kapoor stays with Bloom and, having nowhere else to go, Din sleeps with Gazelle. In the film's lightest, most celebratory scene, all three couples make love in their respective beds. Briskly edited with increasingly frantic cross-cutting, the three-cornered love scene is accompanied by the old Motown song "My Girl" (Smokey Robinson, Ronald White). Adding to the surreal quality of the film is a group of reggae singers, The Ghetto Lites, who stand outside Gift's trailer and sing their soulful version of the song. The scene ends with a horizontal split-screen showing all three couples on screen simultaneously, layered one above the other. The decline of the British empire proves too much for everybody, especially Kapoor and Din, who are both caught between two worlds. Kapoor's daily routine grows increasingly bizarre as he is haunted by a Pakistani specter—a victim of torture who wears a head bandage and sports a bloody, empty eye socket. He is the past, the "Marley's ghost" that rattles chains of guilt and drives Kapoor to the edge. The picture then ends as Kapoor hangs himself in his bedroom, leaving Din and Barber sitting in the middle of their apartment cradled in each other's arms and crying.

SAMMY AND ROSIE GET LAID, the second Frears-Kureishi collaboration, is a triumph of biting satire that approaches Kureishi's stated aim to "get as much filth and anarchy into the cinema as possible." An outspoken opponent of Margaret Thatcher's right-wing politics, Kureishi attacks her Britain on all fronts. In SAMMY AND ROSIE GET LAID, Thatcher's Britain, contrary to her belief, is not all royal weddings, Westminster Abbey, and Buckingham Palace. Instead, London is characterized by its unemployment, suffering, discontent, racial prejudice (the riots begin when an older black woman is mistakenly killed by an overzealous police officer), and hypocritical sexual stands. Thatcher's parliamentary address promises to put an end to urban blight, and Kureishi illustrates her method in a scene in which the squatters, instead of receiving assistance, are bulldozed out of their makeshift homes by city workers who are backed by money hungry, opportunistic real estate developers. Essentially this is a screenwriter's film (the opening credits read: SAMMY AND ROSIE GET LAID by Hanif Kureishi), which is, in one respect, its fault and a fault that also befalls MY BEAUTIFUL LAUNDRETTE. In an effort to retain Kureishi's often overly literary style, the filmmaking itself suffers. Although there are some brilliant directorial touches, the film is never as anarchic as one would expect. It is the dialog that has bite in SAMMY AND ROSIE GET LAID, not the filmmaking, and, with only a few exceptions, the ideas would be just as pointed if they were printed instead of filmed. While director Frears is clearly a prolific and immense talent (he has released THE HIT, MY BEAUTIFUL LAUNDRETTE, and PRICK UP YOUR EARS in less than four years—all of them critically acclaimed) he hasn't yet produced that unqualified masterpiece that seems to be lurking at the edges of his previous films. He must, however, be commended for his continual display of gutsiness in his choice of material and his decision to remain within the liberating limitations of low-budget filmmaking. (This film was made for $2 million—a miniscule budget for a director who could command much more, but one which enables him to turn a profit more easily.)

In addition to the no-holds-barred scripting and the craftsmanlike direction, the film is filled with excellent performances (as is MY BEAUTIFUL LAUNDRETTE). Din, who had a small part in the previous Frears-Kureishi collaboration, is marvelous as he gradually sheds his desensitized observer facade to face his father's past and his country's future. Barber, a plainly pretty Englishwoman who appeared in Nicolas Roeg's CASTAWAY and in WHITE CITY, the hour-long Pete Townshend music video, is equally talented and brings a likable quality to a character who is often despicable. Rounding out the cast are the venerable Indian matinee idol Kapoor, who here sheds his romantic image; the accomplished Bloom, who is warm and maturely sexy as Kapoor's former love interest and his symbolic connection with old England; the perky Gazelle, whose crass American opportunism is played with an innocent tone; and Gift (the lead singer of the British band Fine Young Cannibals), a handsome actor with a sculpted face whose initially mysterious character unfortunately grows less interesting as the film progresses. As if the subject matter wasn't controversial and offensive enough, the title alone caused a stir. Deemed "salacious" (oddly, PRICK UP YOUR EARS received no such condemnation) by the Motion Picture Association of America (MPAA), it was denied registration, thereby leaving it unprotected from copyright infringement. For the first time in the MPAA's half-century history, an MPAA member—Cinecom, the film's distributor—resigned from the association, leaving all other upcoming Cinecom film titles unregistered. The only noticeable effect can be seen in the film's print ads, many of which have obscured the last two words of the title. The resulting ad reads only SAMMY AND ROSIE, leaving the bottom half of the title appearing as if it has been ripped from the ad. *(Brief nudity, sexual situations, drug use, excessive profanity, violence.)*

p, Tim Bevan, Sarah Radclyffe; d, Stephen Frears; w, Hanif Kureishi; ph, Oliver

Stapleton; m, Stanley Myers; ed, Mick Audsley; prod d, Hugo Lyczyc Wyhowski; cos, Barbara Kidd.

Drama **(PR:O MPAA:R)**

SAMSARAM OKA CHADARANGAM (1987, India)

Sarat Babu, Suhasini.

A family that has been split apart is reunited through the efforts of a diligent daughter-in-law. (In Telugu.)

p, M. Balasubramaniam, M.S. Guhan, M. Saravanar; d, S.P. Mutteraman.

(PR:NR MPAA:NR)

SAPPORO STORY† (1987, Hong Kong) 98m D&B-Loong Hsiang/D&B c

Su Ming Ming, Olivia Cheng.

This feature from Hong Kong takes yet another look at the sad, sordid life of women who have been forced into prostitution and are unable to free themselves from its hold. Ming is from Taiwan, Cheng is from Hong Kong, and both have ended up in Japan and, for different reasons, have turned to hooking. Ming has turned pro to please the pimp she has fallen for and Cheng is turning tricks because she has built up a huge gambling debt. Deep down, both just want to go home, but instead their fortunes continue to decline as they move from plying their trade in fancy nightclubs to a provincial cat house. (In Cantonese and Japanese; English and Chinese subtitles.)

p, Wang Hing Hsiang, John Sham, Wong Wah Kay; d, Wong Wah Kay.

Drama **(PR:NR MPAA:NR)**

SARABA ITOSHIKI HITO YO† (1987, Jap.) 102m Shochiku Fuji-Burning c (Trans: The Heartbreak Yakuza)

Hiromi Go *(Shuji)*, Mariko Ishihara *(Hitomi)*, Kazuya Kimura *(Tetsuo)*, Koichi Sato *(Yoshimasa)*, Reiko Nanjo *(Yumiko)*, Daisuke Shima *(Mashiba)*, Kaku Takashina *(Nitta)*, Akira Emoto *(Kato)*, Rikiya Yasuoka *(Kiuchi)*, Chin Naito *(Restaurant Manager)*, Yuya Uchida *(Officer Yamamura)*.

Violent and sentimental *yakusa* film starring Japanese pop idol Hiromi Go as a soft-hearted mob hit man who makes the mistake of sparing the life of one of the rival mobsters (Rikiya Yasuoka) he was supposed to kill in a gangland massacre. The survivor of the shootout immediately plots his revenge on Go, despite the fact that the heads of the rival gangs are in the midst of negotiating a peace. Meanwhile, Go spots his long-lost childhood sweetheart, Mariko Ishihara, working as a hotel waitress at the wedding reception of his boss's daughter. Although he tries to stay away from her because he is now a bad man, Go eventually falls back into love with the sweet and innocent Ishihara. Advised to stay underground because Yasuoka is gunning for him, Go ignores the advice and takes Ishihara dancing at a popular *yakuza* night spot. There they are ambushed and both severely wounded in withering gunfire. The couple survive their wounds, but Go is permanently blinded. Rejecting his life of crime for the love of Ishihara, Go vows to leave the mob, but not before settling a few scores. Director Harada is a devotee of American filmmakers Sam Fuller and Sam Peckinpah and the musical score for this film, composed by Toshihiro Nakanishi, harkens back to the scores Ennio Morricone wrote for Sergio Leone.

p, Yoshinori Moniwa; d&w, Masato Harada; ph, Junichi Fujisawa; m, Toshihiro Nakanishi; ed, Tomoyo Oshima; art d, Yuji Maruyama.

Crime **(PR:NR MPAA:NR)**

SASHSHENNYI FONAR† (1987, USSR) 88m Armenfilm-Studio A-Bek Nasarian/Mosfilm c (Trans: The Lit Lantern)

Vladimir Kotscharian *(Vano)*, Violetta Geworkian *(Vera)*, Absalom Loria *(Merktum)*, Leonid Sarkisov *(Gasparelli)*, Genrich Alaverdian, Karlos Martirosian, Manvel Dawlabetkian, J. Grabbe, A. Belliawski, M. Gluski, V. Ferapontov.

Made in 1983 but receiving its first Western showing at the 1987 Berlin Film Festival, this Soviet meditation on the artist's role in society is only the second film directed by Armenian painter Agassi Aivasian. Kotscharian plays an artist who manages a store for its wealthy owner. Instead of concentrating on the operation of the shop, he occupies himself with sketches or loses himself in aesthetic reverie. As a result, the store's owner, Loria, fires him, much to the disappointment of Kotscharian's wife. At the prompting of friends, Kotscharian tries to win back his job by giving Loria a painting he has done. Loria is touched and welcomes back Kotscharian only to give him the sack again for another transgression.

d&w, Agassi Aivasian; ph, Levon Atoyanz; m, Tigran Mansurian; ed, I. Mikaelian; art d, Grigor Torosian, W. Panosian; cos, S. Tonoian.

Drama **(PR:NR MPAA:NR)**

SATURDAY NIGHT AT THE PALACE** (1987, South Africa) 88m Davnic c

Bill Flynn *(Forcie)*, John Kani *(September, Head Waiter)*, Paul Slabolepszy *(Vince)*, Joanna Weinberg.

Based on a play by Paul Slabolepszy, who also wrote the screenplay and stars here, this film presents a look at the turmoil in South Africa. Slabolepszy plays an unemployed racist lout, whose obnoxious behavior and failure to pay his share of the rent cause his housemates to decide to toss him out. The task of telling Slabolepszy falls on his best friend, Flynn, a milquetoast who idolizes Clint Eastwood. In another part of Johannesburg, Kani, a black man, prepares for his last shift at Rocco's Burger Palace before traveling to his Zulu homeland to see his family, whom he has been away from for two years. The film cuts back and forth between these characters as Kani carries out his duties as the drive-in's crew chief and the white men go to a party, where Flynn makes shy conversation with a woman only to have her disappear into the back seat of a car for a romp with the drunken Slabolepszy. Later, with Slabolepszy as a passenger, Flynn heads home on his motorcycle, but stops at the nearly deserted Rocco's, claiming engine trouble. The truth is he doesn't want to tell his friend that he has been kicked out and tries to get him to phone one of the other housemates to receive the news. Meanwhile, Kani, the last person left at Rocco's, is trying to close up. When the pay phone doesn't work and Kani refuses to serve him (insisting that the drive-in is closed), Slabolepszy turns hostile and directs his pent-up wrath toward the black man. Slabolepszy manages to get hold of Kani's keys and begins tearing up Rocco's. Flynn sympathizes with Kani, but other than making a few discouraging comments, he does nothing to stop Slabolepszy. After being thoroughly humiliated, Kani attacks Slabolepszy, but doesn't slit his throat when the opportunity arises. Later, while staging an arm-wrestling contest for the keys, Slabolepszy, who now knows that he has lost his home, claps Kani into the handcuffs Flynn uses as a lock for his motorcycle. The vicious racist continues to taunt Kani, and when Flynn's protests grow more vehement, Slabolepszy tells him that he's had his way with the woman that Flynn was so fond of at the party. In a rage, Flynn grabs Kani's knife and stabs and kills Slabolepszy. As the realization of what he has done hits him, the panicked Flynn decides to pin the murder on Kani. "It's not my fault. I didn't do anything," Flynn cries before running off.

The political message of SATURDAY NIGHT AT THE PALACE is obvious. With the main characters functioning as representatives of the three factions of South African society, the tragedy of apartheid is played out in microcosm at Rocco's Burger Palace. The symbolism is transparent. Slabolepszy is the heinous proponent of apartheid, Kani is his and its victim, and Flynn represents those South Africans who may be opposed to the institutionalized class system but whose passive acceptance of it allows it to continue. Flynn's final words are an indictment of this latter group. It *is* their fault precisely because they haven't done anything. The problem with the film is not its intent or its political analysis; it is that the characters are such obvious symbols. There is little depth to any of them and as a result the conflicts between them are not as compelling or tension-filled as they should be. While it is difficult to argue with Slabolepszy's portrayal of Vince as an unredeemable monster, a more complex depiction might have been more enlightening. Kani, on the other hand, is too decent, too perfect. Black South Africans in the plays of Athol Fugard ("Master Harold and the Boys," "A Lesson From the Aloes") are real people with both good and bad characteristics and because of this their trampled dignity and their struggles to overcome the inhumanity perpetrated upon them affect us much more profoundly. Though Flynn is somewhat complex, he is still more a *study* in contradictions than a man with contradictory feelings. Though director Davies has taken great pains to avoid merely filming a stage play—particularly in the cinematic elements he introduces in the opening section before the conflict at the drive-in—SATURDAY NIGHT AT THE PALACE is occasionally caught with its theatrical roots showing. Too often the dialog has the well-formed quality that works on stage but that calls too much attention to itself in film. Slabolepszy's play was produced in London's West End and a number of European cities as well as in South Africa. The film was shown at US festivals in 1987. *(Profanity, violence.)*

p&d, Robert Davies; w, Paul Slabolepszy, Bill Flynn (based on the play by Paul Slabolepszy); ph, Robert Davies (Irene color); m, Johnny Cleff; ed, Lena Farugia, Carla Sandrock; art d, Wayne Attrill, Sandy Attrill.

Drama **(PR:C MPAA:NR)**

SCHLOSS & SIEGEL† (1987, Ger.) 80m Frankfurt Filmwerkstatt/Export c (Trans: Lock & Seal)

Karl-Heinz Maslo *(Michael)*, Christiane Carstens *(Babsi)*, Susanne Bredehoft *(Andy)*, Geraldine Blecker *(Susan)*, Gerd Knebel *(Klaus)*, Karl Heuer *(Gerd)*.

Scripted by British actress/singer Geraldine Blecker, who based the story on her personal experiences with the West German penal system, this bittersweet comedy presents the unlikely romance between a pair of prison inmates. No, not the usual unlikely romance between prison inmates: These two are incarcerated in different prisons and know each other only as pen pals. *He* is Maslo, a convict who has become a jailhouse lawyer, and *She* is the diminutive Carstens. After falling in love with each other through their letters, all they want of the penal system is a chance to meet, and the film details their efforts to persuade prison officials to allow them to do that. Ultimately, they win two fleeting, supervised hours together. Transferred from 16mm to 35mm, this is the first feature film for director Ulmke.

p, Michael Smeaton; d, Heidi Ulmke; w, Geraldine Blecker, Heidi Ulmke; ph, Jorg Jeshel; m, Peter W. Schmitt; ed, Susanne Hartmann; art d, Klaus Wischmann.

Comedy/Drama **(PR:NR MPAA:NR)**

SCUOLA DI LADRI 2† (1987, It.) C.G. Silver-Maura/CDI (Trans: School for Thieves 2)

Paolo Villaggio *(Dalmazio Siraghi)*, Massimo Boldi *(Egisto Siraghi)*, Enrico Maria Salerno *(Uncle)*, Florence Guerin *(Susanna)*.

Villaggio and Boldi re-create their original roles as the Siraghi cousins, a pair of ineffectual thieves, in this sequel to the crime comedy SCUOLA DI LADRI (1986). As the film opens, Boldi has been released from a mental institution and Villaggio has been freed from prison. The first order of business is hooking up with another cousin, but when they go to meet him, they find Guerin, his daughter, in his place. Not much later, their uncle, Salerno—who prepared the cousins for a heist and then made off with the loot himself in the original—appears on the scene. With Salerno and Guerin acting as the brains of the outfit, the cousins are back in the robbery game. They blow an armored-car holdup; however, they are luckier with a train robbery and the spoils from it make it possible for them to undertake a big operation, the shipboard theft of some jewels. Villaggio and Boldi nab the precious stones, but Salerno and Guerin make off with them. At the film's end, though, it appears as if the inept cousins are closer to the jewels then Salerno and Guerin would ever guess.

d, Neri Parenti; w, Laura Toscano, Franco Marotta, Neri Parenti; ph, Alessandro d'Eva; m, Bruno Zambrini; ed, Sergio Montanari.

Comedy/Crime **(PR:NR MPAA:NR)**

SDELKA† (1987, USSR) 87m Central Studios of Films for Children and Youth/Sovexportfilm c (Trans: The Deal)

Elgudzha Burduli, Boris Plotnikov, Giya Lezhava, Vladimir Soshalsky.

Translated as "The Deal," this Soviet feature set in Latin America focuses on the agreement that is struck between a rebel leader in exile and a truck driver. Their homeland is ruled by a military junta and the leader has done his best to advance the struggle against the oppressive regime from the safety of a neighboring country, but events necessitate his clandestine return. He cuts a deal with the trucker to allow him to make one of the daily freight runs between the two countries so that he can enter his homeland undetected. Promised a large payment, the driver agrees, but more than that, he also comes to know and respect the political leader, and, moved by his bravery and conviction, the trucker dedicates his life to the struggle.

d, Mikahil Vedyshev; w, Remiz Fataliev; ph, Mikhail Yakovitch; m, Rivas Arancibia, Nelson Adonias; art d, Anatoly Anfilov.

Drama **(PR:NR MPAA:NR)**

SEA AND POISON, THE† (1987, Jap.) 121m Sea and Poison Committee/Nippon Herald bw (UNI TO DOKUYAKU)

Eiji Okuda *(Suguro)*, Ken Watanabe *(Toda)*, Mikio Narita *(Shibata)*, Ken Nishida *(Asai)*, Shigeru Kamiyama *(Prof. Gondo)*, Masumi Okada *(Hattori [Investigator])*, Kyoko Kishida *(Old Woman)*, Kie Nigishi *(Ueda)*, Hiroshi Kusano *(Tanaka)*, Rancho Tsuji *(Mural)*, Masatane Tsugayama *(Miyasaki)*, Yuimi Kuroki *(Mrs. Tabe)*, Akiko Togawa *(Her Mother)*, Mariko Oishi *(Her Sister)*, Maria Watanabe *(Hilda)*, Eagle Galley *(American Prisoner)*, Takahiro Tamura *(Prof. Hashimoto)*.

Described as "harrowing" by many a critic who has seen it, Japanese director Kei Kumai's film SEA AND POISON investigates a long-buried incident in recent Japanese history that many would prefer to be forgotten. Based on a novel written about the case in 1948 by author Shusaku Endo (who refused to let the issue die), the film dramatizes horrific medical experiments performed during WW II on eight healthy American B-29 crewmen at the University Hospital at Kyushu in 1945. The story unfolds shortly after WW II as American occupation officials interview three participants in the operations: two interns (Okuda and Watanabe) and a nurse (Nigishi). Through their testimony it is revealed that two rival surgical teams were performing difficult operations under less than optimum conditions. One team performed lung surgery on the wife of an important naval officer and the patient died on the table. Afraid to reveal the truth, they moved the corpse to post-op and waited until the next day to announce that the patient died from complications *after the operation was completed*. Shortly thereafter the military ordered the doctors to perform vivisection experiments on the eight captured Americans—all of whom die in agony. Although several surgeons and interns are horrified by the military's orders, none is willing to sacrifice his career by disobeying. In the end, 25 of the participants are convicted of war crimes by the Allied Military Tribunal and imprisoned. Ironically, just a few years later—during the Korean War—the 25 were released to promote goodwill between the US and Japan, now allies against the spread of communism. Director Kumai, whose films have always tackled sensitive social and political issues, bought the rights to the book in 1960 and tried in vain to persuade Japanese investors to finance the film. It took him 15 years to find anyone willing to help bring this atrocity out of the closet and force the public to deal with it. The most controversial aspect of this film is Kumai's decision to show the appalling operations in ultra-realistic detail—to make the audience suffer as much as the victims. The only concession Kumai has made to the viewer is that he shot the film in black and white, thus erecting a small barrier (or distancing device) to the gruesomeness that took place at University Hospital in Kyushu in 1945.

p, Kanou Otsuka, Takayoshi Miyagawa; d&w, Kei Kumai (based on the novel by Shusaku Endo); ph, Masao Tochizawa; m, Teizo Matsumura; ed, Osamu Inoue; prod d, Takeo Kimura.

Drama **(PR:NR MPAA:NR)**

SEASON OF DREAMS (SEE: STACKING, 1987)

SECRET OF MY SUCCESS, THE* (1987) 110m Rastar/UNIV c

Michael J. Fox *(Brantley Foster)*, Helen Slater *(Christy Wills)*, Richard Jordan *(Howard Prescott)*, Margaret Whitton *(Vera Prescott)*, John Pankow *(Fred Melrose)*, Christopher Murney *(Barney Rattigan)*, Gerry Bamman *(Art Thomas)*, Fred Gwynne *(Donald Davenport)*, Carol-Ann Susi *(Jean)*, Elizabeth Franz *(Grace Foster)*, Drew Snyder *(Burt Foster)*, Susan Kellerman *(Maureen)*, Barton Heyman *(Arnold Forbush)*, Mercedes Ruehl *(Sheila)*, Ira B. Wheeler *(Owens)*, Ashley J. Laurence *(Fletcher)*, Rex Robbins *(McMasters)*, Christopher Durang *(Davis)*, MacIntyre Dixon *(Ferguson)*, Bill Fagerbakke *(Ron)*, Jack Davidson *(Davidson)*, John Bowman *(Proctor)*, Jeff Brooks, Ascanio Sharpe, Don Amendolia *(Executives)*, Judith Malina *(Mrs. Meachum)*, Mary Catherine Wright *(Research Department Clerk)*, Joseph Ragno *(Shipping Executive)*, Burke Pearson *(Fired Executive)*, Ray Ramirez *(Liquor Store Owner)*, Gloria Irizarry *(Wife of Liquor Store Owner)*, Mark Margolis, Rick Aviles *(Maintenance Men)*, John C. Capodice *(Man in KRS Building)*, Sally-Jane Heit *(Woman In KRS Building)*, Richard Arthur Gallo *(Harried KRS Executive)*, Luis Ramos *(Cuban)*.

This weak office comedy, which recycles HOW TO SUCCEED IN BUSINESS WITHOUT REALLY TRYING, has little to recommend it except an empathetic performance from Fox. The gentle little TV actor is churning out predictable but likable performances for just too many films. In SECRET OF MY SUCCESS Fox is a Kansas farm boy who sets off to take a bite out of the Big Apple, telling his mother that he intends to have "a meaningful relationship with a beautiful woman," a typically naive remark and wholly ignored by his mom whose only concern is that he take along an iron so he won't "walk around wrinkled in New York." Upon arriving in the big town, Fox, in true grit yuppy ingenuity, hits up relative Jordan for a job with his large corporation and gets a lowly position in the mail room. Fox's ambitions soar and he blurts, "I can do anything if I get the chance!" He spots attractive Slater, a rising junior executive, but she turns up her pert nose at mailboy Fox and he resolves to get ahead fast. He locates a deserted office in the corporate building and moves in, making himself an executive and creating important work by which to impress Slater. Meanwhile, to pay the rent for his hovel-like room, infested with roaches and rats, he must keep the mailroom job and is constantly running back and forth, changing clothes to maintain appearances for his self-created dual role. Slater is impressed with Fox, the newly-appointed executive, even though she can't figure out what it is he does for the firm. She, however, is Jordan's mistress and Jordan's seething wife Whitton, quickly and accurately interpreting matters, seduces gullible Fox, not unlike the manner in which Dustin Hoffman was dragged to bed in THE GRADUATE. Matters and cheating lovers all come together at a country party where the whole seamy mess is sorted out and Fox emerges the wiser man.

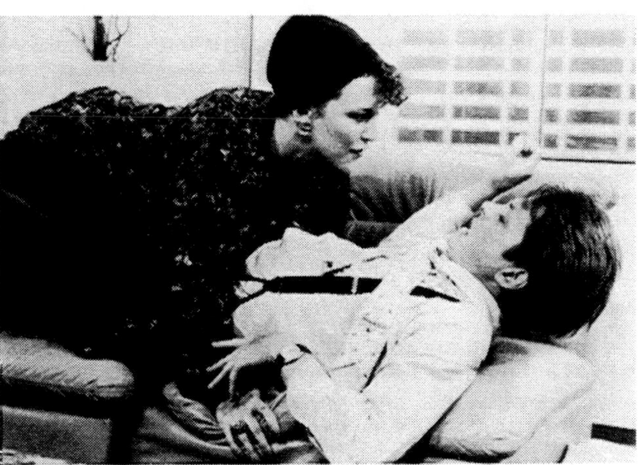

Witlessly directed, all the business canards and stereotypes are represented in this lackluster production. Jordan, as the ruthless corporate tyrant, overplays his predictable role and Slater is empty-headed while Whitton schemes out loud too much. Only Fox is worth watching, but his role is more suited to a one-act play (far, far off-Broadway). The promiscuity displayed in this film seems to say that the producers have never heard of AIDS, which has drastically changed the yuppy world Fox is supposed to represent. No one is really funny here and the lines ring hollow and forced: "Something happens to a man when he puts on a necktie; it cuts off all the oxygen to his brain." Right from the beginning there is a mercenary strain to this film. Fox does not enter New York City as a wide-eyed Andy Hardy in search of pure adventure but as a youth callously eyeing a future bank account and salivating over sexual conquests to come, despite the contemptuous mouthings about "meaningful relationships." This characterization is a cynical disservice done to Fox and the viewer by a miserable script. An amoral profile that sets the wrong standards for youngsters. *(Sexual situations.)*

p&d, Herbert Ross; w, Jim Cash, Jack Epps, Jr., A.J. Carothers (based on a story by A.J. Carothers); ph, Carlo Di Palma; m, David Foster; ed, Paul Hirsch; prod d, Edward Pisoni, Peter Larkin; md, Tommy Mottola, Jeb Brien; set d, Susan Bode; cos, Joseph G. Aulisi; m/l, Siobhan Fahey, Ollie Marland, Paul Waller, David Foster, Jack Blades, Tom Keane, Michael Landau, Pat Benatar, Khris McDaniels, Holly Knight, Tito Puente, Francisco Cruz, Kimberley Rew, Ira Newborn, Danny Peck, Tim DuBois, David Cumming, Jeff Nead, Robert Marcial, John Williams, Boris Blank, Dieter Meier; makeup, Fern Buchner; stunts, Vic Magnotta.

Comedy **(PR:O MPAA:PG-13)**

SEKUNDA NA PODVIG† (1987, N. Korea/USSR) 134m Mosfilm-Korean Studio/Sovexportfilm c (Trans: Seconds Make a Hero)

Andrei Martynov, Chkhve Chkhan Su, Oleg Anofriyev, Li Yen Ir, Natalia Arinbasarova, Irina Shevchuk, Marina Levtova.

Celebrating the wartime comradeship between a Korean soldier and a Soviet soldier, this wide-screen tale of heroism recounts four memorable meetings between them. The first occurs in 1941 at the Soviet-Korean border, where they talk briefly before the Korean returns to the fight against the invading Japanese. In 1945, after the Soviets have entered the war in Asia, they come together to fight side by side against the Japanese. After WW II, in 1946, they again encounter each other in Pyongyang; this time the Soviet throws his body over a grenade, saving many Korean lives. The last meeting, which sparks the flashback remembrances of the first three, occurs when the Soviet returns to Korea years later to be honored as a great hero by the North Korean government.

d, Eldor Urazbayev, Om Ghil Sen; w, Alexander Borodyansky, Pek In Chzhun; ph, Elizbar Karavayev, Chon Ik Khan; m, Eduard Artemyev, Ko Su Yen; art d, Konstantin Forestenko, Kim Chkhol Khon.

War **(PR:NR MPAA:NR)**

SEMBRA MORTO . . . ME E SOLO SVENUTO† (1987, It.) Tecno Image-RAITRE/Mikado (Trans: He Seems to Be Dead . . . But He Has Simply Fainted)

Sergio Castellitto, Marina Confalone, Anita Zagaria, Mario Prosperi, Claudio Spadaro, Marco Giardina, Paolo Porto, Prospero Richelmy.

A brother and sister share an apartment and go happily about their business—he dognaping pedigree pooches and holding them for ransom, she working as a typist—until a neighbor enters their lives and turns their world upside down. The neighbor turns out to be a cocaine dealer, and the sister, who has become his lover, runs away with him when the cops show up. Literally left holding the bag, her brother not only fools the police, but, years later, goes on to become a bigwig in the local mob. His past catches up to him, however, when, while taking his pregnant sister to the hospital, he is shot and killed by one of the dog owners he blackmailed so long ago.

d, Felice Farina; w, Gianni Di Gregorio, Sergio Castellitto, Felice Farina; ph, Renato Tafuri; m, Lamberto Macchi; ed, Roberto Schiavone.

Drama **(PR:NR MPAA:NR)**

SENTIMENTALNOE PUTESHESTVIE NA KARTOSHKU† (1987, USSR) 82m Lenfilm/Sovexportfilm c (Trans: A Sentimental Trip to a Farm)

Filipp Yankovsky, Angelica Nevolina, Pyotr Semak.

A variation on the popular boy-meets-tractor format, this Soviet coming-of-age film follows a city-dwelling student on "a sentimental trip to a farm." Working there on the potato harvest, he not only learns the virtues of hard work, but also comes to recognize just how complex and confusing relationships between people can be, particularly when you love someone who doesn't love you back.

d, Dmitry Dolinin; w, Andrei Smirnov; ph, Vladimir Ivanov; m, Vitaly Chernetsky; art d, Boris Burmistrov.

Drama **(PR:NR MPAA:NR)**

SENTIMIENTOS: MIRTA DE LINIERS A ESTAMBUL*½** (1987, Arg.) 100m Clip S.C.I./Magia c (Trans: Feelings: Mirta From Liniers To Istanbul)

Emilia Mazer *(Mirta)*, Saim Urgay *(Mirta's Turkish Husband)*, Norberto Diaz *(Enrique)*, Arturo Bonin, Victor Laplace, Marla Vaner, Guillermo Battaglia, Elvia Andreoli, Cristina Banegas, Marcelo Alfaro, Ricardo Bartis.

A young woman comes to terms with herself and her life in this touching romance from Argentina. The story opens in Istanbul, where Mazer, an Argentinian woman, tells Urgay, her Turkish husband, about the one great love of her past. The film flashes back five years to 1975. Mazer, who lives with her parents in the Liniers neighborhood of Buenos Aires, is an anthropology student at a local university. The campus is swept by unrest, for the government is teetering and leftist students feel their day is coming soon. Diaz, a member of the radical group, finds himself hopelessly attracted to this politically naive girl. He begins courting her, while trying to raise Mazer's social conscience. The two become lovers and contemplate marriage, but Argentina's political situation forces them to change their plans. Diaz and his comrades are victims of increasingly brutal harassment from government police. Rather than risk death in Argentina, Diaz seeks exile in Stockholm, Sweden. Wanting to be with the man she loves, Mazer leaves Argentina as well, reuniting with Diaz a few months later. At first their new life in Sweden seems idyllic. They live with other Argentinian exiles in an old house, and begin learning the Swedish language. Gradually they begin drifting apart as Diaz grows frustrated with his inactivity. At a party, Mazer, tired of Diaz ignoring her, meets Urgay and engages in a mild flirtation. Later, Diaz decides to travel to Spain and, while he's away, Mazer runs into Urgay again. He tells her of his own difficulties as a Turkish exile. The two fall in love and begin sleeping together. One night Diaz unexpectedly returns and finds his house is empty. When Mazer returns in the morning, they argue. Diaz demands she remain faithful to him, but Mazer knows her life has changed for good. She marries Urgay and they have a child. Eventually Urgay takes her to his homeland, where she is introduced to Urgay's revolutionary friends. One of them reminds Mazer of her old love, a man whose influence she cannot shake. Diaz still thinks of Mazer as well, though he remains in Stockholm plying his trade as a street musician.

Based very loosely on a real-life case, MIRTA . . . is a sensitive tale which takes many turns. It begins as a story of political unrest, then shifts into a romantic comedy, before returning to serious elements. Somehow Diaz and Mazer find time to fall in love, even though the world around them is changing dramatically. The tonal shift from turmoil at home to the new life in Sweden is sudden, but works well. The troubles of Buenos Aires are contrasted with the formal air of Stockholm, as characters adjust and examine their lives. Mazer, just 22 when this was made, carries the film with great heart. She is introduced as an unworldly girl, curious about life. Swept up by Diaz, then forced to make decisions on her own, the character experiences enormous emotional growth. Mazer handles these monumental changes skillfully, creating a woman with whom audiences can empathize. Her performance is a beautiful portrait, and Mazer undoubtedly has great potential in Argentina's growing film industry. While co-directors Coscia and Saura intelligently develop this highly personal story against a background brimming with social concerns, the pair often sabotage the film by using an intrusive music score. The soundtrack is heavy on heart-tugging chords during times of great emotion, while lighter moments are reminiscent of American made-for-television movie scores. The story and performances are strong enough to carry their own emotional weight without an obvious soundtrack to emphasize feelings.

p, Jose Luis Rey Lago; d, Jorge Coscia, Guillermo Saura; w, Jorge Coscia; ph, Diego Bonacinn; m, Leo Sujatovich; ed, Dario Tedesco, Susana Nadal; set d&cos, Guillermo Palacios.

Drama/Romance **(PR:O MPAA:NR)**

SEPPAN† (1987, Swed.) 100m SVT 1-Swedish Film Institute c

Nina Lager, Lil Trulsson, Sofie Mallstrom, Jesper Lager, Jani Niemimaa.

Made for Swedish television but also given a theatrical release, this film attempts to present the mysteries of life as seen from the perspective of children. Director Fagerstrom-Olsson does so by focusing on a group of kids who live in a one-industry suburb of Stockholm.

d, Agneta Fagerstrom-Olsson.

Drama **(PR:NR MPAA:NR)**

SEPTEMBER**** (1987) 82m Orion c

Denholm Elliott *(Howard)*, Dianne Wiest *(Stephanie)*, Mia Farrow *(Lane)*, Elaine Stritch *(Diane)*, Sam Waterston *(Peter)*, Jack Warden *(Lloyd)*, Ira Wheeler *(Mr. Raines)*, Jane Cecil *(Mrs. Raines)*, Rosemary Murphy *(Mrs. Mason)*.

Falling somewhere between the bleak philosophy of INTERIORS and the entertaining philosophy of HANNAH AND HER SISTERS is SEPTEMBER, Woody Allen's second film of 1987 (RADIO DAYS was released in January). Strongly influenced by Ingmar Bergman, INTERIORS explored some very heady issues raised during a family crisis and, as a result, held little appeal for those who expected Allen's comic antics. With HANNAH, Allen explored some of the same themes as INTERIORS but presented them with a lighter tone, giving the film greater mass appeal, no doubt enhanced by his own funny performance. After a nostalgic trip down memory lane with RADIO DAYS (which featured only Allen's voice), Allen doubled back on his audience with SEPTEMBER—another film about family relationships. While only two characters in SEPTEMBER are blood relatives, there is a closeness and warmth to the relationships that one associates with family. Set entirely in one location—a country home somewhere in Vermont—the film is more than a look at a "family"; it is a look at a small universe of people. Visually removed from the outside world (no exteriors are shown), these characters exist only within the walls of this house. As one of the characters states, the universe is "haphazard, morally neutral, and unimaginatively violent." That description is meant to describe galaxies light-years away, but it also applies to the lead characters, who struggle with their interdependence. Set during August—as September approaches, bringing to an end the wistful summer—the film centers on the mother-daughter relationship of Stritch and Farrow. Stritch is an aging sex symbol who has survived the traumas of her past by letting them bounce off her tough veneer. Farrow is still struggling with an incident that occurred years before, when, as a 14-year-old, she allegedly shot and killed her mother's gangster boy friend. (Although never referred to by name, this incident is nearly identical to the Lana Turner/Cheryl Crane/Johnny Stompanato Hollywood scandal of 1958.) The house belongs to Farrow and she is playing host to her mother and her mother's most recent love Warden, a likable physicist who finds the energetic Stritch a pleasing respite from quarks and photons. Living near Farrow is Waterston, an advertising copywriter who is trying to write a novel about "survivors" based on the life of his blacklisted father. Wiest plays Farrow's good friend, a mother and wife who seeks an escape but doesn't have the courage to pursue it to its conclusion. Rounding out the cast is Elliott, a neighbor who has helped Farrow through a nervous breakdown and a suicide attempt, growing very close to her in the process. No romantic promises are fulfilled, however, as each character's love goes unrequited. Elliott is in love with Farrow and doesn't want her to relocate. Farrow is in love with Waterston, who insists their tryst earlier in the summer was a result of their mutual confusion—her breakdown and his recent divorce. Waterston is in love with Wiest and tries to persuade her to leave her family and travel to Paris with him. Finally, Wiest lacks the nerve to drastically change her life, abandon her husband, and destroy her friendship with Farrow, who knows nothing of the budding relationship between Wiest and Waterston. Farrow, a floundering non-artist who has tried various means of expression to find herself, has decided to sell the house and move to New York City. She has hopes of starting her life anew and building her relationship with Waterston. Waterston is as artistically impotent as Farrow. He has tried to begin his novel about his father but is unable to bring it all together. Instead, he entertains thoughts of hack-writing the biography of Stritch's eventful life. Farrow's already tragic life soon takes an even more tragic turn. While the house is being shown to potential buyers, Farrow accidentally discovers Waterston and Wiest embracing. The real estate agent continues the house tour while Farrow sits in shock on the couch. As she listens to Wiest and Waterston explain themselves, Farrow is told by an enthusiastic Stritch that she

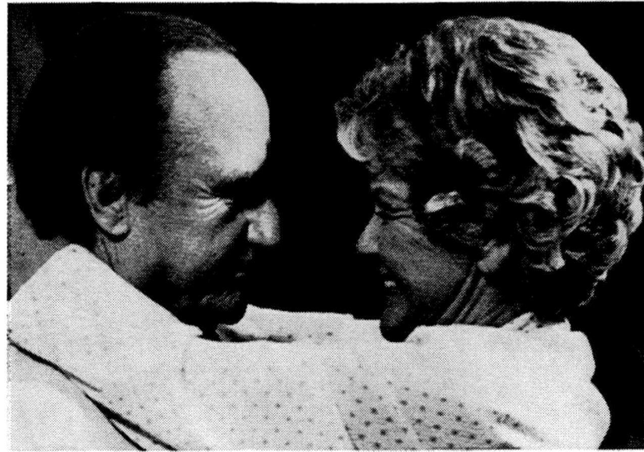

has decided to stay on in the house with Warden. Stritch then denies ever giving Farrow the house, arguing that since she and Farrow's father bought the house many years ago it is rightfully hers. Completely broken, Farrow lashes out at her mother, accusing her of killing her gangster boy friend and insisting that she took the blame for her mother's crime. Stritch finally relents, lets Farrow keep the house, and leaves for Florida with Warden—patching up the hard feelings before going. Despite everyone's efforts, none of the romances works out and Farrow and Wiest are left alone with their friendship and the future.

After a string of crowd pleasers such as BROADWAY DANNY ROSE, PURPLE ROSE OF CAIRO, HANNAH AND HER SISTERS, and RADIO DAYS, it comes as no surprise that Woody Allen should receive the customary critical lambasting that he has with SEPTEMBER. Despite the excellent acting and direction, most critics found little worth in SEPTEMBER. Some even called it his worst film to date; others labeled Allen a junior Ingmar Bergman or berated him for not making a comedy. Whether or not Allen should make comedies or tragedies is irrelevant when it comes to the subject of Allen's command of the filmmaking process. Like only a handful of established American filmmakers (Steven Spielberg and Martin Scorsese among them), Allen displays in his body of work a distinct directorial talent and an overflowing love of cinema. Still infatuated with the language of cinema, Allen has tried in SEPTEMBER to make a film with commercial and artistic appeal. Drawing inspiration from the stories of Russian authors Anton Chekhov and Ivan Turgenev, the filmmaking style of European directors (the moral tone and conversation here are closer to Eric Rohmer than Ingmar Bergman), and the Hollywood gossip surrounding the Lana Turner incident, Allen has come up with a directorial stance that is becoming more personal with each film he makes. His direction is beautifully controlled in the same transcendent way as a Robert Bresson or an Andrei Tarkovsky (who, perhaps not coincidentally, shot his final feature, THE SACRIFICE, in Sweden with much of Bergman's cast and crew).

Although SEPTEMBER seems perfectly realized, it is actually Allen's second version of the film. When he began the film it starred a different group of actors. While Farrow and Wiest were both involved from the start, the supporting cast went through some drastic changes. The Waterston role was originally filled by Christopher Walken (ANNIE HALL), but when he and Allen realized they weren't clicking on the character, Allen replaced him with Sam Shepard. Stritch's role was initially played by Maureen O'Sullivan (Farrow's real-life mother), and Charles Durning had Elliott's part as the neighbor. Elliott, in turn, was cast as Stritch's physicist husband. After finishing principal shooting, Allen discovered in the editing room that the film was not coming together as planned. (His technique of shooting long takes with little or no "coverage" means that if a scene falters because of the script or acting it cannot be "saved" in the editing.) When Allen decided to reshoot, he found much of his cast unable to commit to an additional three months. Both Shepard and Durning had to begin work on other projects, and O'Sullivan was battling pneumonia. In the final cast Elliott switched parts, thereby allowing Warden to play against type as the physicist. While it's a common occurrence for Allen to reshoot as much as half of a film (THE PURPLE ROSE OF CAIRO, for example), SEPTEMBER is an exception to his usual methods. Even so, the budget was barely over $10 million (two-thirds the cost of the average Hollywood feature) and the film cost only 20 percent more than expected. SEPTEMBER is a beautiful, carefully composed film—its painterly lighting reminiscent of Jan Vermeer and its very controlled compositions recalling Edvard Munch. Much of the film's look can be credited to Di Palma, whose camerawork seems to benefit from the single-location limitations. (The "Vermont house" was actually a set created in New York's Astoria Studios.) Wiest, who turns in a performance that surpasses even her Oscar-winning supporting role in HANNAH AND HER SISTERS, and Stritch, as the strong-willed survivor, create the most powerful characters in the film. Farrow, whose remarkable range can be seen by contrasting SEPTEMBER, THE PURPLE ROSE OF CAIRO, and RADIO DAYS, shines in a difficult role that calls for her to be acted *upon*. Elliott, Warden, and Waterston, while all very good in their roles, aren't given the same amount of attention as Allen's female characters. Heard underneath many of the scenes are a number of jazz selections ranging from Irving Berlin's "What'll I Do" to Art Tatum's "Body and Soul." *(Profanity, adult situations.)*

p, Robert Greenhut; d&w, Woody Allen; ph, Carlo Di Palma (Du Art color); ed, Susan E. Morse; prod d, Santo Loquasto; art d, Speed Hopkins; set d, George DeTitta, Jr.; cos, Jeffrey Kurland.

Drama (PR:A MPAA:PG)

SEREBRYANAYA PRYAZHA KAROLINY† (1987, USSR) 76m Tallinnfilm/Sovexportfilm c (Trans: Caroline's Silver Yarn)

Katrin Bagala, Martin Weinmann, Reine Aren.

With plenty of songs and adventure, this filmed fairy tale from the Soviet Union follows the exploits of a persnickety princess who turns up her nose at all of her suitors including the ruler of a nearby kingdom. Though her angry father, the king, prohibits her from leaving the castle, the princess is enticed outside the gates by the melody played by an impoverished wanderer, whom she runs away with. During the course of their eventful travels, the princess grows into a kind, generous soul and she and the wanderer fall in love. Eventually, she learns that her companion is the king she spurned earlier, but now, faced with returning to his opulent castle or continuing to live the simple life, the happy couple chooses the latter.

d, Helle Murdmaa; w, Helle Murdmaa, Vladislav Korzhetz; ph, Ago Ruus; m, Olva Ekhala; art d, Ronald Kolman.

Children's/Musical (PR:NR MPAA:NR)

SERPENT'S WAY, THE*½** (1987, Swed.) 112m Svensk Filmindustri-Swedish Film Institute-SVT 1-Crescendo Film/Svensk Filmindustri c (ORMENS VAG PA HALLEBERGET)

Stina Ekblad *(Tea)*, Stellan Skarsgard *(Karl Orsa)*, Reine Brynolfsson *(Jani)*, Pernilla W. Ostergren *(Eva)*, Tomas von Bromssen *(Jakob)*, Pernilla Wahlgren *(Johanna)*, Ernst Gunther *(Ol Karlsa)*, Birgitta Ulfsson *(Grandma)*, Nils Brandt *(Grandpa)*, Johan Widerberg *(Jani as a Child)*, Melinda Kinnaman *(Eva as a Child)*, Amelia Glas-Drake *(Tilda)*, Lisa Tonnerfors *(Sara)*, Emma Tonnerfors *(Rakel)*.

Bo Widerberg's emotionally powerful depiction of depressed conditions and sexual exploitation in 19th-century Sweden is a beautiful, evocative film of human resilience and nobility. Ekblad must regularly give herself to her landlord, Skarsgard, in order to pay the rent. He fathers several of her children, but does not relieve her poverty nor does she allow him to emotionally participate in the family. Ekblad endures her circumstances stoically, never questioning her suffering. It is God's will and she has little choice. Finding love with a romantic dreamer, Ekblad has a few moments of respite. The rent is paid and the family is happy. But her lover is arrested for thievery, and Ekblad shoulders her burden once again, giving Skarsgard her body but not her soul. Disaster after disaster strikes the family, but Ekblad finds comfort in her Bible and faith in God. When her son finally strikes back against the landlord, the very earth seems to rebel against this human action. A small earthquake tears the house from its foundations, the landlord and the family meeting a common death.

This is a film of man's ultimate helplessness in God's universe and the strength necessary to endure it. Ekblad and Skarsgard give restrained yet powerful performances. Skarsgard manages to show the vulnerability and pain in this devil of a man. Visual metaphors are beautifully rich and the cinematography powerfully evocative. In an interview after completing the film, Widerberg stated his purpose was to "provide an arena for the training and nurturing of the heart." This he has done and done well. Released in Sweden in 1986, and shown on the US festival circuit in 1987. *(Sexual situations, nudity.)*

p, Goran Lindstrom; d&w, Bo Widerberg (based on the novel by Torgny Lindgren); ph, Jorgen Persson, Rolf Lindstrom, Olof Johnsson (Eastmancolor); m, Stefan Nilsson; ed, Bo Widerberg; art d, Pelle Johansson, Kicki Ilander; makeup, Horst Stadlinger, Siw Jarbyn.

Drama (PR:O MPAA:NR)

SEVEN YEARS ITCH† (1987, Hong Kong) 98m Cinema City/Golden Princess c

Raymond Wong, Sylvia Chang, Li Chi, Eric Tsang.

A sex comedy from Hong Kong starring Raymond Wong as a businessman who has maintained a happy co-habitation with his faithful girlfriend for the last seven years. Although they are not officially married, the couple live as man and wife and both refrain from flirting with others. Wong has a wandering eye for attractive ladies however, and while on a business trip to Singapore he meets a sexy young woman, Li Chi, who is definitely trying to seduce him. What Wong does not know is that the woman is a thief who has dumped her loot in his luggage when she was being followed by suspicious police back at the airport. Li Chi's efforts to get the jewels back and Wong's misinterpretation of her attentions propels the film into the realm of the screwball bedroom farce. Written and produced by the star, Raymond Wong.

p, Raymond Wong; d, Johnny To; w, Raymond Wong; ph, Paul Chan; m, Anders G. Nelson; ed, David Wu; art d, Raymond Chan.

Comedy (PR:NR MPAA:NR)

SEVERNY ANEKDOT† (1987 USSR) 98m Mosfilm c (Trans: A Bad Joke)

Evstigneev Sergachev *(Pseudonimov)*.

Made in 1965 but quashed by Soviet censors, SEVERNY ANEKDOT was finally pulled from the vaults and released this year in the rush of relative artistic freedom that has come with *glasnost*. Basically a farce, the film stars Sergachev as a poor bridegroom about to marry his rather unattractive bride. The guests at the raucous affair are a gang of rowdy peasants, but their good time is quelled upon the arrival of a mysterious figure known as His Excellency who sets about intimidating everyone at the function. Meanwhile, the newlyweds have a fight just prior to a trip to the conjugal bed and the groom winds up sleeping next to one of the drunken guests. Filmed on sets full of painted shadows and warped perspectives, directors Alov and Naumov employed a variety of strange lenses during the lengthy wedding and reception scenes to give their film a surreal, nightmarish quality.

d&w, Alexander Alov, Vladimir Naumov; ph, Anatoli Kuznetsov; m, Nikolai Karetnikov.

Comedy **(PR:NR MPAA:NR)**

SEZON CHUDES† (1987, USSR) 91m Odessa/Sovexportfilm c (Trans: Season Of Miracles)

Arunas Storpirstis, Alla Pugacheva, Mikhail Boyarsky.

A young painter moves from the city to the country so that he can concentrate on his work in more idyllic surroundings. His peace and quiet is shattered, however, when a circus family moves in nearby and begin to noisily practice their new act. Although he is infuriated by their intrusion at first, the painter becomes inspired by the colorful troupe and begins a new series of paintings.

d, Georgy Ungwald-Khilkevich; w, Sergei Abramov; ph, Gennady Karyuk; m, Yury Chernavsky; art d, Igor Bryl.

Drama **(PR:NR MPAA:NR)**

SHADEY** (1987, Brit.) 90m Film Four/Skouras c

Antony Sher *(Oliver Shadey)*, Billie Whitelaw *(Dr. Cloud)*, Patrick Macnee *(Sir Cyril Landau)*, Leslie Ash *(Carol Landau)*, Bernard Hepton *(Capt. Amies)*, Larry Lamb *(Dick Darnley)*, Katherine Helmond *(Lady Constance Landau)*, Jon Cartwright *(Shulman)*, Jessie Birdsall *(Carl)*, Oliver Pierre *(Manson)*, Stephen Persaud *(Winston)*, Basil Henson *(The Bishop)*, Madhav Sharma *(Male Orator)*, Susan Engel *(Female Orator)*, Jane Myerson *(Penelope)*, Simon Prebble *(Hotel Manager)*, Zabu *(Hotel Maid)*, Rita Keegan *(The Minder)*, Zohra Segal *(Indian Lady)*, Bill Bingham *(T.V. Interviewer)*, Jonathan Perkins/Silver Spurs *(Pop Group)*.

Scripted by British playwright Snoo Wilson, this black comedy is long on surrealism but short on laughs. Sher plays a bankrupt London auto mechanic who longs to trade his tools for a frilly white dress, a parasol, and a seat on a rowboat; but before he can undergo the sex-change operation he wants so badly, he has to come up with 12,000 pounds sterling. He does, however, possess one very special resource, a prodigious mental telepathy that allows him not only to read people's thoughts and picture occurrences thousands of miles away, but also to transfer those images to film. When fortune brings wealthy industrialist and peer of the realm Macnee into his auto repair shop, Sher is waiting with a proposition and a demonstration of his gift. Convinced of Sher's abilities but uncertain of their worth, Macnee makes an agreement with Whitelaw, a butch secret servicewoman: Macnee makes Sher available to the intelligence organization and they cede to him two floors of offices they are vacating. This is most unfortunate for Sher, as Whitelaw and her fifth-estate comrade Hepton are determined to use him to gain insights into recent developments in Russian submarines. Sher, a confirmed pacifist, has already insisted that he will not allow his talent to be used for military ends. Whitelaw and Hepton also believe that Sher's telepathy has somehow been developed because of his tremendous yearning to change sexes, and that if he gets the operation his powers will vanish. Poor Sher is forced to do their bidding. Word gets out about British intelligence's find, and soon there are foreign agents lurking everywhere, all of them anxious to get their hands on Sher. The only person who seems to understand his plight is Ash, Macnee's daughter, a beautiful model saddled with caring for her loony, agoraphobic mother, Helmond. Ash's engagement party (she's due to marry the Australian director of a rock video in which she has performed) is crawling with spies waiting for the appearance of Sher, who is one step ahead of them and uses his telepathy to goad Helmond into castrating him with one fell swoop of a knife. Shortly thereafter, Macnee is kidnaped by terrorists, but before Sher will help find him, he wangles a wig, undergarments, a nice dress, and lovely restaurant meal from Whitelaw and Hepton. Returning that evening, Sher is set upon by the foreign agents and leads them on an unconventional chase in an elevator, going up and down, up and down, until the lift suddenly becomes luminous and shoots right through the building's roof. The final scene is a lyrical re-creation of the calendar photograph Sher has longed to be a part of since the film's start. While Helmond, now living in a "home," looks on from the shore, the camera glides down from on high to reveal Ash happily poised in the bow of the rowboat afloat on a tranquil pond. The camera then moves to reveal the woman beneath the parasol, Sher, a picture of genteel elegance.

The biggest problem with SHADEY—and there are several—is that it just isn't very funny. Granted it is intended as black humor, but there isn't even much here to smile at knowingly. That said, there are a couple of memorable moments. In one, Macnee returns home to discover that Ash hasn't been keeping a very good eye on Helmond, whose dress and mouth are covered with coal dust. "You let her eat coal!" he says disgustedly. "Again!" In the other, a South African foreign agent corners a vicar and questions him about what he perceives to be latent homosexual tendencies in Christianity. Screenwriter Wilson is well known in Britain for his surreal plays ("The Beast," "The Glad Hand"), and it has been said that he delights in the unexpected, that his plays may, at first, seem to be about nothing, but on second look have very much to say indeed. In SHADEY he has unquestionably come up with an interesting premise; however, the dreamscape he creates from it offers little that one can get a hold of, even by free

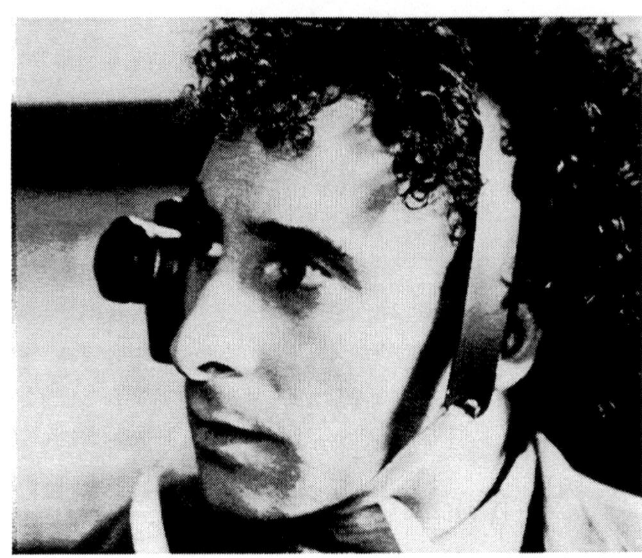

associating away. Perhaps repeated viewing would help, but it seems unlikely. Director Saville (a veteran of British TV and a former actor) and cinematographer Deakins (1984) employ plenty of fluid camera movement, but while it makes the film more interesting to look at, it does little to enhance our understanding. As the film's title character, Sher affects a set-upon, clever innocence. Wearing a bow-tie and a Richard Simmons' haircut, he is partly in the tradition of the great silent comedians, partly like a subdued Pee Wee Herman, and not wholly successful. Though he hasn't been given much by the script, he, nonetheless, appears to have been miscast. Sher, a newcomer to motion pictures, is an accomplished stage actor, having achieved the distinction of being the first performer to win Britain's two biggest dramatic awards in the same year: the Olivier Award for his performance in Harvey Fierstein's "Torch Song Trilogy" and the *Evening Standard* Award for his much-lauded portrayal of the hunched-back king in the Royal Shakespeare Company's "Richard III," which he worked on while filming SHADEY. Macnee (TV's Mr. Steed on "The Avengers") turns in the best of the other performances, which are competent but unexceptional. Helmond, an American best known for her TV work ("Soap," "Who's the Boss"), is becoming a familiar face in British films, or at least in those directed by Terry Gilliam (TIME BANDITS, BRAZIL). She is convincing enough as the crazy Lady Landau, but is given so little to work with that it is difficult to understand exactly why she is in the film, though her situation is not unique. Working with a budget of only about $1.5 million, SHADEY's creators had to come up with an innovative way to give Sher's visions a dreamlike quality. The process they came up with involved the transfer of the negative to video tape, then back to negative, and finally stop-printing the result. *(Violence, sexual situations, brief nudity)*.

p, Otto Plaschkes; d, Philip Saville; w, Snoo Wilson; ph, Roger Deakins; m, Colin Towns; ed, Chris Kelly; prod d, Norman Garwood; set d, Maggie Gray, cos, Tudor George; makeup, Sandra Exelby.

Comedy **Cas.** **(PR:C MPAA:PG-13)**

SHADOWS OF THE PEACOCK† (1987, Aus.) 90m Laughing Kookaburra-Australian European Finance Corp. c

Wendy Hughes *(Maria McEvoy)*, John Lone *(Raka)*, Steven Jacobs *(George McEvoy)*, Peta Toppano *(Judy)*, Rod Mullinar *(Terry)*, Gillian Jones *(Mitty)*, Claudia Karvan *(Julia McEvoy)*, Rebecca Smart *(Tessa)*, Matthew Taylor *(Simon)*, Vithawat Bunnag *(Sali)*, Prasert *(Kasem)*, Lynda Stoner *(Beth Mason)*, Dibbs Mather *(Rev. Whitely)*, Don Pascoe *(Senator Blayney)*, Jan Boreham *(Nun)*, Ruth Caro *(Nurse)*, Marjorie Child *(Maria's Mother)*.

An exotic romance picture starring Hughes as a Sydney housewife whose life is collapsing around her. Shortly after her beloved father's death she learns that her lawyer husband, Jacobs, has been secretly maintaining a girlfriend on the side. Distraught, Hughes takes the advice of a woman friend and accompanies her on a vacation in Phuket, Thailand. There she meets a beguiling Balinese dancer, Lone, who has exiled himself from his native land. Far away from her troubles in Sydney, Hughes falls in love with Lone and has an affair with the dancer. She stays in Thailand longer than anticipated, putting a further strain on her marriage, but in the end she decides to return to her husband and try to salvage the relationship. Shot before actor Lone went to China to work with Bernardo Bertolucci on THE LAST EMPEROR, this may eventually see a limited release in the US.

p, Jane Scott; d, Phillip Noyce; w, Jan Sharp, Anne Brooksbank; ph, Peter James; m, William Motzing; ed, Franz Vandenburg; prod d, Judith Russell; cos, Clarissa Patterson.

Drama **(PR:NR MPAA:NR)**

SHE MUST BE SEEING THINGS† (1987) 90m McLaughlin c

Sheila Dabney, Lois Weaver, Kyle DeCamp, John Erdman.

This feature, screened at the 11th Annual San Francisco International Lesbian and Gay Film Festival, follows the story of Weaver, a lesbian filmmaker who is working on a new project. Dabney is her lover, a successful lawyer, who is prone to jealousy and flighty trips of imagination. While Weaver continues working on her film, Dabney learns to deal with her lover's flirtatious nature.

p,d&w, Sheila McLaughlin; ph, Mark Daniels; m, John Zorn; ed, Ila Von Hasperg; art d, Leigh Kyle.

Drama **(PR:NR MPAA:NR)**

SHEELA† (1987, India)

Sahila Chaddha, Charan Raj, Nana Patekar, Amrit Pal.

Using a not-unfamiliar premise, this film focuses on the fortunes of a young girl who is raised by apes after she is deserted in the wilds of the jungle. (In Hindi.)

p, Dwarakish; d, Deepak Balraj; m, Bappi Lahiri.

Adventure **(PR:NR MPAA:NR)**

SHEERE SANGGY† (1987, Iran) 93m Farabi c (Trans: Stony Lion)

Ali Nassirian, Ezzatollah Entezami, Ali Reza Shoja Noori, Valiollah Shirandami, Hamid Jabeli, Ataollah Zahed, Shamssi Fazlollahi, Azita Lachini, Fahimeh Rastgar, Sogand Rahmani.

The mysterious death of an Englishman sends up sparks that ignite a tribal blood feud in this Iranian epic. A shepherd finds the body of the dead Western engineer and sees that he is buried. When the British authorities demand that the killer be brought to justice, the head of a tribe that works on the oil pipelines sends for the shepherd. Thinking that the shepherd will easily be able to explain his role in the affair, the head of another tribe encourages him to submit to questioning. When the shepherd is made the scapegoat, war breaks out between the tribes.

p, Massood Jafari Jozani, Ali Reza Shoja Noori; d&w, Massood Jafari Jozani; ph, Mahmoud Kalari; m, Fareidoun Shahbazian; ed, Ruhollah Emami; makeup, Iraj Safdari.

Action **(PR:NR MPAA:NR)**

SHELLEY† (1987, Can.) 80m Films Transit-Face to Face/Modern Cinema Mkt. c

Robyn Stevan, Ian Tracey, Diana Stevan, Christianne Hirt.

Teen film, shot on 16mm in the "After School Special" mold, starring Stevan as a 15-year-old who runs away from home to escape the sexual advances of her stepfather. The young girl falls in with the wrong crowd and winds up in a quagmire of drugs and prostitution until she is rescued by a sympathetic social worker who encourages Stevan to return home and bring her stepfather up on child-molestation charges. The case goes to trial and the stepfather is convicted and sentenced. Stevan is finally reunited with her mother.

p,d&w, Christian Bruyere; ph, Tom Turnbull; m, Michael Conway Baker; ed, Jane Morrison, Doris Dyck.

Drama **(PR:NR MPAA:PG)**

SHINRAN: SHIRO MICHI† (1987, Jap.) 127m Shochiku-Nichiei-Kinema Tokyo c (Trans: Shinran: Path To Purity)

Junkyu Moriyama *(Shinran [Zenshin])*, Michio Ogusu *(Asa)*, Shigeru Izumiya *(Ijika)*, Guto Ishimatsu *(Atota)*, Hosei Komatau *(Renshe Utsunemiya)*, Ako *(Shiina)*, Masayo Asada *(Ogure)*, Miki Odagiri *(Woman From Inada)*, Senas Nakahara *(Lady-in-Waiting)*, Izumi Hara *(Ayai)*, Mako Mideri *(Chiyo)*, Tetsuro Tamba, Kantaro Suga.

Film biography of Buddhist religious leader Shinran, founder of the Shinshu sect in the late 12th century. Born Kenshin-Daishi to a court nobleman in 1173, Shihran (played by Moriyama) grew up during a period of upheaval in Japan as the samurai of the Genji clan took control of the country and hunted down members of the deposed Heike Clan and beheaded them. Unable to bear the horrible violence he witnesses all around him, 13-year-old Moriyama enters the priesthood. As he grows older, Moriyama becomes a force in Buddhism, allowing priests to marry and have children. He and his wife Ogusu have children of their own, but their youngest boy dies in an epidemic and Moriyama insists on cremating the body on a funeral pyre over his wife's objections. This decision destroys his marriage. Despite many obstacles and set-backs, Moriyama's spiritualism succeeds in establishing a loyal flock among the Japanese peasants. The $7 million budget for this film is surprisingly expensive for a Japanese production, especially when one considers that Akira Kurosawa had to seek foreign investment to raise $11 million for his masterpiece RAN.

p, Kiyoshi Fujimoto; d, Rentaro Mikuni; w, Don Fujita, Rentaro Mikuni (based on the book by Rentaro Mikuni); ph, Yoshi Yamazaki; m, YAS-KAZ; ed, Osamu Inoue; art d, Takee Kimura.

Biography/Historical **(PR:NR MPAA:NR)**

SHUTO SHOSHITU (SEE: TOKYO BLACKOUT, 1987, Jap.)

SHY PEOPLE† (1987) 118m Golan-Globus/Cannon c

Jill Clayburgh *(Diana Sullivan)*, Barbara Hershey *(Ruth Sullivan)*, Martha Plimpton *(Grace Sullivan)*, Merritt Butrick *(Mike)*, John Philbin *(Tommy Sullivan)*, Pruitt Taylor Vince *(Paul Sullivan)*, Don Swayze *(Mark Sullivan)*, Michael Audley *(Louie)*, Brad Leland *(Larry)*, Paul Landry *(Jake)*, Mare Winningham *(Ruth's Daughter)*.

Barbara Hershey won the Best Actress Award at the Cannes Film Festival for her performance in SHY PEOPLE, which was directed by Soviet-emigree Konchalovsky, his fourth American film in three years (MARIA'S LOVERS, RUNAWAY TRAIN, DUET FOR ONE). Set mostly in the Louisiana bayous, the film begins in Manhattan as freelance writer Clayburgh begins research for an article on family trees for *Cosmopolitan* magazine. Using her own heritage as a base, Clayburgh decides to go down to Louisiana in an effort to track down a great uncle who lives in the bayous. Hoping the change of scenery will be good for her jaded and cocaine-addicted daughter, Plimpton, Clayburgh drags the rebellious teenager along. Upon arriving in the swamps, Clayburgh discovers that her uncle

had disappeared 15 years before, leaving behind a wife, Hershey, and four boys, now grown. The cultural gap between sophisticated Manhattanite Clayburgh and backwoods child-bride Hershey is wide and during the course of the film the women learn much from each other. Whereas Clayburgh has had difficulty controlling her daughter, Hershey rules with an iron hand and keeps her troublesome son (Philbin) locked in the shed. Before long the encroachment of civilization represented by Clayburgh collides with the forces of nature and tragedy results. Screened for one week on one screen in Los Angeles to qualify for

Academy Award nominations, SHY PEOPLE will receive a general release in 1988.

p, Menahem Golan, Yoram Globus; d, Andrei Konchalovsky; w, Gerard Brach, Andrei Konchalovsky, Marjorie David (based on a story by Andrei Konchalovsky); ph, Chris Menges (Rank Color); m, Tangerine Dream; ed, Alain Jakubowicz; prod d, Steve Marsh; art d, Leslie McDonald; set d, Leslie Morales.

Drama **(PR:NR MPAA:R)**

SI LE SOLEIL NE REVENAIT PAS† (1987, Switz./Fr.) 116m JMH Television Suisse Romande-Marion's-Sara-Canal Plus/Sara-CDF c (Trans: If the Sun Never Returns)

Charles Vanel *(Anzevui)*, Catherine Mouchet *(Isabelle Antide)*, Philippe Leotard *(Arlettaz)*, Raoul Billery *(Denis Revaz)*, Claude Evrard *(Follonier)*.

The setting is a village in the Swiss mountains which spends six months in darkness each winter. In the winter of 1937, a village elder predicts the sun won't reappear in spring. The movie then focuses on how various residents of the village react to this portent of doom. The film is based on a novel by Charles Ferdinand Ramuz, which has long been popular in Switzerland. The doom-saying elder is played by Vanel, who is now 95 years old and who has been making movies since 1930.

p, Jean-Marc Henchoz, Sylvette Frydman; d&w, Claude Goretta (based on the novel by Charles Ferdinand Ramuz); ph, Bernard Zitzermann (Eastmancolor); m, Antoine Auberson; ed, Eliane Guignet; makeup, Valerie de Buck.

Drama **(PR:NR MPAA:NR)**

SIBAJI† (1987, S. Korea) 95m Shin Han c (Trans: Contract Mother)

Kang Soo-yeon *(Onyia)*, Lee Goo-soon *(Sangkyu)*, Han Eun-jin *(Old Lady)*, Bang Hee *(Yoon Ssi)*, Yoon Yang-Ha *(Chi-ho)*.

After 12 years of trying, Kang Soo-yeon has been unable to provide her husband, Lee Goo-soon, with a child. Feeling he must have an heir, and with the wife's blessing, Lee Goo-soon finds a 17-year-old girl who agrees to bear his child and never see it again after it is born. The girl moves into the house, and the baby-making efforts eventually pay off, with the girl being thrown off the estate once an heir is produced, though she has fallen in love with Lee Goo-soon. A year later and still despairing, she kills herself.

d, Tarun Majumdar; w, Anjan Chowdhury.

Drama **(PR:NR MPAA:NR)**

SICILIAN, THE** (1987) 115m Gladden/FOX c

Christophe [Christopher] Lambert *(Salvatore Giuliano)*, Terence Stamp *(Prince Borsa)*, Joss Ackland *(Don Masino Croce)*, John Turturro *(Aspanu Pisciotta)*, Richard Bauer *(Prof. Hector Adonis)*, Barbara Sukowa *(Camilla, Duchess)*, Giulia Boschi *(Giovanna Ferra)*, Ray McAnally *(Minister Trezza)*, Barry Miller *(Dr. Nattore)*, Andreas Katsulas *(Passatempo)*, Michael Wincott *(Cpl. Silvestro Canio)*, Derrick Branche *(Terranova)*, Richard Venture *(Cardinal of Palermo)*, Ramon Bieri *(Quintana)*, Stanko Molnar *(Silvio Ferra)*, Oliver Cotton *(Comdr. Roccofino)*, Joe Regalbuto *(Father Doldana)*, Tom Signorelli *(Abbot Manfredi)*, Aldo Ray *(Don Siano of Bisacquino)*, Nicholas Kepros *(University President)*, Justin Clark *(Boy)*, Trevor Ray *(Frisella the Barber)*.

They should have titled this film "Highlights From Michael Cimino's THE SICILIAN" because its production company, Gladden Entertainment, denied the director his final cut and arbitrarily removed more than 30 minutes from the director's original cut. What is left of Cimino's film lurches along from scene to scene with little regard for pacing, nuance, or even narrative coherence. The result is a wholly confusing, vague, and unsatisfying mess. This truncated version is reminiscent of the crude hatchet jobs performed on Sam Peckinpah's westerns MAJOR DUNDEE, THE WILD BUNCH, PAT GARRETT AND BILLY THE KID and Sergio Leone's ONCE UPON A TIME IN AMERICA, and Gladden Entertainment shows nothing but contempt for the paying customer by using tactics that make the final product nearly incoherent. Although the inexpert cuts certainly damage the film, it is also apparent that THE SICILIAN was never going to be a great film. There are simply too many glaring problems that can be attributed to the director himself—especially in the misguided casting. Intact, THE SICILIAN may be a *good* film, but in its current form it is a very bad film with moments of brilliance (Cimino's 147-minute cut is being released in Europe). Based on the best-selling novel by Mario Puzo, THE SICILIAN tells the story of real-life Sicilian folk hero Salvatore Giuliano, a mountain bandit who became a Robin Hood figure to the peasants of Sicily shortly after WW II. Played in stoic fashion by French actor Lambert, Giuliano robs wealthy landowners who are under the protection of the Mafia and then turns over a third of the proceeds to the peasants, urging them to buy land with the money. As ruthless as he is generous, Lambert does not hesitate to execute those who would seek to betray him. Obsessed with his own myth, the bandit fails to realize that his successes are directly attributable to the benign tolerance of an all-powerful Mafia don played superbly by Ackland. Although they have never met, the don has strong paternal feelings for the bandit and hopes to someday persuade Lambert to leave the mountains and become his son (Ackland's own son has rejected his heritage to become an entomologist in Brazil). Ackland uses his vast power to persuade the government in Rome, the Vatican, and the Sicilian police to leave the problem of Lambert to him. Unfortunately, as a major election draws near, the government fears that Lambert's version of land reform will drive the peasants to the Communist party and enable the Reds to win. After a series of betrayals by the government and the church, Lambert finds himself cornered and looks for a way out. Ackland offers a sure pardon to Lambert if the bandit will see to it that the Communists lose the election. Planning to simply scare the Communists by firing over their heads during a pre-election rally, Lambert is shocked when one of his men opens fire on the crowd killing many, including his brother-in-law. Betrayed by his men and discredited with the people, Lambert is forced to accept Ackland's offer of safe passage to America. Although his wife makes it to the US safely, Lambert is murdered by his best friend, Turturro, and his body dumped in the town square where it is shot several more times by the police who take credit for the killing.

Awash in controversy from the moment shooting was completed, THE SICILIAN seemed doomed from the start. Before signing Cimino, Gladden Entertainment head David Begelman (who is very controversial in his own right) stipulated that the director of the infamous disaster HEAVEN'S GATE stick to the script and keep the final cut to a maximum of two hours. It is hard to fathom why Begelman even chose the notoriously difficult Cimino to direct yet another big-budget epic that could easily run over two hours. When the film was finished, Begelman acceded to a cut that would run two hours and five minutes. Cimino delivered both a two-hour version *and* a 147-minute version. Convinced that Cimino purposely did an inferior job on the two-hour cut in an effort to persuade the studio to release the longer version, Begelman withdrew the director's right to final cut and had the film edited down to two hours without Cimino's participation. Cimino went to the courts and sued Begelman on a variety of counts, including failure to pay him $250,000 outstanding from his $2.5 million fee for directing the picture and a request for an additional $5 million in damages. Meanwhile, another storm was brewing over the screenplay credit. Screenwriter/novelist Steve Shagan had done an adaptation of Puzo's novel that both Begelman and Cimino had found unsatisfactory. Cimino then took the script to author Gore Vidal who, according to him, then wrote "six or seven" drafts, each very different from the Shagan version. Cimino approved of a final draft written by Vidal and began production with Vidal periodically phoning in rewrites when needed. Shagan, however, claimed sole credit for the script and the Writers Guild of America found in his favor. Furious over what he considered an obvious case of Hollywood insiders favoring one of their own (Shagan has strong connections in the Writers Guild), Vidal has filed suit against the Writers Guild and claims to have gotten a surprising amount of support from fellow members of the WGA. As far as Shagan is concerned, the final film's structure is "slavishly loyal" to his first draft. He calls Vidal's suit a "rich man's toy" that could destroy the guild through infighting and class distinctions—in that rich writers can afford to lose a protest but working writers cannot (both men are quoted from interviews in *American Film*, November, 1987). As of this writing both Cimino and Vidal's cases are still pending.

Controversy aside, THE SICILIAN has other problems. Although the finer points of characterization and plot development are no doubt lying on the cutting room floor, Cimino must take responsibility for some of the most grievous errors in the film—namely the cast, few of whom are Italian, let alone Sicilian (almost everyone has blue eyes, a rarity in Sicily). As the bandit Giuliano, French actor Lambert looks the part, but fails to infuse the role with an energy and passion necessary to pull it off. Worse still are such British luminaries as Terence Stamp, playing a fey Sicilian prince, and Ray McAnally as an Italian government official; respected German actress Barbara Sukowa playing, of all things, the *American* wife of Stamp; and American bit players Bieri, Signorelli, Miller, Regalbuto, and Venture playing a variety of Mafiosi, priests, and professors, all with clashing American accents. Most distressing of all is a cameo by the almost unrecognizable Aldo Ray, hidden beneath a hat and dark glasses, as a Mafia don who appears in only two scenes and never utters a word before being executed by Lambert's men. None of these actors are *bad*, they are simply miscast. Why Cimino chose a mostly Anglo-American cast and ignored the scores of fine Italian actors available is a mystery. However, there are a few exceptional performances. Young American actor Turturro, last seen as the pool player Paul Newman dumps in favor of Tom Cruise in THE COLOR OF MONEY, is excellent as Lambert's closest friend and associate. Better yet is British stage and screen actor Ackland as Don Masino Croce. Ackland makes the most of his role and luckily it appears that most of his scenes have made it into the final cut intact. Wisely underplaying and finely nuanced, Ackland manages to appear extremely dangerous, yet sympathetic, eccentric, and human, thus creating the only truly vivid character in the film. It is a pity that such a fine performance is trapped in what will prove to be a quickly forgotten film.

As is to be expected in a Cimino film, the production design and cinematography are excellent. Cimino once again proves his superior eye for composition, especially in the wide screen format, and creates several memorable scenes. One can hardly go wrong shooting on location in photogenic Sicily, and Cimino does not disappoint, using the rugged mountains, golden wheat fields, and narrow streets of Palermo to breathtaking advantage. Visually, Cimino is a top-notch filmmaker. Unfortunately, as is the case in all his films, he proves to have a chaotic narrative sense. Alternating between simplemindedness and pomposity, Cimino never gets a handle on his main character and opts for mythmaking instead of insight. For those interested in a more coherent and detailed telling of the story of Giuliano, it was filmed once before by Italian director Francesco Rosi, in 1961, as SALVATORE GIULIANO. *(Graphic violence, gore effects, nudity, profanity.)*

p, Michael Cimino, Joann Carelli; d, Michael Cimino; w, Steve Shagan (based on the novel by Mario Puzo); ph, Alex Thomson (Widescreen, Technicolor); m, David Mansfield; ed, Francoise Bonnot; prod d, Wolf Kroeger; art d, Stefano Ortolani; set d, Joseph Mifsud Chevalier; cos, Wayne Finkelman.

Biography **(PR:O MPAA:R)**

SIDSTE AKT† (1987, Den.) 104m Nordisk-Danish Film Institute/Nordisk c (Trans: Final Curtain; Waiting in the Wings)

Birgitte Federspiel *(Lotta)*, Mime Fonss *(May)*, Kirsten Rolffes *(Miss Archie)*, Holger Juul Hansen *(Perry)*, Ebbe Rode *(Mr. Osborne)*, Lily Broberg *(Molly)*, Erni Arneson *(Bonnie)*, Else Petersen *(Sarita)*, Elin Reimer *(Elvira)*, Tove Maes *(Ester)*, Jytte Breuning *(Cora)*, Lisbeth Movin *(Board Chairman)*, Berthe Quistgaard *(Martha)*, Anne Marie Helger *(Journalist)*, Axel Strobye, Vera Gebuhr, Helle Merete Jensen, Gerda Gilboe.

Based on Noel Coward's play "Waiting in the Wings," and retaining its English character names, this Danish drama is set in a home for retired actresses. These elderly thesps are anxiously anticipating the construction of a glass veranda, but the home's governing body doesn't share the ladies' sense of urgency and won't consent to the addition. Meanwhile, one particularly well-known former actress takes up residence. Anxious to get her not-so-well-known story, a newspaper sends a reporter, and even promises to deliver the sought-after veranda if he can talk with the star. Directed by Edward Fleming (OPERATION LOVEBIRDS, 1967, Den.), SIDSTE AKT features some of the Danish stage and screen's finest mature actresses: Birgitte Federspiel (HUNGER, 1968, Den.), Kirsten Rolffes (EPILOGUE, 1967, Den.), Mime Fonss, and Berthe Quistgaard.

d&w, Edward Fleming (based on the play "Waiting in the Wings" by Noel Coward); ph, Claus Loof (Eastmancolor); ed, Grete Moldrup; prod d, Hanning Bahs; cos, Annelise Hauberg, Ole Glasner, Pia Myrdal.

Drama (PR:A MPAA:NR)

SIEKIEREZADA† (1987, Pol.) 82m Zespoly Filmowe-Perspektiva/Film Polski c (AKA: AXILIAD)

Edward Zentara *(Jan Pradera, Poet)*, Daniel Olbrychski *(Katny)*, Ludwig Pak *(Peresada)*.

A prize winner at the Berlin Film Festival, this Polish allegory tells the story of a poet who tries to get back in touch with nature and himself by relocating to a small village on the edge of a great forest. Boarding with an old woman, the poet (Zentara) takes a job as a lumberjack, but, still haunted by his past, he finds that even his new environment fails to make him feel fulfilled. Before long, Olbrychski, another man much like Zentara, arrives and takes up residence. Zentara sees himself in the new arrival, and, recognizing his own futile search in Olbrychski's actions, the poet commits suicide. SIEKEIREZADA is based on a novel by Edward Stachura, who, like the poet in his story, took his own life.

d&w, Witold Leszczynski (based on the novel by Edward Stachura); ph, Jerzy Lukaszewicz; m, Jerzy Satanowski, Antonio Vivaldi; ed, Lucja Osko; art d, Maciej Putowski.

Drama (PR:NR MPAA:NR)

SIERRA LEONE† (1987, Ger.) 92m Bayerische Rundfunk/Filmverlag der Autoren c

Christian Redl *(Fred)*, Ann-Gisel Glass *(Alma)*, Rita Russek *(Vera)*, Constanze Engelbrecht *(Rita)*, Andras Fricsay, Gotfried Breitfuss, Hans Eckart-Eckhart, Nikolaus Dutsch, Mehmet Bademsoy.

Beginning with footage of West Africa, this road film focuses on the return of its working-class hero to his native Germany. After toiling abroad for three years, Redl comes home to find that neither his wife nor his former mistress want to have anything to do with him. He takes to the autobahns of northern Germany and in his wanderings meets hotel clerk Glass, who joins him in his travels through the industrial wasteland, but is unable to alleviate the emptiness Redl feels.

p, Uwe Schrader, Sylvia Koller; d&w, Uwe Schrader; ph, Klaus Muller-Laue; m, Bulent Ersoy, Garnet Mimms and the Enchanters, Tony Christie, Don Gibson, Samime Sanay; ed, Klaus Muller-Laue; set d, Brigit Gruse, Renate Langer; cos, Brigit Gruse.

Drama (PR:NR MPAA:NR)

SIESTA† (1987) 97m Lorimar c

Ellen Barkin *(Claire)*, Gabriel Byrne *(Augustine)*, Julian Sands *(Kit)*, Isabella Rossellini *(Marie)*, Martin Sheen *(Del, Claire's Husband)*, Alexi Sayle *(Cabbie)*, Grace Jones *(Conchita)*, Jodie Foster *(Nancy)*, Anastassia Stakis *(Desdra)*, Gary Cady *(Roger)*.

Receiving a limited release on both coasts, SIESTA was one of the most-talked-about films of the year and one of the most panned. Directed by Lambert, the rock video maker who contributed to "Madonnamania" by directing the singer's best and most popular videos—"Borderline," "Like a Virgin," and "Material Girl"—SIESTA is a hallucinatory, metaphoric, nonlinear story of a disturbed woman who is driven to destruction by *l'amour fou*. Barkin plays a daredevil skydiver whose upcoming jump—into the mouth of an active volcano—is being promoted by her husband, Sheen. She, instead, opts for a different jump—flying off to Spain and chasing after trapeze artist Byrne, a former lover who has since married Rossellini. The film skips around over a period of five days, beginning with a corpselike Barkin lying at the end of an airport runway. By the end, Barkin has crossed paths with artsy British socialites Sands and Foster, the mysterious Jones, and cabbie-from-hell Sayle. Although SIESTA is Lambert's first feature, it is not her first feature directing job. She had previously been hired to direct Prince's UNDER THE CHERRY MOON, but she and Prince parted ways after two weeks of production. The script was written by Knop (cowriter of 9½ WEEKS) from a novel by Patrice Chaplin, daughter-in-law of Charlie. The lead role was originally meant for Madonna, but she felt that doing a nude scene (after all her *Playboy* and *Penthouse* publicity) would work against her career ambitions.

p, Gary Kurfirst, Chris Brown; d, Mary Lambert; w, Patricia Louisianna Knop (based on the novel by Patrice Chaplin); ph, Bryan Loftus, Michael Lund; m, Marcus Miller; ed, Glenn A. Morgan; prod d, John Beard; art d, Jose Marie Tapiador, Jon Hutman; set d, Kara Lindstrom; cos, Marlene Stewart.

Drama (PR:NR MPAA:R)

SILENT NIGHT, DEADLY NIGHT PART II zero (1987) 88m Ascot Entertainment Group-Silent Night Releasing c

Eric Freeman, James L. Newman, Elizabeth Clayton, Jean Miller.

All is not calm, all is not bright in this alleged sequel to the infamous 1984 Tri-Star release. Least bright are the filmmakers who thought they could capitalize on the controversy surrounding the original movie. This is not so much a sequel as it is a rerun of the first film, as a great deal of footage from the earlier movie appears in this. It is even poorer than its predecessor in every way. The acting is blah, the script is lame, the direction is dumb, and the editing is as pretentious as anything you may have ever seen. The anger at the original's producers centered on the fact that Santa Claus was portrayed as a maniac, whacking people with an axe, causing gore galore, and, in general, insuring any little children who were mistakenly taken to see it of bad dreams until they turn 65. In the first film, two young children's parents are murdered by a killer in a Kris Kringle outfit. The killer is actually the older brother and his actions cause his younger sibling to be sent to an orphanage where he grows up under the care of a frigid mother superior (played by Lilyan Chauvin) and emerges as a certified bedbug himself. It's now years later and Freeman realizes it's Christmas Eve. Does that awaken a lust for blood in the nutso youth? You bet. He repeats his horrible past to a kindly analyst, then knocks the doc off. What follows is an orgy of bloodletting as Freeman dons his red-and-white costume and departs on a murderous Yuletide rampage. The ways in which Freeman kills are ingenious as well as disgusting. He blows off the top of a man's head by cramming live battery chargers down the guy's gullet; he impales a hit man with an umbrella, then opens it up. If the writers had taken as much care with the dialog and the plot as they did with the murders, the movie might have risen from dreadful to mediocre. Making a "sequel" to an awful picture is chancy and the sequel had better be superior. If possible, this was worse. By using so much footage from the first film, this hardly even qualifies as a full movie itself. This picture is little more than recycled trash and deserves to be burned. The stars were virtual unknowns and if they keep accepting jobs like this, they will stay that way. *(Graphic violence.)*

p, Lawrence Appelbaum; d, Lee Harry; w, Lee Harry, Joseph H. Earle (based on a story by Lee Harry, Joseph H. Earle, Dennis Paterson, Lawrence Appelbaum and a character created by Michael Hickey, Paul Caimi); ph, Harvey Genkins (United color); m, Michael Armstrong.

Horror (PR:O MPAA:R)

SINFIN, LA MUERTA NO ES NINGUNA SOLUCION† (1987, Arg.) 86m Aquilea c (Trans: Sinfin, Death Is No Solution)

Alberto Ure, Lorenzo Quinteros, Susana Tanco, Jorge Marrale, Cristina Banegas, Leal Rey, Jose Maria Gutierrez, Monica Galan, Carlos Giordano, Aldo Barbero.

A madman film producer assembles a cast of actors for an adaptation of the Julio Cortazar story "Casa Tomada," which is to be filmed inside a gothic mansion. The catch is that the actors must sign a contract in which they agree to stay in the mansion for the film's duration. Supernatural occurrences arise and the cast soon realizes they cannot leave the movie set. Something of a cross between Luis Bunuel's EXTERMINATING ANGEL and THE DISCREET CHARM OF THE BOURGEOISIE, Raul Ruiz's DANS UN MIROIR, and R.W. Fassbinder's BEWARE THE HOLY WHORE.

d, Cristian Pauls; w, Alan Pauls, Cristian Pauls; ph, Hugo Colace; ed, Pablo Mari; prod d&cos, Horacio Gallo.

Drama (PR:NR MPAA:NR)

SINVERGUENZA . . . PERO HONRADO† (1987, Mex.) 96m Cumbre/Peliculas Mexicanas c (Trans: Shameless . . . But Honorable)

Vicente Fernandez *(Alberto)*, Blanca Guerra *(Carmen)*, Cecilia Camacho *(Cecilia)*, Manuel Capetillo *(Flavio)*, Pedro Weber [Chatanooga] *(Don Pepe)*, Carmelita Gonzalez *(Dona Carmen)*, Guillermo Murray *(Ramon)*, Alicia Encines, Carmelina Encines, Raul Araiza, Jr., Aurora Alonso, Antonio Miguel, Xerardo Moscoso, Irma Infante, Tito Guillen.

A sequel to EL SINVERGUENZA, this comedy revolves around popular Mexican crooner and comedic actor Fernandez. In the original he was hired to pose as the husband of a friend's mistress, Guerra. However, he fell in love with her, they married, and he became stepdad to four kids. In this film he is forced to come to terms with what it *really* means to be a family man.

d, Rafael Villasenor Kuri; w, Adolfo Torres Portillo; ph, Javier Cruz; m, Carlos Torres; ed, Max Sanchez; md, Fernando Mendez.

Comedy/Musical (PR:NR MPAA:NR)

SITTING IN LIMBO† (1987, Can.) 96m National Film Board of Canada/The Other Cinema

Pat Dillon, Fabian Gibbs, Sylvie Clarke, Debbie Grant.

Shot exclusively with a hand-held camera, this low-budget, documentary-like Canadian film was named Best Canadian Film by the international critics at the 1986 Montreal World Film Festival. Set in Montreal, it is the story of two black college students who leave school to set up housekeeping when the woman, Dillon, becomes pregnant. Her boy friend, Gibbs, is a grudging provider at first, not particularly anxious about getting a job. Eventually, though, he does find work and they settle into a basement apartment filled with rented furnishings. Before long, however, the pressures of being a grown-up becomes too much for Gibbs, and he is left without a job or a family. SITTING IN LIMBO was released in Britain in 1987.

p, David Wilson, John N. Smith; d, John N. Smith; w, David Wilson, John N. Smith; ph, Barry Perles, Andreas Poulsson; ed, David Wilson.

Drama **(PR:NR MPAA:NR)**

SKAZKA O PREKRASNOY AYSULU† (1987, USSR) 71m Kazakhfilm/ Sovexportfilm c (Trans: The Tale Of Beautiful Aisulu)

Saule Zhumartova, Sagui Ashimov, Kenes Nurlanov, Raisa Mukhamedjarova.

This Soviet retelling of a Central Asian fairy tale revolves around a handsome khan who, while wandering in the forest, hears an enchanting melody played by the son of a shepherd. The boy invites the chieftain home, introduces him to his beautiful sister, and it is love at first sight. The khan's sister is opposed to her brother's marriage to this unsuitable girl, but she says nothing until he is away fighting a war. Then she sends him false information, claiming that his beloved has given birth and attempted to drown her babies in the river. In the end, however, the khan learns the truth and the story delivers a happily-ever-after finale.

d, Victor Chugunov, Rustem Tazhibaev; w, Nina Davydova, Rustem Tazhibaev, Victor Chugunov; ph, Alexei Berkovich; m, Baigali Serkebaev; prod d, Vladimir Trapeznikov.

Fantasy **(PR:NR MPAA:NR)**

SKORBNOE BESCHUVSTVIE† (1987, USSR) 95m Lenfilm/Sovexportfilm c (Trans: Heartless Grief)

Ramaz Cchikvadze *(Shotover)*, Alla Osipenko *(Ariadna)*, Tat'jana Egoreva *(Hesione)*, Dimitrij Brjancev *(Hector)*, Vladimor Zamanskij *(Mazzini)*, Viktorija Amitova *(Ellie)*, Il'ja Rivin *(Mangan)*, Irina Sokolova *(Nurse Guinness)*, Vadim Zuk *(Dr. Knife)*, Andrej Resetin *(Randall)*, P. Pribytko, L. An, J. Simonov.

George Bernard Shaw's play "Heartbreak House" was the inspiration for this big-budget, wide-screen Soviet feature made after the advent of *glasnost*. Set during WW I in a large country home that purposefully resembles an ark, the film focuses on a gathering of family and friends who, like the symbolic characters in Shaw's play, pass their time flirting and philosophizing, seemingly oblivious to the earth-shaking events occurring elsewhere: in the film, WW I; in "Heartbreak House," the threat of war. Intercut with these discussions is documentary footage of the war and Mr. Shaw himself, and director Sokurov adds more than a few surreal occurrences. The harsh reality of a world turned upside down by war finally intrudes on the self-contained environment when a German dirigible drops a bomb on the house.

d, Aleksandr Sokurov; w, Jurij Arabov (based on the play "Heartbreak House" by George Bernard Shaw); ph, Sergej Jurizdickkij (CinemaScope); ed, Leda Semenova; prod d&cos, Elena Amsinskaja; ch, J. Mjacin.

Fantasy **(PR:NR MPAA:NR)**

SKYTTURNAR† (1987, Iceland) 80m Icelandic Film Corp.-Icelandic Film Fund/Icelandic Film Corp. c (AKA: WHITE WHALES)

Thorarinn Thorarinsson *(Grimur)*, Eggert Gudmundsson *(Bubbi)*, Hronn Steingrimsdottir, Balduin Halldorsson, Helgi Bjornsson, Harald G. Haraldsson, Guddbjorg Thoroddsen.

This is the feature film debut for Icelandic director Fridriksson, who, at age 32, has already helmed four documentaries, including "Rock in Reykjavik," a study of rock music culture in Iceland, and "Iceland Cowboys." In this film, which has also been released as WHITE WHALES, Fridriksson uses a real-life occurrence as the basis for his story. The whaling season is coming to an end and two sailors, Thorarinsson and Gudmundsson, return to port knowing that they will have to find some other kind of employment until the whaling ships are ready to set sail again. Before their boat reaches port, Thorarinsson receives a message from the woman he has been living with telling him that her husband has moved back in and that the seaman needn't bother coming home. When they reach shore, Thorarinsson and Gudmundsson head for Reykjavik, where they begin a bar-hopping spree that only succeeds in getting them progressively drunker and thrown out of one establishment after another. They visit Thorarinsson's grandmother, but because they are so drunk, she is anything but happy to see them. Even the police tell the beached whalers that they have to leave their jail cell, that it is not a hotel room. Finally, feeling alienated from humanity, the two seamen break into a sporting goods store, and after they have armed themselves with rifles, a bloody shoot-out with the police ensues. SKYTTURNAR received the enthusiastic support of Icelandic director Hrafa Gunnlaugsson, whose 1985 adventure WHEN THE RAVEN FLIES helped bring the Icelandic cinema to international attention.

p&d, Fridrik Thor Fridriksson; w, Fridrik Thor Fridriksson, Einar Karason; ph, Ari Kristinsson (Agfacolor); m, Hilmar Oern Hilmarsson, Bubbi Morthens, Sykurmolarnir; ed, Tomas Gislason, Jens Bidstrup.

Drama **(PR:NR MPAA:NR)**

SLAMDANCE*** (1987, US/Brit.) 99m Sho/Island-Zenith c

Tom Hulce *(C.C. Drood)*, Mary Elizabeth Mastrantonio *(Helen Drood)*, Adam Ant *(Jim)*, Judith Barsi *(Bean Drood)*, Rosalind Chao *(Mrs. Bell)*, Sasha Delgado *(Girl at Nursery)*, Joshua Caceras *(Boy at Nursery)*, Don Opper *(Buddy)*, John Doe *(Gilbert)*, Marty Levy *(Detective)*, Jon C. Slade *(Junkie)*, Julian Deyer *(Cop at Police Station)*, Dennis Hayden *(Mean Drunk)*, Harry Dean Stanton *(Smiley)*, Robert Beltran *(Frank)*, Virginia Madsen *(Yolanda)*, Herta Ware *(Mrs. Raines, C.C's Landlady)*, Marc Anthony Thompson *(Bartender)*, Lin Shaye *(Librarian)*, Michael Ennis *(Morgue Clerk)*, Lisa Niemi *(Ms. Schell)*, Jerris L. Poindexter *(Party Cop)*, Christopher Keene *(Cop on Street)*, Millie Perkins *(Bobbie Nye)*, Laura Campbell *(Pat Minninger)*, Philip Granger *(George)*, John Fleck *(Opera Singer)*, Buckley Norris *(Minister)*, Frazer Smith *(Radio DJ)*.

Taking a break from what he calls his "Chinese stuff," director Wayne Wang (CHAN IS MISSING, DIM SUM) grabbed at the biggest budget he's ever had, $4.5 million, and came up with this stylish murder mystery featuring Academy Award nominees Thomas Hulce and Mary Elizabeth Mastrantonio. Written by writer/actor Don Opper, SLAMDANCE features Hulce as a down-on-his-luck cartoonist who is separated from his wife (Mastrantonio) and his child (Barsi) because of a brief affair with the icily beautiful Madsen. A physical and mental wreck incapable of meeting his deadlines, Hulce is suddenly kidnaped by a gun-toting thug, Opper, and his associate Doe (from the L.A. punk band X), who demand to know where he has hidden a package. Totally ignorant of what they want, Hulce takes a brief beating in the back seat of a car before he manages to fling himself out of the moving vehicle. Later, at the police station, Hulce finds himself in handcuffs and being interrogated by detective Stanton as a prime suspect in the murder of Madsen. Hulce confesses his affair with the deceased and admits that he had agreed to leave town with her but backed down at the last minute. Insisting he knows nothing about the murder and with no evidence against him, Hulce is released. Back at his apartment, Hulce receives a package from his eccentric old landlady (Ware). Sent by Madsen, the package is filled with incriminating sexual photos showing Madsen and several prominent local politicians. Before Hulce can take a good look, however, Opper steps out of the shadows and snatches the package. By now Hulce is obsessed with Madsen's murder and begins his own investigation. He discovers that Doe is a cop and that he and Stanton are somehow involved in the conspiracy and Hulce is the fall guy. Further digging reveals that Madsen was a high-priced call girl, and after meeting one of her coworkers, she wound up dead in Hulce's apartment with all the evidence pointing toward him. Eventually Hulce discovers that Madsen was the lover of powerful local female politician Perkins, and that Opper, the real killer, is her hired thug. Opper, however, had deep feelings for Madsen and instead of knocking off Hulce as he was ordered to do by Perkins, he kills himself. Although alive, Hulce finds himself in an impossible position, for the true culprit is dead and has left no proof of his guilt. Hiding out and desperate for help, Hulce begs Mastrantonio to bring him a change of clothes and some money. She does, but she also calls Stanton, who has grown tired of his own complicity and seeks to help clear Hulce. Unfortunately, Doe arrives on the scene as well and shoots Stanton. Hulce and Doe struggle for a gun and Doe is killed. Now a cop killer, Hulce devises a way to get himself out of this mess. He goes back to the car where Opper's body sits, knocks out the corpse's teeth, inserts his own back plate, removes Opper's belongings and replaces them with his own, and then sets the car on fire, making it appear that he (Hulce) has committed suicide. After Hulce's funeral, his wife and child get inside a limo driven by Hulce himself and the trio drive off to start a new life.

Opper's convoluted script, full of flashbacks, is modern *film noir* and Wang directs it as such, highlighting Hulce's alienation, obsession, and entrapment through claustrophobic, dark, and moody urban visuals. The ill-defined and sometimes confusing plot (the title refers to the violent and chaotic style of punk dancing and is a metaphor for Hulce's predicament) is not as important as conveying the dislocation, helplessness, and entanglement felt by the main character. While Wang, cinematographer Mokri, and production designer Zanetti do a superior job of evoking the traditional style, Wang also includes some of the keenly observed and offbeat moments of character that mark his previous work. Hulce is noncommittal, part child and part man, and during moments of high tension he frequently removes himself from the situation and sees the black humor and irony—as if he is merely one of his own cartoon characters. These moments are usually followed by the same burst of insane laughter that erupts when he has drawn a cartoon that amuses him. Hulce seeks to piece together the puzzle through his art, and his obsession leads him to make dozens of drawings and paintings of Madsen's dead body surrounded by her faceless killers (these later incriminate him when discovered by the police). He is also intrigued by the ghostly Opper and, at one point, dyes his hair and assumes the man's identity in order to crash a party thrown by Perkins. Hulce's strange journey is one that teaches him commitment, a virtue espoused, oddly enough, by Opper. By the end of the film Hulce has learned to commit to himself and his family and is able to start his life anew.

Wang infuses his film with interesting characters, and while some of the seemingly major players may be a bit obtuse (Doe, Stanton, Adam Ant), other minor characters are remarkably well observed, especially Hulce's nearly deaf landlady who is so lonely that she pilfers her tenant's mail and pretends it has been sent to her (both she and Hulce live vicariously through others, he via his cartoon characters, she via her tenants). The performances are uniformly good. Hulce lends a goofy credibility to the whole affair, Mastrantonio conveys a remarkable amount of depth to a character that is given too little screen time, Opper is effectively creepy, Madsen makes a perfect *film noir* icon, and Perkins, Doe, and Adam Ant are memorable as well. Regrettably, Stanton is given so little to do here that SLAMDANCE is the biggest waste of his considerable talent since John Carpenter's CHRISTINE. Although average viewers may find the plot a bit too opaque, knowledgeable fans of *film noir* will find much of interest here. Songs include, "Bing Can't Walk" (Stan Ridgway, performed by Ridgway, Mitchell Froom), "For Sentimental Reasons" (Deek Watson, William Best, performed by Eddie Howard), "Art Life" (Maggie Song, John Dentino, Tom Corey, John Berardi, performed by The Fibonaccis), "High Hopes" (Tim Scott, performed by Scott), "My Heart at Thy Sweet Voice" (Camille Saint-Saens, performed by Adelaide Sinclair, Nolan Van Way). *(Graphic violence, full frontal nudity, profanity).*

p, Rubert Harvey, Barry Opper; d, Wayne Wang; w, Don Opper; ph, Amir Mokri (DeLuxe Color); m, Mitchell Froom; ed, Lee Percy; prod d, Eugenio Zanetti; art d, Philip Dean Foreman; set d, Michael C. Marcus; cos, Malissa Daniel; ch, David Titchnell; makeup, Sheri Short; spec eff, Jerry Williams.

Mystery/Thriller **(PR:O MPAA:R)**

SLAMMER GIRLS† (1987) 80m Platinum/Lightning-Vestron c

Devon Jenkin *(Melody)*, Jeff Eagle *(Harry Wiener)*, Jane Hamilton [Veronica Hart] *(Miss Crabapples, Prison Matron)*, Ron Sullivan *(Gov. Caldwell)*, Tally Brittany, Darcy Nychols, Stasia Micula [Samantha Fox], Sharon Cain, Beth Broderick, Sharon Kelly, Kim Kafkaloff [Sheri St. Claire], Philip Campanaro, Michael Hentzman, Louis Bonanno, Janice Doskey, Jane Kreisel, Captain Haggerty.

One of several 1987 attempts by porno director Chuck Vincent to make it in the mainstream market, this send-up of women's prison films features a cast dotted with adult film stars. Jenkin is sent up river after her failed attempt on the life of governor Sullivan (fans of X rated films may recognize him as director Henri Pachard). Though Jenkin wasn't able to kill Sullivan, she did manage to make a eunuch of him. Behind bars, Jenkin is repeatedly set upon by her fellow inmates, and particularly menaced by Hamilton (better known as porno star Veronica Hart), one of the matrons. A deep, dark secret links all of these events, and journalist Eagle, who masquerades as a woman and infiltrates the slammer, discovers it: Sullivan is Jenkin's father and Hamilton her mother. Shot in 1985, SLAMMER GIRLS was exhibited regionally in a few theaters before entering the home video market.

p&d, Chuck Vincent; w, Craig Horrall, Chuck Vincent, Rick Marx, Larue Watts; ph, Larry Revene; m, Ian Shaw, Kai Joffe; ed, Marc Ubell [Chuck Vincent]; cos, Eddie Heath.

Prison **Cas.** **(PR:NR MPAA:R)**

SLATE, WYN & ME† (1987, Aus.) 90m Hemdale-Intl.Film Mgmt.-Ukiyo/Hemdale c

Sigrid Thornton *(Blanche McBride)*, Simon Burke *(Wyn Jackson)*, Martin Sacks *(Slate Jackson)*, Tommy Lewis *(Morgan)*, Lesley Baker *(Molly)*, Harold Baigent *(Sammy)*, Michelle Torres *(Daphne)*, Murray Fahey *(Martin)*, Taya Straton *(Pippa)*, Julia MacDougall *(Del Downer)*, Peter Cummins *(Old Man Downer)*, Reg Gorman *(Sgt. Wilkinson)*, Warren Owens *(Tommy)*, Eric MacPhan, Simon Westaway *(Policemen)*, Kurt von Schneider *(Truck Driver)*.

Reminiscent of BADLANDS and BONNIE AND CLYDE, this Hemdale production tells the story of two down-and-out Australian brothers—Sacks, a Vietnam veteran, and Burke (THE DEVIL'S PLAYGROUND)—who rob a small-town bank and accidentally shoot a policeman. Thornton (THE MAN FROM SNOWY RIVER), the cop's pretty young schoolteacher friend, witnesses the shooting and the brothers toss her in the trunk of their car as they begin their flight into the Outback, planning to kill her later. They have a change of heart, however. Burke, in particular, begins to take an interest in her, though she makes several unsuccessful attempts to escape. Realizing she isn't going to be able to run away, Thornton begins playing mind games with her captors as they continue their cross-country journey, doggedly pursued by the authorities. At first she cuddles up to the very receptive Burke, but later she turns her attention to Sacks. He becomes infatuated with her, and Burke flies into a jealous rage, forcing her to leave at gunpoint. Soon after, the police arrive and kill Sacks. They apprehend Burke but he escapes and, after recovering the robbery loot, wanders the country until he eventually locates Thornton. He is determined to kill her, but she tells him she is carrying Sacks' baby and Burke leaves her untouched when she promises she will wait for him. Written and directed by Don McLennan, who helmed the excellent HARD KNOCKS (1980, Aus.), this received a scant US theatrical release, but the curious can watch it on videocassette.

p, Tom Burstall; d, Don McLennan; w, Don McLennan (based on the novel *Slate and Wyn and Blanche McBride* by Georgia Savage); ph, David Connell (Panavision, Eastmancolor); m, Peter Sullivan; ed, Peter Friedrich; prod d, Paddy Reardon; cos, Jeanie Cameron; makeup, Felicity Schoeffel; spec eff, Brian Pierce, Peter Stubbs.

Drama **Cas.** **(PR:NR MPAA:NR)**

SLAUGHTER HIGH½** (1987) 88m Vestron c

Caroline Munro *(Carol)*, Simon Scuddamore *(Marty)*, Carmine Iannaccone *(Skip)*, Donna Yaeger *(Stella)*, Gary Hartman *(Joe)*, Billy Martin *(Frank)*, Michael Saffran *(Ted)*, John Segal *(Carl)*, Kelly Baker *(Nancy)*, Sally Cross *(Susan)*, Josephine Scandi *(Shirley)*, Marc Smith *(Coach)*, Dick Randall *(Manny)*, Jon Clark *(Digby)*.

A group of high-school kids, the elite clique of the popular and successful, make nerd Scuddamore the butt of their humiliating April Fool's Day gags. When one trick in the science lab turns bad, Scuddamore is horribly scalded with acid. Years pass and the same group of students is invited to the shuttered high school for a reunion. There they find no party, and later, no exit. One by one they are done away with in gruesome fashion until it slowly begins to dawn on them that they are being victimized by Scuddamore. They make efforts to escape, but eventually they are all dead. Scuddamore takes off his mask and begins laughing with delight at his accomplishment, but then the ghosts of his victims begin to torment him and chase after him. He wakes up in the hospital, his face heavily bandaged, with a nurse trying to calm him. Seems he's in the insane asylum and undergoing plastic surgery. The film ends as he makes his escape, apparently to go make his dream a reality. Superficially indistinguishable from the usual run of this type of film, SLAUGHTER HIGH is a superior example. The high-school revenge plot is always potent, for who wasn't humiliated during those years, and who didn't dream of wreaking a nasty revenge? The story line is as direct as can be and little time is wasted with extraneous subplots. Very effective use is made of the location, a decaying old school building that would give anyone the creeps. Good performances by Scuddamore, Iannaccone, and veteran B-movie starlet Munro further enhance the film. The effects are rather good but not too gross, tending to be almost comic. (One fellow's stomach explodes when he downs an entire can of beer in one swallow.) Cowriters/directors Dugdale, Ezra, and Litten definitely know what they're doing and may be names to look for in the future. *(Gore effects, violence, nudity, substance abuse, excessive profanity.)*

p, Steve Minasian, Dick Randall; d&w, George Dugdale, Mark Ezra, Peter Litten; ph, Alain Pudney; m, Harry Manfredini; ed, Jim Connock; prod d, Geoff Sharpe; cos, Lee Scott; spec eff, Coast to Coast Productions, Peter Litten; makeup, Alison Hall, Craig Berkely.

Horror (PR:O MPAA:R)

SLAVE GIRLS FROM BEYOND INFINITY† (1987) 72m Titan/Urban Classics c

Elizabeth Cayton *(Daria)*, Cindy Beal *(Tisa)*, Brinke Stevens *(Shela)*, Don Scribner *(Zed)*, Carl Horner *(Rik)*, Kirk Graves *(Vak)*, Randolph Roehbling *(Krel)*.

The emphasis in this low-budget space adventure is on its scantily clad female stars. After escaping confinement, Cayton, Beal, and Stevens crash-land on a planet that hunter Scribner prowls in search of human quarry, attended by Graves and Roehbling, his android assistants. In various states of undress, the three beauties try to avoid Scribner and his high-tech weaponry, eventually getting the best of him. Trotting out a marketing device that hasn't been used much in recent years, the distributors released SLAVE GIRLS FROM BEYOND INFINITY and CREEPOZOIDS as a double bill. However, the release was a limited one, and most folks are likely to see SLAVE GIRLS on a double bill with whatever ever else they decide to play on their VCR.

p, Ken Dixon, John Eng, Mark Wolf; d&w, Ken Dixon; ph, Ken Wiatrak, Thomas Callaway (Foto-Kem Color); m, Carl Dante; ed, Bruce Stubblefield, James A. Stewart; md, Jonathan Scott Bogner; art d, Escott Norton; spec eff, Mark Wolf, John Eng, John Buechler, Joe Reader, David Cohen; stunts, Mike Cooper, Greg Cooper.

Adventure/Science Fiction (PR:NR MPAA:R)

SLEDY OBOROTNYA† (1987, Arg./USSR) 93m Lithuanian Films-V/O Sovinfilm-Aries Cinematografica/Sovexportfilm c (Trans: The Werewolf's Tracks)

Sergei Shakurov, Mihai Volontir, Jurate Onaitite, Liliana Lavalie.

Filled with intrigue, this Soviet-Argentine thriller set in a fictitious Latin American country features a Soviet journalist as its hero and a closet Nazi as its villain. A wealthy Latin American industrialist with a reputation for fairness suddenly finds his life threatened. The industrialist believes that his godfather and benefactor, another man of great wealth, has been using him to advance his nefarious goals. He hires a photographer to get pictures of a secret meeting his godfather is conducting, but the spy is captured, though not before hiding the photographic evidence, which comes into the possession of the Soviet journalist. He passes it on to the industrialist, who is killed the same evening, leaving it up to the journalist to put together the clues which identify the godfather as a Nazi war criminal.

d, Almantas Grikyavicus; w, Alexander Lapshin, Vladimir Vesensky; ph, Donatas Pecura; m, Juozas Sirvinskas; art d, Mikhail Malkov.

Thriller (PR:NR MPAA:NR)

SLEEP WELL, MY LOVE† (1987, Brit./Swed.) 97m Planborg/Bell c

Debra Beaumont *(Siska Torot)*, Mark Burns *(Her Father)*, Fiona Curzon *(Her Mother)*, Pedrag Bjelac *(The Stud)*, Norman Bowler *(Tom Berto)*, Michael Gothard *(The Hitman)*, Pedrag Bjelac *(The Stud)*, Carl Duering, Lidija Jenko.

Mom wants to make a pauper of Dad, Dad wants Mom dead, and their daughter succeeds in killing both of them in this cheery British-Swedish soap opera set in Yugoslavia. The not-so-happy family—Mom Curzon, ex-husband Burns, and 16-year-old daughter Beaumont—are guests at a posh Yugoslavian hotel. Burns and Beaumont have been sleeping together, and Curzon, who knows all about it, has been trying to blackmail her ex; hence he takes out a contract on her. Before either of them gets satisfaction, however, Beaumont, who has the hots for one of Curzon's lovers, kills both of her parents. Featuring both British and Yugoslavian actors, SLEEP WELL, MY LOVE was directed by Swedish veteran Arne Mattson (THE DOLL, 1964; WOMAN OF DARKNESS, 1968; MY FATHER'S MISTRESS, 1970).

p, Conny Planborg; d, Arne Mattson; w, Jonathan Rumbold (based on a story by Ernest Hotch); ph, Tomislav Pinter (Eastmancolor); m, Alfi Kabiljo; ed, Derek Trigg; prod d, Zeljko Senecic.

Romance/Thriller (PR:NR MPAA:NR)

SLEEPING BEAUTY† (1987) 90m Golan-Globus/Cannon c

Morgan Fairchild *(Queen)*, David Holliday *(King)*, Tahnee Welch *(Rosebud)*, Nicholas Clay *(Prince)*, Sylvia MIles *(Red Fairy)*, Kenny Baker *(Elf)*, Jane Weidlin *(White Fairy)*, Julian Chagrin *(Court Advisor)*.

Morgan Fairchild stars in this Cannon-produced version of Charles Perrault's delightful fairy tale about the beautiful princess who, as a result of a magic spell, is doomed to sleep for 100 years unless a noble prince can reach her with a spell-breaking kiss. Clay plays the prince who does just that after braving the imposing forest that surrounds the castle where Fairchild sleeps. The story was first brought to the screen as an excellent animated feature by Walt Disney in 1959.

p, Menahem Golan, Yoram Globus; d, David Irving; w, Michael Berz (based on a story by Charles Perrault); ph, David Gurfinkel; ed, Tova Neeman; prod d, Marek Dobrowlski; cos, Debbie Leon.

Children's/Fantasy (PR:NR MPAA:NR)

SLUCHAYNYE PASSAZHIRY† (1987, USSR) 79m Lenfilm/Sovexportfilm c (Trans: Chance Passengers)

Vladimir Gostyukhin, Larisa Grebenschikova, Zinaida Sharko, Nikolai Grinko.

When confronted with an emergency, a gruff, unscrupulous truck driver proves to have a heart of gold. He encounters a teacher and a group of kids from an orphanage stranded by the roadside, and, showing a compassionate side that is usually buried deep in his personality, he gives them a ride to town. En route, one of the kids becomes sick and the trucker rushes to the nearest hospital; however, the truck breaks down on the middle of a bridge. One by one, the trucker carries his passengers through the icy water to safety. Then, miraculously, he starts the engine and he and his "chance passengers" are off to the hospital, where he passes out only after his heroic feat is accomplished.

d, Mikhail Ordovsky; w, Yuri Sbitnev; ph, Vladimir Burykin; art d, Boris Burmistrov.

Drama (PR:NR MPAA:NR)

SLUMBER PARTY MASSACRE II½** (1987) 90m Concorde/EM c

Crystal Bernard *(Courtney)*, Jennifer Rhodes *(Mrs. Bates)*, Kimberly McArthur *(Amy)*, Patrick Lowe *(Matt)*, Juliette Cummins *(Sheila)*, Heidi Kozak *(Sally)*, Cynthia Eilbacher *(Valerie)*, Atanas Ilitch *(The Driller Killer)*, Joel Hoffman *(T.J.)*, Marshall La Plante *(Car Driver)*, Don Daniel *(Mr. Damnkids)*, Michael Delano *(Officer Kroeger)*, Hamilton Mitchell *(Officer Voorhies)*.

The original SLUMBER PARTY MASSACRE is one of the few films in the slasher genre directed and written by women (Amy Jones and Rita Mae Brown, respectively). This one carries on that vaguely feminist tradition, having been produced, directed, and written by Deborah Brock. The film gets underway as Bernard, the sister of the girl who survived SPM I, goes off on a weekend trip with the other members of her all-girl rock band. They are going to stay at the new condominium owned by one girl's father, and some boys are going to join them. Bernard is plagued by dreams in which a black-leather-clad rockabilly singer with an auger at the end of his guitar attacks her and her friends. She repeatedly wakes up hysterical and her friends begin to grow upset with her. Suddenly, though, he actually appears, gleefully drilling the boys and girls while doing little dance steps. At one point he even looks straight into the camera and says, "This is the fun part," before launching into a musical number called "Buzz, Buzz," culminating in another girl with a gaping hole in her chest. Bernard manages to escape the house and runs through a number of new home construction sites before she finds an oxy-acetylene cutting torch and sets the killer on fire. The ending is one of those Oh-it-was-only-a-dream-no-it-wasn't-yes-it-was-no-you're-really-insane things so familiar to horror aficionados, but it doesn't detract from the film.

Atanas Ilitch is the killer, and probably the most entertaining slasher ever to grace the screen. It's sort of like Elvis Presley playing Norman Bates, complete with musical numbers. Usually it is no mystery why some films go straight to video without theatrical release, but this film is far above the caliber of most straight-to video releases. Perhaps on tape it will gain the cult audience this original and funny horror film deserves. *(Gore effects, brief nudity, sexual situations, substance abuse, profanity.)*

p, Deborah Brock, Don Daniel; d&w, Deborah Brock; ph, Thomas Callaway; art d, Frank Novak; set d, Rozanne Taucher; cos, Nadine Reimers; spec eff, Margaret Bessera, Bill Corso, J. Scott Coulter, John Criswell, Jeff Farley, Hal Miles, Robert Standlee; m/l, John Coinman, Kristi Callan, Kelly Callan, Michael Monagan, Gregory Lee Schilling, Heidi Rodewald, John Jake Logan, Sterling E. Smith; makeup, Susan Reiner.

Horror Cas. (PR:O MPAA:NR)

SNAYPERY† (1987, USSR) 100m Kazakhfilm/Sovexportfilm c (Trans: Snipers)

Aiturgan Temirova, Marina Yakovleva, Vera Glagoleva, Yuosas Kiselus.

Soviet biopic focuses on Aliya Moldagulova, a 17-year-old WW II hero who lied about her age to get into the army and then underwent the rigorous training necessary to become a sniper. When her battalion commander fell in battle against the Germans, she rallied the troops to continue their assault. Though killed in that same battle, she was posthumously honored as a Hero of the Soviet.

d, Bolotbek Shamshiyev; w, M. Simashko, S. Askarov, B. Shamshiyev; ph, Murat Aliyev, Marat Duganov; m, Viktor Lebedev; art d, Alexander Chertovich.

Biography (PR:NR MPAA:NR)

SNOW QUEEN, THE† (1987, Fin.) 90m Neofilmi/Finnkino c (LUMIKUNINGATAR)

Outi Vainionkulma *(Greta)*, Sebastian Kaatrasalo *(Kaj)*, Satu Silvo *(The Snow Queen)*, Tuula Nyman, Esko Hukkanen, Pirjo Bergstrom, Markko Huhtamo, Antti Litja, Elina Salo. Marja Pyykko.

This Finnish version of Hans Christian Andersen's classic fairy tale is both an allegory of the eternal battle between good and evil and the story of the redemptive power of true love. Silvo is the wicked Snow Queen, but she aspires to an even more regal and malevolent title—the Queen of Darkness. Before she is able

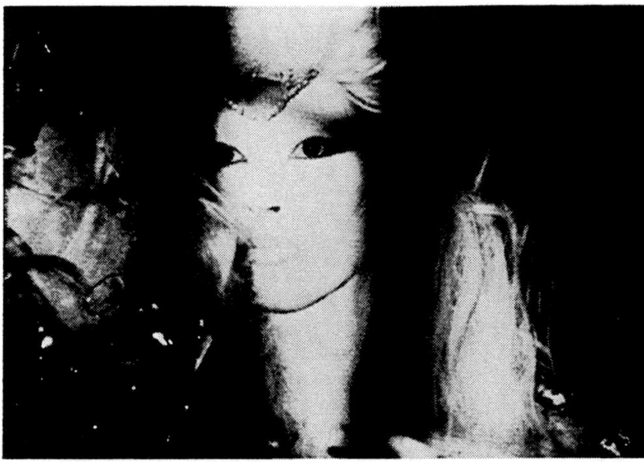

to make the world her icy dominion, Silvo must first possess the mystical powers of the Green Gemstone. To get the gem, she needs the assistance of an innocent child. Kaatrasalo fits the bill perfectly. Silvo literally freezes the boy's heart and then takes him with her as she pursues her evil design. Vainionkulma is the little girl who loves Kaatrasalo, and she follows Silvo to the ends of the earth, or at least to the Snow Queen's castle in the frozen North. There, the glow of Vainionkulma's love melts the evil in Kaatrasalo's heart. The boy is saved and the world is no longer threatened by Silvo's tyranny. Producer-director-writer Hartzell is no stranger to the children's genre, having previously made award-winning shorts and animated flims. THE SNOW QUEEN won the Anjalankoski prize as the best Finnish film of 1986. A Russian-made animated version of Andersen's tale was released in 1959.

p,d&w, Paivi Hartzell (based on the fairy tale by Hans Christian Andersen); ph, Henrik Paersch; m, Jukka Linkola; ed, Anne Lakanen, Olli Soinio; prod d, Reija Hirvikoski; spec eff, Jukka Ruohomaki, Antti Kari, Lauri Pitkanen.

Childrens's **(PR:NR MPAA:NR)**

SNOW WHITE† (1987) 83m Golan-Globus/Cannon c

Diana Rigg *(Mean Queen)*, Billy Barty *(Iddy)*, Sarah Patterson *(Snow White at 16)*, Nicola Stapleton *(Snow White at 7)*, Mike Edmunds *(Biddy)*, Ricardo Gil *(Kiddy)*, Malcolm Dixon *(Diddy)*, Gary Friedkin *(Fiddy)*, Tony Cooper *(Liddy)*, Douglas Sheldon *(King)*, Dorit Adi, Ian James Wright, Annon Meskin.

Though one would think Walt Disney's 1937 animated masterpiece SNOW WHITE AND THE SEVEN DWARFS is pretty much the definitive cinematic statement of the classic Brothers Grimm tale, other filmmakers have taken on the story, and now Cannon takes its shot. This live-action musical version stars Sarah Patterson (who made such a splash in THE COMPANY OF WOLVES [1985]) as the title beauty and also features Diana Rigg in the hammy part as the wicked queen. SNOW WHITE seems like a good candidate for videocassette release.

p, Menahem Golan, Yoram Globus; d&w, Michael Berz; art d, Etan Levy.

Children's **(PR:NR MPAA:NR)**

SO VIELE TRAUME† (1987, E. Ger.) 82m Defa Studio-Gruppe Babelsberg/Defa Aussenhandel c (Trans: So Many Dreams)

Jutta Wachowiak *(Christine Kluver)*, Peter Rene Ludicke *(Ludwig Grabner)*, Dagmar Manzel *(Claudia Seydel)*, Hieko Hehlman *(Gunnar Kluver)*, Thomas Hinrich, Gudron Okras, Christine Harbort.

A mother and daughter reunite during a party thrown in honor of the mother's work as a midwife. The daughter, Manzel, has returned unexpectedly to lash out against her mother, Wachowiak, because the latter let her husband take custody of the young Manzel. The third episode in Carow's trilogy of independent, modern women.

d, Heiner Carow; w, Heiner Carow, Wolfram Witt, Erika Richter (based on documentary material collected by Imma Luning); ph, Peter Ziesche (Orwocolor); m, Stefan Carow; ed, Evelyn Carow; prod d, Christopher Schneider; cos, Regina Viertel.

Drama **(PR:NR MPAA:NR)**

SOFIA*½** (1987, Arg.) 100m Rosafrey y Susy Surany y Asociados/Rosafrey c (Trans: Sophia)

Dora Baret *(Sofia)*, Alejandro Milrud *(Pedro)*, Graciela Dufau *(Pedro's Mother)*, Hector Alterio *(Pedro's Father)*, Lito Cruz, Monica Villa.

Another superb entry from Argentina—a country which has recently pumped some new blood into world cinema. After an impressive showing last year led by MAN FACING SOUTHEAST, BAD COMPANY, A KING AND HIS MOVIE, and NIGHTMARE'S PASSENGERS, The Argentinian film industry delivers another vital piece of work in SOFIA. It stars Milrud as Pedro, a middle-class 17-year-old who turns his back on his family, friends, and school in order to help Baret, an emotionally and physically weary woman who is being hunted by the intolerant, government-backed militia during the dark days of junta rule. The political climate in Argentina is volatile—subversives are found dead in the streets, airports and train stations are crowded with heavily armed guards, and citizens are routinely apprehended if caught without their identification papers. Milrud's friends and classmates, however, are primarily concerned with losing their virginity to a local prostitute—a group activity in which Milrud decides not to take part. One evening Baret, looking helpless and frightened, takes Milrud's arm and solicits his help in escaping the attention of some guards. Moments later she disappears without even giving her name. Over the next few days, the smitten Milrud spots Baret wandering through the streets, riding the bus, and talking in a telephone booth. He finally catches up to her in a church where she collapses from exhaustion. After finding her a place to sleep for the evening, Milrud offers her safe haven in his parents' second home. She explains that she is wanted by the government as a subversive because of her involvement with a Communist. She has no idea of her lover's whereabouts and wants only to escape from Argentina. Milrud finds himself infatuated with Baret, skipping school and staying away from home for days at a time. After Baret spurns Milrud's first sexual advance, the jilted teenager heads home, leaving Baret behind in his parents' house. His parents realize that he is involved with some girl, but have no idea that she is twice his age and wanted by the government. He eventually returns to Baret, who offers herself to him, teaching the virginal youngster how to love a woman. The pair become lovers and Milrud makes plans to escape to Europe with Baret. After efforts to contact Baret's former friends fail, Milrud steals his parents' passports. The boy's father, Alterio, then confronts Baret. In an effort to keep his son out of trouble, Alterio pressures Baret to leave, giving her some money and a promise that he will not notify the authorities. However, Milrud tracks down Baret, bringing her the news that a friend has arranged for a safe passage out of the country. At the last minute Milrud realizes that Baret has been set up. As she is taken away by armed guards, Milrud can do nothing but hopelessly give chase.

Merging elements of romance, drama, politics, and comedy, SOFIA is a skillfully crafted, superbly acted picture which concentrates more on its characters' dilemmas and emotions than on the larger issue of Argentinian politics. Instead of becoming immersed in political details or propaganda, director Doria crafts a moving story about the opposing forces pulling at a young man. Rather than accept the choices that are offered him by his family, his friends, and the government, Milrud chooses to exercise his individual freedoms. He skips school, risks arrest by the militia, and refuses to be brainwashed by officials who tell him to inform on subversives. Instead of acting as part of a group (be it his school, friends, or family), Milrud takes his chances outside of government and socially imposed rules. He helps Baret not because of her political convictions but because she, too, is an individual fighting a struggle. Instead of fighting alone, Baret and Milrud find understanding and companionship in each other. Both actors turn in arresting performances—Baret portraying a frightened woman who tries to hide her fear, and Milrud an idealistic youngster who makes every effort to be brave and comforting. Besides being a very fine actor, the somewhat gawky Milrud is blessed with a sense of comic timing which reminds the audience (and Baret) that there is still a boyish quality which undermines his efforts at manhood. Deserving special mention are Dufau and Alterio as Milrud's parents—a middle-class couple who are learning to cope with their son's restlessness and individuality. Although they set certain rules and attempt to be strict, they love him too much to oppose his actions. One of the film's finest scenes is Alterio's confrontation with Baret. Although he pressures the woman to leave his son, there is a certain reluctance in his doing so. He understands her loneliness and fear, even offering her a friendly pat on the shoulder as a way of expressing his good will. His main concern, however, is the safety of his son and he makes it clear that, although he sympathizes with Baret, he will fight to keep Milrud from harm. SOFIA is a coming-of-age film in which the main characters have substantive problems, as opposed to the Brat-Packers in John Hughes' films who worry about their high-school prom. *(Brief nudity, sexual situations.)*

p, Diana Frey; d, Alejandro Doria; w, Alejandro Doria, Jacobo Langsner (based on a story idea by Miguel Rodriguez); ph, Miguel Rodriguez; m, Luis Maria Serra, Edvard Grieg.

Drama/Romance **(PR:O MPAA:NR)**

SOIGNE TA DROITE† (1987, Fr./Switz.) 82m Gaumont-JLG-Xanadu c (Trans: Keep Up Your Right)

Jean-Luc Godard *(The Idiot/The Prince)*, Jacques Villeret *(The Individual)*, Francois Perier *(The Man)*, Jane Birkin *(The Cricket)*, Michel Galabru *(The Admiral)*, Dominique Lavanant *(The Admiral's Wife)*, Jacques Rufus *(The Policeman)*, Pauline Lafont *(The Golfer)*, Catherine Ringer, Frederic Chichin *(Musicians)*, Isabelle Sadoyan, Laurence Masliah, Rita Mitsouko.

Although it was shot after Godard's much-publicized Cannon venture KING LEAR, SOIGNE TA DROITE is the first of the two films to see a theatrical release. (KING LEAR played only the Toronto Festival of Festivals in 1987 and will not receive a theatrical showing until early 1988.) Here Godard again stretches the limitations of cinema through three interwoven stories: a group of plane passengers travel through the air under the care of a suicidal pilot; a hapless worker looks for friendship with a number of couples; and a group of musicians rehearse for a recording session. Godard, with his playfully irreverent sense of humor, gives cinematography credit to Mr. Eastman and sound credit to Mr. Dolby.

d&w, Jean-Luc Godard; ph, Caroline Champetier (Eastmancolor); m, les Rita Mitsouko; ed, Jean-Luc Godard.

Drama **(PR:NR MPAA:NR)**

SOLDATI: 365 GIORNI ALL' ALBA† (1987, It.) 100m Reteitalia-Numero Uno/CIDIF c (Trans: Soldiers: 365 Till Dawn)

Claudio Amendola *(Claudio Scanna)*, Massimo Dapporto *(Sgt. Fili)*, Agostina

Belli *(Mrs. Fili)*, Claudio Botosso *(The Doctor)*, Alessandro Benvenuti, Manlio Dovi, Ernesto Lama, Roberto Cavosi, Ugo Conti, Ivo Garrani, Antonella Ponziani.

A young Italian army recruit, Amendola, must serve his mandatory year of military service and in the process incurs the wrath of his cruel drill sergeant, Dapporto. The sergeant tries to destroy Amendola's strong will by assigning him to bathroom duty for his entire stay, but the recruit cannot be broken. Directed by Marco Risi, son of veteran director Dino Risi.

p, Claudio Bonivento; d, Marco Risi; w, Marco Modugno, Marco Risi, Stefano Sudrie, Furio Scarpelli; ph, Giuseppe Berardini (Eastmancolor); m, Manuel De Sica; ed, Claudio Di Mauro.

Drama **(PR:NR MPAA:NR)**

SOME KIND OF WONDERFUL*** (1987) 93m PAR c

Eric Stoltz *(Keith Nelson)*, Mary Stuart Masterson *(Watts/"Drummer Girl")*, Lea Thompson *(Amanda Jones)*, Craig Sheffer *(Hardy Jenns)*, John Ashton *(Cliff Nelson)*, Elias Koteas *(Skinhead)*, Molly Hagan *(Shayne)*, Maddie Corman *(Laura Nelson)*, Jane Elliot *(Carol Nelson)*, Candace Cameron *(Cindy Nelson)*, Chynna Philips *(Mia)*.

This virtual remake of last year's John Hughes-Howard Deutch teenage angst epic PRETTY IN PINK overcomes its lack of originality via an interesting gender change and superior performances from Masterson and Stoltz. This time out Stoltz is the Molly Ringwald character. Quiet, shy, and an aspiring artist from the wrong side of the tracks, Stoltz is in love from afar with Thompson (in the Andrew McCarthy role), a beautiful working-class girl from his neighborhood who has somehow been accepted by the rich "preppies" at school. What Stoltz fails to realize, however, is that his best friend since childhood, tomboy drummer Masterson (taking the Jon Cryer part), has blossomed into a winsome young woman herself and has a desperate crush on him. Much to Stoltz's surprise, Thompson agrees to go on a date with him. However, unbeknownst to Stoltz, she is using him to get back at her vile ultra-snobby boy friend Sheffer (filling the generic James Spader role) who has been taking her for granted. Although it breaks her heart to see him mooning over such a vapid prom-queen type and despite her efforts to convince him he is being used, Masterson agrees to help Stoltz make his date a success. In the most emotionally powerful scene to appear in *any* John Hughes film, Masterson tries to teach Stoltz how to kiss. Affecting an air of indifference, Masterson coaches the somewhat dim Stoltz in the fine art of necking. As their lips touch Masterson's facade melts and her passion for the boy takes over. He, on the other hand, continues to believe that what is taking place is merely an academic exercise and does not surrender to her yearning. Frustrated by his lack of response, Masterson abruptly breaks the clinch and walks off, angry and embarrassed, mumbling to Stoltz that he did just fine. In a misguided effort to really impress Thompson, Stoltz withdraws his college savings and spends it on a pair of diamond earrings, a limo, and first-class accommodations for their big night out. In a strange fit of masochism, Masterson agrees to act as the couple's chauffeur so she can watch the depressing proceedings. As the date unfolds, Thompson, who is touched by Stoltz's lavish attentions, has a fit of the guilties and confesses to Stoltz that she has used him. Stoltz is unfazed by the revelation; after all, he had been warned. Instead of mutual recriminations, the pair discuss the value of being true to yourself, the horrors of peer pressure, not forgetting your roots, and other such things teens talk about in John Hughes movies. Thompson decides not to go back to the smug Sheffer, but then advises Stoltz that he should take a few steps back and look at Masterson's obvious attributes and devotion. Finally the dunderhead realizes what true love is, and in a surprisingly touching finale, he gives the diamond earrings to Masterson and they kiss for real this time.

While SOME KIND OF WONDERFUL deserves some healthy contempt for its cribbed screenplay, the superb performances simply overpower the usual annoying Hughesisms. Stoltz, who played the horribly deformed Rocky Dennis in MASK, turns in a restrained, realistic portrayal of a somewhat insecure teenager whose confidence in himself grows during the course of the film. Thankfully bereft of some of the typical fashion and attitude baggage found in most of Hughes' films, Stoltz comes across as a fairly normal guy who isn't so alienated by his lack of popularity that he feels compelled to draw negative attention to

himself—he's basically a loner. Thompson is quite good in what could easily have become a thankless role. She parlays her beauty into something more complex than the average good-looking high-school ditz character normally found in films of this type. There is enough substance in her performance to provide a solid basis for Stoltz's crush so that he doesn't appear to be just a lovesick dolt. But far and away, this is Masterson's film. An amazingly mature young actress, Masterson skillfully brings subtlety, depth, and nuance to her character that most assuredly do not exist in Hughes' tired screenplay. Her scenes with Stoltz are some of the most refreshingly honest and emotionally complex interactions to hit the screen in quite some time. She is simply the most vibrant, interesting, and natural teenager to be found in John Hughes' entire *ouvre*. Although Molly Ringwald exudes a likable naturalness, her performances seem more instinct than acting—she is a teenage *star*. Masterson, on the other hand, is a supremely intelligent *actress* who delves inside her roles and discovers what makes them tick. The difference between Ringwald and Masterson is the difference between raw personality and applied expertise. The Hughes teen-machine owes this young actress a big debt, for what is wonderful about SOME KIND OF WONDERFUL is not his lazy screenplay, but Mary Stuart Masterson's virtuoso performance. As usual there are a bevy of hip pop tunes on the soundtrack with the Lick The Tins version of "Can't Help Falling in Love" (George Weiss, Hugo Peretti, Luigi Creatore) and "Amanda Jones" (Mick Jagger, Keith Richards) used to good effect. *(Profanity.)*

p, John Hughes; d, Howard Deutch; w, John Hughes; ph, Jan Kiesser (Technicolor); m, Stephen Rague, John Musser; ed, Bud Smith, Scott Smith; prod d, Josan Russo; art d, Greg Pickrell; set d, Linda Spheeris; cos, Marilyn Vance-Straker.

Romance **Cas.** **(PR:C MPAA:PG-13)**

SOMEONE TO LOVE† (1987) 109m International Rainbow c

Orson Welles *(Danny's Friend)*, Henry Jaglom *(Danny Sapir)*, Andrea Marcovicci *(Helen Eugene)*, Michael Emil *(Mickey Sapir)*, Sally Kellerman *(Edith Helm)*, Oja Kodar *(Yelena)*, Stephen Bishop *(Blue)*, Dave Frishberg *(Harry)*, Geraldine Baron, Ronee Blakley, Barbara Flood, Pamela Goldblum, Robert Hallak, Kathryn Harrold, Monte Hellman, Jeremy Paul Kagan, Michael Kaye, Miles Kreuger, Amnon Meskin, Sunny Meyer, Peter Rafelson, Ora Rubens, Ketherine Wallach.

This feature by Hollywood independent Jaglom will best be remembered as the final film role for Orson Welles, Jaglom's longtime friend. Jaglom stars as a film director who invites friends to a St. Valentine's Day party. The guests arrive at a splendiferous old theater in Santa Monica, California (the Mayfair Music Hall) unaware of Jaglom's real intentions—to film people and ask them, "Why are you alone?" Some guests leave, others toss the question off with a flip answer, while others respond openly and emotionally. By the end of the film, Welles offers his comments on the question, calls "Cut" to the cameraman, and bursts into his charming laugh. Besides Welles and Jaglom, the cast includes Welles' steady companion Kodar, singer Marcovicci, Sally Kellerman, and directors Monte Hellman and Jeremy Paul Kagan. SOMEONE TO LOVE was shown in the "Un Certain Regard" section of the Cannes Film Festival and at the AFI Festival, but despite Welles' appearance hasn't received much of an arthouse showing.

p, M.H. Simonsons; d&w, Henry Jaglom; ph, Hanania Baer.

Comedy/Drama **(PR:NR MPAA:NR)**

SOMEONE TO WATCH OVER ME*** (1987) 106m COL c

Tom Berenger *(Mike Keegan)*, Mimi Rogers *(Claire Gregory)*, Lorraine Bracco *(Ellie Keegan)*, Jerry Orbach *(Lt. Garber)*, John Rubinstein *(Neil Steinhart)*, Andreas Katsulas *(Joey Venza)*, Tony DiBenedetto *(T.J.)*, James Moriarty *(Koontz)*, Mark Moses *(Win Hockings)*, Daniel Hugh Kelly *(Scotty)*, Harley Cross *(Tommy Keegan)*, Joanne Baron *(Helen Greening)*, Anthony Bishop *(Waiter)*, David Berman *(Cop #1)*, Sharon Brecke *(Bimbo)*, Peter Carew *(Doorman)*, Christopher Cass *(Rookie Cop)*, Jim Paul Eilers *(Sparks)*, Susi Gilder *(Pretty Young Thing)*, Mary Gillis *(Mary the Maid)*, Billy Kane *(Brooklyn)*, Helen Lambros *(Met Benefactress)*, Jack McGee *(Bartender)*, Meg Mundy *(Antonia)*, Jeff Nielsen *(Tie Salesman)*, Harlan Cary Poe *(Killer)*, Marilyn Rockafel-

low *(Marge)*, Helen Tran *(Vietnamese Girl)*, Harvey Vernon *(Giddings)*, Mark Voland *(Plainclothesman)*.

Hot on the heels of the surprise hit FATAL ATTRACTION comes yet another film about a happily married man who strays from the marital bed, SOMEONE TO WATCH OVER ME. Set in New York City, the film stars Berenger as a beat cop who has recently been promoted to detective. Married to spunky ex-cop Bracco, Berenger makes his home in Queens and worries that the neighborhood is becoming a place where he doesn't want to raise his young son, Cross. Meanwhile, just across the river in Manhattan, wealthy socialite Rogers witnesses the murder of one of her oldest friends. The killer, Katsulas, sees Rogers and tries to kill her as well, but she escapes and alerts the police. Ignoring the advice of her snooty boy friend Rubinstein, Rogers agrees to identify the killer once he is caught. Because Katsulas is known to have connections in organized crime, the police put a 24-hour watch on Rogers and beg her to stay in her swank Fifth Avenue apartment. Much to his chagrin, Berenger is given the 8:00 p.m. to 4:00 a.m. shift. Although cold and aloof at first, Rogers begins to warm to the handsome, shy, and somewhat dim-witted detective. Berenger is bored by the assignment, but intrigued with Roger's beauty, independence, and basic decency amid the decadent splendor of her surroundings. The two grow close, and when Katsulas is captured and then subsequently freed on a technicality, the distraught Rogers turns to Berenger. In the heat of the moment their repressed feelings for each other turn passionate and they begin an affair. Despite the fact that he loves his wife and feels guilty, Berenger cannot tear himself away from Rogers, whom he has fallen in love with, too. Eventually the suspicious Bracco realizes that her husband is having an affair with the rich society woman and kicks him out of the house, telling him she may take him back if he returns for her and not just for their child's sake. The affair affects his job as well, for Berenger spends the night with Rogers as a civilian while another cop, DiBenedetto, covers for him. That night Katsulas sends an assassin to kill Rogers, but the intruder happens upon DiBenedetto first and shoots him. Berenger hears the commotion and kills the assassin. For this he is suspended and told to stay away from Rogers as long as she is under police protection. After learning that Berenger and Rogers are having an affair, Katsulas kidnaps Berenger's son and holds the boy and his mother hostage. Ignoring police procedure, Berenger rushes home with Rogers (who refuses to stay behind) and confronts the killer, who demands Rogers in exchange for the detective's family. With another cop disguised as Rogers, Berenger manages to fool Katsulas long enough for the quick-thinking Cross to toss Bracco her gun. Bracco kills Katsulas, saving the lives of her son and husband. Back outside, Rogers and Berenger go their separate ways, knowing that their relationship will never work. Tentatively, Berenger returns to his family to find that they will take him back.

Although both FATAL ATTRACTION and SOMEONE TO WATCH OVER ME have some major problems in the plot plausibility department, the latter is superior because the emphasis is on the people involved in the romantic triangle and not the machinations of a contrived story line. Once the situation is established, director Scott explores the complicated emotions that tie the characters together and seems disinterested with genre expectations. FATAL ATTRACTION, on the other hand, throws characterization to the wind and instead goes for slasher-film shock and suspense. The problem with both films is that neither manages to incorporate both halves of their plots into a satisfying whole. Perhaps much of the credit for what works in SOMEONE TO WATCH OVER ME should go to the excellent cast. Berenger is superb as the emotionally confused detective who finds himself in love with two very different women. In contrast to Michael Douglas' character in FATAL ATTRACTION, Berenger maintains viewer sympathy throughout his sensitive portrayal and the extramarital romance is something that occurs naturally, without either party really looking for it. Rogers proves here that she can handle a lead role with class and aplomb. She is breathtakingly beautiful, and her performance is quiet, subtle, and nuanced as she humanizes what could have been a cold and thankless role. Bracco, however, steals the picture with her charming, dignified, and tough performance as Berenger's no-nonsense wife who can make it on her own if need be. She, too, could have simply allowed a stereotyped role do most of the work, but instead she infuses the part with an energy and wit that is refreshing to watch. It is to the credit of director Scott and his actors that all the characters involved in this romantic triangle remain sympathetic and realistic throughout—no one here is merely selfish, just plain "perfect," or a pathetic lunatic.

Unfortunately, SOMEONE TO WATCH OVER ME fails when it tries to be a thriller. Katsulas is nothing but a boogeyman who pops up when needed to warp the narrative in a new direction. His characterization is inconsistent (he seems both very clever and very stupid, but never the psycho he's supposed to be), and the climax is as annoyingly contrived and illogical as the conclusion of the Berenger/Rogers affair is pat. Scott, in his first film with a contemporary setting, does his usually superior job on the visuals, contrasting the "real" workaday world of Queens with the glittering glamour of midtown Manhattan. The two "different worlds" are shown in the opening credits sequence during one magnificent helicopter shot that starts at the beautiful Chrysler Building at night and ends at Berenger's house in Queens. Surprisingly, the art gallery where the initial murder takes place was filmed in the indoor-swimming-pool room of the *Queen Mary* (docked in Long Beach, California) because of its opulent art-deco decor. Songs include "Someone to Watch Over Me" (George and Ira Gershwin, performed by Sting; Gene Ammons with Richard Wyands, Doug Watkins, J.C. Heard; Roberta Flack), "Johnny Come Home" (David Steele, Roland Gift, performed by Fine Young Cannibals), "Suspicious Minds" (Mark James, performed by Fine Young Cannibals), "Eight Little Notes" (Audrey Hall, performed by Hall), "Cry" (Churchill Kohlman, performed by Johnny Ray), "Freedom Overspill" (Steve Winwood, George Flemming, James Hooker, performed by Winwood), "What More Can I Ask" (Ray Noble, Anona Winn, performed by Noble and his Orchestra), Aria from "La Wally" (Alfredo Catalani, performed by Wilhelminia Wiggans Fernandez with the London Symphony Orchestra), "Marie, Marie" (Dave Alvin, performed by The Blasters), "Viens Mallika" (Leo Delibes, performed by Mady Mesple), "Smoke Gets in Your Eyes" (Jerome Kern, Otto Harbach, performed by Irene Dunne), "Memories of Green" (Vangelis, performed by The New American Orchestra), "Walk Right In" (Gus Cannon, H. Woods, performed by Tex Beneke). *(Graphic violence, adult situations, sexual situations, profanity.)*

p, Thierry de Ganay, Harold Schneider; d, Ridley Scott; w, Howard Franklin; ph, Steven Poster (Deluxe Color); m, Michael Kamen; ed, Claire Simpson; prod d, Jim Bissell; art d, Chris Burian-Mohr, Jay Moore; set d, Jim Teegarden, Ann Harris; cos, Colleen Atwood; m/l, George Gershwin, Ira Gershwin, David Steele, Roland Gift, Mark James, Audrey Hall, Churchill Kohlman, Steve Winwood, George Flemming, James Hooker, Ray Noble, Anona Winn, Alfredo Catalani, Dave Alvin, Leo Delibes, Jerome Kern, Otto Harbach, Vangelis, Gus Cannon, H. Woods; makeup, Rick Sharp, Alan Weisinger; stunts, Glenn Wilder, Ronnie Rondell.

Thriller/Romance **(PR:O MPAA:R)**

SOMETHING SPECIAL!½** (1987) 90m Imagewworks-CRC-Cinema Group/Concorde-Cinema Group c (AKA: WILLY MILLY)

Pamela Segall *(Milly/Willy Niceman)*, Eric Gurry *(Alfie Bensdorf)*, Mary Tanner *(Stephanie)*, Patty Duke *(Mrs. Doris Niceman)*, John Glover *(Mr. Fred Niceman)*, Seth Green *(Malcolm, Stephanie's Brother)*, John David Cullum *(Tom)*, Jeb Ellis-Brown *(Harry Harl)*, Taryn Grimes *(Cynthia Harl)*, Corey Parker *(Lopez)*, Bobby Emmrich *(Luke)*, Mike McGehee *(Smiley)*, Robin Jackson *(Witch)*, Charles Darden *(Mailman)*, Lori Werner *(Drum Majorette)*, Kim Minard *(Marsha)*, Kelliene Fisher *(Luke's Girl)*, Vickie Ackerman *(Smiley's Girl)*, Leonard O. Shinew, Gladys Hollyfield *(Lawn Sale Couple)*, Diane Bogino, Milton Chaikin *(Doctors)*.

The story of a 14-year-old girl (Segall) who envies boys, believing that their lives are simpler and more interesting than those of girls. As the film opens, Green, brother of Segall's best friend Tanner, is traveling the neighborhood, swapping and selling various items. He supplies Segall with lenses for her telescope, then sells her what he says is "eclipse powder," claiming that her "deepest, darkest heart's desire" will be realized if she uses the powder during an upcoming eclipse. She follows his instructions, then wakes up to find she has grown a penis. Naturally, her parents, Duke and Glover, are shocked. Segall asks if she can be both a boy and a girl, but Glover says she must chose one or the other. She flips a letter on a bulletin board and it ends up a "W," so she becomes "Willy" instead if "Milly." Under her male identity, she enrolls in a new high school, making friends with the wheelchair-bound Gurry, but running afoul of the class bully, Ellis-Brown. She begins to adapt to her male life-style, picking up swearing, girl-watching, and boxing tips from her father. Segall encourages Gurry to get some physical therapy to improve his condition, but Gurry refuses because he fears failure. Gurry drives around in a dilapidated van, and one day is pursued by Ellis-Brown in his white sports car. This leads to an accident in which the grill of Ellis-Brown's car is damaged. Gurry tries to make amends by providing Ellis-Brown with a new grill, but the bully is not appeased, and demands additional recompense from Gurry and his friends, at one point forcing them to spruce up his girl friend's house. In the meantime, Gurry is upset because of the "unnatural" feelings he is beginning to have for Segall, and he tries to end the friendship. Eventually, a confrontation arises between Ellis-Brown and Segall. Segall beats the villain, and Gurry's pals rally to defeat Ellis-Brown's cohorts. Segall then tries to tell Gurry that she once was a girl, but Gurry can't be convinced. Segall seeks Green to help her out of her predicament. He's not home, but Tanner gives her a rock and some instructions on what to do with it. At midnight, Segall, along with Tanner, ventures to the top of her parents' house, throws the rock as high as she can and makes a wish. The following evening, Segall, a female once more, goes to a local dance where she meets Gurry, who is now on crutches, and the sparks fly. An enjoyable, low-key film, SOMETHING SPECIAL boasts some fine acting from its teenage cast. Segall handles well both her female and male roles. As the parents, Duke and Glover go somewhat over the top, a rather unwelcome contrast to the reserve exercised by their younger colleagues. *(Profanity.)*

p, M. David Chilewich, Fred Berner; d, Paul Schneider; w, Walter Carbone,

Carla Reuben (based on the story "Willy Milly" by Alan Friedman); ph, Dominique Chapuis (Du-Art Color); m, David McHugh; ed, Michael R. Miller; prod d, Nora Chavooshian; set d, Lynn Wolverton; cos, Maureen O'Leary; m/l, Gary Frischer, John Finley, David McHugh; makeup, Lynn Barber Rosenthal; spec eff, Lenna Kaleva; stunts, Don Ruffin.

Comedy **(PR:C MPAA:PG-13)**

SOMMARKVALLAR PA JORDEN (SEE: NAGRA SOMMARKVALLAR PA JORDEN, 1987, Swed.)

SOMMER† (1987, Ger.) 105m Munich TV and Film Academy/Anderer Blick bw (Trans: Summer)

Michael Schech *(Father)*, Philipp Rankl *(Sebastian)*, Barbara vom Baur *(Woman)*, Lene Beyer *(Maid)*.

Far from being a vacation, the summer of the title is one spent by a devoted father, Schech, with his autistic son Rankl. Schech takes the son out of the sterility of a clinic and brings him to an invigorating Alpine resort in the hope that he can reach a point of communication with the faraway boy.

p&d, Philip Groning; w, Philip Groning, Ralf Zoller, Nicolas Humbert; ph, Ernst Kubiza; ed, Philip Groning; art d, Pavel Pitner.

Drama **(PR:NR MPAA:NR)**

SON URFALI† (1987, Turkey) 95m Candemir c (Trans: The Last Man Of Urfa)

Talat Bulut *(Sehmus)*, Nur Surer *(Girl Friend)*, Savas Yurttas.

Bulut plays a country laborer who travels to Istanbul with the hope of becoming a famous singer, but instead takes a job with a construction crew. His co-workers support his dream, helping him raise the money for a talent contest entry fee. They do so, but at the cost of providing a sick worker with money for medical care. It is then revealed that the contest was fixed and Bulut had no chance at all of winning.

d, Omer Ugur; w, Omer Ugur, Cemal Gozutuk; ph, Umit Ardabak; m, Haluk Ozkan.

Drama **(PR:NR MPAA:NR)**

SON V RUKU, ILI CHEMODON† (1987, USSR) 76m Lenfilm/ Sovexportfilm c (Trans: A Dream Comes True Or The Valise . . .)

Vladimir Basov, Irina Malysheva, Olga Volkova, Earnest Romanov, Natalya Fateyeva.

When a young journalist has his poems chosen for publication, his former girlfriend returns to him. He, however, rejects her and decides that his poetry should be destroyed, not printed. After surviving these personal traumas, he meets an attractive young nurse and starts life anew.

d, Earnest Yasan; w, Vladimir Lobanov; ph, Vladimir Burykin; m, Vadim Bibergan; art d, Viktor Amelchenko.

Comedy **(PR:NR MPAA:NR)**

SOPERNITSY† (1987, USSR) 109m Lenfilm/Sovexportfilm c (Trans: Rivals)

Larisa Guzeeva, Yuri Demich, Oleg Shtefanko, Georgy Vitzin.

A young championship swimmer becomes involved in canoeing and windsurfing at the suggestion of her supportive coach, who wants her to prolong her competitive career.

d, Victor Sadovsky; w, Valentin Ezhov, Victor Sadovsky; ph, Victor Karasev; m, Vladimir Shainsky; art d, Boris Burmistrov.

Sports **(PR:NR MPAA:NR)**

SOROBANZUKU† (1987, Jap.) 108m Fuji TV/Toho c (Trans: All For Business' Sake; AKA: THE MERCENARIES)

Takaashi Ishibashi, Noritake Kinashi, Narumi Yasuda, Kaoru Kobayashi.

A satire on the hyper-competitiveness of the Japanese advertising industry from prolific young director Morita (THE FAMILY GAME), who shoots the entire film as if it were a television commercial. Ishibashi and Kinashi star as two young ad executives from Japan's number two agency, To. The ambitious pair become determined to overthrow the number one agency, Ra, and its fierce director. They are aided by the beautiful Yasuda, the Ra director's former lover. To circumvent his rival's plot, the Ra director attempts to merge both the Ra and To agencies and then fire Ishibashi and Kinashi. Luckily, the clever ad men are able to stop the merger and defeat the evil director. A Japanese television production, SOROBANZUKU was shown at film festivals in North America in 1987.

p, Masaru Kakutani; d&w, Yoshimitsu Morita; ph, Yonezo Maeda; ed, Akira Suzuki.

Comedy **(PR:NR MPAA:NR)**

SOTTO IL RISTORANTE CINESE† (1987, It.) 89m ReteItalia S.p.A-Bozzetto Int'l./D.M.V. c (Trans: Under the Chinese Restaurant)

Claudio Botosso *(Ivan Rosco)*, Amanda Sandrelli *(Eva)*, Nancy Brilli *(Ursula Bridge)*, Bernard Blier *(Eva's Father)*, Claudia Lawrence *(Ivan's Mother)*, Giuseppe Cederna, Cinzia Monreale, Massimiliano Brambilla, Maurizio Solda, Haruhiko Yamanouchi, Sergio Cannonieri, Loredana Butt, Almina De Sanzio, Andrea Dugoni, Marco Marelli.

This romantic comedy enters the realm of science fiction when Botosso, a young man who has inadvertently gotten mixed up in a bank robbery, discovers another world in the basement of a Chinese laundry. After witnessing a holdup he flees from the stick-up men, seeking refuge in the basement of the restaurant. There he finds a fantastic beach populated by inventor Blier and Sandrelli, his daughter. As if it isn't strange enough to find a beach in a basement, this piece of waterfront property is part of another planet and is watched over by two suns. Sandrelli falls for Botosso and follows him back out through the door when he leaves. There is a little problem, though; Botosso is engaged. However, before the film's end, Botosso and Sandrelli are a couple, in this world; Blier and Botosso's ballerina mother, Lawrence, are together in the world behind the door; and Botosso's shrewish fiancee, Brilli, is lost in a world far away.

d, Bruno Bozzetto; w, Bruno Bozzetto, Fabio Comana; ph, Agostino Castiglioni; m, Ugo De Rossi; ed, Roberto Frattini; art d, Carmelo Patrono.

Comedy/Romance/Science Fiction **(PR:NR MPAA:NR)**

SOTTOZERO† (1987, It.) Numero Uno-Reteitalia/CIDIF (Trans: Below Zero)

Jerry Cala, Angelo Infanti, Annie Papa, Antonella Interlenghi.

An Italian family man leaves his job at the factory and takes part-time work on an oil rig off the coast of Norway. He cannot speak the language, and struggles through the sub-zero temperatures, but the good pay helps him to suffer through the experience. His loneliness subsides when he meets a fellow Italian, and the two become fast friends.

d, Gianluigi Polidoro; w, Rodolfo Sonego; ph, Roberto Forges Davanzati; m, Umberto Smaila; ed, Raimondo Crociani.

Drama **(PR:NR MPAA:NR)**

SOUCHASTNIKI† (1987, USSR) 100m Gorky/Sovexportfilm c (Trans: Accessories)

Leonid Filatov, Sergei Kiltakov, Natalia Vilkina.

Focusing on a newly released convict and the court officer who tries to help him readjust to society, this Soviet psychological drama demonstrates the tenuousness of the ex-con's return to the outside world. Temptations and pitfalls wait everywhere for the former criminal, and the importance of the strong, but understanding, guiding hand provided by the probation officer is driven home.

d, Ina Tumanyan; w, Ina Tumanyan, Alexander Shpeer; ph, Valery Ginzburg; m, Yevgeny Gevorkyan; art d, Viktor Sofronov.

Drama **(PR:NR MPAA:NR)**

SOUS LE SOLEIL DE SATAN† (1987, Fr.) 98m Erato-A2-Flach-Action-CNC-SOFICA/Gaumont c (Trans: Under The Sun Of Satan)

Gerard Depardieu *(Father Donissan)*, Sandrine Bonnaire *(Mouchette)*, Maurice Pialat *(Menu-Segrais)*, Alain Arthur *(Marquis de Cadignan)*, Yann Dedet *(Gallet)*, Brigitte Legendre *(Mouchette's Mother)*, Jean-Claude Bourliat *(Malorthy)*, Jean-Christophe Bouvet, Philippe Pallut.

After gaining a critical following with his films, A NOS AMOURS and POLICE, director Maurice Pialat returns with an adaptation of the 1926 novel by Georges Bernanos, whose writings have previously been filmed by Robert Bresson as DIARY OF A COUNTRY PRIEST and MOUCHETTE. Depardieu stars as a country priest who is driven by his devotion to God—a devotion which is tested when he meets Bonnaire, a promiscuous teenager who is pregnant by one man and mistress to another. When she kills the man who impregnated her, Depardieu tries to bring her back into the faith. Instead, she kills herself. As Depardieu carries on he is confronted by the half-hearted devotion of his superior, Pialat, and the devil incarnate, Bouvet. After exploring family life in A NOS AMOUR (which starred his discovery—Bonnaire) and police life in POLICE (which starred Depardieu and featured Bonnaire in a small part), Pialat has turned to a different world to tackle the religious and philosophical questions concerning God, the Devil, faith, and redemption. While Bresson's style is one of controlled reverence (ala Carl Dreyer), Pialat's is a more frantic, claustrophobic one in which he makes great use of tight close-ups, handheld camerawork, and brutally emotional acting. SOUS LE SOLEIL DE SATAN took the Palme d'Or for Best Film at the Cannes Film Festival, becoming the first French picture in 21 years (since A MAN AND A WOMAN) to do so. Since it was the festival's 40th anniversary, some believed that the jury was prejudiced towards awarding a French film with the top honor, citing numerous other films which were supposedly more deserving—the Soviet REPENTANCE or Wim Wender's DER HIMMER UBER BERLIN. Accepting his award to an outburst of booing, Pialat raised his first in the air and lashed out: "You don't like me, well, I don't like you either." Although A NOS AMOURS and POLICE received US art house releases, no distributor picked up SOUS LE SOLEIL DE SATAN for a 1987 US release.

p, Claude Abeille; d, Maurice Pialat; w, Sylvie Danton, Maurice Pialat (based on the novel by Georges Bernanos); ph, Willy Kurant (Fuji, Agfacolor); m, Henri Dutilleux; ed, Yann Dedet; prod d, Katia Vischkof; cos, Gil Noir.

Drama/Religious **(PR:NR MPAA:NR)**

SPACE RAGE** (1987) 77m Vestron c

Richard Farnsworth *(The Colonel)*, Michael Pare *(Grange)*, John Laughlin *(Walker)*, Lee Purcell *(Maggie)*, William Windom *(Gov. Tovah)*, Lewis Van

Bergen *(Drago)*, Dennis Redfield *(Quinn)*, Hank Worden *(Old Codger)*, Frank Doubleday *(Brain Surgeon)*, Harold Sylvester *(Max Bryson)*, Wolfe Perry *(Billy Boy)*, Ricky Supiran *(Kirk)*, Nick Palmisano *(Carny)*, Rick Weber *(Nose)*, Eddy Pansullo *(Mean Guard)*, Paul Linke *(Duffy)*, Gene Hartline *(Bubba)*, Alan Graf *(Tiny)*, Paul Keith *(Dr. Wahlberg)*, R.J. Ganzert *(Talahassee)*, Bob Lesser *(Salesman)*, George Fisher, Tom Rosales *(Felons)*, Victory Palmisano *(Little Girl)*, Esther Palmisano *(Mother)*, James Faracci *(Driver)*, Jim Bentley *(Bob Smith)*, Susan Madigan *(Mary Smith)*, William Cowley *(Charlie)*, Dorothy Dells *(Judge)*, Carl Strano *(Prosecutor)*.

Two hundred years in the future, a ruthless bank robbery is foiled and the desperate robber (Pare) is banished from the Earth and taken to the penal mining colony of New Botany Bay on Proxima Centauri 3. There he quickly makes himself the leader of the prisoners and plots an escape. Also on the planet is Laughlin, the top bounty hunter around, who fetches the prisoners when they run away, and Farnsworth, a old codger who was once the best cop in Los Angeles before he got a knife in his stomach one night and retired. Pare makes his bid for freedom, taking planet governor Windom hostage and killing Laughlin's wife. Laughlin goes after the escapees and kills several before taking a bullet in his shoulder. He manages to drive his buggy to Farnsworth's house, and the old man is forced to put on his old uniform and take a hand in stopping them himself. Pare and his cohorts manage to reach the shuttle docking port and rig it with explosives, threatening to destroy it if any cops come near. Farnsworth sneaks in under cover of darkness, and he and another bounty hunter (Redfield) pick off the escapees one by one. Redfield is killed by Pare and it finally comes down to him and Farnsworth. The old man's gun is empty and Pare comes after him with a knife, but Farnsworth manages to reload in time and shoots Pare. This film represented an attempt by video distributor Vestron to get into production, but the project turned into a quagmire, as they had to go back for extensive reshoots just to get a coherent, if brief, 77-minute film. It also went through a number of title changes, including "A Dollar a Day," "Trackers: 2180," "Trackers," and "The Last Frontier." It actually played a theater in Connecticut in 1985 and a few more in 1986 before finally making it to video tape and general release. An uneasy blend of science fiction and western, the film does have some things going for it that make it worth investigating. Michael Pare, usually cast as a hero, is a terrific villain, reminiscent of James Remar's Ganz in 48 HOURS. Farnsworth is a little ridiculous as he goes through the obligatory arming-up scene, but his is always a welcome presence in any movie. The hard rock soundtrack is a bad idea, but the action scenes are mostly well done, and the film has some dark humor as well. None of this is to recommend the film highly, but science-fiction fans could do worse, and western fans have to take what they can get, even if it's set on a distant planet. *(Graphic violence, excessive profanity.)*

p, Morton Reed, Eric Barrett; d, Conrad E. Palmisano, Peter McCarthy; w, Jim Lenahan (based on a story by Morton Reed); ph, Timothy Suhrstedt, Tom Richmond (Deluxe Color); m, Billy Ferrick, Zander Schloss; ed, W. Peter Miller, Arthur Bressan, Jr.; art d, Cliff Cunningham, William Pomeroy, Richard Rollison; set d, Diana Allen Williams; cos, Theda Deramus; spec eff, Roger George, Frank DeMarco; m/l, Chris O'Connor, Steve Wyn, Jeff Stephens, Ian List and the Spikes, the Jazz Butcher, Sean O'Hagan, Couglan, Ken Spykes; stunts, Bruce Paul Barbour, Rick Barker; makeup, Dathryn Logan.

Science Fiction **Cas.** **(PR:O MPAA:R)**

SPACEBALLS** (1987) 96m MGM-Brookfilms/MGM-UA c

Mel Brooks *(President Skroob/Yogurt)*, John Candy *(Barf the Mawg, Co-Pilot)*, Rick Moranis *(Lord Dark Helmet)*, Bill Pullman *(Lone Starr, Space Bum)*, Daphne Zuniga *(Princess Vespa)*, Dick Van Patten *(King Roland, Ruler of Druidia)*, George Wyner *(Col. Sandurz)*, Michael Winslow *(Radar Technician)*, Joan Rivers *(Voice of Dot Matrix)*, Lorene Yarnell *(Dot Matrix, Droid Maid)*, John Hurt *(Himself)*, Sal Viscuso *(Radio Operator)*, Ronny Graham *(Minister)*, Jm J. Bullock *(Prince Valium)*, Leslie Bevis *(Commanderette Zircon)*, Jim Jackman *(Maj. A———)*, Michael Pniewski *(Laser Gunner)*, Sandy Helberg *(Dr. Schlotkin)*, Stephen Tobolowsky *(Captain of the Guard)*, Jeff MacGregor *(Snotty)*, Henry Kaiser *(Magnetic Beam Operator)*, Denise Gallup *(Charlene)*, Dian Gallup *(Marlene)*, Rhonda Shear *(Woman in Diner)*, Robert Prescott *(Sand Cruiser Driver)*, Jack Riley *(TV Newsman)*, Tom Dreesen *(Megamaid Guard)*, Rudy DeLuca *(Vinnie)*, Ken Olfson *(Head Usher)*, Bryan O'Byrne *(Organist)*, Wayne Wilson *(Trucker in Cap)*, Ira Miller *(Short Order Cook)*, Earl Finn *(Guard with Captain)*, Mitchell Bock *(Video Operator)*, Tommy Swerdlow *(Troop Leader)*, Tim Russ *(Trooper)*, Deanna Booher *(Bearded Lady)*, Johnny Silver *(Caddy)*, Brenda Strong *(Nurse)*, Gail Barle, Dey Young *(Waitresses)*, Tony Griffin, Rick Ducommun *(Prison Guards)*, Ed Gale, Felix Silla, Tony Cox, Antonio Hoyos, Arturo Gil, John Kennedy Hayden *(The Dinks)*, Dom De Luise *(The Voice of Pizza the Hutt)*.

Vaudeville pratfalls, sight gags and ribald one-liners have always been Brooks' mainstay. He has strung such chestnut ploys together in the past (YOUNG FRANKENSTEIN, THE PRODUCERS, BLAZING SADDLES) with great and biting wit and produced winners. Here the beads of his humor are loose, tossed haphazardly from Brooks' gag bag and they roll out ineffectively in a spoof of the Star Wars films. The weak satire also comes much too late to reach a responsive audience. The plot, such as it is, offers pretty princess Zuniga, daughter of Van Patten, the kindly king of the planet, as a kidnap victim of evil Dark Helmet (Moranis). Space adventurer Pullman and his sidekick Candy are assigned to retrieve Zuniga and thus begins a ridiculous odyssey through space with blazing rockets, death rays, and firefights among the stars, resulting in a slaphappy ending.

This is a formula film for Brooks, one that has long ago worn out its welcome with viewers and only Brooks shines momentarily as the president of the planet Spaceball and, in a dual role, as that of his crinkled, ancient adviser Yogurt, a

reprise of Brooks' 2000-year-old-man, who teaches Pullman the secrets of "The Schwartz." Candy mocks himself too much as the half-dog, half-man sidekick and completely destroys his best line: "I'm my own best friend." But then there is really little good to go bad here since it's mostly forced humor all the way, a film that rarely measures up to adequate kitsch. Van Patten is so bland, so boring, and so innocuous as to cause the viewer to question how this character could ever occupy a throne; his personality is more akin to an empty-headed salesman peddling used spaceships. Brooks claimed to have worked on the script for more than two years, but it sounds and looks like it was banged out in one night at a Hollywood cocktail party to amuse his guests. The production cost about $22 million, an enormous waste of money for a bad joke. Aimed at younger audiences, SPACEBALLS misses its mark. Brooks doesn't seem to realize that the slapstick era he so long enjoyed is over. But, through miserable box office showings for SPACEBALLS, he has undoubtedly and grimly realized that the youthful special effects fanatics who made the Star Wars films bonanzas take those technological marvel movies very seriously. The crude humor here is often distasteful for younger viewers. Songs include: "Spaceballs" (Jeff Pescetto, Clyde Lieberman, Mel Brooks; performed by The Spinners), "My Mind Has a Heart of Its Own" (Gloria Sklerov, Lenny Macaluso; performed by Kim Carnes, Jeffrey Osborne), "Heartstrings" (performed by Berlin), "Good Enough" (performed by Van Halen), "Raise Your Hands" (Jon Bon Jovi, Richie Sambora; performed by Jon Bon Jovi), "Hot Together" (performed by The Pointer Sisters), "Wanna Be Loved By You" (performed by Ladyfire). *(Profanity.)*

p&d, Mel Brooks; w, Mel Brooks, Thomas Meehan, Ronny Graham; ph, Nick McLean (Metrocolor); m, John Morris; ed, Conrad Buff IV; prod d, Terence Marsh; art d, Harold Michelson; set d, John Franco, Jr.; cos, Donfeld; m/l, Jeff Pescetto, Clyde Lieberman, Mel Brooks, Gloria Sklerov, Lenny Macaluso, Jon Bon Jovi, Richie Sambora; spec eff, Peter Albiez, Richard Ratliff, Rick Lazzarini, Craig Boyajian, Apogee, Inc., Robert Shepherd, Percy Angress, Industrial Light and Magic; stunts, Richard Warlock; makeup, Ben Nye, Jr.

Comedy **(PR:C MPAA:PG)**

SPARVAGN TILL HAVET† (1987, Swed.) 75m Alexandersson & De Geer Bildproduktion c (Trans: A Tram To The Sea)

Mikael Samuelsson *(Manfred)*, Christine Floderer, Ellen Lamm, Lovisa Lamm.

Samuelsson stars as an emotionally troubled filmmaker who is haunted by one memory—dropping his father's ashes on the floor of a tram. To cope with his problem he tries to make a film called A TRAM TO THE SEA.

d, Hakan Alexandersson.

Drama **(PR:NR MPAA:NR)**

SPECTERS† (1987, It.) 90m Reteitalia-Trio Cinema & TV/Intra c (SPETTRI)

John Pepper *(Marcus)*, Katrine Michelsen *(Alex)*, Donald Pleasence *(Prof. Lasky, Archaeologist)*, Massimo de Rossi, Riccardo De Torrebruna, Lavinia Grizi, Riccardo Parisio Perroti, Laurentina Guidotti, Giovanni Tamberi.

Donald Pleasence stars in this Italian horror feature as an archaeology professor who is involved in the study of the catacombs below Rome. He and his assistants, including Pepper, happen upon the Tomb of Domitiana, which has not been visited since the 19th century. There they encounter a force of absolute evil, but it takes the indiscriminate excavations of the workers who are constructing Rome's new subway to loose the malevolent specters of centuries past upon the unsuspecting Roman populace. Michelsen, a beautiful young woman, falls prey to the evil force. Hurricanes, earthquakes, and mysterious deaths follow. Even zoo animals sense that evil is all around them. Only by sealing the evil in its tomb can Rome and the world be saved.

p, Maurizio Tedesco; d, Marcello Avallone; w, Marcello Avallone, Maurizio Tedesco, Andrea Purgatori, Dardano Sarchetti (based on a story by Marcello Avallone, Maurizio Tedesco, Andrea Purgatori); ph, Silvano Ippoliti (Luciano Vittori color); m, Lele Marchitelli, Daniele Rea; ed, Andriano Tagliano; art d, Carmelo Agate; spec eff, Sergio Stivaletti; makeup, Dante Trani.

Horror **(PR:NR MPAA:NR)**

SPIRALE† (1987, Fr.) 90m T. Films-TFI/UGC c (Trans: Spiral)

Richard Berry *(Jerome)*, Claire Nebout *(Simorre)*, Tcheky Karyo *(Kino)*, Jean Bouise *(Jean-Francois)*, Beatrice Camurat *(Fabienne)*, Judith Magre *(Falconetti)*, Alexandre Mnouchkine *(Stadler)*, Vanessa Lhoste *(Valerie)*, Peter Hudson *(Gordon)*.

From the director of the comically pretentious L'ANNEE DES MEDUSAS, the Valerie Kaprisky sex-as-art film of 1984 which saw a US release in 1987, comes another tale of sexual obsession set in the south of France. Berry is vacationing on the beaches when he meets Nebout, a mysterious woman who holds a dangerous fascination over him. He follows her to her yacht which awaits in the Mediterranean and is introduced to her colorful and eccentric friends. As the title implies, she leads Berry into a downward spiral of sexuality and obsession. Alexandre Mnouchkine, who has been producing films in France since the 1940s, stars as one of Nebout's circle.

d&w, Christopher Frank; ph, Robert Fraisse (Eastmancolor); m, Michel Legrand; ed, Nathalie Lafaurie; art d, Dominique Andre.

Drama **(PR:O MPAA:NR)**

SPORTLOTO—82† (1987, USSR) 94m Mosfilm/Sovexportfilm c (Trans: Sports Lottery—82)

Alghis Arlauskas, Svetlana Amanova, Mikhail Pugovkin, Mikhail Kokshenov, Nina Grebeshkova.

Four passengers on the Moscow-Yuzhnogorsk train are, coincidentally, reading the same detective novel. One of them buys a lottery ticket during a short depot stop, placing the stub in her book. Naturally her ticket is the big winner. She picks up the wrong book, however, and is unable to collect her 20 thousand rubles. What follows is her misadventures while trying to track down the other passengers.

d, Leonid Gaidai; w, Vladlen Bakhnov, Leonid Gaidai; ph, Sergei Poluyanov, Vitaly Abramov.

Comedy **(PR:NR MPAA:NR)**

SQUARE DANCE** (1987) 112m Michael Nesmith-NBC/Island c

Jason Robards, Jr. *(Dillard)*, Jane Alexander *(Juanelle)*, Winona Ryder *(Gemma Dillard)*, Rob Lowe *(Rory)*, Deborah Richter *(Gwen)*, Guich Koock *(Frank)*, Elbert Lewis *(Beecham)*, Charlotte Stanton *(Aggie)*, J. David Moeller *(Dub Mosley)*, Dixie Taylor *(Dolores)*, Irma P. Hall *(Preacher Dixon)*, Barbara Britt *(Miss Lawson)*, Brad Leland *(Drunk Cowboy)*, Dee Pyland *(May Tompkins)*, Gwen Little *(Doreen Hadley)*, Jim Bynum *(Jack Springer)*, Linda Nye *(Eunice Tanner)*, Newt Davis *(Bubba Springer)*, Harlan Jordan *(Ray Ferrys)*, Dennis Letts *(Bob Hadley)*, Annabelle Weenick *(Mrs. Weeks)*, Liz Williams *(Miss Harley)*, Tracey D. Adkins, E.J. Bodin III, Steven Grisaffe, Benny Sonnier, Kip Sonnier *(Bayou Band Members)*, Stephanie Binford, Barbara McCauley *(School Girls)*.

Using the familiar positions of the square dance as its central metaphor, this coming-of-age story set is sincere but unexceptional. Ryder (LUCAS' winsome lass), a God-fearing 13-year-old, lives more or less contentedly with her crotchety grandfather, Robards, on his chicken farm in Twilight, Texas. One morning, she is surprised by her mother, Alexander, who left her in Robards' care many years before, but has come to take Ryder back with her to Ft. Worth. When Ryder wants no part of this, Alexander leaves her address and departs without seeing Robards, her father. With old memories stirred up, Robards recalls happier times when he and his late wife were the king and queen of the local square dance. He teaches Ryder the positions and the steps, explaining that "home" is the spot to which one returns after swinging one's partner, promenading, or do-si-doing. Some time later, Lewis, an old black man who is Ryder's friend, is accidentally buried under a huge heap of garbage at the town dump. Searchers give up, leaving Lewis for dead. Ryder desperately perseveres and becomes outraged when Robards, a childhood friend of Lewis but now a racist, refuses to help. They argue bitterly and she steals away, making her way to Ft. Worth and the apartment Alexander shares with husband Koock over the gas station he runs. Ryder isn't the first female to flee Robards' household; Alexander left at the age of 15 and her mother had done the same.

Alexander works in a beauty parlor and dreams of the better life awaiting her when the West Texas land they've invested in brings in a gusher. She drinks, dances, and carries on with the truck drivers who frequent the Stagecoach Bar, all of which is tolerated by the hard-working, silent-but-strong Koock. Ryder, who gets a new hair style and begins going without her glasses, frequently asks Alexander about the identity of her father, who Robards has told her was killed in Vietnam. She falls into a kind of puppy-love with Lowe, a mentally retarded man several years her senior. When the West Texas land proves to be without oil, all hell breaks loose. In a loud argument, Alexander blames Koock for dashing her dreams, and Ryder tries to smooth things over with Bible quotations. Angry at Ryder's piety, Alexander tells her that her father could have been anyone of a half dozen guys, that all she remembers is Ryder's arrival put an end to her good times. Fleeing the apartment, Ryder goes to the beauty parlor, where she finds Alexander's slatternly friend Richter making love to Lowe. Feeling that he has betrayed Ryder's love, Lowe tries to cut off his penis and is taken to a hospital where he will, in all likelihood, remain permanently. Alexander takes Ryder back to Twilight, and she discovers that Lewis is *alive*, rescued by his old friend Robards. Ryder asks Robards if she looks like her grandmother. "Yes ma'am, you do," he answers and they begin to square dance. The camera pulls back through the screen door, past Lewis (playing his harmonica on the front porch), up into the sky and looks down on the house—make that home.

Based on a novel that was partly inspired by the Texas boyhood of screenwriter

Hines, SQUARE DANCE is a slow-moving slice-of-life affair. Director Petrie's last film, the Genie-winning BAY BOY, was in a similar vein, drawing upon his youth in Nova Scotia. Like it, this film meanders along randomly, unfolding as life itself does. Yet there is an underlying—though easily identifiable—symbolic structure to it, the square dance. At the heart of the film is the idea of leaving and returning to home, though what Petrie and Hines are saying about this is less clear. By calling their hometown Twilight, the filmmakers seem to imply the passing of the time and place where such "homes" can exist. They may also intend to show that while some can go home again, those who are unable to (Alexander) are condemned to a life of rootlessness and pipe dreams. For this notion to be plausible, though, there seems to be a necessary corollary: that the return trip need not necessarily be undertaken physically, that "home" need only be a place where one can go in his mind, as Robards does, remembering happier times in the past. This may or may not be the filmmakers' message, for it is mixed in with Ryder's coming-of-age experiences, a subplot dealing with race, Alexander's promiscuousness, and Lowe's disability. Life is a jumble of such experiences, but art can be frustrating and unsatisfying when it takes this approach. SQUARE DANCE suffers from this and a center that is a little too soft.

The performances are generally good, with Ryder (a real-life 10th grader) convincing as the young girl whose summer is filled with changes. Four-time Oscar nominee Alexander takes a low-key approach, preventing the predictable golden heart of her character from overwhelming her cynical side, the good-time girl who knows her looks and youth are fading. Robards turns in an extremely nuanced performance as the curmudgeon with his own heart of gold heart. Lowe, performing in a role Emilo Estevez had been interested in until given the opportunity to make WISDOM, proves he is more than just a pretty face, though after 112 minutes, his mannerisms and speech appear a little too studied. To prepare for his audition, Lowe worked with a voice therapist, then visited a hospital for the developmentally disabled and mightily impressed Petrie. Richter and Koock turn in solid performances in supporting roles. Alexander also acted as the film's co-executive producer, working for three years with "Hill Street Blues" regular Charles Haid to bring Hines' novel to the screen. After a number of deals fell through, SQUARE DANCE was finally financed by Mike Nesmith's Pacific Arts company in association with NBC Productions (their first feature film endeavor). Except for Robards, the actors worked for deferred payments. The film was made in 38 days on a budget of approximately $4.3 million. *(Profanity, adult and sexual situations.)*

p&d, Daniel Petrie; w, Alan Hines (based on his novel); ph, Jacek Laskus (Allied color); m, Bruce Broughton; ed, Bruce Green; prod d, Jan Scott; set d, Erica Rogalla; cos, Elizabeth McBride; makeup, Carla Palmer; spec eff, Jack Bennett.

Drama **Cas.** **(PR:C MPAA:PG-13)**

SQUEEZE, THE** (1987) 101m Tri-Star-ML Delphi Premier/Tri-Star c

Michael Keaton *(Harry Berg)*, Rae Dawn Chong *(Rachel Dobs)*, John Davidson *(Honest Tom T. Murray, Lottery Host)*, Ric Abernathy *(Bouncer)*, Danny Aiello, III *(Ralph Vigo)*, Bobby Bass *(Poker Player)*, Leslie Bevis *(Gem Vigo)*, Jophrey Brown *(Poker Player)*, Lou Criscoulo *(Kurt)*, Ray Gabriel *(Security Guard)*, George Gerdes *(Joe, Rigaud's Henchman)*, Ronald Guttman *(Rigaud)*, Paul Herman *(Freddy)*, Richard E. Huhn *(Police Clerk)*, John Dennis Johnston *(Nick)*, Jeffrey Josephson *(Al)*, Liane Langland *(Hilda, Harry's Ex-Wife)*, Diana Lewis, Andrew Magarian, Peg Shirley *(Reporters)*, Meat Loaf *(Titus)*, Frank Lugo *(Detective)*, Pat MacNamara *(Arnold Drisco)*, Mick Muldoon *(Ticket Seller)*, Jack Murray *(Hotel Resident)*, Joe Pantoliano *(Norman)*, Richard Portnow *(Ruben)*, Gerald J. Quimby *(Capt. Jack)*, John S. Rushton *(Bouncer)*.

This troubled production went through two producers, two directors, two female leads, the death of a stuntman, an extra $10 million not originally budgeted, and a last minute title change just for the honor of bombing at the box office during a highly competitive summer. A failed attempt to combine laughs with brutally violent action, THE SQUEEZE stars Keaton as a starving New York City artist in the midst of building a giant dinosaur out of hundreds of old television sets. His ex-wife, Langland, sweet-talks him into going to her apartment to pick up a package. At the apartment he discovers a dead man in the closet. Without calling the police, Keaton takes the package and discovers that it contains a strange electromagnetic device that is sought after by gangsters who are anxious to fix the upcoming $50 million lottery drawing with the help of the drawing's corrupt

television host, Davidson. Hooking up with dedicated "skip tracer" Chong—who is after him to pay his alimony—Keaton tries to fend off Mafia muscle-man Meat Loaf (who sweats constantly). Being a compulsive gambler, Keaton can't resist the chance to walk off with the $50 million, but when the bad guys kidnap Chong (with whom he has fallen in love), he decides to blow the lid off the scam and spoil things for both himself and the gangsters.

Confused, poorly paced, and badly directed, THE SQUEEZE was definitely more trouble than it was worth. Actress Jenny Wright (OUT OF BOUNDS, NEAR DARK) originally was cast as the skip tracer and much of the film was shot before she was fired and replaced by Chong. This of course required all the scenes Wright had appeared in to be reshot. During the production, veteran stuntman Vic Magnotta drowned while performing a car stunt in which the auto was driven off a Hoboken pier and plunged into the Hudson River (he was apparently pinned in the car). When the disastrous production was finally finished the budget had ballooned from $12 million to over $22 million. The original title, "Skip Tracer," was changed when it was discovered that there was a 1979 Canadian film of the same name. The fact that the publicity department felt compelled to send out press releases explaining just what a "skip tracer" was certainly contributed to the last minute switch. In addition to the poorly conceived script and the totally lackluster direction by Roger (LASSITER) Young, there is little chemistry between the leads. The normally buoyant Keaton seems bored—probably because he had to do several scenes twice with two different actresses—and desperately tries to clue the audience in on his misery by mugging at the camera. Chong, as usual, tries hard but there isn't much for her to do. The fact that Hollywood is still very skittish when it comes to interracial romance doesn't help the actors either. Former rock star Meat Loaf hams it up nicely as the sweaty menace, and the scene where Chong fends him off with the pinnacle of a large statuette of the Empire State Building elicits some chuckles. Most surprisingly perennial television personality Davidson really sinks his teeth into the role of the smarmy Lotto host—not unlike the role that would be honed to perfection by Richard Dawson in THE RUNNING MAN. A pathetic failure at the box office, THE SQUEEZE doesn't have a chance of breaking even, despite cable and home video sales. *(Graphic violence, profanity.)*

p, Rupert Hitzig, Michael Tannen; d, Roger Young; w, Daniel Taplitz; ph, Arthur Albert (Duart Color); m, Miles Goodman; ed, Harry Keramidas; prod d, Simon Waters; art d, Christopher Nowak; set d, Ted Glass; cos, Jane Greenwood; spec eff, Gary Elmendorf, John Gray, Steve Kirshoff; makeup, Kathryn Bihr; stunts, Victor Magnotta.

Thriller **(PR:O MPAA:PG-13)**

STABILIZER, THE† (1987, Indonesia) 90m Punjabi Bros./Parkit Films-Jakarta c

Peter O'Brian *(Peter Goldson, "The Stabilizer")*, Gillie Beanz *(Silvia Nash)*, Craig Gavin *(Gregg Rainmaker)*, Barry Capry *(Captain Johnny)*, Dana Christina *(Christina Provost)*.

An English-language actioner in which FBI agent O'Brian tracks down a gang of international drugdealers who have kidnapped a powerful scientist. Filled with the usual trademarks of the genre—car chases, explosions, gunblasts, and bone-crunching karate moves.

d, Arizal; w, John Rust, Deddy Armand; ph, Bambang Trimakno (Eastmancolor); m, GSD'Arto; ed, Benny Ms; m/l, Wayne O'Holmes, Elliot Solomen.

Action/Adventure **(PR:O MPAA:NR)**

STACKING½** (1987) 97m Nepenthe/Spectrafilm c

Christine Lahti *(Kathleen Morgan)*, Frederic Forrest *(Buster McGuire)*, Megan Follows *(Anna Mae Morgan)*, Jason Gedrick *(Gary Connaloe)*, Ray Baker *(Dan Morgan)*, Peter Coyote *(Photographer)*, James Gammon *(Clate Connaloe)*, Kaiulani Lee *(Connie Van Buskirk)*, Jacqueline Brookes *(Mrs. Connaloe)*, Irene Dailey *(Mrs. McGuire)*, Pat Goggins *(Auctioneer)*, Darrin Schreder *(Duane Connaloe)*, Pat Ponich *(Stella Martindale)*, Jess Schwidde *(Bartender)*, Amy Krempasky *(Nurse)*, Eric Hendricks *(Len Diltz)*, Mark Jenkins *(Harry Van Buskirk)*.

Set under Montana's big sky in 1954, STACKING is the often compelling story of a young girl's coming of age, her mother's coming to terms with herself, and an alcohol-drenched farmhand's redemption. Follows, the star of PBS' "Anne of Green Gables," plays a 14-year-old whose family is battling to keep the farm that has been theirs for three generations and that was once the largest in the county. An accident has put her father, Baker, in the hospital, but he is equally incapacitated by his self-pity and belief that fate and his dead father have conspired to prevent him from being successful. Lahti (SWING SHIFT), Follows' mother, has fought the good fight long enough. Still very attractive, she longs for the world outside the tiny Montana town where she pushes coffee and pie at the cafe. Only Follows is willing to continue the struggle. Enlisting the help of Forrest (THE ROSE, APOCALYPSE NOW), her father's former farmhand, she sets about converting an old truck into a stacker—a forklift-like vehicle used to stack bales of hay. Forrest, who is almost never without a bottle of beer, was involved with Lahti in the old days, before he lost her to Baker. Now Forrest helps Follows partly out a sense of loyalty to Baker that no one else understands and partly because he hopes for a reconciliation with Lahti. Each passing day, Lahti grows more anxious to leave. Coyote (JAGGED EDGE, A MAN IN LOVE), a handsome motorcycle-riding photographer, stops in town long enough to take Lahti's picture and to ask her if she wants to come with him to California. She almost accepts. Meanwhile, Gedrick (IRON EAGLE), an 18-year-old who lives and works on his family's nearby spread, is in hot pursuit of the blossoming Follows. When Lahti prepares to depart in the night, Follows shows her the stacker, which she hopes will earn them enough to keep the farm. (Follows has contracted with Gammon, Gedrick's father, to do his stacking.) Instead of prompting Lahti to stay, this shows her that Follows is strong-willed enough not to fall into the stifling dependency that afflicts the girls who grow up in this environment and which Lahti wants to escape. Not long afterwards, Lahti is gone. Follows turns to Forrest, but he only wishes that Lahti had asked him to go with her. That night, Follows confronts her father at the hospital, bitterly calling both him and Lahti quitters. At a dance, she finds Gedrick, but a drunken Forrest cuts in and escorts her to his pickup. There he forces her to kiss him. At first Follows resists, then she begins to give herself over to him. Confused and disgusted with himself, Forrest leaves her. The next day Follows is back in the fields, ready to stack. Atop the mountain of hay bales she finds Forrest. "Are you just gonna stand there diddling the dog all day, or are we gonna stack?" he asks her as the film ends.

Without the fine performances of Follows and Forrest, this Martin Rosen-directed film might have been little more than a slow-moving meditation on the embattled family farmer, which, in essence, it is. However, the wonderful chemistry between Follows and Forrest invests the story with a poignancy that the screenplay only barely provides. Peaches-and-cream pretty and open-faced innocent, Follows (who is actually 19) delivers an excellent performance as the headstrong girl on the edge of maturity. Forrest, playing a paunchy, world-weary loser is the perfect foil for her. He provides Follows with the knowledge and sweat to make stacking a reality, and she helps him to regain his self-respect. Lahti also delivers a capable performance, but though she effectively conveys the suffocating frustration her Kathleen feels, her performance is not nearly as captivating as her wonderful work in Bill Forsyth's HOUSEKEEPING, also released in 1987. Gedrick and Baker are unexceptional in support, and Coyote's cameo is convincing but brief. (Reportedly he was slated to direct a Rosen-produced film tentatively titled "Heaven Before I Die" this year.)

STACKING is the first live-action feature as a director for Rosen, who produced SMOOTH TALK and wrote, directed, and produced the animated features WATERSHIP DOWN and THE PLAGUE DOGS. The deliberate pace he gives his film is appropriate for its slice-of-life insights but occasionally the narrative thrust becomes bogged down. This may be screenwriter Jenkins' fault as much it is Rosen's, as her screenplay doesn't always seem to know whose story this is. The photography is excellent, taking full advantage of the purple mountain majesty and amber waves of grain. The film's country-tinged score, composed by Patrick Gleeson and performed by Michael Hedges and The Kronos Quartet (the New Wave classical musicians who are as likely to play Jimi Hendrix as Stockhausen), is equally effective. Songs and musical numbers include: "Uke Pick Waltz," "Barlow Knife" (traditional), and "Dream Chaser" (Brent Maher, Jeff Bullock, performed by Lisa Silver). Originally titled "Season of Dreams," STACKING was given a workshop staging by the Sundance Institute and produced in cooperation with American Playhouse. Its subject matter and treatment should fit comfortably in the context of PBS, on which, as an American Playhouse production, it will likely be shown. *(Adult situations.)*

p, Martin Rosen, Peter Burrell, Patrick Markey; d, Martin Rosen; w, Victoria Jenkins; ph, Richard Bowen (DuArt color); m, Patrick Gleeson; ed, Patrick Dodd; prod d, David Wasco; art d, Sharon Seymour; set d, Sandy Reynolds Wasco; cos, Linda Bass; m/l, Brent Maher, Jeff Bullock; stunts, Loren Janes; makeup, Natalie Mucyn.

Drama **(PR:A-C MPAA:PG)**

STADTRAND† (1987, Ger.) 100m North Rhine-Westphalla Filmburo c (Trans: On the Outskirts)

Leon Boden *(Franz)*, Bruno Peters *(Father)*, Rudolf W. Marnitz *(Insurance Detective)*, Herman Brood, Susanne Kieselstein.

Produced, written, and directed by a filmmaker with a last name that is shockingly familiar—Fuhrer—this German picture tells the story of an educated but unemployed young man who lives in poverty in the heavily industrial Ruhr Valley. Unable to find work in his chosen field, the young man, Boden, takes a job at a gas station, and one night he is accosted by a wounded robber who is fleeing the police. After forcing Boden to treat his wounds, the robber moves on, only to be shot by the police; however, Boden learns that the money the crook stole is still unaccounted for. Searching the garage, he finds the robber's stash and begins using it to satisfy his heart's desire. Soon, though, nosy insurance investigator Marnitz arrives on the scene, and Boden, determined to protect his newfound wealth, kills him. In the end, Boden's fortune goes up in the smoke of a fire that claims his apartment and the box in which he has hidden the loot.

p,d,&w, Volker Fuhrer; ph, Arthur Ahrweiler; m, Bernhard Voss; ed, Wolfgang Gessat; art d, Ralph Eue, Joe Liebetanz.

Crime **(PR:NR MPAA:NR)**

STAKEOUT*½** (1987) 115m Touchstone-Silver Screen Partners III/BV c

Richard Dreyfuss *(Chris Leece)*, Emilio Estevez *(Bill Reimers)*, Madeleine Stowe *(Maria McGuire)*, Aidan Quinn *(Richard "Stick" Montgomery)*, Dan Lauria *(Phil Coldshank)*, Forest Whitaker *(Jack Pismo)*, Ian Tracey *(Caylor Reese)*, Earl Billings *(Capt. Giles)*, Jackson Davies *(FBI Agent Lusk)*, J.J. Makaro, Scott Andersen, Tony Pantages, Beatrice Boepple.

It doesn't matter that this film is a traditional cop vs killer picture since it is presented in very human terms and sparkles with top-flight performances from Dreyfuss, Estevez, and Stowe. Dreyfuss, in gray-haired middle age, is excellent as a plainclothes detective on the Seattle police force, a man with a thankless job and an empty life, until he and Estevez are assigned to stakeout the home of a young woman, Stowe, who had once been the girl friend of a much wanted fugitive. The film opens with Stowe's old boy friend, a vicious hoodlum, Quinn, creating a disturbance in his prison cell which causes a riot in the cell block, all of

this timed to coincide with the arrival of an accomplice driving a delivery truck to the prison. Quinn, slightly wounded in the mock fight with his cellmate, is taken to the prison infirmary where, with the help of his henchman, he escapes while hiding in a box-like contraption affixed to the underpinnings of the truck. Meanwhile, the excitable Dreyfuss, a recovering alcoholic whose girl friend has just left him, joins reliable, cautious Estevez in trying to capture a wanted felon on the Seattle docks. The quarry escapes after a harrowing chase through the fisheries, with Estevez driving a forklift into the bay waters and Dreyfuss jumping in to save his partner. The two are later assigned to a night-time stakeout of Stowe's apartment, moving into a deserted house across the street and watching her through powerful telescopes and binoculars. They while away the hours with innocuous word games dealing with classic movies and the Kennedy assassination. When the tall, dark-haired, beautiful Stowe arrives, Dreyfuss becomes excited. He later climbs a telephone pole to set up a phone tap on her line and then, pretending to be a phone repairman, goes into her apartment to plant bugs in her phones. Stowe and Dreyfuss are quickly attracted to each other but Dreyfuss backs off nervously. Later he meets Stowe at a grocery store where he is buying food for him and his partner and she talks him into giving her a lift when her bicycle gets a flat tire. He not only carries her groceries up to her second-floor apartment but accepts a dinner invitation from Stowe while Estevez, watching, fumes and worries about Dreyfuss compromising their position. Dreyfuss learns from Stowe that she has a young brother who is in jail for a minor offense and he later gets the youth released, along with finding him a job. Dreyfuss and Stowe fall in love and Dreyfuss, much to the consternation of his partner, leaves the stakeout shift to Estevez one night and wakes up in Stowe's bed, horrified to realize that the daytime shift of police is now across the street. He escapes Stowe's apartment by dressing in her hat and shawl, leading police to chase him through alleyways. He is rescued by a disgusted Estevez without being detected. Further complicating matters is escaped killer Quinn who is heading for Seattle and Stowe. He has hidden the loot from his last job in a chair in her apartment and intends to retrieve the money and his girl before leaving the state. In a wild, running gun battle along wilderness roads, Quinn crashes his car into a river and is believed drowned. Police close the case on Quinn and call off the stakeout. Dreyfuss confesses to Stowe that he is a detective and she explodes, quitting him. When Dreyfuss returns to her apartment to try to make amends he finds Quinn there. The killer has survived the river and holds Stowe at gunpoint. Posing as a parole violator, Dreyfuss tells Quinn he is being tailed by Estevez, whom Quinn has spotted outside the apartment. Quinn captures Estevez and takes him, Dreyfuss, and Stowe to a dock where a huge powerboat arrives, driven by an accomplice, the very suspect who had eluded Dreyfuss and Estevez at the film's opening. Dreyfuss and Estevez attack Quinn and the accomplice and both men capture the bad guys, but not until Dreyfuss has a knock-down, slam-bang battle with Quinn through a treacherous lumber mill amidst huge logs and giant buzz saws whirring lethally. Stowe, in the end, aids Dreyfuss in subduing Quinn and winds up in the detective's arms, which is where she wants to be.

STAKEOUT is a well-handled, quick-paced and often funny film that accurately details the humdrum routine of police work. Director Badham expertly mixes just the right amount of action with a very delightful romance between the generously emotional Stowe and the sympathetic, likable Dreyfuss. It's a touching, naturally developed relationship, free from the synthetic red-hot passion of a one-night stand. In fact, this aspect of the well-balanced STAKEOUT is a gem set in the most dangerous area of any film, the middle, so charming that the real and coming menace of Quinn is all but forgotten and all the more frightening when the psychopath, like a bad dream, finally does arrive. Seattle, where the entire film was shot, is stunningly scenic, an unusual and refreshing locale which gives STAKEOUT, in the scenes involving Quinn's manic escape from a police dragnet, a distinctive and realistic look and feel in this superior crime drama. This film is a virtuoso return for Dreyfuss who is absolutely captivating in his role, a down-to-earth portrayal laced with just the right blend of humor, assurance, and introspection. Badham, who directed Dreyfuss in WHOSE LIFE IS IT, ANYWAY? in a period of personal crisis for the actor, remarked that "the actor I worked with on STAKEOUT is like a totally different human being. He's healthier, with a mind that's so much sharper and more focused." Dreyfuss' dedication to his role in STAKEOUT is evident and he makes the most out of it with great skill and care. *(Violence, profanity.)*

p, Jim Kouf, Cathleen Summers; d, John Badham; w, Jim Kouf; ph, John Seale (Deluxe Color); m, Arthur B. Rubinstein; ed, Tom Rolf, Michael Ripps; prod d, Philip Harrison; art d, Richard Hudolin, Michael Ritter; set d, Rose Marie McSherry, Leslie Beale.

Crime/Drama **(PR:O MPAA:R)**

STANISLAW I ANNA† (1987, Pol.) 73m Zespoly Filmowe-Oko c (Trans: Stanislaw and Anna)

Anna Kazmierczak *(Anna Oswiecimowie)*, Waldemar Kownacki *(Stanislaw Oswiecimowie)*, Mieczyslaw Voit *(Anna and Stanislaw's Father)*, Anna Milewska *(Anna's Mother)*, Ernest Bryll *(Narrator)*.

One of the recurring subjects in Polish art, music, and literature in the last two

centuries is the myth of Stanislaw and Anna Oswiecimowie, real-life half-siblings who lived in the 17th Century and who, according to legend, were lovers despite the taboo of incest. Director Konrad's film borrows language from great Polish literary works and images from traditional visual representations of the legend to explore the story of the famous lovers and, in so doing, to make a statement on love in any age. The film features a score by Mieczyslaw Karlowicz, including his piece named for the legendary lovers, and also incorporates modern dance.

d, Kazimierz Konrad, Piotr Stefaniak; w, Pawel Chynowski, Kazimierz Konrad; ph, Jerzy Stawicki; m, Mieczyslaw Karlowicz; ed, Zenon Piorecki; set d, Jerzy Skrzepinski.

Romance **(PR:NR MPAA:NR)**

STAR QUEST† (1987, Jap.) Gainax-Bandai c (aka: THE WINGS OF HONNEAMISE- ROYAL SPACE FORCE)

A feature-length English-dubbed Japanese cartoon which received a glitzy premiere ala the Hollywood style of old. Geared towards adults, the story is set on another planet—one which is in the throes of war and fearing an enemy invasion. The film's hero, Randy, is an enthusiastic young man who aspires to be a fighter pilot, but is instead shuffled in to a space research program. When his girlfriend questions the morality of spending gargantuan amounts of money on research while others are homeless, sick and starving, Randy too begins to doubt his government. He has a change of heart, however, when his services are desperately needed in order to launch the latest, most advanced rocket into orbit before the enemy attack.

p, Toshio Okada; d, Yoshiyuki Sadamoto.

Animation/Science-Fiction **(PR:NR MPAA:NR)**

STARAYA AZBUKA† (1987, USSR) 84m Mosfilm/Sovexportfilm c (Trans: Old Primer)

Vyacheslav Baranov, Valentin Smirnitsky, Svetlana Tormakhova, Anastasia Nemolyaeva.

Subtitled "A Village Teacher's Letters to Lev Nikolaevich Tolstoy," this children's film shows the world through the curious eyes of youngsters.

d, Victor Prokhorov; w, Alexander Alexandrov, Anton Vasiliev (based on the short stories by Lev Nikolaevich Tolstoy); ph, Oleg Martynov; m, Alexander Goldshtein; prod d, Valentin Konovalov.

Children's **(PR:NR MPAA:NR)**

STARLIGHT HOTEL*** (1987, New Zealand) 93m Mirage/Challenge-New Zealand Film Commission c

Greer Robson *(Kate Marshall)*, Peter Phelps *(Patrick Dawson)*, Marshall Napier *(Det. Wallace)*, The Wizard *(Spooner)*, Alice Fraser *(Aunt)*, Patrick Smyth *(Uncle)*, Bruce Phillips *(Dave Marshall)*, Elrich Hooper *(Principal)*, John Watson *(Mr. Curtis)*, Mervyn Glue *(Skip)*, Shirley Kelly *(Mrs. Skip)*, Bill Walker *(John Repo-man)*, John Waite *(Jack Repo-man)*, Donogh Rees *(Helen)*, Timothy Lee *(Maxwell)*, Peter Dennet *(Des)*, Teresa Bonney *(Melissa)*, Duncan Anderson *(Railway Clerk)*, Russell Gibson *(Railway Worker)*, Ken Cook *(Constable Bonnet)*, Gary McCormick *(Constable Murphy)*, Lex Matheson *(Constable Willis)*, Norm Forsey *(Farmer)*, Craig Stewart *(Farmhand)*, Craig Halkett *(Farmer's Son)*, Geoffrey Wearing *(Mr. Jamieson)*, Sherril Cooper *(Flora Peters)*, Louise Petherbridge *(Chairwoman)*, David Telford *(Guard)*, Patrick Pointer *(Station Master)*, Glennis Woods *(Tea Lady)*.

Sort of a Kiwi version of PAPER MOON, this beautifully photographed film set in Depression-era New Zealand is a story of improbable companionship. Robson (SMASH PALACE) is a 13-year-old living in a rural community on the picturesque South Island. Her mother is dead and her unemployed father relocates to Wellington on the North Island, leaving Robson in the care of an aunt who fails to understand the frustration and discomfort Robson experiences at school. When the situation becomes more than she can take, Robson runs away, bound for Christchurch, where she hopes to hop a boat to Wellington and her father. En route she encounters Phelps, an emotionally scarred WW I veteran and Robin Hood type who attempted to reclaim "the people's" furniture from a repossession agent. The agent, who was injured in that struggle, is in now in critical condition, and a nationwide manhunt is on for Phelps. At first, he reluctantly allows Robson to tag along, then he realizes she will make a useful cover for his escape. As they travel through the beautiful country, pursued by one particularly zealous detective, their relationship deepens. One close call follows another. In a port city, they are separated. A friend of Phelps' can get him on a ship to Australia if he will leave right away, but the fugitive is worried about Robson. In his frantic search for her, Phelps even visits a constabulary, where his impatient demands for assistance get him tossed—unidentified—into a Salvation Army mission that is taking the jail's overflow. There he encounters Robson, and after making their escape, they are back on the road again. After a chance encounter with the woman Phelps loved before the war but who jilted him, and a trip to Robson's mother's grave, which the girl has never seen, their luck runs out. Trying to flee, Phelps is shot and plummets from a high bridge to the river below, presumably dead. Robson falls, too, but she is fished out of the water by the police, who take her to Christchurch and put her on a ship to Wellington. As she boards, she hears an explosion that she knows to be the diversion Phelps had planned to use to hop a ship to escape. She searches the vessel and finds him hiding. They say their heartfelt goodbyes and exchange their most treasured possessions, her harmonica and the St. Christopher medal his girl had given him before the war. In Wellington, Robson is greeted by her father. At the fadeout, she stares back at the ship, knowing that it will take Phelps to safety in Sydney.

Although there are a number of improbable or at least fortuitous occurrences that conveniently advance the plot of STARLIGHT HOTEL (which takes its name from sleeping under the night sky), it remains an engaging story of an unlikely friendship. Hindin Miller's screenplay, adapted from his own best-selling novel *The Dream Monger,* is flawed, but the likable central characters he has created are so compelling the audience wants to believe that their adventure could have happened exactly as it is portrayed. Director Pillsbury (THE SCARECROW) unfolds the tale at a surprisingly leisurely pace, considering that this is, at least partly, a chase film. It develops in fits and starts; slow sections that concentrate on character development quickly give way to tense moments where capture seems inevitable. Certainly life on the run is not always literally that, and the film's structure and pace give a very real feel to the cross-country journey. What really makes the film work are the performances by Robson and Phelps. Gruff but clear-eyed, Phelps lets us in on Patrick's fundamental decency right from the start. He is an angry young man, but he is righteously indignant. His hostility towards those who piously sent him to war seems a little acute given that WW I ended twelve years previously, but his anger at those who have taken advantage of the Depression hardship of others is more plausible and well conveyed. More important, his gradual warming to Robson is wholly believable. Robson's performance is equally effective, capturing the independence and indomitable spirit that a girl willing to undertake such a trip would have to possess, while also preserving the innocence and naivety that keep her 13-year-old from being overly capable or self-assured. Had their performances been weaker, the story might easily have been lost in the gorgeous photography of the magnificent New Zealand countryside and the film become a travelog, albeit a breathtakingly beautiful one. Mirage Films had initially planned to shoot most of STARLIGHT HOTEL near its North Island base with a second-unit venturing south to provide the local color. However, even though they realized it would require considerable extra expense, Mirage decided the incredible natural beauty of the South Island would immeasurably enhance the film, and they shot the entire film there.

p, Larry Parr, Finola Dwyer; d, Sam Pillsbury; w, Grant Hinden Miller (based on his novel *The Dream Monger*); ph, Warrick Attewell; ed, Mike Horton; prod d, Mike Beacroft; art d, Roger Guise; cos, Barbara Darragh; makeup, Viv Mepham.

Drama **(PR:A MPAA:NR)**

STEEL DAWN† (1987) 100m Vestron-Silver Lion c

Patrick Swayze *(Nomad)*, Lisa Niemi *(Kasha)*, Christopher Neame *(Sho)*, Brion James *(Tark)*, John Fujioka *(Cord)*, Brett Hool *(Jux, Kasha's Son)*, Anthony Zerbe *(Damnil)*, Marcel Van Heerden *(Lann)*, James Whyle *(Tooey)*, Russell Savadier *(Off)*.

A post-nuclear holocaust variation on SHANE featuring DIRTY DANCING star Swayze as a sword-wielding martial-arts expert known as "Nomad" who wanders the desert wasteland chopping up various mutant-types. Hired by the town of Meridian to be their "Peacemaker" (read: sheriff), Swayze finds himself in the midst of a water-rights battle between wealthy landowner Zerbe and spunky widow Niemi (Mrs. Swayze in real life). Conveniently, Zerbe is the very man responsible for the murder of Swayze's mentor, Fujioka, so now the nomad can kill two birds with one stone: avenge his mentor's death and defend the helpless maiden. Vestron, which also released the surprise hit DIRTY DANCING, gave this a scant play-off late in 1987 prior to general release on home video.

p, Lance Hool, Conrad Hool; d, Lance Hool; w, Doug Lefler; ph, George Tirl (CFI Color); m, Brian May; ed, Mark Conte; prod d, Alex Tavoularis; art d, Hans Van Den Zanden; set d, Lindy Steinman; cos, Poppy Cannon; spec eff, Joe Quinlivan; stunts, John Barrett.

Action **Cas.** **(PR:NR MPAA:R)**

STEELE JUSTICE* (1987) 95m Atlantic c

Martin Kove *(John Steele)*, Sela Ward *(Tracy)*, Ronny Cox *(Bennett)*, Bernie Casey *(Reese)*, Joseph Campanella *(Harry)*, Soon-Teck Oh *(Gen. Bon Soong*

Kwan), Jan Gan Boyd *(Cami Van Minh)*, David Froman *(Kelso)*, Sarah Douglas *(Kay)*, Kimiko Hiroshige *(Grandmother)*, Sheila Gale *(Anchorwoman)*, Robert Kim *(Lee Van Minh)*, Peter Kwong *(Pham)*, Eric Lee *(New Thug)*, Al Leong *(Long Hair)*, Shannon Tweed *(Angela)*, Marc Tubert *(Roger)*, Irene Tsu *(Xua Chan)*, David Lander *(Army Guard)*, Willie Wong *(Young Tough)*, Bond Bradigan, Robyn Ray *(Reporters)*, Big Bull Bates *(Baldy)*, Asher Brauner, Joseph Hiev *(Mob Thugs)*, Ruth Britt *(City Official)*, Phil Fondacaro *(Dan the Bartender)*, Kevin Gage *(Army Sergeant)*, Phil Fravel, Dean Ferrandini *(Cops)*, Alan Johnson *(Doctor)*, Tak Kubota *(Gold Tooth)*, James E. Picciolo *(Prisoner)*, Gerry Rand *(Policeman)*, John Michael Ryan *(Hovercraft Driver)*, Ping Wu *(Chemist)*, April Tran *(Tattoo Man)*, Kenneth H. Chamitoff *(Soldier)*, Chris Hillman and the Desert Rose Band, Astrid Plane.

Unintentionally hilarious RAMBO-inspired actioner featuring the muscle-bound Kove as John Steele, a Vietnam vet having trouble adjusting to postwar life in sunny Southern California. Having lost both his wife (Ward) and his job as a policeman to an alcohol problem instigated by his endless nightmares about Vietnam, Kove seeks solace with the family of his best buddy in "the 'Nam," South Vietnamese soldier-turned-refugee, Kim. Things go from bad to worse for the hapless Kove, as Kim and his family are brutally murdered by Vietnamese drug kingpin Oh, the very same corrupt South Vietnamese general who shot Kove and left him for dead during the fall of Saigon in 1975 (on the very last day of the war no less!). Miraculously, Kim's 16-year-old daughter (played by Boyd, who is at least 10 years older than called for by the role) survives the slaughter. The noble Kove takes her under his wing and vows to avenge her family. Sensing danger, Oh dispatches an elite hit squad of Ninjas to dissuade Kove. There is a bloody and inadvertently hilarious gun battle in the lobby of a swank hotel where Kove's wife Ward is directing pop star Astrid Plane's latest rock video. As the chorus line collapses under a hail of bullets (choreographed by Jeff Kutash), Plane continues to warble her hit tune and Ward continues filming. Incredibly, this scene is topped later when Kove is hit with a poisoned dart. Ripping off his shirt, Kove sucks the venom from the wound, cuts it open with a knife, and then cauterizes the bloody mess with a hot skillet. Find *that* recipe in your "Frugal Gourmet" cookbook. Needless to say Kove eventually corners the bad guy and dispenses his special brand of "Steele Justice" (nice title tie-in, eh?).

Filled with enough cliche characters to stock a small lake, STEELE JUSTICE could almost be mistaken for a parody of the muscle-headed macho-man genre. Kove, known to television viewers as detective Victor Isbecki on "Cagney and Lacey," makes Stallone look like Olivier—no mean feat. Failing to give the impression that he is capable of crossing a street by himself, let alone taking on the entire Vietnamese crime syndicate, Kove merely blunders through the film spouting inane dialog and showing off his nicely pumped pectorals. (For a broken down alcoholic who cannot maintain a marriage or a job, Kove certainly finds plenty of time to work off those brewskis.) Just to detail the collection of stock characters played by semi-talented actors: Cox plays a police chief who is indistinguishable from the one he plays in BEVERLY HILLS COP parts I and II; Casey is Kove's wise-cracking cop buddy; former playmate of the year Tweed is an unlikely Mafia don (she inherited the post); Douglas is the sexy district attorney; and Campanella is a suave bad guy. If it wasn't for the unintentionally uproarious scenes, most viewers would swear that they've seen this film before. What should not go unnoticed, however, is that in an effort to promote fairness, the villains in STEELE JUSTICE are not vile, mean-spirited, ruthless, and corrupt *North* Vietnamese Communists, but vile, mean-spirited, ruthless, and corrupt *South* Vietnamese refugees. So much for knee-jerk accusations of anti-commie xenophobia. *(Graphic violence, profanity.)*

p, John Strong; d&w, Robert Boris; ph, John M. Stephens (United Color); m, Misha Segal; ed, John O'Connor, Steve Rosenblum; prod d, Richard N. McGuire; set d, John Nelson Tichler; cos, Leslie Wilshire; ch, Jeff Kutash; spec eff, James Wayne Beauchamp; makeup, Carla Roseto Kabrizi, Greg Johnson.

Action/Crime **(PR:O MPAA:R)**

STEPFATHER, THE*½** (1987) 90m ITC/New Century-Vista c

Terry O'Quinn *(Jerry Blake, the Stepfather/Henry Morrison/Bill Hodgkins)*, Jill Schoelen *(Stephanie Maine, Jerry's Step-Daughter)*, Shelley Hack *(Susan Blake, Jerry's Wife)*, Charles Lanyer *(Dr. Bondurant, Stephanie's Psychiatrist)*, Stephen Shellen *(Jim Ogilvie)*, Stephen E. Miller *(Al Brennan)*, Robyn Stevan *(Karen)*, Jeff Schultz *(Paul Baker)*, Lindsay Bourne *(Art Teacher)*, Anna Hagan *(Mrs. Leitner)*, Gillian Barber *(Anne Barnes)*, Blu Mankuma *(Lt. Jack Wall)*, Jackson Davies *(Mr. Chesterton)*, Sandra Head *(Receptionist)*, Gabrielle Rose *(Dorothy)*, Richard Sargent *(Mr. Anderson)*, Rochelle Greenwood *(Mr. Anderson)*, Don S. Williams *(Mr. Stark)*, Don MacKay *(Joe)*, Dale Wilson *(Frank)*, Gary Hetherington *(Herb)*, Andrew Snider *(Mr. Grace)*, Marie Stillin *(Mrs. Fairfax)*, Paul Batten *(Mr. Fairfax)*, Sheila Paterson *(Dr. Barbara Faraden)*.

Just when you thought slasher movies were wholly irredeemable, director Joseph Ruben comes along to prove there is some intelligent life in this otherwise bereft sub-genre. Featuring a fascinating script, some taut direction, and an absolutely absorbing performance by O'Quinn, THE STEPFATHER is not just another slice-and-dice thriller. Loosely based on a real-life case, the film begins in a picturesque suburb during fall. The leaves have turned and blow about the lawn of an immaculate suburban home. Inside the house a rugged-looking bearded man, O'Quinn, washes his hands at the bathroom sink. Upon closer observation we see that he is washing blood from his hands. He opens a suitcase and removes a suit wrapped in plastic. He removes his glasses and wedding ring and throws them into the empty suitcase. After taking a shower he cuts his hair and shaves his beard. He then puts on the sweater, suit, and tie and appears to be a completely different person. He moves into the hallway and finds a toy boat on the floor. Shaking his head in disappointment and disgust, O'Quinn puts the boat in a crowded toy box and closes the lid. As he walks downstairs we see pictures on the wall of O'Quinn, his wife, and his children. As he goes farther down the stairs we see that some of the pictures are askew. There is a bloody handprint on the wall. At the bottom of the stairs lies a little girl, murdered. A few feet away O'Quinn's entire family lies dead. O'Quinn leaves the house, picks up the newspaper, and walks off whistling "Camptown Races." One year later O'Quinn is in a new suburb, with a new job, a new wife (Hack) and teenage stepdaughter (Schoelen). Hack, a recently widowed woman who was completely charmed by the friendly O'Quinn, is so in love with her new husband that she makes a supreme effort at affording him the "perfect" household he so desires. Schoelen, however, does not like her stepfather and finds his endless banal chatter about family life strange and unrealistic—it is as if the man really believes in the world of "Leave It To Beaver," "Ozzie and Harriet," and "Father Knows Best." As Schoelen becomes increasingly rebellious toward O'Quinn, the family seems to come apart. After witnessing several incidents that seem to indicate her stepfather is crazy, Schoelen tries to convince therapist Lanyer that O'Quinn is not what he seems. Lanyer investigates and is killed by O'Quinn, who does a fine job of covering up the crime. At the same time, O'Quinn's brother-in-law from his previous marriage (Shellen) has come close to tracking him down. Finally too "disappointed" with his family to continue, O'Quinn quits his job without telling Hack and begins forming a new identity in another town (he changes his appearance during his ferry-boat commute from one town to the other). Once he has gotten a job and established residency in his new town, O'Quinn plans to "discipline" Hack and Schoelen by killing them. His plan goes a bit awry when Hack learns that he has quit his job. When confronted, O'Quinn mistakenly refers to himself by his new name and momentarily loses track of his identity, "Wait a minute . . . Who am I here?" Upon remembering who he is supposed to be, he smiles, thanks Hack for reminding him (she calls him by name), and then calmly bashes her in the head with the phone. He then goes after Schoelen, but the doorbell rings. Shellen barges in the door, but before he can draw his gun O'Quinn kills him. O'Quinn then goes upstairs to kill Schoelen, but the plucky girl fends him off long enough for Hack to retrieve the dead Shellen's gun and shoot her husband. Schoelen stabs her stepfather for good measure and O'Quinn dies with a look of astonishment on his face.

Fitting in nicely among such examinations of the seedy underbelly of "perfect" family life as Hitchcock's SHADOW OF A DOUBT and David Lynch's BLUE VELVET, THE STEPFATHER was a surprise hit with the critics, but failed to catch on with the public due to an ever-changing advertising campaign and a poor distribution pattern. Executives at New Century/Vista snapped up the independ-

ent film for distribution, but then didn't know how to market it. The first ad campaign showed the bearded O'Quinn staring at his clean-shaved image in the foggy bathroom mirror with the words "Who am I here?" scrawled on the condensation. When this ad failed to draw an audience, a new one showed the three different faces of O'Quinn, with Schoelen in the background holding a piece of broken mirror with which to defend herself. Also included were critical blurbs from Judith Crist and Bruce Williamson. When this failed, a third ad was run showing Schoelen cuddling a dog with O'Quinn holding a butcher knife silhouetted in the background. On this ad a blurb from Pauline Kael appeared. Ironically, although the distributor did not want to promote their film as a slasher movie, this third and most exploitative ad proved to be the most effective and has remained the definitive graphic on ads, posters, and the video cassette box. Although the last part of THE STEPFATHER disintegrates into some typical slasher movie conventions and a plethora of clumsy Hitchcock homages, the majority of the film is *definitely not* typical. Fueled by an intense and intricate performance by journeyman actor O'Quinn, the movie is a fascinating examination of America's predilection for superficial appearances over genuine substance. O'Quinn's psychotic character is the consummate actor, one who masks his crazed state with an air of friendliness and easy charm. It is this false veneer of bliss that O'Quinn strives for—one that has been spoon-fed to his diseased mind via television. O'Quinn wants the perfect television family, but when reality rears its ugly head and day-to-day problems cannot be dealt with in a matter of minutes, O'Quinn's repressed rage erupts and he kills his family (effectively "canceling" his home-made tv show) before moving on to the next one. Director Ruben and his screenwriters do a superb job making this procedure plausible and O'Quinn's preparations for establishing a new identity are as intriguing as they are chilling. Enough praise cannot be heaped on O'Quinn's performance for he is able to shift psychological gears in a matter of seconds, reeling from the pleasant "Father Knows Best" facade to dangerous psychopath and back again with sinister ease. His straight-faced spouting of sitcom platitudes is as frightening as it is funny. Schoelen is also terrific as the rebellious teenager who senses that all is not right with O'Quinn. Determined and intelligent, Schoelen is not your average slasher-movie victim. This young actress perfectly conveys the claustrophobic fear she has for her stepfather and makes the viewer share in her apprehension and frustration with a situation over which she has little control. Hack is also perfectly cast as the frightened widow grateful for the protection and security a husband provides. Hack, a rather bland model and television actress, fits in perfectly with the O'Quinn character's vision of what a television wife should be like. In addition to the fine casting, Ruben fills the film with insightful and darkly humorous little moments such as O'Quinn disgustedly putting away the toy boat at the beginning of the film—a little indiscretion which was no doubt symptomatic of O'Quinn's growing "disappointment" with his first family; and a scene where O'Quinn sits enraptured by a rerun of "Mr. Ed." Ruben takes the time to discover such moments and in doing so enriches a movie which could have easily become just another mechanical stalk-and-slash exercise. *(Graphic violence, nudity, profanity.)*

p, Jay Benson; d, Joseph Ruben; w, Donald E. Westlake (based on a story by Carolyn Lefcourt, Brian Garfield, Donald E. Westlake); ph, John W. Lindley; m, Patrick Moraz; ed, George Bowers; prod d, James William Newport; art d, David Willson; set d, Kimberley Richardson; cos, Mina Mittelman; m/l, M. Grombacher, N. Geraldo, C. Amphlett, M. McEntee, Patrick Moraz, John McBurnie.

Thriller **Cas.** **(PR:O MPAA:R)**

STORY OF DR. SUN YAT-SEN, THE† (1987, Taiwan/Hong Kong) 200m Taiwan-Hong Kong-First Films/Golden Princess c

Lam Wei-sung, Alex Man, Hui Ying-Hung, Leung Ka-yen.

One of two biographies of Dr. Sun Yat-sen, this Hong Kong-Taiwanese co-production, like its Chinese counterpart DR. SUN YAT-SEN, follows the leader's life from his early revolutionary days to his 1911 election as provisional President of the new Chinese Republic to his death in 1925.

d, Ting Shang-zi.

Biography **(PR:NR MPAA:NR)**

STRAIGHT TO HELL* (1987, Brit.) 86m Initial Pictures/Island c

Sy Richardson *(Norwood)*, Joe Strummer *(Simms)*, Dick Rude *(Willy)*, Courtney Love *(Velma)*, Zander Schloss *(Karl)*, Del Zamora *(Poncho)*, Luis Contreras *(Sal)*, Jim Jarmusch *(Mr. Amos Dade)*, Miguel Sandoval *(George)*, Jennifer Balgobin *(Fabienne)*, Bill Yaeger *(Frank)*, Sue Kiel *(Leticia)*, Michele Winstanley *(Louise)*, Edward Tudorpole *(Rusty)*, Xander Berkeley *(Preacher)*, Fox Harris *(Kim Blousson)*, Dennis Hopper *(I.G. Farben)*, Grace Jones *(Sonya)*, Graham Fletcher Cook *(Whitey/Jeeves)*, Spider Stacy *(Angel Eyes)*, Shane MacGowan *(Bruno)*, Jem Finer *(Granpa)*, Terry Woods *(Tom)*, Cait O'Riordan *(Slim)*, Kathy Burke *(Sabrina)*, James Fearnley *(Jimmy)*, Sara Sugarman *(Chuch)*, Juan Torres *(Churbo)*, Anne-Marie Ruddock *(Molly)*, Sharon Bailey *(Porter)*, Andrew Rankin *(Lance)*, Frank Murray *(Biff)*, Philip Chevron *(Ed)*, Elvis Costello *(Hives, the Butler)*, Jose Pomedio Monedero *(Gomez)*, Ed Pansullo *(Mac MacMahon)*, The Pogues *(The MacMahons)*, Turnham Green *(McGee)*, Charlie Braun *(Blacksmith McMahon)*, Sean Madigan, Paul Wood *(Jarheads)*, Chalkie Davis *(Branding Victim)*, Linda the Dog *(Weiner)*.

A combination of the punk sensibility of Alex Cox's first film, REPO MAN, and the spaghetti westerns of Sergio Leone, STRAIGHT TO HELL sure seems like it was a lot more fun to make than it is to watch. This haphazard parody was budgeted at $1 million, scripted in three days, and filmed in four weeks. It features a hipper-than-hip crowd of music and film personalities that includes Joe Strummer (formerly of the punk band The Clash), Elvis Costello (singer/songwriter *extraordinaire*), Grace Jones (former disco queen and intimidating costar of A VIEW TO A KILL and VAMP), The Pogues (folksy Irish rock band), Jim Jarmusch (director of STRANGER THAN PARADISE and DOWN BY LAW) and Dennis Hopper (the guiding light of everybody on the fringe). Director Cox apparently had some time on his hands between the completion of SID AND NANCY and the commencement of WALKER, so he shipped off with his friends to Tabernas, near Almeria in southeast Spain (one of Leone's favorite locales), and made a movie.

The incredibly convoluted plot begins as three hired guns—brawny, stoic Richardson, baby-faced Rude, and disheveled Strummer—botch a hit. To offset their failure, they decide to rob a bank, making their getaway in a battered Fiat with Love, Richardson's blonde, obnoxious, and pregnant girl friend (apparently modeled after the Chloe Webb character in SID AND NANCY). In the middle of the desert, the car breaks down and the dusty, sweaty foursome walk aimlessly. They stumble upon a lawless town ruled by the nasty, trigger-happy MacMahon clan (played by The Pogues). Although they are warned by a local barkeep to get out of town, they ignore the advice. The following morning, a showdown takes place. It's right about here that everything seems to go haywire, as if Cox decided to bail out and let the lunatics run the asylum. The members of the MacMahon gang, it is soon revealed, are a bunch of no-good . . . coffee addicts. They like to cavort, shoot guns, drink coffee (which is poured by their ever-present servant, Costello), and sing songs ("Danny Boy" seems to be their favorite). They also like to humiliate Karl, a hot dog vendor (played with a certain charm by Schloss), eventually forcing him to also sing a song, "Ketchup Y Salsa." Meanwhile, Strummer has eyes for Balgobin, the curvaceous wife of storekeeper Sandoval, and Rude has fallen in love with the seductive, money-hungry Winstanley. There's also a bounty hunter, Tudorpole, who comes to El Blanco to capture the McMahons. Into the midst of all this sexual tension, gunfighting, and coffee addiction comes American businessman Hopper and his sweetheart Jones. The imperialistic Hopper immediately has ideas of his own for El Blanco, stating: "This is such a lovely town. Just needs a little sprucin' up . . . A 7-11, an AM-PM Mini Mart, and it'll be just like America. 'Course there'll have to be some changes made." He then supplies Richardson, Strummer, and Rude with some heavy artillery to battle the MacMahons. Enter Jarmusch, the threesome's frog-voiced former employer, who is determined to get vengeance for their bungled hit. By time the final gun battle rolls around nearly everyone has died an amusing death, leaving Hopper to begin his community development project. Making movies fast and cheap is not a new idea for filmmakers. Edgar G. Ulmer made a

career of it, peaking in 1946 with DETOUR; Jean-Luc Godard did it throughout the 1960s in France; and R.W. Fassbinder did the same in Germany in the 1970s. Unfortunately, the recent trend in Hollywood has been to spend months or maybe years on a film, filling it with special effects, and paying large salaries that satisfy actors' overblown egos. After REPO MAN and SID AND NANCY (two of the freshest and most energetic films in recent memory), one hoped that Cox would find much success in his attempt at cranking out a fast and cheap production. No such luck, however. STRAIGHT TO HELL is one of the most boring, incomprehensible, and self-indulgent films in some time. Not since the days of the acid-trip films of the 1960s has a film seemed as much like an inside joke as STRAIGHT TO HELL does. It amounts to nothing more than a home movie, of interest only to the people involved in its making. At best, it will achieve cult status, playing midnight shows to audiences who will delight in seeing Elvis Costello with his coffee pot, or Joe Strummer trying to twirl a gun, or Grace Jones donning a curly black wig, or Jim Jarmusch getting shot right between the eyes. STRAIGHT TO HELL gets a pat on the head for good intentions, but that just isn't enough here. The only real standouts in the film are Sy Richardson (who costarred in REPO MAN and SID AND NANCY) and the dusty, heat-shimmering camerawork of Richmond, which expertly mimics the spaghetti-western style. The film's credits end with the promise of another Cox production, entitled BACK TO HELL, but that seems to be more a threat than a promise. *(Violence, sexual situations.)*

p, Eric Fellner; d, Alex Cox; w, Dick Rude, Alex Cox; ph, Tom Richmond; m, The Pogues, Pray For Rain; ed, Dave Martin; prod d, Andrew McAlpine; art d, Caroline Hanania; cos, Pam Tait; spec eff, Juan Ramon Molina; m/l, Jerry Leiber, Mike Stoller, Joe Strummer, Les Reed, Barry Mason, MacManus, Dan Wul, Zander Schloss, Miguel Sandoval, Fearnley, Rankin, Mussorgsky, Finer, MacGowan; makeup, Morag Ross.

Western/Comedy **Cas.** **(PR:O MPAA:R)**

STRAKH† (1987, USSR) 88m Riga Film/Sovexportfilm c (Trans: Fear)

Eduard Pavuls, Zane Jansevskaya, Aigar Vilims.

A farmer in WW II Latvia is caught between the warring Soviet troops and the retreating Nazis when his son, a deserter from the German army, hides in his father's shed. To complicate matters, the farmer's daughter hides a wounded Soviet pilot, with whom she's fallen in love, in the hayloft.

d, Gunar Tselinsky; w, Vladimir Kaiaks; ph, Mik Zvirbulis; m, Imant Kalnins; art d, Icar Antone.

Drama/War **(PR:NR MPAA:NR)**

STRANDED**½ (1987) 80m New Line c

Ione Skye *(Deirdre Clark)*, Joe Morton *(Sheriff McMahon)*, Maureen O'Sullivan *(Grace Clark)*, Susan Barnes *(Helen Anderson)*, Cameron Dye *(Lt. Scott)*, Michael Greene *(Vernon Burdett)*, Brendan Hughes *(Prince)*, Gary Swanson *(Sergeant)*, Flea *(Jester)*, Spice Williams *(Warrior)*, Florence Sschauffler *(Queen)*, Dennis Vero *(Sir)*, Scott Rosenfeld *(News Reporter)*.

A simple but sophisticated science fiction film set during one evening in a remote North Carolina farmhouse, STRANDED stars Skye as a 17-year-old girl who has been living with her grandmother, O'Sullivan, ever since the recent death of her parents. The relationship between Skye and O'Sullivan is strained, but strengthens when they are visited by five aliens on the run from an assassin. The aliens take refuge in the farmhouse, holding Skye and O'Sullivan hostage. When a friend of Skye's comes to visit he shoots one of the aliens and is then killed by a laser blast. The alien dies, causing panic and sadness among the other aliens. Determined to avenge the boy's death is his angry redneck father Greene. After a policeman is killed during an attempted raid, sheriff Morton, a black, arrives on the scene. He is determined to handle the situation as a normal hostage crisis—in an orderly fashion to prevent any harm to Skye or O'Sullivan. He is met with opposition from some of the white members of his police force and from Greene, who has returned to the scene with an armed posse and wants to storm the farmhouse. Inside, Skye and O'Sullivan have gained the trust of the aliens and have learned to communicate telepathically. Skye and alien Hughes share a mutual, non-physical attraction to one another, while O'Sullivan makes friends with a playful, curious alien called Jester (played by Flea, the bass player for the band Red Hot Chili Peppers). Morton enters the house and sympathizes with the harmless, but frightened, aliens' plight. He cannot, however, promise to help them escape, since they've killed, albeit inadvertently, two humans. Assistance arrives from the Department of Defense in the form of Barnes, a bureaucratic official who is more concerned with capturing the aliens than with the safety of the hostages. Frustrated, Greene tries to gun down Morton, who is forced to take refuge inside the farmhouse. Greene begins shooting wildly, killing another alien in the process. Hughes flees into the woods with Skye, while O'Sullivan hides in the house. It is then revealed that Barnes is not a DOD official but the feared assassin. She guns down another of the aliens, kills Greene during a showdown, and nearly kills Morton. In the meantime, Hughes is preparing to return to the skies. Barnes is about to kill him, but is gunned down by a shotgun-wielding O'Sullivan. Hughes softly bids farewell to Skye and, with the last surviving alien, Flea, returns to outer space.

STRANDED, unlike so many other sci-fi and fantasy films, is a believable human drama set within the framework of the fantastic. Described by director Fuller as reminiscent of the Humphrey Bogart-Fredric March vehicle THE DESPERATE HOURS, the film takes a fantasy situation and places it in rural America. The focus is not on the aliens (they speak no discernable language and their background is barely detailed) but on the humans they affect. Fuller, formerly a photojournalist and documentary filmmaker, clearly is fascinated with the parallel drama taking place outside the house between Morton and the locals. In the Hitchcockian sense, the aliens are the "MacGuffin"—that which draws the audience in to the story, but which is not what the film is about. STRANDED is not about aliens, but about alienation. Skye is alienated by her grandmother, stranded in backwoods North Carolina after the death of her parents. Morton is a black sheriff fighting the alienation of his police force and of the locals—none of whom are accustomed to taking orders from a black man. Also setting STRANDED apart from the rest of the crop are some exceptional performances, most notably Morton's. Probably best known as the alien in THE BROTHER FROM ANOTHER PLANET, he is perfectly cast as the alienated sheriff who understands the aliens' position. O'Sullivan, last seen in HANNAH AND HER SISTERS, turns in a wonderful performance, communicating more with her eyes than in her speech. Skye, an untrained actress fresh from her success in RIVER'S EDGE, is one of the most natural performers to wander onto the screen in some time. Coming across remarkably well are the aliens, especially Hughes and Flea who seem "human" despite their elaborate makeup. Filmed for less than $3 million, the film looks as if it cost much more thanks to the cinematography of Jur (DIRTY DANCING); the alien creations by Oscar-winner Burke (QUEST FOR FIRE); the subtle special effects; and the alien's artificial language consisting of nonsense phonetics designed by sound effects editor Dane Davis. Only a short sequence which takes place on the aliens' home planet is substandard technically. Released regionally in 1987, before getting a wider release in 1988. *(Violence, mild profanity.)*

p, Scott Rosenfelt, Mark Levinson; d, Tex Fuller; w, Alan Castle; ph, Jeff Jur (United Color); m, Stacy Widelitz; ed, Stephen E. Rivkin; set d, Lisette Thomas; spec eff, Allen Hall; stunts, John Branagan, Michelle Burke.

Science Fiction **(PR:A-C MPAA:PG-13)**

STRANGER, THE* (1987, US/Arg.) 88m Tusitala-Nolin Co./COL c

Bonnie Bedelia *(Alice Kildee)*, Peter Riegert *(Dr. Harris Kite)*, Barry Primus *(Sgt. Drake)*, David Spielberg *(Hobby)*, Marcos Woinski *(Macaw)*, Julio de Grazia *(Jay)*, Cecilia Roth *(Anita)*, Arturo Maly, Ricardo Darin, Adrian Ghio, Tito Mendoza, Federico Luppi, Marina Magali, Ernesto Larrese, Sacha Favelevic.

Reminiscent of Hitchcock's SPELLBOUND, this lackluster thriller revolves around a psychiatrist's attempts to cure an amnesiac in order to get to the bottom or a murder she has witnessed. The film opens in a isolated country house where Bedelia witnesses a brutal murder and then flees. One of the killers shoots at her and the screen goes blank. Bedelia reappears on a small-town street, jumps into her car, and speeds off, pursued by another vehicle. Her car swerves off the highway, overturns, and bursts into flames, but, unbeknownst to her assailants, Bedelia escapes from the wreckage. She ends up in a hospital where she is treated by psychiatrist Riegert. Bedelia, who doesn't know her own identity, is able to describe the murder, but doesn't remember where it occurred or who was involved. No similar homicide has been reported, and investigating cop Primus releases Bedelia's photo and story to the press. Before long, shadowy characters start appearing. De Grazia, the owner of a small airport, contracts Spielberg to kill Bedelia. He also picks up the marker for Riegert's $62,000 gambling debt and tries to blackmail the psychiatrist into cooperating. Meanwhile, Spielberg assumes the identity of the amnesia specialist whom he has killed. Against this backdrop, Riegert endeavors to cure Bedelia's amnesia. Well enough to leave the hospital, Bedelia goes to the home of Riegert's nurse girl friend, where Spielberg makes an unsuccessful attempt on her life. Acting on a hunch, Riegert takes Bedelia to see a film called "Deadly." On the screen is the murder she had seen, and the pieces of the psychological puzzle come together. Bedelia had been working at de Grazia's airport, and Darin, an undercover drug enforcement agent, enlisted her help in obtaining some microfilm that exposed de Grazia's drug-smuggling operation. Bedelia had given the evidence to Darin at the theater during "Deadly," but Spielberg and his cohorts were there, too. They murdered Darin and chased Bedelia until her car overturned. In her disturbed state, she substituted the onscreen murder for the real-life events. After making this discovery, Riegert and Bedelia are abducted by de Grazia and company, but they get the drop on their captors and send them to meet their maker. Doctor and patient have been falling for each other all along, and the film ends with their clinch.

Not to be confused with Albert Camus' novel of the same name, this Argentine-made, English-language film nonetheless leaves the viewer pondering at least one important existential question: What would possess anyone to sit through this movie? Bedelia's subconscious fusion of the murder in "Deadly" with Darin's death and her blocking of the events leading up to it give the story an inspired twist, but there isn't much else to recommend the film. Riegert, Bedelia, and Primus, the frustrated cop, do their best to make something of their roles, but they have been given so little that their efforts are futile. The dialog is weak and occasionally atrocious, and the screenplay is full of implausibilities, not the least of which is Riegert's miraculously quick cure of Bedelia. If drugs, hypnotism, and Dr. Freud's methods worked this well, we'd be a very healthy society indeed. The direction of THE STRANGER is not particularly successful either, and what tension there is is sporadic and predictable. When Bedelia is left alone in the house, the question is not whether Spielberg will come for her, but which of her shoulders he will appear over. The film's sound quality is also uneven and bothersome, though "Mirrors and Lights" (Mark Mueller, Craig Safan, performed by Debbie Davis), the song heard during the murder scene in "Deadly" and repeated throughout the film, comes through unmercifully loud and clear. *(Brief nudity, sexual situations, violence.)*

p, Hugo Lamonica; d, Adolfo Aristarain; w, Dan Gurskis; ph, Horacio Maira; m, Craig Safan; ed, Eduardo Lopez; set d, Abel Facello; cos, Felix Sanchez Plaza.

Crime/Drama **(PR:O MPAA:R)**

STRANNAYAR ISTORIYAR DOKTORA DZHEKILA I MISTERA KHAIDA† (1987, USSR) 92m Mosfilm/Sovexportfilm c (Trans: The Strange Case of Dr. Jekyll and Mr. Hyde)

Innokenti Smoktunovsky *(Dr. Henry Jekyll)*, Alexander Feklistov *(Edward Hyde)*, Anatoly Adoskin *(Utterson)*, Bruno Freinlich *(Poole)*, Alla Budnitskaya *(Diana)*.

Robert Louis Stevenson's classic tale is given a faithful treatment in this Soviet adaptation which uses two different actors to portray the split personality of the drug-addicted Dr. Henry Jekyll.

d, Alexander Orlov; w, Alexander Orlov, Georgy Kapralov (based on the novel by Robert Louis Stevenson); ph, Valery Shuvalov (Sovcolor); m, Eduard Artemyev; prod d, Igor Lemeshev.

Mystery/Thriller **(PR:NR MPAA:NR)**

STRATEGIJA SVRAKE† (1987, Yugo.) 113m Forum c (Trans: The Magpie's Strategy)

Predrag-Pepi Lakovic *(Budimir Sarenac)*, Zvonko Lepetic *(Grandson)*, Radmila Zivkovic *(Slavica)*, Boro Stjepanovic, Sukrana Gusani.

A series of comic misadventures results when a hard-drinking, loyal Communist, Lakovic, invites a family of gypsies into his backyard to watch the funeral of Marshal Tito. Lakovic so enjoys the gypsy family, that he invites them to stay and live in his backyard, over the very vocal protests of his own family.

d, Zlatko Lavanic; w, Mladen Materic, Emir Kusturica; ph, Danijal Sukalo; m, Braca Vranesevic; ed, Zoltan Wagner; art d, Predrag Lukovac.

Comedy **(PR:NR MPAA:NR)**

STREET SMART*½ (1987) 95m Golan-Globus/Cannon c

Christopher Reeve *(Jonathan Fisher)*, Morgan Freeman *(Fast Black)*, Kathy Baker *(Punchy)*, Mimi Rogers *(Alison Parker)*, Jay Patterson *(Leonard Pike)*, Andre Gregory *(Ted Avery)*, Anna Maria Horsford *(Harriet)*, Frederick Rolf *(Joel Davis)*, Erik King *(Reggie)*, Michael J. Reynolds *(Art Sheffield)*, Shari Hilton *(Darlene)*, Donna Bailey *(Yvonne)*, Ed Van Nuys *(Judge)*, Daniel Nalrach *(Singer)*, Rick Aviles *(Solo)*, Les Carlson *(Marty)*, Bill Torre *(Hotel Clerk)*, Richard Mullaly *(Suburban John)*, Marie Barrientos *(Hispanic Prostitute)*, Eddie Earl Hatch *(Flashy Man)*, Joe Dorian Clark *(Transvestite)*, Grace Garland *(Black Prostitute)*, Wally Martin *(Lowlife)*, Robert Morelli *(Undercover Cop)*, Shawn Laurence *(Bartender)*, Kelly Ricard *(Woman Magistrate)*, David Glen *(Jay)*, Ulla Moreland *(Ted's Wife)*, Francisco Gonzales *(Pablo)*, Lynne Adams, Claudette Roach, Rudi Adler, Melba Archer, Ian Beaton, Victor Bowen, Lois Dellar, Chui-

Lin Mark, Manon Vallee, Carole Zelles *(Reporters)*, Danny Brainin *(T.V. Cameraman)*, Ernest Deveaux *(Kid)*, Walter Allen Bennet, Jr. *(Ball Player)*, Steve Michaels *(Taxi Inspector)*, Margarita Stocker *(Intellectual Woman)*, Eve Napier *(Trish)*, Ruth Dahan *(Mrs. Silverbeard)*, Vera Miller, Nadia Rona *(Party Guests)*, Terry Haig *(Marshall)*, Donald Lamoureux *(Prison Reporter)*, Carol Ann Francis *(Susan)*, Ann Pearl Gary, Emmanuelle LaSalle *(Waitresses)*.

There is a glibness and calculating coldness about this film, a smugness of script and haughtiness of direction that will be felt by even the average viewer. Again we take a tour through the seamy side of lower New York into the world of pimps and prostitutes. Reeve is a lazy, unimaginative journalist who gets a cushy assignment from a posh magazine to write about the lifestyle of a pimp. When he can't find the right role model, Reeve creates a fictional portrait which is published and receives widespread accolades. In addition, he is given new and lucrative TV assignments to do more along the same line. This editorial approach disgusts Reeve's girl friend Rogers but it pays well and Reeve continues fabricating stories about the lowlifes. In the process, he learns more about the ladies of the night and their main men as he begins to move through their netherworld of drugs and vice and violence. Then a frightening menace enters Reeve's life in the person of Freeman, a vicious, high-powered pimp who is being charged with murder. Freeman's prosecutors have identified Reeve's article as being a profile of Freeman and they demand Reeve's notes. He has none but is afraid to admit he made up the story. His publisher comes to the rescue, screaming freedom of the press. Freeman tells Reeve that if he doesn't create false notes, clearing him of the murder charge, there will be another murder very soon with Reeve as the victim. To complicate matters, Reeve briefly falls in love with noble hooker Baker. Eventually, he makes up the phony editorial notes and turns them over to help the killer. But, relying on his newfound "street smarts," he traps Freeman by setting him up for a hit by another pimp who wants to replace him.

The film is slickly produced and Freeman's murderous pimp role is acted with frightening realism but Reeve merely walks stoically through his role, his emotions as dead as his character's lack of commitment. Nothing of value is promoted here and no character is redeemable, except for pathetic tart Baker and she is shown as a mere love sop. The viewer cannot help but feel that the entire production was just another excuse to parade one sexual indignity after another in a story that has no intention but to shock and pander. The real pimp here is the movie itself. Shot in New York City and Montreal. Songs include "Publico Oyente" (Ray Perez), "Only In Your Arms" (Michael Bishop, Paul Chisten), "Peanut Butter" (S. Dunbar), "(You Make Me Feel Like) A Natural Woman" (Gerry Goffin, Carole King, Jerry Wexler, performed by Aretha Franklin), "The Last Time (I Get Burned Like This)" (Robert Cray, performed by The Robert Cray Band), "Payin' For It Now" (D. Amy, Robert Cray, performed by The Robert Cray Band), "Romance Without Finance," "Street Beat" (Robert Irving III), "Salsa Suite Part II" (Larry Harlow, performed by Larry Harlow & Orchestra), "Nadie Podra Querete Como Yo" (Rosa Soy, performed by Larry Harlow & Orchestra). *((Profanity, violence.)*

p, Menahem Golan, Yoram Globus; d, Jerry Schatzberg; w, David Freeman; ph, Adam Holender (TVC Color); m, Robert Irving, III, Miles Davis; ed, Priscilla Nedd; prod d, Dan Leigh; art d, Serge Jacques; set d, Raymond Larose, Katherine Mathewson; cos, Jo Ynocenio.

Crime/Drama **Cas.** **(PR:O MPAA:R)**

STREET TRASH** (1987) 91m Chaos/Lightning c

Mike Lackey *(Fred)*, Vic Noto *(Bronson)*, Bill Chepil *(Bill the Cop)*, Mark Sferrazza *(Kevin, Fred's Brother)*, Jane Arakawa *(Wendy)*, Nicole Potter *(Winette)*, R.L. Ryan *(Frank Schnizer)*, Clarenze Jarmon *(Burt)*, Bernard Perlman *(Wizzy)*, Miriam Zucker *(Drunken Wench)*, M. D'Jango Krunch *(Ed)*, James Lorinz *(Doorman)*, Morty Storm *(Black Suit)*, Tony Darrow *(Nick Duran)*, Frank Farel, Roy Frumkes.

Judging a film like STREET TRASH is quite problematic. Normally one would not hesitate to praise the debut of an interesting new young talent, a director who can take a budget of less than $100,000 and produce a remarkably professional-looking film that contains sequences of cinematic excitement and verve. Unfortunately, STREET TRASH also happens to be one of the most repugnant exploitation movies ever filmed, one that offends the sensibilities and will shock even the most hardened veteran of so-called "cult" films. This movie "pushes the envelope" of bad taste and is perhaps the most revoltingly funny film since John Waters' PINK FLAMINGOS. As "Midnight Movies" go, STREET TRASH is the most fiercely original and inventive in years, although only those with strong stomachs should dare to investigate. Inspired by Akira Kurosawa's DODES'KA-DEN, the film is set among the homeless of Brooklyn and concentrates on a group of winos living in a trash heap just outside a junkyard. Virtually plotless, the action loosely revolves around a case of contaminated wine a local liquor-store owner has discovered while cleaning his basement and sold to the derelicts for $1 a bottle. Unbeknownst to both the seller and the buyers of said "Tenafly Viper" is that one sip from the bottle and the unfortunate drinker literally melts into a puddle of paint goo (the well-executed gore effects are colorfully cartoonish and relatively inoffensive). The junkyard is dominated by a wacko Vietnam veteran (Noto) who looks like a refugee from Wes Craven's THE HILLS HAVE EYES, is subject to 'Nam flashbacks (staged inventively by director Muro), and carries a knife made from a human femur bone. The ostensible "heroes" of STREET TRASH are a pair of homeless siblings: 1960s hippie Lackey and his teenage brother Sferrazza. They simply try to scratch out a meager existence and steer clear of the dangerously psychotic Noto. When the body of the girl friend of local would-be mobster Darrow is found near the junkyard (she was gang-raped and murdered by the bums—one of the film's most repulsive scenes), plainclothes cop Chepil investigates. He interrogates Darrow and his smart-ass doorman Lorinz, only to find Darrow intends to have the doorman killed for not keeping an eye on his girl. The unfazed Lorinz, who is fed up with his pompous boss, lets loose a litany of clever insults upon Darrow in a dull monotone (easily the funniest scene in the movie). Eventually, Chepil's investigation leads him to the junkyard and a violent confrontation with Noto. Chepil is killed in the battle and Noto continues his rampage until the resourceful Sferrazza manages to decapitate the marauding veteran with a flying propane tank. The film ends with Lorinz tied to a chair and about to be executed by Darrow. Still not intimidated, Lorinz continues his stream of insults and then has a hearty laugh as Darrow takes a sip of the deadly "Tenafly Viper," and melts. Lorinz turns to Darrow's goons and states, "Hey, I guess I'm the 'Don' now, huh?"

An unabashed celebration of bad taste, STREET TRASH has something to offend everyone. The film began life as a 10-minute short made while director Muro was a student at New York City's School for the Visual Arts. Muro was encouraged by his instructor, Frumkes, to expand the concept to feature length and re-shoot on 35mm stock. Frumkes himself took on the writing and producing chores. STREET TRASH is shot surprisingly well (on location at the junkyard owned by Muro, Sr.), with myriad movements that would seem cost-prohibitive on a $100,000 budget. The filmmakers were able to attain this degree of professionalism because the industrious 21-year-old Muro owned and operated his own steadicam—an expensive, delicate, and complicated piece of equipment that enables the cinematographer supreme mobility while maintaining a smooth, gliding shot (infinitely better than the jerky movement seen in hand-held shots). As a director/cinematographer Muro seems most influenced by EVIL DEAD director Sam Raimi, and has a good eye for composition, movement, and color. Muro knows how to effectively stage a wide variety of scenes, and if he can graduate from sophomoric gore to something more mature he may develop into a significant talent. No amount of technical proficiency, however, will dissuade the protectors of public decency from declaring that all the prints of STREET TRASH should be taken out and burned. Frankly, it is difficult to defend Muro other than to state that this film was made for a certain audience and that audience will not take it as seriously as its detractors. Trying to apply generally accepted critical standards to self-consciously fashioned cult films such as STREET TRASH is missing the point. This is renegade cinema, made to offend the establishment. The fact that STREET TRASH is so very offensive says much about what young talent must do to get noticed. The plethora of gore films on the market is a testament to just how difficult it is for independent filmmakers to raise money. Horror films always make money, therefore investors will only put up money for horror films. While 99 percent of these films are junk, there is that one percent made by talented people looking for a break. Some continue to make superior horror films, while others use horror as a springboard to more acceptable filmmaking. In spite of all the excessive gore, misogyny, and shock humor (mostly based on bodily functions), Muro does seem to have some compassion for the homeless. There is a definite sense of community in the junkyard and a certain repulsive nobility to its cast of characters. The disgust-factor in STREET SMART is directly attributable to the hopelessly nightmarish existence these characters lead. As reprehensible as this film may be, it at least acknowledges the plight of the homeless—something mainstream films have ignored. Once again: This is easily one of the most offensive films ever made and potential viewers are strongly cautioned. *(Graphic violence, gore effects, full frontal nudity, sexual situations, excessive profanity, substance abuse.)*

p, Roy Frumkes; d, Jim Muro; w, Roy Frumkes; ph, David Sperling (Technicolor); m, Rick Ulfik; ed, Dennis Werner; prod d, Robert Marcucci; art d, Denise Labelle, Tom Molinelli; cos, Michele Leifer; spec eff, Jennifer Aspinall; makeup, Mike Lackey.

Comedy/Horror **(PR:O MPAA:NR)**

STREGATI† (1987, It.) 95m Union P.N.-C.G. Silver Film/COL c (Trans: Bewitched)

Francesco Nuti *(Lorenzo)*, Ornella Muti *(Anna)*, Novello Novelli, Alex Partexano, Sergio Solli.

Comedian Francesco Nuti directs himself in this romance about a self-proclaimed Don Juan of Genoa, Nuti, who is determined to bed a mysterious and beautiful stranger, Muti. Nuti poses as a cab driver and takes Muti to the misty port where he succeeds in seducing her. Much to his surprise, Nuti actually falls in love with Muti, but she soon ends their brief encounter by informing him that she is to be married the very next day. The lovers part at the train station, never to see each other again. Nuti and Muti co-starred in the 1985 Italian box office hit, TUTTA COLPA DEL PARADISO (Blame It On Paradise), also directed by Nuti.

p, Gianfranco Piccioli; d, Francesco Nuti; w, Vincenzo Cerami, Giovanni Veronesi, Francesco Nuti; ph, Giuseppe Ruzzolini (Luciano Vittori color); m, Giovanni Nuti; ed, Sergio Montanari; art d, Ugo Chiti.

Romance **(PR:NR MPAA:NR)**

STRIKE COMMANDO† (1987, It.) 102m Flora Film c

Reb Brown *(Michael Ramsom)*, Christopher Connelly *(Col. Radek)*, Loes Kamma *(Olga)*, Alan Collins *(Le Duc)*, Alex Vitale *(Jakoda)*, Edison Navarro *(Lao)*, Karen Lopez *(Cho-Li)*, Juliet D. Lee *(Diem)*.

Italian-produced RAMBO rip-off featuring Brown as a muscle-bound member of an elite fighting unit known as the "Strike Commando Force." The unit is sent on a dangerous mission in Vietnam, only to be shot to pieces, with Brown the sole survivor. While he is nursed back to health by the local villagers, Brown spies Soviet advisors milling about the area and hightails it home to headquarters. Brown's superiors send him back to obtain reconnaissance photos of the Russians, but the bare-chested zealot gets himself involved in a one-on-one showdown with head Russkie Vitale. Shown in Kansas City prior to home video release.

p, Franco Gaudenzi; d, Vincent Dawn [Bruno Mattei]; w, Clyde Anderson (based on a story by Clyde Anderson, Vincent Dawn [Bruno Mattei]); ph, Richard Gras (Telecolor); m, Lou Ceccarelli; ed, Vincent Dawn [Bruno Mattei]; art d, Bart Scavya.

Action **Cas.** **(PR:NR MPAA:NR)**

STRIPPED TO KILL** (1987) 84m Concorde c

Kay Lenz *(Cody/Sunny)*, Greg Evigan *(Sgt. Heineman)*, Norman Fell *(Ray)*, Tracy Crowder *(Fanny)*, Athena Worthey *(Zeena)*, Carlye Byron *(Cinnamon)*, Debbie Nassar *(Dazzle)*, Lucia Nagy Lexington *(Brandy)*, Michelle Foreman *(Angel)*, Pia Kamakahi *(Eric/Roxanne)*, Tom Ruben *(Mobile Entrepreneur)*, Diana Bellamy *(Shirl)*, Peter Scranton *(Pocket)*, Brad David Berwick *(Derek)*, J. Bartell *(Margolin)*, Debra Lamb *(Amateur Dancer)*, Jon Lee Freels *(Punk)*, Andy Ruben.

A fairly effective low-budget crime thriller set in a striptease club that actually manages to develop some interesting characters amid the exploitative bump-and-grind. Lenz stars as a tough female cop assigned to solve a series of murders that have left several strippers dead. Convinced by her male partner (Evigan) that the only way to crack the case is for her to go undercover and pose as a stripper, Lenz auditions for club owner Fell at an amateur night contest. Nervous and barely able to dance, she cleverly employs props and sets, and *acts* rather than dances her way through the routine. Fell hires her and soon Lenz is nosing around in the personal lives of the other strippers, while Evigan keeps an eye on the sometimes weird patrons. As the investigation continues, Lenz loses her inhibitions, becoming more relaxed on stage, and actually begins to enjoy stripping before a frenzied crowd. Evigan is disturbed by this and urges her to abandon the case. After several more murders and a frustrating series of false leads, Lenz finally stumbles upon the killer—Kamakahi, one of the strippers. In a bizarre confrontation, Kamakahi tries to kill Lenz, but she counters and stabs the dancer in the chest. To Lenz's astonishment, Kamakahi survives by simply peeling off her foam rubber breasts and revealing that she is actually a he. As it turns out, the villain is really Kamakahi's brother. Orphans who had clung to each other for years, the brother went insane when his sister announced her intention to move in with her lesbian lover. Outraged because she had promised that they would "never be apart," the brother killed his sister and took her identity (yes, it's all very implausible, but actress Kamakahi—who plays both parts—somehow manages to pull it off). Just when Lenz looks doomed, Evigan kills the crazed Kamakahi.

Although its brief running time is padded with innumerable strip routines, STRIPPED TO KILL does spin a moderately interesting tale of mystery and repressed lust. The rapport between Lenz and her partner Evigan is crucial to the success of the film, and the actors rise to the occasion. The script by the husband and wife team of Katt Shea Ruben and Andy Ruben sees the cops masking their love for each other in a veil of professionalism that is only broken when Lenz begins stripping. Unable to express their mutual sexual attraction on the job, Lenz subliminally begins to seduce her partner from the stripper's runway. Lenz's repressed sexuality, now unleashed, threatens to take over her psyche, while Evigan is relegated to the uncomfortable position of culpable voyeur. Luckily, the case is solved before the partners sink too deep into the seedy quagmire, and the experience actually serves to bring their feelings for each other out into the open. Director Ruben, an attractive former actress who most recently appeared in BARBARIAN QUEEN and PSYCHO III (and other fairly exploitative films), demonstrates a keen understanding of low-budget filmmaking and a good visual sense. She walks the fine line between exploration and exploitation, bringing some insight and intelligence to her film while giving the drive-in crowd what they want. Considering that such remarkable American directors as Francis Coppola, Martin Scorsese, and Jonathan Demme paid their dues with exploitation films, perhaps Ruben, if she has aspirations for something better, may someday bring her talents into the mainstream. Songs include "Deny the Night" (Andy Ruben, John O'Kennedy, performed by Larry Streicher), "Bottom Line" (David Russo, performed by John E. Jones), "Fire Dance," "Rickshaw Suite," "It's Been So Long" (O'Kennedy), "Something Special" (Ed Martel), "Run Through the Night," "The Edge of Love" (Gail Lennon, Clyde Liebermann, performed by Lennon), "A Night Like Any Other Night" (O'Kennedy, performed by Darryl

Phinnessee, Anita Sherman), "California Plates" (Mark McKinnis, performed by McKinnis), "Once You've Tried It" (Larry Brown, Steve Sykes, performed by Anita-Marie Brown), "Dream Come True" (Ken Fake, performed by Brown). *(Adult situations, graphic violence, nudity, sexual situations, profanity.)*

p, Andy Ruben, Mark Byers, Matt Leipzig; d, Katt Shea Ruben; w, Katt Shea Ruben, Andy Ruben; ph, John Leblanc (Film House Group color); m, John O'Kennedy; ed, Zach Staenberg; art d, Paul Raubertas; ch, Ted Lin; m/l, Andy Ruben, John O'Kennedy, David Russio, Ed Martel, Gail Lennon, Clyde Liebermann, Mark McKinnis, Larry Brown, Steve Sykes, Ken Fake; makeup, Michael Westmore; spec eff, Roger George; stunts, John Stewart.

Thriller **Cas.** **(PR:O MPAA:R)**

STRIT OG STUMME† (1987, Den.) 81m Metronome-Dansk Tegnefilm Kompagni-Danish Film Institute/Metronome Film c (Trans: Subway To Paradise)

Voices: Berthe Boelsgaard, Jesper "Gokke" Schou, Annemarie Helger, Jess Ingerslev, Per Pallesen, Claus Ryskjar, Berthe Qvistgaard.

Animated children's film about a small family of humans who have been forced to live in the sewers of an unnamed big city after pollution has killed all animal and plant life on the surface. Although the tiny band dreams of someday returning to an above-ground paradise—a magic bird will show them the path—they are oppressed by a malevolent rat dictator (wearing a Stetson hat and toting a pair of Smith & Wesson six-shooters, obviously an American rat) who refuses anyone the chance to see daylight again. Eventually the clever humans are able to avoid their rat captors and follow the magic bird to the surface where they are stunned to find a beautifully regenerated Earth.

p, Tivi Magnusson; d, Jannik Hastrup; w, Bent Haller, Jannik Hastrup; ph, Jakob Koch; m, Fuzzy.

Animation/Children's **(PR:NR MPAA:NR)**

STUDENT CONFIDENTIAL† (1987) 94m Troma c

Eric Douglas *(Johnny Warshetsky)*, Marlon Jackson *(Joseph Williams)*, Susan Scott *(Susan Bishop)*, Elizabeth Singer *(Elaine Duvat)*, Ronee Blakley *(Jenny Selden)*, Richard Horian *(Michael Drake)*, Paula Sorenson *(Carla)*, John Milford *(Mr. Warshetsky)*, Kip King *(Milton Goldman)*, Sarina Grant *(Mrs. Williams)*, Billy Jean Thomas *(Maggie Murkill)*, Joel Mills *(Rob)*, Corwyn Anthony *(Greg)*, Katherine Kriss, Mindy Levy *(Elaine's Friends)*, Ed Karvoski, Paul La Greca, Shawn Lieber *(Johnny's Friends)*, Andre Rosey Brown *(Stick)*, Daniel Morong, John Williamette *(Hoodlums)*, Nadia Cota, Jace Julee, Tara Wade *(Prostitutes)*, Robert Varney *(Superintendent)*, Joan McGough *(Old Woman)*.

Bargain-basement Troma release which lasted one week in New York City stars Kirk Douglas' youngest son, Eric, Michael Jackson's brother Marlon, and former *Playboy* Playmate Scott as three brilliant-but-troubled teens who are counseled by multimillionaire Horian (the writer/director/producer/editor/composer of STUDENT CONFIDENTIAL). Horian coaxes the kids to come out of their shells and helps bolster their self-confidence, but his own life is troubled. When his marriage collapses, he attempts suicide, and it's up to the kids to save him. *Auteur* Horian used to be a successful consumer electronics designer before he began making films, so perhaps it is appropriate that more people will see his movie on home video than did in the theater.

p,d&w, Richard Horian; ph, James Dickson (Deluxe color); m, Richard Horian; ed, Richard Horian; prod d, David Wasco; art d, Robert Joyce; cos, Cassandra Voison; makeup, Nina Kent.

Drama **(PR:NR MPAA:R)**

STUPEN† (1987, USSR) 89m Gruziafilm/Sovexportfilm c (Trans: The Stage)

Merab Ninidze, Irina Chichinadze, Nana Tarkhan-Mouravi, Ninel Chankvetadze, Ramaz Giorgobiani.

A young man who is dissatisfied with his life moves out of the house of his father and takes his own apartment. The change of living quarters does not make him any happier, however, for he continues to hang out with the same friends and talk about the same things. When his favorite school teacher dies, the young man is inspired to follow in his footsteps and move into the mountains to become a small village school teacher.

d, Alexander Rekhviashvili; w, Alexander Rekhviashvili, David Gubinishvili; ph, Archil Filipashvili; art d, Noshrevan Nikoladze, Guiya Laperadze.

Drama **(PR:NR MPAA:NR)**

SUCCESSFUL MAN, A½** (1987, Cuba) 116m ICAIC c (UN HOMBRE DE EXITO)

Cesar Evora, Raquel Revuelta, Daisy Granados, Jorge Trinchet, Mabel Roche, Rubens De Falco.

A film with epic aspirations, A SUCCESSFUL MAN follows the lives of two brothers through 30 years of political unrest in Cuba. As the film opens, in 1932, the wealthy brothers are idealistic young students. However, they soon choose different paths. One deepens his idealism through a commitment to radical action; the other chooses to aspire to wealth and power, and is corrupted in the process. Both end in tragedy. The radical is gunned down by government forces, and the capitalist brother finds himself alienated from his wife and beyond the reach of human contact. The atmosphere of Havana is beautifully evoked in each decade in this lavish production. Fascinated with the glitter of the sophisticated set in prerevolutionary Cuba, its costumes, sets, and art direction are exquisite. The film's problems are partly the result of its poorly focused script. Characters are not fleshed out and key emotional points are lost. While hoping to trace the decline of the bourgeoisie that led to the Cuban Revolution, the film never clearly defines this point. The conflict between corruption and conscience further suffers from hackneyed directorial choices. Director Humberto Solas scripted for a large ensemble of secondary characters and assembled a top-notch cast to portray them; then he failed to use them. Though the film attempts to achieve complexity, it becomes hopelessly muddled and ends in confusion. Cuban political events are inserted by the use of grainy black-and-white footage, but without a clear context they only serve to confuse US audiences. A SUCCESSFUL MAN received a film festival showing in the US in 1987.

p, Humberto Hernandez; d, Humberto Solas; w, Juan Iglesias, Humberto Solas; ph, Livio Delgado; m, Luigi Nono; ed, Nelson Rodriguez.

Drama **(PR:O MPAA:NR)**

SUFRE MAMON† (1987, Span.) 97m "G" P.C. c (Trans: Suffer Mammon)

David Summers *(David)*, Javier Molina *(Javi)*, Daniel Mezquita *(Dani)*, Rafael Gutierrez *(Rafa)*, Marta Madruga *(Patty)*, Gerardo Ortega *(Riky)*, Curro M. Summers, Antonio Gamero, Luis Escobar.

Sort of an Iberian equivalent of 1987's THE ALLNIGHTER in that Spanish filmmaker Manuel Summers directs his rock star son David just as Tamar Simon Hoffs directed her daughter Susanna, lead singer of the Bangles. SUFRE MAMON also stars the rest of David's popular Spanish band, Los Hombres G., and is enlivened by several of their songs. At the center of the film are the attempts by David and company, playing students, to form (no, not an oil cartel) a rock band. Their efforts are complicated by the presence of a gang of wealthy neo-fascist classmates with a built-in antagonism for our heroes. Meantime, David is unlucky at love, though wiser for the experience.

d, Manuel Summers; w, Francisco Tomas, Manuel Summers; ph, Tote Tenas; m, David Summers; ed, Elena Sainz de Rozas; set d, Gumersindo Andres.

Comedy/Musical **(PR:NR MPAA:NR)**

SUICIDE CLUB, THE* (1987) 90m Suicide Prods. c

Mariel Hemingway *(Sasha Michaels)*, Robert Joy *(Michael Collins)*, Lenny Henry *(Cam)*, Madeleine Potter *(Nancy)*, Michael O'Donaghue *(Mervin)*, Anne Carlisle *(Catherine)*, Sullivan Brown *(Brian)*, Leta McCarty *(Cowgirl)*.

A living hell of baroque tedium, THE SUICIDE CLUB is the story of what happens when bored, drugged-out rich kids decide to dress up and play games. Hemingway stars as an heiress who has been teetering on the edge of a mental breakdown ever since the suicide of her brother. Because of her instability her relationship with boy friend Joy is falling apart. When the pair spend a night out at a posh (seemingly private) restaurant with a thoroughly obnoxious wealthy young couple, things start taking an odd turn. Waiter/friend Henry whisks Hemingway off, leaving Joy alone at the table without enough money to pay the bill. In a chauffeured limousine, Henry takes Hemingway to a private costume party in a gothic mansion. The guests are an under-thirty group of the idle rich who dress in elaborate costumes and assume pretentious poses. This is no ordinary party, however. When the guests get bored, *really* bored, they partake in a lethal card game in which the "winner" must swallow a poisonous drink. Naturally, Hemingway wants to play—apparently in a twisted effort to understand her dead brother's decision. Joy eventually tracks her down and almost everyone is killed off by the picture's end.

Based on Robert Louis Stevenson's *The Suicide Club* short story collection, the film quickly becomes almost unwatchable because of director Bruce's peculiar decision to have his characters speak in a stilted Old English which is more suited to the period of Stevenson's story than to the present. Besides the leaden dialog, the direction is flat and uninspired. The restaurant scene is filmed in a continuous (sub-Di Palma) dolly shot which revolves nonstop around the four characters at their dinner table. It is so head-spinning it even gives one cocaine-sniffing character a nosebleed. A low-budget exercise in amateurish literary adaptation, THE

SUICIDE CLUB rates attention only because it stars Hemingway in a less-than-noteworthy performance. Perhaps Hemingway and Crisman, her husband-the film's coproducer, should concentrate their efforts on running their New York restaurant. The Stevenson story was previously filmed in 1919 in Germany as UNHEIMLICHE GESCHICTEN and again in 1932 under the same title. In 1936, Robert Montgomery and Rosalind Russell starred in a 1936 MGM adaptation entitled TROUBLE FOR TWO. THE SUICIDE CLUB was shown at film festivals in Montreal and Chicago. *(Sexual situations, drug use, profanity, violence.)*

p, James Bruce, Steve Crisman, Sam Waksal, Paula Herold, Mariel Hemingway; d, James Bruce; w, Matthew Gaddis, Suzan Kouguell, Carl Caportoto (based on a story by Robert Louis Stevenson); ph, Frank Prizzi (Du Art Color); m, Joel Diamond; ed, James Bruce, Keith Rouse; prod d, Steven McCabe; cos, Natasha Landau.

Drama (PR:C MPAA:NR)

SULLIVAN'S PAVILION† (1987) 83m Adirondack Alliance c

Polly Sullivan, Tate Sullivan, Katie Sullivan, Kirk Sullivan, Ricky Sullivan, Fred G. Sullivan *(Themselves)*, Jon Granik *(Bear/Narrator)*, James R. Hogue *(Conrad P. Drizzle)*, Jan Jalenak *(The Temptress)*, Judith Mayes *(Sister Mary Anthony)*, Don Samuels *(The Cretin Beer Lover)*, Roberta Schwebel *(Gillian Solomon, M.D.)*.

Independent filmmaker Fred G. Sullivan goes autobiographical in his latest movie. Starring Sullivan and his family, it details the travails of being an independent filmmaker. Infused with a self-deprecating comedic air, the film follows Sullivan as he and his ever-patient wife Polly raise their four children in the Adirondack Mountains. When Fred isn't making movies, he works as a lumberjack and tries to fend off the bill collectors. His one feature film, a wilderness adventure entitled COLD RIVER (1982), was panned by the critics and bombed at the box office, causing the fortyish Sullivan to wonder if he should keep trying. While exploring his past, Sullivan presents pictures of his parents, re-creates his college years, has a look at his stint in the Army, and screens his Super 8 home movies. The filmmaking bug has bitten Sullivan hard and he will carry on, despite the incredulous looks he gets from friends, family, and neighbors. Part documentary, part fanciful rumination on life, SULLIVAN'S PAVILION played at the US Film Festival and was given a token release in Los Angeles.

p,d&w, Fred G. Sullivan; ph, Hal Landen (DuArt Color); m, Kenneth Higgins, James Calabrese; ed, Fred G. Sullivan; art d, Susan Neal; cos, Carol Gabridge.

Biography/Comedy (PR:NR MPAA:PG)

SUMMER CAMP NIGHTMARE** (1987) 87m Butterfly/Concorde (AKA: THE BUTTERFLY REVOLUTION) c

Chuck Connors *(Mr. Warren)*, Charles Stratton *(Franklin Reilly)*, Harold B. Pruett *(Chris Wade)*, Adam Carl *(Donald Poultry)*, Tom Fridley *(John Mason)*, Melissa Brennan *(Heather)*, Stuart Rogers *(Stanley Runk)*, Shawn McLemore *(Hammond Pimpernic)*, Samantha Newark *(Debbie)*, Nancy Calabrese *(Trixie)*, Michael Cramer *(Jerome Blackridge)*, Rick Fitts *(Ed Heinz)*, Doug Toby *(Manuel Rivas)*, Shirley Mitchell *(Mrs. Knute)*, Chris Hubbell *(Jack Caldwell)*, Scott Curtis *(Peter)*, Jennifer McGrath *(Laurie)*, John Louis *(Paul Indian)*, Brad Kestin *(GoGo)*, Tina Blum *(Nurse Newman)*, Tom Rayhall *(Detective Stone)*, Wade Crow *(Wade)*, Rick Dorio *(Cop)*, Bradley Lieberman *(Guard)*, David Hern *(TV Preacher)*, Linda Nichols, Nicole Nourmand, Desiree Simpers, Mindy McEnnan, Danielle Rioux *(Girls)*, John Mannger *(Counselor)*, Christopher Gosch *(Kid)*, Sally Piper *(Woman Counselor)*, Tony Willard *(Fat Camper)*, Christianna Hillman *(Girl at Camper)*.

A peaceful summer camp turns into the scene of violent revolt in this odd youth drama. Packaged like a routine Spam-in-a-cabin horror film, it has more in common with a TV "Afterschool Special." Camp North Pines is suffering severe budget cutbacks, so the full-time staff is minimal and headed by Connors, a strict disciplinarian who allows only religious broadcasting to be viewed on TV, bans rock music and contact with the girls at Camp South Pines, and institutes a kind of camp punishment cell. The campers grow restless, and under the leadership of the charismatic Stratton, they get hold of a gun and lock up Connors and the other adults. Stratton appoints a revolutionary council and is soon giving speeches from the balcony while the crowd chants his name. Next, the campers seize control of the girls camp, and it's party time as the action turns to some heavy petting. Connors is bought in and tormented, and on the way back to the jail, he is accidentally killed. Stratton keeps the death secret and continues his reign. One of his cohorts rapes a girl, and when he survives the "Ordeal" of crossing a rickety rope bridge, the enraged girls drag him off into the woods and lynch him. Now Stratton's megalomania is evident. The young character who functions as narrator (Carl) tries to get word out but is caught. When an attempt is made to force him to cross the bridge, the younger campers rise up against the leaders. The police finally arrive and put an end to the fascist regime. There are some interesting ideas at work here, and, with more focus on the issues and less on the lascivious doings of the campers, this could have been akin to *Animal Farm* or *The Lord of the Flies*. Stratton is very good as the leader of the rebellion, but the whole thing falls flat as the result of Dragin's limp direction, which never gets to the heart of the issues. Cowriter Spheeris is well known for her pictures that show some insight into alienated youth (SUBURBIA, DUDES), but her work here is unextraordinary. *(Violence, adult situations, substance abuse.)*

p, Robert T. Crow, Emilia Lesniak-Crow, Andy Howard; d, Bert L. Dragin; w, Bert L. Dragin, Penelope Spheeris (based on the novel *The Butterfly Revolution* by William Butler); ph, Don Burgess (United Color); m, Ted Neeley, Gary Chase; ed, Michael Spence; prod d, Richard McGuire; art d, Barry Franenberg; set d, Jennifer Pray; m/l, Doug Toby, Ted Neeley, Gary Chase, Robert Dragin, Lee Ving; stunts, John Branagan; makeup, Ferri Sorel, Christ Reusch.

Drama Cas. (PR:C MPAA:PG-13)

SUMMER HEAT** (1987) 90m Atlantic c

Lori Singer *(Roxanna "Roxy" Walston)*, Anthony Edwards *(Aaron Walston)*, Bruce Abbott *(Jack Ruffin)*, Clu Gulager *(Will Stanton, Undertaker)*, Kathy Bates *(Ruth Stanton)*, Jessie Kent *(Baby Walston)*, Noble Willingham *(Strother)*, Nesbitt Blaisdell *(Bass)*, Matt Almond *(Neb)*, Jane Cecil *(Georgeanna, Roxy's Grandmother)*, Miriam Byrd-Nethery *(Aunt Patty)*, Jessica Leigh Mann *(Callie)*, Michael Mattick *(Raider)*, Conrad McLaren *(Mr. Tatie)*, Julia Beals Williams *(Old Mama)*, Charmaine Mancil *(Gyp)*, Chris Bass Randolph *(Estelle)*, Robert Albertia *(Tarboro Sheriff)*, Pat Miller *(Tarboro Deputy)*, Charlie Baxter *(Georgia Sheriff)*, Lynne Anchors Hurder *(Cabin Owner)*, Laurens Moore *(Dr. Best)*, Richard Emery *(D.A.)*, Mert Hatfield *(Mr. Martin)*, Joe Inscoe *(Mr. Hodges)*, Phil Uhler *(Mr. Riley)*, E. Pat Hall *(Bailiff)*, Duke Ernsberger, Robin Dale Robertson, Tony Marando *(Reporters)*, Rachel M. Joyner *(Court Clerk)*, Dr. Charles H. Gleason *(Judge)*, Dorothy McGuire *(Narrator)*.

Written and directed by Michie Gleason, a woman who worked as an assistant to the producer on Terrence Malick's DAYS OF HEAVEN, SUMMER HEAT tries hard to capture the transcendental essence of Malick's work but instead comes up with a drab and monotonous film that desperately yearns to be considered art. Based on Louise Shivers' novel *Here To Get My Baby Out of Jail*, the film is set in 1937 and stars Singer as a bored young South Carolina farm wife raising a 22-month-old daughter while her hard-working husband, Edwards, tends to his tobacco fields. Although Edwards is pleasant and decent, Singer has come to view their sexual relations as passionless and mechanical. When Edwards hires handsome young stranger Abbott to help with the tobacco harvest, it is only a matter of time until Singer strays from the conjugal bed. One day while Edwards is out on an errand, Abbott literally pounces on Singer in the fields and she gives herself to him willingly. As the months go by, Singer and Abbott consummate their lust at every opportunity. Their passions come to an abrupt end, however, when during one of their trysts the unwatched baby accidentally spills a pot of boiling water on herself and must be rushed to the hospital. Singer is aghast at the result of her lust and vows to forget Abbott and patch up her marriage. Edwards, who has suspected the affair all along, finally does something about it and decides to fire Abbott. On what is to be his last night of work, Abbott lures Edwards behind the barn and kills him with a shovel. He takes it on the lam with the confused Singer and her baby. Abbott is caught quickly and Singer is charged as a co-conspirator in the murder. At the trial Singer is forced to detail her sexual relations with Abbott for the jury. Abbott clears Singer of any wrong doing by declaring that she knew nothing of his plans and that he forced her to run away with him. At trial's end Abbott is sent to the gas chamber and Singer acquitted. Rather than go to hide in another town, Singer decides to stay home and ride out the townsfolk's gossip and derision.

SUMMER HEAT plays like James M. Cain on downers. All the elements for a steamy, lusty, erotic period piece are in place, but director Gleason presents them in such a deadly dull manner that there is no sense of urgency or passion. She and cinematographer Davis linger lovingly on all the details of South Carolina farm life circa 1937 in a vain effort to capture the magic of DAYS OF HEAVEN (the plots of both films are virtually identical). Every scene is ridiculously overlit, brimming with either a warm orange glow or cool dark blues. The latest trend in cinematography, the subtle use of smoke to diffuse light, is so over-used and inexpertly employed that it appears as if there is a fire somewhere in the house (one waits to hear the sound of a smoke-alarm). Worse than the visuals is the acting. As scripted the three main characters are terribly one-dimensional with little or no motivation. Although Edwards manages to make something of his part, Singer and Abbott are nothing more than mannequins and utterly fail to heat up the screen. From the moment he wanders in, Abbott's character is instantly transparent and the actor does nothing to dissuade the audience from thinking otherwise. Even weaker is Singer. She goes through the entire film with a vague look on her face and even at the end, when she is supposed to be finally taking some control over her life, she has that same vapid expression. If the film was supposed to be some sort of feminist version of a James M. Cain story,

Singer fails to convey any sort of liberated, or even enlightened, attitude. The entire film is lifeless. Only Clu Gulager as Singer's mortician father manages to inject a semblance of reality into the movie. In a scant amount of screen time Gulager steals the film—not exactly difficult when everyone else is a blank-eyed zombie. *(Nudity, sexual situations.)*

p, William Tennant; d&w, Michie Gleason (based on the novel *Here to Get My Baby Out of Jail* by Louise Shivers); ph, Elliot Davis (CFI color); m, Steve Tyrell; ed, Mary Bauer; prod d, Marsha Hinds; art d, Bo Johnson; set d, Jan K. Bergstrom; cos, Anthony Marando; makeup, Christa Reusch; m/l, Will Jennings, Barry Mann, Georges Delerue.

Drama **(PR:O MPAA:R)**

SUMMER SCHOOL* (1987) 98m PAR c

Mark Harmon *(Freddy Shoop)*, Kirstie Alley *(Robin Bishop, History Teacher)*, Robin Thomas *(Phil Gills, Vice Principal)*, Patrick Laborteaux *(Kevin Winchester)*, Courtney Thorne-Smith *(Pam House)*, Dean Cameron *(Francis "Chainsaw" Gremp)*, Gary Riley *(Dave Frazier)*, Kelly Minter *(Denise Green)*, Ken Olandt *(Larry Kazamias)*, Shawnee Smith *(Rhonda Altobello)*, Richard Horvitz *(Alan Eakian)*, Fabiana Udenio *(Anna-Maria Mazarelli)*, Frank McCarthy *(Principal Kelban)*, Amy Stock *(Kim, Freddy's Girl Friend)*, Duane Davis *(Jerome Watkins)*, Lillian Adams *(Grandma Eakian)*, Bo *(Wondermutt)*, Carl Reiner.

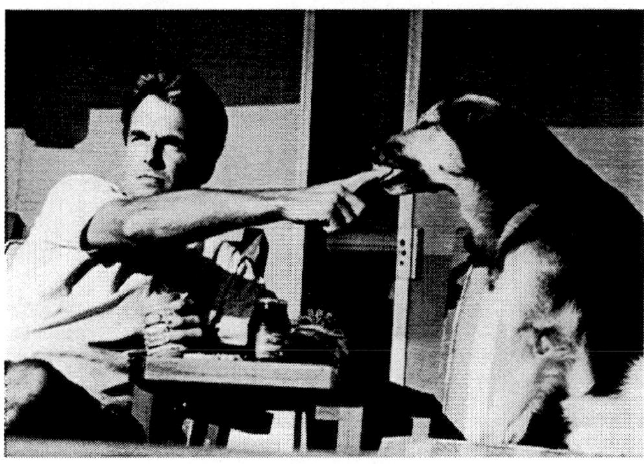

A three "T" film—tame, tepid, and talky—SUMMER SCHOOL is the brain child of Carl Reiner, who directed this ambiguous summerfest notion, a film with less urgency than a recess bell. Harmon, who peddles Coors beer on TV, is a lazy teacher looking forward to his Hawaiian vacation. Then he learns he must teach Reiner's summer school class of lag-behinds. Reiner is seen at the beginning of the film winning a lottery and is off to enjoy life, deserting his class. Harmon hates the idea of trying to educate misfits, and is none too happy about missing his vacation, having become a teacher so he would have his summers free. The class itself is made up of the usual teenage stereotypes, Riley and Cameron (two slasher movie freaks who are forever reenacting the TEXAS CHAIN-SAW MASSACRE debacle), Smith (a resentful teenager who is pregnant), Minter (a hostile minority student), and Thorne-Smith (a mindless surfing girl with a giant crush on Harmon). To alleviate his boredom, Harmon directs his attention to Alley, the sexy but prim-and-proper teacher next door. He makes a play for her but she rebuffs him, considering him inferior material, a disinterested and incompetent teacher, which he is. But, through classroom scenes, field trips, and other adventures, Harmon grows closer to his students and eventually shapes them up. He realizes that Minter's cause of discontent is her dyslexic condition and helps others deal with such problems as persecution and alcoholism. As Harmon rejuvenates his students he also nourishes his own interest in teaching. This emotional and intellectual metamorphosis brings Alley to Harmon's side in the end for a happy, clinching finish. There are a number of cute moments and too many clutching laughs but the humor here is mostly at the expense of the teenagers who are portrayed as oafs and nitwits. Reiner's direction is anemic and what he apparently thinks is funny—the endless reenactment of massacre films, for instance—is not worthy of first-class macabre comedy. As a B movie, SUMMER SCHOOL is simply a failure.

p, George Shapiro, Howard West; d, Carl Reiner; w, Jeff Franklin (based on a story by Stuart Birnbaum, David Dashev, Jeff Franklin); ph, David M. Walsh (Panavision); m, Danny Elfman; ed, Bud Molin; prod d, David L. Snyder; art d, Joe Wood; set d, John Warnke; cos, Ray Summers; makeup, Rick Baker.

Comedy **(PR:C MPAA:PG-13)**

SUPERFANTAGENIO (SEE: ALADDIN, 1987, It.)

SUPERFANTOZZI† (1987, It.) 85m Scena Film/Medusa c

Paolo Villaggio *(Ugo Fantozzi)*, Liu Bosisio *(Pina)*, Fernando Plinio *(Mariangela)*, Luc Merenda *(Adam, etc)*, Eva Lena *(Eve, etc)*.

The seventh in the Fantozzi series sees comedian Villaggio's popular *schlemiel* character in various incarnations throughout history beginning with Adam and Eve and into the 21st century. Villaggio and his ugly wife Bosisio turn out to be God's first try at creating humans. Disatisfied with the results, God tries a second time and produces Merenda and Lena—a handsome couple. This couple plagues Villaggio and his hopeless family throughout the ages, always reaping the good things in life while they get the shaft. Other time periods include much of the New Testament, the French revolution, and the Jazz Age.

p, Augusto Caminito; d, Neri Parenti; w, Leo Benvenuti, Piero De Bernardi, Alessandro Bencivenni, Domenico Saverni, Villaggio Parenti; ph, Cristiano Pogany (Eastmancolor); m, Fred Bongusto.

Comedy **(PR:NR MPAA:NR)**

SUPERMAN IV: THE QUEST FOR PEACE* (1987) 89m Cannon/WB c

Christopher Reeve *(Superman/Clark Kent)*, Gene Hackman *(Lex Luthor)*, Jackie Cooper *(Perry White)*, Marc McClure *(Jimmy Olsen)*, Jon Cryer *(Lenny)*, Sam Wanamaker *(David Warfield)*, Mark Pillow *(Nuclear Man)*, Mariel Hemingway *(Lacy Warfield)*, Margot Kidder *(Lois Lane)*.

The first few films in this series were both amusing and produced with high technical values, but, as this poorly scripted, anemic production, the fourth in the string, embarrassingly shows, the SUPERMAN saga has been worn out. The plot is wrapped around a devoutly wished generality, that the world get rid of nuclear weapons. Reeve, in his Clark Kent/Superman role, receives a request from a 13-year-old to end nuclear proliferation and the Man of Steel goes into action (prompted by a thought that has never occurred to him until this time). He rounds up every nuclear missile in the world, bagging them in a huge net in space and then, wielding this ungodly arsenal as would a discus thrower, he hurls the mammoth net bag into the sun for a resounding explosion bright enough to deepen the suntans of any beach lounger. But all is not well on Reeve's home front. His paper, *The Daily Planet*, has been bought by unscrupulous media magnate Wanamaker who is only interested in turning the newspaper into a sleazy tabloid peddling sensational headlines and peek-a-boo flesh shots. This is quickly demonstrated by one of the *Planet's* headlines reading: "Summit Kaput—Is World on Brink?" And next to this is a photo of a girl in a revealing

bathing suit. Wanamaker doesn't really care for Reeve, the idealistic reporter, and is curious about why Reeve never lists air-travel costs on his expense vouchers. Hemingway, Wanamaker's sexy daughter, however, has eyes for the black-haired, soft-spoken Reeve and has reporter Lois Lane (Kidder) fix her up with him. Kidder dates Reeve as Superman, while Hemingway dates him as Clark Kent, this doubling providing a few chuckles as Reeve does a balancing act. His problems increase when his old nemesis, Lex Luthor (Hackman), reappears in a conspiracy with jingoistic US and Russian generals, set upon bringing about nuclear holocaust. Using a hair from Reeve's head, Hackman creates a worthy opponent for Superman, Nuclear Man, a solar-energized invention, who is not-too-convincingly played by beefcaker Pillow. The mighty pair square off and battle through the world's spectacular monuments, blowing over the Great Wall of China, causing Vesuvius to erupt, and kidnaping the Statue of Liberty. The two titans hold their final battle on the moon and Reeve emerges triumphant.

The plot is for the simpleminded, a lot of it written by Reeve himself. Initially, he had so many long-winded speeches that Warner Brothers cut the film down drastically, giving it a truncated look. In addition, the star was the subject of a $45 million suit from screenwriter Barry Taff who claimed that he submitted a story treatment to Reeve which contained all the basic plots and scenes used in SUPERMAN IV. Reeve is his usual stoic self here and does what is expected, even though he vowed in 1983 that he would never again strip away Clark Kent's suit and emerge in Superman garb. Kidder appears briefly in the film, as does Hemingway who gets to show some leg but no acting ability. Wanamaker glides about with a smirk on his face which may or may not have been a silent comment on the film, while Hackman infrequently flits before the cameras to utter lines about Reeve being so much a workaholic that he never "smells the roses." Director Furie (IRON EAGLE) shows little restraint here and no sense of the wry humor prevalent in the earlier films of the series, using a heavy and expeditious hand that produces scenes of pure lead. The special effects, especially when Reeve is airborne, are decidedly on the cheap side, the hallmark of the Golan-Globus operation. This film, originally at 150 minutes, is an obvious grab at the series' reputation for creating box-office bonanzas. This one failed to glean the pot at the end of the rainbow and deservedly so. *(Violence)* p, Menahem Golan, Yoram Globus; d, Sidney J. Furie; w, Lawrence Konner, Mark Rosenthal (based on a story by Lawrence Konner, Mark Rosenthal, Christopher Reeve); ph, Ernest Day (JDC Widescreen, Rank Color); m, John Williams, Alexander Courage; ed, John Shirley; prod d, John Graysmark; md, Alexander Courage; art d, Leslie Tomkins; set d, Peter Young; cos, John Bloomfield; spec eff, John Evans, Richard Conway, Harrison Ellenshaw.

Adventure/Fantasy Cas. (PR:C MPAA:PG)

SUPERNATURALS, THE** (1987) 80m Republic Ent. Intl. c

Maxwell Caulfield *(Lt. Ray Ellis)*, Nichelle Nichols *(Sgt. Leona Hawkins)*, Talia Balsam *(Pvt. Angela Lejune)*, Bradford Bancroft *(Pvt. Tom Weir)*, LeVar Burton *(Pvt. Michael Osgood)*, Bobby Di Cicco *(Pvt. Tim Cort)*, Margaret Shendal *(Melanie)*, Patrick Davis *(Old Man)*, James Kirkwood *(Captain)*, Scott Jacoby *(Pvt. Chris Mendez)*, Richard Pachorek *(Pvt. Ralph Sedgewick)*, John Zarchen *(Pvt. Julius Engel)*, Robert Barron *(Old Vet)*, Chad Sheets *(Jeremy)*, Mark Schneider, Jesse Lawrence Ferguson *(Recruits)*, David Ault *(Soldier on Horse)*, Frank Caggiano, Greg Landerer, Gary Bentley *(Union Soldiers)*, Laura Francis *(Townswoman)*, Nicky Blair *(Townsman)*.

A surprisingly well acted and thoughtfully directed horror picture, THE SUPERNATURALS avoids many of the exploitative traps of recent entries in the genre. The film opens in Alabama at the close of the Civil War as a Union officer is leading a group of captured Confederates back to camp. A mine field blocks their path, however, causing the sadistic officer to take drastic action. As their terrified families look on, the captured troops, including the preteen Sheets, are forced to march across the mine field. One by one they are blown to bits. Only Sheets makes it through. His horrified mother runs to his aid, stepping on a mine in the process. The scene then shifts to 1985 as a group of Army trainees is being led on a survival mission through the Alabama woodlands by tough female sergeant Nichols. Strange occurrences soon follow: Caulfield sees a ghostly woman (Shendal) appear and disappear; Di Cicco finds a human skull; unexplained winds and scorched earth baffle the recruits; and an underground bunker is found. The trouble starts when the cocky Di Cicco places the skull on a tree trunk, dresses it with a pair of sunglasses, and fires a round of bullets into it. His desecration of the dead is mysteriously avenged when, the following morning, he is found with a bullet wound to the head. Other unexplained murders occur, with the unseen attackers terrorizing the recruits' bivouac. When a deep fog descends on the camp, the recruits are at their most vulnerable. Only then do they see their attackers—skeletal Confederate soldiers who have risen from their graves to continue their Civil War battles. Caulfield saves the day when he pleads with a frail, bearded old man (Davis) who is actually Sheets grown old. Shendal, as it so happens, is the young boy's beautifully preserved mother, who loves Caulfield because he is apparently her reincarnated husband. With the help of Davis, the Confederate dead are returned to their graves. Only Caulfield, Nichols, and pretty young recruit Balsam (who loves Caulfield) survive the attack, leaving the three of them better friends and soldiers.

While most recent horror entries thrive on excessive gore, gratuitous nudity, amateurish acting, and tepid direction, THE SUPERNATURALS (despite its nondescript title) proves to be an entertaining time if one can ignore the ridiculous premise. Displaying professional technical qualities, the film also boasts some superb performances. Caulfield (previously seen in GREASE II, 1984's ELECTRIC DREAMS, and 1985's THE BOYS NEXT DOOR) is a likable, attractive leading man who handles his role well. He receives fine support from Burton (of TV's "Roots" fame), Di Cicco (THE PHILADELPHIA EXPERIMENT and SPLASH, both 1984), Nichols (STAR TREK IV), Balsam, and Bancroft. Director Mastroianni's greatest success comes in his decision to keep the Confederate attackers out of sight for most of the picture. As in the great Val Lewton/Jacques Tourneur films of the 1940s (CAT PEOPLE and I WALKED WITH A ZOMBIE), the greatest fear comes from an unseen attacker. THE SUPERNATURALS is effectively creepy when characters are getting picked off one by one with little or no explanation. It loses its strength in the climactic attack by revealing too much of the murderous Confederates. Its strength lies in strong characterizations and a fairly concise script that leaves no room for gore or nudity. *(Excessive profanity, violence.)*

p, Michael S. Murphey, Joel Soisson; d, Armand Mastroianni; w, Michael S. Murphey, Joel Soisson; ph, Peter Collister; m, Robert O. Ragland; art d, Jo Ann Chorney; set d, Alexandra Kicenik; cos, Gale Viola; spec eff, Gregory Landerer, Mark Shostrom; makeup, Daniel Marc.

Science Fiction/Thriller Cas. (PR:O MPAA:R)

SURE DEATH 4† (1987, Jap.) 131m Shochiku-Asahi c

Makoto Fujita *(Mondo Nakamura)*, Mitsuko Baisyo *(Ofuku)*, Hiroyuki Sanada *(Ukyonosuke Okuda)*, Kin Sugai *(Sen)*.

This film is the fourth in a series based on a Japanese television program. Posing as a cowardly samurai, the detective hero tracks down a rogue band of samurai. Shown at the Tokyo International Film Festival, this feature was directed by Kinji Fukasaku, whose HOUSE ON FIRE was also screened there.

d, Kinju Fukasaku; w, Tatsuo Nogami, Kinji Fukasaku, Akira Nakahara; ph, Koh Ishihara; m, Masaaki Hirao.

Action (PR:NR MPAA:NR)

SURF NAZIS MUST DIE** (1987) 95m Institute/Troma c

Gail Neely, Robert Harden, Barry Brenner, Dawn Wildsmith, Michael Sonye, Joel Hile, Gene Mitchell, Tom Shell, Bobbie Bresee.

You have to be in the right mood to appreciate this bargain-basement picture that is long on wackiness and short on money. It also boasts one of the strangest titles ever to come out of any movie company, even such a Grade B house as Troma which has issued such features as I WAS A TEENAGE TV TERRORIST and THE CURSE OF THE CANNONBALL CONFEDERATES. The earthquake has devastated California (we mean the BIG ONE) and law and order has gone the way of the dodo. Brenner is the leader of the local neo-Nazis. They live in a Hitler-type bunker on the beach, ride surf boards that are equipped with sophisticated weaponry, sport Hell's Angels-type tattoos, and brandish the steel one might find in a Hoffritz store. The beach is up for grabs and there are various

gangs who want control of the sandy turf. Brenner (who has taken the name of "Adolf") has an equally nutso girl friend known as "Eva" played by Wildsmith (there's not a smidgeon of subtlety in the movie). Bresee is a typical upwardly mobile Southern California mom who regularly visits her analyst and is miffed that her son, Shell, is fascinated with the Swastika Corps. When young Harden gets killed by the Nazis, his rotund, cigar-chomping mama, Neely (seen earlier this year in MILLION DOLLAR MYSTERY), comes out of the retirement home where she had been playing penny-ante cards and sawing down trees (a slam at Mr. T. who moved to a fabulous North Shore estate in Illinois and promptly razed a stand of trees) to wreak havoc and exact revenge on the Nazis. The conclusion is a tribute to low-budget filmmaking as Neely, a woman so large that it takes two men and a small boy just to *look* at her, dons red-rimmed sunglasses, picks up a gun that Clint Eastwood would have enjoyed, and goes hunting for the rats who killed her boy.

Lots of laughs, some fine darts tossed at fascism, Southern California customs, and the USA in general, a tongue firmly embedded in the cheek, and a fairly good score all add up to make this a sleeper and a picture that will take its place with ATTACK OF THE KILLER TOMATOES, PLAN 9 FROM OUTER SPACE and THE ROCKY HORROR PICTURE SHOW as a cult movie for years to come. Director George has a career in front of him as does Ayre, the screenwriter. The language, mayhem and several other tasteless moments make this unworthy for children. But if your sense of humor has the slightest warp in it, you may thoroughly enjoy SURF NAZIS MUST DIE. The unpretentiousness of it sort of sneaks up on one like the second kamikaze at the local watering hole. *(Profanity, violence.)*

p, Robert Tinnell; d, Peter George; w, Jon Ayre; ph, Rolf Kesterman; m, Jon McCallum; ed, Craig Colton; art d & cos, Byrnadette diSanto.

Comedy (PR:C-O MPAA:R)

SURFER, THE† (1987, Aus.) 96m Frontier-Producers Circle/Hemdale c

Gary Day *(Sam Barlow)*, Gosia Dobrowolska *(Gina)*, Rod Mullinar *(Hagan)*, Tony Barry *(Calhoun)*, Gerard MacGuire *(Jack)*, Kris McQuade *(Trish)*, Stephen Leeder *(Slaney)*, David Glendenning *(Murph)*.

The press release for this Aussie thriller called it "a treacherous love story," and Day plays the title surfer whose attempts to get to the bottom of a friend's murder are both aided and complicated by the beautiful Dobrowolska (SILVER CITY, 1985; AROUND THE WORLD IN EIGHTY DAYS, 1986). A Vietnam vet, Day lives the easy life, renting surfboards, chairs, and umbrellas on a beach, until he learns his best pal has been killed, most likely by Vietnamese sent to keep him from telling what he knows about a plot to extort money from a government official. Dobrowolska appears from nowhere and, after presenting Day with the lead he needs to pick up the trail of the murderers, joins him in his dangerous cross-country pursuit of them. Not too surprisingly, along the way they fall in love. This is the second feature film for director Shields, who previously helmed HOSTAGE (1983).

p, James M. Vernon, Frank Shields; d, Frank Shields; w, David Marsh; ph, Michael Edols (Eastmancolor); m, Davood Tabrizi; ed, Greg Bell; prod d, Martin O'Neill.

Romance/Thriller Cas. (PR:NR MPAA:NR)

SURRENDER**½** (1987) 96m Cannon/WB c

Sally Field *(Daisy Morgan, Artist)*, Michael Caine *(Sean Stein, Mystery Novelist)*, Steve Guttenberg *(Marty Caesar, Attorney)*, Peter Boyle *(Jay Bass, Sean's Attorney)*, Julie Kavner *(Ronnie)*, Jackie Cooper *(Ace Morgan)*, Louise Lasser *(Joyce)*, Iman *(Hedy)*.

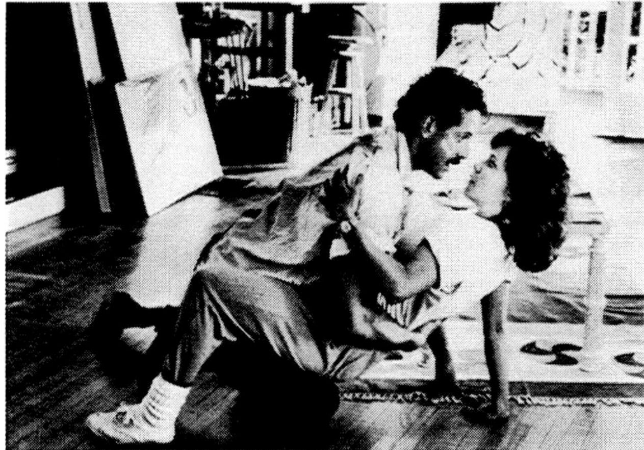

A frothy comedy that harks back to the days when it was "Will she or won't she?" for Doris Day as she snappily protected her presumed virginity back in the 1950s, SURRENDER brings that hoary plot into the 1980s and manages to evoke a number of good belly laughs along the way, but not enough of them to make up for the long dry periods. Field is a pushing-40 artist who makes a meager living turning out motel art on what is darn close to an assembly line. She has a relationship with ultimate yuppie Guttenberg, a lawyer who feels that money isn't everything, it's the *only* thing. While at a museum cocktail party, Field and the other guests are forced to take off all their clothing when some machine gun-carrying criminals enter and tie people together. Field happens to be coupled with Caine, a supremely successful mystery novelist (sort of the Robert Ludlum of the private eye genre). Caine has troubles of his own. He's been married and divorced a few times, is paying alimony and palimony, and is terrified of women. He is so fearful of the fairer sex that when he is standing in a lobby and two elevator doors open, one revealing a gorgeous blonde and the other containing a man with an angry dog, Caine opts for the canine over the cutie. Field and Caine are forced to spend hours coupled together. They toss off quips, zing each other, and it's a sure bet, from the start, that they'll wind up as a duo. Caine is afraid to reveal his real identity and the extent of his monetary success, as he fears that Field might just be another one of the many who want to pick his pocket and leave him emotionally wrung out. He pretends to be a starving writer, which is a weak plot point as it seems everyone would know such a best-selling author's face. A courtship begins and there are some very funny moments along the way. On their first date, Caine arrives several hours early, explaining that he had no place better to go and asking if they could start their date right now instead of waiting? Conveniently, Guttenberg disappears long enough for the romance to flourish, until Field discovers that Caine has been sailing under a false flag. She's insulted that he didn't trust her enough to tell her the truth. All of that is cleared up when Field becomes wealthy in her own right by hitting a $2 million slot machine jackpot in Nevada. Now that Field has her own money, Caine understands that she loves him for him and not his filthy lucre.

Boyle does a good job (and looks great in a wig) as Caine's tired but amiable attorney, and Guttenberg, who must be at least 10 years younger than Field, shows that his career didn't stop with the POLICE ACADEMY pictures. The opening nude scene took three days to lens and the extras were culled from a local nudist colony because the regular contingent of extras who usually work these pictures were unwilling to doff their gear. There are a few extraneous sequences such as one on a mountaintop with a Shirley MacLaine communion with a wild wolf, plus a few seconds with an armed and dangerous transvestite hooker. Kavner is the logical successor to Eve Arden and plays the fast-talking best friend with the same kind of verve the queen of best friends did for so many years. Field's character is fresh in that she is a true woman of the 1980s because she has refused to commit to anyone or anything for many years. Caine, who seems to just keep on working, may be a bit long in the tooth to play this role, although he brings it off most of the time with his customary charm. Writer/director Belson (SMILE, "The Dick Van Dyke Show," and many other TV programs) takes the easy way out a few too many times. His writing, while a cut above many of the other alleged comedies of 1987 (see LIKE FATHER, LIKE SON; better yet, don't see it), is still rooted in the television format, so he feels obligated to toss in jokes where there should be none and visual gags where they are out of order, almost as though he's trying to keep the audience from getting up to go to the refrigerator during a commercial break. And yet, for all its faults, SURRENDER is, for the most part, a neat romantic comedy which has been made for people above the age of acne and heavy metal. For that alone, Belson is to be lauded. The money in the Nevada scene is, by the way, real—a total of 23,800 $5 bills, which may be more than this picture will take in. Randy Newman sings his own very apt theme song, "It's Money That I Love," which sets the tone for the piece. *(Sexual situations.)*

p, Aaron Spelling, Alan Greisman; d&w, Jerry Belson; ph, Juan Ruiz Anchia

(TVC Color); m, Michel Columbier; ed, Wendy Greene Briemont; prod d, Lilly Kilvert; art d, Jon Hutman; set d, Richard Mays.

Comedy (PR:A-C MPAA:PG)

SURVIVAL GAME† (1987) 91m Trans World Ent. c

Mike Norris *(Mike Falcon)*, Deborah Goodrich *(C.J. Forrest)*, Seymour Cassel *(Dave Forrest)*, Ed Bernard *(Sugar Bear)*, Jon Sharp *(Charles)*, Rick Grassi *(Ice)*, Arlene Golonka *(Mike's Mom)*, Michael Halton *(Harlan)*.

Chuck Norris' son Mike stars as an expert survival game player (you've seen those adults who run around the woods on the weekend shooting each other with paint-guns) who meets cute-young-thing Goodrich when the pair experience a fender bender. Norris learns that Goodrich's father (Cassel) has just been released from prison after serving 17 years on drug charges from the 1960s. It seems Cassel sold massive amounts of a hallucinogenic dubbed "Forrest Fire" and both the FBI and Cassel's former partners are convinced that he's got $2 million stashed away somewhere. Predictably, Cassel and Goodrich are kidnaped, giving Norris ample opportunity to apply his survival game strategies in real life. Considering that SURVIVAL GAME received its world premiere at a multi-plex cinema in the Bronx, it comes as no surprise that the rest of the country will have to wait until the movie hits the video rental shelves.

p, Gideon Amir; d, Herb Freed; w, Herb Freed, Susannah de Nimes, P.W. Swann (based on a story by Herb Freed); ph, Avraham Karpick; m, Tom Simonec, Michael Linn; ed, Charles Simmons, Karen Gebura; prod d, Diana Morris; fight coordinator, Aaron Norris.

Action (PR:NR MPAA:R)

SUSPECT**½** (1987) 118m Tri-Star-ML Delphi Premier/Tri-Star c

Cher *(Kathleen Riley, Public Defender)*, Dennis Quaid *(Eddie Sanger, Lobbyist)*, Liam Neeson *(Carl Wayne Anderson)*, John Mahoney *(Judge Matthew Helms)*, Joe Mantegna *(Assistant U.S. Attorney Charlie Stella)*, Philip Bosco *(Assistant U.S. Attorney General Paul Gray)*, E. Katherine Kerr *(Congressperson Grace Comisky)*, Fred Melamed *(Morty Rosenthal)*, Lisbeth Bartlett *(Marilyn)*, Paul D'Amato *(Michael)*, Bernie McInerney *(Walter Abbott, Eddie's Senior Partner)*, Thomas Barbour *(Justice Lowell)*, Katie O'Hare *(Elizabeth Quinn)*, Rosemary Knower *(Justice Lowell's Secretary)*, Aaron Schwartz *(Forensic Pathologist)*, Lloyd White *(Detective)*, Myra Taylor *(April)*, Bill Cobbs *(Arraignment Judge Franklin)*, Sam Gray *(Judge Louis Weiss)*, Richard Gant *(Everett Bennett)*, Sandi Ross *(Doris, Video Typist)*, Paul de la Rosa *(Helms' Court Clerk)*, Siona Dixon *(Helms' Court Steno)*, Gene Mack, Jim Walton *(Helms' Court Marshals)*, Stefan Graham *(Marvin Johnson)*, Robert Walsh *(Club Congressman)*, Edwin M. Adams *(Congressman)*, Michael Beach *(Parking Lot Attendant)*, Prudence Barry *(Bag Lady at River)*, Carl Jackson *(Depot Derelict)*, Billy Williams *(Dr. Alan Alpert)*, Tony Craig *(Hotel Marshal)*, Jaye Tyrone Stewart *(Jailer)*, Paul Hjelmervik *(Court Marshal)*, Ralph Cosham *(Judge Ansel Stewart)*, Wendy E. Taylor *(Security Guard)*, R.C. Coleman *(Arraignment Court Clerk)*, Djanet Sears *(Message Clerk)*, Jack Jessop *(Mr. Davis)*, Diane Marie L. Tomajczyk *(Secretary)*, Ewart Everard Williams *(Anthony Hall)*, Greg McKinney *(Plainsclothes Cop)*, Michael Emmett *(Waiter)*, Darryl Palmer *(Assistant U.S. Attorney)*, David Lyle *(Morty's Assistant)*, Sandra Bowie, Fred Strother *(Public Defender's Office Clients)*.

This tension-filled courtroom drama set in Washington, D.C., pairs Cher with one of 1987's hottest leading men, Dennis Quaid (THE BIG EASY, INNERSPACE). The film opens with the suicide of Supreme Court justice Barbour. Then the young Justice Department employee to whom he had given privileged information is discovered dead in the Potomac River. Her purse is found in the possession of Neeson, and the violent street person is charged with her murder. Cher, an overworked, under-loved public defender, is appointed as counsel for the deaf-mute Vietnam veteran. Mahoney, a judge who is under consideration for nomination to a circuit court, asks to preside over Neeson's trial, as he assumes it will be cut and dried and leave him free to assume his prestigious new bench. The trial begins with Mantegna (HOUSE OF GAMES) as the prosecuting attorney. Quaid, a lobbyist for the dairy industry, is called to serve on the jury. He realizes Cher is overlooking a key fact that could free her client, and though it's illegal, he contacts her. Determined to see justice done and more than a little attracted to

Cher, Quaid begins his own investigation, supplying a reluctant Cher with information. He turns up a cufflink similar to those given as souvenirs by the President and begins to suspect that Bosco, the assistant attorney general, is involved. One night, D'Amato, a street person who witnessed the murder and has been summoned to appear in court, attacks Cher. Quaid is close at hand and fights him off. Later, Quaid finds D'Amato murdered. After breaking into Justice Department files, Quaid and Cher determine that the murders must be connected with something the dead Justice Department worker learned about Barbour and Bosco. On a hunch, Cher goes to the victim's car, which is still in the parking lot where the murder took place. She finds a cassette containing Barbour's confession that he accepted a bribe and obstructed justice while trying a vote fraud case in a lower court. Cher immediately goes to Mahoney's home to present him with the evidence, but Bosco is there as a dinner guest, and, making excuses, she departs. Later, she returns to the empty courthouse to retrieve a document and is chased through the eerie halls by a knife-totting assailant (Bosco?). At the last moment, she is rescued by Quaid. The next day, as Bosco enters the courtroom, Cher calls Mahoney to the stand. While he refuses to testify and attempts to declare a mistrial, she makes public her accusation that Mahoney—who had also been involved in the scandalous vote fraud case—is the murderer. With the case won and Neeson a free man, Quaid and Cher are free to tamper with each other all that they want.

SUSPECT is almost a *well-made* mystery. The pieces of its puzzle are nicely laid out and the film is punctuated by several tense moments. However, there are some glaring implausibilities, particularly in the final reel, that lead to a solution which while it may not exactly come from left field would certainly send the shortstop out on the outfield grass. The initial premise—that a juror would become as involved in a case as Quaid does—is dramatically plausible since Quaid believes strongly in democratic principles, but will skirt the rules a little to achieve what he perceives to be the greater good. To secure an influential swing vote for the All-American dairy industry, he sleeps with a congresswoman; to see an innocent go free, he illegally aids Cher. Mahoney's role as the murderer is tipped early on by the judge's anxiousness to preside over Neeson's trial. What *is* dramatically unsatisfying is the final clue. It seems highly unlikely that the victim's car would remain at the murder site for weeks. The topper, though, is the cassette that is cleverly hidden in the tape player. What are the chances of the police failing to find it? It is as if the final piece in a jigsaw puzzle that just won't come together is discovered in someone's shoe. Nonetheless, there are several nice touches in the film. Most notably, the cufflink that Quaid acquires turns out to be gold plate, like those available to any tourist in the nation's capital, and not a gift from the President. It has absolutely nothing to do with the murder, but it pushes Cher and Quaid in the right direction just the same. Likewise, Bosco is not strictly a red herring.

Despite the script's plausibility problems, SUSPECT is well handled by four-time Oscar-nominated director Yates (BULLITT, THE DRESSER, BREAKING AWAY). While the situation prevents Quaid and Cher from being together long enough for sparks to really fly, the near-fatal attraction between these two people whose personal lives are on hold is believable. Quaid invests his smooth-talking lobbyist with a sincerity and integrity that transcends his lobbyist's veneer. Though Cher has been better, she brings cautious vulnerability to her role. Her world-weary lawyer suffers from a kind of compassion fatigue but she keeps plugging anyway. Neeson makes a suitably sympathetic, if overly soulful, victim, Mahoney gives his judge a threatening tinge, and Bosco and Mantegna are competent. There is no question that SUSPECT is capable of putting a lump in one's throat; the problem is that it's a little hard to swallow. *(Violence, profanity, sexual situations.)*

p, Daniel A. Sherkow; d, Peter Yates; w, Eric Roth; ph, Billy Williams (Technicolor); m, Michael Kamen; ed, Ray Lovejoy; prod d, Stuart Wurtzel; art d, Steve Sardanis, Tony Hall; set d, Arthur Jeph Parker, Steve Shewchuk; cos, Rita Ryack; spec eff, Jim Fredburg, Joe Ramsey; makeup, Richard Dean, Leonard Engleman, Irene Kent; stunts, Jeff Smolek.

Crime/Drama **(PR:O MPAA:R)**

SUTRADHAR† (1987, India)

Nana Patekar, Smita Patil, Girish Karnad, Nilu Phule.

The old adage that power corrupts is proven once again in this Indian film about the moral downfall that accompanies the ascent of a basically honest man. (In Hindi.)

p, Vasudev Deshingkar; d, Chandrakant Joshi; m, Sudheer Moghe.

Drama **(PR:NR MPAA:NR)**

SVART GRYNING† (1987, Swed./Arg.) 100m Crescendo Film-G C Productiones c (Trans: Why)

Thomas Hellberg, Bibi Andersson, Grynet Mollvig-Lewenhaupt, Arturo Bonin.

Based on the real-life disappearance of a Swedish journalist , this Swedish-Argentinian coproduction examines the horrible reality behind the thousands of similar disappearances that occurred during the dark days of the rule of the military dictatorship in Argentina. The inspiration for this story, a female reporter, traveled to Argentina to try to discover what had happened to the thousands of missing people and experienced first hand the fate that befell most of them—death.

d, Carlos Lemos.

Drama/Mystery **(PR:NR MPAA:NR)**

SVIDANIE NA MLECHNOM PUTI† (1987, USSR) 91m Riga Film/ Sovexportfilm c (Trans: The Date In The Milky Way)

Inara Slutskaya *(Astra)*, Nina Ilyina, Yelena Skorokhodova, Yelena Kazarinova.

Set in the last year of WW II in Latvia, where the Soviets are rolling back the

Nazi forces, this wartime romance tells the story of two lovers whom the war has separated for three years. During that time Slutskaya, an interpreter for a special propaganda unit, and her fiance have only been able to imagine each other when they stared heavenward at the Milky Way. Now the higher-ups have given Slutskaya permission to be reassigned to a unit that is only a few miles away from where her fiance is serving.

d, Ian Streich; w, Ingrida Sokolova; ph, Valdis Eglitis; m, Martina Brauns; art d, Viktor Shildknecht.

Romance/War **(PR:NR MPAA:NR)**

SWEET COUNTRY** (1987) 147m Playmovie/Cinema Group c

Jane Alexander *(Anna Willing)*, John Cullum *(Ben Willing)*, Carole Laure *(Eva Araya)*, Franco Nero *(Paul)*, Joanna Pettet *(Monica Araya)*, Randy Quaid *(Juan)*, Irene Papas *(Mrs. Araya)*, Jean-Pierre Aumont *(Mr. Araya)*, Pierre Vaneck *(Father Venegas)*, Katia Dandoulaki *(Nun)*.

Set in Chile against the backdrop of the September 1973 Rightist military coup that followed the assassination of Leftist president Salvador Allende, SWEET COUNTRY explores the emotional turmoil that befalls two families living under military rule. At the center of the story, which opens in New York in the 1980s, is Alexander, an American who lived in Chile during the political upheaval. She attends the screening of a smuggled documentary on the Chilean government's oppressive tactics, and her past is recalled when she is approached by Nero, with whom she had a one-night affair in 1973 and whom she suspects of betraying her to the junta. When a letter bomb explodes during the screening, Alexander is hospitalized and Nero remains at her side as they talk about the past. The scene then shifts to Chile, 1973. Alexander lives just outside the city with her husband, university professor Cullum. When the political situation begins to flare up, Alexander insists that they return to the US. Cullum, however, foresees no danger and decides that they should stay. Among their friends are two divorced sisters, Pettet and Laure, who has served as the secretary to Allende's wife. Because of Laure's political connections she is detained by the junta. Taking a special liking to Laure is Quaid, a leering military policeman who blackmails her into sleeping with him. In the meantime, Alexander sides with a freedom-fighting nun, Dandoulaki, and takes an active part in a political assassination. After learning of Laure's situation, Alexander arranges for her safe passage out of Chile. They are discovered by the junta, and in the process, both Laure and Cullum are savagely gunned down. Thinking that Nero, who she has discovered may be a spy, has informed the authorities, Alexander leaves Chile without her husband or lover.

A talky, uninvolving movie, SWEET COUNTRY has its share of problems and hardly, if ever, approaches the level of intensity reached by such films as Costa-Gavras' STATE OF SIEGE (which also deals with the Chilean situation), Z, or MISSING. While the story (from a novel by Caroline Richards, but scripted by Cacoyannis) is potentially explosive, the film's uneven pacing and the superhistrionic gesticulations of the actors undermine its value. Alexander, who was so good in TESTAMENT and KRAMER VS. KRAMER, comes through the film unscathed with a fine performance, as does Nero. Papas, dressed in mourning black, is excellent but hardly on screen as Laure and Pettet's mother. Aumont, who according to the credits plays Papas' husband, has had his part so reduced in the editing that he is practically absent from the film. The rest of the cast seems as if they've been filmed during an acting workshop. Given a great deal to say, but very little to do, the actors simply walk around the set making exaggerated gestures—pointing, putting their hands on their hips, tapping their heads, and holding one another's hands. Even if the acting was of the highest caliber, nothing could explain Cacoyannis' peculiar casting. Blonde, fair-skinned Pettet is supposed to be the Chilean sister of dark-haired, olive-skinned Laure and the daughter of Papas. In one of the worst casting decisions of the year (rivaled by Terence Stamp as the Sicilian prince in Michael Cimino's THE SICILIAN), Cacoyannis has Randy Quaid playing a Chilean officer. Quaid, who is excellent when properly cast (THE LAST DETAIL or THE LONG RIDERS) might as well be doing an episode of "Saturday Night Live" with his performance as "Juan" (pronounced very deliberately by Quaid as "Hwan"). Not only is he a full head taller than any other officer in Chilean history, but he slips in and out of his accent with great frequency. It's an unfortunate casting decision which makes Quaid look amateurish and undermines the threatening demeanor that his character is supposed to have. One of the film's only effective scenes is a Chilean officer's mass degradation of a group of imprisoned women. For the pleasure of his MP's, the officer calls the prisoners into a gymnasium and orders them to undress. He then makes the women, their bodies bruised and covered with cigarette burns, get down on their knees and fake orgasms. This is supposed to stimulate the men (one of them snaps and begins to fire his pistol wildly into the air) and humiliate the women. While the scene employs some awkward slow-motion shots of the battered women wandering around aimlessly, it is a powerful portrayal of sadism. In filming the scene, Cacoyannis cast a number of women who had never before appeared in a film—average women who were students, secretaries, or housewives. The result is a shockingly frank scene in which modest women who have never before appeared on camera are forced to undress in front of actors, camera, and crew, unrehearsed. Cacoyannis felt that "their lack of artifice, the spirituality of their spontaneous reactions, would transcend physical realism, the way certain paintings can." Originally screened at 147 minutes, the film emerged on videotape at 120 minutes. *(Graphic violence, nudity, sexual situations, profanity.)*.

p, Michael Cacoyannis, Costas Alexakis; d&w, Michael Cacoyannis (based on a novel by Caroline Richards); ph, Andreas Bellis; m, Stavros Xarhakos; ed, Dinos Katsourides, Michael Cacoyannis; set d, Antonis Kyriakoulis.

Drama **Cas.** **(PR:O MPAA:R)**

SWEET LORRAINE*** (1987) 91m Autumn Pictures/Angelika c

Maureen Stapleton *(Lillian Garber)*, Trini Alvarado *(Molly, Lillian's Granddaughter)*, Lee Richardson *(Sam, Cook)*, John Bedford Lloyd *(Jack, Handyman)*, Freddie Roman *(Phil Allen)*, Giancarlo Esposito *(Howie)*, Edith Falco *(Karen)*, Todd Graff *(Leonard)*, Evan Handler *(Bobby)*, Tamara Tunie *(Julie)*, Ben Lin *(Chinese Cook)*.

The title has nothing to do with the song but it is indicative of the nature of this soft, sugary film. After many years of being overlooked, the Catskill Mountains were rediscovered in 1987 with not one but two movies about the area known as "The Borscht Belt" and "The Jewish Alps." The other one is DIRTY DANCING, which is set in a different era. For many decades, the Catskills had been the vacation playground for New Yorkers. It was just two hours away by car, the hotels ranged from plain to plush and the food was always plentiful. Many of the best entertainers in the world began their careers at the small hotels, including Jerry Lewis, Jackie Mason, and Danny Kaye. The Lorraine Hotel is about 80 years old and is just hanging on. This film takes place in the last year that the hotel will be open. New Yorkers have forsworn the Catskills in favor of cruises, flights to the Caribbean or Europe. The smaller hotels are on their way out and being purchased for razing as the real estate under the inns is more valuable than the hostelries. Stapleton is the owner of the Lorraine and she sees the writing on the wall. The place needs major renovation and she hasn't the heart nor the cash to continue. There is an offer to buy the place and she is impaled on the horns of a dilemma. Good sense dictates she take the offer and wash her hands of the place, but there are other elements with which to contend. The chef, Richardson, who would like to keep the place open, has been Stapleton's veteran lover. Every year, their romance is rekindled from Decoration Day through Labor Day. Stapleton's granddaughter, Alvarado, is hurt by the fact that her parents have just divorced so she comes to the Lorraine for solace and to get her mind off her family woes. Alvarado is a pampered princess who has never really worked and once she gets into the machinations of the hotel, she learns a great deal about what hard labor is. She also has a summer fling with the handsome jack-of-all-trades, Lloyd. With a few nice scenes involving the ethnically mixed staff (particularly Chinese cook Ben Lin), and a particularly good performance by long-time Catskills performer Freddie Roman as the hotel's good-natured social director, SWEET LORRAINE meanders all over the place with not much of a plot beyond a depiction of the day-to-day problems of running a kosher hotel that is about to go under. In the end, Stapleton decides to take the buyer's offer.

The movie is, at times, funny, sentimental, charming and quite authentic, right down to the table settings. It is also remarkably free of the cliches one associates with the locations. While not as good as Frank Gilroy's THE GIG (a 1986 movie about musicians in the area) and DIRTY DANCING, it is still a movie one should see, particularly if a person spent any time at all in one of these hotels. Stapleton is quite believable, somewhat more so than Alvarado, who was last seen in RICH KIDS. Roman is a delight, never stooping to the obvious, a tribute to the multi-layered script. Don't bother looking for the "Lorraine." The film was shot at the Heiden Hotel in South Fallsburg, which has since been torn down. Director Gomer had more than a passing knowledge of the place as his grandfather had been an employee there and he spent many summers as a child at the Heiden and eventually married the granddaughter of one of the people who built the place. The subtleties of the movie may be lost on people not familiar with the milieu. *(Profanity.)*

p&d, Steve Gomer; w, Michael Zettler, Shelly Altman (based on a story by Michael Zettler, Shelly Altman, George Malko); ph, Rene Ohashi; m, Richard Robbins; ed, Laurence Solomon; prod d, David Gropman; art d, Karen Schulz; set d, Richard Hoover; cos, Cynthia Flynt.

Drama **(PR:C MPAA:PG-13)**

SWEET REVENGE**½ (1987) 78m Motion Picture Corp. of America/Concorde c

Nancy Allen *(Jillian Grey)*, Ted Shackelford *(Boone)*, Martin Landau *(Cicero)*, Sal Landi *(Gil)*, Michele Little *(Lee)*, Gina Gershon *(K.C.)*, Lotis Key *(Sonya)*, Stacey Adams *(Tina)*, Leo Martinez *(Buddha)*, Angelo Castro, Jr. *(Ricardo)*, Ramon D'Salva *(Dok)*, Paul Holme *(Auction M.C.)*, Jaimie Grey *(Ruth Arras)*, Betty Mae Piccio *(Mai)*, Crispin Medina *(Tak)*, Richard King *(Tho)*, Ronnie Lazaro *(Jimmy Lee)*, Jeffrey Hammett *(Frank)*, Ernie David *(Fat Man)*, Tony Gonzalez *(Count)*, Cecile G. Krevoy *(Countess)*, Billy Gyenes *(1st Mate)*, John Kater *(Derelict)*.

Allen is a TV reporter investigating a series of mysterious disappearances of beautiful young women from the streets of Los Angeles. However, she falls victim to the same fate and is kidnaped (along with three others) and taken to the Far East to be sold by a white slavery operation headed by Landau. The women make several attempts to escape, receiving a little help from Shackelford, a counterfeit perfume smuggler with his own grudge against Landau. One of the girls is killed, Allen and the two others are recaptured, and Shackelford is nabbed as well. During the auction of the girls, Allen grabs an M-16 and opens fire, sending Arab princes and Texas oil tycoons scrambling for cover. The girls flee, liberating Shackelford, who helps them elude the pursuers and reach comparative safety on an island owned by a black marketeer friend of his. He agrees to help them, despite the large price on their heads, as long as they help him with a little piracy. The plot sidetracks for 20 minutes of meaningless action until they return to find their benefactor's island under attack by Landau's helicopters. Shackelford's friend gives his buddy and the three women arms and sends them away. They attack Landau's stronghold, encountering little opposition from his men. Landau escapes capture once and makes for a helicopter, but his two most trusted killers—Key and Landi—turn on him, take his money, and fly away with Landau hanging off the landing gear begging to be let inside. Landi opens the door and steps on Laudau's fingers and he falls to his death. Key shoots Landi in the head, and Shackelford tells Allen to push a button that explodes the helicopter. Back in the US, Allen is greeted by swarms of reporters, and her little daughter runs into her arms. Produced (executively) by Roger Corman, this is a serviceable action-adventure with an excellent cast (for this sort of thing). Allen is surprisingly tough (as she subsequently was in ROBOCOP), while Shackelford is virtually a revelation as the relaxed, wisecracking scent runner. Landau has long since mastered suave villainy. Perhaps most interesting is Key, an exotic Eurasian whose only previous credit is BLACK MAMA, WHITE MAMA. Her first scenes, as she executes Allen's crew and an informant, are shot in slow-motion to make her seem almost like a fantasy—a mannequin with a gun. Together, these actors make up one of the best ensembles ever to take the law into their own hands in a third world country. Songs include: "The Night Will Never End," "Brax" (Ron Arlis, performed by Arlis). *(Violence, brief nudity, adult situations, profanity.)*

p, Brad Krevoy, Steven Stabler; d, Mark Sobel; w, Steven Krauzer, Tim McCoy (based on a original story by Michael Jones, Randy Kornfield); ph, Shane Kelly (Eastmancolor); m, Ernest Troost; ed, Michael S. Murphy; prod d, Vic Dabao; set d, Josie Camposano; cos, Bong Reyes; makeup, Heather Fraker, Violy Puzon, Amparo.

Action/Adventure Cas. (PR:O MPAA:R)

SWORN BROTHERS† (1987, Hong Kong) 98m Bo Ho Film-Movie Impact/ Golden Harvest c

Lau Tak Wah, Cheung Kowk Keung, Vivien Siu, Tung Biu.

Hong Kong cops-and-robbers film very similar to A BETTER TOMORROW (1987) which sees step-brothers on opposite sides of the law. The orphaned Lau Tak Wah is taken in by policeman Tung Biu who raises the unfortunate boy along side his own son Cheung Kowk Keung. Lau grows up to be a mob hit-man while Cheung follows in his father's footsteps. Despite his love for his step-brother, Cheung becomes determined to bring Lau in. The film ends in a bloody gun battle in downtown Hong Kong.

d&w, David Lai (based on a story by Manfred Wong); m, Chris Babida; art d, Tony Au.

Crime (PR:NR MPAA:NR)

SZAMARKOHOGES (SEE: WHOOPING COUGH, 1987, Hung.)

SZORNYEK EVADJA† (1987, Hung.) 88m Mafilm-Dialog Studio c (Trans: Season of Monsters)

Gyorgy Cserhalmi *(Dr. Bardocz)*, Ferenc Kallai *(Kovacs, Teacher)*, Jozsef Madaras *(Prof. Komondi)*, Juli Nyako *(Kato)*, Katarzyna Figura *(Annabella)*, Erzsi Cserhalmi *(The Girl in Leather)*, Bela Tarr *(The Disciple in White)*, Lajos Balazsovits *(Zimmermann)*, Andras Balint *(Prof. Zoltai)*, Andras Kozak *(Col. Antal)*, Miklos B. Szekely *(The Deaf-Mute)*.

Miklos Jancso, one of Hungary's most important directors in the 1960s and early 1970s, focuses his stylish camera on the story of the suicide of a Hungarian professor who has returned to his homeland after living in the US. Balint gives a TV interview upon his arrival, and then kills himself in a hotel room. He leaves behind a note for physician Cserhalmi, a former classmate, who is horrified when he reads it. Meanwhile, at a lakeside house, Kallai, a teacher, is celebrating his 60th birthday in the company of former students who come from all over to be with him. Into the midst of this celebration come Cserhalmi, and Kozak, the police colonel who is investigating Balint's suicide. A number of strange occurrences follow and suspicious eyes are cast on Madaras, a professor and late arrival at the party. Finally, Madaras and Cserhalmi, ideological opposites from the word go, take up daggers.

d, Miklos Jancso; w, Gyula Hernadi, Miklos Jancso; ph, Janos Kende (Eastmancolor); m, Zoltan Simon; ed, Zsuzsa Csakany; art d&cos, Tamas Banovich; m/l, Zoltan Simon, Tamas Cseh.

Drama (PR:NR MPAA:NR)

T

T. DAN SMITH† (1987, Brit.) 86m Amber-British Film-Channel 4 Television/BFI c

T. Dan Smith, Jack Johnston, Ken Sketheway, Dennis Skinner, George Vickers *(Themselves)*, Art Davies *(Councillor Alan Deal)*, Dave Hill *(Jack Cross)*, Christopher Northey *(Jeremy Maudsley-Long)*, Murray Martin *(Murray)*, Steve Trafford *(Steve)*, Harry Herring *(Councillor Albert)*, Cilla Mason *(Councillor Edith)*, Elizabeth Mansfield *(Newscaster)*, Ralph Nossek *(Home Secretary)*, Ray Stubbs *(Resident and Paper Seller)*, Amber Styles *(Cleaner)*, Kay Wight *(Alan Deal's Wife)*, Norma Day, Gwen Doran, Brian Hogg, Joseph Neatrour, Max Roberts, Bob White, Lee Ross, Paul Heslop, Alan Twelvetree, Nigel Stanger.

Combining documentary and fictional sections, this British film focuses on its historical title character, a Newcastle politician who was sent to prison for six years in 1974 for his involvement in an influence-peddling scandal. T. Dan Smith served as both the mayor and the leader of the city council in Newcastle in the 1960s, and during his tenure sweeping redevelopment took place in that city in Northeastern England. The son of a mine worker and a self-made success in the paint business, Smith branched out into public relations work while serving in his elective offices. One of his clients, John Poulson, a wealthy architect and real estate developer, was nailed for corruption and bribery in 1973, and Smith took a fall with him. The film is divided into four components: 1) interviews with the real Smith (and his contemporaries), who avers that he was merely the fall guy, set up by British intelligence agents who were trying to protect more important officials like then Home Secretary Reginald Maudling; 2) documentary footage dealing with Smith; 3) the self-conscious ruminations and investigations of two of the filmmakers, Martin and Trafford, as they walk through the film; 4) a contemporary fictional drama that mirrors the Poulson scandal. In the latter, Davies portrays a public relations man who is the leader of the city council and the chairman of the housing committee. One of his clients, a construction company headed by Hill, comes under investigation. Hill tries to coerce Davies into tampering with the investigative process and Davies does everything he can to keep his involvement with the company from coming under public scrutiny. In the meantime, Northey, the local member of Parliament, who is also up to his ears in the construction corruption, persuades the home secretary to help out the beleaguered Hill. Davies ends up taking the rap for all the venality. Amber Films, which produced the project, is a movie-making collective dedicated to documenting working class life in the north of England. Both Poulson and Maudling are now dead.

p,w,ph&ed, Elaine Drainville, Vivienne Dawson, Dave Eadington, Richard Grassick, Ellin Hare, Sirkka-Liisa Konttinen, Pat McCarthy, Murray Martin, Jane Neatrour, Lorna Powell, Peter Roberts, Ray Stubbs, Judith Tomlinson, Steve Trafford; m, Ray Stubbs.

Docu-drama **(PR:NR MPAA:NR)**

TA PAIDIA TIS CHELIDONAS† (1987, Gr.) 118m Greek Film Center-Costas Vrettakos-ERT 1 c (Trans: The Children of the Swallow)

Alekos Alexandrakis *(Markianos)*, Mary Chronopoulou *(Fotini)*, Vassilis Diamantopoulos *(Spyros)*, Ilias Logothetis *(Panos)*, Stelios Lionakis *(Sotiris)*, Stephanos Iineos *(Iason)*, Maria Martica *(Akrivi)*, Lefteris Voyatzis *(Anguelos)*, Peris Michailidis, Vladimiros Kuriakidis, Phaedra Noutsou.

One of the big prize winners at the Thessaloniki Film Festival, this entry follows a young television director who tries to track down a family of six brothers and sisters for a documentary series. The family is spread throughout the world, from Athens to Germany to Canada. He is able to speak with everyone except Voyatzis, who has chosen to live in isolation and will not cooperate. When Voyatzis dies, the family gathers for his funeral, thereby allowing the director to film everyone in a single place. In his first feature Vrettakos, an award-winning documentary filmmaker, has employed his former techniques and experience to create the document of a Greek family through different periods of that country's recent history. TA PAIDIA TIS CHELIDONAS shared both the prize for Best Picture and Best Screenplay, and won for Best Actress (Mary Chronopoulou), Best Supporting Actor (Vassilis Diamantopoulos), Best Supporting Actress (Maria Martica), and Best Sound (Marinos Athanassopoulos).

d, Costas Vrettakos; w, Costas Vrettakos, Soula Drakopoulou (based on the novel by Dionyssis Chronopoulos); ph, Aris Stavrou; m, Giorgos Tsangaris; ed, Christos Sarantsoglou; art d, Thalia Istikopoulou; cos, Fani Tsouloyanni.

Drama **(PR:NR MPAA:NR)**

TAKAYA ZHESTOKAYA IGRA—KHOKKEY† (1987, USSR) 80m Mosfilm/Sovexportfilm c (Trans: This Tough Game Hockey)

Vladimir Gostyukhin, Vladimir Samoylov, Evgeny Gerasimov, Tatyana Tashkova.

In their attempt to have a championship hockey team, the coach and team captain go head-to-head over team strategy. The coach believes that the end justifies the means and wants to win at all costs, the team captain, however, is concerned with upholding his, and the team's, personal integrity.

d, Andrey Razumovsky; w, Vladimir Dvortsov, Zinovy Yuryev; ph, Boris Brozhovsky; m, Igor Yefremov; art d, Nikolay Usachev, Victor Zenkov.

Drama **(PR:NR MPAA:NR)**

TAKETORI MONOGATARI (SEE: PRINCESS FROM THE MOON, 1987, Jap.)

TALE OF RUBY ROSE, THE*** (1987, Aus.) 101m Seon Film/Hemdale c

Melita Jurisic *(Ruby Rose)*, Chris Haywood *(Henry Rose)*, Rod Zuanic *(Gem)*, Martyn Sanderson *(Bennett)*, Sheila Florance *(Grandma)*.

A gorgeously envisioned Australian film about a woman's perilous trip through both her subconscious and the highlands of Tasmania in 1933. Jurisic lives in the rugged, remote highlands with her stoic Welsh immigrant husband, Haywood, and Zuanic, a homeless boy who has become a member of their family. The men snare and skin wallabies and opossums—though Zuanic has anything but the killer instinct—and Jurisic keeps the home fires burning (literally, to dry the skins). Years before, Haywood came to work on Jurisic's father's farm in the valley. They fell in love, but her father opposed their marriage, and the scandalized couple moved to the highland wilderness. Haywood returns to the valley to trade, but Jurisic has never gone back. Although she functions contentedly in the daytime, Jurisic is terrified of the dark, convinced that it brings evil and death. She has pieced together her own religion based on the struggle between light and darkness. Barely literate, she has compiled a scrapbook "bible" consisting of her own rudimentary writings and illustrations from books and cards sent to her by the grandmother she hardly knows. She recites a litany of her own creation and uses candles and white powder to ward off evil. However, she is convinced that they are no longer protecting her. One day Haywood and Zuanic depart to check their traps, leaving Jurisic alone, frightened, and haunted by the nightmarish vision of the attack of a snapping creature. Looking for answers and help, she begins a dangerous journey down to the valley. Along the way, she encounters Sanderson, an old neighbor, who dies in her presence. She loads the body on his horse and continues her descent. After a stop at a logging camp, she makes it to her father's house, where Florance, her grandmother, is waiting full of tenderness. They share a bath together, and, for this moment, Jurisic knows the gentle love that has been missing in her life. Returning from a musical performance, Jurisic finds Florance dead. Her father returns, and after listening to her tales of evil darkness, he explains that when she was an infant, an animal had climbed up through a hole in the floor and into her crib. Having exorcised the darkness in her soul, Jurisic begins the trip home. On the way, she has a fall and lies helplessly in a crevice. Haywood and Zuanic, who have been searching for her, find her and take her home in a stretcher as she clutches a picture of Jesus ripped from her scrapbook.

From its sweeping flight through the snow-covered highlands to its grainy closing shot of Jurisic in the stretcher, the cinematography of THE TALE OF RUBY ROSE is stunning. Director Scholes and cinematographer Mason continually employ inventive camera placement and movement, and the rocky highlands and verdant valleys—cloaked in mist, blanketed in snow, or imposed upon by huge cloud banks—are spectacular. Just as important and nearly as well rendered is Jurisic's internal landscape. Isolated from society first by her overprotective father and then by a husband who has no interest in the past, she is persecuted by a terror she can't understand. Scholes' film is a kind of psychological mystery. Early on, the audience should be able to guess that a traumatic experience is at the root of Jurisic's paranoia, but Scholes' accomplishment is the way he captures the details that lead to her self-discovery—her harsh environment, her relationship with the brusque but devoted Haywood, her attempts to protect Zuanic from harm, the power of her imagination as stimulated by her grandmother's cards and books. Jurisic's performance is often almost catatonic, though there are moments of animated panic. In both cases, her actions seem right for the part. She is, after all, a woman who is paralyzed by fear. She is taking on a powerful demon and the system of beliefs she has constructed is no longer adequate to the task. Haywood also gives a strong performance as a man who, though his manner is rough, dreams of creating a little utopia in the wilderness for his family. In smaller roles, Zuanic and Sanderson are adequate, but Florence gives a memorable performance as the woman so long denied the opportunity to know the granddaughter she has loved so much from afar. The contrast between her worldliness and Zuanic's cloistered ignorance brings the tragedy of Jurisic's life into bold relief. THE TALE OF RUBY ROSE was seen by festival audiences in the US in 1987. *(Nudity.)*

p, Bryce Menzies, Andrew Wiseman; d&w, Roger Scholes; ph, Steve Mason (Eastmancolor); m, Paul Schutze; art d, Bryce Perrin.

Drama **(PR:C MPAA:NR)**

TALKING WALLS** (1987) 83m NW c (AKA: MOTEL VACANCY)

Stephen Shellen *(Paul Barton)*, Marie Laurin *(Jeanne)*, Barry Primus *(Prof. Hirsh)*, Karen Lee Hopkins *(Luna)*, Sybil Danning *(Bathing Beauty)*, Don Davis *(Don)*, Rae Davis *(Rae)*, Hector Elias *(Roberto)*, Bobby Ettienne *(Butterfly)*, June Wilkerson *(Blonde)*, Sally Kirkland *(Hooker)*, Marshall Efron *(Erwin)*, Don Calfa *(Andre)*, Donna Ponterotto *(Betsy)*, Marty Brill *(Floyd)*, Eileen Barnett *(Judy)*, John Moschitta, Jr. *(Hal)*, Jill Choder *(Naomi)*, Richard Hochberg *(Harold)*, Carole Ita White *(Spring)*, La Cage Aux Folles: Clay Morse *(Barbara)*, James Segovia *(Liza)*, Michael Andrews *(Ann)*, Kelly Lawrence *(Julie)*, Jace Peters *(Manager)*; Hunter Von Leer *(James)*, Susan Wolf *(Brenda)*, Richard Partlow *(Chuck)*, Kathy Cherry *(Rosalie)*, Peter Liapus *(Will)*, Elizabeth Carder *(Bored Girl)*, Will Nye *(Everett)*, Gary Gayle *(Karate Man)*, Diane Gayle *(Karate Woman)*, Twink Caplan, Norman Klar, Jeremy Whelan, Christina Smith, Andrew Block, Mickey Jonas, Anne Bloom, Judy Baldwin, Richard Stockinger,

Loutz Gage, Randy Paul, Barbara Townsend, Bart Bartolo, David Ruprecht, Nicholas Earl Holden, Kathi Sawyer Young, Danny Rogers, Brad Gorman, John Brown, Mimi Maynard.

In 1986, documentary filmmaker Ross McElree released SHERMAN'S MARCH, an unusual film portraying one man's search for love and romance in the age of nuclear war. Rather than set himself apart from the action, McElree became the subject of his film, ruminating on the emotional difficulties of life while using the camera to record his daily encounters. SHERMAN'S MARCH was a consistently absorbing achievement, reflecting on both the nature of love and the cinema. TALKING WALLS, which was shot in 1982, though unreleased until this year, takes a similar approach to the subject of romance, yet unlike SHERMAN'S MARCH, this fictional exploration is a disappointing mess.

The premise is a simple one. Shellen is a sociology student working on his master's thesis for professor Primus. Rather than take the traditional route, Shellen plans to make videotapes that probe the secret behind successful relationships between men and women. He lives in a place called The Total Media Hotel, run by Don and Rae Davis, a genial older couple. In return for room and board Shellen takes care of all of the motel's video equipment, thus giving him complete access to the machinery he needs to perform his study. Each room of the motel has a theme—the Car Room, the Sheep Room, the Shoe Room, etc.—and by using one way mirrors, Shellen soon is able to monitor the goings-on. Still, he cannot figure out the key to successful relationships, and pours out his feelings to his camera. After an unhappy fling with Hopkins, a girl studying to be a sex therapist, Shellen takes his video camera around campus. In so doing, he meets Laurin, a French art student, with whom Shellen falls madly in love. She is also attracted to him, but finds his reliance on the camera annoying. Using a high-tech camera that records body hot spots, Shellen tries to determine where Laurin's erogenous zones are located. This doesn't help him, though, because Laurin is tired of his incessant filming. Shellen prepares to apologize, but while watching his video monitor at the motel, he is horrified to learn that Laurin is sleeping with Primus. Without direction in either his thesis or personal life, Shellen feels like his world is slipping out of control. Eventually Laurin grows tired of Primus, and Shellen watches as she angrily throws the teacher out of the motel room. Quick as a wink, Shellen is there to comfort her, thus learning that true love is the secret behind successful relationships.

Shellen gives a wonderfully manic performance, interacting with his camera like a man possessed. He is unafraid to express his inner thoughts, whether emotional musing or adrenalin charged tirades. At one point Shellen tells his camera, "I'm getting as crazy as those cartoon characters. You know, those ones, those mad scientist types." When TALKING WALLS plays on that high energy level, the film is paradoxically fascinating and uncomfortable to watch. What we witness is a man who is becoming one with his camera, allowing himself to be swallowed by his vision. One scene, in which Shellen contemplates his romantic nature, could easily have come from SHERMAN'S MARCH: the topic, Shellen's angst, and the subjective camerawork are that close to the documentary's honesty. Unfortunately TALKING WALLS shies away from this intriguing approach. In the first place, the idea of a kindly owner of a kinky motel giving a college student complete access to thousands of dollars worth of video equipment is wholly ridiculous. Even if this was remotely believable, the film still wouldn't succeed. Director Verona goes heavy on the cheesecake sex, exploiting it for laughs rather than looking beneath the surface (it should come as no surprise to exploitation fans that B actress Sybil Danning has a bit part in the film). Both Shellen and the point of the film become lost in its technology as the focus veers from comedy to psychology to formula romance. Though Verona initially makes good use of the subjective camera, he loses confidence in the idea and presents no less than four musical interludes. This radically alters the film's tone and destroys TALKING WALLS' original concept. Like Shellen, the other cast members don't appear to be "acting"; however, the ensemble is not a good one. Laurin has a sweet smile and is fine as the romantic interest, but her French accent is atrocious. Primus is adequate as the teacher, but his consistently angry mood doesn't give the character much depth. It's a shame this film never really comes together. Had TALKING WALLS gone for the unusual rather than the mundane, this could have been a really weird and engrossing B picture. Songs include: "Talking Walls," "Luna," "Can't Hold Back" (Richard Glasser, Sam Kunin, performed by Glasser), "Better in the Backseat," "Losing Side of Love," "Once Burned" (Glasser, Kunin, performed by Joey Toronto), "Making It with You Baby" (Glasser, Kunin, performed by Glasser, Didi Carr), "Bedtime Lovin'" (Glasser, Kunin, performed by Carr), "Ain't Got Time to Take My Shoes Off Mama" (Glasser, Paul Baker, performed by Maxie Anderson). *(Profanity, nudity, sexual situations.)*

p, Philip A. Waxman; d, Stephen Verona; w, Stephen Verona (based on the novel *The Motel Tapes* by Mike McGrady); ph, Scott Miller; m, Richard Glasser; ed, Jonathan Lawton; art d, Rick Carter; cos, Irene Tsu; m/l, Richard Glasser, Sam Kunin, Paul Baker; makeup, Richard Arrington.

Comedy/Drama **Cas.** **(PR:O MPAA:NR)**

TALMAE WA POMDARI† (1987, N. Korea) 83m Korean Feature Film Studio c (Trans: Talmae And Pomdari)

Kim Yong Suk *(Talmae)*, Gho Myong Son *(Pomdari)*, Choe Chang Su *(Imdon)*, Yu Wom Jun *(General Hong)*.

Set in historical Korea, this widescreen epic stars Kim Yong Suk and Gho Myong Son as a pair of warrior lovers who want to live a quiet family life now that the war has ended. Son, a great warrior, has proven his heroics, and now it is Suk's turn. When her father is killed, she goes into martial arts training and avenges his death. The final film from veteran director Yun Ryong Gyu.

d, Yun Ryong Gyu; w, Kim Sung Gu; ph, Pak Gyong Won; m, Chon Chang Il.

Historical/Romance **(PR:NR MPAA:NR)**

TAMAS† (1987, India) 150m Blaze c

Om Puri, Deepa Sahi, Amrish Puri, A.K. Hangal, Dina Pathak, Uttara Baokar, Saeed Jaffrey, Surekha Sikhri.

A drama set during the Partition of India—the 1947 provision in which Punjab and Bengal were split between Pakistan and India as a result of an act of the British Parliament. The result was a massive outbreak of violence in which a half-million people were killed within six months and the religious separation of Hindus, Sikhs, and Muslims was widened even further. The film's director has stated that the film "recreates the immense human tragedy caused by the cynical manipulation of religious sentiments of various communities to achieve narrow political objectives." Appearing in the film is one of India's top actors, Saeed Jaffrey, who was seen on US screens most recently in MY BEAUTIFUL LAUNDRETTE.

d, Govind Nihalani; w, Govind Nihalani, Bhisham Sahni (based on a novel by Bhisham Sahni); ph, V.K. Murthy, Govind Nihalani; m, Singh Bandhu, Vanraj Bhatia; ed, Shutanu Gupta; art d, Nitish Roy.

Drama/Historical **(PR:NR MPAA:NR)**

TANDEM† (1987, Fr.) 92m Cinea-Hachette Premiere-Films A2/AMLF c (Trans: Duo)

Gerard Jugnot *(Rivetot)*, Jean Rochefort *(Mortez)*, Sylvie Granotier *(Bookseller)*, Julie Jezequel *(Waitress)*, Jean-Claude Dreyfus *(Councillor)*.

A buddy picture starring Rochefort as a veteran radio show host and Jugnot as his confidante/chauffeur/sound recordist. Together they travel through the provinces, generating a new show from each location. Along the way, Jugnot learns that the show is to be cancelled and does all he can to keep the devastating news from Rochefort.

p, Philippe Carcassonne, Rene Cleitman; d, Patrice Leconte; w, Patrice Leconte, Patrick Dewolf; ph, Denis Lenoir (Eastmancolor); m, Francois Bernheim; ed, Joelle Hache; art d, Ivan Maussion.

Comedy/Drama **(PR:NR MPAA:NR)**

TANT QU'IL AURA DES FEMMES† (1987, Fr.) 85m Hugo Films-Labbefilms-AAA/AAA c (Trans: As Long As There Are Women)

Roland Giraud *(Sam)*, Fanny Cottencon *(Vanessa)*, Marianne Basler *(Joanna)*, Fiona Gelin *(Elodie)*, Martin Lamotte *(Sacha)*, Philippe Lavil *(Jeremie)*, Nicole Jamet *(Madam Lebeuf)*, Florent Ginisty *(Thomas)*, Camille Raymond *(Alice)*.

Giraud is a philandering screenwriter who is best friends with ex-wife Cottencon, lives with lover Gelin, and is tempted by sexy new arrival Basler. Surrounded by beautiful women, Giraud's self-control is put through the wringer, especially when he runs off to Mexico with Basler.

p, Evelyne Gelin, Xavier Gelin; d&w, Didier Kaminka; ph, Eduardo Suerra; m, Jean-Claude Petit; ed, Minique Prim; art d, Loula Morin.

Comedy/Romance **(PR:NR MPAA:NR)**

TANTSPLOSHCHADKA† (1987, USSR) 85m Mosfilm/Sovexportfilm c (Trans: The Dance)

Alexandra Yakovleva, Yevgeny Dvorzhetsky, Lyudmila Shevel, Anna Nazaryeva, Sergei Gazarov.

A young engineer is sent by his bosses to a small seaside town to begin construction of a new facility. He has been expressly ordered to supervise the demolition of a dance pavilion that has much sentimental value to the townsfolk. Although at first he is determined to follow orders, he soon learns how much the pavilion means to the citizens and he fights to keep the structure from being demolished.

d, Samson Samsonov; w, Arkady Inin, Samson Samsonov; ph, Viktor Shestoperov; m, Yevgeny Doga; art d, Yevgeny Markovich.

Drama **(PR:NR MPAA:NR)**

TAROT***   (1987, Ger.) 115m Moana-Anthea/AAA Classic c

Vera Tschechowa *(Charlotte, Actress)*, Hanns Zischler *(Edouard)*, Rudiger Vogler *(Otto)*, Katharina Bohm *(Ottilie)*, William Berger *(Mittler)*, Kerstin Eiblmaier, Peter Moland, George Tabori.

Reteaming the lead actors of Wim Wenders' KINGS OF THE ROAD—Rudiger Vogler and Hanns Zischler—TAROT is an adaptation of Goethe's *Elective Affinities* which explores the interrelationships of four characters living along the Alz River in the German countryside. Zischler is a film director who restlessly passes the days between projects. In the hope of finding a picture to shoot in the spring, he invites screenwriter Vogler to come to his country estate and collaborate on a script. In the meantime, Zischler's longtime companion Tschechowa is struggling over an unfinished novel. Into this group comes Tschechowa's pretty teenage niece, Bohm, a classical guitar student who aspires to become a music instructor. The Zischler-Vogler collaboration goes nowhere, with each half distressed at his own creative inability. When Vogler reads Tschechowa's manuscript and expresses his admiration, Zischler enthusiastically decides that Vogler and Tschechowa should collaborate on the script, which he will direct and in which Tschechowa will star. Meanwhile, Berger, Tschechowa's literary agent, peddles the manuscript and searches for financial backing for the film. While things seem to fall into place professionally and artistically, they are not so orderly on a personal level. Zischler and Tschechowa finally decide to marry, but the following morning they are ready for a divorce after Tschechowa learns that her husband has asked Bohm to star in his film. Zischler grows increasingly insolent and ruthless. One evening, after being offered a month-long directing job in Africa, Zischler asks Bohm to leave town with him, maliciously and falsely claiming that he and Tschechowa have agreed to divorce. Bohm, instead, decides to await his return, fearing that she will hurt Tschechowa. When Zischler returns, neither Bohm nor Vogler want to speak to him. Tschechowa, however, attempts to rekindle their love. She also tells him that she is pregnant with his child. Soon afterwards, Zischler, having landed a deal to direct a television mini-series, drags Vogler off to an island retreat to work on the screenplay. While they are away, Tschechowa gives birth to a son, who dies a short time later. When Zischler returns, he stops by the child's grave but feels no sorrow, and even berates his wife for her "sentimentality." Disgusted, Vogler (who earlier proposed to Tschechowa) turns his back on Zischler. Bohm then refuses Zischler's request to leave with him. A tragic turn of events follows as Bohm is struck and killed by a truck, and Zischler dies of an apparent heart attack in a hotel room. Vogler and Tschechowa are left with their sorrow, quietly contemplating whether they should move in together.

An intellectual discourse on life, love, morality, and the secrets of the future, TAROT uses as its center a set of tarot cards which reveal the player's inner self. For these four characters the drama of life is left up to fate. Tschechowa relies on the cards, Bohm has dreams which later come true, and Vogler's favorite answer to questions is "Only the gods know." It is Zischler who habitually upsets the course of events—creating his own real-life dramas when he has nothing else to do. Just when everything seems to be going smoothly, he declares his love for Bohm and jeopardizes both his marriage and his friendship with Vogler. Although the entire film is acted without emotion (as if the characters are playing intellectual games with one another), all the performances are compelling. Zischler makes the most of his thoroughly reprehensible character in a role which earns him no sympathy. Vogler is a joy as the charming and occasionally witty screenwriter—an extension, of sorts, of his KINGS OF THE ROAD character. Tschechowa garners the most sympathy as the saintly woman who understands Zischler and remains devoted to him despite her attraction to Vogler, and who remains a true friend to Bohm despite her niece's involvement with Zischler. It is Bohm who has the oddest effect on the group. Although she attempts to remain uninvolved (keeping her distance from Zischler for fear of the consequences and taking no active part in his new film), Bohm is the catalyst for most of the film's tragedy—being ultimately responsible for the infant's death and for Zischler's emotional withdrawal.

The blame for the film's faults, however, must be laid at director Thome's feet. Too often the script and performances fluctuate between naturalism and a nonrealistic, detached tone which resembles aloof intellectualism. While this sort of cool melodrama works well in the films of R.W. Fassbinder, here it seems at odds with the more earthy Rohmeresque structure. While Thome's picture lacks the improvisational energy of Rohmer's direction and the youthful exuberance of such Rohmer stars as Beatrice Romand or Pascale Ogier, it does succeed in combining the tone of a Rohmer "Moral Tale" with the Germanic philosophy of Goethe's writing. While Rohmer's films are decidedly French, Thome has made a Rohmer film which is decidedly German. In an effort to clearly align himself with Rohmer, Thome includes a scene between Pascale Ogier and Fabrice Luchini from Rohmer's 1984 film, FULL MOON IN PARIS. Released in Germany in 1986 and shown the same year at the Cannes Film Festival's "Directors Fortnight," TAROT hit the US festival circuit in 1987. *(Nudity.)*

d, Rudolph Thome; w, Hans Zihlmann (based on the novel *Elective Affinities* by Johann Wolfgang von Goethe); ph, Martin Schafer; m, Christoph Oliver; ed, Dorte Volz; art d, Anamarie Michnevich; cos, Gioia Raspe.

Drama   **(PR:C MPAA:NR)**

TAXI NACH KAIRO†   (1987, Ger.) 90m Frank Ripploh/Senator Filmverleih c (Trans: Taxi to Cairo)

Frank Ripploh *(Frank)*, Christine Neubauer *(Klara)*, Udo Schenk *(Eugen)*, Bernd Broaderup *(Bernd)*, Nina Schuehly *(Mother)*, Domenica Niehoff *(Psychotherapist)*, Burkhard Driest *(Vice Squad Officer)*.

Gay German writer-director-actor Ripploh's sequel to his comedy TAXI ZUM KLO, which was a surprise hit on the US art-house circuit in 1981. This one begins where the last left off with promiscuous schoolteacher Ripploh and his faithful lover, Broaderup, finally kaput. Broaderup has been so frustrated by his relationship with Ripploh that he's gone from gay to straight. When Ripploh's nagging mother accidentally walks in on her son engaging in a bit of gay S&M, she insists he get married immediately or be cut out of her will. Ripploh meets an eccentric actress, Neubauer, and persuades her to pose as his bride. She moves in with him at a house in the country and they become fast, but platonic, friends. Unfortunately, both fall in love with their handsome neighbor, Schenk, and the film becomes a bi-sexual bedroom farce. Eventually heterosexual friendship wins out, with Ripploh and Neubauer heading out into the North Sea bound for Cairo.

p&d, Frank Ripploh; w, Tamara Kafka, Frank Ripploh; ph, Dodo Simoncic; m, Peter Breiner; ed, Peter R. Adam, Peter Clausen; art d, Hans Zillmann.

Comedy   **(PR:NR MPAA:NR)**

TAXING WOMAN, A*½**   (1987, Jap.) 127m Itami-New Century/Japanese Films c (MARUSA NO ONNA)

Nobuko Miyamoto *(Ryoko Itakura, Tax Inspector)*, Tsutomu Yamazaki *(Hideki Gondo)* Masahiko Tsugawa *(Assistant Chief Inspector Hanamura)*, Hideo Murota *(Ishii, Motel President)*, Shuji Otaki *(Tsuyuguchi, Tax Office Manager)*, Daisuke Yamashita *(Taro Gondo)*, Shinsuke Ashida, Keiju Kobayashi, Mariko Okada, Kiriko Shimizu, Kazuyo Matsui, Yasuo Daichi, Kinzo Sakura, Hajimeh Asoh, Shiro Ito, Eitaro Ozawa.

Continuing his series of energetic, incisive and very funny examinations of modern Japanese culture (burial rites in THE FUNERAL, food in TAMPOPO), director Juzo Itami now turns his unique cinematic gaze on that most sacred of current Nipponese obsessions—money. Part social satire, part procedural drama, A TAXING WOMAN takes its title from dedicated tax agent Miyamoto, a spunky, freckled woman with a Louise Brooks haircut and a cowlick her superiors continually remind her to tame. Capitalizing on her unassuming and demure looks, Miyamoto encourages tax cheats to let their guard down as she investigates their books. Well versed in the clever methods of tax evasion, she swiftly uncovers her quarry's secrets and suddenly bites like a pit bull, refusing to let go until the penalties are paid. One particularly vexing case involves the multimillion-dollar empire of "adult motel" tycoon Yamazaki. Although cursed with a lame leg, Yamazaki is suave, cool, and very clever. Using his vast influence, Yamazaki launders his money through the *yakuza* (gangsters), phony corporations, real estate, and even his mistress, hoarding his booty in a huge safe hidden behind the bookcase in his house. When Miyamoto first begins her investigation, Yamazaki does not feel threatened, confident he can manipulate any woman to his will. Unfortunately for him, however, Miyamoto is even more clever and dedicated than he when it comes to the pursuit of money. Utilizing the expansive resources of the Japanese Tax Office, a raid involving more than 100 agents and state-of-the-art technology is launched against Yamazaki's home, offices, *yakuza* connections, and banks in an effort to expose all of his hidden income. Eventually the humbled Yamazaki admits defeat and in a fit of deep admiration, asks Miyamoto to become his wife. Although flattered, Miyamoto turns the handsome tax cheat down, for she is already married to the relentless pursuit of hidden income.

In TAMPOPO, Itami relied heavily on an inventive Bunuelian structure that allowed him the freedom to suddenly shift gears and follow some delightfully vivid minor characters within the context of his main narrative. A TAXING WOMAN, however, is much more traditionally structured and is very reminiscent of such classic Akira Kurosawa procedural dramas as STRAY DOG, HIGH AND LOW, and THE BAD SLEEP WELL. We follow Miyamoto step by step as she meticulously investigates potential tax cheats, be they ma-and-pa grocers or bankers. While this approach makes for some fascinating drama, it also allows Itami to introduce his trademark bit players and biting satiric edge. Although not as out-and-out loopy as TAMPOPO, there are a few such moments, such as when Yamazaki seals a particularly lucrative deal and does a hilarious celebratory dance, and when Miyamoto finally outwits an arrogant *pachinko* parlor owner and his face suddenly turns beet red. What A TAXING WOMAN does best is examine the Japanese obsession with acquiring wealth and keeping as much of it as possible. Itami sees the entire society as money mad—everyone is a tax cheat—but even more manic than the populace are those sworn to expose them. The tax investigators are seen as zealous soldiers who live off the thrill of the hunt. Despite rain, sleet, or snow, the tax agents happily pick through garbage dumps, don disguises, spy, make secret videotapes, strip search, and launch invasions of military proportions. Both sides in the game are shown to be supremely clever, as the cheats invent new methods of deception as fast as the agents can uncover them. The boundless energy of the Japanese seems to be what really fascinates Itami, regardless of his subject matter. If the films of Yasujiro Ozu are revered for their portrayal of traditional Japanese family life, then Itami is well on his way to becoming the leading chronicler of life in modern-day Japan. In all his films there is a vibrant spark of wit, cleverness, and verve that makes his work unique and endearing. Again Itami presents a parade of lively characters who remain memorable whether onscreen for one hour or one minute. Miyamoto (the director's wife) and Yamazaki continue to make a terrific team, as they did in THE FUNERAL and TAMPOPO, infusing their roles with detail and nuance rarely found in the films of any country. A TAXING WOMAN was a smash hit in Japan, and Itami has already gone into production on a sequel which once again features Miyamoto, this time pitting the plucky tax investigator against a religious cult. *(Nudity, sexual situations.)*

p, Yasushi Tamaoki, Seigo Hosogoe; d&w, Juzo Itami; ph, Yonezo Maeda; m, Toshiyuki Honda; ed, Akira Suzuki; art d, Shuji Nakamura.

Comedy/Drama   **(PR:C-O MPAA:NR)**

TAYNAYA PROGULKA† (1987, USSR) 83m Gorky/Sovexportfilm c (Trans: Secret Walk)

Mirdza Martinson, Murat Manbetov, Andrei Troitsky, Sergei Barchuk, Vladimir Shikhov.

A WW II thriller which is loosely based on the autobiography of Soviet war scout Sharshen Usubaliev. The Usabaliev character is assigned the task of guiding a female secret service agent across occupied territory to the front line so that she can obtain information pertaining to Nazi plans for the Eastern Front war. The scout and six of his men risk life and limb to complete their mission, and by the time they have guided the spy to her rendezvous on the Baltic, only he and one other scout remain. On their return trip, however, both scouts are killed.

d, Valery Mikhailovsky; w, Yefim Klenov, Sharshen Usubaliev; ph, Boris Seredin; m, Veniamin Basner; art d, Marc Gorelik.

War **(PR:NR MPAA:NR)**

TAYNOE PUTESHESTVIE EMIRA† (1987, USSR) 88m Uzbekfilm/Sovexportfilm c (Trans: The Emir's Secret Voyage)

Gulnara Abdurakhmanova, Ivan Agafonov, Galina Yatskina, Mashrabdjan Kimsanov, Shukhrat Irgashev.

Historical melodrama set in Turkestan which sees a young Emir fall in love with an innocent shepherd's daughter. The impetuous ruler has the girl taken to his palace, but his caravan is ambushed by enemies not far from the girl's home and a bloody fight ensues. Discovering that her parents were killed in the battle, the girl flees and is taken in by a Russian locomotive driver. The driver and his kindly wife adopt the girl, but their happiness is destroyed when, once again, evil forces conspire to enslave her.

d, Farid Davletshin; w, Boris Saakov; ph, Yury Lyubimov; m, Felix Yanov-Yanovsky; art d, Igor Gulenko.

Drama **(PR:NR MPAA:NR)**

TAYNY MADAM VONG† (1987, USSR) 91m Kazakhfilm/Sovexportfilm c (Trans: The Mystery Of The Pirate Queen)

Serik Kanakbayev, Irina Miroshnichenko, Armen Djigarkhanyan.

A heroic Soviet merchant marine, played by Olympic boxer Serik Kanakbayev, does battle with a group of vicious modern-day pirates who are searching for a secret treasure hidden somewhere in Southeast Asia.

d, Stepan Puchinyan; w, Stanislav Govorukhin, Stepan Puchinyan; ph, Abiltai Kasteyev, Igor Vovnyanko; m, Andrei Gevorgyan; art d, Mikhail Garakanidze.

Action/Adventure **(PR:NR MPAA:NR)**

TEEN WOLF TOO* (1987) 95m Atlantic c

Jason Bateman *(Todd Howard)*, Kim Darby *(Prof. Brooks)*, John Astin *(Dean Dunn)*, Paul Sand *(Coach Finstock)*, James Hampton *(Uncle Howard)*, Mark Holton *(Chubby)*, Estee Chandler *(Nicki)*, Robert Neary *(Gustavson)*, Stuart Fratkin *(Stiles)*, Beth Ann Miller *(Lisa)*, Rachel Sharp *(Emily)*.

TEEN WOLF, the 1985 hit that starred Michael J. Fox, has taken in more than $50 million, and visions of overflowing box-office cash boxes must have danced in the heads of the makers of this carbon copy sequel. Eighteen-year-old Jason Bateman, the teen heartthrob star of TV's "Valerie," plays the cousin of Fox's original teenage werewolf. Bateman, who, as far as he knows, isn't a victim of the family curse, is off to Hamilton University on a boxing scholarship. The catch is that Bateman isn't a boxer. Sand, the beleaguered coach of Hamilton's hapless boxing team, has gotten Bateman the free ride because he knows of Fox's lupine-fostered athletic prowess and he hopes Bateman is similarly gifted. Bateman, on the other hand, would rather devote his time to his studies. Meanwhile, tyrannical dean of men Astin puts pressure on Bateman to prove that his scholarship is warranted. After some pathetic efforts in the ring, Bateman discovers that he, too, is a werewolf. Hair grows all over his body, fangs sprout, his eyes glow red, and he becomes both an unstoppable pugilist and the big man/wolf on campus. In the process Bateman becomes caught up in his celebrity. He begins keeping company with shallow hussy Miller and turns his back on buddies Holton (reprising his character from TEEN WOLF) and Fratkin. He also stops doing his schoolwork, much to the dismay of professor Darby and Chandler, a cute classmate who has fallen for the bespectacled, bookish version of Bateman and sees that the hirsute hero is a phony. Before Bateman becomes a lost cause he is visited by his uncle, Hampton, who played Fox's werewolf dad in the original. Hampton puts his nephew back on the to-thine-own-self-be-true path and teaches him a few tricks for his big upcoming match. Darby gives Bateman a chance to take a makeup exam so he can salvage a passing grade. After studying all night and taking the test, Bateman dashes off for his big fight, which he wins without the aid of his lupine powers. Chandler is back in his corner and Darby, who turns out to have her own pair of glowing red eyes, holds Astin at bay.

It's hard to imagine a more calculated sequel than TEEN WOLF TOO. The narrative structure is almost identical to its precursor except the high-school environment has been replaced by a college one that is preposterously unlike any institution of higher education and boxing has replaced basketball as the featured sport. Like Fox in the original, Bateman was this year's model when it came to bankable young TV leading men. Although he has an endearing presence, Bateman doesn't infuse his role with the naive charm Fox brought to the original. There was an innocence to the original that kept its message from being simplistic, and Fox's struggles with his changing body and personality became a metaphor for the confusion of adolescence. Unfortunately, the sequel is predictable and not very funny, though adolescents will find more to laugh at here than adults. Bateman's performance is unexceptional and it seems unlikely this will prove to be the vehicle that will launch him to the successful heights Fox has attained. (It should be remembered, however, that though TEEN WOLF was shot before BACK TO THE FUTURE, it was the latter film that sent Fox's stock soaring.) As for the other performances, Chandler is appropriately sweet as Bateman's redemptive love interest and Hampton is steady as the voice of reason. Astin overplays his nasty administrator, Darby quivers with intensity in a superfluous role, and Sand fails to exploit the comic possibilities that writer Jay Tarses found in the coach in TEEN WOLF. Although Bateman had to endure makeup sessions that lasted more than three hours, the special effects in TEEN WOLF TOO are hardly spectacular. The producer for the $3 million film was Kent Bateman, father of Jason and Justine Bateman, who plays Fox's sister of the TV hit "Family Ties." *(Sexual situations.)*

p, Kent Bateman; d, Christopher Leitch; w, R. Timothy Kring (based on a story by Joseph Loeb III, Matthew Weisman); ph, Jules Brenner (Consolidated Film Labs Color); m, Mark Goldenberg; ed, Steven Polivka, Kim Secrist, Harvey Rosenstock, Raja Gosnell; art d, Peg McClellan.

Comedy **(PR:A-C MPAA:PG)**

TEL AVIV—BERLIN† (1987, Israel) 96m Tel Aviv-Berlin LTD c

Shmuel Vilozny *(Benjamin)*, Rivka Noiman *(Leah)*, Anat Harpazy *(Gusu)*, Joseph Carmon *(Jacob Miller)*.

Vilozny is a concentration camp survivor who has escaped his native Germany in 1942 and emigrated to Tel Aviv. While recovering in hospital from his arduous journey, Vilozny falls in love with his nurse, Noiman, a Polish Jew who has also escaped and come to Tel Aviv. Soon they are married and the proud parents of a baby daughter. By 1948, however, Vilozny finds himself longing for the intellectual stimulation of Berlin, while his small-town wife is content with life in Israel. Vilozny further isolates himself from his wife by surrounding himself with prewar Berlin memorabilia, including clothes, furniture, records, and art. A threat to their marriage arises in the form of beautiful former-Berliner Harpazy, whom Vilozny becomes intellectually and physically attracted to. To make matters worse, Vilozny discovers that one of the *kapos* of his concentration camp—the man responsible for the death of his father—has escaped to Tel Aviv and become a blacksmith. Vilozny's obessions with both another woman and vengeance threaten to destroy his new life.

p, Smadar Azriely; d&w, Tzipi Trope; ph, Gadi Danzig; ed, Rachel Yaguil; m, Shalom Weinstein; art d, Eli Landau; cos, Dafna Hendly.

Drama **(PR:NR MPAA:NR)**

TELEFTAIO STICHIMA† (1987, Gr.) Greek Film Center c (Trans: The Last Wager)

Daniel Olbrychski, Katerina Razelou, Christos Tsangas, Eva Kotamanidou, Mary Iglesi, Nikos Papaconstantinou, Nikos Lykomitros, Antonis Vlissidis, Maria Spantidaki.

Political thriller about a former leader of a militant group who undergoes an ideological crisis that isolates him from his comrades and wife. When he is wrongly incriminated in a series of assassinations and is jailed, he finally snaps out of his malaise and experiences a rebirth of conscience.

d&w, Costas Zirinis; ph, Tassos Alexakis; ed, Aristides Karides-Fuchs; art d, Tassos Zografos.

Thriller **(PR:NR MPAA:NR)**

TEMA† (1987, USSR) 98m Mosfilm/Sovexportfilm-Intl. Film Exchange c (Trans: The Theme)

Mikhail Ulyanov *(Kim Yesenin)*, Inna Churikova *(Sasha Nikolayeva)*, Stanislav Lyubshin *(Gravedigger)*, Yevgeni Vesnik *(Igor)*, Yevgeniya Nechaeva *(Mariya Aleksandrova)*, Natalya Selezyova *(Svetlana)*.

Made in 1979 and not released theatrically until 1987, TEMA stars Ulyanov as a popular Soviet playwright who realizes that he has not written anything of worth in years. Still, however, he remains a success. Hoping to regain some of his initial inspiration, he and an admiring female student retreat to a friend's rural home. Here Ulyanov meets Churikova (the director's wife and frequent star), a tour guide with whom he becomes infatuated. As they talk, Ulyanov learns that Churikova was once a great admirer of his, but now thinks he has sold out to government pressure and expectations. Instead of acting angrily, he becomes intrigued with Churikova because of her honesty. He falls deeply in love with her, only to learn that she is already involved with a young Jewish writer who refuses to bow to the Soviet authorities. Shown briefly in the market at the 1986 Karlovy Vary Film Festival, TEMA received a tremendous amount of attention in 1987 as one of the dozen shelved Soviet films to be liberated by *glasnost*. It won the Golden Bear as best film of the Berlin Film Festival, and received a US arthouse release. (In Russian, English subtitles.)

d, Gleb Panfilov; w, Gleb Panfilov, Alexander Chervinsky; ph, Leonid Kalashnikov; m, Vadim Bibergan; art d, Marksen Gaukman-Sverdlov.

Drama **(PR:NR MPAA:NR)**

TENEREZZA† (1987, It.) AFC Cinematografica c

Massimo Dapporto, Francesca Ferre, Mattia Sbragia, Orchidea De Santis.

A bachelor wanting a child but not a wife finds a prostitute willing to go along with the scheme. Once pregnant, the prostitute has second thoughts about giving up the child, much to the bachelor's chagrin. The man's servant, a homosexual, gets involved and settles the matter.

d&w, Enzo Millioni; ph, Carmillio Barzoni; ed, Otello Colangeli.

Drama **(PR:NR MPAA:NR)**

TENKU NO SHIRO LAPUTA (SEE: LAPUTA: CASTLES IN THE SKY, 1987, Jap.)

TENTAZIONE† (1987, It.) Cine Decima S.r.l./Film Int'l. c (Trans: Temptation)

Katrine Michelsen, Antonio Marsina, Olivia Link, Marzio Honorato.

Bizarre crime drama which sees an attractive widow who owns her own publicity agency fall in love with an ambitious employee. Although they plan to wed, the groom is suddenly distracted by a beautiful and equally ambitious model. The two begin a torrid affair and hatch a plan to kill their boss. The widow survives the attempt on her life and goes on the counter-attack by inviting her attempted killers to dinner, where she poisons them.

d&w, Sergio Bergonzelli (from a story by Sergio Bergonzelli, Enzo Gallo); ph, Roberto Girometti; m, Fabio Frizzi; ed, Sergio Bergonzelli, Luigi Gorini.

Crime/Thriller **(PR:NR MPAA:NR)**

TERESA† (1987, It.) 100m Intl. Dean-Dean-Reteitalia/Medusa c

Serena Grandi *(Teresa)*, Luca Barbareschi *(Gino)*, Eros Pagni *(Nabucco)*.

Grandi is the brawny independent woman whose truck driver husband dies and leaves her indebted to trucking firm owner Pagni. Rather than give in to Pagni, she assumes her husband's route, driving all over Italy with her co-driver Barbareschi. She and Barbareschi fall in love, despite Pagni's unfailing admiration. The jealous Barbareschi leaves, but they later reunite. Grandi now becomes the obsession of another, and once again the jealous Barbareschi leaves. Although Grandi still loves her co-driver, she decides to marry for money not love. While at the altar, however, she changes her mind and runs off with the waiting Barbareschi.

p, Pio Angeletti, Adriano De Micheli; d, Dino Risi; w, Bernardino Zapponi, Graziano Diana, Dino Risi; ph, Blasco Giurato (Eastmancolor); m, Claudio Maioli; ed, Alberto Galliti; art d, Fabio Vitale.

Romance **(PR:NR MPAA:NR)**

TERIREM† (1987, Gr.) 85m Greek Film Center c

Antonis Kafetzopoulos, Olia Lazaridou, Vassia Panagopoulou, Sophocles Pepas.

A young couple travel the country and entertain villagers by staging shadow-puppet shows, a dying art. The wife has been struck mute by a brain tumor which will someday kill her. In one small village they visit an old woman who has visions which lead her nephew to find an ancient icon buried in a field. He sells the icon to a pair of smugglers and they in turn murder the old woman because she knows too much. Meanwhile, the wife confesses to her husband that she has been unfaithful. He leaves her and begins an affair of his own. The despondent wife attempts suicide, but she is saved by a sympathetic monk. The wife attends the old woman's funeral and now she is the one who sees visions. The visions lead her to the spot where the icon was found and the monks find the bones of what they believe to be their patron saint buried at the site. The husband's affair goes badly and he returns to his wife to mend fences when he discovers that her tumor has been miraculously cured and her speech restored.

d&w, Apostolos C. Doxiadis; ph, Andreas Bellis; m, Dionyssis Savvopoulos; ed, G. Mavropsaridis, G. Panoussopoulos; art d, Alexis Kyritsopoulos.

Drama **(PR:NR MPAA:NR)**

TERMINAL EXPOSURE† (1987) 103m Omega c

Mark Hennessy, Scott King, Hope-Marie Carlton, Steve Donmeyer, Joe Phelan, Tara Buckman, Christina Cardan, Ted Lange, Patrick St. Esprit.

Michelangelo Antonioni's BLOW UP is the unlikely inspiration for this low-budget crime thriller shot in Venice Beach and Las Vegas. Hennessy and King play two California beach bums who spend most of their time snapping photos of scantily clad girls. One fine day they discover that they have inadvertently photographed a murder and the only clues they have are the face of the victim and the exquisite rear end of the murderess (*Playboy* playmate Hope-Marie Carlton), which sports a rose tattoo. Soon the photographer "dudes" find themselves emersed in a complicated web of intrigue involving strippers, hired assassins, surfers, blackmailers, skateboards, jet-skis, and the local mob. Given a brief play-off in Los Angeles early in 1987, TERMINAL EXPOSURE will no doubt debut nationally on home video.

p&d, Nico Mastorakis; w, Nico Mastorakis, Kirk Ellis (based on a story by Nico Mastorakis); ph, Cliff D. Ralke (Technicolor); m, Hans Zimmer; ed, Nico Mastorakis, Roger Tweten; prod d, Patricia Hall.

Crime **(PR:NR MPAA:NR)**

TERMINUS† (1987, Fr./Ger.) 115m CAT-Films du Cheval de Fer-Initial Groupe-CLB-Films A2/Hemdale c

Karen Allen *(Gus)*, Johnny Hallyday *(Stump [Manchot])*, Jurgen Prochnow *(Doctor/Monsieur/"Little Brother" Driver)*, Gabriel Damon *(Mati)*, Julie Glenn *(Princess)*, Louise Vincent *(Voice of "Monster")*, Dieter Schidor, Janos Kulka, Dominique Valera, Jean-Luc Montama, David Jalil, Andre Nocquet.

A futuristic international road game, computer-programmed trucks, and death-defying truck drivers add up to TERMINUS, directed by former cinematographer Glenn (DAY FOR NIGHT, STATE OF SEIGE, A LITTLE ROMANCE, COUP DE TORCHON). Allen is a Sigourney Weaveresque competitor who is put behind the wheel of "The Monster," a truck whose computer program has been designed by young whiz Damon. A malfunction sets her steering off-course into a wasteland overrun with sadistic thugs. She is captured, tortured, and killed (one-third of the way into the film). Taking over in the driver's seat is Hallyday, a fellow driver who met her briefly once while they were both in prison. In order to finish the competition, Hallyday must battle murderous hordes, other vehicles involved in the sport, and the demented organizer of the games, Prochnow. Although the film stars Johnny Hallyday, one of France's biggest pop singing stars, TERMINUS died a quick death at Paris theaters. Hemdale has acquired the US distribution rights, but with Allen dying in the first 40 minutes it doesn't seem to have much of an audience. Filmed both in French and English versions with a $6 million budget.

p, Anne Francois; d, Pierre-William Glenn; w, Patrice Duvic, Pierre-William Glenn, (based on an original story by Alain Gillot); ph, Jean-Claude Vicquery (Fujicolor); m, David Cunningham; ed, Thierry Derocles; art d, Alain Challier; cos, Jacqueline Moreau; makeup, Muriel Baurens; spec eff, Jacques Gastineau, Frederic Gastineau; stunts, Michel Norman;

Action/Science Fiction **(PR:NR MPAA:PG)**

TERNOSECCO† (1987, It.) C.G. Silver-RETEITALIA/Columbia Pictures Italia c (Trans: Jackpot)

Giancarlo Giannini, Victoria Abril, Lino Troisi, Franco Angrisano, Ugo Calise, Armando Brancia.

Giannini directs and stars in this crime drama about a man who marries the daughter of the local lottery merchant. When his father-in-law is found strangled, Giannini is accused of the crime and thrown in prison. While serving his sentence Giannini meets and befriends a powerful *Cammora* (Mafia) chieftain. The two grow very close, and when the man is poisoned and dies, Giannini inherits the throne. Once out of prison Giannini uses his power to go after rival gangs. Despite his successes, Giannini realizes that he cannot rid his town of all evil influences or, in fact, keep his wife from cheating on him. Seeking solace, Giannini returns to prison and the cell his friend had occupied.

d, Giancarlo Giannini; w, Lino Jannuzzi, Giancarlo Giannini; ph, Marcello Gatti (Technicolor); m, Antonio Infantino; ed, Franco Fraticelli.

Crime **(PR:NR MPAA:NR)**

TERRORIZERS, THE½** (1987, Taiwan) 109m Central Motion Picture c (KONBU FINZE)

Miaw Chian-Ren [Cora Miao], Lil Lih-Chyun, Jin Shyh-Jye, Wang An.

The third feature from director Yang is a ponderous, confusing, and overly complicated drama which presents three couples from very different backgrounds whose destinies collide through a series of coincidences. The film opens as the police raid the apartment hideout of a street gang. In a nearby apartment, a young photographer hears the commotion and runs out to get some good pictures. One member of the gang is killed, one is captured, and the teenaged girl friend of the captured man escapes with a twisted ankle. The photographer manages to get several pictures of the girl as she limps off. Later, the girl is picked up at a clinic by her estranged mother and is taken home where she is locked in her room. Bored, the girl begins making prank phone calls while her mother is at work. Meanwhile, the photographer becomes obsessed with the girl and plasters pictures of her all around his apartment. This causes a fight with his live-in girl friend and he leaves her to rent the apartment where the shoot-out took place. In another part of town we meet a married couple whose union is on the verge of collapse. The husband is a dull hospital employee who is jockeying for a promotion to section chief, while his wife is a successful novelist suffering writer's block. Bored with her husband, the novelist resumes an old affair. One day the phone rings and it is the gang girl making a prank call. The girl implies that she is having an affair with the woman's husband and tells the novelist to meet her at the apartment where the shoot-out took place. The novelist goes to the apartment, only to find the confused photographer. Although she has no proof that her husband is cheating, she moves out. The incident provides enough inspiration for her to write a novel about a similar situation which climaxes with the husband killing his wife, his lover, and then himself. The book is a hit and the writer wins several awards, although her husband hasn't read it. Meanwhile, the girl and her boy friend reunite and hit the streets. The girl pretends she is a prostitute, picks up men, and takes them to a hotel room where her boy friend suddenly appears and relieves the "johns" of their billfolds. At the same time, the photographer recognizes the novelist from a newspaper article and realizes that her book is partly based on the incident at his front door. He calls to tell her the truth, but gets the husband instead and tells him. Later that morning, the husband learns that he has failed to get his long-awaited promotion and his mind snaps. Convinced that his wife's book is true, he gets drunk, borrows a friend's pistol, and kills his boss. He then shoots his wife's lover, but cannot bring himself to kill her. Instead he wanders the city streets and is eventually picked up by the gang girl, who takes him to a hotel. Before her boy friend can burst in, there is a gunshot from the bathroom. As it turns out, the preceding torrent of violence was merely a dream/fantasy and the husband simply blew his brains out alone in his friend's bath, leaving all the other characters very much alive.

Although intelligently photographed and at times fairly interesting, THE TER-

RORIZERS moves at a very slow pace and is heavy on "atmosphere." Lengthy close-ups of dripping gutters, shots of empty rooms that seem to last an eternity, people silently staring out of windows, and lots and lots of strained silence are the order of the day here. There is a bare minimum of dialog, but unfortunately most of it comes from the novelist who constantly informs her husband and others that "fiction isn't reality" and no one should confuse the two (the photographer's girl friend echoes these sentiments as well). Yang drives this point home by fooling the audience into believing that the climactic slaughter fulfills the novel's prophecy and then revealing that it was all merely a dream/fantasy. While the "message" may be a bit mundane, the portrayal of several different strata of Taiwanese society is fascinating. The girl gang member, who is said to be Amerasian, is as cold and amoral as they come. She is a truly frightening character who barely says a word throughout the entire film. Also shown as cold and distant are the married couple. Both are so self-absorbed and career-minded that there is almost no communication between them and they play out their lives amid an tastefully designed, immaculately clean environment that is positively sterile. Only the struggling photographer—an observer who becomes an unwitting participant—seems to have a conscience, and it moves him to go back to his girl friend and start anew. Although much of the significance and subtlety of THE TERRORIZERS is no doubt lost on Western eyes, there is enough that is accessible to make a viewing worthwhile for those with patience enough to stay with it. There is little music in the film save for a recording of "Smoke Gets in Your Eyes" as performed by The Platters. *(Graphic violence, adult situations, profanity in subtitles.)*

p, Hsu Kuo-Liang; d, Edward Yang [Yang Dechang]; w, Sheau Yee, Edward Yang; ph, Chang Chan [Chang Yian]; ed, Liao Ching Sung; art d, Lai Ming-Tang.

Drama **(PR:O MPAA:NR)**

TERUG NAAR OEGSTGEEST† (1987, Neth.) 95m Movies Film Prods./Meteor Film c (Trans: Return to Oegstgeest)

Tom Jansen *(Father)*, Geert de Jong *(Mother)*, Cas Enklaar *(Jan)*, Leen Jongewaard *(Uncle Louis)*, Elise Hoomans *(Mother as Old Woman)*.

The latest feature from promising young Dutch director Van Gogh is an adaptation of what has been thought to be an unfilmable novel by Jan Wolkers (first published in 1965, now in its 28th edition). Anchored in the 1960s while the middle-aged main character tends to his dying father, the film unfolds in a series of flashbacks to his youth at the beginning of WW II. The contradictory Calvinist upbringing which combined moments of harsh discipline with moments of tenderness only serves to confuse Enklaar, who plays the main character as a young boy. He has a love-hate relationship with his demanding father, a lower middle-class grocer and patriarch of 11 children. Enklaar feels similarly about his older brother who always seems to be better at things than he is, reaping all the praise and attention. The youngster vents his frustrations on bugs and salamanders, controlling their fate as his father controls his. When Enklaar's brother is sent off to war and killed, the boy begins to comprehend the world around him and questions his faith in God.

p, Chris Brouwer, Haig Balian; d&w, Theo Van Gogh (based on the novel by Jan Wolkers); ph, Marc Felperlaan (Fuji AX); m, Rainer Hensel; ed, Willem Hoogenboom; art d, Harry Ammerlaan.

Drama **(PR:NR MPAA:NR)**

TESTAMENT D'UN POETE JUIF ASSASSINE† (1987, Fr.) 87m Feeling-La SEPT-Images des Anges-TF 1-Swan c (Trans: Testament of a Murdered Jewish Poet)

Michel Jonasz *(Paltiel Krossover)*, Erland Josephson *(Zupanev)*, Wojtek Pszoniak *(The judge)*, Philippe Leotard *(Bernard Hauptmann)*, Vincent David *(Grisha Kossover)*, Anne Zacharias *(Inge)*, Anne Wiazemsky *(Raissa Krossover)*, Moscu Alcalay *(Paltiel's Father)*, Laszlo Szabo *(Paul Hamburger)*.

Based on the novel by Elie Wiesel, this film stars French pop singer Jonasz as a Rumanian Jew of the 1950s who is sent to prison under Stalin, where he stays until his death. There he is forced by authorities to write his memoirs, which are later discovered by court registrar Josephson. Filmed in a flashback style as the son reads his father's writings while the prison is being destroyed by a wrecking crew.

p, Hubert Niogret; d, Franck Cassenti; w, Annie Mercier, Franck Cassenti (based on the novel by Elie Wiesel); ph, Patrick Blossier (Eastmancolor); m, Gabriel Yared; ed, Annie Mercier; art d, Yves Brover.

Drama **(PR:NR MPAA:NR)**

TESTET† (1987, Swed.) 92m A.Z.-Swedish Film Institute/Sandrews c (Trans: The Test)

Ann Zacharias *(The Woman)*, Jean-Francois Garreaud *(The Man)*.

Feminist *auteur* Zacharias wrote, produced, and directed this drama that examines how a man and woman react to the woman's unplanned pregnancy. (In French.)

p,d&w, Ann Zacharias; ph, Hans Schott (Eastmancolor); m, Eva Dahlgren, Andres Glenmark; ed, Jean-Paul Vauban; prod d, Ann Zacharias.

Drama **(PR:NR MPAA:NR)**

THEOFILOS† (1987, Gr.) 115m Greek Film Center c

Dimitris Katalifos, Stamatis Fassoulis, Dimitris Kaberidis, Irene Hadziconstanti, Thodoros Exarchos, Manos Stallakis.

A biography of Greek painter Theofilos Hadjimikhail (1868-1934), a man who rejected European influences in favor of the ancient Greek culture of myths and heroes. Hadjimikhail's work went unnoticed until after his death in the 1930s when art critic Stratis Elefteriadis brought his paintings to world prominence. Director Papastathis won the First Prize at the Thessaloniki Film Festival in 1972 for his documentary LETTERS FROM AMERICA.

p,d&w, Lakis Papastathis; ph, Thodoros Margas; m, Giorgios Papadakis; ed, Vagelis Goussias; art d&cos, Julia Stavridou.

Biography **(PR:NR MPAA:NR)**

THEY STILL CALL ME BRUCE½** (1987) 91m Ji Hee-Panda/Shapiro c

Johnny Yune *(Bruce Won)*, Robert Guillaume *(V.A. Officer)*, Pat Paulsen *(Psychiatrist)*, David Mendenhall *(Orphan)*, Carl Bensen *(Mr. B.)*, Joey Travolta, Bethany Wright, Don Gibb.

A sequel to THEY CALL ME BRUCE, this one is funnier and faster-moving than the first and proves that it is possible to make a follow-up film superior to the original. Yune, a "Seoul Man" comic who came to this country as a singer and made his living doing songs of all nations before discovering that he could also make people laugh, plays the role of a recently arrived Korean who has come to Texas to hand over a priceless gift to the G.I. who saved his life during the late unlamented Korean conflict. His command of English is feeble and that leaves a lot of room for humor as he mistakes US expressions and has verbal fun with them. Once in Houston, he goes to the Veterans Administration where he meets Guillaume (TV's "Benson" and a pal of Yune's), who gives Yune a list of people named "W. Brown" for him to trace. Yune has an antique vase about five centuries old and he is sworn to deliver it to the man who helped him so many years ago. In the course of events, he gets into trouble with some local Longhorn mobsters led by Bensen. He tries to help prostitute Wright, who works for Bensen, and gets mauled for his attempts. Soon enough, he winds up at a karate studio where he is hired to be a figurehead because the studio is in financial trouble, as it is run by a Caucasian. Although he has no ability in marital arts, he manages to fake it well enough, even in a climactic televised bout against a behemoth. He meets orphan Mendenhall and thus begins a relationship not unlike the one between Pat Morita and Ralph Macchio in both KARATE KID movies. Lots of quick sight gags and nonstop plays on words as Yune manages to fall in love with Wright, defeat the gangsters, help Mendenhall, and save the day.

Yune's deadpan delivery is perfect for the material (which he co-authored with director Orr) and the pace, which sometimes flags, is perked up by the uncredited supervision of Igo Kantor, the master editor who has saved many a movie in his day and takes no billing on screen. Pat Paulsen does a cute bit as a psychiatrist and John Travolta's brother, Joey, shows that he has a career in front of him. In essence it's a burlesque of all the Bruce Lee movies ever made. Several rip-offs starring people named "Bruce Li" or "Bruce Le" were shot, but those were straight chopsockey flicks. This one wants to be funny and is. The music by Morton Stevens helps to keep matters moving. The executive producer was Korean millionairess Ji Hee Choi, who is a pal of Yune's. In late 1987, yet another sequel was planned. If it is as superior to this one as THEY STILL CALL ME BRUCE is to its predecessor, audiences will be in for many laughs. *(Profanity, comic violence.)*

p,d&w, Johnny Yune, James Orr; ph, R. Michael Delahoussaye; m, Morton Stevens; ed, Roy Watts; art d, Jeff McManus.

Comedy **(PR:A-C MPAA:PG)**

THIN LINE, THE† (1987) 90m Bayani c

Andreas O. Loucka, Joseph Orlando, Jay Gonzalez *(Mr. Lee)*, Terri Prinz, Matt Mitler, Jill Cumer, Donna Davidge, Joseph Pacifico III, Francis Reilly, Greg Zaragoza.

"Like tightrope walkers without a net" the pair this film focuses on—a cop-turned-private eye and transsexual hooker—"precariously balance on the thin line," or so says the press release for this New York-made story of patient revenge. Gonzalez plays an ex-cop whose best friend, another policeman, was killed when both were on stakeout trying to nab an international creep. Two years later, Gonzalez, now a private investigator, goes under cover as a house detective at the hotel where his friend was killed and he was wounded, knowing that eventually the thug will return. Meanwhile, a transsexual prostitute who frequents the same hotel, tries to turn around her life. Eventually both end up in the same hotel room when Gonzalez rushes in to investigate her brutal murder of a john who went too far. This event is the beginning of the end for the prostitute, but it provides Gonzalez with a needed alibi: he has only moments before butchered the thug, who finally returned to the scene of the crime.

p, Ben Jordan; d, Andreas O. Loucka; w, Ben Jordan; ph, Renato Tonelli.

Crime **(PR:NR MPAA:NR)**

THIRTHAM† (1987, India)

Nedumudi Venu, Pallavi Joshi, Sari, Surasu, Murali, Thilakan.

A young man's alcoholism threatens to destroy his marriage. (In Malayalam.)

p, S. Prakash; d, Mohan.

Drama **(PR:NR MPAA:NR)**

THIRTY MILLION RUSH, THE† (1987, Hong Kong) 98m Cinema City Co. Ltd./Golden Princess c

Karl Maka, Lin Ching Hsia, Paula Tsui, Eric Tsang, Mark Cheng, Wong Ching, Lau Kar Leung.

A wild caper comedy from Hong Kong starring Tsang as a bank employee who cannot resist the fact that his financial institution plans to keep 30,000,000 in old bank notes locked up in a cremation station over the weekend to await destruction the following Monday. With dreams of an instant fortune dancing in his head, Tsang recruits old friends Cheng and Leung to help him plan a robbery. Unfortunately for the conspirators, a dedicated nun, Lin Ching Hsia, has gotten wind of the plan and sets out on a holy mission to stop the robbery and save their souls.

p, Wellington Fung; d, Karl Maka; ph, Bob Thompson, Andrew Lau; m, Alvin Kwok; ed, Tony Chow, Wong Ming Lam; art d, Vincent Wai.

Comedy/Crime **(PR:NR MPAA:NR)**

THIRUMATHI ORU VEGUMATHI† (1987,India) c

Pandya, S.V. Sekhar, Jayashree, Kokila, Kalpana.

(In Tamil.)

p, K. Balachander; d, Visu; m, Shanker Ganesh.

Drama **(PR:NR MPAA:NR)**

THIS IS NOT OUR DESTINATION† (1987, India) 132m c

Manohar Singh *(Shamsher Singh)*, Habib Tanvir *(Akhtor Baig)*, B.M. Shah *(Murli Manohar Joshi)*.

This directorial debut for Sudhir Mishra focuses on the experiences of three aging Indians who participated in the struggle for independence. As the three classmates return to celebrate the 100th anniversary of their alma mater, student demonstrations are taking place in the city. Singh, Tanvir, and Shah travel from Bombay to their old university in Rajpur and eventually each of them admits that he temporarily turned traitor for the British at one point. Meanwhile, in a show of solidarity, students join factory workers who are striking because unsafe conditions have led to a fire that killed many of their coworkers. Push comes to shove and the protesters attack the building and the thugs who protect it for the management, leaving the elderly trio to wonder if things have really changed in the 40 years since independence was won.

p,d&w, Sudhir Mishra; ph, Devlin Bose; m, Rajat Dholakla, prod d, Robin Das.

Drama **(PR:NR MPAA:NR)**

THOSE DEAR DEPARTED† (1987, Aus.) 90m Village-Roadshow c

Garry McDonald *(Max Falcon)*, Pamela Stephenson *(Marilyn Falcon)*, Su Cruickshank *(Norda Thompson)*, Marian Dworakowski *(Richard Kowalski)*, John Clarke *(Inspector Jerry)*, Ignatius Jones *(Phil Rene)*, Antonia Murphy *(Phoebe Furlong)*, Graeme Blundell *(Dr. Howie)*, Arthur Dignam *(The Producer)*, Jonathon Biggins *(Sgt. Steve)*, Patrick Cook *(Tristan)*, Maureen O'Shaughnessy *(Bronwyn)*.

A ghost story/comedy from down under, THOSE DEAR DEPARTED offers, among other amusements, a musical-within-the-film based on the life of Sigmund Freud. Its star, McDonald (a well-know Aussie television comedian), has several scrapes with death, but, though he doesn't know it, these aren't accidents. His wife, Stephenson, and their chauffeur, Dworakowski, who also happens to be her lover, are trying to get McDonald out of the way. After flubbing an assassination attempt, failing to do him in with a giant phallus, and poisoning McDonald's manager (Cruickshank) instead of the star, they finally eliminate McDonald from their lives . . . or do they? The actor finds himself in an odd theater-like place that is neither heaven nor earth, a place where souls like him with unresolved business back in the mortal world prepare to stage comebacks of sorts. Accompanied by his similarly stranded father and Cruickshank, McDonald heads earthward as a ghost and pays back the adulterous murderers in full.

p, Phillip Emanuel; d, Ted Robinson; ph, David Burr (Eastmancolor); m, Phil Scott; ed, Robert Gibson; prod d, Roger Ford.

Comedy **(PR:NR MPAA:NR)**

THOU SHALT NOT KILL . . . EXCEPT† (1987) 94m Action Pictures Prod./Filmworld c

Brian Schulz *(Sgt. Jack Stryker)*, John Manfredi *(Miller)*, Robert Rickman *(Jackson)*, Tim Quill *(Tyler)*, Sam Raimi *(Cult Leader)*, Cheryl Hanson *(Sally, Stryker's Girl)*, Perry Mallette *(Otis)*, Rick Hudson *(Kennel Owner)*, Connie Craig, Ivih Fraser, Terry Brumfield *(Cult Girls)*, Ted Raimi *(Rubber Mask)*, Al Johnson *(Huge Biker)*, Kirk Haas *(Leather Vest)*, Glen Barr *(Archer)*, Gary O'Conner *(Green)*, Sayle Jackunas *(Eddie Munster)*, Dave Gerney *(Van Crazy)*, Scott Mitchell *(Philo Crazy)*.

Independent gore film from Detroit, produced by the EVIL DEAD team and featuring EVIL DEAD director Sam Raimi in a supporting role. Vietnam veteran Schulz returns from the front to renew his relationship with his sweetheart, Hanson. Their happiness is shattered, however, when Hanson is kidnaped by a Charles Manson-type family of hippies led by Raimi. Predictably, it is up to Schulz and his Army buddies to hunt down the creeps and rescue Hanson. Filmed in Michigan during the summer of 1985, THOU SHALT NOT KILL . . . EXCEPT received a regional release in Detroit in 1987 and will surely find its audience on home video.

p, Scott Spiegel; d, Josh Becker; w, Josh Becker, Scott Spiegel (based on a story by Josh Becker, Sheldon Lettich, Bruce Campbell); m, Joseph Lo Duca; spec eff, Gary Jones.

Horror **(PR:NR MPAA:NR)**

THREE BEWILDERED PEOPLE IN THE NIGHT† (1987) 92m Desperate Pictures bw

Darcy Marta *(Alicia)*, Mark Howell *(David)*, John Lacques *(Craig)*.

An unexpected prizewinner at the Locarno Film Festival, this ultra-low-budget American independent film (shot for $3,000) is about the interconnected lives of three people in their mid-twenties who struggle with their ideas of life, love, sex, work, and art. Marta is a video artist who lives with journalist/actor Lacques and whose best friend is homosexual performance artist Howell. As the characters wander during the night from coffee shops to galleries to apartments to vacant streets, their personal lives get more and more tangled, leading to heterosexual versus homosexual pressures. Shot on a 16mm Bolex camera without synchronous sound, this film marks another success for the anti-Hollywood movement of independent filmmakers (Jon Jost and Jim Jarmusch have had similar triumphs). The Locarno Film Festival showered THREE BEWILDERED PEOPLE with awards: the International Jury presented a Bronze Leopard to producer/director/writer/photographer/editor Araki for "his artistic use of technical means," the FIPRESCI jury awarded it a shared first prize for a "debuting filmmaker whose invention transcends his material means," and the Youth Jury awarded it the second prize for "its challenge to conventional production means." The film has received only festival showings in the US. *(Sexual situations, profanity.)*

d,w,ph&ed, Gregg Araki.

Drama **(PR:O MPAA:NR)**

THREE FOR THE ROAD* (1987) 88m Vista/New Century-Vista c

Charlie Sheen *(Paul Tracy)*, Kerri Green *(Robin Kitteridge)*, Alan Ruck *(Tommy "T.S.")*, Sally Kellerman *(Blanche, Robin's Mother)*, Blair Tefkin *(Missy)*, Raymond J. Barry *(Sen. Kitteridge)*, Alexa Hamilton *(Virginia)*, Bert Remsen *(Stu)*, James Avery *(Clarence)*.

Like a pair of well-worn, scuffed shoes, THREE FOR THE ROAD begs for feet and movement and gets neither from unimaginative director Norton who has hacked out such mediocrities as MORE AMERICAN GRAFFITI. Sheen, who made this film before PLATOON, is the ambitious junior aide to senator Barry and doesn't question his mentor's slippery machinations, not the least of which concerns his teenage daughter, Green. Barry asks Sheen to drive Green, a troublesome girl, to a southern psychiatric clinic which is no more than a reformatory, to get her out of his hair so that she won't cause him embarrassment in an upcoming political campaign. Sheen blithely accepts the assignment and takes off with Green in Barry's Mercedes-Benz. With them goes Sheen's friend Ruck and for most of the movie these two are plagued by the antics of Green who keeps trying to escape from them. Sheen actually has a pair of handcuffs to restrain Green, given him by the cruel Barry who turns out to be a child beater. Instead of delivering Green to the reformatory, Sheen finds compassion for the girl, a rather sweet young lady who obviously posed no threat whatsoever to Barry, and takes her to her loving and understanding mother, Kellerman. There's not much more to this empty-headed programmer except that Sheen gives a commendable performance with what little characterization is provided by the lame script. Green is fetching and Ruck engaging, but Norton's inept direction undoes their efforts. Not worth the effort. *(Profanity.)*

p, Herb Jaffe, Mort Engelberg; d, B.W.L. Norton; w, Richard Martini, Tim Metcalfe, Miguel Tejada-Flores (based on a story by Richard Martini); ph, Steve Posey (DeLuxe color); m, Barry Goldberg; ed, Christopher Greenbury; prod d, Linda Allen; art d, William Buck; set d, Linda Allen; cos, Hillary Wright.

Drama **Cas.** **(PR:C MPAA:PG)**

THREE KINDS OF HEAT† (1987) 87m Cannon c (AKA: FIREWORKS)

Robert Ginty *(Elliot Cromwell)*, Victoria Barrett *(Sgt. Terry O'Shea)*, Shakti *(Maj. Shan)*, Sylvester McCoy *(Harry Pimm)*, Barry Foster *(George Norris)*, Jeannie Brown *(Angelica)*, Paul Gee, Malcolm Connell, Trevor Martin, Mary Tamm, Keith Edwards, Jack Hedley, Bridget Khan.

The first film shot at Britain's famed Elstree Studios since Cannon purchased the lot, THREE KINDS OF HEAT never found a theatrical release and instead went straight to home video late in 1987. Ginty stars as a state department agent who must team up with female New York City cop Barrett and Hong Kong policewoman Shakti to track down dangerous Chinese mobster, McCoy. The action begins in New York and moves to London before climaxing with a shoot-out in a warehouse full of explosives. Writer-director Stevens made his name in television with such shows as "Outer Limits," "Name of the Game," and "It Takes a Thief."

p, Michael J. Kagan; d&w, Leslie Stevens; ph, Terry Cole (Rank Color); m, Michael Bishop, Scott Page; ed, Bob Dearberg; prod d, Duncan Cameron; art d, Alan Hunter Craig; set d, Robyn Hamilton-Doney; spec eff, John Gant; stunts, Peter Diamond.

Action/Crime **Cas.** **(PR:NR MPAA:R)**

THREE MEN AND A BABY½** (1987) 99m Touchstone-Silver Screen Partners III-Jean Francois Lepetit-Interscope Communications/BV c

Tom Selleck *(Peter Mitchell, Architect)*, Steve Guttenberg *(Michael Kellam, Cartoonist)*, Ted Danson *(Jack Holden, Actor)*, Nancy Travis *(Sylvia, Actress)*, Margaret Colin *(Rebecca)*, Lisa Blair, Michelle Blair *(Mary, Baby)*, Celeste Holm *(Mrs. Holden, Jack's Mother)*, Philip Bosco *(Detective Melkowitz)*, Derek de Lint *(Jan Clopatz, Conductor)*, Paul Guilfoyle *(Vince)*, Alexandra Amini *(Patty)*, Francine Beers *(Woman at Gift Shop)*, Barbara Budd *(Dramatic Actress)*, Michael Burgess *(Handsome Man at Party)*, Claire Cellucci *(Angelyne)*, Eugene Clark *(Man at Party)*, Michele Duquet *(Tawnya)*, David Ferry *(Telephone Installer)*, David Foley *(Grocery Store Clerk)*, Cynthia Harris *(Mrs. Hathaway)*, Earl Hindman *(Satch)*, Mario Joyner *(Cab Driver)*, Edward D. Murphy *(Security Guard)*, Jaqueline Murphy *(Gate Attendant)*, Colin Quinn *(Gift Shop Clerk)*, Thomas Quinn *(Mounted Policeman)*, Jackie Richardson *(Edna)*, John Gould Rubin *(Paul Milner)*, Camilla Scott *(Cherise)*, Daniele Scott *(Swimming Instructor)*, Sharolyn Sparrow *(Vanessa)*, Louise Vallance *(Sally)*, Jonathan Whitaker *(Adam)*, Christine Kossak *(One of Jack's Girls)*, Gary Klar, Joe Lynn *(Detectives)*.

Selleck, Danson, and Guttenberg are three swinging bachelors who share an opulent penthouse apartment in Manhattan. Selleck and Guttenberg are successful career men, the former a busy architect, the latter a cartoonist, the creator of a popular comic strip called "Johnny Cool." Danson is a not-so-successful actor, but of the three, he's the biggest hit with the ladies. After a title sequence which establishes that the bachelors all enjoy lives of unending frolic, the film opens in the apartment with a huge party in progress. One of the guests is a director of television commercials for whom Danson has worked and who asks a little favor of the actor. The director has to leave town early the next day (Sunday) and won't be home to accept a package. He asks if it's all right if the package is delivered to Danson's apartment and kept until Thursday when it will be picked up, an arrangement Danson finds agreeable. The next morning, however, Danson departs for the airport to catch a plane to Turkey where he will spend the next 10 weeks making a film. He has forgotten to tell his roommates about the package, so he calls from the airport to let them know it's coming, instructing them to "toss it aside" until it's picked up on Thursday. Shortly thereafter, Selleck opens the front door and is stunned to find a baby girl in a bassinet. He quickly closes the door and summons the sleeping Guttenberg to the scene. Upon further investigation, they find a note informing them that Danson is the father of the child and the mother, someone named Sylvia, is leaving it in his care. Selleck and Guttenberg assume this is the "package" Danson was talking about and are appalled at his cavalier attitude toward the matter. The baby begins crying and panic swiftly sets in as the two bachelors realize they've got to take care of the child. Selleck bolts for the supermarket to get food and other baby supplies, while Guttenberg vainly tries to stem the flow of tears. While Selleck is out, Harris, the building's manager, visits the apartment and gives Guttenberg a small package which has arrived in the lobby for Danson. Guttenberg is too preoccupied with quieting the child to pay much attention, and simply tosses the package aside, forgetting about it. Selleck returns with bags full of baby food, formula, bottles, child-rearing books, and diapers, and the two men immediately begins a hands-on course in baby care. Naturally, this begins with a disastrous attempt at diaper changing, and includes some rather unorthodox bathing and feeding procedures. They put all the other aspects of their lives on hold and somehow survive the ordeal until Thursday arrives and two men show up at the apartment to pick up the "package." Selleck and Guttenberg turn the child over to the visitors, who seem bewildered but depart. An uneasy Selleck then sits down on the sofa and finds there, behind a cushion, the package which Harris had given to Guttenberg on Sunday. He shows it to Guttenberg, and they simultaneously realize the mistake they've made. Selleck takes the package and bolts from the apartment and down the stairs after the baby. Along the way he trips, the package opens, and little packets filled with white powder fall out. He stuffs the packets in his suit pocket and gets outside in time to find the two men struggling to figure out how to get the bassinet into their sports car. A mounted policemen arrives and, noting that the car is parked illegally, asks the driver for his registration. The two men quickly drive off, leaving Selleck with the baby. The officer now wants to see Selleck's identification and accompanies him to his apartment where Selleck has left his wallet. While retrieving his wallet, Selleck gives the drugs to Guttenberg, telling him to hide them. In the meantime, Bosco, a police sergeant who seems to have been tailing the men who came for the package, arrives and begins questioning Selleck. He finally leaves, but it's apparent that the surrogate fathers are now suspected of being part of a drug ring. Further adding to their troubles, the drug smugglers believe they have been double-crossed, and while Selleck and Guttenberg are out, they ransack the apartment looking for the real package. Before any of this can be resolved, Danson returns, his film part and his stay in Turkey cut short. At first he denies being the baby's father, but then he recalls that a year and a half earlier he had done a play in England and had a brief fling there with an actress named Sylvia. Guttenberg and Selleck are still angry at Danson over the turmoil his indiscretion has caused and they quickly shift responsibility for the baby's care to him. He looks to his mother, Holm, for help, but she declines, telling him he's been running from responsibility all his life, and now it's time to stop running. Much like his roommates, Danson's a little uncomfortable and unsure of himself with the child, but it's soon apparent that all three are growing quite attached to the baby and taking more than a little pleasure in caring for her. They still have the cops and the drug smugglers to worry about, however. They concoct a scheme whereby they hand over the drugs to the criminals in a meeting which Guttenberg captures on videotape and during which the dialog makes it apparent they are free from guilt. The crooks are arrested, the tape exonerates the three heroes, and all is well, until Mom returns. Sylvia (Travis) shows up at the apartment to explain that she found the demands of trying to care for the child while struggling to make it as an actress were too much, which is why she abandoned the baby. But being away from the baby was unbearable and she now plans to return to England and move in with her parents while pursuing her career. Though saddened, the three bachelors see mother and child off in a taxi then repair to the apartment to drown their sorrows. That evening, Danson decides he can't let the baby go and the three men dash off to the airport, only to arrive just as the flight to London is departing. The sullen trio returns to the apartment, where they find Travis and baby waiting. All agree they want to keep the baby and they invite Travis to move in as well, so, at the film's end, it's a happy three men, a woman, and a baby.

In remaking the 1985 French film TROIS HOMMES ET UN COUFFIN (Three Men and a Cradle), which was nominated for an Academy Award for Best Foreign Film, director Nimoy (STAR TREK IV: THE VOYAGE HOME) and screenwriters Cruickshank and Orr (TOUGH GUYS) strived to make this movie as faithful as possible to the original. One wonders why. The French film came complete with the farcical subplot involving the drugs and the cops, and, while it may have worked in the original, it is completely useless here, serving only to bog the film down for long passages. Not that there's anything of great consequence going on in the rest of the film, but what is there is cute and cute is what this movie is all about. In fact, it is relentless in its pursuit of cute, offering us scenes such as Selleck reading, in very hushed tones, an account of a boxing match from a sports magazine as his version of a "bedtime story"; Danson showering with the baby and singing "My Girl" to her; the baby wearing a tiny pink hard hat when she accompanies Selleck to one of his building sites; and the high point of heart-tugging cuteness, when all three men gather around the crib one evening and sing the baby to sleep with a rendition of "Goodnight Sweetheart." It's all very calculated, but in this instance the calculations were evidently correct, as the film proved to be enormously popular with the movie-going public. As for the leads, they acquit themselves fairly well. The babies (the child was portrayed by twins Lisa and Michelle Blair) are, in a word, cute. Guttenberg seems to function best within an ensemble (see DINER), so this was a good opportunity for him and he does well as the most emotional member of the group. The roles Selleck and Danson play are largely extensions of their television characters, which is understandable since much of the film's popularity is no doubt derived from curious TV fans who want to see how Thomas Magnum (Selleck's character on "Magnum, P.I.") and Sam Malone (Danson's character on "Cheers") are going to act around a baby. Danson, who is missing for much of the film, plays the vain, irresponsible, and not-too-bright ladies' man quite well, and here also shows he can do cute when there's a baby in the vicinity. Clearly the biggest winner in all this, though, is Selleck. Films in which he has starred (HIGH ROAD TO CHINA, LASSITER, RUNAWAY) could only charitably be labeled disappointing, but now he has a certified hit on his hands. Much of the credit for the picture's success is due him and a good deal of critical praise has come his way. Though tall, athletic, and handsome, he does maintain a certain appealing modesty and warmth, and that, along with his knack for light comedy, were all put to good use in this vehicle, and will certainly be exploited in other projects. Of course, the overwhelming box-office success of this film virtually assures a sequel will be made, so look for "Three Men and a Toddler" or something of that ilk to be making the rounds in the near future. *(Mild profanity, sexual situations.)*

p, Ted Field, Robert W. Cort, Edward Teets; d, Leonard Nimoy; w, James Orr, Jim Cruickshank (based on the French film TROIS HOMMES ET UN COUFFIN by Coline Serreau); ph, Adam Greenberg (Deluxe Color); m, Marvin Hamlisch; ed, Michael A. Stevenson; prod d, Peter Larkin; art d, Dan Yarhi; set d, Hilton Rosemarin, Justin Scoppa, Jr.; cos, Larry Wells; spec eff, Michael Kavanagh; makeup, Barbara Palmer, Lon Bentley, Barbara Kelly.

Comedy **(PR:A-C MPAA:PG)**

THREE O'CLOCK HIGH** (1987) 97m UNIV c

Casey Siemaszko *(Jerry Mitchell)*, Anne Ryan *(Franny Perrins)*, Stacey Glick *(Brei Mitchell)*, Jonathan Wise *(Vincent Costello)*, Richard Tyson *(Buddy Revell)*, Jeffrey Tambor *(Mr. Rice)*, Liza Morrow *(Karen Clarke)*, John P. Ryan *(Mr. O'Rourke)*, Philip Baker Hall *(Detective Mulvahill)*.

The ingredients here include: the hottest new director in Hollywood; the flashy camerawork of the hottest new cinematographer in Hollywood; a pulsating technopop soundtrack; an accomplished cast of young actors; the moral support of Steven Spielberg; the financial backing of Universal Studios. There's only one thing missing—a script. All this adds up to THREE O'CLOCK HIGH, the debut feature from *wunderkind* 25-year-old Phil Joanou. The story, for what it's worth, is about a nerdy high school kid, Siemaszko, who works for the school newspaper. His first assignment is to cover the arrival of a new student. Normally, the arrival of a new student is not news, but this student would make The Terminator cower in the corner. Played by Tyson as a leather-jacketed Charlie Manson sort of bully, the new kid has a violent reputation which has led to his dismissal from several schools. Weaver High, however, has no objections to accepting the lad. When Siemaszko approaches Tyson for an interview, he touches the lug's arm as a gesture of friendship, unaware that Tyson HATES to be touched. Tyson informs the wimpy cub reporter that he'll meet him at 3 o'clock in the school parking lot for a fight. The rest of the film is HIGH NOON meets THE BREAKFAST CLUB—Siemaszko nervously awaiting the 3 o'clock bell while a number of generic subplots with generic high schoolers pad out the running time. Siemaszko tries desperately to get out of the showdown. He makes an effort to hire a jock bodyguard, then tries to get himself in detention, all to no avail. Finally the clock strikes 3:00. The showdown begins. Siemaszko puts on a pair of brass knuckles and clobbers his Goliath. That's all folks!

Obviously aware that he was hung out to dry with an awful, non-existent script, Joanou tries to make up for this handicap with some startling camerawork by Barry Sonnenfeld (BLOOD SIMPLE, RAISING ARIZONA). The camera zooms, tracks, dollies, and pans with fierce speed. Fast-motion and slow-motion are used to full effect. Exaggerated lighting and odd camera angles are ever present. Much of it is overdone and flashy in an irresponsible film school manner, but the result is one in which Joanou's visual style transcends the vapid script. Unlike the recent success stories of Spike Lee (who privately funded SHE'S GOTTA HAVE IT) or Robert Townsend (who charged his film on a wallet full of credit cards)—both of whom were courted by Hollywood *after* their first features—Joanou was being dubbed "the next Spielberg" even *before* his first film. As a student as USC in 1984, Joanou shook things up with his student film LAST CHANCE DANCE, a 31-minute movie which he was pressured into cutting to 20 minutes to meet with department guidelines. After bending the rules a bit too much, USC tried to keep Joanou from entering his film in the school's industry screening. Joanou hired a lawyer and was able to reverse USC's decision. As a result, his film was seen by Steven Spielberg's story editor. Spielberg then hired Joanou to direct two episodes of his television series "Amazing Stories"—"The Mission" and "The Doll," the latter earning John Lithgow an Emmy. On Spielberg's advice, Joanou accepted Universal's offer to direct a script (then called "After School") which was brought to the studio by Aaron Spelling. While not eager to work as a director-for-hire, Joanou accepted—a decision which may not have been the wisest, but which at least gave him experience that most 25-year-olds never get. Filmed for $5.9 million at Ogden High School in Ogden, Utah, the film is one of the best examples of "style over content" ever. One only hopes that, in the future, Joanou will have a script to work with, instead of an overextended sketch for a television show. *(Violence, profanity.)*

p, David E. Vogel; d, Phil Joanou; w, Richard Christian Matheson, Thomas Szollosi; ph, Barry Sonnenfeld; m, Tangerine Dream; ed, Joe Anne Fogle; prod d, Bill Matthews, Tom Bugenhaven.

Comedy **(PR:C MPAA:PG-13)**

THROW MOMMA FROM THE TRAIN**½ (1987) 88m Orion c

Danny DeVito *(Owen Lift)*, Billy Crystal *(Larry Donner)*, Anne Ramsey *(Momma)*, Kim Greist *(Beth)*, Kate Mulgrew *(Margaret, Larry's Ex-Wife)*, Branford Marsalis *(Lester)*, Rob Reiner *(Joel)*, Bruce Kirby, Oprah Winfrey, Joey DePinto, Annie Ross, Raye Birk.

The diminutive Danny DeVito has catapulted from television star to mega-hit movie star (ROMANCING THE STONE, RUTHLESS PEOPLE, TIN MEN) and now adds directing to his list of accomplishments. Making a surprisingly assured directorial debut that is hampered only by a weak script, DeVito stars as a childlike 40-year-old bachelor whose life is totally dominated by his mean-spirited mother, Ramsey. DeVito has become so frustrated with his momma that he imagines poisoning her soda and plunging a pair of scissors into her ear. Harboring a desire to be a writer, DeVito enrolls in a creative writing class at the local junior college. The course is taught by Crystal, a hapless would-be writer whose ex-wife (Mulgrew) ran off with his only completed manuscript, sold it as her own, and is now a millionaire living in Hawaii and making appearances on "Oprah!" Ever since his divorce Crystal has been gripped by a crippling bout of writer's block which has left him unable to complete the sentence "The night was . . . " Perpetually distracted from his class and his girl friend (Greist), Crystal has little interest in the pesky DeVito's dogged attempts at prose (basically three-page murder mysteries with only two characters). Finally setting aside some time to counsel DeVito on the fundamentals of character motivation and plausible plots, Crystal recommends that he see Hitchcock's STRANGERS ON A TRAIN for inspiration. DeVito is enthralled with the movie and delighted by the way the characters "swap" murders, with each of them killing someone the other wants dead, thus committing an unmotivated crime that cannot be traced. Recalling Crystal's hatred for his ex-wife (he had publicly exclaimed that he wished "she were dead"), DeVito gets it into his head that the teacher has offered to "swap" murders with him: DeVito's momma for Crystal's ex-wife. Without so much as discussing it with Crystal, DeVito runs off to Hawaii and pushes Mulgrew off a ferry boat. Horrified when he learns of the deed (because he's the main suspect in his ex-wife's disappearance), Crystal attempts to distance himself from the crazy little man but instead finds himself holed up at DeVito's house to avoid the police. Strangely, the more time Crystal spends with DeVito, the more he comes to like the pathetic, childlike man. He also grows to hate the whining, demanding, and vulgar Ramsey. Crystal finally decides to make a dash for Mexico, but finds himself sharing a compartment with DeVito and Ramsey. When Ramsey nonchalantly comes up with a finish for the sentence Crystal has been trying to write for months ("The night was . . . sultry"), his mind snaps and he tries to kill the old woman by throwing her from the train. After years of fantasizing her death, DeVito is suddenly faced with the reality of his momma's impending demise and has a change of heart. He runs off to save her, only to find that Crystal has gotten a grip on himself and decided not to kill her after all. Crystal accidentally falls off the train, and after awakening in a hospital bed, he finds that Mulgrew is not dead after all, but had been rescued by a fisherman. Inspired by his bizarre escapade with DeVito, Crystal pounds out a novel based on the incident and one year later the book becomes a big hit. DeVito, whose momma subsequently died of natural causes, also writes a book, a children's pop-up book detailing how he and Crystal became lifelong friends.

After beginning as a promising black comedy, THROW MOMMA FROM THE TRAIN deteriorates into a repetitive and ultimately treacly affair that betrays the brazen nastiness with which it began. Veteran television writer Silver's script merely spins its wheels after the supposed murder of Mulgrew. Despite its brief running time, the film seems much longer because not much happens in the last 45 minutes other than Crystal's attempts to delay killing DeVito's momma. Much to his credit, director DeVito does what he can with the material, contributing a surprisingly mature visual style to the proceedings (a good deal of credit must also go to RAISING ARIZONA cinematographer Sonnenfeld). Filmed in the style of Hitchcock, but with few of the shot-for-shot *hommages* that so many other filmmakers resort to, DeVito's film demonstrates a good understanding of the medium, and he contributes several clever transition sequences that are technically dazzling. DeVito also includes some inspired nuttiness that adds a much needed spark to the comedic proceedings, including the scene at the breakfast table where he conks Crystal on the head with a frying pan (used in the trailer), a running gag involving a variety of bizarre Hawaiian phone booths, and DeVito's hilarious throwaway line—"Look! Cows!"—when he spots a billboard for a local dairy during a discussion of mayhem and murder.

DeVito also does a nice job modulating his own performance, managing to evoke sympathy for his loony character without relying too heavily on simple sentimentality. Crystal, sadly, is hampered by a script that limits him to spells of griping, whining, and full-blown hysteria. Ramsey, who was so memorable in a brief appearance as Nick Nolte's mother in WEEDS, makes an unforgettably hateful wretch (although the filmmakers inject her with small doses of saccharine to make her more palatable). Mulgrew does a superb job as the smug ex-wife and saxophonist/composer Marsalis is likable as Crystal's buddy. Greist is wasted, as usual, in a small role that does not allow her much screen time. A runaway hit at the box office, THROW MOMMA FROM THE TRAIN will certainly allow DeVito the chance to direct again. *(Adult situations, sexual situations, cartoon violence, profanity.)*

p, Larry Brezner; d, Danny DeVito; w, Stu Silver; ph, Barry Sonnenfeld (CFI Color); m, David Newman; ed, Michael Jablow; prod d, Ida Random; art d, William Elliott; set d, Anne D. McCulley; cos, Marilyn Vance-Straker.

Comedy **(PR:C-O MPAA:PG-13)**

THUNDER WARRIOR II† (1987) 93m Fulvia Films Intl./Trans World Ent. c

Mark Gregory *(Thunder)*, Bo Svenson *(Sheriff Roger)*, Raimund Harmstorf *(Rusty)*, Karen Reel *(Sheena)*, William Rice, Vic Roych, Clayton Tevis, Mike Bower, Rex Blackwell, Dennis O'Reilly.

The sequel to last year's straight-to-home-video release sees imprisoned Indian chief Gregory pardoned by the governor of Arizona for crimes committed in THUNDER WARRIOR I and appointed deputy sheriff to sheriff Svenson, the very man who had tracked him down. Svenson, however, is not the real problem, for his other deputy, Harmstorf, is a vile and corrupt creature who leads a profitable drug smuggling ring on the side. When Gregory comes close to uncovering the scheme, Harmstorf frames the Indian for murder and has him sent back to prison. Not one to take things lying down, Gregory escapes and goes after Harmstorf, precipitating many a chase scene through picturesque Monument Valley. Be warned that Italian "Larry Ludman" (Fabrizio De Angelis) has THUNDER WARRIOR III already in production.

d, Larry Ludman [Fabrizio De Angelis]; w, David Parker, Jr., Larry Ludman [Fabrizio De Angelis]; ph, Sergio D'Offizi (Technicolor); m, Walter Ritz; ed, Albert Moryalty; art d, Alexander M. Colby; stunts, Alain Petit.

Action **Cas.** **(PR:NR MPAA:NR)**

TICKET* (1987, S. Korea) 100m Jimi/Motion Picture Promotion Corp. c

Kim Ji-Mi, An So-Young, Lee Heh-Young, Chun Se-Young.

Three adolescent girls from Seoul become prostitutes in a small Korean fishing village, working out of a quaintly disguised teahouse near the harbor. The strict madam (Kim Ji-Mi) informs them that their primary duty is to satisfy the sexual demands of her "tickets," the bored fishermen of the town. Immediately, the young girls are turned loose in an attempt to enliven the lackluster trade. Although quite immature, two of the girls adapt to the demands of the life-style with relative ease. The third, however, is prone to fits of depression and violence, and yearns to be with her boy friend, a student at a distant university. When he occasionally slips into town, she is completely absorbed with him and ignores her job. Kim Ji-Mi reacts harshly when she learns of the new girl's unwillingness to perform during these periods, and metes out additional "tickets" as punishment. When the student informs his girl friend that he is dropping out of school and will be forced to stop his visits, she becomes disconsolate. Only the closeness she develops with the other girls saves her from complete despair. Her two friends from Seoul, on the other hand, view their employment as a stepping stone to the glamourous film industry. Yet their inexperience frequently leaves them unprepared for the duplicity of the shadowy adult world. One of them is mistakenly led to believe she will gain instant stardom if she sleeps with an aging actor, while the other is tricked by a "ticket" in a hotel room, and left to pay the bill. The girls become increasingly restless with their work and Kim Ji-Mi's unrelenting demands. The would-be actresses squabble over the affections of a favorite client, while their lovelorn friend retreats into solitude when she learns that she is pregnant and has contracted a form of venereal disease. Kim Ji-Mi instructs her to have an abortion once the disease has been cured so she can continue working, but the madam is dismayed when there are no more requests for the young prostitute's services. Kim Ji-Mi then receives a unexpected sum of money from a mysterious former lover whom she has not seen in ten years. When she meets him on a hillside above Seoul, she learns the gift is an attempt to compensate her for his lack of attention, though he is unwilling to rekindle the affair. Kim Ji-Mi rejects the money and later drunkenly returns to her girls. In the meantime, the student orders his distraught girl friend to abort the child, then strikes her when she refuses. An angered Kim Ji-Mi charges after him, forcibly removes him from a bus, and shoves him into the nearby harbor, where she thrashes him until he sinks into the depths of the sea. Later, Kim Ji-Mi is visited by one of the girls as she lies in a hospital bed recovering from her nervous breakdown. Her conscience is soothed when she learns that not only have all the girls persevered during her absence but that her victim has miraculously survived the attack and is now repentant.

Im Kwon-t'aek, a frequent director of South Korean films, has attempted to fashion a look at prostitution—one of only a handful of options, the film suggests, for adolescent employment in South Korea. While the film offers some interesting plot devices, it does so without concern for credibility and behavioral insight. Instead, the director and scriptwriter Song Kil-han have opted for a stereotypical approach to the tale that features superficial characters, obvious dialog, and an endless supply of blatant reaction shots. The universally substandard acting only serves to call attention to the inadequacies of the script. Nonetheless, the film successfully captures the tawdriness and tedium of the life-style. The striking colors and congested compositions create an evocative atmosphere and enhance the characters' feelings of entrapment but, in the end, fail to enliven an otherwise lackluster tale.

p, Jin Sung-man; d, Im Kwon-t'aek; w, Song Kil-han; ph, Gu Jung-mo.

Drama **(PR:O MPAA:NR)**

TIERRA DE VALIENTES† (1987, Mex.) 85m Produciones del Rey/Peliculas Mexicanas c (Trans: Land of the Brave)

Juan Valentin *(Rodrigo Pineda)*, Pedro Infant, Jr. *(Gregorio Solorio)*, Patricia Rivera *(Esperanza)*, Fernando Casanova *(Chamuco)*, Roberto Canedo *(Don Bruno Ortiz)*, Noe Murayama *(El Licenciado)*, Victor Alcocer *(Antonio Alvarez)*, Chayito Valdez, Dacia Gonzalez, Alfredo Gutierrez.

With a strong the-people-united-will-never-be-defeated political message at its heart, this Mexican feature presents two men's struggle to organize the long-exploited farmers in their hometown. Both of the organizers have returned home after long absences: Valentin has been working without papers in the States and Infante, Jr. has been studying agriculture at the university. They put to use the lessons they have learned and pull the farmers together to triumph over the unscrupulous Canedo.

p, Arnulfo Delgado; d, Luis Quintanila Rico; w, Jose Luis Rauda Delgado (based on a story by Estela Inda); ph, Antonio Ruiz; m, Rafael Carrion; ed, Angel Camacho.

Drama **(PR:NR MPAA:NR)**

TILINTEKO† (1987, Fin.) 70m Villealfa c (Trans: The Final Arrangement)

Juhani Niemela, Esko Nikkari, Kaija Pakarinen, Seppo Maki.

Two men rob a postal van and immediately after the robbery one of the thieves shoots the other in the back and leaves him for dead. The wounded thief survives and is arrested, but he refuses to identify his accomplice. After serving his prison term, the revenge-seeking man tracks down his traitorous partner and discovers that he has become a successful politician who is running for a seat in Parliament.

p, Aki Kaurismaki; d, Veikko Aaltonen; w, Veikko Aaltonen, Aki Kaurismaki; ph, Timo Salminen, Timo Markko; m, Leo Friman; ed, Juha Jeromaa.

Crime **(PR:NR MPAA:NR)**

TIME FOR DYING, A† (1987,Phil.) Roadshow Films Int'l. c

Charito Solis, Rod Webb, Yoshinori Mori, Rick Bacher.

A World War II adventure set on a small island of the Philippines which is run by a guerillas' stronghold. When a sadistic American pilot crash lands, a bloody battle rages between the Japanese forces (who are looking for submarine installations) and the American-led guerillas.

[no credits available]

War **(PR:NR MPAA:NR)**

TIME GUARDIAN, THE† (1987, Aus.) 85m Hemdale FGH-Chateau Prod. Investments-Jen-Diki/Hemdale c

Tom Burlinson *(Ballard)*, *Nikki Coghill (Annie)*, Carrie Fisher *(Petra)*, Dean Stockwell *(Boss)*, Henry Salter *(Prenzler)*, Jo Flemming *(Tanel)*, Tim Robertson *(Sgt. McCarthy)*, Jim Holt *(Rafferty)*.

Big budget Aussie science fiction film which begins in the 24th century as a tumultuous battle is being fought between the citizens of a large city and a vicious horde of invaders known as the Jen-didi. The humans' only hope is to transport their city to safety *back in time*. Fisher, an expert on the 20th century, and Burlinson, a brave warrior, are sent back to 20th century Australia to scout a good desert location for the city from the future. Unfortunately, the horrid Jen-didi give chase through time and Fisher is mortally wounded. The time-travelers land in the small town of Midas, where Burlison meets a woman geologist (Coghill) and persuades her that he is a warrior from the future. She agrees to help him and during the course of their travails they fall in love. Not surprisingly, Coghill accompanies Burlinson back to the 24th century, and it is she who slays the head baddie of the Jen-didis. THE TIME GUARDIAN, written by director Hannant and film critic John Baxter (author of *Science Fiction in the Cinema*), reportedly suffered some last-minute tinkering by producers who had stripped Hannant of his right to final cut and dispatched editor Prowse to direct the filming of additional scenes. Although the film was originally announced to run 100 minutes, the final cut comes in at 85 minutes, lending further credence to stories of hasty re-shooting and editing.

p, Norman Wilkinson, Robert Lagettie, Harley Manners; d, Brian Hannant; w,

Brian Hannant, John Baxter; ph, Geoff Burton; m, Allan Zavod; ed, Andrew Prowse; prod d, George Liddle; spec eff, Andrew Mason, Ted Price.

Science Fiction **(PR:NR MPAA:NR)**

TIME WARP TERROR (SEE: BLOODY NEW YEAR, 1987, Brit.)

TIN MEN*** (1987) 112m Touchstone-Silver Screen Partners II/BV c

Richard Dreyfuss *(Bill "BB" Babowsky)*, Danny DeVito *(Ernest Tilley)*, Barbara Hershey *(Nora Tilley)*, John Mahoney *(Moe, Partner to "BB")*, Jackie Gayle *(Sam, Tilley's Partner)*, Stanley Brock *(Gil)*, Seymour Cassel *(Cheese)*, Bruno Kirby *(Mouse)*, J.T. Walsh *(Wing)*, Richard Portnow *(Carly)*, Matt Craven *(Looney)*, Alan Blumenfeld *(Stanley)*, Brad Sullivan *(Masters)*, Michael Tucker *(Bagel)*, Deirdre O'Connell *(Nellie)*, Sheila McCauley *(Ada)*, Michael S. Willis *(Mr. Shubner)*, Penny Nichols *(Mrs. Shubner)*, Susan Duvall *(Suburban Housewife)*, David DeBoy *(Suburban Husband)*, Florence Moody *(Diner Waitress)*, Myron Citrenbaum *(Murray)*, Ralph Tabakin *(Mr. Hudson)*, Norma Posner *(Mrs. Hudson)*, Walt MacPherson *(Cadillac Salesman)*, William C. Godsey *(Belvedere Hotel Barman)*, Sharon Ziman, Lois Raymond Munchel, Kathy Jones *(Mason Dixon Operators)*, Cindy Geppi, Ellen Sills, Mary Morgan, Marcia Herr *(Social Security Girls)*, Karen Barth, Sharon Crofoot, Geri Lynn Kelbaugh, Lisa Ford, Rebecca Lucia Weidner, Patricia Pohlman, Shirley Ann Wilson *(Gibraltar Operators)*, Josh Billings, Jeffrey Moser *(Men at Crash)*, Freddie Stevens *(Piano Bar Crooner)*, Bill Danoff *(Police Officer)*, Katherine Ellis *(Ruthie)*, Eva Jean Berg *(Woman at Smorgasbord)*, Todd Jackson *(Young Boy)*, Barbara Rappaport *(Coffee Shop Waitress)*, Theodore Goldman *(Pool Hall Worker)*, Kathleen Goldpaugh *(Arguing Wife)*, Brian Costantini *(Arguing Husband)*.

Barry Levinson returns to the same territory and to the same eating establishment he portrayed so well in DINER. This time, it's with somewhat lesser success but TIN MEN still stands above most of the alleged comedies released in 1987. Dreyfuss and DeVito are two men in the same scam business in 1963 Baltimore. They both sell aluminum siding to unsuspecting home owners, using a multitude of lies and canards to gull their potential buyers. The men in the business all drive Cadillacs and keep up garish fronts, all the more to convince their clients of their legitimacy. Dreyfuss takes delivery of his new gas-guzzler and backs out of the Caddy dealership, only to be slammed into by DeVito, who has just finished an argument with his wife, Hershey. The simple automobile accident begins to escalate into a full-scaled war. DeVito's rage is fueled by the fact that Hershey is bored with him, that he is in the midst of a hassle with the IRS and that he is, in general, disappointed with himself and his lot in life. Dreyfuss, who is the state of the art in nattiness, is one of the best Tin Men in Baltimore and is also somewhat unhappy because he knows, deep in his heart, that he is not doing a good deed when he sells the aluminum siding at inflated prices to cover his commissions and those of his "bird dog." The two men begin harassing each other, smashing the other's car, etc. Then Dreyfuss gets the bright idea to hit DeVito where it really hurts. He follows Hershey to a supermarket and begins to use his charm to seduce her. Once that's done, he gleefully calls DeVito to tell him and DeVito is thrilled to have her off his hands. It is only then that Dreyfuss, a lifelong bachelor, realizes that he is in love with Hershey. In the meantime, DeVito's life takes a tumble. When a Maryland commission is established to investigate these scam artists, DeVito's boss, Walsh, sacrifices DeVito to the investigators. Further, he loses his beloved long-finned Caddie to the IRS. In the end, both DeVito and Dreyfuss meet at the government hearing and drive off together, talking vaguely about getting into the car business together and selling a new item called a Volkswagen.

That's the basic plot but there are many stops along the way that are delightful and moving. In DINER, several young men would meet and talk about their girls, football, their prospects, and the other things the occupy the minds of men in their twenties. Several scenes in TIN MEN take place in the same diner, but on the other side. There is even one character who appears in both pictures. This is Tucker, playing the role of "Bagel." Tucker is a Baltimorean and long-time pal of Levinson's who spent years trying to rid himself of his "Bal'mer" accent and had to relearn it for the part. DeVito's accent is flawless and stands out among the others. Although there are many funny moments in the picture, the most hilarious ones are when veteran comic Jackie Gayle is on screen. Gayle plays DeVito's partner and his monologue on why Lorne Greene was 50 and had three sons who were over 40 on "Bonanza" is hysterical. Many of the words out of Gayle's mouth are from his nightclub act, tried and true material that has convulsed many a Las Vegas audience. It works and Gayle, who had previously been one of the roundtable comics in BROADWAY DANNY ROSE and had also appeared in THE TEMPEST and THE SEVEN MINUTES, should start to work regularly in movies now that producers have noted his split-second timing. Some of the other excellent smaller parts were played by Brock, Cassel, and Mahoney as cronies of Dreyfuss and DeVito. Also helping to establish the era are various mentions of the people of the day as well as music by Jo Stafford, Nat Cole, Johnny Mathis, and Frank Sinatra. Hershey is superb and adds another finely-etched portrait in her acting gallery. Dreyfuss seems to be emerging as a slightly-younger version of Paul Newman. He looks like him, walks like him and, if a wise producer spots the similarity, should be cast as Newman's younger brother in some upcoming project. All the details are accurate, down to the thin row house in which DeVito and Hershey reside. One more funny moment is when the salesmen talk in earnest about the acts appearing on "The Ed Sullivan Show," (a program on which Gayle appeared) and the various merits of Latino ventriloquist Senor Wences versus the myriad jugglers Sullivan favored. There will be a comparison to David Mamet's play "Glengarry Glen Ross" as well as Arthur Miller's "Death of a Salesman." They do have some similarities but "Glengarry Glen Ross" was mean-spirited and dealt with real estate men and if one were to cut the filthy language, that play might have run 20 minutes. While Miller's play was a tear-jerker, TIN MEN is a laugh-jerker most of the time. A few flaws pop up. Since aluminum siding was, at best, a small business at the time, it's hard to believe that Dreyfuss and DeVito didn't know each other at all, mainly because all of DeVito's pals knew who Dreyfuss was immediately. Also, Hershey's move from DeVito to Dreyfuss happens too quickly and her response, once she learns that she has been little more than a pawn in the chess match between her husband and her lover doesn't feel honest. Walsh, who plays DeVito's boss was in "Glengarry Glen Ross" and played the crew's boss, the same role he does here. Hershey, after years of inactivity, has come back with a flourish, appearing in HANNAH AND HER SISTERS and HOOSIERS as well as this. TIN MEN was made for about $10 million and should reap large rewards for the Touchstone subsidiary of Buena Vista (Disney) as well as for director/writer Levinson, whose voice can be heard in this as the Memorial Stadium announcer. In two previous films, his voice was heard—as a TV announcer in DINER and the stadium announcer in THE NATURAL. Seeing TIN MEN is like chewing half a stick of gum. It's sweet, but not satisfying and one wishes there had been more. *(Profanity, sexual situations.)*

p, Mark Johnson; d&w, Barry Levinson; ph, Peter Sova; m, David Steele, Andy Cox; ed, Stu Linder; prod d, Peter Jamison; set d, Philip Abramson; cos, Gloria Gresham; makeup, Irving Buchman.

Comedy **Cas.** **(PR:C-O MPAA:R)**

TISZTA AMERIKA† (1987, Hung./Jap.) 113m Young Cinema/Mafilm-Hunnia/Mokep, Hungarofilm c (Trans: Just Like America)

Andor Lukats *(Frigyes Tolgyesi)*, Trula Hoosier *(Jude)*, Stafford Ashani *(David)*, Erika Bodnar *(Tolgyesi's Wife)*, Antal Marton Jr. *(Tolgyesi's Son)*, Adam Szirtes *(Tolgyesi's Father-in-Law)*, Gyorgy Cserhalmi *(Tolgyesi's Brother-in-Law)*.

An unlikely drama starring Lukats as a Hungarian family man vacationing in the US with his wife and young son. In New York City he becomes intrigued with two black "three card monte" players (Ashani and Hoosier) and ditches his family just before they are to leave to return to Budapest. Alone in the Big Apple, Lukats locates the black street hustlers and although he doesn't speak a word of English, he hangs out with them and becomes their friend. Unfortunately, Ashani and Hoosier are being pursued by two mysterious thugs who want to kill them. After many narrow escapes, the hunters finally get their prey, but Lukats escapes. Having learned how to say only "ham and eggs," Lukats wanders the city living like a bum. Luckily, these three words bring him to the attention of a compassionate waitress who helps the Hungarian out whenever she can. Meanwhile, back in Budapest, Lukats' father-in-law sells the family car and flies to N.Y.C. to bring Lukats back. Without a clue as to the wayward Hungarian's whereabouts, the father-in-law finds Lukats and tries to persuade him to return to his family. Although Lukats is resistent, the duo wander N.Y.C. together and have a splendid time. Just before they are to go to the airport, the killers suddenly appear and toss Lukats off a bridge and into the East River. Director Gothar is best known in the US for his 1981 film TIME STANDS STILL.

p, Yoram Mandel; d, Peter Gothar; w, Peter Esterhazy, Peter Gothar; ph, Zoltan David (Eastmancolor); m, Gyorgy Selmeczi; ed, Maria Nagy; cos, Merrill Stringer, Andrea Flesch.

Drama **(PR:NR MPAA:NR)**

TO DENDRO POU PLIGONAME (SEE: TREE WE HURT, THE, 1987, Gr.)

TO MARKET, TO MARKET† (1987, Aus.) 85m Goosey Ltd.-Film Victoria c

Philip Quast *(Edward Riat)*, Marcus Gollings *(Edward Riat, Age 13)*, Noel Trevarthan *(William Riat Sr.)*, Kate Reid *(Jackie)*, Maureen Edwards *(Mother)*, Tony Llewellyn-Jones *(Richard)*, Genevieve Picot *(Susanna)*, Wayne Cull *(William Riat, Jr.)*.

This backhanded swipe at the moral bankruptcy of the Australian Establishment is the directorial debut for Virginia Rouse, who worked as an assistant for director Paul Cox (MAN OF FLOWERS, CACTUS). Quast plays the grown-up version of Gollings, who is seen early in the film as a student at a school where upper-class consciousness and racism go hand in hand. In keeping with his privileged upbringing Quast assumes his place in the family business, although beneath his compliant surface he longs to live a more compassionate life. Quast's older brother asks his help in some illegal financial dealings which, unbeknownst to Quast, involve the fruits of drug smuggling. Though he is reticent, Quast agrees and ends up taking a fall; however, he ends up a winner, nonetheless, when he bids adieu to the family business and the family that forced him into a mold he never fit.

p,d&w, Virginia Rouse; ph, Jaems Grant (Fujicolor); m, Ben Fitzgerald, Kate Reid, Fincina Hopgood, Gustav Mahler, Johannes Brahms; ed, Tony Paterson; art d, Virginia Rouse.

Drama **(PR:NR MPAA:NR)**

TODA LA VIDA† (1987, Mex.) 91m Producciones Esme-Hermes Int'l.-Alianza Cinematografica Mexicana/Peliculas Mexicanas c (Trans: All Life Long)

Roberto [Flaco] Guzman *(Poncho)*, Jorge Luke *(Jorge)*, Rebeca Silva *(Lola)*, Manuel [Flaco] Ibanez *(Lalo)*, Diana Ferreti *(Leticia)*, Charlie Valentino, Jose Magana, Maricarmen Resendess, Carlos Yustis, Alejandro Peniche, Yirah Aparicio.

Based on a popular Mexican song, this comedy follows two men who spend all their time drinking, bowling, and carousing with loose women while ignoring their true sweethearts who sit at home and wait for their return. Finally fed up with the men's antics, the faithful girl friends decide to make the boys jealous by hanging out in bars like they do.

p, Carlos Vasallo; d, Victor Manuel [Guero] Castro; w, Fernando Galiana; ph, Raul Dominguez; m, Carlos Torres Marin; ed, Max Sanchez.

Comedy **(PR:NR MPAA:NR)**

TOKYO BLACKOUT† (1987, Jap.) 120m Kansai-Tokuma-Daiei c (SHUTO SHOSHITSU)

Tsunehiko Watase *(Tatsuya Asakura, Electric Co. Section Director)*, Yuko Natori *(Mariko Koide, TV Newscaster)*, Shinji Yamashita *(Yohsuke Tamiya, TV Reporter)*, Yoko Ishino *(Mieko Matsunaga)*, Shuji Ohtaki *(Professor Seiichiroh Ohtawara)*, Isao Natsuyagi *(Eiji Sakuma)*, Ichiro Zaitsu *(Kawamura)*, Osamu of the Bonchi *(Koyama)*, Fuyukaze Matsumura *(Yutaka Matsuo)*, Ittoku Kishibe *(Yasuhara)*, Norihei Miki *(Matsukichi Kimura)*, Raita Ryu *(Horie)*, Tetsuroh Tamba *(Nakata)*.

The city of Tokyo, the nerve center of Japan, is suddenly cut off from the rest of the world by a giant impenetrable cloud that envelopes the entire metropolis. While the Soviets and Americans scramble to maintain their respective interests in the area, a team of scientists tries to decipher the riddle of the cloud. Based on the best-selling novel by popular science fiction author Sakyo Komatsu, this film, from the director of TORA! TORA! TORA!, was screened at the World Film Festival in Montreal. Music composed by the decidedly un-Japanese Maurice Jarre.

p, Katsumi Mizoguchi, Motoki Kasahara; d, Toshio Masuda; w, Hiroyasu Yamaura, Toshio Masuda (based on the novel *Disappearance Of The Capitol* by Sakyo Komatsu; ph, Masahiko Iimura (VistaVision); m, Maurice Jarre; ed, Toshio Taniguchi; md, Kazu Matsui; art d, Juichi Ikuno; spec eff, Teruyoshi Nakano.

Science Fiction **(PR:NR MPAA:NR)**

TOO MUCH† (1987) 89m Golan-Globus/Cannon c

Bridgette Andersen *(Suzy/Narrator)*, Masato Fukazama *(Too Much)*, Hiroyuki Watanabe *("Uncle" Tetsuro)*, Char Fontana *(Prof. Finkel)*, Uganda *(Bernie, Finkel's Henchman)*.

Another Cannon-produced kiddie film that received only a scant release in places like Boca Raton, Florida in preparation for an eventual segue to home video. Andersen stars as a little girl accompanying her parents on a business trip to Japan. There she is given a toy robot by her father's business associate, Watanabe. The girl and the robot become fast friends and the machine refuses to leave the girl's side when she is due to return to the US. The girl and the robot run away together and are helped by a young Japanese boy. The trio is pursued not only by the girl's parents, but by an evil scientist (Fontana) and his bumbling assistant (Uganda). Eventually the kids and the robot are cornered in a Tokyo department store, but other toy robots and hundreds of Japanese kids arrive on the scene to help out the plucky little robot and his American friend. Oddly, French writer-director Rochat's previous film was the less-than-wholesome THE STORY OF O, PART II.

p, Menahem Golan, Yoram Globus; d, Eric Rochat; w, Eric Rochat, Joan Laine; ph, Daisaku Kimura (Imagica Color); m, George S. Clinton; ed, Alain Jakubowicz; art d, Tsuneo Kantake; spec eff, Osamu Kung.

Children's **(PR:NR MPAA:PG)**

TOO OUTRAGEOUS† (1987, Can.) 105m Spectrafilm c

Craig Russell *(Robin Turner)*, Hollis McLaren *(Liza Connors)*, David McIlwraith *(Bob)*, Ron White *(Luke)*, Lynne Cormack *(Betty Treisman)*, Michael J. Reynolds *(Lee Sturges)*, Timothy Jenkins *(Rothchild)*, Paul Eves *(Tony Sparks)*, Frank Pellegrino *(Manuel)*, Norma Dell'Agnese *(Homeless Lady)*, Norman Duttweiler *(Man in Drag)*, Kent Staines *(Waiter)*, Rusty Ryan *(Jack Rabbit)*, Doug Millar *(Audience Member)*, Kate Davis *(Receptionist)*, Doug Paulson *(40-year-old Executive)*, George Hevenor *(60-year-old Executive)*, Jimmy James *(Marilyn Monroe Impersonator)*, Barry Flatman *(Phil Kennedy)*, Ray Paisley *(Chuck)*, Raymond Accolas *(French Director)*, Linda Goranson *(Hospital Receptionist)*, Doug Inear *(M.C)*.

The sequel to the surprise cult hit of 1977, OUTRAGEOUS, picks up the characters ten years later as female impersonator Russell is on the verge of becoming a star. Russell shares a loft in New York City's Greenwich Village with his best friend McLaren a straight, female schizophrenic who has channeled her psychosis into creative writing and attained a small amount of success. Although Russell is content to play gay drag-houses in the Village, his act, which includes impersonations of such female stars as Barbra Streisand, Mae West, Tina Turner, Peggy Lee, Ella Fitzgerald, and Bette Midler, catches the attention of a pair of high-powered talent agents, Cormack and Reynolds. The two not only want to represent Russell, but "own" him as well. The agents set about toning down Russell's outrageous act to make it more acceptable to a non-gay audience. Russell and his entourage, which includes McLaren, manager McIlwraith, and accompanist White, return to their hometown of Toronto to work on the new act. In Toronto, McLaren finds herself a boy friend (the relationship ends tragically) and it is learned that accompanist White has contracted AIDS. McIlwraith, who is White's lover, leaves the troupe to care for White, and Russell finds himself alone and insecure about the new direction of his career. Depressed and moody, Russell meets handsome hustler Eves and they become lovers. Russell's new-found happiness is only temporary, for he learns that Eves was hired by Cormack to placate him. Not willing to pay the price of mass acceptance, Russell purposely ruins his big audition before major Broadway backers and goes back to the loft he shares with McLaren. Loosely based on star Russell's trouble adjusting to fame after being thrust into the limelight upon the success of the original OUTRAGEOUS, TOO OUTRAGEOUS was shown at the Toronto Festival of Festivals and received a very selective release pattern from its distributor, Spectrafilm.

p, Roy Krost; d&w, Dick Benner; ph, Fred Guthe; m, Russ Little; ed, George Appleby; art d, Andris Hausmanis; set d, Liz Calderhead, Marlene Graham; cos, Alisa Alexander; makeup, Inge Klaudi.

Drama **(PR:NR MPAA:NR)**

TORA-SAN'S BLUEBIRD FANTASY† (1987, Jap.) 102m Shochiku Co. Inc. c (OTOKOWA TSURAIYO: SHIAWASENO AOI TORI)

Kiyoshi Atsumi, Eysuko Shiomi, Chieko Shiomi, Tsuyoshi Nagabuchi, Masami Shimojo, Chieko Misaki, Chieko Baisho, Gin Maeda, Chishu Ryu, Hisao Dazai.

The 37th installment of the film series that the *Guinness Book of World Records* has declared as the longest running sequelization in film history once again features Kiyoshi Atsumi as Japan's favorite nonconformist, Tora-San. Wearing his trademark brown-check suit and battered pork-pie hat, Atsumi wanders the countryside selling trinkets at local festivals. In this episode, as in all the others, Atsumi falls hopelessly in love with a beautiful young girl (Shiomi) only to lose her to a younger and more handsome man. Within these simple plots director Yamada and writer Asama insert dozens of hilarious situations—all of which show Atsumi breaking staid Japanese traditions. This formula has proven amazingly effective—the series has been seen by 60 million people and has grossed over $600 million at the box office. Director Yamada has helmed every episode and actor Atsumi has starred in each. In addition, the actors who play Atsumi's embarrassed family, Masami Shimojo, Chieko Misaki, Chieko Baisho, and Gin Maeda, have repeated their roles throughout the series. For a look at a non-TORA-SAN film directed by Yamada and featuring Atsumi, see FINAL TAKE, THE GOLDEN AGE OF THE MOVIES (1987).

p, Shunichi Kobayasahi; d, Yoji Yamada; w, Yoji Yamada, Yoshitaka Asama; ph, Tetsuo Takaba; m, Naozumi Yamamoto; art d, Mitsuo Dekawa.

(PR:NR MPAA:NR)

TOUGH COP† (1987, Phil.) F. Puzon c

Rom Kristoff, Jimi B. Jr., Anthony East, Kenneth Peerless, Michael Monty, Mel Davidson, Warren McLean, Ingrid Erlandson.

A former Green Beret recruits expert crime fighters from throughout the US to form an elite fighting force designed to rid Miami of its powerful drug kingpins and arms merchants.

p, Pierre C. Lee; d&w, Dominic Elmo Smith (based on a story by Bobby A. Suarez); ph, John Perreira; ed, Amang Sanchez; prod d, John Paul Pinzon; art d, Jennifer Lee; set d, Awie Vasquez; cos, Dannah Faith; spec eff, Joe Carmona; makeup, Francis Perez; stunts, Roland Falcis, Jolly Joqueta.

Action/Crime **(PR:NR MPAA:NR)**

TOUGH GUYS DON'T DANCE**½ (1987) 108m Golan-Clobus/Cannon c

Ryan O'Neal *(Tim Madden)*, Isabella Rossellini *(Madeline)*, Debra Sandlund *(Patty Lareine)*, Wings Hauser *(Regency)*, John Bedford Lloyd *(Wardley Meeks III)*, Clarence Williams III *(Bolo)*, Lawrence Tierney *(Dougy Madden)*, Penn Jillette *(Big Stoop)*, Frances Fisher *(Jessica Pond)*, R. Patrick Sullivan *(Lonny Pangborn)*, Stephen Morrow *(Stoodie)*, John Snyder *(Spider)*.

Based on the best-selling Norman Mailer novel of 1984, this curious crime drama marks the author's fourth venture into filmmaking. In 1968, Mailer made his first step with WILD 90, an improvised free-for-all in which he starred as one of three hoods holed up in a warehouse. He followed with BEYOND THE LAW, another improvised piece with Mailer starring as the police captain of a Manhattan precinct house. The final installment of his 16mm ego-trip trilogy was MAIDSTONE, an excessive political drama which left Mailer $300,000 in debt. TOUGH GUYS DON'T DANCE differs from his three previous films. With Cannon producing in association with Francis Coppola and Tom Luddy of Zoetrope Studios, Mailer found himself in the throes of professional Hollywood filmmaking—no cinema-verite, no improvised script, and no unrehearsed or amateur acting. The story is a terribly convoluted one which rivals THE BIG SLEEP in its incomprehensibility. (The novel took Mailer two months to write, while the script took him six months.) Set in Provincetown, Massachusetts, the story involves drug dealing, decapitation, divorce, dishonor, deception, and very little dancing. O'Neal is a failed, alcoholic writer who, years before, moved to Provincetown after destroying his relationship with Rossellini, the only woman he ever loved. He then married a wealthy, but trashy, southern belle, Sandlund, who raked in a fortune when she split from her suicidal, decadent first husband,

Lloyd. O'Neal can't get his life together, and when Sandlund takes off, he hits the bottle even harder and turns to a sleazy former porn star, Fisher, for romance. It's not long before O'Neal is caught up in a murder mystery which he cannot piece together. He wakes up one morning to find two severed heads where his drug stash used to be. Although he had previously wondered about his ability to commit murder, he never felt that he could do it. Since he can't remember anything that happened to him the previous night, he begins to think he might be guilty of the murders. Moreover, if it wasn't him, there are plenty of other people in town who would gladly frame him for the crime, including the corrupt, cocaine-dealing police chief Hauser. O'Neal, turns to his father for help. Played by Tierney, O'Neal's father is the epitome of the "tough guy," a cancer-ridden rock of a man who agrees to help O'Neal dump the heads into a nearby river. The more O'Neal probes into the mysterious goings-on, the greater his involvement becomes, until, by the film's end, nearly everyone has been killed off. Only O'Neal and Rossellini survive the mayhem. Reunited with his true love, O'Neal is back at square one.

Described by Mailer as "a murder mystery, a suspense tale, a film of horror, and a comedy of manners," TOUGH GUYS DON'T DANCE is all of those and none of those. It's set up like a mystery, but is not mysterious. Instead, it is incomprehensible. It attempts to be suspenseful, but succeeds only at being intriguing. Its horror comes only in its bastardization of genre expectations, and its comedy is perhaps unintentional. Like the filmmakers of the French New Wave, Mailer uses the *film noir* genre as a skeleton on which to hang the flesh of his personality—the personal signature. TOUGH GUYS DON'T DANCE is not about police corruption and underworld criminal activities, but about O'Neal's need for love from Rossellini and his need for acceptance from Tierney. Less interesting as a film than it is as a part of Mailer's career, TOUGH GUYS DON'T DANCE is another chapter from a life in the limelight which began at age 25 with the overwhelming success of his war novel, *The Naked and the Dead*. In 1987, after such a varied career in the public eye, Mailer should not be seen as a filmmaker, but as someone who, among other things, has the capacity to make films. At this point, he can barely even be seen as a writer, since he has become an icon of American culture.

The genesis of TOUGH GUYS DON'T DANCE is nearly as twisted as the film's plot. It was during the 1985 Cannes Film Festival that the now-legendary contract for Cannon's production of Jean-Luc Godard's KING LEAR was signed on a paper napkin at a cafe. (KING LEAR received a film festival showing in 1987, but received no theatrical release.) The contract called for Godard to film the classic Shakespearean work, which would star Woody Allen and feature a script by Norman Mailer. Leaping at the opportunity, Mailer offered Cannon a deal to film *Tough Guys Don't Dance*. Although producer Jeremy Thomas (THE LAST EMPEROR) had wanted to film the novel under Nicolas Roeg's direction, Cannon agreed to give Mailer a $5 million budget to direct it himself. With the help of executive producers Francis Coppola and Tom Luddy, Mailer was able to secure one of Hollywood's top cameramen, John Bailey (credited as visual consultant), whose previous work includes CAT PEOPLE, MISHIMA, and SILVERADO. Also on board were costume designer Michael Kaplan (BLADERUNNER), editor Debra McDermott (AMADEUS), and composer Angelo Badalamenti (BLUE VELVET). The excellent cast includes the gorgeous Rossellini (after her brilliant BLUE VELVET performance), O'Neal (who hasn't had a role this challenging since BARRY LYNDON), former Hollywood great Tierney (1945's DILLINGER and 1947's BORN TO KILL), and newcomer Sandlund, Mailer's discovery. TOUGH GUYS DON'T DANCE is not a great film, nor is it an awful film. It *is* a film which, by its very nature as a Norman Mailer work, demands attention and discussion. Not surprisingly, when a film dares to do something different, as this one does, it becomes the target of vicious criticism and misunderstanding. Shown out of competition at the Cannes Film Festival, it was greeted by jeers and laughter, and its theatrical release was equally unsuccessful. *(Violence, nudity, excessive profanity, sexual situations, adult situations, substance abuse).*

p, Menahem Golan, Yoram Globus; d&w, Norman Mailer (based on his novel); ph, John Bailey (TVC Color); m, Angelo Badalamenti; ed, Debra McDermott; prod d, Armin Ganz; set d, Gretchen Rau; cos, Michael Kaplan.

Crime **(PR:O MPAA:R)**

TRAGICO TERREMOTO EN MEXICO† (1987, Mex.) 96m Produciones Metropolitan/Peliculas Mexicanas c (Trans: Tragic Earthquake in Mexico)

Miguel Angel Rodriguez *(Miguel)*, Mario Almada *(Don Nacho)*, Diana Golden *(Paty)*, Charito Granados *(Sarah)*, Pedro Weber [Chatanooga] *(Solorio)*, Alejandra Meyer *(Christina)*, Oscar Fentanes *(Chucho)*, Sergio Ramos [Comanche] *(Tepo)*, Isauro Espinoza, Victor Lozaya, Oscar Cadedo, Blanca Lidia, Maria A. Murillo.

Low-budget disaster film wich exploits the tragic earthquake that destroyed much of Mexico City on September 19, 1985. Like the dozens of American disaster films before it, TRAGICO TERREMOTO EN MEXICO introduces a variety of cliched characters and then leaves the audience in suspense as to who will die and who will survive the disaster. The climactic devastation takes place inside three small rooms of the Centro Medico hospital, thus avoiding costly special effects. The only hint of wide-spread destruction comes from real-life news footage of the event.

p, Ignacio Garcia Gardelle; d, Francisco Guerrero; w, Reyes Bercini (based on an idea by Ignacio Garcia Gardelle); ph, Agustin Lara Alvarado; m, Jep Epstein; ed, Jorge Pina.

Drama **(PR:NR MPAA:NR)**

TRAIN OF DREAMS*½** (1987, Can.) 89m National Film Board c

Jason St. Amour *(Tony Abruzzi)*, Marcella Santa Maria *(Mrs. Abruzzi)*, Fred Ward *(The Teacher)*, Christopher Neil *(Nicky Abruzzi)*, David Linesky *(Tony's Lawyer)*, Milton Hartman *(Crown Attorney)*, Basil Danchyshyn *(Judge)*, Sarah Casey *(Girl at Party)*.

Using a predominantly nonprofessional cast, this outstanding documentary-like Canadian feature pulls no punches in its poignant depiction of youth gone bad. St. Amour plays a 17-year-old unemployed dropout who drifts into crime, "an angry young man who is unwilling to take responsibility for his actions." As the film opens he and a group of his street tough friends mug a man in an alley. From this point on the film cuts back and forth between St. Amour's two-year detention in a correctional institution for young offenders and the actions that brought him there. Deserted by his father at an early age, he constantly battles with his mother, Santa Maria, who is incapable of handling him. She tries again and again to talk with him, but he is beyond reach. Finally, he explodes and bashes her. At her wits end, she calls the police and he is institutionalized. At the correctional facility, St. Amour finds himself set upon not only by an endless parade of psychologists, social workers, and administrators, but also by a group of tough punks who, without reason, make life difficult for him, beating the hell out of him on occasion. Yet throughout all of this, St. Amour retains his "attitude," his cynical disdain for those who try to help—"who don't know what it's like, who weren't there, who go home at night." Ward, a teacher at the facility, tries to use poetry to bring hope into the lives of these young men who have forgotten how to dream or have never had that luxury. For a long time, St. Amour, like many of the others in Ward's class, refuses to take the teacher's attempts seriously. They respond to his requests for poems with angry profanity-laden ditties. Gradually, Ward begins to connect with St. Amour. He is the first person to whom St. Amour is willing to tell his story; a bond begins to form between them. One day, Ward plays Billie Holliday's "Don't Worry About Me" to the class, and St. Amour is the only one to recognize the pain in the song's denial of concern. With Ward's help, St. Amour comes to realize that he is his own worst enemy. Good behavior wins St. Amour a weekend at home, and while there, he even tries to clean up the act of his 10-year-old brother, Neil, who seems to be following in his footsteps. The film ends with St. Amour back in the common room at the correctional center, his face momentarily lost among all the other dead-end kids, but suddenly coming into focus. On the soundtrack, the song by Three O'Clock Train that has been repeated throughout the film is heard: "Train of pride/Train of heartache/Train of twisted self-esteem/Careful train/Afraid of breaking/You're riding on the train of dreams." It may be that St. Amour has been given back his dreams.

This synopsis may well sound like any number of sentimentalized, implausible, moralizing teen redemption films, but none of these adjectives applies to TRAIN OF DREAMS, and it is far from certain that St. Amour has been permanently saved from the fate for which he seemed headed. The sense of reality here is almost palpable. Director Smith, a veteran documentary maker, presents his story without passing judgement. Everyone—St. Amour, his mother, the courts, the correctional institute—is a part of the problem and a part of the solution. Cutting abruptly between St. Amour's life at the institution and his life outside, Smith puts us both in the boy's shoes and inside his head. Given Smith's documentary-like approach, there is little fancy camerawork here and occasionally some of the non-professional actors appear a bit self-conscious, but, for the most part, the performances are extremely convincing. At the center of the film is St. Amour's extraordinary performance. Stocky, pimply, and buzz-haired, he looks nothing like the actors usually cast in such parts. Although he, too, is a non-professional, St. Amour is *there* every moment he is onscreen. With little gestures, and smirks, the way he carries himself, and his distant intensity, he is every inch an unrepentant punk. Most often, he is sullen and laconic and just wants to be left alone. At other times, his pent-up energy and frustration explode. It is difficult to like him or even to feel sorry for him at the start of the film, but gradually he reveals little pieces of the troubled, intelligent, sensitive person within him. Because he does this so skillfully we are surprised to find ourselves feeling so deeply for him. Even in his about-face (if we can call it that) he conveys a realistic tentativeness, as if he knows how he shouldn't behave but is uncertain of how to act in its stead. However, the plausibility of St. Amour's transformation would be suspect if it were not for Ward's terrific portrayal of the man who finally reaches him. Ward is no miracle worker, but he is a man with a faith in the transcendent power of art and imagination, and he invests his character with unquestionable reality. He asks his students to appreciate and write poetry and they respond with hilarious profanities, certainly the poetry such angry kids would create. What makes Ward's character so believable is the way that he goes with the flow, recognizing the humor in the situation and patiently persevering. But the really impressive thing about their performances is that, like the rest of the actors in the film, they improvised from a guideline script. *(Nudity, excessive profanity, substance abuse.)*

p, Sam Grana; d, John N. Smith; w, John N. Smith, Sally Bochner, Sam Grana; ph, David de Volpi; m, Malcolm Mackenzi, Jr.; ed, John N. Smith.

Docu-drama **(PR:C-O MPAA:NR)**

TRAVELLING AVANT† (1987, Fr.) 114m Erato/JCT Prods-Sofinergie et Sofica Creations/UGC c (Trans: Dolly In)

Thierry Fremont *(Nino)*, Simon de la Brosse *(Donald)*, Anne-Gisel Glass *(Barbara)*, Sophie Minet *(Angele)*, Laurence Cote *(Janine)*, Luc Lavandier *(Gilles)*, Nathalie Mann *(Vicky)*, Jacques Serre *(Uncle Roger)*, Alix de Konopka *(Wanda)*.

Set in France during the late 1940s, this film features a poor boy (Fremont) and a rich-kid (de la Brosse) who have one thing in common: a passion for movies. The dedicated young film buffs become fast friends and attempt to form a film society. Their individual ambitions begin to tear their friendship apart, however, when de la Brosse loses interest in the project because he has ambitions to become a real filmmaker and not merely a fan. A further wedge is driven between the two when a girl movie buff, Glass, comes between them. Although she at first falls for the more handsome de la Brosse, she eventually finds true love with Fremont.

p, Claude Abeille; d&w, Jean-Charles Tacchella; ph, Jacques Assuerus (Fujicolor); m, Raymond Allessandrini; ed, Marie-Aimee Debril; art d, Georges Levy.

Drama **(PR:NR MPAA:NR)**

TREE WE HURT, THE½** (1986, Gr.) 75m Greek Film Center c (TO DENDRO POU PLIGONAME)

Yannis Avdeliodis, Nikos Mioteris, Marina Delivoria, Takis Agoris, Demos Avdeliodis.

A nostalgic remembrance of those childhood summers that seemed to last forever, THE TREE WE HURT follows two young boys on the Greek isle of Chios in 1960 as they while away the weeks before entering the fifth grade. Director Avdeliodis concentrates on the games, stunts, and pranks pulled by the neighborhood boys as they try to escape the chores that their parents assign them. Episodes include a battle with a nest of angry wasps, the taunting of the village idiot, a skirmish with some adults from a nearby hamlet, a sneaky foray into an orchard that results in the boys getting sick on hastily gobbled plums, the adoption of a dog that has wandered in from another village only to have its mean-spirited owner arrive months later and take it away, and the earning of a few extra drachma by serving as altar boys during funeral processions. The summer brings young love to one of the boys when relatives from the city come to the village on a visit and bring their beautiful daughter. The pair flirt innocently for days, and even manage to hold hands once, until the visit is over and back to the city she goes. The injured tree of the title refers to the process of slashing gum trees to extract the gum, a ritual performed by the women of the village every summer.

Although the scenery is undeniably beautiful and the young actors charming, THE TREE WE HURT tries much too hard to capture the feel of such Francois Truffaut classics as THE 400 BLOWS and SMALL CHANGE without ever realizing the nuances, keen observation, or depth of character that Truffaut evokes. Extremely brief at its 75-minute running time, Avdeliodis pads his film with some annoyingly contrived stylistic tricks (such as showing multiple takes of the same action) that seem gratuitous and out of place. There is no narrative drive here, and although that is not necessarily a problem, the vignettes themselves are poorly developed and do not amount to much. Upon the introduction of the young girl, the narration intones that the boys' relationship suddenly changes, but it does not. There is absolutely no indication that the arrival of a girl on the scene has the slightest effect on the camaraderie of the boys. Avdeliodis fails to integrate his vignettes into a larger whole that gathers strength from the sum of its parts, and that is why the film fails to be totally engaging. Once the end credits roll, THE TREE WE HURT becomes as hazy and inconsequential as most memories of early childhood. Shown at film festivals in the US in 1987.

p,d&w, Demos Avdeliodis; ph, Philippos Koutsaftis; m, Demetris Papademetriou; ed, Costas Foundas; cos, Maria Avdeliodis.

Drama (PR:A MPAA:NR)

TRESPASSES† (1987) 100m XIT/Shapiro c

Robert Kuhn *(Franklin Ramsey)*, Van Brooks *(Richard)*, Mary Pillot *(Sharon Rae, Richard's Wife)*, Adam Roarke, Lou Diamond Phillips *(Drifters)*, Ben Johnson *(August Klein)*, Deborah Neumann *(Catherine)*, Thom Meyer *(Johnny Ramsey, Franklin's Son)*, Marina Rice *(Johnny's Girlfriend)*, KaRan Reed *(Robin)*, George Sledge *(Gibby)*, Lou Perry, John Henry Faulk.

Notable only because LA BAMBA star Lou Diamond Phillips co-wrote the script and has a supporting role here, TRESPASSES was filmed in 1983, never received a theatrical release, and instead debuted on home video. Shot in Texas, the film opens as Kuhn, a cattle farmer, and his son Meyer battle two drifters (Phillips and Roarke) who are raping neighboring farm-woman Pillot. Meyer is killed by Phillips and the drifters escape. Six months later Pillot's banker-father, Johnson, dies and leaves his son-in-law, Brooks, in charge of the business. Meanwhile, Pillot and Kuhn have become close since the rape incident and they begin an affair. When Brooks learns of this, he unknowingly hires fugitives Phillips and Roarke to poison Kuhn's cattle. Kuhn catches the drifters in the act and kills them. Eventually Brooks' plot is revealed and the banker kills himself. Actor Kuhn also served as executive producer.

p, Loren Bivens, Richard Rosetta; d, Adam Roarke, Loren Bivens; w, Loren Bivens, Lou Diamond Phillips, Jo Carol Pierce; ph, Monte Dhooge, Phil Curry (Allied/WBS Color); m, Wayne Bell, Chuck Pennell; ed, Sherri Galloway; art d, Becky Block, Lisa Kight.

Crime Cas. (PR:NR MPAA:R)

TRINAJSTATA GODENICA NA PRINCA† (1987, Bulg.) 88m Bulgariafilm c (Trans: The Thirteenth Bride of the Prince)

Georgi Partsalev, Tatyana Lolova, Nickolai Tsankov, Georgi Mamalev.

Strange amalgamation of traditional fairy tale and modern science fiction which sees the elders of a mythical kingdom grappling with a sticky problem. The heir to the throne, ugly young Prince Alfonso, must marry the even uglier Princess Rosalia. In an effort to produce a more aesthetically pleasing heir, the elders kidnap a beautiful peasant girl and force her to act as a surrogate bride. The girl's betrothed, however, doesn't take this lying down and teams up with a local Robin Hood-type to rescue her. Enter aliens from outer space and a magic potion and the result is a wild children's film from Bulgaria that reportedly enthralled the 2,000 kids that watched it at the Berlin Film Festival.

d, Ivanka Grubcheva; w, the Mormarev Bros.; ph, Grisha Wegenstein; m, Georgi Genkov; art d, Valentin Mladenova.

Children's (PR:NR MPAA:NR)

TRIUMPH DE GERECHTEN† (1987, Ger.) 81m Bierbichler c (Trans: Triumph of the Just)

Josef Bierbichler *(The Ape)*, Felix von Manteuffel *(Emperor Maximilian)*, Edgar Liegl *(The Intellectual)*.

A meditation on the nature of war, this German film based on a short story by Oskar Maria Graf, flashes from the overwhelming destructive capabilities of modern warfare to the less sophisticated but equally horrifying way in which war was waged more than 300 years ago during Germany's Thirty Years War (1618-1648).

d&w, Josef Bierbichler (based on a short story by Oskar Maria Graf); ph, Jorg Schmidt-Reitwein; m, Rudolf Gregor Knabl; ed, Christian Virmond; set d, Hans Reindl; cos, Ann Poppel, Vroni Reindl.

Drama (PR:NR MPAA:NR)

TROUBLE WITH DICK, THE½** (1987) 93m Frolix c

Tom Villard *(Dick Kendred)*, Susan Dey *(Diane)*, Elaine Giftos *(Sheila Dibble, Landlady)*, Elizabeth Gorcey *(Haley Dibble, Landlady's Daughter)*, David Clennon *(Lars)*, Jack Carter *(Samsa)*, Marianne Muellerleile *(Betty)*.

This promising feature film debut from writer-director Gary Walkow is a low-budget comedy about a rather uncinematic subject—writer's block. Villard stars as a struggling writer of "literary science fiction" who has not had a hit for several years. Resisting publishers' demands that he make his writing more commercial (i.e., more sex and violence), Villard finds his mailbox full of rejection notices. Dey, an old college flame, suggests Villard move into the boarding house where she lives because the rent would be cheaper and the atmosphere more conducive to writing (a rock band practices next door to his current apartment). Needing a change and eager for the chance to rekindle his romance with Dey, Villard moves in. Unfortunately he soon learns that Dey isn't interested in anything beyond a platonic relationship. Uninspired and romantically frustrated, Villard becomes embroiled in trysts with both his divorcee landlady (Giftos) and her horny teenaged daughter (Gorcey). The continual literary rejections combined with daily bedroom antics (neither woman is aware that he is sleeping with the other) sap what little energy Villard had for his writing and he degenerates into a semi-zombie who lies in bed all day waiting for his paramours to come home and have their way with him. Intercut with this are scenes from the novel Villard would like to write, *The Galactic Chain Gang*. In them, Clennon, an escaped prisoner from an intergalactic penal colony, wanders the desert wasteland armed with a smart-ass ray gun that talks back to him. After fending off attacks from a variety of strange creatures, Clennon is befriended by a beautiful female escapee (Muellerleile) who, after gaining his confidence, turns out to be one of his tormentors in disguise. After spending weeks in a catatonic state, Giftos announces to Villard that she has sold the house and everyone must move. With Dey, Giftos, and Gorcey gone, Villard finally snaps out of his malaise and motivates himself to move out just as the exterminators have sealed off the house and piped in deadly gas to fumigate it. Back to normal, Villard finds the inspiration to complete his novel, but wisely declines Dey's offer to move in with her and two new female roommates.

A surprise hit that was the cowinner of the Grand Prize at the US Film Festival, THE TROUBLE WITH DICK is a consistently funny little film that contains several winning performances. Villard is suitably likable as the frustrated author suffering from a crippling bout of writer's block, Dey is splendid as his sympathetic college chum, Giftos is appropriately flighty as the aerobics instructor-cum-landlady who fancies herself an artist and sprinkles her speech with French colloquialisms, and Gorcey is wonderful as the oversexed cheerleader who treats the zoned-out Villard like a new puppy. Director Walkow has great sympathy for all his characters and does a fine job of capturing the internal rhythms of a household containing three strong-willed women. The jockeying-for-power interplay between mother Giftos and daughter Gorcey with the hapless Villard as their pawn is well detailed, realistic, and very funny. Also amusing are the science-fiction scenes wherein Clennon goes through paces similar to his creator's, albeit allegorically. Walkow understands the limitations of low-budget filmmaking and uses his two settings (the house and the desert) to good advantage, creating a feeling of claustrophobia without ever becoming repetitive or boring. Although popular at festivals, wide distribution seems unlikely and the film may go the home video route. *(Sexual situations, profanity.)*

p, Gary Walkow, Leslie Robins; d&w, Gary Walkow; ph, Daryl Studebaker; m, Roger Bourland; ed, G.A. Walkowishky; prod d, Eric Jones, Pui Pui Li; cos, Ted Sewell; spec eff, James Zarlengo.

Comedy (PR:O MPAA:NR)

TROUBLE WITH SPIES, THE† (1987) 91m Brigade/DEG-HBO c

Donald Sutherland *(Appleton Porter)*, Ned Beatty *(Harry Lewis)*, Ruth Gordon *(Mrs. Arkwright)*, Lucy Gutteridge *(Mona Smith, Hotel Owner)*, Michael Hordern *(Jason Lock)*, Robert Morley *(Angus Watkins)*, Gregory Sierra *(Capt. Sanchez)*, Suzanne Danielle *(Maria Sola)*, Fima Noveck *(Col. Novikov)*.

Shot for HBO back in 1984 but never shown on cable, THE TROUBLE WITH SPIES was directed by veteran hack Kennedy and finally picked up by DEG for a disastrous theatrical release in 1987. Sutherland stars as a bumbling British secret agent in the Inspector Clouseau mold. His disgusted superiors send him on a mission (his first) to the island of Ibiza where he is to try to locate a missing agent. In reality Sutherland's bosses have sent him to Ibiza as bait for Soviet spies who are known to be developing a truth serum to be used against enemy agents. Since the dim-witted Sutherland knows nothing, the Soviet's will learn nothing from him. At Ibiza, Sutherland checks into the Royal Rose Hotel and immediately runs into the usual collection of eccentric guest stars including, Beatty, Gordon (in her last role), Hordern, and Danielle. Of course, one of them is a Soviet spy and as it turns out, just as inept as Sutherland. Much to their surprise, the two spies learn that they are being used by their governments, so they team up to do battle against their respective agencies. THE TROUBLE WITH SPIES died a very quick death at the box office and now, ironically, it will probably be shown on the very cable station that produced it and then declined to show it in 1984.

p,d&w, Burt Kennedy (based on the novel *Apple Pie In The Sky* by Marc Lovell); ph, Alex Phillips (Eastmancolor); m, Ken Thorne; ed, Warner E. Leighton; prod d, Jose Maria Tapiador.

Comedy/Spy (PR:NR MPAA:PG)

TRUE COLORS† (1987, Hong Kong) 95m Cinema City/Golden Princess c

Raymond Wong, Ti Lung, Lin Ching Hsia, Gary Lim.

After spending several months in hiding, gangster Ti Lung returns to Hong Kong planning to resume his relationships with girlfriend Lin Ching Hsia and his buddy Raymond Wong. Unfortunately, Lin Ching Hsia is now married to a vicious rival gangster and Wong has become a priest. When the rival gangster and his goons kill the rebellious Lin Ching Hsia, Ti Lung seeks bloody retribution. Beautiful actress Lin Ching Hsia, who appeared in PEKING OPERA BLUES, and actor Ti Lung, who appeared in A BETTER TOMORROW, have become well known among international film festival goers for their critically-praised aforementioned efforts.

d, Kirk Wong; w, Raymond Wong; ph, Henry Chan; m, Danny Chung, ed, Johnson Chow; art d, Andy Li.

Crime (PR:NR MPAA:NR)

TUESDAY WEDNESDAY† (1987, Can.) 82m Pickwauket Films c

Jon Alexander *(Phillip Blayney)*, Liz Dufresne *(Evelyn)*, Penny Belmont *(Tina)*.

The devastating effects of alcoholism are explored in this first feature which stars Alexander as a drinker who accidentally kills a child during a drunken stupor. Unable to live with his guilty conscience, he returns to the town where the accident occurred and meets with the boy's grieving mother, Dufresne.

p&d, John Pedersen; w, John Pedersen, David Adams Richards; ph, John Clement; m, Mark Carmody; ed, John Pedersen; prod d&cos, Ilkay Silk.

Drama **(PR:NR MPAA:NR)**

TUNDA BAIDA† (1987, India)

Uttam, Aparajita, Ajit Das.

[No plot available.]

d, Govind Tej; (based on a novel by Kanhu Charan).

Drama **(PR:NR MPAA:NR)**

TURNAROUND† (1987, Norway) 90m Rose Prod. A-S-Major c

Doug McKeon, Eddie Albert, Gayle Hunnicutt, Ramon Sheen, Jonna Lee, Ed Bishop, Edward McClarty

Filmed in both Norway and Long Island, New York, and featuring an international cast, TURNAROUND is a strange revenge film which sees a vicious motorcycle gang destroy the home of a young man during a Christmas party. The young man's grandfather happens to be a world-famous magician and on New Year's Eve, the bikers are lured to the magician's house and terrorized by a series of clever and frightening illusions.

p, Stuart Lyons; d, Ola Solum; w, Sandra K. Bailey (based on a story by Ray Selfe); ph, Odd Geir Saether; m, Mark Shreeve, Andy Richards; m/l, Midge Ure, Daniel Mitchell.

Thriller **(PR:NR MPAA:NR)**

TVOYO MIRNOE NEBO† (1987, USSR) 76m A.Dovzhenko Kiev Film Studio c (Trans: Your Peaceful Sky)

Emmanuel Vitorgan *(Mikhail Samarin)*, Lyudmilla Yaroshenko *(Tatyana Gudunova)*.

A Soviet scientist, Vitorgan, is obsessed with his work on "Screen," an air defense system which is still in the prototype stages and rapidly falling behind in its production schedule. With the help of fellow scientist, Yaroshenko, the project is completed and, in the process, the pair fall in love.

d, Isaac Shmaruk, Vladimir Gorpenko; w, Alexander Belyaev; ph, Alexei Prokopenko; m, Marc Fradkin; art d, Georgy Prokopets.

Drama **(PR:NR MPAA:NR)**

UV

U IME NARODA† (1987, Yugo.) 121m Zeta-Avala Pro-Film-Centar-Montex/Cannon Group c (Trans: In the Name of the People)

Miodrag Krivokapic *(Milutin)*, Savina Gersak *(Marinka)*, Petar Bozovic, Vesna Pecanac.

Covering some of the same ground that Emir Kusturica traversed in his award-winning 1985 film WHEN FATHER WAS AWAY ON BUSINESS, Zivko Nikolic's U IME NARODA deals with how the manipulation of power for selfish or vengeful reasons affects individuals in 1960s Yugoslavia. Set in a poor section of Montenegro, the film focuses primarily on Krivokapic, a supervisor in a factory who protests when his boss is wrongfully arrested. For his expressing of outrage, Krivokapic is first given a lesser job and then fired when he lends a helping hand to his former boss' family. Ultimately, the boss returns, with nothing said of the matter, but Krivokapic, being a man of his convictions, refuses to become a part of the system again.

d, Zivko Nikolic; w, Zivko Nikolic, Dragan Nikolic; ph, Savo Jovanovic; m, Vuk Kulenovic; art d, Bosko Odalovic.

Drama **(PR:NR MPAA:NR)**

UCHENIK LEKARIA (1987, USSR) 88m Gorki/Sovexportfilm c (Trans: Doctor's Apprentice)

Oleg Kazancheyev, Natalya Vavilova, Oleg Golubitsky, Mikhail Gluzsky.

A peasant boy with the power to heal the sick is taken into the home of a famous doctor who treats the Czar. The boy is told to keep secret his powers, but defies orders and risks his position in order to treat his girl friend's ailing mother.

d, Boris Rytsarev; w, Isay Kuznetsov; ph, Andrey Kirillov; m, Mikhael Tariverdiyev; art d Nikolay Terekhov.

Children's **(PR:NR MPAA:NR)**

UHOHO TANKENTAI† (1987, Jap.) 100m New Century Prods. & Dirs./Toho c (Trans: The Hours of Wedlock)

Yukiyo Toake *(Tokiko)*, Kunie Tanaka *(Kazuya)*, Mariko Fuji.

A family drama starring Tanaka as a scientist who must live at the laboratory where he works, which is located quite a distance from his home where his journalist wife, Toake, and two sons reside. Tanaka visits his family only rarely, and on one such visit he confesses to his wife that he has taken a mistress at the lab. Angry and hurt, Toake begins to flirt with the idea of taking on a lover herself. The boys are shocked by their father's revelation and the elder son takes it upon himself to find the mistress and confront her, while the younger son runs off to live with his grandparents. After much angst, a repentant Tanaka ends the affair and asks his family for forgiveness. Screenplay by prolific young director Morita (THE FAMILY GAME, SOROBANZUKU)

p, Yutaka Okada; d, Kichitaro Negishi; w, Yoshimitsu Morita (based on a book by Agata Hikari), ph, Osamu Maruike; m, Saeko Suzuki; ed, Akimasa Kawashima.

Drama **(PR:NR MPAA:NR)**

ULTIMAX FORCE† (1987, Phil.) F. Puzon Film Ent. c

Arnold Nicholas, Jeremy Ladd, Patrick Scott, Vincent Giffin, Vivian Cheung, Rey Vhen, Eric Hahns, Brad Collins, Audrey Miller, Debbie Henson, Sauro Cotoco.

A force of Americans fights their way through the jungles of Vietnam to rescue POWs from a camp run by a sadistic colonel. Besides saving the prisoners, the leader of the American force has a personal vendetta with the colonel—one which is settled in a final deadly showdown.

p, Conrad C. Puzon, Pierre C. Lee; d, Wilfred Milan; w, Joe Avalon; ph, Joe Tunes; ed, Mark Tarnate; prod d, Ronnie Cross; md, Willie Cruz; art d, Benjie Kamaya; spec eff, Edilbert Noelgas; stunts, Roland Falcis; makeup, Francis Perez.

Action/War **(PR:NR MPAA:NR)**

ULTIMO MINUTO† (1987, Ital.) 105m Duea-DMV-RAI-TV Channel 1/Sacis c (Trans: The Last Minute)

Ugo Tognazzi *(Walter Ferroni)*, Lino Capolicchio *(Pres. Di Carlo)*, Diego Abatantuono *(Duccio)*, Elena Sofia Ricci *(Marta)*, Nick Novecento *(Hotel Boy)*, Cinzia De Ponti *(Mrs. Di Carlo)*, Massimo Bonetti, Vittorio Valerio, Marcello Ghinfanti, Nino Prester, Cesare Barbetti.

The latest film from one of Italy's most popular directors, ULTIMO MINUTO is set in the world of soccer and stars veteran actor Tognazzi as a devoted general manager. Caught in a powerplay with the younger, less enthusiastic team owner, Capolicchio, Tognazzi loses his job right before his team enters the playoffs. He still manages, however, to exert his influence and, despite one player's attempt to throw the game, lead the team to an unexpected win. In a supporting role is the late Nick Novecento, a 23-year-old actor whom Avati discovered and cast in a number of his previous films.

p, Antonio Avati; d, Pupi Avati; w, Pupi Avati, Italo Ciucci, Antonio Avati; ph, Pasquale Rachini (Technovision, Eastmancolor); m, Riz Ortolani; ed, Amedeo Salfa; art d, Giuseppe Pirrotta.

Drama **(PR:NR MPAA:NR)**

UM FILM 100% BRAZILEIRO† (1987, Braz.) 80m Embrafilme-Grupo Novo de Cinema c (Trans: A 100% Brazilian Film)

Paulo Cesar Pereiro, Odete Lara, Maria Gladys, Guara Rodrigues, Luiza Clotilde, Wilson Grey, Kimura Schettino, Jesus Pingo.

The stories of two visitors to Rio during Carnivale are paralleled as both—a Parisian artist of the 1920s and a poet of the 1980s—encounter unique characters, beautiful Brazilian women, storytellers, musicians, and the exoticism of Rio de Janeiro.

p, Tarcisio Vidigal; d, Jose Sette; w, Jose Sette (based on a work by Blaise Cendrars); ph, Jose de Barros; m, Luiz Eca; ed, Jose Tavares de Barros, Amauri Alves; prod d, Mario Drummond, Fernando Tavares.

Drama **(PR:NR MPAA:NR)**

UM TREM PARA AS ESTRELAS† (1987, Braz.) 103m CDK-Chrysalide/Embrafilme c (Trans: A Train for the Stars)

Guilherme Fontes *(Vinicius)*, Milton Goncalves *(Freitas)*, Taumaturgo Ferreira *(Drimi)*, Ana Beatriz Wiltgen *(Nicinha)*, Ze Trindade, Miriam Pires, Tania Boscoli, Jose Wilker, Betty Faria, Daniel Filho, Cazuza.

Top Brazilian director Diegues follows his sweeping epic QUILOMBO with this more intimate picture about a young man, Fontes, who embarks on a seemingly futile search for his missing girlfriend. Without help from the girl's parents, the police, or the newspapers, Fontes wanders through the streets of Rio de Janeiro looking for clues and encountering a variety of seedy underworld characters.

d, Carlos Diegues; w, Carlos Diegues, Carlos Lombardi; ph, Edgar Moura; m, Gilberto Gil; ed, Gilberto Santeiro, Dominique Boischot; art d, Lia Renha.

Drama **(PR:NR MPAA:NR)**

UMMADI MOGUDU† (1987, India)

Sobhan Babu, Radhika, Keerthi.

[No plot information available.] (In Telugu.)

p, P.V.V. Satyanarayana; d, B. Bhaskara Rao.

Drama **(PR:NR MPAA:NR)**

UN AMOUR A PARIS† (1987, Fr.) 83m Prods. de la Lune c (Trans: A Romance in Paris)

Karim Allaoui *(Ali)*, Catherine Wilkening *(Marie)*, Daniel Cohn-Bendit *(Benoit)*, Sophie Vigneaud *(Justine)*, Juliet Berto *(Monika)*, Isabelle Weingarten, Xavier Maly, Jim Adhi Lima, Zaira Ben Badis, Attica Guedj, Michel Such, Mostefa Djadjam, Etienne Draber, Muriel Combeau.

A romantic comedy with a tragic end that stars Allaoui as a French-born Arab recently released from jail who falls in love with Wilkening, an Algerian who has moved to Paris as a model. Allaoui's big plan is to collect his share of the robbery money and escape to Houston where he can join NASA. When Allaoui goes to collect his money he is gunned down and, as he dies, he watches the space shuttle Challenger explode before his eyes. In a cameo role is Daniel Cohn-Bendit, the disruptive political organizer of the student uprisings in May 1968 and a temporary collaborator of Jean-Luc Godard's during the filming of WIND FROM THE EAST.

d&w, Merzak Allouache; ph, Jean-Claude Larrieu (Fujicolor); m, Jean Marie Senia; ed, Marie Josee Audiard; art d, Bruno Held.

Romance **(PR:NR MPAA:NR)**

UN HOMBRE DE EXITO (SEE: SUCCESSFUL MAN, A, 1987, Cuba)

UN HOMME AMOUREUX (SEE: MAN IN LOVE, A, 1987, Fr.)

UN RAGAZZO DI CALABRIA† (1987, Ital./Fr.) 106m Italian Intl-U.P. Schermo Video-Carthage-Canal Plus Prods.-General Image-RAI-l/Sacis Intl. c (Trans: A Boy from Calabria)

Santo Polimeno *(Mimi)*, Diego Abatatuono *(Nicola)*, Gian Maria Volonte *(Felice)*, Theresa Liotard *(Mariuccia)*, Giada Faggioli *(Crisolinda)*, Enzo Ruoti, Jean Masrevery.

Polimeno, "A Boy from Calabria," watches the 1960 Rome Olympics on the only black-and-white television in his village and is inspired by the heroics of barefooted Ethiopian marathoner Abebe Bikila. All he wants to do is take off his own shoes and run, but his father, Abatatuono, a guard at a mental institution, is determined that his son do better in life than he has, and so he forbids the boy to run, demanding that he concentrate on his schoolwork. Volonte, a crippled old bus driver, is more sympathetic to the boy's cause and helps him to train. Polimeno's mother, Liotard, also understands her son's dreams of athletic glory and takes his side when Abatatuono castigates Polimeno for overlooking his chores and homework. Abatatuono is determined to get the boy on the right track and forces him to spend a night in the mental hospital in the hopes of shocking the youngster into his senses. Nevertheless, Polimeno perseveres, and after winning some local races, he goes to a big youth competition in Rome. Directed by veteran Italian filmmaker Luigi Comencini, UN RAGAZZO DE CALABRIA is based on an autobiographical story by Demetrio Casile, who himself dreamed of track-and-field greatness when he was a boy in the mountains of southern Calabria.

p, Fulvio Lucisano; d, Luigi Comencini; w, Luigi Comencini, Ugo Pirro, Francesca Comencini (based on a screenplay by Demetrio Casile); ph, Franco Di Giacomo (Eastman Kodak); m, Antonio Vivaldi; ed, Nino Baragli; art d, Ranieri Cochetti.

Drama **(PR:NR MPAA:NR)**

UN SABADO MAS† (1987, Mex.) 96m Cinematografica Tabasco Prods./ Peliculas Mexicanas c (Trans: One More Saturday)

Pedrito Fernandez *(Martin)*, Tatiana *(Tania)*, Jose Elias Moreno *(Isauro [Grande])*, Gilberto Trujillo *(Diego)*, Adela Noriega *(Lucia)*, Jorge Pais, Jaime Santos, Alfredo Garcia Marquez.

Young Mexican pop star Fernandez stars as a motorcycle racer who desperately wants to beat his rival, spoiled rich kid Trujillo. To humiliate Trujillo even more, Fernandez wants to win over Trujillo's pretty girlfriend, Tatiana. Filled with racing and musical numbers, UN SABADO MAS was shown in New York neighborhood theaters.

p, Daniel Galindo; d, Sergio Vejar; w, Kiki Galindo Ripoll; ph, Luis Medina; m, Jorge Zarzosa; ed, Jose Li-Ho.

Drama/Musical **(PR:NR MPAA:NR)**

UN TASSINARO A NEW YORK† (1987, It.) 87m Italian Int'l. Film Prod. c (Trans: A Taxi Driver in New York)

Alberto Sordi *(Pietro, Roman Taxi Driver)*, Anna Longhi *(Teresa, His Wife)*, Dom DeLuise *(Miami Police Chief)*, George Gaynes, Giorgio Gobbi, Sasha D'Ark, Chase Rundolf, Bruno Corazzari.

Sordi and Longhi are a husband and wife from Rome who pay a visit to their student son in New York City, quickly falling prey to some of the Big Apple's less-desirables. Sordi witnesses a Mafia hit and spends the rest of the time dodging their pursuit. He takes to driving a taxi and works his way down to Miami where he meets (are you ready for this!?) police chief Dom DeLuise, who enlists the cabbie's aid in catching the mobsters.

p, Fulvio Lucisano; d, Alberto Sordi; w, Alberto Sordi, Rodolfo Sonego; ph, Giuseppe Ruzzolini; ed, Tatiana Casini Morigi.

Comedy **(PR:NR MPAA:NR)**

UN ZOO LA NUIT (SEE: NIGHT ZOO, 1987, Can.)

UNA CASA IN BILICO† (1987, It.) Angio Film (Trans: A House on the Brink)

Marina Vlady, Riccardo Cucciolla, Luigi Pistilli, Stefania Graziosi, Armando Bandini.

Three older people share a house and establish a deep relationship which enables them to deal with their insecurities and gives them the strength to deal with the outside world.

d, Antonietta De Lillo, Giorgio Magliulo; w, Giuditta Rinaldi, Antonietta De Lillo, Giorgio Magliulo; ph, Giorgio Magliulo; m, Franco Piersanti; ed, Mirco Garrone.

Drama **(PR:NR MPAA:NR)**

UNA DONNA DA SCOPRIRE† (1987, It.) Gico Cinematografica/FOX (Trans: A Woman to Discover)

Marina Suma *(Donna)*, Jean Marie Marion, Antonio Marsina, Agostina Belli.

An emotionally distraught and alcoholic singer, Suma, struggles to cut the bonds with her possessive and overbearing manager. With the encouragement of her photographer lover and her best friend, she finds the strength to defy her manager and embark on a new career. Her manager, however, refuses to be abandoned and guns her down on stage during her opening night performance.

d, Riccardo Sesani; w, Roberto Leoni; ph, Sandro Mancori; m, Sangy, The Creatures, Carjamming; ed, Alberto Moriani.

Drama **(PR:NR MPAA:NR)**

UNA PURA Y DOS CON SAL† (1987, Mex.) 87m Cima Films/Peliculas Mexicanas c (Trans: One Straight and Two With Salt)

Vicente Fernandez *(Don Rogelio Andrade)*, Blanca Guerra *(Aurelia Reyes)*, Lalo el Mimo *(Celayo)*, Irma Porter *(Diana)*, Oscar Traven.

Fernandez stars as a divorced philanderer whose daughter comes to visit him in the hope of bringing her parents together. Filmed in a flashback style in which Fernandez, in between his singing of ranchero tunes, remembers his early meetings with and subsequent marriage to his wife. Shown at neighborhood theaters in New York.

p, Vicente Fernandez; d, Rafael Vilasenor Kuri; w, Adolfo Torres Portillo; ph, Javier Cruz; m, Carlos Torres; ed, Max Sanchez.

Comedy/Drama **(PR:NR MPAA:NR)**

UNDER COVER½** (1987) 94m Golan-Globus/Cannon c

David Neidorf *(Sheffield)*, Jennifer Jason Leigh *(La Rue)*, Barry Corbin *(Sgt. Irwin Lee)*, David Harris *(Lucas)*, Kathleen Wilhoite *(Corrinne)*, Brad Leland *(Drug Dealer)*, David Denney, Mark Holton, Carmen Argenziano.

UNDER COVER is a fairly intriguing cop film once it gets past a cliched opening. Neidorf, a Baltimore undercover policeman, is disturbed by the death of his partner, who was killed while trying to infiltrate the high-school drug scene in Port Allen, South Carolina. Neidorf heads south and joins the same undercover squad. Though Neidorf almost blows his cover, he's helped out by Leigh, a local cop also assigned to the duty. However, the trail quickly leads to Corbin, the unit's boss and Leigh's mentor. Leigh turns up evidence which exonerates Corbin, but Neidorf is not convinced. After a gun is found in the home of Harris, a black youth who has become Neidorf's friend, it appears the crime has been solved. A drug raid is conducted at the school, and Harris is among those arrested. But a slip of Corbin's tongue again piques Neidorf's curiosity. Eventually he and Leigh discover that Corbin is as corrupt as they come, while local drug dealer Leland appears to be both Corbin's silent partner and the sought-after trigger man. In a dockside shoot-out Leland is killed by the Baltimore detective and Corbin is shot by Leigh before he can gun down Neidorf. The case is solved, Harris is freed, and Neidorf heads back home.

At first this appears to be nothing more than a series of crime film conventions strung together without much imagination. Neidorf's opening scene with his Baltimore chief is painfully familiar, with every word and nuance in its proper place. Once the story gets to Port Allen, UNDER COVER turns into a modern REEFER MADNESS, displaying a laughable view of the law trying to combat teenage drug fiends. Then something rather unexpected happens. The film actually grows interesting as the plot takes some unusual twists. Director Stockwell (who appeared onscreen in such films as RADIOACTIVE DREAMS and TOP GUN) takes some chances, with most of them paying off nicely. He works like a magician, misdirecting audience attention while slowly building up a few neat surprises. Neidorf, like the story, begins as a movie stereotype, but he gradually creates a character of some depth. Though high schoolers would never accept him as one of their own, Neidorf does his best to affect adolescence, which leads to a few humorous moments. Leigh, who deserved more screen time than she's given, also gives an interesting performance and builds a nice chemistry with Neidorf. It's a credit to all involved that an obvious romance between these colleagues never arises. The southern locale and police corruption angle may remind some of THE BIG EASY (though set in South Carolina, UNDER COVER, was also shot in Louisiana), but this is hardly a clone of that better-known film. Although it isn't a knock-out, when it gets going, UNDER COVER delivers an unexpected punch. Songs include: "Gotta Have You" (Michael Bishop, Steve Page, performed by The Lucas Sisters), "Absolute Reality" (Ed MacDonald, Mike Peters, performed by The Alarm), "I Need a Disguise" (Tom Kelly, Billy Steinberg, Susanna Hoffs, performed by Belinda Carlisle), "Revenge" (performed by Agent Orange), "Keeping the Tradition Alive," "Honky Tonk Special" (Paul Marshall, Butch Hendrix, performed by Hendrix), "Why" (Heidi Rodewald, performed by Wednesday Week), "Blood and Roses" (Pat DiNizio, performed by The Smithereens), "You're All I Need" (Craig Behrhorst, Carl Albert, Chris Atchison, performed by Ruffians), "Missionary" (Heidi Rodewald, David Nolte, Kent Fuher, performed by Wednesday Week), "Talk Dirty to Me" (performed by Poison), "Lift Him Up" (Bobby McGee, performed by The Bobby McGee Inspirational Chorale), "Love Shy," "You Lied Your Way," "It Comes and Goes" (Sandy Rogers, performed by Rogers), "Waitin' Up" (George Highfill, performed by Highfill), "Heartbreak Train" (Albert Lee, Rosie Flores, Pleasant Gehmen, performed by Lee, Flores). *(Violence, adult situations.)*

p, Menahem Golan, Yoram Globus; d, John Stockwell; w, John Stockwell, Scott

Fields; ph, Alexander Gruszynski; m, Todd Rundgren; ed, Sharyn L. Ross; prod d, Becky Block; stunts, Greg Walker.

Crime **Cas.** **(PR:O MPAA:R)**

UGIORNI, UNOTTI† (1987, It.) Filmirage/Real Film (Trans: Eleven Days, Eleven Nights; AKA: UNDICI GIORNI, UNDICI NOTTE)

Jessica Moore *(Sarah Asproon)*, Joshua McDonald *(Michael Terenzi)*, Mary Sillers, Tom Mojack.

While completing her book "Sarah Asproon and her 100 Men," author Moore realizes there have only been 99 men in her life. Searching for one more, she finds McDonald, a man who is engaged to be married in 11 days. After 11 days and nights of passionate romance, McDonald, as agreed, heads for the altar with his fiancee.

d, Joe D'Amato; w, Sarah Aspron, Clyde Anderson; ph, Federico Slonisco; m, Piero Montanari; ed, Kathleen Stratton.

Romance **(PR:NR MPAA:NR)**

UNE FLAMME DANS MON COEUR† (1987, Fr./Switz.) 112m Garance-La Sept-Filmograph/Bac bw (Trans: A Flame in my Heart)

Myriam Mezieres *(Mercedes)*, Aziz Kabouche *(Johnny)*, Benoit Regent *(Pierre)*, Biana, Jean-Yves Berthelot, Jean-Gabriel Nordmann.

Swiss filmmaker Tanner (JONAH WHO WILL BE 25 IN THE YEAR 2000; IN THE WHITE CITY) directs scriptwriter Mezieres in this tale of an attractive woman who leaves her live-in boyfriend and becomes frighteningly obsessed with Kabouche, a journalist whom she notices during a subway ride. Kabouche is a consummate professional who refuses to let anything stand in the way of his vocation. Mezieres, however, has difficulty coping with his frequent trips away from home. Desperately in need of his love, she becomes absorbed in her own sexuality. He finally agrees to bring her along on an assignment in Cairo, but before long she disappears into the night.

p, Paolo Branco; d, Alain Tanner; w, Myriam Mezieres, Alain Tanner; ph, Acacio de Almeida; m, Johann Sebastian Bach; ed, Laurent Uhler.

Drama **(PR:NR MPAA:NR)**

UNFINISHED BUSINESS . . . * (1987) 65m American Film Institute (Directing Workshop for Women) c

Viveca Lindfors *(Helena)*, Peter Donat *(Ferenzy)*, Gina Hecht *(Vickie, Jonathan's Wife)*, James Morrison *(Jonathan, Helena's Son)*, Anna Devere Smith *(Anna)*, Haley Taylor-Block *(Kristina)*, Herriett Guiar *(Cynthia)*, James Ward *(Chauffeur)*, Chuck Cochran *(Manager)*.

Swedish actress Viveca Lindfors, a former bombshell who has taken the usual route down to cameos in horror films, here takes up direction herself, funded by the American Film Institute's Directing Workshop for Women. Shot on video and transferred to film, UNFINISHED BUSINESS is the story of a stage actress, Lindfors, who is preparing for a production of "Brecht on Brecht." Into her rehearsal and life walks Donat, a Hungarian who left her 15 years before to return to Europe, where he now runs a state-subsidized theater. He also brings his mistress. There are a number of confrontations and lingering close-ups showing what the decades have done to Lindfors. Donat wants to come back to her now, and as the film ends, it looks like she will accept him. It is probably a good thing that no one will ever give Lindfors this kind of money again, so that audiences will be spared having to endure this kind of pretentious, arty drivel again. The video-to-film process assures the poorest kind of visual quality, and little effort seems to have been made with the lighting. There are incomprehensible fade-outs and jump cuts, and the performances are the kind that remind one of why some actors are such dull, trivial people in real life. *(Adult situations, brief nudity, profanity.)*

p, Dale Ann Stieber, Chrisann Verges, Suzanne Kent; d&w, Viveca Lindfors; ph, Sean McLin; m, Patricia Lee Stotter, Don Rebic, Matt Sullivan; ed, Dale Ann Stieber, Sharyn C. Blumenthal; prod d, Johanna Leovey; cos, Marty Rodenbush.

Drama **(PR:C-O MPAA:NR)**

UNI TO DOKUYAKU (SEE: SEA AND POISON, THE, 1987, Jap.)

UNTOUCHABLES, THE** (1987) 119m PAR c

Kevin Costner *(Eliot Ness)*, Sean Connery *(James Malone)*, Charles Martin Smith *(Oscar Wallace)*, Andy Garcia *(George Stone)*, Robert De Niro *(Al Capone)*, Richard Bradford *(Mike)*, Jack Kehoe *(Walter Payne)*, Brad Sullivan *(George)*, Billy Drago *(Frank Nitti)*, Patricia Clarkson *(Catherine Ness)*, Vito D'Ambrosio *(Bowtie Driver)*, Steven Goldstein *(Scoop)*, Peter Aylward *(Lt. Alderson)*, Don Harvey *(Preseuski)*, Robert Swan *(Mountie Captain)*, John J. Walsh *(Bartender)*, Del Close *(Alderman)*, Colleen Bade *(Mrs. Blackmer)*, Greg Noonan *(Rangemaster)*, Sean Grennan *(Cop Cousin)*, Vince Viverito, Sr. *(Italian Waiter)*, Kevin Michael Doyle *(Williamson)*, Mike Bacarella *(Overcoat Hood)*, Michael P. Byrne *(Ness's Clerk)*, Kaitlin Montgomery *(Ness's Daughter)*, Aditra Kohl *(Blackmer Girl)*, Charles Keller Watson, Larry Branderburg, Chelcie Ross, Tim Gamble *(Reporters)*, Sam Smiley, Pat Billingsley *(Bailiffs)*, John Bracci *(Fat Man)*, Jennifer Anglim *(Woman in Elevator)*, Eddie Minasian *(Butler)*, Tony Mockus, Sr. *(Judge)*, Will Zahrn *(Defense Attorney)*, Louis Lanciloti *(Barber)*, Vince Viverito, Valentino Cimo, Joe Greco, Clem Caserta, Bob Martana, Joseph Scianablo, George Spataro *(Bodyguards)*, Melody Rae *(Union Station Woman)*, Robert Miranda *(Gunned Head)*, James Guthrie *(Pagliacci)*, Basil Reale *(Hotel Clerk)*.

It's only wishful thinking on the part of Paramount's publicity department that its box office bruiser, THE UNTOUCHABLES, has anything to do with the facts it purports to depict. The film, other than the infamous real-life people it fictionalizes, has little to recommend it. Director De Palma ignores the true story of the Al Capone mob in Chicago and opts for his usual bloodbath techniques, along with some embarrassingly amateurish efforts to mimic such master filmmakers as Sergei Eisenstein. THE UNTOUCHABLES shows at the beginning Chicago crime kingpin Al Capone (De Niro) emerging from his lavish suite of rooms in, presumably, the old Lexington Hotel, to step into a barbershop, his own, to have a shave from his personal barber while expansively answering questions from slavish newspaper reporters. In his interview, De Niro points out in czar-like fashion how he is only providing people with what they demand—booze—and, as a bootlegger, he is breaking a bad law to fill a public need. The other side of the Capone/De Niro portrait shows his henchmen killing rival gangsters battling over Chicago's lucrative bootleg empire, including the bombing of a speakeasy where the owners refuse to peddle De Niro's brew. Here director De Palma is at his most manipulative and sleazy, showing a young girl discovering a package left in the speakeasy, picking it up and running after the man who has left it, only to be blown to pieces with the saloon. Into this violent atmosphere steps mild-mannered family man Costner, essaying T-Man Eliot Ness, made famous by Robert Stack's four-year presence on TV (1959-63) in the television series of the enormously profitable and technically superb "The Untouchables." Costner, who bears some resemblance to the original Eliot Ness, is shown pensively considering his new assignment to smash Capone's bootleg empire. He enters his office and is looked upon by other federal investigators as an ineffectual college boy. But Costner is saved from making one mistake after another by recruiting a wily Chicago street cop, Connery, after he criticizes one of Costner's fouled up booze raids. Connery knows the ins and outs of the Chicago underworld, and recognizes many in Capone's army of thugs on sight. He joins Costner only on the proviso that the federal agent play it his way: "He (Capone) hurts one of yours, you kill one of his!" It's warfare, Connery intones, and to the death. More recruits are added, including Smith, an accountant who learns how to use a shotgun, and young Italian rookie detective Garcia, these forming the nucleus of what will later be known as "the untouchables," law men who cannot be bought or corrupted by De Niro and his ilk. Successful raids against Capone breweries are made and De Niro shows his resentment by uttering veiled, smiling threats when leaving the opera or attending other galas. He is ever the expansive, generous crime lord, acting as if he is above the law, that he is an untouchable too. Smith finally realizes that the raids against De Niro's booze strongholds are pointless. He will merely open up new ones. The only way to get De Niro behind bars, Smith reasons, is to obtain documentary information about the crime boss' income and convict and imprison him for tax evasion. To that end the lawmen find themselves in Canada, following De Niro henchmen who are about to take possession of several truckloads of prized Canadian hooch. The gangsters are trapped at the border by Costner, Connery and others, including a contingent of Northwest Mounted Police, and a wild shootout occurs where several gangsters are killed and one of De Niro's top lieutenants is captured and brought to a small cabin for interrogation. He only sneers and demands a lawyer. Connery tells Costner he knows how to break the man's dogmatic belief in the code of silence. Connery steps outside and picks up the body of a dead gangster, shouting for him to give information about De Niro. The hoodlum inside the cabin, believing the gangster is still alive, sees Connery put a pistol into the man's mouth, and pull the trigger, blowing the corpse's head off. When Connery steps inside the cabin and tells the gangster that he will do the same thing to him unless he talks, the De Niro lieutenant caves in, telling Costner he will not only inform on De Niro but provide information in written form that will send the gang chief away to prison. (The whole Canadian episode of the film where the lawmen race about on horseback wielding submachineguns is as preposterous and unthinkably forced as the posturing and unbelievable Mamet script.) The informant and Smith are waylaid in a government building elevator, both killed by De Niro hitman Drago, playing the part of the real-life Frank "The Enforcer" Nitti. Costner, Connery, and Garcia then go after another De Niro aide who possesses documents that will seal De Niro's fate in court. Meanwhile, De Niro, seeing the erosion of his criminal empire, begins to clean his house of defectors, giving a banquet for one lieutenant and then beating his brains out with a baseball bat (an event, based on fact, and earlier depicted in PARTY GIRL, in which Lee J. Cobb, playing a

Capone role model, does the same thing, and THE ST. VALENTINE'S DAY MASSACRE in which Jason Robards, Jr., playing Capone, dispatches several unfaithful henchmen. In reality, Capone murdered John Scalise, Albert Anselmi, and Joseph "Hop Toad" Guinta by crushing their heads with a baseball bat while giving them a party at his citadel, The Hawthorn Hotel in Cicero, but the year was 1930, not years later, as indicated in this inaccurate film.) Connery locates the much-wanted witness against De Niro and is murdered for his efforts by Drago. Connery's death scene is the epitome of De Palma's type of filmmaking, gory, bloody, offensive to young and old, as the mortally wounded cop crawls the distance of his entire apartment leaving a trail of blood. Later, Costner corners Drago atop what is supposed to be a federal detention center (it's the Chicago Library's cultural center) and when Drago sneers at him, smugly saying that Connery "bled like a pig" before dying, Costner, up to then showing restraint, explodes and shoves Drago off the building to a screaming death, crashing through the top of a car. (Of course, this, too, is utter myth created by Mamet, a Chicago-based writer who should know better; Frank Nitti committed suicide in 1943 rather than be indicted on federal charges and face certain imprisonment.) Costner, in one of the final scenes of the film, in order to protect the life of the witness whose testimony and documents will send De Niro to jail, shoots it out with a gang of De Niro thugs at Union Station, a stagy scene which is supposed to be fraught with jeopardy in that a child in a baby buggy is in the line of fire. (Again, the unimaginative De Palma can only reach back to the past for his visual climax by blatantly lifting the Odessa steps sequence from Sergei Eisenstein's masterpiece, THE BATTLESHIP POTEMKIN.) Costner and Garcia manage to shoot all the gangsters, save the child and its mother, and deliver the witness. His testimony then leads to De Niro's conviction. The courtroom scenes depicting De Niro on trial and how he explodes when convicted, slapping his attorneys, bailiffs, screaming, and trying to attack Costner, who is on-hand to savor the victory, is also pure myth. Capone never showed such violence in court. Also, although Costner is shown confronting the mob kingpin in the movie several times, in real life Eliot Ness and Alphonse "Scarface" Capone never met and Ness had nothing to do with getting evidence on Capone which sent him to prison (first to Atlanta, then to Alcatraz when "the Rock" opened up in 1934) for income tax evasion. The whole thing is sloppy, a stew brewed by Mamet and served steaming hot by De Palma as true crime history, which it certainly is not. There is something cartoonish about THE UNTOUCHABLES, with De Niro doing an impersonation of Rod Steiger's excellent portrayal of Scarface in CAPONE. The actor put on 30 pounds and studied Capone's movements and voice in newsreels and tapes, but his exaggerated movements and jaw-jutting delivery do little to capture the real Al Capone. Costner is a specter, stoic, unresponsive, a weak-chinned, uncoordinated actor whose rise to stardom, beyond the backing of such $30 million turkeys as this, is inexplicable. There is no command to his voice or delivery and he registers only one emotion with a nerveless face, stupefaction, as if he has been injected with novocaine before each take. The real Ness was reserved and kept a low profile, but Costner's interpretation of this modest lawman is one of dreary indifference, without the forcefulness the role demands, without empathy as Ness' experiences dictated, and without belief in a savage time where stark realism was present in every raw hour of the Great Depression. De Palma's slam-bang style remains unchanged and he still reaches for the buckets of blood when faced with having to present a powerful scene. He continues to show nothing but hack techniques glossed over with expensive production sets, costuming, and props. ***(Graphic violence, profanity.)***

p, Art Linson; d, Brian De Palma; w, David Mamet; ph, Stephen H. Burum (Technicolor); m, Ennio Morricone; ed, Jerry Greenberg, Bill Pankow; art d, William A. Elliott; set d, E.C. Chen, Steven P. Sardanis, Gil Clayton, Nicholas Laborczy; cos, Marilyn Vance-Straker; stunts, Gary Hymes.

Crime **(PR:O MPAA:R)**

UPPU† (1987, India) (Trans: Salt)

Mohammad *(Abu)*, Vijayan Kottarathil *(Moosa)*, Sree Raman *(Kazi)*, Madhavan *(Moidutty)*, Jayalalitha *(Amina)*.

Deeply rooted in Muslim law and reflecting the huge role it plays in the life of Kerala Muslims, this Malayalam-language film is a kind of before and after look at a woman who, bowing to the dictates of her religion, divorces the man she loves to marry another to the seeming benefit of everyone but her. At the behest of Raman, Jayalalitha reluctantly divorces Mohammad so that she may wed Madhavan, a man of great wealth who has shared it with his community. Years later, Madhavan is dead; Jayalalitha has two spoiled, unruly teenage children; and her aging father, Kottarathil, ineptly manages the family finances for her. After years of unhappily adhering to tradition, Jayalalitha leaves her household to rejoin Mohammad, and the film ends as she and her beloved former husband perish in a fire in his humble hut. (In Malayalam.)

p, K.M.A. Rahim; d, Pavithran; w, K.M.A. Rahim; ph, Madhu Ambat; m, Saratchandra Marathe.

Drama **(PR:NR MPAA:NR)**

URSULA† (1987, Fin.) 100m Filminor c

Ville Virtanen *(Marten)*, Heidi Kilpelainen *(Ursula)*, Petri Aalto *(Harri)*, Tomi Salmela, Ahmed Riza, Chris af Enehielm, Pekka Uotila, Eija Vilpas, Johan Donner, Raine Salo.

Drifting almost as aimlessly as the characters at its center, Finnish director Jaakko Pyhala's film follows the fortunes of a raven-haired 18-year-old beauty, Kilpelainen, and her 30-year-old companions: Virtanen, who loves Kilpelainen, and Aalto who loves drugs and money. The *action* moves from Helsinki to Copenhagen to Berlin as Kilpelainen and Virtanen, unable to think of anything better to do, join Aalto in transporting drugs. Although they are eventually caught, the film makes no attempt to pass judgement on their actions or lifestyle.

p, Heikki Takkinen; d&w, Jaakko Pyhala (based on the novel *Puuluola* by Kim Weckstrom); ph, Pertti Mutanen (Eastmancolor); m, Antti Hytti, Raine Salo, Giuseppe Verdi; set d, Jaakko Pyhala.

Drama **(PR:NR MPAA:NR)**

USODNI TELEFON† (1987, Yugo.) 74m E Motion-Skuc-TDS SKD Brut-Filmoteka 16 bw (Trans: The Fatal Telephone)

Miran Sustersic, Vinoi Vogue-Anzlovar.

Helmed by 22-year-old first-timer Kozole, this low-budget Slovenian effort is about a couple of budding filmmakers who are determined to make a picture that is an hour and a half long. Once they have enough footage, the would-be Makavejev's, Sustersic and Vogue-Anzlovar, have to come up with a soundtrack for it, and their eclectic solution includes everything from taped performances by rock bands to intimate telephone conversations. Shot on 16mm black-and-white stock, USODNI TELEFON is one of the first independently produced films to be made in Yugoslavia.

d&w, Damjan Kozole; ph, Andrej Lupinc; m, Otroci Socializma; ed, Vesna Lazeta; art d, Roman Bahovec.

Drama **(PR:NR MPAA:NR)**

UTOLSO KEZIRAT† (1987, Hung.) Mafilm-Dialog (Trans: Last Manuscript)

Jozef Kroner, Alexander Barbini.

An analysis of social and political concerns in Hungary in 1955. The film is based on a novel by Tibor Dery which, written in 1955, predicted the 1956 uprising in Hungary, and was on the banned list in Hungary until recently. In 1971, Makk adapted a Dery novel for his movie LOVE, which won the special jury prize at Cannes.

d, Karoly Makk; w, (based on the novel *A Merry Funeral* by Tibor Dery).

Drama **(PR:NR MPAA:NR)**

UTRO OBRECHENNOGO PRIISKA† (1987, USSR) 91m Mosfilm/ Sovexportfilm c (Trans: The Dawn of the Doomed Gold-Mine)

Dalvin Scherbakov, Ivan Lapikiv, Igor Kvasha, Galina Levina.

In 1918, only months after the October Revolution, the embattled Soviet government struggles to maintain power. The Siberian gold deposits are beginning to dwindle and the government, anxious to replenish its coffers, sends a young Bolshevik engineer to increase production in another gold-mining region where the mines' former owners have taken drastic measures to prevent a government takeover.

d, Arya Dashiev; w, Vladimir Meetypov, Arya Dashiev; ph, Yuri Gantman; m, Yevgeny Ptichkin; art d, Ivan Plastinkin.

Drama **(PR:NR MPAA:NR)**

UUNO TURHAPURO MUUTTAA MAALLE† (1987, Fin.) 105m Filmituotanto Spede Pasanen Oy c (Trans: Numbskull Emptybrook Back in the Country)

Vesa-Matti Loiri, Marjatta Raita, Tapio Hamalainen, Marita Nordberg, Spede Pasanen, Simo Salminen, Helge Herala, Marja Korhonen.

In order to get away from his maddening son-in-law, a man moves out of his daughter's house and buys a home in the country. He finds peace and tranquility in his new home until he learns the route for a new highway runs right through his property. A battle begins to save the house, with the despised son-in-law getting involved and saving the day.

d&w, Ere Kokkonen; ph, Juha Jalasti; m, Jaakko Salo; ed, Eva Jaakontalo; set d, Kristine Elo, Vesa Tapola.

Comedy **(PR:NR MPAA:NR)**

UVEK SPREMNE ZENE† (1987, Yugo.) 107m Danas-Croatia-Smart Egg c (Trans: Woman's Day)

Mirjana Karanovic, Radmila Zivkovic, Tanja Boskovic, Dara Dokic, Cvijeta Mesic, Ksenija Pajic.

Seriocomic Yugoslav film in which Fate confronts seven plucky women with one disheartening experience after another. When their boss doesn't pay them what they are due, seven female farmhands steal a tractor and head off with the intention of finding some way to get jobs in Germany. That failing, they do whatever it takes to survive—working in factories, smuggling, and even streetwalking—but despite their determination, they are repaid only with grief, disaster, and pain . . . yet they refuse to give up.

d, Branko Baletic; w, Milan Secerovic, Branko Baletic; ph, Zivko Zalar; m, Zoran Simjanovic; art d, Nemanja Petrovic.

Comedy **(PR:NR MPAA:NR)**

V STRELYAYUSHCHEY GLUSHI† (1987, USSR) 87m Sverdlovsk/ Sovexportfilm c (Trans: Shooting in the Back-Country)

Sergei Koltakov, Viktor Smirnov, Natalia Akimova, Ivan Agafonov.

Set in 1918, "Shooting in the Back-Country" deals with a commissar's attempts to persuade the citizens of a village to give their grain over to the government before an army unit arrives to take it by force if necessary. However, the villagers can't give what they don't have, since the kulaks (wealthy peasants) have already appropriated all of their harvest. The kulaks then slaughter the detachment that was to have joined the commissar, but when they prepare to do away with him too, the villagers, whom he has won over, come to his defense.

d, Vladimir Khotinenko; w, Anatoly Protsenko; ph, Vladimir Makeranets; m, Boris Petrov; art d, Mikhail Rosenstein.

Drama **(PR:NR MPAA:NR)**

V TALOM SNEGE ZVON RUCHIA† (1987, USSR) 87m Tadjikfilm/ Sovexportfilm c (Trans: Ringing Streams in Thawing Snow)

Mukhitdin Salokhov, Shodi Davronov, Sher Abdulaikhasov, Sergei Lesnoy.

A group of WW II veterans have a reunion every May 9 in Moscow, though their numbers continually dwindle. The film focuses on one of the veterans and the numerous hardships he has faced since the end of the war.

d, Davlat Khudonazarov; w, Gavkhar Surmanov, Valery Talvik; ph, Valery Vilensky; m, Eduard Artyomyev; art d, Sergei Ramonkulov.

Drama **(PR:NR MPAA:NR)**

V.Y. VIHDOINKIN YHDESSA† (1987, Fin.) 90m Skandia Filmi Oy c (Trans: Together at Last)

Pirkka-Pekka Petelius, Sarianna Salminen, Pirkko Uitto, Jari Pehkonen, Mikko Kivinen, Martti Tsokkinen.

A Christmas gift, a sweater "made with love," sends its lonely recipient (Petelius) on an exhaustive search for the woman who has given it to him without signing her name to the card. Petelius looks everywhere for a clue to the identity of his secret admirer, but as the night wears on, he finds himself farther from her and deeper in trouble. In his travels he becomes involved with an unusual holdup gang—a female Santa who is three sheets to the wind and a bunch of jobless kids. This is the first feature film directed by Kyronseppa and the first big film role for Petelius, though both worked together in Finnish TV.

d&w, Kari Kyronseppa; ph, Henrik Paersch; ed, Olli Soinio.

Comedy **(PR:NR MPAA:NR)**

VA DE NUEZ† (1987, Mex.) 95m Diplaf-Producciones Chimalistac/ Peliculas Nacionales c (Trans: Once Again)

Rafael Sanchez Navarro *(Pepe Reyes)*, Patricia Reyes Spindola *(Manuela Reyes)*, Alejandro Parodi, Jorge Zepeda.

Director Gurrola has taken a novel cinematic approach to what is basically a public service-type subject: population control. His main characters—created by screenwriter Jorge Patino—are a young married couple who are frustrated by their inability to have children. The situation becomes doubly disappointing because the rest of their community is producing large families. He directs commercials, while she studies film theory. Their different attitudes toward filmmaking become a catalyst for arguments about what is really eroding their marriage—mutual recriminations over their failed attempts at parenthood. Director Gurrola offers up a variety of different images: commericials, videos, and even scenes from one of his previous films LLAMANME MIKE (Call Me Mike) to act as counterpoint to the emotions felt by the characters. This film was co-produced by the Mexican state family planning organization Desarrollo de Investigacion para la Planeacion Familiar.

p, Hugo Scherer, Gonzalo Infante; d, Alfredo Gurrola; w, Jorge Patino; ph, Miguel Garzon; m, Amparo Rubin; ed, Sergio Soto.

Drama **(PR:NR MPAA:NR)**

VALET GIRLS* (1987) 82m Lexyn/Empire c

Meri D. Marshall *(Lucy)*, April Stewart *(Rosalind)*, Mary Kohnert *(Carnation)*, Christopher Weeks *(Dirk Zebra)*, Patricia Scott Michel *(Tina Zebra)*, Jon Sharp *(Lindsay Brawnsworth)*, Michael Karm *(Alvin Sunday)*, Steve Lyon *(Ike)*, Randy Gallion *(Ramon)*, Stuart Fratkin *(Dash)*, John Terlesky *(Archie Lee Samples)*, Jeanne Byron *(Edie)*, Charles Cooper *(Victor)*, Kenny Sachia *(Tim Cheeseman)*, Tony Cox *(Sammy Rudenko)*, Richard Erdman *(Waiter)*, Rick Leiberman *(Charles Dunson)*, Bridget Sienna *(Yolanda)*, Matt Landers *(Danny)*, Elizabeth Lamers *(Grunting Greta)*, Elsie Richards *(Cindy)*, Rebecca Cruz *(Egypt Von Sand Dunes)*, Valerie Richards *(Busty Girl)*, Janette Caldwell *(Beautiful Girl)*, Kim Gillingham *(Madonna Wannabe)*, Pinky *(New Wave Clone)*, Victor Carron *(Mexican Bus Boy)*, Bob Parr, John Parr *(The Grunts/New Psychotics)*, Magie Song, Louis Molind, John Denting, Joe Berardi, Tom Corey *(Sexy Holiday)*.

Marshall is an aspiring singer who works for "Valet Girls," a professional car parking service used by a variety of Los Angeles clients. Along with her friend Stewart, a U.C.L.A. psychology student with an affected English accent, Marshall makes trouble for her slimy boss, Landers. Meanwhile, at the posh estate of talent agent Weeks, a swanky party is being held. Essentially the soiree is a simple excuse for Weeks and his Hollywood pals Karm and Sharp to pick up young girls for easy sex. When Weeks finds his current valets Lyon, Gallion, and Fratkin have been making fancy with his guests as well, the three car parkers are fired. Of course the Valet Girls, whose number now includes naive Southern belle Kohnert, are hired and the three jobless boys decide to get revenge. At Weeks' next party, Marshall manages to get an opportunity to sing and is consequently noticed by a powerful agent. But Marshall really wants to attract the attention of Karm, who is a well-known rock star. Unable to see a thing without her glasses (at least when it makes for an easy laugh), Marshall accidentally corners the wrong man. Good thing too, for Karm is only interested in one thing and it sure isn't music. Lyon, Gallion, and Fratkin manage to crash the party and destroy any semblance of order. This leads to the Valet Girls being fired, and the former employees are put back on the job. The girls decide to get revenge, not only on the rival car parkers, but on the sleazy show biz folks who frequent Weeks' abode as well. Joining them in this plot is Weeks' long-suffering wife Michel, who has had enough of her husband's philandering. Naturally the girls are victorious, and the film ends with them spray painting the bare bottoms of Lyon, Gallion, and Fratkin as the boys cling to the famous letters overlooking Hollywood Hills.

To be sure, this is a typical teen sex comedy, full of inane jokes, sniggering sexual humor, and an occasional bared breast. Still, there's something slightly cheerful to the stupidity, and that alone makes this more tolerable than most in the genre. Marshall is a lively actress, and surprisingly sings rather well. VALET GIRLS' worst element is its preoccupation with drug humor. Cocaine, quaaludes, and alcohol are all in abundance, as is a mysterious gas party goers periodically suck on for cheap laughs. Songs include: "Flyin' High," 'Heartless Love," "Valet Girls Theme Song," "Reachin' Up," (performed by Meri D. Marshall), "Slow Beautiful Sex" (performed by the Fibonaccis), "Grunt" (performed by Elizabeth Lamers), "Purple Haze" (performed by the Fibonaccis), "Day After Day" (performed by Passion to Pass), "Video Love" (performed by T&W), "Wilshire Girls & Rocks" (performed by Monopoly), "Party Line" (performed by Alan Alvarez, Steve Melson, Mike Melson, Ethan James, Craig Back). *(Nudity, sexual situations, profanity.)*

p, Dennis Murphy; d, Rafal Zielinski; w, Clark Carlton; ph, Nicholas Von Sternberg (United color); m, Robert Parr; ed, Akiko B. Metz; art d, Dins Danielsen; cos, Kathie Clark; ch, Damita Jo Freeman; stunts, Dan Bradley.

Comedy **Cas.** **(PR:O MPAA:NR)**

VALENTIN I VALENTINA† (1987, USSR) 93m Mosfilm/Sovexportfilm c (Trans: Valentin and Valentina)

Marina Zudina, Nikolai Stetsky, Tatyana Doronina, Nina Ruslanova.

A "Romeo and Juliet" tale about two 18-year-olds who fall in love despite the objections of their parents.

d, Georgy Natanson; w, Mikhail Roschin, Georgy Natanson (based on the play by Mikhail Roschin); ph, Viktor Yakushev; m, Yevgeny Doga; art d, Georgy Kolganov.

Romance **(PR:NR MPAA:NR)**

VALHALLA½** (1987, Den.) 88m Swan-Interpresse Metronome-Palle Fogtdal-Danish Film Institute/J&M c

Voices Of: Stephen Thorne *(Thor)*, Allan Corduner *(Loke)*, Suzanne Jones *(Roskva)*, Alexander Jones *(Chalfe)*, Michael Elphick *(Udgaardsloki)*, John Hollis *(Hymer)*, Mark Jones *(Odin)*, Thomas Eje *(Quark)*, Benny Hansen, Jesper Klein, Percy Edwards.

This animated feature, based on a popular Danish comic strip, is the most expensive film ever made in Denmark. Four years in the making, released in Denmark in 1986, the time and money spent certainly shows. The design is lush and the feature populated by lively characters, often recalling the best work of the Disney Studios. Unfortunately VALHALLA lacks a linear plot line, instead developing its story as a series of loosely knit set pieces. As a result, this project achieves only middling success.

The story opens as Thor the God of Thunder arrives with his sidekick Loke at the home of a simple peasant family. Thor sacrifices one of his flying goats for the evening meal, instructing everyone not to break the bones. These will be wrapped in the goat's skin, and Thor will magically return the beast to its original form the following morning. Loke tricks Chalfe, the family's young son, into eating some of the bone marrow and the rejuvenated goat is consequently crippled. As punishment Thor takes Chalfe to be his houseboy. Chalfe's sister Roskva sneaks along, and the two children are soon kept busy in Thor's household. Loke has a troll as his companion, a troublesome creature named Quark. Quark causes untold mayhem which naturally makes Thor angry. Roskva, tired of Thor's orders, goes to the head god to ask for help. She is joined by Quark, for the two are quickly becoming good friends. But Quark's inquisitive nature only causes more trouble and Roskva is dismissed. She goes into the woods with Quark, and Chalfe decides to join her. The group builds a tree house where they live contentedly for some time, until Thor arrives to take them home. The thunder god decides to take Quark back to Udgaard, the land of giants and monsters from which the little troll originates. Upon arrival, Thor meets his old rival, the Giant King. A contest is held between the two, and Thor is tricked by his foe. He is killed, but Chalfe's belief magically brings Thor back to life. The group returns home, and a reformed Quark is accepted back into the fold.

This is a confusing tale which develops in a helter skelter fashion. The story skips from one event to another, hastily resolving situations if not ignoring denouements altogether. Furthermore, the story lacks any real central conflict to link the episodic structure. However, the film is not without some merit. Technically the film is a marvel to look at. Backgrounds are stylized paintings which give a certain moody look to events, and the characters are lively. The mythical creatures depicted here differ dramatically in size, shape, and personality. Quark, as expected, is designed to be an appealing scene stealer, but he certainly does get some tough competition. One marvelous sequence, in which we first see the Udgaard, owes a debt to the famous bar scene from George Lucas' STAR WARS as a myriad creatures guzzle beer in a mutant's tavern. Another outstanding moment would have made Disney proud. As Roskva and Chalfe sit whistling in their new tree home, Quark joins in, pounding out a rhythm with some old bones. The scene turns into a lively musical number with enormous appeal. It's a shame VALHALLA's story doesn't live up to its technical qualities. This could have been something really special.

d, Peter Madsen; w, Peter Madsen, Henning Kure (based on Nordic myths and on characters from "Valhalla" comic strip by Peter Madsen, Henning Kure, Hans Rancke-Madsen, Per Vadmand, Soren Hakonsson); m, Ron Goodwin; ed, Lidia Sablone; art d, Peter Madsen.

Animated **(PR:AA MPAA:NR)**

VAMPIRES IN HAVANA*** (1987, Cuba) 80m Instituto del Arte y Industria Cinematograficos-Television Espanola-Durnoik Produktion c (VAMPIROS EN LA HABANA)

This witty animated spoof of vampire and gangster movies originally was screened in its native Cuba in 1985. The film saw some festival screenings, then received a more widespread release along animation circuits in 1987. The story follows a group of Mafioso vampires headquartered in Chicago during the 1930s. They are at war with their rivals in Dusseldorf, as both gangs are after a secret formula developed by a Cuban scientist. The elixir's of value because it allows vampires to survive in sunlight. Pepito, the Cuban scientist's nephew, is a trumpet player who inevitably gets caught up in these monster-Mafia wars. Though he doesn't realize it, Pepito is a vampire who has been given the serum ever since his childhood.

Padron, a well-known cartoonist in his native land, uses a minimalist animation style that often recalls the simplicity of Jay Ward's "Rocky and Bullwinkle" series. Like that classic television cartoon, VAMPIRES IN HAVANA is easy on the eye and offers some marvelous satirical writing. Padron also has a gift for crude sexual humor, making his caricatures fun without being degrading. Though the animation quality isn't up to FRITZ THE CAT, VAMPIRES IN HAVANA is a much better work in the full realization of its humor. Padron understands that cartoons shouldn't be classified as strictly for children, and he has created a work of enormous fun. *(Profanity, sexual situations.)*

p, Paco Prats; d&w, Juan Padron; ph, Adalberto Hernandez, Julio Simoneau; m, Rembert Egues; ed, Rosa Maria Carreras; prod d, Juan Padron; anim, Mario Garcia-Montes, Joses Reyes, Noel Lima.

Animation/Comedy **(PR:C-O MPAA:NR)**

VAN GELUK GESPROKEN† (1987, Neth.) 99m Verenigde Nederlandsche/ Cannon Tuschinski c (Trans: Count Your Blessings)

Mirjam Sternheim *(Martje)*, Marijke Veugelers *(Karin)*, Gerard Thoolen *(Sjef)*, Peter Tuinman *(Leo)*, Loudi Nijhoff *(Mother Kalk)*, Aart Lamberts *(Kalk)*, Michiel Romeyn *(Harrie)*, Olga Zuiderhoek, Arend Jan Heerma van Voss.

Chosen by the Dutch for consideration as Best Foreign-Language Film at this year's Academy Awards was director Verhoeff's (SIGN OF THE BEAST, DE DROOM) latest film, which examines the lives of the residents of an apartment building in a typical neighborhood in Amsterdam. Although there are many characters, the film concentrates on the landlord's daughter, Sternheim, who is in the midst of an unhappy romance. Other residents include a bachelor who has let his own life go while struggling to keep his ailing mother out of the hospital, and a blue-collar family experiencing financial problems. Actress Sternheim is a newcomer to the screen who was discovered by director Verhoeff—in fabled fashion—when he saw her in a cafe.

p, Rob Houwer; d, Pieter Verhoeff; w, Jean van de Velde, Pieter Verhoeff (based on a novel by Marijke Howeler); ph, Paul van den Bos (Eastmancolor); m, Cees Bijlstra; ed, Ot Louw; art d, Dorus van der Linden.

Drama **(PR:NR MPAA:NR)**

VAN PAEMEL FAMILY, THE† (1987, Bel.) 90m Kunst Nkino/ FlandersFilm Int. c (HET GEZIN VAN PAEMEL)

Senne Rouffaer, Chris Boni, Thom Hoffman, Marijke Pinoy, Ille Geldhof.

Belgian historical drama set in Flanders circa 1885 where Flemish peasants, inspired by the American Revolution, plan a revolt against their French oppressors. Released domestically in 1986, this film received its American premiere at the 1987 American Film Institute European Community Film Festival. (In Flemish and French with English subtitles).

p, Jan van Raemdorick; d, Paul Cammermans; w, Hugo Claus (based on the play by Cyriel Buysse); ph, Lex Wertwyn; m, Daniel Schell; ed, Henri Arissman; prod d, Philippe Graffe.

Historical **(PR:NR MPAA:NR)**

VARJOJA PARATIISISSA† (1987, Fin.) 73m Villealfa Film/Finnkino c (Trans: Shadows in Paradise)

Matti Pellonpaa *(Nikander)*, Kati Outinen *(Ilona)*, Kylli Kongas *(Ilona's Girlfriend)*, Sakari Kuosmanen *(Melartin)*, Esko Nikkari *(Co-worker)*, Pekka Laiho *(Shop Steward)*, Jukka-Pekka Palo *(Third Man)*.

A romantic comedy about a lowly Helsinki garbage collector, Pellonpaa, and a homely supermarket checkout girl, Outinen, who find a new lease on life when they become friends. Both lonely, uneducated, and economically dispensible, the two make tenative stabs at establishing a romance but they both are too shy to initiate anything serious. When Outinen is fired from her job, she rebels by stealing from the store. She runs to Pellonpaa for help and they check into a countryside hotel. Pellonpaa returns the stolen goods to the supermarket and asks Outinen to move in with him, which she does. Although their relationship is platonic at first, they are eventually drawn together because of their mutual feelings of helplessness in a cold and indifferent world. Together they find new strength in their romance and go off to nearby Estonia on a honeymoon of sorts.

d&w, Aki Kaurismaki; ph, Timo Salminen (Eastmancolor); ed, Raija Talvio; set d, Pertti Hilkamo; cos, Tuula Hilkamo.

Romance **(PR:NR MPAA:NR)**

VEC VIDJENO† (1987, Yugo.) 104m Art Film-80 CFS Avala-Croatia-Smart Egg/Smart Egg c (Trans: Deja Vu)

Mustafa Nadarevic *(Mihailo)*, Anica Dobra *(Olga)*, Miroslav Mandic *(Zoran)*, Petar Bozovic.

Psychological thriller that turns into a slasher film starring Nadarevic as a lonely middle-aged piano teacher who was kept from realizing his brilliant potential as a concert pianist because of a traumatic family life that continues to reoccur in his mind via flashbacks. His life changes when he meets the sexy young Dobra, a leggy blonde who arrives at the school to teach a modeling course. Something of a nymphomaniac, Dobra seduces the befuddled Nadarevic, much to the chagrin of the other males at the school. Dobra's rabid sexuality is actually a means of escape from her drunken father and ill brother, but Nadarevic comes to see his new lover as a substitute for his mother—who had commited suicide. When Dobra decides to leave him, Nadarevic experiences a deja vu of the loss of his mother and goes mad and slaughters Dobra's family with a knife. Stylishly directed, VEC VIDJENO may find a wide audience on the international film festival circuit.

d&w, Goran Markovic; ph, Zivko Zalar; m, Zoran Simjanovic; prod d, Slobodan Rundo.

Thriller **(PR:NR MPAA:NR)**

VEIVISEREN (SEE: OFELAS, 1987, Nor.)

VELIKIY POKHOD ZA NEVESTOY† (1987, USSR) 94m Gruziafilm/Sovexportfilm c (Trans: In Search of the Bride)

Guram Pirtskhalava, Mikhail Kherkhedlidze, Tamara Skhirtladze, Tristan Saralidze, Leila Shotadze.

Rivalries between proud villages in Soviet Georgia threaten to explode when a girl from one village refuses to marry a boy from another. The boy's village, Chokhi, considers itself to be the best in the area and they take the girl's rebuff to be an insult. In retaliation they plan to start a campaign against other nearby villages to prove their superiority. A comedic look at Georgian villages derived from folk tales and legends.

d&w, Goderdzi Chokheli; ph, Igor Amasiysky; m, Nodar Gabuniya; art d, Revaz Mirzashvili.

Comedy **(PR:NR MPAA:NR)**

VENGEANCE IS MINE† (1987, Phil.) Roadshow c

Rudy Fernandez *(Ador Ronquillo)*.

The RAMBO of the Phillipines, Rudy Fernandez, once again stars as a trigger-happy innocent who, according to the press release, " . . . Was Trampled Upon, Abused . . . Been Pushed Too Far, Now He Has Crossed The Point Of No Return . . . ," by bad guys who force him to seek a bloody vengeance, this time for the death of his father.

[No credits available.]

Action **(PR:NR MPAA:NR)**

VENNER FOR ALTID† (1987, Den.) 95m Nordisk Film-Danish Film Institute/Nordisk c (Trans: Friends Forever)

Claus Bender Mortensen *(Kristian)*, Thomas Sigsgaard *(Patrick)*, Thomas Elholm *(Henrik)*, Lill Lindfors *(Ayoe)*, Morten Stig Kristensen *(Mads)*, Christine Skou *(Anette)*, Rita Angela *(High School Principal)*, Carsten Morch, Stefan Henszelman, Jens Ravn, Ulla Nielsen, Christian Kamienski, Claus Steenstrup Nielsen, Mourad Slimani, Lone Wassard, Christine Seedorf.

A story of adolescence in 1980s Denmark from young director Henszelman which stars Mortensen as the 16-year-old new kid in town. Attending his new school he becomes friends with two very different youngsters—the tough gangleader Sigsgaard and the independent Elholm. He sides with Sigsgaard, but gradually their friendship is tested when he learns that his friend is gay. Another test comes when the gang gets deeper into delinquency, violence, and criminal acts, prompting both Mortensen and Sigsgaard to drop out. Sexual growth comes for Mortensen when he falls for schoolmate Skou, a lovely blonde, and later has an encounter with older pop singer Lindfors. His knowledge of the world and its often unfair authoritarianism develops when he and Skou lead a student revolt against their hypocritical schoolmaster. A first feature from Henszelman who previously won an award with his short film "Venner For Altid," which served as the basis for this film. Shown in the US under the title FRIENDS FOREVER as part of the Chicago International Film Festival.

p, Gerd Roos, Max Hansen, Vibeke Pedersen, Thomas Heinesen; d, Stefan Henszelman; w, Stefan Henszelman, Alexander Korschen; ph, Marcel Berga (Eastmancolor); m, Morti Vizki, Christian Skeel, Kim Sagild; ed, Stefan Henszelman, Camilla Skousen, Simon Koch, Jutta Fischer; prod d, Lars Rune Nilsson; cos, Bente Ranning, Jane Wessely, Lars Andersen.

Drama **(PR:C-O MPAA:NR)**

VERA*** (1987, Braz.) 92m Nexus Cinema and Video-Embrafilme/Kino Int. c

Ana Beatriz Nogueira *(Vera)*, Raul Cortez *(Professor Paulo Trauberg)*, Aida Leiner *(Clara)*, Carlos Kroeber *(Orphanage Director)*, Cida Almeida *(Paizao)*, Adriana Abujamra *(Telma)*, Imara Reis *(Helena Trauberg)*, Norma Blum *(Izolda)*, Abram Faarc, Liana Duval *(Librarians)*.

Despite her reluctance to leave, 18-year-old Nogueira is released from the orphanage where she has been incarcerated for many years. She is helped by a kindly professor, who enables her to find work in a library research center and offers her lodging in his home. At his dinner table, she silently broods throughout the meal, awkwardly asking who will take responsibility for her. The professor's well-intentioned response, that people should look out for each other, fails to alleviate her fears. That night, a nightmare takes her back to the orphanage. In flashback, she relives the harsh experiences which led her to assume a masculine personality, enabling her to wield a certain amount of control over her compatriots. On one occasion, the director organizes a school dance and invites the members of a nearby boys' orphanage to join in the festivities, undermining the symbolic masculinity of Nogueira. In the outside world, her obsession with the trappings of manhood alienates her coworkers at the library. She does, however, develop an intense platonic relationship with a beautiful coworker (Leiner). Leiner insists that Nogueira must be willing to expose herself if their relationship is to be a mutual expression of love. But the experience of nakedness creates a profound sense of shame for Nogueira, causing her to flee. As her feelings of alienation decline, she seeks out the librarian to reveal her decision to leave—to come to terms with her sexuality by undergoing a sex change. Unexpectedly she races into the bathroom only to be confronted with her menstrual cycle, the undeniable and immutable evidence of her womanhood.

VERA is a portrait of the quintessential outcast—the painful incomprehension of her solitary experience, the single-minded focus of her fantasized escape, and the damning evidence of her inescapable existence. Nogueira, who was 18 years old at the time of the filming, gives a performance that displays an extraordinary range and talent, and for which she won the Best Actress prize at the 1987 Berlin Film Festival. A fragile determination propels her existence outside the orphanage. Her movements are awkward, almost bovine, and her eyes suspicious, continually darting away from making contact as she attempts to exist in a non-regimented world of freedom. But, in reality, she has done nothing more than exchange her legitimate prison environment for a more subtle and chilling one on the outside. The glass mazes of the library walkways display her in an open cage to the outside world, like a rare species that has just become available for microscopic viewing. It is a tribute to the ability of the youthful Nogueira, though, that she is able to portray Vera not as a laboratory animal, but as a human being who " . . . behaves like anyone else in the world, where labels are continually applied." "Her problem is not sexual ambiguity. Vera is not male or female, transsexual or lesbian," director Sergio Toledo has stated about the focus of his first feature film. "Her problem is how she thinks of male behavior. I am fascinated by what makes her feel the need to negate her own body and build a masculine personality." *(Nudity, sexual situations, adult situations.)*

p,d&w, Sergio Toledo; ph, Rodolfo Sanchez; m, Arrigo Barnabe; ed, Tercio G. da Mota; prod d, Rene Silber; set d, Naum Alvez de Souza, Simone Raskin.

Drama **(PR:O MPAA:NR)**

VERMISCHTE NACHRICHTEN† (1987, Ger.) 103m Kairos/Filmverlag der Autoren c (Trans: Odds and Ends)

Marita Breuer *(Restless Woman)*, Rosel Zech *(Successful Man)*, Sabine Wegner *(African Female)*, Andre Jung *(Max the Waiter)*, Sabina Trooger *(Announcer)*.

The politically oriented Kluge directs this compilation of short segments (hence the title "Odds and Ends") about daily life in Germany, most of which were culled from brief news items. Relating to everything from racism to useless statistics about waiters (most carry trays with their left hand), the film also includes an episode by Volker Schlondorff (THE TIN DRUM) about a meeting between former West German chancellor Helmut Schmidt and East German leader Erich Honecker. Actress Rosel Zech, who here is cast as "a successful man," is best remembered by US audiences for her lead performance in R.W. Fassbinder's VERONIKA VOSS.

p, Alexander Kluge; d&w, Alexander Kluge, (contributing one segment) Volker Schlondorff; ph, Werner Luring, Thomas Mauch; ed, Beate Mainka-Jellinghaus, Jane Seitz; art d, Jurgen Schell.

Docu-drama **(PR:NR MPAA:NR)**

VERNEHMUNG DER ZEUGEN† (1987, E. Ger.) 76m Defa Spielfilme c (Trans: Interrogation of the Witness)

Rene Steinke *(Maximilian)*, Mario Gericke *(Rainer)*, Anne Kasprzik *(Viola)*, Johanna Schall, Christine Schorn.

Crime thriller which opens on the dead body of a teenage boy with the mother of his killer openly confessing her son's guilt. At the same time the murderer, Steinke, is attempting suicide by taking an overdose of pills. His life is saved, however, and through flashbacks we learn of the events leading up to the tragedy. Months earlier Steinke was forced to move from Berlin to the country to live with his mother and her new husband. Resentful, Steinke takes out his rage on his family and new classmates, quickily becoming an arrogant bully. His best friend is Gericke, the son of a destitute alchoholic who joins Steinke in his domination of their classmates. The boys' friendship is threatened, however, when both fall for the pretty Kasprzik. Steinke becomes convinced that Gericke and Kasprzik have become lovers and in a fit of insane jealousy, he stabs his friend.

d, Gunther Scholz; w, Manfred Richter, Gunther Scholz; ph, Claus Neumann; m, Friedbert Wissmann; ed, Thea Richter; art d, Harri Lenpold.

Drama **(PR:NR MPAA:NR)**

VERSTECKTE LIEBE† (1987, Ger.) 80m Pro-ject Filmproduktion-Filmverlag der Autoren-Bayerischer Rundfunk bw (Trans: Secret Love)

Peter Cieslinki *(Stranger)*, Dimitra Spanou *(The Girl)*, Jorgos Balasis, Nikos Pekidou *(Boys)*, Nektaria Nikolakakis *(Little Waitress)*, Michaelis Georgulakis *(Priest)*.

Lolitaesque tale about a 30-year-old German author who becomes sexually obsessed with an 11-year-old neighbor girl he meets while trying to get over his writer's block in Greece.

p,d&w, Gottfried Junker; ph, Egon Werdin; m, Chris Heyne; ed, Peter R. Adam.

Romance **(PR:NR MPAA:NR)**

VIA MONTENAPOLEONE† (1987, It.) 92m C.G. Silver Film-Video 80-Reteitalia/COL c

Renee Simonsen *(Elena)*, Carol Alt *(Margherita)*, Luca Barbareschi *(Guido)*, Fabrizio Bentivoglio *(Roberto)*, Corinne Clery *(Chiara)*, Marisa Berenson *(Fabrizio's Mother)*, Valentina Cortese *(Guido's Mother)*, Daniel Gelin, Antonio Ballerio, Paolo Rossi, Sharon Gusberti.

Beautiful faces and tortured relationships fill this Italian potboiler in which the private dramas of a number of characters are woven into the world of high fashion Milan style. Alt plays a housewife whose search for excitement and employment leads her onto a fashion-show ramp and into the arms of Bentivoglio, pregnancy puts an end to the one-night stands of photographer Simonsen, and Berenson becomes the lover of one of her son's friends, Clery. Directed and coscripted by the recently prolific Carlo Vanzina.

p, Mario Gori, Vittorio Cecchi Gori; d, Carlo Vanzina; w, Carlo Vanzina, Enrico Vanzina, Jaja Fiastri; ph, Luigi Kuveiller (Cinecitta Color); m, Beppe Cantarelli; ed, Ruggero Mastroianni; art d, Mario Chiari.

Drama **(PR:NR MPAA:NR)**

VIAJE AL PARAISO† (1987, Mex.) 89m Instituto Mexicano de Cinematografia/Peliculas Mexicanas c (Trans: Trip to Paradise)

Ernesto Gomez Cruz *(Victor)*, Jose Carlos Ruiz *(Pajaro)*, Marla Rojo *(Queta)*, Alejandro Parodi *(Ramiro)*, Jorge Zepeda *(Felipe)*, Gina Morett *(Julia)*, Jorge Balzaretti, Lolo Navarro, Salvador Sanchez, Demian Bichir, Juan Pelaez, Rodrigo Puebla.

Focusing on a crass Mexico City family's trip to the hinterlands, director Retes sends up the values and behavior of the Mexican middle class. The always bickering bunch's holiday is severely disrupted by an encounter with a group of revolutionaries, and through the course of film the family encounters symbolic figures from a cross-section of the establishment, all convinced that they know the way to paradise.

d&w, Ignacio Retes; ph, Guadalupe Garcia; m, Leonardo Velazquez; ed, Jesus Paredes.

Comedy **(PR:NR MPAA:NR)**

VICTORIA† (1987, Swed.) 100m Film AB c

Micaela Jolin, Stephan Schwartz, Sigmar Solbach, Christiane Horbiger, Gustaf Kleen, Hans-Christian Blech.

Bo Widerberg, who also directed 1987's excellent THE SERPENT'S WAY, turns again to the 19th Century for a love story that crosses class lines. While THE SERPENT'S WAY also deals with class and love, its heroine, Stina Ekblad, is driven by economic dependency into a physical relationship with her landlord that is without even a hint of romance. In VICTORIA, the setting is picturesque northern Norway, and the love between Schwartz, the son of a lowly miller, and Jolin, the daughter of a wealthy landowner, is deep-felt and all-encompassing but not enough to overcome the class divisions that prevent their happiness.

p&d, Bo Widerberg.

Romance **(PR:NR MPAA:NR)**

VIDEO DEAD, THE** (1987) 90m Interstate 5-Highlight/Manson Intl. c

Roxanna Augeson *(Zoe Blair)*, Rocky Duvall *(Jeff Blair)*, Michael St. Michaels *(Henry Jordan)*, Thaddeus Gogas, Douglas Bell *(Deliverymen)*, Al Millan *(Taxi Driver)*, Lory Ringuette, George Kernan *(Movers)*, Sam David McClelland *(Joshua Daniels)*, Jennifer Miro *(The Woman)*, Libby Russler *(Maria)*, Vickie Bastel *(April Ellison)*, Garrett Dressler *(Mr. Ellison)*, Melissa Martin *(B-Movie Housewife)*, Cliff Watts *(The Garbageman)*, Muffie Greco *(Beverly Turchow)*, Walter Garrett *(Abe Turchow)*, Jo Ann Peterson *(Mrs. Blair)*, Don Clelland *(Mr. Blair)*, Carl Solomon *(Hospital Attendant)*, Bachelor *(Chocolate, the Dog)*, The Undead: Jack Stellman *(Jack)*, Diane Hadley *(The Bride)*, Patrick Treadway *(Jimmy D.)*, Al Millan *(Ironhead)*, Lory Ringuette *(Half Creeper)*, Stephen Bianchi, Maurice Diller, Anthony Ferrante, Cliff Gardener, Joanne Jarvis, Mark Rosseau.

A television set arrives at the house of a writer. That night it switches itself on and runs a black-and-white horror film, "Zombie Blood Nightmare," in which the dead rise up from their graves and shamble through the woods to attack the living. Smoke starts to come out of the screen and several of the zombies emerge from the set, killing the writer. A few months later the house has new occupants, Augeson and Duvall, teenagers whose parents still haven't arrived. Duvall finds the TV in the attic and hauls it down. That night he turns it on and the movie runs again; however, it soon is interrupted as a most unwholesome woman appears on the screen and starts speaking directly to Duvall. Next, she emerges from the set and makes love to him. She goes back into the TV and is laughing at him from inside when a man appears behind her and slits her throat. He explains to Duvall that she was one of the zombies and tells him to take the set to the basement and put a mirror against the screen. Meanwhile, the zombies in the woods are attacking and killing the neighbors. A Texan, McClelland, shows up and explains that the set was his, and that it is evil. He had shipped it to an occult studies institute, but it was mistakenly delivered to their house. Augeson refuses to believe him until one of the living dead enters the house and carries away Duvall's girl friend. The next morning Duvall and McClelland go out to hunt them down, but both end up as victims. Back at the house as dusk approaches, Augeson sees the zombies approaching and, realizing that she doesn't have a chance except to show no fear, she invites them all in for dinner. They want to dance, so she leads them into the basement, where she manages to trap them. They go crazy and start to eat each other. Augeson leaves the house, her mind gone, and is put in the hospital in a catatonic state. Her parents come to visit and leave her a gift. They wheel the TV into the room and the orderly switches it on to the movie as he leaves. Zombies are something of a growth industry these days, and this is an interesting addition to the genre. The film has a good deal of dark humor and actually manages to create some suspense, no small achievement anymore. Released straight to video, it is at least as good as anything that makes it to the theaters and a long life as a rental item seems guaranteed. *(Gore effects, brief nudity, substance abuse, excessive profanity.)*

p,d&w, Robert Scott; ph, Greg Becker; m, Stuart Rabinowitsk, Kevin McMahon, Leonard Marcel; ed, Bob Sarles; prod d, Katalin Rogers; set d, Elizabeth Bordock; cos, Andrea Nemerson, Edward Richards; spec eff, Dale Hall, jr.; m/l, Leonard Marcel, Kevin McMahon, Stuart Rabinowitsk, Deborah Iyall, Larry Good, Ken Lauber, Jonathan Daniel.

Horror **Cas.** **(PR:O MPAA:NR)**

VILAMBARAM† (1987, India) G.R. International

Balachandra Menon, Ashokan, Soman, Saritha, Ambika, Sari, Thilakan, Jalaja.

When a secretary commits suicide, her boss is thought to be the cause, but investigation reveals his innocence.

d, Balachandra Menon.

Drama **(PR:NR MPAA:NR)**

VINA LEYTENANTA NEKRASOVA† (1987, USSR) 92m Uzbekfilm/Sovexportfilm c (Trans: Lieutenant Nekrasov's Fault)

Aleksei Zharkov, Andrei Tolubeev, Liudmila Volosach, Aleksandr Kuzin.

In the final days of WW II, a Soviet pilot, outraged by his navigator's cowardice, leaves him behind enemy lines. The flyer's impetuous actions lead to a court-martial and, consumed with guilt, he returns to his village and undergoes self-imposed punishment for years. All during this time he writes countless letters trying to locate the wronged navigator to win his forgiveness. His greatest punishment, however, is that he is no longer able to fly, and when the opportunity presents itself, he moves to remote Uzbekistan to take a job testing ejection seats, convinced that it will lead to his return to the air.

d, Roald Batyrov; w, Eduard Volodarsky; ph, Aleksandr Pann, Miron Penson; m, Nikolai Karetnikov; art d, Eduard Avanesov.

Drama **(PR:NR MPAA:NR)**

VINCENT—THE LIFE AND DEATH OF VINCENT VAN GOGH† (1987, Aus./Neth.) 103m Illumination-Look-Ozfilms-Dasha/Seawell c

Voice of Vincent: John Hurt.

Both Paul Gauguin and his one-time roommate Vincent Van Gogh were the subjects of films in 1987. In WOLF AT THE DOOR, Donald Sutherland portrayed Gauguin as he returned to Paris after his first stay in Tahiti, and in this film Australian director Paul Cox uses Van Gogh's own words and paintings and the places that inspired them to communicate the philosophical and emotional essence of the brilliant expressionist painter who took his own life at the age of 37. John Hurt (THE ELEPHANT MAN, THE HIT) narrates from Van Gogh's impassioned letters to his brother Theo and Cox (MAN OF FLOWERS, MY FIRST WIFE) uses his camera like a paintbrush to evoke the world as Van Gogh saw it. In interviews, Cox—who emigrated to Australia from the Netherlands in 1976—has expressed his dislike for Vincente Minnelli's Van Gogh biopic, LUST FOR LIFE (1956), and though he has dramatized some scenes of the life that surrounded the painter, the focus of Cox's film is on what Van Gogh thought and saw and how he tried to capture it. A Dutch-Australian coproduction, VINCENT—THE LIFE AND DEATH OF VINCENT VAN GOGH received only festival showings in the US in 1987.

p, Tony Llewellyn-Jones; d&w, Paul Cox (based on the letters of Vincent Van Gogh); ph, Paul Cox (Fujicolor); m, Antonio Vivaldi, Gioacchino Rossini, Norman Kaye; ed, Paul Cox; prod d, Neil Angwin; cos, Jennie Tate, Beverly Boyd.

Biography **(PR:NR MPAA:NR)**

VIOLINS CAME WITH THE AMERICANS, THE† (1987) 94m Sun and Moon Prods. c

Mila Burnette *(Annie Adams)*, Joaquim de Almeida *(David Garcia)*, Jose Ferrer *(Don Fulhencio)*, Maria Norman, Kevin Conway, Norma Candal, Alba Oms.

An independent feature out of New York which received a showing at the American Film Institute's independent film festival, VIOLINS attempts to address the issues facing Puerto Rican Americans. Burnette is a woman disenchanted with her marriage and her life in midtown Manhattan. She packs her bags and returns home to the financially crippled South Bronx where she organizes the tenants of a tenement and eventually falls in love with a Puerto Rican attorney, de Almeida. Although VIOLINS is an independent film, it does boast two internationally known actors—Jose Ferrer and Portuguese star Joaquim de Almeida, the costar of this year's film by the Taviani Brothers, GOOD MORNING, BABYLON.

p, David Greene; d, Kevin Conway; w, M. Quiros [Mila Burnette]; ph, Benjamin Davis (Technicolor); m, Fred Weinberg; ed, John Tintori; set d, Sue Raney.

Drama **(PR:NR MPAA:NR)**

VIOS KE POLITIA† (1987, Gr.) 105m Greek Film Center-Stefi II-Home Video Hellas-Spentzos Film c (Trans: Living Dangerously)

Giorgos Kimoulis, Dimitris Kalivocas, Giorgos Kotanidis, Pavlos Kontoyannidis, Vana Barba, Takis Moschos, Dimitris Poulikakos, Alkis Panayotidis, Thanassis Papageorgiou.

The Greek government receives a broad lampooning in this offbeat comedy by popular director Nicos Perakis. Kimoulis, an employee of the Greek Telecommunications Organization, enters the office of that organization's head, Kalivocas, and connects an explosive device to his personal computer, demanding that he be permitted to address a nationwide TV audience during the broadcast of the final match of the World Cup soccer championship or else he will blow the building sky high. While Kalivocas buys time, the police begin an investigation of the terrorist group of which Kimoulis claims to be a member. Their probing into Kimoulis' background includes the interrogation of his old army buddies, all engaged in a variety of pursuits, but none of whom are able to offer any clues to the nature of Kimoulis' actions. The police then persuade Kimoulis' chums to help in dealing with him, and the whole affair ends in an uproar that makes clear the ideological confrontation that is at the center of contemporary Greek life.

p,d&w, Nicos Perakis; ph, Giorgos Panoussopoulos; m, Nicos Mamagakis; ed, Yannis Tsitsopoulos; art d&cos, Aphrodite Kotzia.

Comedy **(PR:NR MPAA:NR)**

VIRAGAYA† (1987, Sri Lanka) 180m Dilini c (Trans: The Way of the Lotus)

Sanath Gunatilaka *(Aravinda)*, Sriyani Amarasena *(Sarojini)*, Douglas Ranasinghe *(Siridasa)*, Sabita Perera *(Bathee)*, Somalatha Subasingha *(Mother)*, Asoka Peiris, Sunethra Sarachchandra.

Depending on one's worldview, this drama based on a classic Sri Lankan novel is either about self-acceptance of one's fate and equanimity in the face of misfortune or proof of the truism "nice guys finish last." Told in flashback, the story follows the kind, otherworldly Gunatilaka as he experiences and passively accepts one indignity after another. He gives up the woman he loves to his best friend, allows his sister to force both him and his mother to leave their own home, and is unable to consummate the love he feels for the beautiful young woman whom he adopts as his daughter. Eventually all of this stoic suffering comes to an end with his death.

p, Chandra Mallawarachchi; d&w, Tisssa Abeysekara (based on a novel by Martin Wickramasinghe); ph, Lal Wickremarachchi; m, Sarath Fernando; ed, Lal Piyasena; art d, K.A. Milton Perera.

Romance **(PR:NR MPAA:NR)**

VIRGIN QUEEN OF ST. FRANCIS HIGH, THE* (1987, Can.) 94m Pioneer Pictures-American Artists Corp./Crown Intl. c

Joseph R. Straface *(Mike)*, Stacy Christensen *(Diane)*, J.T. Wotton *(Charles)*, Anna-Lisa Iapaolo *(Judy)*, Lee Barringer *(Randy)*, Bev Wotton *(Diane's Mother)*.

A teen sex comedy without any sex is the angle of this low-low-budget Canadian entry which popped up in the marketplace during the interim between Thanksgiving and Christmas releases. In the typical fashion, Straface stars as a nerdy high-school kid whose heart skips a beat when he lays eyes on Christensen, the prettiest, most virginal girl at St. Francis High. Nicknamed "Snow White" because she's saving *It* for marriage, Christensen sends her male classmates' hormones spinning. At a local drinking hole, class bully Barringer bets Straface $2,000 that the nerdy kid can't get Christensen up to Paradise Bungalows—the lover's lane for the St. Francis kids. Christensen agrees to accompany Straface but only on the condition that she retain her "Snow White" morality. While at Paradise Bungalows, the sexually aware teens pass the time not by playing under the sheets, but by playing a friendly game of Monopoly. In a reversal of the teen-sex-comedy formula, this one ends not with physical groping but with friendship, as Christensen remains seated on her throne of virginity. Directed, written, and edited by Lucente, the film suffers from wretched sound recording and post-dubbing, poor photography and lighting, a nonstop music track (undoubtedly used to cover up the sound problems), and some amateurish acting. Straface, the director's cousin, tries his best but doesn't have the strength to carry the film. Despite the technical problems and its exploitative title, VIRGIN QUEEN does display a positive morality for teenagers. If it's morality you're looking for, however, two better films are this year's MEATBALLS III, a Canadian teen sex comedy starring Patrick Dempsey that is similar to VIRGIN QUEEN, and 1986's overlooked SEVEN MINUTES IN HEAVEN, which is far superior to most teen pictures. *(Sexual situations.)*

d&w, Francesco Lucente; ph, Joseph Bitonti, Kevin Alexander; m, Danny Lowe, Brad Steckel, Brian Island; ed, Francesco Lucente.

Romance **(PR:A MPAA:PG)**

VISA U.S.A.*** (1987, Columbia/Cuba) 90m Focine-ICAIC c

Armando Gutierrez *(Adolfo)*, Marcela Agudelo *(Patricia)*, Raul Eguron Cuesta *(Adolfo's Father)*, Lucy Martinez Tello *(Adolfo's Mother)*, Elios Fernandez *(Patricia's Father)*, Vicky Hernandez *(Patricia's Mother)*, Diego Alvarez *(Pedro Guillermo)*, Maria Lucia Castrillion *(Adriana)*, Gellver de Currea Lugo *(Moncho)*, Gerardo Calero *(Felmo)*.

Gutierrez yearns to escape his father's chicken farm and realize his ambition as a successful radio announcer in the U.S. Spinning records at a local store and tutoring two high school girls in English in order to practice, he saves enough to achieve his goal. The tutoring he has done for free, and he has fallen in love with Agudelo, one of his students. He wins her from her more wealthy suitor, much to the alarm of her upper middle class parents.

Gutierrez's visa is denied; his brother remained in the States illegally and the Immigration Bureau fears Gutierrez has a similar plan. Ashamed, Gutierrez hides his failure and determines to enter the States illegally. Accidently learning of Gutierrez's rejection, Agudelo's father decides to send her to an aunt in New York, knowing that Gutierrez cannot follow. Elated, Agudelo tells Gutierrez of her plans to travel with him and be together in New York.

Desperate now in his attempt to obtain an illegal visa, he travels to Cartagena a week early on the pretext of obtaining his announcer's license. With the help of his friend, Alvarez, he overcomes several obstacles in contacting the traffickers in false passports. Once done, he spends nearly all his money on the phony documents. His resourceful friend keeps them afloat while they await the falsified papers and the departure date by making car repairs. Alvarez remarks that for the money spent in getting to the U.S. they could have opened a successful business in their home town.

Gutierrez's false passport is discovered at the airport. After a frantic chase, Gutierrez escapes by hiding amidst cargo crates filled with baby chicks, waiting to be shipped.

Dejected, Gutierrez returns home. Agudelo and Alvarez are waiting for him. Agudelo has given up her own trip in order to stay with him. Reunited, the three friends happily face the future together.

Lisandro Duque has a fine light touch and tells his story of young love and early disillusionment with a tenderness devoid of sentimentality. The delicacy of the feelings between the lovers pursued in the full rush of their innocence gives a power and rare believability to the portrayal of young adults. A fine script nicely directed, the film suffers technically towards the end. The camera fails to conquer the high tech space of the airport; lighting and compositions become vague. As this is the climatic scene the moment loses power, consequently the resolution seems abrupt. Otherwise, a satisfying film, well acted and storied.

Recipient of the Best Film award at the Cartagena film festival. Originally released in 1986, VISA U.S.A. received US film festival showings this year.

p, Guillermo Calle Delgado; d, Lisandro Duque; w, Martha Elena Restrepo; ph, Raul Perez Ureta; m, Leo Brouwer; ed, Nelson Rodriguez.

Drama **(PR:C MPAA:NR)**

VLCI BOUDA (SEE: WOLF'S HOLE, 1987, Czech.)

VO VREMENA VOLCHYIKA ZAKONOV† (1987, USSR) 83m Tallinfilm/Sovexportfilm c (Trans: When Man Was Wolf to Man)

Arvo Kukumyagi, Regina Razuma, Egon Nuter, Yuri Kryukov, Yuri Yarvet.

Based on an ancient legend set in Estonia in the 14th century, the story concerns a handsome young man who rescues a beautiful damsel who is about to be attacked by a bear. The two fall in love, but their love is doomed. Their families are feuding and the girl's brother has promised her hand to a wealthy land owner.

d, Olav Neuland; w, Arvo Walton; ph, Edward Oya, Victor Shkolnikov; m, Sven Grunberg; art d, Pryit Vakher.

Romance **(PR:NR MPAA:NR)**

VOLNY UMIRAYUT NA BEREGU† (1987, USSR) 80m Kirgizfilm/Sovexportfilm c (Trans: Waves Die on the Shore)

Suymenkul Chokomorov, Idris Nogaibaev, Gulsara Azhibekova, Eugeniya Pleshkite.

Soviet drama about two brothers from the Central Asian republic of Kirgiz who end up on different sides of the Iron Curtain after serving in the army during WW II. The younger of the two returns to their village; the other, a prisoner of war, remains in the West after fighting is over, wandering at first and then settling down in Munich. Both start families, but the brother who goes home starts his with his sibling's ex-wife and child. When the older brother visits Kirgiz as a tourist he learns that his daughter (who was born after he left to soldier) has become a popular singer and that he is a grandfather. Full of memories of his family and home back in Kirgiz, he returns to Germany only to be shot.

d, Tynchylyk Razzakov; w, Aleksandr Gorokhov, Bazarkul Sagambekov; ph, Bekbolot Aidaraliev; m, Victor Sumarokov; art d, Zholtzotbek Kasymaliev.

Drama/War **(PR:NR MPAA:NR)**

VROEGER IS DOOD† (1987, Neth.) 90m Linden/The Movies c (Trans: What's Past is Dead; AKA: BYGONES)

Jasperina de Jong *(Inez)*, Max Croiset *(Father)*, Elise Hoomans *(Mother)*.

Basing her film on an autobiographical novel by Inez van Dullemen, first-time feature director Ine Schenkkan tackles the subject of aging and its impact on both the aged and their families. Playing the author, de Jong sits at a typewriter and the events of the story are shown in flashback as she tries to commit them to paper. Middle-aged, with a family of her own, de Jong also looks after parents. Her father becomes increasingly infirm and has to be institutionalized, but her mother, valuing her independence, insists on living at home. As the film progresses, she, too, is put in a home and dies before her husband does, though not before she is given a chance to say good-bye to him. BYGONES is the film debut for de Jong, who has made a name for herself in Holland as a cabaret performer.

p, Jos van der Linden; d&w, Ine Schenkkan (based on a novel by Inez van Dullemen); ph, Geert Giltay (Kodak Color); m, Simon Burger; ed, Jorge Hoogland; art d, Freek Biesiot.

Drama **(PR:NR MPAA:NR)**

VOENNO-POLEVOI ROMAN† (1987, USSR) 92m Odessa/Sovexportfilm c (Trans: War-Time Romance)

Nikolai Burliayev, Natalia Andreichenko, Inna Churikova, Victor Proskurin.

A wartime infatuation turns into lasting love in this romance from the USSR. In the last years of WW II, a Soviet soldier is captivated by the singing voice of a beautiful female comrade-in-arms. Years later on the streets of Moscow, he hears that voice again but is surprised to see it emanating from the worn-out street vender the beautiful girl has become. Still full of love for her, he rescues her from this dismal existence.

d&w, Pyotr Todorovsky; ph, Valery Blinov; m, Igor Kontyukov, Pyotr Todorovsky; art d, Valentin Konovalov.

Romance **(PR:NR MPAA:NR)**

VOT MOYA DEREVNYA† (1987, USSR) 92m Mosfilm/Sovexportfilm c (Trans: This is My Neck of the Woods)

Alexei Buldakov, Larisa Grebenschikova, Natalia Yegorova.

Seriocomic social problem film that deals with the clash of industry and agriculture in a small Soviet town. The chairman of a collective farm does his damnedest to come up with a way to maintain the townspeople's interest in tilling the land when a huge new construction project is undertaken in his neck of the woods.

d&w, Viktor Tregubovich; ph, Vladimir Burykin; m, Alexei Rybnikov; art d, Viktor Amelnikov.

Comedy **(PR:NR MPAA:NR)**

VREMYA ZHELANIY† (1987, USSR) 98m Mosfilm/Sovexportfilm c (Trans: Time of Desire)

Vera Alentova, Anatoli Papanov, Vladislav Strzhelchik, Tatiana Egorova, Eduard Izotov.

An ambitious 30-year-old woman marries a considerably older man and, obsessed with owning *things*, pushes him to improve his position in the world. He puts his nose to the grindstone and they begin to accumulate possessions, but he is too old for the stressful life he has taken on and dies of a heart attack. And let that be a lesson to her!

d, Yuli Raisman; w, Anatoli Grebnev; ph, Nikolai Olonovski; m, Alexander Belyaiev; art d, Tatiana Lapshina.

Drama **(PR:NR MPAA:NR)**

VYKUP† (1987, USSR) 91m Mosfilm/Sovexportfilm c (Trans: The Ransom)

Boris Scherbakov, Emmanuil Vitorgan, Irina Metlitskaya, Sergei Priselkov.

An avalanche makes the highway impassable, forcing two truck drivers to take refuge in an inn. It turns out the avalanche was caused by terrorists in an effort to isolate the inn and a nearby children's sanitorium. Both the inn and the sanitorium will be destroyed unless a huge ransom is paid to the terrorists, but the brave and clever truck drivers defeat the terrorists and save everyone.

d, Alexander Gordon; w, Alexander Bulganin, Nikolai Ivanov; ph, Vyacheslav Semin; m, Nikolai Sidelnikov; art d, Georgy Kalganov.

Drama **(PR:NR MPAA:NR)**

VZLOMSHCHIK† (1987, USSR) 83m Lenfilm/The Other Cinema c (Trans: Burglar)

Oleg Elykomov *(Senka Laushkin)*, Konstantin Kinchev, Y. Teapnik, S. Gaitan, P. Petrenko, Mikahil Parfyonov, Pyotr Semak, Vladimir Dyatlov, R. Abbasov, S. Bulinenkova, T. Gasan-Zade, E. Gits, S. Danilov, A. Yevgenyev, V. Zhuravlyova, V. Ivanov, A. Kolebanov, Yu. Katsuk, A. Klyuchnikov, V. Lugovoy, K. Medvedyev, O. Miliutin, N. Nekrasov, A. Panov, A. Rakhov, S. Rogozhin, P. Samoilov, E. Sooster, L. Fyodorov, G. Chepishchev, A. Chetvertkov, M. Shadrin, T. Sharkova, The Alicia, Auction, Avia, Pinocchio, Coffee, Presence.

Like a number of other Gorbachev era films, VZLOMSHCHIK is concerned with the nature of life for young people in the Soviet Union. Elykomov, a 12-year-old, lives with his father and older brother, a rock musician. Since the death of Elykomov's mother, his father has taken to drinking and is often not at home. Elykomov idolizes his brother, tagging along with him through the city streets and accompanying him to one of his band's performances. Elykomov becomes upset when he learns that his father plans to marry a woman he has been seeing, but later she comes to the boy and lovingly seeks his acceptance. Meanwhile, his brother is in hot water. For some time he has been borrowing a synthesizer from a friend, but the friend wants the instrument back and suggests that if the musician wants to keep it, he should steal the community center's synthesizer. When Elykomov learns of this, he is determined to keep his brother out of trouble. After the community center officials turn a deaf ear to his warnings, Elykomov becomes the burglar of the translated title and steals the instrument himself, only to eventually confess his crime.

d, Valery Ogorodnikov; w, Valery Priyomykhov; ph, Valery Mironov; m, Viktor Kisin; prod d, Viktor Ivanov; art d, E. Nikolayeva; cos, N. Abdulayevoi; spec eff, L. Pestov; makeup, L. Zavyalovoi.

Drama **(PR:NR MPAA:NR)**

W STARYM DWORKU† (1987, Pol.) 99m Zespoly Filmowe c (Trans: In an Old Manor House)

Beata Tyszkiewicz *(Anastasia)*, Grazyna Szapotowska *(Annette Nevermore)*, Gustaw Holubek *(Tadzeus)*, Jerzy Bonczak.

Tyszkiewicz plays the mistress of a wacky house in Poland at the turn of the century. She's having a very obvious affair with her stepson, prompting her husband to kill her. She then returns to the house as a ghost, and begins offering advice to her remaining family members on affairs of the heart. Her two daughters commit suicide in order to join their mother, and the whole mess is so disconcerting to the men of the house they murder Tyszkiewicz a few more times. At the climax, a mob destroys the house. Based on a play by playwright and painter Witkiewicz.

d&w, Andrzej Kotkowski (based on the play by Stanislaw Ignacy Witkiewicz); ph, Witold Adamek; m, Zbigniew Raj; ed, Jaroslaw Wolejko; art d, Malgorzata Zaleska.

Comedy **(PR:NR MPAA:NR)**

W ZAWIESZENIU† (1987, Pol.) 93m Zespoly Filmowe-Zodiak/Film Polski c (Trans: Suspended)

Krystyna Janda *(Anna Mroczynska, Nurse)*, Jerzy Radziwilowicz *(Marcel Wysocki)*, Slawa Kwasniewska *(Anna's Mother)*, Andrzej Lapicki *(Ruczynski)*, Boguslaw Linda *(The Lieutenant)*, Bozena Dykiel *(Fela)*.

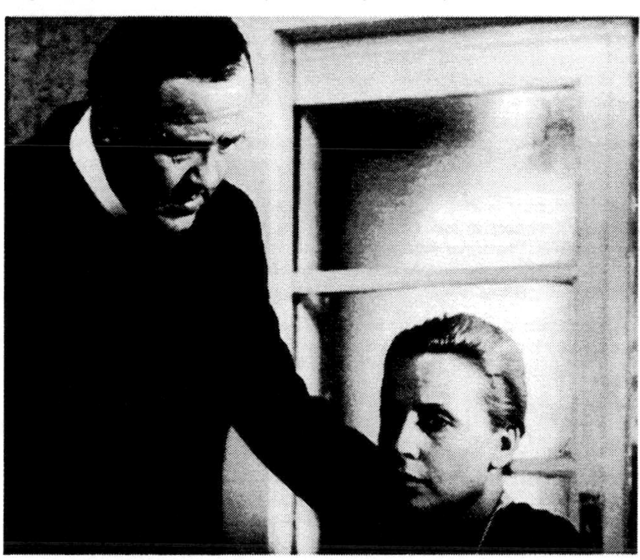

Janda and her lover, Radziwilowicz, are separated during WW II but reunite in 1951 when he is a fugitive from the government. She hides him in her cellar for five years, and bears his child during that time. With the arrival of a new regime in 1956, Radziwilowicz turns himself in and is acquitted at his trial. Screened at the Gdansk Film Festival.

d, Waldemar Krzystek; w, Malgorzata Kopernik, Waldemar Krzystek; ph, Dariusz Kuc; m, Jerzy Satanowski; ed, Krzysztof Osiecki; art d, Tadeusz Kosarewicz.

Romance/Thriller **(PR:NR MPAA:NR)**

WAITING FOR THE MOON*** (1987) 88m New Front-Laboratory for Icon and Idiom-A.B.-American Playhouse-Societe Francaise de Production-ARD-Degeto-Channel Four/Skouras c

Linda Hunt *(Alice B. Toklas)*, Linda Bassett *(Gertrude Stein)*, Bernadette Lafont *(Fernande Olivier)*, Bruce McGill *(Ernest Hemingway)*, Jacques Boudet *(Guillaume Apollinaire)*, Andrew McCarthy *(Henry Hopper)*.

WAITING FOR THE MOON is a quasi biography about Gertrude Stein and Alice B. Toklas that contains almost no factual information. Instead it is an attempt to document the spirit of Stein and Toklas, one of the most famous literary couples of this century. American expatriates living in Paris during the artistically explosive 1920s, Stein and Toklas were at the center of celebrity. The 1967 *Time* obituary for Toklas read: "Their Left Bank apartment was the living room of the Lost Generation," a description that does not exaggerate. Rather than concentrate on facts, director Godmilow, together with her coscreenwriter Magill, probes the mystique that surrounded the pair. Hunt plays the diminutive and possessive Toklas, who, while not as talented as Stein, is perhaps the more interesting character, having lived in her companion's shadow for nearly 40 years. Playing Stein is Bassett (a stage performer in her screen debut), whose physical

presence is greater than Hunt's and whose features are more feminine than those of the real Stein.

As the film opens, Hunt and Bassett are sitting outdoors in the sunny, flowery backyard of their beautiful country home in Bilignin proofreading pages for Stein's latest book. Shortly afterwards, Hunt's trust in her companion is broken when she learns that Bassett has kept secret a doctor's report that says she suffers from a fatal (unnamed) disease. Eventually Bassett is told she has been misdiagnosed and the couple settle their differences. Rather than follow a linear narrative, however, the film is broken down into five days chosen from a three-month period. Set almost exclusively in the French countryside, the action takes place as Hunt and Bassett set out in their Model-A Ford. Early on they pick up a hitchhiking American, McCarthy, who is on his way to Spain to fight in the Civil War. They also meet with Lafont, as Picasso's mistress-of-the-hour Fernande Olivier; Boudet, as poet Guillaume Apollinaire; and McGill, as a drunken Ernest Hemingway, whom they rescue from a bordello. By the film's end, McCarthy has been killed at war, Apollinaire has been poisoned by mushrooms, and Hunt and Bassett are back to proofreading. There is an addition to their household, however—the illegitimate child of Apollinaire who is left in their care.

While most biographers go to great lengths to inform their audience of their subjects' lives, Godmilow and Magill have taken an opposite stance. They tell us, for example, that the incidents take place in 1936, yet Apollinaire died in 1918—not because he ingested poison mushrooms but from a war wound from which he never recovered. The filmmakers have even included in their press release a "Page for the Literal-Minded," which explains what is fact and what is poetic license. To the amusement of a few, and to the shock of many, there is almost nothing factual in WAITING FOR THE MOON. The pages that are being proofread in the film are not Stein's writing but were created by Magill "in the style of Stein;" a play that is rehearsed was also penned by Magill; the cubist paintings on the wall of the couple's salon are fakes; Stein and Toklas were in their fifties in 1936, but appear younger here; Stein "may have been ill in 1936," though not as she appears in the film; Picasso had split from Fernande over 20 years earlier; and Stein and Toklas never cared for a son of Apollinaire's. Not even their Model-A Ford is real; it's played by a Renault. Omitted is any reference to the fact that Stein and Toklas, while famous among literary circles, are almost equally celebrated as being one of the most famous homosexual couples in history—a fact that Godmilow feels is important to the relationship but does not "define."

Of her rather unorthodox method of documentation, Godmilow has said, "We're trying to find new ways to deal with history, literature, *and* film." What is so admirable about WAITING FOR THE MOON is that Godmilow and Magill are trying to capture the spirit that made Stein and Toklas such mythical literary figures. The fact that Stein did not write the words that are being proofread does not make her own accomplishments any less great, nor does it make Godmilow's portrait of her any less potent. For those familiar with the Lost Generation of the 1920s, these lies make the film even more interesting, adding a playful and mischievous edge. It is the same scandalous spirit that surrounded Stein when she wrote *The Autobiography of Alice B. Toklas*. What is especially interesting about these lies is that most audiences are unfamiliar with Stein and company and, therefore, don't even realize they are being fooled by Godmilow and McGill. The PBS American Playhouse style of the film (it was funded in part by and broadcast on PBS less than two months after its theatrical release) adds a sense of respectability to the film, since most people associate public TV with education and factualism. While it is clearly Godmilow and Magill's intention to blur the definition of documentary, their style can also been seen as a drawback. Unfortunately, WAITING FOR THE MOON does not have the cinematographic invention that parallels the literary innovation of Stein's work. While the script and factual details are poetic invention, the visuals are too straightforward and conventional to be seen in the same deconstructive, cubist light of Godmilow's documentary techniques.

WAITING FOR THE MOON does boast some superb performances, most notably the chameleonlike Hunt, still best remembered for her role as Billy Kwan, the male Eurasian in 1982's THE YEAR OF LIVING DANGEROUSLY. The only character that seems out of place is McGill's Hemingway. He is written with the power of hindsight (one scene has him pretending to shoot himself in the head with a fountain pen) and appears one-sided—an obnoxious, drunken oaf who doesn't seem like he could write his name, much less a great novel. Originally intended as a personal, low-budget production (Godmilow and Magill hoped to shoot it for $5,000 under the title "The Trail of the Lonesome Pine"), the script caught the attention of Robert Redford's Sundance Institute, for whom Arthur Penn worked as a consultant on the film's development. The budget eventually grew to $950,000 (Hunt was paid the union scale of $1,370 weekly, plus a share of the profits) with financial assistance coming from PBS, French, German, and British television, and Skouras Pictures, who released the film theatrically. Sharing the grand prize honors at the United States Film Festival in Park City, Utah (with Gary Walkow's THE TROUBLE WITH DICK), WAITING FOR THE MOON performed dismally at the box office during its art-house release and received a lambasting from most critics. Includes the song "The Trail of the Lonesome Pine" (Harry Carroll, Ballard MacDonald).

p, Sandra Schulberg; d, Jill Godmilow; w, Mark Magill (based on a story by Jill Godmilow, Mark Magill); ph, Andre Neau; Michael Sahl; ed, George Klotz; prod d, Patrice Mercier; cos, Elizabeth Tavernier; m/l, Ballard MacDonald, Harry Carroll.

Biography/Drama (PR:A MPAA:PG)

WALK LIKE A MAN zero (1987) 86m MGM/MGM-UA c

Howie Mandel *(Bobo Shand)*, Christopher Lloyd *(Reggie Henry)*, Cloris Leachman *(Margaret Shand)*, Colleen Camp *(Rhonda Shand)*, Amy Steel *(Penny)*.

This picture's title has nothing to do with the song of the same name by The Four Seasons. Matter of fact, this picture has very little to do with anything. It uses plots and ploys from several other films to no advantage. Canadian comic Mandel, who stars in TV's "St. Elsewhere," is a 28-year-old who was lost in the woods as a child and raised by a pack of wolves (see THE WILD CHILD, Truffaut's superb film on the subject). Had they but eaten him on the spot, there would have been no need for this film. When found by animal behaviorist Steel, Mandel is returned to civilization in the hope that he can be tamed. As he is being domesticated, Mandel gets the chance to demonstrate his acting skills by licking the faces of the people he likes, walking around on all fours, hopping, and generally acting stupidly. Mandel's human family learns that he is still alive and in the process of being de-wolfed. This manifests another problem. He is from a wealthy family and stands to inherit $30 million once he's normal (see GREYSTOKE: THE LEGEND OF TARZAN with Chris Lambert). Mandel's brother, Lloyd, will do just about anything to cheat his brother out of the inheritance (this plot appears in so many movies it would take weeks to note the titles). Lloyd is a gambling degenerate who is unwilling to give up the money he thought he would get. He needs it to pay for his habit and for his wife's habit. Camp is an alcoholic and Lloyd needs money to keep her in booze. If she can't lay her hands on the real stuff, she's the kind of person who'll down anything from lighter fluid to Vitalis hair oil. Leachman is Mandel's dippy mother and this role may mark the nadir of her stellar career. The plot mainly concerns Steel's attempts to transform Mandel into a human being while Lloyd attempts to get rid of his unwanted sibling.

Mandel, who really should concentrate on drama, treats the audience to endless demonstrations of drooling, licking, sniffing, and scratching and it's not a pretty sight. Director Mel Frank (a veteran of many movie wars who should have known better than to get involved with this bow-wow) has said that he thought Mandel's doglike movements were terrific. Frank has worked with some of the legends, like Danny Kaye (THE COURT JESTER) and Bing Crosby (WHITE CHRISTMAS), and he was also responsible for the very funny A TOUCH OF CLASS. Lloyd proved he could be funny in TV's "Taxi" as well as in BACK TO THE FUTURE, and Leachman was hilarious in YOUNG FRANKENSTEIN. So why is this so devastatingly awful? First, there's the script by Robert Klane, who has written some very funny novels, including *Where's Poppa?* and *The Horse Is Dead*. Klane also was the executive producer, and in that capacity, he should have fired the screenwriter. Whereas much of his other work is fresh and original (if sometimes tasteless), this is a melange of many stories and adds nothing to his reputation. Mandel's first movie, A FINE MESS, should have clearly shown that he is better at serious acting and that his comedic talents are limited. *(Profanity.)*

p, Leonard Kroll; d, Melvin Frank; w, Robert Klane; ph, Victor J. Kemper (Metrocolor); m, Lee Holdridge; ed, Bill Butler, Steve Butler; prod d, Bill Malley; set d, Richard J. Lawrence.

Comedy (PR:A-C MPAA:PG)

WALK ON THE MOON, A*** (1987) 95m Benenson-Midwest c

Kevin Anderson *(Everett Jones)*, Terry Kinney *(Lew Ellis)*, Laila Robins *(Marty Ellis)*, Patrice Martinez *(India)*, Pedro Armendariz [, Jr.] *(Doctor)*, Roberto Sosa *(Candy)*.

A small Colombian village in 1969 is the backdrop for this surprisingly moving and superbly acted drama about American idealism in the midst of seemingly futile struggles. It is a time of war in Vietnam, a time of shattered dreams after the deaths of Bobby Kennedy and Martin Luther King, and a time for revolution with young people listening to The Beatles and The Rolling Stones. One alternative, however, is the Peace Corps. The bushy-haired Anderson stars as a college graduate who is in Colombia with grand ideas of bringing a backwards village at the foot of the Andes into the modern world. Crammed into his footlocker are books; a ham radio; and a film projector, complete with footage of the White House, John and Jackie Kennedy, and hydroelectric generators. The villagers, however, are simple people who pay little attention to Anderson's master plan of irrigating the farmers' fields—especially since it never rains in the village. Anderson is eventually greeted by Kinney and Robins, the married pair of volunteers whose two-year stint is nearly finished, as is their marriage. Robins, the village schoolteacher, is having an affair with Armendariz, the local medico. Kinney has nearly lost all touch with reality, spending his days hitting rocks with his baseball bat or constructing a gigantic kite to carry him through the air. Originally as idealistic as Anderson, Kinney gave up all hope of bringing modernization to the village after the farmer's co-op he began ended in total failure. As a result he has turned his back on everyone, especially Robins, who he forbids to even trespass on his property. Anderson does his best to battle the obstacles. He goes on medical rounds with Armendariz, helps Robins with her schoolchildren, and puts into motion his plans for an electricity-generating waterwheel. He also meets Martinez, a pretty villager who lives with her adolescent brother, Sosa, a youngster obsessed with American culture. Anderson and Martinez begin falling deeply in love, but in the process alienate Sosa. When Anderson and Martinez marry, Kinney is seen reminiscing about the better times he had with Robins. She, however, cannot put up with his volatile personality. Eventually, the rains come, putting Anderson's waterwheel in motion. In the middle of a torrential downpour, the village square lights up with electricity. The waters rushing down the Andes soon grow fierce, causing furious flood waters to rage through the farmlands. Both Martinez and Sosa are carried off in the current as Anderson tries desperately to save his drowning wife. The following morning he awakens in the mud. He continues his trek down the river, obsessed with finding Martinez and driven half-mad by the emotional and physical toll. Kinney and Robins search the flooded banks for Anderson, but instead find and rekindle their long-lost romance. Anderson is finally located in a sanatorium, having suffered a breakdown. With time Anderson recovers from the loss of Martinez, sees Kinney and Robins off to the airport for their return home, and becomes a valuable asset to the village. As the film ends, Anderson is cultivating the now-fertile farmland which was sowed naturally by the flood waters.

Produced independently in 1985, A WALK ON THE MOON benefits from a fine script, inspired acting, generous use of an authentic location and its inhabitants, and sincere, earthy direction. It is the second film from Raphael Silver, who debuted in 1978 with the prison-yard drama ON THE YARD and acted as producer on wife Joan Micklin Silver's film HESTER STREET. Seeing release only at film festivals throughout the year, A WALK ON THE MOON is a small film which centers on three characters in a simple village, but which also has a broader scope that addresses the idealistic climate of America in the 1960s. The title comes from the July, 1969, landing of astronauts on the moon, opening up a new frontier for the United States. Paralleling Neil Armstrong's "giant leap" are the steps taken by the idealistic Anderson in the barren Colombian village he enters. Anderson, who was also seen this year in ORPHANS, is exceptional, as is Kinney, his beaten Peace Corps predecessor. Both actors are veterans of Chicago's famed Steppenwolf Theater group (appearing together in the stage production of "Orphans") and this is reflected in the rapport that exists between their characters. Holding her own with these two performers is Robins, whose tough-spirited character is a perfect foil for the defeated Kinney. The pretty Martinez also does a wonderful job as the simple villager who captures Anderson's love and attention. The major fault is the reliance on Anderson's narration to supply the audience with information that is either unnecessary or that could be better given visually. *(Brief nudity, profanity, adult situations.)*

p, Dina Silver; d, Raphael Silver; w, William B. Mai; ph, Adam Greenberg (Duart Color); m, Paul Chihara; ed, Peter Frank; prod d, Holger Gross.

Drama (PR:O MPAA:NR)

WALKER*** (1987) 95m Edward R. Pressman-Incine/UNIV-Northern Dist. Partners c

Ed Harris *(William Walker)*, Richard Masur *(Ephraim Squier)*, Rene Auberjonois *(Maj. Siegfried Henningson)*, Keith Szarabajka *(Timothy Crocker)*, Sy Richardson *(Capt. Hornsby)*, Xander Berkeley *(Bryon Cole)*, John Diehl *(Stebbins)*, Peter Boyle *(Commodore Cornelius Vanderbilt)*, Marlee Matlin *(Ellen Martin)*, Alfonso Arau *(Raousset)*, Pedro Armendariz, Jr., *(Munoz)*, Roberto Lopez Espinoza *(Mayorga)*, Gerrit Graham *(Norvell Walker)*, William O'Leary *(James Walker)*, Blanca Guerra *(Yrena)*, Alan Bolt *(Don Domingo)*, Miguel Sandoval *(Parker French)*, Joe Strummer *(Faucet)*, Rene Assa *(Dr. Jones)*, Bennet Guillory *(Achilles Kewen)*, Norbert Weisser *(Prange)*, Bruce Wright *(Anderson)*, Richard Edson *(Turley)*, Charley Braun *(Bruno Van Namzer)*, Linda Callahan *(Mrs. Bingham)*, Milton Selzer *(Judge)*, Richard Zobel *(Lemuel)*, Ren Woods *(Alta Kewen)*, Frederick Neumann *(Wiley Marshall)*, David Hayman *(Father Rossiter)*, Edward Tudor Pole *(Doubleday)*, Sharon Barr *(Darlene)*, Kathy Burke *(Annie Mae)*, Fox Harris *(District Attorney)*, Enrique Beraza *(Corral)*, Luis Contreras *(Benito)*, Ed Pansullo *(Maj. Angus)*, Jack Slater *(Sanders)*, Spider Stacey *(Davenport)*, Del Zamora *(Padre Vigil)*, Biff Yeager *(Rudler)*, William Utay *(Fry)*, George Belanger *(Assistant Deputy)*, Zander Schloss *(Huey)*, William Rothlein *(Dewey)*, David Chung *(Lul)*, Paulino Rodriguez *(Castellon)*, Dick Rude *(Washburn)*, Rudy Wurlitzer *(Morgan)*, Bob Tzudiker *(Garrison)*, Nestor Mendez Garcia *(Mendez)*, Rick Barker *(Breckenridge)*, J.D. Silvester *(Huston)*, Robert Dickman *(Company Man)*, Joe Celeste *(Jury Foreman)*, Martin Aylett, Ramon Alvarez, Raymund Kettless, Tom Collins *(Reporters)*, Louis Mathews *(Priest)*, Dexter Taylor *(Liverpool)*, Michele Winstanely *(Maid)*.

Brutally reviled by the vast majority of American film critics, this distinctly odd, at times confused, but nonetheless wildly creative and compelling political cartoon from SID AND NANCY director Alex Cox is far from a total washout. An agitprop treatise on the United States' ongoing military intrusions into Nicaragua (invasions and occupations in 1855, 1912, and 1926, and the current US-funded *contra* war), Cox's film examines the problem by dramatizing the career of William Walker, a bizarre historical figure who has been all but forgotten in the US, but one who continues to serve as a vivid symbol of Yankee oppression for the people of Central America. Instead of presenting WALKER in generic historical-epic fashion with the hope the audience would make the connection between the events of 1855 and 1987 unaided, Cox and screenwriter Wurlitzer (PAT GARRETT AND BILLY THE KID, TWO-LANE BLACKTOP) provide a

strange hodgepodge of past and present. They insert such anachronisms as modern slang, a computer, a Mercedes-Benz, a Zippo lighter, *Time*, *Newsweek*, and *People* magazines, and even a helicopter during key moments in the film. Added to this melange is violence from the Sam Peckinpah/Sergio Leone school and sophomoric humor that alternates between incisiveness and vulgarity. The result is a truly unique movie universe where all history takes place in a discontinuous time warp.

Born in Nashville in 1824, William Walker was a mass of contradictions. A doctor, a lawyer, a newspaper editor, a slave holder, an abolitionist, and a supporter of universal suffrage, Walker became obsessed with Manifest Destiny and took up the mantle of rogue adventurer. The film opens as Walker (played with a manic intensity by Ed Harris) is forced to withdraw his troop of mercenaries after a disastrous invasion of Mexico. Brought to trial for this incursion, Harris is acquitted by a sympathetic jury. Soon after, he finds himself being courted by Masur, an emissary of the ultimate robber baron, Cornelius Vanderbilt (Boyle), who wants him to "stabilize" Nicaragua for his own business pursuits. Masur's overtures only anger Harris' beautiful fiancee Matlin, who is deaf. Hopelessly in love with a woman who is his moral and intellectual superior, Harris has learned sign language to communicate with her. In a meeting with Boyle, Harris declines to lead the invasion of Nicaragua because Matlin would not approve. Upon his return home, however, Harris is shocked to learn that Matlin has died of cholera. His conscience dead, Harris is determined to bring democracy to the heathens ("It is the God-given right for the American people to dominate the Western Hemisphere," he trumpets). Harris assembles a rag-tag group of mercenaries (58 in all) whom he calls "The Immortals," invades Nicaragua with the support of that country's Liberal party, and defeats the army. He then sets up a puppet government, installs a Nicaraguan as president, and declares himself commander of the armed forces. But when the new president tries to betray his sponsor, Harris has him executed and after a mock election declares himself president of Nicaragua. Ignoring all the noble democratic principles he has espoused, Harris institutes a repressive, fascist government. Public floggings and executions are the order of the day and several Immortals are among the victims. As his power and fame increase (including cover stories in the aforementioned US magazines), Harris sinks deeper and deeper into madness and his men run wild. Desperate for support from the southern states of the US, Harris rejects his abolitionist views and installs slavery in Nicaragua. He also courts American investors, and in a suicidal move, eliminates Boyle's trade routes by seizing the

robber baron's fleet. By 1857, Boyle, the Central American states, and the disgruntled Immortals have had quite enough of Harris. Unable to hold back an attacking force of united Central American states supported by Boyle, Harris and his remaining Immortals burn Granada and regroup in a cathedral. Suddenly, a helicopter lands in the square and modern-day Marines fan out to evacuate the US citizens among the Immortals and their allies (shades of the fall of Saigon). Harris is left behind. Three years later he is executed in Honduras after trying to mount another invasion of Nicaragua.

WALKER has dismayed critics on both ends of the political spectrum and at all points in between. The right can easily dismiss the film as hopelessly biased, vulgar, incoherent, and dishonest propaganda, while the left is angry that Cox has not used this golden opportunity to present their anti-contra views in a sanitized manner that promotes "correctness" of thought while offending no one. Those who are apolitical see it as just another example of indulgent, haphazard, and irresponsible filmmaking. Granted, some charges are valid, but what makes WALKER so fascinating is its total refusal to play by anyone's rules—cinematic or political. In addition to venting his spleen over the horrors of Manifest Destiny and the Reagan administration's foreign policy, Cox appears to be striving for cinematic anarchy. The very fact that he somehow bamboozled $5 million out of Universal to make a film as gleefully subversive as this must warm the cockles of any rebellious young filmmaker's heart. Yes, WALKER plays like the crazed ramblings of an over-zealous smart-ass, but at least this film is *about something*. There is an overwhelming passion here, however misguided it may seem. In an era when Hollywood is devoid of creativity and the market is dominated by pointless sequels, dull remakes, vapid comedies, and hollow exercises in style, WALKER offers us a plethora of ideas that cascade onto the screen and crash in a pool of giddy chaos. Out of this chaos spring some undeniably powerful moments and a chillingly successful juxtaposition of the events of 1855 and 1987. Shot well before the Iran-contra hearings made Oliver North a star, the parallels between William Walker and the lieutenant colonel are all the more eerie. Cox sees Walker as a man whose fervent belief in the justice, humanity, and correctness of his mission blinds him to the fact that he is perverting his own dearly held ideals to achieve his goal. (It is no coincidence that Marlon Brando's very similar character in the unjustly forgotten BURN! is named Sir William Walker. That film and WALKER would make a great revival house double bill.) Cox is both intrigued and repelled by this moral arrogance and his lyrical treatment of violence, a la Peckinpah, may be an attempt to convey the seductive power of such righteousness (why not enjoy the killing if God is on your side?). Some critics charge that Cox never gets inside the head of William Walker. On the contrary, the entire movie seems as if it is being seen through Harris' steely blue eyes. Walker's own book, *The War in Nicaragua*, is written both in first and third person, an oddity that is reflected in Harris' narration and dialog (most of his speeches are direct transcriptions of Walker's words). Walker was a dynamic mass of intellectual confusion and moral contradictions and so is this movie.

Shot almost entirely in Nicaragua with the full support of the Sandinista government (they exercised no censorship over the script or final cut—if they had the film would no doubt be more coherent, effective propaganda), WALKER garnered much media attention during its filming. Journalists from around the world flocked to the set for a glimpse at post-Somoza life in Nicaragua. The cast and crew all worked for much less money than usual because they believed in Cox and the political message he was espousing. Reportedly, Ed Harris turned down a $750,000 part to play Walker for $50,000. Because of the Reagan administration's economic embargo on Nicaragua, the production had to have supplies shipped from Mexico and London, and there were no Hollywood-style amenities for the cast and crew. Early reports from the set decried the fact that Nicaraguan extras were being paid less than their European counterparts, but eventually all players were paid the same rate. Fearing that Universal would interfere with the post-production, Cox stayed in Nicaragua to edit the film, as did ex-Clash member Joe Strummer, who composed a superbly evocative score for the film (see People To Watch). Although WALKER's value as anti-contra, pro-Sandinista propaganda is dubious at best, the scores of lengthy feature articles about the production--most of which describe life under the Sandinistas as hard, but not oppressive or unpleasant—have done more to enlighten North Americans than the film possibly could. Viewers should expect no answers from WALKER. Alex Cox sprang from the punk generation and his films convey that sensibility. He is a cynic who presents the situation in Nicaragua with a rueful resignation that provokes a visionary mixture of bemusement, disgust, awe, and outrage at what history has repeatedly failed to teach us. *(Graphic violence, sexual situations, excessive profanity, brief nudity.)*

p, Lorenzo O'Brien, Angel Flores Marini; d, Alex Cox; w, Rudy Wurlitzer; ph, David Bridges; m, Joe Strummer; ed, Carlos Puente Ortega, Alex Cox; prod d, Bruno Rubeo; art d, Cecilia Montiel, Jorge Sainz; set d, Bryce Perrin, Suzie Frischette; cos, Theda Deramus, Pam Tait; spec eff, Marcellino Pacheco Guzman; stunts, Rick Barker; makeup, Morag Ross.

Historical **(PR:O MPAA:R)**

WALL STREET*** (1987) 124m American Ent./FOX c

Charlie Sheen *(Bud Fox)*, Michael Douglas *(Gordon Gekko)*, Martin Sheen *(Carl Fox)*, Terence Stamp *(Sir Larry Wildman)*, Sean Young *(Kate Gekko)*, Daryl Hannah *(Darien Taylor)*, Sylvia Miles *(Realtor)*, James Spader *(Roger Barnes)*, Hal Holbrook *(Lou Mannheim)*, Saul Rubinek *(Harold Salt)*, John McGinley, Frankin Cover, James Karen, Richard Dysart, Josh Mostel, Millie Perkins, Annie McEnroe, Monique van Vooren.

Once again, writer/director Oliver Stone has proven to have an uncanny knack for anticipating public interest in the subjects he chooses. Last time out it was Vietnam, and PLATOON swept the Academy Awards, grossing over $150 million. This time, in WALL STREET, Stone takes on the much-publicized insider trading scandals. Unfortunately, Stone's proclivity for blatant melodrama—forgivable in the chaotic jungles of Vietnam—nearly overwhelms WALL STREET. This is an old-fashioned liberal morality play that could have been written and directed by one of the Hollywood Ten in the late 1940s with John Garfield in the Charlie Sheen role. Set in 1985, the film follows the hectic career of young Wall Street broker Sheen as he scrambles to make his first million. His idol is ruthless big-time corporate raider Douglas, a man who gobbles up companies by the dozen and then sells them for a quick profit, moving tens of millions of dollars on an hourly basis. Sheen's dream is to get in with Douglas and become one of his brokers. Sheen's father (played by his real-life father, Martin) is a blue-collar airline mechanic and the local representative of his union. Learning from his father that the federal courts are about to vindicate the airline in an accident case—a decision that will improve the airline's business—young Sheen uses this inside information to "bag" Douglas. Intrigued by the tip, Douglas authorizes Sheen to buy up loads of the airline's stock before the news hits the papers. Everything goes off as young Sheen has predicted, and Douglas makes yet another fortune. Much to his surprise, Sheen is rewarded with a gorgeous blonde hooker in a stretch limo. With the promise of big financial rewards negating his momentary apprehension about breaking the law, Sheen willingly goes to work for Douglas and violates nearly every ethical statute of the business world. Sheen's rise to the top is rapid, and he finds himself spending several hundred thousand dollars on a fashionable East Side high-rise condo and even more on the interior decorating engineered by the vapid, social-climbing Hannah. But Sheen doesn't have time to enjoy the spoils of victory, for there is money to be made 24 hours a day. Thinking he can help his father's ailing airline, Sheen persuades Douglas to buy the company, assuring him that he will get the support of the various unions in restructuring the company and making it profitable. Douglas, Sheen, and the representatives of the airline unions meet, and Douglas makes his pitch: Cut salaries and benefits, fire current management, expand routes, and after a few years of profitability, salaries and benefits will be restored. The elder Sheen scoffs at the proposal and says that Douglas is obviously after the company's assets. Much to his son's horror, he refuses to support the buy-out. Despite this reversal, Douglas sets out to buy the company. The younger Sheen soon learns his father was right: Douglas intends to fold the company, sell the fleet, and develop the valuable real estate. Shocked that Douglas would use him and his father to liquidate the airline for immediate capital gain, Sheen confronts the corporate raider and demands an explanation. Douglas merely informs Sheen that this is how the game is played. Spurred by his father's sudden

heart attack, young Sheen undergoes an awakening of conscience and decides to get back at Douglas by helping rival corporate raider Stamp (a benevolent man intent on helping ailing companies with good earning potential) gain possession of the airline. The trick works and Douglas loses a small fortune on the deal ("So I only make $10 million instead of $60 million," he says). Sheen's triumph is short-lived, however, for federal agents arrive to arrest him on insider trading charges. To help his own case and further erode Douglas' credibility, Sheen agrees to be "wired" and secretly tapes Douglas making admissions of wrongdoing. Secure in the knowledge that his father (who has recovered) forgives him, young Sheen walks up the steps of the courthouse to pay the penalty for his unscrupulous greed.

With WALL STREET, director Stone intentionally set out to make a good-old-fashioned liberal drama about the evils of unchecked capitalism. The very fact that WALL STREET's last shot is a panoramic view of New York City skyscrapers with the "Halls of Justice" at the bottom of the frame and a huge, imposing "The End" at the top of the frame seems to indicate that Stone meant to harken back to the old films that ended in just such a manner—the big "Crime Doesn't Pay" finish. As self-consciously nostalgic as this approach may be, it still results in a film with few shades of gray and lots of moralizing speeches on everything from judging a man's value by "the size of his wallet" to "greed is good, greed works." Luckily, Stone nearly pulls it off with his usual visual verve and keen casting instincts. Charlie Sheen is fine in what is essentially the same role he had in PLATOON—the young, inexperienced kid whose soul is battled for by the forces of "Good," represented by Martin Sheen, and "Evil," represented by Douglas. Better yet is Douglas, an actor who has finally hit stride this year, capturing much attention for his work here and in FATAL ATTRACTION. His Gordon Gekko is a predatory animal who literally seduces the weak into his lair. His impassioned speech on the virtues of greed (delivered at a meeting of stockholders) is the centerpiece of the film—and its highlight. Both stars are given excellent support from McGinley, Karen, Young (as Douglas' numb wife), Stamp, Miles (as the ultimate Manhattan realtor), Spader, and Mostel (as a broker known as "the Terminator"). Also managing to come across rather well, given that their characters are both ciphers, are Martin Sheen and Hal Holbrook. The elder Sheen transforms Stone's tired speeches on integrity, usefulness, and genuine self-worth into something resembling honest spontaneity and his scenes opposite his son are relaxed and natural. Faring less well is Holbrook, who represents the brokers of the past (Stone's father was a stockbroker for 50 years) and pops up now and again to offer young Sheen sage advice on the glories of sound conservative investment. Hannah, however, is downright awful. Her performance is a total failure and never even approaches the petty, manipulative creature called for by the script. She reportedly had trouble sympathizing with her character and found it hard to play such a shallow, reprehensible person and it shows.

Despite Stone's obviousness, WALL STREET is easier to take than the current school of filmmaking in which creeps are made into heroes and good-old-fashioned values are scoffed at as terminally naive and "unhip." He makes his films for the masses and presents them in a comfortable populist mold. Stone is the Bruce Springsteen of the American cinema—a thinking man with his heart in the right place who skillfully translates his fundamental liberalism into a media event. He sees today's success-hungry young brokers as living in a fantasy world untainted by street crime, poverty, and everyday problems. But theirs is a house of cards, and in October 1987, its very foundation was shaken. Many Wall Street yuppies had their bubbles burst by the stock market crash and now last year's most heralded and financially successful director has taken a shot at their worship of the almighty dollar. While WALL STREET may not have the pure power of SALVADOR or PLATOON, it does prove that Oliver Stone has a good eye for hot topics and is not afraid to tell it as he sees it. *(Profanity, sexual situations.).*

p, Edward R. Pressman, A. Kitman Ho; d, Oliver Stone; w, Oliver Stone, Stanley Weiser; ph, Robert Richardson (Deluxe Color); m, Stewart Copeland; ed, Claire Simpson; prod d, Stephen Hendrickson; art d, John Jay Moore, Hilda Stark; set d, Leslie Bloom, Susan Bode; cos, Ellen Mirojnick.

Drama **(PR:O MPAA:R)**

WANNSEE CONFERENCE, THE*** (1987, Ger./Aust.) 87m Infafilm GmbH-Austrian Television-ORF-Bavarian Broadcasting/Rearguard c (DIE WANNSEEKONFERENZ)

Robert Artzorn *(Hofmann)*, Friedrich Beckhaus *(Muller)*, Gerd Bockmann *(Adolf Eichmann)*, Jochen Busse *(Leibbrandt)*, Hans W. Bussinger *(Luther)*, Harald Dietl *(Meyer, Gauleiter for the Occupied Eastern Territories)*, Peter Fitz *(Dr. Wilhelm Stuckart, Interior Minister)*, Reinhard Glemnitz *(Buhler)*, Dieter Groest *(Neumann)*, Martin Luttge *(Dr. Rudolf Lange, Commander of the Gestapo in Latvia)*, Anita Mally *(Secretary)*, Dietrich Mattausch *(Reinhard Heydrich, Chief of the Security Police)*, Gerd Rigauer *(Schongarth)*, Franz Rudnick *(Kritzinger, Reich Chancellery Representative)*, Gunter Sporrle *(Gerhard Klopfer)*, Rainer Steffen *(Friesler, Justice Minister)*.

A startling re-creation of one of the most harrowing meetings of the 20th Century—the gathering of 14 Nazi officials on Jan 20, 1942, in the Berlin suburb of Wannsee to discuss the "final solution," or the extermination of some 11 million Jews. The film, like the actual meeting, lasts for 85 minutes and takes place (with the exception of some exterior shots of the villa at Am Grossen Wannseestrasse 56-58) in what amounts to a corporate board room. Organized by Reinhard Heydrich, the chief of the Nazi security police and secret service, the meeting was conducted at the request of Adolf Hitler and Hermann Goering in order to secure the cooperation of a number of key German representatives whose participation was necessary to economically annihilate the Jewish race. The most recognizable name of those in attendance is that of Adolf Eichmann, head of the Gestapo's Jewish Department. While not ministers themselves, others were representatives of various departments from Germany's occupied territories. Already devoted to the Nazi idealogy, the conferees did not attend in order to question the morality of the subject, but to discuss the most efficient means of achieving their goal. Heydrich (Mattausch) dominates the meeting with a light but frightening hand. Latvian Gestapo representative Lange (Luttge) is bored and drunk, worried more about his barking, restless dog than the "final solution." Heydrich and Eichmann (Bockmann) pass time by flirting with their secretary (Mally), who reciprocates when she isn't recording the minutes. Various questions are raised concerning what types of poison gas to employ, how to deal with the press, and how to appease the railway workers who are disgusted with inconveniences caused by Jewish corpses. The only voice or conscience or reason is interior minister Stuckart, who argues that half-Jews should be spared since they are also half-Germans. His solution is to sterilize these half-Jews to prevent them from further contaminating Aryan blood. Eighty-five minutes after the start of the meeting, a plan of attack is decided upon, and the film ends as the group readies for lunch.

Made for German and Austrian television and broadcast in 1984, THE WANNSEE CONFERENCE was released in the US thanks to the efforts of longtime Hollywood producer Max Rosenberg, whose Rearguard Pictures supervised the subtitling, the 16mm to 35mm blowup, and the subsequent limited release. The film's production began when its eventual producer, Korytowski, was involved in the making of a documentary on the Eichmann trial. Based on documents kept at Yad Vashem, the Holocaust archives located in Jerusalem, THE WANNSEE CONFERENCE is not an exact re-creation of the actual meeting. Since no transcript exists (only the secretary's minutes), screenwriter Mommertz and director Schirk had to reconstruct dialog and characterizations through extensive research. Resisting any temptation to tack on an epilog or prolog which might have added historical perspective, the filmmakers chose instead to replay the meeting in real time. The effect is an eerie one. Because of the historical cloud that envelops the viewer (characters are barely even identified) the entire situation takes on an absurd quality, as if the participants are discussing the marketing strategy for a new product line. The camera simply wanders around the room, almost without direction, observing from a kind of heavenly distance. What makes the film so memorable are the powerful performances which soon fool the audience into thinking the real event is unfolding before their eyes. Although certain historical events allegedly have been reshaped (according to author Raul Hilberg, writing in the *New York Times*), the effect of the film is undeniably chilling. Whether or not the film is truly cinematic is irrelevant. As the film's producer has stated: "My intention was to make a record for the future . . . Young people must know what Germany was from 1939 to 1945." *(Adult situations.)*

p, Manfred Korytowski; d, Heinz Schirk; w, Paul Mommertz; ph, Horst Schier; ed, Ursula Mollinger; art d, Robert Hofer-Ach, Barbara Siebner; cos, Diemut Remy.

Historical **(PR:A-C MPAA:NR)**

WANTED: DEAD OR ALIVE*½ (1987) 104m NW-Balcour/NW c

Rutger Hauer *(Nick Randall)*, Gene Simmons *(Malak Al Rahim)*, Robert Guillaume *(Philmore Walker)*, Mel Harris *(Terry)*, William Russ *(Danny Quintz)*, Susan McDonald *(Louise Quintz)*, Jerry Hardin *(John Lipton)*, Hugh Gillin *(Patrick Danahy)*, Robert Harper *(Dave Henderson)*, Eli Danker *(Robert Aziz)*, Joe Nasser *(Hassan)*, Suzanne Wouk *(Jamilla)*, Gerald Papasian *(Abdul Renza)*, Nick Faltas *(Amir)*, Hammam Shafie *(Chemical Expert)*, Tyler Tyhurst *(Charlie)*, Ted White *(Pete)*, Neil Sommers *(Hardy)*, Dennis Burkley *(Farnsworth)*, Deedee Rescher *(Mrs. Farnsworth)*, Jesse Aragon *(Luis Sanchez)*, Tu Thuy *(Young Vietnamese Woman)*, Tu Ban Nguyen *(Vietnamese Shop Owner)*, Garry Scott *(Yeshiva Student)*, Tiiu Leek *(Herself)*, Bill Smith *(Himself)*, R.J. Miller *(Mr. Morrison)*, Charles Shapiro *(Usher)*, David E. Boyle *(Police Chief)*, Jeffrey Josephson *(Sgt. Nelson)*, Patrick Puccinelli *(Policeman)*, Jim Edgcomb *(Technician)*, Buddy Farmer, Gary Werntz, Rif Hutton, Richard Partlow, Rick Goldman, George Shannon, Ed Brodow, Patrick Gorman, Hubie Kerns, Jr. *(Agents)*, Danny Costa *(Truck Driver)*, George W. Elam, Ben R. Scott *(Guards)*.

This arthritic story twitches to life in only a few instances and Hauer, one of the better actors on the scene, is generally wasted as a modern-day bounty hunter, an ex-CIA operative who has shunned "the company" and captures bad guys for profit. The film opens with Hauer watching a cowboy fugitive act up in a bar, and then trailing him to a small grocery store where the thug-cowpoke holds up and terrorizes the Oriental owners. Hauer bashes unconscious the cowpoke's friends, enters the store and puts a gun to the head of his prey after shooting up the place. Leading the cowboy, Tyhurst, to his car he states: "Charlie, you smell!" Then he locks him in the trunk of his car and delivers him to the police. He later fills out the appropriate papers for the bounty with his police officer friend Russ in order to collect the $40,000 on Tyhurst's head. He tells Russ that he wants to bring in "a few more bad guys" for the bounty, put the money into his boat and "see the world . . . without a bull's eye on my forehead." He is referring to his action days with the CIA which he is glad are history, yet Russ tells him "you like that bull's eye." Meanwhile, in the guise of a rabbi, Arab terrorist Simmons arrives in Los Angeles to begin a reign of terror and seemingly purposeless killings. He slits the throat of the rabbi who picks him up at the airport, then joins his Arab henchmen to plan the explosions of public buildings. As Hauer meets his sweetheart, Harris, on his boat (he operates out of a garage loft replete with motorcycles, cars, and gun gallery), Simmons and his zealot girlfriend Wouk blow up a movie house (which is not too ironically playing RAMBO) loaded with women and children. More than one hundred are killed and Simmons is identified as the killer, having called authorities before the explosion and leaving his fingerprints on the glass pane of a phone box.

Guillaume, a CIA officer and old friend of Hauer's, arrives at Hauer's boat the next day and asks him to personally find and bring in the terrorist Simmons, offering him $250,000 and a bonus of $50,000 if Simmons is brought in alive. Hauer accepts because Simmons is an old enemy who killed his friends in Beirut years earlier. But, unknown to Hauer, the CIA, and this is without Guillaume's knowledge, is using Hauer as bait to bring Simmons out in the open. CIA boss, Hardin, knows Simmons seethes to take Hauer's life for killing some of *his* old friends. When CIA operative Harper is captured by Arab thugs working for Simmons, he is tortured into telling them where Hauer keeps his boat. By then Hauer has been in a shootout with the Arabs and he soon realizes he is being used as bait, accusing Guillaume of setting him up. To escape CIA surveillance, Hauer persuades his friend Russ to impersonate him and Russ goes on board the boat where he meets girl friend Harris. Just then, with CIA men on the dock, the boat blows up (and an Arab scuba diver surfaces long enough to grin maniacally before swimming off). Both Russ and Harris are dead and when the disgusted Guillaume gets into his car, Hauer—who has witnessed the explosion—is in the back seat of his car. Guillaume swears he knew nothing of the set-up but promises to help him find the Arab terrorists, later calling Hauer with the address of Danker, Simmons' top lieutenant. Hauer goes to the delapidated house, finds Danker's bomb-making apparatus and then waylays Danker when he comes home. He forces him into a metal locker and fires bullets into it until Danker tells him that Simmons can be found in a warehouse. By the time Hauer reaches the warehouse he sees Arab terrorists getting into large drums and these drums being loaded onto a huge flatbed truck. Working his way beneath the flatbed, Hauer rides along with the truck which goes to a refining plant, Simmons, following in a rented armored car. Hauer, once inside the plant, disposes of the truck driver after the cans containing the hidden terrorists have been dropped off. He takes over the truck and greets Simmons as he drives into the plant, ramming the armored car. By then the CIA learns about the plan to explode the chemical plant and kill thirty thousand people. Cops and agents swarm into the plant area just as the terrorists begin popping out of the cans.The Arabs are killed or captured, except Simmons who is tracked through the plant by Hauer. After a shootout, Hauer handcuffs Simmons and stuffs a live grenade in his mouth. He takes the terrorist to CIA officers, telling Guillaume and Hardin he wants his $250,000 sent to Russ' widow. Then he walks up to Simmons and tells the CIA boys that he doesn't want the $50,000 bonus for bringing Simmons in alive, pulling the pin out of the grenade. Everyone runs as Simmons blows up. Hauer, disgusted by the entire episode, walks to a river's edge, sits down, and begins blowing ambiguous notes on a harmonica for the fadeout.

The terrorist theme has been hacked to pieces over the years and we are now left with villains like Simmons, who specializes in such roles, planning to annihilate tens of thousands of people for little or no reason. In WANTED: DEAD OR ALIVE he is a rather monotonous menace who spends most of his time dreaming up torture and mass murder. Hauer is supposed to be the grandson of the original bounty hunter played by Steve McQueen in the black-and-white TV series of yore and Hauer even makes mention of his grandfather while conjuring his past with Harris. There is no character development, only killing machines in action and Hauer is no less ruthless and relentless than he was as the replicant of BLADE RUNNER, although he certainly doesn't have top production people behind him here. The plot is without finesse and director Sherman's energies all go to weaponry, explosives and destructive car chases. The language is gratuitously foul, the acid rock songs distasteful, and no one is developed into any kind of sympathetic character. There are little nods to the Hollywood of yesteryear. Hauer's boat is entitled "H.M.S. Bounty," after the MUTINY ON THE BOUNTY ship. The chemical plant operation is a lift from WHITE HEAT, and the terrorists secreted in the 55-gallon drums is right out of ALI BABA AND THE FORTY THIEVES (yes, there are forty drums). Even LES MISERABLES is tapped for a Hauer escape through the sewers. Guillaume as the halfway decent CIA man is a walk through effort and the dialog could have been written from the rejected pages of any Charlie Chan opus. In the end we have to ask ourselves why did Simmons ever arrive in Los Angeles? What was his purpose? The film's only answer is: To be blown up by a grenade in his mouth. The language is foul, the violence is graphic and blood flows as freely as a water tap left on overnight. Not for youngsters. *(Violence, profanity.)*

p, Robert C. Peters; d, Gary Sherman; w, Michael Patrick Goodman, Brian Taggert, Gary Sherman; ph, Alex Nepomniaschy (CFI Color); m, Joseph Renzetti; ed, Ross Albert; prod d, Paul Eads; art d, Jon Hutman; cos, Tom McKinley; spec eff, Cal Acord; m/l, Joseph Renzetti, Simon Stokes, Jimmie Davis, Charles Mitchell; stunts, Walter Scott; makeup, Jim Gillespie.

Action **(PR:O MPAA:R)**

WAR ZONE (SEE: DEADLINE, Ger./Brit., 1987)

WARDOGS* (1987, Swed.) 83m Walthers c

Tim Earle, Bill Redvers, Sidney Livingstone, Catherine Jeppson, David Gillies, Irene Gronwall, Chris Masters.

When a former soldier's brother disappears in Vietnam, he refuses to believe that he is really dead. He receives a cryptic letter making it official, but that only leads him to dig further. He makes contact with a journalist who is investigating his old commander. The reporter wants to show him a video tape of an assassination performed at a lonely desert gas station by a team of sunglasses-wearing killers in Army uniforms. Before Stewart can get there, though, the reporter is murdered. He recovers the video tape and recognizes not only his old commander, but his brother as well. He locates the base where a secret force is kept pumped full of drugs that make them the perfect soldiers, but he is captured and tortured. He manages to escape with his brother, and they fight a running battle with the rest of the force, finally killing the commander. The brothers go home, but things aren't over. The brother is a killing machine, and when a nosy neighbor tries to corner him in conversation, he grabs a knife and kills her. The government is after him, too. Knowing they can't cure him, they kill him in an attack on the house. This is a Swedish-made film which goes to great lengths to try to like the US. American flags are everywhere, along with Coca-Cola signs, but then the police drive up in a Volvo wagon. The action scenes are rather flat and there is nothing to really recommend this film except for its intriguing story line. The existence of these assassination teams has long been rumored, and the filmmakers manage to make a few points about them, but for a better treatment of similar themes see EXTREME PREJUDICE. *(Violence, profanity.)*

p, Bjorn Carlstroem, Anders Nilsson, Daniel Hubenbecker; d&w, Bjorn Carlstroem, Daniel Hubenbecker; ph, Anders Nilsson; m, Dag Unenge; ed, Andrew Nelson; art d, Karin Lundberg; spec eff, Martin Sundahl, Susanne Apelquist.

Action **Cas.** **(PR:O MPAA:NR)**

WARM NIGHTS ON A SLOW MOVING TRAIN** (1987, Aus.) 92m Western Pacific/Filmpac Holdings c

Wendy Hughes *(The Girl, Art Teacher)*, Colin Friels *(The Man)*, Norman Kaye *(The Salesman)*, John Clayton *(The Football Coach)*, Lewis Fitz-Gerald *(The Girl's Brother)*, Rod Zuanic *(The Soldier)*, Steve J. Spears *(The Singer)*, Grant Tilly *(The Politician)*, Peter Whitford *(The Train Steward)*, Chris Haywood *(The Stationmaster)*, John Flaus *(The Taxi Driver)*, Peter Carmody *(The Second-Class Passenger)*.

A highly polished but uneventful drama which has hints of STRANGERS ON A TRAIN but adheres more closely to the logic of a Harlequin Romance novel. Hughes, Australia's top actress, is a chameleonic prostitute who spends every weekend traveling on the Melbourne-to-Sydney overnight train. Having struck a deal with the steward, Whitford, a hulking, baby-faced homosexual, Hughes finds her customers in the train's piano bar. Changing her appearance to accommodate the clientele, she picks out a target, eyes him throughout the evening, and entices him to approach her. After sharing a few drinks, she invites him back to her sleeping compartment (the "Judy Garland" suite, usually reserved for celebrities who dislike flying). Before getting into bed, however, she warns her men that "it will cost." Her clients are usually a bit surprised when they discover that she's a hooker, but they inevitably pay—determined to make their fantasies come alive. Then, promptly at 3:00 a.m., Hughes kicks her clients out—mainly because she fears she will become involved with them. The following morning, when she runs into her clients in the dining car, she adopts a cold businesslike manner and ignores them. Throughout the course of the film, Hughes' character is revealed. She is an art teacher in a Catholic girls grade school. She is not a nymphomaniac, nor is she a ruthless whore. Rather she is a devoted sister to Fitz-Gerald, a former Olympic-bound sprinter whose career was tragically cut short after an accident left him a paraplegic. Now, to ease the pain and to keep the nights "warm," Fitz-Gerald depends on morphine—an expensive habit which has become a financial burden for Hughes. During one of her train rides, on a particularly slow evening, Hughes is approached by Friels, a cool, well-dressed man who has been eyeing her on previous train trips. She invites him into her suite and they immediately begin to make love. For the first time, Hughes refrains from requesting payment, and even lets Friels stay past the 3:00 a.m. curfew. She realizes that she is falling in love with Friels, but the next morning he is nowhere to be seen. After disappearing for a while, he returns later with a moneymaking proposition for Hughes. She must kill an influential politician, Tilly, who is scheduled to be riding on her train. Friels not only promises her $800,000, but also vows that they will stay together after the assassination. Hughes is at first apprehensive but agrees to take part. She successfully lures Tilly into her suite and, by using a poisoned fake fingernail, kills her target while they make love. No traceable signs of foul play are left by the poison, so it is assumed that he simply had a heart attack while fooling around with an innocent prostitute. Hughes then learns she was just a pawn in Friels' game. He gladly turns over the payment but is quick to break off the romance. The tables are turned on Hughes and she realizes that Friels has done to her what she has been doing to her clients for so long—creating a fantasy relationship in order to accomplish a specific goal. Her next train trip is a different one—riding in a regular seat, she ignores the advances of a fellow passenger.

Written and directed by Bob Ellis, who scripted the successful Paul Cox films MAN OF FLOWERS and MY FIRST WIFE, WARM NIGHTS has an intelligent and insightful screenplay but lacks anything of interest directorially. Handled like a standard made-for-TV film (there is no profanity or nudity), it relies on a repetitive style which employs the same shots and settings for each scene. Events move from the piano bar to Hughes' suite to the dining car and then back again. This is all intercut with the all-too-frequent shots of the sleek silver train slicing through the pitch-black night. The only things that change from scene to scene are Hughes' wig and wardrobe and the clients whom she lures into her bed. There is Clayton, a burly football coach who dreams of writing a Dostoevskian novel and has a terrible habit of singing in the shower; Zuanic, a young soldier who wants to marry Hughes by morning; Spears, a carefree singer who believes that fate will reunite them in the future; and Kaye (the star of MAN OF FLOWERS), a widower and retired salesman who has found God. While all of these characters are sympathetic and interesting, their episodes are streamlined, and as a result, never probe as deep as one would like. The best sequence is one between Hughes and Whitford, the steward, in which he laments over a lover he lost. Instead of making love, they maintain a friendly conversation before retiring to separate bunks. Hughes turns in a masterful performance, switching personalities as effortlessly as she switches wigs. Her character, however, is such a coldhearted vampire that it is difficult to feel compassion for her. In an attempt to give Hughes some redeeming values, she is made a Catholic schoolteacher and even bears the cross of her poor brother's misery. Instead of adding character complexity, these subplots only divert our attention from the more interesting prostitute-clientele relationship. Friels, too, is excellent (having been seen last year in MALCOLM and KANGAROO), but his character is as cold as Hughes. Reportedly, the original version of WARM NIGHTS ran some 40 minutes longer (which would have been a fatal length for the box office) and concentrated even more on Hughes and her clients than the 92-minute version, which truncates the prostitute-client scenes and devotes the energies of the last half of the film to a ridiculous assassination plot. When WARM NIGHTS works, as in the prostitution scenes, it works well, but unfortunately Ellis tries to throw every plot device imaginable into the film, and as a result, ends up with very little. *(Adult situations.)*

p, Ross Dimsey, Patric Juillet; d, Bob Ellis; w, Bob Ellis, Denny Lawrence; ph, Yuri Sokol; m, Peter Sullivan; ed, Tim Lewis; prod d, Tracy Watt; cos, Alexandra Tynan.

Drama **(PR:C MPAA:NR)**

WARRIOR QUEEN* (1987) 79m Lightning/Seymour Borde c

Sybil Danning *(Berenice)*, Donald Pleasence *(Claudius)*, Richard Hill *(Marcus)*, Josephine Jaqueline Jones *(Chloe)*, Tally Chanel *(Vespa)*, Stasia Micula [Samantha Fox] *(Philomena/Augusta)*, Suzanna Smith *(Veneria)*, David Cain Haughton *(Vicca)*, Mario Cruciani *(Roberto)*, Marco Tullio Cau *(Goliath)*.

This costume epic with lots of naked flesh, softcore sex, and special-effects footage of Pompeii being buried in ash is somehow grafted with a gobbledygook plot and some scenes of Donald Pleasence and Sybil Danning to produce one of the silliest sword-and-sandal epics ever to emerge from the Italian peninsula. It is impossible to extract a coherent plot from the film, but apparently Danning is the mistress of the emperor. While vacationing in sunny Pompeii as the guest of mayor Pleasence, she attends a slave auction where she sees one girl sold off to the proprietor of the nicest brothel in town, The House of Venus. Danning later visits her there and tells her that she is not alone and that later she will be free. While we are left to mull over whatever meaning that may have, the action moves to the tiny gladiatorial combat ring, where bruiser Goliath spins a razor- edged frisbee into the guts of his opponent, which then fall out in a steaming pile. More nonsense rounds out the action, with people falling in love and getting attacked and raped in the woods and sword-fights and the like, until finally Vesuvius erupts. Buildings topple, various cast members run around looking for each other, the bad people die horribly, and the good people make it to the safety of the hills. Danning has little more than a few lines and one expression. Pleasence hams up his role and seems to be having a good time, more than anyone watching, certainly. The rest of the cast have the kind of names that look like they're pseudonyms and give performances that reinforce this notion. This is a pretty worthless item, all in all, but if softcore exploitation is what you're after, you can't do much better than WARRIOR QUEEN, just on sheer comic value. This film had a brief release at 69m before the final videocassette outing of 79m with added sex scenes. *(Graphic violence, nudity, sexual situations.)*

p, Harry Alan Towers; d, Chuck Vincent; w, Rick Marx (based on a story by Peter Welbeck [Harry Alan Towers]); ph, Lorenzo Battaglia (TVC Color); m, Ian Shaw, Kai Joffee; ed, Chuck Vincent, Joel Bender, Jim Sanders, Tony Delcampo; prod d&cos, Lucio Parisi.

Drama **(PR:O MPAA:R)**

WARRIORS OF THE APOCALYPSE† (1987) 95m Film Concept c (AKA: SEARCHERS OF THE VOODOO MOUNTAIN; TIME RAIDERS)

Michael James *(Trapper)*, Debrah Moore *(Sheba)*, Franco Guerrero *(Anouk)*, Ken Metcalfe *(Goruk)*, Robert Marius, Charlotte Cain, David Light, Mike Cohen, David Brass, Steven Rogers.

Set 150 years in the future and shot in the Philippines, this English-dubbed ROAD WARRIOR clone chronicles the exploits of James and his nomadic followers as they stumble upon the 100-year-old Guerrero deep in the jungle and then journey with him in search of Voodoo Mountain. With queen Moore at his side, Metcalfe (who also wrote the screenplay) rules over the mountain and the nuclear power plant hidden within it which is operated by slave labor. Guerrero, James, and company liberate the slaves and do away with Metcalfe, but the secret of eternal life vanishes with him. After being exhibited in some regions under the titles "Searchers of the Voodoo Mountain" and "Time Raiders," this was given a home video release under its present title.

p&d, Bobby A. Suarez; w, Ken Metcalfe (based on a story by Bobby A. Suarez); ph, Jun Pereira (Rank Color); m, Ole Hoyer; prod d, Ruben Arthur Nicdao; ch, Franco Guerrero.

Fantasy **Cas.** **(PR:NR MPAA:R)**

WATASHI O SKI NI TSURETETTE† (1987, Jap.) 95m c (Trans: Take Me Out to the Snowland)

Tomoyo Harada *(Yuh Ikegami)*, Hiroshi Mikami *(Fumio Yano)*, Horishi Fuse *(Kazuniko Izumi)*, Hitomi Takahashi *(Hiroke Haneda)*.

Basic teen/ski picture has skiing ace Mikami smitten with snow bunny Harada, but too shy to do anything about it. Interspersed with a lot of ski footage, Mikami finallys gets Harada's attention and she falls for him.

p, Yasushi Mitsui; d, Yasuo Baba; w, Nobuyuki Isshiki; ph, Genkichi Hasegawa; ed, Isao Tomita; art d, Hiroshi Wada.

Romance/Sports **(PR:NR MPAA:NR)**

WATER ALSO BURNS† (1987, Turkey) 115m Young Cinema 85/Toei c

Tarik Akan *(The Director)*, Sahika Tekand *(Wife)*, Nathalie Douberne *(Girlfriend)*.

Ex-convict Akan faces pressure from the government and police, and must deal with his failing marriage, while trying to make a film.

d, Ali Ozgenturk; ph, Ertunc Senkay; m, Sarper Ozhan; ed, Peter Presgodard.

Drama **(PR:NR MPAA:NR)**

WEEDS*½** (1987) 115m Kingsgate/DEG c

Nick Nolte *(Lee Umstetter)*, Lane Smith *(Claude)*, William Forsythe *(Burt the Booster)*, John Toles-Bey *(Navarro)*, Joe Mantegna *(Carmine)*, Ernie Hudson

(Bagdad), Mark Rolston *(Dave)*, J.J. Johnson *(Lazarus)*, Rita Taggart *(Lillian Bingington, Newspaper Critic)*, Orville Stoeber *(Lead Guitar)*, Essex Smith *(Thurman)*, Cyro Baptista *(Percussion)*, Sam L. Waymon *(Keyboard)*, Anne Ramsey *(Mom Umstetter)*, Ray Reinhardt *(Pop Umstetter)*, Amanda Gronich *(Bagdad's Girlfriend)*, Felton Perry *(Associate Warden)*, Barton Heyman, Walter Charles *(Godot Players)*, William Lucas, Reggie Montgomery *(Rabble Rousers)*, Amy C. Bass *(Grad Student)*, Nicholas Wyman *(Associate Warden)*, Richard Olsen *(Derrick Mann)*, Drew Elliot *(Fisher Cobb)*, Charlie Rich *(Himself)*, Arnold Johnson, Gerald Orange, Leonard Johnson, Paul Herman, Frank Gio, Gift Harris, Paul Weeden, Maximo Cerda *(Inmates)*, Richard Portnow, Michael Luciano, Daniel Kent *(Guards)*, Howard Spiegel *(House Manager)*, Louis Criscuolo *(Waiter)*, Denny Burt *(Caterer)*, Raymond Rivera *(Busboy)*, Billy Badalato *(Doorman)*, John Bonitz *(Dean)*, Billy Cross *(Pound Attendant)*, Rhesa Stone *(Saleswoman)*, James Deuter *(Motel Manager)*, Kirsten Baker *(Kirsten)*, John Ring, Robert Miano, Sam Stoneburner *(Parole Board)*.

A pleasant surprise from DEG studios, WEEDS is an offbeat look at the American penal system and the criminals that pass through it. The film boasts superb performances from an ensemble cast led by Nolte as an inmate sentenced to life with no chance of parole for an armed robbery and aggravated assault. Seeing no hope for release, Nolte tries to commit suicide twice and fails. At the urging of his cellmate, Smith, Nolte tries to distract his mind from his fate by reading. Having left school after the sixth grade, Nolte begins educating himself and passes the time by challenging his intellect. After a few years he is discussing the classics of philosophy and literature with other educated inmates, albeit in a uniquely "street" manner. After witnessing a performance of "Waiting for Godot" performed for the prisoners by a local theatre troupe, Nolte is enthralled and inspired. Working diligently, the inmate writes his own play and bases it on the dehumanizing prison experience (although he sets his play in France so the warden won't think that "atrocities are committed in his penal institution"). Nolte is given permission to perform the play for the inmates, and the playwright casts his work with enthusiastic prisoners (with Forsythe, Toles-Bey, Hudson, Rolston, and Johnson acting, while Stoeber, Smith, Baptista, and Waymon provide the music for the songs). The play is a hit with the inmates and Nolte finds himself something of a celebrity. Taggart, a San Francisco drama critic, sees the play and is greatly impressed with both Nolte's writing and acting. She tries to get the prisoner paroled, but her efforts fail. During the ensuing months Nolte loses most of his cast when they finish serving their sentences. Sadly, he sees each one off, only to have the gates slam in his face every time.

Eventually, Taggart's efforts pay off and Nolte is released. The ex-con moves in with Taggart and they begin a romantic relationship. At Taggart's urging, Nolte reassembles his cast—now all ex-cons—and takes his play on the road, playing mostly college towns. At the play's conclusion, he offers a question and answer session during which students can ask the ex-cons about prison life. Now a professional, Nolte is forced to admit to himself and his cast that he plagiarized most of his play from Jean Genet's "Death Watch" and cribbed lines from Saul Bellow as well. With help from Taggart and his loyal cast, Nolte begins to make the play his own, changing the locale from France to America, adding more songs, and bringing his own experience into the material. Tragically, key cast member Toles-Bey is killed in a car accident and the troupe is forced to cast an obscure New York actor, Mantegna, to replace him. Since Mantegna is not an ex-con, Nolte invents a criminal history for the actor so it will look good in the program bios. After several misadventures, the troupe finally makes it to off-Broadway where they perform the play for influential New York critics. Unfortunately, the most influential critic, Elliot, is unimpressed and gives the play a "nice-try-but-no-cigar" review. Crushed, Nolte and the troupe agree to a performance at a New York state prison. The play, now changed to explicitly reflect life in American prisons, captures the imagination of the inmates and they begin to get rowdy. When the panicky warden stops the play and tries to get the inmates to leave the auditorium, a riot erupts. Still dressed in their prison uniform costumes, Nolte and his troupe try to make their way through the violent chaos, but guards mistake them for inmates and begin beating them. When Nolte is felled by a brutal guard, Forsythe comes to his defense and is killed by a vicious blow to the head. Eventually, the riot is quelled and the actors sorted out from the inmates. The ensuing publicity gives Nolte's play a new lease on life, and public demand causes it to be booked for a limited run on Broadway.

Based loosely on the real-life saga of inmate Rick Cluchey, WEEDS (the title is Nolte's metaphor for how society perceives prisoners) is a fascinating, touching, funny, and at times brutal look at the wreckage of the American penal system and how, in spite of it all, some inmates can emerge from it to lead meaningful and productive lives. While pulling no punches when it comes to the harsh realities of the situation, the film's message is ultimately a hopeful one. The inmate actors involved in the play share a strong sense of self-worth and discover their humanity while functioning as a close-knit group. When a member falters or appears ready to give up and return to a life of crime, the others work to bolster his confidence and reconfirm their devotion to the project and each other. It is important to these men to communicate—first to fellow inmates, and then to the outside world—that prisoners are human beings who feel loneliness, desperation, fear, anger, and sadness. Although they freely admit their crimes, the inmates insist that the rest of the world should not turn a blind eye to their existence. Other seemingly incongruous aspects of prison life are represented as well. In one of the Q & A sessions, Forsythe, a habitual shoplifter, confesses that he sometimes misses the regimented prison life. He admits that before serving time he "wasn't very good at planning [his] days." The rough transition from inmate to citizen is detailed as well. Nearly all the ex-cons continue to carry handguns (a parole violation), but none, including Nolte, can explain why they feel it necessary. It also takes another inmate, Toles-Bey, to make Nolte realize that by plagiarizing much of the play the public is " . . . gonna say you just been doin' your thing . . . stealin'," thus eroding any credibility the project possesses. WEEDS shows the rehumanizing process as slow and painful, but well worth the effort. The script, authored by director Hancock and his wife, Tristan, falters at times by slipping into cliches—all the more dismaying when most of the film constantly surprises. Fortunately, the excellent cast pulls the film through some rough spots. Nolte is superb as he moves from hopeless, suicidal convict to successful actor/playwright who refuses to forget his roots. It is a skillful and detailed performance filled with intelligence and nuance. Toles-Bey (in his film debut), veteran Smith, Forsythe, Hudson, Rolston, and Johnson (an ex-con also making his film debut) are impressive as well, and it is their ensemble performance, full of life and humor, that makes WEEDS so watchable. Taggart scores memorably, although her character is given little to do once Nolte is released from prison.

Most of the prison scenes were shot in Illinois' notoriously tough Stateville Correctional Center, with inmates playing extras. Fearing that even under the most controlled situations, trouble might flare up among the inmates, prison officials could not promise the film crew protection and gave the go-ahead with an "at your own risk" disclaimer. Cast members were instructed to dress down, carry little cash, and not play "movie star" when dealing with the inmates. Surprisingly, all the various racial tensions and gang rivalries were put aside by the inmates and they gave the film their wholehearted support and enthusiasm—there was no trouble during the shoot. Nolte, however, preferred to have a guard dressed as a convict near him at all times to act as a bodyguard during the riot scene. Ironically, one inmate fooled the film people into thinking he was a prison employee and asked to be dropped off in the parking lot. The prisoner escaped, but was recaptured shortly thereafter. The film has several original songs including "I Wanna Go Home," "Weeds," "Burn" (Melissa Etheridge, performed by the cast), "Body Search" (Orville Stoeber, Etheridge, performed by the cast), "Lock & Key" (Richard Peaslee, Stoeber, Adrian Mitchell, performed by the cast), "Pimp Song," "Prick or a Noose" (Stoeber, performed by the cast). Other songs include "Impossible Dream" (Joe Darion, Mich Leigh, performed by Ernie Hudson), "Behind Closed Doors" (Kenny O'Dell, performed by Charlie Rich), "I Can't Help Myself (Sugar Pie, Honey Bunch)" (Eddie Holland, Brian Holland, Lamont Dozier, performed by The Four Tops). Perhaps the biggest disappointment of the film is a shockingly bad soft-rock score by Angelo Badalamenti, the same man who had composed a superb symphonic score for David Lynch's BLUE VELVET. Most startling, however, is the fact that the memorable theme "Mysteries of Love" (Lynch, Badalamenti) from BLUE VELVET is used, in its entirety, over the scene where the play incites the prison riot. *(Graphic violence, nudity, sexual situations, adult situations, profanity.)*

p, Bill Badalato; d, John Hancock; w, Dorothy Tristan, John Hancock; ph, Jan Weincke (Technicolor); m, Angelo Badalamenti; ed, Dennis O'Connor; prod d, Joseph T. Garrity; art d, Pat Tagliaferro; set d, Francine Mercadante; cos, Mary Kay Stolz; spec eff, Mike Menzel, Marvin Gardner, Rick Barefoot; ch, Jerry

Evans; m/l, Melissa Etheridge, Orville Stoeber; stunts, Joe Dunne; makeup, Edouard F. Henriques.

Drama **(PR:O MPAA:R)**

WEEKEND† (1987, USSR) 92m Mosfilm/Sovexportfilm c

Alla Demifova, Alexey Batalov, Vladislav Strzhelchik, Darya Mikhaylova, Mikhail Neganov.

d&w, Igor Talankin (based on a story by Yuri Nagibin); ph, Gueorgy Rerberg; m, Alfred Shnitke; art d, Valery Filippov.

Drama **(PR:NR MPAA:NR)**

WELCOME MARIA† (1987, Mex.) 79m Peliculas Mexicanas c

Maria Victoria *(Marla)*, Allison Ernand *(Meche)*, Bob Copeland *(Ezekiah)*, Christian Canada *(Miguelito)*.

A woman and her son leave Mexico and enter the US illegally to search for the woman's husband, missing for two years. Against the backdrop of the problems faced by illegals, the woman finds her husband in Los Angeles, where he has a new life with an American wife. Moreno, the film's producer, is the son of well-known Mexican comedian Cantinflas.

p, Mario Arturo Moreno; d, Juan Lopez Moctezuma; w, Juan Lopez Moctezuma, Ruben Arvizu; ph, Nadine Markova; m, Miguel Angel Alonso; ed, Jerome F. Brady.

Drama **(PR:NR MPAA:NR)**

WERYFIKACJA† (1987, Pol.) 100m Karol Irzykowskic (Trans: Verification)

Marek Kondrat *(Mark Labus)*, Jan Englert *(Janusz Malicki)*.

During martial law in Poland, journalist Kondrat loses his job on a weekly newspaper. He leaves Warsaw and travels the country, seeking out old friends as he re-examines his life and goals.

d&w, Miroslaw Gronowski; ph, Jacek Mieroslawski; m, Przemyslaw Gintrowski; ed, Halina Prugar-Ketling; set d, Barbara Nowak.

Drama **(PR:NR MPAA:NR)**

WHALES OF AUGUST, THE*** (1987) 90m Alive-Circle-Nelson/Alive c/b&w

Bette Davis *(Libby Strong)*, Lillian Gish *(Sarah Webber)*, Vincent Price *(Mr. Nikolai Maranov)*, Ann Sothern *(Tisha Doughty)*, Harry Carey, Jr. *(Joshua Brackett)*, Frank Grimes *(Mr. Beckwith)*, Frank Pitkin *(Old Randall)*, Mike Bush *(Young Randall)*, Margaret Ladd *(Young Libby)*, Tisha Sterling *(Young Tisha)*, Mary Steenburgen *(Young Sarah)*.

Featuring two of filmdom's most legendary leading ladies, 91-year-old Lillian Gish and 79-year-old Bette Davis, as well as distinguished septuagenarian stars Ann Sothern and Vincent Price, and famed John Ford ensemble member Harry Carey, Jr., THE WHALES OF AUGUST is a wistful meditation on old age. The film opens with sepiatone footage of three young women in billowy dresses frolicking on the beach of a small Maine island, with a weathered house on the cliff above. The camera comes to rest on a buoy bobbing in the ocean. Slowly color seeps onto the screen. It is many years later, 1954, and the young ladies have grown aged. Davis (played by Margaret Ladd in the initial scene) and her younger sister Gish (Mary Steenburgen as a young woman) have returned to the island from Philadelphia for the summer, just as they have for the past 60 years. Davis is now blind and Gish has cheerfully looked after her for 15 years. As girls they had stood on the cliffs and watched for whales headed for warmer waters at the end of the summer. Now the whales come no more. Gish still anticipates their

appearance and would like local handyman Carey to put in a new picture window, but Davis, who has grown bitter and cynical, thinks it would be frivolous and vetoes the idea. Increasingly obsessed with her imminent death, Davis spends most of the day in a rocking chair caustically trying to deflate her more active sister's cheery disposition. "Busy, busy, busy, busy," Davis chides Gish. Sothern (played by her daughter, Tisha Sterling, in the opening sequence), their lifelong friend and the island's resident busybody, pays them a visit. With Davis out on the porch, Sothern tries to persuade Gish to put Davis in her daughter's care, not to return to Philadelphia, and to move in with her. Gish is hesitant, but for perhaps the first time she begins weighing the possibility. Price, a courtly relic of imperial Russia, stops by the house as he returns from fishing. He offers the sisters his catch and Gish invites him to return for dinner. Bathed in moonlight, they share the meal and memories; however, Davis behaves less than civilly. The little get together ends with Price embarrassed and Gish angry. When Davis has gone to bed, Gish celebrates her wedding anniversary. Decorating a table with one white rose and one red one, she lovingly contemplates a photo of her beloved husband Philip, who was killed in WW I. (Earlier, Davis has warmly stroked a lock of her own late husband's hair against her cheek.) For 15 years after Philip's death, Davis and her husband had looked after the emotionally devastated Gish. Now, it strikes Gish that she has been minding Davis for 15 years. They are even. To separate from Davis might cause some financial problems for Gish, but she is no longer morally obligated to stay with her. Later that night Davis awakes from a nightmare screaming for Gish, who comforts her. The following day, Sothern returns with real estate agent Grimes. He begins to appraise the house, but Gish stops him. Shaken by the sudden tangibility of giving up the house and flabbergasted by Sothern's presumptuousness, Gish dismisses Grimes and, with a look that could kill, forever quashes the possibility of moving in with her old friend. Carey returns for a tool he has left behind and Davis, who has witnessed Gish's encounter with Grimes, asks the handyman when he can begin installing the new picture window. The sisters make a slow walk to the edge of the cliff. As they stare out at the ocean, still looking for the whales that will never return, the film ends.

With its extraordinary cast, THE WHALES OF AUGUST would have made cinema history even if its script had been taken from a cereal box. In fact, the screenplay, adapted by David Berry from his own largely autobiographical stage play, isn't one of the film's stronger elements. Suffering from heavy-handed symbolism and offering few real insights, it nonetheless provides the blueprint from which these exceptional actors are able to build their performances. Nothing much happens in the two-day period in which the story transpires, at least not when measured against the standards of the average film. However, British director Lindsay Anderson, making his first American feature, has put the film's emphasis on acting and character. It is a mistake, though, to see the film only as a grand final showcase for its marvelous cast. At the heart of acting is character, and, more than anything else, character is determined by relationships. At the center of THE WHALES OF AUGUST is a captivating character study of the relationship between two very different women, sisters who have lived together for most of their lives, both loving and enduring each other. In essence, Davis has given up on life. Gish, on the other hand, still joyfully embraces it, and the story's central conflict is whether Gish will remain with Davis. For all of their differences, there is still a strong bond between them, their shared past. Gish evokes it when she decides to keep the house, and Davis, recognizing this, makes the important symbolic gesture of accepting the picture window.

Both of these cinematic *grande dames* give wonderful performances. It is impossible to divorce either of them from their film pasts, but though the baggage they bring with them as icons enriches their portrayals, their acting and not their resumes defines their characters. Gish, who began her career when the cinema was still in its infancy and for whom D.W. Griffith literally invented the close-up, still possesses a gentle beauty that radiates from her soul. Even though she has grown a bit jowly and her movements have slowed, there is still something waiflike about her. She brings grace and quiet dignity to her Sarah. After suffering a stroke and undergoing a mastectomy four years before the filming of THE WHALES OF AUGUST, Davis remains the sardonic queen bee. She invests her infirm Libby with toughness, spitting out sentences in the famous manner that dates back to her first film, BAD SISTER (1931). Playing a blind woman, she is denied the use of her famous eyes. However, she compensates with some wonderful acting choices, not the least of which is the aggressive way she rocks her chair, a terrific physicalization of the energy and frustration Libby can no longer express with her body. Wearing a red wig and using a high-pitched voice, the now round-faced Sothern is excellent as the buoyant friend. She provides the film's lighter moments—gossiping, flirting with Price, and arriving at the house with a cane in one hand and freshly picked blueberries in the other—but her deep-felt sorrow at the loss of her driver's license is among the picture's most touching events. The 78-year-old Sothern is best remembered as a comedienne, particularly as the dizzy blonde heroine in the "Maisie" films of the 1940s. After having two TV shows in the 1950s and 1960s, she broke her back in an on-stage accident in 1974, and THE WHALES OF AUGUST marks her return to films. Seventy-six-year-old Price, long known as a horror star, played opposite Davis in THE PRIVATE LIVES OF ELIZABETH AND ESSEX in 1939. This is his first non-horror role in 25 years, but he is less successful than his costars. His character never completely comes into focus, partly because his Russian accent is unconvincing. Clattering his tools, slamming doors, and deflecting insults, Carey, the youngster of the group at 65, gives an assured performance as the handyman.

THE WHALES OF AUGUST doesn't much resemble director Anderson's best-known films—THIS SPORTING LIFE, IF . . . , O LUCKY MAN!—but he has pointed out that even his satires are grounded in a fondness for humanity. His real achievement here is that he lets the film unfold at a pace appropriate for the lives of the characters. Neither the narrative nor the actors are rushed, and there is little fancy camerawork. Anderson and cinematographer Fash simply turn their cameras on the expressive faces of the actors and the sea and let the performers and nature do the rest. Fash was determined to capture the ever-shifting light playing upon the ocean, and his wonderful seascapes provide a striking counterpart to the human drama. The film was shot on location on Cliff Island off Portland, Maine, in the fall of 1986. All of the production's supplies had to be brought in by ferry and the living quarters for the actors were hardly lavish. Since they had to wait for the summer residents to depart, shooting didn't begin until early fall and the weather was changeable and occasionally rough. Anderson's shooting schedule took into consideration the needs of his mature cast, but all of these legendary performers worked with less rest than they were used to on the rugged eight-week shoot.

The $3 million film was the brainchild of coproducer Mike Kaplan. In 1967, while working as a publicist for MGM, he met Gish when she costarred with Richard Burton and Elizabeth Taylor in THE COMEDIANS. Kaplan was enchanted with Gish and determined to find a film that would be a perfect vehicle for her. In 1981, he saw the Trinity Square Theater's world premiere production of Berry's play and was convinced that he had found the right material. He took Gish to see an off-Broadway production of it and she agreed to star in the film. Kaplan was equally certain that Davis would be perfect for the role of Libby, but when he offered her the role, she turned it down, saying, "Who cares about these two old dames?" Five years later, when the production had finally come together, Gish was still willing to do the role, though she wondered if she would have the necessary stamina. When Davis was shown a completed screenplay, she changed her mind. The two-time Oscar winner returned to the movies (and Maine, where she had lived for 10 years with Gary Merrill) after working on TV for 10 years. This is Davis' 100th film and 105th for Gish. Its New York premiere was held on Gish's birthday. Because she doesn't have a birth certificate, her age has been estimated at from 88 to 93, but she celebrated that birthday as her 91st. THE WHALES OF AUGUST has more than a few problems, but anyone interested in the art of acting, the history of the cinema, or in seeing an unpatronizing portrait of elderly characters will find the film rewarding.

p,, Carolyn Pfeiffer, Mike Kaplan; d, Lindsay Anderson; w, David Berry (based on his play); ph, Mike Fash (CFI color); m, Alan Price; ed, Nicolas Gaster; md, Derek Wadsworth; prod d, Jocelyn Herbert; art d, K.C. Fox, Bob Fox; set d, Sosie Hublitz; cos, Rudy Dillon, Julie Weiss; makeup, Julie Hewett, Toni Trimble.

Drama **(PR:A-C MPAA:NR)**

WHEELS OF TERROR† (1987, US/Brit.) 101m Panorama/Manley c

David Carradine *(Col. von Weisshagen)*, Don W. Moffett *(Capt. von Barring)*, Keith Szarabajka *("Old Man")*, Bruce Davison *(Porta)*, Jay O. Sanders *(Tiny)*, David Patrick Kelly *(The Legionnaire)*, Slavko Stimac *(Sven)*, Andrija Maricic *(Stege)*, Boris Komnenic *(Bauer)*, Bane Vidakovic *(Muller)*, Oliver Reed *(The General)*, Irena Prosen *(The Madam)*, Svetlana, Gordana Les, Lidija Pletl, Annie Korzen.

A WW II war picture with a comic touch from director Hessler, whose two most recent films have been adroitly directed martial arts pictures—PRAY FOR DEATH and RAGE OF HONOR. Although the title makes this one sound like a racing drama, it is really about a squad of German prisoners on a suicide mission to destroy a Soviet railroad bridge ala A BRIDGE TOO FAR. It's 1943 and these Germans function on their own—they've had enough of the Russian enemy, the Nazi party, and especially Hitler. All they want to do is blow up a bridge. Along the way they encounter the usual war film contrivances—death, violence, ambushes, pretty maidens, and good old-fashioned male-bonding. Released in Europe with the video market seeming its most likely outlet in the US.

p, Just Betzer, Benni Korzen; d, Gordon Hessler; w, Nelson Gidding (based on a novel by Sven Hassel); ph, George Nikolic (Eastmancolor); m, Ole Hoyer; ed, Bob Gordon; prod d, Vladislav Lasic.

War **(PR:NR MPAA:NR)**

WHEN THE WIND BLOWS**** (1987, Brit.) 85m Meltdown-British Screen-Film Four Intl.-TVC London-Penguin Books/Recorded Releasing c

Voices Of: Peggy Ashcroft *(Hilda Bloggs)*, John Mills *(Jim Bloggs)*, Robin Houston *(Announcer)*, James Russell, David Dundas, Matt Irving.

With its striking simplicity, WHEN THE WIND BLOWS is a deeply moving parable of nuclear holocaust. Unlike the realistic television films "The Day After" or "Threads," this story is told through animation, following the story of a retired English couple who must deal with the post-nuclear winter.

James Bloggs (voiced by John Mills) and his wife Hilda (voiced by Peggy Ashcroft) live in a small cottage located in the British countryside. While Hilda happily toils at her housework, James returns home from his daily trip into the nearby town. He brings with him some pamphlets printed by the government, designed to instruct citizens in proper home defense during a nuclear attack. World tensions have been building, according to radio reports, and war is imminent. James carefully builds a regulation shelter using household materials, while Hilda fusses about. She doesn't understand why her husband is going to all this bother and scolds him repeatedly. James responds by quoting her the facts as stated in the government pamphlets, and continues with his work. A few days later a bulletin comes over the radio announcing a nuclear strike has been launched. Hilda wants to bring in her washing off the line, but James angrily tells her there is not time for that. The bomb goes off, destroying the England James and Hilda love so dearly. After the atomic blast James and Hilda begin adjusting to the post-nuclear world. Hilda is surprised to see what a mess her house has been turned into, while James faithfully continues heeding the government instructions. Electricity, water, and all communications have been cut off, while their beloved vegetable garden has been completely destroyed. Still, James and Hilda are convinced this situation is merely a temporary crisis, and like WW II, one they can stick out until things get back to normal. Gradually, radiation begins taking its toll on the couple. Hilda grows sickly, but James tries to keep up her spirits, explaining her problems are typical for a woman her age. He too becomes ill, but still remains certain things will get better. Husband and wife decide to cuddle up together and James begins to pray. Not knowing any one prayer, his words are a mixture of various psalms, and Hilda is touched by what her dearest companion has said.

The characters of James and Hilda are a comical pair, whose faith in everyday routine gives these catastrophic events a strong sense of pathos. The situation grows more desperate as the small, but important details of their lives slowly slip out of their control. These developments are handled with a gentle, sympathetic humor that subtly brings out the hopelessness in their plight. When James first tries to explain how they'll be unable to use the toilet in the days after the bomb, Hilda grows indignant. War or not, she intends on keeping a certain decorum. This becomes a running joke, until Hilda sees a rat climbing up the toilet bowl. A minor annoyance turns into personal tragedy as Hilda's vestiges of pride are shattered. James' staunch belief in the government pamphlets works in a similar way. He quotes Hilda passage after passage, convinced these instructions are their saving grace. They had listened to authorities during WW II with England emerging victorious, and James is convinced their leaders will guide them through a wartime crisis once more. Like Hilda's need for decorum, James' confidence in the pamphlets begins humorously before harsh reality settles in.

Mills and Ashcroft are perfectly cast in their cartoon roles. Drawn as round, jovial caricatures, these two fine actors bring out the humanity in James and Hilda. They deliver their lines quietly, in an understated manner, with a rapport that could only exist between a long married couple. A variety of animation styles are used in WHEN THE WIND BLOWS with often striking visual effect. James and Hilda's house is a miniature set, while the characters are animated over this background by cels. This combination gives the film a slightly three dimensional look. At times the camera merely explores the destroyed set while Mills and Ashcroft are heard on the soundtrack discussing how to deal with their growing troubles. Other sequences, such as single shots depicting the war's buildup, use model animation and there's also stock footage of WW II employed during James and Hilda's reminiscing.

WHEN THE WIND BLOWS marks the reuniting of an excellent creative team. Raymond Briggs, on whose book this film is based, had previously written the popular children's story of innocence nurtured and lost, "The Snowman." This was made as a short film in 1982, with Jimmy T. Murakami serving as supervising director. He took over full directing chores for this work, while Briggs again supplied the screenplay (Briggs also adapted this story as a radio drama). David Bowie, who served as narrator for THE SNOWMAN, provided the title song here, while Roger Waters, of "Pink Floyd" fame, wrote the musical score and closing theme. Together this talented group has produced an eloquent work. Originally shown in England in 1986, WHEN THE WIND BLOWS was awarded the Getz World Peace Prize at the 1987 Chicago Film Festival. *(Adult situations.)*

p, John Coates; d, Jimmy T. Murakami; w, Raymond Briggs (based on his book); m, Roger Waters; ed, John Cary; md, Ray Williams; art d, Richard Fawdry; spec eff, Stephen Weston; m/l, David Bowie, Roger Waters, Genesis, Paul Hardcastle, Squeeze, Hugh Cornwall, Glenn Tilbrook, Pete Hammond, Erdal Kizilcay.

Animation **(PR:C MPAA:NR)**

WHISTLE BLOWER, THE½** (1987, Brit.) 104m Portreeve Ltd./Hemdale c

Michael Caine *(Frank Jones)*, James Fox *(Lord)*, Nigel Havers *(Robert Jones)*, Felicity Dean *(Cynthia Goodburn)*, John Gielgud *(Sir Adrian Chapple)*, Gordon Jackson *(Bruce)*, Barry Foster *(Charles Greig)*, Kenneth Colley *(Bill Pickett)*, Dinah Stabb *(Rose)*, Andrew Hawkins *(Allen Goodburn)*, Trevor Cooper *(Inspector Bourne)*, James Simmons *(Mark)*, Katherine Reeve *(Tiffany)*, Bill Wallis *(Dodgson)*, David Langton *(Secretary to the Cabinet)*, Arturo Venegas *(Alex)*, Peter Miles *(Stephen Kedge)*, Susan Porrett *(Security Officer)*, Gregory Floy *(Coroner's Officer)*, Joe Dunlop *(Policeman)*, Peter Mackriel *(Flecker)*, Doyle Richmond *(American Interrogator)*, Carmel Cryan *(Anne, Frank's Secretary)*, Renny Krupinski *(Contact Prisoner)*, Ralph Nossek *(Makeup Man)*, Andrew Bradford *(Prison Officer)*, David Shaughnessey *(Medical Officer)*, Patrick Holt

(Irate Driver), Julian Battersby *(Doctor)*, John Gill *(Clergyman)*, David Telfer *(Ticket Collector)*, Sevilla Delofski *(Russian Woman)*, Peter Hutchinson *(Bank Manager)*, Jan Carey *(Miss Donald)*, Pamela Collins *(Sloane Ranger)*.

Despite a superb performance from the incredibly prolific Michael Caine, THE WHISTLE BLOWER is a ponderous affair that, while intellectually interesting, fails miserably on a cinematic level. The slow, confusing, and convoluted opening introduces widower Caine, a Korean War veteran, patriot, and struggling business machine salesman who goes to visit his son, Havers, on his birthday. Havers is an idealistic young man who works as a Russian translator at GCHQ (Government Communications Headquarters), British intelligence's listening center. He confides to his father that ever since a Russian mole was discovered on the staff, GCHQ has been encouraging employees to spy on one another, worried that the paranoid Americans will panic and withdraw their support of British intelligence operations. Several days later, two GCHQ employees suspected of being Soviet agents are found dead—killed in apparent accidents. Havers is convinced that his superiors have allowed the CIA to "plug the leaks" (i.e., had the men murdered) and tells his father that he hates how the "secret world" of espionage has "put out the light of the ordinary world." Havers reveals that he's considering blowing the whistle on the entire sordid operation. Caine is aghast that his son would consider quitting such a secure job and chalks up Havers' dissatisfaction to youthful idealism. Little do they know that GCHQ spies have eavesdropped on their entire conversation.

Meanwhile, the Russian mole is fooled into revealing the identity of his British superior. Much to GCHQ's surprise, the head Soviet spy is Gielgud, a respected member of the upper class and trusted agent of British intelligence. Knowing that this information will surely alarm the Americans, GCHQ head Fox decides to quash any dissent within the department. The next day, Havers is found dead after an apparent fall from his apartment rooftop. A distraught Caine begins to suspect that GCHQ may be responsible, and after failing to come up with any other reasonable explanation, he agrees to talk to the liberal journalist that Havers was scheduled to meet with on the day he died. The excited journalist sees a chance to blow the lid off British intelligence, but Caine protests that he "hasn't the stomach for revolution," and only wants to learn the truth about his son's death. Soon after their meeting, the journalist dies in a mysterious automobile accident and Caine becomes convinced that his son's allegations are true. Seeking information, Caine inebriates his old war buddy Foster—now a highly placed intelligence agent—and learns that Foster set up Havers so that GCHQ could protect Gielgud. Now determined to blow the whistle himself, Caine decides to confront Gielgud and extract a confession. Unfortunately, Fox warns Caine that Havers' lover, Dean, and her young daughter will be harmed if the information is ever made public. Caine goes to Gielgud's flat anyway and is outraged to find him very smug and condescending. Gielgud delights in the fact that he can be a Soviet agent while continuing to enjoy his privileged aristocratic life-style in Britain. At gunpoint, Caine forces Gielgud to write a full confession. When Caine pockets the confession, Gielgud makes a grab for the pistol and it goes off, killing him. With the now-useless confession in his pocket, Caine wanders through the crowd at the annual Remembrance Day ceremony in Whitehall.

Perhaps because Americans are more used to cinematic portrayals of government involvement in corruption, deceit, conspiracy, and murder is why THE WHISTLE BLOWER seems so strangely uninvolving. Bond's script and Langton's direction are so very proper, restrained, and subdued that the viewer has trouble maintaining much interest in revelations that should really be news to no one. Not that every spy film needs James Bond-type action to be successful, but THE WHISTLE BLOWER is mainly dialog with little visual nuance. It may have been more engaging as a radio play. As is typical of British productions, the film is brimming with fine acting. Unfortunately, solid performances are not always enough. THE WHISTLE BLOWER is incredibly lifeless. Scene after scene of characters speaking quietly to each other in sincere tones while standing in studies, apartments, offices, fields, racetracks, and restaurants may be how these things happen in real life, but they do not make a gripping movie. As a film, THE WHISTLE BLOWER suffers from the same sense of resigned stasis that Britain has been mired in for the last 30 years. *(Mild violence, adult situations.)*

p, Geoffrey Reeve; d, Simon Langton; w, Julian Bond (based on the novel by John Hale); ph, Fred Tammes (Technicolor); m, John Scott; ed, Robert Morgan; md, John Scott; prod d, Morley Smith; art d, Chris Burke; cos, Raymond Hughes; makeup, Magdelen Gaffney, Sallie Evans.

Spy/Drama **Cas.** **(PR:A MPAA:PG)**

WHITE MISCHIEF† (1987, Brit.) 107m Goldcrest-Umbrella-Power Tower/COL c

Sarah Miles *(Alive)*, Joss Ackland *(Broughton)*, John Hurt *(Colville)*, Greta Scacchi *(Diana)*, Charles Dance *(Erroll)*, Susan Fleetwood *(Gwladys)*, Jacqueline Pearce *(Idina)*, Catherine Neilson *(June)*, Murray Head *(Lizzie)*, Ray McAnally *(Morris)*, Geraldine Chaplin *(Nina)*, Trevor Howard *(Soames)*.

The film opens in 1940 with husband and wife Ackland (THE SICILIAN) and Scacchi (THE COCA-COLA KID) leaving their home in England for the British colony of Nairobi. Once in Africa, Scacchi falls for Dance, making plans to run away with him, until he is murdered. Though there are a number of suspects, including several of Ackland's former mistresses, Ackland is charged with the murder, but acquitted. WHITE MISCHIEF follows a storyline based on an actual unsolved murder case as it attempts to depict the seamy side of life in the British colonies in Africa. The producer-director team of Perry and Radford previously worked together on 1984.

p, Simon Perry; d, Michael Radford; w, Michael Radford, Jonathan Gems (based on the book by James Fox); ph, Robert Deakins; m, George Fenton; ed, Tom Priestley; prod d, Roger Hall; art d, Len Huntingford; cos, Marit Allen.

Drama **(PR:NR MPAA:NR)**

WHITE OF THE EYE† (1987, Brit./US) 110m Cannon Screen Ent./Cannon c

David Keith *(Paul White)*, Cathy Moriarty *(Joan White)*, Art Evans *(Charles Mendoza)*, Alan Rosenberg *(Mike Desantes)*, Alberta Watson *(Ann Mason)*, Michael Greene *(Phil Ross)*, Danko Gurovich *(Arnold White)*, William Schilling *(Harold Gideon)*, David Chow *(Fred Hoy)*, Danielle Smith *(Danielle White)*, China Cammell *(Ruby Hoy)*, Mark Hayashi.

David Keith (AN OFFICER AND A GENTLEMAN, INDEPENDENCE DAY), who played the white knight from the TVA battling a plague from outer space in this year's THE CURSE, plays a psychotic serial killer in this British financed thriller. The action is set in a small Arizona town where Keith works as a stereo specialist, installing fancy sound systems for wealthy customers. When the victims of a rash of murders all turn out to be people for whom Keith has worked, he becomes the most likely suspect, but the police find it hard to believe that this family man could possibly be a killer. He and wife Moriarty have a 9-year-old daughter, but their shaky marriage is based on twisted passion. Well before the film is over, Keith makes it known that he is, in fact, the slasher, and he begins terrorizing his own wife and child. As the film moves toward its climax, Rosenberg enters the picture; years before, Moriarty had passed through the small Arizona town on the way to meet then-boy friend Rosenberg in California, but she never made it there. Now, the brain-damaged Rosenberg, who has been working as a garbage collector, reappears and kicks the action into even higher gear. Both Cathy Moriarty (RAGING BULL, NEIGHBORS) and director Donald Cammell (PERFORMANCE, THE BAD SEED) have long been missing in action and WHITE OF THE EYE marks their return to moviemaking.

p, Cassian Elwes, Brad Wyman; d, Donald Cammell; w, China Cammell, Donald Cammell (based on the novel *Mrs. White* by Margaret Tracy); ph, Larry McConkey, Alan Jones (Consolidated Color); m, Nick Mason, Rick Penn; ed, Terry Rawlings; prod d, Philip Thomas; md, George Fenton; spec eff, Thomas Ford; stunts, Dan Bradley.

Thriller **(PR:NR MPAA:R)**

WHITE PHANTOM† (1987) 89m Bonaire/Spectrum Ent. c

Jay Roberts, Jr. *(Willi)*, Page Leong *(Mai Lin)*, Jimmy Lee *(Hanzo)*, Bo Svenson *(Col. Slater)*, H. F. Chiang *(Bookstore Owner)*, Kathy McClure *(Daughter)*.

This straight-to-video martial arts workout stars Bo Svenson as the colonel assigned to recover plutonium stolen from American scientists. Enough of the dangerous commodity has been taken to create a very big bang. The culprits are a gang of Ninjas who do the dirty work for a Japanese gangster family, the Sakuras. In Taiwan, Svenson seeks the help of Roberts, who offers his chops and kicks in the service of the forces of good. Leong also goes undercover to get the goods on the Sakuras and dances up a storm in the process.

p, Roy McAree, K.L. Lim; d, Dusty Nelson; w, David Hamilton, Chris Gallagher (based on a story by Dusty Nelson); ph, Alan Brennecke; m, Robert J. Resetar, Kevin Klingler, Bob Mamet; ed, Carole A. Kenneally; ch, Jimmy Lee, Page Leong; stunts, T.H. Lai.

Martial Arts Cas. (PR:NR MPAA:NR)

WHITE WATER SUMMER** (1987) 90m COL c

Kevin Bacon *(Vic)*, Sean Astin *(Alan Block/Narrator)*, Jonathan Ward *(Mitch)*, K.C. Martel *(George)*, Matt Adler *(Chris)*, Caroline McWilliams *(Virginia Block)*, Charles Siebert *(Jerry Block)*, Joseph Piassarelli *(Storekeeper)*.

Astin is a city kid with an aversion to the strenuous life who is forced by his parents to go on a three-week camping trip. Joining him on the trip is Bacon, a gung-ho type who takes it as his personal duty to teach Astin self confidence. As the trip commences, Astin repeatedly makes mistakes that earn him the contempt of the other campers. Bacon becomes rougher and rougher on him as Astin's resolve not to follow stiffens. They reach a mountain they are to climb, but when they come to a section they must traverse by swinging on a rope, Astin freezes and ends up dangling. When he refuses to try to help himself, Bacon leads the others away. Eventually Astin makes it across alone, and when he reaches the others, they join him in walking away from Bacon, headed for home. Bacon follows them and a fight follows in which Bacon is pushed over a cliff and breaks his leg. The others go for help while Astin stays with Bacon, and when his condition worsens, Astin carries him to a canoe and they start for civilization. Over a waterfall they fall out of the canoe and barely survive, but a helicopter comes along to rescue them.

A troubled production that saw Astin age from 13 to 16 before it wrapped and that required going to summery New Zealand when winter closed the mountains in the US, WHITE WATER SUMMER was originally titled RITES OF SUMMER, but apparently never saw a theatrical release under any name. Little wonder, since it plays no better than a bad after school special. None of the characters is the least bit sympathetic; Astin needs a swift kick in the pants rather than affectionate guidance, while Bacon is positively neurotic in his love of the outdoors. Just what audience the filmmakers were aiming at is a mystery, though the film may have therapeutic value as an anaesthetic. *(Mild profanity.)*

p, Mark Tarlov; d, Jeff Bleckner; w, Manya Starr, Ernest Kinoy; ph, John Alcott (Technicolor); m, Michael Boddicker; ed, David Ray; art d, Jeffrey L. Goldstein; set d, Bruce Gibeson; cos, Thomas Dawson; m/l, Bruce Hornsby, John Hornsby, Steve Perry, Jonathan Cain, Neil Schon, Ian Astbury, Billy Duffy, Nicholas Eede, Michael Boddicker, Kaylee Adams, Charlie Mitchell, Mike Slamer, Roy Ward, Mark Luttrelle, Mark Boals; makeup, Dan Streipke.

Drama (PR:C MPAA:PG)

WHITE WHALES (SEE: SKYTTURNER, 1987, Iceland)

WHO'S THAT GIRL½** (1987) 94m WB c

Madonna *(Nikki Finn)*, Griffin Dunne *(Loudon Trutt)*, Haviland Morris *(Wendy Worthington)*, John McMartin *(Simon Worthington)*, Robert Swan *(Detective Bellson)*, Drew Pillsbury *(Detective Doyle)*, Coati Mundi *(Raoul)*, Dennis Burkley *(Benny)*, John Mills *(Montgomery Bell)*, Jim Dietz *(Buck)*, Robert Cornthwaite *(Minister)*, Bibi Besch *(Mrs. Worthington)*; Wendy's Friends: Cecile Callan *(Sandy)*, Karen Baldwin *(Heather)*, Kimberlin Brown *(Rachel)*, Crystal Carson *(Denise)*, Elaine Wilkes *(Holly)*; Tony La Fortezza, Thomas Pinnock, Alvin Hammer *(Cabbies)*, Sean Sullivan *(Gun Dealer)*, Helen Lloyd Breed *(Co-op Chairperson)*, Dalton Dearborn, Robert E. Weil *(Co-op Members)*, Albert Popwell *(Parole Chairman)*, Alice Nunn *(Parole Member)*, Gary Basaraba *(Shipping Clerk)*, Ron Taylor, Stanley Tucci *(Dock Workers)*, Mike Starr *(Shipping Coworker)*, Dwight Crawford *(Bicycle Messenger)*, Laura Drake *(Shitley)*, Efrat Lavie *(Entourage Saleswoman)*, Mary Gillis *(Gown Woman)*, Roy Brocksmith *(Crystal Salesman)*, Ted Hayden *(Flatware Salesman)*, Deryl Carroll *(Florist)*, Beatrice Colen *(Secretary)*, Susan Bugg *(Law Secretary)*, Robert Clotworthy *(Lawyer)*, Lexie Shine *(Judy)*, Faith Minton *(Donovan)*, Judy Kerr *(Prison Officer)*, Darwin Carson *(Prison Reception Guard)*, Andre Rosey Brown *(Record Store Security Guard)*, Brad Rearden *(Record Store Cashier)*, Bert Rosario *(Greasy Guy)*, Patrick McCord *(Traffic Cop)*, Liz Sheridan, Shari Summers *(Nurses)*, Glen Plummer, Lance Slaughter, Alon Williams, Mario Gardner, Dennis Brown *(Harlem Kids)*, Carmen Filpi, Robert Benjamin Pope *(Street Bums)*, Gerald Orange *(Drunk in Harlem Hallway)*, Shelly Lipkin *(Tiffany Salesman)*, Ellen Crawford *(Tiffany Saleswoman)*, Pat Romano, Gary Tacon *(Rolls Royce Thiefs)*, Jinaki *(Lady on Bus)*, Glen Chin *(Bank Guard)*, Lloyd Kino *(Bank Officer)*, Clive Rosengren *(Bus Driver)*, Scott Harms, Christian Letelier, Sanders Cupac *(Motorcycle Cops)*, Meilani Figalan *(Amazon Woman)*, Phil Romano *(Fencing Opponent)*, Lea Lashaway *(Screaming Woman)*, Michael Scott Henderson *(Raoul's Driver)*, Marilyn Ammons *(Prison)*, Murray *(Cougar)*.

Madonna, the "boy-toy" singing idol and star of last year's box-office bomb

SHANGHAI SURPRISE, proves again that she understands the meaning of the term "star vehicle." The public, however, couldn't care less about a new Madonna film. Apparently they have heard too many of her songs and seen too many of the accompanying videos to shell out $5 plus for her film. Like SHANGHAI SURPRISE, WHO'S THAT GIRL was savaged by critics who seem to have a personal stake in keeping Madonna off the big screen. And like SHANGHAI SURPRISE, WHO'S THAT GIRL isn't all that bad. Perhaps if more film reviewers had a historical perspective of the genre of screwball comedies, then WHO'S THAT GIRL would be less of a puzzlement. Madonna, looking like Jean Harlow or Marilyn Monroe incarnate and sounding like a cross between Judy Holliday and Betty Boop, is a New *Yawk* petty thief whose blatant disregard for the law landed her in jail for four years after being wrongly accused of killing her boy friend. After an energetic animated credit sequence, the film opens with her release as she plans to hunt down the men who set her up. She must first find a safe-deposit box (she has the key, but doesn't know the bank or box number to which it belongs) that contains information on the high-powered figure behind her beau's murder. Starring opposite Madonna is Dunne, a reserved, bespectacled yuppie lawyer who is one day away from marrying Morris, the pampered daughter of McMartin, a filthy rich lawyer who also happens to be Dunne's boss. Although Dunne already has a terribly busy schedule which includes picking up his wedding ring from Cartier's and delivering a rare cougar (a Patagonian Felis Concolor, for the curious) to eccentric animal breeder Mills, he is ordered by McMartin to meet Madonna at the prison gates and escort her to the bus station. With the caged cougar, nicknamed Murray, occupying the backseat of his convertible Rolls Royce, Dunne picks up Madonna. He soon realizes that he is in over his preppie head. Before the day is over, Madonna has caused numerous traffic accidents, sent Dunne to the hospital, purchased a gun from a Harlem weapons dealer, left the Rolls to be stripped and spray-painted by ghetto kids, let Murray loose, and stolen from Cartier's. Of course, Dunne has fallen in love with her. After missing the last bus to Philadelphia, Dunne is stuck with Madonna. He agrees to help her clear her name by locating the safe-deposit box. While trying to find Murray, who has run away, they also hunt down Mundi, a sleazy little crook who was involved with the murder. Madonna and Dunne finally discover the box number and the bank, but the doors close before they arrive. Dunne is now stuck with Madonna until morning. In the meantime, Dunne's life grows more frantic and madcap. Mundi kidnaps Morris and her entire bridal party; Dunne tries to pass Madonna off as his high-society wife at an interview with the all-too-respectable board of a co-op; and Dunne and Madonna deliver Murray to Mills' wildlife sanctuary, located in his Manhattan penthouse. Lost in Mills' man-made forest, Dunne and Madonna spend the night together. In the morning, Dunne helps Madonna get to the bank and, without looking at the contents of the safe-deposit box, bids her farewell at the bus depot. He heads to his wedding while a teary-eyed Madonna takes a Greyhound out of town. Looking through her papers, she discovers that the killer is McMartin. She hijacks the bus and heads for the wedding, exposing McMartin as the culprit to all the wedding guests just before the vows are exchanged. After some silly gunplay, Dunne and Madonna declare their love for each other and leave town on the next bus.

Grossing a dismal 5 million in its first 10 days, WHO'S THAT GIRL (there is no question mark) was one of this year's unqualified flops—on a par with Beatty and Hoffman's ISHTAR and Stallone's OVER THE TOP, both of which are, perhaps not coincidentally, star vehicles. Decades ago a famous actor could appear on the screen in just about anything and still garner a respectable box-office showing. With the advent of video, however, movie audiences have become more discriminating when the critics pan a film. (Exceptions certainly do exist. The pathetic BEVERLY HILLS COP II with Eddie Murphy hit paydirt because of the Sequel Axiom of "diminishing quality, increasing return".) The Madonna Phenomenon—hit singles, sellout concerts, endless magazine cover stories and articles (including nude layouts), and a fashion craze of Madonna wanna-be's—has inexplicably failed to cross over to the movie industry. Her major drawback is her choice of material. Both SHANGHAI SURPRISE and WHO'S THAT GIRL are throwbacks to old Hollywood filmmaking—an adventure and a screwball comedy—and therein lies the lack of commercial appeal. In a time when audiences want little more than BEVERLY HILLS COP II and TOP GUN, a BRINGING UP BABY-inspired comedy has little hope. Borrowing heavily from the past (Howard Hawks, Jean Harlow, Marilyn Monroe), WHO'S THAT GIRL has found the right role models but doesn't know what to do with them. While the script is filled with witty lines, fast-paced overlapping dialogue, and screwball situations, it too often sinks to POLICE ACADEMY-style stupidity. Director Foley, who made his mark with the gripping but overly flashy AT CLOSE RANGE (and also directed two Madonna videos, "Papa Don't Preach" and "True Blue"), doesn't seem to have a clue about screwball comedy. (Perhaps if Peter Bogdanovich were at the helm things would be better.)

The only reason WHO'S THAT GIRL works at all is because of Madonna and Dunne. A natural in front of the camera, Madonna has developed a persona which appeals to both men and boys, women and girls. Like Marilyn Monroe (from whom Madonna has borrowed some fashion ideas in the film), Madonna is a sassy, brassy sexual toy that males wish they could have and females wish they could be. Like other screwball actresses—Harlow, Rosalind Russell, Katharine Hepburn—Madonna has an aura of helplessness that transforms itself into an ability to control disastrous situations and the feelings of men. The other essential ingredient to Madonna's success in the film is Dunne. He is the perfect Cary Grant straight man who attempts to organize and plan his life, but is constantly detoured by the unpredictable nature of the female. While Dunne is the symbol of everything orderly in life, Madonna is the embodiment of disorder, and one cannot exist without the other. If only Madonna and Dunne had an intelligent script and some inspired direction, then WHO'S THAT GIRL could have been a screwball classic. Instead it proves the statement that "Those who aspire to stupidity, often achieve it." Like LA BAMBA, the film was released in English and in Spanish (as QUIEN ES ESA CHICA), both versions making it to video. Although she does not sing onscreen, four Madonna songs are included on the soundtrack: "Who's That Girl," "The Look of Love" (Madonna, Patrick Leonard), "Causing a Commotion" and "Can't Stop" (Madonna, Stephen Bray). Other songs included are "Step By Step" (Jay King, Denzil Foster, Thomas McElroy, David Agent, performed by Club Nouveau), "Best Thing Ever" (Green Gartside, David Gamson, performed by Scritti Politti), "Turn It Up" (Michael Davidson, Frederic Mercer, performed by Davidson), "24 Hours" (Mary Kessler, Joey Wilson, performed by Duncan Faure), "El Coco Loco (So So Bad)" (Coati Mundi, performed by Mundi). *(Some profanity, comic violence.)*

p, Rosilyn Heller, Bernard Williams; d, James Foley; w, Andrew Smith, Ken Finkleman (based on a story by Andrew Smith); ph, Jan DeBont (Technicolor); m, Stephen Bray, Patrick Leonard; ed, Pembroke Herring; prod d, Ida Random; art d, Don Woodruff, Jack Blackman; set d, Cloudia, Lee Bloom; cos, Deborah Lynn Scott; m/l, Madonna, Patrick Leonard, Stephen Bray, Jay King, Denzil Foster, Thomas McElroy, David Agent, Green Gartside, David Gamson, Michael Davidson, Frederic Mercer, Mary Kessler, Joey Wilson, Coati Mundi; stunts, Bud Davis; makeup, Ed Ternes, Scott Eddo.

Comedy Cas. (PR:A MPAA:PG)

WHOOPING COUGH**** (1987, Hung.) 90m Mafilm-Hunnia Studio c (SZAMARKOHOGES)

Marcell Toth *(Tomi)*, Eszter Karasz *(Annamari)*, Dezso Garas *(Father)*, Judit Hernadi *(Mother)*, Mari Torocsik *(Grandmother)*, Anna Feher *(The Maid)*, Karoly Eperjes *(Akos)*.

On May 1, 1956, Torocsik is the custodian of a rooftop air raid siren. She tells her ten-year-old grandson, Toth, they must remain vigilant in case they come under attack from the imperialist troops. In October 1956, the calm has been shattered and Budapest is in the midst of a bloody uprising. A curfew is imposed as gunfire resounds throughout the city and families seal themselves behind closed doors. Torocsik is now engrossed in reading and rarely ventures out of doors. Her grandson is ecstatic about the state of insurrection because his school has been shut down until the curfew is lifted. He is confined to his home with the remainder of his family, which includes his father, Garas, who has lost his management job because he struck an employee, and his mother, Hernadi, who has secretly begun an affair. His eight-year-old sister, Karasz, leaves the family in a perpetual state of bewilderment with her obscene and slanderous remarks. At one point, Toth decides to break into the school building to retrieve his grandmother's typewriter, which he had earlier smuggled out of his home. He is apprehended by the brutal custodian and beaten for stealing what appears to be school property. Back home, Karasz's sudden coughing fit leads to fears of whooping cough, and a doctor is summoned. The doctor, a young and attractive female, examines Karasz and finds her free of the disease. She then examines Toth, an experience which leads to the boy's sexual awakening. The children then take advantage of a rare opportunity to enjoy the outdoors by undertaking a rail journey with a group of their school friends on a borrowed flat car. They glide along through the forest until a group of soldiers opens fire on them, killing one of their classmates. Meanwhile, Garas longs for his wife, who has left him to spend the night with her lover. His mother-in-law surprisingly treats him with a rare display of affection, thus enabling him to endure the loneliness until his repentant wife returns the following morning. After the insurrection has been quelled, Torocsik is unjustly jailed for allegedly printing subversive material with her typewriter. When she is released, she marches directly to the roof of her building and pulls the alarm, setting off a violent and deafening wail.

"Most people wanted to survive the shooting outside the house. They wanted to survive history and go beyond it," explains Peter Gardos about the focus of his second feature film, a charmingly astute portrait of a small world turned upside down by the cataclysmic events of 1956. His story follows the exploits of an ordinary family, one of the multitude of fearful ones during the uprising, who shut their doors and windows to the terror of the outside world. In his earlier film, THE PHILADELPHIA ATTRACTION (1985), Gardos explored the obsessive yearnings and the accompanying solitariness of the artist; in WHOOPING COUGH he focuses on the frustrated artistic inclinations of a common man, who rarely explores either of these leanings. The bond of Garas' family loosens as its individual members compromise their commitment to the unit. The delight he feels over his artistic intents forces him to experience the pain of vulnerability when he's greeted with criticism from his judgmental family. Eventually his children arrive at the painful realization that he and the members of the family are just ordinary people and that their attempts at displaying creativity produce little more than hollow failures. Yet, unbeknownst to any of them, it is their ordinary actions that produce the real artistic creativity. Winner of the top prize at the 1987 Chicago International Film Festival. *(Nudity, sexual situations, adult situations.)*

d, Peter Gardos; w, Andras Osvat, Peter Gardos; ph, Tibor Mathe (Eastmancolor); m, Janos Novak; ed, Maria Rigo; prod d, Jozsef Romvari; cos, Agnes Gyarmathy.

War/Drama (PR:O MPAA:NR)

WHOOPS APOCALYPSE† (1987, Brit.) 89m Picture Partnership/ITC Entertainment c

Loretta Swit *(Barbara Adams)*, Peter Cook *(Sir Mortimer Chris)*, Michael Richards *(Lacrobat)*, Rik Mayall *(Specialist Catering Commander)*, Ian Richardson *(Rear Adm. Bendish)*, Alexei Sayle *(Himself)*, Herbert Lom *(Gen. Mosquera)*, Joanne Pearce *(Princess Wendy)*, Christopher Malcolm *(Gallagher)*, Ian McNeice *(Thrush)*, Daniel Benzali *(William Kubert, U.S. Defense Secretary)*, Shane Rimmer *(Marvin Gelber, U.S. Secretary of State)*, Richard Wilson *(Nigel Lipman, Foreign Secretary and Crucifee)*, Richard Pearson *(Michael Sumpter, Defence Secretary and Crucifee)*, Stuart Saunders *(Governor of Santa Maya)*, Graeme Garden *(Man Who Takes a Long Time to Walk to the Phone/Man Who Takes a Long Time to Walk to a Different Phone)*, Marc Smith *(Dan Hickey, TV Anchorman)*, John Benfield, Ben Robertson *(Secret Servicemen)*, Alex Davion *(Maguadoran General)*, Phil Marquis *(Rock Pit Guard)*, Murray Hamilton *(Former President Jack "Kill the Commies" Preston)*, Robert Arden, Blain Fairman, Christopher Muncker *(White House Reporters)*, Dan Fitzgerald *(Foyer Guard)*, Spunky Spaniel *(Himself)*, D.L. Blakely *(Window Cleaner)*, Raymond Forshion *(Conference Guard)*, John Sessions *(Mr. Sweetzer)*, Tristram Jellinek *(Dickie, a Close Friend)*, Christopher Coll *(Flag Lt. Gerald Beaverstone)*, Maria Whittaker, Karen Kelly *(Pin-Up Girls)*, T.R. Durphy, Don Wellington *(Student Protestors)*, Joy Lynn Frasca *(Cute Little Girl Who Gets Socked in the Face)*, Simon Dormandy *(Soldier Parted from His Loved Ones)*, Paul Beech *(Doctor)*, Nick Copping *(Teapot Stirrer)*, Ken Jones *(Man on Cliff/Man off Cliff)*, John Cassidy *(Virgil Grodd, American Intelligence)*, Manolo Coego *(Granny Buyer)*, Ruben Rabasa *(Granny Vendor)*, Robert Blythe *(Guard with Egg in Mouth)*, Suzanne Mitzi, Christine Peak *(Topless Dancers)*, Terry Taplin *(Ed Rosario)*, Micky O'Donoughue *(Hypnotised Serviceman, Chicken)*, John Darrell *(Hypnotized Serviceman, Stripper)*, Ron Webster *(Soldier at Concert)*, Garry Martin *(Purveyor of Rambograms)*, Clifton James *(Maxton S. Pluck)*, Czeslaw Grocholski *(President Trezhnikov)*, Leon Lissek, Michael Poole *(Politburo Members)*, Christopher Rozycki *(Russian Doctor)*, Ed Bishop *(Wink Perelman, TV Interviewer)*, John Archie, Robert Goodman *(U.S. Sailors)*, Harold Bergman *(Desk Clerk)*, Iris Acker *(Woman in Boarding-House)*, Richard Murdoch *(Cabinet Minister Who Should Have Kept His Mouth Shut)*, Barbara Keogh, Elizabeth Proud *(Women at Wax Museum)*, Gavin Richards *(Donald, Vol-au-vents)*, John Blundell *(Douglas, Cucumber Sandwiches)*, Daniel Peacock *(Dominic, Petits Fours)*, Robert Bathurst *(Damien, Getting His Leg Sawn Off)*, Sharon Boyce, Emma Bryant, Lorraine Doyle, Jenny Drummond, Helen Kennedy, Wendy Millward, Tracy Smith, Laura Wynne *(Dancers)*.

Less DR. STRANGELOVE than FAIL SAFE given the AIRPLANE treatment, this British satire of international politics lampoons the Falklands War, the volatile situation in Central America, and the threat of nuclear war. Maguadora, a Central American country ruled by bellicose right-wing dictator Lom (the PINK PANTHER films), invades the neighboring nation of Santa Maya, a British protectorate. The British prime minister, Cook—who makes Peter O'Toole's 14th Earl of Gurney in THE RULING CLASS look like a pillar of sanity—orders a task force to retake Santa Maya. It does, and, riding on a sudden crest of domestic popularity, the bonkers Cook determines that an overabundance of "pixies" are the cause of British unemployment and orders their extermination. All of this sits very badly with British cabinet members, who, even with the CIA's help, are unable to eliminate Cook. Meanwhile, the enraged Lom orders international terrorist Richards to kidnap British princess Pearce, prompting Cook to threaten nuclear retaliation. By this time the Soviets have lined up behind Maguadora, which up until this point, has been a US ally. The American president, Swit, who took over the office when her predecessor (a former circus clown) died, doesn't know what to do. Eventually, it is determined that Richards is holding Pearce in London at the Wax Museum. The SAS manages to free her, but Cook demands that the nuclear strike be carried out anyway.

WHOOPS APOCALYPSE, which received its major UK release in 1987, is loosely based on the British TV series that was penned by the film's screenwriters, Andrew Marshall and David Renwick. The most notable change from the TV to the film version is the shift of the political crisis from the Middle East to Latin America. Fans of British television will also note the presence of popular funnymen Rik Mayall and Alexei Sayle (THE BRIDE, GORKY PARK).

p, Brian Eastman; d, Tom Bussmann; w, Andrew Marshall, David Renwick; ph, Ron Robson (Rank Color); m, Patrick Gowers; ed, Peter Boyle; prod d, Tony Noble; art d, David McHenry, Mark Harrington; set d, Ted O'Neill; cos, Liz Waller; makeup Kezia DeWinne; ch, Libby Roberts; spec eff, Peter Hutchinson.

Comedy (PR:NR MPAA:NR)

WIERNA RZEKA† (1987, Pol.) 140m Zespoly Filmowe-"X" Film Unit/ Film Polski c (Trans: The Faithful River)

Malgorzata Pieczynska *(Miss Salomea Brynicka)*, Olgierd Lukaszewicz *(Duke*

Janusz Odrowaz), Franciszek Pieczka *(Szczepan, Salomea's Servant),* Maria Homerska *(Duchess, Duke Odrowaz's Mother),* Henryk Bista *(Doctor),* Henry Machalica *(Major),* Wojciech Wysocki *(Wiesnicyn),* Jerzy Turek.

A love affair set against the backdrop of battles between Russian Cossacks and Polish nationals in Poland in 1863. Lukaszewicz plays a nationalist wounded in battle and taken in by Pieczynska, who nurses him back to health. They fall in love with each other, but when he has fully recovered, his mother arrives and spirits him away, leaving Pieczynska with a sack of gold coins, which she throws in the river. Based on a classic Polish tale, the film was shot in 1983 but was not shown until four years later when it was screened at the Gdansk Film Festival.

d, Tadeusz Chmielewski; w, Halina Chmielewska, Tadeusz Chmielewski (based on the novel by Stefan Zeromski); ph, Jerzy Stawicki; m, Jerzy Matuszkiewicz; ed, Miroslawa Garlicka; art d, Bogdan Solle.

Romance **(PR:NR MPAA:NR)**

WILD FORCE† (1987, Phil.) Sunny/Davian c

Yusuf Salim, Robert Talby.

Perhaps more aptly titled "The Dirty Half Dozen Plus One," this Filipino action film revolves around the efforts of seven commandos to infiltrate the stronghold of a renegade commander who has taken a United Nations scientist and his secretary hostage. Chosen because they are the best and dirtiest fighters available, this suicide squad made up of six men and one woman is a collection of criminals and mercenaries. Calling themselves the "Wild Force," the warriors overcome harsh terrain and overwhelming opposition to accomplish their mission.

d, Ruben De Guzman.

Action **(PR:NR MPAA:NR)**

WILD PAIR, THE* (1987) 88m Sarlui-Diamant/Trans World Ent. c (AKA: DEVIL'S ODDS)

Beau Bridges *(Joe Jennings),* Bubba Smith *(Benny Avalon),* Lloyd Bridges *(Col. Hester),* Gary Lockwood *(Capt. Kramer),* Raymond St. Jacques *(Ivory),* Danny De La Paz *(Tucker),* Lela Rochon *(Debby),* Ellen Geer *(Fern Willis),* Angelique De Windt *(Nadine Jackson),* Creed Bratton *(Dalton),* Randy Boone *(Farkas),* Greg Finley *(Sgt. Peterson),* Andrew Parks *(Hanks).*

Smith is a local cop who works with ghetto kids and rarely takes off his sweats, while Beau Bridges is an FBI agent attempting to catch drug dealer St. Jacques. They are teamed together unwillingly and each refuses to respect or trust the other. Beau Bridges learns that St. Jacques is controlled by a paramilitary organization that finances its right-wing fantasies with cocaine trafficking. To get to the group he sets up a large buy from St. Jacques, then steals the drugs. Both men dodge several attempts on their lives before Beau Bridges is captured and Smith's girl friend and pet cat are murdered. Smith figures out that his own boss is on the take and has been tipping off the criminals, so he beats some information out of him then twists his neck till it snaps. Beau Bridges is tortured by Lloyd Bridges (also seen is his grandson, offering us three generations of Bridges in one film—our cup runneth over) for information and is about to be killed when Smith launches a one-man attack that frees him. Using a handful of grenades, submachine guns, and an armored car, the two destroy the base, and Smith kills the senior Bridges in a hand-to-hand confrontation. The film ends with Beau Bridges buying Smith a new cat as a going away gift.

Anyone who has ever had trouble distinguishing Beau from Jeff Bridges need only see THE WILD PAIR to clear up all doubt. Jeff is the talented, good-looking one. Beau has put on some weight in the last few years, mostly around the jowls. Smith should stick to less demanding roles, at least until he learns to enunciate his words a little better. The strangest thing about this film, though, is the sad sight of Lloyd Bridges, once the dashing hero of the old "Sea Hunt" TV series, reduced to playing toy soldiers with his grandson. This barely saw a theatrical release in 1987, going straight to second-run houses. *(Brief nudity, violence, adult situations, substance abuse, profanity.)*

p, Paul Mason, Randall Torno; d, Beau Bridges; w, Joseph Gunn (based on a story by Joseph Gunn, John Crowther); ph, Peter Stein; m, John Debney; ed, Christopher Holmes, Scott Conrad; prod d, Stephen Berger.

Crime **(PR:O MPAA:R)**

WILD THING* (1987, US/Can.) 92m Atlantic Ent. Group-Filmline Intl./ Atlantic c

Rob Knepper *(Wild Thing),* Kathleen Quinlan *(Jane, Social Worker),* Robert Davi *(Chopper, Biker),* Maury Chaykin *(Detective Trask),* Betty Buckley *(Leah, Bag Lady),* Guillaume Lemay-Thivierge *(Wild Thing 10 Years Old),* Robert Bednarski *(Free/Wild Thing at 3 Years, son of Hud and Laurie),* Clark Johnson *(Winston),* Sean Hewitt *(Father Quinn),* Teddy Abner *(Rasheed),* Cree Summer Francks *(Lisa),* Shawn Levy *(Paul),* Rod Torchia *(Hud),* Christine Jones *(Laurie),* Robert Austern *(Wiz, Hitchhiker),* Tom Rack *(Braindrain),* Alexander Chapman *(Shakes, Junkie),* Robert Ozores *(El Borracho, Wino),* Lorena Gale *(Scooter),* Sonny Forbes *(Doowop),* Johnny O'Neil *(Worker),* Alastair Chartey *(Blood Andrew),* Richard Raybourne *(Blood Eric),* Freddie James *(Blood Flash),* George Popovich *(Cab Driver),* Ken Roberts *(Bugs),* Ron Lea *(Dink),* Jose Miguel Luis *(Luis),* Claire Rodger *(Kelly),* Lynne Adams *(Edwina),* Elizabeth Turbide *(Stacey),* Diana Sookedeo *(Kim),* Mitsumi Takahashi *(Katie Nagasaki),* Doug Price *(Cousin Louie),* Michael Hunter, Susan Seymour *(Teenagers),* Wally Martin *(Desk Clerk),* Audie Grant *(Runaway Boy),* Jodie Resther *(School Girl),* Carol Ann Francis *(Lady),* Douglas Leopold *(Gay Man),* Patricia Hanganu *(Girl),* Neil Kroetsch *(Photographer),* Harry Stanjofski *(Sgt. Matty),* Tyrone Benskin *(Det. Maury),* Neil Affleck *(Det. Walt),* Arthur Corber *(Doctor),* Griffith Brewer *(Wino),* Anthony Sherwood *(Will),* Joe Cazalet *(Chuckie),* Arthur Holden *(Gay Bar Manager),* Donald Lamoreux *(Orderly),* Sandra Blackie *(Sid),* Ray Roth *(Nino),* Real Andrews *(Raul),* Bonnie Beck *(Barbara),* Jeffrey Chong *(Joey),* Richard Campbell *(Kenny),* Leon Darnell Ramsoondar *(Dennis).*

A thoroughly uninvolving attempt to urbanize the Tarzan legend that plays as corny cross between a comic-book tale and a television cop show. The film opens in 1969 to the strains of the hippie anthem "White Rabbit" as a VW bus rolls through the countryside. Hippie mom, hippie dad, and their 3-year-old hippie son are all out for a quiet drive when, against mom's better vibes, they pick up a hitchhiker. It turns out that this hitchhiker is a former employee of drug dealer Davi. Davi and his corrupt policeman cohort, Chaykin, catch up with the former employee and kill him. To get rid of any witnesses, they also kill the hippie parents, while the little tyke hides in the back of the VW. He scurries away from the killers and escapes by jumping into a sewer drainage canal, apparently drowning. Later, he washes ashore and is found by Buckley, an ultracounterculture bag lady. She takes the little fellow in and teaches him about the "Company" (society), including the nasty "blue coats" (police) and the even nastier "white coats" (doctors and pschologists) who "scramble your eggs" (use electroshock and perform lobotomies, something this bag lady experienced years ago). Buckley soon dies, but not before teaching her adopted son how to live on the streets by eating rats and pigeons and stealing fruit from local vendors. Eventually the present day rolls around and our young hippie has grown up into a local legend called "Wild Thing," now played by Knepper. He lives in an especially unsafe part of town called "The Zone," which is known for its astronomical crime rate and colorful graffiti. He's a cross between Robin Hood and Spiderman, sneaking around by night, unseen, swinging down to the street from the roofs of tenement buildings in order to give drunken bums and destitute children unexpected dinners. Enter Quinlan, a well-groomed social worker named Jane (as in "Me Tarzan, You ...) who is immediately accosted by a couple of thugs who work for (you guessed it) Davi, the drug dealer who many years ago killed Knepper's parents and now is the most powerful person in The Zone. (Chaykin has also risen in the ranks and is now a corrupt police chief.) Knepper comes to Quinlan's rescue and soon everyone is talking about how "Wild Thing" saved her life. It doesn't take Quinlan and Knepper long to meet again and become romantically drawn to each other. In the meantime, both Knepper and Quinlan get pulled deeper and deeper into the drug-dealing/police corruption connection in The Zone. Davi and Chaykin soon realize that Knepper is the little hippie that escaped their grasp years before, and set out to kill him. When Quinlan is kidnaped by Davi, Knepper comes to her rescue, kills the bad guys, and then disappears into a nearby canal. Some assume that Knepper has drowned, while others continue to propagate the legend of "Wild Thing."

Penned by John Sayles, sometime respected director (this year's MATEWAN, for example), sometime slumming screenwriter (PIRANHA, ALLIGATOR), WILD THING held the promise of being an interesting synthesis of the nature-loving attitude of the free-spirited 1960s and the desensitized, corrupt ways of the urban ghetto of the 1980s. Knepper's "Wild Thing" character is the ultimate hippie love-child who has made it through the vacuous 1970s and the yuppified 1980s without losing the 1960s ideal of freedom. A "wild child," Knepper lives off the land, even though the land is now covered with cement and garbage. He is a Tarzan living in an asphalt jungle, swinging from rooftops instead of treetops. This cross-culturization should make for an interesting film, especially given Sayles' past efforts--the 1960s reminiscence of RETURN OF THE SECAUCUS SEVEN and the environmental adaptation of THE BROTHER FROM ANOTHER PLANET. WILD THING, however, is a gross misfire. Instead of addressing any of these issues, it simply settles for standard action fare. More attention is paid to where Davi hides his drugs, than to how the displaced Knepper survives in his environment. While WILD THING may have had good intentions at its inception, it is nothing but a lamebrained farce about urban corruption. All the attention is directed toward the film's criminal elements—the part about a "wild child" living in the city is, unfortunately, incidental. Knepper

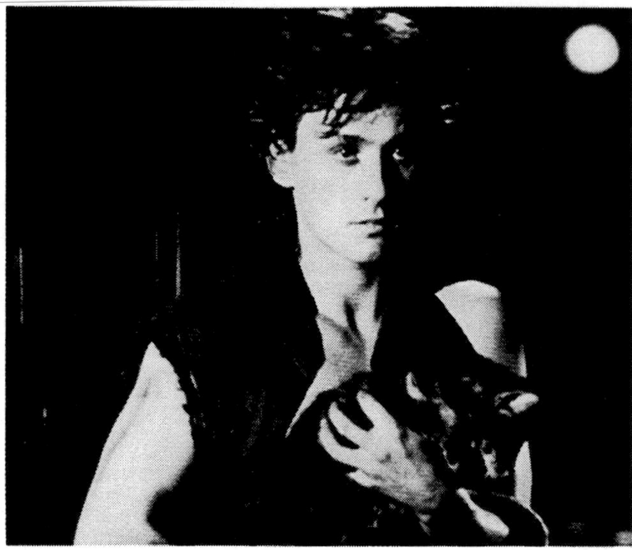

is given very little to do as "Wild Thing," only occassionaly uttering a few words, but more often screeching and hissing like an angry cat. Quinlan's character is the stereotypical social worker, and Buckley's bag lady is so exaggerated that critique is pointless. Only Davi manages to give some life to his otherwise standard performance. This time out the fault rests clearly with the empty script and the spotty direction by first-timer Reid. Songs include: "Wild Thing" (Chip Taylor, performed by The Troggs), "White Rabbit" (Grace Slick, performed by Jefferson Airplane), "Dreamer" (Roger Hodgson, Richard Davies, performed by Supertramp), "Business Lady" (Barry Goffing, performed by Goffing), "The Dancer" (Guy Moon, Jonathan Bogner, Wayne Ward, Peter Penn, performed by Crescendo), "Show Some Emotion" (John Modell, performed by X-Ray Tango), "Tuff Stuff" (Only Child, performed by Only Child), "Crossbow and Fowl's Paradise" (David Kirby, Richard Kosinski, performed by Kirby, Kosinski), "Hollywood Story" (Kirby, Moon, performed by Kirby, Moon), "Trembling Hills" (Kirby, performed by Kirby). *(Violence, drug use, profanity.)*

p, David Calloway, Nicolas Clermont; d, Max Reid; w, John Sayles (based on a story by John Sayles, Larry Stamper); ph, Rene Verzier (Sona color); m, George S. Clinton; ed, Battle Davis, Steven Rosenblum; prod d, John Meighen, Jocelyn Joli; cos, Paul-Andre Guerin; spec eff, Jacques Godbout; m/l, Chip Taylor, Grace Slick, Roger Hodgson, Richard Davies, Barry Goffing, Guy Moon, Jonathan Bogner, Wayne Ward, Peter Penn, John Modell, David Kirby, Richard Kosinski; makeup, Marie-Angele Breitner-Protat; stunts, Peter Cox.

Crime/Drama Cas. (PR:C-O MPAA:PG-13)

WIMPS† (1987) 84m Platinum-Vestron c

Louis Bonanno *(Francis)*, Deborah Blaisdell *(Roxanne)*, Jim Abele *(Charles Conrad)*, Jane Hamilton [Veronica Hart] *(Tracy)*, Eddie Prevot, Derrick R. Roberts, Philip Campanero, Michael Heintzman, Jeanne Marie, Gretchen Kingsley, Lori Stewart, Annie Sprinkle, Carmel Pugh, Siobhan Hunter.

This Chuck Vincent-directed modern-day retelling of "Cyrano de Bergerac" met with one rather large problem in 1987: ROXANNE, the Steve Martin-Daryl Hannah box-office hit which covered the same ground. Though it was filmed first, WIMPS went straight to videocassette. In this version Bonanno plays a wimpy college freshman who gets into a fraternity dominated by football players because his father is one of the school's gridiron legends. He is coerced into helping Abele, the team's star quarterback, both with his studies and in his attempts to romance Blaisdell, a pretty librarian named Roxanne. By the finale Abele's questionable intentions are revealed and Bonanno and Blaisdell end up in each other's arms. Blaisdell may be more familiar to some as Tracy Adams, the name she uses when appearing in adult films.

p&d, Chuck Vincent; w, Chuck Vincent, Craig Horrall; ph, Larry Revene; m, Ian Shaw, Kai Joffe; ed, Marc Ubell [Chuck Vincent], James Davalos; art d, D. Gary Phelps.

Comedy Cas. (PR:NR MPAA:R)

WIND, THE*½** (1987) 93m Omega c

Meg Foster *(Sian Anderson)*, Wings Hauser *(Phil)*, David McCallum *(John)*, Robert Morley *(Elias Appleby)*, Steve Railsback *(Kesner)*, Michael Yannatos *(Policeman)*, Summer Thomas *(Sian's Friend)*, John Michaels, Tracy Young *(Newlyweds)*, Dina Yannou *(Elias' Wife)*.

Foster is a writer of trashy novels who decides to take a break from her life in the Hollywood hills with boy friend McCallum. She rents a villa on a remote Greek island for the winter. The man renting her the place is Morley, an eccentric Englishman with a condescending attitude. He shows her about the place and leaves her with a dire warning about the fierce winds that blow at night, sometimes with fatal results. She settles down and tries to begin working on her next book, but she hears a noise downstairs. It is Hauser, the caretaker, a former seaman and mercenary at the end of his tether. Later that night, while Foster writes, Morley tells Hauser to pack his bags and get out. Hauser beats him to death with a poker and buries him in the yard. Foster sees him through her window and goes out to investigate. She finds the body and goes back inside, trying to figure out how to call for help. Speaking no Greek, she is only able to call McCallum in Los Angeles and have him call back for help. Meanwhile, Foster comes to the conclusion that Hauser knows she knows and he is taking his time and enjoying terrorizing her. She survives a number of attacks from various quarters (Hauser has many ways in and out of the house). Morley's Greek wife comes looking for him and falls victim, as does Railsback, another American sent up to check things out after a call from McCallum. Finally Foster sets a trap that sends a heavy shutter crashing onto Hauser when he tries to come through the window, impaling him on his own scythe. The morning is starting to break and Foster tries to make her way down to the village, but Hauser, driven only by his madness, appears again and chases her to the highest point on the mountain. She cowers on the ground as he raises the sickle above his head, when a final gust of wind blows, picking Hauser up and dashing him on the rocks far below.

An entertaining, suspenseful drama that merited a theatrical release but apparently never received one, THE WIND benefits most from excellent performances by Foster and Hauser. She is a level-headed woman who is no idiot, a rare commodity in a film like this. She more than holds her own against Hauser, and only the fact that he won't die keeps the film from ending half an hour sooner. Hauser gives an even better performance, not as a supernatural slasher with some childhood sexual trauma leading him to butchery for the sake of butchery, but as a man with a drinking problem whose slide to the bottom turns to murder when he sees his last hope, his caretaking job, snatched away. The other cast members have little to do but die or move the plot along, though Morley is as delightful as ever. Shot on the island of Monemvassia off the coast of Greece, the scenery is spectacular and nicely enhances the atmosphere. The cinematography is superb, adding to the sense of menace without being ostentatious. For the killer winds that howl throughout the night, five giant wind machines and three helicopters were required, while lighting in a building with no electricity required even more ingenuity. The musical score is also excellent, particularly the creepy electronic compositions of Hans Zimmer which add tremendously to the atmosphere. With THE WIND, producer-writer-director Mastorakis proves he can make as good a film as anyone, and better than most. *(Violence, profanity.)*

p&d, Nico Mastorakis; w, Nico Mastorakis, Fred C. Perry (based on a story by Nico Mastorakis); ph, Andrew Bellis (Technicolor); m, Stanley Myers, Hans Zimmer; ed, Nico Mastorakis, Bruce Cannon; prod d, Lester Gallagher; art d, Dotty Engfeld, G. Koliopandos, Lenny Schultz; cos, Richard Abramson; spec eff, L. Ludovik, A. Bellek, M. Samiotis; makeup, A. Kouroupou.

Thriller Cas. (PR:O MPAA:NR)

WINNERS TAKE ALL** (1987) 105m Apollo-Embassy Home Entertainment/Manson c

Don Michael Paul *(Rick Melon)*, Kathleen York *(Judy McCormick)*, Robert Krantz *("Bad" Billy Robinson)*, Deborah Richter *(Cindy Wickes)*, Peter DeLuise *(Wally Briskin)*, Courtney Gains *(Goose Trammel)*, Paul Hampton *(Frank Bushing, Biker Team Manager)*, Gerardo Mejia *(Johnny Rivera)*, Tony Longo *("Bear" Nolan)*, Isabel Grandin *(Peggy Nolan)*, Broc Glover *(Carl)*, Roger Hampton *(Mongrel)*, Virgil Frye *(Sam)*, Noon Orsatti *(Brendt)*, Clarke Coleman *(Kenny)*, Barbie Langmack *(Amy)*, Bevie Langmack *(Angie)*, Arthur Abelson *(Art the Cameraman)*, Jeff MacGregor *(Indian Head Announcer)*, Brian Libby *(Bus Driver)*, Denisa Allan *(Model)*, Robert Ruth *(Guard)*, Geoff Witcher *(Interviewer)*, Sean McGraw *(Official)*, Michael T. Laide, Brad Leland *(Scrutineers)*, Jerry Nelson *(Head Official)*, Jeff Imada *(Japanese Rider)*, Bryan J. Thompson, Paul Sherrod, Richard Epper *(Riders)*, Kimberly LaBelle, Irene Jacobs, Robin Stille, Stephanie Hershey, Kathleen Kinmont *(Party Girls)*, Michael Yama *(Japanese Rep)*, Jack Eiseman *(Party Dude)*, Steve Clawson *(Spectator)*, David Stanfield, Rick Johnson, David Bailey, Larry Huffman *(Themselves)*.

Finding personal salvation through sporting events is by now a well-worn theme in the post-ROCKY movie world. Though WINNERS TAKE ALL starts off as an interesting character study, the film fails to deliver on its initial promise as it eventually capitulates to formula development. Krantz is a top motorcycle racer who rides for a corporate-sponsored team. Hampton, the team's devious manager, is taking his boys on a tour of rural America which brings Krantz back to the small town where he grew up. There he is reunited with Paul, his best friend and constant rival ever since grammar school. Paul is now dating Krantz's former flame Richter, but this fickle girl quickly returns to the successful racer. Old jealousies rise and Paul decides to challenge Krantz in motorcross racing. Also entering the competition is York, a tough young woman whose mechanical knowledge surprises Paul. Before the race begins, a fight breaks out when Paul's buddies DeLuise and Gains look at the bikes of Krantz's teammates. Krantz and Paul enter into the fray, spurred on by Richter's fleeting affections. During the competition Paul has a bad accident, which ultimately leads him to rethink his plans for the future. Krantz, in the meantime, has to deal with trouble he is getting from fellow teammate Mejia, an ambitious racer who will do anything to get ahead. After the race, Krantz leaves town with Richter in tow, while Paul enrolls in community college. There he once more runs into York, who convinces Paul he shouldn't be discouraged from racing. With York as his mechanic, Paul decides to enter an important competition which is to be held in Dallas. DeLuise and Gains join the pair in training, and Paul develops a tentative romantic interest in his coach. The quartet heads down to Dallas, where they meet fellow competitor Longo and his wife Grandin. Longo, who is aptly nicknamed "Bear," is a wild but friendly man, whose rambunctious personality can only be controlled by Grandin. Paul qualifies for the main event, and the night before the big race a party is held for all competitors and their respective crews. Paul and York finally admit to their mutual attraction and end up in bed together. That night

Mejia destroys Paul's bike, but friends rally to build a new machine out of spare parts. During the big race Longo attacks Mejia when he sees the single-minded racer is about to engage in some underhanded tactics. A huge fight ensues, which results in the suspension of most of the competitors, including Paul, Krantz, and Longo. But these motorcrossers are an honorable bunch, and they decide to hold their own race in a remote rural area. The event finally comes down to a one-on-one challenge between Paul and Krantz. Paul, to no one's surprise, finally beats his old friend. The two mend their tattered friendship, and with York, decide to form their own motorcross team.

Unlike other films of this nature, the characters here are well developed. Paul, Krantz, and York give good performances while Richter comes off like the quintessential small town party girl. Hampton is another standout as the well-dressed but oily team promoter. When director Kiersch sticks to depictions of small town life or friendship bonding, WINNERS TAKE ALL is fairly engaging. The look and ambience are completely accurate, displaying an insider's understanding of this world. Unfortunately these elements are usually subordinated to genre cliches or countless shots of motorcycles raising dirt. Once Kiersch gets past introducing us to his characters' milieu, he goes right for the obvious, reducing the film to another simple-minded sports drama. Songs include: "Don't Look Back," (performed by Moon Calhoun), "The Long Ride," (performed by Deke Richards, Tony Martin, Jr.) "Lady Killer," (performed by Deke Richards), "Love or Illusion," (performed by Deke Richards), "When Your Old Man's Gone," (performed by Leon Rubenhold), "Skydance," (performed by Tony Martin, Jr.). *(Profanity, sexual situations.)*

p, Christopher W. Knight, Tom Tatum; d, Fritz Kiersch; w, Ed Turner (based on a story by Tom Tatum, Christopher W. Knight); ph, Fred V. Murphy II (Deluxe color); m, Doug Timm; ed, Lorenzo De Stefano; prod d, Steve P. Sardanis; set d, Tom Talbert; cos, Darryl Levine; makeup, Kristine Chadwick, Elaine Offers; m/l, Doug Tim, Randy Peterson, Deke Richards, Tony Martin, Jr., Chris Lussier, Leon Rubenhold.

Drama **Cas.** **(PR:C MPAA:PG-13)**

WINTER TAN, A† (1987, Can.) 91m Ontario Film Dev.-Telefilm Canada-Canada Council-Ontario Arts Council c

Jackie Burroughs *(Maryse Holder)*, Erando Gonzalez *(Miguel Novaro)*, Javier Torres *(Lucio Salvador)*, Anita Olanick *(Pam)*, Diane 'Aquila *(Edith)*, Fernando Perez de Leon, Dulce Kuri, Ruben Dario Hernandez, Abraham Hernandez Castillo, Maricarmen Dominguez, Reyna Lobato Mariche, John Frizzell, John Walker, Jorge Galcedo, Luis Lobato, Servando Gaja, Alberta Chalulas, Librado Jiminez.

Based on the letters of Maryse Holder, a feminist from New York who both reveled in life and had a kind of death wish, this is the story of the lustful trip to Mexico that eventually brought about her death. Burroughs, who wrote the screenplay and codirected, stars as Holder, and, addressing the camera directly, she recites from the letters as the film slides into flashbacks of the trip to sunny Mexico. Burroughs' days and nights are full of sexual longing and satisfaction. Under the influence of drugs, alcohol, and her libido, she prowls beaches and nightclubs for sexual partners, and one-night stand follows one-night stand until she meets Gonzalez. He treats her with little respect, but this only intensifies her obsession with him, and, in the end, the combination of her attraction and his revulsion leads to her tragic demise.

p, Louise Clark; d, Louise Clark, Jackie Burroughs, John Frizzell, John Walker, Aerlyn Weissman; w, Jackie Burroughs (based on the book *Give Sorrow Words* by Maryse Holder); ph, John Walker; m, Ahmend Hassan, John Lang; ed, Alan Lee, Susan Martin.

Biography **(PR:NR MPAA:NR)**

WISH YOU WERE HERE½** (1987, Brit.) 92m Zenith-Working Title/Atlantic c

Emily Lloyd *(Lynda)*, Tom Bell *(Eric)*, Clare Clifford *(Mrs. Parfitt)*, Barbara Durkin *(Valerie)*, Geoffrey Hutchings *(Hubert)*, Charlotte Barker *(Gillian)*, Chloe Leland *(Margaret)*, Trudy Cavanagh *(Tap Dancing Lady)*, Jesse Birdsall *(Dave)*, Geoffrey Durham *(Harry Figgis)*, Pat Heywood *(Aunt Millie)*, Heathcote Williams *(Dr. Holroyd)*, Charlotte Ball *(Lynda, age 11)*, Abigail Leland *(Margaret, age 7)*, *Susan Skippr (Lynda's Mother)*, Sheila Kelley (Joan Figgis), Neville Smith *(Cinema Manager)*, Marjorie Sudell *(Lady With Hurt Knee)*, Lee Whitlock *(Brian)*, Frederick Hall *(Passenger With Umbrella)*, Bob Flag *(Mental Patient)*, William Lawford *(Uncle Brian)*, Pamela Duncan *(Mrs. Hartley)*, David Hatton *(Shop Van Customer)*, Ben Daniels *(Policeman)*, Val McLane *(Maisie Mathews)*, Kim McDermott *(Vickie)*, Barrie Houghton *(Cafe Manager)*, Jim Dowdall *(Cook)*, Danielle Phelps *(The Baby)*, George *(Mitch The Dog)*.

A standard British lament of postwar adolescence which has found an audience in the US on the strength of its sexually spunky lead, 15-year-old newcomer Lloyd. Living on the British seaside during the mid-1950s, Lloyd attracts the attention of her puritanical neighbors by openly displaying her sexuality. She shamelessly bicycles past gawking men, lifting her skirt to her thighs and giving them an eyeful. She fancies herself as having Betty Grable legs, marvels at the shape of her own breasts, and swears like a lorry driver—"Up your bum" being her favorite expression. Her mother has been dead for some time (the title is a reference to this loss) and her father, Hutchings, cannot cope with raising a daughter, especially one who consistently embarrasses him. To appease Hutchings, she studies to become a hairdresser, but that effort ends when she scorches a customer's hair. She then takes a job at the local bus depot, though this career move, too, is short lived. She gets herself (and nearly all of her co-workers) fired when, realizing her sexual hold over men, she stands atop a desk, hikes her skirt up, and models her new lingerie for the cheering bus drivers. Eventually she has her first sexual encounter with Birdsall, a teenager who strains for a continental image by wearing silk pajamas and puffing on a cigarette holder. Birdsall proves to be an unsatisfactory lover and Lloyd next meets the sleazy but oddly magnetic Bell, a 40ish friend of her father. Although she initially teases Bell, she gives in to his persistance and her own curiosity. Inevitably finding herself pregnant, she defies convention by temporarily leaving town to have the baby out of wedlock. Some months later she triumphantly returns—a proud mother. Although she seems happy, one can't help but see her future as a gloomy one.

WISH YOU WERE HERE, like numerous recent British films (MR. LOVE, FRENCH LESSON, David Puttnam's "First Love" series), is a slice-of-life comedy/drama about exceptionally average folks. Unfortunately, the result is a rather ordinary coming-of-age picture which throws in some standard traumas—mum is dead, dad isn't loving, adults don't understand, and, as the final straw, pregnancy. What sets WISH YOU WERE HERE apart is Emily Lloyd. Previously unknown, she sparkles on screen and carries the weight of the entire picture with her lovely smile. Bubbling with energy, she exudes a combination of innocence and sexiness—the type of teenage girl Vladimir Nabokov would have called a "nymphet." Although first-time director Leland (he scripted MONA LISA and this year's PERSONAL SERVICES) has a gold mine in Lloyd, he clutters the film with grotesque, Fellini-esque characters that give this small British town a surrealistic circus quality. The honesty and simplicity of Lloyd's performance directly contrasts the film's surreal atmosphere. Leland overwhelms his film with quirky yet empty symbolism (Lloyd likes to wear a WW II gas mask). The film is inexplicably framed by a freakish street performer who does a little song-and-dance. Although the audience is apparently supposed to draw significance from this scene, the effect is one of befuddlement as we are jarred from the reality of Lloyd, the young mother. Having proven himself to be a talented script writer, it is a disappointment that Leland has resorted to such a tired vehicle in WISH YOU WERE HERE. Lloyd receives ample support from her co-stars, especially in Bell's perversely creepy performance. Perhaps the film's finest scene is a very funny battle of wits between Lloyd and Williams, a frizzy-haired psychiatrist who tries to get his patient to reveal her sexual amorality. Sitting in his cozy office, he has her utter all the obscenities she knows, in alphabetical order. When he finally gets to "F," he becomes frustrated that Lloyd doesn't respond with the proper (and obvious) four-letter word. After only a few moments, Lloyd has completely turned the tables on Williams calling him "a dirty old bugger" when he exclaims that he wants to hear her swear. *(Sexual situations, brief nudity, profanity.)*

p, Sarah Radclyffe; d&w, David Leland; ph, Ian Wilson (Technicolor); m, Stanley Myers; ed, George Akers; prod d, Caroline Amies; art d, Nigel Phelps; stunts, Jim Dowdall; cos, Shuna Harwood; makeup, Jenny Shircore.

Drama **(PR:C-O MPAA:R)**

WITCH HUNT† (1987, Aus.) 92m Documentary c

Jaye Paul *(Chris Naki)*, Bill Brady *(Inspector Thomas)*, Danny Carett *(George Theodorakis)*, Stavros Economidis *(Matthew Argias)*, Nancy Carvana *(Angela Argias)*, Leslie Dayman *(David Rofe, Q.C.)*, George Donikian *(Presenter)*.

Australian docu-drama based on a 1978 mass arrest of Sydney's Greek community. More than 1,000 Greek immigrants and some of the physicians who cared for them were accused of defrauding the Australian welfare system and nabbed in one huge police operation. Director Chobocky interviews many of those actually accused (there were never any convictions) as well as some of those responsible for the action, and actors re-create the incident.

p&d, Barbara A. Chobocky; w, Barbara A. Chobocky, Jeffrey Bruer; m, Thomas Mexis; ed, Jeffrey Bruer.

Docu-drama **(PR:NR MPAA:NR)**

WITCHBOARD** (1987) 98m Paragon Arts/Cinema Group c

Todd Allen *(Jim Morar)*, Tawny Kitaen *(Linda Brewster)*, Steven Nichols *(Brandon Sinclair)*, Kathleen Wilhoite *(Zarabeth)*, Burke Byrnes *(Lt. Dewhurst)*, Rose Marie *(Mrs. Moses)*, James W. Quinn *(Lloyd)*, Judy Tatum *(Dr. Gelineau)*,

Gloria Hayes *(Wanda)*, J.P. Luebsen *(Malfeitor)*, Susan Nickerson *(Chris)*, Ryan Carroll *(Roger)*, Kenny Rhodes *(Mike)*, Clare Bristol *(Anchorwoman)*.

An ambitious little horror film that rejects the current trend in graphic violence (dubbed "splatter" by critics) and instead spins a spooky tale of the supernatural, WITCHBOARD opens at a party thrown by Kitaen and her live-in boy friend Allen. The party goes badly because of the tension between Allen and his former best friend Nichols (their friendship shattered over Kitaen). Nichols produces a ouija board and regales the guests with tales of contacting the dead. While Allen scoffs, Nichols entices Kitaen to join him in an attempt to contact the spirit of David, a 10-year-old who died in a boating accident 30 years previously. The couple succeed in contacting the spirit, but Allen's disbelief annoys David and the spell is abruptly broken. When the party breaks up, Nichols forgets to take the ouija board home and Kitaen finds herself drawn to it. Breaking one of the rules of the ouija board (don't use it alone), Kitaen contacts David by herself and the helpful spirit informs her that the diamond ring she lost is caught in the bathroom drain. Meanwhile, at the construction site where Allen works, his friend and coworker Quinn is killed in an accident that almost takes Allen's life. Over the next few days Kitaen becomes more and more obsessed by the ouija board and her behavior becomes erratic. A worried Allen finally turns to Nichols for help. Nichols brings a goofy punkish spiritualist, Wilhoite, to chase the spirit away. Later that evening Wilhoite is killed. Allen and Nichols decide to take a trip to Big Bear, the site of David's death, to look for clues. Just as they begin to realize that it was an evil spirit pretending to be David that contacted Kitaen, another "accident" occurs and Nichols is killed (the victims are all done in by an ax blow, and the accidents are designed to disguise this). Allen eventually learns that their house was once owned by an infamous ax murderer, Luebsen, and it is his spirit that is trying to possesses Kitaen. Allen races home only to discover that Luebsen has taken over Kitaen's body. After a brutal battle with the possessed Kitaen, Allen manages to destroy the ouija board—thus closing the portal of evil and restoring Kitaen to normal.

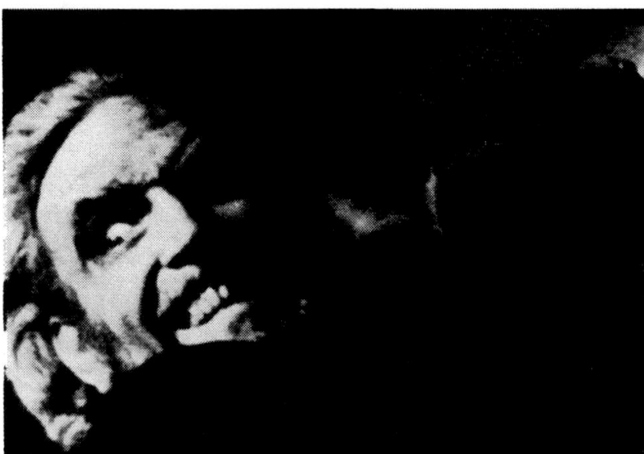

In a period in which most horror films introduce cardboard characters only moments before killing them in a variety of disgusting ways, WITCHBOARD takes the high road and actually tries to develop relatively complex relationships between the main characters. Allen's character, in particular, is much more interesting than the average low-budget horror film protagonist. He's somewhat self-destructive (smoking and drinking too much, working at a high-risk job), jealous, and hides his inability to care behind a cynical sense of humor. It is revealed that he dropped out of medical school because he couldn't cultivate enough compassion to treat patients. Although Kitaen loves him and tells him so often, Allen cannot bring himself to tell her the same. The arrival of the evil in WITCHBOARD serves to bring Allen's repressed compassion to the surface and forces him to prove his love for Kitaen and his friend Nichols. While the film suffers at times from some clumsy scripting, weak (but not bad) acting, and a cliche presentation, WITCHBOARD still *tries* to be something more than just a scary thrill ride (the gore and violence are definitely de-emphasized). First-time feature director-writer Tenney (whose USC Film School project WAR GAMES won a student Emmy Award) imbues his film with a surprisingly slick sense of style and employs some clever camerawork when the narrative warrants it, refusing to bore the viewer with endless evil-point-of-view shots favored by so many other horror directors. Overall, the performances he elicits from his cast are solid, if undistinguished. Allen and Nichols are fine, but Wilhoite nearly steals the film in her brief appearance as the eccentric young punk spiritualist. Perhaps Tenney's greatest directorial achievement is the fact that he coaxed a decent performance from the red-maned Kitaen, an actress who had previously turned in some pathetic thesping in such drivel as BACHELOR PARTY, THE PERILS OF GWENDOLINE, and the straight-to-video INSTANT JUSTICE. Unfortunately, WITCHBOARD died a quick death at the box office, but it may find new life on videocassette. *(Profanity, violence, brief gore effects, brief nudity.)*

p, Gerold Geoffray; d&w, Kevin S. Tenney; ph, Roy H. Wagner; m, Dennis Michael Tenney; ed, Daniel Duncan, Stephen J. Waller; art d, Sarah Burdick; set d, Laura Call, Patricia Fuenzalida; cos, Merrill Greene; spec eff, Tassilo Baur; makeup, John Blake; stunts, Chuck Couch, Buck McDancer.

Horror **Cas.** **(PR:O MPAA:R)**

WITCHES OF EASTWICK, THE** (1987) 118m WB c

Jack Nicholson *(Daryl Van Horne)*, Cher *(Alexandra Medford)*, Susan Sarandon *(Jane Spofford)*, Michelle Pfeiffer *(Sukie Ridgemont)*, Veronica Cartwright *(Felicia Alden)*, Richard Jenkins *(Clyde Alden)*, Keith Jochim *(Walter Neff)*, Carel Struycken *(Fidel)*, Helen Lloyd Breed *(Mrs. Biddle)*, Caroline Struzik *(Carol Medford)*, Becca Lish *(Mrs. Neff)*, Ruth Maynard *(Mrs. Biddle's Friend)*, Carole Ita White *(Cashier)*, Margot Dionne *(Nurse)*, John Blood *(Deli Counterman)*, Ron Campbell *(Ice-Cream Counterman)*, Eugene Boles *(Minister)*, Lansdale Chatfield, James T. Boyle *(Doctors)*, Michele Sincavage, Nicol Sincavage, Heather Coleman, Carolyn Ditmars, Cynthia Ditmars, Christine Ditmars *(Ridgemont Children)*, Craig Burket, Abraham Mishkind, Christopher Verrette *(String Quartet)*, Babbie Green, Jane A. Johnston, Merrily Horowitz, Harriet Medin *(Women at Market)*, Corey Carrier, Kate Barret, Dan Edson, Anthony Falco, Kevin Goodwin, Tara Halfpenny, David Hazel, Melanie Hewitt, Matt Kane, Anne Lindgren, Jessica Macdonald, Corinna Minnar, Scott Nickerson, Stephen Oakes, Ann Senechal, James Staunton, Amy Warner *(Lenox School Band)*.

Witches, warlocks and spiritual malcontents of all sorts have always made good film fare, the most notable being the Fredric March-Veronica Lake vehicle I MARRIED A WITCH and BELL, BOOK AND CANDLE with James Stewart and Kim Novak. This production, however, combines witchcraft of the white or good type with Satanism and sex, or pedestrian male wish fulfillment. Little of director Miller's effort pays off, with much ado about Nicholson, the satyr-like devil who seduces three local ladies, endowing them with powers that prove his own undoing. Cher, Sarandon, and Pfeiffer are all recently divorced and living in the small New England town of Eastwick. Cher is a sculptress making big-breasted, obese female plaster figures; Sarandon is a high school music teacher; Pfeiffer works for the town's weekly newspaper. Into this peaceful community comes balding, eccentric, beer-barreled Nicholson, fabulously rich, a man of mystery whose name cannot be remembered by all who meet him. He buys a sprawling mansion on the hill overlooking the town and turns it into a sumptuous, if not garish, palace. Cher is the first to be taken into Nicholson's Borgia bed, impregnated by this charming, conniving creature from Hell. Next Nicholson spellbinds naive Sarandon by driving her to a crescendo of emotion while she flails away at her cello. The final lady to fall into his sexual snare is Pfeiffer. All three move in with Nicholson, discovering unusual powers. They can fly or float motionless in the air and Nicholson endows them with more sinister powers, such as causing endless vomiting on the part of those they dislike. One of these is Cartwright, Pfeiffer's boss. Cartwright becomes aware of the goings-on at the infamous mansion. The mansion had long been deserted, mainly due to its unsavory past as the site, hundreds of years earlier, where notorious witches were burned. Misfortune follows Cartwright. She first breaks her leg and later turns into a raving lunatic who hounds her milquetoast husband Jenkins mercilessly, warning that the little town is being corrupted by Nicholson and friends. Cartwright publishes an article in her paper which turns the townsfolk against the women. They are now ostracized, called sluts by their neighbors. Loving Nicholson has its drawbacks. They strike back at Cartwright, causing her to become a screaming, screeching shrike to Jenkins who has had enough one day and reaches for a poker, bashing in his wife's brains. At Cartwright's funeral, Cher, Sarandon, and Pfeiffer, suddenly aware they are playing with the supernatural, become frightened, acting like terrified school girls, racing to their respective homes and refusing to have anything more to do with Nicholson. Try as he might, Nicholson cannot get his witch creations to return to him. He goes to Cher's shack and she tells him to go away, that "you hurt people." Sarandon isn't home to Nicholson and Pfeiffer simply pulls a door shade down in front of his frowning face. He takes his revenge by visiting upon these hapless ladies their worst fears, snakes, pain and other maladies. To ease Pfeiffer's intense pain, Cher and Sarandon return to Nicholson's fold and soon Pfeiffer joins them. Nicholson is satanically edified when entering his bed chamber to find all three long-legged ladies scantily clad and inviting him with their bodies. But this is all according to their plan. Sending Nicholson to town to buy exotic foods to feed appetites gone awry through pregnancy, the women frantically prepare a wax doll and begin to punish it, causing the unsuspecting Nicholson to be blown, feather-encrusted, through the town of Eastwick. He sails straight into the church and there offends the faithful by regurgitating upon them while going through a tirade on women. He tells the vomit-splashed churchgoers to "pay no attention to that—a cheap trick—I taught it to them!" The horrified faithful, of course, have no idea of what he means. Nicholson raves on about women, asking if there is not a cure for them, some sort of inoculation that will make men immune from their machinations. He blames their wily natures on God and shouts in what is undoubtedly his most histrionic performance to date (or that of any other actor in the last decade): "You think God doesn't make mistakes? But when he does they call it NATURE!" He then heads for the mansion, driving his Rolls Royce crazily down country roads as the women begin sticking pins into the wax doll, causing Nicholson to flip and lurch about while driving and almost crashing his car. By the time he reaches the mansion, the women take refuge in one room into which Nicholson, seen from behind, is about to enter. He first straightens his broken neck, recalling the nightmarish 360-degree neck and head turn by Linda Blair in THE EXORCIST, and reaches forth with a claw-like hand on the door knob but the witches seize the doll and smash it. The mansion shakes and rolls and Nicholson then appears outside the huge windows as a giant, hideous ogre full of rage, reaching an enormous hand through the wall in an attempt to crush the cowering women (a scene lifted right out of THE THIEF OF BAGHDAD). In a desperate moment, the wax doll is set on fire and the giant snarling, roaring monster outside is set ablaze and is reduced to a gnat bearing Nicholson's distorted face floating in the air to suddenly pop into nothingness as would a bubble. The three supposedly good witches are shown 18 months later living in high style in the mansion, each with a baby boy, products of their frolicking fornication with Devil Nicholson. He appears once more on a giant wall with

many TV screens and beckons his boys to crawl forward to him. Cher, Sarandon, and Pfeiffer rush into the room and, with a simple switching of a remote control unit, turn him off and go about their business. Cute.

The whole thing is a feeble attempt to present the battle of the sexes with a spiritual-satanic motif. The special effects add to the sinister elements of the yarn but Nicholson's performance is so offbeat and so extravagant (he is obviously out of directorial control here and allowed to do exactly as he pleases) it is less riveting than if he had opted to show some restraint. He is ungainly and so overweight as to appear funny without intent. His hooded eye look, borrowed from THE SHINING and PRIZZI'S HONOR, is overused and he ends up appearing clownish, not devilish. Sarandon is the best of the three witches, but all look and act alike, remaining true to their initial stereotypes as black widow divorcees. Cher is the weakest of the lot, registering a monotone delivery. The story is jagged and the viewer is left to wonder what the fuss was all about. The film tries to be truly evil, or present evil, in depicting Cartwright's gruesome end, a blood-splattered wall representing her fate at the hands of a henpecked husband. Not funny. The production values are good, like the foundation of a solid house, but the furnishings never arrive. Instead, we get an ugly little man wearing a series of strange-looking hats with all of his expression in his arched eyebrows. Moreover, promiscuity and fear of the AIDS threat are totally ignored. Miller, who directed the ultraviolent ROAD WARRIOR, saves his last shot for a massive blowout of special effects and camp horror and even the spectacular cannot put the pieces in working order. The prim and proper New England town where the film was shot on location is Cohasset, Massachusetts. Nicholson, who was allowed free reign with his outrageous character, enjoyed making the film, spoofing the subject all the way, but Sarandon, an avowed political and social activist, expressed her considerable anger when the role first promised to her, that of the sculptress, went to Cher. But in the end result, the actress' discontent means nothing; all three female leads are interchangeable and all of them are essentially meaningless, as was Updike's intent when writing the novel upon which the film was based. *(Sexual situations, violence.)*

p, Neil Canton, Peter Guber, Jon Peters; d, George Miller; w, Michael Cristofer (based on the novel by John Updike); ph, Vilmos Zsigmond (Panavision, Technicolor); m, John Williams; ed, Richard Francis-Bruce, Hubert C. De La Bouillerie; prod d, Polly Platt; md, John Williams; art d, Mark Mansbridge, Dave Howard Stein; set d, Robert Sessa, Stan Tropp; cos, Aggie Guerard Rodgers; spec eff, Mike Lanteri, Rob Bottin; anim, Ellen Lichtwardt, John Armstrong, Chris Green; makeup, Ben Nye III, Leonard Engleman; stunts, Alan Gibbs.

Horror/Comedy Cas. (PR:O MPAA:R)

WITH LOVE TO THE PERSON NEXT TO ME† (1987, Aus.) 98m Standard c

Kim Gyngell *(Wallace)*, Paul Chubb *(Sid)*, Barry Dickins *(Bodger)*, Sally McKenzie *(Gail)*, Beverley Gardner *(Irene)*, Phil Motherwell *(Drunken Passenger)*.

The first feature film from Aussie documentary-maker Brian McKenzie, WITH LOVE TO THE PERSON NEXT TO ME is slice-of-drama from the perspective of a melancholy cab driver (Gyngell). He lives in a run-down apartment near the waterfront and passes his time listening to the tape recordings he makes of his taxi passengers. Life is not much more fulfilling for his neighbor, McKenzie, whose unloving boy friend, Chubb, and his crony, Dickins, load their place with stolen goods until the police put an end to their thievery. McKenzie copes by moving away; all Wallace can think of to do is to tell his story to his tape recorder.

p, John Cruthers; d&w, Brian McKenzie; ph, Ray Argall (Fujicolor); ed, Ray Argall, David Greig; prod d, Kerith Holmes.

Drama (PR:NR MPAA:NR)

WITHNAIL AND I*** (1987, Brit.) 108m Handmade/Cineplex Odeon c

Richard E. Grant *(Withnail)*, Paul McGann *(Marwood [I])*, Richard Griffiths *(Monty)*, Ralph Brown *(Danny)*, Michael Elphick *(Jake)*, Daragh O'Mallery *(Irishman)*, Michael Wardle *(Issac Parkin)*, Una Brandon-Jones *(Mrs. Parkin)*, Noel Johnson *(General)*, Irene Sutcliffe *(Waitress)*.

A hilarious black comedy and already something of a cult favorite, WITHNAIL AND I is the directorial debut for Robinson, the Oscar-nominated screenwriter of THE KILLING FIELDS. It opens with a slow pan around a cluttered, refuse-ridden flat in North London that resembles an archeological dig. This confused mess is home for two out-of-work actors: gaunt, sarcastic, vaguely aristocratic, and, above all, dissipated Grant—the Withnail of the title—and handsome, bespectacled McGann, whose name is Marwood but is more readily identifiable as *I* because his journal notations, heard in voice-over, serve as the film's narration. It is 1969, some 90 days before the end of that cataclysmic decade, and as McGann observes, he and his friend are "drifting into the arena of the unwell." The amphetamine-popping Grant hasn't slept for 60 hours, his agent seems to have forgotten about him, and he is freezing in their cold apartment. McGann is in little better shape, but he has resolved to try to turn his life around, having recently auditioned for a part in a provincial theater production. They visit Grant's wealthy eccentric uncle Griffiths in hopes of getting the use of his country cottage for a weekend away to "rejuvenate." The rotund Griffiths, a one-time actor who has decorated his home with potted vegetables, is particularly taken with McGann and gives Grant the keys to his cottage near Penrith, in the Lake District. With "All Along the Watchtower" (Bob Dylan, performed by Jimi Hendrix) blaring on the soundtrack, McGann and Grant drive north in a battered Jaguar, arriving at the cottage only to find it a rustic version of their own flat—ice cold, damp, totally without provisions. The next morning, wearing plastic bags to cover his feet, McGann sets about coming up with food and firewood, but is turned away by a neighbor who tells him to talk to her son, the farmer. Grant and McGann go "fishing" in a stream: McGann acts as spotter and Grant blasts away with a shotgun. Finally, they see the farmer. "Are you the farmer?" the wild-eyed, out-of-it Grant repeatedly beckons. "Of course he's the bloody farmer," McGann admonishes. "Stop saying that!" Eventually the farmer brings them firewood and a chicken. Returning from the village, where he has called his agent and haughtily turned down the opportunity to understudy a role, Grant fails to close the gate that encloses the farmer's pasture and a bull gets out. As he has done so many times before, Grant leaves McGann holding the bag (in this case, full of groceries), vaulting to safety over a stone wall, and McGann is forced to chase the bull back into the pasture.

That night, at the pub, Grant and McGann have a drunken run-in with Elphick, a poacher who refuses to sell them either the dead eel or the pheasant he produces from under his clothing. Grant irks the poacher, who promises he'll come looking for them. En route to the cottage, Grant screams out to the echoing hills that he's not afraid of anyone, that he'll be a star one day. But, as has already become plain, Grant is afraid of his own shadow (or, perhaps more poignantly, the shadowy existence that has become his reality). Terrified, he insists that McGann let him sleep in the same bed with him. Later, they hear someone trying to break in. The bedroom door slowly opens, but it is only Griffiths. Grant has told his uncle, who is gay, that McGann is also gay (he isn't, neither is Grant), and Griffiths has come to woo the innocent-looking lad. Much of the next day is taken up with a sumptuous lunch, including plenty of fine wine—to Grant's delight—and many longing looks from Griffiths—to McGann's extreme discomfiture. McGann is anxious to get back to London but Grant is inclined to stay. That night, Griffiths comes to McGann's bedroom intent on seduction (Grant is passed out in another room). After much stammering, McGann persuades the ever-advancing Griffiths that Grant, too, is gay and that the two of them haven't slept apart for six years. At this, Griffiths retreats, not wanting to come between them. He departs in the night, leaving behind a touching note. The next morning a telegram arrives. McGann has a callback for the part for which he auditioned. Driving back to London, the inebriated Grant zigzags between lanes and is hauled over by the police. Grant confidently refuses a breathalizer test and at the station he attempts to cheat his way through a urinalysis by employing a hidden tank-and-tube contraption that funnels child's urine into the sample beaker. Not surprisingly, he's caught. Returning to their flat they are greeted by Brown, a drug dealer friend and self-styled philosopher-mystic whose permanently dilated pupils are the worn road maps of too many journeys to the center of his mind. He tells them they are about to be evicted. McGann learns he didn't get the role; instead, he has gotten the lead. Later, when McGann, his hair chopped short, prepares to depart for Manchester and the play, Grant offers him a parting drink. McGann isn't interested. With a wine bottle in one hand and an umbrella in the other, Grant accompanies him in a downpour through Regents Park on the way to the train station. McGann tells Grant he wants to go on alone, and after their farewells, he does just that, leaving Grant to deliver an emotional recitation of Hamlet's speech to Rosencrantz and Gildenstern (Act II, Scene II: "I have of late, but wherefore I know not, lost all my mirth, forgone all custom of exercises . . . ").

WITHNAIL AND I is a very funny, intelligent, and finally touching film. At its core are Grant and McGann, two men after the same brass ring, a successful acting career. Together they have grasped feebly for it from a dizzying merry-go-round of self-indulgence, drugs, and booze that may or may not be as much a product of the times as of their personalities. They are both intelligent, but Grant is more obvious about his smarts, routinely slinging wisecracks; McGann, on the other hand, is still-water thoughtful. He finds the humility, self-control, and the self-confidence to get off the merry-go-round that has made a prisoner of Grant. McGann matures, Grant doesn't, and, in the end, he is an empathetic figure. Along the way, though, there are plenty of laughs from the rapid-fire repartee, strange characters, and Monty Pythonesque moments of Robinson's script. Robinson, a former actor, adapted the screenplay from his own autobiographical novel written in 1970. After the success of his THE KILLING FIELDS screenplay, he was reputedly given a relatively free hand with this film and occasionally it suffers from the excesses of a writer-director who is too close to his material and unable to let go of any of it. There are scenes and dialog that could have been left out and that slow the pace of the film and there is nothing very exciting about Robinson's use of the camera. However, these deficiencies are compensated for by the richness of script and the performances.

Griffiths, who was so good in A PRIVATE FUNCTION, is even better here. He is both silly and touching, balancing the grandiose gestures and nose-crinkling stares of a stage poof with the more stately sensitivity of genuine romantic. His ability to make that transition keeps the last half of the film from gravitating into homophobic nonsense. Robinson was determined to use new faces for his leads. Grant had only limited experience on the English stage before winning his role; McGann came to his after British stage and TV work. Both are excellent. Beneath his bleary-eyed, haughty flippancy Grant conveys the pain of one who will never reach his dreams and knows it. McGann is alternately put-upon, frantic, and introspective, but at the heart of his performance is the sensitivity and quiet determination that make his maturation believable. Brown and Elphick also turn in fine performances in smaller roles. Before production on the film began, some suggested it would have a better box-office success if its setting were changed to San Francisco's Haight-Ashbury to make the most of its 1960s theme, but Robinson held firm, wanting to preserve the Britishness he felt was essential to understanding the characters. In the end, however, the setting seems secondary to the characters. And though it is flawed, WITHNAIL AND I remains a funny, fascinating character study. *(Sexual situations, excessive profanity.)*

p, Paul M. Heller; d&w, Bruce Robinson (based on a novel by Bruce Robinson); ph, Peter Hannan; m, David Dundas; ed, Alan Strachan; prod d, Michael Pickwoad; art d, Henry Harris; cos, Andrea Galer; m/l, Bob Dylan.

Drama **(PR:O MPAA:R)**

WITNESS TO A KILLING† (1987, Sri Lanka) 71m Taprobane c

Razi Anwer *(Salinda)*, Tony Ranasinghe *(Father)*, Swineetha Weerasinghe *(Mother)*, Ravindra Randeniya *(Killer)*, Anoja Weerasinghe *(Killer's Wife)*.

Variation on the "boy who cried wolf" theme in which a boy who has a habit of telling fibs witnesses a murder but can't convince anybody that the crime actually happened. The killer knows the boy speaks the truth, and he's out to silence him. Screened at the Tokyo International Film Festival. (In English.)

p, Jayantha Jayatilaka; d&w, Chandran Rutnam; ph, Daryn Okada (Yangtze Color); m, Sarath Fernando; ed, Cladwin Fernando; art d, Errol Kelly.

Thriller **(PR:NR MPAA:NR)**

WOLF AT THE DOOR, THE**½ (1987, Fr./Den.) 102m Dagmar-Henning Dam Kargaard-Cameras Continentales-Famous French Films-TF-1-Danish Film Institute-Danish Radio & TV-French Ministry of Cultural Affairs/Manson c (OVIRI)

Donald Sutherland *(Paul Gauguin)*, Valerie Morea *(Annah-la-Javanaise)*, Max von Sydow *(August Strindberg)*, Sofie Graboel *(Judith Molard)*, Merete Voldstedlund *(Mette Gauguin)*, Jorgen Reenberg *(Edward Brandes)*, Yves Barsack *(Edgar Degas)*, Thomas Antoni *(Jourdan)*, Fanny Bastien *(Juliette Huet)*, Jean Yanne *(William Molard)*, Ghita Norby *(Ida Molard)*, Kristina Dubin *(Aline Gauguin)*, Henrik Larsen *(Julien Leclercq)*, Bill Dunn, Morten Grunwald, Hans Henrik Lehrfeldt, Jean-Claude Flamant, Solbjorg Hojfeldt, Jesper Bruun Rasmussen, Anthony Michael, Chili Turell.

Painter Paul Gauguin, like so many brilliant artists, went through life defending his work to deaf ears only to have his talents recognized after death. THE WOLF AT THE DOOR focuses on one short period in the life of Gauguin—1893-94—when the Danish artist had returned to Paris after a hiatus in Tahiti. Arriving from the islands with a collection of canvases, Gauguin (played by Sutherland) believes he can set the art world afire with his florid and colorful depictions of native girls. An exhibition of his works fails miserably, however, as most of the patrons are shocked by Gauguin's unconventional methods. Only the established and respected artist Edgar Degas (Barsack) sees the talent. He purchases one of the paintings and tells Sutherland that he "paints like a wolf."

When Sutherland is not painting, he is either entertaining a small circle of artists and intellectuals or carrying on with one of his many female interests. His loves include his stoic Danish wife, Voldstedlund, whom he left behind with their children; a former mistress, Bastien, with whom he has had a child; a young Javanese model, Morea; and Graboel, a pretty 14-year-old neighbor who desperately wants Sutherland, but reminds the artist too much of his own daughter. Sutherland tries to put away enough money to return to Tahiti, dreaming of

establishing an artist's colony with his Parisian friends—a dream they all share, temporarily. He even tries to convince his intellectual rival, writer August Strindberg (von Sydow), to try island life. Strindberg, however, already feels that European women are uncivilized and has no intentions of surrounding himself with Tahitian "savages." As the days pass, Sutherland begins to break away from all the women in his life. His arrival in Denmark upsets the very controlled life of Voldstedlund, his inability to commit to a relationship causes the faithful Bastien to leave, and his ill-treatment of Morea sends her packing, taking with her the money he had saved for his ticket to Tahiti. Only Graboel is left. She makes an advance towards Sutherland but he cannot shake the image of the daughter he left behind in Denmark. Upon discovering Morea has taken his money, Sutherland sells his most valued possessions—three paintings by his deceased friend Vincent van Gogh—and with the money returns to Tahiti.

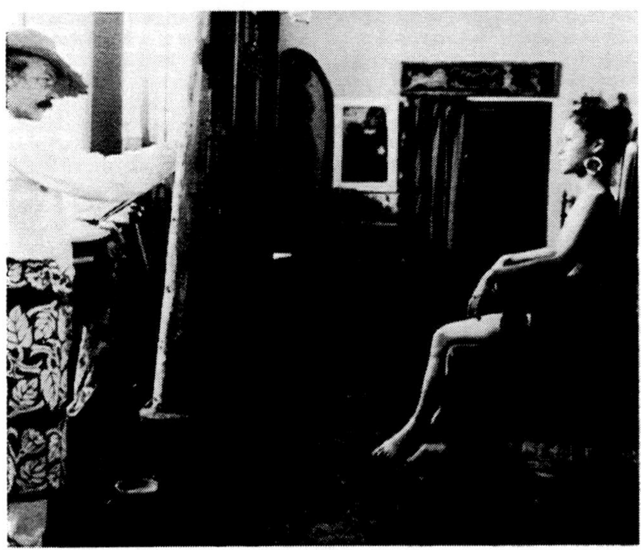

A respectful and restrained portrait of Gauguin, THE WOLF AT THE DOOR is unfortunately too tame to depict the ferocity of its title or the image of Gauguin's artistic and personal spontaneity. While there is much to enjoy in the film—Sutherland's performance, the warm photography, Graboel's charmingly intimate performance—there is very little passion on the screen. An exotic and driven man, Gauguin is given very little chance to live in director Carlsen's world. Sutherland has a natural way of wearing his ratty full-length leather jacket and his weather-beaten straw hat, as if the actor is not merely portraying Gauguin but is possessed by him. Sutherland's Gauguin is not a madman artist but a real person who is driven by an inner struggle. (Although the film barely mentions it, Gauguin was a banker and family man in Denmark until his mid-30's when he opted for the very different life of an artist living in Tahiti with a 13-year-old native bride.) It is not because of Sutherland's performance that THE WOLF AT THE DOOR is without passion, but because of a "Masterpiece Theater" style script and Carlsen's tame direction. THE WOLF AT THE DOOR is an unexceptional look at an exceptional man. Gauguin, along with many of his contemporaries, altered the way people see by creating art that challenged the rules. Carlsen, however, has delivered a film which is anything but challenging. Instead of bringing Gauguin and his art to life, Carlsen has made him lifeless. The original script was written by Carlsen and Jean-Claude Carriere (Luis Bunuel's former collaborator) in French, and Carlsen had hoped to sign Sutherland for the part, though Sutherland is not fluent in French. Gaumont was determined to cast a Frenchman for the role, but when Gaumont eventually dropped out the script was rewritten, with Carlsen's blessings, by British playwright Christopher Hampton and Sutherland got the role. Hampton's script is filled with rather uninspired speeches about art (the conversations between Gauguin and Strindberg are taken verbatim from their correspondence, but they seem stilted on the screen) and Gauguin's sexual appetite.

While the film strives to convey the almost emotionless relationship between artist and model, Carlsen seems to make an extra effort to exploit the models' nudity. Nudity which is treated casually by the actors is given a voyeuristic treatment by the camera. Four fine performances are given by the actresses portraying the women in the artist's life. Voldstedlund wears well the stoic mask of Gauguin's wife, Bastien is excellent as the former mistress who is still in love with Gauguin, and Morea appears to have walked right out of Gauguin's "Annah-la-Javanaise." But, it is Graboel, as the neighbor girl who harbors a deep, unrequited love for Gauguin, who shines the brightest. A Swede, heretofore unseen in the US, Graboel is a young beauty with a simple face who perfectly combines childlike innocence with womanly sensuality. THE WOLF AT THE DOOR, released in Europe in 1986, is Carlsen's 14th film (his first in English) and his first to receive attention in US theaters. Gauguin's life has been brought to the screen twice before in Hollywood—Anthony Quinn played him in an Oscar-winning performance opposite Kirk Douglas as Vincent van Gogh in 1956's LUST FOR LIFE and George Sanders played a thinly-veiled Gauguin in the MOON AND THE SIXPENCE, the 1942 adaptation of W. Somerset Maugham's novel. *(Nudity, sexual situations.)*

p&d, Henning Carlsen; w, Christopher Hampton (based on a story by Henning Carlsen, Jean-Claude Carriere); ph, Mikael Salomon (Eastmancolor); m, Ole Schmidt; ed, Janus Billeskov Jansen; art d, Andre Guerin, Karl-Otto Hedal; cos, Charlotte Clason, Ole Glaesner, Annelise Hauberg; makeup, Birte Christensen, Birthe Lyngsoe.

Biography **Cas.** **(PR:C-O MPAA:R)**

WOLF'S HOLE** (1987, Czech.) 92m Barrandov c (VLCI BOUDA; AKA: WOLF'S CHALET; WOLF'S LAIR)

Miroslav Machacek *(Daddy)*, Stepankova Cervenkova *(Babeta)*, Tomas Palaty *(Dingo)*, Rita Dudusova *(Gitka)*, Hana Mrozkovy *(Lenka)*, Ivana Mrozkovy *(Linda)*, Radka Slavikova *(Emilka)*, Jitka Zelenkova *(Brona)*, Simona Rackova *(Gaba)*, Frantisek Stanek *(Petr)*, Jan Bidlas *(Jan)*, Petr Horacek *(Alan)*, Norbert Pycha *(Marcipan)*, Roman Fiser *(Jozka)*, Jan Kacer *(Jan's Father)*, Nina Diviskova *(Jan's Mother)*, Jiri Krampol *(Alan's Father)*, Antonin Vrablik *(Lumberjack)*.

Czech director Chytilova, one of the driving forces of the Czech new wave in the 1960s, presents a dim-witted, poorly constructed political allegory and disguises it as a cross between a slasher film and science fiction. Ten Czech teenagers from different schools are mysteriously selected to participate in a ski seminar high in the mountains. On the big day, however, 11 kids show up with invitations. Because a recent avalanche has cut off the lodge from the rest of the world with only a limited supply of food, the kids are warned by their three strange "instructors" that they will either all have to pull together and sacrifice to make ends meet, or single out someone to leave. The leader (Machacek), who likes to be refered to as "Dad," extols the virtues of unity and discipline and subjects the teens to a series of situations designed to test their character. Palaty, an even more sinister-looking adult, is the ski instructor, and the beautiful blonde Cervenkova is in charge of meals. During the seminar strange things begin to happen. Late at night several teens notice both Palaty and Cervenkova, dressed only in their underclothes, thrashing around in a snowbank. One girl spots a list that does indeed have all eleven names on it, but Machacek swears her to silence. After much eerie music, ominous time-lapse shots of ice freezing, and countless sudden zoom-ins of the mountains, the instructors reveal themselves to be aliens from outer space who plan to take over the world by sowing dissention among the human race. Machacek announces that the teens will be allowed to leave if they merely sacrifice one of their number. Only a few of the kids take this seriously and the aliens watch closely as tension mounts—at one point or another, almost all the teens announce they want to kill someone in a moment of anger. Eventually the more savvy teens are able to convince the rest of the group that their instructors are indeed aliens and the kids run to a large ski-lift to escape. Unfortunately, 11 people are simply too heavy for the lift to work. Nobly, one unpopular girl offers to sacrifice her little dog and one of the boys volunteers to stay behind. Putting their differences aside, the teens strip off their expensive ski pants, jackets, boots, scarves, toys, drugs, and cigarettes, thus allowing all of them to escape—including the dog.

This is a silly and ponderous film. Combine nearly a dozen rowdy teenagers at a remote recreational camp with a trio of bizarre counselors whose every appearance is accompanied by foreboding music and you've got the ingredients of an average American slasher movie. If there's one good thing to say about American slasher movies, it's that they are totally devoid of pompous allegory and symbolism; WOLF'S HOLE isn't. After the first 15 minutes of this film any viewer with a brain in his skull should become painfully aware of the message director Chytilova keeps driving home in scene after scene. Regrettably, her attempts at genre conventions are unimaginative, repetitive, and poorly executed (this is one of those films where the villain continually pops up to scare the victims—either from behind doors, in shadows, or, most often, just out of frame). While the teens' performances run the range from annoying to competent, the aliens seem as if they were snatched from a silent movie. Pasty-faced and bug-eyed, they all sneer knowingly and have short tempers. Palaty is especially ridiculous because he seems to be doing a parody of Dwight Frye's maniacal Renfield from DRACULA (1931). The screenplay is a perturbing mess of obtuse metaphor and doesn't even provide the slightest explanation of how the aliens really plan to take over the Earth: Are they going to take every teenager on the face of the Earth on a ski trip and trick them all into betraying one another? Better yet, the aliens could simply bore the world to death with this film. Shown at film festivals in the US in 1987. *(Profanity in subtitles, substance abuse.)*

d, Vera Chytilova; w, Daniela Fischerova, Vera Chytilova; ph, Jaromir Sofr; m, Michael Kocab; ed, Jiri Brozek; art d, Ludvik Siroky; cos, Sarka Hejnova; makeup, Jana Dolejsi.

Science Fiction **(PR:C MPAA:NR)**

WONDER WOMEN† (1987, Hong Kong) 98m D&B c

Dodo Cheng, Cecilia Yip, Michael Wong.

Cheng and Yip are a couple of young women who are out to climb the ladder to fame and fortune. They enter a beauty contest and, though neither makes it to the finals, they become close friends. Their friendship is tested later when they both fall for the same guy, only to find he's not interested in either one of them. Former actor Kam Kwok-leung made his writing/directing debut with this film, which proved to be quite successful at the box offices in Hong Kong.

d&w, Kam Kwok-leung; m, George Lam.

Drama **(PR:NR MPAA:NR)**

WRONG COUPLES, THE† (1987, Hong Kong) 98m D&B c

Richard Ng, Josephine Siu Fong Fong, Paul Chiang, Pauline Kwan, Maggie Li, Dennis Li.

Hong Kong version of THE GOODBYE GIRL (1977) in which sailor Ng returns from the sea to find his wife has deserted him and rented their apartment to Fong Fong. Though neither is fond of the arrangement at first, they eventually fall in love as Ng fights for custody of his daughter, Kwan. A big star in Hong Kong in the 1960s when she was a teenager, this film was something of a comeback for Fong Fong.

p, John Sham; d, John Chiang; w, John Chan; ph, Yee Tung Lung; art d, Fong Ying.

Comedy **(PR:NR MPAA:NR)**

YA LYUBIL VAC BOLSHE ZHIZNI† (1987, USSR) 86m Azerbaijanfilm/Sovexportfilm c (Trans: I Loved You More Than Life)

Ramiz Kovruzov.

Soviet WW II hero Maj. Gen. Azi Aslanov, who was only 30 years old when he gave his life for his country, is the subject of this film biography. Focusing on his short but distinguished military career, the picture includes both his exploits as commander of a tank brigade facing the Nazis and quieter moments with his family on the homefront.

d, Rasim Izmailov; w, Ramiz Fataliyev; ph, Valery Kerimov; m, Akshin Alizade; art d, Nadir Zeinalov.

Biography **(PR:NR MPAA:NR)**

YA TEBYA POMNYU† (1987, USSR) 93m Uzbek/Sovexportfilm c (Trans: I Remember You)

Vyacheslav Bogachev, Guli Tashbayeva, Lilia Gritsenko

A veterinarian whose father died during WW II near Leningrad decides to trek across the Soviet Union and find his grave. This odyssey takes him to unfamiliar places and introduces him to a variety of people, each of whom share their remembrances of the war. In the process of learning about his father, the son also learns much about himself. Made in 1985 but held from release until 1987. Shown in the US at the San Francisco Film Festival.

d&w, Ali Khamrayev; ph, Rifkat Ibragimov; art d, Rustam Khamdamov.

Drama **(PR:NR MPAA:NR)**

YA YEY NRAVLYUS† (1987, USSR) 75m Tadjikfilm Studio/Sovexportfilm c (Trans: She Likes Me)

Niyezakhmad Musoyev, Bakhrom Akramov, Gamida Omarova.

Two medical students finish their studies and begin their professional lives—one works for an ambulance company and the other in scientific research. They both fall in love with the same girl, but only one becomes engaged to her. Before the wedding, however, it is revealed that the husband-to-be has had an affair, leaving the other to finally profess his love for the jilted bride.

d, Anvar Turayev; w, Rustam Ibragimbekov, Viktor Bagdasarov; ph, Alexander Shabatayev; m, Gennady Alexandrov; art d, Sergei Ramonkulov.

Romance **(PR:NR MPAA:NR)**

YAGUAR† (1987, USSR) 89m Mosfilm/Sovexportfilm c (Trans: The Jaguar)

Sergei Veksler, Artem Kaminsky, Sergei Gazarov, Yanina Khachaturova.

Set in an unidentified South American country under fascist rule, this film follows the lives of the students at a military training school—a microcosm of their country. The most feared young man among them is called "The Jaguar"—a sly, powerful and dictatorial ruler who abuses everyone around him. As the students would like to do to their country's government, they topple this fascist Jaguar by revealing his true nature as a murderer.

d, Sebastian Alarcon; w, Sebastian Alarcon, Tatyana Yakovleva; ph, Anatoly Ivanov; m, Sebastian Alarcon, Viktor Babushkin; art d, Irina Shreter.

Drama **(PR:NR MPAA:NR)**

YALDEI STALIN† (1987, Israel) 90m Doron Eran c (Trans: Stalin's Kids)

Shmuel Shilo, Yosi Kanz, Hugu Yarden, Rashel Dobson.

Kibbutz life and political beliefs are examined in this picture about a naive group of cobblers who firmly believe that Joseph Stalin's leadership will bring liberation and contentment to everyone. With the renouncement at the 20th Congress of the Communist Party of Stalin's purges, the cobblers' wrong-headed beliefs are silenced.

p, Doron Eran; d&w, Nadav Levitan; ph, Gadi Danzig; m, Antonin Dvorak; ed, Shimon Tamir; art d, Ela Sakagu.

Comedy **(PR:NR MPAA:NR)**

YAM DAABO† (1987, Burkina Faso) 80m Les Films de l'Avenir c (Trans: The Choice)

Aoua Guiraud, Bologo Moussa, Assita Quedraogo, Fatimata Quedraogo, Oumarou Quedraogo, Rasmane Quedraogo, Salif Quedraogo.

An ethnographic drama filmed with non-professional actors who star as a family from the barren countryside who travel to the city with the hope that life there will be a richer one. Their visit begins on a sad note when their youngest child gets struck and killed by a car. Later, however, their unfailing optimism leads them to a simple, more prosperous life. The first fiction feature from Ouedraogo, an award-winning documentary filmmaker.

d&w, Idrissa Ouedraogo; ph, Jean Monsigny, Sekou Ouedraogo, Issaka Thiombiano; m, Francis Bebey; ed, Arnaud Blin.

Drama **(PR:NR MPAA:NR)**

YEAR MY VOICE BROKE, THE† (1987, Aus.) 103m Kennedy-Miller c

Noah Taylor *(Danny Embling)*, Loene Carmen *(Freya Olson)*, Ben Mendelsohn *(Trevor)*, Graeme Blundell *(Nils Olson)*, Lynette Curran *(Anne Olson)*, Malcolm Robertson *(Bruce Embling)*, Judi Farr *(Sheila Embling)*, Tim Robertson *(Bob Leishman)*, Bruce Spence *(Jonah)*, Harold Hopkins *(Tom Alcock)*, Nick Tate *(Sgt. Pierce)*, Vincent Ball *(Headmaster)*, Anja Coleby *(Gail Olson)*, Kylie Ostara *(Alison)*, Kelly Dingwall *(Barry)*, Dorothy St. Heaps *(Mrs. Beal)*, Coleen Clifford *(Gran Olson)*, Kevin Manser *(Mr. Keith)*, Mary Regan *(Miss McColl)*, Queenie Ashton *(Mrs. O'Neil)*, Helen Lomas *(Sally)*, Emma Lyle *(Lisa)*, Louise Birgan *(Lyn)*, Matthew Ross *(Malseed)*, Allan Penney *(Martin)*, Robert Carlton *(Pierdon)*.

Named as Best Film at the Australian Film Awards, THE YEAR MY VOICE BROKE is an adolescent drama set in a rural town in 1962 which revolves around two teens—Taylor and Carmen—who have been friends all their life. Taylor's parents run the neighborhood pub, while Carmen's own the local cafe, and the youngsters have, as a result, spent much time together. They begin drifting apart as they get older. Carmen becomes infatuated with an older boy, Mendelsohn, a macho football coach who is tough competition for the smaller Taylor. Carmen grows up quickly when she gets pregnant by Mendelsohn. As the local scandal becomes more and more intense, Carmen sees a move to the city as her only way out, leaving behind the boy who was once her closest friend. THE YEAR MY VOICE BROKE (co-produced by George Miller of MAD MAX fame) also received awards for Best Director, Best Screenplay and Best Supporting Actor (Mendelsohn). The film's eligibility was initially questioned because THE YEAR MY VOICE BROKE was originally filmed as a television production, an objection which was successfully argued against.

p, George Miller, Doug Mitchell, Terry Hayes; d&w, John Duigan; ph, Geoff Burton; m, Christine Woodruff; ed, Neil Thumpston; prod d, Roger Ford.

Drama **(PR:NR MPAA:NR)**

YEAR OF AWAKENING, THE½** (1987, Span.) 120m Iberoamericana de TV c (EL ANO DE LAS LUCES)

Jorge Sanz *(Manolo)*, Maribel Verdu *(Maria Jesus)*, Manuel Alexandre *(Emilio)*, Rafaela Aparicio *(Rafaela)*, Lucas Martin *(Jesus)*, Veronica Forque *(Irene)*, Santiago Ramos, Chus Lampreave, Jose Sazatornil, Pedro Reyes, Violeta Cela, Miguel Angel Rellan.

The territory of awakening adolescent sexuality is an area often explored by filmmakers around the world. This bittersweet comedy from Spain takes a look at one boy's initiation to passion, setting the story within a sanitarium for young boys. Sanz is a handsome 15-year-old youth who, with his younger brother, is sent to the institution. They've been placed there by a third brother, an older sibling who can no longer look after the orphaned boys since he is a soldier fighting in WW II. Sanz, who towers above the rest of the children, is allowed to study on his own, though he must sleep in the regular dormitories. Nurses assigned to the wards must also sleep with the children, though they are separated by a modest screen. Sanz takes to watching the silhouette of his nurse as she undresses, fueling his adolescent fantasies. He masturbates while watching this nightly display, and studiously chronicles each orgasm on a calendar. Sanz becomes a lively flirt with staff members, an activity encouraged by the sanitarium's roguish caretaker. When his current nurse must take leave due to family illness, Sanz is heartbroken. She is soon forgotten though, when Verdu, the pretty niece of a local priest, is hired as a replacement. Verdu is just a few years older than Sanz, and the boy becomes hopelessly smitten with her. He gives Verdu a kiss in secret, but she angrily threatens to tell her boy friend. Sanz sends her a note, saying she should go ahead and tell if she wants. Of course Verdu has no boy friend, and the two begin a clandestine romance. Verdu reveals to Sanz that the priest is really her father, not her uncle. Eventually their affair is uncovered. Verdu and Sanz run off and make love, hoping that she will become pregnant. This way, Verdu insists, her family will insist that Sanz marry her. But Verdu is removed from her position, while Sanz is taken by his older brother who plans to put the errant youth into a reformatory. When Sanz's car accidentally passes Verdu and her family on the street, the boy bolts from the auto. He and Verdu grasp each other in a passionate embrace, but the lovers are forcibly separated. Sanz's brother drives into the night, and tears slowly roll down the broken-hearted adolescent's cheeks.

Sanz is fine in the lead, sensitively portraying the difficulties encountered within a young man's burgeoning sexuality. He is both brash and shy, maintaining an aggressive air that is not without a sense of innocence. His chemistry with Verdu is endearing as the two naive teenagers enter their tentative romance. Trueba directs with sensitivity, showing an understanding of what his protagonist is undergoing. Unlike so many American films dealing with adolescents, Trueba injects humor without exploiting the situation for easy laughs. Unfortunately Trueba has nothing really new to say about the subject. There is a certain predictability to the film which slightly undermines Trueba's obvious good intentions. Originally released in Spain in 1986, THE YEAR OF AWAKENING premiered in the US in 1987.

p, Andres Vicente Gomez; d, Fernando Trueba; w, Rafael Azcona, Fernando Trueba; ph, Juan Amoros (Eastmancolor); m, Francisco Guerrero; ed, Carmen Frias; set d, Josep Rosell.

Comedy/Romance **(PR:O MPAA:NR)**

YEELEN† (1987, Mali) 105m Les Films Cisse-Atriascop-Midas-Government of Mali-CNC-UTA-WDR TV-Fuji c (Trans: Brightness)

Issiaka Kane *(Nianankoro, the Son)*, Aoua Sangare *(Young Wife)*, Niamanto Sanogo *(Father)*, Balla Moussa Keita *(Peul King)*, Soumba Traore *(Mother)*, Ismaila Sarr *(Uncle)*, Youssouf Tenin Cisse *(Young Boy)*.

Described by *Cahiers Du Cinema* as a "film of grace," this entry from Mali was shown in competition at the 1987 Cannes Film Festival where it garnered much attention for its combination of mythology, ethnography, and documentation (its use of talking head interviews). Set in the past, YEELEN is a film about the tensions between father and son, and about one's quest for knowledge, or "brightness." Kane plays Nianankoro, the young tribe member who is about to be shown the secrets of "Komo"—the ancestral knowledge of his Bambara tribe. His father, Sanogo, is an all-powerful magician who tries to prevent his son from gaining knowledge and, thereby, becoming an equal. Sanogo (a real-life shaman) sets out to find his son, tracking him down with a magical pylon. Kane is armed with a wing which gives him his own powers. When the two finally meet for their showdown, the mystical powers of the pylon and the wing collide in a spectacular burst of light. The film then shifts to the present day as a young boy discovers two spheres buried in the sand on the spot where his father and grandfather did battle, acquiring the knowledge of his ancestors. Equally as compelling as the odyssey of the film's characters is the director's attempt to get his film made. Photographed deep in the desert, YEELEN experienced numerous difficulties ranging from the death of a principal actor (Sarr) to the departure of one cameraman (Ferragut) to desperate attempts to find additional financing. By the picture's completion, money from France, Germany, and Japan had been poured into the project. Shown at the New York Film Festival. (In Bambara; English subtitles.)

d&w, Souleymane Cisse; ph, Jean-Noel Ferragut, Jean-Michel Humeau (Fujicolor); m, Michel Portal; ed, Dounamba Coulibaly, Andree Davanture, Marie-Catherine Miqueau, Jenny Frenck, Seipati Bulane; art d & cos, Kossa Mody Keita.

Drama/Fantasy **(PR:NR MPAA:NR)**

YEHOSHUA—YEHOSHUA† (1987, Israel) 90m Doron Eran c (Trans: Joshua—Joshua)

Osi Hilel, Avri Gilad, Mati Seri, Duvi Koen.

An unhappy writer tries to use his imagination to create a better life for himself, but fails. Fortunately, things take a turn for the better in his real world, and he finds happiness.

p, Doron Eran; d, Avi Cohen; w, Itzhak Ginsberg; ph, Yoav Kosh; ed, Lina Kadish; art d, Tali Farchi.

Comedy **(PR:NR MPAA:NR)**

YENETHLIA POLI† (1987, Gr.) 85m Greek Film Center c (Trans: Birthday Town)

Takis Moschos, Michelle Valley, Costas Tsapekos, Tatiana Papamoschou, George Sarri, Christoforos Nezer.

Moschos, a Greek businessman, returns to his hometown, Thessaloniki, which is preparing to celebrate 2,300 years of existence. Existence is the operable concept here, as Moschos is overcome with existential dread, lost in the void created by his inability to believe in the values that carried him through most of his life. He has returned home looking for *something*, but is unforthcoming with his old friends Valley and Tsapekos, who sense that something is very wrong but are unable to help him. Tsapekos, an architect, is organizing a pageant to commemorate the city's birthday, and Papamoschou, a young beauty, is its star. Moschos is immediately taken with her and joins the cast; however, when he asks her to leave the city with him, she refuses and he sinks even deeper into the abyss of his private despair.

p&d, Takis Papayannidis; w, Takis Papayannidis, Thanassis Valtinos; ph, Lefteris Pavlopoulos; m, Thomas Sliomis; ed, Yannis Tsitsopoulos; art d, Simos Karafilis.

Drama **(PR:NR MPAA:NR)**

YER DEMIR, GOK BAKIR† (1987, Turk./Ger.) 104m Interfilm-Road Movies-WDR c (Trans: Iron Earth, Copper Sky)

Rutkay Aziz, Macide Tanir, Yavuzer Cetinkaya, Eray Ozbal, Serap Aksoy, Tuncay Akca, Melih Cardak, Dilek Damlacik, Ingeborg Carstens, Ugur Esen, Hulya Guler.

Directorial debut of film music composer Omer Zulfu Livaneli is set in a remote snowbound village in the Anatolian region of Turkey. Because the villagers have had a bad year and earned little money, they fear the arrival of the landlord who is due to collect the rent. In desperation they turn to the hated local headman, the landlord's enforcer, for help. One villager, a rogue named Tashbash, refuses to grovel and makes his feelings known. When another villager sees a vision in the mountains and claims that it was a local saint appearing in the form of the rebellious Tashbash, the rest of the peasants take it as a sign from God and turn to him. Although Tashbash thinks their superstitions ridiculous, in time he comes to believe that he is actually a saint. Director Livaneli also wrote the script and composed the music. Co-produced by German director Wim Wenders.

p, Ulker Livaneli, Wim Wenders; d&w, Omer Zulfu Livaneli (based on the novel by Yashmar Kemal); ph, Jurgen Jurges; m, Omer Zulfu Livaneli; ed, Bettina Bohler; prod d, Gurel Yontan; cos, Yudum Yontan.

Drama **(PR:NR MPAA:NR)**

YERBA SANGRIENTE† (1987, Mex.) 97m Peliculas Rodriguez/Peliculas Mexicanas c (Trans: Bloody Weed)

Alvaro Zermeno *(Meleton Garcia "Norteno")*, Juan Valentin *(Salvador)*, Rosenda Bernal *(Alegria)*, Noe Murayama *(El Diablo)*, Ruben Rojo *(Giovanni Rosetti)*, Cuitlahuac Cui *(Pepe)*, Arturo Martinez, Marta Elena Cervantes.

Quickie exploitation film thrown together on a low budget to capitalize on the story of a real-life marijuana plantation that was discovered in Chihuahua in 1984. The film focuses on Zermeno, a farm worker who is conned into recruiting thousands of innocent laborers on the pretext that they will be picking cotton. In reality, they are kidnapped by an Italian mafioso (the real crooks were actually Mexican) who uses brutal tactics to enslave the workers, forcing them to harvest his massive marijuana crop. Eventually an intrepid reporter, Valentin, exposes the operation. Strangely, producer-director Rodriguez's brother, Robert, produced yet another film version of these events on a larger budget and released it only a few months after YERBA SANGRIENTE had left the theaters.

p, Ismael Rodriguez Jr.; d, Ismael Rodriguez; w, Jorge Manriquez, Ismael Rodriguez; ph, Fernando Alvarez Colin; m, Ernesto Cortazar; ed, Rogelio Zuniga.

Crime **(PR:NR MPAA:NR)**

YI LOU YI† (1987, Hong Kong) 81m Films Creative c (Trans: Reunion)

Pau Wai-leung *(Chak)*, Yiu Hin-shui, Cheng Hon-ki, Joanna Lai, Bo Bo, Sze Ku, Lui Tak.

An independently produced low-budget effort starring Pau Wai-leung as a sullen, unemployed man who lives a bleak existence. Accompanied by his young son, Pau Wai-leung goes to visit his estranged wife and tries to negotiate a reconcilliation. She refuses and the scene turns ugly as they begin to fight. Pau Wai-leung starts a fire in the apartment and in the midst of the chaos the wife accidentally kills the little boy. Pau Wai-leung retaliates by stabbing his wife to death, a crime which gets him sent to prison.

d, Kwan Park-huen; w, Thomas Pang, Kwan Park-huen; ph, Herman Yau; m, Herman Yau, Roland Morales; ed, Kwan Park-huen; prod d, Mango Kwan.

Drama **(PR:NR MPAA:NR)**

YINGXIONG BENSE (SEE: BETTER TOMORROW, 1987, Hong Kong)

YO, EL EJECUTOR† (1987, Mex.) 95m Cinematografica Sol/Peliculas Mexicanas c (Trans: I, The Executioner)

Valentin Trujillo *(Valente Carrera "Thompson")*, Patricia Maria *(Amy Samanta)*, Mario Almada *(Captain)*, Pedro Weber [Chatanuga] *(Padrino)*, Gabriela Ruffo *(Lupita)*, Rene Cardona Sr., Victoria Ruffo.

Popular action hero Trujillo once again directs himself in this shoot-em-up where he plays a secret agent well schooled in the art of killing. Shot on locations in Los Angeles, Washington, DC, Brazil, and Acapulco. Trujillo sets about dispatching a small army of bad guys while trying to keep his identity a secret from pretty reporter Maria who writes for a Spanish-language newspaper in Los Angeles.

p, Gilberto de Anda; d, Valentin Trujillo; w, Valentin Trujillo, Ramon Obon; ph, Antonio de Anda; m, Kiko Campos; ed, Sergio Soto.

Action **(PR:NR MPAA:NR)**

YOSHIWARA ENJO† (1987, Jap.) 133m Toei c (Trans: Tokyo Bordello)

Yuko Natori, Jinpachi Nezu, Sayoko Ninomiya, Mariko Fuji, Mineko Nishikawa.

Set during the years 1907-11 when prostitution was still legal in the famed Yoshiwara brothel district of Tokyo, this film follows a young girl who is sold into prostitution to pay off her father's debts. Although she resists the lifestyle at first and deserts her very first customer, the girl is slowly weaned into the profession by an older geisha who introduces her to the ways of the flesh. Eventually the girl's stock rises and she soon becomes the most sought-after geisha in Tokyo. Unfortunately, tragedy strikes the district in 1911 when a massive fire erupts and destroys most of the brothels.

p, Shigeru Okada; d, Hideo Gosha; w, Sadao Nakajima (based on the book *Yoshiwara Conflagration* by Shinichi Saito); ph, Fujio Morita; m, Masaru Sato; ed, Isamu Ichida; prod d, Yoshinobu Nishioka.

Drama **(PR:NR MPAA:NR)**

YOU TALKIN' TO ME?† (1987) 97m Second Generation/MGM-UA c

Jim Youngs *(Bronson Green)*, James Noble *(Peter Archer)*, Mykel T. Williamson *(Thatcher Marks)*, Faith Ford *(Dana Archer)*, Bess Motta *(Judith Margolis)*, Rex Ryon *(Kevin)*, Brian Thompson *(James)*, Alan King *(Himself)*.

The directorial debut of Charles Winkler, son of high-powered producer Irwin Winkler (the ROCKY films, ROUND MIDNIGHT), YOU TALKIN' TO ME? stars Youngs (younger brother of John Savage) as a New York actor who is obsessed with fellow actor Robert DeNiro, especially his performance in Martin Scorsese's TAXI DRIVER. When not auditioning for work, Youngs sits in revival houses watching TAXI DRIVER over and over, memorizing DeNiro's dialog and mannerisms. Fed up with the lack of work in the Big Apple, Youngs and his best friend, Williamson, a black model also struggling to find work, decide to move to Los Angeles in search of fame and fortune. Although Williamson gets lucky and lands a job that results in his face being plastered on billboards extolling the virtues of milk, Youngs finds that L.A. casting directors are not interested in his "ethnic" looks and New York intensity. He winds up driving a cab to make ends meet. Frustrated, Youngs finally gives in and dyes his dark hair blond, dons Hawaiian shirts, and begins talking as if he grew up in the valley ("dude" is the operative word here). Although this change of personality causes his actress girl friend Motta (of "20 Minute Workout" fame) to dump him, his new blond locks attract Ford, a Hollywood brat who is impressed with Youngs' heroics when he foils an armed robbery in a surfer emporium. Ford introduces her new beau to her wealthy right-wing father, Noble, a racist who produces syndicated television shows extolling the virtues of extreme conservatism. Impressed with Youngs' bravery, Noble puts the actor on his television show and makes him a star. Unfortunately, Youngs' newfound fame goes to his head and alienates best friend Williamson. Youngs' bubble finally bursts, however, when Noble spots Williamson's picture on a billboard and becomes incensed that a black man is representing "white" milk. Noble has his neo-Nazi goons kidnap Williamson and tie him to one of the billboards. He then has white paint dumped on him, but Youngs reverts to his TAXI DRIVER sensibilities and intervenes.

YOU TALKIN' TO ME was made independently for less than $1 million using money raised by Winkler and producer Polaire without help from Winkler's father. It received favorable notices at the Montreal World and Deauville American Film Festivals, but was lambasted during its brief run in New York City. Because of the bad press the national release planned by MGM/UA never materialized and the film seems destined to go the cable/home video route.

p, Michael Polaire; d&w, Charles Winkler; ph, Paul Ryan; m, Joel McNeely; ed, David Handman.

Drama **(PR:NR MPAA:R)**

ZABOU† (1987, Ger.) 102m Bavaria Atelier-Neue Constantin-WDR/Neue Constantin c/bw

Gotz George *(Schimanski)*, Claudia Messner *(Conny/Zabou)*, Eberhard Feik *(Thanner)*, Wolfram Berger *(Hocks)*, Hannes Jaenicke *(Melting)*, Dieter Pfaff *(Schafer)*, Klaus Lage *(Cook)*, Annette Kreft *(Hostess)*.

The third feature film version of the popular German television crime series "Tatort" featuring the show's star, Gotz George, as merciless police commissioner Schimanski. In this installment, George sets his sights on his city's drug problem, specifically the illicit goings-on at a flashy new nightclub called Sunflash which is owned by sleazy former porn-house manager Berger. Together with his lieutenant, Feik, George begins a shakedown of the establishment. At Sunflash George is shocked to discover that Messner, the daughter of a former flame, is working for Berger as a dancer and calls herself "Zabou." Addicted to drugs and a seedy lifestyle, Messner—who harbored an adolescent crush on George years before—isn't interested in the commissioner's efforts to rehabilitate her. While battling drug runners and corrupt cops, George must grapple with his feelings toward Messner—some of which have evolved from paternal to sexual.

p, Gunter Rohrbach; d, Hajo Gies; w, Martin Gies, Axel Gotz; ph, Axel Block; m, Klaus Lage; ed, Hannes Nikel; art d, Jan Kott; cos, Rosemarie Hettmann; spec eff, Heinz Ludwig; m/l, Klaus Lage, Joe Cocker; stunts, Francois Doge.

Crime **(PR:NR MPAA:NR)**

ZARTLICHE CHAOTEN† (1987, Ger.) 90m Karl Spiehs/Tivoli c (Trans: Without You)

Thomas Gottschalk *(Ricky)*, Helmut Fischer *(Schmidgruber)*, Michael Winslow *(Walker)*.

A trio of goofballs stumbles through Germany trying to win over a beautiful woman who wants little to do with them. Gottschalk, a popular German funnyman, stars along with Austrian actor Fischer, and black American actor Winslow, who is best known as that wacky character in the POLICE ACADEMY films who is a human sound effects machine.

p, Karl Spiehs; d, Franz Josef Gottlieb; w, Thomas Gottschalk; ph, Klaus Werner; ed, Ute Albrecht-Lovell; art d, Josef Sanktjohanser.

Comedy **(PR:NR MPAA:NR)**

ZAVTRA BILA VOINA† (1987, USSR) 91m Gorky/Sovexportfilm c/bw (Trans: Tomorrow There Came War)

Sergei Nikonenko, Nina Ruslanova, Vladimir Zamansky, Irina Chernichenko, Natalia Negoda.

Set on the eve of WW II, this film examines the lives of several Soviet youths as they struggle to make sense of Stalinism. One girl, Iskara, lives with a mother too absorbed in communist party literature to pay much attention to her blossoming daughter. Although just as dedicated to the party as her mother, Iskara is a bit more pragmatic and refuses to condemn the bourgeois father of one of her friends—even after he has been arrested. When her friend commits suicide rather than face having to testify against her father, Iskara defies her mother and makes an impassioned speech at the funeral. Soon after the war begins and Iskara watches her friends march off to fight Hitler's army. In an epilogue the fate of all the youths is shown, including the hanging of both Iskara and her mother by the Nazis.

d, Yuri Kara; w, Boris Vasiliev; ph, Vadim Semenovykh; art d, Anatoli Kochurov.

War/Drama **(PR:NR MPAA:NR)**

ZAWGAT RAGOL MOHIM† (1987, Egypt) 114m El-Alamia c (Trans: Wife of an Important Man)

Ahmed Zaki *(Hisham)*, Mervet Amin *(Mona)*, Zizi Mustafa *(Samiha)*, Ali Ghandour *(Ismail)*, Hassan Houssny, Nahid Samir.

Amin is a good-hearted liberal girl living in a small Egyptian town in 1975. She is engaged to a handsome young police officer, Zaki, and when he is promoted to the Secret Police they are married and move to a swank apartment in Cairo. Although Amin is willing to behave as a proper housewife, she balks at having to entertain officials that she knows to be corrupt. By 1977 Zaki has become a brutish, violent, oppressive fascist who zealously puts down civil disorders by the most fierce means possible. Eventually his rabid behavior gets him discharged from the force. Having genuinely believed that he was serving the best interest of his country, Zaki is incredulous at the dismissal. During an arguement with Amin, Zaki's mind finally snaps and he tries to shoot her, killing her father by mistake. Zaki then turns his gun on himself and commits suicide. Director Khan frequently explores controversial Egyptian social problems with a liberal bias.

p, Hussein Kalla; d, Mohammed Khan; w, Raouf Tawfik; ph, Moheen Ahmed; m, George Kazazian; ed, Nadia Chukri; art d, Onsy Abuseif.

Drama **(PR:NR MPAA:NR)**

ZEGEN† (1987, Jap.) 124m Imamura/Toei c (Trans: The Pimp)

Ken Ogata *(Iheiji Muraoka "Zegen")*, Mitsuko Baisho *(Shiho)*, Norihei Miki *(Tomenaga "Bizenya")*, Taiji Tonoyama *(Shimada "The Barber")*, Mami Kumagaya *(Iheiji's last wife, Kino)*, Ko Chun-Hsiung *("Boss" Wang)*.

Shohei Imamura, one of Japan's most original filmmakers and the director of 1984's brilliant picture THE BALLAD OF NARAYAMA, returns with this biography of Iheiji Muraoka, a wealthy and powerful pimp known as "Zegen." Starting his life as a Hong Kong castaway, he became a devoted patriot who saw as his duty the formulation of a system of brothels throughout the country. For nearly forty years, from 1902 to 1941, he lived a comfortable, but lazy existence as the reigning king of the prostitution trade. Starring as Zegen is Ken Ogata, the exceptionally talented actor who played the title character in 1985's MISHIMA. Shown in competition at the Cannes Film Festival.

p, Yoshiniko Sugiyama, Kunio Tokoshige, Jire Ooba; d, Shohei Imamura; w, Shohei Imamura, Kote Okabe; ph, Masao Techizawa; m, Shinichiro Ikaba; art d, Yoshimaga Yokeo.

Biography **(PR:NR MPAA:NR)**

ZEMLYA I ZOLOTO† (1987, USSR) 80m Armenfilm/Sovexportfilm c (Trans: Land and Gold)

Azat Sherentz, Anaid Gukasyan, Evard Abalyan.

An Armenian village just before the outbreak of WW II is the setting for this drama. The film centers on one particular house, depicting the joys, sorrows, and concerns of the residents. When war breaks out, many of the villagers are called to serve and to die in the battles, and the film recounts the impact this has on the village.

d, Armen Manaryan, Henry Markaryan; w, Shagen Tatikyan; ph, Vrez Petrosyan; m, Stepan Shakaryan; art d, Stepan Andranikyan.

Drama/War **(PR:NR MPAA:NR)**

ZERO BOYS, THE*½ (1987) 89m Omega-Forminx/Omega Ent. c

Daniel Hirsch *(Steve)*, Kelli Maroney *(Jamie)*, Nicole Rio *(Sue)*, Tom Shell *(Larry)*, Jared Moses *(Rip)*, Crystal Carson *(Trish)*, Joe Phelan *(Killer)*, Gary Jochimsen *(Killer No.2)*, John Michaels *(Casey)*, Elise Turner *(Victim)*, T.K. Webb *(Killer No.3)*, Steve Shaw *(Coach)*, Jason Picketts, Stephen Kay, Neil Weiss, Dennis Ott, Patrick Hirsch *(Soldiers)*, Henry Donenfeld *(Snake Man)*, Trudy Ames *(Secretary)*, Angelia High, Jessica Tress, Christina Cardan *(Spectators)*.

What would have happened if three champion survival game players (you know, those paint-gun warriors) and their girl friends had stumbled upon the remote California cabin where Leonard Lake and his accomplice Charles Ng tortured and murdered dozens of men and women, including Lake's own brother? Well, that's the unlikely premise for this lame combination of shoot'em up and slasher film. Hirsch, Shell, and Moses are the title team in paint-gun wars, and their weekend trip takes a turn for the worse when they enter an empty house up in the hills. Before long, strange things start to happen: their truck won't start, and they see flitting figures with big knives through the trees. When they spot an area with skeletons littering the ground, they know they are in trouble. In the house, they find a body in a trunk and a head in the icebox. In the barn they find a torture chamber and a video set-up. One girl is abducted and tortured, then returned barely alive. The truck suddenly starts working again and they flee through dense fog. One of the guys gets a crossbow bolt through his back, and another girl falls into a pit of pungi stakes. They manage to kill two attackers, but the open ending reveals another up in a tree. There is some potential in this premise, but director-writer-producer Mastorakis never manages to create more than fleeting tension and the film degenerates into a routine Spam-in-a-cabin knife opus. Only Hirsch gives some semblance of a performance and Maroney, memorable in NIGHT OF THE COMET and CHOPPING MALL, shows more girth and less talent with each role. Joe Phelan, who plays "Killer," briefly glimpsed standing in a tree at the close, is praised in the press release as "a charismatic actor" who is Martin Sheen's brother and Emilio Estevez's uncle, and that is about as close to real talent as this film gets. Shot in 1985, it was released unrated and went straight to video in 1987. *(Graphic violence, sexual situations, profanity.)*

p&d, Nico Mastorakis; w, Nico Mastorakis, Fred C. Perry (based on a story by Nico Mastorakis); ph, Steve Shaw (United color); m, Stanley Myers, Hans Zimmer; ed, George Rosenberg; art d, Gregory Melton; cos, Richard Abramson; makeup, June Brickman; stunts, Vince Deadrick, Jr.

Action **Cas.** **(PR:C-O MPAA:NR)**

ZHELEZNOE POLE† (1987, USSR) 85m Sverdlovsk Film Studio/Sovexportfilm c (Trans: The Iron Field)

Pyotr Velyaminov, Valentin Titova.

A plea for pacifism conveyed in the form of a remembrance of things past experienced by a Soviet engineer who returns to his home town on his 60th birthday and begins to recall his pre-war youth. Fueled by nostalgia, the engineer and a WW II buddy travel to a town where they had fought many battles. There they encounter a West German tourist—also a veteran—who cannot forget the past. The men realize that as long as memories of war exist, peace is in danger and new wars must be avoided at any cost.

d, Yaropolk Lapshin; w, Alexander Rekemchuk; ph, Igor Lukshin; m, David Tukhmanov; art d, Yury Istratov.

Drama **(PR:NR MPAA:NR)**

ZIMATAR† (1987, Phil.) Roadshow

Ace Vergel, Al Tantay, Michael De Mesa, J.C. Bonnin.

Fairy tale about a king who has three sons but wants a daughter. He has taken a second wife in hopes she will bear him a daughter, but the baby she is still-born, prompting a lady-in-waiting to subsitute her own baby, another male. Disappointed with another son, the king consults a sorcerer who tells him that the queen, by drinking the nectar of a magic flower, will be able to give birth to a daughter. The king goes off in search of the flower and offends a forest goddess, who turns him into a tree stump. One-by-one, the king's sons attempt to complete the mission and suffer similar fates. Years pass, and the youngest boy goes out in search of the king and his three sons. He pleases the forest goddess and is able to find the magic flower and rescue the king and his sons.

d, Ric Santiago, Jose F. Sibal; w, Ped Tiangco; m, Carlos Rodriguez.

Fantasy **(PR:NR MPAA:NR)**

ZINA-ZINULYA† (1987, USSR) 88m Mosfilm/Sovexportfilm c

Viktor Pavlov, Vladimir Gostyukhin, Alexander Zbruyev, Tatiana Agafonova, Yelena Mayorova, Svetlana Tormakhova.

A woman construction foreman in charge of concrete shipments finds her strict management style is anathema to many of the corrupt male workers. One such worker becomes angry when she thwarts a scheme of his and gets revenge by charging that she had given him the wrong directions for a delivery. Outraged, the foreman demands a formal apology and goes off to sit in the forest until it is forthcoming. She spends the whole night in the forest and undergoes some self-evaluation. She even considers suicide, but in the end she become determined to stick to her principles.

d, Pavel Chukhrai; w, Alexander Gelman; ph, Nikolai Nemolyayev; m, Mark Minkov; art d, Sovet Agoyan.

Drama **(PR:NR MPAA:NR)**

ZISCHKE† (1987, Ger.) 91m Backhaus-Krieger/Ingefilm Medienvertrieb bw

David Strempel, Amira Ghazalla, Michael Altmann, Amado Meaini.

Strempel is a West German teenager who finds himself abandoned by his mother when she runs off with her American G.I. boyfriend. Tired of her abuse, Strempel decides to take a trip, and while scrounging around Berlin for the trainfare he discovers a pair of forged passports which could snare a good price. Unfortunately the documents belong to pretty Lebanese actress Ghazalla, who had obtained the passports so that her brothers could illegally cross from East to West Berlin. Unbeknownst to both Ghazalla and Strempel, a pair of corrupt immigration officials are closing in on them.

d&w, Martin Theo Krieger; ph, Claus Deubel; ed, Raimund Maria Barthelmes.

Drama **(PR:NR MPAA:NR)**

ZIVOT RADNIKA† (1987, Yugo.) 97m Forum c (Trans: A Worker's Life)

Istref Begoli *(Musa Sokolovic)*, Mira Banjac *(Zilha)*, Emir Hadzihafizbegovic *(Sead)*, Anica Dobra *(Mira)*, Boro Stjepanovic, Dragan Maksimovic, Zvonko Lepetic, Mladen Nelevic, Zeljko Nincic.

The dark, depressing life of an aging Yugoslavian worker is told in this debut feature from Mandic which stars Begoli as a miller who loses his desire to work after a disheartening strike. His son is also unemployed and must resort to stealing in order to put food on the table. Driven into deep depression, Begoli can no longer stand his life and throws his wife and son out into the street. His wife eventually dies, while Begoli is wrongly imprisoned for rape. Begoli must now live his life alone—without family, friends, or money.

p, Mirza Pasic; d, Miroslav Mandic; w, Haris Kulenovic, Miroslav Mandic, Emir Kusturica; ph, Vilko Filac; m, Zoran Simjanovic; ed, Andrija Zafranovic.

Drama **(PR:NR MPAA:NR)**

ZJOEK† (1987, Neth.) 90m Allart/Haagse c

Hans Dagelet *(Solomon Sjerasjevski)*, Felix-Jan Kuypers *(Ljova Zasetsky)*, Guusje van Tilborgh *(Olga)*, Rudolf Lucieer *(Alexander R. Luria)*, Maarten Wansink, Coby Stunnenburg, Anke Lankreyer, Henk Hofstede.

Set in 1943 on the Russian front, this Dutch entry (subtitled "The Art of Forgetting") tells the story of an injured soldier who has lost his memory and a mnemonist who helps him try to regain it. Based on two books of research by Soviet neuro-psychologist Alexander R. Luria—"The Mind of a Mnemonist" and "The Man with the Shattered World"—the film explores the process of memory as the Luria character (played by Lucieer) enlists the aid of a "memory man" entertainer, Dagelet, to help the officer, Kuypers, relearn basic skills of remembering. Kuypers' condition is so extreme that he can no longer associate words with their meanings, or even remember the way back to his own home. By contrast, Dagelet's condition is so extreme that he is cursed with remembering everything with equal clarity and lacking the ability to forget. The word "Zjoek" is Russian for "beetle," though it is also used to mean "the fear of memory loss." It takes on a symbolic meaning in the film as Dagelet the mnemonist has an irrational fear of beetles.

p, Kees Kasander, Denis Wigman; d, Eric van Zuylen; w, Marietta de Vries (based on *The Mind of a Mnemonist* and *The Man with the Shattered World* by Alexander R. Luria); ph, Witold Sobocinski, Piotr Sobocinski; m, Henk Hofstede; ed, Jan Dop.

Drama **(PR:NR MPAA:NR)**

ZLOTA MAHMUDIA† (1987, Pol./Bulgaria) 84m Zespoly-Bojana c (Trans: The Golden Mahmudia)

Zdzislaw Kozien *(Georgi)*, Leon Niemczyk *(Angel)*, Rafal Wegrzyniak *(Stas)*, Norbert Kliszczewski *(Peter)*.

Two youngsters vacationing at the Black Sea sneak onto a mysterious ship and spy the peculiar activities of a treasure-seeking crew. They are discovered and tossed into prison as the ship heads for an unchartered island. The boys' parents put together an expedition and, after numerous adventures, the marauding treasure hunters are apprehended and the mystery of the secret cove is solved.

d&w, Kazimierz Tarnas (based on the novel by Leslaw Bartelski); ph, Zdzislaw Kaczmarek; m, Seweryn Krajewski; ed, Zbigniew Osinski.

Children's **(PR:NR MPAA:NR)**

ZLOTY POCIAG† (1987, Pol./Rum.) 158m Zespoly-Profil-Romaniafilm c (Trans: The Train of Gold)

Matica Popescu *(Muntianu)*, Waclaw Ulewicz *(Maj. Bobruk)*, Ewa Kuklinska *(Renata)*, Gheorghe Cozorici *(Armand Calinescu)*, Tomasz Zaliwski *(Gorski)*, Jerzi Molga.

Recalling John Frankenheimer's 1965 film THE TRAIN, this Polish-Romanian co-production tells the WW II story of a Polish train stocked with the country's national assets which are being transported to Romania. Beginning the odyssey in 1939, the train is under the constant threat of sabotage by Nazi troops, but with the combined efforts of Polish and Romanian officials it arrives, eight years later, in the port at Constanta. From there the treasures are shipped to Britain and, after the war's end, delivered back to their homeland.

d, Bohdan Poreba; w, Ioan Grigorescu; ph, Marian Stanciu, Nicolae Girardi; m,

Cornelia Tautu; ed, Jerzy Pekalski; art d, Jaroslaw Switoniak, Victor Tapu; cos, Ileana Oroveanu, Anna Szczek.

War **(PR:NR MPAA:NR)**

ZOEKEN NAAR EILEEN (SEE: LOOKING FOR EILEEN, 1987, Neth.)

ZOMBIE HIGH† (1987) 91m Cinema Group c

Virginia Madsen *(Andrea Miller)*, Richard Cox *(Prof. Philo)*, Kay Kuter *(Dean Eisner)*, James Wilder *(Barry)*, Sherilynn Fenn *(Suzi)*, Paul Feig *(Emerson)*, T. Scott Coffey *(Felner)*, Paul Williams *(Ignatius)*, Henry Sutton *(Bell)*, Clare Carey *(Mary Beth)*.

Madsen stars as one of the first coeds to be allowed to enroll in previously all-male prep school, Ettinger Academy. Much to the dismay of the girls, all of the boys seem to be bland, boring types only interested in their studies. The curious Madsen investigates and uncovers a plot by the school's instructors to gain immortality by lobotomizing the student body and using the brain matter to make a serum that promotes everlasting life. Not content to merely lobotomize the teens, the faculty replaces their missing brain tissue with special quartz crystals that respond to the ever-present classical music that is heard throughout the campus. This enables the teachers to control the students at all times. The unlikely feature film debut of stage director Ron Link, ZOMBIE HIGH was given a brief run in Los Angeles before being released on home video in 1988.

p, Marc Toberoff, Aziz Ghazal; d, Ron Link; w, Tim Doyle, Elizabeth Passerelli, Aziz Ghazal; ph, David Lux, Brian Coyne (Film House Color); m, Daniel May; ed, Shawn Hardin, James Whitney; prod d, Matthew Kozinets; art d, Hisham Abed; set d, Martin Jones, Todd Stevens; spec eff, Chris Biggs, Mark Messenger.

Horror **(PR:NR MPAA:R)**

ZNAK BEDY† (1987, USSR) 151m Byelarusfilm/Sovexportfilm c (Trans: The Sign of Disaster)

Nina Ruslanova, Gennady Barbuk, Vladimir Gostyukhin.

A Soviet farmer and his wife must contend with the intrusion of Nazi troops on their farm during WW II. Although the husband tries to compromise with the invaders, the wife is defiant—milking their cow in the grass so as to deny the Nazis milk, tossing their rifles down the well, and hiding a bomb for future use. Eventually the husband joins his wife's struggle, feeling it is better to die for the motherland than to capitulate.

d, Mikhai Ptashuk; w, Yevgeny Grigoryev, Oscar Nikich (based on the story by Vasil Bykov); ph, Tatiana Loginova; m, Oleg Yanchenko; art d, Vladimir Dementyev.

War **(PR:NR MPAA:NR)**

ZNAY NASHIKH† (1987, USSR) 88m Kazakhfilm Studio/Sovexportfilm c (Trans: That's Us)

Aleukhan Bekbulatov, Dimitry Zolotukhin, Alexander Furachev, Soslan Andiyev, Fedor Sukhov, Yelena Akifyeva.

The story of 19th century wrestlers Khadji Mukan and Ivan Poddubny as they make their way through fairs and exhibitions to get to the 1904 World Championship in Paris where Poddubny is awarded the first prize and Grand Gold Medal, while Mukan wins the second prize and Small Gold Medal.

d, Sultan Khodjikov; w, Rustem Khodjikov, Sultan Khodjikov; ph, Iskander Tynyshpayev, Alexander Nilov; m, Murad Kazhlayev; art d, Viktor Lednev.

Sports/Biographical **(PR:NR MPAA:NR)**

ZOLOTAYA BABA† (1987, USSR) 79m Sverdlovsk/Sovexportfilm c (Trans: The Golden Woman)

Sergei Parfenov, Albert Filozov, Lyudmila Nikolayeva.

Adaptation of an ancient feudal legend which sees Ivashka, a brave young man who hopes to marry his sweetheart, try to win his freedom from his employer by searching for the mythical "Golden Woman," an icon rumored to bring its holder happiness and wealth. Ivashka sets out on the arduous journey, which will bring him face-to-face with the evil shaman who guards the coveted icon. Along the way Ivashka saves the life of another young man who repays him by guiding the way to the shaman's lair. They succeed in capturing the icon and Ivashka returns home, but instead of turning the prize over to his greedy employer, he gives it to the entire tribe. The angry man steals the icon, but he is struck dead and the treasure sinks to the bottom of the river. Ivashka and his beloved are finally reunited.

d, Viktor Kobzev; w, Sergei Plekhanov; ph, Rudolf Mescheryagin; m, Algis Paulavicus; art d, Valery Kukenkov.

Fantasy **(PR:NR MPAA:NR)**

ZOMBIE NIGHTMARE† (1987) 83m Gold-Gems c

Adam West *(Capt. Churchman)*, Jon-Mikl Thor *(Tony Washington)*, Tia Carrere *(Amy)*, Manuska Rigaud *(Molly)*, Frank Dietz *(Frank)*, Linda Singer *(Maggie)*, Francesca Bonacorsa *(Tony's Wife)*, Linda Smith, John Fasano.

This ludicrous-sounding horror film, which failed to get a theatrical release and instead went the straight-to-home-video route, stars blond-maned Canadian heavy-metal singer Thor (see: ROCK 'N' ROLL NIGHTMARE) as a hapless man who is killed by some irresponsible teenagers in a hit-and-run accident. Thor's widow, Bonacorsa, summons a mysterious Haitian woman (Rigaud) to perform a Macumba ceremony to bring Thor back to life so that he can teach those darn kids a lesson they'll never forget. The trick works, but Rigaud sends the zombiefied Thor (using *zombiefied* to describe Thor will seem kinda redundant to anyone who has seen his performance in ROCK 'N' ROLL NIGHTMARE) to kill those who had raped her many years before, including current police chief Adam "Batman" West. Since the rapists were members of a baseball team in their youth, Thor bludgeons them to death with a baseball bat. Cute. As was the case in ROCK AND ROLL NIGHTMARE, the multi-talented Thor provides the music here as well.

p, Pierre Grise; d, Jack Bravman; w, David Wellington; ph, Robert Racine (Bellevue Pathe Color); m, Jon-Mikl Thor; ed, David Franko; art d, David Blanchard.

Horror **Cas.** **(PR:NR MPAA:R)**

ZONTIK DLYA NOVOBRACHNYKH† (1987, USSR) 89m Mosfilm/Sovexportfilm c (Trans: Umbrella for the Newlyweds)

Alexi Batalov, Nijole Ozelite, Nikita Mikhailovsky.

An older couple, Vera and Dmitry, are vacationing in a small resort town when they meet a pair of young lovers who have run away from home because their parents where opposed to marriage. Sympathetic to the youngsters' plight, the couple take them in and all four enjoy a splendid holiday together, with the younger couple coming to look upon Vera and Dmitry as family. When the holiday is over, however, we learn that the older couple is not married at all. Dmitry is married to another and has three children, while Vera lives with her mother. The lovers steal precious moments to be together. Shaken by the experience with the young couple, Vera and Dmitry decide they can no longer deceive their families and they stop seeing each other. Not long thereafter, the younger couple—now married—want to visit their surrogate family on New Year's Day. So as not to disappoint the newlyweds, Dmitry and Vera once again pretend to be a happily married couple—taking the chance that this latest charade will change their lives forever.

d, Rodion Nakhapetov; w, Ramiz Fatallyev; ph, Vladimir Shevtsik; m, Isaak Schwarz; art d, Yury Kladiyenko.

Romance **(PR:NR MPAA:NR)**

ZUHANAS KOZBEN† (1987, Hung.) 115m Dialog-Mafilm c (Trans: The Fall)

Atilla Kaszas *(Wolf)*, Judit Pogany *(Nora, English Teacher)*, Peter Rudolf *(Gyuri, Taxi Driver)*, Hilda Harsing *(Zsuzsa)*, Adel Kovats *(Ildiko, Ballet Dancer)*, Tamas Vegvari *(Nora's Husband)*, Geza Balkay *(Torok)*, Zbigniew Zapasiewicz *(English Choreographer)*.

Film noir Hungarian-style starring Kaszas as a small-time crook who makes a living selling stolen VCRs and bootlegged videotapes. Kaszas hires a middle-aged English teacher, Pogany, to perform the voice-over dubbing of an illicit copy of THE TEXAS CHAINSAW MASSACRE. Pogany is attracted to the much-younger Kaszas and agrees to help him. When local mob types give Kaszas a brutal beating, Pogany tends his wounds and winds up seducing him in his car. Knowing that Kaszas is really in love with a beautiful ballerina who is cheating on him, Pogany decides to kill them both by driving the car into the Danube. Rudolf, a local cabbie with love problems of his own (his story is seen parallel to Kaszas), sees the car take the plunge and rescues the couple, sacrificing his own life in the process.

d&w, Tamas Tolmar; ph, Emil Novak (Eastmancolor); m, Gyorgy Selmeczy, Peter Peterdi; ed, Peter Timar; prod d, Laszlo Gardonyi; cos, Zsuzsa Partenyi.

Drama **(PR:NR MPAA:NR)**

ZYCIE WEWNETRZNE† (1987, Pol.) 89m Karol Irzykowski c (Trans: Inner Life)

Wojciech Wysocki *(Mikhail)*, Joanna Sienkiewicz *(Mikhail's Wife)*, Maria Probosz *(Eve)*, Jolanta Nowak *(Blondeve)*, Antonina Gordon-Gorecka, Henryk Bista.

The second feature from MADHOUSE (1984) director Koterski is a black comedy starring Wysocki as a pathetic little white-collar worker who compensates for his impotence by treating those less powerful than he like dirt. His life is a routine. Every day he comes home to his drab apartment, takes out the garbage, tinkers around the house, reads the paper, eats a dinner of cold cuts in front of the television, and starts pointless arguments with his mousey wife, Sienkiewicz. At night he has erotic dreams featuring the various neighbor women that he has nothing but contempt for during the day. An allegory for life in the Eastern bloc, director Koterski reportedly elicits excellent performances from Wysocki and Sienkiewicz, and adds touches of surrealism to his drab brew.

d&w, Marek Koterski; ph, Jacek Blawut; m, Johann Sebastian Bach; ed, Miroslawa Garlicka; set d, Wojciech Saloni-Marczewski.

Comedy/Drama **(PR:NR MPAA:NR)**

ZYGFRYD† (1987, Pol.) 93m Zespoly-Tor/Film Polski c (Trans: Siegfried)

Gustaw Holoubek *(Zygfryd, Circus Acrobat)*, Tomasz Hudziec *(Stefan Drawicz)*, Maria Pakulnis *(Maria, Waldo's Wife)*, Jan Nowicki *(Waldo, Circus Owner)*.

Feature debut of director Domalik takes place in Southern Poland circa 1936 and stars Hudziec as a cynical intellectual who no longer finds solace in the arts and has since become a recluse. One day he goes to the circus and sees Holoubek, a magnificent young acrobat who is the embodiment of life. Hudziec befriends the acrobat and introduces him to the intellectual world, teaching the boy art and philosophy. Unfortunately, these new thoughts despoil the purity of Holoubek's natural physical talents. Holoubek finds that circus life is no longer enough for him and he ends it all by falling from the top of his acrobatic ladder.

d&w, Andrzej Domalik (based on a short story by J. Iwaszkiewicz); ph, Grzegorz Kedzierski (Agfacolor); m, Jerzy Satanowski; ed, Malgorzata Domalik; art d, Jerzy Sajko.

Drama **(PR:NR MPAA:NR)**

People to Watch

Suzy Amis

Making a smashing impression in an otherwise listless film is no mean feat, but newcomer Suzy Amis did just that in THE BIG TOWN. Although saddled with the cliched role of the "good" girl competing with "bad" girl Diane Lane for the affections of Matt Dillon, Amis brought a freshness and intelligence to her performance that wasn't in the script. Playing a young woman raising a child by herself, she made her character lively, sexy, self-confident, independent, and capable. Her relaxed, direct, and wholly natural performance was in direct contrast with the rest of the cast of THE BIG TOWN, most of whom seemed resigned to playing their parts just as artificially as the synthetic script dictated. Born in Oklahoma, Amis became a fashion model when she turned 17 and soon after turned to acting. She landed a supporting role in the 1985 film FANDANGO, and followed that appearance with a stint in the off-Broadway play "Fresh Horses," garnering favorable notices. As an actress Amis demonstrates a depth of understanding and a subtlety of character rarely seen on the screen today. Without resorting to histrionics, she elicits sympathy and emotion, drawing the audience to her. Amis' acting is perfectly suited to the camera and her wholesome good looks will allow her to play a wide range of characters and escape the typecasting that plagues some of her more "glamourous" contemporaries. Amis is married to Sam Robards (actor son of Jason Robards, Jr. and Lauren Bacall), whom she met on the set of FANDANGO.

Kevin Anderson

Bursting onto the screen with thundering ferocity, ORPHANS costar Kevin Anderson did something very few actors are capable of doing—he stole scenes from Albert Finney and Matthew Modine, both of whom turned in some of their finest work to date. Undergoing a physical and mental transformation in the film, Anderson begins as a hyperactive, long-haired "wild child" and develops into a clean-cut, self-assured young man. Beginning on the Chicago stage (he played John F. Kennedy in a local production) and studying at the Goodman School of Drama, Anderson made his first film appearance as one of Tom Cruise's friends in RISKY BUSINESS. This was followed by a role in an independently produced teen comedy called PINK NIGHTS, which received a 1986 Chicago Film Festival showing and a limited release from New World in 1987. However, it wasn't until he joined Chicago's Steppenwolf Theatre Company that Anderson's career began to skyrocket. He costarred in the company's production of Lyle Kessler's "Orphans," which was later staged in New York and London, with Anderson in the cast both times. It was Albert Finney's love of the play, Alan Pakula's determination, and their mutual admiration for Anderson that brought him and "Orphans" to the screen. Although he has a soft voice and delicate features, Anderson is an emotional powerhouse who explodes on the screen in a remarkable display of physical acting. He appeared this year on the festival circuit in A WALK ON THE MOON, a 1960s drama about Peace Corps volunteers in South America which also starred former Steppenwolf actor Terry Kinney.

Anne Archer

After years of pursuing an acting career that never really sparked, Anne Archer decided to retire to have a child. Two years later she re-entered the business and wound up with a strong supporting role in one of the most successful films of the year, FATAL ATTRACTION. As Michael Douglas' beautiful and vivacious wife—the perfect lover, mother, and homemaker—Archer brought life to a role that has traditionally been mundane and thankless. Perhaps she played her part too well, for Archer is such a desirable mate that most men would think Douglas insane for straying from his marital bed for the likes of the obviously deranged Glenn Close. Although some of the scripting and direction of her character is questionable, Archer rises above the material and turns in a strong, dignified portrayal of a woman who has been unjustly betrayed and then plunged into a nightmare of her husband's making. Born to actor parents John Archer and Marjorie Lord, Anne knew early that she would pursue acting, but never harbored any illusions that it would be an easy or secure life. With forgettable roles in such dreary films as CANCEL MY RESERVATION (1972), ALL-AMERICAN BOY (1973), HERO AT LARGE (1980), and RAISE THE TITANIC (1980), Archer seemed doomed to career limbo until director Adrian Lyne saw her on television in "Falcon Crest" and decided that she would be a nice change from the dowdy actresses usually cast as cheated-on spouses. Lyne was right. So right that he lost any sympathy for his main character, Michael Douglas. With FATAL ATTRACTION nearing the $130 million mark at the box office and Archer getting raves for her performance, her long-stalled career has finally taken off.

Clive Barker

With the release of his series of short story collections entitled *Books of Blood*, British horror author Clive Barker has rapidly risen in prominence and popularity, prompting even Stephen King to hail him as "the future of the horror genre." Disappointed with the quality of film adaptations of his work (chiefly UNDERWORLD and RAWHEAD REX), Barker decided to try directing and the result was the disappointing but nonetheless interesting HELLRAISER. Thematically HELLRAISER is far ahead of the rest of the pack of horror films, but in his zeal to deliver some purely gut-wrenching thrills, Barker failed to tap the strength of his fiction—tightly constructed narratives and well-delineated characters—and transfer it to the screen. Visually, however, Barker demonstrates a surprising amount of imagination and skill, albeit of the grotesque variety. There are powerful images in HELLRAISER that viewers will be unlikely to forget. Born in Liverpool in 1952, Barker grew up on a steady diet of comic books and Edgar Allan Poe. While still only a teenager Barker began writing plays and stories. Eventually he moved to London where he became a playwright specializing in works of the macabre. In 1984 the first three volumes of his *Books of Blood* were published. Both critically acclaimed and popular, the short story collections brought Barker much publicity. Three more collections of stories were followed by the novel *The Damnation Game*, which made it to the *New York Times* best-seller list, and then in the fall of 1987 came a second novel, *Weaveworld*. Brought in on a budget of $3 million dollars, HELLRAISER garnered mixed reviews but was a financial success. Undoubtedly there will be more horror films from Barker and his debut, although flawed, shows signs of great chills to come.

Emmanuelle Beart

Fawnlike and *angelic* are but two of the adjectives which have been aptly used to describe Emmanuelle Beart, the 22-year-old French star of this year's MANON OF THE SPRING and DATE WITH AN ANGEL. As Manon, the star of the second part of JEAN DE FLORETTE, Beart played the

Amis

Anderson

Archer

Barker

Beart

Bracco

Cooper

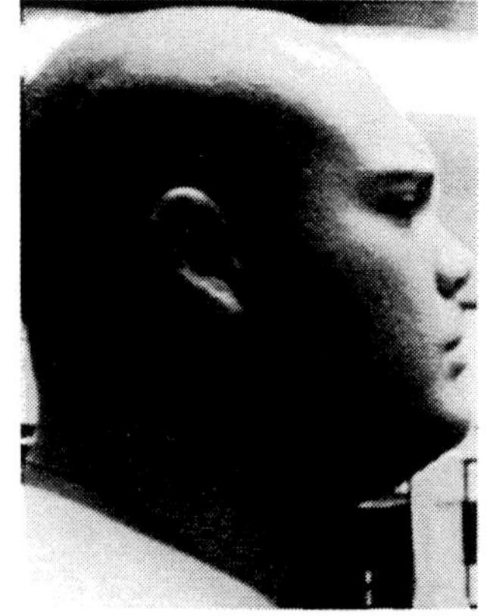
D'Onofrio

wood nymph/shepherdess who captures the heart of Daniel Auteuil and brings about his demise and that of his malevolent father Montand. In MANON, Beart does not so much *act* as rely on her physically commanding presence. Likewise in DATE WITH AN ANGEL she captures the viewer's attention with her vibrant face, her aura of heavenly innocence, and her graceful movement. Without speaking a word (though she makes otherworldly sounds), using physical acting, Beart communicates with her costar Michael Knight. Born in St. Tropez to pop singer Guy Beart and model Genevieve, Beart spent her childhood on a farm in the Midi section of France. At age 13, she had a small part in the film DEMAIN LES MOMES. At age 16 Beart moved to Montreal where she was employed as an au pair. Her interest in acting was renewed when she was approached on the street by Robert Altman, who offered her a part in a since-abandoned project called "The Eggs of Easter." She returned to Paris after three years in Montreal, took an acting course, and was soon offered film roles. She played a nubile nymphet in 1983's PREMIERS DESIRS, by soft-core photographer David Hamilton, and the following year appeared in Jean-Pierre Dougnac's L'AMOUR INTERDIT, which earned Beart a Cesar nomination as Most Promising Newcomer. In 1985 she appeared (with MANON costar Daniel Auteuil, her real-life companion) in Edouard Molinaro's L'AMOUR EN DOUCE, earning her second Cesar nomination. Finally, in 1986, she won the Cesar for Best Actress for MANON OF THE SPRING. Not limiting her acting to motion pictures, she took a stage role this year in the late Jean Anouilh's "La Repetition."

Kathryn Bigelow

One of the most auspicious directing debuts of the year belongs to Kathryn Bigelow for her genre-hybrid vampire film NEAR DARK. With its clever script (cowritten with THE HITCHER screenwriter Eric Red) and sumptuous visuals, NEAR DARK proved to be one of the most original and exciting films of the year. Combining a painter's eye (she studied at the San Francisco Art Institute) with a B-movie sensibility (she taught a course on the subject at the California Institute of the Arts), Bigelow blurs the lines between film genres and delivers a work that is entirely unique. By rethinking genre conventions, she breathes new life into a tired old standby. Destroying any notion that a woman cannot direct violent action, Bigelow proves that she has learned well from role models ranging from John Ford and Howard Hawks to Sam Peckinpah and James Cameron. The shootouts in NEAR DARK are as thrilling and as skillfully choreographed as the best of the entire macho oeuvre. Bigelow will never be pegged as a "woman's" director and from what she has said in interviews that suits her just fine, for she is after a commonality of vision that is not based on gender. Although NEAR DARK is her *solo* directing debut, she also codirected the fascinating biker picture THE LOVELESS in 1982. That film caught the eye of director Walter Hill and he arranged for Bigelow to develop projects at Universal. After developing several scripts for various studios, Bigelow met Red and together they wrote NEAR DARK. Over the course of one weekend, executive producer Edward S. Feldman read the script and decided to fund the project with Bigelow at the helm. The $6 million NEAR DARK is sure to turn a profit and Bigelow hopes to direct another biker movie and a gangster film in the near future.

Lorraine Bracco

One of the year's most pleasant surprises was the completely captivating performance of Lorraine Bracco as Tom Berenger's spunky wife in SOMEONE TO WATCH OVER ME. Handed what very well could have been a thankless role as the cheated-on wife, Bracco turned in a feisty and sensitive portrayal of a sexy, witty, tough woman who is willing to forgive her philandering husband —but only on her own terms. Her realistic, no-nonsense performance (she even gets to deck Berenger during an argument) is so good that she manages to steal the film from Berenger and Mimi Rogers, both of whom turn in excellent performances as well. Raised in Brooklyn, Bracco has had an amazingly diverse career, beginning with her success as a fashion model in America and Europe. In France she appeared on the covers of *Elle*, *Cosmopolitan*, and *Depeche Mode*, and in several television commercials. After a brief try at film acting in DUO SUR CANAPE, she became a Paris disk jockey then produced and conducted interviews for a French television special which examined how fashion and music interrelate. Bracco then returned to film acting and was featured in Lina Wertmuller's CAMORRA. This year she appeared in Ridley Scott's SOMEONE TO WATCH OVER ME and had a small part as a hooker in James Toback's THE PICK-UP ARTIST. She also participated in a theater workshop production at the Lincoln Center opposite husband Harvey Keitel, Madonna, and Sean Penn under the direction of playwright David Rabe. A many-faceted talent, Lorraine Bracco could someday become a force to be reckoned on both sides of the camera.

Chris Cooper

Conveying the kind of sincerity, integrity, and soft-spoken strength that made Gary Cooper and Henry Fonda film icons, Chris Cooper demonstrated an extraordinary screen presence in his role as the pacifist union organizer in MATEWAN, John Sayles' film about the 1920s West Virginia Coal Wars. Part Joe Hill, part Tom Joad, Joe Kenehan is the embodiment of populist activism and idealism—Cooper's chiseled features and unaffected folksiness are perfectly suited to the role. Underplaying to great effect, he brought a quiet intensity and charisma to his compassionate but resolute character. Cooper's explanation of his conversion to pacifism to James Earl Jones, the miner sent to kill him when he has been framed as a union spy, is one of 1987's most memorable screen moments. Hailing from Kansas City, Missouri, Cooper drew on his familiarity with the people of the Ozark Mountains, gained by doing construction work, to inform his understanding of MATEWAN's West Virginia miners. Cooper, 36, came to MATEWAN with primarily a stage background, though he had appeared in BAD TIMING and UNDERTOW. After serving in the Coast Guard reserve and then graduating from the University of Missouri, he went to New York City and worked a variety of jobs between roles in such off-Broadway productions as "The Ballad of Soapy Smith" and "A Different Moon." He also appeared in "Of the Fields Lately" on Broadway, in the 1985 London revival of "Sweet Bird of Youth," and as Sam Cranshaw on the TV soap opera "The Edge of Night." Cooper was one of the first actors Sayles auditioned for the role of Joe Kenehan, and the actor's striking presence remained with the director throughout the audition process, just as Cooper's memorable performance remains with those who have seen MATEWAN.

Vincent D'Onofrio

Not since Robert De Niro's weight gain for RAGING BULL has an actor's metamorphosis been as amazing as Vincent D'Onofrio's as Pvt. "Gomer Pyle" Dawson in Stanley Kubrick's FULL METAL JACKET. As Pvt. Pyle, D'Onofrio is a 280-pound blubbering country bumpkin who is turned into a leering, maniacal killing machine by his brutal Marine drill instructor. In another picture released this year, ADVENTURES IN BABYSITTING, the 6-foot-3 D'Onofrio is the 210-pound, muscular "Thor" whose curly hair hangs down to his shoulders. This ability to transform himself physically, combined with his perceptiveness as an actor, is what makes his future so promising. 27-year-old, Brooklyn-born D'Onofrio has been seen in a number of Off-Broadway productions, including "Open Admissions," and has appeared on an episode of TV's "The Equalizer" as a retarded man accused of murder. It was his Pvt. Pyle, however, that deservedly earned him international praise. D'Onofrio initially plays the character as a likable oaf who has trouble in boot camp from day one. As his DI's hatred for him grows stronger, so, too, does Pvt. Pyle's hatred for the DI and, eventually, for everyone around him. In two scenes—the pep talk about great Marines and Pvt. Pyle's murder/suicide—D'Onofrio is simply frightening as his devastating facial expressions are augmented by Kubrick's direction and masterful use of lighting. With D'Onofrio's acting talent and his ability to take on any number of physical characteristics, there's no predicting the direction that his promising career could take.

Patrick Dempsey

A 21-year-old native of Maine, Patrick Dempsey is a newcomer to film who made quite a showing this year in three films—IN THE MOOD, as the legendary "Woo-Woo Kid;" MEATBALLS III, as a awkward kid who gets help from porn queen-turned-angel Sally Kellerman; and CAN'T BUY ME LOVE, as another nerdy type who struggles to be accepted in his high school. Although Dempsey appeared in HEAVEN HELP US in 1985, his first film was actually MEATBALLS III, which was duly shelved for three years before its theatrical release this year. While the film itself is a rather dismal attempt at the teen sex comedy genre, Dempsey's fresh performance saves it from being a total waste. The same can be said for CAN'T BUY ME LOVE, another teen sex comedy that misfires but which is redeemed by Dempsey. It is in IN THE MOOD that Dempsey, who some have likened to John Cusack, shows his best work as Sonny "The Woo-Woo Kid" Wisecarver, the 15-year-old hero of the 1940s who charmed the hearts of many when he ran off with two women in their twenties, marrying one of them. Born in Turner, Maine, Dempsey began his acting career during high school in a Maine Acting Company production of "On Golden Pond" in which he played Billy. After a stint with Monmoth Theater, a Shakespearean repertory company, Dempsey was offered a role in a road-show production of "Torch Song Trilogy" which took him to San Francisco. MEATBALLS III followed; then came the International Tour Company's production of "Brighton Beach Memoirs." Some television roles also came his way—a made-for-cable TV Disney film and a six-week shot as Damon on the weekly series "Fast Times at Ridgemont High," which earned him an Emmy nomination. The energetic and seemingly effortless acting ability he displays will certainly keep him on the big screen for years to come, hopefully in roles more akin to IN THE MOOD than CAN'T BUY ME LOVE.

Robert Downey, Jr.

Although he has been in films since he was a child, Robert Downey came to the forefront only this year with two exceptionally powerful performances. He costarred with Molly Ringwald in THE PICK-UP ARTIST as Jack Jericho, a self-assured New Yorker who compulsively tries to pick up pretty women. Combining a young stud image with the poetic sensitivity of Francois Truffaut's Antoine Doinel, Downey created in Jack Jericho one of the few *romantics* in recent films. As Julian Wells in LESS THAN ZERO, Downey played a bored rich kid whose charm has always helped him to survive but who finally realizes his life has run completely afoul. Digging deep under the scum of a decadent life-style, Downey plays an out-of-control drug addict, yet still manages to make him sympathetic. No stranger to motion pictures, Downey is the son of Robert Downey, the 1960s avant-garde filmmaker who directed such underground classics as CHAFED ELBOWS (1967) and PUTNEY SWOPE (1969). After appearing on screen for the first time at age 5 as an adopted puppy in his father's POUND, Downey then had a small part in 1972's GREASER'S PALACE, also directed by his father. A few more small roles followed in Downey's teen years, including one in John Sayles' BABY IT'S YOU. Things started to roll for Downey in 1985. He was part of the least-spectacular "Saturday Night Live" cast and appeared in TO LIVE AND DIE IN L.A., WEIRD SCIENCE, and TUFF TURF (along with James Spader, who co-starred in LESS THAN ZERO). Downey also gained some recognition last year as Rodney Dangerfield's son in BACK TO SCHOOL, but not until this year did he display his superior acting talents.

Dempsey

Downey

Forsythe

William Forsythe

Although he has performed in several films and television shows during the last few years and appeared in over 60 plays (Off-Broadway, summer stock, touring companies), character actor William Forsythe has suddenly been "discovered" by Hollywood. Cast in no less than three films this year, Forsythe has demonstrated an incredible range of talent that belies his somewhat hulking appearance. In EXTREME PREJUDICE he played an intelligent, brave, and honorable member of a elite squad of military assassins who discover that they have been betrayed by their leader. In RAISING ARIZONA Forsythe proved to be equally adept at comedy, playing the dim-witted prison escapee who, along with his former cellmate Goodman, develops a genuine soft-spot for the baby that they kidnap. In the underrated WEEDS, Forsythe turned in what may be his best performance thus far as the compulsive shoplifter who finds rehabilitation via acting in fellow convict Nick Nolte's prison play. Forsythe has the ability to infuse his outlaw characters with a sensitivity and humanity that forces viewers to understand and sympathize with him. Perhaps the greatest testament to his skill as an actor is the difference between his character in last year's LIGHTSHIP and this year's RAISING ARIZONA. Ostensibly the same character in both films, that of an imbecilic criminal, Forsythe is downright scary in LIGHTSHIP and hilarious in RAISING ARIZONA, while never losing sight of the very human aspects of both characters. Born in Brooklyn, New York, Forsythe turned to acting at a young age as an escape from the more vile distractions of his Flatbush neighborhood. Now that casting agents, critics, and audiences alike have embraced this multi-faceted actor, perhaps he will get a chance to expand his repertoire even further and continue to surprise.

Grey

Hunt

Hunter

Lloyd

Jennifer Grey

The daughter of actor Joel Grey and singer-actress Jo Wilder, and granddaughter of Borsch Belt comedian Mickey Katz, 27-year-old Jennifer Grey is hardly a stranger to show business. She began dancing at age 6 (when her father was appearing on Broadway in "Cabaret") and spent much time in the wings watching her father's performances. At age 18 she danced in a Dr. Pepper commercial, and then worked as an understudy in the Off-Broadway production of "Album." After appearing in some "After School Specials" on TV, Grey landed her first film role as a friend of Daryl Hannah in 1984's RECKLESS. That same year she also appeared (briefly) in THE COTTON CLUB as Nicolas Cage's girl and in the survivalist fantasy RED DAWN, which featured her DIRTY DANCING costar Patrick Swayze. In 1986 she landed supporting roles in AMERICAN FLYERS and, most memorably, in FERRIS BUELLER'S DAY OFF as Matthew Broderick's spiteful sister. Although the films Grey has appeared in have received attention, little notice has come her way. With her starring role in DIRTY DANCING—a blockbuster hit which earned Grey excellent reviews—she has finally found a place for herself in Hollywood. A superb actress, she conveys, with equal ability, both virginal naivete and passionate intensity. Her character grows from a sweet, idealistic "daddy's girl" into an experienced woman whose views become more jaded and realistic. Rather than run with the "Brat Pack," as do so many of her less-talented contemporaries, Grey remains independent and intent on taking well-scripted and thoughtful roles.

Helen Hunt

After receiving some attention as Kathleen Turner's daughter in last year's PEGGY SUE GOT MARRIED, 23-year-old Helen Hunt turned in an especially memorable performance this year in PROJECT X. Starring opposite Matthew Broderick and numerous chimpanzees, Hunt plays a graduate student whose research in primate language studies has been cut off financially. Although animals are known scene-stealers, Hunt dominates the screen with a quality that is simultaneously intelligent, aggressive, sensual, and vulnerable. A veteran of television films, she started at a young age in 1973's "Pioneer Woman." Often playing someone's young daughter, she eventually landed better parts, and starred in 1981's "The Miracle of Kathy Miller." In 1983 she was in three quality made-for-TV films—"Quarterback Princess," "Choice of the Heart" (about the murder of Maryknoll nuns in El Salvador), and "Bill: On His Own" (which cast Hunt opposite Mickey Rooney and earned her a critical rave from the *New York Times* describing her as "a young Meryl Streep"). Hunt also had television roles on such programs as "The Mary Tyler Moore Show," "Swiss Family Robinson," and "St. Elsewhere." Although she appeared in the 1977 disaster film ROLLERCOASTER, Hunt did very little film work until 1985. That year she was seen in two theatrical releases—the peppy teen comedy GIRLS JUST WANT TO HAVE FUN and the futuristic sci-fi film TRANCERS—neither of which is especially memorable. Her supporting role in PEGGY SUE GOT MARRIED proved that she belonged on the big screen. It was in PROJECT X, however, that she really got a chance to shine. Although her part is relatively small (the film revolves around Broderick), she invests it with such genuine and honest emotions that one can't help but remember her.

Holly Hunter

Hailing from a 250-acre farm in Conyers, Georgia, Holly Hunter, a 29-year-old, 5-foot-2 actress with a southern twang, has quickly found herself among the ranks of film's top actresses. In addition to appearing as Nicolas Cage's police officer-turned-kidnaper wife in RAISING ARIZONA, Hunter grabbed one of the year's most sought-after Hollywood roles. In BROADCAST NEWS, directed by James (TERMS OF ENDEARMENT) Brooks, Hunter starred opposite William Hurt after beating out such big names as Sigourney Weaver, Elizabeth McGovern, Mary Beth Hurt, Christine Lahti, and Judy Davis. Hunter decided in high school (where she appeared in "Oklahoma" and "The Boyfriend") that she wanted to pursue acting. Four years of schooling at Pittsburgh's Carnegie-Mellon University led to a move to New York. In just three weeks she landed her first acting job—a small part in the 1981 slasher film THE BURNING. An audition for THE POPE OF GREENWICH VILLAGE followed. Although she didn't get the part, she did meet playwright Beth Henley and, as a result, appeared on Broadway in three Henley plays—"Crimes of the Heart," "Miss Firecracker Contest," and "The Wake of Jamey Foster." Costarring roles followed in Jonathan Demme's SWING SHIFT (though she has been nearly edited out), Jenny Bowen's 1985 Sundance Institute production ANIMAL BEHAVIOR, and the CBS television film A GATHERING OF OLD MEN, which was directed by Volker Schlondorff and received a European theatrical release. In RAISING ARIZONA she is superb as the simple but fiercely determined small-town newlywed who *will* have a baby—even if it means stealing one. Armed with some sharp comic timing, Hunter gets a great deal of mileage out of the line "Turn to the right!" which she barks repeatedly at Cage during a police mug shot session.

Neal Jimenez

It's a rare occurrence when a screenplay written by a student as a class assignment makes its way to the screen, but Neal Jimenez's script for RIVER'S EDGE is not your average student script. Written in 1981 while Jimenez was an undergraduate at UCLA, the script takes the pulse of today's disillusioned American youth in a writing style that is part-social examination, part-surrealism, and part-black comedy. Based on a celebrated murder case in Milpitas, California, RIVER'S EDGE tells the story of a tightly knit group of high school friends who are emotionally unable to care when one friend kills another. Adding to its complexity is the inclusion of a 1960s biker/murderer character (Dennis Hopper) whose values, albeit peculiar ones, contrast the frightening *lack* of values in today's youth. Jimenez's second feature-length script, "The River," as it was then called, initially received only a C+ grade from his instructor, before a rewrite earned him an A+. From there the script was passed throughout Hollywood and eventually reached Midge Sanford and Sarah Pillsbury, the producing team who delivered DESPERATELY SEEKING SUSAN. Two years after their initial reading of the script, Sanford/Pillsbury combined all the elements to make RIVER'S EDGE—Hemdale, director Tim Hunter, and box-office name Dennis Hopper. The 27-year-old Jimenez, who lost the use of his legs after a hiking accident, has since co-scripted the 1986 film WHERE THE RIVER RUNS BLACK.

Emily Lloyd

In what has to rank as one of film's most astounding debuts, the effervescent 16-year-old Londoner Emily Lloyd, star of WISH YOU WERE HERE, became a press sensation overnight for her natural performance and brassy personality. The granddaughter of British stage actor Charles Lloyd Pack and daughter of Roger Lloyd Pack, a leading member of the National Theatre Company, Lloyd came to WISH YOU WERE HERE with a minimum of acting experience. Determined from a young age to be a professional actress, she eventually persuaded her reluctant parents to allow her to attend drama school. Prior to WISH YOU WERE HERE her only real role was as a young boy in a drama workshop adaptation of Barry Hines' novel *Kes*. Lloyd forged ahead, and after two unsuccessful auditions, she read for the casting director of WISH YOU WERE HERE. Although the reading was initially a failure, she returned a second time on the urging of her father's agent. Screenwriter and director David Leland narrowed the field to five actresses before finally deciding on Lloyd, a decision which turned her into an international sensation and, ultimately, saved an otherwise mediocre film from obscurity. With the now-famous line "Up your bum!" and the sassy, sexy, devil-may-care attitude of a Lolita-like nymphet, Lloyd captured the viewer's attention and imagination. Both on and off the screen her candor is refreshing. She shocks the uptight locals in the film with her promiscuous ways, and unsettles others with her determination to remain a fun-loving, irreverent teenager. Lloyd is blessed with presence—a quality which cannot be learned and has little or nothing to do with her acting ability (which seems considerable) or the quality of her films. The only question is whether Lloyd can improve on such a stunning debut.

David Mamet

At age 39, Pulitzer Prize winner David Mamet has already joined the pantheon of American playwrights (his ouevre includes "American Buffalo," "Glengarry Glen Ross," "Sexual Perversity in Chicago," "The Water Engine," "A Life in the Theatre"), but this year he set his sights on cinematic greatness and made a stunning directorial debut with the stylish HOUSE OF GAMES. Though he has never been enamored of Hollywood, Mamet wrote the screenplays for THE VERDICT and Bob Rafelson's remake of THE POSTMAN ALWAYS RINGS TWICE, and in 1987 he also scripted THE UNTOUCHABLES for Brian De Palma. Born and bred in Chicago, where he made his reputation in the theater, Mamet was already familiar with much of the lore surrounding Al Capone and Eliot Ness. The film was not intended as a remake of the popular TV series of the same name, and Mamet attempted to invest the historical characters and the story with mythic qualities. As with HOUSE OF GAMES, his screenplay reflects his wonderful ear for the way people talk and his adeptness at capturing both the humor and pungency of colloquial speech. HOUSE OF GAMES was made on a considerably smaller budget than THE UNTOUCHABLES and starred Mamet's wife, Lindsay Crouse, and longtime associates Joe Mantegna and Mike Nussbaum. Originally, it was to have been helmed by Peter Yates, but after the first production deal fell through, Mamet took on the directing chores himself and approached the project with meticulous preparation. The result is not only a tightly scripted, exceptionally *well-made* film, but also a visually stunning one. Because of the positive reaction to it, soon after, Mamet went into production on his second directorial project, THINGS CHANGE, cowritten with Shel Silverstein.

Joe Mantegna

Known primarily for his outstanding work in the plays of David Mamet, veteran Chicago actor Joe Mantegna made notable appearances in three films in 1987: WEEDS, SUSPECT, and Mamet's impressive directorial debut, HOUSE OF GAMES. Although his two supporting roles (as an Off-Broadway actor drafted by playwright Nick Nolte to replace one of his cast of ex-cons in WEEDS, and as the aggressive prosecuting attorney in SUSPECT) were remarkably assertive, Mantegna's most powerful screen performance came when his friend Mamet handed the actor his first starring role in HOUSE OF GAMES. No one—including Mamet's actress wife Lindsay Crouse—handles Mamet's distinctive staccato dialog as well as Mantegna does. As Mike, the consummate con man, Mantegna creates the quintessential Mametian character: a quick-witted, street-smart student of human nature who is ready, willing, and able to pounce on his victims while maintaining that his deceptions are "only business." Mantegna and Mamet, who were born only two weeks apart, have known each other for 15 years and worked together frequently. The first highlight of their collaboration came when Mantegna won a Tony Award for his role in Mamet's Pulitzer Prize-winning play "Glengarry Glen Ross." Although Mamet had no control over the casting of a potential film adaptation of the play, he wrote two screenplays with Mantegna in mind. Vowing not to make the films without Mantegna in the lead, Mamet got both HOUSE OF GAMES and his next film, THINGS CHANGE, produced. The 40-year-old Mantegna garnered rave reviews for his performance in HOUSE OF GAMES and offers have been pouring in. After THINGS CHANGE he plans to star in Mamet's next stage play, "Speed the Plow," with more movie roles to follow. In HOUSE OF GAMES Mantegna says, "Everybody gets something out of every transaction." In this case Mantegna finally has gotten his long overdue popular recognition, and the audience has been introduced to an exciting new actor.

Mamet

Mantegna

Douglas Milsome

For his first major outing as a director of photography, Douglas Milsome found himself standing beside Stanley Kubrick on the director's first film in seven years, FULL METAL JACKET. Kubrick's well-deserved reputation as a master of composition and lighting was made possible by the expertise of the late John Alcott (who died July 28, 1986), Kubrick's cameraman since 1971. It is only natural, then, that a student of Alcott's, Milsome, should follow in his mentor's footsteps. Milsome began his film career as a focus puller for Alcott on A CLOCKWORK ORANGE (1971) and BARRY LYNDON (1975). By 1980's THE SHINING, Milsome had moved up to first assistant and was allowed to shoot first unit photography after Alcott left for another project. "I'd like to carry on where John stopped," Milsome told *American Cinematographer* magazine. Judging from his work on FULL METAL JACKET (with which he was involved for a year and a half), Milsome has clearly done so. Meticulously photographed in a grainy documentary-style color, the film, in technical terms, is perhaps the best crafted motion picture in recent memory. Ranging from the fluorescent lighting of the boot camp barracks to the surreal lighting effects of Pvt. Pyle's murder/suicide to the haunting Tet Offensive and its numerous tracking shots, the talent of Milsome is visible throughout FULL METAL JACKET. In 1983, during the seven-year period between THE SHINING and FULL METAL JACKET, Milsome shot a feature in New Zealand called WILD HORSES. One can only hope that more of his work will hit the screen before the

Phillips

Roebuck (see River's Edge cast)

Miller (see River's Edge cast)

Rogers

next Kubrick film—whenever it may be.

Lou Diamond Phillips

Twenty-five-year-old Lou Diamond Phillips made a big splash in 1987 with his winning portrayal of 1950s rock 'n' roll idol Ritchie Valens in the surprise summer hit LA BAMBA. Although he bears little resemblance to the real-life Valens, Phillips (who gained 15 pounds for the role) exudes an enthusiasm and wholesome charm that audiences found irresistible. Director Luis Valdez picked the young actor from the more than 500 candidates that auditioned. Phillips overcame a potential stumbling block—the fact that he is not a singer—by listening to Valens' songs (as performed by Los Lobos) on a Walkman for two weeks solid until he became familiar with every note and vocal intonation. Then when it came time to lip-sync the tunes for the cameras, Phillips performed flawlessly. A Navy brat of Filipino, Hispanic, Hawaiian, and Cherokee descent, Phillips took the role because for him it represented the first truly positive Hollywood film about Hispanics in the US. Indeed, the success of LA BAMBA was the inspiration for a flurry of newspaper and magazine articles about the new, more affirmative attitude Hollywood has adopted toward Hispanics. Among the items pinpointed were the crop of promising young Hispanic stars (Andy Garcia, Julie Carmen, Elizabeth Pena, Esai Morales, Jimmy Smits) and the previously untapped Hispanic market just waiting for films that address their interests and concerns. A veteran stage actor as well as a movie star, Phillips will next appear in WALKING ON WATER, which teams him with "Miami Vice" star Edward James Olmos and THE UNTOUCHABLES' Andy Garcia.

RIVER'S EDGE cast

In a film that features as many superb performances as RIVER'S EDGE does it is not possible to single out any one actor. Not since Francis Ford Coppola's 1983 film THE OUTSIDERS have so many promising new performers appeared together so early in their careers. With the exception of Crispin Glover (who attracted attention as Michael J. Fox's father in BACK TO THE FUTURE), the cast of RIVER'S EDGE is made up of a group of unknowns fast on their way to successful careers—Keanu Reeves, Ione Skye [Leitch], Daniel Roebuck, Josh Richman, Joshua Miller, and Roxana Zal. Reeves is the film's conscience—the one character who is caught between his loyalty to Glover and Roebuck and his own sense of morality. Born in Beirut, Lebanon, Reeves' minimal film experience includes the Rob Lowe film YOUNGBLOOD and FLYING. Ione Skye (who has dropped the Leitch from her name since the release of RIVER'S EDGE) is the 16-year-old daughter of 1960s pop singer Donovan, and, until RIVER'S EDGE, she had no intent of pursuing an acting career. Spotted by director Tim Hunter in a fashion layout in the *L.A. Weekly*, Skye was chosen for the role of Clarissa, the best friend of the murdered girl. She also appeared in the science-fiction film STRANDED, another 1987 release. Roebuck's background is a most peculiar one. In RIVER'S EDGE he plays the cold, unredeemable killer Samson, but prior to the film he was pursuing a career in comedy. Hyped by his managers as a John Candy type, Roebuck was doing stand-up routines before landing the lead in the forgettable 1985 film CAVE GIRL. Roebuck also appeared this year in PROJECT X and opposite Jon Cryer in DUDES. Richman, who has had small roles in MODERN GIRLS, THRASHIN', and THE ALLNIGHTER, plays Tony, a hard-edged kid who is more concerned with his guitar playing than the murder. Zal, a 16-year-old actress previously seen in TABLE FOR FIVE and TESTAMENT, and an Emmy-award winner for the television film SOMETHING ABOUT AMELIA, appears as the tough but naive "Maggie," who, like Clarissa, doesn't know where to turn. Lastly, there is 11-year-old Joshua Miller, the son of actor/playwright Jason Miller. Cast as Reeves's little brother, Miller turns in a haunting portrayal of a disturbed, androgynous youngster who is so obsessed with Glover's code of friendship that he nearly kills his own brother for not abiding by it. What makes these performances so potent is the cast's ability to bring a sense of realism to their roles. Unlike the homogeneous, suburbanized Brat Pack stars, these kids have a ring of truth, as if they were a group of "burn-outs" picked off the street and put before the cameras. Their mannerisms, language, and attitude are as real as anything ever put on screen, and it is this talent which insures that they will continue to be seen.

Mimi Rogers

Until her memorable performance in SOMEONE TO WATCH OVER ME, actress Mimi Rogers' principal notoriety had come from her marriage to heartthrob actor Tom Cruise earlier in the year. Far from a novice, Rogers has appeared in the films BLUE SKIES AGAIN (1983) and GUNG HO (1986), been a regular cast member in the television series "Paper Dolls" and "The Rousers," and has had guest shots on several shows including "Magnum P.I.," "Hart to Hart," and "Hill Street Blues." Not until this year, however, has she had the chance to make a name for herself in theatrical films. Early in 1987 Rogers appeared as Christopher Reeve's girl friend in the little-seen STREET SMART, then came her much-publicized marriage to Cruise, and following that, her widely praised performance as the glamourous socialite in SOMEONE TO WATCH OVER ME. In both of her films this year, Rogers has portrayed a strong, intelligent, independent woman who finds herself in a situation beyond her control. In STREET SMART she watched journalist Reeve slide further and further away from her as he became mired in deceit, corruption, and venality while pursuing success as a sensationalistic television reporter. Whereas she was the personification of the earthy, upwardly mobile N.Y.C. professional in that film, Rogers' next role, in SOMEONE TO WATCH OVER ME, called for her to convey the aloof glamour of the Fifth Avenue bourgeoisie. Proper, elegant, and very alluring, Rogers managed to find basic decency and a touching humanity in a character that could have easily been a dull cliche. An intelligent actress with a natural beauty that enables her to play a variety of roles, Mimi Rogers should prove to be a major talent in the years to come.

Joseph Ruben

Hampered by a haphazard marketing strategy, Joseph Ruben's THE STEPFATHER seemed doomed to the obscurity of video shelves. It was released in only a few markets over a period of six months with the ad campaign changing radically in virtually every market. Critics and audiences who actually managed to see Ruben's movie found a genuinely intelligent, gripping, and ultimately disturbing little psycho-thriller that is definitely *not* just another slasher film. From its slow, shocking opening to its breathless conclusion, THE STEPFATHER demonstrates that a unique hand was at the helm. Ruben improved upon the screenplay written by Donald Westlake (from a story by Carolyn Lefcourt and Brian Garfield) which tells the chilling story of a man who seems calm and charming on the outside, but in reality is a violent psychopath who feels compelled to kill those who do not fit into his idealized vision of the American Family. Ruben, who previously directed the very interesting DREAMSCAPE (1984), knows how to visualize a story as well. THE STEPFATHER begins as a Norman Rockwell painting and slowly becomes dark and menacing until, in the end, it explodes into an Hitchcockian nightmare. Although his film is violent, Ruben understands that implied violence is much more powerful than graphic bloodletting. The director gets more visceral impact out of a two-by-four suddenly slicing a diagonal line across the frame and then impacting off-screen, than he would have if he had opted for a stiff, clinical, gore-effects close-up. Ruben can handle actors as well, eliciting great performances from Shelly Hack, newcomer Jill Schoelen, and a superbly creepy Terry O'Quinn as the madman. With any luck Hollywood will realize the financial failure of THE STEPFATHER was due to bad marketing and recognize Joseph Ruben as a potential powerhouse.

John Patrick Shanley

An acclaimed Off-Broadway playwright ("Danny and the Deep Blue Sea"), 36-year-old John Patrick Shanley made an auspicious debut as a screenwriter this year with a pair of well-crafted but unconventional screenplays—MOONSTRUCK for Norman Jewison and FIVE CORNERS (given a festival release in 1987) for Tony Bill. Both films are characterized by distinctive, unusual tones, due in no small part to the scripts by the "Bard from the Bronx." MOONSTRUCK is a hybrid of profound emotion and humor. FIVE CORNERS, set in 1964 in the Bronx of Shanley's youth, is a strangely affecting symbiotic mix of humor and violence. Both films benefit from the screenwriter's finely observed detailing of environment: the ethnicity of Italian-American Brooklyn in MOONSTRUCK, the period atmosphere of a blue-collar Bronx neighborhood at the outset of the civil rights era in FIVE CORNERS. Shanley has a strong sense of the essence of character, but he also has a prodigious gift for conveying it through exacting particularization. His wonderful, revealing, funny dialog resounds with verisimilitude. Bill was so captivated by a Shanley monolog he heard as an audition piece that he sought out the playwright. When the producer-director found him, Shanley had his first original screenplay, FIVE CORNERS, ready and waiting. Shanley, whose father was an Irish Catholic immigrant, grew up in the Bronx where he also became familiar with the ins and outs of Italian-American culture. The New York University graduate's newest screenplay is entitled THE JANUARY MAN.

Elena Sofonova

Blessed with the beautiful, deep-set "dark eyes" of the movie of the same name, 31-year-old Elena Sofonova made a lasting impression on US art house audiences this year as the naive Russian woman who captures the heart of Marcello Mastroianni. With a fragile quality that reminds one of Audrey Hepburn in ROMAN HOLIDAY, Sofonova brings to life a carefully scripted character whose complexities are gradually revealed to both Mastroianni and the audience. It is to Sofonova's credit that she can play not just the innocent beauty, but also the secretive woman that hides behind that innocence. More than just beautiful, Sofonova is a graceful and talented actress. In 1974, at the age of 17, Sofonova decided she wanted to pursue the career for which her father—Soviet actor Vsevolod Sofonov—had become famous. Since then she has appeared in some 20 Soviet films, only this year gaining deserved international exposure in DARK EYES, an Italian production filmed in both Italy and the USSR by Soviet director Nikita Mikhalkov. Her greatest success in her own country came in 1985 in Igor Maslennikov's WINTER CHERRIES, in which she played a divorced mother attempting to adjust to a life of independence. What makes Sofonova so special in DARK EYES is her ability to play off of Mastroianni without being overshadowed by his excellent performance and romantic charm. Of their working relationship and the differences in their acting styles, Sofonova has said: "We [Soviet actors] are taught to play through a long scene in which there are several transitions from one mood to another. For Marcello this was incomprehensible. He likes to play the various fragments and then splice it together."

Joe Strummer [John Mellors]

In London, 1976, Joe Strummer, along with three fellow musicians, formed one of rock music's premier punk bands, The Clash. By the end of that year they were signed by CBS Records and were recording such songs as "White Riot" and "I'm So Bored With The U.S.A." Within a few years, The Clash was getting assimilated into the mainstream, had a Top-40 single, and by 1985 had disbanded. Perhaps the apex of their career was a three-record set entitled "Sandinista," which introduced to many listeners the political and social turmoil that was occurring in Nicaragua. Eleven years after The Clash's birth, the 34-year-old Strummer has again become a musical force—this time with the superb score for Alex Cox's WALKER, a filmed-in-Nicaragua tale of American imperialism. Drawing on influences as diverse as Latino rhythms, his rock-and-roll roots, and Ennio Morricone's spaghetti western soundtracks, Strummer has composed a haunting score which recalls his compositions from "Sandinista." While this is his first soundtrack, it is not Strummer's introduction to film. In 1980, The Clash starred in a part-fiction/part-concert film called RUDE BOY. They also appeared, very briefly, in a street scene in Martin Scorsese's KING OF COMEDY. It is through his association with Alex Cox, however, that Strummer has again made a mark. Strummer wrote the anthem for Cox's SID AND NANCY, "Love Kills," for which Cox then directed a rock video. Strummer has also appeared as an actor in both Cox films released this year—STRAIGHT TO HELL (a title taken from a song by The Clash) and, very briefly, WALKER.

D.B. Sweeney

With strong performances in two starring roles this year, 26-year-old D.B. Sweeney emerged as one of Hollywood's most endearing new leading men. In Francis Ford Coppola's much-maligned GARDENS OF STONE, he plays an idealistic young Army recruit who has known for his whole life that, like his father, he was born to soldier. Itching for combat duty, he is instead assigned to the company that watches over Arlington National Cemetery. In The Old Guard he enjoys the comradeship of James Caan and James Earl Jones before he departs to fight and die in Vietnam. Sweeney invests his character with wholly believable brashness and determination yet undercuts it with the naivete the role demands. In NO MAN'S LAND he is a green cop given the task of infiltrating the car theft ring run by Charlie Sheen. The impressionable Sweeney becomes friends with rich kid Sheen and is seduced by life in the fast lane. Matching Sheen's excellent performance, Sweeney makes his young policeman's confusion palpable, capturing both

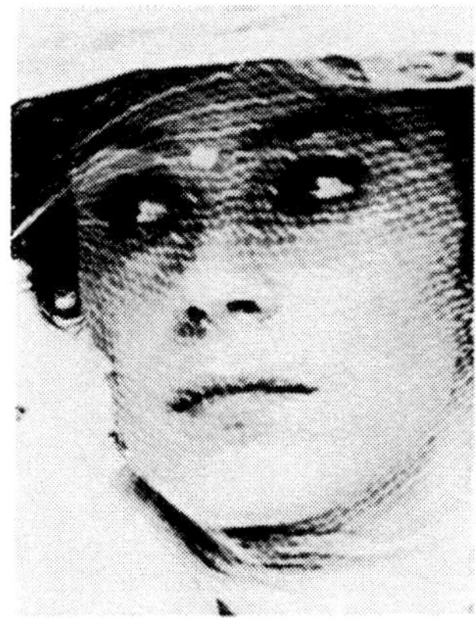

Sofonova

Strummer

Sweeney

Townsend

Vance

Washington

the exuberance and remorse that accompanies his initiation into a world of moral uncertainty and betrayal. In both roles Sweeney conveys the kind of profound sincerity that should keep him working for a long time to come. A native New Yorker, Sweeney attended Tulane and New York Universities, and though he didn't win many roles in student productions, after his graduation he was cast in a Broadway production of "The Caine Mutiny Court Martial." He also appeared off-Broadway in "Short Change" and did guest shots on TV's "The Edge of Night" and "Spenser: For Hire." His other film credits include POWER, CAPTIVE HEARTS, and FIRE WITH FIRE. In 1987 Sweeney was also hard at work on EIGHT MEN OUT, John Sayles' upcoming film about the 1919 "Black Sox" World Series scandal. In it Sweeney, a talented baseball player who recently tried out at the San Francisco Giants rookie camp, portrays the infamous "Say it ain't so" slugger Shoeless Joe Jackson. It seems likely that more big roles will follow.

Robert Townsend

A veteran stand-up comic and character actor, Chicago-born Robert Townsend burst upon the scene as a director with his hilarious semi-autobiographical comedy HOLLYWOOD SHUFFLE. Having grown increasingly frustrated with the stereotyped roles Hollywood was offering him (pimps, thieves, street hustlers, slaves), Townsend decided to make his own film, a satire on Hollywood's attitudes toward blacks. Using money he had saved from his roles in STREETS OF FIRE, A SOLDIER'S STORY, RATBOY, ODD JOBS, and AMERICAN FLYERS, Townsend scraped together $60,000 and recruited actor friends to appear with him in the film he cowrote with his buddy Keenen Ivory Wayans. HOLLYWOOD SHUFFLE was filmed in fourteen days over a two-and-a-half-year period. Townsend rented two vans (one for equipment, the other for his actors) and shot his film on weekends utilizing the hit-and-run method—that is, pulling up to a location, leaping out of the vans, shooting a scene, and leaving before the police arrived seeking expensive permits. Just in case they did get caught, Townsend bought his crew UCLA t-shirts so they could claim that they were shooting a student film. The $60,000 ran out before his ideas did, so he applied for dozens of credit cards and finished the film on $40,000 worth of plastic. Luckily, the Samuel Goldwyn Company loved the rough cut of the film and put up an additional $750,000 for post-production and paid Townsend's huge credit card bills. Much to everyone's surprise, this quirky, ultra-low-budget film was a hit with the critics and audiences alike and easily turned a profit. Townsend promoted the film (and himself) heavily, focusing attention on the plight of black actors. Also released this year was EDDIE MURPHY RAW, a concert film directed by Townsend which is sure to make big money. A talented triple threat (actor/writer/director) who has become a proven financial success, Robert Townsend will definitely be someone worth watching.

Courtney B. Vance

Standing out from a cast of promising young newcomers is never easy, especially in an episodic war film like HAMBURGER HILL, but 26-year-old Courtney B. Vance came through with flying colors. As the outspoken medic Doc, Vance turned in a vivid, emotional portrayal of a man who must do everything from lecturing new recruits on the art of brushing their teeth to mending the wounds of his fallen comrades under heavy enemy fire. Vance's Doc is a passionate man whose growing frustration with the awful waste of life he sees takes the form of angry outbursts at the mindless bureaucracy that has dropped these men into the midst of such insanity. He is also the combat veteran among the company's "bloods" (black soldiers) and at first resents being forced to defend "The United States of White America." Eventually his displaced anger at his white comrades evolves into an understanding that the white soldiers, too, are ". . . all good dumb niggers on this hill." With the rain, smoke, and mud the soldiers must slog through during the course of HAMBURGER HILL, all the men seem to become one. It is truly an ensemble performance, but when Vance is on screen, all eyes are riveted on him, such is the intensity of his performance. A veteran stage actor with a degree in history from Harvard, and a MFA degree from the Yale Drama School, Vance was nominated for a Tony Award for his performance in the Pulitzer Prize- and Tony Award-winning play "Fences." He was also a member of the Boston Shakespeare Company and has performed several plays at the Eugene O'Neill Theatre Center. An actor with the credentials and talent to make waves on stage and screen, Courtney B. Vance will be around for quite some time.

Denzel Washington

After his memorable secondary role as the angry private in an era before the ascendancy of black militancy in A SOLDIER'S STORY (1984) and his strong supporting work in POWER (1986), Denzel Washington was given a major role in CRY FREEDOM and made the most of it. Many found his portrayal of Stephen Biko, the martyred leader of South Africa's Black Consciousness movement, to be the best thing about Richard Attenborough's much-discussed film, despite the fact that Washington is killed before the picture is half over. His Biko radiates intelligence, pride, charisma, strength, and hope and would have done so even without Attenborough's lighting and camera-angle embellishments. Washington's greatest triumph, though, is his transcendence of a script which seemingly calls for an otherworldly Biko. With many small touches, he reminds us of Biko's humanity, that he was a man, albeit a great man, but not a saint. Attenborough had hoped to cast a South African in the role, and auditioned actors in Africa, the US, Britain, Canada, and Germany. Finally, recalling Washington's work in A SOLDIER'S STORY, Attenborough cast him without even asking him to audition. Washington put on 20 pounds and had the caps on his teeth removed to create a gap so that he would more closely resemble the slain political leader. Though he may be best known to some as a regular on TV's "St. Elsewhere," it seems likely that Washington will become increasingly familiar as a leading man on the big screen.

Abbas, Khwaja Ahmad

Died 1 June 1987, Bombay, India; age 74.

Filmmaker/Writer/Journalist

Wrote scripts for films directed by Raj Kapoor as well as 75 books in Urdu and English, including his autobiography, *I Am Not an Island: An Experiment in Autobiography, The Mad, Mad World of Indian Cinema*, and biographies of Indira Gandhi, Nikita Khrushchev, and cosmonaut Yuri Gagarin, all in English. Was paid $75 for his first film script, "Naya Sansar." Other screenplays, noted for their progressiveness and deep social content, include: NAI DUNIYA; NAI KAHANI; ZINDAGI ZINDAGI; BOBBY; ACHANAK. Among the films he directed are GYARA HAZAR LADKIYAN; SHEHAR AUR SAPNA; BAMBAI RAAT KI BAHON MEIN; SAAT HINDUSTANI; NAXALITES; and children's films EID MUBARAK; BHARAT DARSHAN; LAV KUSH.

Abel, Robert

Died 22 March 1987, Miami, Fla.; age 74.

Screenwriter/Boxer

To keep a career as a fighter secret from his mother in South Philadelphia, he signed a contract that kept him boxing on the West Coast until he retired from the ring after winning 32 of 34 bouts. He studied writing and drama and proved to be equally prolific in those areas, receiving credit on over 20 films including BREAKDOWN, adapted from his play "The Samson Slasher," which had a boxing background, and ROAR OF THE CROWD, featuring Howard Duff. Other films include THE GREENWOOD TREE; UNDER THE GREENWOOD TREE; THE PRIME TIME.

Abel, Walter

Born 6 June 1898, St. Paul, Minn.; died 26 March 1987, Essex, Conn.

Actor

In a career spanning 50 years, he appeared on Broadway and in more than 80 films including OUT OF A CLEAR SKY (film debut, 1918); LILIOM; THE THREE MUSKETEERS (in the role of D'Artagnan, costarring with Paul Lukas and Margot Grahame); THE LADY CONSENTS; TWO IN THE DARK; THE WITNESS CHAIR; SECOND WIFE; Fritz Lang's 1936 classic FURY; WE WENT TO COLLEGE; PORTIA ON TRIAL; WISE GIRL; GREEN LIGHT; LAW OF THE UNDERWORLD; RACKET BUSTERS; MEN WITH WINGS; KING OF THE TURF. Other films include ARISE MY LOVE; MICHAEL SHAYNE, PRIVATE DETECTIVE; MIRACLE ON MAIN STREET; DANCE, GIRL, DANCE; WHO KILLED AUNT MAGGIE?; HOLD BACK THE DAWN; BEYOND THE BLUE HORIZON; STAR SPANGLED RHYTHM; HOLIDAY INN; MR. SKEFFINGTON; THE AFFAIRS OF SUSAN; KISS AND TELL; SKYLARK; GLAMOUR BOY; WAKE ISLAND; SO PROUDLY WE HAIL; FIRED WIFE; AN AMERICAN ROMANCE; FOLLOW THE BOYS; DUFFY'S TAVERN; THE KIDS FROM BROOKLYN; 13 RUE MADELEINE; DREAM GIRL; THE FABULOUS JOE; THAT LADY IN ERMINE; SO THIS IS LOVE; NIGHT PEOPLE; ISLAND IN THE SKY; THE INDIAN FIGHTER; THE STEEL JUNGLE; BERNARDINE; RAINTREE COUNTY; HANDLE WITH CARE. During the 1960s he was president of the American National Theater and Academy. His remaining film roles were scarce: THE CONFESSION; Edward Dmytryk's 1965 classic MIRAGE; NIGHT OF THE DARK FULL MOON; QUICK, LET'S GET MARRIED; SILENT NIGHT, BLOODY NIGHT. His final picture was THE ULTIMATE SOLUTION OF GRACE QUIGLEY, 1984. He was vice president of the Screen Actors Guild in the 1950s when Ronald Reagan was the guild's president.

Abbott, Tom

Died 8 April 1987, New York, N.Y.; age 52.

Stage Director/Choreographer

Studied at the School of American Ballet. He appeared in the original Broadway production and the film version of WEST SIDE STORY. Assisted choreographer Jerome Robbins in the original Broadway production of "Fiddler on the Roof"; choreographed the film version and restaged the show in Tel Aviv, London, Amsterdam, Hamburg, and Oslo, plus its New York revivals in 1976-77 and 1981. He assisted on a revival of "The Concert" for the New York City Ballet, with whom he was professionally associated, and on The Royal Ballet's production of that work. Other ballets he restaged include "Afternoon of a Faun," "Moves," "In G Major," and "New York: Opus Jazz." He was most recently involved in directing and choreographing "Fiddler" in Vienna and for the Australian Opera, and producing a revival of "The Concert" in Melbourne.

Abraham, John

Died 30 May 1987, Calcutta, India; age 49.

Director

Founder of "Odessa," a film movement that involved the masses in rural areas by showing quality films to the public at large. For six years he went from village to village beating a drum to raise contributions not exceeding 100 rupees to make his last film, AMMA ARIYAN (AKA: FOR MOTHER TO KNOW), which won him the 1987 National Special Jury Prize. Other films include VIDYARTHIKALE ITHILE ITHILE; CHERIYACHANTE KROORA KRITHYANGAL; and AGRAHARATHIL KAZHUTHAI, winner of a national award in Tamil.

Abramson, Philip

Died 5 July 1987, Sherman Oaks, Calif., age 54.

Set Designer

A native of Omaha, Nebr., and a graduate of UCLA, he received an Academy Award nomination in 1978 for CLOSE ENCOUNTERS OF THE THIRD KIND. Other films on which he worked are: CAMELOT; BULLITT; FINIAN'S RAINBOW; ASH WEDNESDAY; LE MANS; A SEPARATE PEACE; THE DROWNING POOL; JAWS 2; JAWS 3-D; RAGING BULL; YOUNG DOCTORS IN LOVE; SHARKEY'S MACHINE; THE REIVERS; MONTE WALSH; THE SPORTING CLUB; FUZZ; THEY ONLY KILL THEIR MASTERS; THE OTHER SIDE OF THE MOUNTAIN; REFLECTION OF FEAR; HARD TO HOLD; THE LEGEND OF THE LONE RANGER.

Adams, Peter

Born 22 Sept. 1917, Los Angeles, Calif.; died 9 January 1987, Beverly Hills, Calif.

Film/Stage/TV Actor

A descendant of an old California family, he began a 50-year acting career while a student at Williams College. His films include: DONOVAN'S BRAIN; WAR OF THE WORLDS; RUBY GENTRY; FLAT TOP; FIGHTING MAN; SILENT FEAR; JAILHOUSE ROCK; PROJECT MOONBASE; THE COURT MARTIAL OF BILLY MITCHELL; FLAME OF THE ISLANDS; THE SCARLET COAT; HELL ON DEVIL'S ISLAND; OMAR KHAYYAM; THE BIG FISHERMAN. He toured nationally with Claudette Colbert in "Community of Two" and "Marriage Go Round." Among his television credits were roles in the old "Zorro" and such early shows as "Lux Video Theatre," "The Life of Riley," "Perry Mason," and "Alfred Hitchcock Presents." Most recently he had appeared on television's "Dallas" and "General Hospital."

Alderman, John

Died 12 Jan. 1987; age 53.

Actor

Appeared on the big screen in PORK CHOP HILL; THE THRILL OF IT ALL; HOT SPUR; THE PICK-UP; THE FABULOUS BASTARD FROM CHICAGO; STARLET; THAR SHE BLOWS; TWO ROSES AND A GOLDEN-ROD; DIAMOND STUD; THE HARD ROAD; TRADER HORNEE; ESCAPE FROM THE PLANET OF THE APES; THE PINK ANGELS; THE LAST MOVIE; CLEOPATRA JONES; STACEY!; THE EROTIC ADVENTURES OF ZORRO; THIS IS A HIJACK; DANDY; DIVORCE LAS VEGAS STYLE; LITTLE MISS INNOCENCE; BLACK SAMSOM; THE BLACK GODFATHER; THE ALPHA INCIDENT; CANNONBALL; THE SWINGING BARMAIDS; C.B. HUSTLERS; NEW YEAR'S EVIL; THE STUNT MAN; and the TV films, "The Screaming Woman," "Nowhere to Hide," "Mr. Horn," "The Ordeal of Patty Hearst," "Angel on My Shoulder," "Mickey Spillane's Margin for Murder," "Kung Fu: The Movie."

Allegret, Yves

Born 13 Oct. 1907, Paris; died 31 January 1987, Paris, France.

Director

Launched the career of Simone Signoret to whom he was married from 1944 to 1949. He was considered a leading figure of post-WW II French cinema and directed his first film in the early 1930s, working as assistant to Jean Renoir before gaining recognition with UNE SI JOLIE PETITE PLAGE, considered by many to be his finest work. Other films include DEDEE D'ANVERS; MANAGES; JEUNES TIMIDES; LA BOITE AUX REVES; LES DEMONS DE L'AUBE; LES MIRACLES N'ONT LIEU QU'UNE FOIS; NEZ DE CUIR; MAM'ZELLE NITOUCHE; LES ORGUEILLEUX (his most successful film; written by Jean-Paul Sartre); QUAND LE FEMME S'EN MELE; LA FILLE DE HAMBOURG; L'AMBITIEUSE; JOHNNY BANCO; L'INVASION; CONFESSIONS OF A NEWLYWED; DESPERATE DECISION; PORT OF DESIRE. He was to have received a career achievement French Cesar award at the Palais des Congres March 7.

Allen, Irving [Irving Applebaum]

Born 1905, Lemburg, Poland; died 17 Dec. 1987, Los Angeles, Calif.

Film Producer

Though born in Poland, he attended college at Georgetown University and went to Hollywood in 1926. He began his film career as an apprentice editor at Universal, working on ALL QUIET ON THE WESTERN FRONT. He became an independent producer in 1940, making shorts, including "40 Boys and a Song" which garnered an Academy Award nomination. After WW II he went to Europe where he produced an Academy Award-winning documentary, "Climbing

Astaire

the Matterhorn." He returned to Hollywood in 1965 and began producing the "Matt Helm" spy spoof series, starring Dean Martin. Among his films are: GENGHIS KHAN; STRANGE VOYAGE; AVALANCHE (1946); HIGH CONQUEST; SIXTEEN FATHOMS DEEP; THE MAN ON THE EIFFEL TOWER; NEW MEXICO; SLAUGHTER TRAIL; THE BLACK KNIGHT; HELL BELOW ZERO; PARATROOPER; COCKLESHELL HEROES; PRIZE OF GOLD; ZARAK; FIRE DOWN BELOW; HIGH FLIGHT; PICKUP ALLEY; THE MAN INSIDE; TANK FORCE; THE BANDIT OF ZHOBE; THE ROAD TO HONG KONG; THE LONG SHIPS; THE SILENCERS; MURDERERS' ROW; HAMMERHEAD; THE WRECKING CREW; THE DESPERADOES; CROMWELL.

Allen, Vera

Died 10 August 1987, Croton-on-Hudson, N.Y.; age 89.

Stage/Film/Radio/TV Actress

Graduated from Barnard College and began her stage career in the early 1920s, appearing in "The Dybbuk," "The Critic," and "Grand Street Follies" at the Neighborhood Playhouse in New York. On Broadway she appeared in "The Silver Cord," "Susan and God," "The Philadelphia Story," "At Home Abroad," "The Show Is On," "The Two Mrs. Carrols," and "Ladies of the Corridor." On screen she played opposite Will Rogers in DOCTOR BULL. She was active in Actors Equity and was a president of the American Theater Wing.

Amen, Carol

Died 11 July 1987, Sunnyside, Calif.; age 53.

Writer

Died 10 days after holding a "She Lives Until She Dies" party for friends at her home. Wrote a three-page story called "Last Testament," published in 1981, describing how a small Northern California town coped after a nuclear explosion. It was adapted into the 1983 film TESTAMENT.

Amendt, Rudolph

Died 27 March 1987, Woodland Hills, Calif.; age 91.

Stage/Film Actor

Born in Germany, he began his career with the Rhinehart Theaters in Berlin following his graduation from Heidelberg. He came to Hollywood in 1930 and appeared in many films, usually as a German military officer, until his retirement in 1963. Among his films are STAMBOUL QUEST; WHEN STRANGERS MARRY; THE FOUNTAIN; THE GOLDEN ARROW; WE'RE IN THE LEGION NOW; THE MAD EMPRESS.

Anand, Inder Raj

Died 6 March 1987, Bombay, India; age 68.

Playwright/Screenwriter

Starting as a publicist at the Bombay Talkies in 1944, he became a writer for Prithvi Theaters. Most notable among his plays is "Deewar." His work included nearly 50 scripts for Raj Kapoor's films, as well as dialog for numerous others.

Andre, Michel

Died 10 Nov. 1987, Paris, France; age 74.

Actor/Playwright

The son of actor Marcel Andre, he was born in Paris in 1912 and played in the company of Louis Jouvet, under whom he studied. His theatrical career was interrupted by WW II, during which he was held in a German prison camp. From this experience he wrote the scenario for and acted in THE ESCAPEES, which was included in the 1955 Cannes festival program. His farce A QUIET CORNER was awarded the Tristan Bernard prize in 1954, and he appeared in the 1948 production of THE IDIOT.

Anstey, Edgar F.

Died 26 Sept. 1987, London, England; age 80.

Documentarian

His career, beginning in the 1930s, included four years with the old "March of Time" theatrical news documentaries, first as an anchor of London operations, and then as foreign editor based in New York. For a brief period of time he served as a film critic for *The Spectator*, a weekly journal of commentary, and was in charge of the film unit of the British Transport Commission, one of whose propaganda efforts, directed by John Schlesinger, was a 1961 profile of London's Waterloo rail station called TERMINUS, which won the Best Short prize at the Venice Film Festival. Along with John Grierson, Arthur Elton, Basil Wright, and others, he was one of the revered pioneers of the British documentary school famed for its impressionistic techniques and gritty realism. His WILD WINGS won the 1966 Academy Award for best nonfiction short. Other prize-winning documentaries were JOURNEY INTO SPRING, BETWEEN THE TIDES, and UNDER NIGHT STREETS.

Argento, Salvatore

Died 19 April 1987, Rome, Italy; age 73.

Film Producer

As a public relations executive for Unitalia, the government organization for promoting cinema exports, he was a key figure in introducing and popularizing Italian films and performers around the world. He first entered production as a line producer working for Dino De Laurentiis. Other films he coproduced include KISS THE GIRLS AND MAKE THEM DIE; ARABELLA; COMMANDMENTS FOR A GANGSTER; PROBABILITY ZERO. Under the Seda banner he produced the distinctive thrillers of his son Dario, including THE BIRD WITH THE CRYSTAL PLUMAGE; CAT O'NINE TAILS; FOUR FLIES ON GREY VELVET; DEEP RED; SUSPIRIA. He later formed Sigma and Intersound, which produced Dario's films INFERNO and TENEBRAE.

Arliss, Leslie

Died 30 Dec. 1987, London, England; age 86.

Screenwriter/Director

Began as a journalist in South Africa before returning to England and collaborating on screenplays for the Elstree lot. Pre-WW II writing credits are TONIGHT'S THE NIGHT; ORDERS IS ORDERS; JACK AHOY; HEAT WAVE; RHODES OF AFRICA; PASTOR HALL. He switched to directing in 1941 with THE FARMER'S WIFE; IDOL OF PARIS; THE NIGHT HAS EYES; THE WOMAN'S ANGLE; A MAN ABOUT THE HOUSE; MISS TULIP STAYS THE NIGHT; SEE HOW THEY RUN. He produced as well as directed and wrote SAINTS AND SINNERS. His other films include: JOSSER ON THE RIVER; WHY SAPS LEAVE HOME; MY OLD DUTCH; ROAD HOUSE; ALL IN; EVERYBODY DANCE; WHERE THERE'S A WILL; WINDBAG THE SAILOR; SEZ O'REILLY TO MACNAB; COME ON GEORGE; TOO DANGEROUS TO LIVE; FOR FREEDOM; THE SECOND MR. BUSH; SOUTH AMERICAN GEORGE; TERROR HOUSE; THE MAN IN GREY; THE SAINT MEETS THE TIGER; SOMEWHERE IN FRANCE; THE WICKED LADY; A LADY SURRENDERS; TOP OF THE FORM; DESTINATION MILAN; FOREVER MY HEART.

Arnaud, Georges [Henri Girard]

Born 16 July 1917, France, Died 4 March 1987, Barcelona, Spain.

Writer

Author of *The Wages of Fear*, a novel about men who drove nitroglycerine-laden trucks over dangerous roads. The novel sold an estimated 2 million copies worldwide and was turned into a film classic by director Georges-Henri Clouzot which won the Grand Prix of the 1953 Cannes Film Festival. Accused of murdering his father, Georges Girard, Foreign Ministry official and noted historian, and an aunt in 1941, he spent 19 months in jail before being declared innocent in 1943. This experience left him so embittered with the police and judicial system he stayed away from Paris for many years. He later became a leading supporter of the Algerian independence movement during its war against France in the 1950s and was given a suspended two-year prison term for supporting the Algerian rebels. He wrote several other novels and travel books, and, at the time of his death, was working on a novel, *An Executioner in the Streets*, tentatively slated for publication in September 1987. Films he worked on include SIN ON THE BEACH; THE WAGES OF FEAR; SORCERER.

Ashman, Gene

Died 23 Oct. 1987, Burbank, Calif; age 58.

Costumer

A career which started at Western Costume in 1952 culminated in his becoming president of Motion Picture Costumers Local 705 at the time of his death. He worked at various studios over the years and headed the costume department at EUE Screen Gems for 14 years. Among the movies he worked on are HEAD; GETTING STRAIGHT; THE LIBERATION OF L.B. JONES. He was head costumer throughout the run of "The Monkees" television series and last worked on "The Bronx Zoo."

Astaire, Fred [Frederick Austerlitz]

Born 10 May 1899, Omaha, Nebr.; died 22 June 1987, Los Angeles, Calif.

Dancer/Actor/Choreographer

The man who George Balanchine called "the most interesting, the most inventive, the most elegant dancer of our time" began his 50-year dancing career at age seven touring the vaudeville circuit with his sister Adele as a dancing partner. Their first appearance on film is believed to be in 1915 with Mary Pickford in FANCHON THE CRICKET. Their act broke up after his sister's marriage. He was given a small part opposite Joan Crawford in DANCING LADY even though the famous verdict brought by his first screen test was: "Can't act. Slightly bald. Can dance a little." He next landed a role costarring with Ginger Rogers in FLYING DOWN TO RIO (the first movie wherein he wore a top hat and tails). In 1946 Astaire announced his retirement, but two years later he replaced the ailing Gene Kelly as Judy Garland's partner in a triumphant comeback, EASTER PARADE. He appeared in six Emmy Award-winning specials and made his dramatic debut in Stanley Kramer's ON THE BEACH. He received an Academy Award nomination for best supporting actor in THE TOWERING INFERNO. In 1949 he was honored with a special Academy Award for "his unique contribution to films." The American Film Institute presented him with its Lifetime Achievement Award in 1981 and his last performance was in the 1982 movie GHOST STORY. He was a brilliant choreographer whose unstinting perfectionism set the standard for film musicals. Among his films are: THE GAY DIVORCEE; ROBERTA; TOP HAT; FOLLOW THE FLEET; SWING TIME; A DAMSEL IN DISTRESS; SHALL WE DANCE; CAREFREE; THE STORY OF VERNON AND IRENE CASTLE; BROADWAY MELODY OF 1940; SECOND CHORUS; YOU'LL NEVER GET RICH; HOLIDAY INN; YOU WERE NEVER LOVELIER; THE SKY'S THE LIMIT; YOLANDA AND THE THIEF; ZIEGFELD FOLLIES; BLUE SKIES; THE BARKLEYS OF BROADWAY; LET'S DANCE; THREE LITTLE WORDS; ROYAL WEDDING; THE BELLE OF NEW YORK; THE BAND WAGON; DADDY LONG LEGS; FUNNY FACE; SILK STOCKINGS; THE PLEASURE OF HIS COMPANY; THE NOTORIOUS LANDLADY; PARIS WHEN IT SIZZLES; FINIAN'S RAINBOW; MIDAS RUN; THE AMAZING DOBERMANS; THE PURPLE TAXI; GHOST STORY.

Astor, Mary [Lucile Langhanke]

Born 3 May 1906, Quincy, Ill.; died 25 Sept. 1987, Woodland Hills, Calif.

Film Actress/Writer

Made her silent film debut in 1920 with the Famous Players-Lasky and made more than 100 movies over a 45-year period, winning a supporting-actress Oscar for her role opposite Bette Davis in THE GREAT LIE. She was best known for her role as the duplicitous Brigid O'Shaughnessy in THE MALTESE FALCON with Humphrey Bogart. Her private life was as dramatic as her movie career and in 1936 she was the center of a scandal involving custody of her four-year-old daughter. She was married three times and plagued by family members who lived lavishly on her salary. Her personal problems and financial pressures were worsened by a long-time drinking problem. In 1959, at the urging of a priest-psychologist who was her therapist, she published her autobiography *My Story* which was praised for its style and uncompromising insights. Encouraged, she began writing novels and in 1971 completed a successful memoir on movie making, *A Life on Film*, wherein she deplored a "poverty of spirit" in many contemporary movies, writing that "whatever we did—we old movie makers—we gave people a lot of fun. Through depressions and wars and calamities, we gave them the sense of glory, of a future that would be braver than today." She retired to the Motion Picture Country Home in Woodland Hills in 1974. Her films include: HOLIDAY (1930); LADIES LOVE BRUTES; THE LASH; RUNAWAY BRIDE; BEHIND OFFICE DOORS; OTHER MEN'S WOMEN; THE ROYAL BED; SIN SHIP; SMART WOMAN (1931); WHITE SHOULDERS; THE LOST SQUADRON; MEN OF CHANCE; RED DUST; A SUCCESSFUL CALAMITY; THOSE WE LOVE; CONVENTION CITY; JENNIE GERHARDT; THE KENNEL MURDER CASE; THE LITTLE GIANT; THE WORLD CHANGES; THE CASE OF THE HOWLING DOG; EASY TO LOVE; THE MAN WITH TWO FACES; RETURN OF THE TERROR; UPPER WORLD; DINKY; I AM A THIEF; MAN OF IRON; PAGE MISS GLORY; RED HOT TIRES; STRAIGHT FROM THE HEART; AND SO THEY WERE MARRIED; DODSWORTH; LADY FROM NOWHERE; THE MURDER OF DR. HARRIGAN; TRAPPED BY TELEVISION; THE HURRICANE; THE PRISONER OF ZENDA; LISTEN, DARLING; NO TIME TO MARRY; PARADISE FOR THREE; THERE'S ALWAYS A WOMAN; WOMAN AGAINST WOMAN; MIDNIGHT; BRIGHAM YOUNG—FRONTIERSMAN; TURNABOUT; THE GREAT LIE; ACROSS THE PACIFIC; IN THIS OUR LIFE; THE PALM BEACH STORY; THOUSANDS CHEER; YOUNG IDEAS; BLONDE FEVER; MEET ME IN ST. LOUIS; CLAUDIA AND DAVID; CASS TIMBERLANE; CYNTHIA; DESERT FURY; ACT OF VIOLENCE; ANY NUMBER CAN PLAY; LITTLE WOMEN; A KISS BEFORE DYING; THE POWER AND THE PRIZE; THE DEVIL'S HAIRPIN; THIS HAPPY FEELING; STRANGER IN MY ARMS; RETURN TO PEYTON PLACE; HUSH . . . HUSH SWEET CHARLOTTE. Among her silent films are: JOHN SMITH; THE MAN WHO PLAYED GOD; SECOND FIDDLE; SUCCESS; BEAU BRUMMEL; THE FIGHTING AMERICAN; THE FIGHTING COWARD; INEZ FROM HOLLYWOOD; OH DOCTOR; THE PRICE OF A PARTY; DON Q, SON OF ZORRO; THE PACE THAT THRILLS; DON JUAN; FOREVER AFTER; THE ROUGH RIDERS; THE SEA TIGER; THE SUNSET DERBY; NEW YEAR'S EVE; THE BRIGHT SHAWL; HOLLYWOOD; PURITAN PASSIONS; UNGUARDED WOMEN; ENTICEMENT; PLAYING WITH SOULS; SCARLET SAINT; HIGH STEPPERS; THE WISE GUY; NO PLACE TO GO; ROSE OF THE GOLDEN WEST; TWO ARABIAN KNIGHTS; DRESSED TO KILL; DRY MARTINI; HEART TO HEART; ROMANCE OF THE UNDERWORLD; SAILORS' WIVES; THREE-RING MARRIAGE; THE WOMAN FROM HELL.

Attaway, Ruth

Died 21 Sept. 1987, New York, N.Y., age 77.

Stage/Film Actress

Born in Greenville, Mississippi, she graduated from University of Illinois. Made her Broadway debut in 1936 in "You Can't Take It with You." Appeared on Broadway, off-Broadway, and in summer stock productions for 40 years. Member of the Repertory Society of Lincoln Center from 1964 to 1967 and the first director of the New York Players Guild, a black repertory theater company formed in New York in 1945. Worked in radio and television and between jobs worked as a social worker with the American Red Cross and the state of New York. Films include PORGY AND BESS; RAINTREE COUNTY; THE TAKING OF PELHAM ONE, TWO, THREE; THE PRESIDENT'S LADY; THE YOUNG DON'T CRY; PIE IN THE SKY; CONRACK; BEING THERE.

Avakian, Aram

Died 17 Jan. 1987, New York, N.Y., age 60.

Film Editor/Director

Born in New York, a graduate of Yale University, he also attended the Sorbonne in Paris, France. Known primarily for his editing of Edward R. Murrow's "See It Now" series, he also codirected, with Bert Stern, as well as edited "Jazz on a Summer Day," one of the first feature-length music festival documentaries. Films he edited include: THE MIRACLE WORKER; LILITH; ANDY; MICKEY ONE; YOU'RE A BIG BOY NOW; THE NEXT MAN; HONEYSUCKLE ROSE. He cowrote (with Terry Southern) and directed END OF THE ROAD, starring his wife at the time, Dorothy Tristan, and directed LAD: A DOG; COPS AND ROBBERS; 11 HARROWHOUSE. Head of the film department at the State University College at Purchase from 1983 to 1986.

Bailey, Bruce R.

Died 16 June 1987, Burbank, Calif.; age mid-80s.

Still Photographer

Began his career in the 1920s as an extra and bit player in the silents WINGS and WHAT PRICE GLORY, then turned to publicity photography for films and newspapers. In the 1950s he was a newsreel cameraman but switched to still photography, and at one time was photo editor for *Screen Guide* magazine. He was the recipient of a special Academy Award in 1955 for his development of the process that allowed the restoration of the historical "paper films" for the Motion Picture Academy and Library of Congress. Among the movies he worked on are, THE SAND PEBBLES; THE ONLY GAME IN TOWN; SILVER STREAK; THE DRIVER.

Bailey, Sherwood

Born 6 Aug. 1923, Long Beach, Calif.; died 6 Aug. 1987, Newport Beach, Calif.

Actor

Appeared as the freckle-faced, red-haired Spud in the OUR GANG movies from 1922 to 1944. Films include: TOO MANY PARENTS; YOUNG THOMAS EDISON; THE BIG STAMPEDE; THE MYSTERIOUS RIDER; THE LOUDSPEAKER; PADDY O'DAY; THE DEVIL IS A SISSY; GIRL LOVES BOY; QUALITY STREET; SHALL WE DANCE; QUICK MONEY; KING OF THE UNDERWORLD. Grew up to become a civil engineer.

Baird, Bil

Died 18 March 1987, New York, N.Y.; age 82.

Puppeteer

He studied stage design and became an apprentice to leading puppeteer Tony Sarg in the late 1920s. Appeared with his creations Charlemagne the Lion and Slugger Ryan on Jack Paar's "The Morning Show," Ed Sullivan, and Sid Caesar's "Show of Shows." Received an Emmy nomination for the 1958 "Art Carney Meets Peter and the Wolf." His puppets appeared as the dancing goats in THE SOUND OF MUSIC.

Baldwin, James

Born 2 Aug. 1924, Harlem, New York, N.Y.; died 30 Nov. 1987, St Paul De Vence, France.

Writer

GO TELL IT ON THE MOUNTAIN (1984) is based on his first novel (which was grew out of his early experiences as a young storefront preacher) originally published in 1953. Some of his other important books are *The Fire Next Time*, *Notes of a Native Son*, *Tell Me How Long the Train's Been Gone*, *Evidence of Things Not Seen*, *Harlem Quartet*, as well as various volumes of essays and a play, "Blues for Mr. Charlie." Was the recipient of various awards, active in civil rights, and moved to France as a protest against his perception of racism in the US.

Baring, Aubrey

Born 3 May 1912, London, England; died June 1987, London, England.

Producer

Astor

Blakely

Served with the Royal Air Force in WW II and was an early associate of Alexander Korda, producing British films FOOLS RUSH IN; SNOWBOUND; CAIRO ROAD; THE SPIDER AND THE FLY; APPOINTMENT IN LONDON; SO LITTLE TIME; THE GOLDEN MASK; THEY WHO DARE; THE KEY (1958); TROUBLE IN THE SKY; THE WRONG ARM OF THE LAW; ABOMINABLE SNOWMAN; CONE OF SILENCE. Former chairman of Twickenham Studios, he left the film industry to become head of an electronics firm.

Barnes, Paul

Died 19 Jan. 1987, Burbank, Calif.; age 61.

Production Designer/Art Director

His artwork was first noticed in a college production by an executive of a CBS station and he was hired and quickly transferred to network operations in New York. Noted for his art direction in the formative years of TV; his work covered seven seasons on "Your Hit Parade," three seasons each for "The Bell Telephone Hour" and "The Garry Moore Show," and two for "The Perry Como Hour." He won the first Emmy given for art direction on a variety show for his work during the 1956 "Hit Parade" season, that series' first year in color. Collected nine Emmy nominations for his 11 years of art direction on "The Carol Burnett Show." His films include JAMBOREE, LET'S ROCK, and THE LAST MILE, on which he was production designer.

Bass, Alfie

Born 8 Apr. 1921, London, England; died 15 July 1987, London, England.

Comic Actor

He ran the gamut from Cockney to Shakespeare, working on the stage in "Hamlet," "King John," "The Merchant of Venice," "Taming of the Shrew," and "The Winter's Tale," and performing in the films ALFIE, MOONRAKER, and THE LAVENDER HILL MOB. Born in the Cockney heartland of London, he first worked professionally in a 1939 Unity Theater production of "Plant in the Sun" with Paul Robeson, and gained early screen experience during the war in British army documentaries. Other movies include: HELL; HEAVEN OR HOBOKEN; JOHNNY FRENCHMAN; HOLIDAY CAMP; THE MONKEY'S PAW; BOYS IN BROWN; THE HASTY HEART; IT ALWAYS RAINS ON SUNDAY; MAN ON THE RUN; THE GALLOPING MAJOR; HIGH TREASON; POOL OF LONDON; BRANDY FOR THE PARSON; FOUR AGAINST FATE; MADE IN HEAVEN; OUTPOST IN MALAYA; TREASURE HUNT; YOU CAN'T BEAT THE IRISH; TOP OF THE FORM; BLACKOUT; MAKE ME AN OFFER; THE PASSING STRANGER; THE NIGHT MY NUMBER CAME UP; THE SQUARE RING; SVENGALI; THE ANGEL WHO PAWNED HER HARP; BEHIND THE HEADLINES; CASH ON DELIVERY; CHILD IN THE HOUSE; JUMPING FOR JOY; A KID FOR TWO FARTHINGS; A TOUCH OF THE SUN; CARRY ON ADMIRAL; NO ROAD BACK; TIME IS MY ENEMY; HELL DRIVERS; I ONLY ASKED; A TALE OF TWO CITIES; THE MILLIONAIRESS; HELP; A FUNNY THING HAPPENED ON THE WAY TO THE FORUM; THE SANDWICH MAN; CARNABY, M.D.; THE FEARLESS VAMPIRE KILLERS, OR PARDON ME BUT YOUR TEETH ARE IN MY NECK; A CHALLENGE FOR ROBIN HOOD; THE FIXER; UP THE JUNCTION; THE MAGNIFICENT SEVEN DEADLY SINS; REVENGE OF THE PINK PANTHER.

Baum, Lal

Died 21 July 1987, Los Angeles, Calif.; age 49.

Actor/Producer/Director

Acted in the TV series "All in the Family," and "High Chapparal," and produced and directed the documentary "Run Up Pikes Peak." Appeared in the film CHANDLER (1971).

Beard, Cecil

Died 28 Dec. 1987, Silver City, N. Mex.; age 79.

Film Cartoonist

A Texas native, he moved to Hollywood in 1937 and began a career with Walt Disney, working on such animated features as SNOW WHITE and BAMBI. He also served as secretary of the Screen Cartoonists Guild before moving to New Mexico in 1979, where he continued working as a freelance artist.

Bennet, Spencer Gordon

Died 8 Oct. 1987, Santa Monica, Calif., age 94.

Director

In his 30-year career he directed more than 100 movies, most of them action-packed serials that kept crowds coming back to theaters to follow the adventures of their heros. With co-director Thomas Carr, he directed the first SUPERMAN films in 1948. His other enduring film characters included Batman, Robin, and Captain Video. He was born in New York City and got into the business as a stunt man. Among his films: NIGHT ALARM; ACROSS THE PLAINS; OKLAHOMA TERROR; RIDERS OF THE FRONTIER; THE FUGITIVE SHERIFF; HEROES OF THE RANGE; RANGER COURAGE; THE RANGERS STEP IN; RECKLESS RANGER; RIO GRANDE RANGER; RIDING THE CHEROKEE TRAIL; MOJAVE FIREBRAND; TUCSON RAIDERS; REQUIEM FOR A GUNFIGHTER; ROGUE OF THE RIO GRANDE; 99 WOUNDS; JUSTICE TAKES A HOLIDAY; FEROCIOUS PAL; THE FIGHTING ROOKIE; GET THAT MAN; RESCUE SQUAD; WESTERN COURAGE; THE CATTLE THIEF; THE UNKNOWN RANGER; LAW OF THE RANGER; WESTBOUND STAGE; THEY RAID BY NIGHT; LONE TEXAS RANGER; SAVAGE MUTINY. Among his silent films, BEHOLD THE MAN; THE FIGHTING MARINE; HAWK OF THE HILLS; MARKED MONEY.

Bennett, Michael [Michael Bennett DiFiglia]

Died 2 July 1987, Tucson, Ariz.; age 44.

Stage Director/Choreographer

Mastermind behind "A Chorus Line," the longest-running musical in Broadway history.

Benson, Harry C.

Died 24 Apr. 1987, Los Angeles, Calif.; age 75.

Actor

Entered acting after a long career in the liquor business, playing mostly grandfather-type roles in television shows like "Fairie Tale Theater," "Hell Town," "The Dukes of Hazzard," "Gidget," "Finders of Lost Loves." He also had a role in the film ICE PIRATES.

Bernard, Bruno

Died 3 June 1987, Los Angeles, Calif.; age 75.

Photographer

He was a pin-up publisher and film-lore scholar who escaped Hitler's Germany in 1937. After earning a doctorate in criminal psychology, he discovered he could make a living at his hobby, photography, in which he had no formal training. He had two good teachers, he claimed in an interview: "Trial and error." Among the most famous of his photographs was his shot of Marilyn Monroe, skirt swirling around her legs while she stood on a subway grid in New York City, a promo for the movie THE SEVEN YEAR ITCH. He was credited with introducing Monroe to the agent who negotiated her first picture contract with 20th Century-Fox. Years later she signed one of his 10 books on photography, "Remember Bernie, you started it all." Known as "Bernard of Hollywood," he spent three decades photographing most of Hollywood's major personalities. In 1986 he became the first still photographer to be honored by the Academy of Motion Picture Arts and Sciences, where a retrospective of his work was shown. "Requiem for Marilyn," a book he compiled, is due to be published in 1988.

Blache, Irwin

Died 16 Jan. 1987, New Orleans, Louisiana; age 77.

Cameraman

He had more than 200 camera-crew credits, including TOYS IN THE ATTIC; MANDINGO; BLINDFOLD; THE HORSE SOLDIERS; THE CINCINNATI KID; CREATURE FROM THE BLACK LAGOON; THE GREATEST SHOW ON EARTH; THE ALAMO.

Blakely, Colin

Born 23 Sept. 1930, Bangor, County Down, Northern Ireland; died 7 May 1987, London, England.

Actor

Born in Northern Ireland, he worked at theaters in Belfast and Wales and made his first stage appearance in London at the Royal Court Theater in 1959 in Sean O'Casey's "Cock-a-Doodle-Dandy." One of his last appearances was in "Paradise Postponed," a British television mini-series based on the book by John Mortimer. He had appeared in the early 1960s with the Royal Shakespeare Company in "As You Like It" and "Richard III," and spent the rest of that decade with the National Theatre. Among his films are: SATURDAY NIGHT AND SUNDAY MORNING; THE HELLIONS; THE PASSWORD IS COURAGE; THIS SPORTING LIFE; THE LONG SHIPS; NEVER PUT IT IN WRITING; UNDERWORLD INFORMERS; THE COUNTERFEIT CONSTABLE; A MAN FOR ALL SEASONS; THE SPY WITH A COLD NOSE; THE DAY THE FISH CAME OUT; CHARLIE BUBBLES; THE VENGEANCE OF SHE; ALFRED THE GREAT; DECLINE AND FALL . . . OF A BIRD WATCHER; THE PRIVATE LIFE OF SHERLOCK HOLMES; SOMETHING TO HIDE; YOUNG WINSTON; THE NATIONAL HEALTH, OR NURSE NORTON'S AFFAIR; MURDER ON THE ORIENT EXPRESS; GALILEO; THE PINK PANTHER STRIKES AGAIN; EQUUS; THE BIG SLEEP; ALL THINGS BRIGHT AND BEAUTIFUL; THE DOGS OF WAR; NIJINSKY; LOOPHOLE; EVIL UNDER THE SUN; RED MONARCH.

Blakely, Gene

Died 23 Nov. 1987, Creston, Iowa; age 66.

Stage/Film Actor

Appeared in Chicago theater before debuting on Broadway in "Brighten the Corner" (1945); other plays include "The Traitor," "Mr. Barry's Etchings," "A Mighty Man Is He," "Calculated Risk," "Weekend," "Red Gloves," "The Male Animal," "The Desperate Hours," "Teahouse of the August Moon." His films include BATTLE OF THE CORAL SEA; EVERYTHING'S DUCKY; THAT DARN CAT; THE SAND PEBBLES; BEACH RED; THE PRISONER OF SECOND AVENUE; USED CARS as well as the TV-film "September Gun"; appeared in a regular part on the 1953-1954 daytime soap, "Three Steps to Heaven" and had occasional parts on such series as "Bewitched," "The Mary Tyler Moore Show," and "Maude."

Blasetti, Alessandro

Born 3 July 1900, Rome, Italy; died 2 Feb. 1987, Rome, Italy.

Director

Born in Rome and educated as a lawyer, this versatile stylist was, with Mario Camerini, one of the leading Italian filmmakers of the 1930s and a patriarchal figure on the Italian cinema scene in his later years. After law school, his interest turned to journalism and he became film critic of the daily *L'Impero*, later starting his own monthly, *Lo Schermo*, which became *Cinematografo* in 1928. At the same time he joined forces with the likes of Goffredo Allesandrini and Umberto Barbaro to form the Augustus cooperative which produced his first picture, SOLE. In 1952 he introduced the genre of the film broken down into episodes, which became a staple of Italian production during the next two decades. Among his movies are: AN ADVENTURE OF SALVATOR ROSA; BELLISSIMA; FATHER'S DILEMMA; TIMES GONE BY; LUCKY TO BE A WOMAN; THREE FABLES OF LOVE; A VERY HANDY MAN; FABIOLA; TOO BAD SHE'S BAD.

Bloch, Bertram

Died 12 June 1987, New York, N.Y.; age 95.

Playwright/Novelist/Story Editor

Continued to live in Manhattan while working as Eastern story director for Fox and MGM, responsible for buying the stories that ultimately became such movie classics as GRAND HOTEL, ALL ABOUT EVE, and BUS STOP. He was co-author, with George Brewer, Jr., of the Broadway play "Dark Victory," which became a Warner Bros. picture. In addition, he co-authored with Thomas Mitchell "Glory Hallelujah" in 1926 and on his own wrote "Even in Egypt," "Jewel Robbery," and "Spring Again." He also wrote the novels *Mrs. Hulett*, *The Little Laundress*, *The Fearful Knight*, and *The Only Nellie Fayle*. He was a cofounder of the Screen Writers Guild and a longtime member of the Dramatists Guild.

Bocchicchio, Alfeo

Died 18 Apr. 1987, Woodland Hills, Calif.

Art Director

Born in Italy, raised in Pittsburgh, trained as an architect, he worked as a carpenter at Republic Studios upon moving to Los Angeles. He was a designer at Disneyland, designed the MCA building in Toronto, and supervised the interior design for MCA's Universal City headquarters. Though most of his work was for television, films he worked on are: SNOWFIRE; LITTLE CIGARS; SCREAM BLACULA SCREAM; SLAUGHTER'S BIG RIP-OFF; RING OF TERROR.

Boland, Joseph

Died 21 June 1987; age 83.

Actor

He appeared on the original "Tonight Show" with Steve Allen and in "Love of Life" and "Playhouse 90." His movie roles include parts in ADVISE AND CONSENT and THE ROPE DANCERS.

Bolger, Ray [Raymond Wallace Bolger]

Born 10 Jan. 1904, Boston, Mass.; died 15 Jan. 1987, Los Angeles, Calif.

Dancer/Comedian

The last major surviving cast member of the 1939 classic THE WIZARD OF OZ, his stage, screen, and TV career spanned six decades. He first performed in an amateur show put on by the insurance company for which he worked. Stardom came in 1936 when he appeared in "On Your Toes," a Broadway musical choreographed by George Balanchine. This brought him to Hollywood's attention and film appearances in THE GREAT ZIEGFELD; ROSALIE; SWEETHEARTS; THE WIZARD OF OZ; SUNNY. His last feature was THAT'S DANCING (1985), in which he narrated a scarecrow dance scene from the WIZARD OF OZ. It was in the Broadway hit "Where's Charley?" that he immortalized the song "Once in Love with Amy," which became his signature song. He was elected to the Theater Hall of Fame in 1980 and didn't stop performing until 1984 when his leg gave out after a performance. Films include: FOUR JACKS AND A JILL; FOREVER AND A DAY; STAGE DOOR CANTEEN; THE HARVEY GIRLS; LOOK FOR THE SILVER LINING; WHERE'S CHARLEY?; APRIL IN PARIS; BABES IN TOYLAND; THE DAYDREAMER; THE ENTERTAINER; JUST YOU AND ME, KID; THE RUNNER STUMBLES.

Bolger

Bond, Henry

Born 5 Jan. 1927, Long Beach, Calif.; died 3 Jan. 1987, Hollywood, Calif.

Fan

A diminutive man, instantly recognizable in his baseball cap, multicolor shirt, and string tie, he was known as "Preview Henry" to preview audiences and studio executives alike. He became a fixture at practically every preview, usually accompanied by his 80-year-old mother, who died six years ago after being beaten by intruders who broke into their Hollywood home. He appeared in three pictures: as a crowd extra in IT'S A MAD, MAD, MAD, MAD WORLD and HELLO, DOLLY and as an onlooker watching an operation in YOUNG DOCTORS IN LOVE.

Booker, Bernice Ingalls

Died 25 Feb. 1987, Jacksonville, Fla.; age 91.

Silent Film Actress

She was discovered along with Theda Bara in Ohio in the early 1900s, and went on to costar opposite Bara in five silent motion pictures for Fox Films before it became 20th Century-Fox. Three of the movies are in the film archives of the Museum of Modern Art in New York, the most significant of which is A FOOL THERE WAS, touted as being comparable in importance to D.W. Griffith's BIRTH OF A NATION. Her other films include: BUTTERFLY ON THE WHEEL; M'LISS; GODMAN and BIRTH OF A RACE. She was a great-great-cousin of Laura Ingalls Wilder, author of the classic books on which the series "Little House on the Prairie" is based. Her son, Bob Booker, is a TV producer, packager, and writer.

Bookwalter, DeVeren

Died 23 July 1987, New York, N.Y.; age 47.

Actor/Director

He produced, directed, and played the title role in a 1975-76 version of "Cyrano de Bergerac" at the Globe Theater, for which he received three awards from the Los Angeles Drama Critics Circle. He made his New York professional debut in 1962 in a production of "Macbeth" by the New York Shakespeare Festival. He made film appearances in THE OMEGA MAN and THE ENFORCER and performed on television.

Borgani, Nick

Died 11 March 1987.

Actor

Appeared in CASBAH; SEPTEMBER AFFAIR; ST. VALENTINE'S DAY MASSACRE.

Bowers, William

Born 17 Jan. 1916, Las Cruces, N. Mex.; died 27 Mar. 1987, Woodland Hills, Calif.

Screenwriter

Was a reporter for the Long Beach *Independent-Press-Telegram* when he wrote his first stage play, "Where Do We Go From Here," which led to writing for radio in New York. He turned to film writing after working as Hollywood correspondent for the National Education Association and received two Academy Award nominations, for THE GUNFIGHTER and THE SHEEPMAN. At the urging of his friend Francis Ford Coppola, he appeared as an actor in one film, GODFATHER II, playing the role of the chairman of the Senate investigating committee. Films include: MY FAVORITE SPY; SEVEN DAYS LEAVE; ADVENTURES OF A ROOKIE; HIGHER AND HIGHER; SING YOUR WAY HOME; THE FABULOUS SUZANNE; NIGHT AND DAY; LADIES' MAN; SOMETHING IN THE WIND; THE WEB; THE WISTFUL WIDOW OF WAGON GAP; BLACK BART; THE COUNTESS OF MONTE CRISTO; JUNGLE PATROL; LARCENY; RIVER LADY; THE GAL WHO TOOK THE WEST; CONVICTED; MRS. O'MALLEY AND MR. MALONE; CRY DANGER; THE MOB; ASSIGNMENT PARIS; SPLIT SECOND; SHE COULDN'T SAY NO; FIVE AGAINST THE HOUSE; TIGHT SPOT; THE BEST THINGS IN LIFE ARE FREE; MY MAN GODFREY (1957); IMITATION GENERAL; THE LAW AND JAKE WADE; -30-; ALIAS JESSE JAMES; THE LAST TIME I SAW ARCHIE; ADVANCE TO THE REAR; WAY . . . WAY OUT; THE RIDE TO HANGMAN'S TREE; SUPPORT YOUR LOCAL SHERIFF.

Breslow, Lou

Born 18 July 1900, Boston, Mass.; died 10 Nov. 1987, Woodland Hills, Calif.

Screenwriter

Although born in Boston, he came to California as a youngster and worked as an extra. After jobs as cameraman and story consultant, he rose to become one of the major screenwriters (first for Fox/20th Century, then Paramount) during the golden days of Hollywood for such top personalities as the Marx Brothers, Laurel and Hardy, Abbott and Costello, W.C. Fields, Red Skelton, Bob Hope, Ronald

Reagan, and the Three Stooges. His film credits (either for original scripting or in collaboration specializing in humor) include: DUCK SOUP; HORSE FEATHERS (the previous two went uncredited); NO GREATER LOVE (1932); RACKETY RAX; SITTING PRETTY (1933); GIFT OF GAB; NO MORE WOMEN (1934); MUSIC IS MAGIC; PADDY O'DAY; SILK HAT KID; $10 RAISE; THIS IS THE LIFE (1935); CHARLIE CHAN AT THE RACE TRACK; FIFTEEN MAIDEN LANE; HIGH TENSION; LITTLE MISS NOBODY; THIRTY SIX HOURS TO KILL; BIG TOWN GIRL; DANGEROUSLY YOURS (1937); THE HOLY TERROR (1937); MIDNIGHT TAXI (1937); ONE MILE FROM HEAVEN; SING AND BE HAPPY; TIME OUT FOR ROMANCE; BATTLE OF BROADWAY; CITY STREETS (1938); FIVE OF A KIND; INTERNATIONAL SETTLEMENT; MR. MOTO TAKES A CHANCE; UP THE RIVER (1938); HOLLYWOOD CAVALCADE; IT COULD HAPPEN TO YOU (1939); PACK UP YOUR TROUBLES (1939); 20,000 MEN A YEAR; SAILOR'S LADY; SHOOTING HIGH; GREAT GUNS; SLEEPERS WEST; A-HAUNTING WE WILL GO; BLONDIE GOES TO COLLEGE; WHISPERING GHOSTS; GOOD LUCK, MR. YATES; THE HEAT'S ON; SOMETHING TO SHOUT ABOUT; FOLLOW THE BOYS (1944); ABBOTT AND COSTELLO IN HOLLYWOOD; MURDER, HE SAYS; MERTON OF THE MOVIES; SECOND CHANCE (1947); DON'T TRUST YOUR HUSBAND; ON OUR MERRY WAY; AND BABY MAKES THREE; NEVER A DULL MOMENT (1950); BEDTIME FOR BONZO; MY FAVORITE SPY (1951); REUNION IN RENO; YOU NEVER CAN TELL (1951, also directed); BACK AT THE FRONT; STEEL TOWN; THE CROOKED WEB. Work in television included scripts for "Ford Theater" and "Damon Runyon Theatre."

Bressan, Arthur J., Jr.

Died 29 July 1987, New York, N.Y.; age 44.

Filmmaker

A life-long film buff, he received degrees from Iona College and New York University and briefly taught school before moving to San Francisco in the late 1960s. His first job was editing a legal defense film for 15 native Americans who had occupied Alcatraz Island, where he later filmed sex scenes for his 1979 prison picture, FORBIDDEN LETTERS. He alternated between gay adult features and serious non-explicit fare and in 1977 produced, directed, and edited the documentary GAY U.S.A. His last film, BUDDIES, released in 1985, was a drama about AIDS support-group volunteers. Already suffering from AIDS himself, he made his last public appearance at the Alliance of Gay & Lesbian Artists awards ceremony where he was honored. Other films include: COMING OUT; PASSING STRANGERS; ABUSE; PLEASURE BEACH; THANK YOU, MR. PRESIDENT; DADDY DEAREST; SPACE RAGE.

Bromley, Sydney

Died 16 Aug. 1987.

Film/Stage/TV Actor

Noted for playing rural types in film comedies, though he essayed a number of Shakespearean roles on stage. Films include: DEMOBBED; BRIEF ENCOUNTER; LOYAL HEART; THE DARK ROAD; TO THE PUBLIC DANGER; THE MARK OF CAIN; DEVIL'S HARBOR; BLONDE BLACKMAILER; THE LOVE MATCH; SAINT JOAN; THE CONCRETE JUNGLE; THE PIPER'S TUNE; NIGHT CREATURES; PARANOIAC; FATHER CAME TOO; DIE, MONSTER, DIE; CARRY ON COWBOY; OPERATION THIRD FORM; THE CHRISTMAS TREE; THE FEARLESS VAMPIRE KILLERS, OR PARDON ME BUT YOUR TEETH ARE IN MY NECK; HALF A SIXPENCE; PREHISTORIC WOMEN; SMASHING TIME; A LITTLE OF WHAT YOU FANCY; ISLAND OF THE BURNING DAMNED; MACBETH (1971); NO SEX PLEASE-WE'RE BRITISH; FRANKENSTEIN AND THE MONSTER FROM HELL; ROBIN HOOD JUNIOR; CANDLESHOE; CROSSED SWORDS; AN AMERICAN WEREWOLF IN LONDON; DRAGONSLAYER; THE NEVERENDING STORY; PIRATES. Appeared in a number of British TV efforts as well as the American mini-series "Anastasia: The Mystery of Anna."

Brown, Clarence

Born 10 May 1890, Clinton, Mass.; died 17 Aug. 1987, Santa Monica, Calif.

Director

Greta Garbo's favorite director graduated from the University of Tennessee with two degrees in engineering, but his interest in motion pictures led him to the Peerless Studio in Fort Lee, N.J., where he talked his way into a job as assistant to Maurice Tourneur with whom he worked for five years and to whom, he claimed long after retirement, he owed everything. His first solo film was DON'T MARRY FOR MONEY in 1923, and in 1925 he directed Rudolph Valentino in THE EAGLE. He was closely associated with Louis B. Mayer and spent 27 years at MGM Studios. He was nominated six times for an Academy Award and retired in 1953, one of the wealthiest men in show business due to his astute real estate investments. Films include: WONDER OF WOMEN; ANNA CHRISTIE; NAVY BLUES; ROMANCE; A FREE SOUL; INSPIRATION; POSSESSED; EMMA; LETTY LYNTON; THE SON-DAUGHTER; LOOKING FORWARD; NIGHT FLIGHT; CHAINED; FIFTEEN WIVES; SADIE MCKEE; AH, WILDERNESS!; ANNA KARENINA (1935); THE GORGEOUS HUSSY; WIFE VERSUS SECRETARY; CONQUEST; OF HUMAN HEARTS; IDIOT'S DELIGHT; THE RAINS CAME; EDISON, THE MAN; COME LIVE WITH ME; THEY MET IN BOMBAY; THE HUMAN COMEDY; THE WHITE CLIFFS OF DOVER; SONG OF LOVE; INTRUDER IN THE DUST; THE SECRET GARDEN; TO PLEASE A LADY; ANGELS IN THE OUTFIELD; PLYMOUTH ADVENTURE; WHEN IN ROME; NEVER LET ME GO. Silents: THE LAST OF THE MOHICANS; THE ACQUITTAL; THE SIGNAL TOWER; THE EAGLE; THE GOOSE WOMAN; FLESH AND THE DEVIL; KIKI; A WOMAN OF AFFAIRS; THE TRAIL OF '98; THE GREAT REDEEMER; BUTTERFLY; SMOULDERING FIRES; THE LIGHT IN THE DARK.

Brown, Vivian

Died 13 June 1987, Los Angeles, Calif.; age 62.

Actress

Her feature film credits include FRIENDS; EARTHQUAKE; 3 O'CLOCK HIGH. Among her many television credits are "Down to Earth," "Hitchcock Presents," "Benson," "Lou Grant," and telefilms "Eye of the Hawk," "Facts of Life Goes to Paris," and "The Money Changers."

Bruck, Karl

Died 21 Aug. 1987, Los Angeles, Calif.; age 81.

Actor

A native of Vienna, he came to the US after losing his family in the Holocaust and being imprisoned himself. In Europe he had appeared as Hamlet and in "Faust," "Six Characters in Search of an Author," and "Journey's End," among other stage productions. He was well known to daytime soap opera fans for more than a decade as Maistro Ernesto Fautsch on "The Young and the Restless," and was seen regularly on TV shows such as "The Fugitive," "Star Trek," "Mission Impossible," "It Takes a Thief," and "Love Boat." His film credits include appearances in ESCAPE FROM THE PLANET OF THE APES; THE BIRDMEN; PAINT YOUR WAGON.

Bryson, Winifred

Died 20 Aug. 1987; age 94.

Silent Film Actress

Appeared in A HEART TO LET; HER FACE VALUE; THE GREAT NIGHT; SOUTH OF SUVA; SUZANNA; CRASHIN' THRU; THE HUNCHBACK OF NOTRE DAME (1923, with the legendary Lon Chaney, Sr.); PLEASURE MAD; THUNDERING DAWN; TRUXTON KING; BEHIND THE CURTAIN; BROKEN BARRIERS; DON'T DOUBT YOUR HUSBAND; FLIRTING WITH LOVE; THE LAW FORBIDS; THE LOVER OF CAMILLE; THE AWFUL TRUTH (1925); ADORATION.

Burnell, Peter

Died 5 Jan. 1987, Chicago, Ill.; age 44.

Actor

Born in Johnstown, N.Y., he graduated from Columbia University and made his Broadway debut in "In Praise of Love," with Rex Harrison and Julie Harris. Other New York stage roles include "Flying Blind," "Bohemian Heaven," "Ubu Roi," "Ubu Bound," and appearances with the New York Shakespeare Festival, Chelsea Theater, Manhattan Theater Club, and Circle Repertory Co. He was featured for five years on the daytime serial "The Doctors," and made other TV appearances as well as appearing in the 20th Century Fox feature WITHOUT A TRACE.

Burton, Russ J.

Died 22 Apr. 1987, Santa Barbara, Calif.; age 70.

Novelist/Playwright/Screenwriter/Publicist

A friend of Ernest Hemingway, he wrote many short stories, novels, and plays and worked in all areas of TV and motion picture publicity. He was a former public relations director at KCET, a member of Governor Pat Brown's campaign press staff, and worked at the Art Jacobs Public Relations Agency and Universal Studios.

Butler, Ralph

Died 6 March 1987, Woodland Hills, Calif.; age 74.

Screenwriter

He began his career in 1929 for Hal Roach and is credited with writing the screenplay for TOPPER. During WW II he served as a projectionist/cameraman for the US Army in New Guinea on Gen. Douglas MacArthur's staff.

Butterfield, Paul

Died 4 May 1987, North Hollywood, Calif.; age 44.

Musician

Raised in Chicago, he was trained in classical flute, but became enamored of the harmonica, which he mastered sufficiently by age 16 to play with Howlin' Wolf, Otis Rush, Buddy Guy, and other local stars in Chicago clubs. He formed his Butterfield Blues Band and cut his first album in 1965. In 1967, he expanded his group to include a horn section and opened up his sound to incorporate elements of rock, jazz, and folk as well as blues. Supplied the music for 1973's STEELYARD BLUES.

Calapristi, Samuel [Santo]

Died 27 Apr. 1987, Springfield, Pa.; age 90.

Actor

An extra and bit player in silents and talkies who sometimes served as Ronald Colman's stand-in. He continued to work in films and television for 50 years.

Caldwell, Erskine

Born 17 Dec. 1903, Coweta County, Ga.; died 11 Apr. 1987, Paradise Valley, Ariz.

Novelist/Screenwriter

His "Tobacco Road" was adapted for the stage by Jack Kirkland and ran seven and a half years on Broadway starting in 1933. Darryl F. Zanuck made the less successful film version in 1941, tacking on a happy ending which enraged the author. His accounts of deprivation and depravity in the Depression-era Deep South brought him fame and notoriety and "Tobacco Road" and "God's Little Acre" were two of the biggest sellers of all time. He wrote 24 novels, 10 short-story collections, an autobiography, a dozen works of nonfiction, and worked for five years writing Hollywood scripts. Among his works adapted for film are TOBACCO ROAD; VOLCAN; GOD'S LITTLE ACRE; CLAUDELLE ENGLISH.

Carroll, Madeleine [Marie-Madeleine Bernadette O'Carroll]

Born 26 Feb. 1906, Birmingham, England; died 2 Oct. 1987, Marbella, Spain.

Actress

She graduated from Birmingham University with a degree in French and her first jobs were modeling hats and teaching French. Her acting debut was as a French maid with a touring company in England. She went on to appear in a score of British movies, with leading roles in THE 39 STEPS and SECRET AGENT. In 1936 she went to Hollywood where she was put under contract to Walter Wanger and 20th Century-Fox. During WW II her sister was killed in a German air raid on London and she went back to England where she did war-relief work. She earned the rank of captain and received the Medal of Freedom for her nursing service. In 1946, France awarded her the Legion of Honor for her work as a liaison between US Army forces and French Resistance forces. Among her films are: THE AMERICAN PRISONER; ATLANTIC; THE CROOKED BILLET; ESCAPE; KISSING CUP'S RACE; THE SCHOOL FOR SCANDAL; YOUNG WOODLEY; "W" THE PLAN; FASCINATION; FRENCH LEAVE; MADAME GUILLOTINE; THE WRITTEN LAW; SLEEPING CAR; I WAS A SPY; THE WORLD MOVES ON; THE DICTATOR; THE CASE AGAINST MRS. AMES; THE GENERAL DIED AT DAWN; LLOYDS OF LONDON; THE SECRET AGENT; IT'S ALL YOURS; ON THE AVENUE; THE PRISONER OF ZENDA; BLOCKADE; CAFE SOCIETY; HONEYMOON IN BALI; MY SON, MY SON!; NORTHWEST MOUNTED POLICE; SAFARI; ONE NIGHT IN LISBON; VIRGINIA; MY FAVORITE BLONDE; HIGH FURY; DON'T TRUST YOUR HUSBAND; THE FAN; BAHAMA PASSAGE. Her silent films were THE FIRST BORN and THE GUNS OF LOOS.

Caruso, Enrico, Jr.

Born 7 Sept. 1904; died 9 Apr. 1987, Jacksonville, Fla.

Actor/Singer

Son of the great tenor, he moved to Hollywood after his father's death and starred in two Spanish-language films, THE FORTUNE TELLER and THE SINGER OF NAPLES. Like his father, he was a tenor and in the late 1930s sang regularly in California. After WW II, he gave up singing permanently and, under the name of Henry De Costa, worked as a department head for the import-export firm of Dunnington & Arnold until 1971. At the time of his death, he had completed a book of memoirs entitled *Enrico Caruso, My Father and My Family,* with Andrew Farkas.

Caspary, Vera

Born 13 Nov. 1899, Chicago, Ill.; died 13 June 1987, New York, N.Y.

Novelist/Screenwriter

A writer whose body of work included 18 published novels, 10 screenplays, and four stage plays, she was known for the deep and enigmatic female characters about whom she wrote. Most notable among her novels was *Laura,* a mystery story that became a classic as a novel, a movie, and a Broadway play. She left school at 18 to become an advertising copywriter for a Chicago mail-order company, writing novels in her free time. Her career in Hollywood began with Paramount in 1932 when she wrote the story for THE NIGHT OF JUNE 13TH. Among the other films she wrote or adapted for the screen are: WORKING GIRLS; PRIVATE SCANDAL; SUCH WOMEN ARE DANGEROUS; I'LL LOVE YOU ALWAYS; PARTY WIRE; EASY LIVING; SCANDAL STREET; SERVICE DE LUXE; SING, DANCE, PLENTY HOT; LADY FROM LOUISIANA; LADY BODYGUARD; LAURA; BEDELIA; OUT OF THE BLUE; A LETTER TO THREE WIVES; THREE HUSBANDS; I CAN GET IT FOR YOU WHOLESALE; THE BLUE GARDENIA; GIVE A GIRL A BREAK; LES GIRLS; BACHELOR IN PARADISE.

Chaney, Harold Lee

Died 4 Jan. 1987, Los Angeles, Calif.; age 59.

Photographer

He was a pioneer in time-lapse photography and inventor of dissolve-lapse photography, and had his own production company, Folmagic, in Hollywood for over 20 years. He won an Emmy in 1977 for film sound editing on the series "Police Story," and worked over the years at most of the major studios, including Warner Bros., Columbia, Paramount, and 20th Century Fox. Earlier in his career he was a screenwriter for Disney.

Chew, Virgilia

Born 9 July 1905, Houston, Tex.; died 23 July 1987, Englewood, N.J.

Stage Actress

She began her career in the Broadway production of "Ethan Frome," starring Raymond Massey and Ruth Gordon. She followed that with the original production of "Little Women," "Life with Father" (in Chicago with Lillian Gish), and a London production of "The Eve of St. Mark." Appeared in the film version of Tennessee Williams' "Orpheus," titled THE FUGITIVE KIND. Her last major stage appearance was in a 1970s road production of "The Rose Tattoo" starring Maureen Stapleton.

Chilberg, John E.

Died 2 March 1987, Los Angeles, Calif.; age 57.

Art Director

Worked on BATTLESTAR GALACTICA, STAR TREK III: THE SEARCH FOR SPOCK, and AVALANCHE EXPRESS, but was mostly noted for his work in television on such shows as "McMillan and Wife," "Rich Man, Poor Man," "Baretta," "Chicago Story," "Dynasty," and "Hotel."

Chissell, Noble LaPorte ("Kid")

Died 8 Nov. 1987 Toluca Lake, Calif.

Actor/Stuntman/Boxer

As a teenager he sparred with Bob Hope when the future comedian was an aspiring boxer named Packey East. He appeared on stage in vaudeville and as a stuntman in hundreds of Westerns. He was the technical adviser on the film THEY SHOOT HORSES DON'T THEY? and appeared in HOME IN INDIANA. Some of his other films are: EX-CHAMP; KNOCKOUT; MY BUDDY; SONG OF ARIZONA; A LIKELY STORY; GRAND CANYON; SORROWFUL JONES; JEALOUSY (1945); THE SET-UP (1949); THE HELLCATS; MACHISMO-40 GRAVES FOR 40 GUNS; DILLINGER.

Christy, Ann [Gladys Cronin]

Born 31 May 1909, Logansport, Ill.; died 14 Nov. 1987.

Actress

Winning a beauty contest was the start of her show business career, leading to a contract with Christie Comedies and a part opposite Bing Crosby in one of his first films for Mack Sennett. Her other films include: THE KID SISTER; SPEEDY; THE WATER HOLE; JUST OFF BROADWAY; THE LARIAT KID; THE FOURTH ALARM; BEHIND STONE WALLS. In 1933, she left films for marriage.

Clark, Janet

Died 12 July 1987, Los Angeles, Calif. age, mid-60s.

Actress

Her most recent appearances were in the television series "Gloria" and "Growing Pains." She was the daughter of character actor and producer Edward Clark.

Clarens, Carlos [Carlos Figueradoy Clarens]

Born 7 July 1936, Havana, Cuba; died 8 Feb. 1987, New York, N.Y., age 56.

Film Critic/Historian/Teacher

Born in Havana and educated at Havana and Columbia universities and the Sorbonne, he wrote film criticism for many leading journals, including *Cahiers du Cinema*, *Films In Review*, *The Seventh Art*, *Sight and Sound*, *Film Comment*, and *The Village Voice.* In his early years he worked as an assistant to directors Jacques Demy, Agnes Varda, and Robert Bresson, did casting chores for Francis Coppola, and wrote English subtitles for many foreign films, among them Franco Zeffirelli's LA TRAVIATA. He appeared in two movies,

Coco

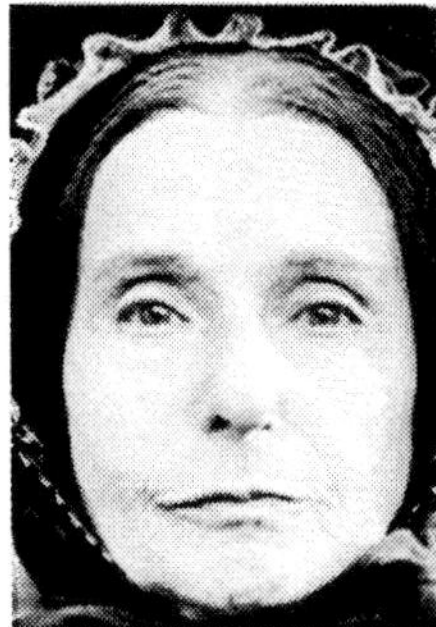
Patience Collier

LIONS LOVE and FLACONS D'OR, and in recent years had taught on crime films at New York's School of Visual Arts and was co-owner with Howard Mandelbaum of Phototeque, a stills service. His books include *An Illustrated History of the Horror Film*, published in 1967 and considered the definitive study of the genre, *Crime Movies*, published in 1980, and a study of George Cukor.

Cockrell, Frank M.

Died 13 Apr. 1987, Boones Mill, Va.; age 80.

Film/TV Writer

He began his career writing for *Liberty* magazine and *The Saturday Evening Post*, then went to Hollywood to work for Harold Lloyd writing screenplays. He continued to write for a number of different studios until WW II, in which he served as a Marine combat photographer. He was cited for extraordinary bravery on Iwo Jima, where he filmed some of the heaviest battles of the Pacific campaign. He wrote extensively for television, including many episodes for "Alfred Hitchcock Presents," "G.E. Theater," "Batman," and "Outer Limits." Among the movies he wrote for are: AGE OF CONSENT; THE SPORT PARADE; THE FAMILY SECRET; RHUBARB; INFERNO; THE RAID; ON THE THRESHOLD OF SPACE; WALKING ON AIR; PROFESSOR BEWARE; THE PROFESSIONALS; LADY IN A JAM; DARK WATERS.

Coco, James

Born 21 Mar. 1930, New York, N.Y.; died 25 Feb. 1987, New York, N.Y.

Actor

He first came to public attention during the late 1960s for his television commercials. His performance in the play "Next" won critical accolades and the notice of Neil Simon, who became a close friend and often wrote parts for him into his plays. His Broadway appearances included "Last of the Red Hot Lovers," "Man of La Mancha," and "You Can't Take It with You." Throughout his career he won several Obie awards, a Drama Desk award, and an Emmy. Films include: ENSIGN PULVER; GENERATION; THE STRAWBERRY STATEMENT; TELL ME THAT YOU LOVE ME, JUNIE MOON; A NEW LEAF; SUCH GOOD FRIENDS; MAN OF LA MANCHA; THE WILD PARTY; MURDER BY DEATH; BYE BYE MONKEY!; CHARLESTON; THE CHEAP DETECTIVE; SCAVENGER HUNT; WHOLLY MOSES; ONLY WHEN I LAUGH; THE MUPPETS TAKE MANHATTAN.

Coe, Peter

Died 25 May 1987, England; age 59.

Stage Director/Film Actor

His career peaked in 1961 when he had three hits running simultaneously in London's West End—"The Miracle Worker," "The World of Suzie Wong," and "Oliver." He staged musicals and dramas around the world but was best known for his direction of the Broadway production of "Oliver!" He began his career as an actor in the late 1950s after studying at the London Academy of Music and Dramatic Art. His version of Henry Fielding's 18th Century play "Lock Up Your Daughters" established him as a director. Films include: GUNG HO!; FOLLOW THE BOYS; GYPSY WILDCAT; HOUSE OF FRANKENSTEIN; THE MUMMY'S CURSE; MY OWN TRUE LOVE; SANDS OF IWO JIMA; SWORD IN THE DESERT; ROCKY MOUNTAIN; DIPLOMATIC COURIER; HELLGATE; ROAD TO BALI; THE WILD BLUE YONDER; ARROWHEAD; DESERT LEGION; FLIGHT TO TANGIER; THE HINDU; ALASKA SEAS; PASSION; ESCAPE TO BURMA; SHOTGUN; SMOKE SIGNAL; THE TEN COMMANDMENTS; HELL SHIP MUTINY; LOUISIANA HUSSY; OKEFENOKEE; THE PRIZE; THE SECRET INVASION; TOBRUK; LOCK UP YOUR DAUGHTERS; VIGILANTE FORCE.

Colby, Robert

Died 10 March 1987, New York, N.Y.; age 64.

Composer/Theatrical Producer/Music Publisher

A graduate of the University of Mississippi, he served in the Navy during WW II before moving to New York to study at the Julliard School of Music. He formed the Croma Music Co. and wrote songs for Barbra Streisand, Nancy Wilson, Ella Fitzgerald, Steve Lawrence and Eydie Gorme, Maurice Chevalier, Cab Calloway and others. On stage he produced "The Male of the Species," in London and Australia, "Kennedy's Children" on Broadway, and, with David Merrick, Tennessee Williams' "The Red Devil Battery Sign." He was also involved in the production of the movie CHOPPER SQUAD.

Collier, Patience [Renee Ritcher]

Born 19 Aug. 1910, London, England; died 13 July 1987, London, England.

Actress

Her early work with the Royal Shakespeare Company and British National Theatre included "The Cherry Orchard," "Wars of the Roses," "King Lear," and a Peter Brook production of the "The Hostage" in New York. She appeared in numerous TV dramas and on over 2,000 radio shows. Her most impressive screen effort was as the malevolent Mrs. Poulteney in THE FRENCH LIEUTENANT'S WOMAN. Films include: THE THIRD SECRET; THE WILD AFFAIR; BABY LOVE; DECLINE AND FALL . . . OF A BIRD WATCHER; HOUSE OF CARDS; PERFECT FRIDAY; THINK DIRTY; FIDDLER ON THE ROOF; COUNTESS DRACULA; THE NATIONAL HEALTH, OR NURSE NORTON'S AFFAIR.

Collier, William "Buster"

Born 12 Feb. 1902, New York, N.Y.; died 6 Feb. 1987, San Francisco, Calif.

Actor

The son of William Collier, a star of both stage and film, he began his acting career at age four, appearing in his father's play "Caught in the Rain." His first film role came at the age of 14, in 1914, and he subsequently went on to play juvenile leads throughout the 1920s. Living up to his image as one of the leading young romantic actors of his time, he made headlines with his New Year's Eve marriage to a Ziegfeld girl, Marie Stevens, with William Randolph Hearst as his best man. When his acting career ended in the 1940s he became an agent at the William Morris Agency where he managed to lure top film stars including Mary Pickford, Wallace Beery, and Clark Gable to do spots on "The Lux Radio Theater." Among his movies: THE LION AND THE MOUSE; WOMEN THEY TALK ABOUT; THE BACHELOR GIRL; THE COLLEGE COQUETTE; THE DONOVAN AFFAIR; HARDBOILED ROSE; NEW ORLEANS; ONE STOLEN NIGHT; TWO MEN AND A MAID; FOX MOVIETONE FOLLIES OF 1930; LUMMOX; MELODY MAN; RAIN OR SHINE; A ROYAL ROMANCE; THE BIG GAMBLE; BROADMINDED; CIMARRON; LITTLE CAESAR; THE SECRET WITNESS; SOUL OF THE SLUMS; THE COUNTY FAIR; DANCERS IN THE DARK; EXPOSED; THE FIGHTING GENTLEMAN; FILE 113; THE PHANTOM EXPRESS; BEHIND JURY DOORS; FORGOTTEN; MARK IT PAID; THE STORY OF TEMPLE DRAKE; ALL OF ME; THE PEOPLE'S ENEMY; PUBLIC STENOGRAPHER; BEWARE OF BACHELORS; SPEED DEMON; REDUCING; SPORTING CHANCE. Silent films in which he appeared are: EVERYBODY'S SWEETHEART; THE SOUL OF YOUTH; AT THE STAGE DOOR; THE HEART OF MARYLAND; CARDIGAN; THE ENEMIES OF WOMEN; LOYAL LIVES; PLEASURE MAD; THE LIGHTHOUSE BY THE SEA; THE DEVIL'S CARGO; EVE'S SECRET; THE RECKLESS SEX; THE RAINMAKER; BACKSTAGE; CONVOY; STRANDED; THE SUNSET DERBY; THE FLOATING COLLEGE; A NIGHT OF MYSTERY; SO THIS IS LOVE; THE TRAGEDY OF YOUTH; THE BUGLE CALL; THE AGE OF DESIRE; FOOL'S HIGHWAY; LEAVE IT TO GERRY; THE VERDICT; GOD GAVE ME TWENTY CENTS; THE LADY OF THE HAREM; THE LUCKY LADY; THE WANDERER; THE BROKEN GATE; THE COLLEGE WIDOW; DEARIE; THE DESIRED WOMAN; THE RED SWORD; TIDE OF EMPIRE; THE SECRETS OF PARIS; THE GIRL FROM PORCUPINE.

Connor, Velma

Died 19 July 1987, Los Angeles, Calif.; age 81.

Vaudeville Performer

Together with her twin sister Thelma, who died in 1981, she had an illustrious career in vaudeville. Starting with Gus Edwards in 1921, and featured in the Ziegfield Follies, the girls were known as the Connor Twins and were credited with being the first flappers. At the height of the Depression they worked the Orpheum Circuit under the banner of the Federal Theater Project. In films, the sisters appeared in MILLION DOLLAR BABY in 1932, but on her own Velma appeared in PIRATES OF LOVE; RECKLESS; THE LEATHER PUSHERS; THE SCRAPPIN' KID; THE TERROR.

Cook, Mark

Died 8 Feb. 1987, Los Angeles, Calif.; age 86.

Violinist/Actor

Served for many years as supervisor of choral conductors for the Los Angeles Bureau of Music and played bit parts in dozens of Hollywood films. In 1983 he received an award from Los Angeles Mayor Tom Bradley for outstanding service to Artists of the Future.

Cooper, Olive

Died 12 June 1987, Los Angeles, Calif., age 94.

Stage Actress/Screenwriter

Began her show business career as a child screen actress in San Francisco. She went to Republic Studios in 1937 as a screenwriter and over the next 13 years wrote 34 pictures, most of them westerns, including musicals starring Gene Autry or Roy Rogers. She was frequently employed as a script doctor and at different periods of her life served as an officer of the Screen Writers Guild. The late director George Stevens was her nephew. Films include: CONFIDENTIAL; HOT TIP; STREAMLINE EXPRESS; DANCING FEET; FOLLOW YOUR HEART; HEARTS IN BONDAGE; LAUGHING IRISH EYES; NAVY BORN; THE RETURN OF JIMMY VALENTINE; HAPPY-GO-LUCKY; JIM HANVEY, DETECTIVE; JOIN THE MARINES; LADY BEHAVE; RHYTHM IN THE CLOUDS;

ANNABEL TAKES A TOUR; ORPHANS OF THE STREET; SHE MARRIED A COP; THE BORDER LEGION (1940); YOUNG BILL HICKOK; DOWN MEXICO WAY; THE GREAT TRAIN ROBBERY (1941); ICE-CAPADES; IN OLD CHEYENNE (1941); ROBIN HOOD OF THE PECOS; SHERIFF OF TOMBSTONE; THE SINGING HILL; CALL OF THE CANYON; COWBOY SERENADE; IDAHO; KING OF THE COWBOYS; NOBODY'S DARLING; SHANTYTOWN; MY BEST GAL; SONG OF NEVADA; THREE LITTLE SISTERS; SWINGIN' ON A RAINBOW; THE BAMBOO BLONDE; SIOUX CITY SUE; BANDIT KING OF TEXAS; THE BIG SOMBRERO; OUTCASTS OF THE TRAIL; HILLS OF OKLAHOMA.

Coromina, Pepon

Died 25 Dec. 1987, Barcelona, Spain; age 41.

Producer

Headed Figaro Films and produced ANGUISH (directed by Bigas Luna).

Costello, Carole

Died 29 March 1987, Los Angeles, Calif.; age 48.

Talent Coordinator

The daughter of Lou Costello, she appeared in numerous Abbott and Costello films before embarking on a career as a nightclub singer, then talent coordinator for Mark Goodson Productions. She was married to Craig Martin, son of Dean Martin.

Couch, Charles "Chuck"

Died 23 Dec. 1987, Hollywood, Calif.; age 78.

Animation Creative Director

Worked mainly for Disney (1927-1933; 1935-1942) on Mickey Mouse (story director and supervisor) and Donald Duck (creative director) cartoons. Handled the creative segment directing and supervising chores on FANTASIA and BAMBI. Also worked for Screen Gems and Walter Lantz (doing the creative direction on Woody Woodpecker cartoons).

Council, Elizabeth [Elizabeth Council Crafts]

Died 3 Feb. 1987, New York, N.Y.; age 79.

Stage/Film Actress

She appeared on Broadway in "The Bad Seed," and toured with the Eva Le Gallienne National Repertory Theater in "Hedda Gabler" and "She Stoops to Conquer." Appeared in the film I PASSED FOR WHITE and on television frequently, including "Guiding Light," "Robert Montgomery Presents," "The Verdict Is Yours," "The Sid Caesar Show" and numerous commercials.

Crawley, F.R. "Budge"

Died 13 May, 1987; age 75.

Film Producer

His most notable achievement in a 48-year career with a total of 235 US and international awards was the Academy Award he received for his coproducing chores on THE MAN WHO SKIED DOWN EVEREST. Other notable efforts include THE LOON'S NECKLACE and NEWFOUNDLAND SCENE, both done by Crawley Films, a production firm he founded with his wife.

Crespinel, William [William Thomas Crespinel]

Born 9 July, 1890, Weymouth, England; died 19 Jun. 1987, Laguna Beach, Calif.

Film Company Executive/Inventor

His career, which spanned more than 40 years, began in 1906 with Kinemacolor in his native England; he then transferred to their New York facility in 1912. Did the photography for J. Stuart Blackton's GLORIOUS ADVENTURE in 1921. Was an innovator in developing a process that would let any camera use color film, and after he founded Cinecolor in 1932, broadened it into a three-color system from the prevailing two-color process. Retired as president in 1948.

Culver, Calvin [John Calvin Culver]

Died 10 Aug. 1987, Inverness, Fla.

Film/Stage Actor

Started out as a teacher before switching to acting in gay pornography films. Also appeared on stage, working in Florida community theaters. Prior to his death he had been working on videos promoting safe sex.

Da Pron, Louis F.

Born 3 Feb. 1913, Hammond, Ind.; died 21 July 1987, Westlake, Calif.

Choreographer/Teacher

Danced and choreographed for film and television from 1935 until the 1970s. He operated the Louis DaPron School of Dance in Canoga Park and taught tap classes at the California Dance Theatre in Agoura Hills. He signed on with Paramount Pictures in 1936 and made five pictures in 18 months. In 1941 he choreographed Donald O'Connor in WHEN JOHNNY COMES MARCHING HOME for Universal Pictures and began an association with the actor-dancer that continued through 13 movies. He moved to television in the 1950s, worked on "The Perry Como Show" for five years, and was nominated for an Emmy for his choreography on Milton Berle's "Texaco Star Theater." Films include: MELODY LANE; SWEETHEART OF THE CAMPUS; SWING IT SOLDIER; ALWAYS A BRIDESMAID; FOLLOW THE BAND; HE'S MY GUY; HOW'S ABOUT IT?; MOONLIGHT IN VERMONT; MR. BIG; SHE'S FOR ME; TOP MAN; THE MERRY MONAHANS; THE SINGING SHERIFF; THIS IS THE LIFE; HER LUCKY NIGHT; GIRL ON THE SPOT; SLIGHTLY SCANDALOUS; ARE YOU WITH IT?; THERE'S A GIRL IN MY HEART; YES SIR, THAT'S MY BABY; ONE TOO MANY; WALKING MY BABY BACK HOME; THE BIG BROADCAST OF 1937; COLLEGE HOLIDAY; THREE CHEERS FOR LOVE; ALL-AMERICAN SWEETHEART; HIDEAWAY GIRL; GO WEST, YOUNG LADY; ROOKIES ON PARADE; SAN ANTONIO ROSE; HOW'S ABOUT IT?; NIGHT CLUB GIRL; PATRICK THE GREAT; PENTHOUSE RHYTHM; THAT NIGHT WITH YOU; FEUDIN', FUSSIN' AND A-FIGHTIN'; THE KETTLES IN THE OZARKS.

Damon, Cathryn

Died 4 May 1987, Los Angeles, Calif.; age 56.

Stage/TV Actress

Winner of an Emmy in 1980 as Best Actress in A Comedy Series for her performance as Mary Campbell in "Soap," she moved to New York from Seattle at 16 to pursue a career in ballet. She spent two years with the Ballet Repertory Co., followed by two years as a soloist with the Metropolitan Opera Ballet, then turned to Broadway where she appeared in 11 shows, including "Flora, The Red Menace," "The Prisoner of Second Avenue," "Last of the Red Hot Lovers," "Foxy," "Sweet Bird of Youth," and "Passion". She appeared extensively in off-Broadway productions before her television career gained impetus. Her feature films include HOW TO BEAT THE HIGH COST OF LIVING and SHE'S HAVING A BABY.

Dana

Dana, Viola [Virginia Flugrath]

Born 28 June 1897, Brooklyn, N.Y.; died 3 July 1987, Woodland Hills, Calif.

Silent Film Actress

Began her career at 16 on Broadway and got her big break in films after starring in the 1913 Broadway hit "Poor Little Rich Girl." She went on to become one of the silent screen's most familiar ingenues after signing a long-term contract with Metro Pictures, which later became part of Metro-Goldwyn-Mayer. At her peak she was earning $1,750 a week but her voice was not suited for sound pictures and after a brief stint in vaudeville she retired. She was married twice, to director John H. Collins and screen cowboy Maurice (Lefty) Flynn. Her sister was screen star Shirley Mason. Silent films include: GLADIOLA; THE HOUSE OF THE LOST CORD; THE INNOCENCE OF RUTH; ALADDIN'S OTHER LAMP; THE GIRL WITHOUT A SOUL; FALSE EVIDENCE; A CHORUS GIRL'S ROMANCE; DANGEROUS TO MEN; HOME STUFF; LIFE'S DARN FUNNY; THE OFFSHORE PIRATE; JUNE MADNESS; SEEING'S BELIEVING; CRINOLINE AND ROMANCE; HER FATAL MILLIONS; IN SEARCH OF A THRILL; A NOISE IN NEWBORO; THE SOCIAL CODE; ALONG CAME RUTH; MERTON OF THE MOVIES; OPEN ALL NIGHT; REVELATION; AS MAN DESIRES; FORTY WINKS; THE GREAT LOVE; THE NECESSARY EVIL; THE ICE FLOOD; THE SILENT LOVER; WILD OATS LANE; HOME STRUCK; NAUGHTY NANETTE; SALVATION JANE; ONE SPLENDID HOUR; THE CHILDREN OF EVE; COHEN'S LUCK; ON DANGEROUS PATHS; THE SLAVEY STUDENT; THE COSSACK WHIP; THE FLOWER OF NO MAN'S LAND; THE GATES OF EDEN; THE LIGHT OF HAPPINESS; BLUE JEANS; GOD'S LAW AND MAN'S; LADY BARNACLE; THE MORTAL SIN; THREADS OF FATE; BREAKERS AHEAD; FLOWER OF THE DUSK; THE ONLY ROAD; OPPORTUNITY; RIDERS OF THE NIGHT; THE WINDING TRAIL; THE GOLD CURE; JEANNE OF THE GUTTER; THE MICROBE; THE PARISIAN BRIDE; BLACKMAIL; CINDERELLA'S TWIN; THE WILLOW TREE; THE MATCHBREAKER; PUPPETS OF FATE; THERE ARE NO VILLAINS; THE FIVE DOLLAR BABY; THE FOURTEENTH LOVER; GLASS HOUSES; LOVE IN THE DARK; THEY LIKE 'EM ROUGH; ROUGED LIPS; THE BEAUTY PRIZE; DON'T DOUBT YOUR HUSBAND; THE HEART BANDIT; WINDS OF CHANCE; BIGGER THAN BARNUM'S; BRED IN OLD KENTUCKY; KOSHER KITTY KELLY; THE LURE OF THE NIGHT CLUB; THAT CERTAIN THING; TWO SISTERS.

Dandridge, Ruby

Died 17 October 1987, age 87.

Actress/Singer

The mother of Broadway and film singer/actress Dorothy Dandridge, she began her career as a singer on stage before moving on to film, radio, and television. She made her film debut in 1942 in

GALLANT LADY and then went on to make NIGHT FOR CRIME; PRISON GIRL; CABIN IN THE SKY; CORREGIDOR; MELODY PARADE; NEVER A DULL MOMENT; LADIES OF WASHINGTON; JUNIOR MISS; SARATOGA TRUNK; HOME IN OKLAHOMA; INSIDE JOB; THREE LITTLE GIRLS IN BLUE; THE ARNELO AFFAIR; DEAD RECKONING; MY WILD IRISH ROSE; TAP ROOTS; FATHER IS A BACHELOR; HOLE IN THE HEAD. Her television appearances included "Beulah" with Judy Canova and "Life with Father" with Leon Ames.

Davis, Art

Died 16 Jan. 1987, age unknown.

Actor

Appeared in many B westerns as a member of the Frontier Marshals with Lee Powell and Bill ("Cowboy Rambler") Boyd. He was also in films with Tim McCoy, Gene Autry, Johnny Mack Brown. Was popular with western fans as he actively participated in various conventions. Films include: SAGEBRUSH TROUBADOUR; ROOTIN' TOOTIN' RHYTHM; SPRINGTIME IN THE ROCKIES; IN EARLY ARIZONA; PHANTOM GOLD; PIONEER TRAIL; CODE OF THE CACTUS; SIX-GUN RHYTHM; PRAIRIE PALS; RAIDERS OF THE WEST; ROLLING DOWN THE GREAT DIVIDE; TEXAS MAN HUNT; BUGS BUNNY'S THIRD MOVIE—1001 RABBIT TALES; ALONG THE SUNDOWN TRAIL; TUMBLEWEED TRAIL.

Dawson, Hal K.

Died 17 Feb. 1987, Loma Linda, Calif., age 90.

Stage/Film/TV Actor

He appeared in many New York stage plays including "Machinal" with Clark Gable. He roomed with Gable for the duration of the play, and later they made several motion pictures together. He made his film debut in 1933 and appeared in several Alfred Hitchcock thrillers. Aside from his many character and comedy parts in films and on stage, he appeared in more than 100 television shows, including "Alfred Hitchcock Presents," "Lassie," "Carol Burnett & Friends," and "Mannix." He was a member of the Pioneers of Radio Club and a lifetime member of the Masquers Club, in which he was active for 45 years. Films include: THE FIREBIRD; DR. SOCRATES; MUSIC IS MAGIC; PADDY O'DAY; CHINA CLIPPER; EVERYBODY'S OLD MAN; LIBELED LADY; MY AMERICAN WIFE; PUBLIC ENEMY'S WIFE; WEDDING PRESENT; CAFE METROPOLE; DANGER—LOVE AT WORK; LIFE BEGINS IN COLLEGE; LOVE AND HISSES; ON AGAIN-OFF AGAIN; SECOND HONEYMOON; VOGUES OF 1938; WELLS FARGO; WE'RE ON THE JURY; WIFE, DOCTOR AND NURSE; BOY MEETS GIRL; INTERNATIONAL SETTLEMENT; JUST AROUND THE CORNER; KEEP SMILING; SWEETHEARTS; YOU AND ME; BLACKMAIL (1939); FOR LOVE OR MONEY; THE GREAT VICTOR HERBERT; HOTEL FOR WOMEN; I STOLE A MILLION; ICE FOLLIES OF 1939; THE LADY'S FROM KENTUCKY; ROSE OF WASHINGTON SQUARE; THE STORY OF VERNON AND IRENE CASTLE; TWO BRIGHT BOYS; BLONDIE ON A BUDGET; DOCTOR TAKES A WIFE; THE GREAT PROFILE; LILLIAN RUSSELL; PUBLIC DEB NO.1; STAR DUST; TIN PAN ALLEY; TWO GIRLS ON BROADWAY; WE WHO ARE YOUNG; CRACKED NUTS; A GIRL, A GUY AND A GOB; HELLZAPOPPIN'; OBLIGING YOUNG LADY; SAN ANTONIO ROSE; WASHINGTON MELODRAMA; WEEKEND IN HAVANA; YOU'LL NEVER GET RICH; BABY FACE MORGAN; LIFE BEGINS AT 8:30; THE MAD MARTINDALES; THE MAGNIFICENT DOPE; MY FAVORITE SPY (1942); SONG OF THE ISLANDS; CONEY ISLAND; HI DIDDLE DIDDLE; MR. LUCKY; RIDING HIGH; SWEET ROSIE O'GRADY; WHAT A WOMAN!; GREENWICH VILLAGE; HENRY ALDRICH'S LITTLE SECRET; DIAMOND HORSESHOE; DOLL FACE; GUEST WIFE; THE KID FROM BROOKLYN; ONE MORE TOMORROW; BLONDIE'S BIG MOMENT; THE FABULOUS DORSEYS; A LIKELY STORY; THE SHOCKING MISS PILGRIM; VARIETY GIRL; APARTMENT FOR PEGGY; B.F.'S DAUGHTER; CHICKEN EVERY SUNDAY; THE FLAME; LET'S LIVE A LITTLE; MR. BLANDINGS BUILDS HIS DREAM HOUSE; THAT WONDERFUL URGE; YOU GOTTA STAY HAPPY; SLIGHTLY FRENCH; YOU'RE MY EVERYTHING; DALLAS; TO PLEASE A LADY; WABASH AVENUE; DOUBLE DYNAMITE; RHUBARB; SUPERMAN AND THE MOLE MEN; CAPTIVE CITY; IT GROWS ON TREES; PARK ROW; THE GLENN MILLER STORY; THE COUNTRY GIRL; THE YELLOW MOUNTAIN; FOXFIRE; A LAWLESS STREET; THREE FOR THE SHOW; LOVING YOU; THE TIN STAR; CATTLE EMPIRE; THE LAST HURRAH; THE ALLIGATOR PEOPLE; FACE OF A FUGITIVE; THE RAT RACE.

Decae, Henri

Born 1915, France; died 7 Mar. 1987, Paris, France, age 71.

Cinematographer

Popular during the French New Wave period of the late 1950s and early 1960s, he worked for Francois Truffaut (THE 400 BLOWS), Claude Chabrol (LE BEAU SERGE; LES COUSINS; A DOUBLE TOUR; LES BONNES FEMMES), Jacques Baratier (DRAGEES AU POIVRE), and Louis Malle (ASCENSEUR POUR L'ECHAFAUD; LES AMANTS; VIE PRIVEE; VIVE MARIA; LE VOLEUR). His first color feature, PLEIN SOLEIL, was acclaimed for its cinematography and his landmark black-and-white work was the Oscar-winning SUNDAYS AND CYBELE. He directed and lensed short subjects during WW II and began his career as chief cameraman with Jean-Pierre Melville, for whom he shot LE SILENCE DEL LA MER; LES ENFANTS TERRIBLES; BOB LE FLAMBEUR; LEON MORIN PRETRE; L'AINE DES FERCHAUX; LE SAMOURAI; LE CERCLE ROUGE. He also lensed a long list of US and British productions including: FRANTIC; PURPLE NOON; WEB OF PASSION; SEVEN CAPITAL SINS; A VERY PRIVATE AFFAIR; THE DAY AND THE HOUR; JOY HOUSE; SWEET AND SOUR; CIRCLE OF LOVE; HOTEL PARADISO; THE SUCKER; WEEKEND AT DUNKIRK; THE COMEDIANS; THE NIGHT OF THE GENERALS; THE THIEF OF PARIS; DIABOLICALLY YOURS; CASTLE KEEP; HELLO-GOODBYE; THE ONLY GAME IN TOWN; THE SICILIAN CLAN; DELUSIONS OF GRANDEUR; THE LIGHT AT THE EDGE OF THE WORLD; THE GODSON; THE ADVENTURES OF RABBI JACOB; TWO PEOPLE; OPERATION DAYBREAK; SEVEN NIGHTS IN JAPAN; BOBBY DEERFIELD; AN ALMOST PERFECT AFFAIR; THE ISLAND; EXPOSED.

DeFore, Jimmy

Died 24 Jan. 1987, Newport Beach, Calif.; age 63.

Dancer/Choreographer

As a teenager he performed at a ballroom in Kansas City where Red Skelton was m.c., and both were urged by an agent to seek work on the West Coast. He became a contract dancer at RKO, and had a principal dancing role in an Astaire-Rogers film. He later appeared in Broadway productions of "Guys and Dolls," "Copa," "Pajama Game," and "Pal Joey." He moved to Newport Beach in 1976 and opened the Jimmy DeFore Dance Center, which has become the home of the South Coast Ballet.

DeLiagre, Alfred

Died 3 March 1987, New York, N.Y.; age 82

Broadway Producer/Director

The man Katharine Hepburn once called "the last of the gentleman producers" enjoyed several mini-careers before choosing the legitimate theater as his lifelong vocation. He had a brief stint in journalism, conducting interviews with Mahatma Gandhi and Kaiser Wilhelm; played a bit role in the Marx Brothers film COCONUTS; founded the Aviation Country Club in Hicksville, where he taught, flew, and met fellow aviators Charles Lindbergh and Amelia Earhart; studied drama at Yale with Monty Woolley. His stage productions include "Deathtrap," the longest-running Broadway comedy thriller ever, "Voice of the Turtle," "Madwoman of Chaillot," the Pulitzer Prize-winning "J.B.," the Tony Award-winning reproduction of "On Your Toes," and the Drama Critics Circle Award-winning musical "The Golden Apple."

Dempster, Hugh

Born 3 Aug. 1900, London, England; died 30 Apr. 1987, Chicago, Ill.

Film/Stage Actor

Born in London and a Royal Air Force veteran of WW II, his stage credits include dozens of productions stretching from London's West End to Broadway, but he is best known for his portrayal of Col. Pickering in "My Fair Lady," which he performed more than 2,500 times on tour. Among his many film credits are: LORD BABS; MUSIC HATH CHARMS; THE SCARLET PIMPERNEL; THE STUDENT'S ROMANCE; APRIL BLOSSOMS; MARIGOLD; ME AND MY PAL; GARRISON FOLLIES; THREE SILENT MEN; BELL-BOTTOM GEORGE; CANDLES AT NINE; HE SNOOPS TO CONQUER; HEAVEN IS ROUND THE CORNER; JOHNNY IN THE CLOUDS; SCHOOL FOR SECRETS; THE TROJAN BROTHERS; WALTZ TIME; ANNA KARENINA (1948); VICE VERSA; THE FAN; WHILE THE SUN SHINES; THE WINSLOW BOY; A CHRISTMAS CAROL (1951); FLESH AND BLOOD; HAPPY GO LOVELY; PAUL TEMPLE'S TRIUMPH; BABES IN BAGDAD; THE FRIGHTENED BRIDE; MOULIN ROUGE (1952); THE DETECTIVE (1954); HEATWAVE; THE EXTRA DAY; THE CURSE OF FRANKENSTEIN.

Devlin, William

Died 25 Jan. 1987, Somerset, England; age 75.

Actor

Born in Aberdeen, Scotland, he performed at the Old Vic, the Abbey Theatre in Dublin, and the Shakespeare Memorial Theater in Stratford-on-Avon. His US work included "King Lear" and "Macbeth" on the Boston stage and a 1948 Broadway production of "You Never

Can Tell." Apart from a role in the 1950 Walt Disney version of TREASURE ISLAND, he never pursued a movie career.

Dietz, James

Died 22 Apr. 1987, Los Angeles, Calif.; age 27.

Actor

He had a prominent role in WHO'S THAT GIRL and was seen in HOT RESORTS. He also made numerous commercials.

Dobson, James

Died 6 Dec. 1987, Hollywood, Calif.

Actor

Born in Tennessee, moved to Hollywood where he picked up an interest in acting which led first to a Broadway acting career in such productions as "Love on Leave," "The Day Will Come," "Life with Father," "A Story for Strangers," "Mr. Adam." He was one of the voices of the title character in the popular "Archie Andrews" radio show and also appeared on "The Right to Happiness." His films include BOOMERANG; THEY LIVE BY NIGHT; ON MOONLIGHT BAY; THE WEST POINT STORY; FLYING LEATHERNECKS; THE TANKS ARE COMING; FOR MEN ONLY; I DREAM OF JEANIE; OKINAWA; THE ROSE BOWL STORY; CULT OF THE COBRA; FRIENDLY PERSUASION; THE STORM RIDER; THE TALL STRANGER; JET ATTACK; ARMORED COMMAND; CAPTAIN SINDBAD; COME FLY WITH ME; HARLOW (1965); MUTINY IN OUTER SPACE; COUNTRY BOY; TRACK OF THUNDER; A DREAM OF KINGS; THE UNDEFEATED; WHAT'S THE MATTER WITH HELEN? Later worked in various TV episodes, especially on "Love Boat," and was the dialog director for "McMillan and Wife."

Donovan, King

Died 30 June 1987, Branford, Conn., age 69.

Actor/Comedian

His 50-year stage, film, and television career included more than 30 shows with his wife, comedienne Imogene Coca. His Broadway debut was in 1948 in "The Vigil," and during the 1950s he appeared in the TV series "Love That Bob," "The George Burns and Gracie Allen Show," "Please Don't Eat the Daisies," and "Daktari." His final appearance was in 1982 with his wife in NOTHING LASTS FOREVER. Films include: THE MAN FROM TEXAS; OPEN SECRET; SHOCKPROOF; CARGO TO CAPETOWN; KISS TOMORROW GOODBYE; MYSTERY STREET; ONE WAY STREET; THE REDHEAD AND THE COWBOY; SIDE STREET; STORM WARNING; THE SUN SETS AT DAWN; ANGELS IN THE OUTFIELD; THE ENFORCER (1951); LITTLE BIG HORN; THE PRINCE WHO WAS A THIEF; THE SCARF; TAKE CARE OF MY LITTLE GIRL; THE UNKNOWN MAN; THE MERRY WIDOW (1952); SALLY AND SAINT ANNE; SINGIN' IN THE RAIN; SOMETHING TO LIVE FOR; THE BEAST FROM 20,000 FATHOMS; EASY TO LOVE; FOREVER FEMALE; HALF A HERO; THE KID FROM LEFT FIELD; THE MAGNETIC MONSTER; THE MISSISSIPPI GAMBLER (1953); THREE SAILORS AND A GIRL; TUMBLEWEED; BROKEN LANCE; PRIVATE HELL 36; RIDERS TO THE STARS; THE BAMBOO PRISON; THE SEVEN LITTLE FOYS; INVASION OF THE BODY SNATCHERS (1956); THE IRON SHERIFF; THE DEFIANT ONES; THE PERFECT FURLOUGH; THE HANGING TREE; PROMISES, PROMISES; THE BIRDS AND THE BEES.

Dorn, Harding

Died 18 Feb. 1987, New York, N.Y.; age 63.

Dancer/Stage Director/Choreographer

He danced with the Ballet Russe de Monte Carlo in the 1940s and 1950s, and directed, choreographed, or was associate producer on about 20 regional and touring stage productions. He choreographed and provided musical staging for over 100 others, including creating original ballets. On TV he performed on "Kojak" and "Queen of the Stardust Ballroom." Films he worked on are: THREE DAYS OF THE CONDOR; DEATH WISH; REPORT TO THE COMMISSIONER; THE STEPFORD WIVES; THE REINCARNATION OF PETER PROUD, and AARON LOVES ANGELA.

Drake, Ken

Died 30 Jan. 1987, Springville, Calif., age 65.

Stage/TV/Film Actor

A graduate of Pasadena Playhouse and member of the Stage Society in the early 1950s, he was a regular on the TV series "Not For Hire." He also appeared in episodes of "Bonanza," "Gunsmoke," "Sea Hunt," "Flipper," "Highway Patrol," "The Man From U.N.C.L.E.," and others. He was married for 19 years to *Los Angeles Times* drama critic Sylvie Drake. Among his movies: I BURY THE LIVING; CRIME AND PUNISHMENT USA; THE NEW INTERNS; THE BIGAMIST; TWELVE O'CLOCK HIGH; BUTCH CASSIDY AND THE SUNDANCE KID; THE GREAT NORTHFIELD MINNESOTA RAID.

Drew, Max [Guy Morton]

Died 8 Jan. 1987, Sherman Oaks, Calif.; age 40.

Actor

He studied with the Royal Shakespeare Co. in London for two years and spent two years with the Berkeley Shakespeare Festival. He last appeared on stage in "Night Sweat," a play about AIDS that ran in Hollywood for four months. His only film appearance was in CUTTER'S WAY.

Dunlap, Romola Remus

Died 17 Feb. 1987, Chicago, Ill.; age unknown.

Silent Film Actress

The original "Dorothy" was cast by author L. Frank Baum himself to play the starring role in his classic THE WIZARD OF OZ (1925). She skipped school to perform and was paid $5 a day for her work in the film which was one of the first color movies, the celluloid reels having been sent to France, where each frame was hand-colored. She also appeared in the movies THE FOUR-FOOTED HERO and MARY: TEN NIGHTS IN A BAR ROOM, but when Chicago's movie industry moved west to Hollywood, her parents refused to let her go along. She later performed in vaudeville and taught music and dance in Chicago.

Donovan

Dunn, Clara Whips

Died 1987, Atlanta, Ga.; age 90.

Actress

Performed in 10 feature films as well as many one-woman shows.

Egan, Richard

Born 29 July 1921, San Francisco, Calif.; died 16 June 1987, Santa Monica, Calif.

Stage/Film/TV Actor

A graduate of the University of San Francisco, he joined the Army in 1942 and taught judo and saw active duty in the Philippines. He was discovered by a Warner Bros. talent scout in 1949 at Stanford University where he had appeared in numerous plays on campus while earning his M.A. in theater history and dramatic literature. Prior to joining the Fox roster of performers in the early 1950s, where he was touted as a young Clark Gable, he performed on stage in classics such as "The Miser," "Richard III," "Twelfth Night," and comedies "Room Service," and "The Circle." His TV appearances included "Empire," "Redigo," and the soap opera series "Capitol." In between film and TV acting assignments he toured in stage productions of "I Ought to Be in Pictures," "Hanky Panky," and "Strike a Match." His films include: THE DAMNED DON'T CRY; THE GOOD HUMOR MAN; HIGHWAY 301; KANSAS RAIDERS; THE KILLER THAT STALKED NEW YORK; UNDERCOVER GIRL; WYOMING MAIL; BRIGHT VICTORY; FLAME OF ARABY; THE GOLDEN HORDE; HOLLYWOOD STORY; UP FRONT; THE BATTLE AT APACHE PASS; BLACKBEARD THE PIRATE; CRIPPLE CREEK; THE DEVIL MAKES THREE; ONE MINUTE TO ZERO; THE GLORY BRIGADE; THE KID FROM LEFT FIELD; SPLIT SECOND; WICKED WOMAN; DEMETRIUS AND THE GLADIATORS; GOG; KHYBER PATROL; SEVEN CITIES OF GOLD; UNDERWATER; UNTAMED; THE VIEW FROM POMPEY'S HEAD; VIOLENT SATURDAY; LOVE ME TENDER; TENSION AT TABLE ROCK; SLAUGHTER ON TENTH AVENUE; THE HUNTERS; VOICE IN THE MIRROR; A SUMMER PLACE; THESE THOUSAND HILLS; ESTHER AND THE KING; POLLYANNA; THE 300 SPARTANS; VALLEY OF MYSTERY; CHUBASCO; THE DESTRUCTORS; THE BIG CUBE; MOONFIRE; DAY OF THE WOLVES; THE AMSTERDAM KILL; THE SWEET CREEK COUNTY WAR; THE LEFT HAND OF GEMINI; KINO, THE PADRE ON HORSEBACK.

Egan

Elkerbout, Ben

Died 6 July 1987, Amsterdam, Netherlands; age 46.

Documentary/Feature Filmmaker

Started out as a reporter (specializing in Mideast and international affairs, interviewed Golda Meir and Mao Tse Tung) for a Dutch TV station, rising through the ranks to the position of deputy managing director; then worked for Belbo, a documentary film company, for which he directed THE MULTINATIONALS and RED DENNY. Had recently directed his first feature film DREAMERS.

Elston, Robert

Died 10 Dec. 1987, Amsterdam, Netherlands; age 55.

Actor

Mainly a stage actor, made his debut in "Maybe Tuesday" (1958); Broadway stage efforts include: "Spoon River Anthology," "Tall Story," "Vivat! Vivat! Regina!" Appeared in several films including MARK OF THE WITCH. He founded various theater groups and teaching of the dramatic art, directing, and cowriting were among his other talents. TV efforts include the TV film "A Private Battle," the mini-series "George Washington," and the soaps "Love of Life" and "As the World Turns."

Fong

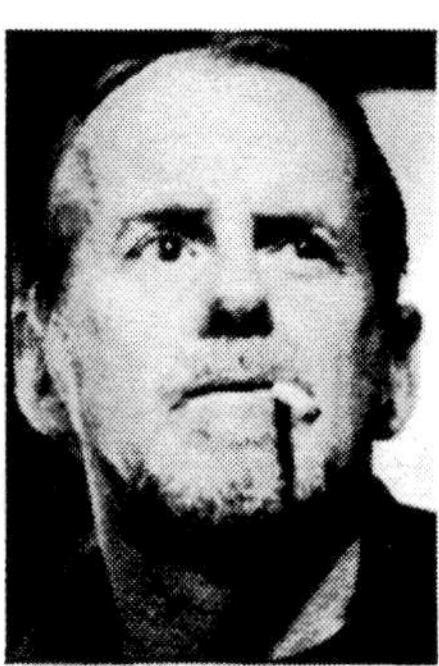

Fosse

England, Don [Don Torrillo]

Died 4 Feb. 1987, Los Angeles, Calif.; age 57.

Actor/Dancer

Appeared as a baby in DRACULA (1931), which featured Bela Lugosi's definitive portrayal of the vampire. After reaching manhood, appeared as a dancer in BRIGADOON; A STAR IS BORN (1954); THE RELUCTANT DEBUTANTE; THE COUNTRY GIRL. He switched to acting and appeared in THE FORTUNE and THE PRISONER OF SECOND AVENUE. Also worked in summer stock, TV (a regular part on "Taxi"), and Las Vegas, and played engagements at fairs.

Ensor, David

Died 5 Feb. 1987; age 80.

Film/TV Actor

Appeared in such British films as THE MAN WITH THE GREEN CARNATION; INFORMATION RECEIVED; THE POT CARRIERS.

Evans, Wilbur

Born 5 Aug. 1905, Philadelphia, Pa.; died 31 May 1987, Elmer, New Jersey.

Stage/Film Actor-Singer

Started his singing career with oratorio societies and symphony orchestras in 1927, winning the Atwater-Kent Foundation radio-singing contest, which led to a regular spot on the program until 1931. Made his Broadway debut in "The Merry Widow" (1942); other stage spots included: "The New Moon," "Mexican Hayride," "Up in Central Park," "Desert Song," a London production of "South Pacific" with Mary Martin. Appeared in HER FIRST ROMANCE (1940) and MAN WITH A MILLION. Became director of Valley Forge Music Fair in 1955 and also taught voice and musical comedy technique in Philadelphia, Pa.

Evers, Ann

Died 4 June 1987; age unknown.

Film/Stage Actress

Acted in character parts (usually as a maid or nurse) on stage in "Mr. Big" and in these films: FORGOTTEN FACES; A SON COMES HOME; ANYTHING FOR A THRILL; FRONTIER TOWN; IF I WERE KING; THE MAD MISS MANTON; MARIE ANTOINETTE; RIDERS OF THE BLACK HILLS; BEAUTY FOR THE ASKING; GUNGA DIN; SHE HAS WHAT IT TAKES; SOMEONE TO REMEMBER; CASANOVA BROWN.

Faulkner, Ralph B.

Died 28 Jan. 1987, Burbank, Calif.; age 95.

Fencing Master/Actor

Started out as a silent screen actor in such efforts as ANNE OF LITTLE SMOKY; APRIL SHOWERS (1923); LOVING LIES; MY NEIGHBOR'S WIFE; GOD OF MANKIND; suffered a knee injury during this period and took up fencing to strengthen it, gaining such expertise that he won a French amateur championship in 1932 and was a member of the US Olympic fencing team in 1928 and 1932; established his own fencing school, teaching such luminaries of the screen as Errol Flynn, Ronald Colman, Douglas Fairbanks, Jr., Basil Rathbone (one of his top pupils), Louis Hayward, Danny Kaye, Cornel Wilde (another Olympic contender), and Tony Curtis. Sound films in which he appeared are: THE THREE MUSKETEERS (1935); THE PRISONER OF ZENDA (1937); THE STAR MAKER.

Feder, Sidney

Died 27 May 1987, Los Angeles, Calif.; age 81.

Theater Owner/Film Producer

Coproduced THIS IS RUSSIA, a 1957 documentary, as well as having a hand in the financing for the Arch Oboler-produced/directed/written 3-D BWANA DEVIL in 1953. With his three brothers, owned a three-theater chain in California.

Fletcher, Tex [Jerry Bisceglia]

Died 18 March 1987, Newburgh, New York; age 78.

Film Actor

Appeared in one western in 1939, SIX GUN RHYTHM, made just before his production company, Grand National, went out of business. He had a some success on radio and in recordings, and became a security guard in later years.

Fong, Benson

Born 10 Oct. 1916, Sacramento, Calif.; died 1 Aug. 1987, Los Angeles, Calif.

Film/TV Actor

A grocer in Sacramento, he was asked by Paramount in 1943 if he would like to be in a movie. His 40-year career ranged from playing one of Charlie Chan's sons to the "Old One" on the "Kung Fu" TV series. At the suggestion of his friend Gregory Peck, he opened "Au Fong's" restaurant in Hollywood in 1946, and eventually four more on Sunset Boulevard. Besides his regular role on the "Kung Fu" series, he appeared on television in "Family in Blue," "Moonlight," and "The Glitter Dome." His movies include: CHARLIE CHAN AT THE OPERA; BEHIND THE RISING SUN; CHARLIE CHAN IN THE SECRET SERVICE; THE CHINESE CAT; DESTINATION TOKYO; DRAGON SEED; THE KEYS OF THE KINGDOM; THE PURPLE HEART; THIRTY SECONDS OVER TOKYO; UP IN ARMS; BACK TO BATAAN; CHINA SKY; FIRST YANK INTO TOKYO; NOB HILL; THE SCARLET CLUE; THE SHANGHAI COBRA; DARK ALIBI; DECEPTION; THE RED DRAGON; CALCUTTA; HAZARD; WOMEN IN THE NIGHT; BOSTON BLACKIE'S CHINESE VENTURE; CHINATOWN AT MIDNIGHT; THREE HUSBANDS; KOREA PATROL; PEKING EXPRESS; BACK AT THE FRONT; DRAGONFLY SQUADRON; HIS MAJESTY O'KEEFE; CONQUEST OF SPACE; THE LEFT HAND OF GOD; THE SCARLET HOUR; FIVE GATES TO HELL; WALK LIKE A DRAGON; FLOWER DRUM SONG; GIRLS! GIRLS! GIRLS!; OUR MAN FLINT; THE LOVE BUG; CHARLEY VARRICK; THE STRONGEST MAN IN THE WORLD; OLIVER'S STORY; S.O.B.; JINXED; A TIME FOR LOVE; HE IS MY BROTHER.

Forbes, Murray M.

Died 27 Jan. 1987, Los Angeles, Calif.; age 80.

Radio Actor/Author

Mainly noted for the character of Willie Fitz (as well as a minor character, Hunkins) on the 30-year run of "Ma Perkins" on radio, he also wrote a thriller novel, *Hollow Triumph*, which was turned into a 1948 film starring Paul Henreid and Joan Bennett. Other radio appearances include "Guiding Light," "Today's Children," "Foxes of Flatbush," "Lonely Women" and "The Story of Mary Marlin" after a 1931 start on "The General Tire Show" in his native Chicago.

Fosse, Robert Louis

Born 23 June 1927, Chicago, Ill.; died 23 Sept. 1987, Washington, D.C.

Choreographer/Director

He achieved the unmatched feat of winning an Oscar, a Tony, and an Emmy in a single year for directing CABARET, Broadway's "Pippin," and the Liza Minnelli TV special "Liza with a *Z*. The son of a vaudeville entertainer, he began performing on the vaudeville circuit as a child and by the age of 13 was a seasoned veteran. He loved staging more than performing, however, and moved to New York where he bluffed his way into being hired by George Abbott as choreographer for "Pajama Game," proving his worth by winning a Tony. In all, he received nine Tonys, three Emmys, and an Oscar. In 1979 he made ALL THAT JAZZ, a semi-autobiographical film portrait of a director-choreographer who dies of a heart attack, which won nine Oscar nominations. He collapsed the evening of the National Theater's revival premiere of "Sweet Charity," one of his most enduring choreographic creations. Among his movies: GIVE A GIRL A BREAK; KISS ME KATE; MY SISTER EILEEN; THE PAJAMA GAME; DAMN YANKEES; SWEET CHARITY; LENNY; THE LITTLE PRINCE; HOW TO SUCCEED IN BUSINESS WITHOUT REALLY TRYING; THIEVES; STAR 80.

Franju, Georges

Born 12 April 1912, Fougeres, Brittany, France; died 5 November 1987, Paris, France

Director/Screenwriter

Called by French film historian Georges Sadoul "a filmmaker with a mocking sense of anarchic black humor and a feeling for unusual atmospheres," Franju began his film career at an early age when, in 1934, he made a documentary called LE METRO with Henri Langlois. The following year he, with the help of his good friend Langlois, helped to form a film club called "Le Cercle du Cinema," which later evolved into the famous Cinematheque Francaise. From 1938 until the end of the war, Franju served as the secretary of the International Federation of Film Archives (F.I.A.F.). In 1945, he served as secretary of Jean Painleve's Institut de Cinematographie Scientifique. The first of his films was LE SANG DES BETES (1949; The Blood of the Beasts), followed in 1952 by HOTEL DES INVALIDES, and LE GRAND MELIES. By 1958, he began making fiction films, beginning with LA TETE CONTRE LES MURS (THE KEEPERS in the U.S.) Among his other films are LES YEUX SANS VISAGE (released in the U.S. as THE HORROR CHAMBER OF DR. FAUSTUS); LA FAUTE DE L'ABBE MOURET; THOMAS L'IMPOSTEUR; PLEINS FEUX SUR L'ASSASSIN (aka: SPOTLIGHT ON MURDER); THERESE DESQUEROUX (aka: THERESE); JUDEX; THOMAS L'IMPOSTEUR (aka: THOMAS THE IMPOSTER), LES RIDEAUX BLANCS (for French television); MARCEL ALLAIN (for French television); LA FAUTE DE L'ABBE MOURET (aka: THE DEMISE OF FATHER MOURET); L'HOMME SANS VISAGE (aka: SHADOWMAN).

Fraser, Bill

Born 5 June 1907, Perth, Scotland; died 5 Sept. 1987, Hertfordshire, England.

Film/Stage/TV Actor

Was a classical character actor in both the Royal Shakespeare and National Theater companies as well as heading his own company early in his career. Spent his WW II service producing shows for servicemen. His films (in which he essayed mainly comic small parts) include: THE COMMON TOUCH; SCOTLAND YARD INSPECTOR; THE CAPTAIN'S PARADISE; MEET MR. LUCIFER; TERROR ON A TRAIN; TONIGHT AT 8:30; THE BAREFOOT CONTESSA; DUEL IN THE JUNGLE; ALIAS JOHN PRESTON; CHARLEY MOON; JUMPING FOR JOY; JUST MY LUCK; SECOND FIDDLE (1957); ANOTHER TIME, ANOTHER PLACE; THE MAN WHO LIKED FUNERALS; ORDERS ARE ORDERS; THE FAST LADY; WHAT A CRAZY WORLD; THE AMERICANIZATION OF EMILY; I'VE GOTTA HORSE; JOEY BOY; MASQUERADE (1965); DIAMONDS FOR BREAKFAST; THE BEST HOUSE IN LONDON; CAPTAIN NEMO AND THE UNDERWATER CITY; ALL THE WAY UP; UP POMPEII; UP THE CHASTITY BELT; UP THE FRONT; LOVE THY NEIGHBOR (1973); THAT'S YOUR FUNERAL; MOMENTS; EYE OF THE NEEDLE; WAGNER; PIRATES. Appeared on TV in "Bootsie and Snudge," "Rumpole of the Bailey," and "The Corn Is Green" (the Katharine Hepburn version and one of the last directorial efforts of George Cukor), which was shown theatrically in Britain.

Freedman, Ben

Died 13 June 1987, Los Angeles, Calif.; age 83.

Actor

His main job was as a manager for the employment department for the state of California. Also did some stage work, appeared in LAST OF THE RED HOT LOVERS and SAVE THE TIGER, as well as such TV series as "Barney Miller" and "Baretta."

Fregonese, Hugo

Born 8 Apr. 1908, Mendoza, Argentina; died 17 Jan. 1987, Buenos Aires, Argentina.

Director

Began his career in 1935 when Columbia Pictures hired him as an adviser on films with Latin American themes. He returned to his native Argentina in the 1940s to direct his own movies including DONDE MUEREN LAS PALABRAS, PAMPA BARBARA and APENAS UN DELINQUENTE. He also directed in West Germany, Spain, and Britain. Among his American movies are: ONE WAY STREET; SADDLE TRAMP; APACHE DRUMS; MARK OF THE RENEGADE; MY SIX CONVICTS; UNTAMED FRONTIER; BLOWING WILD; DECAMERON NIGHTS; MAN IN THE ATTIC; THE RAID; BLACK TUESDAY; HARRY BLACK AND THE TIGER; THE BEASTS OF MARSEILLES; MARCO POLO; DR. MABUSE'S RAYS OF DEATH; SAVAGE PAMPAS; ASSIGNMENT TERROR.

Froehlich, Gustav

Born 21 March 1902, Hanover, Germany; died 22 Dec. 1987, Lugano, Switzerland.

Actor/Director

Started out as a journalist and editor before switching to the acting on stage and screen in the mid-1920s. Appeared in such films as FREISENBLUT; METROPOLIS (his most noted part, as the youthful protagonist); EVA AND THE GRASSHOPPER; THE MEISTERSINGER; HOMECOMING; HURRAH I'M ALIVE; THE BURNING HEART; THE IMMORTAL VAGABOND; ZWEI MENSCHEN; VORUNTERSUCHUNG; KISMET (German version of the Otis Skinner film); GLORIA; LIEBESLIED, MEIN LEOPOLD, EIN WALZER VOM STRAUSS; LIEBESKOMMANDO; KAISERWALTER; WHAT WOMEN DREAM; THE NIGHT OF THE GREAT LOVE; DER FLUCHTLING AUS CHIKAGO; STRADIVARI; BARCAROLE; LIEBESLEUTE; INKOGNITO; MINOR LOVE AND THE REAL THING; DER GROSSE KONIG; FAMILIE BUCHHOLZ; DER GROSSE FALL; SECRETS OF A SOUL; THE SINNER; HOUSE OF LIFE; BALL DER NATIONEN. His directorial credits include: RAKOCZY-MARSCH (which he codirected with Stefan Szekely as well as acted in), LIEBE UND TROMPETENLANG; WEGE IM ZWIELICHT; TORREANI (also acted in the last three); LEB' WOHL CHRISTINA (also coscripted); DER BAGNOSTRAFLING; DIE LUGE (also wrote the last two); SEINE TOCHTER IST DER PETER.

Gaines, Lee [Otho Lee Gaines]

Died 15 July 1987, Helsinki, Finland; age 73.

Singer

Organized the Delta Rhythm Boys in college, a singing group which appeared in approximately 35 feature or short musical films in the 1940s and 1950s including: CRAZY HOUSE; HI' YA, SAILOR; SO'S YOUR UNCLE; HI' GOOD-LOOKIN'; NIGHT CLUB GIRL; RECKLESS AGE; FOLLOW THE BOYS; WEEKEND PASS; EASY TO LOOK AT. Some of their classic recordings are: "Dry Bones," "Take the A Train" (Gaines did the lyrics for this one as well as for "Just a-Sittin' and a-Rockin" by Duke Ellington), "It's Only a Paper Moon" (with Ella Fitzgerald). Worked with such top musical performers as Count Basie, Charlie Barnet, Les Paul, and Fred Astaire.

Ganzert, R.J.

Died 20 Jan. 1987.

Film Actor

Appeared in two Clint Eastwood films, ESCAPE FROM ALCATRAZ and HONKYTONK MAN.

Geraghty, Maurice

Born 29, Sept. 1908, Rushville, Ind.; died 30 June 1987, Palm Springs, Calif.

Film/TV Producer-Director-Writer

A native of Rushville, Indiana, he was the son of screenwriter Tom Geraghty, and the brother of silent film star Carmelita Geraghty and writer Gerald Geraghty. After graduating from Princeton in 1928 he went to work as a western story supervisor at Republic for three years. He scripted 20 features from 1937 through the mid 1950s. At RKO he produced much of the FALCON series, wrote and directed THE SWORD OF MONTE CRISTO, and wrote the story for Elvis Presley's first film, LOVE ME TENDER. He wrote and directed for the television series "Lassie," "Laramie," "Beacon Street," "87th Precinct," "Daniel Boone," "Bonanza," and "The Virginian." His movies include: HILLS OF OLD WYOMING; TROUBLE AT MIDNIGHT; WESTBOUND LIMITED; LAW OF THE PLAINS; THE MYSTERIOUS RIDER (1938); SILVER ON THE SAGE; APACHE TRAIL; THE FALCON'S BROTHER; WEST OF TOMBSTONE; THE FALCON AND THE CO-EDS; THE FALCON IN DANGER; THE FALCON STRIKES BACK; GOOD MORNING, JUDGE; ACTION IN ARABIA; THE FALCON IN HOLLYWOOD; THE FALCON IN MEXICO; CHINA SKY; THE FALCON IN SAN FRANCISCO; WHIPLASH; WHO KILLED "DOC" ROBBIN?; CALAMITY JANE AND SAM BASS; RED CANYON; THE SWORD OF MONTE CRISTO; TOMAHAWK; ROSE OF CIMARRON; ROBBER'S ROOST; LOVE ME TENDER; MOHAWK.

Gessner, Adrienne

Died 23 June 1987; age 90.

Actress

This Austrian native appeared in NO TIME FOR FLOWERS; STOLEN IDENTITY; A BREATH OF SCANDAL.

Gibson, Alan

Born 28 Apr. 1938, Canada; died 5 July 1987, London, England.

Director

Studied with the Bristol Old Vic rep company in England and was staff producer-director at BBC-TV, responsible for such productions as "A Woman Called Golda," "Churchill and the Generals," "Playboy of the Western World," and "Love Doesn't Grow on Trees." Among his movies are: DURING ONE NIGHT; JOURNEY INTO MIDNIGHT; GOODBYE GEMINI; CRESCENDO; DRACULA A.D. 1972; CHECKERED FLAG OR CRASH; COUNT DRACULA AND HIS VAMPIRE BRIDE; THE TWO FACES OF EVIL.

Gibson, Wynne [Winifred Gibson]

Born 3 July, 1905, New York, N.Y.; died 15 May 1987, Laguna Niguel, Calif.

Film/Stage Actress

After running away from home in New York at 16 to become a chorus girl on Broadway, she worked in vaudeville, theater, and on tour until moving to Hollywood where she made more than 40 films over the next 14 years. She later appeared on radio and television on such shows as "Studio One" and "Martin Kane." She was on the board of Actors Equity and was chairwoman of the Equity Library Theater. Her movies include: NOTHING BUT THE TRUTH; CHILDREN OF PLEASURE; THE FALL GUY; CITY STREETS; THE GANG BUSTER; JUNE MOON; KICK IN; MAN OF THE WORLD; ROAD TO RENO; THE DEVIL IS DRIVING; IF I HAD A MILLION; LADIES OF THE BIG HOUSE; LADY AND GENT; NIGHT AFTER NIGHT; THE STRANGE CASE OF CLARA DEANE; TWO KINDS OF WOMEN; AGGIE APPLEBY; MAKER OF MEN; THE CRIME OF THE CENTURY; EMERGENCY CALL; THE CAPTAIN HATES THE SEA; THE CROSBY CASE; GAMBLING; I GIVE MY LOVE; SLEEPERS EAST; ADMIRALS ALL; ANY MAN'S WIFE; COME CLOSER, FOLKS; THE CROUCHING BEAST; MICHAEL O'HALLORAN; RACKETEERS IN EXILE; TRAPPED BY G-MEN; FLIRTING WITH FATE; GANGS OF NEW YORK; CAFE HOSTESS; FORGOTTEN GIRLS; A MIRACLE ON MAIN STREET; MY SON IS GUILTY; DOUBLE CROSS; A MAN'S WORLD; THE FALCON STRIKES BACK; MYSTERY BROADCAST.

Gimbel, Peter R.

Died 12 July 1987, New York, N.Y.; age 59.

Documentary Cinematographer

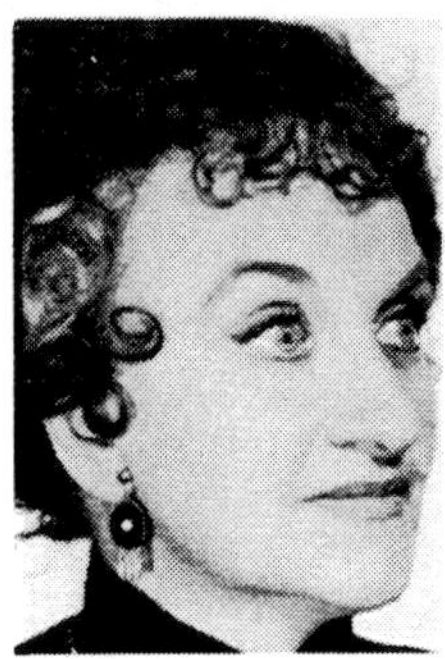

Gingold

Gleason

A native of New York City, his father was Bernard F. Gimbel of the Gimbels and Saks Fifth Ave. store chains. Started out as an investment banker. When the Italian luxury liner *Andrea Doria* sank in 1956, he did some scuba diving at the wreck site, coming up with pictures that were featured in *Life* magazine, launching a career which included assignments for *Time*, *National Geographic*, and *Encyclopedia Brittanica*; later did the main job of producing, directing, writing, and performing for the noted documentary about great white sharks, BLUE WATER, WHITE DEATH. Worked on two more films about the *Andrea Doria* that were presented on TV in 1975 and 1981.

Gingold, Hermione Ferdinanda

Born 9 Dec. 1897, London, England; died 24 May 1987, New York, N.Y.

Stage/Film Actress-Comedienne

Her stage debut was in a kindergarten production of "Henry VIII," and by 14 she had appeared in "Where the Rainbow Ends" with Noel Coward. During WW II she gained an international reputation playing to US servicemen in the hit London revue "Sweet and Low." After appearing in Shakespearean plays at the Old Vic and starring in British revues and on BBC radio and television, she came to the US and began her theater career in the production of "It's About Time" in Cambridge, Mass. She won the Broadway theater's Donaldson Award in 1954 and appeared in such hits as "Oh, Dad, Poor Dad, Mama's Hung You in the Closet and I'm Feelin' So Sad" in 1963 and "A Little Night Music" in 1973. Her TV credits include "The Ed Sullivan Show," "The Jack Paar Show," "Omnibus," and "Person to Person." She is fondly remembered for her nostalgic duet with Maurice Chevalier in the classic screen musical GIGI. Other films include: DANCE PRETTY LADY; SOMEONE AT THE DOOR; MERRY COMES TO STAY; MEET MR. PENNY; THE BUTLER'S DILEMMA; THE PICKWICK PAPERS; THE SLASHER; THE ADVENTURES OF SADIE; AROUND THE WORLD IN 80 DAYS; BELL, BOOK AND CANDLE; THE NAKED EDGE; GAY PURR-EE; THE MUSIC MAN; I'D RATHER BE RICH; HARVEY MIDDLEMAN, FIREMAN; MUNSTER, GO HOME; PROMISE HER ANYTHING; THOSE FANTASTIC FLYING FOOLS; A LITTLE NIGHT MUSIC; GARBO TALKS.

Ginsberg, Claire

Died 1 July 1987.

Actress

Started in the acting profession at the age of 53 and appeared in the film, MICROWAVE MASSACRE. Appeared on TV in "One Day at a Time" and "Big Shamus, Little Shamus," the Brian Dennehy starrer. Her stage credits include: "Third Best Sport," "The Shadow Box" and an eight-hour play, "Anzac."

Gladwin, Joe

Died 11 March 1987, Manchester, England; age 82.

TV/Radio/Film Actor

Like many British comedians, he got his start in the British music halls, later going into such films as A KIND OF LOVING; NIGHT MUST FALL (1964); CHARLIE BUBBLES; THE MIND OF MR. SOAMES; THE RECKONING; THE LITTLE HORSE THIEVES; NEAREST AND DEAREST; YANKS. He is probably best known in Britain for his continuing role in the BBC series "Last of the Summer Wine."

Gleason, Jackie [Herbert John Gleason]

Born 26 Feb. 1916, Brooklyn, N.Y.; died 24 June 1987, Fort Lauderdale, Fla.

TV/Film Actor-Comedian

"The Great One's" career spanned six decades—he was a nightclub comic in the 1930s, a character actor under contract to Warner Bros. and 20th Century-Fox in the 1940s, a star of a network television series in the 1950s and 1960s, and reemerged as a late blooming star of the movies in the 1970s and 1980s. He was best known, however, for his role as Ralph Kramden on "The Honeymooners," which began as a weekly half-hour TV series and developed a following that has lasted 30 years. Though he couldn't read music or play a musical instrument, he composed, arranged, and conducted 38 record albums. He was awarded a Tony for his Broadway stage work and an Academy Award nomination for his performance in THE HUSTLER, but never received an Emmy Award. His movies include: NAVY BLUES; ALL THROUGH THE NIGHT; ORCHESTRA WIVES; SPRINGTIME IN THE ROCKIES; TRAMP, TRAMP, TRAMP; THE DESERT HAWK; THE HUSTLER; GIGOT; REQUIEM FOR A HEAVYWEIGHT; PAPA'S DELICATE CONDITION; SOLDIER IN THE RAIN; SKIDOO; DON'T DRINK THE WATER; HOW TO COMMIT MARRIAGE; HOW DO I LOVE THEE?; MR. BILLION; SMOKEY AND THE BANDIT; SMOKEY AND THE BANDIT II; THE TOY; SMOKEY AND THE BANDIT-PART 3; THE STING II.

Golden, Ray

Died 12 Nov. 1987; age 81.

Screenwriter/Stage Producer

Wrote screenplays for both the Marx and Ritz Brothers comedy teams. For the stage, both produced and wrote revues.

Golland, Joseph

Died 17 Nov. 1987, Vancouver, British Columbia; age unknown.

Actor

Had a 30-year career in film in Canada and the US, and did numerous TV commercials. His films include: THE TRAP (1967); THE VISITOR (1973); BEAR ISLAND. Appeared as Albert Einstein in the TV miniseries "A Man Called Intrepid"; other TV films include: "Love, Mary," "Love Is Never Silent," "I-Man," "The Christmas Star," and "Nobody's Child." Was in the midst of filming a John Travolta film, THE EXPERTS, when he died of a heart attack.

Goodman, Jack

Died 7 Apr. 1987, Evanston, Ill.; age 89.

Restaurateur/Actor

Was a restaurant operator at various locations in Chicagoland from the late 1920s until his retirement in 1970. Appeared in the Warren Beatty film MICKEY ONE, which was partially shot at one of his restaurants.

Goodwin, Harold

Born 1 Dec. 1902, Peoria, Ill.; died 13 July 1987, Woodland Hills, Calif.

Actor/Dialog Director

Not to be confused with the British character actor of the same name, he gained his initial acting experience in local Los Angeles theater and moved on to silent films with LITTLE ORPHAN (1915); then went on to make THE SAWDUST RING; SET FREE (1918); HEART O' THE HILLS (1919). His early years in silents were his most successful and included starring parts at Fox Studios, Universal, and R-C. Other silents include PUPPY LOVE; THE WINNING GIRL; SWEET LAVANDER; OVERLAND RED; SUDS; LOVETIME; OLIVER TWIST, JR.; THE ROAD DEMON; HEARTS OF YOUTH; THE FLIRT (1922); THE BOOTLEGGER'S DAUGHTER; KISSED; MAN TO MAN (1922); THE ROSARY; SEEING'S BELIEVING; TRACKED TO EARTH; ALICE ADAMS (1923); BROADWAY GOLD; BURNING WORDS; THE RAMBLIN' KID; GENTLE JULIA; KINDLED COURAGE; THE WANTERS; HIT AND RUN; IN LOVE WITH LOVE; THAT FRENCH LADY; THE ARIZONA EXPRESS; MADONNA OF THE STREETS (1924); RIDERS OF THE PURPLE SAGE (1925); THE TALKER; THE MIDSHIPMAN; THE BETTER 'OLE (1926); THE FLAMING FRONTIER (1926); THE HONEYMOON EXPRESS; SECRET ORDERS (1926); COLLEGE (1927); SNOWBOUND; TARZAN AND THE GOLDEN LION; WHEN A DOG LOVES; THE CAMERAMAN; THE CHEER LEADER; HER SUMMER HERO. His sound films include: FLIGHT (1929); ALL QUIET ON THE WESTERN FRONT; THE MIGHTY; THE WIDOW FROM CHICAGO; DIRIGIBLE; GRAFT; THE LAWYER'S SECRET; HAT CHECK GIRL; MOVIE CRAZY; SKY BRIDE; SYMPHONY OF SIX MILLION; HALLELUJAH, I'M A BUM; PLEASURE; STRAWBERRY ROAN (1933); LONE COWBOY; SHE WAS A LADY; SMOKING GUNS (1934); WAGON WHEELS; THE CRUSADES; ROMANCE IN MANHATTAN; WESTERN FRONTIER; THE DARK HOUR; THEODORA GOES WILD; BREAKFAST FOR TWO; A FIGHT TO THE FINISH; IT HAPPENED IN HOLLYWOOD; ALEXANDER'S RAGTIME BAND; CITY GIRL (1938); MY LUCKY STAR (1938); BOY FRIEND (1939); JESSE JAMES (1939); SECOND FIDDLE (1939); SUSANNAH OF THE MOUNTIES; TOO BUSY TO WORK; UNION PACIFIC; YOUNG MR. LINCOLN; CHARLIE CHAN AT THE WAX MUSEUM; RAGTIME COWBOY JOE; TEXAS RANGERS RIDE AGAIN; VIVA CISCO KID; FORCED LANDING; INTERNATIONAL LADY; TANKS A MILLION; YOU'LL NEVER GET RICH; BUCK PRIVATES; ABOUT FACE (1942); QUIET PLEASE, MURDER; HAY FOOT; HE HIRED THE BOSS; FRONTIER GAL; SHE GETS HER MAN (1945); DON'T GAMBLE WITH STRANGERS; LOVER COME BACK (1946); RIDE THE PINK HORSE; SLAVE GIRL; THE BOLD FRONTIERSMAN; CARSON CITY RAIDERS; FAMILY HONEYMOON; KISS THE BLOOD OFF MY HANDS; RIVER LADY; THE LADY GAMBLES; LAW OF THE GOLDEN WEST; TOKYO JOE; THE GREAT RUPERT; I WAS A SHOPLIFTER; THE KID FROM TEXAS; THE VANISHING WESTERNER; COMIN' ROUND THE MOUNTAIN; ABBOTT AND COSTELLO MEET THE INVISIBLE MAN; DOUBLE DYNAMITE; HERE COME THE NELSONS; ABBOTT AND COSTELLO GO TO MARS; MA AND PA KETTLE ON VACATION; THE REDHEAD FROM WYOMING; MA AND PA KETTLE AT WAIKIKI; ABBOTT AND COSTELLO MEET THE KEYSTONE KOPS; JOE BUTTERFLY; NIGHT PASSAGE; PORTRAIT IN BLACK; MOVE OVER, DARLING; FATE IS THE HUNTER; MORITURI.

Gould-Porter, Arthur

Died 2 Jan. 1987, Los Angeles, Calif.; age 81.

Actor/Composer

His career began in England and spanned several decades. He was a composer of show tunes and appeared in such television productions as "G.E. Theater," "The Man from U.N.C.L.E.," "Alfred Hitchcock Presents," "Gomer Pyle," and "The Wild, Wild West," but is probably best remembered for his role as the original butler on the television series "The Beverly Hillbillies." His film credits include: NIGHTMARE (1942); NORTHERN PURSUIT; JANE EYRE (1944); THE WHITE CLIFFS OF DOVER; A DOUBLE LIFE; KISS THE BLOOD OFF MY HANDS; KIND LADY; AGAINST ALL FLAGS; ROGUE'S MARCH; DANGEROUS WHEN WET; ABBOTT AND COSTELLO MEET DR. JEKYLL AND MR. HYDE; SO THIS IS PARIS (1954); LADY GODIVA (1955); THE VIRGIN QUEEN (1955); THREE NUTS IN SEARCH OF A BOLT; TORN CURTAIN; THE KARATE KILLERS; THE GIRLS OF PLEASURE ISLAND; DARLING LILI; THE IRON CURTAIN; PIRATES OF TORTUGA; ASSAULT ON A QUEEN; BEDKNOBS AND BROOMSTICKS.

Grasso, Sal

Died 12 Sep. 1987, Burbank, Calif.; age 50.

Art Director/Director

Started out as an assistant to Ann Sothern before switching to art direction on such films as FROGS; THE KILLING KIND; CONCRETE JUNGLE; SEXTETTE; SEVEN; MALIBU EXPRESS; HARD TICKET TO HAWAII; later became a director of adult or gay-oriented films, using the name of Steve Scott.

Gray, Harriette Ann

Died 20 Apr. 1987, Columbia, Mo.; age 73.

Choreographer/Dancer/Teacher/Actress

At first associated with a dance company, she worked from 1941 to 1951 in Hollywood where she was an assistant choreographer at Columbia, and danced in the 1947 Rita Hayworth film DOWN TO EARTH as well as other Columbia films. Later worked at Warner Bros. and United Artists and taught dancing at Universal; in later years taught and ran her own regional dance company.

Greene, Lorne

Born 12 Feb. 1915, Ottawa, Ontario; died 11 Sept. 1987, Santa Monica Calif.

TV/Film/Stage/Radio Actor

Best known as patriarch Ben Cartwright on the 14-year television series "Bonanza," he began his professional radio career while still a student at Queen's University and subsequently became Canada's leading newscaster. In the early 1950s he moved to New York and appeared on live TV productions as well as on Broadway with Katharine Cornell in "Prescott Proposals." He was deeply committed to environmental and wildlife causes and served as chairman of the National Wildlife Federation. Among his films are: THE SILVER CHALICE; TIGHT SPOT; AUTUMN LEAVES; THE HARD MAN; PEYTON PLACE; THE BUCCANEER (1958); THE GIFT OF LOVE; THE LAST OF THE FAST GUNS; THE TRAP (1959); THE ERRAND BOY; EARTHQUAKE; TIDAL WAVE; BATTLESTAR GALACTICA; MISSION GALACTICA: THE CYLON ATTACK; CONQUEST OF THE EARTH; KLONDIKE FEVER; HEIDI'S SONG; HIGH COUNTRY CALLING.

Greenwood, Joan

Born 4 Mar. 1921, London, England; died 28 Feb. 1987, London, England.

Stage/Film Actress

Best known for her comedy performances, she costarred with Alec Guinness in KIND HEARTS AND CORONETS, THE MAN IN THE WHITE SUIT, and THE DETECTIVE (1954). She made her London stage debut at 18 and was cast by Leslie Howard as his leading lady in the film THE GENTLE SEX after he saw her in a production of "The Women." For most of her career she alternated between the London stage and film work, first appearing on the Broadway stage in 1954 in T.S. Eliot's "The Confidential Clerk." Among her movies are: HE FOUND A STAR; MY WIFE'S FAMILY; THE GENTLE SEX; THEY KNEW MR. KNIGHT; FRENZY (1946); A GIRL IN A MILLION; BAD SISTER (1947); THE OCTOBER MAN; THE SMUGGLERS; THE BAD LORD BYRON; SARABAND; TIGHT LITTLE ISLAND; FLESH AND BLOOD; MR. PEEK-A-BOO; THE IMPORTANCE OF BEING EARNEST; YOUNG WIVES' TALE; LOVERS, HAPPY LOVERS!; MOONFLEET; STAGE STRUCK; MYSTERIOUS ISLAND (1961); TOM JONES; THE MOON-SPINNERS; THE AMOROUS MR. PRAWN; GIRL STROKE BOY; THE UNCANNY; THE WATER BABIES; THE HOUND OF THE BASKERVILLES (1980); WAGNER.

Groesse, Paul

Born 28 Feb. 1906, Hungary; died 4 May 1987, Woodland Hills, Calif.

Art Director

A native of Hungary, he came to the US at age six, studied at Northwestern University, and graduated from Yale in 1930. He worked as an architect in Chicago and was a designer of the Century of Progress Exposition until joining MGM in the mid-1930s. He was nominated for 11 Academy Awards, winning for PRIDE AND PREJUDICE; THE YEARLING; LITTLE WOMEN. Other movies featuring his work are: MANNEQUIN (1937); THE SHINING HOUR; LADY OF THE TROPICS; I TAKE THIS WOMAN; TORTILLA FLAT; LASSIE, COME HOME; MADAME CURIE; THIRTY SECONDS OVER TOKYO; THE VALLEY OF DECISION; THE SEA OF GRASS; A DATE WITH JUDY; LUXURY LINER (1948); THE STRATTON STORY; ANNIE GET YOUR GUN; GROUNDS FOR MARRIAGE; MR. IMPERIUM; NO QUESTIONS ASKED; TOO YOUNG TO KISS; THE MERRY WIDOW (1952); GIVE A GIRL A BREAK; LILI; RHAPSODY; HIT THE DECK (1955); THE CATERED AFFAIR; SPRING REUNION; UNTIL THEY SAIL; HANDLE WITH CARE (1958); THE GAZEBO; THE WORLD, THE FLESH, AND THE DEVIL; THE WRECK OF THE MARY DEARE; ADVENTURES OF A YOUNG MAN; THE MUSIC MAN; TWILIGHT OF HONOR; HONEYMOON HOTEL (1964); ONCE A THIEF (1965); MISTER BUDDWING; IN THE HEAT OF THE NIGHT.

Greene

Greenwood

Gunzburg, Roy

Died 4 Jan. 1987.

Film Actor

Appeared in HAWMPS and DEATH VALLEY (1982). His small-screen efforts include the TV movies "The Gun and the Pulpit," "Killing Stone," and "September Gun."

Grzimek, Bernhard

Died 13 March 1987, Frankfurt, Germany; age 77.

Documentary Filmmaker

A native of Neisse, Germany, he studied veterinary medicine and zoology in college and assumed the leadership of the Frankfurt zoo in 1945, making it into one of the world's best. This led him into documentary filmmaking. Focusing on animal behavior, he created the Oscar-winning SERENGETI MUST NOT DIE. He also produced a book about the film that was translated into 36 languages and a 14-volume animal wildlife encyclopedia. Another documentary, NO PLACE FOR WILD ANIMALS, won prizes in Germany. He presided over one of the longest-running TV shows in Germany, "A Place for Animals."

Haack, Morton

Born 26 Jun. 1924, Los Angeles, Calif; died 22 Mar. 1987, Rome, Italy.

Costume Designer

Nominated for Academy Awards for THE UNSINKABLE MOLLY BROWN; PLANET OF THE APES; and WHAT'S THE MATTER WITH HELEN? Other films include: COME SEPTEMBER; WILD HERITAGE; PLEASE DON'T EAT THE DAISIES; JUMBO; WALK, DON'T RUN.

Haifetz, Jascha

Born 2 Feb. 1901, Vilna, Russia; died 11 Dec. 1987, Los Angeles, Calif.

Violinist

The preeminent classical violinist of the first half of the 20th Century, he grew up in Russia and gained worldwide respect for his playing while still a child, making his US debut in 1917 at Carnegie Hall. His pure use of technique and musicianship was acclaimed throughout his concert and recording career. He appeared in THEY SHALL HAVE MUSIC and CARNEGIE HALL. One of his wives was silent screen star Florence Vidor.

Hallenbeck, E. Darrell

Died 31 Jan. 1987, Northridge, Calif.; age 64.

Production Manager/Film/TV Director

Started his show business career in 1942 as a messenger at MGM and went on to become a director, handling such TV shows as "Gunsmoke," "The Virginian," "The Man from U.N.C.L.E.," "The Girl from U.N.C.L.E.," "Tarzan," "The Green Hornet." Did production management or associate producer chores on such films as ALL THE PRESIDENT'S MEN; DRUM; THE JAZZ SINGER (1980); TRENCHCOAT; BABY; MY SCIENCE PROJECT; ABOUT LAST NIGHT; also produced TOY SOLDIERS and directed ONE OF OUR SPIES IS MISSING (episodes of "The Man From Uncle" which were spliced together and released theatrically).

Hamilton, Marc

Died 12 May 1987, Burbank, Calif.; age 64.

Actor

He appeared in such films as THIS ISLAND EARTH; GIANT; THE GREAT LOCOMOTIVE CHASE; MAN FROM DEL RIO; THE MOLE PEOPLE. TV appearances include roles in "Death

Hartman

Hayes

Hayworth

Valley Days" and "The Life and Legend of Wyatt Earp." Appeared on stage in "The Big Two" as well as Mae West's "Diamond Lil."

Handl, Irene

Born 27 Dec. 1901; died 29 Nov. 1987, London, England.

Actress/Comedienne

One of Britain's best-loved actresses, she perfected the role of a slightly eccentric cockney old lady, but didn't begin her career until she was nearly 40, and then appeared in stage plays, films, and television comedies as well as becoming an accomplished writer. Among her movies are: MISSING—BELIEVED MARRIED (1937); STRANGE BOARDERS; MRS. PYM OF SCOTLAND YARD; DR. O'DOWD; THE FUGITIVE (1940); GASBAGS; GEORGE AND MARGARET; NIGHT TRAIN; THE GIRL IN THE NEWS; THE FLEMISH FARM; GET CRACKING; I'LL WALK BESIDE YOU; IT'S IN THE BAG (1943); MILLIONS LIKE US; RHYTHM SERENADE; GIVE US THE MOON; KISS THE BRIDE GOODBYE; UNCENSORED; WELCOME, MR. WASHINGTON; BRIEF ENCOUNTER; FOR YOU ALONE; GREAT DAY (1945); MR. EMMANUEL; THE GAY INTRUDERS; I'LL TURN TO YOU; THE HILLS OF DONEGAL; CODE OF SCOTLAND YARD; THE FOOL AND THE PRINCESS; THE CARDBOARD CAVALIER; DARK SECRET; FOR THEM THAT TRESPASS; HER MAN GILBEY; THE HISTORY OF MR. POLLY; SILENT DUST; TEMPTATION HARBOR; ADAM AND EVELYNE; THE PERFECT WOMAN; STAGE FRIGHT; ONE WILD OAT; TREASURE HUNT; MEET MR. LUCIFER; MR. POTTS GOES TO MOSCOW; THE WEDDING OF LILLI MARLENE; BURNT EVIDENCE; DUEL IN THE JUNGLE; MAD ABOUT MEN; THE WEAK AND THE WICKED; YOUNG WIVES' TALE; A KID FOR TWO FARTHINGS; WHO DONE IT? (1956); BROTHERS IN LAW; THE SILKEN AFFAIR; SMALL HOTEL; HAPPY IS THE BRIDE; IT'S NEVER TOO LATE; THE KEY; LAW AND DISORDER; THE CROWNING TOUCH; I'M ALL RIGHT, JACK; LEFT, RIGHT AND CENTRE; CARRY ON CONSTABLE; DESERT MICE; DOCTOR IN LOVE; FRENCH MISTRESS; INN FOR TROUBLE; MAKE MINE MINK; MAN IN A COCKED HAT; NEXT TO NO TIME; SCHOOL FOR SCOUNDRELS; BEWARE OF CHILDREN; CALL ME GENIUS; DOUBLE BUNK; THE NIGHT WE GOT THE BIRD; NOTHING BARRED; THE PURE HELL OF ST. TRINIAN'S; TWO-WAY STRETCH; UPSTAIRS AND DOWNSTAIRS; WATCH IT, SAILOR; WEEKEND WITH LULU; MAKE MINE A DOUBLE; HEAVENS ABOVE; JUST FOR FUN; MORGAN; THE WRONG BOX; SMASHING TIME; LIONHEART; THE MINI-AFFAIR; THE ITALIAN JOB; WONDERWALL; DOCTOR IN TROUBLE; ON A CLEAR DAY YOU CAN SEE FOREVER; THE PRIVATE LIFE OF SHERLOCK HOLMES; THE LAST REMAKE OF BEAU GESTE; STAND UP VIRGIN SOLDIERS; THE HOUND OF THE BASKERVILLES (1980).

Hartman, Elizabeth

Born 23 Dec. 1941, Youngstown, Ohio, died 10 June 1987, Pittsburgh, Pa.

Film/Stage Actress

She won quick fame in 1966 with an Academy Award nomination for her role in the film A PATCH OF BLUE, then went on to make THE GROUP; YOU'RE A BIG BOY NOW; THE FIXER; THE BEGUILED; WALKING TALL. Appeared on Broadway in a revival of Thornton Wilder's "Our Town." Other films include: FULL MOON HIGH; THE SECRET OF NIMH.

Hassinger, Jim

Died 5 Aug. 1987, West Los Angeles, Calif.; age 61.

Film/TV Set Decorator

Worked both in films (DOCTOR DOLITTLE; STAR!; VALLEY OF THE DOLLS; PLANET OF THE APES; HELLO, DOLLY; THE OCTAGON) and TV ("Ozzie and Harriet," "The Red Skelton Show," "Lost in Space," "The Mary Tyler Moore Show," "Trapper John, M.D.," "The Doris Day Show," and several Judy Garland specials.

Hayes, Bernadene

Died 29 Aug. 1987, Los Angeles, Calif., age 75.

Film/Stage/Radio Actress

One-time "Queen of Radio" moved to Los Angeles from Chicago, where she had trained as a singer. She landed roles opposite Clark Gable and Gene Kelly and performed on Broadway with Buddy Ebsen in the hit play "Goodnight Ladies." Films include: TRIGGER TOM; THE HUMAN SIDE; FOLIES BERGERE (1935); THE JUDGMENT BOOK; LOVE IN BLOOM; SHE GETS HER MAN; ABSOLUTE QUIET; THE ACCUSING FINGER; GREAT GUY; PAROLE; ALONG CAME LOVE; THE EMPEROR'S CANDLESTICKS; GIRL LOVES BOY; RUSTLER'S VALLEY; NORTH OF THE RIO GRANDE; SWEETHEART OF THE NAVY; THAT'S MY STORY; TROUBLE AT MIDNIGHT; MY OLD KENTUCKY HOME; PRISON NURSE; YOU AND ME; THE DAY THE BOOKIES WEPT; HEROES IN BLUE; IDIOT'S DELIGHT; KING OF CHINATOWN; LUCKY NIGHT; PANAMA LADY; SOME LIKE IT HOT (1939); SAILOR'S LADY; SANTA FE MARSHAL; THE DEADLY GAME (1941); THE GAY VAGABOND; SING FOR YOUR SUPPER; I LIVE ON DANGER; NAZI AGENT; THIS GUN FOR HIRE; MR. WINKLE GOES TO WAR; DON'T GAMBLE WITH STRANGERS; THE CRIMSON KEY; DICK TRACY'S DILEMMA; LIVING IN A BIG WAY; THE 13TH HOUR; WOMEN IN THE NIGHT; CAUGHT (1949); BUNCO SQUAD; WICKED WOMAN (1953).

Hayworth, Rita [Margarita Carmen Cansino]

Born 17 Oct. 1918, New York, N.Y.; died 14 May 1987, New York, N.Y.

Film Actress

One of the great beauties of the screen, she was particularly popular during WW II and for some time was the leading box-office attraction for Columbia Pictures. Descending from a long line of Spanish dancers called the Dancing Cansinos, she began lessons at six and made her professional debut at 14. She kept her real name, Rita Cansino, during her first 10 movies until meeting her first husband, Edward Judson, who transformed her from a raven-haired Latin to an auburn-haired cosmopolitan. Her breakthrough came in 1941 when she was chosen as Fred Astaire's new partner for the Cole Porter musical YOU'LL NEVER GET RICH. She was married five times—to Judson, Orson Welles, Prince Aly Khan, singer Dick Haymes, and producer James Hill. "They fell in love with Gilda and woke up with me," was her rueful commentary on her men. Her movies include: CRIMINALS OF THE AIR; THE GAME THAT KILLS; GIRLS CAN PLAY; PAID TO DANCE; THE SHADOW (1937); CONVICTED (1938); JUVENILE COURT; RENEGADE RANGER; THERE'S ALWAYS A WOMAN; WHO KILLED GAIL PRESTON?; HOMICIDE BUREAU; THE LONE WOLF SPY HUNT; ONLY ANGELS HAVE WINGS; SPECIAL INSPECTOR; ANGELS OVER BROADWAY; BLONDIE ON A BUDGET; THE LADY IN QUESTION; MUSIC IN MY HEART; SUSAN AND GOD; AFFECTIONATELY YOURS; BLOOD AND SAND; THE STRAWBERRY BLONDE; MY GAL SAL; TALES OF MANHATTAN; YOU WERE NEVER LOVELIER; COVER GIRL; TONIGHT AND EVERY NIGHT; GILDA; DOWN TO EARTH; THE LADY FROM SHANGHAI; THE LOVES OF CARMEN; AFFAIR IN TRINIDAD; MISS SADIE THOMPSON; SALOME (1953); FIRE DOWN BELOW; PAL JOEY; SEPARATE TABLES; THE STORY ON PAGE ONE; THEY CAME TO CORDURA; THE HAPPY THIEVES; CIRCUS WORLD; THE MONEY TRAP; THE POPPY IS ALSO A FLOWER; THE ROVER; SONS OF SATAN; THE NAKED ZOO; ROAD TO SALINA; THE WRATH OF GOD.

Hein, Keith

Died 8 July 1987, Los Angeles, Calif.; age 46.

Film/TV Set Decorator

Worked in his specialty for stage, film (THE LADY IN RED; THE OSTERMAN WEEKEND; THE AVIATOR) and TV (mainly on "Hallmark Hall of Fame" productions).

Hiestand, John "Bud"

Died 5 Feb. 1987.

Actor

Started his career as a stage actor in Los Angeles, then went into radio, working on "Amos 'n' Andy," "The Fred Allen Show," and the Burns and Allen, Jack Benny, and Mel Blanc shows. Films include: LOVE AND HISSES; NAVY BLUE AND GOLD; A SLIGHT CASE OF MURDER; SWING, SISTER, SWING; SECOND FIDDLE (1939); THE MAN I MARRIED; THE GREAT AMERICAN BROADCAST; I WANTED WINGS; REMEMBER THE DAY; RISE AND SHINE; THE HUCKSTERS; YOU'RE MY EVERYTHING; MISTER 880; THE GLASS WEB; GOOD MORNING, MISS DOVE; THE MAN FROM BUTTON WILLOW; THE STEAGLE. Did character parts on such TV outings as "Bachelor Father," "Hazel," "The Donna Reed Show," "Room for One More" and handled announcing chores on "Ford Theater," "Hogan's Heroes," "Green Acres," "The Smothers Brothers Show," "The Waltons," and various "Charlie Brown" specials.

Hirszman, Leon

Born 22 Nov. 1937, Rio de Janeiro, Brazil; died 15 Sep. 1987, Rio de Janeiro, Brazil.

Director

Was active in the film club movement in his native Brazil that emphasized the production of films reflecting Brazilian culture, mores, and history. Feature films include: THE DEAD WOMAN; THE GIRL FROM IPANEMA; WHAT COUNTRY IS THIS?; ABC DA GREVE; SAO BERNARDO; THEY DON'T WEAR BLACK TIE (won two awards at the Venice Film Festival) and IMAGES OF THE UNCONSCIOUS (unreleased at his death).

Hobley, McDonald

Died 30 July 1987, Bournemouth, England; age 70.

Actor

A TV announcer and a comedy panel-show host in his native England as well as appearing in NO PLACE FOR JENNIFER; MEET MR. LUCIFER; MAN OF THE MOMENT; CHECKPOINT; THE ENTERTAINER (1960). Also appeared on stage in "No Sex, Please, We're British" and "40 Years On."

Holcombe, Harry

Died 15 Sept. 1987, Valencia, Calif., age 80.

Radio/Film/Stage Actor

Began his radio career in Chicago and later directed programs including "Tena and Tim," "Dr. I.Q.," and Benny Goodman's radio show, "Camel Caravan." In later years he appeared in television commercials. Among his films are: THE SILENCERS; THE YOUNG SAVAGES; THE COUCH; FOLLOW THAT DREAM; THE MANCHURIAN CANDIDATE; KING KONG VERSUS GODZILLA; SUMMER MAGIC; THE UNSINKABLE MOLLY BROWN; HARLOW; THE MONKEY'S UNCLE; THE FORTUNE COOKIE; THE GRADUATE; GAILY, GAILY; GETTING STRAIGHT; THE HAWAIIANS; FOXY BROWN; ESCAPE TO WITCH MOUNTAIN; PSYCHIC KILLER; EMPIRE OF THE ANTS; FUN WITH DICK AND JANE.

Howard, Noel

Born 25 Dec. 1920, Paris, France; died 7 Feb. 1987, Los Angeles, Calif.

Director/Second Unit Director/Author

Studied painting in France and the US before entering WW II as a pilot. Was introduced to Hollywood after the war by Victor Fleming, the director who engaged him as technical adviser on JOAN OF ARC. He then worked as a stuntman on THE THREE MUSKETEERS (1948) before using his abilities mainly as a second unit director on such films as THE DESERT FOX, THE SNIPER; LES MISERABLES (1952); DECISION BEFORE DAWN; ACT OF LOVE; THE JOURNEY; THE LAND OF THE PHARAOHS; THE SPIRIT OF ST. LOUIS; HOLIDAY IN PARIS; LOVE IN THE AFTERNOON; PHAEDRA; THE HAPPY ROAD; GIGI; SOLOMON AND SHEBA; KING OF KINGS (1961); LAWRENCE OF ARABIA; 55 DAYS AT PEKING; A FLEA IN HER EAR; codirected MARCO THE MAGNIFICENT and had sole directorial charge on D'OU VIENS TU, JOHNNY?, and CAN YOU HEAR THE DOGS BARKING?

Huston, John

Born 5 Aug. 1906, Nevada, Mo.; died 28 Aug. 1987, Middletown, R.I.

Director/Screenwriter/Actor

Among the many achievements of this legendary director and scenarist who made THE MALTESE FALCON was the fact that he directed the Academy Award-winning performances of his father, Walter, in THE TREASURE OF SIERRA MADRE in 1948 and his daughter Anjelica in PRIZZI'S HONOR in 1985. A sickly child, he spent his youth shuttling between his actor father and his journalist mother, Rhea Gore. By the time he reached adulthood he had been a boxer, an opera singer, a cavalry lieutenant, actor, writer, sculptor, painter, newspaper reporter, and combat cameraman. With THE MALTESE FALCON he graduated from screenwriter to director. He won two Oscars, for writing and directing THE TREASURE OF SIERRA MADRE, and was nominated for many more. At the age of 79 he received the New York Film Critics award as best director of 1985 for PRIZZI'S HONOR; was the 1983 recipient of the American Film Institute's Life Achievement Award and was presented with the 1964 Lauren Award of the Writers Guild. He was the subject of an homage at the Cannes Film Festival in 1979. His final film, completed just before his death, was THE DEAD, based on a short story by James Joyce, with an adaptation and screenplay by his son Tony, and starring his daughter Anjelica. He was married five times, he said, to "a schoolgirl, a gentle-woman, a movie star, a ballerina, and a crocodile." Other movies he acted in, directed, or wrote: A HOUSE DIVIDED; LAW AND ORDER (1932); MURDERS IN THE RUE MORGUE (1932); DEATH DRIVES THROUGH; IT HAPPENED IN PARIS (1935); THE AMAZING DR. CLITTERHOUSE; JEZEBEL; JUAREZ; DR. EHRLICH'S MAGIC BULLET; HIGH SIERRA; ACROSS THE PACIFIC; IN THIS OUR LIFE; THE KILLERS (1946); THE STRANGER (1946); THREE STRANGERS; KEY LARGO; WE WERE STRANGERS; THE ASPHALT JUNGLE; THE AFRICAN QUEEN; THE RED BADGE OF COURAGE; MOULIN ROUGE; BEAT THE DEVIL; MOBY DICK (1956); HEAVEN KNOWS, MR. ALLISON; THE BARBARIAN AND THE GEISHA; THE ROOTS OF HEAVEN; THE UNFORGIVEN; THE MISFITS; FREUD; THE CARDINAL; THE LIST OF ADRIAN MESSENGER; THE NIGHT OF THE IGUANA; THE BIBLE . . . IN THE BEGINNING; CASINO ROYALE; REFLECTIONS IN A GOLDEN EYE; CANDY; DE SADE; SINFUL DAVEY; A WALK WITH LOVE AND DEATH; THE KREMLIN LETTER; THE DESERTER; MAN IN THE WILDERNESS; FAT CITY; THE LIFE AND TIMES OF JUDGE ROY BEAN; BATTLE FOR THE PLANET OF THE APES; THE MACKINTOSH MAN; CHINATOWN; BREAKOUT (1975); THE MAN WHO WOULD BE KING; THE WIND AND THE LION; ANGELA (1977); TENTACLES; JAGUAR LIVES; WINTER KILLS; WISE BLOOD; PHOBIA; THE VISITOR; HEAD ON (1981); VICTORY; ANNIE; CANNERY ROW; LOVESICK; YOUNG GIANTS; UNDER THE VOLCANO; THE BRIDGE IN THE JUNGLE.

Hutton, Marion [Marion Hutton Schoen]

Died 9 Jan. 1987, Kirkland, Wash.; age 67.

Singer/Actress

The sister of Betty Hutton, she was one of the top vocalists with Glenn Miller in the late 1930s and early 1940s. She popularized such melodies as "Kalamazoo," "Chattanooga Choo-Choo," "Don't Sit Under the Apple Tree," "Moonlight Serenade," "I'll Be Seeing You" and appeared in the following films: ORCHESTRA WIVES; CRAZY HOUSE; BABES ON SWING STREET; IN SOCIETY; LOVE HAPPY. She performed with top entertainers like Perry Como, Bob Hope, and Jack Carson. After retirement in 1954, developed an alcohol problem which she overcame and spent her later years setting up programs to help other people, mainly women, with their addiction.

Ishihara, Yujiro

Died 17 July 1987, Tokyo, Japan; age 52.

Actor/Singer/Producer

Made his movie debut in 1956. Movies include: ALONE ON THE PACIFIC; THOSE MAGNIFICENT MEN IN THEIR FLYING MACHINES; OR HOW I FLEW FROM LONDON TO PARIS IN 25 HOURS AND 11 MINUTES; TUNNEL TO THE SUN; UNDER THE BANNER OF SAMURAI; TENCHU!

Jacks, Robert L.

Born 14 June 1927, Oxnard, Calif.; died 26 Aug. 1987, Los Angeles, Calif.

Film/TV Producer

One-time son-in-law of Darryl F. Zanuck produced numerous westerns and adventure films mostly for 20th Century-Fox as well as such successful TV productions as "Eight is Enough," "The Waltons" (for which he won an Emmy), and "The Dukes of Hazard." Among his movies are: LURE OF THE WILDERNESS; THE DESERT RATS; MAN IN THE ATTIC; MAN ON A TIGHTROPE; GORILLA AT LARGE; PRINCE VALIANT; PRINCESS OF THE NILE; THE RAID; WHITE FEATHER; BANDIDO; THE KILLER IS LOOSE; MAN FROM DEL RIO; THE PROUD ONES; THE UNDEFEATED.

Jaidev

Died 6 Jan. 1987, Bombay, India; age 68.

Music Director

Although he was born in Nairobi, Kenya, he worked in India. He was involved with 26 films, starting in 1951. His pictures include: MAITI GHAR (the first Nepali-language film); RESHAMAUR SERA; GAMAN; ANKAHEE.

Jameson, Joyce [Joyce Beverly Jameson]

Born 26 Sept. 1932, Chicago, Ill.; died 16 Jan. 1987.

Film/TV Actress-Comedienne

Her film break came in 1951 as a member of the chorus in SHOWBOAT. She started her career with the Billy Barnes Revue and was married to Barnes at that time. During the late 1950s she appeared on the "Steve Allen Show." Other television credits include appearances in "Columbo," "The Love Boat," "The Fall Guy," "Baretta," and "Barney Miller." Among her movies are: SHOW BOAT (1951); THE SON OF DR. JEKYLL; THE STRIP; PROBLEM GIRLS; PHFFFT!; GANG BUSTERS; CRIME AGAINST JOE; TIP ON A DEAD JOCKEY; THE APARTMENT; TALES OF TERROR; THE BALCONY; THE COMEDY OF TERRORS; GOOD NEIGHBOR SAM; BOY, DID I GET A WRONG NUMBER!; THE SPLIT; COMPANY OF KILLERS; THE OUTLAW JOSEY WALES; SCORCHY; HARDBODIES.

Jarrett, Art [Jr.]

Born 1909, New York, N.Y.; died 23 July 1987, Los Angeles, Calif.

Band Leader/Singer/Film Actor

Started his show business career as a singer-guitarist and worked with such bands as Earl Burnett, Red Nichols, Isham Jones, Phil Harris, and Ted Weems. Did such films as ACE OF ACES; DANCING LADY; SITTING PRETTY (1933); THE GAY DIVORCEE; HOLLYWOOD PARTY; LET'S FALL IN LOVE; RIP TIDE; MY LUCKY STAR; TRIGGER PALS; THE TATTOOED STRANGER.

Jeffries, Lang

Died 12 Feb. 1987, Huntington Beach, Calif.; age 55.

Actor

Holcombe

Huston

Jameson

Kaye

Muscular hero in films of the 1960s (mostly European minor-league efforts). They include: THE REVOLT OF THE SLAVES; DON'T KNOCK THE TWIST; MISSION STARDUST; FIGHT FOR ROME; THE SPY STRIKES SILENTLY; LOTUS FOR MISS KWAN; ALONE AGAINST ROME; MARK DONAN-AGENT Z-7; OPERATION OCEAN; THE HOTHEADS; REQUIEM FOR A GRINGO; A SOLDIER NAMED JOE; THE JUNKMAN. Before he entered films, he had a costarring part on a 1958 syndicated TV series, "Rescue 8," and was formerly married to Rhonda Fleming. After an early 1970s retirement, he returned to the US and worked in boat and real estate sales.

Jefferies, Phil

Died 6 Apr. 1987, Burbank, Calif., age 61.

Production Designer

After serving in the Army during WW II, he became junior illustrator at Universal, then moved to Warner Bros. He received an Oscar nomination for his work on TOM SAWYER (1973). His movies include: THE MANCHURIAN CANDIDATE; THIS PROPERTY IS CONDEMNED; OH DAD, POOR DAD, MAMA'S HUNG YOU IN THE CLOSET AND I'M FEELIN' SO SAD; THE ST. VALENTINE'S DAY MASSACRE; WALKING TALL, PART II; WUSA; CONQUEST OF THE PLANET OF THE APES; THE COWBOYS; HUCKLEBERRY FINN (1974); THE ISLAND OF DR. MOREAU; MASS APPEAL; ST. IVES; DAMIEN-OMEN II; AN OFFICER AND A GENTLEMAN.

Johnson, Edgar

Died 13 June 1987, Los Angeles, Calif.; age 59.

Actor/Extra/Dancer/Musician

Worked in three areas of show business: films (many of these, including MY FAIR LADY), local theater, and TV ("Cheers"). He was active in trade organizations, especially the Academy of Science Fiction, Fantasy and Horror Films (of which he was the general secretary for a five years).

Johnson, June [June Johnson May]

Born 28 May 1918, St. Louis, Mo.; died 14 July 1987, Las Vegas, Nev.

Actress

Active from a very early age in stage, film, radio, and TV. Her stage efforts include: "Funzapoppin," "Pardon Our French," "Hell'z-a-Splashin." Films are: ROSE BOWL; THE MANDARIN MYSTERY; ANYTHING FOR A THRILL; DOUBLE DANGER; VIVACIOUS LADY; LONE STAR RAIDERS; GANGS OF SONORA; PALS OF THE PECOS. She was related to Chic Johnson of Olsen and Johnson fame and appeared in many of their productions.

Jones, Paul R.

Died 24 Feb. 1987, New Milford, Conn.; age 77.

Stage Actor/Film Producer-Writer-Director

Debuted on stage at age three in his native Denver, Colorado, and went on to child parts in film, eventually doing some work on Broadway in "Caesar and Cleopatra" (with Helen Hayes) and "Courage" (which ran for three years). Using the name John Byrd, appeared in a production of "Hamlet" produced by and starring Leslie Howard as well as in the musical "Bloomer Girl." For 26 years with the US Navy, he served as producer, director, and writer of service films which featured stars such as Celeste Holm, Douglas Fairbanks, Jr., and others. He retired from the Navy in 1979 and worked in local theater.

Josefberg, Milton

Died 14 Dec. 1987, Burbank, Calif.; age 76.

Writer

Mainly noted for his radio writing for Bob Hope and Jack Benny (authored a book about him), as well as for writing and producing "All in the Family" episodes. Supplied the script for one film, ICE-CAPADES.

Jutra, Claude

Died 23 Apr. 1987, Quebec; age 56

Director

The body of this award-winning French-Canadian filmmaker, probably best known as a leading Canadian exponent of *cinema verite*, was pulled from the St. Lawrence River, where police believe it had been since his disappearance five months earlier. He was known to have suffered from Alzheimer's disease and his death was attributed to probable suicide. A former medical student who turned to drama at Montreal's Theater of the New World; his best-known films are the semi-autobiographical A TOUT PRENDRE (1963) and MON ONCLE ANTOINE (1971), the latter declared the best-ever Canadian film by an international film panel in 1984. His films include: KAMOURASKA; TWO SOLITUDES; BY DESIGN. Films by others in which he acted were: ACT OF THE HEART; THE RAPE OF A SWEET YOUNG GIRL; LA FLEUR AUX DENTS; TILL DEATH DO US PART.

Kahl, Milton

Died 19 Apr. 1987, Mill Valley, Calif., age 78.

Animator

One of the "nine old men" of animation, a select group of artists and draftsmen Walt Disney assembled in the 1930s. He was involved with Disney's first animated feature film, SNOW WHITE, in 1937 and was animation director on many of Disney's most successful films. He joined Disney after a lucrative commercial art career in the San Francisco area and was admired for his distinctive style. Films include: THE THREE CABALLEROS; MAKE MINE MUSIC; SONG OF THE SOUTH; SO DEAR TO MY HEART; ALICE IN WONDERLAND (1951); PETER PAN; LADY AND THE TRAMP; ONE HUNDRED AND ONE DALMATIANS; THE SWORD AND THE STONE; MARY POPPINS; THE JUNGLE BOOK; ROBIN HOOD (1973); THE RESCUERS; PINOCCHIO; BAMBI; THE ARISTOCATS.

Kaye, Danny [David Daniel Kominski]

Born 18 Jan. 1913, Brooklyn, N.Y.; died 3 Mar. 1987, Los Angeles, Calif.

Film/TV/Stage Actor-Singer-Comedian

Began his career as a "tummler" on the Borscht Belt. He tried a mixed bag of jobs, all dismal failures, until his Broadway debut in 1940 when he met and married lyricist Sylvia Fine, the "brains" behind his subsequent success. He was almost as well known for his offstage interests through his charity work with UNICEF. He won a special Oscar in 1954, Emmys in 1964 and 1975, the Motion Picture Academy's Jean Hersholt Humanitarian Award in 1982 and Danish knighthood in 1983. His movies include: UP IN ARMS; WONDER MAN; THE KID FROM BROOKLYN; THE SECRET LIFE OF WALTER MITTY; A SONG IS BORN; THE INSPECTOR GENERAL; IT'S A GREAT FEELING; ON THE RIVIERA; HANS CHRISTIAN ANDERSEN; KNOCK ON WOOD; WHITE CHRISTMAS; THE COURT JESTER; ME AND THE COLONEL; MERRY ANDREW; THE FIVE PENNIES; ON THE DOUBLE; THE MAN FROM THE DINERS'CLUB; THE MADWOMAN OF CHAILLOT.

Kaye, Nora [Nora Koreff]

Born 1920, New York City, NY; died 28 Feb. 1987, Santa Monica, Calif.

Dancer/Choreographer/Film Producer

Of Russian descent, she studied with Michel Fokine, a prominent ballet dancer, and at the Metropolitan Opera Ballet School. She worked with George Ballanchine and had 24 ballets created especially for her talents. Starting out with small roles, she became the premier ballerina for the American Ballet Theater and the New York City Ballet, working in both classical and modern roles. "Pillar of Fire" was the ballet that put her over the top in her profession. She was married to Herbert Ross, the film director and choreographer, and was an integral part of some of his later projects. She was executive producer on THE TURNING POINT, coproducer of both NIJINSKY and PENNIES FROM HEAVEN (1981), associate producer on THE SECRET OF MY SUCCESS, and co-executive producer on the recently completed Mikhail Baryshnikov dance film, GISELLE. At one time she was married to Isaac Stern.

Kaye, Sammy

Born 13 March 1910, Rocky River, Ohio.

Orchestra Leader/Film Actor

Leader of a dance band which peaked in popularity from the late 1930s through the 1940s, he was in the business for 50 years. Known by its slogan, "Swing and Sway with Sammy Kaye," the band featured a mellow sound with the brasses predominating, and used prominent vocalists such as Charlie Wilson, Tommy Ryan, Don Cornell, and Tony Alamo. Following his first big hit in 1937, his version of the title song from the Eleanor Powell-Nelson Eddy musical ROSALIE, his organization put forward such hits as "(There'll Be Bluebirds Over) the White Cliffs of Dover," "My Buddy," "There Goes That Song Again," "Harbor Lights," "There Will Never Be Another You," "Remember Pearl Harbor" (the last written by Kaye the same evening of the day that the naval base was bombed in 1941). Widely heard over radio through both "The Chesterfield Supper Club" and "So You Want to Lead a Band?," his band appeared in the films ICELAND and SONG OF THE OPEN ROAD.

Keller, Harry

Born 22 Feb. 1913, Los Angeles, Calif.; died 19 Jan. 1987, Los Angeles, Calif.

Film Producer/Director/Editor

Began as a film editor in 1936, made his directing debut in 1949 with THE BLONDE BANDIT, and in the late 1960s also produced films. His television credits included directing 40 installments of "The Loretta Young" show. Among his movies are: INSIDE INFORMATION; MYSTERY OF THE WHITE ROOM; THE WITNESS VANISHES; BLACK HILLS EXPRESS; CANYON CITY; DAYS OF OLD CHEYENNE; DEATH VALLEY MANHUNT; KING OF

THE COWBOYS; THE MAN FROM THUNDER RIVER; RAIDERS OF SUNSET PASS; CALIFORNIA JOE; CODE OF THE PRAIRIE; FIREBRANDS OF ARIZONA; THE LARAMIE TRAIL; MOJAVE FIREBRAND; SHERIFF OF SUNDOWN; STAGECOACH TO MONTEREY; TUCSON RAIDERS; GRISSLY'S MILLIONS; SONG OF MEXICO; STEPPIN' IN SOCIETY; UTAH; A GUY COULD CHANGE; MY PAL TRIGGER; PASSKEY TO DANGER; SPECTER OF THE ROSE; SUN VALLEY CYCLONE; THE CATMAN OF PARIS; ANGEL AND THE BADMAN; NORTHWEST OUTPOST; ROBIN HOOD OF TEXAS; RUSTLERS OF DEVIL'S CANYON; SADDLE PALS; TWILIGHT ON THE RIO GRANDE; HOMICIDE FOR THREE; MADONNA OF THE DESERT; MOONRISE; SON OF GOD'S COUNTRY; THE RED MENACE; THE RED PONY; ROSE OF THE YUKON; THE STREETS OF SAN FRANCISCO; TOO LATE FOR TEARS; THE ARIZONA COWBOY; THE BLONDE BANDIT; BORDERLINE (1950); COVERED WAGON RAID; HIT PARADE OF 1951; LONELY HEARTS BANDITS; THE SHOWDOWN (1950); TARNISHED; BELLE LE GRAND; THE DAKOTA KID; DESERT OF LOST MEN; FORT DODGE STAMPEDE; BLACK HILLS AMBUSH; CAPTIVE OF BILLY THE KID; LEADVILLE GUNSLINGER; ROSE OF CIMARRON; THUNDERING CARAVANS; BANDITS OF THE WEST; EL PASO STAMPEDE; MARSHAL OF CEDAR ROCK; RED RIVER SHORE; SAVAGE FRONTIER; THE PHANTOM STALLION; THE UNGUARDED MOMENT; MAN AFRAID; QUANTEZ; DAY OF THE BAD MAN; THE FEMALE ANIMAL; STEP DOWN TO TERROR; TOUCH OF EVIL; VOICE IN THE MIRROR; SEVEN WAYS FROM SUNDOWN; TAMMY, TELL ME TRUE; SIX BLACK HORSES; TAMMY AND THE DOCTOR; THE BRASS BOTTLE; KITTEN WITH A WHIP; SEND ME NO FLOWERS; MIRAGE; THAT FUNNY FEELING; TEXAS ACROSS THE RIVER; IN ENEMY COUNTRY; SKIN GAME; STIR CRAZY; STRIPES; HANKY-PANKY; THE MAN WHO WASN'T THERE; COMMANDO CODY.

Kenna, Peter

Died 27 Nov. 1987, Sydney, Australia; age 57.

Screenwriter/Actor

Worked in radio and stage in his native Australia before becoming a playwright, eventually turning out 18 plays. Supplied the script for the 1987 Australian release THE GOOD WIFE (see: Film Reviews).

Kennedy, Madge

Born 19 Apr. 1891, Chicago, Ill.; died 9 June 1987, Woodland Hills, Calif.

Film/Stage Actress

One of the longest surviving members of the movie industry, her career ranged from the Broadway stage of 1910 to the movie MARATHON MAN in 1976. In 1923 she starred in the Broadway production of "Poppy," in which she was billed over costar W.C. Fields. She left motion pictures in 1926 after making several silent films; continued to work on the stage until making a movie comeback in 1952. Her movies include: THE MARRYING KIND; MAIN STREET TO BROADWAY; THE RAINS OF RANCHIPUR; THE CATERED AFFAIR; LUST FOR LIFE; THREE BAD SISTERS; HOUSEBOAT; A NICE LITTLE BANK THAT SHOULD BE ROBBED; NORTH BY NORTHWEST; PLUNDERERS OF PAINTED FLATS; LET'S MAKE LOVE; THEY SHOOT HORSES, DON'T THEY; THE BABY MAKER; THE DAY OF THE LOCUST; MARATHON MAN. Among her silent films are: BABY MINE; THE FAIR PRETENDER; OUR LITTLE WIFE; A PERFECT LADY; DAUGHTER OF MINE; DOLLARS AND SENSE; THE TRUTH; NEARLY MARRIED; THE DANGER GAME; FRIEND HUSBAND; THE KINGDOM OF YOUTH; THE SERVICE STAR; DAY DREAMS; LEAVE IT TO SUSAN; STRICTLY CONFIDENTIAL; THROUGH THE WRONG DOOR; THE BLOOMING ANGEL; THE GIRL WITH A JAZZ HEART; HELP YOURSELF; THE HIGHEST BIDDER; OH MARY BE CAREFUL; THE PURPLE HIGHWAY; THREE MILES OUT; BAD COMPANY; LYING WIVES; SCANDAL STREET; OH BABY.

Kezer, Glenn B.

Born 1923; died 26 March 1987, Okemah, Okla.

Actor

Appeared on stage in "Walk in Darkness," "The Trial of Lee Harvey Oswald," "The Other Man," "Oh, Say Can You See L A," "The Firebugs," "The David Show," "Promenade," "My Fair Lady," "Camelot," "Little Murders." His TV efforts include the 1984 mini-series "Master of the Game" as well as regular appearances on "Guiding Light," "As the World Turns," "Another World." His films include: POWER; NO WAY TO TREAT A LADY; IRISH WHISKEY REBELLION; WEREWOLF OF WASHINGTON.

Kidd, Jonathan [Kurt Richards]

Died 15 Dec. 1987, Los Angeles, Calif.; age 73.

Actor

Used his real name for such stage efforts as "Miss Swan Expects" (1939), "Hamlet," "Counsellor-at-Law," "Wallflower," "The Edge of the Sword," "A Streetcar Named Desire." Under the name of Kidd, had roles in such cinematic efforts as MACABRE; WINK OF AN EYE; SEVEN THIEVES; CAN-CAN; THE 7TH COMMANDMENT; OPERATION EICHMANN; THE ONE AND ONLY GENUINE ORIGINAL FAMILY BAND; THE DAY OF THE LOCUST. His TV work included the telefilms "Thursday's Game," "Young Pioneers," "The Great Cash Giveaway Getaway" as well as parts in "Perry Mason," "Mannix," "Rawhide," "Dr. Kildare," "General Hospital."

Kleban, Ed

Died 28 Dec. 1987, New York City, N.Y.; age 48.

Lyricist

Did the lyrics for the Pulitzer Prize-winning musical "A Chorus Line," which was filmed in 1985 by Sir Richard Attenborough. A former record producer, he also taught at a musical theater workshop.

Knight, Esmond

Born 4 May 1906, East Sheen, Surrey, England; died 23 Feb. 1987, Egypt.

Film/Stage Actor

Died on location while making a film version of "The Balkan Trilogy." He was born in a London suburb and made his stage debut in 1925. His acting career spanned more than 60 years and was almost ended when he was blinded in WW II, but partial sight was restored and he went on to make many more films. Among his movies are: DEADLOCK (1931); ROMANY LOVE; 77 PARK LANE; THE RINGER (1932); THE BERMONDSEY KID; THE BLUE SQUADRON; FATHER AND SON (1934); GIRLS WILL BE BOYS; LEST WE FORGET (1934); STRAUSS' GREAT WALTZ; WOMANHOOD; CRIME UNLIMITED; DANDY DICK; SOME DAY; BLACK ROSES; A CLOWN MUST LAUGH; THE VICAR OF BRAY; WEDDINGS ARE WONDERFUL; THE ARSENAL STADIUM MYSTERY; BLACKOUT (1940); FINGERS (1940); THIS ENGLAND; A CANTERBURY TALE; THE HALF-WAY HOUSE; THE SILVER FLEET; HENRY V; BLACK NARCISSUS; THE END OF THE RIVER (1951); HOLIDAY CAMP; THE RED SHOES; THE INHERITANCE (1951); THE RIVER (1951); GIRDLE OF GOLD; THE WILD HEART; THE STEEL KEY; RICHARD III; THE PRINCE AND THE SHOWGIRL; MISSILE FROM HELL; PEEPING TOM; THE SPY WHO CAME IN FROM THE COLD; THE WINTER'S TALE; ANNE OF THE THOUSAND DAYS; WHERE'S JACK?; THE BOY WHO TURNED YELLOW; ROBIN AND MARIAN; THE ELEMENT OF CRIME.

Knight, June

Died 16 June 1987, Los Angeles, Calif.; age 74.

Stage/Film Actress

Entered films in 1933 after appearing on Broadway in Ziegfeld's "Hot Cha." A child performer in revues in Los Angeles and a former dance partner of Jack Holland, she worked for Universal through the 1930s, appearing in such films as LADIES MUST LOVE; TAKE A CHANCE; CROSS COUNTRY CRUSADE; GIFT OF GAB; WAKE UP AND DREAM; BROADWAY MELODY OF 1936; BREAK THE NEWS; VACATION FROM LOVE; THE HOUSE ACROSS THE BAY; THE LILAC DOMINO.

Knuth, Gustav

Died 1 Feb. 1987, Zurich, Switzerland; age 85.

Actor

Was active in theater in his native Germany and did at least one play in the US, "Alcestiade," in 1957. Made his film debut in THE AMMON KING (1935) and had a good career in such efforts as THE RATS; THE BEGGAR STUDENT; A DAY WILL COME; HIPPODROME; THE HOUSE OF THE THREE GIRLS; FOREVER MY LOVE; THE GIRL AND THE LEGEND; HEIDI (1968); THE BRAZEN WOMEN OF BALZAC. Appeared on TV in "All My Animals," "Salto Mortale," "The Iron Gustav." Received various honors in his 50-year career, including the Ernst Lubitsch Award.

Korngold, George

Died 25 Nov. 1987, Los Angeles, Calif.; age 58.

Music Editor/Record Producer

Closely connected with producing musical scores written by his father, Erich Wolfgang Korngold, for some of the best Warner Brothers epics of the 1930s and 1940s, including KINGS ROW and THE SEA HAWK. Handled the music editing chores on such films as THE FURY; THE LAST EMBRACE; FEDORA; THE TURNING POINT; HOPSCOTCH; OUTLAND; PENNIES FROM HEAVEN (1981).

Lake

LeRoy

Kuhn, Rodolfo

Died 3 Jan. 1987, Valle de Bravo, Mexico; age 53.

Film/TV Director

His first effort was LOS JOVENES VIEJOS (1961), followed by PAJARITO GOMEZ (codirected with Hector Pelegrini); UFA CON EL SEXO; EL SENOR GALINDEZ. Some of his films were banned by the Argentine government because of their criticism of militarism, forcing him to do most of his work in Europe and Spain.

Lake, Arthur [Arthur Silverlake]

Born 17 Apr. 1905, Corbin, Ky.; died 9 Jan. 1987, Indian Wells, Calif.

Actor

Portrayed Dagwood Bumstead, long-suffering husband to Penny Singleton's "Blondie," for over two dozen years. Born into a circus family, his father and uncle toured as "The Flying Silverlakes," an aerial act, and at age three he joined his sister and parents in a vaudeville routine. He made his film debut at age 12 and performed in westerns, but when he heard that Columbia was looking for someone to play Dagwood Bumstead, he was determined to get the part and succeeded with the intercession of Marion Davies and William Randolph Hearst, whose newspapers ran the "Blondie" strip. His movies include: THE AIR CIRCUS; DANCE HALL; ON WITH THE SHOW; TANNED LEGS; CHEER UP AND SMILE; SHE'S MY WEAKNESS; INDISCREET (1931); MIDSHIPMAN JACK; GIRL O' MY DREAMS; ORCHIDS TO YOU; THE SILVER STREAK (1935); WOMEN MUST DRESS; IT'S A GREAT LIFE (1936); ANNAPOLIS SALUTE; EXILED TO SHANGHAI; TOPPER; 23 1/2 HOURS LEAVE; BLONDIE; DOUBLE DANGER; EVERYBODY'S DOING IT; I COVER CHINATOWN; THERE GOES MY HEART; BLONDIE BRINGS UP BABY; BLONDIE MEETS THE BOSS; BLONDIE TAKES A VACATION; BLONDIE HAS SERVANT TROUBLE; BLONDIE ON A BUDGET; BLONDIE PLAYS CUPID; BLONDIE GOES LATIN; BLONDIE IN SOCIETY; BLONDIE FOR VICTORY; BLONDIE GOES TO COLLEGE; BLONDIE'S BLESSED EVENT; THE DARING YOUNG MAN (1942); FOOTLIGHT GLAMOUR; IT'S A GREAT LIFE (1943); THE GHOST THAT WALKS ALONE; SAILOR'S HOLIDAY; 3 IS A FAMILY; THE BIG SHOW-OFF; LEAVE IT TO BLONDIE; BLONDIE KNOWS BEST; BLONDIE'S LUCKY DAY; LIFE WITH BLONDIE; BLONDIE IN THE DOUGH; BLONDIE'S ANNIVERSARY; BLONDIE'S BIG MOMENT; BLONDIE'S HOLIDAY; BLONDIE'S REWARD; BLONDIE'S SECRET; SIXTEEN FATHOMS DEEP; BLONDIE HITS THE JACKPOT; BLONDIE'S BIG DEAL; BEWARE OF BLONDIE; BLONDIE'S HERO. Silents include: SKINNER'S DRESS SUIT (1926); THE IRRESISTIBLE LOVER; HAROLD TEEN (1928); STOP THAT MAN.

Lapenieks, Vilis

Born 10 Nov. 1931, Riga, Latvia; died 3 July, 1987, North Hollywood, Calif.

Cinematographer

A native of Latvia, where his parents had been involved in the creation of the local film industry, he emigrated to the US during WW II and graduated from the University of Southern California film school. He worked closely with John and Robert Kennedy and Hubert Humphrey as a newsreel-documentary cameraman and much of his footage was included in the films THE MAKING OF THE PRESIDENT; FOUR DAYS IN NOVEMBER; CAPTAINS AND KINGS; THE LEE HARVEY OSWALD STORY. Aside from his work on documentaries, he worked on the television series "Kojak," "Toma," and "M*A*S*H," and was cinematographer on low-budget, independent features such as FALLGUY; WALK THE ANGRY BEACH; THIRD OF A MAN; NIGHT TIDE; SHELL SHOCK; VOYAGE TO THE PREHISTORIC PLANET; DEATHWATCH; MOTHER GOOSE A GO-GO; IF IT'S TUESDAY, THIS MUST BE BELGIUM; I LOVE MY WIFE; CISCO PIKE; NEWMAN'S LAW; CAPONE; TWO; THE HIDEOUS SUN DEMON; QUEEN OF BLOOD; EEGAH!.

Laurence, Margaret Wemyss

Born 1926; died 5 Jan. 1987, Lakefield, Ontario.

Novelist

Author of the novel *A Jest of God* (1966), which was made into RACHEL, RACHEL in 1968, starring Joanne Woodward and directed by Paul Newman. Her other books include: *New Wind in a Dry Land*, *A Tree for Poverty*, *The Tomorrow-Tamer*.

Lawrence, Jay

Died 18 June 1987; age 63.

Film Actor/Comedian

The brother of Larry Storch and a big band performer (with Louis Armstrong, Vaughn Monroe), he appeared in THE MAN FROM TUMBLEWEEDS; KING OF DODGE CITY; STALAG 17; THE BIG CHASE; RIDING SHOTGUN; A LAWLESS STREET; WALK THE DARK STREET; THE HALLIDAY BRAND; TRAIN RIDE TO HOLLYWOOD; THE DARK.

Le Bret, Robert Favre

Born 1904, Paris, France; died 28 Apr. 1987, Bougy Villars, Switzerland.

Film Festival Founder

The founder and longtime head of the Cannes Film Festival died just before that festival's 40th anniversary celebration. Started out as a journalist, worked for the French tourism bureau, and served as secretary general of the Paris Ballet. His experience led him to believe that a film festival would be a good thing both for French tourism and the cinema industry. His diplomacy enabled him to guide the festival through its growing pains, bringing it to its current preeminence.

Learn, Bessie [Betty Robbins]

Born 30 Aug. 1888, San Diego, Calif.; died 5 Feb. 1987, Burbank, Calif.

Silent Film Actress

Her active years were spent with the Edison Film Co., which produced films from 1912 through 1916. Appeared in THROUGH TURBULENT WATERS and THE GIRL OF THE GYPSY CAMP.

Leighton, Ava

Died 27 Aug. 1987, New York, N.Y.; age unknown.

Film Producer

Worked with Radley Metzger, the producer/director of the film company they founded (Audobon Films), which distributed some of the more offbeat films released in recent years. She served as coproducer on THERESE AND ISABELLE; CAMILLE 2000; THE LICKERISH QUARTET; SCORE; THE IMAGE; plus some films that Metzger directed under the name of Henry Paris, such as THE OPENING OF MISTY BEETHOVEN and THE PRIVATE AFTERNOONS OF PAMELA MANN. In recent years, founded two film distribution companies.

Leland, David

Died 17 Apr. 1987, Hollywood, Calif.; age 65.

Actor/Tour Manager

Appeared in films (THE HOUR BEFORE THE DAWN; NOTHING BUT TROUBLE), on stage ("Frankie and Johnnie," "The Ponder Heart") and TV ("Cheyenne," "Sugarfoot") before becoming the tour manager for singer Robert Goulet.

Lenard, Grace

Died 7 Apr. 1987, Lakeview Terrace, Calif.; age mid-60s.

Actress

Appeared in the following B films from the 1940s and 1950s: GIRLS OF THE ROAD; SECRETS OF A MODEL; THEY KNEW WHAT THEY WANTED; HONOLULU LU; PARIS CALLING; PLAYMATES; BROADWAY (1942); A MAN'S WORLD; THE SILVER BULLET; STRICTLY IN THE GROOVE; MAN FROM FRISCO; ONCE UPON A TIME (1944); SUNDOWN VALLEY; JOHNNY STOOL PIGEON; I WAS A COMMUNIST FROM THE F.B.I.; QUEEN FOR A DAY; ABBOTT AND COSTELLO GO TO MARS; FOXFIRE.

Leon, Jerry

Died 2 Feb. 1987, New York, N.Y.; age 52.

Actor

A former New York City police detective, he used his years of experience on the job as a technical adviser on THE FRENCH CONNECTION; later appeared onscreen in the films THE SEVEN UPS and BOOK OF NUMBERS. Had a role on the popular "Kojak" TV series.

LeRoy, Mervyn

Born 15 Oct. 1900, San Francisco, Calif.; died 13 Sept. 1987, Beverly Hills, Calif.

Producer/Director

The man who introduced Ronald Reagan to Nancy Davis saw his father's department store destroyed by the 1906 earthquake, and was selling newspapers at the age of 12 before beginning a career as an actor in 1912. By 1944 he had organized his own production company in Burbank after working for MGM and Warner Bros. While at Warner Bros. in 1931 he made LITTLE CAESAR and he is recognized as having launched the gangster cycle. Though he didn't direct THE WIZARD OF OZ, he was the producer and initiated the project. He received a special Oscar in 1945 for a short documentary, THE HOUSE I LIVE IN, and in 1975 won the Irving G. Thalberg Memorial Academy Award for career achievements. Among his movies are: WITHOUT RESERVATIONS; BROADWAY BABIES; HOT STUFF; LITTLE JOHNNY JONES; NUMBERED MEN; PLAYING AROUND; SHOW GIRL IN HOLLYWOOD; TOP SPEED; BROADMINDED; FIVE STAR FINAL; GENTLEMAN'S FATE; LITTLE CAESAR; LOCAL BOY MAKES GOOD; TO-

NIGHT OR NEVER; TOO YOUNG TO MARRY; BIG CITY BLUES; HEART OF NEW YORK; I AM A FUGITIVE FROM A CHAIN GANG; THREE ON A MATCH; TWO SECONDS; ELMER THE GREAT; GOLD DIGGERS OF 1933; HARD TO HANDLE; TUGBOAT ANNIE; HAPPINESS AHEAD; HEAT LIGHTNING; I FOUND STELLA PARISH; OIL FOR THE LAMPS OF CHINA; PAGE MISS GLORY; SWEET ADELINE; ANTHONY ADVERSE; THREE MEN ON A HORSE; THE GREAT GARRICK; THE KING AND THE CHORUS GIRL; MR. DODD TAKES THE AIR; THEY WON'T FORGET; DRAMATIC SCHOOL; FOOLS FOR SCANDAL; AT THE CIRCUS; STAND UP AND FIGHT; THE WIZARD OF OZ; ESCAPE (1940); WATERLOO BRIDGE; BLOSSOMS IN THE DUST; UNHOLY PARTNERS; JOHNNY EAGER; RANDOM HARVEST; MADAME CURIE; THIRTY SECONDS OVER TOKYO; DESIRE ME; HOMECOMING; ANY NUMBER CAN PLAY; EAST SIDE, WEST SIDE; LITTLE WOMEN (1949); LOVELY TO LOOK AT; MILLION DOLLAR MERMAID; LATIN LOVERS; ROSE MARIE (1954); MISTER ROBERTS; STRANGE LADY IN TOWN; THE BAD SEED; TOWARD THE UNKNOWN; HOME BEFORE DARK; NO TIME FOR SERGEANTS; THE FBI STORY; WAKE ME WHEN IT'S OVER; THE DEVIL AT FOUR O'CLOCK; A MAJORITY OF ONE; GYPSY; MARY, MARY; MOMENT TO MOMENT. Silents include: BROKEN DISHES; ELLA CINDERS; IRENE (1926); FLYING ROMEOS; HAROLD TEEN (1928); OH, KAY; NAUGHTY BABY; NO PLACE TO GO.

Lescoulie, Jack

Born 17 May 1912, Sacramento, Calif.; died 9 July 1987, Memphis, Tenn.

TV Announcer/Interviewer

Second banana to Dave Garroway on the original "Today Show" when it premiered on 14 Jan. 1952. Movies he appeared in include: OKLAHOMA RENEGADES; EMERGENCY LANDING; A GIRL, A GUY AND A GOB; THE SLEEPING CITY.

Levine, Joseph E.

Born 9 Sept. 1905, Boston, Mass.; died 31 July 1987, Greenwich, Conn.

Producer/Distributor

Known as the "Boston Barnum," this self-made tycoon became the leading independent producer of the late 1960s, and through the years presented, produced, and acquired or distributed 498 motion pictures —from HERCULES to the early Fellini masterpieces, to THE GRADUATE, THE LION IN WINTER, and A BRIDGE TOO FAR. He first became involved in film in 1945 with the establishment of his own independent Embassy Pictures, which released profitable B pictures. Movies he produced include: THE FABULOUS WORLD OF JULES VERNE; THE WONDERS OF ALADDIN; SEVEN CAPITAL SINS; CONTEMPT; THE CARPETBAGGERS; WHERE LOVE HAS GONE; HARLOW; MAGIC; TATTOO.

Levinson, Richard Leighton

Born 7 Aug. 1934, Philadelphia, Pa.; died 12 Mar. 1987, Los Angeles, Calif.

Film/TV Writer-Producer

With William Link, he created a standard of excellence in TV writing that far exceeded the norm. Started his writing career on the paper of a suburban Philadelphia junior high school with friend and fellow student Link. Later in college, they wrote musical shows, radio scripts, and short stories. After military service, he took a job with the Philadelphia CBS outlet, working on set placement and weather programs. When Link finished his military stint, both he and Levinson went to Los Angeles and sold a play, "Chain of Command," to the Desilu Playhouse. From there they wrote for TV series such as "Alfred Hitchcock Presents," "Dr. Kildare," and "The Fugitive," then created series such as "Mannix," "McCloud," "Ellery Queen," and "Murder, She Wrote." Their play "Prescription: Murder" was developed as the TV series "Columbo," starring Peter Falk. Their telefilms include: "Istanbul Express," "Prescription: Murder," "The Whole World Is Watching," "My Sweet Charlie" (which was released theatrically and garnered a TV Emmy), "Two on a Bench," "Ransom for a Dead Man," "That Certain Summer," "Savage" (directed by Steven Spielberg), "Tenafly" (turned into a short-lived series); "The Gun," "The Execution of Private Slovik" (which received several Emmy nominations and won a Peabody Award), "Ellery Queen: Too Many Suspects," "The Storyteller," "Murder by Natural Causes," "Crisis at Central High," "Take Your Best Shot," "Rehearsal for Murder," "Prototype," "The Guardian," "Guilty Conscience," "Vanishing Act." With his partner, he wrote the screenplay or story for two films, THE HINDENBURG and ROLLERCOASTER.

Lewis, David [David Levy]

Born 14 Dec. 1903, Trinidad, Colo.; died 13 Mar. 1987, Los Angeles, Calif.

Producer

Raised in Seattle, he began his career in motion pictures in the early 1930s as a script reader and Irving Thalberg's personal assistant at MGM. After Thalberg's death he joined Warner Bros. as associate producer to Hal B. Wallis. By the 1940s he was receiving full production credit. He retired from filmmaking in the early 1960s and spent some years packaging productions in Rome, Paris, and London. Among his movies: FLYING DEVILS; SON OF THE BORDER; TWO ALONE; MEN ARE SUCH FOOLS; SECRETS OF AN ACTRESS; THE SISTERS; DARK VICTORY; EACH DAWN I DIE; ALL THIS AND HEAVEN TOO; IN THIS OUR LIFE; TILL WE MEET AGAIN (1944); IT'S A PLEASURE; TOMORROW IS FOREVER; THE OTHER LOVE; ARCH OF TRIUMPH; THE END OF THE AFFAIR; RAINTREE COUNTY; THE SEVENTH SIN.

Liberace

Liberace [Wladziu Valentino Liberace]

Born 16 May 1919, West Allis, Wis.; died 4 Feb. 1987, Palm Springs, Calif.

Entertainer/Musician

The "Sultan of Schmaltz's" flamboyant manner and extravagant clothes attracted adoring female fans more than his talents as a musician. His shtick as a pianist was to play a mixture of abridged, romanticized versions of classics and popular, sentimental tunes interspersed with jokes and chatter. His syndicated television show was one of the most popular attractions of the 1950s and he was a top club and concert attraction for 35 years. He grew up in Milwaukee where his father encouraged him to become an undertaker. His mother was a friend of the great pianist Paderewski, who served as a key role model in his life and encouraged him to become a musician. It was in 1940 while playing to a sniggering, sophisticated cafe society crowd in the Persian Room of the Plaza Hotel in New York that he developed his manner of disarming his audience by saying what they were thinking and heckling himself. He published three books: *Liberace Cooks! Recipes from His Seven Dining Rooms*, an autobiography, *Liberace*, and a coffee table book, *The Things I Love*. Among the movies he appeared in are: SOUTH SEA SINNER; SINCERELY YOURS; THE LOVED ONE; WHEN THE BOYS MEET THE GIRLS.

Lipton, Rex

Died 3 Nov. 1987; age unknown.

Film Editor

Worked for various studios, starting with Monogram and moving on to Pine-Thomas, Republic, Paramount, 20th Century Fox, and Universal. Had full editorial credit on mostly B fare such as GIGANTIS; THUNDER IN CAROLINA; FLIGHT OF THE LOST BALLOON; THE GUN HAWK; TERRIFIED!

Livadary, John Paul

Born 29 Apr. 1899, Constantinople, Turkey; died 7 Apr. 1987, Balboa Island, Calif.

Sound Technician

Born in Turkey to French parents, he studied medicine at the University of Athens, served in the US Army during WW I, and graduated from MIT. He was hired by Columbia in 1928 at the advent of the sound era and, as head of the studio's sound department, was a leading innovator. He won Academy Awards for THE JOLSON STORY in 1946 and FROM HERE TO ETERNITY in 1953. He was also nominated on 14 other occasions. He received four Scientific or Technical Academy Awards and retired in 1959. Movies he worked on include: LOVE ME FOREVER; MR. DEEDS GOES TO TOWN; LOST HORIZON (1937); YOU CAN'T TAKE IT WITH YOU; MR. SMITH GOES TO WASHINGTON; TOO MANY HUSBANDS; THE MEN IN YOUR LIFE; YOU WERE NEVER LOVELIER; SAHARA (1943); COVER GIRL; A SONG TO REMEMBER; THE CAINE MUTINY; THE EDDY DUCHIN STORY; THE STUDENT TEACHERS; PAL JOEY.

Livingston, Jerry [Jerry Levinson]

Born 25 Mar. 1909, Denver, Colo.; died 2 July 1987, Los Angeles, Calif.

Composer

Prolific composer for films and television, he scored Walt Disney's film CINDERELLA, which featured his songs "Bibbidi Bobbidi Boo" and "A Wish Your Heart Makes." Other hit songs he wrote include "Mairzy Doats," "The Twelfth of Never," "I Had Too Much to Dream Last Night," "Blue and Sentimental," and "It's the Talk of the Town." For television he wrote the title songs for "77 Sunset Strip," "Hawaiian Eye," and "Lawman". Among his chief collaborators were Mack David, Helen Deutsch, Milton Drake, Ralph Freed, Al Hoffman, Bob Merrill, Mitchell Parish, and Paul Francis Webster.

Locke, Harry

Born 1915, London, England; died 1987, London, England.

Actor

British actor who specialized in lower-class parts like porters and cab drivers in such films as PICCADILLY INCIDENT; PANIC AT

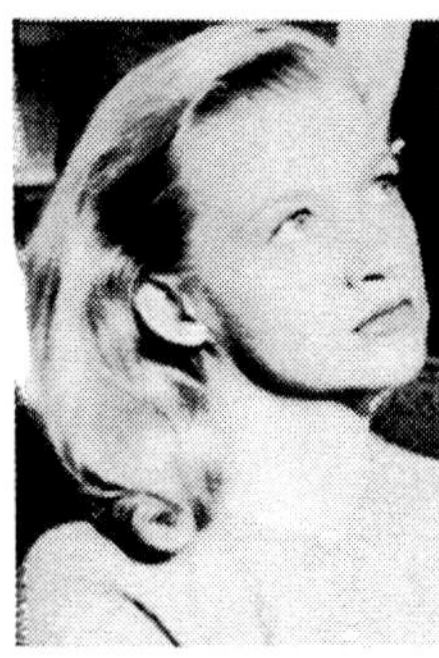

Lonergan

MADAM TUSSAUD'S; PASSPORT TO PIMLICO; PRIVATE ANGELO; NO ROOM AT THE INN; TREASURE ISLAND (1950); FATHER'S DOING FINE; JUDGMENT DEFERRED; TREAD SOFTLY; TERROR ON A TRAIN; ANGELS ONE FIVE; DEVIL ON HORSEBACK; DOCTOR IN THE HOUSE; PARATROOPER; THE NAKED HEART; A KID FOR TWO FARTHINGS; THE TECKMAN MYSTERY; A YANK IN ERMINE; BLONDE SINNER; THE BABY AND THE BATTLESHIP; DOCTOR AT LARGE; REACH FOR THE SKY; THE SILKEN AFFAIR; THE THIRD KEY; TOWN ON TRIAL; WOMEN IN A DRESSING GOWN; ALL AT SEA (1958); CARRY ON NURSE; UPSTAIRS AND DOWNSTAIRS; I'M ALL RIGHT, JACK; NOWHERE TO GO; THE CAPTAIN'S TABLE; LIGHT UP THE SKY; MAN IN A COCKED HAT; THE MAN IN THE BACK SEAT; WATCH IT SAILOR!; KILL OR CURE; THE L-SHAPED ROOM; TIARA TAHITI; CROOKS ANONYMOUS; PLAY IT COOL; TWO AND TWO MAKE SIX; HEAVENS ABOVE; MAID FOR MURDER; THE SMALL WORLD OF SAMMY LEE; THE DEVIL-SHIP PIRATES; A HOME OF YOUR OWN; WHAT A CRAZY WORLD; GO KART GO; IN THE DOGHOUSE; YOUNG AND WILLING (1964); THE AMOROUS MR. PRAWN; THE LEGEND OF YOUNG DICK TURPIN; THE EARLY BIRD; OPERATION SNAFU; THE FAMILY WAY; ALFIE; HALF A SIXPENCE; MISTER TEN PERCENT; ARABESQUE; CARRY ON DOCTOR; NEVER BACK LOSERS; THE SKY BIKE; CLUE OF THE TWISTED CANDLE; CARRY ON AGAIN, DOCTOR; OH! WHAT A LOVELY WAR; ON THE RUN; SUBTERFUGE; TALES FROM THE CRYPT; THE CREEPING FLESH.

Loman, Stan

Died 27 Aug. 1987, Hollywood, Fla.; age 68.

Actor/Cruise Ship Performer

The main thrust of his career was as a cruise ship performer, although he did appear in both the stage and film versions of "This Is Your Army."

Lonergan, Lenore

Born 2 June 1928, Ohio; died 31 Aug. 1987, Stuart, Fla.

Actress

She was known for her spirited portrayals of juveniles in the 1930s and 1940s, a talent no doubt inherited from her grandfather, father, and brother who were also in the theater. Her stage debut was at the age of six in "Mother Lode" and in 1939 she played Katharine Hepburn's younger sister in "The Philadelphia Story." She also played juvenile roles in "Junior Miss," and "Dear Ruth," and appeared in the films, TOM, DICK AND HARRY; THE LADY SAYS NO; WESTWARD THE WOMEN; WHISTLE AT EATON FALLS.

Ludlam, Charles

Died 28 May 1987, New York City, N.Y.; age 44.

Actor

Started his own theater company in his hometown, Northport, N.Y., then went to New York City to inaugurate the Ridiculous Theater Company, writing, directing, and acting in productions such as "The Mystery of Irma Vep," "Camille," "Conquest of the Universe or When Queens Collide," and "The Artificial Jungle." His group specialized in satirical parodies done in an outrageous format. Film roles include: LUPE; UNDERGROUND AND EMIGRANTS; IMPOSTORS; THE BIG EASY; FOREVER, LULU. Received four Obie awards for his theater work, and taught acting at the college level.

Lundmark, William

Died 15 Feb. 1987.

Actor

Appeared in FROM HERE TO ETERNITY; MAN CRAZY; PEYTON PLACE.

MacAdam, Michael R.

Died 7 Apr. 1987, San Gabriel, Calif.; age 77.

TV/Film Editor

Mostly worked on TV although he did co-edit JET PILOT and edited BACKTRACK (shown first as a episode of "The Virginian"). Other TV efforts include "G.E. Theater," "Bachelor Father," "The Munsters," "The Virginan," "Riverboat," "Wagon Train," "Marcus Welby."

MacGibbon, Harriet E.

Died 8 Feb. 1987, Beverly Hills, Calif.; age 81.

Actress

A Chicago native, she started on Broadway in 1923 in "Beggar on Horseback," and appeared in "Howdy King," "Ringside," "The Marriage Bed," "Houseparty," "Midnight," "Lightnin'," "Two on an Island," and "Cloud 7," and toured in "I Am a Camera," which starred Julie Harris in one of her most famous stage roles. Appeared on the screen in CRY FOR HAPPY; A MAJORITY OF ONE; THE FOUR HORSEMEN OF THE APOCALYPSE (1962); SON OF FLUBBER; FLUFFY. TV appearances included "The Judge and Jake Wyler" and "The Best Place to Be." Her most frequent TV exposure besides guest appearances in series episodes was a regular part in "The Beverly Hillbillies."

Mackay, Fulton

Died 6 June 1987, London, England, age 64.

Film/Stage Actor

After volunteering for the Royal Air Force in 1941, he enrolled in the Royal Academy of Dramatic Art in London and spent nine seasons with the Citizen's Theater. He was also a founder of the Scottish Actors Co., for which he both acted and directed. Most of his career was in theater and television. He appeared in the films THE BRAVE DON'T CRY; I'M A STRANGER; THE LAST MOMENT; SCOTCH ON THE ROCKS; A PRIZE OF ARMS; GUMSHOE; NOTHING BUT THE NIGHT; DOING TIME; BRITTANIA HOSPITAL; LOCAL HERO.

MacLean, Alistair

Born 1922, Scotland; died 2 Feb. 1987, Munich, Ger.

Novelist/Screenwriter

Born in the Scottish Highlands, he served in the Royal Navy and taught English near Glasgow before winning a short story contest which led a publisher to encourage him to write a novel. The result was *H.M.S. Ulysses*, and the start of a successful new career writing novels that were "conceived in such cinematic terms, they hardly needed to be adapted for the screen," according to Elliott Kastner, the American film producer who talked him into writing his first screenplay. He wrote 29 books, most of which sold in the millions and many of which were made into films, including: THE GUNS OF NAVARONE; THE SECRET WAYS; WHERE EAGLES DARE; PUPPET ON A CHAIN; WHEN EIGHT BELLS TOLL; FEAR IS THE KEY; CARAVAN TO VACCARES; BREAKHEART PASS; GOLDEN RENDEZVOUS; FORCE 10 FROM NAVARONE; BEAR ISLAND.

Magnotta, Victor

Died 8 Jan. 1987, Hoboken, N.J.; age 45.

Stuntman/Stunt Coordinator

One of Hollywood's top stuntmen, he not only did stunts, but coordinated them and handled second-unit directing and some acting. Appeared in, stunted for, or worked on WHO'S THAT KNOCKING AT MY DOOR?; TAXI DRIVER; SOMEBODY KILLED HER HUSBAND; SIMON; VOICES; THE WARRIORS; THE WANDERERS; DRESSED TO KILL; RAGING BULL; THE CHOSEN; ENDLESS LOVE; FORT APACHE, THE BRONX; RAGTIME; ROLLOVER; A STRANGER IS WATCHING; WOLFEN; AMITYVILLE II: THE POSSESSION; THE WORLD ACCORDING TO GARP; FIGHTING BACK; THE BOUNTY; EASY MONEY; THE SOLDIER; I AM THE CHEESE; SLAYGROUND; BEAT STREET; COTTON CLUB; AFTER HOURS; ALAMO BAY; FIRSTBORN; MOSCOW ON THE HUDSON; THE MUPPETS TAKE MANHATTAN; SPLASH; KEY EXCHANGE; HIGHLANDER; LEGAL EAGLES; SQUEEZE. TV films include "Mickey Spillane's Mike Hammer: More Than Murder" and "Finnegan Begin Again." Had been a colonel in the Marine Corps (receiving a number of medals) and played football for the Los Angeles Rams. Was killed on the set of SQUEEZE while doing a car stunt.

Mamoulian, Rouben

Born 8 Oct. 1897, Tiflis, USSR; died 4 Dec. 1987, Los Angeles, Calif.

Director

Last of the 10 directors responsible for founding the Directors Guild of America, he arrived in New York in 1926 and applied at the Theatre Guild, where he was told he was "not the type" to direct an American play. Undeterred, he began teaching and producing plays for the Guild and the next year directed the Guild's widely acclaimed Broadway play "Porgy," and in 1935 directed the musical version. He was known for innovative techniques in his films. Among his films: APPLAUSE; CITY STREETS; DR. JEKYLL AND MR. HYDE (1932); LOVE ME TONIGHT; QUEEN CHRISTINA; SONG OF SONGS; WE LIVE AGAIN; BECKY SHARP; THE GAY DESPERADO; HIGH, WIDE AND HANDSOME; GOLDEN BOY; THE MARK OF ZORRO; BLOOD AND SAND (1941); RINGS ON HER FINGERS; SUMMER HOLIDAY; SILK STOCKINGS.

Mandell, Daniel

Died 8 June 1987, Huntington Beach, Calif., age 92.

Film Editor

Won Oscars for PRIDE OF THE YANKEES, BEST YEARS OF OUR LIVES, and THE APARTMENT and was nominated for five others during his Hollywood career. Born in New York City, he quit school to tour with Ringling Brothers Circus as a vaudeville comedy acrobat with his brother. He was hired by Samuel Goldwyn's technical staff and his first film for the company was THESE THREE in 1935. Other films include: DEVOTION (1931); REBOUND; A

WOMAN COMMANDS; MELODY LANE (1929); SHOW BOAT (1929); HOLIDAY (1930); SIN TAKES A HOLIDAY; SWING HIGH; BEYOND VICTORY; THE ANIMAL KINGDOM; COUNSELLOR-AT-LAW; I'LL TELL THE WORLD; WAKE UP AND DREAM; THE GOOD FAIRY; HIS NIGHT OUT; KING SOLOMON OF BROADWAY; DODSWORTH; DEAD END; WOMAN CHASES MAN; YOU ONLY LIVE ONCE (1937); THE REAL GLORY; WUTHERING HEIGHTS; THE WESTERNER (1940); THE LITTLE FOXES; MEET JOHN DOE; THE NORTH STAR; THEY GOT ME COVERED; ARSENIC AND OLD LACE; THE PRINCESS AND THE PIRATE; UP IN ARMS; WONDER MAN; THE KID FROM BROOKLYN; ENCHANTMENT; A SONG IS BORN; MY FOOLISH HEART; ROSEANNA McCOY; EDGE OF DOOM; I WANT YOU; A MILLIONAIRE FOR CHRISTY; VALENTINO; HANS CHRISTIAN ANDERSEN; RETURN TO PARADISE; GUYS AND DOLLS; THE SHARKFIGHTERS; WITNESS FOR THE PROSECUTION; PORGY AND BESS; ONE, TWO, THREE; IRMA LA DOUCE; KISS ME, STUPID; THE FORTUNE COOKIE; ONE-TRICK PONY. Among his silent films are LOVE ME AND THE WORLD IS MINE and SILKS AND SADDLES.

Mann, Jerry

Died 6 Dec. 1987; age 77.

Actor/Vaudeville Artist

Started in show business at age nine imitating Eddie Cantor in both revues and nightclubs as well as doing his bit with the USO during the WW II years. Toured in "Oklahoma" and appeared in "How to Succeed in Business Without Really Trying," "Bells Are Ringing," and a revival of "Knickerbocker Holiday" which starred Burt Lancaster. Films include: UNDERWORLD, U.S.A; THE MALTESE BIPPY; SWEET CHARITY; HOW TO SEDUCE A WOMAN; ROCKY. Seen on TV in "MacMillan and Wife," "The Debbie Reynolds Show," and the TV film "The Big Rip-Off."

Markstein, George

Died 15 Jan. 1987, London, England; age 57.

Screenwriter/Author

Started his career as a journalist before becoming the screenwriter of such films as ROBBERY; THE ODESSA FILE; THE FINAL OPTION. In 1975, started turning out thrillers like *Soul Hunters, The Cooler, Chance Awakening, Man from Yesterday, Tara Kane*, and *Traitor for a Cause*. Had a hand in creating the critically acclaimed Patrick McGoohan TV series "The Prisoner," as well as "Special Branch."

Marquand, Richard

Died 4 Sept. 1987, London, England; age 49.

Director

Began his career in London in BBC-TV's documentary department where he worked closely with British author James Cameron and made numerous highly successful documentaries and dramas. Two of his efforts, "Search for the Nile" and "Big Henry and the Polka Dot Kid," won Emmys and he was nominated for the documentary "Mr. Nixon's Secret Legacy" and the telefilm "Luke Was There." His first feature film was THE LEGACY, which was followed by the 1979 docu-drama "Birth of the Beatles," shown on TV in the US but released theatrically throughout the rest of the world. After his 1981 film, EYE OF THE NEEDLE, he was chosen by George Lucas to direct RETURN OF THE JEDI, one of the most successful films of all time. His most recent films are JAGGED EDGE, UNTIL SEPTEMBER, and the unreleased HEARTS OF FIRE.

Martin, Dean Paul

Born 17 Nov. 1951, Santa Monica, Calif.; died 25 Mar. 1987, San Bernardino, Calif.

Musician/Athlete/Pilot/Actor

Eldest son of entertainer Dean Martin, he died in the crash of the F4-C Phantom jet he was flying during a routine training mission. He became a pilot in the Air National Guard in 1980. He originally pursued a career in rock music forming a band with Desi Arnaz, Jr. in the 1960s which toured the world and had several hit records, then he took up tennis, playing many major tournaments. In 1979 he made his acting debut in the feature film PLAYERS, for which he won a Golden Globe nomination for Male Newcomer of the Year. Other films included MADE IN USA and BACKFIRE.

Martin, Quinn

Born 22 May 1922, New York, N.Y.; died 5 Sept. 1987, Santa Fe, Calif.

Producer

President and CEO of QM Productions, which for nearly two deacdes produced such classic television series as "The Untouchables," "The FBI," The Fugitive," "The Streets of San Francisco," "Cannon," and "Barnaby Jones" and in TV's golden age was responsible for a group of presentations on "Playhouse 90." Son of film editor and producer Martin Cohn, he became an apprentice editor at MGM after graduating from the University of California at Berkeley, and soon began writing scripts and producing at Desilu Productions. His films include: BLONDIE GOES LATIN; THE SCARFACE MOB (reedited episodes of the TV pilot released theatrically); THE MEPHISTO WALTZ.

Martin, Vivian

Died 16 Mar. 1987, New York, N.Y.; age 95.

Stage/Silent Film Actress

She made her stage debut in 1901 in a production of "Cyrano de Bergerac," and at age 12 played the title role in "Little Lord Fauntleroy." Her only performance in talkies was the 1935 production of FOLIES BERGERE. The silent films in which she appeared include: THE WISHING RING; THE ARRIVAL OF PERPETUA; THE LITTLE MADEMOISELLE; LITTLE MISS BROWN; A KISS FOR SUSIE; MOLLY ENTANGLED; JANE GOES A'WOOING; LITTLE COMRADE; LOUISIANA; OVER NIGHT; HER FATHER'S SON; MERELY MARY ANN; A MODERN THELMA; THE RIGHT DIRECTION; THE STRONGER LOVE; THE FAIR BARBARIAN; FORBIDDEN PATHS; THE GIRL AT HOME; GIVING BECKY A CHANCE; LITTLE MISS OPTIMIST; THE SPIRIT OF ROMANCE; SUNSET TRAIL; THE TROUBLE BUSTER; THE WAX MODEL; HER COUNTRY FIRST; MIRANDY SMILES; A PETTICOAT PILOT; UNCLAIMED GOODS; VIVIETTE; HIS OFFICIAL FIANCEE; THE HOME TOWN GIRL; AN INNOCENT ADVENTURESS; THE THIRD KISS; YOU NEVER SAID SUCH A GIRL; HUSBANDS AND WIVES; THE SONG OF THE SOUL; MOTHER ETERNAL; PARDON MY FRENCH; SOILED.

Marvin, Lee

Born 19 Feb. 1924, New York, N.Y.; died 29 Aug. 1987, Tucson, Ariz.

Actor

The gravel-voiced tough guy was born into a well-to-do New York City family. He was sent to a succession of exclusive Eastern boarding schools, and after being expelled from many of them, he quit school and joined the Marines. After 21 landings on Pacific islands as a scout sniper he was felled by a Japanese bullet, causing a spine injury that kept him hospitalized for 13 months. His move to Hollywood came after more than 200 featured roles in television dramas. His first starring role in film came with CAT BALLOU, for which he won an Academy Award. He gained headlines as a defendant in a historic "palimony" suit filed by his former live-in mate. Though he epitomized the uncompromising rugged tough guy with a "killer instinct," he wryly insisted he had only two expressions: "Hat on and hat off." Among his films are: YOU'RE IN THE NAVY NOW; DIPLOMATIC COURIER; THE DUEL AT SILVER CREEK; EIGHT IRON MEN; HANGMAN'S KNOT; WE'RE NOT MARRIED; THE BIG HEAT; DOWN AMONG THE SHELTERING PALMS; THE GLORY BRIGADE; GUN FURY; SEMINOLE; THE STRANGER WORE A GUN; THE WILD ONE; THE CAINE MUTINY; GORILLA AT LARGE; THE RAID; BAD DAY AT BLACK ROCK; I DIED A THOUSAND TIMES; A LIFE IN THE BALANCE; NOT AS A STRANGER; PETE KELLY'S BLUES; SHACK OUT ON 101; VIOLENT SATURDAY; ATTACK!; PILLARS OF THE SKY; THE RACK; SEVEN MEN FROM NOW; RAINTREE COUNTY; THE MISSOURI TRAVELER; RIDE LONESOME; THE COMANCHEROS; THE MAN WHO SHOT LIBERTY VALANCE; DONOVAN'S REEF; THE KILLERS (1964); SHIP OF FOOLS; THE PROFESSIONALS; THE DIRTY DOZEN; POINT BLANK; HELL IN THE PACIFIC; SERGEANT RYKER; PAINT YOUR WAGON; MONTE WALSH; POCKET MONEY; PRIME CUT; EMPEROR OF THE NORTH POLE; THE ICEMAN COMETH; THE KLANSMAN; THE SPIKES GANG; THE GREAT SCOUT AND CATHOUSE THURSDAY; SHOUT AT THE DEVIL; AVALANCHE EXPRESS; THE BIG RED ONE; DEATH HUNT; GORKY PARK.

Mason, Brewster

Died 14 Aug. 1987; age 65.

Actor

Attended the Royal Academy of Dramatic Art in his native England and appeared on stage in "The Affair," "Hamlet," "The Merry Wives of Windsor," "Henry VIII." Some of his films include MACBETH (1963); PRIVATE POTTER; QUATERMASS CONCLUSION. After he became a member of the Royal Shakespeare Company, he toured Europe and the Orient, eventually coming to the US to direct New England Shakespeare festivals and then to teach acting in California.

Maureen, Mollie

Died 26 Jan. 1987.

Actress

This British actress made her mark on TV, landing a regular part in "Crossroads." Appeared in THE PRIVATE LIFE OF SHERLOCK HOLMES; CURSE OF THE PINK PANTHER; THE WICKED LADY (1983).

Marquand

Dean Paul Martin

Vivian Martin

Marvin

Meyer

Maysles, David

Born 10 Jan. 1932, Brookline, Mass; died 3 Jan. 1987, New York, N.Y.

Documentary Filmmaker

Along with his brother Albert he is credited with being among the founders of the cinema verite style of filmmaking, which uses lightweight, handheld cameras to capture slices of daily life rather than delivering static interviews and narration. He began his career as an assistant to the producer on the Marilyn Monroe pictures BUS STOP and THE PRINCE AND THE SHOWGIRL, and in 1962 formed a film company with his brother and produced SHOWMAN, a documentary about mogul Joseph E. Levine. The brothers went on to make some two dozen nonfiction features and telefilms over their 30-year career, plus many corporate films and TV commercials to finance their feature projects. Among the best-known of their documentaries are SALESMAN, which chronicles the adventures of four bible salesmen; GIMME SHELTER, a record of the latter part of the Rolling Stones' 1969 American tour; and GREY GARDENS, about the reclusive aunt and cousin of Jacqueline Kennedy Onassis. His 1974 film, VALLEY CURTAIN, the first of a trilogy of films about Christo's work, was nominated for an Academy Award. Other films include: PSYCHIATRY IN RUSSIA; PRIMARY; YANKI NO!; SIX IN PARIS; MONTEREY POP; YOUTH IN POLAND; WHAT'S HAPPENING: THE BEATLES IN THE USA; MEET MARLON BRANDO; WITH LOVE FROM TRUMAN; RUNNING FENCE.

McDermid, Finlay

Died 2 Mar. 1987, Woodland Hills, Calif.; age 82.

Story Editor/Writer

Worked more than 20 years at Warner Bros. in the capacity of story editor and screenwriter. Handled the cowriting chores on a Randolph Scott western, THE BOUNTY HUNTER.

McGrath, Pat

Died 2 June 1987, Los Angeles, Calif.; age 46.

Costumer

Received an Emmy in 1986 for supervising the men's costumes on "North and South, Book I." In later years worked on such television shows as "Cannon," "The Streets of San Francisco," "Barnaby Jones," and "Most Wanted." Her film credits include: THE PROFESSIONALS; CAMELOT; DIVORCE AMERICAN STYLE; THE BALLAD OF CABLE HOGUE; JUNIOR BONNER.

McKay, Scott [Carl Gose]

Born 28 May 1915, Pleasantville, Ia.; died 16 March 1987, New York, N.Y.

Actor

From his first theatrical job as a stooge for a magician touring Iowa, he went on to Broadway where he performed in more than 25 productions. He appeared frequently on radio and television and his movie credits include: GUEST IN THE HOUSE; THIRTY SECONDS OVER TOKYO; KISS AND TELL; DUEL IN THE SUN; THE GENIE; THE FRONT; THE BELL JAR; YOU BETTER WATCH OUT; THE BLACK CAT.

McKenzie, Ella [Ella Gilbert Sweeney]

Died 25 Apr. 1987, Hollywood, Calif.; age unknown.

Actress

She came from a family of actors and as a child appeared in over 100 films, working with Charlie Chaplin, Ben Turpin, and Will Rogers, as well as her first husband, comic actor Billy Gilbert. Among her films: THE LAST WARNING (1929); ALICE ADAMS (1935); THE MAN FROM GUN TOWN; PALM SPRINGS; RIDERS OF THE DAWN.

McLaren, Norman

Born 11 Apr. 1914, Stirling, Scotland; died 27 Jan. 1987, Montreal, Quebec.

Animator

Pioneered such techniques as drawing directly on celluloid, synthetic sound, three-dimensional animation, and stop-action. He went to work for the British General Post Office Film Unit on animated films and the war documentaries that would make them famous, then, in 1942, immigrated to Canada where he was a founding member of Canada's National Film Board. He received this year the first Life Achievement Award in Animation from the Seventh World Festival of Animated Films held in Zagreb, Yugoslavia. Among his films: BEGONE DULL CARE (winner at the Venice Film Festival), NEIGHBORS (winner of an Oscar in 1957); PAX DE DEUX; BLINKITY BLANK; RHYTHEMITC; A CHAIRY TALE; SHORT AND SUITE; CANON; MOSAIC. His last film was NARCISSUS, released in 1983. He received a special Genie Award in Canada in 1984.

Meyer, Andrew C.

Died 8 Mar. 1987, Los Angeles, Calif.; age 43.

Writer/Director

At first associated with Andy Warhol, he directed the shorts "Match Girl," "An Early Clue to the New Direction," "Annunciation," and "Flower Child," which received considerable notice and gave him the opportunity to direct the cult film NIGHT OF THE COBRA WOMAN. His other films are THE SKY PIRATE and TIDAL WAVE. Appeared in DOCUMENTEUR—AN EMOTION PICTURE (a documentary helmed by Agnes Varda), wrote articles for film magazines, did assistant editing, and lectured on film.

Meyer, Emile

Died 19 Mar. 1987, Covington, La., age 76.

Actor

He was discovered in New Orleans by Elia Kazan in 1950, when the director was filming PANIC IN THE STREETS and cast him it. Before that he had worked as a longshoreman, paymaster, trucker, insurance salesman, safety engineer, and cabbie. He appeared in the TV series "Bonanza," "Death Valley Days," "The Lawman," and "Dennis the Menace" and the movies THE BIG NIGHT; CATTLE QUEEN; THE GUY WHO CAME BACK; THE MOB; THE PEOPLE AGAINST O'HARA; BLOODHOUNDS OF BROADWAY; CARBINE WILLIAMS; HURRICANE SMITH; WE'RE NOT MARRIED; THE WILD NORTH; THE FARMER TAKES A WIFE (1953); SHANE; DRUMS ACROSS THE RIVER; THE HUMAN JUNGLE; RIOT IN CELL BLOCK 11; SHIELD FOR MURDER; SILVER LODE; THE BLACKBOARD JUNGLE; THE GIRL IN THE RED VELVET SWING; THE MAN WITH THE GOLDEN ARM; MAN WITH THE GUN; STRANGER ON HORSEBACK; THE TALL MEN; WHITE FEATHER; THE MAVERICK QUEEN; RAW EDGE; BABY FACE NELSON; BADLANDS OF MONTANA; THE DELICATE DELINQUENT; GUN THE MAN DOWN; PATHS OF GLORY; SWEET SMELL OF SUCCESS; THE CASE AGAINST BROOKLYN; THE FIEND WHO WALKED THE WEST; GOOD DAY FOR A HANGING; THE LINEUP (1958); REVOLT IN THE BIG HOUSE; KING OF THE WILD STALLIONS; THE GIRL IN LOVER'S LANE; THE THREAT; YOUNG JESSE JAMES; MOVE OVER, DARLING; TAGGART; YOUNG DILLINGER; HOSTILE GUNS; A TIME FOR KILLING; THE OUTFIT; MACON COUNTY LINE.

Meyer, Joseph

Born 12 Mar. 1894, Modesto, Calif.; died 22 Jun. 1987, New York City, N.Y.

Composer

Took up the study of the violin in Paris, returning to the US in 1908 to play in cafes. After WW I service, began his lengthy songwriting career, penning such popular hits as "California, Here I Come," "If You Knew Susie" (popularized by Eddie Cantor), "Crazy Rhythm," "A Cup of Coffee, a Sandwich and You." Wrote for the following stage shows: "Battling Buttler," "Big Boy," "Gay Paree," "Andre Charlot Revue of 1925," "Sweetheart Time," "Ziegfeld Follies of 1934," "New Faces of 1936." Contributed to such films as THOSE THREE FRENCH GIRLS; GEORGE WHITE'S SCANDALS OF 1935; POSSESSED; WAY OUT WEST; DANCING SWEETIES.

Millakowsky, Herman

Died 12 Feb. 1987, Beverly Hills, Calif.; age 95.

Producer

A native of Germany, he spent time in the fields of journalism and banking before starting his film production career in the 1920s, in Germany (PRIVATE SECRETARY), launching such future directors as Billy Wilder, William Wyler, Max Ophuls, Joe Pasternak, and Hermann Kosterlitz [Henry Koster]. The rise of the Nazi regime in the 1930s prompted his to move to Paris for such efforts as YOSHIWARA;THE VOLGA BOATMAN; DARK EYES; THE POSTMASTER'S DAUGHTER; GENERAL MOBILIZATON. The eruption of WW II caused him to leave France for the US, where he went to Hollywood for three films, WOMEN IN BONDAGE; FACES IN THE FOG; MURDER IN THE FOG. After WW II, returned to Europe and did FEAR, with Ingrid Bergman, the last of the nearly 60 films he produced.

Minor, Michael

Died 4 May 1987, Los Angeles, Calif., age 46.

Art Director

An Emmy Award winner for art direction and visual effects, he worked extensively with set design and construction. He was the art director and visual effects designer on STAR TREK II—THE WRATH OF KHAN. He was staff art director for Fantasy II and Coast Special Effects, where he worked on the development of effects for over 100 commercials. The films he worked on include: STAR TREK—THE MOTION PICTURE; REMO WILLIAMS: THE ADVENTURE BEGINS; THE MAN WHO SAW TOMORROW; SPACEHUNTER, ADVENTURES IN THE FORBIDDEN ZONE; AIRPLANE II: THE SEQUEL; VIRUS; THE BIG EASY; BEASTMASTER; BRUBAKER; THE CAT FROM OUTER SPACE; PETE'S DRAGON.

Mirel, Amelia [Alma Ruggiero; Alma Bambu]

Died 14 Jun. 1987, Buenos Aires, Argentina; age 78

Silent Film Actress

Was active in the Argentine silent film industry in such films as FAUSTO (1922) and CRIOLLO VIEJO (1925) until sound came, forcing her to switch to the stage and to change her name to Alma Bambu. Later became a singer in France and then did radio work in Argentina.

Miranov, Andrei A.

Died 17 Aug. 1987, Riga, Latvia, USSR; age 46.

Actor

Popular leading actor on both stage and screen had roles in MY FRIEND, IVAN LAPSHIN, and THE DIAMOND HAND.

Montgomery, Earl

Born 17 Apr. 1921, Memphis, Tenn.; died 4 Mar. 1987, Los Angeles, Calif.

Film/Stage Actor

He first appeared on stage opposite Charles Laughton performing in Brecht's "Galileo," in New York. Over the years he was seen in City Center productions of "Love's Labour's Lost" and "The Merchant of Venice" and with the Lincoln Center Repertory Theater Company in "The Caucasian Chalk Circle" and "The Alchemist." Other credits include "A Visit to a Small Planet," "Becket," "Summer and Smoke," and Jean Anouilh's "Rehearsal." He was last seen on Broadway in 1973 in "The Waltz of the Toreadors." He was a founder-member of the Association of Producing Artists, a group of actors who took the classics on tour. He began acting on television in its infancy, starting with "Love of Life" in 1952. Among films he appeared in are: ACT ONE; THE DETECTIVE (1968); ROCKY II; F.I.S.T.; HEAVEN CAN WAIT (1978); NAVY BORN; SEED OF INNOCENCE.

Moore, James

Died 8 Apr. 1987, Hollywood, Calif., age 72.

Film/Television Editor

He began his career as a messenger at Warner Bros. in 1932 and remained at the studio for 27 years. He eventually became head of Warner Bros. television post-production department and oversaw editing of all the studio's TV series. In 1960 he moved to MGM, and later Universal. Films he edited include: FANTASIA; THE SECRET SEVEN; THUNDER OVER THE PLAINS; THE BOY FROM OKLAHOMA; PHANTOM OF THE RUE MORGUE (1954); THE RIVER CHANGES; THE SINISTER URGE; THE LOSERS (1970); THE TANKS ARE COMING; THIS WOMAN IS DANGEROUS.

Moore, Phil

Born 20 Feb. 1918, Portland, Ore.; died 13 May 1987, Los Angeles, Calif.

Composer/Conductor/Arranger

Believed to be the first black man to work for a Hollywood studio music department, he was hired as a rehearsal pianist by MGM in 1941 and worked there for five years, while at the same time freelancing scoring jobs for RKO, Columbia, and Paramount. With his wife he founded Get Your Act Together, Hollywood school for singers. Among his vocal pupils were: Mae West, Lucille Ball, Ann Sothern, Red Skelton, Lena Horne, Judy Garland, Dorothy Dandridge, Johnny Mathis, Marilyn Monroe, Goldie Hawn, Diahann Carroll and The Supremes. Films for which he conducted music are: A DAY AT THE RACES; CABIN IN THE SKY; PANAMA HATTIE; KISMET (1944); BROADWAY MELODY; ZIEGFELD GIRL; PRESENTING LILY MARS; THE PALM BEACH STORY; THIS GUN FOR HIRE; MY FAVORITE BLONDE.

Morrison, Jane

Died 21 Jan. 1987, Nairobi, Kenya; age 39.

Film Producer/Writer/Director

After college, she had a hand in setting up repertory theaters and writing workshops before getting into the production, direction, and writing of documentaries and shorts. She did one fiction film, THE TWO WORLDS OF ANGELITA.

Moustache [Francois-Alexandre Galepides]

Died 25 Mar. 1987, Paris, France; age 58.

Actor/Entertainer/Jazz Drummer

Born in Paris, son of Greek parents, he was an outstanding personality of Parisian nightlife for three decades. He began his career as a jazz drummer and host of several supper clubs, and in 1953 formed his own orchestra. He counted among his intimate friends Frank Sinatra, Darryl F. Zanuck, Brigitte Bardot, Charlie Chaplin, and James Jones. The movies he appeared in are PARIS BLUES; IN THE FRENCH STYLE; CIRCUS WORLD; HOW TO STEAL A MILLION; A FLEA IN HER EAR; MAYERLING; SILVER BEARS; LOVE IN THE AFTERNOON.

Munch, Richard

Died 6 June 1987, Malaga, Spain; age 71.

Director/Actor

Born in Giessen, Germany, he worked in the German Theater in Hamburg with the celebrated Gustaf Grundgens and with the Vienna Burg Theater. He won the German Film Prize for his role in THE WONDER OF MALACHIAS. Other films include: THE LONGEST DAY; THE YOUNG GO WILD; THE RESTLESS NIGHT; THE VISIT; THE TRAIN; THE BRIDGE AT REMAGEN.

Muse, Kenneth L.

Died 26 July 1987, Templeton, Calif.; age 75.

Animator

Worked for Walt Disney, MGM, and Hanna-Barbera drawing such well-known characters as Mickey Mouse, Tom & Jerry, the Jetsons, the Flintstones, Scooby-Doo, Yogi Bear. Handled the animation for the dancing mouse who appeared opposite Gene Kelly in a noted sequence from ANCHORS AWEIGH.

Myrow, Josef

Born 28 Feb. 1910, Russia; died 24 Dec. 1987, Los Angeles, Calif.

Songwriter

Came to the US in 1912, earning a living as a pianist with symphony orchestras in Cleveland and Philadelphia. Handled musical programming and directing for Philadelphia radio stations. Started out composing for revues in New York and Florida nightclubs. Some of his standards include "The Five O'Clock Whistle," "On the Boardwalk in Atlantic City," "You Do," "Kokomo, Indiana," "You Make Me Feel So Young," with input from such collaborators as Mack Gordon, Johnny Mercer, Kim Gannon, Eddie DeLange. Supplied scores and tunes for such films as THREE LITTLE GIRLS IN BLUE; IF I'M LUCKY; ONE MORE TOMORROW; MOTHER WORE TIGHTS; WHEN MY BABY SMILES AT ME; IT HAPPENS EVERY SPRING; THE BEAUTIFUL BLONDE FROM BASHFUL BEND; WABASH AVENUE; I LOVE MELVIN; THE GIRL NEXT DOOR; THE FRENCH LINE; BUNDLE OF JOY.

Negri, Pola [Barbara Apollonia Chalupiec]

Born 31 Dec. 1899, Warsaw, Poland; died 1 Aug. 1987, San Antonio, Tex.

Silent Film Star

Well known in German films before being lured to the US by producer Adolph Zukor in 1921. Her dramatic image on screen in the US was mirrored in her volatile relationship with Charlie Chaplin and a much-publicized affair with Rudolph Valentino, after whose death she went into seclusion, only to emerge a year later to marry a destitute Georgian prince, Serge Mdivani, thus incurring the wrath of the Valentino worshippers. Among her American movies are: THE WAY OF LOST SOULS; THE WOMAN HE SCORNED; A WOMAN COMMANDS; MOSCOW-SHANGHAI; HI, DIDDLE DIDDLE; THE MOON-SPINNERS. Silents include PASSION; ONE ARABIAN NIGHT; FORBIDDEN PARADISE (1924); THE CHARMER; EAST OF SUEZ; GOOD AND NAUGHTY; BARBED WIRE (1927); THE WOMAN ON TRIAL; THE SECRET HOUR; THREE SINNERS; SLAVE OF PASSION, SLAVE OF VICE; GYPSY BLOOD; LAST PAYMENT; SUMURUN; VENDETTA (1921); THE DEVILS'S PAWN; THE RED PEACOCK; BELLA DONNA (1923); THE CHEAT; THE SPANISH DANCER; LILY OF THE DUST; MEN; SHADOWS OF PARIS; FLOWER OF NIGHT; A WOMAN OF THE WORLD (1925); THE CROWN OF LIES; HOTEL IMPERIAL (1927); LOVES OF AN ACTRESS; THE WOMAN FROM MOSCOW.

Nelson, Ralph

Born 12 Aug. 1916, New York, N.Y; died 21 December 1987, Santa Monica, Calif.

Director

At the age 15 he won both a *New York Times* oratory contest and a judge's description as "potentially the most dangerous juvenile criminal" in that city, for a series of gang fights. By his next birthday he had been jailed in 12 states for vagrancy and suspicion of burglary. He arrived in Los Angeles hidden on a freight train, but was soon back in jail and told to get out of town in 90 days. Saved by the Union Rescue Mission, he returned to New York to finish school. He studied acting and went to work as a "gofer" for various producers and actors. He directed both film and television versions of REQUIEM FOR A HEAVYWEIGHT, winning an Emmy, and received an Oscar nomination for the movie LILIES OF THE FIELD. He directed more than 1,000 television shows. In the theater he understudied Leslie Howard as "Hamlet," and appeared on stage with Alfred Lunt and Lynn Fontanne's company where he met his first wife Celeste Holm. Among his other films: SOLDIER IN THE RAIN; FATE IS THE HUNTER; FATHER GOOSE; ONCE A THIEF; DUEL AT DIABLO; COUNTERPOINT; CHARLY; SOLDIER BLUE; TICK . . . TICK . . . TICK . . . ; FLIGHT OF THE DOVES; THE WRATH OF GOD; THE WILBY CONSPIRACY;

Negri

Page

Patrick

EMBRYO; A HERO AIN'T NOTHING BUT A SANDWICH; YOU CAN'T GO HOME AGAIN.

Oboler, Arch

Died 19 Mar. 1987, Los Angeles, Calif., age 78.

Film/Radio Producer-Writer

Though his greatest achievements were in radio, he worked in film as writer-producer-director. His 1945 MGM feature BEWITCHED was a forerunner of the split-personality melodramas, and BWANA DEVIL the first commercial success using 3-D. He is mostly remembered, though, as the producer-director and macabre voice of "Lights Out," network radio's classic late night series, and for his use of realistic sound effects. His movies were: ESCAPE (1940); GANGWAY FOR TOMORROW; BEWITCHED; STRANGE HOLIDAY (1945); THE ARNELO AFFAIR; ON OUR MERRY WAY; FIVE; BWANA DEVIL; THE TWONKY; ONE PLUS ONE; THE BUBBLE.

Ondra, Anny [Anna Sophie Ondrakowa]

Born 15 May 1903, Tarnow, Poland; died 28 Feb. 1987, Hamburg, West Germany.

Actress

Started in Czech films at the age of 15 working for producer-director Gaustav Machaty and also appeared in Austrian, German, and British efforts. Her credits include: WOMAN WITH SMALL FEET; SONG OF GOLD; DRATENICEK; GILLY IN PRAGUE; DER ERSTE KUSS; GOD'S CLAY; GLORIOUS YOUTH; THE MANXMAN; BLACKMAIL (her voice was dubbed for this early Alfred Hitchcock talkie), BABY, KIKI; EINE NACHT IM PARADIES; DIE VOM RUMMELPLATZ; POLISH BLOOD; KNOCKOUT; DONOGOO TONKA; THE IRRESISTIBLE MAN; GENERAL HOUSECLEANING; SCHON MUSS MAN SEIN. Her first husband was Karel Lamac (the director with whom she made approximately 70 films) and her second was Max Schmeling, the world champion boxer who had two famous bouts with Joe Louis.

Orlando, Don

Died 10 Dec. 1987; age 75.

Actor

An extra and minor-part player who was born in Italy, he appeared in PALS OF THE SADDLE; ROMANCE OF THE ROCKIES; TORRID ZONE; LAW OF THE TROPICS; FIXED BAYONETS; KANSAS CITY CONFIDENTIAL; PARK ROW; HELL AND HIGH WATER (1954); HELL'S ISLAND; WALK THE DARK STREET; DOMINO KID; RUN OF THE ARROW; 20 MILLION MILES TO EARTH; ANNIVERSARY WALTZ. "Tugboat Annie" is one of his many TV credits. In later years, he became a real estate broker.

Page, Geraldine

Born 22 Nov. 1924, Kirksville, Mo.; died 13 June 1987, New York, N.Y.

Film/Stage Actress

She won the Best Actress Oscar for her screen role in 1985's THE TRIP TO BOUNTIFUL, after seven unsuccessful nominations. Primarily known as a theater actress, she was first noticed in 1952 in an off-Broadway revival of Tennessee Williams' "Summer and Smoke." Her Broadway debut was in "Midsummer." Her characters were often Southerners, projecting an air of vulnerability and torment. Despite a successful Hollywood career, she remained a strong supporter of repertory theater throughout her life, often acting in their productions at a low salary and in supporting roles. She won two Emmy awards for her television performances in Truman Capote's "A Christmas Memory" and "The Thanksgiving Visitor." She was married, for the second time, to actor Rip Torn. Movies she appeared in are: TOYS IN THE ATTIC; HONDO; TAXI; SUMMER AND SMOKE; SWEET BIRD OF YOUTH; DEAR HEART; YOU'RE A BIG BOY NOW; THE HAPPIEST MILLIONAIRE; MONDAY'S CHILD; TRUMAN CAPOTE'S TRILOGY; WHAT EVER HAPPENED TO AUNT ALICE; THE BEGUILED; J.W. COOP; PETE 'N' TILLIE; HAPPY AS THE GRASS WAS GREEN; THE DAY OF THE LOCUST; NASTY HABITS; THE RESCUERS; THE THREE SISTERS (1977); HAZEL'S PEOPLE; INTERIORS; HARRY'S WAR; HONKY TONK FREEWAY; I'M DANCING AS FAST AS I CAN; THE POPE OF GREENWICH VILLAGE.

Packer, Peter

Died 13 Feb. 1987; age 81.

Novelist/Screenwriter/TV Writer

A native of London who came to the US in his early adult years and wrote stories that appeared in such magazines as *The New Yorker*, *Collier's*, and *Esquire*. Wrote several novels—*Big Valley*, *Bonanza*, *Lost in Space*, *Broken Arrow*, *The Massie Case*—as well as scripts for TV ("Stalk the Wild Child," a telefilm) and the big screen (SEVENTH CAVALRY).

Paige, Robert [David Carlyle]

Died 21 Dec. 1987; age 77.

Actor

He was a leading man in B films and musicals for Universal Pictures in the 1940s, sometimes appearing under the name David Carlyle. He also worked as a television newscaster for ABC and served as co-host of the quiz show "The Big Payoff" with Bess Myerson. His films include: HIGHWAY PATROL; I STAND ACCUSED; THE LADY OBJECTS; THE LAST WARNING; THE MAIN EVENT; THERE'S ALWAYS A WOMAN; WHEN G-MEN STEP IN; WHO KILLED GAIL PRESTON?; DEATH OF A CHAMPION; HOMICIDE BUREAU; DANCING ON A DIME; EMERGENCY SQUAD; GOLDEN GLOVES; OPENED BY MISTAKE; PAROLE FIXER; WOMEN WITHOUT NAMES; DON'T GET PERSONAL; HELLZAPOPPIN'; MELODY LANE; THE MONSTER AND THE GIRL; SAN ANTONIO ROSE; ALMOST MARRIED; GET HEP TO LOVE; JAIL HOUSE BLUES; PARDON MY SARONG; WHAT'S COOKIN'?; YOU'RE TELLING ME; COWBOY IN MANHATTAN; CRAZY HOUSE; FIRED WIFE; FRONTIER BADMEN; GET GOING; HI, BUDDY; HI'YA CHUM; HOW'S ABOUT IT?; KEEP 'EM SLUGGING; MR. BIG; SON OF DRACULA; FOLLOW THE BOYS; HER PRIMITIVE MAN; SHADY LADY; TANGIER; THE RED STALLION; THE FLAME; BLONDE ICE; THE GREEN PROMISE; ABBOTT AND COSTELLO GO TO MARS; SPLIT SECOND; THE MARRIAGE-GO-ROUND; BYE BYE BIRDIE; MEDIUM COOL. Under the name of David Carlyle he appeared in CAIN AND MABEL; CHEROKEE STRIP; THE KID COMES BACK; MEET THE BOY FRIEND; ONCE A DOCTOR; RHYTHM IN THE CLOUDS; SMART BLONDE; TALENT SCOUT.

Parker, Raymond D.

Died 19 Oct. 1987, Harrison, N.Y.; age 75.

Film/Stage Actor-Director-Producer

Appeared onscreen in FRESHMAN YEAR; HIS EXCITING NIGHT; THE LAST WARNING; LETTER OF INTRODUCTION; LITTLE TOUGH GUY; SERVICE DE LUXE; SWING THAT CHEER; EAST SIDE OF HEAVEN; FOR LOVE OR MONEY (1939); THE HOUSE OF FEAR (1939); SOCIETY SMUGGLERS. His stage efforts include: "Star Wagon," "The World of Carl Sandburg," "Sabrina Fair," and tours with "Wait Until Dark," "Teahouse of the August Moon," "Barefoot in the Park." Was involved with "Mister Roberts" to a great extent, as a actor with the 1950 national tour and the 1956 Broadway revival, and then produced, directed, and acted in his own touring company's productions.

Patrick, Dorothy [Dorothy Davis]

Died 31 May 1987, Los Angeles, Calif.; age 65.

Actress

Born in Boniface, Manitoba, she started her career as a model in New York and at one time was the Chesterfield girl. After winning the Jesse Lasky "Gateway to Hollywood" contest in 1939, she was offered a film contract but turned it down to wed New York Ranger hockey hall-of-famer Lynn Patrick. She later moved to Hollywood and performed in such films as: UP IN ARMS; BOY'S RANCH; THE MIGHTY MC GURK; TILL THE CLOUDS ROLL BY; THE HIGH WALL; NEW ORLEANS; ALIAS A GENTLEMAN; COME TO THE STABLE; FOLLOW ME QUIETLY; BELLE OF OLD MEXICO; THE BLONDE BANDIT; DESTINATION BIG HOUSE; FEDERAL AGENT AT LARGE; HOUSE BY THE RIVER; LONELY HEARTS BANDITS; TARNISHED; UNDER MEXICALI STARS; 711 OCEAN DRIVE; THE BIG GUSHER; THE BAD AND THE BEAUTIFUL; DESERT PASSAGE; ROAD AGENT; SCARAMOUCHE; SINGIN' IN THE RAIN; HALF A HERO; MAN OF CONFLICT; SAVAGE FRONTIER; TANGIER INCIDENT; TORCH SONG; MEN OF THE FIGHTING LADY; THE OUTLAW STALLION; THUNDER PASS; LAS VEGAS SHAKEDOWN; VIOLENT SATURDAY; THE PEACEMAKER.

Pierce, Arthur C.

Died 17 Nov. 1987, Mesquite, Tex.; age 64.

Screenwriter/Cameraman/Director/Actor

Started his career as a cameraman in the Naval Intelligence photographic division based in Hawaii during WW II, later winning awards for work on such documentaries as THE FIGHTING LADY and SILENT SERVICE. Went to Hollywood to turn out B-level science-fiction scripts for such films as THE COSMIC MAN; BEYOND THE TIME BARRIER; INVASION OF THE ANIMAL PEOPLE; THE HUMAN DUPLICATORS; MUTINY IN OUTER SPACE (also coproduced the last two films); CYBORG 2087; DESTINATION INNER SPACE; LAS VEGAS HILLBILLYS (directed only); WOMEN OF THE PREHISTORIC PLANET (also directed); THE DESTRUCTORS; INVISIBLE STRANGLER.

Pinheiro, Victor

Died 5 Mar. 1987, Los Angeles, Calif.; age 58.

Actor

After immigrating from England and making a short stopover in New York, he came to California to start the first repertory company to present one-man shows dealing with historical personages such as Benjamin Franklin, Richard Henry Dana, Stephen A. Douglas, and Ulysses S. Grant. Also appeared on TV ("The Young and the Restless," "Kids Are People Too") and in films (BILLY JACK GOES TO WASHINGTON and ALEX AND THE GYPSY).

Pokras, Abel

Born 22 Apr. 1919; died 22 Apr. 1987.

Dancer

Appeared on stage ("Something for the Boys," "Sugar," "Lady in the Dark," "How to Succeed in Business Without Really Trying," "No, No, Nanette"), in films (STAR OF INDIA; DANCIN'; HEART BEAT) and TV ("Al Hirt Show," "Ed Sullivan Show"). Later worked in local theater as a choreographer and served as an executive secretary to such show business personalities as Herschel Bernardi, Howard Keel, and Larry Parks.

Preston, Robert [Robert Preston Meservey]

Born 8 June 1918, Newton Highlands, Mass.; died 21 Mar. 1987, Santa Barbara, Calif.

Actor

He was raised in Hollywood and after high school joined a repertory company headed by Tyrone Power's mother, before being signed by Paramount Pictures at the age of 19. Though best known for his Broadway legitimate achievements, his film career was lengthy and he is best remembered for his portrayal of the fast-talking, warm-hearted con man from Gary, Ind., Prof. Harold Hill, in THE MUSIC MAN. Of his career which spanned nearly half a century, he mused: "I'd get the best role in every B picture and the second best in the A pictures." Among those pictures: ILLEGAL TRAFFIC; KING OF ALCATRAZ; BEAU GESTE (1939); DISBARRED; UNION PACIFIC; MOON OVER BURMA; NORTHWEST MOUNTED POLICE; TYPHOON; LADY FROM CHEYENNE; MIDNIGHT ANGEL; NIGHT OF JANUARY 16TH; PARACHUTE BATTALION; NIGHT PLANE FROM CHUNGKING; PACIFIC BLACKOUT; REAP THE WILD WIND; STAR SPANGLED RHYTHM; THIS GUN FOR HIRE; WAKE ISLAND; THE MACOMBER AFFAIR; VARIETY GIRL; WILD HARVEST; BIG CITY (1948); BLOOD ON THE MOON; WHISPERING SMITH; THE LADY GAMBLES; TULSA; THE SUNDOWNERS (1950); BEST OF THE BADMEN; MY BROTHER, THE OUTLAW; WHEN I GROW UP; CLOUDBURST; THE LAST FRONTIER; THE DARK AT THE TOP OF THE STAIRS; HOW THE WEST WAS WON; THE MUSIC MAN; ALL THE WAY HOME; ISLAND OF LOVE; CHILD'S PLAY; JUNIOR BONNER; MAME; SEMI-TOUGH; S.O.B.; VICTOR/VICTORIA; THE LAST STARFIGHTER.

Priest, Natalie

Died 7 July 1987; age 68.

Actress

Was active in radio and TV commercial work. Appeared on stage ("God Bless You, Harold Fineberg," "Yentl," "The Respectful Prostitute," and a one-woman show, "Looking Forward"), TV ("Miss Susan," "Edge of Night," "As the World Turns," "Ryan's Hope,") and in the films THE WRONG MAN and PATERNITY.

Quaid, Buddy

Died 8 Feb. 1987.

Actor

Appeared in LOCAL HERO (1983).

Qualen, John [John Oleson]

Born 8 Dec. 1899, Vancouver, British Columbia; died 12 Sept. 1987, Torrance, Calif.

Actor

His career in New York began when he told a producer he could play Norwegian character parts and was cast as the Norwegian janitor in the Pulitzer Prize-winning play "Street Scene." But probably his best-known role was that of the overwhelmed father of the Dionne Quintuplets in three movies. Other notable roles he played were Muley Graves in THE GRAPES OF WRATH; the mild, tormented killer in HIS GIRL FRIDAY; and the sailor Axel Larson in THE LONG VOYAGE HOME. Among the other films in his long career are: ARROWSMITH; COUNSELLOR-AT-LAW; THE DEVIL'S BROTHER; LET'S FALL IN LOVE; OUR DAILY BREAD; SERVANTS' ENTRANCE; NIGHTS IN HOLLYWOOD; BLACK FURY; CHASING YESTERDAY; DOUBTING THOMAS; THE FARMER TAKES A WIFE (1935); GREAT HOTEL MURDER; MAN OF IRON (1935); ORCHIDS TO YOU; SILK HAT KID; THE THREE MUSKETEERS (1935); THUNDER IN THE NIGHT; CHEERS OF THE CROWD; THE COUNTRY DOCTOR (1936); GIRLS' DORMITORY; MEET NERO WOLFE; REUNION (1936); RING AROUND THE MOON; THE ROAD TO GLORY; WHIPSAW; WIFE VERSUS SECRETARY; ANGEL'S HOLIDAY; FIFTY ROADS TO TOWN; FIT FOR A KING; NOTHING SACRED; SEVENTH HEAVEN (1937); SHE HAD TO EAT; BAD MAN OF BRIMSTONE; THE CHASER; FIVE OF A KIND; JOY OF LIVING; THE MAD MISS MANTON; THE TEXANS; HONEYMOON IN BALI; OUTSIDE THE LAW (1938); LET US LIVE; MICKEY, THE KID; STAND UP AND FIGHT; STRANGE CASE OF DR. MEADE; THUNDER AFLOAT; ANGELS OVER BROADWAY; BABIES FOR SALE; BLONDIE ON A BUDGET; KNUTE ROCKNE—ALL AMERICAN; ON THEIR OWN; SKI PATROL; YOUTH WILL BE SERVED; THE DEVIL AND DANIEL WEBSTER; MILLION DOLLAR BABY; MODEL WIFE; NEW WINE; OUT OF THE FOG; THE SHEPHERD OF THE HILLS (1941); ARABIAN NIGHTS (1942); CASABLANCA; JUNGLE BOOK (1942); LARCENY, INC.; TORTILLA FLAT; SWING SHIFT MAISIE; AN AMERICAN ROMANCE; DARK WATERS; THE IMPOSTER; ADVENTURE; CAPTAIN KIDD; RIVER GANG; ROUGHLY SPEAKING; THE FUGITIVE (1947); HIGH CONQUEST; SONG OF SCHEHERAZADE; ALIAS A GENTLEMAN; ON OUR MERRY WAY; HOLLOW TRIUMPH; MY GIRL TISA; SIXTEEN FATHOMS DEEP; THE BIG STEAL; CAPTAIN CHINA; BUCCANEER'S GIRL; FLYING MISSILE; THE JACKPOT; WOMAN ON THE RUN; BELLE LE GRAND; GOODBYE, MY FANCY; HANS CHRISTIAN ANDERSEN; AMBUSH AT TOMAHAWK GAP; I, THE JURY; THE HIGH AND THE MIGHTY; THE OTHER WOMAN (1954); PASSION (1954); THE STUDENT PRINCE; AT GUNPOINT; THE SEA CHASE; UNCHAINED (1955); JOHNNY CONCHO; THE SEARCHERS; THE BIG LAND; THE GUN RUNNERS; MY WORLD DIES SCREAMING; REVOLT IN THE BIG HOUSE; ANATOMY OF A MURDER; HELL BENT FOR LEATHER; NORTH TO ALASKA; TWO RODE TOGETHER; THE MAN WHO SHOT LIBERTY VALANCE; THE PRIZE; CHEYENNE AUTUMN; SEVEN FACES OF DR. LAO; THOSE CALLOWAYS; I'LL TAKE SWEDEN; A PATCH OF BLUE; THE SONS OF KATIE ELDER; BIG HAND FOR THE LITTLE LADY; THE ADVENTURES OF BULLWHIP GRIFFIN; FIRECREEK; P.J.; HAIL, HERO!; FRASIER, THE SENSUOUS LION.

Preston

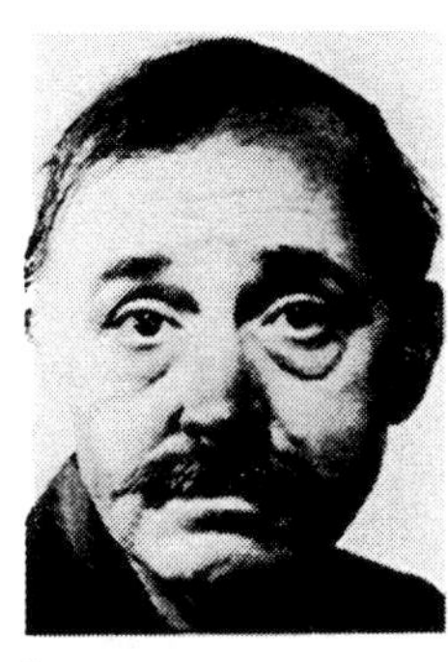

Qualen

Rabin, Jack

Died 25 June 1987; age 73.

Special Effects Artist

Supplied the special effects (sometimes coproducing or writing) for the following films: HE WALKED BY NIGHT; HOME OF THE BRAVE; ROCKETSHIP X-M; UNKNOWN WORLD; MAN FROM PLANET X; CAT WOMEN OF THE MOON; INVADERS FROM MARS; PARIS MODEL; ROBOT MONSTER; THE NIGHT OF THE HUNTER; WORLD WITHOUT END; HELL BOUND; THE INVISIBLE BOY; KRONOS; VOODOO ISLAND; DESERT HELL; FORT BOWIE; MACABRE; THE MONSTER FROM GREEN HELL; WAR OF THE SATELLITES; THE THIRTY FOOT BRIDE OF CANDY ROCK; THE ATOMIC SUBMARINE; THE BEES; DEATHSPORT.

Ramos Da Silva, Fernando

Died 25 Aug. 1987, Sao Paulo, Brazil.

Actor

The child star of Hector Babenco's film PIXOTE, a story of youthful Brazilian street criminals, was killed in a shootout with police after allegedly resisting arrest following an assault. He asserted, after two previous arrests for minor offenses, that he was constantly harassed by the police because they could not distinguish him from the role he played in the film. He had just returned to Sao Paulo from the northeast, where he had been acting in a play called "Atalipa My Love." In it he played a hired assassin.

Ramsey, Thea

Died 9 July 1987, New York, N.Y.; age 37.

Actress/Cabaret Performer

She appeared on stage at Light Opera of Manhattan and in several off-Broadway shows and summer stock and dinner theater productions. From 1975 to 1980 she teamed with David Rambo in a cabaret act. Movies in which she appeared include THE EYES OF LAURA MARS and HEADIN' FOR BROADWAY.

Reid, Roy

Died 19 Nov. 1987, El Monte, Calif.; age 95.

Producer/Distributor

President of Headliner Productions and a veteran independent film producer-distributor, he started his show business career as a booker of vaudeville acts. He helped organize and opened one of the first distribution exchanges on the old Film Row on Cordova Street.

Renoir, Marguerite Houlle

Died July 1987, Paris, France, age 82.

Film Editor

She began her career at age 15 hand-coloring silent films at the Pathe labs and was soon to share the life of Jean Renoir both privately and professionally, editing all of his now classic productions from the late 1920s until the eve of WW II. She retained his name, though they were never married, and later collaborated with Jacques Becker. Her

Rey

films are: THE CRIME OF MONSIEUR LANGE; GRAND ILLUSION; LA BETE HUMAINE; LA MARSEILLAISE; THE RULES OF THE GAME; ANTOINE ET ANTOINETTE; WAYS OF LOVE; EDWARD AND CAROLINE; ALI BABA; CASQUE D'OR; GINA; MODIGLIANI OF MONTPARNASSE; THE NIGHT WATCH; THANK HEAVEN FOR SMALL FAVORS; MASCULINE FEMININE; BOUDU SAVED FROM DROWNING; TONI; SOLO; LA CHIENNE; DEATH IN THE GARDEN.

Rey, Alejandro

Born 8 Feb. 1930, Buenos Aires; died 21 May 1987, Los Angeles, Calif.

Actor

Best known for his work on TV, especially his role as the charitable playboy disco owner opposite Sally Field in TV's "The Flying Nun," he also directed for television. Among the movies in which he appeared: END OF INNOCENCE; BATTLE AT BLOODY BEACH; FUN IN ACAPULCO; SYNANON; BLINDFOLD; THE WILD PACK; MR. MAJESTYK; BREAKOUT; HIGH VELOCITY; THE SWARM; CUBA; SUNBURN; THE NINTH CONFIGURATION; THE STEPMOTHER; MOSCOW ON THE HUDSON.

Rhodes

Rey, Henri-Francois

Died 22 July 1987, Paris, France; age 68.

Novelist/Journalist/Screenwriter

In addition to his novels, he wrote several film scripts in the 1950s, notably for director Yves Ciampi: LES HEROS SONT FATIGUES, L'ESCLAVE, LE VENT SE LEVE. He also produced for radio and television in France and Switzerland in the years after WW II, and in recent years wrote a cinema column for the French daily *Le Figaro*.

Rhodes, Grandon

Died 9 June 1987, Encino, Calif., age 82.

Film/Stage/TV Actor

Along with his wife, actress Ruth Lee, he appeared on the stage in "The Night of January 16," "Three Men on a Horse," and "I Remember Mama." He had continuing roles on TV as the doctor on "Bonanza" and the judge on "Perry Mason." Among the more than 40 films he made are: SHIP AHOY; SHADOW OF A DOUBT; HOLLYWOOD AND VINE; THE DOUGHGIRLS; FOLLOW THE BOYS; THE IMPOSTER; LADIES COURAGEOUS; LADY IN THE DARK; SENSATIONS OF 1945; MAGNIFICENT DOLL; BORN TO KILL; RIDE THE PINK HORSE; SONG OF MY HEART; TOO MANY WINNERS; BLONDIE'S SECRET; THE GENTLEMAN FROM NOWHERE; LARCENY; ROAD HOUSE; WALK A CROOKED MILE; ALL THE KING'S MEN; AND BABY MAKES THREE; CANADIAN PACIFIC; THE CLAY PIGEON; DANCING IN THE DARK; MISS MINK OF 1949; SLATTERY'S HURRICANE; STREETS OF LAREDO; TELL IT TO THE JUDGE; TUCSON; WHITE HEAT; THE EAGLE AND THE HAWK (1950); LYING MISSILE; THE LOST VOLCANO; STORM WARNING; TRIPOLI; WOMAN FROM HEADQUARTERS; BORN YESTERDAY; CRIMINAL LAWYER (1951); DETECTIVE STORY; THE GUY WHO CAME BACK; TAKE CARE OF MY LITTLE GIRL; CRIPPLE CREEK; THE SNIPER; A BLUEPRINT FOR MURDER; A HOUSE OF WAX; ON TOP OF OLD SMOKY; SO BIG (1953); THREE SAILORS AND A GIRL; HUMAN DESIRE; SECRET OF THE INCAS; A STAR IS BORN (1954); A MAN ALONE; REVENGE OF THE CREATURE; TEXAS LADY; TRIAL; EARTH VS. THE FLYING SAUCERS; THESE WILDER YEARS; JAILHOUSE ROCK; THE WAYWARD GIRL; THE 27TH DAY; THE NOTORIOUS MR. MONKS; THE BRAMBLE BUSH; OKLAHOMA TERRITORY; TESS OF THE STORM COUNTRY (1961).

Rorke

Rich, Buddy [Bernard Rich]

Born 30 June 1917, Brooklyn, N.Y.; died 2 Apr. 1987, Los Angeles, Calif.

Drummer

He began his career as a vaudeville song-and-dance prodigy known as "Baby Traps the Drum Wonder," making his professional debut when he was just 18 months old. By the time he was 15, his $1,000-a-week salary made him second only to Jackie Coogan as the highest-paid child performer. He played with bands fronted by well-known jazzmen Joe Marsala, Bunny Berigan, Benny Carter, Artie Shaw, and Tommy Dorsey. He performed extensively with Jazz at the Philharmonic, an assemblage of top jazzmen that toured in the 1940s, then gave up the group to join Harry James' Band. He formed his own band, for the second time, in the 1960s, becoming a favorite on the college concert circuit. Appeared in the film HOW'S ABOUT IT? (1943).

Richards, Keith

Died 23 Mar. 1987; age 72.

Actor

Appeared in minor parts in these films: BUY ME THAT TOWN; NOTHING BUT THE TRUTH; ONE NIGHT IN LISBON; SECRETS OF THE WASTELAND; SKYLARK; WEST POINT WIDOW; THE FOREST RANGERS; HENRY ALDRICH GETS GLAMOUR; THE LADY HAS PLANS; LUCKY JORDAN; THE PALM BEACH STORY; REAP THE WILD WIND; STAR SPANGLED RHYTHM; STREET OF CHANCE; TAKE A LETTER, DARLING; WAKE ISLAND; AERIAL GUNNER; ALASKA HIGHWAY; LOST CANYON; NO TIME FOR LOVE; THE MIRACLE OF MORGAN'S CREEK; DANGER WOMAN; QUEEN OF THE AMAZONS; ROAD TO THE BIG HOUSE; SEVEN WERE SAVED; TWILIGHT ON THE RIO GRANDE; THE GAY RANCHERO; SONS OF ADVENTURE; TAP ROOTS; WALK A CROOKED MILE; CAPTAIN CHINA; DUKE OF CHICAGO; SHADOWS OF THE WEST; TRAIL'S END; THE BLONDE BANDIT; NORTH OF THE GREAT DIVIDE; SPOILERS OF THE PLAINS; TALES OF ROBIN HOOD; WHEN WORLDS COLLIDE; THE GREATEST SHOW ON EARTH; BLADES OF THE MUSKETEERS; REBEL CITY; AT GUNPOINT; YAQUI DRUMS; THE BUSTER KEATON STORY; UNTAMED YOUTH; AMBUSH AT CIMARRON PASS; THE GAMBLER WORE A GUN; INCIDENT IN AN ALLEY.

Riggle, Louise.

Died 5 July 1987, New York, N.Y.; age 78.

Actress

An extra who appeared in THE COTTON CLUB, HAIR, and several Woody Allen films, including HANNAH AND HER SISTERS.

Rios, Elvira [Elvira Gallegos]

Born 16 Nov. 1914, Mexico City, Mexico; died 13 Jan. 1987, Mexico City, Mexico.

Actress/Singer

A popular radio performer in Mexico known as "The Voice of Smoke," she toured extensively in Brazil, Argentina, Europe, and the US. She appeared in Mexican musicals of the 1940s, and in Hollywood, she acted in the Paramount features ENCHANTMENT OF THE TROPICS and LONG VOYAGE HOME.

Rocha, Victoria Joan

Died 12 Mar. 1987, Scottsdale, Ariz.; age 33

Actress/Comedienne

As a stand-up performer, she appeared in comedy clubs around the country and on television. Her movies include FALLING IN LOVE AGAIN and WAR BABIES.

Roediger, Rolf

Died 24 Dec. 1987, Los Angeles, Calif.; age 57.

Puppetmaker

A native of Germany and former ballet dancer, he moved to Los Angeles in 1957 and joined Sid and Marty Krofft Productions as head of their puppet and costume character department. He worked on the "Les Poupees de Paris" puppet shows which performed at four World's Fairs and built the animated characters for many rides at the Six Flags theme parks, and was also involved in television, most notably with the Krofft's production of "H.R. Pufnstuf."

Rogers, Charles Benton.

Died 11 May 1987.

Set Builder

He worked in Hollywood from the 1920s through the 1950s, building special sets, boats, cars, and other props for most studios. He appeared in one film, the 1928 Laurel and Hardy classic TWO TARS.

Rorke, Hayden

Born 23 Oct. 1910, Brooklyn, N.Y.; died 19 Aug. 1987, Toluca Lake, Calif.

Stage/Film/TV Actor

He studied at the American Academy of Dramatic Arts and was the last surviving member of Walter Hampton's repertory company. While serving in the Army during WW II he appeared in both the road company and film version of THIS IS THE ARMY. During a career that spanned six decades, he appeared in 243 plays, 70 Broadway productions, 53 motion pictures, guest-starring roles in over 400 series segments, miniseries, and movies for television, the most notable of which was his on-going role as Dr. Bellows on 140 episodes of "I Dream of Jeanie." Movies in which he appeared are: LUST FOR GOLD; ROPE OF SAND; SWORD IN THE DESERT; DOUBLE CROSSBONES; KIM; THE MAGNIFICENT YANKEE; AN AMERICAN IN PARIS; FATHER'S LITTLE DIVIDEND; FRANCIS GOES TO THE RACES; INSIDE STRAIGHT; THE LAW AND THE LADY; THE PRINCE WHO WAS A THIEF; STARLIFT; WHEN WORLDS COLLIDE; ROGUE'S MARCH; ROOM FOR ONE MORE; SKIRTS AHOY!; WILD STALLION; ABOVE AND BEYOND; CONFIDENTIAL CONNIE; THE GIRL NEXT DOOR; PROJECT MOONBASE; THE ROBE; SOUTH SEA WOMAN; THE STORY OF THREE LOVES; DRUM BEAT; LUCKY ME; THE ETERNAL SEA; THE RESTLESS YEARS; THIS HAPPY FEELING; PILLOW TALK; STRANGER IN MY ARMS; MIDNIGHT LACE; PARRISH; POCKETFUL OF MIRACLES; TAMMY, TELL ME TRUE; SPENCER'S MOUNTAIN;

THE THRILL OF IT ALL; A HOUSE IS NOT A HOME; I'D RATHER BE RICH; THE NIGHT WALKER; THE UNSINKABLE MOLLY BROWN; YOUNGBLOOD HAWKE.

Rose, William

Born 1918, died 10 Feb. 1987, Isle of Jersey, U.K.

Screenwriter

A native of Jefferson City, Missouri, he went to Canada at the outset of WW II to join the Canadian Black Watch; served in Scotland and Europe, and it was to Scotland and Pinewood Studios he returned after the war, upon deciding to become a screenwriter. During his collaboration with director Alexander Mackendrick he wrote the screenplay for the classic black comedy THE LADYKILLERS, based on a dream he had. While continuing to live in England, he began writing for Hollywood in the 1960s and was nominated three times for Oscars. He finally received an Academy Award for best original screenplay for Stanley Kramer's GUESS WHO'S COMING TO DINNER. In 1973 he received the Writer's Guild of America's top honor, the Laurel Award. Among his movies: ESTHER WATERS; LUCKY NICK CAIN; MANIACS ON WHEELS; OPERATION X; GLORY AT SEA; BACHELOR IN PARIS; GENEVIEVE; HIGH AND DRY; THE LIGHT TOUCH; DECISION AGAINST TIME; THE SMALLEST SHOW ON EARTH; DAVY; IT'S A MAD, MAD, MAD, MAD WORLD; THE RUSSIANS ARE COMING, THE RUSSIANS ARE COMING; THE FLIM-FLAM MAN; THE SECRET OF SANTA VITTORIA.

Rosenberg, Edgar

Died 14 Aug. 1987, Philadelphia, Pa.; age 62.

TV Executive/Producer

Husband of comedienne Joan Rivers, he was born in Germany and lived in Denmark and then in South Africa to escape the Nazis. Educated at Rugby and Cambridge he moved to the US and worked as an assistant to the late Manny Sachs at NBC. As an executive at the network he worked on "The Pinky Lee Show," "The Milton Berle Show," and "Your Hit Parade." He formed the Telson Production Co., and after marrying Rivers, spent most of his time as her manager. He also produced the Rivers-directed "Rabbit Test" for TV in 1978.

Rosenthal, Sandy

Died 27 Dec. 1987, Tucson, Ariz.; age 63.

Actor/Director

Founder and onetime artistic director of the Arizona Theater Co., for whom he directed 29 plays. As an actor, he appeared on television in "Bonanza" and "Little House on the Prairie," and in the film RAGE.

Rouse, Russell

Died 2 Oct. 1987, Santa Monica, Calif.; age 74.

Director/Screenwriter

Worked his way up through the ranks as stagehand, props handler and junior writer to win an Academy Award for his screenplay for PILLOW TALK. He cowrote with Clarence Greene the suspense thriller D.O.A., which is currently being remade as a vehicle for Dennis Quaid. In 1951 he was nominated for a Best Screenplay Oscar for THE WELL, a portrait of a small town racked by racial tension. Other films include: NOTHING BUT TROUBLE; THE TOWN WENT WILD; GREAT PLANE ROBBERY; THE THIEF; WICKED WOMAN; NEW YORK CONFIDENTIAL; FASTEST GUN ALIVE; HOUSE OF NUMBERS; THUNDER IN THE SUN; A HOUSE IS NOT A HOME; THE OSCAR; THE CAPER OF THE GOLDEN BULLS; COLOR ME DEAD.

Roussin, Andre

Died 3 Nov. 1987, Paris, France; age 76.

Playwright/Actor

Born in Marseilles in 1911, he formed a theatrical company with Louis Ducreux for which he acted and wrote plays. It toured France and North Africa at the end of WW II. By 1945 he had two plays produced in Paris: "Jean-Baptiste, The Poorly Loved" and "A Grown-Up Girl with No Problems." In 1947 he staged "The Little Hut," which ran six years in the City of Light. Other plays include "The Ostrich Eggs," "Nina," "Bobosse," "The Good-Looking Antonio," and "The Private Life of Helen of Troy." He was elected to the French Academy in 1973, and his recent satirical one-acter, "The Little Cat is Dead," continues its engagement at the Theatre Gaveau.

Rowan, Dan Hale

Born 2 July 1922, Beggs, Okla.; died 22 Sept. 1987, Englewood, Fla.

Comedian

The only child of two carnival workers who died when he was young, he was raised in an orphanage in Pueblo, Colorado. He moved to Hollywood and found work at Paramount, first in the mailroom, then as a junior writer. He quit to become a pilot in the Air Corps during WW II and was shot down in New Guinea. Upon discharge, he returned to Los Angeles as co-owner of a foreign car dealership and met Dick Martin, a bartender who was to become his lifelong partner. They worked in clubs throughout the country and starred in two uninspired feature films, ONCE UPON A HORSE and THE MALTESE BIPPY. Their biggest success was with the TV comedy series "Laugh-In," which brought a fresh, fast-paced, irreverent approach to the variety-show format. The weekly show was introduced in 1968 and last aired on May 14, 1973, winning 28 honors and awards, including seven Emmys. He wrote a book entitled *A Friendship*, a compilation of the correspondence he carried on for seven years with prolific mystery writer John D. MacDonald. At the time of his death he had completed his first novel, a spy thriller, which he had planned to have published late in 1987.

Salt, Waldo

Born 18 Oct. 1914, Chicago, Ill; died 7 Mar. 1987, Los Angeles, Calif.

Screenwriter

He entered Stanford University at age 14 and, after graduating in 1934, went to work for MGM as a junior writer. After refusing to testify before the House Un-American Activities Committee, he was blacklisted for 12 years and did not resume his career until the 1960s during which he won an Academy Award for his adaptation of James Leo Herlihy's novel *Midnight Cowboy*, a film that also brought him a Writers Guild Award. In 1978 he shared an Oscar for the screenplay of COMING HOME. His other movies are: SHOPWORN ANGEL; THE PHILADELPHIA STORY; THE WILD MAN OF BORNEO; TONIGHT WE RAID CALAIS; MR. WINKLE GOES TO WAR; RACHEL AND THE STRANGER; THE FLAME AND THE ARROW; TARAS BULBA; FLIGHT FROM ASHIYA; WILD AND WONDERFUL; THE GANG THAT COULDN'T SHOOT STRAIGHT; SERPICO; THE DAY OF THE LOCUST.

Sampson

Sampson, Will

Born 1935, Okmulgee, Okla.; died 3 June 1987, Houston, Tex.

Actor

A full-blooded Muscogee-Creek Indian with the name Kva-Kvna, meaning left-handed, he was born in Okmulgee, Oklahoma. He began painting as a child and was discovered at an art show in Washington by a member of Michael Douglas' staff who was told to keep his eye out for a big Indian. The result was the casting of the 6-foot-7 painter as the silent strongman mental patient in ONE FLEW OVER THE CUCKOO'S NEST, for which he won critical praise. He appeared on the television series "Vegas" and other productions. Among the movies he made are: BUFFALO BILL AND THE INDIANS, OR SITTING BULL'S HISTORY LESSON; THE OUTLAW JOSEY WALES; ORCA; THE WHITE BUFFALO; FISH HAWK.

Santoro, Dean

Died 10 June 1987, Sherman Oaks, Calif.; age 49

TV/Stage Actor

Longtime activist in performing arts unions, he served as campaign manager for Ed Asner in his successful bid for the SAG presidency. Performed off-Broadway in "Hadrian VII" and "Borstal Boy" and was in the cast of the soap opera "As the World Turns" for four years. Appeared in more than 50 regional theater productions and many television series.

Sapir, Richard Ben

Died 1987, Boston, Mass.; age 50.

Writer

Worked as a reporter before he turned to writing novels. His books include *Brescio*, *The Far Arena*, *Spies*, *The Body*, and *Quest*. He coauthored more than 60 mysteries in the "Destroyer" series and one of his novels was made into the 1985 movie REMO WILLIAMS, THE ADVENTURE BEGINS.

Saunders, Russell

Died 27 Apr. 1987, Burbank, Calif.; age 81.

Production Manager/Assistant Director

Worked at Warner Bros. for 30 years, under the tutelage of director Raoul Walsh. Among the films he worked on as a unit production manager or assistant director are BONNIE AND CLYDE; BATTLE CRY; PT109; THE LONGEST YARD; THE WAY WE WERE; LOST HORIZONS; HATARI; THE CHASE; BAND OF ANGELS; STRIPES; AMITYVILLE HORROR; HIGH SIERRA; THEY DIED WITH THEIR BOOTS ON; THE STALKING MOON; THE LIBERATION OF L.B. JONES; THE SHOOTIST; THE DRIVER; BRUBAKER.

Scholz, Walter

Died 24 Sept. 1987; age 44.

Stage Director

He directed several plays including the 1981 New York production of Daniel Berrigan's "Trial of the Catonsville Nine." For the Shakespeare Society of America he directed "Timon of Athens," "Coriolanus," and "The Two Nobel Kinsman," which was nominated for a Los Angeles Drama Critics Award. He was associate producer of Kurt Vonnegut's "Happy Birthday, Wanda June," and, as an actor, appeared in a European production of Arthur Miller's "The Price."

Scott

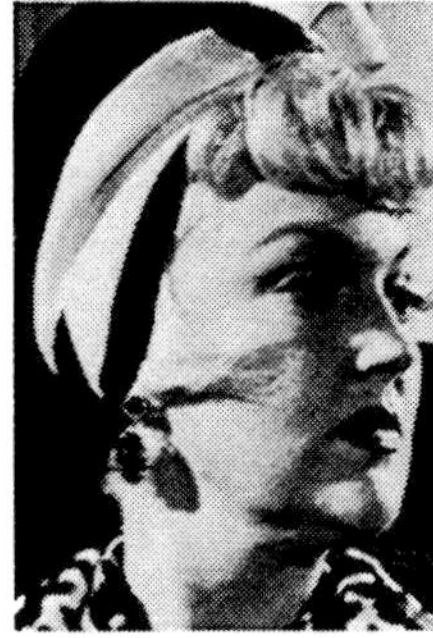
Shawlee

Shawn

Scott, Randolph Crane

Born 23 Jan. 1898, Orange County, Va.; died 2 Mar. 1987, Los Angeles, Calif.

Actor

Attended Georgia Tech and the University of North Carolina, and upon arrival in Hollywood was introduced by a family friend to Howard Hughes. He enrolled in the Pasadena Playhouse and began his career as a romantic lead, but his square-jawed countenance and poker-faced stare became prototypes for the generation of western heros who followed him. Though he never won an Oscar, he praised the western as "the mainstay of the film industry" and the type of movies families could see and enjoy. He appeared in close to 100 movies from 1929 to 1962, including a few war epics and musicals. His movies include: THE VIRGINIAN (1929); WOMEN MEN MARRY; HOT SATURDAY; A SUCCESSFUL CALAMITY; WILD HORSE MESA (1932); BROKEN DREAMS; COCKTAIL HOUR; HELLO, EVERYBODY; HERITAGE OF THE DESERT (1933); ISLAND OF LOST SOULS; MAN OF THE FOREST (1933); MURDERS IN THE ZOO; SUNSET PASS (1933); SUPERNATURAL; TO THE LAST MAN (1933); THE LAST ROUND-UP (1934); THE THUNDERING HERD (1934); WAGON WHEELS; HOME ON THE RANGE (1935); ROBERTA; ROCKY MOUNTAIN MYSTERY; SHE (1935); SO RED THE ROSE; VILLAGE TALE; AND SUDDEN DEATH; FOLLOW THE FLEET; GO WEST, YOUNG MAN (1936); THE LAST OF THE MOHICANS (1936); HIGH, WIDE AND HANDSOME; REBECCA OF SUNNYBROOK FARM (1938); THE ROAD TO RENO; THE TEXANS; COAST GUARD; FRONTIER MARSHAL (1939); JESSE JAMES; SUSANNAH OF THE MOUNTIES; 20,000 MEN A YEAR; MY FAVORITE WIFE; VIRGINIA CITY; WHEN THE DALTONS RODE; BELLE STARR; PARIS CALLING; WESTERN UNION; PITTSBURGH; THE SPOILERS (1942); TO THE SHORES OF TRIPOLI; BOMBARDIER; CORVETTE K-225; THE DESPERADOES; GUNG HO (1943); BELLE OF THE YUKON; FOLLOW THE BOYS; CHINA SKY; ABILENE TOWN; BADMAN'S TERRITORY; HOME SWEET HOMICIDE; CHRISTMAS EVE; THE GUNFIGHTERS; TRAIL STREET; ALBUQUERQUE; CORONER CREEK; RETURN OF THE BADMEN; CANADIAN PACIFIC; THE DOOLINS OF OKLAHOMA; FIGHTING MAN OF THE PLAINS; THE WALKING HILLS; THE CARIBOO TRAIL; COLT .45; THE NEVADAN; FORT WORTH; MAN IN THE SADDLE; SANTA FE; STARLIFT; SUGARFOOT; CARSON CITY; HANGMAN'S KNOT; THE MAN BEHIND THE GUN; THE STRANGER WORE A GUN; THUNDER OVER THE PLAINS; THE BOUNTY HUNTER; RIDING SHOTGUN; A LAWLESS STREET; RAGE AT DAWN; TALL MAN RIDING; TEN WANTED MEN; SEVEN MEN FROM NOW; SEVENTH CAVALRY; DECISION AT SUNDOWN; SHOOT-OUT AT MEDICINE BEND; THE TALL T; BUCHANAN RIDES ALONE; RIDE LONESOME; WESTBOUND; COMANCHE STATION; RIDE THE HIGH COUNTRY. His one silent film was THE FAR CALL.

Seidl, Lea [Caroline Mayrseidl]

Died 4 Jan. 1987, London, England; age 91.

Actress/Singer

She made her stage debut in Vienna in 1917 and moved to England in 1930, appearing in a succession of musical hits including "Frederica," "Dancing City," "No Sky is Blue," and "The White Horse Inn." Her screen credits include WAR AND PEACE; I AM A CAMERA; CANDLELIGHT IN ALGERIA; THE WOMAN'S ANGLE; I AIM AT THE STARS; GREAT CATHERINE.

Sessa, Robert

Died 23 May 1987, Canoga Park, Calif.

Set Designer

He worked for Universal, Disney, and Aaron Spelling, designing sets for PALE RIDER; HEARTBREAK RIDGE; WITCHES OF EASTWICK; THE MAN WITH TWO BRAINS.

Shankar

Died 26 Apr. 1987, Bombay, India; age 65.

Music Director

A native of Hyderabad, he started his career with Prithvi Theaters founded by Prithviraj Kapoor, father of Raj Kapoor, filmmaker and studio owner. He scored music for Raj Kapoor's BARSAAT.

Shaw, T. Rodger.

Died 4 Sept. 1987, France; age 39.

Animatronics Engineer

A sculptor, he began his film career making background robots for STAR WARS and worked as a propmaker on VALENTINO, MONTY PYTHON'S LIFE OF BRIAN, FORCE 10 FROM NAVARONE, and ALIEN, then became an animatronics technician, building Landstriders in the film THE DARK CRYSTAL and working on TIME BANDITS, INDIANA JONES AND THE TEMPLE OF DOOM; GREYSTOKE: THE LEGEND OF TARZAN, LORD OF THE APES (for which he was also chief primate effects technician). He also created creatures for INDIANA JONES; THE COMPANY OF WOLVES; PRINCESS BRIDE; HYPER SAPIEN.

Shawlee, Joan [Joan Fulton]

Born 5 Mar. 1929, Forest Hills, N.Y.; died 22 Mar. 1987, Los Angeles, Calif.

Actress

A former model, nightclub entertainer, and dancer in New York City, she came to Hollywood at the urging of comic Lou Costello to work for Universal. She portrayed zany and often bawdy characters in some of film's most memorable comedies of the 1940s and 1950s, including Sweet Sue, the leader of the all-girl band in Billy Wilder's SOME LIKE IT HOT. She made her film debut at the age of 13 as a starlet in A STAR IS BORN with Judy Garland. Her other movies are: THIS LOVE OF OURS; SMASH-UP, THE STORY OF A WOMAN; PREHISTORIC WOMEN; WOMAN ON THE RUN; TWO TICKETS TO BROADWAY; THE MARRYING KIND; SOMETHING FOR THE BIRDS; ALL ASHORE; FROM HERE TO ETERNITY; LOOSE IN LONDON; ABOUT MRS. LESLIE; CASANOVA'S BIG NIGHT; FRANCIS JOINS THE WACS; PRIDE OF THE BLUE GRASS; BOWERY TO BAGDAD; A FAREWELL TO ARMS (1957); THE APARTMENT; CRITIC'S CHOICE; IRMA LA DOUCE; THE WILD ANGELS; THE RELUCTANT ASTRONAUT; THE ST. VALENTINE'S DAY MASSACRE; TONY ROME; LIVE A LITTLE, LOVE A LITTLE; ONE MORE TRAIN TO ROB; WILLARD; FAREWELL, MY LOVELY; FLASH AND THE FIRECAT; BUDDY BUDDY; CITY HEAT; BORN FOR TROUBLE; GUERILLAS IN PINK LACE.

Shawn, Dick [Richard Schulefand]

Born 1 Dec. 1923, Buffalo, N.Y.; died 17 Apr. 1987, San Diego, Calif.

Film/TV/Stage Actor-Comedian

Collapsed while performing in front of an audience of college students, many of whom thought it part of his act. A rubbery faced comic who was a favorite among comedians, he began his film career in 1956, after performing in cabarets and nightclubs. He appeared on stage and television but is most remembered for his role as Adolf Hitler in Mel Brooks' comedy THE PRODUCERS. His other films include: THE OPPOSITE SEX; WAKE ME WHEN IT'S OVER; THE WIZARD OF BAGHDAD; IT'S A MAD, MAD, MAD, MAD WORLD; A VERY SPECIAL FAVOR; PENELOPE; WAY . . . WAY OUT; WHAT DID YOU DO IN THE WAR, DADDY?; THE HAPPY ENDING; LOOKING UP; LOVE AT FIRST BITE; YOUNG WARRIORS.

Shearing, Renee C.

Died 9 Mar. 1987, San Francisco, Calif.; age 86.

Actress

A native of Stratford-upon-Avon, England, she acted in pictures from 1933 to 1942, her major role coming in MOTHER'S DARLING. Her WAC career, which mostly involved arranging base and hospital shows, extended 21 years.

Sherdeman, Ted

Born 21 June 1909, Lincoln, Neb.; died 22 Aug. 1987, Santa Ana, Calif.

Screenwriter

Born in Lincoln, Nebraska, educated at the University of Nebraska and Creighton, he worked for NBC in Hollywood and Chicago. He rose to the rank of colonel in the Army in WW II and thereafter worked as a radio producer for Lennen & Mitchell from 1945 to 1948. For television he worked on "Wagon Train," "Dick Powell's Zane Grey Theater," "Hazel," "My Favorite Martian," "Bewitched," "Family Affair," and "The Flying Nun." Among his movies are: LUST FOR GOLD; BREAKTHROUGH (1950); SCANDAL SHEET (1952); THE WINNING TEAM; THE EDDIE CANTOR STORY; RIDING SHOTGUN; THEM!; THE MC CONNELL STORY; AWAY ALL BOATS; TOY TIGER; MARACAIBO; ST. LOUIS BLUES (1958); A DOG OF FLANDERS (1959); HELL TO ETERNITY; THE BIG SHOW (1961); MISTY; ISLAND OF THE BLUE DOLPHINS; AND NOW MIGUEL; LATITUDE ZERO; MY SIDE OF THE MOUNTAIN.

Shoup, Howard

Died 29 May, 1987, Woodland Hills, Calif., age 83

Costumer

He was nominated for five Academy Awards, recipient of the Adrian Award in 1986, the Friendly House Award in 1965, and the Best Costume Award in 1966, and was a founding member of the Costumers Guild. Among the movies he designed costumes for are: THE PERFECT SPECIMEN; SAN QUENTIN (1937); WEST OF SHANGHAI; WINE, WOMEN AND HORSES; GIRLS ON PROBATION; MEN ARE SUCH FOOLS; RACKET BUSTERS; SERGEANT MURPHY; SWING YOUR LADY; TORCHY BLANE IN CHINATOWN; TORCHY GETS HER MAN; WHEN WERE YOU BORN?; EACH DAWN I DIE; NAUGHTY BUT NICE; NO

PLACE TO GO; BROTHER ORCHID; MURDER IN THE AIR; TORRID ZONE; CITY FOR CONQUEST; FOOTSTEPS IN THE DARK; NAVY BLUES; STRANGE ALIBI; CAPTAINS OF THE CLOUDS; JACKASS MAIL; NAZI AGENT; SEVEN SWEETHEARTS; DU BARRY WAS A LADY; THE YOUNGEST PROFESSION; THE MIGHTY MCGURK; OCEAN BREAKERS; THE JAZZ SINGER (1953); SO BIG (1953); THE COURT-MARTIAL OF BILLY MITCHELL; THE MC CONNELL STORY; PETE KELLY'S BLUES; SINCERELY YOURS; YOUNG AT HEART; BUNDLE OF JOY; SERENADE; BOMBERS B-52; THE UNHOLY WIFE; THE DEEP SIX; HOME BEFORE DARK; I MARRIED A WOMAN; MARJORIE MORNINGSTAR; ONIONHEAD; THE HELEN MORGAN STORY; ISLAND OF LOST WOMEN; WESTBOUND; THE YOUNG PHILADELPHIANS; THE BRAMBLE BUSH; CASH MCCALL; ICE PALACE; OCEAN'S ELEVEN; THE RISE AND FALL OF LEGS DIAMOND; CLAUDELLE INGLISH; FEVER IN THE BLOOD; PARRISH; PORTRAIT OF A MOBSTER; SUSAN SLADE; GYPSY (1962); ROME ADVENTURE; WALL OF NOISE; A DISTANT TRUMPET; KISSES FOR MY PRESIDENT; YOUNGBLOOD HAWKE; A RAGE TO LIVE; COOL HAND LUKE; THE COOL ONES; HOTEL; OH DAD, POOR DAD, MAMA'S HUNG YOU IN THE CLOSET AND I'M FEELIN' SO SAD.

Shyer, James Wilson

Died 2 July 1987, Los Angeles, Calif.; age 61.

Assistant Director

He began his career as an assistant director working for Universal Pictures and Walt Disney Productions on several motion pictures including IMITATION OF LIFE; WRITTEN ON THE WIND; OPERATION PETTICOAT; THE GREAT TRAIN ROBBERY. During the 1960s and 1970s he served as first assistant director on many films and television series.

Silverthorn, Richard Jay

Died 23 Mar. 1987; age 35.

Actor/Author/Filmmaker

Graduated from the USC film school and went on to star in Frank LaLoggia's FEAR NO EVIL. In addition to acting, he demonstrated skills in special effects, makeup artistry, cinematography, film editing, and sound recording. His horror novel *Lucifer* was published by Avon Books in 1987.

Sims, Glenn Michael

Died 1 Aug. 1987, Richardson, Tex.; age 25.

Gymnast

A champion gymnast who appeared in the 1986 film AMERICAN ANTHEM, he was shot to death while pursuing purse snatchers in a Dallas suburb.

Sirk, Douglas [Detlef Sierck]

Born 26 Apr. 1900, Hamburg, Germany; died 14 Jan. 1987, Lugano, Switzerland.

Director

He first made his reputation in the theater in Germany in the 1920s. In the 1930s he felt the limitations imposed by the Nazis on theater work were too great, and he became involved in filmmaking. He directed his first American film, HITLER'S MADMAN in 1943. Among his other movies are LA HABANERA; SUMMER STORM; A SCANDAL IN PARIS; LURED; SLEEP, MY LOVE; SHOCKPROOF; SLIGHTLY FRENCH; MYSTERY SUBMARINE; THE FIRST LEGION; THE LADY PAYS OFF; THUNDER ON THE HILL; WEEKEND WITH FATHER; HAS ANYBODY SEEN MY GAL?; MEET ME AT THE FAIR; NO ROOM FOR THE GROOM; ALL I DESIRE; TAKE ME TO TOWN; MAGNIFICENT OBSESSION (1954); SIGN OF THE PAGAN; TAZA, SON OF COCHISE; ALL THAT HEAVEN ALLOWS; CAPTAIN LIGHTFOOT; NEVER SAY GOODBYE; THERE'S ALWAYS TOMORROW; WRITTEN ON THE WIND; BATTLE HYMN; INTERLUDE (1957); THE TARNISHED ANGELS; A TIME TO LOVE AND A TIME TO DIE; IMITATION OF LIFE (1959).

Slater, Patrick Scott

Died 30 Aug. 1987, New York City, N.Y.; age 42.

Film/TV Actor

After serving in the Marine Corps in Vietnam, he took up acting, studying at the American Academy of Dramatic Arts. He frequently appeared on the soap operas, was seen on some prime-time shows, did commercials, and had parts in the films JUST TELL ME WHAT YOU WANT; TOOTSIE; HELLO AGAIN; WALL STREET.

Smalls, Charlie

Died 27 Aug. 1987, Bruges, Belgium; age 43.

Composer/Lyricist

A New York native, he gave his first piano concert at age 5 and enrolled at the Julliard music school at 11. He was a pianist with the New York Jazz Repertory Company and toured with Harry Belafonte and Hugh Masekela. He came to prominence in 1975 when "The Wiz," a musical version of L. Frank Baum's "Wonderful Wizard of Oz" with a black cast, opened at the Majestic Theater. It was made into a film in 1978. He had finished writing the songs for a new musical, "Miracles," shortly before his death. The show is based on the H.G. Wells novel *The Man Who Could Work Miracles.*

Spinell, Mary [Filomena M. Spagnuolo]

Died 30 July 1987, New York, N.Y., age 83.

Actress

Mother of actor Joe Spinell; appeared in nearly 50 films including THE GODFATHER films, NEXT STOP, GREENWICH VILLAGE; GLORIA; TEMPEST (1982); MOSCOW ON THE HUDSON; NUNZIO; EASY MONEY; and with her son in THE LAST HORROR SHOW.

Spratley, Thomas Reay

Died 10 June 1987, Encino, Calif., age 74.

Actor/Singer

Early in his career he appeared on stage in "South Pacific," "How to Succeed in Business Without Really Trying," and "Plaza Suite." He was seen on television in "Highway to Heaven," "Dynasty," "Dallas," "The Adams Chronicles," and "Charlie's Angels." Among his film credits: THE HOSPITAL; THE STING; WHERE THE LILIES BLOOM; THE SUNSHINE BOYS; THE MAN WITH TWO BRAINS; MAX DUGAN RETURNS; SUDDEN IMPACT; CITY HEAT; PROTOCOL; BANANAS; THE STEPFORD WIVES; LOVE STORY (1970); MOMMIE DEAREST; FERRIS BUELLER'S DAY OFF.

Springs, Jimmy

Died 4 Oct. 1987, Philadelphia, Pa.; age 75.

Singer

Lead singer of the Red Caps vocal group for over 30 years, he also toured in vaudeville and performed on the radio on Gene Autry's "National Barn Dance" show. His group appeared in motion pictures including the Bing Crosby film DOUBLE OR NOTHING.

Smith, Jack G., [Sr.]

Died 20 Mar. 1987, Los Angeles, Calif.; age 90.

Actor/Technical Director

A former California horse-racing official who served as technical director on many racetrack movies and, as a young man, worked as an extra.

Snyder, Billy [William]

Died Nov. 1987, Las Vegas, Nev.; age 81

Actor

The onetime stand-in for George Raft started out as a vaudeville singer and bit actor in films before moving to Las Vegas in 1955, eventually becoming executive host at the Dunes, the Sahara, and the Frontier. Among his films: TWENTY MILLION SWEETHEARTS; YOU'RE OUT OF LUCK; HIT THE HAY; SO DARK THE NIGHT; TANGIER; CAMPUS SLEUTH; FRENCH LEAVE; SMART POLITICS; YOU WERE MEANT FOR ME; ABBOTT AND COSTELLO MEET THE KILLER, BORIS KARLOFF; THE RECKLESS MOMENTS; SCENE OF THE CRIME; THE SET-UP; THE JOKER IS WILD; THE TATTERED DRESS; GANG WAR; THE LINEUP; PEPE.

Stewart, Michael

Born 1 Aug. 1924, New York, N.Y.; Died 20 Sept. 1987, New York, N.Y.

Lyricist

In a career that started in 1953, he wrote numerous books and lyrics for Broadway musicals, including "I Love My Wife," "Barnum," "Hello Dolly," and "42nd Street," in collaboration with Mark Bramble. Considered one of the most successful musical authors of the modern Broadway period, he also helped write Sid Caesar's "Your Show of Shows" in the 1950s.

Stone, Grant H. "Jimmy"

Died 7 May 1987, Woodland Hills, Calif.; age 85.

Cameraman

He was commanding officer of the first motion picture unit out of Hal Roach Studios during WW II and was the cameraman on the pilot for "I Love Lucy," all "The Lone Ranger" series, THE WIZARD OF OZ, FOR WHOM THE BELL TOLLS, MIRACLE ON 34TH STREET, and the original ADVENTURES OF ROBIN HOOD, starring Errol Flynn.

Strauss, Helen M.

Died 1987, New York City, N.Y.; age 83.

Literary Agent

Dynamic and controversial, she created the literary department at the William Morris Agency and became a major influence in the world of books, motion pictures, and theater. A resident of Manhattan, she began her career with the story department of Paramount Pictures

Taylor

Teasdale

before joining the Morris agency in 1944. Her client list included James Michener, Robert Penn Warren, Ralph Ellison, Archibald MacLeish, Gore Vidal, Justice William O. Douglas, and Frank Yerby. She was credited with originating the idea for "The King and I," the musical by Richard Rodgers and Oscar Hammerstein II. She produced THE INCREDIBLE SARAH, a 1976 film starring Glenda Jackson as Sarah Bernhardt.

Subba Rao, B.A.

Died 13 Mar. 1987, Hyderabad, India; age 71.

Director

He won the Andhra Pradesh government's Raghupathi Venkiah Naidue Award in 1983 for his contribution to the Telugu film industry. He was also director of the Andhra Pradesh Film Development Corp. Among the films he directed are PALLETURIPILLA; RAU PEDA; CHENCHULAKSUMI.

Sullivan, Maxine [Marietta Williams]

Died 7 Apr. 1987, Bronx, N.Y.; age 75.

Singer

Her swinging version of "Loch Lomond" in 1937 launched a career that lasted 50 years. She married bassist John Kirby in 1938 and, with his band, became the star of the weekly NBC Radio series, "Flow Gently Sweet Rhythm." She performed on Broadway with Louis Armstrong and Benny Goodman in a swing version of "A Midsummer Night's Dream" called "Swingin' the Dream," and appeared in two films, GOING PLACES and ST. LOUIS BLUES. In 1979 she was nominated for a Tony for her performance in "My Old Friend."

Surendranath

Died 11 Sept, 1987, Bombay, India; age 76.

Actor/Singer

He was a lawyer before starting his film career in 1936. He acted and sang in more than 60 films. Though he gave up his film career in 1963, he continued singing and recording until his death.

Susskind, David

Born 19 Dec. 1920, New York, N.Y.; died 22 Feb. 1987, New York, N.Y.

Stage/TV/Film Producer

A familiar public figure, particularly in New York, the combative television talk-show host produced TV shows that won 27 Emmy awards and three Peabody awards. Though considered one of the pioneers of the television talk-show format, his career began as a press agent in Hollywood with Warner Bros. and then Universal Pictures. His film production credits include: EDGE OF THE CITY; A RAISIN IN THE SUN; REQUIEM FOR A HEAVYWEIGHT; ALL THE WAY HOME; LOVERS AND OTHER STRANGERS; THE PURSUIT OF HAPPINESS (1971); ALICE DOESN'T LIVE HERE ANYMORE; ALL CREATURES GREAT AND SMALL; SIMON.

Sutherland, Esther

Died 31 Dec. 1987, Los Angeles, Calif.; age 54.

Actress/Musician/Singer

Born in New York and educated at Julliard, she appeared on stage in "Under Papa's Picture," "Get on Board," "Lenny," and "Funny You Should Ask." She was featured in many TV series including "The Jeffersons," "Hill Street Blues," "Lou Grant," "Archie Bunker's Place," and "Kojak." Among her film credits are: RIVERRUN; BLACK BELT JONES; TRUCK TURNER; THE COMMITMENT; THE GOODBYE GIRL; NINE TO FIVE; STIR CRAZY; YOUNG DOCTORS IN LOVE.

Tanzman, Alexandre

Died 15 Nov. 1987, Paris, France; age 89.

Pianist/Conductor

He composed numerous symphonic, string quartet, ballet, and operatic works. His rare film assignments included the memorable score for Julien Duvivier's 1932 classic POLI DU CARLITTE and Jean Epstein's LA CHATELAINE DU LIBAN.

Taylor, Kent [Louis Weiss]

Born 11 May 1906, Nashua, Ia.; died 9 Apr. 1987, North Hollywood, Calif.

Actor

Star of the popular 1950s television series "Boston Blackie," he went to Hollywood after high school graduation. After some work as an extra, he was signed by Paramount and appeared in 30 films by 1935. Among his films: HUSBAND'S HOLIDAY; BLONDE VENUS; DANCERS IN THE DARK; DEVIL AND THE DEEP; FORGOTTEN COMMANDMENTS; IF I HAD A MILLION; MERRILY WE GO TO HELL; THE SIGN OF THE CROSS; TWO KINDS OF WOMEN; CRADLE SONG; I'M NO ANGEL; A LADY'S PROFESSION; THE MYSTERIOUS RIDER; THE STORY OF TEMPLE DRAKE; SUNSET PASS (1933); UNDER THE TONTO RIM (1933); WHITE WOMAN; DAVID HARUM; DEATH TAKES A HOLIDAY; DOUBLE DOOR; LIMEHOUSE BLUES; MANY HAPPY RETURNS; MRS. WIGGS OF THE CABBAGE PATCH (1934); COLLEGE SCANDAL; THE COUNTY CHAIRMAN; SMART GIRL; TWO FISTED; WITHOUT REGRET; THE ACCUSING FINGER; FLORIDA SPECIAL; MY MARRIAGE; RAMONA (1936); SKY PARADE; A GIRL WITH IDEAS; LADY FIGHTS BACK; LOVE IN A BUNGALOW; PRESCRIPTION FOR ROMANCE; WHEN LOVE IS YOUNG; WINGS OVER HONOLULU; THE JURY'S SECRET; THE LAST EXPRESS; ESCAPE TO PARADISE; FIVE CAME BACK; FOUR GIRLS IN WHITE; GRACIE ALLEN MURDER CASE; PIRATES OF THE SKIES; THREE SONS; GIRL FROM AVENUE A; GIRL IN 313; I TAKE THIS WOMAN; I'M STILL ALIVE; MEN AGAINST THE SKY; SUED FOR LIBEL; TWO GIRLS ON BROADWAY; REPENT AT LEISURE; WASHINGTON MELODRAMA; ARMY SURGEON; FRISCO LIL; HALF WAY TO SHANGHAI; MISSISSIPPI GAMBLER (1942); TOMBSTONE, THE TOWN TOO TOUGH TO DIE; BOMBER'S MOON; ALASKA; ROGER TOUHY, GANGSTER; THE DALTONS RIDE AGAIN; DANGEROUS MILLIONS; DEADLINE FOR MURDER; SMOOTH AS SILK; TANGIER; YOUNG WIDOW; THE CRIMSON KEY; SECOND CHANCE (1947); HALF PAST MIDNIGHT; FEDERAL AGENT AT LARGE; TRIAL WITHOUT JURY; WESTERN PACIFIC AGENT; PAYMENT ON DEMAND; SEEDS OF DESTRUCTION; PLAYGIRL; SECRET VENTURE; FRONTIER GAMBLER; GHOST TOWN (1956); THE PHANTOM FROM 10,000 LEAGUES; SLIGHTLY SCARLET (1956); TRACK THE MAN DOWN; THE IRON SHERIFF; FORT BOWIE; GANG WAR; WALK TALL; THE PURPLE HILLS; THE BROKEN LAND; THE FIREBRAND; THE CRAWLING HAND; THE DAY MARS INVADED EARTH; HARBOR LIGHTS; LAW OF THE LAWLESS; FORT COURAGEOUS; BRIDES OF BLOOD; THE MIGHTY GORGA; SATAN'S SADISTS; HELL'S BLOODY DEVILS; BRAIN OF BLOOD.

Teasdale, Verree

Born 15 Mar. 1905, Spokane, Wash.; died 17 Feb. 1987.

Stage/Film Actress

The widow of Adolphe Menjou was born in Spokane, Washington, and trained for the stage at the New York School of Expression before appearing on Broadway in 1924. She appeared regularly on the stage until making her screen debut in 1929. She continued to perform in films through the early 1940s. Among her films: SYNCOPATION (1929); THE SAP FROM SYRACUSE; PAYMENT DEFERRED; SKYSCRAPER SOULS; LOVE, HONOR, AND OH BABY; LUXURY LINER (1933); ROMAN SCANDALS; TERROR ABOARD; THEY JUST HAD TO GET MARRIED; DESIRABLE; DOCTOR MONICA; FASHIONS OF 1934; THE FIREBIRD; GOODBYE LOVE; MADAME DU BARRY (1934); A MODERN HERO; A MIDSUMMER NIGHT'S DREAM (1935); THE MILKY WAY (1936); FIRST LADY; FIFTH AVENUE GIRL; TOPPER TAKES A TRIP; I TAKE THIS WOMAN (1940); LOVE THY NEIGHBOR (1940); TURNABOUT; COME LIVE WITH ME.

Teichmann, Howard M.

Born 22 Jan. 1916, Chicago, Ill.; died 7 July 1987, New York, N.Y.

Playwright/Biographer

After graduating from the University of Wisconsin he began his professional career as stage manager for Orson Welles' Mercury Theater of the Air, writing scripts and producing shows. He served as senior editor for the Office of War Information and continued writing for radio and television in its early days. Together with George S. Kaufman, he scored a major hit with the 1953 comedy "The Solid Gold Cadillac," which was made into a 1956 film starring Judy Holiday. He wrote the 1957 stage adaptation of Nathaneal West's "Miss Lonelyhearts," as well as four well-received biographies: *George S. Kaufman: An Intimate Portrait*, *Smart Aleck: The Wit, World and Life of Alexander Woolcott*, *Alice: The Life and Times of Alice Roosevelt Longworth*, and *Fonda, My Life*, on which he collaborated with Henry Fonda. For 40 years he was professor of English at Barnard College, where he specialized in teaching writing for the stage, screen, radio, and television.

Telford, Frank

Died 19 May 1987, Los Angeles, Calif.; age 72.

Radio/TV Producer-Director-Writer

A combat correspondent for NBC and *Life* magazine during WW II, he also worked as a producer and director for radio and television. Among the feature films on which he worked are: THE BAMBOO SAUCER; SERGEANT RYKER; HELLO DOWN THERE.

Terry, Alice [Alice Frances Taafe]

Born 24 July 1899, Vincennes, Ind.; died 22 Dec. 1987, North Hollywood, Calif.

Silent Film Actress

Silent screen star began her career in 1916 with two pictures—THE BUGLE CALL and NOT MY SISTER—for D.W. Griffith's Triangle Studios, but her real fame came in the films she did in the 1920s for her director husband Rex Ingram. Acting opposite Ramon Novarro in THE ARAB and Rudolph Valentino in THE FOUR HORSEMAN, she provided the perfect cool foil for their hot Latin temperaments. She and Ingram moved to Nice, on the French Riviera, in the 1920s and set up their own studio there, but returned to the US at the outset of WW II. Her other films include: STRICTLY BUSINESS, THE BOTTOM OF THE WELL, OLD WIVES FOR NEW; THE CLARION CALL; THIN ICE; SHORE ACRES; HEARTS ARE TRUMPS; THE CONQUERING POWER; TURN TO THE RIGHT; THE PRISONER OF ZENDA; WHERE THE PAVEMENT ENDS; SCARAMOUCHE; SACKCLOTH AND SCARLET; THE GREAT DIVIDE; CONFESSIONS OF A QUEEN; ANY WOMAN; MARE NOSTRUM; THE MAGICIAN; LOVERS?; THE GARDEN OF ALLAH; THE THREE PASSIONS; ASILO NAVAL.

Texas, Temple

Died 18 June 1987; age 63.

Actress

Appeared on stage in "It Takes Two," "The Girl From Nantucker," "Pipe Dream" and was seen in KISS OF DEATH (1947).

Thatcher, Heather

Died February 1987, age early 90s, London, England.

Actress

A British musical comedy star of the theater, she had a sporadic career in English films before coming to Hollywood in the 1930s where she was in demand for her eccentric characterizations. Her films include: THE PLAYTHING; A WARM CORNER; BUT THE FLESH IS WEAK; IT'S A BOY; LOYALTIES; THE PRIVATE LIFE OF DON JUAN; THE DICTATOR (1935); MAMA STEPS OUT; THE THIRTEENTH CHAIR; TOVARICH; FOOLS FOR SCANDAL; GIRLS' SCHOOL; IF I WERE KING (1938); BEAU GESTE (1939); MAN HUNT (1941); JOURNEY FOR MARGARET; THE MOON AND SIXPENCE; SON OF FURY; THIS ABOVE ALL; THE UNDYING MONSTER; WE WERE DANCING; FLESH AND FANTASY; GASLIGHT (1944); ANNA KARENINA (1948); DEAR MR. PROHACK; THE GAY LADY; ENCORE; FATHER'S DOING FINE; THE HOUR OF THIRTEEN; DUEL IN THE JUNGLE; THE DEEP BLUE SEA; JOSEPHINE AND MEN; WILL ANY GENTLEMAN? Silent films include THE KEY TO THE WORLD; THE FIRST MEN IN THE MOON; THE GREEN TERROR; PALLARD THE PUNTER; THE LITTLE HOUR OF PETER WELLS.

Tibbles, George

Died 14 Feb. 1987, Palm Springs, Calif., age 73.

Writer/Songwriter/Playwright/Producer

Creator of the "Woody Woodpecker Song," cowritten with Ramey Idriss, which earned him an Academy Award nomination in 1948. He began his career as a musician performing in the late 1930s in nightclubs. He was writer and producer for television's long-running series "My Three Sons," as well as writing for other hit shows, among them "Leave it to Beaver," "The Munsters," and "Maude." He had a dozen plays in regional and dinner theaters including "Beloved Enemies," "Never Get Smart with an Angel," and "Leonardo the Florentine." Movies on which he worked are MUNSTER GO HOME; TAMMY AND THE MILLIONAIRE; HOW TO FRAME A FIGG.

Torres, Raquel [Paula Marie Osterman]

Born 11 Nov. 1908, Hermosillo, Mexico; died 10 Aug. 1987, Malibu, Calif.

Actress

At the age of 19, she appeared in MGM's first feature fully synchronized for dialog, music, and effects, the 1928 release of Woody Van Dyke's WHITE SHADOWS IN THE SOUTH SEAS. She was married to New York stockbroker Stephen Ames, who later produced films at RKO and MGM. Her other films include: THE SEA BAT; UNDER A TEXAS MOON; ALOHA; DUCK SOUP; SO THIS IS AFRICA; THE WOMAN I STOLE; RED WAGON; and a silent film, THE DESERT RIDER (1949).

Tosh, Peter [Winston Hubert MacIntosh]

Born 9 Oct. 1944, Westmoreland, Jamaica; died 1987, Kingston, Jamaica.

Singer/Songwriter

Jamaican reggae singer/songwriter shot during an armed robbery at his home. He founded the Wailers with Bob Marley and Neville "Bunny Wailer" Livingston in 1963, and wrote some of the group's most political material. On his own, he recorded a string of highly political albums, including the pro-marijuana "Legalize It." In 1978 he toured the US as an opening act for the Rolling Stones, an association that also saw him release several albums on the Stones' record label. His most recent album, "No Nuclear War," was released in July.

Triest, Frank

Died 30 Jan. 1987.

Actor

Appeared in LIARS DICE (1980).

Troughton, Patrick G.

Died 28 Mar. 1987, Columbus, Ga., age 67.

Actor

Appeared in the long-running British television program "Dr. Who," from 1966 to 1968, and died of a heart attack while making a personal appearance tour at a "Dr. Who" convention. His career included many appearances on English TV and among his films are: ESCAPE (1948); HAMLET; CHANCE OF A LIFETIME (1950); TREASURE ISLAND (1950); HER PANELLED DOOR; THE FRANCHISE AFFAIR; WHITE CORRIDORS; THE BLACK KNIGHT; RICHARD III; THE CURSE OF FRANKENSTEIN; THE MOONRAKER; THE PHANTOM OF THE OPERA (1962); JASON AND THE ARGONAUTS; THE GORGON; THE BLACK TORMENT; THE VIKING QUEEN; THE SCARS OF DRACULA; FRANKENSTEIN AND THE MONSTER FROM HELL; THE OMEN; SINBAD AND THE EYE OF THE TIGER and A HITCH IN TIME.

Torres

Tunick, Irve

Born 27 July 1912, New York, N.Y.; died Sept. 1987, Carmel, N.Y.

Scriptwriter

Founder and former president of the eastern region of the Television Writers of America, he began his career writing radio scripts and, during WW II moved to Washington where he wrote films used by the government to promote the war effort. He became a scriptwriter in the developing TV industry and wrote for a wide range of television shows and series including "Studio One," "The Armstrong Circle Theater," "Bonanza," "Witness," and "The F.B.I." He wrote one feature film, MURDER INC., released in 1960. He received the Robert E. Sherwood and George Foster Peabody Awards for achievements in the scriptwriting field.

Valenty, Lili

Died 11 Mar. 1987, Hollywood, Calif., age 86.

Film/TV Actress

A well-known stage star in Germany, she moved to New York when Hitler rose to power, appearing in 20 Broadway plays and countless radio shows. She had a recurring role in the television series "Bonanza" and also was featured in such shows as "Vegas," "Falcon Crest," "Hart to Hart," and "Little House on the Prairie." Among the films she made are: WILD IS THE WIND; CAN-CAN; SPARTACUS; ROME ADVENTURE; THE STORY OF RUTH; CHUBASCO; IT HAPPENED IN ATHENS; GIRLS, GIRLS, GIRLS; ONCE A THIEF; THE BABYMAKER; THE HARRAD SUMMER; TELL ME A RIDDLE.

Valenzuela, Connie

Died 18 Oct. 1987, Watsonville, Calif.; age 72.

Mother of the late 1950s rock singer Ritchie Valens, who was killed in a plane crash in 1959, at the age of 17, along with Buddy Holly, and whose climb to success was chronicled in the movie LA BAMBA (in which she appeared). She worked as a waitress, a farm worker, a bartender, and a house cleaner.

Van Den Boezem, Nick

Died August, 1987, Amsterdam, Netherlands; age 63.

Director

Worked for national broadcaster VARA, specializing in directing Dutch-language dramas. He was also involved in directing and designing theater shows.

Van der Linden, Charles Huguenot

Died 20 July 1987, Jubbega, Netherlands; age 78.

Filmmaker

His documentary short "This Tiny World" won a 1982 Academy Award and in 1963 he won the Berlin festival's Best Documentary prize for his short "Building Game," which also received an Academy Award nomination.

Ventura, Lino [Lino Borrini]

Born 14 July 1919, Parma, Italy; died 23 Oct. 1987, Saint-Cloud, France.

Actor

One of Europe's most popular screen personalities, the taciturn leading man's powerful presence and dramatic subtlety enhanced even the most routine melodrama. He dropped out of school at eight and worked at various occupations, eventually turning to the ring as a prizefighter. He entered French films in 1953 and was frequently employed in tough-guy roles, often as a gangster. His films include: THE GORILLA GREETS YOU; MISTRESS OF THE WORLD; FRANTIC; MODIGLIANI OF MONTPARNASSE; THE DEVIL AND THE TEN COMMANDMENTS; THREE PENNY OPERA

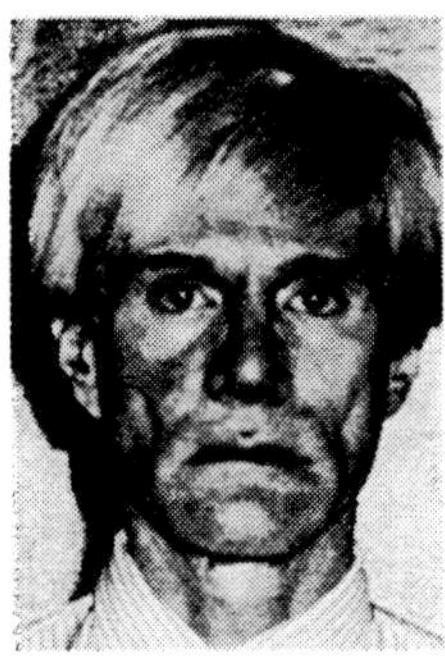

Warhol

(1963); GREED IN THE SUN; TAXI FOR TOBRUK; THE LAST ADVENTURE; WISE GUYS (1969); THE SICILIAN CLAN; THE VALACHI PAPERS; THREE TOUGH GUYS; A BUTTERFLY ON THE SHOULDER; THE MEDUSA TOUCH; THE ANGRY MAN; SUNDAY LOVERS; THE INQUISITOR; LES MISERABLES (1982); JIG SAW.

Vernon, Jackie [Ralph Verrone]

Died 10 Nov. 1987, Hollywood, Calif.; age 63.

Comedian

Began his comedy career in the early 1950s performing in small nightclubs around the country until discovered by Steve Allen, who launched his career with an appearance on the late-night television show "Celebrity Talent Scouts." He played the role of the hapless loser and appeared on the "Tonight Show" with Johnny Carson, "The Dean Martin Show," and "The Ed Sullivan Show." His standup routines were popular in Las Vegas showrooms and on television. Among the movies in which he appeared are: THE MONITORS; THE GANG THAT COULDN'T SHOOT STRAIGHT; MICROWAVE MASSACRE.

Victor, Paula

Died 17 Mar. 1987, Woodland Hills, Calif; age 71.

Actress

She began her acting career at 18 and wrote an advice to the lovelorn column in the *Philadelphia Ledger*. She did radio work in her native Philadelphia and later in New York, where she also acted in small theaters. She moved to Los Angeles in the early 1950s and appeared in numerous radio dramas, commercials, and TV series. Film credits include PETE 'N' TILLIE; GREAT WHITE HOPE; FLICKS; HAIL HERO.

Villa, Claudio

Died 7 Feb. 1987, Padua, Italy; age 61.

Singer

He won the San Remo Song Festival four times during the 1950s and 1960s, when he sold millions of records and became known as "The Little King" *(Il Reuccio)* of Italian popular music. He appeared, mainly in singing roles in about two dozen films, from Mario Soldati's BOTTA E RISPOSTA to Renzo Arbore's FFSS.

Volkie, Ralph

Died 6 Mar. 1987, Hollywood, Calif.; age 76.

Actor/Film Fight Coordinator

He was a trainer for five world championship boxers and his expertise was used in the film industry by actors and directors, including Robert Mitchum, Robert Ryan, Dick Powell, and Robert Aldrich. In 1954 he became John Wayne's personal trainer, and remained with the star until his death in 1979. Movies in which he appeared include: EAST OF THE RIVER; TALK OF THE TOWN; JOHNNY O'CLOCK; LEATHER GLOVES; A SOUTHERN YANKEE; WHIPLASH; A DANGEROUS PROFESSION; KNOCK ON ANY DOOR; THE UNDERCOVER MAN; NEW MEXICO; SLAUGHTER TRAIL; TEN TALL MEN; BLOODHOUNDS OF BROADWAY; BOOTS MALONE; THE LUSTY MEN; SCANDAL SHEET; THE SNIPER; DANGEROUS MISSION; THE FRENCH LINE; AUTUMN LEAVES; SERENADE; CHICAGO CONFIDENTIAL; THE PAJAMA GAME; THE MAN WHO SHOT LIBERTY VALANCE; DONOVAN'S REEF; FOUR FOR TEXAS; MC LINTOCK; THE SONS OF KATIE ELDER; EL DORADO; CHISUM; THE WAR WAGON; TRUE GRIT; RIO LOBO; THE SHOOTIST.

Von Trapp, Baroness Maria Augusta.

Born 26 Jan. 1905, Vienna, Austria; Died 28 Mar. 1987, Morrisville, Vt.

Entertainer

Onetime religious novice who, while tutoring the children of an Austrian war hero, married him and led her singing family in an escape from Nazi-occupied Austria that inspired the stage and screen musical THE SOUND OF MUSIC. Of the screen adaptation she was to say: "The first 10 minutes—the hills and the singing—I would like to see every morning for breakfast."

Waddington, Patrick

Died 4 Feb. 1987, York, England; age 86.

Actor

He played Colonel Pickering in more than 1,000 performances of "My Fair Lady." His first film was a silent, IF YOUTH BUT KNEW, in 1926, followed by LOYALTIES; THE BLACK TULIP; THE LOVES OF MADAME DUBARRY; JOURNEY TOGETHER; SCHOOL FOR SECRETS; THE CLOUDED CRYSTAL; SHOWTIME; IT'S NOT CRICKET; STOP PRESS GIRL; IF THIS BE SIN; THE WOODEN HORSE; THE MOONRAKER; A NIGHT TO REMEMBER; RX MURDER.

Wadhwani, Mohan

Died 14 Apr. 1987, Bombay, India; age 74.

Director

He joined the film division of the Ministry of Information & Broadcasting in 1948 and was promoted to chief producer in 1968. He won more than 30 national and international awards for his films in that division.

Wallerstein, Pearl Avnet

Died 2 Mar. 1987, Burbank, Calif.; age 91.

Actress

Born in New York, she appeared as an extra and in small parts in a number of silent films including THE PERILS OF PAULINE. In 1917, she wed Ruby Wallerstein, an actor on the Yiddish stage. She was the mother of Norm Wallerstein, post-production supervisor for Gladden Entertainment; Rowe Wallerstein, unit manager for Lorimar Pictures; and the late Herb Wallerstein, longtime president and production manager at 20th Century Fox.

Warhol, Andy [Andrew Warhola]

Born 6 Aug. 1927, Pittsburgh, Pa.; died 22 Feb. 1987, New York, N.Y.

Pop Artist/Filmmaker

He graduated from the Carnegie Institute of Technology in 1949 and became a successful commercial artist in New York. His silkscreen prints of Campbell's soup cans and other pop culture artifacts brought him worldwide attention in 1962. He began filmmaking in his New York headquarters called "The Factory." His best-known film was the cult classic CHELSEA GIRLS, which ran 31/2 hours on two screens. Among his other movies are: THE ILLIAC PASSION; LONESOME COWBOYS; L'AMOUR; THE DRIVER'S SEAT; COCAINE COWBOYS; HORSE; POOR LITTLE RICH GIRL.

Watt, Harry

Born 1906; died 2 Apr. 1987, Amersham, England.

Director

Worked with Robert Flaherty and John Grierson before filming his own documentary shorts "Night Mail" and "Target for Tonight" followed by a feature-length semi-documentary, NINE MEN. His films (for which he also handled the writing chores) include: FIDDLERS THREE; THE OVERLANDERS (made in Australia); MASSACRE HILL; IVORY HUNTER (directed only); WEST OF ZANZIBAR; FOUR DESPERATE MEN. Cowrote the script of FOR THOSE IN PERIL.

Weisenborn, Gordon

Died Oct. 1987, Chicago, Ill.; age 64.

Documentary Director

His work on specialized motion pictures won him more than 70 national and international prizes. In the 1940s John Grierson, head of the National Film Board of Canada, considered a pioneer in documentary making, brought him to Canada to work as his assistant and to teach him filmmaking. He returned to Chicago to work as a freelancer.

Werris, Snag [Solomon Samuel]

Died 27 Feb. 1987, Los Angeles, Calif; age 75.

Magician/Comedy Writer

Began his career as a magician, broke into vaudeville at 15, and was hired by Bert Wheeler to write for the Wheeler & Woolsey comedy team. He signed with 20th Century Fox where he wrote FOUR JILLS IN A JEEP; TAKE IT OR LEAVE IT; IF I'M LUCKY; LADIES OF WASHINGTON; CONEY ISLAND; DANCING MASTERS; FRIENDLY NEIGHBORS; PEEPER. In television, he wrote for "The Jackie Gleason Show," "The Red Skelton Comedy Hour," "The Brady Bunch," "Hawaii Five-O," and "All in the Family."

Wescoatt, Rusty

Died 3 Sept. 1987; age 76.

Actor

Film credits include THE MUTINEERS; CAPTIVE GIRL; CHAIN GANG; LAST OF THE BUCCANEERS; PYGMY ISLAND; STATE PENITENTIARY; FURY OF THE CONGO; HURRICANE ISLAND; A YANK IN KOREA; BRAVE WARRIOR; SIGN OF THE PAGAN; THE BIG BLUFF; GANG BUSTERS; TARANTULA; SNOWFIRE; TOUCH OF EVIL; THE SILENT CALL; 20,000 EYES; THE THREE STOOGES MEET HERCULES; BLACK GOLD; THE YOUNG SWINGERS; MORITURI.

Westlund, R. Chris

Died 28 Jan. 1987, age 37

Set Decorator/Production Designer

Born in Burbank, he worked in TV and film, listing among his credits such films as: OH GOD! BOOK II; MIDNIGHT MADNESS; DINER; THE LEGEND OF BILLIE JEAN; THIEF OF HEARTS; LOST BOYS; MIKE'S MURDER; SWING SHIFT; AT CLOSE RANGE.

Wheeler, Hugh

Died 26 July 1987, Pittsfield, Mass.; age 75.

Writer

He won Tony Awards for his books on which the musicals "Sweeney Todd" and "A Little Night Music" were based. A native of London, he came to the US at 19 to collaborate with mystery writer Richard Webb. He wrote 32 novels, 15 novellas, and 80 short stories, and several of the novels were made into films. Among the movies he wrote are FIVE MILES TO MIDNIGHT; SOMETHING FOR EVERYONE; TRAVELS WITH MY AUNT; A LITTLE NIGHT MUSIC; NIJINSKY; CABARET; THE MAN IN THE NET.

Wiard, William

Died 2 July 1987, Pacific Palisades, Calif.; age 59.

Director

He grew up in Beverly Hills and started his career at Universal, where he worked as a film editor through most of the 1950s. He then started directing episodes of television shows. During the mid 1970s he made telefilms. He was called in on short notice to replace the original director on the feature film TOM HORN, but then returned to TV and his telefilms include "Scott Free," "Ski Lift to Death," "This House Possessed," "Fantasies," and "Kicks."

Williams, Emlyn [George Emlyn Williams]

Born 26 Nov. 1905, Pen-y-Ffordd, Flintshire, North Wales; died 25 Sept. 1987, London, England.

Actor/Author/Playwright/Stage Director

First stepped on stage in 1927 in "And So to Bed," continuing his career with "The Mock Emperor," "French Leave," "Monserrat," and "Criminal at Large." Wrote over 20 plays including "Full Moon" (his first), "A Murder Has Been Arranged," "Glamour," "He Was Born Gay," "The Corn Is Green," "The Wind of Heaven," "Trespass," "Accolade," and "Beth." Appeared on the screen (sometimes also handling the writing chores) in CRIMINAL AT LARGE; SALLY BISHOP; FRIDAY THE 13TH; ROAD HOUSE (1934); THE CITY OF BEAUTIFUL NONSENSE; THE DICTATOR; THE IRON DUKE; MEN OF TOMORROW; MY SONG FOR YOU; BROKEN BLOSSOMS (1936); THE CITADEL; NIGHT ALONE; THEY DRIVE BY NIGHT (1938); DEAD MEN TELL NO TALES; JAMAICA INN; THE STARS LOOK DOWN; THE GIRL IN THE NEWS; MAJOR BARBARA; THIS ENGLAND; YOU WILL REMEMBER; HATTER'S CASTLE; THE LAST DAYS OF DOLWYN (also directed Richard Burton's film debut); THREE HUSBANDS; THE SCARF; ANOTHER MAN'S POISON; IVANHOE; THE MAGIC BOX; THE DEEP BLUE SEA; I ACCUSE; BEYOND THIS PLACE; THE WRECK OF THE MARY DEARE; THE L-SHAPED ROOM; EYE OF THE DEVIL; DAVID COPPERFIELD (1970); THE WALKING STICK; DEADLY GAMES. Films he wrote are EVERGREEN; THE DIVINE SPARK; THE MAN WHO KNEW TOO MUCH; NIGHT MUST FALL; LIFE BEGINS AT 8:30; THE CORN IS GREEN; TIME WITHOUT PITY. In later years he appeared in one-man shows that brought the works of Dylan Thomas and Charles Dickens to the stage. Wrote two volumes autobiographies—*George*, *Emlyn*—along with a novel, *Headlong*.

Wilson, Ajita

Died 26 May 1987; age 36.

Actress

Appeared in Italian films; her first performance was in THE NUDE PRINCESS, presumably based on Elisabeth Bagayen, one of the discarded wives of Uganda's strong-arm ruler, Idi Amin. Best known in the US as a pin-up model appearing in men's magazines; her film ORINOCO-PRISON OF SEX was released on video as ESCAPE FFOM HELL, and later re-edited for theatrical release as SAVAGE ISLAND.

Winter, Claude

Died 19 July 1987, Paris, France; age 65.

Producer

Created, with his wife and her sister, the Sofracima Production House in 1959, which was involved in such films as Alain Resnais' LA GUERRE EST FINIE; FLAGRANT DESIR; PRINCESS ACADEMY; THE NOVICE.

Wolcott, Charles

Died 26 Jan. 1987, Haifa, Israel; age 80.

Music Director/Arranger

A graduate of the University of Michigan, he came to Hollywood in 1937 and did arrangements for the "Rudy Vallee Radio Show" and "The Al Jolson Show." During his career, he also worked as an arranger for the bands of Paul Whiteman, Benny Goodman, Johnny Green, and the Dorsey Brothers. He joined the staff at Disney as an arranger and composer, working on cartoon shorts. He was general music director at Disney from 1944 to 1949 and was directly responsible for including the early rock 'n' roll smash "Rock Around the Clock" on the soundtrack of THE BLACKBOARD JUNGLE. His other films include: THE THREE CABALLEROS; MAKE MINE MUSIC; SONG OF THE SOUTH; IT'S A BIG COUNTRY; SKY FULL OF MOON; GABY; NEVER SO FEW; HOME FROM THE HILL; KEY WITNESS.

Yarnell, Gwen

Died 27 Jan. 1987; age 61.

Actress/Producer

Onetime director of children's theaters, she was a comedienne on the "Mike Douglas Show" at its beginning. She appeared in over 30 productions, including the film ONE POTATO, TWO POTATO.

Yin, Pak [Chan Yok-ping]

Died 6 May 1987, Hong Kong; age 67.

Actress

Born in Guangzhou, China, in 1920, she starred in more than 200 Cantonese movies between 1936 and 1964. She formed a film company in Hong Kong in the 1950s and produced many movies, featuring herself as protagonist, often the tragic heroine.

Awards

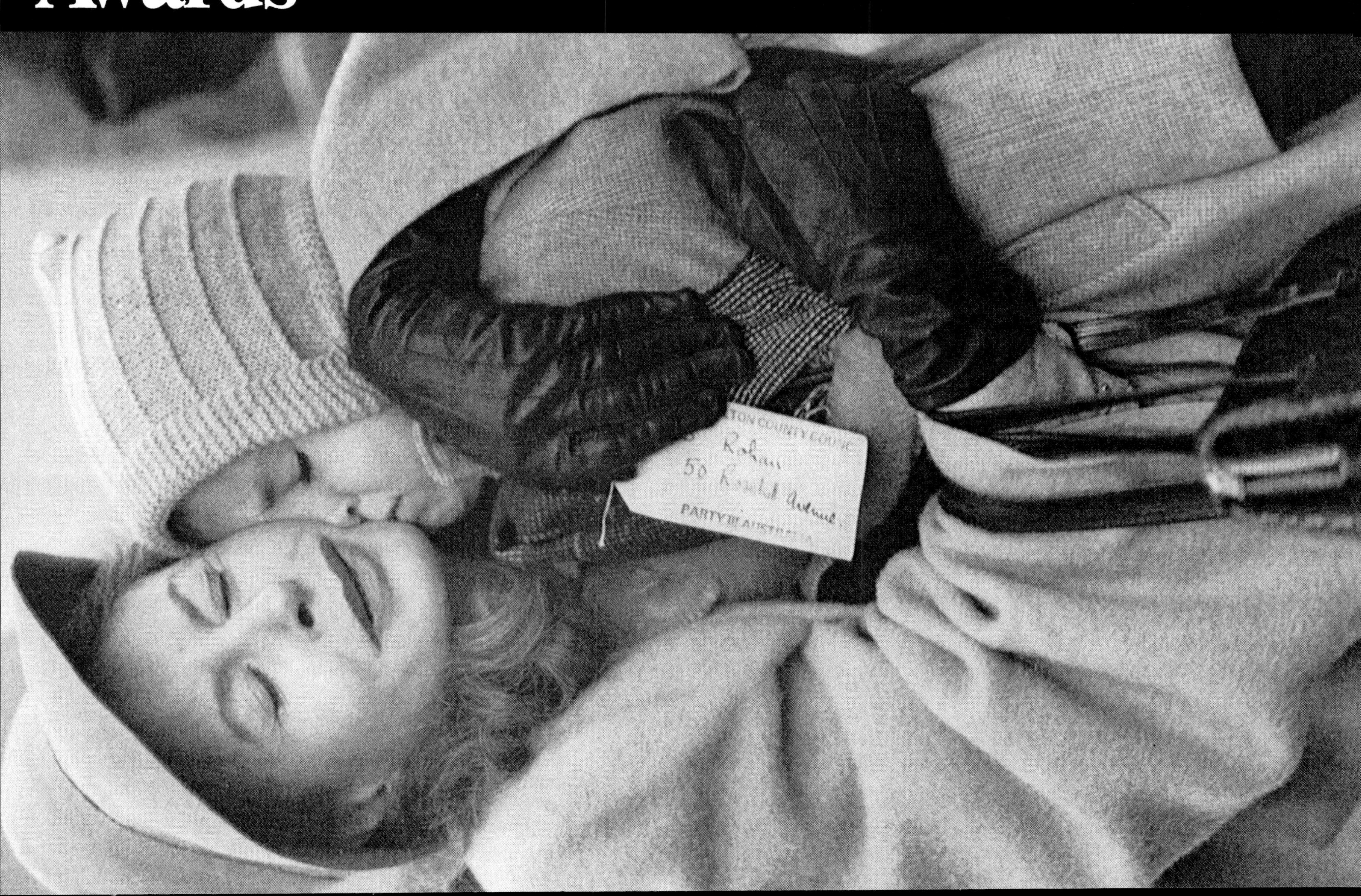

AWARDS INDEX

This section covers the major film industry awards given throughout the world between May, 1987 and April, 1988.

The index includes honors awarded by international, competitive film festivals in Berlin, Cannes, Chicago, Locarno, Montreal, Moscow, Rio De Janeiro, San Sebastian, Tokyo, Siciliy (Taormina), Toronto, Spain (Valladolid), and Venice.

In addition to the festivals, the index includes the awards given by the following organizations: Academy of Motion Picture Arts and Sciences (Oscars), American Society of Cinematographers, Australian Film Institute, French film industry (Cesars), Italian film industry (David Di Donatello awards), Directors Guild of America Awards, French Film Critics, Italian Film Journalists, Academy of Canadian Cinema and Television (Genies), German film industry, the Hollywood Foreign Press Association (Golden Globes), London Film Critics Association, Los Angeles Film Critics Association, National Board of Review (D.W. Griffith Awards), National Society of Film Critics, the New York Film Critics, and the Writers Guild of America.

Where appropriate, winning entries are denoted with an asterisk(*).

60TH AWARDS OF THE ACADEMY OF MOTION PICTURE ARTS AND SCIENCES

Best Picture

BROADCAST NEWS, Twentieth Century Fox. Produced by James L. Brooks, Penney Finkelman Cox.

FATAL ATTRACTION, Paramount. Produced by Stanley R. Jaffe, Sherry Lansing.

HOPE AND GLORY, Columbia. Produced by John Boorman, Michael Dryhurst.

THE LAST EMPEROR, Columbia. Produced by Jeremy Thomas.*

MOONSTRUCK, Metro-Goldwyn-Mayer. Produced by Patrick Palmer, Norman Jewison.

Best Actor

Michael Douglas for WALL STREET. *

William Hurt for BROADCAST NEWS.

Marcello Mastroianni for DARK EYES (It.).

Jack Nicholson for IRONWEED.

Robin Williams for GOOD MORNING VIETNAM.

Best Actress

Cher for MOONSTRUCK. *

Glenn Close for FATAL ATTRACTION.

Holly Hunter for BROADCAST NEWS.

Sally Kirkland for ANNA.

Meryl Streep for IRONWEED.

Best Supporting Actor

Albert Brooks for BROADCAST NEWS.

Sean Connery for THE UNTOUCHABLES.*

Morgan Freeman for STREET SMART.

Vincent Gardenia for MOONSTRUCK.

Denzel Washington for CRY FREEDOM (Brit.).

Best Supporting Actress

Norma Aleandro for GABY—A TRUE STORY.

Anne Archer for FATAL ATTRACTION.

Olympia Dukakis for MOONSTRUCK.*

Anne Ramsey for THROW MOMMA FROM THE TRAIN .

Ann Southern for THE WHALES OF AUGUST.

Best Direction

Bernardo Bertolucci for THE LAST EMPEROR (It., Hong Kong).*

John Boorman for HOPE AND GLORY (Brit.).

Adrian Lynne for FATAL ATTRACTION.

Lasse Hallstrom for MY LIFE AS A DOG (Swed.).

Norman Jewison for MOONSTRUCK.

Best Screenplay Based on Material from Another Medium

James Dearden for FATAL ATTRACTION.

Lasse Hallstrom, Reidar Jonsson, Brasse Brannstrom, Per Berglund for MY LIFE AS A DOG (Swed.).

Tony Huston for THE DEAD.

Stanley Kubrick, Michael Herr, Gustav Hasford for FULL METAL JACKET.

Mark Peploe, Bernardo Bertolucci, Enzo Ungari for THE LAST EMPEROR (It., Hong Kong).*

Best Screenplay Written Directly for the Screen

Woody Allen for RADIO DAYS.

John Boorman for HOPE AND GLORY (Brit.).

James L. Brooks for BROADCAST NEWS.

Louis Malle for AU REVOIR, LES ENFANTS (Fr.).

John Patrick Shanley for MOONSTRUCK.*

Best Cinematography

Michael Ballhaus for BROADCAST NEWS.

Allen Daviau for EMPIRE OF THE SUN.

Philippe Rousselot for HOPE AND GLORY (Brit.).

Vittorio Storaro for THE LAST EMPEROR (It., Hong Kong).*

Haskell Wexler for MATEWAN.

Best Song

Willy DeVille for "Storybook Love" from THE PRINCESS BRIDE.

Harold Faltermeyer, Keith Forsey, Bob Seger for "Shakedown" from BEVERLY HILLS COP II.

George Fenton, Jonas Gwangwa for "Cry Freedom" from CRY FREEDOM (Brit.).

Albert Hammond, Diane Warren for "Nothing's Gonna Stop Us Now" from MANNEQUIN.

Franke Previte, John DeNicola, Donald Markowitz for "(I've Had) The Time of My Life" from DIRTY DANCING.*

Best Original Score

George Fenton, John Gwangwa for CRY FREEDOM (Brit.).

Ennio Morricone for THE UNTOUCHABLES.

Ryuichi Sakamoto, David Byrne, Cong Su for THE LAST EMPEROR (It., Hong Kong).*

John T. Williams for EMPIRE OF THE SUN.

John T. Williams for THE WITCHES OF EASTWICK.

Best Film Editing

Gabriella Cristiani for THE LAST EMPEROR (It., Hong Kong).*

Michael Kahn for EMPIRE OF THE SUN.

Michael Kahn, Peter E. Berger for FATAL ATTRACTION.

Richard Marks for BROADCAST NEWS.

Frank J. Urioste for ROBOCOP.

Best Art Direction—Set Decoration

Santo Loquasto, Carol Joffe, Les Bloom, George DeTitta, Jr. for RADIO DAYS.

Anthony Pratt, Joan Woollard for HOPE AND GLORY (Brit.).

Norman Reynolds, Harry Cordwell for EMPIRE OF THE SUN.

Ferdinando Scarfiotti, Bruno Cesari for THE LAST EMPEROR (It., Hong Kong).*

Patrizia Von Brandenstein, Hal Gausman for THE UNTOUCHABLES.

Best Costume Design

James Acheson for THE LAST EMPEROR (It., Hong Kong).*

Jenny Beavan, John Bright for MAURICE.

Dorothy Jeakins for THE DEAD.

Bob Ringwood for EMPIRE OF THE SUN.

Marilyn Vance-Straker for THE UNTOUCHABLES.

Best Makeup

Rick Baker for HARRY AND THE HENDERSONS.*

Bob Laden for HAPPY NEW YEAR.

Best Sound

Wayne Artman, Tom Beckert, Tom Dahl, Art Rochester for THE WITCHES OF EASTWICK.

Les Fresholtz, Dick Alexander, Vern Poole, Bill Nelson for LETHAL WEAPON.

Robert Knuson, Don Digirolamo, John Boyle, Tony Dawe for EMPIRE OF THE SUN.

Michael J. Kohut, Carlos DeLarios, Aaron Rochin, Robert Wald for ROBOCOP.

Bill Rowe, Ivan Sharrock for THE LAST EMPEROR (It., Hong Kong).*

Best Visual Effects

Joel Hynek, Robert M. Greenberg, Richard Greenberg, Stan Winston for PREDATOR.

Dennis Muren, William George, Harley Jessup, Kenneth Smith for INNERSPACE.*

Best Foreign-Language Film

AU REVOIR, LES ENFANTS (Fr.).

BABETTE'S FEAST (Den.).*

COURSE COMPLETED (Span.).

THE FAMILY (It.).

PATHFINDER (Nor.).

Short Subjects

Best Animated Film

Frederic Back for THE MAN WHO PLANTED TREES.*

Eunice Macaulay for GEORGE AND ROSEMARY.

Bill Plymton for YOUR FACE.

Best Live-Action Film

Robert A. Katz for SHOESHINE.

Jonathan Sanger, Jana Sue Memel for RAY'S MALE HETEROSEXUAL DANCE HALL.*

Ann Wingate for MAKING WAVES.

Documentaries

Best Short Documentary

Deborah Dickson for FRANCES STELOFF: MEMOIRS OF A BOOKSELLER.

Sue Marx, Pamela Conn for YOUNG AT HEART.*

Lynn Mueller for SILVER INTO GOLD.

University of Southern California for IN THE WEE WEE HOURS.

Megan Williams for LANGUAGE SAYS IT ALL.

Best Feature Documentary

Callie Crossley, James A. DeVinney for EYES ON THE PRIZE: AMERICA'S CIVIL RIGHTS YEARS, BRIDGE TO FREEDOM, 1965.

Barbara Herbich, Cyril Christo for A STITCH FOR TIME.

John Junkerman, John Dower for HELLFIRE: A JOURNEY FROM HIROSHIMA.

Aviva Slesin for THE TEN-YEAR LUNCH: THE WIT AND LEGEND OF THE ALGONQUIN ROUND TABLE.*
Robert Stone for RADIO BIKINI.

2ND AMERICAN SOCIETY OF CINEMATOGRAPHERS AWARD

Stephen H. Burum for THE UNTOUCHABLES.
Allen Daviau for EMPIRE OF THE SUN.*
Steven Poster for SOMEONE TO WATCH OVER ME.
Vittorio Storaro for THE LAST EMPEROR.
Haskell Wexler for MATEWAN.

AUSTRALIAN FILM INSTITUTE AWARDS

Best Film
THE YEAR MY VOICE BROKE, produced by George Miller.

Best Direction
John Duigan for THE YEAR MY VOICE BROKE.

Best Actor
Leo McKern for TRAVELLING NORTH.

Best Actress
Judy Davis for HIGH TIDE.

Best Supporting Actor
Ben Mendelsohn for THE YEAR MY VOICE BROKE.

Best Supporting Actress
Jan Adele for HIGH TIDE.

Best Original Screenplay
John Duigan for THE YEAR MY VOICE BROKE.

Best Adapted Screenplay
David Williamson for TRAVELLING NORTH.

Best Cinematography
Steve Dobson for GROUND ZERO.

Best Original Music
Paul Schutze for THE TALE OF RUBY ROSE.

Best Costume Design
Jennie Tate for THE UMBRELLA WOMAN.

Best Editing
David Pulbrook for GROUND ZERO.

Best Production Design
Brian Thomson for GROUND ZERO.

Best Sound
Gary Wilkins, Mark Wasiutak, Craig Carter, Roger Savage for GROUND ZERO.

Best Documentary
PAINTING THE TOWN

Short Film Awards
Best Fiction Film
FEATHERS
Best Experimental Film
PALISADE
Best Animated Film
CRUST

AFI Member's Prize for Excellence in a Feature Film
THE YEAR MY VOICE BROKE, John Duigan.

37TH BERLIN INTERNATIONAL FILM FESTIVAL

Prizes of the International Jury
Golden Bear
THE THEME (USSR), Gleb Panfilov.
Silver Bears
Special Jury Prize
THE SEA AND POISON (Jap.), Kei Kumai.
Best Direction
Oliver Stone for PLATOON (US).
Best Actress
Ana Beatriz Nogueira for VERA (Braz.).
Best Actor
Gian Maria Volonte for THE MORO AFFAIR (It.).
Outstanding Single Achievement
THE YEAR OF AWAKENING, Fernando Trueba (Span.).
For a film which treats an unusual subject in a popular and sensitive way
CHILDREN OF A LESSER GOD, Randa Haines (US).
Alfred Bauer Prize
BAD BLOOD, Leos Carax (Fr.).
Golden Bear for Short Film
CURRICULUM VITAE (Czech.), Pavel Koutsky.
Silver Bear for Short Film
John Lasseter, Bill Reeves for LUXO JR. (US).

FIPRESCI Prize
Best in Competition
THE THEME (USSR), Gleb Panfilov.

CIDALC Prize
THE THEME (USSR), Gleb Panfilov.

Interfilm Jury Prize
THE THEME (USSR), Gleb Panfilov.

BRITISH ACADEMY OF FILM AND TELEVISION AWARDS

Best Picture
A ROOM WITH A VIEW, James Ivory.

Best Actor
Bob Hoskins for MONA LISA.

Best Actress
Maggie Smith for A ROOM WITH A VIEW.

Best Direction
Woody Allen for HANNAH AND HER SISTERS (US).

Best Original Screenplay
Paul Hogan, Ken Shadie, and John Cornell for CROCODILE DUNDEE (Aus.).

Best Adapted Screenplay
Kurt Luedtke for OUT OF AFRICA (US).

Best Supporting Actor
Ray McAnally for THE MISSION.

Best Supporting Actress
Judi Dench for A ROOM WITH A VIEW.

Best Musical Score
Ennio Morricone for THE MISSION.

Best Cinematography
Chris Menges for THE MISSION.

Best Production Design
Gianni Quaranta and Brian Ackland-Snow for A ROOM WITH A VIEW.

Best Costume Design
Jenny Bevan and John Bright for A ROOM WITH A VIEW.

Best Editing
Jim Clark for THE MISSION.

Best Sound
ALIENS (US).

Best Makeup
Shohichiro Meda, Tameyuki Aimi, Chihako Naito, and Noriko Takemizawa for RAN, (Jap./Fr.).

Best Foreign Language Film
RAN (Jap./Fr.), Akira Kurosawa.

British Film Institute Fellowship Award
Federico Fellini.

40TH CANNES INTERNATIONAL FILM FESTIVAL

Prizes of the International Jury
40th Anniversary Prize
Federico Fellini for INTERVISTA (It.).
Golden Palm
UNDER SATAN'S SUN (Fr.), Maurice Pialat.
Special Jury Prize
REPENTANCE (USSR), Tengiz Abuladze.
Jury Prize (ex aequo)
YEELEN (Mali), Souleymane Cisse.
SHINRAN (Jap.), Rentaro Mikuni.

Best Director
Wim Wenders for DER HIMMEL UBER BERLIN (Ger./Fr.).

Best Actor
Marcello Mastroianni for DARK EYES (It.).

Best Actress
Barbara Hershey for SHY PEOPLE (US).

Best Artistic Contribution
Stanley Myers for music for PRICK UP YOUR EARS (Brit.).

Camera D'Or for Best First Feature
Nana Dzhordzhadze for MY ENGLISH GRANDFATHER (USSR).

Short Films
Golden Palm
PALISADE (Aus.) Laurie McInnes.

FIPRESCI Prizes
Best Competing Film
REPENTANCE (USSR), Tengiz Abuladze.

12TH CESAR AWARDS OF THE FRENCH FILM INDUSTRY

Best Film/Best Director
THERESE, Alain Cavalier. Produced by Maurice Bernart.

Best First Feature
LA FEMME DE MA VIE, Regis Wargnier.

Best Foreign Film
THE NAME OF THE ROSE (US), Jean-Jacques Annaud.

Best Actor
Daniel Auteuil for JEAN DE FLORETTE.

Best Actress
Sabine Azema for MELO.

Best Supporting Actor
Pierre Arditi for MELO.

Best Supporting Actress
Emmanuelle Beart for MANON OF THE SPRING.

Best Young Male Hopeful
Isaach de Bankole for BLACK MIC-MAC.

Best Young Female Hopeful
Catherine Mouchet for THERESE.

Best Screenplay
THERESE by Alain Cavalier and Camille de Casabianca.

Best Score
Herbie Hancock for 'ROUND MIDNIGHT (US/Fr.).

Best Cinematography
Philippe Rousselot for THERESE.

Best Production Design
Pierre Guffroy for PIRATES.

Best Sound
Michel Desrois and William Flageollet for 'ROUND MIDNIGHT (US/Fr.).

Best Editing
Isabelle Dedieu for THERESE.

Best Costumes
Anthony Powell for PIRATES.

Best Short Film
LA COULA, Roger Guillot.

Best Poster
BETTY BLUE, designed by Christian Blondel.

Special Career Cesar
Jean-Luc Godard.

23RD CHICAGO INTERNATIONAL FILM FESTIVAL

Prizes of the International Jury
Gold Hugo
Best Feature
WHOOPING COUGH (Hung.), Peter Gardos.
Special Jury Prize
REPENTANCE (USSR), Tengiz Abuladze.
Best Animation
WHEN THE WIND BLOWS (Brit.).
Silver Hugo
Feature Film
BOY SOLDIER (Wales), Karl Francis.
Best Director
Alain Resnais for MELO (Fr.).
Best Actor
Brian Dennehy for THE BELLY OF AN ARCHITECT (Brit.).
Avtandil Makharadze for REPENTENCE (USSR).
Best Actress
Nobuko Miyamoto for A TAXING WOMAN (Jap.).
Artistic Conception
THE BELLY OF AN ARCHITECT (Brit.), Peter Greenaway.

Gold Plaques
Best Performance
Jason St. Amour and Fred Ward for TRAIN OF DREAMS (Can.).

Oscar Getz World Peace Medal
WHEN THE WIND BLOWS (Brit.), Jimmy Murakami.

31ST DAVID DI DONATELLO AWARDS

Awards for Italian Films
Best Picture
LET'S HOPE IT'S A GIRL, Mario Monicelli.
Best Direction
Mario Monicelli for LET'S HOPE IT'S A GIRL.
Best Actor
Marcello Mastroianni for GINGER AND FRED.
Best Actress
Angela Molina for CAMORRA.
Best Supporting Actor
Bernard Blier for LET'S HOPE IT'S A GIRL.
Best Supporting Actress
Athina Cenci for LET'S HOPE IT'S A GIRL.
Best Producer
Giovanni Di Clemente for LET'S HOPE IT'S A GIRL.
Best Cinematography
Giuseppe Lanci for CAMORRA.
Best Screenplay
Mario Monicelli, Tullio Pinelli, Suso Cecchi d'Amici, Leonardo Benvenuti, and Piero De Bernardi for LET'S HOPE IT'S A GIRL.
Best Costume
Danilo Donati for GINGER AND FRED.
Best Set Design
Enrico Job for CAMORRA.
Best Score
Nicola Piovani for GINGER AND FRED. Riz Ortolani for GRADUATION PARTY.
Best Editing
Ruggero Mastroianni for LET'S HOPE IT'S A GIRL.
Best First Film
Enrico Montesano for I LIKE MYSELF.

Foreign Film Awards
Best Picture
OUT OF AFRICA (US), Sidney Pollack.
Best Direction
Akira Kurosawa for RAN (Jap./Fr.).
Best Actor
William Hurt for KISS OF THE SPIDER WOMAN (US/Braz.).
Best Actress
Meryl Streep for OUT OF AFRICA (US).
Best Producer
Steven Spielberg, Frank Marshall, and Kathleen Kennedy for BACK TO THE FUTURE (US).
Best Screenplay
Robert Zemeckis and Bob Gale for BACK TO THE FUTURE (US).

Rene Clair Award
Federico Fellini.

Luchino Visconti Memorial Lifetime Achievement Award
Ingmar Bergman.

39TH DIRECTORS GUILD OF AMERICA AWARDS

Outstanding Feature Film Achievement
Bernardo Bertolucci for THE LAST EMPEROR.*
James L. Brooks for BROADCAST NEWS.
Lasse Hallstrom for MY LIFE AS A DOG.
Adrian Lyne for FATAL ATTRACTION.
Steven Spielberg for EMPIRE OF THE SUN.

D.W. Griffith Award for outstanding achievement and contribution to film
Robert Wise.

Robert B. Aldrich Award
Sheldon Leonard.

Honorary Life Member
Michael Franklin.

FRENCH FILM CRITICS UNION AWARDS

Melies Prize for Best Domestic Film
THERESE, Alain Cavalier.

Moussinac Prize for Best Foreign Film
HANNAH AND HER SISTERS (US), Woody Allen.

Literary Prize
Henri Langlois: 300 Ans de Cinema.

14TH GENIE AWARDS OF THE ACADEMY OF CANADIAN CINEMA AND TELEVISION

Best Picture
FAMILY VIEWING, produced by Atom Egoyan.
I'VE HEARD THE MERMAIDS SINGING, produced by Alexandra Raffe, Patricia Rozema.
LIFE CLASSES, produced by Stephen Reynolds.
TRAIN OF DREAMS, produced by Sam Grana.
NIGHT ZOO, produced by Roger Frappier, Pierre Gendron. *

Best Actor
David Hemblen for FAMILY VIEWING.
Roger Le Bel for NIGHT ZOO. *
Gilles Maheu for NIGHT ZOO.
Jason St. Amour for TRAIN OF DREAMS.

Best Actress
Frederique Collin for MARIE S'EN VA-T-EN VILLE.
Jacinta Cormier for LIFE CLASSES.
Kate Lynch for TAKING CARE.
Sheila McCarthy for I'VE HEARD THE MERMAIDS SINGING. *
Gabrielle Rose for FAMILY VIEWING.

Best Supporting Actor
Hrant Alianak for FAMILY VIEWING.
Leon Dubinsky for LIFE CLASSES.
Germain Houde for NIGHT ZOO. *
Tony Nardi for CONCRETE ANGELS.
Murray Westgate for BLUE CITY SLAMMERS.

Best Supporting Actress
Paule Baillargeon for I'VE HEARD THE MERMAIDS SINGING. *
Jayne Eastwood for NIGHT FRIEND.
Fran Gebhard for BLUE CITY SLAMMERS.
Ann-Marie MacDonald for I'VE HEARD THE MERMAIDS SINGING.
Maruska Stankova for DREAMS BEYOND MEMORY.

Best Direction
Atom Egoyan for FAMILY VIEWING.

Jean-Claude Lauzon for NIGHT ZOO.*
Marquise Lepage for MARIE S'EN VA-T-EN VILLE.
Patricia Rozema for I'VE HEARD THE MERMAIDS SINGING.
John N. Smith for TRAIN OF DREAMS.

Best Cinematography
Michel Brault for THE GREAT LAND OF SMALL.
Guy Dufaux for NIGHT ZOO.*
Douglas Koch for I'VE HEARD THE MERMAIDS SINGING.
Richard Leiterman for THE CLIMB.

Best Screenplay
Sally Bochner, John N. Smith, Sam Grana for TRAIN OF DREAMS.
Atom Egoyan for FAMILY VIEWING.
Jean-Claude Lauzon for NIGHT ZOO.*
William D. MacGillivray for LIFE CLASSES.
Patricia Rozema for I'VE HEARD THE MERMAIDS SINGING.

Best Art Direction/Production Design
Violette Daneau for THE GREAT LAND OF SMALL.
Ronald Fauteux for LE FRERE ANDRE.
Francois Seguin for MARIE S'EN VA-T-EN VILLE.
Jean-Baptiste Tard for NIGHT ZOO.*

Best Film Editing
Michel Arcand for NIGHT ZOO.*
Atom Egoyan, Bruce MacDonald for FAMILY VIEWING.

Best Costume Design
Michele Hamel for THE GREAT LAND OF SMALL.
Martine Matthews, Alexandra Z for I'VE HEARD THE MERMAIDS SINGING.
Andree Morin for NIGHT ZOO.*
Nicole Pelletier for MARIE S'EN VA-T-EN VILLE.
Denis Sperdouklis for LE FRERE ANDRE.

Best Score
Jean Corriveau for NIGHT ZOO.*
Patricia Cullen for THE CARE BEARS—ADVENTURE IN WONDERLAND.
Mychael Danna for FAMILY VIEWING.
Tim McCauley for BLUE CITY SLAMMERS.

Best Original Song
Krezsmir Debski, Howard Forman for "When We're Together" from THE YOUNG MAGICIAN.
William D. MacGillivray for "Mary's Lament" from LIFE CLASSES.
Maribeth Solomon for "Rise and Shine" from THE CARE BEARS-*ADVENTURES IN WONDERLAND.
Robert Stanley, Jean Corriveau, Daniel De Shaimes, Jean-Pierre Bonin for "Lost in a Hurricane" from NIGHT ZOO.*
Guy Trepanier for "The Great Land of Small" from THE GREAT LAND OF SMALL.

Best Sound
Yvon Benoit, Hans-Peter Strobl, Adrian Croll for NIGHT ZOO.*
Michel Charron, Michel Descombes, Andre Gagnon, Jocelyn Caron for THE YOUNG MAGICIAN.
Egidio Coccimiglio, Gordon Thompson, Michele Moses for I'VE HEARD THE MERMAIDS SINGING.
Lars Ekstrom, Tony Van Den Akker, Marvin Berns for HELLO MARY LOU: PROM NIGHT 2.
Daniel Latour, David Appleby for TOO OUTRAGEOUS!

Best Sound Editing
Claude Langlois, Louise Cote, Alain Clavier, Viateur Paiement, Serge Viau for THE YOUNG MAGICIAN.
Robin Leigh, Richard Cadger, Jane Tattersall, Peter McBurnie, Penny Hozy for THE CLIMB.
Marcel Pothier, Diane Boucher, Antoine Morin, Viateur Paiement, Jocelyn Caron for LE FRERE ANDRE.
Peter Thillaye, Marta Sternberg, Peter McBurnie, Nick Rotundo, Peter Jermyn for HELLO MARY LOU: PROM NIGHT 2.
Marcel Pothier, Diane Boucher, Viateur Paiment for NIGHT ZOO.*

Shorts and Documentaries
Best Documentary
THE CANNERIES, directed by Bonni E. Devlin, Stephen Insley.
DANCE FOR MODERN TIMES, produced by Moze Mossanen.
ELEPHANT DREAMS, produced by Martha Davis.
GOD RIDES A HARLEY, produced by Andreas Erne, Stavros C. Stavrides.*
TO HURT AND TO HEAL, produced by Laura Sky.
Best Short Film
FASHION 99, produced by Karen Firus.
FUTURE BLOCK, directed by Kevin McCracken.
GEORGE AND ROSEMARY, directed by David Fine, Alison Snowden.*

GERMAN FILM AWARDS

German Film Prize
ROSA LUXEMBURG, Margarethe von Trotta.

Gold Film Band
Barbara Sukowa for her performance in ROSA LUXEMBURG.

Silver Film Band
THE BLIND DIRECTOR, Alexander Kluge.
MEN, Doris Dorrie.

German Cross of Merit for longstanding service to film and television
Manfred Durniok.

45TH GOLDEN GLOBE AWARDS

Best Motion Picture—Drama
THE LAST EMPEROR, Hemdale/Columbia.

Best Actress—Drama
Sally Kirkland for ANNA.

Best Actor—Drama
Michael Douglas for WALL STREET.

Best Motion Picture—Musical or Comedy
HOPE AND GLORY, Columbia-Nelson Ent./Columbia.

Best Actress—Musical or Comedy
Cher for MOONSTRUCK.

Best Actor—Musical or Comedy
Robin Williams for GOOD MORNING, VIETNAM.

Best Foreign-Language Film
MY LIFE AS A DOG (Swed.), Lasse Hallstrom.

Best Supporting Actress
Olympia Dukakis for MOONSTRUCK.

Best Supporting Actor
Sean Connery for THE UNTOUCHABLES.

Best Director
Bernardo Bertolucci for THE LAST EMPEROR.

Best Screenplay
Mark Peploe, Bernardo Bertolucci, Enzo Ungari for THE LAST EMPEROR.

Best Original Score
Ryuichi Sakamoto, David Byrne, Cong Su, for THE LAST EMPEROR.

Best Original Song
Frank Previte, John DeNicola, Donald Markowitz "(I've Had) The Time of my Life" for DIRTY DANCING.

Cecil B. DeMille Award for Outstanding Contribution to the Entertainment Industry
Clint Eastwood

ITALIAN FILM JOURNALISTS AWARDS

Best Film
LET'S HOPE IT'S A GIRL, Mario Monicelli.

Best Actor
Marcello Mastroianni for GINGER AND FRED.

Best Actress
Giulietta Masina for GINGER AND FRED.

Best Foreign Film
OUT OF AFRICA (US), Sidney Pollack.

Best Foreign Actor
Phillipe Noiret for LET'S HOPE IT'S A GIRL.

Best Foreign Actress
Angela Molina for CAMORRA.

Best Supporting Actress
Isa Danieli for CAMORRA.

Best Debuting Actor
Elvio Porta for CAMORRA.

Best Screenplay
Mario Monicelli, Tullio Pinelli, Suso Cecchi d'Amici, Leonardo Benvenuti, and Piero De Bernardi for LET'S HOPE IT'S A GIRL.

Best Cinematography
Marcello Gatti for INGANNI.

Best Editing
Ruggero Mastroianni for LET'S HOPE IT'S A GIRL.

Best Score
Tony Esposito for CAMORRA.

Best Art Direction
Dante Feretti for GINGER AND FRED.

Best Costume Design
Danilo Donati for GINGER AND FRED.

Best Producer
Fulvio Lucisano.

Special Ribbon for Poetic Subject Matter
INGANNI, Luigi Faccini.

40TH LOCARNO INTERNATIONAL FILM FESTIVAL

Prizes of the International Jury
Golden Leopard
THE JESTER (Port.), Jose Alvaro Morais.
Silver Leopard
THE TERRORIZERS (Taiwan), Edward Yang (Yang De-chang).

Bronze Leopard

ODINOKU GOLOS CELOVEKA (USSR), Aleksandr Solourov.

Arpad Vermes for his performance in HOL VOLT, HOL NEM VOLT (Hung.), Gaula Gazdag.

Gregg Araki, THREE BEWILDERED PEOPLE IN THE NIGHT (US), for his artistic use of technical means.

Special Mentions

SKYTTURNAR (Iceland), Fridrik Thor Fridriksson.

Roland Dubillard for his performance in POISONS (Switz./Fr.).

ROBINSON NO NIWA (Jap.), Masashi Yamamoto.

FIPRESCI Prize

THREE BEWILDERED PEOPLE IN THE NIGHT (US), Gregg Araki.

DOLGIE PROVODY (USSR), Kira Muratova.

International Federation of Art Cinemas Prize

THE JESTER (Port.), Jose Alvaro Morais.

Youth Prizes

First Prize

AVRIL BRISE (Fr.), Liria Begeja.

Second Prize

THREE BEWILDERED PEOPLE IN THE NIGHT (US), Gregg Araki.

Third Prize

POISONS (Switz./Fr.), Pierre Maillard.

LONDON FILM CRITICS AWARDS

Best Picture

HOPE AND GLORY, John Boorman.

Best Director

Stanley Kubrick for FULL METAL JACKET (US).

Best Actor

Sean Connery for THE UNTOUCHABLES (US), and THE NAME OF THE ROSE (US).

Gary Oldman for PRICK UP YOUR EARS.

Best Screenplay

Alan Bennett for PRICK UP YOUR EARS.

Best Foreign-Language Film

JEAN DE FLORETTE (Fr.), Claude Berri.

Best Music

Ennio Morricone for his career volume of work including THE MISSION and THE UNTOUCHABLES (US).

Special Awards for Outstanding Contribution to the Cinema

Pinewood Studios.

Tommy Manderson, makeup artist.

David Rose, executive in charge of film projects for Channel 4.

LOS ANGELES FILM CRITICS ASSOCIATION AWARDS

Best Picture

HOPE AND GLORY (Brit.), John Boorman.

Best Director

John Boorman for HOPE AND GLORY (Brit.).

Best Actor (tie)

Steve Martin for ROXANNE.

Jack Nicholson for IRONWEED and THE WITCHES OF EASTWICK.

Best Actress (tie)

Holly Hunter for BROADCAST NEWS.

Sally Kirkland for ANNA.

Best Foreign Film

AU REVOIR, LES ENFANTS (Fr.), Louis Malle.

Best Supporting Actor

Morgan Freeman for STREET SMART.

Best Supporting Actress

Olympia Dukakis for MOONSTRUCK.

Best Cinematography

Vittorio Storaro for THE LAST EMPEROR.

Best Music

Ryuichi Sakamoto, David Byrne, Cong Su for THE LAST EMPEROR.

Career Achievement Award

Joel McCrea.

Samuel Fuller.

New Generation Award

Pedro Almodovar, director, LAW OF DESIRE (Span.).

Independent/Experimental Film

MALA NOCHE, Gus Van Sant.

Special Awards

Documentary Film

WEAPONS OF THE SPIRIT, Pierre Sauvage.

For Screenings of Independent and Avant-garde Cinema

Film Forum at the Wallenboyd Center.

11TH MONTREAL WORLD FILM FESTIVAL AWARDS

Prizes of the International Jury

Grand Prix of the Americas

THE KID BROTHER (Can./US/Jap.), Claude Gagnon.

Special Jury Award

MY GENERAL (Span.), Jaime de Arminan.

Jury Award

THE BIG PARADE (Chi.), Chen Kaige.

Best Actress

Irina Kupchenko for LONELY WOMAN SEEKS LIFE COMPANION (USSR).

Best Actor

Leo McKern for TRAVELLING NORTH (Aus.).

Short Films

Best Short

SHOESHINE (US), Tom Abrams.

Special Jury Award

GEORGE AND ROSEMARY (Can.), Alison Snowden, David Fine.

Special Award

Eric Rohmer for his work in the series COMEDIES AND PROVERBS on the occasion of the presentation of L'AMI DE MON AMIE.

FIPRESCI Prize

WHOOPING COUGH (Hung.), Peter Gardos.

THE GREAT RACE (Pol.), Jerzy Domaradzki.

Ecumenical Awards

Best Film

FAREWELL, MOSCOW (It.), Mauro Bolognini.

Special Mention

LE GRAND CHEMIN (Fr.), Jean)Loup Hubert.

15TH MOSCOW FILM FESTIVAL

Best Picture

INTERVISTA (It.), Federico Fellini.

Best Actor

Anthony Hopkins for 84 CHARING CROSS ROAD (Brit.).

Best Actress

Dorottya Udvaros for CSOK, ANYU (Hung.).

Special Jury Prize

KURIER (USSR), Karen Shakhnazarov.

BOHATER ROKU (Pol.), Feliks Falk.

FIPRESCI Prize

BOHATER ROKU (Pol.), Feliks Falk.

Children's Film Festival

Gold Prize

THE JOURNEY OF NATTY GANN (US).

Silver Prize

WONDER CHILD (Pol.).

SPEAK BOLDLY (Pol.).

BACH AND BROCCOLI (Can.).

NATIONAL BOARD OF REVIEW D.W. GRIFFITH AWARDS

Best Picture

EMPIRE OF THE SUN, Steven Spielberg.

Best Foreign-Language Film

JEAN DE FLORETTE and MANON OF THE SPRING (Fr.), Claude Berri.

Best Director

Steven Spielberg for EMPIRE OF THE SUN.

Best Actor

Michael Douglas for WALL STREET.

Best Actress

Lillian Gish for THE WHALES OF AUGUST.

Holly Hunter for BROADCAST NEWS.

Best Supporting Actor

Sean Connery for THE UNTOUCHABLES.

Best Supporting Actress

Olympia Dukakis for MOONSTRUCK.

Outstanding Juvenile Performance

Christian Bale for EMPIRE OF THE SUN.

22ND NATIONAL SOCIETY OF FILM CRITICS AWARDS

Best Picture

THE DEAD, John Huston.

Best Director

John Boorman for HOPE AND GLORY.

Best Actor

Steve Martin for ROXANNE.

Best Actress

Emily Lloyd for WISH YOU WERE HERE.

Best Supporting Actor

Morgan Freeman for STREET SMART.

Best Supporting Actress

Kathy Baker for STREET SMART.

Best Screenplay
John Boorman for HOPE AND GLORY.

Best Cinematography
Philippe Rousselot for HOPE AND GLORY.

Special Award
Richard Roud for 18 years of service as director of the New York Film Festival.

53RD NEW YORK FILM CRITICS CIRCLE AWARDS

Best Picture
BROADCAST NEWS, James L. Brooks.

Best Director
James L. Brooks for BROADCAST NEWS.

Best Actress
Holly Hunter for BROADCAST NEWS.

Best Actor
Jack Nicholson for BROADCAST NEWS, IRONWEED, and THE WITCHES OF EASTWICK.

Best Supporting Actress
Vanessa Redgrave for PRICK UP YOUR EARS (Brit.).

Best Supporting Actor
Morgan Freeman for STREET SMART.

Best Foreign Film
MY LIFE AS A DOG (Swed.), Lasse Hallstrom.

Best Screenplay
James L. Brooks for BROADCAST NEWS.

Best Cinematography
Vittorio Storaro for THE LAST EMPEROR.

4TH RIO DE JANEIRO INTERNATIONAL FILM FESTIVAL

Prizes of the International Jury
Golden Toucan for Best Film
OUT OF ROSENHEIM (Ger.), Percy Adlon.
Best Director
Pedro Almodovar for THE LAW OF DESIRE (Span.).
Best Actor
Denes Dobrei for TOLERANCE (Hung.).
Best Actress
Wendy Hughes for WARM NIGHTS ON A SLOW MOVING TRAIN (Aus.).
Special Jury Prize
THE LAST EMPRESS (Chi.), Chen Jialin.
KIN-DZA-DZA (USSR), Georgui Danelia.
Special Jury Mention
MEMORIA VIVA (Braz.), Octavio Bezerra.
Best Short
NIGHT ANGEL (Can.), Jacques Drouin, Bretislav Pojar.
CIDADAO JATOBA (Braz.), Maria Luiza Aboim.

FIPRESCI Prize
BOUBA (Israel), Zeev Revach.

OCIC and CIFEJ Prizes
ANDEJO CUVAR (Yugo.), Goran Paskaljevic.

FIC Prize
OUT OF ROSENHEIM (Ger.), Percy Adlon.

35TH SAN SEBASTIAN INTERNATIONAL FILM FESTIVAL

Prizes of the International Jury
Gold Shell for Best Film
NOCE EN GALILEE (Bel./Fr.), Michel Khleifi.
Best Direction
Dominique Deruddere for LOVE IS A DOG FROM HELL (Bel.).
Best Actor
Imanol Arias for EL LUTE—CAMINA O REVIENTA (Span.).
Best Actress
Victoria Abril for EL LUTE—CAMINA O REVIENTA (Span.).
Silver Shell
CANDY MOUNTAIN (Switz./Can.), Robert Frank and Rudy Wurlitzer.
HIGH SEASON (Brit.), Clare Peploe.

FIPRESCI Prize
STRATEGLIA SURAKE (Yugo.), Zlatco Lavanic.

OCIC Catholic Prize
YER DEMIR, GOK BAKIR (Turkey), Omer Zulfu Livaneli.

Ciga Prize
Alejandro Agresti for EL AMOR ES UNA MUJER GORDA.
Felipe Vega for MIENTRAS HAYA LUZ.

23RD TAORMINA (SICILY) FILM FESTIVAL

GOLDEN CHARYBDIS
NGATI (New Zealand), Barry Barclay.

SILVER CHARYBDIS
YAM DAABO (Burkina Faso), Idrissa Oudraogo.

BRONZE CHARYBDIS
ZYGFRYD (Pol.), Andrzej Domalik.

GOLD POLYPHEMUS MASK
John Kani for SATURDAY NIGHT AT THE PALACE (South Africa).

SILVER POLYPHEMUS MASK
Maria Pakulnis for LA VIE EST BELLE (Bel./Zaire).

BRONZE POLYPHEMUS MASK
All the actresses in LA VIE EST BELLE (Bel./Zaire).

ITALIAN CRITICS AWARD
YAM DAABO (Burkina Faso), Idrissa Oudraogo.

TOKYO INTERNATIONAL FILM FESTIVAL

Grand Prize and Governor's Award
OLD WELL (Chi.), Wu Tianming.

Special Jury Prize
HOUSEKEEPING, Bill Forsyth.

Best Director
Lana Gogoberidze for TURNOVER (USSR).

Best Actor
Zhang Yiou for OLD WELL (Chi.).

Best Actress
Rachel Ward for THE GOOD WIFE (Aus.).

Best Artistic Contribution
John Boorman for HOPE AND GLORY (Brit.).

Best Screenplay
Bill Forsyth for HOUSEKEEPING.

Young Cinema Sakura Gold and Governor's Award
THE KITCHEN TOTO (Brit.), Harry Hook.

Young Cinema Sakura Silver
SWEET LORRAINE (US), Steve Gomer.

FIPRESCI Award
THE MAN WITH THREE COFFINS (S.K.), Lee Chang)ho.

FIPRESCI Special Recognition
OLD WELL (Chi.).

Special Festival Award
John Huston.

12TH TORONTO FESTIVAL OF FESTIVALS

John Labatt Classic Prize for Most Popular Film (Audience Poll)
THE PRINCESS BRIDE (US), Rob Reiner.

Four Seasons International Critics Award
NIGHT ZOO, Jean-Claude Lauzon.

Best Canadian Film
FAMILY VIEWING, Atom Egoyan.

Special Jury Prize
Best Documentary
ARTISTS ON FIRE, Kay Armatage.

32ND VALLADOLID (SPAIN) FILM FESTIVAL

Prizes of the International Jury
Golden Sheaf for Best Picture
ZAVTRA BILA VOINA (USSR), Yuri Kara.
Silver Sheaf
YEELEN (Mali), Souleymane Cisse.

Francois Truffaut Prize for Best First Film
DRAGON'S FOOD (Ger./Switz.), Jan Schutte.
WISH YOU WERE HERE (Brit.), David Leland.

Best Cinematography
Mikael Salomon for BARNDOMMENS GADE (Den.).

Best Actress
Leonor Manso for MADE IN ARGENTINA (Arg.).

Best Actor
Dennis Quaid for THE BIG EASY (US).

Short Film Awards
Golden Sheaf
THE MAN WHO PLANTED TREES (Can.), Frederic Back.
Silver Sheaf
LUXO JR. (US), John Lasseter, Bill Reeves.

44TH VENICE INTERNATIONAL FILM FESTIVAL

Prizes of the International Jury
Golden Lion
AU REVOIR, LES ENFANTS (Fr.), Louis Malle.
Special Jury Award
HIP, HIP, HURRAH! (Swed./Nor./Den.), Kjell Grede.
Silver Lion
MAURICE (Brit.), James Ivory.
LUNGA VITA ALLA SIGNORA! (It.), Ermanno Olmi.

Best Actor
James Wilby for MAURICE (Brit.).
Hugh Grant for MAURICE (Brit.).

Best Actress
Kang Soo-Yeon for SIBAJI (Korea).

Italian Senate Prize
PLUMBUM, OR A DANGEROUS GAME (USSR), Vadim Abdrashitov.

Special Mention
Miklos Jancso "for the coherence with which he carries on and renews his expressive research in a period of rapid evolution of film language."

FIPRESCI Prize
BURGLAR (USSR), Valeri Ogorodnikov.
ANAYURT OTELI (Turkey), Omer Kavur.
LUNGA VITA ALLA SIGNORA! (It.), Ermanno Olmi.

Italian Critics Prize
HOUSE OF GAMES (US), David Mamet.
DRAGON FOOD (Ger./Switz.), Jan Schutte.

Osella Prizes
Best Screenplay
David Mamet for HOUSE OF GAMES (US).
Best Music
Richard Robbins for MAURICE (Brit.).
Best Cinematography
Sten Holmberg for HIP, HIP, HURRAH (Swed./Nor./Den.).
Best Art Direction
Luciano Ricceri for GLI OCCHIALI D'ORO (It./Fr./Yugo.).
Best Costumes
Nana Cecchi for GLI OCCHIALI D'ORO (It./Fr./Yugo.).

40TH WRITERS GUILD OF AMERICA AWARDS

Best Screenplay Written Directly for the Screen
James L. Brooks for BROADCAST NEWS.
John Boorman for HOPE AND GLORY.
Mark Peploe, Bernardo Bertolucci, Enzo Ungari for THE LAST EMPEROR.
John Patrick Shanley for MOONSTRUCK.*
Woody Allen for RADIO DAYS.

Best Screenplay Adapted from Another Medium
James Dearden for FATAL ATTRACTION.
Stanley Kubrick, Michael Herr, Gustav Hasford for FULL METAL JACKET.
William Goldman for THE PRINCESS BRIDE.
Steve Martin for ROXANNE.*
David Mamet for THE UNTOUCHABLES.

Motion Picture Guide Master List

MOTION PICTURE GUIDE MASTER LIST

The following is an alphabetical listing of the titles of all the films in the ten movie entry volumes of the Motion Picture Guide (MPG) (1910–1984). Immediately following this list are listings of all the films which appear in the MPG 1986 Annual (the films of 1985) and the MPG 1987 Annual (the films of 1986).

The list includes the year of release of the film and the parental recommendation (AAA: must for children; AA: good for children; A: acceptable for children; C: cautionary; O: objectionable) for the film. Italics denote that the film is available on cassette.

Those films which do not include a year of release are cross references for films which appear in the volumes under another title. A "SEE:" notation appears with those titles in the MPG volumes to indicate the title under which the film has been reviewed. Those titles which have no PR rating are from the MPG miscellaneous lists. Miscellaneous talkies (1930–1984) are listed in Volume IX. Miscellaneous silents (1910–1929) are listed in Volume X.

-A-

A, 1976
A L'HORIZON DU SUD, 1924
A L'OMBRE DE VATICAN, 1922
A L'OMBRE DES TOMBEAUX, 1927
A LA GARE, 1925
A NOS AMOURS, 1984, O
A NOUS LA LIBERTE, 1931, A
A-HAUNTING WE WILL GO, 1942, AA
AARON LOVES ANGELA, 1975, O
AARON SLICK FROM PUNKIN CRICK, 1952, AA
ABABIAN KNIGHT, AN, 1920, A
ABANDON SHIP, 1957, C-O
ABANDONED, 1953, A
ABANDONMENT, THE, 1916
ABAR—THE FIRST BLACK SUPERMAN, 1977
ABBOTT AND COSTELLO IN HOLLYWOOD, 1945, AAA
ABBOTT AND COSTELLO IN THE FOREIGN LEGION, 1950, A
ABBOTT AND COSTELLO IN THE NAVY
ABBOTT AND COSTELLO LOST IN ALASKA
ABBOTT AND COSTELLO MEET CAPTAIN KIDD, 1952, A
ABBOTT AND COSTELLO MEET DR. JEKYLL AND MR. HYDE, 1954, A
ABBOTT AND COSTELLO MEET FRANKENSTEIN, 1948, A
ABBOTT AND COSTELLO MEET THE INVISIBLE MAN, 1955, A
ABBOTT AND COSTELLO MEET THE KILLER, BORIS KARLOFF, 1949, A
ABBOTT AND COSTELLO MEET THE MUMMY, 1955, A
ABBY, 1974, O
ABC OF LOVE, THE, 1919
ABDICATION, THE, 1974, C-O
ABDUCTION, 1975, O
ABDUCTORS, THE, 1957, A
ABDUCTORS, THE, 1972
ABDUL THE DAMNED, 1935, C
ABDULLAH'S HAREM, 1956, O
ABE LINCOLN IN ILLINOIS, 1940, AA
ABIE'S IMPORTED BRIDE, 1925, A
ABIE'S IRISH ROSE, 1928, A
ABIE'S IRISH ROSE, 1946, C
ABILENE TOWN, 1946, A
ABILENE TRAIL, 1951, A
ABLEMINDED LADY, THE, 1922, A
ABOMINABLE DR. PHIBES, THE, 1971, O
ABOMINABLE SNOWMAN OF THE HIMALAYAS, THE, 1957, A
ABORTION, 1924
ABOUT FACE, 1942, A
ABOUT FACE, 1952, A
ABOUT MRS. LESLIE, 1954, A
ABOUT TRIAL MARRIAGE
ABOVE ALL LAW
ABOVE AND BEYOND, 1953, A
ABOVE SUSPICION, 1943, A
ABOVE THE CLOUDS, 1934, A
ABOVE US THE WAVES, 1956, A
ABRAHAM LINCOLN, 1924, A
ABRAHAM LINCOLN, 1930, AAA
ABRAHAM OUR PATRIARCH, 1933
ABROAD WITH TWO YANKS, 1944, A
ABSENCE OF MALICE, 1981, O
ABSENT, 1928, A
ABSENT-MINDED PROFESSOR, THE, 1961, AAA
ABSENTEE-NRA, THE, 1915, A
ABSINTHE, 1914
ABSOLUTE QUIET, 1936, C
ABSOLUTION, 1981, O
ABSURD—ANTROPOPHAGOUS 2, 1982
ABUSED CONFIDENCE, 1938, C-O
ABYSMAL BRUTE, THE, 1923, A
ACAPULCO GOLD, 1978, O
ACCATTONE!, 1961, O
ACCENT ON LOVE, 1941, A
ACCENT ON YOUTH, 1935, A
ACCEPTABLE LEVELS, 1983, C
ACCESS CODE, 1984
ACCESSION TO THE THRONE, 1913
ACCIDENT, 1967, O
ACCIDENT, 1983
ACCIDENTAL DEATH, 1963, C
ACCIDENTAL HONEYMOON, THE, 1918
ACCIDENTS WILL HAPPEN, 1938, A
ACCOMPLICE, 1946, A
ACCOMPLICE, THE, 1917
ACCORDING TO HOYLE, 1922, A
ACCORDING TO LAW, 1916, C
ACCORDING TO MRS. HOYLE, 1951, A
ACCORDING TO THE CODE, 1916, A
ACCOUNT RENDERED, 1957, A
ACCURSED, THE, 1958, A
ACCUSED
ACCUSED, 1925
ACCUSED, 1936, A
ACCUSED OF MURDER, 1956, A
ACCUSED, THE, 1949, C
ACCUSED, THE, 1953
ACCUSED—STAND UP, 1930, A
ACCUSING FINGER, THE, 1936, A
ACE ELI AND RODGER OF THE SKIES, 1973, A
ACE HIGH, 1918
ACE HIGH, 1969, O
ACE IN THE HOLE
ACE OF ACES, 1933, C
ACE OF ACES, 1982, O
ACE OF ACTION, 1926, A
ACE OF CACTUS RANGE, 1924
ACE OF CADS, THE, 1926, A
ACE OF CLUBS, THE, 1926
ACE OF HEARTS, THE, 1916, C
ACE OF HEARTS, THE, A
ACE OF SPADES, THE, 1935, A
ACE OF THE LAW, A
ACE OF THE SADDLE, 1919
ACE, THE
ACES AND EIGHTS, 1936, A
ACES HIGH, 1977, C
ACES WILD, 1937, A
ACID EATERS, THE, 1968
ACQUITTAL, THE, 1923, A
ACQUITTED, 1929, C
ACQUITTED, A
ACROSS 110TH STREET, 1972, O
ACROSS THE ATLANTIC, 1928
ACROSS THE BADLANDS, 1950, A
ACROSS THE BORDER, 1922
ACROSS THE BRIDGE, 1957, C
ACROSS THE CONTINENT, 1913
ACROSS THE CONTINENT, 1922, A
ACROSS THE DEAD-LINE, 1922, A
ACROSS THE DEADLINE, 1925, AA
ACROSS THE DEADLINE, 1976, AAA
ACROSS THE DIVIDE, 1921
ACROSS THE GREAT DIVIDE, 1921
ACROSS THE GREAT DIVIDE, 1976, AAA
ACROSS THE PACIFIC, 1914
ACROSS THE PACIFIC, 1926, A
ACROSS THE PACIFIC, 1942, A
ACROSS THE PLAINS, 1928
ACROSS THE PLAINS, 1939, A
ACROSS THE RIO GRANDE, 1949, A
ACROSS THE RIVER, 1965, C
ACROSS THE SIERRAS, 1941, A
ACROSS THE SINGAPORE, 1928, A
ACROSS THE WIDE MISSOURI, 1951, A
ACT OF LOVE, 1953, C
ACT OF MURDER, 1965, C
ACT OF MURDER, AN, 1948, C
ACT OF REPRISAL, 1965
ACT OF THE HEART, 1970, O
ACT OF VENGEANCE, 1974, O
ACT OF VIOLENCE, 1949, C
ACT ONE, 1964, A
ACT, THE, 1984, O
ACTION, 1921
ACTION CRAVER, THE, 1927, A
ACTION FOR SLANDER, 1937, A
ACTION GALORE, 1925, A
ACTION IN ARABIA, 1944, A
ACTION IN THE NORTH ATLANTIC, 1943, A
ACTION OF THE TIGER, 1957, A
ACTION STATIONS, 1959, A-C
ACTOR'S REVENGE, AN, 1963, O
ACTORS AND SIN, 1952, C
ACTRESS, THE, 1928, A
ACTRESS, THE, 1953, A
ADA, 1961, C
ADALEN 31, 1969, C
ADAM AND EVA, 1923, A
ADAM AND EVE, 1958, O
ADAM AND EVELYNE, 1950, A
ADAM AND EVIL, 1927, A
ADAM AT 6 A.M., 1970, O
ADAM BEDE, C
ADAM HAD FOUR SONS, 1941, A
ADAM'S RIB, 1923, A
ADAM'S RIB, 1949, A
ADAM'S WOMAN, 1972, C
ADDING MACHINE, THE, 1969, C
ADDRESS UNKNOWN, 1944, A
ADELE, 1919, A
ADELE HASN'T HAD HER SUPPER YET, 1978, C
ADERYN PAPUR, 1984, A-C
ADIEU PHILLIPINE, 1962, C
ADIOS AMIGO, 1975, C
ADIOS GRINGO, 1967, A
ADIOS SABATA, 1971, A
ADMIRABLE CRICHTON, THE, 1918, A
ADMIRABLE CRICHTON, THE, 1957, A
ADMIRAL NAKHIMOV, 1948, C
ADMIRAL WAS A LADY, THE, 1950, A
ADMIRAL'S SECRET, THE, 1934, A
ADMIRALS ALL, 1935, A
ADOLESCENT, THE, 1978, C
ADOLESCENTS, THE, 1967, C
ADOLF HITLER—MY PART IN HIS DOWNFALL, 1973, A
ADOPTED SON, THE, 1917, A
ADOPTION, THE, 1978, O
ADORABLE, 1933, A
ADORABLE CHEAT, THE, 1928, A
ADORABLE CREATURES, 1956, O
ADORABLE DECEIVER, THE, 1926, A
ADORABLE JULIA, 1964, C
ADORABLE LIAR, 1962, C
ADORABLE SAVAGE, THE, 1920
ADORATION, 1928, A
ADRIFT, 1971, O
ADULTERESS, THE, 1959, O
ADULTERESS, THE, 1976
ADULTEROUS AFFAIR, 1966, A
ADVANCE TO THE REAR, 1964, A
ADVENTURE, 1925, A
ADVENTURE, 1945, A
ADVENTURE FOR TWO, 1945, A
ADVENTURE GIRL, 1934
ADVENTURE IN BALTIMORE, 1949, AAA
ADVENTURE IN BLACKMAIL, 1943, A
ADVENTURE IN DIAMONDS, 1940, A
ADVENTURE IN HEARTS, AN, 1919, A

ADVENTURE IN MANHATTAN, 1936, A
ADVENTURE IN MUSIC, 1944
ADVENTURE IN ODESSA, 1954, C
ADVENTURE IN SAHARA, 1938, A
ADVENTURE IN THE HOPFIELDS, 1954, AA
ADVENTURE IN WASHINGTON, 1941, C
ADVENTURE ISLAND, 1947, A
ADVENTURE LIMITED, 1934, A
ADVENTURE MAD, 1928
ADVENTURE OF SALVATOR ROSA, AN, 1940, A
ADVENTURE OF SHERLOCK HOLMES' SMARTER BROTHER, THE, 1975, AA
ADVENTURE SHOP, THE, 1918, A
ADVENTURE'S END, 1937, A
ADVENTURER, THE
ADVENTURER, THE, 1917
ADVENTURER, THE, 1920
ADVENTURER, THE, 1928, A
ADVENTURERS, THE, 1951, C
ADVENTURERS, THE, 1970, O
ADVENTURES AT RUGBY
ADVENTURES IN IRAQ, 1943, A
ADVENTURES IN SILVERADO, 1948, A
ADVENTURES OF A BOY SCOUT, THE, 1915
ADVENTURES OF A MADCAP, 1915
ADVENTURES OF A ROOKIE, 1943, A
ADVENTURES OF A YOUNG MAN, 1962, A
ADVENTURES OF AN OCTOBERITE, THE, 1924
ADVENTURES OF ARSENE LUPIN, 1956, A
ADVENTURES OF BARRY McKENZIE, 1972, C-O
ADVENTURES OF BUCKAROO BANZAI: ACROSS THE 8TH DIMENSION, THE, 1984, C-O
ADVENTURES OF BUFFALO BILL, 1917
ADVENTURES OF BULLWHIP GRIFFIN, THE, 1967, AAA
ADVENTURES OF CAPTAIN FABIAN, 1951, A
ADVENTURES OF CAPTAIN KETTLE, THE, 1922, A
ADVENTURES OF CAROL, THE, 1917, AA
ADVENTURES OF CASANOVA, 1948, A
ADVENTURES OF CHICO, THE, 1938
ADVENTURES OF DON COYOTE, 1947, A
ADVENTURES OF DON JUAN, 1949, A
ADVENTURES OF FRONTIER FREMONT, THE, 1976, AAA
ADVENTURES OF GALLANT BESS, 1948, AAA
ADVENTURES OF GERARD, THE, 1970, A
ADVENTURES OF HAJJI BABA, 1954, C
ADVENTURES OF HAL 5, THE, 1958, A
ADVENTURES OF HUCKLEBERRY FINN
ADVENTURES OF HUCKLEBERRY FINN, THE, 1960, AAA
ADVENTURES OF ICHABOD AND MR. TOAD, 1949, AAA
ADVENTURES OF JACK LONDON
ADVENTURES OF JANE ARDEN, 1939, A
ADVENTURES OF JANE, THE, 1949, A
ADVENTURES OF KITTY COBB, THE, 1914, A
ADVENTURES OF KITTY O'DAY, 1944, A
ADVENTURES OF LUCKY PIERRE, THE, 1961
ADVENTURES OF MARCO POLO, THE, 1938, A
ADVENTURES OF MARK TWAIN, THE, 1944, AAA
ADVENTURES OF MARTIN EDEN, THE, 1942, A
ADVENTURES OF MICHAEL STROGOFF
ADVENTURES OF MR. PICKWICK, THE, 1921, A
ADVENTURES OF PC 49, THE, 1949, A
ADVENTURES OF PICASSO, THE, 1980, O
ADVENTURES OF PINOCCHIO. THE, 1978
ADVENTURES OF PRINCE ACHMED, THE, 1926
ADVENTURES OF QUENTIN DURWARD, THE
ADVENTURES OF ROBIN HOOD, THE, 1938, AAA
ADVENTURES OF ROBINSON CRUSOE, THE, 1954, AA
ADVENTURES OF RUSTY, 1945, A
ADVENTURES OF SADIE, THE, 1955, A
ADVENTURES OF SCARAMOUCHE, THE, 1964, C
ADVENTURES OF SHERLOCK HOLMES, THE, 1939, A
ADVENTURES OF STAR BIRD, 1978
ADVENTURES OF TARTU, 1943, A
ADVENTURES OF THE MASKED PHANTOM, THE, 1939
ADVENTURES OF THE WILDERNESS FAMILY, THE, 1975, AAA
ADVENTURES OF TOM SAWYER, THE, 1938, AAA
ADVENTURES OF YOUNG ROBIN HOOD, 1983
ADVENTURESS, THE, 1946, A
ADVENTUROUS BLONDE, 1937, A
ADVENTUROUS KNIGHTS, 1935
ADVENTUROUS SEX, THE, 1925, A
ADVENTUROUS SOUL, THE, 1927, A
ADVENTUROUS YOUTH, 1928, A
ADVERSARY, THE, 1970
ADVERSARY, THE, 1973, A
ADVICE TO THE LOVELORN, 1933, A
ADVISE AND CONSENT, 1962, C
AELITA, 1929
AERIAL GUNNER, 1943, A
AERODROME, THE, 1983
AFFAIR AT AKITSU, 1980, O
AFFAIR BLUM, THE, 1949, C
AFFAIR IN HAVANA, 1957, O
AFFAIR IN MONTE CARLO, 1953, A
AFFAIR IN RENO, 1957, A
AFFAIR IN TRINIDAD, 1952, C
AFFAIR LAFONT, THE, 1939, O
AFFAIR OF SUSAN, 1935, A
AFFAIR OF THE FOLLIES, AN, 1927, A
AFFAIR OF THE SKIN, AN, 1964, O
AFFAIR OF THREE NATIONS, AN, 1915
AFFAIR TO REMEMBER, AN, 1957, A
AFFAIR WITH A STRANGER, 1953, A
AFFAIRS IN VERSAILLES
AFFAIRS OF A GENTLEMAN, 1934, A
AFFAIRS OF A MODEL, 1952, O
AFFAIRS OF A ROGUE, THE, 1949, A
AFFAIRS OF ADELAIDE, 1949, C
AFFAIRS OF ANATOL, THE, 1921, C
AFFAIRS OF ANNABEL, 1938, A
AFFAIRS OF CAPPY RICKS, 1937, A
AFFAIRS OF CELLINI, THE, 1934, C
AFFAIRS OF DOBIE GILLIS, THE, 1953, A
AFFAIRS OF DR. HOLL, 1954, A
AFFAIRS OF GERALDINE, 1946, A
AFFAIRS OF JIMMY VALENTINE
AFFAIRS OF JULIE, THE, 1958, C
AFFAIRS OF MARTHA, THE, 1942, A
AFFAIRS OF MAUPASSANT, 1938, A
AFFAIRS OF MESSALINA, THE, 1954, O
AFFAIRS OF ROBIN HOOD, THE, 1981
AFFAIRS OF SUSAN, 1945, A
AFFECTIONATELY YOURS, 1941, A
AFFINITIES, 1922
AFGANISTAN, 1929
AFLAME IN THE SKY, 1927, A
AFRAID OF LOVE, 1925, C
AFRAID TO FIGHT, 1922, A
AFRAID TO LOVE, 1927, A
AFRAID TO TALK, 1932, C
AFRICA SCREAMS, 1949, AA
AFRICA—TEXAS STYLE!, 1967, AA
AFRICAN FURY
AFRICAN INCIDENT, 1934
AFRICAN MANHUNT, 1955, A
AFRICAN QUEEN, THE, 1951, AA
AFRICAN TREASURE, 1952, A
AFRICAN, THE, 1983, C
AFTER A MILLION, 1924, A
AFTER BUSINESS HOURS, 1925, A
AFTER DARK, 1915
AFTER DARK, 1915
AFTER DARK, 1923
AFTER DARK, 1924, AA
AFTER FIVE, 1915, A
AFTER HIS OWN HEART, 1919
AFTER MANY DAYS, 1919, C
AFTER MANY YEARS, 1930, A
AFTER MARRIAGE, 1925, A
AFTER MIDNIGHT, 1921, A
AFTER MIDNIGHT, 1927, A
AFTER MIDNIGHT WITH BOSTON BLACKIE, 1943, A
AFTER OFFICE HOURS, 1932, A
AFTER OFFICE HOURS, 1935, A
AFTER SIX DAYS, 1922
AFTER THE BALL, 1914
AFTER THE BALL, 1924, A
AFTER THE BALL, 1932, C
AFTER THE BALL, 1957, A
AFTER THE DANCE, 1935, A
AFTER THE FALL OF NEW YORK, 1984, O
AFTER THE FOG, 1930, C
AFTER THE FOX, 1966, A
AFTER THE REHEARSAL, 1984, C-O
AFTER THE SHOW, 1921, A
AFTER THE STORM, 1928, A
AFTER THE THIN MAN, 1936, A
AFTER THE VERDICT, 1929, A
AFTER THE WAR, 1918
AFTER TOMORROW, 1932, A
AFTER TONIGHT, 1933, A
AFTER YOU, COMRADE, 1967, A
AFTER YOUR OWN HEART, 1921
AFTERGLOW, 1923
AFTERMATH, 1914
AFTERMATH, THE, 1980
AFTERWARDS, 1928, A
AGAINST A CROOKED SKY, 1975, C
AGAINST ALL FLAGS, 1952, A
AGAINST ALL ODDS, 1924, A
AGAINST ALL ODDS, 1984, C-O
AGAINST THE LAW, 1934, C
AGAINST THE TIDE, 1937, A
AGAINST THE WIND, 1948, A
AGATHA, 1979, C
AGATHA CHRISTIE'S ENDLESS NIGHT
AGE FOR LOVE, THE, 1931, A
AGE OF CONSENT, 1932, C
AGE OF CONSENT, 1969, O
AGE OF DESIRE, THE, 1923
AGE OF ILLUSIONS, 1967, O
AGE OF INDISCRETION, 1935, C
AGE OF INFIDELITY, 1958, O
AGE OF INNOCENCE, 1934, C
AGE OF INNOCENCE, 1977, A
AGE OF INNOCENCE, THE, 1924
AGE OF PISCES, 1972
AGE OF THE MEDICI, THE, 1979, C
AGENCY, 1981, O
AGENT 8 3/4, 1963, C
AGENT FOR H.A.R.M., 1966, C
AGGIE APPLEBY, MAKER OF MEN, 1933, A
AGITATOR, THE, 1949, A
AGONY AND THE ECSTASY, THE, 1965, A
AGOSTINO, 1962, C
AGUIRRE, THE WRATH OF GOD, 1977, O
AH YING, 1984, A
AH, WILDERNESS!, 1935, AAA
AHEAD OF THE LAW, 1926, A
AIDA, 1954, A
AIMEZ-VOUS BRAHMS
AIN EL GHEZAL
AIN'T LOVE FUNNY?, 1927, A
AIN'T MISBEHAVIN', 1955, A
AIR CADET, 1951, A
AIR CIRCUS, THE, 1928, A
AIR DEVILS, 1938, A
AIR EAGLES, 1932, C
AIR FORCE, 1943, A
AIR HAWK, THE, 1924, A
AIR HAWKS, 1935, A
AIR HOSTESS, 1933, A
AIR HOSTESS, 1949, A
AIR LEGION, THE, 1929, A
AIR MAIL, 1932, A
AIR MAIL PILOT, THE, 1928, A
AIR MAIL, THE, 1925, A
AIR PATROL, 1962, C
AIR PATROL, THE, 1928, A
AIR POLICE, 1931, A
AIR RAID WARDENS, 1943, AAA
AIR STRIKE, 1955, A
AIRBORNE, 1962, A
AIRPLANE II: THE SEQUEL, 1982, C
AIRPLANE!, 1980, C
AIRPORT, 1970, A
AIRPORT '77, 1977, C
AIRPORT '79
AIRPORT 1975, 1974, C
AL CAPONE, 1959, C-O
AL CHRISTIE'S "MADAME BEHAVE"
AL JENNINGS OF OKLAHOMA, 1951, A
ALABAMA'S GHOST, 1972
ALABASTER BOX, AN, 1917
ALADDIN AND HIS LAMP, 1952, AA
ALADDIN AND THE WONDERFUL LAMP, 1917
ALADDIN FROM BROADWAY, 1917, A
ALADDIN'S OTHER LAMP, 1917, AA
ALAKAZAM THE GREAT!, 1961, AAA
ALAMBRISTA!, 1977, C
ALAMO, THE, 1960, AA
ALARM CLOCK ANDY, 1920, A
ALARM ON 83RD STREET, 1965
ALARM, THE, 1917
ALASKA, 1944, A
ALASKA HIGHWAY, 1943, A
ALASKA PASSAGE, 1959, A
ALASKA PATROL, 1949, A
ALASKA SEAS, 1954, A
ALASKAN, THE, A
ALBANY NIGHT BOAT, THE, 1928, A
ALBERT, R.N., 1953, A
ALBINO, 1980
ALBUQUERQUE, 1948, A
ALCATRAZ ISLAND, 1937, A
ALCHEMIST, THE, 1981
ALERT IN THE SOUTH, 1954, A
ALEX AND THE GYPSY, 1976, C
ALEX IN WONDERLAND, 1970, C
ALEX JOSEPH & HIS WIVES, 1978
ALEX THE GREAT, 1928, A
ALEXANDER GRAHAM BELL
ALEXANDER HAMILTON, 1931, A
ALEXANDER NEVSKY, 1939, C
ALEXANDER THE GREAT, 1956, A
ALEXANDER'S RAGTIME BAND, 1938, AAA
ALF GARNETT SAGA, THE, 1972
ALF 'N' FAMILY, 1968, C
ALF'S BABY, 1953, A
ALF'S BUTTON, 1920, A
ALF'S BUTTON, 1930, AA
ALF'S BUTTON AFLOAT, 1938, A
ALF'S CARPET, 1929, A
ALFIE, 1966, O
ALFIE DARLING, 1975, O
ALFRED THE GREAT, 1969, C
ALFREDO, ALFREDO, 1973, O
ALGIERS, 1938, C
ALGOL, 1920
ALI BABA, 1954, A
ALI BABA AND THE FORTY THIEVES, 1918, A

ALI BABA AND THE FORTY THIEVES, 1944, AAA
ALI BABA GOES TO TOWN, 1937, AAA
ALI BABA NIGHTS, 1953
ALIAS A GENTLEMAN, 1948, A
ALIAS BIG SHOT, 1962, C
ALIAS BILLY THE KID, 1946, AA
ALIAS BOSTON BLACKIE, 1942, A
ALIAS BULLDOG DRUMMOND, 1935, A
ALIAS FRENCH GERTIE, 1930, A
ALIAS JESSE JAMES, 1959, A
ALIAS JIMMY VALENTINE, 1915
ALIAS JIMMY VALENTINE, 1920, A
ALIAS JIMMY VALENTINE, 1928, A
ALIAS JOHN LAW, 1935, A
ALIAS JOHN PRESTON, 1956, A
ALIAS JULIUS CAESAR, 1922, A
ALIAS LADYFINGERS
ALIAS MARY BROWN, 1918, A
ALIAS MARY DOW, 1935, A
ALIAS MARY FLYNN, 1925
ALIAS MARY SMITH, 1932, A
ALIAS MIKE MORAN, 1919, A
ALIAS MISS DODD, 1920
ALIAS MR. TWILIGHT, 1946
ALIAS MRS. JESSOP, 1917, A
ALIAS NICK BEAL, 1949, A
ALIAS PHIL KENNEDY, 1922
ALIAS THE BAD MAN, 1931, A
ALIAS THE CHAMP, 1949, A
ALIAS THE DEACON, 1928, A
ALIAS THE DEACON, 1940, A
ALIAS THE DOCTOR, 1932, A
ALIAS THE LONE WOLF, 1927, A
ALIAS THE NIGHT WIND, 1923, A
ALIBI, 1929, C
ALIBI, 1931, A
ALIBI FOR MURDER, 1936, A
ALIBI IKE, 1935, AA
ALIBI INN, 1935, A
ALIBI, THE, 1916
ALIBI, THE, 1939, C
ALIBI, THE, 1943, C
ALICE ADAMS, 1923, A
ALICE ADAMS, 1935, A
ALICE DOESN'T LIVE HERE ANYMORE, 1975, O
ALICE GOODBODY, 1974
ALICE IN THE CITIES, 1974, A
ALICE IN WONDERLAND, 1916
ALICE IN WONDERLAND, 1931
ALICE IN WONDERLAND, 1933, AAA
ALICE IN WONDERLAND, 1951, AAA
ALICE IN WONDERLAND, 1951, A
ALICE OF WONDERLAND IN PARIS, 1966
ALICE THROUGH A LOOKING GLASS, 1928
ALICE'S ADVENTURES IN WONDERLAND, 1972, A
ALICE'S RESTAURANT, 1969, O
ALICE, OR THE LAST ESCAPADE, 1977, C
ALICE, SWEET ALICE, 1978, O
ALICIA OF THE ORPHANS
ALIEN, 1979, O
ALIEN BLOOD, 1917
ALIEN CONTAMINATION, 1981
ALIEN ENCOUNTER, 1979
ALIEN ENEMY, AN, 1918, C
ALIEN FACTOR, THE, 1978
ALIEN FACTOR, THE, 1984, C
ALIEN SOULS, 1916, A
ALIEN THUNDER, 1975, C
ALIEN ZONE, 1978
ALIEN'S RETURN, THE, 1980
ALIEN, THE, 1915, A
ALIENS
ALIENS FROM ANOTHER PLANET, 1967
ALIENS FROM SPACESHIP EARTH, 1977
ALIKI—MY LOVE, 1963
ALIMONY, 1924, A
ALIMONY, 1949, C
ALIMONY MADNESS, 1933, C
ALISON'S BIRTHDAY, 1979
ALIVE AND KICKING, 1962, AA
ALIVE ON SATURDAY, 1957, A
ALL ABOARD, 1927, A
ALL ABOUT EVE, 1950, A
ALL AMERICAN, THE
ALL AROUND FRYING PAN, 1925
ALL ASHORE, 1953, AA
ALL AT SEA, 1929
ALL AT SEA, 1935, A
ALL AT SEA, 1939, A
ALL AT SEA, 1958, A
ALL AT SEA, 1970, A
ALL BY MYSELF, 1943, A
ALL COPPERS ARE..., 1972
ALL CREATURES GREAT AND SMALL, 1975, AAA
ALL DOLLED UP, 1921, A
ALL FALL DOWN, 1962
ALL FOR A GIRL, 1915, A
ALL FOR A HUSBAND, 1917
ALL FOR A WOMAN, 1921
ALL FOR MARY, 1956, A
ALL HALLOWE'EN, 1952
ALL HANDS ON DECK, 1961, A
ALL I DESIRE, 1953, A
ALL IN, 1936, A
ALL IN A NIGHT'S WORK, 1961, C
ALL MAN, 1916, A
ALL MAN, 1918, A
ALL MEN ARE APES, 1965
ALL MEN ARE ENEMIES, 1934, A
ALL MEN ARE LIARS, 1919, A
ALL MINE TO GIVE, 1957, AA
ALL MY SONS, 1948, C
ALL NEAT IN BLACK STOCKINGS, 1969, C
ALL NIGHT, 1918, A
ALL NIGHT LONG, 1961, C
ALL NIGHT LONG, 1981, C
ALL NUDITY SHALL BE PUNISHED, 1974, O
ALL OF A SUDDEN NORMA, 1919, A
ALL OF A SUDDEN PEGGY, 1920
ALL OF ME, 1934, C
ALL OF ME, 1984, A-C
ALL OVER THE TOWN, 1949, AA
ALL OVER TOWN, 1937, A
ALL QUIET ON THE WESTERN FRONT, 1930, C
ALL RIGHT, MY FRIEND, 1983, A
ALL ROADS LEAD TO CALVARY, 1921, C
ALL SCREWED UP, 1976, O
ALL SORTS AND CONDITIONS OF MEN, 1921, A
ALL SOULS EVE, 1921, A
ALL THAT GLITTERS, 1936, A
ALL THAT HEAVEN ALLOWS, 1955, A
ALL THAT I HAVE, 1951
ALL THAT JAZZ, 1979, O
ALL THAT MONEY CAN BUY
ALL THE BROTHERS WERE VALIANT, 1923, A
ALL THE BROTHERS WERE VALIANT, 1953, A
ALL THE FINE YOUNG CANNIBALS, 1960, C
ALL THE KING'S HORSES, 1935, A
ALL THE KING'S MEN, 1949, C
...ALL THE MARBLES, 1981, C
ALL THE OTHER GIRLS DO!, 1967, C
ALL THE PRESIDENT'S MEN, 1976, C
ALL THE RIGHT MOVES, 1983, C
ALL THE RIGHT NOISES, 1973, O
ALL THE SAD WORLD NEEDS, 1918, A
ALL THE WAY HOME, 1963, A
ALL THE WAY UP, 1970, A
ALL THE WAY, BOYS, 1973, C
ALL THE WINNERS, 1920, A
ALL THE WORLD TO NOTHING, 1919, A
ALL THE WORLD'S A STAGE, 1917, C
ALL THE YOUNG MEN, 1960, A
ALL THE YOUNG WIVES, 1975
ALL THESE WOMEN, 1964, O
ALL THINGS BRIGHT AND BEAUTIFUL, 1979, AAA
ALL THIS AND HEAVEN TOO, 1940, A
ALL THROUGH THE NIGHT, 1942, A
ALL WOMAN, 1918, A
ALL WOMAN, 1967, O
ALL WOMEN HAVE SECRETS, 1939, A
ALL WRONG, 1919, A
ALL'S FAIR IN LOVE, 1921, A
ALL-AMERICAN BOY, THE, 1973, 0
ALL-AMERICAN CHUMP, 1936, A
ALL-AMERICAN CO-ED, 1941, A
ALL-AMERICAN SWEETHEART, 1937, A
ALL-AMERICAN, THE, 1932, A
ALL-AMERICAN, THE, 1953, A
ALL-AROUND REDUCED PERSONALITY—OUTTAKES, THE, 1978, A
ALLEGHENY UPRISING, 1939, A
ALLEGRO NON TROPPO, 1977, A
ALLERGIC TO LOVE, 1943, A
ALLEY CAT, 1984, O
ALLEY CAT, THE, 1929, A
ALLEY OF GOLDEN HEARTS, THE, 1924, A
ALLIES
ALLIGATOR, 1980, O
ALLIGATOR NAMED DAISY, AN, 1957, A
ALLIGATOR PEOPLE, THE, 1959, C
ALLOTMENT WIVES, INC., 1945, A
ALLURING GOAL, THE, 1930, A
ALMA, WHERE DO YOU LIVE?, 1917
ALMIGHTY DOLLAR, THE, 1916
ALMOST A BRIDE
ALMOST A DIVORCE, 1931, A
ALMOST A GENTLEMAN, 1938
ALMOST A GENTLEMAN, 1939, A
ALMOST A HONEYMOON, 1930, A
ALMOST A HONEYMOON, 1938, A
ALMOST A HUSBAND, 1919, A
ALMOST A LADY, 1926, A
ALMOST ANGELS, 1962, AAA
ALMOST HUMAN, 1927
ALMOST HUMAN, 1974, O
ALMOST MARRIED, 1919, A
ALMOST MARRIED, 1932, C
ALMOST MARRIED, 1942, A
ALMOST PERFECT AFFAIR, AN, 1979, C
ALMOST SUMMER, 1978, A
ALMOST TRANSPARENT BLUE, 1980, O
ALMOST YOU, 1984, C
ALOHA, 1931, A
ALOHA OE, 1915
ALOHA, BOBBY AND ROSE, 1975, C
ALOMA OF THE SOUTH SEAS, 1926, A
ALOMA OF THE SOUTH SEAS, 1941, A
ALONE AGAINST ROME, 1963, C
ALONE IN LONDON, 1915, A
ALONE IN NEW YORK, 1914
ALONE IN THE DARK, 1982, O
ALONE IN THE STREETS, 1956, C
ALONE ON THE PACIFIC, 1964, AAA
ALONG CAME JONES, 1945, A
ALONG CAME LOVE, 1937, A
ALONG CAME RUTH, 1924, A
ALONG CAME SALLY, 1933
ALONG CAME SALLY, 1934, A
ALONG CAME YOUTH, 1931, A
ALONG THE GREAT DIVIDE, 1951, C
ALONG THE NAVAJO TRAIL, 1945, A
ALONG THE OREGON TRAIL, 1947, A
ALONG THE RIO GRANDE, 1941, A
ALONG THE SUNDOWN TRAIL, 1942
ALPHA BETA, 1973, C
ALPHA INCIDENT, THE, 1976
ALPHABET CITY, 1984, O
ALPHABET MURDERS, THE, 1966, A
ALPHAVILLE, A STRANGE CASE OF LEMMY CAUTION, 1965, A
ALRAUNE, 1952, O
ALSACE, 1916
ALSINO AND THE CONDOR, 1983, C
ALSTER CASE, THE, 1915, A
ALTAR CHAINS, 1916, C
ALTAR STAIRS, THE, 1922, A
ALTARS OF DESIRE, 1927, A
ALTEMER LE CYNIQUE, 1924
ALTERED STATES, 1980, O
ALTERNATIVE, 1976
ALTERNATIVE MISS WORLD, THE, 1980
ALVAREZ KELLY, 1966, A
ALVIN PURPLE, 1974, C
ALVIN RIDES AGAIN, 1974, O
ALWAYS A BRIDE, 1940, A
ALWAYS A BRIDE, 1954, A
ALWAYS A BRIDESMAID, 1943, A
ALWAYS ANOTHER DAWN, 1948, A
ALWAYS AUDACIOUS, 1920, A
ALWAYS GOODBYE, 193A
ALWAYS GOODBYE, 193A
ALWAYS IN MY HEART, 194A, A
ALWAYS IN THE WAY, 1915
ALWAYS IN TROUBLE, 1938, AA
ALWAYS LEAVE THEM LAUGHING, 1949, A
ALWAYS RIDIN' TO WIN, 1925
ALWAYS THE WOMAN, 1922, A
ALWAYS TOGETHER, 1947, A
ALWAYS VICTORIOUS, 1960, A
AM I GUILTY?, A
AMADEUS, 1984, C
AMANITA PESTILENS, 1963
AMANTI
AMARCORD, 1974, O
AMARILLY OF CLOTHESLINE ALLEY, 1918, A
AMATEUR ADVENTURESS, THE, 1919, A
AMATEUR CROOK, 1937, A
AMATEUR DADDY, 193A
AMATEUR DEVIL, AN, 1921, A
AMATEUR GENTLEMAN, 1936, A
AMATEUR GENTLEMAN, THE, 1920, A
AMATEUR GENTLEMAN, THE, 1926, A
AMATEUR ORPHAN, AN, 1917
AMATEUR WIDOW, AN, 1919, A
AMATEUR WIFE, THE, 1920, A
AMATEUR, THE, 1982, C
AMAZING ADVENTURE, THE
AMAZING COLOSSAL MAN, THE, 195A
AMAZING DOBERMANS, THE, 1976, AAA
AMAZING DR. CLITTERHOUSE, THE, 1938, C
AMAZING GRACE, 1974, A
AMAZING IMPOSTER, THE, 1919, A
AMAZING LOVE SECRET, 1975
AMAZING LOVERS, 1921, A
AMAZING MONSIEUR FABRE, THE, 1952, A
AMAZING MR. BEECHAM, THE, 1949, A
AMAZING MR. BLUNDEN, THE, 197C
AMAZING MR. FORREST, THE, 194A
AMAZING MR. WILLIAMS, 1939, A
AMAZING MR. X, THE
AMAZING MRS. HOLLIDAY, 1943, AAA
AMAZING PARTNERSHIP, THE, 1921, A
AMAZING QUEST OF ERNEST BLISS, THE
AMAZING TRANSPARENT MAN, THE, 1960, C
AMAZING TRANSPLANT, THE, 1970
AMAZING VAGABOND, 1929, A
AMAZING WIFE, THE, A

AMAZON QUEST, 1949, A
AMAZONS, THE, 1917, A
AMBASSADOR BILL, 1933, A
AMBASSADOR'S DAUGHTER, THE, 1956, A
AMBASSADOR, THE, 1984
AMBITION, 1916, A
AMBUSH, 1939, A
AMBUSH, 1950, A
AMBUSH AT CIMARRON PASS, 1958, A
AMBUSH AT TOMAHAWK GAP, 1953, C
AMBUSH BAY, 1966, C
AMBUSH IN LEOPARD STREET, 196C
AMBUSH TRAIL, 1946, A
AMBUSH VALLEY, 1936, A
AMBUSHED, 1926
AMBUSHERS, THE, 1967, A
AME D'ARTISTE, 1925
AMELIE OR THE TIME TO LOVE, 1961, A
AMERICA, 1924, A
AMERICA—THAT'S ALL, 1917
AMERICA, AMERICA, 1963, A
AMERICAN ARISTOCRACY, 1916, A
AMERICAN BEAUTY, 1927, A
AMERICAN BEAUTY, THE, 1916
AMERICAN BUDS, 1918, AA
AMERICAN CITIZEN, AN, 1914
AMERICAN CONSUL, THE, 1917, A
AMERICAN DREAM, AN, 1966, O
AMERICAN DREAMER, 1984, A-C
AMERICAN EMPIRE, 1942, A
AMERICAN FRIEND, THE, 1977
AMERICAN GAME, THE, 1979
AMERICAN GENTLEMAN, AN, 1915
AMERICAN GIGOLO, 1980, O
AMERICAN GRAFFITI, 1973, C
AMERICAN GUERRILLA IN THE PHILIPPINES, AN, 1950, A
AMERICAN HOT WAX, 1978, A
AMERICAN IN PARIS, AN, 1951, AAA
AMERICAN LIVE WIRE, AN, 1918, A
AMERICAN LOVE, 1932, A
AMERICAN MADNESS, 1932, A
AMERICAN MAID, 1917, A
AMERICAN MANNERS, 1924, A
AMERICAN MATCHMAKER, 1940
AMERICAN METHODS, 1917, A
AMERICAN NIGHTMARE, 1984, O
AMERICAN NIGHTMARE, 1981
AMERICAN PLUCK, 1925
AMERICAN POP, 1981, O
AMERICAN PRISONER, THE, 1929, A
AMERICAN RASPBERRY, 1980
AMERICAN ROMANCE, AN, 1944, A
AMERICAN SOLDIER, THE, 1970, C
AMERICAN SUCCESS COMPANY, THE, 1980, C
AMERICAN TABOO, 1984, O
AMERICAN TRAGEDY, AN, 1931, C
AMERICAN VENUS, THE, 1926, A
AMERICAN WAY, THE, 1919, A
AMERICAN WEREWOLF IN LONDON, AN, 1981, O
AMERICAN WIDOW, AN, 1917, A
AMERICAN WIFE, AN, 1965, O
AMERICANA, 1981, C
AMERICANIZATION OF EMILY, THE, 1964, C
AMERICANO, THE, 1917, A
AMERICANO, THE, 1955, A
AMERICATHON, 1979, C
AMES D'ENFANTS, 1929
AMES D'ORIENT, 1919
AMIN—THE RISE AND FALL, 1982, O
AMITYVILLE 3-D, 1983, O
AMITYVILLE HORROR, THE, 1979, O
AMITYVILLE II: THE POSSESSION, 1982, O
AMONG HUMAN WOLVES, 1940, A
AMONG THE LIVING, 1941, C
AMONG THE MISSING, 1934, A
AMONG THE RUINS, 1923
AMONG VULTURES, 1964, A
AMOROUS ADVENTURES OF DON QUIXOTE AND SANCHO PANZA, THE, 1976
AMOROUS ADVENTURES OF MOLL FLANDERS, THE, 1965, C
AMOROUS MR. PRAWN, THE, 1965, A
AMOS 'N' ANDY, 1930, A
AMOUR, AMOUR, 1937, A
AMOURS, DELICES ET ORGUES, 1925
AMPHIBIOUS MAN, THE, 1961, AA
AMPHYTRYON, 1937, A
AMSTERDAM AFFAIR, THE, 1968, C
AMSTERDAM KILL, THE, 1978, O
AMY, 1981, AAA
ANASTASIA, 1956, A
ANATAHAN, 1953, C
ANATOMIST, THE, 1961, C
ANATOMY OF A MARRIAGE (MY DAYS WITH JEAN-MARC AND MY NIGHTS WITH FRANCOISE), 1964, O
ANATOMY OF A MURDER, 1959, C
ANATOMY OF A PSYCHO, 1961, C
ANATOMY OF A SYNDICATE
ANATOMY OF LOVE, 1959, C
ANCE A LA CARTE, 1938, A
ANCE IS SACRED
ANCHORS AWEIGH, 1945, AAA
ANCIENT HIGHWAY, THE, 1925, A
ANCIENT MARINER, THE, 1925, A
AND A STILL, SMALL VOICE, 1918, A
AND BABY MAKES THREE, 1949, A
AND GOD CREATED WOMAN, 1957, O
AND HOPE TO DIE, 1972, C
...AND JUSTICE FOR ALL, 1979, O
AND MILLIONS WILL DIE, 1973, C
AND NOW FOR SOMETHING COMPLETELY DIFFERENT, 1972, PG
AND NOW MIGUEL, 1966, AA
AND NOW MY LOVE, 1975, C
AND NOW THE SCREAMING STARTS, 1973, O
AND NOW TOMORROW, 1944, A
AND NOW TOMORROW, 1952
AND ONE WAS BEAUTIFUL, 1940, A
...AND PIGS MIGHT FLY
AND QUIET FLOWS THE DON, 1960, A
AND SO THEY WERE MARRIED
AND SO THEY WERE MARRIED, 1936, AA
AND SO TO BED, 1965, O
AND SOON THE DARKNESS, 1970, O
AND SUDDEN DEATH, 1936, A
AND SUDDENLY IT'S MURDER!, 1964, C
AND THE ANGELS SING, 1944, A
AND THE LAW SAYS, 1916
AND THE SAME TO YOU, 1960, A
AND THE SHIP SAILS ON, 1983, A
AND THE WALL CAME TUMBLING DOWN, 1984
AND THE WILD, WILD WOMEN, 1961, C-O
AND THEN THERE WERE NONE
AND THEN THERE WERE NONE, 1945, A
AND THERE CAME A MAN, 1968, AAA
AND WOMEN SHALL WEEP, 1960, C
ANDERSON TAPES, THE, 1971, C-O
ANDRE CORNELIS, 1918
ANDRE CORNELIS, 1927
ANDREA, 1979
ANDREI KOZHUKHOV, 1917
ANDREI ROUBLOV, 1973, A
ANDREW'S RAIDERS
ANDROCLES AND THE LION, 1952, A
ANDROID, 1982, O
ANDROMEDA STRAIN, THE, 1971, A
ANDY, 1965, A
ANDY HARDY COMES HOME, 1958, AAA
ANDY HARDY GETS SPRING FEVER, 1939, AAA
ANDY HARDY MEETS DEBUTANTE, 1940, AAA
ANDY HARDY'S BLONDE TROUBLE, 1944, AAA
ANDY HARDY'S DOUBLE LIFE, 1942, AAA
ANDY HARDY'S PRIVATE SECRETARY, 1941, AAA
ANDY WARHOL'S DRACULA, 1974
ANDY WARHOL'S FRANKENSTEIN, 1974
ANGEL, 1937, C
ANGEL, 1982, C
ANGEL, 1984, O
ANGEL AND SINNER, 1947, C
ANGEL AND THE BADMAN, 1947, A
ANGEL BABY, 1961, C
ANGEL CHILD, 1918, A
ANGEL CITIZENS, 1922
ANGEL COMES TO BROOKLYN, AN, 1945, AA
ANGEL ESQUIRE, 1919, A
ANGEL FACE, 1953, C
ANGEL FACTORY, THE, 1917
ANGEL FOR SATAN, AN, 1966
ANGEL FROM TEXAS, AN, 1940, A
ANGEL IN EXILE, 1948, A
ANGEL IN MY POCKET, 1969, AA
ANGEL LEVINE, THE, 1970, A
ANGEL OF BROADWAY, THE, 1927, A
ANGEL OF CROOKED STREET, THE, 1922, A
ANGEL OF H.E.A.T., 1982
ANGEL OF THE WARD, THE, 1915
ANGEL OF VIOLENCE
ANGEL ON MY SHOULDER, 1946, A
ANGEL ON THE AMAZON, 1948, A
ANGEL PASSED OVER BROOKLYN, AN
ANGEL STREET
ANGEL UNCHAINED, 1970, C
ANGEL WHO PAWNED HER HARP, THE, 1956, A
ANGEL WITH THE TRUMPET, THE, 1950, C
ANGEL WORE RED, THE, 1960, A
ANGEL'S HOLIDAY, 1937, A
ANGEL, ANGEL, DOWN WE GO, 1969, O
ANGELA, 1955, A
ANGELA, 1977, O
ANGELE, 1934, C
ANGELIKA
ANGELINA, 1948, C
ANGELO, 1951, C
ANGELO IN THE CROWD, 1952, A
ANGELO MY LOVE, 1983, O
ANGELS, 1976
ANGELS ALLEY, 1948, A
ANGELS BRIGADE, 1980, O
ANGELS DIE HARD, 1970, O
ANGELS FROM HELL, 1968, O
ANGELS HARD AS THEY COME, 1971, O
ANGELS IN DISGUISE, 1949, A
ANGELS IN THE OUTFIELD, 1951, AAA
ANGELS OF DARKNESS, 1956, O
ANGELS OF THE STREETS, 1950, C
ANGELS ONE FIVE, 1954, A
ANGELS OVER BROADWAY, 1940, A
ANGELS WASH THEIR FACES, 1939, A
ANGELS WITH BROKEN WINGS, 1941, A
ANGELS WITH DIRTY FACES, 1938, C
ANGELS' WILD WOMEN, 1972
ANGI VERA, 1980, C
ANGOISSE, 1917
ANGRY BREED, THE, 1969, O
ANGRY GOD, THE, 1948
ANGRY HILLS, THE, 1959, A
ANGRY ISLAND, 1960, A
ANGRY MAN, THE, 1979, C
ANGRY RED PLANET, THE, 1959, A
ANGRY SILENCE, THE, 1960, C
ANIMAL CRACKERS, 1930, AAA
ANIMAL FARM, 1955, A
ANIMAL HOUSE
ANIMAL KINGDOM, THE, 1932, A
ANIMALS, THE, 1971, O
ANITA GARIBALDI, 1954, C
ANKLES PREFERRED, 1927, A
ANN CARVER'S PROFESSION, 1933, A
ANN VICKERS, 1933, A
ANN'S FINISH, 1918, A
ANNA, 1951, C-O
ANNA, 1981, A
ANNA AND THE KING OF SIAM, 1946, A
ANNA ASCENDS, 1922, A
ANNA CHRISTIE, 1923, C
ANNA CHRISTIE, 1930, C
ANNA CROSS, THE, 1954, A
ANNA KARENINA, 1914
ANNA KARENINA, 1935, A
ANNA KARENINA, 1948, A
ANNA LUCASTA, 1949, C
ANNA LUCASTA, 1958, C
ANNA OF BROOKLYN, 1958, C
ANNA OF RHODES, 1950, A
ANNA THE ADVENTURESS, 1920, A
ANNABEL LEE, 1921, A
ANNABEL TAKES A TOUR, 1938, A
ANNABELLE LEE, 1972
ANNABELLE'S AFFAIRS, 1931, A
ANNAPOLIS, 1928, A
ANNAPOLIS FAREWELL, 1935, A
ANNAPOLIS SALUTE, 1937, A
ANNAPOLIS STORY, AN, 1955, A
ANNE AGAINST THE WORLD, 1929, A
ANNE DEVLIN, 1984, C
ANNE OF GREEN GABLES, 1919, A
ANNE OF GREEN GABLES, 1934, A
ANNE OF LITTLE SMOKY, 1921, A
ANNE OF THE INDIES, 1951, A
ANNE OF THE THOUSAND DAYS, 1969, C-O
ANNE OF WINDY POPLARS, 1940, A
ANNE ONE HUNDRED, 1933, A
ANNE-MARIE, 1936, A
ANNEXING BILL, 1918, A
ANNIE, 1982, AAA
ANNIE GET YOUR GUN, 1950, AAA
ANNIE HALL, 1977, C-O
ANNIE LAURIE, 1916
ANNIE LAURIE, 1927, A
ANNIE LAURIE, 1936, A
ANNIE OAKLEY, 1935, AAA
ANNIE, LEAVE THE ROOM, 1935, A
ANNIE-FOR-SPITE, 1917
ANNIVERSARY, THE, 1968, O
ANONYMOUS AVENGER, THE, 1976
ANONYMOUS VENETIAN, THE, 1971, C
ANOTHER CHANCE
ANOTHER COUNTRY, 1984, C
ANOTHER DAWN, 1937, A
ANOTHER FACE, 1935, A
ANOTHER LANGUAGE, 1933, A
ANOTHER MAN'S BOOTS, 1922, A
ANOTHER MAN'S POISON, 1952, C
ANOTHER MAN'S SHOES, 1922
ANOTHER MAN'S WIFE, 1924, A
ANOTHER MAN, ANOTHER CHANCE, 1977, C-O
ANOTHER PART OF THE FOREST, 1948, C
ANOTHER SCANDAL, 1924, A
ANOTHER SHORE, 1948, A
ANOTHER SKY, 1960, A
ANOTHER THIN MAN, 1939, A
ANOTHER TIME, ANOTHER PLACE, 1958, A
ANOTHER TIME, ANOTHER PLACE, 1983, C
ANOTHER TIME, ANOTHER PLACE, 1984, O
ANSWER THE CALL, 1915

ANSWER, THE, 1916, A
ANSWER, THE, 1918, A
ANTARCTICA, 1984, A
ANTHING ONCE, 1917, A
ANTHONY ADVERSE, 1936, A
ANTHONY OF PADUA, 1952, O
ANTI-CLOCK, 1980, C-O
ANTICS OF ANN, THE, 1917, A
ANTIGONE, 1962, A
ANTIQUE DEALER, THE, 1915
ANTOINE ET ANTOINETTE, 1947, A
ANTOINETTE SABRIER, 1927
ANTON THE TERRIBLE, 1916, A
ANTONIO DAS MORTES, 1970, C-O
ANTONY AND CLEOPATRA, 1973, A
ANTS IN HIS PANTS, 1940, AA
ANY BODY...ANY WAY, 1968
ANY GUN CAN PLAY, 1968, C
ANY MAN'S WIFE, 1936, A
ANY NIGHT, 1922
ANY NUMBER CAN PLAY, 1949, A
ANY NUMBER CAN WIN, 1963, A
ANY WEDNESDAY, 1966, C-O
ANY WHICH WAY YOU CAN, 1980, C
ANY WIFE, 1922, C
ANY WOMAN, 1925, A
ANY WOMAN'S MAN
ANYBODY HERE SEEN KELLY?, 1928
ANYBODY'S BLONDE, 1931, A
ANYBODY'S WAR, 1930, A
ANYBODY'S WOMAN, 1930, A
ANYONE CAN PLAY, 1968, O
ANYONE FOR VENICE?
ANYTHING CAN HAPPEN, 1952, A
ANYTHING FOR A SONG, 1947, A
ANYTHING FOR A THRILL, 1937, A
ANYTHING FOR LOVE
ANYTHING GOES, 1936, A
ANYTHING GOES, 1956, A
ANYTHING MIGHT HAPPEN, 1935, A
ANYTHING ONCE, 1925, A
ANYTHING TO DECLARE?, 1939, A
ANZIO, 1968, A
APACHE, 1954, A
APACHE AMBUSH, 1955, A
APACHE CHIEF, 1949, A
APACHE COUNTRY, 1952, A
APACHE DANCER, THE, 1923
APACHE DRUMS, 1951, A
APACHE GOLD, 1965, A
APACHE KID'S ESCAPE, THE, 1930
APACHE KID, THE, 1941, A
APACHE RAIDER, THE, 1928, A
APACHE RIFLES, 1964, A
APACHE ROSE, 1947, A
APACHE TERRITORY, 1958, A
APACHE TRAIL, 1942, A
APACHE UPRISING, 1966, A
APACHE WAR SMOKE, 1952, A
APACHE WARRIOR, 1957, A
APACHE WOMAN, 1955, A
APACHE, THE, 1925, A
APACHE, THE, 1928, A
APACHES OF PARIS, 1928
APACHES OF PARIS, THE, 1915
APARAJITO, 1959, A
APARTMENT 29, 1917, A
APARTMENT FOR PEGGY, 1948, A
APARTMENT ON THE THIRTEENTH FLOOR, 1973
APARTMENT, THE, 1960, C-O
APE CREATURE, 1968
APE MAN, THE, 1943, C
APE WOMAN, THE, 1964, C
APE, THE, 1928, A
APE, THE, 1940, C
APOCALYPSE 3:16, 1964
APOCALYPSE NOW, 1979, O
APOLLO GOES ON HOLIDAY, 1968, A
APOLOGY FOR MURDER, 1945, A
APOSTLE OF VENGEANCE, THE, 1916, A
APPALOOSA, THE, 1966, C
APPASSIONATA, 1929
APPASSIONATA, 1946, A
APPEARANCE OF EVIL, 1918, A
APPEARANCES, 1921, A
APPLAUSE, 1929, A
APPLE DUMPLING GANG RIDES AGAIN, THE, 1979, AA
APPLE DUMPLING GANG, THE, 1975, AAA
APPLE, THE, 1980, C-O
APPLE-TREE GIRL, THE, 1917
APPOINTMENT FOR LOVE, 1941, A
APPOINTMENT FOR MURDER, 1954, C
APPOINTMENT IN BERLIN, 1943, A
APPOINTMENT IN HONDURAS, 1953, A
APPOINTMENT IN LONDON, 1953, A
APPOINTMENT WITH A SHADOW, 1957
APPOINTMENT WITH A SHADOW, 1958, A
APPOINTMENT WITH CRIME, 1945, A
APPOINTMENT WITH DANGER, 1951, C
APPOINTMENT WITH MURDER, 1948, A
APPOINTMENT WITH VENUS
APPOINTMENT, THE, 1969, O
APPRENTICESHIP OF DUDDY KRAVITZ, THE, 1974, A
APRES L'AMOUR, 1948, O
APRIL, 1916
APRIL 1, 2000, 1953, A
APRIL BLOSSOMS, 1937, A
APRIL FOLLY, 1920
APRIL FOOL, 1926, A
APRIL FOOLS, THE, 1969, C
APRIL IN PARIS, 1953, A
APRIL LOVE, 1957, AA
APRIL ROMANCE
APRIL SHOWERS, 1923, A
APRIL SHOWERS, 1948, A
AQUARIAN, THE, 1972
ARAB, THE, 1915, A
ARAB, THE, 1924, A
ARABELLA, 1969, A
ARABESQUE, 1966, C
ARABIA, 1922
ARABIAN ADVENTURE, 1979, AA
ARABIAN LOVE, 1922, A
ARABIAN NIGHTS, 1942, AAA
ARABIAN NIGHTS, 1980, O
ARCADIANS, THE, 1927, A
ARCH OF TRIUMPH, 1948, C
ARCTIC ADVENTURE, 1922
ARCTIC FLIGHT, 1952, A
ARCTIC FURY, 1949, AA
ARCTIC MANHUNT, 1949, A
ARE ALL MEN ALIKE?, 1920, A
ARE CHILDREN TO BLAME?, 1922, A
ARE HUSBANDS NECESSARY?, 1942, A
ARE PARENTS PEOPLE?, 1925, A
ARE THE CHILDREN TO BLAME?
ARE THESE OUR CHILDREN?, 1931, A
ARE THESE OUR PARENTS?, 1944, A
ARE WE CIVILIZED?, 1934, A
ARE YOU A FAILURE?, 1923, A
ARE YOU A MASON?, 1915, A
ARE YOU A MASON?, 1934, A
ARE YOU BEING SERVED?, 1977
ARE YOU LEGALLY MARRIED?, 1919, A
ARE YOU LISTENING?, 1932, A
ARE YOU THERE?, 1930, AA
ARE YOU WITH IT?, 1948, AA
AREN'T MEN BEASTS?, 1937, A
ARENA, 1953, A
ARENA, THE, 1973, O
ARENT WE ALL?, 1932, A
ARENT WE WONDERFUL?, 1959, A
ARGENTINE LOVE, 1924, A
ARGENTINE NIGHTS, 1940, AA
ARGONAUTS OF CALIFORNIA, 1916
ARGUMENT, THE
ARGYLE CASE, THE, 1917, A
ARGYLE CASE, THE, 1929, A
ARGYLE SECRETS, THE, 1948, A
ARIANE, 1931, A
ARIANE, RUSSIAN MAID, 1932, A
ARISE, MY LOVE, 1940, A
ARISTOCATS, THE, 1970, AAA
ARISTOCRACY, 1914
ARIZONA
ARIZONA, 1913
ARIZONA, 1918, A
ARIZONA, 1940, A
ARIZONA BADMAN, 1935, A
ARIZONA BOUND, 1927, A
ARIZONA BOUND, 1941, A
ARIZONA BUSHWHACKERS, 1968, A
ARIZONA CATCLAW, THE, 1919, A
ARIZONA COLT, 1965, C
ARIZONA COWBOY, THE, 1950, A
ARIZONA CYCLONE, 1928, A
ARIZONA CYCLONE, 1934, A
ARIZONA CYCLONE, 1941, A
ARIZONA DAYS, 1928, A
ARIZONA DAYS, 1937, A
ARIZONA EXPRESS, THE, 1924, A
ARIZONA FRONTIER, 1940, A
ARIZONA GANGBUSTERS, 1940, A
ARIZONA GUNFIGHTER, 1937, A
ARIZONA KID, THE, 1929, A
ARIZONA KID, THE, 1930, A
ARIZONA KID, THE, 1939, A
ARIZONA LEGION, 1939, A
ARIZONA MAHONEY, 1936, A
ARIZONA MANHUNT, 1951, A
ARIZONA MISSION
ARIZONA NIGHTS, 1927
ARIZONA NIGHTS, 1934, A
ARIZONA RAIDERS, 1965, A
ARIZONA RAIDERS, THE, 1936, A
ARIZONA RANGER, THE, 1948, A
ARIZONA ROMEO, THE, 1925, AA
ARIZONA ROUNDUP, 1942, A
ARIZONA SPEED, 1928
ARIZONA STAGECOACH, 1942
ARIZONA STREAK, THE, 1926
ARIZONA SWEEPSTAKES, 1926, A
ARIZONA TERRITORY, 1950, A
ARIZONA TERROR, 1931, A
ARIZONA TERRORS, 1942, A
ARIZONA TO BROADWAY, 1933, A
ARIZONA TRAIL, 1943, A
ARIZONA TRAILS, 1935, A
ARIZONA WHIRLWIND, 1944, A
ARIZONA WHIRLWIND, THE, 1927
ARIZONA WILDCAT, 1927, A
ARIZONA WILDCAT, 1938, AA
ARIZONIAN, THE, 1935, A
ARKANSAS JUDGE, 1941, A
ARKANSAS TRAVELER, THE, 1938, A
ARM OF THE LAW, 1932, S
ARMAGEDDON, 1923, A
ARMCHAIR DETECTIVE, THE, 1952, A
ARMED AND DANGEROUS, 1977, A
ARMORED ATTACK
ARMORED CAR, 1937, A
ARMORED CAR ROBBERY, 1950, A
ARMORED COMMAND, 1961, C
ARMS AND THE GIRL
ARMS AND THE GIRL, 1917, A
ARMS AND THE MAN, 1932, A
ARMS AND THE MAN, 1962, A
ARMS AND THE WOMAN, 1916, A
ARMSTRONG'S WIFE, 1915, A
ARMY BOUND, 1952, A
ARMY GAME, THE, 1963, C-O
ARMY GIRL, 1938, A
ARMY SURGEON, 1942, A
ARMY WIVES, 1944, A
ARNELO AFFAIR, THE, 1947, A
ARNOLD, 1973, C
ARNOLD'S WRECKING CO., 1973
AROUND THE CORNER, 1930
AROUND THE TOWN, 1938, A
AROUND THE WORLD, 1943, A
AROUND THE WORLD IN 80 DAYS, 1956, AAA
AROUND THE WORLD UNDER THE SEA, 1966, A
AROUSED, 1968
AROUSERS, THE, 1973, O
ARRANGEMENT, THE, 1969, O
ARREST BULLDOG DRUMMOND, 1939, A
ARREST NORMA MACGREGOR, 1921
ARRIVAL OF PERPETUA, THE, 1915, A
ARRIVEDERCI, BABY!, 1966, C-O
ARROW IN THE DUST, 1954, A
ARROWHEAD, 1953, C
ARROWSMITH, 1931, A
ARSENAL, 1929, A
ARSENAL STADIUM MYSTERY, THE, 1939, A
ARSENE LUPIN, 1916, A
ARSENE LUPIN, 1917, A
ARSENE LUPIN, 1932, A
ARSENE LUPIN RETURNS, 1938, A
ARSENIC AND OLD LACE, 1944, A
ARSON FOR HIRE, 1959, A
ARSON GANG BUSTERS, 1938, A
ARSON RACKET SQUAD, 1938
ARSON SQUAD, 1945, A
ARSON, INC., 1949, A
ART OF LOVE, THE, 1928
ART OF LOVE, THE, 1965, A
ARTHUR, 1931, C
ARTHUR, 1981, C
ARTHUR TAKES OVER, 1948, A
ARTHUR!! ARTHUR?, 1970
ARTIE, THE MILLIONAIRE KID, 1916, A
ARTISTIC TEMPERAMENT, THE, 1919, A
ARTISTS AND MODELS, 1937, AAA
ARTISTS AND MODELS, 1955, A
ARTISTS AND MODELS ABROAD, 1938, A
ARTURO'S ISLAND, 1963, C
ARYAN, THE, 1916, A
AS A MAN LIVES, 1923, A
AS A MAN THINKS, 1919
AS A WOMAN SOWS, 1916, A
AS GOD MADE HER, 1920, A
AS GOOD AS MARRIED, 1937, A
AS HE WAS BORN, 1919, A
AS HUSBANDS GO, 1934, A
AS IN A LOOKING GLASS, 1916, A
AS LONG AS THEYRE HAPPY, 1957, A
AS LONG AS YOU'RE NEAR ME, 1956, A
AS MAN DESIRES, 1925, A
AS MAN MADE HER, 1917
AS MEN LOVE, 1917, A
AS NO MAN HAS LOVED
AS THE DEVIL COMMANDS, 1933, A
AS THE EARTH TURNS, 1934, A
AS THE SEA RAGES, 1960, A
AS THE SUN WENT DOWN, 1915

AS THE SUN WENT DOWN, 1919, A
AS THE WORLD ROLLS ON, 1921
AS YE REPENT
AS YE SOW, 1914, A
AS YOU DESIRE ME, 1932, A
AS YOU LIKE IT, 1936, A
AS YOU WERE, 1951, A
AS YOUNG AS WE ARE, 1958, C
AS YOUNG AS YOU FEEL, 1951, A
ASCENDANCY, 1983, C
ASCENT TO HEAVEN
ASH WEDNESDAY, 1973, C
ASHAMED OF PARENTS, 1921, A
ASHANTI, 1979, O
ASHES, 1922
ASHES AND DIAMONDS, 1961, C
ASHES AND EMBERS, 1982
ASHES OF DESIRE, 1919
ASHES OF EMBERS, 1916, A
ASHES OF HOPE, 1917, A
ASHES OF REVENGE, THE, 1915
ASHES OF VENGEANCE, 1923, A
ASIAN SUN, THE, 1921
ASK A POLICEMAN, 1939, A
ASK ANY GIRL, 1959, A
ASK BECCLES, 1933, A
ASKING FOR TROUBLE, 1942, A
ASPHALT JUNGLE, THE, 1950, C
ASPHYX, THE, 1972, C
ASSASSIN, 1973, C
ASSASSIN FOR HIRE, 1951, C
ASSASSIN OF YOUTH, 1937
ASSASSIN, THE, 1953, A
ASSASSIN, THE, 1961, O
ASSASSINATION BUREAU, THE, 1969, O
ASSASSINATION OF TROTSKY, THE, 1972, O
ASSAULT, 1971, O
ASSAULT OF THE REBEL GIRLS
ASSAULT ON A QUEEN, 1966, A
ASSAULT ON AGATHON, 1976, O
ASSAULT ON PRECINCT 13, 1976, O
ASSAULT WITH A DEADLY WEAPON, 1983
ASSIGNED TO DANGER, 1948, A
ASSIGNMENT ABROAD, 1955
ASSIGNMENT IN BRITTANY, 1943, A
ASSIGNMENT K, 1968, A
ASSIGNMENT OUTER SPACE, 1960, C
ASSIGNMENT REDHEAD
ASSIGNMENT TERROR, 1970, C-O
ASSIGNMENT TO KILL, 1968, C
ASSIGNMENT, THE, 1978
ASSIGNMENT—PARIS, 1952, A
ASSIGNMENT: KILL CASTRO
ASSISTANT, THE, 1982, C
ASSOCIATE, THE, 1982, A
ASTERO, 1960, A
ASTHORE, 1917, C
ASTONISHED HEART, THE, 1950, C
ASTOUNDING SHE-MONSTER, THE, 1958, C
ASTRO-ZOMBIES, THE, 1969, C
ASTROLOGER, THE, 1975
ASTROLOGER, THE, 1979
ASYLUM, 1972, O
ASYLUM FOR A SPY, 1967
ASYLUM OF SATAN, 1972
AT
AT 3:25
AT BAY, 1915
AT DAWN WE DIE, 1943, A
AT DEVIL'S GORGE, 1923, A
AT FIRST SIGHT, 1917
AT GUNPOINT, 1955, A
AT LONG LAST LOVE, 1975, A
AT PINEY RIDGE, 1916
AT SWORD'S POINT, 1951, A
AT THE CIRCUS, 1939, AAA
AT THE CROSSROADS, 1922
AT THE EARTH'S CORE, 1976, C
AT THE EDGE OF THE WORLD, 1929
AT THE END OF THE WORLD, 1921
AT THE GREY HOUSE
AT THE MERCY OF MEN, 1918
AT THE MERCY OF TIBERIUS
AT THE OLD CROSSED ROADS, 1914
AT THE RIDGE, 1931, A
AT THE SIGN OF THE JACK O'LANTERN, 1922
AT THE STAGE DOOR, 1921, A
AT THE STROKE OF NINE, 1957, A
AT THE TORRENT'S MERCY, 1915
AT THE VILLA ROSE, 1920, A
AT WAR WITH THE ARMY, 1950, A
AT YALE
ATCH ME A SPY, 1971, A-C
ATHENA, 1954, A
ATLANTIC, 1929, A
ATLANTIC ADVENTURE, 1935, A
ATLANTIC CITY, 1944, A
ATLANTIC CITY, 1981, C-O
ATLANTIC CONVOY, 1942, A
ATLANTIC FERRY, 1941, A
ATLANTIC FLIGHT, 1937, A
ATLANTIS, 1913
ATLANTIS, THE LOST CONTINENT, 1961, A
ATLAS, 1960, C-O
ATLAS AGAINST THE CYCLOPS, 1963, A
ATLAS AGAINST THE CZAR, 1964, A
ATOLL K
ATOM AGE VAMPIRE, 1961, C
ATOM, THE, 1918, A
ATOMIC AGENT, 1959
ATOMIC BRAIN, THE, 1964, O
ATOMIC CITY, THE, 1952, A
ATOMIC KID, THE, 1954, A
ATOMIC MAN, THE, 1955, A
ATOMIC SUBMARINE, THE, 1960, A
ATOMIC WAR BRIDE, 1966
ATONEMENT, 1920
ATONEMENT OF GOSTA BERLING, THE
ATOR, THE INVINCIBLE, 1984
ATOR: THE FIGHTING EAGLE, 1983
ATRAGON, 1965, A
ATTA BOY, 1926, A
ATTA BOY'S LAST RACE, 1916, A
ATTACK AND RETREAT
ATTACK AT NOON SUNDAY, 1971
ATTACK OF THE 50 FOOT WOMAN, 1958, A
ATTACK OF THE CRAB MONSTERS, 1957, A
ATTACK OF THE GIANT LEECHES, 1959, C-O
ATTACK OF THE KILLER TOMATOES, 1978, C
ATTACK OF THE MAYAN MUMMY, 1963, C
ATTACK OF THE MUSHROOM PEOPLE, 1964, A
ATTACK OF THE PUPPET PEOPLE, 1958, A
ATTACK OF THE ROBOTS, 1967, C
ATTACK ON THE IRON COAST, 1968, A
ATTACK!, 1956, O
ATTEMPT TO KILL, 1961, A
ATTENTION, THE KIDS ARE WATCHING, 1978, C
ATTIC, THE, 1979, C-O
ATTILA, 1958, C
ATTORNEY FOR THE DEFENSE, 1932, A
AU BONHEUR DES DAMES, 1929
AU DELA DES LOIS HUMAINES, 1920
AU HASARD, BALTHAZAR, 1970, C-O
AU PAIR GIRLS, 1973
AU PARADIS DES ENFANTS, 1918
AU SEUIL DU HAREM, 1922
AUCTION BLOCK, THE, 1917, C
AUCTION BLOCK, THE, 1926, A
AUCTION MART, THE, 1920, A
AUCTION OF SOULS, 1922
AUCTION OF VIRTUE, THE, 1917
AUCTIONEER, THE, 1927, A
AUDACIOUS MR. SQUIRE, THE, 1923, A
AUDREY, 1916, A
AUDREY ROSE, 1977, C
AUGUST WEEK-END, 1936, A
AUGUSTINE OF HIPPO, 1973, A
AULD LANG SYNE, 1917, A
AULD LANG SYNE, 1929, A
AULD LANG SYNE, 1937, A
AULD ROBIN GRAY, 1917, A
AULD ROBIN GRAY, 1917
AUNT CLARA, 1954, A
AUNT FROM CHICAGO, 1960, C
AUNT RACHEL, 1920, A
AUNTIE MAME, 1958, A
AUNTIE'S ANTICS, 1929
AURORA LEIGH, 1915
AUSTERLITZ, 1960, A
AUTHOR! AUTHOR!, 1982, A
AUTOCRAT, THE, 1919, A
AUTOPSY, 1980
AUTOUR D'UN BERCEAU, 1925
AUTOUR DU MYSTERE, 1920
AUTUMN, 1916
AUTUMN CROCUS, 1934, A
AUTUMN LEAVES, 1956, C
AUTUMN MARATHON, 1982, A
AUTUMN OF PRIDE, THE, 1921, A
AUTUMN SONATA, 1978, O
AUX JARDINS DE MURCIE, 1923
AVALANCHE, 1928, A
AVALANCHE, 1946, A
AVALANCHE, 1975
AVALANCHE, 1978, O
AVALANCHE EXPRESS, 1979, C
AVALANCHE, THE, 1915
AVALANCHE, THE, 1919, C
AVANTI!, 1972, C
AVE MARIA, 1918, A
AVE MARIA, 1984, O
AVENGER OF THE SEVEN SEAS, 1960
AVENGER OF VENICE, 1965
AVENGER, THE, 1924, A
AVENGER, THE, 1931, A
AVENGER, THE, 1933, A
AVENGER, THE, 1962, C
AVENGER, THE, 1966, C
AVENGERS, THE, 1942, A
AVENGERS, THE, 1950, A
AVENGING CONSCIENCE, THE, 1914, C
AVENGING FANGS, 1927, A
AVENGING HAND, THE, 1915
AVENGING HAND, THE, 1936, A
AVENGING RIDER, THE, 1928, A
AVENGING RIDER, THE, 1943, A
AVENGING SHADOW, THE, 1928, A
AVENGING TRAIL, THE, 1918, A
AVENGING WATERS, 1936, A
AVERAGE WOMAN, THE, 1924, A
AVIATOR SPY, THE, 1914
AVIATOR'S WIFE, THE, 1981, O
AVIATOR, THE, 1929, A
AWAKENING OF BESS MORTON, THE, 1916
AWAKENING OF HELENA RICHIE, THE, 1916
AWAKENING OF JIM BURKE, 1935, A
AWAKENING OF RUTH, THE, 1917
AWAKENING, THE, 1917, C
AWAKENING, THE, 1928, A
AWAKENING, THE, 1938, A
AWAKENING, THE, 1958, AA
AWAKENING, THE, 1980, O
AWAY ALL BOATS, 1956, A
AWAY GOES PRUDENCE, 1920, A
AWAY IN THE LEAD, 1925
AWFUL DR. ORLOFF, THE, 1964, O
AWFUL TRUTH, THE, 1925, A
AWFUL TRUTH, THE, 1929, A
AWFUL TRUTH, THE, 1937, A
AWOL, 1973
AXE, 1977
AYLWIN, 1920, A
AZAIS, 1931, A
AZTEC MUMMY, THE, 1957, O
AZURE EXPRESS, 1938, A

-B-

"B"...MUST DIE, 1973
B. F.'S DAUGHTER, 1948, A
B.J. LANG PRESENTS, 1971
B.S. I LOVE YOU, 1971, O
BAB THE FIXER, 1917
BAB'S BURGLAR, 1917, A
BAB'S CANDIDATE, 1920, A
BAB'S DIARY, 1917, A
BAB'S MATINEE IDOL, 1917
BABBITT, 1924, A
BABBITT, 1934, A
BABBLING TONGUES, 1917, A
BABE COMES HOME, 1927, A
BABE RUTH STORY, THE, 1948, AAA
BABES IN ARMS, 1939, AAA
BABES IN BAGDAD, 1952, A
BABES IN THE WOODS, 1917
BABES IN TOYLAND, 1934, AAA
BABES IN TOYLAND, 1961, AAA
BABES ON BROADWAY, 1941, AAA
BABES ON SWING STREET, 1944, A
BABETTE, 1917
BABETTE GOES TO WAR, 1960, C
BABETTE OF THE BALLY HOO, 1916
BABIES FOR SALE, 1940, C
BABO 73, 1964
BABY AND THE BATTLESHIP, THE, 1957, A
BABY BLUE MARINE, 1976, C
BABY CYCLONE, THE, 1928
BABY DOLL, 1956, O
BABY DOLLS, 1982
BABY FACE, 1933, O
BABY FACE HARRINGTON, 1935, A
BABY FACE MORGAN, 1942, A
BABY FACE NELSON, 1957, O
BABY LOVE, 1969, O
BABY MAKER, THE, 1970, O
BABY MINE, 1917, A
BABY MINE, 1928, A
BABY MOTHER, THE
BABY NEEDS A NEW PAIR OF SHOES, 1974
BABY, IT'S YOU, 1983, C-O
BABY, TAKE A BOW, 1934, AA
BABY, THE, 1973, C-O
BABY, THE RAIN MUST FALL, 1965, C
BABYLON, 1980, O
BABYSITTER, THE, 1969
BACCHANALE, 1970
BACCHANTES, THE, 1963, A
BACHELOR AND THE BOBBY-SOXER, THE, 1947, AAA
BACHELOR APARTMENT, 1931, C
BACHELOR APARTMENTS, 1920
BACHELOR BAIT, 1934, A
BACHELOR BRIDES, 1926
BACHELOR DADDY, 1941, A
BACHELOR DADDY, THE, 1922
BACHELOR FATHER, 1931, A
BACHELOR FLAT, 1962, A
BACHELOR GIRL, THE, 1929, A

BACHELOR HUSBAND, THE, 1920
BACHELOR IN PARADISE, 1961, A
BACHELOR IN PARIS, 1953, A
BACHELOR MOTHER, 1933, C
BACHELOR MOTHER, 1939, A
BACHELOR OF ARTS, 1935, A
BACHELOR OF HEARTS, 1958, A
BACHELOR PARTY, 1984, O
BACHELOR PARTY, THE, 1957, C
BACHELOR'S AFFAIRS, 1932, A
BACHELOR'S BABY, 1932, C
BACHELOR'S BABY, A, 1922
BACHELOR'S BABY, THE, 1927, A
BACHELOR'S CHILDREN, A, 1918
BACHELOR'S CLUB, THE, 1929
BACHELOR'S DAUGHTERS, THE, 1946, A
BACHELOR'S FOLLY
BACHELOR'S PARADISE, 1928, A
BACHELOR'S ROMANCE, THE, 1915
BACHELOR'S WIFE, A, 1919
BACHELORS' CLUB, THE, 1921, A
BACK AT THE FRONT, 1952, A
BACK DOOR TO HEAVEN, 1939, A
BACK DOOR TO HELL, 1964, A
BACK FIRE, 1922, A
BACK FROM ETERNITY, 1956, C
BACK FROM SHANGHAI, 1929
BACK FROM THE DEAD, 1957, C-O
BACK HOME AND BROKE, 1922, A
BACK IN CIRCULATION, 1937, A
BACK IN THE SADDLE, 1941, A
BACK OF THE MAN, 1917
BACK PAGE, 1934
BACK PAY, 1922
BACK PAY, 1930, A
BACK ROADS, 1981, O
BACK ROOM BOY, 1942, A
BACK STREET, 1932, A
BACK STREET, 1941, A
BACK STREET, 1961, A
BACK STREETS OF PARIS, 1962, C-O
BACK TO BATAAN, 1945, A
BACK TO GOD'S COUNTRY, 1919
BACK TO GOD'S COUNTRY, 1927
BACK TO GOD'S COUNTRY, 1953, A
BACK TO LIBERTY, 1927
BACK TO LIFE, 1925
BACK TO NATURE, 1936, A
BACK TO OLD VIRGINIA, 1923
BACK TO THE WALL, 1959, O
BACK TO THE WOODS, 1918
BACK TO YELLOW JACKET, 1922
BACK TRAIL, 1948, A
BACK TRAIL, THE, 1924, A
BACKBONE, 1923
BACKFIRE, 1950, A
BACKFIRE, 1965, C
BACKFIRE!, 1961, A
BACKGROUND, 1953, C
BACKGROUND TO DANGER, 1943, A
BACKLASH, 1947, A
BACKLASH, 1956, A
BACKSTAGE, 1927, A
BACKSTAGE, 1937, A
BACKSTAIRS, 1921
BACKTRACK, 1969, A
BAD AND THE BEAUTIFUL, THE, 1952, C
BAD BASCOMB, 1946, AA
BAD BLONDE, 1953, C
BAD BOY, 1935, A
BAD BOY, 1938, A
BAD BOY, 1939, A
BAD BOY, 1949, A
BAD BOYS, 1917
BAD BOYS, 1983, O
BAD BUNCH, THE, 1976
BAD CHARLESTON CHARLIE, 1973, A
BAD COMPANY, 1925
BAD COMPANY, 1931, A
BAD COMPANY, 1972, A
BAD DAY AT BLACK ROCK, 1955, A
BAD FOR EACH OTHER, 1954, A
BAD GEORGIA ROAD, 1977
BAD GIRL, 1931, C
BAD GIRL, 1959
BAD GUY, 1937, A
BAD LANDS, 1939, A
BAD LANDS, THE, 1925
BAD LITTLE ANGEL, 1939, AA
BAD LORD BYRON, THE, 1949, A
BAD MAN FROM BODIE, 1925
BAD MAN FROM RED BUTTE, 1940, A
BAD MAN OF BRIMSTONE, 1938, A
BAD MAN OF DEADWOOD, 1941, A
BAD MAN'S BLUFF, 1926
BAD MAN'S MONEY
BAD MAN'S RIVER, 1972, A
BAD MAN, THE, 1923
BAD MAN, THE, 1930, A
BAD MAN, THE, 1941, A
BAD MANNERS, 1984, C
BAD MEN OF MISSOURI, 1941, A
BAD MEN OF THE BORDER, 1945, A
BAD MEN OF THE HILLS, 1942, A
BAD MEN OF THUNDER GAP, 1943, A
BAD MEN OF TOMBSTONE, 1949, C
BAD MEN'S MONEY, 1929
BAD NEWS BEARS GO TO JAPAN, THE, 1978, C
BAD NEWS BEARS IN BREAKING TRAINING, THE, 1977, C
BAD NEWS BEARS, THE, 1976, C
BAD ONE, THE, 1930, C
BAD SEED, THE, 1956, C
BAD SISTER, 1931, A
BAD SISTER, 1947, A
BADGE 373, 1973, O
BADGE OF HONOR, 1934, A
BADGE OF MARSHAL BRENNAN, THE, 1957, A
BADGER'S GREEN, 1934, A
BADGER'S GREEN, 1949, A
BADLANDERS, THE, 1958, A
BADLANDS, 1974, O
BADLANDS OF DAKOTA, 1941, A
BADLANDS OF MONTANA, 1957, A
BADMAN'S COUNTRY, 1958, A
BADMAN'S GOLD, 1951, A
BADMAN'S TERRITORY, 1946, A
BAFFLED, 1924, A
BAG AND BAGGAGE, 1923
BAGDAD, 1949, A
BAHAMA PASSAGE, 1941, A
BAILOUT AT 43,000, 1957, A
BAIT, 1950, A
BAIT, 1954, C
BAIT, THE, 1916
BAIT, THE, 1921, A
BAITED TRAP, 1926
BAKER'S HAWK, 1976, A
BAKER'S WIFE, THE, 1940, C
BAL TABARIN, 1952, A
BALACLAVA
BALACLAVA
BALALAIKA, 1939, A
BALCONY, THE, 1963, O
BALKAN EXPRESS, 1983
BALL AT SAVOY, 1936, A
BALL AT THE CASTLE, 1939, A
BALL OF FIRE, 1941, A
BALL OF FORTUNE, THE, 1926
BALLAD IN BLUE
BALLAD OF A GUNFIGHTER, 1964, A
BALLAD OF A HUSSAR, 1963, A
BALLAD OF A SOLDIER, 1960, A
BALLAD OF BILLIE BLUE, 1972
BALLAD OF CABLE HOGUE, THE, 1970, C
BALLAD OF COSSACK GLOOTA, 1938, A
BALLAD OF GREGORIO CORTEZ, THE, 1983, C-O
BALLAD OF JOSIE, 1968, A
BALLAD OF NARAYAMA, 1961, C
BALLAD OF NARAYAMA, THE, 1984, C
BALLERINA, 1950, A
BALLET GIRL, THE, 1916, A
BALLOON GOES UP, THE, 1942, A
BALLYHOO BUSTER, THE, 1928
BALTHAZAR
BALTIC DEPUTY, 1937, A
BALTIMORE BULLET, THE, 1980, C
BAMBI, 1942, AAA
BAMBOLE!, 1965, C
BAMBOO BLONDE, THE, 1946, A
BAMBOO GODS AND IRON MEN, 1974
BAMBOO PRISON, THE, 1955, A
BAMBOO SAUCER, THE, 1968, A
BANANA MONSTER, THE
BANANA PEEL, 1965, C
BANANA RIDGE, 1941, A
BANANAS, 1971, C
BAND OF ANGELS, 1957, A
BAND OF ASSASSINS, 1971
BAND OF OUTSIDERS, 1966, C-O
BAND OF THIEVES, 1962, A
BAND PLAYS ON, THE, 1934, A
BAND WAGGON, 1940, A
BAND WAGON, THE, 1953, A
BANDBOX, THE, 1919
BANDE A PART
BANDIDO, 1956, A
BANDIDOS, 1967, A
BANDIT BUSTER, THE, 1926
BANDIT KING OF TEXAS, 1949, A
BANDIT OF SHERWOOD FOREST, THE, 1946, AA
BANDIT OF ZHOBE, THE, 1959, A
BANDIT QUEEN, 1950, A
BANDIT RANGER, 1942, A
BANDIT TAMER, THE, 1925
BANDIT TRAIL, THE, 1941, A
BANDIT'S BABY, THE, 1925
BANDIT'S DOUBLE, THE, 1917
BANDIT'S SON, THE, 1927, A
BANDIT, THE, 1949, A
BANDITS IN ROME, 1967
BANDITS OF CORSICA, THE, 1953, A
BANDITS OF DARK CANYON, 1947, A
BANDITS OF EL DORADO, 1951, A
BANDITS OF ORGOSOLO, 1964, A
BANDITS OF THE AIR, 1925
BANDITS OF THE BADLANDS, 1945, A
BANDITS OF THE WEST, 1953, A
BANDITS ON THE WIND, 1964, A
BANDOLERO!, 1968, A
BANDOLERO, THE, 1924
BANG BANG KID, THE, 1968, A
BANG THE DRUM SLOWLY, 1973, A
BANG! YOU'RE DEAD, 1954, C
BANG, BANG, YOU'RE DEAD, 1966, A
BANISHED, 1978, C
BANJO, 1947, AA
BANJO ON MY KNEE, 1936, A
BANK ALARM, 1937, A
BANK DICK, THE, 1940, A
BANK HOLIDAY, 1938, C
BANK MESSENGER MYSTERY, THE, 1936, A
BANK RAIDERS, THE, 1958, A
BANK SHOT, 1974, A
BANKER'S DAUGHTER, THE, 1914
BANNERLINE, 1951, A
BANNING, 1967, C
BANTAM COWBOY, THE, 1928, A
BANZAI, 1983, C-O
BAR 20, 1943, A
BAR 20 JUSTICE, 1938, A
BAR 20 RIDES AGAIN, 1936, A
BAR L RANCH, 1930, A
BAR MITSVE, 1935
BAR NOTHIN', 1921, A
BAR SINISTER, THE, 1917, A
BAR SINISTER, THE, 1955, A
BAR Z BAD MEN, 1937, A
BAR-C MYSTERY, THE, 1926
BARABBAS, 1962, C
BARB WIRE, 1922
BARBADOS QUEST
BARBARA, 1970
BARBARA FRIETCHIE, 1915
BARBARA FRIETCHIE, 1924
BARBARELLA, 1968, O
BARBARIAN AND THE GEISHA, THE, 1958, A
BARBARIAN, THE, 1921
BARBARIAN, THE, 1933, C
BARBAROSA, 1982, C
BARBARY COAST, 1935, A
BARBARY COAST GENT, 1944, A
BARBARY PIRATE, 1949, A
BARBARY SHEEP, 1917
BARBED WIRE
BARBED WIRE, 1927, A
BARBED WIRE, 1952, A
BARBER OF SEVILLE, 1949, A
BARBER OF SEVILLE, THE, 1947, A
BARBER OF SEVILLE, THE, 1973, A
BARBER OF STAMFORD HILL, THE, 1963, A
BARBERINA, 1932, A
BARCAROLE, 1935, A
BARDELYS THE MAGNIFICENT, 1926
BARE FISTS, 1919
BARE KNEES, 1928
BARE KNUCKLES, 1921
BARE KNUCKLES, 1977
BARE KNUCKLES, 1978, O
BARE-FISTED GALLAGHER, 1919
BAREE, SON OF KAZAN, 1918
BAREE, SON OF KAZAN, 1925
BAREFOOT BATTALION, THE, 1954, A
BAREFOOT BOY, 1938, A
BAREFOOT BOY, THE, 1923
BAREFOOT CONTESSA, THE, 1954, A
BAREFOOT EXECUTIVE, THE, 1971, AAA
BAREFOOT IN THE PARK, 1967, A
BAREFOOT MAILMAN, THE, 1951, A
BAREFOOT SAVAGE
BARGAIN WITH BULLETS, 1937
BARGAIN, THE, 1914
BARGAIN, THE, 1921
BARGAIN, THE, 1931, A
BARGAINS, 1923
BARGEE, THE, 1964, C
BARKER, THE, 1917
BARKER, THE, 1928
BARKER, THE, 1928, A
BARKLEYS OF BROADWAY, THE, 1949, A
BARN OF THE NAKED DEAD Zero, 1976, O
BARNABY, 1919
BARNABY RUDGE, 1915
BARNACLE BILL, 1935, A
BARNACLE BILL, 1941, A
BARNACLE BILL, 1958
BARNES MURDER CASE, THE, 1930, A

BARNSTORMER, THE, 1922
BARNSTORMERS, THE, 1915
BARNUM WAS RIGHT, 1929, A
BARNYARD FOLLIES, 1940, A
BAROCCO, 1925
BAROCCO, 1976, O
BARON BLOOD, 1972, C
BARON MUNCHAUSEN, 1962, A
BARON OF ARIZONA, THE, 1950, A
BARONESS AND THE BUTLER, THE, 1938, A
BARQUERO, 1970, O
BARRACUDA, 1978, C
BARRANCO, 1932, A
BARRETTS OF WIMPOLE STREET, THE, 1934, A
BARRETTS OF WIMPOLE STREET, THE, 1957, A
BARRICADE, 1939, A
BARRICADE, 1950, A
BARRICADE, THE, 1917
BARRICADE, THE, 1921
BARRIER, 1966, A
BARRIER, THE, 1926, A
BARRIER, THE, 1937, A
BARRIERS BURNED AWAY, 1925
BARRIERS OF FOLLY, 1922
BARRIERS OF SOCIETY, 1916
BARRIERS OF THE LAW, 1925, A
BARRY LYNDON, 1975, C-O
BARRY MC KENZIE HOLDS HIS OWN, 1975
BARS OF HATE, 1936, A
BARS OF IRON, 1920
BARTLEBY, 1970, A
BARTON MYSTERY, THE, 1920
BARTON MYSTERY, THE, 1932, A
BASHFUL BACHELOR, THE, 1942, A
BASHFUL BUCCANEER, 1925, A
BASHFUL ELEPHANT, THE, 1962, A
BASILEUS QUARTET, 1984, O
BASKET CASE, 1982, O
BASKETBALL FIX, THE, 1951, A
BAT PEOPLE, THE, 1974, C
BAT WHISPERS, THE, 1930, A
BAT, THE, 1926, A
BAT, THE, 1959, C
BATAAN, 1943, C
BATHING BEAUTY, 1944, A
BATMAN, 1966, AA
BATTLE AT APACHE PASS, THE, 1952, A
BATTLE AT BLOODY BEACH, 1961, A
BATTLE BENEATH THE EARTH, 1968, A
BATTLE BEYOND THE STARS, 1980, C
BATTLE BEYOND THE SUN, 1963, O
BATTLE CIRCUS, 1953, A
BATTLE CRY, 1955, A
BATTLE CRY, 1959, A
BATTLE CRY OF PEACE, THE, 1915, A
BATTLE CRY, THE
BATTLE FOR MUSIC, 1943, A
BATTLE FOR THE PLANET OF THE APES, 1973, A
BATTLE HELL, 1956, A
BATTLE HYMN, 1957, A
BATTLE IN OUTER SPACE, 1960, A
BATTLE OF ALGIERS, THE, 1967, C
BATTLE OF AUSTERLITZ
BATTLE OF BALLOTS, THE, 1915
BATTLE OF BILLY'S POND, 1976
BATTLE OF BLOOD ISLAND, 1960, A
BATTLE OF BRITAIN, THE, 1969
BATTLE OF BROADWAY, 1938, A
BATTLE OF EL ALAMEIN, 1971
BATTLE OF GALLIPOLI, 1931, A
BATTLE OF GETTYSBURG, 1914, A
BATTLE OF GREED, 1934, A
BATTLE OF HEARTS, 1916
BATTLE OF LIFE, THE, 1916, A
BATTLE OF LOVE'S RETURN, THE, 1971, A
BATTLE OF MONS, 1929
BATTLE OF PARIS, THE, 1929, A
BATTLE OF ROGUE RIVER, 1954, A
BATTLE OF SHILOH, THE, 1914
BATTLE OF THE AMAZONS, 1973, A
BATTLE OF THE BULGE, 1965, A
BATTLE OF THE CORAL SEA, 1959, A
BATTLE OF THE EAGLES, 1981
BATTLE OF THE NERETVA, 1971, A
BATTLE OF THE RAILS, 1949, A
BATTLE OF THE RIVER PLATE, THE
BATTLE OF THE SEXES, THE, 1914, A
BATTLE OF THE SEXES, THE, 1928, A
BATTLE OF THE SEXES, THE, 1960, A
BATTLE OF THE VI
BATTLE OF THE VILLA FIORITA, THE, 1965, A
BATTLE OF THE WORLDS, 1961, A
BATTLE OF WATERLOO, THE, 1913
BATTLE STATIONS, 1956, A
BATTLE STRIPE
BATTLE TAXI, 1955, A
BATTLE ZONE, 1952, A
BATTLE, THE, 1934, A
BATTLEAXE, THE, 1962, A
BATTLEGROUND, 1949, A
BATTLER, THE, 1919
BATTLER, THE, 1925
BATTLES OF CHIEF PONTIAC, 1952, A
BATTLES OF THE CORONEL AND FALKLAND ISLANDS, THE, 1928, A
BATTLESHIP POTEMKIN, THE, 1925, C
BATTLESTAR GALACTICA, 1979, A
BATTLETRUCK, 1982, C
BATTLIN' BILL, 1927
BATTLIN' BUCKAROO, 1924
BATTLING BATES, 1923
BATTLING BELLHOP, THE
BATTLING BOOKWORM, 1928
BATTLING BUCKAROO, 1932, A
BATTLING BUDDY, 1924
BATTLING BUNYON, 1925
BATTLING BURKE, 1928
BATTLING BUTLER, 1926, A
BATTLING FOOL, THE, 1924
BATTLING JANE, 1918
BATTLING KID, 1926
BATTLING KING, 1922
BATTLING MARSHAL, 1950, A
BATTLING MASON, 1924
BATTLING ORIOLES, THE, 1924
BAVU, 1923
BAWBS O' BLUE RIDGE, 1916
BAWDY ADVENTURES OF TOM JONES, THE, 1976, O
BAXTER, 1973, C
BAY BOY, 1984, C
BAY OF ANGELS, 1964, C
BAY OF SAINT MICHEL, THE, 1963, A
BAYOU, 1957, A
BE A LITTLE SPORT, 1919
BE CAREFUL, MR. SMITH, 1935
BE MINE TONIGHT, 1933, A
BE MY GUEST, 1965, A
BE MY VALENTINE, OR ELSE...
BE MY WIFE, 1921
BE YOURSELF, 1930, A
BEACH BALL, 1965, A
BEACH BLANKET BINGO, 1965, A
BEACH BUNNIES, 1977
BEACH COMBER, THE
BEACH GIRLS, 1982, C-O
BEACH GIRLS AND THE MONSTER, THE, 1965, C
BEACH HOUSE, 1982
BEACH HOUSE PARTY
BEACH OF DREAMS, 1921
BEACH PARTY, 1963, A
BEACH PARTY, ITALIAN STYLE
BEACH RED, 1967, A
BEACHCOMBER, THE, 1938, A
BEACHCOMBER, THE, 1955, A
BEACHHEAD, 1954, C
BEADS OF ONE ROSARY, THE, 1982, A
BEALE STREET MAMA, 1946
BEANS, 1918
BEAR ISLAND, 1980, C
BEAR'S WEDDING, THE, 1926
BEAR, THE, 1963, AA
BEAR, THE, 1984, C
BEARCAT, THE, 1922
BEARS AND I, THE, 1974, C
BEARTOOTH, 1978
BEAST FROM 20,000 FATHOMS, THE, 1953, C
BEAST FROM THE HAUNTED CAVE, 1960, C
BEAST IN THE CELLAR, THE, 1971, C
BEAST MUST DIE, THE, 1974, A
BEAST OF BABYLON AGAINST THE SON OF HERCULES
BEAST OF BLOOD, 1970, C-O
BEAST OF BORNEO, 1935
BEAST OF BUDAPEST, THE, 1958, C
BEAST OF HOLLOW MOUNTAIN, THE, 1956, A
BEAST OF MOROCCO
BEAST OF THE CITY, THE, 1932, C-O
BEAST OF THE DEAD
BEAST OF THE YELLOW NIGHT, 1971
BEAST OF YUCCA FLATS, THE, 1961, C
BEAST THAT KILLED WOMEN, 1965
BEAST WITH A MILLION EYES, THE, 1956, A
BEAST WITH FIVE FINGERS, THE, 1946, C
BEAST WITHIN, THE, 1982, O
BEAST, THE, 1916
BEAST, THE, 1975, O
BEASTMASTER, THE, 1982, C
BEASTS, 1983
BEASTS OF BERLIN, 1939, C
BEASTS OF MARSEILLES, THE, 1959, C
BEAT GENERATION, THE, 1959, C
"BEAT" GIRL
BEAT STREET, 1984, A-C
BEAT THE BAND, 1947, A
BEAT THE DEVIL, 1953, A
BEATEN, 1924
BEATING THE GAME, 1921, A
BEATING THE ODDS, 1919
BEATNIKS, THE, 1960, O
BEAU BANDIT, 1930, A
BEAU BROADWAY, 1928
BEAU BROCADE, 1916
BEAU BRUMMEL, 1924, A
BEAU BRUMMELL, 1954, A
BEAU GESTE, 1926, A
BEAU GESTE, 1939, A
BEAU GESTE, 1966, A
BEAU IDEAL, 1931, A
BEAU JAMES, 1957, A
BEAU PERE, 1981, O
BEAU REVEL, 1921, C
BEAU SABREUR, 1928, A
BEAUTE FATALE, 1916
BEAUTE QUI MEURT, 1917
BEAUTIFUL ADVENTURE, 1932, A
BEAUTIFUL ADVENTURE, THE, 1917
BEAUTIFUL AND DAMNED, THE, 1922, A
BEAUTIFUL BLONDE FROM BASHFUL BEND, THE, 1949, A
BEAUTIFUL BUT BROKE, 1944, A
BEAUTIFUL BUT DEADLY
BEAUTIFUL BUT DUMB, 1928, A
BEAUTIFUL CHEAT, THE, 1926, A
BEAUTIFUL CHEAT, THE, 1946, A
BEAUTIFUL CITY, THE, 1925
BEAUTIFUL GAMBLER, THE, 1921, A
BEAUTIFUL JIM
BEAUTIFUL KITTY, 1923, A
BEAUTIFUL LIAR, THE, 1921, A
BEAUTIFUL LIE, THE, 1917
BEAUTIFUL MRS. REYNOLDS, THE, 1918
BEAUTIFUL PRISONER, THE, 1983, C
BEAUTIFUL SINNER, THE, 1924
BEAUTIFUL STRANGER, 1954, C
BEAUTIFUL SWINDLERS, THE, 1967, O
BEAUTIFULLY TRIMMED, 1920
BEAUTY AND BULLETS, 1928, A
BEAUTY AND THE BAD MAN, 1925
BEAUTY AND THE BANDIT, 1946, A
BEAUTY AND THE BARGE, 1937, A
BEAUTY AND THE BEAST, 1947, A
BEAUTY AND THE BEAST, 1963, C
BEAUTY AND THE BODY, 1963
BEAUTY AND THE BOLSHEVIK, 1923
BEAUTY AND THE BOSS, 1932, A
BEAUTY AND THE DEVIL, 1952, A
BEAUTY AND THE ROGUE, 1918
BEAUTY FOR SALE, 1933, A
BEAUTY FOR THE ASKING, 1939, A
BEAUTY FROM NIVERNAISE, THE
BEAUTY IN CHAINS, 1918
BEAUTY JUNGLE, THE, 1966, C
BEAUTY MARKET, THE, 1920
BEAUTY ON PARADE, 1950, A
BEAUTY PARLOR, 1932, A
BEAUTY PRIZE, THE, 1924
BEAUTY PROOF, 1919
BEAUTY SHOP, THE, 1922
BEAUTY SHOPPERS, 1927
BEAUTY'S DAUGHTER, 1935
BEAUTY'S SORROWS, 1931
BEAUTY'S WORTH, 1922
BEBO'S GIRL, 1964, A
BECAUSE, 1918
BECAUSE, 1921
BECAUSE I LOVED YOU, 1930, C
BECAUSE OF EVE, 1948, C-O
BECAUSE OF HIM, 1946, A
BECAUSE OF THE CATS, 1974
BECAUSE OF THE WOMAN, 1917
BECAUSE OF YOU, 1952, A
BECAUSE THEY'RE YOUNG, 1960, C
BECAUSE YOU'RE MINE, 1952, AA
BECKET, 1923
BECKET, 1964, C
BECKONING FLAME, THE, 1916
BECKONING ROADS, 1920
BECKONING TRAIL, THE, 1916
BECKY, 1927
BECKY SHARP, 1935, C
BED AND BOARD, 1971, C
BED AND BREAKFAST, 1930, A
BED AND BREAKFAST, 1936, A
BED AND SOFA, 1926
BED OF ROSES, 1933, A
BED OF VIOLENCE, 1967
BED SITTING ROOM, THE, 1969, C
BEDAZZLED, 1967, C
BEDELIA, 1946, A
BEDEVILLED, 1955, C
BEDFORD INCIDENT, THE, 1965, C
BEDKNOBS AND BROOMSTICKS, 1971, AAA
BEDLAM, 1946, C
BEDROOM EYES, 1984, O
BEDROOM WINDOW, THE, 1924, A
BEDSIDE, 1934, A
BEDSIDE MANNER, 1945, A

BEDTIME FOR BONZO, 1951, AA
BEDTIME STORY, 1938, A
BEDTIME STORY, 1942, A
BEDTIME STORY, 1964, C
BEDTIME STORY, A, 1933, AA
BEEN DOWN SO LONG IT LOOKS LIKE UP TO ME, 1977, A
BEES IN PARADISE, 1944, A
BEES, THE, 1978, C
BEETLE, THE, 1919
BEFORE DAWN, 1933, A
BEFORE HIM ALL ROME TREMBLED, 1947, A
BEFORE I HANG, 1940, A
BEFORE I WAKE
BEFORE MIDNIGHT, 1925
BEFORE MIDNIGHT, 1934, A
BEFORE MORNING, 1933, A
BEFORE THE REVOLUTION, 1964, C
BEFORE THE WHITE MAN CAME, 1920
BEFORE WINTER COMES, 1969, C
BEG, BORROW OR STEAL, 1937, A
BEGGAR GIRL'S WEDDING, THE, 1915
BEGGAR IN PURPLE, A, 1920
BEGGAR OF CAWNPORE, THE, 1916
BEGGAR ON HORSEBACK, 1925, A
BEGGAR PRINCE, THE, 1920
BEGGAR STUDENT, THE, 1931, A
BEGGAR STUDENT, THE, 1958, A
BEGGAR'S HOLIDAY, 1934
BEGGAR'S OPERA, THE, 1953, C
BEGGARS IN ERMINE, 1934, A
BEGGARS OF LIFE, 1928, A-C
BEGGING THE RING, 1979
BEGINNING OF THE END, 1957, C
BEGINNING OR THE END, THE, 1947, A
BEGUILED, THE, 1971, A-O
BEHAVE YOURSELF, 1951, C
BEHEMOTH, THE SEA MONSTER, 1959, A
BEHIND CITY LIGHTS, 1945, A
BEHIND CLOSED DOORS, 1929
BEHIND CLOSED SHUTTERS, 1952, O
BEHIND GREEN LIGHTS, 1935, A
BEHIND GREEN LIGHTS, 1946, A
BEHIND JURY DOORS, 1933, A
BEHIND LOCKED DOORS, 1948, A
BEHIND LOCKED DOORS, 1976, O
BEHIND MASKS, 1921
BEHIND OFFICE DOORS, 1931, A
BEHIND PRISON BARS, 1937
BEHIND PRISON GATES, 1939, A
BEHIND PRISON WALLS, 1943, A
BEHIND SOUTHERN LINES, 1952
BEHIND STONE WALLS, 1932, A
BEHIND THAT CURTAIN, 1929, C
BEHIND THE ALTAR, 1929
BEHIND THE CURTAIN, 1924
BEHIND THE DOOR
BEHIND THE DOOR, 1920
BEHIND THE EIGHT BALL, 1942, A
BEHIND THE EVIDENCE, 1935, A
BEHIND THE FRONT, 1926, A
BEHIND THE HEADLINES, 1937, A
BEHIND THE HEADLINES, 1953
BEHIND THE HEADLINES, 1956, A
BEHIND THE HIGH WALL, 1956, C
BEHIND THE IRON CURTAIN
BEHIND THE IRON MASK, 1977, C
BEHIND THE LINES, 1916
BEHIND THE MAKEUP, 1930, C
BEHIND THE MASK, 1917
BEHIND THE MASK, 1932, C
BEHIND THE MASK, 1946, A
BEHIND THE MASK, 1958, C
BEHIND THE MIKE, 1937, A
BEHIND THE NEWS, 1941, A
BEHIND THE RISING SUN, 1943, C
BEHIND THE SCENES, 1914
BEHIND THE SHUTTERS, 1976
BEHIND TWO GUNS, 1924
BEHIND YOUR BACK, 1937, A
BEHOLD A PALE HORSE, 1964, C
BEHOLD MY WIFE, 1920
BEHOLD MY WIFE, 1935, C
BEHOLD THE MAN, 1921
BEHOLD THIS WOMAN, 1924
BEILIS CASE, THE, 1917
BEING RESPECTABLE, 1924
BEING THERE, 1979, C
BEING, THE, 1983, C
BELA LUGOSI MEETS A BROOKLYN GORILLA, 1952, A
BELGIAN, THE, 1917
BELIEVE IN ME, 1971, O
BELIEVE ME, XANTIPPE, 1918
BELL BOY 13, 1923
BELL FOR ADANO, A, 1945, A
BELL JAR, THE, 1979, O
BELL OF HELL, THE, 1973
BELL' ANTONIO, 1962, C-O
BELL, BOOK AND CANDLE, 1958, A
BELL-BOTTOM GEORGE, 1943, A
BELLA DONNA, 1915
BELLA DONNA, 1923
BELLA DONNA, 1934, A
BELLA DONNA, 1983, C
BELLAMY TRIAL, THE, 1929, C
BELLAMY: MESSAGE GIRL MURDERS, 1980
BELLBOY, THE, 1960, AA
BELLE DE JOUR, 1968, O
BELLE LE GRAND, 1951, A
BELLE OF ALASKA, 1922
BELLE OF BROADWAY, THE, 1926
BELLE OF NEW YORK, THE, 1919
BELLE OF NEW YORK, THE, 1952, A
BELLE OF OLD MEXICO, 1950, A
BELLE OF THE NINETIES, 1934, C
BELLE OF THE SEASON, THE, 1919
BELLE OF THE YUKON, 1944, A
BELLE SOMMERS, 1962
BELLE STARR, 1941, A
BELLE STARR'S DAUGHTER, 1947, A
BELLES OF ST. CLEMENTS, THE, 1936, A
BELLES OF ST. TRINIAN'S, THE, 1954, AA
BELLES ON THEIR TOES, 1952, AAA
BELLISSIMA, 1952, C
BELLMAN, THE, 1947, C
BELLS, 1981, O
BELLS ARE RINGING, 1960, AA
BELLS GO DOWN, THE, 1943, A
BELLS OF CAPISTRANO, 1942, A
BELLS OF CORONADO, 1950, AA
BELLS OF ROSARITA, 1945, AAA
BELLS OF SAN ANGELO, 1947, A
BELLS OF SAN FERNANDO, 1947, A
BELLS OF SAN JUAN, 1922
BELLS OF ST. MARY'S, THE, 1928
BELLS OF ST. MARY'S, THE, 1945, AAA
BELLS, THE, 1914
BELLS, THE, 1918
BELLS, THE, 1926
BELLS, THE, 1931, C
BELONGING, 1922
BELOVED, 1934, A
BELOVED ADVENTURESS, THE, 1917
BELOVED BACHELOR, THE, 1931, A
BELOVED BLACKMAILER, THE, 1918
BELOVED BRAT, 1938, A
BELOVED BRUTE, THE, 1924
BELOVED CHEATER, THE, 1920
BELOVED ENEMY, 1936, C
BELOVED IMPOSTER, 1936, A
BELOVED IMPOSTER, THE, 1918
BELOVED INFIDEL, 1959, A
BELOVED JIM, 1917
BELOVED ROGUE, THE, 1927, A
BELOVED ROGUES, 1917
BELOVED TRAITOR, THE, 1918
BELOVED VAGABOND, THE, 1912
BELOVED VAGABOND, THE, 1923
BELOVED VAGABOND, THE, 1936, A
BELOVED, THE, 1972
BELOW THE BELT, 1980, C
BELOW THE BORDER, 1942, A
BELOW THE DEAD LINE, 1921
BELOW THE DEADLINE, 1929
BELOW THE DEADLINE, 1936, A
BELOW THE DEADLINE, 1946, A
BELOW THE HILL, 1974
BELOW THE LINE, 1925, A
BELOW THE RIO GRANDE, 1923
BELOW THE SEA, 1933, A
BELOW THE SURFACE, 1920
BELPHEGOR THE MOUNTEBANK, 1921
BELSTONE FOX, THE, 1976, AAA
BELT AND SUSPENDERS MAN, THE, 1970
BEN, 1972, A
BEN BLAIR, 1916
BEN HUR, 1959, A
BEN-HUR, 1925, A
BEND OF THE RIVER, 1952, C
BENEATH THE 12-MILE REEF, 1953, A
BENEATH THE CZAR, 1914
BENEATH THE PLANET OF THE APES, 1970, AA
BENEATH WESTERN SKIES, 1944, A
BENGAL BRIGADE, 1954, A
BENGAL TIGER, 1936, A
BENGAZI, 1955, A-C
BENJAMIN, 1968, O
BENJAMIN, 1973, AA
BENJI, 1974, AAA
BENNIE THE HOWL, 1927
BENNY GOODMAN STORY, THE, 1956, AA
BENSON MURDER CASE, THE, 1930, A
BENTLEY'S CONSCIENCE, 1922
BENVENUTA, 1983, C
BEQUEST TO THE NATION
BERKELEY SQUARE, 1933, A
BERLIN AFTER DARK, 1929
BERLIN ALEXANDERPLATZ, 1933, A
BERLIN CORRESPONDENT, 1942, A
BERLIN EXPRESS, 1948, C
BERLIN VIA AMERICA, 1918
BERMONDSEY KID, THE, 1933, A
BERMUDA AFFAIR, 1956, A
BERMUDA MYSTERY, 1944, A
BERNADETTE OF LOURDES, 1962, A
BERNARDINE, 1957, AA
BERSERK, 1967, O
BERTHA, THE SEWING MACHINE GIRL, 1927, A
BESIDE THE BONNIE BRIER BUSH
BEST BAD MAN, THE, 1925
BEST DEFENSE, 1984, O
BEST FOOT FORWARD, 1943, A
BEST FRIENDS, 1975, O
BEST FRIENDS, 1975
BEST FRIENDS, 1982, A
BEST HOUSE IN LONDON, THE, 1969, O
BEST LITTLE WHOREHOUSE IN TEXAS, THE, 1982, O
BEST MAN WINS, 1948, AA
BEST MAN WINS, THE, 1935, A
BEST MAN, THE, 1917
BEST MAN, THE, 1919
BEST MAN, THE, 1964, C
BEST OF ENEMIES, 1933, A
BEST OF ENEMIES, THE, 1962, A
BEST OF EVERYTHING, THE, 1959, C-O
BEST OF LUCK, THE, 1920
BEST OF THE BADMEN, 1951, A
BEST PEOPLE, THE, 1925
BEST THINGS IN LIFE ARE FREE, THE, 1956, AA
BEST WAY, THE, 1978, C
BEST YEARS OF OUR LIVES, THE, 1946, A
BEST, THE, 1979
BETES...COMES LES HOMMES, 1923
BETHUNE, 1977
BETRAYAL, 1929
BETRAYAL, 1932, A
BETRAYAL, 1939, A
BETRAYAL, 1983, O
BETRAYAL FROM THE EAST, 1945, AA
BETRAYAL, THE
BETRAYAL, THE, 1929
BETRAYAL, THE, 1948, A
BETRAYAL, THE, 1958, A
BETRAYAL: THE STORY OF KAMILLA
BETRAYED, 1916
BETRAYED, 1917
BETRAYED, 1954, C
BETRAYED WOMEN, 1955, C
BETSY ROSS, 1917
BETSY'S BURGLAR, 1917
BETSY, THE, 1978, C
BETTA THE GYPSY, 1918
BETTER 'OLE, THE, 1926, A
BETTER A WIDOW, 1969, O
BETTER DAYS, 1927
BETTER HALF, THE, 1918
BETTER LATE THAN NEVER, 1983, C
BETTER MAN WINS, THE, 1922
BETTER MAN, THE, 1914
BETTER MAN, THE, 1915
BETTER MAN, THE, 1921
BETTER MAN, THE, 1926
BETTER TIMES, 1919
BETTER WAY, THE, 1926
BETTER WIFE, THE, 1919
BETTER WOMAN, THE, 1915
BETTINA LOVED A SOLDIER, 1916
BETTY AND THE BUCCANEERS, 1917
BETTY BE GOOD, 1917
BETTY CO-ED, 1946, A
BETTY OF GRAYSTONE, 1916
BETTY TAKES A HAND, 1918
BETTY TO THE RESCUE, 1917
BETWEEN DANGERS, 1927
BETWEEN FIGHTING MEN, 1932, A
BETWEEN FRIENDS, 1924
BETWEEN HEAVEN AND HELL, 1956, A
BETWEEN MEN, 1916
BETWEEN MEN, 1935, A
BETWEEN MIDNIGHT AND DAWN, 1950, C
BETWEEN THE LINES, 1977, C
BETWEEN TIME AND ETERNITY, 1960, A
BETWEEN TWO HUSBANDS, 1922
BETWEEN TWO WOMEN, 1937, C
BETWEEN TWO WOMEN, 1944, A
BETWEEN TWO WORLDS
BETWEEN TWO WORLDS, 1944, A
BETWEEN US GIRLS, 1942, C
BEULAH, 1915
BEVERLY HILLS COP, 1984, O
BEVERLY OF GRAUSTARK, 1926, A
BEWARE, 1919
BEWARE, 1946, A
BEWARE MY BRETHREN, 1972
BEWARE OF BACHELORS, 1928
BEWARE OF BLONDES, 1928

BEWARE OF BLONDIE, 1950, AA
BEWARE OF CHILDREN, 1961, A
BEWARE OF LADIES, 1937, A
BEWARE OF MARRIED MEN, 1928
BEWARE OF PITY, 1946, A
BEWARE OF STRANGERS, 1918
BEWARE OF THE BRIDE, 1920
BEWARE OF THE LAW, 1922
BEWARE OF WINDOWS, 1927
BEWARE SPOOKS, 1939, A
BEWARE THE BLACK WIDOW, 1968
BEWARE! THE BLOB, 1972, A
BEWARE, MY LOVELY, 1952, C
BEWITCHED, 1945, C
BEYOND, 1921, A
BEYOND A REASONABLE DOUBT, 1956, C
BEYOND ALL ODDS, 1926
BEYOND AND BACK, 1978, A
BEYOND ATLANTIS, 1973, O
BEYOND CONTROL, 1971
BEYOND EVIL, 1980, A
BEYOND FEAR, 1977, C
BEYOND GLORY, 1948, A
BEYOND GOOD AND EVIL, 1984, O
BEYOND LONDON LIGHTS, 1928
BEYOND MOMBASA, 1957, A-C
BEYOND PRICE, 1921, A
BEYOND REASON, 1977
BEYOND REASONABLE DOUBT, 1980, C
BEYOND THE BLUE HORIZON, 1942, A
BEYOND THE BORDER, 1925
BEYOND THE CITIES, 1930, A
BEYOND THE CROSSROADS, 1922
BEYOND THE CURTAIN, 1960, A
BEYOND THE DOOR, 1975, O
BEYOND THE DOOR II, 1979, O
BEYOND THE DREAMS OF AVARICE, 1920
BEYOND THE FOG, 1981, O
BEYOND THE FOREST, 1949, C
BEYOND THE LAST FRONTIER, 1943, A
BEYOND THE LAW, 1918
BEYOND THE LAW, 1930
BEYOND THE LAW, 1934, A
BEYOND THE LAW, 1967
BEYOND THE LAW, 1968, C
BEYOND THE LIMIT, 1983, C
BEYOND THE LIVING
BEYOND THE MOON, 1964
BEYOND THE PECOS, 1945, A
BEYOND THE POSEIDON ADVENTURE, 1979, A-C
BEYOND THE PURPLE HILLS, 1950, A
BEYOND THE RAINBOW, 1922
BEYOND THE REEF, 1981, C
BEYOND THE RIO GRANDE, 1930, A
BEYOND THE RIVER, 1922
BEYOND THE ROCKIES, 1926
BEYOND THE ROCKIES, 1932, A
BEYOND THE ROCKS, 1922, A
BEYOND THE SACRAMENTO, 1941, A
BEYOND THE SHADOWS, 1918
BEYOND THE SIERRAS, 1928
BEYOND THE TIME BARRIER, 1960, C
BEYOND THE TRAIL, 1926
BEYOND THE UNIVERSE, 1981
BEYOND THE VEIL, 1925
BEYOND THE WALL
BEYOND THIS PLACE, 1959, C
BEYOND TOMORROW, 1940, A
BEYOND VICTORY, 1931, C
BHOWANI JUNCTION, 1956, C
BIBI, 1977
BIBLE...IN THE BEGINNING, THE, 1966, AA
BICYCLE THIEF, THE, 1949, A-C
BID FOR FORTUNE, A, 1917, A
BIDDY, 1983, A
BIFF BANG BUDDY, 1924
BIG ADVENTURE, THE, 1921
BIG AND THE BAD, THE, 1971, C
BIG BAD MAMA, 1974, O
BIG BAD WOLF, THE, 1968
BIG BEAT, THE, 1958, A
BIG BIRD CAGE, THE, 1972, O
BIG BLOCKADE, THE, 1942, A
BIG BLUFF, THE, 1933, A
BIG BLUFF, THE, 1955, C
BIG BONANZA, THE, 1944, C
BIG BOODLE, THE, 1957, C
BIG BOSS, THE, 1941, A
BIG BOUNCE, THE, 1969, O
BIG BOY, 1930, A
BIG BOY RIDES AGAIN, 1935
BIG BRAIN, THE, 1933, A
BIG BRAWL, THE, 1980, C
BIG BROADCAST OF 1936, THE, 1935, AA
BIG BROADCAST OF 1937, THE, 1936, AA
BIG BROADCAST OF 1938, THE, 1937, AA
BIG BROADCAST, THE, 1932, AA
BIG BROTHER, 1923
BIG BROWN EYES, 1936, A
BIG BUS, THE, 1976, A
BIG BUSINESS, 1930, A
BIG BUSINESS, 1934, A
BIG BUSINESS, 1937, A
BIG BUSINESS GIRL, 1931, A
BIG BUST-OUT, THE, 1973
BIG CAGE, THE, 1933, A
BIG CALIBRE, 1935
BIG CAPER, THE, 1957, C
BIG CARNIVAL, THE, 1951, O
BIG CAT, THE, 1949, C
BIG CATCH, THE, 1968, A
BIG CHANCE, THE, 1933, A
BIG CHANCE, THE, 1957, A
BIG CHASE, THE, 1954, A
BIG CHIEF, THE, 1960, AA
BIG CHILL, THE, 1983, C
BIG CIRCUS, THE, 1959, A
BIG CITY, 1937, A
BIG CITY, 1948, AA
BIG CITY BLUES, C
BIG CITY, THE, 1928, A
BIG CITY, THE, 1963, A
BIG CLOCK, THE, 1948, C
BIG COMBO, THE, 1955, O
BIG COUNTRY, THE, 1958
BIG CUBE, THE, 1969, O
BIG DADDY, 1969, O
BIG DAN, 1923
BIG DAY, THE, 1960, A
BIG DEAL ON MADONNA STREET, THE, 1960, A
BIG DIAMOND ROBBERY, THE, 1929
BIG DOLL HOUSE, THE, 1971, O
BIG DOLL HOUSE, THE, 1971
BIG DRIVE, THE, 1928
BIG EXECUTIVE, 1933, A
BIG FELLA, 1937, A
BIG FIGHT, THE, 1930
BIG FISHERMAN, THE, 1959, A-C
BIG FIX, THE, 1947, A
BIG FIX, THE, 1978, C
BIG FOOT, 1973, O
BIG FRAME, THE, 1953, A
BIG FUN CARNIVAL, THE, 1957
BIG GAMBLE, THE, 1931, A
BIG GAMBLE, THE, 1961, A
BIG GAME, 1921, C
BIG GAME, THE
BIG GAME, THE, 1936, A
BIG GAME, THE, 1972, C
BIG GUNDOWN, THE, 1968, A
BIG GUNS
BIG GUSHER, THE, 1951, A
BIG GUY, THE, 1939, A
BIG HAND FOR THE LITTLE LADY, A, 1966, A
BIG HANGOVER,THE, 1950, A-C
BIG HAPPINESS, 1920
BIG HEART, THE
BIG HEARTED HERBERT, 1934, A
BIG HEAT, THE, 1953, C
BIG HOP, THE, 1928
BIG HOUSE, THE, 1930, C
BIG HOUSE, U.S.A., 1955, O
BIG JACK, 1949, C
BIG JAKE, 1971, O
BIG JIM GARRITY, 1916
BIG JIM McLAIN, 1952, C
BIG JOB, THE, 1965, A
BIG KILLING, THE, 1928
BIG KNIFE, THE, 1955, O
BIG LAND, THE, 1957, A
BIG LEAGUER, 1953, A
BIG LIFT, THE, 1950, A-C
BIG LITTLE PERSON, THE, 1919
BIG MEAT EATER, 1984, O
BIG MONEY, 1918
BIG MONEY, 1930, A
BIG MONEY, THE, 1962, A
BIG MOUTH, THE, 1967, AA
BIG NEWS, 1929, A
BIG NIGHT, THE, 1951, C
BIG NIGHT, THE, 1960, C
BIG NOISE, THE, 1928
BIG NOISE, THE, 1936, A
BIG NOISE, THE, 1944, AA
BIG OPERATOR, THE, 1959, O
BIG PAL, 1925, A
BIG PARADE, THE, 1925, A
BIG PARTY, THE, 1930, A
BIG PAYOFF, THE, 1933, A
BIG POND, THE, 1930, A
BIG PUNCH, THE, 1921, A
BIG PUNCH, THE, 1948, A
BIG RACE, THE, 1934, AA
BIG RED, 1962, AA
BIG RED ONE, THE, 1980, C
BIG SCORE, THE, 1983, C
BIG SEARCH, THE
BIG SHAKEDOWN, THE, 1934, A
BIG SHOT, THE, 1931, A
BIG SHOT, THE, 1937, A
BIG SHOT, THE, 1942, A
BIG SHOW, THE, 1926
BIG SHOW, THE, 1937, A
BIG SHOW, THE, 1961, A
BIG SHOW-OFF, THE, 1945, C
BIG SISTER, THE, 1916
BIG SKY, THE, 1952, A
BIG SLEEP, THE, 1946, C
BIG SLEEP, THE, 1978, C
BIG SOMBRERO, THE, 1949, A
BIG SPLASH, THE, 1935, A
BIG STAKES, 1922
BIG STAMPEDE, THE, 1932, A
BIG STEAL, THE, 1949, C
BIG STORE, THE, 1941, AA
BIG STREET, THE, 1942, A
BIG STUNT, 1925
BIG SWITCH, THE, 1970, O
BIG TIMBER, 1917
BIG TIMBER, 1924
BIG TIMBER, 1950, A-C
BIG TIME, 1929, A
BIG TIME, 1977
BIG TIME OR BUST, 1934, A
BIG TIMER, 1932
BIG TIMERS, 1947
BIG TIP OFF, THE, 1955, C
BIG TOWN, 1932, C
BIG TOWN, 1947, AA
BIG TOWN AFTER DARK, 1947, AA
BIG TOWN CZAR, 1939, C
BIG TOWN GIRL, 1937, A
BIG TOWN IDEAS, 1921, A
BIG TOWN ROUND-UP, 1921
BIG TOWN SCANDAL, 1948, AA
BIG TRAIL, THE, 1930, A
BIG TREES, THE, 1952, A-C
BIG TREMAINE, 1916, A
BIG WEDNESDAY, 1978, A-C
BIG WHEEL, THE, 1949, A-C
BIG ZAPPER, 1974
BIGAMIST, THE, 1916
BIGAMIST, THE, 1921, A
BIGAMIST, THE, 1953, C
BIGGER MAN, THE
BIGGER SPLASH,A, 1984, O
BIGGER THAN BARNUM'S, 1926
BIGGER THAN LIFE, 1956, C
BIGGEST BUNDLE OF THEM ALL, THE, 1968, A
BIGGEST SHOW ON EARTH, THE, 1918
BIJOU, 1972
BIKINI BEACH, 1964, A
BIKINI PARADISE, 1967
BILL AND COO, 1947, AAA
BILL APPERSON'S BOY, 1919
BILL CRACKS DOWN, 1937, A
BILL FOR DIVORCEMENT, A, 1922
BILL HENRY, 1919
BILL OF DIVORCEMENT, 1940, C
BILL OF DIVORCEMENT, A, 1932, A-C
BILL'S LEGACY, 1931, A
BILLIE, 1965, A
BILLION DOLLAR BRAIN, 1967, C
BILLION DOLLAR HOBO, THE, 1977, A
BILLION DOLLAR SCANDAL, 1932, A
BILLION DOLLAR THREAT, THE, 1979
BILLIONS, 1920
BILLY AND THE BIG STICK, 1917
BILLY BUDD, 1962, C
BILLY IN THE LOWLANDS, 1979, A-C
BILLY JACK, 1971, O
BILLY JACK GOES TO WASHINGTON, 1977, C
BILLY JIM, 1922, A
BILLY LIAR, 1963, A-C
BILLY ROSE'S DIAMOND HORSESHOE
BILLY ROSE'S JUMBO
BILLY THE KID, 1930, A
BILLY THE KID, 1941, A
BILLY THE KID IN TEXAS, 1940, A
BILLY THE KID OUTLAWED, 1940
BILLY THE KID RETURNS, 1938, A
BILLY THE KID TRAPPED, 1942, A
BILLY THE KID VS. DRACULA, 1966, A
BILLY THE KID WANTED, 194A
BILLY THE KID'S FIGHTING PALS, 1941, A
BILLY THE KID'S GUN JUSTICE, 1940
BILLY THE KID'S RANGE WAR, 1941, A
BILLY THE KID'S ROUNDUP, 1941, A
BILLY THE KID'S SMOKING GUNS, 1942
BILLY TWO HATS, 1973, O
BILLY'S SPANISH LOVE SPASM, 1915
BIM, 1976
BIMBO THE GREAT, 1961
BING BANG BOOM, 1922
BINGO BONGO, 198A, AA
BINGO LONG TRAVELING ALL-STARS AND MOTOR KINGS, THE, A-C

BIO-HAZARD, 1984
BIOGRAPHY OF A BACHELOR GIRL, 1935, A
BIONIC BOY, THE, 1977, R
BIQUEFARRE, 1983, A
BIRCH INTERVAL, 1976, A
BIRD OF PARADISE, 1932
BIRD OF PARADISE, 1951, C
BIRD OF PREY, A, 1916
BIRD OF PREY, THE, 1918
BIRD WATCH, THE, 1983
BIRD WITH THE CRYSTAL PLUMAGE, THE, 1970, C
BIRDMAN OF ALCATRAZ, 1962, C
BIRDS AND THE BEES, THE, 1965, A
BIRDS COME TO DIE IN PERU, 1968, C
BIRDS DO IT, 1966, A
BIRDS OF A FEATHER, 1931, AA
BIRDS OF A FEATHER, 1935, A
BIRDS OF PREY
BIRDS OF PREY, 1927
BIRDS' CHRISTMAS CAROL, THE, 1917
BIRDS, THE, 1963, C
BIRDS, THE BEES AND THE ITALIANS, THE, 1967, O
BIRDY, 1984, O
BIRTH CONTROL, 1917
BIRTH OF A BABY, 1938, C
BIRTH OF A MAN, THE, 1916
BIRTH OF A NATION, THE, 1915, C
BIRTH OF A RACE, 1919
BIRTH OF A SOUL, THE, 1920
BIRTH OF CHARACTER, THE, 1916
BIRTH OF PATRIOTISM, THE, 1917
BIRTH OF THE BLUES, 1941, A
BIRTHDAY PARTY, THE, 1968, C
BIRTHDAY PRESENT, THE, 1957, C
BIRTHRIGHT, 1924
BIRTHRIGHT, 1939
BISCUIT EATER, THE, 1940, AA
BISCUIT EATER, THE, 1972, AAA
BISHOP MISBEHAVES, THE, 1933, AA
BISHOP MURDER CASE, THE, 1930, A
BISHOP OF THE OZARKS, THE, 1923
BISHOP'S EMERALDS, THE, 1919
BISHOP'S SECRET, THE, 1916
BISHOP'S WIFE, THE, 1947, A
BIT O'HEAVEN, A
BIT OF HEAVEN, A, 1928
BIT OF JADE, A, 1918
BIT OF KINDLING, A, 1917
BITCH, THE, 1979
BITE THE BULLET, 1975, C
BITER BIT, THE, 1937, A
BITS OF LIFE, 1921
BITTER APPLES, 1927
BITTER CREEK, 1954, A
BITTER HARVEST, 1963, C
BITTER RICE, 1950, O
BITTER SPRINGS, 1950, A
BITTER SWEET, 1933, A
BITTER SWEET, 1940, A
BITTER SWEETS, 1928
BITTER TEA OF GENERAL YEN, THE, 1933, C
BITTER TEARS OF PETRA VON KANT, THE, 1970
BITTER TRUTH, 1917
BITTER VICTORY, 1958, C
BITTERSWEET LOVE, 1976, C
BIZARRE, 1969
BIZARRE BIZARRE, 1939, A
BIZET'S CARMEN, 1984, A-C
BLACK 13, 1954, A
BLACK ABBOT, THE, 1934, A
BLACK ACE, THE, 1928
BLACK ACES, 1937, A
BLACK AND WHITE IN COLOR, 1976, C
BLACK ANGEL, 1946, A
BLACK ANGELS, THE, 1970, O
BLACK ARROW, 1948, A
BLACK BAG, THE, 1922
BLACK BANDIT, 1938
BLACK BART, 1948, C
BLACK BEAUTY, 1921, AAA
BLACK BEAUTY, 1933, AAA
BLACK BEAUTY, 1946, AA
BLACK BEAUTY, 1971, AA
BLACK BELLY OF THE TARANTULA, THE, 1972, O
BLACK BELT JONES, 1974, O
BLACK BELT JONES, 1974
BLACK BIRD DESCENDING: TENSE ALIGNMENT, 1977
BLACK BIRD, THE, 1926, A
BLACK BIRD, THE, 1975, A-C
BLACK BOOK, THE, 1949, A
BLACK BOOMERANG, THE, 1925
BLACK BUTTERFLIES, 1928
BLACK BUTTERFLY, THE, 1916
BLACK CAESAR, 1973, O
BLACK CAMEL, THE, 1931, A
BLACK CARGOES OF THE SOUTH SEAS, 1929
BLACK CARRION, 1984
BLACK CASTLE, THE, 1952, C
BLACK CAT, THE, 1934, C
BLACK CAT, THE, 1941, A
BLACK CAT, THE, 1966, O
BLACK CAT, THE, 1984, O
BLACK CHARIOT, 1971
BLACK CHRISTMAS, 1974, O
BLACK CIRCLE, THE, 1919
BLACK COFFEE, 1931, A
BLACK CONNECTION, THE, 1974
BLACK CROOK, THE, 1916
BLACK CYCLONE, 1925, AAA
BLACK DAKOTAS, THE, 1954, A-C
BLACK DEVILS OF KALI, THE
BLACK DIAMOND, THE, 1927
BLACK DIAMONDS, 1932, A
BLACK DIAMONDS, 1940, A
BLACK DOLL, THE, 1938, A
BLACK DRAGONS, 1942, A
BLACK EAGLE, 1948, A
BLACK EYE, 1974, O
BLACK EYES, 1939, A
BLACK FANTASY, 1974
BLACK FEAR, 1915
BLACK FEATHER, 1928
BLACK FIST, 1977
BLACK FOREST, THE, 1954
BLACK FRIDAY, 1916
BLACK FRIDAY, 1940, A
BLACK FURY, 1935, C
BLACK GATE, THE, 1919
BLACK GESTAPO, THE, 1975, O
BLACK GIRL, 1972, A
BLACK GLOVE, 1954, A
BLACK GODFATHER, THE, 1974
BLACK GOLD, 1924
BLACK GOLD, 1928
BLACK GOLD, 1947, A
BLACK GOLD, 1963, A-C
BLACK GUNN, 1972, O
BLACK HAND, THE, 1950, C
BLACK HAND GANG, THE, 1930, A
BLACK HEART, THE, 1915
BLACK HEAT, 1976
BLACK HILLS, 1929
BLACK HILLS, 1948, A
BLACK HILLS AMBUSH, 1952, A-C
BLACK HILLS EXPRESS, 1943, A
BLACK HOLE, THE, 1979, A-C
BLACK HOOKER, 1974
BLACK HORSE CANYON, 1954, A
BLACK ICE, THE, 1957, A
BLACK IS WHITE, 1920
BLACK ISLAND, 1979
BLACK JACK
BLACK JACK, 1927
BLACK JACK, 1973, C
BLACK JACK, 1979, AA
BLACK JESUS, 1971
BLACK JOY, 1977, A-C
BLACK KING, 1932, A
BLACK KLANSMAN, THE, 1966, O
BLACK KNIGHT, THE, 1954, A-C
BLACK LASH, THE, 1952, A
BLACK LEGION, THE, 1937, C
BLACK LIGHTING, 1924
BLACK LIKE ME, 1964, C
BLACK LIMELIGHT, 1938, A
BLACK LOLITA, 1975
BLACK MAGIC, 1929
BLACK MAGIC, 1949, C
BLACK MAMA, WHITE MAMA, 1973, O
BLACK MARBLE, THE, 1980, C-O
BLACK MARKET BABIES, 1946, A
BLACK MARKET RUSTLERS, 1943, A
BLACK MASK, 1935, A
BLACK MEMORY, 1947, A
BLACK MIDNIGHT, 1949, AA
BLACK MOON, 1934, C
BLACK MOON, 1975, C
BLACK NARCISSUS, 1947, A-C
BLACK NIGHT, THE, 1916
BLACK OAK CONSPIRACY, 1977, C
BLACK ORCHID, 1952
BLACK ORCHID, 1959, C
BLACK ORCHIDS, 1917
BLACK ORPHEUS, 1959, C
BLACK OXEN, 1924
BLACK PANTHER'S CUB, THE, 1921
BLACK PANTHER, THE, 1977, O
BLACK PARACHUTE, THE, 1944, A
BLACK PARADISE, 1926
BLACK PATCH, 1957, C
BLACK PEARL, THE, 1928
BLACK PEARL, THE, 1977
BLACK PIRATE, THE, 1926, A
BLACK PIRATES, THE, 1954, C
BLACK PIT OF DOCTOR M, 1958, O
BLACK PLANET, THE, 1982
BLACK RAINBOW, 1966
BLACK RAVEN, THE, 1943, A
BLACK RIDER, THE, 1954, A
BLACK RODEO, 1972, C
BLACK ROOM, THE, 1935, C
BLACK ROOM, THE, 1983
BLACK ROOM, THE, 1984, O
BLACK ROSE, THE, 1950, A
BLACK ROSES, 1921
BLACK ROSES, 1936, A
BLACK SABBATH, 1963, O
BLACK SAIL, THE, 1929
BLACK SAMSON, 1974, O
BLACK SAMURAI, 1977
BLACK SCORPION, THE, 1957, C
BLACK SHADOWS, 1920
BLACK SHAMPOO, 1976, O
BLACK SHEEP, 1921
BLACK SHEEP, 1935, A
BLACK SHEEP OF THE FAMILY, THE, 1916
BLACK SHEEP OF WHITEHALL, THE, 1941, A
BLACK SHEEP, A, 1915
BLACK SHEEP, THE, 1920
BLACK SHIELD OF FALWORTH, THE, 1954, A-C
BLACK SIX, THE, 1974, Adven
BLACK SLEEP, THE, 1956, C
BLACK SPIDER, THE, 1920
BLACK SPIDER, THE, 1983, O
BLACK SPURS, 1965, A
BLACK STALLION RETURNS, THE, 1983, A-C
BLACK STALLION, THE, 1979, AAA
BLACK STARLET, 1974
BLACK STORK, THE, 1917
BLACK STREETFIGHTER, 1976
BLACK SUN, THE, 1979, A
BLACK SUNDAY, 1961, O
BLACK SUNDAY, 1977, C
BLACK SWAN, THE, 1942, A
BLACK TEARS, 1927
BLACK TENT, THE, 1956, A
BLACK THUNDERBOLT, THE, 1922
BLACK TIDE, 1958
BLACK TIGHTS, 1962, A
BLACK TORMENT, 1984
BLACK TORMENT, THE, 1965, A
BLACK TRASH, 1978
BLACK TUESDAY, 1955, C
BLACK TULIP, THE, 1921
BLACK TULIP, THE, 1937, A
BLACK VEIL FOR LISA, A, 1969, C
BLACK WATCH, THE, 1929, C
BLACK WATERS, 1929, A
BLACK WHIP, THE, 195A
BLACK WIDOW, 1951, A
BLACK WIDOW, 1954, C
BLACK WINDMILL, THE, 1974, C
BLACK WOLF, THE, 1917
BLACK ZOO, 1963, C
BLACKBEARD THE PIRATE, 1952, A-C
BLACKBEARD'S GHOST, 1968, AA
BLACKBIRDS, 1920
BLACKBOARD JUNGLE, THE, 1955, C
BLACKENSTEIN, 1973, O
BLACKIE'S REDEMPTION, 1919
BLACKJACK, 1978
BLACKJACK KETCHUM, DESPERADO, 1956, A
BLACKLIST, 1916
BLACKMAIL, 1920
BLACKMAIL, 1929, A
BLACKMAIL, 1939, A
BLACKMAIL, 1947, A
BLACKMAILED, 1951, A
BLACKMAILER, 1936, A
BLACKMAILERS, THE, 1915
BLACKOUT, 1940, A
BLACKOUT, 1950, A
BLACKOUT, 1954, A-C
BLACKOUT, 1978, A-C
BLACKSNAKE, 1973
BLACKWELL'S ISLAND, 1939, A
BLACULA, 1972, O
BLADE, 1973, O
BLADE O' GRASS, 1915
BLADE RUNNER, 1982, O
BLADES OF THE MUSKETEERS, 1953, A
BLADYS OF THE STEWPONY, 1919
BLAME IT ON RIO, 1984, O
BLAME IT ON THE NIGHT, 1984, C
BLAME THE WOMAN, 1932, A
BLANCHE, 1971, PC
BLANCHE FURY, 1948, A-C
BLANCHETTE, 1921
BLANCHEVILLE MONSTER, 1963
BLARNEY, 1926
BLARNEY KISS, 1933, A
BLASPHEMER, THE, 1921
BLAST OF SILENCE, 1961, C
BLAST-OFF
BLAST-OFF GIRLS, 1967
BLASTED HOPES, 1924

BLAZE AWAY, 1922
BLAZE O' GLORY, 1930, A
BLAZE OF GLORY, 1963, A
BLAZE OF NOON, 1947, A-C
BLAZING ACROSS THE PECOS, 1948
BLAZING ARROWS, 1922
BLAZING BARRIERS
BLAZING BARRIERS, 1937, A
BLAZING BULLETS, 1951
BLAZING DAYS, 1927, A
BLAZING FOREST, THE, 1952, A-C
BLAZING FRONTIER, 1944, A
BLAZING GUNS, 1935
BLAZING GUNS, 1943, A
BLAZING JUSTICE, 1936
BLAZING LOVE, 1916
BLAZING MAGNUM, 1976
BLAZING SADDLES, 1974, C-O
BLAZING SIX SHOOTERS, 1940, A
BLAZING SIXES, 1937, A
BLAZING STEWARDESSES, 1975
BLAZING SUN, THE, 1950, A
BLAZING THE WESTERN TRAIL, 1945
BLAZING TRAIL, THE, 1921, A
BLAZING TRAIL, THE, 1949, A
BLEAK HOUSE, 1920
BLEAK HOUSE, 1922
BLEAK MOMENTS, 1972, C
BLESS 'EM ALL
BLESS 'EM ALL, 1949, A
BLESS THE BEASTS AND CHILDREN, 1971, A-C
BLESS THEIR LITTLE HEARTS, 1984, O
BLESS THIS HOUSE, 1972
BLESSED EVENT, 1932, A-C
BLESSURE D'AMOUR, 1916
BLIGHTY, 1927
BLIND ADVENTURE, 1933, A
BLIND ADVENTURE, THE, 1918
BLIND ALIBI, 1938, A
BLIND ALLEY
BLIND ALLEY, 1939, C
BLIND ALLEYS, 1927, A
BLIND BARGAIN, A, 1922, C
BLIND BOY, THE, 1917, A
BLIND CIRCUMSTANCES, 1922
BLIND CORNER
BLIND DATE, 1934, A
BLIND DATE, 1984, O
BLIND DATE, 1959
BLIND DEAD, THE, 1972, O
BLIND DESIRE, 1948, A
BLIND FOLLY, 1939, A
BLIND FOOLS, 1940
BLIND GODDESS, THE, 1926, A
BLIND GODDESS, THE, 1948, A
BLIND HEARTS, 1921, A
BLIND HUSBANDS, 1919, A
BLIND JUSTICE, 1917
BLIND JUSTICE, 1934, A
BLIND LOVE, THE, 1920
BLIND MAN'S BLUFF, 1936, AA
BLIND MAN'S BLUFF, 1952, A
BLIND MAN'S BLUFF, 1967
BLIND MAN'S EYES, 1919
BLIND MAN'S HOLIDAY, 1917
BLIND MAN'S LUCK, 1917
BLIND RAGE, 1978
BLIND SPOT, 1932, A
BLIND SPOT, 1947
BLIND SPOT, 1958, A
BLIND TERROR
BLIND TRAIL, 1926
BLIND WIVES, 1920
BLIND YOUTH, 1920
BLINDFOLD, 1928
BLINDFOLD, 1966, A
BLINDFOLDED, 1918
BLINDING TRAIL, THE, 1919
BLINDMAN, 1972, O
BLINDNESS OF DEVOTION, 1915
BLINDNESS OF DIVORCE, THE, 1918
BLINDNESS OF LOVE, THE, 1916
BLINDNESS OF VIRTUE, THE, 1915
BLINKER'S SPY-SPOTTER, 1971
BLINKEYES, 1922
BLINKY, 1923
BLISS OF MRS. BLOSSOM, THE, 1968, C
BLITHE SPIRIT, 1945, A
BLIZZARD, THE, 1924
BLOB, THE, 1958, A-C
BLOCK BUSTERS, 1944, A
BLOCK SIGNAL, THE, 1926
BLOCKADE, 1928, A
BLOCKADE, 1929, A
BLOCKADE, 1938, A
BLOCKED TRAIL, THE, 1943
BLOCKHEADS, 1938, AAA
BLOCKHOUSE, THE, 1974, A
BLOND CHEAT, 1938, A
BLONDE ALIBI, 1946, A
BLONDE BAIT, 1956, A
BLONDE BANDIT, THE, 1950, A-C
BLONDE BLACKMAILER, 1955, A
BLONDE BOMBSHELL
BLONDE COMET, 1941, A
BLONDE CONNECTION, THE, 1975
BLONDE CRAZY, 1931, A
BLONDE DYNAMITE, 1950, A
BLONDE FEVER, 1944, A
BLONDE FOR A DAY, 1946, A
BLONDE FOR A NIGHT, A, 1928
BLONDE FROM BROOKLYN, 1945, A
BLONDE FROM PEKING, THE, 1968, A
BLONDE FROM SINGAPORE, THE, 1941, A
BLONDE GODDESS, 1982
BLONDE ICE, 1949, C
BLONDE IN A WHITE CAR
BLONDE INSPIRATION, 1941, A
BLONDE NIGHTINGALE, 1931, A
BLONDE OR BRUNETTE, 1927
BLONDE PICKUP, 1955, A
BLONDE RANSOM, 1945, A
BLONDE SAINT, THE, 1926
BLONDE SAVAGE, 1947, A
BLONDE SINNER, 1956, C
BLONDE TROUBLE, 1937, A
BLONDE VAMPIRE, THE, 1922
BLONDE VENUS, 1932, C-O
BLONDES AT WORK, 1938, A
BLONDES BY CHOICE, 1927
BLONDES FOR DANGER, 1938, A
BLONDIE, 1938, AA
BLONDIE BRINGS UP BABY, 1939, AA
BLONDIE FOR VICTORY, 1942, A
BLONDIE GOES LATIN, 1941, AA
BLONDIE GOES TO COLLEGE, 1942, AA
BLONDIE HAS SERVANT TROUBLE, 1940, AA
BLONDIE HITS THE JACKPOT, 1949, AA
BLONDIE IN SOCIETY, 1941, AA
BLONDIE IN THE DOUGH, 1947, AA
BLONDIE JOHNSON, 1933, A
BLONDIE KNOWS BEST, 1946, AA
BLONDIE MEETS THE BOSS, 1939, AA
BLONDIE OF THE FOLLIES, 1932, A-C
BLONDIE ON A BUDGET, 1940, AA
BLONDIE PLAYS CUPID, 1940, AA
BLONDIE TAKES A VACATION, 1939, AA
BLONDIE'S ANNIVERSARY, 1947, AA
BLONDIE'S BIG DEAL, 1949, AA
BLONDIE'S BIG MOMENT, 1947, AA
BLONDIE'S BLESSED EVENT, 1942, AA
BLONDIE'S HERO, 1950, AA
BLONDIE'S HOLIDAY, 1947, AA
BLONDIE'S LUCKY DAY, 1946, AA
BLONDIE'S REWARD, 1948, AA
BLONDIE'S SECRET, 1948, AA
BLOOD, 1974, C
BLOOD ALLEY, 1955, A-C
BLOOD AND BLACK LACE, 1965, O
BLOOD AND GUNS, 1979
BLOOD AND GUTS, 1978, O
BLOOD AND LACE, 1971, O
BLOOD AND ROSES, 1961, C-O
BLOOD AND SAND, 1922, C
BLOOD AND SAND, 1941, C
BLOOD AND SOUL, 1923
BLOOD AND STEEL, 1925
BLOOD AND STEEL, 1959, A
BLOOD ARROW, 1958, A-C
BLOOD BARRIER, THE, 1920
BLOOD BATH, 1966, C
BLOOD BATH, 1976, O
BLOOD BEACH, 1981, C
BLOOD BEAST FROM OUTER SPACE, 1965, C
BLOOD BEAST TERROR, THE, 1967, C
BLOOD BOND, THE, 1925
BLOOD COUPLE, 1974
BLOOD CREATURE
BLOOD DEBTS, 1983
BLOOD DEMON, 1967, O
BLOOD DRINKERS, THE, 1966, P
BLOOD FEAST, 1963, O
BLOOD FEAST, 1976, O
BLOOD FEUD, 1979, O
BLOOD FROM THE MUMMY'S TOMB, 1972, O
BLOOD IN THE STREETS, 1975, C
BLOOD LEGACY
BLOOD MANIA, 1971, O
BLOOD MONEY, 1921
BLOOD MONEY, 1933, C
BLOOD MONEY, 1974, O
BLOOD MONSTER, 1972
BLOOD NEED NOT BE SPILLED, 1917
BLOOD OF A POET, THE, 1930, C
BLOOD OF DRACULA, 1957, O
BLOOD OF DRACULA'S CASTLE, 1967, O
BLOOD OF FRANKENSTEIN, 1970, O
BLOOD OF FU MANCHU, THE, 1968, O
BLOOD OF GHASTLY HORROR
BLOOD OF HIS FATHERS, 1917
BLOOD OF JESUS, 1941
BLOOD OF THE IRON MAIDEN, 1969
BLOOD OF THE TREVORS
BLOOD OF THE VAMPIRE, 1958, O
BLOOD ON MY HANDS
BLOOD ON SATAN'S CLAW, THE, 1970, O
BLOOD ON THE ARROW, 1964, C
BLOOD ON THE MOON, 1948, A
BLOOD ON THE SUN, 1945, C
BLOOD ORANGE, 1953, A
BLOOD ORGY OF THE SHE-DEVILS, 1973, O
BLOOD RELATIVES, 1978, O
BLOOD ROSE, THE, 1970, O
BLOOD SEEKERS, THE, 1971
BLOOD SHIP, THE, 1927
BLOOD SIMPLE, 1984, O
BLOOD SONG, 1982
BLOOD SPATTERED BRIDE, THE, 1974, O
BLOOD SUCKERS
BLOOD TEST, 1923
BLOOD THIRST, 1965
BLOOD TIDE, 1982, O
BLOOD WATERS OF DOCTOR Z, 1982, O
BLOOD WEDDING, 1981, A
BLOOD WILL TELL, 1917
BLOOD WILL TELL, 1927
BLOOD, SWEAT AND FEAR, 1975, C-O
BLOODBATH AT THE HOUSE OF DEATH, 1984, C-O
BLOODBROTHERS, 1978, O
BLOODEATERS, 1980, C
BLOODHOUND, THE, 1925
BLOODHOUNDS OF BROADWAY, 1952, A
BLOODLESS VAMPIRE, THE, 1965
BLOODLINE, 1979, O
BLOODLUST, 1959, O
BLOODRAGE, 1979
BLOODSTALKERS, 1976
BLOODSUCKERS
BLOODSUCKING FREAKS, 1982, O
BLOODTHIRSTY BUTCHERS, 1970, O
BLOODY BIRTHDAY, 1980
BLOODY BROOD, THE, 1959, O
BLOODY EAST, THE, 1915
BLOODY KIDS, 1983, O
BLOODY MAMA, 1970, O
BLOODY PIT OF HORROR, THE, 1965, O
BLOOMFIELD, 1971, C
BLOOMING ANGEL, THE, 1920
BLOSSOM TIME
BLOSSOMS IN THE DUST, 1941, A
BLOSSOMS ON BROADWAY, 1937, A
BLOT, THE, 1921, A
BLOW BUGLES BLOW, 1936
BLOW OUT, 1981, O
BLOW TO THE HEART, 1983, O
BLOW YOUR OWN HORN, 1923
BLOW YOUR OWN TRUMPET, 1958, A
BLOW-UP, 1966, O
BLOWING WILD, 1953, C
BLOWN SKY HIGH, 1984
BLUE, 1968, C
BLUE ANGEL, THE, 1930, O
BLUE ANGEL, THE, 1959, O
BLUE BANDANNA, THE, 1919
BLUE BIRD, THE, 1940, AA
BLUE BIRD, THE, 1976, AA
BLUE BLAZES, 1922
BLUE BLAZES, 1926
BLUE BLAZES RAWDEN, 1918
BLUE BLOOD, 1922
BLUE BLOOD, 1925, A
BLUE BLOOD, 1951, AA
BLUE BLOOD, 1973, C
BLUE BLOOD AND RED, 1916
BLUE BONNET, THE, 1920
BLUE CANADIAN ROCKIES, 1952, A
BLUE COLLAR, 1978, O
BLUE COUNTRY, THE, 1977, C-O
BLUE DAHLIA, THE, 1946, C
BLUE DANUBE, 1932, A
BLUE DANUBE, THE, 1928
BLUE DEMON VERSUS THE INFERNAL BRAINS, 1967, O
BLUE DENIM, 1959, C-O
BLUE EAGLE, THE, 1926
BLUE ENVELOPE MYSTERY, THE, 1916
BLUE EXPRESS, 1929
BLUE FIN, 1978, A
BLUE GARDENIA, THE, 1953, C
BLUE GRASS OF KENTUCKY, 1950, AA
BLUE HAWAII, 1961, A
BLUE IDOL, THE, 1931, A
BLUE JEANS, 1917
BLUE LAGOON, THE, 1949, A-C
BLUE LAGOON, THE, 1980, O
BLUE LAMP, THE, 1950, C
BLUE LIGHT, THE, 1932, A

BLUE MAX, THE, 1966, C
BLUE MONEY, 1975
BLUE MONTANA SKIES, 1939, AA
BLUE MOON, THE, 1920
BLUE MOUNTAIN MYSTERY, THE, 1922
BLUE MURDER AT ST. TRINIAN'S, 1958, AA
BLUE PARROT, THE, 1953, A
BLUE PEARL, THE, 1920
BLUE PETER, THE
BLUE PETER, THE, 1928
BLUE SCAR, 1949, A
BLUE SEXTET, 1972
BLUE SIERRA, 1946, AA
BLUE SKIES, 1929
BLUE SKIES, 1946, AA
BLUE SKIES AGAIN, 1983, A
BLUE SMOKE, 1935, A
BLUE SQUADRON, THE, 1934, A
BLUE STEEL, 1934, A
BLUE STREAK MCCOY, 1920
BLUE STREAK O'NEIL, 1926
BLUE STREAK, THE, 1917
BLUE STREAK, THE, 1926, A
BLUE SUMMER, 1973
BLUE SUNSHINE, 1978, A
BLUE THUNDER, 1983, C
BLUE VEIL, THE, 1947, A
BLUE VEIL, THE, 1951, A
BLUE, WHITE, AND PERFECT, 1941, A
BLUE-EYED MARY, 1918
BLUEBEARD, 1944, A
BLUEBEARD, 1972, O
BLUEBEARD'S 8TH WIFE, 1923
BLUEBEARD'S CASTLE, 1969
BLUEBEARD'S EIGHTH WIFE, 1938, A-C
BLUEBEARD'S SEVEN WIVES, A
BLUEBEARD'S TEN HONEYMOONS, 1960, A-C
BLUEBEARD, 1963
BLUEBEARD, JR.
BLUEBIRD, THE, 1918
BLUEPRINT FOR MURDER, A, 1953, CA
BLUEPRINT FOR ROBBERY, 1961, A
BLUES BROTHERS, THE, 1980, C-O
BLUES BUSTERS, 1950, AA
BLUES FOR LOVERS, 1966, A
BLUES IN THE NIGHT, 1941, A
BLUFF, 1916
BLUFF, 1921
BLUFF, 1924, A
BLUFFER, THE, 1919
BLUME IN LOVE, 1973, O
BLUSHING BRIDE, THE, 1921, A
BLUSHING BRIDES, 1930, A
BMX BANDITS, 1983, AA
BOADICEA, 1926
BOARDING HOUSE, 1984
BOARDING HOUSE BLUES, 1948
BOARDWALK, 1979, C-O
BOASTER, THE, 1926
BOAT FROM SHANGHAI, 1931, A
BOAT, THE
BOATNIKS, THE, 1970, AAA
BOB AND CAROL AND TED AND ALICE, 1969, O
BOB HAMPTON OF PLACER, 1921, A
BOB MATHIAS STORY, THE, 1954, AA
BOB'S YOUR UNCLE, 1941, A
BOB, SON OF BATTLE
BOBBED HAIR, 1922
BOBBED HAIR, 1925
BOBBIE JO AND THE OUTLAW, 1976, C-O
BOBBIE OF THE BALLET, 1916
BOBBIKINS, 1959, A
BOBBY DEERFIELD, 1977, C
BOBBY WARE IS MISSING, 1955, A
BOBO, THE, 1967, A-C
BOCCACCIO, 1936, A
BOCCACCIO '70, 1962, O
BOD SQUAD, THE, 1976
BODEN'S BOY, 1923
BODY AND SOUL, 1920
BODY AND SOUL, 1925
BODY AND SOUL, 1927
BODY AND SOUL, 1931, A
BODY AND SOUL, 1947, C
BODY AND SOUL, 1981, C
BODY BEAUTIFUL, 1928
BODY BENEATH, THE, 1970
BODY DISAPPEARS, THE, 1941, A
BODY DOUBLE, 1984, O
BODY FEVER, 1981
BODY HEAT, 1981, C
BODY IS A SHELL, THE, 1957
BODY PUNCH, THE, 1929
BODY ROCK, 1984, C
BODY SAID NO!, THE, 1950, AA
BODY SNATCHER, THE, 1945, A
BODY STEALERS, THE, 1969, A
BODYGUARD, 1948, A
BODYGUARD, THE, 1976
BODYHOLD, 1950, A
BOEFJE, 1939, AA
BOEING BOEING, 1965, C
BOER WAR, THE, 1914
BOESMAN AND LENA, 1976
BOFORS GUN, THE, 1968, A-C
BOHEMIAN DANCER, 1929
BOHEMIAN GIRL, THE, 1922
BOHEMIAN GIRL, THE, 1936, A
BOHEMIAN RAPTURE, 1948, A
BOILING POINT, THE, 1932, A
BOLD ADVENTURESS, A, 1915
BOLD AND THE BRAVE, THE, 1956, A
BOLD CABALLERO, 1936, A
BOLD EMMETT, IRELAND'S MARTYR, 1915
BOLD FRONTIERSMAN, THE, 1948, A
BOLDEST JOB IN THE WEST, THE, 1971, A-C
BOLERO, 1934, A-C
BOLERO, 1982, A
BOLERO, 1984, O
BOLIBAR, 1928, A
BOLSHEVISM ON TRIAL, 1919
BOLTED DOOR, THE, 1923
BOMB IN THE HIGH STREET, 1961, A
BOMBA AND THE ELEPHANT STAMPEDE
BOMBA AND THE HIDDEN CITY, 1950, A
BOMBA AND THE JUNGLE GIRL, 1952, A
BOMBA ON PANTHER ISLAND, 1949, A
BOMBA THE JUNGLE BOY, 1949, A
BOMBARDIER, 1943, A
BOMBARDMENT OF MONTE CARLO, THE, 1931, A
BOMBAY CLIPPER, 1942, A
BOMBAY MAIL, 1934, A
BOMBAY TALKIE, 1970, C
BOMBAY WATERFRONT, 1952
BOMBER'S MOON, 1943, A
BOMBERS B-52, 1957, A
BOMBS OVER BURMA, 1942, A
BOMBS OVER LONDON, 1937, A
BOMBSHELL, 1933, A-C
BOMBSIGHT STOLEN, 1941, A
BON VOYAGE, 1962, AA
BON VOYAGE, CHARLIE BROWN (AND DON'T COME BACK), 1980, AAA
BONA, 1984, O
BONANZA BUCKAROO, THE, 1926
BONANZA TOWN, 1951, A
BOND BETWEEN, THE, 1917
BOND BOY, THE, 1922
BOND OF FEAR, 1956, A
BOND OF FEAR, THE, 1917
BOND STREET, 1948, A
BOND WITHIN, THE, 1916
BONDAGE, 1917
BONDAGE, 1933, C
BONDAGE OF BARBARA, THE, 1919
BONDAGE OF FEAR, THE, 1917
BONDED WOMAN, THE, 1922
BONDMAN, THE, 1916
BONDMAN, THE, 1929
BONDS OF HONOR, 1919
BONDS OF LOVE, 1919
BONDWOMEN, 1915
BONE, 1972
BONHOMME DE NEIGE, 1917
BONJOUR TRISTESSE, 1958, C-O
BONNE CHANCE, 1935, A
BONNIE AND CLYDE, 1967, O
BONNIE ANNIE LAURIE, 1918
BONNIE BRIER BRUSH, THE, 1921
BONNIE MARY, 1918
BONNIE MAY, 1920
BONNIE PARKER STORY, THE, 1958, O
BONNIE PRINCE CHARLIE, 1923
BONNIE PRINCE CHARLIE, 1948, A
BONNIE SCOTLAND, 1935, AAA
BONNIE'S KIDS, 1973
BONNIE, BONNIE LASSIE, 1919
BONZO GOES TO COLLEGE, 1952, AAA
BOOB, THE, 1926
BOOBY TRAP, 1957, A
BOOGENS, THE, 1982, A
BOOGEY MAN, THE, 1980, O
BOOGEYMAN II, 1983, O
BOOGIE MAN WILL GET YOU, THE, 1942, C
BOOK AGENT, THE, 1917
BOOK OF NUMBERS, 1973, O
BOOLOO, 1938, A
BOOM TOWN, 1940, A
BOOM!, 1968, O
BOOMERANG, 1934, A
BOOMERANG, 1947, C
BOOMERANG, 1960, A-C
BOOMERANG BILL, 1922
BOOMERANG JUSTICE, 1922
BOOMERANG, THE, 1919
BOOMERANG, THE, 1925
BOOT HILL, 1969, A
BOOT HILL BANDITS, 1942
BOOTHILL BRIGADE, 1937, A
BOOTLE'S BABY, 1914
BOOTLEGGER'S DAUGHTER, THE, 1922
BOOTLEGGERS, 1974, A-C
BOOTLEGGERS, THE, 1922
BOOTS, 1919
BOOTS AND SADDLES, 1916
BOOTS AND SADDLES, 1937, A
BOOTS MALONE, 1952, A
BOOTS OF DESTINY, 1937, A
BOOTS TURNER, 1973
BOOTS! BOOTS!, 1934, A
BOP GIRL GOES CALYPSO, 1957, A
BORDER BADMEN, 1945, A
BORDER BANDITS, 1946, A
BORDER BLACKBIRDS, 1927
BORDER BRIGANDS, 1935, A
BORDER BUCKAROOS, 1943, A
BORDER CABALLERO, 1936, A
BORDER CAFE, 1937, A
BORDER CAVALIER, THE, 1927
BORDER CITY RUSTLERS, 1953
BORDER DEVILS, 1932, A
BORDER FENCE, 1951
BORDER FEUD, 1947, A
BORDER FLIGHT, 1936, A
BORDER G-MAN, 1938, A
BORDER GUNS, 1934
BORDER INCIDENT, 1949, C
BORDER INTRIGUE, 1925
BORDER JUSTICE, 1925
BORDER LAW, 1931, A
BORDER LEGION, THE, 1919
BORDER LEGION, THE, 1924
BORDER LEGION, THE, 1930, A
BORDER LEGION, THE, 1940, A
BORDER LUST, 1967
BORDER MENACE, THE, 1934
BORDER OUTLAWS, 1950, A
BORDER PATROL, 1943, A
BORDER PATROL, THE, 1928
BORDER PATROLMAN, THE, 1936, A
BORDER PHANTOM, 1937, A
BORDER RAIDERS, THE, 1918
BORDER RAIDERS, THE, 1921
BORDER RANGERS, 1950
BORDER RIDER, THE, 1924
BORDER RIVER, 1954, A
BORDER ROMANCE, 1930, A
BORDER ROUNDUP, 1942
BORDER SADDLEMATES, 1952, A
BORDER SCOUTS, THE, 1922
BORDER SHERIFF, THE, 1926
BORDER STREET, 1950, A
BORDER TREASURE, 1950, A
BORDER VENGEANCE, 1935
BORDER VENGENCE, 1925
BORDER VIGILANTES, 1941, A
BORDER WHIRLWIND, THE, 1926
BORDER WILDCAT, THE, 1929
BORDER WIRELESS, THE, 1918
BORDER WOLVES, 1938, A
BORDER WOMEN, 1924, A
BORDER, THE, 1982, O
BORDERLAND, 1922
BORDERLAND, 1937, A
BORDERLINE, 1950, A
BORDERLINE, 1980, C
BORDERTOWN, 1935, C
BORDERTOWN GUNFIGHTERS, 1943, A
BORDERTOWN TRAIL, 1944
BORIS GODUNOV, 1959, A
BORN AGAIN, 1978, A
BORN FOR GLORY, 1935, A
BORN FOR TROUBLE, 1955
BORN FREE, 1966, AAA
BORN IN FLAMES, 1983, O
BORN LOSERS, 1967, O
BORN LUCKY, 1932, A
BORN RECKLESS, 1930, C
BORN RECKLESS, 1937, A
BORN RECKLESS, 1959, A
BORN RICH, 1924
BORN THAT WAY, 1937, A
BORN TO BATTLE, 1926
BORN TO BATTLE, 1927
BORN TO BATTLE, 1935
BORN TO BE BAD, 1934, A
BORN TO BE BAD, 1950, A
BORN TO BE LOVED, 1959, A
BORN TO BE WILD, 1938, A
BORN TO DANCE, 1936, A
BORN TO FIGHT, 1938, A
BORN TO GAMBLE, 1935, A
BORN TO KILL, 1947, A
BORN TO KILL, 1975, O
BORN TO LOVE, 1931, A
BORN TO SING, 1942, A
BORN TO SPEED, 1947, A

BORN TO THE SADDLE, 1929
BORN TO THE SADDLE, 1953, A
BORN TO THE WEST, 1926
BORN TO THE WEST, 1937, A
BORN TO WIN, 1971, C
BORN WILD, 1968, C
BORN YESTERDAY, 1951, A
BORROW A MILLION, 1934, A
BORROWED CLOTHES, 1918
BORROWED CLOTHES, 1934, A
BORROWED FINERY, 1925, A
BORROWED HERO, 1941, A
BORROWED HUSBANDS, 1924
BORROWED PLUMAGE, 1917
BORROWED TROUBLE, 1948, A
BORROWED WIVES, 1930, A
BORROWING TROUBLE, 1937, A
BORSALINO, 1970, O
BORSALINO AND CO., 1974, O
BOSS COWBOY, 1934
BOSS LADY, 1982
BOSS NIGGER, 1974, C
BOSS OF BIG TOWN, 1943, A
BOSS OF BOOMTOWN, 1944
BOSS OF BULLION CITY, 1941, A
BOSS OF CAMP 4, THE, 1922
BOSS OF HANGTOWN MESA, 1942, A
BOSS OF LONELY VALLEY, 1937, A
BOSS OF RUSTLER'S ROOST, THE, 1928
BOSS OF THE LAZY Y, THE, 1918
BOSS OF THE RAWHIDE, 1944, A
BOSS RIDER OF GUN CREEK, 1936, A
BOSS'S SON, THE, 1978, A
BOSS, THE, 1915
BOSS, THE, 1956, A
BOSTON BLACKIE, 1923
BOSTON BLACKIE AND THE LAW, 1946, A
BOSTON BLACKIE BOOKED ON SUSPICION, 1945, A
BOSTON BLACKIE GOES HOLLYWOOD, 1942, A
BOSTON BLACKIE'S CHINESE VENTURE, 1949, A
BOSTON BLACKIE'S LITTLE PAL, 1918
BOSTON BLACKIE'S RENDEZVOUS, 1945
BOSTON STRANGLER, THE, 1968
BOSTONIANS, THE, 1984, A-C
BOTANY BAY, 1953, C
BOTH BARRELS BLAZING, 1945
BOTH ENDS OF THE CANDEL
BOTH SIDES OF THE LAW, 1953, A
BOTTLE IMP, THE, 1917
BOTTLE, THE, 1915
BOTTOM OF THE BOTTLE, THE, 1956, A
BOTTOM OF THE WELL, 1917
BOTTOMS UP, 1934, A
BOTTOMS UP, 1960, A
BOUCLETTE, 1918
BOUDOIR DIPLOMAT, 1930, C
BOUDU SAVED FROM DROWNING, 1967, C
BOUGHT, 1931, A-C
BOUGHT AND PAID FOR, 1916
BOUGHT AND PAID FOR, 1922
BOULDER DAM, 1936, A
BOULEVARD NIGHTS, 1979, O
BOUND FOR GLORY, 1976, A-C
BOUND IN MOROCCO, 1918
BOUNDARY HOUSE, 1918
BOUNTIFUL SUMMER, 1951, A
BOUNTY HUNTER, THE, 1954, A
BOUNTY HUNTERS, THE, 1970, A-C
BOUNTY KILLER, THE, 1965, A-C
BOUNTY, THE, 1984, O
BOURBON ST. SHADOWS, 1962
BOWERY AT MIDNIGHT, 1942
BOWERY BATTALION, 1951, A
BOWERY BISHOP, THE, 1924
BOWERY BLITZKRIEG, 1941, A
BOWERY BOMBSHELL, 1946, A
BOWERY BOY, 1940, A
BOWERY BOYS MEET THE MONSTERS, THE, 1954, A
BOWERY BUCKAROOS, 1947, A
BOWERY CHAMPS, 1944, A
BOWERY CINDERELLA, 1927, A
BOWERY TO BAGDAD, 1955, A
BOWERY TO BROADWAY, 1944, A
BOWERY, THE, 1933, A
BOXCAR BERTHA, 1972
BOXER, 1971, A
BOXER, THE
BOXOFFICE, 1982, C-O
BOY AND HIS DOG, A, 1975, O
BOY AND THE BRIDGE, THE, 1959, A
BOY AND THE PIRATES, THE, 1960, AA
BOY CRAZY, 1922
BOY CRIED MURDER, THE, 1966, C-O
BOY, DID I GET A WRONG NUMBER!, 1966, AA
BOY FRIEND, 1939, A
BOY FRIEND, THE, 1926
BOY FRIEND, THE, 1971, A
BOY FROM INDIANA, 1950, A
BOY FROM OKLAHOMA, THE, 1954, A
BOY FROM STALINGRAD, THE, 1943
BOY GIRL, THE, 1917
BOY MEETS GIRL, 1938, A
BOY NAMED CHARLIE BROWN, A, 1969, AAA
BOY OF FLANDERS, A, 1924
BOY OF MINE, 1923, A
BOY OF THE STREETS, 1937, A
BOY OF THE STREETS, A, 1927
BOY OF TWO WORLDS, 1970
BOY ON A DOLPHIN, 1957, C
BOY RIDER, THE, 1927, A
BOY SLAVES, 1938, A
BOY TEN FEET TALL, A, 1965, AAA
BOY TROUBLE, 1939, A
BOY WHO CAUGHT A CROOK, 1961, AA
BOY WHO CRIED WEREWOLF, THE, 1973, A-C
BOY WHO STOLE A MILLION, THE, 1960, AA
BOY WHO TURNED YELLOW, THE, 1972, AA
BOY WITH THE GREEN HAIR, THE, 1949, AA
BOY WITH TWO HEADS, THE, 1974
BOY WOODBURN, 1922
BOY! WHAT A GIRL, 1947, A
BOY'S REFORMATORY, 1939, A
BOY, A GIRL AND A BIKE, A, 1949, A
BOY, A GIRL, AND A DOG, A, 1946, A
BOY, DID I GET A WRONG NUMBER!, 1966, AA
BOY...A GIRL, A, 1969, O
BOYD'S SHOP, 1960, A
BOYS FROM BRAZIL, THE, 1978, C-O
BOYS FROM BROOKLYN, THE
BOYS FROM SYRACUSE, 1940, A
BOYS IN BROWN, 1949, AA
BOYS IN COMPANY C, THE, 1978, O
BOYS IN THE BAND, THE, 1970, O
BOYS OF PAUL STREET, THE, 1969, A
BOYS OF THE CITY, 1940, A
BOYS OF THE OLD BRIGADE, THE, 1916
BOYS OF THE OTTER PATROL, 1918
BOYS TOWN, 1938, AAA
BOYS WILL BE BOYS, 1921
BOYS WILL BE BOYS, 1936, A
BOYS WILL BE GIRLS, 1937, AA
BOYS' NIGHT OUT, 1962, C
BOYS' RANCH, 1946, A
BOYS, THE, 1962, C
BRACE UP, 1918
BRACELETS, 1931, A
BRADY'S ESCAPE, 1984, C
BRAIN EATERS, THE, 1958, C
BRAIN FROM THE PLANET AROUS, THE, 1958, C
BRAIN MACHINE, THE, 1955, A
BRAIN MACHINE, THE, 1972
BRAIN OF BLOOD, 1971, C
BRAIN THAT WOULDN'T DIE, THE, 1959, O
BRAIN, THE, 1965, A
BRAIN, THE, 1969, A
BRAINSTORM, 1965, C
BRAINSTORM, 1983, C-O
BRAINWASH, 1982
BRAINWASHED, 1961, A-C
BRAINWAVES, 1983, O
BRAMBLE BUSH, THE, 1919
BRAMBLE BUSH, THE, 1960, O
BRANCHES, 1971
BRAND, 1915
BRAND OF CAIN, THE, 1935
BRAND OF COWARDICE, 1925
BRAND OF COWARDICE, THE, 1916, A
BRAND OF FEAR, 1949, A
BRAND OF HATE, 1934
BRAND OF LOPEZ, THE, 1920
BRAND OF SATAN, THE, 1917
BRAND OF THE DEVIL, 1944, A
BRAND OF THE OUTLAWS, 1936
BRAND X, 1970
BRAND'S DAUGHTER, 1917
BRAND, THE, 1919
BRANDED, 1920
BRANDED, 1931, A
BRANDED, 1951, A
BRANDED A BANDIT, 1924, A
BRANDED A COWARD, 1935, A
BRANDED A THIEF, 1924
BRANDED MAN, 1922
BRANDED MAN, 1928
BRANDED MEN, 1931, A
BRANDED SOMBRERO, THE, 1928
BRANDED SOUL, A, 1917
BRANDED SOUL, THE, 1920
BRANDED WOMAN, THE, 1920, A
BRANDING BROADWAY, 1918, A
BRANDING FIRE, 1930
BRANDING IRON, THE, 1920, A
BRANDY FOR THE PARSON, 1952, A
BRANDY IN THE WILDERNESS, 1969
BRANNIGAN, 1975, A-C
BRASA DORMIDA, 1928
BRASHER DOUBLOON, THE, 1947, A
BRASIL ANNO 2,000, 1968, A
BRASS, 1923
BRASS BOTTLE, THE, 1914
BRASS BOTTLE, THE, 1923
BRASS BOTTLE, THE, 1964, A
BRASS BOWL, THE, 1924
BRASS BUTTONS, 1919
BRASS CHECK, THE, 1918
BRASS COMMANDMENTS, 1923
BRASS KNUCKLES, 1927
BRASS LEGEND, THE, 1956, A
BRASS MONKEY
BRASS RING, THE, 1975
BRASS TARGET, 1978, A-C
BRAT, THE, 1919, A
BRAT, THE, 1930, A
BRAT, THE, 1931, A
BRAVADOS, THE, 1958, C
BRAVE AND BOLD, 1918, A
BRAVE BULLS, THE, 1951, A
BRAVE DON'T CRY, THE, 1952, A
BRAVE ONE, THE, 1956, AAA
BRAVE WARRIOR, 1952, A
BRAVEHEART, 1925
BRAVEST WAY, THE, 1918, A
BRAWN OF THE NORTH, 1922
BRAZEN BEAUTY, 1918, A
BRAZIL, 1944, A
BREAD, 1918, A
BREAD, 1924
BREAD AND CHOCOLATE, 1978, A
BREAD OF LOVE, THE, 1954, A
BREAD, LOVE AND DREAMS, 1953, O
BREAK IN THE CIRCLE, THE, 1957, A
BREAK OF DAY, 1977, A
BREAK OF HEARTS, 1935, A
BREAK THE NEWS, 1938, A
BREAK THE NEWS TO MOTHER, 1919
BREAK TO FREEDOM
BREAK, THE, 1962, A
BREAK-UP, THE, 1930
BREAKAWAY, 1956, A
BREAKDOWN, 1953, A
BREAKER MORANT, 1980, A-C
BREAKER! BREAKER!, 1977, C
BREAKER, THE, 1916, A
BREAKERS AHEAD, 1918
BREAKERS AHEAD, 1935, A
BREAKERS AHEAD, 1938, A
BREAKFAST AT SUNRISE, 1927
BREAKFAST AT TIFFANY'S, 1961, A
BREAKFAST FOR TWO, 1937, A
BREAKFAST IN BED, 1978, C
BREAKFAST IN HOLLYWOOD, 1946, A
BREAKFAST IN PARIS, 1981
BREAKHEART PASS, 1976, C
BREAKIN', 1984, A-C
BREAKIN' 2: ELECTRIC BOOGALOO, 1984, A-C
BREAKING AWAY, 1979, C-O
BREAKING GLASS, 1980, C-O
BREAKING HOME TIES, 1922
BREAKING INTO SOCIETY, 1923
BREAKING OF BUMBO, 1972
BREAKING POINT, 1976, C-O
BREAKING POINT, THE, 1921, C
BREAKING POINT, THE, 1924, A
BREAKING POINT, THE, 1950, A
BREAKING POINT, THE, 1961, A
BREAKING THE ICE, 1938, A
BREAKING THE SOUND BARRIER, 1952, A
BREAKOUT, 1959
BREAKOUT, 1960, A
BREAKOUT, 1975, C
BREAKOUT, 1984, AA
BREAKTHROUGH, 1950, A
BREAKTHROUGH, 1978, C
BREATH OF A SCANDAL, THE, 1924
BREATH OF LIFE, 1962, A
BREATH OF SCANDAL, A, 1960, A
BREATH OF THE GODS, THE, 1920
BREATHLESS, 1959, O
BREATHLESS, 1983, O
BREATHLESS MOMENT, THE, 1924
BRED IN OLD KENTUCKY, 1926
BRED IN THE BONE, 1915
BREED APART, A, 1984, A-C
BREED OF COURAGE, 1927
BREED OF MEN, 1919, A
BREED OF THE BORDER, 1933, A
BREED OF THE BORDER, THE, 1924
BREED OF THE SEA, 1926
BREED OF THE SUNSETS, 1928, A
BREED OF THE TRESHAMS, THE, 1920
BREED OF THE WEST, 1930
BREEZING HOME, 1937, A
BREEZY, 1973, O
BREEZY BILL, 1930
BREEZY JIM, 1919
BRENDA OF THE BARGE, 1920, A
BREWSTER McCLOUD, 1970, C

BREWSTER'S MILLIONS, 1914, A
BREWSTER'S MILLIONS, 1921, A
BREWSTER'S MILLIONS, 1935, A
BREWSTER'S MILLIONS, 1945, A
BRIBE, THE, 1949, C
BRIDAL CHAIR, THE, 1919, A
BRIDAL PATH, THE, 1959, A
BRIDAL SUITE, 1939, A
BRIDE AND THE BEAST, THE, 1958, C
BRIDE BY MISTAKE, 1944, A
BRIDE CAME C.O.D., THE, 1941, A
BRIDE COMES HOME, 1936, A
BRIDE COMES TO YELLOW SKY, THE
BRIDE FOR A NIGHT, A, 1923, A
BRIDE FOR HENRY, A, 1937, A
BRIDE FOR SALE, 1949, A
BRIDE GOES WILD, THE, 1948, A
BRIDE IS MUCH TOO BEAUTIFUL, THE, 1958, O
BRIDE OF FEAR, THE, 1918, A
BRIDE OF FRANKENSTEIN, THE, 1935, C
BRIDE OF GLOMDAL, THE, 1925
BRIDE OF HATE, THE, 1917, A
BRIDE OF THE DESERT, 1929, A
BRIDE OF THE GORILLA, 1951, A
BRIDE OF THE LAKE, 1934, A
BRIDE OF THE MONSTER, 1955, A
BRIDE OF THE REGIMENT, 1930, A
BRIDE OF THE STORM, 1926, A
BRIDE OF VENGEANCE, 1923
BRIDE OF VENGEANCE, 1949, A
BRIDE WALKS OUT, THE, 1936, A
BRIDE WITH A DOWRY, 1954, A
BRIDE WORE BLACK, THE, 1968, C
BRIDE WORE BOOTS, THE, 1946, A
BRIDE WORE CRUTCHES, THE, 1940, A
BRIDE WORE RED, THE, 1937, A
BRIDE'S AWAKENING, THE, 1918, A
BRIDE'S CONFESSION, THE, 1921
BRIDE'S PLAY, THE, 1922
BRIDE'S SILENCE, THE, 1917, A
BRIDE, THE, 1973, C-O
BRIDEGROOM FOR TWO, 1932, A
BRIDES ARE LIKE THAT, 1936, A
BRIDES OF BLOOD, 1968, O
BRIDES OF DRACULA, THE, 1960, O
BRIDES OF FU MANCHU, THE, 1966, A
BRIDES TO BE, 1934, A
BRIDGE AT REMAGEN, THE, 1969, C
BRIDGE IN THE JUNGLE, THE, 1971
BRIDGE OF SAN LUIS REY, THE, 1929, A
BRIDGE OF SAN LUIS REY, THE, 1944, A
BRIDGE OF SIGHS, 1936, A
BRIDGE OF SIGHS, THE, 1915
BRIDGE OF SIGHS, THE, 1922
BRIDGE OF SIGHS, THE, 1925
BRIDGE ON THE RIVER KWAI, THE, 1957, C
BRIDGE TO THE SUN, 1961, A
BRIDGE TOO FAR, A, 1977, C
BRIDGE, THE, 1961, A
BRIDGES AT TOKO-RI, THE, 1954, A
BRIDGES BURNED, 1917
BRIDGES TO HEAVEN, 1975
BRIEF ECSTASY, 1937, A
BRIEF ENCOUNTER, 1945, A
BRIEF MOMENT, 1933, A
BRIEF RAPTURE, 1952, C
BRIEF VACATION, A, 1975, C
BRIG, THE, 1965
BRIGADIER GERARD, 1915
BRIGADOON, 1954, A
BRIGAND OF KANDAHAR, THE, 1965, A
BRIGAND, THE, 1952, A
BRIGGS FAMILY, THE, 1940, A
BRIGHAM YOUNG—FRONTIERSMAN, 1940, A
BRIGHT COLLEGE YEARS, 1971
BRIGHT EYES, 1934, AAA
BRIGHT LEAF, 1950, A
BRIGHT LIGHTS, 1925, A
BRIGHT LIGHTS, 1931, A
BRIGHT LIGHTS, 1935, A
BRIGHT LIGHTS OF BROADWAY, 1923
BRIGHT ROAD, 1953, A
BRIGHT SHAWL, THE, 1923
BRIGHT SKIES, 1920
BRIGHT VICTORY, 1951, A
BRIGHTHAVEN EXPRESS, 1950
BRIGHTON ROCK, 1947, C
BRIGHTON STRANGLER, THE, 1945, AA
BRIGHTY OF THE GRAND CANYON, 1967, A
BRILLIANT MARRIAGE, 1936, A
BRIMSTONE, 1949, A
BRIMSTONE AND TREACLE, 1982, C
BRING HIM IN, 1921, A
BRING ME THE HEAD OF ALFREDO GARCIA, 1974, O
BRING ON THE GIRLS, 1945, A
BRING YOUR SMILE ALONG, 1955, A
BRINGIN' HOME THE BACON, 1924
BRINGING HOME FATHER, 1917
BRINGING UP BABY, 1938, A
BRINGING UP BETTY, 1919
BRINGING UP FATHER, 1928
BRINGING UP FATHER, 1946, A
BRINK OF LIFE, 1960, C-O
BRINK'S JOB, THE, 1978, A-C
BRINK, THE, 1915
BRITANNIA MEWS
BRITANNIA OF BILLINGSGATE, 1933, A
BRITISH AGENT, 1934, A
BRITISH INTELLIGENCE, 1940, A
BRITTANIA HOSPITAL, 1982, C
BRITTON OF THE SEVENTH, 1916
BROAD COALITION, THE, 1972
BROAD DAYLIGHT, 1922
BROAD ROAD, THE, 1923
BROADMINDED, 1931, A
BROADWAY, 1929, A
BROADWAY, 1942, A
BROADWAY AFTER DARK, 1924, A
BROADWAY AFTER MIDNIGHT, 1927
BROADWAY AND HOME, 1920
BROADWAY ARIZONA, 1917
BROADWAY BABIES, 1929, A
BROADWAY BAD, 1933, A
BROADWAY BIG SHOT, 1942, A
BROADWAY BILL, 1918
BROADWAY BILL, 1934, A
BROADWAY BILLY, 1926, A
BROADWAY BOOB, THE, 1926
BROADWAY BROKE, 1923
BROADWAY BUBBLE, THE, 1920
BROADWAY BUCKAROO, 1921
BROADWAY BUTTERFLY, A, 1925
BROADWAY COWBOY, THE, 1920
BROADWAY DADDIES, 1928
BROADWAY DANNY ROSE, 1984, A-C
BROADWAY DRIFTER, THE, 1927
BROADWAY FEVER, 1929
BROADWAY GALLANT, THE, 1926
BROADWAY GOLD, 1923
BROADWAY GONDOLIER, 1935, A
BROADWAY HOOFER, THE, 1929, A
BROADWAY HOSTESS, 1935, A
BROADWAY JONES, 1917
BROADWAY LADY, 1925
BROADWAY LIMITED, 1941, A
BROADWAY LOVE, 1918
BROADWAY MADNESS, 1927
BROADWAY MADONNA, THE, 1922
BROADWAY MELODY OF '38, 1937, A
BROADWAY MELODY OF 1936, 1935, A
BROADWAY MELODY OF 1940, 1940, A
BROADWAY MELODY, THE, 1929, A
BROADWAY MUSKETEERS, 1938, A
BROADWAY NIGHTS, 1927
BROADWAY OR BUST, 1924
BROADWAY PEACOCK, THE, 1922
BROADWAY RHYTHM, 1944, A
BROADWAY ROSE, 1922, A
BROADWAY SAINT, A, 1919
BROADWAY SCANDAL, 1918, A
BROADWAY SCANDALS, 1929, A
BROADWAY SERENADE, 1939, A
BROADWAY SPORT, THE, 1917
BROADWAY THROUGH A KEYHOLE, 1933, A
BROADWAY TO CHEYENNE, 1932, A
BROADWAY TO HOLLYWOOD, 1933, A
BROKEN ARROW, 1950, A
BROKEN BARRIER
BROKEN BARRIERS, 1919
BROKEN BARRIERS, 1924
BROKEN BARRIERS, 1928
BROKEN BLOSSOMS, 1919, A
BROKEN BLOSSOMS, 1936, A
BROKEN BUTTERFLY, THE, 1919
BROKEN CHAINS, 1916, C
BROKEN CHAINS, 1922
BROKEN CHAINS, 1925
BROKEN COMMANDMENTS, 1919
BROKEN DISHES, 1930
BROKEN DOLL, A, 1921, A
BROKEN DREAMS, 1933, A
BROKEN ENGLISH, 1981, O
BROKEN FETTERS, 1916
BROKEN GATE, THE, 1920
BROKEN GATE, THE, 1927
BROKEN HEARTED, 1929
BROKEN HEARTS, 1926, A
BROKEN HEARTS, 1933
BROKEN HEARTS OF BROADWAY, THE, 1923
BROKEN HEARTS OF HOLLYWOOD, 1926, A
BROKEN HOMES, 1926
BROKEN HORSESHOE, THE, 1953, A
BROKEN JOURNEY, 1948, A
BROKEN LANCE, 1954, A
BROKEN LAND, THE, 1962, A
BROKEN LAW, THE, 1915
BROKEN LAW, THE, 1924
BROKEN LAW, THE, 1926
BROKEN LAWS, 1924
BROKEN LOVE, 1946, A
BROKEN LULLABY, 1932, A
BROKEN MASK, THE, 1928
BROKEN MELODY, 1938, A
BROKEN MELODY, THE, 1916
BROKEN MELODY, THE, 1920
BROKEN MELODY, THE, 1929, A
BROKEN MELODY, THE, 1934, A
BROKEN ROAD, THE, 1921
BROKEN ROMANCE, A, 1929, A
BROKEN ROSARY, THE, 1934, A
BROKEN SHADOWS, 1922
BROKEN SILENCE, THE, 1922
BROKEN SPUR, THE, 1921
BROKEN STAR, THE, 1956, A
BROKEN STRINGS, 1940
BROKEN THREADS, 1917
BROKEN THREADS, 1919
BROKEN TIES, 1918
BROKEN VIOLIN, THE, 1923
BROKEN VIOLIN, THE, 1927
BROKEN WING, THE, 1923
BROKEN WING, THE, 1932, A
BROMLEY CASE, THE, 1920
BRONC BUSTER, THE
BRONC STOMPER, THE, 1928
BRONCHO BUSTER, THE, 1927
BRONCHO TWISTER, 1927, A
BRONCO BILLY, 1980, C
BRONCO BULLFROG, 1972, A
BRONCO BUSTER, 1952, A
BRONENOSETS POTEMKIN
BRONTE SISTERS, THE, 1979, A
BRONX WARRIORS
BRONZE BELL, THE, 1921, A
BRONZE BRIDE, THE, 1917
BRONZE BUCKAROO, THE, 1939, A
BROOD, THE, 1979, C
BROODING EYES, 1926
BROOKLYN ORCHID, 1942, A
BROTH FOR SUPPER, 1919
BROTH OF A BOY, 1959, A
BROTHER ALFRED, 1932, A
BROTHER CARL, 1972
BROTHER FROM ANOTHER PLANET, THE, 1984, O
BROTHER JOHN, 1971, A
BROTHER OF THE WIND, 1972
BROTHER ON THE RUN, 1973
BROTHER ORCHID, 1940, A
BROTHER RAT, 1938, A
BROTHER RAT AND A BABY, 1940, A
BROTHER SUN, SISTER MOON, 1973, A
BROTHER, CRY FOR ME, 1970
BROTHERHOOD OF DEATH, 1976
BROTHERHOOD OF SATAN, THE, 1971, C-O
BROTHERHOOD OF THE YAKUZA
BROTHERHOOD, THE, 1968, C-O
BROTHERLY LOVE, 1928
BROTHERLY LOVE, 1970, O
BROTHERS, 1929
BROTHERS, 1930, A
BROTHERS, 1977, C
BROTHERS, 1984, O
BROTHERS AND SISTERS, 1980, A
BROTHERS DIVIDED, 1919
BROTHERS IN LAW, 1957, A
BROTHERS IN THE SADDLE, 1949, A
BROTHERS KARAMAZOV, THE, 1958, C-O
BROTHERS O'TOOLE, THE, 1973, A
BROTHERS OF THE WEST, 1938, A
BROTHERS RICO, THE, 1957, C
BROTHERS UNDER THE SKIN, 1922
BROTHERS, THE, 1948, A
BROWN DERBY, THE, 1926
BROWN IN HARVARD, 1917
BROWN OF HARVARD, 1926, A
BROWN ON RESOLUTION
BROWN SUGAR, 1922
BROWN SUGAR, 1931, A
BROWN WALLET, THE, 1936, A
BROWNING VERSION, THE, 1951, A
BRUBAKER, 1980, C-O
BRUCE LEE AND I, 1976, C-O
BRUCE LEE—TRUE STORY, 1976, C-O
BRUISED BY THE STORMS OF LIFE, 1918
BRUISER, THE, 1916
BRUSHFIRE, 1962, A
BRUTAL JUSTICE, 1978
BRUTE AND THE BEAST, THE, 1968, C
BRUTE BREAKER, THE, 1919
BRUTE CORPS, 1972
BRUTE FORCE, 1947, C
BRUTE MAN, THE, 1946, A
BRUTE MASTER, THE, 1920
BRUTE, THE, 1925
BRUTE, THE, 1927, A
BRUTE, THE, 1952, C
BUBBLE, THE, 1967, A

BUBBLES, 1920
BUCCANEER'S GIRL, 1950, A
BUCCANEER, THE, 1938, A
BUCCANEER, THE, 1958, A
BUCHANAN RIDES ALONE, 1958, A
BUCHANAN'S WIFE, 1918
BUCK AND THE PREACHER, 1972
BUCK BENNY RIDES AGAIN, 1940, A
BUCK PRIVATES, 1928
BUCK PRIVATES, 1941, AAA
BUCK PRIVATES COME HOME, 1947, AAA
BUCK ROGERS
BUCK ROGERS IN THE 25TH CENTURY, 1979, A-C
BUCKAROO BANZAI
BUCKAROO FROM POWDER RIVER, 1948, A
BUCKAROO KID, THE, 1926
BUCKAROO SHERIFF OF TEXAS, 1951, A
BUCKET OF BLOOD, 1934, O
BUCKET OF BLOOD, A, 1959, A
BUCKIN' THE WEST, 1924
BUCKING BROADWAY, 1918
BUCKING THE BARRIER, 1923
BUCKING THE LINE, 1921
BUCKING THE TIGER, 1921
BUCKING THE TRUTH, 1926, A
BUCKSHOT JOHN, 1915
BUCKSKIN, 1968, A
BUCKSKIN FRONTIER, 1943, A
BUCKSKIN LADY, THE, 1957, A
BUCKTOWN, 1975, C
BUDDHA, 1965, C
BUDDIES, 1983, A
BUDDY BUDDY, 1981, C
BUDDY HOLLY STORY, THE, 1978, A-C
BUDDY SYSTEM, THE, 1984, A-C
BUECHSE DER PANDORA
BUFFALO BILL, 1944, AAA
BUFFALO BILL AND THE INDIANS, OR SITTING BULL'S HISTORY LESSON, 1976, C
BUFFALO BILL IN TOMAHAWK TERRITORY, 1952, A
BUFFALO BILL ON THE U.P. TRAIL, 1926
BUFFALO BILL RIDES AGAIN, 1947, A
BUFFALO BILL, HERO OF THE FAR WEST, 1962, A
BUFFALO GUN, 1961, A
BUFFALO RIDER, 1978
BUG, 1975, A-C
BUGLE CALL, THE, 1916
BUGLE CALL, THE, 1927
BUGLE SOUNDS, THE, 1941, A
BUGLER OF ALGIERS, THE, 1916
BUGLES IN THE AFTERNOON, 1952, A
BUGS BUNNY'S THIRD MOVIE—1001 RABBIT TALES, 1982, AAA
BUGS BUNNY, SUPERSTAR, 1975, AAA
BUGS BUNNY/ROAD-RUNNER MOVIE, THE
BUGSY MALONE, 1976, AAA
BUILD MY GALLOWS HIGH
BUILD THY HOUSE, 1920
BUILDERS OF CASTLES, 1917
BUILT FOR RUNNING, 1924
BULL BUSTER, THE, 1975
BULL DODGER, THE, 1922
BULLDOG BREED, THE, 1960, A
BULLDOG COURAGE, 1922, A
BULLDOG COURAGE, 1935
BULLDOG DRUMMOND, 1923, A
BULLDOG DRUMMOND, 1929, A
BULLDOG DRUMMOND AT BAY, 1937, A
BULLDOG DRUMMOND AT BAY, 1947
BULLDOG DRUMMOND COMES BACK, 1937, A
BULLDOG DRUMMOND ESCAPES, 1937, A
BULLDOG DRUMMOND IN AFRICA, 1938, A
BULLDOG DRUMMOND STRIKES BACK, 1934, A
BULLDOG DRUMMOND STRIKES BACK, 1947
BULLDOG DRUMMOND'S BRIDE, 1939, A
BULLDOG DRUMMOND'S PERIL, 1938, A
BULLDOG DRUMMOND'S REVENGE, 1937, A
BULLDOG DRUMMOND'S SECRET POLICE, 1939, A
BULLDOG EDITION, 1936, A
BULLDOG JACK
BULLDOG PLUCK, 1927, A
BULLDOG SEES IT THROUGH, 1940, A
BULLDOGS OF THE TRAIL, THE, 1915
BULLET CODE, 1940, A
BULLET FOR A BADMAN, 1964, A
BULLET FOR BILLY THE KID, 1963
BULLET FOR JOEY, A, 1955, A
BULLET FOR PRETTY BOY, A, 1970, C
BULLET FOR SANDOVAL, A, 1970, C
BULLET FOR STEFANO, 1950, A
BULLET FOR THE GENERAL, A, 1967, C
BULLET IS WAITING, A, 1954, A
BULLET MARK, THE, 1928, A
BULLET SCARS, 1942, A
BULLET-PROOF, 1920
BULLETS AND BROWN EYES, 1916
BULLETS AND JUSTICE, 1929
BULLETS AND SADDLES, 1943
BULLETS FOR BANDITS, 1942
BULLETS FOR O'HARA, 1941, A
BULLETS FOR RUSTLERS, 1940, A
BULLETS OR BALLOTS, 1936, A
BULLFIGHTER AND THE LADY, 1951, A
BULLFIGHTERS, THE, 1945, A
BULLIN' THE BULLSHEVIKI, 1919, A
BULLITT, 1968, C
BULLSHOT, 1983, A-C
BULLWHIP, 1958, A
BULLY, 1978
BUMMER, 1973
BUNCH OF KEYS, A, 1915
BUNCH OF VIOLETS, A, 1916
BUNCO SQUAD, 1950, A
BUNDLE OF JOY, 1956, A
BUNGALOW 13, 1948, A
BUNKER BEAN, 1936, A
BUNNY LAKE IS MISSING, 1965, C
BUNNY O'HARE, 1971, C
BUNTY PULLS THE STRINGS, 1921, A
BUONA SERA, MRS. CAMPBELL, 1968, C
BURDEN OF PROOF, THE, 1918
BURDEN OF RACE, THE, 1921
BUREAU OF MISSING PERSONS, 1933, A
BURG THEATRE, 1936, A
BURGLAR AND THE LADY, THE, 1914
BURGLAR BY PROXY, 1919
BURGLAR, THE, 1917
BURGLAR, THE, 1956, A
BURGLAR-PROOF, 1920
BURGLARS, THE, 1972, C
BURGOMASTER OF STILEMONDE, THE, 1928
BURIDAN, LE HEROS DE LA TOUR DE NESLE, 1924
BURIED ALIVE, 1939, A
BURIED ALIVE, 1951, C
BURIED ALIVE, 1984, O
BURIED GOLD, 1926
BURIED TREASURE, 1921, A
BURKE AND HARE, 1972, O
BURMA CONVOY, 1941, A
BURN, 1970, O
BURN 'EM UP BARNES, 1921, A
BURN 'EM UP O'CONNER, 1939, A
BURN WITCH BURN, 1962, O
BURNING AN ILLUSION, 1982, C
BURNING BRIDGES, 1928
BURNING CROSS, THE, 1947, C
BURNING DAYLIGHT, 1914
BURNING DAYLIGHT, 1920
BURNING DAYLIGHT, 1928
BURNING GOLD, 1927
BURNING GOLD, 1936, A
BURNING HILLS, THE, 1956, A
BURNING QUESTION, THE
BURNING QUESTION, THE, 1919
BURNING SANDS, 1922, A
BURNING THE CANDLE, 1917
BURNING THE WIND, 1929
BURNING TRAIL, THE, 1925
BURNING UP, 1930, A
BURNING UP BROADWAY, 1928
BURNING WORDS, 1923
BURNING YEARS, THE, 1979, O
BURNING, THE, 1981, O
BURNOUT, 1979
BURNT EVIDENCE, 1954, O
BURNT FINGERS, 1927
BURNT IN, 1920
BURNT OFFERINGS, 1976, C-O
BURNT WINGS, 1916
BURNT WINGS, 1920
BURY ME AN ANGEL, 1972, O
BURY ME DEAD, 1947, C
BURY ME NOT ON THE LONE PRAIRIE, 1941, A
BUS IS COMING, THE, 1971, C-O
BUS RILEY'S BACK IN TOWN, 1965, A
BUS STOP, 1956, A
BUSH CHRISTMAS, 1947, AA
BUSH CHRISTMAS, 1983, AA
BUSH LEAGUER, THE, 1927
BUSH PILOT, 1947
BUSHBABY, THE, 1970, AA
BUSHER, THE, 1919
BUSHIDO BLADE, THE, 1982, O
BUSHRANGER, THE, 1928
BUSHWHACKERS, THE, 1952, A
BUSINESS AND PLEASURE, 1932, A
BUSINESS IS BUSINESS, 1915
BUSINESS OF LIFE, THE, 1918
BUSINESS OF LOVE, THE, 1925
BUSMAN'S HOLIDAY, 1936, A
BUSMAN'S HONEYMOON, 1940, A
BUSSES ROAR, 1942, A
BUSTER AND BILLIE, 1974
BUSTER KEATON STORY, THE, 1957, A
BUSTER, THE, 1923
BUSTIN' LOOSE, 1981, O
BUSTIN' THRU, 1925
BUSTING, 1974, C
BUSYBODY, THE, 1967, A
BUT NOT FOR ME, 1959, A
BUT NOT IN VAIN, 1948, A
BUT THE FLESH IS WEAK, 1932, A
BUT WE'RE AFRAID TO ASK, 1972, O
BUT YOUR TEETH ARE IN MY NECK, THE, 1967, C
BUTCH AND SUNDANCE: THE EARLY DAYS, 1979, C
BUTCH CASSIDY AND THE SUNDANCE KID, 1969, A
BUTCH MINDS THE BABY, 1942, A
BUTCHER BAKER (NIGHTMARE MAKER), 1982, O
BUTCHER, THE
BUTLER'S DILEMMA, THE, 1943, A
BUTLEY, 1974, O
BUTTER AND EGG MAN, THE, 1928
BUTTERCUP CHAIN, THE, 1971, O
BUTTERFIELD 8, 1960, O
BUTTERFLIES ARE FREE, 1972, A
BUTTERFLIES IN THE RAIN, 1926
BUTTERFLY, 1924
BUTTERFLY, 1982, O
BUTTERFLY AFFAIR, THE, 1934
BUTTERFLY GIRL, THE, 1917
BUTTERFLY GIRL, THE, 1921
BUTTERFLY ON THE SHOULDER, A, 1978, C-O
BUTTERFLY RANCH
BUTTERFLY RANGE, 1922
BUTTERFLY, THE, 1915
BUTTONS, 1927
BUY ME THAT TOWN, 1941, A
BUZZARD'S SHADOW, THE, 1915
BUZZY AND THE PHANTOM PINTO, 1941
BUZZY RIDES THE RANGE, 1940
BWANA DEVIL, 1953, A
BY APPOINTMENT ONLY, 1933, A
BY BERWIN BANKS, 1920
BY CANDLELIGHT, 1934, A
BY DESIGN, 1982, O
BY DIVINE RIGHT, 1924
BY HOOK OR BY CROOK
BY HOOK OR CROOK, 1918
BY LOVE POSSESSED, 1961, O
BY PROXY, 1918, A
BY RIGHT OF BIRTH, 1921
BY RIGHT OF POSSESSION, 1917, A
BY RIGHT OF PURCHASE, 1918
BY THE LAW, 1926
BY THE LIGHT OF THE SILVERY MOON, 1953, A
BY THE SHORTEST OF HEADS, 1915
BY THE WORLD FORGOT, 1918, A
BY WHOSE HAND?, 1916, A
BY WHOSE HAND?, 1927, A
BY WHOSE HAND?, 1932, A
BY YOUR LEAVE, 1935, A
BYE BYE BARBARA, 1969, A
BYE BYE BIRDIE, 1963
BYE-BYE BRAVERMAN, 1968, A
BYE-BYE BRASIL, 1980, C-O
BYE-BYE BUDDY, 1929
BYPASS TO HAPPINESS, 1934, A

-C-

C'MON, LET'S LIVE A LITTLE, 1967
C-MAN, 1949, A
C. C. AND COMPANY, 1971, O
C.B. HUSTLERS, 1978
C.H.O.M.P.S., 1979, AAA
C.H.U.D., 1984, O
C.O.D., 1915
C.O.D., 1932, A
C.O.D., 1983
CAARAVAN TRAIL, THE, 1946
CABARET, 1927
CABARET, 1972, CMPAA
CABARET GIRL, THE, 1919, A
CABARET, THE, 1918, A
CABIN IN THE COTTON, 1932, A-C
CABIN IN THE SKY, 1943, AA
CABINET OF CALIGARI, THE, 1962, A
CABINET OF DR. CALIGARI, THE, 1921, A
CABIRIA
CABIRIA, 1914, G
CABOBLANCO, 1981
CACCIA TRAGICA
CACTUS CRANDALL, 1918
CACTUS CURE, THE, 1925
CACTUS FLOWER, 1969, C
CACTUS IN THE SNOW, 1972, A
CACTUS KID, THE, 1934
CACTUS TRAILS, 1925
CACTUS TRAILS, 1927
CADDIE, 1976, C
CADDY SHACK, 1980, C-O
CADDY, THE, 1953, A
CADET GIRL, 1941, A
CADET-ROUSSELLE, 1954, A
CADETS ON PARADE, 1942
CAESAR AND CLEOPATRA, 1946, A
CAESAR THE CONQUEROR, 1963, C
CAFE COLETTE, 1937, A

CAFE DE PARIS, 1938
CAFE ELECTRIC, 1927
CAFE EXPRESS, 1980, C
CAFE FLESH, 1982
CAFE HOSTESS, 1940, A
CAFE IN CAIRO, A, 1924
CAFE MASCOT, 1936, A
CAFE METROPOLE, 1937, A-C
CAFE SOCIETY, 1939, A
CAGE OF EVIL, 1960, A-C
CAGE OF GOLD, 1950, A
CAGE OF NIGHTINGALES, A, 1947, A
CAGED, 1950, O
CAGED FURY, 1948, A
CAGED FURY, 1984, O
CAGED HEAT
CAGED VIRGINS, 1972
CAGED WOMEN, 1984, O
CAGLIOSTRO, 1920
CAGLIOSTRO, 1928
CAGLIOSTRO, 1975, C
CAHILL, UNITED STATES MARSHAL, 1973, C
CAILLAUX CASE, THE, 1918
CAIN AND MABEL, 1936, A
CAIN'S WAY, 1969, O
CAINE MUTINY, THE, 1954, A
CAIO, 1967
CAIRO, 1942, A
CAIRO, 1963, A
CAIRO ROAD, 1950, A
CAL, 1984, O
CALABUCH, 1956, A
CALAMITY JANE, 1953
CALAMITY JANE AND SAM BASS, 1949
CALAMITY THE COW, 1967, AA
CALCULATED RISK, 1963, A
CALCUTTA, 1947, A
CALEB PIPER'S GIRL, 1919
CALENDAR GIRL, 1947, A
CALENDAR, THE, 1931, A
CALENDAR, THE, 1948, A
CALENDER GIRL, THE, 1917
CALGARY STAMPEDE, THE, 1925
CALIBRE 38, 1919
CALIBRE 45, 1924
CALIFORNIA, 1927, A
CALIFORNIA, 1946, A
CALIFORNIA, 1963, A
CALIFORNIA CONQUEST, 1952, A
CALIFORNIA DOLLS
CALIFORNIA DREAMING, 1979, C
CALIFORNIA FIREBRAND, 1948, A
CALIFORNIA FRONTIER, 1938, A
CALIFORNIA GIRLS, 1984, O
CALIFORNIA GOLD RUSH, 1946
CALIFORNIA IN '49, 1924
CALIFORNIA JOE, 1944, A
CALIFORNIA MAIL, THE, 1929
CALIFORNIA MAIL, THE, 1937, A
CALIFORNIA OR BUST, 1927, A
CALIFORNIA PASSAGE, 1950, A
CALIFORNIA ROMANCE, A, 1922, A
CALIFORNIA SPLIT, 1974, C
CALIFORNIA STRAIGHT AHEAD, 1925
CALIFORNIA STRAIGHT AHEAD, 1937
CALIFORNIA SUITE, 1978, A-C
CALIFORNIA TRAIL, THE, 1933, A
CALIFORNIAN, THE, 1937, A
CALIGARI'S CURE, 1983
CALL A MESSENGER, 1939, A
CALL FROM THE WILD, THE, 1921, A
CALL HER SAVAGE, 1932, A
CALL HIM MR. SHATTER, 1976, O
CALL IT A DAY, 1937
CALL IT LUCK, 1934, A
CALL ME BWANA, 1963, A
CALL ME BY MY RIGHTFUL NAME, 1973
CALL ME GENIUS, 1961, A
CALL ME MADAM, 1953, A
CALL ME MAME, 1933
CALL ME MISTER, 1951, A
CALL NORTHSIDE 777, 1948
CALL OF COURAGE, THE, 1925
CALL OF HER PEOPLE, THE, 1917
CALL OF HIS PEOPLE, THE, 1922
CALL OF HOME, THE, 1922
CALL OF THE BLOOD, 1948, A
CALL OF THE CANYON, 1942, A
CALL OF THE CANYON, THE, 1923
CALL OF THE CIRCUS, 1930, A
CALL OF THE CUMBERLANDS, THE, 1915
CALL OF THE DANCE, THE, 1915
CALL OF THE DESERT, 1930
CALL OF THE EAST, THE, 1917
CALL OF THE EAST, THE, 1922, C
CALL OF THE FLESH, 1930, A
CALL OF THE FOREST, 1949
CALL OF THE HEART, 1928
CALL OF THE HILLS, THE, 1923
CALL OF THE JUNGLE, 1944, A
CALL OF THE KLONDIKE, 1950, A
CALL OF THE KLONDIKE, THE, 1926
CALL OF THE MATE, 1924
CALL OF THE NIGHT, 1926
CALL OF THE NORTH, THE, 1914, A
CALL OF THE NORTH, THE, 1921
CALL OF THE PIPES, THE, 1917
CALL OF THE PRAIRIE, 1936, A
CALL OF THE ROAD, THE, 1920
CALL OF THE ROCKIES, 1931
CALL OF THE ROCKIES, 1938, A
CALL OF THE ROCKIES, 1944
CALL OF THE SEA, THE, 1915
CALL OF THE SEA, THE, 1919
CALL OF THE SEA, THE, 1930
CALL OF THE SOUL, THE, 1919
CALL OF THE SOUTH SEAS, 1944, A
CALL OF THE WEST, 1930
CALL OF THE WILD, 1935, AA
CALL OF THE WILD, 1972, A
CALL OF THE WILD, THE, 1914
CALL OF THE WILD, THE, 1923, A
CALL OF THE WILDERNESS, THE, 1926
CALL OF THE YUKON, 1938, A
CALL OF YOUTH, THE, 1920, A
CALL OF YOUTH, THE, 1921
CALL OUT THE MARINES, 1942, A
CALL THE MESQUITEERS, 1938
CALL, THE, 1938, A
CALLAHANS AND THE MURPHYS, THE, 1927, A
CALLAN, 1975
CALLAWAY WENT THATAWAY, 1951
CALLBOX MYSTERY, THE, 1932, A
CALLED BACK, 1914
CALLED BACK, 1933
CALLING ALL CARS, 1935
CALLING ALL CROOKS, 1938, A
CALLING ALL HUSBANDS, 1940, A
CALLING ALL MA'S
CALLING ALL MARINES, 1939, A
CALLING BULLDOG DRUMMOND, 1951, A-C
CALLING DR. DEATH, 1943, A
CALLING DR. GILLESPIE, 1942, A
CALLING DR. KILDARE, 1939, A
CALLING HOMICIDE, 1956
CALLING OF DAN MATTHEWS, THE, 1936
CALLING PAUL TEMPLE, 1948, A
CALLING PHILO VANCE, 1940, A
CALLING THE TUNE, 1936
CALLING WILD BILL ELLIOTT, 1943, A
CALLING, THE
CALLIOPE, 1971
CALM YOURSELF, 1935, A
CALTIKI, THE IMMORTAL, MONSTER, 1959, C
CALVAIRE D'AMOUR, 1923
CALVARY, 1920
CALVERT'S VALLEY, 1922
CALYPSO, 1959, A-C
CALYPSO HEAT WAVE, 1957, A
CALYPSO JOE, 1957, A
CAMBRIC MASK, THE, 1919
CAMEL BOY, THE, 1984, AAA
CAMELOT, 1967, A-C
CAMELS ARE COMING, THE, 1934, A
CAMEO KIRBY, 1923
CAMEO KIRBY, 1930
CAMERA BUFF, 1983, A
CAMERAMAN, THE, 1928, A
CAMERONS, THE, 1974
CAMILLE, 1916
CAMILLE, 1917
CAMILLE, 1921
CAMILLE, 1927, A
CAMILLE, 1937, A-C
CAMILLE 2000, 1969, O
CAMILLE OF THE BARBARY COAST, 1925
CAMMINA CAMMINA, 1983, AA
CAMOUFLAGE KISS, A, 1918
CAMP ON BLOOD ISLAND, THE, 1958
CAMPBELL'S KINGDOM, 1957, A
CAMPBELLS ARE COMING, THE, 1915, A
CAMPER JOHN, 1973
CAMPSITE MASSACRE, 1981
CAMPUS CONFESSIONS, 1938, A
CAMPUS FLIRT, THE, 1926, A
CAMPUS HONEYMOON, 1948
CAMPUS KNIGHTS, 1929, A
CAMPUS RYTHM, 1943, A
CAMPUS SLEUTH, 1948, A
CAMPY KIDS FROM BOOT CAMP, 1942
CAN A WOMAN LOVE TWICE?, 1923
CAN HIERONYMUS MERKIN EVER FORGET MERCY HUMPPE AND FIND TRUE HAPPINESS?, 1969
CAN I DO IT 'TIL I NEED GLASSES?, 1977
CAN SHE BAKE A CHERRY PIE?, 1983, C
CAN THIS BE DIXIE?, 1936, A
CAN YOU HEAR ME MOTHER?, 1935, A
CAN'T HELP SINGING, 1944, A
CAN'T STOP THE MUSIC, 1980, C
CAN-CAN, 1960, A-C
CANADIAN MOUNTIES VS, ATOMIC INVADERS
CANADIAN PACIFIC, 1949, A
CANADIAN, THE, 1926
CANADIANS, THE, 1961, A
CANAL ZONE, 1942, A
CANARIES SOMETIMES SING, 1930, A
CANARIS, 1955, C
CANARY MURDER CASE, THE, 1929, A
CANCEL MY RESERVATION, 1972, A
CANCELLED DEBT, THE, 1927
CANDIDATE FOR MURDER, 1966, A
CANDIDATE, THE, 1964, C
CANDIDATE, THE, 1972, A-C
CANDIDE, 1962, A
CANDLELIGHT IN ALGERIA, 1944, A
CANDLES AT NINE, 1944
CANDLESHOE, 1978, AAA
CANDY, 1968, O
CANDY GIRL, THE, 1917
CANDY KID, THE, 1928
CANDY MAN, THE, 1969
CANDY SNATCHERS, THE, 1974
CANDY STRIPE NURSES, 1974
CANDY TANGERINE MAN, THE, 1975
CANDYTUFT, I MEAN VERONICA, 1921
CANICULE
CANNABIS, 1970, O
CANNERY ROW, 1982, C-O
CANNIBAL ATTACK, 1954, A
CANNIBAL GIRLS, 1973, C
CANNIBALISTIC HUMANOID UNDERGROUND DWELLING
CANNIBALS IN THE STREETS, 1982, O
CANNIBALS, THE, 1970, C-O
CANNON AND THE NIGHTINGALE, THE, 1969
CANNON FOR CORDOBA, 1970, C-O
CANNONBALL, 1976, C
CANNONBALL EXPRESS, 1932
CANNONBALL RUN II, 1984, O
CANNONBALL RUN, THE, 1981, A
CANON CITY, 1948, A
CANTERBURY TALE, A, 1944, A
CANTERVILLE GHOST, THE, 1944, AAA
CANTOR'S DAUGHTER, THE, 1913
CANTOR'S SON, THE, 1937, A
CANVAS KISSER, THE, 1925
CANYON AMBUSH, 1952, A
CANYON CITY, 1943, A
CANYON CROSSROADS, 1955, A
CANYON HAWKS, 1930, A
CANYON OF ADVENTURE, THE, 1928
CANYON OF LIGHT, THE, 1926
CANYON OF MISSING MEN, THE, 1930, A
CANYON OF THE FOOLS, 1923
CANYON PASSAGE, 1946, A
CANYON RAIDERS, 1951, A
CANYON RIVER, 1956, A
CANYON RUSTLERS, 1925
CAP'N ABE'S NIECE
CAPE CANAVERAL MONSTERS, 1960, A
CAPE FEAR, 1962, O
CAPE FORLORN
CAPER OF THE GOLDEN BULLS, THE, 1967, A
CAPETOWN AFFAIR, 1967, C
CAPITAL PUNISHMENT, 1925
CAPITOL, THE, 1920
CAPONE, 1975, O
CAPPY RICKS, 1921, A
CAPPY RICKS RETURNS, 1935, A
CAPRICE, 1913
CAPRICE, 1967, A
CAPRICE OF THE MOUNTAINS, 1916, A
CAPRICES OF KITTY, THE, 1915, A
CAPRICIOUS SUMMER, 1968, C
CAPRICORN ONE, 1978, C
CAPTAIN ALVAREZ, 1914
CAPTAIN APACHE, 1971, C
CAPTAIN APPLEJACK, 1931, A
CAPTAIN BILL, 1935, A
CAPTAIN BLACK JACK, 1952, A
CAPTAIN BLOOD, 1924
CAPTAIN BLOOD, 1935, A
CAPTAIN BOYCOTT, 1947
CAPTAIN CALAMITY, 1936, A
CAPTAIN CARELESS, 1928, A
CAPTAIN CAREY, U.S.A, 1950, A
CAPTAIN CAUTION, 1940, A
CAPTAIN CELLULOID VS THE FILM PIRATES, 1974
CAPTAIN CHINA, 1949, A
CAPTAIN CLEGG
CAPTAIN COURTESY, 1915, A
CAPTAIN COWBOY, 1929
CAPTAIN DIEPPE
CAPTAIN EDDIE, 1945, AA
CAPTAIN FLY-BY-NIGHT, 1922
CAPTAIN FROM CASTILE, 1947
CAPTAIN FROM KOEPENICK, 1933, A

CAPTAIN FROM KOEPENICK, THE, 1956, A
CAPTAIN FURY, 1939, A
CAPTAIN GRANT'S CHILDREN, 1939, AA
CAPTAIN HORATIO HORNBLOWER, 1951, A
CAPTAIN HURRICANE, 1935, A
CAPTAIN IS A LADY, THE, 1940, A
CAPTAIN JANUARY, 1924, A
CAPTAIN JANUARY, 1935, AAA
CAPTAIN JINKS OF THE HORSE MARINES, 1916
CAPTAIN JOHN SMITH AND POCAHONTAS, 1953
CAPTAIN KIDD, 1945, A
CAPTAIN KIDD AND THE SLAVE GIRL, 1954, A
CAPTAIN KIDD, JR., 1919
CAPTAIN KIDDO, 1917
CAPTAIN KRONOS: VAMPIRE HUNTER, 1974, O
CAPTAIN LASH, 1929, A
CAPTAIN LIGHTFOOT, 1955, A
CAPTAIN MACKLIN, 1915
CAPTAIN MIDNIGHT
CAPTAIN MILKSHAKE, 1970, O
CAPTAIN MOONLIGHT, 1940, A
CAPTAIN NEMO AND THE UNDERWATER CITY, 1969, A
CAPTAIN NEWMAN, M.D., 1963, C
CAPTAIN OF HIS SOUL, 1918
CAPTAIN OF THE GRAY HORSE TROOP, THE, 1917, A
CAPTAIN OF THE GUARD, 1930, A
CAPTAIN PIRATE, 1952, A
CAPTAIN SALVATION, 1927, A
CAPTAIN SCARLET VS. THE MYSTERIONS, 1982
CAPTAIN SCARLETT, 1953, A
CAPTAIN SINDBAD, 1963, A
CAPTAIN SIROCCO
CAPTAIN SWAGGER, 1928
CAPTAIN SWIFT, 1914, A
CAPTAIN SWIFT, 1920
CAPTAIN THUNDER, 1931
CAPTAIN TUGBOAT ANNIE, 1945
CAPTAIN'S CAPTAIN, THE, 1919, A
CAPTAIN'S COURAGE, A, 1926, A
CAPTAIN'S KID, THE, 1937, A
CAPTAIN'S ORDERS, 1937
CAPTAIN'S PARADISE, THE, 1953
CAPTAIN'S TABLE, THE, 1936, A
CAPTAIN'S TABLE, THE, 1960, A
CAPTAINS COURAGEOUS, 1937, AAA
CAPTAINS OF THE CLOUDS, 1942, A-C
CAPTIVATION, 1931, A
CAPTIVE, 1980
CAPTIVE CITY, 1952, A
CAPTIVE CITY, THE, 1963, C
CAPTIVE GIRL, 1950, A
CAPTIVE GOD, THE, 1916, A
CAPTIVE HEART, THE, 1948, C
CAPTIVE OF BILLY THE KID, 1952, A
CAPTIVE WILD WOMAN, 1943, A
CAPTIVE WOMEN, 1952, A
CAPTIVE, THE, 1915, A
CAPTURE OF BIGFOOT, THE, 1979
CAPTURE THAT CAPSULE, 1961
CAPTURE, THE, 1950
CAPTURED, 1933, A
CAPTURED IN CHINATOWN, 1935
CAR 99, 1935, A
CAR OF CHANCE, THE, 1917
CAR OF DREAMS, 1935, A
CAR, THE, 1977, C
CARAVAN, 1934, A
CARAVAN, 1946, A
CARAVAN TO VACCARES, 1974, C
CARAVANS, 1978, C
CARBINE WILLIAMS, 1952, A
CARBON COPY, 1981, C
CARD, THE
CARD, THE, 1922
CARDBOARD CAVALIER, THE, 1949, A
CARDBOARD LOVER, THE, 1928
CARDIAC ARREST, 1980, O
CARDIGAN, 1922, A
CARDINAL RICHELIEU, 1935, A
CARDINAL RICHELIEU'S WARD, 1914
CARDINAL, THE, 1936, A
CARDINAL, THE, 1963, C
CAREER, 1939, A
CAREER, 1959, C
CAREER BED, 1972
CAREER GIRL, 1944, A
CAREER GIRL, 1960
CAREER OF KATHERINE BUSH, THE, 1919
CAREER WOMAN, 1936, A
CAREERS, 1929, A
CAREFREE, 1938, A
CAREFUL, HE MIGHT HEAR YOU, 1984, A-C
CAREFUL, SOFT SHOULDERS, 1942, A
CARELESS AGE, 1929, A
CARELESS LADY, 1932, A
CARELESS WOMAN, THE, 1922
CARELESS YEARS, THE, 1957
CARESSED, 1965
CARETAKER, THE
CARETAKERS DAUGHTER, THE, 1952, A
CARETAKERS, THE, 1963, C
CAREY TREATMENT, THE, 1972, C
CARGO TO CAPETOWN, 1950
CARHOPS, 1980
CARIB GOLD, 1955
CARIBBEAN, 1952, A
CARIBBEAN MYSTERY, THE, 1945, A
CARIBOO TRAIL, THE, 1950, A
CARLTON-BROWNE OF THE F.O.
CARMELA, 1949, A
CARMEN
CARMEN, 1915, A
CARMEN, 1916
CARMEN, 1917
CARMEN, 1928
CARMEN, 1931
CARMEN, 1946, A
CARMEN, 1949
CARMEN, 1983, C
CARMEN JONES, 1954, C
CARMEN OF THE KLONDIKE, 1918, A
CARMEN OF THE NORTH, 1920
CARMEN, BABY, 1967, O
CARNABY, M.D., 1967, C
CARNAL KNOWLEDGE, 1971, O
CARNAL MADNESS, 1975
CARNATION KID, 1929
CARNEGIE HALL, 1947, A
CARNIVAL, 1921
CARNIVAL, 1931, A
CARNIVAL, 1935, A
CARNIVAL, 1946, A
CARNIVAL, 1953, A
CARNIVAL BOAT, 1932, A
CARNIVAL GIRL, THE, 1926, A
CARNIVAL IN COSTA RICA, 1947, A
CARNIVAL IN FLANDERS, 1936, A
CARNIVAL LADY, 1933, A
CARNIVAL OF BLOOD, 1976, C
CARNIVAL OF CRIME, 1929
CARNIVAL OF SINNERS, 1947, A
CARNIVAL OF SOULS, 1962, C
CARNIVAL QUEEN, 1937, A
CARNIVAL ROCK, 1957, A
CARNIVAL STORY, 1954, A
CARNY, 1980, O
CAROLINA, 1934, A
CAROLINA BLUES, 1944
CAROLINA CANNONBALL, 1955, A
CAROLINA MOON, 1940, A
CAROLINE CHERIE, 1968, C
CAROLLIE CHERIE, 1951, A
CAROLYN OF THE CORNERS, 1919, A
CAROUSEL, 1956
CARPET FROM BAGDAD, THE, 1915, A
CARPETBAGGERS, THE, 1964, C
CARRIE, 1952, C
CARRIE, 1976, O
CARRINGTON SCHOOL MYSTERY, THE, 1958
CARRINGTON V.C.
CARROTS, 1917
CARRY ON, 1927
CARRY ON 'ROUND THE BEND, 1972
CARRY ON ABROAD, 1974
CARRY ON ADMIRAL, 1957
CARRY ON AGAIN, DOCTOR, 1969, C
CARRY ON BEHIND, 1975
CARRY ON CABBIE, 1963, C
CARRY ON CAMPING, 1969, C
CARRY ON CLEO, 1964, C
CARRY ON CONSTABLE, 1960, C
CARRY ON COWBOY, 1966, A
CARRY ON CRUISING, 1962
CARRY ON DICK, 1975
CARRY ON DOCTOR, 1968, C
CARRY ON EMANUELLE, 1978, O
CARRY ON ENGLAND, 1976, A
CARRY ON GIRLS, 1974
CARRY ON HENRY VIII, 1970, O
CARRY ON JACK, 1963, A
CARRY ON LOVING, 1970, C-O
CARRY ON MATRON, 1973
CARRY ON NURSE, 1959, A
CARRY ON REGARDLESS, 1961, C
CARRY ON SCREAMING, 1966, A
CARRY ON SERGEANT, 1959, A
CARRY ON SPYING, 1964, A
CARRY ON TEACHER, 1962, A
CARRY ON TV
CARRY ON UP THE JUNGLE, 1970, A
CARRY ON VENUS
CARRY ON, UP THE KHYBER, 1968, A
CARS THAT ATE PARIS, THE, 1974, O
CARSON CITY, 1952, A
CARSON CITY CYCLONE, 1943, A
CARSON CITY KID, 1940, AA
CARSON CITY RAIDERS, 1948, A
CARTER CASE, THE, 1947, A
CARTHAGE IN FLAMES, 1961, C-O
CARTOUCHE, 1957, A
CARTOUCHE, 1962, A
CARVE HER NAME WITH PRIDE, 1958, A
CARWASH, 1976, C
CARYL OF THE MOUNTAINS, 1936, AA
CASA MANANA, 1951, A
CASA RICORDI
CASABLANCA, 1942, A
CASANOVA, 1927
CASANOVA, 1976, O
CASANOVA '70, 1965
CASANOVA AND COMPANY
CASANOVA BROWN, 1944, A
CASANOVA IN BURLESQUE, 1944, A
CASANOVA'S BIG NIGHT, 1954, A
CASBAH, 1948, C
CASE AGAINST BROOKLYN, THE, 1958, A
CASE AGAINST FERRO, THE, 1980, C
CASE AGAINST MRS. AMES, THE, 1936, A
CASE AT LAW, A, 1917
CASE FOR PC 49, A, 1951, A
CASE FOR THE CROWN, THE, 1934, A
CASE OF BECKY, THE, 1921
CASE OF CHARLES PEACE, THE, 1949
CASE OF CLARA DEANE, THE, 1932, A
CASE OF DR. LAURENT, 1958
CASE OF GABRIEL PERRY, THE, 1935, A
CASE OF JONATHAN DREW, THE
CASE OF LADY CAMBER, THE, 1920
CASE OF LENA SMITH, THE, 1929
CASE OF MRS. LORING
CASE OF PATTY SMITH, THE, 1962, C-O
CASE OF SERGEANT GRISCHA, THE, 1930
CASE OF THE 44'S, THE, 1964, C
CASE OF THE BLACK CAT, THE, 1936
CASE OF THE BLACK PARROT, THE, 1941, A
CASE OF THE CURIOUS BRIDE, THE, 1935, A
CASE OF THE FRIGHTENED LADY, THE, 1940
CASE OF THE HOWLING DOG, THE, 1934, A
CASE OF THE LUCKY LEGS, THE, 1935, A
CASE OF THE MISSING MAN, THE, 1935, A
CASE OF THE RED MONKEY, 1955, A
CASE OF THE STUTTERING BISHOP, THE, 1937, A
CASE OF THE VELVET CLAWS, THE, 1936, A
CASE VAN GELDERN, 1932, C
CASEY AT THE BAT, 1916
CASEY AT THE BAT, 1927, A
CASEY JONES, 1927
CASEY'S MILLIONS, 1922
CASEY'S SHADOW, 1978, A
CASH McCALL, 1960, C
CASH ON DELIVERY, 1956, A
CASH ON DEMAND, 1962, C
CASINO DE PARIS, 1957, C
CASINO MURDER CASE, THE, 1935, A
CASINO ROYALE, 1967, A
CASQUE D'OR, 1956, C
CASS, 1977
CASS TIMBERLANE, 1947, C
CASSANDRA CROSSING, THE, 1977, C
CASSIDY, 1917, A
CASSIDY OF BAR 20, 1938, A
CAST A DARK SHADOW, 1958, A
CAST A GIANT SHADOW, 1966, A-C
CAST A LONG SHADOW, 1959, C
CASTAWAY COWBOY, THE, 1974, AAA
CASTE, 1930, A
CASTILIAN, THE, 1963, C
CASTLE, 1917
CASTLE IN THE AIR, 1952, A
CASTLE IN THE DESERT, 1942, A
CASTLE KEEP, 1969, C
CASTLE OF BLOOD, 1964, O
CASTLE OF CRIMES, 1940, A
CASTLE OF DREAMS, 1919
CASTLE OF EVIL, 1967, C
CASTLE OF FU MANCHU, THE, 1968, C
CASTLE OF PURITY, 1974, C-O
CASTLE OF TERROR
CASTLE OF THE LIVING DEAD, 1964, C
CASTLE OF THE MONSTERS, 1958, C
CASTLE ON THE HUDSON, 1940, C
CASTLE SINISTER, 1932, C
CASTLE, THE, 1969, C
CASTLES FOR TWO, 1917
CASTLES IN SPAIN, 1920
CASTLES IN THE AIR, 1919
CASTLES IN THE AIR, 1923
CAT AND MOUSE
CAT AND MOUSE, 1958
CAT AND MOUSE, 1978
CAT AND THE CANARY, THE, 1927, A
CAT AND THE CANARY, THE, 1939
CAT AND THE CANARY, THE, 1979, A
CAT AND THE FIDDLE, 1934, A
CAT ATE THE PARAKEET, THE, 1972, A

CAT BALLOU, 1965, A-C
CAT BURGLAR, THE, 1961, C
CAT CREEPS, THE, 1930
CAT CREEPS, THE, 1946, AA
CAT FROM OUTER SPACE, THE, 1978, AAA
CAT GANG, THE, 1959
CAT GIRL, 1957, C
CAT IN THE SACK, THE, 1967, C
CAT MURKIL AND THE SILKS, 1976
CAT O'NINE TAILS, 1971, O
CAT ON A HOT TIN ROOF, 1958, C
CAT PEOPLE, 1942, C
CAT PEOPLE, 1982, O
CAT WOMEN OF THE MOON, 1953, A
CAT'S PAJAMAS, THE, 1926, A
CAT'S PAW, THE, 1934, A
CAT, THE, 1959, C
CAT, THE, 1966
CAT, THE, 1975, C
CATACLYSM, 1980
CATACOMBS
CATALINA CAPER, THE, 1967, A
CATAMOUNT KILLING, THE, 1975, C
CATCH AS CATCH CAN, 1927, A
CATCH AS CATCH CAN, 1937, A
CATCH AS CATCH CAN, 1968, C
CATCH ME IF YOU CAN, 1959
CATCH ME A SPY, 1971, A-C
CATCH MY SMOKE, 1922
CATCH MY SOUL, 1974, C
CATCH US IF YOU CAN
CATCH-22, 1970, O
CATERED AFFAIR, THE, 1956, A
CATHERINE, 1924
CATHERINE & CO., 1976, O
CATHERINE THE GREAT, 1934, C
CATHY'S CHILD, 1979, C
CATHY'S CURSE, 1977, O
CATLOW, 1971
CATMAN OF PARIS, THE, 1946, A
CATSKILL HONEYMOON, 1950
CATSPAW, THE, 1916
CATTLE ANNIE AND LITTLE BRITCHES, 1981, C
CATTLE DRIVE, 1951, AA
CATTLE EMPIRE, 1958
CATTLE KING, 1963, A
CATTLE QUEEN, 1951, A
CATTLE QUEEN OF MONTANA, 1954, A
CATTLE RAIDERS, 1938
CATTLE STAMPEDE, 1943, A
CATTLE THIEF, THE, 1936, A
CATTLE TOWN, 1952, A
CAUGHT, 1931, A
CAUGHT, 1949, C
CAUGHT BLUFFING, 1922
CAUGHT CHEATING, 1931
CAUGHT IN THE ACT, 1918
CAUGHT IN THE ACT, 1941, A
CAUGHT IN THE DRAFT, 1941, AA
CAUGHT IN THE FOG, 1928, A
CAUGHT IN THE NET, 1960, AA
CAUGHT PLASTERED, 1931, A
CAUGHT SHORT, 1930, A
CAULDRON OF BLOOD, 1971, C
CAULDRON OF DEATH, THE, 1979, O
CAUSE FOR ALARM, 1951, C
CAUSE FOR DIVORCE, 1923
CAVALCADE, 1933, A
CAVALCADE OF THE WEST, 1936, A
CAVALIER OF THE STREETS, THE, 1937
CAVALIER OF THE WEST, 1931, A
CAVALIER, THE, 1928, A
CAVALIER, THE, 1928
CAVALLERIA RUSTICANA
CAVALRY, 1936, A
CAVALRY COMMAND, 1963, A
CAVALRY SCOUT, 1951, A
CAVANAUGH OF THE FOREST RANGERS, 1918
CAVE GIRL, THE, 1921
CAVE OF OUTLAWS, 1951, A
CAVE OF THE LIVING DEAD, 1966, A
CAVELL CASE, THE
CAVEMAN, 1981, C
CAVEMAN, THE, 1915
CAVEMAN, THE, 1926, A
CAVERN, THE, 1965, A
CAXAMBU, 1968
CAYMAN TRIANGLE, THE, 1977, C-O
CE COCHON DE MORIN, 1924
CE PAUVRE CHERI, 1923
CECILIA OF THE PINK ROSES, 1918
CECROPIA MOTH, THE, 1916
CEDDO, 1978, C
CEILNG ZERO, 1935
CELEBRATED CASE, A, 1914, A
CELEBRATED SCANDAL, A, 1915
CELEBRITY, 1928
CELESTE, 1982, A
CELESTE OF THE AMBULANCE CORPS, 1916
CELESTIAL CITY, THE, 1929
CELIA, 1949, A
CELINE AND JULIE GO BOATING, 1974, C
CELL 2455, DEATH ROW, 1955, C
CELLAR OF DEATH, THE, 1914
CENSUS TAKER, THE, 1984, O
CENTENNIAL SUMMER, 1946, AA
CENTERFOLD GIRLS, THE, 1974
CENTO ANNI D'AMORE, 1954, C
CENTRAL AIRPORT, 1933, A
CENTRAL PARK, 1932, A
CENTURION, THE, 1962, A
CEREBROS DIABOLICOS, 1966, A
CEREBROS INFERNAL
CEREMONY, THE, 1963, C
CERTAIN RICH MAN, A, 1921
CERTAIN SMILE, A, 1958, C-O
CERTAIN YOUNG MAN, A, 1928
CERTAIN, VERY CERTAIN, AS A MATTER OF FACT... PROBABLE, 1970, O
CERVANTES
CESAR, 1936, A
CESAR AND ROSALIE, 1972, C
CH OF BLUE, A, 1965, A
CHA-CHA-CHA BOOM, 1956
CHACALS, 1918
CHAD HANNA, 1940, A-C
CHAFED ELBOWS, 1967
CHAIN GANG, 1950, C
CHAIN GANG WOMEN, 1972
CHAIN INVISIBLE, THE, 1916
CHAIN LIGHTING, 1927
CHAIN LIGHTNING, 1922, A
CHAIN LIGHTNING, 1950, A
CHAIN OF CIRCUMSTANCE, 1951
CHAIN OF EVENTS, 1958, A-C
CHAIN OF EVIDENCE, 1957, A
CHAIN REACTION, 1980, C
CHAINED, 1927
CHAINED, 1934, C
CHAINED FOR LIFE, 1950, C
CHAINED HEAT, 1983, O
CHAINS OF BONDAGE, 1916
CHAINS OF EVIDENCE, 1920
CHAIRMAN, THE, 1969
CHALICE OF COURAGE, THE, 1915
CHALICE OF SORROW, THE, 1916
CHALK GARDEN, THE, 1964, A
CHALK MARKS, 1924
CHALLENGE, 1974
CHALLENGE ACCEPTED, THE, 1918, A
CHALLENGE FOR ROBIN HOOD, A, 1968, A
CHALLENGE OF CHANCE, THE, 1919, A
CHALLENGE OF MC KENNA, THE, 1983
CHALLENGE OF THE LAW, THE, 1920
CHALLENGE OF THE RANGE, 1949, A
CHALLENGE THE WILD, 1954
CHALLENGE TO BE FREE, 1976, A
CHALLENGE TO LASSIE, 1949, AAA
CHALLENGE TO LIVE, 1964, O
CHALLENGE, THE
CHALLENGE, THE, 1916
CHALLENGE, THE, 1922
CHALLENGE, THE, 1939, A
CHALLENGE, THE, 1948, A
CHALLENGE, THE, 1982, C
CHALLENGERS, THE, 1968
CHAMBER OF HORRORS, 1929
CHAMBER OF HORRORS, 1941, A
CHAMBER OF HORRORS, 1966, O
CHAMBER OF MYSTERY, THE, 1920
CHAMELEON, 1978, C
CHAMP FOR A DAY, 1953, A
CHAMP, THE, 1931, AA
CHAMP, THE, 1979, AA
CHAMPAGNE, 1928, A
CHAMPAGNE CHARLIE, 1936, A
CHAMPAGNE CHARLIE, 1944, A
CHAMPAGNE FOR BREAKFAST, 1935, A
CHAMPAGNE FOR CAESAR, 1950, AAA
CHAMPAGNE MURDERS, THE, 1968, C
CHAMPAGNE WALTZ, 1937, A
CHAMPI TORTU, 1921
CHAMPION, 1949, C
CHAMPION OF LOST CAUSES, 1925, A
CHAMPIONS, 1984, C
CHAN IS MISSING, 1982, C
CHANCE AT HEAVEN, 1933, A
CHANCE MEETING, 1954, A
CHANCE MEETING, 1960, C
CHANCE OF A LIFETIME, 1950, A
CHANCE OF A LIFETIME, THE, 1916
CHANCE OF A LIFETIME, THE, 1943, A
CHANCE OF A NIGHT-TIME, THE, 1931, A
CHANCES, 1931, A
CHANDLER, 1971
CHANDU ON THE MAGIC ISLAND, 1934
CHANDU THE MAGICIAN, 1932, A
CHANEL SOLITAIRE, 1981, C
CHANG, 1927, C
CHANGE FOR A SOVEREIGN, 1937, A
CHANGE OF HABIT, 1969, C-O
CHANGE OF HEART, 1934, A
CHANGE OF HEART, 1938
CHANGE OF HEART, 1943
CHANGE OF HEART, 1962, A
CHANGE OF MIND, 1969, C
CHANGE OF SEASONS, A, 1980, C-O
CHANGE PARTNERS, 1965
CHANGELING, THE, 1980, O
CHANGES, 1969, O
CHANGING HUSBANDS, 1924
CHANGING WOMAN, THE, 1918
CHANNEL CROSSING, 1934, A
CHANNING OF THE NORTHWEST, 1922
CHANNINGS, THE, 1920
CHANSON FILMEES, 1918
CHANT OF JIMMIE BLACKSMITH, THE, 1980, O
CHANTE-LOUVE, 1921
CHAPERON, THE, 1916
CHAPMAN REPORT, THE, 1962, O
CHAPPAQUA, 1967, O
CHAPPY—THAT'S ALL, 1924
CHAPTER IN HER LIFE, A, 1923
CHAPTER TWO, 1979, C
CHARADE, 1953, A
CHARADE, 1963, A-C
CHARGE AT FEATHER RIVER, THE, 1953, C
CHARGE IT, 1921, A
CHARGE IT TO ME, 1919
CHARGE OF THE GAUCHOS, THE, 1928
CHARGE OF THE LANCERS, 1953, A
CHARGE OF THE LIGHT BRIGADE, THE, 1936, A
CHARGE OF THE LIGHT BRIGADE, THE, 1968
CHARGE OF THE MODEL-T'S, 1979, AA
CHARING CROSS ROAD, 1935, A
CHARITY
CHARITY ANN, 1915
CHARITY CASTLE, 1917
CHARITY?, 1916, A
CHARLATAN, THE, 1916
CHARLATAN, THE, 1929, A
CHARLES AND LUCIE, 1982, A
CHARLES XII, PARTS 1 & 2, 1927
CHARLES, DEAD OR ALIVE, 1972
CHARLESTON, 1978, A
CHARLEY AND THE ANGEL, 1973
CHARLEY MOON, 1956, A
CHARLEY VARRICK, 1973, C
CHARLEY', BIG-
CHARLEY'S AUNT, 1925
CHARLEY'S AUNT, 1930
CHARLEY'S AUNT, 1941, AA
CHARLEY-ONE-EYE, 1973, C
CHARLIE BUBBLES, 1968, C
CHARLIE CHAN AND THE CURSE OF THE DRAGON QUEEN, 1981, A
CHARLIE CHAN AT MONTE CARLO, 1937, A
CHARLIE CHAN AT THE CIRCUS, 1936, A
CHARLIE CHAN AT THE OLYMPICS, 1937, A
CHARLIE CHAN AT THE OPERA, 1936, A
CHARLIE CHAN AT THE RACE TRACK, 1936, A
CHARLIE CHAN AT THE WAX MUSEUM, 1940
CHARLIE CHAN AT TREASURE ISLAND, 1939, A
CHARLIE CHAN CARRIES ON, 1931, A
CHARLIE CHAN IN BLACK MAGIC, 1944, A
CHARLIE CHAN IN EGYPT, 1935, A
CHARLIE CHAN IN HONOLULU, 1938, A
CHARLIE CHAN IN LONDON, 1934, A
CHARLIE CHAN IN PANAMA, 1940, A
CHARLIE CHAN IN PARIS, 1935
CHARLIE CHAN IN RENO, 1939, A
CHARLIE CHAN IN RIO, 1941, A
CHARLIE CHAN IN SHANGHAI, 1935, A
CHARLIE CHAN IN THE CITY OF DARKNESS, 1939, A
CHARLIE CHAN IN THE SECRET SERVICE, 1944, A
CHARLIE CHAN ON BROADWAY, 1937, A
CHARLIE CHAN'S CHANCE, 1932, A
CHARLIE CHAN'S COURAGE, 1934, A
CHARLIE CHAN'S GREATEST CASE, 1933, A
CHARLIE CHAN'S MURDER CRUISE, 1940, A
CHARLIE CHAN'S SECRET, 1936, A
CHARLIE CHAN: HAPPINESS IS A WARM CLUE, 1971
CHARLIE MC CARTHY, DETECTIVE, 1939, AAA
CHARLIE, THE LONESOME COUGAR, 1967, AAA
CHARLOTTE, 1917
CHARLOTTE'S WEB, 1973, AAA
CHARLTON-BROWN OF THE F.O.
CHARLY, 1968, A-C
CHARM SCHOOL, THE, 1921, A
CHARMER, THE, 1917
CHARMER, THE, 1925, A
CHARMING DECEIVER, THE, 1921
CHARMING DECEIVER, THE, 1933, A
CHARMING SINNERS, 1929, A
CHARRIOTS OF FIRE, 1981, AAA
CHARRO, 1969, A
CHARTER PILOT, 1940, A

CHARTROOSE CABOOSE, 1960
CHASE A CROOKED SHADOW, 1958, A
CHASE FOR THE GOLDEN NEEDLES
CHASE ME CHARLIE, 1918
CHASE, THE, 1946, A
CHASE, THE, 1966, O
CHASER, THE, 1928, A
CHASER, THE, 1938
CHASERS, THE
CHASING DANGER, 1939, A
CHASING RAINBOWS, 1919
CHASING RAINBOWS, 1930, A
CHASING THE MOON, 1922, A
CHASING THROUGH EUROPE, 1929
CHASING TROUBLE, 1926
CHASING TROUBLE, 1940, A
CHASING YESTERDAY, 1935, A
CHASTITY, 1923
CHASTITY, 1969, C
CHASTITY BELT, THE, 1968, C
CHATEAU HISTORIQUE, 1923
CHATO'S LAND, 1972, O
CHATTANOOGA CHOO CHOO, 1984, A-C
CHATTEL, THE, 1916
CHATTERBOX, 1936, A
CHATTERBOX, 1943, A
CHATTERBOX, 1977
CHE!, 1969, C
CHE?, 1973, O
CHEAP DETECTIVE, THE, 1978, C
CHEAP KISSES, 1924
CHEAPER BY THE DOZEN, 1950, AAA
CHEAPER TO KEEP HER, 1980, O
CHEAPER TO MARRY, 1925
CHEAT, THE, 1915
CHEAT, THE, 1923
CHEAT, THE, 1931, C-O
CHEAT, THE, 1950
CHEATED HEARTS, 1921, A
CHEATED LOVE, 1921
CHEATER REFORMED, THE, 1921, A
CHEATER, THE, 1920
CHEATERS, 1927, A
CHEATERS, 1934, A
CHEATERS AT PLAY, 1932, A
CHEATERS, THE, 1945, A
CHEATERS, THE, 1961, O
CHEATING BLONDES, 1933, A
CHEATING CHEATERS, 1919
CHEATING CHEATERS, 1927, A
CHEATING CHEATERS, 1934
CHEATING HERSELF, 1919
CHEATING THE PUBLIC, 1918
CHECHAHCOS, THE, 1924
CHECK AND DOUBLE CHECK
CHECK YOUR GUNS, 1948, A
CHECKERBOARD, 1969, O
CHECKERED COAT, THE, 1948, A
CHECKERED FLAG OR CRASH, 1978, C
CHECKERED FLAG, THE, 1926
CHECKERED FLAG, THE, 1963, C
CHECKERS, 1913, A
CHECKERS, 1919
CHECKERS, 1937, A
CHECKMATE, 1935, A
CHECKMATE, 1973, O
CHECKMATE, THE, 1917
CHECKPOINT, 1957, A
CHEECH AND CHONG'S NEXT MOVIE, 1980, O
CHEECH AND CHONG'S NICE DREAMS, 1981, O
CHEECH AND CHONG'S THE CORSICAN BROTHERS, 1984, O
CHEER BOYS CHEER, 1939, A
CHEER LEADER, THE, 1928
CHEER THE BRAVE, 1951
CHEER UP AND SMILE, 1930, A
CHEER UP!, 1936, A
CHEERFUL FRAUD, THE, 1927
CHEERFUL GIVERS, 1917
CHEERING SECTION, 1977
CHEERLEADERS BEACH PARTY, 1978
CHEERLEADERS, THE, 1973
CHEERS FOR MISS BISHOP, 1941, A
CHEERS OF THE CROWD, 1936, A
CHELSEA GIRLS, THE, 1967, O
CHELSEA LIFE, 1933, A
CHELSEA STORY, 1951, A
CHEREZ TERNII K SVEZDAM, 1981, A
CHEROKEE FLASH, THE, 1945, A
CHEROKEE KID, THE, 1927
CHEROKEE STRIP, 1937, A
CHEROKEE STRIP, 1940, A
CHEROKEE STRIP, THE, 1925
CHEROKEE UPPRISING, 1950, A
CHERRY HILL HIGH, 1977
CHERRY RIPE, 1921
CHESS PLAYER, THE, 1930
CHESS PLAYERS, THE, 1978, C
CHESTY ANDERSON, U.S. NAVY, 1976, O
CHETNIKS, 1943, A
CHEYENNE, 1929
CHEYENNE, 1947, A
CHEYENNE AUTUMN, 1964, A
CHEYENNE CYCLONE, THE, 1932, A
CHEYENNE KID, THE, 1930, A
CHEYENNE KID, THE, 1933, A
CHEYENNE KID, THE, 1940, A
CHEYENNE RIDES AGAIN, 1937, A
CHEYENNE ROUNDUP, 1943, A
CHEYENNE SOCIAL CLUB, THE, 1970, C
CHEYENNE TAKES OVER, 1947, A
CHEYENNE TORNADO, 1935, A
CHEYENNE TRAILS, 1928
CHEYENNE WILDCAT, 1944, A
CHICAGO, 1928, A
CHICAGO 70, 1970, C
CHICAGO AFTER MIDNIGHT, 1928, A
CHICAGO CALLING, 1951, A
CHICAGO CONFIDENTIAL, 1957
CHICAGO DEADLINE, 1949, A
CHICAGO KID, THE, 1945, A
CHICAGO KID, THE, 1969
CHICAGO SYNDICATE, 1955, A
CHICHINETTE ET CLE, 1921
CHICK, 1928
CHICK, 1936, A
CHICKEN A LA KING, 1928
CHICKEN CASEY, 1917, A
CHICKEN CHRONICLES, THE, 1977, C
CHICKEN EVERY SUNDAY, 1948, A
CHICKEN IN THE CASE, THE, 1921
CHICKEN WAGON FAMILY, 1939, A
CHICKENS, 1921, A
CHICKIE, 1925
CHIEF CRAZY HORSE, 1955, A
CHIEF, THE, 1933, A
CHIFFY KIDS GANG, THE, 1983
CHIGNON D'OR, 1916
CHILD AND THE KILLER, THE, 1959, C
CHILD BRIDE, 1937
CHILD FOR SALE, A, 1920, A
CHILD IN JUDGEMENT, A, 1915
CHILD IN PAWN, A, 1921
CHILD IN THE HOUSE, 1956, A
CHILD IS A WILD THING, A, 1976, O
CHILD IS BORN, A, 1940, A
CHILD IS WAITING, A, 1963, A
CHILD OF DESTINY, THE, 1916
CHILD OF DIVORCE, 1946, A
CHILD OF GOD, A, 1915
CHILD OF M'SIEU, 1919, A
CHILD OF MANHATTAN, 1933, C
CHILD OF MYSTERY, A, 1916
CHILD OF THE BIG CITY, 1914
CHILD OF THE PARIS STREETS, A, 1916
CHILD OF THE PRAIRIE, A, 1925
CHILD OF THE WILD, A, 1917
CHILD THOU GAVEST ME, THE, 1921
CHILD UNDER A LEAF, 1975, O
CHILD'S PLAY, 1954, A
CHILD'S PLAY, 1972
CHILD'S PLAY, 1984
CHILD, THE, 1977, O
CHILDHOOD OF MAXIM GORKY, 1938
CHILDISH THINGS, 1969, O
CHILDREN—FLOWERS OF LIFE, 1919
CHILDREN GALORE, 1954, A
CHILDREN IN THE HOUSE, THE, 1916
CHILDREN NOT WANTED, 1920
CHILDREN OF BABYLON, 1980, O
CHILDREN OF BANISHMENT, 1919
CHILDREN OF CHANCE, 1930, A
CHILDREN OF CHANCE, 1949, A
CHILDREN OF CHANCE, 1950, A
CHILDREN OF CHAOS, 1950, C
CHILDREN OF COURAGE, 1921
CHILDREN OF DESTINY, 1920
CHILDREN OF DIVORCE, 1927
CHILDREN OF DREAMS, 1931, A
CHILDREN OF DUST, 1923
CHILDREN OF EVE, THE, 1915
CHILDREN OF FATE, 1926
CHILDREN OF FATE, 1928
CHILDREN OF GIBEON, THE, 1920
CHILDREN OF GOD'S EARTH, 1983, C
CHILDREN OF HIROSHIMA, 1952, C-O
CHILDREN OF JAZZ, 1923
CHILDREN OF PARADISE, 1945, C
CHILDREN OF PLEASURE, 1930, A
CHILDREN OF RAGE, 1975, O
CHILDREN OF SANCHEZ, THE, 1978, O
CHILDREN OF STORM, 1926
CHILDREN OF THE CORN, 1984, C-O
CHILDREN OF THE DAMNED, 1963, O
CHILDREN OF THE FEUD, 1916
CHILDREN OF THE FOG, 1935
CHILDREN OF THE GHETTO, THE, 1915
CHILDREN OF THE NEW DAY, 1930
CHILDREN OF THE NIGHT, 1921, A
CHILDREN OF THE RITZ, 1929
CHILDREN OF THE SEA, 1926
CHILDREN OF THE WHIRLWIND, 1925
CHILDREN PAY, THE, 1916
CHILDREN SHOULDN'T PLAY WITH DEAD THINGS, 1972, O
CHILDREN'S HOUR, THE, 1961, C
CHILDREN, THE, 1949, AAA
CHILDREN, THE, 1980, O
CHILDRENS GAMES, 1969
CHILL, THE, 1981
CHILLY SCENES OF WINTER, 1982, C
CHILTERN HUNDREDS, THE
CHIMES AT MIDNIGHT, 1967, C
CHIMES, THE, 1914
CHIMMIE FADDEN, 1915, A
CHIMMIE FADDEN OUT WEST, 1915, A
CHINA, 1943, C
CHINA 9, LIBERTY 37, 1978, O
CHINA BOUND, 1929
CHINA CLIPPER, 1936, A
CHINA CORSAIR, 1951, C
CHINA DOLL, 1958, C
CHINA GATE, 1957, C
CHINA GIRL, 1942, A
CHINA IS NEAR, 1968, C-O
CHINA PASSAGE, 1937, A
CHINA SEAS, 1935, A
CHINA SKY, 1945
CHINA SLAVER, 1929
CHINA SYNDROME, THE, 1979, A
CHINA VENTURE, 1953, C
CHINA'S LITTLE DEVILS, 1945, C
CHINATOWN, 1974, O
CHINATOWN AFTER DARK, 1931, A
CHINATOWN AT MIDNIGHT, 1949, C
CHINATOWN CHARLIE, 1928
CHINATOWN NIGHTS, 1929, A
CHINATOWN NIGHTS, 1938, A
CHINATOWN SQUAD, 1935
CHINCERO
CHINESE BOXES, 1984, O
CHINESE BUNGALOW, THE, 1926, A
CHINESE BUNGALOW, THE, 1930, A
CHINESE CAT, THE, 1944, A
CHINESE DEN, THE, 1940, A
CHINESE PARROT, THE, 1927
CHINESE PUZZLE, THE, 1919
CHINESE PUZZLE, THE, 1932, A
CHINESE RING, THE, 1947, A
CHINESE ROULETTE, 1977, O
CHINO, 1976, A-C
CHIP OF THE FLYING U, 1914
CHIP OF THE FLYING U, 1926
CHIP OF THE FLYING U, 1940, A
CHIP OFF THE OLD BLOCK, 1944, A
CHIPS, 1938
CHIQUTTO PERO PICOSO, 1967, A
CHISUM, 1970, A
CHITTY CHITTY BANG BANG, 1968, AAA
CHIVALROUS CHARLEY, 1921
CHIVATO, 1961, A-C
CHLOE IN THE AFTERNOON, 1972, O
CHOCOLATE SOLDIER, THE, 1915
CHOCOLATE SOLDIER, THE, 1941, A
CHOICE OF ARMS, 1983, C
CHOICES, 1981
CHOIRBOYS, THE, 1977, O
CHOOSE ME, 1984, O
CHOPPER SQUAD, 1971
CHOPPERS, THE, 1961, C-O
CHORUS CALL, 1979
CHORUS GIRL'S ROMANCE, A, 1920, A
CHORUS KID, THE, 1928
CHORUS LADY, THE, 1924
CHORUS OF TOKYO, 1931
CHOSEN SURVIVORS, 1974
CHOSEN, THE, 1978, O
CHOSEN, THE, 1982, A
CHOUCHOU POIDS PLUME, 1925
CHOUQUETTE ET SON AS, 1920
CHRIS AND THE WONDERFUL LAMP, 1917, A
CHRISMAS THAT ALMOST WASN'T, THE, 1966, A
CHRIST STOPPED AT EBOLI
CHRISTIAN LICORICE STORE, THE, 1971
CHRISTIAN THE LION, 1976, AAA
CHRISTIAN, THE, 1914, A
CHRISTIAN, THE, 1915
CHRISTIAN, THE, 1923
CHRISTIE JOHNSTONE, 1921
CHRISTINA, 1929
CHRISTINA, 1974, C
CHRISTINE, 1959, C
CHRISTINE, 1983
CHRISTINE JORGENSEN STORY, THE, 1970, O
CHRISTINE KEELER AFFAIR, THE, 1964, O
CHRISTINE OF THE BIG TOPS, 1926
CHRISTINE OF THE HUNGRY HEART, 1924

CHRISTMAS CAROL, A, 1938, AAA
CHRISTMAS CAROL, A, 1951, AAA
CHRISTMAS EVE, 1913
CHRISTMAS EVE, 1947, A
CHRISTMAS HOLIDAY, 1944, A
CHRISTMAS IN CONNECTICUT, 1945, AAA
CHRISTMAS IN JULY, 1940, A
CHRISTMAS KID, THE, 1968, C
CHRISTMAS STORY, A, 1983, A
CHRISTMAS TREE, THE, 1966, AA
CHRISTMAS TREE, THE, 1969, A
CHRISTOPHE COLOMB, 1919
CHRISTOPHER BEAN, 1933, A
CHRISTOPHER COLUMBUS, 1949, A
CHRISTOPHER STRONG, 1933, C
CHRISTUS, 1917
CHROME AND HOT LEATHER, 1971, O
CHRONICLE OF ANNA MAGDALENA BACH, 1968, A-C
CHRONICLE OF THE MAY RAIN, 1924
CHRONICLES OF THE GRAY HOUSE, THE, 1923
CHRONOPOLIS, 1982
CHRYSANTHEMUMS, 1914
CHU CHIN CHOW, 1923
CHU CHIN CHOW, 1934, A
CHU CHU AND THE PHILLY FLASH, 1981, A
CHUBASCO, 1968, A
CHUKA, 1967, C
CHUMP AT OXFORD, A, 1940, A
CHURCH MOUSE, THE, 1934, A
CHUSHINGURA, 1963, C
CIAO MANHATTAN, 1973
CIGARETTE GIRL, 1947, A
CIGARETTE GIRL FROM MOSSELPROM, 1924
CIGARETTE GIRL, THE, 1917
CIGARETTE MAKER'S ROMANCE, A, 1920
CIMARRON, 1931
CIMARRON, 1960, A
CIMARRON KID, THE, 1951, A
CINCINNATI KID, THE, 1965
CINDERELLA, 1915, A
CINDERELLA, 1926
CINDERELLA, 1937, A
CINDERELLA, 1950, AAA
CINDERELLA AND THE MAGIC SLIPPER, 1917
CINDERELLA JONES, 1946
CINDERELLA LIBERTY, 1973, C-O
CINDERELLA MAN, THE, 1918
CINDERELLA OF THE HILLS, 1921
CINDERELLA SWINGS IT, 1942, A
CINDERELLA'S TWIN, 1920
CINDERFELLA, 1960, A
CINDERS, 1926
CINDY AND DONNA, 1971
CINEMA GIRL'S ROMANCE, A, 1915
CINEMA MURDER, THE, 1920
CIPHER BUREAU, 1938, A
CIPHER KEY, THE, 1915
CIRCE THE ENCHANTRESS, 1924
CIRCLE CANYON, 1934, A
CIRCLE OF DANGER, 1951, C
CIRCLE OF DEATH, 1935
CIRCLE OF DECEIT, 1982, O
CIRCLE OF DECEPTON, 1961, C
CIRCLE OF IRON, 1979
CIRCLE OF LOVE, 1965, C-O
CIRCLE OF POWER
CIRCLE OF POWER, 1984
CIRCLE OF TWO, 1980, O
CIRCLE, THE, 1925
CIRCLE, THE, 1959, C
CIRCULAR STAIRCASE, THE, 1915
CIRCUMSTANIAL EVIDENCE, 1954, C
CIRCUMSTANTIAL EVIDENCE, 1920
CIRCUMSTANTIAL EVIDENCE, 1929
CIRCUMSTANTIAL EVIDENCE, 1935
CIRCUMSTANTIAL EVIDENCE, 1945, C
CIRCUS
CIRCUS ACE, THE, 1927, A
CIRCUS BOY, 1947
CIRCUS CLOWN, 1934, A
CIRCUS COWBOY, THE, 1924
CIRCUS CYCLONE, THE, 1925
CIRCUS DAYS, 1923, A
CIRCUS FRIENDS, 1962, AA
CIRCUS GIRL, 1937, A
CIRCUS JIM, 1921
CIRCUS JOYS, 1923
CIRCUS KID, THE, 1928, A
CIRCUS LURE, 1924
CIRCUS MAN, THE, 1914, A
CIRCUS OF FEAR
CIRCUS OF HORRORS, 1960
CIRCUS OF LIFE, THE, 1917
CIRCUS OF LOVE, 1958, C
CIRCUS QUEEN MURDER, THE, 1933, C
CIRCUS ROMANCE, A, 1916
CIRCUS ROOKIES, 1928
CIRCUS SHADOWS, 1935
CIRCUS WORLD, 1964, A
CIRCUS, THE, 1928, A
CISCO KID, 1931, AA
CISCO KID AND THE LADY, THE, 1939, A
CISCO KID RETURNS, THE, 1945, A
CISCO PIKE, 1971, O
CITADEL OF CRIME, 1941, C
CITADEL, THE, 1938, A
CITIES AND YEARS, 1931
CITIZEN KANE, 1941, A
CITIZEN SAINT, 1947, AA
CITIZEN SOLDIER, 1984
CITIZENS BAND, 1977
CITY ACROSS THE RIVER, 1949, C
CITY AFTER MIDNIGHT, 1957, C
CITY BENEATH THE SEA, 1953, C
CITY DESTROYED, A, 1922
CITY GIRL, 1930
CITY GIRL, 1938, C
CITY GIRL, THE, 1984, O
CITY GONE WILD, THE, 1927, A
CITY HEAT, 1984, O
CITY IN DARKNESS
CITY LIGHTS, 1931, A
CITY LIMITS, 1934, A
CITY LIMITS, 1941
CITY LOVERS, 1982, C
CITY NEWS, 1983, C
CITY OF BAD MEN, 1953, A
CITY OF BEAUTIFUL NONSENSE, THE, 1919
CITY OF BEAUTIFUL NONSENSE, THE, 1935, A
CITY OF CHANCE, 1940, C
CITY OF COMRADES, THE, 1919
CITY OF DIM FACE, THE, 1918
CITY OF FAILING LIGHT, THE, 1916
CITY OF FEAR, 1959, C
CITY OF FEAR, 1965, C
CITY OF ILLUSION, THE, 1916
CITY OF MASKS, THE, 1920
CITY OF MISSING GIRLS, 1941
CITY OF PAIN, 1951, C
CITY OF PLAY, 1929, A
CITY OF PURPLE DREAMS, 1928
CITY OF PURPLE DREAMS, THE, 1918, A
CITY OF SECRETS, 1963, O
CITY OF SHADOWS, 1929
CITY OF SHADOWS, 1955, A
CITY OF SILENT MEN, 1921, A
CITY OF SILENT MEN, 1942
CITY OF SONG
CITY OF SONGS
CITY OF TEARS, THE, 1918
CITY OF TEMPTATION, 1929
CITY OF THE DEAD
CITY OF THE DEAD
CITY OF THE WALKING DEAD, 1983, O
CITY OF TORMENT, 1950, C
CITY OF WOMEN, 1980, O
CITY OF YOUTH, 1938, C
CITY OF YOUTH, THE, 1928
CITY ON A HUNT
CITY ON FIRE, 1979, O
CITY PARK, 1934, A
CITY SENTINEL
CITY SPARROW, THE, 1920
CITY STORY, 1954, C
CITY STREETS, 1931, A
CITY STREETS, 1938, A
CITY THAT NEVER SLEEPS, 1953, A
CITY THAT NEVER SLEEPS, THE, 1924
CITY UNDER THE SEA, 1965, A
CITY WITHOUT MEN, 1943, A
CITY, FOR CONQUEST, 1941, A
CITY, THE, 1916
CITY, THE, 1926
CIVILIAN CLOTHES, 1920
CIVILIZATION, 1916, A
CIVILIZATION'S CHILD, 1916
CLAIM, THE, 1918
CLAIR DE FEMME, 1980, O
CLAIRE'S KNEE, 1971, C-O
CLAIRVOYANT, THE, 1935, A
CLAMBAKE, 1967
CLANCY IN WALL STREET, 1930, A
CLANCY STREET BOYS, 1943
CLANCY'S KOSHER WEDDING, 1927, A
CLANDESTINE, 1948, C
CLARENCE, 1922
CLARENCE, 1937, A
CLARENCE AND ANGEL, 1981, C
CLARENCE, THE CROSS-EYED LION, 1965, AAA
CLARETTA AND BEN, 1983, O
CLARION, THE, 1916, A
CLARISSA
CLASH BY NIGHT, 1952
CLASH OF THE TITANS, 1981, AA
CLASH OF THE WOLVES, 1925
CLASS, 1983
CLASS AND NO CLASS, 1921
CLASS ENEMY, 1984, O
CLASS OF '44, 1973, C
CLASS OF '74, 1972
CLASS OF 1984, 1982, O
CLASS OF MISS MAC MICHAEL, THE, 1978, O
CLASSIFIED, 1925
CLASSMATES, 1914, A
CLASSMATES, 1924, A
CLAUDE DUVAL, 1924
CLAUDELLE INGLISH, 1961, C-O
CLAUDIA, 1943, A
CLAUDIA AND DAVID, 1946, AA
CLAUDINE, 1974, A
CLAW MONSTERS, THE, 1966
CLAW, THE, 1918
CLAW, THE, 1927
CLAWS, 1977
CLAWS OF THE HUN, THE, 1918
CLAY, 1964, C-O
CLAY DOLLARS, 1921, A
CLAY PIGEON, 1971, O
CLAY PIGEON, THE, 1949, A
CLAYDON TREASURE MYSTERY, THE, 1938, A
CLEAN GUN, THE, 1917
CLEAN HEART, THE, 1924
CLEAN UP, THE, 1922
CLEAN UP, THE, 1923, A
CLEAN-UP MAN, THE, 1928
CLEAN-UP, THE, 1917
CLEAN-UP, THE, 1929
CLEANING UP, 1933, A
CLEAR ALL WIRES, 1933, A
CLEAR SKIES, 1963, A-C
CLEAR THE DECKS, 1929, A
CLEAR THE DECKS, 1929
CLEARING THE RANGE, 1931, A
CLEARING THE TRAIL, 1928, A
CLEGG, 1969, O
CLEMENCEAU CASE, THE, 1915, A
CLEO FROM 5 TO 7, 1961, C
CLEOPATRA, 1913
CLEOPATRA, 1917
CLEOPATRA, 1934, C
CLEOPATRA, 1963, A-C
CLEOPATRA JONES, 1973, O
CLEOPATRA JONES AND THE CASINO OF GOLD, 1975, O
CLEOPATRA'S DAUGHTER, 1963, C
CLEVER MRS. CARFAX, THE, 1917, A
CLICKING HOOFS, 1926
CLIMAX, THE, 1930
CLIMAX, THE, 1944, A
CLIMAX, THE, 1967, C-O
CLIMBER, THE, 1917
CLIMBERS, THE, 1915, A
CLIMBERS, THE, 1919, A
CLIMBERS, THE, 1927
CLIMBING HIGH, 1938, A
CLINGING VINE, THE, 1926
CLINIC, THE, 1983, O
CLIPPED WINGS, 1938, A
CLIPPED WINGS, 1953, A
CLIVE OF INDIA, 1935, A
CLOAK AND DAGGER, 1946, A
CLOAK AND DAGGER, 1984, C
CLOAK WITHOUT DAGGER
CLOAK, THE, 1926
CLOCK, THE, 1917
CLOCK, THE, 1945
CLOCKMAKER, THE, 1976, O
CLOCKWORK ORANGE, A, 1971, O
CLODHOPPER, THE, 1917
CLOISTER AND THE HEARTH, THE, 1913
CLONES, THE, 1973, A
CLONUS HORROR, THE, 1979, O
CLOPORTES, 1966, C-O
CLOSE CALL FOR BOSTON BLACKIE, A, 1946, A
CLOSE CALL FOR ELLERY QUEEN, A, 1942, A
CLOSE ENCOUNTERS OF THE THIRD KIND, 1977, A
CLOSE HARMONY, 1929, A
CLOSE SHAVE, 1981
CLOSE TO MY HEART, 1951, A
CLOSE TO NATURE, 1917
CLOSE-UP, 1948, A
CLOSED DOORS, 1921
CLOSED GATES, 1927
CLOSED ROAD, THE, 1916
CLOSELY WATCHED TRAINS, 1967, A
CLOSET CASANOVA, THE, 1979
CLOSIN' IN, 1918
CLOSING NET, THE, 1915
CLOTHES, 1920
CLOTHES, 1924
CLOTHES AND THE WOMAN, 1937, A
CLOTHES MAKE THE PIRATE, 1925, A
CLOTHES MAKE THE WOMAN, 1928
CLOUD DANCER, 1980, A
CLOUD DODGER, THE, 1928
CLOUD RIDER, THE, 1925

CLOUDBURST, 1922
CLOUDBURST, 1952, A
CLOUDED CRYSTAL, THE, 1948
CLOUDED MINE, A
CLOUDED NAME, A, 1923
CLOUDED NAME, THE, 1919
CLOUDED YELLOW, THE, 1950, A
CLOUDS OVER EUROPE, 1939, A
CLOUDS OVER ISRAEL, 1966, C-O
CLOVER'S REBELLION, 1917
CLOWN AND THE KID, THE, 1961, A
CLOWN AND THE KIDS, THE, 1968, AA
CLOWN MURDERS, THE, 1976, C
CLOWN MUST LAUGH, A, 1936, A
CLOWN, THE, 1916
CLOWN, THE, 1927
CLOWN, THE, 1927, C
CLOWN, THE, 1953, A
CLUB HAVANA, 1946, A
CLUB OF THE BIG DEED, THE, 1927
CLUB, THE, 1980, C
CLUE OF THE CIGAR BAND, THE, 1915
CLUE OF THE MISSING APE, THE, 1953, AA
CLUE OF THE NEW PIN, THE, 1929, A
CLUE OF THE NEW PIN, THE, 1929
CLUE OF THE NEW PIN, THE, 1961, A-C
CLUE OF THE SILVER KEY, THE, 1961, A-C
CLUE OF THE TWISTED CANDLE, 1968, A
CLUE, THE, 1915
CLUNY BROWN, 1946, A
CLUTCH OF CIRCUMSTANCE, THE, 1918
CO-RESPONDENT, THE, 1917
COACH, 1978, C-O
COAL KING, THE, 1915
COAL MINER'S DAUGHTER, 1980, A-C
COALS OF FIRE, 1918
COAST GUARD, 1939, A
COAST GUARD PATROL, THE, 1919
COAST OF FOLLY, THE, 1925
COAST OF OPPORTUNITY, THE, 1920
COAST OF SKELETONS, 1965, A
COAST PATROL, THE, 1925
COAST TO COAST, 1980
COAX ME, 1919
COBBLER, THE
COBRA, 1925, A
COBWEB, THE, 1917
COBWEB, THE, 1955, A
COCAINE
COCAINE COWBOYS, 1979, O
COCAINE FIENDS, 1937
COCK O' THE NORTH, 1935
COCK O' THE WALK, 1930
COCK OF THE AIR, 1932, A
COCK-EYED WORLD, THE, 1929, C
COCKEYED CAVALIERS, 1934, A
COCKEYED COWBOYS OF CALICO COUNTY, THE, 1970, AA
COCKEYED MIRACLE, THE, 1946, AA
COCKFIGHTER
COCKLESHELL HEROES, THE, 1955, A
COCKTAIL HOSTESSES, THE, 1976
COCKTAIL HOUR, 1933, C
COCKTAIL MOLOTOV, 1980, A
COCOANUT GROVE, 1938, AA
COCOANUTS, THE, 1929, A
COCTAILS, 1928
CODE 7, VICTIM 5, 1964, A
CODE NAME TRIXIE
CODE NAME, RED ROSES
CODE OF HONOR
CODE OF HONOR, 1930, A
CODE OF MARCIA GRAY, 1916, A
CODE OF SCOTLAND YARD, 1948, C-O
CODE OF SILENCE, 1960, C
CODE OF THE AIR, 1928
CODE OF THE CACTUS, 1939
CODE OF THE COW COUNTRY, 1927
CODE OF THE FEARLESS, 1939, A
CODE OF THE LAWLESS, 1945, A
CODE OF THE MOUNTED, 1935, A
CODE OF THE NORTHWEST, 1926
CODE OF THE OUTLAW, 1942, A
CODE OF THE PLAINS, 1947
CODE OF THE PRAIRIE, 1944, A
CODE OF THE RANGE, 1927, A
CODE OF THE RANGE, 1937
CODE OF THE RANGERS, 1938, A
CODE OF THE SADDLE, 1947
CODE OF THE SCARLET, THE, 1928
CODE OF THE SEA, 1924, A
CODE OF THE SECRET SERVICE, 1939, A
CODE OF THE SILVER SAGE, 1950, A
CODE OF THE STREETS, 1939, A
CODE OF THE WEST, 1925
CODE OF THE WEST, 1929
CODE OF THE WEST, 1947, A
CODE OF THE WILDERNESS, 1924
CODE OF THE YUKON, 1919
CODE TWO, 1953
CODY, 1977
COEUR DE TITI, 1924
COEUR FIDELE, 1923
COEUR LEGER, 1923
COEURS FAROUCHES, 1923
COFFY, 1973, O
COGNASSE, 1932, A
COHEN'S LUCK, 1915
COHENS AND KELLYS IN AFRICA, THE, 1930, A
COHENS AND KELLYS IN ATLANTIC CITY, THE, 1929, A
COHENS AND KELLYS IN SCOTLAND, THE, 1930, A
COHENS AND KELLYS IN TROUBLE, THE, 1933, A
COHENS AND KELLYS, THE, 1926, A
COHENS AND THE KELLYS IN PARIS, THE, 1928, A
COHENS, AND KELLYS IN HOLLYWOOD, THE, 1932, A
COINCIDENCE, 1921
COLD DECK, THE, 1917
COLD FEET, 1984, C
COLD FURY, 1925
COLD JOURNEY, 1975, C
COLD NERVE, 1925
COLD RIVER, 1982, A
COLD STEEL
COLD SWEAT, 1974, O
COLD TURKEY, 1971, A
COLD WIND IN AUGUST, 1961, O
COLDITZ STORY, THE, 1955, A
COLE YOUNGER, GUNFIGHTER, 1958, A
COLLECTOR, THE, 1965, C
COLLEEN, 1927
COLLEEN, 1936, A
COLLEEN OF THE PINES, 1922
COLLEGE, 1927, A
COLLEGE BOOB, THE, 1926
COLLEGE COACH, 1933, A
COLLEGE CONFIDENTIAL, 1960, C
COLLEGE COQUETTE, THE, 1929, A
COLLEGE DAYS, 1926, A
COLLEGE HERO, THE, 1927
COLLEGE HOLIDAY, 1936, A
COLLEGE HUMOR, 1933
COLLEGE IS A NICE PLACE, 1936
COLLEGE LOVE, 1929, A
COLLEGE LOVERS, 1930, A
COLLEGE ORPHAN, THE, 1915
COLLEGE RHYTHM, 1934, A
COLLEGE SCANDAL, 1935, A
COLLEGE SWEETHEARTS, 1942, A
COLLEGE SWING, 1938, A
COLLEGE WIDOW, THE, 1915
COLLEGE WIDOW, THE, 1927
COLLEGIATE, 1926
COLLEGIATE, 1936, A
COLLISION, 1932, A
COLLISION COURSE
COLONEL BLIMP, 1945, A
COLONEL BLOOD, 1934, A
COLONEL BOGEY, 1948, A
COLONEL CHABERT, 1947, A
COLONEL EFFINGHAM'S RAID, 1945, A
COLONEL MARCH INVESTIGATES, 1952, A
COLONEL NEWCOME THE PERFECT GENTLEMAN, 1920
COLOR ME BLOOD RED, 1965, O
COLOR ME DEAD, 1969
COLOR OF POMEGRANATES, THE, 1980, C-O
COLORADO, 1915
COLORADO, 1921
COLORADO, 1940, A
COLORADO AMBUSH, 1951, A
COLORADO KID, 1938, A
COLORADO PIONEERS, 1945
COLORADO PLUCK, 1921
COLORADO RANGER, 1950, A
COLORADO SERENADE, 1946, A
COLORADO SUNDOWN, 1952, A
COLORADO SUNSET, 1939, A
COLORADO TERRITORY, 1949, A
COLORADO TRAIL, 1938, A
COLOSSUS AND THE AMAZONS, 1960
COLOSSUS OF NEW YORK, THE, 1958, A
COLOSSUS OF RHODES,1THE, 1961, A
COLOSSUS: THE FORBIN PROJECT, 1969, A
COLT .45, 1950, A
COLT COMRADES, 1943, A
COLUMBUS, 1923
COLUMN SOUTH, 1953, A
COMA, 1978, A
COMANCHE, 1956, A
COMANCHE STATION, 1960, A
COMBAT, 1927
COMBAT SQUAD, 1953, A
COMBAT, THE, 1916
COMBAT, THE, 1926
COME 'N' GET IT
COME ACROSS, 1929
COME AGAIN SMITH, 1919
COME AND GET IT, 1929
COME AND GET IT, 1936, A
COME BACK BABY, 1968, O
COME BACK CIHARLESTON BLUE, 1972, O
COME BACK LITTLE SHEBA, 1952, A-C
COME BACK PETER, 1952, A
COME BACK PETER, 1971
COME BACK TO THE 5 & DIME, JIMMY DEAN, JIMMY DEAN, 1982, O
COME BLOW YOUR HORN, 1963, A-C
COME CLOSER, FOLKS, 1936
COME DANCE WITH ME, 1950
COME DANCE WITH ME, 1960, C-O
COME FILL THE CUP, 1951, C
COME FLY WITH ME, 1963, A
COME LIVE WITH ME, 1941, A
COME NEXT SPRING, 1956, AA
COME ON COWBOYS, 1924
COME ON DANGER, 1942, A
COME ON DANGER!, 1932, A
COME ON GEORGE, 1939, A
COME ON IN, 1918
COME ON OVER, 1922, AA
COME ON RANGERS, 1939, A
COME ON TARZAN, 1933, A
COME ON, COWBOY!, 1948
COME ON, COWBOYS, 1937, A
COME ON, LEATHERNECKS, 1938
COME ON, MARINES, 1934, A
COME ON, THE, 1956, A
COME ONE, COME ALL, 1970
COME OUT FIGHTING, 1945, A
COME OUT OF KITCHEN, 1919
COME OUT OF THE PANTRY, 1935, AA
COME SEPTEMBER, 1961, A
COME SPY WITH ME, 1967, A
COME THROUGH, 1917
COME TO MY HOUSE, 1927
COME TO THE STABLE, 1949, AA
COME-BACK, THE, 1916
COMEBACK TRAIL, THE, 1982, O
COMEBACK, THE, 1982, C
COMEDIANS, THE, 1967, C
COMEDY MAN, THE, 1964, A
COMEDY OF HORRORS, THE, 1964, A
COMES A HORSEMAN, 1978, A-C
COMES MIDNIGHT, 1940
COMET OVER BROADWAY, 1938
COME TOGETHER, 1971
COMFORT AND JOY, 1984, A-C
COMIC, THE, 1969, A
COMIG OUT PARTY, 1934, A
COMIN' AT YA!, 1981, O
COMIN' ROUND THE MOUNTAIN, 1936
COMIN' ROUND THE MOUNTAIN, 1940, AA
COMIN' ROUND THE MOUNTAIN, 1951, AAA
COMIN' THRO' THE RYE, 1916
COMIN' THRO' THE RYE, 1923
COMIN' THRU' THE RYE, 1947, A
COMING AN' GOING, 1926, A
COMING APART, 1969
COMING ATTRACTIONS
COMING HOME, 1978, C-O
COMING OF AGE, 1938, A
COMING OF AMOS, THE, 1925, A
COMING OF THE LAW, THE, 1919
COMING POWER, THE, 1914
COMING THROUGH, 1925
COMING, THE, 1983
COMING-OUT PARTY, A-C
COMMANCHE TERRITORY, 1950, A
COMMANCHEROS, THE, 1961, A
COMMAND DECISION, 1948, A
COMMAND PERFORMANCE, 1931, A
COMMAND PERFORMANCE, 1937, A
COMMAND, THE, 1954, A
COMMANDING OFFICER, THE, 1915, A
COMMANDMENTS, THE, 1956, AA
COMMANDO, 1962, C
COMMANDO CODY, 1953
COMMANDOS STRIKE AT DAWN, THE, 1942
COMMISSIONAIRE, 1933, A
COMMITMENT, THE, 1976, C
COMMITTEE, THE, 1968, C
COMMON CAUSE, THE, 1918
COMMON CLAY, 1919
COMMON CLAY, 1930, A
COMMON GROUND, 1916
COMMON LAW WIFE, 1963, O
COMMON LAW, THE, 1916, A
COMMON LAW, THE, 1923, A
COMMON LAW, THE, 1931
COMMON LEVEL, A, 1920
COMMON PROPERTY, 1919
COMMON SENSE, 1920
COMMON SENSE BRACKETT, 1916
COMMON SIN, THE, 1920
COMMON TOUCH, THE, 1941, A

COMMUNION
COMMUTER HUSBANDS, 1974
COMMUTORS, THE, 1915
COMPANEROS, 1970, C
COMPANION, THE, 1976
COMPANIONATE MARRIAGE, THE, 1928
COMPANIONS IN CRIME, 1954
COMPANY OF KILLERS, 1970, A
COMPANY SHE KEEPS, THE, 1950, C
COMPANYY OF COWARDS
COMPASSION, 1927
COMPELLED, 1960
COMPETITION, THE, 1980, C
COMPLIMENTS OF MR. FLOW, 1941, A
COMPROMISE, 1925, A
COMPROMISED, 1931, A
COMPROMISED DAPHINE
COMPROMISED!, 1931, A
COMPULSION, 1959, C-O
COMPULSORY HUSBAND, THE, 1930, A
COMPULSORY WIFE, THE, 1937, A
COMPUTER FREE-FOR-ALL, 1969, C
COMPUTER WORE TENNIS SHOES, THE, 1970, AAA
COMRADE JOHN, 1915
COMRADE X, 1940, A
COMRADES, 1928
COMRADESHIP, 1919
CON ARTISTS, THE, 1981, O
CON MEN, THE, 1973, A
CONAN THE BARBARIAN, 1982, C-O
CONAN THE DESTROYER, 1984, C
CONCEALED TRUTH, THE, 1915
CONCEIT, 1921
CONCENTRATIN' KID, THE, 1930, A
CONCENTRATION CAMP, 1939, A
CONCERNING MR. MARTIN, 1937, A
CONCERT, THE, 1921
CONCORDE, THE—AIRPORT '79, A-C
CONCRETE JUNGLE, THE, 1962, C
CONCRETE JUNGLE, THE, 1982, O
CONDEMNED, 1923
CONDEMNED, 1929, C
CONDEMNED MEN, 1940
CONDEMNED OF ALTONA, THE, 1963
CONDEMNED TO DEATH, 1932, A
CONDEMNED TO LIFE
CONDEMNED TO LIVE, 1935, A
CONDEMNED WOMEN, 1938, A
CONDOR, 1984
CONDORMAN, 1981, AAA
CONDUCT UNBECOMING, 1975, A-C
CONDUCTOR 1492, 1924
CONDUCTOR, THE, 1981, A-C
CONE OF SILENCE
CONEY ISLAND, 1928
CONEY ISLAND, 1943, A
CONEY ISLAND PRINCESS, A, 1916
CONFESS DR. CORDA, 1960, C
CONFESSION, 1918
CONFESSION, 1937, A
CONFESSION, 1955
CONFESSION, THE, 1920
CONFESSION, THE, 1964
CONFESSION, THE, 1970, C
CONFESSIONAL, THE, 1977, O
CONFESSIONS, 1925
CONFESSIONS FROM A HOLIDAY CAMP, 1977, A
CONFESSIONS OF A CO-ED, 1931, A
CONFESSIONS OF A NAZI SPY, 1939, C
CONFESSIONS OF A NEWLYWED, 1941, A
CONFESSIONS OF A POLICE CAPTAIN, 1971, A
CONFESSIONS OF A POP PERFORMER, 1975, O
CONFESSIONS OF A QUEEN, 1925
CONFESSIONS OF A ROGUE, 1948
CONFESSIONS OF A WIFE, 1928
CONFESSIONS OF A WINDOW CLEANER, 1974, O
CONFESSIONS OF AMANS, THE, 1977, C-O
CONFESSIONS OF AN OPIUM EATER, 1962, C
CONFESSIONS OF BOSTON BLACKIE, 1941, A
CONFESSIONS OF FELIX KRULL, THE, 1957, C-O
CONFESSIONS OF TOM HARRIS, 1972
CONFESSOR, 1973, A
CONFETTI, 1927
CONFIDENCE, 1922
CONFIDENCE, 1980, C-O
CONFIDENCE GIRL, 1952, A
CONFIDENCE MAN, THE, 1924
CONFIDENTIAL, 1935, A
CONFIDENTIAL AGENT, 1945, C
CONFIDENTIAL CONNIE, 1953, A
CONFIDENTIAL LADY, 1939
CONFIDENTIAL REPORT
CONFIDENTIALLY YOURS, 1983, A-C
CONFIRM OR DENY, 1941, A
CONFLAGRATION
CONFLICT, 1937, A
CONFLICT, 1939, O
CONFLICT, 1945, A
CONFLICT OVER WINGS
CONFLICT, THE, 1916
CONFLICT, THE, 1921, A
CONFORMIST, THE, 1971, C
CONGESTION, 1918
CONGO CROSSING, 1956, A
CONGO MAISIE, 1940, A
CONGO SWING
CONGRESS DANCES, 1932
CONGRESS DANCES, 1957
CONJUGAL BED, THE, 1963, O
CONJURE WOMAN, THE, 1926
CONNECTICUT YANKEE AT KING ARTHUR'S COURT, A, 1921, A
CONNECTICUT YANKEE IN KING ARTHUR'S COURT, A, 1949, AAA
CONNECTICUT YANKEE, A, 1931, AAA
CONNECTING ROOMS, 1971, A
CONNECTION, THE, 1962, O
CONQUERED CITY, 1966, C
CONQUERED HEARTS, A
CONQUERING HORDE, THE, 1931, A
CONQUERING POWER, THE, 1921, A
CONQUERING THE WOMAN, 1922
CONQUEROR OF CORINTH
CONQUEROR WORM, THE, 1968, O
CONQUEROR, THE, 1916
CONQUEROR, THE, 1917
CONQUEROR, THE, 1956, A-C
CONQUERORS, THE, 1932, A
CONQUEST, 1929, C
CONQUEST, 1937, C
CONQUEST, 1984, O
CONQUEST OF CANAAN, THE, 1921
CONQUEST OF CHEYENNE, 1946, A
CONQUEST OF COCHISE, 1953, A
CONQUEST OF MYCENE, 1965, A-C
CONQUEST OF SPACE, 1955, A
CONQUEST OF THE AIR, 1940, A
CONQUEST OF THE CAUCASUS, 1913
CONQUEST OF THE EARTH, 1980, A
CONQUEST OF THE PLANET OF THE APES, 1972, A
CONRACK, 1974, A
CONRAD IN QUEST OF HIS YOUTH, 1920
CONSCIENCE, 1915
CONSCIENCE, 1917
CONSCIENCE BAY, 1960, C
CONSCIENCE OF JOHN DAVID, THE, 1916
CONSOLATION MARRIAGE, 1931, A
CONSPIRACY, 1939, A
CONSPIRACY IN TEHERAN, 1948, A
CONSPIRACY OF HEARTS, 1960, AAA
CONSPIRACY Zero, 1930, A
CONSPIRACY, THE, 1914, A
CONSPIRATOR, 1949, A-C
CONSPIRATORS, THE
CONSPIRATORS, THE, 1944, A
CONSTANCE, 1984, O
CONSTANT FACTOR, THE, 1980, C-O
CONSTANT NYMPH, THE, 1928
CONSTANT WOMAN, THE, 1933
CONSTANTINE AND THE CROSS, 1962, C-O
CONTACT MAN, THE
CONTEMPT, 1963, C-O
CONTENDER, THE, 1944, A
CONTEST GIRL
CONTINENTAL DIVIDE, 1981, A-C
CONTINENTAL EXPRESS, 1939, A
CONTINENTAL GIRL, A, 1915
CONTINENTAL TWIST
CONTRABAND
CONTRABAND, 1925
CONTRABAND LOVE, 1931, A
CONTRABAND SPAIN, 1955, A
CONTRACT, THE, 1982
CONVENTION CITY, 1933
CONVENTION GIRL, 1935, A
CONVENTION GIRLS, 1978
CONVERSATION PIECE, 1976, C
CONVERSATION, THE, 1974, A-C
CONVICT 99, 1919
CONVICT 99, 1938, A
CONVICT 993, 1918
CONVICT KING, THE, 1915
CONVICT STAGE, 1965, A
CONVICT'S CODE, 1930, A
CONVICT'S CODE, 1939, A
CONVICTED, 1931, A
CONVICTED, 1938, A
CONVICTED, 1950, A
CONVICTED WOMAN, 1940, A
CONVICTS AT LARGE, 1938, A
CONVICTS FOUR, 1962, A
CONVOY, 1927, A
CONVOY, 1940, A
CONVOY, 1978, C
CONVOY BUDDIES, 1977
COOGAN'S BLUFF, 1968, C-O
COOK OF CANYON CAMP, THE, 1917
COOL AND THE CRAZY, THE, 1958, C-O
COOL BREEZE, 1972, C
COOL HAND LUKE, 1967, C
COOL IT, CAROL!, 1970, O
COOL MIKADO, THE, 1963, A
COOL ONES THE, 1967, A
COOL SOUND FROM HELL, A, 1959
COOL WORLD, THE, 1963, C-O
COOLEY HIGH, 1975
COONSKIN, 1975, C
COP HATER, 1958, C
COP KILLERS, 1984
COP, A, 1973, O
COP, THE, 1928
COP-OUT, 1967, C-O
COPACABANA, 1947, A
COPPER CANYON, 1950, A
COPPER SKY, 1957, A
COPPER, THE, 1930, A
COPPERHEAD, THE, 1920
COPS AND ROBBERS, 1973, A
COPTER KIDS, THE, 1976
COQUETTE, 1929, C
COQUETTE, THE, 1915
CORA, 1915
CORAL, 1915
CORDELIA, 1980, C-O
CORDELIA THE MAGNIFICENT, 1923
CORINTHIAN JACK, 1921
CORKY, 1972
CORKY OF GASOLINE ALLEY, 1951, AA
CORN IS GREEN, THE, 1945, A
CORNBREAD, EARL AND ME, 1975, C
CORNER GROCER, THE, 1917
CORNER IN COLLEENS, A, 1916, A
CORNER IN COTTON, A, 1916
CORNER MAN, THE, 1921
CORNER, THE, 1916
CORNERED, 1924
CORNERED, 1932, A
CORNERED, 1945, C
CORONADO, 1935
CORONER CREEK, 1948
CORPORAL KATE, 1926, A
CORPSE CAME C.O.D., THE, 1947, A
CORPSE GRINDERS, THE, 1972, O
CORPSE OF BEVERLY HILLS, THE, 1965, O
CORPSE VANISHES, THE, 1942, C
CORPUS CHRISTI BANDITS, 1945, A
CORREGIDOR, 1943, C
CORRIDOR OF MIRRORS, 1948, A
CORRIDORS OF BLOOD, 1962, C-O
CORRUPT, 1984, O
CORRUPT ONES, THE, 1967, C
CORRUPTION, 1917
CORRUPTION, 1933, A
CORRUPTION, 1968, O
CORRUPTION OF CHRIS MILLER, THE, 1979, O
CORRUPTION OF THE DAMNED, 1965
CORSAIR, 1931, C
CORSAIR, THE, 1914
CORSICAN BROTHERS, THE, 1920
CORSICAN BROTHERS, THE, 1941, A
CORVETTE K-225, 1943
CORVETTE SUMMER, 1978, C-O
CORVINI INHERITANCE, 1984
COSH BOY
COSMIC MAN, THE, 1959, A
COSMIC MONSTERS, 1958, A
COSMO JONES, CRIME SMASHER, 1943
COSSACK WHIP, THE, 1916
COSSACKS IN EXILE, 1939, A
COSSACKS OF THE DON, 1932, A
COSSACKS, THE, 1928
COSSACKS, THE, 1960
COST OF BEAUTY, THE, 1924
COST OF HATRED, THE, 1917
COST, THE, 1920, A
COSTELLO CASE, THE, 1930, A
COTTAGE ON DARTMOOR
COTTAGE TO LET
COTTER, 1972
COTTON AND CATTLE, 1921
COTTON CLUB, THE, 1984, O
COTTON COMES TO HARLEM, 1970, O
COTTON KING, THE, 1915, A
COTTON QUEEN, 1937, A
COTTONPICKIN' CHICKENPICKERS, 1967, C
COUCH, THE, 1962, C-O
COUNSEL FOR CRIME, 1937
COUNSEL FOR ROMANCE, 1938
COUNSEL FOR THE DEFENSE, 1925
COUNSEL'S OPINION, 1933, A
COUNSELLOR-AT-LAW, 1933, A
COUNT DRACULA, 1971, C-O
COUNT DRACULA AND HIS VAMPIRE BRIDE, 1978, C-O
COUNT FIVE AND DIE, 1958, A
COUNT OF BRAGELONNE, THE
COUNT OF LUXEMBOURG, THE, 1926

COUNT OF MONTE CRISTO, 1976, A
COUNT OF MONTE CRISTO, THE, 1913
COUNT OF MONTE CRISTO, THE, 1934, AAA
COUNT OF MONTE-CRISTO, 1955, A
COUNT OF TEN, THE, 1928
COUNT OF THE MONK'S BRIDGE, THE, 1934
COUNT OF TWELVE, 1955
COUNT THE HOURS, 1953
COUNT THREE AND PRAY, 1955, A
COUNT YORGA, VAMPIRE, 1970, O
COUNT YOUR BLESSINGS, 1959, A-C
COUNT YOUR BULLETS, 1972, O
COUNTDOWN, 1968, A
COUNTDOWN AT KUSINI, 1976, C
COUNTDOWN TO DANGER, 1967, AA
COUNTER BLAST, 1948
COUNTER TENORS, THE
COUNTER-ATTACK, 1945, A
COUNTER-ESPIONAGE, 1942, A
COUNTERFEIT, 1919, A
COUNTERFEIT, 1936, A
COUNTERFEIT COMMANDOS, 1981, O
COUNTERFEIT CONSTBLE, THE, 1966, A-C
COUNTERFEIT KILLER, THE, 1968, A
COUNTERFEIT LADY, 1937, A
COUNTERFEIT LOVE, 1923
COUNTERFEIT PLAN, THE, 1957, A
COUNTERFEIT TRAITOR, THE, 1962, A-C
COUNTERFEITERS OF PARIS, THE, 1962, C
COUNTERFEITERS, THE, 1948, A
COUNTERFEITERS, THE, 1953, A
COUNTERPLOT, 1959, A
COUNTERPOINT, 1967, A-C
COUNTERSPY MEETS SCOTLAND YARD, 1950, A
COUNTESS CHARMING, THE, 1917
COUNTESS DRACULA, 1972, O
COUNTESS FROM HONG KONG, A, 1967, C
COUNTESS OF MONTE CRISTO, THE, 1934, A
COUNTESS OF MONTE CRISTO, THE, 1948, A
COUNTRY, 1984, C
COUNTRY BEYOND, THE, 1926
COUNTRY BEYOND, THE, 1936, A
COUNTRY BLUE, 1975
COUNTRY BOY, 1966, A
COUNTRY BOY, THE, 1915
COUNTRY BRIDE, 1938, A
COUNTRY COUSIN, THE, 1919
COUNTRY CUZZINS, 1972
COUNTRY DANCE
COUNTRY DOCTOR, THE, 1927
COUNTRY DOCTOR, THE, 1936, A
COUNTRY DOCTOR, THE, 1963, A
COUNTRY FAIR, 1941, A
COUNTRY FLAPPER, THE, 1922
COUNTRY GENTLEMEN, 1937, A
COUNTRY GIRL, THE, 1954, A-C
COUNTRY KID, THE, 1923, AA
COUNTRY MAN, 1982, C
COUNTRY MOUSE, THE, 1914, A
COUNTRY MUSIC, 1972
COUNTRY MUSIC HOLIDAY, 1958, A
COUNTRY THAT GOD FORGOT, THE, 1916
COUNTRY TOWN, 1971
COUNTY CHAIRMAN, THE, 1914, A
COUNTY CHAIRMAN, THE, 1935, A
COUNTY FAIR, 1933, A
COUNTY FAIR, 1937
COUNTY FAIR, 1950
COUNTY FAIR, THE, 1920
COUNTY FAIR, THE, 1932, A
COUP DE FOUDRE
COUP DE GRACE, 1978, C
COUP DE TETE
COUP DE TORCHON, 1981, O
COUPLE OF DOWN AND OUTS, A, 1923
COUPLE ON THE MOVE, A, 1928
COURAGE
COURAGE, 1921, A
COURAGE, 1924
COURAGE, 1930, A
COURAGE AND THE MAN, 1915
COURAGE FOR TWO, 1919
COURAGE OF BLACK BEAUTY, 1957, AA
COURAGE OF LASSIE, 1946, AAA
COURAGE OF MARGE O'DOONE, THE, 1920
COURAGE OF SILENCE, THE, 1917
COURAGE OF THE COMMONPLACE, 1917
COURAGE OF THE NORTH, 1935
COURAGE OF THE WEST, 1937, A
COURAGE OF WOLFHEART, 1925
COURAGEOUS AVENGER, THE, 1935, A
COURAGEOUS COWARD, THE, 1919
COURAGEOUS COWARD, THE, 1924
COURAGEOUS DR. CHRISTIAN, THE, 1940, A
COURAGEOUS FOOL, 1925
COURAGEOUS MR. PENN, THE, 1941, A
COURIER OF LYONS, 1938, A
COURRIER SUD, 1937, A
COURT CONCERT, THE, 1936
COURT JESTER, THE, 1956, AAA
COURT MARTIAL, 1954, A
COURT MARTIAL, 1962, A-C
COURT MARTIAL OF MAJOR KELLER, THE, 1961, A-C
COURT-MARTIAL, 1928
COURT-MARTIAL OF BILLY MITCHELL, THE, 1955, A
COURT-MARTIALED, 1915
COURTESAN, THE, 1916
COURTIN' TROUBLE, 1948, A
COURTIN' WILDCATS, 1929, A
COURTNEY AFFAIR, THE, 1947, A
COURTSHIP OF ANDY HARDY, THE, 1942, A
COURTSHIP OF EDDY'S FATHER, THE, 1963, AA
COURTSHIP OF MILES STANDISH, THE, 1923, A
COUSIN KATE, 1921
COUSIN PONS, 1924
COUSIN, COUSINE, 1976
COUSINE DE FRANCE, 1927
COUSINS IN LOVE, 1982, O
COUSINS, THE, 1959, C-O
COVE OF MISSING MEN, 1918
COVENANT WITH DEATH, A, 1966
COVER GIRL, 1944, AA
COVER GIRL KILLER, 1960, C-O
COVER GIRL MODELS, 1975
COVER ME BABE, 1970, O
COVER-UP, 1949, A
COVERED TRAIL, THE, 1924, A
COVERED TRAILER, THE, 1939, AA
COVERED WAGON DAYS, 1940, A
COVERED WAGON RAID, 1950, A
COVERED WAGON TRAILS, 1930, A
COVERED WAGON TRAILS, 1930
COVERED WAGON TRAILS, 1940, A
COVERED WAGON, THE, 1923, A
COVERGIRL, 1984, O
COVERT ACTION, 1980, O
COW AND I. THE, 1961, A
COW COUNTRY, 1953, A
COW TOWN, 1950, A
COWARD, THE, 1914
COWARD, THE, 1915
COWARD, THE, 1927, A
COWARDICE COURT, 1919
COWARDS, 1970, C-O
COWBOY, 1958, A
COWBOY ACE, A, 1921
COWBOY AND THE BANDIT, THE, 1935, A
COWBOY AND THE BLONDE, THE, 1941, A
COWBOY AND THE COUNTESS, THE, 1926
COWBOY AND THE FLAPPER, THE, 1924
COWBOY AND THE INDIANS, THE, 1949
COWBOY AND THE KID,THE, 1936, A
COWBOY AND THE LADY, THE, 1915
COWBOY AND THE LADY, THE, 1922
COWBOY AND THE LADY, THE, 1938, A
COWBOY AND THE OUTLAW, THE, 1929
COWBOY AND THE PRIZEFIGHTER, 1950, A
COWBOY AND THE SENORITA, 1944, A
COWBOY BLUES, 1946, A
COWBOY CANTEEN, 1944, A
COWBOY CAVALIER, 1929
COWBOY CAVALIER, 1948, A
COWBOY CAVALIER, THE, 1928
COWBOY COMMANDOS, 1943, A
COWBOY COP, THE, 1926
COWBOY COUNSELOR, 1933
COWBOY COURAGE, 1925
COWBOY FROM BROOKLYN, 1938, A
COWBOY FROM LONESOME RIVER, 1944, A
COWBOY FROM SUNDOWN, 1940
COWBOY GRIT, 1925
COWBOY HOLIDAY, 1934, A
COWBOY IN AFRICA
COWBOY IN MANHATTTAN, 1943, A
COWBOY IN THE CLOUDS, 1943, A
COWBOY KID, THE, 1928
COWBOY KING, THE, 1922
COWBOY MILLIONAIRE, 1935, A
COWBOY MUSKETEER, THE, 1925
COWBOY PRINCE, THE, 1924
COWBOY PRINCE, THE, 1930
COWBOY QUARTERBACK, 1939, A
COWBOY SERENADE, 1942, A
COWBOY STAR, THE, 1936, A
COWBOYS FROM TEXAS, 1939, A
COWBOYS, THE, 1972, A-C
COYOTE FANGS, 1924
COYOTE TRAILS, 1935, A
CPTAINN HATES THE SEA, THE, 1934, A
CRAB, THE, 1917, A
CRACK IN THE MIRROR, 1960
CRACK IN THE WORLD, 1965
CRACK O'DAWN, 1925
CRACK-UP, 1946, A
CRACK-UP, THE, 1937, A
CRACKED NUTS, 1931, AA
CRACKED NUTS, 1941, A
CRACKERJACK
CRACKERJACK, THE, 1925
CRACKERS, 1984, A-C
CRACKING UP
CRACKING UP, 1977, O
CRACKLE OF DEATH, 1974
CRACKSMAN, THE, 1963, A
CRADLE BUSTER, THE, 1922, A
CRADLE OF COURAGE, THE, 1920
CRADLE OF THE WASHINGTONS, THE, 1922
CRADLE SNATCHERS, THE, 1927
CRADLE SONG, 1933, A
CRADLE, THE, 1922, A
CRAIG'S WIFE, 1928, A
CRAIG'S WIFE, 1936, A-C
CRAINQUEBILLE, 1922
CRANES ARE FLYING, THE, 1960, A
CRASH, 1977, C-O
CRASH, THE, 1932, A
CRASH DIVE, 1943
CRASH DONOVAN, 1936, A
CRASH DRIVE, 1959, A-C
CRASH LANDING, 1958, A
CRASH OF SILENCE, 1952, A
CRASH, THE, 1928
CRASHIN' THROUGH, 1924
CRASHIN' THRU, 1923, A
CRASHIN' THRU DANGER, 1938, A
CRASHING BROADWAY, 1933, A
CRASHING COURAGE, 1923
CRASHING HOLLYWOOD, 1937, A
CRASHING LAS VEGAS, 1956, A
CRASHING THROUGH, 1928
CRASHING THRU, 1939, A
CRASHING THRU, 1949, A
CRASHOUT, 1955, C
CRATER LAKE MONSTER, THE, 1977, A
CRAVING, THE, 1916
CRAVING, THE, 1918, A
CRAWLING ARM, THE, 1973
CRAWLING EYE, THE, 1958, C
CRAWLING HAND, THE, 1963, A
CRAWLING MONSTER, THE
CRAWLING TERROR, THE, 1958
CRAZE, 1974, C
CRAZIES, THE, 1973, O
CRAZY DESIRE, 1964, C
CRAZY FOR LOVE, 1960, C-O
CRAZY HOUSE, 1943
CRAZY HOUSE, 1975
CRAZY JACK AND THE BOY
CRAZY JOE, 1974, O
CRAZY KNIGHTS, 1944, A
CRAZY MAMA, 1975
CRAZY OVER HORSES, 1951, A
CRAZY PAGE, A, 1926
CRAZY PARADISE, 1965, O
CRAZY PEOPLE, 1934, A
CRAZY QUILT, THE, 1966, A
CRAZY RAY, THE
CRAZY THAT WAY, 1930, A
CRAZY TO MARRY, 1921, A
CRAZY WORLD OF JULIUS VROODER, THE, 1974, C-O
CRAZYLEGS, ALL AMERICAN, 1953
CREAKING STAIRS, 1919
CREAM OF THE EARTH
CREAM OF THE EARTH
CREATION, 1922, A
CREATION OF THE HUMANOIDS, 1962, C
CREATURE CALLED MAN, THE, 1970, C
CREATURE FROM BLACK LAKE, THE, 1976, C
CREATURE FROM THE BLACK LAGOON, 1954, A
CREATURE FROM THE HAUNTED SEA, 1961, C
CREATURE OF DESTRUCTION, 1967
CREATURE OF THE WALKING DEAD, 1960, C
CREATURE WALKS AMONG US, THE, 1956, A
CREATURE WASN'T NICE, THE, 1981, A
CREATURE WITH THE ATOM BRAIN, 1955, O
CREATURE WITH THE BLUE HAND, 1971, O
CREATURE'S REVENGE, THE
CREATURES
CREATURES OF DARKNESS, 1969
CREATURES OF THE PREHISTORIC PLANET
CREATURES THE WORLD FORGOT, 1971, O
CREEPER, THE, 1948, O
CREEPER, THE, 1980, O
CREEPING FLESH, 1973, O
CREEPING TERROR, THE, 1964, C
CREEPS
CREEPSHOW, 1982, O
CREMATOR, THE, 1973, O
CREMATORS, THE, 1972, C
CREPUSCULE D'EPOUVANTE, 1921
CRESCENDO, 1972, A
CREST OF THE WAVE, 1954, A
CRICKET OF THE HEARTH, THE, 1968
CRICKET ON THE HEARTH, THE, 1923

CRICKET, THE, 1917
CRIES AND WHISPERS, 1972, C
CRIES IN THE NIGHT, 1964
CRIES IN THE NIGHT, 1982
CRIME AFLOAT, 1937, A
CRIME AGAINST JOE, 1956
CRIME AND PASSION, 1976, C-O
CRIME AND PUNISHMENT, 1913
CRIME AND PUNISHMENT, 1917, A
CRIME AND PUNISHMENT, 1929
CRIME AND PUNISHMENT, 1935, A
CRIME AND PUNISHMENT, 1935, C
CRIME AND PUNISHMENT, 1948, A
CRIME AND PUNISHMENT, 1975, A
CRIME AND PUNISHMENT, U.S.A., 1959, A
CRIME AND THE PENALTY, 1916
CRIME AT BLOSSOMS, THE, 1933, A
CRIME AT PORTA ROMANA, 1980, O
CRIME AT THE DARK HOUSE, 1940, A-C
CRIME BOSS, 1976, C
CRIME BY NIGHT, 1944, A
CRIME DOCTOR, 1943, A
CRIME DOCTOR'S COURAGE, THE, 1945, A
CRIME DOCTOR'S DIARY, THE, 1949, A
CRIME DOCTOR'S GAMBLE, 1947, A
CRIME DOCTOR'S MAN HUNT, 1946, A
CRIME DOCTOR'S STRANGEST CASE, 1943, A
CRIME DOCTOR'S WARNING, 1945
CRIME DOCTOR, THE, 1934, A
CRIME DOES NOT PAY, 1962, C-O
CRIME IN THE STREETS, 1956, C-O
CRIME NOBOBY SAW, THE, 1937, A
CRIME OF DR. CRESPI, THE, 1936, C
CRIME OF DR. FORBES, 1936, A
CRIME OF DR. HALLET, 1938, A
CRIME OF HELEN STANLEY, 1934
CRIME OF MONSIEUR LANGE, THE, 1936, C-O
CRIME OF PASSION, 1957
CRIME OF PETER FRAME, THE, 1938, A
CRIME OF STEPHEN HAWKE, THE, 1936, A-C
CRIME OF THE CENTURY, 1946
CRIME OF THE CENTURY, THE, 1933, A
CRIME OF THE FUTURE, 1969, O
CRIME OF THE HOUR, 1918
CRIME ON THE HILL, 1933, A
CRIME OVER LONDON, 1936, A
CRIME PATROL, THE, 1936, A
CRIME RING, 1938, A
CRIME SCHOOL, 1938, AA
CRIME TAKES A HOLIDAY, 1938, A
CRIME UNLIMITED, 1935, A
CRIME WAVE, 1954
CRIME WITHOUT PASSION, 1934, A
CRIME, INC., 1945, A
CRIMES OF PASSION, 1984, O
CRIMINAL AT LARGE, 1932, A
CRIMINAL CODE, 1931, A
CRIMINAL CONVERSATION, 1980, C
CRIMINAL COURT, 1946, A
CRIMINAL INVESTIGATOR, 1942
CRIMINAL LAWYER, 1937
CRIMINAL LAWYER, 1951, A
CRIMINAL LIFE OF ARCHIBALDO DE LA CRUZ, THE, 1962, O
CRIMINAL, THE
CRIMINAL, THE, 1916
CRIMINALS OF THE AIR, 1937, A
CRIMINALS WITHIN, 1941, A
CRIMSON ALTAR, THE
CRIMSON BLADE, THE, 1964, A
CRIMSON CANARY, 1945, A
CRIMSON CANDLE, THE, 1934, A-C
CRIMSON CANYON, THE, 1928
CRIMSON CHALLENGE, THE, 1922, A
CRIMSON CIRCLE, THE, 1922, A
CRIMSON CIRCLE, THE, 1930, A
CRIMSON CIRCLE, THE, 1936, A
CRIMSON CITY, THE, 1928, A
CRIMSON CLUE, 1922
CRIMSON CROSS, THE, 1921
CRIMSON CULT, THE, 1970, O
CRIMSON DOVE, THE, 1917, A
CRIMSON EXECUTIONER, THE
CRIMSON GARDENIA, THE, 1919
CRIMSON GHOST, THE
CRIMSON GOLD, 1923
CRIMSON KEY, THE, 1947, A
CRIMSON KIMONO, THE, 1959
CRIMSON PIRATE, THE, 1952
CRIMSON ROMANCE, 1934, C
CRIMSON RUNNER, THE, 1925, A
CRIMSON SHOALS, 1919
CRIMSON SKULL, THE, 1921
CRIMSON TRAIL, THE, 1935
CRIMSON WING, THE, 1915
CRINOLINE AND ROMANCE, 1923, A
CRIPPLE CREEK, 1952, A
CRIPPLED HAND, THE, 1916
CRISIS, 1950, A
CRISIS, THE, 1915
CRISS CROSS, 1949, C
CRITIC'S CHOICE, 1963, A
CRITICAL AGE, THE, 1923, A
CROCODILE, 1979, O
CROISIERES SIDERALES, 1941, A
CROMWELL, 1970, A
CROOK OF DREAMS, 1919
CROOK'S ROMANCE, A, 1921
CROOK, THE, 1971, A
CROOKED ALLEY, 1923
CROOKED ALLEY, 1923, A
CROOKED BILLET, THE, 1930, A
CROOKED CIRCLE, 1932, A
CROOKED CIRCLE, THE, 1958, A-C
CROOKED LADY, THE, 1932, A
CROOKED RIVER, 1950, A
CROOKED ROAD, 1932
CROOKED ROAD, THE, 1940, A
CROOKED ROAD, THE, 5,BC
CROOKED ROMANCE, A, 1917
CROOKED SKY, THE, 1957, A
CROOKED STRAIGHT, 1919
CROOKED STREETS, 1920, A
CROOKED TRAIL, THE, 1936, A
CROOKED WAY, THE, 1949, A-C
CROOKED WEB, THE, 1955, A
CROOKS AND CORONETS
CROOKS ANONYMOUS, 1963, A-C
CROOKS CAN'T WIN, 1928
CROOKS IN CLOISTERS, 1964
CROOKS TOUR, 1940, A
CROOKY, 1915
CROONER, 1932
CROQUETTE, 1927
CROSBY CASE, THE, 1934, A
CROSS AND THE SWITCHBLADE, THE, 1970, A
CROSS BEARER, THE, 1918
CROSS BREED, 1927, A
CROSS CHANNEL, 1955, A-C
CROSS COUNTRY, 1983, O
CROSS COUNTRY CRUISE, 1934, A-C
CROSS COUNTRY ROMANCE, 1940, A
CROSS CREEK, 1983, C
CROSS CURRENTS, 1916
CROSS CURRENTS, 1935, A
CROSS MY HEART, 1937, A
CROSS MY HEART, 1946, A
CROSS OF IRON, 1977, O
CROSS OF LORRAINE, THE, 1943, C-O
CROSS OF THE LIVING, 1963, C-O
CROSS ROADS, 1922
CROSS ROADS, 1930
CROSS STREETS, 1934, A
CROSS-EXAMINATION, 1932, A
CROSS-UP, 1958, A
CROSSED SIGNALS, 1926
CROSSED SWORDS, 1954, A
CROSSED SWORDS, 1978, A
CROSSED TRAILS, 1924
CROSSED TRAILS, 1948, A
CROSSED WIRES, 1923
CROSSFIRE, 1933, A
CROSSFIRE, 1947, C
CROSSING TRAILS, 1921, A
CROSSPLOT, 1969, C
CROSSROADS
CROSSROADS, 1938, A
CROSSROADS, 1942, A
CROSSROADS OF NEW YORK, THE, 1922
CROSSROADS OF PASSION, 1951, A
CROSSROADS TO CRIME, 1960, C
CROSSTALK, 1982, A
CROSSTRAP, 1962, C
CROSSWAYS, 1928
CROSSWINDS, 1951, A
CROUCHING BEAST, THE, 1936, A
CROW HOLLOW, 1952, A-C
CROW'S NEST, THE, 1922
CROWD INSIDE, THE, 1971, C
CROWD ROARS, THE, 1932, A-C
CROWD ROARS, THE, 1938, A
CROWD, THE, 1928, A
CROWDED DAY, THE, 1954, A
CROWDED PARADISE, 1956, C
CROWDED SKY, THE, 1960, A
CROWED HOUR, THE, 1925
CROWN JEWELS, 1918
CROWN OF LIES, THE, 1926
CROWN OF THORNS, 1934
CROWN PRINCE'S DOUBLE, THE, 1916
CROWN VS STEVENS, 1936, A
CROWNING EXPERIENCE, THE, 1960, A
CROWNING GIFT, THE, 1967, A
CROWNING TOUCH, THE, 1959, A
CROXLEY MASTER, THE, 1921
CRUCIAL TEST, THE, 1916
CRUCIBLE OF HORROR, 1971, C
CRUCIBLE OF LIFE, THE, 1918
CRUCIBLE OF TERROR, 1971, O
CRUCIBLE, THE, 1914
CRUCIFIX OF DESTINY, THE, 1920
CRUCIFIX, THE, 1934, A
CRUEL SEA, THE, 1953, A
CRUEL SWAMP
CRUEL TOWER, THE, 1956, A
CRUEL TRUTH, THE, 1927
CRUISE MISSILE, 1978
CRUISE OF THE HELLION, THE, 1927
CRUISE OF THE JASPER B, THE, 1926
CRUISE OF THE MAKE-BELIEVES, THE, 1918
CRUISER EMDEN, 1932, A
CRUISIN' 57, 1975
CRUISIN' DOWN THE RIVER, 1953, A
CRUISING, 1980, O
CRUISKEEN LAWN, 1922
CRUNCH, 1975
CRUSADE AGAINST RACKETS, 1937, A
CRUSADE OF THE INNOCENT, 1922
CRUSADER, THE, 1922
CRUSADER, THE, 1932, A
CRUSADERS OF THE WEST, 1930
CRUSADES, THE, 1935, A
CRUZ BROTHERS AND MISS MALLOY, THE, 1979
CRY BABY KILLER, THE, 1958, C
CRY BLOOD, APACHE, 1970, O
CRY DANGER, 1951, A
CRY DOUBLE CROSS
CRY DR. CHICAGO, 1971, C
CRY FOR HAPPY, 1961, C
CRY FOR JUSTICE, THE, 1919
CRY FOR ME, BILLY
CRY FREEDOM, 1961, A
CRY FROM THE STREET, A, 1959, AAA
CRY HAVOC, 1943, A
CRY IN THE NIGHT, A, 1956, C
CRY MURDER, 1936, A
CRY OF BATTLE, 1963, A
CRY OF THE BANSHEE, 1970, O
CRY OF THE BEWITCHED
CRY OF THE CITY, 1948, C
CRY OF THE HUNTED, 1953, A
CRY OF THE PENGUINS, 1972, A
CRY OF THE WEAK, THE, 1919
CRY OF THE WEREWOLF, 1944, C-O
CRY TERROR, 1958, A-C
CRY TO THE WIND, 1979
CRY TOUGH, 1959, A
CRY UNCLE, 1973
CRY VENGEANCE, 1954, A
CRY WOLF, 1947, A
CRY WOLF, 1968, AA
CRY, THE BELOVED COUNTRY, 1952, A
CRYPT OF DARK SECRETS, 1976
CRYPT OF THE LIVING DEAD, 1973, C
CRYSTAL BALL, THE, 1943
CRYSTAL CUP, THE, 1927, A
CRYSTAL GAZER, THE, 1917
CUB REPORTER, THE, A
CUB, THE, 1915, A
CUBA, 1979, C
CUBA CROSSING, 1980, O
CUBAN FIREBALL, 1951, A
CUBAN LOVE SONG,THE, 1931, A
CUBAN PETE, 1946, A
CUBAN REBEL GIRLS, 1960
CUCKOO CLOCK, THE, 1938, A
CUCKOO IN THE NEST, THE, 1933
CUCKOO PATROL, 1965
CUCKOOS, THE, 1930, AA
CUJO, 1983
CUL-DE-SAC, 1966, C-O
CULPEPPER CATTLE COMPANY, THE, 1972, C
CULT OF THE COBRA, 1955, A-C
CULT OF THE DAMNED
CUMBERLAND ROMANCE, A, 1920, A
CUP FEVER, 1965, AA
CUP OF FURY, THE, 1920
CUP OF KINDNESS, A, 1934, A
CUP OF LIFE, THE, 1915
CUP OF LIFE, THE, 1921
CUP-TIE HONEYMOON, 1948, A
CUPID BY PROXY, 1918, A
CUPID FORECLOSES, 1919
CUPID IN CLOVER, 1929
CUPID'S BRAND, 1921
CUPID'S FIREMAN, 1923
CUPID'S KNOCKOUT, 1926
CUPID'S ROUND-UP, 1918
CUPID'S RUSTLER, 1924
CUPID, THE COWPUNCHER, 1920
CUPS OF SAN SEBASTIAN, THE
CURE FOR LOVE, THE, 1950, A
CURFEW BREAKERS, 1957, C
CURIOUS CONDUCT OF JUDGE LEGARDE, THE, 1915
CURIOUS DR. HUMPP, 1967, O
CURIOUS FEMALE, THE, 1969, O
CURLY TOP, 1935, AAA

CURLYTOP, 1924
CURSE OF BIGFOOT, THE, 1972, C
CURSE OF DRACULA, THE
CURSE OF DRINK, THE, 1922, A
CURSE OF EVE, THE, 1917
CURSE OF FRANKENSTEIN, THE, 1957, O
CURSE OF GREED, THE, 1914
CURSE OF IKU, THE, 1918
CURSE OF KILIMANJARO, 1978
CURSE OF THE AZTEC MUMMY, THE, 1965, A-C
CURSE OF THE BLOOD GHOULS, 1969, O
CURSE OF THE CAT PEOPLE, THE, 1944, C-O
CURSE OF THE CRIMSON ALTAR
CURSE OF THE CRYING WOMAN, THE, 1969, C
CURSE OF THE DEMON, 1958, O
CURSE OF THE DEVIL, 1973, O
CURSE OF THE DOLL PEOPLE, THE, 1968, C-o
CURSE OF THE FACELESS MAN, 1958, C
CURSE OF THE FLY, 1965, C
CURSE OF THE GHOULS
CURSE OF THE GOLEM
CURSE OF THE HEADLESS HORSEMAN, 1972
CURSE OF THE LIVING CORPSE, THE, 1964
CURSE OF THE MAYAN TEMPLE, 1977
CURSE OF THE MOON CHILD, 1972
CURSE OF THE MUMMY'S TOMB, THE, 1965, C
CURSE OF THE MUSHROOM PEOPLE
CURSE OF THE PINK PANTHER, 1983, A
CURSE OF THE STONE HAND, 1965, C
CURSE OF THE SWAMP CREATURE, 1966, C
CURSE OF THE UNDEAD, 1959, C
CURSE OF THE VAMPIRE
CURSE OF THE VAMPIRES, 1970, O
CURSE OF THE VOODOO, 1965, O
CURSE OF THE WEREWOLF, THE, 1961, O
CURSE OF THE WRAYDONS, THE, 1946, A-C
CURSED MILLIONS, 1917
CURTAIN, 1920
CURTAIN AT EIGHT, 1934, A
CURTAIN CALL, 1940, A
CURTAIN CALL AT CACTUS CREEK, 1950, AA
CURTAIN FALLS, THE
CURTAIN RISES, THE, 1939, A
CURTAIN UP, 1952, A
CURTAINS, 1983, O
CURUCU, BEAST OF THE AMAZON, 1956, C
CUSTARD CUP, THE, 1923
CUSTER MASSACRE, THE
CUSTER OF THE WEST, 1968, C
CUSTER'S LAST FIGHT, 1925
CUSTOMARY TWO WEEKS, THE, 1917
CUSTOMS AGENT, 1950, A
CUTTER AND BONE, 1981, O
CUTTING LOOSE, 1980
CY WHITTAKER'S WARD, 1917
CYBORG 2087, 1966, A
CYCLE OF FATE, THE, 1916
CYCLE SAVAGES, 1969, O
CYCLE, THE, 1979, A-C
CYCLES SOUTH, 1971
CYCLONE BLISS, 1921
CYCLONE BOB, 1926
CYCLONE BUDDY, 1924
CYCLONE CAVALIER, 1925
CYCLONE COWBOY, THE, 1927
CYCLONE FURY, 1951
CYCLONE HIGGINS, D.D., 1918
CYCLONE JONES, 1923
CYCLONE KID, 1931, A
CYCLONE KID, THE, 1942, A
CYCLONE OF THE RANGE, 1927, A
CYCLONE OF THE SADDLE, 1935
CYCLONE ON HORSEBACK, 1941, A
CYCLONE PRAIRIE RANGERS, 1944
CYCLONE RANGER, 1935, A
CYCLONE RIDER, THE, 1924
CYCLONE, THE, 1920, A
CYCLOPS, 1957
CYCLOTRODE X, 1946, A
CYNARA, 1932, A-C
CYNTHIA, 1947, AA
CYNTHIA IN THE WILDERNESS, 1916
CYNTHIA'S SISTER, 1975
CYNTHIA-OF-THE-MINUTE, 1920
CYRANO DE BERGERAC, 1950, AA
CYTHEREA, 1924
CYTHEREA, 1924, A
CZAR OF BRODWAY, THE, 1930, A
CZAR WANTS TO SLEEP, 1934, A
CZECH MATE, 1984

-D-

D'ARTAGNAN, 1916
D-DAY, THE SIXTH OF JUNE, 1956, A
D.C. CAB, 1983, C
D.I., THE, 1957, A
D.O.A., 1950, A
D.W. GRIFFITH'S "THAT ROYLE GIRL"
DAD AND DAVE COME TO TOWN, 1938, A
DAD'S ARMY, 1971, A
DAD'S GIRL, 1919
DADDIES, 1924
DADDY, 1917
DADDY, 1923, A
DADDY LONG LEGS, 1919, A
DADDY LONG LEGS, 1931, AAA
DADDY LONG LEGS, 1955, AAA
DADDY'S DEADLY DARLING, 1984, O
DADDY'S GIRL
DADDY'S GIRL, 1918
DADDY'S GONE A-HUNTING, 1925
DADDY'S GONE A-HUNTING, 1969, C
DADDY'S LOVE, 1922
DADDY-O, 1959, C
DAFFODIL KILLER
DAFFY
DAFFY DUCK'S MOVIE: FANTASTIC ISLAND, 1983
DAGGERS OF BLOOD
DAGORA THE SPACE MONSTER, 1964, A
DAISIES, 1967, C-O
DAISY KENYON, 1947, A-C
DAISY MILLER, 1974, C-O
DAKOTA, 1945, A
DAKOTA INCIDENT, 1956, A
DAKOTA KID, THE, 1951, AAA
DAKOTA LIL, 1950, A
DALEKS—INVASION EARTH 2155 A.D., 1966, A
DALLAS, 1950, A
DALTON GANG, THE, 1949, A
DALTON GIRLS, THE, 1957, A
DALTON THAT GOT AWAY, 1960, A
DALTON'S WOMEN, THE, 1950, A
DALTONS RIDE AGAIN, THE, 1945, A
DAM BUSTERS, THE, 1955, A
DAMAGED GOODS, 1915, A
DAMAGED GOODS, 1917
DAMAGED GOODS, 1919
DAMAGED GOODS, 1937, C
DAMAGED HEARTS, 1924
DAMAGED LIVES, 1937, C
DAMAGED LOVE, 1931, C
DAME CHANCE, 1926, A
DAMES, 1934, AA
DAMES AHOY, 1930, AAA
DAMIEN'S ISLAND, 1976
DAMIEN—OMEN II, 1978, O
DAMN CITIZEN, 1958, A
DAMN THE DEFIANT!, 1962, A
DAMN YANKEES, 1958, A
DAMNATION ALLEY, 1977, C
DAMNED DON'T CRY, THE, 1950, A-C
DAMNED, THE
DAMNED, THE, 1948, C
DAMON AND PYTHIAS, 1914, A
DAMON AND PYTHIAS, 1962, A
DAMSEL IN DISTRESS, A, 1919, A
DAMSEL IN DISTRESS, A, 1937, A
DAN, 1914, A
DAN CANDY'S LAW
DAN MATTHEWS, 1936, A
DAN'S MOTEL, 1982, O
DANCE BAND, 1935, A
DANCE HALL, 1929, A
DANCE HALL, 1941, AA
DANCE HALL, 1950, A
DANCE HALL RACKET, 1956
DANCE LITTLE LADY, 1954, A
DANCE MADNESS, 1926
DANCE MAGIC, 1927
DANCE MALL HOSTESS, 1933, A
DANCE OF DEATH, THE, 1938, A
DANCE OF DEATH, THE, 1971, C
DANCE OF LIFE, THE, 1929, A
DANCE OF THE DWARFS, 1983, C
DANCE OF THE VAMPIRES
DANCE PRETTY LADY, 1932, A
DANCE TEAM, 1932, AA
DANCE WITH ME, HENRY, 1956, A
DANCE, CHARLIE, DANCE, 1937, A
DANCE, FOOLS, DANCE, 1931, A-C
DANCE, GIRL, DANCE, 1933, A
DANCE, GIRL, DANCE, 1940, A
DANCER AND THE KING, THE, 1914
DANCER OF BARCELONA, 1929
DANCER OF PARIS, THE, 1926
DANCER OF THE NILE, THE, 1923
DANCER'S PERIL, THE, 1917, A
DANCERS IN THE DARK, 1932, A
DANCERS, THE, 1925
DANCERS, THE, 1930, A
DANCIN' FOOL, THE, 1920
DANCING CHEAT, THE, 1924
DANCING CO-ED, 1939
DANCING DAYS, 1926
DANCING DYNAMITE, 1931, A
DANCING FEET, 1936, A
DANCING GIRL, THE, 1915
DANCING HEART, THE, 1959, A
DANCING IN MANHATTAN, 1945, A
DANCING IN THE DARK, 1949, A
DANCING LADY, 1933, A
DANCING MAN, 1934, A
DANCING MASTERS, THE, 1943, A
DANCING MOTHERS, 1926, A
DANCING ON A DIME, 1940, A
DANCING PIRATE, 1936, A
DANCING SWEETIES, 1930, A
DANCING WITH CRIME, 1947, A
DANCING YEARS, THE, 1950, AA
DANDY, 1973
DANDY DICK, 1935, A
DANDY IN ASPIC, A, 1968, A
DANDY, THE ALL AMERICAN GIRL, 1976, A
DANGER, 1923
DANGER AHEAD, 1921
DANGER AHEAD, 1923
DANGER AHEAD, 1935, A
DANGER AHEAD, 1940, A
DANGER BY MY SIDE, 1962, A-C
DANGER FLIGHT, 1939, AAA
DANGER GAME, THE, 1918
DANGER GIRL, THE, 1926
DANGER IN THE PACIFIC, 1942, A
DANGER IS A WOMAN, 1952, C-O
DANGER ISLAND
DANGER LIGHTS, 1930, AA
DANGER LINE, THE, 1924
DANGER MAN, THE, 1930
DANGER MARK, THE, 1918, A
DANGER ON THE AIR, 1938, A
DANGER ON WHEELS, 1940, A
DANGER PATH, THE
DANGER PATROL, 1928
DANGER PATROL, 1937, A
DANGER POINT, THE, 1922, A
DANGER QUEST, 1926
DANGER RIDER, 1925
DANGER RIDER, 1925
DANGER RIDER, THE, 1928
DANGER ROUTE, 1968, A
DANGER SIGNAL, 1945, A
DANGER SIGNAL, THE, 1915, A
DANGER SIGNAL, THE, 1925
DANGER SIGNALS, 1917
DANGER STREET, 1928
DANGER STREET, 1947, A
DANGER TOMORROW, 1960, A-C
DANGER TRAIL, 1928
DANGER TRAIL, THE, 1917
DANGER TRAILS, 1935, A
DANGER VALLEY, 1921, A
DANGER VALLEY, 1938
DANGER WITHIN
DANGER WITHIN, 1918
DANGER WOMAN, 1946, A
DANGER ZONE, 1951, C
DANGER ZONE, THE, 1918
DANGER ZONE, THE, 1925
DANGER! WOMEN AT WORK, 1943, A
DANGER, GO SLOW, 1918
DANGER—LOVE AT WORK, 1937, A
DANGER: DIABOLIK, 1968, A
DANGEROUS, 1936, A-C
DANGEROUS ADVENTURE, A, 1922
DANGEROUS ADVENTURE, A, 1937, A
DANGEROUS AFFAIR, A, 1919
DANGEROUS AFFAIR, A, 1931, A
DANGEROUS AFTERNOON, 1961, A-C
DANGEROUS AGE, A, 1960, A
DANGEROUS AGE, THE, 1922, A
DANGEROUS APPOINTMENT, 1934
DANGEROUS ASSIGNMENT, 1950
DANGEROUS BLONDE, THE, 1924
DANGEROUS BLONDES, 1943, A
DANGEROUS BUSINESS, 1920
DANGEROUS BUSINESS, 1946, A
DANGEROUS CARGO, 1939, A
DANGEROUS CARGO, 1954, C
DANGEROUS CHARTER, 1962, A
DANGEROUS CORNER, 1935, A
DANGEROUS COWARD, THE, 1924
DANGEROUS CROSSING, 1953, A
DANGEROUS CURVE AHEAD, 1921
DANGEROUS CURVES, 1929, AA
DANGEROUS DAVIES—THE LAST DETECTIVE, 1981, A
DANGEROUS DAYS, 1920
DANGEROUS DUB, THE, 1926
DANGEROUS DUDE, THE, 1926
DANGEROUS EXILE, 1958, A
DANGEROUS FEMALE
DANGEROUS FINGERS
DANGEROUS FISTS, 1925
DANGEROUS FLIRT, THE, 1924
DANGEROUS FRIEND
DANGEROUS FRIENDS, 1926
DANGEROUS GAME, A, 1922

DANGEROUS GAME, A, 1941, A
DANGEROUS GROUND, 1934, A
DANGEROUS HOLIDAY, 1937, AA
DANGEROUS HOUR, 1923, A
DANGEROUS HOURS, 1920
DANGEROUS INNOCENCE, 1925
DANGEROUS INTRIGUE, 1936, A
DANGEROUS INTRUDER, 1945, A
DANGEROUS KISS, THE, 1961, A
DANGEROUS LADY, 1941, A
DANGEROUS LIES, 1921
DANGEROUS LITTLE DEMON, THE, 1922
DANGEROUS LOVE AFFAIR
DANGEROUS MAID, THE, 1923
DANGEROUS MEDICINE, 1938, A
DANGEROUS MILLIONS, 1946, A
DANGEROUS MISSION, 1954, A-C
DANGEROUS MOMENT, THE, 1921
DANGEROUS MONEY, 1924
DANGEROUS MONEY, 1946, A
DANGEROUS MOONLIGHT
DANGEROUS NAN McGREW, 1930, A
DANGEROUS NUMBER, 1937, A
DANGEROUS ODDS, 1925
DANGEROUS PARADISE, 1930, A
DANGEROUS PARADISE, THE, 1920
DANGEROUS PARTNERS, 1945, A
DANGEROUS PASSAGE, 1944, A
DANGEROUS PASTIME, 1922
DANGEROUS PATHS, 1921
DANGEROUS PLEASURE, 1925
DANGEROUS PROFESSION, A, 1949, A
DANGEROUS RELATIONS, 1973
DANGEROUS SEAS, 1931, A
DANGEROUS SECRETS, 1938, A
DANGEROUS TALENT, THE, 1920
DANGEROUS TO KNOW, 1938, A
DANGEROUS TO MEN, 1920, A
DANGEROUS TOYS, 1921
DANGEROUS TRAFFIC, 1926
DANGEROUS TRAILS, 1923
DANGEROUS VENTURE, 1947, A
DANGEROUS VOYAGE
DANGEROUS WATERS, 1919
DANGEROUS WATERS, 1936, A
DANGEROUS WHEN WET, 1953, A
DANGEROUS WOMAN, 1929, A
DANGEROUS YEARS, 1947, A
DANGEROUS YOUTH, 1958, A
DANGEROUSLY THEY LIVE, 1942, A
DANGEROUSLY YOURS, 1933, A
DANGEROUSLY YOURS, 1937, A
DANGERS OF THE ENGAGEMENT PERIOD, 1929
DANIEL, 1983, C
DANIEL BOONE, 1936, AAA
DANIEL BOONE THRU THE WILDERNESS, 1926
DANIEL BOONE, TRAIL BLAZER, 1957, AA
DANIEL DERONDA, 1921
DANIELLA BY NIGHT, 1962, C
DANNY, 1979
DANNY BOY, 1934, A
DANNY BOY, 1941, A
DANNY BOY, 1946, AAA
DANS LA RAFALE, 1916
DANS LES GRIFFES DU MANIAQUE
DANSE MACABRE
DANTE'S INFERNO, 1924, A
DANTE'S INFERNO, 1935
DANTON
DANTON, 1931, A
DANTON, 1983, O
DAPHNE AND THE PIRATE, 1916, A
DAPHNE, THE, 1967, A-C
DARBY AND JOAN, 1919
DARBY AND JOAN, 1937, A
DARBY O'GILL AND THE LITTLE PEOPLE, 1959, AAA
DARBY'S RANGERS, 1958
DAREDEVIL, 1919
DAREDEVIL DRIVERS, 1938, A
DAREDEVIL IN THE CASTLE, 1969, A
DAREDEVIL KATE, 1916
DAREDEVIL'S REWARD, 1928, A
DAREDEVIL, THE, 1918
DAREDEVIL, THE, 1920
DAREDEVIL, THE, 1971
DAREDEVILS OF EARTH, 1936, A
DAREDEVILS OF THE CLOUDS, 1948, A
DARING CABALLERO, THE, 1949, A
DARING CHANCES, 1924, A
DARING DANGER, 1922
DARING DANGER, 1932, A
DARING DAUGHTERS, 1933
DARING DAYS, 1925
DARING DEEDS, 1927
DARING DOBERMANS, THE, 1973, AA
DARING GAME, 1968, A
DARING HEARTS, 1919
DARING LOVE, 1924
DARING OF DIANA, THE, 1916
DARING YEARS, THE, 1923
DARING YOUNG MAN, THE, 1935
DARING YOUNG MAN, THE, 1942, A
DARING YOUTH, 1924, A
DARK ALIBI, 1946, A
DARK ANGEL, THE, 1925, A
DARK ANGEL, THE, 1925
DARK ANGEL, THE, 1935, A
DARK AT THE TOP OF THE STAIRS, THE, 1960, C
DARK AUGUST, 1975
DARK AVENGER, THE
DARK CASTLE, THE, 1915
DARK CITY, 1950, A
DARK COMMAND, THE, 1940, A
DARK CORNER, THE, 1946, C
DARK CRYSTAL, THE, 1982, A
DARK DELUSION, 1947, A
DARK DREAMS, 1971
DARK END OF THE STREET, THE, 1981, O
DARK ENDEAVOUR, 1933
DARK ENEMY, 1984, A
DARK EYES, 1938, O
DARK EYES, 1980
DARK EYES OF LONDON
DARK EYES OF LONDON, 1961, A
DARK HAZARD, 1934, A
DARK HORSE, THE, 1932, A
DARK HORSE, THE, 1946, A
DARK HOUR, THE, 1936, A
DARK INTERVAL, 1950, C
DARK INTRUDER, 1965, C
DARK IS THE NIGHT, 1946, C-O
DARK JOURNEY, 1937, A
DARK LANTERN, A, 1920
DARK LIGHT, THE, 1951, C
DARK MAN, THE, 1951, A
DARK MANHATTAN, 1937, C
DARK MIRROR, THE, 1946, C
DARK MIRROR, THE, A
DARK MOUNTAIN, 1944, A
DARK ODYSSEY, 1961, C
DARK OF THE SUN, 1968, A
DARK PASSAGE, 1947, A
DARK PAST, THE, 1948, A
DARK PLACES, 1974, A
DARK PURPOSE, 1964
DARK RED ROSES, 1930, A
DARK RIVER, 1956, O
DARK ROAD, THE, 1917, A
DARK ROAD, THE, 1948
DARK SANDS, 1938, AA
DARK SECRET, 1949, A
DARK SECRETS, 1923
DARK SHADOWS
DARK SIDE OF TOMORROW, THE, 1970, O
DARK SILENCE, THE, 1916
DARK SKIES
DARK STAIRWAY, THE, 1938, A
DARK STAIRWAYS, 1924, A
DARK STAR, 1975, C
DARK STAR, THE, 1919
DARK STREETS, 1929, A
DARK STREETS OF CAIRO, 1940, A
DARK SUNDAY, 1978
DARK SWAN, THE, 1924
DARK TOWER, THE, 1943
DARK VENTURE, 1956, A
DARK VICTORY, 1939, A
DARK WATERS, 1944, A
DARK WORLD, 1935, A
DARK, THE, 1979, O
DARK, THE
DARKENED ROOMS, 1929
DARKENED SKIES, 1930, A
DARKENING TRAIL, THE, 1915
DARKER THAN AMBER, 1970, O
DARKEST AFRICA, 1936, A
DARKEST HOUR, THE, 1920
DARKEST LONDON, 1915, A
DARKEST RUSSIA, 1917
DARKNESS AND DAYLIGHT, 1923
DARKNESS BEFORE DAWN, THE, 1915
DARKTOWN STRUTTERS, 1975, C
DARLING, 1965, O
DARLING LILI, 1970, C
DARLING MINE, 1920, A
DARLING OF NEW YORK, THE, 1923
DARLING OF PARIS, THE, 1917, A
DARLING OF THE RICH, THE, 1923, A
DARLING, HOW COULD YOU!, 1951, A
DARTS ARE TRUMPS, 1938, A
DARWIN ADVENTURE, THE, 1972, A
DARWIN WAS RIGHT, 1924
DAS BOOT, 1982, C-O
DAS CABINETT DES CALIGARI
DAS LETZTE GEHEIMNIS, 1959, C
DASHING THRU, 1925
DATE AT MIDNIGHT, 1960
DATE BAIT, 1960, O
DATE WITH A DREAM, A, 1948, A
DATE WITH DEATH, A, 1959, A
DATE WITH DISASTER, 1957, C
DATE WITH JUDY, A, 1948, AA
DATE WITH THE FALCON, A, 1941, A
DATELINE DIAMONDS, 1966, A
DAUGHTER ANGELE, 1918
DAUGHTER IN REVOLT, A, 1927, A
DAUGHTER OF CLEOPATRA
DAUGHTER OF DARKNESS, 1948, O
DAUGHTER OF DAWN, THE, 1920
DAUGHTER OF DAWN, THE, 1924
DAUGHTER OF DECEIT, 1977, A-C
DAUGHTER OF DESTINY, 1917
DAUGHTER OF DEVIL DAN, 1921
DAUGHTER OF DR. JEKYLL, 1957, A
DAUGHTER OF ENGLAND, A, 1915
DAUGHTER OF EVE, A, 1919
DAUGHTER OF EVIL, 1930, O
DAUGHTER OF FRANCE, A, 1918
DAUGHTER OF LOVE, A, 1925, A
DAUGHTER OF LUXURY, A, 1922
DAUGHTER OF MACGREGOR, A, 1916
DAUGHTER OF MARYLAND, A, 1917
DAUGHTER OF MATA HARI
DAUGHTER OF MINE, 1919, A
DAUGHTER OF ROSIE O'GRADY, THE, 1950, AA
DAUGHTER OF SHANGHAI, 1937, A
DAUGHTER OF THE CITY, A, 1915
DAUGHTER OF THE CONGO, A, 1930
DAUGHTER OF THE DON, THE, 1917
DAUGHTER OF THE DON, THE, 1918
DAUGHTER OF THE DRAGON, 1931, A
DAUGHTER OF THE GODS, A, 1916
DAUGHTER OF THE JUNGLE, 1949, A
DAUGHTER OF THE LAW, A, 1921
DAUGHTER OF THE OLD SOUTH, A, 1918
DAUGHTER OF THE PEOPLE, A, 1915
DAUGHTER OF THE POOR, A, 1917
DAUGHTER OF THE SANDS, 1952, C-O
DAUGHTER OF THE SEA, A, 1915, A
DAUGHTER OF THE SIOUX, A, 1925
DAUGHTER OF THE SUN GOD, 1962
DAUGHTER OF THE TONG, 1939, A
DAUGHTER OF THE WEST, 1949, A
DAUGHTER OF THE WEST, A, 1918
DAUGHTER OF THE WILDS, 1917
DAUGHTER OF THE WOLF, A, 1919
DAUGHTER OF TWO WORLDS, A, 1920
DAUGHTER OF WAR, A, 1917
DAUGHTER PAYS, THE, 1920, A
DAUGHTERS COURAGEOUS, 1939, A
DAUGHTERS OF DARKNESS, 1971, O
DAUGHTERS OF DESIRE, 1929
DAUGHTERS OF DESTINY, 1954, C
DAUGHTERS OF MEN, A
DAUGHTERS OF PLEASURE, 1924
DAUGHTERS OF SATAN, 1972
DAUGHTERS OF THE NIGHT, 1924
DAUGHTERS OF THE RICH, 1923
DAUGHTERS OF TODAY, 1924, A
DAUGHTERS OF TODAY, 1933, A
DAUGHTERS WHO PAY, 1925, A
DAVID, 1979, C
DAVID AND BATHSHEBA, 1951, C
DAVID AND GOLIATH, 1961
DAVID AND JONATHAN, 1920, A
DAVID AND LISA, 1962, A-C
DAVID COPPERFIELD, 1913
DAVID COPPERFIELD, 1935, A
DAVID COPPERFIELD, 1970, A
DAVID GARRICK, 1913
DAVID GARRICK, 1916
DAVID GOLDER, 1932, A
DAVID HARDING, COUNTERSPY, 1950, A
DAVID HARUM, 1915, A
DAVID HARUM, 1934, A
DAVID HOLZMAN'S DIARY, 1968, C-O
DAVID LIVINGSTONE, 1936, A
DAVY, 1958, A
DAVY CROCKETT, 1916
DAVY CROCKETT AND THE RIVER PIRATES, 1956, AAA
DAVY CROCKETT AT THE FALL OF THE ALAMO, 1926
DAVY CROCKETT, INDIAN SCOUT, 1950, AAA
DAVY CROCKETT, KING OF THE WILD FRONTIER, 1955, AAA
DAWN, 1917, A
DAWN, 1919
DAWN, 1928, C
DAWN, 1979, C
DAWN AT SOCORRO, 1954, A
DAWN EXPRESS, THE, 1942, A
DAWN MAKER, THE, 1916
DAWN OF A TOMORROW, THE, 1915, A
DAWN OF A TOMORROW, THE, 1924
DAWN OF FREEDOM, THE, 1916

DAWN OF LOVE, THE, 1916
DAWN OF REVENGE, 1922
DAWN OF THE DEAD, 1979, O
DAWN OF THE EAST, 1921, A
DAWN OF THE MUMMY, 1981
DAWN OF THE TRUTH, THE, 1920
DAWN OF UNDERSTANDING, THE, 1918
DAWN ON THE GREAT DIVIDE, 1942, A
DAWN OVER IRELAND, 1938, A
DAWN PATROL, THE, 1930, A
DAWN PATROL, THE, 1938, C
DAWN RIDER, 1935, A
DAWN TRAIL, THE, 1931, A
DAWN, THE
DAY AFTER HALLOWEEN, THE, 1981, O
DAY AFTER THE DIVORCE, THE, 1940
DAY AFTER, THE
DAY AND THE HOUR, THE, 1963, A
DAY AT THE BEACH, A, 1970, O
DAY AT THE RACES, A, 1937, AA
DAY DREAMS, 1919
DAY FOR NIGHT, 1973, A-C
DAY IN COURT, A, 1965, O
DAY IN THE DEATH OF JOE EGG, A, 1972, O
DAY IT CAME TO EARTH, THE, 1979
DAY MARS INVADED EARTH, THE, 1963, C
DAY OF ANGER, 1970, O
DAY OF DAYS, THE, 1914, A
DAY OF FAITH, THE, 1923
DAY OF FURY, A, 1956, A
DAY OF RECKONING, 1933, O
DAY OF THE ANIMALS, 1977, C
DAY OF THE BAD MAN, 1958, A
DAY OF THE DOLPHIN, THE, 1973, A
DAY OF THE EVIL GUN, 1968, A
DAY OF THE HANGING, THE
DAY OF THE JACKAL, THE, 1973, C
DAY OF THE LANDGRABBERS
DAY OF THE LOCUST, THE, 1975, C-O
DAY OF THE NIGHTMARE, 1965, C
DAY OF THE OUTLAW, 1959, A
DAY OF THE OWL, THE, 1968, C
DAY OF THE TRIFFIDS, THE, 1963, C
DAY OF THE WOLVES, 1973, A-C
DAY OF TRIUMPH, 1954, A
DAY OF WRATH, 1948, C
DAY SANTA CLAUS CRIED, THE, 1980
DAY SHE PAID, THE, 1919
DAY THAT SHOOK THE WORLD, THE, 1977, A-C
DAY THE BOOKIES WEPT, THE, 1939, A
DAY THE EARTH CAUGHT FIRE, THE, 1961, A
DAY THE EARTH FROZE, THE, 1959, AA
DAY THE EARTH GOT STONED, THE, 1978
DAY THE EARTH STOOD STILL, THE, 1951, A
DAY THE FISH CAME OUT, THE, 1967, C
DAY THE HOTLINE GOT HOT, THE, 1968, A
DAY THE LORD GOT BUSTED, THE, 1976
DAY THE SCREAMING STOPPED, THE
DAY THE SKY EXPLODED, THE, 1958, A
DAY THE SUN ROSE, THE, 1969, A
DAY THE WAR ENDED, THE, 1961, A-C
DAY THE WORLD CHANGED HANDS, THE
DAY THE WORLD ENDED, THE, 1956
DAY THEY ROBBED THE BANK OF ENGLAND, THE, 1960, A
DAY TIME ENDED, THE, 1980, A
DAY TO REMEMBER, A, 1953, A
DAY WILL COME, A, 1960
DAY WILL DAWN, THE
DAY-TIME WIFE, 1939, A-C
DAYBREAK, 1918
DAYBREAK, 1931, A
DAYBREAK, 1940, A
DAYDREAK, 1948, C-O
DAYDREAMER, THE, 1966, AAA
DAYDREAMER, THE, 1975, A
DAYLIGHT ROBBERY, 1964, AA
DAYS AND NIGHTS, 1946, C
DAYS OF 36, 1972, C
DAYS OF BUFFALO BILL, 1946
DAYS OF GLORY, 1944, A
DAYS OF HEAVEN, 1978
DAYS OF JESSE JAMES, 1939, A
DAYS OF OLD CHEYENNE, 1943, A
DAYS OF OUR LIFE, 1914
DAYS OF WINE AND ROSES, 1962, C
DAYTIME WIVES, 1923
DAYTON'S DEVILS, 1968, A
DAYTONA BEACH WEEKEND Zero, 1965
DAZZLING MISS DAVISON, THE, 1917
DE L'AMOUR, 1968, C
DE SADE, 1969, O
DE STILTEROND CHRISTINE M...
DEAD ALIVE, THE, 1916
DEAD AND BURIED, 1981, O
DEAD ARE ALIVE, THE, 1972, O
DEAD CERT, 1974
DEAD CERTAINTY, A, 1920, A
DEAD DON'T DREAM, THE, 1948, A
DEAD END, 1937, C
DEAD END KIDS ON DRESS PARADE, 1939, A
DEAD EYES OF LONDON
DEAD GAME, 1923
DEAD HEART, THE, 1914
DEAD HEAT ON A MERRY-GO-ROUND, 1966, A
DEAD KIDS, 1981, O
DEAD LINE, THE, 1920
DEAD LINE, THE, 1926
DEAD LUCKY, 1960, C
DEAD MAN'S CHEST, 1965, A-C
DEAD MAN'S CURVE, 1928, A
DEAD MAN'S EVIDENCE, 1962
DEAD MAN'S EYES, 1944, A
DEAD MAN'S FLOAT, 1980
DEAD MAN'S GOLD, 1948, A
DEAD MAN'S GULCH, 1943, A
DEAD MAN'S SHOES, 1939, A
DEAD MAN'S TRAIL, 1952, A
DEAD MAN, THE, 1914
DEAD MARCH, THE, 1937, C
DEAD MELODY, 1938, C
DEAD MEN ARE DANGEROUS, 1939, A
DEAD MEN DON'T MAKE SHADOWS, 1970
DEAD MEN DON'T WEAR PLAID, 1982, C
DEAD MEN TELL, 1941, A
DEAD MEN TELL NO TALES, 1920
DEAD MEN TELL NO TALES, 1939
DEAD MEN WALK, 1943, A
DEAD MOUNTAINEER HOTEL, THE, 1979, C
DEAD OF NIGHT, 1946, O
DEAD OF NIGHT, 1972
DEAD OF SUMMER, 1970, C-O
DEAD ON COURSE, 1952, A-C
DEAD ONE, THE, 1961, C
DEAD OR ALIVE, 1921
DEAD OR ALIVE, 1944, A
DEAD OR ALIVE, 1968
DEAD PEOPLE, 1974, O
DEAD PIGEON ON BEETHOVEN STREET, 1972, C
DEAD RECKONING, 1947, C
DEAD RINGER, 1964, A-C
DEAD RUN, 1961, C
DEAD SOUL, THE, 1915
DEAD TO THE WORLD, 1961, A
DEAD WOMAN'S KISS, A, 1951, A
DEAD ZONE, THE, 1983, O
DEAD-SHOT BAKER, 1917
DEADFALL, 1968, C
DEADHEAD MILES, 1982, A-C
DEADLIER SEX, THE, 1920
DEADLIER THAN THE MALE, 1957, C
DEADLIER THAN THE MALE, 1967, C
DEADLIEST SIN, THE, 1956
DEADLINE, 1948, A
DEADLINE, 1984
DEADLINE AT DAWN, 1946, A
DEADLINE AT ELEVEN, 1920
DEADLINE FOR MURDER, 1946, A
DEADLINE, THE, 1932, A
DEADLINE—U.S.A., 1952, C
DEADLOCK, 1931, A
DEADLOCK, 1943, A
DEADLOCK, 1961
DEADLY AFFAIR, THE, 1967, A-C
DEADLY AND THE BEAUTIFUL, 1974
DEADLY AS THE FEMALE
DEADLY AUGUST, 1966
DEADLY BEES,THE, 1967, C
DEADLY BLESSING, 1981, O
DEADLY CHINA DOLL, 1973, O
DEADLY CIRCLE, THE
DEADLY COMPANIONS, THE, 1961, C
DEADLY DECISION
DEADLY DECOYS, THE, 1962, A-C
DEADLY DUO, 1962, A
DEADLY ENCOUNTER, 1979
DEADLY EYES, 1982, O
DEADLY FEMALES, THE, 1976, O
DEADLY FORCE, 1983, O
DEADLY GAME, THE, 1941
DEADLY GAME, THE, 1955, A
DEADLY GAME, THE, 1974
DEADLY GAMES, 1982
DEADLY GAMES, 1980
DEADLY HARVEST, 1972
DEADLY HERO, 1976, O
DEADLY HONEYMOON, 1974
DEADLY IS THE FEMALE
DEADLY MANTIS, THE, 1957, A
DEADLY NIGHTSHADE, 1953, A
DEADLY RECORD, 1959, A
DEADLY SILENCE
DEADLY SPAWN, THE, 1983, O
DEADLY STRANGERS, 1974, C
DEADLY TRACKERS, 1973, O
DEADLY TRAP, THE, 1972
DEADLY WEAPONS, 1974
DEADSHOT CASEY, 1928
DEADWOOD COACH, THE, 1924
DEADWOOD PASS, 1933, A
DEADWOOD '76, 1965, C
DEAF SMITH AND JOHNNY EARS, 1973, C
DEAFULA, 1975
DEAL OF THE CENTURY, 1983, C
DEALING: OR THE BERKELEY-TO-BOSTON FORTY-BRICK
DEAR BRAT, 1951, A
DEAR BRIGETTE, 1965, A
DEAR DETECTIVE, 1978, C
DEAR FOOL, A, 1921
DEAR HEART, 1964, A
DEAR INSPECTOR
DEAR JOHN, 1966
DEAR MARTHA
DEAR MR. PROHACK, 1949, A
DEAR MR. WONDERFUL, 1983, C
DEAR MURDERER, 1947, C
DEAR OCTOPUS
DEAR RUTH, 1947, A
DEAR WIFE, 1949, AA
DEAR, DEAD DELILAH, 1972, O
DEARIE, 1927
DEATH AT A BROADCAST, 1934, A
DEATH AT DAWN, 1924
DEATH BAY, 1926
DEATH BITE
DEATH BLOW
DEATH BY INVITATION, 1971
DEATH COLLECTOR, 1976, O
DEATH CORDS
DEATH CROONS THE BLUES, 1937, A
DEATH CURSE OF TARTU, 1967, C-O
DEATH DANCE, THE, 1918
DEATH DRIVER, 1977
DEATH DRIVES THROUGH, 1935, A
DEATH DRUMS ALONG THE RIVER
DEATH FLIES EAST, 1935, A
DEATH FORCE, 1978
DEATH FROM A DISTANCE, 1936, A
DEATH FROM OUTER SPACE
DEATH GAME, 1977, O
DEATH GOES NORTH, 1939, A
DEATH HUNT, 1981, C
DEATH IN SMALL DOSES, 1957, C
DEATH IN THE AIR, 1937
DEATH IN THE GARDEN, 1977, O
DEATH IN THE SKY, 1937, C
DEATH IN VENICE, 1971, C
DEATH IS A NUMBER, 1951, A-C
DEATH IS A WOMAN
DEATH IS CALLED ENGELCHEN, 1963, C
DEATH JOURNEY, 1976
DEATH KISS, THE, 1933, A
DEATH MACHINES, 1976, O
DEATH MAY BE YOUR SANTA CLAUS, 1969
DEATH OF A BUREAUCRAT, 1979, A-C
DEATH OF A CHAMPION, 1939, A
DEATH OF A CYCLIST
DEATH OF A GUNFIGHTER, 1969, C
DEATH OF A JEW
DEATH OF A SALESMAN, 1952, O
DEATH OF A SCOUNDREL, 1956, C
DEATH OF A STRANGER, 1976
DEATH OF AN ANGEL, 1952, A
DEATH OF HER INNOCENCE
DEATH OF MARIO RICCI, THE, 1983, C
DEATH OF MICHAEL TURBIN, THE, 1954, A
DEATH OF TARZAN, THE, 1968, C
DEATH OF THE APEMAN
DEATH OF THE DIAMOND, 1934, A
DEATH OF THE GODS, 1917
DEATH ON CREDIT, 1976
DEATH ON THE MOUNTAIN, 1961, O
DEATH ON THE NILE, 1978, C
DEATH ON THE SET
DEATH OVER MY SHOULDER, 1958, A-C
DEATH PLAY, 1976, C
DEATH RACE, 1978, C-O
DEATH RACE 2000, 1975, O
DEATH RAY, THE, 1925
DEATH RIDERS, 1976
DEATH RIDES A HORSE, 1969
DEATH RIDES THE PLAINS, 1944, A
DEATH RIDES THE RANGE, 1940, A
DEATH SCREAMS, 1982
DEATH SENTENCE, 1967, O
DEATH SHIP, 1980, O
DEATH SMILES ON A MURDER, 1974
DEATH TAKES A HOLIDAY, 1934, C
DEATH TOOK PLACE LAST NIGHT, 1970, O
DEATH TRAP, 1962, C
DEATH TRAP, 1967
DEATH TRAP, 1976
DEATH TRAP, 1982
DEATH VALLEY, 1927
DEATH VALLEY, 1946, A
DEATH VALLEY, 1982, O

DEATH VALLEY GUNFIGHTER, 1949, A
DEATH VALLEY MANHUNT, 1943, A
DEATH VALLEY OUTLAWS, 1941, A
DEATH VALLEY RANGERS, 1944, A
DEATH VENGEANCE, 1982, O
DEATH WEEKEND
DEATH WISH, 1974
DEATH WISH II, 1982, O
DEATHCHEATERS, 1976, C
DEATHDREAM, 1972, O
DEATHGAMES, 1981
DEATHHEAD VIRGIN, THE, 1974
DEATHLINE, 1973, O
DEATHLOCK, THE, 1915
DEATHMASTER, THE, 1972, O
DEATHSHEAD VAMPIRE
DEATHSPORT, 1978, O
DEATHSTALKER, 1983
DEATHSTALKER, THE, 1984, O
DEATHTRAP, 1982
DEATHWATCH, 1966, O
DEATHWATCH, 1980, O
DEATM GOES TO SCHOOL, 1953, A
DEBT OF HONOR, 1922, A
DEBT OF HONOR, 1936, A
DEBT OF HONOR, A, 1916
DEBT OF HONOR, THE, 1918
DEBT, THE
DEBT, THE, 1917
DEBTOR TO THE LAW, A, 1924
DECAMERON NIGHTS, 1924, A
DECAMERON NIGHTS, 1953, A
DECEIT, 1923
DECEIVER, THE, 1920
DECEIVER, THE, 1931, A
DECEIVERS, THE
DECEMBRISTS, 1927
DECEPTION, 1918
DECEPTION, 1921
DECEPTION, 1933, A
DECEPTION, 1946, A-C
DECIDING KISS, THE, 1918
DECISION AGAINST TIME, 1957
DECISION AT SUNDOWN, 1957, C
DECISION BEFORE DAWN, 1951, A
DECISION OF CHRISTOPHER BLAKE, THE, 1948, A
DECKS RAN RED, THE, 1958, A-C
DECLASSE, 1925
DECLINE AND FALL... OF A BIRD WATCHER, 1969, C
DECOY, 1946, C-O
DECOY FOR TERROR, 1970, O
DECOY, 1963
DECOY, THE, 1916
DEDEE, 1949, C
DEEDS MEN DO, THE
DEEDS OF DARING, 1924
DEEMSTER, THE, 1917
DEEP BLUE SEA, THE, 1955, C
DEEP DESIRE OF GODS
DEEP END, 1970, O
DEEP IN MY HEART, 1954, AA
DEEP IN THE HEART, 1983, O
DEEP IN THE HEART OF TEXAS, 1942, A
DEEP PURPLE, THE, 1915
DEEP PURPLE, THE, 1920
DEEP RED, 1976, O
DEEP SIX, THE, 1958, A
DEEP THRUST—THE HAND OF DEATH, 1973, O
DEEP VALLEY, 1947, C
DEEP WATERS, 1920
DEEP WATERS, 1948, A
DEEP, THE, 1977, O
DEER HUNTER, THE, 1978, O
DEERSLAYER, 1943, A
DEERSLAYER, THE, 1923
DEERSLAYER, THE, 1957, A
DEFEAT OF HANNIHAL, THE, 1937, C
DEFEAT OF THE CITY, THE, 1917
DEFECTOR, THE, 1966, C
DEFENCE OF SEVASTOPOL, 1911
DEFEND MY LOVE, 1956, A-C
DEFEND YOURSELF, 1925
DEFENDERS OF THE LAW, 1931, A
DEFENSE HESTS, THE, 1934, A
DEFENSE OF VOLOTCHAYEVSK, THE, 1938, A
DEFIANCE, 1980, C
DEFIANT DAUGHTERS
DEFIANT ONES, THE, 1958, C
DEFINITE OBJECT, THE, 1920
DEFYING DESTINY, 1923
DEFYING THE LAW, 1922
DEFYING THE LAW, 1924
DEFYING THE LAW, 1935
DEGREE OF MURDER, A, 1969, O
DELAVINE AFFAIR, THE, 1954, A
DELAY IN MARIENBORN
DELAYED ACTION, 1954, A
DELICATE BALANCE, A, 1973, C
DELICATE DELINQUENT, THE, 1957, A
DELICIOUS, 1931, A
DELICIOUS LITTLE DEVIL, THE, 1919
DELIGHTFUL HOGUE, 1929, A
DELIGHTFULLY DANGEROUS, 1945
DELINQUENT DAUGHTERS, 1944, C
DELINQUENT PARENTS, 1938, A
DELINQUENTS, THE, 1957, C
DELIRIUM
DELIRIUM, 1979, O
DELIVER US FROM EVIL, 1975
DELIVERANCE, 1928
DELIVERANCE, 1972, O
DELIVERY BOYS, 1984, O
DELTA FACTOR, THE, 1970, C
DELTA FOX, 1979
DELUGE, 1933, A
DELUGE, THE, 1925
DELUSION
DELUSIONS OF GRANDEUR, 1971, C
DELUXE ANNIE, 1918
DEMENTED, 1980, O
DEMENTIA, 1955, O
DEMENTIA 13, 1963, C
DEMETRIUS AND THE GLADIATORS, 1954, C
DEMI-BRIDE, THE, 1927
DEMI-PARADISE, THE
DEMOBBED, 1944, A
DEMOCRACY, 1918
DEMOCRACY, 1920
DEMOLITION, 1977
DEMON BARBER OF FLEET STREET, THE, 1939
DEMON FOR TROUBLE, A, 1934, A
DEMON FROM DEVIL'S LAKE, THE, 1964, A
DEMON LOVER, THE, 1977, O
DEMON PLANET, THE
DEMON POND, 1980, C
DEMON RIDER, THE, 1925
DEMON SEED, 1977, O
DEMON WITCH CHILD, 1974
DEMON, THE, 1918
DEMON, THE, 1926
DEMON, THE, 1981, O
DEMON, THE, 1965
DEMONIAQUE, 1958, C-O
DEMONIOS EN EL JARDIN
DEMONOID
DEMONS IN THE GARDEN, 1984, O
DEMONS OF LUDLOW, THE, 1983, O
DEMONS OF THE DEAD, 1976
DEMONS OF THE MIND, 1972, O
DEMONSTRATOR, 1971, O
DEMOS
DEN OF DOOM
DENIAL, THE, 1925
DENNY FROM IRELAND, 1918
DENTIST IN THE CHAIR, 1960, A
DENTIST ON THE JOB
DENVER AND RIO GRANDE, 1952, A
DENVER DUDE, THE, 1927
DENVER KID, THE, 1948
DEPARTMENT STORE, 1935, A
DEPORTED, 1950, A
DEPRAVED, THE, 1957, A-C
DEPTH CHARGE, 1960, A-C
DEPUTY DRUMMER, THE, 1935, A
DEPUTY MARSHAL, 1949, A
DER FREISCHUTZ, 1970, A
DER GOLEM
DER LETZTE MANN
DER MUDE TOD
DER VERLORENE SCHATTEN
DERANGED, 1974, O
DERBY DAY
DERBY WINNER, THE, 1915
DERELICT, 1930, A
DERELICT, THE, 1917
DERELICT, THE, 1937, A
DERELICTS, 1917
DERSU UZALA, 1976, A
DES VOLKES HELDENGANG
DESERT ATTACK, 1958, A
DESERT BANDIT, 1941, A
DESERT BLOSSOMS, 1921, A
DESERT BRIDE, THE, 1928
DESERT BRIDGEGROOM, A, 1922
DESERT DEMON, THE, 1925
DESERT DESPERADOES
DESERT DRIVEN, 1923
DESERT DUST, 1917
DESERT DUST, 1927
DESERT FLOWER, THE, 1925, A
DESERT FOX, THE, 1951, A
DESERT FURY, 1947, C
DESERT GOLD, 1919
DESERT GOLD, 1926
DESERT GOLD, 1936, A
DESERT GREED, 1926
DESERT GUNS, 1936, A
DESERT HAWK, THE, 1924
DESERT HAWK, THE, 1950, A
DESERT HELL, 1958, A
DESERT HONEYMOON, A, 1915
DESERT HORSEMAN, THE, 1946, A
DESERT JUSTICE, 1936, A
DESERT LAW, 1918
DESERT LEGION, 1953, A
DESERT LOVE, 1920
DESERT MADNESS, 1925
DESERT MAN, THE, 1917
DESERT MESA, 1935, A
DESERT MICE, 1960, A
DESERT NIGHTS, 1929
DESERT OF LOST MEN, 1951, A
DESERT OF THE LOST, THE, 1927
DESERT OF THE TARTARS, THE, 1976, C
DESERT OUTLAW, THE, 1924
DESERT PASSAGE, 1952, A
DESERT PATROL, 1938, A
DESERT PATROL, 1962, C
DESERT PHANTOM, 1937, A
DESERT PIRATE, THE, 1928, A
DESERT PURSUIT, 1952, A
DESERT RATS, THE, 1953, A
DESERT RAVEN, THE, 1965, A
DESERT RIDER, 1923
DESERT RIDER, THE, 1929, A
DESERT SANDS, 1955, A
DESERT SCORPION, THE, 1920
DESERT SECRET, THE, 1924
DESERT SHEIK, THE, 1924
DESERT SONG, THE, 1929, A
DESERT SONG, THE, 1943, A
DESERT SONG, THE, 1953, A
DESERT TRAIL, 1935, A
DESERT VALLEY, 1926
DESERT VENGEANCE, 1931
DESERT VIGILANTE, 1949, A
DESERT VULTURES, 1930
DESERT WARRIOR, 1961, A
DESERT WOOING, A, 1918
DESERT'S CRUCIBLE, THE, 1922
DESERT'S PRICE, THE, 1926, A
DESERT'S TOLL, THE, 1926, A
DESERTED AT THE ALTAR, 1922, A
DESERTER, 1934, A
DESERTER AND THE NOMADS, THE, 1969, O
DESERTER, THE, 1916
DESERTER, THE, 1971
DESERTERS, 1983
DESERTEUSE, 1917
DESIGN FOR LIVING, 1933, A
DESIGN FOR LOVING, 1962, A
DESIGN FOR MURDER, 1940, C
DESIGN FOR SCANDAL, 1941, A
DESIGNING WOMAN, 1957, A
DESIGNING WOMEN, 1934, A
DESIRABLE, 1934, A
DESIRE
DESIRE, 1923
DESIRE, 1936, A
DESIRE IN THE DUST, 1960, C
DESIRE ME, 1947, A
DESIRE OF THE MOTH, THE, 1917
DESIRE UNDER THE ELMS, 1958, O
DESIRE, THE INTERIOR LIFE, 1980, O
DESIRED WOMAN, THE, 1918, A
DESIRED WOMAN, THE, 1927
DESIREE, 1954, A
DESIREE, 1984, O
DESK SET, 1957, A
DESPAIR, 1978, O
DESPERADO TRAIL, THE, 1965, A
DESPERADO, THE, 1954, A
DESPERADOES ARE IN TOWN, THE, 1956, A
DESPERADOES OF DODGE CITY, 1948, A
DESPERADOES OUTPOST, 1952, A
DESPERADOES, THE, 1943
DESPERADOS, THE, 1969, O
DESPERATE, 1947, C
DESPERATE ADVENTURE, A, 1924
DESPERATE ADVENTURE, A, 1938
DESPERATE CARGO, 1941, A
DESPERATE CHANCE, 1926
DESPERATE CHANCE FOR ELLERY QUEEN, A, 1942, A
DESPERATE CHARACTERS, 1971, A-C
DESPERATE COURAGE, 1928
DESPERATE DECISION, 1954, O
DESPERATE GAME, THE, 1926
DESPERATE HERO, THE, 1920
DESPERATE HOURS, THE, 1955, C
DESPERATE JOURNEY, 1942, A
DESPERATE MAN, THE, 1959, A-C
DESPERATE MOMENT, 1953, A
DESPERATE MOMENT, A, 1926
DESPERATE ODDS, 1925
DESPERATE ONES, THE, 1968, C

DESPERATE SEARCH, 1952
DESPERATE SIEGE
DESPERATE TRAILS, 1921
DESPERATE TRAILS, 1939, A
DESPERATE WOMEN, THE, O
DESPERATE YOUTH, 1921
DESPERATION, 1916
DESPOILER, THE, 1915, A
DESTIN, 1927
DESTINATION 60,000, 1957, A
DESTINATION BIG HOUSE, 1950, A
DESTINATION GOBI, 1953, A
DESTINATION INNER SPACE, 1966, A
DESTINATION MILAN, 1954, A
DESTINATION MOON, 1950, A
DESTINATION MURDER, 1950, C
DESTINATION TOKYO, 1944, A
DESTINATION UNKNOWN, 1933, A
DESTINATION UNKNOWN, 1942, A
DESTINEE, 1926
DESTINEES
DESTINY
DESTINY, 1919
DESTINY, 1921
DESTINY, 1938, A
DESTINY, 1944, A
DESTINY OF A MAN, 1961, A
DESTINY'S ISLE, 1922, A
DESTINY'S SKEIN, 1915
DESTINY'S TOY, 1916
DESTROY ALL MONSTERS, 1969
DESTROY, SHE SAID, 1969, O
DESTROYER, 1943, A
DESTROYERS, THE, 1916
DESTROYING ANGEL, THE, 1915
DESTROYING ANGEL, THE, 1923
DESTRUCTION, 1915, A
DESTRUCTION TEST
DESTRUCTORS, THE, 1968, C
DESTRUCTORS, THE, 1974, C
DESTRY, 1954, A
DESTRY RIDES AGAIN, 1932, A
DESTRY RIDES AGAIN, 1939, A
DETECTIVE BELLI, 1970, O
DETECTIVE CRAIG'S COUP, 1914
DETECTIVE KITTY O'DAY, 1944, A
DETECTIVE STORY, 1951, C
DETECTIVE, THE, 1954, A
DETECTIVE, THE, 1968, C
DETECTIVES, 1928
DETERMINATION, 1920
DETERMINATION, 1922
DETOUR, 1945, O
DETOUR, THE, 1968, A
DETROIT 9000, 1973, O
DEUCE DUNCAN, 1918
DEUCE HIGH, 1926
DEUCE OF SPADES, THE, 1922
DEVIL AND DANIEL WEBSTER, THE, 1941, A
DEVIL AND LEROY BASSETT, THE, 1973
DEVIL AND MAX DEVLIN, THE, 1981, A
DEVIL AND MISS JONES, THE, 1941, A
DEVIL AND THE DEEP, 1932, C
DEVIL AND THE TEN COMMANDMENTS, THE, 1962, C
DEVIL AT FOUR O'CLOCK, THE, 1961, A
DEVIL AT HIS ELBOW, THE, 1916
DEVIL BAT'S DAUGHTER, THE, 1946, A
DEVIL BAT, THE, 1941, A
DEVIL BY THE TAIL, THE, 1969, C
DEVIL CHECKS UP, 1944
DEVIL COMMANDS, THE, 1941, C
DEVIL DANCER, THE, 1927
DEVIL DODGER, THE, 1917, A
DEVIL DOG DAWSON, 1921
DEVIL DOGS, 1928, A
DEVIL DOGS OF THE AIR, 1935, A
DEVIL DOLL, 1964, C
DEVIL DOLL, THE, 1936
DEVIL GIRL FROM MARS, 1954, A
DEVIL GODDESS, 1955
DEVIL GOT ANGRY, THE
DEVIL HAS SEVEN FACES, THE, 1977
DEVIL HORSE, THE, 1926
DEVIL IN LOVE, THE, 1968, C
DEVIL IN SILK, 1968
DEVIL IN THE CASTLE
DEVIL IN THE FLESH, THE, 1949, C
DEVIL IS A SISSY, THE, 1936, A
DEVIL IS A WOMAN, THE, 1935
DEVIL IS A WOMAN, THE, 1975, O
DEVIL IS AN EMPRESS, THE, 1939, A
DEVIL IS DRIVING, THE, 1932, A
DEVIL IS DRIVING, THE, 1937, A
DEVIL MADE A WOMAN, THE, 1962, A
DEVIL MAKES THREE, THE, 1952, A-C
DEVIL MAY CARE, 1929, A
DEVIL MCCARE, 1919
DEVIL MONSTER, 1946
DEVIL NEVER SLEEPS, THE
DEVIL ON DECK, 1932
DEVIL ON HORSEBACK, 1954, A
DEVIL ON HORSEBACK, THE, 1936
DEVIL ON WHEELS, THE, 1947, A
DEVIL PAYS OFF, THE, 1941, A
DEVIL PAYS, THE, 1932, A
DEVIL PROBABLY, THE, 1977, C
DEVIL RIDER, 1971
DEVIL RIDERS, 1944, A
DEVIL RIDES OUT, THE
DEVIL SHIP, 1947, A
DEVIL STONE, THE, 1917
DEVIL STRIKES AT NIGHT, THE, 1959, C
DEVIL THUMBS A RIDE, THE, 1947, A
DEVIL TIGER, 1934, A
DEVIL TIMES FIVE, 1974, C
DEVIL TO PAY, THE, 1920, A
DEVIL TO PAY, THE, 1930, A
DEVIL WITH HITLER, THE, 1942
DEVIL WITH WOMEN, A, 1930, A
DEVIL WITHIN HER, THE, 1976, O
DEVIL WITHIN, THE, 1921
DEVIL WOLF OF SHADOW MOUNTAIN, THE, 1964
DEVIL WOMAN
DEVIL WOMAN, 1976, O
DEVIL'S 8, THE, 1969, C
DEVIL'S AGENT, THE, 1962, C
DEVIL'S ANGEL, THE, 1920
DEVIL'S ANGELS, 1967, O
DEVIL'S APPLE TREE, 1929, A
DEVIL'S ASSISTANT, THE, 1917
DEVIL'S BAIT, 1959, A
DEVIL'S BAIT, THE, 1917
DEVIL'S BEDROOM, THE, 1964, O
DEVIL'S BOND WOMAN, THE, 1916
DEVIL'S BONDMAN, THE
DEVIL'S BOWL, THE, 1923
DEVIL'S BRIDE, THE, 1968, O
DEVIL'S BRIGADE, THE, 1968, C
DEVIL'S BROTHER, THE, 1933, AAA
DEVIL'S CAGE, THE, 1928
DEVIL'S CANYON, 1935
DEVIL'S CANYON, 1953, A
DEVIL'S CARGO, THE, 1925, A
DEVIL'S CARGO, THE, 1948, A
DEVIL'S CHAPLAIN, 1929, A
DEVIL'S CIRCUS, THE, 1926
DEVIL'S CLAIM, THE, 1920
DEVIL'S COMMANDMENT, THE, 1956, O
DEVIL'S CONFESSION, THE, 1921
DEVIL'S DAFFODIL, THE, 1961, A
DEVIL'S DAUGHTER, 1949, A
DEVIL'S DAUGHTER, THE, 1915
DEVIL'S DICE, 1926
DEVIL'S DISCIPLE, THE, 1926
DEVIL'S DISCIPLE, THE, 1959, A
DEVIL'S DOLL
DEVIL'S DOORWAY, 1950, A
DEVIL'S DOORYARD, THE, 1923
DEVIL'S DOUBLE , THE, 1916
DEVIL'S ENVOYS, THE, 1947, A
DEVIL'S EXPRESS, 1975, O
DEVIL'S EYE, THE, 1960, C
DEVIL'S GARDEN, THE, 1920
DEVIL'S GENERAL, THE, 1957, A-C
DEVIL'S GHOST, THE, 1922
DEVIL'S GODMOTHER, THE, 1938, A
DEVIL'S GULCH, THE, 1926
DEVIL'S HAIRPIN, THE, 1957, A
DEVIL'S HAND, THE, 1961, C
DEVIL'S HARBOR, 1954, C
DEVIL'S HENCHMEN, THE, 1949, A
DEVIL'S HOLIDAY, THE, 1930, A
DEVIL'S IMPOSTER, THE
DEVIL'S IN LOVE, THE, 1933, A
DEVIL'S ISLAND, 1926
DEVIL'S ISLAND, 1940, C
DEVIL'S JEST, THE, 1954
DEVIL'S LOTTERY, 1932, A
DEVIL'S MAN, THE, 1967, C
DEVIL'S MASK, THE, 1946, A
DEVIL'S MASTERPIECE, THE, 1927, A
DEVIL'S MATCH, THE, 1923
DEVIL'S MATE, 1933, A
DEVIL'S MAZE, THE, 1929, A-C
DEVIL'S MEN, THE
DEVIL'S MESSENGER, THE, 1962, C
DEVIL'S MISTRESS, THE, 1968, O
DEVIL'S NEEDLE, THE, 1916
DEVIL'S NIGHTMARE, THE, 1971, O
DEVIL'S OWN, THE, 1967, C
DEVIL'S PARTNER, THE, 1923, A
DEVIL'S PARTNER, THE, 1958, C-O
DEVIL'S PARTY, THE, 1938, A
DEVIL'S PASS, THE, 1957
DEVIL'S PASSKEY, THE, 1920, A
DEVIL'S PAWN, THE, 1922
DEVIL'S PAY DAY, THE, 1917
DEVIL'S PIPELINE, THE, 1940, A
DEVIL'S PIT, THE, 1930
DEVIL'S PITCHFORK
DEVIL'S PLAYGROUND, 1937, A
DEVIL'S PLAYGROUND, THE, 1918, A
DEVIL'S PLAYGROUND, THE, 1946, A
DEVIL'S PLAYGROUND, THE, 1976, A
DEVIL'S PLOT, THE, 1948, C
DEVIL'S PRAYER-BOOK, THE, 1916
DEVIL'S PRIZE, THE, 1916
DEVIL'S PROFESSION, THE, 1915
DEVIL'S RAIN, THE, 1975, O
DEVIL'S RIDDLE, THE, 1920
DEVIL'S ROCK, 1938, A
DEVIL'S SADDLE LEGION, THE, 1937, A
DEVIL'S SADDLE, THE, 1927
DEVIL'S SISTERS, THE, 1966, O
DEVIL'S SKIPPER, THE, 1928
DEVIL'S SLEEP, THE, 1951, A
DEVIL'S SPAWN, THE
DEVIL'S SQUADRON, 1936, A
DEVIL'S TEMPLE, 1969, C-O
DEVIL'S TOLL, THE
DEVIL'S TOWER, 1929, A
DEVIL'S TOY, THE, 1916
DEVIL'S TRADEMARK, THE, 1928
DEVIL'S TRAIL, THE, 1919, A
DEVIL'S TRAIL, THE, 1942, A
DEVIL'S TRAP, THE, 1964, A-C
DEVIL'S TWIN, THE, 1927
DEVIL'S WANTON, THE, 1962, C
DEVIL'S WEDDING NIGHT, THE, 1973, O
DEVIL'S WHEEL, THE, 1918
DEVIL'S WHEEL, THE, 1926
DEVIL'S WIDOW, THE, 1972, O
DEVIL'S WOMAN, THE
DEVIL, THE, 1921
DEVIL, THE, 1963, A
DEVIL, THE SERVANT AND THE MAN, THE, 1916
DEVIL-SHIP PIRATES, THE, 1964, C
DEVILS OF DARKNESS, THE, 1965, C
DEVILS, THE, 1971
DEVONSVILLE TERROR, THE, 1983, O
DEVOTION, 1921
DEVOTION, 1931, A
DEVOTION, 1946, A
DEVOTION, 1953, C-O
DEVOTION, 1955, A
DIABOLIC WEDDING, 1972
DIABOLICAL DR. MABUSE, THE
DIABOLICAL DR. Z, THE, 1966, O
DIABOLICALLY YOURS, 1968, C
DIABOLIQUE, 1955, O
DIAGNOSIS: MURDER, 1974, C
DIAL 1119, 1950, C
DIAL 999, 1937
DIAL 999, 1955
DIAL M FOR MURDER, 1954, A-C
DIAL RED O, 1955, C
DIALOGUE, 1967, A
DIAMANT NOIR, 1922
DIAMOND BANDIT, THE, 1924
DIAMOND CARLISLE, 1922
DIAMOND CITY, 1949, A
DIAMOND COUNTRY
DIAMOND CUT DIAMOND
DIAMOND EARRINGS
DIAMOND FRONTIER, 1940
DIAMOND HANDCUFFS, 1928
DIAMOND HEAD, 1962, C
DIAMOND HORSESHOE, 1945, A
DIAMOND HUNTERS
DIAMOND JIM, 1935, A
DIAMOND MAN, THE, 1924
DIAMOND NECKLACE, THE, 1921, A
DIAMOND QUEEN, THE, 1953, A
DIAMOND RUNNERS, THE, 1916
DIAMOND SAFARI, 1958, A
DIAMOND STUD, 1970, C
DIAMOND STUD, 1970
DIAMOND TRAIL, 1933, A
DIAMOND WIZARD, THE, 1954
DIAMONDS, 1975, C
DIAMONDS ADRIFT, 1921, A
DIAMONDS AND CRIME
DIAMONDS AND PEARLS, 1918
DIAMONDS ARE FOREVER, 1971, C
DIAMONDS FOR BREAKFAST, 1968, C
DIAMONDS OF THE NIGHT, 1968, C
DIANA AND DESTINY, 1916
DIANA OF DOBSON'S, 1917
DIANA OF THE CROSSWAYS, 1922
DIANA OF THE FOLLIES, 1916
DIANE, 1955, A-C
DIANE OF STAR HOLLOW, 1921, A
DIANE OF THE GREEN VAN, 1919
DIANE'S BODY, 1969
DIARY FOR MY CHILDREN, 1984, O
DIARY OF A BACHELOR, 1964, O

DIARY OF A BAD GIRL, 1958, C
DIARY OF A CHAMBERMAID, 1946, A
DIARY OF A CHAMBERMAID, 1964, O
DIARY OF A CLOISTERED NUN, 1973, O
DIARY OF A COUNTRY PRIEST, 1954, A
DIARY OF A HIGH SCHOOL BRIDE, 1959, C-O
DIARY OF A LOST GIRL, 1929
DIARY OF A MAD HOUSEWIFE, 1970, C-O
DIARY OF A MADMAN, 1963, C-O
DIARY OF A NAZI, 1943, C
DIARY OF A REVOLUTIONIST, 1932, A
DIARY OF A SCHIZOPHRENIC GIRL, 1970, A
DIARY OF A SHINJUKU BURGLAR, 1969, O
DIARY OF AN ITALIAN, 1972, C
DIARY OF ANNE FRANK, THE, 1959, A
DIARY OF FORBIDDEN DREAMS
DIARY OF MAJOR THOMPSON, THE
DIARY OF OHARU
DICE OF DESTINY, 1920
DICE WOMAN, THE, 1927
DICK BARTON AT BAY, 1950, A
DICK BARTON STRIKES BACK, 1949, A
DICK BARTON—SPECIAL AGENT, 1948, A
DICK CARSON WINS THROUGH, 1917
DICK DEADEYE, 1977
DICK TRACY, 1945, A-C
DICK TRACY MEETS GRUESOME, 1947, A-C
DICK TRACY VS. CUEBALL, 1946, C
DICK TRACY'S DILEMMA, 1947, C
DICK TURPIN, 1925, A
DICK TURPIN, 1933
DICK TURPIN'S RIDE TO YORK, 1922
DICK'S FAIRY, 1921
DICKY MONTEITH, 1922
DICTATOR, THE, 1922, A
DICTATOR, THE, 1935, A
DID I BETRAY?
DID YOU HEAR THE ONE ABOUT THE TRAVELING
DIDN'T YOU HEAR, 1983
DIE FASTNACHTSBEICHTE, 1962, A
DIE FLAMBIERTE FRAU
DIE FLEDERMAUS, 1964, A
DIE GANS VON SEDAN, 1962, A
DIE GEHEIMNISSE EINER SEELE
DIE HAMBURGER KRANKHEIT, 1979, C
DIE LAUGHING, 1980, O
DIE MANNER UM LUCIE, 1931, A
DIE NIBELUNGEN
DIE NIBELUNGEN
DIE SCREAMING, MARIANNE, 1970, O
DIE SISTER, DIE, 1978
DIE UNENDLICHE GESCHICHTE
DIE, BEAUTIFUL MARYANNE, 1969
DIE, DIE, MY DARLING, 1965, O
DIE, MONSTER, DIE, 1965, C
DIFFERENT SONS, 1962, O
DIFFERENT STORY, A, 1978, O
DIFFICULT LOVE, A
DIFFICULT YEARS, 1950, C
DIG THAT JULIET
DIG THAT URANIUM, 1956, A
DIGBY, THE BIGGEST DOG IN THE WORLD, 1974, AAA
DILLINGER, 1945, C-O
DILLINGER, 1973, O
DILLINGER IS DEAD, 1969, O
DIMBOOLA, 1979, O
DIME WITH A HALO, 1963, A
DIMENSION 5, 1966, A
DIMKA, 1964, AA
DIMPLES, 1916, A
DIMPLES, 1936, AAA
DINER, 1982, C-O
DING DONG WILLIAMS, 1946, A
DINGAKA, 1965, A
DINKY, 1935, A
DINNER AT EIGHT, 1933, C
DINNER AT THE RITZ, 1937, A
DINNER FOR ADELE
DINO, 1957, A
DINOSAURUS, 1960, AA
DINTY, 1920, A
DION BROTHERS, THE
DIPLOMACY, 1916
DIPLOMACY, 1926
DIPLOMANIACS, 1933, A
DIPLOMAT'S MANSION, THE, 1961, C
DIPLOMATIC CORPSE, THE, 1958, A
DIPLOMATIC COURIER, 1952, A
DIPLOMATIC LOVER, THE, 1934, A
DIPLOMATIC MISSION, A, 1918
DIPLOMATIC PASSPORT, 1954, A
DIRIGIBLE, 1931, A
DIRT GANG, THE, 1972, O
DIRTIEST GIRL I EVER MET, THE, 1973
DIRTY DINGUS MAGEE, 1970, C
DIRTY DOZEN, THE, 1967, C-O
DIRTY GAME, THE, 1966, C
DIRTY GERTY FROM HARLEM, USA, 1946
DIRTY HANDS, 1976, O
DIRTY HARRY, 1971, O
DIRTY HEROES, 1971, A
DIRTY KNIGHT'S WORK, 1976, C
DIRTY LITTLE BILLY, 1972, C-O
DIRTY MARY, CRAZY LARRY, 1974, O
DIRTY MONEY, 1977, C
DIRTY O'NEIL, 1974, O
DIRTY OUTLAWS, THE, 1971, O
DIRTY TRICKS, 1981, C
DIRTY WORK, 1934, A
DIRTYMOUTH, 1970, O
DISAPPEARANCE OF THE JUDGE, THE, 1919
DISAPPEARANCE, THE, 1981, C
DISASTER, 1948, A
DISBARRED, 1939
DISC JOCKEY, 1951, A
DISC JOCKEY JAMBOREE
DISCARD, THE, 1916
DISCARDED LOVERS, 1932, A
DISCARDED WOMAN, THE, 1920
DISCIPLE OF DEATH, 1972, O
DISCIPLE, THE, 1915
DISCIPLES OF DEATH, 1975
DISCO 9000, 1977
DISCO FEVER, 1978
DISCO GODFATHER, 1979
DISCONTENTED HUSBANDS, 1924
DISCONTENTED WIVES, 1921
DISCORD, 1933, A
DISCOVERIES, 1939, A
DISCREET CHARM OF THE BOURGEOISIE, THE, 1972, C
DISEMBODIED, THE, 1957, C
DISGRACED, 1933, A
DISHONOR BRIGHT, 1936, A
DISHONORED, 1931, C
DISHONORED, 1950, A
DISHONORED LADY, 1947, C
DISHONORED MEDAL, THE, 1914, A
DISILLUSION, 1949, A
DISOBEDIENT, 1953, O
DISORDER, 1964
DISORDER AND EARLY TORMENT, 1977, A
DISORDERLY CONDUCT, 1932, A
DISORDERLY ORDERLY, THE, 1964, A
DISPATCH FROM REUTERS, A, 1940, A
DISPUTED PASSAGE, 1939, A
DISRAELI, 1916
DISRAELI, 1921
DISRAELI, 1929, A
DISTANCE, 1975, O
DISTANT DRUMS, 1951, A
DISTANT JOURNEY, 1950, C
DISTANT TRUMPET, 1952, A
DISTANT TRUMPET, A, 1964, A
DISTRICT ATTORNEY, THE, 1915
DITES 33
DIVA, 1982, C
DIVE BOMBER, 1941, A-C
DIVIDED HEART, THE, 1955, A
DIVIDEND, THE, 1916, A
DIVINE EMMA, THE, 1983, A
DIVINE GIFT, THE, 1918
DIVINE LADY, THE, 1929
DIVINE MR. J., THE, 1974, O
DIVINE NYMPH, THE, 1979
DIVINE SACRIFICE, THE, 1918
DIVINE SINNER, 1928
DIVINE SPARK, THE, 1935, A
DIVINE WOMAN, THE, 1928, A
DIVING GIRLS OF JAPAN
DIVING GIRLS' ISLAND, THE
DIVORCE, 1923, A
DIVORCE, 1945, A
DIVORCE AMERICAN STYLE, 1967, C
DIVORCE AMONG FRIENDS, 1931, C
DIVORCE AND THE DAUGHTER, 1916
DIVORCE COUPONS, 1922
DIVORCE GAME, THE, 1917, A
DIVORCE IN THE FAMILY, 1932, A
DIVORCE MADE EASY, 1929
DIVORCE OF CONVENIENCE, A, 1921
DIVORCE OF LADY X. THE, 1938, A
DIVORCE TRAP, THE, 1919, A
DIVORCE, ITALIAN STYLE, 1962, A
DIVORCED, 1915
DIVORCEE, THE, 1917
DIVORCEE, THE, 1919
DIVORCEE, THE, 1930, C
DIVORCONS, 1915
DIXIANA, 1930, A
DIXIE, 1943, A
DIXIE DUGAN, 1943, A
DIXIE DYNAMITE, 1976, C
DIXIE FLYER, THE, 1926, A
DIXIE HANDICAP, THE, 1925
DIXIE JAMBOREE, 1945, A
DIXIE MERCHANT, THE, 1926
DIZZY DAMES, 1936, A
DIZZY LIMIT, THE, 1930
DJANGO, 1966, O
DJANGO KILL, 1967, O
DK. JEKYLL AND THE WOLFMAN, 1971
DO AND DARE, 1922, A
DO IT NOW, 1924
DO NOT DISTURB, 1965, A
DO NOT THROW CUSHIONS INTO THE RING, 1970, O
DO THE DEAD TALK?, 1920
DO UNTO OTHERS, 1915
DO YOU KEEP A LION AT HOME?, 1966, AA
DO YOU KNOW THIS VOICE?, 1964
DO YOU LIKE WOMEN?
DO YOU LOVE ME?, 1946, A
DO YOUR DUTY, 1928, A
DOBBIN, THE, 1939
DOBERMAN GANG, THE, 1972, C
DOC, 1914
DOC, 1971, O
DOC HOOKER'S BUNCH, 1978
DOC SAVAGE... THE MAN OF BRONZE, 1975, A
DOCK BRIEF, THE
DOCKS OF NEW ORLEANS, 1948, A
DOCKS OF NEW YORK, 1945, A
DOCKS OF NEW YORK, THE, 1928
DOCKS OF SAN FRANCISCO, 1932, A
DOCTEUR LAENNEC, 1949, A
DOCTEUR POPAUL, 1972, O
DOCTOR AND THE BRICKLAYER, THE, 1918
DOCTOR AND THE GIRL, THE, 1949, C
DOCTOR AND THE WOMAN, THE, 1918
DOCTOR AT LARGE, 1957, A
DOCTOR AT SEA, 1955, A
DOCTOR BEWARE, 1951, C
DOCTOR CRIMEN, 1953, C
DOCTOR DEATH: SEEKER OF SOULS, 1973, O
DOCTOR DETROIT, 1983, O
DOCTOR DOLITTLE, 1967
DOCTOR FAUSTUS, 1967, C
DOCTOR FROM SEVEN DIALS, THE
DOCTOR IN CLOVER
DOCTOR IN DISTRESS, 1963, A
DOCTOR IN LOVE, 1960, A
DOCTOR IN THE HOUSE, 1954, A
DOCTOR IN TROUBLE, 1970, A
DOCTOR JACK, 1922, A
DOCTOR MONICA, 1934, A
DOCTOR OF DOOM, 1962, O
DOCTOR OF ST. PAUL, THE, 1969, C
DOCTOR PHIBES RISES AGAIN, 1972, C-O
DOCTOR SYN, 1937, A
DOCTOR TAKES A WIFE, 1940, AA
DOCTOR X, 1932, A
DOCTOR ZHIVAGO, 1965, A-C
DOCTOR'S DIARY, A, 1937, A
DOCTOR'S DILEMMA, THE, 1958, A
DOCTOR'S ORDERS, 1934, A
DOCTOR'S SECRET, 1929, A
DOCTOR'S WOMEN, THE, 1929
DOCTOR, YOU'VE GOT TO BE KIDDING, 1967
DOCTORS AND NURSES, 1983
DOCTORS DON'T TELL, 1941, A
DOCTORS WEAR SCARLET
DOCTORS' WIVES, 1931, C
DOCTORS' WIVES, 1971, O
DOCTORS, THE, 1956, A
DOCUMENT SECRET, 1916
DODESKA-DEN, 1970, C
DODGE CITY, 1939, A
DODGE CITY TRAIL, 1937, A
DODGING A MILLION, 1918
DODGING THE DOLE, 1936, A
DODSWORTH, 1936, A
DOES IT PAY?, 1923
DOG AND THE DIAMONDS, THE, 1962, AA
DOG DAY, 1984, O
DOG DAY AFTERNOON, 1975, O
DOG EAT DOG, 1963
DOG JUSTICE, 1928
DOG LAW, 1928, A
DOG OF FLANDERS, A, 1935, AAA
DOG OF FLANDERS, A, 1959, AAA
DOG OF THE REGIMENT, 1927, A
DOG'S BEST FRIEND, A, 1960, AAA
DOG, A MOUSE AND A SPUTNIK, A
DOGPOUND SHUFFLE, 1975, A
DOGS, 1976, O
DOGS OF HELL
DOGS OF WAR, THE, 1980, O
DOING THEIR BIT, 1918, A
DOING TIME, 1979, A
DOLEMITE, 1975, O
DOLL FACE, 1945, A
DOLL SQUAD, THE, 1973
DOLL THAT TOOK THE TOWN, THE, 1965
DOLL'S EYE, 1982
DOLL'S HOUSE, A, 1917
DOLL'S HOUSE, A, 1918, A

DOLL'S HOUSE, A, 1922
DOLL'S HOUSE, A, 1973
DOLL'S HOUSE, A, 1973, A
DOLL, THE, 1962, A
DOLL, THE, 1964, C
DOLLAR, 1938, A
$ (DOLLARS), 1971, O
DOLLAR AND THE LAW, THE, 1916
DOLLAR DEVILS, 1923, A
DOLLAR DOWN, 1925
DOLLAR FOR DOLLAR, 1920
DOLLAR MARK, THE, 1914, A
DOLLAR-A-YEAR MAN, THE, 1921
DOLLARS AND SENSE, 1920, A
DOLLARS AND THE WOMAN, 1916
DOLLARS AND THE WOMAN, 1920
DOLLARS FOR A FAST GUN, 1969, A
DOLLARS IN SURREY, 1921
DOLLS, THE
DOLLY, 1929
DOLLY DOES HER BIT, 1918
DOLLY GETS AHEAD, 1931, A
DOLLY SISTERS, THE, 1945, AA
DOLLY'S VACATION, 1918, A
DOLORES, 1928
DOLORES, 1949, A
DOLWYN
DOMANI A TROPPO TARDI
DOMBEY AND SON, 1917
DOMENICA D'AGOSTO
DOMESTIC MEDDLERS, 1928
DOMESTIC RELATIONS, 1922
DOMESTIC TROUBLES, 1928
DOMESTIC-AGITATOR, 1920
DOMINANT SEX, THE, 1937, A
DOMINIQUE, 1978
DOMINO KID, 1957, A
DOMINO PRINCIPLE, THE, 1977, O
DON CAESAR DE BAZAN, 1915
DON CHICAGO, 1945, A
DON DARE DEVIL, 1925
DON DESPERADO, 1927
DON GIOVANNI, 1955, A
DON GIOVANNI, 1979, A
DON IS DEAD, THE, 1973, O
DON JUAN, 1926, A
DON JUAN, 1956, A
DON JUAN ET FAUST, 1923
DON JUAN OF THE WEST, 1928
DON JUAN QUILLIGAN, 1945, A
DON JUAN'S THREE NIGHTS, 1926
DON JUAN, 1934
DON MIKE, 1927, A
DON Q, SON OF ZORRO, 1925, A
DON QUICKSHOT OF THE RIO GRANDE, 1923
DON QUIXOTE, 1916
DON QUIXOTE, 1923, A
DON QUIXOTE, 1935, A
DON QUIXOTE, 1961, A
DON QUIXOTE, 1973, A
DON RICARDO RETURNS, 1946, A
DON X, 1925, A
DON'S PARTY, 1976, C-O
DON'T, 1925
DON'T ANSWER THE PHONE, 1980, O
DON'T BE A DUMMY, 1932, A
DON'T BET ON BLONDES, 1935, A
DON'T BET ON LOVE, 1933, A
DON'T BET ON WOMEN, 1931, A
DON'T BLAME THE STORK, 1954, A
DON'T BLAME YOUR CHILDREN, 1922
DON'T BOTHER TO KNOCK, 1952, O
DON'T BOTHER TO KNOCK, 1964
DON'T BUILD YOUR HAPPINESS ON YOUR WIFE AND CHILD (1917, USSR)
DON'T CALL IT LOVE, 1924
DON'T CALL ME A CON MAN, 1966
DON'T CALL ME LITTLE GIRL, 1921, A
DON'T CHANGE YOUR HUSBAND, 1919
DON'T CRY WITH YOUR MOUTH FULL, 1974, A
DON'T CRY, IT'S ONLY THUNDER, 1982, O
DON'T DOUBT YOUR HUSBAND, 1924
DON'T DOUBT YOUR WIFE, 1922
DON'T DRINK THE WATER, 1969, A
DON'T EVER LEAVE ME, 1949, A
DON'T EVER MARRY, 1920
DON'T FENCE ME IN, 1945, A
DON'T GAMBLE WITH LOVE, 1936, A
DON'T GAMBLE WITH STRANGERS, 1946, A
DON'T GET ME WRONG, 1937, A
DON'T GET PERSONAL, 1922, A
DON'T GET PERSONAL, 1936, A
DON'T GET PERSONAL, 1941, A
DON'T GIVE UP THE SHIP, 1959, A
DON'T GO IN THE HOUSE, 1980, O
DON'T GO INTO THE WOODS, 1980
DON'T GO NEAR THE PARK, 1981
DON'T GO NEAR THE WATER, 1975
DON'T JUST LIE THERE, SAY SOMETHING!, 1973
DON'T JUST STAND THERE, 1968, A
DON'T KNOCK THE ROCK, 1956, A
DON'T KNOCK THE TWIST, 1962, A
DON'T LEAVE YOUR HUSBAND
DON'T LET THE ANGELS FALL, 1969, A
DON'T LOOK IN THE BASEMENT, 1973, O
DON'T LOOK NOW, 1969, A
DON'T LOOK NOW, 1973, O
DON'T LOSE YOUR HEAD, 1967, C
DON'T MAKE WAVES, 1967, A
DON'T MARRY, 1928, A
DON'T MARRY FOR MONEY, 1923, A
DON'T NEGLECT YOUR WIFE, 1921
DON'T OPEN THE DOOR, 1974
DON'T OPEN THE WINDOW, 1974, O
DON'T OPEN TILL CHRISTMAS, 1984, O
DON'T PANIC CHAPS!, 1959, A
DON'T PLAY US CHEAP, 1973
DON'T PLAY WITH MARTIANS, 1967, A
DON'T RAISE THE BRIDGE, LOWER THE RIVER, 1968, A
DON'T RUSH ME, 1936, A
DON'T SAY DIE, 1950, A
DON'T SCREAM, DORIS DAYS!
DON'T SHOOT, 1922
DON'T TAKE IT TO HEART, 1944, A
DON'T TALK TO STRANGE MEN, 1962, C
DON'T TELL EVERYTHING, 1921, A
DON'T TELL THE WIFE, 1927
DON'T TELL THE WIFE, 1937, A
DON'T TEMPT THE DEVIL, 1964, A
DON'T TOUCH MY SISTER
DON'T TOUCH THE LOOT
DON'T TOUCH WHITE WOMEN!, 1974, C
DON'T TRUST YOUR HUSBAND, 1948, C
DON'T TURN THE OTHER CHEEK, 1974, C
DON'T TURN'EM LOOSE, 1936, A
DON'T WORRY, WE'LL THINK OF A TITLE, 1966, A
DON'T WRITE LETTERS, 1922
DON'T YOU CRY
DONA FLOR AND HER TWO HUSHANDS, 1977, O
DONATELLA, 1956, A
DONDI, 1961, AAA
DONKEY SKIN, 1975, C-O
DONOVAN AFFAIR, THE, 1929, A
DONOVAN'S BRAIN, 1953, C
DONOVAN'S REEF, 1963, A
DONZOKO
DOOLINS OF OKLAHOMA, THE, 1949, A
DOOMED AT SUNDOWN, 1937, AA
DOOMED BATTALION, THE, 1932, A
DOOMED CARAVAN, 1941
DOOMED CARGO, 1936, A
DOOMED TO DIE, 1940, A
DOOMSDAY, 1928
DOOMSDAY AT ELEVEN, 1963, A-C
DOOMSDAY MACHINE, 1967, A
DOOMSDAY VOYAGE, 1972, O
DOOMWATCH, 1972, C
DOOR BETWEEN, THE, 1917
DOOR THAT HAS NO KEY, THE, 1921
DOOR TO DOOR, 1984, C
DOOR WITH SEVEN LOCKS, THE
DOOR-TO-DOOR MANIAC
DOORSTEPS, 1916, A
DOORWAY TO HELL, 1930, O
DOP DOCTOR, THE
DORA THORNE, 1915
DORIAN GRAY, 1970, O
DORIAN'S DIVORCE, 1916
DORM THAT DRIPPED BLOOD, THE, 1983, O
DORMANT POWER, THE, 1917
DOROTHY VERNON OF HADDON HALL, 1924
DOS COSMONAUTAS A LA FUERZA, 1967, A
DOSS HOUSE, 1933, A-C
DOT AND THE BUNNY, 1983, AA
DOTTED LINE, THE
DOUBLE ACTION DANIELS, 1925
DOUBLE AFFAIR, THE
DOUBLE AGENT 73, 1974
DOUBLE AGENTS, THE
DOUBLE ALIBI, 1940, A
DOUBLE BED, THE, 1965, C
DOUBLE BUNK, 1961, A
DOUBLE CON, THE
DOUBLE CONFESSION, 1953, C
DOUBLE CRIME IN THE MAGINOT LINE, 1939, A
DOUBLE CROSS, 1941, A
DOUBLE CROSS, 1956, A-C
DOUBLE CROSS ROADS, 1930, A
DOUBLE CROSSBONES, 1950, AA
DOUBLE CROSSED, 1917
DOUBLE DANGER, 1938, AA
DOUBLE DARING, 1926
DOUBLE DATE, 1941, AA
DOUBLE DEAL, 1939
DOUBLE DEAL, 1950
DOUBLE DEALING, 1923
DOUBLE DECEPTION, 1963, A-C
DOUBLE DOOR, 1934, C-O
DOUBLE DYNAMITE, 1951, A
DOUBLE EVENT, THE, 1921
DOUBLE EVENT, THE, 1934, A
DOUBLE EXPOSURE, 1944, A
DOUBLE EXPOSURE, 1954, A-C
DOUBLE EXPOSURE, 1982, O
DOUBLE EXPOSURES, 1937, A
DOUBLE FISTED, 1925
DOUBLE HARNESS, 1933, A-C
DOUBLE INDEMNITY, 1944, C
DOUBLE INITIATION, 1970
DOUBLE JEOPARDY, 1955, A
DOUBLE LIFE OF MR. ALFRED BURTON, THE, 1919, A
DOUBLE LIFE, A, 1947, C-O
DOUBLE MAN, THE, 1967, C
DOUBLE MCGUFFIN, THE, 1979, A
DOUBLE NEGATIVE, 1980, O
DOUBLE NICKELS, 1977, C
DOUBLE O, THE, 1921
DOUBLE OR NOTHING, 1937, A
DOUBLE OR QUITS, 1938, A
DOUBLE SPEED, 1920
DOUBLE STANDARD, THE, 1917
DOUBLE STOP, 1968
DOUBLE SUICIDE, 1970, O
DOUBLE TAKE, 1972
DOUBLE TROUBLE, 1915
DOUBLE TROUBLE, 1941, A
DOUBLE TROUBLE, 1967, A
DOUBLE TROUBLE, 1962
DOUBLE WEDDING, 1937, A
DOUBLE, THE, 1916
DOUBLE, THE, 1963, A
DOUBLE-BARRELED JUSTICE, 1925
DOUBLE-BARRELLED DETECTIVE STORY, THE, 1965, A
DOUBLE-DYED DECIEVER, A, 1920
DOUBLE-ROOM MYSTERY, THE, 1917
DOUBLES, 1978, C
DOUBLING FOR ROMEO, 1921, A
DOUBLING WITH DANGER, 1926, A
DOUBTING THOMAS, 1935, A
DOUCE
DOUGH BOYS, 1930, AAA
DOUGHBOYS IN IRELAND, 1943, A
DOUGHGIRLS, THE, 1944, A
DOUGHNUTS AND SOCIETY, 1936, A
DOUGLAS FAIRBANKS IN ROBIN HOOD
DOULOS—THE FINGER MAN, 1964, C
DOVE, THE, 1927
DOVE, THE, 1974, AA
DOWN AMONG THE SHELTERING PALMS, 1953, A
DOWN AMONG THE Z MEN, 1952, A
DOWN ARGENTINE WAY, 1940
DOWN BY THE RIO GRANDE, 1924, A
DOWN CHANNEL, 1929
DOWN DAKOTA WAY, 1949
DOWN GRADE, THE, 1927, A
DOWN HOME, 1920
DOWN IN ARKANSAW, 1938, A
DOWN IN SAN DIEGO, 1941, A
DOWN LAREDO WAY, 1953, A
DOWN MEMORY LANE, 1949, A
DOWN MEXICO WAY, 1941, A
DOWN MISSOURI WAY, 1946, A
DOWN ON THE FARM, 1920
DOWN ON THE FARM, 1938, A
DOWN OUR ALLEY, 1939, A
DOWN OUR STREET, 1932, A
DOWN RIO GRANDE WAY, 1942
DOWN RIVER, 1931, A
DOWN TEXAS WAY, 1942, A
DOWN THE ANCIENT STAIRCASE, 1975, O
DOWN THE STRETCH, 1927, A
DOWN THE STRETCH, 1936, A
DOWN THE WYOMING TRAIL, 1939, A
DOWN THREE DARK STREETS, 1954, C
DOWN TO EARTH, 1917, A
DOWN TO EARTH, 1932, A
DOWN TO EARTH, 1947, A
DOWN TO THE SEA, 1936, A
DOWN TO THE SEA, 1975
DOWN TO THE SEA IN SHIPS, 1923, A
DOWN TO THE SEA IN SHIPS, 1949, AAA
DOWN TO THE SEA IN SHIPS, 1937
DOWN TO THEIR LAST YACHT, 1934, A
DOWN UNDER DONOVAN, 1922
DOWN UNDER THE SEA
DOWN UPON THE SUWANNEE RIVER, 1925, A
DOWNFALL, 1964, C
DOWNHILL
DOWNHILL
DOWNHILL RACER, 1969, C
DOWNSTAIRS, 1932, A
DOWNSTREAM, 1929
DOZENS, THE, 1981, C
DR. BLACK AND MR. HYDE, 1976, O

DR. BLOOD'S COFFIN, 1961, O
DR. BROADWAY, 1942, C
DR. BULL, 1933, A
DR. BUTCHER, M.D., 1982, O
DR. CHRISTIAN MEETS THE WOMEN, 1940
DR. COPPELIUS, 1968, AA
DR. CRIPPEN, 1963, C
DR. CYCLOPS, 1940, A
DR. EHRLICH'S MAGIC BULLET, 1940, A
DR. FRANKENSTEIN ON CAMPUS, 1970
DR. GILLESPIE'S CRIMINAL CASE, 1943, A
DR. GILLESPIE'S NEW ASSISTANT, 1942, A
DR. GOLDFOOT AND THE BIKINI MACHINE, 1965, C
DR. GOLDFOOT AND THE GIRL BOMBS, 1966
DR. HECKYL AND MR. HYPE, 1980, O
DR. JEKYLL AND MR. HYDE, 1920, A
DR. JEKYLL AND MR. HYDE, 1932, O
DR. JEKYLL AND MR. HYDE, 1941
DR. JEKYLL AND SISTER HYDE, 1971, A
DR. JEKYLL'S DUNGEON OF DEATH, 1982, O
DR. JIM, 1921, A
DR. JOSSER KC, 1931, A
DR. KILDARE GOES HOME, 1940, A
DR. KILDARE'S CRISIS, 1940, A
DR. KILDARE'S STRANGE CASE, 1940, A
DR. KILDARE'S VICTORY, 1941, A
DR. KILDARE'S WEDDING DAY, 1941, A
DR. KNOCK, 1936, A
DR. MABUSE'S RAYS OF DEATH, 1964, A
DR. MABUSE, DER SPIELER
DR. MABUSE, THE GAMBLER, 1922
DR. MACDONALD'S SANATORIUM, 1920
DR. MINX, 1975, O
DR. MORELLE—THE CASE OF THE MISSING HEIRESS, 1949, A
DR. NEIGHBOR, 1916
DR. NO, 1962, C
DR. O'DOWD, 1940, A
DR. POPAUL
DR. RAMEAU, 1915
DR. RENAULT'S SECRET, 1942, C
DR. RHYTHM, 1938, AA
DR. SIN FANG, 1937, A
DR. SOCRATES, 1935, A-C
DR. STRANGELOVE: OR HOW I LEARNED TO STOP
DR. SYN, ALIAS THE SCARECROW, 1975, AA
DR. TARR'S TORTURE DUNGEON, 1972, O
DR. TERROR'S GALLERY OF HORRORS, 1967
DR. TERROR'S HOUSE OF HORRORS, 1965, O
DR. WAKE'S PATIENT, 1916
DR. WHO AND THE DALEKS, 1965, A
DRACULA, 1931, C-O
DRACULA, 1969, O
DRACULA, 1979, C
DRACULA A.D. 1972, 1972, O
DRACULA AND SON, 1976, C
DRACULA AND THE SEVEN GOLDEN VAMPIRES, 1978, O
DRACULA HAS RISEN FROM HIS GRAVE, 1968, O
DRACULA SUCKS, 1979
DRACULA TODAY
DRACULA VERSUS FRANKENSTEIN, 1972, O
DRACULA'S DAUGHTER, 1936, O
DRACULA'S DOG, 1978, O
DRACULA'S GREAT LOVE, 1972, O
DRACULA, 1958
DRACULA—PRINCE OF DARKNESS, 1966, O
DRAEGERMAN COURAGE, 1937, A
DRAFT 258, 1917
DRAG, 1929, A
DRAG HARLAN, 1920
DRAGNET, 1954, A
DRAGNET, 1974, A
DRAGNET NIGHT, 1931, A
DRAGNET PATROL, 1932, A
DRAGNET, THE, 1928, A
DRAGNET, THE, 1936
DRAGON DIES HARD, THE, 1974
DRAGON FLIES, THE
DRAGON HORSE, THE
DRAGON INN, 1968, C
DRAGON MASTER
DRAGON MURDER CASE, THE, 1934, A
DRAGON OF PENDRAGON CASTLE, THE, 1950
DRAGON PAINTER, THE, 1919
DRAGON SEED, 1944, A
DRAGON SKY, 1964, A
DRAGON WELLS MASSACRE, 1957, A
DRAGON'S GOLD, 1954
DRAGON, THE, 1916
DRAGONFLY SQUADRON, 1953, A
DRAGONFLY, 1976
DRAGONFLY, THE, 1955, A
DRAGONSLAYER, 1981, C-O
DRAGONWYCH, 1946
DRAGSTRIP GIRL, 1957, A
DRAGSTRIP RIOT, 1958, C
DRAKE CASE, THE, 1929, A
DRAKE THE PIRATE, 1935, A
DRAMA OF JEALOUSY, A
DRAMA OF THE RICH, 1975, A-C
DRAMATIC LIFE OF ABRAHAM LINCOLN, THE
DRAMATIC SCHOOL, 1938, A-C
DRANGO, 1957, A
DRAUGHTSMAN'S CONTRACT, THE, 1983, O
DREADING LIPS, 1958, C
DREAM CHEATER, THE, 1920
DREAM COME TRUE, A, 1963, A
DREAM DOLL, THE, 1917
DREAM GIRL, 1947, A
DREAM GIRL, THE, 1916
DREAM LADY, THE, 1918
DREAM MAKER, THE, 1963, A
DREAM MELODY, THE, 1929, A
DREAM NO EVIL, 1984
DREAM NO MORE, 1950, A
DREAM OF A COSSACK, 1982, A
DREAM OF BUTTERFLY, THE, 1941
DREAM OF KINGS, A, 1969, C
DREAM OF LOVE, 1928
DREAM OF PASSION, A, 1978, C
DREAM OF SCHONBRUNN, 1933, A
DREAM OF THE RED CHAMBER, THE, 1966, A
DREAM ON, 1981, O
DREAM ONE, 1984, A
DREAM OR TWO AGO, A, 1916
DREAM STREET, 1921, A
DREAM TOWN, 1973, C
DREAM WIFE, 1953, A
DREAM WOMAN, THE, 1914
DREAMBOAT, 1952, AA
DREAMER, 1979, A
DREAMER, THE, 1936, A
DREAMER, THE, 1947
DREAMER, THE, 1970, O
DREAMING, 1944, A
DREAMING LIPS, 1937, C
DREAMING OUT LOUD, 1940, A
DREAMS, 1960, C
DREAMS COME TRUE, 1936, A
DREAMS IN A DRAWER, 1957, A
DREAMS OF GLASS, 1969, C
DREAMS OF YOUTH, 1923
DREAMS OF YOUTH, 1928
DREAMS THAT MONEY CAN BUY, 1948, C
DREAMSCAPE, 1984, C-O
DREAMWORLD
DREARY HOUSE, 1928
DREI VON DER TANKSTELLE
DRESS PARADE, 1927, A
DRESSED TO KILL, 1941, A
DRESSED TO KILL, 1946, A
DRESSED TO KILL, 1928
DRESSED TO KILL, 1980, O
DRESSED TO THRILL, 1935, A
DRESSER, THE, 1983, C
DRESSMAKER FROM PARIS, THE, 1925
DREYFUS CASE, THE, 1931, A
DREYFUS CASE, THE, 1940, A
DRIFT FENCE, 1936
DRIFTER, 1975
DRIFTER, THE, 1916, A
DRIFTER, THE, 1929
DRIFTER, THE, 1932
DRIFTER, THE, 1944, A
DRIFTER, THE, 1966, C
DRIFTERS, THE
DRIFTERS, THE, 1919
DRIFTIN' KID, THE, 1941, A
DRIFTIN' RIVER, 1946, A
DRIFTIN' SANDS, 1928, A
DRIFTIN' THRU, 1926
DRIFTING, 1923
DRIFTING, 1932, A
DRIFTING, 1984, O
DRIFTING ALONG, 1946, A
DRIFTING KID, THE, 1928
DRIFTING ON, 1927
DRIFTING SOULS, 1932
DRIFTING WEEDS
DRIFTING WESTWARD, 1939
DRIFTWOOD, 1916
DRIFTWOOD, 1924
DRIFTWOOD, 1928
DRIFTWOOD, 1947, A
DRILLER KILLER, 1979, O
DRINK, 1917
DRIVE A CROOKED ROAD, 1954, C
DRIVE, HE SAID, 1971, O
DRIVE-IN, 1976, O
DRIVE-IN MASSACRE, 1976, O
DRIVEN
DRIVEN, 1923
DRIVEN FROM HOME, 1927, A
DRIVER'S SEAT, THE, 1975, O
DRIVER, THE, 1978, O
DRIVERS TO HELL
DRIVIN' FOOL, THE, 1923
DROLE DE DRADE
DROP DEAD, DARLING
DROP DEAD, MY LOVE, 1968, C
DROP THEM OR I'LL SHOOT, 1969, O
DROPKICK, THE, 1927, A
DROWNING POOL, THE, 1975, C
DRUG MONSTER, THE, 1923
DRUG STORE COWBOY, 1925
DRUG TRAFFIC, THE, 1923, A
DRUGGED WATERS, 1916
DRUM, 1976, O
DRUM BEAT, 1954, A
DRUM TAPS, 1933, A
DRUMMER OF VENGEANCE, 1974, O
DRUMS, 1938, A
DRUMS ACROSS THE RIVER, 1954, A
DRUMS ALONG THE MOHAWK, 1939, AAA
DRUMS IN THE DEEP SOUTH, 1951, A
DRUMS O' VOODOO, 1934
DRUMS OF AFRICA, 1963, A
DRUMS OF DESTINY, 1937, A
DRUMS OF FATE, 1923
DRUMS OF FU MANCHU, 1943, A
DRUMS OF JEOPARDY, 1931, A
DRUMS OF JEOPARDY, THE, 1923
DRUMS OF LOVE, 1928
DRUMS OF TABU, THE, 1967, A
DRUMS OF TAHITI, 1954, A
DRUMS OF THE CONGO, 1942, A
DRUMS OF THE DESERT, 1927
DRUMS OF THE DESERT, 1940, A
DRUNKEN ANGEL, 1948, C
DRUNKENNESS AND ITS CONSEQUENCES, 1913
DRUSILLA WITH A MILLION, 1925
DRY BIKINI, THE
DRY MARTINI, 1928
DRY ROT, 1956
DRY SUMMER, 1967, A
DRY VALLEY JOHNSON, 1917
DRYLANDERS, 1963, A
DU BARRY WAS A LADY, 1943, A
DU BARRY, WOMAN OF PASSION, 1930, A-C
DU RIRE AUX LARMES, 1917
DU SOLLIST NICHT EHEBRECHEN
DUAL ALIBI, 1947
DUB, THE, 1919
DUBARRY, 1915
DUBEAT-E-O, 1984, O
DUBLIN NIGHTMARE, 1958, A-C
DUCH IN ORANGE SAUCE, 1976, C
DUCHESS AND THE DIRTWATER FOX, THE, 1976, C
DUCHESS OF BUFFALO, THE, 1926
DUCHESS OF DOUBT, THE, 1917
DUCHESS OF IDAHO, THE, 1950
DUCHESS OF SEVEN DIALS, THE, 1920
DUCK RINGS AT HALF PAST SEVEN, THE, 1969, O
DUCK SOUP, 1933, AA
DUCK, YOU SUCKER!, 1972, C
DUCKS AND DRAKES, 1921, A
DUDE BANDIT, THE, 1933, A
DUDE COWBOY, 1941, A
DUDE COWBOY, THE, 1926, A
DUDE GOES WEST, THE, 1948, A
DUDE RANCH, 1931, A
DUDE RANGER, THE, 1934, A
DUDE WRANGLER, THE, 1930
DUDES ARE PRETTY PEOPLE, 1942, A
DUDS, 1920
DUE SOLDI DI SPERANZA
DUEL, 1928
DUEL AT APACHE WELLS, 1957, A
DUEL AT DIABLO, 1966, A
DUEL AT EZO, 1970, C
DUEL AT SILVER CREEK, THE, 1952, A
DUEL IN DURANGO
DUEL IN THE JUNGLE, 1954, A
DUEL IN THE SUN, 1946, C-O
DUEL OF CHAMPIONS, 1964, A
DUEL OF THE TITANS, 1963, A
DUEL ON THE MISSISSIPPI, 1955, A
DUEL WITHOUT HONOR, 1953, A
DUEL, THE, 1964, A
DUELLISTS, THE, 1977, O
DUET FOR CANNIBALS, 1969, O
DUET FOR FOUR, 1982, C
DUFFY, 1968, C
DUFFY OF SAN QUENTIN, 1954, A
DUFFY'S TAVERN, 1945, A
DUGAN OF THE BAD LANDS, 1931, A
DUGAN OF THE DUGOUTS, 1928
DUGI BRODOVI
DUKE COMES BACK, THE, 1937, A
DUKE IS THE TOPS, THE, 1938, A
DUKE OF CHICAGO, 1949, A
DUKE OF CHIMNEY BUTTE, THE, 1921
DUKE OF THE NAVY, 1942, A
DUKE OF WEST POINT, THE, 1938, A
DUKE STEPS OUT, THE, 1929, A
DUKE WORE JEANS, THE, 1958, A

DUKE'S SON
DULCIE'S ADVENTURE, 1916
DULCIMA, 1971, A
DULCIMER STREET, 1948, A
DULCINEA, 1962, C
DULCY, 1923, A
DULCY, 1940, A
DUMB GIRL OF PORTICI, 1916, A
DUMBBELLS IN ERMINE, 1930, A
DUMBO, 1941, AAA
DUMMY TALKS, THE, 1943, A
DUMMY, THE, 1917
DUMMY, THE, 1929, A-C
DUNCAN'S WORLD, 1977
DUNE, 1984, C-O
DUNGEON OF DEATH, THE, 1915
DUNGEON, THE, 1922
DUNGEONS OF HARROW, 1964, O
DUNKIRK, 1958, A
DUNWICH HORROR, THE, 1970, C
DUPE, THE, 1916, A
DUPED, 1925
DUPLICITY OF HARGRAVES, THE, 1917
DURAND OF THE BAD LANDS, 1917
DURAND OF THE BAD LANDS, 1925
DURANGO KID, THE, 1940, A
DURANGO VALLEY RAIDERS, 1938, A
DURANT AFFAIR, THE, 1962
DURING ONE NIGHT, 1962, A
DUSK TO DAWN, 1922
DUST, 1916
DUST BE MY DESTINY, 1939, A
DUST FLOWER, THE, 1922, A
DUST OF DESIRE, 1919, A
DUST OF EGYPT, THE, 1915
DUSTY AND SWEETS McGEE, 1971, O
DUSTY ERMINE
DUTCHMAN, 1966, C
DUTY FIRST, 1922
DUTY'S REWARD, 1927
DWELLING PLACE OF LIGHT, THE, 1920
DYBBUK THE, 1938
DYNAMITE, 1930, A
DYNAMITE, 1948, A
DYNAMITE, 1972
DYNAMITE ALLEN, 1921
DYNAMITE BROTHERS, THE, 1974
DYNAMITE CANYON, 1941, A
DYNAMITE DAN, 1924, A
DYNAMITE DELANEY, 1938
DYNAMITE DENNY, 1932, A
DYNAMITE JACK, 1961, A
DYNAMITE JOHNSON, 1978, A
DYNAMITE PASS, 1950, A
DYNAMITE RANCH, 1932
DYNAMITE SMITH, 1924
DYNAMITERS, THE, 1956, A

-E-

E.T. THE EXTRA-TERRESTRIAL, 1982, AAA
EACH DAWN I DIE, 1939, A
EACH MAN FOR HIMSELF
EACH PEARL A TEAR, 1916, A
EACH TO HIS KIND, 1917, A
EADIE WAS A LADY, 1945, A
EAGER BEAVERS
EAGER LIPS, 1927, A
EAGLE AND THE HAWK, THE, 1933, C
EAGLE AND THE HAWK, THE, 1950, A
EAGLE HAS LANDED, THE, 1976
EAGLE IN A CAGE, 1971, A
EAGLE OF THE SEA, THE, 1926
EAGLE OVER LONDON, 1973, C
EAGLE ROCK, 1964, A
EAGLE SQUADRON, 1942, A
EAGLE WITH TWO HEADS, 1948, A
EAGLE'S BROOD, THE, 1936, A
EAGLE'S CLAW, THE, 1924, A
EAGLE'S FEATHER, THE, 1923, A
EAGLE'S MATE, THE, 1914, A
EAGLE'S NEST, 1915
EAGLE'S WING, 1979, A
EAGLE'S WINGS, THE, 1916
EAGLE, THE, 1918, A
EAGLE, THE, 1925, A
EARL CARROLL SKETCHBOOK, 1946, A
EARL CARROLL'S VANITIES, 1945, A
EARL OF CHICAGO, THE, 1940, A
EARL OF PAWTUCKET, THE, 1915, A
EARL OF PUDDLESTONE, 1940, A
EARLY AUTUMN, 1962, C
EARLY BIRD, THE, 1925, A
EARLY BIRD, THE, 1936, A
EARLY BIRD, THE, 1965, A
EARLY BIRDS, 1923
EARLY TO BED, 1933, A
EARLY TO BED, 1936, A
EARLY TO WED, 1926, A
EARLY WORKS, 1970, O
EARRINGS OF MADAME DE..., THE, 1954, C-O
EARTH, 1930, A
EARTH CRIES OUT, THE, 1949, A
EARTH DIES SCREAMING, THE, 1964, A
EARTH ENTRANCED, 1970, C
EARTH VS. THE FLYING SAUCERS, 1956
EARTH VS. THE SPIDER, 1958, A
EARTH WOMAN, THE, 1926
EARTHBOUND, 1920
EARTHBOUND, 1940, A
EARTHBOUND, 1981, C
EARTHLING, THE, 1980, C
EARTHQUAKE, 1974, A
EARTHQUAKE MOTOR, THE, 1917
EARTHWORM TRACTORS, 1936
EASIEST WAY, THE, 1917
EASIEST WAY, THE, 1931, C
EAST CHINA SEA, 1969, C
EAST END CHANT
EAST IS EAST, 1916, A
EAST IS WEST, 1922, A
EAST IS WEST, 1930, C
EAST LYNNE, 1913, A
EAST LYNNE, 1916, A
EAST LYNNE, 1921
EAST LYNNE, 1925
EAST LYNNE, 1931, A
EAST LYNNE ON THE WESTERN FRONT, 1931, A
EAST MEETS WEST, 1936, A
EAST OF BORNEO, 1931, A
EAST OF BROADWAY, 1924, A
EAST OF EDEN, 1955, C-O
EAST OF ELEPHANT ROCK, 1976, O
EAST OF FIFTH AVE., 1933, C
EAST OF JAVA, 1935, A
EAST OF KILIMANJARO, 1962
EAST OF PICADILLY
EAST OF SHANGHAI
EAST OF SUDAN, 1964, A
EAST OF SUEZ, 1925, C
EAST OF SUMATRA, 1953, A
EAST OF THE RIVER, 1940, A
EAST SIDE KIDS, 1940, A
EAST SIDE KIDS MEET BELA LUGOSI, THE
EAST SIDE OF HEAVEN, 1939, A
EAST SIDE SADIE, 1929, A
EAST SIDE, WEST SIDE, 1927
EAST SIDE, WEST SIDE, 1949, A-C
EAST SIDE—WEST SIDE, 1923, C
EASTER SUNDAY
EASTER PARADE, 1948, AAA
EASTWARD HO, 1919
EASY COME, EASY GO, 1928, A
EASY COME, EASY GO, 1947, A
EASY COME, EASY GO, 1967, A
EASY GO
EASY GOING, 1926
EASY GOING GORDON, 1925, A
EASY LIFE, THE, 1963, C
EASY LIFE, THE, 1971, C
EASY LIVING, 1937, A
EASY LIVING, 1949, A
EASY MILLIONS, 1933, A
EASY MONEY, 1917
EASY MONEY, 1922
EASY MONEY, 1925, A
EASY MONEY, 1934
EASY MONEY, 1936, A
EASY MONEY, 1948, A
EASY MONEY, 1983, C-O
EASY PICKINGS, 1927, A
EASY RICHES, 1938, A
EASY RIDER, 1969, O
EASY ROAD, THE, 1921, A
EASY STREET, 1930
EASY TO GET, 1920, A
EASY TO LOOK AT, 1945, A
EASY TO LOVE, 1934, A
EASY TO LOVE, 1953, A
EASY TO MAKE MONEY, 1919, A
EASY TO TAKE, 1936, A
EASY TO WED, 1946, A
EASY VIRTUE, 1927, A
EASY WAY
EAT MY DUST!, 1976, A
EATEN ALIVE, 1976, O
EATING RAOUL, 1982, O
EAVESDROPPER, THE, 1966, C
EBB TIDE, 1922, A
EBB TIDE, 1932, A
EBB TIDE, 1937, A
EBIRAH, HORROR OF THE DEEP
EBOLI, 1980, A
EBONY, IVORY AND JADE, 1977
ECHO MURDERS, THE, 1945, A
ECHO OF A DREAM, 1930, A-C
ECHO OF BARBARA, 1961, C
ECHO OF DIANA, 1963, A-C
ECHO OF YOUTH, THE, 1919
ECHO, THE, 1964, C
ECHOES, 1983, O
ECHOES OF A SUMMER, 1976, A
ECHOES OF SILENCE, 1966, C
ECLIPSE, 1962, C
ECSTACY OF YOUNG LOVE, 1936
ECSTASY, 1940, O
ED HILLS, THE, 1956, A
EDDIE AND THE CRUISERS, 1983, C
EDDIE CANTOR STORY, THE, 1953, AA
EDDIE MACON'S RUN, 1983, A-C
EDDY DUCHIN STORY, THE, 1956, A
EDEN AND RETURN, 1921
EDEN CRIED, 1967, A
EDGAR ALLAN POE'S CASTLE OF BLOOD
EDGAR ALLAN POE'S CONQUEROR WORM
EDGAR ALLAN POE'S "THE OBLONG BOX"
EDGE O'BEYOND, 1919, A
EDGE OF DARKNESS, 1943, A
EDGE OF DIVORCE
EDGE OF DOOM, 1950, C
EDGE OF ETERNITY, 1959, A
EDGE OF FURY, 1958, O
EDGE OF HELL, 1956, A
EDGE OF THE ABYSS, THE, 1915, A
EDGE OF THE CITY, 1957, A
EDGE OF THE LAW, 1917
EDGE OF THE WORLD, THE, 1937, A
EDGE OF YOUTH, THE, 1920
EDGE, THE, 1968, C
EDISON, THE MAN, 1940, AAA
EDITH AND MARCEL, 1984, A
EDMUND KEAN—PRINCE AMONG LOVERS
EDUCATED EVANS, 1936, A
EDUCATING FATHER, 1936, A
EDUCATING RITA, 1983, A
EDUCATION DE PRINCE, 1927
EDUCATION OF ELIZABETH, THE, 1921, A
EDUCATION OF NICKY, THE, 1921, A
EDUCATION OF SONNY CARSON, THE, 1974
EDVARD MUNCH, 1976, C
EDWARD AND CAROLINE, 1952
EDWARD, MY SON, 1949, C
EEGAH!, 1962, C
EERIE WORLD OF DR. JORDAN. THE
EFFECT OF GAMMA RAYS ON MAN-IN-THE-
EFFECTS, 1980, O
EFFI BRIEST, 1974, O
EFFICIENCY EDGAR'S COURTSHIP, 1917, A
EGG AND I, THE, 1947, AAA
EGG CRATE WALLOP, THE, 1919
EGGHEAD'S ROBOT, 1970, A
EGLANTINE, 1972, A
EGON SCHIELE—EXCESS AND PUNISHMENT, 1981, O
EGYPT BY THREE, 1953
EGYPTIAN. THE, 1954, A-C
EIGER SANCTION, THE, 1975, C
EIGHT ARMS TO HOLD YOU
EIGHT BELLS, 1916
EIGHT BELLS, 1935, A
EIGHT GIRLS IN A BOAT, 1932, A
EIGHT GIRLS IN A BOAT, 1934, C
EIGHT IRON MEN, 1952
EIGHT O'CLOCK WALK, 1954, A
EIGHT ON THE LAM, 1967, A
18 MINUTES, 1935
1812, 1912
1812, 1944, A
EIGHTEEN AND ANXIOUS, 1957, C
EIGHTEEN IN THE SUN, 1964, C
80 STEPS TO JONAH, 1969, A
80,000 SUSPECTS, 1963, C
EIGHTH DAY OF THE WEEK, THE, 1959, C-O
EILEEN OF THE TREES
EINE DU BARRY VON HEUTE
EINE LIEBE IN DEUTSCHLAND
EL, 1955, C-O
EL ALAMEIN, 1954, A-C
EL BRUTO
EL CID, 1961
EL CONDOR, 1970, O
EL DIABLO RIDES, 1939, A
EL DORADO, 1967, A-C
EL DORADO PASS, 1949, A
EL GRECO, 1966, A
EL NORTE, 1984, O
EL PASO, 1949, A
EL PASO KID, THE, 1946, A
EL PASO STAMPEDE, 1953, A
EL RELICARIO, 1926
EL SUPER, 1979
EL TOPO, 1971, O
ELDER BROTHER, THE, 1937, A
ELDER MISS BLOSSOM, THE
ELDER VASILI GRYAZNOV, 1924
ELDORADO, 1921
ELECTRA, 1962, A
ELECTRA GLIDE IN BLUE, 1973, C

ELECTRIC BOOGALOO: BREAKIN' 2
ELECTRIC CHAIR, THE, 1977
ELECTRIC DREAMS, 1984, A-C
ELECTRIC HORSEMAN, THE, 1979, A-C
ELECTRONIC MONSTER. THE, 1960, C
ELEMENT OF CRIME, THE, 1984, O
ELEPHANT BOY, 1937, AA
ELEPHANT CALLED SLOWLY, AN, 1970, A
ELEPHANT GUN, 1959, A
ELEPHANT MAN, THE, 1980, A-C
ELEPHANT STAMPEDE, 1951, A
ELEPHANT WALK, 1954, A
ELEVENTH COMMANDMENT, 1933, A
ELEVENTH COMMANDMENT, THE, 1924, A
ELEVENTH HOUR, THE, 1922, A
ELEVENTH HOUR, THE, 1923, A
ELEVENTH bEARb THE, 1928
ELI ELI, 1940, A
ELIANE, 1919
ELIMINATOR, THE
ELIMINATOR, THE, 1982
ELINOR NORTON, 1935, A
ELISABETH OF AUSTRIA, 1931, A
ELISABETH REIGNE D'ANGLETERRE
ELISO, 1928
ELIZA COMES TO STAY, 1936, A
ELIZA FRASER, 1976, C
ELIZA'S HOROSCOPE, 1975, O
ELIZABETH OF ENGLAND
ELIZABETH OF LADYMEAD, 1949, A
ELIZABETH THE QUEEN
ELLA CINDERS, 1926, A
ELLERY QUEEN AND THE MURDER RING, 1941, A
ELLERY QUEEN AND THE PERFECT CRIME, 1941, A
ELLERY QUEEN'S PENTHOUSE MYSTERY, 1941, A
ELLERY QUEEN. MASTER DETECTIVE, 1940, A
ELLIE, 1984, O
ELLIS ISLAND, 1936
ELMER, 1977
ELMER AND ELSIE, 1934, A
ELMER GANTRY, 1960, C
ELMER THE GREAT, 1933
ELOPE IF YOU MUST, 1922, A
ELOPEMENT, 1951, A
ELUSIVE CORPORAL, THE, 1963, A
ELUSIVE ISABEL, 1916, A
ELUSIVE PIMPERNEL, THE
ELUSIVE PIMPERNEL, THE, 1919, A
ELVIRA MADIGAN, 1967, O
ELVIS! ELVIS!, 1977, A
ELYSIA, 1933
EMBALMER, THE, 1966, C
EMBARRASSING MOMENTS, 1930, A
EMBARRASSING MOMENTS, 1934, A
EMBARRASSMENT OF RICHES, THE, 1918, A
EMBASSY, 1972, C
EMBERS, 1916
EMBEZZLED HEAVEN, 1959, A
EMBEZZLER, THE, 1954, A
EMBLEMS OF LOVE, 1924
EMBODIED THOUGHT, THE, 1916
EMBRACEABLE YOU, 1948, A
EMBRACERS, THE, 1966, C
EMBRYO, 1976, C
EMERALD OF THE EAST, 1928, A
EMERGENCY, 1962, A
EMERGENCY CALL, 1933, A
EMERGENCY CALL, 1953
EMERGENCY HOSPITAL, 1956, A
EMERGENCY LANDING, 1941, A
EMERGENCY SQUAD, 1940, A
EMERGENCY WARD
EMERGENCY WEDDING, 1950
EMERGENCY! 1953
EMIGRANTS, THE, 1972, A
EMIL, 1938, AA
EMIL AND THE DETECTIVE, 1931, AA
EMIL AND THE DETECTIVES, 1964, AA
EMILY
EMILY, 1976, O
EMMA, 1932, A
EMMA MAE, 1976, O
EMPEROR AND A GENERAL, THE, 1968, O
EMPEROR AND THE GOLEM, THE, 1955, A
EMPEROR AND THE NIGHTINGALE, THE, 1949
EMPEROR JONES, THE, 1933, C
EMPEROR OF PERU
EMPEROR OF THE NORTH POLE, 1973, C
EMPEROR WALTZ, THE, 1948, AA
EMPEROR'S CANDLESTICKS, THE, 1937, A
EMPIRE BUILDERS, 1924
EMPIRE OF DIAMONDS, THE, 1920
EMPIRE OF NIGHT, THE, 1963, C
EMPIRE OF THE ANTS, 1977, C
EMPIRE STRIKES BACK, THE, 1980, A
EMPLOYEE'S ENTRANCE, 1933, A
EMPRESS AND I, THE, 1933, A
EMPRESS WU, 1965, A
EMPRESS, THE, 1917
EMPTY ARMS, 1920
EMPTY CAB, THE, 1918
EMPTY CANVAS, THE, 1964, O
EMPTY CRADLE, THE, 1923
EMPTY HANDS, 1924, A
EMPTY HEARTS, 1924
EMPTY HOLSTERS, 1937
EMPTY POCKETS, 1918
EMPTY SADDLE, THE, 1925
EMPTY SADDLES, 1937, A
EMPTY STAR, THE, 1962, A
EN PLONGEE, 1927
EN RADE, 1927
EN RAEDSOM NAT, 1914
ENCHANTED APRIL, 1935, A
ENCHANTED BARN, THE, 1919
ENCHANTED COTTAGE, THE, 1924, A
ENCHANTED COTTAGE, THE, 1945, A
ENCHANTED FOREST, THE, 1945, AAA
ENCHANTED HILL, THE, 1926, A
ENCHANTED ISLAND, 1958, A
ENCHANTED ISLAND, THE, 1927, A
ENCHANTED VALLEY, THE, 1948, A
ENCHANTING SHADOW, THE, 1965, A
ENCHANTMENT, 1920, A
ENCHANTMENT, 1921, A
ENCHANTMENT, 1948, A
ENCORE, 1951, A
ENCOUNTER WITH THE UNKNOWN, 1973, C
ENCOUNTERS IN SALZBURG, 1964, C
ENCOUNTERS OF THE DEEP, 1984
END OF A DAY, THE, 1939, A
END OF A PRIEST, 1970, C
END OF AUGUST, 1974
END OF AUGUST AT THE HOTEL OZONE, THE, 1967, C
END OF AUGUST, THE, 1982, C-O
END OF BELLE, THE
END OF DESIRE, 1962, A
END OF INNOCENCE, 1960, O
END OF MRS. CHENEY, 1963, A
END OF ST. PETERSBURG, THE, 1927
END OF SUMMER, THE
END OF THE AFFAIR, THE, 1955, A
END OF THE GAME, 1976, C-O
END OF THE GAME, THE, 1919, A
END OF THE LINE, THE, 1959, A-C
END OF THE RAINBOW, THE, 1916
END OF THE RIVER, THE, 1947, A
END OF THE ROAD, 1944, A
END OF THE ROAD, THE, 1915
END OF THE ROAD, THE, 1923
END OF THE ROAD, THE, 1936, A
END OF THE ROAD, THE, 1954, A
END OF THE ROPE, 1923
END OF THE TOUR, THE, 1917
END OF THE TRAIL, 1932, A
END OF THE TRAIL, 1936, A
END OF THE TRAIL, THE, 1916, A
END OF THE WORLD, 1977, C
END OF THE WORLD, 1978, C
END OF THE WORLD, THE, 1930, A
END OF THE WORLD, THE, 1962
END PLAY, 1975, C
END, THE, 1978, O
ENDANGERED SPECIES, 1982, O
ENDGAME, 1984
ENDLESS LOVE, 1981, O
ENDLESS NIGHT, 1971, C
ENDLESS NIGHT, THE, 1963, C
ENDSTATION 13 SAHARA
ENEMIES OF CHILDREN, 1923, A
ENEMIES OF PROGRESS, 1934, A
ENEMIES OF THE LAW, 1931, A
ENEMIES OF WOMEN, THE, 1923, A
ENEMIES OF YOUTH, 1925, A
ENEMY AGENT, 1940
ENEMY AGENTS MEET ELLERY QUEEN, 1942, A
ENEMY BELOW, THE, 1957, A
ENEMY FROM SPACE, 1957, A
ENEMY GENERAL, THE, 1960, A
ENEMY OF MEN, AN, 1925, A
ENEMY OF THE LAW, 1945, A
ENEMY OF THE PEOPLE, AN, 1978, A
ENEMY OF THE POLICE, 1933, A
ENEMY OF WOMEN, 1944, C
ENEMY SEX, THE, 1924, A
ENEMY TO SOCIETY, AN, 1915
ENEMY TO THE KING, AN, 1916
ENEMY, THE
ENEMY, THE, 1916
ENEMY, THE, 1927, C
ENEMY, THE SEA, THE
ENERGETIC EVA, 1916
ENFORCER FROM DEATH ROW, THE, 1978
ENFORCER, THE, 1951, C
ENFORCER, THE, 1976, O
ENGAGEMENT ITALIANO, 1966
ENGINEER PRITE'S PROJECT, 1918
ENGLANO MADE ME, 1973, C
ENGLISH WITHOUT TEARS
ENGLISHMAN'S HOME, AN
ENGLISHMAN'S HONOUR, AN, 1915
ENIGMA, 1983, C
ENJO, 1959, O
ENLIGHTEN THY DAUGHTER, 1917
ENLIGHTEN THY DAUGHTER, 1934, A
ENOCH ARDEN, 1914
ENOCH ARDEN, 1915
ENOUGH ROPE, 1966
ENSIGN PULVER, 1964, A
ENTENTE CORDIALE, 1939, A
ENTER ARSENE LUPIN, 1944, A
ENTER INSPECTOR DUVAL, 1961
ENTER LAUGHING, 1967, A
ENTER MADAME, 1922, A
ENTER MADAME, 1935, A
ENTER THE DEVIL, 1975
ENTER THE DRAGON, 1973, O
ENTER THE NINJA, 1982, O
ENTERTAINER, THE, 1960, A
ENTERTAINER, THE, 1975, A-C
ENTERTAINING MR. SLOANE, 1970, O
ENTICEMENT, 1925
ENTITY, THE, 1982, O
ENTRE NOUS, 1983, C
ENVIRONMENT, 1917
ENVIRONMENT, 1922, A
ENVOY EXTRAORDINARY, THE, 1914
ENVY, 1917, A
EPILOGUE, 1967, A
EPISODE, 1937, A
EQUINOX, 1970, C-O
"E QUUS", 1977, O
ER LOVE A STRANGER, 1958, A
ER WAVE AT A WAC, 1952, A
ERASERHEAD, 1978, O
ERASMUS WITH FRECKLES
ERENDIRA, 1984, O
ERIC SOYA'S "17", 1967, O
ERIK THE CONQUEROR, 1963, C
ERMINE AND RHINESTONES, 1925
ERNEST HEMINGWAY'S ADVENTURES OF A YOUNG MAN
ERNEST HEMINGWAY'S THE KILLERS, 1964
ERNEST MALTRAVERS, 1920
ERNEST MALTRAVERS, 1920, A
ERNESTO, 1979, O
EROICA, 1966, C
EROTIKON, 1920
EROTIKON, 1929
EROTIQUE, 1969, C
ERRAND BOY, THE, 1961, A
ERSTWHILE SUSAN, 1919, A
ESCAPADE, 1932, A
ESCAPADE, 1935, A
ESCAPADE, 1955, A
ESCAPADE IN JAPAN, 1957, A
ESCAPE, 1930, A
ESCAPE, 1940, A
ESCAPE, 1948, A
ESCAPE 2000, 1983, 0
ESCAPE ARTIST, THE, 1982, C
ESCAPE BY NIGHT, 1937, A
ESCAPE BY NIGHT, 1954, A-C
ESCAPE BY NIGHT, 1965, C
ESCAPE DANGEROUS, 1947, A
ESCAPE FROM ALCATRAZ, 1979, C
ESCAPE FROM ANGOLA, 1976
ESCAPE FROM CRIME, 1942, A
ESCAPE FROM DEVIL'S ISLAND, 1935, A
ESCAPE FROM EAST BERLIN, 1962, A
ESCAPE FROM EL DIABLO, 1983
ESCAPE FROM FORT BRAVO, 1953, A
ESCAPE FROM HELL ISLAND
ESCAPE FROM HONG KONG, 1942, A
ESCAPE FROM NEW YORK, 1981, O
ESCAPE FROM RED ROCK, 1958, A
ESCAPE FROM SAN QUENTIN, 1957, A
ESCAPE FROM SEGOVIA, 1984, C
ESCAPE FROM TERROR, 1960, A
ESCAPE FROM THE DARK
ESCAPE FROM THE PLANET OF THE APES, 1971, C
ESCAPE FROM THE SEA, 1968, AA
ESCAPE FROM YESTERDAY, 1939, A
ESCAPE FROM ZAHRAIN, 1962, A
ESCAPE IN THE DESERT, 1945, A
ESCAPE IN THE FOG, 1945, A
ESCAPE IN THE SUN, 1956, A
ESCAPE LIBRE
ESCAPE ME NEVER, 1935, A
ESCAPE ME NEVER, 1947, A
ESCAPE ROUTE
ESCAPE TO ATHENA, 1979, C
ESCAPE TO BERLIN, 1962, A
ESCAPE TO BURMA, 1955, A
ESCAPE TO DANGER, 1943, A
ESCAPE TO GLORY, 1940, A

ESCAPE TO PARADISE, 1939, A
ESCAPE TO THE SUN, 1972, C
ESCAPE TO WITCH MOUNTAIN, 1975, AA
ESCAPE 2000, 1983, O
ESCAPE, THE, 1914, C
ESCAPE, THE, 1926
ESCAPE, THE, 1928, A
ESCAPE, THE, 1939, A
ESCAPED CONVICT, THE, 1927
ESCAPED FROM DARTMOOR, 1930, C
ESCORT FOR HIRE, 1960, A-C
ESCORT WEST, 1959, A
ESMERALDA, 1915, A
ESPIONAGE, 1937, A
ESPIONAGE AGENT, 1939, A
ESSANAY-CHAPLIN REVUE OF 1916, THE, 1916
ESSENTIAL SPARK OF JEWISHNESS, THE, 1912
ESTHER AND THE KING, 1960, A
ESTHER REDEEMED, 1915
ESTHER WATERS, 1948, C
ETERNAL CITY, THE, 1915, A
ETERNAL CITY, THE, 1923
ETERNAL FEMININE, THE, 1931
ETERNAL FLAME, THE, 1922
ETERNAL GRIND, THE, 1916, A
ETERNAL HUSBAND, THE, 1946, C
ETERNAL LIGHT, THE, 1919
ETERNAL LOVE, 1917, A
ETERNAL LOVE, 1929, A
ETERNAL LOVE, 1960, A
ETERNAL MAGDALENE, THE, 1919, A
ETERNAL MASK, THE, 1937, A-C
ETERNAL MELODIES, 1948, A
ETERNAL MOTHER, THE, 1917
ETERNAL MOTHER, THE, 1921
ETERNAL PEACE, 1922
ETERNAL QUESTION, THE, 1916
ETERNAL RETURN, THE, 1943, A
ETERNAL SAPHO, THE, 1916, A
ETERNAL SEA, THE, 1955, A
ETERNAL SIN, THE, 1917, C
ETERNAL STRUGGLE, THE, 1923, A
ETERNAL SUMMER, 1961, A
ETERNAL TEMPTRESS, THE, 1917, A
ETERNAL THREE, THE, 1923, A
ETERNAL TRIANGLE, THE, 1917
ETERNAL WALTZ, THE, 1959, A
ETERNAL WOMAN, THE, 1929, A
ETERNALLY YOURS, 1939, A
ETERNITY OF LOVE, 1961, C
ETHAN, 1971
ETRE AIME POUR SOI-MEME, 1920
ETRE OU NE PAS ETRE, 1922
EUGENE ARAM, 1914, A
EUGENE ARAM, 1915, A
EUGENE ARAM, 1924
EUNION, 1936, A
EUREKA, 1983, O
EUREKA STOCKADE
EUROPE 51
EUROPEANS, THE, 1979, A
EVA, 1918
EVA, 1962, O
EVANGELINE, 1914
EVANGELINE, 1919
EVANGELINE, 1929, A
EVANGELINE, 1929, A
EVANGELIST, THE, 1915
EVE, 1968, A
EVE IN EXILE, 1919
EVE KNEW HER APPLES, 1945, A
EVE OF ST. MARK, THE, 1944, A-C
EVE WANTS TO SLEEP, 1961, A
EVE'S DAUGHTER, 1918, A
EVE'S DAUGHTER, 1916, Brit.
EVE'S LEAVES, 1926
EVE'S LOVER, 1925, A
EVE'S SECRET, 1925, A
EVEL KNIEVEL, 1971
EVELYN PRENTICE, 1934, C
EVEN AS EVE, 1920
EVEN AS YOU AND I, 1917, A
EVEN BREAK, AN, 1917
EVENING CLOTHES, 1927, A
EVENINGS FOR SALE, 1932, A
EVENSONG, 1934, A
EVENT, AN, 1970, C
EVENTS, 1970, O
EVER IN MY HEART, 1933, C
EVER SINCE EVE, 1921
EVER SINCE EVE, 1934, A
EVER SINCE EVE, 1937, A
EVER SINCE VENUS, 1944, A
EVERGREEN, 1934, A
EVERLASTING WHISPER, THE, 1925
EVERY BASTARD A KING, 1968, C
EVERY DAY IS A HOLIDAY, 1966, A
EVERY DAY'S A HOLIDAY, 1938, A
EVERY DAY'S A HOLIDAY, 1965
EVERY DAY'S A HOLIDAY, 1954
EVERY GIRL SHOULD BE MARRIED, 1948, A
EVERY GIRL'S DREAM, 1917
EVERY HOME SHOULD HAVE ONE
EVERY LITTLE CROOK AND NANNY, 1972, C
EVERY MAN A KING
EVERY MAN FOR HIMSELF, 1980, O
EVERY MAN FOR HIMSELF AND GOD AGAINST ALL, 1975, A
EVERY MAN'S WIFE, 1925, A
EVERY MOTHER'S SON, 1919
EVERY MOTHER'S SON, 1926, C
EVERY NIGHT AT EIGHT, 1935, A
EVERY PICTURE TELLS A STORY, 1984, C
EVERY SATURDAY NIGHT, 1936, A
EVERY SPARROW MUST FALL, 1964, C
EVERY WHICH WAY BUT LOOSE, 1978
EVERY WOMAN'S PROBLEM, 1921, A
EVERYBODY DANCE, 1936, A
EVERYBODY DOES IT, 1949, A
EVERYBODY GO HOME!, 1962
EVERYBODY SING, 1938, A
EVERYBODY'S ACTING, 1926
EVERYBODY'S BABY, 1939, A
EVERYBODY'S DANCIN', 1950, A
EVERYBODY'S DOING IT, 1938, A
EVERYBODY'S GIRL, 1918, A
EVERYBODY'S HOBBY, 1939
EVERYBODY'S OLD MAN, 1936, A
EVERYBODY'S SWEETHEART, 1920, A
EVERYDAY, 1976
EVERYMAN'S LAW, 1936, A
EVERYMAN'S PRICE, 1921, A
EVERYTHING BUT THE TRUTH, 1920
EVERYTHING BUT THE TRUTH, 1956, AA
EVERYTHING FOR SALE, 1921
EVERYTHING HAPPENS AT NIGHT, 1939, A
EVERYTHING HAPPENS TO ME, 1938, A
EVERYTHING I HAVE IS YOURS, 1952, A
EVERYTHING IN LIFE, 1936, A
EVERYTHING IS RHYTHM, 1940, A
EVERYTHING IS THUNDER, 1936, A
EVERYTHING OKAY, 1936
EVERYTHING YOU ALWAYS WANTED TO KNOW ABOUT SEX, BUT WERE AFRAID TO ASK
EVERYTHING'S DUCKY, 1961, A
EVERYTHING'S ON ICE, 1939, A
EVERYTHING'S ROSIE, 1931, A
EVERYWOMAN, 1919
EVERYWOMAN'S HUSBAND, 1918
EVICTORS, THE, 1979, O
EVIDENCE, 1915, A
EVIDENCE, 1918, A
EVIDENCE, 1922
EVIDENCE, 1929, A
EVIDENCE OF POWER, 1979
EVIL COME, EVIL GO
EVIL DEAD, THE, 1983, O
EVIL EYE, 1964
EVIL EYE OF KALINOR, THE, 1934
EVIL EYE, THE, 1917
EVIL FINGERS, 1975
EVIL GUN
EVIL IN THE DEEP
EVIL MIND
EVIL OF FRANKENSTEIN, THE, 1964, A
EVIL THAT MEN DO, THE
EVIL THAT MEN DO, THE, 1984, O
EVIL THEREOF, THE, 1916
EVIL UNDER THE SUN, 1982, A
EVIL WOMEN DO, THE, 1916
EVIL, THE, 1978, O
EVILS OF THE NIGHT, 1983
EVILSPEAK, 1982, O
EX-BAD BOY, 1931, A
EX-CHAMP, 1939, A
EX-FLAME, 1931, A
EX-LADY, 1933, A
EX-MRS. BRADFORD, THE, 1936
EXALTED FLAPPER, THE, 1929, A
EXCALIBUR, 1981, C-O
EXCESS BAGGAGE, 1928, A
EXCESS BAGGAGE, 1933, A
EXCHANGE OF WIVES, 1925
EXCITEMENT, 1924, A
EXCITERS, THE, 1923, A
EXCLUSIVE, 1937, A
EXCLUSIVE RIGHTS, 1926
EXCLUSIVE STORY, 1936, A
EXCUSE ME, 1916
EXCUSE ME, 1925
EXCUSE MY DUST, 1920, A
EXCUSE MY DUST, 1951, AAA
EXCUSE MY GLOVE, 1936, A
EXECUTIONER PART II, THE, 1984, O
EXECUTIONER, THE, 1970, C
EXECUTIVE ACTION, 1973, C
EXECUTIVE SUITE, 1954, A
EXILE, 1917
EXILE EXPRESS, 1939, A
EXILE, THE, 1931, C-O
EXILE, THE, 1947
EXILED TO SHANGHAI, 1937, A
EXILES, THE, 1923, A
EXILES, THE, 1966
EXIT SMILING, 1926, A
EXIT THE DRAGON, ENTER THE TIGER, 1977, O
EXIT THE VAMP, 1921, A
EXODUS, 1960, C
EXORCISM AT MIDNIGHT, 1966, C-O
EXORCISM'S DAUGHTER, 1974, O
EXORCIST II: THE HERETIC, 1977, O
EXORCIST, THE, 1973, O
EXOTIC ONES, THE, 1968, O
EXPENSIVE HUSBANDS, 1937, A
EXPENSIVE WOMEN, 1931, C
EXPERIENCE, 1921
EXPERIENCE PREFERRED... BUT NOT ESSENTIAL, 1983, C
EXPERIMENT ALCATRAZ, 1950, A
EXPERIMENT IN TERROR, 1962, C
EXPERIMENT PERILOUS, 1944
EXPERIMENT, THE, 1922, A
EXPERIMENTAL MARRIAGE, 1919
EXPERT'S OPINION, 1935, A
EXPERT, THE, 1932, A
EXPIATION, 1918
EXPIATION, 1922
EXPLOSION, 1969, O
EXPLOSIVE GENERATION, THE, 1961, C
EXPOSED, 1932, A
EXPOSED, 1938, A
EXPOSED, 1947, A
EXPOSED, 1983, O
EXPOSURE, 1932
EXPRESSO BONGO, 1959, C
EXQUISIT THIEF, THE, 1919
EXQUISITE SINNER, THE, 1926, A
EXTERMINATING ANGEL, THE, 1967, O
EXTERMINATOR 2, 1984, O
EXTERMINATOR, THE, 1980, O
EXTERMINATORS, THE, 1965, A-C
EXTORTION, 1938, A
EXTRA DAY, THE, 1956, A
EXTRA EXTRA, 1922
EXTRA GIRL, THE, 1923, A
EXTRAORDINARY ADVENTURES OF MR. WEST IN THE LAND OF THE BOLSHEVIKS (1924, USSR)
EXTRAORDINARY SEAMAN, THE, 1969, A
EXTRAVAGANCE, 1916
EXTRAVAGANCE, 1919, A
EXTRAVAGANCE, 1921
EXTRAVAGANCE, 1930, A
EXTREME CLOSE-UP, 1973
EYE CREATURES, THE, 1965, A-C
EYE FOR AN EYE, AN, 1915
EYE FOR AN EYE, AN, 1966
EYE FOR AN EYE, AN, 1975
EYE FOR AN EYE, AN, 1981, O
EYE FOR EYE, 1918, A
EYE OF ENVY, THE, 1917
EYE OF GOD, THE, 1916
EYE OF THE CAT, 1969, C
EYE OF THE DEVIL, 1967, C
EYE OF THE NEEDLE, 1981, C-O
EYE OF THE NEEDLE, THE, 1965, C
EYE OF THE NIGHT, THE, 1916, A
EYE WITNESS, 1950, A-C
EYEBALL, 1978, O
EYES BEHIND THE STARS, 1972
EYES IN THE NIGHT, 1942, A
EYES OF A STRANGER, 1980, O
EYES OF ANNIE JONES, THE, 1963, A
EYES OF FATE, 1933, A
EYES OF FIRE, 1984, O
EYES OF HELL
EYES OF HOLLYWOOD, 1925
EYES OF JULIA DEEP, THE, 1918, A
EYES OF LAURA MARS, 1978, 0
EYES OF MYSTERY, THE, 1918
EYES OF TEXAS, 1948, A
EYES OF THE AMARYLLIS, THE, 1982, A-C
EYES OF THE DESERT, 1926
EYES OF THE FOREST, 1923
EYES OF THE HEART, 1920, A
EYES OF THE JUNGLE, 1953
EYES OF THE SOUL, 1919
EYES OF THE TOTEM, 1927
EYES OF THE UNDERWORLD, 1929, A
EYES OF THE UNDERWORLD, 1943, A
EYES OF THE WORLD, THE, 1917
EYES OF THE WORLD, THE, 1930, C
EYES OF YOUTH, 1919
EYES RIGHT, 1926, A
EYES THAT KILL, 1947, A
EYES WITHOUT A FACE
EYES, THE MOUTH, THE, 1982
EYES, THE SEA AND A BALL, 1968, A

EYEWITNESS, 1956, A
EYEWITNESS, 1981, O
EYEWITNESS, 1970

-F-

F MAN, 1936, A
F.I.S.T., 1978, A-C
F.J. HOLDEN, THE, 1977, O
F.P. 1, 1933
F.P. 1 DOESN'T ANSWER, 1933, A
FABIAN OF THE YARD, 1954, A
FABIENNE, 1920
FABIOLA, 1923
FABIOLA, 1951, A-C
FABLE, A, 1971, O
FABULOUS ADVENTURES OF MARCO POLO, THE
FABULOUS BARON MUNCHAUSEN, THE
FABULOUS DORSEYS, THE, 1947, A
FABULOUS JOE, THE, 1946
FABULOUS SENORITA, THE, 1952, A
FABULOUS SUZANNE, THE, 1946, A
FABULOUS TEXAN, THE, 1947, A
FABULOUS WORLD OF JULES VERNE, THE, 1961, AA
FACE A L'OCEAN, 1920
FACE AT THE WINDOW, THE, 1920, A
FACE AT THE WINDOW, THE, 1932, C
FACE AT THE WINDOW, THE, 1939, C
FACE AT YOUR WINDOW, 1920
FACE BEHIND THE MASK, THE, 1941, C
FACE BEHIND THE SCAR, 1940, A
FACE BETWEEN, THE, 1922
FACE IN THE CROWD, A, 1957, C
FACE IN THE DARK, 1918
FACE IN THE FOG, 1922
FACE IN THE FOG, A, 1936, A
FACE IN THE NIGHT
FACE IN THE RAIN, A, 1963, A
FACE IN THE SKY, 1933, A
FACE OF A FUGITIVE, 1959, A
FACE OF A STRANGER, 1964, A-C
FACE OF ANOTHER, THE, 1967, O
FACE OF EVE, THE
FACE OF EVIL
FACE OF FEAR
FACE OF FEAR, 1964
FACE OF FIRE, 1959, C
FACE OF FU MANCHU, THE, 1965, O
FACE OF MARBLE, THE, 1946, A
FACE OF TERROR, 1964, C
FACE OF THE SCREAMING WEREWOLF, 1959, A
FACE OF THE WORLD, 1921
FACE ON THE BARROOM FLOOR, THE, 1923
FACE ON THE BARROOM FLOOR, THE, 1932, A
FACE TO FACE, 1920
FACE TO FACE, 1952, A
FACE TO FACE, 1967, O
FACE TO FACE, 1976, O
FACE TO THE WIND
FACE VALUE, 1918
FACE VALUE, 1927
FACE, THE
FACELESS MAN, THE
FACELESS MEN, THE
FACELESS MONSTERS
FACES, 1934, A
FACES, 1968, O
FACES IN THE DARK, 1960, A
FACES IN THE FOG, 1944, A
FACES OF CHILDREN
FACING THE MUSIC, 1933
FACING THE MUSIC, 1941, A
FACTORY MAGDALEN, A, 1914, A
FACTS OF LIFE, THE
FACTS OF LIFE, THE, 1960, A
FACTS OF LOVE, 1949, A
FACTS OF MURDER, THE, 1965, O
FADE TO BLACK, 1980
FADE-IN, 1968
FADED FLOWER, THE, 1916
FAGASA, 1928
FAHRENHEIT 451, 1966, C
FAIL SAFE, 1964, C
FAILURE, THE
FAILURE, THE, 1915
FAINT PERFUME, 1925
FAIR AND WARMER, 1919
FAIR BARBARIAN, THE, 1917
FAIR CHEAT, THE, 1923
FAIR CO-ED, THE, 1927, A
FAIR ENOUGH, 1918, A
FAIR EXCHANGE, 1936, A
FAIR IMPOSTER, A, 1916
FAIR LADY, 1922
FAIR MAID OF PERTH, THE, 1923
FAIR PLAY, 1925, A
FAIR PRETENDER, THE, 1918, A
FAIR WARNING, 1931, A
FAIR WARNING, 1937, A
FAIR WEEK, 1924
FAIR WIND TO JAVA, 1953, A
FAIRY AND THE WAIF, THE, 1915
FAIRY TALES, 1979
FAITH
FAITH, 1916
FAITH, 1919
FAITH, 1920, A
FAITH AND ENDURIN', 1918
FAITH AND FORTUNE, 1915
FAITH FOR GOLD, 1930
FAITH HEALER, THE, 1921, A
FAITH OF A CHILD, THE, 1915
FAITH OF THE STRONG, 1919
FAITHFUL, 1936, A
FAITHFUL CITY, 1952, A
FAITHFUL HEART, 1933, A
FAITHFUL HEART, THE
FAITHFUL HEART, THE, 1922
FAITHFUL HEARTS
FAITHFUL IN MY FASHION, 1946, A
FAITHFUL WIVES, 1926
FAITHLESS, 1932
FAITHLESS LOVER, 1928
FAITHLESS SEX, THE, 1922
FAKE'S PROGRESS, 1950, A
FAKE, THE, 1927, C
FAKE, THE, 1953, A
FAKE-OUT, 1982
FAKER, THE, 1929
FAKERS, THE
FAKING OF THE PRESIDENT, THE, 1976
FALCON AND THE CO-EDS, THE, 1943, A
FALCON FIGHTERS, THE, 1970, C
FALCON IN DANGER, THE, 1943, A
FALCON IN HOLLYWOOD, THE, 1944, A
FALCON IN MEXICO, THE, 1944, A
FALCON IN SAN FRANCISCO, THE, 1945, A
FALCON OUT WEST, THE, 1944
FALCON STRIKES BACK, THE, 1943, A
FALCON TAKES OVER, THE, 1942, A
FALCON'S ADVENTURE, THE, 1946, A
FALCON'S ALIBI, THE, 1946, A
FALCON'S BROTHER, THE, 1942, A
FALCON'S GOLD, 1982
FALL GIRL, THE
FALL GUY, 1947, C
FALL GUY, THE
FALL GUY, THE, 1930, A
FALL OF A NATION, THE, 1916
FALL OF A SAINT, THE, 1920
FALL OF EVE, THE, 1929, A
FALL OF ROME, THE, 1963, C
FALL OF THE HOUSE OF USHER, THE
FALL OF THE HOUSE OF USHER, THE, 1928
FALL OF THE HOUSE OF USHER, THE, 1952, C
FALL OF THE HOUSE OF USHER, THE, 1980, O
FALL OF THE ROMAN EMPIRE, THE, 1964, O
FALL OF THE ROMANOFFS, THE, 1917
FALLEN ANGEL, 1945, A
FALLEN ANGEL, THE, 1918
FALLEN ANGELS
FALLEN IDOL, A, 1919
FALLEN IDOL, THE, 1949, A
FALLEN SPARROW, THE, 1943, C
FALLEN STAR, A, 1916
FALLGUY, 1962
FALLING FOR YOU, 1933
FALLING IN LOVE
FALLING IN LOVE, 1984, C
FALLING IN LOVE AGAIN, 1980, C
FALLS, THE, 1980
FALSE ALARM, THE, 1926
FALSE AMBITION, 1918
FALSE BRANDS, 1922, A
FALSE CODE, THE, 1919
FALSE COLORS, 1914, A
FALSE COLORS, 1943, A
FALSE EVIDENCE, 1919, A
FALSE EVIDENCE, 1922, A
FALSE EVIDENCE, 1937, A-C
FALSE FACE
FALSE FACES, 1919, A
FALSE FACES, 1932, A
FALSE FACES, 1943, A
FALSE FATHERS, 1929, A
FALSE FRIEND, THE, 1917, A
FALSE FRIENDS, 1926
FALSE FRONTS, 1922
FALSE GODS, 1919
FALSE KISSES, 1921
FALSE MADONNA, 1932, A
FALSE MAGISTRATE, THE, 1914
FALSE MORALS, 1927
FALSE PARADISE, 1948, A
FALSE PLAY
FALSE PRETENSES, 1935, A
FALSE PRIDE, 1926
FALSE RAPTURE, 1941, A
FALSE ROAD, THE, 1920
FALSE SHAME
FALSE TRAILS, 1924
FALSE WIRELESS, THE, 1914
FALSE WITNESS
FALSE WOMEN, 1921
FALSTAFF
FAME, 1936, A
FAME, 1980, C
FAME AND FORTUNE, 1918, A
FAME IS THE SPUR, 1947, A
FAME STREET, 1932, A
FAMILY AFFAIR, 1954
FAMILY AFFAIR, A, 1937, AAA
FAMILY CLOSET, THE, 1921
FAMILY CUPBOARD, THE, 1915, A
FAMILY DIARY, 1963, A
FAMILY DOCTOR
FAMILY ENFORCER, 1978
FAMILY GAME, THE, 1984, C
FAMILY HONEYMOON, 1948, A
FAMILY HONOR, 1973, O
FAMILY HONOR, THE, 1917
FAMILY HONOR, THE, 1920
FAMILY JEWELS, THE, 1965, A
FAMILY KILLER, 1975
FAMILY LIFE, 1971, O
FAMILY NEXT DOOR, THE, 1939, A
FAMILY PLOT, 1976, C
FAMILY SECRET, THE, 1924, A
FAMILY SECRET, THE, 1951, A
FAMILY SKELETON, THE, 1918, A
FAMILY STAIN, THE, 1915
FAMILY UPSTAIRS, THE, 1926
FAMILY WAY, THE, 1966, O
FAMILY, THE, 1974, O
FAMILY—PART TWO, 1978, AAA
FAMOUS FERGUSON CASE, THE, 1932, A
FAMOUS MRS. FAIR, THE, 1923
FAN FAN, 1918
FAN'S NOTES, A, 1972, C
FAN, THE, 1949, A
FAN, THE, 1981, C-O
FANATIC
FANATIC, THE
FANATICS, 1917
FANCHON THE CRICKET, 1915, A
FANCY BAGGAGE, 1929, A
FANCY DRESS, 1919, A
FANCY PANTS, 1950, A
FANDANGO, 1970, O
FANFAN THE TULIP, 1952, A
FANGELSE
FANGS, 1974
FANGS OF DESTINY, 1927
FANGS OF FATE, 1925
FANGS OF FATE, 1928
FANGS OF JUSTICE, 1926, A
FANGS OF THE ARCTIC, 1953, A
FANGS OF THE WILD, 1928, A
FANGS OF THE WILD, 1954, A
FANGS OF THE WOLF, 1924
FANGS OF WOLFHEART, 1925
FANNY, 1948, A-C
FANNY, 1961, A-C
FANNY AND ALEXANDER, 1983, C-O
FANNY BY GASLIGHT
FANNY FOLEY HERSELF, 1931, A
FANNY HAWTHORNE, 1927
FANNY HILL: MEMOIRS OF A WOMAN OF PLEASURE, 1965, O
FANTAISIE DE MILLARDAIRE, 1919
FANTASIA, 1940, AAA
FANTASIES, 1981, O
FANTASM, 1976, O
FANTASMA, 1914
FANTASTIC COMEDY, A, 1975, C
FANTASTIC INVASION OF THE PLANET EARTH, THE
FANTASTIC INVENTION, THE
FANTASTIC PLANET, 1973, A
FANTASTIC THREE, THE, 1967, A
FANTASTIC VOYAGE, 1966, A
FANTASTICA, 1980, C-O
FANTASY MAN, 1984, C
FANTOMAS, 1966
FANTOMAS STRIKES BACK, 1965, A
FANTOMAS, THE CROOK DETECTIVE, 1914
FANTOMAS, THE FALSE MAGISTRATE
FAR CALL, THE, 1929, A
FAR COUNTRY, THE, 1955, A
FAR CRY, THE, 1926, A
FAR FROM DALLAS, 1972, C
FAR FROM POLAND, 1984, C
FAR FROM THE MADDING CROWD, 1915, A
FAR FROM THE MADDING CROWD, 1967
FAR FRONTIER, THE, 1949, A
FAR HORIZONS, THE, 1955, A
FAR SHORE, THE, 1976, O
FAR WESTERN TRAILS, 1929

FARARUV KONEC
FAREWELL AGAIN
FAREWELL PERFORMANCE, 1963, A-C
FAREWELL TO ARMS, A, 1932, A
FAREWELL TO ARMS, A, 1957, C
FAREWELL TO CINDERELLA, 1937, A
FAREWELL TO LOVE, 1931, A
FAREWELL, DOVES, 1962
FAREWELL, FRIEND, 1968, O
FAREWELL, MY BELOVED, 1969, O
FAREWELL, MY LOVELY, 1975, C-O
FAREWELL, MY LOVELY, 1944
FARGO, 1952, A
FARGO EXPRESS, 1933, A
FARGO KID, THE, 1941, A
FARGO, 1964
FARM GIRL
FARMER IN THE DELL, THE, 1936
FARMER TAKES A WIFE, THE, 1935, A
FARMER TAKES A WIFE, THE, 1953, A
FARMER'S DAUGHTER, THE, 1928
FARMER'S DAUGHTER, THE, 1940, A
FARMER'S DAUGHTER, THE, 1947, AA
FARMER'S OTHER DAUGHTER, THE, 1965, A
FARMER'S WIFE, THE, 1928, A
FARMER'S WIFE, THE, 1941, A
FARMER, THE, 1977, O
FASCINATING YOUTH, 1926
FASCINATION, 1922
FASCINATION, 1931
FASCIST, THE, 1965, A
FASHION HOUSE OF DEATH
FASHION MADNESS, 1928
FASHION MODEL, 1945, A
FASHION ROW, 1923
FASHIONABLE FAKERS, 1923
FASHIONS FOR WOMEN, 1927
FASHIONS IN LOVE, 1929, A-C
FASHIONS OF 1934, 1934, A
FAST AND FEARLESS, 1924
FAST AND FURIOUS, 1927
FAST AND FURIOUS, 1939
FAST AND LOOSE, 1930, A
FAST AND LOOSE, 1939, A
FAST AND LOOSE, 1954, A
FAST AND SEXY, 1960, A
FAST AND THE FURIOUS, THE, 1954, A
FAST BREAK, 1979, A
FAST BULLETS, 1936
FAST CHARLIE... THE MOONBEAM RIDER, 1979, C
FAST COMPANIONS, 1932, A
FAST COMPANY, 1918
FAST COMPANY, 1929, A
FAST COMPANY, 1938
FAST COMPANY, 1953, A
FAST COMPANY, 1979
FAST FIGHTIN', 1925
FAST KILL, 1973
FAST LADY, THE, 1963, A
FAST LIFE, 1929, A
FAST LIFE, 1932
FAST MAIL, THE, 1922
FAST ON THE DRAW, 1950, A
FAST SET, THE, 1924
FAST TIMES AT RIDGEMONT HIGH, 1982, O
FAST WORKER, THE, 1924
FAST WORKERS, 1933, A
FAST-WALKING, 1982, O
FASTEST GUITAR ALIVE, THE, 1967, A
FASTEST GUN ALIVE, 1956, A
FASTEST GUN, THE
FAT ANGELS, 1980, C
FAT CHANCE, 1982
FAT CITY, 1972, C
FAT MAN, THE, 1951
FAT SPY, 1966, A
FATAL 30, THE, 1921
FATAL DESIRE, 1953, C
FATAL FINGERS, 1916, A
FATAL GAMES, 1983
FATAL HOUR, THE, 1920
FATAL HOUR, THE, 1937, A
FATAL HOUR, THE, 1940, A
FATAL LADY, 1936
FATAL MARRIAGE, THE
FATAL MISTAKE, THE, 1924
FATAL NIGHT, THE, 1915
FATAL NIGHT, THE, 1948
FATAL PLUNGE, THE, 1924
FATAL WITNESS, THE, 1945
FATALNA KLATWA, 1913
FATE, 1921
FATE AND THE CHILD, 1917
FATE IS THE HUNTER, 1964, A
FATE OF A FLIRT, THE, 1925
FATE TAKES A HAND, 1962, A
FATE'S BOOMERANG, 1916
FATE'S PLAYTHING, 1920, A
FATHER, 1967, A
FATHER AND SON, 1916
FATHER AND SON, 1929, A
FATHER AND SON, 1934, A
FATHER AND THE BOYS, 1915
FATHER BROWN
FATHER BROWN, DETECTIVE, 1935, A
FATHER CAME TOO, 1964
FATHER DEAR FATHER, 1973
FATHER FROST, 1924
FATHER GOOSE, 1964, AAA
FATHER IS A BACHELOR, 1950, A
FATHER IS A PRINCE, 1940, A
FATHER MAKES GOOD, 1950, A
FATHER O'FLYNN, 1919, A
FATHER O'FLYNN, 1938, A
FATHER OF A SOLDIER, 1966, C
FATHER OF THE BRIDE, 1950, AA
FATHER SERGIUS, 1918
FATHER STEPS OUT, 1937, A
FATHER STEPS OUT, 1941
FATHER TAKES A WIFE, 1941, A
FATHER TAKES THE AIR, 1951, A
FATHER TOM, 1921
FATHER WAS A FULLBACK, 1949, A
FATHER'S DILEMMA, 1952, A
FATHER'S DOING FINE, 1952, A
FATHER'S LITTLE DIVIDEND, 1951
FATHER'S SON, 1931, A
FATHER'S SON, 1941, A
FATHER'S WILD GAME, 1950, A
FATHERHOOD, 1915
FATHERS AND SONS, 1960, A
FATHERS OF MEN, 1916
FATHOM, 1967, A
FATSO, 1980, A
FATTY FINN, 1980, A-C
FAUBOURG MONTMARTE, 1924
FAUSSES INGENUES
FAUST, 1922
FAUST, 1926, C
FAUST, 1963, A
FAUST, 1964, A
FAVOR TO A FRIEND, A, 1919
FAZIL, 1928
FBI CODE 98, 1964, A
FBI CONTRO DR. MABUSE
FBI GIRL, 1951
FBI STORY, THE, 1959, C
FEAR, 1946, C
FEAR, 1956, O
FEAR AND DESIRE, 1953, C
FEAR CHAMBER, THE, 1968, C
FEAR CITY, 1984, O
FEAR EATS THE SOUL, 1974, O
FEAR FIGHTER, THE, 1925
FEAR IN THE NIGHT, 1947, C-O
FEAR IN THE NIGHT, 1972, C
FEAR IS THE KEY, 1973, C
FEAR MARKET, THE, 1920
FEAR NO EVIL, 1981, O
FEAR NO MORE, 1961, C
FEAR NOT, 1917
FEAR O' GOD, 1926, A
FEAR O'GOD, 1926
FEAR SHIP, THE, 1933, A
FEAR STRIKES OUT, 1957, C
FEAR WOMAN, THE, 1919
FEAR, THE, 1967, O
FEAR-BOUND, 1925
FEARLESS DICK, 1922
FEARLESS FAGAN, 1952, AA
FEARLESS FRANK, 1967
FEARLESS LOVER, THE, 1925, A
FEARLESS RIDER, THE, 1928
FEARLESS VAMPIRE KILLERS, OR PARDON ME
FEARMAKERS, THE, 1958, A
FEAST OF FLESH
FEAST OF LIFE, THE, 1916
FEATHER IN HER HAT, A, 1935, A
FEATHER YOUR NEST, 1937, A
FEATHER, THE, 1929, A
FEATHERED SERPENT, THE, 1934, A
FEATHERED SERPENT, THE, 1948, A
FEATHERTOP, 1916
FECONDITE, 1929
FEDERAL AGENT, 1936, A
FEDERAL AGENT AT LARGE, 1950, A
FEDERAL BULLETS, 1937, A
FEDERAL FUGITIVES, 1941, A
FEDERAL MAN, 1950, A
FEDERAL MAN-HUNT, 1939, A
FEDERICO FELLINI'S 8 1/2
FEDORA, 1918
FEDORA, 1946, A
FEDORA, 1978, C
FEEDBACK, 1979, C
FEEL MY PULSE, 1928
FEELIN' GOOD, 1966, A
FEELIN' UP, 1983
FEET FIRST, 1930, A
FEET OF CLAY, 1917
FEET OF CLAY, 1924
FEET OF CLAY, 1960, A
FELIANA L'ESPIONNE, 1924
FELIX O'DAY, 1920
FELLER NEEDS A FRIEND, 1932, A
FELLINI SATYRICON, 1969, C-O
FELLINI'S CASANOVA
FELLINI'S ROMA
FEMALE, 1933, A
FEMALE ANIMAL, THE, 1958
FEMALE BUNCH, THE, 1969, O
FEMALE BUTCHER, THE, 1972, O
FEMALE FIENDS, 1958, A
FEMALE FUGITIVE, 1938, A
FEMALE JUNGLE, THE, 1955, C
FEMALE OF THE SPECIES, 1917, A
FEMALE ON THE BEACH, 1955, A-C
FEMALE PRINCE, THE, 1966, C
FEMALE PRISONER, THE
FEMALE RESPONSE, THE, 1972, O
FEMALE SWINDLER, THE, 1916
FEMALE TRAP, THE
FEMALE TROUBLE, 1975, O
FEMALE, THE, 1924
FEMALE, THE, 1960, C
FEMININE TOUCH, THE
FEMININE TOUCH, THE, 1941, A
FEMMES D'UN ETE
FEMMINA, 1968, C
FEMMINE DI LUSSO
FENCE RIDERS, 1950, A
FERN, THE RED DEER, 1977
FERNANDEL THE DRESSMAKER, 1957, A
FEROCIOUS PAL, 1934, AAA
FERRAGUS, 1923
FERRY ACROSS THE MERSEY, 1964, A
FERRY TO HONG KONG, 1959, A
FETTERED, 1919
FETTERED WOMAN, THE, 1917
FEU, 1927
FEU MATHIAS PASCAL
FEUD GIRL, THE, 1916
FEUD MAKER, 1938, A
FEUD OF THE RANGE, 1939, A
FEUD OF THE TRAIL, 1938
FEUD OF THE WEST, 1936, A
FEUD WOMAN, THE, 1926
FEUD, THE, 1919
FEUDIN' FOOLS, 1952, A
FEUDIN' RHYTHM, 1949
FEUDIN', FUSSIN' AND A-FIGHTIN', 1948, A
FEVER HEAT, 1968, A
FEVER IN THE BLOOD, A, 1961, A
FEW BULLETS MORE, A, 1968, A
FFOLKES, 1980, C
FIANCAILLES, 1926
FIANCES, THE, 1964, A
FIASCO IN MILAN, 1963, A
FIBBERS, THE, 1917
FICKLE FINGER OF FATE, THE, 1967, A
FICKLE WOMAN
FICKLE WOMEN, 1920, A
FIDDLER ON THE ROOF, 1971, AAA
FIDDLERS THREE, 1944, A
FIDDLIN' BUCKAROO, THE, 1934, A
FIDELIO, 1961, A
FIDELIO, 1970, A
FIDELITE, 1924
FIELD OF HONOR, THE, 1917
FIELD OF HONOR, THE, 1922, A
FIELDS OF HONOR
FIELDS OF HONOR, 1918
FIEND, 1980, O
FIEND OF DOPE ISLAND, 1961, C
FIEND WHO WALKED THE WEST, THE, 1958, O
FIEND WITH THE SYNTHETIC BRAIN
FIEND WITHOUT A FACE, 1958, C-O
FIEND, THE, 1971
FIENDISH GHOULS, THE
FIENDISH PLOT OF DR. FU MANCHU, THE, 1980, C
FIENDS OF HELL, 1914
FIENDS, THE
FIERCEST HEART, THE, 1961, A
FIERY SPUR
FIESTA, 1947, A
FIEVRE, 1921
15 FROM ROM
50,000 B.C. (BEFORE CLOTHING), 1963, O
52 MILES TO MIDNIGHT
52 MILES TO TERROR
52ND STREET, 1937, A
55 DAYS AT PEKING, 1963
FIFTEEN MAIDEN LANE, 1936, A
FIFTEEN WIVES, 1934, A
FIFTH AVENUE, 1926
FIFTH AVENUE GIRL, 1939, A
FIFTH AVENUE MODELS, 1925

FIFTH COMMANDMENT, THE, 1915
FIFTH COMMANDMENT, THE, 1927
FIFTH FLOOR, THE, 1980, O
FIFTH FORM AT ST. DOMINIC'S, THE, 1921
FIFTH HORSEMAN IS FEAR, THE, 1968, C
FIFTH HORSEMAN, THE, 1924
FIFTH MAN, THE, 1914
FIFTH MUSKETEER, THE
FIFTY CANDLES, 1921, A
FIFTY FATHOMS DEEP, 1931, A
FIFTY MILLION FRENCHMEN, 1931, AA
FIFTY ROADS TO TOWN, 1937, A
FIFTY-FIFTY, 1916
FIFTY-FIFTY, 1925
FIFTY-FIFTY GIRL, THE, 1928, A
FIFTY-SHILLING BOXER, 1937, A
FIG LEAVES, 1926
FIGARO, 1929
FIGHT FOR FREEDOM, A OR EXILED TO SIBERIA, 1914
FIGHT FOR HONOR, A, 1924
FIGHT FOR LIFE, THE, 1940
FIGHT FOR LOVE, A, 1919
FIGHT FOR MILLIONS, THE, 1913
FIGHT FOR ROME, 1969, A
FIGHT FOR THE 'ULTIMATUM' FACTORY, 1923
FIGHT FOR THE GLORY, 1970, C
FIGHT FOR YOUR LADY, 1937, A
FIGHT FOR YOUR LIFE Zero, 1977, O
FIGHT NEVER ENDS, THE, 1947
FIGHT TO THE FINISH, A, 1925
FIGHT TO THE FINISH, A, 1937, A
FIGHT TO THE LAST, 1938, C
FIGHT, THE, 1915
FIGHTER ATTACK, 1953, A
FIGHTER PILOTS, 1977
FIGHTER SQUADRON, 1948, A
FIGHTER'S PARADISE, 1924, A
FIGHTER, THE, 1921, A
FIGHTER, THE, 1952, A
FIGHTERS IN THE SADDLE
FIGHTERS OF THE SADDLE, 1929
FIGHTIN' COMEBACK, THE, 1927
FIGHTIN' DEVIL, 1922
FIGHTIN' MAD, 1921
FIGHTIN' ODDS, 1925
FIGHTIN' REDHEAD, THE, 1928
FIGHTIN' THRU, 1924
FIGHTING 69TH, THE, 1940, A
FIGHTING ACE, THE
FIGHTING AMERICAN, THE, 1924, A
FIGHTING BACK
FIGHTING BACK, 1917
FIGHTING BACK, 1948, A
FIGHTING BACK, 1983, C
FIGHTING BILL CARSON, 1945, A
FIGHTING BILL FARGO, 1942, A
FIGHTING BLACK KINGS, 1977
FIGHTING BLADE, THE, 1923
FIGHTING BOB, 1915, A
FIGHTING BOOB, THE, 1926, A
FIGHTING BREED, THE, 1921, A
FIGHTING BUCKAROO, THE, 1926
FIGHTING BUCKAROO, THE, 1943, A
FIGHTING CABALLERO, 1935, A
FIGHTING CARAVANS, 1931, A
FIGHTING CHAMP, 1933, A
FIGHTING CHANCE, THE, 1920
FIGHTING CHANCE, THE, 1955
FIGHTING CHEAT, THE, 1926, A
FIGHTING COAST GUARD, 1951, A
FIGHTING COBBLER, THE, 1915
FIGHTING CODE, THE, 1934, A
FIGHTING COLLEEN, A, 1919
FIGHTING COURAGE, 1925
FIGHTING COWARD, THE, 1924, A
FIGHTING COWBOY, 1930
FIGHTING COWBOY, 1933, A
FIGHTING CRESSY, 1919
FIGHTING CUB, THE, 1925, A
FIGHTING DEATH, 1914
FIGHTING DEMON, THE, 1925
FIGHTING DEPUTY, THE, 1937, A
FIGHTING DESTINY, 1919
FIGHTING DEVIL DOGS, 1938
FIGHTING DOCTOR, THE, 1926
FIGHTING EAGLE, THE, 1927
FIGHTING EDGE, 1926, A
FIGHTING EDGE, THE, 1926
FIGHTING FAILURE, THE, 1926
FIGHTING FATE, 1925
FIGHTING FATHER DUNNE, 1948, A
FIGHTING FOOL, THE, 1932, A
FIGHTING FOOLS, 1949, A
FIGHTING FOR GOLD, 1919
FIGHTING FOR JUSTICE, 1924
FIGHTING FOR JUSTICE, 1932
FIGHTING FOR LOVE, 1917, A
FIGHTING FRONTIER, 1943, AA
FIGHTING FRONTIERSMAN, THE, 1946
FIGHTING FURY
FIGHTING FURY, 1924
FIGHTING GENTLEMAN, THE, 1932, A
FIGHTING GOB, THE, 1926
FIGHTING GRIN, THE, 1918
FIGHTING GRINGO, THE, 1917
FIGHTING GRINGO, THE, 1939, A
FIGHTING GUARDSMAN, THE, 1945, A
FIGHTING GUIDE, THE, 1922
FIGHTING HEART, A, 1924
FIGHTING HEART, THE, 1925
FIGHTING HEARTS, 1922
FIGHTING HERO, 1934, A
FIGHTING HOMBRE, THE, 1927
FIGHTING HOPE, THE, 1915
FIGHTING JACK, 1926
FIGHTING JIM GRANT, 1923
FIGHTING KENTUCKIAN, THE, 1949, A
FIGHTING KENTUCKIANS, THE, 1920
FIGHTING KID, THE, 1922
FIGHTING LADY, 1935
FIGHTING LAWMAN, THE, 1953, A
FIGHTING LEGION, THE, 1930, A
FIGHTING LOVE, 1927
FIGHTING LOVER, THE, 1921
FIGHTING LUCK, 1926
FIGHTING MAD, 1917
FIGHTING MAD, 1939, A
FIGHTING MAD, 1948, A
FIGHTING MAD, 1957, A-C
FIGHTING MAD, 1976, C
FIGHTING MAN OF THE PLAINS, 1949, A
FIGHTING MARINE, THE, 1926
FIGHTING MARSHAL, THE, 1932, AA
FIGHTING MUSTANG, 1948
FIGHTING O'FLYNN, THE, 1949, A
FIGHTING ODDS, 1917, A
FIGHTING PARSON, THE, 1933, A
FIGHTING PEACEMAKER, THE, 1926
FIGHTING PILOT, THE, 1935
FIGHTING PIMPERNEL, THE, 1950, A
FIGHTING PIONEERS, 1935, A
FIGHTING PLAYBOY, 1937, A
FIGHTING PRINCE OF DONEGAL, THE, 1966, AAA
FIGHTING RANGER, 1926
FIGHTING RANGER, THE, 1922
FIGHTING RANGER, THE, 1934, A
FIGHTING RANGER, THE, 1948, A
FIGHTING REDHEAD, THE, 1950, A
FIGHTING RENEGADE, 1939, AA
FIGHTING ROMEO, THE, 1925
FIGHTING ROOKIE, THE, 1934, A
FIGHTING SAP, THE, 1924
FIGHTING SEABEES, THE, 1944, C
FIGHTING SHADOWS, 1935, A
FIGHTING SHEPHERDESS, THE, 1920
FIGHTING SHERIFF, THE, 1925
FIGHTING SHERIFF, THE, 1931, A
FIGHTING SMILE, THE, 1925, A
FIGHTING STALLION, THE, 1926
FIGHTING STALLION, THE, 1950, A
FIGHTING STOCK, 1935, A
FIGHTING STRAIN, THE, 1923
FIGHTING STRANGER, THE, 1921
FIGHTING STREAK, THE, 1922
FIGHTING SULLIVANS, THE
FIGHTING TERROR, THE, 1929, A
FIGHTING TEXAN, 1937, A
FIGHTING TEXANS, 1933, A
FIGHTING THE FLAMES, 1925
FIGHTING THOROBREDS, 1926
FIGHTING THOROUGHBREDS, 1939, A
FIGHTING THREE, THE, 1927
FIGHTING THROUGH, 1934
FIGHTING THRU, 1931, A
FIGHTING TO LIVE, 1934
FIGHTING TROOPER, THE, 1935, A
FIGHTING TROUBLE, 1956, A
FIGHTING VALLEY, 1943, A
FIGHTING VIGILANTES, THE, 1947, A
FIGHTING WILDCATS, THE, 1957, A-C
FIGHTING YOUTH, 1925
FIGHTING YOUTH, 1935, A
FIGUREHEAD, THE, 1920
FIGURES DON'T LIE, 1927
FIGURES IN A LANDSCAPE, 1970, C
FILE 113, 1932, A
FILE OF THE GOLDEN GOOSE, THE, 1969, C
FILE ON THELMA JORDAN, THE, 1950, A-C
FILES FROM SCOTLAND YARD, 1951, A
FILLE D'ARTISTE, 1916
FILLE DE RIEN, 1921
FILLING HIS OWN SHOES, 1917
FILM WITHOUT A NAME, 1950, A
FINAL APPOINTMENT, 1954, A
FINAL ASSIGNMENT, 1980, C
FINAL CHAPTER—WALKING TALL, 1977, O
FINAL CHORD, THE, 1936, C
FINAL CLOSEUP, THE, 1919
FINAL COLUMN, THE, 1955, A
FINAL COMEDOWN, THE, 1972, O
FINAL CONFLICT, THE, 1981, O
FINAL COUNTDOWN, THE, 1980, C
FINAL CURTAIN, THE, 1916, A
FINAL CUT, THE, 1980, O
FINAL EDITION, 1932, A
FINAL EXAM, 1981, O
FINAL EXTRA, THE, 1927
FINAL HOUR, THE, 1936, A
FINAL JUDGEMENT, THE, 1915
FINAL OPTION, THE, 1983, O
FINAL PAYMENT, THE, 1917
FINAL PROGRAMME, THE
FINAL RECKONING, THE, 1932, A
FINAL TERROR, THE, 1983, O
FINAL TEST, THE, 1953, A
FINAL WAR, THE, 1960, C
FINALLY SUNDAY
FINCHE DURA LA TEMPESTA
FIND THE BLACKMAILER, 1943, A
FIND THE LADY, 1936, A
FIND THE LADY, 1956, A
FIND THE WITNESS, 1937, A
FIND THE WOMAN, 1918
FIND THE WOMAN, 1922
FIND YOUR MAN, 1924
FINDERS KEEPERS, 1921
FINDERS KEEPERS, 1928
FINDERS KEEPERS, 1951, AA
FINDERS KEEPERS, 1966, A
FINDERS KEEPERS, 1984, C-O
FINDERS KEEPERS, LOVERS WEEPERS, 1968, O
FINE CLOTHES, 1925
FINE FEATHERS, 1915, A
FINE FEATHERS, 1915
FINE FEATHERS, 1921, A
FINE FEATHERS, 1937
FINE MADNESS, A, 1966, C
FINE MANNERS, 1926, A
FINE PAIR, A, 1969, C
FINGER MAN, 1955, A
FINGER OF GUILT, 1956, A
FINGER ON THE TRIGGER, 1965, A
FINGER POINTS, THE, 1931, C
FINGER PRINTS, 1923, A
FINGER PRINTS, 1927
FINGERMAN, THE, 1963, C
FINGERPRINTS DON'T LIE, 1951, A
FINGERS, 1940, A
FINGERS, 1978, O
FINGERS AT THE WINDOW, 1942, C
FINIAN'S RAINBOW, 1968
FINISHING SCHOOL, 1934, A
FINN AND HATTIE, 1931, A
FINNEGAN'S BALL, 1927, A
FINNEGANS WAKE, 1965, A
FINNEY, 1969, A
FINNIS TERRAE, 1929
FINO A FARTI MALE, 1969, O
FIRE AND ICE, 1983, C
FIRE AND STEEL, 1927
FIRE AND SWORD, 1914, A
FIRE AND SWORD, 1982
FIRE BRIDE, THE, 1922
FIRE BRIGADE, THE, 1926
FIRE CAT, THE, 1921
FIRE DOWN BELOW, 1957, C
FIRE EATER, THE, 1921
FIRE FLINGERS, THE, 1919
FIRE HAS BEEN ARRANGED, A, 1935, A
FIRE IN THE FLESH, 1964, A
FIRE IN THE STONE, THE, 1983, AA
FIRE IN THE STRAW, 1943, A
FIRE MAIDENS FROM OUTER SPACE, 1956, A
FIRE OVER AFRICA, 1954, A
FIRE OVER ENGLAND, 1937
FIRE PATROL, THE, 1924
FIRE RAISERS, THE, 1933
FIRE SALE, 1977, A-C
FIRE WITHIN, THE, 1964, O
FIREBALL 590, 1966, A
FIREBALL JUNGLE, 1968, C
FIREBALL, THE, 1950, A
FIREBIRD 2015 AD, 1981, O
FIREBIRD, THE, 1934, A
FIREBRAND JORDAN, 1930, A
FIREBRAND TREVISON, 1920
FIREBRAND, THE, 1918
FIREBRAND, THE, 1922
FIREBRAND, THE, 1962, C
FIREBRANDS OF ARIZONA, 1944, A
FIRECHASERS, THE, 1970, C
FIRECRACKER, 1981, 0
FIRECREEK, 1968, C
FIRED WIFE, 1943
FIREFLY OF FRANCE, THE, 1918
FIREFLY OF TOUGH LUCK, THE, 1917

FIREFLY, THE, 1937, A
FIREFOX, 1982, C
FIREMAN SAVE MY CHILD, 1954, A
FIREMAN'S BALL, THE, 1968, C
FIREMAN, SAVE MY CHILD, 1927, A
FIREMAN, SAVE MY CHILD, 1932, A
FIREPOWER, 1979, O
FIRES OF CONSCIENCE, 1916, A
FIRES OF FATE, 1923, A
FIRES OF FATE, 1932, A
FIRES OF INNOCENCE, 1922, A
FIRES OF REBELLION, 1917
FIRES OF YOUTH, 1917
FIRES OF YOUTH, 1918
FIRES OF YOUTH, 1924
FIRES ON THE PLAIN, 1962, O
FIRESTARTER, 1984, O
FIRETRAP, THE, 1935
FIRING LINE, THE, 1919
FIRM MAN, THE, 1975, C
FIRM OF GIRDLESTONE, THE, 1915, A
1ST NOTCH, THE, 1977
FIRST 100 YEARS, THE, 1938, A
FIRST A GIRL, 1935, A
FIRST AID, 1931, A
FIRST AND THE LAST, THE
FIRST AUTO, THE, 1927
FIRST BABY, 1936, A
FIRST BLOOD, 1982, O
FIRST BORN, THE, 1921
FIRST BORN, THE, 1928
FIRST COMES COURAGE, 1943, A
FIRST DEADLY SIN, THE, 1980, O
FIRST DEGREE, THE, 1923
FIRST FAMILY, 1980, O
FIRST GENTLEMAN, THE
FIRST GREAT TRAIN ROBBERY, THE
FIRST HUNDRED YEARS
FIRST KISS, THE, 1928
FIRST LADY, 1937, A
FIRST LAW, THE, 1918
FIRST LEGION, THE, 1951, A
FIRST LOVE, 1921
FIRST LOVE, 1939, A
FIRST LOVE, 1970, C-O
FIRST LOVE, 1977, O
FIRST MAN INTO SPACE, 1959, A
FIRST MARINES
FIRST MEN IN THE MOON, 1964, A
FIRST MEN IN THE MOON, THE, 1919
FIRST MONDAY IN OCTOBER, 1981
FIRST MRS. FRASER, THE, 1932, A
FIRST NAME: CARMEN, 1984, O
FIRST NIGHT, 1937, A
FIRST NIGHT, THE, 1927
FIRST NUDIE MUSICAL, THE, 1976, O
FIRST OF THE FEW, THE
FIRST OFFENCE, 1936, A
FIRST OFFENDERS, 1939
FIRST REBEL, THE
FIRST SPACESHIP ON VENUS, 1960, A
FIRST START, 1953, A
FIRST TASTE OF LOVE, 1962, C
FIRST TEXAN, THE, 1956
FIRST TIME ROUND, 1972
FIRST TIME, THE, 1952, A
FIRST TIME, THE, 1969, C
FIRST TIME, THE, 1978, O
FIRST TIME, THE, 1983, O
FIRST TO FIGHT, 1967, C
FIRST TRAVELING SALESLADY, THE, 1956, A
FIRST TURN-ON?, THE, 1984, O
FIRST WIFE
FIRST WOMAN, THE, 1922
FIRST YANK INTO TOKYO, 1945, C
FIRST YEAR, THE, 1926, A
FIRST YEAR, THE, 1932
FIRSTBORN, 1984, C
FISH HAWK, 1981, AA
FISH THAT SAVED PITTSBURGH, THE, 1979
FISHERMAN'S WHARF, 1939, AA
FIST IN HIS POCKET, 1968, O
FIST OF FEAR, TOUCH OF DEATH, 1980, O
FIST OF FURY
FISTFUL OF CHOPSTICKS, A
FISTFUL OF DOLLARS, A, 1964, C
FISTFUL OF DYNAMITE, A
FISTS OF FURY, 1973
FIT FOR A KING, 1937, A
FITZCARRALDO, 1982, C
FITZWILLY, 1967
$5,000 REWARD
$5,000 REWARD, 1918
$5,000,000 COUNTERFEITING PLOT, THE, 1914, A
$50,000 Reward, 1924
5 MINUTES TO LOVE
5 SINNERS, 1961, C-O
5,000 FINGERS OF DR. T. THE, 1953, AAA
FIVE, 1951, C
FIVE AGAINST THE HOUSE, 1955, C
FIVE AND TEN, 1931, A
FIVE AND TEN CENT ANNIE, 1928
FIVE ANGLES ON MURDER, 1950, A
FIVE ANGRY WOMEN, 1975
FIVE ASHORE IN SINGAPORE
FIVE BAD MEN, 1935
FIVE BLOODY GRAVES
FIVE BOLD WOMEN, 1960, A
FIVE BRANDED WOMEN, 1960, C
FIVE CAME BACK, 1939, A
FIVE CARD STUD, 1968, C
FIVE DAYS
FIVE DAYS FROM HOME, 1978, C
FIVE DAYS ONE SUMMER, 1982, A
FIVE DAYS TO LIVE, 1922
FIVE DOLLAR BABY, THE, 1922
FIVE EASY PIECES, 1970, C-O
FIVE FAULTS OF FLO, THE, 1916
FIVE FINGER EXERCISE, 1962, A
FIVE FINGERS, 1952, A
FIVE FINGERS OF DEATH, 1973, O
FIVE GATES TO HELL, 1959, O
FIVE GIANTS FROM TEXAS, 1966, C
FIVE GOLDEN DRAGONS, 1967, O
FIVE GOLDEN HOURS, 1961, A
FIVE GRAVES TO CAIRO, 1943, A
FIVE GUNS TO TOMBSTONE, 1961, A
FIVE GUNS WEST, 1955, A
FIVE LITTLE PEPPERS AND HOW THEY GREW, 1939, AA
FIVE LITTLE PEPPERS AT HOME, 1940, AA
FIVE LITTLE PEPPERS IN TROUBLE, 1940, A
FIVE MAN ARMY, THE, 1970, C
FIVE MILES TO MIDNIGHT, 1963, O
FIVE MILLION YEARS TO EARTH, 1968, A
FIVE MINUTES TO LIVE, 1961, C
FIVE NIGHTS, 1915
FIVE OF A KIND, 1938, AA
FIVE OF THE JAZZBAND
FIVE ON THE BLACK HAND SIDE, 1973, A
FIVE PENNIES, THE, 1959, A
FIVE POUND MAN, THE, 1937, C
FIVE SINISTER STORIES, 1919
FIVE STAR FINAL, 1931, C
FIVE STEPS TO DANGER, 1957, A
FIVE THE HARD WAY, 1969, O
FIVE THOUSAND AN HOUR, 1918
FIVE TO ONE, 1963, C
FIVE WEEKS IN A BALLOON, 1962, A
FIVE WILD GIRLS, 1966, O
FIXATION
FIXED BAYONETS, 1951, A
FIXED BY GEORGE, 1920
FIXER DUGAN, 1939, A
FIXER, THE
FIXER, THE, 1968, O
FLAG LIEUTENANT, THE, 1919
FLAG LIEUTENANT, THE, 1926
FLAG LIEUTENANT, THE, 1932
FLAME, 1975
FLAME AND THE ARROW, THE, 1950, A
FLAME AND THE FLESH, 1954, C
FLAME BARRIER, THE, 1958, C
FLAME IN THE HEATHER, 1935, A
FLAME IN THE STREETS, 1961, A
FLAME OF ARABY, 1951
FLAME OF CALCUTTA, 1953, A
FLAME OF HELLGATE, THE, 1920
FLAME OF LIFE, THE, 1923
FLAME OF LOVE, THE, 1930, A
FLAME OF NEW ORLEANS, THE, 1941, A-C
FLAME OF PASSION, THE, 1915
FLAME OF SACRAMENTO
FLAME OF STAMBOUL, 1957, A
FLAME OF THE ARGENTINE, 1926
FLAME OF THE BARBARY COAST, 1945, A
FLAME OF THE DESERT, 1919
FLAME OF THE ISLANDS, 1955, A
FLAME OF THE WEST, 1945, A
FLAME OF THE YUKON, THE, 1917
FLAME OF THE YUKON, THE, 1926
FLAME OF TORMENT
FLAME OF YOUTH, 1920
FLAME OF YOUTH, 1949, A
FLAME OF YOUTH, THE, 1917
FLAME OVER INDIA, 1960, A
FLAME OVER VIETNAM, 1967, A
FLAME WITHIN, THE, 1935, C
FLAME, THE, 1920
FLAME, THE, 1948, A
FLAMENCA LA GITANE, 1928
FLAMES, 1917, A
FLAMES, 1926
FLAMES, 1932, A
FLAMES OF CHANCE, THE, 1918, A
FLAMES OF DESIRE, 1924
FLAMES OF FEAR, 1930, A
FLAMES OF JOHANNIS, THE, 1916
FLAMES OF PASSION, 1922, A
FLAMES OF PASSION, 1923
FLAMES OF THE FLESH, 1920, A
FLAMES OF WRATH, 1923
FLAMING BARRIERS, 1924, A
FLAMING BULLETS, 1945, A
FLAMING CLUE, THE, 1920
FLAMING CRISIS, THE, 1924
FLAMING DESIRE
FLAMING FEATHER, 1951, A
FLAMING FOREST, THE, 1926
FLAMING FORTIES, THE, 1924
FLAMING FRONTIER, 1958
FLAMING FRONTIER, 1968, A
FLAMING FRONTIER, THE, 1926
FLAMING FURY, 1926
FLAMING FURY, 1949, A
FLAMING GOLD, 1934, A
FLAMING GUNS, 1933, A
FLAMING HEARTS, 1922
FLAMING HOUR, THE, 1922
FLAMING LEAD, 1939, A
FLAMING OMEN, THE, 1917
FLAMING PASSION
FLAMING SIGNAL, 1933, A
FLAMING STAR, 1960, C-O
FLAMING SWORD, 1915
FLAMING TEEN-AGE, THE, 1956, A
FLAMING URGE, THE, 1953
FLAMING WATERS, 1925, A
FLAMING YOUTH, 1923
FLAMINGO, 1947
FLAMINGO AFFAIR, THE, 1948, A
FLAMINGO KID, THE, 1984, C
FLAMINGO ROAD, 1949, C
FLANAGAN BOY, THE
FLANNELFOOT, 1953, A
FLAP, 1970, A
FLAPPER WIVES, 1924
FLAPPER, THE, 1920, A
FLARE-UP SAL, 1918
FLAREUP, 1969, O
FLASH AND THE FIRECAT, 1976
FLASH GORDON, 1936, AAA
FLASH GORDON, 1980, AA
FLASH O'LIGHTING, 1925
FLASH OF FATE, THE, 1918
FLASH OF GREEN, A, 1984, A-C
FLASH OF THE FOREST, 1928
FLASH THE SHEEPDOG, 1967, AA
FLASH, THE, 1923
FLASHDANCE, 1983
FLASHING FANGS, 1926
FLASHING GUNS, 1947, A
FLASHING HOOFS, 1928
FLASHING SPURS, 1924
FLASHING STEEDS, 1925
FLASHLIGHT, THE, 1917, A
FLASHPOINT, 1984, O
FLAT TOP, 1952, A
FLAT TWO, 1962, A-C
FLATTERY, 1925
FLATTERY, 1925, A
FLAVOR OF GREEN TEA OVER RICE, THE
FLAW, THE, 1933, A
FLAW, THE, 1955, A
FLAXY MARTIN, 1949, A
FLEA IN HER EAR, A, 1968, C
FLEDGLINGS, 1965, O
FLEET'S IN, THE, 1928
FLEET'S IN, THE, 1942, AA
FLEETWING, 1928
FLEMISH FARM, THE, 1943, A
FLESH, 1932, C
FLESH AND BLOOD, 1922
FLESH AND BLOOD, 1951, C
FLESH AND BLOOD SHOW, THE, 1974, O
FLESH AND FANTASY, 1943, A-C
FLESH AND FLAME
FLESH AND FURY, 1952, A
FLESH AND SPIRIT, 1922
FLESH AND THE DEVIL, 1926, A
FLESH AND THE FIENDS, THE
FLESH AND THE SPUR, 1957, C
FLESH AND THE WOMAN, 1954, O
FLESH EATERS, THE, 1964, O
FLESH FEAST, 1970, O
FLESH GORDON, 1974
FLESH IS WEAK, THE, 1957, O
FLESH MERCHANT, THE, 1956, O
FLESHBURN, 1984, O
FLETCH, 1984, C
FLEUR D'AMOUR, 1927
FLEUR DE PARIS, 1916
FLICK
FLICKER UP, 1946
FLIGHT, 1929, A
FLIGHT, 1960
FLIGHT ANGELS, 1940, A

FLIGHT AT MIDNIGHT, 1939, A
FLIGHT COMMAND, 1940, A
FLIGHT COMMANDER, THE, 1927
FLIGHT FOR FREEDOM, 1943, A
FLIGHT FROM ASHIYA, 1964, A
FLIGHT FROM DESTINY, 1941
FLIGHT FROM FOLLY, 1945, A
FLIGHT FROM GLORY, 1937, A
FLIGHT FROM SINGAPORE, 1962, A
FLIGHT FROM TERROR
FLIGHT FROM TREASON, 1960
FLIGHT FROM VIENNA, 1956, A
FLIGHT INTO NOWHERE, 1938
FLIGHT LIEUTENANT, 1942, A
FLIGHT NURSE, 1953, A
FLIGHT OF THE DOVES, 1971, AA
FLIGHT OF THE DUCHESS, THE, 1916
FLIGHT OF THE EAGLE, 1983, A-C
FLIGHT OF THE LOST BALLOON, 1961, C
FLIGHT OF THE PHOENIX, THE, 1965, C
FLIGHT OF THE SANDPIPER, THE
FLIGHT THAT DISAPPEARED, THE, 1961, A
FLIGHT TO BERLIN, 1984, O
FLIGHT TO FAME, 1938, A
FLIGHT TO FURY, 1966, C
FLIGHT TO HONG KONG, 1956, C
FLIGHT TO MARS, 1951, A
FLIGHT TO NOWHERE, 1946, C
FLIGHT TO TANGIER, 1953, A
FLIM-FLAM MAN, THE, 1967, A
FLIPOTTE, 1920
FLIPPER, 1963, AAA
FLIPPER'S NEW ADVENTURE, 1964, AAA
FLIRT, THE, 1916
FLIRT, THE, 1922, A
FLIRTATION WALK, 1934, AA
FLIRTING WIDOW, THE, 1930, A
FLIRTING WITH DANGER, 1935, A
FLIRTING WITH DEATH, 1917
FLIRTING WITH FATE, 1916, A
FLIRTING WITH FATE, 1938, A
FLIRTING WITH LOVE, 1924
FLITTERWOCHEN IN DER HOLLE
FLOATING COLLEGE, THE, 1928, A
FLOATING DUTCHMAN, THE, 1953, A
FLOATING WEEDS, 1970, A
FLOOD, 1915
FLOOD TIDE, 1935, A
FLOOD TIDE, 1958, C
FLOOD, THE, 1931, A
FLOOD, THE, 1963, AA
FLOODGATES, 1924
FLOODS OF FEAR, 1958, A
FLOODTIDE, 1949, A
FLOOR ABOVE, THE, 1914, A
FLOOR BELOW, THE, 1918
FLORENCE NIGHTINGALE, 1915
FLORENTINE DAGGER, THE, 1935, A
FLORIAN, 1940, AAA
FLORIDA ENCHANTMENT, A, 1914, A
FLORIDA SPECIAL, 1936, A
FLORINE LA FLEUR DU VALOIS, 1926
FLORODORA GIRL, THE, 1930, A
FLOTSAM, 1921
FLOWER DRUM SONG, 1961, A
FLOWER OF DOOM, THE, 1917
FLOWER OF FAITH, THE, 1916
FLOWER OF NIGHT, 1925
FLOWER OF NO MAN'S LAND, THE, 1916
FLOWER OF THE DUSK, 1918
FLOWER OF THE NORTH, 1921
FLOWER THIEF, THE, 1962, O
FLOWERS ARE LATE, THE, 1917
FLOWERS FOR THE MAN IN THE MOON, 1975, A
FLOWING GOLD, 1921
FLOWING GOLD, 1924, A
FLOWING GOLD, 1940, A
FLUCHT NACH BERLIN
FLUFFY, 1965, AAA
FLUSH, 1981
FLY AWAY PETER, 1948, A
FLY BY NIGHT, 1942, A
FLY GOD, THE, 1918, A
FLY ME, 1973
FLY NOW, PAY LATER, 1969, O
FLY, RAVEN, FLY
FLY, THE, 1958, O
FLY-AWAY BABY, 1937, A
FLYIN' COWBOY, THE, 1928
FLYIN' THRU, 1925
FLYING ACE, 1928
FLYING BLIND, 1941, A
FLYING BUCKAROO, THE, 1928
FLYING CADETS, 1941, A
FLYING COLORS, 1917
FLYING DEUCES, THE, 1939, AAA
FLYING DEVILS, 1933, A
FLYING DOCTOR, THE, 1936, A
FLYING DOWN TO RIO, 1933, A
FLYING DUTCHMAN, THE, 1923
FLYING EYE, THE, 1955, AA
FLYING FEET, THE, 1929, A
FLYING FIFTY-FIVE, 1939, A
FLYING FIFTY-FIVE, THE, 1924, A
FLYING FISTS, THE, 1938, A
FLYING FONTAINES, THE, 1959, A
FLYING FOOL, 1925
FLYING FOOL, 1929, A
FLYING FOOL, THE, 1931, A
FLYING FORTRESS, 1942, A
FLYING FROM JUSTICE, 1915, A
FLYING GUILLOTINE, THE, 1975, O-C
FLYING HIGH, 1926
FLYING HIGH, 1931, A
FLYING HOOFS, 1925
FLYING HORSEMAN, THE, 1926
FLYING HOSTESS, 1936, A
FLYING IRISHMAN, THE, 1939, A
FLYING LARIATS, 1931
FLYING LEATHERNECKS, 1951, C
FLYING LUCK, 1927
FLYING MAIL, THE, 1926
FLYING MARINE, THE, 1929, A
FLYING MATCHMAKER, THE, 1970, A
FLYING MISSILE, 1950, A
FLYING PAT, 1920, A
FLYING ROMEOS, 1928, A
FLYING SAUCER, THE, 1950, A
FLYING SAUCER, THE, 1964, A
FLYING SCOT, THE
FLYING SCOTSMAN, THE, 1929, A
FLYING SERPENT, THE, 1946, C
FLYING SORCERER, THE, 1974
FLYING SQUAD, THE, 1929
FLYING SQUAD, THE, 1932, A
FLYING SQUAD, THE, 1940, A
FLYING SQUADRON, 1952
FLYING TIGERS, 1942, C
FLYING TORPEDO, THE, 1916, A
FLYING TWINS, THE, 1915
FLYING U RANCH, THE, 1927
FLYING WILD, 1941, A
FLYING WITH MUSIC, 1942, A
FM, 1978, C
FOES, 1977, C
FOG, 1934, A
FOG 1966
FOG BOUND, 1923
FOG ISLAND, 1945, A
FOG OVER FRISCO, 1934
FOG, THE, 1923, A
FOG, THE, 1980, C-O
FOGGY HARBOR, 1923
FOLIES BERGERE, 1958, C
FOLIES DERGERE, 1935, A
FOLKS AT THE RED WOLF INN
FOLKS FROM WAY DOWN EAST, 1924
FOLLIES GIRL, 1943, A
FOLLIES GIRL, THE, 1919, A
FOLLOW A STAR, 1959, A
FOLLOW ME, 1969
FOLLOW ME QUIETLY, 1949, C
FOLLOW ME, BOYS!, 1966, AA
FOLLOW THAT CAMEL, 1967, A
FOLLOW THAT DREAM, 1962, A
FOLLOW THAT HORSE!, 1960, A
FOLLOW THAT MAN, 1961, A
FOLLOW THAT WOMAN, 1945, A
FOLLOW THE BAND, 1943, A
FOLLOW THE BOYS, 1944, AA
FOLLOW THE BOYS, 1963, A
FOLLOW THE FLEET, 1936, AA
FOLLOW THE GIRL, 1917
FOLLOW THE HUNTER
FOLLOW THE LEADER, 1930, A
FOLLOW THE LEADER, 1944, A
FOLLOW THE SUN, 1951, A
FOLLOW THRU, 1930, A
FOLLOW YOUR HEART, 1936, A
FOLLOW YOUR STAR, 1938, A
FOLLY OF DESIRE, THE OR THE SHULAMITE, 1916
FOLLY OF REVENGE, THE, 1916
FOLLY OF VANITY, THE, 1924
FOLLY OF YOUTH, 1925
FOLLY TO BE WISE, 1953, A
FOND MEMORIES, 1982, C
FOOD FOR SCANDAL, 1920, A
FOOD GAMBLERS, THE, 1917
FOOD OF THE GODS, THE, 1976, O
FOOL AND HIS MONEY, A, 1920
FOOL AND HIS MONEY, A, 1925
FOOL AND THE PRINCESS, THE, 1948, A
FOOL KILLER, THE, 1965, O
FOOL THERE WAS, A, 1915, A-C
FOOL THERE WAS, A, 1922
FOOL'S AWAKENING, A, 1924
FOOL'S GOLD, 1919
FOOL'S GOLD, 1946
FOOL'S PARADISE, 1921
FOOL'S PROMISE, A, 1921
FOOL'S REVENGE, THE, 1916
FOOL, THE, 1925
FOOLIN' AROUND, 1980, C
FOOLISH AGE, THE, 1921
FOOLISH HUSBANDS, 1948
FOOLISH LIVES, 1922
FOOLISH MATRONS, THE, 1921
FOOLISH MEN AND SMART WOMEN, 1924
FOOLISH MONTE CARLO, 1922
FOOLISH MOTHERS, 1923
FOOLISH TWINS, THE, 1923
FOOLISH VIRGIN, THE, 1917
FOOLISH VIRGIN, THE, 1924
FOOLISH WIVES, 1920, C
FOOLS, 1970, O
FOOLS AND RICHES, 1923
FOOLS AND THEIR MONEY, 1919
FOOLS FIRST, 1922
FOOLS FOR LUCK, 1917
FOOLS FOR LUCK, 1928
FOOLS FOR SCANDAL, 1938, A
FOOLS IN THE DARK, 1924
FOOLS OF DESIRE, 1941, C
FOOLS OF FASHION, 1926
FOOLS OF FORTUNE, 1922, A
FOOLS OF PASSION, 1926
FOOLS RUSH IN, 1949, A
FOOLS' HIGHWAY, 1924
FOOLS' PARADE, 1971
FOOT STEPS OF CAPTAIN KIDD, THE, 1917
FOOTFALLS, 1921
FOOTLIGHT FEVER, 1941, A
FOOTLIGHT GLAMOUR, 1943
FOOTLIGHT PARADE, 1933
FOOTLIGHT RANGER, THE, 1923
FOOTLIGHT SERENADE, 1942, A
FOOTLIGHTS, 1921
FOOTLIGHTS AND FOOLS, 1929, A
FOOTLIGHTS AND SHADOWS, 1920
FOOTLIGHTS OF FATE, THE, 1916
FOOTLOOSE, 1984, A-C
FOOTLOOSE HEIRESS, THE, 1937, A
FOOTLOOSE WIDOWS, 1926
FOOTSTEPS IN THE DARK, 1941, A
FOOTSTEPS IN THE FOG, 1955, A
FOOTSTEPS IN THE NIGHT, 1932, A
FOOTSTEPS IN THE NIGHT, 1957, A
FOOTSTEPS ON THE MOON, 1973
FOR A DOLLAR IN THE TEETH
FOR A FEW BULLETS MORE
FOR A FEW DOLLARS MORE, 1967, C
FOR A FISTFUL OF DOLLARS
FOR A WOMAN'S FAIR NAME, 1916
FOR ALIMONY ONLY, 1926
FOR ALL ETERNITY, 1917
FOR ANOTHER WOMAN, 1924
FOR ATT INTE TALA OM ALLA DESSA KVINNOR
FOR BEAUTY'S SAKE, 1941, A
FOR BETTER FOR WORSE
FOR BETTER FOR WORSE, 1954
FOR BETTER, FOR WORSE, 1919
FOR BIG STAKES, 1922
FOR FIVE THOUSAND DOLLARS A YEAR, 1915
FOR FRANCE, 1917
FOR FREEDOM, 1919
FOR FREEDOM, 1940, A
FOR HE'S A JOLLY BAD FELLOW
FOR HEAVEN'S SAKE, 1926, A
FOR HEAVEN'S SAKE, 1950, A
FOR HER FATHER'S SAKE, 1921
FOR HER PEOPLE, 1914
FOR HIS MOTHER'S SAKE, 1922
FOR HIS SAKE, 1922
FOR HUSBANDS ONLY, 1918
FOR KING AND COUNTRY, 1914
FOR LADIES ONLY, 1927
FOR LIBERTY, 1918
FOR LOVE AND MONEY, 1967, O
FOR LOVE OF IVY, 1968, A
FOR LOVE OF MONEY
FOR LOVE OF SERVICE, 1922
FOR LOVE OF YOU, 1933, A
FOR LOVE OR MONEY, 1934, A
FOR LOVE OR MONEY, 1939, A
FOR LOVE OR MONEY, 1963, A
FOR ME AND MY GAL, 1942, A
FOR MEMBERS ONLY, 1960
FOR MEN ONLY, 1952, A
FOR PETE'S SAKE, 1977, C
FOR PETE'S SAKE!, 1966, A
FOR SALE, 1918
FOR SALE, 1924
FOR SINGLES ONLY, 1968
FOR THE DEFENCE, 1916
FOR THE DEFENSE, 1922
FOR THE DEFENSE, 1930, A-C
FOR THE FIRST TIME, 1959, A

FOR THE FREEDOM OF IRELAND, 1920
FOR THE FREEDOM OF THE EAST, 1918
FOR THE FREEDOM OF THE WORLD, 1917
FOR THE LOVE O'LIL, 1930, A
FOR THE LOVE OF BENJI, 1977, AAA
FOR THE LOVE OF MARY, 1948, A
FOR THE LOVE OF MIKE, 1927
FOR THE LOVE OF MIKE, 1933, A
FOR THE LOVE OF MIKE, 1960, AAA
FOR THE LOVE OF RUSTY, 1947, AAA
FOR THE SERVICE, 1936, A
FOR THE SOUL OF RAFAEL, 1920
FOR THEM THAT TRESPASS, 1949, A
FOR THOSE IN PERIL, 1944, A
FOR THOSE WE LOVE, 1921
FOR THOSE WHO THINK YOUNG, 1964, A
FOR VALOR, 1937, A
FOR VALOUR, 1917
FOR VALOUR, 1928
FOR WHOM THE BELL TOLLS, 1943, C
FOR WIVES ONLY, 1926
FOR WOMAN'S FAVOR, 1924
FOR YOU ALONE, 1945, A
FOR YOU I DIE, 1947, A
FOR YOU MY BOY, 1923
FOR YOUR DAUGHTER'S SAKE
FOR YOUR EYES ONLY, 1981, A
FORBID THEM NOT, 1961
FORBIDDEN, 1919
FORBIDDEN, 1919
FORBIDDEN, 1932, A-C
FORBIDDEN, 1949, A-C
FORBIDDEN, 1953, A
FORBIDDEN ADVENTURE, THE, 1915, A
FORBIDDEN ALLIANCE
FORBIDDEN CARGO, 1925
FORBIDDEN CARGO, 1925
FORBIDDEN CARGO, 1954, A
FORBIDDEN CARGOES, 1925, A
FORBIDDEN CITY, THE, 1918
FORBIDDEN CITY, THE, 1918
FORBIDDEN COMPANY, 1932, A
FORBIDDEN FIRE, 1919
FORBIDDEN FIRE, 1919
FORBIDDEN FRUIT, 1916
FORBIDDEN FRUIT, 1916
FORBIDDEN FRUIT, 1921
FORBIDDEN FRUIT, 1921
FORBIDDEN FRUIT, 1959, C
FORBIDDEN GAMES, 1953, C
FORBIDDEN GRASS, 1928
FORBIDDEN GRASS, 1928
FORBIDDEN HEAVEN, 1936, A
FORBIDDEN HOURS, 1928
FORBIDDEN HOURS, 1928
FORBIDDEN ISLAND, 1959, C
FORBIDDEN JOURNEY, 1950, A
FORBIDDEN JUNGLE, 1950, A
FORBIDDEN LESSONS, 1982
FORBIDDEN LOVE, 1921
FORBIDDEN LOVE, 1921
FORBIDDEN LOVE, 1927
FORBIDDEN LOVE, 1927
FORBIDDEN LOVE AFFAIR
FORBIDDEN LOVER, 1923
FORBIDDEN LOVER, 1923
FORBIDDEN MUSIC, 1936, A
FORBIDDEN PARADISE
FORBIDDEN PARADISE, 1922
FORBIDDEN PARADISE, 1922
FORBIDDEN PARADISE, 1924, C
FORBIDDEN PATH, THE, 1918
FORBIDDEN PATH, THE, 1918
FORBIDDEN PATHS, 1917
FORBIDDEN PATHS, 1917
FORBIDDEN PLANET, 1956, C
FORBIDDEN RANGE, THE, 1923
FORBIDDEN RANGE, THE, 1923
FORBIDDEN RELATIONS, 1983, O
FORBIDDEN ROOM, THE, 1914
FORBIDDEN ROOM, THE, 1914
FORBIDDEN ROOM, THE, 1919
FORBIDDEN ROOM, THE, 1919
FORBIDDEN STREET, THE
FORBIDDEN TERRITORY, 1938
FORBIDDEN THING, THE, 1920
FORBIDDEN THING, THE, 1920
FORBIDDEN TRAIL, 1936, A
FORBIDDEN TRAIL, THE, 1923
FORBIDDEN TRAIL, THE, 1923
FORBIDDEN TRAILS, 1920
FORBIDDEN TRAILS, 1920
FORBIDDEN TRAILS, 1928
FORBIDDEN TRAILS, 1928
FORBIDDEN TRAILS, 1941, A
FORBIDDEN UNDER THE CENSORSHIP OF THE KING, 1973
FORBIDDEN VALLEY, 1920
FORBIDDEN VALLEY, 1920
FORBIDDEN VALLEY, 1938, AA
FORBIDDEN WATERS, 1926
FORBIDDEN WATERS, 1926
FORBIDDEN WOMAN, THE, 1920, A
FORBIDDEN WOMAN, THE, 1927
FORBIDDEN WOMAN, THE, 1927
FORBIDDEN WORLD, 1982, O
FORBIDDEN ZONE, 1980
FORBIN PROJECT, THE
FORBRYDELSENS ELEMENT
FORCE 10 FROM NAVARONE, 1978, A-C
FORCE BEYOND, THE, 1978, C
FORCE DE LA VIE, 1920
FORCE DE LA VIE, 1920
FORCE FOUR, 1975
FORCE OF ARMS, 1951, A
FORCE OF EVIL, 1948, C
FORCE OF IMPULSE, 1961, A
FORCE OF ONE, A, 1979, C-O
FORCE: FIVE, 1981, O
FORCED ENTRY, 1975, O
FORCED LANDING, 1935, A
FORCED LANDING, 1941
FORCED VENGEANCE, 1982, O
FORCES' SWEETHEART, 1953, A
FORDINGTON TWINS, THE, 1920
FORDINGTON TWINS, THE, 1920
FOREFEIT, THE, 1919
FOREFEIT, THE, 1919
FOREIGN AFFAIR, A, 1948
FOREIGN AFFAIRES, 1935, A
FOREIGN AGENT, 1942, A
FOREIGN CORRESPONDENT, 1940, A
FOREIGN DEVILS, 1927, A
FOREIGN INTRIGUE, 1956, C
FOREIGN LEGION, THE, 1928
FOREIGNER, THE, 1978, C
FOREMAN OF BAR Z RANCH, THE, 1924
FOREMAN WENT TO FRANCE, THE
FOREPLAY, 1975, O
FOREST HAVOC, 1926
FOREST KING, THE, 1922
FOREST ON THE HILL, THE, 1919
FOREST RANGERS, THE, 1942, A
FOREST RIVALS, 1919
FOREST, THE, 1983, O
FOREVER, 1921
FOREVER AFTER, 1926, A
FOREVER AMBER, 1947, C-O
FOREVER AND A DAY, 1943, A
FOREVER DARLING, 1956, A
FOREVER ENGLAND
FOREVER FEMALE, 1953, A
FOREVER MY HEART, 1954, C
FOREVER MY LOVE, 1962, A
FOREVER YOUNG, 1984, C
FOREVER YOUNG, FOREVER FREE, 1976, AAA
FOREVER YOURS, 1937, A
FOREVER YOURS, 1945, A
FORGED BRIDE, THE, 1920
FORGED PASSPORT, 1939, A
FORGER, THE, 1928
FORGET ME NOT
FORGET-ME-NOT, 1922
FORGET-ME-NOTS, 1917
FORGIVE AND FORGET, 1923
FORGIVE US OUR TRESPASSES, 1919
FORGIVEN, OR THE JACK O'DIAMONDS, 1914, A
FORGOTTEN, 1914
FORGOTTEN, 1933, A
FORGOTTEN COMMANDMENTS, 1932, A
FORGOTTEN FACES, 1928
FORGOTTEN FACES, 1936, A
FORGOTTEN GIRLS, 1940, A
FORGOTTEN LAW, THE, 1922
FORGOTTEN WOMAN, 1921
FORGOTTEN WOMAN, THE, 1939, A
FORGOTTEN WOMEN, 1932, A
FORGOTTEN WOMEN, 1949, A
FORGOTTEN, THE, 1912
FORLORN RIVER, 1926
FORLORN RIVER, 1937, AA
FORMULA, THE, 1980, C
FORSAKEN GARDEN, THE
FORSAKING ALL OTHERS, 1922
FORSAKING ALL OTHERS, 1935, A
FORT ALGIERS, 1953, A
FORT APACHE, 1948, A
FORT APACHE, THE BRONX, 1981, O
FORT BOWIE, 1958, A
FORT COURAGEOUS, 1965, A
FORT DEFIANCE, 1951, A
FORT DOBBS, 1958, A
FORT DODGE STAMPEDE, 1951, AA
FORT FRAYNE, 1926
FORT GRAVEYARD, 1966, C
FORT MASSACRE, 1958
FORT OSAGE, 1952, A
FORT SAVAGE RAIDERS, 1951, A
FORT TI, 1953, AA
FORT UTAH, 1967, A
FORT VENGEANCE, 1953, A
FORT WORTH, 1951, A
FORT YUMA, 1955, A
FORTRESS IN THE SUN, 1978
FORTRESS OF THE DEAD, 1965
FORTRESS, THE, 1979, C
FORTUNATE FOOL, THE, 1933, A
FORTUNATE YOUTH, THE, 1916
FORTUNE AND MEN'S EYES, 1971, O
FORTUNE AT STAKE, A, 1918
FORTUNE COOKIE, THE, 1966, A-C
FORTUNE HUNTER, THE, 1914, A
FORTUNE HUNTER, THE, 1920
FORTUNE HUNTER, THE, 1927, A
FORTUNE HUNTERS, THE, 1914
FORTUNE IN DIAMONDS
FORTUNE IS A WOMAN
FORTUNE LANE, 1947, AA
FORTUNE OF CHRISTINA McNAB, THE, 1921
FORTUNE TELLER, THE, 1920
FORTUNE TELLER, THE, 1961, A-C
FORTUNE'S CHILD, 1919, A
FORTUNE'S FOOL, 1922
FORTUNE'S MASK, 1922
FORTUNE, THE, 1975, C
FORTUNES OF CAPTAIN BLOOD, 1950, A
FORTUNES OF FIFI, THE, 1917
'49 -'17, 1917
.45 CALIBRE WAR, 1929
40 GUNS TO APACHE PASS, 1967, A
40-HORSE HAWKINS, 1924
40TH DOOR, THE, 1924
42ND STREET, 1933, A
45 FATHERS, 1937, AA
45 MINUTES FROM BROADWAY, 1920
47 SAMURAI
48 HOURS, 1944
48 HOURS, 1982, O
48 HOURS TO ACAPULCO, 1968, C
48 HOURS TO LIVE, 1960, A
48, AVENUE DE L'OPERA, 1917
4D MAN, 1959, A
FORTY ACRE FEUD, 1965, A
FORTY CARATS, 1973, A-C
FORTY DEUCE, 1982, O
FORTY GUNS, 1957, A-C
FORTY LITTLE MOTHERS, 1940, A
FORTY NAUGHTY GIRLS, 1937, A
FORTY NINTH PARALLEL
FORTY POUNDS OF TROUBLE, 1962, AAA
FORTY THIEVES, 1944, A
FORTY THOUSAND HORSEMEN, 1941, A
FORTY WINKS, 1925, A
FORTY-FIRST, THE, 1927
FORTY-FIVE CALIBRE ECHO, 1932
FORTY-NINE DAYS, 1964, A
FORTY-NINERS, THE, 1932, A
FORTY-NINTH MAN, THE, 1953, A
FORTYNINERS, THE, 1954, A
FORWARD PASS, THE, 1929
FOUL PLAY, 1920
FOUL PLAY, 1978, A-C
FOUND ALIVE, 1934, A
FOUND GUILTY, 1922
FOUNDATIONS OF FREEDOM. THE, 1918, A
FOUNDLING, THE, 1916
FOUNTAIN OF LOVE, THE, 1968, C
FOUNTAIN, THE, 1934, A
FOUNTAINHEAD, THE, 1949, A
FOUR AGAINST FATE, 1952, A
FOUR AGAINST THE DESERT, 1979
FOUR AROUND THE WOMAN, 1921
FOUR BAGS FULL, 1957, A
FOUR BOYS AND A GUN, 1957, C
FOUR COMPANIONS, THE, 1938, A
FOUR CORNERED TRIANGLE
FOUR DARK HOURS
FOUR DAUGHTERS, 1938, A
FOUR DAYS, 1951, A
FOUR DAYS IN JULY, 1984, C-O
FOUR DAYS LEAVE, 1950
FOUR DAYS OF NAPLES, THE, 1963, A
FOUR DAYS WONDER, 1936, AA
FOUR DESPERATE MEN, 1960, C
FOUR DEUCES, THE, 1976, O
FOUR DEVILS, 1929, A
FOUR FACES WEST, 1948, A
FOUR FAST GUNS, 1959, A
FOUR FEATHERS, 1915, A
FOUR FEATHERS, 1929, A
FOUR FEATHERS, THE, 1921
FOUR FEATHERS, THE, 1939, A
FOUR FLIES ON GREY VELVET, 1972, C
FOUR FLUSHER, THE, 1919
FOUR FOR TEXAS, 1963
FOUR FOR THE MORGUE, 1962, C
FOUR FRIENDS, 1981

FOUR FRIGHTENED PEOPLE, 1934, C
FOUR FROM NOWHERE, THE, 1925
FOUR GIRLS IN TOWN, 1956, A
FOUR GIRLS IN WHITE, 1939, A
FOUR GUNS TO THE BORDER, 1954, A
FOUR HEARTS, 1922
FOUR HORSEMEN OF THE APOCALYPSE, THE, 1921, A
FOUR HORSEMEN OF THE APOCALYPSE, THE, 1962, A
FOUR HOURS TO KILL, 1935, A
FOUR HUNDRED BLOWS, THE, 1959, A-C
FOUR IN A JEEP, 1951, A
FOUR IN THE MORNING, 1965, C
FOUR JACKS AND A JILL, 1941, A
FOUR JILLS IN A JEEP, 1944, A
FOUR JUST MEN, THE
FOUR JUST MEN, THE, 1921
FOUR KINDS OF LOVE
FOUR MASKED MEN, 1934, A
FOUR MEN AND A PRAYER, 1938, A
FOUR MEN IN A VAN, 1921, A
FOUR MOTHERS, 1941, A
FOUR MUSKETEERS, THE, 1975, A-C
FOUR NIGHTS OF A DREAMER, 1972, O
FOUR POSTER, THE, 1952, A
FOUR RODE OUT, 1969, O
FOUR SEASONS, THE, 1981, C
FOUR SIDED TRIANGLE, 1953
FOUR SKULLS OF JONATHAN DRAKE, THE, 1959, C-O
FOUR SONS, 1928, A
FOUR SONS, 1940, A
FOUR WALLS, 1928, A
FOUR WAYS OUT, 1954, C
FOUR WIVES, 1939, A
FOUR'S A CROWD, 1938, A
FOUR-FOOTED RANGER, THE, 1928
FOURFLUSHER, THE
FOURFLUSHER, THE, 1928
FOURTEEN HOURS, 1951, C
FOURTEEN, THE, 1973, A
FOURTEENTH LOVER, THE, 1922
FOURTEENTH MAN, THE, 1920
FOURTH ALARM, THE, 1930, A
FOURTH COMMANDMENT, THE, 1927
FOURTH ESTATE, THE, 1916
FOURTH FOR MARRIAGE, A
FOURTH HORSEMAN, THE, 1933, AA
FOURTH MAN, THE, 1984, O
FOURTH MARRIAGE OF DAME MARGARET
FOURTH MUSKETEER, THE, 1923
FOURTH SQUARE, THE, 1961, A-C
FOX AFFAIR, THE, 1978
FOX AND HIS FRIENDS, 1976, O
FOX AND THE HOUND, THE, 1981, AAA
FOX FARM, 1922, A
FOX MOVIETONE FOLLIES, 1929, A
FOX MOVIETONE FOLLIES OF 1930, 1930, A
FOX STYLE, 1973
FOX WITH NINE TAILS, THE, 1969
FOX WOMAN, THE, 1915
FOX, THE, 1921
FOX, THE, 1967, O
FOXES, 1980, O
FOXES OF HARROW, THE, 1947, A
FOXFIRE, 1955, C
FOXHOLE IN CAIRO, 1960, A
FOXTROT, 1977, C-O
FOXY DROWN, 1974, O
FOXY LADY, 1971, A
FQIEDA, 1947, A
FRA DIAVOLO
FRAGE 7
FRAGMENT OF AN EMPIRE, 1930
FRAGMENT OF FEAR, 1971, C-O
FRAGRANCE OF WILD FLOWERS, THE, 1979, C
FRAIL WOMEN, 1932, C
FRAILTY, 1921, C
FRAME UP, THE, 1917, A
FRAME UP, THE, 1923
FRAME-UP THE, 1937, A
FRAME-UP, THE
FRAME-UP, THE, 1915
FRAMED, 1927
FRAMED, 1930, A
FRAMED, 1940
FRAMED, 1947, C
FRAMED, 1975
FRAMEUP, THE, 1916
FRAMING FRAMERS, 1918
FRANCES, 1982
FRANCHETTE; LES INTRIGUES, 1969, O
FRANCHISE AFFAIR, THE, 1952, A
FRANCIS, 1949
FRANCIS COVERS THE BIG TOWN, 1953, AA
FRANCIS GOES TO THE RACES, 1951, AA
FRANCIS GOES TO WEST POINT, 1952, AA
FRANCIS IN THE HAUNTED HOUSE, 1956
FRANCIS IN THE NAVY, 1955, AA
FRANCIS JOINS THE WACS, 1954, AA
FRANCIS OF ASSISI, 1961, A
FRANCOISE
FRANK'S GREATEST ADVENTURE
FRANKENSTEIN, 1931, C-O
FRANKENSTEIN 1970, 1958, C
FRANKENSTEIN AND THE MONSTER FROM HELL, 1974, O
FRANKENSTEIN CONQUERS THE WORLD, 1964, C
FRANKENSTEIN CREATED WOMAN, 1965, O
FRANKENSTEIN MEETS THE SPACE MONSTER, 1965, C
FRANKENSTEIN MEETS THE WOLF MAN, 1943, C
FRANKENSTEIN MUST BE DESTROYED!, 1969, C-O
FRANKENSTEIN VS. THE GIANT DEVILFISH
FRANKENSTEIN'S BLOODY TERROR, 1968, C
FRANKENSTEIN'S DAUGHTER, 1958, C-O
FRANKENSTEIN'S ISLAND, 1982
FRANKENSTEIN, THE VAMPIRE AND CO., 1961, C
FRANKENSTEIN-ITALIAN STYLE, 1977, O
FRANKIE AND JOHNNY, 1936, A-C
FRANKIE AND JOHNNY, 1966, A
FRANKWEILER, 1973, AA
FRANTIC, 1961, C
FRASIER, THE SENSUOUS LION, 1973, AA
FRATERNITY ROW, 1977, O
FRAU IM MOND
FRAULEIN, 1958, C
FRAULEIN DOKTOR, 1969, C-O
FREAKS, 1932, O
FREAKS!, 1966
FREAKY FRIDAY, 1976, AA
FRECKLED RASCAL, THE, 1929, A
FRECKLES, 1917
FRECKLES, 1928
FRECKLES, 1935, A
FRECKLES, 1960, A
FRECKLES COMES HOME, 1942, A
FREDDIE STEPS OUT, 1946, A
FREDDY UNTER FREMDEN STERNEN, 1962, A
FREE AIR, 1922
FREE AND EASY, 1930, A
FREE AND EASY, 1941, A
FREE AND EQUAL, 1924
FREE FOR ALL, 1949, A
FREE GRASS, 1969, O
FREE KISSES, 1926
FREE LIPS, 1928, A
FREE LOVE, 1930
FREE SOUL, A, 1931, C
FREE SPIRIT
FREE TO LOVE, 1925
FREE, BLONDE AND 21, 1940, A
FREE, WHITE AND 21, 1963, C
FREEBIE AND THE BEAN, 1974, O
FREEDOM FOR US
FREEDOM OF THE PRESS, 1928, A
FREEDOM OF THE SEAS, 1934, A
FREEDOM RADIO
FREEDOM TO DIE, 1962, A
FREEWHEELIN', 1976, A
FREEZE BOMB, 1980
FREEZE OUT, THE, 1921
FREIBURG PASSION PLAY, 1924
FREIGHTERS OF DESTINY, 1932, A
FRENCH CANCAN, 1956, A
FRENCH CONNECTION 11, 1975, O
FRENCH CONNECTION, THE, 1971, O
FRENCH CONSPIRACY, THE, 1973, A
FRENCH DOLL, THE, 1923, A
FRENCH DRESSING, 1927, C
FRENCH DRESSING, 1964, A
FRENCH GAME, THE, 1963, C
FRENCH HEELS, 1922
FRENCH KEY, THE, 1946, A
FRENCH LEAVE, 1937, A
FRENCH LEAVE, 1948, A
FRENCH LIEUTENANT'S WOMAN, THE, 1981, O
FRENCH LINE, THE, 1954
FRENCH MISTRESS, 1960, A
FRENCH POSTCARDS, 1979
FRENCH QUARTER, 1978, O
FRENCH TOUCH, THE, 1954, A
FRENCH WAY, THE, 1952, A
FRENCH WAY, THE, 1975, O
FRENCH WITHOUT TEARS, 1939, A
FRENCH, THEY ARE A FUNNY RACE, THE, 1956, A
FRENCHIE, 1950, A
FRENCHMAN'S CREEK, 1944, A
FRENZIED FLAMES, 1926
FRENZY, 1946
FRENZY, 1972, C-O
FRESH EVERY HOUR
FRESH FROM PARIS, 1955, A
FRESHIE, THE, 1922, A
FRESHMAN LOVE, 1936, A
FRESHMAN YEAR, 1938, A
FRESHMAN, THE
FRESHMAN, THE, 1925, A
FREUD, 1962, A-C
FRIC FRAC, 1939, A
FRIDAY FOSTER, 1975, O
FRIDAY ON MY MIND, 1970
FRIDAY THE 13TH, 1916, A
FRIDAY THE 13TH, 1934, A
FRIDAY THE 13TH, 1980, O
FRIDAY THE 13TH PART II, 1981, O
FRIDAY THE 13TH PART III, 1982, O
FRIDAY THE 13TH—THE FINAL CHAPTER, 1984, O
FRIDAY THE 13TH... THE ORPHAN, 1979, O
FRIEND HUSBAND, 1918
FRIEND OF THE FAMILY, 1965, A
FRIEND OR FOE, 1982
FRIEND WILL COME TONIGHT, A, 1948, A
FRIEND WILSON'S DAUGHTER, 1915
FRIENDLIEST GIRLS IN THE WORLD, THE
FRIENDLY ENEMIES, 1925
FRIENDLY ENEMIES, 1942, A
FRIENDLY HUSBAND, A, 1923, A
FRIENDLY KILLER, THE, 1970, C-O
FRIENDLY NEIGHBORS, 1940, A
FRIENDLY PERSUASION, 1956, A
FRIENDS, 1971, O
FRIENDS AND HUSBANDS, 1983, C
FRIENDS AND LOVERS
FRIENDS AND LOVERS, 1931, A
FRIENDS AND NEIGHBORS, 1963, A
FRIENDS FOR LIFE, 1964, A
FRIENDS OF EDDIE COYLE, THE, 1973, O
FRIENDS OF MR. SWEENEY, 1934
FRIGHT
FRIGHT, 1971, O
FRIGHTENED BRIDE, THE, 1952, A
FRIGHTENED CITY, THE, 1961, A
FRIGHTENED LADY
FRIGHTENED LADY, THE
FRIGHTENED MAN, THE, 1952, A
FRIGHTMARE, 1974, O
FRIGHTMARE, 1983, O
FRIGID WIFE
FRINGE OF SOCIETY, THE, 1918
FRISCO JENNY, 1933, A
FRISCO KID, 1935, A
FRISCO KID, THE, 1979, C
FRISCO LILL, 1942, A
FRISCO SAL, 1945, A
FRISCO SALLY LEVY, 1927
FRISCO TORNADO, 1950, A
FRISCO WATERFRONT, 1935, A
FRISKY, 1955, A
FRISKY MRS. JOHNSON, THE, 1920
FRIVOLOUS SAL, 1925
FRIVOLOUS WIVES, 1920
FROG, THE, 1937, A
FROGGY'S LITTLE BROTHER
FROGMEN, THE, 1951
FROGS, 1972, C
FROM A BROADWAY TO A THRONE, 1916
FROM A ROMAN BALCONY, 1961, C
FROM BEYOND THE GRAVE, 1974, C
FROM BROADWAY TO CHEYENNE, 1932
FROM HEADQUARTERS, 1919
FROM HEADQUARTERS, 1929
FROM HEADQUARTERS, 1933, A
FROM HELL IT CAME, 1957, C
FROM HELL TO HEAVEN, 1933, C
FROM HELL TO TEXAS, 1958, C
FROM HELL TO VICTORY, 1979, C
FROM HERE TO ETERNITY, 1953, C-O
FROM NASHVILLE WITH MUSIC, 1969
FROM NOON TO THREE, 1976, C
FROM NOW ON, 1920
FROM RAGS TO RICHES
FROM RUSSIA WITH LOVE, 1963, A
FROM SHOPGIRL TO DUCHESS, 1915
FROM SPARKS—FLAMES, 1924
FROM THE DESK OF MARGARET TYDING, 1958
FROM THE EARTH TO THE MOON, 1958
FROM THE GROUND UP, 1921, A
FROM THE LIFE OF THE MARIONETTES, 1980, O
FROM THE MANGER TO THE CROSS, 1913, A
FROM THE MIXED-UP FILES OF MRS. BASIL E.
FROM THE TERRACE, 1960, C
FROM THE VALLEY OF THE MISSING, 1915
FROM THE WEST, 1920
FROM THIS DAY FORWARD, 1946, A
FROM TOP TO BOTTOM, 1933, A
FROM TWO TO SIX, 1918
FROMONT JEUNNE ET RISLER AINE, 1921
FRONT LINE KIDS, 1942, AA
FRONT PAGE STORY, 1954, A
FRONT PAGE STORY, A, 1922, A
FRONT PAGE WOMAN, 1935, A
FRONT PAGE, THE, 1931
FRONT PAGE, THE, 1974, C-O
FRONT, THE, 1976, C
FRONTIER AGENT, 1948, A

FRONTIER BADMEN, 1943, A
FRONTIER CRUSADER, 1940
FRONTIER DAYS, 1934, A
FRONTIER FEUD, 1945
FRONTIER FIGHTERS, 1947
FRONTIER FUGITIVES, 1945
FRONTIER FURY, 1943, A
FRONTIER GAL, 1945, A
FRONTIER GAMBLER, 1956
FRONTIER GUN, 1958, A
FRONTIER GUNLAW, 1946
FRONTIER HELLCAT, 1966, A
FRONTIER INVESTIGATOR, 1949, A
FRONTIER JUSTICE, 1936, A
FRONTIER LAW, 1943, A
FRONTIER MARSHAL, 1934, A
FRONTIER MARSHAL, 1939, A
FRONTIER MARSHAL IN PRAIRIE PALS
FRONTIER OF THE STARS, THE, 1921
FRONTIER OUTLAWS, 1944, A
FRONTIER OUTPOST, 1950, A
FRONTIER PHANTOM, THE, 1952, A
FRONTIER PONY EXPRESS, 1939
FRONTIER REVENGE, 1948, A
FRONTIER SCOUT, 1939, A
FRONTIER TOWN, 1938, A
FRONTIER TRAIL, THE, 1926
FRONTIER UPRISING, 1961, A
FRONTIER VENGEANCE, 1939, A
FRONTIER WOMAN, 1956
FRONTIERS OF '49, 1939, A
FRONTIERSMAN, THE, 1927
FRONTIERSMAN, THE, 1938, A
FRONTIERSMAN, THE, 1968
FROU FROU, 1914
FROU-FROU, 1955, A
FROZEN ALIVE, 1966, A
FROZEN DEAD, THE, 1967, C
FROZEN FATE, 1929
FROZEN GHOST, THE, 1945
FROZEN JUSTICE, 1929, A
FROZEN LIMITS, THE, 1939, A
FROZEN RIVER, 1929, A
FROZEN SCREAM, 1980
FROZEN WARNING, THE, 1918
FRUIT IS RIPE, THE, 1961, C
FRUIT OF DIVORCE, THE
FRUITFUL VINE, THE, 1921
FRUITS OF DESIRE, THE, 1916, A
FRUITS OF PASSION, 1919
FRUSTRATIONS, 1967, O
FU MANCHU AND THE KISS OF DEATH
FUEGO
FUEL OF LIFE, 1917
FUGITIVE AT LARGE, 1939, A
FUGITIVE FROM A PRISON CAMP, 1940, A
FUGITIVE FROM JUSTICE, A, 1940, A
FUGITIVE FROM MATRIMONY, 1919
FUGITIVE FROM SONORA, 1943, A
FUGITIVE GIRLS, 1975
FUGITIVE IN THE SKY, 1937
FUGITIVE KILLER, 1975
FUGITIVE KIND, THE, 1960, C
FUGITIVE LADY, 1934, C
FUGITIVE LADY, 1951, O
FUGITIVE LOVERS, 1934
FUGITIVE OF THE PLAINS, 1943
FUGITIVE ROAD, 1934, A
FUGITIVE SHERIFF, THE, 1936
FUGITIVE VALLEY, 1941, A
FUGITIVE, THE, 1916
FUGITIVE, THE, 1925
FUGITIVE, THE, 1933, A
FUGITIVE, THE, 1940, A
FUGITIVE, THE, 1947, C
FUGITIVES, 1929, A
FUGITIVES FOR A NIGHT, 1938, C
FULL CIRCLE, 1935, A
FULL CIRCLE, 1977, O
FULL CONFESSION, 1939, C
FULL HOUSE, A, 1920
FULL MOON HIGH, 1982, A-C
FULL MOON IN PARIS, 1984, O
FULL OF LIFE, 1956, A
FULL OF PEP, 1919
FULL SPEED, 1925
FULL SPEED AHEAD, 1936, A
FULL SPEED AHEAD, 1939, A
FULL TREATMENT, THE
FULLER BRUSH GIRL, THE, 1950, AAA
FULLER BRUSH MAN, 1948, AAA
FULLER REPORT, THE, 1966
FUN AND FANCY FREE, 1947, AAA
FUN AND GAMES, 1973
FUN AT ST. FANNY'S, 1956, AA
FUN HOUSE, THE, 1977
FUN IN ACAPULCO, 1963, A
FUN LOVING
FUN ON A WEEKEND, 1979, AA
FUN ON THE FARM, 1926
FUN WITH DICK AND JANE, 1977, C-O
FUNDOSHI ISHA
FUNERAL FOR AN ASSASSIN, 1977
FUNERAL HOME, 1982, O
FUNERAL IN BERLIN, 1966, C
FUNHOUSE, THE, 1981, O
FUNNY FACE, 1957, AA
FUNNY FARM, THE, 1982, C
FUNNY GIRL, 1968
FUNNY LADY, 1975, A
FUNNY MONEY, 1983, O
FUNNY PARISHIONER, THE
FUNNY THING HAPPENED ON THE WAY TO THE FORUM,
FUNNY THING HAPPENED ON THE WAY TO THE FORUM, A, 1966, C
FUNNYMAN, 1967, C
FUOCO FATUO
FUR COLLAR, THE, 1962
FURESSHUMAN WAKADISHO
FURIA, 1947, O
FURIES, THE, 1930, A
FURIES, THE, 1950, C
FURIN KAZAN
FURNANCE, THE, 1920
FURTHER ADVENTURES OF THE FLAG LIEUTENANT, 1927, A
FURTHER ADVENTURES OF THE WILDERNESS
FURTHER EXPLOITS OF SEXTON BLAKE, THE -MYSTERY OF THE S.S. OLYMPIC, THE (1919, Brit.)
FURTHER UP THE CREEK!, 1958
FURY, 1922
FURY, 1936, C
FURY AND THE WOMAN, 1937, A
FURY AT FURNACE CREEK, 1948, A
FURY AT GUNSIGHT PASS, 1956, O
FURY AT SHOWDOWN, 1957, O
FURY AT SMUGGLERS BAY, 1963, A
FURY BELOW, 1938, A
FURY IN PARADISE, 1955, A
FURY OF HERCULES, THE, 1961, A
FURY OF THE CONGO, 1951, AA
FURY OF THE JUNGLE, 1934, O
FURY OF THE PAGANS, 1963, C
FURY OF THE VIKINGS
FURY OF THE WILD, 1929
FURY ON THE BOSPHOROUS, 1965
FURY, THE, 1978, O
FUSS AND FEATHERS, 1918
FUSS OVER FEATHERS, 1954, AAA
FUTARI NO MUSUCKO
FUTUREWORLD, 1976, C
FUZZ, 1972, O
FUZZY PINK NIGHTGOWN, THE, 1957, A
FUZZY SETTLES DOWN, 1944, A
FYRE, 1979

-G-

G-MAN'S WIFE
G-MEN, 1935, A
G.I. BLUES, 1960, A
G.I. EXECUTIONER, THE, 1971
G.I. HONEYMOON, 1945
G.I. JANE, 1951, A
G.I. WAR BRIDES, 1946, A
GABLE AND LOMBARD, 1976, O
GABLES MYSTERY, THE, 1931, A
GABLES MYSTERY, THE, 1938, A
GABRIEL OVER THE WHITE HOUSE, 1933, C
GABRIELA, 1984, O
GABY, 1956, A
GAIETY GEORGE
GAIETY GIRL, THE, 1924
GAIETY GIRLS, THE, 1938, A
GAILY, GAILY, 1969, C-O
GAL WHO TOOK THE WEST, THE, 1949, A
GAL YOUNG UN, 1979
GALAXINA, 1980
GALAXY EXPRESS, 1982, A
GALAXY OF TERROR, 1981, O
GALIA, 1966, C
GALILEO, 1968, A
GALILEO, 1975
GALLANT BESS, 1946
GALLANT BLADE, THE, 1948, A
GALLANT DEFENDER, 1935, A
GALLANT FOOL, THE, 1926, A
GALLANT FOOL, THE, 1933, A
GALLANT HOURS, THE, 1960, A
GALLANT JOURNEY, 1946, A
GALLANT LADY, 1934, A
GALLANT LADY, 1942, A
GALLANT LEGION, THE, 1948, A
GALLANT ONE, THE, 1964, A
GALLANT SONS, 1940, A
GALLERY OF HORRORS
GALLEY SLAVE, THE, 1915
GALLIPOLI, 1981, A-C
GALLOPER, THE, 1915
GALLOPIN' THROUGH
GALLOPING ACE, THE, 1924, A
GALLOPING COWBOY, THE, 1926
GALLOPING DEVIL, THE
GALLOPING DEVILS, 1920
GALLOPING DUDE
GALLOPING DYNAMITE, 1937, A
GALLOPING FISH, 1924
GALLOPING FURY, 1927
GALLOPING GALLAGHER, 1924, A
GALLOPING GOBS, THE, 1927, A
GALLOPING JINX, 1925
GALLOPING KID, THE, 1922, A
GALLOPING KID, THE, 1932
GALLOPING LOVER, THE, 1929
GALLOPING MAJOR, THE, 1951
GALLOPING ON, 1925
GALLOPING ROMEO, 1933, A
GALLOPING THRU, 1923, A
GALLOPING THRU, 1932, A
GALLOPING THUNDER, 1927
GALLOPING THUNDER, 1946
GALLOPING VENGENCE, 1925
GALS, INCORPORATED, 1943, A
GAMBIT, 1966
GAMBLE FOR LOVE, A, 1917
GAMBLE IN LIVES, A, 1920
GAMBLE IN SOULS, A, 1916
GAMBLE WITH HEARTS, A, 1923, A
GAMBLER AND THE LADY, THE, 1952, A
GAMBLER FROM NATCHEZ, THE, 1954
GAMBLER OF THE WEST, THE, 1915
GAMBLER WORE A GUN, THE, 1961, A
GAMBLER'S ADVOCATE, 1915
GAMBLER'S CHOICE, 1944, A
GAMBLER, THE, 1958, C
GAMBLER, THE, 1974, O
GAMBLERS ALL, 1919
GAMBLERS, THE, 1914
GAMBLERS, THE, 1919
GAMBLERS, THE, 1929, A
GAMBLERS, THE, 1969, A
GAMBLERS, THE 1948
GAMBLIN' MAN
GAMBLING, 1934, A
GAMBLING DAUGHTERS, 1941, A
GAMBLING FOOL, THE, 1925
GAMBLING HOUSE, 1950, A
GAMBLING IN SOULS, 1919, A
GAMBLING LADY, 1934, A
GAMBLING ON THE HIGH SEAS, 1940, A
GAMBLING SAMURAI, THE, 1966, C
GAMBLING SEX, 1932, A
GAMBLING SHIP, 1933, A
GAMBLING SHIP, 1939, A
GAMBLING TERROR, THE, 1937, A
GAMBLING WITH SOULS, 1936
GAMBLING WIVES, 1924, A
GAME CHICKEN, THE, 1922
GAME FIGHTER, A, 1924
GAME FOR SIX LOVERS, A, 1962, A
GAME FOR THREE LOSERS, 1965, A
GAME FOR VULTURES, A, 1980, O
GAME IS OVER, THE, 1967, O
GAME OF CHANCE, A, 1932, A
GAME OF DANGER
GAME OF DEATH, A, 1945, A
GAME OF DEATH, THE, 1979, O
GAME OF LIBERTY, THE
GAME OF LIFE, THE, 1922, A
GAME OF LOVE, THE, 1954, C
GAME OF TRUTH, THE, 1961, C
GAME OF WITS, A, 1917
GAME SHOW MODELS, 1977
GAME THAT KILLS, THE, 1937, A
GAME WITH FATE, A, 1918
GAME'S UP, THE, 1919
GAMEKEEPER, THE, 1980, A
GAMERA THE INVINCIBLE, 1966, A
GAMERA VERSUS BARUGON, 1966, A
GAMERA VERSUS GAOS, 1967, A
GAMERA VERSUS GUIRON, 1969, A
GAMERA VERSUS MONSTER K, 1970, A
GAMERA VERSUS VIRAS, 1968
GAMERA VERSUS ZIGRA, 1971, A
GAMES, 1967, O
GAMES FOR SIX LOVERS
GAMES MEN PLAY, THE, 1968, O
GAMES THAT LOVERS PLAY, 1971, O
GAMES, THE, 1970
GAMESTERS, THE, 1920
GAMLET
GAMMA PEOPLE, THE, 1956, A
GAMMERA THE INVINCIBLE
GANDHI, 1982, A
GANG BULLETS, 1938, A
GANG BUSTER, THE, 1931, A
GANG BUSTERS, 1955, A

GANG SHOW, THE
GANG THAT COULDN'T SHOOT STRAIGHT, THE, 1971
GANG WAR, 1928
GANG WAR, 1940, C
GANG WAR, 1958, C-O
GANG WAR, 1962, A
GANG'S ALL HERE, 1941, A
GANG'S ALL HERE, THE
GANG'S ALL HERE, THE, 1943, A
GANG, THE, 1938, A
GANGA
GANGS INCORPORATED
GANGS OF CHICAGO, 1940, A
GANGS OF NEW YORK, 1938, A
GANGS OF SONORA, 1941, A
GANGS OF THE WATERFRONT, 1945, A
GANGSTER STORY, 1959, A
GANGSTER VIP, THE, 1968, C
GANGSTER'S BOY, 1938, A
GANGSTER'S BRIDE, THE
GANGSTER'S DEN, 1945
GANGSTER'S ENEMY NO. 1
GANGSTER'S REVENGE
GANGSTER, THE, 1947, C
GANGSTERS OF NEW YORK, THE, 1914, O
GANGSTERS OF THE FRONTIER, 1944, A
GANGSTERS, THE, 1914
GANGWAY, 1937, A
GANGWAY FOR TOMORROW, 1943, A
GANJA AND HESS, 1973, O
GAOL BREAK, 1936, A
GAOLBREAK, 1962, A
GAP, THE
GAPPA THE TRIFIBIAN MONSTER, 1967
GARAKUTA
GARBAGE MAN, THE, 1963, C
GARBO TALKS, 1984, C
GARDEN MURDER CASE, THE, 1936
GARDEN OF ALLAH, THE, 1916
GARDEN OF ALLAH, THE, 1927
GARDEN OF ALLAH, THE, 1936, C
GARDEN OF EDEN, 1954, O
GARDEN OF EDEN, THE, 1928
GARDEN OF EVIL, 1954, C
GARDEN OF KNOWLEDGE, THE, 1917, O
GARDEN OF LIES, THE, 1915
GARDEN OF RESURRECTION, THE, 1919, A
GARDEN OF THE DEAD, 1972, O
GARDEN OF THE FINZI-CONTINIS, THE, 1976, C
GARDEN OF THE MOON, 1938, A
GARDEN OF WEEDS, THE, 1924
GARDENER, THE
GARDIENS DE PHARE, 1929
GARMENT JUNGLE, THE, 1957, A
GARMENTS OF YOUTH, 1921
GARNET BRACELET, THE, 1966, A
GARRISON FOLLIES, 1940, A
GARRISON'S FINISH, 1923, A
GARRYOWEN, 1920
GARTER GIRL, THE, 1920
GARU, THE MAD MONK
GAS, 1981, O
GAS HOUSE KIDS, 1946, A
GAS HOUSE KIDS GO WEST, 1947, A
GAS HOUSE KIDS IN HOLLYWOOD, 1947, A
GAS PUMP GIRLS, 1979
GAS, OIL AND WATER, 1922
GAS-S-S-S!, 1970, O
GASBAGS, 1940
GASLIGHT, 1940, C
GASLIGHT, 1944, C
GASOLINE ALLEY, 1951, AA
GASOLINE COWBOY, 1926
GASOLINE GUS, 1921, A
GASU NINGEN DAIICHIGO
GATE CRASHER, THE, 1928, A
GATE OF FLESH, 1964, O
GATE OF HELL, 1954, C-O
GATES OF BRASS, 1919
GATES OF DOOM, THE, 1917
GATES OF DUTY, 1919
GATES OF EDEN, THE, 1916
GATES OF GLADNESS, 1918
GATES OF HELL, THE, 1983, O
GATES OF PARIS, 1958, C
GATES OF THE NIGHT, 1950, C-O
GATES TO PARADISE, 1968, C
GATEWAY, 1938
GATEWAY OF THE MOON, THE, 1928, A
GATEWAY TO GLORY, 1970, C
GATHERING OF EAGLES, A, 1963, A
GATLING GUN, THE, 1972, C
GATOR, 1976, C
GATOR BAIT, 1974, O
GAUCHO SERENADE, 1940, A
GAUCHO, THE, 1928, A
GAUCHOS OF EL DORADO, 1941, A
GAUNT STRANGER, THE
GAUNTLET, THE, 1920
GAUNTLET, THE, 1977, O
GAVILAN, 1968, C
GAWAIN AND THE GREEN KNIGHT, 1973, C-O
GAY ADVENTURE, THE, 1936
GAY ADVENTURE, THE, 1953, A
GAY AMIGO, THE, 1949, A
GAY AND DEVILISH, 1922, A
GAY BLADES, 1946, A
GAY BRIDE, THE, 1934, A-C
GAY BUCKAROO, THE, 1932, A
GAY CABALLERO, THE, 1932
GAY CABALLERO, THE, 1940, A
GAY CAVALIER, THE, 1946
GAY CITY, THE
GAY CORINTHIAN, THE, 1924, A
GAY DECEIVER, THE, 1926
GAY DECEIVERS, THE, 1969, O
GAY DECEPTION, THE, 1935, A
GAY DEFENDER, THE, 1927
GAY DESPERADO, THE, 1936, A
GAY DIPLOMAT, THE, 1931, A
GAY DIVORCEE, THE, 1934, AA
GAY DOG, THE, 1954
GAY FALCON, THE, 1941, A
GAY IMPOSTERS, THE
GAY INTRUDERS, THE, 1946, A
GAY INTRUDERS, THE, 1948, A
GAY LADY, THE, 1949, A
GAY LADY, THE, 1935
GAY LORD QUEX, THE, 1917, A-C
GAY LORD QUEX, THE, 1920
GAY LORD WARING, THE, 1916
GAY LOVE, 1936, A
GAY NINETIES
GAY OLD BIRD, THE, 1927, A
GAY OLD DOG, 1936, A
GAY OLD DOG, THE, 1919
GAY PURR-EE, 1962, AAA
GAY RANCHERO, THE, 1948, A
GAY RETREAT, THE, 1927, A
GAY SENORITA, THE, 1945, A
GAY SISTERS, THE, 1942, A-C
GAY VAGABOND, THE, 1941, A
GAYEST OF THE GAY, THE, 1924
GAZEBO, THE, 1959
GEARED TO GO, 1924, A
GEEK MAGGOT BINGO, 1983, O
GEHEIMINISSE IN GOLDEN NYLONS
GEISHA BOY, THE, 1958, A
GEISHA GIRL, 1952, A
GEISHA, A, 1978, A
GELIEBTE BESTIE
GELIGNITE GANG
GEN TO FUDO-MYOH
GENDARME OF ST. TROPEZ, THE, 1966, O
GENE AUTRY AND THE MOUNTIES, 1951, A
GENE KRUPA STORY, THE, 1959, A-C
GENERAL CRACK, 1929, A.C
GENERAL CUSTER AT LITTLE BIG HORN, 1926
GENERAL DIED AT DAWN, THE, 1936, C
GENERAL JOHN REGAN, 1921, A
GENERAL JOHN REGAN, 1933, A
GENERAL MASSACRE, 1973, O
GENERAL POST, 1920, A
GENERAL SPANKY, 1937, AA
GENERAL SUVOROV, 1941, A
GENERAL, THE, 1927, A
GENERALE DELLA ROVERE, 1960, C
GENERALS OF TOMORROW
GENERALS WITHOUT BUTTONS, 1938, A
GENERATION, 1969, C
GENEVIEVE, 1923
GENEVIEVE, 1953
GENGHIS KHAN
GENIE, THE, 1953, A
GENIUS AT WORK, 1946, A
GENIUS, THE, 1976, C
GENTLE ANNIE, 1944, A
GENTLE ART OF MURDER
GENTLE CREATURE, A, 1971, C
GENTLE CYCLONE, THE, 1926
GENTLE GANGSTER, A, 1943, A
GENTLE GIANT, 1967, AAA
GENTLE GUNMAN, THE, 1952, C
GENTLE INTRUDER, THE, 1917
GENTLE JULIA, 1923, A
GENTLE JULIA, 1936
GENTLE PEOPLE AND THE QUIET LAND, THE, 1972, A
GENTLE RAIN, THE, 1966, O
GENTLE SEX, THE, 1943, A
GENTLE TERROR, THE, 1962, A
GENTLE TOUCH, THE, 1956, A
GENTLE TRAP, THE, 1960, A
GENTLEMAN AFTER DARK, A, 1942, A
GENTLEMAN AT HEART, A, 1942, A
GENTLEMAN CHAUFFEUR
GENTLEMAN FROM AMERICA, THE, 1923
GENTLEMAN FROM ARIZONA, THE, 1940, A
GENTLEMAN FROM CALIFORNIA, THE
GENTLEMAN FROM DIXIE, 1941, A
GENTLEMAN FROM INDIANA, A, 1915
GENTLEMAN FROM LOUISIANA, 1936, A
GENTLEMAN FROM MISSISSIPPI, THE, 1914, A
GENTLEMAN FROM NOWHERE, THE, 1948, A
GENTLEMAN FROM TEXAS, 1946, A
GENTLEMAN JIM, 1942, A
GENTLEMAN JOE PALOOKA
GENTLEMAN MISBEHAVES, THE, 1946, A
GENTLEMAN OF FRANCE, A, 1921
GENTLEMAN OF LEISURE, A, 1923, A
GENTLEMAN OF PARIS, A, 1927
GENTLEMAN OF PARIS, A, 1931, A
GENTLEMAN OF QUALITY, A, 1919
GENTLEMAN OF VENTURE
GENTLEMAN PREFFERED, A, 1928
GENTLEMAN RIDER, THE
GENTLEMAN ROUGHNECK, THE, 1925
GENTLEMAN UNAFRAID, 1923
GENTLEMAN'S AGREEMENT, 1935, A
GENTLEMAN'S AGREEMENT, 1947, A
GENTLEMAN'S AGREEMENT, A, 1918
GENTLEMAN'S FATE, 1931, C
GENTLEMAN'S GENTLEMAN, A, 1939, A
GENTLEMEN ARE BORN, 1934, A
GENTLEMEN IN BLUE, THE, 1917
GENTLEMEN MARRY BRUNETTES, 1955, A
GENTLEMEN OF THE NAVY
GENTLEMEN OF THE PRESS, 1929, A
GENTLEMEN PREFER BLONDES, 1928, A
GENTLEMEN PREFER BLONDES, 1953, A
GENTLEMEN WITH GUNS, 1946, A
GENUINE, 1920
GEO, LE MYSTERIEUX, 1917
GEORDIE
GEORG, 1964, C
GEORGE, 1973, A
GEORGE AND MARGARET, 1940, A
GEORGE AND MILDRED, 1980
GEORGE IN CIVVY STREET, 1946, A
GEORGE RAFT STORY, THE, 1961, A
GEORGE TAKES THE AIR
GEORGE WASHINGTON CARVER, 1940, A
GEORGE WASHINGTON COHEN, 1928
GEORGE WASHINGTON SLEPT HERE, 1942, A
GEORGE WASHINGTON, JR., 1924
GEORGE WHITE'S 1935 SCANDALS, 1935, A
GEORGE WHITE'S SCANDALS, 1934, AA
GEORGE WHITE'S SCANDALS, 1945, A
GEORGIA ROSE, 1930
GEORGIA, GEORGIA, 1972, O
GEORGY GIRL, 1966, A-C
GERALD CRANSTON'S LADY, 1924
GERALDINE, 1929, A
GERALDINE, 1953, A
GERM, THE, 1923
GERMAN SISTERS, THE, 1982, C-O
GERMANY IN AUTUMN, 1978, O
GERMANY PALE MOTHER, 1984, O
GERMANY, YEAR ZERO, 1949
GERMINAL, 1963, A
GERONIMO, 1939, C
GERONIMO, 1962, C
GERT AND DAISY CLEAN UP, 1942, A
GERT AND DAISY'S WEEKEND, 1941, A
GERTRUD, 1966, A
GERVAISE, 1956, C-O
GESTAPO
GET BACK, 1973, C
GET CARTER, 1971, O
GET CHARLIE TULLY, 1976, C
GET CRACKING, 1943, A
GET CRAZY, 1983, O
GET DOWN AND BOOGIE, 1977
GET GOING, 1943, A
GET HEP TO LOVE, 1942, A
GET MEAN, 1976, C
GET OFF MY FOOT, 1935, A
GET ON WITH IT, 1963, A
GET OUT OF TOWN
GET OUT YOUR HANDKERCHIEFS, 1978, O
GET OUTTA TOWN, 1960, C
GET THAT GIRL, 1932, C
GET THAT GIRL, 1936
GET THAT MAN, 1935, A
GET TO KNOW YOUR RABBIT, 1972, 0
GET YOUR MAN, 1921, A
GET YOUR MAN, 1927
GET YOUR MAN, 1934
GET YOURSELF A COLLEGE GIRL, 1964, A
GET-AWAY, THE, 1941
GET-RICH-QUICK WALLINGFORD, 1921
GETAWAY, THE, 1972, O
GETTING 'EM RIGHT, 1925
GETTING AWAY WITH MURDER
GETTING EVEN, 1981, C
GETTING GERTIE'S GARTER, 1927

GETTING GERTIE'S GARTER, 1945, A
GETTING HER MAN, 1924
GETTING IT ON, 1983
GETTING MARY MARRIED, 1919, A
GETTING OF WISDOM, THE, 1977, C
GETTING OVER, 1981, A-C
GETTING STRAIGHT, 1970, C-0
GETTING TOGETHER, 1976, O
GETTING WASTED, 1980
GHARBAR
GHARE BAIRE
GHASTLY ONES, THE, 1968, O
GHETTO FREAKS
GHETTO SHAMROCK, THE, 1926
GHIDRAH, THE THREE-HEADED MONSTER, 1965, A
GHOST AND MR. CHICKEN, THE, 1966, A
GHOST AND MRS. MUIR, THE, 1942, A
GHOST AND THE GUEST, 1943, A
GHOST BREAKER, 1914
GHOST BREAKER, THE, 1922
GHOST BREAKERS, THE, 1940
GHOST CAMERA, THE, 1933, A
GHOST CATCHERS, 1944, A
GHOST CHASERS, 1951, A
GHOST CITY, 1921
GHOST CITY, 1932, A
GHOST CLUB, THE, 1914
GHOST COMES HOME, THE, 1940, A
GHOST CREEPS, THE
GHOST DANCE, 1982
GHOST DANCE, 1984, O
GHOST DIVER, 1957, A
GHOST FLOWER, THE, 1918
GHOST GOES WEST, THE, 1936, A
GHOST GOES WILD, THE, 1947, A
GHOST GUNS, 1944, A
GHOST HOUSE, THE, 1917
GHOST IN THE GARRET, THE, 1921
GHOST IN THE INVISIBLE BIKINI, 1966, C
GHOST IN THE NOONDAY SUN, 1974
GHOST OF A CHANCE, A, 1968
GHOST OF CROSSBONES CANYON, THE, 1952
GHOST OF DRAGSTRIP HOLLOW, 1959, C
GHOST OF FRANKENSTEIN, THE, 1942, C
GHOST OF HIDDEN VALLEY, 1946, A
GHOST OF JOHN HOLLING
GHOST OF OLD MORRO, THE, 1917
GHOST OF ROSY TAYLOR, THE, 1918
GHOST OF ST. MICHAEL'S. THE, 1941, A
GHOST OF THE CHINA SEA, 1958, A
GHOST OF THE RANCHO, THE, 1918
GHOST OF TOLSTON'S MANOR, THE, 1923
GHOST OF ZORRO, 1959
GHOST PATROL, 1936, A
GHOST PATROL, THE, 1923
GHOST RIDER, THE, 1925
GHOST RIDER, THE, 1935, A
GHOST RIDER, THE, 1943
GHOST SHIP, 1953, A
GHOST SHIP, THE, 1943, C
GHOST STORIES
GHOST STORY, 1974
GHOST STORY, 1981, O
GHOST TALKS, THE, 1929, A
GHOST THAT NEVER RETURNS, THE, 1930
GHOST THAT WALKS ALONE, THE, 1944, A
GHOST THAT WILL NOT RETURN, THE
GHOST TOWN, 1937, A
GHOST TOWN, 1956
GHOST TOWN GOLD, 1937, A
GHOST TOWN LAW, 1942, C
GHOST TOWN RENEGADES, 1947, A
GHOST TOWN RIDERS, 1938, A
GHOST TRAIN, THE, 1927, A
GHOST TRAIN, THE, 1933, A
GHOST TRAIN, THE, 1941, A
GHOST VALLEY, 1932, A
GHOST VALLEY RAIDERS, 1940, A
GHOST WALKS, THE, 1935
GHOST, THE, 1965, O
GHOSTBUSTERS, 1984, A-C
GHOSTS, 1915
GHOSTS IN THE NIGHT
GHOSTS OF BERKELEY SQUARE, 1947, A
GHOSTS OF HANLEY HOUSE, THE, 1974
GHOSTS OF YESTERDAY, 1918
GHOSTS ON THE LOOSE, 1943, A
GHOSTS THAT STILL WALK, 1977
GHOSTS, ITALIAN STYLE, 1969, C
GHOUL IN SCHOOL, THE
GHOUL, THE, 1934, C
GHOUL, THE, 1975, O
GIANT, 1956, A
GIANT BEHEMOTH, THE
GIANT CLAW, THE, 1957, A
GIANT FROM THE UNKNOWN, 1958, C
GIANT GILA MONSTER, THE, 1959, A
GIANT LEECHES, THE
GIANT OF HIS RACE, A, 1921
GIANT OF MARATHON, THE, 1960, O
GIANT OF METROPOLIS, THE, 1963, A
GIANT SPIDER INVASION, THE, 1975, A
GIANTS A' FIRE
GIBRALTAR
GIBRALTAR ADVENTURE
GIDEON OF SCOTLAND YARD, 1959, A
GIDEON'S DAY
GIDGET, 1959
GIDGET GOES HAWAIIAN, 1961, A
GIDGET GOES TO ROME, 1963, A
GIFT
GIFT FOR HEIDI, A, 1958
GIFT GIRL, THE, 1917
GIFT HORSE, THE
GIFT O' GAB, 1917
GIFT OF GAB, 1934
GIFT OF LOVE, THE, 1958, A
GIFT SUPREME, THE, 1920
GIFT, THE
GIFT, THE, 1983, O
GIGANTES PLANETARIOS, 1965
GIGANTIS, 1959, A
GIGI, 1958, A
GIGOLETTE, 1920
GIGOLETTE, 1935, A-C
GIGOLETTES OF PARIS, 1933, A
GIGOLO, 1926
GIGOT, 1962, A
GILBERT AND SULLIVAN
GILDA, 1946, C
GILDED BUTTERFLY, THE, 1926, A
GILDED CAGE, THE, 1916, A
GILDED CAGE, THE, 1954, A
GILDED DREAM, THE, 1920, A
GILDED FOOL, THE, 1915
GILDED HIGHWAY, THE, 1926, A
GILDED LIES, 1921
GILDED LILY, THE, 1921, A
GILDED LILY, THE, 1935, AA
GILDED SPIDER, THE, 1916, A
GILDED YOUTH, A, 1917
GILDERSLEEVE ON BROADWAY, 1943, A
GILDERSLEEVE'S BAD DAY, 1943, A
GILDERSLEEVE'S GHOST, 1944, A
GIMME AN 'F', 1984, O
GIMMIE, 1923, A
GINA, 1961, C
GINGER, 1919
GINGER, 1935, A
GINGER, 1947, A
GINGER, 1972
GINGER IN THE MORNING, 1973, A
GINGHAM GIRL, THE, 1927
GINSBERG THE GREAT, 1927, A
GION MATSURI
GIORDANO BRUNO, 1973, O
GIORNI DI FUOCO
GIPSY BLOOD
GIPSY CAVALIER, A, 1922
GIRARA, 1967, G
GIRDLE OF GOLD, 1952, A
GIRL AGAINST NAPOLEON, A
GIRL ALASKA, THE, 1919
GIRL AND THE CRISIS, THE, 1917
GIRL AND THE GAMBLER, THE, 1939, A
GIRL AND THE GENERAL, THE, 1967, C
GIRL AND THE HUGLER, THE, 1967, AA
GIRL AND THE JUDGE, THE, 1918
GIRL AND THE LEGEND, THE, 1966, A
GIRL AND THE PALIO, THE
GIRL ANGLE, THE, 1917
GIRL AT BAY, A, 1919
GIRL AT HOME, THE, 1917
GIRL BY THE ROADSIDE, THE, 1918
GIRL CAN'T HELP IT, THE, 1956, C
GIRL CAN'T STOP, THE, 1966, C
GIRL CRAZY, 1932, A
GIRL CRAZY, 1943, AAA
GIRL CRAZY, 1965
GIRL DODGER, THE, 1919
GIRL DOWNSTAIRS, THE, 1938, A
GIRL FEVER, 1961, A
GIRL FOR JOE, A
GIRL FRIEND, THE, 1935, A
GIRL FRIENDS, THE
GIRL FROM ALASKA, 1942
GIRL FROM AVENUE A, 1940, A
GIRL FROM BEYOND, THE, 1918
GIRL FROM BOHEMIA, THE, 1918
GIRL FROM CALGARY, 1932, A
GIRL FROM CARTHAGE, THE, 1924
GIRL FROM CHICAGO, THE, 1927, A
GIRL FROM CHINA, THE
GIRL FROM CONEY ISLAND, THE
GIRL FROM DOWNING STREET, THE, 1918, A
GIRL FROM GAY PAREE, THE, 1927
GIRL FROM GOD'S COUNTRY, 1940, A
GIRL FROM GOD'S COUNTRY, THE, 1921
GIRL FROM HAVANA, 1940, A
GIRL FROM HAVANA, THE, 1929, A
GIRL FROM HIS TOWN, THE, 1915, A
GIRL FROM HONG KONG, 1966, A
GIRL FROM IRELAND
GIRL FROM JONES BEACH, THE, 1949, AA
GIRL FROM LORRAINE, A, 1982, O
GIRL FROM MANDALAY, 1936, A
GIRL FROM MANHATTAN, 1948, A
GIRL FROM MAXIM'S. THE, 1936, A
GIRL FROM MEXICO, 1930
GIRL FROM MEXICO, THE, 1939, A
GIRL FROM MISSOURI, THE, 1934
GIRL FROM MONTEREY, THE, 1943, A
GIRL FROM MONTMARTRE, THE, 1926
GIRL FROM NOWHERE, THE, 1919
GIRL FROM NOWHERE, THE, 1921
GIRL FROM PARIS, THE
GIRL FROM PETROVKA, THE, 1974, A
GIRL FROM POLTAVA, 1937, A
GIRL FROM PORCUPINE, THE, 1921
GIRL FROM RECTOR'S, THE, 1917
GIRL FROM RIO, THE, 1927, A
GIRL FROM RIO, THE, 1939, A
GIRL FROM ROCKY POINT, THE, 1922
GIRL FROM SAN LORENZO, THE, 1950, A
GIRL FROM SCOTLAND YARD, THE, 1937, A
GIRL FROM STARSHIP VENUS, THE, 1975, O
GIRL FROM TENTH AVENUE, THE, 1935, A
GIRL FROM THE MARSH CROFT, THE, 1935, A
GIRL FROM THE OUTSIDE, THE, 1919
GIRL FROM THE WEST, 1923, A
GIRL FROM TOBACCO ROW, THE, 1966
GIRL FROM TRIESTE, THE, 1983, C
GIRL FROM VALLADOLIO, 1958, A
GIRL FROM WOOLWORTH'S, THE, 1929, A
GIRL GAME, 1968, C
GIRL GETTERS, THE, 1966, C
GIRL GLORY, THE, 1917
GIRL GRABBERS, THE, 1968, O
GIRL HABIT, 1931, A
GIRL HAPPY, 1965, A
GIRL HE DIDN'T BUY, THE, 1928
GIRL HE LEFT BEHIND, THE, 1956, A
GIRL HUNTERS, THE, 1963, C-O
GIRL I ABANDONED, THE, 1970, C-O
GIRL I LEFT BEHIND ME, THE, 1915
GIRL I LOVED, THE, 1923
GIRL I MADE, THE
GIRL IN 313, 1940, A
GIRL IN 419, 1933
GIRL IN A MILLION, A, 1946, A
GIRL IN BLACK STOCKINGS, 1957
GIRL IN BLUE, THE, 1974
GIRL IN BOHEMIA, A, 1919
GIRL IN DANGER, 1934, A
GIRL IN DISTRESS, 1941, A
GIRL IN EVERY PORT, A, 1928, A
GIRL IN EVERY PORT, A, 1952, A
GIRL IN GOLD BOOTS, 1968, O
GIRL IN HIS HOUSE, THE, 1918
GIRL IN HIS POCKET
GIRL IN HIS ROOM, THE, 1922
GIRL IN LOVER'S LANE, THE, 1960
GIRL IN NUMBER 29, THE, 1920
GIRL IN OVERALLS, THE
GIRL IN PAWN
GIRL IN POSSESSION, 1934, A
GIRL IN ROOM 13, 1961, A
GIRL IN ROOM 17, THE
GIRL IN THE BIKINI, THE, 1958
GIRL IN THE CASE, 1944, A
GIRL IN THE CHECKERED COAT, THE, 1917
GIRL IN THE CROWD, THE, 1934, A
GIRL IN THE DARK, THE, 1918, A
GIRL IN THE FLAT, THE, 1934, A
GIRL IN THE GLASS CAGE, THE, 1929, A
GIRL IN THE HEADLINES, THE
GIRL IN THE INVISIBLE BIKINI, THE
GIRL IN THE KREMLIN, THE, 1957, A
GIRL IN THE LEATHER SUIT
GIRL IN THE LIMOUSINE, THE, 1924
GIRL IN THE NEWS, THE, 1941, A
GIRL IN THE NIGHT, THE, 1931, A
GIRL IN THE PAINTING, THE, 1948, A
GIRL IN THE PICTURE, THE, 1956, A
GIRL IN THE PULLMAN, THE, 1927
GIRL IN THE RAIN, 1927
GIRL IN THE RAIN, THE, 1920
GIRL IN THE RED VELVET SWING, THE, 1955, C
GIRL IN THE SHOW, THE, 1929, A
GIRL IN THE STREET, 1938, A
GIRL IN THE TAXI, 1937, A
GIRL IN THE TAXI, THE, 1921
GIRL IN THE WEB, THE, 1920
GIRL IN THE WOODS, 1958
GIRL IN TROUBLE, 1963, C
GIRL IN WHITE, THE, 1952, A
GIRL IS MINE, THE, 1950, A

GIRL LIKE THAT, A, 1917
GIRL LOVES BOY, 1937
GIRL MADNESS
GIRL MERCHANTS
GIRL MISSING, 1933, A
GIRL MOST LIKELY, THE, 1957, AA
GIRL MUST LIVE, A, 1941, A
GIRL NAMED MARY, A, 1920
GIRL NAMED TAMIRO, A, 1962, A
GIRL NEXT DOOR, THE, 1953, A
GIRL O' MY DREAMS, 1935, A
GIRL O'DREAMS, THE, 1918
GIRL OF GOLD, THE, 1925
GIRL OF LONDON, A, 1925, A
GIRL OF LOST LAKE, THE, 1916
GIRL OF MY DREAMS
GIRL OF MY DREAMS, THE, 1918
GIRL OF MY HEART, 1920, A
GIRL OF THE GOLDEN WEST, 1930, A
GIRL OF THE GOLDEN WEST, THE, 1915, A
GIRL OF THE GOLDEN WEST, THE, 1923, A
GIRL OF THE GOLDEN WEST, THE, 1938, AA
GIRL OF THE GYPSY CAMP, THE, 1925
GIRL OF THE LIMBERLOST, 1934, A
GIRL OF THE LIMBERLOST, A, 1924
GIRL OF THE LIMBERLOST, THE, 1945, A
GIRL OF THE MOORS, THE, 1961, C-O
GIRL OF THE MOUNTAINS, 1958, C-O
GIRL OF THE NIGHT, 1960, C-O
GIRL OF THE NILE, THE, 1967
GIRL OF THE OZARKS, 1936, A
GIRL OF THE PORT, 1930, A
GIRL OF THE RIO, 1932, A
GIRL OF THE SEA, 1920
GIRL OF THE SUNNY SOUTH, THE, 1913
GIRL OF THE TIMBER CLAIMS, THE, 1917
GIRL OF THE WEST, 1925
GIRL OF THE YEAR
GIRL OF TODAY, THE, 1918
GIRL ON A CHAIN GANG, 1966, O
GIRL ON A MOTORCYCLE, THE, 1968, O
GIRL ON APPROVAL, 1962, A
GIRL ON THE BARGE, THE, 1929, A
GIRL ON THE BOAT, THE, 1962, A
GIRL ON THE BRIDGE, THE, 1951, A
GIRL ON THE CANAL, THE, 1947, A
GIRL ON THE FRONT PAGE, THE, 1936, A
GIRL ON THE MOON, THE
GIRL ON THE PIER, THE, 1953, A
GIRL ON THE RUN, 1961, A
GIRL ON THE SPOT, 1946, A
GIRL ON THE STAIRS, THE, 1924, A
GIRL OVERBOARD, 1929, A
GIRL OVERBOARD, 1937, A
GIRL PHILIPPA, THE, 1917
GIRL PROBLEM, THE, 1919
GIRL RUSH, 1944, A
GIRL RUSH, THE, 1955, A
GIRL SAID NO, THE, 1930
GIRL SAID NO, THE, 1937, A
GIRL SHY, 1924, A
GIRL SMUGGLERS, 1967, O
GIRL STROKE BOY, 1971, C
GIRL SWAPPERS, THE
GIRL THIEF, THE, 1938, AA
GIRL TROUBLE, 1933
GIRL TROUBLE, 1942, A
GIRL WAS YOUNG, THE
GIRL WHO CAME BACK, THE, 1918
GIRL WHO CAME BACK, THE, 1923
GIRL WHO CAME BACK, THE, 1935, A
GIRL WHO COULDN'T GROW UP, THE, 1917
GIRL WHO COULDN'T QUITE, THE, 1949, A
GIRL WHO COULDN'T SAY NO, THE, 1969, A
GIRL WHO DARED, THE
GIRL WHO DARED, THE, 1920, A
GIRL WHO DARED, THE, 1944, A
GIRL WHO DID NOT CARE, THE
GIRL WHO DIDN'T THINK, THE, 1917
GIRL WHO DOESN'T KNOW, THE, 1917
GIRL WHO FORGOT, THE, 1939, A
GIRL WHO HAD EVERYTHING, THE, 1953, A
GIRL WHO KNEW TOO MUCH, THE, 1969, O
GIRL WHO LOVES A SOLDIER, THE, 1916, A
GIRL WHO RAN WILD, THE, 1922
GIRL WHO STAYED AT HOME, THE, 1919, A
GIRL WHO TOOK THE WRONG TURNING, THE, 1915, A
GIRL WHO WON OUT, THE, 1917
GIRL WHO WOULDN'T QUIT, THE, 1918, A
GIRL WHO WOULDN'T WORK, THE, 1925, A
GIRL WHO WRECKED HIS HOME, THE, 1916
GIRL WITH A JAZZ HEART, THE, 1920
GIRL WITH A PISTOL, THE, 1968, A
GIRL WITH A SUITCASE, 1961, A
GIRL WITH GREEN EYES, 1964, A-C
GIRL WITH IDEAS, A, 1937
GIRL WITH NO REGRETS, THE, 1919
GIRL WITH THE CHAMPAGNE EYES, THE, 1918
GIRL WITH THE FABULOUS BOX, THE, 1969
GIRL WITH THE GOLDEN EYES, THE, 1962, C
GIRL WITH THE GREEN EYES, THE, 1916
GIRL WITH THE HAT-BOX, 1927
GIRL WITH THE JAZZ HEART, THE, 1920
GIRL WITH THE RED HAIR, THE, 1983, A
GIRL WITH THREE CAMELS, THE, 1968, A
GIRL WITHOUT A ROOM, 1933, A
GIRL WITHOUT A SOUL, THE, 1917, A
GIRL WOMAN, THE, 1919
GIRL'S DESIRE, A, 1922
GIRL'S FOLLY, A, 1917, A
GIRL, A GUY AND A GOB, A, 1941, A
GIRL, THE BODY, AND THE PILL, THE, 1967, O
GIRL-SHY COWBOY, THE, 1928
GIRLFRIENDS, 1978, A-C
GIRLS, 1919
GIRLS ABOUT TOWN, 1931
GIRLS ARE FOR LOVING, 1973
GIRLS AT SEA, 1958, A
GIRLS CAN PLAY, 1937, A
GIRLS DEMAND EXCITEMENT, 1931, A
GIRLS DISAPPEAR
GIRLS DON'T GAMBLE, 1921, A
GIRLS FOR RENT, 1974
GIRLS FROM THUNDER STRIP, THE, 1966, O
GIRLS GONE WILD, 1929, A
GIRLS HE LEFT BEHIND, THE
GIRLS IN ACTION
GIRLS IN ARMS
GIRLS IN CHAINS, 1943, A
GIRLS IN PRISON, 1956, C
GIRLS IN THE NIGHT, 1953, C
GIRLS IN THE STREET, 1937, A
GIRLS IN UNIFORM,, 1932
GIRLS IN UNIFORM, 1965
GIRLS MEN FORGET, 1924
GIRLS NEVER TELL
GIRLS NEXT DOOR, THE, 1979
GIRLS NIGHT OUT, 1984, O
GIRLS OF 42ND STREET, 1974
GIRLS OF LATIN QUARTER, 1960, A
GIRLS OF PLEASURE ISLAND, THE, 1953, A
GIRLS OF SPIDER ISLAND
GIRLS OF THE BIG HOUSE, 1945, A
GIRLS OF THE ROAD, 1940, C
GIRLS ON PROBATION, 1938, A
GIRLS ON THE BEACH, 1965, A
GIRLS ON THE LOOSE, 1958
GIRLS PLEASE!, 1934, A
GIRLS UNDER TWENTY-ONE, 1940, A
GIRLS WHO DARE, 1929, A
GIRLS WILLS BE BOYS, 1934, A
GIRLS! GIRLS! GIRLS!, 1962, A
GIRLS' DORMITORY, 1936, A
GIRLS' SCHOOL, 1938, A
GIRLS' SCHOOL, 1950, A
GIRLS' TOWN, 1942, A
GIRLS' TOWN, 1959, C
GIRLS, THE, 1972, O
GIRLY
GIRO CITY, 1982, C
GIT ALONG, LITTLE DOGIES, 1937, A
GIT!, 1965
GITANELLA, 1924
GIU LA TESTA
GIULIETTA DEGLI SPIRITI
GIULIO CEASRE IL CONQUISTATORE DELLE GALLIE
GIULLI, 1927
GIUSEPPE VENDUTO DAI FRATELLI
GIVE A DOG A HONE, 1967, A
GIVE A GIRL A BREAK, 1953, A
GIVE AND TAKE
GIVE AND TARE, 1929, A
GIVE HER A RING, 1936, A
GIVE HER THE MOON, 1970, A
GIVE ME A SAILOR, 1938, A
GIVE ME MY CHANCE, 1958, C
GIVE ME THE STARS, 1944, A
GIVE ME YOUR HEART, 1936, A
GIVE MY REGARDS TO BROAD STREET, 1984, A-C
GIVE MY REGARDS TO BROADWAY, 1948, A
GIVE OUT, SISTERS, 1942, A
GIVE US THE MOON, 1944, A
GIVE US THIS DAY
GIVE US THIS DAY, 1913
GIVE US THIS NIGHT, 1936, A
GIVE US WINGS, 1940, A
GIVE'EM HELL, HARRY!, 1975, A
GIVEN WORD, THE, 1964, A
GIVING BECKY A CHANCE, 1917
GLAD EYE, THE, 1920
GLAD EYE, THE, 1927
GLAD RAG DOLL, THE, 1929, O
GLAD TIDINGS, 1953, A
GLADIATOR OF ROME, 1963, C
GLADIATOR, THE, 1938, AAA
GLADIATORERNA
GLADIATORS 7, 1964, O
GLADIATORS, THE, 1970, C-O
GLADIOLA, 1915, A
GLAMOROUS NIGHT, 1937, C
GLAMOUR, 1931, A
GLAMOUR, 1934, C
GLAMOUR BOY, 1941, AA
GLAMOUR BOY, 1940
GLAMOUR FOR SALE, 1940, A
GLAMOUR GIRL, 1938, A
GLAMOUR GIRL, 1947, A
GLASS ALIBI, THE, 1946, A
GLASS BOTTOM BOAT, THE, 1966, A
GLASS CAGE, THE
GLASS CAGE, THE, 1964, O
GLASS HOUSES, 1922
GLASS HOUSES, 1972, O
GLASS KEY, THE, 1935, C
GLASS KEY, THE, 1942, O
GLASS MENAGERIE, THE, 1950, A
GLASS MOUNTAIN, THE, 1950, A
GLASS OF WATER, A, 1962, A
GLASS SLIPPER, THE, 1955, A
GLASS SPHINX, THE, 1968, A
GLASS TOMB, THE, 1955, A
GLASS TOWER, THE, 1959, A
GLASS WALL, THE, 1953, A
GLASS WEB, THE, 1953, A
GLEAM O'DAWN, 1922, A
GLEN AND RANDA, 1971
GLEN OR GLENDA, 1953, O
GLENISTER OF THE MOUNTED, 1926
GLENN MILLER STORY, THE, 1953, AAA
GLENROWAN AFFAIR, THE, 1951, C
GLIMPSE OF PARADISE, A, 1934, A
GLIMPSES OF THE MOON, THE, 1923
GLITTERBALL, THE, 1977
GLOBAL AFFAIR, A, 1964, A
GLOIRE ROUGE, 1923
GLORIA, 1980, O
GLORIANA, 1916
GLORIFYING THE AMERICAN GIRL, 1930
GLORIOUS ADVENTURE, THE, 1918
GLORIOUS ADVENTURE, THE, 1922, A
GLORIOUS FOOL, THE, 1922
GLORIOUS LADY, THE, 1919
GLORIOUS SACRIFICE
GLORIOUS TRAIL, THE, 1928
GLORIOUS YOUTH, 1928
GLORY, 1917
GLORY, 1955, AAA
GLORY ALLEY, 1952, C
GLORY AT SEA, 1952, A
GLORY BOY, 1971, O
GLORY BRIGADE, THE, 1953, C
GLORY GUYS, THE, 1965, C
GLORY OF CLEMENTINA, THE, 1922
GLORY OF FAITH, THE, 1938, A
GLORY OF LOVE, THE
GLORY OF YOLANDA, THE, 1917
GLORY STOMPERS, THE, 1967, O
GLORY TRAIL, THE, 1937, A
GLOVE, THE, 1979
GLOVE, THE, 1980, O
GLOW OF LIFE, THE, 1918
GLOWING AUTUMN, 1981, A-C
GNOME-MOBILE, THE, 1967, AAA
GO AND GET IT, 1920
GO CHASE YOURSELF, 1938, A
GO DOWN DEATH, 1944
GO FOR A TAKE, 1972
GO FOR BROKE, 1951, A
GO GET 'EM GARRINGER, 1919
GO GET HIM, 1921
GO INTO YOUR DANCE, 1935, A
GO KART GO, 1964, AAA
GO NAKED IN THE WORLD, 1961, O
GO STRAIGHT, 1921
GO STRAIGHT, 1925
GO TELL IT ON THE MOUNTAIN, 1984, A
GO TELL THE SPARTANS, 1978, O
GO TO BLAZES, 1962, A
GO WEST, 1925, A
GO WEST, 1940, A
GO WEST, YOUNG LADY, 1941, A
GO WEST, YOUNG MAN, 1919, A
GO WEST, YOUNG MAN, 1936, C
GO, JOHNNY, GO!, 1959, A
GO, MAN, GO!, 1954, A
GO-BETWEEN, THE, 1971, A-C
GO-GET-'EM HAINES, 1936
GO-GETTER, THE, 1923
GO-GETTER, THE, 1937, A
GO-GO SET
GOAT GETTER, 1925, A
GOAT, THE, 1918
GOBEN NO TSUBAKI
GOBS AND GALS, 1952, A
GOD AND THE MAN, 1918, A

GOD BLESS DR. SHAGETZ, 1977
GOD BLESS OUT RED, WHITE AND BLUE, 1918
GOD FORGIVES—I DON'T!, 1969, O
GOD GAME, THE
GOD GAVE HIM A DOG
GOD GAVE ME TWENTY CENTS, 1926
GOD IN THE GARDEN, THE, 1921, A
GOD IS MY CO-PILOT, 1945, A
GOD IS MY PARTNER, 1957, A
GOD IS MY WITNESS, 1931, A
GOD OF LITTLE CHILDREN, 1917
GOD OF MANKIND, 1928
GOD OF VENGEANCE, THE, 1914
GOD TOLD ME TO, 1976, O
GOD'S BLOODY ACRE, 1975
GOD'S CLAY, 1919
GOD'S CLAY, 1928
GOD'S COUNTRY, 1946, A
GOD'S COUNTRY AND THE LAW, 1921
GOD'S COUNTRY AND THE MAN, 1931, A
GOD'S COUNTRY AND THE MAN, 1937, A
GOD'S COUNTRY AND THE WOMAN, 1916
GOD'S COUNTRY AND THE WOMAN, 1937
GOD'S CRUCIBLE, 1917
GOD'S CRUCIBLE, 1921
GOD'S GIFT TO WOMEN, 1931, A
GOD'S GOLD, 1921
GOD'S GOOD MAN, 1921
GOD'S GREAT WILDERNESS, 1927
GOD'S GUN, 1977, O
GOD'S HALF ACRE, 1916, A
GOD'S LAW AND MAN'S, 1917
GOD'S LITTLE ACRE, 1958, O
GOD'S MAN, 1917
GOD'S OUTLAW, 1919, A
GOD'S PRODIGAL, 1923
GOD'S STEPCHILDREN, 1937
GOD'S WITNESS, 1915
GOD, MAN AND DEVIL, 1949
GODDESS OF LOST LAKE, THE, 1918
GODDESS OF LOVE, THE, 1960, O
GODDESS, THE, 1958, C-O
GODDESS, THE, 1962
GODFATHER, THE, 1972, O
GODFATHER, THE, PART II, 1974, O
GODLESS GIRL, THE, 1929, C
GODLESS MEN, 1921
GODS MUST BE CRAZY, THE, 1984, C
GODS OF FATE, 1916
GODSEND, THE, 1980, O
GODSON, THE, 1972, C-O
GODSPELL, 1973, C
GODY MOLODYYE
GODZILLA
GODZILLA TAI MOTHRA
GODZILLA VERSUS THE COSMIC MONSTER, 1974, C
GODZILLA VERSUS THE SEA MONSTER, 1966, C
GODZILLA VERSUS THE SMOG MONSTER, 1972
GODZILLA VS. MEGALON, 1976, C
GODZILLA VS. THE THING, 1964, C
GODZILLA'S REVENGE, 1969
GODZILLA, RING OF THE MONSTERS, 1956, C
GOFORTH
GOG, 1954, A
GOHA, 1958, O
GOIN' ALL THE WAY, 1982
GOIN' COCONUTS, 1978, AAA
GOIN' DOWN THE ROAD, 1970, O
GOIN' HOME, 1976, AAA
GOIN' SOUTH, 1978, O
GOIN' TO TOWN, 1935, C
GOIN' TO TOWN, 1944, A
GOING APE!, 1981, A
GOING BERSERK, 1983, O
GOING CROOKED, 1926
GOING GAY
GOING HIGHBROW, 1935, A
GOING HOLLYWOOD, 1933, A
GOING HOME, 1971, O
GOING IN STYLE, 1979, C
GOING MY WAY, 1944, AAA
GOING PLACES, 1939, A
GOING PLACES, 1974, O
GOING SOME, 1920
GOING STEADY, 1958, A
GOING STRAIGHT, 1916
GOING STRAIGHT, 1933, A
GOING THE LIMIT, 1925, A
GOING THE LIMIT, 1926
GOING TO TOWN
GOING UP, 1923
GOING WILD, 1931, A
GOJIRA TAI MOSUHA
GOJUMAN-NIN NO ISAN
GOKE, BODYSNATCHER FROM HELL, 1968, O
GOLD, 1932, A
GOLD, 1934, C
GOLD, 1974, O
GOLD AND GRIT, 1925
GOLD AND THE GIRL, 1925, A
GOLD AND THE WOMAN, 1916
GOLD CURE, THE, 1919
GOLD CURE, THE, 1925
GOLD DIGGERS IN PARIS, 1938, A
GOLD DIGGERS OF 1933, 1933, A
GOLD DIGGERS OF 1935, 1935, A
GOLD DIGGERS OF 1937, 1936, A
GOLD DIGGERS OF BROADWAY, 1929, A
GOLD DIGGERS, THE, 1923, A
GOLD DIGGERS, THE, 1984
GOLD DUST GERTIE, 1931
GOLD EXPRESS, THE, 1955, A
GOLD FEVER, 1952, A
GOLD FOR THE CAESARS, 1964, C
GOLD FROM WEEPAH, 1927
GOLD GRABBERS, 1922
GOLD GUITAR, THE, 1966, A
GOLD HEELS, 1924
GOLD HUNTERS, THE, 1925
GOLD IS WHERE YOU FIND IT, 1938
GOLD MADNESS, 1923, A
GOLD MINE IN THE SKY, 1938, A
GOLD OF NAPLES, 1957, C-O
GOLD OF THE SEVEN SAINTS, 1961, A
GOLD RACKET, THE, 1937, A
GOLD RAIDERS, THE, 1952
GOLD RUSH, THE, 1925, A
GOLD WEST, THE, 1932
GOLDEN ARROW, THE, 1936, A
GOLDEN ARROW, THE, 1964, A
GOLDEN ARROW, THE, 1949
GOLDEN BED, THE, 1925
GOLDEN BEETLE, THE, 1914
GOLDEN BIRD, THE
GOLDEN BLADE, THE, 1953, A
GOLDEN BOX, THE, 1970
GOLDEN BOY, 1939, A
GOLDEN BULLET
GOLDEN CAGE, THE, 1933, A
GOLDEN CALF, THE, 1930, AA
GOLDEN CHANCE, THE, 1915, A
GOLDEN CLAW, THE, 1915
GOLDEN CLOWN, THE, 1927
GOLDEN COACH, THE, 1953, A-C
GOLDEN COCOON, THE, 1926
GOLDEN DAWN, 1930, A
GOLDEN DAWN, THE, 1921
GOLDEN DEMON, 1956, C-O
GOLDEN DISK
GOLDEN DREAMS, 1922
GOLDEN EARRINGS, 1947, C
GOLDEN EYE, THE
GOLDEN FETTER, THE, 1917
GOLDEN FLAME, THE, 1923
GOLDEN FLEECE, THE, 1918
GOLDEN FLEECING, THE, 1940, A
GOLDEN GALLOWS, THE, 1922
GOLDEN GATE GIRL, 1941, C
GOLDEN GIFT, THE, 1922, A
GOLDEN GIRL, 1951, AA
GOLDEN GLOVES, 1940, A
GOLDEN GLOVES STORY, THE, 1950, A
GOLDEN GLOVES, 1939
GOLDEN GOAL, THE, 1918
GOLDEN GOD, THE, 1917
GOLDEN GODDESS, THE, 1916
GOLDEN GOOSE, THE, 1966
GOLDEN HANDS OF KURIGAL, THE, 1949
GOLDEN HARVEST, 1933, A
GOLDEN HAWK, THE, 1952, A
GOLDEN HEAD, THE, 1965, A
GOLDEN HEIST, THE
GOLDEN HELMET
GOLDEN HOOFS, 1941, AAA
GOLDEN HORDE, THE, 1951, A
GOLDEN IDIOT, THE, 1917
GOLDEN IDOL, THE, 1954, AA
GOLDEN IVORY
GOLDEN LADY, THE, 1979, O
GOLDEN LINK, THE, 1954, A
GOLDEN MADONNA, THE, 1949, A
GOLDEN MARIE
GOLDEN MASK, THE, 1954, A
GOLDEN MISTRESS, THE, 1954, A
GOLDEN MOUNTAINS, 1958, A
GOLDEN NEEDLES, 1974, O
GOLDEN NYMPHS, THE
GOLDEN PLAGUE, THE, 1963, A
GOLDEN PRINCESS, THE, 1925
GOLDEN RABBIT, THE, 1962, A
GOLDEN RENDEZVOUS, 1977, O
GOLDEN ROSARY, THE, 1917
GOLDEN RULE KATE, 1917
GOLDEN SALAMANDER, 1950, A
GOLDEN SEA, THE, 1919
GOLDEN SEAL, THE, 1983, AAA
GOLDEN SHACKLES, 1928
GOLDEN SHOWER, THE, 1919
GOLDEN SILENCE, 1923
GOLDEN SNARE, THE, 1921
GOLDEN STALLION, THE, 1949, A
GOLDEN STRAIN, THE, 1925
GOLDEN THOUGHT, A, 1924
GOLDEN TRAIL, THE, 1920
GOLDEN TRAIL, THE, 1927
GOLDEN TRAIL, THE, 1940, A
GOLDEN TRAIL, THE 1937
GOLDEN VOYAGE OF SINBAD, THE, 1974, AAA
GOLDEN WEB, THE, 1920
GOLDEN WEB, THE, 1926
GOLDEN WEST, THE, 1932, A
GOLDEN YUKON, THE, 1927
GOLDENGIRL, 1979, O
GOLDFINGER, 1964, C-O
GOLDFISH, THE, 1924, A
GOLDIE, 1931
GOLDIE GETS ALONG, 1933, A
GOLDSTEIN, 1964, O
GOLDTOWN GHOST RIDERS, 1953, A
GOLDWYN FOLLIES, THE, 1938, A
GOLEM, 1980, C
GOLEM, THE, 1914
GOLEM, THE, 1937, C
GOLEM: HOW HE CAME INTO THE WORLD, THE, 1920, C
GOLF WIDOWS, 1928
GOLFO
GOLGOTHA, 1937
GOLIATH AGAINST THE GIANTS, 1963, A
GOLIATH AND THE BARBARIANS, 1960, A
GOLIATH AND THE DRAGON, 1961, A
GOLIATH AND THE SINS OF BABYLON, 1964, A
GOLIATH AND THE VAMPIRES, 1964, C
GOLIATHON, 1979, C
GONE ARE THE DAYS, 1963, A
GONE IN 60 SECONDS, 1974, C
GONE TO EARTH
GONE TO GROUND, 1976
GONE TO THE DOGS, 1939, A
GONE WITH THE WEST, 1976
GONE WITH THE WIND, 1939, A
GONG SHOW MOVIE, THE, 1980, C
GONKS GO BEAT, 1965
GONZAQUE, 1923
GOOD AND EVIL, 1921
GOOD AND NAUGHTY, 1926, A
GOOD AS GOLD, 1927
GOOD BAD BOY, 1924
GOOD BAD GIRL, THE, 1931, C
GOOD BAD MAN, THE, 1916, A
GOOD BEGINNING, THE, 1953, A
GOOD COMPANIONS, 1933, A
GOOD COMPANIONS, THE, 1957, A
GOOD DAME, 1934, A
GOOD DAY FOR A HANGING, 1958, A
GOOD DAY FOR FIGHTING
GOOD DIE YOUNG, THE, 1954, C
GOOD DISSONANCE LIKE A MAN, A, 1977, C
GOOD EARTH, THE, 1937, A
GOOD FAIRY, THE, 1935, A
GOOD FELLOWS, THE, 1943, A
GOOD FOR NOTHING, THE, 1917
GOOD GIRLS GO TO PARIS, 1939, A
GOOD GRACIOUS ANNABELLE, 1919
GOOD GUYS AND THE BAD GUYS, THE, 1969, A-C
GOOD GUYS WEAR BLACK, 1978, O
GOOD HUMOR MAN, THE, 1950, A
GOOD INTENTIONS, 1930, A
GOOD LITTLE DEVIL, A, 1914, A
GOOD LOSER, THE, 1918
GOOD LUCK, MISS WYCKOFF, 1979, O
GOOD LUCK, MR. YATES, 1943, A
GOOD MEN AND BAD, 1923
GOOD MEN AND TRUE, 1922
GOOD MORNING JUDGE, 1928
GOOD MORNING, BOYS
GOOD MORNING, DOCTOR
GOOD MORNING, JUDGE, 1943, A
GOOD MORNING, MISS DOVE, 1955, A
GOOD MORNING... AND GOODBYE, 1967, O
GOOD NEIGHBOR SAM, 1964
GOOD NEWS, 1930, A
GOOD NEWS, 1947, AA
GOOD NIGHT, PAUL, 1918, A
GOOD OLD DAYS, THE, 1939, A
GOOD OLD SOAR, THE, 1937, A
GOOD PROVIDER, THE, 1922
GOOD REFERENCES, 1920
GOOD SAM, 1948, A
GOOD SOLDIER SCHWEIK, THE, 1963
GOOD SPORT, 1931, A
GOOD TIME CHARLEY, 1927
GOOD TIME GIRL, 1950, O
GOOD TIMES, 1967, A
GOOD WOMEN, 1921
GOOD, THE BAD, AND THE BEAUTIFUL, THE, 1975
GOOD, THE BAD, AND THE UGLY, THE, 1967, O

GOOD-BAD WIFE, THE, 1921
GOOD-BY GIRLS, 1923
GOOD-BYE KISS, THE, 1928, A
GOOD-BYE, BILL, 1919, A
GOOD-FOR-NOTHING, THE, 1914, A
GOODBYE, 1918
GOODBYE AGAIN, 1933, A
GOODBYE AGAIN, 1961, C
GOODBYE BROADWAY, 1938, A
GOODBYE BRUCE LEE: HIS LAST GAME OF DEATH
GOODBYE CHARLIE, 1964, C
GOODBYE COLUMBUS, 1969, O
GOODBYE CRUEL WORLD, 1983
GOODBYE EMMANUELLE, 1980, O
GOODBYE FRANKLIN HIGH, 1978, A
GOODBYE GEMINI, 1970, O
GOODBYE GIRL, THE, 1977, C
GOODBYE LOVE, 1934, A
GOODBYE MR. CHIPS, 1939, AAA
GOODBYE MR. CHIPS, 1969, A
GOODBYE PEOPLE, THE, 1984, A-C
GOODBYE PORK PIE, 1981, C
GOODBYE TO THE HILL
GOODBYE, MOSCOW, 1968, O
GOODBYE, MY FANCY, 1951, A
GOODBYE, MY LADY, 1956, AA
GOODBYE, NORMA JEAN, 1976, O
GOODNIGHT SWEETHEART, 1944, A
GOODNIGHT VIENNA
GOODNIGHT, LADIES AND GENTLEMEN, 1977, C-O
GOONA-GOONA, 1932
GOOSE AND THE GANDER, THE, 1935, A
GOOSE GIRL, THE, 1915, A
GOOSE GIRL, THE, 1967, C-O
GOOSE HANGS HIGH, THE, 1925
GOOSE STEP
GOOSE STEPS OUT, THE, 1942, A
GOOSE WOMAN, THE, 1925, C
GORATH, 1964, C
GORBALS STORY, THE, 1950, C
GORDEYEV FAMILY, THE, 1961, O
GORDON IL PIHATA NERO
GORDON'S WAR, 1973, O
GORGEOUS HUSSY, THE, 1936, AA
GORGO, 1961, C
GORGON, THE, 1964
GORILLA, 1964, C
GORILLA AT LARGE, 1954, C
GORILLA GREETS YOU, THE, 1958, C
GORILLA MAN, 1942, A
GORILLA SHIP, THE, 1932, A
GORILLA, 1944
GORILLA, THE, 1927
GORILLA, THE, 1931, A
GORILLA, THE, 1939, A
GORKY PARK, 1983, O
GORP, 1980, O
GOSH, 1974
GOSPEL ACCORDING TO ST. MATTHEW, THE, 1966, A
GOSPEL ROAD, THE, 1973, A
GOSSIP, 1923
GOT IT MADE, 1974
GOT WHAT SHE WANTED, 1930, A
GOUPI MAINS ROUGES
GOVERNMENT GIRL, 1943, A
GOVERNOR'S BOSS, THE, 1915, A
GOVERNOR'S LADY, THE, 1923
GOWN OF DESTINY, THE, 1918
GOYOKIN, 1969, O
GRACE QUIGLEY
GRACIE ALLEN MURDER CASE, 1939, A
GRAD NIGHT, 1980
GRADUATE, THE, 1967, A
GRADUATION DAY, 1981
GRAFT, 1931, C
GRAFTERS, 1917
GRAIL, THE, 1923
GRAIN OF DUST, THE, 1928, A
GRAN VARIETA, 1955, A
GRANATOVYY BRASLET, 1966
GRAND BABYLON HOTEL, THE, 1916
GRAND CANARY, 1934, A
GRAND CANYON, 1949, A
GRAND CANYON TRAIL, 1948, A
GRAND CENTRAL MURDER, 1942, A
GRAND DUCHESS AND THE WAITER, THE, 1926, A
GRAND DUKE AND MR. PIMM
GRAND ESCAPADE, THE, 1946, A
GRAND EXIT, 1935, A
GRAND FINALE, 1936, A
GRAND HOTEL, 1932, A
GRAND ILLUSION, 1938, A
GRAND JURY, 1936, A
GRAND JURY, 1977
GRAND JURY SECRETS, 1939, A
GRAND LARCENY, 1922
GRAND MANEUVER, THE, 1956, C
GRAND NATIONAL NIGHT
GRAND OLD GIRL, 1935, A
GRAND OLE OPRY, 1940, A
GRAND PARADE, THE, 1930, A
GRAND PASSION, THE, 1918
GRAND PRIX, 1934, A
GRAND PRIX, 1966, O
GRAND SLAM, 1933, A
GRAND SLAM, 1968, A-C
GRAND SUBSTITUTION, THE, 1965, C
GRAND THEFT AUTO, 1977
GRANDAD RUDD, 1935, A
GRANDEE'S RING, THE, 1915
GRANDEUR ET DECADENCE, 1923
GRANDMA'S BOY, 1922, A
GRANDPA GOES TO TOWN, 1940, A
GRANDVIEW, U.S.A., 1984, O
GRANNY GET YOUR GUN, 1940, A
GRAPES OF WRATH, 1940, A
GRASP OF GREED, THE, 1916
GRASS EATER, THE, 1961, C
GRASS IS GREENER, THE, 1960, A
GRASS IS SINGING, THE
GRASS IS SINGING, THE, 1982, A
GRASS ORPHAN, THE, 1922
GRASSHOPPER, THE, 1970, O
GRAUSTARK, 1915
GRAUSTARK, 1925
GRAVE OF THE VAMPIRE, 1972, O
GRAVE ROBBERS FROM OUTER SPACE
GRAVESIDE STORY, THE
GRAVEYARD OF HORROR, 1971, O
GRAVY TRAIN, THE, 1974, O
GRAY DAWN, THE, 1922
GRAY HORIZON, THE, 1919
GRAY HORROR, THE, 1915
GRAY LADY DOWN, 1978, C
GRAY TOWERS MYSTERY, THE, 1919
GRAY WOLF'S GHOST, THE, 1919
GRAYEAGLE, 1977, C
GRAZIE ZIA
GRAZIELLA, 1926
GREASE, 1978, A
GREASE 2, 1982, C-O
GREASED LIGHTING, 1919
GREASED LIGHTING, 1928
GREASED LIGHTNING, 1977, C
GREASER'S PALACE, 1972, C
GREAT ACCIDENT, THE, 1920
GREAT ADVENTURE, THE, 1915, A
GREAT ADVENTURE, THE, 1918, A
GREAT ADVENTURE, THE, 1921
GREAT ADVENTURE, THE, 1955, AAA
GREAT ADVENTURE, THE, 1976, A
GREAT AIR ROBBERY, THE, 1920
GREAT ALLIGATOR, 1980, O
GREAT ALONE, THE, 1922
GREAT AMERICAN BROADCAST, THE, 1941, A
GREAT AMERICAN BUGS BUNNY-ROAD RUNNER CHASE, 1979, AAA
GREAT AMERICAN PASTIME, THE, 1956, A
GREAT ARMORED CAR SWINDLE, THE, 1964
GREAT AWAKENING, THE
GREAT BALLOON ADVENTURE, THE
GREAT BANK HOAX, THE, 1977, C
GREAT BANK ROBBERY, THE, 1969, A
GREAT BARRIER, THE
GREAT BIG THING, A, 1968, C
GREAT BIG WORLD AND LITTLE CHILDREN, THE, 1962, A
GREAT BRADLEY MYSTERY, THE, 1917
GREAT BRAIN MACHINE, THE
GREAT BRAIN, THE, 1978, AA
GREAT BRITISH TRAIN ROBBERY, THE, 1967, A
GREAT CALL OF THE WILD, THE, 1976
GREAT CARUSO, THE, 1951, A
GREAT CATHERINE, 1968, AA
GREAT CHICAGO CONSPIRACY CIRCUS, THE
GREAT CITIZEN, THE, 1939
GREAT COMMANDMENT, THE, 1941, A
GREAT COUP, A, 1919
GREAT DAN PATCH, THE, 1949, AA
GREAT DAWN, THE, 1947, A
GREAT DAY, 1945, A
GREAT DAY IN THE MORNING, 1956, A
GREAT DAY, THE, 1921
GREAT DAY, THE, 1977
GREAT DECEPTION, THE, 1926
GREAT DEFENDER, THE, 1934, A
GREAT DIAMOND MYSTERY, THE, 1924
GREAT DIAMOND ROBBERY, 1953, A
GREAT DIAMOND ROBBERY, THE, 1914
GREAT DICTATOR, THE, 1940, AAA
GREAT DIVIDE, THE, 1916
GREAT DIVIDE, THE, 1925
GREAT DIVIDE, THE, 1930, A
GREAT DREAM, THE
GREAT ESCAPE, THE, 1963, A
GREAT EXPECTATIONS, 1917, A
GREAT EXPECTATIONS, 1934, AA
GREAT EXPECTATIONS, 1946, AAA
GREAT EXPECTATIONS, 1975, AAA
GREAT FEED, THE
GREAT FLAMARION, THE, 1945, A-C
GREAT FLIRTATION, THE, 1934, A
GREAT GABBO, THE, 1929, C
GREAT GAMBINI, THE, 1937, A
GREAT GAME, THE, 1918, A
GREAT GAME, THE, 1930, A
GREAT GAME, THE, 1953, A
GREAT GARRICK, THE, 1937, A
GREAT GATSBY, THE, 1926, A
GREAT GATSBY, THE, 1949, A
GREAT GATSBY, THE, 1974
GREAT GAY ROAD, THE, 1931, A
GREAT GEORGIA BANK HOAX
GREAT GILBERT AND SULLIVAN, THE, 1953, AAA
GREAT GILDERSLEEVE, THE, 1942, A
GREAT GOD GOLD, 1935, A
GREAT GUNDOWN, THE, 1977, O
GREAT GUNFIGHTER, THE
GREAT GUNS, 1941, AAA
GREAT GUY, 1936, A
GREAT GUY ROAD, THE, 1920
GREAT HADIO MYSTERY, THE
GREAT HOPE, THE, 1954, C
GREAT HOSPITAL MYSTERY, THE, 1937, A
GREAT HOTEL MURDER, 1935, A
GREAT IMPERSONATION, THE, 1921
GREAT IMPERSONATION, THE, 1935, A
GREAT IMPERSONATION, THE, 1942, A
GREAT IMPOSTER, THE, 1918
GREAT IMPOSTOR, THE, 1960, A
GREAT JASPER, THE, 1933
GREAT JESSE JAMES RAID, THE, 1953, A
GREAT JEWEL ROBBER, THE, 1950, A
GREAT JEWEL ROBBERY, THE, 1925
GREAT JOHN L. THE, 1945, A
GREAT K & A TRAIN ROBBERY, THE, 1926, A
GREAT LEAP, THE, 1914, A
GREAT LESTER BOGGS, THE, 1975
GREAT LIE, THE, 1941, A
GREAT LOCOMOTIVE CHASE, THE, 1956, AA
GREAT LOVE, THE, 1918, A
GREAT LOVE, THE, 1925, A
GREAT LOVER, THE, 1920
GREAT LOVER, THE, 1931, A
GREAT LOVER, THE, 1949, A
GREAT MACARTHY, THE, 1975, C-O
GREAT MAGARAZ, THE, 1915
GREAT MAIL ROBBERY, THE, 1927, A
GREAT MAN VOTES, THE, 1939, A
GREAT MAN'S LADY, THE, 1942, A
GREAT MAN, THE, 1957, A
GREAT MANHUNT, THE, 1951, A
GREAT MANHUNT, THE, 1949
GREAT MCGONAGALL, THE, 1975, O
GREAT MEN AMONG US, 1915
GREAT MIKE, THE, 1944, A
GREAT MISSOURI RAID, THE, 1950, A
GREAT MOMENT, THE, 1921
GREAT MOMENT, THE, 1944, A
GREAT MONKEY RIP-OFF, THE, 1979
GREAT MORGAN, THE, 1946
GREAT MR. HANDEL, THE, 1942, A
GREAT MR. NOBODY, THE, 1941, A
GREAT MUPPET CAPER, THE, 1981
GREAT McGINTY, THE, 1940, A
GREAT NIGHT, THE, 1922, A
GREAT NORTHFIELD, MINNESOTA RAID, THE, 1972, O
GREAT O'MALLEY, THE, 1937, A
GREAT PHYSCIAN, THE, 1913
GREAT PLANE ROBBERY, 1950, A
GREAT PLANE ROBBERY, THE, 1940, A
GREAT POISON MYSTERY, THE, 1914
GREAT PONY RAID, THE, 1968, AA
GREAT POWER, THE, 1929, A
GREAT PRINCE SHAN, THE, 1924
GREAT PROBLEM, THE, 1916
GREAT PROFILE, THE, 1940, A
GREAT RACE, THE, 1965, A-C
GREAT REDEEMER, THE, 1920
GREAT RIDE, THE, 1978
GREAT RIVIERA BANK ROBBERY, THE, 1979
GREAT ROAD, THE, 1927
GREAT ROMANCE, THE, 1919
GREAT RUBY, THE, 1915
GREAT RUPERT, THE, 1950
GREAT SANTINI, THE, 1979
GREAT SCHNOZZLE, THE
GREAT SCOUT AND CATHOUSE THURSDAY, THE, 1976, O
GREAT SENSATION, THE, 1925
GREAT SHADOW, THE, 1920, A
GREAT SINNER, THE, 1949, A
GREAT SIOUX MASSACRE, THE, 1965, A
GREAT SIOUX UPRISING, THE, 1953, A
GREAT SKYCOPTER RESCUE, THE, 1982

GREAT SMOKEY ROADBLOCK, THE, 1978, C
GREAT SPY CHASE, THE, 1966
GREAT SPY MISSION, THE
GREAT ST. LOUIS BANK ROBBERY, THE, 1959, C-O
GREAT ST. TRINIAN'S TRAIN ROBBERY, THE, 1966, AA
GREAT STAGECOACH ROBBERY, 1945, A
GREAT STUFF, 1933, A
GREAT SWINDLE, THE, 1941, A
GREAT TEXAS DYNAMITE CHASE, THE, 1976, O
GREAT THAIN ROBBERY, THE, 1941, A
GREAT TRAIN ROBBERY, THE, 1979, A
GREAT TURF MYSTERY, THE, 1924
GREAT VAN ROBBERY, THE, 1963, O
GREAT VICTOR HERBERT, THE, 1939, AAA
GREAT VICTORY, WILSON OR THE KAISER?, THE, 1918
GREAT WALDO PEPPER, THE, 1975, C
GREAT WALL OF CHINA, THE, 1970
GREAT WALL, THE, 1965, O
GREAT WALTZ, THE, 1938, AA
GREAT WALTZ, THE, 1972, AA
GREAT WAR, THE, 1927
GREAT WAR, THE, 1961, O
GREAT WELL, THE
GREAT WHITE HOPE, THE, 1970, C-O
GREAT WHITE TRAIL, THE, 1917
GREAT WHITE WAY, THE, 1924
GREAT WHITE, THE, 1982, O
GREAT YEARNING, THE, 1930, A
GREAT ZIEGFELD, THE, 1936, AAA
GREAT, MEADOW, THE, 1931
GREATER ADVISOR, THE, 1940
GREATER CLAIM, THE, 1921
GREATER GLORY, THE, 1926
GREATER LAW, THE, 1917, A
GREATER LOVE HATH NO MAN, 1915
GREATER LOVE, THE, 1919
GREATER NEED, THE, 1916, A
GREATER PROFIT, THE, 1921
GREATER SINNER, THE, 1919
GREATER THAN A CROWN, 1925
GREATER THAN ART, 1915
GREATER THAN FAME, 1920, A
GREATER THAN LOVE, 1920
GREATER THAN MARRIAGE, 1924
GREATER WILL, THE, 1915
GREATER WOMAN, THE, 1917
GREATEST BATTLE ON EARTH, THE
GREATEST BATTLE ON EARTH, THE
GREATEST LOVE OF ALL, THE, 1925
GREATEST LOVE, THE, 1920
GREATEST LOVE, THE, 1954, C
GREATEST MENACE, THE, 1923
GREATEST POWER, THE, 1917
GREATEST QUESTION, THE, 1920, A
GREATEST SHOW ON EARTH, THE, 1952
GREATEST SIN, THE, 1922
GREATEST STORY EVER TOLD, THE, 1965
GREATEST THING IN LIFE, THE, 1918, AAA
GREATEST TRUTH, THE, 1922
GREATEST WISH IN THE WORLD, THE, 1918, A
GREATEST, THE, 1977, C-O
GREATHEART, 1921
GREED, 1917
GREED, 1925, C
GREED IN THE SUN, 1965, O
GREED OF WILLIAM HART, THE, 1948, C-O
GREEK STREET
GREEK TYCOON, THE, 1978, C
GREEKS HAD A WORD FOR THEM, 1932, A
GREEN ICE, 1981
GREEN BERETS, THE, 1968, C
GREEN BUDDHA, THE, 1954, A
GREEN CARAVAN, THE, 1922, A
GREEN CARNATION
GREEN CLOAK, THE, 1915
GREEN COCKATOO, THE, 1947, A
GREEN DOLPHIN STREET, 1947, A-C
GREEN EYE OF THE YELLOW GOD, THE, 1913
GREEN EYES, 1918
GREEN EYES, 1934, A
GREEN FIELDS, 1937, A
GREEN FINGERS, 1947, A
GREEN FIRE, 1955, C
GREEN FLAME, THE, 1920, A
GREEN FOR DANGER, 1946, A
GREEN GLOVE, THE, 1952, A
GREEN GOD, THE, 1918
GREEN GODDESS, THE, 1923
GREEN GODDESS, THE, 1930, A
GREEN GRASS OF WYOMING, 1948, AA
GREEN GRASS WIDOWS, 1928
GREEN GROW THE RUSHES, 1951, A
GREEN HELL, 1940, A
GREEN HELMET, THE, 1961, A
GREEN ICE, 1981, C
GREEN LIGHT, 1937, A
GREEN MAN, THE, 1957, A
GREEN MANSIONS, 1959, A
GREEN MARE, THE, 1961, O
GREEN ORCHARD, THE, 1916
GREEN PACK, THE, 1934, C
GREEN PASTURES, 1936, AA
GREEN PROMISE, THE, 1949, A
GREEN ROOM, THE, 1979, C-O
GREEN SCARF, THE, 1954, A
GREEN SLIME, THE, 1969, C
GREEN SPIDER, THE, 1916
GREEN STOCKINGS, 1916
GREEN SWAMP, THE, 1916
GREEN TEMPTATION, THE, 1922
GREEN TERROR, THE, 1919
GREEN TREE, THE, 1965, A
GREEN YEARS, THE, 1946, A
GREEN-EYED BLONDE, THE, 1957, C
GREEN-EYED MONSTER, THE, 1916
GREEN-EYED MONSTER, THE, 1921
GREENE MURDER CASE, THE, 1929, A
GREENGAGE SUMMER, THE
GREENWICH VILLAGE, 1944, A
GREENWICH VILLAGE STORY, 1963, C
GREENWOOD TREE, THE, 1930, A
GREGORIO, 1968
GREGORY'S GIRL, 1982
GREH, 1962, O
GRELL MYSTERY, THE, 1917
GREMLINS, 1984, O
GRENDEL GRENDEL GRENDEL, 1981, AAA
GRETCHEN, THE GREENHORN, 1916, A
GRETNA GREEN, 1915
GREY DAWN, THE
GREY DEVIL, THE, 1926, A
GREY FOX, THE, 1983, C
GREY PARASOL, THE, 1918
GREY STREAK, THE, 1927
GREY VULTURE, THE, 1926
GREYFRIARS BOBBY, 1961, AAA
GREYHOUND LIMITED, THE, 1929, A
GREYHOUND, THE, 1914, A
GREYSTOKE: THE LEGEND OF TARZAN
GREYSTOKE: THE LEGEND OF TARZAN, LORD OF THE APES, 1984, C
GRIBICHE, 1926
GRIDIRON FLASH, 1935, A
GRIEF STREET, 1931, A
GRIFFON OF AN OLD WARRIOR, 1916
GRIGSBY
GRIM COMEDIAN, THE, 1921
GRIM GAME, THE, 1919, A
GRIM JUSTICE, 1916
GRIM REAPER, THE, 1981, O
GRINGO, 1963
GRINNING GUNS, 1927
GRIP, 1915
GRIP OF IRON, THE, 1913
GRIP OF IRON, THE, 1920
GRIP OF JEALOUSY, THE, 1916
GRIP OF THE STRANGLER
GRIP OF THE YUKON, THE, 1928
GRISSLY'S MILLIONS, 1945, A
GRISSOM GANG, THE, 1971, C-O
GRIT, 1924, A
GRIT OF A JEW, THE, 1917, A
GRIT WINS, 1929, A
GRITOS EN LA NOCHE
GRIZZLY, 1976, C
GROOM WORE SPURS, THE, 1951, A
GROOVE ROOM, THE, 1974
GROOVE TUBE, THE, 1974, O
GROUCH, THE, 1961, A
GROUND ZERO, 1973, O
GROUNDS FOR DIVORCE, 1925
GROUNDS FOR MARRIAGE, 1950, A
GROUNDSTAR CONSPIRACY, THE, 1972, C
GROUP MARRIAGE, 1972
GROUP, THE, 1966, O
GROUPIE GIRL
GROVE, THE
GROWING BETTER, 1923
GROWING PAINS
GROWN-UP CHILDREN, 1963, A
GRUB STAKE, THE, 1923
GRUESOME TWOSOME, 1968, O
GRUMPY, 1923
GRUMPY, 1930, A
GUADALAJARA, 1943, A
GUADALCANAL DIARY, 1943, C
GUARD THAT GIRL, 1935, A
GUARDIAN OF THE WILDERNESS, 1977, AAA
GUARDIAN, THE, 1917
GUARDIANS OF THE WILD, 1928
GUARDING BRITAIN'S SECRETS
GUARDSMAN, THE, 1927
GUARDSMAN, THE, 1931, A
GUDRUN
GUERILLAS IN PINK LACE, 1964
GUERRE SECRET
GUERRILLA GIRL, 1953, C
GUESS WHAT HAPPENED TO COUNT DRACULA, 1970, O
GUESS WHAT WE LEARNED IN SCHOOL TODAY?, 1970, O
GUESS WHAT!?!
GUESS WHO'S COMING TO DINNER, 1967, C
GUEST AT STEENKAMPSKRAAL, THE, 1977, O
GUEST HOUSE, THE
GUEST IN THE HOUSE, 1944, A
GUEST OF HONOR, 1934, A
GUEST WIFE, 1945, A
GUEST, THE, 1963, C
GUEST, THE, 1984, O
GUESTS ARE COMING, 1965, A
GUEULE D'ANGE
GUIDE FOR THE MARRIED MAN, A, 1967, C
GUIDE, THE, 1965, A
GUILE OF WOMEN, 1921, A
GUILT, 1930, A
GUILT, 1967, O
GUILT IS MY SHADOW, 1950, O
GUILT IS NOT MINE, 1968, A
GUILT OF JANET AMES, THE, 1947, A
GUILT OF SILENCE, THE, 1918
GUILTY, 1922
GUILTY AS CHARGED
GUILTY AS HELL, 1932, A
GUILTY BYSTANDER, 1950, C
GUILTY CONSCIENCE, A, 1921
GUILTY GENERATION, THE, 1931
GUILTY HANDS, 1931, C
GUILTY MAN, THE, 1918
GUILTY MELODY, 1936, A
GUILTY OF LOVE, 1920, C
GUILTY OF TREASON, 1950, C
GUILTY ONE, THE, 1924
GUILTY OR NOT GUILTY, 1932
GUILTY PARENTS, 1934, C
GUILTY TRAILS, 1938, A
GUILTY, THE, 1947, C
GUILTY?, 1930, A
GUILTY?, 1956, A
GUINEA PIG, THE
GUINGUETTE, 1959, C
GULF BETWEEN, THE, 1918
GULLIVER IN LILLIPUT, 1923
GULLIVER'S TRAVELS, 1939, AAA
GULLIVER'S TRAVELS, 1977
GULLIVER'S TRAVELS BEYOND THE MOON, 1966, AAA
GUMBALL RALLY, THE, 1976, A
GUMBO YA-YA
GUMS, 1976
GUMSHOE, 1972, C
GUN BATTLE AT MONTEREY, 1957, C
GUN BELT, 1953, A
GUN BROTHERS, 1956, A
GUN CODE, 1940, A
GUN CRAZY, 1949, O
GUN DUEL IN DURANGO, 1957, A
GUN FEVER, 1958
GUN FIGHT, 1961, C
GUN FOR A COWARD, 1957, O
GUN FURY, 1953, A
GUN GLORY, 1957, A
GUN GOSPEL, 1927
GUN GRIT, 1936
GUN HAND, THE
GUN HAWK, THE, 1963, C
GUN JUSTICE, 1934, A
GUN LAW, 1929, A
GUN LAW, 1933, A
GUN LAW, 1938, A
GUN LAW JUSTICE, 1949, A
GUN LORDS OF STIRRUP BASIN, 1937, A
GUN MAN FROM BODIE, THE, 1941, A
GUN MOLL
GUN MOLL, 1938
GUN PACKER, 1938, A
GUN PLAY, 1936, A
GUN RANGER, THE, 1937, A
GUN RIDERS, THE, 1969, O
GUN RUNNER, 1949, A
GUN RUNNER, 1969, O
GUN RUNNER, THE
GUN RUNNER, THE, 1928, A
GUN RUNNERS, THE, 1958, A
GUN SHY, 1922
GUN SMOKE, 1931, A
GUN SMOKE, 1936, A
GUN SMOKE, 1945
GUN SMUGGLERS, 1948, A
GUN STREET, 1962
GUN TALK, 1948, A
GUN THAT WON THE WEST, THE, 1955, C
GUN THE MAN DOWN, 1957, C
GUN TOWN, 1946, A
GUN WOMAN, THE, 1918

GUN, THE, 1978, O
GUN-FIGHTIN' GENTLEMAN, A, 1919
GUN-HAND GARRISON, 1927
GUNFIGHT AT ABILENE
GUNFIGHT AT COMANCHE CREEK, 1964, A
GUNFIGHT AT DODGE CITY, THE, 1959
GUNFIGHT AT RED SANDS
GUNFIGHT AT THE O.K. CORRAL, 1957, C
GUNFIGHT IN ABILENE, 1967, C
GUNFIGHT, A, 1971, O
GUNFIGHTER, THE, 1917
GUNFIGHTER, THE, 1923
GUNFIGHTER, THE, 1950
GUNFIGHTERS OF ABILENE, 1960, A
GUNFIGHTERS OF CASA GRANDE, 1965, C
GUNFIGHTERS, THE, 1947, A
GUNFIRE, 1935
GUNFIRE, 1950, A
GUNFIRE AT INDIAN GAP, 1957, A
GUNG HO!, 1943, C
GUNGA DIN, 1939, C
GUNMAN FROM BODIE
GUNMAN HAS ESCAPED, A, 1948
GUNMAN'S CODE, 1946, A
GUNMAN'S WALK, 1958, C
GUNMAN, THE, 1952
GUNMEN FROM LAREDO, 1959, O
GUNMEN OF ABILENE, 1950, A
GUNMEN OF THE RIO GRANDE, 1965, C
GUNN, 1967, C
GUNNAR HEDE'S SAGA, 1922
GUNNERS AND GUNS, 1935
GUNNING FOR JUSTICE, 1948, A
GUNNING FOR VENGEANCE, 1946
GUNPLAY, 1951, A
GUNPOINT, 1966, A
GUNPOINT!
GUNRUNNERS, THE
GUNS, 1980, O
GUNS A'BLAZING
GUNS ALONG THE BORDER, 1952
GUNS AND GUITARS, 1936, A
GUNS AND THE FURY, THE, 1983, O
GUNS AT BATASI, 1964, C
GUNS FOR HIRE, 1932
GUNS FOR SAN SEBASTIAN, 1968, O
GUNS IN THE AFTERNOON
GUNS IN THE DARK, 1937, A
GUNS IN THE HEATHER, 1968, AA
GUNS OF A STRANGER, 1973, A
GUNS OF DARKNESS, 1962, C
GUNS OF DIABLO, 1964, C
GUNS OF FORT PETTICOAT, THE, 1957, A
GUNS OF HATE, 1948, A
GUNS OF LOOS, THE, 1928
GUNS OF NAVARONE, THE, 1961
GUNS OF THE BLACK WITCH, 1961, C
GUNS OF THE LAW, 1944, A
GUNS OF THE MAGNIFICENT SEVEN, 1969, C
GUNS OF THE PECOS, 1937, A
GUNS OF THE TIMBERLAND, 1960, A
GUNS OF THE TREES, 1964, O
GUNS OF WYOMING
GUNS, GIRLS AND GANGSTERS, 1958, C
GUNS, SIN AND BATHTUB GIN
GUNSAULUS MYSTERY, THE, 1921
GUNSIGHT RIDGE, 1957, A
GUNSLINGER, 1956, C
GUNSLINGERS, 1950, A
GUNSMOKE, 1947
GUNSMOKE, 1953, A
GUNSMOKE IN TUCSON, 1958, A
GUNSMOKE MESA, 1944, A
GUNSMOKE ON THE GUADALUPE, 1935
GUNSMOKE RANCH, 1937, A
GUNSMOKE TRAIL, 1938, A
GURU, THE, 1969
GURU, THE MAD MONK, 1971
GUS, 1976, AAA
GUSARSKAYA BALLADA
GUTS IN THE SUN, 1959, O
GUTTER GIRLS, 1964, O
GUTTER MAGDALENE, THE, 1916
GUTTERSNIPE, THE, 1922
GUV'NOR, THE
GUY CALLED CAESAR, A, 1962, A
GUY COULD CHANGE, A, 1946, A
GUY FAWKES, 1923
GUY FROM HARLEM, THE, 1977
GUY NAMED JOE, A, 1943, A
GUY WHO CAME BACK, THE, 1951, A
GUY, A GAL AND A PAL, A, 1945, A
GUYANA, CULT OF THE DAMNED, 1980, O
GUYS AND DOLLS, 1955, A
GWENDOLINE
GWYNETH OF THE WELSH HILLS, 1921
GYPSY, 1937, A
GYPSY, 1962, C
GYPSY AND THE GENTLEMAN, THE, 1958, O
GYPSY BLOOD, 1921
GYPSY COLT, 1954
GYPSY FURY, 1950, C
GYPSY GIRL, 1966
GYPSY MELODY, 1936, A
GYPSY MOTHS, THE, 1969, O
GYPSY OF THE NORTH, 1928, A
GYPSY PASSION, 1922
GYPSY ROMANCE, THE, 1926
GYPSY TRAIL, THE, 1918
GYPSY WILDCAT, 1944, A
GYPSY'S TRUST, THE, 1917

-H-

H-MAN, THE, 1959, O
H.A.R.M. MACHINE, THE
H.E.A.L.T.H.
H.M. PULHAM, ESQ., 1941, A
H.M.S. DEFIANT
H.M.S. PINAFORE, 1951
H.O.T.S., 1979, O
HA' PENNY BREEZE, 1950, A
HABIT, 1921
HABIT OF HAPPINESS, THE, 1916, A
HACELDAMA, 1919
HADAKA NO SHIMA
HADAKA NO TAISHO
HADLEY'S REBELLION, 1984, C
HAGBARD AND SIGNE, 1968, C-O
HAHAKIRI, 1963, O
HAIL, 1973, O
HAIL AND FAREWELL, 1936, A
HAIL MAFIA, 1965, O
HAIL THE CONQUERING HERO, 1944, A
HAIL THE HERO, 1924
HAIL THE WOMAN, 1921
HAIL TO THE CHIEF
HAIL TO THE RANGERS, 1943, A
HAIL, HERO!, 1969, C
HAINE, 1918
HAIR, 1979, C-O
HAIR OF THE DOG, 1962, A
HAIR TRIGGER BAXTER, 1926, A
HAIR TRIGGER CASEY, 1922
HAIR-TRIGGER CASEY, 1936
HAIRPINS, 1920, A
HAIRY APE, THE, 1944, A
HAKUCHI
HAKUJA DEN
HALCON Y LA PRESA, EL
HALDANE OF THE SECRET SERVICE, 1923, A
HALF A BRIDE, 1928, A
HALF A CHANCE, 1920
HALF A HERO, 1953, AA
HALF A HOUSE, 1979
HALF A ROGUE, 1916
HALF A SINNER, 1934, A
HALF A SINNER, 1940, A
HALF A SIXPENCE, 1967, A
HALF A TRUTH, 1922, A
HALF AN HOUR, 1920
HALF ANGEL, 1936, C
HALF ANGEL, 1951, A
HALF BREED, THE, 1916
HALF BREED, THE, 1922
HALF HUMAN, 1955, C-O
HALF MILLION BRIBE, THE, 1916
HALF PAST MIDNIGHT, 1948, A
HALF PINT, THE, 1960, AAA
HALF SHOT AT SUNRISE, 1930, A
HALF WAY TO HEAVEN, 1929, A
HALF WAY TO SHANGHAI, 1942, C
HALF-A-DOLLAR BILL, 1924
HALF-BREED, THE, 1952, A
HALF-MARRIAGE, 1929
HALF-NAKED TRUTH, THE, 1932, A
HALF-WAY GIRL, THE, 1925
HALF-WAY HOUSE, THE, 1945, C
HALFBREED, 1919
HALFWAY TO HELL, 1957
HALLELUJAH, 1929, A
HALLELUJAH AND SARTANA, SON OF...GOD, 1972
HALLELUJAH THE HILLS, 1963, C
HALLELUJAH TRAIL, THE, 1965, A
HALLELUJAH, I'M A BUM, 1933, A
HALLIDAY BRAND, THE, 1957, C
HALLOWEEN, 1978, O
HALLOWEEN II, 1981, O
HALLOWEEN III: SEASON OF THE WITCH, 1982, O
HALLS OF ANGER, 1970, O
HALLS OF MONTEZUMA, 1951, C
HALLUCINATION GENERATION, 1966, C
HALLUCINATORS, THE
HAM AND EGGS
HAM AND EGGS AT THE FRONT, 1927, A
HAMBONE AND HILLIE, 1984, A
HAMILE, 1965, C
HAMLET, 1913, A
HAMLET, 1921
HAMLET, 1948, A
HAMLET, 1962, A
HAMLET, 1964, A
HAMLET, 1966, C
HAMLET, 1969, A
HAMLET, 1976
HAMMER, 1972, O
HAMMER THE TOFF, 1952, A
HAMMERHEAD, 1968, C
HAMMERSMITH IS OUT, 1972, C
HAMMETT, 1982, C
HAMNSTED
HAMP
HAMPSTER OF HAPPINESS
HANA TO NAMIDA TO HONOO
HAND AT THE WINDOW, THE, 1918
HAND IN HAND, 1960
HAND IN THE TRAP, THE, 1963, C
HAND INVISIBLE, THE, 1919
HAND OF DEATH, 1962
HAND OF DESTINY, THE, 1914
HAND OF JUSTICE, THE, 1915
HAND OF NIGHT, THE, 1968, C
HAND OF PERIL, THE, 1916
HAND OF THE HUN, THE, 1917
HAND OF THE LAW, THE, 1915
HAND THAT ROCKS THE CRADLE, THE, 1917
HAND, THE, 1960, C
HAND, THE, 1981, O
HANDCUFFED, 1929, A
HANDCUFFS OR KISSES, 1921
HANDCUFFS, LONDON, 1955
HANDGUN
HANDICAP, THE, 1925
HANDLE WITH CARE
HANDLE WITH CARE, 1922, A
HANDLE WITH CARE, 1932, A
HANDLE WITH CARE, 1935, A
HANDLE WITH CARE, 1958, A
HANDLE WITH CARE, 1964, A
HANDS ACROSS THE BORDER, 1926, A
HANDS ACROSS THE BORDER, 1943, A
HANDS ACROSS THE ROCKIES, 1941
HANDS ACROSS THE TABLE, 1935, A
HANDS DOWN, 1918
HANDS OF A STRANGER, 1962, C
HANDS OF DESTINY, 1954, A
HANDS OF NARA, THE, 1922
HANDS OF ORLAC, THE, 1925
HANDS OF ORLAC, THE, 1964, A
HANDS OF THE RIPPER, 1971, O
HANDS OF THE STRANGLER
HANDS OFF, 1921
HANDS OFF, 1927
HANDS UP, 1917
HANDS UP, 1926, A
HANDSOME BRUTE, THE, 1925, A
HANDSOME SERGE
HANDY ANDY, 1921, A
HANDY ANDY, 1934, A
HANG YOUR HAT ON THE WIND, 1969, AA
HANG'EM HIGH, 1968, C
HANG-UP, THE, 1969
HANGAR 18, 1980, A
HANGING JUDGE, THE, 1918, A
HANGING TREE, THE, 1959, C
HANGING WOMAN, THE, 1976
HANGMAN WAITS, THE, 1947, C
HANGMAN'S HOUSE, 1928
HANGMAN'S KNOT, 1952, C
HANGMAN'S WHARF, 1950, A
HANGMAN, THE, 1959
HANGMEN ALSO DIE, 1943
HANGOVER
HANGOVER SQUARE, 1945, C
HANGUP, 1974
HANK WILLIAMS STORY, THE
HANK WILLIAMS: THE SHOW HE NEVER GAVE, 1982, C
HANKY-PANKY, 1982, A-C
HANNAH K., 1983, C
HANNAH LEE, 1953, A
HANNAH—QUEEN OF THE VAMPIRES, 1972
HANNIBAL, 1960, A
HANNIBAL BROOKS, 1969, C
HANNIE CALDER, 1971, 0
HANOI HANNA—QUEEN OF CHINA
HANOVER STREET, 1979, C
HANS BRINKER AND THE SILVER SKATES, 1969
HANS CHRISTIAN ANDERSEN, 1952
HANSEL AND GRETEL, 1954, AA
HANSEL AND GRETEL, 1965, AA
HANTISE, 1922
HAPPENING, THE, 1967, C
HAPPIDROME, 1943
HAPPIEST DAYS OF YOUR LIFE, 1950, A
HAPPIEST MILLIONAIRE, THE, 1967, AA
HAPPILY EVER AFTER
HAPPINESS

HAPPINESS, 1917
HAPPINESS, 1924
HAPPINESS A LA MODE, 1919
HAPPINESS AHEAD, 1928
HAPPINESS AHEAD, 1934, A
HAPPINESS C.O.D., 1935, A
HAPPINESS CAGE, THE, 1972, C
HAPPINESS OF THREE WOMEN, THE, 1917
HAPPINESS OF THREE WOMEN, THE, 1954, A
HAPPINESS OF US ALONE, 1962, A
HAPPY, 1934, A
HAPPY ALEXANDER
HAPPY ANNIVERSARY, 1959, C
HAPPY AS THE GRASS WAS GREEN, 1973, A
HAPPY BIRTHDAY TO ME, 1981, O
HAPPY BIRTHDAY, DAVY, 1970, O
HAPPY BIRTHDAY, GEMINI, 1980
HAPPY BIRTHDAY, WANDA JUNE, 1971
HAPPY DAYS, 1930, A
HAPPY DAYS ARE HERE AGAIN, 1936, A
HAPPY DEATHDAY, 1969, C
HAPPY END, 1968, C-O
HAPPY ENDING, THE, 1925
HAPPY ENDING, THE, 1931, A
HAPPY ENDING, THE, 1969, C
HAPPY EVER AFTER
HAPPY EVER AFTER, 1932, A
HAPPY FAMILY, THE
HAPPY FAMILY, THE, 1936, A
HAPPY GO LOVELY, 1951, A
HAPPY GO LUCKY, 1943, AA
HAPPY GYPSIES
HAPPY HOOKER GOES TO HOLLYWOOD, THE, 1980, O
HAPPY HOOKER GOES TO WASHINGTON, THE, 1977, O
HAPPY HOOKER, THE, 1975, O
HAPPY IS THE BRIDE, 1958, A
HAPPY LAND, 1943, A
HAPPY LANDING, 1934, A
HAPPY LANDING, 1938, A
HAPPY MOTHER'S DAY... LOVE, GEORGE, 1973, C
HAPPY ROAD, THE, 1957
HAPPY THIEVES, THE, 1962, C
HAPPY THOUGH MARRIED, 1919
HAPPY TIME, THE, 1952, AAA
HAPPY WARRIOR, THE, 1917
HAPPY WARRIOR, THE, 1925
HAPPY YEARS, THE, 1950
HAPPY-GO-LUCKY, 1937, A
HAR HAR DU DITT LIV
HARAKIRI, 1919
HARASSED HERO, THE, 1954, A
HARBOR LIGHT YOKOHAMA, 1970, C-O
HARBOR LIGHTS, 1963
HARBOR OF MISSING MEN, 1950
HARBOR PATROL, 1924
HARBOUR LIGHTS, THE, 1914
HARBOUR LIGHTS, THE, 1923
HARD BOILED, 1919
HARD BOILED, 1926
HARD BOILED HAGGERTY, 1927
HARD BOILED MAHONEY, 1947, A
HARD BUNCH, THE
HARD CASH, 1921
HARD CHOICES, 1984, O
HARD CONTRACT, 1969
HARD COUNTRY, 1981, O
HARD DAY'S NIGHT, A, 1964, A
HARD DRIVER
HARD FEELINGS, 1981
HARD FISTS, 1927
HARD GUY, 1941, A
HARD HITTIN' HAMILTON, 1924
HARD HOMBRE, 1931, A
HARD KNOCKS, 1980, O
HARD MAN, THE, 1957
HARD ON THE TRAIL
HARD PART BEGINS, THE, 1973, C
HARD RIDE, THE, 1971, C
HARD ROAD, THE, 1970, O
HARD ROCK BREED, THE, 1918
HARD ROCK HARRIGAN, 1935, A
HARD STEEL, 1941
HARD TIMES, 1915, A
HARD TIMES, 1975, A-C
HARD TO GET, 1929, A
HARD TO GET, 1938, A
HARD TO HANDLE, 1933, A
HARD TO HOLD, 1984, A-C
HARD TRAIL, 1969
HARD WAY TO DIE, A, 1980
HARD WAY, THE, 1916, A
HARD WAY, THE, 1942, A-C
HARD WAY, THE, 1980
HARD, FAST, AND BEAUTIFUL, 1951, A
HARD-BOILED CANARY
HARDBODIES, 1984, O
HARDBOILED, 1929, A
HARDBOILED ROSE, 1929, A
HARDCORE, 1979, O
HARDER THEY COME, THE, 1973, C
HARDER THEY FALL, THE, 1956, O
HARDLY WORKING, 1981
HARDYS RIDE HIGH, THE, 1939, AAA
HAREM BUNCH; OR WAR AND PIECE, THE, 1969, C-O
HAREM GIRL, 1952, A
HAREM HOLIDAY
HARISCHANDRA, 1913
HARLEM AFTER MIDNIGHT, 1934
HARLEM GLOBETROTTERS, THE, 1951, A
HARLEM IS HEAVEN, 1932, A
HARLEM ON THE PRAIRIE, 1938, A
HARLEM RIDES THE RANGE, 1939, A
HARLEQUIN, 1980, C-O
HARLOW, 1965, C
HARMON OF MICHIGAN, 1941, A
HARMONY AT HOME, 1930, A
HARMONY HEAVEN, 1930, A
HARMONY LANE, 1935, A
HARMONY ROW, 1933, A
HARMONY TRAIL
HAROLD AND MAUDE, 1971, A-C
HAROLD ROBBINS' THE BETSY
HAROLD TEEN, 1928, A
HAROLD TEEN, 1934, A
HARP IN HOCK, A, 1927
HARP KING, THE, 1920
HARP OF BURMA, 1967
HARPER, 1966, C
HARPER MYSTERY, THE, 1913
HARPER VALLEY, P.T.A., 1978, C
HARPOON, 1948, A
HARRAD EXPERIMENT, THE, 1973, O
HARRAD SUMMER, THE, 1974, O
HARRIET AND THE PIPER, 1920
HARRIET CRAIG, 1950, A-C
HARRIGAN'S KID, 1943, A
HARRY AND SON, 1984, C
HARRY AND TONTO, 1974, C
HARRY AND WALTER GO TO NEW YORK, 1976, C
HARRY BLACK AND THE TIGER, 1958, C
HARRY FRIGG
HARRY IN YOUR POCKET, 1973, C
HARRY TRACY—DESPERADO, 1982, C
HARRY'S WAR, 1981, C
HARSH FATHER, THE, 1911
HARUM SCARUM, 1965, A
HARVARD, HERE I COME, 1942, A
HARVEST, 1939, O
HARVEST MELODY, 1943, A
HARVEST MOON, THE, 1920
HARVEST OF HATE, THE, 1929, A
HARVESTER, THE, 1927
HARVESTER, THE, 1936, A
HARVEY, 1950, A
HARVEY GIRLS, THE, 1946, AAA
HARVEY MIDDLEMAN, FIREMAN, 1965, C
HAS ANYBODY SEEN MY GAL?, 1952, A
HAS MAN THE RIGHT TO KILL?, 1919
HAS THE WORLD GONE MAD, 1923, A
HASHIMURA TOGO, 1917
HASSAN, TERRORIST, 1968, O
HASTY HEART, THE, 1949, A
HAT CHECK GIRL, 1932
HAT CHECK HONEY, 1944, A
HAT, COAT AND GLOVE, 1934, A
HATARI!, 1962, A
HATCHET FOR A HONEYMOON, 1969, O
HATCHET MAN, THE, 1932, C-O
HATE, 1917
HATE, 1922
HATE FOR HATE, 1967, C
HATE IN PARADISE, 1938
HATE SHIP, THE, 1930, A
HATE TRAIL, THE, 1922
HATE WITHIN
HATER OF MEN, 1917, A
HATFUL OF RAIN, A, 1957, C
HATRED, 1941, A
HATS OFF, 1937, A
HATS OFF TO RHYTHM
HATTER'S CASTLE, 1948, C
HATTER'S GHOST, THE, 1982
HAUNTED, 1976, O
HAUNTED AND THE HUNTED
HAUNTED BEDROOM, THE, 1919
HAUNTED CASTLE, THE, 1921
HAUNTED GOLD, 1932, A
HAUNTED HONEYMOON
HAUNTED HOUSE OF HORROR
HAUNTED HOUSE, THE, 1917
HAUNTED HOUSE, THE, 1928, A
HAUNTED HOUSE, THE, 1940, A
HAUNTED MANOR, THE, 1916
HAUNTED MINE, THE, 1946
HAUNTED PAJAMAS, 1917, A
HAUNTED PALACE, THE, 1963
HAUNTED RANCH, THE
HAUNTED RANCH, THE, 1943, A
HAUNTED RANGE, THE, 1926, A
HAUNTED SHIP, THE, 1927
HAUNTED STRANGLER, THE, 1958, O
HAUNTED TRAILS, 1949
HAUNTING OF CASTLE MONTEGO
HAUNTING OF JULIA, THE, 1981, O
HAUNTING OF M, THE, 1979, C
HAUNTING OF ROSALIND, THE, 1973
HAUNTING SHADOWS, 1920
HAUNTING, THE, 1963, C-O
HAUNTS, 1977, O
HAVANA ROSE, 1951, A
HAVANA WIDOWS, 1933, A
HAVE A HEART, 1934
HAVE A NICE WEEKEND, 1975, O
HAVE ROCRET, WILL TRAVEL, 1959, A
HAVING A WILD WEEKEND, 1965
HAVING WONDERFUL CRIME, 1945, A
HAVING WONDERFUL TIME, 1938, A
HAVOC, 1925
HAVOC, THE, 1916
HAWAII, 1966, C
HAWAII BEACH BOY
HAWAII CALLS, 1938, A
HAWAIIAN BUCKAROO, 1938, A
HAWAIIAN NIGHTS, 1939, A
HAWAIIAN NIGHTS, 1934
HAWAIIANS, THE, 1970, C
HAWK OF POWDER RIVER, THE, 1948, A
HAWK OF THE HILLS, 1929
HAWK OF WILD RIVER, THE, 1952, A
HAWK THE SLAYER, 1980, A
HAWK'S NEST, THE, 1928
HAWK, THE, 1917
HAWK, THE, 1935
HAWKS AND THE SPARROWS, THE, 1967, C
HAWLEY'S OF HIGH STREET, 1933, A
HAWMPS!, 1976
HAWTHORNE OF THE U.S.A., 1919, A
HAXAN
HAY FOOT, 1942, A
HAY FOOT, STRAW FOOT, 1919
HAY, HAY, HAY, 1983
HAZARD, 1948, A
HAZARDOUS VALLEY, 1927, A
HAZEL KIRKE, 1916
HAZEL'S PEOPLE, 1978, C
HAZING, THE, 1978, C
HE COMES UP SMILING, 1918
HE COULDN'T SAY NO, 1938, A
HE COULDN'T TAKE IT, 1934
HE FELL IN LOVE WITH HIS WIFE, 1916
HE FOUND A STAR, 1941, A
HE HIRED THE BOSS, 1943, A
HE IS MY BROTHER, 1976
HE KNEW WOMEN, 1930, A
HE KNOWS YOU'RE ALONE, 1980, O
HE LAUGHED LAST, 1956, A
HE LEARNED ABOUT WOMEN, 1933
HE LOVED AN ACTRESS, 1938, A
HE MARRIED HIS WIFE, 1940, A
HE RAN ALL THE WAY, 1951
HE RIDES TALL, 1964, A
HE SNOOPS TO CONQUER, 1944, A
HE STAYED FOR BREAKFAST, 1940, A
HE WALKED BY NIGHT, 1948
HE WAS HER MAN, 1934, A-C
HE WHO GETS SLAPPED, 1916
HE WHO GETS SLAPPED, 1924, A
HE WHO LAUGHS LAST, 1925
HE WHO RIDES A TIGER, 1966, A
HE WHO SHOOTS FIRST, 1966, C
HE'S A COCKEYED WONDER, 1950, A
HE'S A PRINCE
HE'S MY GUY, 1943, A
HE, SHE OR IT!
HE-MAN'S COUNTRY, A, 1926, A
HEAD, 1968, A
HEAD FOR THE DEVIL
HEAD FOR THE HILLS
HEAD MAN, THE, 1928, A
HEAD OF A TYRANT, 1960
HEAD OF JANUS, THE, 1920
HEAD OF THE FAMILY, 1933, A
HEAD OF THE FAMILY, 1967
HEAD OF THE FAMILY, THE, 1922, A
HEAD OF THE FAMILY, THE, 1928, A
HEAD OFFICE, 1936, A
HEAD ON, 1971, O
HEAD ON, 1981
HEAD OVER HEELS
HEAD OVER HEELS, 1922
HEAD OVER HEELS IN LOVE, 1937
HEAD THAT WOULDN'T DIE
HEAD WINDS, 1925
HEAD, THE, 1961, O

HEADIN' EAST, 1937, A
HEADIN' FOR BROADWAY, 1980, C
HEADIN' FOR DANGER, 1928
HEADIN' FOR GOD'S COUNTRY, 1943, A
HEADIN' FOR THE RIO GRANDE, 1937, A
HEADIN' FOR TROUBLE, 1931, A
HEADIN' HOME, 1920
HEADIN' NORTH, 1921
HEADIN' NORTH, 1930, A
HEADIN' SOUTH, 1918, A
HEADIN' THROUGH, 1924
HEADIN' WEST, 1922
HEADIN' WESTWARD, 1929, A
HEADING FOR HEAVEN, 1947, A
HEADING WEST, 1946
HEADLESS EYES, THE, 1983
HEADLESS GHOST, THE, 1959, A
HEADLESS HORSEMAN, THE, 1922
HEADLEYS AT HOME, THE, 1939, A
HEADLINE, 1943, A
HEADLINE CRASHER, 1937, A
HEADLINE HUNTERS, 1955, A
HEADLINE HUNTERS, 1968, AAA
HEADLINE SHOOTER, 1933, A
HEADLINE WOMAN, THE, 1935, A
HEADLINES, 1925
HEADMASTER, THE, 1921
HEADS UP, 1925, A
HEADS UP, 1930, A
HEADS UP, CHARLIE, 1926
HEADS WE GO
HEADS WIN, 1919
HEALER, THE, 1935, A
HEALTH, 1980, C-O
HEAR ME GOOD, 1957, A
HEAR THE PIPERS CALLING, 1918
HEARSE, THE, 1980, A
HEART AND SOUL, 1917
HEART AND SOUL, 1950, A
HEART BANDIT, THE, 1924
HEART BEAT, 1979, O
HEART BUSTER, THE, 1924
HEART IN PAWN, A, 1919
HEART IS A LONELY HUNTER, THE, 1968, O
HEART LIKE A WHEEL, 1983, C
HEART LINE, THE, 1921
HEART O' THE HILLS, 1919
HEART O' THE WEST
HEART OF A CHILD, 1958
HEART OF A CHILD, THE, 1915
HEART OF A CHILD, THE, 1920
HEART OF A CLOWN
HEART OF A COWARD, THE, 1926, A
HEART OF A FOLLIES GIRL, THE, 1928, A
HEART OF A FOOL
HEART OF A GIRL, 1918
HEART OF A GYPSY, THE, 1919
HEART OF A HERO, THE, 1916
HEART OF A LION, THE, 1918
HEART OF A MAN, THE, 1959, A
HEART OF A NATION, THE, 1943, A
HEART OF A PAINTED WOMAN, THE, 1915
HEART OF A ROSE, THE, 1919
HEART OF A SIREN, 1925
HEART OF A TEMPTRESS
HEART OF A TEXAN, THE, 1922
HEART OF A WOMAN, THE, 1920
HEART OF ALASKA, 1924
HEART OF ARIZONA, 1938, A
HEART OF BROADWAY, THE, 1928
HEART OF EZRA GREER, THE, 1917
HEART OF GOLD, 1919
HEART OF HUMANITY, THE, 1919
HEART OF JENNIFER, THE, 1915
HEART OF JUANITA, 1919
HEART OF LINCOLN, THE, 1922
HEART OF MARYLAND, THE, 1915
HEART OF MARYLAND, THE, 1921, A
HEART OF MARYLAND, THE, 1927
HEART OF MIDLOTHIAN, THE, 1914
HEART OF NEW YORK, 1932, A
HEART OF NEW YORK, THE, 1916
HEART OF NORA FLYNN, THE, 1916
HEART OF PARIS, 1939, A
HEART OF PAULA, THE, 1916
HEART OF RACHAEL, THE, 1918
HEART OF ROMANCE, THE, 1918
HEART OF SALOME, THE, 1927
HEART OF SISTER ANN, THE, 1915
HEART OF TARA, THE, 1916
HEART OF TEXAS RYAN, THE, 1917
HEART OF THE BLUE RIDGE, THE, 1915, A
HEART OF THE GOLDEN WEST, 1942, A
HEART OF THE HILLS, THE, 1916
HEART OF THE MATTER, THE, 1954, A-C
HEART OF THE NORTH, 1938, A
HEART OF THE NORTH, THE, 1921
HEART OF THE RIO GRANDE, 1942, A
HEART OF THE ROCKIES, 1937, A
HEART OF THE ROCKIES, 1951, A
HEART OF THE STAG, 1984, O
HEART OF THE SUNSET, 1918
HEART OF THE WEST
HEART OF THE WEST, 1937, A
HEART OF THE WILDS, 1918
HEART OF THE YUKON, THE, 1927
HEART OF TWENTY, THE, 1920
HEART OF VIRGINIA, 1948, A
HEART OF WETONA, THE, 1919
HEART OF YOUTH, THE, 1920
HEART PUNCH, 1932, A
HEART RAIDER, THE, 1923, A
HEART SONG, 1933, A
HEART SPECIALIST, THE, 1922
HEART STRINGS, 1917
HEART STRINGS, 1920
HEART THIEF, THE, 1927
HEART TO HEART, 1928
HEART TO LET, A, 1921
HEART TROUBLE, 1928, A
HEART WITHIN, THE, 1957, A
HEART'S CRUCIBLE, A, 1916
HEART'S DESIRE, 1917
HEART'S DESIRE, 1937, A
HEART'S HAVEN, 1922
HEART'S REVENGE, A, 1918
HEARTACHES, 1915
HEARTACHES, 1947, A
HEARTACHES, 1981, O
HEARTBEAT, 1946, A
HEARTBEEPS, 1981
HEARTBOUND, 1925
HEARTBREAK, 1931, A
HEARTBREAK KID, THE, 1972, C-O
HEARTBREAK MOTEL, 1978
HEARTBREAKER, 1983, C
HEARTBREAKERS, 1984, C-O
HEARTLAND, 1980, A
HEARTLESS HUSBANDS, 1925
HEARTS ADRIFT, 1914, A
HEARTS AFLAME, 1923
HEARTS AND FISTS, 1926, A
HEARTS AND FLOWERS, 1914
HEARTS AND MASKS, 1921
HEARTS AND SADDLES, 1919
HEARTS AND SPANGLES, 1926
HEARTS AND SPURS, 1925
HEARTS AND THE HIGHWAY, 1915
HEARTS ARE TRUMPS, 1920
HEARTS ASLEEP, 1919
HEARTS DIVIDED, 1936, A
HEARTS IN BONDAGE, 1936, A
HEARTS IN DIXIE, 1929, A
HEARTS IN EXILE, 1929, A
HEARTS O' THE RANGE, 1921
HEARTS OF HUMANITY, 1932, A
HEARTS OF HUMANITY, 1936, A
HEARTS OF LOVE, 1918
HEARTS OF MEN, 1915
HEARTS OF MEN, 1919, A
HEARTS OF MEN, 1928
HEARTS OF MEN, THE
HEARTS OF OAK, 1924, A
HEARTS OF THE WEST, 1925
HEARTS OF THE WEST, 1975, A
HEARTS OF THE WOODS, 1921
HEARTS OF THE WORLD, 1918, A
HEARTS OF YOUTH, 1921
HEARTS OR DIAMONDS?, 1918
HEARTS THAT ARE HUMAN, 1915
HEARTS UNITED, 1914
HEARTS UP, 1920
HEARTSEASE, 1919
HEARTSTRINGS, 1917
HEARTSTRINGS, 1923, A
HEAT, 1970, O
HEAT, 1972
HEAT AND DUST, 1983, C
HEAT LIGHTNING, 1934, A
HEAT OF DESIRE, 1984, O
HEAT OF MIDNIGHT, 1966, O
HEAT OF THE SUMMER, 1961, A
HEAT WAVE, 1935, A
HEAT'S ON, THE, 1943, A-C
HEATWAVE, 1954, A
HEATWAVE, 1983, O
HEAVEN CAN WAIT, 1943, A
HEAVEN CAN WAIT, 1978, C
HEAVEN IS ROUND THE CORNER, 1944, A
HEAVEN KNOWS, MR. ALLISON, 1957, A
HEAVEN ON EARTH, 1927
HEAVEN ON EARTH, 1931, A
HEAVEN ON EARTH, 1960, A
HEAVEN ONLY KNOWS, 1947, A
HEAVEN SENT
HEAVEN WITH A BARBED WIRE FENCE, 1939, A
HEAVEN WITH A GUN, 1969, C
HEAVEN'S GATE, 1980, O
HEAVENLY BODY, THE, 1943, A
HEAVENLY DAYS, 1944, A
HEAVENS ABOVE!, 1963, AA
HEAVY METAL, 1981, O
HEAVY TRAFFIC, 1974
HEDDA, 1975, A-C
HEDDA GABLER, 1917
HEEDLESS MOTHS, 1921
HEIDI, 1937, AAA
HEIDI, 1954, AAA
HEIDI, 1968, AAA
HEIDI AND PETER, 1955, AAA
HEIDI'S SONG, 1982, AA
HEIGHTS OF DANGER, 1962, A
HEIGHTS OF HAZARDS, THE, 1915
HEINZELMANNCHEN
HEIR OF THE AGES, THE, 1917
HEIR TO JENGHIS-KHAN, THE, 1928
HEIR TO JENGHIZ KHAN, THE
HEIR TO THE HOORAH, THE, 1916
HEIR TO TROUBLE, 1936, A
HEIR-LOONS, 1925
HEIRESS AT "COFFEE DAN'S", THE, 1917
HEIRESS FOR A DAY, 1918
HEIRESS, THE, 1949, A
HEIRLOOM MYSTERY, THE, 1936, A
HEIST, THE, 1979, A
HELD BY THE ENEMY, 1920
HELD BY THE LAW, 1927, A
HELD FOR RANSOM, 1914
HELD FOR RANSOM, 1938, A
HELD IN TRUST, 1920
HELD IN TRUST, 1949, A
HELD TO ANSWER, 1923, A
HELDEN
HELDEN—HIMMEL UND HOLLE
HELDINNEN, 1962, A
HELDORADO
HELEN MORGAN STORY, THE, 1959, A
HELEN OF FOUR GATES, 1920
HELEN OF TROY
HELEN OF TROY, 1956, A
HELEN'S BABIES, 1924, A
HELENE OF THE NORTH, 1915
HELICOPTER SPIES, THE, 1968, A
HELIOTROPE, 1920
HELL AND HIGH WATER, 1933, A
HELL AND HIGH WATER, 1954, A
HELL BELOW, 1933, A
HELL BELOW ZERO, 1954, A
HELL BENT, 1918
HELL BENT FOR 'FRISCO, 1931, A
HELL BENT FOR GLORY
HELL BENT FOR LEATHER, 1960, A
HELL BENT FOR LOVE, 1934, A
HELL BOATS, 1970, A
HELL BOUND, 1931, A
HELL BOUND, 1957, A
HELL CANYON OUTLAWS, 1957, A
HELL CAT, THE, 1918
HELL CAT, THE, 1934, A
HELL DIGGERS, THE, 1921
HELL DIVERS, 1932
HELL DRIVERS, 1958, A
HELL FIRE AUSTIN, 1932, A
HELL HARBOR, 1930
HELL HATH NO FURY, 1917
HELL HOUSE GIRLS, 1975
HELL IN KOREA, 1956, C
HELL IN NORMANDY, 1968
HELL IN THE CITY
HELL IN THE HEAVENS, 1934, A
HELL IN THE PACIFIC, 1968, O
HELL IS A CITY, 1960, A
HELL IS EMPTY, 1967, C
HELL IS FOR HEROES, 1962, C
HELL IS SOLD OUT, 1951, A
HELL MORGAN'S GIRL, 1917
HELL NIGHT, 1981, O
HELL ON DEVIL'S ISLAND, 1957, A
HELL ON EARTH, 1934, A
HELL ON FRISCO BAY, 1956, C
HELL ON WHEELS, 1967, A
HELL RAIDERS, 1968, A-C
HELL RAIDERS OF THE DEEP, 1954, A
HELL RIVER, 1977
HELL ROARIN' REFORM, 1919
HELL SHIP MUTINY, 1957, A
HELL SHIP, THE, 1920
HELL SHIP, THE, 1923
HELL SQUAD, 1958, A
HELL TO ETERNITY, 1960, A
HELL TO MACAO
HELL UP IN HARLEM, 1973, O
HELL WITH HEROES, THE, 1968, C
HELL'S 400, 1926
HELL'S ANGELS, 1930, C
HELL'S ANGELS ON WHEELS, 1967, O
HELL'S ANGELS '69, 1969, O

HELL'S BELLES, 1969, O
HELL'S BLOODY DEVILS, 1970, O
HELL'S BOARDER
HELL'S BORDER, 1922
HELL'S CARGO, 1935, A
HELL'S CARGO, 1939
HELL'S CHOSEN FEW, 1968, O
HELL'S CRATER, 1918
HELL'S CROSSROADS, 1957, A
HELL'S END, 1918
HELL'S FIVE HOURS, 1958, A
HELL'S HALF ACRE, 1954, A
HELL'S HEADQUARTERS, 1932
HELL'S HEROES, 1930, A
HELL'S HIGHROAD, 1925
HELL'S HIGHWAY, 1932, A
HELL'S HINGES, 1916, A
HELL'S HOLE, 1923
HELL'S HORIZON, 1955, A
HELL'S HOUSE, 1932, A
HELL'S ISLAND, 1930, A
HELL'S ISLAND, 1955
HELL'S KITCHEN, 1939, A
HELL'S OASIS, 1920
HELL'S OUTPOST, 1955, A
HELL'S PLAYGROUND, 1967, A
HELL'S RIVER
HELL'S VALLEY, 1931
HELL, HEAVEN OR HOBOKEN, 1958, A
HELL-BENT FOR HEAVEN, 1926
HELL-SHIP MORGAN, 1936
HELL-TO-PAY AUSTIN, 1916, A
HELLBENDERS, THE, 1967, A
HELLCAT, THE, 1928
HELLCATS OF THE NAVY, 1957, A
HELLCATS, THE, 1968, O
HELLDORADO, 1935, A
HELLDORADO, 1946, A
HELLER IN PINK TIGHTS, 1960, C
HELLFIGHTERS, 1968, A
HELLFIRE, 1949, A
HELLFIRE CLUB, THE, 1963, C
HELLGATE, 1952, A
HELLHOUNDS OF THE WEST, 1922
HELLION, THE, 1919
HELLION, THE, 1924
HELLIONS, THE, 1962, O
HELLO ANNAPOLIS, 1942, A
HELLO BEAUTIFUL
HELLO BILL, 1915
HELLO CHEYENE, 1928
HELLO DOWN THERE, 1969
HELLO GOD, 1951, A
HELLO LONDON, 1958
HELLO SISTER, 1930, A
HELLO SISTER!, 1933, C-O
HELLO SUCKER, 1941, A
HELLO SWEETHEART, 1935, A
HELLO TROUBLE, 1932, A
HELLO, DOLLY!, 1969, AAA
HELLO, ELEPHANT, 1954
HELLO, EVERYBODY, 1933, A
HELLO, FRISCO, HELLO, 1943, A
HELLO—GOODBYE, 1970, O
HELLSHIP BRONSON, 1928
HELLZAPOPPIN', 1941, A
HELP HELP POLICE, 1919
HELP I'M INVISIBLE, 1952, A
HELP ME...I'M POSSESSED, 1976
HELP WANTED, 1915
HELP WANTED—MALE, 1920, A
HELP YOURSELF, 1920
HELP YOURSELF, 1932, A
HELP!, 1965, A
HELTER SKELTER, 1949, A
HEMINGWAY'S ADVENTURES OF A YOUNG MAN
HENNESSY, 1975, C
HENRIETTE'S HOLIDAY, 1953, C
HENRY ALDRICH FOR PRESIDENT, 1941, A
HENRY ALDRICH GETS GLAMOUR, 1942, A
HENRY ALDRICH HAUNTS A HOUSE, 1943, A
HENRY ALDRICH PLAYS CUPID, 1944, A
HENRY ALDRICH SWINGS IT, 1943, A
HENRY ALDRICH'S LITTLE SECRET, 1944, A
HENRY ALDRICH, BOY SCOUT, 1944, A
HENRY ALDRICH, EDITOR, 1942, A
HENRY AND DIZZY, 1942, A
HENRY GOES ARIZONA, 1939, A
HENRY LIMPET
HENRY STEPS OUT, 1940, A
HENRY V, 1946, A
HENRY VIII
HENRY VIII AND HIS SIX WIVES, 1972, A
HENRY'S NIGHT IN, 1969
HENRY, KING OF NAVARRE, 1924
HENRY, THE RAINMAKER, 1949, A
HENTAI, 1966, O
HER ACCIDENTAL HUSBAND, 1923
HER ADVENTUROUS NIGHT, 1946, A
HER AMERICAN HUSBAND, 1918
HER AMERICAN PRINCE, 1916
HER ATONEMENT, 1915
HER BELOVED ENEMY, 1917
HER BELOVED VILLIAN, 1920
HER BENNY, 1920
HER BETTER SELF, 1917
HER BIG ADVENTURE, 1926
HER BIG NIGHT, 1926
HER BITTER CUP, 1916
HER BLEEDING HEART, 1916
HER BODY IN BOND, 1918
HER BODYGUARD, 1933, A
HER BOY, 1915, A
HER BOY, 1918
HER CARDBOARD LOVER, 1942, A
HER CODE OF HONOR, 1919
HER CONDONED SIN
HER COUNTRY FIRST, 1918
HER COUNTRY'S CALL, 1917
HER CROSS, 1919
HER DEBT OF HONOR, 1916
HER DECISION, 1918
HER DOUBLE CROSS, 1917
HER DOUBLE LIFE, 1916
HER ELEPHANT MAN, 1920, A
HER ENLISTED MAN
HER EXCELLENCY, THE GOVERNOR, 1917
HER FACE VALUE, 1921
HER FATAL MILLIONS, 1923, A
HER FATHER SAID NO, 1927
HER FATHER'S GOLD, 1916
HER FATHER'S KEEPER, 1917
HER FATHER'S SON, 1916
HER FAVORITE HUSBAND
HER FIGHTING CHANCE, 1917, A
HER FINAL RECKONING, 1918
HER FIRST AFFAIR, 1947, A
HER FIRST AFFAIRE, 1932, A
HER FIRST BEAU, 1941, A
HER FIRST ELOPEMENT, 1920
HER FIRST MATE, 1933, A
HER FIRST ROMANCE, 1940
HER FIRST ROMANCE, 1951
HER FIVE-FOOT HIGHNESS, 1920, A
HER FORGOTTEN PAST, 1933, A
HER GAME, 1919
HER GILDED CAGE, 1922, A
HER GOOD NAME, 1917
HER GREAT CHANCE, 1918, A
HER GREAT HOUR, 1916
HER GREAT MATCH, 1915
HER GREAT PRICE, 1916
HER GREATEST BLUFF, 1927
HER GREATEST LOVE, 1917
HER GREATEST PERFORMANCE, 1916
HER HALF BROTHER
HER HAPPINESS, 1915
HER HERITAGE, 1919, A
HER HIGHNESS AND THE BELLBOY, 1945, A
HER HONOR THE GOVERNOR, 1926
HER HONOR THE MAYOR, 1920
HER HOUR, 1917
HER HUSBAND LIES, 1937, A
HER HUSBAND'S AFFAIRS, 1947, A
HER HUSBAND'S FRIEND, 1920
HER HUSBAND'S HONOR, 1918
HER HUSBAND'S SECRET, 1925
HER HUSBAND'S SECRETARY, 1937, A
HER HUSBAND'S TRADEMARK, 1922
HER IMAGINARY LOVER, 1933, A
HER INDISCRETIONS, 1927
HER INSPIRATION, 1918
HER JUNGLE LOVE, 1938, A
HER KIND OF MAN, 1946, A
HER KINGDOM OF DREAMS, 1919
HER LAST AFFAIRE, 1935, A
HER LIFE AND HIS, 1917
HER LONELY SOLDIER, 1919, A
HER LORD AND MASTER, 1921
HER LOVE STORY, 1924
HER LUCKY NIGHT, 1945, A
HER MAD BARGAIN, 1921, A
HER MAD NIGHT, 1932, A
HER MAJESTY, 1922
HER MAJESTY LOVE, 1931, A
HER MAN, 1918
HER MAN, 1924, A
HER MAN, 1930, C
HER MAN GILBEY, 1949, A
HER MAN O'WAR, 1926
HER MARKET VALUE, 1925
HER MARRIAGE LINES, 1917
HER MARRIAGE VOW, 1924
HER MARTYRDOM, 1915
HER MASTER'S VOICE, 1936, A
HER MATERNAL RIGHT, 1916
HER MISTAKE, 1918
HER MOMENT, 1918
HER MOTHER'S SECRET, 1915
HER NAMLESS CHILD, 1915
HER NEW YORK, 1917
HER NIGHT OF NIGHTS, 1922
HER NIGHT OF ROMANCE, 1924
HER NIGHT OUT, 1932, A
HER OFFICAL FATHERS, 1917
HER ONE MISTAKE, 1918
HER ONLY WAY, 1918
HER OWN FREE WILL, 1924, A
HER OWN MONEY, 1922
HER OWN PEOPLE, 1917
HER OWN STORY, 1922
HER OWN STORY, 1926
HER OWN WAY, 1915
HER PANELLED DOOR, 1951, A
HER PENALTY, 1921
HER PRICE, 1918
HER PRIMITIVE MAN, 1944, A
HER PRIVATE AFFAIR, 1930, A
HER PRIVATE LIFE, 1929, A
HER PROPER PLACE, 1915
HER PURCHASE PRICE, 1919
HER RECKONING, 1915
HER REDEMPTION
HER REPUTATION, 1923
HER REPUTATION, 1931, A
HER RESALE VALUE, 1933, A
HER RIGHT TO LIVE, 1917
HER SACRIFICE, 1917
HER SACRIFICE, 1926
HER SECOND CHANCE, 1926
HER SECOND HUSBAND, 1918
HER SECOND MOTHER, 1940
HER SECRET, 1917
HER SECRET, 1919, A
HER SECRET, 1933
HER SHATTERED IDOL, 1915
HER SILENT SACRIFICE, 1917
HER SISTER, 1917
HER SISTER FROM PARIS, 1925
HER SISTER'S GUILT, 1916
HER SISTER'S SECRET, 1946, A
HER SOCIAL VALUE, 1921
HER SON, 1920
HER SOUL'S INSPIRATION, 1917
HER SPLENDID FOLLY, 1933, A
HER STORY, 1920, A
HER STORY, 1922
HER STRANGE DESIRE, 1931, A
HER STRANGE WEDDING, 1917
HER STURDY OAK, 1921
HER SUMMER HERO, 1928
HER TEMPORARY HUSBAND, 1923
HER TEMPTATION, 1917
HER TWELVE MEN, 1954, A
HER UNBORN CHILD, 1933
HER UNWILLING HUSBAND, 1920
HER VOCATION, 1915
HER WAYWARD SISTER, 1916
HER WEDDING NIGHT, 1930, A
HER WILD OAT, 1927
HER WINNING WAY, 1921, A
HERBIE GOES BANANAS, 1980, AAA
HERBIE GOES TO MONTE CARLO, 1977, AAA
HERBIE RIDES AGAIN, 1974, AAA
HERCULE CONTRE MOLOCH
HERCULES, 1959, C-O
HERCULES, 1983, A
HERCULES AGAINST THE MOON MEN, 1965, A
HERCULES AGAINST THE SONS OF THE SUN, 1964, A
HERCULES AND THE CAPTIVE WOMEN, 1963
HERCULES AND THE PRINCESS OF TROY, 1966
HERCULES AND THE TYRANTS OF BABYLON, 1964
HERCULES IN NEW YORK, 1970, A
HERCULES IN THE HAUNTED WORLD, 1964, C
HERCULES IN VALE OF WOE, 1962
HERCULES THE INVINCIBLE, 1963
HERCULES UNCHAINED, 1960, A
HERCULES VS-THE GIANT WARRIORS, 1965, A
HERCULES' PILLS, 1960, C
HERCULES, PRISONER OF EVIL, 1967
HERCULES, SAMSON & ULYSSES, 1964, A
HERE COME THE CO-EDS, 1945, AAA
HERE COME THE GIRLS, 1953, A
HERE COME THE HUGGETTS, 1948, A
HERE COME THE JETS, 1959
HERE COME THE MARINES, 1952
HERE COME THE NELSONS, 1952, A
HERE COME THE TIGERS, 1978, C
HERE COME THE WAVES, 1944, A
HERE COMES CARTER, 1936, A
HERE COMES COOKIE, 1935, A
HERE COMES ELMER, 1943, A
HERE COMES HAPPINESS, 1941, A
HERE COMES KELLY, 1943, A
HERE COMES MR. JORDAN, 1941, A
HERE COMES SANTA CLAUS, 1984, AAA

HERE COMES THAT NASHVILLE SOUND
HERE COMES THE BAND, 1935, A
HERE COMES THE BRIDE, 1919
HERE COMES THE GROOM, 1934, A
HERE COMES THE GROOM, 1951, A
HERE COMES THE NAVY, 1934, A
HERE COMES THE SUN, 1945, A
HERE COMES TROUBLE, 1936, A
HERE COMES TROUBLE, 1948, A
HERE HE COMES, 1926
HERE I AM A STRANGER, 1939, A
HERE IS A MAN
HERE IS MY HEART, 1934, A
HERE SURRENDER, 1916
HERE WE GO AGAIN, 1942, AA
HERE WE GO ROUND THE MULBERRY BUSH, 1968, C
HERE'S FLASH CASEY, 1937, A
HERE'S GEORGE, 1932, A
HERE'S THE KNIFE, DEAR: NOW USE IT
HERE'S TO ROMANCE, 1935, A
HERE'S YOUR LIFE, 1968, C-O
HEREDITY, 1918
HERETIC
HERITAGE, 1915
HERITAGE, 1920
HERITAGE, 1935, A
HERITAGE OF HATE, THE, 1916
HERITAGE OF THE DESERT, 1933, A
HERITAGE OF THE DESERT, 1939, A
HERITAGE OF THE DESERT, THE, 1924
HERKER VON LONDON, DER
HERO, 1982, C
HERO AIN'T NOTHIN' BUT A SANDWICH, A, 1977
HERO AT LARGE, 1980, A
HERO FOR A DAY, 1939, A
HERO FOR A NIGHT, A, 1927
HERO OF BABYLON, 1963, A
HERO OF OUR TIME, A, 1969
HERO OF SUBMARINE D-2, THE, 1916
HERO OF THE BIG SNOWS, A, 1926
HERO OF THE CIRCUS, THE, 1928
HERO OF THE HOUR, THE, 1917
HERO ON HORSEBACK, A, 1927
HERO'S ISLAND, 1962, A
HERO, THE
HERO, THE, 1923, A
HEROD THE GREAT, 1960, C
HEROES, 1977, A
HEROES AND HUSBANDS, 1922
HEROES ARE MADE, 1944, C-O
HEROES DIE YOUNG, 1960, C
HEROES FOR SALE, 1933, A
HEROES IN BLUE, 1927
HEROES IN BLUE, 1939, A
HEROES IN THE NIGHT, 1927
HEROES OF TELEMARK, THE, 1965, C
HEROES OF THE ALAMO, 1938, A
HEROES OF THE HILLS, 1938, A
HEROES OF THE RANGE, 1936, A
HEROES OF THE SADDLE, 1940, A
HEROES OF THE SEA, 1941
HEROES OF THE STREET, 1922
HEROES THREE, 1984
HEROES, THE
HEROES, THE, 1975
HEROIC LOVER, THE, 1929, A
HEROINA, 1965, C
HEROS SANS RETOUR
HEROSTRATUS, 1968, C
HEROWORK, 1977
HERR ARNES PENGAR
HERR DOKTOR, 1917
HERRSCHER OHNE KRONE
HERS TO HOLD, 1943, A
HESPER OF THE MOUNTAINS, 1916
HESTER STREET, 1975, C
HEX, 1973, O
HEY BABE?, 1984, A
HEY BOY! HEY GIRL!, 1959, A
HEY HEY COWBOY, 1927, A
HEY RUBE, 1928, A
HEY THERE, IT'S YOGI BEAR, 1964, AAA
HEY! HEY! U.S.A., 1938, A
HEY, GOOD LOOKIN', 1982, O
HEY, LET'S TWIST!, 1961, A
HEY, ROOKIE, 1944
HI DIDDLE DIDDLE, 1943, A
HI GAUCHO!, 1936, A
HI IN THE CELLAR
HI' YA, SAILOR, 1943, A
HI'YA, CHUM, 1943, A
HI, BUDDY, 1943, A
HI, GANG!, 1941, A
HI, GOOD-LOOKIN', 1944, A
HI, MOM!, 1970, O
HI, NEIGHBOR, 1942, A
HI, NELLIE!, 1934, A
HI-DE-HO, 1947, A
HI-JACKED, 1950, A
HI-JACKERS, THE, 1963, A
HI-JACKING RUSTLERS, 1926
HI-RIDERS, 1978, O
HI-YO SILVER, 1940, AA
HIAWATHA, 1913
HIAWATHA, 1952, AAA
HICKEY AND BOGGS, 1972, C
HICKVILLE TO BROADWAY, 1921
HIDDEN ACES, 1927
HIDDEN CHILDREN, THE, 1917
HIDDEN CODE, THE, 1920
HIDDEN DANGER, 1949, A
HIDDEN ENEMY, 1940, A
HIDDEN EYE, THE, 1945, A
HIDDEN FEAR, 1957, C
HIDDEN FIRES, 1918
HIDDEN FORTRESS, THE, 1959, C
HIDDEN GOLD, 1933, A
HIDDEN GOLD, 1940, A
HIDDEN GUNS, 1956, C
HIDDEN HAND, THE, 1916
HIDDEN HAND, THE, 1942, C
HIDDEN HOMICIDE, 1959, C
HIDDEN LAW, THE, 1916
HIDDEN LIGHT, 1920
HIDDEN LOOT, 1925
HIDDEN MENACE, THE, 1925
HIDDEN MENACE, THE, 1940, A
HIDDEN PEARLS, 1918
HIDDEN POWER, 1939, A
HIDDEN ROOM OF 1,000 HORRORS
HIDDEN ROOM, THE, 1949, A
HIDDEN SCAR, THE, 1916, A
HIDDEN SPRING, THE, 1917
HIDDEN TRUTH, THE, 1919
HIDDEN VALLEY, 1932, A
HIDDEN VALLEY OUTLAWS, 1944, A
HIDDEN VALLEY, THE, 1916
HIDDEN WAY, THE, 1926
HIDDEN WOMAN, THE, 1922
HIDE AND SEEK, 1964, A
HIDE IN PLAIN SIGHT, 1980, C
HIDE-OUT, 1934, A
HIDE-OUT, THE, 1930, A
HIDEAWAY, 1937, A
HIDEAWAY GIRL, 1937, A
HIDEAWAYS, THE
HIDEOUS SUN DEMON, THE, 1959, C
HIDEOUT, 1948, C
HIDEOUT, 1949, A
HIDEOUT IN THE ALPS, 1938, A
HIDEOUT IN THE SUN, 1960
HIDEOUT, THE, 1956, C
HIDING PLACE, THE, 1975, C-O
HIER ET AUJOURD'HUI, 1918
HIGGINS FAMILY, THE, 1938, A
HIGH, 1968, O
HIGH AND DRY, 1954, A
HIGH AND HANDSOME, 1925, A
HIGH AND LOW, 1963, C-O
HIGH AND THE MIGHTY, THE, 1954, A
HIGH ANXIETY, 1977, C
HIGH BARBAREE, 1947, A
HIGH BRIGHT SUN, THE
HIGH COMMAND, 1938, A
HIGH COMMISSIONER, THE, 1968, C-O
HIGH CONQUEST, 1947, A
HIGH COST OF LOVING, THE, 1958, A
HIGH COUNTRY CALLING, 1975
HIGH COUNTRY ROMANCE, 1915
HIGH COUNTRY, THE, 1981, A
HIGH EXPLOSIVE, 1943, A
HIGH FINANCE, 1917
HIGH FINANCE, 1933, A
HIGH FLIGHT, 1957, A
HIGH FLYER, THE, 1926
HIGH FLYERS, 1937, A
HIGH FURY, 1947, A
HIGH GEAR, 1933, A
HIGH GEAR JEFFREY, 1921
HIGH HAND, THE, 1915
HIGH HAND, THE, 1926
HIGH HAT, 1927
HIGH HAT, 1937, A
HIGH HEELS, 1921, A
HIGH HELL, 1958, C
HIGH INFIDELITY, 1965, O
HIGH JINKS IN SOCIETY, 1949, A
HIGH JUMP, 1959, A
HIGH LONESOME, 1950, A
HIGH NOON, 1952, C
HIGH PLAINS DRIFTER, 1973, O
HIGH PLAY, 1917
HIGH POCKETS, 1919
HIGH POWERED, 1945, A
HIGH PRESSURE, 1932, A
HIGH RISK, 1981, O
HIGH ROAD TO CHINA, 1983, C
HIGH ROAD, THE, 1915
HIGH ROLLING, 1977, O
HIGH SCHOOL, 1940, A
HIGH SCHOOL BIG SHOT, 1959, C
HIGH SCHOOL CAESAR, 1960, C
HIGH SCHOOL CONFIDENTIAL, 1958, O
HIGH SCHOOL GIRL, 1935, A
HIGH SCHOOL HELLCATS, 1958, O
HIGH SCHOOL HERO, 1927
HIGH SCHOOL HERO, 1946, A
HIGH SCHOOL HONEYMOON
HIGH SEAS, 1929, A
HIGH SIERRA, 1941, C
HIGH SIGN, THE, 1917
HIGH SOCIETY, 1932
HIGH SOCIETY, 1955, AA
HIGH SOCIETY, 1956, A
HIGH SOCIETY BLUES, 1930, A
HIGH SPEED, 1917, A
HIGH SPEED, 1920
HIGH SPEED, 1924
HIGH SPEED, 1932, A
HIGH SPEED LEE, 1923
HIGH STAKES, 1918
HIGH STAKES, 1931, A
HIGH STEPPERS, 1926
HIGH TENSION, 1936, A
HIGH TERRACE, 1957, A
HIGH TIDE, 1918
HIGH TIDE, 1947, A
HIGH TIDE AT NOON, 1957, A
HIGH TIME, 1960, A
HIGH TREASON, 1929, A
HIGH TREASON, 1937, A
HIGH TREASON, 1951, A
HIGH VELOCITY, 1977, C
HIGH VOLTAGE, 1929, A
HIGH WALL, THE, 1947, C
HIGH WIND IN JAMAICA, A, 1965, A
HIGH YELLOW, 1965, C-O
HIGH, WIDE AND HANDSOME, 1937, A
HIGH-BALLIN', 1978, C
HIGH-POWERED RIFLE, THE, 1960, A
HIGHBINDERS, THE, 1926
HIGHER AND HIGHER, 1943, A
HIGHEST BID, THE, 1916
HIGHEST BIDDER, THE, 1921
HIGHEST LAW, THE, 1921
HIGHEST TRUMP, THE, 1919
HIGHLAND FLING, 1936, A
HIGHLY DANGEROUS, 1950, A
HIGHPOINT, 1984, C
HIGHWAY 13, 1948, A
HIGHWAY 301, 1950, C
HIGHWAY DRAGNET, 1954, A
HIGHWAY OF HOPE, THE, 1917
HIGHWAY PATROL, 1938, A
HIGHWAY PICKUP, 1965, C
HIGHWAY TO BATTLE, 1961, A
HIGHWAY TO HELL, 1984, O
HIGHWAY WEST, 1941, A
HIGHWAYMAN RIDES, THE
HIGHWAYMAN, THE, 1951, C
HIGHWAYS BY NIGHT, 1942, A
HIJACK, 1975
HIKEN
HIKEN YABURI, 1969, C
HILARY'S BLUES, 1983
HILDA CRANE, 1956, A
HILDE WARREN AND DEATH, 1916
HILDUR AND THE MAGICIAN, 1969, AAA
HILL 24 DOESN'T ANSWER, 1955, A
HILL BILLY, THE, 1924
HILL IN KOREA, A
HILL, THE, 1965, O
HILLBILLY BLITZKRIEG, 1942, A
HILLBILLYS IN A HAUNTED HOUSE, 1967, A
HILLCREST MYSTERY, THE, 1918
HILLS HAVE EYES, THE, 1978, O
HILLS OF DONEGAL, THE, 1947, A
HILLS OF HATE, 1921
HILLS OF HOME, 1948, AAA
HILLS OF KENTUCKY, 1927, A
HILLS OF MISSING MEN, 1922, A
HILLS OF OKLAHOMA, 1950, A
HILLS OF OLD WYOMING, 1937, A
HILLS OF PERIL, 1927
HILLS OF UTAH, 1951, A
HILLS RUN RED, THE, 1967, C
HIM
HINDENBURG, THE, 1975, C
HINDERED, 1974
HINDLE WAKES
HINDLE WAKES, 1918
HINDLE WAKES, 1931, A
HINDLE WAKES, 1952
HINDU TOMB, THE
HINDU, THE, 1953, AA
HINOTORI, 1980, O

HINTON'S DOUBLE, 1917
HIPPODROME, 1961, C-O
HIPPOLYT, THE LACKEY, 1932, A
HIPS, HIPS, HOORAY, 1934, A
HIRED GUN
HIRED GUN, 1952
HIRED GUN, THE, 1957, A
HIRED HAND, THE, 1971, A
HIRED KILLER, THE, 1967, C
HIRED MAN, THE, 1918
HIRED WIFE, 1934, A
HIRED WIFE, 1940, A
HIRELING, THE, 1973, C
HIROSHIMA, MON AMOUR, 1959, C-O
HIS AND HERS, 1961, A
HIS AND HIS
HIS BACK AGAINST THE WALL, 1922
HIS BIRTHRIGHT, 1918
HIS BONDED WIFE, 1918
HIS BRIDAL NIGHT, 1919
HIS BROTHER'S GHOST, 1945, A
HIS BROTHER'S KEEPER, 1921
HIS BROTHER'S KEEPER, 1939, A-C
HIS BROTHER'S WIFE, 1916
HIS BROTHER'S WIFE, 1936, A-C
HIS BUDDY'S WIFE, 1925
HIS BUTLER'S SISTER, 1943, A
HIS CALL
HIS CAPTIVE WOMAN, 1929, A
HIS CHILDREN'S CHILDREN, 1923
HIS COUNTRY'S HONOUR
HIS DARKER SELF, 1924, A
HIS DAUGHTER'S DILEMMA, 1916
HIS DAUGHTER'S SECOND HUSBAND, 1916
HIS DEAREST POSSESSION, 1919
HIS DEBT, 1919
HIS DIVORCED WIFE, 1919
HIS DOG, 1927
HIS DOUBLE LIFE, 1933, A
HIS ENEMY THE LAW, 1918
HIS ENEMY'S DAUGHTER
HIS ENEMY'S DAUGHTER
HIS EXCELLENCY, 1952, A
HIS EXCITING NIGHT, 1938, A
HIS EYES, 1916
HIS FAMILY TREE, 1936, A
HIS FATHER'S SON, 1917, A
HIS FATHER'S WIFE, 1919
HIS FIGHTING BLOOD, 1935, A
HIS FIRST COMMAND, 1929, A
HIS FIRST FLAME, 1927
HIS FOREIGN WIFE, 1927
HIS FORGOTTEN WIFE, 1924
HIS GIRL FRIDAY, 1940, C
HIS GLORIOUS NIGHT, 1929
HIS GRACE GIVES NOTICE, 1924
HIS GRACE GIVES NOTICE, 1933, A
HIS GREAT CHANCE, 1923
HIS GREAT TRIUMPH, 1916
HIS GREATEST BATTLE, 1925
HIS GREATEST GAMBLE, 1934, A
HIS GREATEST SACRIFICE, 1921
HIS HOUR, 1924, A
HIS HOUSE IN ORDER, 1920
HIS HOUSE IN ORDER, 1928, A
HIS JAZZ BRIDE, 1926, A
HIS KIND OF WOMAN, 1951, C-O
HIS LAST BULLET, 1928
HIS LAST DEFENCE, 1919
HIS LAST DOLLAR, 1914, A
HIS LAST HAUL, 1928
HIS LAST RACE, 1923
HIS LAST TWELVE HOURS, 1953, A
HIS LORDSHIP, 1932, A
HIS LORDSHIP GOES TO PRESS, 1939, A
HIS LORDSHIP REGRETS, 1938, A
HIS LORDSHIP, 1936
HIS LUCKY DAY, 1929, A
HIS MAJESTY AND CO, 1935, A
HIS MAJESTY BUNKER BEAN
HIS MAJESTY BUNKER BEAN, 1918
HIS MAJESTY BUNKER BEAN, 1925
HIS MAJESTY O'KEEFE, 1953, A
HIS MAJESTY THE AMERICAN, 1919, A
HIS MAJESTY THE OUTLAW, 1924
HIS MAJESTY, KING BALLYHOO, 1931, A
HIS MAJESTY, THE SCARECROW OF OZ, 1914
HIS MASTER'S VOICE, 1925, A
HIS MOTHER'S BOY, 1917
HIS MYSTERY'S GIRL, 1923
HIS NEW YORK WIFE, 1926
HIS NIBS, 1921
HIS NIGHT OUT, 1935, A
HIS OFFICIAL FIANCEE, 1919
HIS OLD-FASHIONED DAD, 1917
HIS OTHER WIFE, 1921
HIS OTHER WOMAN
HIS OWN HOME TOWN, 1918
HIS OWN LAW, 1920
HIS OWN LAW, 1924
HIS OWN PEOPLE, 1918
HIS PAJAMA GIRL, 1921
HIS PARISIAN WIFE, 1919
HIS PEOPLE, 1925
HIS PICTURE IN THE PAPERS, 1916
HIS PRIVATE LIFE, 1928
HIS PRIVATE SECRETARY, 1933, A
HIS RISE TO FAME, 1927
HIS ROBE OF HONOR, 1918, A
HIS ROYAL HIGHNESS, 1918
HIS ROYAL HIGHNESS, 1932, A
HIS SECRETARY, 1925, A
HIS SISTER'S CHAMPION, 1916
HIS SUPREME MOMENT, 1925
HIS SUPREME SACRIFICE, 1922
HIS SWEETHEART, 1917
HIS TEMPORARY WIFE, 1920
HIS TIGER LADY, 1928
HIS TURNING POINT, 1915
HIS VINDICATION, 1915
HIS WIFE, 1915
HIS WIFE'S FRIEND, 1920
HIS WIFE'S GOOD NAME, 1916
HIS WIFE'S HUSBAND, 1913
HIS WIFE'S HUSBAND, 1922
HIS WIFE'S HUSBAND, 1922
HIS WIFE'S MONEY, 1920
HIS WIFE'S MOTHER, 1932, A
HIS WIFE'S LOVER, 1931
HIS WOMAN, 1931, A
HIS, HERS AND THEIRS
HISTOIRE D'ADELE H
HISTOIRE D'AIMER
HISTORY IS MADE AT NIGHT, 1937, C
HISTORY OF MR. POLLY, THE, 1949, A
HISTORY OF THE WORLD, PART 1, 1981, C-O
HIT, 1973, O
HIT AND RUN, 1924
HIT AND RUN, 1957, C
HIT AND RUN, 1982
HIT MAN, 1972, O
HIT OF THE SNOW, 1928
HIT OF THE SNOW, 1928
HIT OR MISS, 1919
HIT PARADE OF 1941, 1940, A
HIT PARADE OF 1943, 1943, A
HIT PARADE OF 1947, 1947, A
HIT PARADE OF 1951, 1950, A
HIT PARADE, THE, 1937, A
HIT THE DECK, 1930, A
HIT THE DECK, 1955, AA
HIT THE HAY, 1945, A
HIT THE ICE, 1943, A
HIT THE ROAD, 1941
HIT THE SADDLE, 1937, A
HIT-THE-TRAIL HOLLIDAY, 1918
HITCH HIKE LADY, 1936, A
HITCH HIKE TO HEAVEN, 1936, A
HITCH IN TIME, A, 1978, AA
HITCH-HIKER, THE, 1953, C-O
HITCHHIKE TO HAPPINESS, 1945, A
HITCHHIKE TO HELL, 1978
HITCHHIKERS, THE, 1972, O
HITCHIN' POSTS, 1920
HITLER, 1962, C
HITLER GANG, THE, 1944, A
HITLER'S CHILDREN, 1942, C
HITLER'S GOLD
HITLER'S MADMAN, 1943, A
HITLER, A FILM FROM GERMANY
HITLER—DEAD OR ALIVE, 1942, A
HITLER: THE LAST TEN DAYS, 1973, C
HITOKIRI
HITTER, THE, 1979
HITTIN' THE TRAIL, 1937, A
HITTING A NEW HIGH, 1937, A
HITTING THE HIGH SPOTS, 1918
HITTING THE TRAIL, 1918
HIYA, CHUM
HO, 1968, O
HOA-BINH, 1971, C-O
HOARDED ASSETS, 1918
HOAX, THE, 1972, C
HOBBS IN A HURRY, 1918
HOBSON'S CHOICE, 1920
HOBSON'S CHOICE, 1931, A
HOBSON'S CHOICE, 1954, A
HOEDOWN, 1950, A
HOFFMAN, 1970, A
HOG WILD, 1980, O
HOGAN'S ALLEY, 1925
HOLD 'EM YALE, 1928, A
HOLD BACK THE DAWN, 1941, A
HOLD BACK THE NIGHT, 1956, A
HOLD BACK TOMORROW, 1955, O
HOLD EVERYTHING, 1930, AA
HOLD ME TIGHT, 1933, A
HOLD MY HAND, 1938, A
HOLD ON, 1966, A
HOLD THAT BABY!, 1949, A
HOLD THAT BLONDE, 1945, A
HOLD THAT CO-ED, 1938, A
HOLD THAT GHOST, 1941, AAA
HOLD THAT GIRL, 1934, A
HOLD THAT HYPNOTIST, 1957, A
HOLD THAT KISS, 1938, A
HOLD THAT LINE, 1952, A
HOLD THAT LION, 1926
HOLD THAT RIVER, 1936
HOLD THAT WOMAN, 1940, A
HOLD THE PRESS, 1933, C
HOLD YOUR BREATH, 1924
HOLD YOUR HORSES, 1921
HOLD YOUR MAN, 1929, C
HOLD YOUR MAN, 1933, C
HOLD'EM JAIL, 1932, A
HOLD'EM NAVY!, 1937, A
HOLD'EM YALE, 1935
HOLD-UP A LA MILANAISE
HOLE IN THE HEAD, A, 1959
HOLE IN THE WALL, 1929, A-C
HOLE IN THE WALL, THE, 1921
HOLIDAY, 1930, A
HOLIDAY, 1938, A
HOLIDAY AFFAIR, 1949, A
HOLIDAY CAMP, 1947, C
HOLIDAY FOR HENRIETTA, 1955, A
HOLIDAY FOR LOVERS, 1959, A
HOLIDAY FOR SINNERS, 1952, C
HOLIDAY IN HAVANA, 1949, A
HOLIDAY IN MEXICO, 1946, A
HOLIDAY IN SPAIN
HOLIDAY INN, 1942, A
HOLIDAY ON THE BUSES, 1974
HOLIDAY RHYTHM, 1950, A
HOLIDAY WEEK, 1952, A
HOLIDAY'S END, 1937, A
HOLIDAYS WITH PAY, 1948, A
HOLLOW OF HER HAND, THE
HOLLOW TRIUMPH, 1948, A
HOLLY AND THE IVY, THE, 1954, A
HOLLYWOOD, 1923
HOLLYWOOD 90028, 1973
HOLLYWOOD AND VINE, 1945, AA
HOLLYWOOD BARN DANCE, 1947, A
HOLLYWOOD BOULEVARD, 1936, A
HOLLYWOOD BOULEVARD, 1976, O
HOLLYWOOD CANTEEN, 1944, A
HOLLYWOOD CAVALCADE, 1939, A
HOLLYWOOD COWBOY, 1937, A
HOLLYWOOD COWBOY, 1975
HOLLYWOOD HIGH, 1976
HOLLYWOOD HIGH, 1977, O
HOLLYWOOD HIGH PART II, 1984, O
HOLLYWOOD HOODLUM
HOLLYWOOD HOT TUBS, 1984, O
HOLLYWOOD HOTEL, 1937, AA
HOLLYWOOD KNIGHT, 1979
HOLLYWOOD KNIGHTS, THE, 1980, O
HOLLYWOOD MAN, THE, 1976
HOLLYWOOD MYSTERY, 1934, C
HOLLYWOOD OR BUST, 1956, A
HOLLYWOOD PARTY, 1934, AAA
HOLLYWOOD REPORTER, THE, 1926
HOLLYWOOD ROUNDUP, 1938, A
HOLLYWOOD SPEAKS, 1932, C-O
HOLLYWOOD STADIUM MYSTERY, 1938, A
HOLLYWOOD STORY, 1951, A
HOLLYWOOD STRANGLER MEETS THE SKIDROW SLASHER, THE, 1979
HOLLYWOOD STRANGLER, THE
HOLLYWOOD THRILL-MAKERS, 1954
HOLLYWOOD THRILLMAKERS
HOLOCAUST 2000
HOLY INNOCENTS, THE, 1984, O
HOLY MATRIMONY, 1943, A
HOLY MOUNTAIN, THE, 1973, O
HOLY ORDERS, 1917, A
HOLY SINNER, THE, 1929
HOLY TERROR
HOLY TERROR, A, 1931, A
HOLY TERROR, THE, 1937, A
HOMBRE, 1967, C
HOMBRE Y EL MONSTRUO, EL
HOME, 1915
HOME, 1916, A
HOME, 1919
HOME AND AWAY, 1956, A
HOME AND THE WORLD, THE, 1984, C
HOME AT SEVEN
HOME BEFORE DARK, 1958, C
HOME FOR TANYA, A, 1961, A
HOME FREE ALL, 1983, A
HOME FREE ALL, 1984, O
HOME FROM HOME, 1939
HOME FROM THE HILL, 1960, O
HOME IN INDIANA, 1944

HOME IN OKLAHOMA, 1946, A
HOME IN SAN ANTONE, 1949
HOME IN WYOMIN', 1942, A
HOME IS THE HERO, 1959, C
HOME JAMES, 1928
HOME MADE, 1927
HOME MAKER, THE, 1925
HOME MOVIES, 1979
HOME OF THE BRAVE, 1949, C
HOME ON THE HANGE, 1946, A
HOME ON THE PRAIRIE, 1939, A
HOME ON THE RANGE, 1935, A
HOME STRETCH, THE, 1921
HOME STRUCK, 1927, A
HOME STUFF, 1921, A
HOME SWEET HOME, 1914, A
HOME SWEET HOME, 1945, A
HOME SWEET HOME, 1981, O
HOME SWEET HOMICIDE, 1946, AAA
HOME TALENT, 1921
HOME TO DANGER, 1951, A
HOME TOWN GIRL, THE, 1919
HOME TOWN STORY, 1951, C
HOME TOWNERS, THE, 1928, A
HOME TRAIL, THE, 1918
HOME WANTED, 1919
HOME, SWEET HOME, 1933, A
HOME-KEEPING HEARTS, 1921
HOMEBODIES, 1974, O
HOMEBREAKER, THE, 1919
HOMECOMING, 1929
HOMECOMING, 1948, A
HOMECOMING, THE, 1973, C
HOMEMAKER, THE, 1919
HOMER, 1970, C
HOMER COMES HOME, 1920
HOMESICK, 1928, A
HOMESPUN FOLKS, 1920
HOMESPUN VAMP, A, 1922, A
HOMESTEADER, THE, 1922
HOMESTEADERS OF PARADISE VALLEY, 1947, A
HOMESTEADERS, THE, 1953, A
HOMESTRETCH, THE, 1947, A
HOMETOWN U.S.A., 1979, C
HOMEWARD BORNE, 1957
HOMEWARD BOUND, 1923
HOMEWORK, 1982, O
HOMICIDAL, 1961, O
HOMICIDE, 1949, C
HOMICIDE BUREAU, 1939, O
HOMICIDE FOR THREE, 1948, C
HOMICIDE SQUAD, 1931, A
HONDO, 1953, C
HONEST HUTCH, 1920
HONEST MAN, AN, 1918
HONESTY-THE BEST POLICY, 1926
HONEY, 1930, A
HONEY BEE, THE, 1920
HONEY POT, THE, 1967, A
HONEYBABY, HONEYBABY, 1974, C
HONEYCHILE, 1951, A
HONEYMOON, 1929, A
HONEYMOON, 1947, A
HONEYMOON ABROAD, 1929
HONEYMOON ADVENTURE, A
HONEYMOON AHEAD, 1927, A
HONEYMOON AHEAD, 1945, A
HONEYMOON DEFERRED, 1940, A
HONEYMOON DEFERRED, 1951, A
HONEYMOON EXPRESS, THE, 1926
HONEYMOON FLATS, 1928, A
HONEYMOON FOR THREE, 1935, A
HONEYMOON FOR THREE, 1941, A
HONEYMOON HATE, 1927
HONEYMOON HOTEL, 1946, A
HONEYMOON HOTEL, 1964, C
HONEYMOON IN BALI, 1939, A
HONEYMOON KILLERS, THE, 1969, O
HONEYMOON LANE, 1931, A
HONEYMOON LIMITED, 1936, A
HONEYMOON LODGE, 1943, A
HONEYMOON MACHINE, THE, 1961, A
HONEYMOON MERRY-GO-ROUND, 1939, AA
HONEYMOON OF HORROR, 1964, O
HONEYMOON OF TERROR, 1961, O
HONEYMOON RANCH, 1920
HONEYMOON'S OVER, THE, 1939, C
HONEYMOON, THE, 1917
HONEYMOONS WILL KILL YOU, 1966
HONEYPOT, THE, 1920
HONEYSUCKLE ROSE, 1980, C
HONG KONG, 1951, A
HONG KONG AFFAIR, 1958, A
HONG KONG CONFIDENTIAL, 1958, A
HONG KONG NIGHTS, 1935, A
HONKERS, THE, 1972, C
HONKY, 1971, O
HONKY TONK, 1929, A
HONKY TONK, 1941, C
HONKY TONK FREEWAY, 1981, C
HONKYTONK MAN, 1982, A-C
HONNEUR D'ARTISTE, 1917
HONOLULU, 1939, A
HONOLULU LU, 1941, A
HONOLULU-TOKYO-HONG KONG, 1963, A
HONOR AMONG LOVERS, 1931, A
HONOR AMONG MEN, 1924
HONOR BOUND, 1920
HONOR BOUND, 1928
HONOR FIRST, 1922
HONOR OF HIS HOUSE, THE, 1918
HONOR OF MARY BLAKE, THE, 1916
HONOR OF THE FAMILY, 1931, A
HONOR OF THE MOUNTED, 1932, A
HONOR OF THE PRESS, 1932, A
HONOR OF THE RANGE, 1934, A
HONOR OF THE WEST, 1939, A
HONOR SYSTEM, THE, 1917, A
HONOR THY NAME, 1916
HONOR'S ALTAR, 1916
HONOR'S CROSS, 1918
HONORABLE ALGY, THE, 1916
HONORABLE FRIEND, THE, 1916
HONOUR IN PAWN, 1916
HONOURABLE MURDER, AN, 1959, C
HONOURS EASY, 1935, A
HOOCH, 1977
HOODLUM EMPIRE, 1952, A
HOODLUM PRIEST, THE, 1961, C
HOODLUM SAINT, THE, 1946, A
HOODLUM THE, 1919, A
HOODLUM, THE, 1951, C
HOODMAN BLIND
HOODMAN BLIND, 1913
HOODMAN BLIND, 1923
HOODOO ANN, 1916
HOODOO RANCH, 1926
HOODWINK, 1981, C
HOOF MARKS, 1927
HOOFBEATS OF VENGEANCE, 1929, A
HOOK AND HAND, 1914
HOOK AND LADDER, 1924, A
HOOK AND LADDER NO. 9, 1927, A
HOOK, LINE AND SINKER, 1930, A
HOOK, LINE AND SINKER, 1969, A
HOOK, THE, 1962, C
HOOKED GENERATION, THE, 1969, O
HOOP-LA, 1919
HOOPER, 1978, A
HOOPLA, 1933, C
HOORAY FOR LOVE, 1935, A
HOOSIER HOLIDAY, 1943, A
HOOSIER ROMANCE, A, 1918
HOOSIER SCHOOLBOY, 1937, A
HOOSIER SCHOOLMASTER, 1914, A
HOOSIER SCHOOLMASTER, 1935, A
HOOSIER SCHOOLMASTER, THE, 1924
HOOTENANNY HOOT, 1963, A
HOOTS MON!, 1939, A
HOP, THE DEVIL'S BREW, 1916, A
HOPALONG CASSIDY, 1935, A
HOPALONG CASSIDY RETURNS, 1936
HOPALONG RIDES AGAIN, 1937, A
HOPE
HOPE CHEST, THE, 1918
HOPE OF HIS SIDE, 1935, A
HOPE, THE, 1920
HOPELESS ONES, THE
HOPPER, THE, 1918
HOPPITY GOES TO TOWN
HOPPY SERVES A WRIT, 1943, A
HOPPY'S HOLIDAY, 1947, A
HOPSCOTCH, 1980, C
HORIZONS WEST, 1952, A
HORIZONTAL LIEUTENANT, THE, 1962, A
HORLA, THE
HORN BLOWS AT MIDNIGHT, THE, 1945, AAA
HORNET'S NEST, 1923
HORNET'S NEST, 1970, O
HORNET'S NEST, THE, 1919
HORNET'S NEST, THE, 1955, A
HOROSCOPE, 1950, O
HORRIBLE DR. HICHCOCK, THE, 1964
HORRIBLE HOUSE ON THE HILL, THE
HORRIBLE MILL WOMEN, THE
HORROR CASTLE, 1965, O
HORROR CHAMBER OF DR. FAUSTUS, THE, 1962, O
HORROR CREATURES OF THE PREHISTORIC PLANET
HORROR EXPRESS, 1972, C
HORROR HIGH, 1974, O
HORROR HOSPITAL, 1973
HORROR HOTEL, 1960, C
HORROR HOTEL, 1976
HORROR HOUSE, 1970, O
HORROR ISLAND, 1941, A
HORROR MANIACS
HORROR OF DRACULA, THE, 1958, O
HORROR OF FRANKENSTEIN, THE, 1970
HORROR OF IT ALL, THE, 1964, A
HORROR OF PARTY BEACH, THE, 1964, C
HORROR OF THE BLOOD MONSTERS, 1970, O
HORROR OF THE STONE WOMEN
HORROR OF THE ZOMBIES, 1974, C
HORROR ON SNAPE ISLAND
HORROR PLANET, 1982, O
HORRORS OF SPIDER ISLAND
HORRORS OF THE BLACK MUSEUM, 1959, O
HORRORS OF THE BLACK ZOO
HORSE, 1965
HORSE FEATHERS, 1932, A
HORSE IN THE GRAY FLANNEL SUIT, THE, 1968, AAA
HORSE NAMED COMANCHE, A
HORSE OF PRIDE, 1980, A
HORSE ON BROADWAY, A, 1926
HORSE SENSE, 1924
HORSE SHOES, 1927
HORSE SOLDIERS, THE, 1959, C
HORSE'S MOUTH, THE, 1953, A
HORSE'S MOUTH, THE, 1958, A
HORSE, MY HORSE
HORSE, THE, 1984, O
HORSEMAN OF THE PLAINS, A, 1928
HORSEMEN OF THE SIERRAS, 1950, A
HORSEMEN, THE, 1971, C
HORSEPLAY, 1933, A
HORSESHOE LUCK, 1924
HOSPITAL MASSACRE, 1982, O
HOSPITAL MASSACRE, 1984, O
HOSPITAL, THE, 1971, C
HOSTAGE, THE, 1917
HOSTAGE, THE, 1956, A
HOSTAGE, THE, 1966, A
HOSTAGES, 1943, A
HOSTILE COUNTRY, 1950, A
HOSTILE GUNS, 1967, A
HOSTILE WITNESS, 1968, A
HOT AND DEADLY, 1984, O
HOT ANGEL, THE, 1958, C
HOT BLOOD, 1956, A
HOT BOX, THE, 1972, O
HOT CAR GIRL, 1958, O
HOT CARGO, 1946, A
HOT CARS, 1956, A
HOT CHILD, 1974
HOT CURVES, 1930, A
HOT DOG...THE MOVIE, 1984, O
HOT ENOUGH FOR JUNE
HOT FOR PARIS, 1930, A
HOT FRUSTRATIONS
HOT HEELS, 1928
HOT HEIRESS, 1931, A
HOT HORSE
HOT HOURS, 1963, O
HOT ICE, 1952
HOT IN PARADISE
HOT LEAD, 1951, A
HOT LEAD AND COLD FEET, 1978, AA
HOT MILLIONS, 1968, C
HOT MONEY, 1936, A
HOT MONEY GIRL, 1962, C
HOT MONTH OF AUGUST, THE, 1969
HOT MOVES, 1984, O
HOT NEWS, 1928, A
HOT NEWS, 1936, A
HOT NEWS, 1953, A
HOT OFF THE PRESS, 1935
HOT PEPPER, 1933, A
HOT POTATO, 1976, O
HOT PURSUIT, 1981
HOT RHYTHM, 1944, A
HOT ROCK, THE, 1972, A-C
HOT ROD, 1950, A
HOT ROD GANG, 1958, A
HOT ROD GIRL, 1956, A
HOT ROD HULLABALOO, 1966, C
HOT ROD RUMBLE, 1957, C
HOT RODS TO HELL, 1967, C-O
HOT SATURDAY, 1932, A
HOT SHOTS, 1956, A
HOT SPELL, 1958, C-O
HOT SPOT
HOT SPUR, 1968, O
HOT STEEL, 1940, A
HOT STUFF, 1929, A
HOT STUFF, 1979, C
HOT SUMMER IN BAREFOOT COUNTY, 1974
HOT SUMMER NIGHT, 1957, A
HOT SUMMER WEEK, 1973, O
HOT T-SHIRTS, 1980
HOT TIMES, 1974, O
HOT TIP, 1935, A
HOT TOMORROWS, 1978, C
HOT WATER, 1924, A
HOT WATER, 1937, A
HOTEL, 1967, A

HOTEL BERLIN, 1945, A
HOTEL CONTINENTAL, 1932, A
HOTEL FOR WOMEN, 1939, A
HOTEL HAYWIRE, 1937, A
HOTEL IMPERIAL, 1927
HOTEL IMPERIAL, 1939, A
HOTEL MOUSE, THE, 1923, A
HOTEL NEW HAMPSHIRE, THE, 1984, C-O
HOTEL PARADISO, 1966
HOTEL RESERVE, 1946, A
HOTEL SAHARA, 1951, A
HOTEL SPLENDIDE, 1932, A
HOTEL VARIETY, 1933, A
HOTHEAD, 1963, C
HOTSPRINGS HOLIDAY, 1970, A
HOTTENTOT, THE, 1922
HOTTENTOT, THE, 1929, A
HOTWIRE, 1980
HOUDINI, 1953, A
HOUND OF THE BASKERVILLES, 1932, A
HOUND OF THE BASKERVILLES, THE, 1914
HOUND OF THE BASKERVILLES, THE, 1917
HOUND OF THE BASKERVILLES, THE, 1921
HOUND OF THE BASKERVILLES, THE, 1929
HOUND OF THE BASKERVILLES, THE, 1939, A
HOUND OF THE BASKERVILLES, THE, 1959, C
HOUND OF THE BASKERVILLES, THE, 1980, C
HOUND OF THE BASKERVILLES, THE, 1983, C
HOUND OF THE SILVER CREEK, THE, 1928
HOUND-DOG MAN, 1959, A
HOUNDS... OF NOTRE DAME, THE, 1980
HOUR BEFORE THE DAWN, THE, 1944, A
HOUR OF DECISION, 1957, A
HOUR OF GLORY, 1949
HOUR OF RECKONING, THE, 1927
HOUR OF THE GUN, 1967, C
HOUR OF THE TRIAL, THE, 1920
HOUR OF THE WOLF, THE, 1968, O
HOUR OF THIRTEEN, THE, 1952, A
HOURS OF LONELINESS, 1930, C
HOURS OF LOVE, THE, 1965, A
HOUSE ACROSS THE BAY, THE, 1940, A
HOUSE ACROSS THE LAKE, THE
HOUSE ACROSS THE STREET, THE, 1949, A
HOUSE AND THE BRAIN, THE, 1973
HOUSE AT THE END OF THE WORLD
HOUSE AT THE END OF THE WORLD
HOUSE BEHIND THE CEDARS, THE, 1927
HOUSE BROKEN, 1936
HOUSE BUILT UPON SAND, THE, 1917
HOUSE BY THE CEMETERY, THE, 1984, O
HOUSE BY THE LAKE, THE, 1977, O
HOUSE BY THE RIVER, 1950, C
HOUSE CALLS, 1978, C
HOUSE DIVIDED, A, 1919
HOUSE DIVIDED, A, 1932, C
HOUSE IN MARSH ROAD, THE, 1960
HOUSE IN NIGHTMARE PARK, THE
HOUSE IN THE SNOW-DRIFTS, THE, 1928
HOUSE IN THE SQUARE, THE
HOUSE IN THE WOODS, THE, 1957, C
HOUSE IS NOT A HOME, A, 1964, O
HOUSE NEXT DOOR, THE, 1914, A
HOUSE OF 1,000 DOLLS, 1967, O
HOUSE OF A THOUSAND CANDLES, THE, 1915
HOUSE OF A THOUSAND CANDLES, THE, 1936, A
HOUSE OF BAMBOO, 1955, C
HOUSE OF BLACKMAIL, 1953, C
HOUSE OF CARDS, 1969, C
HOUSE OF CARDS, 1934
HOUSE OF CONNELLY
HOUSE OF CRAZIES
HOUSE OF DANGER, 1934, A
HOUSE OF DARK SHADOWS, 1970, C-O
HOUSE OF DARKENED WINDOWS, THE, 1925
HOUSE OF DARKNESS, 1948, O
HOUSE OF DEATH, 1932, C
HOUSE OF DRACULA, 1945, A
HOUSE OF DREAMS, 1933
HOUSE OF DREAMS, 1963
HOUSE OF ERRORS, 1942, A
HOUSE OF EVIL, 1968, O
HOUSE OF EXORCISM, THE, 1976, O
HOUSE OF FEAR, 1929
HOUSE OF FEAR, THE, 1915
HOUSE OF FEAR, THE, 1939, A
HOUSE OF FEAR, THE, 1945, A
HOUSE OF FRANKENSTEIN, 1944, A
HOUSE OF FREAKS, 1973, O
HOUSE OF FRIGHT, 1961
HOUSE OF GLASS, THE, 1918
HOUSE OF GOD, THE, 1979
HOUSE OF GOD, THE, 1984, O
HOUSE OF GOLD, THE, 1918
HOUSE OF GREED, 1934, A
HOUSE OF HORROR, 1929
HOUSE OF HORRORS, 1946, C
HOUSE OF INTRIGUE, THE, 1959, A
HOUSE OF LIES, THE, 1916
HOUSE OF LIFE, 1953
HOUSE OF LONG SHADOWS, THE, 1983, O
HOUSE OF MARNEY, 1926
HOUSE OF MIRRORS, THE, 1916
HOUSE OF MIRTH, THE, 1918
HOUSE OF MORTAL SIN, THE
HOUSE OF MYSTERY, 1934, A
HOUSE OF MYSTERY, 1941, A
HOUSE OF MYSTERY, 1961, C
HOUSE OF MYSTERY, THE, 1938
HOUSE OF NUMBERS, 1957, A
HOUSE OF PERIL, THE, 1922
HOUSE OF PLEASURE
HOUSE OF PSYCHOTIC WOMEN, THE, 1973, O
HOUSE OF ROTHSCHILD, THE, 1934, A
HOUSE OF SCANDAL, THE, 1928
HOUSE OF SECRETS, 1929, O
HOUSE OF SECRETS, 1956
HOUSE OF SECRETS, THE, 1937, A
HOUSE OF SEVEN CORPSES, THE, 1974, C-O
HOUSE OF SEVEN GABLES
HOUSE OF SEVEN JOYS
HOUSE OF SHADOWS, 1977
HOUSE OF SHAME, THE, 1928
HOUSE OF SILENCE, THE, 1918
HOUSE OF STRANGE LOVES, THE, 1969, C
HOUSE OF STRANGERS, 1949, C
HOUSE OF TEARS, THE, 1915
HOUSE OF TEMPERLEY, THE, 1913, A
HOUSE OF THE ARROW, THE, 1930, A
HOUSE OF THE ARROW, THE, 1953, A
HOUSE OF THE ARROW, THE, 1940
HOUSE OF THE BLACK DEATH, 1965, O
HOUSE OF THE DAMNED, 1963, C
HOUSE OF THE DEAD, 1980
HOUSE OF THE GOLDEN WINDOWS, THE, 1916
HOUSE OF THE LIVING DEAD, 1973, C
HOUSE OF THE LOST CORD, THE, 1915, A
HOUSE OF THE MISSING GIRLS, 1974
HOUSE OF THE SEVEN GABLES, THE, 1940, A
HOUSE OF THE SEVEN HAWKS, THE, 1959, A
HOUSE OF THE SPANIARD, THE, 1936, A
HOUSE OF THE THREE GIRLS, THE, 1961, A
HOUSE OF THE TOLLING BELLS, THE, 1920
HOUSE OF TOYS, THE, 1920
HOUSE OF TRENT, THE, 1933, A
HOUSE OF UNREST, THE, 1931, A
HOUSE OF USHER, 1960, O
HOUSE OF WAX, 1953, C
HOUSE OF WHIPCORD, 1974, O
HOUSE OF WHISPERS, THE, 1920
HOUSE OF WOMEN, 1962, O
HOUSE OF YOUTH, THE, 1924, A
HOUSE ON 56TH STREET, THE, 1933, C
HOUSE ON 92ND STREET, THE, 1945, A
HOUSE ON CEDAR HILL, THE, 1926
HOUSE ON HAUNTED HILL, 1958, C
HOUSE ON SKULL MOUNTAIN, THE, 1974, C
HOUSE ON SORORITY ROW, THE, 1983, O
HOUSE ON STRAW HILL, THE, 1976
HOUSE ON TELEGRAPH HILL, 1951, C
HOUSE ON THE FRONT LINE, THE, 1963, A
HOUSE ON THE MARSH, THE, 1920, A
HOUSE ON THE SAND, 1967, C
HOUSE ON THE SQUARE, THE
HOUSE ON TRUBNAYA SQUARE, 1928
HOUSE OPPOSITE, THE, 1917
HOUSE OPPOSITE, THE, 1931, A
HOUSE RENT PARTY, 1946
HOUSE THAT CRIED MURDER, THE
HOUSE THAT DRIPPED BLOOD, THE, 1971, O
HOUSE THAT JAZZ BUILT, THE, 1921
HOUSE THAT SCREAMED, THE, 1970, O
HOUSE THAT VANISHED, THE, 1974, O
HOUSE WHERE DEATH LIVES, THE, 1982
HOUSE WHERE DEATH LIVES, THE, 1984, O
HOUSE WHERE EVIL DWELLS, THE, 1982, O
HOUSE WITH AN ATTIC, THE, 1964, A
HOUSE WITH THE GOLDEN WINDOWS, THE, 1916
HOUSE WITHOUT CHILDREN, THE, 1919
HOUSEBOAT, 1958, A
HOUSEHOLDER, THE, 1963, A
HOUSEKEEPER'S DAUGHTER, 1939, A
HOUSEMASTER, 1938, A
HOUSEWIFE, 1934, A
HOUSTON STORY, THE, 1956, A
HOVERBUG, 1970, AA
HOW ABOUT US?
HOW BAXTER BUTTED IN, 1925
HOW COME NOBODY'S ON OUR SIDE?, 1975, A
HOW COULD YOU UNCLE?, 1918
HOW COULD YOU, CAROLINE?, 1918
HOW COULD YOU, JEAN?, 1918
HOW DO I LOVE THEE?, 1970, C
HOW DO YOU DO?, 1946, A
HOW GREEN WAS MY VALLEY, 1941, A
HOW I WON THE WAR, 1967, C
HOW KITCHENER WAS BETRAYED, 1921
HOW LOW CAN YOU FALL?
HOW MANY ROADS
HOW MEN LOVE WOMEN, 1915
HOW MOLLY MADE GOOD, 1915, A
HOW MOLLY MALONE MADE GOOD
HOW NOT TO ROB A DEPARTMENT STORE, 1965, A
HOW SWEET IT IS, 1968, C-O
HOW THE WEST WAS WON, 1962, AAA
HOW TO BE VERY, VERY, POPULAR, 1955, A
HOW TO BEAT THE HIGH COST OF LIVING, 1980, A
HOW TO COMMIT MARRIAGE, 1969, A
HOW TO EDUCATE A WIFE, 1924
HOW TO FRAME A FIGG, 1971, AA
HOW TO HANDLE WOMEN, 1928
HOW TO MAKE A DOLL, 1967
HOW TO MAKE A MONSTER, 1958, C
HOW TO MAKE IT
HOW TO MARRY A MILLIONAIRE, 1953, A
HOW TO MURDER A RICH UNCLE, 1957, A
HOW TO MURDER YOUR WIFE, 1965, A
HOW TO SAVE A MARRIAGE—AND RUIN YOUR LIFE, 1968, A
HOW TO SCORE WITH GIRLS, 1980
HOW TO SEDUCE A PLAYBOY, 1968, C
HOW TO SEDUCE A WOMAN, 1974, O
HOW TO STEAL A MILLION, 1966, A
HOW TO STUFF A WILD BIKINI, 1965, A
HOW TO SUCCEED IN BUSINESS WITHOUT REALLY
HOW TO UNDRESS IN FRONT OF YOUR HUSBAND, 1937
HOW WILLINGLY YOU SING, 1975, A-C
HOW WOMEN LOVE, 1922
HOW'S ABOUT IT?, 1943, A
HOW'S CHANCES
HOWARD CASE, THE, 1936, A
HOWARDS OF VIRGINIA, THE, 1940, A
HOWDY BROADWAY, 1929
HOWLING, THE, 1981, O
HOWZER, 1973, A
HT CARGO, 1936, A
HU-MAN, 1975, C
HUCK AND TOM, 1918, A
HUCKLEBERRY FINN, 1920, A
HUCKLEBERRY FINN, 1931, AAA
HUCKLEBERRY FINN, 1939, AAA
HUCKLEBERRY FINN, 1960
HUCKLEBERRY FINN, 1974, AAA
HUCKSTERS, THE, 1947, A
HUD, 1963, O
HUDDLE, 1932, A
HUDSON'S BAY, 1940, A
HUE AND CRY, 1950, A
HUGGETTS ABROAD, THE, 1949, A
HUGHES AND HARLOW: ANGELS IN HELL, 1978
HUGO THE HIPPO, 1976
HUGON THE MIGHTY, 1918
HUGS AND KISSES, 1968, O
HUK, 1956, O
HULA, 1927
HULDA FROM HOLLAND, 1916
HULLABALOO, 1940, A
HULLABALOO OVER GEORGIE AND BONNIE'S PICTURES, 1979
HUMAN BEAST, THE
HUMAN CARGO, 1929
HUMAN CARGO, 1936, A
HUMAN COLLATERAL, 1920
HUMAN COMEDY, THE, 1943, A
HUMAN CONDITION, THE, 1959
HUMAN DESIRE, 1954, C
HUMAN DESIRE, THE, 1919
HUMAN DESIRES, 1924, A
HUMAN DRIFTWOOD, 1916
HUMAN DUPLICATORS, THE, 1965, A
HUMAN EXPERIMENTS, 1980, O
HUMAN FACTOR, THE, 1975, O
HUMAN FACTOR, THE, 1979, C
HUMAN GORILLA, 1948
HUMAN HEARTS, 1922
HUMAN HIGHWAY, 1982, O
HUMAN JUNGLE, THE, 1954, A
HUMAN LAW, 1926
HUMAN MONSTER, THE, 1940, O
HUMAN ORCHID, THE, 1916
HUMAN PASSIONS, 1919
HUMAN SIDE, THE, 1934, A
HUMAN STUFF, 1920, A
HUMAN SUFFERING, 1923
HUMAN TARGETS, 1932
HUMAN TERROR, THE, 1924
HUMAN TORNADO, THE, 1925
HUMAN TORNADO, THE, 1976, O
HUMAN VAPOR, THE, 1964, A
HUMAN WRECKAGE, 1923
HUMANITY, 1917
HUMANITY, 1933, A
HUMANIZING MR. WINSBY, 1916
HUMANOID, THE, 1979, C
HUMANOIDS FROM THE DEEP, 1980, O
HUMDRUM BROWN, 1918

HUMMING BIRD, THE, 1924
HUMONGOUS, 1982, O
HUMORESQUE, 1920
HUMORESQUE, 1946, A-C
HUMPHREY TAKES A CHANCE, 1950, A
HUN WITHIN, THE, 1918, A
HUNCH, THE, 1921, A
HUNCH, THE, 1967, AA
HUNCHBACK AND THE DANCER, THE, 1920
HUNCHBACK OF NOTRE DAME, THE, 1923, A
HUNCHBACK OF NOTRE DAME, THE, 1939, A-C
HUNCHBACK OF NOTRE DAME, THE, 1957, A-C
HUNCHBACK OF ROME, THE, 1963, C
HUNCHBACK OF THE MORGUE, THE, 1972, O
HUNDRA, 1984, C
HUNDRED HOUR HUNT, 1953, A
HUNDRED POUND WINDOW, THE, 1943, A
HUNDRETH CHANCE, THE, 1920
HUNGARIAN NABOB, THE, 1915
HUNGER, 1968, O
HUNGER OF THE BLOOD, THE, 1921
HUNGER, THE, 1983, O
HUNGRY EYES, 1918
HUNGRY HEART, A, 1917
HUNGRY HEART, THE, 1917
HUNGRY HEARTS, 1922, A
HUNGRY HILL, 1947, C
HUNGRY WIVES, 1973, O
HUNS WIHIN OUR GATES, 1918
HUNS, THE, 1962
HUNT THE MAN DOWN, 1950, A
HUNT TO KILL
HUNT, THE, 1967, O
HUNTED
HUNTED IN HOLLAND, 1961, AA
HUNTED MEN, 1930, A
HUNTED MEN, 1938, A
HUNTED WOMAN, THE, 1916
HUNTED WOMAN, THE, 1925
HUNTED, THE
HUNTED, THE, 1948, A
HUNTER OF THE APOCALYPSE
HUNTER, THE, 1980, C
HUNTERS OF THE GOLDEN COBRA, THE, 1984, A
HUNTERS, THE, 1958, A-C
HUNTIN' TROUBLE, 1924
HUNTING IN SIBERIA, 1962, A
HUNTING OF THE HAWK, THE, 1917
HUNTING PARTY, THE, 1977, O
HUNTINGTOWER, 1927, A
HUNTRESS OF MEN, THE, 1916
HUNTRESS, THE, 1923, A
HURRAY FOR BETTY BOOP, 1980
HURRICANE, 1929, A
HURRICANE, 1979
HURRICANE HAL, 1925
HURRICANE HORSEMAN, 1925
HURRICANE HORSEMAN, 1931, A
HURRICANE HUTCH IN MANY ADVENTURES, 1924
HURRICANE ISLAND, 1951
HURRICANE KID, THE, 1925, A
HURRICANE SMITH, 1942, A
HURRICANE SMITH, 1952, A
HURRICANE'S GAL, 1922
HURRICANE, THE, 1926, A
HURRICANE, THE, 1937, A
HURRICANE, THE 1964
HURRY SUNDOWN, 1967, O
HURRY UP OR I'LL BE 30, 1973, C
HURRY, CHARLIE, HURRY, 1941, A
HUSBAND AND WIFE, 1916
HUSBAND HUNTER, THE, 1920
HUSBAND HUNTER, THE, 1920
HUSBAND HUNTERS, 1927, A
HUSBAND'S HOLIDAY, 1931, A
HUSBANDS, 1970, C
HUSBANDS AND LOVERS, 1924, A
HUSBANDS AND WIVES, 1920
HUSBANDS FOR RENT, 1927, A
HUSH, 1921
HUSH MONEY, 1921, A
HUSH MONEY, 1931, A
HUSH-A-BYE MURDER
HUSH... HUSH, SWEET CHARLOTTE, 1964, O
HUSHED HOUR, THE, 1920
HUSSY, 1979
HUSTLE, 1975, O
HUSTLER SQUAD, 1976
HUSTLER SQUAD, THE
HUSTLER, THE, 1961, C
HUTCH OF THE U.S.A., 1924
HUTCH STIRS 'EM UP, 1923, A
HUTCH—U.S.A.
HVEM ER HUN?, 1914
HYDE PARK CORNER, 1935, A
HYPERBOLOID OF ENGINEER GARIN, THE, 1965, A
HYPNOTIC EYE, THE, 1960, O
HYPNOSIS, 1966, C-O
HYPNOTIST, THE
HYPNOTIZED, 1933, A
HYPOCRISY, 1916
HYPOCRITE, THE, 1921
HYPOCRITES, 1914, A
HYPOCRITES, THE
HYPOCRITES, THE, 1923
HYSTERIA, 1965, O
HYSTERICAL, 1983, O

-I-

I ACCUSE
I ACCUSE
I ACCUSE, 1916
I ACCUSE, 1958, A
I ACCUSE MY PARENTS, 1945, A
I ADORE YOU, 1933, A
I AIM AT THE STARS, 1960, A
I AM A CAMERA, 1955, A
I AM A CRIMINAL, 1939, A
I AM A FUGITIVE FROM A CHAIN GANG, 1932, 0
I AM A GROUPIE, 1970, O
I AM A THIEF, 1935, A
I AM CURIOUS GAY
I AM FRIGID...WHY?, 1973
I AM GUILTY, 1921
I AM NOT AFRAID, 1939, A
I AM SUZANNE, 1934, A
I AM THE CHEESE, 1983, A
I AM THE LAW, 1922
I AM THE LAW, 1938, A
I AM THE MAN, 1924
I AM THE WOMAN, 1921
I BECAME A CRIMINAL, 1947, A
I BELIEVE, 1916
I BELIEVE, 1918
I BELIEVE IN YOU, 1953, A
I BELIEVED IN YOU, 1934, A
I BOMBED PEARL HARBOR, 1961, A
I BURY THE LIVING, 1958, A
I CALL FIRST
I CAN EXPLAIN, 1922
I CAN GET IT FOR YOU WHOLESALE, 1951, A
I CAN'T ... I CAN'T
I CAN'T ESCAPE, 1934, A
I CAN'T GIVE YOU ANYTHING BUT LOVE, BABY, 1940, A
I CHANGED MY SEX
I CHEATED THE LAW, 1949, A
I COLTELLI DEL VENDICATORE
I COMPAGNI
I CONFESS, 1953, A
I CONQUER THE SEA, 1936, A
I COULD GO ON SINGING, 1963, A
I COULD NEVER HAVE SEX WITH ANY MAN WHO HAS SO LITTLE REGARD FOR MY HUSBAND, 1973, O
I COVER BIG TOWN, 1947, A
I COVER CHINATOWN, 1938, A
I COVER THE UNDERWORLD, 1955, A
I COVER THE UNDERWORLD
I COVER THE WAR, 1937, A
I COVER THE WATERFRONT, 1933, A
I CROSSED THE COLOR LINE
I DEAL IN DANGER, 1966, A
I DEMAND PAYMENT, 1938, A
I DIDN'T DO IT, 1945, A
I DIED A THOUSAND TIMES, 1955, A-C
I DISMEMBER MAMA, 1974, O
I DON'T CARE GIRL, THE, 1952, A
I DON'T WANT TO BE BORN
I DOOD IT, 1943, A
I DREAM OF JEANIE, 1952, A
I DREAM TOO MUCH, 1935, A
I DRINK YOUR BLOOD, 1971, O
I EAT YOUR SKIN, 1971, O
I ESCAPED FROM DEVIL'S ISLAND, 1973, O
I ESCAPED FROM THE GESTAPO, 1943, A
I EVEN MET HAPPY GYPSIES, 1968, A
I FLUNKED, BUT..., 1930
I FOUND STELLA PARISH, 1935, A
I GIORNI DELL'IRA
I GIVE MY HEART
I GIVE MY LOVE, 1934, A
I HAD SEVEN DAUGHTERS
I HATE BLONDES, 1981, A
I HATE MY BODY, 1975, A
I HATE WOMEN, 1934
I HATE YOUR GUTS
I HAVE LIVED, 1933, A
I HAVE SEVEN DAUGHTERS
I HEAR YOU CALLING ME, 1919
I KILLED EINSTEIN, GENTLEMEN, 1970, A
I KILLED GERONIMO, 1950, A
I KILLED THAT MAN, 1942, A
I KILLED THE COUNT
I KILLED WILD BILL HICKOK, 1956, A
I KNOW WHERE I'M GOING, 1947, A
I LED TWO LIVES
I LIKE IT THAT WAY, 1934, A
I LIKE MONEY, 1962, A
I LIKE YOUR NERVE, 1931, A
I LIVE FOR LOVE, 1935, A
I LIVE FOR YOU
I LIVE IN FEAR, 1967, A
I LIVE IN GROSVENOR SQUARE
I LIVE MY LIFE, 1935, A
I LIVE ON DANGER, 1942, A
I LIVED WITH YOU, 1933, A
I LOVE A BANDLEADER, 1945, A
I LOVE A MYSTERY, 1945, A
I LOVE A SOLDIER, 1944, A
I LOVE IN JERUSALEM
I LOVE MELVIN, 1953, A
I LOVE MY WIFE, 1970, O
I LOVE THAT MAN, 1933, A
I LOVE TROUBLE, 1947, A
I LOVE YOU, 1918, A
I LOVE YOU
I LOVE YOU AGAIN, 1940, A
I LOVE YOU, ALICE B. TOKLAS, 1968, O
I LOVE YOU, I KILL YOU, 1972, O
I LOVE YOU, I LOVE YOU NOT
I LOVED A WOMAN, 1933, A
I LOVED YOU WEDNESDAY, 1933, A
I MARRIED A COMMUNIST
I MARRIED A DOCTOR, 1936, A
I MARRIED A MONSTER FROM OUTER SPACE, 1958, O
I MARRIED A NAZI
I MARRIED A SPY, 1938, A
I MARRIED A WITCH, 1942, A
I MARRIED A WOMAN, 1958, A
I MARRIED AN ANGEL, A
I MARRIED TOO YOUNG
I MET A MURDERER, 1939, C-O
I MET HIM IN PARIS, 1937, A
I MET MY LOVE AGAIN, 1938, A
I MISS YOU, HUGS AND KISSES, 1978, C-O
I MISTERI DELLA GIUNGLA NERA
I NEVER PROMISED YOU A ROSE GARDEN, 1977, O
I NEVER SANG FOR MY FATHER, 1970, A-C
I NUOVI BARBARI
I NUOVI MOSTRI
I ONLY ASKED, 1958, A
I OUGHT TO BE IN PICTURES, 1982, C
I PASSED FOR WHITE, 1960, A
I PROMISE TO PAY, 1937, A
I PROMISE TO PAY, 1962
I REMEMBER LOVE, 1981
I REMEMBER MAMA, 1948, AAA
I RING DOORBELLS, 1946, A
I SAILED TO TAHITI WITH AN ALL GIRL CREW, 1969, A
I SAW WHAT YOU DID, 1965, C-O
I SEE A DARK STRANGER
I SEE ICE, 1938, A
I SELL ANYTHING, 1934, A
I SENT A LETTER TO MY LOVE, 1981, A
I SHALL RETURN
I SHOT BILLY THE KID, 1950, A
I SHOT JESSE JAMES, 1949, A
I SPIT ON YOUR GRAVE, 1962, O
I SPIT ON YOUR GRAVE, 1983, O
I SPY, 1933, A
I SPY, YOU SPY
I STAND ACCUSED, 1938, A
I STAND CONDEMNED, 1936, A
I START COUNTING, 1970, O
I STOLE A MILLION, 1939, A
I SURRENDER DEAR, 1948, A
I TAKE THIS OATH, 1940, A
I TAKE THIS WOMAN, 1931, A
I TAKE THIS WOMAN, 1940, A
I THANK A FOOL, 1962, A-C
I THANK YOU, 1941, A
I TITANI
I TRE VOLTI
I TRE VOLTI DELLA PAURA
I VAMPIRI
I VITELLONI
I WAKE UP SCREAMING, 1942, A
I WALK ALONE, 1948, C
I WALK THE LINE, 1970, A
I WALKED WITH A ZOMBIE, 1943, C-O
I WANNA HOLD YOUR HAND, 1978, A
I WANT A DIVORCE, 1940, A
I WANT HER DEAD
I WANT MY MAN, 1925
I WANT TO BE A MOTHER, 1937
I WANT TO FORGET, 1918, A
I WANT TO LIVE, O
I WANT WHAT I WANT, 1972, O
I WANT YOU, 1951, A
I WANTED WINGS, A
I WAS A CAPTIVE IN NAZI GERMANY, 1936, A
I WAS A COMMUNIST FOR THE F.B.I., C
I WAS A CONVICT, 1939, A
I WAS A MALE WAR BRIDE, A

I WAS A PRISONER ON DEVIL'S ISLAND, 1941, A
I WAS A SHOPLIFTER, 1950, A
I WAS A SPY, 1934, A
I WAS A TEENAGE ALIEN, 1980
I WAS A TEENAGE FRANKENSTEIN, 1958, C-O
I WAS A TEENAGE WEREWOLF, 1957, C-O
I WAS A ZOMBIE FOR THE F.B.I., 1982
I WAS AN ADVENTURESS, 1940, A
I WAS AN AMERICAN SPY, 1951, A
I WAS BORN, BUT..., 1932
I WAS FAITHLESS
I WAS FRAMED, 1942, A
I WAS HAPPY HERE
I WAS MONTY'S DOUBLE
I WILL, 1919
I WILL ...I WILL ...FOR NOW, 1976, C
I WILL REPAY
I WILL REPAY, 1917
I WONDER WHO'S KILLING HER NOW, 1975
I WONDER WHO'S KISSING HER NOW, 1947, A
I WOULDN'T BE IN YOUR SHOES, 1948, A
I'D CLIMB THE HIGHEST MOUNTAIN, 1951, A
I'D GIVE MY LIFE, 1936, A
I'D RATHER BE RICH, 1964, A
I'LL BE SEEING YOU, 1944, A
I'LL BE THERE, 1927
I'LL BE YOUR SWEETHEART, 1945, A
I'LL BE YOURS, 1947, A
I'LL CRY TOMORROW, 1955, A-C
I'LL FIX IT, 1934, A
I'LL GET BY, 1950, A
I'LL GET HIM YET, 1919, A
I'LL GET HIM YET, 1919
I'LL GET YOU, 1953, A
I'LL GET YOU FOR THIS
I'LL GIVE A MILLION, 1938, A
I'LL GIVE MY LIFE, 1959, A
I'LL LOVE YOU ALWAYS, 1935, A
I'LL NAME THE MURDERER, 1936
I'LL NEVER FORGET WHAT'S 'IS NAME, 1967, A-C
I'LL NEVER FORGET YOU, 1951, A
I'LL REMEMBER APRIL, 1945, A
I'LL SAVE MY LOVE
I'LL SAY SO, 1918
I'LL SEE YOU IN MY DREAMS, 1951, A
I'LL SELL MY LIFE, 1941, A
I'LL SHOW YOU THE TOWN, 1925
I'LL STICK TO YOU, 1933, A
I'LL TAKE ROMANCE, 1937, A
I'LL TAKE SWEDEN, 1965, A
I'LL TELL THE WORLD, 1934, A
I'LL TELL THE WORLD, 1945, AA
I'LL TURN TO YOU, 1946, A
I'LL WAIT FOR YOU, 1941, A
I'LL WALK BESIDE YOU, 1943, A
I'M A STRANGER, 1952, A
I'M ALL RIGHT, JACK, 1959, A
I'M AN EXPLOSIVE, 1933, A
I'M CRAZY ABOUT YOU
I'M DANCING AS FAST AS I CAN, 1982, C-O
I'M FROM ARKANSAS, 1944, A
I'M FROM MISSOURI, 1939, A
I'M FROM THE CITY, 1938, A
I'M GLAD MY BOY GREW TO BE A SOLDIER, 1915
I'M GOING TO BE FAMOUS, 1981
I'M GOING TO GET YOU ... ELLIOT BOY, 1971, O
I'M NO ANGEL, 1933, C
I'M NOBODY'S SWEETHEART NOW, 1940, A
I'M STILL ALIVE, 1940, A
I'PAGLIACCI, 1923
I'VE ALWAYS LOVED YOU, 1946, A
I'VE BEEN AROUND, 1935, A
I'VE GOT A HORSE, 1938, A
I'VE GOT YOUR NUMBER, 1934, A
I'VE GOTTA HORSE, 1965, A
I'VE LIVED BEFORE, 1956, A
I, JANE DOE, 1948, A
I, MAUREEN, 1978, A
I, MOBSTER, 1959, C-O
I, MONSTER, 1971, C
I, THE JURY, 1953, C-O
I, THE JURY, 1982, O
I, TOO, AM ONLY A WOMAN, 1963, C
I.N.R.I
IBANEZ' TORRENT
ICARUS XB-1
ICE, 1970, O
ICE CASTLES, 1978, A
ICE COLD IN ALEX
ICE FLOOD, THE, 1926, A
ICE FOLLIES OF 1939, 1939, A
ICE HOUSE, THE, 1969, O
ICE PALACE, 1960, A-C
ICE PIRATES, THE, 1984, A-C
ICE STATION ZEBRA, 1968, A
ICE-CAPADES, 1941, A
ICE-CAPADES REVUE, 1942, A
ICEBOUND, 1924, A
ICED BULLET, THE, 1917, A
ICELAND, 1942, A
ICEMAN, 1984, A-C
ICEMAN COMETH, THE, C
ICEMAN OF THE 16TH PRECINCT, THE, 1963, A
ICHABOD AND MR. TOAD
ICHIJOJI NO KETTO
IDAGINE SU UN CITTADINO AL DI DOPRA DI OGNI SOSPETTO
IDAHO, 1943, A
IDAHO KID, THE, 1937, A
IDAHO RED, 1929, A
IDAHO TRANSFER, 1975, C
IDEA GIRL, 1946, A
IDEAL HUSBAND, AN, 1948, A
IDEAL LODGER, THE, 1957, O
IDEAL LOVE, THE, 1921
IDEAL MARRIAGE, THE, 1970
IDENTIFICATION MARKS: NONE, 1969, A
IDENTIFICATION OF A WOMAN, 1983, C-O
IDENTIKIT
IDENTITY PARADE
IDENTITY UNKNOWN, 1945, A
IDENTITY UNKNOWN, 1960, A
IDIOT'S DELIGHT, 1939, A
IDIOT, THE, 1948, A
IDIOT, THE, 1960, O
IDIOT, THE, 1963, C-O
IDLE HANDS, 1920
IDLE HANDS, 1921, A
IDLE ON PARADE
IDLE RICH, THE, 1921, A
IDLE RICH, THE, 1929, A
IDLE TONGUES, 1924
IDLE WIVES, 1916
IDLER, THE, 1914
IDO ZERO DAISAKUSEN
IDOL DANCER, THE, 1920, A
IDOL OF PARIS, 1948, A
IDOL OF PARIS, THE, 1914
IDOL OF THE CROWDS, 1937, A
IDOL OF THE NORTH, THE, 1921, A
IDOL OF THE STAGE, THE, 1916, A
IDOL ON PARADE, 1959, A
IDOL, THE, 1966, O
IDOLATORS, 1917
IDOLMAKER, THE, 1980, A-C
IDOLS IN THE DUST
IDOLS OF CLAY, 1920
IERI, OGGI E DOMANI
IF, 1916, A
IF ..., 1968, O
IF A MAN ANSWERS, 1962, A
IF EVER I SEE YOU AGAIN, 1978, C
IF FOUR WALLS TOLD, 1922, A
IF HE HOLLERS, LET HIM GO, 1968, O
IF I HAD A MILLION, 1932, A
IF I HAD MY WAY, 1940, A
IF I MARRY AGAIN, 1925, A
IF I WERE BOSS, 1938, A
IF I WERE FREE, 1933, A
IF I WERE KING, 1920
IF I WERE KING, 1938, A
IF I WERE KING, 1930
IF I WERE QUEEN, 1922, A
IF I WERE RICH, 1936, A
IF I WERE SINGLE, 1927, A
IF I'M LUCKY, 1946, A
IF IT'S TUESDAY, THIS MUST BE BELGIUM, 1969, A
IF MARRIAGE FAILS, 1925
IF MY COUNTRY SHOULD CALL, 1916
IF ONLY JIM, 1921, A
IF PARIS WERE TOLD TO US, 1956, A
IF THIS BE SIN, 1950, A
IF THOU WERT BLIND, 1917, A
IF WINTER COMES, 1923
IF WINTER COMES, 1947, A
IF WOMEN ONLY KNEW, 1921, A
IF YOU BELIEVE IT, IT'S SO, 1922, A
IF YOU COULD ONLY COOK, 1936, A
IF YOU COULD SEE WHAT I HEAR, 1982, A
IF YOU DON'T STOP IT, YOU'LL GO BLIND, 1977
IF YOU FEEL LIKE SINGING
IF YOU KNEW SUSIE, 1948, A
IF YOUTH BUT KNEW, 1926, A
IGNORANCE, 1916
IGNORANCE, 1922
IGOROTA, THE LEGEND OF THE TREE OF LIFE, 1970, O
IKARIE XB 1
IKIMONO NO KIROUKU
IKIRU, 1960, A
IL BIDONE
IL BODONE
IL BUONO, IL BRUTTO, IL CATTIVO
IL COBRA
IL CONFORMIST
IL CONTE DI MONTECRISTO
IL DESERTO ROSSO
IL DESTINO
IL DIABOLICO DR. MABUSE
IL DISPREZZO
IL GATTOPARDO
IL GENERALE DELA-ROVERE
IL GIORNO DELLA CIVETTA
IL GIORNO E L'ORA
IL GRIDO, 1962, C
IL MAESTRO
IL MAESTRO DI DON GIOVANNI
IL MAGNIFICO CORNUTO
IL MITO
IL NEMICO DI MIA MOGLIE
IL POZZO DELLE TRE VERITA
IL RE DEI FAISARI
IL SEGNO DI VENERA
IL SEME DELL'UOMO
IL SEPOLCRO DEI RE
IL SOGNO DI BUTTERFLY
IL SUFFIT D'AIMER
IL TESORO DI ROMMEL
IL TROVATORE, 1914
IL VANGELO SECONDE MATTEO
ILL MET BY MOONLIGHT
ILL-STARRED BABBLE, 1915
ILLEGAL, 1932, A
ILLEGAL, 1955, C
ILLEGAL DIVORCE, THE
ILLEGAL ENTRY, 1949, A
ILLEGAL RIGHTS
ILLEGAL TRAFFIC, 1938, A
ILLIAC PASSION, THE, 1968, O
ILLICIT, 1931, C
ILLICIT INTERLUDE, 1954, O
ILLUMINATIONS, 1976, O
ILLUSION, 1929, A
ILLUSION OF BLOOD, 1966, O
ILLUSION OF LOVE, 1929
ILLUSION TRAVELS BY STREETCAR, THE, 1977, C
ILLUSTRATED MAN, THE, 1969, O
ILLUSTRIOUS PRINCE, THE, 1919
ILSA, HAREM KEEPER OF THE OIL SHEIKS, 1976
ILSA, SHE WOLF OF THE SS, 1975
IM LAUF DER ZEIT
IM STAHLNETZ DES DR. MABUSE
IMAGE MAKER, THE, 1917
IMAGE OF DEATH, 1977
IMAGES, 1972, C-O
IMAGINARY BARON, THE, 1927
IMAGINARY SWEETHEART
IMAGO, 1970
IMAR THE SERVITOR, 1914
IMERES TOU 36
IMITATION GENERAL, 1958, A
IMITATION OF LIFE, 1934, A
IMITATION OF LIFE, 1959, A
IMMEDIATE DISASTER
IMMEDIATE LEE, 1916, A
IMMIGRANT, THE, 1915, A
IMMORAL CHARGE, 1962, A
IMMORAL MOMENT, THE, 1967, C
IMMORTAL BACHELOR, THE, 1980, O
IMMORTAL BATTALION, THE
IMMORTAL FLAME, THE, 1916
IMMORTAL GARRISON, THE, 1957, A
IMMORTAL GENTLEMAN, 1935, A
IMMORTAL MONSTER
IMMORTAL SERGEANT, THE, 1943, A
IMMORTAL STORY, THE, 1969, C
IMMORTAL VAGABOND, 1931, A
IMMORTALS OF BONNIE SCOTLAND
IMP, THE, 1920
IMPACT, 1949, A
IMPACT, 1963, C
IMPASSE, 1969, O
IMPASSE DES VERTUS
IMPASSIVE FOOTMAN, THE
IMPATIENT MAIDEN, 1932, C
IMPATIENT YEARS, THE, 1944, A
IMPERFECT LADY, THE, 1947, A
IMPERFECT LADY, THE, 1935
IMPERFECT LOVER, THE, 1921
IMPERIAL VENUS, 1963, A
IMPERSONATION, THE, 1916
IMPERSONATOR, THE, 1962, C
IMPORTANCE OF BEING EARNEST, THE, 1952, A
IMPORTANT MAN, THE, 1961, O
IMPORTANT WITNESS, THE, 1933, A
IMPOSSIBLE CATHERINE, 1919, A
IMPOSSIBLE LOVER
IMPOSSIBLE MRS. BELLEW, THE, 1922, A
IMPOSSIBLE OBJECT, 1973, C-O
IMPOSSIBLE ON SATURDAY, 1966, A
IMPOSSIBLE SUSAN, 1918
IMPOSSIBLE WOMAN, THE, 1919, A
IMPOSSIBLE YEARS, THE, 1968, A
IMPOSTER, THE, 1918, A
IMPOSTER, THE, 1926
IMPOSTER, THE, 1944, A
IMPOSTORS, 1979, O

IMPRESSIVE FOOTMAN, THE
IMPROPER CHANNELS, 1981, C
IMPROPER DUCHESS, THE, 1936, A
IMPULSE, 1922, A
IMPULSE, 1955, C
IMPULSE, 1975, O
IMPULSE, 1984, O
IN
IN A LONELY PLACE, 1950, C
IN A MOMENT OF TEMPTATION, 1927
IN A MONASTERY GARDEN, 1935, A
IN A SECRET GARDEN
IN A YEAR OF THIRTEEN MOONS, 1980, O
IN AGAIN-OUT AGAIN, 1917, A
IN ANOTHER GIRL'S SHOES, 1917
IN BAD, 1918, A
IN BONDAGE, 1919
IN BORROWED PLUMES, 1926, A
IN BRONCHO LAND, 1926
IN CALIENTE, 1935, A
IN CASE OF ADVERSITY
IN CELEBRATION, 1975, O
IN COLD BLOOD, 1967, O
IN DARKNESS WAITING
IN DER HOLLE IST NOCH PLATZ
IN EARLY ARIZONA, 1938, A
IN ENEMY COUNTRY, 1968, A-C
IN EVERY WOMAN'S LIFE, 1924, A
IN FAST COMPANY, 1924, A
IN FAST COMPANY, 1946, A
IN FOLLY'S TRAIL, 1920, A
IN FOR THIRTY DAYS, 1919, A
IN FULL CRY, 1921
IN GAY MADRID, 1930, A
IN GOD WE TRUST, 1980, C-O
IN HARM'S WAY, 1965, A
IN HIGH GEAR, 1924, A
IN HIS BROTHER'S PLACE, 1919
IN HIS GRIP, 1921, A
IN HIS STEPS, 1936, A
IN HOLLAND, 1929
IN HOLLYWOOD WITH POTASH AND PERLMUTTER, 1924, A
IN HONOR'S WEB, 1919
IN JUDGEMENT OF, 1918
IN LIKE FLINT, 1967, A
IN LOVE, 1983
IN LOVE AND WAR, 1958, A
IN LOVE WITH LIFE, 1934, A
IN LOVE WITH LOVE, 1924
IN MACARTHUR PARK, 1977, C-O
IN MIZZOURA, 1914
IN MIZZOURA, 1919
IN MUSIC LAND, 1928
IN NAME ONLY, 1939, A
IN OLD AMARILLO, 1951, A
IN OLD ARIZONA, 1929, A
IN OLD CALIENTE, 1939, A
IN OLD CALIFORNIA, 1929, A
IN OLD CALIFORNIA, 1942, A
IN OLD CHEYENNE, 1931, A
IN OLD CHEYENNE, 1941, A
IN OLD CHICAGO, 1938, A
IN OLD COLORADO, 1941, A
IN OLD KENTUCKY, 1920, A
IN OLD KENTUCKY, 1927, A
IN OLD KENTUCKY, 1935, A
IN OLD LOS ANGELES, 1948
IN OLD MEXICO, 1938, A
IN OLD MISSOURI, 1940, A
IN OLD MONTANA, 1939, A
IN OLD MONTANA, 1939
IN OLD MONTEREY, 1939, A
IN OLD NEW MEXICO, 1945, AA
IN OLD OKLAHOMA, 1943, A
IN OLD SACRAMENTO, 1946, C
IN OLD SANTA FE, 1935, A
IN OUR TIME, 1944, C
IN PARIS, A.W.O.L., 1936
IN PERSON, 1935, A
IN PIENO SOLE
IN PRAISE OF OLDER WOMEN, 1978, O
IN PURSUIT OF POLLY, 1918
IN ROSIE'S ROOM
IN SEARCH OF A HERO, 1926
IN SEARCH OF A HUSBAND, 1915
IN SEARCH OF A SINNER, 1920, A
IN SEARCH OF A THRILL, 1923, A
IN SEARCH OF ANNA, 1978, O
IN SEARCH OF ARCADY, 1919
IN SEARCH OF GOLDEN SKY, 1984
IN SEARCH OF GREGORY, 1970, O
IN SEARCH OF HISTORIC JESUS, 1980, AA
IN SEARCH OF THE CASTAWAYS, 1962, AAA
IN SELF DEFENSE, 1947
IN SLUMBERLAND, 1917
IN SOCIETY, 1921
IN SOCIETY, 1944, AAA
IN SPITE OF DANGER, 1935, A
IN STRANGE COMPANY
IN THE BALANCE, 1917, A
IN THE BISHOP'S CARRIAGE, 1913
IN THE BLOOD, 1923, A
IN THE COOL OF THE DAY, 1963, C
IN THE COUNTRY, 1967, A
IN THE DARK, 1915
IN THE DAYS OF SAINT PATRICK, 1920, A
IN THE DAYS OF THE COVERED WAGON, 1924
IN THE DAYS OF THE MISSIONS
IN THE DAYS OF THE THUNDERING HERD, 1914
IN THE DAYS OF THE THUNDERING HERD
IN THE DEVIL'S BOWL
IN THE DEVIL'S GARDEN
IN THE DIPLOMATIC SERVICE, 1916
IN THE DOGHOUSE, 1964, A
IN THE FALL OF '55 EDEN CRIED
IN THE FIRST DEGREE, 1927
IN THE FRENCH STYLE, 1963, O
IN THE GLOAMING, 1919
IN THE GOOD OLD SUMMERTIME, 1949, AA
IN THE GRIP OF SPIES, 1914
IN THE GRIP OF THE SULTAN, 1915
IN THE HANDS OF THE LAW, 1917
IN THE HANDS OF THE LONDON CROOKS, 1913, A
IN THE HEADLINES, 1929, A
IN THE HEART OF A FOOL, 1920
IN THE HEAT OF THE NIGHT, 1967, C
IN THE HOLLOW OF HER HAND, 1918
IN THE HOUR OF HIS NEED, 1925
IN THE KINGDOM OF OIL AND MILLIONS, 1916
IN THE LINE OF DUTY, 1931, A
IN THE MEANTIME, DARLING, 1944, A
IN THE MONEY, 1934, A
IN THE MONEY, 1958, AA
IN THE NAME OF LIFE, 1947, O
IN THE NAME OF LOVE, 1925, A
IN THE NAME OF THE LAW, 1922
IN THE NAME OF THE PRINCE OF PEACE, 1914
IN THE NAVY, 1941, AAA
IN THE NEXT ROOM, 1930, A
IN THE NICK, 1960, A
IN THE NIGHT
IN THE NIGHT, 1920
IN THE PALACE OF THE KING, 1915
IN THE PALACE OF THE KING, 1923
IN THE PILLORY, 1924
IN THE RAPTURE, 1976
IN THE SHADOW, 1915
IN THE SHADOW OF BIG BEN, 1914
IN THE SOUP, 1936, A
IN THE SPIDER'S WEB, 1924
IN THE STRETCH, 1914, A
IN THE WAKE OF A STRANGER, 1960, C
IN THE WAKE OF THE BOUNTY, 1933, A
IN THE WATER, 1923
IN THE WEB OF THE GRAFTERS, 1916
IN THE WEST, 1923
IN THE WHIRLWIND OF REVOLUTION, 1922
IN THE WHITE CITY, 1983, C-O
IN THE WOODS
IN THE YEAR 2889, 1966, C
IN THIS CORNER, 1948, A
IN THIS OUR LIFE, 1942, C-O
IN TREASON'S GRASP, 1917
IN TROUBLE WITH EVE, 1964, A
IN WALKED EVE
IN WALKED MARY, 1920, A
IN WHICH WE SERVE, 1942, A
IN WRONG, 1919
IN-LAWS, THE, 1979, A
INADMISSIBLE EVIDENCE, 1968, C
INBETWEEN AGE, THE, 1958, A
INBREAKER, THE, 1974, O
INCENDIARY BLONDE, 1945, A
INCENSE FOR THE DAMNED, 1970, O
INCH'ALLAH, 1922
INCHON, 1981, O
INCIDENT, 1948, C
INCIDENT AT MIDNIGHT, 1966, A
INCIDENT AT PHANTOM HILL, 1966
INCIDENT IN AN ALLEY, 1962, A
INCIDENT IN SHANGHAI, 1937, A
INCIDENT, THE, 1967, O
INCOMING FRESHMEN, 1979
INCOMPARABLE BELLAIRS, THE
INCOMPARABLE MISTRESS BELLAIRS, THE, 1914
INCORRIGIBLE, 1980, C
INCORRIGIBLE DUKANE, THE, 1915, A
INCREDIBLE INVASION, THE, 1971, C-O
INCREDIBLE JOURNEY, THE, 1963, AAA
INCREDIBLE MELTING MAN, THE, 1978, O
INCREDIBLE MR. LIMPET, THE, 1964, AAA
INCREDIBLE PETRIFIED WORLD, THE, 1959, A
INCREDIBLE PRAYING MANTIS, THE
INCREDIBLE SARAH, THE, 1976, C
INCREDIBLE SHRINKING MAN, THE, 1957, A
INCREDIBLE SHRINKING WOMAN, THE, 1981, C
INCREDIBLE TWO-HEADED TRANSPLANT, THE, 1971, O
INCREDIBLY STRANGE CREATURES WHO STOPPED LIVING AND BECAME CRAZY MIXED-UP ZOMBIES, THE, 1965, O
INCREDIBLY STRANGE CREATURES, THE
INCUBUS, 1966, O
INCUBUS, THE, 1982, O
INDECENT, 1962, O
INDEPENDENCE DAY, 1976, C-O
INDEPENDENCE DAY, 1983, O
INDESTRUCTIBLE MAN, THE, 1956, A
INDESTRUCTIBLE WIFE, THE, 1919
INDIAN AGENT, 1948, A
INDIAN FIGHTER, THE, 1955, C
INDIAN LOVE CALL
INDIAN LOVE LYRICS, THE, 1923, A
INDIAN PAINT, 1965, AA
INDIAN SCOUT
INDIAN SUMMER
INDIAN SUMMER OF DRY VALLEY JOHNSON, THE, 1917
INDIAN TERRITORY, 1950, A
INDIAN TOMB, THE
INDIAN UPRISING, 1951, A
INDIANA JONES AND THE TEMPLE OF DOOM, 1984, C-O
INDIANAPOLIS SPEEDWAY, 1939, A
INDISCREET, 1931, C
INDISCREET, 1958, A-C
INDISCREET CORINNE, 1917
INDISCRETION, 1917
INDISCRETION, 1921
INDISCRETION OF AN AMERICAN WIFE, 1954, A-C
INDISCRETIONS OF EVE, 1932, A
INEVITABLE, THE, 1917
INEZ FROM HOLLYWOOD, 1924, A
INFAMOUS
INFAMOUS LADY, THE, 1928
INFAMOUS MISS REVELL, THE, 1921, A
INFATUATION, 1915, A
INFATUATION, 1925
INFELICE, 1915
INFERIOR SEX, THE, 1920, A
INFERNAL IDOL
INFERNAL MACHINE, 1933, A
INFERNO, 1953, O
INFERNO, 1980, O
INFERNO DEI MORTI-VIVENTI
INFIDEL, THE, 1922
INFIDELITY, 1917, A
INFINITE SORROW, 1922
INFORMATION KID
INFORMATION RECEIVED, 1962, C
INFORMER, THE, 1929, A
INFORMER, THE, 1935, C
INFORMERS, THE
INFRA SUPERMAN, THE
INFRA-MAN, 1975, C
INGAGI, 1931, C
INGEBORG HOLM, 1913
INGLORIOUS BASTARDS
INHERIT THE WIND, 1960, A
INHERITANCE, 1920
INHERITANCE IN PRETORIA, 1936, C
INHERITANCE, THE, 1951, A
INHERITANCE, THE, 1964, C
INHERITANCE, THE, 1978, O
INHERITED PASSIONS, 1916
INITIATION, THE, 1984, O
INJUN FENDER, 1973, O
INJUSTICE
INN FOR TROUBLE, 1960, A
INN IN TOKYO, AN, 1935
INN OF THE DAMNED, 1974, O
INN OF THE FRIGHTENED PEOPLE
INN OF THE SIXTH HAPPINESS, THE, 1958, AA
INNER CHAMBER, THE, 1915
INNER CHAMBER, THE, 1921, A
INNER CIRCLE, THE, 1946, A
INNER MAN, THE, 1922, A
INNER SANCTUM, 1948, A
INNER SHRINE, THE, 1917
INNER STRUGGLE, THE, 1916
INNER VOICE, THE, 1920
INNERVIEW, THE, 1974, O
INNOCENCE, 1923, A
INNOCENCE IS BLISS
INNOCENCE OF LIZETTE, THE, 1917
INNOCENCE OF RUTH, THE, 1916, A
INNOCENCE UNPROTECTED, 1971, C
INNOCENT, 1918, A
INNOCENT, 1921, A
INNOCENT ADVENTURESS, AN, 1919
INNOCENT AFFAIR, AN
INNOCENT AND THE DAMNED
INNOCENT BYSTANDERS, 1973, O
INNOCENT CHEAT, THE, 1921
INNOCENT LIE, THE, 1916, A

INNOCENT LOVE, 1928
INNOCENT MAGDALENE, AN, 1916, A
INNOCENT MAID, AN, 1934
INNOCENT MEETING, 1959, C
INNOCENT SINNER, THE, 1917, A
INNOCENT SINNERS, 1958, AAA
INNOCENT'S PROGRESS, 1918
INNOCENT, THE, 1979, O
INNOCENTS IN PARIS, 1955, A
INNOCENTS OF CHICAGO, THE
INNOCENTS OF PARIS, 1929, A
INNOCENTS WITH DIRTY HANDS
INNOCENTS, THE, 1961, C-O
INQUEST, 1931, C
INQUEST, 1939, C
INQUISITOR, THE, 1982, C-O
INSECT WOMAN, THE, 1964, C
INSECT, THE
INSEL DER AMAZONEN
INSEMINOID
INSEMINOID, 1980
INSEPARABLES, THE, 1929, A
INSIDE AMY, 1975, O
INSIDE DAISY CLOVER, 1965, O
INSIDE DETROIT, 1955, O
INSIDE INFORMATION
INSIDE INFORMATION, 1934, A
INSIDE INFORMATION, 1939, A
INSIDE JOB, 1946, A
INSIDE LOOKING OUT, 1977, C
INSIDE MOVES, 1980, C
INSIDE OF THE CUP, THE, 1921
INSIDE OUT
INSIDE OUT, 1975, C
INSIDE STORY, 1939, A
INSIDE STORY, THE, 1948, A
INSIDE STRAIGHT, 1951, O
INSIDE THE LAW, 1942, A
INSIDE THE LINES, 1918, A
INSIDE THE LINES, 1930, A
INSIDE THE MAFIA, 1959, O
INSIDE THE ROOM, 1935, C
INSIDE THE WALLS OF FOLSOM PRISON, 1951, C
INSIDIOUS DR. FU MANCHU, THE
INSINUATION, 1922
INSPECTOR CALLS, AN, 1954, O
INSPECTOR CLOUSEAU, 1968, A
INSPECTOR GENERAL, THE, 1937, A
INSPECTOR GENERAL, THE, 1949, AAA
INSPECTOR HORNLEIGH, 1939, A
INSPECTOR HORNLEIGH GOES TO IT
INSPECTOR HORNLEIGH ON HOLIDAY, 1939, A
INSPECTOR MAIGRET
INSPECTOR, THE
INSPIRATION, 1928
INSPIRATION, 1931, C
INSPIRATIONS OF HARRY LARRABEE, 1917
INSTANT COFFEE, 1974
INSTRUCTOR, THE, 1983
INSULT, 1932, C
INSURANCE INVESTIGATOR, 1951, C
INSURRECTION, THE, 1915
INTELLIGENCE MEN, THE
INTENT TO KILL, 1958, A
INTERFERENCE, 1928, A
INTERFERIN' GENT, THE, 1927
INTERIORS, 1978, C-O
INTERLOPER, THE, 1918
INTERLUDE
INTERLUDE, 1957, A
INTERLUDE, 1968, C
INTERMEZZO, 1937, A
INTERMEZZO: A LOVE STORY, 1939, A
INTERNATIONAL CRIME, 1938, A
INTERNATIONAL HOUSE, 1933, A
INTERNATIONAL LADY, 1941, A
INTERNATIONAL MARRIAGE, AN, 1916
INTERNATIONAL POLICE
INTERNATIONAL SETTLEMENT, 1938, A
INTERNATIONAL SQUADRON, 1941, A
INTERNATIONAL VELVET, 1978, AAA
INTERNECINE PROJECT, THE, 1974, O
INTERNES CAN'T TAKE MONEY, 1937, A
INTERNS, THE, 1962, O
INTERPLAY, 1970
INTERPOL
INTERRUPTED HONEYMOON, AN, 1948
INTERRUPTED HONEYMOON, THE, 1936, A
INTERRUPTED JOURNEY, THE, 1949, A-C
INTERRUPTED MELODY, 1955, A
INTERVAL, 1973, C
INTIMACY, 1966, O
INTIMATE LIGHTING, 1969, A
INTIMATE PLAYMATES, THE, 1976
INTIMATE RELATIONS, 1937, A
INTIMATE RELATIONS, 1948
INTIMATE RELATIONS, 1953
INTIMATE STRANGER, THE
INTIMNI OSVETLENI
INTO HER KINGDOM, 1926
INTO NO MAN'S LAND, 1928
INTO THE BLUE
INTO THE NIGHT, 1928, A
INTO THE PRIMITIVE, 1916
INTO THE STRAIGHT, 1950, C
INTOLERANCE, 1916, C
INTRAMUROS
INTRIGUE, 1916
INTRIGUE, 1917
INTRIGUE, 1921
INTRIGUE, 1947, A
INTRIGUE IN PARIS
INTRODUCE ME, 1925, A
INTRODUCTION TO MARRIAGE, 1930
INTRUDER IN THE DUST, 1949, C-O
INTRUDER, THE, 1932, A
INTRUDER, THE, 1955, C
INTRUDER, THE, 1962, C
INTRUSION OF ISABEL, THE, 1919
INVADER, THE
INVADERS FROM MARS, 1953, A
INVADERS, THE, 1929, A
INVADERS, THE, 1941, A
INVASION, 1965, A
INVASION 1700, 1965, C
INVASION EARTH 2150 A.D.
INVASION FORCE
INVASION FROM INNER EARTH, 1977
INVASION FROM THE MOON
INVASION OF ASTRO-MONSTERS
INVASION OF THE ANIMAL PEOPLE, 1962, A
INVASION OF THE ASTROS
INVASION OF THE BEE GIRLS, 1973, O
INVASION OF THE BLOOD FARMERS, 1972, O
INVASION OF THE BODY SNATCHERS, 1956, A
INVASION OF THE BODY SNATCHERS, 1978, C-O
INVASION OF THE BODY STEALERS
INVASION OF THE FLESH HUNTERS, 1981
INVASION OF THE FLYING SAUCERS
INVASION OF THE HELL CREATURES
INVASION OF THE SAUCER MEN, 1957, C
INVASION OF THE STAR CREATURES, 1962, A
INVASION OF THE VAMPIRES, THE, 1961, O
INVASION OF THE ZOMBIES
INVASION QUARTET, 1961, A
INVASION U.S.A., 1952, A
INVESTIGATION OF A CITIZEN ABOVE SUSPICION, 1970, O
INVESTIGATION OF MURDER, AN
INVINCIBLE GLADIATOR, THE, 1963, C
INVINCIBLE SIX, THE, 1970, A
INVISIBLE AGENT, 1942, A
INVISIBLE AVENGER, THE, 1958, A
INVISIBLE BOND, THE, 1920
INVISIBLE BOY, THE, 1957, AA
INVISIBLE CREATURE, THE
INVISIBLE DIVORCE, THE, 1920
INVISIBLE DR. MABUSE, THE, 1965, C
INVISIBLE ENEMY, 1938, A
INVISIBLE ENEMY, THE, 1916
INVISIBLE FEAR, THE, 1921, A
INVISIBLE GHOST, THE, 1941, C
INVISIBLE HORROR, THE
INVISIBLE INFORMER, 1946, A
INVISIBLE INVADERS, 1959, C
INVISIBLE KILLER, THE, 1940, A
INVISIBLE MAN RETURNS, THE, 1940, A
INVISIBLE MAN'S REVENGE, 1944, A
INVISIBLE MAN, THE, 1933, C
INVISIBLE MAN, THE, 1958, A
INVISIBLE MAN, THE, 1963, A
INVISIBLE MENACE, THE, 1938, A
INVISIBLE MESSAGE, THE
INVISIBLE OPPONENT, 1933, A
INVISIBLE POWER
INVISIBLE POWER, THE, 1914
INVISIBLE POWER, THE, 1921, A
INVISIBLE RAY, THE, 1936, C
INVISIBLE STRANGLER, 1984, C-O
INVISIBLE STRIPES, 1940, A
INVISIBLE WALL, THE, 1947, A
INVISIBLE WEB, THE, 1921
INVISIBLE WOMAN, THE, 1941, A
INVITATION, 1952, A
INVITATION TO A GUNFIGHTER, 1964, C
INVITATION TO A HANGING
INVITATION TO HAPPINESS, 1939, A
INVITATION TO MURDER, 1962, C
INVITATION TO THE DANCE, 1956, A
INVITATION TO THE WALTZ, 1935, A
INVITATION, THE, 1975, C-O
IO ... TU ... Y ... ELLA, 1933, A
IOLANTA
IPCRESS FILE, THE, 1965, A-C
IPHIGENIA, 1977, A
IPNOSI
IRELAND'S BORDER LINE, 1939, A
IRENE, 1926, A
IRENE, 1940, A
IRIS, 1915, A
IRISH AND PROUD OF IT, 1938, A
IRISH DESTINY, 1925, A
IRISH EYES, 1918
IRISH EYES ARE SMILING, 1944, A
IRISH FOR LUCK, 1936, A
IRISH GRINGO, THE, 1935
IRISH HEARTS
IRISH HEARTS, 1927, A
IRISH IN US, THE, 1935, A
IRISH LUCK, 1925
IRISH LUCK, 1939, A
IRISH MOTHER, AN
IRISH WHISKEY REBELLION, 1973, C
IRISHMAN, THE, 1978, A MP
IRMA LA DOUCE, 1963, C-O
IRO
IRON ANGEL, 1964, A
IRON COLLAR, THE
IRON CURTAIN, THE, 1948, A
IRON DUKE, THE, 1935, A
IRON FIST
IRON FIST, 1926
IRON GLOVE, THE, 1954, A
IRON HAND, THE, 1916
IRON HEART, THE, 1917
IRON HEART, THE, 1920
IRON HORSE, THE, 1924, A
IRON JUSTICE, 1915, C
IRON KISS, THE
IRON MAIDEN, THE
IRON MAJOR, THE, 1943, A
IRON MAN, THE, 1925, A
IRON MAN, THE, 1931, A
IRON MAN, THE, 1951, C
IRON MASK, THE, 1929, A
IRON MASTER, THE, 1933, A
IRON MISTRESS, THE, 1952, C
IRON MOUNTAIN TRAIL, 1953, A
IRON PETTICOAT, THE, 1956, A
IRON RIDER, THE, 1920
IRON RING, THE, 1917, A
IRON ROAD, THE
IRON SHERIFF, THE, 1957, A
IRON STAIR, THE
IRON STAIR, THE, 1933, A
IRON STRAIN, THE, 1915
IRON TO GOLD, 1922
IRON TRAIL, THE, 1921
IRON WOMAN, THE, 1916
IROQUOIS TRAIL, THE, 1950, A
IRRECONCILABLE DIFFERENCES, 1984, A-C
IRRESISTIBLE FLAPPER, THE, 1919
IRRESISTIBLE LOVER, THE, 1927, A
IS A MOTHER TO BLAME?, 1922
IS DIVORCE A FAILURE?, 1923, A
IS EVERYBODY HAPPY?, 1929, A
IS EVERYBODY HAPPY?, 1943, A
IS LIFE WORTH LIVING?, 1921
IS LOVE EVERYTHING?, 1924, A
IS MATRIMONY A FAILURE?, 1922
IS MONEY EVERYTHING?, 1923, A
IS MY FACE RED?, 1932, A
IS PARIS BURNING?, 1966, A
IS THAT NICE?, 1926, A
IS THERE JUSTICE?, 1931, A
IS THERE SEX AFTER DEATH, 1971
IS THIS TRIP REALLY NECESSARY?, 1970, O
IS WHEN IT SIZZLES, 1964, A
IS YOUR DAUGHTER SAFE?, 1927, C
IS YOUR HONEYMOON REALLY NECESSARY?, 1953, A
IS ZAT SO?, 1927, A
ISAAC LITTLEFEATHERS, 1984, C
ISABEL, 1968, O
ISADORA, 1968, O
ISLAND AT THE TOP OF THE WORLD, THE, 1974, AAA
ISLAND CAPTIVES, 1937, A
ISLAND CLAWS, 1981, O
ISLAND IN THE SKY, 1938, A
ISLAND IN THE SKY, 1953, A
ISLAND IN THE SUN, 1957, C
ISLAND MAN
ISLAND OF ALLAH, 1956, A
ISLAND OF DESIRE, 1952, C
ISLAND OF DESIRE, 1930
ISLAND OF DESIRE, THE, 1917
ISLAND OF DESPAIR, THE, 1926
ISLAND OF DOOM, 1933, A
ISLAND OF DOOMED MEN, 1940, C
ISLAND OF DR. MOREAU, THE, 1977, C
ISLAND OF INTRIGUE, THE, 1919, A
ISLAND OF LOST GIRLS, 1975
ISLAND OF LOST MEN, 1939, A
ISLAND OF LOST SOULS, 1933, C
ISLAND OF LOST WOMEN, 1959, A
ISLAND OF LOVE, 1963, A

ISLAND OF MONTE CRISTO
ISLAND OF PROCIDA, THE, 1952, C
ISLAND OF REGENERATION, THE, 1915, A
ISLAND OF ROMANCE, THE, 1922
ISLAND OF SURPRISE, THE, 1916
ISLAND OF TERROR, 1967, C
ISLAND OF THE BLUE DOLPHINS, 1964, AAA
ISLAND OF THE BURNING DAMNED, 1971, C
ISLAND OF THE BURNING DOOMED
ISLAND OF THE DAMNED, 1976, O
ISLAND OF THE DOOMED, 1968, C
ISLAND OF THE FISHMEN, THE
ISLAND OF WISDOM, THE, 1920
ISLAND RESCUE, 1952, A
ISLAND TRADER, 1982
ISLAND WIVES, 1922
ISLAND WOMAN
ISLAND WOMEN, 1958, A
ISLAND, THE, 1962, C
ISLAND, THE, 1980, O
ISLANDS IN THE STREAM, 1977, C
ISLE OF CONQUEST, 1919, A
ISLE OF DESTINY, 1940, A
ISLE OF DOUBT, 1922
ISLE OF ESCAPE, 1930, C
ISLE OF FORGOTTEN SINS, 1943, A
ISLE OF FORGOTTEN WOMEN, 1927, A
ISLE OF FURY, 1936, A
ISLE OF HOPE, THE, 1925, A
ISLE OF INTRIGUE, THE, 1918
ISLE OF LIFE, THE, 1916
ISLE OF LOST MEN, 1928, A
ISLE OF LOST SHIPS, 1929, A
ISLE OF LOST SHIPS, THE, 1923, A
ISLE OF LOST WRANGLERS
ISLE OF LOVE, THE, 1916
ISLE OF LOVE, THE, 1922
ISLE OF MISSING MEN, 1942, A
ISLE OF OBLIVION, 1917
ISLE OF RETRIBUTION, THE, 1926, A
ISLE OF SIN, 1963, C-O
ISLE OF THE DEAD, 1945, C
ISLE OF THE SNAKE PEOPLE
ISN'T IT ROMANTIC?, 1948, A
ISN'T LIFE A BITCH?
ISN'T LIFE WONDERFUL, 1924, A
ISN'T LIFE WONDERFUL, 1953, A
ISOBEL, 1920, A
ISTANBUL, 1957, A
IT, 1927, A
IT, 1967, O
IT AIN'T EASY, 1972, C-O
IT AIN'T HAY, 1943, AAA
IT ALL CAME TRUE, 1940, A-C
IT ALWAYS RAINS ON SUNDAY, 1949, C
IT CAME FROM BENEATH THE SEA, 1955, A
IT CAME FROM OUTER SPACE, 1953, A
IT CAME WITHOUT WARNING
IT CAN BE DONE, 1921, A
IT CAN BE DONE, 1929, A
IT CAN'T LAST FOREVER, 1937, A
IT COMES UP LOVE, 1943, A
IT COMES UP MURDER
IT CONQUERED THE WORLD, 1956, A
IT COULD HAPPEN TO YOU, 1937, A
IT COULD HAPPEN TO YOU, 1939, A
IT COULDN'T HAVE HAPPENED
IT COULDN'T HAVE HAPPENED—BUT IT DID, 1936, A
IT FELL FROM THE SKY, 1980, C
IT GROWS ON TREES, 1952, A
IT HAD TO BE YOU, 1947, A
IT HAD TO HAPPEN, 1936, A
IT HAPPENED AT THE INN, 1945, A
IT HAPPENED AT THE WORLD'S FAIR, 1963, A
IT HAPPENED HERE, 1966, C
IT HAPPENED IN ATHENS, 1962, A
IT HAPPENED IN BROAD DAYLIGHT, 1960, A
IT HAPPENED IN BROOKLYN, 1947, A
IT HAPPENED IN CANADA, 1962, A
IT HAPPENED IN FLATBUSH, 1942, A
IT HAPPENED IN GIBRALTAR, 1943, A
IT HAPPENED IN HARLEM, 1945
IT HAPPENED IN HOLLYWOOD
IT HAPPENED IN HOLLYWOOD, 1937, A
IT HAPPENED IN HONOLULU, 1916
IT HAPPENED IN NEW YORK, 1935, A
IT HAPPENED IN PARIS, 1919
IT HAPPENED IN PARIS, 1935, A
IT HAPPENED IN PARIS, 1953, A
IT HAPPENED IN PARIS, 1938
IT HAPPENED IN PARIS, 1940
IT HAPPENED IN ROME, 1959, A
IT HAPPENED IN SOHO, 1948, C
IT HAPPENED ON 5TH AVENUE, 1947, A
IT HAPPENED ONE NIGHT, 1934, A
IT HAPPENED ONE SUMMER
IT HAPPENED ONE SUNDAY, 1944, A
IT HAPPENED OUT WEST, 1923
IT HAPPENED OUT WEST, 1937, A
IT HAPPENED TO ADELE, 1917
IT HAPPENED TO JANE, 1959, A
IT HAPPENED TO ONE MAN, 1941, A
IT HAPPENED TOMORROW, 1944, A
IT HAPPENS EVERY SPRING, 1949, AAA
IT HAPPENS EVERY THURSDAY, 1953, A
IT HAPPENS IN ROME
IT HURTS ONLY WHEN I LAUGH
IT IS FOR ENGLAND
IT IS THE LAW, 1924, A
IT ISN'T BEING DONE THIS SEASON, 1921
IT ISN'T DONE, 1937, A
IT LIVES AGAIN, 1978, O
IT LIVES BY NIGHT
IT MIGHT HAPPEN TO YOU, 1920
IT MUST BE LOVE, 1926, A
IT ONLY HAPPENS TO OTHERS, 1971, C
IT ONLY TAKES 5 MINUTES
IT PAYS TO ADVERTISE, 1919
IT PAYS TO ADVERTISE, 1931, A
IT RAINED ALL NIGHT THE DAY I LEFT, 1978
IT SEEMED LIKE A GOOD IDEA AT THE TIME, 1975, O
IT SHOULD HAPPEN TO YOU, 1954, A
IT SHOULDN'T HAPPEN TO A DOG, 1946, A
IT SHOULDN'T HAPPEN TO A VET
IT STALKED THE OCEAN FLOOR
IT STARTED AT MIDNIGHT
IT STARTED IN NAPLES, 1960, C
IT STARTED IN PARADISE, 1952, A
IT STARTED IN THE ALPS, 1966, A
IT STARTED WITH A KISS, 1959, C
IT STARTED WITH EVE, 1941, A
IT TAKES A THIEF, 1960, C
IT TAKES ALL KINDS, 1969, C
IT THE TERROR FROM BEYOND SPACE, 1958, C
IT THE VAMPIRE FROM BEYOND SPACE
IT WON'T RUB OFF, BABY
IT'S A 2'6" ABOVE THE GROUND WORLD, 1972, O
IT'S A BEAR, 1919, A
IT'S A BET, 1935, A
IT'S A BIG COUNTRY, 1951, AA
IT'S A BIKINI WORLD, 1967, A
IT'S A BOY, 1934, A
IT'S A COP, 1934, A
IT'S A DATE, 1940, A
IT'S A DEAL, 1930, A-C
IT'S A DOG'S LIFE
IT'S A GIFT, 1934, AAA
IT'S A GRAND LIFE, 1953, A
IT'S A GRAND OLD WORLD, 1937, A
IT'S A GREAT DAY, 1956, A
IT'S A GREAT FEELING, 1949, A
IT'S A GREAT LIFE, 1920
IT'S A GREAT LIFE, 1930, A
IT'S A GREAT LIFE, 1936, A
IT'S A GREAT LIFE, 1943, AA
IT'S A JOKE, SON, 1947, A
IT'S A KING, 1933, A
IT'S A MAD, MAD, MAD, MAD WORLD, 1963, AAA
IT'S A PLEASURE, 1945, A
IT'S A SMALL WORLD, 1935, A
IT'S A SMALL WORLD, 1950, A
IT'S A WISE CHILD, 1931, A
IT'S A WONDERFUL DAY, 1949, A
IT'S A WONDERFUL LIFE, 1946, AAA
IT'S A WONDERFUL WORLD, 1939, A
IT'S A WONDERFUL WORLD, 1956, A
IT'S ALIVE, 1968, C
IT'S ALIVE, 1974, O
IT'S ALIVE II
IT'S ALL HAPPENING
IT'S ALL IN YOUR MIND, 1938
IT'S ALL OVER TOWN, 1963, A
IT'S ALL YOURS, 1937, A
IT'S ALWAYS FAIR WEATHER, 1955, A
IT'S EASY TO MAKE MONEY, 1919
IT'S GREAT TO BE ALIVE, 1933, A
IT'S GREAT TO BE YOUNG, 1946, A
IT'S GREAT TO BE YOUNG, 1956, A
IT'S HAPPINESS THAT COUNTS, 1918, A
IT'S HARD TO BE GOOD, 1950, A
IT'S HOT IN HELL
IT'S HOT IN PARADISE, 1962, C
IT'S IN THE AIR, 1935, A
IT'S IN THE AIR, 1940, A
IT'S IN THE BAG, 1936, A
IT'S IN THE BAG, 1943, A
IT'S IN THE BAG, 1945, A
IT'S IN THE BLOOD, 1938, A
IT'S LOVE AGAIN, 1936, A
IT'S LOVE I'M AFTER, 1937, A
IT'S MAGIC
IT'S MY LIFE
IT'S MY TURN, 1980, C
IT'S NEVER TOO LATE, 1958, A
IT'S NEVER TOO LATE, 1984, O
IT'S NEVER TOO LATE TO MEND, 1917
IT'S NEVER TOO LATE TO MEND, 1937, A
IT'S NO LAUGHING MATTER, 1915, A
IT'S NOT CRICKET, 1937, A
IT'S NOT CRICKET, 1949, A
IT'S NOT THE SIZE THAT COUNTS, 1979, O
IT'S ONLY MONEY, 1962, A
IT'S ONLY MONEY, 1951
IT'S SAM SMALL AGAIN
IT'S THAT MAN AGAIN, 1943, A
IT'S THE OLD ARMY GAME, 1926, A
IT'S TOUGH TO BE FAMOUS, 1932, A
IT'S TRAD, DAD
IT'S TURNED OUT NICE AGAIN
IT'S WHAT'S HAPPENING
IT'S YOU I WANT, 1936, A
ITALIAN CONNECTION, THE, 1973, O
ITALIAN JOB, THE, 1969, A
ITALIAN MOUSE, THE
ITALIAN SECRET SERVICE, 1968, C
ITALIAN STRAW HAT, AN, 1927, A
ITALIAN, THE, 1915, A
ITALIANI BRAVA GENTE
ITALIANO BRAVA GENTE, 1965, A
ITCHING PALMS, 1923
IVAN GROZNYI
IVAN THE TERRIBLE, PART 1, 1947, A
IVAN'S CHILDHOOD
IVAN'S CHILDHOOD
IVANHOE, 1913, A
IVANHOE, 1952, A
IVANHOE
IVANOVO DETSTVO
IVORY HUNTER, 1952, A
IVORY HUNTERS, THE
IVORY SNUFF BOX, THE, 1915, A
IVORY-HANDLED GUN, 1935, A
IVY, 1947, A
IVY LEAGUE KILLERS, 1962

-J-

J'ACCUSE, 1919
J'ACCUSE, 1939, C-O
J'AI TUE, 1924
J'AVAIS SEPT FILLES
J'IRAI CRACHER SUR VOS TOMBES
J-MEN FOREVER, 1980, C
J.C., 1972
J.D.'S REVENGE, 1976, O
J.R.
J.W. COOP, 1971, A
JABBERWOCKY, 1977, O
JACK, 1925
JACK AHOY, 1935, A
JACK AND JILL, 1917, A
JACK AND THE BEANSTALK, 1917, A
JACK AND THE BEANSTALK, 1952, AAA
JACK AND THE BEANSTALK, 1970, AA
JACK CHANTY, 1915
JACK FROST, 1966, AAA
JACK KNIFE MAN, THE, 1920, A
JACK LONDON, 1943, A
JACK LONDON'S KLONDIKE FEVER
JACK MCCALL, DESPERADO, 1953, A
JACK O' CLUBS, 1924, A
JACK O'HEARTS, 1926, A
JACK OF ALL TRADES
JACK OF DIAMONDS, 1967, A
JACK OF DIAMONDS, THE, 1949, A
JACK OF HEARTS
JACK RIDER, THE, 1921, A
JACK SLADE, 1953, C
JACK SPURLOCK, PRODIGAL, 1918, A
JACK STRAW, 1920, A
JACK TAR, 1915, A
JACK THE GIANT KILLER, 1962, AA
JACK THE RIPPER, 1959, O
JACK'S WIFE
JACK, SAM AND PETE, 1919, A
JACKALS, THE, 1967, A
JACKASS MAIL, 1942, A
JACKIE, 1921
JACKIE ROBINSON STORY, THE, 1950, AA
JACKPOT, 1960, A
JACKPOT, 1982
JACKPOT, THE, 1950, A
JACKSON COUNTY JAIL, 1976, O
JACKTOWN, 1962, A
JACOB TWO-TWO MEETS THE HOODED FANG, 1979, AAA
JACQUELINE, 1956, A
JACQUELINE SUSANN'S ONCE IS NOT ENOUGH
JACQUELINE, OR BLAZING BARRIERS, 1923, A
JACQUES BREL IS ALIVE AND WELL AND LIVING IN PARIS, 1975, A
JACQUES LANDAUZE, 1919
JACQUES OF THE SILVER NORTH, 1919
JADA, GOSCIE, JADA
JADE CASKET, THE, 1929
JADE CUP, THE, 1926

JADE HEART, THE, 1915
JADE MASK, THE, 1945, A
JAFFERY, 1915
JAGA WA HASHITTA
JAGUAR, 1956, A
JAGUAR, 1980, C
JAGUAR LIVES, 1979, C
JAGUAR'S CLAWS, 1917
JAIL BAIT, 1954, C
JAIL BAIT, 1977, O
JAIL BUSTERS, 1955, AA
JAIL HOUSE BLUES, 1942, A
JAILBIRD, THE, 1920, A
JAILBIRDS, 1939, A
JAILBIRDS, 1931
JAILBREAK, 1936, A
JAILBREAKERS, THE, 1960, A
JAILHOUSE ROCK, 1957, A
JAK BYC KOCHANA
JAKE THE PLUMBER, 1927, A
JALNA, 1935, A
JALOPY, 1953, AA
JALSAGHAR
JAM SESSION, 1944, A
JAMAICA INN, 1939, C
JAMAICA RUN, 1953, A
JAMAICAN GOLD, 1971
JAMBOREE
JAMBOREE, 1944, A
JAMBOREE, 1957, A
JAMES BROTHERS, THE
JAMESTOWN, 1923, A
JAN OF THE BIG SNOWS, 1922
JANE, 1915
JANE AUSTEN IN MANHATTAN, 1980, A
JANE EYRE, 1914
JANE EYRE, 1921, A
JANE EYRE, 1935, A
JANE EYRE, 1944, A
JANE EYRE, 1971, A
JANE GOES A' WOOING, 1919, A
JANE SHORE
JANE STEPS OUT, 1938, A
JANICE MEREDITH, 1924, A
JANIE, 1944, AA
JANIE GETS MARRIED, 1946, A
JANITOR, THE
JAPANESE NIGHTINGALE, A, 1918
JAPANESE WAR BRIDE, 1952, A
JASON AND THE ARGONAUTS, 1963, AA
JASPER LANDRY'S WILL
JASSY, 1948, A
JAVA HEAD, 1923, A
JAVA HEAD, 1935, C
JAVA SEAS
JAWS, 1975, C-O
JAWS 3-D, 1983, C-O
JAWS II, 1978, A-C
JAWS OF DEATH, THE
JAWS OF HELL, 1928
JAWS OF JUSTICE, 1933, A
JAWS OF SATAN, 1980, O
JAWS OF STEEL, 1927, A
JAWS OF THE JUNGLE, 1936, C
JAYHAWKERS, THE, 1959, A
JAZZ AGE, THE, 1929
JAZZ BABIES, 1932, A
JAZZ BOAT, 1960, A
JAZZ CINDERELLA, 1930, A
JAZZ GIRL, THE, 1926, A
JAZZ HEAVEN, 1929, A
JAZZ HOUNDS, THE, 1922
JAZZ MAD, 1928
JAZZ SINGER, THE, 1927, A
JAZZ SINGER, THE, 1953, A
JAZZ SINGER, THE, 1980, C
JAZZBAND FIVE, THE, 1932, A
JAZZBOAT
JAZZLAND, 1928, A
JAZZMAN, 1984, C
JAZZMANIA, 1923, A
JE T'AIME, 1974, C
JE T'AIME, JE T'AIME, 1972, C
JE VOUS SALUE, MAFIA
JEALOUS HUSBANDS, 1923, A
JEALOUSY
JEALOUSY, 1916
JEALOUSY, 1929, C
JEALOUSY, 1931, A
JEALOUSY, 1934, C
JEALOUSY, 1945, A
JEAN D'AGREVE, 1922
JEAN MARC OR CONJUGAL LIFE
JEAN O' THE HEATHER, 1916
JEANNE DORE, 1916
JEANNE EAGELS, 1957, C
JEANNE OF THE GUTTER, 1919
JEANNIE
JEDDA, THE UNCIVILIZED, 1956, A
JEDER FUR SICH UND GOTT GEGEN ALLE
JEEPERS CREEPERS, 1939, A
JEKYLL AND HYDE, 1982, O
JEKYLL AND HYDE PORTFOLIO, THE
JEKYLL AND HYDE TOGETHER AGAIN, 1972
JEKYLL'S INFERNO
JELF'S
JENIFER HALE, 1937, A
JENNIE
JENNIE, 1941, A
JENNIE GERHARDT, 1933, A
JENNIE LESS HA UNA NUOVA PISTOLA
JENNIE, WIFE/CHILD, 1968
JENNIFER, 1953, A
JENNIFER, 1978, C-O
JENNIFER (THE SNAKE GODDESS)
JENNIFER ON MY MIND, 1971, O
JENNY, 1969, A
JENNY BE GOOD, 1920, A
JENNY LAMOUR, 1948, A
JENNY LIND
JENSEITS DES RHIENS
JEOPARDY, 1953, A
JEREMIAH JOHNSON, 1972, C-O
JEREMY, 1973, A
JERICHO
JERK, THE, 1979, O
JERRICO, THE WONDER CLOWN
JERUSALEM DELIVERED, 1918
JERUSALEM FILE, THE, 1972, C
JES' CALL ME JIM, 1920
JESS, 1914
JESS OF MOUNTAIN COUNTRY, 1914
JESSE AND LESTER, TWO BROTHERS IN A PLACE CALLED TRINITY, 1972, A
JESSE JAMES, 1927, A
JESSE JAMES, 1939, A
JESSE JAMES AS THE OUTLAW, 1921, A
JESSE JAMES AT BAY, 1941, A
JESSE JAMES MEETS FRANKENSTEIN'S DAUGHTER, 1966, A
JESSE JAMES UNDER THE BLACK FLAG, 1921, A
JESSE JAMES VERSUS THE DALTONS, 1954, A
JESSE JAMES' WOMEN, 1954, A
JESSE JAMES, JR., 1942, A
JESSE'S GIRLS, 1975
JESSICA, 1962, C
JESSICA, 1970
JESSIE'S GIRLS, 1976, O
JEST OF GOD, A
JESUS, 1979, A
JESUS CHRIST, SUPERSTAR, 1973, A
JESUS OF NAZARETH, 1928
JESUS TRIP, THE, 1971, C
JET ATTACK, 1958, A
JET JOB, 1952, A
JET MEN OF THE AIR
JET OVER THE ATLANTIC, 1960, A
JET PILOT, 1957, C
JET SQUAD
JET STORM, 1961, A
JETLAG, 1981, C
JETSTREAM
JEU DE MASSACRE
JEUNE FILLE, UN SEUL AMOUR, UNE
JEUNES FILLES EN UNIFORME
JEUX D'ADULTES
JEUX PRECOCES
JEW AT WAR, A, 1931
JEW SUSS
JEWEL, 1915
JEWEL IN PAWN, A, 1917
JEWEL ROBBERY, 1932, A
JEWEL, THE, 1933, A
JEWELS OF BRANDENBURG, 1947, A
JEWELS OF DESIRE, 1927, A
JEWISH DAUGHTER, 1933
JEWISH FATHER, 1934
JEWISH KING LEAR, 1935
JEWISH LUCK, 1925
JEWISH MELODY, THE, 1940
JEZEBEL, 1938, A
JEZEBELS, THE
JIG SAW, 1965, A
JIG SAW, 1979
JIGGS AND MAGGIE IN COURT, 1948
JIGGS AND MAGGIE IN JACKPOT JITTERS, 1949
JIGGS AND MAGGIE IN SOCIETY, 1948, AA
JIGGS AND MAGGIE OUT WEST, 1950, AA
JIGOKUHEN
JIGOKUMEN
JIGSAW, 1949, A
JIGSAW, 1968, O
JIGSAW MAN, THE, 1984, C
JIGSAW, 1965
JILT, THE, 1922, A
JILTED JANET, 1918
JIM BLUDSO, 1917
JIM GRIMSBY'S BOY, 1916, A
JIM HANVEY, DETECTIVE, 1937, A
JIM LA HOULETTE, ROI DES VOLEURS, 1926
JIM THE CONQUEROR, 1927, A
JIM THE MAN, 1967
JIM THE PENMAN, 1921, A
JIM THORPE—ALL AMERICAN, 1951, A
JIM, THE PENMAN, 1915
JIM, THE WORLD'S GREATEST, 1976, A
JIMMIE'S MILLIONS, 1925, A
JIMMY, 1916, A
JIMMY AND SALLY, 1933, A
JIMMY BOY, 1935, A
JIMMY ORPHEUS, 1966, C
JIMMY THE GENT, 1934, A
JIMMY THE KID, 1982, A
JIMMY VALENTINE
JIMMY'S MILLIONS
JIMMY, THE BOY WONDER, 1966
JINCHOGE
JINX, 1919
JINX JUMPER, THE, 1917
JINX MONEY, 1948, A
JINXED, 1982, O
JITTERBUGS, 1943, AAA
JIVARO, 1954, A
JIVE JUNCTION, 1944, A
JIVE TURKEY, 1976
JO THE CROSSING SWEEPER, 1918, C
JOAN AT THE STAKE, 1954, A
JOAN BEDFORD IS MISSING
JOAN OF ARC, 1948, A
JOAN OF FLANDERS
JOAN OF OZARK, 1942, A
JOAN OF PARIS, 1942, A
JOAN OF PLATTSBURG, 1918, A
JOAN OF THE ANGELS, 1962, O
JOAN OF THE WOODS, 1918, O
JOAN THE WOMAN, 1916, C
JOANNA, 1925, A
JOANNA, 1968, O
JOAQUIN MARRIETA
JOB LAZADASA
JOCASTE, 1927
JOCELYN, 1922
JOCK PETERSEN
JOCKEY OF DEATH, THE, 1916
JOE, 1970, O
JOE AND ETHEL TURP CALL ON THE PRESIDENT, 1939, A
JOE AND MAXI, 1980
JOE BUTTERFLY, 1957, A
JOE DAKOTA, 1957, C
JOE HILL, 1971, C
JOE KIDD, 1972, C
JOE LOUIS STORY, THE, 1953, A
JOE MACBETH, 1955, C
JOE NAVIDAD
JOE PALOOKA
JOE PALOOKA IN FIGHTING MAD
JOE PALOOKA IN HUMPHREY TAKES A CHANCE
JOE PALOOKA IN THE BIG FIGHT, 1949, AA
JOE PALOOKA IN THE COUNTERPUNCH, 1949, AAA
JOE PALOOKA IN THE KNOCKOUT, 1947
JOE PALOOKA IN THE SQUARED CIRCLE, 1950, A
JOE PALOOKA IN TRIPLE CROSS, 1951, AA
JOE PALOOKA IN WINNER TAKE ALL, 1948, AA
JOE PALOOKA MEETS HUMPHREY, 1950, AA
JOE PALOOKA, CHAMP, 1946, AA
JOE PANTHER, 1976, AAA
JOE SMITH, AMERICAN, 1942, A
JOE'S BED-STUY BARBERSHOP: WE CUT HEADS, 1983
JOE, EL IMPLACABLE
JOEY, 1977
JOEY BOY, 1965, O
JOHANNA ENLISTS, 1918
JOHANNES, FILS DE JOHANNES, 1918
JOHANSSON GETS SCOLDED, 1945, A
JOHN AND JULIE, 1957, AAA
JOHN AND MARY, 1969, O
JOHN BARLEYCORN, 1914, A
JOHN ERMINE OF THE YELLOWSTONE, 1917
JOHN FORREST FINDS HIMSELF, 1920
JOHN GLAYDE'S HONOR, 1915, A
JOHN GOLDFARB, PLEASE COME HOME, 1964, A-C
JOHN HALIFAX, GENTLEMAN, 1915, A
JOHN HALIFAX—GENTLEMAN, 1938, A
JOHN HERIOT'S WIFE, 1920, A
JOHN LOVES MARY, 1949, A
JOHN MEADE'S WOMAN, 1937, C
JOHN NEEDHAM'S DOUBLE, 1916, A
JOHN OF THE FAIR, 1962, AAA
JOHN PAUL JONES, 1959, A
JOHN PETTICOATS, 1919
JOHN SMITH, 1922, A
JOHN WESLEY, 1954, AAA
JOHNNY ALLEGRO, 1949, A-C
JOHNNY ANGEL, 1945, A
JOHNNY APOLLO, 1940, A

JOHNNY BANCO, 1969, O
JOHNNY BELINDA, 1948, C-O
JOHNNY COME LATELY, 1943, A
JOHNNY COMES FLYING HOME, 1946, A
JOHNNY CONCHO, 1956, A
JOHNNY COOL, 1963, O
JOHNNY DANGEROUSLY, 1984, C
JOHNNY DARK, 1954, A
JOHNNY DOESN'T LIVE HERE ANY MORE, 1944, A
JOHNNY DOUGHBOY, 1943, AA
JOHNNY EAGER, 1942, C
JOHNNY FIRECLOUD, 1975
JOHNNY FRENCHMAN, 1946, A
JOHNNY GET YOUR GUN, 1919, A
JOHNNY GET YOUR HAIR CUT, 1927, A
JOHNNY GOT HIS GUN, 1971, O
JOHNNY GUITAR, 1954, C
JOHNNY HAMLET, 1972, O
JOHNNY HOLIDAY, 1949, A
JOHNNY IN THE CLOUDS, 1945, A
JOHNNY NOBODY, 1965, O
JOHNNY NORTH
JOHNNY O'CLOCK, 1947, A
JOHNNY ON THE RUN, 1953, AAA
JOHNNY ON THE SPOT, 1954, A
JOHNNY ONE-EYE, 1950, A
JOHNNY ORO
JOHNNY RENO, 1966, O
JOHNNY RING AND THE CAPTAIN'S SWORD, 1921, A
JOHNNY ROCCO, 1958, A
JOHNNY STEALS EUROPE, 1932, A
JOHNNY STOOL PIGEON, 1949, C
JOHNNY THE GIANT KILLER, 1953, AA
JOHNNY TIGER, 1966, A
JOHNNY TREMAIN, 1957, AAA
JOHNNY TROUBLE, 1957, A
JOHNNY VAGABOND
JOHNNY VIK, 1973, C
JOHNNY YUMA, 1967, O
JOHNNY, YOU'RE WANTED, 1956, A
JOHNNY-ON-THE-SPOT, 1919, A
JOHNSTOWN FLOOD, THE, 1926, A
JOHNSTOWN MONSTER, THE, 1971
JOI-UCHI
JOIN THE MARINES, 1937, A
JOKE OF DESTINY LYING IN WAIT AROUND THE CORNER LIKE A STREET BANDIT, A, 1984, C
JOKE OF DESTINY, A
JOKER IS WILD, THE, 1957, C
JOKER, THE, 1961, O
JOKERS, THE, 1967, A-C
JOKES MY FOLKS NEVER TOLD ME, 1979
JOLLY BAD FELLOW, A, 1964, C
JOLLY GENIE, THE, 1964
JOLLY OLD HIGGINS
JOLSON SINGS AGAIN, 1949, A
JOLSON STORY, THE, 1946, A
JOLT, THE, 1921, A
JONAH—WHO WILL BE 25 IN THE YEAR 2000, 1976, C
JONAS: QUI AURA 25 ANS EN L'AN 2000
JONATHAN, 1973, O
JONATHAN LIVINGSTON SEAGULL, 1973, A
JONES FAMILY IN HOLLYWOOD, THE, 1939, A
JONI, 1980, A
JONIKO
JONIKO AND THE KUSH TA KA, 1969, AAA
JORDAN IS A HARD ROAD, 1915, A
JORY, 1972, A
JOSEPH AND HIS BRETHREN
JOSEPH AND HIS BRETHREN, 1915
JOSEPH ANDREWS, 1977, O
JOSEPH IN THE LAND OF EGYPT, 1914
JOSEPH IN THE LAND OF EGYPT, 1932
JOSEPH SOLD BY HIS BROTHERS
JOSEPHINE AND MEN, 1955, A
JOSETTE, 1938, A
JOSHUA, 1976, O
JOSSELYN'S WIFE, 1919
JOSSELYN'S WIFE, 1926, A
JOSSER IN THE ARMY, 1932, A
JOSSER JOINS THE NAVY, 1932, A
JOSSER ON THE FARM, 1934, A
JOSSER ON THE RIVER, 1932, A
JOTAI
JOUR DE FETE, 1952, A
JOURNAL OF A CRIME, 1934, C
JOURNEY, 1977, O
JOURNEY AHEAD, 1947, A
JOURNEY AMONG WOMEN, 1977, O
JOURNEY BACK TO OZ, 1974, AAA
JOURNEY BENEATH THE DESERT, 1967, A
JOURNEY FOR MARGARET, 1942, AA
JOURNEY INTO DARKNESS, 1968, A
JOURNEY INTO FEAR, 1942, A
JOURNEY INTO FEAR, 1976, O
JOURNEY INTO LIGHT, 1951, C
JOURNEY INTO MIDNIGHT, 1968, A
JOURNEY INTO NOWHERE, 1963, O
JOURNEY THROUGH ROSEBUD, 1972, O
JOURNEY TO FREEDOM, 1957, A
JOURNEY TO ITALY
JOURNEY TO LOVE, 1953, A
JOURNEY TO SHILOH, 1968, C
JOURNEY TO THE BEGINNING OF TIME, 1966, AAA
JOURNEY TO THE CENTER OF THE EARTH, 1959, AAA
JOURNEY TO THE CENTER OF TIME, 1967, A
JOURNEY TO THE FAR SIDE OF THE SUN, 1969, A
JOURNEY TO THE LOST CITY, 1960, A
JOURNEY TO THE SEVENTH PLANET, 1962, C
JOURNEY TOGETHER, 1946, A
JOURNEY'S END, 1918, A
JOURNEY'S END, 1930, C
JOURNEY'S END, THE, 1921, A
JOURNEY, THE, 1959, A-C
JOURNEYS FROM BERLIN—1971, 1980, O
JOVITA, 1970, O
JOY, 1983, O
JOY AND THE DRAGON, 1916, A
JOY GIRL, THE, 1927, A
JOY HOUSE, 1964, O
JOY IN THE MORNING, 1965, O
JOY OF LEARNING, THE
JOY OF LIVING, 1938, A
JOY OF SEX, 1984, O
JOY PARADE, THE
JOY RIDE, 1935, A
JOY RIDE, 1958, C
JOY RIDE TO NOWHERE, 1978
JOY STREET, 1929, A
JOYOUS ADVENTURES OF ARISTIDE PUJOL, THE, 1920, A
JOYOUS LIAR, THE, 1919, A
JOYOUS TROUBLEMAKERS, THE, 1920, A
JOYRIDE, 1977, O
JOYSTICKS, 1983, O
JUAREZ, 1939, A
JUAREZ AND MAXIMILLIAN
JUBAL, 1956, C
JUBILEE, 1978, O
JUBILEE TRAIL, 1954, A
JUBILEE WINDOW, 1935, A
JUBILO, 1919, A
JUCKLINS, THE, 1920
JUD, 1971, O
JUDAS CITY
JUDAS WAS A WOMAN
JUDEX, 1966, C
JUDGE AND THE ASSASSIN, THE, 1979, C
JUDGE AND THE SINNER, THE, 1964, C
JUDGE HARDY AND SON, 1939, AAA
JUDGE HARDY'S CHILDREN, 1938, AAA
JUDGE HER NOT, 1921, A
JUDGE NOT, 1920, A
JUDGE NOT OR THE WOMAN OF MONA DIGGINGS, 1915, A
JUDGE PRIEST, 1934, AAA
JUDGE STEPS OUT, THE, 1949, A
JUDGE, THE, 1949, O
JUDGED BY APPEARANCES, 1916
JUDGEMENT, 1922
JUDGEMENT HOUSE, THE, 1917
JUDGEMENT, THE
JUDGMENT AT NUREMBERG, 1961, C
JUDGMENT BOOK, THE, 1935
JUDGMENT DEFERRED, 1952, A
JUDGMENT IN THE SUN
JUDGMENT OF THE HILLS, 1927, A
JUDGMENT OF THE STORM, 1924, A
JUDITH, 1965, C-O
JUDITH OF BETHULIA, 1914, C
JUDITH OF THE CUMBERLANDS, 1916, A
JUDO SAGA, 1965, C
JUDO SHOWDOWN, 1966, C
JUDY FORGOT, 1915, A
JUDY GOES TO TOWN
JUDY OF ROGUES' HARBOUR, 1920, A
JUDY'S LITTLE NO-NO, 1969, O
JUGGERNAUT, 1937, O
JUGGERNAUT, 1974, A-C
JUGGERNAUT, THE, 1915, A
JUGGLER, THE, 1953, C-O
JUKE BOX JENNY, 1942, AA
JUKE BOX RACKET, 1960, A
JUKE BOX RHYTHM, 1959, A
JUKE GIRL, 1942, A
JUKE JOINT, 1947
JULES AND JIM, 1962, C-O
JULES OF THE STRONG HEART, 1918, A
JULES VERNE'S ROCKET TO THE MOON
JULIA, 1977, A-C
JULIA MISBEHAVES, 1948, A
JULIA, DU BIST ZAUBER-HAFT
JULIE, 1956, A
JULIE DARLING, 1982, O
JULIE THE REDHEAD, 1963, A
JULIET OF THE SPIRITS, 1965, A-C
JULIETTA, 1957, A
JULIUS CAESAR, 1914
JULIUS CAESAR, 1952, A
JULIUS CAESAR, 1953, C
JULIUS CAESAR, 1970, A
JULY PORK BELLIES
JUMBO, 1962, AA
JUMP, 1971, A
JUMP FOR GLORY
JUMP INTO HELL, 1955, A
JUMPING FOR JOY, 1956, A
JUMPING JACKS, 1952, A
JUNCTION 88, 1940
JUNCTION CITY, 1952, A
JUNE BRIDE, 1948, A
JUNE FRIDAY, 1915, A
JUNE MADNESS, 1922, A
JUNE MOON, 1931, A
JUNGE LORD, DER
JUNGE SCHRIE MORD, EIN
JUNGE TORLESS, DER
JUNGLE ATTACK
JUNGLE BOOK, 1942, AAA
JUNGLE BOOK, THE, 1967, AAA
JUNGLE BRIDE, 1933, A
JUNGLE CAPTIVE, 1945, A
JUNGLE CHILD, THE, 1916, A
JUNGLE FIGHTERS
JUNGLE FLIGHT, 1947, A
JUNGLE GENTS, 1954, AA
JUNGLE GODDESS, 1948, A
JUNGLE GODS, 1927
JUNGLE HEAT, 1957, A
JUNGLE HELL, 1956
JUNGLE ISLAND
JUNGLE JIM, 1948, AAA
JUNGLE JIM IN THE FORBIDDEN LAND, 1952, AAA
JUNGLE LOVERS, THE, 1915
JUNGLE MAN, 1941, A
JUNGLE MAN-EATERS, 1954, AAA
JUNGLE MANHUNT, 1951, AAA
JUNGLE MOON MEN, 1955, AAA
JUNGLE OF CHANG, 1951, A
JUNGLE PATROL, 1948, A
JUNGLE PRINCESS, THE, 1923
JUNGLE PRINCESS, THE, 1936, A
JUNGLE QUEEN, 1946
JUNGLE RAMPAGE
JUNGLE SIREN, 1942, A
JUNGLE STREET
JUNGLE STREET GIRLS, 1963, A
JUNGLE TERROR
JUNGLE TRAIL OF THE SON OF TARZAN, 1923
JUNGLE TRAIL, THE, 1919, A
JUNGLE VIRGIN
JUNGLE WARRIORS, 1984, O
JUNGLE WOMAN
JUNGLE WOMAN, 1944, A
JUNGLE WOMAN, THE, 1926, A
JUNGLE, THE, 1914, A
JUNGLE, THE, 1952, AA
JUNIOR ARMY, 1943, AA
JUNIOR BONNER, 1972, A-C
JUNIOR MISS, 1945, AAA
JUNIOR PROM, 1946, AA
JUNKET 89, 1970, AAA
JUNKMAN, THE, 1982, C-O
JUNO AND THE PAYCOCK, 1930, A
JUPITER, 1952, A
JUPITER MENACE, THE, 1982
JUPITER'S DARLING, 1955, A
JURY OF FATE, THE, 1917
JURY OF ONE
JURY OF THE JUNGLE
JURY'S EVIDENCE, 1936, A
JURY'S SECRET, THE, 1938, A
JUST A BIG, SIMPLE GIRL, 1949, A
JUST A GIGOLO, 1931, A
JUST A GIGOLO, 1979, O
JUST A GIRL, 1916, A
JUST A MOTHER, 1923
JUST A SONG AT TWILIGHT, 1922, A
JUST A WIFE, 1920
JUST A WOMAN, 1925, A
JUST ACROSS THE STREET, 1952, A
JUST AROUND THE CORNER, 1921, A
JUST AROUND THE CORNER, 1938, AAA
JUST BE THERE, 1977
JUST BEFORE DAWN, 1946, A
JUST BEFORE DAWN, 1980, O
JUST BEFORE NIGHTFALL, 1975, A-C
JUST DECEPTION, A, 1917, C
JUST FOR A SONG, 1930, A
JUST FOR FUN, 1963, AA
JUST FOR THE HELL OF IT, 1968, O
JUST FOR THE HELL OF IT, 1968
JUST FOR TONIGHT, 1918, A
JUST FOR YOU, 1952, A
JUST GREAT

JUST IMAGINE, 1930, A
JUST JIM, 1915, A
JUST JOE, 1960, A
JUST LIKE A WOMAN, 1923, A
JUST LIKE A WOMAN, 1939, A
JUST LIKE A WOMAN, 1967, C
JUST LIKE HEAVEN, 1930, A
JUST MARRIED, 1928, A
JUST ME, 1950, A
JUST MY LUCK, 1933, A
JUST MY LUCK, 1936
JUST MY LUCK, 1957, A
JUST OFF BROADWAY, 1924, A
JUST OFF BROADWAY, 1929, A
JUST OFF BROADWAY, 1942, A
JUST ONCE MORE, 1963, O
JUST ONE MORE
JUST OUT OF COLLEGE, 1921, A
JUST OUT OF REACH, 1979, C
JUST OUTSIDE THE DOOR, 1921
JUST PALS, 1920
JUST PLAIN FOLKS, 1925
JUST SMITH
JUST SQAW, 1919
JUST SUPPOSE, 1926, A
JUST SYLVIA, 1918, A
JUST TELL ME WHAT YOU WANT, 1980, C
JUST TELL ME YOU LOVE ME, 1979
JUST THE TWO OF US, 1975
JUST THE WAY YOU ARE, 1984, C
JUST THIS ONCE, 1952, A
JUST TO BE LOVED
JUST TONY, 1922, A
JUST TRAVELIN', 1927
JUST WILLIAM, 1939, AA
JUST WILLIAM'S LUCK, 1948, A
JUST YOU AND ME, KID, 1979, C
JUSTE AVANT LA NUIT
JUSTICE, 1914
JUSTICE, 1914, A
JUSTICE, 1917
JUSTICE CAIN
JUSTICE D'ABORD, 1921
JUSTICE FOR SALE
JUSTICE OF THE FAR NORTH, 1925, A
JUSTICE OF THE RANGE, 1935, A
JUSTICE TAKES A HOLIDAY, 1933, A
JUSTINE, 1969, C
JUSTINE, 1969, O
JUVENILE COURT, 1938, A
JUVENILE JUNGLE, 1958, A
JUVENTUD A LA IMTEMPERIE

-K-

K—THE UNKNOWN, 1924, A
KADOYNG, 1974, AAA
KAGEMUSHA, 1980, C
KAGI
KAHUNA!, 1981
KAIDAN
KAIJU DAISENSO
KAIJU SOSHINGEKI
KAISER'S FINISH, THE, 1918, A
KAISER'S SHADOW, THE, 1918, A
KAISER, BEAST OF BERLIN, THE, 1918, A
KAITEI GUNKA
KAJA, UBIT CU TE
KAJIKKO
KALEIDOSCOPE, 1966, A-C
KALIA MARDAN, 1919
KAMIGAMI NO FUKAKI YOKUBO
KAMIKAZE '89, 1983, O
KAMILLA, 1984, A-C
KAMOURASKA, 1973, O
KANAL, 1961, C
KANCHENJUNGHA, 1966, A
KANGAROO, 1952, A
KANGAROO KID, THE, 1950, A
KANGAROO, THE, 1914
KANOJO
KANSAN, THE, 1943, A
KANSAS CITY BOMBER, 1972, O
KANSAS CITY CONFIDENTIAL, 1952, C-O
KANSAS CITY KITTY, 1944, A
KANSAS CITY PRINCESS, 1934, A
KANSAS CYCLONE, 1941, A
KANSAS PACIFIC, 1953, A
KANSAS RAIDERS, 1950, A
KANSAS TERRITORY, 1952, A
KANSAS TERRORS, THE, 1939, A
KAPHETZOU
KAPITANLEUTENANT PRIEN—DER STIER VON SCAPA FLOW
KAPO, 1964, O
KARAMAZOV, 1931, C
KARAMI-AI
KARATE KID, THE, 1984, A-C
KARATE KILLERS, THE, 1967, A
KARATE, THE HAND OF DEATH, 1961, C
KARE JOHN
KAREN, THE LOVEMAKER, 1970, O
KARIN, INGMAR'S DAUGHTER, 1920
KARL XII
KARMA, 1933, A
KATE PLUS TEN, 1938, A
KATERINA IZMAILOVA, 1969, A
KATHLEEN, 1938, A
KATHLEEN, 1941, AAA
KATHLEEN MAVOUREEN, 1938
KATHLEEN MAVOURNEEN, 1919, A
KATHLEEN MAVOURNEEN, 1930, A
KATHY O', 1958, A
KATHY'S LOVE AFFAIR
KATIA
KATIE DID IT, 1951, A
KATINA
KATKA'S REINETTE APPLES, 1926
KATOK I SKRIPKA
KATORGA, 1928
KAWAITA MIZUUMI
KAYA, I'LL KILL YOU, 1969, A
KAZABLAN, 1974, A
KAZAN, 1921
KAZAN, 1949, AA
KEAN, 1924
KEAN—THE MADNESS OF GENIUS
KEELER AFFAIR, THE
KEEP 'EM FLYING, 1941, AAA
KEEP 'EM ROLLING, 1934, A
KEEP 'EM SLUGGING, 1943, AA
KEEP FIT, 1937, A
KEEP GOING, 1926
KEEP HIM ALIVE
KEEP IT CLEAN, 1956, A
KEEP IT COOL
KEEP IT QUIET, 1934, A
KEEP IT UP, JACK!, 1975
KEEP MOVING, 1915, A
KEEP MY GRAVE OPEN, 1980, O
KEEP OFF! KEEP OFF!, 1975
KEEP PUNCHING, 1939
KEEP SMILING, 1925, A
KEEP SMILING, 1938, A
KEEP SMILING, 1938
KEEP TO THE RIGHT, 1920
KEEP YOUR POWDER DRY, 1945, A
KEEP YOUR SEATS PLEASE, 1936, A
KEEP, THE, 1983, O
KEEPER OF THE BEES, 1935, A
KEEPER OF THE BEES, 1947, A
KEEPER OF THE BEES, THE, 1925
KEEPER OF THE DOOR, 1919, A
KEEPER OF THE FLAME, 1942, A
KEEPER, THE, 1976, A
KEEPERS OF YOUTH, 1931, A
KEEPING COMPANY, 1941, A
KEEPING ON, 1981
KEEPING UP WITH LIZZIE, 1921, A
KEITH OF THE BORDER, 1918
KEK BALVANY
KELLY, 1981
KELLY AND ME, 1957, AA
KELLY OF THE SECRET SERVICE, 1936, A
KELLY OF THE U.S.A.
KELLY THE SECOND, 1936, A
KELLY'S HEROES, 1970, C-O
KEMPO SAMURAI
KENNEDY SQUARE, 1916, A
KENNEL MURDER CASE, THE, 1933, A
KENNER, 1969, C
KENNY AND CO., 1976, C
KENT THE FIGHTING MAN, 1916
KENT, THE FIGHTING MAN, 1916, A
KENTUCKIAN, THE, 1955, A
KENTUCKIANS, THE, 1921, A
KENTUCKY, 1938, AA
KENTUCKY BLUE STREAK, 1935, A
KENTUCKY CINDERELLA, A, 1917, A
KENTUCKY COLONEL, THE, 1920
KENTUCKY COURAGE
KENTUCKY DAYS, 1923, A
KENTUCKY DERBY, THE, 1922, A
KENTUCKY FRIED MOVIE, THE, 1977, O
KENTUCKY HANDICAP, 1926, A
KENTUCKY JUBILEE, 1951, A
KENTUCKY KERNELS, 1935, A
KENTUCKY MINSTRELS, 1934, A
KENTUCKY MOONSHINE, 1938, AAA
KENTUCKY PRIDE, 1925
KENTUCKY RIFLE, 1956, A
KENYA—COUNTRY OF TREASURE, 1964
KEPT HUSBANDS, 1931, C
KES, 1970, C
KETTLE CREEK
KETTLES IN THE OZARKS, THE, 1956, AAA
KETTLES ON OLD MACDONALD'S FARM, THE, 1957, AAA
KETTO GENRYU JIMA
KEY LARGO, 1948, C
KEY MAN, THE, 1957, A
KEY OF THE WORLD, THE, 1918
KEY TO HARMONY, 1935, A
KEY TO POWER, THE, 1918
KEY TO THE CITY, 1950, A
KEY TO YESTERDAY, THE, 1914
KEY WITNESS, 1947, C
KEY WITNESS, 1960, O
KEY, THE, 1934, A
KEY, THE, 1958, O
KEYHOLE, THE, 1933, A
KEYS OF THE KINGDOM, THE, 1944, A
KEYS OF THE RIGHTEOUS, THE, 1918
KEYS, THE, 1917
KHARTOUM, 1966, C
KHYBER PATROL, 1954, A
KIBITZER, THE, 1929, A
KICK BACK, THE, 1922, A
KICK IN, 1917, A
KICK IN, 1922, A
KICK IN, 1931, C
KICK-OFF, THE, 1926, A
KICKING THE MOON AROUND
KID BLUE, 1973, C
KID BOOTS, 1926, A
KID BROTHER, THE, 1927, A
KID CANFIELD THE REFORM GAMBLER, 1922, A
KID COLOSSUS, THE
KID COMES BACK, THE, 1937, A
KID COURAGEOUS, 1935, A
KID DYNAMITE, 1943, AA
KID FOR TWO FARTHINGS, A, 1956, A
KID FROM AMARILLO, THE, 1951, A
KID FROM ARIZONA, THE, 1931, A
KID FROM BOOKLYN, THE, 1946, AA
KID FROM BROKEN GUN, THE, 1952, A
KID FROM CANADA, THE, 1957, AA
KID FROM CLEVELAND, THE, 1949, A
KID FROM GOWER GULCH, THE, 1949, A
KID FROM KANSAS, THE, 1941, C
KID FROM KOKOMO, THE, 1939, A
KID FROM LEFT FIELD, THE, 1953, AAA
KID FROM NOT SO BIG, THE, 1978
KID FROM SANTA FE, THE, 1940, AA
KID FROM SPAIN, THE, 1932, AA
KID FROM TEXAS, THE, 1939, AAA
KID FROM TEXAS, THE, 1950, C
KID GALAHAD, 1937, A-C
KID GALAHAD, 1962, A
KID GLOVE KILLER, 1942, C
KID GLOVES, 1929, C
KID IS CLEVER, THE, 1918
KID MILLIONS, 1934, AAA
KID MONK BARONI, 1952, C
KID NIGHTINGALE, 1939, A
KID RANGER, THE, 1936, A
KID RIDES AGAIN, THE, 1943, A
KID RODELO, 1966, C
KID SISTER, THE, 1927, A
KID SISTER, THE, 1945, A
KID VENGEANCE, 1977, C
KID'S CLEVER, THE, 1929, A
KID'S LAST FIGHT, THE
KID'S LAST RIDE, THE, 1941, A
KID, THE, 1916, A
KID, THE, 1921, AA
KIDCO, 1984, C
KIDDER & KO., 1918
KIDNAP OF MARY LOU, THE
KIDNAPPED, 1917, A
KIDNAPPED, 1938, AAA
KIDNAPPED, 1948, AAA
KIDNAPPED, 1960, AAA
KIDNAPPED, 1971, AA
KIDNAPPED, 1934
KIDNAPPERS, THE, 1964, A
KIDNAPPERS, THE, 1953
KIDNAPPING OF THE PRESIDENT, THE, 1980, O
KIEV COMEDY, A, 1963, C
KIGEKI DAI SHOGEKI
KIKI, 1926, A
KIKI, 1931, A
KIL 1
KILDARE OF STORM, 1918, A
KILL
KILL, 1968, C
KILL A DRAGON, 1967, O
KILL AND GO HIDE
KILL AND KILL AGAIN, 1981, O
KILL BABY KILL, 1966, O
KILL CASTRO
KILL HER GENTLY, 1958, O
KILL KILL KILL, 1972, O
KILL ME TOMORROW, 1958, C
KILL OR BE KILLED, 1950, C
KILL OR BE KILLED, 1967, C
KILL OR BE KILLED, 1980, C
KILL OR CURE, 1962, C

KILL SQUAD, 1982, O
KILL THE GOLDEN GOOSE, 1979
KILL THE UMPIRE, 1950, AA
KILL THEM ALL AND COME BACK ALONE, 1970, O
KILL, THE, 1968, O
KILL, THE, 1973
KILL-JOY, THE, 1917
KILLER APE, 1953, AA
KILLER AT LARGE, 1936, O
KILLER AT LARGE, 1947, O
KILLER BATS
KILLER BEHIND THE MASK, THE
KILLER DILL, 1947, C
KILLER DILLER, 1948
KILLER DINO
KILLER ELITE, THE, 1975, O
KILLER FISH, 1979, O
KILLER FORCE, 1975, O
KILLER GRIZZLY
KILLER INSIDE ME, THE, 1976, O
KILLER IS LOOSE, THE, 1956, O
KILLER LEOPARD, 1954, A
KILLER McCOY, 1947, A
KILLER ON A HORSE
KILLER SHARK, 1950, A
KILLER SHREWS, THE, 1959, C
KILLER THAT STALKED NEW YORK, THE, 1950, O
KILLER WALKS, A, 1952, A
KILLER WITH A LABEL
KILLER'S CAGE
KILLER'S CARNIVAL, 1965
KILLER'S DELIGHT, 1978
KILLER'S KISS, 1955, C
KILLER'S MOON, 1978
KILLER, THE
KILLER, THE
KILLER, THE, 1921, C
KILLERS ARE CHALLENGED
KILLERS FROM KILIMANJARO
KILLERS FROM SPACE, 1954, A
KILLERS OF KILIMANJARO, 1960, A
KILLERS OF THE PRAIRIE
KILLERS OF THE WILD, 1940, AAA
KILLERS THREE, 1968, O
KILLERS, THE, 1946, C
KILLERS, THE, 1964, C-O
KILLERS, THE, 1984, O
KILLING AT OUTPOST ZETA, THE, 1980
KILLING FIELDS, THE, 1984, O
KILLING GAME, THE, 1968, C
KILLING GROUND, THE, 1972
KILLING HEAT, 1984, O
KILLING HOUR, THE, 1982, O
KILLING KIND, THE, 1973, O
KILLING OF A CHINESE BOOKIE, THE, 1976, C
KILLING OF ANGEL STREET, THE, 1983, A
KILLING TOUCH, THE, 1983
KILLING URGE
KILLING, THE, 1956, C
KILLPOINT, 1984, O
KILMENY, 1915, A
KILROY ON DECK
KILROY WAS HERE, 1947, AA
KILTIES THREE, 1918, A
KIM, 1950, AA
KIMBERLEY JIM, 1965, A
KIN FOLK
KIND HEARTS AND CORONETS, 1949, A-C
KIND LADY, 1935, A
KIND LADY, 1951, O
KIND OF LOVING, A, 1962, A-C
KIND STEPMOTHER, 1936, AAA
KINDLED COURAGE, 1923, A
KINDLING, 1915, A
KINDRED OF THE DUST, 1922, A
KINFOLK, 1970, O
KING AND COUNTRY, 1964, C
KING AND FOUR QUEENS, THE, 1956, A
KING AND I, THE, 1956, AAA
KING AND THE CHORUS GIRL, THE, 1937, AA
KING ARTHUR WAS A GENTLEMAN, 1942, A
KING BLANK, 1983, O
KING CHARLES, 1913, A
KING COBRA
KING COWBOY, 1928
KING CREOLE, 1958, A
KING DINOSAUR, 1955, AA
KING FOR A NIGHT, 1933, C
KING FRAT, 1979
KING IN NEW YORK, A, 1957, A
KING IN SHADOW, 1961, A
KING KELLY OF THE U.S.A, 1934, A
KING KONG, 1933, A-C
KING KONG, 1976, C-O
KING KONG ESCAPES, 1968, C
KING KONG VERSUS GODZILLA, 1963, C
KING KONG'S COUNTERATTACK
KING LEAR, 1916, A
KING LEAR, 1971, C
KING MONSTER, 1977
KING MURDER, THE, 1932, 0
KING OEDIPUS
KING OF AFRICA
KING OF ALCATRAZ, 1938, C
KING OF BURLESQUE, 1936, A
KING OF CHINATOWN, 1939, O
KING OF COMEDY, THE, 1983, C
KING OF CRIME, THE, 1914
KING OF DIAMONDS, THE, 1918, A
KING OF DODGE CITY, 1941, A
KING OF GAMBLERS, 1937, A
KING OF HEARTS, 1936, AA
KING OF HEARTS, 1967, C
KING OF HOCKEY, 1936, AA
KING OF KINGS, 1961, AA
KING OF KINGS, THE, 1927, AA
KING OF MARVIN GARDENS, THE, 1972, C-O
KING OF PARIS, THE, 1934, A
KING OF THE ALCATRAZ
KING OF THE ARENA, 1933, A
KING OF THE BANDITS, 1948, A
KING OF THE BULLWHIP, 1950, C
KING OF THE CASTLE, 1925, A
KING OF THE CASTLE, 1936, A
KING OF THE CORAL SEA, 1956, C
KING OF THE COWBOYS, 1943, AAA
KING OF THE DAMNED, 1936, C
KING OF THE GAMBLERS, 1948, A
KING OF THE GRIZZLIES, 1970, AAA
KING OF THE GYPSIES, 1978, O
KING OF THE HERD, 1927, A
KING OF THE ICE RINK
KING OF THE JUNGLE, 1933, A
KING OF THE JUNGLELAND
KING OF THE KHYBER RIFLES, 1953, A
KING OF THE KHYBER RIFLES, 1929
KING OF THE LUMBERJACKS, 1940, A
KING OF THE MOUNTAIN, 1981, O
KING OF THE MOUNTAIN, 1964
KING OF THE NEWSBOYS, 1938, A
KING OF THE PACK, 1926
KING OF THE PECOS, 1936, A
KING OF THE PEOPLE, A, 1917
KING OF THE RITZ, 1933, A
KING OF THE ROARING TWENTIES—THE STORY OF ARNOLD ROTHSTEIN, 1961, C
KING OF THE RODEO, 1929, A
KING OF THE ROYAL MOUNTED, 1936, A
KING OF THE SADDLE, 1926, A
KING OF THE SIERRAS, 1938, A
KING OF THE STALLIONS, 1942, A
KING OF THE TURF, 1939, A
KING OF THE TURF, THE, 1926, A
KING OF THE UNDERWORLD, 1939, A-C
KING OF THE UNDERWORLD, 1952, A
KING OF THE WILD
KING OF THE WILD HORSES, 1947, A
KING OF THE WILD HORSES, THE, 1924, A
KING OF THE WILD HORSES, THE, 1934, A
KING OF THE WILD STALLIONS, 1959, AAA
KING OF THE ZOMBIES, 1941, C
KING ON MAIN STREET, THE, 1925
KING RAT, 1965, O
KING RICHARD AND THE CRUSADERS, 1954, A
KING SOLOMON OF BROADWAY, 1935, A
KING SOLOMON'S MINES, 1937, A
KING SOLOMON'S MINES, 1950, A
KING SOLOMON'S TREASURE, 1978, A
KING SPRUCE, 1920, A
KING STEPS OUT, THE, 1936, A
KING TUT-ANKH-AMEN'S EIGHTH WIFE, 1923, A
KING'S CREEK LAW, 1923, A
KING'S CUP, THE, 1933, A
KING'S DAUGHTER, THE, 1916, A
KING'S GAME, THE, 1916, A
KING'S HIGHWAY, THE, 1927
KING'S JESTER, THE, 1947, O
KING'S OUTCAST, THE
KING'S PIRATE, 1967, A
KING'S RHAPSODY, 1955, A
KING'S ROMANCE, THE
KING'S ROW, 1942, C-O
KING'S THIEF, THE, 1955, A
KING'S VACATION, THE, 1933, A
KING, MURRAY, 1969, O
KING, QUEEN, JOKER, 1921, A
KING, QUEEN, KNAVE, 1972, O
KING, THE
KINGDOM OF HUMAN HEARTS, THE, 1921
KINGDOM OF LOVE, THE, 1918, A
KINGDOM OF THE SPIDERS, 1977, C
KINGDOM OF TWILIGHT, THE, 1929
KINGDOM OF YOUTH, THE, 1918
KINGDOM WITHIN, THE, 1922, A
KINGFISH CAPER, THE, 1976, A
KINGFISHER CAPER, THE
KINGFISHER'S ROOST, THE, 1922, A
KINGFISHER, THE, 1982
KINGS AND DESPERATE MEN, 1984, C
KINGS GO FORTH, 1958, A
KINGS OF THE HILL, 1976
KINGS OF THE ROAD, 1976, C
KINGS OF THE SUN, 1963, O
KINKAID, GAMBLER, 1916, A
KINKY COACHES & THE POM POM PUSSYCATS, THE, 1981
KINO, THE PADRE ON HORSEBACK, 1977
KINSMAN, THE, 1919
KIPPERBANG, 1984, A-C
KIPPS
KIPPS, 1921, A
KIRA KIRALINA, 1927
KIRI NI MUSEBU YORU
KIRLIAN WITNESS, THE, 1978, O
KIRU
KISENGA, MAN OF AFRICA, 1952, C
KISMET, 1916
KISMET, 1920, A
KISMET, 1930, A
KISMET, 1944, A
KISMET, 1955, A
KISS AND KILL
KISS AND MAKE UP, 1934, A
KISS AND TELL, 1945, A
KISS BARRIER, THE, 1925, A
KISS BEFORE DYING, A, 1956, A
KISS BEFORE THE MIRROR, THE, 1933, A
KISS DADDY GOODBYE, 1981
KISS FOR CINDERELLA, A, 1926, A
KISS FOR CORLISS, A, 1949, A
KISS FOR SUSIE, A, 1917, A
KISS FROM EDDIE, A
KISS HER GOODBYE, 1959
KISS IN A TAXI, A, 1927
KISS IN THE DARK, A, 1925, A
KISS IN THE DARK, A, 1949, A
KISS IN TIME, A, 1921, A
KISS ME
KISS ME AGAIN, 1925, A
KISS ME AGAIN, 1931, A
KISS ME DEADLY, 1955, O
KISS ME GOODBYE, 1935, A
KISS ME GOODBYE, 1982, C
KISS ME KATE, 1953, AA
KISS ME, SERGEANT, 1930, A
KISS ME, STUPID, 1964, C
KISS MY BUTTERFLY
KISS MY GRITS, 1982
KISS OF DEATH, 1916
KISS OF DEATH, 1947, C-O
KISS OF EVIL, 1963, C
KISS OF FIRE, 1955, A
KISS OF FIRE, THE, 1940, A
KISS OF HATE, THE, 1916
KISS OF THE TARANTULA, 1975, O
KISS OF THE VAMPIRE, THE
KISS OR KILL, 1918
KISS THE BLOOD OFF MY HANDS, 1948, C-O
KISS THE BOYS GOODBYE, 1941, A
KISS THE BRIDE GOODBYE, 1944, A
KISS THE GIRLS AND MAKE THEM DIE, 1967, O
KISS THE GIRLS AND SEE THEM DIE, 1968
KISS THE OTHER SHEIK, 1968, C
KISS THEM FOR ME, 1957, A
KISS TOMORROW GOODBYE, 1950, C-O
KISS, THE, 1916, A
KISS, THE, 1921
KISS, THE, 1929, A
KISSED, 1922, A
KISSES, 1922, A
KISSES FOR BREAKFAST, 1941, A
KISSES FOR MY PRESIDENT, 1964, A
KISSES FOR THE PRESIDENT
KISSIN' COUSINS, 1964, A
KISSING BANDIT, THE, 1948, A
KISSING CUP, 1913
KISSING CUP'S RACE, 1920
KISSING CUP'S RACE, 1920, A
KISSING CUP'S RACE, 1930, A
KIT CARSON, 1928, A
KIT CARSON, 1940, A
KIT CARSON OVER THE GREAT DIVIDE, 1925
KITCHEN, THE, 1961, A
KITTEN WITH A WHIP, 1964, C-O
KITTY, 1929, A
KITTY, 1929
KITTY, 1945, A
KITTY AND THE BAGMAN, 1983, O
KITTY CAN'T HELP IT, 1975
KITTY FOYLE, 1940, A-C
KITTY KELLY, M.D., 1919
KITTY MACKAY, 1917
KIVALINA OF THE ICE LANDS, 1925
KLANSMAN, THE, 1974, C
KLAUN FERDINAND A RAKETA
KLEINES ZELT UND GROSSE LIEBE
KLONDIKE, 1932, A

KLONDIKE ANNIE, 1936, A-C
KLONDIKE FEVER, 1980, A
KLONDIKE FURY, 1942, A
KLONDIKE KATE, 1944, A
KLUTE, 1971, O
KNACK ... AND HOW TO GET IT, THE, 1965, C
KNACK, THE
KNAVE OF DIAMONDS, THE, 1921
KNAVE OF HEARTS
KNAVE OF HEARTS, THE, 1919, A
KNICKERBOCKER BUCKAROO, THE, 1919, A
KNICKERBOCKER HOLIDAY, 1944, A
KNIFE FOR THE LADIES, A, 1973
KNIFE IN THE BODY, THE
KNIFE IN THE WATER, 1963, O
KNIFE, THE, 1918, A
KNIGHT ERRANT, THE, 1922
KNIGHT IN LONDON, A, 1930, A
KNIGHT OF THE EUCHARIST, 1922, A
KNIGHT OF THE PLAINS, 1939, A
KNIGHT OF THE RANGE, A, 1916, A
KNIGHT OF THE WEST, A, 1921, A
KNIGHT WITHOUT ARMOR, 1937, A
KNIGHTRIDERS, 1981, C
KNIGHTS FOR A DAY, 1937, A
KNIGHTS OF THE BLACK CROSS
KNIGHTS OF THE RANGE, 1940, A
KNIGHTS OF THE ROUND TABLE, 1953, A
KNIGHTS OF THE SQUARE TABLE, 1917
KNIGHTS OF THE TEUTONIC ORDER, THE, 1962, A
KNIVES OF THE AVENGER, 1967, A
KNOCK, 1926
KNOCK, 1955, A
KNOCK ON ANY DOOR, 1949, C
KNOCK ON THE DOOR, THE, 1923, A
KNOCK ON WOOD, 1954, A
KNOCKING AT HEAVEN'S DOOR, 1980
KNOCKNAGOW, 1918, A
KNOCKOUT, 1941, A
KNOCKOUT KID, THE, 1925, A
KNOCKOUT REILLY, 1927, A
KNOCKOUT, THE, 1923, A
KNOCKOUT, THE, 1925, A
KNOW YOUR MEN, 1921, A
KNOWING MEN, 1930, A
KNUTE ROCKNE—ALL AMERICAN, 1940, AA
KOENIGSMARK, 1923
KOENIGSMARK, 1935, A
KOGDA DEREVYA BYLI BOLSHIMI
KOHAYAGAWA-KE NO AKI
KOJIRO, 1967, A
KOKKINA PHANARIA
KOKOSEI BANCHO
KOL MAMZER MELECH
KOL NIDRE, 1939
KOLBERG, 1945, O
KOLYBELNAYA
KOMMANDO SINAI
KONA COAST, 1968, C
KONEC SPRNA V HOTELU OZON
KONGA, 1961, C
KONGA, 1939
KONGA, THE WILD STALLION, 1939, AA
KONGI'S HARVEST, 1971
KONGO, 1932, O
KONSKA OPERA
KOREA PATROL, 1951, C
KORT AR SOMMAREN
KOSHER KITTY KELLY, 1926
KOSHOKU ICHIDAI ONNA
KOTCH, 1971, A-C
KOTO
KOTO NO TAIYO
KRADETSUT NA PRASKOVI
KRAKATIT, 1948, C
KRAKATOA, EAST OF JAVA, 1969, A
KRALJ PETROLEJA
KRAMER VS. KRAMER, 1979, A
KRASNAYA PALATKA
KREMLIN LETTER, THE, 1970, C-O
KREUTZER SONATA, THE, 1915
KRIEGSGERICHT
KRIEMHILD'S REVENGE, 1924, C
KRIEMHILDS RACHE
KRIVI PUT
KRONOS, 1957, A
KRONOS, 1974
KRUEZER EMDEN
KRULL, 1983, A
KULTUR, 1918
KUMONOSUJO
KUNG FU HALLOWEEN, 1981
KUNGSLEDEN
KUNISADA CHUJI
KURAGEJIMA—LEGENDS FROM A SOUTHERN ISLAND, 1970, O
KUREIZI OGON SAKUSEN
KUROBE NO TAIYO
KUROENKO, 1968, O
KVARTERET KORPEN
KVINNORS VANTAN
KWAIDAN, 1965, O
KYOMO WARE OZORANI ARI
KYONETSU NO KISETSU
KYUBI NO KITSUNE TO TOBIMARU

-L-

L' APACHE, 1919
L'ABBE CONSTANTIN, 1925
L'ABSOLUTION, 1922
L'ACCUSATEUR, 1920
L'ADOLESCENT
L'AFFAIRE DE LA RUE DE LOUREINE, 1923
L'AFFAIRE DU COURRIER DE LYON, 1923
L'AFFICHE, 1925
L'AFRICAN
L'AGE D'OR, 1979, C
L'AGONIE DE JERUSALEM, 1926
L'AGONIE DES AIGLES, 1921
L'ALIBI, 1917
L'AMANT DE LADY CHATTERLEY
L'AME DE PIERRE, 1918
L'AME DE PIERRE, 1928
L'AME DU BRONZE, 1918
L'AME DU MOTEUR: LE CARBURATEUR, 1926
L'AMI FRITZ, 1920
L'AMORE
L'AMORE DIFFICILE
L'AMOUR, 1973, O
L'AMOUR PAR TERRE
L'ANATRA ALL'ARANCIA
L'ANEE DERNIERE A MARIENBAD
L'ANGOISSANTE AVENTURE, 1920
L'ANNIVERSAIRE, 1916
L'APPEL DU SANG, 1920
L'APRE LUTTE, 1917
L'ARGENT, 1929
L'ARGENT, 1984, O
L'ARLESIENNE, 1922
L'ARMEE DES OMBRES, 1969, C
L'ARPETE, 1929
L'ARRIVISTE, 1924
L'AS DES AS
L'ASSASSIN HABITE AU 21
L'ASSOCIE
L'ASSOMOIR, 1921
L'ATALANTE, 1947, C
L'ATLANTIDE, 1921
L'ATLANTIDE, 1932, Ger.
L'ATLANTIDE, 1967, Fr./Ital.
L'ATRE, 1923
L'ATTENTAT
L'AUBERGE ROUGE, 1923
L'AUTRE, 1917
L'AUTRE AILE, 1924
L'AVENTURE, 1923
L'AVENTURE DES MILLIONS, 1916
L'AVENTURIER, 1924
L'AVEU
L'AVOCAT, 1925
L'AVVENTURA, 1960, A
L'AVVENTURIERO
L'ECLIPSE
L'ECLISSE
L'ECOLE BUISSONIERE
L'ECUYERE, 1922
L'ELISIR D'AMORE
L'EMPIRE DU DIAMENT, 1921
L'EMPREINTE, 1916
L'EMPRISE, 1924
L'ENFANCE NUE
L'ENFANT DU CARNAVAL, 1921
L'ENGRENAGE, 1919
L'ENGRENAGE, 1923
L'ENIGMATIQUE MONSIEUR PARKES, 1930, A
L'ENIGME, 1919
L'ENIGME, 1919
L'ENIGME DU MONT AGEL, 1924
L'ENVOLEE, 1921
L'EPAVE, 1917
L'EPERVIER, 1924
L'EPINGLE ROUGE, 1921
L'ESPION
L'ESPIONE, 1923
L'ESPIONE AUX YEUX NOIRS, 1926
L'ETAU, 1920
L'ETE DE LA SAINT MARTIN, 1920
L'ETE MEURTRIER
L'ETERNEL FEMININE, 1921
L'ETOILE DU NORD, 1983, O
L'ETRANGE AVENTURE DU DOCTEUR WORKS, 1921
L'ETRANGER
L'EVANGILE SELON SAINT MATTHIEU
L'EVASION, 1922
L'EVEIL, 1924
L'HEURE TRAGIQUE, 1916
L'HEUREUX MORT, 1924
L'HOMME AU CHAPEAU ROND
L'HOMME DE RIO
L'HOMME DES BALEARES, 1925
L'HOMME DU LARGE, 1920
L'HOMME DU MINNESOTA
L'HOMME DU TRAIN 117, 1923
L'HOMME EN COLERE
L'HOMME ET LA POUPEE, 1921
L'HOMME INUSABLE, 1923
L'HOMME MERVEILLEUX, 1922
L'HOMME QUI AIMAT LES FEMMES
L'HOMME QUI REVIENT DE LION, 1917
L'HOMME SAN VISAGE, 1919
L'HOMME Z L'HISPANO, 1927
L'IBIS BLEU, 1919
L'IDEE DE FRANCOISE, 1923
L'IDIOT
L'IDOLE BRISEE, 1920
L'ILE D'AMOUR, 1928
L'ILE DE LA MORT, 1923
L'ILE ENCHANTEE, 1927
L'IMAGE, 1926
L'IMMORTELLE, 1969, C
L'INCONNU, 1921
L'INHUMAINE, 1923
L'INONDATION, 1924
L'INSIGNE MYSTERIEUX, 1922
L'INSTINCT, 1917
L'INSTINCT EST MAITRE, 1917
L'INTRIGO
L'INVITATION AU VOYAGE, 1927
L'IRONIE DU DESTIN, 1924
L'IRONIE DU SORT, 1924
L'OBSTACLE, 1918
L'OCCIDENT, 1928
L'OEIL DE SAINT-YVES, 1919
L'OEIL DU MALIN
L'OEILLET BLANC, 1923
L'OMBRE DECHIREE, 1921
L'OMBRE DU BONHEUR, 1924
L'OMBRE DU PECHE, 1922
L'OR ET L'AMOUR
L'ORAGE, 1917
L'ORAGE, 1917
L'ORDONNANCE, 1921
L'ORDONNANCE, 1921
L'OURAGAN SUR LA MONTAGE, 1922
L'OURAGAN SUR LA MONTAGE, 1922
L'OURS
L'ULTIMO UOMO DELLA TERRA
L'UN ET L'AUTRE
L'UNE CHANTE L'AUTRE PAS
L'UOMO DALLE DUE OMBRE
L-SHAPED ROOM, THE, 1962, C
LA BABY SITTER, 1975, O
LA BAI DES ANGES
LA BALANCE, 1983, O
LA BATAILLE, 1923
LA BATAILLE DU RAIL
LA BEAUTE DU DIABLE
LA BELLA MUGNAIA
LA BELLE AMERICAINE, 1961, A
LA BELLE CAPTIVE
LA BELLE DAME SANS MERCI, 1920
LA BELLE EQUIPE
LA BELLE ET LA BETE
LA BELLE ET LE CAVALIER
LA BELLE NIVERNAISE, 1923
LA BELLE RUSSE, 1919
LA BETE HUMAINE, 1938, A
LA BETE TRAQUEE, 1923
LA BISBETICA DOMATA
LA BLESSURE, 1925
LA BOHEME
LA BOHEME, 1926
LA BOHEME, 1965, A
LA BONNE HOTESE, 1918
LA BONNE SOUPE, 1964, C
LA BOUM, 1983, A
LA BOUQUETIERE DES INNOCENTS, 1922
LA BOURASQUE, 1920
LA BRIERE, 1925
LA CAGE, 1975, C
LA CAGE AUX FOLLES, 1979, O
LA CAGE AUX FOLLES II, 1981, C-O
LA CALOMNIE, 1917
LA CALVAIRE DE DONA PISA, 1925
LA CASSE
LA CHAMBRE VERTE
LA CHASSE A L'HOMME
LA CHATELAINE DU LIBAN, 1926
LA CHAUSSEE DES GEANTS, 1926
LA CHAUSSEE DES GEANTS, 1926
LA CHEVAUCHE BLANCHE, 1923
LA CHEVRE AUX PIEDS D'OR, 1926
LA CHIENNE, 1975, C-O
LA CHINOISE, 1967, C-O
LA CHUTE DE LA MAISON USHER
LA CIBLE, 1925
LA CIGARETTE, 1919

LA CINEMA AU SERVICE DE L'HISTOIRE, 1927
LA CINTURA DI CASTITA
LA CIQUILLE ET LE CLERGYMAN, 1928
LA CITE FOUDROYEE, 1924
LA CITTA PRIGIONIERA
LA CITTA SI DIFENDE
LA CLE DE VOUTE, 1925
LA COLLECTIONNEUSE, 1971, C-O
LA CONGA NIGHTS, 1940, A
LA CONGIUNTURA
LA CORDE AU COU, 1926
LA COURSE AU FLAMBEAU, 1925
LA CROISADE, 1920
LA CROIX DES VIVANTS
LA CUCARACHA, 1961, A
LA DAME MASQUEE, 1924
LA DANSEUSE ORCHIDEE, 1928
LA DANSEUSE VOILEE, 1917
LA DECADE PRODIGIEUSE
LA DENTELLIERE
LA DETTE, 1920
LA DETTE DE SANG, 1923
LA DISTANCE, 1918
LA DIVINE CROISIERE, 1928
LA DIXIEME SYMPHONIE, 1918
LA DOLCE VITA, 1961, C
LA DOUBLE EXISTENCE DE LORD SAMSEY, 1924
LA DOULEUR, 1925
LA DUBARRY, 1914
LA FABULEUSE AVENTURE DE MARCO POLO
LA FAUTE D'ODETTE MARECHAL, 1920
LA FAUTE DE MONIQUE, 1928
LA FAUTEUIL 47, 1926
LA FEE DES NEIGES, 1920
LA FEMME AUX BOTTES ROUGES
LA FEMME AUX DEUX VISAGES, 1920
LA FEMME D'A COTE
LA FEMME DE MON POTE
LA FEMME DE NULLE PART, 1922
LA FEMME DU BOULANGERS
LA FEMME ET LE PANTIN, 1929
LA FEMME INCONNUE, 1923
LA FEMME INFIDELE, 1969, C
LA FEMME NUE
LA FEMME REVEE, 1929
LA FEMME SU VOISIN, 1929
LA FERME DU PENDU, 1946, C
LA FETE A HENRIETTE
LA FETE ESPAGNOLE, 1919
LA FEU FOLLET
LA FIANCEE DU DISPARU, 1921
LA FILLE BIEN GARDEE, 1924
LA FILLE DE L'EAU, 1924
LA FILLE DE MATA HARI, n(SE
LA FILLE DE PUISATIER
LA FILLE DES CHIFFONNIERS, 1922
LA FILLE DU DIABLE
LA FILLE DU PEUPLE, 1920
LA FILLE SANS VOILE
LA FIN DE MONTE, 1927
LA FIN DU MONDE
LA FLAMBEE DE REVES, 1924
LA FLAMME, 1925
LA FLAMME CACHE, 1918
LA FLUTE A SIX SCHTROUMPFS
LA FOLIE DES VAILLANTS, 1925
LA FOLIE DU DOUTE, 1923
LA FOLLE DES GRANDEURS
LA FONTAINE DES AMOURS, 1924
LA FORET QUI TUE, 1924
LA FORTUNA DI ESSERE DONNA
LA FUGA, 1966, O
LA FUGITIVE, 1918
LA FUGUE DE LILY, 1917
LA GALERIE DES MONSTRES, 1924
LA GLU, 1927
LA GOSSELINE, 1923
LA GOUTTE DE SANG, 1924
LA GRANDE BOUFFE, 1973, C-O
LA GRANDE BOURGEOISE, 1977, C
LA GRANDE ILLUSION
LA GRANDE PASSION, 1928
LA GUERRE EST FINIE, 1967, C-O
LA GUITARE ET LA JAZZ BAND, 1922
LA HABANERA, 1937, A
LA HIJA DEL ENGANO
LA HURLE, 1921
LA JALOUSIE DU BARBOUILLE, 1929
LA JOVEN
LA JUSTICIERE, 1925
LA KERMESSE HEROIQUE
LA LA LUCILLE, 1920
LA LAMA NEL CORPO
LA LEGENDE DE SOEUR BEATRIX, 1923
LA LINEA DEL CIELO
LA LUNE DANS LE CANIVEAU
LA LUTTE POUR LA VIE, 1920
LA MADONE DES SLEEPINGS, 1928
LA MAIN QUI A TUE, 1924
LA MAISON D'ARGILE, 1918
LA MAISON DU MALTAIS, 1927
LA MAISON DU SOLEIL, 1929
LA MAISON VIDE, 1921
LA MALDICION DE LA MOMIA AZTECA
LA MAMAM ET LA PUTAIN
LA MANDARINE
LA MANDRAGOLA
LA MARCA DEL MUERTO
LA MARCHAND DE PLAISIR, 1923
LA MARCHE DU DESTIN, 1924
LA MARCHE NUPTIALE, 1929
LA MARCHE TRIOMPHALE, 1916
LA MARIE DU PORT, 1951, C
LA MARIEE ETAIT EN NOIR
LA MARSEILLAISE, 1920
LA MARSEILLAISE, 1938, A
LA MARTYRE DE STE. MAXENCE, 1927
LA MASCOTTE DES POILUS, 1918
LA MATERNELLE, 1925
LA MATERNELLE, 1933, A
LA MEILLEURE MAITRESSE, 1929
LA MERVELILLEUSE VIE DE JEANNE D'ARC, 1929
LA MONTEE VERS L'ACROPOLE, 1920
LA MORT DU SOLEIL, 1922
LA MORT EN CE JARDIN
LA MORTADELLA
LA MORTE EN DIRECT
LA MORTE RISALE A IERI SERA
LA MORTE VIENE DALLA SPAZIO
LA MUERTA EN EST JARDIN
LA NAVE DE LOS MONSTRUOS, 1959, C-O
LA NEUVAINE DE COLETTE, 1925
LA NIEGE SUR LE PAS, 1924
LA NOTTE, 1961, C-O
LA NOTTE BRAVA, 1962, O
LA NOUVELLE ANTIGONE, 1916
LA NUIT AMERICAINE
LA NUIT DE LA REVANCHE, 1924
LA NUIT DE SAINT JEAN, 1922
LA NUIT DE VARENNES, 1983, O
LA NUIT DES GENERAUX
LA NUIT DU 11 SEPTEMBRE, 1922
LA NUIT DU 13, 1921
LA NUIT EST A NOUS, 1927
LA NUIT ROUGE, 1924
LA P'TITE DU SIXIEME, 1917
LA PAIX CHEZ SOI, 1921
LA PARISIENNE, 1958, C-O
LA PART DE L'OMBRE
LA PASSANTE, 1983, C
LA PEAU DOUCE
LA PENTE, 1928
LA PERE GORIOT, 1921
LA PERMISSION
LA PETIT SIRENE, 1984, C
LA PETITE CAFE
LA PETITE CHOCOLATIERE, 1927
LA PLANETE SAUVAGE
LA PORTEUSE DE PAIN, 1923
LA POSSESSION, 1929
LA POUPEE
LA POUPEE, 1920
LA POUPEE, 1920, A
LA PREUVE, 1921
LA PRINCESSE AUX CLOWNS, 1925
LA PRINCESSE MANDANE, 1928
LA PRISE DE POUVOIR PAR LOUIS XIV
LA PRISONNIERE, 1969, O
LA PROIE, 1917
LA PROIE DU VENT, 1927
LA PROMISE DE L'AUBE
LA PROVINCIALE
LA QUESTION
LA RAFALE, 1920
LA RESIDENCIA
LA RESURRECTION DU BOUIF, 1922
LA REVANCHE DU MAUDIT, 1929
LA RIPOSTE, 1922
LA RONDE, 1954, O
LA RONDE INFERNALE, 1927
LA ROSE ESCORCHEE
LA ROUE, 1923
LA ROUTE DE DEVOIR, 1918
LA ROUTE EST BELLE
LA RUE DES AMOURS FACILES
LA RUE DU PAVE D'AMOUR, 1923
LA RUSE, 1922
LA SIGNORA SENZA CAMELIE
LA SIN-VENTURA, 1922
LA SIRENE DE PIERRE, 1922
LA SIRENE DES TROPIQUES, 1928
LA SIRENE DU MISSISSIPPI
LA STRADA, 1956, A-C
LA STRADA PER FORT ALAMO
LA SULTANE DE L'AMOUR, 1919
LA SUPREME EPOEE, 1919
LA SYMPHONIE PASTORALE
LA SYMPHONIE PATHETIQUE, 1929
LA TENDA ROSSA
LA TENTATION, 1929
LA TERRA TREMA, 1947, A
LA TERRAZA
LA TERRE, 1921
LA TERRE DU DIABLE, 1921
LA TERRE PROMISE, 1925
LA TOSCA, 1918
LA TRAVIATA, 1968, A
LA TRAVIATA, 1982, A
LA TRUITE
LA VACCA E IL PRIGIONIERO
LA VACHE ET LE PRISONNIER
LA VALLEE DES PHARAOHS
LA VENGANZA DEL SEXO
LA VENGEANCE DE MALLET, 1920
LA VERITE, 1922
LA VESTALE DU GANGE, 1927
LA VIA LATTEA
LA VIACCIA, 1962, C-O
LA VICTOIRE EN CHANTANT
LA VIE CONTINUE, 1982, A
VIE D'UNE REINE, 1917
LA VIE DE BOHEME, 1916
LA VIE DE CHATEAU, 1967, A
LA VIE DEVANT SOI
LA VIE EST UN ROMAN
LA VIE MIRACULEIUSE DE THERESE MARTIN, 1929
LA VIERGE FOLLE, 1929
LA VIOLENZA E L'MORE
LA VIRGEN DE LA CARIDAD, 1930
LA VISITA, 1966, O
LA VIVANTE EPINGLE, 1921
LA VOGLIA MATTA
LA VOIE LACTEE
LA VOIX DE LA MER, 1921
LA VOYANTE, 1923
LA ZOME DE LA MORT, 1917
LABBRA ROSSE
LABORATORY, 1980
LABOUR LEADER, THE, 1917, A
LABURNUM GROVE, 1936, A
LABYRINTH
LABYRINTH, THE, 1915
LACE, 1928
LACEMAKER, THE, 1977, O
LACKEY AND THE LADY, THE, 1919
LACOMBE, LUCIEN, 1974, O
LAD AND THE LION, THE, 1917
LAD FROM OUR TOWN, 1941, A
LAD, THE, 1935, A
LAD: A DOG, 1962, AAA
LADDER JINX, THE, 1922
LADDER OF LIES, THE, 1920
LADDIE, 1920
LADDIE, 1926
LADDIE, 1935, AAA
LADDIE, 1940, AAA
LADDIE BE GOOD, 1928, A
LADIES AND GENTLEMEN, THE FABULOUS STAINS, 1982, O
LADIES AT EASE, 1927, A
LADIES AT PLAY, 1926, A
LADIES BEWARE, 1927
LADIES COURAGEOUS, 1944, A
LADIES CRAVE EXCITEMENT, 1935, A
LADIES IN DISTRESS, 1938, A
LADIES IN LOVE, 1930, A
LADIES IN LOVE, 1936, A
LADIES IN RETIREMENT, 1941, C
LADIES IN WASHINGTON
LADIES LOVE BRUTES, 1930, A
LADIES LOVE DANGER, 1935, A
LADIES MAN, THE, 1961, A
LADIES MUST DRESS, 1927, A
LADIES MUST LIVE, 1921
LADIES MUST LIVE, 1940, A
LADIES MUST LOVE, 1933, A
LADIES MUST PLAY, 1930, A
LADIES OF LEISURE, 1926
LADIES OF LEISURE, 1930, A-C
LADIES OF THE BIG HOUSE, 1932, A
LADIES OF THE CHORUS, 1948, A
LADIES OF THE JURY, 1932, A
LADIES OF THE MOB
LADIES OF THE MOB, 1928, A
LADIES OF THE NIGHT CLUB, 1928
LADIES OF THE PARK, 1964, C
LADIES OF WASHINGTON, 1944, A
LADIES SHOULD LISTEN, 1934, A
LADIES THEY TALK ABOUT, 1933, A
LADIES TO BOARD, 1924, A
LADIES WHO DO, 1964, A
LADIES' DAY, 1943, A
LADIES' MAN, 1931, C
LADIES' MAN, 1947, A
LADIES' NIGHT IN A TURKISH BATH, 1928
LADS OF THE VILLAGE, THE, 1919
LADY AND GENT, 1932, A

LADY AND THE BANDIT, THE, 1951, A
LADY AND THE BEARD, THE, 1931
LADY AND THE BURGLAR, THE, 1915
LADY AND THE DOCTOR, THE
LADY AND THE MOB, THE, 1939, A
LADY AND THE MONSTER, THE, 1944, C
LADY AND THE OUTLAW, THE
LADY AND THE TRAMP, 1955, AAA
LADY AT MIDNIGHT, 1948, A
LADY AUDLEY'S SECRET, 1920
LADY BARNACLE, 1917
LADY BE CAREFUL, 1936, A
LADY BE GAY
LADY BE GOOD, 1928, A
LADY BE GOOD, 1941, A
LADY BEHAVE, 1937, A
LADY BEWARE
LADY BODYGUARD, 1942, A
LADY BY CHOICE, 1934, A
LADY CAROLINE LAMB, 1972, A
LADY CHASER, 1946, A
LADY CHATTERLEY'S LOVER, 1959, A
LADY CHATTERLEY'S LOVER, 1981, O
LADY CHATTERLY VS. FANNY HILL, 1980
LADY CLARE, THE, 1919
LADY COCOA, 1975
LADY CONFESSES, THE, 1945, A
LADY CONSENTS, THE, 1936, A
LADY CRAVED EXCITEMENT, THE, 1950, A
LADY DANCES, THE
LADY DOCTOR, THE, 1963, C
LADY DRACULA, THE, 1974, O
LADY ESCAPES, THE, 1937, A
LADY EVE, THE, 1941, A
LADY FIGHTS BACK, 1937, A
LADY FOR A DAY, 1933, A
LADY FOR A NIGHT, 1941, A
LADY FRANKENSTEIN, 1971, O
LADY FREDERICK
LADY FROM BOSTON, THE
LADY FROM CHEYENNE, 1941, A
LADY FROM CHUNGKING, 1943, A
LADY FROM HELL, THE, 1926, A
LADY FROM LISBON, 1942, A
LADY FROM LONGACRE, THE, 1921
LADY FROM LOUISIANA, 1941, A
LADY FROM NOWHERE, 1931, A
LADY FROM NOWHERE, 1936, A
LADY FROM SHANGHAI, THE, 1948, C
LADY FROM TEXAS, THE, 1951, A
LADY FROM THE SEA, THE, 1929, A
LADY GAMBLES, THE, 1949, A
LADY GANGSTER, 1942, A
LADY GENERAL, THE, 1965, A
LADY GODIVA, 1955, A
LADY GODIVA RIDES AGAIN, 1955, A
LADY GREY, 1980, O
LADY HAMILTON
LADY HAMILTON, 1969, O
LADY HAS PLANS, THE, 1942, A
LADY ICE, 1973, CA
LADY IN A CAGE, 1964, O
LADY IN A JAM, 1942, A
LADY IN CEMENT, 1968, O
LADY IN DANGER, 1934, A
LADY IN DISTRESS, 1942, A
LADY IN ERMINE, THE, 1927
LADY IN LOVE, A, 1920, A
LADY IN QUESTION, THE, 1940, A
LADY IN RED, THE, 1979, O
LADY IN SCARLET, THE, 1935, A
LADY IN THE CAR WITH GLASSES AND A GUN, THE, 1970, O
LADY IN THE DARK, 1944, A
LADY IN THE DEATH HOUSE, 1944, A
LADY IN THE FOG
LADY IN THE IRON MASK, 1952, A
LADY IN THE LAKE, 1947, A
LADY IN THE LIBRARY, THE, 1917
LADY IN THE MORGUE, 1938, A
LADY IS A SQUARE, THE, 1959, A
LADY IS FICKLE, THE, 1948, A
LADY IS WILLING, THE, 1934, A
LADY IS WILLING, THE, 1942, A
LADY JANE GREY, 1936, A
LADY JENNIFER, 1915
LADY KILLER, 1933, A
LADY KILLERS, THE
LADY L, 1965, C
LADY LIBERTY, 1972, C
LADY LIES, THE, 1929, A
LADY LUCK, 1936, A
LADY LUCK, 1946, A
LADY MISLAID, A, 1958, A
LADY NOGGS-PEERESS, 1929, A
LADY OBJECTS, THE, 1938, A
LADY OF BURLESQUE, 1943, C
LADY OF CHANCE, A, 1928, A
LADY OF DECEIT
LADY OF MONZA, THE, 1970, O
LADY OF MYSTERY
LADY OF QUALITY, A, 1913
LADY OF QUALITY, A, 1924
LADY OF RED BUTTE, THE, 1919
LADY OF SCANDAL, THE, 1930, A
LADY OF SECRETS, 1936, A
LADY OF THE BOULEVARDS
LADY OF THE DUGOUT, 1918
LADY OF THE HAREM, THE, 1926
LADY OF THE LAKE, THE, 1928, A
LADY OF THE NIGHT, 1925, A
LADY OF THE PAVEMENTS, 1929, A
LADY OF THE PHOTOGRAPH, THE, 1917
LADY OF THE ROSE
LADY OF THE SHADOWS
LADY OF THE TROPICS, 1939, C
LADY OF VENGEANCE, 1957, A
LADY ON A TRAIN, 1945, A
LADY ON THE TRACKS, THE, 1968, A
LADY OSCAR, 1979, C
LADY OWNER, THE, 1923
LADY PAYS OFF, THE, 1951, A
LADY POSSESSED, 1952, A
LADY RAFFLES, 1928
LADY REFUSES, THE, 1931, A
LADY REPORTER
LADY ROBINHOOD, 1925, A
LADY ROSE'S DAUGHTER, 1920
LADY SAYS NO, THE, 1951, A
LADY SCARFACE, 1941, A
LADY SINGS THE BLUES, 1972, O
LADY SURRENDERS, A, 1930, A
LADY SURRENDERS, A, 1947, A
LADY TAKES A CHANCE, A, 1943, A
LADY TAKES A FLYER, THE, 1958, A
LADY TAKES A SAILOR, THE, 1949, A
LADY TETLEY'S DEGREE, 1920
LADY TO LOVE, A, 1930, A
LADY TUBBS, 1935, A
LADY VANISHES, THE, 1938, A
LADY VANISHES, THE, 1980, C
LADY WANTS MINK, THE, 1953, A
LADY WHO DARED, THE, 1931, A
LADY WHO LIED, THE, 1925
LADY WINDERMERE'S FAN, 1916
LADY WINDERMERE'S FAN, 1925, A
LADY WINDERMERE'S FAN
LADY WITH A LAMP, THE, 1951, A
LADY WITH A PAST, 1932, A
LADY WITH RED HAIR, 1940, A
LADY WITH THE DOG, THE, 1962, A
LADY WITH THE LAMP, THE
LADY WITHOUT CAMELLIAS, THE, 1981, C-O
LADY WITHOUT PASSPORT, A, 1950, A
LADY'S FROM KENTUCKY, THE, 1939, A
LADY'S MORALS, A, 1930, A
LADY'S NAME, A, 1918
LADY'S PROFESSION, A, 1933, A
LADY, LET'S DANCE, 1944, A
LADY, STAY DEAD, 1982, O
LADY, THE, 1925
LADYBIRD, THE, 1927, A
LADYBUG, LADYBUG, 1963, C
LADYFINGERS, 1921
LADYKILLERS, THE, 1956, A-C
LAFAYETTE, 1963, AA
LAFAYETTE ESCADRILLE, 1958, A
LAFAYETTE, WE COME, 1918
LAFFIN' FOOL, THE, 1927, A
LAHOMA, 1920
LAILA
LAIR OF THE WOLF, THE, 1917
LAKE OF DRACULA, 1973, O
LAKE PLACID SERENADE, 1944, A
LAKE, THE, 1970, O
LAMA NEL CORPO, LA
LAMB AND THE LION, THE, 1919
LAMB, THE, 1915, A
LAMBETH WALK, THE, 1940, A
LAMENT OF THE PATH, THE
LAMP IN ASSASSIN MEWS, THE, 1962, A
LAMP IN THE DESERT, 1922
LAMP OF DESTINY, 1919
LAMP STILL BURNS, THE, 1943, A
LAMPLIGHTER, THE, 1921, A
LANCASHIRE LASS, A, 1915
LANCASHIRE LUCK, 1937, A
LANCELOT AND GUINEVERE
LANCELOT DU LAC
LANCELOT OF THE LAKE, 1975, C
LANCER SPY, 1937, A
LAND AND THE LAW
LAND BEYOND THE LAW, 1937, A
LAND BEYOND THE LAW, THE, 1927
LAND JUST OVER YONDER, THE, 1916
LAND O' LIZARDS, 1916
LAND OF FIGHTING MEN, 1938, A
LAND OF FURY, 1955, A
LAND OF HOPE AND GLORY, 1927, A
LAND OF HOPE, THE, 1921
LAND OF HUNTED MEN, 1943, A
LAND OF JAZZ, THE, 1920
LAND OF LONG SHADOWS, 1917
LAND OF MISSING MEN, THE, 1930, A
LAND OF MY FATHERS, 1921
LAND OF MYSTERY, THE, 1920
LAND OF NO RETURN, THE, 1981, A
LAND OF OZ
LAND OF PROMISE, THE, 1917
LAND OF SIX GUNS, 1940
LAND OF THE LAWLESS, 1927
LAND OF THE LAWLESS, 1947, A
LAND OF THE MINOTAUR, 1976, O
LAND OF THE MISSING MEN
LAND OF THE OPEN RANGE, 1941, A
LAND OF THE OUTLAWS, 1944, A
LAND OF THE PHARAOHS, 1955, A-C
LAND OF THE SILVER FOX, 1928, AA
LAND OF THE SIX GUNS, 1940, A
LAND OF WANTED MEN, 1932, A
LAND RAIDERS, 1969, C
LAND THAT TIME FORGOT, THE, 1975, A
LAND UNKNOWN, THE, 1957, A
LAND WE LOVE, THE
LAND WITHOUT MUSIC
LANDFALL, 1953, A
LANDLOPER, THE, 1918
LANDLORD, THE, 1970, C
LANDON'S LEGACY, 1916
LANDRU, 1963, O
LANDRUSH, 1946, A
LANDSLIDE, 1937, A
LANE THAT HAD NO TURNING, THE, 1922
LANGTAN
LARAMIE, 1949, A
LARAMIE KID, THE, 1935
LARAMIE MOUNTAINS, 1952, A
LARAMIE TRAIL, THE, 1944, A
LARCENY, 1948, A-C
LARCENY IN HER HEART, 1946, A
LARCENY LANE
LARCENY ON THE AIR, 1937, A
LARCENY STREET, 1941, A
LARCENY WITH MUSIC, 1943, A
LARCENY, INC., 1942, A
LARGE ROPE, THE
LARGE ROPE, THE, 1953, A
LARIAT KID, THE, 1929, A
LARIATS AND SIXSHOOTERS, 1931
LARMES DE CROCODILE, 1916
LAS CUATRO VERDADES
LAS RATAS NO DUERMEN DE NOCHE, 1974, O
LAS VEGAS 500 MILLIONS
LAS VEGAS FREE-FOR-ALL, 1968, C
LAS VEGAS HILLBILLYS, 1966, A
LAS VEGAS LADY, 1976, A
LAS VEGAS NIGHTS, 1941, A
LAS VEGAS SHAKEDOWN, 1955, A
LAS VEGAS STORY, THE, 1952, A
LASCA, 1919
LASCA OF THE RIO GRANDE, 1931, A
LASCIVIOUSNESS OF THE VIPER, THE, 1920
LASERBLAST, 1978, C
LASH OF DESTINY, THE, 1916
LASH OF JEALOUSY, THE
LASH OF PINTO PETE, THE, 1924
LASH OF POWER, THE, 1917
LASH OF THE LAW, 1926
LASH OF THE PENITENTES
LASH OF THE WHIP, 1924, A
LASH, THE, 1916
LASH, THE, 1930, A
LASH, THE, 1934, C
LASKY JEDNE PLAVOLASKY
LASS O' THE LOOMS, A, 1919, A
LASSIE FROM LANCASHIRE, 1938, AA
LASSIE'S GREAT ADVENTURE, 1963, AAA
LASSIE, COME HOME, 1943, AAA
LASSIE, THE VOYAGER, 1966
LASSITER, 1984, O
LAST ACT OF MARTIN WESTON, THE, 1970, C
LAST ACT, THE, 1916
LAST ADVENTURE, THE, 1968, A
LAST ADVENTURERS, THE, 1937, A
LAST AFFAIR, THE, 1976, O
LAST ALARM, THE, 1926, A
LAST ALARM, THE, 1940
LAST AMERICAN HERO, THE, 1973, C
LAST AMERICAN VIRGIN, THE, 1982, O
LAST ANGRY MAN, THE, 1959, A
LAST ASSIGNMENT, THE, 1936
LAST BANDIT, THE, 1949, A
LAST BARRICADE, THE, 1938, C
LAST BATTLE, THE
LAST BLITZKRIEG, THE, 1958, A
LAST BRIDGE, THE, 1957, O
LAST CARD, THE, 1921

LAST CASTLE, THE
LAST CHALLENGE, THE, 1916
LAST CHALLENGE, THE, 1967, A
LAST CHANCE, THE, 1921, A
LAST CHANCE, THE, 1926, A
LAST CHANCE, THE, 1937, A
LAST CHANCE, THE, 1945, A
LAST CHAPTER, THE, 1915, A
LAST CHASE, THE, 1981, A
LAST COMMAND, THE, 1928, A
LAST COMMAND, THE, 1955, A
LAST COMMAND, THE, 1942
LAST CONCERT, THE, 1915
LAST COUPON, THE, 1932, A
LAST CROOKED MILE, THE, 1946, A
LAST CURTAIN, THE, 1937, A
LAST DANCE, THE, 1930, A
LAST DAY OF THE WAR, THE, 1969, A
LAST DAYS OF BOOT HILL, 1947, A
LAST DAYS OF DOLWYN, THE, 1949
LAST DAYS OF MAN ON EARTH, THE, 1975, O
LAST DAYS OF MUSSOLINI, 1974, A
LAST DAYS OF PLANET EARTH
LAST DAYS OF POMPEII, THE, 1935, A
LAST DAYS OF POMPEII, THE, 1960, A
LAST DAYS OF SODOM AND GOMORRAH, THE
LAST DETAIL, THE, 1973, O
LAST DOOR, THE, 1921
LAST EDITION, THE, 1925, A
LAST EGYPTIAN, THE, 1914, A
LAST EMBRACE, 1979, O
LAST ESCAPE, THE, 1970, A
LAST EXPRESS, THE, 1938, A
LAST FEELINGS, 1981
LAST FIGHT, THE, 1983
LAST FIGHT, THE, 1983, O
LAST FLIGHT OF NOAH'S ARK, THE, 1980, AA
LAST FLIGHT, THE, 1931, A
LAST FOUR DAYS, THE
LAST FRONTIER UPRISING, 1947, A
LAST FRONTIER, THE, 1926
LAST FRONTIER, THE, 1955, A
LAST GAME, THE, 1964, C
LAST GAME, THE, 1983
LAST GANGSTER, THE, 1937, A
LAST GANGSTER, THE, 1944
LAST GENERATION, THE, 1971
LAST GENTLEMAN, THE, 1934, A
LAST GLORY OF TROY
LAST GRAVE, THE
LAST GREAT TREASURE, THE
LAST GRENADE, THE, 1970, C
LAST GUNFIGHTER, THE
LAST GUNFIGHTER, THE, 1961, A
LAST HARD MEN, THE, 1976, O
LAST HERO
LAST HILL, THE, 1945, A
LAST HOLIDAY, 1950, A
LAST HORROR FILM, THE, 1984, O
LAST HORSEMAN, THE, 1944, A
LAST HOUR, THE, 1923
LAST HOUR, THE, 1930, A
LAST HOUSE ON DEAD END STREET, 1977, O
LAST HOUSE ON THE LEFT, 1972, O
LAST HOUSE ON THE LEFT, PART II
LAST HUNT, THE, 1956, C
LAST HUNTER, THE, 1984, O
LAST HURRAH, THE, 1958, A
LAST JOURNEY, THE, 1936, A
LAST KIDS ON EARTH, THE, 1983
LAST LAP, 1928
LAST LAUGH, THE, 1924, A
LAST LOAD, THE, 1948, AAA
LAST MAN, 1932, A
LAST MAN ON EARTH, THE, 1924
LAST MAN ON EARTH, THE, 1964, O
LAST MAN TO HANG, THE, 1956, C
LAST MAN, THE, 1916
LAST MAN, THE, 1924
LAST MAN, THE, 1968, C
LAST MARRIED COUPLE IN AMERICA, THE, 1980, O
LAST MERCENARY, THE, 1969, C
LAST METRO, THE, 1981, C-O
LAST MILE, THE, 1932, A
LAST MILE, THE, 1959, C
LAST MOMENT, THE, 1923
LAST MOMENT, THE, 1928
LAST MOMENT, THE, 1954, A
LAST MOMENT, THE, 1966
LAST MOMENT, THE, 1976
LAST MOVIE, THE, 1971, O
LAST MUSKETEER, THE, 1952, A
LAST MUSKETEER, THE, 1952
LAST NIGHT AT THE ALAMO, 1984, O
LAST OF HIS PEOPLE, THE, 1919
LAST OF MRS. CHEYNEY, THE, 1929, A
LAST OF MRS. CHEYNEY, THE, 1937, A
LAST OF SHEILA, THE, 1973, C
LAST OF SUMMER
LAST OF THE AMERICAN HOBOES, THE, 1974
LAST OF THE BADMEN, 1957, A
LAST OF THE BUCCANEERS, 1950, A
LAST OF THE CARNABYS, THE, 1917
LAST OF THE CAVALRY, THE
LAST OF THE CLINTONS, THE, 1935, A
LAST OF THE COMANCHES, 1952, A
LAST OF THE COWBOYS, THE
LAST OF THE DESPERADOES, 1956, A
LAST OF THE DUANES, 1930, A
LAST OF THE DUANES, 1941, A
LAST OF THE DUANES, THE, 1919
LAST OF THE DUANES, THE, 1924
LAST OF THE FAST GUNS, THE, 1958, A
LAST OF THE INGRAHAMS, THE, 1917, A
LAST OF THE KNUCKLEMEN, THE, 1981, A
LAST OF THE LONE WOLF, 1930, A
LAST OF THE MAFFIA, THE, 1915
LAST OF THE MOHICANS, THE, 1920, A
LAST OF THE MOHICANS, THE, 1936, A
LAST OF THE PAGANS, 1936, A
LAST OF THE PONY RIDERS, 1953, A
LAST OF THE RED HOT LOVERS, 1972, A
LAST OF THE REDMEN, 1947, AA
LAST OF THE REDSKINS
LAST OF THE RENEGADES, 1966, A
LAST OF THE SECRET AGENTS?, THE, 1966, A
LAST OF THE VIKINGS, THE, 1962, A
LAST OF THE WARRENS, THE, 1936, A
LAST OF THE WILD HORSES, 1948, A
LAST OUTLAW, THE, 1927
LAST OUTLAW, THE, 1936, A
LAST OUTPOST, THE, 1935, A
LAST OUTPOST, THE, 1951, A
LAST PAGE, THE
LAST PARADE, THE, 1931, A
LAST PAYMENT, 1921
LAST PERFORMANCE, THE, 1929, C
LAST PICTURE SHOW, THE, 1971, C-0
LAST PLANE OUT, 1983
LAST PORNO FLICK, THE, 1974, O
LAST POSSE, THE, 1953, A
LAST POST, THE, 1929, C
LAST REBEL, THE, 1918
LAST REBEL, THE, 1961, C
LAST REBEL, THE, 1971, C
LAST REMAKE OF BEAU GESTE, THE, 1977, C
LAST REUNION, 1978
LAST RHINO, THE, 1961, AAA
LAST RIDE, THE, 1932, A
LAST RIDE, THE, 1944, A
LAST RITES, 1980, O
LAST ROMAN, THE
LAST ROSE OF SUMMER, THE, 1920, A
LAST ROSE OF SUMMER, THE, 1937, A
LAST ROUND-UP, THE, 1934, A
LAST ROUND-UP, THE, 1947, AA
LAST ROUNDUP, THE, 1929, A
LAST RUN, THE, 1971, A
LAST SAFARI, THE, 1967, A
LAST SENTENCE, THE, 1917
LAST SHOT YOU HEAR, THE, 1969, C
LAST STAGE, THE
LAST STAGECOACH WEST, THE, 1957, A
LAST STAND, THE, 1938, A
LAST STARFIGHTER, THE, 1984, C
LAST STOP ON THE NIGHT TRAIN, 1976
LAST STOP, THE, 1949, O
LAST STRAW, THE, 1920, A
LAST SUMMER, 1969, O
LAST SUNSET, THE, 1961, C-O
LAST TANGO IN ACAPULCO, THE, 1975
LAST TEN DAYS, THE, 1956, A
LAST THREE, 1942
LAST TIDE, THE, 1931
LAST TIME I SAW ARCHIE, THE, 1961, A
LAST TIME I SAW PARIS, THE, 1954, A
LAST TOMAHAWK, THE, 1965, A
LAST TOMB OF LIGEIA
LAST TRAIL, 1921, A
LAST TRAIL, THE, 1927, A
LAST TRAIL, THE, 1934, A
LAST TRAIN FROM BOMBAY, 1952, A
LAST TRAIN FROM GUN HILL, 1959, C
LAST TRAIN FROM MADRID, THE, 1937, A
LAST TYCOON, THE, 1976, C
LAST UNICORN, THE, 1982, AAA
LAST VALLEY, THE, 1971, A
LAST VICTIM, THE
LAST VOLUNTEER, THE, 1914, A
LAST VOYAGE, THE, 1960, A
LAST WAGON, THE, 1956, C
LAST WALTZ, THE, 1927
LAST WALTZ, THE, 1936, A
LAST WAR, THE, 1962, C
LAST WARNING, THE, 1929, A
LAST WARNING, THE, 1938, A
LAST WARRIOR, THE
LAST WAVE, THE, 1978, A
LAST WHITE MAN, THE, 1924
LAST WILL OF DR. MABUSE, THE
LAST WINTER, THE, 1983
LAST WITNESS, THE, 1925, A
LAST WOMAN OF SHANG, THE, 1964, A
LAST WOMAN ON EARTH, THE, 1960, A
LAST WORD, THE, 1979, A
LAST YEAR AT MARIENBAD, 1962, C
LATE AT NIGHT, 1946, A
LATE AUTUMN, 1973, A
LATE EDWINA BLACK, THE
LATE EXTRA, 1935, A
LATE GEORGE APLEY, THE, 1947, A
LATE LIZ, THE, 1971, A
LATE MATTHEW PASCAL, THE, 1925
LATE SHOW, THE, 1977, A-C
LATEST FROM PARIS, THE, 1928, A
LATIN LOVE, 1930, A
LATIN LOVERS, 1953, A
LATIN QUARTER
LATITUDE ZERO, 1969, AAA
LAUGH AND GET RICH, 1931, A
LAUGH IT OFF, 1939, A
LAUGH IT OFF, 1940, A
LAUGH PAGLIACCI, 1948, A
LAUGH YOUR BLUES AWAY, 1943, A
LAUGH, CLOWN, LAUGH, 1928, A
LAUGHING ANNE, 1954, A
LAUGHING AT DANGER, 1924, A
LAUGHING AT DANGER, 1940, A
LAUGHING AT DEATH, 1929
LAUGHING AT LIFE, 1933, A
LAUGHING AT TROUBLE, 1937, A
LAUGHING BILL HYDE, 1918
LAUGHING BOY, 1934, A
LAUGHING CAVALIER, THE, 1917
LAUGHING IN THE SUNSHINE, 1953, A
LAUGHING IRISH EYES, 1936, A
LAUGHING LADY, THE, 1930, A
LAUGHING LADY, THE, 1950, A
LAUGHING POLICEMAN, THE, 1973, O
LAUGHING SINNERS, 1931, C
LAUGHTER, 1930, A-C
LAUGHTER AND TEARS, 1921, A
LAUGHTER HOUSE, 1984, C
LAUGHTER IN HELL, 1933, A
LAUGHTER IN PARADISE, 1951, AA
LAUGHTER IN THE AIR
LAUNDRY GIRL, THE
LAURA, 1944, A
LAUTLOSE WAFFEN
LAVENDER AND OLD LACE, 1921, A
LAVENDER BATH LADY, THE, 1922, A
LAVENDER HILL MOB, THE, 1951, A
LAVIRINT SMRTI
LAW AND DISORDER, 1940, A
LAW AND DISORDER, 1958, A
LAW AND DISORDER, 1974, O
LAW AND JAKE WADE, THE, 1958, A
LAW AND LAWLESS, 1932, A
LAW AND LEAD, 1937, A
LAW AND ORDER, 1932, A
LAW AND ORDER, 1940, A
LAW AND ORDER, 1942, A
LAW AND ORDER, 1953, A
LAW AND ORDER, 1936
LAW AND ORDER, 1936
LAW AND THE LADY, THE, 1924
LAW AND THE LADY, THE, 1951, A
LAW AND THE MAN, 1928
LAW AND THE OUTLAW, 1925
LAW AND THE WOMAN, THE, 1922
LAW AND TOMBSTONE, THE
LAW BEYOND THE RANGE, 1935, A
LAW COMES TO GUNSIGHT, THE, 1947
LAW COMES TO TEXAS, THE, 1939, A
LAW COMMANDS, THE, 1938, A
LAW DECIDES, THE, 1916
LAW DEMANDS, THE
LAW DEMANDS, THE, 1924
LAW DIVINE, THE, 1920
LAW FOR TOMBSTONE, 1937, A
LAW FORBIDS, THE, 1924, A
LAW HUSTLERS, THE
LAW IN HER HANDS, THE, 1936, A
LAW IS THE LAW, THE, 1959, A
LAW MEN, 1944, A
LAW OF COMPENSATION, 1927
LAW OF COMPENSATION, THE, 1917
LAW OF FEAR, 1928
LAW OF MEN, THE, 1919
LAW OF NATURE, THE, 1919
LAW OF THE 45'S, 1935
LAW OF THE BADLANDS, 1950, A
LAW OF THE BARBARY COAST, 1949, A
LAW OF THE CANYON, 1947
LAW OF THE GOLDEN WEST, 1949, A
LAW OF THE GREAT NORTHWEST, THE, 1918
LAW OF THE JUNGLE, 1942, A

LAW OF THE LAND, THE, 1917, A
LAW OF THE LASH, 1947, A
LAW OF THE LAWLESS, 1964, A
LAW OF THE LAWLESS, THE, 1923, A
LAW OF THE MOUNTED, 1928, A
LAW OF THE NORTH, 1932, AA
LAW OF THE NORTH, THE, 1917
LAW OF THE NORTH, THE, 1918
LAW OF THE NORTH, THE, 1918
LAW OF THE NORTHWEST, 1943, A
LAW OF THE PAMPAS, 1939, A
LAW OF THE PANHANDLE, 1950, A
LAW OF THE PLAINS, 1929
LAW OF THE PLAINS, 1929
LAW OF THE PLAINS, 1938, A
LAW OF THE RANGE, 1941, A
LAW OF THE RANGE, THE, 1928, A
LAW OF THE RANGER, 1937, A
LAW OF THE RIO
LAW OF THE RIO GRANDE, 1931, A
LAW OF THE SADDLE, 1944, A
LAW OF THE SEA, 1932, A
LAW OF THE SNOW COUNTRY, THE, 1926, A
LAW OF THE TEXAN, 1938, A
LAW OF THE TIMBER, 1941, A
LAW OF THE TONG, 1931, A
LAW OF THE TROPICS, 1941, A
LAW OF THE UNDERWORLD, 1938, A
LAW OF THE VALLEY, 1944, A
LAW OF THE WEST, 1932
LAW OF THE WEST, 1949, A
LAW OF THE WILD, 1941
LAW OF THE YUKON, THE, 1920
LAW OF THE YUKON, THE, 1920
LAW OR LOYALTY, 1926
LAW OR LOYALTY, 1926
LAW RIDES AGAIN, THE, 1943, A
LAW RIDES WEST, THE
LAW RIDES, THE, 1936, A
LAW RUSTLERS, THE, 1923
LAW RUSTLERS, THE, 1923
LAW THAT DIVIDES, THE, 1919
LAW THAT DIVIDES, THE, 1919
LAW THAT FAILED, THE, 1917
LAW THAT FAILED, THE, 1917
LAW UNTO HIMSELF, A, 1916
LAW UNTO HIMSELF, A, 1916
LAW VS. BILLY THE KID, THE, 1954, A
LAW WEST OF TOMBSTONE, THE, 1938, A
LAW'S LASH, THE, 1928
LAW'S OUTLAW, THE, 1918
LAW, THE, 1940
LAW, THE, 1958
LAWBREAKERS, THE, 1960
LAWFUL CHEATERS, 1925, A
LAWFUL LARCENY, 1923, A
LAWFUL LARCENY, 1930, A
LAWLESS BORDER, 1935, A
LAWLESS BREED, THE, 1946, AA
LAWLESS BREED, THE, 1952, A
LAWLESS CLAN
LAWLESS CODE, 1949, A
LAWLESS COWBOYS, 1952, A
LAWLESS EIGHTIES, THE, 1957, C
LAWLESS EMPIRE, 1946, A
LAWLESS FRONTIER, THE, 1935, A
LAWLESS LAND, 1937, A
LAWLESS LEGION, THE, 1929, A
LAWLESS LOVE, 1918
LAWLESS MEN, 1924
LAWLESS NINETIES, THE, 1936, A
LAWLESS PLAINSMEN, 1942, A
LAWLESS RANGE, 1935, A
LAWLESS RIDER, THE, 1954, A
LAWLESS RIDERS, 1936, A
LAWLESS STREET, A, 1955, A
LAWLESS TRAILS, 1926
LAWLESS VALLEY, 1932
LAWLESS VALLEY, 1938, A
LAWLESS WOMAN, THE, 1931, A
LAWLESS, THE, 1950, A-C
LAWMAN, 1971, C
LAWMAN IS BORN, A, 1937, A
LAWRENCE OF ARABIA, 1962, C
LAWTON STORY, THE, 1949, A
LAWYER MAN, 1933, A
LAWYER'S SECRET, THE, 1931, A
LAWYER, THE, 1969, O
LAXDALE HALL
LAY THAT RIFLE DOWN, 1955, A
LAZARILLO, 1963, A
LAZY BONES
LAZY LIGHTNING, 1926, A
LAZY RIVER, 1934, A
LAZYBONES, 1925, A
LAZYBONES, 1935, A
LE 15E PRELUDE DE CHOPIN, 1922
LE AMICHE, 1962, C
LE AVVENTURE E GLI AMORI DI MIGUEL CERVANTES
LE BAL, 1984, A
LE BANDEAU SUR LES YEUX, 1917
LE BEAU MARIAGE, 1982, C-O
LE BEAU SERGE, 1959, C-O
LE BLE EN HERBE
LE BLED, 1929
LE BON PLAISIR, 1984, A-C
LE BONHEUR, 1966, C
LE BONHEUR CONJUGAL, 1922
LE BONHEUR DES AUTRES, 1919
LE BONHEUR DU JOUR, 1927
LE BOUCHER, 1971, O
LE BRASIER ARDENT, 1923
LE CABINET DE L'HOMME NOIR, 1924
LE CALVAIRE D'UNE REINE, 1919
LE CAPITAINE FRACASSE, 1929
LE CAPORAL EPINGLE
LE CARILLON DE MINUIT, 1922
LE CARNIVAL DES VERITES, 1920
LE CAVE SE REBIFFE
LE CERVEAU
LE CHANSON DU FEU, 1917
LE CHANT DE L'AMOUR TRIOMPHANT, 1923
LE CHARME DISCRET DE LA BOURGEOISIE
LE CHAT
LE CHAT DANS LE SAC
LE CHAUFFEUR DE MADEMOISELLE, 1928
LE CHEMIN D'ERONA, 1921
LE CHEMINEAU, 1917
LE CHEMINEAU, 1926
LE CHEVAL D'ORGEUIL
LE CHEVALIER DE GABY, 1920
LE CHIFFONNIER DE PARIS, 1924
LE CIEL EST A VOUS, 1957, A
LE CLOCHARD
LE COFFRET DE JADE
LE COMTE DE MONTE CRISTO
LE COMTE KOSTIA, 1925
LE CORBEAU
LE CORNIAUD
LE COSTAUD DES EPINETTES, 1923
LE COUPABLE, 1917
LE COUR DES GUEUX, 1925
LE CRABE TAMBOUR, 1984, O
LE CREPUSCULE DE COEUR, 1916
LE CRIME DE LORD ARTHUR SAVILLE, 1922
LE CRIME DE MONSIEUR LANGE
LE CRIME DES HOMMES, 1923
LE CRIME DU BOUIF, 1921
LE DANGER VIENT DE L'ESCAPE
LE DEDALE, 1917
LE DEDALE, 1927
LE DELAI, 1918
LE DENIER MILLIARDAIRE, 1934, A
LE DERNIER COMBAT, 1984, O
LE DESERT DES TARTARES
LE DESERT ROUGE
LE DESTIN EST MAITRE, 1920
LE DIABLE AU COEUR, 1928
LE DIABLE AU CORPS
LE DIABLE DANS LA VILLE, 1925
LE DIABLE PAR LA QUEUE
LE DIABLE PROBABLEMENT
LE DIABOLIQUE DOCTEUR MABUSE
LE DIAMANT VERT, 1917
LE DIEU DU HASARD, 1919
LE DISTRAIT
LE DOUBLE AMOUR, 1925
LE DROIT A LA VIE, 1917
LE DROIT DE TUER, 1920
LE FANTOME DE LA LIBERTE
LE FANTOME DU MOULIN ROUGE, 1925
LE FARCEUR
LE FATE
LE FERME DU CHOQUART, 1922
LE GAI SAVOIR, 1968, A
LE GAMIN DE PARIS, 1923
LE GARDIN DU FEU, 1924
LE GENDARME ET LES EXTRATERRESTRES, 1978, C
LE GENTILHOMME COMMERCANT, 1918
LE GENTLEMAN DE COCODY
LE GEOLE, 1921
LE GORILLE A MORDU L'ARCHEVEQUE
LE GRAND CHEF
LE GRAND JEU
LE JARDIN SUR L'ORONTE, 1925
LE JEUNE FOLLE
LE JOUER D'ECHECS
LE JOUER D'ECHES
LE JOUEUR
LE JOUR ET L'HEURE
LE JOUR SE LEVE
LE JOURNAL D'UNE CURE DE CAMPAGNE
LE JUGE ET L'ASSASSIN
LE JUIF ERRANT, 1926
LE LAC D'ARGENT, 1922
LE LION DES MOGOLS, 1924
LE LONG DES TROITTORS
LE LOTUS D'OR, 1916
LE LYS ROUGE, 1920
LE MAGNIFIQUE
LE MALHEUR QUI PASSE, 1916
LE MANOIR DE LA PEUR, 1927
LE MANS, 1971, A
LE MARIAGE DE FIGARO
LE MARIAGE DE MADEMOISELLE BEULEMANS, 1927
LE MARIAGE DE ROSINE, 1925
LE MAUVAIS GARCON, 1923
LE MENEUR DE JOIES, 1929
LE MEPRIS
LE MERAVIGLIOSE AVVENTURE DI MARCO POLO
LE MERCENARIRE
LE MERCHANT HOMME, 1921
LE MEURTIER DE THEODORE, 1921
LE MILLION
LE MIRACLE DES LOUPS
LE MIROIR A DEUX FACES
LE MONDAT
LE MONDE TREMBLERA, 1939, A
LE MYSTERE DE LA TOUR EIFFEL, 1927
LE NEGRE BLANC, 1925
LE NOCTURNE, 1917
LE NOCTURNE, 1919
LE NOEL D'UN VAGABOND, 1918
LE NOEL DU PERE LATHUILE, 1922
LE NOTTI BIANCHE
LE PASSAGER, 1928
LE PASSAGER DE LA PLUIE
LE PASSE DE MONIQUE, 1918
LE PASSE MURAILLE
LE PAYS BLEU
LE PENSEUR, 1920
LE PERE TRANQUILLE
LE PETIT CAFE, 1919
LE PETIT CHOSE, 1923
LE PETIT MOINEAU DE PARIS, 1923
LE PETIT SOLDAT, 1965, C
LE PETIT THEATRE DE JEAN RENOIR, 1974, C
LE PLAISIR, 1954, C-O
LE PORION, 1921
LE PREMIERE IDYLLE DE BOUCOT, 1920
LE PRINCE CHARMANT, 1925
LE PRINCE JEAN, 1928
LE PUITS AUX TROIS VERITES
LE QUATTRO VERITA
LE RAVIN SANS FOND, 1917
LE RAYON INVISIBLE
LE REFLET DE CLAUDE MERCOEUR, 1923
LE REMOUS, 1920
LE RETOUR AUX CHAMPS, 1918
LE REVE, 1921
LE REVEIL, 1925
LE REVEIL DE MADDALONE, 1924
LE ROI DE CAMARGUE, 1921
LE ROI DE CIRQUE, 1925
LE ROI DE COEUR
LE ROI DE LA MER, 1917
LE ROI DE LA VITESSE, 1923
LE ROMAN D'UN JEUNE HOMME PAUVRE, 1927
LE ROMAN D'UN SPAHI, 1917
LE ROMAN D'UN TRICHEUR
LE ROUBLE A DEUX FACES
LE ROUGE AUX LEVRES
LE ROUGE ET LA NOIR
LE ROUTE DE CORINTH
LE SANG D'ALLAH, 1922
LE SANG D'UN POETE
LE SANG DES FINOEL, 1922
LE SCANDALE, 1918
LE SECRET DE CARGO, 1929
LE SECRET DE POLICHINELLE, 1923
LE SECRET DE ROSETTE LAMBERT, 1920
LE SECRET DU 'LONE STAR', 1920
LE SENS DE LA MORT, 1921
LE SERPENT
LE SIEGE DES TROIS, 1918
LE SILENCE EST D'OR
LE SOUFFLE AU COEUR
LE SOUS MARIN DE CRISTAL, 1928
LE TABLIER BLANC, 1917
LE TALISON, 1921
LE TAXI 313 x 7, 1922
LE TEMPS DES ASSASSINS
LE TESTAMENT DU DR. MABUSE
LE TOCSIN, 1920
LE TONNERRE, 1921
LE TORNOI, 1928
LE TORRENT, 1918
LE TOURBILLON DE PARIS, 1928
LE TRAIN SANS YEUX, 1928
LE TRAITEMENT DU HOQUET, 1918
LE VALSE DE L'ADIEU, 1928
LE VENENOSA, 1928
LE VENT D'EST
LE VERTIGE, 1917
LE VERTIGE, 1926

LE VICOMTE REGLE SES COMPTES
LE VIOL, 1968, O
LE VOILE BLEU
LE VOLEUR
LE VOYAGE EN AMERIQUE
LE VOYAGE IMAGINAIRE, 1926
LE VOYOU
LEAD KINDLY LIGHT
LEAD LAW
LEAD, KINDLY LIGHT, 1918, A
LEADBELLY, 1976, C-O
LEADVILLE GUNSLINGER, 1952, A
LEAGUE OF FRIGHTENED MEN, 1937, A
LEAGUE OF GENTLEMEN, THE, 1961, A-C
LEAH KLESCHNA, 1913
LEAH'S SUFFERING, 1917
LEAP INTO LIFE, 1924
LEAP INTO THE VOID, 1982, O
LEAP OF FAITH, 1931, A
LEAP TO FAME, 1918, A
LEAP YEAR, 1921
LEAP YEAR, 1932, A
LEARN, BABY, LEARN
LEARNIN' OF JIM BENTON, THE, 1917
LEARNING TO LOVE, 1925, A
LEARNING TREE, THE, 1969, O
LEASE OF LIFE, 1954, A
LEATHER AND NYLON, 1969, A-C
LEATHER BOYS, THE, 1965, O
LEATHER BURNERS, THE, 1943, A
LEATHER GLOVES, 1948, A
LEATHER SAINT, THE, 1956, A
LEATHER-PUSHERS, THE, 1940, A
LEATHERNECK, THE, 1929, A
LEATHERNECKING, 1930, A
LEATHERNECKS HAVE LANDED, THE, 1936, A
LEAVE HER TO HEAVEN, 1946, O
LEAVE IT TO BLANCHE, 1934, A
LEAVE IT TO BLONDIE, 1945, A
LEAVE IT TO GERRY, 1924
LEAVE IT TO HENRY, 1949, A
LEAVE IT TO ME, 1920
LEAVE IT TO ME, 1933, A
LEAVE IT TO ME, 1937, A
LEAVE IT TO SMITH, 1934, A
LEAVE IT TO SUSAN, 1919
LEAVE IT TO THE IRISH, 1944, A
LEAVE IT TO THE MARINES, 1951, A
LEAVENWORTH CASE, THE, 1923
LEAVENWORTH CASE, THE, 1936, A
LEAVES FROM SATAN'S BOOK, 1921
LEAVES OF MEMORY, 1914
LEBENSBORN
LEBENSZEICHEN
LEDA
LEECH WOMAN, THE, 1960, C
LEECH, THE, 1921, A
LEFT HAND BRAND, THE, 1924
LEFT HAND OF GEMINI, THE, 1972
LEFT HAND OF GOD, THE, 1955, A
LEFT, RIGHT AND CENTRE, 1959, A
LEFT-HANDED, 1972
LEFT-HANDED GUN, THE, 1958, C
LEFT-HANDED LAW, 1937, A
LEFT-HANDED WOMAN, THE, 1980, C-O
LEFTOVER LADIES, 1931, A
LEGACY, 1963
LEGACY, 1976, O
LEGACY OF A SPY
LEGACY OF BLOOD, 1973, O
LEGACY OF BLOOD, 1978, O
LEGACY OF HORROR, 1978
LEGACY OF MAGGIE WALSH
LEGACY OF SATAN, 1973
LEGACY OF THE 500,000, THE, 1964, A
LEGACY, THE, 1979, O
LEGAL LARCENY
LEGALLY DEAD, 1923, A
LEGEND IN LEOTARDS
LEGEND OF A BANDIT, THE, 1945, A
LEGEND OF ALFRED PACKER, THE, 1979
LEGEND OF BLOOD MOUNTAIN, THE, 1965
LEGEND OF BLOOD MOUNTAIN, THE, 1965, O
LEGEND OF BOGGY CREEK, THE, 1973, A-C
LEGEND OF CHAMPIONS, 1983
LEGEND OF COUGAR CANYON, 1974, A
LEGEND OF EARL DURAND, THE, 1974
LEGEND OF FRANK WOODS, THE, 1977
LEGEND OF FRENCHIE KING, THE, 1971, C
LEGEND OF GOSTA BERLING, 1928
LEGEND OF HELL HOUSE, THE, 1973, C
LEGEND OF HILLBILLY JOHN, THE
LEGEND OF HOLLYWOOD, THE, 1924, A
LEGEND OF HORROR, 1972
LEGEND OF LOBO, THE, 1962, AA
LEGEND OF LYLAH CLARE, THE, 1968, A-C
LEGEND OF NIGGER CHARLEY, THE, 1972, C
LEGEND OF ROBIN HOOD, THE
LEGEND OF SPIDER FOREST, THE, 1976, C
LEGEND OF THE BAYOU
LEGEND OF THE JUGGLER, 1978
LEGEND OF THE LONE RANGER, THE, 1981, C
LEGEND OF THE LOST, 1957, C
LEGEND OF THE SEA WOLF
LEGEND OF THE SEVEN GOLDEN VAMPIRES, THE
LEGEND OF THE TREE OF LIFE
LEGEND OF THE WEREWOLF, 1974
LEGEND OF THE WILD, 1981
LEGEND OF THE WOLF WOMAN, THE, 1977, O
LEGEND OF TOM DOOLEY, THE, 1959, A
LEGEND OF WITCH HOLLOW
LEGENDARY CURSE OF LEMORA
LEGION OF DEATH, THE, 1918
LEGION OF LOST FLYERS, 1939, A
LEGION OF MISSING MEN, 1937, A
LEGION OF TERROR, 1936, A
LEGION OF THE CONDEMNED, 1928
LEGION OF THE DOOMED, 1958, A
LEGION OF THE LAWLESS, 1940, A
LEGIONNAIRES IN PARIS, 1927
LEGIONS OF THE NILE, 1960, A
LEMON DROP KID, THE, 1934, A
LEMON DROP KID, THE, 1951, A
LEMON GROVE KIDS MEET THE MONSTERS, THE, 1966, C
LEMONADE JOE, 1966, A
LEMORA THE LADY DRACULA
LENA RIVERS, 1914
LENA RIVERS, 1925
LENA RIVERS, 1932, A
LEND ME YOUR EAR
LEND ME YOUR HUSBAND, 1924, A
LEND ME YOUR HUSBAND, 1935, A
LEND ME YOUR NAME, 1918
LEND ME YOUR WIFE, 1935, A
LENNY, 1974, C-O
LEO AND LOREE, 1980, A
LEO CHRONICLES, THE, 1972
LEO THE LAST, 1970, O
LEONOR, 1977, O
LEOPARD IN THE SNOW, 1979, A
LEOPARD LADY, THE, 1928, A
LEOPARD MAN, THE, 1943, O
LEOPARD WOMAN, THE, 1920
LEOPARD'S BRIDE, THE, 1916
LEOPARD, THE, 1963, A-C
LEOPARDESS, THE, 1923
LEPKE, 1975, O
LES ABYSSES, 1964, O
LES AMANTS
LES AMANTS DE VERONE
LES AMOURS DE ROCAMBOLE, 1924
LES ANGES DU PECHE
LES AVENTURES EXTRAORDINAIRES DE CERVANTES
LES BAS FONDS
LES BELLES-DE-NUIT, 1952, C
LES BICHES, 1968, O
LES BLEUS DE L'AMOUR, 1918
LES CAMARADES
LES CAPRICES DE MARIE
LES CARABINIERS, 1968, O
LES CHASSEUR DE CHEZ MAXIM'S, 1927
LES CHERES IMAGES, 1920
LES CHOSES DE LA VIE
LES CINQ GENTLEMEN MAUDITS, 1919
LES CLANDESTINS
LES CLOCHES DE CORNEVILLE, 1917
LES COMPERES, 1984, A
LES CONTES LES MILLES ET UNE NUITS, 1922
LES COUSINS
LES CREATURES, 1969, A
LES DAMES DE BOIS DE BOULOGNE
LES DAMES DE CROIX-MORT, 1917
LES DEMOISELLES DE ROCHEFORT
LES DEMONS DE MINUIT
LES DERNIERES VACANCES, 1947, A-C
LES DEUX AMOURS, 1917
LES DEUX BAISERS, 1920
LES DEUX GOSSES, 1924
LES DEUX MARQUISES, 1916
LES DEUX TIMIDES, 1929
LES DIABOLIQUES
LES DIEUX ONT SOIF, 1926
LES DOIGTS CROISES
LES ECRITS RESTENT, 1917
LES ELUS DE LA MER, 1925
LES ENFANTS DU PARADIS
LES ENFANTS TERRIBLES, 1952, A-C
LES ESPIONS
LES FELINS
LES FEMMES COLLANTES, 1920
LES FEMMES DES AUTRES, 1920
LES FOURCHAMBAULT, 1929
LES FRERES CORSES, 1917
LES GARCONS
LES GAULOISES BLEUES, 1969, A
LES GIRLS, 1957, A
LES GRANDES MANOEUVRES
LES GRANDS, 1924
LES HERITIERS DE L'ONCLE JAMES, 1924
LES HOMMES EN BLANC
LES INNOCENTS AUX MAINS SALES
LES JEUX INTERDIT
LES JEUX SONT FAITS, 1947, A-C
LES LACHES VIVENT D'ESPOIR
LES LARMES DU PARDON, 1919
LES LETTRES DE MON MOULIN
LES LIAISONS DANGEREUSES, 1961, O
LES LIENS DE SANG
LES LOUVES
LES LOUVES, 1925
LES MAINS FLETRIES, 1920
LES MAINS SALES, 1954, A-C
LES MAITRES DU TEMPS, 1982, A
LES MAUDITS
LES MISERABLES, 1918, A
LES MISERABLES, 1927
LES MISERABLES, 1935, A
LES MISERABLES, 1936, A
LES MISERABLES, 1952, A
LES MISERABLES, 1982, A
LES MORTS QUI PARLENT, 1920
LES MOUTTES, 1919
LES MYSTERES SU CIEL, 1920
LES NOCES DU SABLE
LES NOUVEAUX MESSIEURS, 1929
LES NUITS DE CARNAVAL, 1922
LES NUITS DE L'EVPOUVANTE
LES NUITS DE LA PLEINE LUNE
LES OGRESSES
LES OMBRES QUI PASSANT, 1924
LES OPPRIMES, 1923
LES PARENTS TERRIBLES, 1950, A
LES PEMPS DES AMANTS
LES PERLES DES COURONNE
LES PETITES MARIONETTES, 1918
LES PETITS, 1925
LES PETROLEUSES
LES PORTES DE LA NUIT
LES PREMIERES ARMES DE ROCAMBOLE, 1924
LES QUATRES CENTS COUPS
LES QUATRES VERITES
LES RANTZAU, 1924
LES RIPOUX
LES ROQUEVILLARD, 1922
LES SOEURS ENNEMIES, 1917
LES SOMNAMBULES
LES TERRES D'OR, 1925
LES TITANS
LES TRANSATLANTIQUES, 1928
LES TRAVAILLEURS DE LA MER, 1918
LES TRICHEURS
LES TRIPES AU SOLIEL
LES TROIS COURONNES DU MATELOT
LES TROIS GANTS DE LA DAMES EN NOIR, 1920
LES TROIS MASQUES, 1921
LES VACANCES DE MONSIEUR HULOT
LES VALSEUSES
LES VISITEURS DU SOIR
LES VOLEURS DE GLOIRE, 1926
LES YEUX D L'AIME, 1922
LES YEUX SANS VISAGE
LESBIAN TWINS
LESNAYA PESNYA
LESS THAN KIN, 1918
LESS THAN THE DUST, 1916
LESSON IN LOVE, A, 1960, C
LESSON, THE, 1917
LESSONS IN LOVE, 1921, A
LEST WE FORGET, 1918
LEST WE FORGET, 1934, C
LET 'EM HAVE IT, 1935, A
LET 'ER BUCK, 1925, A
LET 'ER GO GALLEGHER, 1928, A
LET FREEDOM RING, 1939, A
LET GEORGE DO IT, 1938
LET GEORGE DO IT, 1940, A
LET HIM BUCK, 1924
LET IT RAIN, 1927, A
LET JOY REIGN SUPREME, 1977, C
LET KATHY DO IT, 1916
LET ME EXPLAIN, DEAR, 1932, A
LET NO MAN PUT ASUNDER, 1924
LET NO MAN WRITE MY EPITAPH, 1960, A
LET THE BALLOON GO, 1977, A
LET THE PEOPLE LAUGH
LET THE PEOPLE SING, 1942, A
LET THEM LIVE, 1937, A
LET US BE GAY, 1930, A
LET US LIVE, 1939, A
LET WOMEN ALONE, 1925
LET'S BE FAMOUS, 1939, A
LET'S BE FASHIONABLE, 1920
LET'S BE HAPPY, 1957, A
LET'S BE RITZY, 1934, A
LET'S DANCE, 1950, A

LET'S DO IT
LET'S DO IT AGAIN, 1953, A
LET'S DO IT AGAIN, 1975, A
LET'S ELOPE, 1919
LET'S FACE IT, 1943, A
LET'S FALL IN LOVE, 1934, A
LET'S FINISH THE JOB, 1928
LET'S GET A DIVORCE, 1918
LET'S GET MARRIED, 1926, A
LET'S GET MARRIED, 1937, A
LET'S GET MARRIED, 1960, A
LET'S GET TOUGH, 1942, A
LET'S GO, 1923
LET'S GO COLLEGIATE, 1941, A
LET'S GO GALLAGHER, 1925
LET'S GO NATIVE, 1930, A
LET'S GO NAVY, 1951, A
LET'S GO PLACES, 1930, A
LET'S GO STEADY, 1945, A
LET'S GO, YOUNG GUY, 1967, A
LET'S HAVE A MURDER
LET'S HAVE FUN
LET'S HAVE FUN, 1943
LET'S KILL UNCLE, 1966, C
LET'S LIVE A LITTLE, A
LET'S LIVE AGAIN, 1948, A
LET'S LIVE TONIGHT, 1935, A
LET'S LOVE AND LAUGH
LET'S MAKE A MILLION, 1937, A
LET'S MAKE A NIGHT OF IT, 1937, A
LET'S MAKE IT LEGAL, 1951, A
LET'S MAKE LOVE, 1960, AA
LET'S MAKE MUSIC, 1940, A
LET'S MAKE UP, 1955, A
LET'S MAKE WHOOPEE
LET'S PRETEND
LET'S ROCK, 1958, A
LET'S SCARE JESSICA TO DEATH, 1971, C
LET'S SING AGAIN, 1936, A
LET'S TALK ABOUT WOMEN, 1964, C
LET'S TALK IT OVER, 1934, A
LET'S TRY AGAIN, 1934, A
LETTER FOR EVIE, A, 1945, A
LETTER FROM A NOVICE
LETTER FROM AN UNKNOWN WOMAN, 1948, A
LETTER FROM KOREA
LETTER OF INTRODUCTION, 1938, A
LETTER THAT WAS NEVER SENT, THE, 1962, A
LETTER TO THREE WIVES, A, 1948, A
LETTER, THE, 1929, A
LETTER, THE, 1940, A
LETTERS FROM MY WINDMILL, 1955, A
LETTING IN THE SUNSHINE, 1933, A
LETTY LYNTON, 1932, A-C
LETYAT ZHURAVIT
LEVIATHAN, 1961, O
LEW TYLER'S WIVES, 1926
LI'L ABNER, 1940, AAA
LI'L ABNER, 1959, AA
LI-HANG LE CRUEL, 1920
LIANG SHAN-PO YU CHU YING-TAI
LIANNA, 1983, O
LIAR'S DICE, 1980, O
LIAR'S MOON, 1982, O
LIAR, THE, 1918
LIARS, THE, 1964, A
LIBEL, 1959, A
LIBELED LADY, 1936, A
LIBERATION OF L.B. JONES, THE, 1970, O
LIBERTINE, THE, 1916
LIBERTY HALL, 1914
LIBIDO, 1973, O
LICENSED TO KILL
LICENSED TO LOVE AND KILL, 1979
LIDO MYSTERY, THE
LIE DETECTOR, THE
LIE, THE, 1918
LIEBESSPIELE
LIES, 1983
LIES, 1984, C
LIES MY FATHER TOLD ME, 1960, A
LIES MY FATHER TOLD ME, 1975, A
LIEUT. DANNY, U.S.A., 1916, A
LIEUTENANT DARING RN AND THE WATER RATS, 1924, A
LIEUTENANT DARING, RN, 1935, A
LIEUTENANT WORE SKIRTS, THE, 1956, A
LIFE, 1920
LIFE, 1928, A
LIFE AFTER DARK
LIFE AND DEATH OF COLONEL BLIMP, THE
LIFE AND DEATH OF LIEUTENANT SCHMIDT, 1917
LIFE AND LEGEND OF BUFFALO JONES, THE, 1976
LIFE AND LOVES OF BEETHOVEN, THE, 1937, A
LIFE AND LOVES OF MOZART, THE, 1959, C
LIFE AND PASSION OF CHRIST, 1921
LIFE AND TIMES OF CHESTER-ANGUS RAMSGOOD, THE, 1971, C
LIFE AND TIMES OF GRIZZLY ADAMS, THE, 1974, AAA
LIFE AND TIMES OF JUDGE ROY BEAN, THE, 1972, C
LIFE AT STAKE, A
LIFE AT THE TOP, 1965, C
LIFE BEGINS, 1932, C
LIFE BEGINS ANEW, 1938, A
LIFE BEGINS AT 17, 1958, C
LIFE BEGINS AT 40, 1935, AAA
LIFE BEGINS AT 8:30, 1942, A
LIFE BEGINS AT COLLEGE
LIFE BEGINS FOR ANDY HARDY, 1941, A
LIFE BEGINS IN COLLEGE, 1937, AA
LIFE BEGINS TOMORROW, 1952, C
LIFE BEGINS WITH LOVE, 1937, A
LIFE DANCES ON, CHRISTINE
LIFE FOR A LIFE, A, 1916
LIFE FOR RUTH
LIFE GOES ON, 1932, A-C
LIFE GOES ON, 1938
LIFE IN DANGER, 1964, A
LIFE IN DEATH, 1914
LIFE IN EMERGENCY WARD 10, 1959, C
LIFE IN HER HANDS, 1951, C
LIFE IN THE BALANCE, A, 1955, O
LIFE IN THE ORANGE GROVES, 1920
LIFE IN THE RAW, 1933, A
LIFE IS A BED OF ROSES, 1984, C
LIFE IS A CIRCUS, 1962, A
LIFE LINE, THE, 1919
LIFE LOVE DEATH, 1969, O
LIFE MASK, THE, 1918
LIFE OF A COUNTRY DOCTOR, 1961, A
LIFE OF A LONDON ACTRESS, THE, 1919
LIFE OF AN ACTRESS, 1927
LIFE OF AN ACTRESS, THE, 1915
LIFE OF BRIAN
LIFE OF EMILE ZOLA, THE, 1937, AA
LIFE OF GENERAL VILLA, THE, 1914
LIFE OF GENEVIEVE, THE, 1922
LIFE OF HER OWN, A, 1950, A-C
LIFE OF JIMMY DOLAN, THE, 1933, A
LIFE OF JOHN BUNYAN-PILGRIM'S PROGRESS, 1912
LIFE OF LORD KITCHENER, THE, 1917
LIFE OF MOSES, 1909
LIFE OF OHARU, 1964, C
LIFE OF RILEY, THE, 1927
LIFE OF RILEY, THE, 1949, A
LIFE OF ROBERT BURNS, THE, 1926, A
LIFE OF SHAKESPEARE, THE
LIFE OF THE COUNTRY DOCTOR
LIFE OF THE PARTY, 1934, A
LIFE OF THE PARTY, THE, 1920
LIFE OF THE PARTY, THE, 1930, A
LIFE OF THE PARTY, THE, 1937, A
LIFE OF VERGIE WINTERS, THE, 1934, C
LIFE OF "BIG TIM" SULLIVAN, THE, 1914
LIFE OR HONOR?, 1918
LIFE POD, 1980
LIFE RETURNS, 1939, C
LIFE STORY OF DAVID LLOYD GEORGE, THE, 1918
LIFE STUDY, 1973, O
LIFE UPSIDE DOWN, 1965, C
LIFE WITH BLONDIE, 1946, AAA
LIFE WITH FATHER, 1947, AAA
LIFE WITH HENRY, 1941, AAA
LIFE WITH THE LYONS
LIFE WITHOUT SOUL, 1916, A
LIFE'S A FUNNY PROPOSITION, 1919
LIFE'S A STAGE, 1929
LIFE'S BLIND ALLEY, 1916
LIFE'S CROSSROADS, 1928
LIFE'S DARN FUNNY, 1921, A
LIFE'S GREATEST GAME, 1924
LIFE'S GREATEST PROBLEM, 1919
LIFE'S GREATEST QUESTION, 1921
LIFE'S MOCKERY, 1928
LIFE'S SHADOWS, 1916
LIFE'S SHOP WINDOW, 1914
LIFE'S TEMPTATIONS, 1914
LIFE'S TWIST, 1920
LIFE'S WHIRLPOOL, 1916, A
LIFE'S WHIRLPOOL, 1917, A
LIFEBOAT, 1944, A
LIFEGUARD, 1976, C
LIFEGUARDSMAN, THE, 1916
LIFESPAN, 1975, C
LIFT, THE, 1965, O
LIFT, THE, 1983, C
LIFTED VEIL, THE, 1917
LIFTING SHADOWS, 1920, A
LIGEA
LIGHT
LIGHT, 1915
LIGHT ACROSSS THE STREET, THE, 1957, O
LIGHT AT DUSK, THE, 1916, A
LIGHT AT THE EDGE OF THE WORLD, THE, 1971, O
LIGHT BLUE
LIGHT FANTASTIC, 1964, A
LIGHT FANTASTIC, THE
LIGHT FINGERS, 1929, A
LIGHT FINGERS, 1957, A
LIGHT IN DARKNESS, 1917
LIGHT IN THE CLEARING, THE, 1921
LIGHT IN THE DARK, THE, 1922, A
LIGHT IN THE FOREST, THE, 1958, AAA
LIGHT IN THE PIAZZA, 1962, A
LIGHT IN THE WINDOW, THE, 1927, A
LIGHT OF HAPPINESS, THE, 1916
LIGHT OF HEART, THE
LIGHT OF THE WESTERN STARS, THE, 1925
LIGHT OF VICTORY, 1919, A
LIGHT OF WESTERN STARS, THE, 1918
LIGHT OF WESTERN STARS, THE, 1930, A
LIGHT OF WESTERN STARS, THE, 1940, A
LIGHT THAT FAILED, THE, 1916
LIGHT THAT FAILED, THE, 1923
LIGHT THAT FAILED, THE, 1939, A
LIGHT TOUCH, THE, 1951, C
LIGHT TOUCH, THE, 1955, A
LIGHT UP THE SKY, 1960, A
LIGHT WITHIN, THE
LIGHT WITHIN, THE, 1918
LIGHT WOMAN, A
LIGHT WOMAN, A, 1920
LIGHT YEARS AWAY, 1982, C
LIGHT, THE, 1916
LIGHT, THE, 1919
LIGHTHOUSE, 1947, A
LIGHTHOUSE BY THE SEA, THE, 1924, A
LIGHTHOUSE KEEPER'S DAUGHTER, THE
LIGHTING, 1927
LIGHTING BILL, 1926
LIGHTNING BOLT, 1967, A
LIGHTING RIDER, THE, 1924
LIGHTING SPEED, 1928
LIGHTNIN', 1925
LIGHTNIN', 1930, A
LIGHTNIN' CRANDALL, 1937, A
LIGHTNIN' IN THE FOREST, 1948, C
LIGHTNIN' JACK, 1924
LIGHTNIN' SHOT, 1928
LIGHTNIN' SMITH RETURNS, 1931
LIGHTNING BILL CARSON, 1936, A
LIGHTNING BOLT, 1967, A
LIGHTNING CARSON RIDES AGAIN, 1938
LIGHTNING CONDUCTOR, 1938, A
LIGHTNING CONDUCTOR, THE, 1914, A
LIGHTNING FLYER, 1931, A
LIGHTNING GUNS, 1950, A
LIGHTNING LARIATS, 1927, A
LIGHTNING RAIDERS, 1945, A
LIGHTNING RANGE, 1934, A
LIGHTNING REPORTER, 1926, A
LIGHTNING ROMANCE, 1924, A
LIGHTNING STRIKES TWICE, 1935, A
LIGHTNING STRIKES TWICE, 1951, C
LIGHTNING STRIKES WEST, 1940, A
LIGHTNING SWORDS OF DEATH
LIGHTNING TRIGGERS, 1935
LIGHTS AND SHADOWS
LIGHTS O' LONDON, THE, 1914
LIGHTS OF HOME, THE, 1920
LIGHTS OF NEW YORK, 1928, A
LIGHTS OF NEW YORK, THE, 1916, A
LIGHTS OF NEW YORK, THE, 1922
LIGHTS OF OLD BROADWAY, 1925
LIGHTS OF OLD SANTA FE, 1944, A
LIGHTS OF THE DESERT, 1922, A
LIGHTS OF VARIETY
LIGHTS OUT
LIGHTS OUT, 1923
LIKE A CROW ON A JUNE BUG, 1972, C
LIKE A TURTLE ON ITS BACK, 1981, O
LIKE FATHER LIKE SON, 1961, C
LIKE FATHER, LIKE SON, 1965
LIKE WILDFIRE, 1917
LIKELY LADS, THE, 1976, A
LIKELY STORY, A, 1947, A
LIKENESS OF THE NIGHT, THE, 1921, A
LILA, 1962
LILA, 1968
LILA—LOVE UNDER THE MIDNIGHT SUN
LILAC DOMINO, THE, 1940, A
LILAC SUNBONNET, THE, 1922
LILAC TIME, 1928, A
LILACS IN THE SPRING
LILI, 1953, AA
LILI MARLEEN, 1981, O
LILI MARLENE
LILIES OF THE FIELD, 1930, O
LILIES OF THE FIELD, 1934, A
LILIES OF THE FIELD, 1963, A
LILIOM, 1930, C
LILIOM, 1935, A
LILITH, 1964, C
LILLI MARLENE, 1951, C
LILLIAN RUSSELL, 1940, A

LILLIES OF THE FIELD, 1924
LILLIES OF THE STREETS, 1925
LILLY TURNER, 1933, C
LILY AND THE ROSE, THE, 1915, A
LILY CHRISTINE, 1932, C
LILY OF KILARNEY
LILY OF KILLARNEY, 1929
LILY OF LAGUNA, 1938, C
LILY OF POVERTY FLAT, THE, 1915
LILY OF THE ALLEY, 1923, A
LILY OF THE DUST, 1924
LILY, THE, 1926
LIMBO
LIMBO, 1972, O
LIMBO LINE, THE, 1969, O
LIMEHOUSE BLUES, 1934, A-C
LIMELIGHT, 1952, A
LIMELIGHT, 1937
LIMIT, THE, 1972, C
LIMITE, 1930
LIMITED MAIL, THE, 1925
LIMONADOVY JOE
LIMOUSINE LIFE, 1918
LIMPING MAN, THE, 1931, A
LIMPING MAN, THE, 1936, A
LIMPING MAN, THE, 1953, A
LINCOLN CONSPIRACY, THE, 1977, A
LINCOLN HIGHWAYMAN, THE, 1920
LINDA, 1929, A
LINDA, 1960, A
LINDA BE GOOD, 1947, A
LINDA LOVELACE FOR PRESIDENT, 1975
LINE
LINE ENGAGED, 1935, A
LINE OF DUTY
LINE, THE, 1982, C
LINEUP, THE, 1934, A
LINEUP, THE, 1958, O
LINGERIE, 1928, A
LINKED BY FATE, 1919
LINKS OF JUSTICE, 1958, A
LIOLA
LION AND THE HORSE, THE, 1952, A
LION AND THE LAMB, 1931, A
LION AND THE MOUSE, THE, 1914
LION AND THE MOUSE, THE, 1919
LION AND THE MOUSE, THE, 1928, A
LION HAS WINGS, THE, 1940, A
LION HUNTERS, THE, 1951, AA
LION IN THE STREETS, A
LION IN WINTER, THE, 1968, A
LION IS IN THE STREETS, A, 1953, A
LION MAN, THE, 1936
LION OF SPARTA
LION OF ST. MARK, 1967, A
LION OF THE DESERT, 1981, O
LION'S BREATH, THE, 1916
LION'S BRIDE, THE, 1914
LION'S DEN, THE, 1919
LION'S DEN, THE, 1936, A
LION'S MOUSE, THE, 1922, A
LION, THE, 1962, A
LIONHEART, 1968, AA
LIONHEART, 1970
LIONS FOR BREAKFAST, 1977
LIONS LOVE, 1969, O
LIONS OF ST. PETERSBURG, THE, 1971
LIPS OF BLOOD, 1972
LIPSTICK, 1965, C-O
LIPSTICK, 1976, O
LIQUID GOLD, 1919
LIQUID SKY, 1982, O
LIQUIDATOR, THE, 1966, C
LISA, 1962, O
LISA, 1977
LISA AND THE DEVIL
LISA, TOSCA OF ATHENS, 1961, A
LISBON, 1956, O
LISBON STORY, THE, 1946, A
LISETTE, 1961, C
LIST OF ADRIAN MESSENGER, THE, 1963, A
LISTEN LESTER, 1924
LISTEN TO THE CITY, 1984, O
LISTEN, DARLING, 1938, AAA
LISTEN, LET'S MAKE LOVE, 1969, O
LISZTOMANIA, 1975, O
LITTLE 'FRAID LADY, THE, 1920, A
LITTLE ACCIDENT, 1930, A
LITTLE ACCIDENT, 1939, A
LITTLE ADVENTURESS, THE, 1927
LITTLE ADVENTURESS, THE, 1938, AA
LITTLE AMERICAN, THE, 1917
LITTLE ANGEL, 1961, A
LITTLE ANGEL OF CANYON CREEK, THE, 1914, A
LITTLE ANNIE ROONEY, 1925, A
LITTLE ARK, THE, 1972, AAA
LITTLE AUSTRALIANS, 1940, C
LITTLE BALLERINA, THE, 1951, AAA
LITTLE BIG HORN, 1927, A
LITTLE BIG HORN, 1951, C
LITTLE BIG MAN, 1970, C-O
LITTLE BIG SHOT, 1935, AAA
LITTLE BIG SHOT, 1952, A
LITTLE BIT OF BLUFF, A, 1935, A
LITTLE BIT OF FLUFF, A
LITTLE BIT OF FLUFF, A, 1919
LITTLE BIT OF HEAVEN
LITTLE BIT OF HEAVEN, A, 1940, AAA
LITTLE BOSS, THE, 1919
LITTLE BOSS, THE, 1927
LITTLE BOY BLUE, 1963, A
LITTLE BOY LOST, 1953, A
LITTLE BOY SCOUT, THE, 1917
LITTLE BREADWINNER, THE, 1916
LITTLE BROTHER OF GOD, 1922
LITTLE BROTHER OF THE RICH, A, 1915
LITTLE BROTHER OF THE RICH, A, 1919
LITTLE BROTHER, THE, 1917, A
LITTLE BUCKAROO, THE, 1928
LITTLE CAESAR, 1931, C
LITTLE CHEVALIER, THE, 1917
LITTLE CHILD SHALL LEAD THEM, A
LITTLE CHILD SHALL LEAD THEM, A, 1919
LITTLE CHURCH AROUND THE CORNER, 1923, A
LITTLE CHURCH AROUND THE CORNER, THE, 1915
LITTLE CIGARS, 1973, A
LITTLE CLOWN, THE, 1921, A
LITTLE COLONEL, THE, 1935, AAA
LITTLE COMRADE, 1919, A
LITTLE CONVICT, THE, 1980, AA
LITTLE DAMOZEL, THE, 1916
LITTLE DAMOZEL, THE, 1933, A
LITTLE DARLINGS, 1980, O
LITTLE DETECTIVES, THE, 1983
LITTLE DIPLOMAT, THE, 1919
LITTLE DOLLY DAYDREAM, 1938, AA
LITTLE DOOR INTO THE WORLD, THE, 1923, A
LITTLE DORRIT, 1920
LITTLE DRAGONS, THE, 1980, A-C
LITTLE DRUMMER GIRL, THE, 1984, C-O
LITTLE DUCHESS, THE, 1917
LITTLE EGYPT, 1951, A
LITTLE EVA ASCENDS, 1922, A
LITTLE EVE EDGARTON, 1916
LITTLE FAUSS AND BIG HALSY, 1970, O
LITTLE FELLER, THE, 1979
LITTLE FIREBRAND, THE, 1927
LITTLE FOOL, THE, 1921
LITTLE FOXES, THE, 1941, A-C
LITTLE FRENCH GIRL, THE, 1925
LITTLE FRIEND, 1934, C
LITTLE FUGITIVE, THE, 1953, A
LITTLE GEL
LITTLE GIANT, 1946, A
LITTLE GIANT, THE, 1926
LITTLE GIANT, THE, 1933, A
LITTLE GIRL IN A BIG CITY, A, 1925
LITTLE GIRL NEXT DOOR, THE, 1916
LITTLE GIRL NEXT DOOR, THE, 1923
LITTLE GIRL THAT HE FORGOT, THE, 1914
LITTLE GIRL WHO LIVES DOWN THE LANE, THE, 1977, O
LITTLE GIRL, BIG TEASE, 1977
LITTLE GRAY LADY, THE, 1914, A
LITTLE GREY MOUSE, THE, 1920
LITTLE GYPSY, THE, 1915
LITTLE HOUR OF PETER WELLS, THE, 1920
LITTLE HUMPBACKED HORSE, THE, 1962, A
LITTLE HUT, THE, 1957, A
LITTLE INTRUDER, THE, 1919
LITTLE IODINE, 1946, A
LITTLE IRISH GIRL, THE, 1926, A
LITTLE ITALY, 1921
LITTLE JOE, THE WRANGLER, 1942, A
LITTLE JOHNNY JONES, 1923
LITTLE JOHNNY JONES, 1930, A
LITTLE JOURNEY, A, 1927, A
LITTLE JUNGLE BOY, 1969, A
LITTLE KIDNAPPERS, THE, 1954, AAA
LITTLE LADY EILEEN, 1916
LITTLE LAURA AND BIG JOHN, 1973, O
LITTLE LIAR, THE, 1916, A
LITTLE LORD FAUNTLEROY, 1914, A
LITTLE LORD FAUNTLEROY, 1921, A
LITTLE LORD FAUNTLEROY, 1936, AAA
LITTLE LOST SISTER, 1917
LITTLE MADEMOISELLE, THE, 1915, A
LITTLE MALCOLM, 1974, C
LITTLE MAN, WHAT NOW?, 1934, A
LITTLE MARTYR, THE, 1947, A
LITTLE MARY SUNSHINE, 1916
LITTLE MAYORESS, THE
LITTLE MEENA'S ROMANCE, 1916
LITTLE MEG'S CHILDREN, 1921
LITTLE MELODY FROM VIENNA, 1948, A
LITTLE MEN, 1935, A
LITTLE MEN, 1940, AA
LITTLE MERMAID, THE, 1979
LITTLE MICKEY GROGAN, 1927
LITTLE MINISTER, THE, 1921
LITTLE MINISTER, THE, 1922
LITTLE MINISTER, THE, 1934, A
LITTLE MISS BIG, 1946, A
LITTLE MISS BROADWAY, 1938, A
LITTLE MISS BROADWAY, 1947, A
LITTLE MISS BROWN, 1915, A
LITTLE MISS DEVIL, 1951, A
LITTLE MISS FORTUNE, 1917
LITTLE MISS GROWN-UP, 1918
LITTLE MISS HAPPINESS, 1916
LITTLE MISS HAWKSHAW, 1921
LITTLE MISS HOOVER, 1918, A
LITTLE MISS INNOCENCE, 1973
LITTLE MISS LONDON, 1929
LITTLE MISS MARKER, 1934, AAA
LITTLE MISS MARKER, 1980, C
LITTLE MISS MOLLY, 1940, A
LITTLE MISS NO-ACCOUNT, 1918
LITTLE MISS NOBODY, 1917
LITTLE MISS NOBODY, 1923
LITTLE MISS NOBODY, 1933, A
LITTLE MISS NOBODY, 1936, AA
LITTLE MISS OPTIMIST, 1917
LITTLE MISS REBELLION, 1920, A
LITTLE MISS ROUGHNECK, 1938, AA
LITTLE MISS SMILES, 1922, A
LITTLE MISS SOMEBODY, 1937, A
LITTLE MISS THOROUGHBRED, 1938, AA
LITTLE MISTER JIM, 1946, A
LITTLE MOTHER, 1973, O
LITTLE MOTHER, THE, 1922
LITTLE MURDERS, 1971, O
LITTLE NAPOLEON, THE, 1923
LITTLE NELLIE KELLY, 1940, A
LITTLE NIGHT MUSIC, A, 1977, C
LITTLE NUNS, THE, 1965, A
LITTLE OF WHAT YOU FANCY, A, 1968, A
LITTLE OLD NEW YORK, 1923
LITTLE OLD NEW YORK, 1940, A
LITTLE ONES, THE, 1965, AA
LITTLE ORPHAN, 1915
LITTLE ORPHAN ANNIE, 1932, AAA
LITTLE ORPHAN ANNIE, 1938, A
LITTLE ORPHAN, THE, 1917
LITTLE ORPHANT ANNIE, 1919
LITTLE ORVIE, 1940, AA
LITTLE PAL, 1915, A
LITTLE PATRIOT, A, 1917, A
LITTLE PEOPLE, THE, 1926
LITTLE PIRATE, THE, 1917
LITTLE PRINCE, THE, 1974, AAA
LITTLE PRINCESS, THE, 1917
LITTLE PRINCESS, THE, 1939, AAA
LITTLE RED DECIDES, 1918
LITTLE RED MONKEY
LITTLE RED RIDING HOOD, 1917
LITTLE RED RIDING HOOD, 1963, A
LITTLE RED RIDING HOOD AND HER FRIENDS, 1964, A
LITTLE RED RIDING HOOD AND THE MONSTERS, 1965, C
LITTLE RED SCHOOLHOUSE, 1936, AA
LITTLE RED SCHOOLHOUSE, THE, 1923
LITTLE ROBINSON CRUSOE, 1924
LITTLE ROMANCE, A, 1979, A
LITTLE ROWDY, THE, 1919
LITTLE RUNAWAY, THE, 1918
LITTLE SAMARITAN, THE, 1917
LITTLE SAVAGE, THE, 1929, A
LITTLE SAVAGE, THE, 1959, A
LITTLE SCHOOL MA'AM, THE, 1916, A
LITTLE SEX, A, 1982, O
LITTLE SHEPARD OF KINGDOM COME, THE, 1920
LITTLE SHEPHERD OF BARGIAN ROW, THE, 1916
LITTLE SHEPHERD OF KINGDOM COME, 1961, A
LITTLE SHEPHERD OF KINGDOM COME, THE, 1928
LITTLE SHOES, 1917
LITTLE SHOP OF HORRORS, 1961, C-O
LITTLE SISTER
LITTLE SISTER OF EVERYBODY, A, 1918
LITTLE SISTERS, 1972
LITTLE SNOB, THE, 1928
LITTLE SOLDIER, THE
LITTLE STRANGER, 1934, A
LITTLE SUNSET, 1915
LITTLE TERROR, THE, 1917
LITTLE THEATER OF JEAN RENOIR, THE
LITTLE TOKYO, U.S.A., 1942, A
LITTLE TOUGH GUY, 1938, A
LITTLE TOUGH GUYS IN SOCIETY, 1938, A
LITTLE WANDERER, THE, 1920
LITTLE WELSH GIRL, THE, 1920
LITTLE WHITE SAVAGE, THE, 1919
LITTLE WILD GIRL, THE, 1928, A
LITTLE WILDCAT, 1922, A
LITTLE WILDCAT, THE, 1928, A
LITTLE WOMEN, 1917

LITTLE WOMEN, 1919
LITTLE WOMEN, 1933, AAA
LITTLE WOMEN, 1949, AA
LITTLE WORLD OF DON CAMILLO, THE, 1953, A
LITTLE YANK, THE, 1917
LITTLE YELLOW HOUSE, THE, 1928
LITTLEST HOBO, THE, 1958, AAA
LITTLEST HORSE THIEVES, THE, 1977, AAA
LITTLEST OUTLAW, THE, 1955, AAA
LITTLEST REBEL, THE, 1914
LITTLEST REBEL, THE, 1935, AAA
LITTLEST SCOUT, 1919
LIVE A LITTLE, LOVE A LITTLE, 1968, A
LIVE A LITTLE, STEAL A LOT
LIVE AGAIN, 1936, A
LIVE AND LAUGH, 1933
LIVE AND LET DIE, 1973, C
LIVE AND LET LIVE, 1921
LIVE FAST, DIE YOUNG, 1958, A
LIVE FOR LIFE, 1967, A
LIVE IT UP
LIVE NOW—PAY LATER, 1962, A
LIVE SPARKS, 1920
LIVE TO LOVE
LIVE TODAY FOR TOMORROW
LIVE WIRE HICK, A, 1920
LIVE WIRE, THE, 1925
LIVE WIRE, THE, 1937, A
LIVE WIRES, 1921, A
LIVE WIRES, 1946, A
LIVE YOUR OWN WAY, 1970, A
LIVE, LOVE AND LEARN, 1937, A
LIVELY SET, THE, 1964, A
LIVER EATERS, THE
LIVES OF A BENGAL LANCER, 1935, A
LIVING
LIVING BETWEEN TWO WORLDS, 1963, A
LIVING COFFIN, THE, 1965, C
LIVING CORPSE, A, 1918
LIVING CORPSE, A, 1931
LIVING CORPSE, THE, 1940, A
LIVING DANGEROUSLY, 1936, A
LIVING DEAD AT MANCHESTER MORGUE
LIVING DEAD MAN, THE
LIVING DEAD, THE, 1936, A
LIVING FREE, 1972, A
LIVING GHOST, THE, 1942, A
LIVING HEAD, THE, 1969, O
LIVING IDOL, THE, 1957, C-O
LIVING IN A BIG WAY, 1947, A
LIVING IT UP, 1954, A
LIVING LEGEND, 1980, O
LIVING LIES, 1922
LIVING ON LOVE, 1937, A
LIVING ON VELVET, 1935, A
LIVING ORPHAN, THE, 1939
LIVING VENUS, 1961, O
LIVINGSTONE, 1925, A
LIZA, 1976, O
LIZZIE, 1957, C
LJUBAVNI SLUJAC ILI TRAGEDIJA SLUZBENICE P.T.T.
LLANO KID, THE, 1940, A
LLOYDS OF LONDON, 1936, A
LO STRANIERO
LOADED DICE
LOADED DICE, 1918
LOADED DOOR, THE, 1922, A
LOADED GUNS, 1975
LOADED PISTOLS, 1948, A
LOAN SHARK, 1952, A
LOCAL BAD MAN, 1932, A
LOCAL BOY MAKES GOOD, 1931, A
LOCAL COLOR, 1978, O
LOCAL HERO, 1983, A-C
LOCH NESS HORROR, THE, 1983
LOCK UP YOUR DAUGHTERS, 1969, C-O
LOCK YOUR DOORS
LOCKED DOOR, THE, 1929, A
LOCKED DOORS, 1925
LOCKED HEART, THE, 1918
LOCKED LIPS, 1920
LOCKER 69, 1962, A
LOCKET, THE, 1946, C
LOCKSMITH AND CHANCELLOR, 1923
LOCO LUCK, 1927
LODGE IN THE WILDERNESS, THE, 1926, A
LODGER, THE
LODGER, THE, 1926, A
LODGER, THE, 1944, C-O
LODGER: A STORY OF THE LONDON FOG, THE
LOGAN'S RUN, 1976, A
LOLA, 1914, A
LOLA, 1961, C
LOLA, 1971, C-O
LOLA, 1982, O
LOLA MONTES, 1955, C
LOLA'S MISTAKE
LOLA, 1933
LOLITA, 1962, C-O
LOLLIPOP, 1966, O
LOLLIPOP COVER, THE, 1965, A
LOLLIPOP, 1976
LOLLY MADONNA WAR, THE
LOLLY-MADONNA XXX, 1973, A
LOMBARDI, LTD., 1919
LONDON, 1926, A
LONDON AFTER MIDNIGHT, 1927, A
LONDON BELONGS TO ME
LONDON BLACKOUT MURDERS, 1942, A
LONDON BY NIGHT, 1937, A
LONDON CALLING
LONDON FLAT MYSTERY, A, 1915
LONDON MELODY, 1930, A
LONDON MELODY, 1938
LONDON NIGHTHAWKS, 1915
LONDON PRIDE, 1920, A
LONDON TOWN
LONDON'S ENEMIES, 1916, A
LONE AVENGER, THE, 1933, A
LONE BANDIT, THE, 1934
LONE CHANCE, THE, 1924
LONE CLIMBER, THE, 1950, AAA
LONE COWBOY, 1934, A
LONE EAGLE, THE, 1927, A
LONE FIGHTER, 1923
LONE GUN, THE, 1954, A
LONE HAND SAUNDERS, 1926
LONE HAND TEXAN, THE, 1947, A
LONE HAND TEXAS, 1924
LONE HAND WILSON, 1920
LONE HAND, THE, 1920, A
LONE HAND, THE, 1922
LONE HAND, THE, 1953, A
LONE HORSEMAN, THE, 1923
LONE HORSEMAN, THE, 1929, A
LONE PATROL, THE, 1928
LONE PRAIRIE, THE, 1942, A
LONE RANGER AND THE LOST CITY OF GOLD, THE, 1958, AA
LONE RANGER, THE, 1955, AA
LONE RIDER AMBUSHED, THE, 1941, A
LONE RIDER AND THE BANDIT, THE, 1942, A
LONE RIDER CROSSES THE RIO, THE, 1941, A
LONE RIDER FIGHTS BACK, THE, 1941, A
LONE RIDER IN BORDER ROUNDUP, 1942
LONE RIDER IN CHEYENNE, THE, 1942, A
LONE RIDER IN FRONTIER FURY, THE, 1941
LONE RIDER IN GHOST TOWN, THE, 1941, A
LONE RIDER RIDES ON, THE, 1941
LONE RIDER, THE, 1922
LONE RIDER, THE, 1927
LONE RIDER, THE, 1930, A
LONE RIDER, THE, 1934
LONE STAR, 1916
LONE STAR, 1952, A
LONE STAR COUNTRY, 1983
LONE STAR LAW MEN, 1942, A
LONE STAR LAWMAN
LONE STAR MOONLIGHT, 1946
LONE STAR PIONEERS, 1939, A
LONE STAR RAIDERS, 1940, A
LONE STAR RANGER, 1942, A
LONE STAR RANGER, THE, 1919
LONE STAR RANGER, THE, 1923
LONE STAR RANGER, THE, 1930, A
LONE STAR RUSH, THE, 1915
LONE STAR TRAIL, THE, 1943, A
LONE STAR VIGILANTES, THE, 1942, A
LONE TEXAN, 1959, A
LONE TEXAS RANGER, 1945, A
LONE TRAIL, THE, 1932, A
LONE TROUBADOR, THE
LONE WAGON, THE, 1924, A
LONE WOLF AND HIS LADY, THE, 1949, A
LONE WOLF IN LONDON, 1947, A
LONE WOLF IN MEXICO, THE, 1947, A
LONE WOLF IN PARIS, THE, 1938, A
LONE WOLF KEEPS A DATE, THE, 1940, A
LONE WOLF MEETS A LADY, THE, 1940, A
LONE WOLF McQUADE, 1983, C-O
LONE WOLF RETURNS, THE, 1926
LONE WOLF RETURNS, THE, 1936, A
LONE WOLF SPY HUNT, THE, 1939, A
LONE WOLF STRIKES, THE, 1940, A
LONE WOLF TAKES A CHANCE, THE, 1941, A
LONE WOLF'S DAUGHTER, THE, 1919
LONE WOLF'S DAUGHTER, THE, 1929, A
LONE WOLF'S DAUGHTER, THE, 1939
LONE WOLF, THE, 1917
LONE WOLF, THE, 1924
LONELINESS OF THE LONG DISTANCE RUNNER, THE, 1962, C-O
LONELY ARE THE BRAVE, 1962, C
LONELY GUY, THE, 1984, O
LONELY HEART, 1921
LONELY HEART BANDITS
LONELY HEARTS, 1983, O
LONELY HEARTS BANDITS, 1950, A
LONELY HEARTS KILLER
LONELY HEARTS KILLERS
LONELY LADY OF GROSVENOR, THE, 1922
LONELY LADY, THE, 1983, O
LONELY LADY, THE, 1955
LONELY LANE, 1963, O
LONELY MAN, THE, 1957, A
LONELY MAN, THE, 1969
LONELY ROAD, THE
LONELY ROAD, THE, 1923, A
LONELY STAGE
LONELY TRAIL, THE, 1922
LONELY TRAIL, THE, 1936, A
LONELY WIVES, 1931, A
LONELY WOMAN, THE
LONELY WOMAN, THE, 1918
LONELYHEARTS, 1958, C
LONER, THE
LONERS, THE, 1972, O
LONESOME, 1928, A
LONESOME CHAP, THE, 1917
LONESOME CORNERS, 1922
LONESOME COWBOYS, 1968, O
LONESOME HEART, 1915
LONESOME LADIES, 1927
LONESOME TOWN, 1916
LONESOME TRAIL, 1945
LONESOME TRAIL, THE, 1930, A
LONESOME TRAIL, THE, 1955, A
LONG ABSENCE, THE, 1962, A
LONG AGO, TOMORROW, 1971, C
LONG AND THE SHORT AND THE TALL, THE, 1961, A
LONG ARM OF MANNISTER, THE, 1919
LONG ARM, THE
LONG CHANCE, THE, 1915
LONG CHANCE, THE, 1922, A
LONG CORRIDOR
LONG DARK HALL, THE, 1951, A-C
LONG DAY'S DYING, THE, 1968, C-O
LONG DAY'S JOURNEY INTO NIGHT, 1962, C
LONG DISTANCE
LONG DUEL, THE, 1967, A
LONG GOOD FRIDAY, THE, 1982, O
LONG GOODBYE, THE, 1973, O
LONG GRAY LINE, THE, 1955, A
LONG HAUL, THE, 1957, A
LONG IS THE ROAD, 1948, A
LONG JOHN SILVER, 1954, A
LONG JOHN SILVER RETURNS TO TREASURE ISLAND
LONG KNIFE, THE, 1958, C
LONG LANE'S TURNING, THE, 1919
LONG LIVE THE KING, 1923, A
LONG LOOP ON THE PECOS, THE, 1927
LONG LOOP, THE
LONG LOST FATHER, 1934, A
LONG MEMORY, THE, 1953, A
LONG NIGHT, THE, 1947, A
LONG NIGHT, THE, 1976, A
LONG ODDS, 1922, A
LONG PANTS, 1927, A
LONG RIDE FROM HELL, A, 1970, O
LONG RIDE HOME, THE
LONG RIDE, THE
LONG RIDERS, THE, 1980, O
LONG ROPE, THE, 1961, A
LONG SHADOW, THE, 1961, A
LONG SHIPS, THE, 1964, C
LONG SHOT, 1981, C
LONG SHOT, THE, 1939, A
LONG TRAIL, THE, 1917
LONG VOYAGE HOME, THE, 1940, A
LONG WAIT, THE, 1954, A
LONG WEEKEND, 1978, C-O
LONG, DARK NIGHT, THE
LONG, HOT SUMMER, THE, 1958, A-C
LONG, LONG TRAIL, THE, 1929, A
LONG, LONG TRAIL, THE, 1942
LONG, LONG TRAILER, THE, 1954, A
LONGEST DAY, THE, 1962, C
LONGEST NIGHT, THE, 1936, A
LONGEST SPUR
LONGEST YARD, THE, 1974, O
LONGHORN, THE, 1951, A
LONGING FOR LOVE, 1966, O
LONGSHOT, 1982
LONNIE, 1963, C
LOOK BACK IN ANGER, 1959, C-O
LOOK BEFORE YOU LAUGH
LOOK BEFORE YOU LOVE, 1948, A
LOOK DOWN AND DIE, MEN OF STEEL
LOOK FOR THE SILVER LINING, 1949, A
LOOK IN ANY WINDOW, 1961, A
LOOK OUT FOR LOVE
LOOK OUT GIRL, THE, 1928
LOOK OUT SISTER, 1948, A
LOOK UP AND LAUGH, 1935, A

LOOK WHO'S LAUGHING, 1941, A
LOOK YOUR BEST, 1923
LOOKER, 1981, O
LOOKIN' FOR SOMEONE
LOOKIN' GOOD
LOOKIN' TO GET OUT, 1982, O
LOOKING FOR DANGER, 1957, A
LOOKING FOR LOVE, 1964, A
LOOKING FOR MR. GOODBAR, 1977, C-O
LOOKING FOR TROUBLE, 1926, A
LOOKING FOR TROUBLE, 1934, A
LOOKING FOR TROUBLE, 1931
LOOKING FORWARD, 1933, A
LOOKING GLASS WAR, THE, 1970, C
LOOKING ON THE BRIGHT SIDE, 1932, A
LOOKING UP, 1977, C
LOOKS AND SMILES, 1982, C
LOONEY, LOONEY, LOONEY BUGS BUNNY MOVIE, THE, 1981
LOONIES ON BROADWAY
LOOPED FOR LIFE, 1924
LOOPHOLE, 1954, A
LOOPHOLE, 1981, C
LOOSE ANKLES, 1930, A
LOOSE CONNECTIONS, 1984, C
LOOSE ENDS, 1930, A
LOOSE ENDS, 1975, C
LOOSE IN LONDON, 1953, A
LOOSE PLEASURES
LOOSE SHOES, 1980, C
LOOT, 1919
LOOT, 1971, C
LOOTERS, THE, 1955, A
LOPERJENTEN
LORD AND LADY ALGY, 1919
LORD BABS, 1932, A
LORD BYRON OF BROADWAY, 1930, A
LORD CAMBER'S LADIES, 1932, A
LORD CHUMLEY, 1914
LORD EDGEWARE DIES, 1934, A
LORD GAVE, THE
LORD JEFF, 1938, AA
LORD JIM, 1925, A
LORD JIM, 1965, A
LORD LOVE A DUCK, 1966, A
LORD LOVELAND DISCOVERS AMERICA, 1916
LORD LOVES THE IRISH, THE, 1919, A
LORD MOUNTDRAGO
LORD OF THE FLIES, 1963, A-C
LORD OF THE JUNGLE, 1955, A
LORD OF THE MANOR, 1933, A
LORD OF THE RINGS, THE, 1978, A
LORD RICHARD IN THE PANTRY, 1930, A
LORD SHANGO, 1975, O
LORDS OF DISCIPLINE, THE, 1983, O
LORDS OF FLATBUSH, THE, 1974, C
LORDS OF HIGH DECISION, THE, 1916
LORELEI OF THE SEA, 1917
LORNA DOONE, 1920
LORNA DOONE, 1927, A
LORNA DOONE, 1935, A
LORNA DOONE, 1951, A
LORRAINE OF THE LIONS, 1925
LORSQU'UNE FEMME VENT, 1919
LOS AMANTES DE VERONA
LOS AMIGOS
LOS ASTRONAUTAS, 1960, A
LOS AUTOMATAS DE LA MUERTE, 1960, A
LOS INVISIBLES, 1961, A
LOS OLVIDADOS, 1950, O
LOS PLATILLOS VOLADORES, 1955, A
LOS SANTOS INOCENTES
LOSER TAKE ALL
LOSER TAKES ALL, 1956, A
LOSER'S END, 1934
LOSER'S END, THE, 1924, A
LOSERS, THE, 1968, O
LOSERS, THE, 1970, O
LOSIN' IT, 1983, O
LOSING GAME, THE
LOSING GROUND, 1982
LOSS OF FEELING, 1935, A
LOSS OF INNOCENCE, 1961, C
LOSS OF THE BIRKENHEAD, THE, 1914
LOST
LOST, 1983
LOST—A WIFE, 1925
LOST AND FOUND
LOST AND FOUND, 1979, A-C
LOST AND FOUND ON A SOUTH SEA ISLAND, 1923
LOST AND WON, 1915
LOST AND WON, 1917
LOST ANGEL, 1944, A
LOST AT SEA, 1926
LOST AT THE FRONT, 1927
LOST ATLANTIS
LOST BATALLION, THE, 1919
LOST BATTALION, 1961, A
LOST BATTALION, THE, 1921
LOST BOUNDARIES, 1949, A
LOST BRIDEGROOM, THE, 1916, A
LOST CANYON, 1943, A
LOST CHORD, THE, 1917, A
LOST CHORD, THE, 1925
LOST CHORD, THE, 1937, A
LOST CITY, THE, 1982
LOST COMMAND, THE, 1966, A-C
LOST CONTINENT, 1951, A
LOST CONTINENT, THE, 1968, A
LOST EXPRESS, THE, 1926
LOST FACE, THE, 1965, C
LOST HAPPINESS, 1948, A
LOST HONEYMOON, 1947, A
LOST HONOR OF KATHARINA BLUM, THE, 1975, C
LOST HORIZON, 1937, A
LOST HORIZON, 1973, A
LOST HOUSE, THE, 1915
LOST ILLUSION, THE
LOST IN A BIG CITY, 1923
LOST IN A HAREM, 1944, A
LOST IN ALASKA, 1952, AAA
LOST IN THE DARK, 1914
LOST IN THE LEGION, 1934, A
LOST IN THE STARS, 1974, A
LOST IN THE STRATOSPHERE, 1935, A
LOST IN TRANSIT, 1917
LOST JUNGLE, THE, 1934, A
LOST LADY, A, 1924, A
LOST LADY, A, 1934, A
LOST LADY, THE
LOST LAGOON, 1958, A
LOST LEADER, A, 1922
LOST LIMITED, THE, 1927, A
LOST MAN, THE, 1969, C
LOST MEN
LOST MISSILE, THE, 1958, A
LOST MOMENT, THE, 1947, A
LOST MONEY, 1919
LOST ON THE WESTERN FRONT, 1940, A
LOST ONE, THE, 1951, C
LOST PARADISE, THE, 1914
LOST PATROL, THE, 1929, A
LOST PATROL, THE, 1934, C
LOST PEOPLE, THE, 1950, A
LOST PRINCESS, THE, 1919
LOST RANCH, 1937, A
LOST RIVER
LOST ROMANCE, THE, 1921
LOST SEX, 1968, O
LOST SHADOW, THE, 1921
LOST SOULS, 1961, O
LOST SQUADRON, THE, 1932, C
LOST STAGE VALLEY
LOST TRAIL, THE, 1926
LOST TRAIL, THE, 1945, A
LOST TREASURE OF THE AMAZON
LOST TRIBE, THE, 1924
LOST TRIBE, THE, 1949, A
LOST VOLCANO, THE, 1950, AA
LOST WEEKEND, THE, 1945, C-O
LOST WOMEN
LOST WORLD OF LIBRA, THE, 1968
LOST WORLD OF SINBAD, THE, 1965, A
LOST WORLD, THE, 1925, A
LOST WORLD, THE, 1960, A
LOST ZEPPELIN, 1930, A
LOST ZEPPELIN, THE, 1929
LOST, LONELY AND VICIOUS, 1958, A
LOST-BAG BLUES, 1971
LOTNA, 1966, C
LOTTERY BRIDE, THE, 1930, A
LOTTERY LOVER, 1935, A
LOTTERY MAN, THE, 1916
LOTTERY MAN, THE, 1919
LOTUS BLOSSOM, 1921
LOTUS BLOSSOM, 1921
LOTUS EATER, THE, 1921
LOTUS LADY, 1930, A
LOTUS WOMAN, THE, 1916
LOUDEST WHISPER, THE
LOUDSPEAKER, THE, 1934, A
LOUDWATER MYSTERY, THE, 1921
LOUIE, THERE'S A CROWD DOWNSTAIRS
LOUISA, 1950, A
LOUISE, 1940, A
LOUISIANA, 1919, A
LOUISIANA, 1947, A
LOUISIANA GAL
LOUISIANA HAYRIDE, 1944, A
LOUISIANA HUSSY, 1960, C
LOUISIANA PURCHASE, 1941, A
LOUISIANA STORY, 1948, AAA
LOUISIANA TERRITORY, 1953, A
LOUISIANE, 1984, A-C
LOULOU, 1980, O
LOVABLE AND SWEET
LOVABLE CHEAT, THE, 1949, A
LOVE, 1916, A
LOVE, 1920
LOVE, 1927, C
LOVE, 1972, C
LOVE, 1982, C
LOVE 'EM AND LEAVE 'EM, 1926
LOVE -HATE -DEATH, 1918
LOVE A LA CARTE, 1965, O
LOVE AFFAIR, 1932, A
LOVE AFFAIR, 1939, A
LOVE AFFAIR OF THE DICTATOR, THE
LOVE AFFAIR; OR THE CASE OF THE MISSING SWITCHBOARD OPERATOR, 1968, O
LOVE AFLAME, 1917, A
LOVE AFTER DEATH, 1968
LOVE AMONG THE MILLIONAIRES, 1930, A
LOVE AND AMBITION, 1917
LOVE AND ANARCHY, 1974, O
LOVE AND BULLETS, 1979, C
LOVE AND DEATH, 1975, A-C
LOVE AND GLORY, 1924
LOVE AND HATE, 1916
LOVE AND HISSES, 1937, A
LOVE AND JOURNALISM, 1916
LOVE AND KISSES, 1965, A
LOVE AND KISSES
LOVE AND LARCENY, 1963, A
LOVE AND LARCENY, 1983
LOVE AND LEARN, 1928, A
LOVE AND LEARN, 1947, A
LOVE AND MARRIAGE, 1966, C
LOVE AND MONEY, 1982, O
LOVE AND PAIN AND THE WHOLE DAMN THING, 1973, C
LOVE AND SACRIFICE
LOVE AND SACRIFICE, 1936
LOVE AND THE DEVIL, 1929
LOVE AND THE FRENCHWOMAN, 1961, C-O
LOVE AND THE LAW, 1919
LOVE AND THE MIDNIGHT AUTO SUPPLY, 1978, C-O
LOVE AND THE WOMAN, 1919
LOVE AT FIRST BITE, 1979, C
LOVE AT FIRST SIGHT, 1930, A
LOVE AT FIRST SIGHT, 1977, A
LOVE AT NIGHT, 1961, C-O
LOVE AT SEA, 1936, A
LOVE AT SECOND SIGHT
LOVE AT THE WHEEL, 1921, A
LOVE AT TWENTY, 1963, C
LOVE AUCTION, THE, 1919, A
LOVE BAN, THE
LOVE BANDIT, THE, 1924
LOVE BEFORE BREAKFAST, 1936, A
LOVE BEGINS AT TWENTY, 1936, A
LOVE BIRDS, 1934, A
LOVE BOUND, 1932, A
LOVE BRAND, THE, 1923
LOVE BUG, THE, 1968, AAA
LOVE BURGLAR, THE, 1919
LOVE BUTCHER, THE, 1982, O
LOVE CAGE, THE
LOVE CALL, THE, 1919
LOVE CAPTIVE, THE, 1934, A
LOVE CHARM, THE, 1921, A
LOVE CHEAT, THE, 1919
LOVE CHILD, 1982, O
LOVE CHILDREN
LOVE COMES ALONG, 1930, A
LOVE COMES QUIETLY, 1974
LOVE CONTRACT, THE, 1932, A
LOVE CRAZY, 1941, A
LOVE CYCLES, 1969, C
LOVE DARES ALL
LOVE DEFENDER, THE, 1919
LOVE DOCTOR, THE, 1917
LOVE DOCTOR, THE, 1929, A
LOVE ETERNAL
LOVE ETERNE, THE, 1964, A
LOVE EXPERT, THE, 1920
LOVE FACTORY, 1969, C-O
LOVE FEAST, THE, 1966, O
LOVE FINDS A WAY
LOVE FINDS ANDY HARDY, 1938, AA
LOVE FLOWER, THE, 1920, A
LOVE FROM A STRANGER, 1937, C
LOVE FROM A STRANGER, 1947, A
LOVE GAMBLE, THE, 1925
LOVE GAMBLER, THE, 1922, A
LOVE GIRL, THE, 1916, A
LOVE GOD?, THE, 1969, A
LOVE HABIT, THE, 1931, A
LOVE HAPPY, 1949, A
LOVE HAS MANY FACES, 1965, C
LOVE HERMIT, THE, 1916
LOVE HOUR, THE, 1925
LOVE HUNGER, 1965, O
LOVE HUNGER, THE, 1919
LOVE HUNGRY, 1928
LOVE IN 4 DIMENSIONS, 1965, C
LOVE IN A BUNGALOW, 1937, A

LOVE IN A FOUR LETTER WORLD, 1970, O
LOVE IN A GOLDFISH BOWL, 1961, A
LOVE IN A HOT CLIMATE, 1958, A
LOVE IN A HURRY, 1919, A
LOVE IN A TAXI, 1980, A
LOVE IN A WOOD, 1915, A
LOVE IN BLOOM, 1935, A
LOVE IN COLD BLOOD
LOVE IN EXILE, 1936, A
LOVE IN GERMANY, A, 1984, O
LOVE IN HIGH GEAR, 1932
LOVE IN LAS VEGAS
LOVE IN MOROCCO, 1933, A
LOVE IN PAWN, 1953, A
LOVE IN THE AFTERNOON, 1957, A
LOVE IN THE DARK, 1922
LOVE IN THE DESERT, 1929, A
LOVE IN THE ROUGH, 1930, A
LOVE IN THE WELSH HILLS, 1921
LOVE IN THE WILDERNESS, 1920
LOVE IN WAITING, 1948, A
LOVE INSURANCE, 1920
LOVE IS A BALL, 1963, A
LOVE IS A CAROUSEL, 1970, O
LOVE IS A DAY'S WORK
LOVE IS A FUNNY THING, 1970, C
LOVE IS A HEADACHE, 1938, A
LOVE IS A MANY-SPLENDORED THING, 1955, A
LOVE IS A RACKET, 1932, A
LOVE IS A SPLENDID ILLUSION, 1970, O
LOVE IS A WEAPON
LOVE IS A WOMAN, 1967, C
LOVE IS AN AWFUL THING, 1922, A
LOVE IS BETTER THAN EVER, 1952, A
LOVE IS LIKE THAT, 1933, A
LOVE IS LIKE THAT, 1930
LOVE IS LOVE, 1919
LOVE IS MY PROFESSION, 1959, O
LOVE IS NEWS, 1937, A
LOVE IS ON THE AIR, 1937, A
LOVE ISLAND, 1952, A
LOVE ITALIAN STYLE
LOVE KISS, THE, 1930, A
LOVE LAUGHS AT ANDY HARDY, 1946, A
LOVE LETTER, THE, 1923, A
LOVE LETTERS, 1917
LOVE LETTERS, 1924
LOVE LETTERS, 1945, A
LOVE LETTERS, 1983, C
LOVE LETTERS OF A STAR, 1936, A
LOVE LIAR, THE, 1916, A
LOVE LIES, 1931, A
LOVE LIGHT, THE, 1921, A
LOVE LOTTERY, THE, 1954, A
LOVE MACHINE, THE, 1971, O
LOVE MADNESS
LOVE MADNESS, 1920
LOVE MAGGY, 1921
LOVE MAKERS, THE
LOVE MAKES 'EM WILD, 1927, A
LOVE MART, THE, 1927
LOVE MASK, THE, 1916
LOVE MASTER, THE, 1924
LOVE MATCH, THE, 1955, A
LOVE MATES, 1967, A
LOVE MATES, THE
LOVE ME, 1918
LOVE ME AND THE WORLD IS MINE, 1928, A
LOVE ME DEADLY, 1972, O
LOVE ME FOREVER, 1935, A
LOVE ME OR LEAVE ME, 1955, A
LOVE ME TENDER, 1956, A
LOVE ME TONIGHT, 1932, A
LOVE MERCHANT, THE, 1966, O
LOVE MERCHANTS
LOVE NEST, 1951, A
LOVE NEST, THE, 1922
LOVE NEST, THE, 1933, A
LOVE NET, THE, 1918
LOVE NEVER DIES, 1916
LOVE NEVER DIES, 1921
LOVE NOW . . . PAY LATER, 1966, C
LOVE NOW . . . PAY LATER, O
LOVE OF A STATE COUNCILLOR, 1915
LOVE OF AN ACTRESS, THE, 1914
LOVE OF JEANNE NEY, THE, 1927
LOVE OF PAQUITA, THE, 1927
LOVE OF SUNYA, THE, 1927
LOVE OF THREE QUEENS
LOVE OF WOMEN, 1924
LOVE OF WOMEN, THE, 1915
LOVE ON A BET, 1936, A
LOVE ON A BUDGET, 1938, A
LOVE ON A PILLOW, 1963, O
LOVE ON SKIS, 1933, A
LOVE ON THE DOLE, 1945, A
LOVE ON THE GROUND, 1984, C
LOVE ON THE RIO GRANDE, 1925
LOVE ON THE RIVIERA, 1964, C
LOVE ON THE RUN, 1936, A
LOVE ON THE RUN, 1980, A-C
LOVE ON THE SPOT, 1932, A
LOVE ON TOAST, 1937, A
LOVE ON WHEELS, 1932, A
LOVE ONE ANOTHER, 1922
LOVE OR FAME, 1919
LOVE OR JUSTICE, 1917
LOVE OR MONEY, 1920
LOVE OVER THE NIGHT, 1928
LOVE PARADE, THE, 1929, A-C
LOVE PAST THIRTY, 1934, A
LOVE PIKER, THE, 1923
LOVE PILL, THE, 1971
LOVE PIRATE, THE, 1923
LOVE PLAY
LOVE PROBLEMS, 1970, C
LOVE RACE
LOVE RACE, THE, 1931, A
LOVE RACKET, THE, 1929, A
LOVE REDEEMED
LOVE ROBOTS, THE, 1965, C
LOVE ROOT, THE
LOVE ROUTE, THE, 1915
LOVE SLAVES OF THE AMAZONS, 1957, A
LOVE SPECIAL, THE, 1921
LOVE SPECIALIST, THE, 1959, A
LOVE STARVED
LOVE STORM, THE, 1931, A
LOVE STORY
LOVE STORY, 1949, C
LOVE STORY, 1970, A-C
LOVE STORY OF ALIETTE BRUNTON, THE, 1924
LOVE STREAMS, 1984, C
LOVE SUBLIME, A, 1917
LOVE SWINDLE, 1918, A
LOVE TAKES FLIGHT, 1937, A
LOVE TEST, THE, 1935, A
LOVE THAT BRUTE, 1950, A
LOVE THAT DARES, THE, 1919
LOVE THAT LIVES, THE, 1917
LOVE THIEF, THE, 1916
LOVE THIEF, THE, 1926
LOVE THRILL, THE, 1927
LOVE THY NEIGHBOR, 1940, A
LOVE THY NEIGHBOUR, 1973
LOVE TIME, 1934, A
LOVE TOY, THE, 1926, A
LOVE TRADER, 1930, A
LOVE TRAIL, THE, 1916
LOVE TRAP, THE, 1923
LOVE TRAP, THE, 1929, A
LOVE UNDER FIRE, 1937, A
LOVE UNDER THE CRUCIFIX, 1965, A
LOVE UNDER THE ELMS, 1973
LOVE UP THE POLE, 1936, A
LOVE WAGER, THE, 1927
LOVE WAGER, THE, 1933, A
LOVE WALTZ, THE, 1930, A
LOVE WANGA, 1942
LOVE WATCHES, 1918
LOVE WITH THE PROPER STRANGER, 1963, C
LOVE WITHOUT QUESTION, 1920
LOVE'S A LUXURY
LOVE'S BATTLE, 1920
LOVE'S BLINDNESS, 1926, A
LOVE'S BOOMERANG, 1922
LOVE'S CONQUEST, 1918
LOVE'S CROSS ROADS, 1916
LOVE'S CRUCIBLE, 1916
LOVE'S CRUCIBLE, 1922
LOVE'S FLAME, 1920
LOVE'S GREATEST MISTAKE, 1927
LOVE'S HARVEST, 1920
LOVE'S INFLUENCE, 1922
LOVE'S LARIAT, 1916
LOVE'S LAW, 1917
LOVE'S LAW, 1918
LOVE'S MASQUERADE, 1922
LOVE'S OLD SWEET SONG, 1917, A
LOVE'S OLD SWEET SONG, 1923
LOVE'S OLD SWEET SONG, 1933, A
LOVE'S OPTION, 1928
LOVE'S PAY DAY, 1918
LOVE'S PENALTY, 1921, A
LOVE'S PILGRIMAGE TO AMERICA, 1916
LOVE'S PRISONER, 1919
LOVE'S PROTEGE, 1920
LOVE'S REDEMPTION, 1921, A
LOVE'S TOLL, 1916, A
LOVE'S WHIRLPOOL, 1924
LOVE'S WILDERNESS, 1924, A
LOVE, HATE AND A WOMAN, 1921
LOVE, HONOR AND ?, 1919
LOVE, HONOR AND BEHAVE, 1920
LOVE, HONOR AND BEHAVE, 1938, A
LOVE, HONOR AND GOODBYE, 1945, A
LOVE, HONOR AND OBEY, 1920, A
LOVE, HONOR AND OH, BABY, 1940, A
LOVE, HONOR, AND OH BABY, 1933, A
LOVE, LIFE AND LAUGHTER, 1934, A
LOVE, LIVE AND LAUGH, 1929, A
LOVE, SOLDIERS AND WOMEN
LOVE, THE ITALIAN WAY, 1964, C
LOVE, THE ONLY LAW
LOVE, VAMPIRE STYLE, 1971
LOVE—TAHITI STYLE
LOVE-INS, THE, 1967, C
LOVEBOUND, 1923
LOVED ONE, THE, 1965, C
LOVELESS, THE, 1982, O
LOVELETTERS FROM TERALBA ROAD, 1977
LOVELINES, 1984, O
LOVELORN, THE, 1927, A
LOVELY BUT DEADLY, 1983
LOVELY MARY, 1916
LOVELY TO LOOK AT
LOVELY TO LOOK AT, 1952, A
LOVELY WAY TO DIE, A, 1968, C
LOVELY WAY TO GO, A
LOVEMAKER, THE
LOVEMAKERS, THE
LOVER BOY
LOVER COME BACK, 1931, A
LOVER COME BACK, 1946, A
LOVER COME BACK, 1961, A
LOVER FOR THE SUMMER, A
LOVER OF CAMILLE, THE, 1924
LOVER'S ISLAND, 1925, A
LOVER'S LANE, 1924, A
LOVER'S NET, 1957, C
LOVER'S OATH, A, 1925, A
LOVER, WIFE
LOVERS AND LIARS, 1981, O
LOVERS AND LOLLIPOPS, 1956, A
LOVERS AND LUGGERS, 1938, A
LOVERS AND OTHER STRANGERS, 1970, C
LOVERS COURAGEOUS, 1932, A
LOVERS IN ARABY, 1924
LOVERS IN LIMBO
LOVERS IN QUARANTINE, 1925
LOVERS LIKE US
LOVERS MUST LEARN
LOVERS OF LISBON
LOVERS OF MONTPARNASSE, THE
LOVERS OF TERUEL, THE, 1962, A
LOVERS OF TOLEDO, THE, 1954, A
LOVERS OF VERONA, THE, 1951, A
LOVERS ON A TIGHTROPE, 1962, A
LOVERS' ROCK, 1966, A
LOVERS, HAPPY LOVERS, 1955, C
LOVERS, THE, 1959, O
LOVERS, THE, 1972, C
LOVERS?, 1927
LOVES AND ADVENTURES IN THE LIFE OF SHAKESPEARE (1914, Brit.)
LOVES AND TIMES OF SCARAMOUCHE, THE, 1976, C
LOVES OF A BLONDE, 1966, A
LOVES OF A DICTATOR
LOVES OF AN ACTRESS, 1928
LOVES OF ARIANE, THE
LOVES OF CARMEN, 1927
LOVES OF CARMEN, THE, 1948, C
LOVES OF COLLEEN BAWN, THE, 1924
LOVES OF EDGAR ALLAN POE, THE, 1942, A
LOVES OF HERCULES, THE, 1960, A
LOVES OF ISADORA, THE
LOVES OF JOANNA GODDEN, THE, 1947, A
LOVES OF LETTY, THE, 1920
LOVES OF MADAME DUBARRY, THE, 1938, A
LOVES OF MARY, QUEEN OF SCOTS, THE, 1923
LOVES OF RICARDO, THE, 1926, A
LOVES OF ROBERT BURNS, THE, 1930, A
LOVES OF SALAMMBO, THE, 1962, A
LOVES OF THREE QUEENS, THE, 1954, A
LOVESICK, 1983, C
LOVETIME, 1921
LOVEY MARY, 1926
LOVIN' FOOL, THE, 1926
LOVIN' MOLLY, 1974, O
LOVIN' THE LADIES, 1930, A
LOVING, 1970, C
LOVING COUPLES, 1966, O
LOVING COUPLES, 1980, O
LOVING FOOL, THE
LOVING LIES, 1924
LOVING MEMORY, 1970, O
LOVING YOU, 1957, A
LOW BLOW, THE, 1970
LOWER DEPTHS, THE, 1937, C
LOWER DEPTHS, THE, 1962, C
LOWLAND CINDERELLA, A, 1921
LOYAL HEART, 1946, AAA
LOYAL LIVES, 1923, A
LOYALTIES, 1934, A
LOYALTY, 1918
LOYALTY OF LOVE, 1937, A
LSD, I HATE YOU

LT. ROBIN CRUSOE, U.S.N., 1966, AAA
LUCETTE, 1924
LUCI DEL VARIETA
LUCIANO, 1963, C
LUCIFER COMPLEX, THE, 1978
LUCIFER PROJECT, THE
LUCIFER'S WOMEN, 1978
LUCK, 1923, A
LUCK AND PLUCK, 1919, A
LUCK AND SAND, 1925
LUCK IN PAWN, 1919
LUCK OF A SAILOR, THE, 1934, A
LUCK OF GERALDINE LAIRD, THE, 1920
LUCK OF GINGER COFFEY, THE, 1964, A-C
LUCK OF ROARING CAMP, THE, 1937, A
LUCK OF THE GAME
LUCK OF THE IRISH, 1948, A
LUCK OF THE IRISH, THE, 1920
LUCK OF THE IRISH, THE, 1937, A
LUCK OF THE NAVY
LUCK OF THE NAVY, THE, 1927
LUCK OF THE TURF, 1936, A
LUCK TOUCHED MY LEGS, 1930
LUCKIEST GIRL IN THE WORLD, THE, 1936, A
LUCKY
LUCKY 13
LUCKY BOOTS
LUCKY BOY, 1929, A
LUCKY BRIDE, THE, 1948, AA
LUCKY CARSON, 1921
LUCKY CISCO KID, 1940, A
LUCKY DAN, 1922
LUCKY DAYS, 1935, A
LUCKY DAYS, 1943
LUCKY DEVIL, 1925
LUCKY DEVILS, 1933, A
LUCKY DEVILS, 1941, C
LUCKY DOG, 1933, AAA
LUCKY FOOL, 1927
LUCKY GIRL, 1932, A
LUCKY HORSESHOE, THE, 1925, A
LUCKY IN LOVE, 1929, A
LUCKY JADE, 1937, A
LUCKY JIM, 1957, C
LUCKY JORDAN, 1942, A
LUCKY LADIES, 1932, A
LUCKY LADY, 1975, C-O
LUCKY LADY, THE, 1926
LUCKY LARKIN, 1930
LUCKY LARRIGAN, 1933, A
LUCKY LEGS, 1942, A
LUCKY LOSER, 1934, A
LUCKY LOSERS, 1950, C
LUCKY LUCIANO
LUCKY LUKE, 1971, A
LUCKY MASCOT, THE, 1951, A
LUCKY ME, 1954, A
LUCKY NICK CAIN, 1951, A
LUCKY NIGHT, 1939, A
LUCKY NUMBER, THE, 1933, A
LUCKY PARTNERS, 1940, A
LUCKY RALSTON
LUCKY SPURS, 1926
LUCKY STAR, 1929, A
LUCKY STAR, THE, 1980, A
LUCKY STIFF, THE, 1949, A
LUCKY SWEEP, A, 1932, A
LUCKY TERROR, 1936, A
LUCKY TEXAN, THE, 1934, A
LUCKY TO BE A WOMAN, 1955, C-O
LUCKY TO ME, 1939, AA
LUCRECE BORGIA, 1953, O
LUCRETIA BORGIA
LUCRETIA LOMBARD, 1923
LUCREZIA BORGIA, 1937, A
LUCY GALLANT, 1955, C
LUDWIG, 1973, O
LUGGAGE OF THE GODS, 1983, C
LULLABY, 1961, A
LULLABY OF BROADWAY, THE, 1951, A
LULLABY, THE
LULLABY, THE, 1924, A
LULU, 1962, O
LULU, 1978, O
LULU BELLE, 1948, A
LUM AND ABNER ABROAD, 1956, AA
LUMBERJACK, 1944, A
LUMIERE, 1976, O
LUMIERE D'ETE, 1943, C
LUMMOX, 1930, A
LUNA, 1979, O
LUNATIC AT LARGE, THE, 1921
LUNATIC AT LARGE, THE, 1927
LUNCH HOUR, 1962, C
LUNCH ON THE GRASS
LUNCH WAGON, 1981, O
LUNCH WAGON GIRLS
LUNG-MEN K'O-CHAN
LUPE, 1967, O
LURE OF A WOMAN, THE, 1921
LURE OF AMBITION, 1919
LURE OF CROONING WATER, THE, 1920
LURE OF EGYPT, THE, 1921
LURE OF GOLD, 1922, A
LURE OF HEART'S DESIRE, THE, 1916
LURE OF JADE, THE, 1921
LURE OF LONDON, THE, 1914, A
LURE OF LOVE, THE, 1924, A
LURE OF LUXURY, THE, 1918
LURE OF MILLIONS, 1915
LURE OF NEW YORK, THE, 1913
LURE OF THE ISLANDS, 1942, A
LURE OF THE JUNGLE, THE, 1970, AAA
LURE OF THE MASK, THE, 1915
LURE OF THE MINE, 1929
LURE OF THE NIGHT CLUB, THE, 1927
LURE OF THE SWAMP, 1957, C
LURE OF THE TRACK, 1925
LURE OF THE WASTELAND, 1939, A
LURE OF THE WEST, 1925
LURE OF THE WILD, THE, 1925, A
LURE OF THE WILDERNESS, 1952, C
LURE OF THE YUKON, 1924, A
LURE OF YOUTH, THE, 1921, A
LURE, THE, 1914, A
LURE, THE, 1933, A
LURED, 1947, A
LURING LIGHTS, 1915
LURING LIPS, 1921
LURING SHADOWS, 1920
LUST FOR A VAMPIRE, 1971, O
LUST FOR EVIL
LUST FOR GOLD, 1949, O
LUST FOR LIFE, 1956, C
LUST OF EVIL
LUST OF THE AGES, THE, 1917
LUST OF THE RED MAN, THE, 1914
LUST TO KILL, 1960
LUSTY BRAWLERS
LUSTY MEN, THE, 1952, C
LUTHER, 1974, C
LUTRING
LUV, 1967, A-C
LUXURY, 1921
LUXURY GIRLS, 1953, C
LUXURY LINER, 1933, A
LUXURY LINER, 1948, A
LYCANTHROPUS
LYDIA, 1941, A
LYDIA, 1964, O
LYDIA ATE THE APPLE
LYDIA BAILEY, 1952, A
LYDIA GILMORE, 1916
LYING LIPS, 1916
LYING LIPS, 1921, A
LYING LIPS, 1939
LYING TRUTH, THE, 1922, A
LYING WIVES, 1925
LYNCHING, 1968
LYONS IN PARIS, THE, 1955, A
LYONS MAIL, THE, 1916
LYONS MAIL, THE, 1931, A
LYSISTRATA

-M-

M, 1933, O
M, 1951, C
M, 1970, C-O
M'BLIMEY, 1931, A
M'LISS, 1915
M'LISS, 1918, A
M'LISS, 1936, A
M'LORD OF THE WHITE ROAD, 1923
M. LECOQ, 1915
M.A.R.S.
M★A★S★H, 1970, C-O
M3: THE GEMINI STRAIN, 1980
MA AND PA KETTLE, 1949, A
MA AND PA KETTLE AT HOME, 1954, A
MA AND PA KETTLE AT THE FAIR, 1952, A
MA AND PA KETTLE AT WAIKIKI, 1955, A
MA AND PA KETTLE BACK ON THE FARM, 1951, A
MA AND PA KETTLE GO TO PARIS
MA AND PA KETTLE GO TO TOWN, 1950
MA AND PA KETTLE ON VACATION, 1953, A
MA BARKER'S KILLER BROOD, 1960, O
MA NUIT CHEZ MAUD
MA POMME
MA TANTE D'HONFLEUR, 1923
MA, HE'S MAKING EYES AT ME, 1940, A
MAARAKAT ALGER
MABUL, 1927
MAC ARTHUR, 1977, A
MACABRE, 1958, C
MACAO, 1952, C
MACARIO, 1961, AA
MACBETH, 1916
MACBETH, 1916
MACBETH, 1948, A
MACBETH, 1950
MACBETH, 1963, A
MACBETH, 1971, O
MACDONALD OF THE CANADIAN MOUNTIES
MACHETE, 1958, A
MACHINE GUN KELLY, 1958, C-O
MACHINE GUN MAMA, 1944, A
MACHINE GUN McCAIN, 1970, O
MACHISMO—40 GRAVES FOR 40 GUNS, 1970, O
MACHISTE AGAINST THE CZAR
MACHO CALLAHAN, 1970, O
MACISTE IN HELL, 1926
MACISTE NELLA TERRA DEI CICLOPI
MACK, THE, 1973, O
MACKENNA'S GOLD, 1969, C
MACKINTOSH & T.J., 1975, C-O
MACKINTOSH MAN, THE, 1973, C
MACOMBER AFFAIR, THE, 1947, C
MACON COUNTY LINE, 1974, O
MACUMBA LOVE, 1960, A
MACUSHLA, 1937, A
MAD ABOUT MEN, 1954, A
MAD ABOUT MONEY
MAD ABOUT MUSIC, 1938, A
MAD ADVENTURES OF RABBI JACOB, THE, 1973, C
MAD ADVENTURES OF "RABBI" JACOB, THE, 974,
MAD AT THE WORLD, 1955, C
MAD ATLANTIC, THE, 1967, O
MAD BOMBER, THE, 1973, O
MAD BUTCHER, THE, 1972
MAD CAGE, THE
MAD DANCER, 1925, A
MAD DOCTOR OF BLOOD ISLAND, THE, 1969, O
MAD DOCTOR OF MARKET STREET, THE, 1942, A
MAD DOCTOR, THE, 1941, A
MAD DOG
MAD DOG COLL, 1961, C
MAD DOG MORGAN, 1976, O
MAD EMPRESS, THE, 1940, A
MAD EXECUTIONERS, THE, 1965, O
MAD GAME, THE, 1933, A
MAD GENIUS, THE, 1931, A-C
MAD GHOUL, THE, 1943, C
MAD HATTER, THE
MAD HATTERS, THE, 1935, A
MAD HOLIDAY, 1936, A
MAD HOUR, 1928
MAD LITTLE ISLAND, 1958, A
MAD LOVE, 1935, C
MAD LOVER, THE
MAD MAGAZINE PRESENTS UP THE ACADEMY
MAD MAGICIAN, THE, 1954, C
MAD MARRIAGE, THE, 1921, A
MAD MARRIAGE, THE, 1925
MAD MARTINDALES, THE, 1942, A
MAD MASQUERADE
MAD MAX, 1979, O
MAD MAX 2
MAD MEN OF EUROPE, 1940, A
MAD MISS MANTON, THE, 1938, A-C
MAD MONSTER PARTY, 1967, AA
MAD MONSTER, THE, 1942, A
MAD PARADE, THE, 1931, A
MAD QUEEN, THE, 1950, A
MAD ROOM, THE, 1969, O
MAD WEDNESDAY, 1950, A
MAD WHIRL, THE, 1925
MAD YOUTH, 1940, A
MAD, MAD MOVIE MAKERS, THE
MADALENA, 1965, A
MADAM SATAN
MADAM WHO?, 1917
MADAME, 1963, A-C
MADAME AKI, 1963, O
MADAME BEHAVE, 1925
MADAME BOVARY, 1949, A
MADAME BUTTERFLY, 1915, A
MADAME BUTTERFLY, 1932, A
MADAME BUTTERFLY, 1955, A
MADAME CURIE, 1943, AAA
MADAME DE
MADAME DEATH, 1968, O
MADAME DU BARRY, 1934, A
MADAME DU BARRY, 1954, C
MADAME DUBARRY
MADAME DUBARRY, 1918
MADAME ET SON FILLEUL, 1919
MADAME FLIRT, 1923
MADAME FRANKENSTEIN
MADAME GUILLOTINE, 1931, A
MADAME JEALOUSY, 1918
MADAME JULIE
MADAME LA PRESIDENTE, 1916
MADAME LOUISE, 1951, A
MADAME PEACOCK, 1920
MADAME PIMPERNEL
MADAME POMPADOUR, 1927, A
MADAME RACKETEER, 1932, A

MADAME RECAMIER, 1928
MADAME ROSA, 1977, O
MADAME SANS-GENE, 1923
MADAME SANS-GENE, 1925
MADAME SANS-GENE
MADAME SATAN, 1930, A
MADAME SHERRY, 1917
MADAME SPHINX, 1918
MADAME SPY, 1918, A
MADAME SPY, 1934, A
MADAME SPY, 1942, A
MADAME WANTS NO CHILDREN, 1927
MADAME WHITE SNAKE, 1963, C
MADAME X, 1916
MADAME X, 1920
MADAME X, 1929, A
MADAME X, 1937, A
MADAME X, 1966, A
MADCAP
MADCAP BETTY, 1915, A
MADCAP MADGE, 1917
MADCAP OF THE HOUSE, 1950, A
MADCAP, THE, 1916
MADCHEN FUR DIE MAMBO-BAR
MADCHEN IN UNIFORM
MADDEST CAR IN THE WORLD, THE, 1974, AAA
MADDEST STORY EVER TOLD, THE
MADE, 1972, C
MADE FOR EACH OTHER, 1939, AA
MADE FOR EACH OTHER, 1971, C
MADE FOR LOVE, 1926
MADE IN HEAVEN, 1921, A
MADE IN HEAVEN, 1952, A
MADE IN ITALY, 1967, C
MADE IN PARIS, 1966, A
MADE IN U.S.A., 1966, C
MADE ON BROADWAY, 1933, A
MADE-TO-ORDER HERO, A, 1928
MADELEINE, 1950, A
MADELEINE IS, 1971, O
MADEMOISELLE, 1966, C
MADEMOISELLE DE LA SEIGLIERE, 1921
MADEMOISELLE DOCTEUR
MADEMOISELLE FIFI, 1944, A
MADEMOISELLE FRANCE
MADEMOISELLE JOSETTE MA FEMME, 1926
MADEMOISELLE MIDNIGHT, 1924
MADEMOISELLE MODISTE, 1926
MADHOUSE, 1974, C
MADHOUSE, 1982
MADIGAN, 1968, C
MADIGAN'S MILLIONS, 1970, A
MADISON AVENUE, 1962, A
MADISON SQUARE GARDEN, 1932, A
MADLY, 1970, O
MADMAN, 1982, O
MADMAN OF LAB 4, THE, 1967, A
MADMEN OF MANDORAS
MADNESS OF HELEN, THE, 1916
MADNESS OF LOVE, THE, 1922
MADNESS OF THE HEART, 1949, A
MADNESS OF YOUTH, 1923, A
MADONNA OF AVENUE A, 1929, A
MADONNA OF THE DESERT, 1948, A
MADONNA OF THE SEVEN MOONS, 1945, C
MADONNA OF THE STREETS, 1924
MADONNA OF THE STREETS, 1930, A
MADONNA'S SECRET, THE, 1946, A
MADONNAS AND MEN, 1920, C
MADRON, 1970, O
MADWOMAN OF CHAILLOT, THE, 1969, A
MAEDCHEN IN UNIFORM, 1932, C
MAEDCHEN IN UNIFORM, 1965, C
MAELSTROM, THE, 1917
MAEVA, 1961, O
MAEVA—PORTRAIT OF A TAHITIAN GIRL
MAFIA, •(19, C
MAFIA GIRLS, THE, 1969, C-O
MAFIA JUNCTION, 1977
MAFIA, THE, 1972, C
MAFIOSO, 1962, C
MAFU CAGE, THE, 1978, O
MAG WHEELS, 1978
MAGDA, 1917
MAGDALENE OF HILLS, A, 1917
MAGGIE PEPPER, 1919
MAGGIE, THE
MAGIC, 1978, O
MAGIC BOW, THE, 1947, A
MAGIC BOX, THE, 1952, AA
MAGIC BOX, THE, 1965
MAGIC BOY, 1960, A
MAGIC CARPET, THE, 1951, A
MAGIC CHRISTIAN, THE, 1970, C-O
MAGIC CHRISTMAS TREE, 1964, A
MAGIC CLOAK OF OZ, THE, 1914
MAGIC CUP, THE, 1921
MAGIC EYE, THE, 1918
MAGIC FACE, THE, 1951, A
MAGIC FIRE, 1956, A
MAGIC FLAME, THE, 1927
MAGIC FOUNTAIN, THE, 1961, A
MAGIC GARDEN OF STANLEY SWEETHART, THE, 1970, O
MAGIC GARDEN, THE
MAGIC GARDEN, THE, 1927
MAGIC NIGHT, 1932, A
MAGIC OF LASSIE, THE, 1978, AA
MAGIC PONY, 1979
MAGIC SKIN, THE, 1915
MAGIC SPECTACLES, 1961, O
MAGIC SWORD, THE, 1962, A
MAGIC TOWN, 1947, AA
MAGIC VOYAGE OF SINBAD, THE, 1962, A
MAGIC WEAVER, THE, 1965, A
MAGIC WORLD OF TOPO GIGIO, THE, 1961, A
MAGICAL SPECTACLES
MAGICIAN OF LUBLIN, THE, 1979, C
MAGICIAN, THE, 1926
MAGICIAN, THE, 1959, C
MAGNET, THE, 1950, A
MAGNETIC MONSTER, THE, 1953, C
MAGNIFICENT ADVENTURE, THE, 1952
MAGNIFICENT AMBERSONS, THE, 1942, A
MAGNIFICENT BANDITS, THE, 1969, C
MAGNIFICENT BRUTE, THE, 1921
MAGNIFICENT BRUTE, THE, 1936, A
MAGNIFICENT CONCUBINE, THE, 1964, A
MAGNIFICENT CUCKOLD, THE, 1965, A
MAGNIFICENT DOLL, 1946, A
MAGNIFICENT DOPE, THE, 1942, A
MAGNIFICENT FLIRT, THE, 1928, A
MAGNIFICENT FRAUD, THE, 1939, A
MAGNIFICENT LIE, 1931, A
MAGNIFICENT MATADOR, THE, 1955, A
MAGNIFICENT MEDDLER, THE, 1917
MAGNIFICENT OBSESSION, 1935, A
MAGNIFICENT OBSESSION, 1954, A
MAGNIFICENT ONE, THE, 1974, A
MAGNIFICENT OUTCAST
MAGNIFICENT ROGUE, THE, 1946, A
MAGNIFICENT ROUGHNECKS, 1956, A
MAGNIFICENT SEVEN DEADLY SINS, THE, 1971, A-C
MAGNIFICENT SEVEN RIDE, THE, 1972, A
MAGNIFICENT SEVEN, THE, 1960, C
MAGNIFICENT SEVEN, THE, 1954
MAGNIFICENT SHOWMAN, THE
MAGNIFICENT SINNER, 1963, A
MAGNIFICENT TRAMP, THE, 1962, A
MAGNIFICENT TWO, THE, 1967, A
MAGNIFICENT YANKEE, THE, 1950, AA
MAGNUM FORCE, 1973, C-O
MAGOICHI SAGA, THE, 1970, C
MAGUS, THE, 1968, C
MAHANAGAR
MAHLER, 1974, A-C
MAHOGANY, 1975, C
MAID AND THE MARTIAN, THE
MAID FOR MURDER, 1963, A
MAID HAPPY, 1933, A
MAID OF BELGIUM, THE, 1917
MAID OF CEFN YDFA, THE, 1914
MAID OF SALEM, 1937, A
MAID OF THE MOUNTAINS, THE, 1932, A
MAID OF THE WEST, 1921, A
MAID TO ORDER, 1932, A
MAID'S NIGHT OUT, 1938, A
MAIDEN FOR A PRINCE, A, 1967, A
MAIDEN, THE, 1961, A
MAIDS, THE, 1975, C
MAIDSTONE, 1970, C
MAIGRET LAYS A TRAP, 1958, C
MAIL ORDER BRIDE, 1964, A
MAIL TRAIN, 1941, A
MAILBAG ROBBERY, 1957, A-C
MAILMAN, THE, 1923, A
MAIN ATTRACTION, THE, 1962, A
MAIN CHANCE, THE, 1966, A
MAIN EVENT, THE, 1927
MAIN EVENT, THE, 1938, A
MAIN EVENT, THE, 1979, A-C
MAIN STREET, 1923
MAIN STREET, 1956, A
MAIN STREET AFTER DARK, 1944, A
MAIN STREET GIRL
MAIN STREET KID, THE, 1947, A
MAIN STREET LAWYER, 1939, A
MAIN STREET TO BROADWAY, 1953, A
MAIN STREET, 1936
MAIN THING IS TO LOVE, THE, 1975, C
MAINSPRING, THE, 1916
MAINSPRING, THE, 1917
MAIS OU ET DONC ORNICAR, 1979, C
MAISIE, 1939, A
MAISIE GETS HER MAN, 1942, A
MAISIE GOES TO RENO, 1944, A
MAISIE WAS A LADY, 1941, A
MAISIE'S MARRIAGE, 1923
MAITRE EVORA, 1921
MAJDHAR, 1984, C
MAJESTY OF THE LAW, THE, 1915
MAJIN, 1968, A
MAJIN, THE HIDEOUS IDOL
MAJIN, THE MONSTER OF TERROR
MAJOR AND THE MINOR, THE, 1942, A
MAJOR BARBARA, 1941, A
MAJOR DUNDEE, 1965, C-O
MAJORITY OF ONE, A, 1961, A
MAKE A FACE, 1971, C
MAKE A MILLION, 1935, A
MAKE A WISH, 1937, A
MAKE AND BREAK
MAKE BELIEVE BALLROOM, 1949, A
MAKE HASTE TO LIVE, 1954, A
MAKE IT THREE, 1938, A
MAKE LIKE A THIEF, 1966, A
MAKE ME A STAR, 1932, A
MAKE ME AN OFFER, 1954, A
MAKE MINE A DOUBLE, 1962, A
MAKE MINE A MILLION, 1965, A
MAKE MINE MINK, 1960, A
MAKE MINE MUSIC, 1946, AA
MAKE WAY FOR A LADY, 1936, A
MAKE WAY FOR LILA, 1962, A
MAKE WAY FOR TOMORROW, 1937, A
MAKE YOUR OWN BED, 1944, A
MAKE-BELIEVE WIFE, THE, 1918
MAKE-UP, 1937, A
MAKER OF MEN, 1931, A
MAKERS OF MEN, 1925
MAKING A MAN, 1922, A
MAKING GOOD
MAKING GOOD
MAKING GOOD, 1923
MAKING IT, 1971, O
MAKING LOVE, 1982, O
MAKING OF A LADY, THE
MAKING OF BOBBY BURNIT, THE, 1914
MAKING OF MADDALENA, THE, 1916
MAKING OF O'MALLEY, THE, 1925
MAKING OVER OF GEOFFREY MANNING, THE, 1915
MAKING THE GRADE, 1921, A
MAKING THE GRADE, 1929, A
MAKING THE GRADE, 1984, O
MAKING THE HEADLINES, 1938, A
MAKING THE VARSITY, 1928, A
MAKO: THE JAWS OF DEATH, 1976, C
MAKUCHI
MALACHI'S COVE, 1973, AAA
MALAGA, 1962, A
MALAGA, 1954
MALATESTA'S CARNIVAL, 1973, O
MALAY NIGHTS, 1933, A
MALAYA, 1950, A
MALCOLM STRAUSS' SALOME
MALDONE, 1928
MALE AND FEMALE, 1919, A
MALE AND FEMALE
MALE AND FEMALE SINCE ADAM AND EVE, 1961, A
MALE ANIMAL, THE, 1942, A
MALE COMPANION, 1965, A
MALE HUNT, 1965, A
MALE SERVICE, 1966, O
MALE WANTED, 1923
MALEFICES
MALENCONTRE, 1920
MALENKA, THE VAMPIRE, 1972, O
MALEVIL, 1981, C
MALIBU
MALIBU BEACH, 1978, C
MALIBU HIGH, 1979, O
MALICE
MALICIOUS, 1974, O
MALIZIA
MALOU, 1983, C
MALPAS MYSTERY, THE, 1967, A
MALPERTIUS, 1972, C
MALTA STORY, 1954, A-C
MALTESE BIPPY, THE, 1969, A
MALTESE FALCON, THE, 1931, A
MALTESE FALCON, THE, 1941, A
MAMA LOVES PAPA, 1933, A
MAMA LOVES PAPA, 1945, A
MAMA RUNS WILD, 1938, A
MAMA STEPS OUT, 1937, A
MAMA'S AFFAIR, 1921
MAMA'S DIRTY GIRLS, 1974
MAMA'S GONE A-HUNTING, 1976
MAMAN COLIBRI, 1929
MAMBA, 1930, A
MAMBO, 1955, C
MAME, 1974, A
MAMI
MAMMA DRACULA, 1980, O
MAMMA ROMA, 1962, C
MAMMY, 1930, A
MAN ABOUT THE HOUSE, 1974

MAN ABOUT THE HOUSE, A, 1947, A
MAN ABOUT TOWN, 1932, A
MAN ABOUT TOWN, 1939, AA
MAN ABOUT TOWN, 1947, A
MAN ABOVE THE LAW, 1918, A
MAN ACCUSED, 1959, C
MAN AFRAID, 1957, A
MAN AGAINST MAN, 1961, C
MAN AGAINST WOMAN, 1932, A
MAN ALIVE, 1945, A
MAN ALONE, A, 1955, A
MAN ALONE, THE, 1923
MAN AND A WOMAN, A, 1966, A-C
MAN AND BEAST, 1917
MAN AND BOY, 1972, A
MAN AND HIS ANGEL, 1916
MAN AND HIS MATE
MAN AND HIS MATE, A, 1915, A
MAN AND HIS MONEY, A, 1919
MAN AND HIS SOUL, 1916
MAN AND HIS WOMAN, 1920, C
MAN AND MAID, 1925, A
MAN AND THE BEAST, THE, 1951, A
MAN AND THE MOMENT, THE, 1918, C
MAN AND THE MOMENT, THE, 1929, A
MAN AND THE MONSTER, THE, 1965, A
MAN AND THE WOMAN, A, 1917, A
MAN AND WIFE, 1923
MAN AND WOMAN, 1920
MAN AND WOMAN, 1921
MAN AT LARGE, 1941, A
MAN AT SIX
MAN AT THE CARLTON TOWER, 1961, C
MAN AT THE TOP, 1973, A
MAN BAIT, 1926, A
MAN BAIT, 1952, A
MAN BEAST, 1956, A
MAN BEHIND THE CURTAIN, THE, 1916
MAN BEHIND THE DOOR, THE, 1914, A
MAN BEHIND THE GUN, THE, 1952, A
MAN BEHIND THE MASK, THE, 1936, A
MAN BEHIND "THE TIMES", THE, 1917
MAN BENEATH, THE, 1919
MAN BETRAYED, A, 1937, A
MAN BETRAYED, A, 1941, A
MAN BETWEEN, THE, 1923
MAN BETWEEN, THE, 1953, A
MAN BY THE ROADSIDE, THE, 1923
MAN CALLED ADAM, A, 1966, C
MAN CALLED BACK, THE, 1932, C
MAN CALLED DAGGER, A, 1967, A
MAN CALLED FLINTSTONE, THE, 1966, AAA
MAN CALLED GANNON, A, 1969, A
MAN CALLED HORSE, A, 1970, O
MAN CALLED NOON, THE, 1973, C
MAN CALLED PETER, THE, 1955, AA
MAN CALLED SLEDGE, A, 1971, O
MAN CALLED SULLIVAN, A
MAN COULD GET KILLED, A, A
MAN CRAZY, 1927, A
MAN CRAZY, A
MAN DETAINED, C
MAN EATER, 1958
MAN EATER OF HYDRA
MAN ESCAPED, A, A
MAN FOLLOWING THE SUN
MAN FOR ALL SEASONS, A, A
MAN FOR HANGING, A, 1972
MAN FOUR-SQUARE, A, 1926, A
MAN FOUR-SQUARE, THE
MAN FRIDAY, A-C
MAN FROM ARIZONA, THE, 1932
MAN FROM BEYOND, THE, 1922, A
MAN FROM BITTER RIDGE, THE, 1955, A
MAN FROM BITTER ROOTS, THE, 1916
MAN FROM BLACK HILLS, THE, 1952, A
MAN FROM BLANKLEY'S, THE, 1930, A
MAN FROM BROADWAY, 1924
MAN FROM BRODNEY'S, THE, 1923
MAN FROM BUTTON WILLOW, THE, AA
MAN FROM C.O.T.T.O.N.
MAN FROM CAIRO, THE, 1953, A
MAN FROM CHEYENNE, A
MAN FROM CHICAGO, THE, A
MAN FROM COCODY, A
MAN FROM COLORADO, THE, 1948, A-C
MAN FROM DAKOTA, THE, 1940, A
MAN FROM DEATH VALLEY, THE, 1931, A
MAN FROM DEL RIO, 1956, A
MAN FROM DOWN UNDER, THE, 1943, A-C
MAN FROM DOWNING STREET, THE, 1922
MAN FROM FRISCO, 1944, A
MAN FROM FUNERAL RANGE, THE, 1918
MAN FROM GALVESTON, THE, 1964, A
MAN FROM GLENGARRY, THE, 1923
MAN FROM GOD'S COUNTRY, 1924
MAN FROM GOD'S COUNTRY, 1958, A
MAN FROM GUN TOWN, THE, 1936, A
MAN FROM HARDPAN, THE, 1927, A
MAN FROM HEADQUARTERS, 1928, A
MAN FROM HEADQUARTERS, 1942, A
MAN FROM HELL'S EDGES, 1932, A
MAN FROM HELL'S RIVER, THE, 1922
MAN FROM HELL, THE, 1934, A
MAN FROM HOME, THE, 1914, A
MAN FROM HOME, THE, 1922
MAN FROM HONG KONG, 1975, O
MAN FROM LARAMIE, THE, 1955, C
MAN FROM LONE MOUNTAIN, THE, 1925
MAN FROM LOST RIVER, THE, 1921
MAN FROM MANHATTAN, THE, 1916
MAN FROM MARS, THE
MAN FROM MEDICINE HAT, THE
MAN FROM MEXICO, THE, 1914
MAN FROM MONTANA, 1941, A
MAN FROM MONTANA, THE, 1917, A
MAN FROM MONTEREY, THE, 1933, A
MAN FROM MONTREAL, THE, 1940, A
MAN FROM MOROCCO, THE, 1946, A
MAN FROM MUSIC MOUNTAIN, 1938, A
MAN FROM MUSIC MOUNTAIN, 1943, A
MAN FROM NEVADA, THE
MAN FROM NEVADA, THE, 1929
MAN FROM NEW MEXICO, THE, 1932, A
MAN FROM NEW YORK, THE, 1923
MAN FROM NOWHERE, A, 1920
MAN FROM NOWHERE, THE, 1916
MAN FROM NOWHERE, THE, 1930
MAN FROM NOWHERE, THE, 1976
MAN FROM NOWHERE, THE
MAN FROM O.R.G.Y., THE, 1970, O
MAN FROM OKLAHOMA, THE, 1926
MAN FROM OKLAHOMA, THE, 1945, AAA
MAN FROM OREGON, THE, 1915
MAN FROM PAINTED POST, THE, 1917, A
MAN FROM PLANET X, THE, 1951, A
MAN FROM RAINBOW VALLEY, THE, 1946, A
MAN FROM RED GULCH, THE, 1925
MAN FROM SNOWY RIVER, THE, 1983, C
MAN FROM SONORA, 1951
MAN FROM SUNDOWN, THE, 1939, A
MAN FROM TANGIER
MAN FROM TEXAS, THE, 1921
MAN FROM TEXAS, THE, 1939, A
MAN FROM TEXAS, THE, 1948, A
MAN FROM THE ALAMO, THE, 1953, A
MAN FROM THE BIG CITY, THE
MAN FROM THE BLACK HILLS, 1952
MAN FROM THE DINERS' CLUB, THE, 1963, A
MAN FROM THE EAST, A, 1974, C-O
MAN FROM THE EAST, THE, 1961, A
MAN FROM THE FIRST CENTURY, THE, 1961, A
MAN FROM THE FOLIES BERGERE, THE
MAN FROM THE PAST, THE
MAN FROM THE RIO GRANDE, THE, 1926
MAN FROM THE RIO GRANDE, THE, 1943, A
MAN FROM THE WEST, THE, 1926
MAN FROM THUNDER RIVER, THE, 1943, A
MAN FROM TORONTO, THE, 1933, A
MAN FROM TUMBLEWEEDS, THE, 1940, A
MAN FROM UTAH, THE, 1934, A
MAN FROM WYOMING, A, 1930, A
MAN FROM WYOMING, THE, 1924, A
MAN FROM YESTERDAY, THE, 1932, A
MAN FROM YESTERDAY, THE, 1949, O
MAN GETTER, THE
MAN GETTER, THE, 1923
MAN GOES THROUGH THE WALL, A
MAN HATER, THE, 1917, C
MAN HE FOUND, THE
MAN HUNT, 1933, A
MAN HUNT, 1936, A
MAN HUNT, 1941, A
MAN HUNT, THE, 1918, A
MAN HUNTER, THE, 1919
MAN HUNTER, THE, 1930, A
MAN HUNTERS, 1923
MAN HUNTERS OF THE CARIBBEAN, 1938, A
MAN I KILLED
MAN I LOVE, THE, 1929, A
MAN I LOVE, THE, 1946, A
MAN I MARRIED, THE, 1940, A
MAN I MARRY, THE, 1936, A
MAN I WANT, THE, 1934, A
MAN IN A COCKED HAT, 1960, A
MAN IN A LOOKING GLASS, A, 1965
MAN IN BLACK, THE, 1950, C-O
MAN IN BLUE, THE, 1925
MAN IN BLUE, THE, 1937, A
MAN IN GREY, THE, 1943, A-C
MAN IN HALF-MOON STREET, THE, 1944, A
MAN IN HIDING
MAN IN HOBBLES, THE, 1928, A
MAN IN MOTLEY, THE, 1916
MAN IN OUTER SPACE
MAN IN POSSESSION, THE
MAN IN POSSESSION, THE, 1915
MAN IN POSSESSION, THE, 1931, A-C
MAN IN THE ATTIC, 1953, C
MAN IN THE ATTIC, THE, 1915
MAN IN THE BACK SEAT, THE, 1961, A
MAN IN THE DARK, 1953, A
MAN IN THE DARK, 1963, A
MAN IN THE DINGHY, THE, 1951, A
MAN IN THE GLASS BOOTH, THE, 1975, A
MAN IN THE GREY FLANNEL SUIT, THE, 1956, A
MAN IN THE IRON MASK, THE, 1939, A
MAN IN THE MIDDLE, 1964, A-C
MAN IN THE MIRROR, THE, 1936, A
MAN IN THE MOON, 1961, A
MAN IN THE MOONLIGHT MASK, THE, 1958, A
MAN IN THE MOONLIGHT, THE, 1919
MAN IN THE NET, THE, 1959, A
MAN IN THE OPEN, A, 1919, A
MAN IN THE ROAD, THE, 1957, A
MAN IN THE ROUGH, 1928, A
MAN IN THE SADDLE, 1951, A
MAN IN THE SADDLE, THE
MAN IN THE SADDLE, THE, 1926
MAN IN THE SHADOW, 1957, A
MAN IN THE SHADOW, THE, 1926
MAN IN THE SHADOWS, THE, 1915
MAN IN THE SKY
MAN IN THE STORM, THE, 1969, A
MAN IN THE TRUNK, THE, 1942, A
MAN IN THE VAULT, 1956, A
MAN IN THE WATER, THE, 1963, A
MAN IN THE WHITE SUIT, THE, 1952, A
MAN IN THE WILDERNESS, 1971, O
MAN INSIDE, THE, 1916
MAN INSIDE, THE, 1958, C
MAN IS ARMED, THE, 1956, A
MAN IS TEN FEET TALL, A
MAN KILLER
MAN LIFE PASSED BY, THE, 1923
MAN MAD
MAN MADE MONSTER, 1941, A
MAN MISSING
MAN MUST LIVE, THE, 1925
MAN NEXT DOOR, THE, 1923
MAN NOBODY KNOWS, THE, 1925
MAN O' WARS MAN, THE, 1914
MAN OF A THOUSAND FACES, 1957, A
MAN OF ACTION, 1933
MAN OF ACTION, THE, 1923
MAN OF AFFAIRS, 1937, A
MAN OF AFRICA, 1956, A
MAN OF BRONZE
MAN OF BRONZE, THE, 1918
MAN OF CONFLICT, 1953, A
MAN OF CONQUEST, 1939, A
MAN OF COURAGE, 1922
MAN OF COURAGE, 1943, A
MAN OF EVIL, 1948, A
MAN OF FLOWERS, 1984, O
MAN OF HIS WORD, A, 1915
MAN OF HONOR, A, 1919
MAN OF IRON
MAN OF IRON, 1935, A
MAN OF IRON, 1981, C
MAN OF IRON, A
MAN OF LA MANCHA, 1972, C
MAN OF MARBLE, 1979, C-O
MAN OF MAYFAIR, 1931, A
MAN OF MUSIC, 1953, A
MAN OF MYSTERY, THE, 1917
MAN OF NERVE, A, 1925, A
MAN OF QUALITY, A, 1926
MAN OF SENTIMENT, A, 1933, A
MAN OF SHAME, THE, 1915
MAN OF SORROW, A, 1916
MAN OF STONE, THE, 1921
MAN OF THE FAMILY
MAN OF THE FOREST, 1926
MAN OF THE FOREST, 1933, A
MAN OF THE FOREST, THE, 1921
MAN OF THE HOUR
MAN OF THE HOUR, THE, 1940, A
MAN OF THE MOMENT, 1935, A
MAN OF THE MOMENT, 1955, A
MAN OF THE PEOPLE, 1937, A
MAN OF THE WEST, 1958, C-O
MAN OF THE WORLD, 1931, A
MAN OF TWO WORLDS, 1934, A
MAN OF VIOLENCE, 1970, O
MAN ON A MISSION, 1965
MAN ON A STRING, 1960, A
MAN ON A SWING, 1974, C
MAN ON A TIGHTROPE, 1953, A
MAN ON A TIGHTROPE, 1949
MAN ON AMERICA'S CONSCIENCE, THE
MAN ON FIRE, 1957, A
MAN ON THE BOX, THE, 1914
MAN ON THE BOX, THE, 1925, A
MAN ON THE EIFFEL TOWER, THE, 1949, A
MAN ON THE FLYING TRAPEZE, THE, 1935, A
MAN ON THE PROWL, 1957, A

MAN ON THE RUN, 1949, A
MAN ON THE RUN, 1964
MAN ON THE SPYING TRAPEZE, 1965
MAN OR GUN, 1958, A
MAN OUTSIDE, 1965
MAN OUTSIDE, THE, 1933, A
MAN OUTSIDE, THE, 1968, A
MAN POWER, 1927
MAN RUSTLIN', 1926
MAN SHE BROUGHT BACK, THE, 1922
MAN STOLEN, 1934, A
MAN TAMER, THE, 1921
MAN THE ARMY MADE, A, 1917, A
MAN THERE WAS, A, 1917
MAN THEY COULD NOT HANG, THE, 1939, C
MAN THEY COULDN'T ARREST, THE, 1933, A
MAN TO MAN, 1922, A
MAN TO MAN, 1931, A
MAN TO REMEMBER, A, 1938, A
MAN TRACKERS, THE, 1921
MAN TRAIL, THE, 1915
MAN TRAILER, THE, 1934, A
MAN TRAP, THE, 1917
MAN TROUBLE, 1930, A
MAN UNCONQUERABLE, THE, 1922
MAN UNDER COVER, THE, 1922
MAN UPSTAIRS, THE, 1926
MAN UPSTAIRS, THE, 1959, A
MAN WANTED, 1922
MAN WANTED, 1932, A
MAN WHO BEAT DAN DOLAN, THE, 1915
MAN WHO BOUGHT LONDON, THE, 1916
MAN WHO BROKE THE BANK AT MONTE CARLO, THE, 1935, A
MAN WHO CAME BACK, THE, 1924
MAN WHO CAME BACK, THE, 1931, C
MAN WHO CAME FOR COFFEE, THE, 1970, O
MAN WHO CAME TO DINNER, THE, 1942, A
MAN WHO CHANGED HIS MIND
MAN WHO CHANGED HIS NAME, THE, 1928, A
MAN WHO CHANGED HIS NAME, THE, 1934, A
MAN WHO CHANGED, THE
MAN WHO CHEATED HIMSELF, THE, 1951, A
MAN WHO COULD CHEAT DEATH, THE, 1959, C
MAN WHO COULD NOT LOSE, THE, 1914, A
MAN WHO COULD WORK MIRACLES, THE, 1937, A
MAN WHO COULD'T BEAT GOD, THE, 1915
MAN WHO COULDN'T WALK, THE, 1964, A
MAN WHO CRIED WOLF, THE, 1937, A
MAN WHO DARED, THE, 1920
MAN WHO DARED, THE, 1933, AA
MAN WHO DARED, THE, 1939, A
MAN WHO DARED, THE, 1946, A
MAN WHO DIED TWICE, THE, 1958, A
MAN WHO FELL TO EARTH, THE, 1976, C-O
MAN WHO FIGHTS ALONE, THE, 1924
MAN WHO FINALLY DIED, THE, 1967, A
MAN WHO FORGOT, THE, 1917, A
MAN WHO FORGOT, THE, 1919
MAN WHO FOUND HIMSELF, THE, 1915
MAN WHO FOUND HIMSELF, THE, 1925
MAN WHO FOUND HIMSELF, THE, 1937, A
MAN WHO HAD EVERYTHING, THE, 1920
MAN WHO HAD POWER OVER WOMEN, THE, 1970, C
MAN WHO HAUNTED HIMSELF, THE, 1970, A
MAN WHO KILLED BILLY THE KID, THE, 1967, A
MAN WHO KNEW TOO MUCH, THE, 1935, C
MAN WHO KNEW TOO MUCH, THE, 1956, A
MAN WHO LAUGHS, THE, 1927, C
MAN WHO LAUGHS, THE, 1966, O
MAN WHO LIES, THE, 1970, C
MAN WHO LIKED FUNERALS, THE, 1959, A
MAN WHO LIVED AGAIN, THE, 1936, A
MAN WHO LIVED TWICE, 1936, A
MAN WHO LOST HIMSELF, THE, 1920
MAN WHO LOST HIMSELF, THE, 1941, A
MAN WHO LOST HIS WAY, THE
MAN WHO LOVED CAT DANCING, THE, 1973, C-O
MAN WHO LOVED REDHEADS, THE, 1955, A
MAN WHO LOVED WOMEN, THE, 1977, O
MAN WHO LOVED WOMEN, THE, 1983, O
MAN WHO MADE DIAMONDS, THE, 1937, A
MAN WHO MADE GOOD, THE, 1917, A
MAN WHO MADE GOOD, THE, 1917
MAN WHO MARRIED HIS OWN WIFE, THE, 1922
MAN WHO NEVER WAS, THE, 1956, A
MAN WHO PAID, THE, 1922
MAN WHO PAWNED HIS SOUL
MAN WHO PLAYED GOD, THE, 1922, A
MAN WHO PLAYED GOD, THE, 1932, A
MAN WHO PLAYED SQUARE, THE, 1924
MAN WHO RECLAIMED HIS HEAD, THE, 1935, A
MAN WHO RETURNED TO LIFE, THE, 1942, A
MAN WHO SAW TOMORROW, THE, 1922, A
MAN WHO SAW TOMORROW, THE, 1981
MAN WHO SHOT LIBERTY VALANCE, THE, 1962, A
MAN WHO STAYED AT HOME, THE, 1915
MAN WHO STAYED AT HOME, THE, 1919
MAN WHO STOLE THE SUN, THE, 1980, C
MAN WHO STOOD STILL, THE, 1916
MAN WHO TALKED TOO MUCH, THE, 1940, A
MAN WHO TALKS TO WHALES, THE, 1976
MAN WHO THOUGHT LIFE, THE, 1969, A
MAN WHO TOOK A CHANCE, THE, 1917
MAN WHO TURNED TO STONE, THE, 1957, C
MAN WHO TURNED WHITE, THE, 1919, A
MAN WHO UNDERSTOOD WOMEN, THE, 1959, A-C
MAN WHO VANISHED, THE, 1915
MAN WHO WAGGED HIS TAIL, THE, 1961, A
MAN WHO WAITED, THE, 1922
MAN WHO WALKED ALONE, THE, 1945, A
MAN WHO WALKED THROUGH THE WALL, THE, 1964, A
MAN WHO WAS AFRAID, THE, 1917
MAN WHO WAS NOBODY, THE, 1960, C
MAN WHO WAS SHERLOCK HOLMES, THE, 1937, A
MAN WHO WASN'T THERE, THE, 1983, C
MAN WHO WATCHED TRAINS GO BY, THE
MAN WHO WOKE UP, THE, 1918
MAN WHO WON, THE, 1918
MAN WHO WON, THE, 1919
MAN WHO WON, THE, 1923
MAN WHO WON, THE, 1933, A
MAN WHO WOULD BE KING, THE, 1975, A-C
MAN WHO WOULD NOT DIE, THE, 1916
MAN WHO WOULD NOT DIE, THE, 1975, C
MAN WHO WOULDN'T DIE, THE, 1942, A
MAN WHO WOULDN'T TALK, THE, 1940, A
MAN WHO WOULDN'T TALK, THE, 1958, A
MAN WHO WOULDN'T TELL, THE, 1918
MAN WHO, THE, 1921, A
MAN WITH 100 FACES, THE, 1938, A
MAN WITH A CLOAK, THE, 1951, A
MAN WITH A GUN, 1958, C
MAN WITH A MILLION, 1954, A
MAN WITH BOGART'S FACE, THE, 1980, A-C
MAN WITH CONNECTIONS, THE, 1970, C
MAN WITH MY FACE, THE, 1951, A
MAN WITH NINE LIVES, THE, 1940, A
MAN WITH THE BALLOONS, THE, 1968, A
MAN WITH THE DEADLY LENS, THE
MAN WITH THE ELECTRIC VOICE, THE
MAN WITH THE GLASS EYE, THE, 1916
MAN WITH THE GOLDEN ARM, THE, 1955, O
MAN WITH THE GOLDEN GUN, THE, 1974, A
MAN WITH THE GREEN CARNATION, THE, 1960, A
MAN WITH THE GUN, 1955, C
MAN WITH THE ICY EYES, THE, 1971
MAN WITH THE MAGNETIC EYES, THE, 1945, C
MAN WITH THE SYNTHETIC BRAIN
MAN WITH THE TRANSPLANTED BRAIN, THE, 1972, A
MAN WITH THE X-RAY EYES, THE
MAN WITH THE YELLOW EYES
MAN WITH THIRTY SONS, THE
MAN WITH TWO BRAINS, THE, 1983, O
MAN WITH TWO FACES, THE, 1934, A-C
MAN WITH TWO HEADS, THE, 1972, O
MAN WITH TWO LIVES, THE, 1942, A
MAN WITH TWO MOTHERS, THE, 1922
MAN WITH X-RAY EYES, THE
MAN WITHIN, THE, 1948
MAN WITHIN, THE, 1975
MAN WITHOUT A BODY, THE, 1957, A
MAN WITHOUT A CONSCIENCE, THE, 1925
MAN WITHOUT A COUNTRY, THE, 1917
MAN WITHOUT A COUNTRY, THE, 1925
MAN WITHOUT A FACE, 1964
MAN WITHOUT A FACE, THE, 1935, A
MAN WITHOUT A FACE, THE, 1975
MAN WITHOUT A GUN
MAN WITHOUT A HEART, THE, 1924
MAN WITHOUT A SOUL, THE
MAN WITHOUT A STAR, 1955, C
MAN WITHOUT DESIRE, THE, 1923, A
MAN WORTH WHILE, THE, 1921, A
MAN'S AFFAIR, A, 1949, A
MAN'S BEST FRIEND, 1935
MAN'S CASTLE, A, 1933, A
MAN'S COUNTRY, 1938, A
MAN'S COUNTRY, A, 1919
MAN'S DESIRE, 1919
MAN'S FATE, 1917
MAN'S FAVORITE SPORT (?), 1964, A
MAN'S FIGHT, A, 1927
MAN'S GAME, A, 1934, A
MAN'S HERITAGE
MAN'S HOME, A, 1921, A
MAN'S HOPE, 1947, A
MAN'S LAND, A, 1932, A
MAN'S LAW AND GOD'S, 1922, A
MAN'S LAW, A, 1917
MAN'S MAKING, THE, 1915
MAN'S MAN, A, 1917
MAN'S MAN, A, 1929, A
MAN'S MATE, A, 1924
MAN'S PAST, A, 1927
MAN'S PLAYTHING, 1920
MAN'S PREROGATIVE, A, 1915, A
MAN'S SHADOW, A, 1920, C
MAN'S SIZE, 1923
MAN'S WOMAN, 1917
MAN'S WORLD, A, 1918
MAN'S WORLD, A, 1942, A
MAN, A WOMAN AND A KILLER, A, 1975, O
MAN, A WOMAN, AND A BANK, A, 1979, C
MAN, THE, 1925
MAN, THE, 1972, A
MAN, WOMAN AND CHILD, 1983, A
MAN, WOMAN AND SIN, 1927
MAN, WOMAN AND WIFE, 1929
MAN, WOMAN, MARRIAGE
MAN—WOMAN—MARRIAGE, 1921
MAN-EATER
MAN-EATER OF HYDRA
MAN-EATER OF KUMAON, 1948, A
MAN-KILLER
MAN-MADE WOMEN, 1928, A
MAN-PROOF, 1938, A
MAN-TRAP, 1961, A
MANAGER OF THE B&A, THE, 1916
MANCHESTER MAN, THE, 1920, A
MANCHU EAGLE MURDER CAPER MYSTERY, THE, 1975, A
MANCHURIAN CANDIDATE, THE, 1962, C-O
MANDABI, 1970, A
MANDALAY, 1934, A-C
MANDARIN MYSTERY, THE, 1937, A
MANDARIN'S GOLD, 1919
MANDINGO, 1975, O
MANDRAGOLA, 1966, A
MANDRAGOLA/THE LOVE ROOT
MANDY
MANFISH, 1956, A
MANGANINNIE, 1982, A
MANGO TREE, THE, 1981, O
MANHANDLED, 1924
MANHANDLED, 1949, A
MANHANDLERS, THE, 1975
MANHATTAN, 1924, A
MANHATTAN, 1979, C
MANHATTAN ANGEL, 1948, A
MANHATTAN BUTTERFLY, 1935
MANHATTAN COCKTAIL, 1928, A
MANHATTAN COCKTAIL, 1928
MANHATTAN COWBOY, 1928, A
MANHATTAN HEARTBEAT, 1940, A
MANHATTAN KNIGHT, A, 1920
MANHATTAN KNIGHTS, 1928, A
MANHATTAN LOVE SONG, 1934, A
MANHATTAN MADNESS, 1916, A
MANHATTAN MADNESS, 1925
MANHATTAN MADNESS, 1936
MANHATTAN MADNESS, 1943, Brit.
MANHATTAN MELODRAMA, 1934, A
MANHATTAN MERRY-GO-ROUND, 1937, A
MANHATTAN MOON, 1935, A
MANHATTAN MUSIC BOX
MANHATTAN PARADE, 1931, A
MANHATTAN SHAKEDOWN, 1939, A
MANHATTAN TOWER, 1932, A
MANHUNT
MANHUNT
MANHUNT IN SPACE, 1954
MANHUNT IN THE JUNGLE, 1958, A
MANHUNTER, 1983
MANIA, 1961, O
MANIAC, 1934, O
MANIAC, 1963, C
MANIAC, 1977, C
MANIAC, 1980, O
MANIAC MANSION, 1978, O
MANIAC, 1978, Ital.
MANIACS ARE LOOSE, THE
MANIACS ON WHEELS, 1951, A
MANICURE GIRL, THE, 1925
MANILA CALLING, 1942, A
MANINA
MANIPULATOR, THE, 1972
MANITOU, THE, 1978, C
MANJI
MANNEQUIN, 1926
MANNEQUIN, 1933, A
MANNEQUIN, 1937, A
MANNER MUSSEN SO SIEN
MANNISKOR MOTS OCH LJUV MUSIK UPPSTAR I HJARTAT
MANNY'S ORPHANS
MANOLETE, 1950, A
MANOLIS, 1962, A
MANON, 1950, A
MANON 70, 1968, O
MANON LESCAUT, 1914, A
MANON LESCAUT, 1926
MANOS, THE HANDS OF FATE, 1966, C
MANPOWER, 1941, A

MANSION OF ACHING HEARTS, THE, 1925
MANSION OF THE DOOMED, 1976, O
MANSLAUGHTER, 1922
MANSLAUGHTER, 1930, A
MANSON MASSACRE, THE, 1976
MANSTER, THE, 1962, A
MANSTER—HALF MAN, HALF MONSTER, THE
MANTIS IN LACE, 1968, O
MANTLE OF CHARITY, THE, 1918
MANTRAP, 1926
MANTRAP, 1953
MANTRAP, 1961
MANTRAP, THE, 1943, A
MANUELA
MANULESCU, 1933, A
MANUSCRIPT FOUND IN SARAGOSSA
MANXMAN, THE, 1916
MANXMAN, THE, 1929, A
MANY A SLIP, 1931, A
MANY HAPPY RETURNS, 1934, A
MANY RIVERS TO CROSS, 1955, A
MANY TANKS MR. ATKINS, 1938, A
MANY WATERS, 1931, A
MAOS SANGRENTAS
MARA MARU, 1952, A
MARA OF THE WILDERNESS, 1966, A
MARACAIBO, 1958, A
MARAT/SADE
MARATHON MAN, 1976, O
MARAUDERS, THE, 1947, A
MARAUDERS, THE, 1955, A
MARAUDERS, THE, 1962
MARBLE HEART, THE, 1915
MARBLE HEART, THE, 1916
MARCELLINI MILLIONS, THE, 1917
MARCH HARE, THE, 1919, A
MARCH HARE, THE, 1921
MARCH HARE, THE, 1956, A
MARCH OF THE SPRING HARE, 1969, O
MARCH OF THE WOODEN SOLDIERS, THE
MARCH ON PARIS 1914—OF GENERALOBERST ALEXANDER VON KLUCK—AND HIS MEMORY OF JESSIE HOLLADAY, 1977, C
MARCH OR DIE, 1977, C-O
MARCHA O MUERE
MARCHANDES D'ILLUSIONS
MARCHANDS DE FILLES
MARCIA O CREPA
MARCO, 1973, A
MARCO POLO, 1962, A
MARCO POLO JUNIOR, 1973, A
MARCO THE MAGNIFICENT, 1966, C
MARCUS GARLAND, 1925
MARDI GRAS, 1958, A
MARDI GRAS MASSACRE, 1978, O
MARE NOSTRUM, 1926, A
MARGARET DAY
MARGEM, A
MARGIE, 1940, A
MARGIE, 1946, AAA
MARGIN FOR ERROR, 1943, A
MARGIN, THE,, 1969, A
MARIA CANDELARIA
MARIA CHAPDELAINE
MARIA ELENA
MARIA MARTEN
MARIA MARTEN, 1928
MARIA ROSA, 1916
MARIA, THE WONDERFUL WEAVER
MARIAGE A L'ITALIENNE
MARIAGE D'AMOUR, 1917
MARIANNE
MARIANNE, 1929, A
MARIE ANTOINETTE, 1938, A
MARIE DES ILES
MARIE GALANTE, 1934, A
MARIE OF THE ISLES, 1960, A
MARIE WALEWSKA
MARIE, LTD., 1919
MARIE-ANN, 1978, A
MARIGOLD, 1938, A
MARIGOLD MAN, 1970, C
MARIGOLDS IN AUGUST, 1980, C
MARIGOLDS IN AUGUST, 1984, A
MARILYN, 1953, O
MARINE BATTLEGROUND, 1966, A
MARINE RAIDERS, 1944, A
MARINES ARE COMING, THE, 1935, A
MARINES ARE HERE, THE, 1938, A
MARINES COME THROUGH, THE, 1943, A
MARINES FLY HIGH, THE, 1940, A
MARINES, LET'S GO, 1961, A
MARION DE LORME, 1918
MARIONETTES, THE, 1918
MARIUS, 1933, C
MARIZINIA, 1962, A
MARIZINIA, THE WITCH BENEATH THE SEA
MARJORIE MORNINGSTAR, 1958, A-C
MARK IT PAID, 1933, A
MARK OF CAIN, THE, 1916
MARK OF CAIN, THE, 1917
MARK OF CAIN, THE, 1948, A
MARK OF THE APACHE
MARK OF THE AVENGER
MARK OF THE BEAST, 1923
MARK OF THE CLAW
MARK OF THE DEVIL, 1970, O
MARK OF THE DEVIL II, 1975, O
MARK OF THE GORILLA, 1950, A
MARK OF THE GUN, 1969
MARK OF THE HAWK, THE, 1958, A
MARK OF THE LASH, 1948, A
MARK OF THE PHOENIX, 1958, C
MARK OF THE RENEGADE, 1951, A
MARK OF THE SPUR, 1932
MARK OF THE VAMPIRE, 1935, C
MARK OF THE VAMPIRE, 1957
MARK OF THE WHISTLER, THE, 1944, A
MARK OF THE WITCH, 1970, C
MARK OF ZORRO, 1920, A
MARK OF ZORRO, THE, 1940, A
MARK TWAIN, AMERICAN, 1976
MARK, THE, 1961, A
MARKED BULLET, THE
MARKED CARDS, 1918
MARKED FOR MURDER, 1945, A
MARKED GIRLS, 1949, A
MARKED MAN, A, 1917
MARKED MAN, THE
MARKED MEN, 1920
MARKED MEN, 1940, A
MARKED MONEY, 1928, A
MARKED ONE, THE, 1963, A
MARKED TRAILS, 1944, A
MARKED WOMAN, 1937, C
MARKED WOMAN, THE, 1914
MARKET OF SOULS, THE, 1919
MARKET OF VAIN DESIRE, THE, 1916, A
MARKETA LAZAROVA, 1968, O
MARKO POLO
MARKOPOULOS PASSION, THE
MARKSMAN, THE, 1953, C
MARLIE THE KILLER, 1928
MARLOWE, 1969, A
MARNIE, 1964, C
MAROC 7, 1967, A
MAROONED, 1933, C
MAROONED, 1969, A
MAROONED HEARTS, 1920
MARQUIS DE SADE: JUSTINE
MARQUIS PREFERRED, 1929
MARQUITTA, 1927
MARRIAGE, 1927
MARRIAGE BARGAIN, THE, 1935
MARRIAGE BOND, THE, 1916
MARRIAGE BOND, THE, 1932, A
MARRIAGE BY CONRACT, 1928
MARRIAGE BY CONTRACT, 1928, A
MARRIAGE CAME TUMBLING DOWN, THE, 1968, A
MARRIAGE CHANCE, THE, 1922
MARRIAGE CHEAT, THE, 1924
MARRIAGE CIRCLE, THE, 1924, A
MARRIAGE CLAUSE, THE, 1926, A
MARRIAGE FOR CONVENIENCE, 1919
MARRIAGE FORBIDDEN
MARRIAGE IN THE SHADOWS, 1948, A
MARRIAGE IN TRANSIT, 1925
MARRIAGE IS A PRIVATE AFFAIR, 1944, A
MARRIAGE LIE, THE, 1918
MARRIAGE LINES, THE, 1921
MARRIAGE MAKER, THE, 1923
MARRIAGE MARKET, THE, 1917
MARRIAGE MARKET, THE, 1923
MARRIAGE MORALS, 1923
MARRIAGE OF A YOUNG STOCKBROKER, THE, 1971, A
MARRIAGE OF BALZAMINOV, THE, 1966, A
MARRIAGE OF CONVENIENCE, 1970, A
MARRIAGE OF CONVENIENCE, 1934
MARRIAGE OF CORBAL
MARRIAGE OF FIGARO, THE, 1963, A
MARRIAGE OF FIGARO, THE, 1970, A
MARRIAGE OF KITTY, THE, 1915, A
MARRIAGE OF MARIA BRAUN, THE, 1979, O
MARRIAGE OF MOLLY-O, THE, 1916
MARRIAGE OF THE BEAR, THE, 1928
MARRIAGE OF WILLIAM ASHE, THE, 1916
MARRIAGE OF WILLIAM ASHE, THE, 1921, A
MARRIAGE ON APPROVAL, 1934, A
MARRIAGE ON THE ROCKS, 1965, A-C
MARRIAGE PIT, THE, 1920
MARRIAGE PLAYGROUND, THE, 1929, A
MARRIAGE PRICE, 1919, A
MARRIAGE RING, THE, 1918
MARRIAGE SPECULATION, THE, 1917
MARRIAGE SYMPHONY
MARRIAGE WHIRL, THE, 1925
MARRIAGE, A, 1983, C
MARRIAGE—ITALIAN STYLE, 1964, O
MARRIAGE-GO-ROUND, THE, 1960, A
MARRIAGES ARE MADE, 1918
MARRIED ALIVE, 1927, A
MARRIED AND IN LOVE, 1940, A
MARRIED BACHELOR, 1941, A
MARRIED BEFORE BREAKFAST, 1937, A
MARRIED BUT SINGLE
MARRIED COUPLE, A, 1969, O
MARRIED FLAPPER, THE, 1922
MARRIED FLIRTS, 1924, A
MARRIED FOR MONEY, 1915
MARRIED IN HASTE, 1919
MARRIED IN HASTE, 1931
MARRIED IN HASTE, 1934
MARRIED IN HOLLYWOOD, 1929, A
MARRIED IN NAME ONLY, 1917
MARRIED LIFE, 1920
MARRIED LIFE, 1921
MARRIED LOVE
MARRIED PEOPLE, 1922
MARRIED TO A MORMAN, 1922, A
MARRIED TOO YOUNG, 1962, A
MARRIED VIRGIN, THE, 1918
MARRIED WOMAN, THE, 1965, C
MARRIED?, 1926
MARRY IN HASTE, 1924, A
MARRY ME, 1925
MARRY ME, 1932, A
MARRY ME, 1949, A
MARRY ME AGAIN, 1953, A
MARRY ME MARRY ME, 1969, A
MARRY THE BOSS' DAUGHTER, 1941, A
MARRY THE GIRL, 1928, A
MARRY THE GIRL, 1935, A
MARRY THE GIRL, 1937, A
MARRY THE POOR GIRL, 1921
MARRYING KIND, THE, 1952, A
MARRYING MONEY, 1915
MARRYING WIDOWS, 1934, C
MARS CALLING
MARS NEEDS WOMEN, 1966, A
MARSCHIER ODER KREIPER
MARSE COVINGTON, 1915
MARSEILLAISE
MARSEILLES CONTRACT, THE
MARSHAL OF AMARILLO, 1948, A
MARSHAL OF CEDAR ROCK, 1953, A
MARSHAL OF CRIPPLE CREEK, THE, 1947, A
MARSHAL OF GUNSMOKE, 1944, A
MARSHAL OF HELDORADO, 1950, A
MARSHAL OF LAREDO, 1945, A
MARSHAL OF MESA CITY, THE, 1939, A
MARSHAL OF MONEYMINT, THE, 1922, A
MARSHAL OF RENO, 1944, A
MARSHAL'S DAUGHTER, THE, 1953, A
MARSHALS IN DISGUISE, 1954
MARSHMALLOW MOON
MARTA OF THE LOWLANDS, 1914
MARTHA'S VINDICATION, 1916, A
MARTHE, 1919
MARTIAN IN PARIS, A, 1961, A
MARTIN, 1979, O
MARTIN LUTHER, 1953, AA
MARTIN LUTHER, HIS LIFE AND TIME, 1924
MARTIN ROUMAGNAC
MARTINACHE MARRIAGE, THE, 1917
MARTY, 1955, A
MARTYR SEX, THE, 1924
MARTYR, THE, 1976, C
MARTYRDOM OF PHILLIP STRONG, THE, 1916
MARTYRE, 1926
MARTYRS OF LOVE, 1968, A
MARTYRS OF THE ALAMO, THE, 1915, A
MARUJA
MARVELOUS MACISTE, THE, 1918
MARVIN AND TIGE, 1983, C
MARX BROTHERS AT THE CIRCUS
MARX BROTHERS GO WEST
MARY
MARY BURNS, FUGITIVE, 1935, A
MARY ELLEN COMES TO TOWN, 1920
MARY HAD A LITTLE, 1961, C
MARY JANE'S PA, 1917
MARY JANE'S PA, 1935, A
MARY LATIMER, NUN, 1920, A
MARY LAWSON'S SECRET, 1917
MARY LOU, 1948, A
MARY MORELAND, 1917
MARY NAMES THE DAY
MARY OF SCOTLAND, 1936, A
MARY OF THE MOVIES, 1923
MARY POPPINS, 1964, AAA
MARY REGAN, 1919
MARY RYAN, DETECTIVE, 1949, C
MARY STEVENS, M.D., 1933, A
MARY'S ANKLE, 1920
MARY'S LAMB, 1915
MARY, MARY, 1963, A-C

MARY, MARY, BLOODY MARY, 1975, O
MARY, QUEEN OF SCOTS, 1971, A-C
MARY-FIND-THE-GOLD, 1921
MARYA-ISKUSNITSA
MARYJANE, 1968, O
MARYLAND, 1940, A
MARYSE, 1917
MAS ALLA DE LAS MONTANAS
MASCULINE FEMININE, 1966, C-O
MASK OF DIIJON, THE, 1946, A-C
MASK OF DIMITRIOS, THE, 1944, A
MASK OF DUST
MASK OF FU MANCHU, THE, 1932, C
MASK OF FURY
MASK OF KOREA, 1950, A
MASK OF LOPEZ, THE, 1924
MASK OF RICHES
MASK OF THE AVENGER, 1951, A
MASK OF THE DRAGON, 1951, A
MASK OF THE HIMALAYAS
MASK OF THE KU KLUX KLAN, THE, 1923
MASK, THE, 1918
MASK, THE, 1921, A
MASK, THE, 1961, O
MASKED ANGEL, 1928, A
MASKED AVENGER, THE, 1922, A
MASKED BRIDE, THE, 1925
MASKED DANCER, THE, 1924
MASKED EMOTIONS, 1929, A
MASKED HEART, THE, 1917
MASKED LOVER, THE, 1928
MASKED PIRATE, THE
MASKED RAIDERS, 1949, A
MASKED RIDER, THE, 1916
MASKED RIDER, THE, 1941, A
MASKED STRANGER
MASKED WOMAN, THE, 1927
MASKS AND FACES, 1917
MASKS OF THE DEVIL, THE, 1928
MASOCH, 1980, O
MASON OF THE MOUNTED, 1932, A
MASQUE OF THE RED DEATH, THE, 1964, C
MASQUERADE, 1965, A
MASQUERADE BANDIT, THE, 1926
MASQUERADE IN MEXICO, 1945, C
MASQUERADE OF THIEVES, 1973
MASQUERADE, 1929, A
MASQUERADER, THE, 1922
MASQUERADER, THE, 1933, A
MASQUERADERS, THE, 1915, A
MASS APPEAL, 1984, C
MASSACRE, 1934, A
MASSACRE, 1956, A
MASSACRE AT CENTRAL HIGH, 1976, O
MASSACRE AT FORT HOLMAN
MASSACRE AT GRAND CANYON, 1965
MASSACRE AT THE ROSEBUD
MASSACRE CANYON, 1954, A
MASSACRE HILL, 1949, A
MASSACRE IN ROME, 1973, C
MASSACRE RIVER, 1949, A
MASSIVE RETALIATION, 1984, O
MASTER AND MAN, 1915
MASTER AND MAN, 1929
MASTER AND MAN, 1934, A
MASTER CRACKSMAN, THE, 1914, A
MASTER GUNFIGHTER, THE, 1975, C
MASTER MAN, THE, 1919
MASTER MIND, THE, 1914, A
MASTER MIND, THE, 1920, A
MASTER MINDS, 1949, A
MASTER OF BALLANTRAE, THE, 1953, A
MASTER OF BANKDAM, THE, 1947, C
MASTER OF BEASTS, THE, 1922
MASTER OF CRAFT, A, 1922, A
MASTER OF GRAY, THE, 1918
MASTER OF HIS HOME, 1917
MASTER OF HORROR, 1965, C-O
MASTER OF LASSIE
MASTER OF LOVE, THE, 1919
MASTER OF MEN, 1933, A
MASTER OF MEN, A, 1917
MASTER OF TERROR
MASTER OF THE HOUSE, 1925
MASTER OF THE HOUSE, THE, 1915
MASTER OF THE ISLANDS
MASTER OF THE RANGE, 1928
MASTER OF THE WORLD, 1935, A
MASTER OF THE WORLD, 1961, A
MASTER PASSION, THE, 1917
MASTER PLAN, THE, 1955, A
MASTER RACE, THE, 1944, C
MASTER SHAKESPEARE, STROLLING PLAYER, 1916
MASTER SPY, 1964, A
MASTER STROKE, A, 1920, A
MASTER TOUCH, THE, 1974, C
MASTERMIND, 1977, A
MASTERS OF MEN, 1923
MASTERSON OF KANSAS, 1954, A
MATA HARI, 1931, A
MATA HARI, 1965, C
MATA HARI'S DAUGHTER, 1954, A
MATALOS Y VUELVE
MATCH KING, THE, 1932, C
MATCH-BREAKER, THE, 1921
MATCH-MAKERS, THE, 1916
MATCHLESS, 1967, C
MATCHLESS, 1974, O
MATCHMAKER, THE, 1958, A
MATCHMAKING OF ANNA, THE, 1972, O
MATE DOMA IVA?
MATE OF THE SALLY ANN, THE, 1917
MATER DOLOROSA, 1917
MATERNAL SPARK, THE, 1917
MATERNITY, 1917
MATHIAS SANDORF, 1963, A
MATILDA, 1978, A
MATINEE IDOL, 1933, A
MATINEE IDOL, THE, 1928, A
MATINEE LADIES, 1927, A
MATING CALL, THE, 1928
MATING GAME, THE, 1959, A
MATING OF MARCELLA, THE, 1918
MATING OF MARCUS, THE, 1924, A
MATING OF MILLIE, THE, 1948, A
MATING OF THE SABINE WOMEN, THE
MATING SEASON, THE, 1951, A
MATING, THE, 1915
MATING, THE, 1918
MATKA JOANNA OD ANIOLOW
MATRIMANIAC, THE, 1916, A
MATRIMONIAL BED, THE, 1930, A
MATRIMONIAL MARTYR, A, 1916
MATRIMONIAL PROBLEM, A
MATRIMONIAL WEB, THE, 1921
MATRIMONIO ALL'ITALIANA
MATRIMONY, 1915
MATT, 1918
MATTER OF CHOICE, A, 1963, A
MATTER OF CONVICTION, A
MATTER OF DAYS, A, 1969, O
MATTER OF INNOCENCE, A, 1968, A
MATTER OF LIFE AND DEATH, A
MATTER OF LOVE, A, 1979
MATTER OF MORALS, A, 1961, O
MATTER OF MURDER, A, 1949, A
MATTER OF RESISTANCE, A
MATTER OF TIME, A, 1976, A-C
MATTER OF WHO, A, 1962, A
MAUPRAT, 1926
MAURIE, 1973, A
MAURIE, 1973
MAUSOLEUM, 1983, O
MAVERICK QUEEN, THE, 1956, A
MAVERICK, THE, 1952, A
MAX DUGAN RETURNS, 1983, A
MAXIME, 1962, A
MAXWELL ARCHER, DETECTIVE, 1942, C
MAY BLOSSOM, 1915, A
MAY MORNING, 1970
MAYA, 1966, A
MAYA, 1982, C
MAYBE IT'S LOVE, 1930, A
MAYBE IT'S LOVE, 1935, A
MAYBLOSSOM, 1917
MAYERLING, 1937, C-O
MAYERLING, 1968, C
MAYFAIR GIRL, 1933, A
MAYFAIR MELODY, 1937, A
MAYHEM
MAYOR OF 44TH STREET, THE, 1942, A
MAYOR OF CASTERBRIDGE, THE, 1921
MAYOR OF FILBERT, THE, 1919
MAYOR OF HELL, THE, 1933, C
MAYOR'S NEST, THE, 1932, A
MAYOR'S NEST, THE, 1941
MAYTIME, 1923
MAYTIME, 1937, A
MAYTIME IN MAYFAIR, 1952, A
MAZE, THE, 1953, C
MAZEL TOV, 1924
MAZEL TOV OU LE MARIAGE
MAZEL TOV, JEWS, 1941
MC CABE AND MRS. MILLER, 1971, O
MC CONNELL STORY, THE, 1955, A
MC CORD
MC CULLOCHS, THE
MC FADDEN'S FLATS, 1935, A
MC GLUSKY THE SEA ROVER
MC GUIRE, GO HOME, 1966, A
MC HALE'S NAVY, 1964, A
MC HALE'S NAVY JOINS THE AIR FORCE, 1965, A
MC KENNA OF THE MOUNTED, 1932, A
MC KENZIE BREAK, THE, 1970, C
MC LINTOCK, 1963, A
MC MASTERS, THE, 1970, O
MC Q, 1974, O
MC VICAR, 1982, C
MCFADDEN FLATS, 1927
MCGUIRE OF THE MOUNTED, 1923
ME, 1970, A
ME AND CAPTAIN KID, 1919
ME AND GOTT
ME AND M'PAL, 1916
ME AND MARLBOROUGH, 1935, A
ME AND ME MOKE
ME AND MY BROTHER, 1969, O
ME AND MY GAL, 1932, A
ME AND MY PAL, 1939, A
ME AND THE COLONEL, 1958, A
ME UND GOTT, 1918
ME, GANGSTER, 1928
ME, NATALIE, 1969, C
MEA CULPA, 1919
MEAL, THE, 1975, O
MEAN DOG BLUES, 1978, O
MEAN FRANK AND CRAZY TONY, 1976, O
MEAN JOHNNY BARROWS, 1976, O
MEAN MOTHER, 1974
MEAN STREETS, 1973, O
MEANEST GAL IN TOWN, THE, 1934, A
MEANEST MAN IN THE WORLD, THE, 1923
MEANEST MAN IN THE WORLD, THE, 1943, A
MEANWHILE BACK AT THE RANCH
MEANWHILE, FAR FROM THE FRONT
MEASURE OF A MAN, THE, 1916, A
MEASURE OF A MAN, THE, 1924, A
MEAT CLEAVER MASSACRE, 1977
MEATBALLS, 1979, C
MEATBALLS PART II, 1984, C
MEATEATER, 1979
MECHANIC, THE, 1972, O
MED MORD I BAGAGET
MEDAL FOR BENNY, A, 1945, A
MEDAL FOR THE GENERAL
MEDALS
MEDDLER, THE, 1925, A
MEDDLIN' STRANGER, THE, 1927
MEDDLING WOMEN, 1924
MEDEA, 1971, O
MEDIATOR, THE, 1916, A
MEDICINE BEND, 1916
MEDICINE MAN, THE, 1917
MEDICINE MAN, THE, 1930, A
MEDICINE MAN, THE, 1933, A
MEDICO OF PAINTED SPRINGS, THE, 1941, A
MEDIUM COOL, 1969, O
MEDIUM, THE, 1951, A
MEDJU JASTREBOVIMA
MEDUSA TOUCH, THE, 1978, C
MEET BOSTON BLACKIE, 1941, A
MEET DANNY WILSON, 1952, A
MEET DR. CHRISTIAN, 1939, A
MEET JOHN DOE, 1941, A
MEET MAXWELL ARCHER
MEET ME AFTER THE SHOW, 1951, A
MEET ME AT DAWN, 1947, A
MEET ME AT THE FAIR, 1952, A
MEET ME IN LAS VEGAS, 1956, A
MEET ME IN MOSCOW, 1966, A
MEET ME IN ST. LOUIS, 1944, AAA
MEET ME ON BROADWAY, 1946, A
MEET ME TONIGHT
MEET MISS BOBBY SOCKS, 1944, A
MEET MISS MARPLE
MEET MR. CALLAGHAN, 1954, A
MEET MR. LUCIFER, 1953, A
MEET MR. MALCOLM, 1954, A
MEET MR. PENNY, 1938, A
MEET MY SISTER, 1933, A
MEET NERO WOLFE, 1936, A
MEET SEXTON BLAKE, 1944, A
MEET SIMON CHERRY, 1949, A
MEET THE BARON, 1933, A
MEET THE BOY FRIEND, 1937, A
MEET THE CHUMP, 1941, A
MEET THE DUKE, 1949, A
MEET THE GIRLS, 1938, A
MEET THE MAYOR, 1938, A
MEET THE MISSUS, 1937, A
MEET THE MISSUS, 1940, A
MEET THE MOB, 1942, A
MEET THE NAVY, 1946, A
MEET THE NELSONS
MEET THE PEOPLE, 1944, A
MEET THE PRINCE, 1926
MEET THE PRINCE, 1926
MEET THE STEWARTS, 1942, A
MEET THE WIFE, 1931, A
MEET THE WILDCAT, 1940, A
MEET WHIPLASH WILLIE
MEETING AT MIDNIGHT
MEETINGS WITH REMARKABLE MEN, 1979, A
MEFIEZ-VOUS DE VOTRE BONNE, 1920
MEG, 1926, A
MEG O' THE WOODS, 1918
MEG OF THE SLUMS, 1916

MEGAFORCE, 1982, C
MEGLIO VEDOVA
MEIN KAMPF—MY CRIMES, 1940, C
MELANIE, 1982, A
MELBA, 1953, A
MELINDA, 1972, O
MELISSA OF THE HILLS, 1917
MELODIE EN SOUS-SOL
MELODIES, 1926
MELODY, 1971, AAA
MELODY AND MOONLIGHT, 1940, A
MELODY AND ROMANCE, 1937, A
MELODY CLUB, 1949, A
MELODY CRUISE, 1933, A
MELODY FOR THREE, 1941, A
MELODY FOR TWO, 1937, A
MELODY GIRL
MELODY IN SPRING, 1934, A
MELODY IN THE DARK, 1948, A
MELODY INN
MELODY LANE, 1929, A
MELODY LANE, 1941, A
MELODY LINGERS ON, THE, 1935, A
MELODY MAKER, 1946
MELODY MAKER, THE, 1933, A
MELODY MAN, 1930, A
MELODY OF LIFE
MELODY OF LOVE, 1954, A
MELODY OF LOVE, THE, 1928, A
MELODY OF MY HEART, 1936, A
MELODY OF THE PLAINS, 1937, A
MELODY OF YOUTH
MELODY PARADE, 1943, A
MELODY RANCH, 1940, A
MELODY TIME, 1948, AAA
MELODY TRAIL, 1935, AA
MELON AFFAIR, THE, 1979
MELTING MILLIONS, 1917
MELTING POT, THE
MELTING POT, THE, 1915
MELVIN AND HOWARD, 1980, C-O
MELVIN, SON OF ALVIN, 1984, O
MEMBER OF THE JURY, 1937, A
MEMBER OF THE TATTERSALL'S, A, 1919
MEMBER OF THE WEDDING, THE, 1952, A
MEMED MY HAWK, 1984, C
MEMENTO MEI, 1963, C
MEMOIRS, 1984, O
MEMOIRS OF A SURVIVOR, 1981, C
MEMOIRS OF PRISON, 1984, O
MEMORIAS DO CARCERE
MEMORY EXPERT, THE
MEMORY FOR TWO
MEMORY LANE, 1926, A
MEMORY OF LOVE, 1949
MEMORY OF US, 1974, A
MEN, 1924
MEN AGAINST THE SKY, 1940, A
MEN AGAINST THE SUN, 1953, A
MEN AND WOMEN, 1925
MEN ARE CHILDREN TWICE, 1953, A
MEN ARE LIKE THAT, 1930, A
MEN ARE LIKE THAT, 1931, A
MEN ARE NOT GODS, 1937, A-C
MEN ARE SUCH FOOLS, 1933, A
MEN ARE SUCH FOOLS, 1938, A
MEN BEHIND BARS
MEN CALL IT LOVE, 1931, C
MEN IN EXILE, 1937, A
MEN IN HER DIARY, 1945, A
MEN IN HER LIFE, 1931, A
MEN IN HER LIFE, THE, 1941, A
MEN IN THE RAW, 1923
MEN IN WAR, 1957, A-C
MEN IN WHITE, 1934, A
MEN LIKE THESE
MEN MUST FIGHT, 1933, A
MEN OF ACTION, 1935
MEN OF AMERICA, 1933, A
MEN OF BOYS TOWN, 1941, AA
MEN OF CHANCE, 1932, A
MEN OF DARING, 1927
MEN OF DESTINY
MEN OF IRELAND, 1938, A
MEN OF SAN QUENTIN, 1942, A
MEN OF SHERWOOD FOREST, 1957, A
MEN OF STEEL, 1926
MEN OF STEEL, 1932, A
MEN OF STEEL, 1937
MEN OF STEEL, 1980
MEN OF TEXAS, 1942, A
MEN OF THE DEEP
MEN OF THE DESERT, 1917
MEN OF THE FIGHTING LADY, 1954, A
MEN OF THE HOUR, 1935, A
MEN OF THE NIGHT, 1926
MEN OF THE NIGHT, 1934, A
MEN OF THE NORTH, 1930, A
MEN OF THE PLAINS, 1936, A
MEN OF THE SEA, 1938, A
MEN OF THE SEA, 1951, A
MEN OF THE SKY, 1931, A
MEN OF THE TENTH
MEN OF THE TIMBERLAND, 1941, A
MEN OF TOMORROW, 1935, A
MEN OF TWO WORLDS
MEN OF YESTERDAY, 1936, A
MEN OF ZANSIBAR, THE, 1922
MEN ON CALL, 1931, A
MEN ON HER MIND, 1944, A
MEN ON HER MIND, 1935
MEN PREFER FAT GIRLS, 1981, C
MEN SHE MARRIED, THE, 1916, A
MEN WHO FORGET, 1923
MEN WHO HAVE MADE LOVE TO ME, 1918
MEN WITH WINGS, 1938, A
MEN WITHOUT HONOUR, 1939, A
MEN WITHOUT LAW, 1930, A
MEN WITHOUT NAMES, 1935, A
MEN WITHOUT SOULS, 1940, A
MEN WITHOUT WOMEN, 1930, A
MEN WOMEN LOVE, 1926
MEN WOMEN LOVE
MEN, THE, 1950, C
MEN, WOMEN AND MONEY, 1919
MEN, WOMEN AND MONEY, 1924
MENACE, 1934, A
MENACE IN THE NIGHT, 1958, A
MENACE OF THE MUTE, THE, 1915
MENACE, 1934, Brit.
MENACE, THE, 1918
MENACE, THE, 1932, A-C
MENACING PAST, THE, 1922
MENILMONTANT, 1926
MENNESKER MODES OG SOD MUSIK OPSTAR I HJERTET
MENSCHEN AM SONNTAG
MENSCHEN IM NETZ
MENTIONED IN CONFIDENCE, 1917
MEPHISTO, 1981, O
MEPHISTO WALTZ, THE, 1971, C-O
MERCENARIES, THE
MERCENARY, THE, 1970, C
MERCHANT OF SLAVES, 1949, C
MERCHANT OF VENICE, THE, 1914
MERCHANT OF VENICE, THE, 1916, A
MERCY ISLAND, 1941, A
MERCY PLANE, 1940, A
MERELY MARY ANN, 1916
MERELY MARY ANN, 1920
MERELY MARY ANN, 1931, A
MERELY MR. HAWKINS, 1938, A
MERELY MRS. STUBBS, 1917
MERELY PLAYERS, 1918
MERES FRANCAISES, 1917
MERMAID, THE, 1966, A
MERMAIDS OF TIBURON, THE, 1962, A-C
MERRILL'S MARAUDERS, 1962, C-O
MERRILY WE GO TO HELL, 1932, A-C
MERRILY WE LIVE, 1938, A
MERRY ANDREW, 1958, AA
MERRY CAVALIER, THE, 1926
MERRY CHRISTMAS MR. LAWRENCE, 1983, O
MERRY COMES TO STAY, 1937, A
MERRY COMES TO TOWN
MERRY FRINKS, THE, 1934, A
MERRY MONAHANS, THE, 1944, A
MERRY WIDOW, THE, 1925, C
MERRY WIDOW, THE, 1934, A-C
MERRY WIDOW, THE, 1952, A
MERRY WIVES OF RENO, THE, 1934, A
MERRY WIVES OF TOBIAS ROUKE, THE, 1972, A
MERRY WIVES OF WINDSOR, THE, 1952, A
MERRY WIVES OF WINDSOR, THE, 1966, A
MERRY WIVES, THE, 1940, C
MERRY-GO-ROUND, 1948, A
MERRY-GO ROUND, THE, 1919
MERRY-GO-ROUND, 1923, A
MERRY-GO-ROUND OF 1938, 1937, A
MERTON OF THE MOVIES, 1924, A
MERTON OF THE MOVIES, 1947, A
MES FEMMES AMERICAINES
MESA OF LOST WOMEN, THE, 1956, A
MESDAMES ET MESSIEURS
MESQUITE BUCKAROO, 1939, A
MESSAGE FROM MARS, A, 1913, A
MESSAGE FROM MARS, A, 1921
MESSAGE FROM SPACE, 1978, A
MESSAGE OF HOPE, THE, 1923
MESSAGE OF THE MOUSE, THE, 1917
MESSAGE TO GARCIA, A, 1916
MESSAGE TO GARCIA, A, 1936, A
MESSAGE, THE
MESSALINA, 1924
MESSALINE, 1952, A
MESSENGER OF PEACE, 1950, A
MESSENGER OF THE BLESSED VIRGIN, 1930
MESSIAH OF EVIL
METAL MESSIAH, 1978
METALSTORM: THE DESTRUCTION OF JARED-SYN, 1983, C
METAMORPHOSES, 1978, A
METAMORPHOSIS, 1951
METEMPSYCO
METEOR, 1979, C
METEOR MONSTER
METROPOLIS, 1927, A
METROPOLITAN, 1935, A
METROPOLITAN SYMPHONY, 1929
MEURTRE EN 45 TOURS
MEXICALI KID, THE, 1938, A
MEXICALI ROSE, 1929, A
MEXICALI ROSE, 1939, A
MEXICAN HAYRIDE, 1948, A
MEXICAN MANHUNT, 1953, A
MEXICAN SPITFIRE, 1939, A
MEXICAN SPITFIRE AT SEA, 1942, A
MEXICAN SPITFIRE OUT WEST, 1940, A
MEXICAN SPITFIRE SEES A GHOST, 1942, A
MEXICAN SPITFIRE'S BABY, 1941, A
MEXICAN SPITFIRE'S BLESSED EVENT, 1943, A
MEXICAN SPITFIRE'S ELEPHANT, 1942, A
MEXICAN, THE
MEXICANA, 1945, A
MEXICO IN FLAMES, 1982, O
MI MUJER ES DOCTOR
MIAMI, 1924
MIAMI EXPOSE, 1956, A
MIAMI RENDEZVOUS
MIAMI STORY, THE, 1954, A
MIARKA, LA FILLE A L'OURSE
MIARKA, THE DAUGHTER OF THE BEAR
MICE AND MEN, 1916, A
MICHAEL, 1924
MICHAEL AND MARY, 1932, A
MICHAEL O'HALLORAN, 1923
MICHAEL O'HALLORAN, 1937, A
MICHAEL O'HALLORAN, 1948, A
MICHAEL SHAYNE, PRIVATE DETECTIVE, 1940, A
MICHAEL STROGOFF, 1960, A
MICHAEL STROGOFF, 1937
MICHEL STROGOFF, 1926
MICHELINE, 1920
MICHELLE, 1970, C
MICHIGAN KID, THE, 1928, A
MICHIGAN KID, THE, 1947, A
MICKEY, 1919, A
MICKEY, 1948, A
MICKEY ONE, 1965, C-O
MICKEY, THE KID, 1939, A
MICKI AND MAUDE, 1984, C
MICROBE, THE, 1919
MICROSCOPE MYSTERY, THE, 1916
MICROSCOPIA
MICROWAVE MASSACRE, 1983, O
MID-DAY MISTRESS, 1968, O
MIDAREGUMO
MIDARERU
MIDAS RUN, 1969, C
MIDAS TOUCH, THE, 1940, A
MIDCHANNEL, 1920
MIDDLE AGE CRAZY, 1980, O
MIDDLE AGE SPREAD, 1979, O
MIDDLE COURSE, THE, 1961, A
MIDDLE OF THE NIGHT, 1959, A-C
MIDDLE PASSAGE, 1978
MIDDLE WATCH, THE, 1930, A
MIDDLE WATCH, THE, 1939, A
MIDDLEMAN, THE, 1915
MIDDLETON FAMILY AT THE N.Y. WORLD'S FAIR, 1939, A
MIDINETTE, 1917
MIDLANDERS, THE, 1920
MIDNIGHT, 1922
MIDNIGHT, 1934, A
MIDNIGHT, 1939, A
MIDNIGHT, 1983, O
MIDNIGHT ACE, THE, 1928
MIDNIGHT ADVENTURE, THE, 1928
MIDNIGHT ALARM, THE, 1923
MIDNIGHT ALIBI, 1934, A
MIDNIGHT ANGEL, 1941, A
MIDNIGHT AT MADAME TUSSAUD'S
MIDNIGHT AT MAXIM'S, 1915
MIDNIGHT AT THE WAX MUSEUM, 1936, A
MIDNIGHT AUTO SUPPLY
MIDNIGHT BELL, A, 1921
MIDNIGHT BRIDE, THE, 1920
MIDNIGHT BURGLAR, THE, 1918
MIDNIGHT CLUB, 1933, A
MIDNIGHT COURT, 1937, A
MIDNIGHT COWBOY, 1969, O
MIDNIGHT DADDIES, 1929, A
MIDNIGHT EPISODE, 1951, A
MIDNIGHT EXPRESS, 1978, O
MIDNIGHT EXPRESS, THE, 1924, A
MIDNIGHT FACES, 1926

MIDNIGHT FIRES
MIDNIGHT FLOWER, THE, 1923
MIDNIGHT FLYER, THE, 1925
MIDNIGHT FOLLY, 1962, C
MIDNIGHT GAMBOLS, 1919
MIDNIGHT GIRL, THE, 1925
MIDNIGHT GUEST, THE, 1923
MIDNIGHT INTRUDER, 1938, A
MIDNIGHT KISS, THE, 1926
MIDNIGHT LACE, 1960, C
MIDNIGHT LADY, 1932, A
MIDNIGHT LIFE, 1928, A
MIDNIGHT LIMITED, 1926
MIDNIGHT LIMITED, 1940, A
MIDNIGHT LOVERS, 1926
MIDNIGHT MADNESS, 1918
MIDNIGHT MADNESS, 1928, A
MIDNIGHT MADNESS, 1980, C
MIDNIGHT MADONNA, 1937, A
MIDNIGHT MAN, 1917
MIDNIGHT MAN, THE, 1974, O
MIDNIGHT MANHUNT
MIDNIGHT MARY, 1933, A-C
MIDNIGHT MEETING, 1962, A
MIDNIGHT MELODY
MIDNIGHT MENACE
MIDNIGHT MESSAGE, THE, 1926, A
MIDNIGHT MOLLY, 1925
MIDNIGHT MORALS, 1932, A
MIDNIGHT MYSTERY, 1930, A
MIDNIGHT ON THE BARBARY COAST, 1929
MIDNIGHT PATROL, THE, 1918, A
MIDNIGHT PATROL, THE, 1932, A
MIDNIGHT PHANTOM, THE, 1935
MIDNIGHT PLEASURES, 1975, O
MIDNIGHT PLOWBOY, 1973
MIDNIGHT RAIDERS
MIDNIGHT ROMANCE, A, 1919, A
MIDNIGHT ROSE, 1928
MIDNIGHT SECRETS, 1924
MIDNIGHT SHADOW, 1939
MIDNIGHT SHADOWS, 1924
MIDNIGHT SPECIAL, 1931, A
MIDNIGHT STAGE, THE, 1919
MIDNIGHT STORY, THE, 1957, A
MIDNIGHT SUN, THE, 1926
MIDNIGHT TAXI, 1937, A
MIDNIGHT TAXI, THE, 1928, A
MIDNIGHT THIEVES, 1926
MIDNIGHT TRAIL, THE, 1918
MIDNIGHT WARNING, THE, 1932, A
MIDNIGHT WATCH, THE, 1927, A
MIDSHIPMAID GOB, 1932, A
MIDSHIPMAN EASY
MIDSHIPMAN JACK, 1933, A
MIDSHIPMAN, THE, 1925
MIDSHIPMAN, THE
MIDSTREAM, 1929, A
MIDSUMMER MADNESS, 1920, C
MIDSUMMER NIGHT'S DREAM, A, 1928
MIDSUMMER NIGHT'S DREAM, A, 1966, A
MIDSUMMER NIGHT'S DREAM, A, 1969, A
MIDSUMMER NIGHT'S DREAM, A, 1984, O
MIDSUMMER NIGHT'S SEX COMEDY, A, 1982, C-O
MIDSUMMER'S NIGHT'S DREAM, A, 1935, A
MIDSUMMERS NIGHT'S DREAM, A, 1961, AAA
MIDWAY, 1976, A
MIDWIFE, THE, 1961, A
MIGHT AND THE MAN, 1917
MIGHT MAKES RIGHT
MIGHTY BARNUM, THE, 1934, A
MIGHTY CRUSADERS, THE, 1961, A
MIGHTY DEBRAU, THE, 1923
MIGHTY GORGA, THE, 1969, A
MIGHTY JOE YOUNG, 1949, A
MIGHTY JUNGLE, THE, 1965, A
MIGHTY LAK' A ROSE, 1923
MIGHTY MCGURK, THE, 1946, A
MIGHTY MOUSE IN THE GREAT SPACE CHASE, 1983, AAA
MIGHTY TREVE, THE, 1937, AAA
MIGHTY TUNDRA, THE
MIGHTY URSUS, 1962, A
MIGHTY WARRIOR, THE
MIGHTY, THE, 1929, A
MIGNON, 1915
MIKADO, THE, 1939, A
MIKADO, THE, 1967, AAA
MIKE, 1926, A
MIKE'S MURDER, 1984, O
MIKEY AND NICKY, 1976, C-O
MILADY, 1923
MILADY O' THE BEAN STALK, 1918
MILCZACA GWIAZDA
MILDRED PIERCE, 1945, A
MILE A MINUTE
MILE A MINUTE LOVE, 1937, A
MILE A MINUTE MORGAN, 1924
MILE-A-MINUTE KENDALL, 1918
MILE-A-MINUTE MAN, THE, 1926
MILE-A-MINUTE ROMEO, 1923
MILESTONES, 1916
MILESTONES, 1920
MILESTONES, 1975, C
MILESTONES OF LIFE, 1915
MILITARY ACADEMY, 1940, A
MILITARY ACADEMY WITH THAT TENTH AVENUE GANG, 1950, A
MILITARY POLICEMAN
MILITARY SECRET, 1945, A
MILKMAN, THE, 1950, A
MILKY WAY, THE, 1922
MILKY WAY, THE, 1936, AA
MILKY WAY, THE, 1969, C
MILL OF THE STONE WOMEN, 1963, O
MILL ON THE FLOSS, 1939, A
MILL ON THE FLOSS, THE, 1915
MILL-OWNER'S DAUGHTER, THE, 1916
MILLER'S WIFE, THE, 1957, O
MILLERSON CASE, THE, 1947, A
MILLIE, 1931, A
MILLIE'S DAUGHTER, 1947, A
MILLION A MINUTE, A, 1916
MILLION BID, A, 1914
MILLION BID, A, 1927
MILLION DOLLAR BABY, 1935, A
MILLION DOLLAR BABY, 1941, A
MILLION DOLLAR COLLAR, THE, 1929, A
MILLION DOLLAR DOLLIES, THE, 1918
MILLION DOLLAR DUCK
MILLION DOLLAR HANDICAP, THE, 1925
MILLION DOLLAR HAUL, 1935
MILLION DOLLAR KID, 1944, A
MILLION DOLLAR LEGS, 1932, A
MILLION DOLLAR LEGS, 1939, A
MILLION DOLLAR MANHUNT, 1962, A
MILLION DOLLAR MERMAID, 1952, A
MILLION DOLLAR MYSTERY, 1927
MILLION DOLLAR PURSUIT, 1951, A
MILLION DOLLAR RACKET
MILLION DOLLAR RANSOM, 1934, A
MILLION DOLLAR ROBBERY, THE, 1914, A
MILLION DOLLAR WEEKEND, 1948, A
MILLION EYES OF SU-MURU, THE, 1967, A
MILLION FOR LOVE, A, 1928, A
MILLION FOR MARY, A, 1916
MILLION POUND NOTE
MILLION TO BURN, A, 1923
MILLION TO ONE, A, 1938, A
MILLION, THE, 1915
MILLION, THE, 1931, A
MILLIONAIRE BABY, THE, 1915
MILLIONAIRE COWBOY, THE, 1924
MILLIONAIRE FOR A DAY
MILLIONAIRE FOR A DAY, A, 1921
MILLIONAIRE FOR CHRISTY, A, 1951, A
MILLIONAIRE KID, 1936, A
MILLIONAIRE MERRY-GO-ROUND
MILLIONAIRE ORPHAN, THE, 1926
MILLIONAIRE PIRATE, THE, 1919
MILLIONAIRE PLAYBOY, 1940, A
MILLIONAIRE PLAYBOY, 1937
MILLIONAIRE POLICEMAN, THE, 1926
MILLIONAIRE VAGRANT, THE, 1917
MILLIONAIRE'S DOUBLE, THE, 1917
MILLIONAIRE, THE, 1921, A
MILLIONAIRE, THE, 1931, A
MILLIONAIRES, 1926
MILLIONAIRES IN PRISON, 1940, A
MILLIONAIRESS, THE, 1960, A
MILLIONARE, THE, 1927
MILLIONS, 1936, A
MILLIONS IN THE AIR, 1935, A
MILLIONS LIKE US, 1943, A
MILLS OF THE GODS, 1935, A
MILLSTONE, THE, 1917
MILOSC DWUDZIESTOLATKOW
MILPITAS MONSTER, THE, 1980
MIMI, 1935, A
MIMI TROTTIN, 1922
MIN AND BILL, 1930, A
MIN VAN BALTHAZAR
MINAMI NO SHIMA NI YUKI GA FURA
MIND BENDERS, THE, 1963, C-O
MIND OF MR. REEDER, THE
MIND OF MR. SOAMES, THE, 1970, A
MIND OVER MOTOR, 1923, A
MIND READER, THE, 1933, A
MIND SNATCHERS, THE
MIND THE PAINT GIRL, 1919
MIND YOUR OWN BUSINESS, 1937, A
MIND-THE-PAINT-GIRL, 1916
MINDWARP: AN INFINITY OF TERROR
MINE OF MISSING MEN, 1917
MINE OWN EXECUTIONER, 1948, C-O
MINE TO KEEP, 1923
MINE WITH THE IRON DOOR, THE, 1924
MINE WITH THE IRON DOOR, THE, 1936, A
MINESWEEPER, 1943, A
MINI WEEKEND
MINI-AFFAIR, THE, 1968, A
MINI-SKIRT MOB, THE, 1968, O
MINISTRY OF FEAR, 1945, C
MINIVER STORY, THE, 1950, A
MINNESOTA CLAY, 1966, C
MINNIE, 1922
MINNIE AND MOSKOWITZ, 1971, C
MINOTAUR, 1955
MINOTAUR, 1976
MINOTAUR, THE, 1961, A
MINOTAUR, WILD BEAST OF CRETE
MINSTREL BOY, THE, 1937, A
MINSTREL MAN, 1944, A
MINTS OF HELL, THE, 1919
MINUIT...PLACE PIGALLE, 1928
MINUTE TO PRAY, A SECOND TO DIE, A, 1968, C
MINX, THE, 1969, O
MIO FIGILIO NERONE
MIR VKHODYASHCHEMU
MIRACLE BABY, THE, 1923
MIRACLE CAN HAPPEN, A
MIRACLE IN HARLEM, 1948, A
MIRACLE IN MILAN, 1951, A
MIRACLE IN SOHO, 1957, A
MIRACLE IN THE RAIN, 1956, A
MIRACLE IN THE SAND
MIRACLE KID, 1942, A
MIRACLE MAKERS, THE, 1923, A
MIRACLE MAN, THE, 1919, A
MIRACLE MAN, THE, 1932, A
MIRACLE OF FATIMA
MIRACLE OF LIFE
MIRACLE OF LIFE, THE, 1915
MIRACLE OF LIFE, THE, 1926
MIRACLE OF LOVE, A, 1916
MIRACLE OF LOVE, THE, 1920
MIRACLE OF MANHATTAN, THE, 1921
MIRACLE OF MONEY, THE, 1920
MIRACLE OF MORGAN'S CREEK, THE, 1944, C
MIRACLE OF OUR LADY OF FATIMA, THE, 1952, A
MIRACLE OF SAN SEBASTIAN
MIRACLE OF SANTA'S WHITE REINDEER, THE, 1963, A
MIRACLE OF THE BELLS, THE, 1948, A
MIRACLE OF THE HILLS, THE, 1959, A
MIRACLE OF THE WHITE REINDEER, THE
MIRACLE OF THE WHITE STALLIONS, 1963, AA
MIRACLE OF WOLVES, THE, 1925
MIRACLE ON 34TH STREET, THE, 1947, AAA
MIRACLE ON MAIN STREET, A, 1940, A
MIRACLE WOMAN, THE, 1931, A-C
MIRACLE WORKER, THE, 1962, A
MIRACLE, THE, 1912
MIRACLE, THE, 1959, A
MIRACLE, THE, 1948
MIRACLE-MAKER, 1922
MIRACLES DO HAPPEN, 1938, A
MIRACLES FOR SALE, 1939, A
MIRACOLO A MILANO
MIRACULOUS JOURNEY, 1948, A
MIRAGE, 1965, A-C
MIRAGE, 1972, C
MIRAGE, THE, 1920, A
MIRAGE, THE, 1924
MIRANDA, 1949, A
MIRANDY SMILES, 1918
MIRELE EFROS, 1912
MIRELE EFROS, 1939
MIRIAM
MIRIAM ROZELLA, 1924, C
MIRROR CRACK'D, THE, 1980, A-C
MIRROR HAS TWO FACES, THE, 1959, A
MIRROR OF LIFE, THE, 1916
MIRROR, THE, 1917
MIRRORS, 1978
MIRRORS, 1984, O
MIRTH AND MELODY
MISADVENTURES OF MERLIN JONES, THE, 1964, AAA
MISBEHAVING HUSBANDS, 1941, A
MISBEHAVING LADIES, 1931, A
MISCHIEF, 1931, A
MISCHIEF, 1969, A
MISCHIEF MAKER, THE, 1916, A
MISERICORDE, 1917
MISFIT EARL, A, 1919
MISFIT WIFE, THE, 1920
MISFITS, THE, 1961, C
MISHPACHAT SIMCHON
MISLEADING LADY, THE, 1916
MISLEADING LADY, THE, 1920
MISLEADING LADY, THE, 1932, A
MISLEADING WIDOW, THE, 1919
MISMATES, 1926
MISS ADVENTURE, 1919
MISS AMBITION, 1918
MISS ANNIE ROONEY, 1942, A

MISS ARIZONA, 1919
MISS BLUEBEARD, 1925, A
MISS BREWSTER'S MILLIONS, 1926, A
MISS CHARITY, 1921
MISS CRUSOE, 1919, A
MISS DECEPTION, 1917
MISS DULCIE FROM DIXIE, 1919, A
MISS EDITH, DUCHESSE, 1928
MISS FANE'S BABY IS STOLEN, 1934, A
MISS FIX-IT
MISS GEORGE WASHINGTON, 1916
MISS GRANT TAKES RICHMOND, 1949, A
MISS HELYETT, 1927
MISS HOBBS, 1920, A
MISS INNOCENCE, 1918
MISS JACKIE OF THE ARMY, 1917
MISS JACKIE OF THE NAVY, 1916
MISS JESSICA IS PREGNANT, 1970, O
MISS JUDE
MISS LESLIE'S DOLLS, 1972
MISS LONDON LTD., 1943, A
MISS LULU BETT, 1921
MISS MELODY JONES, 1973
MISS MEND, 1926
MISS MINK OF 1949, 1949, A
MISS MISCHIEF MAKER, 1918
MISS MUERTE
MISS NOBODY, 1917
MISS NOBODY, 1920
MISS NOBODY, 1926, A
MISS PACIFIC FLEET, 1935, A
MISS PAUL REVERE, 1922
MISS PEASANT, 1916
MISS PETTICOATS, 1916
MISS PILGRIM'S PROGRESS, 1950, A
MISS PINKERTON, 1932, A
MISS PRESIDENT, 1935, A
MISS ROBIN CRUSOE, 1954, A
MISS ROBIN HOOD, 1952, A
MISS ROBINSON CRUSOE, 1917
MISS ROVEL, 1920
MISS SADIE THOMPSON, 1953, O
MISS SUSIE SLAGLE'S, 1945, A
MISS TATLOCK'S MILLIONS, 1948, A
MISS TULIP STAYS THE NIGHT, 1955, A
MISS U.S.A., 1917
MISS V FROM MOSCOW, 1942, A
MISSILE FROM HELL, 1960, A
MISSILE TO THE MOON, 1959, A
MISSING, 1918
MISSING, 1982, A-C
MISSING CORPSE, THE, 1945, A
MISSING DAUGHTERS, 1924
MISSING DAUGHTERS, 1939, A
MISSING EVIDENCE, 1939, A
MISSING GIRLS, 1936, A
MISSING GUEST, THE, 1938, A
MISSING HUSBANDS
MISSING IN ACTION, 1984, O
MISSING JUROR, THE, 1944, A
MISSING LADY, THE, 1946, A
MISSING LINK, THE, 1927
MISSING LINKS, THE, 1916
MISSING MILLION, THE, 1942, A
MISSING MILLIONS, 1922, A
MISSING NOTE, THE, 1961, AA
MISSING PEOPLE, THE, 1940, A
MISSING PERSONS
MISSING REMBRANDT, THE, 1932, A
MISSING TEN DAYS, 1941, A
MISSING THE TIDE, 1918, C
MISSING WITNESS
MISSING WITNESSES, 1937, A
MISSING WOMEN, 1951, A
MISSING, BELIEVED MARRIED, 1937, A
MISSION BATANGAS, 1968, A
MISSION BLOODY MARY, 1967, A
MISSION GALACTICA: THE CYLON ATTACK, 1979, A
MISSION HILL, 1982
MISSION IN MOROCCO, 1959
MISSION MARS, 1968, A
MISSION OF THE SEA HAWK, 1962
MISSION OVER KOREA, 1953, A
MISSION STARDUST, 1968, A
MISSION TO DEATH, 1966
MISSION TO HELL
MISSION TO HONG KONG
MISSION TO MOSCOW, 1943, A
MISSION, THE, 1984, O
MISSION: MONTE CARLO, 1981
MISSIONARY, THE, 1982, O
MISSISSIPPI, 1935, A
MISSISSIPPI GAMBLER, 1929, A
MISSISSIPPI GAMBLER, 1942, A
MISSISSIPPI GAMBLER, THE, 1953, C
MISSISSIPPI MERMAID, 1970, A
MISSISSIPPI RHYTHM, 1949, A
MISSISSIPPI SUMMER, 1971, C
MISSISSIPPI, 1931
MISSOURI BREAKS, THE, 1976, C-O
MISSOURI OUTLAW, A, 1942, A
MISSOURI TRAVELER, THE, 1958, A
MISSOURIANS, THE, 1950, A
MIST IN THE VALLEY, 1923
MISTAKEN ORDERS, 1926
MISTER 44, 1916
MISTER 880, 1950, AA
MISTER ANTONIO, 1929, A
MISTER BROWN, 1972, C
MISTER BUDDWING, 1966, C
MISTER CINDERELLA, 1936, A
MISTER CINDERS, 1934, A
MISTER CORY, 1957, A
MISTER FREEDOM, 1970, A
MISTER HOBO, 1936, A
MISTER MOSES, 1965, A
MISTER ROBERTS, 1955, A
MISTER ROCK AND ROLL, 1957, A
MISTER SCARFACE, 1977
MISTER TEN PERCENT, 1967, A
MISTER V
MISTER, YOU ARE A WIDOWER
MISTERIOUS DE ULTRATUMBA
MISTRESS FOR THE SUMMER, A, 1964, C
MISTRESS NELL, 1915, A
MISTRESS OF ATLANTIS, THE, 1932, A
MISTRESS OF SHENSTONE, THE, 1921, A
MISTRESS OF THE APES, 1981, O
MISTRESS OF THE WORLD, 1959, A
MISTRESS PAMELA, 1974
MISTY, 1961, AAA
MISUNDERSTOOD, 1984, C
MIT EVA DIE SUNDE AN
MITCHELL, 1975, O
MITYA, 1927
MIVTZA KAHIR
MIX ME A PERSON, 1962, C
MIXED BLOOD, 1916
MIXED BLOOD, 1984, O
MIXED COMPANY, 1974, C
MIXED DOUBLES, 1933, A
MIXED FACES, 1922, A
MLLE PAULETTE, 1918
MOANA, 1926
MOB TOWN, 1941, A
MOB, THE, 1951, C-O
MOBS INC, 1956, A
MOBY DICK, 1930
MOBY DICK, 1956, C
MOCCASINS, 1925
MOCKERY, 1927, C
MODEL AND THE MARRIAGE BROKER, THE, 1951, A
MODEL FOR MURDER, 1960, A
MODEL FROM MONTMARTE, THE, 1928
MODEL MURDER CASE, THE, 1964, A
MODEL SHOP, THE, 1969, C-O
MODEL WIFE, 1941, A
MODEL'S CONFESSION, THE, 1918
MODELS, INC., 1952, C
MODERATO CANTABILE, 1964, C
MODERN CAIN, A, 1925
MODERN CINDERELLA, A, 1917, A
MODERN DAUGHTERS, 1927
MODERN DAY HOUDINI, 1983
MODERN DU BARRY, A, 1928
MODERN ENOCH ARDEN, A, 1916
MODERN HERO, A, 1934, A
MODERN HERO, A 1941
MODERN HUSBANDS, 1919
MODERN JEAN VAL JEAN; OR A FRAME UP, A, 1930
MODERN LORELEI, A
MODERN LOVE, 1918
MODERN LOVE, 1929, A
MODERN MADNESS
MODERN MAGDALEN, A, 1915
MODERN MARRIAGE, 1923, A
MODERN MARRIAGE, A, 1962, O
MODERN MATRIMONY, 1923
MODERN MEPHISTO, A, 1914
MODERN MIRACLE, THE
MODERN MONTE CRISTO, A, 1917, A
MODERN MOTHER GOOSE, 1917
MODERN MOTHERS, 1928
MODERN MUSKETEER, A, 1917, A
MODERN OTHELLO, A, 1917
MODERN PROBLEMS, 1981, A-C
MODERN ROMANCE, 1981, C
MODERN SALOME, A, 1920, C
MODERN THELMA, A, 1916
MODERN TIMES, 1936, A
MODERN YOUTH, 1926
MODESTY BLAISE, 1966, A
MODIGLIANI OF MONTPARNASSE, 1961, A
MOGAMBO, 1953, A
MOGLIAMANTE
MOHAMMAD, MESSENGER OF GOD, 1976, C-O
MOHAN JOSHI HAAZIR HO, 1984, A
MOHAWK, 1956, A
MOHICAN'S DAUGHTER, THE, 1922
MOI AUSSI, J'ACCUSE, 1920
MOJAVE FIREBRAND, 1944, A
MOJAVE KID, THE, 1927
MOKEY, 1942, A
MOLE PEOPLE, THE, 1956, A
MOLE, THE
MOLESTER, THE
MOLLY
MOLLY AND I, 1920
MOLLY AND LAWLESS JOHN, 1972, A
MOLLY AND ME, 1929, A
MOLLY AND ME, 1945, A
MOLLY BAWN, 1916, A
MOLLY ENTANGLED, 1917, A
MOLLY LOUVAIN
MOLLY MAGUIRES, THE, 1970, C-O
MOLLY MAKE-BELIEVE, 1916
MOLLY O', 1921, A
MOLLY OF THE FOLLIES, 1919, A
MOLLY, GO GET 'EM, 1918
MOLLYCODDLE, THE, 1920, A
MOM AND DAD, 1948, O
MOMENT BEFORE, THE, 1916
MOMENT BY MOMENT, 1978, O
MOMENT OF DANGER
MOMENT OF INDISCRETION, 1958, A
MOMENT OF TERROR, 1969, C
MOMENT OF TRUTH
MOMENT OF TRUTH, THE, 1965, A
MOMENT TO MOMENT, 1966, A
MOMENTS, 1974, O
MOMMAN, LITTLE JUNGLE BOY
MOMMIE DEAREST, 1981, C-O
MON COEUR AU RALENTI, 1928
MON CURE CHEZ LES PAUVRES, 1925
MON CURE CHEZ LES RICHES, 1925
MON ONCLE
MON ONCLE, 1925
MON ONCLE ANTOINE
MON ONCLE BENJAMIN, 1923
MON ONCLE D'AMERIQUE, 1980, C
MON PREMIER AMOUR
MONA KENT
MONASTERY GARDEN
MONDAY'S CHILD, 1967, A-C
MONDO TRASHO, 1970, O
MONEY, 1915
MONEY, 1921
MONEY AND THE WOMAN, 1940, A
MONEY CHANGERS, THE, 1920
MONEY CORRAL, THE, 1919, A
MONEY FOR JAM
MONEY FOR NOTHING, 1932, A
MONEY FOR SPEED, 1933, A
MONEY FROM HOME, 1953, A
MONEY GOD, OR DO RICHES BRING HAPPINESS, THE, 1914
MONEY HABIT, THE, 1924, A
MONEY IN MY POCKET, 1962
MONEY ISN'T EVERYTHING
MONEY ISN'T EVERYTHING, 1918
MONEY ISN'T EVERYTHING, 1925, A
MONEY JUNGLE, THE, 1968, A
MONEY LENDER, THE, 1914
MONEY MAD, 1918
MONEY MAD, 1934, A
MONEY MADNESS, 1917
MONEY MADNESS, 1948, A
MONEY MAGIC, 1917, A
MONEY MANIAC, THE, 1921
MONEY MASTER, THE, 1915
MONEY MEANS NOTHING, 1932, A
MONEY MEANS NOTHING, 1934, A
MONEY MILL, THE, 1917
MONEY MONEY MONEY, 1923, A
MONEY MOVERS, 1978, O
MONEY ON THE STREET, 1930, A
MONEY ORDER, THE
MONEY TALKS, 1926
MONEY TALKS, 1933, A
MONEY TO BURN, 1922
MONEY TO BURN, 1926
MONEY TO BURN, 1940, A
MONEY TO BURN, 1981
MONEY TRAP, THE, 1966, C
MONEY, MONEY, MONEY
MONEY, THE, 1975, O
MONEY, WOMEN AND GUNS, 1958, A
MONGOLS, THE, 1966, A
MONGREL, 1982, O
MONITORS, THE, 1969, C
MONKEY BUSINESS, 1931, A
MONKEY BUSINESS, 1952, A
MONKEY GRIP, 1983, A
MONKEY HUSTLE, THE, 1976, C-O
MONKEY IN WINTER, A, 1962, A
MONKEY ON MY BACK, 1957, C
MONKEY TALKS, THE, 1927, A

MONKEY'S PAW, THE, 1923, A
MONKEY'S PAW, THE, 1933, C
MONKEY'S PAW, THE, 1948, A
MONKEY'S UNCLE, THE, 1965, AAA
MONKEYS, GO HOME, 1967, AAA
MONNA VANNA, 1923
MONOLITH MONSTERS, THE, 1957, A
MONOPOLIST, THE, 1915
MONSEIGNEUR, 1950, A
MONSIEUR, 1964, A
MONSIEUR BEAUCAIRE, 1924, A
MONSIEUR BEAUCAIRE, 1946, A
MONSIEUR COGNAC
MONSIEUR FABRE
MONSIEUR HULOT'S HOLIDAY
MONSIEUR LE DIRECTEUR, 1924
MONSIEUR LEBIDOIS PROPRIETAIRE, 1922
MONSIEUR LEBUREAU, 1920
MONSIEUR RIPOIS
MONSIEUR VERDOUX, 1947, O
MONSIEUR VINCENT, 1949, A
MONSIGNOR, 1982, O
MONSOON, 1953, C
MONSTER, O
MONSTER A GO-GO, 1965, C
MONSTER AND THE GIRL, THE, 1914
MONSTER AND THE GIRL, THE, 1941, C
MONSTER BARAN, THE
MONSTER CLUB, THE, 1981, C
MONSTER FROM THE GREEN HELL, 1958, A
MONSTER FROM THE OCEAN FLOOR, THE, 1954, A
MONSTER FROM THE SURF
MONSTER ISLAND, 1981, C
MONSTER MAKER, 1954
MONSTER MAKER, THE, 1944, C
MONSTER MEETS THE GORILLA
MONSTER OF HIGHGATE PONDS, THE, 1961, AAA
MONSTER OF LONDON CITY, THE, 1967, O
MONSTER OF PIEDRAS BLANCAS, THE, 1959, C
MONSTER OF TERROR
MONSTER OF THE ISLAND, 1953, A
MONSTER OF THE WAX MUSEUM
MONSTER ON THE CAMPUS, 1958, C
MONSTER THAT CHALLENGED THE WORLD, THE, 1957, A
MONSTER WALKED, THE
MONSTER WALKS, THE, 1932, A
MONSTER WANGMAGWI, 1967, A
MONSTER YONGKARI
MONSTER ZERO, 1970, A
MONSTER, 1980
MONSTER, THE, 1925, A
MONSTERS ARE LOOSE
MONSTERS FROM THE MOON
MONSTERS FROM THE UNKNOWN PLANET, 1975, A
MONSTROID, 1980
MONSTROSITY
MONTANA, 1950, A
MONTANA BELLE, 1952, A
MONTANA BILL, 1921
MONTANA DESPERADO, 1951, A
MONTANA INCIDENT, 1952
MONTANA JUSTICE
MONTANA KID, THE, 1931, A
MONTANA MIKE
MONTANA MOON, 1930, A
MONTANA TERRITORY, 1952, A
MONTE CARLO, 1926
MONTE CARLO, 1930, AA
MONTE CARLO BABY, 1953, A
MONTE CARLO MADNESS
MONTE CARLO NIGHTS, 1934, A
MONTE CARLO OR BUST
MONTE CARLO STORY, THE, 1957, A
MONTE CASSINO, 1948, A
MONTE CRISTO, 1912
MONTE CRISTO, 1922
MONTE CRISTO'S REVENGE
MONTE WALSH, 1970, C
MONTE-CRISTO, 1929
MONTENEGRO, 1981, O
MONTENEGRO—OR PIGS AND PEARLS
MONTMARTE ROSE, 1929
MONTPARNASSE 19
MONTREAL MAIN, 1974, O
MONTY PYTHON AND THE HOLY GRAIL, 1975, O
MONTY PYTHON'S LIFE OF BRIAN, 1979, O
MONTY PYTHON'S THE MEANING OF LIFE, 1983, O
MONTY WORKS THE WIRES, 1921, A
MOON AND SIXPENCE, THE, 1942, A
MOON IN THE GUTTER, THE, 1983, O
MOON IS BLUE, THE, 1953, A-C
MOON IS DOWN, THE, 1943, C
MOON MADNESS, 1920, C
MOON MARIGOLDS, THE, 1972, C
MOON OF ISRAEL, 1927
MOON OVER BURMA, 1940, A
MOON OVER HARLEM, 1939
MOON OVER HER SHOULDER, 1941, A
MOON OVER LAS VEGAS, 1944, AA
MOON OVER MIAMI, 1941, A
MOON OVER MONTANA, 1946
MOON OVER THE ALLEY, 1980, O
MOON PILOT, 1962, AAA
MOON WALK
MOON ZERO TWO, 1970, A
MOON'S OUR HOME, THE, 1936, A
MOON-SPINNERS, THE, 1964, AAA
MOONBEAM MAN, THE
MOONCHILD, 1972, O
MOONFIRE, 1970, O
MOONFLEET, 1955, A
MOONLIGHT AND CACTUS, 1944, A
MOONLIGHT AND HONEYSUCKLE, 1921
MOONLIGHT AND MELODY
MOONLIGHT AND PRETZELS, 1933, A
MOONLIGHT FOLLIES, 1921
MOONLIGHT IN HAVANA, 1942, A
MOONLIGHT IN HAWAII, 1941, A
MOONLIGHT IN VERMONT, 1943, A
MOONLIGHT MASQUERADE, 1942, A
MOONLIGHT MURDER, 1936, A
MOONLIGHT ON THE PRAIRIE, 1936, A
MOONLIGHT ON THE RANGE, 1937, A
MOONLIGHT RAID
MOONLIGHT SONATA, 1938, A
MOONLIGHTER, THE, 1953, A
MOONLIGHTING, 1982, C
MOONLIGHTING WIVES, 1966, O
MOONRAKER, 1979, A
MOONRAKER, THE, 1958, A
MOONRISE, 1948, C
MOONRUNNERS, 1975, A
MOONSHINE COUNTY EXPRESS, 1977, C
MOONSHINE MENACE, THE, 1921
MOONSHINE MOUNTAIN, 1964, A
MOONSHINE TRAIL, THE, 1919
MOONSHINE VALLEY, 1922, A
MOONSHINE WAR, THE, 1970, C
MOONSHINER'S WOMAN, 1968, O
MOONSHOT
MOONSPINNERS, THE
MOONSTONE, THE, 1915
MOONSTONE, THE, 1934, A
MOONTIDE, 1942, A
MOONWOLF, 1966, A
MORAL CODE, THE, 1917
MORAL COURAGE, 1917
MORAL DEADLINE, THE, 1919
MORAL FABRIC, THE, 1916
MORAL FIBRE, 1921, A
MORAL LAW, THE, 1918
MORAL SINNER, THE, 1924
MORAL SUICIDE, 1918
MORALIST, THE, 1964, A
MORALS, 1921, A
MORALS FOR MEN, 1925
MORALS FOR WOMEN, 1931, A
MORALS OF HILDA, THE, 1916
MORALS OF MARCUS, THE, 1936, A
MORALS OF WEYBURY, THE, 1916
MORALS SQUAD, 1960
MORAN OF THE LADY LETTY, 1922, A
MORAN OF THE MARINES, 1928
MORAN OF THE MOUNTED, 1926
MORD UND TOTSCHLAG
MORDEI HA'OR
MORDER UNTER UNS
MORE, 1969, O
MORE AMERICAN GRAFFITI, 1979, C
MORE DEAD THAN ALIVE, 1968, C
MORE DEADLY THAN THE MALE, 1919
MORE DEADLY THAN THE MALE, 1961, C
MORE EXCELLENT WAY, THE, 1917
MORE PAY—LESS WORK, 1926
MORE THAN A MIRACLE, 1967, O
MORE THAN A SECRETARY, 1936, A
MORE THE MERRIER, THE, 1943, A
MORE TO BE PITIED THAN SCORNED, 1922
MORE TROUBLE, 1918, A
MORE TRUTH THAN POETRY, 1917
MORGAN, 1966, C
MORGAN LA SIRENE
MORGAN THE PIRATE, 1961, A
MORGAN'S LAST RAID, 1929, A
MORGAN'S MARAUDERS, 1929, A
MORGAN'S RAIDERS, 1918
MORGANE, THE ENCHANTRESS, 1929
MORGANSON'S FINISH, 1926
MORIARTY
MORITURI, 1965, C
MORMON MAID, A, 1917
MORMON PERIL, THE
MORNING CALL
MORNING DEPARTURE
MORNING GLORY, 1933, C
MORNING STAR, 1962, A
MORO WITCH DOCTOR, 1964, C
MOROCCO, 1930, C
MOROZKO
MORTADELLA
MORTAL SIN, THE, 1917
MORTAL STORM, THE, 1940, A
MORTE A VENEZIA
MORTGAGED WIFE, THE, 1918
MORTMAIN, 1915
MORTON OF THE MOUNTED
MORTUARY, 1983, O
MOSCOW, 1927
MOSCOW DISTRUSTS TEARS
MOSCOW DOES NOT BELIEVE IN TEARS, 1980, A
MOSCOW IN OCTOBER, 1927
MOSCOW NIGHTS
MOSCOW ON THE HUDSON, 1984, C-O
MOSCOW SHANGHAI, 1936, A
MOSCOW—CASSIOPEIA, 1974, A
MOSES, 1976, A
MOSES AND AARON, 1975, C
MOSQUITO SQUADRON, 1970, A
MOSS ROSE, 1947, A
MOST BEAUTIFUL AGE, THE, 1970, C
MOST DANGEROUS GAME, THE, 1932, C-O
MOST DANGEROUS MAN ALIVE, THE, 1961, A
MOST DANGEROUS MAN IN THE WORLD, THE
MOST IMMORAL LADY, A, 1929, A
MOST PRECIOUS THING IN LIFE, 1934, A
MOST WANTED MAN, THE, 1962, A
MOST WONDERFUL EVENING OF MY LIFE, THE, 1972, A
MOSURA
MOTEL HELL, 1980, O
MOTEL, THE OPERATOR, 1940, C
MOTELE THE WEAVER
MOTH AND RUST, 1921
MOTH AND THE FLAME, THE, 1915, A
MOTH, THE, 1917
MOTH, THE, 1934, A
MOTHER, 1914, A
MOTHER, 1920
MOTHER, 1926
MOTHER, 1927
MOTHER AND DAUGHTER, 1965, A
MOTHER AND SON, 1931, A
MOTHER AND THE WHORE, THE, 1973, C
MOTHER CAREY'S CHICKENS, 1938, A
MOTHER DIDN'T TELL ME, 1950, A
MOTHER ETERNAL, 1921
MOTHER GOOSE A GO-GO, 1966, A
MOTHER HEART, THE, 1921
MOTHER INSTINCT, THE, 1917
MOTHER IS A FRESHMAN, 1949, A
MOTHER JOAN OF THE ANGELS?
MOTHER KNOWS BEST, 1928, A
MOTHER KNOWS BEST, 1949
MOTHER KUSTERS GOES TO HEAVEN, 1976, C-O
MOTHER LODE, 1982, C
MOTHER LOVE AND THE LAW, 1917
MOTHER MACHREE, 1922
MOTHER MACHREE, 1928
MOTHER O' MINE, 1921
MOTHER O'MINE, 1917
MOTHER OF DARTMOOR, THE, 1916
MOTHER OF HIS CHILDREN, THE, 1920
MOTHER OUGHT TO MARRY
MOTHER RILEY, 1952, A
MOTHER RILEY JOINS UP, 1939, A
MOTHER RILEY MEETS THE VAMPIRE
MOTHER RILEY'S JUNGLE TREASURE, 1951, A
MOTHER RILEY, HEADMISTRESS, 1950, A
MOTHER SHOULD BE LOVED, A, 1934
MOTHER SIR
MOTHER SUPERIOR
MOTHER WORE TIGHTS, 1947, A
MOTHER'S BOY, 1929, A
MOTHER'S DAY, 1980, O
MOTHER'S HEART, A, 1914
MOTHER'S MILLIONS
MOTHER'S ORDEAL, A, 1917
MOTHER'S SECRET, A, 1918
MOTHER'S SIN, A, 1918
MOTHER, I NEED YOU, 1918
MOTHER, JUGS & SPEED, 1976, O
MOTHERHOOD, 1915, C
MOTHERHOOD, 1917
MOTHERHOOD; LIFE'S GREATEST MIRACLE, 1928
MOTHERLOVE, 1916
MOTHERS CRY, 1930, A
MOTHERS OF MEN, 1917
MOTHERS OF MEN, 1920
MOTHERS OF TODAY, 1939, C
MOTHERS-IN-LAW, 1923, A
MOTHRA, 1962, A
MOTHS, 1913
MOTION TO ADJOURN, A, 1921
MOTIVE FOR REVENGE, 1935, A
MOTIVE WAS JEALOUSY, THE, 1970, C
MOTOR MADNESS, 1937, A

MOTOR PATROL, 1950, A
MOTOR PSYCHO, 1965, O
MOTORCYCLE GANG, 1957, C-O
MOTORING, 1927, A
MOTORING THRU SPAIN, 1929
MOTSART I SALVERI
MOUCHETTE, 1970, C
MOULDER OF MEN, 1927
MOULIN ROUGE, 1928, C
MOULIN ROUGE, 1934, A
MOULIN ROUGE, 1944, A
MOULIN ROUGE, 1952, A-C
MOUNTAIN CHARLIE, 1982
MOUNTAIN DESPERADOES
MOUNTAIN DEW, 1917
MOUNTAIN EAGLE, THE
MOUNTAIN EAGLE, THE
MOUNTAIN FAMILY ROBINSON, 1979, A
MOUNTAIN JUSTICE, 1930, A
MOUNTAIN JUSTICE, 1937, A
MOUNTAIN MADNESS, 1920
MOUNTAIN MAN
MOUNTAIN MEN, THE, 1980, O
MOUNTAIN MOONLIGHT, 1941, A
MOUNTAIN MUSIC, 1937, A
MOUNTAIN RAT, THE, 1914, A
MOUNTAIN RHYTHM, 1939, A
MOUNTAIN RHYTHM, 1942, AAA
MOUNTAIN ROAD, THE, 1960, A
MOUNTAIN WOMAN, THE, 1921
MOUNTAIN, THE, 1935, A
MOUNTAIN, THE, 1956, A
MOUNTAINS O'MOURNE, 1938, A
MOUNTAINS OF MANHATTAN, 1927
MOUNTED FURY, 1931, A
MOUNTED STRANGER, THE, 1930, A
MOURNING BECOMES ELECTRA, 1947, C
MOURNING SUIT, THE, 1975, C
MOUSE AND HIS CHILD, THE, 1977, A
MOUSE AND THE WOMAN, THE, 1981, O
MOUSE ON THE MOON, THE, 1963, AA
MOUSE THAT ROARED, THE, 1959, AAA
MOUTH TO MOUTH, 1978, C
MOUTHPIECE, THE, 1932, A
MOVE, 1970, C
MOVE OVER, DARLING, 1963, A
MOVIE CRAZY, 1932, A
MOVIE MOVIE, 1978, A-C
MOVIE STAR, AMERICAN STYLE, OR, LSD I HATE YOU, 1966, C
MOVIE STRUCK
MOVIE STUNTMEN, 1953, A
MOVIEMAKERS, 1970
MOVIETONE FOLLIES OF 1929
MOVIETONE FOLLIES OF 1930
MOVING FINGER, THE, 1963, C
MOVING GUEST, THE, 1927
MOVING IMAGE, THE, 1920
MOVING IN SOCIETY
MOVING TARGET, THE
MOVING VIOLATION, 1976, C
MOZAMBIQUE, 1966, A
MOZART
MOZART, 1940, A
MOZART STORY, THE, 1948, A
MR. ACE, 1946, A
MR. AND MRS. NORTH, 1941, A
MR. AND MRS. SMITH, 1941, A
MR. ARKADIN, 1962, C
MR. ASHTON WAS INDISCREET
MR. BARNES OF NEW YORK, 1914, A
MR. BARNES OF NEW YORK, 1922
MR. BELVEDERE GOES TO COLLEGE, 1949, A
MR. BELVEDERE RINGS THE BELL, 1951, A
MR. BIG, 1943, A
MR. BILL THE CONQUEROR
MR. BILLINGS SPENDS HIS DIME, 1923, A
MR. BILLION, 1977, A
MR. BINGLE, 1922
MR. BLANDINGS BUILDS HIS DREAM HOUSE, 1948, A
MR. BOGGS STEPS OUT, 1938, A
MR. BROWN COMES DOWN THE HILL, 1966, A
MR. BUG GOES TO TOWN, 1941, AAA
MR. CELEBRITY, 1942, A
MR. CHEDWORTH STEPS OUT, 1939, A
MR. CHUMP, 1938, A
MR. COHEN TAKES A WALK, 1936, A
MR. DEEDS GOES TO TOWN, 1936, A
MR. DENNING DRIVES NORTH, 1953, A
MR. DISTRICT ATTORNEY, 1941, A
MR. DISTRICT ATTORNEY, 1946, A
MR. DISTRICT ATTORNEY IN THE CARTER CASE
MR. DODD TAKES THE AIR, 1937, A
MR. DOLAN OF NEW YORK, 1917
MR. DOODLE KICKS OFF, 1938, A
MR. DRAKE'S DUCK, 1951, A
MR. DREW
MR. DYNAMITE, 1935, A
MR. DYNAMITE, 1941, A
MR. EMMANUEL, 1945, A
MR. FAINTHEART
MR. FIX-IT, 1918, A
MR. FORBUSH AND THE PENGUINS
MR. FOX OF VENICE
MR. GILFIL'S LOVE STORY, 1920
MR. GOODE, THE SAMARITAN, 1916
MR. GREX OF MONTE CARLO, 1915
MR. GRIGGS RETURNS
MR. H. C. ANDERSEN, 1950, A
MR. HEX, 1946, A
MR. HOBBS TAKES A VACATION, 1962, AA
MR. HORATIO KNIBBLES, 1971
MR. HOT SHOT
MR. HULOT'S HOLIDAY, 1954, AAA
MR. IMPERIUM, 1951, A
MR. INNOCENT
MR. INVISIBLE
MR. JIM—AMERICAN, SOLDIER, AND GENTLEMAN
MR. JUSTICE RAFFLES, 1921, A
MR. KINGSTREET'S WAR, 1973
MR. KLEIN, 1976, C
MR. LEMON OF ORANGE, 1931, A
MR. LIMPET
MR. LOGAN, USA, 1918
MR. LORD SAYS NO, 1952, A
MR. LUCKY, 1943, A
MR. LYNDON AT LIBERTY, 1915
MR. MAGOO'S HOLIDAY FESTIVAL, 1970, AAA
MR. MAJESTYK, 1974, C
MR. MOM, 1983, A-C
MR. MOTO AND THE PERSIAN OIL CASE
MR. MOTO IN DANGER ISLAND, 1939, A
MR. MOTO ON DANGER ISLAND
MR. MOTO TAKES A CHANCE, 1938, A
MR. MOTO TAKES A VACATION, 1938, A
MR. MOTO'S GAMBLE, 1938, A
MR. MOTO'S LAST WARNING, 1939, A
MR. MUGGS RIDES AGAIN, 1945, A
MR. MUGGS STEPS OUT, 1943, A
MR. MUSIC, 1950, A
MR. NOBODY, 1927, A
MR. OPP, 1917
MR. ORCHID, 1948, A
MR. PATMAN, 1980, C
MR. PEABODY AND THE MERMAID, 1948, AA
MR. PEEK-A-BOO, 1951
MR. PERRIN AND MR. TRAILL, 1948, A
MR. PIM PASSES BY, 1921
MR. POTTER OF TEXAS, 1922
MR. POTTS GOES TO MOSCOW, 1953, A
MR. PULVER AND THE CAPTAIN
MR. QUILP, 1975, A
MR. QUINCEY OF MONTE CARLO, 1933, A
MR. RADISH AND MR. CARROT
MR. RECKLESS, 1948, A
MR. REEDER IN ROOM 13
MR. RICCO, 1975, C
MR. ROBINSON CRUSOE, 1932, A
MR. SARDONICUS, 1961, C
MR. SATAN, 1938, A
MR. SCOUTMASTER, 1953, A
MR. SEBASTIAN
MR. SKEFFINGTON, 1944, C
MR. SKITCH, 1933, A
MR. SMITH CARRIES ON, 1937, A
MR. SMITH GOES GHOST, 1940
MR. SMITH GOES TO WASHINGTON, 1939, AAA
MR. SOFT TOUCH, 1949, A
MR. STRINGFELLOW SAYS NO, 1937, A
MR. SUPERINVISIBLE, 1974, AAA
MR. SYCAMORE, 1975, A
MR. TOPAZE
MR. UNIVERSE, 1951, A
MR. WALKIE TALKIE, 1952, A
MR. WASHINGTON GOES TO TOWN, 1941, A
MR. WHAT'S-HIS-NAME, 1935, A
MR. WINKLE GOES TO WAR, 1944, A
MR. WISE GUY, 1942, A
MR. WONG AT HEADQUARTERS
MR. WONG IN CHINATOWN, 1939, A
MR. WONG, DETECTIVE, 1938, A
MR. WU, 1919, A
MR. WU, 1927, C
MRS. BALFANE, 1917
MRS. BLACK IS BACK, 1914, A
MRS. BROWN, YOU'VE GOT A LOVELY DAUGHTER, 1968, A
MRS. CASSELL'S PROFESSION, 1915
MRS. DANE'S CONFESSION, 1922
MRS. DANE'S DANGER, 1922
MRS. DANE'S DEFENCE, 1933, A
MRS. DANE'S DEFENSE, 1918
MRS. FITZHERBERT, 1950, A
MRS. GIBBONS' BOYS, 1962, A
MRS. LEFFINGWELL'S BOOTS, 1918
MRS. LORING'S SECRET
MRS. MIKE, 1949, A
MRS. MINIVER, 1942, A
MRS. O'MALLEY AND MR. MALONE, 1950, A
MRS. PARKINGTON, 1944, A
MRS. PLUM'S PUDDING, 1915
MRS. POLLIFAX-SPY, 1971, A
MRS. PYM OF SCOTLAND YARD, 1939, A
MRS. SLACKER, 1918, A
MRS. SOFFEL, 1984, C
MRS. TEMPLE'S TELEGRAM, 1920
MRS. THOMPSON, 1919, A
MRS. WARREN'S PROFESSION, A
MRS. WIGGS OF THE CABBAGE PATCH, 1914
MRS. WIGGS OF THE CABBAGE PATCH, 1919
MRS. WIGGS OF THE CABBAGE PATCH, 1934, A
MRS. WIGGS OF THE CABBAGE PATCH, 1942, AA
MS. 45, 1981, O
MUCEDNICI LASKY
MUCH TOO SHY, 1942, A
MUD
MUD HONEY
MUDDY RIVER, 1982, A
MUDHONEY
MUDLARK, THE, 1950, A
MUERTO 4-3-2-1-0
MUG TOWN, 1943, A
MUGGER, THE, 1958, A
MUHOMATSU NO ISSHO
MULE TRAIN, 1950, A
MULHALL'S GREAT CATCH, 1926
MUM'S THE WORD, 1918
MUMMY AND THE HUMMINGBIRD, THE, 1915
MUMMY'S BOYS, 1936, A
MUMMY'S CURSE, THE, 1944, A
MUMMY'S GHOST, THE, 1944, A
MUMMY'S HAND, THE, C
MUMMY'S SHROUD, THE, 1967, C
MUMMY'S TOMB, THE, 1942, C
MUMMY, THE, 1932, C-O
MUMMY, THE, 1959, C
MUMSIE, 1927, A
MUMSY, NANNY, SONNY, AND GIRLY, 1970, O
MUMU, 1961, A
MUNECOS INFERNALES
MUNITION GIRL'S ROMANCE, A, 1917, A
MUNKBROGREVEN
MUNSTER, GO HOME, 1966, A
MUPPET MOVIE, THE, 1979, AA
MUPPETS TAKE MANHATTAN, THE, 1984, AAA
MURDER, 1930, A
MURDER A LA MOD, 1968, C
MURDER AHOY, 1964, A
MURDER AMONG FRIENDS, 1941, A
MURDER AT 3 A.M., 1953, A
MURDER AT 45 R.P.M., 1965, A
MURDER AT COVENT GARDEN, 1932, A
MURDER AT DAWN, 1932, A
MURDER AT GLEN ATHOL, 1936, A
MURDER AT MIDNIGHT, 1931, A
MURDER AT MONTE CARLO, 1935, A
MURDER AT SCOTLAND YARD, 1952
MURDER AT SITE THREE, 1959, A
MURDER AT THE BASKERVILLES, 1941, A
MURDER AT THE BURLESQUE
MURDER AT THE CABARET, 1936, A
MURDER AT THE GALLOP, 1963, A
MURDER AT THE INN, 1934, A
MURDER AT THE VANITIES, 1934, A
MURDER AT THE WINDMILL
MURDER BY AGREEMENT
MURDER BY AN ARISTOCRAT, 1936, A
MURDER BY CONTRACT, 1958, C
MURDER BY DEATH, 1976, C
MURDER BY DECREE, 1979, C-O
MURDER BY INVITATION, 1941, A
MURDER BY MAIL
MURDER BY PHONE
MURDER BY PROXY
MURDER BY ROPE, 1936, A
MURDER BY TELEVISION, 1935, A
MURDER BY THE CLOCK, 1931, C
MURDER CAN BE DEADLY, 1963, A
MURDER CLINIC, THE, 1967, C
MURDER CZECH STYLE, 1968, A
MURDER FOR SALE
MURDER GAME, THE, 1966, A
MURDER GOES TO COLLEGE, 1937, A
MURDER IN EDEN, 1962, A
MURDER IN GREENWICH VILLAGE, 1937, A
MURDER IN MISSISSIPPI, 1965, C
MURDER IN MOROCCO
MURDER IN REVERSE, 1946, A
MURDER IN SOHO
MURDER IN THE AIR, 1940, A
MURDER IN THE BIG HOUSE
MURDER IN THE BIG HOUSE, 1942, A
MURDER IN THE BLUE ROOM, 1944, A
MURDER IN THE CATHEDRAL, 1952, A
MURDER IN THE CLOUDS, 1934, A
MURDER IN THE FAMILY, 1938, A

MURDER IN THE FLEET, 1935, A
MURDER IN THE FOOTLIGHTS
MURDER IN THE MUSEUM, 1934, C
MURDER IN THE MUSIC HALL, 1946, O
MURDER IN THE NIGHT, 1940, O
MURDER IN THE OLD RED BARN, 1936, O
MURDER IN THE PRIVATE CAR, 1934, A
MURDER IN THORTON SQUARE
MURDER IN TIMES SQUARE, 1943, O
MURDER IN TRINIDAD, 1934, O
MURDER IS MY BEAT, 1955, O
MURDER IS MY BUSINESS, 1946, O
MURDER IS NEWS, 1939, O
MURDER MAN, 1935, C
MURDER MISSISSIPPI
MURDER MOST FOUL, 1964, A
MURDER OF DR. HARRIGAN, THE, 1936, O
MURDER OF GENERAL GRYAZNOV, THE, 1921
MURDER ON A BRIDLE PATH, 1936, O
MURDER ON A HONEYMOON, 1935, A
MURDER ON APPROVAL, 1956, C
MURDER ON DIAMOND ROW, 1937, C
MURDER ON LENOX AVENUE, 1941
MURDER ON MONDAY, 1953, C
MURDER ON THE BLACKBOARD, 1934, A
MURDER ON THE BRIDGE
MURDER ON THE CAMPUS, 1934, A
MURDER ON THE CAMPUS, 1963, A
MURDER ON THE HIGH SEAS, 1938
MURDER ON THE ORIENT EXPRESS, 1974, C
MURDER ON THE ROOF, 1930, A
MURDER ON THE RUNAWAY TRAIN
MURDER ON THE SECOND FLOOR, 1932, A
MURDER ON THE SET, 1936, A
MURDER ON THE WATERFRONT, 1943, A
MURDER ON THE YUKON, 1940, A
MURDER OVER NEW YORK, 1940, A
MURDER REPORTED, 1958, O
MURDER RING, THE
MURDER SHE SAID, 1961, A
MURDER SOCIETY, THE
MURDER TOMORROW, 1938, A
MURDER WILL OUT, 1930, A
MURDER WILL OUT, 1939, A
MURDER WILL OUT, 1953, A
MURDER WITH MUSIC, 1941
MURDER WITH PICTURES, 1936, A
MURDER WITHOUT CRIME, 1951, A
MURDER WITHOUT TEARS, 1953, A
MURDER, HE SAYS, 1945, A
MURDER, INC.
MURDER, INC., 1960, O
MURDER, MY SWEET, 1945, C-O
MURDERER AMONG US
MURDERER DMITRI KARAMAZOV, THE
MURDERER LIVES AT NUMBER 21, THE, 1947, A
MURDERER, THE
MURDERERS AMONG US, 1948, O
MURDERERS ARE AMONGST US
MURDERERS' ROW, 1966, C
MURDERS IN THE RUE MORGUE, 1932, C
MURDERS IN THE RUE MORGUE, 1971, O
MURDERS IN THE ZOO, 1933, O
MURDOCK TRIAL, THE, 1914
MURIEL, 1963, A
MURIEL, OU LE TEMPS D'UN RETOUR
MURIETA, 1965, O
MURMUR OF THE HEART, 1971, O
MURPH THE SURF, 1974, C
MURPHY'S WAR, 1971, C-O
MURRI AFFAIR, THE
MUSCLE BEACH PARTY, 1964, AA
MUSEUM MYSTERY, 1937, A
MUSHROOM EATER, THE, 1976, O
MUSIC AND MILLIONS
MUSIC BOX KID, THE, 1960, C
MUSIC FOR MADAME, 1937, A
MUSIC FOR MILLIONS, 1944, AA
MUSIC GOES 'ROUND, THE, 1936, A
MUSIC HALL, 1934, A
MUSIC HALL PARADE, 1939, A
MUSIC HATH CHARMS, 1935, A
MUSIC IN MANHATTAN, 1944, A
MUSIC IN MY HEART, 1940, A
MUSIC IN THE AIR, 1934, A
MUSIC IS MAGIC, 1935, A
MUSIC LOVERS, THE, 1971, O
MUSIC MACHINE, THE, 1979, O
MUSIC MAKER, THE, 1936, A
MUSIC MAN, 1948, AA
MUSIC MAN, THE, 1962, AAA
MUSIC MASTER, THE, 1927
MUSIC ROOM, THE, 1963, A
MUSICAL MUTINY, 1970, A
MUSIK I MORKER
MUSS 'EM UP, 1936, A
MUST WE MARRY?, 1928
MUSTANG, 1959, A
MUSTANG COUNTRY, 1976, A
MUSUME TO WATASHI
MUTANT
MUTATIONS, THE, 1974, O
MUTE APPEAL, A, 1917
MUTHERS, THE, 1976
MUTINEERS, THE
MUTINEERS, THE, 1949, A
MUTINY, 1917
MUTINY, 1925, A
MUTINY, 1952, A
MUTINY AHEAD, 1935, A
MUTINY IN OUTER SPACE, 1965, A
MUTINY IN OUTER SPACE, 1958
MUTINY IN THE ARCTIC, 1941, A
MUTINY IN THE BIG HOUSE, 1939, A
MUTINY OF THE ELSINORE, THE, 1920
MUTINY OF THE ELSINORE, THE, 1939, A
MUTINY ON THE BLACKHAWK, 1939, A
MUTINY ON THE BOUNTY, 1935, A
MUTINY ON THE BOUNTY, 1962, C-O
MUTINY ON THE SEAS
MY AIN FOLK, 1944, A
MY AIN FOLK, 1974, A
MY AMERICAN UNCLE
MY AMERICAN WIFE, 1923, A
MY AMERICAN WIFE, 1936, A
MY APPLE
MY BABY IS BLACK, 1965, A
MY BEST FRIEND'S GIRL, 1984, O
MY BEST GAL, 1944, A
MY BEST GIRL, 1915
MY BEST GIRL, 1927, A
MY BILL, 1938, A
MY BLOOD RUNS COLD, 1965, O
MY BLOODY VALENTINE, 1981, O
MY BLUE HEAVEN, 1950, A
MY BODY HUNGERS, 1967, O
MY BODYGUARD, 1980, A
MY BOY, 1922, A
MY BOYS ARE GOOD BOYS, 1978, A
MY BREAKFAST WITH BLASSIE, 1983, O
MY BRILLIANT CAREER, 1980, O
MY BROTHER HAS BAD DREAMS, 1977, O
MY BROTHER JONATHAN, 1949, A
MY BROTHER TALKS TO HORSES, 1946, AAA
MY BROTHER'S KEEPER, 1949, A
MY BROTHER'S WEDDING, 1983, A
MY BROTHER, THE OUTLAW, 1951, A
MY BUDDY, 1944, A
MY CHILDHOOD, 1972, A
MY COUNTRY FIRST, 1916
MY COUSIN, 1918, A
MY COUSIN RACHEL, 1952, A
MY DAD, 1922, A
MY DARLING CLEMENTINE, 1946, A
MY DAUGHTER JOY
MY DAYS WITH JEAN MARC
MY DEAR MISS ALDRICH, 1937, A
MY DEAR SECRETARY, 1948, A-C
MY DEATH IS A MOCKERY, 1952, C-O
MY DINNER WITH ANDRE, 1981, A-C
MY DOG RUSTY, 1948, AAA
MY DOG SHEP, 1948
MY DOG, BUDDY, 1960, C
MY DREAM IS YOURS, 1949, A
MY ENEMY, THE SEA
MY FAIR LADY, 1964, AA
MY FATHER'S HOUSE, 1947, A
MY FATHER'S MISTRESS, 1970, C
MY FAVORITE BLONDE, 1942, A
MY FAVORITE BRUNETTE, 1947, A
MY FAVORITE SPY, 1942, A
MY FAVORITE SPY, 1951, A
MY FAVORITE WIFE, 1940, A
MY FAVORITE YEAR, 1982, C
MY FIGHTING GENTLEMAN, 1917
MY FIRST LOVE, 1978, O
MY FOOLISH HEART, 1949, A-C
MY FORBIDDEN PAST, 1951, C
MY FOUR YEARS IN GERMANY, 1918, A
MY FRIEND FLICKA, 1943, AAA
MY FRIEND FROM INDIA, 1927
MY FRIEND IRMA, 1949, A
MY FRIEND IRMA GOES WEST, 1950, A
MY FRIEND THE KING, 1931, A
MY FRIEND, THE DEVIL, 1922
MY FRIENDS NEED KILLING, 1984
MY GAL LOVES MUSIC, 1944, A
MY GAL SAL, 1942, A
MY GEISHA, 1962, A
MY GIRL TISA, 1948, A
MY GIRLFRIEND'S WEDDING, 1969
MY GUN IS QUICK, 1957, O
MY HANDS ARE CLAY, 1948, A
MY HEART BELONGS TO DADDY, 1942, A
MY HEART GOES CRAZY, 1953, A
MY HEART IS CALLING, 1935, A
MY HERO
MY HOBO, 1963, A
MY HOME TOWN, 1925
MY HOME TOWN, 1928, A
MY HUSBAND'S FRIEND, 1918
MY HUSBAND'S FRIEND, 1922
MY HUSBAND'S OTHER WIFE, 1919
MY HUSBAND'S WIVES, 1924, A
MY IRISH MOLLY
MY KIND OF TOWN, 1984, A
MY KINGDOM FOR A COOK, 1943, A
MY LADY FRIENDS, 1921
MY LADY INCOG, 1916, A
MY LADY OF WHIMS, 1925
MY LADY'S DRESS, 1917
MY LADY'S GARTER, 1920
MY LADY'S LATCHKEY, 1921
MY LADY'S LIPS, 1925
MY LADY'S SLIPPER, 1916
MY LAST DUCHESS
MY LEARNED FRIEND, 1943, A
MY LIFE IS YOURS
MY LIFE TO LIVE, 1963, A
MY LIFE WITH CAROLINE, 1941, A-C
MY LIPS BETRAY, 1933, A
MY LITTLE BOY, 1917
MY LITTLE CHICKADEE, 1940, A
MY LITTLE SISTER, 1919
MY LORD CONCEIT, 1921
MY LORD THE CHAUFFEUR, 1927, A
MY LOVE CAME BACK, 1940, A
MY LOVE FOR YOURS
MY LOVE LETTERS
MY LOVER, MY SON, 1970, O
MY LUCKY STAR, 1933, A
MY LUCKY STAR, 1938, A
MY MADONNA, 1915
MY MAIN MAN FROM STONY ISLAND
MY MAN, 1924
MY MAN, 1928, A
MY MAN AND I, 1952, A
MY MAN GODFREY, 1936, A
MY MAN GODFREY, 1957, A
MY MARGO, 1969, C
MY MARRIAGE, 1936, A
MY MOTHER, 1933, A
MY NAME IS IVAN, 1963, O
MY NAME IS JULIA ROSS, 1945, A
MY NAME IS LEGEND, 1975
MY NAME IS NOBODY, 1974, O
MY NAME IS PECOS, 1966, C
MY NAME IS ROCCO PAPALEO
MY NEIGHBOR'S WIFE, 1925
MY NEW PARTNER, 1984, O
MY NIGHT AT MAUD'S, 1970, A
MY NIGHT WITH MAUD
MY NIGHTS WITH FRANCOISE
MY OFFICIAL WIFE, 1914
MY OFFICIAL WIFE, 1926
MY OLD DUCHESS, 1933, A
MY OLD DUTCH, 1915, A
MY OLD DUTCH, 1926
MY OLD DUTCH, 1934, A
MY OLD KENTUCKY HOME, 1922
MY OLD KENTUCKY HOME, 1938, A
MY OLD MAN'S PLACE
MY OUTLAW BROTHER
MY OWN PAL, 1926
MY OWN TRUE LOVE, 1948, A
MY OWN UNITED STATES, 1918
MY PAL, 1925
MY PAL GUS, 1952, A
MY PAL TRIGGER, 1946, AAA
MY PAL, THE KING, 1932, A
MY PAL, WOLF, 1944, A
MY PARTNER, 1916
MY PARTNER MR. DAVIS
MY PAST, 1931, A
MY PLEASURE IS MY BUSINESS, 1974
MY REPUTATION, 1946, A-C
MY SEVEN LITTLE SINS, 1956, A
MY SIDE OF THE MOUNTAIN, 1969, AAA
MY SIN, 1931, A-C
MY SISTER AND I, 1948, C
MY SISTER EILEEN, 1942, AA
MY SISTER EILEEN, 1955, AA
MY SISTER, MY LOVE
MY SIX CONVICTS, 1952, A-C
MY SIX LOVES, 1963, AA
MY SON, 1925, A
MY SON ALONE
MY SON IS A CRIMINAL, 1939, A
MY SON IS GUILTY, 1940, C
MY SON NERO
MY SON, JOHN, 1952, C
MY SON, MY SON, 1940, A
MY SON, THE HERO, 1943, A
MY SON, THE HERO, 1963, A
MY SON, THE VAMPIRE, 1963, A
MY SONG FOR YOU, 1935, A
MY SONG GOES ROUND THE WORLD, 1934, A

MY SOUL RUNS NAKED
MY SWEETHEART, 1918
MY TEENAGE DAUGHTER
MY THIRD WIFE BY GEORGE
MY THIRD WIFE GEORGE, 1968, A
MY TRUE STORY, 1951, A
MY TUTOR, 1983, O
MY TWO HUSBANDS
MY UNCLE, 1958, AAA
MY UNCLE ANTOINE, 1971, C
MY UNCLE FROM AMERICA
MY UNCLE, MR. HULOT
MY UNIVERSITY
MY UNMARRIED WIFE, 1918
MY WAY, 1974, A
MY WAY HOME, 1978, C
MY WEAKNESS, 1933, AAA
MY WIDOW AND I, 1950, C
MY WIFE, 1918
MY WIFE AND I, 1925
MY WIFE'S BEST FRIEND, 1952, A
MY WIFE'S ENEMY, 1967, A
MY WIFE'S FAMILY, 1932, A
MY WIFE'S FAMILY, 1941, A
MY WIFE'S FAMILY, 1962, A
MY WIFE'S HUSBAND, 1965, A
MY WIFE'S LODGER, 1952, A
MY WIFE'S RELATIVES, 1939, AAA
MY WILD IRISH ROSE, 1922
MY WILD IRISH ROSE, 1947, A
MY WOMAN, 1933, A
MY WORLD DIES SCREAMING, 1958, C
MYRT AND MARGE, 1934, A
MYRTE AND THE DEMONS, 1948
MYSTERE D'UNE VIE, 1917
MYSTERIANS, THE, 1959, A
MYSTERIES, 1979, C
MYSTERIES OF INDIA, 1922
MYSTERIES OF LONDON, THE, 1915
MYSTERIOUS AVENGER, THE, 1936, A
MYSTERIOUS CLIENT, THE, 1918
MYSTERIOUS CROSSING, 1937, A-C
MYSTERIOUS DESPERADO, THE, 1949, A
MYSTERIOUS DOCTOR, THE, 1943, C
MYSTERIOUS DR. FU MANCHU, THE, 1929, A
MYSTERIOUS GOODS, 1923
MYSTERIOUS HOUSE OF DR. C., THE, 1976, A
MYSTERIOUS INTRUDER, 1946, A
MYSTERIOUS INVADER, THE
MYSTERIOUS ISLAND, 1929, A
MYSTERIOUS ISLAND, 1941, A
MYSTERIOUS ISLAND, 1961, AA
MYSTERIOUS ISLAND OF CAPTAIN NEMO, THE, 1973, AA
MYSTERIOUS ISLAND, THE 1973
MYSTERIOUS LADY, THE, 1928, A
MYSTERIOUS MISS TERRY, THE, 1917
MYSTERIOUS MISS X, THE, 1939, A
MYSTERIOUS MR. DAVIS, THE, 1936, A
MYSTERIOUS MR. MOTO, 1938, A
MYSTERIOUS MR. MOTO OF DEVIL'S ISLAND
MYSTERIOUS MR. NICHOLSON, THE, 1947, A
MYSTERIOUS MR. REEDER, THE, 1940, A-C
MYSTERIOUS MR. TILLER, THE, 1917
MYSTERIOUS MR. VALENTINE, THE, 1946, A
MYSTERIOUS MR. WONG, 1935, C
MYSTERIOUS MRS. M, THE, 1917
MYSTERIOUS MRS. MUSSLEWHITE, THE
MYSTERIOUS RIDER, 1921
MYSTERIOUS RIDER, THE, 1927
MYSTERIOUS RIDER, THE, 1933, A
MYSTERIOUS RIDER, THE, 1938, A
MYSTERIOUS RIDER, THE, 1942, A
MYSTERIOUS SATELLITE, THE, 1956, A
MYSTERIOUS STRANGER, 1982
MYSTERIOUS STRANGER, THE, 1925
MYSTERIOUS STRANGER, THE 1937
MYSTERIOUS STRANGER, THE 1945
MYSTERIOUS WITNESS, THE, 1923, A
MYSTERY AT MONTE CARLO
MYSTERY AT THE BURLESQUE, 1950, A
MYSTERY AT THE VILLA ROSE, 1930, A
MYSTERY BRAND, THE, 1927
MYSTERY BROADCAST, 1943, A
MYSTERY CLUB, THE, 1926
MYSTERY HOUSE, 1938, A
MYSTERY IN MEXICO, 1948, A
MYSTERY IN SWING, 1940
MYSTERY JUNCTION, 1951, A
MYSTERY LAKE, 1953, A
MYSTERY LINER, 1934, A
MYSTERY MAN, 1944, A
MYSTERY MAN, THE, 1935, A
MYSTERY MANSION, 1984, C
MYSTERY OF A GIRL, THE, 1918
MYSTERY OF A HANSOM CAB, THE, 1915
MYSTERY OF A LONDON FLAT, THE
MYSTERY OF DIAMOND ISLAND, THE
MYSTERY OF EDWIN DROOD, THE, 1914
MYSTERY OF EDWIN DROOD, THE, 1935, C
MYSTERY OF KASPAR HAUSER, THE
MYSTERY OF MARIE ROGET, THE, 1942, A
MYSTERY OF MR. BERNARD BROWN, 1921, A
MYSTERY OF MR. WONG, THE, 1939, A
MYSTERY OF MR. X, THE, 1934, C
MYSTERY OF NO. 47, THE, 1917
MYSTERY OF RICHMOND CASTLE, THE, 1913
MYSTERY OF ROOM 13, 1941, A
MYSTERY OF ROOM 13, THE, 1915
MYSTERY OF SOULS, THE, 1911
MYSTERY OF THE 13TH GUEST, THE, 1943, A
MYSTERY OF THE BLACK JUNGLE, 1955, A
MYSTERY OF THE DIAMOND BELT, 1914
MYSTERY OF THE FATAL PEARL, THE, 1914
MYSTERY OF THE GLASS COFFIN, THE, 1912
MYSTERY OF THE GOLDEN EYE, THE, 1948, A
MYSTERY OF THE HOODED HORSEMEN, THE, 1937, A
MYSTERY OF THE LOST RANCH, THE, 1925
MYSTERY OF THE MARIE CELESTE
MYSTERY OF THE OLD MILL, THE, 1914
MYSTERY OF THE PINK VILLA, THE, 1930, A
MYSTERY OF THE PINK VILLA, THE, 930,
MYSTERY OF THE POISON POOL, THE, 1914, A
MYSTERY OF THE WAX MUSEUM, THE, 1933, C
MYSTERY OF THE WENTWORTH CASTLE, THE
MYSTERY OF THE WHITE ROOM, 1939, A
MYSTERY OF THE YELLOW ROOM, THE, 1919
MYSTERY OF THUG ISLAND, THE, 1966, A
MYSTERY OF TUT-ANK-AMEN'S EIGHTH WIFE, THE
MYSTERY ON BIRD ISLAND, 1954, A
MYSTERY ON MONSTER ISLAND
MYSTERY PLANE, 1939, A
MYSTERY RANCH, 1932, A
MYSTERY RANCH, 1934
MYSTERY RANGE, 1937, A
MYSTERY RIDER, 1928
MYSTERY ROAD, THE, 1921
MYSTERY SEA RAIDER, 1940, A
MYSTERY SHIP, 1941, A
MYSTERY STREET, 1950, C
MYSTERY SUBMARINE, 1950, A
MYSTERY SUBMARINE, 1963, A
MYSTERY TRAIN, 1931, A
MYSTERY VALLEY, 1928
MYSTERY WOMAN, 1935, A
MYSTIC CIRCLE MURDER, 1939, A
MYSTIC FACES, 1918
MYSTIC HOUR, THE, 1917
MYSTIC HOUR, THE, 1934, A
MYSTIC MIRROR, THE, 1928
MYSTIC, THE, 1925
MYSTIFIERS, THE
MYSTIQUE, 1981, O
MYTH, THE, 1965, O

-N-

N CITY, 1946, O
N. P., 1971, A
NA SEMI VETRAKH
NABONGA, 1944, A
NACHTS, WENN DER TEUFEL KAM
NACKT UNTER WOLFEN
NADA
NADA GANG, THE, 1974, A
NADA MAS QUE UNA MUJER, 1934, A
NADIA, 1984, C
NAGANA, 1933, A
NAGOOA
NAIDRA, THE DREAM WOMAN, 1914
NAKED ALIBI, 1954, A
NAKED AMONG THE WOLVES, 1967, C
NAKED AND THE DEAD, THE, 1958, O
NAKED ANGELS, 1969, O
NAKED APE, THE, 1973, C
NAKED AUTUMN, 1963, A
NAKED BRIGADE, THE, 1965, A
NAKED CHILDHOOD
NAKED CITY, THE, 1948, C
NAKED DAWN, THE, 1955, A
NAKED EARTH, THE, 1958, A
NAKED EDGE, THE, 1961, A-C
NAKED EVIL
NAKED FACE, THE, 1984, C
NAKED FLAME, THE, 1970, C
NAKED FURY, 1959, C
NAKED FURY, THE, 1964
NAKED GENERAL, THE, 1964, A
NAKED GODDESS, THE
NAKED GUN, THE, 1956
NAKED HEART, THE, 1955, A
NAKED HEARTS, 1916, A
NAKED HILLS, 1956
NAKED HOURS, THE, 1964, C
NAKED IN THE SUN, 1957, C
NAKED ISLAND
NAKED JUNGLE, THE, 1953, A-C
NAKED KISS, THE, 1964, O
NAKED LOVERS, THE
NAKED MAJA, THE, 1959, A
NAKED NIGHT, THE, 1956, O
NAKED PARADISE, 1957, A
NAKED PREY, THE, 1966, O
NAKED RIVER, 1977
NAKED RUNNER, THE, 1967, A-C
NAKED SET
NAKED SPUR, 1968
NAKED SPUR, THE, 1953, A-C
NAKED STREET, THE, 1955, C
NAKED TEMPTATION
NAKED TEMPTRESS, THE
NAKED TRUTH, THE
NAKED TRUTH, THE
NAKED TRUTH, THE
NAKED TRUTH, THE, 1914
NAKED UNDER LEATHER
NAKED WITCH, THE, 1964, C
NAKED WOMAN, THE, 1950, A
NAKED WORLD OF HARRISON MARKS, THE, 1967, O
NAKED YOUTH, 1961, C-O
NAKED YOUTH, 1961
NAKED ZOO, THE, 1970, C
NAM ANGELS
NAME FOR EVIL, A, 1970, C-O
NAME OF THE GAME IS KILL, THE, 1968, C
NAME THE MAN, 1924
NAME THE WOMAN, 1928, A
NAME THE WOMAN, 1934, A
NAMELESS
NAMELESS MEN, 1928, A
NAMONAKU MAZUSHIKU UTSUKUSHIKU
NAMU, THE KILLER WHALE, 1966, A
NAMUS, 1926
NAN O' THE BACKWOODS, 1915
NAN OF MUSIC MOUNTAIN, 1917, A
NAN WHO COULDN'T BEAT GOD, THE, 1915
NANA, 1926
NANA, 1934, C
NANA, 1957, A-C
NANA, 1983, O
NANCE, 1920
NANCY COMES HOME, 1918, A
NANCY DREW AND THE HIDDEN STAIRCASE, 1939, AA
NANCY DREW, TROUBLE SHOOTER, 1939, AA
NANCY DREW—DETECTIVE, 1938, AA
NANCY DREW—REPORTER, 1939, AA
NANCY FROM NOWHERE, 1922, A
NANCY GOES TO RIO, 1950, A
NANCY STEELE IS MISSING, 1937, A
NANCY'S BIRTHRIGHT, 1916, A
NANETTE OF THE WILDS, 1916, A
NANNY, THE, 1965, O
NANTAS, 1924
NAPLES AU BAISER DE FEU, 1925
NAPLO GYERMEKEIMNEK
NAPOLEON, 1927, A
NAPOLEON, 1955, A
NAPOLEON AND JOSEPHINE, 1924
NAPOLEON AND SAMANTHA, 1972, AAA
NARAYAMA-BUSHI-KO
NARAYANA, 1920
NARCO MEN, THE, 1969, O
NARCOTIC, THE, 1937
NARCOTICS STORY, THE, 1958, O
NARK, THE
NARROW CORNER, THE, 1933, C
NARROW MARGIN, THE, 1952, A
NARROW PATH, THE, 1916
NARROW PATH, THE, 1918, A
NARROW STREET, THE, 1924, A
NARROW TRAIL, THE, 1917
NARROW VALLEY, THE, 1921, A
NARROWING CIRCLE, THE, 1956, C
NASHVILLE, 1975, C-O
NASHVILLE GIRL
NASHVILLE REBEL, 1966, A
NASILJE NA TRGU
NASTY HABITS, 1976, C
NASTY RABBIT, THE, 1964, A
NATASHA ROSTOVA, 1915
NATCHEZ TRACE, 1960, C
NATE AND HAYES, 1983, C
NATHALIE, 1958, A
NATHALIE GRANGER, 1972, C
NATHALIE, AGENT SECRET, 1960, A
NATHANIEL HAWTHORNE'S "TWICE TOLD TALES"
NATION AFLAME, 1937, A
NATION'S PERIL, THE, 1915, A
NATIONAL BARN DANCE, 1944, A
NATIONAL HEALTH, OR NURSE NORTON'S AFFAIR, THE, 1973, C
NATIONAL LAMPOON'S ANIMAL HOUSE, 1978, C
NATIONAL LAMPOON'S CLASS REUNION, 1982, O
NATIONAL LAMPOON'S VACATION, 1983, C-O
NATIONAL VELVET, 1944, AAA
NATIVE COUNTRY, 1923

NATIVE LAND, 1942
NATIVE SON, 1951, C-O
NATSUKASHIKI FUE YA TAIKO
NATTLEK
NATTVARDSGASTERNA
NATURAL BORN SALESMAN
NATURAL ENEMIES, 1979, O
NATURAL LAW, THE, 1917
NATURAL, THE, 1984, C
NATURE GIRL, THE, 1919
NATURE MAN, THE, 1915
NATURE OF THE BEAST, THE, 1919, A
NATURE'S GENTLEMAN, 1918
NATURE'S MISTAKES
NAUGHTY, 1927
NAUGHTY ARLETTE, 1951, C-O
NAUGHTY BABY, 1929, A
NAUGHTY BUT NICE, 1927
NAUGHTY BUT NICE, 1939, A
NAUGHTY CINDERELLA, 1933, A
NAUGHTY DUCHESS, THE, 1928
NAUGHTY FLIRT, THE, 1931, A
NAUGHTY GIRLS ON THE LOOSE, 1976
NAUGHTY HUSBANDS, 1930
NAUGHTY MARIETTA, 1935, A
NAUGHTY NANETTE, 1927, A
NAUGHTY NINETIES, THE, 1945, AAA
NAUGHTY NYMPHS, 1974
NAUGHTY SCHOOL GIRLS, 1977
NAUGHTY STEWARDESSES, THE, 1973
NAUGHTY WIVES, 1974
NAUGHTY, NAUGHTY, 1918, A
NAULAHKA, THE, 1918, A
NAVAJO, 1952, A
NAVAJO JOE, 1967, C
NAVAJO KID, THE, 1946, A
NAVAJO RUN, 1966, C
NAVAJO TRAIL RAIDERS, 1949, A
NAVAJO TRAIL, THE, 1945, A
NAVAL ACADEMY, 1941, A
NAVIGATOR, THE, 1924, A
NAVY BLUE AND GOLD, 1937, A
NAVY BLUES, 1930, A
NAVY BLUES, 1937, A
NAVY BLUES, 1941, A
NAVY BORN, 1936, A
NAVY BOUND, 1951, A
NAVY HEROES, 1959, A
NAVY LARK, THE, 1959, A
NAVY SECRETS, 1939, A
NAVY SPY, 1937, A
NAVY STEPS OUT, THE
NAVY VS. THE NIGHT MONSTERS, THE, 1966, C
NAVY WAY, THE, 1944, A
NAVY WIFE, 1936, A
NAVY WIFE, 1956, A
NAZARIN, 1968, A
NE'ER-DO-WELL, THE, 1916, A
NE'ER-DO-WELL, THE, 1923
NEAR LADY, THE, 1923, A
NEARER MY GOD TO THEE, 1917
NEARLY A KING, 1916, A
NEARLY A LADY, 1915, A
NEARLY MARRIED, 1917
'NEATH BROOKLYN BRIDGE, 1942, A
'NEATH THE ARIZONA SKIES, 1934, A
'NEATH WESTERN SKIES, 1929
NEBO ZOVYOT
NEBRASKAN, THE, 1953, A
NECESSARY EVIL, THE, 1925, A
NECK AND NECK, 1931, A
NECKLACE OF RAMESES, THE, 1914
NECROMANCY, 1972, C
NED KELLY, 1970, C
NED MCCOBB'S DAUGHTER, 1929, A
NEDRA, 1915
NEE, 1957, A
NEEKA, 1968
NEFERTITE, REGINA DEL NILO
NEGATIVES, 1968, C
NEGLECTED WIVES, 1920, A
NEGLECTED WOMEN, 1924
NEHEZELETUEK
NEIGE
NEIGHBORHOOD HOUSE, 1936
NEIGHBORS, 1918, A
NEIGHBORS, 1981, O-C
NEIGHBORS' WIVES, 1933
NEITHER BY DAY NOR BY NIGHT, 1972, A
NEITHER THE SEA NOR THE SAND, 1974, A
NELL GWYN, 1935, A-C
NELL GWYNNE, 1914, A
NELL GWYNNE, 1926, A
NELL OF THE CIRCUS, 1914, A
NELLA CITTA L'INFERNO
NELLIE, THE BEAUTIFUL CLOAK MODEL, 1924, A
NELLY'S VERSION, 1983, A
NELSON, 1918, A
NELSON, 1926, A
NELSON AFFAIR, THE, 1973, C
NELSON TOUCH, THE
NEMO
NENE, 1924
NEON PALACE, THE, 1970, A
NEPTUNE DISASTER, THE
NEPTUNE FACTOR, THE, 1973, A
NEPTUNE'S DAUGHTER, 1914, A
NEPTUNE'S DAUGHTER, 1949, A
NERO, 1922, A
NERO'S BIG WEEKEND
NERO'S MISTRESS, 1962, C
NERVOUS WRECK, THE, 1926, A
NEST OF NOBLEMEN, A, 1915
NEST OF THE CUCKOO BIRDS, THE, 1965, C
NEST OF VIPERS, 1979, O
NEST, THE, 1927, A
NEST, THE, 1982, A
NESTING, THE, 1981, O
NET, THE
NET, THE, 1916, A
NET, THE, 1923, A
NETS OF DESTINY, 1924, A
NETWORK, 1976, C
NEUNZIG MINUTEN NACH MITTER NACHT
NEURASTHENIA, 1929
NEUTRAL PORT, 1941, A
NEUTRON CONTRA EL DR. CARONTE, 1962, A
NEUTRON EL ENMASCARADO NEGRO, 1962, A
NEVADA, 1927, A
NEVADA, 1936, A
NEVADA, 1944, A
NEVADA BADMEN, 1951, A
NEVADA BUCKAROO, THE, 1931
NEVADA CITY, 1941, A
NEVADA SMITH, 1966, C
NEVADAN, THE, 1950, A
NEVER A DULL MOMENT, 1943, A
NEVER A DULL MOMENT, 1950, A
NEVER A DULL MOMENT, 1968, A
NEVER BACK LOSERS, 1967, A
NEVER CRY WOLF, 1983, C
NEVER FEAR, 1950, A
NEVER GIVE A SUCKER A BREAK
NEVER GIVE A SUCKER AN EVEN BREAK, 1941, A
NEVER GIVE AN INCH
NEVER LET GO, 1960, C
NEVER LET ME GO, 1953, A
NEVER LOOK BACK, 1952, A
NEVER MENTION MURDER, 1964, A
NEVER NEVER LAND, 1982
NEVER ON SUNDAY, 1960, O
NEVER PUT IT IN WRITING, 1964, A
NEVER SAY DIE, 1924, A
NEVER SAY DIE, 1939, A
NEVER SAY DIE, 1950
NEVER SAY GOODBYE, 1946, A
NEVER SAY GOODBYE, 1956, A
NEVER SAY NEVER AGAIN, 1983, A
NEVER SAY QUIT, 1919, A
NEVER SO FEW, 1959, C
NEVER STEAL ANYTHING SMALL, 1959, C
NEVER STEAL ANYTHING WET
NEVER TAKE CANDY FROM A STRANGER, 1961, C-O
NEVER TAKE NO FOR AN ANSWER, 1952, A
NEVER TAKE SWEETS FROM A STRANGER
NEVER THE TWAIN SHALL MEET, 1925, A
NEVER THE TWAIN SHALL MEET, 1931, A
NEVER TO LOVE
NEVER TOO LATE, 1925
NEVER TOO LATE, 1935
NEVER TOO LATE, 1965, A
NEVER TROUBLE TROUBLE, 1931, A
NEVER TRUST A GAMBLER, 1951, A
NEVERENDING STORY, THE, 1984, C
NEW ADAM AND EVE, THE, 1915
NEW ADVENTURES OF DON JUAN
NEW ADVENTURES OF DR. FU MANCHU, THE
NEW ADVENTURES OF GET-RICH-QUICK WALLINGFORD, THE, 1931, A
NEW ADVENTURES OF TARZAN, 1935, A
NEW BABYLON, THE, 1929
NEW BARBARIANS, THE, 1983, O
NEW BROOMS, 1925, A
NEW CENTURIONS, THE, 1972, O
NEW CHAMPION, 1925, A
NEW CLOWN, THE, 1916, A
NEW COMMANDMENT, THE, 1925, A
NEW DAY AT SUNDOWN, 1957
NEW DISCIPLE, THE, 1921, A
NEW EARTH, THE, 1937, A
NEW FACE IN HELL
NEW FACES, 1954, A
NEW FACES OF 1937, 1937, A
NEW FRONTIER, 1939, A
NEW FRONTIER, THE, 1935, A
NEW GENTLEMEN, THE
NEW GIRL IN TOWN, 1977, C-O
NEW HORIZONS, 1939, A
NEW HOTEL, THE, 1932
NEW HOUSE ON THE LEFT, THE, 1978
NEW INTERNS, THE, 1964, C
NEW INVISIBLE MAN, THE
NEW KIND OF LOVE, A, 1963, A-C
NEW KLONDIKE, THE, 1926, A
NEW LAND, THE, 1973, A
NEW LEAF, A, 1971, C-O
NEW LIFE STYLE, THE, 1970, O
NEW LIVES FOR OLD, 1925, A
NEW LOVE, 1968, O
NEW LOVE FOR OLD, 1918, A
NEW MEXICO, 1951, A
NEW MINISTER, 1922
NEW MONSTERS, THE
NEW MOON, 1930, A
NEW MOON, 1940, A
NEW MOON, THE, 1919, A
NEW MORALS FOR OLD, 1932, A
NEW MOVIETONE FOLLIES OF 1930, THE
NEW ONE-ARMED SWORDSMAN, THE
NEW ORLEANS, 1929, A
NEW ORLEANS, 1947, A
NEW ORLEANS AFTER DARK, 1958, C
NEW ORLEANS UNCENSORED, 1955, A
NEW SCHOOL TEACHER, THE, 1924
NEW TEACHER, THE, 1922, A
NEW TEACHER, THE, 1941
NEW TOYS, 1925
NEW WINE, 1941, A
NEW WIZARD OF OZ, THE
NEW YEAR'S EVE, 1923
NEW YEAR'S EVE, 1929, A
NEW YEAR'S EVIL, 1980, O
NEW YORK
NEW YORK, 1916, A
NEW YORK, 1927, A
NEW YORK APPELLE SUPER DRAGON
NEW YORK CONFIDENTIAL, 1955, C
NEW YORK IDEA, THE, 1920, A
NEW YORK LUCK, 1917
NEW YORK NIGHTS
NEW YORK NIGHTS, 1929, A
NEW YORK NIGHTS, 1984
NEW YORK PEACOCK, THE, 1917, A
NEW YORK TOWN, 1941, A
NEW YORK, NEW YORK, 1977, C
NEWLY RICH, 1931, AA
NEWMAN SHAME, THE, 1977
NEWMAN'S LAW, 1974, A
NEWS HOUNDS, 1947, A
NEWS IS MADE AT NIGHT, 1939, A
NEWS PARADE, THE, 1928, A
NEWSBOY'S HOME, 1939, A
NEWSFRONT, 1979, C
NEXT CORNER, THE, 1924
NEXT IN LINE
NEXT MAN, THE, 1976, O
NEXT OF KIN, 1942, A
NEXT OF KIN, 1983, O
NEXT ONE, THE, 1982, C
NEXT STOP, GREENWICH VILLAGE, 1976, C
NEXT TIME I MARRY, 1938, A
NEXT TIME WE LOVE, 1936, A
NEXT TO NO TIME, 1960, A
NEXT VICTIM, 1971
NEXT VOICE YOU HEAR, THE, 1950
NEXT!, 1971, O
NIAGARA, 1953, C
NICE GIRL LIKE ME, A, 1969, C
NICE GIRL?, 1941, A
NICE LITTLE BANK THAT SHOULD BE ROBBED, A, 1958, A
NICE PEOPLE, 1922, A
NICE PLATE OF SPINACH, A
NICE WOMAN, 1932, A
NICHOLAS AND ALEXANDRA, 1971, C
NICHOLAS NICKLEBY, 1947, A
NICHT VERSOHNT ODER "ES HILFT NUR GEWALT, WO GEWALT HERRSCHT"
NICK CARTER IN PRAGUE
NICK CARTER, MASTER DETECTIVE, 1939, A
NICKEL QUEEN, THE, 1971, A
NICKEL RIDE, THE, 1974, C
NICKELODEON, 1976, C
NICOLE, 1972
NIGGER, THE, 1915
NIGHT, 1923
NIGHT AFFAIR, 1961, A
NIGHT AFTER NIGHT, 1932, C
NIGHT AFTER NIGHT AFTER NIGHT, 1970
NIGHT ALARM, 1935, A
NIGHT ALONE, 1938, A
NIGHT AMBUSH, 1958, A
NIGHT AND DAY, 1933, A
NIGHT AND DAY, 1946, A
NIGHT AND THE CITY, 1950, O
NIGHT ANGEL, THE, 1931, A
NIGHT AT EARL CARROLL'S, A, 1940, A

NIGHT AT THE OPERA, A, 1935, A
NIGHT AT THE RITZ, A, 1935, A
NIGHT BEAT, 1932, A
NIGHT BEAT, 1948, A
NIGHT BEFORE CHRISTMAS, A, 1963, A
NIGHT BEFORE THE DIVORCE, THE, 1942, A
NIGHT BIRD, THE, 1928
NIGHT BIRDS, 1931, A
NIGHT BOAT TO DUBLIN, 1946, A
NIGHT BRIDE, THE, 1927, A
NIGHT CALL NURSES, 1974, O
NIGHT CALLER FROM OUTER SPACE
NIGHT CALLER, THE
NIGHT CARGOES, 1963
NIGHT CHILD, 1975, O
NIGHT CLUB
NIGHT CLUB GIRL, 1944, A
NIGHT CLUB GIRL, 1947
NIGHT CLUB HOSTESS
NIGHT CLUB LADY, 1932, A
NIGHT CLUB MURDER
NIGHT CLUB QUEEN, 1934, A
NIGHT CLUB SCANDAL, 1937, A
NIGHT CLUB, THE, 1925, A
NIGHT COMERS, THE, 1971, C-O
NIGHT COMES TOO SOON, 1948, C
NIGHT COURT, 1932, A
NIGHT CRAWLERS, THE
NIGHT CREATURE, 1979, A
NIGHT CREATURES, 1962, A
NIGHT CROSSING, 1982, C
NIGHT CRY, THE, 1926, A
NIGHT DIGGER, THE, 1971, O
NIGHT EDITOR, 1946, A
NIGHT ENCOUNTER, 1963, A
NIGHT EVELYN CAME OUT OF THE GRAVE, THE, 1973, O
NIGHT EXPRESS, THE
NIGHT FIGHTERS, THE, 1960, A
NIGHT FLIGHT, 1933, A
NIGHT FLIGHT FROM MOSCOW
NIGHT FLOWERS, 1979, O
NIGHT FLYER, THE, 1928, A
NIGHT FOR CRIME, A, 1942, A
NIGHT FREIGHT, 1955, A
NIGHT FULL OF RAIN, A
NIGHT GAMES, 1966, O
NIGHT GAMES, 1980, O
NIGHT GOD SCREAMED, THE, 1975
NIGHT HAIR CHILD, 1971, O
NIGHT HAS A THOUSAND EYES, 1948, C
NIGHT HAS EYES, THE
NIGHT HAWK, THE, 1921
NIGHT HAWK, THE, 1924
NIGHT HAWK, THE, 1938, A
NIGHT HEAVEN FELL, THE, 1958, O
NIGHT HOLDS TERROR, THE, 1955, C
NIGHT HORSEMAN, THE, 1921, A
NIGHT HUNT
NIGHT IN BANGKOK, 1966, A
NIGHT IN CAIRO, A
NIGHT IN CASABLANCA, A, 1946, A
NIGHT IN HAVANA
NIGHT IN HEAVEN, A, 1983, O
NIGHT IN HONG KONG, A, 1961, A
NIGHT IN JUNE, A, 1940, A
NIGHT IN MONTMARTE, A, 1931, A
NIGHT IN NEW ARABIA, A, 1917
NIGHT IN NEW ORLEANS, A, 1942, A
NIGHT IN PARADISE, A, 1946, A
NIGHT INTO MORNING, 1951, A
NIGHT INVADER, THE, 1943, C
NIGHT IS ENDING, THE
NIGHT IS MY FUTURE, 1962, A
NIGHT IS OURS, 1930, A
NIGHT IS THE PHANTOM
NIGHT IS YOUNG, THE, 1935, A
NIGHT JOURNEY, 1938, A
NIGHT KEY, 1937, A
NIGHT LIFE, 1927, A
NIGHT LIFE IN HOLLYWOOD, 1922, A
NIGHT LIFE IN RENO, 1931
NIGHT LIFE OF NEW YORK, 1925, A
NIGHT LIFE OF THE GODS, 1935, A
NIGHT LIKE THIS, A, 1932, A
NIGHT MAIL, 1935, C
NIGHT MAYOR, THE, 1932
NIGHT MESSAGE, THE, 1924
NIGHT MONSTER, 1942, A
NIGHT MOVES, 1975, C
NIGHT MUST FALL, 1937, O
NIGHT MUST FALL, 1964, O
NIGHT MY NUMBER CAME UP, THE, 1955, A-C
NIGHT NURSE, 1931, A-C
NIGHT NURSE, THE, 1977
NIGHT OF A THOUSAND CATS, 1974, O
NIGHT OF ADVENTURE, A, 1944, A
NIGHT OF ANUBIS
NIGHT OF BLOODY HORROR, 1969, O
NIGHT OF DARK SHADOWS, 1971, C
NIGHT OF EVIL, 1962, C
NIGHT OF JANUARY 16TH, 1941, A
NIGHT OF JUNE 13, 1932, A
NIGHT OF LOVE, THE, 1927, A
NIGHT OF LUST, 1965, C
NIGHT OF MAGIC, A, 1944, A
NIGHT OF MYSTERY, 1937, A
NIGHT OF MYSTERY, A, 1928, A
NIGHT OF NIGHTS, THE, 1939, A
NIGHT OF PASSION
NIGHT OF SAN LORENZO, THE
NIGHT OF TERROR, 1933, A
NIGHT OF TERRORS
NIGHT OF THE ASKARI, 1978, C
NIGHT OF THE ASSASSIN, THE, 1972
NIGHT OF THE BEAST
NIGHT OF THE BIG HEAT
NIGHT OF THE BLOOD BEAST, 1958, A
NIGHT OF THE BLOODY APES, 1968, O
NIGHT OF THE CLAW
NIGHT OF THE COBRA WOMAN, 1974, O
NIGHT OF THE COMET, 1984, C-O
NIGHT OF THE DARK FULL MOON
NIGHT OF THE DEMON
NIGHT OF THE DEMON
NIGHT OF THE DEMON, 1980
NIGHT OF THE EAGLE
NIGHT OF THE FLESH EATERS
NIGHT OF THE FOLLOWING DAY, THE, 1969, O
NIGHT OF THE FULL MOON, THE, 1954, C
NIGHT OF THE GARTER, 1933, A
NIGHT OF THE GENERALS, THE, 1967, O
NIGHT OF THE GHOULS, 1959
NIGHT OF THE GRIZZLY, THE, 1966, A
NIGHT OF THE HOWLING BEAST, 1977
NIGHT OF THE HUNTER, THE, 1955, O
NIGHT OF THE IGUANA, THE, 1964, O
NIGHT OF THE JUGGLER, 1980, O
NIGHT OF THE LAUGHING DEAD
NIGHT OF THE LEPUS, 1972, C
NIGHT OF THE LIVING DEAD, 1968, O
NIGHT OF THE PARTY, THE, 1934, A
NIGHT OF THE PROWLER, 1962
NIGHT OF THE PROWLER, THE, 1979, O
NIGHT OF THE QUARTER MOON, 1959, C
NIGHT OF THE SEAGULL, THE, 1970, C
NIGHT OF THE SHOOTING STARS, THE, 1982, O
NIGHT OF THE SILICATES
NIGHT OF THE SORCERORS, 1970
NIGHT OF THE STRANGLER, 1975
NIGHT OF THE TIGER, THE
NIGHT OF THE WITCHES, 1970, O
NIGHT OF THE ZOMBIES, 1981, O
NIGHT OF THE ZOMBIES, 1983, O
NIGHT OUT, A, 1916, A
NIGHT OWL, THE, 1926, A
NIGHT PARADE, 1929, A
NIGHT PASSAGE, 1957, A
NIGHT PATROL, 1984, O
NIGHT PATROL, THE
NIGHT PATROL, THE, 1926, A
NIGHT PEOPLE, 1954, A
NIGHT PLANE FROM CHUNGKING, 1942, A
NIGHT PORTER, THE, 1974, O
NIGHT RAIDERS, 1952, A
NIGHT RIDE, 1930, A
NIGHT RIDE, 1937, C
NIGHT RIDER, THE, 1932, A
NIGHT RIDERS OF MONTANA, 1951, A
NIGHT RIDERS, THE, 1920
NIGHT RIDERS, THE, 1939, A
NIGHT ROSE, THE, 1921
NIGHT RUNNER, THE, 1957, A
NIGHT SCHOOL, 1981, O
NIGHT SHADOWS, 1984, O
NIGHT SHIFT, 1982, C
NIGHT SHIP, THE, 1925, A
NIGHT SONG, 1947, A
NIGHT SPOT, 1938, A
NIGHT STAGE TO GALVESTON, 1952, A
NIGHT THE CREATURES CAME
NIGHT THE LIGHTS WENT OUT IN GEORGIA, THE, 1981, C
NIGHT THE SILICATES CAME
NIGHT THE SUN CAME OUT, THE
NIGHT THE WORLD EXPLODED, THE, 1957, A
NIGHT THEY KILLED RASPUTIN, THE, 1962, C
NIGHT THEY RAIDED MINSKY'S, THE, 1968, C-O
NIGHT THEY ROBBED BIG BERTHA'S, THE, 1975, O
NIGHT TIDE, 1963, C
NIGHT TIME IN NEVADA, 1948, A
NIGHT TO DISMEMBER, A, 1983
NIGHT TO REMEMBER, A, 1942, A
NIGHT TO REMEMBER, A, 1958, A
NIGHT TRAIN, 1940, A
NIGHT TRAIN FOR INVERNESS, 1960, C
NIGHT TRAIN TO MEMPHIS, 1946, A
NIGHT TRAIN TO MUNDO FINE, 1966, A
NIGHT TRAIN TO MUNICH
NIGHT TRAIN TO PARIS, 1964, A
NIGHT UNTO NIGHT, 1949, A
NIGHT VISITOR, THE, 1970, C
NIGHT WAITRESS, 1936, A
NIGHT WALK
NIGHT WALKER, THE, 1964, C
NIGHT WAS OUR FRIEND, 1951, C-O
NIGHT WATCH, 1973, C
NIGHT WATCH, THE, 1926, A
NIGHT WATCH, THE, 1928, C
NIGHT WATCH, THE, 1964, A
NIGHT WE DROPPED A CLANGER, THE
NIGHT WE GOT THE BIRD, THE, 1961, C
NIGHT WIND, 1948, A
NIGHT WITHOUT PITY, 1962
NIGHT WITHOUT SLEEP, 1952, C
NIGHT WITHOUT STARS, 1953, A
NIGHT WON'T TALK, THE, 1952, C
NIGHT WORK, 1930, A
NIGHT WORK, 1939, A
NIGHT WORKERS, THE, 1917, A
NIGHT WORLD, 1932, A
NIGHT, THE
NIGHTBEAST, 1982, C-O
NIGHTBIRDS OF LONDON, THE, 1915
NIGHTFALL, 1956, A
NIGHTFLIGHT FROM MOSCOW
NIGHTHAWKS, 1978, O
NIGHTHAWKS, 1981
NIGHTINGALE SANG IN BERKELEY SQUARE, A, 1979
NIGHTINGALE, THE, 1914, A
NIGHTKILLERS, 1983
NIGHTMARE
NIGHTMARE, 1942, C
NIGHTMARE, 1956, C
NIGHTMARE, 1963, O
NIGHTMARE, 1981, O
NIGHTMARE ALLEY, 1947, C-O
NIGHTMARE BLOOD BATH, 1971
NIGHTMARE CASTLE, 1966, C
NIGHTMARE CITY
NIGHTMARE COUNTY, 1977
NIGHTMARE HONEYMOON, 1973, O
NIGHTMARE IN BLOOD, 1978, O
NIGHTMARE IN THE SUN, 1964, O
NIGHTMARE IN WAX, 1969, O
NIGHTMARE ON ELM STREET, A, 1984, O
NIGHTMARE WEEKEND
NIGHTMARES, 1983, O
NIGHTS IN A HAREM
NIGHTS OF CABIRIA, 1957, C
NIGHTS OF LUCRETIA BORGIA, THE, 1960, A
NIGHTS OF PRAGUE, THE, 1968, C
NIGHTS OF SHAME, 1961, O
NIGHTS WHEN THE DEVIL CAME
NIGHTSONGS, 1984, C
NIGHTWING, 1979, O
NIHON NO ICHIBAN NAGAI HI
NIJINSKY, 1980, C-O
NIKKI, WILD DOG OF THE NORTH, 1961, AAA
NIKOLAI STAVROGIN, 1915
NIKUTAI NO GAKKO
NINA, THE FLOWER GIRL, 1917, A
NINE, 1920
NINE AND THREE-FIFTHS SECONDS, 1925, A
NINE DAYS A QUEEN
NINE DAYS OF ONE YEAR, 1964, O
NINE FORTY-FIVE, 1934, A
NINE GIRLS, 1944, C
NINE HOURS TO RAMA, 1963, C
NINE LIVES ARE NOT ENOUGH, 1941, A
NINE LIVES OF FRITZ THE CAT, THE, 1974
NINE MEN, 1943, A
NINE MILES TO NOON, 1963, C
9/30/55, 1977, C
NINE O'CLOCK TOWN, A, 1918, A
NINE POINTS OF THE LAW, 1922
NINE TILL SIX, 1932, A
NINE TO FIVE, 1980, C-O
1984, 1956, A-C
1941, 1979, C-O
1900, 1976, C-O
1990: BRONX WARRIORS, 1983, C
90 DEGREES IN THE SHADE, 1966, O
99 AND 44/100% DEAD, 1974, C-O
99 RIVER STREET, 1953, C
99 WOUNDS, 1931, A
92 IN THE SHADE, 1975, C
NINE-TENTHS OF THE LAW, 1918
NINETEEN AND PHYLLIS, 1920, A
NINETY AND NINE, THE, 1916
NINETY AND NINE, THE, 1922, A
NINGEN NO JOKEN
NINGEN NO JOKEN II
NINGEN NO JOKEN III
NINJA III—THE DOMINATION, 1984, O
NINJA MISSION, 1984
NINJUTSU, SORYU HIKEN

NINOTCHKA, 1939
NINTH CIRCLE, THE, 1961, O
NINTH CONFIGURATION, THE, 1980, O
NINTH GUEST, THE, 1934, A
NINTH HEART, THE, 1980, A
NINTH OF JANUARY, 1925
NIOBE, 1915, A
NIPPER, THE
NIPPON KONCHUKI
NIPPON NO ICHIBAN NAGAI HI
NITCHEVO, 1926
NITWITS, THE, 1935, A
NIX ON DAMES, 1929, A
NO BABIES WANTED, 1928, A
NO BLADE OF GRASS, 1970, O
NO BRAKES
NO CHILDREN WANTED, 1918
NO CONTROL, 1927, A
NO DEADLY MACHINE
NO DEFENSE, 1921
NO DEFENSE, 1929, A
NO DEPOSIT, NO RETURN, 1976, AAA
NO DIAMONDS FOR URSULA, 1967
NO DOWN PAYMENT, 1957, C
NO DRUMS, NO BUGLES, 1971, A
NO ESCAPE, 1934, C
NO ESCAPE, 1936, C
NO ESCAPE, 1953, O
NO ESCAPE, 1943
NO EXIT, 1930
NO EXIT, 1962, O
NO FUNNY BUSINESS, 1934, A
NO GREATER GLORY, 1934, A
NO GREATER LOVE, 1915
NO GREATER LOVE, 1932, A
NO GREATER LOVE, 1944, O
NO GREATER LOVE THAN THIS, 1969, C
NO GREATER LOVE, 1931
NO GREATER LOVE, 1970
NO GREATER SIN
NO GREATER SIN, 1941, A
NO HANDS ON THE CLOCK, 1941, A
NO HAUNT FOR A GENTLEMAN, 1952, A
NO HIGHWAY
NO HIGHWAY IN THE SKY, 1951, A
NO HOLDS BARRED, 1952, A
NO KIDDING
NO KNIFE
NO LADY, 1931, A
NO LEAVE, NO LOVE, 1946, A
NO LIMIT, 1931, A
NO LIMIT, 1935, A
NO LIVING WITNESS, 1932, A
NO LONGER ALONE, 1978, C
NO LOVE FOR JOHNNIE, 1961, O
NO LOVE FOR JUDY, 1955
NO MAN IS AN ISLAND, 1962, C
NO MAN OF HER OWN, 1933, A
NO MAN OF HER OWN, 1950, A
NO MAN WALKS ALONE
NO MAN'S GOLD, 1926, A
NO MAN'S LAND
NO MAN'S LAND, 1918
NO MAN'S LAND, 1964, O
NO MAN'S LAW, 1925
NO MAN'S LAW, 1927, A
NO MAN'S RANGE, 1935, A
NO MAN'S WOMAN, 1921, A
NO MAN'S WOMAN, 1955, C
NO MARRIAGE TIES, 1933, A
NO MERCY MAN, THE, 1975, O
NO MINOR VICES, 1948, A
NO MONKEY BUSINESS, 1935, A
NO MORE EXCUSES, 1968
NO MORE LADIES, 1935, C
NO MORE ORCHIDS, 1933, A
NO MORE WOMEN, 1924, A
NO MORE WOMEN, 1934, A
NO MOTHER TO GUIDE HER, 1923, C
NO NAME ON THE BULLET, 1959, A
NO ONE MAN, 1932, A
NO ORCHIDS FOR MISS BLANDISH, 1948, O
NO OTHER WOMAN, 1928, A
NO OTHER WOMAN, 1933, A
NO PARKING, 1938, A
NO PLACE FOR A LADY, 1943, A
NO PLACE FOR JENNIFER, 1950, A
NO PLACE LIKE HOMICIDE
NO PLACE TO GO, 1927
NO PLACE TO GO, 1939, A
NO PLACE TO HIDE, 1956, A
NO PLACE TO HIDE, 1975, C-O
NO PLACE TO LAND, 1958, A-C
NO QUESTIONS ASKED, 1951, A
NO RANSOM, 1935, A
NO RESTING PLACE, 1952, A
NO RETURN ADDRESS, 1961, A
NO ROAD BACK, 1957, A
NO ROOM AT THE INN, 1950, A
NO ROOM FOR THE GROOM, 1952, A
NO ROOM TO DIE, 1969, O
NO ROSES FOR OSS 117, 1968, C
NO SAD SONGS FOR ME, 1950, A-C
NO SAFETY AHEAD, 1959, C
NO SEX PLEASE—WE'RE BRITISH, 1979, C
NO SLEEP TILL DAWN
NO SMALL AFFAIR, 1984, O
NO SMOKING, 1955, A
NO SURVIVORS, PLEASE, 1963, C
NO TIME FOR BREAKFAST, 1978, O
NO TIME FOR COMEDY, 1940, A
NO TIME FOR ECSTASY, 1963, O
NO TIME FOR FLOWERS, 1952, A
NO TIME FOR LOVE, 1943, A
NO TIME FOR SERGEANTS, 1958, A
NO TIME FOR TEARS, 1957, A
NO TIME FOR TEARS, 1951
NO TIME TO BE YOUNG, 1957, O
NO TIME TO DIE
NO TIME TO KILL, 1963, C
NO TIME TO MARRY, 1938, A
NO TOYS FOR CHRISTMAS
NO TRACE, 1950, A
NO TREE IN THE STREET, 1964, A
NO TRESPASSING, 1922, A
NO WAY BACK, 1949, C
NO WAY BACK, 1976, O
NO WAY OUT, 1950, A
NO WAY OUT, 1975, O
NO WAY TO TREAT A LADY, 1968, C-O
NO WOMAN KNOWS, 1921, A
NO, MY DARLING DAUGHTER, 1964, A
NO, NO NANETTE, 1930, A
NO, NO NANETTE, 1940, A
NO-GOOD GUY, THE, 1916
NO-GUN MAN, THE, 1924, A
NO. 13 DEMON STREET
NO. 5 JOHN STREET, 1921, A
NO. 96, 1974, C
NO. 99, 1920
NOAH'S ARK, 1928, A-C
NOB HILL, 1945, A
NOBI
NOBODY, 1921, A
NOBODY HOME
NOBODY IN TOYLAND, 1958, A
NOBODY LIVES FOREVER, 1946, A
NOBODY LOVES A DRUNKEN INDIAN
NOBODY LOVES A FLAPPING EAGLE
NOBODY RUNS FOREVER
NOBODY WAVED GOODBYE, 1965, C
NOBODY'S BABY, 1937, A
NOBODY'S BRIDE, 1923, A
NOBODY'S CHILD, 1919, A
NOBODY'S CHILDREN, 1926
NOBODY'S CHILDREN, 1940, AAA
NOBODY'S DARLING, 1943, A
NOBODY'S FOOL, 1921, A
NOBODY'S FOOL, 1936, A
NOBODY'S GIRL, 1920
NOBODY'S KID, 1921, A
NOBODY'S MONEY, 1923, A
NOBODY'S PERFECT, 1968, A
NOBODY'S PERFEKT, 1981, C
NOBODY'S WIDOW, 1927, A
NOBODY'S WIFE, 1918, A
NOBORIRYU TEKKAHADA
NOCTURNA, 1979, O
NOCTURNE, 1946, C
NOISE IN NEWBORO, A, 1923, A
NOISY NEIGHBORS, 1929, A
NOMADIC LIVES, 1977
NOMADS OF THE NORTH, 1920, A
NOMANDIE, 1931
NON TIRATE IL DIAVOLO PER LA CODA
NON-CONFORMIST PARSON, A, 1919
NON-STOP FLIGHT, THE, 1926, A
NON-STOP NEW YORK, 1937, A
NONE BUT THE BRAVE, 1928, A
NONE BUT THE BRAVE, 1963, C
NONE BUT THE BRAVE, 1965, O
NONE BUT THE BRAVE, 1960
NONE BUT THE LONELY HEART, 1944, A
NONE SHALL ESCAPE, 1944, A
NONE SO BLIND, 1923
NONENTITY, THE, 1922, A
NOON SUNDAY, 1971
NOOSE
NOOSE FOR A GUNMAN, 1960, A
NOOSE FOR A LADY, 1953, A
NOOSE HANGS HIGH, THE, 1948, AAA
NOOSE, THE, 1928, C
NOR THE MOON BY NIGHT
NORA INU
NORA PRENTISS, 1947, A
NORAH O'NEALE, 1934, A
NORMA RAE, 1979, A-C
NORMAN CONQUEST, 1953, A
NORMAN LOVES ROSE, 1982, O
NORMAN...IS THAT YOU?, 1976, C
NORSEMAN, THE, 1978, C
NORTH AVENUE IRREGULARS, THE, 1979, A
NORTH BY NORTHWEST, 1959, A
NORTH DALLAS FORTY, 1979, C-O
NORTH FROM LONE STAR, 1941, A
NORTH OF '36, 1924, A
NORTH OF ALASKA, 1924
NORTH OF ARIZONA, 1935
NORTH OF FIFTY-THREE, 1917
NORTH OF HUDSON BAY, 1923, A
NORTH OF NEVADA, 1924, A
NORTH OF NOME, 1925
NORTH OF NOME, 1937, A
NORTH OF SHANGHAI, 1939, A
NORTH OF THE GREAT DIVIDE, 1950
NORTH OF THE RIO GRANDE, 1922, A
NORTH OF THE RIO GRANDE, 1937, A
NORTH OF THE ROCKIES, 1942
NORTH OF THE YUKON, 1939, A
NORTH SEA HIJACK
NORTH SEA PATROL, 1939, A
NORTH STAR, 1925
NORTH STAR, THE, 1943, A-C
NORTH STAR, THE, 1982
NORTH TO ALASKA, 1960, A
NORTH TO THE KLONDIKE, 1942, A
NORTH WEST FRONTIER
NORTH WIND'S MALICE, THE, 1920, A
NORTHEAST TO SEOUL, 1974
NORTHERN CODE, 1925, A
NORTHERN FRONTIER, 1935, A
NORTHERN LIGHTS, 1914
NORTHERN LIGHTS, 1978, A
NORTHERN PATROL, 1953, A
NORTHERN PURSUIT, 1943, A
NORTHFIELD CEMETERY MASSACRE, THE
NORTHVILLE CEMETERY MASSACRE, THE, 1976
NORTHWEST MOUNTED POLICE, 1940, A
NORTHWEST OUTPOST, 1947, A
NORTHWEST PASSAGE, 1940, A-C
NORTHWEST RANGERS, 1942, A
NORTHWEST STAMPEDE, 1948, A
NORTHWEST TERRITORY, 1952, A
NORTHWEST TRAIL, 1945, A
NORWOOD, 1970, A
NOSE ON MY FACE, THE
NOSFERATU, A SYMPHONY OF HORROR
NOSFERATU, A SYMPHONY OF TERROR
NOSFERATU, THE VAMPIRE, 1922, C
NOSFERATU, THE VAMPIRE, 1979, C-O
NOSFURATU, EINE SYMPHONIE DES GRAUENS
NOSTALGHIA, 1984, O
NOT A DRUM WAS HEARD, 1924
NOT A HOPE IN HELL, 1960
NOT A LADIES MAN, 1942
NOT AGAINST THE FLESH
NOT AS A STRANGER, 1955, A-C
NOT BUILT FOR RUNNIN', 1924
NOT DAMAGED, 1930, C
NOT EXACTLY GENTLEMEN
NOT FOR HONOR AND GLORY
NOT FOR PUBLICATION, 1927
NOT FOR PUBLICATION, 1984, C-O
NOT FOR SALE, 1924
NOT FOR SALE, 1924, A
NOT GUILTY, 1915
NOT GUILTY, 1919, A
NOT GUILTY, 1921, A
NOT MINE TO LOVE, 1969, A
NOT MY DAUGHTER, 1975
NOT MY SISTER, 1916, A
NOT NEGOTIABLE, 1918
NOT NOW DARLING, 1975, O
NOT OF THIS EARTH, 1957
NOT ON YOUR LIFE
NOT ON YOUR LIFE, 1965, C-O
NOT ONE TO SPARE
NOT QUITE A LADY, 1928, A
NOT QUITE DECENT, 1929, A
NOT RECONCILED, OR "ONLY VIOLENCE HELPS WHERE IT RULES", 1969, C
NOT SO DUMB, 1930, A
NOT SO DUSTY, 1936, A
NOT SO DUSTY, 1956, A
NOT SO LONG AGO, 1925, A
NOT SO QUIET ON THE WESTERN FRONT, 1930, A
NOT TONIGHT HENRY, 1961
NOT WANTED, 1949, A
NOT WANTED ON VOYAGE, 1957, A
NOT WANTED ON VOYAGE, 1938, Brit.
NOT WITH MY WIFE, YOU DON'T!, 1966, A
NOTCH NUMBER ONE, 1924
NOTEBOOKS OF MAJOR THOMPSON
NOTHING BARRED, 1961, A
NOTHING BUT A MAN, 1964, A
NOTHING BUT LIES, 1920
NOTHING BUT THE BEST, 1964, C

NOTHING BUT THE NIGHT, 1975, A
NOTHING BUT THE TRUTH, 1920, A
NOTHING BUT THE TRUTH, 1929, A
NOTHING BUT THE TRUTH, 1941, A
NOTHING BUT TROUBLE, 1944, AA
NOTHING ELSE MATTERS, 1920
NOTHING LASTS FOREVER, 1984, C
NOTHING LIKE PUBLICITY, 1936, A
NOTHING PERSONAL, 1980, A-C
NOTHING SACRED, 1937, A
NOTHING TO BE DONE, 1914
NOTHING TO LOSE
NOTHING TO WEAR, 1928, A
NOTHING VENTURE, 1948, AAA
NOTORIETY, 1922, A
NOTORIOUS, 1946, A
NOTORIOUS AFFAIR, 1930, A
NOTORIOUS BUT NICE, 1934, A
NOTORIOUS CLEOPATRA, THE, 1970, O
NOTORIOUS GALLAGHER
NOTORIOUS GENTLEMAN, 1945, C
NOTORIOUS GENTLEMAN, A, 1935, A
NOTORIOUS LADY, THE, 1927, A
NOTORIOUS LANDLADY, THE, 1962, A-C
NOTORIOUS LONE WOLF, THE, 1946, A
NOTORIOUS MISS LISLE, THE, 1920, A
NOTORIOUS MR. MONKS, THE, 1958, C
NOTORIOUS MRS. CARRICK, THE, 1924, A
NOTORIOUS MRS. SANDS, THE, 1920, A
NOTORIOUS SOPHIE LANG, THE, 1934, A
NOTRA PAUVRE COEUR, 1916
NOTRE DAME D'AMOUR, 1922
NOTRE DAME DE PARIS
NOTTI BIANCHE, LA
NOUS IRONS A PARIS, 1949, A
NOVEL AFFAIR, A, 1957, A
NOW ABOUT ALL THESE WOMEN
NOW AND FOREVER, 1934, A
NOW AND FOREVER, 1956, A
NOW AND FOREVER, 1983, O
NOW BARABBAS
NOW BARABBAS WAS A ROBBER, 1949, A
NOW I LAY ME DOWN
NOW I'LL TELL, 1934, A-C
NOW IT CAN BE TOLD
NOW OR NEVER, 1935
NOW THAT APRIL'S HERE, 1958, A
NOW WE'RE IN THE AIR, 1927, A
NOW YOU SEE HIM, NOW YOU DON'T, 1972, AAA
NOW, VOYAGER, 1942, A-C
NOWHERE TO GO, 1959, A
NOZ W WODZIE
NTH COMMANDMENT, THE, 1923, A
NTOM SUBMARINE, THE, 1941, A
NUDE BOMB, THE, 1980, A
NUDE HEAT WAVE
NUDE IN A WHITE CAR, 1960, C
NUDE IN HIS POCKET, 1962, A
NUDE ODYSSEY, 1962, A
NUDE...SI MUORE
NUDES ON CREDIT
NUGGET IN THE ROUGH, A, 1918
NUGGET NELL, 1919, A
NUISANCE, THE, 1933, A
NUIT DE VARENNES, LA
NUITS ROUGES
NUMBER 17, 1920, A
NUMBER ONE, 1969, C
NUMBER ONE, 1984, C
NUMBER SEVENTEEN, 1928, A
NUMBER SEVENTEEN, 1932, A
NUMBER SIX, 1962, A
NUMBER TWO, 1975
NUMBERED MEN, 1930, A
NUMBERED WOMAN, 1938
NUMERO DEUX
NUN AND THE SERGEANT, THE, 1962, A
NUN AT THE CROSSROADS, A, 1970, A
NUN OF MONZA, THE
NUN'S STORY, THE, 1959, A
NUN, THE, 1971, C
NUNZIO, 1978, O
NUR TOTE ZEUGEN SCHWEIGEN
NUREMBERG, 1961
NURSE AND MARTYR, 1915
NURSE EDITH CAVELL, 1939, A
NURSE FROM BROOKLYN, 1938, A
NURSE MARJORIE, 1920, A
NURSE ON WHEELS, 1964, O
NURSE SHERRI, 1978, O
NURSE'S SECRET, THE, 1941, A
NURSEMAID WHO DISAPPEARED, THE, 1939, A
NURSES FOR SALE, 1977
NUT FARM, THE, 1935, A
NUT, THE, 1921, A
NUT-CRACKER, THE, 1926, A
NUTCRACKER, 1982, O
NUTCRACKER, 1984
NUTCRACKER FANTASY, 1979, AAA
NUTTY PROFESSOR, THE, 1963, A
NUTTY, NAUGHTY CHATEAU, 1964, C
NVUIIRANDO NO WAKADAISHO
NYMPH, 1974
NYMPH OF THE FOOTHILLS, A, 1918
NYMPH OF THE WOODS, A
NYUJIRANDO NO WAKADAISHO

-O-

O LUCKY MAN!, 1973, O
O SLAVNOSTI A HOSTECH
O'FLYNN, THE
O'HARA'S WIFE, 1983, C
O'LEARY NIGHT
O'MALLEY OF THE MOUNTED, 1921, A
O'MALLEY OF THE MOUNTED, 1936, A
O'MALLEY RIDES ALONE, 1930
O'RILEY'S LUCK
O'ROURKE OF THE ROYAL MOUNTED
O'SHAUGHNESSY'S BOY, 1935, A
O, MY DARLING CLEMENTINE, 1943, A
O. HENRY'S FULL HOUSE, 1952, AAA
O.K. CONNERY
O.M.H.S.
O.S.S., 1946, C
O.U. WEST, 1925
OAD BACK,THE, 1937, A
OAKDALE AFFAIR, THE, 1919, A
OASIS OF FEAR, 1973
OASIS, THE, 1984, O
OATH OF THE BIBLE, THE
OATH OF VENGEANCE, 1944
OATH, THE, 1921
OATH-BOUND, 1922, A
OBEAH, 1935
OBEY THE LAW, 1926
OBEY THE LAW, 1933, A
OBEY YOUR HUSBAND, 1928, A
OBJECT—ALIMONY, 1929, A
OBJECTIVE 500 MILLION, 1966, C
OBJECTIVE, BURMA!, 1945, C
OBLIGIN' BUCKAROO, THE, 1927
OBLIGING YOUNG LADY, 1941, A
OBLONG BOX, THE, 1969, O
OBSESSED, 1951, C
OBSESSION
OBSESSION, 1954, C
OBSESSION, 1968, C
OBSESSION, 1976, C
OBVIOUS SITUATION, AN
OCCASIONALLY YOURS, 1920, A
OCCHI SENZA VOLTO
OCEAN BREAKERS, 1949, A
OCEAN WAIF, THE, 1916
OCEAN'S ELEVEN, 1960, A
OCHAZUKE NO AJI
OCTAGON, THE, 1980, O
OCTAMAN, 1971, O
OCTOBER
OCTOBER, 1928
OCTOBER MAN, THE, 1948, A
OCTOBER MOTH, 1960, O
OCTOMAN
OCTOPUSSY, 1983, C
ODD ANGRY SHOT, THE, 1979, C
ODD COUPLE, THE, 1968, A
ODD JOB, THE, 1978, O
ODD MAN OUT, 1947, C-O
ODD OBSESSION, 1961, O
ODDO, 1967
ODDS AGAINST
ODDS AGAINST HER, THE, 1919, A
ODDS AGAINST TOMORROW, 1959, C
ODE TO BILLY JOE, 1976, O
ODESSA FILE, THE, 1974, C
ODETTE, 1951, A-C
ODISSEA NUDA
ODONGO, 1956, A
ODYSSEY OF THE NORTH, AN, 1914, A
ODYSSEY OF THE PACIFIC, 1983, AA
OEDIPUS REX, 1957, A
OEDIPUS THE KING, 1968
OEVIL'S HAND, THE
OF BEDS AND BROADS
OF FLESH AND BLOOD, 1964, C
OF HUMAN BONDAGE, 1934, C-O
OF HUMAN BONDAGE, 1946, O
OF HUMAN BONDAGE, 1964, O
OF HUMAN HEARTS, 1938, A
OF LOVE AND DESIRE, 1963, O
OF MICE AND MEN, 1939, O
OF STARS AND MEN, 1961, AAA
OF UNKNOWN ORIGIN, 1983, O
OF WAYWARD LOVE, 1964, O
OFF LIMITS, 1953, A
OFF THE BEATEN TRACK
OFF THE DOLE, 1935, A
OFF THE HIGHWAY, 1925, A
OFF THE RECORD, 1939, A
OFF THE WALL, 1977, C
OFF THE WALL, 1983, O
OFF TO THE RACES, 1937, A
OFF YOUR ROCKER, 1980
OFF-SHORE PIRATE, THE, 1921, A
OFFBEAT, 1961, A
OFFENDERS, THE, 1924, A
OFFENDERS, THE, 1980, O
OFFENSE, THE, 1973, O
OFFERING, THE, 1966, C
OFFICE GIRL, THE, 1932, A
OFFICE GIRLS, 1974
OFFICE PICNIC, THE, 1974, C
OFFICE SCANDAL, THE, 1929, A
OFFICE WIFE, THE, 1930, A
OFFICER 13, 1933, A
OFFICER 444, 1926
OFFICER 666, 1914
OFFICER 666, 1920
OFFICER AND A GENTLEMAN, AN, 1982, O
OFFICER AND THE LADY, THE, 1941, A
OFFICER JIM, 1926, A
OFFICER O'BRIEN, 1930, A
OFFICER'S MESS, THE, 1931, A
OGGI, DOMANI E DOPODOMANI, 1968
OGNUNO PER SE
OGRE AND THE GIRL, THE, 1915
OGUE SONG, THE, 1930, A
OH BILLY BEHAVE, 1926
OH BOY!, 1938, A
OH BROTHERHOOD
OH CE BAISER, 1917
OH DAD, POOR DAD, MAMA'S HUNG YOU IN THE CLOSET AND I'M FEELIN' SO SAD, 1967, C
OH DADDY!, 1935, A
OH DOCTOR, 1937, A
OH GOD! BOOK II, 1980, A-C
OH GOD! YOU DEVIL, 1984, A-C
OH JOHNNY, HOW YOU CAN LOVE!, 1940, A
OH MARY BE CAREFUL, 1921
OH MY DARLING CLEMENTINE
OH NO DOCTOR!, 1934
OH ROSALINDA, 1956, A
OH WHAT A DUCHESS!
OH! CALCUTTA!, 1972, O
OH! FOR A MAN!, 1957
OH! SAILOR, BEHAVE!, 1930, AAA
OH! SUSANNA, 1951, A
OH! THOSE MOST SECRET AGENTS
OH! WHAT A LOVELY WAR, 1969, A-C
OH, ALFIE
OH, BABY, 1926
OH, BOY, 1919, A
OH, DOCTOR, 1924, A
OH, FOR A MAN!, 1930, A
OH, GOD!, 1977, A-C
OH, HEAVENLY DOG!, 1980, A
OH, JO, 1921
OH, JOHNNY, 1919, A
OH, KAY, 1928, A
OH, LADY, LADY, 1920, A
OH, MABEL BEHAVE, 1922
OH, MEN! OH, WOMEN!, 1957, A-C
OH, MR. PORTER!, 1937, A
OH, SUSANNA, 1937, A
OH, WHAT A NIGHT, 1926, A
OH, WHAT A NIGHT, 1935, A
OH, WHAT A NIGHT, 1944, A
OH, WHAT A NURSE, 1926, A
OH, YEAH!, 1929, A
OH, YOU BEAUTIFUL DOLL, 1949, A
OH, YOU TONY, A
OH, YOU WOMEN, 1919
OHAYO, 1962, A
OIL, 1977
OIL AND ROMANCE, 1925
OIL FOR THE LAMPS OF CHINA, 1935, A
OIL GIRLS, THE
OIL RAIDER, THE, 1934
OIL TOWN
OISEAUX DE PASSAGE, 1925
OKAY AMERICA, 1932, A
OKAY BILL, 1971, O
OKAY FOR SOUND, 1937, A
OKEFENOKEE, 1960
OKINAWA, 1952, A
OKLAHOMA, 1955, AAA
OKLAHOMA ANNIE, 1952, A
OKLAHOMA BADLANDS, 1948, A
OKLAHOMA BLUES, 1948, A
OKLAHOMA COWBOY, AN, 1929
OKLAHOMA CRUDE, 1973, O
OKLAHOMA CYCLONE, 1930, A
OKLAHOMA FRONTIER, 1939
OKLAHOMA JIM, 1931, A
OKLAHOMA JUSTICE, 1951, A
OKLAHOMA KID, THE, 1929, A
OKLAHOMA KID, THE, 1939, A
OKLAHOMA RAIDERS, 1944, A

OKLAHOMA RENEGADES, 1940, A
OKLAHOMA SHERIFF, THE, 1930, A
OKLAHOMA TERRITORY, 1960, A
OKLAHOMA TERROR, 1939, A
OKLAHOMA WOMAN, THE, 1956, C
OKLAHOMAN, THE, 1957, A
OLD ACQUAINTANCE, 1943, A-C
OLD AGE HANDICAP, 1928, A
OLD AND NEW, 1930
OLD ARM CHAIR, THE, 1920, A
OLD BARN DANCE, THE, 1938, A
OLD BILL AND SON, 1940, A
OLD BILL OF PARIS
OLD BILL THROUGH THE AGES, 1924, A
OLD BONES OF THE RIVER, 1938, A
OLD BOYFRIENDS, 1979, O
OLD CHISHOLM TRAIL, 1943, A
OLD CLOTHES, 1925, A
OLD CODE, THE, 1928, A
OLD CORRAL, THE, 1937, A
OLD CORRAL, THE, 1936
OLD COUNTRY, THE, 1921, A
OLD CURIOSITY SHOP, THE, 1913, A
OLD CURIOSITY SHOP, THE, 1921, A
OLD CURIOSITY SHOP, THE, 1935, A
OLD CURIOSITY SHOP, THE, 1975
OLD DAD, 1920
OLD DARK HOUSE, THE, 1932, A
OLD DARK HOUSE, THE, 1963, A
OLD DRACULA, 1975, C
OLD ENGLISH, 1930, A
OLD ENOUGH, 1984, C
OLD FAITHFUL, 1935, A
OLD FASHIONED BOY, AN, 1920, A
OLD FASHIONED YOUNG MAN, AN, 1917
OLD FOLKS AT HOME, THE, 1916, A
OLD FOOL, THE, 1923
OLD FRONTIER, THE, 1950, A
OLD GREATHEART
OLD GROUCHY
OLD HARTWELL'S CUB, 1918
OLD HEIDELBERG, 1915
OLD HOME WEEK, 1925, A
OLD HOMESTEAD, THE, 1916
OLD HOMESTEAD, THE, 1922
OLD HOMESTEAD, THE, 1935, A
OLD HOMESTEAD, THE, 1942, A
OLD HUTCH, 1936, A
OLD IRON, 1938, A
OLD IRONSIDES, 1926, A
OLD LADY 31, 1920
OLD LOS ANGELES, 1948, A
OLD LOUISIANA, 1938, A
OLD LOVES AND NEW, 1926, A
OLD LOVES FOR NEW, 1918
OLD MAC, 1961
OLD MAID'S BABY, THE, 1919, A
OLD MAID, THE, 1939, C
OLD MAN AND THE BOY, THE
OLD MAN AND THE SEA, THE, 1958, A
OLD MAN RHYTHM, 1935, A
OLD MAN, THE, 1932, A
OLD MOTHER RILEY, 1937, A
OLD MOTHER RILEY AT HOME, 1945, A
OLD MOTHER RILEY CATCHES A QUISLING
OLD MOTHER RILEY IN BUSINESS, 1940, A
OLD MOTHER RILEY IN PARIS, 1938
OLD MOTHER RILEY IN SOCIETY, 1940, A
OLD MOTHER RILEY MEETS THE VAMPIRE
OLD MOTHER RILEY MP, 1939, A
OLD MOTHER RILEY OVERSEAS, 1943, A
OLD MOTHER RILEY'S CIRCUS, 1941, A
OLD MOTHER RILEY'S GHOSTS, 1941, A
OLD MOTHER RILEY'S NEW VENTURE
OLD MOTHER RILEY, DETECTIVE, 1943, A
OLD NEST, THE, 1921
OLD OAKEN BUCKET, THE, 1921
OLD OKLAHOMA PLAINS, 1952, A
OLD OVERLAND TRAIL, 1953, A
OLD ROSES, 1935, A
OLD SAN FRANCISCO, 1927, A
OLD SCHOOL TIE, THE
OLD SHATTERHAND, 1968, A
OLD SHOES, 1927, A
OLD SOAK, THE, 1926, A
OLD SOLDIERS NEVER DIE, 1931, A
OLD SPANISH CUSTOM, AN, 1936, A
OLD SPANISH CUSTOMERS, 1932, A
OLD ST. PAUL'S
OLD SUREHAND, 1. TIEL
OLD SWEETHEART OF MINE, AN, 1923
OLD SWIMMIN' HOLE, THE, 1921, A
OLD SWIMMIN' HOLE, THE, 1941, A
OLD TESTAMENT, 1963
OLD TEXAS TRAIL, THE, 1944, A
OLD WEST, THE, 1952, A
OLD WIVES FOR NEW, 1918, C
OLD WIVES' TALE, THE, 1921, A
OLD WOOD CARVER, THE, 1913
OLD WYOMING TRAIL, THE, 1937, A
OLD YELLER, 1957, A
OLD-FASHIONED GIRL, AN, 1948, A
OLD-FASHIONED WAY, THE, 1934, A
OLDEST CONFESSION, THE
OLDEST LAW, THE, 1918, C
OLDEST PROFESSION, THE, 1968, O
OLE REX, 1961
OLGA'S GIRLS, 1964, O
OLIVE TREES OF JUSTICE, THE, 1967, A
OLIVER TWIST, 1912
OLIVER TWIST, 1916, A
OLIVER TWIST, 1922, A
OLIVER TWIST, 1933, A
OLIVER TWIST, 1951, AA
OLIVER TWIST, JR., 1921, A
OLIVER!, 1968, AAA
OLIVER'S STORY, 1978, C
OLLY, OLLY, OXEN FREE, 1978, A
OLSEN'S BIG MOMENT, 1934, A
OLSEN'S NIGHT OUT
OLTRAGGIO AL PUDORE
OLTRE IL BENE E IL MALE
OLYMPIC HERO, THE, 1928, A
OLYMPIC HONEYMOON
OMAHA TRAIL, THE, 1942, A
OMAR KHAYYAM, 1957, A
OMAR THE TENTMAKER, 1922
OMBRE BIANCHE
OMEGA MAN, THE, 1971, C
OMEGANS, THE, 1968
OMEN, THE, 1976, O
OMICRON, 1963, A
OMOO OMOO, THE SHARK GOD, 1949, A
ON A CLEAR DAY YOU CAN SEE FOREVER, 1970, AA
ON AGAIN—OFF AGAIN, 1937, A
ON AN ISLAND WITH YOU, 1948, A
ON ANY STREET
ON APPROVAL, 1930, A
ON APPROVAL, 1944, A
ON BITTER CREEK, 1915
ON BORROWED TIME, 1939, A
ON DANGEROUS GROUND, 1917
ON DANGEROUS GROUND, 1951, C
ON DANGEROUS PATHS, 1915
ON DRESS PARADE
ON FRIDAY AT ELEVEN
ON GOLDEN POND, 1981, A-C
ON GUARD
ON HER BED OF ROSES, 1966, C
ON HER HONOR, 1922
ON HER MAJESTY'S SECRET SERVICE, 1969, C
ON HER WEDDING NIGHT, 1915, A
ON HIS MAJESTY'S SECRET SERVICE
ON HIS OWN, 1939, A
ON LEAVE, 1918, A
ON MOONLIGHT BAY, 1951, AAA
ON MY WAY TO THE CRUSADES, I MET A GIRL WHO...
ON NE BADINE PAS AVEC L'AMOUR, 1924
ON OUR LITTLE PLACE
ON OUR MERRY WAY, 1948, A
ON OUR SELECTION, 1930, A
ON PROBATION
ON PROBATION, 1924, A
ON PROBATION, 1935, A
ON RECORD, 1917, A
ON SECRET SERVICE, 1933
ON SECRET SERVICE, 1936
ON SPECIAL DUTY
ON STAGE EVERYBODY, 1945, A
ON SUCH A NIGHT, 1937, A
ON THE AIR, 1934, A
ON THE AIR LIVE WITH CAPTAIN MIDNIGHT, 1979
ON THE AVENUE, 1937
ON THE BANKS OF ALLAN WATER, 1916, A
ON THE BANKS OF THE WABASH, 1923, A
ON THE BEACH, 1959, O
ON THE BEAT, 1962, A
ON THE BREAD LINE, 1915
ON THE BRINK
ON THE BUSES, 1972, C
ON THE CARPET
ON THE COMET, 1970, A
ON THE DIVIDE, 1928, A
ON THE DOTTED LINE
ON THE DOUBLE, 1961, A
ON THE FIDDLE
ON THE GO, 1925, A
ON THE GREAT WHITE TRAIL, 1938, A
ON THE HIGH CARD, 1921
ON THE HIGH SEAS, 1922, A
ON THE ISLE OF SAMOA, 1950, A
ON THE JUMP, 1918
ON THE LAM, 1972
ON THE LEVEL, 1917
ON THE LEVEL, 1930, A
ON THE LINE, 1984, O
ON THE LOOSE, 1951, A
ON THE MAKE
ON THE NICKEL, 1980, O
ON THE NIGHT OF THE FIRE
ON THE NIGHT STAGE, 1915
ON THE OLD SPANISH TRAIL, 1947, A
ON THE QUIET, 1918, A
ON THE RIGHT TRACK, 1981, C
ON THE RIVERA, 1951, A
ON THE ROAD AGAIN
ON THE RUN, 1958, A
ON THE RUN, 1967, A
ON THE RUN, 1969, A
ON THE RUN, 1983, C
ON THE SHELF
ON THE SPANISH MAIN, 1917
ON THE SPOT, 1940, A
ON THE STEPS OF THE ALTAR, 1916
ON THE STEPS OF THE THRONE, 1913
ON THE STROKE OF NINE
ON THE STROKE OF THREE, 1924, A
ON THE STROKE OF TWELVE, 1927
ON THE SUNNY SIDE, 1942, AA
ON THE SUNNYSIDE, 1936, A
ON THE THRESHOLD, 1925
ON THE THRESHOLD OF SPACE, 1956, A
ON THE TOWN, 1949, A
ON THE WARSAW HIGHROAD, 1916
ON THE WATERFRONT, 1954, O
ON THE YARD, 1978, O
ON THEIR OWN, 1940, A
ON THIN ICE, 1925, A
ON THIN ICE, 1933
ON TIME, 1924, A
ON TO RENO, 1928, A
ON TOP OF OLD SMOKY, 1953, A
ON TOP OF THE WORLD
ON TRIAL, 1917, A
ON TRIAL, 1928, A
ON TRIAL, 1939, A
ON VELVET, 1938
ON WINGS OF SONG
ON WITH THE DANCE, 1920, A
ON WITH THE SHOW, 1929, A
ON YOUR BACK, 1930, A
ON YOUR TOES, 1927
ON YOUR TOES, 1939, A
ON ZE BOULEVARD, 1927, A
ON-THE-SQUARE GIRL, THE, 1917
ONCE, 1974, C
ONCE A CROOK, 1941, A
ONCE A DOCTOR, 1937, A
ONCE A GENTLEMAN, 1930, A
ONCE A JOLLY SWAGMAN
ONCE A LADY, 1931, A
ONCE A PLUMBER, 1920, A
ONCE A RAINY DAY, 1968, A
ONCE A SINNER, 1931, A
ONCE A SINNER, 1952, A
ONCE A THIEF, 1935, A
ONCE A THIEF, 1950, A
ONCE A THIEF, 1965, C
ONCE A THIEF, 1961
ONCE ABOARD THE LUGGER, 1920, A
ONCE AND FOREVER, 1927
ONCE BEFORE I DIE, 1967, C
ONCE IN A BLUE MOON, 1936, A
ONCE IN A LIFETIME, 1925
ONCE IN A LIFETIME, 1932, A
ONCE IN A MILLION
ONCE IN A NEW MOON, 1935, A
ONCE IN PARIS, 1978, C
ONCE IS NOT ENOUGH, 1975, O
ONCE MORE, MY DARLING, 1949, A
ONCE MORE, WITH FEELING, 1960, A-C
ONCE THERE WAS A GIRL, 1945, C
ONCE TO EVERY BACHELOR, 1934, A
ONCE TO EVERY WOMAN, 1920
ONCE TO EVERY WOMAN, 1934, A
ONCE UPON A COFFEE HOUSE, 1965, A
ONCE UPON A DREAM, 1949, A
ONCE UPON A HONEYMOON, 1942, A
ONCE UPON A HORSE, 1958, A
ONCE UPON A SCOUNDREL, 1973, A
ONCE UPON A SUMMER
ONCE UPON A THURSDAY
ONCE UPON A TIME
ONCE UPON A TIME, 1918, A
ONCE UPON A TIME, 1922, A
ONCE UPON A TIME, 1922
ONCE UPON A TIME, 1944, A
ONCE UPON A TIME IN AMERICA, 1984, O
ONCE UPON A TIME IN THE WEST, 1969
ONCE YOU KISS A STRANGER, 1969, O
ONDATA DI CALORE
100 MEN AND A GIRL, 1937, AAA
100 RIFLES, 1969, O
1001 ARABIAN NIGHTS, 1959, AA
1 2 3 MONSTER EXPRESS, 1977, C
$100 A NIGHT, 1968, C

ONE A MINUTE, 1921, A
ONE AGAINST MANY, 1919
ONE AGAINST SEVEN
ONE AND ONLY GENUINE ORIGINAL FAMILY BAND, THE, 1968, AA
ONE AND ONLY, THE, 1978, C
ONE APRIL 2000, 1952, A
ONE ARABIAN NIGHT, 1921, A
ONE ARABIAN NIGHT, 1923
ONE ARMED EXECUTIONER, 1980
ONE AWAY, 1980
ONE BIG AFFAIR, 1952, A
ONE BODY TOO MANY, 1944, A
ONE BORN EVERY MINUTE
ONE BRIEF SUMMER, 1971
ONE CHANCE IN A MILLION, 1927, A
ONE CHANCE TO WIN, 1976
ONE CLEAR CALL, 1922, A
ONE COLUMBO NIGHT, 1926, A
ONE CROWDED NIGHT, 1940, A
ONE DANGEROUS NIGHT, 1943, A
ONE DARK NIGHT, 1939, A
ONE DARK NIGHT, 1983, C
ONE DAY, 1916, A
ONE DAY IN THE LIFE OF IVAN DENISOVICH, 1971, A
ONE DEADLY SUMMER, 1984, O
ONE DESIRE, 1955, AA
ONE DOWN TWO TO GO, 1982, O
ONE EIGHTH APACHE, 1922
ONE EMBARRASSING NIGHT, 1930, A
ONE EXCITING ADVENTURE, 1935, A
ONE EXCITING NIGHT, 1922, A
ONE EXCITING NIGHT, 1945, A
ONE EXCITING NIGHT, 1946
ONE EXCITING WEEK, 1946, A
ONE FAMILY, 1930
ONE FATAL HOUR
ONE FLEW OVER THE CUCKOO'S NEST, 1975, O
ONE FOOT IN HEAVEN, 1941, AA
ONE FOOT IN HELL, 1960, A
ONE FOR ALL
ONE FOR THE BOOKS
ONE FRIGHTENED NIGHT, 1935, A
ONE FROM THE HEART, 1982, O
ONE GIRL'S CONFESSION, 1953, C
ONE GLORIOUS DAY, 1922
ONE GLORIOUS NIGHT, 1924
ONE GLORIOUS SCRAP, 1927, A
ONE GOOD TURN, 1936, A
ONE GOOD TURN, 1955, A
ONE HEAVENLY NIGHT, 1931, A
ONE HORSE TOWN
ONE HOUR, 1917
ONE HOUR BEFORE DAWN, 1920
ONE HOUR LATE, 1935, A
ONE HOUR OF LOVE, 1927, A
ONE HOUR PAST MIDNIGHT, 1924
ONE HOUR TO DOOM'S DAY
ONE HOUR TO LIVE, 1939
ONE HOUR WITH YOU, 1932, A-C
ONE HUNDRED AND ONE DALMATIANS, 1961, AAA
$100 A NIGHT, 1968, C
100 MEN AND A GIRL, 1937, AAA
ONE HUNDRED PERCENT PURE
100 RIFLES, 1969, O
125 ROOMS OF COMFORT, 1974, O
ONE HYSTERICAL NIGHT, 1930, A
ONE IN A MILLION, 1935, A
ONE IN A MILLION, 1936, AA
ONE INCREASING PURPOSE, 1927
ONE IS A LONELY NUMBER, 1972, C
ONE IS GUILTY, 1934
ONE JUMP AHEAD, 1955, A
ONE JUST MAN, 1955, A
ONE LAST FLING, 1949, A
ONE LAST RIDE, 1980
ONE LAW FOR BOTH, 1917, A
ONE LAW FOR THE WOMAN, 1924, A
ONE LIFE
ONE LITTLE INDIAN, 1973, AA
ONE MAD KISS, 1930, A
ONE MAN, 1979, C
ONE MAN AGAINST THE ORGANIZATION, 1977
ONE MAN DOG, THE, 1929, A
ONE MAN GAME, A, 1927
ONE MAN IN A MILLION, 1921
ONE MAN JURY, 1978, O
ONE MAN JUSTICE, 1937, A
ONE MAN TRAIL, 1926
ONE MAN'S JOURNEY, 1933, A
ONE MAN'S LAW, 1940, A
ONE MAN'S WAY, 1964, A
ONE MILE FROM HEAVEN, 1937, A
ONE MILLION B.C., 1940, A-C
ONE MILLION DOLLARS, 1915, A
ONE MILLION DOLLARS, 1965, A
$1,000,000 DUCK, 1971, AA
$1,000,000 RACKET, 1937, A
ONE MILLION IN JEWELS, 1923, A
ONE MILLION YEARS B.C., 1967, A
ONE MINUTE TO PLAY, 1926, A
ONE MINUTE TO ZERO, 1952, A
ONE MOMENT'S TEMPTATION, 1922
ONE MORE AMERICAN, 1918, A
ONE MORE RIVER, 1934, A
ONE MORE SPRING, 1935, A
ONE MORE TIME, 1970, A
ONE MORE TOMORROW, 1946, A
ONE MORE TRAIN TO ROB, 1971, A
ONE MYSTERIOUS NIGHT, 1944, A
ONE NEW YORK NIGHT, 1935, A
ONE NIGHT AT SUSIE'S, 1930, A
ONE NIGHT IN LISBON, 1941, A
ONE NIGHT IN PARIS, 1940, A
ONE NIGHT IN ROME, 1924
ONE NIGHT IN THE TROPICS, 1940, A
ONE NIGHT OF LOVE, 1934, A
ONE NIGHT STAND, 1976, O
ONE NIGHT WITH YOU, 1948, A
ONE NIGHT...A TRAIN, 1968, C
ONE OF MANY, 1917, C
ONE OF MILLIONS, 1914
ONE OF OUR AIRCRAFT IS MISSING, 1942, A
ONE OF OUR DINOSAURS IS MISSING, 1975, AA
ONE OF OUR GIRLS, 1914, A
ONE OF OUR SPIES IS MISSING, 1966, A
ONE OF THE BEST, 1927, A
ONE OF THE BRAVEST, 1925, A
ONE OF THE FINEST, 1919
ONE OF THE MANY
ONE OF THOSE THINGS, 1974
ONE ON ONE, 1977, A
ONE PAGE OF LOVE, 1979
ONE PLUS ONE, 1961, C-O
ONE PLUS ONE, 1969, O
ONE POTATO, TWO POTATO, 1964, C
ONE PRECIOUS YEAR, 1933, A
ONE PUNCH O'DAY, 1926, A
ONE RAINY AFTERNOON, 1936, A
ONE ROMANTIC NIGHT, 1930, A
ONE RUSSIAN SUMMER, 1973
ONE SHOT RANGER, 1925
ONE SHOT ROSS, 1917, A
ONE SINGS, THE OTHER DOESN'T, 1977, C-O
ONE SPLENDID HOUR, 1929, A
ONE SPY TOO MANY, 1966, A
ONE STEP TO HELL, 1969, C
ONE STOLEN NIGHT, 1923, A
ONE STOLEN NIGHT, 1929, A
ONE SUMMER LOVE, 1976, C
ONE SUMMER'S DAY, 1917, A
ONE SUNDAY AFTERNOON, 1933, A
ONE SUNDAY AFTERNOON, 1948, A
ONE THAT GOT AWAY, THE, 1958, A
ONE THIRD OF A NATION, 1939, A
1,000 CONVICTS AND A WOMAN, 1971, O
$1,000 A MINUTE, 1935, A
$1,000 A TOUCHDOWN, 1939, A
1,000 PLANE RAID, 1969, A
1,000 SHAPES OF A FEMALE, 1963, A
1001 ARABIAN NIGHTS, 1959, AA
ONE THOUSAND DOLLARS, 1918
ONE THRILLING NIGHT, 1942, A
ONE TOO MANY, 1950, A
ONE TOUCH OF NATURE, 1917
ONE TOUCH OF SIN, 1917
ONE TOUCH OF VENUS, 1948, A
ONE, TWO, THREE, 1961, A
123 MONSTER EXPRESS, 1977, C
ONE WAY OUT
ONE WAY OUT, 1955, A
ONE WAY PASSAGE, 1932, A
ONE WAY PENDULUM, 1965, A
ONE WAY STREET, 1925
ONE WAY STREET, 1950, A
ONE WAY TICKET TO HELL, 1955
ONE WAY TO LOVE, 1946, A
ONE WAY TRAIL, THE, 1931, A
ONE WAY WAHINI, 1965, C-O
ONE WEEK OF LIFE, 1919
ONE WEEK OF LOVE, 1922, A
ONE WILD NIGHT, 1938, A
ONE WILD OAT, 1951, A
ONE WILD WEEK, 1921, A
ONE WISH TOO MANY, 1956, A
ONE WITH THE FUZZ, THE
ONE WOMAN IDEA, THE, 1929
ONE WOMAN TO ANOTHER, 1927, A
ONE WOMAN'S STORY, 1949, A
ONE WOMAN, THE, 1918
ONE WONDERFUL NIGHT, 1914
ONE WONDERFUL NIGHT, 1922
ONE YEAR LATER, 1933, A
ONE YEAR TO LIVE, 1925, A
ONE-EYED JACKS, 1961, O
ONE-EYED SOLDIERS, 1967, C
ONE-MAN LAW, 1932
ONE-MAN MUTINY
ONE-MAN TRAIL, THE, 1921
ONE-PIECE BATHING SUIT, THE
ONE-ROUND HOGAN, 1927, A
ONE-THING-AT-A-TIME O'DAY, 1919
ONE-TRICK PONY, 1980, O
ONE-WAY TICKET, 1935, A
ONE-WAY TRAIL, THE, 1920
ONEICHAN MAKARI TORU
ONI NO SUMU YAKATA
ONI SHLI NA VOSTOK
ONIBABA, 1965, C
ONIMASA, 1983, O
ONION FIELD, THE, 1979, C-O
ONIONHEAD, 1958, A
ONKEL TOMS HUTTE
ONLY 38, 1923, A
ONLY A MILL GIRL, 1919, A
ONLY A SHOP GIRL, 1922, A
ONLY A WOMAN, 1966, A
ONLY ANGELS HAVE WINGS, 1939, A
ONLY EIGHT HOURS
ONLY GAME IN TOWN, THE, 1970, C
ONLY GIRL, THE
ONLY GOD KNOWS, 1974, A
ONLY MAN, THE, 1915
ONLY ONCE IN A LIFETIME, 1979, C
ONLY ONE NIGHT, 1942, C
ONLY ROAD, THE, 1918
ONLY SAPS WORK, 1930, A
ONLY SON, THE, 1914, A
ONLY THE BEST
ONLY THE BRAVE, 1930, A
ONLY THE FRENCH CAN
ONLY THE VALIANT, 1951, A
ONLY THING YOU KNOW, THE, 1971, C
ONLY THING, THE, 1925
ONLY TWO CAN PLAY, 1962, C
ONLY WAY HOME, THE, 1972, C
ONLY WAY OUT IS DEAD, THE, 1970
ONLY WAY OUT, THE, 1915
ONLY WAY, THE, 1926, A
ONLY WAY, THE, 1970, A
ONLY WHEN I LARF, 1968, A
ONLY WHEN I LAUGH, 1981, C
ONLY WOMAN, THE, 1924, A
ONLY YESTERDAY, 1933, C
ONNA GA KAIDAN O AGARUTOKI
ONNA GOROSHI ABURA JIGOKU
ONNA NO MIZUUMI
ONNA NO NAKANI IRU TANIN
ONNA NO REKISHI
ONNA NO UZU TO FUCHI TO NAGARE
ONNA NO ZA
ONNA UKIYOBURO
ONSEN GERIRA DAI SHOGEKI
ONWARD CHRISTIAN SOLDIERS, 1918, A
OOH, YOU ARE AWFUL
OPEN ALL NIGHT, 1924, A
OPEN ALL NIGHT, 1934, O
OPEN COUNTRY, 1922, C
OPEN DOOR, THE, 1919
OPEN PLACES, 1917
OPEN RANGE, 1927
OPEN ROAD, THE, 1940, A
OPEN SEASON, 1974, O
OPEN SECRET, 1948, A
OPEN SWITCH, THE, 1926
OPEN THE DOOR AND SEE ALL THE PEOPLE, 1964, A
OPEN TRAIL, THE
OPEN YOUR EYES, 1919, C
OPENED BY MISTAKE, 1940, A
OPENED SHUTTERS, 1921
OPENED SHUTTERS, THE, 1914, A
OPENING NIGHT, 1977, C
OPENING NIGHT, THE, 1927
OPERACION GOLDMAN
OPERACION LOTO AZUL
OPERATION AMSTERDAM, 1960, A
OPERATION BIKINI, 1963, A
OPERATION BLUE BOOK
OPERATION BOTTLENECK, 1961, A
OPERATION BULLSHINE, 1963, A
OPERATION CAMEL, 1961, A
OPERATION CIA, 1965, A
OPERATION CONSPIRACY, 1957, A
OPERATION CROSS EAGLES, 1969, A
OPERATION CROSSBOW, 1965, A
OPERATION CUPID, 1960, A
OPERATION DAMES, 1959, C
OPERATION DAYBREAK, 1976, A
OPERATION DELILAH, 1966, A
OPERATION DIAMOND, 1948, A
OPERATION DIPLOMAT, 1953, A
OPERATION DISASTER, 1951, A
OPERATION EICHMANN, 1961, A
OPERATION ENEMY FORT, 1964
OPERATION GANYMED, 1977

OPERATION HAYLIFT, 1950, A
OPERATION KID BROTHER, 1967, A
OPERATION LOTUS BLEU
OPERATION LOVEBIRDS, 1968, A
OPERATION M
OPERATION MAD BALL, 1957, A
OPERATION MANHUNT, 1954, A
OPERATION MASQUERADE
OPERATION MERMAID
OPERATION MURDER, 1957, A
OPERATION PACIFIC, 1951, A
OPERATION PETTICOAT, 1959, A
OPERATION SAN GENNARO
OPERATION SECRET, 1952, A
OPERATION SNAFU, 1965, A
OPERATION SNAFU, 1970
OPERATION SNATCH, 1962, A
OPERATION ST. PETER'S, 1968, A
OPERATION STOGIE, 1960
OPERATION THIRD FORM, 1966, AA
OPERATION THUNDERBOLT, 1978, C
OPERATION UNDER COVER
OPERATION WAR HEAD
OPERATION X, 1951, A-C
OPERATION X, 1963, C
OPERATOR 13, 1934, A
OPERAZIA GOLDMAN
OPERAZIONE CROSSBOW
OPERAZIONE PARADISO
OPERAZIONE PAURA
OPERETTA, 1949, A
OPHELIA, 1964, C
OPIATE '67, 1967, C
OPPORTUNITY, 1918
OPPOSITE SEX, THE, 1956, A
OPTIMIST, THE
OPTIMISTIC TRAGEDY, THE, 1964, A
OPTIMISTS OF NINE ELMS, THE
OPTIMISTS, THE, 1973, A
OR POUR LES CESARS
ORA PRO NOBIS, 1917, A
ORACLE, THE
ORAZIO E COURIAZI
ORBITA MORTAL
ORCA, 1977, C
ORCHESTRA WIVES, 1942, A
ORCHIDS AND ERMINE, 1927
ORCHIDS TO YOU, 1935, A
ORDEAL BY INNOCENCE, 1984, C
ORDEAL OF ELIZABETH, THE, 1916
ORDEAL OF ROSETTA, THE, 1918
ORDEAL, THE, 1914, C
ORDEAL, THE, 1922, C
ORDER OF DEATH
ORDER TO KILL, 1974
ORDERED TO LOVE, 1963, O
ORDERS ARE ORDERS, 1959, A
ORDERS IS ORDERS, 1934, A
ORDERS TO KILL, 1958, A
ORDERS, THE, 1977, C-O
ORDET, 1957, A-C
ORDINARY PEOPLE, 1980, O
OREGON PASSAGE, 1958, A
OREGON TRAIL, 1945, A
OREGON TRAIL SCOUTS, 1947, A
OREGON TRAIL, THE, 1936, A
OREGON TRAIL, THE, 1959, A
ORFEU NEGRO
ORGANIZATION, THE, 1971, C
ORGANIZER, THE, 1964, A
ORGY OF BLOOD
ORGY OF THE DEAD, 1965, O
ORGY OF THE GOLDEN NUDES
ORIENT EXPRESS, 1934, A
ORIENT EXPRESS, 1952
ORIENTAL DREAM
ORIGINAL OLD MOTHER RILEY, THE
ORLAK, THE HELL OF FRANKENSTEIN, 1960, C-O
ORPHAN OF THE PECOS, 1938, A
ORPHAN OF THE RING
ORPHAN OF THE SAGE, 1928, A
ORPHAN OF THE WILDERNESS, 1937, A
ORPHAN SALLY, 1922
ORPHAN, THE, 1920
ORPHAN, THE, 1979
ORPHANS OF THE GHETTO, 1922
ORPHANS OF THE NORTH, 1940
ORPHANS OF THE STORM, 1922, A
ORPHANS OF THE STREET, 1939, AAA
ORPHEE
ORPHEUS, 1950, A
OSAKA MONOGATARI
OSCAR WILDE, 1960, C
OSCAR, THE, 1966, A
OSETROVNA
OSS 117—MISSION FOR A KILLER, 1966, C
OSSESSIONE, 1959, C
OSTATNI ETAP
OSTERMAN WEEKEND, THE, 1983, C-O
OSTRE SLEDOVANE VLAKY
OTCHI TCHORNIA
OTCHIY DOM
OTEL U POGIBSHCHEGO ALPINISTA
OTETS SOLDATA
OTHELLO, 1914
OTHELLO, 1922
OTHELLO, 1955, C
OTHELLO, 1960, A
OTHELLO, 1965, A
OTHER GIRL, THE, 1916
OTHER HALF, THE, 1919
OTHER KIND OF LOVE, THE, 1924, A
OTHER LOVE, THE, 1947, A
OTHER MAN'S WIFE, THE, 1919, A
OTHER MAN, THE, 1918, A
OTHER MEN'S DAUGHTERS, 1918, A
OTHER MEN'S DAUGHTERS, 1923
OTHER MEN'S SHOES, 1920
OTHER MEN'S WIVES, 1919
OTHER MEN'S WOMEN, 1931, A-C
OTHER ONE, THE, 1967, C
OTHER PEOPLE'S BUSINESS
OTHER PEOPLE'S MONEY, 1916
OTHER PEOPLE'S SINS, 1931, A
OTHER PERSON, THE, 1921, A
OTHER SELF, THE, 1918
OTHER SIDE OF BONNIE AND CLYDE, THE, 1968
OTHER SIDE OF MIDNIGHT, THE, 1977, O
OTHER SIDE OF PARADISE, THE
OTHER SIDE OF THE DOOR, THE, 1916
OTHER SIDE OF THE MOUNTAIN, THE, 1975
OTHER SIDE OF THE MOUNTAIN—PART 2, THE, 1978, A
OTHER SIDE OF THE UNDERNEATH, THE, 1972, O
OTHER SIDE, THE, 1922
OTHER TOMORROW, THE, 1930, A
OTHER WOMAN'S STORY, THE, 1925
OTHER WOMAN, THE, 1918
OTHER WOMAN, THE, 1921
OTHER WOMAN, THE, 1931, A
OTHER WOMAN, THE, 1954, C-O
OTHER WOMEN'S CLOTHES, 1922
OTHER WOMEN'S HUSBANDS, 1926
OTHER, THE, 1912
OTHER, THE, 1972, O
OTKLONENIE
OTLEY, 1969, C
OTOKO TAI OTOKO
OTROKI VO VSELENNOI
OTTO E MEZZO
OUANGA, 1936, A
OUR BETTER SELVES, 1919
OUR BETTERS, 1933, C
OUR BLUSHING BRIDES, 1930, A
OUR DAILY BREAD, 1934, A
OUR DAILY BREAD, 1950, O
OUR DANCING DAUGHTERS, 1928, A
OUR FIGHTING NAVY
OUR GIRL FRIDAY
OUR HEARTS WERE GROWING UP, 1946, A
OUR HEARTS WERE YOUNG AND GAY, 1944, A
OUR HITLER, A FILM FROM GERMANY, 1980, O
OUR HOSPITALITY, 1923, A
OUR LADY OF FATIMA
OUR LEADING CITIZEN, 1922, A
OUR LEADING CITIZEN, 1939, A
OUR LITTLE GIRL, 1935, AAA
OUR LITTLE WIFE, 1918, A
OUR MAN IN HAVANA, 1960, A
OUR MAN IN JAMAICA, 1965
OUR MAN IN MARRAKESH, 1966
OUR MAN IN MARRAKESH, 1967
OUR MAN IN THE CARIBBEAN, 1962
OUR MEN IN BAGHDAD, 1967
OUR MISS BROOKS, 1956, AA
OUR MISS FRED, 1972, C
OUR MODERN MAIDENS, 1929, A
OUR MODERN MAIDENS, 1929, A
OUR MOTHER'S HOUSE, 1967, O
OUR MRS. McCHESNEY, 1918, A
OUR MUTUAL FRIEND, 1921
OUR NEIGHBORS—THE CARTERS, 1939, AAA
OUR RELATIONS, 1936, AA
OUR SILENT LOVE, 1969, A
OUR TIME, 1974, A
OUR TOWN, 1940, A
OUR VERY OWN, 1950, A
OUR VINES HAVE TENDER GRAPES, 1945, A
OUR WIFE, 1941, A
OUR WINNING SEASON, 1978, C
OURSELVES ALONE
OUT, 1982, C-O
OUT ALL NIGHT, 1927, A
OUT ALL NIGHT, 1933, A
OUT CALIFORNIA WAY, 1946, A
OUT OF A CLEAR SKY, 1918, A
OUT OF IT, 1969, A
OUT OF LUCK, 1919, A
OUT OF LUCK, 1923, A
OUT OF SEASON, 1975, C-O
OUT OF SIGHT, 1966, A
OUT OF SINGAPORE, 1932, C
OUT OF THE BLUE, 1931, A
OUT OF THE BLUE, 1947, A
OUT OF THE BLUE, 1982, O
OUT OF THE CHORUS, 1921
OUT OF THE CLOUDS, 1921
OUT OF THE CLOUDS, 1957, A
OUT OF THE DARKNESS, 1958
OUT OF THE DARKNESS, 1979
OUT OF THE DEPTHS, 1921
OUT OF THE DEPTHS, 1946, A
OUT OF THE DRIFTS, 1916, A
OUT OF THE DUST, 1920, C
OUT OF THE FOG, 1919
OUT OF THE FOG, 1941, C
OUT OF THE FOG, 1962
OUT OF THE FRYING PAN
OUT OF THE NIGHT
OUT OF THE NIGHT, 1918
OUT OF THE PAST, 1927, C
OUT OF THE PAST, 1933
OUT OF THE PAST, 1947, C
OUT OF THE RUINS, 1915
OUT OF THE RUINS, 1928
OUT OF THE SHADOW
OUT OF THE SHADOW, 1919, A
OUT OF THE SHADOWS, 1920
OUT OF THE SILENT NORTH, 1922, A
OUT OF THE STORM, 1920, A
OUT OF THE STORM, 1926
OUT OF THE STORM, 1948, A
OUT OF THE TIGER'S MOUTH, 1962, A
OUT OF THE WEST, 1926, A
OUT OF THE WRECK, 1917
OUT OF THIN AIR, 1969
OUT OF THIS WORLD, 1945, A
OUT OF TOWNERS, THE, 1970, A
OUT OF TOWNERS, THE, 1964
OUT TO WIN, 1923, A
OUT WEST WITH THE HARDYS, 1938, AAA
OUT WEST WITH THE PEPPERS, 1940, AAA
OUT WITH THE TIDE, 1928, A
OUT YONDER, 1920, A
OUTBACK, 1971, O
OUTBREAK OF HOSTILITIES, 1979
OUTCAST, 1917
OUTCAST, 1922
OUTCAST, 1928, C
OUTCAST, 1937, A
OUTCAST LADY, 1934, A
OUTCAST OF BLACK MESA, 1950, A
OUTCAST OF THE ISLANDS, 1952, A
OUTCAST SOULS, 1928
OUTCAST, THE, 1915
OUTCAST, THE, 1934, A
OUTCAST, THE, 1954, A
OUTCAST, THE, 1951
OUTCASTS OF POKER FLAT, THE, 1919, A
OUTCASTS OF POKER FLAT, THE, 1937, A
OUTCASTS OF POKER FLAT, THE, 1952, A
OUTCASTS OF THE CITY, 1958, A
OUTCASTS OF THE TRAIL, 1949, A
OUTCRY, 1949, C-O
OUTCRY, THE
OUTER GATE, THE, 1937, A
OUTFIT, THE, 1973, C-O
OUTLAND, 1981, O
OUTLAW AND HIS WIFE, THE, 1918
OUTLAW AND THE LADY, THE
OUTLAW BLUES, 1977, A
OUTLAW BRAND, 1948, A
OUTLAW COUNTRY, 1949, A
OUTLAW DEPUTY, THE, 1935, A
OUTLAW DOG, THE, 1927, A
OUTLAW EXPRESS, 1938, A
OUTLAW EXPRESS, THE, 1926
OUTLAW GOLD, 1950, A
OUTLAW JOSEY WALES, THE, 1976, O
OUTLAW JUSTICE, 1933, A
OUTLAW MOTORCYCLES, 1967
OUTLAW OF THE PLAINS, 1946, A
OUTLAW QUEEN, 1957
OUTLAW REFORMS, THE, 1914, A
OUTLAW RIDERS, 1971
OUTLAW ROUNDUP, 1944
OUTLAW RULE, 1935
OUTLAW STALLION, THE, 1954, A
OUTLAW TAMER, THE, 1934
OUTLAW TERRITORY
OUTLAW TRAIL, 1944, A
OUTLAW TREASURE, 1955, A
OUTLAW WOMEN, 1952, A
OUTLAW'S DAUGHTER, THE, 1925, A
OUTLAW'S DAUGHTER, THE, 1954, A
OUTLAW'S PARADISE, 1927
OUTLAW'S PARADISE, 1939, A

OUTLAW'S SON, 1954
OUTLAW'S SON, 1957, A
OUTLAW, THE, 1943, O
OUTLAW: THE SAGE OF GISLI, 1982, C
OUTLAWED, 1921
OUTLAWED, 1929, A
OUTLAWED GUNS, 1935, A
OUTLAWS IS COMING, THE, 1965, A
OUTLAWS OF BOULDER PASS, 1942
OUTLAWS OF PINE RIDGE, 1942, A
OUTLAWS OF RED RIVER, 1927, A
OUTLAWS OF SANTA FE, 1944, A
OUTLAWS OF SONORA, 1938, A
OUTLAWS OF STAMPEDE PASS, 1943, A
OUTLAWS OF TEXAS, 1950, A
OUTLAWS OF THE CHEROKEE TRAIL, 1941, A
OUTLAWS OF THE DESERT, 1941, A
OUTLAWS OF THE ORIENT, 1937, A
OUTLAWS OF THE PANHANDLE, 1941, A
OUTLAWS OF THE PRAIRIE, 1938, A
OUTLAWS OF THE RANGE, 1936
OUTLAWS OF THE RIO GRANDE, 1941, A
OUTLAWS OF THE ROCKIES, 1945, A
OUTLAWS OF THE SEA, 1923, A
OUTLAWS OF THE WEST
OUTLAWS' HIGHWAY, 1934
OUTPOST IN MALAYA, 1952, A
OUTPOST IN MOROCCO, 1949, A
OUTPOST OF HELL, 1966, A
OUTPOST OF THE MOUNTIES, 1939, A
OUTRAGE, 1950, C
OUTRAGE, THE, 1964, C
OUTRAGEOUS!, 1977, O
OUTRIDERS, THE, 1950, A
OUTRIDERS, THE, 1950
OUTSIDE CHANCE, 1978
OUTSIDE IN, 1972
OUTSIDE MAN, THE, 1973, C
OUTSIDE OF PARADISE, 1938, A
OUTSIDE THE 3-MILE LIMIT, 1940, A
OUTSIDE THE LAW
OUTSIDE THE LAW, 1921, A
OUTSIDE THE LAW, 1930, A
OUTSIDE THE LAW, 1938
OUTSIDE THE LAW, 1956, A
OUTSIDE THE WALL, 1950, A
OUTSIDE THESE WALLS, 1939, A
OUTSIDE WOMAN, THE, 1921, A
OUTSIDER IN AMSTERDAM, 1983, O
OUTSIDER, THE, 1917
OUTSIDER, THE, 1926, A
OUTSIDER, THE, 1933, A
OUTSIDER, THE, 1940, A
OUTSIDER, THE, 1949, A
OUTSIDER, THE, 1962, A-C
OUTSIDER, THE, 1980, O
OUTSIDERS, THE, 1983, C
OUTSIDERS, THE, 1964, Fr.
OUTWARD BOUND, 1930, C
OUTWITTED, 1917, A
OUTWITTED, 1925, A
OVAL DIAMOND, THE, 1916, A
OVER 21, 1945, C
OVER MY DEAD BODY, 1942, A
OVER NIAGRA FALLS, 1914
OVER NIGHT, 1915
OVER SHE GOES, 1937, A
OVER THE BORDER, 1922, A
OVER THE BORDER, 1950, A
OVER THE BROOKLYN BRIDGE, 1984, O
OVER THE EDGE, 1979, O
OVER THE GARDEN WALL, 1919
OVER THE GARDEN WALL, 1934, A
OVER THE GARDEN WALL, 1950, A
OVER THE GOAL, 1937, A
OVER THE HILL
OVER THE HILL, 1917
OVER THE HILL, 1931, C
OVER THE HILL TO THE POORHOUSE, 1920, A
OVER THE MOON, 1940, A
OVER THE ODDS, 1961, A
OVER THE RIVER, A
OVER THE SANTA FE TRAIL, 1947
OVER THE STICKS, 1929, A
OVER THE TOP, 1918
OVER THE WIRE, 1921
OVER THERE, 1917
OVER-EXPOSED, 1956, C
OVER-UNDER, SIDEWAYS-DOWN, 1977, C
OVERALLS, 1916, A
OVERCOAT, THE
OVERCOAT, THE, 1916
OVERLAND BOUND, 1929, A
OVERLAND EXPRESS, THE, 1938, A
OVERLAND LIMITED, THE, 1925, A
OVERLAND MAIL, 1939, A
OVERLAND MAIL ROBBERY, 1943, A
OVERLAND PACIFIC, 1954, A
OVERLAND RED, 1920, A
OVERLAND RIDERS, 1946, A
OVERLAND STAGE COACH
OVERLAND STAGE RAIDERS, 1938, A
OVERLAND STAGE, THE, 1927
OVERLAND STAGECOACH, 1942
OVERLAND TELEGRAPH, 1951, A
OVERLAND TELEGRAPH, THE, 1929, A
OVERLAND TO DEADWOOD, 1942
OVERLAND TRAILS, 1948
OVERLANDERS, THE, 1946, C
OVERLORD, 1975, O
OVERNIGHT, 1933, C
OVERSEXED, 1974
OVERTURE TO GLORY, 1940, C
OWD BOB
OWD BOB, 1924, C
OWL AND THE PUSSYCAT, THE, 1970, C
OX-BOW INCIDENT, THE, 1943, C-O
OXFORD BLUES, 1984, O
OYSTER PRINCESS, THE, 1919
OZ

-P-

P'TANG, YANG, KIPPERBANG
P.C. JOSSER, 1931, A
P.J., 1968, O
P.O.W., THE, 1973, C
PACE THAT KILLS, THE, 1928
PACE THAT THRILLS, THE, 1925, A
PACE THAT THRILLS, THE, 1952, C
PACIFIC ADVENTURE, 1947, A
PACIFIC BLACKOUT, 1942, A
PACIFIC DESTINY, 1956, A
PACIFIC LINER, 1939, C
PACIFIC RENDEZVOUS, 1942, A
PACK TRAIN, 1953, A
PACK UP YOUR TROUBLES, 1932, AAA
PACK UP YOUR TROUBLES, 1939
PACK UP YOUR TROUBLES, 1940, A
PACK, THE, 1977, O
PACO, 1976
PAD, THE...(AND HOW TO USE IT), 1966, O
PADDY, 1970, O
PADDY O'DAY, 1935, A
PADDY O'HARA, 1917
PADDY, THE NEXT BEST THING, 1923, A
PADDY, THE NEXT BEST THING, 1933, A
PADLOCKED, 1926
PADRE PADRONE, 1977, C
PAGAN GOD, THE, 1919
PAGAN HELLCAT
PAGAN ISLAND, 1961, A
PAGAN LADY, 1931, A
PAGAN LOVE, 1920
PAGAN LOVE SONG, 1950, A
PAGAN PASSIONS, 1924
PAGAN, THE, 1929
PAGE MISS GLORY, 1935, A
PAGE MYSTERY, THE, 1917
PAGE OF MADNESS, A
PAGES OF LIFE, 1922, A
PAGLIACCI
PAGLIACCI, 1923
PAI-SHE CHUAN
PAID, 1930, A
PAID BACK, 1922, A
PAID IN ADVANCE, 1919
PAID IN ERROR, 1938, A
PAID IN FULL, 1914
PAID IN FULL, 1919
PAID IN FULL, 1950, A
PAID TO DANCE, 1937, C
PAID TO KILL, 1954, C
PAID TO LOVE, 1927
PAINT AND POWDER, 1925
PAINT YOUR WAGON, 1969, C
PAINTED ANGEL, THE, 1929, A
PAINTED BOATS
PAINTED DESERT, THE, 1931, A
PAINTED DESERT, THE, 1938, A
PAINTED FACES, 1929, A
PAINTED FLAPPER, THE, 1924, A
PAINTED HILLS, THE, 1951, AAA
PAINTED LADY, THE, 1924
PAINTED LIE, THE, 1917
PAINTED LILY, THE, 1918
PAINTED LIPS, 1918
PAINTED MADONNA, THE, 1917
PAINTED PEOPLE, 1924, A
PAINTED PICTURES, 1930, A
PAINTED PONIES, 1927, A
PAINTED POST, 1928
PAINTED SMILE, THE
PAINTED SOUL, THE, 1915, C
PAINTED TRAIL, 1928
PAINTED TRAIL, THE, 1938, A
PAINTED VEIL, THE, 1934, A
PAINTED WOMAN, 1932, A
PAINTED WORLD, THE, 1919
PAINTING THE CLOUDS WITH SUNSHINE, 1951, A
PAINTING THE TOWN, 1927, A
PAIR OF BRIEFS, A, 1963, A
PAIR OF CUPIDS, A, 1918, A
PAIR OF HELLIONS, A, 1924
PAIR OF SILK STOCKINGS, A, 1918, A
PAIR OF SIXES, A, 1918, A
PAIR OF SPECTACLES, A, 1916
PAISA
PAISAN, 1948, C
PAJAMA GAME, THE, 1957, A
PAJAMA PARTY, 1964, AA
PAJAMA PARTY IN THE HAUNTED HOUSE
PAJAMAS, 1927, A
PAL FROM TEXAS, THE, 1939, A
PAL JOEY, 1957, C
PAL O'MINE, 1924
PALACE AND FORTRESS, 1924
PALACE OF NUDES, 1961, C
PALACE OF PLEASURE, THE, 1926
PALACE OF THE DARKENED WINDOWS, THE, 1920
PALACES, 1927
PALAIS DE DANSE, 1928, A
PALAVER, 1926
PALE ARROW
PALEFACE, THE, 1948, A
PALISER CASE, THE, 1920
PALLARD THE PUNTER, 1919
PALLET ON THE FLOOR, 1984, O
PALM BEACH, 1979, O
PALM BEACH GIRL, THE, 1926
PALM BEACH STORY, THE, 1942, A
PALM SPRINGS, 1936, A
PALM SPRINGS AFFAIR
PALM SPRINGS WEEKEND, 1963, C
PALMY DAYS, 1931, A
PALOMINO, THE, 1950, AAA
PALOOKA, 1934, AA
PALS, 1925
PALS FIRST, 1918
PALS FIRST, 1926
PALS IN BLUE, 1924
PALS IN PARADISE, 1926
PALS IN PERIL, 1927
PALS OF THE GOLDEN WEST, 1952, A
PALS OF THE PECOS, 1941, A
PALS OF THE PRAIRIE, 1929, A
PALS OF THE RANGE, 1935, A
PALS OF THE SADDLE, 1938, A
PALS OF THE SILVER SAGE, 1940, A
PALS OF THE WEST, 1922
PAMELA'S PAST, 1916
PAMPA SALVAJE
PAMPERED YOUTH, 1925
PAN-AMERICANA, 1945, A
PANAMA FLO, 1932, A
PANAMA HATTIE, 1942, A
PANAMA LADY, 1939, A
PANAMA PATROL, 1939, A
PANAMA RED, 1976
PANAMA SAL, 1957, A
PANAMINT'S BAD MAN, 1938, A
PANCHO VILLA, 1975, C
PANCHO VILLA RETURNS, 1950, A
PANDA AND THE MAGIC SERPENT, 1961, A
PANDEMONIUM, 1982, C
PANDORA AND THE FLYING DUTCHMAN, 1951, A-C
PANDORA'S BOX, 1929, C
PANHANDLE, 1948, A
PANIC
PANIC, 1966, A
PANIC BUTTON, 1964, A
PANIC IN NEEDLE PARK, 1971, O
PANIC IN THE CITY, 1968, O
PANIC IN THE PARLOUR, 1957
PANIC IN THE STREETS, 1950, C
PANIC IN YEAR ZERO!, 1962, O
PANIC ON THE AIR
PANIC ON THE TRANS-SIBERIAN TRAIN
PANIQUE, 1947, C
PANTHEA, 1917
PANTHER ISLAND
PANTHER WOMAN, THE, 1919
PANTHER'S CLAW, THE, 1942, A
PANTHER'S MOON
PANTS, 1917
PAPA HULIN, 1916
PAPA SOLTERO, 1939
PAPA'S DELICATE CONDITION, 1963, A
PAPER BULLETS, 1941, A
PAPER CHASE, THE, 1973, A-C
PAPER DOLL'S WHISPER OF SPRING, A, 1926
PAPER GALLOWS, 1950, A
PAPER LION, 1968, A
PAPER MOON, 1973, C
PAPER ORCHID, 1949, C
PAPER PEOPLE, THE, 1969
PAPER TIGER, 1975, A-C
PAPERBACK HERO, 1973, O

PAPILLON, 1920
PAPILLON, 1973, O
PAR DESSUS LE MUR, 1923
PAR LE FER ET PAR LE FEU
PAR OU T'ES RENTRE? ON T'A PAS VUE SORTIR, 1984, A
PARACHUTE BATTALION, 1941
PARACHUTE JUMPER, 1933, A
PARACHUTE NURSE, 1942, A
PARADE D'AMOUR
PARADE OF THE WEST, 1930, A
PARADES, 1972, O
PARADINE CASE, THE, 1947, A-C
PARADISE, 1926, A
PARADISE, 1928, A
PARADISE, 1982, O
PARADISE ALLEY, 1931, A
PARADISE ALLEY, 1962
PARADISE ALLEY, 1978, O
PARADISE AND PURGATORY, 1912
PARADISE CANYON, 1935, A
PARADISE EXPRESS, 1937, A
PARADISE FOR THREE, 1938, A
PARADISE FOR TWO
PARADISE FOR TWO, 1927
PARADISE GARDEN, 1917, C
PARADISE IN HARLEM, 1939
PARADISE ISLAND, 1930, A
PARADISE ISLE, 1937, A
PARADISE LAGOON
PARADISE POUR TOUS, 1982, C-O
PARADISE ROAD
PARADISE WITHOUT ADAM, 1918
PARADISE, HAWAIIAN STYLE, 1966, A
PARADISIO, 1962
PARADISO DELL'UOMO
PARALLAX VIEW, THE, 1974, O
PARALLELS, 1980, A-C
PARANOIA, 1968
PARANOIA, 1968
PARANOIAC, 1963, O
PARASITE, 1982, O
PARASITE MURDERS, THE
PARASITE, THE, 1925
PARATROOP COMMAND, 1959, A
PARATROOPER, 1954, A
PARBESZED
PARDNERS, 1917
PARDNERS, 1956, A
PARDON MY BRUSH, 1964
PARDON MY FRENCH, 1921
PARDON MY FRENCH, 1951, A
PARDON MY GUN, 1930, A
PARDON MY GUN, 1942, A
PARDON MY NERVE, 1922, A
PARDON MY PAST, 1945, A
PARDON MY RHYTHM, 1944, A
PARDON MY SARONG, 1942, AAA
PARDON MY STRIPES, 1942, A
PARDON MY TRUNK
PARDON OUR NERVE, 1939, A
PARDON US, 1931, AAA
PAREMA, CRERATURE FROM THE STARWORLD, 1922
PARENT TRAP, THE, 1961, AA
PARENTAGE, 1918
PARENTS ON TRIAL, 1939, A
PARIS, 1924
PARIS, 1926
PARIS, 1929, A
PARIS AFTER DARK, 1923
PARIS AFTER DARK, 1943, A
PARIS ASLEEP
PARIS AT MIDNIGHT, 1926
PARIS AU MOIS D'AOUT
PARIS BELONGS TO US, 1962, A-C
PARIS BLUES, 1961, O
PARIS BOUND, 1929, A
PARIS BRULE-T-IL?
PARIS CALLING, 1941, A
PARIS DOES STRANGE THINGS, 1957, A
PARIS EN CINQ JOURS, 1926
PARIS EROTIKA
PARIS EXPRESS, THE, 1953, A
PARIS FOLLIES OF 1956, 1955, A
PARIS GIRLS, 1929
PARIS GREEN, 1920, A
PARIS HOLIDAY, 1958, A
PARIS HONEYMOON, 1939, A
PARIS IN SPRING, 1935, A
PARIS IN THE MONTH OF AUGUST, 1968, A
PARIS INTERLUDE, 1934, A
PARIS IS OURS
PARIS LOVE SONG
PARIS MODEL, 1953, A
PARIS NOUS APPARTIENT
PARIS OOH-LA-LA!, 1963, O
PARIS PICK-UP, 1963, C
PARIS PLANE, 1933, A
PARIS PLAYBOYS, 1954, A
PARIS QUI DORT, 1924
PARIS UNDERGROUND, 1945, A
PARIS VU PAR
PARIS WAS MADE FOR LOVERS
PARIS, TEXAS, 1984, C-O
PARISH PRIEST, THE, 1921
PARISIAN COBBLER, 1928
PARISIAN LOVE, 1925
PARISIAN NIGHTS, 1925
PARISIAN ROMANCE, A, 1916
PARISIAN ROMANCE, A, 1932, A
PARISIAN SCANDAL, A, 1921
PARISIAN TIGRESS, THE, 1919
PARISIAN, THE, 1931, A
PARISIENNE
PARK AVENUE LOGGER, 1937, A
PARK PLAZA 605
PARK ROW, 1952, A
PARLIAMO DI DONNE
PARLOR, BEDROOM AND BATH, 1920
PARLOR, BEDROOM AND BATH, 1931, A
PARMI LES VAUTOURS
PARNELL, 1937, A-C
PAROLE, 1936, A
PAROLE FIXER, 1940, A
PAROLE GIRL, 1933, A
PAROLE RACKET, 1937, A
PAROLE, INC., 1949, A
PAROLED FROM THE BIG HOUSE, 1938, A
PAROLED—TO DIE, 1938, A
PAROXISMUS
PARRISH, 1961, A
PARSIFAL, 1983, A
PARSON AND THE OUTLAW, THE, 1957, A
PARSON OF PANAMINT, THE, 1916, A
PARSON OF PANAMINT, THE, 1941, A
PARSON'S WIDOW, THE, 1920
PART 2, SOUNDER
PART 2, WALKING TALL
PART TIME WIFE, 1930, A
PART TIME WIFE, THE, 1925
PART-TIME WIFE, 1961
PARTED BY THE SWORD, 1915
PARTED CURTAINS, 1921
PARTING OF THE TRAILS, 1930
PARTINGS, 1962, A
PARTLY CONFIDENTIAL
PARTNER, THE, 1966, A
PARTNERS, 1932, A
PARTNERS, 1976, C
PARTNERS, 1982, O
PARTNERS AGAIN, 1926, A
PARTNERS AT LAST, 1916
PARTNERS IN CRIME, 1928, A
PARTNERS IN CRIME, 1937, A
PARTNERS IN CRIME, 1961
PARTNERS IN FORTUNE
PARTNERS IN TIME, 1946, A
PARTNERS OF FATE, 1921
PARTNERS OF THE NIGHT, 1920, A
PARTNERS OF THE PLAINS, 1938, A
PARTNERS OF THE SUNSET, 1922
PARTNERS OF THE SUNSET, 1948, A
PARTNERS OF THE TIDE, 1921, A
PARTNERS OF THE TRAIL, 1931, A
PARTNERS OF THE TRAIL, 1944, A
PARTNERS THREE, 1919
PARTS: THE CLONUS HORROR
PARTY CRASHERS, THE, 1958, A
PARTY GIRL, 1930, A
PARTY GIRL, 1958, C
PARTY GIRLS FOR THE CANDIDATE
PARTY HUSBAND, 1931, A
PARTY PARTY, 1983, C
PARTY WIRE, 1935, A
PARTY'S OVER, THE, 1966, O
PARTY, THE, 1968, A
PAS DE MENTALITE
PAS QUESTION LE SEMEDI
PASAZERKA
PASQUALE, 1916
PASQUALINO SETTEBELLEZZE
PASQUALINO: SEVEN BEAUTIES
PASS TO ROMANCE
PASSAGE FROM HONG KONG, 1941, A
PASSAGE HOME, 1955, A
PASSAGE OF LOVE
PASSAGE TO INDIA, A, 1984, C
PASSAGE TO MARSEILLE, 1944, A
PASSAGE WEST, 1951, A
PASSAGE, THE, 1979, O
PASSAGES FROM JAMES JOYCE'S FINNEGANS WAKE
PASSENGER TO LONDON, 1937, A
PASSENGER, THE, 1970, O
PASSENGER, THE, 1975, C
PASSERS-BY, 1916
PASSERS-BY, 1920
PASSIN' THROUGH
PASSING FANCY, 1933
PASSING OF MR. QUIN, THE, 1928, A
PASSING OF THE OKLAHOMA OUTLAWS, THE, 1915
PASSING OF THE THIRD FLOOR BACK, THE, 1918
PASSING OF THE THIRD FLOOR BACK, THE, 1936, A
PASSING OF WOLF MACLEAN, THE, 1924
PASSING SHADOWS, 1934, A
PASSING SHOW, THE
PASSING STRANGER, THE, 1954, A
PASSING THROUGH, 1977, O
PASSING THRU, 1921
PASSION, 1917
PASSION, 1920, A
PASSION, 1954, A
PASSION, 1968, O
PASSION, 1983, O
PASSION FLOWER, 1930, A
PASSION FLOWER, THE, 1921
PASSION FOR LIFE, 1951, A
PASSION FRUIT, 1921
PASSION HOLIDAY, 1963, C
PASSION IN THE SUN, 1964, O
PASSION ISLAND, 1927, A
PASSION ISLAND, 1943, A
PASSION OF A WOMAN TEACHER, THE, 1926
PASSION OF ANNA, THE, 1970, C
PASSION OF JOAN OF ARC, THE, 1928, A
PASSION OF LOVE, 1982, O
PASSION OF SLOW FIRE, THE, 1962, C
PASSION OF ST. FRANCIS, 1932
PASSION OF THE SUN
PASSION PIT, THE, 1965
PASSION PIT, THE, 1969
PASSION SONG, THE, 1928
PASSION STREET, U.S.A., 1964, C
PASSION'S PATHWAY, 1924
PASSION'S PLAYGROUND, 1920
PASSION, 1969
PASSIONATE ADVENTURE, THE, 1924, C
PASSIONATE DEMONS, THE, 1962, A
PASSIONATE FRIENDS, THE
PASSIONATE FRIENDS, THE, 1922, A
PASSIONATE PILGRIM, THE, 1921
PASSIONATE PLUMBER, 1932, A
PASSIONATE QUEST, THE, 1926
PASSIONATE SENTRY, THE, 1952, C
PASSIONATE STRANGER, THE
PASSIONATE STRANGERS, THE, 1968, C
PASSIONATE SUMMER, 1959, A
PASSIONATE SUNDAY
PASSIONATE THIEF, THE, 1963, A
PASSIONATE YOUTH, 1925, A
PASSIONE D'AMORE
PASSIONNEMENT, 1921
PASSKEY TO DANGER, 1946, A
PASSOVER PLOT, THE, 1976, C
PASSPORT HUSBAND, 1938, A
PASSPORT TO ADVENTURE
PASSPORT TO ALCATRAZ, 1940, A
PASSPORT TO CHINA, 1961, A
PASSPORT TO DESTINY, 1944, A
PASSPORT TO HEAVEN, 1943
PASSPORT TO HELL, 1932, A
PASSPORT TO HELL, 1940
PASSPORT TO OBLIVION
PASSPORT TO PARADISE, 1932
PASSPORT TO PIMLICO, 1949, A
PASSPORT TO SHAME
PASSPORT TO SUEZ, 1943, A
PASSPORT TO TREASON, 1956, A
PASSWORD IS COURAGE, THE, 1962, A
PAST OF MARY HOLMES, THE, 1933, A
PASTEBOARD CROWN, A, 1922
PASTEBOARD LOVER, THE
PASTEUR, 1922
PASTEUR, 1936, A
PASTOR HALL, 1940, A
PAT AND MIKE, 1952, A
PAT GARRETT AND BILLY THE KID, 1973, C
PATATE
PATCH
PATCHWORK GIRL OF OZ, THE, 1914, A
PATENT LEATHER KID, THE, 1927
PATENT LEATHER PUG, THE, 1926
PATERNITY, 1981, C
PATH FORBIDDEN, THE, 1914
PATH OF DARKNESS, THE, 1916
PATH OF GLORY, THE, 1934, A
PATH OF HAPPINESS, THE, 1916
PATH SHE CHOSE, THE, 1920
PATH TO THE RAINBOW, THE, 1915
PATHER PANCHALI, 1958, A
PATHFINDER, THE, 1952, A
PATHS OF FLAME, 1926
PATHS OF GLORY, 1957, C
PATHS TO PARADISE, 1925, A
PATIENT IN ROOM 18, THE, 1938, A
PATIENT VANISHES, THE, 1947, A

PATRICIA BRENT, SPINSTER, 1919, A
PATRICIA GETS HER MAN, 1937, A
PATRICK, 1979, O
PATRICK THE GREAT, 1945, A
PATRIOT AND THE SPY, THE, 1915
PATRIOT, THE, 1916, A
PATRIOT, THE, 1928, C
PATSY, 1917
PATSY, 1921, A
PATSY, THE, 1928
PATSY, THE, 1964, A
PATTERN FOR PLUNDER
PATTERN OF EVIL
PATTERNS, 1956, A
PATTERNS OF POWER
PATTON, 1970, C
PAUL AND MICHELLE, 1974, O
PAUL SLEUTH AND THE MYSTIC SEVEN
PAUL STREET BOYS, 1929
PAUL TEMPLE RETURNS, 1952, A
PAUL TEMPLE'S TRIUMPH, 1951, A
PAULA
PAULA, 1915, A
PAULA, 1952, A
PAULINE A LA PLAGE
PAULINE AT THE BEACH, 1983, O
PAUPER MILLIONAIRE, THE, 1922
PAWN OF FATE, THE, 1916
PAWN OF FORTUNE, THE, 1914
PAWN TICKET 210, 1922, A
PAWN, THE, 1968
PAWNBROKER, THE, 1965, C
PAWNED, 1922
PAWNS OF MARS, 1915
PAWNS OF PASSION, 1929
PAWS OF THE BEAR, 1917, A
PAX DOMINE, 1923
PAY AS YOU ENTER, 1928
PAY BOX ADVENTURE, 1936, A
PAY DAY, 1918
PAY DIRT, 1916
PAY ME, 1917
PAY OFF, THE, 1926
PAY OFF, THE, 1930, A
PAY OR DIE, 1960, C
PAY OR DIE, 1982
PAY THE DEVIL
PAYABLE ON DEMAND, 1924
PAYDAY, 1972, O
PAYING HIS DEBT, 1918
PAYING THE LIMIT, 1924, A
PAYING THE PIPER, 1921
PAYING THE PRICE, 1916
PAYING THE PRICE, 1924
PAYING THE PRICE, 1927
PAYMENT DEFERRED, 1932, A
PAYMENT GUARANTEED, 1921
PAYMENT IN BLOOD, 1968, O
PAYMENT ON DEMAND, 1951, A-C
PAYMENT, THE, 1916
PAYOFF, THE, 1935, A
PAYOFF, THE, 1943, A
PAYROLL, 1962, A
PEACE FOR A GUNFIGHTER, 1967, C
PEACE KILLERS, THE, 1971, O
PEACE OF ROARING RIVER, THE, 1919
PEACE TO HIM WHO ENTERS, 1963, A
PEACEFUL PETERS, 1922, A
PEACEFUL VALLEY, 1920
PEACEMAKER
PEACEMAKER, THE, 1922
PEACEMAKER, THE, 1956, A
PEACH O' RENO, 1931, A
PEACH THIEF, THE, 1969, C
PEACOCK ALLEY, 1922, A
PEACOCK ALLEY, 1930, A
PEACOCK FAN, 1929, A
PEACOCK FEATHERS
PEACOCK FEATHERS, 1925
PEAKS OF DESTINY, 1927
PEARL OF ANTILLES, THE, 1915
PEARL OF DEATH, THE, 1944, A
PEARL OF LOVE, THE, 1925
PEARL OF PARADISE, THE, 1916
PEARL OF THE SOUTH PACIFIC, 1955, A
PEARL OF THE SOUTH SEAS, 1927, A
PEARL OF TLAYUCAN, THE, 1964, A
PEARL, THE, 1948, A
PEARLS BRING TEARS, 1937, A
PEARLS OF DEATH, 1914
PEARLS OF THE CROWN, 1938, A
PEAU D'ESPION
PEAU DE BANANE
PEAU DE PECHE, 1929
PECCATORI IN BLUE-JEANS
PECHEUR D'ISLANDE, 1924
PECK O' PICKLES, 1916
PECK'S BAD BOY, 1921, A
PECK'S BAD BOY, 1934, AAA
PECK'S BAD BOY WITH THE CIRCUS, 1938, AAA
PECK'S BAD GIRL, 1918, A
PECOS DANDY, THE, 1934
PECOS KID, THE, 1935
PECOS RIVER, 1951, A
PEDDLER OF LIES, THE, 1920
PEDDLER, THE, 1917
PEDDLIN' IN SOCIETY, 1949, A
PEDESTRIAN, THE, 1974, C
PEEK-A-BOO, 1961, O
PEEP BEHIND THE SCENES, A, 1918, A
PEEP BEHIND THE SCENES, A, 1929, A
PEEPER, 1975, A
PEEPING TOM, 1960, O
PEER GYNT, 1915
PEER GYNT, 1965, A
PEG O' MY HEART, 1919
PEG O' MY HEART, 1922
PEG O' MY HEART, 1933, A
PEG O' THE SEA, 1917
PEG OF OLD DRURY, 1936, A
PEG OF THE PIRATES, 1918, A
PEGEEN, 1920
PEGGY, 1916, A
PEGGY, 1950, A
PEGGY DOES HER DARNDEST, 1919
PEGGY LEADS THE WAY, 1917
PEGGY OF THE SECRET SERVICE, 1925
PEGGY PUTS IT OVER, 1921
PEGGY REBELS
PEGGY, THE WILL O' THE WISP, 1917
PEKING BLONDE
PEKING EXPRESS, 1951, A
PEKING MEDALLION, THE
PELL STREET MYSTERY, THE, 1924, A
PELVIS, 1977
PEN VULTURE, THE
PEN VULTURES, 1918
PENAL CODE, THE, 1933, A
PENAL SERVITUDE
PENALTY OF FAME
PENALTY, THE, 1920, A
PENALTY, THE, 1941, C
PENDULUM, 1969, A-C
PENELOPE, 1966, A
PENGUIN POOL MURDER, THE, 1932, A
PENGUIN POOL MYSTERY, THE
PENITENTE MURDER CASE, THE, 1936, O
PENITENTES, THE, 1915, A
PENITENTIARY, 1938, A
PENITENTIARY, 1979, O
PENITENTIARY II, 1982, O
PENN OF PENNSYLVANIA
PENNIES FROM HEAVEN, 1936, A
PENNIES FROM HEAVEN, 1981, C-O
PENNILESS MILLIONAIRE, THE, 1921, A
PENNINGTON'S CHOICE, 1915, A
PENNY OF TOP HILL TRAIL, 1921
PENNY PARADISE, 1938, A
PENNY PHILANTHROPIST, THE, 1917
PENNY POINTS TO PARADISE, 1951
PENNY POOL, THE, 1937, A
PENNY PRINCESS, 1953, A
PENNY SERENADE, 1941, A
PENNYWHISTLE BLUES, THE, 1952, A
PENROD, 1922, A
PENROD AND HIS TWIN BROTHER, 1938, AAA
PENROD AND SAM, 1923, A
PENROD AND SAM, 1931, AAA
PENROD AND SAM, 1937, AAA
PENROD'S DOUBLE TROUBLE, 1938, AAA
PENTHOUSE, 1933, A
PENTHOUSE PARTY, 1936, A
PENTHOUSE RHYTHM, 1945, A
PENTHOUSE, THE, 1967, O
PEOPLE AGAINST O'HARA, THE, 1951, C
PEOPLE ARE FUNNY, 1945, A
PEOPLE MEET AND SWEET MUSIC FILLS THE HEART, 1969, O
PEOPLE NEXT DOOR, THE, 1970, O
PEOPLE ON SUNDAY, 1929
PEOPLE THAT SHALL NOT DIE, A, 1939
PEOPLE THAT TIME FORGOT, THE, 1977, AA
PEOPLE TOYS
PEOPLE VS. DR. KILDARE, THE, 1941, A
PEOPLE VS. JOHN DOE, THE, 1916
PEOPLE VS. NANCY PRESTON, THE, 1925
PEOPLE WHO OWN THE DARK, 1975, O
PEOPLE WILL TALK, 1935, A
PEOPLE WILL TALK, 1951, A-C
PEOPLE'S ENEMY, THE, 1935, A
PEPE, 1960, AAA
PEPE LE MOKO, 1937, C
PEPPER, 1936, AAA
PEPPER AND HIS WACKY TAXI, 1972
PEPPERMINT SODA, 1979, C
PEPPY POLLY, 1919
PER IL BENE E PER IL MALE
PER QUALCHE DOLLARO IN PIU
PER UN PUGNO DI DOLLARI, O
PERCH OF THE DEVIL, 1927
PERCY, 1925
PERCY'S PROGRESS
PERFECT 36, A, 1918
PERFECT ALIBI, THE, 1924
PERFECT ALIBI, THE, 1931, A
PERFECT CLOWN, THE, 1925
PERFECT CLUE, THE, 1935, A
PERFECT COUPLE, A, 1979, A-C
PERFECT CRIME, O
PERFECT CRIME, A, 1921, A
PERFECT CRIME, THE, 1928, A-C
PERFECT CRIME, THE, 1937, A
PERFECT CRIME, THE, 1934
PERFECT DREAMER, THE, 1922
PERFECT FLAPPER, THE, 1924
PERFECT FLAW, THE, 1934
PERFECT FRIDAY, 1970, C
PERFECT FURLOUGH, THE, 1958, A
PERFECT GENTLEMAN, A, 1928
PERFECT GENTLEMAN, THE, 1935, A
PERFECT KILLER, THE, 1977
PERFECT LADY, A, 1918, A
PERFECT LADY, THE, 1931
PERFECT LOVER, THE, 1919, C
PERFECT MARRIAGE, THE, 1946, A
PERFECT SAP, THE, 1927
PERFECT SET-UP, THE
PERFECT SNOB, THE, 1941, A
PERFECT SPECIMEN, THE, 1937, A
PERFECT STRANGERS
PERFECT STRANGERS, 1950, A
PERFECT STRANGERS, 1984, O
PERFECT UNDERSTANDING, 1933, A-C
PERFECT WEEKEND, A
PERFECT WOMAN, THE, 1920
PERFECT WOMAN, THE, 1950, A
PERFECTIONIST, THE, 1952, A
PERFORMANCE, 1970
PERFORMERS, THE, 1970, C
PERIL FOR THE GUY, 1956, A
PERIL OF THE RAIL, 1926
PERILOUS HOLIDAY, 1946, A
PERILOUS JOURNEY, 1983
PERILOUS JOURNEY, A
PERILOUS JOURNEY, A, 1953, A
PERILOUS VALLEY, 1920
PERILOUS WATERS, 1948, A
PERILS OF DIVORCE, 1916
PERILS OF GWENDOLINE IN THE LAND OF THE YIK-YAK, THE
PERILS OF GWENDOLINE, THE, 1984, O
PERILS OF PARIS
PERILS OF PAULINE, THE, 1947, A
PERILS OF PAULINE, THE, 1967, A
PERILS OF PORK PIE, THE, 1916
PERILS OF TEMPTATION, THE, 1915
PERILS OF THE COAST GUARD, 1926, A
PERILS OF THE WEST, 1922
PERIOD OF ADJUSTMENT, 1962, A-C
PERIWINKLE, 1917
PERJURY, 1921
PERMANENT VACATION, 1982, C
PERMETTE SIGNORA CHE AMI VOSTRA FIGLIA
PERMISSION TO KILL, 1975, C
PERNICKETY POLLY ANN
PERPETUA
PERRY RHODAN-SOS AUS DEM WELTALLO
PERSECUTION, 1974, C
PERSECUTION AND ASSASSINATION OF JEAN-PAUL MARAT AS PERFORMED BY THE INMATES OF THE ASYLUM OF CHARENTON UNDER THE DIRECTION OF THE MARQUIS DE SADE, 1967, C
PERSECUTION OF HASTA VALENCIA
PERSISTENT LOVERS, THE, 1922
PERSONA, 1967, O
PERSONAL AFFAIR, 1954, C
PERSONAL BEST, 1982, C-O
PERSONAL COLUMN
PERSONAL COLUMN, 1939, C
PERSONAL HONOR
PERSONAL MAID, 1931, A
PERSONAL MAID'S SECRET, 1935, A
PERSONAL PROPERTY, 1937, A
PERSONAL SECRETARY, 1938, A
PERSONALITY, 1930, A
PERSONALITY KID, 1946, AA
PERSONALITY KID, THE, 1934, A
PERSONALS, THE, 1982, C
PERSONS IN HIDING,, 1939
PERSONS UNKNOWN
PERSUADER, THE, 1957, A
PERSUASIVE PEGGY, 1917, A
PERVYY DEN MIRA
PEST IN FLORENZ, 1919
PEST, THE, 1919, A
PETAL ON THE CURRENT, THE, 1919, C
PETE 'N' TILLIE, 1972, A-C

PETE KELLY'S BLUES, 1955, C
PETE'S DRAGON, 1977, AAA
PETER IBBETSON
PETER IBBETSON, 1935, A
PETER PAN, 1924, A
PETER PAN, 1953, AAA
PETER RABBIT AND TALES OF BEATRIX POTTER, 1971, AA
PETER THE CRAZY
PETER THE GREAT, 1923
PETERSEN, 1974, C
PETERVILLE DIAMOND, THE, 1942, A
PETEY WHEATSTRAW, 1978, O
PETIT ANGE, 1920
PETIT ANGE ET SON PANTIN, 1923
PETIT HOTEL A LOUER, 1923
PETITE FILLE, 1928
PETRIFIED FOREST, THE, 1936
PETS, 1974
PETTICOAT FEVER, 1936, A
PETTICOAT LARCENY, 1943, A
PETTICOAT LOOSE, 1922
PETTICOAT PILOT, A, 1918
PETTICOAT PIRATES, 1961, A
PETTICOAT POLITICS, 1941, A
PETTICOATS AND BLUEJEANS
PETTICOATS AND POLITICS, 1918
PETTIGREW'S GIRL, 1919
PETTY GIRL, THE, 1950, A
PETTY STORY, THE, 1974
PETULIA, 1968, C
PEYTON PLACE, 1957, C
PHAEDRA, 1962, C
PHANTASM, 1979, O
PHANTOM BROADCAST, THE, 1933, A
PHANTOM BUCCANEER, THE, 1916
PHANTOM BULLET, THE, 1926
PHANTOM BUSTER, THE, 1927
PHANTOM CARRIAGE, THE, 1921
PHANTOM CHARIOT, THE
PHANTOM CITY, THE, 1928
PHANTOM COWBOY, THE, 1935
PHANTOM COWBOY, THE, 1941, A
PHANTOM EXPRESS, THE, 1925
PHANTOM EXPRESS, THE, 1932, A
PHANTOM FIEND, 1966
PHANTOM FIEND, THE, 1935, A
PHANTOM FLYER, THE, 1928
PHANTOM FORTUNES, THE, 1916
PHANTOM FROM 10,000 LEAGUES, THE, 1956, A
PHANTOM FROM SPACE, 1953, A
PHANTOM GOLD, 1938, A
PHANTOM HONEYMOON, THE, 1919
PHANTOM HORSEMAN, THE
PHANTOM HORSEMAN, THE, 1924
PHANTOM HUSBAND, A, 1917
PHANTOM IN THE HOUSE, THE, 1929, A
PHANTOM JUSTICE, 1924
PHANTOM KID, THE, 1983
PHANTOM KILLER, 1942, A
PHANTOM LADY, 1944, C
PHANTOM LIGHT, THE, 1935, C
PHANTOM MELODY, THE, 1920
PHANTOM OF 42ND STREET, THE, 1945, A
PHANTOM OF CHINATOWN, 1940, A
PHANTOM OF CRESTWOOD, THE, 1932, A
PHANTOM OF LIBERTY, THE, 1974, O
PHANTOM OF PARIS, 1942
PHANTOM OF PARIS, THE, 1931, A
PHANTOM OF SANTA FE, 1937
PHANTOM OF SOHO, THE, 1967, C
PHANTOM OF TERROR, THE
PHANTOM OF THE AIS
PHANTOM OF THE DESERT, 1930, A
PHANTOM OF THE FOREST, THE, 1926
PHANTOM OF THE JUNGLE, 1955, A
PHANTOM OF THE MOULIN ROUGE, THE
PHANTOM OF THE NORTH, 1929, A
PHANTOM OF THE OPERA, 1943, A
PHANTOM OF THE OPERA, THE, 1925, A
PHANTOM OF THE OPERA, THE, 1929, A
PHANTOM OF THE OPERA, THE, 1962, C-O
PHANTOM OF THE PARADISE, 1974, C
PHANTOM OF THE PLAINS, 1945, A
PHANTOM OF THE RANGE, 1928, A
PHANTOM OF THE RANGE, THE, 1938, A
PHANTOM OF THE RUE MORGUE, 1954, C
PHANTOM OF THE TURF, 1928
PHANTOM PATROL, 1936, A
PHANTOM PICTURE, THE, 1916, A
PHANTOM PLAINSMEN, THE, 1942, A
PHANTOM PLANET, THE, 1961, A
PHANTOM PRESIDENT, THE, 1932, A
PHANTOM RAIDERS, 1940, A
PHANTOM RANCHER, 1940, A
PHANTOM RANGER, 1938, A
PHANTOM RANGER, THE
PHANTOM RIDER, THE, 1929, A
PHANTOM RIDERS, THE, 1918
PHANTOM SHADOWS, 1925
PHANTOM SHIP, 1937, A
PHANTOM SHOTGUN, THE, 1917
PHANTOM SPEAKS, THE, 1945, A
PHANTOM STAGE, THE, 1939, A
PHANTOM STAGECOACH, THE, 1957, A
PHANTOM STALLION, THE, 1954, A
PHANTOM STOCKMAN, THE, 1953
PHANTOM STRIKES, THE, 1939, A
PHANTOM THIEF, THE, 1946, A
PHANTOM THUNDERBOLT, THE, 1933, A
PHANTOM TOLLBOOTH, THE, 1970, AAA
PHANTOM VALLEY, 1948, A
PHANTOM'S SECRET, THE, 1917
PHANTOM, THE, 1916
PHANTOM, THE, 1922
PHAR LAP, 1984, C
PHARAOH'S CURSE, 1957, A
PHAROAH'S WOMAN, THE, 1961, A
PHASE IV, 1974, A
PHENIX CITY STORY, THE, 1955, C
PHFFFT!, 1954, A
PHIL-FOR-SHORT, 1919
PHILADELPHIA EXPERIMENT, THE, 1984, C
PHILADELPHIA HERE I COME, 1975
PHILADELPHIA STORY, THE, 1940
PHILIP
PHILIP HOLDEN -WASTER, 1916
PHILO VANCE RETURNS, 1947, A
PHILO VANCE'S GAMBLE, 1947, A
PHILO VANCE'S SECRET MISSION, 1947, A
PHOBIA, 1980, O
PHOBIA, 1981
PHOELIX, 1979
PHOENIX CITY STORY
PHONE CALL FROM A STRANGER, 1952, A-C
PHONY AMERICAN, THE, 1964, A
PHROSO, 1922
PHYLLIS OF THE FOLLIES, 1928, A
PHYNX, THE, 1970, C
PHYSICIAN, THE, 1928, C
PIAF—THE EARLY YEARS, 1982, A-C
PICCADILLY, 1932, A-C
PICCADILLY INCIDENT, 1948, A
PICCADILLY JIM, 1920
PICCADILLY JIM, 1936, A
PICCADILLY NIGHTS, 1930
PICCADILLY THIRD STOP, 1960, A
PICK A STAR, 1937, AAA
PICK-UP, 1933, A
PICK-UP, 1975
PICK-UP SUMMER, 1981, O
PICKPOCKET, 1963, A
PICKUP, 1951, A
PICKUP ALLEY, 1957, A
PICKUP IN ROME
PICKUP ON 101, 1972, C
PICKUP ON SOUTH STREET, 1953, C
PICKWICK PAPERS, THE, 1952, AA
PICNIC, 1955, A
PICNIC AT HANGING ROCK, 1975, C-O
PICNIC ON THE GRASS, 1960, C
PICTURE BRIDES, 1934, A
PICTURE MOMMY DEAD, 1966, O
PICTURE OF DORIAN GRAY, THE, 1915
PICTURE OF DORIAN GRAY, THE, 1916, C
PICTURE OF DORIAN GRAY, THE, 1917
PICTURE OF DORIAN GRAY, THE, 1945, C
PICTURE SHOW MAN, THE, 1980, A
PICTURE SNATCHER, 1933, A-C
PICTURES, 1982, A-C
PIDGIN ISLAND, 1916
PIE IN THE SKY, 1964, A
PIECE OF THE ACTION, A, 1977, C
PIECES, 1983, O
PIECES OF DREAMS, 1970, C
PIED PIPER MALONE, 1924
PIED PIPER OF HAMELIN, THE, 1917
PIED PIPER, THE, 1942, C
PIED PIPER, THE, 1972, C
PIED PIPER, THE, 1968
PIEGES
PIEL DE VERANO
PIER 13, 1940, A
PIER 13, 1932
PIER 23, 1951, A
PIER 5, HAVANA, 1959, A
PIERRE ET JEAN, 1924
PIERRE OF THE PLAINS, 1914, A
PIERRE OF THE PLAINS, 1942, A
PIERROT LE FOU, 1968, O
PIERROT PIERRETTE, 1924
PIGEON THAT TOOK ROME, THE, 1962, C
PIGEONS
PIGS, 1984, C
PIGS, THE
PIGSKIN PARADE, 1936, A
PIKOVAJA DAMA
PIKOVAYA DAMA
PILGRIM LADY, THE, 1947, A
PILGRIM, FAREWELL, 1980, C
PILGRIM, THE, 1923, A
PILGRIMAGE, 1933, A-C
PILGRIMAGE, 1972, C
PILGRIMS OF THE NIGHT, 1921
PILL, THE
PILLAR OF FIRE, THE, 1963, A
PILLARS OF SOCIETY, 1916
PILLARS OF SOCIETY, 1920
PILLARS OF SOCIETY, 1936, A
PILLARS OF THE SKY, 1956, A
PILLORY, THE, 1916
PILLOW OF DEATH, 1945, A
PILLOW TALK, 1959, A
PILLOW TO POST, 1945
PILOT NO. 5, 1943, A
PILOT, THE, 1979, C
PIMPERNEL SMITH, 1942, A
PIMPERNEL SVENSSON, 1953, A
PIMPLE'S THREE WEEKS, 1915
PIN UP GIRL, 1944, A
PINBALL PICK-UP
PINBALL SUMMER
PINCH HITTER, THE, 1917, A
PINCH HITTER, THE, 1925
PINK ANGELS, THE, 1971
PINK FLOYD—THE WALL, 1982, O
PINK GODS, 1922
PINK JUNGLE, THE, 1968, A
PINK MOTEL, 1983, O
PINK PANTHER STRIKES AGAIN, THE, 1976, A
PINK PANTHER, THE, 1964, A
PINK STRING AND SEALING WAX, 1950, A
PINK TIGHTS, 1920, A
PINKY, 1949, A
PINOCCHIO, 1940, AAA
PINOCCHIO, 1969, AA
PINOCCHIO IN OUTER SPACE, 1965, AA
PINOCCHIO'S GREATEST ADVENTURE, 1974
PINOCCHIO'S STORYBOOK ADVENTURES, 1979
PINTO, 1920
PINTO BANDIT, THE, 1944, A
PINTO CANYON, 1940, AA
PINTO KID, THE, 1928
PINTO KID, THE, 1941, A
PINTO RUSTLERS, 1937, A
PIONEER BUILDERS
PIONEER DAYS, 1940, A
PIONEER JUSTICE, 1947, A
PIONEER MARSHAL, 1950, A
PIONEER SCOUT, THE, 1928, A
PIONEER TRAIL, 1938, A
PIONEER TRAILS, 1923
PIONEER'S GOLD, 1924
PIONEER, GO HOME
PIONEERS OF THE FRONTIER, 1940, A
PIONEERS OF THE WEST, 1927
PIONEERS OF THE WEST, 1929
PIONEERS OF THE WEST, 1940, A
PIONEERS, THE, 1941, A
PIPE DREAMS, 1976, C
PIPER'S PRICE, THE, 1917
PIPER'S TUNE, THE, 1962, AA
PIPER, THE
PIPES OF PAN, THE, 1923, C
PIPPI IN THE SOUTH SEAS, 1974, AAA
PIPPI ON THE RUN, 1977, AAA
PIRAHANA II: FLYING KILLERS
PIRANHA, 1978, O
PIRANHA II: THE SPAWNING, 1981, O
PIRANHA, PIRANHA, 1972
PIRATE AND THE SLAVE GIRL, THE, 1961, A
PIRATE HAUNTS, 1917
PIRATE MOVIE, THE, 1982, C
PIRATE OF THE BLACK HAWK, THE, 1961, A
PIRATE SHIP
PIRATE, THE, 1948, A
PIRATES OF BLOOD RIVER, THE, 1962, A
PIRATES OF CAPRI, THE, 1949, A
PIRATES OF MONTEREY, 1947, A
PIRATES OF PENZANCE, THE, 1983, A
PIRATES OF THE PRAIRIE, 1942, A
PIRATES OF THE SEVEN SEAS, 1941, A
PIRATES OF THE SKIES, 1939, A
PIRATES OF THE SKY, 1927, A
PIRATES OF TORTUGA, 1961, A
PIRATES OF TRIPOLI, 1955, A
PIRATES ON HORSEBACK, 1941, A
PISTOL FOR RINGO, A, 1966, C
PISTOL HARVEST, 1951, A
PISTOL PACKIN' MAMA, 1943, A
PISTOLERO
PIT AND THE PENDULUM, THE, 1961, C
PIT OF DARKNESS, 1961, A
PIT STOP, 1969, O
PIT, THE
PIT, THE, 1915
PIT, THE, 1984

PIT-BOY'S ROMANCE, A, 1917
PITFALL, 1948, C
PITFALL, THE, 1915
PITFALLS OF A BIG CITY, 1919
PITFALLS OF PASSION, 1927
PITTSBURGH, 1942, A
PITTSBURGH KID, THE, 1941, A
PITY ME NOT, 1960
PIXOTE, 1981, O
PIZZA TRIANGLE, THE, 1970, O
PLACE BEYOND THE WINDS, THE, 1916
PLACE CALLED GLORY, A, 1966
PLACE CALLED TRINITY, A, 1975
PLACE FOR LOVERS, A, 1969, C-O
PLACE IN THE SUN, A, 1916, C
PLACE IN THE SUN, A, 1951, C
PLACE OF HONOUR, THE, 1921, A
PLACE OF ONE'S OWN, A, 1945, A
PLACE OF THE HONEYMOONS, THE, 1920
PLACE TO GO, A, 1964, A
PLACE WITHOUT PARENTS, A, 1974
PLACES IN THE HEART, 1984, A-C
PLAGUE, 1978, C
PLAGUE DOGS, THE, 1982
PLAGUE DOGS, THE, 1984, C-O
PLAGUE OF THE ZOMBIES, THE, 1966, C
PLAGUE-M3: THE GEMINI STRAIN
PLAIN JANE, 1916
PLAINS OF HEAVEN, THE, 1982
PLAINSMAN AND THE LADY, 1946, A
PLAINSMAN, THE, 1937, C
PLAINSMAN, THE, 1966, A
PLAINSMAN, THE, 1964
PLAINSONG, 1982
PLAN 9 FROM OUTER SPACE, 1959, A
PLANET OF BLOOD, 1965
PLANET OF BLOOD, 1966
PLANET OF DINOSAURS, 1978, A
PLANET OF HORRORS
PLANET OF STORMS
PLANET OF THE APES, 1968, C
PLANET OF THE VAMPIRES, 1965, C
PLANET ON THE PROWL
PLANETS AGAINST US, THE, 1961, C
PLANK, THE, 1967, A
PLANTER'S WIFE, THE
PLANTER, THE, 1917
PLANTS ARE WATCHING US, THE
PLASTERED IN PARIS, 1928
PLASTIC AGE, THE, 1925, A
PLASTIC DOME OF NORMA JEAN, THE, 1966, C
PLATINUM BLONDE, 1931, A
PLATINUM HIGH SCHOOL, 1960, A
PLAY DEAD, 1981
PLAY DIRTY, 1969, C
PLAY GIRL, 1932, A
PLAY GIRL, 1940, A
PLAY GIRL, THE, 1928, A
PLAY IT AGAIN, SAM, 1972, C
PLAY IT AS IT LAYS, 1972, O
PLAY IT COOL, 1963, A
PLAY IT COOL, 1970, C
PLAY IT COOLER, 1961
PLAY MISTY FOR ME, 1971, O
PLAY SAFE, 1927, A
PLAY SQUARE, 1921
PLAY UP THE BAND, 1935
PLAYBACK, 1962, A
PLAYBOY OF PARIS, 1930, A
PLAYBOY OF THE WESTERN WORLD, THE, 1963, C
PLAYBOY, THE, 1942, AA
PLAYERS, 1979, O
PLAYERS, 1980
PLAYGIRL, 1954, A
PLAYGIRL AFTER DARK
PLAYGIRL AND THE WAR MINISTER, THE
PLAYGIRL KILLER
PLAYGIRL, 1968
PLAYGIRLS AND THE BELLBOY, THE, 1962, O
PLAYGIRLS AND THE VAMPIRE, 1964, O
PLAYGROUND, THE, 1965, O
PLAYING AROUND, 1930, A
PLAYING DEAD, 1915
PLAYING DOUBLE, 1923, A
PLAYING THE GAME
PLAYING THE GAME, 1918, A
PLAYING WITH FIRE, 1916
PLAYING WITH FIRE, 1921
PLAYING WITH SOULS, 1925
PLAYMATES, 1941, A
PLAYMATES, 1969, O
PLAYMATES, 1971
PLAYTHING OF BROADWAY, THE, 1921
PLAYTHING, THE, 1929, A
PLAYTHINGS, 1918
PLAYTHINGS OF DESIRE, 1924, A
PLAYTHINGS OF DESTINY, 1921, A
PLAYTHINGS OF HOLLYWOOD, 1931
PLAYTIME, 1963, C
PLAYTIME, 1973, AAA
PLAZA SUITE, 1971, A-C
PLEASANTVILLE, 1976, A
PLEASE BELIEVE ME, 1950, A
PLEASE DON'T EAT MY MOTHER, 1972
PLEASE DON'T EAT THE DAISIES, 1960, A
PLEASE GET MARRIED, 1919
PLEASE HELP EMILY, 1917
PLEASE MURDER ME, 1956, A
PLEASE SIR, 1971, A
PLEASE STAND BY, 1972, C
PLEASE TEACHER, 1937, A
PLEASE TURN OVER, 1960, C
PLEASE! MR. BALZAC, 1957, C
PLEASE, NOT NOW!, 1963, C
PLEASURE, 1933, A
PLEASURE BEFORE BUSINESS, 1927
PLEASURE BUYERS, THE, 1925
PLEASURE CRAZED, 1929, A
PLEASURE CRUISE, 1933, A
PLEASURE DOING BUSINESS, A, 1979
PLEASURE GARDEN, THE, 1925, A
PLEASURE GIRL
PLEASURE GIRLS, THE, 1966, C
PLEASURE LOVER
PLEASURE LOVERS, THE, 1964, C
PLEASURE MAD, 1923, C
PLEASURE OF HIS COMPANY, THE, 1961, A
PLEASURE PLANTATION, 1970, O
PLEASURE SEEKERS, 1920
PLEASURE SEEKERS, THE, 1964, A
PLEASURES AND VICES, 1962, C
PLEASURES OF THE FLESH, THE, 1965, C
PLEASURES OF THE RICH, 1926, A
PLEBIAN, 1915
PLEDGEMASTERS, THE, 1971, O
PLEIN SOLEIL
PLEIN SUD
PLEURE PAS LA BOUCHE PLEINE
PLEYDELL MYSTERY, THE, 1916, A
PLOT THICKENS, THE, 1936, A
PLOT THICKENS, THE, 1935
PLOT TO KILL ROOSEVELT, THE
PLOTTERS, THE, 1966
PLOUGH AND THE STARS, THE, 1936, A
PLOUGHMAN'S LUNCH, THE, 1984, O
PLOUGHSHARE, THE, 1915
PLOW GIRL, THE, 1916, A
PLOW WOMAN, THE, 1917
PLUCKED, 1969, C-O
PLUMBER, THE, 1980, C-O
PLUNDER, 1931, A
PLUNDER OF THE SUN, 1953, A
PLUNDER ROAD, 1957, A
PLUNDERER, THE, 1915, A
PLUNDERER, THE, 1924
PLUNDERERS OF PAINTED FLATS, 1959, A
PLUNDERERS, THE, 1948, A
PLUNDERERS, THE, 1960, A
PLUNGE INTO DARKNESS, 1977
PLUNGER, THE, 1920
PLUNGING HOOFS, 1929, A
PLYMOUTH ADVENTURE, 1952, AA
POACHER'S DAUGHTER, THE, 1960
POCATELLO KID, 1932, A
POCKET MONEY, 1972, A-C
POCKETFUL OF MIRACLES, 1961, AA
POCO—LITTLE DOG LOST, 1977
POCOMANIA, 1939, C
POE'S TALES OF HORROR
POET'S PUB, 1949, A
POI TI SPOSERO
POIL DE CAROTTE, 1926
POIL DE CAROTTE, 1932, A
POINT BLANK, 1967, O
POINT BLANK, 1962
POINT OF TERROR, 1971, O
POINT OF VIEW, THE, 1920
POINTED HEELS, 1930, A
POINTING FINGER, THE, 1919
POINTING FINGER, THE, 1922, A
POINTING FINGER, THE, 1934, A
POINTS WEST, 1929, A
POISON, 1924, A
POISON PEN, 1941, A
POISON PEN, THE, 1919
POISONED DIAMOND, THE, 1934
POISONED PARADISE: THE FORBIDDEN STORY OF MONTE CARLO, 1924
POITIN, 1979, A
POKER FACES, 1926
POLAR STAR, THE, 1919, A
POLICE ACADEMY, 1984, O
POLICE BULLETS, 1942, A
POLICE CALL, 1933, A
POLICE CAR 17, 1933
POLICE CONNECTION: DETECTIVE GERONIMO
POLICE COURT
POLICE DOG, 1955, A
POLICE DOG STORY, THE, 1961, A
POLICE NURSE, 1963
POLICE PATROL, THE, 1925, A
POLICE PYTHON 357, 1976, C
POLICEWOMAN, 1974
POLIKUSHKA, 1919
POLITIC FLAPPER, THE
POLITICAL ASYLUM, 1975, A
POLITICAL PARTY, A, 1933, A
POLITICIANS, THE, 1915
POLITICS, 1931, A
POLK COUNTY POT PLANE, 1977
POLLY ANN, 1917
POLLY FULTON
POLLY OF THE CIRCUS, 1917, A
POLLY OF THE CIRCUS, 1932, A
POLLY OF THE FOLLIES, 1922
POLLY OF THE MOVIES, 1927
POLLY OF THE STORM COUNTRY, 1920, A
POLLY PUT THE KETTLE ON, 1917
POLLY REDHEAD, 1917
POLLY WITH A PAST, 1920
POLLYANNA, 1920, A
POLLYANNA, 1960, AAA
POLO JOE, 1936, A
POLTERGEIST, 1982, C-O
POLYESTER, 1981, O
POM POM GIRLS, THE, 1976
POMOCNIK
PONCOMANIA
PONJOLA, 1923
PONTIUS PILATE, 1967, A
PONY EXPRESS, 1953, A
PONY EXPRESS RIDER, 1926, A
PONY EXPRESS RIDER, 1976, A
PONY EXPRESS, THE, 1925, A
PONY POST, 1940, A
PONY SOLDIER, 1952, A
POOKIE
POOL OF FLAME, THE, 1916
POOL OF LONDON, 1951, A
POOR ALBERT AND LITTLE ANNIE
POOR BOOB, 1919
POOR COW, 1968, C
POOR GIRL'S ROMANCE, A, 1926
POOR GIRLS, 1927
POOR LITTLE PEPPINA, 1916
POOR LITTLE RICH GIRL, 1936, A
POOR LITTLE RICH GIRL, 1965
POOR LITTLE RICH GIRL, A, 1917, A
POOR MEN'S WIVES, 1923, A
POOR MILLIONAIRE, THE, 1930
POOR NUT, THE, 1927
POOR OLD BILL, 1931, A
POOR OUTLAWS, THE
POOR PRETTY EDDIE, 1975
POOR RELATION, A, 1921
POOR RELATIONS, 1919, A
POOR RICH MAN, THE, 1918
POOR RICH, THE, 1934, A
POOR SCHMALTZ, 1915
POOR SIMP, THE, 1920
POOR WHITE TRASH
POOR WHITE TRASH II
POOR, DEAR MARGARET KIRBY, 1921
POP ALWAYS PAYS, 1940, A
POPDOWN, 1968
POPE JOAN, 1972, C
POPE OF GREENWICH VILLAGE, THE, 1984, O
POPE ONDINE STORY, THE
POPEYE, 1980, A
POPI, 1969, A
POPIOL Y DIAMENT
POPPIES OF FLANDERS, 1927, A
POPPY, 1917
POPPY, 1936, A
POPPY GIRL'S HUSBAND, THE, 1919, A
POPPY IS ALSO A FLOWER, THE, 1966, C
POPPY TRAIL, THE, 1920
POPSY POP, 1971, A
POPULAR SIN, THE, 1926
POR MIS PISTOLAS, 1969, A
POR UN PUNADO DE DOLARES
PORCELAIN LAMP, THE, 1921
PORGY AND BESS, 1959, A-C
PORI, 1930
PORK CHOP HILL, 1959, C
PORKY'S, 1982, O
PORKY'S II: THE NEXT DAY, 1983, O
PORRIDGE
PORT AFRIQUE, 1956, A
PORT DES LILAS
PORT O' DREAMS
PORT OF 40 THIEVES, THE, 1944, A
PORT OF CALL, 1963, C
PORT OF DESIRE, 1960, C
PORT OF DOOM, THE, 1913
PORT OF ESCAPE, 1955, A
PORT OF HATE, 1939, A

PORT OF HELL, 1955, A
PORT OF LOST DREAMS, 1935, A
PORT OF LOST SOULS, 1924
PORT OF MISSING GIRLS, 1938, A
PORT OF MISSING GIRLS, THE, 1928
PORT OF MISSING MEN, 1914, A
PORT OF MISSING WOMEN, THE, 1915
PORT OF NEW YORK, 1949, A
PORT OF SEVEN SEAS, 1938, A
PORT OF SHADOWS, 1938, A
PORT OF SHAME
PORT SAID, 1948, A
PORT SINISTER, 1953, A
PORTIA ON TRIAL, 1937, A
PORTLAND EXPOSE, 1957, A
PORTNOY'S COMPLAINT, 1972, O
PORTRAIT FROM LIFE
PORTRAIT IN BLACK, 1960, A-C
PORTRAIT IN SMOKE, 1957, O
PORTRAIT IN TERROR, 1965
PORTRAIT OF A HITMAN, 1984
PORTRAIT OF A MOBSTER, 1961, C
PORTRAIT OF A SINNER, 1961, C
PORTRAIT OF A WOMAN, 1946, A
PORTRAIT OF ALISON
PORTRAIT OF CHIEKO, 1968, A
PORTRAIT OF CLARE, 1951, A
PORTRAIT OF HELL, 1969, A
PORTRAIT OF INNOCENCE, 1948, A
PORTRAIT OF JASON, 1967
PORTRAIT OF JENNIE, 1949, A
PORTRAIT OF LENIN, 1967, A
PORTRAIT OF MARIA, 1946, C
PORTRAIT OF THE ARTIST AS A YOUNG MAN, A, 1979, A
PORTS OF CALL, 1925, A
POSEIDON ADVENTURE, THE, 1972, A
POSITIONS
POSITIONS OF LOVE
POSSE, 1975, C
POSSE FROM HEAVEN, 1975
POSSE FROM HELL, 1961, A
POSSESSED, 1931, A-C
POSSESSED, 1947, A-C
POSSESSION, 1919, A
POSSESSION, 1922
POSSESSION, 1981, O
POSSESSION OF JOEL DELANEY, THE, 1972, O
POST OFFICE INVESTIGATOR, 1949, A
POSTAL INSPECTOR, 1936, A
POSTMAN ALWAYS RINGS TWICE, THE, 1946, O
POSTMAN ALWAYS RINGS TWICE, THE, 1981, O
POSTMAN DIDN'T RING, THE, 1942, A
POSTMAN GOES TO WAR, THE, 1968, A
POSTMAN'S KNOCK, 1962, A
POSTMARK FOR DANGER, 1956, A
POSTORONNIM VKHOD VOSPRESHCHEN
POT CARRIERS, THE, 1962, A
POT LUCK, 1936, A
POT LUCK PARDS, 1924
POT O' GOLD, 1941, A
POT! PARENTS! POLICE!, 1975
POT-LUCK PARDS
POTASH AND PERLMUTTER, 1923
POTEMKIN
POTIPHAR'S WIFE
POTLUCK PARDS, 1934
POTS AND PANS PEGGIE, 1917
POTTER'S CLAY, 1922, A
POTTERS, THE, 1927, A
POTTERY GIRL'S ROMANCE, A, 1918
POUR EPOUSER GABY, 1917
POUR UNE NUIT, 1921
POURQUOI PAS!, 1979, C
POVERTY OF RICHES, THE, 1921, A
POWDER, 1916
POWDER MY BACK, 1928, A
POWDER RIVER, 1953, A
POWDER RIVER RUSTLERS, 1949, A
POWDER TOWN, 1942, A
POWDERSMOKE RANGE, 1935, A
POWER, 1928
POWER, 1934, A
POWER AND GLORY
POWER AND THE GLORY, THE, 1918
POWER AND THE GLORY, THE, 1933
POWER AND THE PRIZE, THE, 1956, A
POWER DIVE, 1941, A
POWER DIVINE, THE, 1923
POWER OF A LIE, THE, 1922
POWER OF DARKNESS, THE, 1918
POWER OF DECISION, THE, 1917, A
POWER OF EVIL, 1929
POWER OF EVIL, THE, 1916
POWER OF JUSTICE
POWER OF LIFE, THE, 1938
POWER OF LOVE, THE, 1922
POWER OF POSSESSION
POWER OF RIGHT, THE, 1919, A
POWER OF SILENCE, THE, 1928
POWER OF THE PRESS, 1943, A
POWER OF THE PRESS, THE, 1914
POWER OF THE PRESS, THE, 1928, A
POWER OF THE WEAK, THE, 1926, A
POWER OF THE WHISTLER, THE, 1945, A
POWER OVER MEN, 1929, A
POWER PLAY, 1978, C
POWER WITHIN, THE, 1921
POWER, THE, 1968, A
POWER, THE, 1984, O
POWERFORCE, 1983, O
POWERS GIRL, THE, 1942, A
POWERS THAT PREY, 1918
POZEGNANIA
PRACTICALLY YOURS, 1944, A
PRAIRIE BADMEN, 1946, A
PRAIRIE EXPRESS, 1947, A
PRAIRIE GUNSMOKE, 1942
PRAIRIE JUSTICE, 1938, A
PRAIRIE KING, THE, 1927
PRAIRIE LAW, 1940, A
PRAIRIE MOON, 1938
PRAIRIE MYSTERY, THE, 1922
PRAIRIE OUTLAWS, 1948
PRAIRIE PALS, 1942
PRAIRIE PIONEERS, 1941, A
PRAIRIE PIRATE, THE, 1925
PRAIRIE RAIDERS, 1947
PRAIRIE ROUNDUP, 1951, A
PRAIRIE RUSTLERS, 1945, A
PRAIRIE SCHOONERS, 1940, A
PRAIRIE STRANGER, 1941, A
PRAIRIE THUNDER, 1937, A
PRAIRIE TRAILS, 1920
PRAIRIE WIFE, THE, 1925, A
PRAIRIE, THE, 1948, A
PRAISE AGENT, THE, 1919, A
PRANKS, 1982
PRATLDWANDI
PRAYING MANTIS, 1982, C
PREACHERMAN, 1971, O
PREACHERMAN MEETS WIDDERWOMAN, 1973
PRECIOUS JEWELS, 1969
PRECIOUS PACKET, THE, 1916
PREHISTORIC MAN, THE, 1924, A
PREHISTORIC PLANET WOMEN
PREHISTORIC WOMEN, 1950, C
PREHISTORIC WOMEN, 1967, O
PREHISTORIC WORLD
PREJUDICE, 1922
PREJUDICE, 1949, A
PRELUDE TO ECSTASY, 1963, C
PRELUDE TO FAME, 1950, A
PRELUDE TO TAURUS, 1972
PREMATURE BURIAL, THE, 1962, C
PREMIERE
PREMONITION, 1972
PREMONITION, THE, 1976, C
PRENON: CARMEN
PREP AND PEP, 1928, A
PREPARED TO DIE, 1923, A
PREPPIES
PREPPIES, 1984, O
PRES DE CRIME, 1921
PRESCOTT KID, THE, 1936
PRESCRIPTION FOR ROMANCE, 1937, A
PRESENT ARMS
PRESENTING LILY MARS, 1943, A
PRESIDENT VANISHES, THE, 1934, A
PRESIDENT'S ANALYST, THE, 1967, O
PRESIDENT'S LADY, THE, 1953, A-C
PRESIDENT'S MYSTERY, THE, 1936, A
PRESIDENT, THE, 1918
PRESS FOR TIME, 1966, A
PRESSURE, 1976, C
PRESSURE OF GUILT, 1964, C
PRESSURE POINT, 1962, C
PRESTIGE, 1932, A
PRESUMPTION OF STANLEY HAY, MP, THE, 1925, A
PRETENDER, THE, 1918
PRETENDER, THE, 1947, A
PRETENDERS, THE, 1915
PRETENDERS, THE, 1916, A
PRETTY BABY, 1950, A
PRETTY BABY, 1978, O
PRETTY BOY FLOYD, 1960, C-O
PRETTY BUT WICKED, 1965, O
PRETTY CLOTHES, 1927, A
PRETTY LADIES, 1925, A
PRETTY MAIDS ALL IN A ROW, 1971, O
PRETTY MRS. SMITH, 1915, A
PRETTY POISON, 1968, C-O
PRETTY POLLY
PRETTY SISTER OF JOSE, 1915, A
PRETTY SMOOTH, 1919
PREVIEW MURDER MYSTERY, 1936, A
PREY OF THE DRAGON, THE, 1921
PREY, THE, 1920
PREY, THE, 1984, O
PRICE FOR FOLLY, A, 1915, A
PRICE MARK, THE, 1917, A
PRICE OF A GOOD TIME, THE, 1918
PRICE OF A PARTY, THE, 1924, A
PRICE OF A SONG, THE, 1935, A
PRICE OF APPLAUSE, THE, 1918
PRICE OF DIVORCE, THE, 1928
PRICE OF FAME, THE, 1916
PRICE OF FEAR, THE, 1928
PRICE OF FEAR, THE, 1956, A
PRICE OF FLESH, THE, 1962, O
PRICE OF FOLLY, THE, 1937, A
PRICE OF FREEDOM, THE
PRICE OF HAPPINESS, THE, 1916
PRICE OF HER HONOR, THE, 1927
PRICE OF HER SILENCE, THE, 1915
PRICE OF HER SOUL, THE, 1917
PRICE OF JUSTICE, THE, 1914
PRICE OF JUSTICE, THE, 1915
PRICE OF MALICE, THE, 1916
PRICE OF PLEASURE, THE, 1925
PRICE OF POSSESSION, THE, 1921
PRICE OF POWER, THE, 1916
PRICE OF POWER, THE, 1916
PRICE OF POWER, THE, 1969, C
PRICE OF PRIDE, THE, 1917
PRICE OF REDEMPTION, THE, 1920
PRICE OF SILENCE, THE, 1916
PRICE OF SILENCE, THE, 1917
PRICE OF SILENCE, THE, 1920, A
PRICE OF SILENCE, THE, 1960, A
PRICE OF SUCCESS, THE, 1925
PRICE OF THINGS, THE, 1930, A
PRICE OF WISDOM, THE, 1935, A
PRICE OF YOUTH, THE, 1922
PRICE SHE PAID, THE, 1917
PRICE SHE PAID, THE, 1924
PRICE WOMAN PAYS, THE, 1919
PRICE, THE, 1915
PRIDE, 1917
PRIDE AND PREJUDICE, 1940, A
PRIDE AND THE MAN, 1917
PRIDE AND THE PASSION, THE, 1957, C
PRIDE OF DONEGAL, THE, 1929, A
PRIDE OF JENNICO, THE, 1914, A
PRIDE OF KENTUCKY
PRIDE OF MARYLAND, 1951, A
PRIDE OF NEW YORK, THE, 1917
PRIDE OF PALOMAR, THE, 1922, A
PRIDE OF PAWNEE, THE, 1929
PRIDE OF ST. LOUIS, THE, 1952, AA
PRIDE OF SUNSHINE ALLEY, 1924, A
PRIDE OF THE ARMY, 1942, AA
PRIDE OF THE BLUE GRASS, 1954, A
PRIDE OF THE BLUEGRASS, 1939, AA
PRIDE OF THE BOWERY, 1941, A
PRIDE OF THE BOWERY, THE, 1946
PRIDE OF THE CLAN, THE, 1917, A
PRIDE OF THE FANCY, THE, 1920, A
PRIDE OF THE FORCE, THE, 1925, A
PRIDE OF THE FORCE, THE, 1933, A
PRIDE OF THE LEGION, THE, 1932, A
PRIDE OF THE MARINES, 1936, A
PRIDE OF THE MARINES, 1945, C
PRIDE OF THE NAVY, 1939, A
PRIDE OF THE NORTH, THE, 1920, A
PRIDE OF THE PLAINS, 1944, A
PRIDE OF THE WEST, 1938, A
PRIDE OF THE YANKEES, THE, 1942, AAA
PRIEST OF LOVE, 1981, O
PRIEST OF ST. PAULI, THE, 1970, C
PRIEST'S WIFE, THE, 1971, O
PRIMA DELLA REVOLUTIONA
PRIMA DONNA'S HUSBAND, THE, 1916
PRIMAL LAW, THE, 1921
PRIMAL LURE, THE, 1916, A
PRIME CUT, 1972, O
PRIME MINISTER, THE, 1941, A
PRIME OF MISS JEAN BRODIE, THE, 1969, C
PRIME TIME, THE, 1960, O
PRIMITIVE CALL, THE, 1917
PRIMITIVE LOVE, 1927
PRIMITIVE LOVE, 1966, O
PRIMITIVE LOVER, THE, 1922
PRIMITIVE WOMAN, THE, 1918
PRIMITIVES, THE, 1962, A
PRIMROSE PATH, 1940, C
PRIMROSE PATH, THE, 1915
PRIMROSE PATH, THE, 1925
PRIMROSE PATH, THE, 1934, A
PRIMROSE RING, THE, 1917
PRINCE AND BETTY, THE, 1919
PRINCE AND THE BEGGARMAID, THE, 1921, C
PRINCE AND THE DANCER, 1929
PRINCE AND THE PAUPER, THE, 1915, A
PRINCE AND THE PAUPER, THE, 1929
PRINCE AND THE PAUPER, THE, 1937, AAA
PRINCE AND THE PAUPER, THE, 1969, AA

PRINCE AND THE PAUPER, THE, 1978
PRINCE AND THE SHOWGIRL, THE, 1957, A
PRINCE CHAP, THE, 1916
PRINCE CHAP, THE, 1920
PRINCE EMBETE, 1920
PRINCE IN A PAWNSHOP, A, 1916, A
PRINCE OF A KING, A, 1923
PRINCE OF ARCADIA, 1933, AA
PRINCE OF AVENUE A., THE, 1920, A
PRINCE OF BROADWAY, THE, 1926
PRINCE OF DIAMONDS, 1930, A
PRINCE OF FOXES, 1949, C
PRINCE OF GRAUSTARK, THE, 1916
PRINCE OF HEADWAITERS, THE, 1927
PRINCE OF HEARTS, THE, 1929
PRINCE OF HIS RACE, THE, 1926
PRINCE OF INDIA, A, 1914, A
PRINCE OF LOVERS, A, 1922
PRINCE OF PEACE, THE, 1951, AAA
PRINCE OF PEANUTS
PRINCE OF PEP, THE, 1925
PRINCE OF PILSEN, THE, 1926, A
PRINCE OF PIRATES, 1953, A
PRINCE OF PLAYERS, 1955, C
PRINCE OF TEMPTERS, THE, 1926
PRINCE OF THE BLUE GRASS
PRINCE OF THE CITY, 1981, O
PRINCE OF THE PLAINS, 1927
PRINCE OF THE PLAINS, 1949, A
PRINCE OF THE SADDLE, 1926
PRINCE OF THIEVES, THE, 1948, A
PRINCE THERE WAS, A, 1921, A
PRINCE VALIANT, 1954, AA
PRINCE WHO WAS A THIEF, THE, 1951, A
PRINCE ZILAH, 1926
PRINCESS AND THE MAGIC FROG, THE, 1965, AAA
PRINCESS AND THE PIRATE, THE, 1944, A
PRINCESS AND THE PLUMBER, THE, 1930, A
PRINCESS CHARMING, 1935, A
PRINCESS COMES ACROSS, THE, 1936, A
PRINCESS FROM HOBOKEN, THE, 1927, A
PRINCESS JONES, 1921
PRINCESS O'HARA, 1935, A
PRINCESS O'ROURKE, 1943, A
PRINCESS OF BAGDAD, 1913
PRINCESS OF BROADWAY, THE, 1927
PRINCESS OF HAPPY CHANCE, THE, 1916, A
PRINCESS OF NEW YORK, THE, 1921
PRINCESS OF PARK ROW, THE, 1917
PRINCESS OF PATCHES, THE, 1917
PRINCESS OF THE DARK, 1928
PRINCESS OF THE DARK, A, 1917
PRINCESS OF THE NILE, 1954, AA
PRINCESS OLALA
PRINCESS ROMANOFF, 1915
PRINCESS VIRTUE, 1917
PRINCESS' NECKLACE, THE, 1917
PRINCESS, THE
PRINCESSE LULU, 1924
PRINCESSE MASHA, 1927
PRINSESSAN
PRINTEMPS D'AMOUR, 1927
PRINTER'S DEVIL, THE, 1923
PRIORITIES ON PARADE, 1942, A
PRISCA, 1921
PRISM, 1971, C
PRISM, 1971
PRISON BREAK, 1938, A
PRISON BREAKER, 1936, A
PRISON CAMP
PRISON FARM, 1938, A
PRISON GIRL, 1942, A
PRISON NURSE, 1938, A
PRISON SHADOWS, 1936, A
PRISON SHIP, 1945, C
PRISON TRAIN, 1938, A
PRISON WARDEN, 1949, A
PRISON WITHOUT BARS, 1939, A
PRISON WITHOUT WALLS, THE, 1917
PRISONER IN THE HAREM, THE, 1913
PRISONER OF CORBAL, 1939, C
PRISONER OF JAPAN, 1942, A
PRISONER OF SECOND AVENUE, THE, 1975, A-C
PRISONER OF SHARK ISLAND, THE, 1936, A
PRISONER OF THE CANNIBAL GOD, 1978
PRISONER OF THE IRON MASK, 1962, A
PRISONER OF THE PINES, 1918, A
PRISONER OF THE VOLGA, 1960, C
PRISONER OF WAR, 1954, C
PRISONER OF WAR, THE, 1918
PRISONER OF ZENDA, THE, 1915, A
PRISONER OF ZENDA, THE, 1922, A
PRISONER OF ZENDA, THE, 1937, A
PRISONER OF ZENDA, THE, 1952
PRISONER OF ZENDA, THE, 1979, A
PRISONER, THE, 1923, A
PRISONER, THE, 1955, C
PRISONERS, 1929, A
PRISONERS, 1975
PRISONERS IN PETTICOATS, 1950, A
PRISONERS OF LOVE, 1921, C
PRISONERS OF THE CASBAH, 1953, A
PRISONERS OF THE SEA, 1929
PRISONERS OF THE STORM, 1926
PRIVATE AFFAIRS, 1925
PRIVATE AFFAIRS, 1940, A
PRIVATE AFFAIRS OF BEL AMI, THE, 1947, A
PRIVATE AFFAIRS, 1935
PRIVATE ANGELO, 1949, A
PRIVATE BENJAMIN, 1980, O
PRIVATE BUCKAROO, 1942, A
PRIVATE COLLECTION, 1972, O
PRIVATE DETECTIVE, 1939, A
PRIVATE DETECTIVE 62, 1933, A
PRIVATE DUTY NURSES, 1972, O
PRIVATE ENTERPRISE, A, 1975, A
PRIVATE EYES, 1953, A
PRIVATE EYES, THE, 1980, A
PRIVATE FILES OF J. EDGAR HOOVER, THE, 1978, C
PRIVATE HELL 36, 1954, C
PRIVATE INFORMATION, 1952, A
PRIVATE IZZY MURPHY, 1926, A
PRIVATE JONES, 1933, A
PRIVATE LESSONS, 1981, O
PRIVATE LIFE
PRIVATE LIFE OF DON JUAN, THE, 1934, A
PRIVATE LIFE OF HELEN OF TROY, THE, 1927
PRIVATE LIFE OF HENRY VIII, THE, 1933, A-C
PRIVATE LIFE OF LOUIS XIV, 1936, A
PRIVATE LIFE OF SHERLOCK HOLMES, THE, 1970, C
PRIVATE LIVES, 1931, A
PRIVATE LIVES OF ADAM AND EVE, THE, 1961
PRIVATE LIVES OF ELIZABETH AND ESSEX, THE, 1939, A
PRIVATE NAVY OF SGT. O'FARRELL, THE, 1968, A
PRIVATE NUMBER, 1936, A
PRIVATE NURSE, 1941, A
PRIVATE PARTS, 1972, O
PRIVATE PEAT, 1918, A
PRIVATE POOLEY, 1962, C
PRIVATE POTTER, 1963, A-C
PRIVATE PROPERTY, 1960, O
PRIVATE RIGHT, THE, 1967
PRIVATE ROAD, 1971, O
PRIVATE SCANDAL, 1934, A
PRIVATE SCANDAL, A, 1921, A
PRIVATE SCANDAL, A, 1932, A
PRIVATE SCHOOL, 1983, O
PRIVATE SECRETARY, THE, 1935, A
PRIVATE SNUFFY SMITH
PRIVATE WAR OF MAJOR BENSON, THE, 1955, A
PRIVATE WORE SKIRTS, THE
PRIVATE WORLDS, 1935, A-C
PRIVATE'S AFFAIR, A, 1959, A
PRIVATE'S PROGRESS, 1956, A
PRIVATES ON PARADE, 1982, O
PRIVATES ON PARADE, 1984, O
PRIVATKLINIK PROF. LUND
PRIVILEGE, 1967, A
PRIVILEGED, 1982, C-O
PRIZE FIGHTER, THE, 1979, C
PRIZE OF ARMS, A, 1962, A
PRIZE OF GOLD, A, 1955, A
PRIZE, THE, 1952, A
PRIZE, THE, 1963, C
PRIZED AS A MATE!
PRIZEFIGHTER AND THE LADY, THE, 1933, A
PRO, THE
PROBATION, 1932, A
PROBATION WIFE, THE, 1919
PROBLEM GIRLS, 1953, A
PROCES DE JEANNE D'ARC
PRODIGAL DAUGHTER, THE, 1916
PRODIGAL DAUGHTERS, 1923
PRODIGAL GUN
PRODIGAL JUDGE, THE, 1922
PRODIGAL LIAR, THE, 1919
PRODIGAL SON, THE, 1923, A
PRODIGAL SON, THE, 1935
PRODIGAL SON, THE, 1964, C
PRODIGAL WIFE, THE, 1918, C
PRODIGAL, THE, 1931, A
PRODIGAL, THE, 1955, A-C
PRODIGAL, THE, 1984, A
PRODUCERS, THE, 1967, O
PROFESSIONAL BLONDE
PROFESSIONAL BRIDE
PROFESSIONAL GUN, A
PROFESSIONAL SOLDIER, 1936, A
PROFESSIONAL SWEETHEART, 1933, A
PROFESSIONALS, THE, 1960
PROFESSIONALS, THE, 1966, O
PROFESSOR BEWARE, 1938, A
PROFESSOR CREEPS, 1942
PROFESSOR TIM, 1957, A
PROFILE, 1954, A
PROFILE OF TERROR, THE
PROFIT AND THE LOSS, 1917, A
PROFITEER, THE, 1919
PROFITEERS, THE, 1919
PROFLIGATE, THE, 1917, C
PROHIBITION, 1915, C
PROJECT M7, 1953, A
PROJECT MOONBASE, 1953, A
PROJECT X, 1949, A
PROJECT X, 1968
PROJECT: KILL, 1976, O
PROJECTED MAN, THE, 1967, A
PROJECTIONIST, THE, 1970, A-C
PROLOGUE, 1970, C
PROM NIGHT, 1980, O
PROMISE AT DAWN, 1970, A
PROMISE HER ANYTHING, 1966, A
PROMISE HER ANYTHING, 1963
PROMISE OF A BED, A
PROMISE, THE, 1917
PROMISE, THE, 1969, A
PROMISE, THE, 1979, A-C
PROMISED LAND, THE, 1925
PROMISES IN THE DARK, 1979, C
PROMISES, PROMISES, 1963, O
PROMOTER, THE, 1952, A
PROPER TIME, THE, 1959
PROPERTY, 1979
PROPHECIES OF NOSTRADAMUS, 1974, C
PROPHECY, 1979, C-O
PROPHET'S PARADISE, THE, 1922
PROPHET, THE, 1976
PROSPERITY, 1932, A
PROSTITUTE, 1980, O
PROSTITUTION, 1965, C
PROTECT US, 1914
PROTECTION, 1929, A
PROTECTORS, BOOK 1, THE, 1981, O
PROTECTORS, THE
PROTOCOL, 1984, A-C
PROUD AND THE DAMNED, THE, 1972, C-O
PROUD AND THE PROFANE, THE, 1956, A-C
PROUD FLESH, 1925, A
PROUD HEART
PROUD ONES, THE, 1956, A
PROUD REBEL, THE, 1958, A
PROUD RIDER, THE, 1971, C
PROUD VALLEY, THE, 1941, A
PROUD, DAMNED AND DEAD
PROVIDENCE, 1977, O
PROWL GIRLS, 1968
PROWLER, THE, 1951, C-O
PROWLER, THE, 1981, O
PROWLERS OF THE NIGHT, 1926, A
PROWLERS OF THE SEA, 1928
PROXIES, 1921
PRUDENCE AND THE PILL, 1968, O
PRUDENCE ON BROADWAY, 1919
PRUDENCE THE PIRATE, 1916
PRUDES FALL, THE, 1924, A
PRUNELLA, 1918, A
PRUSSIAN CUR, THE, 1918
PSI FACTOR, 1980
PSYCH-OUT, 1968, O
PSYCHE 59, 1964, C
PSYCHIC KILLER, 1975, O
PSYCHIC LOVER, THE
PSYCHIC, THE, 1979, O
PSYCHO, 1960, O
PSYCHO A GO-GO!, 1965, O
PSYCHO FROM TEXAS, 1982, O
PSYCHO II, 1983, O
PSYCHO KILLERS
PSYCHO LOVER, 1969
PSYCHO SISTERS, 1972
PSYCHO-CIRCUS, 1967, O
PSYCHOMANIA, 1964, O
PSYCHOMANIA, 1974, O
PSYCHOPATH, THE, 1966, O
PSYCHOPATH, THE, 1973, O
PSYCHOTRONIC MAN, THE, 1980, O
PSYCHOUT FOR MURDER, 1971, O
PSYCOSISSIMO, 1962, O
PT 109, 1963, A
PT RAIDERS
PT RAIDERS
PUBERTY BLUES, 1983, O
PUBLIC AFFAIR, A, 1962, C
PUBLIC BE DAMNED, 1917
PUBLIC BE HANGED, THE
PUBLIC COWBOY NO. 1, 1937, A
PUBLIC DEB NO. 1, 1940, C
PUBLIC DEFENDER, 1917
PUBLIC DEFENDER, THE, 1931, A
PUBLIC ENEMIES, 1941, A
PUBLIC ENEMY'S WIFE, 1936, A
PUBLIC ENEMY, THE, 1931, O
PUBLIC EYE, THE, 1972, A
PUBLIC HERO NO. 1, 1935, A
PUBLIC LIFE OF HENRY THE NINTH, THE, 1934
PUBLIC MENACE, 1935, C

PUBLIC NUISANCE NO. 1, 1936, A
PUBLIC OPINION, 1916
PUBLIC OPINION, 1935, A
PUBLIC PIGEON NO. 1, 1957, A
PUBLIC PROSECUTOR, 1917
PUBLIC STENOGRAPHER, 1935, C
PUBLIC WEDDING, 1937, A
PUBLICITY MADNESS, 1927
PUDD'NHEAD WILSON, 1916
PUDDIN' HEAD, 1941, AAA
PUEBLO TERROR, 1931
PUFNSTUF, 1970, AAA
PULCINELLA, 1925
PULGARCITO
PULP, 1972, C
PULSE OF LIFE, THE, 1917
PUMA MAN, THE, 1980
PUMPKIN, 1928
PUMPKIN EATER, THE, 1964
PUNCH AND JUDY MAN, THE, 1963, A
PUNISHMENT PARK, 1971, O
PUO UNA MORTA RIVIVERE PER AMORE?
PUPPET CROWN, THE, 1915, A
PUPPET MAN, THE, 1921, C
PUPPET ON A CHAIN, 1971, O
PUPPETS, 1926, A
PUPPETS OF FATE
PUPPETS OF FATE
PUPPETS OF FATE, 1921
PUPPY LOVE, 1919
PURCHASE PRICE, THE, 1932, O
PURE GRIT, 1923, A
PURE HELL OF ST. TRINIAN'S, THE, 1961, C
PURE S, 1976, O
PURITAN PASSIONS, 1923
PURITY, 1916
PURLIE VICTORIOUS
PURPLE CIPHER, THE, 1920, A
PURPLE DAWN, 1923
PURPLE GANG, THE, 1960, O
PURPLE HAZE, 1982, O
PURPLE HEART DIARY, 1951, A
PURPLE HEART, THE, 1944, C-O
PURPLE HEARTS, 1984, C-O
PURPLE HIGHWAY, THE, 1923
PURPLE HILLS, THE, 1961, O
PURPLE LADY, THE, 1916
PURPLE LILY, THE, 1918
PURPLE MASK, THE, 1955, A
PURPLE NOON, 1961, O
PURPLE PLAIN, THE, 1954, A-C
PURPLE RAIN, 1984, O
PURPLE RIDERS, THE
PURPLE TAXI, THE, 1977
PURPLE V, THE, 1943, O
PURPLE VIGILANTES, THE, 1938, A
PURSE STRINGS, 1933, A
PURSUED, 1925
PURSUED, 1934, A
PURSUED, 1947, C-O
PURSUERS, THE, 1961, A
PURSUING VENGEANCE, THE, 1916, A
PURSUIT, 1935, A
PURSUIT, 1975, O
PURSUIT OF D.B. COOPER, THE, 1981, C
PURSUIT OF HAPPINESS, THE, 1934, C
PURSUIT OF HAPPINESS, THE, 1971, O
PURSUIT OF PAMELA, THE, 1920, C
PURSUIT OF THE GRAF SPEE, 1957, A
PURSUIT OF THE PHANTOM, THE, 1914, A
PURSUIT TO ALGIERS, 1945, A
PUSHER, THE, 1960, O
PUSHERS, THE
PUSHING UP DAISIES, 1971
PUSHOVER, 1954, A
PUSHOVER, THE
PUSS AND KRAM
PUSS OCH KRAM
PUSS 'N' BOOTS, 1964, AAA
PUSS 'N' BOOTS, 1967, AAA
PUSSYCAT ALLEY, 1965, O
PUSSYCAT, PUSSYCAT, I LOVE YOU, 1970, O
PUSUIT OF POLLY
PUT 'EM UP, 1928
PUT ON THE SPOT, 1936, A
PUT UP OR SHUT UP, 1968, O
PUT UP YOUR HANDS, 1919
PUTNEY SWOPE, 1969, O
PUTTIN' ON THE RITZ, 1930, A
PUTTING IT OVER, 1919, A
PUTTING IT OVER, 1922, A
PUTTING ONE OVER, 1919
PUTTING THE BEE IN HERBERT, 1917
PUTYOVKA V ZHIZN
PUZZLE OF A DOWNFALL CHILD, 1970, O
PYGMALION, 1938, A
PYGMY ISLAND, 1950, A
PYRAMID, THE, 1976
PYRO, 1964, O
PYRO-THE THING WITHOUT A FACE
PYX, THE, 1973, O

-Q-

Q, 1982, O
Q PLANES
Q-SHIPS
QUACKSER FORTUNE HAS A COUSIN IN THE BRONX, 1970, A-C
QUADROON, 1972, O
QUADROPHENIA, 1979, O
QUAI DE GRENELLE
QUAI DES BRUMES
QUALIFIED ADVENTURER, THE, 1925, A
QUALITY OF FAITH, THE, 1916
QUALITY STREET, 1927, A
QUALITY STREET, 1937, A
QUAND NOUS ETIONS DEUX, 1929
QUANDO EL AMOR RIE, 1933
QUANTEZ, 1957, A
QUANTRILL'S RAIDERS, 1958, A
QUARANTINED RIVALS, 1927
QUARE FELLOW, THE, 1962, C-O
QUARTERBACK, THE, 1926, A
QUARTERBACK, THE, 1940, A
QUARTET, 1949, C
QUARTET, 1981, C
QUATERMASS AND THE PIT
QUATERMASS CONCLUSION, 1980, C
QUATERMASS EXPERIMENT, THE
QUATERMASS II
QUATRE-VINGT TREIZE, 1921
QUE LA BETE MEURE
QUE LA FETE COMMENCE
QUEBEC, 1951, A
QUEEN BEE
QUEEN BEE, 1955, C
QUEEN BOXER, THE, 1973
QUEEN CHRISTINA, 1933, A
QUEEN ELIZABETH, 1912, A
QUEEN FOR A DAY, 1951, A
QUEEN HIGH, 1930, A
QUEEN KELLY, 1929, A
QUEEN MOTHER, THE, 1916, A
QUEEN O' DIAMONDS, 1926, A
QUEEN O' TURF, 1922
QUEEN OF ATLANTIS
QUEEN OF BABYLON, THE, 1956, A
QUEEN OF BLOOD, 1966, O
QUEEN OF BROADWAY, 1942, A
QUEEN OF BROADWAY, 1943
QUEEN OF BURLESQUE, 1946, C
QUEEN OF CLUBS
QUEEN OF CRIME
QUEEN OF DESTINY
QUEEN OF HEARTS, 1936, A
QUEEN OF HEARTS, THE, 1918
QUEEN OF MY HEART, 1917, C
QUEEN OF OUTER SPACE, 1958, A
QUEEN OF SHEBA, 1953, C
QUEEN OF SHEBA MEETS THE ATOM MAN, THE, 1963
QUEEN OF SHEBA, THE, 1921, C
QUEEN OF SIN AND THE SPECTACLE OF SODOM AND GOMORRAH, THE (1923, Aust.)
QUEEN OF SIN, THE
QUEEN OF SPADES, 1925
QUEEN OF SPADES, 1948, A-C
QUEEN OF SPADES, 1961, C
QUEEN OF SPADES, THE, 1916
QUEEN OF SPIES
QUEEN OF THE AMAZONS, 1947, A
QUEEN OF THE CANNIBALS
QUEEN OF THE CHORUS, 1928
QUEEN OF THE MOB, 1940, C
QUEEN OF THE MOULIN ROUGE, 1922
QUEEN OF THE NIGHTCLUBS, 1929, A-C
QUEEN OF THE NILE, 1964, C
QUEEN OF THE PIRATES, 1961, C
QUEEN OF THE SCREEN, 1916
QUEEN OF THE SEA, 1918
QUEEN OF THE SEAS, 1960
QUEEN OF THE SMUGGLERS, THE, 1914
QUEEN OF THE WEST
QUEEN OF THE WICKED, 1916, A
QUEEN OF THE YUKON, 1940, A
QUEEN WAS IN THE PARLOUR, THE
QUEEN X, 1917
QUEEN'S AFFAIR, THE
QUEEN'S EVIDENCE, 1919, A
QUEEN'S GUARDS, THE, 1963, C
QUEEN'S HUSBAND, THE
QUEEN'S SECRET, THE, 1919
QUEEN'S SWORDSMEN, THE, 1963, AAA
QUEENIE, 1921, A
QUEENS, THE, 1968, O
QUEER CARGO
QUEI DISPERATI CHE PUZZANO DI SUDORE E DI MORTE
QUEI TEMERARI SULLE LORO PAZZE, SCATENATE, SCALCINATE CARRIOLE
QUEIMADA
QUELLA VILLA ACCANTO AL CIMITERO
QUELLI CHE NON MUOIONO
QUELQU'UN DERRIERE LA PORTE
QUELQUES JOURS PRES
QUEMADA!
QUENTIN DURWARD, 1955, A
QUERELLE, 1983, O
QUERY, 1945, O
QUEST FOR FIRE, 1982, O
QUEST FOR LOVE, 1971, C
QUEST OF LIFE, THE, 1916, A
QUEST OF THE SACRED GEM, THE, 1914
QUEST, THE, 1915
QUESTI FANTASMI
QUESTION 7, 1961, C
QUESTION OF ADULTERY, A, 1959, C
QUESTION OF HONOR, A, 1922, A
QUESTION OF SILENCE, 1984, O
QUESTION OF SUSPENSE, A, 1961, C
QUESTION OF TRUST, A, 1920, A
QUESTION, THE, 1916, C
QUESTION, THE, 1917
QUESTION, THE, 1977, O
QUESTIONE DI PELLE
QUI A TUE, 1919
QUICK ACTION, 1921
QUICK AND THE DEAD, THE, 1963, O
QUICK CHANGE, 1925
QUICK GUN, THE, 1964, A
QUICK MILLIONS, 1931, C
QUICK MILLIONS, 1939, A
QUICK MONEY, 1938, A
QUICK ON THE TRIGGER, 1949, A
QUICK TRIGGER LEE, 1931
QUICK TRIGGERS, 1928
QUICK, BEFORE IT MELTS, 1964, A
QUICK, LET'S GET MARRIED, 1965, C
QUICKENING FLAME, THE, 1919
QUICKER'N LIGHTNIN', 1925, A
QUICKSAND, 1950, C
QUICKSANDS, 1917
QUICKSANDS, 1918, A
QUICKSANDS, 1923
QUICKSANDS OF LIFE, 1915
QUIEN SABE?
QUIET AMERICAN, THE, 1958, A
QUIET DAY IN BELFAST, A, 1974, C
QUIET GUN, THE, 1957, A
QUIET MAN, THE, 1952, A
QUIET PLACE IN THE COUNTRY, A, 1970, O
QUIET PLEASE, 1938, A
QUIET PLEASE, MURDER, 1942, A
QUIET WEDDING, 1941, A
QUIET WEEKEND, 1948, A
QUIET WOMAN, THE, 1951, A
QUILLER MEMORANDUM, THE, 1966, C
QUINCANNON, FRONTIER SCOUT, 1956, A
QUINCY ADAMS SAWYER, 1922
QUINCY ADAMS SAWYER AND MASON'S CORNER FOLKS (1912)
QUINTET, 1979, C-O
QUITTER, THE
QUITTER, THE, 1916
QUITTER, THE, 1929
QUITTERS, THE, 1934
QUO VADIS, 1951
QUO VADIS?, 1913, A
QUO VADIS?, 1925

-R-

R.P.M., 1970, C
R.S.V.P., 1921
R.S.V.P., 1984
RABBI AND THE SHIKSE, THE, 1976, A
RABBIT TEST, 1978, C-O
RABBIT TRAP, THE, 1959, A
RABBIT, RUN, 1970, O
RABBLE, THE, 1965, A
RABID, 1976, O
RACCONTI D'ESTATE
RACE FOR LIFE, A, 1928
RACE FOR LIFE, A, 1955, A
RACE FOR THE YANKEE ZEPHYR
RACE FOR YOUR LIFE, CHARLIE BROWN, 1977, AAA
RACE GANG
RACE STREET, 1948, C
RACE SUICIDE, 1916
RACE WILD, 1926
RACE WITH THE DEVIL, 1975, C
RACE, THE, 1916, A
RACERS, THE, 1955, A
RACETRACK, 1933, A
RACHEL AND THE STRANGER, 1948, A
RACHEL CADE
RACHEL'S MAN, 1974
RACHEL, RACHEL, 1968, A-C

RACING BLOOD, 1926
RACING BLOOD, 1938, A
RACING BLOOD, 1954, A
RACING FEVER, 1964, C
RACING FOOL, THE, 1927
RACING FOR LIFE, 1924, A
RACING HEARTS, 1923, A
RACING LADY, 1937, A
RACING LUCK, 1924
RACING LUCK, 1935, A
RACING LUCK, 1948, A
RACING LUCK, 1935
RACING ROMANCE, 1926, A
RACING ROMANCE, 1927
RACING ROMANCE, 1937, A
RACING ROMEO, 1927, A
RACING STRAIN, 1919
RACING STRAIN, THE, 1933, A
RACING WITH THE MOON, 1984, C
RACING YOUTH, 1932
RACK, THE, 1956, A
RACKET MAN, THE, 1944, A
RACKET, THE, 1928, A
RACKET, THE, 1951, C
RACKETEER ROUND-UP, 1934
RACKETEER, THE, 1929, A
RACKETEERS IN EXILE, 1937, A
RACKETEERS OF THE RANGE, 1939, A
RACKETY RAX, 1932, A
RACQUET, 1979, O
RADAN
RADAR SECRET SERVICE, 1950, A
RADIO CAB MURDER, 1954, A
RADIO CITY REVELS, 1938, A
RADIO FLYER, THE, 1924
RADIO FOLLIES, 1935, A
RADIO LOVER, 1936, A
RADIO MURDER MYSTERY, THE
RADIO ON, 1980, C
RADIO PARADE OF 1935
RADIO PATROL, 1932, A
RADIO PIRATES, 1935, A
RADIO REVELS OF 1942
RADIO STAR, THE
RADIO STARS ON PARADE, 1945, A
RADIO-MANIA, 1923
RADIOGRAFIA D'UN COLPO D'ORO
RADISHES AND CARROTS
RADON
RADON THE FLYING MONSTER
RAFFERTY AND THE GOLD DUST TWINS, 1975, C-O
RAFFICA DI COLTELLI
RAFFLES, 1930, A
RAFFLES, 1939, A
RAFFLES, THE AMATEUR CRACKSMAN, 1917
RAFFLES, THE AMATEUR CRACKSMAN, 1925, A
RAFTER ROMANCE, 1934, A
RAG DOLL
RAG MAN, THE, 1925, A
RAGE, 1966, C
RAGE, 1972, C
RAGE, 1984
RAGE AT DAWN, 1955, A
RAGE IN HEAVEN, 1941, C
RAGE OF PARIS, THE, 1921, A
RAGE OF PARIS, THE, 1938, A
RAGE OF THE BUCCANEERS, 1963, A
RAGE TO LIVE, A, 1965, C
RAGE WITHIN, THE
RAGE, 1976
RAGE, THE, 1963
RAGGED ANGELS
RAGGED EARL, THE, 1914
RAGGED EDGE, THE, 1923, A
RAGGED HEIRESS, THE, 1922, A
RAGGED MESSENGER, THE, 1917, C
RAGGED PRINCESS, THE, 1916
RAGGED ROBIN, 1924
RAGGEDY ANN AND ANDY, 1977, AAA
RAGGEDY MAN, 1981, C
RAGGEDY QUEEN, THE, 1917
RAGING BULL, 1980, O
RAGING MOON, THE
RAGING TIDE, THE, 1951, A
RAGING WATERS
RAGMAN'S DAUGHTER, THE, 1974, C
RAGS, 1915, A
RAGS TO RICHES, 1922, A
RAGS TO RICHES, 1941, A
RAGTIME, 1927, A
RAGTIME, 1981, C
RAGTIME COWBOY JOE, 1940, A
RAID ON ROMMEL, 1971, C
RAID, THE, 1954, A-C
RAIDERS FROM BENEATH THE SEA, 1964, A
RAIDERS OF ATLANTIS, 1983
RAIDERS OF LEYTE GULF, 1963, A
RAIDERS OF OLD CALIFORNIA, 1957, A
RAIDERS OF RED GAP, 1944, A
RAIDERS OF SAN JOAQUIN, 1943, A
RAIDERS OF SUNSET PASS, 1943, A
RAIDERS OF THE BORDER, 1944, A
RAIDERS OF THE DESERT, 1941, A
RAIDERS OF THE LOST ARK, 1981, C-O
RAIDERS OF THE RANGE, 1942, A
RAIDERS OF THE SEVEN SEAS, 1953, A
RAIDERS OF THE SOUTH, 1947, A
RAIDERS OF THE WEST, 1942, A
RAIDERS OF TOMAHAWK CREEK, 1950, A
RAIDERS, THE, 1916
RAIDERS, THE, 1921, A
RAIDERS, THE, 1952, A
RAIDERS, THE, 1964, A
RAIL RIDER, THE, 1916
RAILROAD MAN, THE, 1965, A
RAILROAD WORKERS, 1948, A
RAILROADED, 1923, A
RAILROADED, 1947, C
RAILROADER, THE, 1919
RAILS INTO LARAMIE, 1954, A
RAILWAY CHILDREN, THE, 1971, A
RAIN, 1932, C-O
RAIN FOR A DUSTY SUMMER, 1971, C
RAIN OR SHINE, 1930, A
RAIN PEOPLE, THE, 1969, C-O
RAINBOW, 1921, A
RAINBOW 'ROUND MY SHOULDER, 1952, A
RAINBOW BOYS, THE, 1973, A
RAINBOW BRIDGE, 1972
RAINBOW GIRL, THE, 1917
RAINBOW ISLAND, 1944, A
RAINBOW JACKET, THE, 1954, A
RAINBOW MAN, 1929, A
RAINBOW ON THE RIVER, 1936, A
RAINBOW OVER BROADWAY, 1933, A
RAINBOW OVER TEXAS, 1946, A
RAINBOW OVER THE RANGE, 1940, A
RAINBOW OVER THE ROCKIES, 1947, A
RAINBOW PRINCESS, THE, 1916, A
RAINBOW RANCH, 1933, A
RAINBOW RANGE, 1929
RAINBOW RANGERS, 1924, A
RAINBOW RILEY, 1926
RAINBOW TRAIL, 1932, A
RAINBOW TRAIL, THE, 1918
RAINBOW TRAIL, THE, 1925, A
RAINBOW VALLEY, 1935, A
RAINBOW'S END, 1935, A
RAINBOW, THE, 1917
RAINBOW, THE, 1929
RAINBOW, THE, 1944, C
RAINMAKER, THE, 1926, A
RAINMAKER, THE, 1956, A
RAINMAKERS, THE, 1935, A
RAINS CAME, THE, 1939, A
RAINS OF RANCHIPUR, THE, 1955
RAINTREE COUNTY, 1957, C
RAISE MARX AND PASS THE AMMUNITION, 1970, A
RAISE THE ROOF, 1930
RAISE THE TITANIC, 1980, A-C
RAISIN IN THE SUN, A, 1961, A
RAISING A RIOT, 1957, A
RAISING THE ROOF, 1971
RAISING THE WIND, 1933
RAISING THE WIND, 1962
RAJAH'S AMULET, THE
RAKE'S PROGRESS, THE
RAKU FIRE, 5m
RALLY 'ROUND THE FLAG, BOYS!, 1958, C
RAMBLIN' GALOOT, THE, 1926
RAMBLIN' KID, THE, 1923
RAMBLING RANGER, THE, 1927
RAMON, 1972
RAMONA, 1916, A
RAMONA, 1928, A
RAMONA, 1936, A
RAMPAGE, 1963, A
RAMPAGE AT APACHE WELLS, 1966, A
RAMPANT AGE, THE, 1930, A
RAMPARTS WE WATCH, THE, 1940, A
RAMROD, 1947, A
RAMRODDER, THE, 1969, O
RAMSBOTTOM RIDES AGAIN, 1956, A
RAMSHACKLE HOUSE, 1924, A
RAMUNTCHO, 1919
RANCHERS AND RASCALS, 1925
RANCHERS, THE, 1923
RANCHO DELUXE, 1975
RANCHO GRANDE, 1938, A
RANCHO GRANDE, 1940, A
RANCHO NOTORIOUS, 1952, A
RANDOLPH FAMILY, THE, 1945, A
RANDOM HARVEST, 1942, A
RANDY RIDES ALONE, 1934, A
RANDY STRIKES OIL
RANGE BEYOND THE BLUE, 1947, A
RANGE BLOOD, 1924
RANGE BOSS, THE, 1917
RANGE BUSTERS, THE, 1940, A
RANGE BUZZARDS, 1925
RANGE COURAGE, 1927
RANGE DEFENDERS, 1937, A
RANGE FEUD, THE, 1931, A
RANGE JUSTICE, 1925
RANGE JUSTICE, 1949, A
RANGE LAND, 1949, A
RANGE LAW, 1931, A
RANGE LAW, 1944, A
RANGE PATROL, THE, 1923
RANGE PIRATE, THE, 1921
RANGE RAIDER, THE, 1927
RANGE RENEGADES, 1948, A
RANGE RIDERS
RANGE RIDERS, THE, 1927, A
RANGE TERROR, THE, 1925
RANGE VULTURES, 1925
RANGE WAR, 1939, A
RANGE WARFARE, 1935
RANGELAND, 1922
RANGER AND THE LADY, THE, 1940, A
RANGER AND THE LAW, THE, 1921
RANGER BILL, 1925
RANGER COURAGE, 1937, A
RANGER OF CHEROKEE STRIP, 1949, A
RANGER OF THE BIG PINES, 1925, A
RANGER OF THE NORTH, 1927, A
RANGER'S CODE, THE, 1933, A
RANGER'S OATH, 1928
RANGER'S ROUNDUP, THE, 1938, A
RANGER, THE, 1918
RANGERS OF CHEROKEE STRIP
RANGERS OF FORTUNE, 1940, AA
RANGERS RIDE, THE, 1948, A
RANGERS STEP IN, THE, 1937, A
RANGERS TAKE OVER, THE, 1942
RANGLE RIVER, 1939, A
RANGO, 1931, A
RANI RADOVI
RANK OUTSIDER, 1920, A
RANKS AND PEOPLE, 1929
RANSOM, 1928, A
RANSOM, 1956, A
RANSOM, 1975
RANSOM, 1977
RANSOM, THE, 1916, A
RANSON'S FOLLY, 1915, A
RANSON'S FOLLY, 1926, A
RAPE KILLER, THE, 1976
RAPE OF MALAYA
RAPE OF THE SABINES, THE
RAPE SQUAD
RAPE, THE, 1965, O
RAPE, THE, 1968
RAPID FIRE ROMANCE, 1926
RAPTURE, 1950, A
RAPTURE, 1965, C
RAQ LO B'SHABBAT
RARE BREED, 1984, A
RARE BREED, THE, 1966, A
RARIN' TO GO, 1924
RASCAL, 1969, AAA
RASCALS, 1938, AA
RASHOMON, 1951, A-C
RASPOUTINE, 1954, C
RASPUTIN
RASPUTIN, 1929
RASPUTIN, 1930
RASPUTIN, 1932, A
RASPUTIN, 1939, A
RASPUTIN AND THE EMPRESS, 1932, C
RASPUTIN THE MAD MONK, 1932
RASPUTIN, THE BLACK MONK, 1917
RASPUTIN, THE HOLY SINNER
RASPUTIN—THE MAD MONK, 1966, C
RAT, 1960, A
RAT FINK, 1965, C
RAT PFINK AND BOO BOO, 1966, A
RAT RACE, THE, 1960, A
RAT SAVIOUR, THE, 1977
RAT, THE, 1925, A
RAT, THE, 1938, A
RATATAPLAN, 1979, A
RATCATCHER, THE
RATED AT $10,000,000, 1915
RATIONING, 1944, A
RATON PASS, 1951, A
RATS, 1984
RATS ARE COMING! THE WEREWOLVES ARE HERE!, THE, 1972, O
RATS OF TOBRUK, 1951, A
RATS, THE, 1955, A
RATS, THE, 1982
RATTLE OF A SIMPLE MAN, 1964, C
RATTLER, THE, 1925
RATTLERS, 1976, C
RATTLERS, 1976
RAUTHA SKIKKJAN

RAVAGER, THE, 1970, O
RAVAGERS, THE, 1965, A
RAVAGERS, THE, 1979, A
RAVEN'S END, 1970, A
RAVEN, THE, 1915
RAVEN, THE, 1935, A
RAVEN, THE, 1948, A
RAVEN, THE, 1963, C
RAVISHING IDIOT, A, 1966, A
RAW COURAGE, 1984, O
RAW DEAL, 1948, A-C
RAW DEAL, 1977, A
RAW EDGE, 1956, A
RAW FORCE, 1982, O
RAW MEAT
RAW TIMBER, 1937, A
RAW WEEKEND, 1964, O
RAW WIND IN EDEN, 1958, A
RAWHIDE, 1926
RAWHIDE, 1938, A
RAWHIDE, 1951
RAWHIDE HALO, THE
RAWHIDE KID, THE, 1928, A
RAWHIDE MAIL, 1934
RAWHIDE RANGERS, 1941, A
RAWHIDE ROMANCE, 1934
RAWHIDE TERROR, THE, 1934
RAWHIDE TRAIL, THE, 1950
RAWHIDE TRAIL, THE, 1958, A
RAWHIDE YEARS, THE, 1956, A
RAYMIE, 1960, AAA
RAZOR'S EDGE, THE, 1946
RAZOR'S EDGE, THE, 1984, C-O
RAZORBACK, 1984, O
RE-CREATION OF BRIAN KENT, THE, 1925
RE-UNION
RE: LUCKY LUCIANO, 1974, O
REACH FOR GLORY, 1963, A
REACH FOR THE SKY, 1957, A
REACHING FOR THE MOON, 1917, A
REACHING FOR THE MOON, 1931, A
REACHING FOR THE SUN, 1941, A
REACHING OUT, 1983, O
READIN' 'RITIN' 'RITHMETIC, 1926
READY FOR LOVE, 1934, A
READY FOR THE PEOPLE, 1964, A
READY MONEY, 1914, A
READY, WILLING AND ABLE, 1937, A
REAL ADVENTURE, THE, 1922, A
REAL BLOKE, A, 1935, A
REAL FOLKS, 1918, A
REAL GLORY, THE, 1939, A
REAL GONE GIRLS, THE
REAL LIFE, 1979, C
REAL LIFE, 1984, C
REAP THE WILD WIND, 1942, A
REAPERS, THE, 1916
REAR WINDOW, 1954, C
REASON TO LIVE, A REASON TO DIE, A, 1974, A
REASON WHY, THE, 1918
REASONABLE DOUBT, 1936
REBECCA, 1940, C
REBECCA OF SUNNYBROOK FARM, 1917, A
REBECCA OF SUNNYBROOK FARM, 1932, A
REBECCA OF SUNNYBROOK FARM, 1938, AAA
REBECCA THE JEWESS, 1913, C
REBEL ANGEL, 1962, C
REBEL CITY, 1953, A
REBEL GLADIATORS, THE, 1963, A
REBEL IN TOWN, 1956, A
REBEL ROUSERS, 1970, O
REBEL SET, THE, 1959, A
REBEL SON, THE, 1939, A
REBEL WITH A CAUSE
REBEL WITHOUT A CAUSE, 1955, C-O
REBEL, THE
REBEL, THE, 1933, A
REBELLION, 1936
REBELLION, 1938, A
REBELLION, 1967, C
REBELLION IN CUBA, 1961
REBELLION OF THE HANGED, THE, 1954, C
REBELLIOUS BRIDE, THE, 1919
REBELLIOUS DAUGHTERS, 1938
REBELLIOUS ONE, THE
REBELS AGAINST THE LIGHT, 1964, A
REBELS DIE YOUNG
REBORN, 1978
REBOUND, 1931, A
REBUS, 1969
RECAPTURED LOVE, 1930, A
RECEIVED PAYMENT, 1922
RECESS, 1967, A
RECKLESS, 1935, A
RECKLESS, 1984, O
RECKLESS AGE, 1944, A
RECKLESS AGE, THE, 1924, A
RECKLESS AGE, THE, 1958
RECKLESS BUCKAROO, THE, 1935
RECKLESS CHANCES
RECKLESS COURAGE, 1925
RECKLESS GAMBLE, A, 1928
RECKLESS HOUR, THE, 1931, A
RECKLESS LADY, THE, 1926, C
RECKLESS LIVING, 1931, A
RECKLESS LIVING, 1938, A
RECKLESS MOLLYCODDLE, THE, 1927
RECKLESS MONEY, 1926
RECKLESS RIDER, THE, 1932
RECKLESS RIDING BILL, 1924
RECKLESS ROMANCE, 1924, A
RECKLESS SEX, THE, 1925, A
RECKLESS SPEED, 1924
RECKLESS WIVES, 1921
RECKLESS YOUTH, 1922, A
RECKONING DAY, THE, 1918, A
RECLAIMED, 1918
RECLAMATION, THE, 1916
RECOIL, THE, 1917
RECOIL, THE, 1921
RECOIL, THE, 1922
RECOIL, THE, 1924, C
RECOMPENSE, 1925, C
RECORD 413, 1936, A
RECORD CITY, 1978, A-C
RECORD OF A LIVING BEING
RED, 1970, C
RED ACES, 1929
RED AND THE BLACK, THE, 1954, A
RED AND THE WHITE, THE, 1969, A
RED BADGE OF COURAGE, THE, 1951, C
RED BALL EXPRESS, 1952, A
RED BEARD, 1966, C-O
RED BERET, THE
RED BLOOD, 1926
RED BLOOD AND BLUE, 1925
RED BLOOD OF COURAGE, 1935, A
RED CANYON, 1949, A
RED CLAY, 1927
RED CLOAK, THE, 1961, A
RED COURAGE, 1921
RED DANCE, THE, 1928
RED DANUBE, THE, 1949, A
RED DAWN, 1984, O
RED DESERT, 1949, A
RED DESERT, 1965, O
RED DICE, 1926, A
RED DRAGON, THE, 1946, A
RED DRESS, THE, 1954, A
RED DUST, 1932, C
RED ENSIGN
RED FOAM, 1920
RED FORK RANGE, 1931, A
RED GARTERS, 1954, A
RED GOLD, 1930
RED HAIR, 1928, A
RED HANGMAN, THE
RED HEAD, 1934, A
RED HEAD, THE
RED HEADED WOMAN, 1932, A
RED HOT DOLLARS, 1920, A
RED HOT HOOFS, 1926
RED HOT LEATHER, 1926
RED HOT RHYTHM, 1930, A
RED HOT ROMANCE, 1922, A
RED HOT SPEED, 1929, A
RED HOT TIRES, 1925
RED HOT TIRES, 1935, A
RED HOUSE, THE, 1947, A
RED IMPS, 1923
RED INN, THE
RED KIMONO, 1925, A
RED LANE, THE, 1920, A
RED LANTERN, THE, 1919
RED LANTERNS, 1965, C
RED LIGHT, 1949, A-C
RED LIGHTS, 1923, A
RED LIGHTS AHEAD, 1937
RED LILY, THE, 1924
RED LINE 7000, 1965, C
RED LION, 1971, A
RED LIPS, 1928, A
RED LIPS, 1964, O
RED LOVE, 1925
RED MAJESTY, 1929
RED MANTLE, THE
RED MARK, THE, 1928, A
RED MENACE, THE, 1949, A
RED MILL, THE, 1927, A
RED MONARCH, 1983, C
RED MORNING, 1935, A
RED MOUNTAIN, 1951, A-C
RED ON RED
RED OVER RED
RED PEACOCK, THE, 1922
RED PEARLS, 1930, A
RED PLANET MARS, 1952, A
RED PONY, THE, 1949, AA
RED POTTAGE, 1918, A
RED RAIDERS, THE, 1927
RED RIDER, THE, 1925
RED RIDERS OF CANADA, 1928
RED RIVER, 1948, A
RED RIVER RANGE, 1938, A
RED RIVER RENEGADES, 1946, A
RED RIVER ROBIN HOOD, 1943, A
RED RIVER SHORE, 1953, A
RED RIVER VALLEY, 1936, A
RED RIVER VALLEY, 1941, A
RED ROCK OUTLAW, 1950
RED ROPE, THE, 1937, A
RED ROSES OF PASSION, 1967
RED RUNS THE RIVER, 1963, A
RED SALUTE, 1935, A
RED SAUNDERS PLAYS CUPID
RED SHEIK, THE, 1963, A
RED SHOES, THE, 1948, A
RED SIGNALS, 1927
RED SKIES OF MONTANA, 1952, A
RED SKY AT MORNING, 1971, C
RED SNOW, 1952, A
RED STALLION IN THE ROCKIES, 1949, AA
RED STALLION, THE, 1947, A
RED SUN, 1972, A
RED SUNDOWN, 1956, A
RED SWORD, THE, 1929
RED TENT, THE, 1971, A
RED TOMAHAWK, 1967, A
RED TRAIL, 1923
RED VIPER, THE, 1919
RED VIRGIN, THE, 1915
RED WAGON, 1936, A
RED WARNING, THE, 1923
RED WIDOW, THE, 1916, A
RED WINE, 1928, A
RED WOMAN, THE, 1917
RED ZONE CUBA, 1972
RED, HOT AND BLUE, 1949, A
RED, INN, THE, 1954, A
RED, RED HEART, THE, 1918, A
RED, WHITE AND BLACK, THE, 1970, C
RED, WHITE AND BLUE BLOOD, 1918
RED-DRAGON, 1967, A
RED-HAIRED ALIBI, THE, 1932, A
RED-HAIRED CUPID, A, 1918
REDEEMED, 1915
REDEEMER, THE
REDEEMER, THE, 1965, A
REDEEMER, THE, 1978, O
REDEEMING LOVE, THE, 1917
REDEEMING SIN, THE, 1925, A
REDEEMING SIN, THE, 1929, A
REDEMPTION, 1917
REDEMPTION, 1930, A
REDEMPTION OF DAVE DARCEY, THE, 1916
REDEMPTION OF HIS NAME, THE, 1918
REDHEAD
REDHEAD, 1919
REDHEAD, 1941, A
REDHEAD AND THE COWBOY, THE, 1950, A
REDHEAD FROM MANHATTAN, 1954
REDHEAD FROM WYOMING, THE, 1953, A
REDHEADS ON PARADE, 1935, A
REDHEADS PREFERRED, 1926, A
REDNECK, 1975
REDNECK MILLER, 1977
REDS, 1981, C-O
REDSKIN, 1929
REDUCING, 1931, A
REDWOOD FOREST TRAIL, 1950, A
REED CASE, THE, 1917
REEFER MADNESS, 1936, C-O
REET, PETITE AND GONE, 1947
REFEREE, THE, 1922, A
REFLECTION OF FEAR, A, 1973, C
REFLECTIONS, 1984, C
REFLECTIONS FROM A BRASS BED, 1976
REFLECTIONS IN A GOLDEN EYE, 1967, O
REFORM
REFORM CANDIDATE, THE, 1915
REFORM GIRL, 1933, A
REFORM SCHOOL, 1939, A
REFORM SCHOOL GIRL, 1957, A
REFORMATORY, 1938, A
REFORMER AND THE REDHEAD, THE, 1950, A
REFUGE, 1923
REFUGE, 1981, O
REFUGEE, THE
REG'LAR FELLERS, 1941, A
REGAL CAVALCADE, 1935, A
REGENERATES, THE, 1917
REGENERATING LOVE, THE, 1915
REGENERATION, 1923
REGENERATION, THE, 1915
REGGIE MIXES IN, 1916, A
REGISTERED NURSE, 1934, A
REGULAR FELLOW, A, 1919

REGULAR FELLOW, A, 1925, A
REGULAR GIRL, A, 1919
REGULAR SCOUT, A, 1926, A
REHEARSAL FOR A CRIME
REIGN OF TERROR
REINCARNATE, THE, 1971, C
REINCARNATION OF PETER PROUD, THE, 1975, C-O
REIVERS, THE, 1969, C
REJECTED WOMAN, THE, 1924, A
REJUVINATION OF AUNT MARY, THE, 1914
REJUVINATION OF AUNT MARY, THE, 1927
REKOPIS ZNALEZIONY W SARAGOSSIE
RELAZIONI PERICOLOSE
RELENTLESS, 1948, A
RELIGIOUS RACKETEERS
RELUCTANT ASTRONAUT, THE, 1967, A
RELUCTANT BRIDE
RELUCTANT DEBUTANTE, THE, 1958, A
RELUCTANT DRAGON, THE, 1941, AAA
RELUCTANT HEROES, 1951, A
RELUCTANT SAINT, THE, 1962, A
RELUCTANT WIDOW, THE, 1951, A
REMAINS TO BE SEEN, 1953, A
REMARKABLE ANDREW, THE, 1942, A
REMARKABLE MR. KIPPS, 1942, A
REMARKABLE MR. PENNYPACKER, THE, 1959, A
REMBRANDT, 1936, A
REMEDY FOR RICHES, 1941, A
REMEMBER, 1926
REMEMBER LAST NIGHT, 1935, A
REMEMBER MY NAME, 1978, O
REMEMBER PEARL HARBOR, 1942, A
REMEMBER THAT FACE
REMEMBER THE DAY, 1941, A
REMEMBER THE NIGHT, 1940, A
REMEMBER WHEN
REMEMBER?, 1939, A
REMEMBRANCE, 1922
REMEMBRANCE, 1927
REMEMBRANCE, 1982, C-O
REMITTANCE WOMAN, THE, 1923
REMODELING HER HUSBAND, 1920
REMORQUES
REMORSELESS LOVE, 1921
REMOTE CONTROL, 1930, A
REMOVALISTS, THE, 1975, C
RENAISSANCE AT CHARLEROI, THE, 1917
RENALDO AND CLARA, 1978, O
RENDEZ-VOUS, 1932, A
RENDEZVOUS, 1935, A
RENDEZVOUS 24, 1946, A
RENDEZVOUS AT MIDNIGHT, 1935, A
RENDEZVOUS WITH ANNIE, 1946, A
RENDEZVOUS, 1951
RENDEZVOUS, THE, 1923, A
RENEGADE GIRL, 1946, A
RENEGADE GIRLS, 1974, O
RENEGADE HOLMES, M.D., 1925
RENEGADE POSSE
RENEGADE RANGER, 1938, A
RENEGADE TRAIL, 1939, A
RENEGADE, THE, 1943
RENEGADES, 1930, A
RENEGADES, 1946, A
RENEGADES OF SONORA, 1948, A
RENEGADES OF THE RIO GRANDE, 1945, A
RENEGADES OF THE SAGE, 1949, A
RENEGADES OF THE WEST, 1932, A
RENFREW OF THE ROYAL MOUNTED, 1937, A
RENFREW OF THE ROYAL MOUNTED ON THE GREAT WHITE TRAIL
RENFREW ON THE GREAT WHITE TRAIL
RENO, 1923, A
RENO, 1930, A
RENO, 1939, A
RENO AND THE DOC, 1984, O
RENO DIVORCE, A, 1927
RENONCEMENT, 1917
RENT CONTROL, 1981, C
RENT FREE, 1922
RENTADICK, 1972, O
RENTED
REPEAT PERFORMANCE, 1947, A
REPENT AT LEISURE, 1941, A
REPENTANCE, 1922, A
REPLICA OF A CRIME
REPO MAN, 1984, O
REPORT ON TH EPARTY AND THE GUESTS, A, 1968, A
REPORT TO THE COMMISSIONER, 1975, C
REPORTED MISSING, 1922, A
REPORTED MISSING, 1937, A
REPRIEVE
REPRIEVED
REPRISAL, 1956, A
REPTILE, THE, 1966, C
REPTILICUS, 1962, A
REPULSION, 1965, O
REPUTATION
REPUTATION, 1917
REPUTATION, 1921, A
REQUIEM FOR A GUNFIGHTER, 1965, A
REQUIEM FOR A HEAVYWEIGHT, 1962, C
REQUIEM FOR A SECRET AGENT, 1966, A
REQUINS, 1917
RESCUE SQUAD, 1935, A
RESCUE SQUAD, THE, 1963, A
RESCUE, THE, 1917, A
RESCUE, THE, 1929, A
RESCUERS, THE, 1977, AAA
RESCUING ANGEL, THE, 1919
RESERVED FOR LADIES, 1932, AA
RESPECTABLE BY PROXY, 1920
RESPONDENT, THE
REST CURE, THE, 1923, A
REST IS SILENCE, THE, 1960, C
RESTITUTION, 1918
RESTLESS
RESTLESS BREED, THE, 1957, A
RESTLESS NIGHT, THE, 1964, C
RESTLESS ONES, THE, 1965, A
RESTLESS SEX, THE, 1920
RESTLESS SOULS, 1919
RESTLESS SOULS, 1922
RESTLESS WIVES, 1924
RESTLESS YEARS, THE, 1958, A
RESTLESS YOUTH, 1928
RESURRECTION, 1912
RESURRECTION, 1918
RESURRECTION, 1927
RESURRECTION, 1931, A
RESURRECTION, 1963, A
RESURRECTION, 1980, C
RESURRECTION OF LOVE, 1922
RESURRECTION OF ZACHARY WHEELER, THE, 1971, A
RESURRECTION SYNDICATE
RETALIATION, 1929
RETENEZ MOI...OU JE FAIS UN MALHEUR
RETRIEVERS, THE
RETURN FROM THE ASHES, 1965, A
RETURN FROM THE PAST
RETURN FROM THE SEA, 1954, A
RETURN FROM WITCH MOUNTAIN, 1978, AA
RETURN OF 18 BRONZEMEN, 1984
RETURN OF A MAN CALLED HORSE, THE, 1976, C
RETURN OF A STRANGER, 1962, C
RETURN OF A STRANGER, 1940
RETURN OF BOSTON BLACKIE, THE, 1927
RETURN OF BULLDOG DRUMMOND, THE, 1934, A
RETURN OF CAPTAIN INVINCIBLE, THE, 1983, C
RETURN OF CAROL DEANE, THE, 1938, A
RETURN OF CASEY JONES, 1933, A
RETURN OF COUNT YORGA, THE, 1971, C
RETURN OF DANIEL BOONE, THE, 1941, A
RETURN OF DR. FU MANCHU, THE, 1930, A
RETURN OF DR. MABUSE, THE, 1961, C
RETURN OF DR. X, THE, 1939, C
RETURN OF DRACULA, THE, 1958
RETURN OF EVE, THE, 1916
RETURN OF FRANK JAMES, THE, 1940, A
RETURN OF GILBERT AND SULLIVAN, 1952
RETURN OF JACK SLADE, THE, 1955, A
RETURN OF JESSE JAMES, THE, 1950, A
RETURN OF JIMMY VALENTINE, THE, 1936, A
RETURN OF MARTIN GUERRE, THE, 1983, C
RETURN OF MARY, THE, 1918
RETURN OF MAURICE DONNELLY, THE, 1915
RETURN OF MAXWELL SMART, THE
RETURN OF MONTE CRISTO, THE, 1946, A
RETURN OF MR. H, THE
RETURN OF MR. MOTO, THE, 1965, A
RETURN OF OCTOBER, THE, 1948, A
RETURN OF OLD MOTHER RILEY, THE
RETURN OF PETER GRIMM, THE, 1926, A
RETURN OF PETER GRIMM, THE, 1935, A
RETURN OF RAFFLES, THE, 1932, A
RETURN OF RIN TIN TIN, THE, 1947, AA
RETURN OF RINGO, THE, 1966, A
RETURN OF RUSTY, THE, 1946
RETURN OF SABATA, 1972, C
RETURN OF SOPHIE LANG, THE, 1936, A
RETURN OF TARZAN, THE, 1920
RETURN OF THE APE MAN, 1944, A
RETURN OF THE BADMEN, 1948, C
RETURN OF THE BLACK EAGLE, 1949, A
RETURN OF THE CISCO KID, 1939, A
RETURN OF THE CORSICAN BROTHERS
RETURN OF THE DRAGON, 1974, O
RETURN OF THE DURANGO KID, 1945
RETURN OF THE FLY, 1959, A
RETURN OF THE FROG, THE, 1938, A
RETURN OF THE FRONTIERSMAN, 1950, A
RETURN OF THE JEDI, 1983, A-C
RETURN OF THE LASH, 1947, A
RETURN OF THE LIVING DEAD
RETURN OF THE LONE WOLF
RETURN OF THE PINK PANTHER, THE, 1975, A-C
RETURN OF THE PRODIGAL, THE
RETURN OF THE RANGERS, THE, 1943, A
RETURN OF THE RAT, THE, 1929, A
RETURN OF THE SCARLET PIMPERNEL, 1938, A
RETURN OF THE SECAUCUS SEVEN, 1980, O
RETURN OF THE SEVEN, 1966, A
RETURN OF THE SOLDIER, THE, 1983, C
RETURN OF THE TERROR, 1934, C
RETURN OF THE TEXAN, 1952, A
RETURN OF THE TIGER, 1979
RETURN OF THE VAMPIRE, THE, 1944, A
RETURN OF THE VIGILANTES, THE
RETURN OF THE WHISTLER, THE, 1948, A
RETURN OF WILD BILL, THE, 1940, A
RETURN OF WILDFIRE, THE, 1948, A
RETURN OF "DRAW" EGAN, THE, 1916
RETURN TO BOGGY CREEK, 1977, AA
RETURN TO CAMPUS, 1975, C
RETURN TO MACON COUNTY, 1975, C-O
RETURN TO PARADISE, 1953, A
RETURN TO PEYTON PLACE, 1961, A
RETURN TO SENDER, 1963, A
RETURN TO THE HORRORS OF BLOOD ISLAND
RETURN TO THE LAND OF OZ, 1971
RETURN TO TREASURE ISLAND, 1954, A
RETURN TO WARBOW, 1958, A
RETURN TO YESTERDAY, 1940, A
RETURN, THE, 1980, C
RETURNING, THE, 1983, O
REUBEN, REUBEN, 1983, O
REUNION, 1932, A
REUNION IN FRANCE, 1942, A
REUNION IN RENO, 1951, A
REUNION IN VIENNA, 1933, A-C
REUNION, THE, 1977
REVEILLE, 1924
REVEILLE WITH BEVERLY, 1943, A
REVEILLE-TOI ET MEURS
REVELATION, 1918
REVELATION, 1924, A
REVELATIONS, 1916
REVENGE, 1918
REVENGE, 1928
REVENGE AT EL PASO, 1968, A
REVENGE AT MONTE CARLO, 1933, A
REVENGE IS MY DESTINY, 1971
REVENGE OF DRACULA
REVENGE OF FRANKENSTEIN, THE, 1958, C
REVENGE OF GENERAL LING
REVENGE OF KING KONG
REVENGE OF MILADY, THE
REVENGE OF THE BLOOD BEAST, THE
REVENGE OF THE CHEERLEADERS, 1976, O
REVENGE OF THE CREATURE, 1955, A
REVENGE OF THE DEAD
REVENGE OF THE DEAD, 1975
REVENGE OF THE GLADIATORS, 1962
REVENGE OF THE GLADIATORS, 1965, A
REVENGE OF THE LIVING DEAD
REVENGE OF THE NERDS, 1984, C-O
REVENGE OF THE NINJA, 1983, A
REVENGE OF THE PINK PANTHER, 1978, A-C
REVENGE OF THE SCREAMING DEAD
REVENGE OF THE SHOGUN WOMEN, 1982, O
REVENGE OF THE ZOMBIES, 1943, A
REVENGE OF UKENO-JO, THE
REVENGE RIDER, THE, 1935, A
REVENGE, 1936
REVENGE, 1971
REVENGE, 1979
REVENGEFUL SPIRIT OF EROS, THE, 1930
REVENGERS, THE, 1972, A-C
REVENUE AGENT, 1950, A
REVERSE BE MY LOT, THE, 1938, A
REVOLT, 1916
REVOLT AT FORT LARAMIE, 1957, A
REVOLT IN CANADA, 1964
REVOLT IN THE BIG HOUSE, 1958, A
REVOLT IN THE DESERT, 1932
REVOLT OF JOB, THE, 1984, O
REVOLT OF THE BOYARS, THE
REVOLT OF THE MERCENARIES, 1964, A
REVOLT OF THE ROBOTS
REVOLT OF THE SLAVES, THE, 1961, C
REVOLT OF THE ZOMBIES, 1936, C
REVOLUTION
REVOLUTIONARY, THE, 1970, A-C
REVOLUTIONIST, 1917
REVOLUTIONIST, THE, 1914
REVOLUTIONS PER MINUTE
REWARD OF FAITH, 1929
REWARD OF PATIENCE, THE, 1916
REWARD OF THE FAITHLESS, THE, 1917
REWARD, THE, 1915, A
REWARD, THE, 1965, A
REY DE AFRICA
RHAPSODIE IN BLEI
RHAPSODY, 1954, A
RHAPSODY IN BLUE, 1945, AA

RHINESTONE, 1984, C
RHINO, 1964, A
RHINOCEROS, 1974, A-C
RHODES, 1936, A
RHODES OF AFRICA
RHUBARB, 1951, A
RHYTHM HITS THE ICE
RHYTHM IN THE AIR, 1936, A
RHYTHM IN THE CLOUDS, 1937, A
RHYTHM INN, 1951, A
RHYTHM OF THE ISLANDS, 1943, A
RHYTHM OF THE RIO GRANDE, 1940, A
RHYTHM OF THE SADDLE, 1938, A
RHYTHM ON THE RANGE, 1936, A
RHYTHM ON THE RANGE, 1932
RHYTHM ON THE RIVER
RHYTHM ON THE RIVER, 1940, A
RHYTHM PARADE, 1943, A
RHYTHM RACKETEER, 1937, A
RHYTHM ROMANCE
RHYTHM ROUND-UP, 1945
RHYTHM SERENADE, 1943, A
RICE GIRL, 1963, C-O
RICH AND FAMOUS, 1981, O
RICH AND STRANGE, 1932, C
RICH ARE ALWAYS WITH US, THE, 1932, A
RICH BRIDE, THE
RICH BUT HONEST, 1927
RICH GIRL, POOR GIRL, 1921
RICH KIDS, 1979, C
RICH MAN'S DAUGHTER, A, 1918
RICH MAN'S FOLLY, 1931, A
RICH MAN'S PLAYTHING, A, 1917
RICH MAN, POOR GIRL, 1938, A
RICH MAN, POOR MAN, 1918
RICH MEN'S SONS, 1927
RICH MEN'S WIVES, 1922, A
RICH PEOPLE, 1929, A
RICH SLAVE, THE, 1921
RICH, FULL LIFE, THE
RICH, YOUNG AND DEADLY
RICH, YOUNG AND PRETTY, 1951, A-C
RICHARD, 1972, C
RICHARD III, 1913
RICHARD III, 1956, A-C
RICHARD TAUBER STORY, THE
RICHARD THE BRAZEN, 1917
RICHARD'S THINGS, 1981, O
RICHARD, THE LION-HEARTED, 1923
RICHELIEU
RICHELIEU, 1914
RICHES AND ROMANCE
RICHEST GIRL IN THE WORLD, THE, 1934, A
RICHEST GIRL, THE, 1918
RICHEST MAN IN THE WORLD, THE
RICHEST MAN IN TOWN, 1941, A
RICHTOFEN, 1932
RICKSHAW MAN, THE, 1960, C-O
RICOCHET, 1966, C
RICOCHET ROMANCE, 1954, AAA
RIDDLE GAWNE, 1918
RIDDLE OF THE SANDS, THE, 1984, C
RIDDLE RANCH, 1936
RIDDLE TRAIL, THE, 1928
RIDDLE: WOMAN, THE, 1920, A
RIDE 'EM COWBOY, 1936, A
RIDE 'EM COWBOY, 1942, AAA
RIDE 'EM COWGIRL, 1939, A
RIDE 'EM HIGH, 1927
RIDE A CROOKED MILE, 1938, C
RIDE A CROOKED TRAIL, 1958, A-C
RIDE A NORTHBOUND HORSE, 1969, AA
RIDE A VIOLENT MILE, 1957, C
RIDE A WILD PONY, 1976, AAA
RIDE BACK, THE, 1957, C
RIDE BEYOND VENGEANCE, 1966, O
RIDE CLEAR OF DIABLO, 1954, C
RIDE FOR YOUR LIFE, 1924, A
RIDE HIM, COWBOY, 1932, A
RIDE IN A PINK CAR, 1974
RIDE IN THE WHIRLWIND, 1966, C
RIDE LONESOME, 1959, C
RIDE ON VAQUERO, 1941, A
RIDE OUT FOR REVENGE, 1957, C
RIDE THE HIGH COUNTRY, 1962, C
RIDE THE HIGH IRON, 1956, A
RIDE THE HIGH WIND, 1967, A
RIDE THE MAN DOWN, 1952, C
RIDE THE PINK HORSE, 1947, C
RIDE THE TIGER, 1971
RIDE THE WILD SURF, 1964, A
RIDE TO HANGMAN'S TREE, THE, 1967, A
RIDE, KELLY, RIDE, 1941, A
RIDE, RANGER, RIDE, 1936, A
RIDE, RYDER, RIDE!, 1949, A
RIDE, TENDERFOOT, RIDE, 1940, A
RIDE, VAQUERO!, 1953, A
RIDER FROM NOWHERE
RIDER FROM TUCSON, 1950, A
RIDER IN THE NIGHT, THE, 1968, C
RIDER OF DEATH VALLEY, 1932, A
RIDER OF MYSTERY RANCH, 1924
RIDER OF THE KING LOG, THE, 1921
RIDER OF THE LAW, 1919
RIDER OF THE LAW, 1927
RIDER OF THE LAW, THE, 1935, A
RIDER OF THE PLAINS, 1931, A
RIDER ON A DEAD HORSE, 1962, C
RIDER ON THE RAIN, 1970, C
RIDERS AT NIGHT, 1923
RIDERS FROM NOWHERE, 1940, A
RIDERS FROM THE DUSK
RIDERS IN THE SKY, 1949, A
RIDERS OF BLACK HILLS
RIDERS OF BLACK MOUNTAIN, 1941, A
RIDERS OF BLACK RIVER, 1939, A
RIDERS OF BORDER BAY, 1925
RIDERS OF DESTINY, 1933, A
RIDERS OF MYSTERY, 1925, A
RIDERS OF PASCO BASIN, 1940, A
RIDERS OF RIO, 1931
RIDERS OF THE BADLANDS, 1941, A
RIDERS OF THE BLACK HILLS, 1938, A
RIDERS OF THE CACTUS, 1931, A
RIDERS OF THE DARK, 1928
RIDERS OF THE DAWN, 1920, A
RIDERS OF THE DAWN, 1937, A
RIDERS OF THE DAWN, 1945, A
RIDERS OF THE DEADLINE, 1943, A
RIDERS OF THE DESERT, 1932, A
RIDERS OF THE DUSK, 1949, A
RIDERS OF THE FRONTIER, 1939, A
RIDERS OF THE GOLDEN GULCH, 1932, A
RIDERS OF THE LAW, 1922
RIDERS OF THE LONE STAR, 1947
RIDERS OF THE NIGHT, 1918
RIDERS OF THE NORTH, 1931, A
RIDERS OF THE NORTHLAND, 1942, A
RIDERS OF THE NORTHWEST MOUNTED, 1943, A
RIDERS OF THE PONY EXPRESS, 1949
RIDERS OF THE PURPLE SAGE, 1918
RIDERS OF THE PURPLE SAGE, 1925, A
RIDERS OF THE PURPLE SAGE, 1931, A
RIDERS OF THE PURPLE SAGE, 1941, A
RIDERS OF THE RANGE, 1923
RIDERS OF THE RANGE, 1949, A
RIDERS OF THE RIO GRANDE, 1929, A
RIDERS OF THE RIO GRANDE, 1943, A
RIDERS OF THE ROCKIES, 1937, A
RIDERS OF THE SAGE, 1939
RIDERS OF THE SAND STORM, 1925
RIDERS OF THE SANTA FE, 1944, A
RIDERS OF THE STORM, 1929
RIDERS OF THE WEST, 1927
RIDERS OF THE WEST, 1942, A
RIDERS OF THE WHISTLING PINES, 1949, A
RIDERS OF THE WHISTLING SKULL, 1937, A-C
RIDERS OF VENGEANCE
RIDERS OF VENGEANCE, 1919, A
RIDERS OF VENGEANCE, 1928
RIDERS TO THE STARS, 1954, A
RIDERS UP, 1924
RIDGEWAY OF MONTANA, 1924, A
RIDIN' COMET, 1925
RIDIN' DEMON, THE, 1929
RIDIN' DOUBLE
RIDIN' DOWN THE CANYON, 1942, A
RIDIN' DOWN THE TRAIL, 1947, A
RIDIN' EASY, 1925
RIDIN' FOOL, 1924
RIDIN' FOOL, THE, 1931
RIDIN' FOR JUSTICE, 1932, A
RIDIN' GENT, A, 1926
RIDIN' KID, 1930
RIDIN' KID FROM POWDER RIVER, THE, 1924
RIDIN' LAW, 1930, A
RIDIN' LUCK, 1927
RIDIN' MAD, 1924, A
RIDIN' ON, 1936
RIDIN' ON A RAINBOW, 1941, A
RIDIN' PRETTY, 1925
RIDIN' RASCAL, THE, 1926
RIDIN' ROMEO, A, 1921
RIDIN' ROWDY, THE, 1927
RIDIN' STRAIGHT, 1926
RIDIN' STREAK, THE, 1925
RIDIN' THE LONE TRAIL, 1937, A
RIDIN' THE OUTLAW TRAIL, 1951, A
RIDIN' THE TRAIL, 1940
RIDIN' THE WIND, 1925, A
RIDIN' THROUGH
RIDIN' THRU, 1923
RIDIN' THRU, 1935
RIDIN' THUNDER, 1925
RIDIN' WEST, 1924
RIDIN' WILD, 1922, A
RIDIN' WILD, 1925
RIDING AVENGER, THE, 1936, A
RIDING DEMON
RIDING DOUBLE, 1924
RIDING FOOL, 1924
RIDING FOR FAME, 1928
RIDING FOR LIFE, 1926
RIDING HIGH, 1937, A
RIDING HIGH, 1943, A
RIDING HIGH, 1950, A
RIDING ON, 1937, A
RIDING ON AIR, 1937, AA
RIDING RENEGADE, THE, 1928
RIDING RIVALS, 1926
RIDING ROMANCE, 1926
RIDING SHOTGUN, 1954, A
RIDING SPEED, 1934, A
RIDING TALL
RIDING THE CALIFORNIA TRAIL, 1947
RIDING THE CHEROKEE TRAIL, 1941, A
RIDING THE SUNSET TRAIL, 1941, A
RIDING THE WIND, 1942, A
RIDING THROUGH NEVADA, 1942
RIDING THUNDER
RIDING TO FAME, 1927
RIDING TORNADO, THE, 1932, A
RIDING WEST, 1944, A
RIDING WILD, 1935
RIDING WITH DEATH, 1921, A
RIDING WITH DEATH, 1976
RIEL, 1979
RIFF RAFF GIRLS, 1962, O
RIFF-RAFF, 1936, A
RIFFRAFF, 1947, A
RIFIFFI A TOKYO
RIFIFI, 1956, A-C
RIFIFI FOR GIRLS
RIFIFI FRA LE DONNE
RIFIFI IN PARIS
RIFIFI IN TOKYO, 1963, A-C
RIFIFI INTERNAZIONALE
RIGHT AGE TO MARRY, THE, 1935, A
RIGHT APPROACH, THE, 1961, A
RIGHT CROSS, 1950, A-C
RIGHT DIRECTION, THE, 1916
RIGHT ELEMENT, THE, 1919
RIGHT HAND OF THE DEVIL, THE, 1963, C
RIGHT MAN, THE
RIGHT MAN, THE, 1925
RIGHT OF MARY BLAKE, THE, 1916
RIGHT OF THE STRONGEST, THE, 1924
RIGHT OF WAY, THE, 1915
RIGHT OF WAY, THE, 1920
RIGHT OF WAY, THE, 1931, A
RIGHT OFF THE BAT, 1915
RIGHT STUFF, THE, 1983, A-C
RIGHT THAT FAILED, THE, 1922, A
RIGHT TO BE HAPPY, THE, 1917
RIGHT TO HAPPINESS, THE, 1919
RIGHT TO LIE, THE, 1919, A
RIGHT TO LIVE, THE, 1921
RIGHT TO LIVE, THE, 1933, A
RIGHT TO LIVE, THE, 1935, A
RIGHT TO LIVE, THE, 1945
RIGHT TO LOVE, THE, 1920
RIGHT TO LOVE, THE, 1931, C
RIGHT TO ROMANCE, 1933, A-C
RIGHT TO STRIKE, THE, 1923
RIGHT TO THE HEART, 1942, A
RIGHT WAY, THE, 1921, A
RIGHTS OF MAN, THE, 1915
RIGOLETTO, 1949, A
RILEY OF THE RAINBOW DIVISION, 1928
RILEY THE COP, 1928, A
RILKA, 1918
RIM OF HELL, 1970
RIM OF THE CANYON, 1949, A
RIMFIRE, 1949, A
RIMROCK JONES, 1918
RING AND THE MAN, THE, 1914, A
RING AROUND THE CLOCK, 1953, A
RING AROUND THE MOON, 1936, A
RING OF BRIGHT WATER, 1969, A
RING OF FEAR, 1954, A
RING OF FIRE, 1961, A-C
RING OF SPIES
RING OF SPIES, 1964, A
RING OF TERROR, 1962, A
RING OF THE BORGIAS, THE, 1915
RING TWENTIES, THE, 1939, C
RING UP THE CURTAIN
RING, THE, 1927, A
RING, THE, 1952, A
RING-A-DING RHYTHM, 1962, A
RINGER, THE, 1928, A
RINGER, THE, 1932, A
RINGER, THE, 1953, A
RINGING THE CHANGES, 1929
RINGO AND HIS GOLDEN PISTOL, 1966, A
RINGS ON HER FINGERS, 1942, A
RINGSIDE, 1949, A

RINGSIDE MAISIE, 1941, A
RINGTAILED RHINOCEROS, THE, 1915
RINTY OF THE DESERT, 1928
RIO, 1939, A
RIO 70, 1970, C
RIO ABAJO
RIO BRAVO, 1959, A
RIO CONCHOS, 1964
RIO GRANDE, 1920
RIO GRANDE, 1939, A
RIO GRANDE, 1949
RIO GRANDE, 1950, A
RIO GRANDE PATROL, 1950, A
RIO GRANDE RAIDERS, 1946, A
RIO GRANDE RANGER, 1937, A
RIO GRANDE ROMANCE, 1936, A
RIO LOBO, 1970, A
RIO RATTLER, 1935
RIO RITA, 1929, A
RIO RITA, 1942, AAA
RIO VENGENCE
RIOT, 1969, O
RIOT AT LAUDERDALE
RIOT IN CELL BLOCK 11, 1954, C
RIOT IN JUVENILE PRISON, 1959, C
RIOT ON PIER 6
RIOT ON SUNSET STRIP, 1967, C
RIOT SQUAD, 1933
RIOT SQUAD, 1941, A
RIOTOUS BRUIN, THE
RIP OFF, 1977
RIP ROARIN' BUCKAROO, 1936
RIP ROARIN' ROBERTS, 1924
RIP ROARING LOGAN, 1928
RIP ROARING RILEY, 1935
RIP SNORTER, THE, 1925
RIP TIDE, 1934, A
RIP VAN WINKLE, 1914, A
RIP VAN WINKLE, 1921, A
RIP-OFF, 1971, O
RIP-TIDE, THE, 1923, A
RIPPED-OFF, 1971
RISATE DI GIOLA
RISE AGAINST THE SWORD, 1966, A
RISE AND FALL OF LEGS DIAMOND, THE, 1960, C
RISE AND RISE OF MICHAEL RIMMER, THE, 1970, C
RISE AND SHINE, 1941, A
RISE OF CATHERINE THE GREAT
RISE OF HELGA, THE
RISE OF JENNIE CUSHING, THE, 1917, C
RISE OF LOUIS XIV, THE, 1970, A
RISE OF SUSAN, THE, 1916
RISING DAMP, 1980, C
RISING GENERATION, THE, 1928
RISING OF THE MOON, THE, 1957, A
RISING TO FAME
RISK, THE, 1961, A
RISKY BUSINESS, 1920
RISKY BUSINESS, 1926
RISKY BUSINESS, 1939, A
RISKY BUSINESS, 1983, O
RISKY ROAD, THE, 1918, A
RITA, 1963, C
RITEN
RITUAL, THE, 1970, O
RITUALS
RITZ, THE, 1976, C-O
RITZY, 1927
RIVAL OF PERPETUA, THE, 1915
RIVALEN DER MANEGE
RIVALS, 1933
RIVALS, 1972, O
RIVALS, THE, 1963, A
RIVER BEAT, 1954, A
RIVER CHANGES, THE, 1956, A
RIVER GANG, 1945, A
RIVER HOUSE GHOST, THE, 1932, A
RIVER HOUSE MYSTERY, THE, 1935, A
RIVER LADY, 1948, A
RIVER NIGER, THE, 1976, O
RIVER OF EVIL, 1964
RIVER OF FOREVER, 1967, A-C
RIVER OF LIGHT, THE, 1921
RIVER OF MISSING MEN
RIVER OF NO RETURN, 1954, A
RIVER OF POISON
RIVER OF ROMANCE, 1929, A
RIVER OF ROMANCE, THE, 1916
RIVER OF STARS, THE, 1921
RIVER OF UNREST, 1937, A
RIVER RAT, THE, 1984, A
RIVER WOLVES, THE, 1934, A
RIVER WOMAN, 1929
RIVER WOMAN, THE, 1928, A
RIVER'S EDGE, THE, 1957
RIVER'S END, 1931, A
RIVER'S END, 1940, A
RIVER'S END, THE, 1920
RIVER, THE, 1928, A
RIVER, THE, 1951, A
RIVER, THE, 1961
RIVER, THE, 1984, A-C
RIVERBOAT RHYTHM, 1946, A
RIVERRUN, 1968, O
RIVERSIDE MURDER, THE, 1935, A
ROAD AGENT, 1926
ROAD AGENT, 1941, A
ROAD AGENT, 1952, A
ROAD BETWEEN, THE, 1917
ROAD CALLED STRAIGHT, THE, 1919
ROAD DEMON, 1938
ROAD DEMON, THE, 1921
ROAD GAMES, 1981, O
ROAD GANG, 1936
ROAD GANGS, ADVENTURES IN THE CREEP ZONE
ROAD HOME, THE, 1947, A
ROAD HOUSE, 1928, A
ROAD HOUSE, 1934
ROAD HOUSE, 1948, C
ROAD HUSTLERS, THE, 1968, C
ROAD IS FINE, THE, 1930, A
ROAD MOVIE, 1974, O
ROAD OF AMBITION, THE, 1920
ROAD OF DEATH, 1977
ROAD REBELS, 1963
ROAD SHOW, 1941, A
ROAD THROUGH THE DARK, THE, 1918
ROAD TO ALCATRAZ, 1945, A
ROAD TO ARCADY, THE, 1922
ROAD TO BALI, 1952
ROAD TO BROADWAY, THE, 1926
ROAD TO DENVER, THE, 1955, A
ROAD TO DIVORCE, THE, 1920
ROAD TO ETERNITY, 1962, O
ROAD TO FORT ALAMO, THE, 1966, C
ROAD TO FORTUNE, THE, 1930, A
ROAD TO FRANCE, THE, 1918
ROAD TO FRISCO
ROAD TO GLORY, THE, 1926
ROAD TO GLORY, THE, 1936, A-C
ROAD TO HAPPINESS, 1942, A
ROAD TO HONG KONG, THE, 1962, AA
ROAD TO LIFE, 1932, A
ROAD TO LONDON, THE, 1921, A
ROAD TO LOVE, THE, 1916
ROAD TO MANDALAY, THE, 1926, C
ROAD TO MOROCCO, 1942, AA
ROAD TO NASHVILLE, 1967
ROAD TO PARADISE, 1930, A
ROAD TO RENO, 1931, A
ROAD TO RENO, THE, 1938, A
ROAD TO RIO, 1947, AA
ROAD TO ROMANCE, THE, 1927
ROAD TO RUIN, 1934, O
ROAD TO RUIN, THE, 1913, A
ROAD TO RUIN, THE, 1928
ROAD TO SALINA, 1971, O
ROAD TO SHAME, THE, 1962, C-O
ROAD TO SINGAPORE, 1931, A
ROAD TO SINGAPORE, 1940, AA
ROAD TO THE BIG HOUSE, 1947, A
ROAD TO UTOPIA, 1945, AA
ROAD TO YESTERDAY, THE, 1925
ROAD TO ZANZIBAR, 1941, AA
ROAD WARRIOR, THE, 1982, O
ROAD, THE
ROADBLOCK, 1951, A
ROADHOUSE 66, 1984, C
ROADHOUSE GIRL
ROADHOUSE MURDER, THE, 1932, A
ROADHOUSE NIGHTS, 1930, A
ROADIE, 1980, A-C
ROADRACERS, THE, 1959, A
ROADS OF DESTINY, 1921
ROADSIDE IMPRESARIO, A, 1917
ROAMIN' WILD, 1936
ROAMING COWBOY, THE, 1937, A
ROAMING LADY, 1936, A
ROAR, 1981, A
ROAR OF THE CROWD, 1953, A
ROAR OF THE DRAGON, 1932, A
ROAR OF THE PRESS, 1941, A
ROARIN' BRONCS, 1927
ROARIN' GUNS, 1936, A
ROARIN' LEAD, 1937, A
ROARING ADVENTURE, A, 1925
ROARING BILL ATWOOD, 1926
ROARING CITY, 1951, A
ROARING FIRES, 1927
ROARING FORTIES, THE
ROARING FRONTIERS, 1941
ROARING GUNS, 1930
ROARING RAILS, 1924, A
ROARING RANCH, 1930, A
ROARING RANGERS, 1946
ROARING RIDER, 1926
ROARING ROAD, 1926
ROARING ROAD, THE, 1919, A
ROARING ROADS, 1935
ROARING SIX GUNS, 1937, A
ROARING TIMBER, 1937, A
ROARING TIMBERS
ROARING WESTWARD, 1949, A
ROB ROY
ROB ROY, 1922, A
ROB ROY, THE HIGHLAND ROGUE, 1954, A
ROBBER SYMPHONY, THE, 1937, A
ROBBERS OF THE RANGE, 1941
ROBBERS' ROOST, 1933, A
ROBBERY, 1967, A-C
ROBBERY UNDER ARMS, 1958, A
ROBBERY WITH VIOLENCE, 1958, A
ROBBO
ROBBY, 1968, AA
ROBE, THE, 1953, A
ROBERT'S ADVENTURE IN THE GREAT WAR, 1920
ROBERTA, 1935, A
ROBES OF SIN, 1924
ROBIN, 1979
ROBIN AND MARIAN, 1976, A-C
ROBIN AND THE SEVEN HOODS, 1964, A-C
ROBIN HOOD, 1913
ROBIN HOOD, 1922, A
ROBIN HOOD, 1973, AAA
ROBIN HOOD OF EL DORADO, 1936, C
ROBIN HOOD OF MONTEREY, 1947
ROBIN HOOD OF THE PECOS, 1941, A
ROBIN HOOD OF THE RANGE, 1943, A
ROBIN HOOD, 1938
ROBIN HOOD, 1952
ROBIN HOOD, JR., 1923
ROBIN OF TEXAS, 1947, A
ROBINSON CRUSOE
ROBINSON CRUSOE, 1916
ROBINSON CRUSOE, 1927, A
ROBINSON CRUSOE AND THE TIGER, 1972
ROBINSON CRUSOE ON MARS, 1964, A
ROBINSON CRUSOELAND
ROBINSON SOLL NICHT STERBEN
ROBO DE DIAMANTES
ROBO NO ISHI
ROBOT MONSTER, 1953, A
ROBOT VS. THE AZTEC MUMMY, THE, 1965, O
ROCAMBOLE, 1923
ROCCO AND HIS BROTHERS, 1961, C
ROCCO E I SUOI FRATELLI
ROCCO PAPALEO, 1974, O
ROCK 'N' ROLL HIGH SCHOOL, 1979, C
ROCK 'N' RULE, 1983
ROCK ALL NIGHT, 1957, A
ROCK AROUND THE CLOCK, 1956, A
ROCK AROUND THE WORLD, 1957, A
ROCK BABY, ROCK IT, 1957, A
ROCK ISLAND TRAIL, 1950, A
ROCK OF AGES, 1918
ROCK RIVER RENEGADES, 1942, A
ROCK YOU SINNERS, 1957, A
ROCK, PRETTY BABY, 1956, A
ROCK, ROCK, ROCK!, 1956, A
ROCK-A-BYE BABY, 1958, A
ROCKABILLY BABY, 1957, A
ROCKABYE, 1932, A
ROCKERS, 1980, O
ROCKET ATTACK, U.S.A., 1961
ROCKET FROM CALABUCH, THE
ROCKET MAN, THE, 1954, A
ROCKET TO NOWHERE, 1962, AAA
ROCKET TO THE MOON
ROCKETS GALORE
ROCKETS IN THE DUNES, 1960, AA
ROCKETSHIP X-M, 1950, A
ROCKIN' IN THE ROCKIES, 1945, A
ROCKING HORSE WINNER, THE, 1950, C-O
ROCKING MOON, 1926
ROCKS OF VALPRE, THE
ROCKS OF VALPRE, THE, 1919
ROCKY, 1948, A
ROCKY, 1976, A-C
ROCKY HORROR PICTURE SHOW, THE, 1975, O
ROCKY II, 1979, A-C
ROCKY III, 1982, A-C
ROCKY MOUNTAIN, 1950, A
ROCKY MOUNTAIN MYSTERY, 1935, A
ROCKY MOUNTAIN RANGERS, 1940, A
ROCKY RHODES, 1934, A
RODAN, 1958, A
RODEO, 1952, A
RODEO KING AND THE SENORITA, 1951, A
RODEO MIXUP, A, 1924
RODEO RHYTHM, 1941, AA
ROGER LA HONTE, 1922
ROGER TOUHY, GANGSTER!, 1944, A
ROGUE AND GRIZZLY, THE, 1982
ROGUE AND RICHES, 1920
ROGUE COP, 1954, C
ROGUE IN LOVE, A, 1916
ROGUE IN LOVE, A, 1922, A

ROGUE OF THE RANGE, 1937, A
ROGUE OF THE RIO GRANDE, 1930, A
ROGUE RIVER, 1951, A
ROGUE'S GALLERY, 1968
ROGUE'S GALLERY, 1942
ROGUE'S MARCH, 1952, A
ROGUE'S ROMANCE, A, 1919
ROGUE'S WIFE, A, 1915
ROGUE'S YARN, 1956, A
ROGUE, THE, 1976
ROGUES AND ROMANCE, 1920
ROGUES GALLERY, 1945, A
ROGUES OF LONDON, THE, 1915, A
ROGUES OF PARIS, 1913
ROGUES OF SHERWOOD FOREST, 1950, A
ROGUES OF THE TURF, 1923
ROGUES' REGIMENT, 1948, A
ROGUES' TAVERN, THE, 1936, A
ROLL ALONG, COWBOY, 1938, A
ROLL ON
ROLL ON TEXAS MOON, 1946, A
ROLL, THUNDER, ROLL, 1949, A
ROLL, WAGONS, ROLL, 1939, A
ROLLED STOCKINGS, 1927, A
ROLLER BOOGIE, 1979, C
ROLLERBALL, 1975, O
ROLLERCOASTER, 1977, C-O
ROLLIN' HOME TO TEXAS, 1941, A
ROLLIN' PLAINS, 1938, A
ROLLIN' WESTWARD, 1939, A
ROLLING CARAVANS, 1938, A
ROLLING DOWN THE GREAT DIVIDE, 1942, A
ROLLING HOME, 1926, A
ROLLING HOME, 1935, A
ROLLING HOME, 1948
ROLLING IN MONEY, 1934, A
ROLLING ROAD, THE, 1927
ROLLING STONES, 1916
ROLLING THUNDER, 1977, O
ROLLOVER, 1981, O
ROMA, 1972, O
ROMA CONTRO ROMA
ROMA RIVUOLE CESARE
ROMA, CITTA APERTA
ROMAINE KALBRIS, 1921
ROMAN HOLIDAY, 1953, A
ROMAN SCANDALS, 1933, A-C
ROMAN SPRING OF MRS. STONE, THE, 1961, C
ROMANCE, 1920
ROMANCE, 1930, A
ROMANCE AND ARABELLA, 1919, A
ROMANCE AND BRIGHT LIGHTS
ROMANCE AND RHYTHM
ROMANCE AND RICHES, 1937, A
ROMANCE AND RUSTLERS, 1925
ROMANCE FOR THREE
ROMANCE IN FLANDERS, A, 1937, Brit.
ROMANCE IN MANHATTAN, 1935, A
ROMANCE IN RHYTHM, 1934
ROMANCE IN THE DARK, 1938, A
ROMANCE IN THE RAIN, 1934, A
ROMANCE LAND, 1923, A
ROMANCE OF A HORSE THIEF, 1971, A
ROMANCE OF A MILLION DOLLARS, THE, 1926
ROMANCE OF A ROGUE, 1928
ROMANCE OF A RUSSIAN BALLERINA, 1913
ROMANCE OF ANNIE LAURIE, THE, 1920
ROMANCE OF BILLY GOAT HILL, A, 1916
ROMANCE OF HAPPY VALLEY, A, 1919, A
ROMANCE OF LADY HAMILTON, THE, 1919
ROMANCE OF OLD BAGDAD, A, 1922
ROMANCE OF RIO GRANDE
ROMANCE OF ROSY RIDGE, THE, 1947, A
ROMANCE OF SEVILLE, A, 1929, A
ROMANCE OF TARZAN, THE, 1918, A
ROMANCE OF THE AIR, A, 1919, A
ROMANCE OF THE LIMBERLOST, 1938, A
ROMANCE OF THE MAYFAIR, A, 1925
ROMANCE OF THE NAVY, A, 1915
ROMANCE OF THE NILE, 1924
ROMANCE OF THE REDWOODS, 1939, A
ROMANCE OF THE REDWOODS, A, 1917, A
ROMANCE OF THE RIO GRANDE, 1929, A
ROMANCE OF THE RIO GRANDE, 1941, A
ROMANCE OF THE ROCKIES, 1938, A
ROMANCE OF THE UNDERWORLD, 1928
ROMANCE OF THE UNDERWORLD, A, 1918
ROMANCE OF THE WASTELAND, 1924
ROMANCE OF THE WEST, 1946, A
ROMANCE OF WASTDALE, A, 1921
ROMANCE ON THE BEACH
ROMANCE ON THE HIGH SEAS, 1948, A
ROMANCE ON THE RANGE, 1942, A
ROMANCE ON THE RUN, 1938, A
ROMANCE PROMOTORS, THE, 1920
ROMANCE RANCH, 1924, A
ROMANCE RIDES THE RANGE, 1936, A
ROMANCE ROAD, 1925, A
ROMANCING THE STONE, 1984, C-O
ROMANOFF AND JULIET, 1961, A
ROMANTIC ADVENTURESS, A, 1920
ROMANTIC AGE, THE, 1927
ROMANTIC AGE, THE, 1934
ROMANTIC AGE, THE, 1949, Brit.
ROMANTIC COMEDY, 1983, A-C
ROMANTIC ENGLISHWOMAN, THE, 1975, O
ROMANTIC JOURNEY, THE, 1916
ROMANTIC ROGUE, 1927
ROMANY LASS, A
ROMANY LOVE, 1931
ROMANY RYE, THE, 1915
ROMANY, THE, 1923
ROME ADVENTURE, 1962, A
ROME EXPRESS, 1933, A
ROME WANTS ANOTHER CAESAR, 1974, A
ROME, OPEN CITY
ROMEO AND JULIET, 1916, A
ROMEO AND JULIET, 1916
ROMEO AND JULIET, 1936, C
ROMEO AND JULIET, 1954, A
ROMEO AND JULIET, 1955, A
ROMEO AND JULIET, 1966, A
ROMEO AND JULIET, 1968, A-C
ROMEO AND JULIET, 1968, C
ROMEO IN PYJAMAS
ROMEO, JULIET AND DARKNESS
ROMMEL'S TREASURE, 1962, A
ROMMEL-DESERT FOX
ROMOLA, 1925, A
ROMOLO E REMO
ROOF TREE, THE, 1921
ROOF, THE, 1933, A
ROOGIE'S BUMP, 1954, A
ROOK, THE
ROOKERY NOOK
ROOKIE COP, THE, 1939, A
ROOKIE FIREMAN, 1950, A
ROOKIE'S RETURN, THE, 1921, A
ROOKIE, THE, 1959, A
ROOKIES
ROOKIES, 1927
ROOKIES COME HOME
ROOKIES IN BURMA, 1943, A
ROOKIES ON PARADE, 1941, A
ROOM 43, 1959, A
ROOM AND BOARD, 1921
ROOM AT THE TOP, 1959, O
ROOM FOR ONE MORE, 1952, AA
ROOM FOR TWO, 1940, A
ROOM IN THE HOUSE, 1955, A
ROOM SERVICE, 1938, A
ROOM TO LET, 1949, A
ROOM UPSTAIRS, THE, 1948, C
ROOMATES, 1969
ROOMMATES, 1962, AA
ROOMMATES, 1971, O
ROOMMATES, THE, 1973, O
ROONEY, 1958, A
ROOSTER COGBURN, 1975, A
ROOT OF ALL EVIL, THE, 1947, A
ROOT OF EVIL, THE, 1919
ROOTIN' TOOTIN' RHYTHM, 1937, A
ROOTS OF HEAVEN, THE, 1958, C
ROPE, 1948, C-O
ROPE OF FLESH, 1965, O
ROPE OF SAND, 1949
ROPE, 1965
ROPED, 1919
ROPED BY RADIO, 1925
ROPIN' RIDIN' FOOL, A, 1925
ROSALEEN DHU, 1920
ROSALIE, 1937, A
ROSARY, THE, 1915
ROSARY, THE, 1922
ROSARY, THE, 1931
ROSE BOWL, 1936, A
ROSE BOWL STORY, THE, 1952, A
ROSE FOR EVERYONE, A, 1967, O
ROSE FRANCE, 1919
ROSE IN THE DUST, 1921
ROSE MARIE, 1936, AA
ROSE MARIE, 1954, AA
ROSE O' PARADISE, 1918
ROSE O' THE RIVER
ROSE O' THE SEA, 1922
ROSE OF BLOOD, THE, 1917
ROSE OF CIMARRON, 1952, A
ROSE OF GRENADE, 1916
ROSE OF KILDARE, THE, 1927
ROSE OF NOME, 1920
ROSE OF PARIS, THE, 1924, A
ROSE OF SANTA ROSA, 1947
ROSE OF THE ALLEY, 1916
ROSE OF THE BOWERY, 1927
ROSE OF THE DESERT, 1925
ROSE OF THE GOLDEN WEST, 1927
ROSE OF THE RANCHO, 1914, A
ROSE OF THE RANCHO, 1936, A
ROSE OF THE RIO GRANDE
ROSE OF THE RIO GRANDE, 1938, A
ROSE OF THE RIVER, 1919
ROSE OF THE SOUTH, 1916
ROSE OF THE TENEMENTS, 1926
ROSE OF THE WEST, 1919
ROSE OF THE WORLD, 1918, A
ROSE OF THE WORLD, 1925, A
ROSE OF THE YUKON, 1949, A
ROSE OF TRALEE, 1938, A
ROSE OF TRALEE, 1942, A
ROSE OF WASHINGTON SQUARE, 1939, A
ROSE TATTOO, THE, 1955, C-O
ROSE, THE, 1979, O
ROSE-MARIE, 1928
ROSEANNA McCOY, 1949, AA
ROSEBUD, 1975, C
ROSEBUD BEACH HOTEL, 1984, C-O
ROSELAND, 1977, C
ROSEMARY, 1915
ROSEMARY, 1960, C
ROSEMARY CLIMBS THE HEIGHTS, 1918
ROSEMARY'S BABY, 1968, O
ROSEMARY'S KILLER
ROSEN FUR DEN STAATSANWALT
ROSES ARE RED, 1947, A
ROSES BLOOM TWICE, 1977
ROSES FOR THE PROSECUTOR, 1961, A
ROSES OF PICARDY, 1918
ROSES OF PICARDY, 1927, A
ROSIE THE RIVETER, 1944, A
ROSIE!, 1967, A
ROSITA, 1923, A
ROSMUNDA E ALBOINO
ROSSINI, 1948, A
ROSSITER CASE, THE, 1950, A
ROTHSCHILD, 1938, A
ROTTEN APPLE, THE, 1963, O
ROTTEN TO THE CORE, 1956, C
ROTTERS, THE, 1921
ROTWEILER: DOGS OF HELL, 1984, O
ROUGE AND RICHES, 1920
ROUGED LIPS, 1923
ROUGH AND READY, 1918, A
ROUGH AND READY, 1927
ROUGH AND READY, 1930
ROUGH AND THE SMOOTH, THE
ROUGH COMPANY
ROUGH CUT, 1980, C
ROUGH DIAMOND, THE, 1921
ROUGH GOING, 1925
ROUGH HOUSE ROSIE, 1927, A
ROUGH LOVER, THE, 1918, A
ROUGH NIGHT IN JERICHO, 1967, O
ROUGH RIDERS OF CHEYENNE, 1945, A
ROUGH RIDERS OF DURANGO, 1951, A
ROUGH RIDERS' ROUNDUP, 1939, A
ROUGH RIDERS, THE, 1927, A
ROUGH RIDIN', 1924
ROUGH RIDIN' JUSTICE, 1945
ROUGH RIDIN' RED, 1928
ROUGH RIDIN' RHYTHM, 1937, A
ROUGH RIDING RANGER, 1935, A
ROUGH RIDING ROMANCE, 1919
ROUGH RIDING ROMEO
ROUGH ROMANCE, 1930, A
ROUGH SHOD, 1925, A
ROUGH SHOD FIGHTER, A, 1927
ROUGH SHOOT
ROUGH STUFF, 1925
ROUGH WATERS, 1930
ROUGH, TOUGH AND READY, 1945, A
ROUGH, TOUGH WEST, THE, 1952, A
ROUGHLY SPEAKING, 1945
ROUGHNECK, THE, 1919
ROUGHNECK, THE, 1924, A
ROUGHSHOD, 1949, A
ROULETTE, 1924, A
ROUND TRIP, 1967, C
ROUND UP, THE, 1920, A
ROUND UP, THE, 1969, O
ROUNDERS, THE, 1965, A-C
ROUNDING UP THE LAW, 1922
ROUNDTRIP
ROUNDUP TIME IN TEXAS, 1937
ROUNDUP, THE, 1941, A
ROUSTABOUT, 1964, A
ROVER, THE, 1967, C
ROVIN' TUMBLEWEEDS, 1939
ROVING ROGUE, A
ROWDY, THE, 1921, A
ROWDYMAN, THE, 1973, C
ROXIE HART, 1942, A
ROYAL AFFAIR, A, 1950, A
ROYAL AFFAIRS IN VERSAILLES, 1957, A
ROYAL AFRICAN RIFLES, THE, 1953, A
ROYAL AMERICAN, THE, 1927
ROYAL BED, THE, 1931, A
ROYAL BOX, THE, 1914

ROYAL BOX, THE, 1930, A
ROYAL CAVALCADE
ROYAL DEMAND, A, 1933, A
ROYAL DEMOCRAT, A, 1919
ROYAL DIVORCE, A, 1923
ROYAL DIVORCE, A, 1938, A
ROYAL EAGLE, 1936, A
ROYAL FAMILY OF BROADWAY, THE, 1930, A
ROYAL FAMILY, A, 1915, A
ROYAL FLASH, 1975, A-C
ROYAL FLUSH
ROYAL GAME, THE
ROYAL HUNT OF THE SUN, THE, 1969, A
ROYAL LOVE, 1915
ROYAL MOUNTED PATROL, THE, 1941
ROYAL OAK, THE, 1923, A
ROYAL PAUPER, THE, 1917
ROYAL RIDER, THE, 1929, A
ROYAL ROMANCE, 1917
ROYAL ROMANCE, A, 1930, A
ROYAL SCANDAL, 1929
ROYAL SCANDAL, A, 1945, C-O
ROYAL TRACK, THE
ROYAL WALTZ, THE, 1936, A
ROYAL WEDDING, 1951, A
ROZMARNE LETO
RUBA AL PROSSIMO TUO
RUBBER GUN, THE, 1977, C
RUBBER HEELS, 1927
RUBBER RACKETEERS, 1942, A
RUBBER TIRES, 1927, A
RUBE, THE, 1925
RUBY, 1971, C
RUBY, 1977, O
RUBY GENTRY, 1952, C-O
RUBY VIRGIN, THE
RUCKUS, 1981, C
RUDDIGORE, 1967
RUDE BOY, 1980, O
RUDYARD KIPLING'S JUNGLE BOOK
RUE CASES NEGRES
RUE DE LA PAIX, 1927
RUGGED O'RIORDANS, THE, 1949, A
RUGGED PATH, THE, 1918
RUGGED WATER, 1925, A
RUGGLES OF RED GAP, 1918
RUGGLES OF RED GAP, 1923, A
RUGGLES OF RED GAP, 1935, A
RULER OF THE ROAD, 1918
RULER OF THE WORLD
RULERS OF THE SEA, 1939, A
RULES OF THE GAME, THE, 1939, C
RULING CLASS, THE, 1972, O
RULING PASSION, THE, 1916
RULING PASSION, THE, 1922, A
RULING VOICE, THE, 1931, A
RUM RUNNERS, THE, 1923
RUMBA, 1935, A
RUMBLE FISH, 1983, O
RUMBLE ON THE DOCKS, 1956, A
RUMMY, THE, 1916
RUMPELSTILSKIN, 1915
RUMPELSTILTSKIN, 1965, A
RUMPELSTILZCHEN
RUN ACROSS THE RIVER, 1961, A
RUN FOR COVER, 1955, A-C
RUN FOR THE HILLS, 1953, A
RUN FOR THE ROSES, 1978, C
RUN FOR THE SUN, 1956, A
RUN FOR YOUR MONEY, A, 1950, A
RUN FOR YOUR WIFE, 1966, C
RUN HERO RUN
RUN HOME SLOW, 1965
RUN LIKE A THIEF
RUN LIKE A THIEF, 1968, C
RUN OF THE ARROW, 1957, C-O
RUN ON GOLD, A
RUN SHADOW RUN
RUN SILENT, RUN DEEP, 1958, A-C
RUN WILD, RUN FREE, 1969, A
RUN WITH THE DEVIL, 1963, A
RUN WITH THE WIND, 1966, O
RUN, ANGEL, RUN, 1969, O
RUN, RUN, JOE!, 1974
RUN, STRANGER, RUN
RUNAROUND, THE, 1931, A
RUNAROUND, THE, 1946, A
RUNAWAY, 1971
RUNAWAY, 1984, C-O
RUNAWAY BRIDE, 1930, A
RUNAWAY BUS, THE, 1954, A
RUNAWAY DAUGHTER
RUNAWAY DAUGHTERS, 1957, A
RUNAWAY DAUGHTERS, 1968
RUNAWAY EXPRESS, THE, 1926
RUNAWAY GIRL, 1966, C
RUNAWAY GIRLS, 1928, A
RUNAWAY LADIES, 1935, A
RUNAWAY PRINCESS, THE, 1929
RUNAWAY QUEEN, THE, 1935, A
RUNAWAY RAILWAY, 1965, AA
RUNAWAY ROMANY, 1917
RUNAWAY WIFE, THE, 1915
RUNAWAY, THE, 1917
RUNAWAY, THE, 1926, A
RUNAWAY, THE, 1964, A
RUNNER STUMBLES, THE, 1979, C
RUNNERS, 1983, A
RUNNING, 1979, C
RUNNING BRAVE, 1983, C
RUNNING FIGHT, THE, 1915, A
RUNNING HOT, 1984, O
RUNNING MAN, THE, 1963, A-C
RUNNING SCARED
RUNNING SCARED, 1972, C-O
RUNNING SCARED, 1980
RUNNING TARGET, 1956, A
RUNNING WATER, 1922, A
RUNNING WILD, 1927
RUNNING WILD, 1955, A
RUNNING WILD, 1973
RUNNING WITH THE DEVIL, 1973
RUPERT OF HENTZAU, 1915, A
RUPERT OF HENTZAU, 1923, A
RUSE OF THE RATTLER, THE, 1921
RUSH, 1984, C-O
RUSH HOUR, THE, 1927, A
RUSLAN I LUDMILA, 1915
RUSSIA, 1929
RUSSIA—LAND OF TOMORROW, 1919
RUSSIAN ROULETTE, 1975, C
RUSSIANS ARE COMING, THE RUSSIANS ARE COMING, THE, 1966, A
RUSTLE OF SILK, THE, 1923
RUSTLER'S END, THE, 1928
RUSTLER'S HIDEOUT, 1944, A
RUSTLER'S PARADISE, 1935, A
RUSTLER'S RANCH, 1926, A
RUSTLER'S ROUNDUP, 1946, A
RUSTLER'S VALLEY, 1937, A
RUSTLERS, 1949, A
RUSTLERS OF DEVIL'S CANYON, 1947, A
RUSTLERS OF THE BADLANDS, 1945
RUSTLERS OF THE NIGHT, 1921
RUSTLERS ON HORSEBACK, 1950, A
RUSTLERS' ROUNDUP, 1933, A
RUSTLING A BRIDE, 1919
RUSTLING FOR CUPID, 1926
RUSTY LEADS THE WAY, 1948, A
RUSTY RIDES ALONE, 1933, A
RUSTY SAVES A LIFE, 1949, A
RUSTY'S BIRTHDAY, 1949, A
RUTHLESS, 1948, A
RUTHLESS FOUR, THE, 1969, C
RUUSUJEN AIKA
RUY BLAS, 1948, A
RX MURDER, 1958, A
RYAN'S DAUGHTER, 1970, O
RYMDINVASION I LAPPLAND
RYSOPIS

-S-

S, 1974, C
S.O.B., 1981, O
S.O.S., 1928
S.O.S. COAST GUARD, 1937
S.O.S. ICEBERG, 1933, A
S.O.S. PACIFIC, 1960, A
S.O.S. PERILS OF THE SEA, 1925
S.O.S. TIDAL WAVE, 1939, A
S.T.A.B., 1976, O
S.W.A.L.K.
SA GOSSE, 1919
SA TETE, 1930
SAADIA, 1953, A
SABA, 1929
SABAKA
SABALEROS
SABATA, 1969, C
SABINA, THE, 1979, O
SABLE BLESSING, THE, 1916
SABLE LORCHA, THE, 1915, A
SABLES, 1928
SABOTAGE, 1937, O
SABOTAGE, 1939, A
SABOTAGE AT SEA, 1942, A
SABOTAGE SQUAD, 1942, A
SABOTAGE, 1932, Brit.
SABOTEUR, 1942, A
SABOTEUR, CODE NAME MORITURI
SABRA, 1970, C
SABRE AND THE ARROW, THE
SABRE JET, 1953, A
SABRINA, 1954, A
SABRINA FAIR
SABU AND THE MAGIC RING, 1957, A
SACCO AND VANZETTI, 1971, C
SACKCLOTH AND SCARLET, 1925
SACRED AND PROFANE LOVE, 1921
SACRED FLAME, THE, 1919
SACRED FLAME, THE, 1929, A
SACRED FLAME, THE, 1935
SACRED GROUND, 1984, C
SACRED HEARTS, 1984, A
SACRED KNIVES OF VENGEANCE, THE, 1974, O
SACRED RUBY, THE, 1920
SACRED SILENCE, 1919, A
SACRIFICE, 1917
SACRIFICE, 1929
SACRIFICE OF HONOR, 1938, A
SAD HORSE, THE, 1959, AA
SAD SACK, THE, 1957, A
SAD SACK, THE, 1963
SADDLE ACES, 1935
SADDLE BUSTER, THE, 1932, A
SADDLE CYCLONE, 1925
SADDLE HAWK, THE, 1925
SADDLE JUMPERS, 1927
SADDLE KING, THE, 1929
SADDLE LEATHER LAW, 1944
SADDLE LEGION, 1951, A
SADDLE MATES, 1928
SADDLE MOUNTAIN ROUNDUP, 1941, A
SADDLE PALS, 1947, A
SADDLE SERENADE, 1945
SADDLE THE WIND, 1958, A
SADDLE TRAMP, 1950, A
SADDLEMATES, 1941, A
SADDLES AND SAGEBRUSH, 1943
SADIE GOES TO HEAVEN, 1917
SADIE LOVE, 1920
SADIE MCKEE, 1934, A
SADIE THOMPSON, 1928, C
SADIE THOMPSON, 1928, C
SADIST THE, 1963, A
SADKO
SAFARI, 1940, A
SAFARI, 1956, A
SAFARI 3000, 1982, A-C
SAFARI DRUMS, 1953, A
SAFE AFFAIR, A, 1931, A
SAFE AT HOME, 1962, A
SAFE FOR DEMOCRACY
SAFE GUARDED, 1924
SAFE IN HELL, 1931, A
SAFE PLACE, A, 1971, A
SAFECRACKER, THE, 1958, A
SAFETY CURTAIN, THE, 1918
SAFETY FIRST, 1926, A
SAFETY IN NUMBERS, 1930, A
SAFETY IN NUMBERS, 1938, A
SAFETY LAST, 1923, A
SAFFO, VENERE DE LESBO
SAGA OF DEATH VALLEY, 1939, A
SAGA OF DRACULA, THE, 1975, O
SAGA OF GOSTA BERLING, THE, 1924
SAGA OF HEMP BROWN, THE, 1958, A
SAGA OF THE FLYING HOSTESS
SAGA OF THE ROAD, THE
SAGA OF THE VAGABONDS, 1964, A
SAGA OF THE VIKING WOMEN AND THEIR VOYAGE TO THE WATERS OF THE, 1957, A
SAGE BRUSH HAMLET, A, 1919
SAGE HEN, THE, 1921
SAGE-BRUSH LEAGUE, THE, 1919
SAGEBRUSH FAMILY TRAILS WEST, THE, 1940, A
SAGEBRUSH GOSPEL, 1924
SAGEBRUSH HEROES, 1945
SAGEBRUSH LADY, THE, 1925
SAGEBRUSH LAW, 1943, A
SAGEBRUSH POLITICS, 1930, A
SAGEBRUSH TRAIL, 1934, A
SAGEBRUSH TRAIL, THE, 1922
SAGEBRUSH TROUBADOR, 1935, A
SAGEBRUSHER, THE, 1920
SAGINAW TRAIL, 1953, A
SAGITTARIUS MINE, THE, 1972
SAHARA, 1919, C
SAHARA, 1943, C
SAHARA, 1984, C
SAHARA LOVE, 1926
SAID O'REILLY TO MACNAB
SAIGON, 1948, A
SAIKAKU ICHIDAI ONNA
SAIL A CROOKED SHIP, 1961, A
SAIL INTO DANGER, 1957, A
SAILING ALONG, 1938, A
SAILOR BE GOOD, 1933, A
SAILOR BEWARE, 1951, A
SAILOR BEWARE?
SAILOR FROM GIBRALTAR, THE, 1967, O
SAILOR IZZY MURPHY, 1927, A
SAILOR OF THE KING, 1953, A
SAILOR TAKES A WIFE, THE, 1946, A
SAILOR TRAMP, A, 1922
SAILOR WHO FELL FROM GRACE WITH THE SEA, THE, 1976, O

SAILOR'S DON'T CARE, 1940, A
SAILOR'S HOLIDAY, 1944, A
SAILOR'S LADY, 1940, A
SAILOR'S LUCK, 1933, A
SAILOR'S RETURN, THE, 1978, O
SAILOR'S SWEETHEART, A, 1927, A
SAILOR-MADE MAN, A, 1921, A
SAILORS DON'T CARE, 1928
SAILORS ON LEAVE, 1941, A
SAILORS THREE
SAILORS' HOLIDAY, 1929, A
SAILORS' WIVES, 1928
SAINT AND THE BRAVE GOOSE, THE, 1981
SAINT IN LONDON, THE, 1939, A
SAINT IN NEW YORK, THE, 1938, A
SAINT IN PALM SPRINGS, THE, 1941, A
SAINT JACK, 1979, O
SAINT JOAN, 1957, A-C
SAINT MEETS THE TIGER, THE, 1943, A
SAINT STRIKES BACK, THE, 1939, A
SAINT TAKES OVER, THE, 1940, A
SAINT'S ADVENTURE, THE, 1917
SAINT'S DOUBLE TROUBLE, THE, 1940, A
SAINT'S GIRL FRIDAY, THE, 1954, A
SAINT'S RETURN, THE
SAINT'S VACATION, THE, 1941, A
SAINT, DEVIL AND WOMAN, 1916
SAINTED DEVIL, A, 1924, A
SAINTED SISTERS, THE, 1948, A
SAINTLY SINNER, THE, 1917
SAINTLY SINNERS, 1962, A
SAINTS AND SINNERS, 1916
SAINTS AND SINNERS, 1949, A
SAJENKO THE SOVIET, 1929
SAL OF SINGAPORE, 1929, A
SALAMANDER, THE, 1915, A
SALAMANDER, THE, 1916
SALAMANDER, THE, 1983, O
SALAMMBO
SALAMMBO, 1925
SALARIO PARA MATAR
SALESLADY, 1938, A
SALESLADY, THE, 1916
SALESLADY?, 1968, A-C
SALLAH, 1965, C
SALLY, 1925, A
SALLY, 1929, A
SALLY AND SAINT ANNE, 1952, A
SALLY BISHOP, 1916
SALLY BISHOP, 1923
SALLY BISHOP, 1932, O
SALLY CASTLETON, SOUTHERNER, 1915
SALLY FIELDGOOD & CO., 1975, C-O
SALLY IN A HURRY, 1917
SALLY IN OUR ALLEY, 1916
SALLY IN OUR ALLEY, 1927, A
SALLY IN OUR ALLEY, 1931, A
SALLY OF THE SAWDUST, 1925, A
SALLY OF THE SCANDALS, A
SALLY OF THE SUBWAY, 1932, C
SALLY SHOWS THE WAY
SALLY'S HOUNDS, 1968, C
SALLY'S IRISH ROGUE
SALLY'S SHOULDERS, 1928
SALLY, IRENE AND MARY, 1925
SALLY, IRENE AND MARY, 1938, A
SALOME, 1919
SALOME, 1922, A
SALOME, 1923
SALOME, 1953, C
SALOME OF THE TENEMENTS, 1925
SALOME, WHERE SHE DANCED, 1945, C
SALOMY JANE, 1914, A
SALOMY JANE, 1923, A
SALOON BAR, 1940, C
SALT & PEPPER, 1968, C
SALT AND THE DEVIL
SALT IN THE WOUND, 1972
SALT LAKE RAIDERS, 1950, A
SALT LAKE TRAIL, 1926
SALT OF THE EARTH, 1917
SALT OF THE EARTH, 1954, C
SALT TO THE DEVIL, 1949, A
SALTO, 1966, O
SALTY, 1975, A
SALTY O'ROURKE, 1945, A-C
SALTY SAUNDERS, 1923
SALUTE, 1929, A
SALUTE FOR THREE, 1943, A
SALUTE JOHN CITIZEN, 1942, A
SALUTE THE TOFF, 1952, A
SALUTE TO A REBEL
SALUTE TO COURAGE
SALUTE TO ROMANCE
SALUTE TO THE MARINES, 1943, C
SALVAGE, 1921, A
SALVAGE GANG, THE, 1958, AA
SALVARE LA FACCIA
SALVATION HUNTERS, THE, 1925, A
SALVATION JANE, 1927, A
SALVATION JOAN, 1916
SALVATION NELL, 1921, A
SALVATION NELL, 1931, A
SALVATORE GIULIANO, 1966, O
SALZBURG CONNECTION, THE, 1972, C
SAM COOPER'S GOLD
SAM MARLOW, PRIVATE EYE
SAM SMALL LEAVES TOWN, 1937, A
SAM WHISKEY, 1969, C-O
SAM'S BOY, 1922
SAM'S SON, 1984, A-C
SAM'S SONG, 1971, O
SAMANTHA
SAMAR, 1962, C
SAMARITAN, THE
SAME TIME, NEXT YEAR, 1978, A-C
SAMMY GOING SOUTH
SAMMY SOMEBODY, 1976
SAMMY STOPS THE WORLD, 1978, C
SAMPO
SAMSON, 1914, A
SAMSON, 1915
SAMSON, 1961, A
SAMSON AND DELILAH, 1922
SAMSON AND DELILAH, 1949, C
SAMSON AND THE SEA BEAST, 1960
SAMSON AND THE SEVEN MIRACLES OF THE WORLD, 1963, A
SAMSON AND THE SLAVE QUEEN, 1963, A
SAMSON IN THE WAX MUSEUM
SAMSON VS. THE GIANT KING
SAMURAI
SAMURAI, 1945, A-C
SAMURAI, 1955, O
SAMURAI (PART II), 1967, C-O
SAMURAI (PART III), 1967, C-O
SAMURAI ASSASSIN, 1965, O
SAMURAI BANNERS
SAMURAI FROM NOWHERE, 1964, C
SAMURAI PIRATE
SAN ANTONE, 1953, C
SAN ANTONE AMBUSH, 1949, A
SAN ANTONIO, 1945, A-C
SAN ANTONIO KID, THE, 1944, A
SAN ANTONIO ROSE, 1941, A
SAN DEMETRIO, LONDON, 1947, C
SAN DIEGO, I LOVE YOU, 1944, A
SAN FERNANDO VALLEY, 1944, A
SAN FERRY ANN, 1965, A
SAN FRANCISCO, 1936, A
SAN FRANCISCO DOCKS, 1941, A
SAN FRANCISCO NIGHTS, 1928
SAN FRANCISCO STORY, THE, 1952, A
SAN QUENTIN, 1937, C
SAN QUENTIN, 1946, A
SANCTUARY, 1916, A
SANCTUARY, 1961, O
SAND, 1920, A
SAND, 1949, A
SAND BLIND, 1925
SAND CASTLE, THE, 1961, AAA
SAND PEBBLES, THE, 1966, C-O
SANDA TAI GAILAH
SANDAI KAIJU CHIKYU SAIDAI NO KESSEN
SANDERS, 1963, A
SANDERS OF THE RIVER, 1935, A-C
SANDFLOW, 1937, A
SANDOKAN THE GREAT, 1964, A
SANDPIPER, THE, 1965, C-O
SANDPIT GENERALS, THE
SANDRA, 1924
SANDRA, 1966, O
SANDS OF BEERSHEBA, 1966, O
SANDS OF FATE, 1914
SANDS OF IWO JIMA, 1949, C
SANDS OF SACRIFICE, 1917
SANDS OF THE DESERT, 1960, A
SANDS OF THE KALAHARI, 1965, O
SANDS OF TIME, THE, 1919
SANDU FOLLOWS THE SUN, 1965, AAA
SANDWICH MAN, THE, 1966, A
SANDY, 1918
SANDY, 1926, A
SANDY BURKE OF THE U-BAR-U, 1919
SANDY GETS HER MAN, 1940, AAA
SANDY IS A LADY, 1940, AAA
SANDY TAKES A BOW
SANDY THE SEAL, 1969, AAA
SANG D'UN POETE
SANG ET LUMIERES
SANGAREE, 1953, C
SANITORIUM
SANJURO, 1962, C
SANS FAMILLE, 1925
SANSHO THE BAILIFF, 1969, A
SANSONE
SANTA, 1932, O
SANTA AND THE THREE BEARS, 1970, AAA
SANTA CLAUS, 1960, AAA
SANTA CLAUS CONQUERS THE MARTIANS, 1964, C-O
SANTA FE, 1951, A
SANTA FE BOUND, 1937, A
SANTA FE MARSHAL, 1940, A
SANTA FE PASSAGE, 1955, O
SANTA FE PETE, 1925
SANTA FE RIDES, 1937
SANTA FE SADDLEMATES, 1945, A
SANTA FE SATAN
SANTA FE SCOUTS, 1943, A
SANTA FE STAMPEDE, 1938, C
SANTA FE TRAIL, 1940, C
SANTA FE TRAIL, THE, 1930, A
SANTA FE UPRISING, 1946, A
SANTA'S CHRISTMAS CIRCUS, 1966, AAA
SANTEE, 1973, O
SANTIAGO, 1956, A
SANTO AND THE BLUE DEMON VS. THE MONSTERS
SANTO CONTRA BLUE DEMON EN LA ATLANTIDA, 1968, O
SANTO CONTRA EL CEREBRO DIABOLICO, 1962, C
SANTO CONTRA EL DOCTOR MUERTE, 1974, O
SANTO CONTRA LA HIJA DE FRANKENSTEIN, 1971, O
SANTO CONTRA LA INVASION DE LOS MARCIANOS, 1966, O
SANTO EN EL MUSEO DE CERA, 1963, O
SANTO VERSUS THE MARTIAN INVASION
SANTO VS. FRANKENSTEIN'S DAUGHTER
SANTO Y BLUE DEMON CONTRA LOS MONSTRUOS ZERO, 1968, O
SAP FROM ABROAD, THE
SAP FROM SYRACUSE, THE, 1930, A
SAP, THE, 1926
SAP, THE, 1929, A
SAPHEAD, THE, 1921, A
SAPHO
SAPHO, 1917
SAPPHIRE, 1959, A
SAPPHO, 1913
SAPS AT SEA, 1940, A
SARABA MOSUKUWA GURENTAI
SARABAND, 1949, A
SARABAND FOR DEAD LOVERS
SARACEN BLADE, THE, 1954, A
SARAGOSSA MANUSCRIPT, THE, 1972, A
SARAH AND SON, 1930, A
SARAH AND THE SQUIRREL, 1983
SARATI-LE-TERRIBLE, 1923
SARATOGA, 1937, A
SARATOGA TRUNK, 1945, A-C
SARDINIA: RANSOM, 1968, C
SARDONICUS
SARGE GOES TO COLLEGE, 1947, A
SARONG GIRL, 1943, A
SARUMBA, 1950, A
SASAKI KOJIRO
SASAYASHI NO JOE
SASKATCHEWAN, 1954, A-C
SASOM I EN SPEGEL
SASQUATCH, 1978, A
SATAN AND THE WOMAN, 1928
SATAN BUG, THE, 1965, A
SATAN IN HIGH HEELS, 1962, O
SATAN IN SABLES, 1925
SATAN JUNIOR, 1919
SATAN MET A LADY, 1936, A
SATAN NEVER SLEEPS, 1962, C
SATAN SANDERSON, 1915
SATAN TOWN, 1926
SATAN TRIUMPHANT, 1917
SATAN'S BED, 1965, O
SATAN'S BLACK WEDDING, 1976
SATAN'S CHEERLEADERS, 1977, O
SATAN'S CHILDREN, 1975
SATAN'S CLAW
SATAN'S CRADLE, 1949, A
SATAN'S HARVEST, 1970
SATAN'S MISTRESS, 1982, O
SATAN'S PAWN
SATAN'S PRIVATE DOOR, 1917
SATAN'S SADIST, 1969, O
SATAN'S SATELLITES, 1958, AA
SATAN'S SISTER, 1925, A
SATAN'S SKIN
SATAN'S SLAVE, 1976, O
SATANAS, 1919
SATANIC RITES OF DRACULA, THE
SATANIST, THE, 1968
SATELLITE IN THE SKY, 1956, A
SATIN GIRL, THE, 1923
SATIN MUSHROOM, THE, 1969, C
SATIN WOMAN, THE, 1927
SATURDAY ISLAND
SATURDAY NIGHT, 1922, A
SATURDAY NIGHT AND SUNDAY MORNING, 1961, O
SATURDAY NIGHT AT THE BATHS, 1975, O

SATURDAY NIGHT BATH IN APPLE VALLEY
SATURDAY NIGHT FEVER, 1977, C-O
SATURDAY NIGHT IN APPLE VALLEY, 1965, C
SATURDAY NIGHT KID, THE, 1929, A
SATURDAY NIGHT OUT, 1964, A
SATURDAY NIGHT REVUE, 1937, A
SATURDAY THE 14TH, 1981, A
SATURDAY'S CHILDREN, 1929, A
SATURDAY'S CHILDREN, 1940, A
SATURDAY'S HERO, 1951, A
SATURDAY'S HEROES, 1937, A
SATURDAY'S MILLIONS, 1933, A
SATURN 3, 1980, C
SATYRICON
SAUCE FOR THE GOOSE, 1918
SAUL AND DAVID, 1968, A
SAUTERELLE
SAUVE QUI PEUT/LA VIE
SAVAGE ABDUCTION, 1975, O
SAVAGE AMERICAN, THE
SAVAGE BRIGADE, 1948, A
SAVAGE DAWN, 1984, O
SAVAGE DRUMS, 1951, A
SAVAGE EYE, THE, 1960, C-O
SAVAGE FRONTIER, 1953, A
SAVAGE GIRL, THE, 1932, A
SAVAGE GOLD, 1933, C
SAVAGE GUNS, THE, 1962, A
SAVAGE HARVEST, 1981, A
SAVAGE HORDE, THE, 1950, A
SAVAGE INNOCENTS, THE, 1960, A
SAVAGE IS LOOSE, THE, 1974, C
SAVAGE MESSIAH, 1972, O
SAVAGE MUTINY, 1953, A
SAVAGE OF THE SEA, 1925
SAVAGE PAMPAS, 1967, C
SAVAGE PASSIONS, 1927
SAVAGE SAM, 1963, A
SAVAGE SEASON, 1970
SAVAGE SEVEN, THE, 1968, O
SAVAGE SISTERS, 1974, O
SAVAGE STREETS, 1984, O
SAVAGE WEEKEND, 1983, O
SAVAGE WILD, THE, 1970, A
SAVAGE WILDERNESS
SAVAGE WOMAN, THE, 1918
SAVAGE!, 1973
SAVAGE, THE, 1917
SAVAGE, THE, 1926
SAVAGE, THE, 1953, A
SAVAGE, THE, 1975, C
SAVAGE?, 1962, A
SAVAGES, 1972, O
SAVAGES FROM HELL, 1968, O
SAVANNAH SMILES, 1983, AA
SAVE A LITTLE SUNSHINE, 1938, A
SAVE THE TIGER, 1973, C-O
SAVED BY RADIO, 1922
SAVED FROM THE HAREM, 1915
SAVED FROM THE SEA, 1920
SAVING THE FAMILY NAME, 1916, A
SAVVA, 1919
SAWDUST, 1923, A
SAWDUST AND TINSEL
SAWDUST DOLL, THE, 1919
SAWDUST PARADISE, THE, 1928
SAWDUST RING, THE, 1917
SAWDUST TRAIL, 1924, A
SAXON CHARM, THE, 1948, A
SAY HELLO TO YESTERDAY, 1971, C
SAY IT AGAIN, 1926
SAY IT IN FRENCH, 1938, A
SAY IT WITH DIAMONDS, 1927
SAY IT WITH DIAMONDS, 1935, A
SAY IT WITH FLOWERS, 1934, A
SAY IT WITH MUSIC, 1932, A
SAY IT WITH SABLES, 1928
SAY IT WITH SONGS, 1929, A
SAY ONE FOR ME, 1959, C
SAY YOUNG FELLOW, 1918, A
SAYONARA, 1957, C
SAYS O'REILLY TO MCNAB
SCALAWAG, 1973, A
SCALAWAG BUNCH, THE, 1976
SCALES OF JUSTICE, THE, 1914, A
SCALLYWAG, THE, 1921
SCALP MERCHANT, THE, 1977
SCALPEL, 1976, O
SCALPHUNTERS, THE, 1968, C-O
SCALPS, 1983, O
SCAMP, THE
SCANDAL, 1915, A
SCANDAL, 1917
SCANDAL, 1929, A
SCANDAL, 1964, A
SCANDAL '64
SCANDAL AT SCOURIE, 1953, A
SCANDAL FOR SALE, 1932, A
SCANDAL IN DENMARK, 1970, O
SCANDAL IN PARIS, 1929
SCANDAL IN PARIS, A, 1946, A
SCANDAL IN SORRENTO, 1957, O
SCANDAL INCORPORATED, 1956, A
SCANDAL MONGERS, 1918
SCANDAL PROOF, 1925
SCANDAL SHEET, 1931, A
SCANDAL SHEET, 1940, A
SCANDAL SHEET, 1952, C
SCANDAL STREET, 1925
SCANDAL STREET, 1938, A
SCANDAL, THE, 1923, A
SCANDAL?, 1929
SCANDALOUS, 1984, C
SCANDALOUS ADVENTURES OF BURAIKAN, THE, 1970, C
SCANDALOUS JOHN, 1971, AA
SCANDALOUS TONGUES, 1922
SCANDALS
SCANDALS OF PARIS, 1935, A
SCANNERS, 1981, O
SCAPEGOAT, THE, 1959, A
SCAPPAMENTO APERTO
SCAR HANAN, 1925
SCAR OF SHAME, THE, 1927
SCAR, THE
SCAR, THE, 1919
SCARAB, 1982, O
SCARAB MURDER CASE, THE, 1936, A
SCARAB RING, THE, 1921, A
SCARAMOUCHE, 1923, A
SCARAMOUCHE, 1952, A
SCARAMOUCHE, 1964
SCARECROW, 1973, C-O
SCARECROW IN A GARDEN OF CUCUMBERS, 1972, C
SCARECROW, THE, 1982, C
SCARED STIFF, 1945, A
SCARED STIFF, 1953, A
SCARED TO DEATH, 1947, A
SCARED TO DEATH, 1981, O
SCAREHEADS, 1931, A
SCAREMAKER, THE
SCARF, THE, 1951, A
SCARFACE, 1932, O
SCARFACE, 1983, O
SCARFACE MOB, THE, 1962, A
SCARLET AND GOLD, 1925
SCARLET ANGEL, 1952, A
SCARLET BLADE, THE
SCARLET BRAND, 1932, A
SCARLET BUCCANEER, THE
SCARLET CAMELLIA, THE, 1965, C
SCARLET CAR, THE, 1918
SCARLET CAR, THE, 1923, A
SCARLET CLAW, THE, 1944, A
SCARLET CLUE, THE, 1945, A
SCARLET COAT, THE, 1955, A
SCARLET CRYSTAL, THE, 1917
SCARLET DAREDEVIL, THE, 1928
SCARLET DAWN, 1932, A
SCARLET DAYS, 1919, A
SCARLET DOVE, THE, 1928, A
SCARLET DROP, THE, 1918
SCARLET EMPRESS, THE, 1934, C
SCARLET HONEYMOON, THE, 1925
SCARLET HOUR, THE, 1956, A
SCARLET KISS, THE, 1920
SCARLET LADY, THE, 1922
SCARLET LADY, THE, 1928, A
SCARLET LETTER, THE, 1917
SCARLET LETTER, THE, 1926, A
SCARLET LETTER, THE, 1934, A
SCARLET LILY, THE, 1923, A
SCARLET OATH, THE, 1916
SCARLET PAGES, 1930, A
SCARLET PIMPERNEL, THE, 1917
SCARLET PIMPERNEL, THE, 1935, A
SCARLET RIVER, 1933, A
SCARLET ROAD, THE, 1916, A
SCARLET ROAD, THE, 1918
SCARLET SAINT, 1925
SCARLET SEAS, 1929, A
SCARLET SHADOW, THE, 1919
SCARLET SIN, THE, 1915, A
SCARLET SPEAR, THE, 1954, A
SCARLET STREET, 1945, C
SCARLET THREAD, 1951, A
SCARLET TRAIL, THE, 1919
SCARLET WEB, THE, 1954, A
SCARLET WEEKEND, A, 1932, A
SCARLET WEST, THE, 1925
SCARLET WOMAN, THE, 1916
SCARLET WOOING, THE, 1920
SCARLET YOUTH, 1928
SCARRED, 1984, O
SCARRED HANDS, 1923
SCARS OF DRACULA, THE, 1970, O
SCARS OF HATE, 1923
SCARS OF JEALOUSY, 1923, A
SCATTERBRAIN, 1940, A
SCATTERGOOD BAINES, 1941, A
SCATTERGOOD MEETS BROADWAY, 1941, A
SCATTERGOOD PULLS THE STRINGS, 1941, A
SCATTERGOOD RIDES HIGH, 1942, A
SCATTERGOOD SURVIVES A MURDER, 1942, A
SCAVENGER HUNT, 1979, C
SCAVENGERS, THE, 1959, A
SCAVENGERS, THE, 1969, O
SCENE OF THE CRIME, 1949, A
SCENES FROM A MARRIAGE, 1974, C-O
SCENIC ROUTE, THE, 1978, A
SCENT OF A WOMAN, 1976, O
SCENT OF MYSTERY, 1960, A
SCHATTEN UBER TIRAN-KOMMANDO SINAI
SCHEHERAZADE, 1965, A
SCHEMERS, THE, 1922
SCHIZO, 1977, O
SCHIZOID, 1980, O
SCHLAGER-PARADE, 1953, A
SCHLOCK, 1973, A
SCHNEEWEISSCHEN UND ROSENROT
SCHNEEWITTCHEN UND DIE SIEBEN ZWERGE
SCHNOOK, THE (SEE: SWINGIN' ALONG, 1962)
SCHOOL DAYS, 1921, A
SCHOOL FOR BRIDES, 1952, A
SCHOOL FOR DANGER, 1947, A
SCHOOL FOR GIRLS, 1935, A
SCHOOL FOR HUSBANDS, 1939, A
SCHOOL FOR HUSBANDS, A, 1917
SCHOOL FOR RANDLE, 1949, A
SCHOOL FOR SCANDAL, THE, 1914
SCHOOL FOR SCANDAL, THE, 1923
SCHOOL FOR SCANDAL, THE, 1930, A
SCHOOL FOR SCOUNDRELS, 1960, AA
SCHOOL FOR SECRETS, 1946, A
SCHOOL FOR SEX, 1966, O
SCHOOL FOR SEX, 1969, O
SCHOOL FOR STARS, 1935, A
SCHOOL FOR UNCLAIMED GIRLS, 1973, O
SCHOOL FOR VIOLENCE
SCHOOL FOR WIVES, 1925
SCHOOL OF LOVE
SCHOOLBOY PENITENTIARY
SCHOOLGIRL DIARY, 1947, A
SCHOOLMASTER, THE
SCHOONER GANG, THE, 1937, A
SCHWARZE NYLONS-HEISSE NACHTE
SCHWEIK'S NEW ADVENTURES, 1943, A
SCHWESTERN, ODER DIE BALANCE DES GLUECKS
SCIENTIFIC CARDPLAYER, THE, 1972, A
SCINTILLATING SIN
SCIPIO
SCOBIE MALONE, 1975, O
SCOFFER, THE, 1920
SCOOP, THE, 1934, A
SCOOP, THE,
SCORCHER, THE, 1927
SCORCHING FURY, 1952
SCORCHY, 1976, O
SCORE, 1973
SCORING, 1980
SCORPIO, 1973, C
SCORPIO SCARAB, THE, 1972
SCORPION WITH TWO TAILS, 1982
SCORPION'S STING, THE, 1915
SCOTCH ON THE ROCKS, 1954, A
SCOTLAND YARD, 1930, A
SCOTLAND YARD, 1941, A
SCOTLAND YARD COMMANDS, 1937, A
SCOTLAND YARD DRAGNET, 1957, A
SCOTLAND YARD HUNTS DR. MABUSE, 1963, A
SCOTLAND YARD INSPECTOR, 1952, A
SCOTLAND YARD INVESTIGATOR, 1945, A
SCOTLAND YARD MYSTERY, THE
SCOTT JOPLIN, 1977, C
SCOTT OF THE ANTARCTIC, 1949, A
SCOUNDREL IN WHITE
SCOUNDREL, THE, 1935, C
SCOURGE, THE
SCOUTS OF THE AIR
SCRAGS, 1930
SCRAMBLE, 1970, AAA
SCRAMBLED WIVES, 1921
SCRAP IRON, 1921
SCRAP OF PAPER, THE, 1920
SCRAPPER, THE, 1922, A
SCRAPPIN' KID, THE, 1926
SCRATCH HARRY, 1969, O
SCRATCH MY BACK, 1920
SCREAM AND DIE
SCREAM AND SCREAM AGAIN, 1970, O
SCREAM BLACULA SCREAM, 1973, O
SCREAM BLOODY MURDER, 1972, O
SCREAM BLOODY MURDER, 1973
SCREAM FOR HELP, 1984, O
SCREAM FREE
SCREAM IN THE DARK, A, 1943, A
SCREAM IN THE NIGHT, 1943, A

SCREAM IN THE NIGHT, A, 1919
SCREAM IN THE STREETS, A, 1972
SCREAM OF FEAR, 1961, C
SCREAM OF THE BUTTERFLY, 1965, O
SCREAM, BABY, SCREAM, 1969, O
SCREAMERS, 1978, A
SCREAMING EAGLES, 1956, A
SCREAMING HEAD, THE
SCREAMING MIMI, 1958, O
SCREAMING SKULL, THE, 1958, A
SCREAMS OF A WINTER NIGHT, 1979, A
SCREAMTIME, 1983
SCREWBALLS, 1983, O
SCROOGE, 1935, AA
SCROOGE, 1970, AAA
SCROOGE, 1951, Brit.
SCRUBBERS, 1984, O
SCRUFFY, 1938, AA
SCUDDA-HOO? SCUDDA-HAY?, 1948, A
SCULPTOR'S DREAM, 1929
SCUM, 1979, O
SCUM OF THE EARTH, 1963, O
SCUM OF THE EARTH, 1976, O
SCUSI, FACCIAMO L'AMORE?
SCUTTLERS, THE, 1920
SE PERMETTETE, PARLIAMO DI DONNE
SE TUTTE LE DONNE DEL MONDO
SEA BAT, THE, 1930, A
SEA BEAST, THE, 1926, A
SEA CHASE, THE, 1955, A-C
SEA DEVILS, 1931, A
SEA DEVILS, 1937, A
SEA DEVILS, 1953, A
SEA FEVER
SEA FLOWER, THE, 1918
SEA FURY, 1929, A
SEA FURY, 1959, A
SEA GHOST, THE, 1931, A
SEA GOD, THE, 1930, A
SEA GULL, THE, 1968, A-C
SEA GYPSIES, THE, 1978, AAA
SEA HAWK, THE, 1924
SEA HAWK, THE, 1940, A
SEA HORNET, THE, 1951, A
SEA HORSES, 1926, A
SEA LEGS, 1930, A
SEA LION, THE, 1921, A
SEA MASTER, THE, 1917
SEA NYMPHS
SEA OF GRASS, THE, 1947, A-C
SEA OF LOST SHIPS, 1953, A
SEA OF SAND
SEA PANTHER, THE, 1918
SEA PIRATE, THE, 1967, A
SEA PROWLERS
SEA RACKETEERS, 1937, A
SEA RIDER, THE, 1920
SEA SHALL NOT HAVE THEM, THE, 1955, A-C
SEA SPOILERS, THE, 1936, A
SEA TIGER, 1952, A
SEA TIGER, THE, 1927, A
SEA URCHIN, THE, 1926
SEA WAIF, THE, 1918
SEA WALL, THE
SEA WIFE, 1957, A
SEA WOLF, THE, 1920
SEA WOLF, THE, 1926
SEA WOLF, THE, 1930, A
SEA WOLF, THE, 1941, C
SEA WOLVES, THE, 1981, A
SEA WOMEN, THE
SEA WYF AND BUSCUIT
SEA-WOLF, THE, 1913, A
SEABO, 1978, O
SEAFIGHTERS, THE
SEAGULLS OVER SORRENTO
SEAL OF SILENCE, THE, 1918
SEALED CARGO, 1951, A
SEALED ENVELOPE, THE, 1919
SEALED HEARTS, 1919
SEALED LIPS, 1915, A
SEALED LIPS, 1925
SEALED LIPS, 1941, A
SEALED LIPS, 1933
SEALED VALLEY, THE, 1915, A
SEALED VERDICT, 1948, A
SEANCE ON A WET AFTERNOON, 1964, C
SEARCH AND DESTROY, 1981, C
SEARCH FOR BEAUTY, 1934, A
SEARCH FOR BRIDEY MURPHY, THE, 1956, A
SEARCH FOR DANGER, 1949, A
SEARCH FOR THE EVIL ONE, 1967
SEARCH FOR THE MOTHER LODE
SEARCH OF THE CASTAWAYS
SEARCH, THE, 1948, A
SEARCHERS, THE, 1956, C
SEARCHING WIND, THE, 1946, A-C
SEAS BENEATH, THE, 1931, A
SEASIDE SWINGERS, 1965, AA
SEASON FOR LOVE, THE, 1963, A-C
SEASON OF PASSION, 1961, C
SEASON OF THE WITCH
SEATED AT HIS RIGHT, 1968, O
SEATS OF THE MIGHTY, THE, 1914, A
SEAWEED CHILDREN, THE
SEAWOLF, 1974
SEBASTIAN, 1968, A
SECLUDED ROADHOUSE, THE, 1926
SECOND BEST BED, 1937, A
SECOND BEST SECRET AGENT IN THE WHOLE WIDE WORLD, THE, 1965, A-C
SECOND BUREAU, 1936, A
SECOND BUREAU, 1937, A
SECOND CHANCE, 1947, A
SECOND CHANCE, 1950
SECOND CHANCE, 1953, A-C
SECOND CHANCES
SECOND CHOICE, 1930, A
SECOND CHORUS, 1940, A
SECOND COMING OF SUZANNE, THE, 1974, C
SECOND COMING, THE
SECOND FACE, THE, 1950, A
SECOND FIDDLE, 1923, A
SECOND FIDDLE, 1939, A
SECOND FIDDLE, 1957, A
SECOND FIDDLE TO A STEEL GUITAR, 1965, A
SECOND FLOOR MYSTERY, THE, 1930, A
SECOND GREATEST SEX, THE, 1955, A
SECOND HAND LOVE, 1923, A
SECOND HAND ROSE, 1922, A
SECOND HAND WIFE, 1933, A
SECOND HONEYMOON, 1930
SECOND HONEYMOON, 1931, A
SECOND HONEYMOON, 1937, C
SECOND HOUSE FROM THE LEFT
SECOND IN COMMAND, THE, 1915, A
SECOND MATE, THE, 1929
SECOND MATE, THE, 1950, A
SECOND MR. BUSH, THE, 1940, A
SECOND MRS. TANQUERAY, THE, 1916
SECOND MRS. TANQUERAY, THE, 1952, A
SECOND STORY MURDER, THE
SECOND THOUGHTS, 1983, C
SECOND THOUGHTS, 1938
SECOND TIME AROUND, THE, 1961, A
SECOND TIME LUCKY, 1984, C
SECOND TO NONE, 1926
SECOND WIFE, 1930, A
SECOND WIFE, 1936, A
SECOND WIND, 1976, A
SECOND WIND, A, 1978, C
SECOND WOMAN, THE, 1951, A-C
SECOND YOUTH, 1924, A
SECOND-HAND HEARTS, 1981, A-C
SECONDS, 1966, C
SECRET AGENT, 1933, A
SECRET AGENT FIREBALL, 1965, A-C
SECRET AGENT OF JAPAN, 1942, A
SECRET AGENT SUPER DRAGON, 1966, A
SECRET AGENT THE, 1936, C
SECRET BEYOND THE DOOR, THE, 1948, C
SECRET BRIDE, THE, 1935, A
SECRET BRIGADE, THE, 1951, A
SECRET CALL, THE, 1931, A
SECRET CAVE, THE, 1953, A
SECRET CEREMONY, 1968, O
SECRET CODE, THE, 1918
SECRET COMMAND, 1944, A
SECRET DIARY OF SIGMUND FREUD, THE, 1984, O
SECRET DOCUMENT—VIENNA, 1954, A
SECRET DOOR, THE, 1964, A
SECRET ENEMIES, 1942, A
SECRET ENEMY
SECRET EVIDENCE, 1941, A
SECRET FILE OF HOLLYWOOD
SECRET FILE: HOLLYWOOD, 1962, A-C
SECRET FLIGHT
SECRET FOUR, THE, 1940, A
SECRET FOUR, THE, 1952
SECRET FURY, THE, 1950, A
SECRET GAME, THE, 1917, A
SECRET GARDEN, THE, 1919
SECRET GARDEN, THE, 1949, AA
SECRET GIFT, THE, 1920
SECRET HEART, THE, 1946, C
SECRET HONOR, 1984, C
SECRET HONOR: A POLITICAL MYTH
SECRET HONOR: THE LAST TESTAMENT OF RICHARD M. DIXON
SECRET HOUR, THE, 1928, A
SECRET INTERLUDE, 1936
SECRET INTERLUDE, 1955
SECRET INVASION, THE, 1964, A
SECRET JOURNEY
SECRET KINGDOM, THE
SECRET LIFE OF AN AMERICAN WIFE, THE, 1968, C-O
SECRET LIFE OF WALTER MITTY, THE, 1947, A
SECRET LIVES
SECRET LOVE, 1916, A
SECRET MAN, THE, 1917
SECRET MAN, THE, 1958, A
SECRET MARK OF D'ARTAGNAN, THE, 1963, A
SECRET MARRIAGE, 1919
SECRET MENACE, 1931, A
SECRET MISSION, 1944, A
SECRET MISSION, 1949, A
SECRET MOTIVE
SECRET OF BLACK CANYON, THE, 1925
SECRET OF BLACK MOUNTAIN, THE, 1917
SECRET OF BLOOD ISLAND, THE, 1965, A
SECRET OF CONVICT LAKE, THE, 1951, A
SECRET OF DEEP HARBOR, 1961, C
SECRET OF DORIAN GRAY, THE
SECRET OF DR. ALUCARD, THE
SECRET OF DR. KILDARE, THE, 1939, A
SECRET OF EVE, THE, 1917
SECRET OF G.32
SECRET OF LINDA HAMILTON
SECRET OF MADAME BLANCHE, THE, 1933, A
SECRET OF MAGIC ISLAND, THE, 1964, AAA
SECRET OF MONTE CRISTO, THE, 1961, A
SECRET OF MY SUCCESS, THE, 1965, A-C
SECRET OF NAVAJO CAVE, 1976
SECRET OF NIMH, THE, 1982, AA
SECRET OF OUTER SPACE ISLAND
SECRET OF OUTLAW FLATS, 1953
SECRET OF SANTA VITTORIA, THE, 1969, A
SECRET OF ST. IVES, THE, 1949, A
SECRET OF STAMBOUL, THE, 1936, A
SECRET OF THE BLACK WIDOW, 1964
SECRET OF THE BLUE ROOM, 1933, A
SECRET OF THE CHATEAU, 1935, A
SECRET OF THE CHINESE CARNATION, THE, 1965
SECRET OF THE DESERT, 1916
SECRET OF THE FOREST, THE, 1955, AA
SECRET OF THE HILLS, THE, 1921, A
SECRET OF THE INCAS, 1954, A
SECRET OF THE LOCH, THE, 1934, A
SECRET OF THE MOOR, THE, 1919
SECRET OF THE MOUNTAIN, THE, 1914
SECRET OF THE PUEBLO, THE, 1923
SECRET OF THE PURPLE REEF, THE, 1960, A
SECRET OF THE SACRED FOREST, THE, 1970, A
SECRET OF THE STORM COUNTRY, THE, 1917
SECRET OF THE SWAMP, THE, 1916
SECRET OF THE TELEGIAN, THE, 1961, A
SECRET OF THE WHISTLER, 1946, A
SECRET OF TREASURE MOUNTAIN, 1956, A
SECRET ORCHARD, 1915, A
SECRET ORDERS, 1926
SECRET PARTNER, THE, 1961, A
SECRET PASSION, THE
SECRET PATROL, 1936, A
SECRET PEOPLE, 1952, A
SECRET PLACE, THE, 1958, A
SECRET PLACES, 1984, C
SECRET ROOM, THE, 1915
SECRET SCROLLS (PART I), 1968, A-C
SECRET SCROLLS (PART II), 1968, A-C
SECRET SERVICE, 1919
SECRET SERVICE, 1931, A
SECRET SERVICE INVESTIGATOR, 1948, A
SECRET SERVICE OF THE AIR, 1939, A
SECRET SEVEN, THE, 1915
SECRET SEVEN, THE, 1940, A
SECRET SEVEN, THE, 1966, A
SECRET SINNERS, 1933, A
SECRET SIX, THE, 1931, C
SECRET SORROW, 1921
SECRET STRANGER, THE
SECRET STRINGS, 1918
SECRET STUDIO, THE, 1927
SECRET TENT, THE, 1956, A
SECRET VALLEY, 1937, A
SECRET VENTURE, 1955, A
SECRET VOICE, THE, 1936, A
SECRET WAR OF HARRY FRIGG, THE, 1968, A-C
SECRET WAR, THE
SECRET WAYS, THE, 1961, A-C
SECRET WEAPON, THE
SECRET WITNESS, THE, 1931, A
SECRET WOMAN, THE, 1918
SECRET WORLD, 1969, C
SECRET, THE, 1955, A
SECRET, THE, 1979, C-O
SECRETARY OF FRIVOLOUS AFFAIRS, THE, 1915
SECRETARY, THE, 1971
SECRETS, 1924
SECRETS, 1933, A-C
SECRETS, 1971, O
SECRETS, 1984, A-C
SECRETS D'ALCOVE, 1954, C
SECRETS OF A CO-ED, 1942, A
SECRETS OF A MODEL, 1940, C
SECRETS OF A NURSE, 1938, A
SECRETS OF A SECRETARY, 1931, A

SECRETS OF A SORORITY GIRL, 1946, A
SECRETS OF A SOUL
SECRETS OF A SOUL, 1925
SECRETS OF A WINDMILL GIRL, 1966, O
SECRETS OF A WOMAN'S TEMPLE, 1969, O
SECRETS OF AN ACTRESS, 1938, A-C
SECRETS OF CHINATOWN, 1935, A
SECRETS OF HOLLYWOOD, 1933
SECRETS OF MONTE CARLO, 1951, A
SECRETS OF PARIS, THE, 1922, A
SECRETS OF SCOTLAND YARD, 1944, A
SECRETS OF SEX, 1970, O
SECRETS OF THE CITY
SECRETS OF THE FRENCH POLICE, 1932, A
SECRETS OF THE LONE WOLF, 1941, A
SECRETS OF THE MARIE CELESTE, THE
SECRETS OF THE NIGHT, 1925
SECRETS OF THE ORIENT, 1932
SECRETS OF THE RANGE, 1928
SECRETS OF THE UNDERGROUND, 1943, A
SECRETS OF THE WASTELANDS, 1941, A
SECRETS OF WOMEN, 1961, C
SECRETS OF WU SIN, 1932, A
SECRETS, 1941
SECTOR 13, 1982
SECURITY RISK, 1954, A
SEDDOK, L'EREDE DI SATANA
SEDMI KONTINENT
SEDMIKRASKY
SEDUCED AND ABANDONED, 1964, C
SEDUCERS, THE, 1962, C
SEDUCTION BY THE SEA, 1967, C
SEDUCTION OF JOE TYNAN, THE, 1979, C-O
SEDUCTION, THE, 1982, O
SEE AMERICA THIRST, 1930, A
SEE HERE, PRIVATE HARGROVE, 1944, A
SEE HOW THEY RUN, 1955, A
SEE MY LAWYER, 1921
SEE MY LAWYER, 1945, A
SEE NO EVIL, 1971, C
SEE YOU IN HELL, DARLING
SEE YOU IN JAIL, 1927
SEE YOU LATER, 1928
SEED, 1931, A
SEED OF INNOCENCE, 1980, O
SEED OF MAN, THE, 1970, C-O
SEED OF TERROR
SEEDS OF DESTRUCTION, 1952, A
SEEDS OF EVIL, 1981, O
SEEDS OF FREEDOM, 1929
SEEDS OF FREEDOM, 1943, A
SEEDS OF VENGEANCE, 1920
SEEING IS BELIEVING, 1934, A
SEEING IT THROUGH
SEEING IT THROUGH, 1920
SEEING'S BELIEVING, 1922, A
SEEKERS, THE
SEEKERS, THE, 1916
SEEMS LIKE OLD TIMES, 1980, A-C
SEGRETI CHE SCOTTANO
SEI DONNE PER L'ASSASSINO
SEISHUN MONOTOGARI
SEISHUN ZANKOKU MONOTOGARI
SEIZURE, 1974, C
SELF DEFENSE, 1933
SELF MADE WIDOW, 1917
SELF STARTER, THE, 1926
SELF-MADE FAILURE, A, 1924
SELF-MADE LADY, 1932, A
SELF-MADE MAN, A, 1922
SELF-MADE WIFE, THE, 1923
SELF-PORTRAIT, 1973, O
SELF-SERVICE SCHOOLGIRLS, 1976
SELFISH WOMAN, THE, 1916
SELFISH YATES, 1918
SELL 'EM COWBOY, 1924
SELL OUT, THE, 1976, C
SELLERS OF GIRLS, 1967, O
SELLOUT, THE, 1951, A
SEMBAZURU
SEMI-TOUGH, 1977, C-O
SEMINOLE, 1953, C
SEMINOLE UPRISING, 1955, A
SEN NOCI SVATOJANSKE
SEN YAN'S DEVOTION, 1924
SENATOR WAS INDISCREET, THE, 1947, A
SENATOR, THE, 1915, A
SEND FOR PAUL TEMPLE, 1946, A
SEND ME NO FLOWERS, 1964, A
SENDER, THE, 1982, O
SENGOKU GUNTO-DEN
SENGOKU YARO
SENIOR PROM, 1958, A
SENIORS, THE, 1978, O
SENIORS, THE, 1978
SENJO NI NAGARERU UTA
SENOR AMERICANO, 1929, A
SENOR DAREDEVIL, 1926
SENOR JIM, 1936
SENORA CASADA NECEISITA MARIDO, 1935, A
SENORITA, 1927
SENORITA FROM THE WEST, 1945, A
SENSATION, 1936, A
SENSATION HUNTERS, 1934, A
SENSATION HUNTERS, 1945, A
SENSATION SEEKERS, 1927, A
SENSATION, 1970
SENSATIONS
SENSATIONS OF 1945, 1944, A
SENSO, 1968, A
SENSUALITA, 1954, A
SENSUOUS VAMPIRES
SENTENCE SUSPENDED
SENTENCED FOR LIFE, 1960, A
SENTENZA DI MORTE
SENTIMENTAL BLOKE, 1932, A
SENTIMENTAL JOURNEY, 1946, A
SENTIMENTAL LADY, THE, 1915, A
SENTIMENTAL TOMMY, 1921
SENTINEL, THE, 1977, O
SEPARATE PEACE, A, 1972, A
SEPARATE TABLES, 1958, A-C
SEPARATE WAYS, 1981, O
SEPARATION, 1968, A
SEPARATION, 1977
SEPIA CINDERELLA, 1947, A
SEPPUKU
SEPT FOIS FEMME
SEPT HOMMES EN OR
SEPTEMBER 30, 1955
SEPTEMBER AFFAIR, 1950, A
SEPTEMBER STORM, 1960, A
SEQUEL TO THE DIAMOND FROM THE SKY, 1916
SEQUOIA, 1934, A
SERAFINO, 1970, A
SERDTSE MATERI
SERENA, 1962, A-C
SERENADE, 1921
SERENADE, 1927
SERENADE, 1956, A
SERENADE FOR TWO SPIES, 1966, A
SERENADE OF THE WEST, 1937
SERENADE OF THE WEST, 1942
SERENITY, 1962, A
SERGE PANIN, 1922
SERGEANT BERRY, 1938, A
SERGEANT DEADHEAD, 1965, A
SERGEANT DEADHEAD THE ASTRONAUT
SERGEANT JIM, 1962, A
SERGEANT MADDEN, 1939, A
SERGEANT MIKE, 1945, A
SERGEANT MURPHY, 1938, A
SERGEANT RUTLEDGE, 1960, C
SERGEANT RYKER, 1968, A
SERGEANT STEINER
SERGEANT WAS A LADY, THE, 1961, A
SERGEANT YORK, 1941, A
SERGEANT, THE, 1968, O
SERGEANTS 3, 1962, A
SERIAL, 1980, O
SERIOUS CHARGE
SERPENT ISLAND, 1954, A
SERPENT OF THE NILE, 1953, A
SERPENT'S EGG, THE, 1977, O
SERPENT'S TOOTH, THE, 1917
SERPENT, THE, 1916, C
SERPENT, THE, 1973, A-C
SERPENTS OF THE PIRATE MOON, THE, 1973, O
SERPICO, 1973, C-O
SERVANT IN THE HOUSE, THE, 1920
SERVANT QUESTION, THE, 1920
SERVANT, THE, 1964, C
SERVANTS' ENTRANCE, 1934, A
SERVICE
SERVICE DE LUXE, 1938, A
SERVICE FOR LADIES
SERVICE FOR LADIES, 1927
SERVICE STAR, THE, 1918
SERVING TWO MASTERS, 1921
SERYOZHA
SESSION WITH THE COMMITTEE
SET FREE, 1918
SET FREE, 1927
SET, THE, 1970, O
SET-UP, THE, 1926
SET-UP, THE, 1949, C
SET-UP, THE, 1963, A
SETTE CONTRO LA MORTE
SETTE DONNE PER I MAC GREGOR
SETTE PISTOLE PER I MAC GREGOR
SETTE UOMINI D'ORO
SETTE VOLTE DONNA
SETTE WINCHESTER PER UN MASSACRO
SETTLED OUT OF COURT, 1925
SEVEN, 1979, O
SEVEN AGAINST THE SUN, 1968, A
SEVEN ALONE, 1975, AA
SEVEN ANGRY MEN, 1955, A
SEVEN BAD MEN
SEVEN BEAUTIES, 1976, O
SEVEN BRAVE MEN, 1936, A
SEVEN BRIDES FOR SEVEN BROTHERS, 1954, AA
SEVEN BROTHERS MEET DRACULA, THE
SEVEN CAPITAL SINS, 1962, O
SEVEN CHANCES, 1925, A
SEVEN CITIES OF GOLD, 1955, A-C
SEVEN CITIES TO ATLANTIS
SEVEN DARING GIRLS, 1962, A
SEVEN DAYS, 1925
SEVEN DAYS ASHORE, 1944, A
SEVEN DAYS IN MAY, 1964, C
SEVEN DAYS LEAVE, 1930, A
SEVEN DAYS LEAVE, 1942, A
SEVEN DAYS TO NOON, 1950, C
SEVEN DEADLY SINS, THE, 1953, A
SEVEN DIFFERENT WAYS
SEVEN DOORS OF DEATH, 1983
SEVEN DOORS TO DEATH, 1944, A
SEVEN DWARFS TO THE RESCUE, THE, 1965, A
SEVEN FACES, 1929, A
SEVEN FACES OF DR. LAO, 1964, A
SEVEN FOOTPRINTS TO SATAN, 1929, C
SEVEN GOLDEN MEN, 1969, A
SEVEN GRAVES FOR ROGAN
SEVEN GUNS FOR THE MACGREGORS, 1968, A
SEVEN GUNS TO MESA, 1958, A
SEVEN HILLS OF ROME, THE, 1958, A
SEVEN KEYS, 1962, A
SEVEN KEYS TO BALDPATE, 1917
SEVEN KEYS TO BALDPATE, 1925
SEVEN KEYS TO BALDPATE, 1930, A
SEVEN KEYS TO BALDPATE, 1935, A
SEVEN KEYS TO BALDPATE, 1947, A
SEVEN LITTLE FOYS, THE, 1955, AAA
SEVEN MEN FROM NOW, 1956, A
SEVEN MILES FROM ALCATRAZ, 1942, A
SEVEN MINUTES, THE, 1971, O
SEVEN NIGHTS IN JAPAN, 1976, C
SEVEN REVENGES, THE, 1967, C
SEVEN SAMURAI, THE, 1956, C
SEVEN SEAS TO CALAIS, 1963, A
SEVEN SECRETS OF SU-MARU, THE
SEVEN SINNERS, 1925
SEVEN SINNERS, 1940, A
SEVEN SINNERS, 1936
SEVEN SISTERS
SEVEN SISTERS, THE, 1915, A
SEVEN SLAVES AGAINST THE WORLD, 1965, A
SEVEN SWANS, THE, 1918
SEVEN SWEETHEARTS, 1942, A
SEVEN TASKS OF ALI BABA, THE, 1963, A
SEVEN THIEVES, 1960, A-C
SEVEN THUNDERS
SEVEN TIMES SEVEN, 1973
SEVEN UPS, THE, 1973, C
SEVEN WAVES AWAY
SEVEN WAYS FROM SUNDOWN, 1960, A
SEVEN WERE SAVED, 1947, A
SEVEN WOMEN, 1966, C
SEVEN WOMEN FROM HELL, 1961, A
SEVEN YEAR ITCH, THE, 1955, A-C
SEVEN YEARS BAD LUCK, 1921
SEVEN-PER-CENT SOLUTION, THE, 1977, C
SEVENTEEN, 1916
SEVENTEEN, 1940, A
SEVENTH BANDIT, THE, 1926
SEVENTH CAVALRY, 1956, A
SEVENTH CONTINENT, THE, 1968, A
SEVENTH CROSS, THE, 1944, C
SEVENTH DAWN, THE, 1964, A-C
SEVENTH DAY, THE, 1922, A
SEVENTH HEAVEN, 1927, A
SEVENTH HEAVEN, 1937, A-C
SEVENTH JUROR, THE, 1964, A
SEVENTH NOON, THE, 1915
SEVENTH SEAL, THE, 1958, C
SEVENTH SHERIFF, THE, 1923, A
SEVENTH SIN, THE, 1917
SEVENTH SIN, THE, 1957, A
SEVENTH SURVIVOR, THE, 1941, A
SEVENTH VEIL, THE, 1946, A-C
SEVENTH VICTIM, THE, 1943, A
SEVENTH VOYAGE OF SINBAD, THE, 1958, AA
SEVENTY DEADLY PILLS, 1964, AA
SEVERED ARM, 1973
SEVERED HEAD, A, 1971, O
SEX, 1920, A
SEX AGENT
SEX AND THE SINGLE GIRL, 1964, C
SEX AND THE TEENAGER
SEX AT NIGHT
SEX DU JOUR, 1976
SEX IS A WOMAN
SEX KITTENS GO TO COLLEGE, 1960, A
SEX LURE, THE, 1916
SEX MADNESS, 1929
SEX MADNESS, 1937

SEX RACKETEERS, THE
SEXORCISTS, THE
SEXTETTE, 1978, C
SEXTON BLAKE AND THE BEARDED DOCTOR, 1935, A
SEXTON BLAKE AND THE HOODED TERROR, 1938, A
SEXTON BLAKE AND THE MADEMOISELLE, 1935, A
SEXY GANG
SEZ O'REILLY TO MACNAB, 1938, A
SFIDA A RIO BRAVO
SGT. PEPPER'S LONELY HEARTS CLUB BAND, 1978, A
SH? THE OCTOPUS, 1937, A
SHABBY TIGER, THE
SHACK OUT ON 101, 1955, A
SHACKLED, 1918
SHACKLED BY FILM, 1918
SHACKLED LIGHTING, 1925
SHACKLES OF FEAR, 1924
SHACKLES OF GOLD, 1922, A
SHACKLES OF TRUTH, 1917
SHADES OF SILK, 1979, O
SHADOW AND THE MISSING LADY, THE, MISS, A
SHADOW BETWEEN, THE, 1920
SHADOW BETWEEN, THE, 1932, A
SHADOW IN THE SKY, 1951, A
SHADOW LAUGHS, 1933
SHADOW MAN, 1953, A
SHADOW OF A DOUBT, 1935, A
SHADOW OF A DOUBT, 1943, C
SHADOW OF A MAN, 1955, A-C
SHADOW OF A WOMAN, 1946, A
SHADOW OF CHIKARA
SHADOW OF DOUBT, THE, 1916
SHADOW OF EGYPT, THE, 1924, A
SHADOW OF EVIL, 1921
SHADOW OF EVIL, 1967, A
SHADOW OF FEAR, 1956, A
SHADOW OF FEAR, 1963, A
SHADOW OF LIGHTING RIDGE, THE, 1921
SHADOW OF MIKE EMERALD, THE, 1935, A
SHADOW OF NIGHT, THE
SHADOW OF ROSALIE BYRNES, THE, 1920
SHADOW OF SUSPICION, 1944, A
SHADOW OF TERROR, 1945, A
SHADOW OF THE CAT, THE, 1961, A
SHADOW OF THE DESERT
SHADOW OF THE EAGLE, 1955, A
SHADOW OF THE EAST, THE, 1924
SHADOW OF THE HAWK, 1976, A
SHADOW OF THE LAW, 1930, A
SHADOW OF THE LAW, THE, 1926
SHADOW OF THE PAST, 1950, A
SHADOW OF THE THIN MAN, 1941, A
SHADOW ON THE WALL, 1950, A
SHADOW ON THE WALL, THE, 1925
SHADOW ON THE WINDOW, THE, 1957, A
SHADOW RANCH, 1930, A
SHADOW RANGER, 1926
SHADOW RETURNS, THE, 1946, A
SHADOW STRIKES, THE, 1937, A
SHADOW VALLEY, 1947, A
SHADOW VERSUS THE THOUSAND EYES OF DR. MABUSE, THE
SHADOW WARRIOR, THE
SHADOW, THE, 1916
SHADOW, THE, 1921
SHADOW, THE, 1936, A
SHADOW, THE, 1937, A
SHADOWED, 1946, A
SHADOWED EYES, 1939, A-C
SHADOWMAN, 1974, A
SHADOWS, 1915
SHADOWS, 1919
SHADOWS, 1922, A
SHADOWS, 1931, A-C
SHADOWS, 1960, O
SHADOWS AND SUNSHINE, 1916
SHADOWS FROM THE PAST, 1915
SHADOWS GROW LONGER, THE, 1962, A
SHADOWS IN AN EMPTY ROOM
SHADOWS IN THE NIGHT, 1944, A
SHADOWS OF CHINATOWN, 1926
SHADOWS OF CONSCIENCE, 1921, A
SHADOWS OF DEATH, 1945, A
SHADOWS OF FEAR
SHADOWS OF FORGOTTEN ANCESTORS, 1967, A
SHADOWS OF OUR FORGOTTEN ANCESTORS
SHADOWS OF PARIS, 1924
SHADOWS OF SING SING, 1934, A
SHADOWS OF SINGAPORE
SHADOWS OF SUSPICION, 1919
SHADOWS OF THE MOULIN ROUGE, THE, 1914
SHADOWS OF THE NIGHT, 1928, A
SHADOWS OF THE NORTH, 1923
SHADOWS OF THE ORIENT, 1937, A
SHADOWS OF THE PAST, 1919
SHADOWS OF THE SEA, 1922, A
SHADOWS OF THE WEST, 1921
SHADOWS OF THE WEST, 1949, A
SHADOWS OF TOMBSTONE, 1953, A
SHADOWS OF YOSHIWARA, THE
SHADOWS ON THE RANGE, 1946
SHADOWS ON THE SAGE, 1942, A
SHADOWS ON THE STAIRS, 1941, A
SHADOWS OVER CHINATOWN, 1946, A
SHADOWS OVER SHANGHAI, 1938, A
SHADY LADY, 1945, A
SHADY LADY, THE, 1929, A
SHAFT, 1971, O
SHAFT IN AFRICA, 1973, O
SHAFT'S BIG SCORE, 1972, O
SHAGGY, 1948, AA
SHAGGY D.A., THE, 1976, AAA
SHAGGY DOG, THE, 1959, AAA
SHAKE HANDS WITH MURDER, 1944, A
SHAKE HANDS WITH THE DEVIL, 1959, C
SHAKE, RATTLE, AND ROCK?, 1957, A
SHAKEDOWN, 1936, A
SHAKEDOWN, 1950, C
SHAKEDOWN, 1934
SHAKEDOWN, THE, 1929, A
SHAKEDOWN, THE, 1960, C
SHAKESPEARE WALLAH, 1966, A
SHAKIEST GUN IN THE WEST, THE, 1968, A
SHALAKO, 1968, O
SHALIMAR, 1978
SHALL THE CHILDREN PAY?
SHALL WE DANCE, 1937, A
SHALL WE FORGIVE HER?, 1917
SHAM, 1921, A
SHAME
SHAME, 1918
SHAME, 1921, A
SHAME, 1968, O
SHAME OF MARY BOYLE, THE
SHAME OF PATTY SMITH, THE
SHAME OF THE JUNGLE, 1980
SHAME OF THE SABINE WOMEN, THE, 1962, A
SHAME, SHAME, EVERYBODY KNOWS HER NAME, 1969, O
SHAMEFUL BEHAVIOR?, 1926
SHAMELESS OLD LADY, THE, 1966, A
SHAMPOO, 1975, O
SHAMROCK AND THE ROSE, THE, 1927
SHAMROCK HANDICAP, THE, 1926
SHAMROCK HILL, 1949, AA
SHAMS OF SOCIETY, 1921, A
SHAMUS, 1959, AA
SHAMUS, 1973, C
SHAN-KO LIEN
SHANE, 1953, C
SHANGHAI, 1935, A
SHANGHAI BOUND, 1927
SHANGHAI CHEST, THE, 1948, A
SHANGHAI COBRA, THE, 1945, A
SHANGHAI DOCUMENT, A, 1929
SHANGHAI DRAMA, THE, 1945, A
SHANGHAI EXPRESS, 1932, O
SHANGHAI GESTURE, THE, 1941, C
SHANGHAI LADY, 1929, A
SHANGHAI MADNESS, 1933, A
SHANGHAI ROSE, 1929
SHANGHAI STORY, THE, 1954, A
SHANGHAIED, 1927
SHANGHAIED LOVE, 1931, A
SHANGRI-LA, 1961, O
SHANKS, 1974, A
SHANNON OF THE SIXTH, 1914
SHANNONS OF BROADWAY, THE, 1929, A
SHANTY TRAMP, 1967, O
SHANTYTOWN, 1943, A
SHANTYTOWN HONEYMOON, 1972
SHAPE OF THINGS TO COME, THE, 1979, A
SHARE AND SHARE ALIKE, 1925
SHARE OUT, THE, 1966, A
SHARK, 1970, C
SHARK GOD, THE
SHARK MASTER, THE, 1921, A
SHARK MONROE, 1918
SHARK REEF
SHARK RIVER, 1953, A
SHARK WOMAN, THE, 1941, A
SHARK'S TREASURE, 1975, A
SHARK, THE, 1920
SHARKFIGHTERS, THE, 1956, A
SHARKY'S MACHINE, 1928, O
SHARP SHOOTERS, 1928, A
SHARPSHOOTERS, 1938, A
SHATTER
SHATTERED DREAMS, 1922
SHATTERED FAITH, 1923
SHATTERED IDOLS, 1922, A
SHATTERED IDYLL, A, 1916
SHATTERED LIVES, 1925
SHATTERED REPUTATIONS, 1923, A
SHATTERHAND
SHE, 1916
SHE, 1917
SHE, 1925
SHE, 1935, A
SHE, 1965, A-C
SHE, 1983
SHE ALWAYS GETS THEIR MAN, 1962, A
SHE AND HE, 1967, A
SHE AND HE, 1969, O
SHE ASKED FOR IT, 1937, A
SHE BEAST, THE, 1966, C
SHE CAME TO THE VALLEY, 1979
SHE COULDN'T HELP IT, 1921
SHE COULDN'T SAY NO, 1930, A
SHE COULDN'T SAY NO, 1939, A
SHE COULDN'T SAY NO, 1941, A
SHE COULDN'T SAY NO, 1954, A
SHE COULDN'T TAKE IT, 1935, A
SHE DANCES ALONE, 1981, A
SHE DEMONS, 1958, A
SHE DEVIL, 1940
SHE DEVIL, 1957, A
SHE DEVIL, THE, 1918
SHE DIDN'T SAY NO?, 1962, A
SHE DONE HIM WRONG, 1933, C
SHE FREAK, 1967, O
SHE GETS HER MAN, 1935, A
SHE GETS HER MAN, 1945, A
SHE GOES TO WAR, 1929, A
SHE GOT HER MAN
SHE GOT WHAT SHE WANTED, 1930, A
SHE HAD TO CHOOSE, 1934, A
SHE HAD TO EAT, 1937, A
SHE HAD TO SAY YES, 1933, A
SHE HAD TO SAY YES, 1954
SHE HAS WHAT IT TAKES, 1943, A
SHE HIRED A HUSBAND, 1919
SHE KNEW ALL THE ANSWERS, 1941, A
SHE KNEW WHAT SHE WANTED, 1936, A
SHE KNOWS Y'KNOW, 1962, C
SHE LEARNED ABOUT SAILORS, 1934, A
SHE LEFT WITHOUT HER TRUNKS, 1916
SHE LET HIM CONTINUE
SHE LOVED A FIREMAN, 1937, A
SHE LOVES AND LIES, 1920, A
SHE LOVES ME NOT, 1934, A
SHE MADE HER BED, 1934, A
SHE MAN, THE, 1967, C
SHE MARRIED A COP, 1939, A
SHE MARRIED AN ARTIST, 1938, A
SHE MARRIED HER BOSS, 1935, A
SHE MONSTER OF THE NIGHT
SHE PLAYED WITH FIRE, 1957, C
SHE SHALL HAVE MURDER, 1950, A
SHE SHALL HAVE MUSIC, 1935, A
SHE SHOULD HAVE SAID NO, 1949
SHE SHOULDA SAID NO
SHE STEPS OUT
SHE STOOPS TO CONQUER, 1914
SHE WANTED A MILLIONAIRE, 1932, A
SHE WAS A HIPPY VAMPIRE
SHE WAS A LADY, 1934, A
SHE WAS ONLY A VILLAGE MAIDEN, 1933, A
SHE WENT TO THE RACES, 1945, A
SHE WHO DARES
SHE WOLVES, 1925
SHE WORE A YELLOW RIBBON, 1949, A
SHE WOULDN'T SAY YES, 1945, A
SHE WROTE THE BOOK, 1946, A
SHE'LL FOLLOW YOU ANYWHERE, 1971
SHE'LL HAVE TO GO
SHE'S A SHEIK, 1927, A
SHE'S A SOLDIER TOO, 1944, A
SHE'S A SWEETHEART, 1944, A
SHE'S BACK ON BROADWAY, 1953, A
SHE'S DANGEROUS, 1937, A
SHE'S FOR ME, 1943, A
SHE'S GOT EVERYTHING, 1938, A
SHE'S IN THE ARMY, 1942, A
SHE'S MY BABY, 1927
SHE'S MY LOVELY
SHE'S MY WEAKNESS, 1930, A
SHE'S NO LADY, 1937, A
SHE'S TOO MEAN TO ME, 1948
SHE'S WORKING HER WAY THROUGH COLLEGE, 1952, A
SHE-CREATURE, THE, 1956, A
SHE-DEVIL ISLAND, 1936, A
SHE-DEVILS ON WHEELS, 1968, O
SHE-GODS OF SHARK REEF, 1958, A
SHE-WOLF OF LONDON, 1946, A
SHE-WOLF, THE, 1931, A
SHE-WOLF, THE, 1963, A
SHEBA, 1919
SHEBA BABY, 1975, C
SHED NO TEARS, 1948, A
SHEENA, 1984, C-O
SHEEP TRAIL, 1926
SHEEPDOG OF THE HILLS, 1941, A

SHEEPMAN, THE, 1958, A
SHEER BLUFF, 1921, A
SHEFFIELD BLADE, A, 1918, A
SHEHERAZADE
SHEIK OF ARABY, THE, 1922
SHEIK OF MOJAVE, THE, 1928
SHEIK STEPS OUT, THE, 1937, A
SHEIK'S WIFE, THE
SHEIK, THE, 1921, A
SHEILA LEVINE IS DEAD AND LIVING IN NEW YORK, 1975, A-C
SHELL FORTY-THREE, 1916
SHELL GAME, THE, 1918
SHELL SHOCK, 1964, C
SHELL SHOCKED SAMMY, 1923
SHELTERED DAUGHTERS, 1921
SHENANDOAH, 1965, C
SHENANIGANS
SHEP COMES HOME, 1949, AA
SHEPHERD GIRL, THE, 1965, A
SHEPHERD KING, THE, 1923
SHEPHERD LASSIE OF ARGYLE, THE, 1914
SHEPHERD OF THE HILL, THE, 1928
SHEPHERD OF THE HILLS, THE, 1920
SHEPHERD OF THE HILLS, THE, 1941, A
SHEPHERD OF THE HILLS, THE, 1964, A
SHEPHERD OF THE OZARKS, 1942, A
SHEPPER-NEWFOUNDER, THE
SHERIFF OF CIMARRON, 1945, A
SHERIFF OF FRACTURED JAW, THE, 1958, A
SHERIFF OF HOPE ETERNAL, THE, 1921
SHERIFF OF LAS VEGAS, 1944, A
SHERIFF OF MEDICINE BOW, THE, 1948
SHERIFF OF REDWOOD VALLEY, 1946, A
SHERIFF OF SAGE VALLEY, 1942, A
SHERIFF OF SUN-DOG, THE, 1922
SHERIFF OF SUNDOWN, 1944, A
SHERIFF OF TOMBSTONE, 1941, A
SHERIFF OF WICHITA, 1949, A
SHERIFF'S GIRL, 1926
SHERIFF'S LASH, THE, 1929
SHERIFF'S LONE HAND, THE
SHERIFF'S SECRET, THE, 1931
SHERIFF'S SON, THE, 1919
SHERLOCK BROWN, 1921, A
SHERLOCK HOLMES, 1916
SHERLOCK HOLMES, 1922, A
SHERLOCK HOLMES, 1932, A
SHERLOCK HOLMES AND THE DEADLY NECKLACE, 1962, A
SHERLOCK HOLMES AND THE SECRET CODE
SHERLOCK HOLMES AND THE SECRET WEAPON, 1942, A
SHERLOCK HOLMES AND THE SPIDER WOMAN, 1944, A
SHERLOCK HOLMES AND THE VOICE OF TERROR, 1942, A
SHERLOCK HOLMES FACES DEATH, 1943, O
SHERLOCK HOLMES GROSSTER FALL
SHERLOCK HOLMES IN WASHINGTON, 1943, A
SHERLOCK HOLMES' FATAL HOUR, 1931, A
SHERLOCK HOLMES, 1939
SHERLOCK, JR., 1924, A
SHERRY, 1920
SHICHININ NO SAMURAI
SHIELD FOR MURDER, 1954, A
SHIELD OF FAITH, THE, 1956, A
SHIELD OF HONOR, THE, 1927, A
SHIELD OF SILENCE, THE, 1925
SHIFTING SANDS, 1918
SHIFTING SANDS, 1922
SHILLINGBURY BLOWERS, THE, 1980, A
SHIN NO SHIKOTEI
SHINBONE ALLEY, 1971, A
SHINE GIRL, THE, 1916
SHINE ON, HARVEST MOON, 1938, A
SHINE ON, HARVEST MOON, 1944, A
SHINEL
SHINING ADVENTURE, THE, 1925
SHINING HOUR, THE, 1938, A-C
SHINING STAR
SHINING VICTORY, 1941, A
SHINING, THE, 1980, C-O
SHINJU TEN NO AMIJIMA
SHIP AHOY, 1942, A
SHIP CAFE, 1935, A
SHIP COMES IN, A, 1928
SHIP FROM SHANGHAI, THE, 1930, A
SHIP OF CONDEMNED WOMEN, THE, 1963, A
SHIP OF DOOM, THE, 1917
SHIP OF FOOLS, 1965, C
SHIP OF LOST MEN, THE, 1929
SHIP OF SOULS, 1925
SHIP OF WANTED MEN, 1933, A
SHIP THAT DIED OF SHAME, THE, 1956, A
SHIP WAS LOADED, THE
SHIPBUILDERS, THE, 1943, A
SHIPMATES, 1931, A
SHIPMATES FOREVER, 1935, A
SHIPMATES O' MINE, 1936, A
SHIPS OF HATE, 1931, A
SHIPS OF THE NIGHT, 1928
SHIPS THAT PASS IN THE NIGHT, 1921, A
SHIPS WITH WINGS, 1942, A
SHIPWRECK
SHIPWRECKED, 1926
SHIPYARD SALLY, 1940, A
SHIRALEE, THE, 1957, C
SHIRAZ, 1929
SHIRIKURAE MAGOICHI
SHIRLEY, 1922
SHIRLEY KAYE, 1917
SHIRLEY OF THE CIRCUS, 1922, A
SHIRLEY THOMPSON VERSUS THE ALIENS, 1968, O
SHIRO TO KURO
SHIVERS
SHIVERS, 1984, C
SHLOSHA YAMIN VE' YELED
SHNEI KUNI LEMEL
SHOCK, 1934, C
SHOCK, 1946, O
SHOCK CORRIDOR, 1963, O
SHOCK HILL, 1966
SHOCK PUNCH, THE, 1925
SHOCK TREATMENT, 1964, O
SHOCK TREATMENT, 1973, O
SHOCK TREATMENT, 1981, O
SHOCK TROOPS, 1968, O
SHOCK WAVES, 1977, O
SHOCK, 1979
SHOCK, THE, 1923, A
SHOCKER
SHOCKING MISS PILGRIM, THE, 1947, A
SHOCKING NIGHT, A, 1921, A
SHOCKPROOF, 1949, C
SHOD WITH FIRE, 1920
SHOE SHINE, 1947, C
SHOEBLACK OF PICCADILLY, THE, 1920, A
SHOEMAKER AND THE ELVES, THE, 1967, AAA
SHOES, 1916
SHOES OF THE FISHERMAN, THE, 1968, A
SHOES THAT DANCED, THE, 1918
SHOGUN ASSASSIN, 1980, O
SHOGUN ISLAND
SHONEN SSARUTOBI SASUKE
SHOOT, 1976, O
SHOOT FIRST, 1953, C-O
SHOOT FIRST, DIE LATER, 1973
SHOOT FIRST, LAUGH LAST, 1967, O
SHOOT IT: BLACK, SHOOT IT: BLUE, 1974, O
SHOOT LOUD, LOUDER... I DON'T UNDERSTAND, 1966, O
SHOOT OUT, 1971, C
SHOOT OUT AT BIG SAG, 1962, C
SHOOT THE MOON, 1982, C-O
SHOOT THE PIANO PLAYER, 1962, C
SHOOT THE SUN DOWN, 1981
SHOOT THE WORKS, 1934, A
SHOOT TO KILL, 1947, C
SHOOT TO KILL, 1961, A
SHOOT-OUT AT MEDICINE BEND, 1957, A
SHOOTIN' FOR LOVE, 1923, A
SHOOTIN' IRONS
SHOOTIN' IRONS, 1927, A
SHOOTIN' SQUARE, 1924
SHOOTING HIGH, 1940, A
SHOOTING OF DAN MCGREW, THE, 1915, A
SHOOTING OF DAN MCGREW, THE, 1924
SHOOTING STARS, 1928
SHOOTING STRAIGHT, 1927
SHOOTING STRAIGHT, 1930, A
SHOOTING, THE, 1971, O
SHOOTIST, THE, 1976, O
SHOOTOUT
SHOOTOUT AT MEDICINE BEND
SHOP ANGEL, 1932, C
SHOP AROUND THE CORNER, THE, 1940, A
SHOP AT SLY CORNER, THE
SHOP GIRL, THE
SHOP ON HIGH STREET, THE
SHOP ON MAIN STREET, THE, 1966, C-O
SHOPGIRLS; OR, THE GREAT QUESTION, 1914
SHOPSOILED GIRL, THE, 1915, A
SHOPWORN, 1932, A
SHOPWORN ANGEL, 1938, A
SHOPWORN ANGEL, THE, 1928, A
SHORE ACRES, 1914
SHORE ACRES, 1920
SHORE LEAVE, 1925, A
SHORT CUT TO HELL, 1957, O
SHORT EYES, 1977, O
SHORT GRASS, 1950, C
SHORT IS THE SUMMER, 1968, O
SHORT SKIRTS, 1921
SHOT AT DAWN, A, 1934, C
SHOT GUN PASS
SHOT IN THE DARK, A, 1933, A
SHOT IN THE DARK, A, 1935, C
SHOT IN THE DARK, A, 1964, A-C
SHOT IN THE DARK, THE, 1941, C
SHOT IN THE NIGHT, A, 1923
SHOTGUN, 1955, O
SHOTGUN PASS, 1932, A
SHOTGUN WEDDING, THE, 1963, A-C
SHOULD A BABY DIE?, 1916
SHOULD A DOCTOR TELL?, 1923
SHOULD A DOCTOR TELL?, 1931, C
SHOULD A GIRL MARRY?, 1929, A
SHOULD A GIRL MARRY?, 1939, A
SHOULD A HUSBAND FORGIVE?, 1919
SHOULD A MOTHER TELL?, 1915
SHOULD A WIFE FORGIVE?, 1915, A
SHOULD A WIFE WORK?, 1922, A
SHOULD A WOMAN DIVORCE?, 1914, A
SHOULD A WOMAN TELL?, 1920, C
SHOULD HUSBANDS WORK?, 1939, AAA
SHOULD LADIES BEHAVE?, 1933, C-O
SHOULD SHE OBEY?, 1917
SHOULDER ARMS, 1917
SHOUT AT THE DEVIL, 1976, C
SHOUT, THE, 1978, O
SHOW BOAT, 1929, A
SHOW BOAT, 1936, A
SHOW BOAT, 1951, A
SHOW BUSINESS, 1944, AAA
SHOW FLAT, 1936, A
SHOW FOLKS, 1928, A
SHOW GIRL, 1928, A
SHOW GIRL IN HOLLYWOOD, 1930, A
SHOW GIRL, THE, 1927, A
SHOW GOES ON, THE, 1937, A
SHOW GOES ON, THE, 1938, C
SHOW OFF, THE, 1926
SHOW PEOPLE, 1928, A
SHOW THEM NO MERCY, 1935, C
SHOW, THE, 1927
SHOW-DOWN, THE, 1917
SHOW-OFF, THE, 1934, A
SHOW-OFF, THE, 1946, A
SHOWDOWN, 1963, A
SHOWDOWN, 1973, A
SHOWDOWN AT ABILENE, 1956, A
SHOWDOWN AT BOOT HILL, 1958, A
SHOWDOWN FOR ZATOICHI, 1968, C-O
SHOWDOWN, THE, 1928
SHOWDOWN, THE, 1940, A
SHOWDOWN, THE, 1950, A
SHOWDOWN, THE, 1940
SHOWGIRL IN HOLLYWOOD
SHOWOFF
SHOWTIME, 1948, A
SHRIEK IN THE NIGHT, A, 1933, A
SHRIEK OF ARABY, THE, 1923
SHRIEK OF THE MUTILATED, 1974, O
SHRIKE, THE, 1955, C
SHRINE OF HAPPINESS, THE, 1916
SHUBIN
SHULAMIS, 1931
SHULMATE, THE, 1915
SHUT MY BIG MOUTH, 1942, AAA
SHUT MY BIG MOUTH, 1946
SHUTTERED ROOM, THE, 1968, C-O
SHUTTLE OF LIFE, THE, 1920
SHUTTLE, THE, 1918
SI JAMAIS JE TE PINCE, 1920
SI PARIS NOUS ETAIT CONTE
SI VERSAILLES M'ETAIT CONTE
SIAVASH IN PERSEPOLIS, 1966, C
SIBERIA, 1926, A
SICILIAN CLAN, THE, 1970, O
SICILIAN CONNECTION, THE, 1977, O
SICILIANS, THE, 1964, A
SICK ABED, 1920
SICKLE AND HAMMER, 1921
SICKLE OR THE CROSS, THE, 1951
SIDDHARTHA, 1972, C
SIDE SHOW, 1931, A
SIDE STREET, 1929, A
SIDE STREET, 1950, C
SIDE STREET ANGEL, 1937, A
SIDE STREETS, 1934, A
SIDECAR RACERS, 1975, A
SIDEHACKERS, THE
SIDELONG GLANCES OF A PIGEON KICKER, THE, 1970, O
SIDESHOW, 1950, C
SIDESHOW OF LIFE, THE, 1924, A
SIDESHOW, THE, 1928
SIDEWALKS OF LONDON, 1940, AA
SIDEWALKS OF NEW YORK, 1923
SIDEWALKS OF NEW YORK, 1931, AAA
SIDEWINDER ONE, 1977, C
SIDNEY SHELDON'S BLOODLINE
SIEGE, 1925
SIEGE, 1983, O
SIEGE AT RED RIVER, THE, 1954, C
SIEGE OF FORT BISMARK, 1968, C-O

SIEGE OF HELL STREET, THE
SIEGE OF PINCHGUT
SIEGE OF RED RIVER, THE
SIEGE OF SIDNEY STREET, THE, 1960, O
SIEGE OF SYRACUSE, 1962, C
SIEGE OF THE SAXONS, 1963, A
SIEGFRIED, 1924, C
SIEGFRIED'S DEATH
SIEGFRIEDS TOD
SIERRA, 1950, A
SIERRA BARON, 1958, A
SIERRA DE TERUEL
SIERRA PASSAGE, 1951, A
SIERRA STRANGER, 1957, C
SIERRA SUE, 1941, A
SIETE HOMBRES DE ORO
SIGHT UNSEEN, A, 1914
SIGMA III, 1966
SIGN, 1932, C-O
SIGN INVISIBLE, THE, 1918
SIGN OF AQUARIUS, 1970, O
SIGN OF FOUR, THE, 1932, C
SIGN OF FOUR, THE, 1983, C
SIGN OF THE CACTUS, THE, 1925
SIGN OF THE CLAW, THE, 1926
SIGN OF THE FOUR, THE, 1923
SIGN OF THE GLADIATOR, 1959, C
SIGN OF THE PAGAN, 1954, C
SIGN OF THE POPPY, THE, 1916
SIGN OF THE RAM, THE, 1948, A
SIGN OF THE ROSE, THE, 1922, A
SIGN OF THE SPADE, THE, 1916
SIGN OF THE VIRGIN, 1969, O
SIGN OF THE WOLF, 1941, AAA
SIGN OF VENUS, THE, 1955, C
SIGN OF ZORRO, THE, 1960, AAA
SIGN ON THE DOOR, THE, 1921
SIGNAL 7, 1984, O
SIGNAL FIRES, 1926
SIGNAL TOWER, THE, 1924, A
SIGNALS-AN ADVENTURE IN SPACE, 1970, A
SIGNED JUDGEMENT
SIGNORA SENZA CAMELIE
SIGNORE E SIGNORI
SIGNPOST TO MURDER, 1964, O
SIGNS OF LIFE, 1981, O
SILAS MARNER, 1916
SILAS MARNER, 1922
SILENCE, 1926
SILENCE, 1931, O
SILENCE, 1974, AAA
SILENCE HAS NO WINGS, 1971, A
SILENCE OF DEAN MAITLAND, THE, 1934, C-O
SILENCE OF DR. EVANS, THE, 1973, C
SILENCE OF MARTHA, THE
SILENCE OF THE DEAD, THE, 1913
SILENCE OF THE NORTH, 1981, C
SILENCE SELLERS, THE, 1917
SILENCE, THE, 1964, O
SILENCERS, THE, 1966, 0
SILENT ACCUSER, THE
SILENT ACCUSER, THE, 1914
SILENT ACCUSER, THE, 1924
SILENT AVENGER, THE, 1927
SILENT BARRIER, THE, 1920
SILENT BARRIERS, 1937, A
SILENT BATTLE, THE
SILENT BATTLE, THE, 1916
SILENT CALL, THE, 1921, A
SILENT CALL, THE, 1961, A
SILENT CODE, THE, 1935
SILENT COMMAND, THE, 1915
SILENT COMMAND, THE, 1923, A
SILENT CONFLICT, 1948, A
SILENT DEATH
SILENT DUST, 1949, A
SILENT ENEMY, THE, 1930, C
SILENT ENEMY, THE, 1959, C
SILENT EVIDENCE, 1922, A
SILENT FLUTE, THE
SILENT GUARDIAN, THE, 1926
SILENT HERO, THE, 1927
SILENT HOUSE, THE, 1929
SILENT INVASION, THE, 1962, A
SILENT LADY, THE, 1917
SILENT LIE, THE, 1917
SILENT LOVER, THE, 1926, A
SILENT MADNESS, 1984, O
SILENT MAN, THE, 1917
SILENT MASTER, THE, 1917
SILENT MEN, 1933
SILENT MOVIE, 1976, A-C
SILENT NIGHT, BLOODY NIGHT, 1974, O
SILENT NIGHT, DEADLY NIGHT, 1984, O
SILENT NIGHT, EVIL NIGHT
SILENT ONE, THE, 1984, A
SILENT PAL, 1925
SILENT PARTNER, 1944, C
SILENT PARTNER, THE, 1917
SILENT PARTNER, THE, 1923, A
SILENT PARTNER, THE, 1979, C-O
SILENT PASSENGER, THE, 1935, A
SILENT PLAYGROUND, THE, 1964, C-O
SILENT POWER, THE, 1926, A
SILENT RAGE, 1982, O
SILENT RAIDERS, 1954, C
SILENT RIDER, THE, 1918
SILENT RIDER, THE, 1927
SILENT RUNNING, 1972, C
SILENT SANDERSON, 1925
SILENT SCREAM, 1980, O
SILENT SENTINEL, 1929
SILENT SHELBY
SILENT SHELDON, 1925
SILENT STAR
SILENT STRANGER, THE, 1924
SILENT STRANGER, THE, 1975
SILENT STRENGTH, 1919
SILENT TRAIL, 1928
SILENT VOICE, THE
SILENT VOICE, THE, 1915, A
SILENT VOW, THE, 1922, A
SILENT WATCHER, THE, 1924
SILENT WIRES, 1924
SILENT WITNESS, 1942
SILENT WITNESS, THE, 1917
SILENT WITNESS, THE, 1932, C
SILENT WITNESS, THE, 1962, O
SILENT WOMAN, THE, 1918
SILENT YEARS, 1921
SILHOUETTES, 1982, C
SILICATES
SILK BOUQUET, THE, 1926
SILK EXPRESS, THE, 1933, A
SILK HAT KID, 1935, A
SILK HOSIERY, 1920
SILK HUSBANDS AND CALICO WIVES, 1920
SILK LEGS, 1927, A
SILK NOOSE, THE, 1950, A
SILK STOCKING SAL, 1924
SILK STOCKINGS, 1927
SILK STOCKINGS, 1957, A
SILK-LINED BURGLAR, THE, 1919
SILKEN AFFAIR, THE, 1957, A
SILKEN SHACKLES, 1926
SILKEN SKIN
SILKEN TRAP, THE
SILKS AND SADDLES, 1929, A
SILKS AND SADDLES, 1938
SILKS AND SATINS, 1916
SILKWOOD, 1983, C-O
SILLY BILLIES, 1936, A
SILVER BANDIT, THE, 1950, A
SILVER BEARS, 1978, C
SILVER BLAZE
SILVER BRIDGE, THE, 1920
SILVER BULLET, THE, 1935
SILVER BULLET, THE, 1942, C
SILVER CANYON, 1951, A
SILVER CAR, THE, 1921, A
SILVER CHAINS
SILVER CHALICE, THE, 1954, A
SILVER CITY, 1951, C
SILVER CITY, 1948
SILVER CITY BONANZA, 1951, A
SILVER CITY KID, 1944, A
SILVER CITY RAIDERS, 1943, A
SILVER COMES THROUGH, 1927, A
SILVER COMES THRU
SILVER CORD, 1933, A
SILVER DARLINGS, THE, 1947, A
SILVER DEVIL
SILVER DOLLAR, 1932, A
SILVER DREAM RACER, 1982, C
SILVER DUST, 1953, C
SILVER FINGERS, 1926
SILVER FLEET, THE, 1945, A
SILVER GIRL, THE, 1919
SILVER GREYHOUND, THE, 1919
SILVER HORDE, THE, 1920
SILVER HORDE, THE, 1930, A
SILVER KEY, THE
SILVER KING COMES THRU
SILVER KING, THE, 1919
SILVER KING, THE, 1929
SILVER LINING, 1932, A
SILVER LINING, THE, 1919
SILVER LINING, THE, 1921, A
SILVER LINING, THE, 1927
SILVER LODE, 1954, A
SILVER ON THE SAGE, 1939, A
SILVER QUEEN, 1942, A
SILVER RAIDERS, 1950, A
SILVER RANGE, 1946
SILVER RIVER, 1948, A
SILVER SKATES, 1943, A
SILVER SLAVE, THE, 1927, A
SILVER SPOON, THE, 1934, A
SILVER SPURS, 1922
SILVER SPURS, 1936, A
SILVER SPURS, 1943, A
SILVER STALLION, 1941, A
SILVER STAR, THE, 1955, A
SILVER STREAK, 1976, C
SILVER STREAK, THE, 1935, A
SILVER THREADS AMONG THE GOLD, 1915, A
SILVER TOP, 1938, A
SILVER TRAIL, THE, 1937, A
SILVER TRAILS, 1948, A
SILVER TREASURE, THE, 1926
SILVER VALLEY, 1927, A
SILVER WHIP, THE, 1953, A
SILVER WINGS, 1922, A
SILVERSPURS
SIMBA, 1955, O
SIMCHON FAMILY, THE, 1969, C
SIMON, 1980, A-C
SIMON AND LAURA, 1956, C-O
SIMON THE JESTER, 1915, C
SIMON THE JESTER, 1925
SIMON, KING OF THE WITCHES, 1971, O
SIMONE, 1918
SIMONE, 1926
SIMP, THE, 1921
SIMPLE CASE OF MONEY, A, 1952, A
SIMPLE SIMON, 1922
SIMPLE SIS, 1927
SIMPLE SOULS, 1920
SIMPLE TAILOR, THE, 1934
SIMPLETTE, 1919
SIMPLY IRRESISTIBLE, 1983
SIMPLY TERRIFIC, 1938, A
SIN, 1915, C
SIN, THE
SIN CARGO, 1926
SIN FLOOD
SIN FLOOD, THE, 1922
SIN NOW...PAY LATER
SIN OF HAROLD DIDDLEBOCK, THE
SIN OF MADELON CLAUDET, THE, 1931, C
SIN OF MARTHA QUEED, THE, 1921, A
SIN OF MONA KENT, THE, 1961, O
SIN OF NORA MORAN, 1933, A
SIN ON THE BEACH, 1964, O
SIN SHIP, 1931, A
SIN SISTER, THE, 1929, A
SIN TAKES A HOLIDAY, 1930, A
SIN THAT WAS HIS, THE, 1920, C
SIN TOWN, 1929
SIN TOWN, 1942, A
SIN WOMAN, THE, 1917
SIN YE DO, THE, 1916
SIN YOU SINNERS, 1963, O
SIN'S PAYDAY, 1932, A
SINAI COMMANDOS: THE STORY OF THE SIX DAY WAR, 1968, C
SINAIA
SINBAD AND THE EYE OF THE TIGER, 1977, AAA
SINBAD THE SAILOR, 1947, A
SINCE YOU WENT AWAY, 1944, A
SINCERELY YOURS, 1955, A
SINEWS OF STEEL, 1927
SINFONIA PER DUE SPIE
SINFONIA PER UN MASSACRO
SINFUL DAVEY, 1969, O
SINFUL DWARF, THE, 1973
SING A JINGLE, 1943, A
SING ALONG WITH ME, 1952, A
SING AND BE HAPPY, 1937, A
SING AND LIKE IT, 1934, A
SING AND SWING, 1964, C
SING ANOTHER CHORUS, 1941, A
SING AS WE GO, 1934, A
SING AS YOU SWING, 1937, A
SING FOR YOUR SUPPER, 1941, AA
SING ME A LOVE SONG
SING ME A LOVE SONG, 1936, A
SING ME A SONG OF TEXAS, 1945
SING SING NIGHTS, 1935, C
SING SINNER, SING, 1933, C
SING WHILE YOU DANCE, 1946, A
SING WHILE YOU'RE ABLE, 1937, A
SING YOU SINNERS, 1938, AA
SING YOUR WAY HOME, 1945, A
SING YOUR WORRIES AWAY, 1942, A
SING, BABY, SING, 1936, A
SING, BOY, SING, 1958, C
SING, COWBOY, SING, 1937, A
SING, DANCE, PLENTY HOT, 1940, A
SING, NEIGHBOR, SING, 1944, A
SINGAPORE, 1947, A
SINGAPORE MUTINY, THE, 1928
SINGAPORE WOMAN, 1941, A
SINGAPORE, SINGAPORE, 1969, C
SINGED, 1927, A
SINGED WINGS, 1915
SINGED WINGS, 1922, A

SINGER AND THE DANCER, THE, 1977, C
SINGER JIM MCKEE, 1924, A
SINGER NOT THE SONG, THE, 1961, O
SINGIN' IN THE CORN, 1946, A
SINGIN' IN THE RAIN, 1952, A
SINGING BLACKSMITH, 1938, C
SINGING BUCKAROO, THE, 1937, AA
SINGING COP, THE, 1938, A
SINGING COWBOY, THE, 1936, A
SINGING COWGIRL, THE, 1939, A
SINGING FOOL, THE, 1928, A
SINGING GUNS, 1950, A
SINGING HILL, THE, 1941, AA
SINGING IN THE DARK, 1956, A
SINGING KID, THE, 1936, A
SINGING MARINE, THE, 1937, A
SINGING NUN, THE, 1966, A
SINGING ON THE TRAIL, 1946
SINGING OUTLAW, 1937, A
SINGING PRINCESS, THE, 1967, A
SINGING RIVER, 1921, A
SINGING SHERIFF, THE, 1944, A
SINGING SPURS, 1948
SINGING TAXI DRIVER, 1953, A
SINGING THROUGH, 1935, A
SINGING VAGABOND, THE, 1935, A
SINGLE CODE, THE, 1917
SINGLE GIRLS, 1973
SINGLE HANDED, 1923
SINGLE LIFE, 1921
SINGLE MAN, A, 1929, A
SINGLE MAN, THE, 1919, A
SINGLE ROOM FURNISHED, 1968, O
SINGLE SHOT PARKER
SINGLE SIN, 1931, A
SINGLE STANDARD, THE, 1914
SINGLE STANDARD, THE, 1929, A
SINGLE TRACK, THE, 1921, A
SINGLE WIVES, 1924
SINGLE-HANDED
SINGLE-HANDED SANDERS, 1932, A
SINGLETON'S PLUCK
SINISTER HANDS, 1932, A
SINISTER HOUSE
SINISTER JOURNEY, 1948, A
SINISTER MAN, THE, 1965, C
SINISTER STREET, 1922
SINISTER URGE, THE, 1961, O
SINK THE BISMARCK!, 1960, A
SINKING OF THE LUSITANIA, THE, 1918
SINLESS SINNER, A
SINNER, THE
SINNER OR SAINT, 1923
SINNER TAKE ALL, 1936, C
SINNER'S BLOOD, 1970
SINNER'S HOLIDAY, 1930, A
SINNER'S PARADE, 1928, A
SINNERS, 1920
SINNERS, THE
SINNERS GO TO HELL
SINNERS IN HEAVEN, 1924, A
SINNERS IN LOVE, 1928, A
SINNERS IN PARADISE, 1938, C
SINNERS IN SILK, 1924
SINNERS IN THE SUN, 1932, C
SINS OF DORIAN GRAY, 1982
SINS OF HER PARENT, 1916
SINS OF JEZEBEL, 1953, C
SINS OF LOLA MONTES, THE
SINS OF MAN, 1936, A
SINS OF MEN, 1916
SINS OF RACHEL, THE, 1975
SINS OF RACHEL CADE, THE, 1960, O
SINS OF ROSE BERND, THE, 1959
SINS OF ROZANNE, 1920, A
SINS OF SOCIETY, 1915, A
SINS OF ST. ANTHONY, THE, 1920
SINS OF THE BORGIAS
SINS OF THE CHILDREN, 1918
SINS OF THE CHILDREN, 1930, A
SINS OF THE FATHER, 1928
SINS OF THE FATHERS, 1928, A
SINS OF THE FATHERS, 1948, C
SINS OF THE MOTHERS, 1915, A
SINS OF THE PARENTS, 1914
SINS OF YOUTH, THE, 1919
SINS THAT YE SIN, THE, 1915
SINS YE DO, THE, 1924
SINTHIA THE DEVIL'S DOLL, 1970
SIOUX BLOOD, 1929, A
SIOUX CITY SUE, 1946, A
SIR ARNE'S TREASURE, 1920
SIR GAWAIN AND THE GREEN KNIGHT
SIR HENRY AT RAWLINSON END, 1980, O
SIR LUMBERJACK, 1926
SIR OR MADAM, 1928
SIR, YOU ARE A WIDOWER, 1971, O
SIREN, THE, 1917
SIREN, THE, 1927
SIREN CALL, THE, 1922, A
SIREN OF ATLANTIS, 1948, A
SIREN OF BAGDAD, 1953, A
SIREN OF SEVILLE, THE, 1924
SIREN'S SONG, THE, 1919
SIRENE DU MISSISSIPPI
SIRENS OF THE SEA, 1917
SIROCCO, 1951, A
SIROCCO D'HIVER
SIS HOPKINS, 1919
SIS HOPKINS, 1941, A
SISSI
SISTER AGAINST SISTER, 1917
SISTER KENNY, 1946, A
SISTER OF SIX, A, 1916
SISTER TO ASSIST 'ER, A, 1922, A
SISTER TO ASSIST 'ER, A, 1927, A
SISTER TO ASSIST'ER, A, 1930, A
SISTER TO ASSIST'ER, A, 1938, A
SISTER TO ASSIST'ER, A, 1948, A
SISTER TO JUDAS, 1933
SISTER TO SALOME, A, 1920
SISTER-IN-LAW, THE, 1975, O
SISTERS, 1922, C
SISTERS, 1930, A
SISTERS, 1973, O
SISTERS, THE, 1938, A
SISTERS, THE, 1969, C
SISTERS OF DEATH, 1976
SISTERS OF EVE, 1928
SISTERS, OR THE BALANCE OF HAPPINESS, 1982, O
SISTERS UNDER THE SKIN, 1934, C
SIT TIGHT, 1931, A
SITTING BULL, 1954, C
SITTING BULL—THE HOSTILE SIOUX INDIAN CHIEF, 1914
SITTING BULL AT THE "SPIRIT LAKE MASSACRE", 1927
SITTING DUCKS, 1979, C
SITTING ON THE MOON, 1936, A
SITTING PRETTY, 1933, A
SITTING PRETTY, 1948, AAA
SITTING TARGET, 1972, O
SITUATION HOPELESS—BUT NOT SERIOUS, 1965, A
SIX BEST CELLARS, THE, 1920
SIX BLACK HORSES, 1962, A
SIX BRIDGES TO CROSS, 1955, A
SIX CYLINDER LOVE, 1923
SIX CYLINDER LOVE, 1931, A
SIX DAYS, 1923, A
SIX DAYS A WEEK, 1966, O
SIX FEET FOUR, 1919
SIX FEMMES POUR L'ASSASSIN
SIX GUN GOLD, 1941, A
SIX GUN GOSPEL, 1943, A
SIX GUN JUSTICE, 1935
SIX GUN MAN, 1946, A
SIX GUN MESA, 1950
SIX GUN SERENADE, 1947, A
SIX HOURS TO LIVE, 1932, C
SIX IN PARIS, 1968, C-O
SIX INCHES TALL
SIX LESSONS FROM MADAME LA ZONGA, 1941, A
SIX MEN, THE, 1951, A
SIX OF A KIND, 1934, A
SIX P.M., 1946, A
SIX PACK, 1982, C
SIX PACK ANNIE, 1975, O
SIX SHOOTIN' ROMANCE, A, 1926
SIX SHOOTIN' SHERIFF, 1938, A
SIX WEEKS, 1982, C
SIX-DAY BIKE RIDER, 1934, A
SIX-FIFTY, THE, 1923
SIX-GUN DECISION, 1953
SIX-GUN LAW, 1948, AA
SIX-GUN RHYTHM, 1939, A
SIX-GUN TRAIL, 1938
SIX-SHOOTER ANDY, 1918
SIXTEEN
SIXTEEN CANDLES, 1984, A-C
SIXTEEN FATHOMS DEEP, 1934, A
SIXTEEN FATHOMS DEEP, 1948, A
SIXTEENTH WIFE, THE, 1917
SIXTH AND MAIN, 1977, C
SIXTH COMMANDMENT, THE, 1924
SIXTH MAN, THE
SIXTH OF JUNE, THE
SIXTH OF THE WORLD, A, 1926
SIXTY CENTS AN HOUR, 1923, A
SIXTY GLORIOUS YEARS, 1938, A
SKAMMEN
SKATEBOARD, 1978, C
SKATEBOARD MADNESS, 1980
SKATETOWN, U.S.A., 1979, A
SKATING-RINK AND THE VIOLIN, THE
SKAZA O KONKE-GORBUNKE
SKEDADDLE GOLD, 1927
SKELETON ON HORSEBACK, 1940, C
SKETCHES OF A STRANGLER
SKEZAG, 1971
SKI BATTALION, 1938, C
SKI BUM, THE, 1971, O
SKI FEVER, 1969, C
SKI PARTY, 1965, A
SKI PATROL, 1940, A
SKI RAIDERS, THE
SKI TROOP ATTACK, 1960, C
SKID KIDS, 1953, AAA
SKID PROOF, 1923, A
SKIDOO, 1968, C
SKIES ABOVE
SKIMPY IN THE NAVY, 1949, A
SKIN DEEP, 1922
SKIN DEEP, 1929, C
SKIN DEEP, 1978, O
SKIN GAME, 1971, C
SKIN GAME, THE, 1920
SKIN GAME, THE, 1931, C
SKIN GAME, THE, 1965, O
SKINNER STEPS OUT, 1929, A
SKINNER'S BABY, 1917
SKINNER'S BIG IDEA, 1928, A
SKINNER'S BUBBLE, 1917
SKINNER'S DRESS SUIT, 1917, A
SKINNER'S DRESS SUIT, 1926, A
SKINNING SKINNERS, 1921
SKIP TRACER, THE, 1979, C
SKIPALONG ROSENBLOOM, 1951, A
SKIPPER SURPRISED HIS WIFE, THE, 1950, A
SKIPPER'S WOOING, THE, 1922, A
SKIPPY, 1931, AAA
SKIRTS, 1921
SKIRTS, 1928
SKIRTS AHOY?, 1952, A
SKULL, THE, 1965, O
SKULL AND CROWN, 1938, AAA
SKULLDUGGERY, 1970, C
SKUPLIJACI PERJA
SKY ABOVE HEAVEN, 1964, C
SKY BANDITS, THE, 1940, A
SKY BEYOND HEAVEN
SKY BIKE, THE, 1967, AAA
SKY BRIDE, 1932, A
SKY CALLS, THE, 1959, A
SKY COMMANDO, 1953, A
SKY DEVILS, 1932, A
SKY DRAGON, 1949, A
SKY FULL OF MOON, 1952, A
SKY GIANT, 1938, A
SKY HAWK, 1929, A
SKY HIGH, 1922, A
SKY HIGH, 1952, A
SKY HIGH CORRAL, 1926
SKY IS RED, THE, 1952, O
SKY IS YOURS, THE
SKY LINER, 1949, A
SKY MONSTER, THE, 1914
SKY MURDER, 1940, A
SKY PARADE, 1936, A
SKY PATROL, 1939, A
SKY PILOT, THE, 1921, A
SKY PIRATE, THE, 1926
SKY PIRATE, THE, 1970, C
SKY PIRATES, 1977
SKY RAIDER, THE, 1925
SKY RAIDERS, 1931, A
SKY RAIDERS, THE, 1938, A
SKY RIDER, THE, 1928, A
SKY RIDERS, 1976, C
SKY SKIDDER, THE, 1929, A
SKY SPIDER, THE, 1931, A
SKY TERROR
SKY WEST AND CROOKED
SKY'S THE LIMIT, 1925
SKY'S THE LIMIT, THE, 1937, A
SKY'S THE LIMIT, THE, 1943, A
SKY-EYE, 1920
SKY-HIGH SAUNDERS, 1927, A
SKYBOUND, 1935
SKYDIVERS, THE, 1963, C
SKYJACKED, 1972, A
SKYLARK, 1941, A
SKYLARKS, 1936, A
SKYLIGHT ROOM, THE, 1917
SKYLINE, 1931, A
SKYLINE, 1984, C
SKYROCKET, THE, 1926, A
SKYSCRAPER, 1928
SKYSCRAPER SOULS, 1932, A
SKYSCRAPER WILDERNESS
SKYWATCH
SKYWAY, 1933, A
SKYWAYMAN, THE, 1920
SLA FORST, FREDE?
SLACKER, THE, 1917
SLADE
SLAM BANG JIM
SLAMMER

SLAMS, THE, 1973, O
SLANDER, 1916
SLANDER, 1956, A
SLANDER HOUSE, 1938, A
SLANDER THE WOMAN, 1923, A
SLANDER THE WOMAN, 1923, A
SLANDERERS, THE, 1924
SLAP IN THE FACE, 1974
SLAP SHOT, 1977, O
SLAPSTICK OF ANOTHER KIND, 1984, A-C
SLASHER, THE, 1953, O
SLASHER, THE, 1975, O
SLATTERY'S HURRICANE, 1949, C
SLAUGHTER, 1972, O
SLAUGHTER, THE, 1913
SLAUGHTER HOTEL, 1971, O
SLAUGHTER IN SAN FRANCISCO, 1981, O
SLAUGHTER OF THE VAMPIRES, THE
SLAUGHTER ON TENTH AVENUE, 1957, A-C
SLAUGHTER TRAIL, 1951, A
SLAUGHTER'S BIG RIP-OFF, 1973, O
SLAUGHTERDAY, 1981
SLAUGHTERHOUSE-FIVE, 1972, O
SLAVE, THE, 1917
SLAVE, THE, 1918
SLAVE, THE, 1963, A
SLAVE GIRL, 1947, A
SLAVE GIRL OF BABYLON, 1962
SLAVE GIRLS
SLAVE GIRLS OF SHEBA, 1960
SLAVE MARKET, THE, 1917
SLAVE OF DESIRE, 1923, A
SLAVE OF FASHION, A, 1925
SLAVE OF PASSION, SLAVE OF VICE, 1914
SLAVE OF THE CANNIBAL GOD, 1979, O
SLAVE OF VANITY, A, 1920
SLAVE SHIP, 1937, A
SLAVER, THE, 1927
SLAVERS, 1977, O
SLAVES, 1969, O
SLAVES OF BABYLON, 1953, A
SLAVES OF BEAUTY, 1927, A
SLAVES OF DESTINY, 1924, A
SLAVES OF PRIDE, 1920
SLAVES OF SCANDAL, 1924
SLAVEY STUDENT, THE, 1915
SLAYER, THE, 1982, O
SLAYGROUND, 1984, O
SLEEP, MY LOVE, 1948, A
SLEEPAWAY CAMP, 1983, O
SLEEPER, 1973, A-C
SLEEPERS EAST, 1934, A
SLEEPERS WEST, 1941, A
SLEEPING BEAUTY, 1959, AAA
SLEEPING BEAUTY, 1965, AAA
SLEEPING BEAUTY, THE, 1966, AAA
SLEEPING CAR, 1933, A
SLEEPING CAR MURDER THE, 1966, C-O
SLEEPING CAR TO TRIESTE, 1949, A
SLEEPING CARDINAL, THE
SLEEPING CITY, THE, 1950, C
SLEEPING DOGS, 1977, C
SLEEPING FIRES, 1917
SLEEPING LION, THE, 1919
SLEEPING MEMORY, A, 1917
SLEEPING PARTNER, 1961
SLEEPING PARTNERS, 1930, A
SLEEPING PARTNERS, 1964
SLEEPING TIGER, THE, 1954, C
SLEEPLESS NIGHTS, 1933, A
SLEEPWALKER, THE, 1922, A
SLEEPY LAGOON, 1943, A
SLEEPYTIME GAL, 1942, A
SLENDER THREAD, THE, 1965, C
SLEPOY MUZYKANT
SLEUTH, 1972, C-O
SLIDE, KELLY, SLIDE, 1927, A
SLIGHT CASE OF LARCENY, A, 1953, A
SLIGHT CASE OF MURDER, A, 1938, A
SLIGHTLY DANGEROUS, 1943, A
SLIGHTLY FRENCH, 1949, A
SLIGHTLY HONORABLE, 1940, A
SLIGHTLY MARRIED, 1933, A
SLIGHTLY SCANDALOUS, 1946, A
SLIGHTLY SCARLET, 1930, A
SLIGHTLY SCARLET, 1956, C
SLIGHTLY TEMPTED, 1940, A
SLIGHTLY TERRIFIC, 1944, A
SLIGHTLY USED, 1927, A
SLIM, 1937, A
SLIM CARTER, 1957, A
SLIM FINGERS, 1929, A
SLIM PRINCESS, THE, 1915, A
SLIM PRINCESS, THE, 1920
SLIM SHOULDERS, 1922, A
SLIME PEOPLE, THE, 1963, A
SLINGSHOT, 1971
SLINGSHOT KID, THE, 1927
SLIPPER AND THE ROSE, THE, 1976, AAA
SLIPPER EPISODE, THE, 1938, A
SLIPPY MCGEE, 1923, A
SLIPPY MCGEE, 1948, A
SLIPSTREAM, 1974, O
SLITHER, 1973, C
SLITHIS, 1978, C
SLOGAN, 1970, C
SLOTH, 1917
SLOW AS LIGHTING, 1923
SLOW DANCING IN THE BIG CITY, 1978, C
SLOW DYNAMITE, 1925
SLOW MOTION
SLOW MOVES, 1984, O
SLOW RUN, 1968, O
SLUMBER PARTY '57, 1977, O
SLUMBER PARTY IN A HAUNTED HOUSE
SLUMBER PARTY IN HORROR HOUSE
SLUMBER PARTY MASSACRE, THE, 1982, O
SLUMS OF TOKYO, 1930
SMALL BACHELOR, THE, 1927
SMALL BACK ROOM, THE
SMALL CHANGE, 1976, C
SMALL CIRCLE OF FRIENDS, A, 1980, O
SMALL HOTEL, 1957, A
SMALL HOURS, THE, 1962, O
SMALL MAN, THE, 1935, A
SMALL MIRACLE, THE
SMALL TOWN BOY, 1937, A
SMALL TOWN DEB, 1941, A
SMALL TOWN GIRL, 1936, A
SMALL TOWN GIRL, 1953, A
SMALL TOWN GIRL, A, 1917
SMALL TOWN GUY, THE, 1917
SMALL TOWN IDOL, A, 1921, A
SMALL TOWN IN TEXAS, A, 1976, C
SMALL TOWN LAWYER
SMALL TOWN STORY, 1953, A
SMALL VOICE, THE
SMALL WORLD OF SAMMY LEE, THE, 1963, C
SMALLEST SHOW ON EARTH, THE, 1957, A
SMART ALEC, 1951, A
SMART ALECKS, 1942, A
SMART BLONDE, 1937, A
SMART GIRL, 1935, A
SMART GIRLS DON'T TALK, 1948, A
SMART GUY, 1943, A
SMART MONEY, 1931, A
SMART POLITICS, 1948, A
SMART SET, A, 1919
SMART SET, THE, 1928, A
SMART SEX, THE, 1921
SMART WOMAN, 1931, A
SMART WOMAN, 1948, A
SMARTEST GIRL IN TOWN, 1936, A
SMARTY, 1934, A
SMASH AND GRAB
SMASH PALACE, 1982, O
SMASH-UP, THE STORY OF A WOMAN, 1947, C
SMASHED BACK, 1927
SMASHING BARRIERS, 1923
SMASHING BIRD I USED TO KNOW, THE
SMASHING THE CRIME SYNDICATE
SMASHING THE MONEY RING, 1939, A
SMASHING THE RACKETS, 1938, A
SMASHING THE SPY RING, 1939, A
SMASHING THROUGH
SMASHING THROUGH, 1918
SMASHING THROUGH, 1928, A
SMASHING TIME, 1967, C
SMELL OF HONEY, A SWALLOW OF BRINE? A, 1966, O
SMELL OF HONEY? THE
SMILE, 1975, C-O
SMILE ORANGE, 1976, C
SMILE, BROTHER, SMILE, 1927, A
SMILES, 1919
SMILES ARE TRUMPS, 1922, A
SMILES OF A SUMMER NIGHT, 1957, A
SMILEY, 1957, A
SMILEY GETS A GUN, 1959, A
SMILIN' AT TROUBLE, 1925, A
SMILIN' GUNS, 1929
SMILIN' ON, 1923
SMILIN' THROUGH, 1922
SMILIN' THROUGH, 1932, A
SMILIN' THROUGH, 1941, A
SMILING ALL THE WAY, 1921
SMILING ALONG, 1938, A
SMILING AT TROUBLE
SMILING AT TROUBLE
SMILING BILLY, 1927
SMILING EARTH, THE, 1925
SMILING GHOST, THE, 1941, A
SMILING IRISH EYES, 1929, A
SMILING JIM, 1922
SMILING LIEUTENANT, THE, 1931, A-C
SMILING TERROR, THE, 1929
SMILING THROUGH
SMITH, 1917
SMITH, 1969, A
SMITH'S WIVES, 1935, A
SMITHEREENS, 1982, O
SMITHY, 1933, A
SMITHY, 1946, A
SMOKE BELLEW, 1929, A
SMOKE EATERS, THE, 1926
SMOKE IN THE WIND, 1975, C
SMOKE JUMPERS
SMOKE LIGHTNING, 1933
SMOKE SIGNAL, 1955, A
SMOKE TREE RANGE, 1937, A
SMOKESCREEN, 1964, A
SMOKEY AND THE BANDIT, 1977, C-O
SMOKEY AND THE BANDIT II, 1980, C-O
SMOKEY AND THE BANDIT—PART 3, 1983, C-O
SMOKEY AND THE GOODTIME OUTLAWS, 1978
SMOKEY AND THE HOTWIRE GANG, 1980
SMOKEY BITES THE DUST, 1981, C
SMOKEY SMITH, 1935, A
SMOKING GUNS, 1927
SMOKING GUNS, 1934, A
SMOKING TRAIL, THE, 1924
SMOKY, 1933, A
SMOKY, 1946, A
SMOKY, 1966, A
SMOKY CANYON, 1952, A
SMOKY MOUNTAIN MELODY, 1949, A
SMOKY RIVER SERENADE, 1947
SMOKY TRAILS, 1939, A
SMOOTH AS SATIN, 1925
SMOOTH AS SILK, 1946, A
SMORGASBORD, 1983, C
SMOULDERING EMBERS, 1920
SMOULDERING FIRES, 1925
SMUDGE, 1922
SMUGGLED CARGO, 1939, A
SMUGGLERS, THE, 1916
SMUGGLERS, THE, 1948, A
SMUGGLERS, THE, 1969, C
SMUGGLER'S GOLD, 1951, A
SMUGGLER'S ISLAND, 1951, A
SMUGGLERS' COVE, 1948, A
SMURFS AND THE MAGIC FLUTE, THE, 1984, AAA
SNAFU, 1945, A
SNAIL, THE, 1918
SNAKE PEOPLE, THE, 1968, O
SNAKE PIT, THE, 1948, C
SNAKE RIVER DESPERADOES, 1951, A
SNAKE WOMAN, THE, 1961, C
SNAP JUDGEMENT, 1917
SNAPSHOT
SNARE, THE, 1918, A
SNARES OF PARIS, 1919
SNARL OF HATE, THE, 1927
SNARL, THE, 1917
SNEAK, THE, 1919
SNIPER'S RIDGE, 1961, A
SNIPER, THE, 1952, O
SNITCHING HOUR, THE, 1922
SNOB, THE, 1921
SNOB, THE, 1924, A
SNOB BUSTER, THE, 1925
SNOBS, 1915, A
SNOOPY, COME HOME, 1972, AAA
SNORKEL, THE, 1958, A
SNOUT, THE
SNOW, 1983, O
SNOW BRIDE, THE, 1923
SNOW COUNTRY, 1969, O
SNOW CREATURE, THE, 1954, A
SNOW DEMONS
SNOW DEVILS, THE, 1965, A
SNOW DOG, 1950, AA
SNOW IN THE DESERT, 1919
SNOW IN THE SOUTH SEAS, 1963, C
SNOW JOB, 1972, A
SNOW MAIDEN, THE, 1914
SNOW QUEEN, THE, 1959, AAA
SNOW TREASURE, 1968, A
SNOW WHITE, 1916
SNOW WHITE, 1917
SNOW WHITE, 1965, AAA
SNOW WHITE AND ROSE RED, 1966, AAA
SNOW WHITE AND THE SEVEN DWARFS, 1937, AAA
SNOW WHITE AND THE THREE CLOWNS
SNOW WHITE AND THE THREE STOOGES, 1961, A
SNOWBALL, 1960, A
SNOWBALL EXPRESS, 1972, AAA
SNOWBIRD, THE, 1916
SNOWBLIND, 1921, A
SNOWBOUND, 1927
SNOWBOUND, 1949, A
SNOWDRIFT, 1923
SNOWED UNDER, 1936, A
SNOWFIRE, 1958, AAA
SNOWMAN
SNOWS OF KILIMANJARO, THE, 1952, C
SNOWSHOE TRAIL, THE, 1922

SNUFFY SMITH
SNUFFY SMITH, YARD BIRD, 1942, A
SO BIG, 1924, A
SO BIG, 1932, A
SO BIG, 1953, A
SO BRIGHT THE FLAME
SO DARK THE NIGHT, 1946, C
SO DEAR TO MY HEART, 1949, AAA
SO ENDS OUR NIGHT, 1941, A
SO EVIL MY LOVE, 1948, C
SO EVIL SO YOUNG, 1961, A
SO FINE, 1981, C-O
SO GOES MY LOVE, 1946, A
SO IT'S SUNDAY, 1932, A
SO LITTLE TIME, 1953, A
SO LONG AT THE FAIR, 1951, A
SO LONG LETTY, 1920
SO LONG LETTY, 1929, A
SO LONG PHILIPPINE
SO LONG, BLUE BOY, 1973, O
SO PROUDLY WE HAIL, 1943, A
SO RED THE ROSE, 1935, A
SO THIS IS AFRICA, 1933, A
SO THIS IS ARIZONA, 1922, A
SO THIS IS COLLEGE, 1929, A
SO THIS IS LONDON, 1930, A
SO THIS IS LONDON, 1940, A
SO THIS IS LOVE, 1928, A
SO THIS IS LOVE, 1953, A
SO THIS IS MARRIAGE, 1924
SO THIS IS NEW YORK, 1948, A
SO THIS IS PARIS, 1926, A
SO THIS IS PARIS, 1954, A
SO THIS IS WASHINGTON, 1943, A
SO THIS WAS PARIS
SO WELL REMEMBERED, 1947, A-C
SO YOU WON'T TALK, 1940, A
SO YOU WON'T TALK?, 1935, A
SO YOUNG, SO BAD, 1950, A
SO'S YOUR AUNT EMMA
SO'S YOUR OLD MAN, 1926, A
SO'S YOUR UNCLE, 1943, A
SOAK THE RICH, 1936, A
SOAP GIRL, THE, 1918
SOAPBOX DERBY, 1958, AAA
SOB SISTER, 1931, A
SOCIAL AMBITION, 1918
SOCIAL BRIARS, 1918
SOCIAL BUCCANEER, THE, 1916
SOCIAL CELEBRITY, A, 1926, A
SOCIAL CODE, THE, 1923, A
SOCIAL ENEMY NO. 1
SOCIAL ERROR, 1935
SOCIAL EXILE, THE
SOCIAL HIGHWAYMAN, THE, 1916
SOCIAL HIGHWAYMAN, THE, 1926, A
SOCIAL HYPOCRITES, 1918
SOCIAL LEPER, THE, 1917
SOCIAL LION, THE, 1930, A
SOCIAL PIRATE, THE, 1919
SOCIAL QUICKSANDS, 1918
SOCIAL REGISTER, 1934, A
SOCIAL SECRETARY, THE, 1916, A
SOCIETY DOCTOR, 1935, A
SOCIETY EXILE, A, 1919
SOCIETY FEVER, 1935, A
SOCIETY FOR SALE, 1918
SOCIETY GIRL, 1932, A
SOCIETY LAWYER, 1939, A
SOCIETY SCANDAL, A, 1924, A
SOCIETY SECRETS, 1921
SOCIETY SENSATION, A, 1918
SOCIETY SMUGGLERS, 1939, A
SOCIETY SNOBS, 1921, A
SOCIETY WOLVES, 1916
SOCIETY'S DRIFTWOOD, 1917
SOD SISTERS, 1969, O
SODA WATER COWBOY, 1927
SODOM AND GOMORRAH, 1962, C
SODOMA E GOMORRA
SOFI, 1967, A
SOFIA, 1948, A
SOFT BEDS AND HARD BATTLES
SOFT BODY OF DEBORAH, THE
SOFT BOILED, 1923
SOFT CUSHIONS, 1927, A
SOFT LIVING, 1928
SOFT SHOES, 1925
SOFT SKIN AND BLACK LACE
SOFT SKIN ON BLACK SILK, 1964, O
SOFT SKIN, THE, 1964, C-O
SOFT WARM EXPERIENCE, A
SOGEKI
SOGGY BOTTOM U.S.A., 1982, C
SOHO CONSPIRACY, 1951, A
SOHO INCIDENT
SOIL
SOILED, 1924
SOIREE DE REVEILLON, 1922

SOL MADRID, 1968, C
SOLANGE DU DA BIST
SOLARIS, 1972, C
SOLD, 1915, A
SOLD APPETITE, THE, 1928
SOLD AT AUCTION, 1917, O
SOLD FOR MARRIAGE, 1916
SOLDATERKAMMERATER PA VAGT
SOLDIER, THE, 1982, O
SOLDIER AND A MAN, A, 1916, A
SOLDIER AND THE LADY, THE, 1937, C
SOLDIER BLUE, 1970, O
SOLDIER IN LOVE
SOLDIER IN SKIRTS
SOLDIER IN THE RAIN, 1963, C
SOLDIER NAMED JOE, A, 1970
SOLDIER OF FORTUNE, 1955, C
SOLDIER OF LOVE
SOLDIER OF ORANGE, 1979, O
SOLDIER'S OATH, A, 1915
SOLDIER'S PLAYTHING, A, 1931, A
SOLDIER'S PRAYER, A, 1970, C
SOLDIER'S SONS, 1916
SOLDIER'S STORY, A, 1984, C
SOLDIER'S STORY, THE, 1981
SOLDIER'S TALE, THE, 1964, A
SOLDIER, SAILOR, 1944, A
SOLDIERS, THE
SOLDIERS 3
SOLDIERS AND WOMEN, 1930, A
SOLDIERS OF CHANCE, 1917
SOLDIERS OF FORTUNE
SOLDIERS OF FORTUNE, 1914
SOLDIERS OF FORTUNE, 1919
SOLDIERS OF PANCHO VILLA, THE
SOLDIERS OF THE KING
SOLDIERS OF THE STORM, 1933, A
SOLDIERS THREE, 1951, A
SOLE SURVIVOR, 1984, O
SOLID GOLD CADILLAC, THE, 1956, A
SOLIMANO IL CONQUISTATORE
SOLITAIRE MAN, THE, 1933, A
SOLITARY CHILD, THE, 1958, A
SOLITARY SIN, THE, 1919
SOLNTSE SVETIT VSEM
SOLO, 1970, O
SOLO, 1978, O
SOLO CONTRO ROMA
SOLO FOR SPARROW, 1966, A
SOLOMON AND SHEBA, 1959, C
SOLOMON IN SOCIETY, 1922
SOLOMON KING, 1974, O
SOLUTION BY PHONE, 1954, A
SOMBRERO, 1953, A-C
SOMBRERO KID, THE, 1942, A
SOME ARTIST, 1919
SOME BLONDES ARE DANGEROUS, 1937, A
SOME BOY, 1917
SOME BRIDE, 1919
SOME CALL IT LOVING, 1973, O
SOME CAME RUNNING, 1959, C
SOME DAY, 1935, A
SOME GIRLS DO, 1969, C
SOME KIND OF A NUT, 1969, C
SOME KIND OF A NUT, 1959
SOME KIND OF HERO, 1982, O
SOME LIAR, 1919
SOME LIKE IT COOL, 1979, O
SOME LIKE IT HOT, 1939, A
SOME LIKE IT HOT, 1959, C
SOME MAY LIVE, 1967, A
SOME MOTHER'S BOY, 1929
SOME OF MY BEST FRIENDS ARE..., 1971, O
SOME PEOPLE, 1964, A
SOME PUN'KINS, 1925
SOME WAITER, 1916
SOME WILL, SOME WON'T, 1970, A
SOMEBODY ELSE'S CHILDREN
SOMEBODY KILLED HER HUSBAND, 1978, A
SOMEBODY LOVES ME, 1952, A
SOMEBODY UP THERE LIKES ME, 1956, C
SOMEBODY'S DARLING, 1925
SOMEBODY'S MOTHER, 1926
SOMEHOW GOOD, 1927, A
SOMEONE, 1968, O
SOMEONE AT THE DOOR, 1936, A
SOMEONE AT THE DOOR, 1950, A
SOMEONE BEHIND THE DOOR, 1971, C
SOMEONE IN THE HOUSE, 1920
SOMEONE MUST PAY, 1919
SOMEONE TO LOVE, 1928
SOMEONE TO REMEMBER, 1943, A
SOMETHING ALWAYS HAPPENS, 1928
SOMETHING ALWAYS HAPPENS, 1934, A
SOMETHING BIG, 1971, A
SOMETHING CREEPING IN THE DARK, 1972
SOMETHING DIFFERENT, 1920
SOMETHING FOR EVERYONE, 1970, O
SOMETHING FOR THE BIRDS, 1952, A

SOMETHING FOR THE BOYS, 1944, A
SOMETHING IN THE CITY, 1950, A
SOMETHING IN THE WIND, 1947, A
SOMETHING IS OUT THERE
SOMETHING MONEY CAN'T BUY, 1952, A
SOMETHING OF VALUE, 1957, O
SOMETHING SHORT OF PARADISE, 1979, C-O
SOMETHING TO DO, 1919
SOMETHING TO HIDE, 1972, C-O
SOMETHING TO LIVE FOR, 1952, A
SOMETHING TO SHOUT ABOUT, 1943, A
SOMETHING TO SING ABOUT, 1937, A
SOMETHING TO THINK ABOUT, 1920, A
SOMETHING WAITS IN THE DARK
SOMETHING WEIRD, 1967, O
SOMETHING WICKED THIS WAY COMES, 1983, C
SOMETHING WILD, 1961, A
SOMETHING'S ROTTEN, 1979, C
SOMETIMES A GREAT NOTION, 1971, O
SOMETIMES GOOD, 1934, A
SOMEWHERE I'LL FIND YOU, 1942, A
SOMEWHERE IN BERLIN, 1949, A
SOMEWHERE IN CAMP, 1942, A
SOMEWHERE IN CIVVIES, 1943, A
SOMEWHERE IN ENGLAND, 1940, A
SOMEWHERE IN FRANCE, 1916
SOMEWHERE IN FRANCE, 1943, A
SOMEWHERE IN GEORGIA, 1916
SOMEWHERE IN POLITICS, 1949, A
SOMEWHERE IN SONORA, 1927, A
SOMEWHERE IN SONORA, 1933, A
SOMEWHERE IN THE NIGHT, 1946, C
SOMEWHERE IN TIME, 1980, C
SOMEWHERE ON LEAVE, 1942, A
SOMMARLEK
SOMME, THE, 1927, A
SON ADVENTURE, 1919
SON COMES HOME, A, 1936, A
SON CRIME, 1921
SON DESTIN, 1919
SON HEROS, 1917
SON OF A BADMAN, 1949, A
SON OF A GUN, 1926
SON OF A GUN, THE, 1919
SON OF A GUNFIGHTER, 1966, A
SON OF A SAILOR, 1933, A
SON OF A STRANGER, 1957, O
SON OF ALI BABA, 1952, A
SON OF BELLE STARR, 1953, A
SON OF BILLY THE KID, 1949, A
SON OF BLOB
SON OF CAPTAIN BLOOD, THE, 1964, A
SON OF DAVID, A, 1920
SON OF DAVY CROCKETT, THE, 1941, A
SON OF DR. JEKYLL, THE, 1951, A
SON OF DRACULA, 1943, C
SON OF DRACULA, 1974, C
SON OF ERIN, A, 1916
SON OF FLUBBER, 1963, AAA
SON OF FRANKENSTEIN, 1939, C
SON OF FURY, 1942, A
SON OF GOD'S COUNTRY, 1948, A
SON OF GODZILLA, 1967, C
SON OF GREETINGS
SON OF HIS FATHER, A, 1925
SON OF HIS FATHER, THE, 1917
SON OF INDIA, 1931, A
SON OF INGAGI, 1940, A
SON OF KISSING CUP, 1922
SON OF KONG, 1933, A
SON OF LASSIE, 1945, AAA
SON OF MADAME SANS GENE, 1924
SON OF MINE
SON OF MONGOLIA, 1936, A
SON OF MONTE CRISTO, 1940, A
SON OF OKLAHOMA, 1932, A
SON OF PALEFACE, 1952, A
SON OF ROARING DAN, 1940, A
SON OF ROBIN HOOD, 1959, A
SON OF RUSTY, THE, 1947
SON OF SAMSON, 1962, A
SON OF SATAN, A, 1924
SON OF SINBAD, 1955, A
SON OF SONTAG, THE, 1925
SON OF SPARTACUS
SON OF STRIFE, A, 1917
SON OF THE BLOB
SON OF THE BORDER, 1933, A
SON OF THE DESERT, A, 1928
SON OF THE GODS, 1930, A
SON OF THE GOLDEN WEST, 1928
SON OF THE HILLS, A, 1917
SON OF THE IMMORTALS, A, 1916
SON OF THE LAND, 1931
SON OF THE NAVY, 1940, A
SON OF THE PLAINS, 1931, A
SON OF THE RED CORSAIR, 1963, A
SON OF THE REGIMENT, 1948, A
SON OF THE RENEGADE, 1953, A

SON OF THE SAHARA, A, 1924
SON OF THE SHEIK, 1926, A
SON OF THE WOLF, THE, 1922, A
SON OF WALLINGFORD, THE, 1921
SON-DAUGHTER, THE, 1932, A
SONG AND DANCE MAN, THE, 1926
SONG AND DANCE MAN, THE, 1936, A
SONG AND THE SILENCE, THE, 1969, A
SONG AT EVENTIDE, 1934, C
SONG FOR MISS JULIE, A, 1945, A
SONG FOR TOMORROW, A, 1948, A
SONG FROM MY HEART, THE, 1970, A
SONG IS BORN, A, 1948, A
SONG O' MY HEART, 1930, A
SONG OF ARIZONA, 1946, A
SONG OF BERNADETTE, THE, 1943, AAA
SONG OF CHINA, 1936
SONG OF FREEDOM, 1938, A
SONG OF HATE, THE, 1915, A
SONG OF IDAHO, 1948, A
SONG OF INDIA, 1949, A
SONG OF KENTUCKY, 1929, A
SONG OF LIFE, THE, 1922, A
SONG OF LIFE, THE, 1931, A
SONG OF LOVE, 1947, A
SONG OF LOVE, THE, 1923, A
SONG OF LOVE, THE, 1929, A
SONG OF MEXICO, 1945, A
SONG OF MY HEART, 1947, A
SONG OF NEVADA, 1944, A
SONG OF NORWAY, 1970, A
SONG OF OLD WYOMING, 1945, A
SONG OF PARIS
SONG OF RUSSIA, 1943, A
SONG OF SCHEHERAZADE, 1947, A
SONG OF SIXPENCE, A, 1917
SONG OF SOHO, 1930, A
SONG OF SONGS, 1933, A-C
SONG OF SONGS, 1935
SONG OF SONGS, THE, 1918
SONG OF SURRENDER, 1949, A
SONG OF TEXAS, 1943, A
SONG OF THE BUCKAROO, 1939, A
SONG OF THE CABELLERO, 1930, A
SONG OF THE CITY, 1937, A
SONG OF THE DRIFTER, 1948, A
SONG OF THE EAGLE, 1933, A
SONG OF THE FLAME, 1930, A
SONG OF THE FOREST, 1963, A
SONG OF THE FORGE, 1937, A
SONG OF THE GRINGO, 1936, A
SONG OF THE ISLANDS, 1942, A
SONG OF THE LITTLE ROAD
SONG OF THE LOON, 1970, O
SONG OF THE OPEN ROAD, 1944, A
SONG OF THE PLOUGH
SONG OF THE PRAIRIE, 1945
SONG OF THE RANGE, 1944
SONG OF THE ROAD, 1937, A
SONG OF THE ROAD, 1940
SONG OF THE ROAD, THE, 1958
SONG OF THE SADDLE, 1936, A
SONG OF THE SARONG, 1945, A
SONG OF THE SIERRAS, 1946, A
SONG OF THE SIERRAS, 1947
SONG OF THE SOUL, THE, 1918
SONG OF THE SOUL, THE, 1920
SONG OF THE SOUTH, 1946, AAA
SONG OF THE THIN MAN, 1947, A
SONG OF THE TRAIL, 1936, A
SONG OF THE WAGE SLAVE, THE, 1915, C
SONG OF THE WASTELAND, 1947, A
SONG OF THE WEST, 1930, A
SONG OF TRIUMPHANT LOVE, 1915
SONG OVER MOSCOW, 1964, A
SONG TO REMEMBER, A, 1945, A
SONG WITHOUT END, 1960, A
SONG YOU GAVE ME, THE, 1934, A
SONGS AND BULLETS, 1938, A
SONGS AND SADDLES, 1938
SONGWRITER, 1984, C-O
SONIA, 1921
SONIA, 1928
SONNY, 1922, A
SONNY AND JED, 1974, O
SONNY BOY, 1929, A
SONORA KID, THE, 1927, A
SONORA STAGECOACH, 1944, A
SONS AND LOVERS, 1960, C
SONS AND MOTHERS, 1967, A
SONS O' GUNS, 1936, A
SONS OF ADVENTURE, 1948, A
SONS OF GOOD EARTH, 1967, A-C
SONS OF KATIE ELDER, THE, 1965, A
SONS OF MATTHEW
SONS OF NEW MEXICO, 1949, A
SONS OF SATAN, 1969, C
SONS OF SATAN, THE, 1915
SONS OF STEEL, 1935, A
SONS OF THE DESERT, 1933, A
SONS OF THE LEGION, 1938, A
SONS OF THE LEGION, 1933
SONS OF THE MUSKETEERS
SONS OF THE PIONEERS, 1942, A
SONS OF THE SADDLE, 1930, A
SONS OF THE SEA, 1925
SONS OF THE SEA, 1939, A
SONS OF THE SEA, 1941
SONS OF THE WEST, 1922
SOOKY, 1931, A
SOONER OR LATER, 1920
SOPHIE LANG
SOPHIE LANG GOES WEST, 1937, A
SOPHIE'S CHOICE, 1982, O
SOPHIE'S PLACE, 1970, C
SOPHIE'S WAYS, 1970, O
SOPHOMORE, THE, 1929, A
SORCERER, 1977, O
SORCERERS, THE, 1967, C
SORCERESS, 1983, O
SORORITY GIRL, 1957, C
SORORITY HOUSE, 1939, A
SORRELL AND SON, 1927
SORRELL AND SON, 1934, A
SORROWFUL JONES, 1949, A
SORROWS OF HAPPINESS, 1916
SORROWS OF LOVE, THE, 1916
SORROWS OF SATAN, 1926, A
SORROWS OF SATAN, THE, 1917
SORRY YOU'VE BEEN TROUBLED
SORRY, WRONG NUMBER, 1948, C
SORYU HIKEN
SOTTO IL TALLONE
SOUFFLE AU COUER, LE
SOUHVEZDI PANNY
SOUL ADRIFT, A
SOUL AND BODY, 1921
SOUL ENSLAVED, A, 1916
SOUL FOR SALE, A, 1915
SOUL FOR SALE, A, 1918
SOUL HARVEST, THE
SOUL IN TRUST, A, 1918
SOUL KISS
SOUL MARKET, THE, 1916
SOUL MASTER, THE, 1917
SOUL MATES, 1916
SOUL MATES, 1925, A
SOUL OF A CHILD, THE, 1916
SOUL OF A MAN, THE, 1921
SOUL OF A MONSTER, THE, 1944, A
SOUL OF A WOMAN, THE, 1915
SOUL OF A WOMAN, THE, 1922
SOUL OF BROADWAY, THE, 1915, A
SOUL OF BRONZE, THE, 1921
SOUL OF BUDDHA, THE, 1918
SOUL OF FRANCE, 1929
SOUL OF GUILDA LOIS, THE
SOUL OF KURA SAN, THE, 1916
SOUL OF MAGDALEN, THE, 1917
SOUL OF MEXICO, 1932
SOUL OF NIGGER CHARLEY, THE, 1973, O
SOUL OF SATAN, THE, 1917
SOUL OF THE BEAST, 1923, A
SOUL OF THE SLUMS, 1931, A
SOUL OF YOUTH, THE, 1920, A
SOUL SOLDIERS
SOUL WITHOUT WINDOWS, A, 1918
SOUL'S AWAKENING, A, 1922
SOUL'S CRUCIFIXION, A, 1919
SOUL'S CYCLE, THE, 1916
SOUL-FIRE, 1925
SOULS ADRIFT, 1917
SOULS AFLAME, 1928, A
SOULS AT SEA, 1937, A
SOULS FOR SABLES
SOULS FOR SABLES, 1925
SOULS FOR SALE
SOULS FOR SALE, 1923, A
SOULS IN BONDAGE, 1916
SOULS IN BONDAGE, 1923
SOULS IN CONFLICT, 1955, A
SOULS IN PAWN, 1917
SOULS OF MEN, 1921
SOULS OF SIN
SOULS OF SIN, 1949
SOULS ON THE ROAD, 1921
SOULS TRIUMPHANT, 1915
SOUND AND THE FURY, THE, 1959, C-O
SOUND BARRIER, THE
SOUND OF FURY, THE, 1950, C
SOUND OF HORROR, 1966, C
SOUND OF LIFE, THE, 1962, A
SOUND OF MUSIC, THE, 1965, AAA
SOUND OF TRUMPETS, THE, 1963, A
SOUND OFF, 1952, A
SOUNDER, 1972, AAA
SOUNDER, PART 2, 1976, AA
SOUNDS OF HORROR, 1968
SOUP FOR ONE, 1982, O
SOUP TO NUTS, 1930, A
SOUP TO NUTS, 1982
SOURCE, THE, 1918
SOURDOUGH, 1977, AA
SOUS LA MENACE, 1916
SOUS LES TOITS DE PARIS
SOUTH AMERICAN GEORGE, 1941, A
SOUTH OF ALGIERS
SOUTH OF ARIZONA, 1938, A
SOUTH OF CALIENTE, 1951, A
SOUTH OF DEATH VALLEY, 1949, A
SOUTH OF DIXIE, 1944, A
SOUTH OF HELL MOUNTAIN, 1971
SOUTH OF MONTEREY, 1946
SOUTH OF NORTHERN LIGHTS, 1922, A
SOUTH OF PAGO PAGO, 1940, A
SOUTH OF PANAMA, 1928
SOUTH OF PANAMA, 1941, A
SOUTH OF RIO, 1949, A
SOUTH OF SANTA FE, 1924
SOUTH OF SANTA FE, 1932, A
SOUTH OF SANTA FE, 1942, A
SOUTH OF SONORA, 1930, A
SOUTH OF ST. LOUIS, 1949, A
SOUTH OF SUEZ, 1940, A
SOUTH OF SUVA, 1922, A
SOUTH OF TAHITI, 1941, A
SOUTH OF THE BORDER, 1939, A
SOUTH OF THE CHISHOLM TRAIL, 1947
SOUTH OF THE EQUATOR, 1924
SOUTH OF THE RIO GRANDE, 1932, A
SOUTH OF THE RIO GRANDE, 1945, A
SOUTH PACIFIC, 1958, A
SOUTH PACIFIC TRAIL, 1952, A
SOUTH RIDING, 1938, A
SOUTH SEA BUBBLE, A, 1928
SOUTH SEA LOVE, 1923, A
SOUTH SEA LOVE, 1927
SOUTH SEA ROSE, 1929, A
SOUTH SEA SINNER, 1950, A
SOUTH SEA WOMAN, 1953, A
SOUTH SEAS FURY
SOUTH TO KARANGA, 1940, A
SOUTHERN COMFORT, 1981, O
SOUTHERN DOUBLE CROSS, 1973
SOUTHERN JUSTICE, 1917
SOUTHERN LOVE
SOUTHERN MAID, A, 1933, A
SOUTHERN PRIDE, 1917
SOUTHERN ROSES, 1936, A
SOUTHERN STAR, THE, 1969, C
SOUTHERN YANKEE, A, 1948, AAA
SOUTHERNER, THE, 1945, A
SOUTHERNER, THE, 1931
SOUTHSIDE 1-1000, 1950, A
SOUTHWARD HO?, 1939, A
SOUTHWEST PASSAGE, 1954, A
SOUTHWEST TO SONORA
SOWERS AND REAPERS, 1917
SOWERS, THE, 1916
SOWING THE WIND, 1916
SOWING THE WIND, 1921
SOYLENT GREEN, 1973, C
SPACE AMOEBA, THE, 1970, A
SPACE CHILDREN, THE, 1958, A
SPACE CRUISER, 1977, A
SPACE DEVILS
SPACE FIREBIRD 2772, 1979, A
SPACE HUNTER: ADVENTURES IN THE FORBIDDEN ZONE
SPACE INVASION FROM LAPLAND
SPACE MASTER X-7, 1958, A
SPACE MEN
SPACE MEN APPEAR IN TOKYO
SPACE MISSION OF THE LOST PLANET
SPACE MONSTER, 1965, A
SPACE RAIDERS, 1983, C
SPACE RIDERS, 1984
SPACE SHIP, THE, 1935, A
SPACE STATION X
SPACE STATION X-14
SPACED OUT, 1981, O
SPACEFLIGHT IC-1, 1965, A
SPACEHUNTER: ADVENTURES IN THE FORBIDDEN ZONE, 1983, C
SPACEMAN AND KING ARTHUR, THE
SPACEMEN SATURDAY NIGHT
SPACESHIP
SPACESHIP TO VENUS
SPACEWAYS, 1953, A
SPAN OF LIFE, THE, 1914
SPANGLES, 1926
SPANGLES, 1928
SPANIARD'S CURSE, THE, 1958, A
SPANIARD, THE, 1925
SPANISH AFFAIR, 1958, A
SPANISH CAPE MYSTERY, 1935, A
SPANISH DANCER, THE, 1923

SPANISH EYES, 1930, A
SPANISH FLY, 1975, O
SPANISH GARDENER, THE, 1957, A
SPANISH JADE, 1922
SPANISH JADE, THE, 1915
SPANISH MAIN, THE, 1945, A
SPANISH SWORD, THE, 1962, A
SPARA FORTE, PIU FORTE...NON CAPISCO
SPARE A COPPER, 1940, A
SPARE THE ROD, 1961, A
SPARK DIVINE, THE, 1919
SPARKLE, 1976, C-O
SPARKS OF FLINT, 1921
SPARROWS, 1926, C
SPARROWS, 1926, C
SPARROWS CAN'T SING, 1963, A
SPARTACUS, 1960, C
SPARTAKIADA, 1929
SPASMO, 1976
SPASMS, 1983, O
SPATS TO SPURS
SPAWN OF THE DESERT, 1923, A
SPAWN OF THE NORTH, 1938, A
SPEAK EASILY, 1932, A
SPEAKEASY, 1929, A
SPECIAL AGENT, 1935, A-C
SPECIAL AGENT, 1949, A
SPECIAL AGENT K-7, 1937, A
SPECIAL DAY, A, 1977, C
SPECIAL DELIVERY, 1927, A
SPECIAL DELIVERY, 1955, A
SPECIAL DELIVERY, 1976, C
SPECIAL EDITION, 1938, A
SPECIAL EFFECTS, 1984, O
SPECIAL INSPECTOR, 1939, A
SPECIAL INVESTIGATOR, 1936, A
SPECIALIST, THE, 1975, O
SPECKLED BAND, THE, 1931, A
SPECTER OF FREEDOM, THE
SPECTER OF THE ROSE, 1946, C
SPECTOR OF FREEDOM
SPECTRE HAUNTS EUROPE, A, 1923
SPECTRE OF EDGAR ALLAN POE, 1973
SPECTRE OF EDGAR ALLAN POE, THE, 1974, O
SPEED, 1925
SPEED, 1936, A
SPEED BRENT WINS
SPEED CLASSIC, THE, 1928
SPEED COP, 1926, A
SPEED CRAZED, 1926, A
SPEED CRAZY, 1959, C
SPEED DEMON, 1933
SPEED DEMON, THE, 1925
SPEED DEVILS, 1935, A
SPEED GIRL, THE, 1921, A
SPEED KING, 1923, A
SPEED LIMIT 65
SPEED LIMIT, THE, 1926
SPEED LIMITED, 1940, A
SPEED LOVERS, 1968, A
SPEED MAD, 1925, A
SPEED MADNESS, 1925
SPEED MADNESS, 1932, A
SPEED MANIAC, THE, 1919
SPEED REPORTER, 1936, A
SPEED REPORTER, THE 1931
SPEED SPOOK, THE, 1924
SPEED TO BURN, 1938, A
SPEED TO SPARE, 1937, A
SPEED TO SPARE, 1948, A
SPEED WILD, 1925
SPEED WINGS, 1934, A
SPEEDING HOOFS, 1927
SPEEDING THROUGH, 1926
SPEEDING VENUS, THE, 1926
SPEEDTRAP, 1978, A
SPEEDWAY, 1929
SPEEDWAY, 1968, A
SPEEDY, 1928, A
SPEEDY MEADE, 1919
SPEEDY SMITH, 1927
SPEEDY SPURS, 1926
SPELL OF AMY NUGENT, THE, 1945, A
SPELL OF THE HYPNOTIST, 1956, A
SPELL OF THE YUKON, THE, 1916
SPELLBINDER, THE, 1939, A
SPELLBOUND
SPELLBOUND, 1916
SPELLBOUND, 1945, A-C
SPENCER'S MOUNTAIN, 1963, C
SPENDER OR THE FORTUNES OF PETER, THE, 1915
SPENDER, THE, 1919
SPENDERS, THE, 1921
SPENDTHRIFT, 1936, A
SPENDTHRIFT, THE, 1915, A
SPERMULA, 1976, O
SPESSART INN, THE, 1961, A
SPETTERS, 1983, O
SPHINX, 1981, C
SPHINX, THE, 1916
SPHINX, THE, 1933, A
SPICE OF LIFE, 1954, A
SPIDER, THE, 1916, C
SPIDER, THE, 1931, A
SPIDER, THE, 1940, A
SPIDER, THE, 1945, A
SPIDER, THE, 1958, A
SPIDER AND THE FLY, THE, 1916
SPIDER AND THE FLY, THE, 1952, A
SPIDER AND THE ROSE, THE, 1923, A
SPIDER BABY, OR THE MADDEST STORY EVER TOLD
SPIDER BABYZERO, 1968, O
SPIDER WEBS, 1927, A
SPIDER WOMAN
SPIDER WOMAN STRIKES BACK, THE, 1946, A
SPIDER'S WEB, THE, 1927
SPIDER'S WEB, THE, 1960, A
SPIDER'S WEB, THE, 1962
SPIDERS, THE, 1919
SPIELER, THE, 1929, A
SPIES, 1929, A
SPIES A GO-GO
SPIES AT WORK
SPIES OF THE AIR, 1940, A
SPIKES GANG, THE, 1974, C
SPIN A DARK WEB, 1956, A
SPIN OF A COIN
SPINAL TAP
SPINDLE OF LIFE, THE, 1917, A
SPINNER O' DREAMS, 1918
SPINOUT, 1966, A
SPIONE UNTER SICHE
SPIRAL BUREAU, THE, 1974
SPIRAL ROAD, THE, 1962, A
SPIRAL STAIRCASE, THE, 1946, C
SPIRAL STAIRCASE, THE, 1975, C-O
SPIRIT AND THE FLESH, THE, 1948, A
SPIRIT IS WILLING, THE, 1967, A
SPIRIT OF '17, THE, 1918
SPIRIT OF '76, THE, 1917
SPIRIT OF CULVER, THE, 1939, A
SPIRIT OF GOOD, THE, 1920
SPIRIT OF NOTRE DAME, THE, 1931, A
SPIRIT OF ROMANCE, THE, 1917
SPIRIT OF ST. LOUIS, THE, 1957, AAA
SPIRIT OF STANFORD, THE, 1942, A
SPIRIT OF THE BEEHIVE, THE, 1976, C
SPIRIT OF THE CONQUEROR, OR THE NAPOLEON OF LABOR, THE (1915)
SPIRIT OF THE DEAD
SPIRIT OF THE PEOPLE
SPIRIT OF THE U.S.A., THE, 1924
SPIRIT OF THE WEST, 1932, A
SPIRIT OF THE WIND, 1979, C
SPIRIT OF WEST POINT, THE, 1947, A
SPIRIT OF YOUTH, 1937, A
SPIRIT OF YOUTH, THE, 1929
SPIRITISM, 1965, C
SPIRITS OF THE DEAD, 1969, O
SPIRITUALIST, THE, 1948, A
SPITE BRIDE, THE, 1919
SPITE MARRIAGE, 1929, A
SPITFIRE, 1922
SPITFIRE, 1934, A
SPITFIRE, 1943, A
SPITFIRE, THE, 1914
SPITFIRE, THE, 1924, A
SPITFIRE OF SEVILLE, THE, A
SPITTIN' IMAGE, 1983
SPLASH, 1984, A-C
SPLATTER UNIVERSITY, 1984, O
SPLENDID COWARD, THE, 1918
SPLENDID CRIME, THE, 1926
SPLENDID FELLOWS, 1934, A
SPLENDID FOLLY, 1919
SPLENDID HAZARD, A, 1920
SPLENDID LIE, THE, 1922, A
SPLENDID ROAD, THE, 1925, A
SPLENDID ROMANCE, THE, 1918
SPLENDID SIN, THE, 1919, C
SPLENDID SINNER, THE, 1918
SPLENDOR, 1935, A
SPLENDOR IN THE GRASS, 1961, C
SPLINTERS, 1929, A
SPLINTERS IN THE AIR, 1937, A
SPLINTERS IN THE NAVY, 1931, A
SPLIT IMAGE, 1982, O
SPLIT SECOND, 1953, A
SPLIT, THE, 1968, O
SPLIT, THE, 1962
SPLITFACE
SPLITTING THE BREEZE, 1927, A
SPLITTING UP, 1981, C
SPLITZ, 1984, O
SPOILED ROTTEN, 1968, C-O
SPOILERS OF THE FOREST, 1957, A
SPOILERS OF THE NORTH, 1947, A
SPOILERS OF THE PLAINS, 1951, A
SPOILERS OF THE RANGE, 1939, A
SPOILERS OF THE WEST, 1927
SPOILERS, THE, 1914, A
SPOILERS, THE, 1923
SPOILERS, THE, 1930, A
SPOILERS, THE, 1942, A
SPOILERS, THE, 1955, C
SPOILS OF THE NIGHT, 1969, C-O
SPOOK BUSTERS, 1946, A
SPOOK CHASERS, 1957, A
SPOOK RANCH, 1925, A
SPOOK TOWN, 1944, A
SPOOK WHO SAT BY THE DOOR, THE, 1973, O
SPOOKS RUN WILD, 1941, A
SPORT OF A NATION
SPORT OF KINGS, 1947, A
SPORT OF KINGS, THE, 1921, A
SPORT OF KINGS, THE, 1931, A
SPORT OF THE GODS, THE, 1921
SPORT PARADE, THE, 1932, A
SPORTING AGE, THE, 1928
SPORTING BLOOD, 1916
SPORTING BLOOD, 1931, A
SPORTING BLOOD, 1940, A
SPORTING CHANCE, 1931, A
SPORTING CHANCE, A, 1919
SPORTING CHANCE, A, 1945, A
SPORTING CHANCE, THE, 1925
SPORTING CLUB, THE, 1971, O
SPORTING DOUBLE, A, 1922
SPORTING DUCHESS, THE, 1915
SPORTING DUCHESS, THE, 1920
SPORTING GOODS, 1928, A
SPORTING INSTINCT, THE, 1922
SPORTING LIFE
SPORTING LIFE, 1918
SPORTING LIFE, 1925
SPORTING LOVE, 1936, A
SPORTING LOVER, THE, 1926
SPORTING VENUS, THE, 1925
SPORTING WEST, 1925
SPORTING WIDOW, THE
SPORTING YOUTH, 1924
SPORTS KILLER, THE, 1976
SPORTSMAN'S WIFE, A, 1921
SPOT
SPOT OF BOTHER, A, 1938, A
SPOTLIGHT SADIE, 1919
SPOTLIGHT SCANDALS, 1943, A
SPOTLIGHT, THE, 1927
SPOTS ON MY LEOPARD, THE, 1974, A
SPOTTED LILY, THE, 1917
SPREADING DAWN, THE, 1917, A
SPREADING EVIL, THE, 1919
SPRING, 1948, A
SPRING AFFAIR, 1960, A
SPRING AND PORT WINE, 1970, C-O
SPRING BREAK, 1983, O
SPRING COMES WITH THE LADIES, 1932
SPRING FEVER, 1927
SPRING FEVER, 1983, C
SPRING HANDICAP, 1937, A
SPRING IN PARK LANE, 1949, A
SPRING IN THE AIR, 1934, A
SPRING IS HERE, 1930, A
SPRING MADNESS, 1938, A
SPRING MEETING, 1941, A
SPRING NIGHT, SUMMER NIGHT
SPRING PARADE, 1940, A
SPRING REUNION, 1957, A
SPRING SHOWER, 1932, A
SPRING SONG
SPRING TONIC, 1935, A
SPRINGFIELD RIFLE, 1952, A
SPRINGTIME, 1915, A
SPRINGTIME, 1948, A
SPRINGTIME FOR HENRY, 1934, A
SPRINGTIME IN TEXAS, 1945
SPRINGTIME IN THE ROCKIES, 1937, A
SPRINGTIME IN THE ROCKIES, 1942, A
SPRINGTIME IN THE SIERRAS, 1947, A
SPRINGTIME ON THE VOLGA, 1961, A
SPUDS, 1927, A
SPURS, 1930, A
SPURS AND SADDLES, 1927
SPURS OF SYBIL, THE, 1918
SPUTNIK, 1960, A
SPY 13
SPY 77
SPY BUSTERS
SPY CHASERS, 1956, A
SPY FOR A DAY, 1939, A
SPY HUNT, 1950, A
SPY IN BLACK, THE
SPY IN THE GREEN HAT, THE, 1966, A
SPY IN THE PANTRY
SPY IN THE SKY, 1958, A
SPY IN WHITE, THE

SPY IN YOUR EYE, 1966, A
SPY OF MME. POMPADOUR, 1929
SPY OF NAPOLEON, 1939, A
SPY RING, THE, 1938, A
SPY SHIP, 1942, A
SPY SQUAD, 1962
SPY TODAY, DIE TOMORROW, 1967
SPY TRAIN, 1943, A
SPY WHO CAME IN FROM THE COLD, THE, 1965, A-C
SPY WHO LOVED ME, THE, 1977, C
SPY WITH A COLD NOSE, THE, 1966, A
SPY WITH MY FACE, THE, 1966, A
SPY, THE, 1914
SPY, THE, 1917
SPY, THE, 1931
SPYASHCHAYA KRASAVITSA
SPYLARKS, 1965, A
SPYS
SQUAD CAR, 1961, A
SQUADRON 633, 1964, A-C
SQUADRON LEADER X, 1943, A
SQUADRON OF HONOR, 1938, A
SQUALL, THE, 1929, A
SQUANDERED LIVES, 1920
SQUARE CROOKS, 1928
SQUARE DANCE JUBILEE, 1949, A
SQUARE DANCE KATY, 1950, A
SQUARE DEAL MAN, THE, 1917
SQUARE DEAL SANDERSON, 1919
SQUARE DEAL, A, 1917
SQUARE DEAL, A, 1918
SQUARE DECEIVER, THE, 1917
SQUARE JOE, 1921
SQUARE JUNGLE, THE, 1955, A
SQUARE OF VIOLENCE, 1963, A
SQUARE PEG, THE, 1958, A
SQUARE RING, THE, 1955, A
SQUARE ROOT OF ZERO, THE, 1964, C
SQUARE SHOOTER, 1935
SQUARE SHOOTER, THE
SQUARE SHOOTER, THE, 1920
SQUARE SHOULDERS, 1929, A
SQUARED CIRCLE, THE
SQUARES, 1972, A
SQUATTER'S DAUGHTER, 1933, A
SQUAW MAN'S SON, THE, 1917
SQUAW MAN, THE, 1914, A
SQUAW MAN, THE, 1918
SQUAW MAN, THE, 1931, A
SQUEAKER, THE, 1930, A
SQUEAKER, THE, 1937
SQUEALER, THE, 1930, A
SQUEEZE A FLOWER, 1970, A
SQUEEZE PLAY, 1981, O
SQUEEZE, THE, 1977, O
SQUEEZE, THE, 1980, O
SQUIBS, 1921, A
SQUIBS, 1935, A
SQUIBS WINS THE CALCUTTA SWEEP, 1922, A
SQUIBS' HONEYMOON, 1926, A
SQUIBS, MP, 1923, A
SQUIRE OF LONG HADLEY, THE, 1925
SQUIRE PHIN, 1921
SQUIRM, 1976, C
SQUIZZY TAYLOR, 1984, O
SSSSNAKE
SSSSSSSS, 1973, C
ST. BENNY THE DIP, 1951, A
ST. ELMO, 1923, A
ST. GEORGE AND THE 7 CURSES
ST. HELENS, 1981, A
ST. IVES, 1976, O
ST. LOUIS BLUES, 1939, A
ST. LOUIS BLUES, 1958, A
ST. LOUIS KID, THE, 1934, A
ST. LOUIS WOMAN, 1935
ST. MARTIN'S LANE
ST. VALENTINE'S DAY MASSACRE, THE, 1967, O
STABLE COMPANIONS, 1922
STABLEMATES, 1938, A
STACEY AND HER GANGBUSTERS
STACEY?, 1973, O
STACKED CARDS, 1926
STACY'S KNIGHTS, 1983, C
STADIUM MURDERS, THE
STAGE COACH DRIVER, 1924
STAGE DOOR, 1937, A-C
STAGE DOOR CANTEEN, 1943, A
STAGE FRIGHT, 1950, A-C
STAGE FROM BLUE RIVER
STAGE KISSES, 1927, A
STAGE MADNESS, 1927, A
STAGE MOTHER, 1933, A
STAGE ROMANCE, A, 1922
STAGE STRUCK, 1917
STAGE STRUCK, 1925
STAGE STRUCK, 1936, A
STAGE STRUCK, 1948, C
STAGE STRUCK, 1958, A-C
STAGE TO BLUE RIVER, 1951, A
STAGE TO CHINO, 1940, A
STAGE TO MESA CITY, 1947, A
STAGE TO THUNDER ROCK, 1964, A
STAGE TO TUCSON, 1950, A
STAGE WHISPERS
STAGECOACH, 1939, C
STAGECOACH, 1966, A-C
STAGECOACH BUCKAROO, 1942, A
STAGECOACH DAYS, 1938, A
STAGECOACH DRIVER, 1951
STAGECOACH EXPRESS, 1942, A
STAGECOACH KID, 1949, A
STAGECOACH LINE
STAGECOACH OUTLAWS, 1945, A
STAGECOACH TO DANCER'S PARK, 1962, A
STAGECOACH TO DENVER, 1946, A
STAGECOACH TO FURY, 1956, A
STAGECOACH TO HELL
STAGECOACH TO MONTEREY, 1944, A
STAGECOACH WAR, 1940, A
STAGEFRIGHT, 1983
STAIN IN THE BLOOD, THE, 1916
STAIN, THE, 1914, A
STAINLESS BARRIER, THE, 1917
STAIRCASE, 1969, C-O
STAIRS OF SAND, 1929, A
STAIRWAY FOR A STAR, 1947
STAIRWAY TO HEAVEN, 1946, A
STAKEOUT ON DOPE STREET, 1958, C
STAKEOUT?, 1962, A
STAKING HIS LIFE, 1918
STALAG 17, 1953, C
STALKER, 1982, C
STALKING MOON, THE, 1969, A
STALLION CANYON, 1949, A
STALLION ROAD, 1947, A
STAMBOUL, 1931, A
STAMBOUL QUEST, 1934, A
STAMPEDE, 1930
STAMPEDE, 1936, A
STAMPEDE, 1949, A
STAMPEDE THUNDER, 1925
STAMPEDE, 1960
STAMPEDE, THE, 1921
STAMPEDED
STAMPEDIN' TROUBLE, 1925
STAND AND DELIVER
STAND AND DELIVER, 1928, A
STAND AT APACHE RIVER, THE, 1953, A
STAND BY ALL NETWORKS, 1942
STAND BY FOR ACTION, 1942, A
STAND EASY
STAND UP AND BE COUNTED, 1972, C
STAND UP AND CHEER, 1934, A
STAND UP AND FIGHT, 1939, A-C
STAND UP VIRGIN SOLDIERS, 1977, O
STAND-IN, 1937, A
STANDING ROOM ONLY, 1944, A
STANLEY
STANLEY, 1973, O
STANLEY AND LIVINGSTONE, 1939, AA
STAR 80, 1983, O
STAR CHAMBER, THE, 1983, C-O
STAR CHILD
STAR CRASH
STAR DUST
STAR DUST, 1940, A
STAR DUST TRAIL, THE, 1924
STAR FELL FROM HEAVEN, A, 1936, AAA
STAR FOR A NIGHT, 1936, A
STAR IN THE DUST, 1956, A
STAR IN THE WEST
STAR INSPECTOR, THE, 1980, A
STAR IS BORN, A, 1937, C
STAR IS BORN, A, 1954, A-C
STAR IS BORN, A, 1976, C-O
STAR MAIDENS, 1976
STAR MAKER, THE, 1939, AA
STAR ODYSSEY, 1978
STAR OF HONG KONG, 1962, A
STAR OF INDIA, 1956, A
STAR OF INDIA, THE, 1913
STAR OF MIDNIGHT, 1935, A
STAR OF MY NIGHT, 1954, C
STAR OF TEXAS, 1953, A
STAR OF THE CIRCUS
STAR PACKER, THE, 1934, A
STAR PILOT, 1977, A
STAR REPORTER, 1939, A
STAR REPORTER, THE, 1921
STAR ROVER, THE, 1920
STAR SAID NO, THE
STAR SPANGLED GIRL, 1971, A
STAR SPANGLED RHYTHM, 1942, A
STAR TREK II: THE WRATH OF KHAN, 1982, A
STAR TREK III: THE SEARCH FOR SPOCK, 1984, A-C
STAR TREK: THE MOTION PICTURE, 1979, A
STAR WARS, 1977, A-C
STAR WITNESS, 1931, A
STAR!, 1968, A-C
STAR, THE, 1953, A
STARBIRD AND SWEET WILLIAM, 1975
STARCRASH, 1979, C
STARDUST, 1921, A
STARDUST, 1974, O
STARDUST MEMORIES, 1980, C
STARDUST ON THE SAGE, 1942, A
STARDUST, 1938
STARFIGHTERS, THE, 1964, A
STARHOPS, 1978, O
STARK FEAR, 1963, C
STARK LOVE, 1927
STARK MAD, 1929, A
STARK RAVING MAD, 1983
STARLIFT, 1951, A
STARLIGHT OVER TEXAS, 1938, A
STARLIGHT SLAUGHTER
STARLIGHT'S REVENGE, 1926
STARLIGHT, THE UNTAMED, 1925
STARLIT GARDEN, THE, 1923
STARMAN, 1984, C
STARS AND STRIPES FOREVER, 1952, AAA
STARS ARE SINGING, THE, 1953, A
STARS IN MY CROWN, 1950, A
STARS IN YOUR BACKYARD
STARS IN YOUR EYES, 1956, A
STARS LOOK DOWN, THE, 1940, A-C
STARS ON PARADE, 1944, A
STARS OVER ARIZONA, 1937, A
STARS OVER BROADWAY, 1935, A
STARS OVER TEXAS, 1946, A
STARSHIP INVASIONS, 1978, AA
STARSTRUCK, 1982, C
START CHEERING, 1938, A
START THE REVOLUTION WITHOUT ME, 1970, C-O
STARTING OVER, 1979, C-O
STARTING POINT, THE, 1919, A
STASTNY KONEC
STATE DEPARTMENT—FILE 649, 1949, A
STATE FAIR, 1933, A
STATE FAIR, 1945, A
STATE FAIR, 1962, A
STATE OF SIEGE, 1973, C
STATE OF THE UNION, 1948, A
STATE OF THINGS, THE, 1983, A
STATE PENITENTIARY, 1950, A
STATE POLICE, 1938, A
STATE POLICE 1948
STATE SECRET
STATE STREET SADIE, 1928, C
STATE TROOPER, 1933, A
STATE'S ATTORNEY, 1932, A
STATELESS
STATELINE MOTEL, 1976, O
STATION CONTENT, 1918
STATION MASTER, THE, 1928
STATION SIX-SAHARA, 1964, C
STATION WEST, 1948, A
STATUE, THE, 1971, O
STAVISKY, 1974, C
STAY AWAY, JOE, 1968, A
STAY HOME
STAY HUNGRY, 1976, O
STAYING ALIVE, 1983, C
STEADFAST HEART, THE, 1923, A
STEADY COMPANY, 1932, A
STEAGLE, THE, 1971, O
STEALERS, THE, 1920
STEAMBOAT BILL, JR., 1928, A
STEAMBOAT ROUND THE BEND, 1935, A
STEEL, 1980, C
STEEL AGAINST THE SKY, 1941, A
STEEL ARENA, 1973, C
STEEL BAYONET, THE, 1958, A
STEEL CAGE, THE, 1954, A
STEEL CLAW, THE, 1961, A
STEEL FIST, THE, 1952, A
STEEL HELMET, THE, 1951, C
STEEL HIGHWAY, THE
STEEL JUNGLE, THE, 1956, A
STEEL KEY, THE, 1953, A
STEEL KING, THE, 1919
STEEL LADY, THE, 1953, A
STEEL PREFERRED, 1926
STEEL TOWN, 1952, A
STEEL TRAP, THE, 1952, A
STEELHEART, 1921, A
STEELYARD BLUES, 1973, C
STEFANIA, 1968, O
STEFANIE IN RIO, 1963
STELLA, 1921
STELLA, 1950, A
STELLA DALLAS, 1925, A
STELLA DALLAS, 1937, A
STELLA MARIS, 1918, A
STELLA MARIS, 1925, A

STELLA PARISH
STELLA STAR
STELLE OF THE ROYAL MOUNTED, 1925
STEP BY STEP, 1946, A
STEP DOWN TO TERROR, 1958, A
STEP LIVELY, 1944, A
STEP LIVELY, JEEVES, 1937, A
STEP ON IT, 1922, A
STEPAN KHALTURIN, 1925
STEPCHILD, 1947, A
STEPCHILDREN, 1962, A
STEPFORD WIVES, THE, 1975, A-C
STEPHANIA
STEPHEN STEPS OUT, 1923, A
STEPMOTHER, THE, 1914
STEPMOTHER, THE, 1973
STEPPE, THE, 1963, A
STEPPENWOLF, 1974, O
STEPPIN' IN SOCIETY, 1945, A
STEPPIN' OUT, 1925
STEPPING ALONG, 1926, A
STEPPING FAST, 1923, A
STEPPING INTO SOCIETY
STEPPING LIVELY, 1924
STEPPING OUT, 1919
STEPPING OUT, 1931
STEPPING SISTERS, 1932, A
STEPPING STONE, THE, 1916
STEPPING TOES, 1938, A
STEPS TO THE MOON, 1963, A
STEPTOE AND SON, 1972, A-C
STEREO, 1969, O
STERILE CUCKOO, THE, 1969, C
STEVIE, 1978, A
STEVIE, SAMSON AND DELILAH, 1975
STICK 'EM UP, 1950, A
STICK TO YOUR GUNS, 1941, A
STICK TO YOUR STORY, 1926
STICK UP, THE, 1978, A
STICKS
STIGMA, 1972, O
STIGMATIZED ONE, THE
STILETTO, 1969, O
STILL ALARM, THE, 1926
STILL OF THE NIGHT, 1982, O
STILL ROOM IN HELL
STILL SMOKIN', 1983, O
STILL WATERS, 1915, A
STILL WATERS RUN DEEP, 1916, A
STING II, THE, 1983, C
STING OF DEATH, 1966, C
STING OF THE LASH, 1921, A
STING OF THE SCORPION, THE, 1923, A
STING OF VICTORY, THE, 1916
STING, THE, 1973, C
STINGAREE, 1934, A
STINGRAY, 1978, C
STIR, 1980, O
STIR CRAZY, 1980, C-O
STIRRUP CUP SENSATION, THE, 1924
STITCH IN TIME, A, 1919
STITCH IN TIME, A, 1967, A
STOCK CAR, 1955, A
STOCKS AND BLONDES, 1928, A
STOKER, THE, 1932, A
STOKER, THE, 1935, A
STOLEN AIRLINER, THE, 1962, AA
STOLEN ASSIGNMENT, 1955, A
STOLEN BRIDE, THE, 1927, A
STOLEN CHILD, THE, 1923
STOLEN DIRIGIBLE, THE, 1966, AAA
STOLEN FACE, 1952, A
STOLEN GOODS, 1915
STOLEN HARMONY, 1935, A
STOLEN HEAVEN, 1931, A
STOLEN HEAVEN, 1938, A
STOLEN HEIRLOOMS, THE, 1915
STOLEN HOLIDAY, 1937, A
STOLEN HONOR, 1918
STOLEN HONOURS, 1914
STOLEN HOURS, 1918
STOLEN HOURS, 1963, A-C
STOLEN IDENTITY, 1953, A
STOLEN KISS, THE, 1920
STOLEN KISSES, 1929, A
STOLEN KISSES, 1969, O
STOLEN LIFE, 1939, A
STOLEN LIFE, A, 1946, A-C
STOLEN LOVE, 1928
STOLEN MASTERPIECE, THE, 1914
STOLEN MOMENTS, 1920
STOLEN ORDERS, 1918
STOLEN PARADISE, 1941
STOLEN PARADISE, THE, 1917
STOLEN PLANS, THE, 1962, AA
STOLEN PLAY, THE, 1917
STOLEN PLEASURES, 1927, A
STOLEN RANCH, THE, 1926
STOLEN SACRIFICE, THE, 1916
STOLEN SECRETS, 1924
STOLEN SWEETS, 1934, A
STOLEN TIME
STOLEN TREATY, THE, 1917
STOLEN TRIUMPH, THE, 1916
STOLEN VOICE, 1915, A
STOLEN WEALTH
STONE, 1974, O
STONE BOY, THE, 1984, C
STONE COLD DEAD, 1980, O
STONE KILLER, THE, 1973, O
STONE OF SILVER CREEK, 1935, A
STONE RIDER, THE, 1923
STONY ISLAND, 1978, C
STOOGE, THE, 1952, A
STOOGES GO WEST
STOOL PIGEON, 1928
STOOL PIGEON, THE
STOOLIE, THE, 1972, C
STOP AT NOTHING, 1924
STOP FLIRTING, 1925
STOP ME BEFORE I KILL?, 1961, C
STOP PRESS GIRL, 1949, A
STOP THAT CAB, 1951, A
STOP THAT MAN, 1928, A
STOP THE WORLD—I WANT TO GET OFF, 1966, A
STOP THIEF, 1915
STOP THIEF, 1920, A
STOP TRAIN 349, 1964, A
STOP, LOOK, AND LISTEN, 1926
STOP, LOOK, AND LOVE, 1939, A
STOP, YOU'RE KILLING ME, 1952, A
STOPOVER FOREVER, 1964, A
STOPOVER TOKYO, 1957, A
STORIA DI UNA DONNA
STORIES FROM A FLYING TRUNK, 1979, AA
STORK, 1971, O
STORK BITES MAN, 1947, A
STORK CLUB, THE, 1945, A
STORK PAYS OFF, THE, 1941, A
STORK TALK, 1964, O
STORK'S NEST, THE, 1915, A
STORM AT DAYBREAK, 1933, A
STORM BOY, 1976, AAA
STORM BREAKER, THE, 1925
STORM CENTER, 1956, A
STORM DAUGHTER, THE, 1924, A
STORM FEAR, 1956, A
STORM GIRL, 1922
STORM IN A TEACUP, 1937, A
STORM IN A WATER GLASS, 1931, A
STORM OVER AFRICA
STORM OVER ASIA, 1929, A
STORM OVER BENGAL, 1938, A
STORM OVER LISBON, 1944, A
STORM OVER THE ANDES, 1935, A
STORM OVER THE NILE, 1955, A
STORM OVER THE PACIFIC
STORM OVER TIBET, 1952, A
STORM OVER WYOMING, 1950, A
STORM PLANET, 1962, A
STORM RIDER, THE, 1957, A
STORM SIGNAL, 1966
STORM WARNING, 1950, C-O
STORM WITHIN, THE
STORM, THE, 1916
STORM, THE, 1922, A
STORM, THE, 1930, A
STORM, THE, 1938, A
STORMBOUND, 1951, A
STORMSWEPT, 1923, A
STORMY, 1935, A
STORMY CROSSING, 1958, A-C
STORMY KNIGHT, A, 1917
STORMY SEAS, 1923, A
STORMY TRAILS, 1936, A
STORMY WATERS, 1928, A
STORMY WATERS, 1946, A
STORMY WEATHER, 1935, A
STORMY WEATHER, 1943, A
STORY OF A CHEAT, THE, 1938, O
STORY OF A CITIZEN ABOVE ALL SUSPICION
STORY OF A DRAFT DODGER
STORY OF A LOVE STORY
STORY OF A TEENAGER
STORY OF A THREE DAY PASS, THE, 1968, O
STORY OF A WOMAN, 1970, O
STORY OF ADELE H., THE, 1975, C-O
STORY OF ALEXANDER GRAHAM BELL, THE, 1939, AA
STORY OF ARNOLD ROTHSTEIN
STORY OF CINDERELLA, THE
STORY OF DAVID, A, 1960, A
STORY OF DR. EHRLICH'S MAGIC BULLET, THE
STORY OF DR. WASSELL, THE, 1944, A-C
STORY OF ESTHER COSTELLO, THE, 1957, C
STORY OF FLOATING WEEDS, A, 1934
STORY OF G.I. JOE, THE, 1945, A-C
STORY OF GILBERT AND SULLIVAN, THE
STORY OF JOSEPH AND HIS BRETHREN THE, 1962, A
STORY OF LOUIS PASTEUR, THE, 1936, AA
STORY OF MANDY, THE
STORY OF MANKIND, THE, 1957, A
STORY OF MOLLY X, THE, 1949, A
STORY OF MONTE CRISTO, THE
STORY OF ROBIN HOOD AND HIS MERRIE MEN, THE
STORY OF ROBIN HOOD, THE, 1952, AAA
STORY OF RUTH, THE, 1960, A
STORY OF SEABISCUIT, THE, 1949, A
STORY OF SEVEN WHO WERE HANGED, 1920
STORY OF SHIRLEY YORKE, THE, 1948, A
STORY OF SUSAN, THE, 1916
STORY OF TEMPLE DRAKE, THE, 1933, O
STORY OF THE BLOOD RED ROSE, THE, 1914
STORY OF THE COUNT OF MONTE CRISTO, THE, 1962, A
STORY OF THE CRUELTIES OF YOUTH, A
STORY OF THE ROSARY, THE, 1920
STORY OF THREE LOVES, THE, 1953, A
STORY OF VERNON AND IRENE CASTLE, THE, 1939, A
STORY OF VICKIE, THE, 1958, A
STORY OF WILL ROGERS, THE, 1952, A
STORY ON PAGE ONE, THE, 1959, C
STORY WITHOUT A NAME
STORY WITHOUT A NAME, THE, 1924
STORY WITHOUT WORDS, 1981, A
STORYVILLE, 1974
STOWAWAY, 1932, A
STOWAWAY, 1936, AAA
STOWAWAY GIRL, 1957, A
STOWAWAY GIRL, THE, 1916
STOWAWAY IN THE SKY, 1962, AA
STRAIGHT FROM PARIS, 1921
STRAIGHT FROM THE HEART, 1935, A
STRAIGHT FROM THE SHOULDER, 1921
STRAIGHT FROM THE SHOULDER, 1936, A
STRAIGHT IS THE WAY, 1921, A
STRAIGHT IS THE WAY, 1934, A
STRAIGHT JACKET, 1980
STRAIGHT ON TILL MORNING, 1974, O
STRAIGHT ROAD, THE, 1914, A
STRAIGHT SHOOTER, 1940, A
STRAIGHT SHOOTIN', 1927
STRAIGHT SHOOTING, 1917
STRAIGHT THROUGH, 1925
STRAIGHT TIME, 1978, O
STRAIGHT TO HEAVEN, 1939, A
STRAIGHT WAY, THE, 1916
STRAIGHT, PLACE AND SHOW, 1938, A
STRAIGHTAWAY, 1934, A
STRAIGHTFORWARD BOY, A, 1929
STRAIT-JACKET, 1964, O
STRAITJACKET, 1963
STRANDED, 1916
STRANDED, 1927, A
STRANDED, 1935, A
STRANDED, 1965, O
STRANDED IN ARCADY, 1917
STRANDED IN PARIS
STRANDED IN PARIS, 1926
STRANDED, 1967
STRANGE ADVENTURE, 1932, A
STRANGE ADVENTURE, A, 1956, A
STRANGE ADVENTURES OF MR. SMITH, THE, 1937, A
STRANGE AFFAIR, 1944, A
STRANGE AFFAIR OF UNCLE HARRY, THE
STRANGE AFFAIR, THE, 1968, O
STRANGE AFFECTION, 1959, A
STRANGE ALIBI, 1941, A
STRANGE AWAKENING, THE
STRANGE BARGAIN, 1949, A
STRANGE BEDFELLOWS, 1965, A-C
STRANGE BEHAVIOR
STRANGE BOARDERS, 1938, A
STRANGE BORDER, THE, 1920
STRANGE BREW, 1983, C
STRANGE CARGO, 1929, A
STRANGE CARGO, 1936, A
STRANGE CARGO, 1940, C
STRANGE CASE OF CLARA DEANE, THE, 1932, A
STRANGE CASE OF DISTRICT ATTORNEY M., 1930
STRANGE CASE OF DR. MANNING, THE, 1958, A
STRANGE CASE OF DR. MEADE, 1939, A
STRANGE CASE OF DR. RX, THE, 1942, A
STRANGE CASE OF PHILIP KENT, THE, 1916
STRANGE CONFESSION
STRANGE CONFESSION, 1945, A
STRANGE CONQUEST, 1946, A
STRANGE CONSPIRACY, THE
STRANGE DEATH OF ADOLF HITLER, THE, 1943, A
STRANGE DECEPTION, 1953, O
STRANGE DOOR, THE, 1951, A
STRANGE EVIDENCE, 1933, A
STRANGE EXPERIMENT, 1937, A

STRANGE FACES, 1938, A
STRANGE FASCINATION, 1952, A
STRANGE FETISHES OF THE GO-GO GIRLS
STRANGE FETISHES, THE, 1967, O
STRANGE GAMBLE, 1948, A
STRANGE HOLIDAY, 1945, A
STRANGE HOLIDAY, 1969, A
STRANGE IDOLS, 1922
STRANGE ILLUSION, 1945, A
STRANGE IMPERSONATION, 1946, A
STRANGE INCIDENT
STRANGE INTERLUDE, 1932, C
STRANGE INTERVAL
STRANGE INTRUDER, 1956, A
STRANGE INVADERS, 1983, O
STRANGE JOURNEY, 1946, A
STRANGE JOURNEY, 1966
STRANGE JUSTICE, 1932, A
STRANGE LADY IN TOWN, 1955, A
STRANGE LAWS
STRANGE LOVE OF MARTHA IVERS, THE, 1946, C
STRANGE LOVE OF MOLLY LOUVAIN, THE, 1932, A
STRANGE LOVERS, 1963, O
STRANGE MR. GREGORY, THE, 1945, A
STRANGE MRS. CRANE, THE, 1948, A
STRANGE ONE, THE, 1957, O
STRANGE ONES, THE,
STRANGE PEOPLE, 1933, A
STRANGE RIDER, THE, 1925
STRANGE ROADS
STRANGE SHADOWS IN AN EMPTY ROOM, 1977, O
STRANGE THINGS HAPPEN AT NIGHT, 1979
STRANGE TRANSGRESSOR, A, 1917
STRANGE TRIANGLE, 1946, A
STRANGE VENEGEANCE OF ROSALIE, THE, 1972, C
STRANGE VOYAGE, 1945, A
STRANGE WIVES, 1935, A
STRANGE WOMAN, THE, 1918
STRANGE WOMAN, THE, 1946, C
STRANGE WORLD, 1952, A
STRANGE WORLD OF PLANET X, THE
STRANGER AT MY DOOR, 1950, A
STRANGER AT MY DOOR, 1956, A
STRANGER CAME HOME, THE
STRANGER FROM ARIZONA, THE, 1938, A
STRANGER FROM PECOS, THE, 1943, A
STRANGER FROM PONCA CITY, THE, 1947
STRANGER FROM SANTA FE, 1945
STRANGER FROM SOMEWHERE, A, 1916
STRANGER FROM TEXAS, THE, 1940, A
STRANGER FROM VENUS, THE, 1954, A
STRANGER IN BETWEEN, THE, 1952, A
STRANGER IN CANYON VALLEY, THE, 1921
STRANGER IN HOLLYWOOD, 1968, A-C
STRANGER IN MY ARMS, 1959, A
STRANGER IN THE HOUSE, 1967
STRANGER IN THE HOUSE, 1975
STRANGER IN TOWN, 1932, A
STRANGER IN TOWN, 1957, A
STRANGER IN TOWN, A, 1943, A
STRANGER IN TOWN, A, 1968, C
STRANGER IS WATCHING, A, 1982, O
STRANGER KNOCKS, A, 1963, C
STRANGER OF THE HILLS, THE, 1922
STRANGER ON HORSEBACK, 1955, A
STRANGER ON THE PROWL, 1953, A-C
STRANGER ON THE THIRD FLOOR, 1940, C
STRANGER RETURNS, THE, 1968, A
STRANGER THAN FICTION, 1921, A
STRANGER THAN LOVE
STRANGER THAN PARADISE, 1984, O
STRANGER WALKED IN, A
STRANGER WORE A GUN, THE, 1953, A
STRANGER'S BANQUET, 1922, A
STRANGER'S GUNDOWN, THE, 1974, C
STRANGER'S HAND, THE, 1955, A
STRANGER'S MEETING, 1957, A
STRANGER'S RETURN, 1933, A
STRANGER, THE, 1913
STRANGER, THE, 1924, A
STRANGER, THE, 1946, C
STRANGER, THE, 1967, C-O
STRANGER, THE, 1940
STRANGER, THE, 1962
STRANGERS ALL, 1935, A
STRANGERS AT SUNRISE, 1969
STRANGERS CAME, THE
STRANGERS HONEYMOON
STRANGERS IN LOVE, 1932, A
STRANGERS IN THE CITY, 1962, A
STRANGERS IN THE HOUSE, 1949, C
STRANGERS IN THE NIGHT, 1944, A-C
STRANGERS KISS, 1984, C
STRANGERS MAY KISS, 1931, A
STRANGERS OF THE EVENING, 1932, A
STRANGERS OF THE NIGHT, 1923, A
STRANGERS ON A HONEYMOON, 1937, A
STRANGERS ON A TRAIN, 1951, C-O
STRANGERS WHEN WE MEET, 1960, C
STRANGERS, 1970
STRANGERS, THE, 1955, A
STRANGEST CASE, THE
STRANGLEHOLD, 1931, A
STRANGLEHOLD, 1962, A
STRANGLER OF THE SWAMP, 1945, A
STRANGLER'S WEB, 1966, A-C
STRANGLER, THE, 1941, C
STRANGLER, THE, 1964, C
STRANGLERS OF BOMBAY, THE, 1960, C
STRANGLING THREADS, 1923
STRATEGIC AIR COMMAND, 1955, A
STRATEGY OF TERROR, 1969, A
STRATHMORE, 1915
STRATTON STORY, THE, 1949, AA
STRAUSS' GREAT WALTZ, 1934, A
STRAUSS' SALOME
STRAUSS, THE WALTZ KING, 1929
STRAW DOGS, 1971, O
STRAW MAN, THE, 1953, A
STRAWBERRY BLONDE, THE, 1941, A
STRAWBERRY ROAN, 1933, A
STRAWBERRY ROAN, 1945, A
STRAWBERRY ROAN, THE, 1948, A
STRAWBERRY STATEMENT, THE, 1970, C
STRAWS IN THE WIND, 1924
STRAY DOG, 1963, A-C
STREAK OF LUCK, A, 1925
STREAM OF LIFE, THE, 1919
STREAMERS, 1983, O
STREAMLINE EXPRESS, 1935, A
STREET ANGEL, 1928, A
STREET BANDITS, 1951, A
STREET CALLED STRAIGHT, THE, 1920
STREET CORNER
STREET CORNER, 1948, C
STREET FIGHTER, 1959, A
STREET GANG
STREET GIRL, 1929, A
STREET GIRLS, 1975
STREET IS MY BEAT, THE, 1966, C
STREET LAW, 1981
STREET MUSIC, 1982, A-C
STREET OF ADVENTURE, THE, 1921
STREET OF CHANCE, 1930, A
STREET OF CHANCE, 1942, A
STREET OF DARKNESS, 1958, A
STREET OF FORGOTTEN MEN, THE, 1925
STREET OF ILLUSION, THE, 1928
STREET OF MEMORIES, 1940, A
STREET OF MISSING MEN, 1939, A
STREET OF MISSING WOMEN
STREET OF SEVEN STARS, THE, 1918
STREET OF SHADOWS
STREET OF SIN, THE, 1928, A
STREET OF SINNERS, 1957, A
STREET OF TEARS, THE, 1924
STREET OF WOMEN, 1932, A
STREET PARTNER, THE
STREET PEOPLE, 1976, O
STREET SCENE, 1931, C
STREET SINGER, THE, 1937, A
STREET SONG, 1935, A
STREET WITH NO NAME, THE, 1948, C-O
STREET, THE, 1927
STREETCAR NAMED DESIRE, A, 1951, C-O
STREETFIGHTER, THE
STREETS OF FIRE, 1984, C
STREETS OF GHOST TOWN, 1950, A
STREETS OF HONG KONG, 1979
STREETS OF ILLUSION, THE, 1917
STREETS OF LAREDO, 1949, A-C
STREETS OF LONDON, THE, 1929
STREETS OF NEW YORK, 1939, A
STREETS OF NEW YORK, THE, 1922, A
STREETS OF SAN FRANCISCO, 1949, A
STREETS OF SHANGHAI, 1927
STREETS OF SIN
STREETS OF SINNERS
STRENGTH OF DONALD MCKENZIE, THE, 1916
STRENGTH OF THE PINES, 1922
STRENGTH OF THE WEAK, THE, 1916
STRICTLY CONFIDENTIAL
STRICTLY CONFIDENTIAL, 1919
STRICTLY CONFIDENTIAL, 1959, A
STRICTLY DISHONORABLE, 1931, A-C
STRICTLY DISHONORABLE, 1951, A
STRICTLY DYNAMITE, 1934, A
STRICTLY FOR PLEASURE
STRICTLY FOR THE BIRDS, 1963, C
STRICTLY ILLEGAL, 1935, A
STRICTLY IN THE GROOVE, 1942, A
STRICTLY MODERN, 1930, A
STRICTLY PERSONAL, 1933, A
STRICTLY UNCONVENTIONAL, 1930, A
STRIFE, 1919
STRIFE ETERNAL, THE, 1915
STRIKE, 1925
STRIKE IT RICH, 1933, A
STRIKE IT RICH, 1948, A
STRIKE ME DEADLY
STRIKE ME DEADLY, 1963
STRIKE ME PINK, 1936, A
STRIKE UP THE BAND, 1940, AAA
STRIKE?, 1934, A
STRIKEBOUND, 1984, C-O
STRIKERS, THE
STRIKERS, THE, 1915
STRIKING BACK, 1981
STRING BEANS, 1918
STRIP TEASE MURDER, 1961, C-O
STRIP, THE, 1951, C
STRIP-TEASE
STRIPED STOCKING GANG, THE
STRIPES, 1981, O
STRIPPED FOR A MILLION, 1919
STRIPPER, THE, 1963, O
STRIPTEASE LADY
STRIVING FOR FORTUNE, 1926, A
STROKE OF MIDNIGHT, THE
STROKER ACE, 1983, C
STROMBOLI, 1950, C-O
STRONG BOY, 1929, A
STRONG MAN'S WEAKNESS, A, 1917
STRONG MAN, THE, 1917
STRONG MAN, THE, 1926, A
STRONG MEDICINE, 1981
STRONG WAY, THE, 1918
STRONGER LOVE, THE, 1916
STRONGER SEX, THE, 1931, A
STRONGER THAN DEATH, 1920
STRONGER THAN DESIRE, 1939, A
STRONGER THAN FEAR
STRONGER THAN THE SUN, 1980, A
STRONGER VOW, THE, 1919
STRONGER WILL, THE, 1928
STRONGEST MAN IN THE WORLD, THE, 1975, A
STRONGEST, THE, 1920
STRONGHOLD, 1952, A
STRONGROOM, 1962, A
STRUGGLE EVERLASTING, THE, 1918
STRUGGLE, THE, 1916
STRUGGLE, THE, 1921, A
STRUGGLE, THE, 1931, A-C
STRYKER, 1983, O
STUBBORNESS OF GERALDINE, THE, 1915
STUCK ON YOU, 1983, O
STUCKEY'S LAST STAND, 1980, C
STUD, THE, 1979, O
STUDENT BODIES, 1981, O
STUDENT BODY, THE, 1976, O
STUDENT NURSES, THE, 1970, O
STUDENT OF PRAGUE, THE, 1913
STUDENT OF PRAGUE, THE, 1927, A
STUDENT PRINCE IN OLD HEIDELBERG, THE, 1927
STUDENT PRINCE, THE, 1954, A
STUDENT ROMANCE
STUDENT TEACHERS, THE, 1973, O
STUDENT TOUR, 1934, A
STUDENT'S ROMANCE, THE, 1936, A
STUDIO GIRL, THE, 1918
STUDIO MURDER MYSTERY, THE, 1929, A
STUDIO ROMANCE
STUDS LONIGAN, 1960, A
STUDY IN SCARLET, A, 1914
STUDY IN SCARLET, A, 1933, A
STUDY IN TERROR, A, 1966, A
STUETZEN DER GESELLSCHAFT
STUNT MAN, THE, 1980, O
STUNT PILOT, 1939, A
STUNTS, 1977, C-O
SUB-A-DUB-DUB
SUBJECT WAS ROSES, THE, 1968, C
SUBMARINE, 1928
SUBMARINE ALERT, 1943, A
SUBMARINE BASE, 1943, A
SUBMARINE COMMAND, 1951, A
SUBMARINE D-1, 1937, A
SUBMARINE EYE, THE, 1917
SUBMARINE PATROL, 1938, A
SUBMARINE PIRATE, A, 1915, A
SUBMARINE RAIDER, 1942, A
SUBMARINE SEAHAWK, 1959, A
SUBMARINE ZONE
SUBMERSION OF JAPAN, THE
SUBSTITUTE WIFE, THE, 1925
SUBSTITUTION, 1970, O
SUBTERFUGE, 1969, A
SUBTERRANEANS, THE, 1960, C
SUBURBAN WIVES, 1973, O
SUBURBAN, THE, 1915, A
SUBURBIA, 1984, O
SUBVERSIVES, THE, 1967, C
SUBWAY EXPRESS, 1931, A
SUBWAY IN THE SKY, 1959, C
SUBWAY RIDERS, 1981, O
SUBWAY SADIE, 1926
SUCCESS

SUCCESS, 1923, A
SUCCESS AT ANY PRICE, 1934, A
SUCCESS IS THE BEST REVENGE, 1984, O
SUCCESSFUL ADVENTURE, THE, 1918
SUCCESSFUL CALAMITY, A, 1932, A
SUCCESSFUL FAILURE, A, 1917
SUCCESSFUL FAILURE, A, 1934, A
SUCH A GORGEOUS KID LIKE ME, 1973, O
SUCH A LITTLE PIRATE, 1918
SUCH A LITTLE QUEEN, 1914, A
SUCH A LITTLE QUEEN, 1914, A
SUCH A LITTLE QUEEN, 1921, A
SUCH GOOD FRIENDS, 1971, O
SUCH IS LIFE, 1929
SUCH IS LIFE, 1936, A
SUCH IS THE LAW, 1930, A
SUCH MEN ARE DANGEROUS
SUCH MEN ARE DANGEROUS, 1930, A
SUCH THINGS HAPPEN
SUCH WOMEN ARE DANGEROUS, 1934, A
SUCKER ... OR HOW TO BE GLAD WHEN YOU'VE BEEN HAD, THE
SUCKER MONEY, 1933, A
SUCKER, THE, 1966, A
SUDAN, 1945, A-C
SUDDEN BILL DORN, 1938, A
SUDDEN DANGER, 1955, A
SUDDEN DEATH, 1977
SUDDEN FEAR, 1952, A-C
SUDDEN FURY, 1975, C
SUDDEN GENTLEMAN, THE, 1917
SUDDEN IMPACT, 1983, O
SUDDEN JIM, 1917
SUDDEN MONEY, 1939, A
SUDDEN RICHES, 1916
SUDDEN TERROR, 1970, A
SUDDENLY, 1954, C
SUDDENLY IT'S SPRING, 1947, A
SUDDENLY, A WOMAN, 1967, O
SUDDENLY, LAST SUMMER, 1959, O
SUDS, 1920, A
SUE OF THE SOUTH, 1919
SUED FOR LIBEL, 1940, A
SUENO DE NOCHE DE VERANO
SUEZ, 1938, A
SUGAR CANE ALLEY, 1984, C
SUGAR COOKIES, 1973
SUGAR HILL, 1974, C
SUGARFOOT, 1951, A
SUGARLAND EXPRESS, THE, 1974, C
SUGATA SANSHIRO
SUICIDE BATTALION, 1958, A
SUICIDE CLUB, THE
SUICIDE CLUB, THE, 1914
SUICIDE FLEET, 1931, A
SUICIDE LEGION, 1940, C
SUICIDE MISSION, 1956, C
SUICIDE RUN
SUICIDE SQUADRON, 1942, A
SUITABLE CASE FOR TREATMENT, A
SUITOR, THE, 1963, C
SULEIMAN THE CONQUEROR, 1963, A
SULLIVAN'S EMPIRE, 1967, A
SULLIVAN'S TRAVELS, 1941, C
SULLIVANS, THE, 1944, A
SULT
SULTAN'S DAUGHTER, THE, 1943, A
SULTANA, THE, 1916
SUMARINE X-1, 1969, A
SUMMER AND SMOKE, 1961, C-O
SUMMER BACHELORS, 1926, A
SUMMER CAMP, 1979, O
SUMMER FIRES
SUMMER FLIGHT
SUMMER GIRL, THE, 1916
SUMMER HOLIDAY, 1948, AA
SUMMER HOLIDAY, 1963, A
SUMMER INTERLUDE
SUMMER LIGHTNING, 1933, A
SUMMER LIGHTNING, 1948
SUMMER LOVE, 1958, A
SUMMER LOVERS, 1982, O
SUMMER MADNESS
SUMMER MAGIC, 1963, AAA
SUMMER OF '42, 1971, O
SUMMER OF '64
SUMMER OF SECRETS, 1976, O
SUMMER OF THE SEVENTEENTH DOLL
SUMMER PLACE, A, 1959, C
SUMMER RUN, 1974, A
SUMMER RUN, 1974
SUMMER SCHOOL TEACHERS, 1977, O
SUMMER SOLDIERS, 1972, C
SUMMER STOCK, 1950, A
SUMMER STORM, 1944, C
SUMMER TALES
SUMMER TO REMEMBER, A, 1961, A
SUMMER WISHES, WINTER DREAMS, 1973, A
SUMMER'S CHILDREN, 1979, O
SUMMERDOG, 1977, AAA
SUMMERFIELD, 1977, O
SUMMERPLAY
SUMMERSKIN, 1962, C
SUMMERSPELL, 1983, C
SUMMERTIME, 1955, A-C
SUMMERTIME KILLER, 1973, C
SUMMERTREE, 1971, A
SUMURU
SUMURUN
SUMURUN, 1910
SUMURUN, 1921
SUN ABOVE, DEATH BELOW, 1969, C
SUN ALSO RISES, THE, 1957, C
SUN ALWAYS RISES, THE
SUN COMES UP, THE, 1949, AAA
SUN DEMON, THE
SUN DOG TRAILS, 1923
SUN IS UP, THE
SUN NEVER SETS, THE, 1939, A
SUN RISES AGAIN, THE
SUN SETS AT DAWN, THE, 1950, A
SUN SHINES BRIGHT, THE, 1953, A
SUN SHINES FOR ALL, THE, 1961, A
SUN SHINES FOR EVERYBODY, THE
SUN SHINES, THE, 1939, A
SUN TAN RANCH, 1948
SUN VALLEY CYCLONE, 1946, A
SUN VALLEY SERENADE, 1941, AA
SUN-UP, 1925
SUNA NO KAORI
SUNA NO ONNA
SUNBEAM, THE, 1916
SUNBONNET SUE, 1945, A
SUNBURN, 1979, C
SUNBURST, 1975
SUNDANCE CASSIDY AND BUTCH THE KID, 1975
SUNDAY BLOODY SUNDAY, 1971, O
SUNDAY DINNER FOR A SOLDIER, 1944, A
SUNDAY IN NEW YORK, 1963, C
SUNDAY IN THE COUNTRY, 1975, O
SUNDAY IN THE COUNTRY, A, 1984, A
SUNDAY LOVERS, 1980, O
SUNDAY PUNCH, 1942, A
SUNDAY SINNERS, 1941
SUNDAY TOO FAR AWAY, 1975, C
SUNDAYS AND CYBELE, 1962, C
SUNDOWN, 1924
SUNDOWN, 1941, C
SUNDOWN IN SANTA FE, 1948, A
SUNDOWN JIM, 1942, A
SUNDOWN KID, THE, 1942, A
SUNDOWN ON THE PRAIRIE, 1939, A
SUNDOWN RIDER, THE, 1933, AA
SUNDOWN RIDERS, 1948, A
SUNDOWN SAUNDERS, 1937, A
SUNDOWN SLIM, 1920
SUNDOWN TRAIL, 1931, A
SUNDOWN TRAIL, THE, 1919
SUNDOWN TRAIL, THE, 1975
SUNDOWN VALLEY, 1944, A
SUNDOWNERS, THE, 1950, A
SUNDOWNERS, THE, 1960, A
SUNFLOWER, 1970, A
SUNKEN ROCKS, 1919
SUNLIGHT'S LAST RAID, 1917
SUNNY, 1930, A
SUNNY, 1941, A
SUNNY JANE, 1917
SUNNY SIDE OF THE STREET, 1951, A
SUNNY SIDE UP, 1929, A
SUNNY SKIES, 1930, A
SUNNYSIDE, 1979, O
SUNNYSIDE UP, 1926
SUNRISE AT CAMPOBELLO, 1960, A
SUNRISE TRAIL, 1931, A
SUNRISE—A SONG OF TWO HUMANS, 1927, A
SUNSCORCHED, 1966, O
SUNSET BOULEVARD, 1950, C-O
SUNSET CARSON RIDES AGAIN, 1948
SUNSET COVE, 1978, O
SUNSET DERBY, THE, 1927, A
SUNSET IN EL DORADO, 1945, A
SUNSET IN THE WEST, 1950, A
SUNSET IN VIENNA
SUNSET IN WYOMING, 1941, A
SUNSET JONES, 1921
SUNSET LEGION, THE, 1928, A
SUNSET MURDER CASE, 1941, C
SUNSET OF A CLOWN
SUNSET OF POWER, 1936, A
SUNSET ON THE DESERT, 1942, AA
SUNSET PASS, 1929, A
SUNSET PASS, 1933, A
SUNSET PASS, 1946, A
SUNSET RANGE, 1935, A
SUNSET SERENADE, 1942, A
SUNSET SPRAGUE, 1920
SUNSET TRAIL, 1917
SUNSET TRAIL, 1932, A
SUNSET TRAIL, 1938, A
SUNSET TRAIL, THE, 1924
SUNSHINE AHEAD, 1936, A
SUNSHINE ALLEY, 1917
SUNSHINE AND GOLD, 1917
SUNSHINE BOYS, THE, 1975, A-C
SUNSHINE DAD, 1916
SUNSHINE HARBOR, 1922
SUNSHINE NAN, 1918
SUNSHINE OF PARADISE ALLEY, 1926
SUNSHINE RUN, 1979
SUNSHINE SUSIE
SUNSHINE TRAIL, THE, 1923, A
SUNSTRUCK, 1973, A
SUPER BUG, 1975
SUPER COPS, THE, 1974, O
SUPER DRAGON
SUPER DUDE
SUPER FUZZ, 1981, C
SUPER INFRAMAN, THE
SUPER SEAL, 1976
SUPER SLEUTH, 1937, A
SUPER SPEED, 1925
SUPER SPOOK, 1975, O
SUPER VAN, 1977, C
SUPER WEAPON, THE, 1976
SUPER-JOCKS, THE, 1980
SUPER-SEX, THE, 1922, A
SUPERARGO, 1968, A
SUPERARGO VERSUS DIABOLICUS, 1966, A
SUPERBEAST, 1972, O
SUPERBUG, SUPER AGENT, 1976, AAA
SUPERBUG, THE WILD ONE, 1977
SUPERCHICK, 1973, O
SUPERCOCK, 1975
SUPERDAD, 1974, AAA
SUPERFLY, 1972, O
SUPERFLY T.N.T., 1973, O
SUPERGIRL, 1984, C
SUPERMAN, 1978, AAA
SUPERMAN AND THE MOLE MEN, 1951, A
SUPERMAN AND THE STRANGE PEOPLE
SUPERMAN II, 1980, A
SUPERMAN III, 1983, A
SUPERNATURAL, 1933, A-C
SUPERSNOOPER
SUPERSONIC MAN, 1979, A
SUPERSONIC SAUCER, 1956
SUPERSPEED, 1935, A
SUPERSTITION, 1922
SUPERZAN AND THE SPACE BOY, 1972, AAA
SUPPORT YOUR LOCAL GUNFIGHTER, 1971, A
SUPPORT YOUR LOCAL SHERIFF, 1969, A
SUPPOSE THEY GAVE A WAR AND NOBODY CAME?, 1970, A
SUPREME KID, THE, 1976, C
SUPREME PASSION, THE, 1921
SUPREME SACRIFICE, THE, 1916
SUPREME SECRET, THE, 1958, A
SUPREME TEMPTATION, THE, 1916
SUPREME TEST, THE, 1915
SUPREME TEST, THE, 1923, A
SUPRISES OF AN EMPTY HOTEL, THE, 1916
SUR LA COUR
SUR LA ROUTE DE SALINA
SURABAYA CONSPIRACY, 1975
SURCOUF, LE DERNIER CORSAIRE
SURE FIRE, 1921
SURE FIRE FLINT, 1922, A
SURF II, 1984, O
SURF PARTY, 1964, A
SURF TERROR
SURF, THE
SURFTIDE 77, 1962, O
SURFTIDE 777
SURGEON'S KNIFE, THE, 1957, C
SURGING SEAS, 1924, A
SURPRISE PACKAGE, 1960, C
SURRENDER, 1927
SURRENDER, 1931, A
SURRENDER, 1950, C
SURRENDER—HELL?, 1959, C
SURROGATE, THE, 1984, O
SURVIVAL, 1930
SURVIVAL, 1976, C
SURVIVAL RUN, 1980, O
SURVIVAL, 1962
SURVIVAL, 1965
SURVIVE!, 1977, O
SURVIVOR, 1980, C-O
SURVIVORS, THE, 1983, C-O
SUSAN AND GOD, 1940, A
SUSAN LENOX—HER FALL AND RISE, 1931, C
SUSAN ROCKS THE BOAT, 1916
SUSAN SLADE, 1961, C
SUSAN SLEPT HERE, 1954, C
SUSAN'S GENTLEMAN, 1917
SUSANNA

SUSANNA PASS, 1949, A
SUSANNAH OF THE MOUNTIES, 1939, AAA
SUSIE SNOWFLAKE, 1916
SUSIE STEPS OUT, 1946, A
SUSPECT, 1961
SUSPECT, THE, 1916
SUSPECT, THE, 1944, C
SUSPECTED
SUSPECTED ALIBI
SUSPECTED PERSON, 1943, A
SUSPENCE, 1919
SUSPENDED ALIBI, 1957, A
SUSPENSE, 1930, C
SUSPENSE, 1946, A-C
SUSPICION, 1918
SUSPICION, 1941, A-C
SUSPICIOUS WIFE, A, 1914
SUSPICIOUS WIVES, 1921
SUSPIRIA, 1977, O
SUSUZ YAZ
SUTTER'S GOLD, 1936, A
SUZANNA, 1922, A
SUZANNE, 1916
SUZANNE, 1980, C
SUZY, 1936, C
SVALT
SVEGLIATI E UCCIDI
SVENGALI, 1931, A-C
SVENGALI, 1955, C
SVIRACHUT
SWALLOWS AND AMAZONS, 1977, AAA
SWAMP COUNTRY, 1966, O
SWAMP DIAMONDS
SWAMP FIRE, 1946, A
SWAMP THING, 1982, C
SWAMP WATER, 1941, A
SWAMP WOMAN, 1941, A
SWAMP WOMEN, 1956, A
SWAMP, THE, 1921, A
SWAN LAKE, THE, 1967, AAA
SWAN, THE, 1925
SWAN, THE, 1956, A
SWANEE RIVER, 1931
SWANEE RIVER, 1939, A-C
SWANEE SHOWBOAT, 1939
SWANN IN LOVE, 1984, C-O
SWAP MEET, 1979, O
SWAPPERS, THE, 1970, O
SWARM, THE, 1978, C
SWASHBUCKLER, 1976, O
SWASTIKA SAVAGES
SWAT THE SPY, 1918
SWEATER GIRL, 1942, A
SWEATER GIRLS, 1978
SWEDENHIELMS, 1935, A
SWEDISH MISTRESS, THE, 1964, O
SWEDISH WEDDING NIGHT, 1965, C
SWEENEY, 1977, O
SWEENEY 2, 1978, O
SWEENEY TODD, 1928
SWEENEY TODD. THE DEMON BARBER OF FLEET STREET
SWEEPING AGAINST THE WINDS, 1930
SWEEPINGS, 1933, A
SWEEPSTAKE ANNIE, 1935, A
SWEEPSTAKE RACKETEERS
SWEEPSTAKES, 1931, A
SWEEPSTAKES WINNER, 1939, A
SWEET ADELINE, 1926, A
SWEET ADELINE, 1935, A
SWEET ALOES
SWEET ALYSSUM, 1915
SWEET AND LOWDOWN, 1944, A
SWEET AND SOUR, 1964, A
SWEET AND TWENTY, 1919
SWEET BEAT, 1962, A
SWEET BIRD OF YOUTH, 1962, O
SWEET BODY OF DEBORAH, THE, 1969, O
SWEET BODY, THE
SWEET CHARITY, 1969, A
SWEET COUNTRY ROAD, 1981
SWEET CREEK COUNTY WAR, THE, 1979, A
SWEET DADDIES, 1926
SWEET DEVIL, 1937, A
SWEET DIRTY TONY
SWEET DREAMERS, 1981
SWEET ECSTASY, 1962, C
SWEET GENEVIEVE, 1947
SWEET GEORGIA, 1972
SWEET GINGER BROWN
SWEET HUNTERS, 1969, C
SWEET INNISCARRA, 1934, A
SWEET JESUS, PREACHER MAN, 1973, O
SWEET KILL
SWEET KITTY BELLAIRS, 1916
SWEET KITTY BELLAIRS, 1930, A
SWEET LAVANDER, 1920
SWEET LAVENDER, 1915
SWEET LIGHT IN A DARK ROOM, 1966, A
SWEET LOVE, BITTER, 1967, C
SWEET MAMA, 1930, A
SWEET MUSIC, 1935, A
SWEET NOVEMBER, 1968, A
SWEET REVENGE
SWEET RIDE, THE, 1968, C
SWEET ROSIE O'GRADY, 1926
SWEET ROSIE O'GRADY, 1943, A
SWEET SAVIOR, 1971
SWEET SIXTEEN, 1928, A
SWEET SIXTEEN, 1983, O
SWEET SKIN, 1965, O
SWEET SMELL OF LOVE, 1966, A
SWEET SMELL OF SUCCESS, 1957, C-O
SWEET SOUND OF DEATH, 1965
SWEET STEPMOTHER
SWEET SUBSTITUTE, 1964, C
SWEET SUGAR, 1972, O
SWEET SURRENDER, 1935, A
SWEET SUZY, 1973, O
SWEET TRASH, 1970, O
SWEET VIOLENCE
SWEET WILLIAM, 1980, O
SWEETHEART OF SIGMA CHI, 1933, A
SWEETHEART OF SIGMA CHI, 1946, A
SWEETHEART OF THE CAMPUS, 1941, A
SWEETHEART OF THE DOOMED, 1917
SWEETHEART OF THE FLEET, 1942, A
SWEETHEART OF THE NAVY, 1937, A
SWEETHEARTS, 1919
SWEETHEARTS, 1938, A
SWEETHEARTS AND WIVES, 1930, A
SWEETHEARTS OF THE U.S.A., 1944, A
SWEETHEARTS ON PARADE, 1930, A
SWEETHEARTS ON PARADE, 1953, A
SWEETHEARTS ON PARADE, 1944
SWEETIE, 1929, A
SWELL GUY, 1946, A
SWELL-HEAD, 1935, A
SWELL-HEAD, THE, 1927, A
SWELLHEAD, THE, 1930, A
SWEPT AWAY...BY AN UNUSUAL DESTINY IN THE BLUE SEA OF AUGUST, 1975, O
SWIFT SHADOW, THE, 1927
SWIFT VENGEANCE
SWIFTY, 1936, A
SWIM TEAM, 1979
SWIM, GIRL, SWIM, 1927
SWIMMER, THE, 1968, C
SWINDLE, THE, 1962, A
SWINDLER, THE, 1919
SWING, 1938
SWING AND SWAY
SWING FEVER, 1943, A
SWING HIGH, 1930, A
SWING HIGH, 1944
SWING HIGH, SWING LOW, 1937, A-C
SWING HOSTESS, 1944, A
SWING IN THE SADDLE, 1944, A
SWING IT BUDDY
SWING IT SAILOR, 1937, A
SWING IT SOLDIER, 1941, A
SWING IT, PROFESSOR, 1937, A
SWING OUT THE BLUES, 1943, A
SWING OUT, SISTER, 1945, A
SWING PARADE OF 1946, 1946, A
SWING SHIFT, 1984, A-C
SWING SHIFT MAISIE, 1943, A
SWING THAT CHEER, 1938, A
SWING THE WESTERN WAY, 1947
SWING TIME, 1936, AA
SWING YOUR LADY, 1938, A
SWING YOUR PARTNER, 1943, A
SWING, COWBOY, SWING, 1944
SWING, SISTER, SWING, 1938, A
SWING, TEACHER, SWING
SWINGER'S PARADISE, 1965, A
SWINGER, THE, 1966, A
SWINGIN' AFFAIR, A, 1963, A
SWINGIN' ALONG, 1962, A
SWINGIN' IN THE GROOVE, 1960
SWINGIN' MAIDEN, THE, 1963, A
SWINGIN' ON A RAINBOW, 1945, A
SWINGIN' SUMMER, A, 1965, A
SWINGING BARMAIDS, THE, 1976, O
SWINGING CHEERLEADERS, THE, 1974
SWINGING COEDS, THE, 1976
SWINGING FINK
SWINGING PEARL MYSTERY, THE
SWINGING SET
SWINGING THE LEAD, 1934, A
SWINGTIME JOHNNY, 1944, A
SWIRL OF GLORY
SWISS CONSPIRACY, THE, 1976, C
SWISS FAMILY ROBINSON, 1940, AAA
SWISS FAMILY ROBINSON, 1960, AAA
SWISS HONEYMOON, 1947, A
SWISS MISS, 1938, AAA
SWISS TOUR
SWITCH, THE, 1963, C
SWITCHBLADE SISTERS, 1975, O
SWORD AND THE DRAGON, THE, 1960, A
SWORD AND THE ROSE, THE, 1953, A
SWORD AND THE SORCERER, THE, 1982, O
SWORD IN THE DESERT, 1949, C
SWORD IN THE STONE, THE, 1963, AAA
SWORD OF ALI BABA, THE, 1965, A
SWORD OF DAMOCLES, THE, 1920
SWORD OF DOOM, THE, 1967, C-O
SWORD OF EL CID, THE, 1965, A
SWORD OF FATE, THE, 1921
SWORD OF HONOUR, 1938, A
SWORD OF LANCELOT, 1963, A
SWORD OF MONTE CRISTO, THE, 1951, A
SWORD OF PENITENCE, 1927
SWORD OF SHERWOOD FOREST, 1961, A
SWORD OF THE AVENGER, 1948, A
SWORD OF THE CONQUEROR, 1962, C
SWORD OF THE VALIANT, 1984, C
SWORD OF VALOR, THE, 1924, A
SWORD OF VENUS, 1953, A
SWORDKILL, 1984, C
SWORDS AND THE WOMAN, 1923
SWORDSMAN OF SIENA, THE, 1962, A
SWORDSMAN, THE, 1947, A
SWORN ENEMY, 1936, A
SYBIL, 1921
SYLVIA, 1965, O
SYLVIA AND THE GHOST
SYLVIA AND THE PHANTOM, 1950, A
SYLVIA GRAY, 1914, A
SYLVIA OF THE SECRET SERVICE, 1917
SYLVIA ON A SPREE, 1918
SYLVIA SCARLETT, 1936, A-C
SYLVIE AND THE PHANTOM
SYMBOL OF THE UNCONQUERED, 1921
SYMPATHY FOR THE DEVIL
SYMPHONIE FANTASTIQUE, 1947, A
SYMPHONIE PASTORALE, 1948, C
SYMPHONY FOR A MASSACRE, 1965, A
SYMPHONY IN TWO FLATS, 1930, A
SYMPHONY OF LIFE, 1949, A
SYMPHONY OF LIVING, 1935, A
SYMPHONY OF LOVE AND DEATH, 1914
SYMPHONY OF SIX MILLION, 1932, A
SYMPHONY, THE
SYMPTOMS, 1976, O
SYNANON, 1965, C
SYNCOPATING SUE, 1926, A
SYNCOPATION, 1929, A
SYNCOPATION, 1942, A
SYNDICATE, THE, 1968, A
SYNTHETIC SIN, 1929
SYRIAN IMMIGRANT, THE, 1921
SYSTEM, THE, 1953, A
SYSTEM, THE, 1966
SYV DAGER FOR ELISABETH, 1927
SZEGENYLEGENYEK (NEHEZELETUEK)

-T-

T'OTHER DEAR CHARMER, 1918
T-BIRD GANG, 1959, C
T-MEN, 1947, C
T.A.G.: THE ASSASSINATION GAME, 1982, C
T.N.T (THE NAKED TRUTH), 1924
T.P.A.
T.R. BASKIN, 1971, C
TA CHI
TABLE BAY
TABLE FOR FIVE, 1983, C
TABLE TOP RANCH, 1922
TABLES TURNED, 1915
TABU, 1931, A
TABU (FUGITIVOS DE LAS ISLAS DEL SUR)
TAFFY AND THE JUNGLE HUNTER, 1965, AA
TAGGART, 1964, C
TAHITI HONEY, 1943, A
TAHITI NIGHTS, 1945, A
TAHITIAN, THE, 1956, A
TAIHEIYO HITORIBOTCHI
TAIHEIYO NO ARASHI
TAIL OF THE TIGER, 1984, AA
TAIL SPIN, 1939, A
TAILOR MADE MAN, A, 1922, A
TAILOR MADE MAN, A, 1931, A
TAILOR OF BOND STREET, THE, 1916, A
TAINTED MONEY
TAINTED MONEY, 1924
TAKE A CHANCE, 1933, A
TAKE A CHANCE, 1937, A
TAKE A GIANT STEP, 1959, A
TAKE A GIRL LIKE YOU, 1970, O
TAKE A HARD RIDE, 1975, C
TAKE A LETTER, DARLING, 1942, A
TAKE A POWDER, 1953, A
TAKE ALL OF ME, 1978, O
TAKE CARE OF MY LITTLE GIRL, 1951, A
TAKE DOWN, 1979, C

TAKE HER BY SURPRISE, 1967, A
TAKE HER, SHE'S MINE, 1963, A
TAKE IT ALL, 1966, A
TAKE IT BIG, 1944, A
TAKE IT FROM ME, 1926, A
TAKE IT FROM ME, 1937, A
TAKE IT OR LEAVE IT, 1944, A
TAKE ME AWAY, MY LOVE, 1962, O
TAKE ME BACK TO OKLAHOMA, 1940
TAKE ME HIGH, 1973, A
TAKE ME HOME, 1928, A
TAKE ME OUT TO THE BALL GAME, 1949, AA
TAKE ME OVER, 1963, A
TAKE ME TO PARIS, 1951, A
TAKE ME TO THE FAIR
TAKE ME TO TOWN, 1953, A
TAKE MY LIFE, 1942, A
TAKE MY LIFE, 1948, A
TAKE MY TIP, 1937, A
TAKE OFF THAT HAT, 1938, A
TAKE ONE, 1977
TAKE ONE FALSE STEP, 1949, C
TAKE THE HEIR, 1930
TAKE THE HEIR, 1930, AA
TAKE THE HIGH GROUND, 1953, A
TAKE THE MONEY AND RUN, 1969, C
TAKE THE STAGE
TAKE THE STAND, 1934, A
TAKE THIS JOB AND SHOVE IT, 1981, C-O
TAKE, THE, 1974, C
TAKEN BY SURPRISE
TAKERS, THE
TAKING A CHANCE, 1928
TAKING CHANCES, 1922, A
TAKING OF PELHAM ONE, TWO, THREE, THE, 1974, O
TAKING OFF, 1971, O
TAKING SIDES
TAKING TIGER MOUNTAIN, 1983, O
TALE OF A SHIRT, 1916
TALE OF FIVE CITIES, A
TALE OF FIVE WOMEN, A, 1951, A
TALE OF PRIEST PANKRATI, 1918
TALE OF THE COCK
TALE OF THREE WOMEN, A, 1954, A
TALE OF TWO CITIES, A, 1917, A
TALE OF TWO CITIES, A, 1935, A
TALE OF TWO CITIES, A, 1958, A
TALE OF TWO NATIONS, A, 1917
TALE OF TWO WORLDS, A, 1921, A
TALENT SCOUT, 1937, A
TALES AFTER THE RAIN
TALES FROM THE CRYPT, 1972, C
TALES FROM THE CRYPT PART II
TALES OF 1001 NIGHTS
TALES OF A SALESMAN, 1965, C
TALES OF A TRAVELING SALESMAN
TALES OF BEATRIX POTTER
TALES OF HOFFMANN, THE, 1951, A
TALES OF MANHATTAN, 1942, AA
TALES OF ORDINARY MADNESS, 1983, O
TALES OF PARIS, 1962, A
TALES OF ROBIN HOOD, 1951, A
TALES OF TERROR, 1962, C
TALES OF THE UNCANNY, 1932, C
TALES THAT WITNESS MADNESS, 1973, O
TALISMAN, THE, 1966, C
TALK ABOUT A LADY, 1946, A
TALK ABOUT A STRANGER, 1952, A
TALK ABOUT JACQUELINE, 1942, A
TALK OF A MILLION
TALK OF HOLLYWOOD, THE, 1929, A
TALK OF THE DEVIL, 1937, A
TALK OF THE TOWN, 1918
TALK OF THE TOWN, 1942, AA
TALKER, THE, 1925
TALKING BEAR, THE
TALKING FEET, 1937, A
TALL BLOND MAN WITH ONE BLACK SHOE, THE, 1973, C
TALL HEADLINES
TALL IN THE SADDLE, 1944, A
TALL LIE, THE
TALL MAN RIDING, 1955, A
TALL MEN, THE, 1955, A
TALL STORY, 1960, C
TALL STRANGER, THE, 1957, A
TALL T, THE, 1957, A
TALL TARGET, THE, 1951, A
TALL TEXAN, THE, 1953, A
TALL TIMBER
TALL TIMBERS, 1937, A
TALL TROUBLE, THE
TALL WOMEN, THE, 1967, A
TALL, DARK AND HANDSOME, 1941, A
TALL, TAN AND TERRIFIC, 1946
TAM-LIN
TAMAHINE, 1964, C
TAMANGO, 1959, C
TAMARIND SEED, THE, 1974, C
TAME CAT, THE, 1921
TAMING OF DOROTHY, THE, 1950, A
TAMING OF THE SHREW, THE, 1929, A
TAMING OF THE SHREW, THE, 1967, A-C
TAMING OF THE WEST, THE, 1925
TAMING OF THE WEST, THE, 1939, A
TAMING SUTTON'S GAL, 1957, A
TAMING THE WILD, 1937, A
TAMMY
TAMMY AND THE BACHELOR, 1957, A
TAMMY AND THE DOCTOR, 1963, A
TAMMY AND THE MILLIONAIRE, 1967, A
TAMMY, TELL ME TRUE, 1961, A
TAMPICO, 1944, A
TANGA-TIKA, 1953, A
TANGANYIKA, 1954, A
TANGIER, 1946, A
TANGIER ASSIGNMENT, 1954, A
TANGIER INCIDENT, 1953, A
TANGLE, THE, 1914, A
TANGLED DESTINIES, 1932, A
TANGLED EVIDENCE, 1934, A
TANGLED FATES, 1916, A
TANGLED FORTUNES, 1932
TANGLED HEARTS, 1916
TANGLED HERDS, 1926
TANGLED LIVES, 1917
TANGLED LIVES, 1918
TANGLED TRAILS, 1921
TANGO, 1936, A
TANGO BAR, 1935, A
TANGO CAVALIER, 1923
TANIN NO KAO
TANK, 1984, C
TANK BATTALION, 1958, A
TANK COMMANDO
TANK COMMANDOS, 1959, A
TANK FORCE, 1958, A
TANKS A MILLION, 1941, A
TANKS ARE COMING, THE, 1951, A
TANNED LEGS, 1929, A
TANSY, 1921
TANTE ZITA
TANYA, 1976
TANYA'S ISLAND, 1981, O
TAP ROOTS, 1948, C
TAPS, 1981, C
TAR HEEL WARRIOR, THE, 1917, A
TARAKANOVA, 1930
TARANTULA, 1955, A
TARANTULA, THE, 1916
TARAS BULBA, 1962, A
TARAS FAMILY, THE, 1946, A
TARAWA BEACHHEAD, 1958, A
TARGET, 1952, A
TARGET EAGLE, 1982
TARGET EARTH, 1954, A
TARGET FOR SCANDAL
TARGET HONG KONG, 1952, A
TARGET IN THE SUN
TARGET OF AN ASSASSIN, 1978
TARGET UNKNOWN, 1951, A
TARGET ZERO, 1955, A
TARGET, THE, 1916, A
TARGET: HARRY, 1980, C
TARGETS, 1968, O
TARNISH, 1924
TARNISHED, 1950, A
TARNISHED ANGEL, 1938, A
TARNISHED ANGELS, THE, 1957, C
TARNISHED HEROES, 1961, A
TARNISHED LADY, 1931, A
TARNISHED REPUTATIONS, 1920
TARS AND SPARS, 1946, A
TARTARS, THE, 1962, A
TARTU
TARTUFFE, 1927, A
TARZAN '65
TARZAN '66
TARZAN AND HIS MATE, 1934, A-C
TARZAN AND THE AMAZONS, 1945, A
TARZAN AND THE GOLDEN LION, 1927
TARZAN AND THE GREAT RIVER, 1967, A
TARZAN AND THE GREEN GODDESS, 1938, AA
TARZAN AND THE HUNTRESS, 1947, AA
TARZAN AND THE JUNGLE BOY, 1968, AA
TARZAN AND THE JUNGLE QUEEN
TARZAN AND THE LEOPARD WOMAN, 1946, AA
TARZAN AND THE LOST SAFARI, 1957, AA
TARZAN AND THE MERMAIDS, 1948, AA
TARZAN AND THE SHE-DEVIL, 1953, AA
TARZAN AND THE SLAVE GIRL, 1950, AA
TARZAN AND THE VALLEY OF GOLD, 1966, AA
TARZAN ESCAPES, 1936, A
TARZAN FINDS A SON, 1939, AA
TARZAN GOES TO INDIA, 1962, AA
TARZAN NO. 22
TARZAN OF THE APES, 1918, A
TARZAN THE FEARLESS, 1933, AA
TARZAN THE MAGNIFICENT, 1960, A
TARZAN TRIUMPHS, 1943, AA
TARZAN VERSUS I.B.M.
TARZAN'S DEADLY SILENCE, 1970, AA
TARZAN'S DESERT MYSTERY, 1943, AA
TARZAN'S FIGHT FOR LIFE, 1958, AA
TARZAN'S GREATEST ADVENTURE, 1959, AA
TARZAN'S HIDDEN JUNGLE, 1955, AA
TARZAN'S JUNGLE REBELLION, 1970, AA
TARZAN'S MAGIC FOUNTAIN, 1949, AA
TARZAN'S NEW YORK ADVENTURE, 1942, AA
TARZAN'S PERIL, 1951, A
TARZAN'S REVENGE, 1938, AA
TARZAN'S SAVAGE FURY, 1952, AA
TARZAN'S SECRET TREASURE, 1941, AA
TARZAN'S THREE CHALLENGES, 1963, AA
TARZAN, THE APE MAN, 1932, AA
TARZAN, THE APE MAN, 1959, A
TARZAN, THE APE MAN, 1981, O
TARZANA, THE WILD GIRL, 1973, O
TARZANOVA SMRT
TASK FORCE, 1949, A
TASTE FOR WOMEN, A, 1966, O
TASTE OF BLOOD, A, 1967, O
TASTE OF EXCITEMENT, 1969, C
TASTE OF FEAR
TASTE OF FLESH, A, 1967, O
TASTE OF HELL, A, 1973, C
TASTE OF HONEY, A, 1962, C
TASTE OF HONEY, A SWALLOW OF BRINE? A
TASTE OF HOT LEAD, A
TASTE OF LIFE, A, 1919
TASTE OF MONEY, A, 1960, A
TASTE OF SIN, A, 1983, O
TASTE THE BLOOD OF DRACULA, 1970, O
TATSU, 1962, C
TATTERED DRESS, THE, 1957, C
TATTERLY, 1919, A
TATTLERS, THE, 1920
TATTOO, 1981, O
TATTOOED STRANGER, THE, 1950, O
TAUR THE MIGHTY, 1960
TAVERN KNIGHT, THE, 1920
TAWNY PIPIT, 1947, A
TAXI, 1919
TAXI, 1953, A
TAXI 13, 1928, AAA
TAXI DANCER, THE, 1927, A
TAXI DRIVER, 1976, O
TAXI FOR TOBRUK, 1965, A
TAXI FOR TWO, 1929, A
TAXI MYSTERY, THE, 1926, A
TAXI NACH TOBRUK
TAXI TAXI, 1927, A
TAXI TO HEAVEN, 1944, A
TAXI!, 1932, A
TAZA, SON OF COCHISE, 1954, A
TE QUIERO CON LOCURA, 1935, A
TEA AND RICE, 1964, A
TEA AND SYMPATHY, 1956, C-O
TEA FOR THREE, 1927, A
TEA FOR TWO, 1950, A
TEA LEAVES IN THE WIND
TEA—WITH A KICK, 1923
TEACHER AND THE MIRACLE, THE, 1961, A
TEACHER'S PET, 1958, A
TEACHER, THE, 1974, C
TEACHERS, 1984, C-O
TEAHOUSE OF THE AUGUST MOON, THE, 1956, AA
TEAM-MATES, 1978
TEAR GAS SQUAD, 1940, A
TEARIN' INTO TROUBLE, 1927
TEARIN' LOOSE, 1925
TEARING THROUGH, 1925
TEARS, 1914
TEARS AND SMILES, 1917
TEARS FOR SIMON, 1957, A
TEARS OF HAPPINESS, 1974, A
TEASER, THE, 1925
TEASERS, THE, 1977
TECHNIQUE D'UN MEUTRE
TECKMAN MYSTERY, THE, 1955, A
TECNICA DI UN OMICIDO
TEDDY BEAR, THE
TEEN AGE TRAMP
TEEN KANYA
TEEN-AGE CRIME WAVE, 1955, C
TEEN-AGE STRANGLER, 1967, O
TEENAGE BAD GIRL, 1959, O
TEENAGE CAVEMAN, 1958, A
TEENAGE DELINQUENTS
TEENAGE DOLL, 1957, O
TEENAGE FRANKENSTEIN
TEENAGE GANG DEBS, 1966, O
TEENAGE GRAFFITI, 1977
TEENAGE HITCHHIKERS, 1975
TEENAGE LOVERS
TEENAGE MILLIONAIRE, 1961, A

TEENAGE MONSTER, 1958, A
TEENAGE MOTHER, 1967, O
TEENAGE PSYCHO MEETS BLOODY MARY
TEENAGE REBEL, 1956, A
TEENAGE TEASE, 1983
TEENAGE TEASERS, 1982
TEENAGE THUNDER, 1957, A
TEENAGE ZOMBIES, 1960, C
TEENAGER, 1975
TEENAGERS FROM OUTER SPACE, 1959, A
TEENAGERS IN SPACE, 1975, AA
TEETH, 1924
TEETH OF THE TIGER, THE, 1919
TEHERAN
TEL AVIV TAXI, 1957, A
TELEFON, 1977, C-O
TELEGIAN, THE
TELEGRAPH TRAIL, THE, 1933, A
TELEPHONE BOOK, THE, 1971
TELEPHONE GIRL, THE, 1927, A
TELEPHONE OPERATOR, 1938, A
TELEVISION SPY, 1939, A
TELEVISION TALENT, 1937, A
TELI SIROKKO
TELL ENGLAND
TELL IT TO A STAR, 1945, A
TELL IT TO SWEENEY, 1927
TELL IT TO THE JUDGE, 1949, A
TELL IT TO THE MARINES
TELL IT TO THE MARINES, 1918
TELL IT TO THE MARINES, 1926, A
TELL ME A RIDDLE, 1980, A
TELL ME IN THE SUNLIGHT, 1967, C-O
TELL ME LIES, 1968, O
TELL ME THAT YOU LOVE ME, 1983
TELL ME THAT YOU LOVE ME, JUNIE MOON, 1970, A-C
TELL NO TALES, 1939, A
TELL THEM WILLIE BOY IS HERE, 1969, C
TELL YOUR CHILDREN
TELL-TALE HEART, THE, 1962, O
TELL-TALE HEART, THE, 1934
TELLING THE WORLD, 1928, A
TELLTALE STEP, THE, 1917
TEMPERAMENTAL WIFE, A, 1919
TEMPERED STEEL, 1918
TEMPEST, 1928, A
TEMPEST, 1932, C
TEMPEST, 1958, C
TEMPEST, 1982, C-O
TEMPEST AND SUNSHINE, 1916
TEMPEST, THE, 1980
TEMPETES, 1922
TEMPLE DRAKE
TEMPLE OF DUSK, THE, 1918
TEMPLE OF VENUS, THE, 1923
TEMPLE TOWER, 1930, A
TEMPO DI MASSACRO
TEMPORAL POWER, 1916
TEMPORARY GENTLEMAN, A, 1920
TEMPORARY MARRIAGE, 1923, A
TEMPORARY SHERIFF, 1926
TEMPORARY VAGABOND, A, 1920, A
TEMPORARY WIDOW, THE, 1930, C
TEMPTATION, 1915, A
TEMPTATION, 1916
TEMPTATION, 1923, A
TEMPTATION, 1930
TEMPTATION, 1935, A
TEMPTATION, 1936, A
TEMPTATION, 1946, A
TEMPTATION, 1962, C
TEMPTATION AND THE MAN, 1916
TEMPTATION HARBOR, 1949, A
TEMPTATION OF CARLTON EARLYE, THE, 1923
TEMPTATION'S HOUR, 1916
TEMPTATIONS OF A SHOP GIRL, 1927
TEMPTATIONS OF SATAN, THE, 1914
TEMPTER, THE, 1974, A-C
TEMPTER, THE, 1978, O
TEMPTRESS AND THE MONK, THE, 1963, C
TEMPTRESS, THE, 1920
TEMPTRESS, THE, 1926, A
TEMPTRESS, THE, 1949, A
TEN CENTS A DANCE, 1931, A
TEN CENTS A DANCE, 1945, A
TEN COMMANDMENTS, THE, 1923, A
TEN COMMANDMENTS, THE, 1956, AA
TEN DAYS, 1925
TEN DAYS IN PARIS
TEN DAYS THAT SHOOK THE WORLD, 1927, A
TEN DAYS TO TULARA, 1958, A
TEN DAYS' WONDER, 1972, O
TEN DOLLAR RAISE, THE, 1921, A
$10 RAISE, 1935, A
TEN GENTLEMEN FROM WEST POINT, 1942, A
TEN GLADIATORS, THE, 1960
TEN LAPS TO GO, 1938, A
TEN LITTLE INDIANS, 1965, A
TEN LITTLE INDIANS, 1975, C
TEN LITTLE NIGGERS
TEN MILLION DOLLAR GRAB, 1966
TEN MINUTE ALIBI, 1935, A
TEN MINUTES TO KILL, 1933
TEN MINUTES TO LIVE, 1932
TEN MODERN COMMANDMENTS, 1927
TEN NIGHTS IN A BAR ROOM, 1921
TEN NIGHTS IN A BARROOM
TEN NIGHTS IN A BARROOM, 1926
TEN NIGHTS IN A BARROOM, 1931, A
10 WORTH FREDERICK, 1958, A-C
10 RILLINGTON PLACE, 1971, O
TEN OF DIAMONDS, 1917
TEN SECONDS TO HELL, 1959, A
TEN TALL MEN, 1951, AA
10:30 P.M. SUMMER, 1966, O
TEN THOUSAND BEDROOMS, 1957, A
10,000 DOLLARS BLOOD MONEY, 1966, O
10 TO MIDNIGHT, 1983, O
10 VIOLENT WOMEN, 1982, O
TEN WANTED MEN, 1955, A-C
TEN WHO DARED, 1960, A
TENANT, THE, 1976, O
TENCHU, 1970, O
TENDER COMRADE, 1943, A
TENDER DRACULA OR CONFESSIONS OF A BLOOD DRINKER, 1974
TENDER FLESH, 1976, O
TENDER HEARTS, 1955, A
TENDER HOUR, THE, 1927, A
TENDER IS THE NIGHT, 1961, C
TENDER LOVING CARE, 1974
TENDER MERCIES, 1982, A-C
TENDER SCOUNDREL, 1967, C
TENDER TRAP, THE, 1955, A
TENDER WARRIOR, THE, 1971, AAA
TENDER YEARS, THE, 1947, A-C
TENDERFEET, 1928
TENDERFOOT GOES WEST, A, 1937, A
TENDERFOOT, THE, 1917
TENDERFOOT, THE, 1932, A
TENDERLOIN, 1928, A
TENDERLY
TENDRE POULET
TENDRE VOYOU
TENNESSEE BEAT, THE
TENNESSEE CHAMP, 1954, A
TENNESSEE JOHNSON, 1942, A
TENNESSEE'S PARDNER, 1916, A
TENNESSEE'S PARTNER, 1955, C
TENSION, 1949, O
TENSION AT TABLE ROCK, 1956, A
TENTACLES, 1977, C
TENTACLES OF THE NORTH, 1926
TENTH AVENUE, 1928
TENTH AVENUE ANGEL, 1948, A
TENTH AVENUE KID, 1938, A
TENTH CASE, THE, 1917
TENTH MAN, THE, 1937, A
TENTH VICTIM, THE, 1965, O
TENTH WOMAN, THE, 1924
TENTING TONIGHT ON THE OLD CAMP GROUND, 1943, A
TENTS OF ALLAH, THE, 1923
TEOREMA, 1969, O
TERCENTENARY OF THE ROMANOV DYNASTY'S
TERESA, 1951, A
TERESA RAQUIN, 1915
TERM OF TRIAL, 1962, C
TERMINAL ISLAND, 1973, O
TERMINAL MAN, THE, 1974, C
TERMINAL STATION
TERMINATOR, THE, 1984, O
TERMS OF ENDEARMENT, 1983, A-C
TERRA EM TRANSE
TERRACE, THE, 1964, O
TERREUR, 1924
TERRIBLE BEAUTY, A
TERRIBLE ONE, THE, 1915
TERRIBLE REVENGE, A, 1913
TERRIFIED, 1963, O
TERROR, 1928
TERROR, 1979, O
TERROR ABOARD, 1933, A
TERROR AFTER MIDNIGHT, 1965, C
TERROR AT BLACK FALLS, 1962, C
TERROR AT HALFDAY
TERROR AT MIDNIGHT, 1956, A
TERROR BENEATH THE SEA, 1966, C
TERROR BY NIGHT, 1946, A
TERROR BY NIGHT, 1931
TERROR CASTLE
TERROR CIRCUS
TERROR EN EL ESPACIO
TERROR EYES, 1981, O
TERROR FACTOR, THE
TERROR FROM THE SUN
TERROR FROM THE UNKNOWN, 1983
TERROR FROM THE YEAR 5,000, 1958, A
TERROR FROM UNDER THE HOUSE, 1971, C
TERROR HOUSE, 1942, C
TERROR HOUSE, 1972, O
TERROR IN A TEXAS TOWN, 1958, A
TERROR IN THE CITY
TERROR IN THE CRYPT, 1963
TERROR IN THE HAUNTED HOUSE
TERROR IN THE JUNGLE, 1968, A
TERROR IN THE MIDNIGHT SUN
TERROR IN THE SWAMP, 1984
TERROR IN THE WAX MUSEUM, 1973, C
TERROR IS A MAN, 1959, C
TERROR ISLAND, 1920
TERROR MOUNTAIN, 1928
TERROR OF BAR X, THE, 1927, A
TERROR OF DR. CHANEY, THE
TERROR OF DR. MABUSE, THE, 1965, C
TERROR OF FRANKENSTEIN
TERROR OF GODZILLA
TERROR OF PUEBLO, THE, 1924
TERROR OF SHEBA
TERROR OF THE BLACK MASK, 1967, A
TERROR OF THE BLOODHUNTERS, 1962, A
TERROR OF THE HATCHET MEN
TERROR OF THE MAD DOCTOR, THE
TERROR OF THE PLAINS, 1934
TERROR OF THE TONGS, THE, 1961, O
TERROR OF TINY TOWN, THE, 1938, A
TERROR ON A TRAIN, 1953, A
TERROR ON BLOOD ISLAND
TERROR ON TIPTOE, 1936, A
TERROR ON TOUR, 1980, O
TERROR SHIP, 1954, A
TERROR STREET, 1953, A
TERROR STRIKES, THE
TERROR TRAIL, 1933, A
TERROR TRAIL, 1946
TERROR TRAIN, 1980, O
TERROR, THE, 1917
TERROR, THE, 1920
TERROR, THE, 1926
TERROR, THE, 1928, A
TERROR, THE, 1941, A
TERROR, THE, 1963, C
TERROR-CREATURES FROM THE GRAVE, 1967, O
TERRORE NELLO SPAZIO
TERRORISTS, THE, 1975, C
TERRORNAUTS, THE, 1967, A
TERRORS ON HORSEBACK, 1946, A
TESEO CONTRO IL MINOTAURO
TESHA, 1929, A
TESS, 1980, A-C
TESS OF THE D'URBERVILLES, 1924, A
TESS OF THE STORM COUNTRY, 1914, A
TESS OF THE STORM COUNTRY, 1922, A
TESS OF THE STORM COUNTRY, 1932, A
TESS OF THE STORM COUNTRY, 1961, A
TESSIE, 1925
TEST OF DONALD NORTON, THE, 1926
TEST OF HONOR, THE, 1919
TEST OF LOYALTY, THE, 1918
TEST OF PILOT PIRX, THE, 1978, C
TEST OF WOMANHOOD, THE, 1917
TEST PILOT, 1938, A
TEST, THE, 1915
TEST, THE, 1916
TESTAMENT, 1983, A
TESTAMENT OF DR. MABUSE, THE, 1943, C
TESTAMENT OF DR. MABUSE, THE, 1965
TESTAMENT OF ORPHEUS, 1962, C
TESTIGO PARA UN CRIMEN
TESTIMONY, 1920
TESTING BLOCK, THE, 1920, A
TESTING OF MILDRED VANE, THE, 1918
TEUFEL IN SEIDE
TEVYA, 1939, A
TEX, 1926
TEX, 1982, A
TEX RIDES WITH THE BOY SCOUTS, 1937, A
TEX TAKES A HOLIDAY, 1932, A
TEXAN MEETS CALAMITY JANE, THE, 1950, A
TEXAN'S HONOR, A, 1929
TEXAN, THE, 1920
TEXAN, THE, 1930, A
TEXAN, THE, 1932
TEXANS NEVER CRY, 1951, A
TEXANS, THE, 1938, A
TEXAS, 1922
TEXAS, 1941, A
TEXAS ACROSS THE RIVER, 1966, A
TEXAS BAD MAN, 1932, A
TEXAS BAD MAN, 1953, A
TEXAS BEARCAT, THE, 1925
TEXAS BUDDIES, 1932, A
TEXAS CARNIVAL, 1951, A
TEXAS CHAIN SAW MASSACRE, THE, 1974, O
TEXAS CITY, 1952, A
TEXAS COWBOY, A, 1929

TEXAS CYCLONE, 1932, A
TEXAS DESPERADOS
TEXAS DETOUR, 1978
TEXAS DYNAMO, 1950, A
TEXAS FLASH, 1928
TEXAS GUN FIGHTER, 1932, A
TEXAS JACK, 1935
TEXAS JUSTICE, 1942
TEXAS KID
TEXAS KID, OUTLAW
TEXAS KID, THE, 1944, A
TEXAS LADY, 1955, A
TEXAS LAWMEN, 1951, A
TEXAS LIGHTNING, 1981, O
TEXAS MAN HUNT, 1942, A
TEXAS MARSHAL, THE, 1941, A
TEXAS MASQUERADE, 1944, A
TEXAS PANHANDLE, 1945
TEXAS PIONEERS, 1932, A
TEXAS RAMBLER, THE, 1935
TEXAS RANGER, THE, 1931, A
TEXAS RANGERS RIDE AGAIN, 1940, A
TEXAS RANGERS, THE, 1936, A
TEXAS RANGERS, THE, 1951, A
TEXAS RENEGADES, 1940
TEXAS ROAD AGENT
TEXAS ROSE
TEXAS SERENADE
TEXAS STAGECOACH, 1940, A
TEXAS STAMPEDE, 1939, A
TEXAS STEER, A, 1915
TEXAS STEER, A, 1915
TEXAS STEER, A, 1927, A
TEXAS STREAK, THE, 1926
TEXAS TERROR, 1935, A
TEXAS TERROR, THE, 1926
TEXAS TERRORS, 1940, A
TEXAS TO BATAAN, 1942, A
TEXAS TOMMY, 1928
TEXAS TORNADO, 1934, A
TEXAS TORNADO, THE, 1928
TEXAS TRAIL, 1937, A
TEXAS TRAIL, THE, 1925
TEXAS TROUBLE SHOOTERS, 1942
TEXAS WILDCATS, 1939, A
TEXAS, BROOKLYN AND HEAVEN, 1948, A
TEXICAN, THE, 1966, A
THAIS, 1914, C
THAIS, 1917
THANK EVANS, 1938, A
THANK GOD IT'S FRIDAY, 1978, C
THANK HEAVEN FOR SMALL FAVORS, 1965, A
THANK YOU, 1925
THANK YOU ALL VERY MUCH, 1969, C
THANK YOU, AUNT, 1969, O
THANK YOU, JEEVES, 1936, A
THANK YOU, MR. MOTO, 1937, A
THANK YOUR LUCKY STARS, 1943, A
THANK YOUR STARS
THANKS A MILLION, 1935, A
THANKS FOR EVERYTHING, 1938, A
THANKS FOR LISTENING, 1937, A
THANKS FOR THE BUGGY RIDE, 1928, A
THANKS FOR THE MEMORY, 1938, A
THANOS AND DESPINA, 1970, C
THARK, 1932, A
THAT BRENNAN GIRL, 1946, A
THAT CERTAIN AGE, 1938, A
THAT CERTAIN FEELING, 1956, A
THAT CERTAIN SOMETHING, 1941, A
THAT CERTAIN THING, 1928
THAT CERTAIN WOMAN, 1937, A-C
THAT CHAMPIONSHIP SEASON, 1982, O
THAT COLD DAY IN THE PARK, 1969, O
THAT CURSED WINTER'S DAY, DJANGO & SARTANA TO THE LAST SHOT, 1970
THAT DANGEROUS AGE
THAT DARN CAT, 1965, AAA
THAT DEVIL QUEMADO, 1925
THAT DEVIL, BATEESE, 1918
THAT FORSYTE WOMAN, 1949, A-C
THAT FRENCH LADY, 1924
THAT FUNNY FEELING, 1965, C
THAT GANG OF MINE, 1940, A
THAT GIRL FROM BEVERLY HILLS
THAT GIRL FROM COLLEGE
THAT GIRL FROM PARIS, 1937, A
THAT GIRL IS A TRAMP, 1974
THAT GIRL MONTANA, 1921
THAT GIRL OKLAHOMA, 1926
THAT HAGEN GIRL, 1947, A-C
THAT HAMILTON WOMAN, 1941, A
THAT HOUSE IN THE OUTSKIRTS, 1980, C-O
THAT I MAY LIVE, 1937, A
THAT I MAY SEE, 1953
THAT KIND OF GIRL
THAT KIND OF GIRL, 1963, O
THAT KIND OF WOMAN, 1959, C
THAT LADY, 1955, C
THAT LADY IN ERMINE, 1948, A
THAT LUCKY TOUCH, 1975, A-C
THAT MAD MR. JONES
THAT MAN BOLT, 1973, O
THAT MAN FLINTSTONE
THAT MAN FROM RIO, 1964, A
THAT MAN FROM TANGIER, 1953, A
THAT MAN GEORGE, 1967, A-C
THAT MAN IN ISTANBUL, 1966, A-C
THAT MAN JACK, 1925
THAT MAN MR. JONES
THAT MAN OF MINE, 1947
THAT MAN'S HERE AGAIN, 1937, A
THAT MIDNIGHT KISS, 1949, A
THAT MODEL FROM PARIS, 1926
THAT MURDER IN BERLIN, 1929
THAT NAVY SPIRIT
THAT NAZTY NUISANCE, 1943, A
THAT NIGHT, 1957, A
THAT NIGHT IN LONDON
THAT NIGHT IN RIO, 1941, A-C
THAT NIGHT WITH YOU, 1945, A
THAT NIGHT'S WIFE, 1930
THAT OBSCURE OBJECT OF DESIRE, 1977, O
THAT OLD GANG OF MINE, 1925
THAT OTHER WOMAN, 1942, A
THAT RIVIERA TOUCH, 1968, A
THAT SINKING FEELING, 1979, A
THAT SOMETHING, 1921
THAT SORT, 1916
THAT SPLENDID NOVEMBER, 1971, C-O
THAT SUMMER, 1979, A-C
THAT TENDER AGE
THAT TENDER TOUCH, 1969, O
THAT TENNESSEE BEAT, 1966, A
THAT TEXAS JAMBOREE, 1946
THAT THEY MAY LIVE
THAT TOUCH OF MINK, 1962
THAT TOUCH OF MINK, 1962, C
THAT UNCERTAIN FEELING, 1941, A
THAT WAY WITH WOMEN, 1947, A
THAT WILD WEST, 1924
THAT WOMAN, 1922
THAT WOMAN, 1968, C-O
THAT WOMAN OPPOSITE
THAT WONDERFUL URGE, 1948, A
THAT'LL BE THE DAY, 1974, C
THAT'S A GOOD GIRL, 1933, A
THAT'S GOOD, 1919
THAT'S GRATITUDE, 1934, A
THAT'S MY BABY, 1926, A
THAT'S MY BABY, 1944, A
THAT'S MY BOY, 1932, A
THAT'S MY BOY, 1951, A
THAT'S MY DADDY, 1928
THAT'S MY GAL, 1947, A
THAT'S MY MAN, 1947, A
THAT'S MY STORY, 1937, A
THAT'S MY UNCLE, 1935, A
THAT'S MY WIFE, 1933, A
THAT'S RIGHT—YOU'RE WRONG, 1939, A
THAT'S THE SPIRIT, 1945, A
THAT'S THE TICKET, 1940, A
THAT'S THE WAY OF THE WORLD, 1975, C
THAT'S YOUR FUNERAL, 1974
THEATRE OF BLOOD, 1973, O
THEATRE OF DEATH, 1967, C-O
THEATRE ROYAL, 1943, A
THEATRE ROYAL, 1930
THEIR BIG MOMENT, 1934, A
THEIR COMPACT, 1917
THEIR HOUR, 1928
THEIR MAD MOMENT, 1931
THEIR MUTUAL CHILD, 1920
THEIR NIGHT OUT, 1933, A
THEIR ONLY CHANCE, 1978
THEIR OWN DESIRE, 1929, A
THEIR SECRET AFFAIR
THELMA, 1918
THELMA, 1922, A
THELMA JORDAN
THEM NICE AMERICANS, 1958, A
THEM?, 1954, C
THEN CAME THE WOMAN, 1926
THEN I'LL COME BACK TO YOU, 1916
THEN THERE WERE THREE, 1961, A-C
THEN YOU'LL REMEMBER ME, 1918
THEODORA, 1921
THEODORA GOES WILD, 1936, A
THEOREM
THERE AIN'T NO JUSTICE, 1939, A
THERE ARE NO VILLAINS, 1921
THERE GOES KELLY, 1945, A
THERE GOES MY GIRL, 1937, A
THERE GOES MY HEART, 1938, A
THERE GOES SUSIE
THERE GOES THE BRIDE, 1933, A
THERE GOES THE BRIDE, 1980, C
THERE GOES THE GROOM, 1937, A
THERE IS ANOTHER SUN
THERE IS NO 13, 1977, O
THERE IS STILL ROOM IN HELL, 1963, C-O
THERE WAS A CROOKED MAN, 1962, A
THERE WAS A CROOKED MAN, 1970, C
THERE WAS A YOUNG LADY, 1953, A
THERE WAS A YOUNG MAN, 1937, A
THERE WAS AN OLD COUPLE, 1967, A
THERE YOU ARE, 1926
THERE'S A GIRL IN MY HEART, 1949, A
THERE'S A GIRL IN MY SOUP, 1970, C
THERE'S ALWAYS A THURSDAY, 1957, A
THERE'S ALWAYS A WOMAN, 1938, A
THERE'S ALWAYS TOMORROW
THERE'S ALWAYS TOMORROW, 1956, A
THERE'S ALWAYS VANILLA, 1972, C
THERE'S MAGIC IN MUSIC, 1941, A
THERE'S MILLIONS IN IT, 1924
THERE'S NO BUSINESS LIKE SHOW BUSINESS, 1954, A
THERE'S NO PLACE BY SPACE
THERE'S ONE BORN EVERY MINUTE, 1942, A
THERE'S SOMETHING ABOUT A SOLDIER, 1943, A
THERE'S SOMETHING FUNNY GOING ON
THERE'S THAT WOMAN AGAIN, 1938, AA
THERESE, 1963, O
THERESE AND ISABELLE, 1968, O
THERESE DESQUEYROUX
THERESE RAQUIN, 1928
THERESE UND ISABELL
THESE ARE THE DAMNED, 1965, C
THESE CHARMING PEOPLE, 1931, A
THESE DANGEROUS YEARS
THESE GLAMOUR GIRLS, 1939, A
THESE THIRTY YEARS, 1934, A
THESE THOUSAND HILLS, 1959, A
THESE THREE, 1936, C
THESE WILDER YEARS, 1956, C
THESEUS AGAINST THE MINOTAUR
THEY ALL COME OUT, 1939, A
THEY ALL DIED LAUGHING
THEY ALL KISSED THE BRIDE, 1942, A-C
THEY ALL LAUGHED, 1981, A
THEY ARE GUILTY
THEY ARE NOT ANGELS, 1948, A
THEY ASKED FOR IT, 1939, A
THEY CALL HER ONE EYE, 1974, O
THEY CALL IT SIN, 1932, A
THEY CALL ME BRUCE, 1982, C
THEY CALL ME HALLELUJAH, 1973
THEY CALL ME MISTER TIBBS, 1970, C
THEY CALL ME ROBERT, 1967, A
THEY CALL ME TRINITY, 1971, A
THEY CALLED HIM AMEN, 1972
THEY CAME BY NIGHT, 1940, A
THEY CAME FROM BEYOND SPACE, 1967, A
THEY CAME FROM WITHIN, 1976, O
THEY CAME TO A CITY, 1944, A
THEY CAME TO BLOW UP AMERICA, 1943, A
THEY CAME TO CORDURA, 1959, C-O
THEY CAME TO ROB LAS VEGAS, 1969, O
THEY CAN'T HANG ME, 1955, A
THEY DARE NOT LOVE, 1941, A
THEY DIDN'T KNOW, 1936, A
THEY DIED WITH THEIR BOOTS ON, 1942, A
THEY DON'T WEAR PAJAMAS AT ROSIE'S
THEY DRIVE BY NIGHT, 1938, C
THEY DRIVE BY NIGHT, 1940, A-C
THEY FLEW ALONE
THEY GAVE HIM A GUN, 1937, A
THEY GOT ME COVERED, 1943, A
THEY HAD TO SEE PARIS, 1929, A
THEY JUST HAD TO GET MARRIED, 1933, A
THEY KNEW MR. KNIGHT, 1945, A
THEY KNEW WHAT THEY WANTED, 1940, C
THEY LEARNED ABOUT WOMEN, 1930, A
THEY LIKE 'EM ROUGH, 1922
THEY LIVE BY NIGHT, 1949, C
THEY LIVE IN FEAR, 1944, A
THEY LOVE AS THEY PLEASE
THEY LOVED LIFE
THEY MADE HER A SPY, 1939, A
THEY MADE ME A CRIMINAL
THEY MADE ME A CRIMINAL, 1939, A
THEY MADE ME A FUGITIVE
THEY MADE ME A KILLER, 1946, A
THEY MEET AGAIN, 1941, A
THEY MET AT MIDNIGHT
THEY MET IN A TAXI, 1936, A
THEY MET IN ARGENTINA, 1941, A
THEY MET IN BOMBAY, 1941, A
THEY MET IN THE DARK, 1945, A
THEY MET ON SKIS, 1940, A
THEY MIGHT BE GIANTS, 1971, A
THEY NEVER COME BACK, 1932, A
THEY ONLY KILL THEIR MASTERS, 1972, C
THEY PASS THIS WAY
THEY RAID BY NIGHT, 1942, A
THEY RAN FOR THEIR LIVES, 1968, A

THEY RODE WEST, 1954, A
THEY SAVED HITLER'S BRAIN, 1964, C
THEY SHALL HAVE MUSIC, 1939, A
THEY SHALL PAY, 1921
THEY SHOOT HORSES, DON'T THEY?, 1969, O
THEY WANTED PEACE, 1940, A
THEY WANTED TO MARRY, 1937, A
THEY WENT THAT-A-WAY AND THAT-A-WAY, 1978, C
THEY WERE EXPENDABLE, 1945, A
THEY WERE FIVE, 1938, A
THEY WERE NOT DIVIDED, 1951, A
THEY WERE SISTERS, 1945, A
THEY WERE SO YOUNG, 1955, A
THEY WERE TEN, 1961, A
THEY WHO DARE, 1954, A
THEY WON'T BELIEVE ME, 1947, C
THEY WON'T FORGET, 1937, C
THEY'RE A WEIRD MOB, 1966, A
THEY'RE COMING TO GET YOU, 1976
THEY'RE OFF
THEY'RE OFF, 1917
THEY'RE OFF, 1922
THEY'RE PLAYING WITH FIRE, 1984, O
THIEF, 1916
THIEF, 1981, O
THIEF IN PARADISE, A, 1925
THIEF IN THE DARK, A, 1928
THIEF OF BAGDAD, THE, 1924, A
THIEF OF BAGHDAD, THE, 1940, AAA
THIEF OF BAGHDAD, THE, 1961, A
THIEF OF DAMASCUS, 1952, A
THIEF OF HEARTS, 1984, C-O
THIEF OF PARIS, THE, 1967, A
THIEF OF VENICE, THE, 1952, A
THIEF WHO CAME TO DINNER, THE, 1973, A
THIEF, THE, 1915, A
THIEF, THE, 1920
THIEF, THE, 1952, C
THIEVES, 1919
THIEVES, 1977, A
THIEVES FALL OUT, 1941, A
THIEVES LIKE US, 1974, C
THIEVES' GOLD, 1918
THIEVES' HIGHWAY, 1949, C
THIÈVES' HOLIDAY
THIN AIR
THIN ICE, 1919
THIN ICE, 1937, A
THIN LINE, THE, 1967, C
THIN MAN GOES HOME, THE, 1944, A
THIN MAN, THE, 1934, A
THIN RED LINE, THE, 1964, O
THING THAT CAME FROM ANOTHER WORLD, THE
THING THAT COULDN'T DIE, THE, 1958, C
THING WITH TWO HEADS, THE, 1972, C
THING WITHOUT A FACE, A
THING, THE, 1951, C
THING, THE, 1982, O
THINGS ARE LOOKING UP, 1934, A
THINGS ARE TOUGH ALL OVER, 1982, O
THINGS HAPPEN AT NIGHT, 1948, A
THINGS MEN DO, 1921
THINGS OF LIFE, THE, 1970, C
THINGS TO COME, 1936
THINGS WE LOVE, THE, 1918
THINGS WIVES TELL, 1926
THINK DIRTY, 1970, O
THINK FAST, MR. MOTO, 1937, A
THINK IT OVER, 1917
THIRD ALARM, THE, 1922, A
THIRD ALARM, THE, 1930, A
THIRD ALIBI, THE, 1961, A
THIRD CLUE, THE, 1934, A
THIRD DAY, THE, 1965, C
THIRD DEGREE, THE, 1914
THIRD DEGREE, THE, 1919
THIRD DEGREE, THE, 1926, A
THIRD EYE, THE, 1929
THIRD FINGER, LEFT HAND, 1940, A
THIRD GENERATION, THE, 1915
THIRD GENERATION, THE, 1920
THIRD KEY, THE, 1957, A
THIRD KISS, THE, 1919
THIRD LOVER, THE, 1963, O
THIRD MAN ON THE MOUNTAIN, 1959, A
THIRD MAN, THE, 1950, C
THIRD OF A MAN, 1962, C
THIRD PARTY RISK
THIRD ROAD, THE
THIRD SECRET, THE, 1964, C
THIRD STRING, THE, 1932, A
THIRD TIME LUCKY, 1931, A
THIRD TIME LUCKY, 1950, A
THIRD VISITOR, THE, 1951, A
THIRD VOICE, THE, 1960, O
THIRD WALKER, THE, 1978, C
THIRD WOMAN, THE, 1920
THIRST
THIRST, 1979, O
THIRSTY DEAD, THE, 1975, O
13 EAST STREET, 1952, A
THIRTEEN FIGHTING MEN, 1960, C
THIRTEEN FRIGHTENED GIRLS, 1963, A
THIRTEEN GHOSTS, 1960, A
THIRTEEN HOURS BY AIR, 1936, A
THIRTEEN LEAD SOLDIERS, 1948, A
13 MEN AND A GUN, 1938, A
13 RUE MADELEINE, 1946, A-C
THIRTEEN WEST STREET, 1962, O
THIRTEEN WOMEN, 1932, C
THIRTEEN, THE, 1937, A
THIRTEENTH CANDLE, THE, 1933, A
THIRTEENTH CHAIR, THE, 1919
THIRTEENTH CHAIR, THE, 1930, A
THIRTEENTH CHAIR, THE, 1937, A
THIRTEENTH GREEN, 1954
THIRTEENTH GUEST, THE, 1932, A
THIRTEENTH HOUR, THE, 1927
13TH HOUR, THE, 1947, A
THIRTEENTH JUROR, THE, 1927
THIRTEENTH LETTER, THE, 1951, C
THIRTEENTH MAN, THE, 1937, A
THIRTIETH PIECE OF SILVER, THE, 1920
—30—, 1959, A-C
THIRTY A WEEK, 1918
THIRTY DAYS
THIRTY DAYS, 1922, A
THIRTY FOOT BRIDE OF CANDY ROCK, THE, 1959, AAA
30 IS A DANGEROUS AGE, CYNTHIA, 1968, A-C
39 STEPS, THE, 1935, A
THIRTY NINE STEPS, THE, 1960, C
THIRTY NINE STEPS, THE, 1978, C
THIRTY SECONDS OVER TOKYO, 1944, A
THIRTY-SIX HOURS
36 HOURS, 1965, C
THIRTY SIX HOURS TO KILL, 1936
THIRTY SIX HOURS TO LIVE
THIRTY YEARS BETWEEN, 1921
THIRTY YEARS LATER, 1928
THIRTY YEARS LATER, 1938
THIRTY-DAY PRINCESS, 1934, A
THIS ABOVE ALL, 1942, A
THIS ACTING BUSINESS, 1933, A
THIS ANGRY AGE, 1958, C
THIS COULD BE THE NIGHT, 1957, AA
THIS DAY AND AGE, 1933, A
THIS EARTH IS MINE, 1959, O
THIS ENGLAND, 1941, A
THIS FREEDOM, 1923
THIS GREEN HELL, 1936, A
THIS GUN FOR HIRE, 1942, C-O
THIS HAPPY BREED, 1944, A
THIS HAPPY FEELING, 1958, A
THIS HERO STUFF, 1919, A
THIS IMMORAL AGE
THIS IS A HIJACK, 1973, C
THIS IS ELVIS, 1982, A
THIS IS HEAVEN, 1929, A
THIS IS MY AFFAIR, 1937, A
THIS IS MY LOVE, 1954, O
THIS IS MY STREET, 1964, O
THIS IS NOT A TEST, 1962, A
THIS IS SPINAL TAP, 1984, C-O
THIS IS THE ARMY, 1943, AA
THIS IS THE LIFE, 1917
THIS IS THE LIFE, 1933, A
THIS IS THE LIFE, 1935, A
THIS IS THE LIFE, 1944, A
THIS IS THE NIGHT, 1932, A
THIS ISLAND EARTH, 1955, A
THIS LAND IS MINE, 1943, A
THIS LOVE OF OURS, 1945, C
THIS MAD WORLD, 1930, C
THIS MADDING CROWD, 1964, C
THIS MAN CAN'T DIE, 1970, O
THIS MAN IN PARIS, 1939, A
THIS MAN IS DANGEROUS
THIS MAN IS MINE, 1934, A
THIS MAN IS MINE, 1946, A
THIS MAN IS NEWS, 1939, A
THIS MAN MUST DIE, 1970, O
THIS MAN REUTER
THIS MAN'S NAVY, 1945, AA
THIS MARRIAGE BUSINESS, 1927, A
THIS MARRIAGE BUSINESS, 1938, A
THIS MODERN AGE, 1931, A-C
THIS OTHER EDEN, 1959, A
THIS PROPERTY IS CONDEMNED, 1966, O
THIS REBEL AGE
THIS REBEL BREED, 1960, O
THIS RECKLESS AGE, 1932, A
THIS SAVAGE LAND, 1969, A
THIS SIDE OF HEAVEN, 1934, AA
THIS SIDE OF THE LAW, 1950, C
THIS SPECIAL FRIENDSHIP, 1967, O
THIS SPORTING AGE, 1932, A
THIS SPORTING LIFE, 1963, O
THIS STRANGE PASSION TORMENTS
THIS STUFF'LL KILL YA!, 1971, O
THIS THING CALLED LOVE, 1929, C
THIS THING CALLED LOVE, 1940, O
THIS TIME FOR KEEPS, 1942, A
THIS TIME FOR KEEPS, 1947, AAA
THIS TIME FOREVER, 1981
THIS WAS A WOMAN, 1949, O
THIS WAS PARIS, 1942, C
THIS WAY PLEASE, 1937, AA
THIS WEEK OF GRACE, 1933, A
THIS WINE OF LOVE, 1948, AA
THIS WOMAN, 1924
THIS WOMAN IS DANGEROUS, 1952, A-C
THIS WOMAN IS MINE
THIS WOMAN IS MINE, 1941, A
THIS'LL MAKE YOU WHISTLE, 1938, A
THIS, THAT AND THE OTHER, 1970, O
THISTLEDOWN, 1938, A
THOMAS CROWN AFFAIR, THE, 1968, C
THOMASINE AND BUSHROD, 1974, O
THOR AND THE AMAZON WOMEN, 1960
THORNS AND ORANGE BLOSSOMS, 1922, A
THOROBRED, 1922
THOROUGHBRED, 1932, A
THOROUGHBRED, 1936, C
THOROUGHBRED, THE, 1916
THOROUGHBRED, THE, 1916
THOROUGHBRED, THE, 1925
THOROUGHBRED, THE, 1928
THOROUGHBRED, THE, 1930, A
THOROUGHBREDS
THOROUGHBREDS, 1945, AA
THOROUGHBREDS DON'T CRY, 1937, AA
THOROUGHBREDS, THE, 1977
THOROUGHLY MODERN MILLIE, 1967, A
THOSE CALLOWAYS, 1964, AA
THOSE DARING YOUNG MEN IN THEIR JAUNTY JALOPIES, 1969, A
THOSE DIRTY DOGS, 1974, C
THOSE ENDEARING YOUNG CHARMS, 1945, A
THOSE FANTASTIC FLYING FOOLS, 1967, AAA
THOSE HIGH GREY WALLS, 1939, C
THOSE KIDS FROM TOWN, 1942, A
THOSE LIPS, THOSE EYES, 1980, O
THOSE MAGNIFICENT MEN IN THEIR FLYING MACHINES, ACHI, A
THOSE PEOPLE NEXT DOOR, 1952, A
THOSE REDHEADS FROM SEATTLE, 1953, AA
THOSE THREE FRENCH GIRLS, 1930, A
THOSE WE LOVE, 1932, C
THOSE WERE THE DAYS, 1934, A
THOSE WERE THE DAYS, 1940, A
THOSE WERE THE HAPPY TIMES
THOSE WHO DANCE, 1924
THOSE WHO DANCE, 1930, A
THOSE WHO DARE, 1924
THOSE WHO JUDGE, 1924
THOSE WHO LOVE, 1929, A
THOSE WHO PAY, 1918
THOSE WHO TOIL, 1916
THOSE WITHOUT SIN, 1917, A
THOU ART THE MAN, 1915
THOU ART THE MAN, 1916
THOU ART THE MAN, 1920, A
THOU FOOL, 1926, A
THOU SHALT HONOR THY WIFE
THOU SHALT NOT
THOU SHALT NOT, 1914, A
THOU SHALT NOT, 1919
THOU SHALT NOT COVET, 1916
THOU SHALT NOT KILL, 1915
THOU SHALT NOT KILL, 1939, A
THOU SHALT NOT KILL
THOU SHALT NOT LOVE, 1922
THOU SHALT NOT STEAL, 1917
THOU SHALT NOT STEAL, 1929
THOUGHT, 1916
THOUGHTLESS WOMEN, 1920
THOUSAND AND ONE NIGHTS, A, 1945, A
THOUSAND CLOWNS, A, 1965, A-C
THOUSAND CRANES, 1969, O
THOUSAND DOLLAR HUSBAND, THE, 1916
THOUSAND EYES OF DR. MABUSE, THE, 1960, O
THOUSAND PLANE RAID, THE
THOUSAND TO ONE, A, 1920
THOUSANDS CHEER, 1943, A
THREADS, 1932, A
THREADS OF DESTINY, 1914
THREADS OF FATE, 1917
THREAT, THE, 1949, O
THREAT, THE, 1960, O
THREE, 1967, C
THREE, 1969, O
THREE AGES, THE, 1923, A
THREE BAD MEN, 1926
THREE BAD MEN IN THE HIDDEN FORTRESS
THREE BAD SISTERS, 1956

THREE BITES OF THE APPLE, 1967, A
THREE BLACK TRUMPS, THE, 1915
THREE BLIND MICE, 1938, A
THREE BLONDES IN HIS LIFE, 1961, C
THREE BRAVE MEN, 1957, A
THREE BROADWAY GIRLS
THREE BROTHERS
THREE BROTHERS, 1982, C
THREE BUCKAROOS, THE, 1922
THREE BULLETS FOR A LONG GUN, 1973
THREE CABALLEROS, THE, 1944, AAA
THREE CAME HOME, 1950, O
THREE CAME TO KILL, 1960, C
THREE CARD MONTE, 1978, C
THREE CASES OF MURDER, 1955, A
THREE CHEERS FOR LOVE, 1936, A
THREE CHEERS FOR THE IRISH, 1940, A
THREE COCKEYED SAILORS, 1940, A
THREE COINS IN THE FOUNTAIN, 1954, C
THREE COMRADES, 1938, A
THREE CORNERED FATE, 1954, A
THREE CRAZY LEGIONNAIRES, THE
THREE CROOKED MEN, 1958, A
THREE CROWNS OF THE SAILOR, 1984, O
THREE DARING DAUGHTERS, 1948, A
THREE DAUGHTERS, 1949
THREE DAYS AND A CHILD
THREE DAYS OF THE CONDOR, 1975, C-O
THREE DAYS OF VIKTOR TSCHERNIKOFF, 1968, C
THREE DAYS TO LIVE, 1924
THREE DESPERATE MEN, 1951, A
THREE DIMENSIONS OF GRETA, 1973
THREE DOLLS FROM HONG KONG, 1966, C
THREE DOLLS GO TO HONG KONG
THREE FABLES OF LOVE, 1963, C
THREE FACES EAST, 1926
THREE FACES EAST, 1930, A
THREE FACES OF A WOMAN, 1965, C
THREE FACES OF EVE, THE, 1957, A-C
THREE FACES OF SIN, 1963, O
THREE FACES WEST, 1940, A
THREE FOR BEDROOM C, 1952, A
THREE FOR JAMIE DAWN, 1956, A
THREE FOR THE SHOW, 1955, A
THREE FRIENDS AND AN INVENTION, 1928
THREE GIRLS ABOUT TOWN, 1941, A
THREE GIRLS LOST, 1931, A
THREE GODFATHERS, 1936, A
THREE GODFATHERS, THE, 1916
THREE GODFATHERS, THE, 1948, A
THREE GOLD COINS, 1920
THREE GREEN EYES, 1919
THREE GUNS FOR TEXAS, 1968, A
THREE GUYS NAMED MIKE, 1951, A
THREE HATS FOR LISA, 1965, A
THREE HEARTS FOR JULIA, 1943, A
THREE HOURS, 1927
THREE HOURS, 1944, A
THREE HOURS TO KILL, 1954, A
365 NIGHTS IN HOLLYWOOD, 1934, A
300 SPARTANS, 1962, A
300 YEAR WEEKEND, 1950, A
THREE HUSBANDS, 1950, A
THREE IN EDEN
THREE IN EXILE, 1925
THREE IN ONE, 1956, A
THREE IN THE ATTIC, 1968, O
THREE IN THE CELLAR
THREE IN THE SADDLE, 1945, A
THREE INTO TWO WON'T GO, 1969, O
3 IS A FAMILY, 1944, A
THREE JUMPS AHEAD, 1923
THREE KEYS, 1925
THREE KIDS AND A QUEEN, 1935, A
THREE KINGS, THE, 1929
THREE LEGIONNAIRES, THE, 1937, A
THREE LIGHTS, THE
THREE LITTLE GIRLS IN BLUE, 1946, A
THREE LITTLE SISTERS, 1944, A
THREE LITTLE WORDS, 1950, AA
THREE LIVE GHOSTS, 1922
THREE LIVE GHOSTS, 1929, A
THREE LIVE GHOSTS, 1935, A
THREE LIVES, 1971
THREE LIVES OF THOMASINA, THE, 1963, AAA
THREE LOVES, 1931
THREE LOVES HAS NANCY, 1938, A
THREE MARRIED MEN, 1936, A
THREE MAXIMS, THE
THREE MEN AND A GIRL, 1919
THREE MEN AND A GIRL, 1938
THREE MEN AND A GIRL, 1949, Brit.
THREE MEN FROM TEXAS, 1940, A
THREE MEN IN A BOAT, 1920
THREE MEN IN A BOAT, 1933, A
THREE MEN IN A BOAT, 1958, A
THREE MEN IN A CART, 1929
THREE MEN IN WHITE, 1944, A
THREE MEN ON A HORSE, 1936, A
THREE MEN TO DESTROY, 1980, O
MESQUITEERS, THE, 1936, A
THREE MILES OUT, 1924
THREE MILES UP, 1927
THREE MOUNTED MEN, 1918
THREE MOVES TO FREEDOM, 1960, A
THREE MUSKETEERS, THE, 1914
THREE MUSKETEERS, THE, 1921, A
THREE MUSKETEERS, THE, 1935, A
THREE MUSKETEERS, THE, 1939, A
THREE MUSKETEERS, THE, 1948, C
THREE MUSKETEERS, THE, 1974, C
THREE MUST-GET-THERES, THE, 1922
THREE NIGHTS OF LOVE, 1969, O
THREE NUTS IN SEARCH OF A BOLT, 1964, O
THREE O'CLOCK IN THE MORNING, 1923
THREE OF A KIND, 1936, A
THREE OF A KIND, 1944
THREE OF MANY, 1917
THREE OF US, THE, 1915
THREE ON A COUCH, 1966, A
THREE ON A HONEYMOON, 1934, A
THREE ON A MATCH, 1932, C
THREE ON A MEATHOOK, 1973
THREE ON A SPREE, 1961, A
THREE ON A TICKET, 1947, A
THREE ON THE TRAIL, 1936, A
THREE OUTCASTS, THE, 1929
THREE OUTLAWS, THE, 1956, A
THREE PALS, 1916
THREE PALS, 1926
THREE PASSIONS, THE, 1928
THREE PENNY OPERA, 1963, A
THREE RASCALS IN THE HIDDEN FORTRESS
THREE RING CIRCUS, 1954, A
THREE ROGUES, 1931, A
THREE RUSSIAN GIRLS, 1943, A
THREE SAILORS AND A GIRL, 1953, A
THREE SECRETS, 1950, A
THREE SERGEANTS OF BENGAL, 1965
THREE SEVENS, 1921
THREE SHADES OF LOVE
THREE SILENT MEN, 1940, A
THREE SINNERS
THREE SINNERS, 1928, C
THREE SISTERS, 1974, C
THREE SISTERS, THE, 1930, A
THREE SISTERS, THE, 1969, C
THREE SISTERS, THE, 1977, A
THREE SMART GIRLS, 1937, AA
THREE SMART GIRLS GROW UP, 1939, A
THREE SONS, 1939, A
THREE SONS O'GUNS, 1941, A
THREE SPARE WIVES, 1962, A
THREE STEPS IN THE DARK, 1953, A
THREE STEPS NORTH, 1951, A
THREE STOOGES GO AROUND THE WORLD IN A DAZE, THE, 1963, AA
THREE STOOGES IN ORBIT, THE, 1962, AA
THREE STOOGES MEET HERCULES, THE, 1962, AA
THREE STOOGES VS. THE WONDER WOMEN, 1975, C
THREE STRANGERS, 1946, A-C
THREE STRIPES IN THE SUN, 1955, A
THREE SUNDAYS TO LIVE, 1957, A
THREE SWORDS OF ZORRO, THE, 1960
THREE TALES OF CHEKHOV, 1961, A
3:10 TO YUMA, 1957, O
THREE TEXAS STEERS, 1939, A
THREE THE HARD WAY, 1974, O
THREE TO GO, 1971, A-C
THREE TOUGH GUYS, 1974, C
THREE VIOLENT PEOPLE, 1956, A
THREE WARRIORS, 1977, A
THREE WAX MEN
THREE WAX WORKS
THREE WAY LOVE, 1977
THREE WAY WEEKEND, 1979
THREE WEEK-ENDS, 1928
THREE WEEKS, 1915
THREE WEEKS, 1924
THREE WEEKS IN PARIS, 1925
THREE WEEKS OF LOVE, 1965, A
THREE WEIRD SISTERS, THE, 1948, A
THREE WHO LOVED, 1931, A
THREE WHO PAID, 1923
THREE WHO WERE DOOMED, THE
THREE WISE CROOKS, 1925
THREE WISE FOOLS, 1923, A
THREE WISE FOOLS, 1946, A
THREE WISE GIRLS, 1932, A
THREE WISE GUYS, THE, 1936, A
THREE WITNESSES, 1935, A
THREE WOMEN, 1924
THREE WOMEN, 1977, C
THREE WORD BRAND, 1921
THREE WORLDS OF GULLIVER, THE, 1960, AAA
THREE X GORDON, 1918
THREE YOUNG TEXANS, 1954, A
THREE'S A CROWD, 1927, A
THREE'S A CROWD, 1945, A
THREE'S COMPANY, 1953, A
THREE-CORNERED MOON, 1933, A
THREE-RING MARRIAGE, 1928
THREE-WAY SPLIT, 1970, O
THREEPENNY OPERA, THE, 1931, O
THREES, MENAGE A TROIS, 1968, O
THRESHOLD, 1983, C
THRILL CHASER, THE, 1923
THRILL CHASER, THE, 1928
THRILL HUNTER, THE, 1926
THRILL HUNTER, THE, 1933, A
THRILL KILLERS, THE, 1965, O
THRILL OF A LIFETIME, 1937, A
THRILL OF A ROMANCE, 1945, A
THRILL OF BRAZIL, THE, 1946, A
THRILL OF IT ALL, THE, 1963, A
THRILL OF YOUTH, 1932, C
THRILL SEEKERS
THRILL SEEKERS, THE, 1927
THRILLING YOUTH, 1926
THRONE OF BLOOD, 1961, O
THROUGH A GLASS DARKLY, 1962, O
THROUGH A GLASS WINDOW, 1922
THROUGH DANTE'S FLAMES, 1914
THROUGH DAYS AND MONTHS, 1969, AC
THROUGH DIFFERENT EYES
THROUGH FIRE AND WATER, 1923
THROUGH FIRE TO FORTUNE OR THE SUNKEN VILLAGE, 1914
THROUGH HELL TO GLORY
THROUGH STORMY WATERS, 1920
THROUGH THE BACK DOOR, 1921
THROUGH THE BREAKERS, 1928
THROUGH THE DARK, 1924
THROUGH THE STORM
THROUGH THE STORM, 1922
THROUGH THE TOILS, 1919
THROUGH THE VALLEY OF SHADOWS, 1914
THROUGH THE WALL, 1916
THROUGH THE WRONG DOOR, 1919
THROUGH THICK AND THIN, 1927
THROUGH TURBULENT WATERS, 1915
THROW A SADDLE ON A STAR, 1946
THROW OF THE DICE, 1930
THROWBACK, THE, 1935, A
THROWING LEAD, 1928
THROWN TO THE LIONS, 1916
THRU DIFFERENT EYES, 1929, A
THRU DIFFERENT EYES, 1942, A
THRU THE EYES OF MEN, 1920
THRU THE FLAMES, 1923
THUMB PRINT, THE, 1914
THUMB TRIPPING, 1972, O
THUMBELINA, 1970, AAA
THUMBS DOWN, 1927, A
THUMBS UP, 1943, A
THUNDER, 1929, A
THUNDER ACROSS THE PACIFIC
THUNDER AFLOAT, 1939, A
THUNDER ALLEY, 1967, A
THUNDER AND LIGHTNING, 1977, C
THUNDER AT THE BORDER, 1966, A
THUNDER BAY, 1953, A
THUNDER BELOW, 1932, A
THUNDER BIRDS, 1942, A
THUNDER IN CAROLINA, 1960, A
THUNDER IN DIXIE, 1965, A
THUNDER IN GOD'S COUNTRY, 1951, A
THUNDER IN THE BLOOD, 1962, C
THUNDER IN THE CITY, 1937, A
THUNDER IN THE DESERT, 1938, A
THUNDER IN THE DUST
THUNDER IN THE EAST
THUNDER IN THE EAST, 1953, A
THUNDER IN THE NIGHT, 1935, A
THUNDER IN THE PINES, 1949, A
THUNDER IN THE SUN, 1959, A
THUNDER IN THE VALLEY
THUNDER ISLAND, 1921
THUNDER ISLAND, 1963, A-C
THUNDER MOUNTAIN, 1925
THUNDER MOUNTAIN, 1935, A
THUNDER MOUNTAIN, 1947, A
THUNDER MOUNTAIN, 1964
THUNDER OF DRUMS, A, 1961, A-C
THUNDER ON THE HILL, 1951, A
THUNDER ON THE TRAIL
THUNDER OVER ARIZONA, 1956, A
THUNDER OVER HAWAII
THUNDER OVER SANGOLAND, 1955, A
THUNDER OVER TANGIER, 1957, A
THUNDER OVER TEXAS, 1934, A
THUNDER OVER THE PLAINS, 1953, A
THUNDER OVER THE PRAIRIE, 1941, A
THUNDER PASS, 1954, A
THUNDER PASS,
THUNDER RIDERS, 1928
THUNDER RIVER FEUD, 1942, A

THUNDER ROAD, 1958, C
THUNDER ROCK, 1944, A
THUNDER TOWN, 1946, A
THUNDER TRAIL, 1937, A
THUNDERBALL, 1965, A-C
THUNDERBIRD 6, 1968, A
THUNDERBIRDS, 1952, A
THUNDERBIRDS 6, 1968
THUNDERBIRDS ARE GO, 1968, A
THUNDERBOLT, 1929, A
THUNDERBOLT, 1936, A-C
THUNDERBOLT AND LIGHTFOOT, 1974, O
THUNDERBOLT STRIKES, THE, 1926
THUNDERBOLT'S TRACKS, 1927
THUNDERBOLT, THE, 1919
THUNDERBOLTS OF FATE, 1919
THUNDERCLAP, 1921
THUNDERCLOUD
THUNDERCLOUD, THE, 1919
THUNDERGAP OUTLAWS, 1947
THUNDERGATE, 1923
THUNDERGOD, 1928
THUNDERHEAD-SON OF FLICKA, 1945, AAA
THUNDERHOOF, 1948, A
THUNDERING CARAVANS, 1952, A
THUNDERING DAWN, 1923
THUNDERING FRONTIER, 1940, A
THUNDERING GUN SLINGERS, 1944, A
THUNDERING HERD, THE, 1925
THUNDERING HERD, THE, 1934, A
THUNDERING HOOFS, 1922
THUNDERING HOOFS, 1924
THUNDERING HOOFS, 1941, A
THUNDERING JETS, 1958, A
THUNDERING ROMANCE, 1924
THUNDERING SPEED, 1926
THUNDERING THOMPSON, 1929
THUNDERING THROUGH, 1925
THUNDERING TRAIL, THE, 1951, A
THUNDERING TRAILS, 1943, A
THUNDERING WEST, THE, 1939, A
THUNDERING WHEELS
THUNDERSTORM, 1934, A
THUNDERSTORM, 1956, A
THURSDAY MORNING MURDERS, THE, 1976
THURSDAY'S CHILD, 1943, A
THX 1138, 1971, C
THY NAME IS WOMAN, 1924
THY NEIGHBOR'S WIFE, 1953, C
THY SOUL SHALL BEAR WITNESS
TI-CUL TOUGAS, 1977, C
TIARA TAHITI, 1962, A
...TICK...TICK...TICK..., 1970, A
TICKET OF LEAVE, 1936, A
TICKET OF LEAVE MAN, THE, 1937, A
TICKET TO CRIME, 1934, A
TICKET TO HEAVEN, 1981, C
TICKET TO PARADISE, 1936, A
TICKET TO PARADISE, 1961, A
TICKET TO TOMAHAWK, 1950, A
TICKET-OF-LEAVE MAN, THE, 1918
TICKLE ME, 1965, A
TICKLED PINK
TICKLISH AFFAIR, A, 1963, A
TIDAL WAVE, 1975, A-C
TIDAL WAVE, 1939
TIDAL WAVE, THE, 1918
TIDAL WAVE, THE, 1920
TIDE OF EMPIRE, 1929
TIDES OF BARNEGAT, THE, 1917
TIDES OF FATE, 1917, A
TIDES OF PASSION, 1925
TIE THAT BINDS, THE, 1923, A
TIERRA BRUTAL
TIES OF BLOOD, 1921
TIFFANY JONES, 1976, O
TIFFANY MEMORANDUM, 1966
TIGER AMONG US, THE
TIGER AND THE FLAME, THE, 1955, A-C
TIGER AND THE PUSSYCAT, THE, 1967, A-C
TIGER BAY, 1933, A
TIGER BAY, 1959, A
TIGER BY THE TAIL, 1970, C
TIGER BY THE TAIL, 1958
TIGER FANGS, 1943, A
TIGER FLIGHT, 1965, A
TIGER GIRL, 1955, A
TIGER IN THE SKY
TIGER IN THE SMOKE, 1956, A
TIGER LILY, THE, 1919
TIGER LOVE, 1924
TIGER MAKES OUT, THE, 1967, A-C
TIGER MAN
TIGER MAN, THE, 1918
TIGER OF BENGAL
TIGER OF ESCHNAPUR, THE
TIGER OF THE SEA, THE, 1918
TIGER OF THE SEVEN SEAS, 1964, A
TIGER ROSE, 1923
TIGER ROSE, 1930, A
TIGER SHARK, 1932, A-C
TIGER THOMPSON, 1924
TIGER TRUE, 1921
TIGER WALKS, A, 1964, C
TIGER WOMAN, THE, 1917, A
TIGER WOMAN, THE, 1945, A
TIGER'S CLAW, THE, 1923, A
TIGER'S COAT, THE, 1920
TIGER'S CUB, 1920
TIGHT LITTLE ISLAND, 1949
TIGHT SHOES, 1941, A
TIGHT SKIRTS
TIGHT SKIRTS, LOOSE PLEASURES, 1966, O
TIGHT SPOT, 1955, O
TIGHTROPE, 1984, C-O
TIGHTROPE TO TERROR, 1977
TIGRESS, THE, 1914, A
TIGRESS, THE, 1927
TIGRIS, 1913
TIJUANA STORY, THE, 1957, A
TIKI TIKI, 1971, AAA
TIKO AND THE SHARK, 1966, A
TIKOYO AND HIS SHARK
'TIL WE MEET AGAIN, 1940, A
TILL DEATH, 1978, C-O
TILL DEATH DO US PART
'TILL I COME BACK TO YOU, 1918
TILL MARRIAGE DO US PART, 1979, O
TILL THE CLOUDS ROLL BY, 1946, AA
TILL THE END OF TIME, 1946, A-C
TILL TOMORROW COMES, 1962, C
TILL WE MEET AGAIN, 1922
TILL WE MEET AGAIN, 1936, A
TILL WE MEET AGAIN, 1944, A
TILLERS OF THE SOIL
TILLIE, 1922, A
TILLIE AND GUS, 1933, A
TILLIE THE TOILER, 1927, A
TILLIE THE TOILER, 1941, A
TILLIE WAKES UP, 1917, A
TILLIE'S PUNCTURED ROMANCE, 1914, A
TILLIE'S PUNCTURED ROMANCE, 1928, A
TILLIE'S TOMATO SURPRISE, 1915, A
TILLIE, A MENONITE MAID, 1922
TILLY OF BLOOMSBURY, 1921
TILLY OF BLOOMSBURY, 1931, A
TILLY OF BLOOMSBURY, 1940, A
TILT, 1979, C
TIM, 1981, C
TIM DRISCOLL'S DONKEY, 1955, AA
TIMBER, 1942, A
TIMBER FURY, 1950, A
TIMBER QUEEN, 1944, A
TIMBER STAMPEDE, 1939, A
TIMBER TERRORS, 1935, A
TIMBER TRAIL, THE, 1948, A
TIMBER TRAMPS, 1975
TIMBER WAR, 1936, A
TIMBER WOLF, 1925
TIMBERESQUE, 1937
TIMBERJACK, 1955, A
TIMBERLAND TERROR, 1940
TIMBUCTOO, 1933, A
TIMBUKTU, 1959, A
TIME AFTER TIME, 1979, O
TIME AND THE TOUCH, THE, 1962, C
TIME BANDITS, 1981, A-C
TIME BOMB, 1961, A
TIME BOMB, 1953
TIME FLIES, 1944, A
TIME FOR ACTION
TIME FOR DYING, A, 1971, C
TIME FOR GIVING, A
TIME FOR HEROS, A
TIME FOR KILLING, A, 1967, A
TIME FOR LOVE, A, 1974
TIME FOR LOVING, A, 1971, A-C
TIME GENTLEMEN PLEASE?, 1953, A
TIME IN THE SUN, A, 1970, O
TIME IS MY ENEMY, 1957, A
TIME LIMIT, 1957, C
TIME LOCK, 1959, A
TIME LOCK NO. 776, 1915
TIME LOCKS AND DIAMONDS, 1917
TIME LOST AND TIME REMEMBERED, 1966, A
TIME MACHINE, THE, 1960, A
TIME OF DESIRE, THE, 1957, O
TIME OF FURY, 1968
TIME OF HIS LIFE, THE, 1955, A
TIME OF INDIFFERENCE, 1965, A
TIME OF RETURN, THE
TIME OF ROSES, 1970, C
TIME OF THE HEATHEN, 1962, C
TIME OF THE WOLVES, 1970, O
TIME OF THEIR LIVES, THE, 1946, AAA
TIME OF YOUR LIFE, THE, 1948, A-C
TIME OUT FOR LOVE, 1963, A
TIME OUT FOR MURDER, 1938, A
TIME OUT FOR RHYTHM, 1941, A
TIME OUT FOR ROMANCE, 1937, A
TIME OUT OF MIND, 1947, A
TIME RUNNING OUT, 1950
TIME SLIP, 1981, C
TIME TO DIE, A, 1983, O
TIME TO KILL, 1942, A
TIME TO KILL, A, 1955, A
TIME TO LOVE, 1927, A
TIME TO LOVE AND A TIME TO DIE, A, 1958, A-C
TIME TO REMEMBER, 1962, A
TIME TO RUN, 1974
TIME TO SING, A, 1968, A
TIME TRAP
TIME TRAVELERS, THE, 1964, A
TIME WALKER, 1982, A
TIME WITHOUT PITY, 1957, C
TIME, THE COMEDIAN, 1925
TIME, THE PLACE AND THE GIRL, THE, 1929, A
TIME, THE PLACE AND THE GIRL, THE, 1946, A
TIMERIDER, 1983, C
TIMES GONE BY, 1953, C
TIMES HAVE CHANGED, 1923
TIMES SQUARE, 1929, A
TIMES SQUARE, 1980, O
TIMES SQUARE LADY, 1935, A
TIMES SQUARE PLAYBOY, 1936, A
TIMESLIP
TIMETABLE, 1956, A
TIMID TERROR, THE, 1926
TIMOTHY'S QUEST, 1922, A
TIMOTHY'S QUEST, 1936, A
TIN DRUM, THE, 1979, O
TIN GIRL, THE, 1970, A
TIN GODS, 1926, A
TIN GODS, 1932, A
TIN HATS, 1926
TIN MAN, 1983, A
TIN PAN ALLEY, 1920
TIN PAN ALLEY, 1940, A
TIN STAR, THE, 1957, A
TINDER BOX, THE, 1968, AA
TINGLER, THE, 1959, C
TINKER, 1949, AA
TINKER, 1950
TINKER, TAILOR, SOLDIER, SAILOR, 1918
TINSEL, 1918
TINTED VENUS, THE, 1921
TINTORERA...BLOODY WATERS, 1977, O
TIOGA KID, THE, 1948, A
TIP ON A DEAD JOCKEY, 1957, A-C
TIP-OFF GIRLS, 1938, A
TIP-OFF, THE, 1929
TIP-OFF, THE, 1931, A
TIPPED OFF, 1923, A
TIPTOES, 1927
TIRE AU FLANC
TIRE AU FLANC, 1929
TIRED BUSINESS MAN, THE, 1927
TIREZ SUR LE PIANISTE
'TIS A PITY SHE'S A WHORE, 1973, O
TISH, 1942, A
TIT FOR TAT, 1922
TITANIC, 1953, A-C
TITFIELD THUNDERBOLT, THE, 1953, A
TITLE SHOT, 1982, C
TNT JACKSON, 1975, O
TO A FINISH, 1921
TO ALL A GOODNIGHT, 1980, O
TO BE A CROOK, 1967, A
TO BE A LADY, 1934, A
TO BE A MAN
TO BE FREE, 1972, O
TO BE OR NOT TO BE, 1942, A
TO BE OR NOT TO BE, 1983, C
TO BEAT THE BAND, 1935, A
TO BED OR NOT TO BED
TO BEGIN AGAIN, 1982, C
TO CATCH A COP, 1984, A
TO CATCH A SPY
TO CATCH A THIEF, 1936, A
TO CATCH A THIEF, 1955, C
TO CHASE A MILLION, 1967
TO COMMIT A MURDER, 1970, C
TO DIE IN PARIS, 1968
TO DOROTHY, A SON
TO EACH HIS OWN, 1946, A-C
TO ELVIS WITH LOVE
TO FIND A MAN, 1972, A
TO HAVE AND HAVE NOT, 1944, A-C
TO HAVE AND TO HOLD, 1916
TO HAVE AND TO HOLD, 1922, A
TO HAVE AND TO HOLD, 1951, A
TO HAVE AND TO HOLD, 1963, A
TO HELL AND BACK, 1955, A-C
TO HELL WITH THE KAISER, 1918
TO HELL YOU PREACH, 1972
TO HIM THAT HATH, 1918
TO HONOR AND OBEY, 1917

TO KILL A CLOWN, 1972, C-O
TO KILL A MOCKINGBIRD, 1962, C
TO KILL OR TO DIE, 1973, C
TO LIVE
TO LIVE IN PEACE, 1947, A
TO LOVE, 1964, O
TO LOVE, PERHAPS TO DIE, 1975
TO MARY—WITH LOVE, 1936, A
TO OBLIGE A LADY, 1931, A
TO OUR LOVES
TO PARIS WITH LOVE, 1955, A
TO PLEASE A LADY, 1950, A
TO PLEASE ONE WOMAN, 1920
TO SIR, WITH LOVE, 1967, A
TO THE DEATH, 1917
TO THE DEVIL A DAUGHTER, 1976, O
TO THE ENDS OF THE EARTH, 1948, A-C
TO THE HIGHEST BIDDER, 1918
TO THE LADIES, 1923
TO THE LAST MAN, 1923, A
TO THE LAST MAN, 1933, A
TO THE SHORES OF HELL, 1966, A
TO THE SHORES OF TRIPOLI, 1942, A
TO THE VICTOR, 1938, A
TO THE VICTOR, 1948, A
TO TRAP A SPY, 1966, A
TO WHAT RED HELL, 1929, A
TOAST OF DEATH, THE, 1915
TOAST OF NEW ORLEANS, THE, 1950, A
TOAST OF NEW YORK, THE, 1937, A
TOAST OF THE LEGION
TOAST TO LOVE, 1951, A
TOBACCO ROAD, 1941, A
TOBO, THE HAPPY CLOWN, 1965
TOBOR THE GREAT, 1954, AA
TOBRUK, 1966, A
TOBY TYLER, 1960, AAA
TOBY'S BOW, 1919
TODAY, 1917, A
TODAY, 1930, A
TODAY I HANG, 1942, A
TODAY IT'S ME...TOMORROW YOU?, 1968, C
TODAY WE KILL...TOMORROW WE DIE, 1971
TODAY WE LIVE, 1933, C
TODAY WE LIVE, 1963
TODD KILLINGS, THE, 1971, O
TODD OF THE TIMES, 1919
TOGETHER, 1918
TOGETHER, 1956, A
TOGETHER AGAIN, 1944, A
TOGETHER BROTHERS, 1974, C
TOGETHER FOR DAYS, 1972, C
TOGETHER IN PARIS
TOGETHER WE LIVE, 1935, A
TOGETHERNESS, 1970
TOILER, THE, 1932
TOILERS OF THE SEA, 1923
TOILERS OF THE SEA, 1936, A
TOILERS, THE, 1919
TOILERS, THE, 1928, A
TOKIO SIREN, A, 1920
TOKOLOSHE, 1973
TOKYO AFTER DARK, 1959, A
TOKYO FILE 212, 1951, A
TOKYO JOE, 1949, A
TOKYO MARCH, 1929
TOKYO ROSE, 1945, A
TOKYO STORY, 1972, A
TOL'ABLE DAVID, 1921, A
TOL'ABLE DAVID, 1930, A
TOLD AT THE TWILIGHT, 1917
TOLD IN THE HILLS, 1919
TOLL GATE, THE, 1920
TOLL GATE, THE, 1920, A
TOLL OF LOVE, THE, 1914
TOLL OF MAMON, 1914, A
TOLL OF THE DESERT, 1936, A
TOLL OF THE SEA, THE, 1922
TOM, 1973, O
TOM AND HIS PALS, 1926, A
TOM BROWN OF CULVER, 1932, AA
TOM BROWN'S SCHOOL DAYS, 1940, AA
TOM BROWN'S SCHOOLDAYS, 1916
TOM BROWN'S SCHOOLDAYS, 1951, AA
TOM HORN, 1980, O
TOM JONES, 1917
TOM JONES, 1963, O
TOM SAWYER, 1917
TOM SAWYER, 1930, AAA
TOM SAWYER, 1973, AAA
TOM SAWYER, 1938
TOM SAWYER, DETECTIVE, 1939, A
TOM THUMB, 1958, AAA
TOM THUMB, 1967, A
TOM'S GANG, 1927
TOM, DICK AND HARRY, 1941, A
TOMAHAWK, 1951, A
TOMAHAWK AND THE CROSS, THE
TOMAHAWK TRAIL, 1957, A
TOMAHAWK TRAIL, THE, 1950
TOMB OF LIGEIA, THE, 1965, C
TOMB OF THE CAT
TOMB OF THE LIVING DEAD
TOMB OF THE UNDEAD, 1972, O
TOMB OF TORTURE, 1966, O
TOMBOY, 1940, A
TOMBOY AND THE CHAMP, 1961, A
TOMBOY, THE, 1921
TOMBOY, THE, 1924
TOMBS OF HORROR
TOMBS OF THE BLIND DEAD, 1974
TOMBSTONE CANYON, 1932, A
TOMBSTONE TERROR, 1935, A
TOMBSTONE, THE TOWN TOO TOUGH TO DIE, 1942, A
TOMCAT, THE, 1968, O
TOMCATS, 1977
TOMMY, 1975, C
TOMMY ATKINS, 1928
TOMMY STEELE STORY, THE
TOMMY THE TOREADOR, 1960, A
TOMORROW, 1972, C
TOMORROW AND TOMORROW, 1932, A
TOMORROW AT MIDNIGHT
TOMORROW AT SEVEN, 1933, A
TOMORROW AT TEN, 1964, A
TOMORROW IS ANOTHER DAY, 1951, A
TOMORROW IS FOREVER, 1946, A
TOMORROW IS MY TURN, 1962, C
TOMORROW MAN, THE, 1979
TOMORROW NEVER COMES, 1978, O
TOMORROW THE WORLD, 1944, A
TOMORROW WE LIVE, 1936, C
TOMORROW WE LIVE, 1942, A
TOMORROW'S CHILDREN, 1934
TOMORROW'S LOVE, 1925
TOMORROW'S YOUTH, 1935, A
TONG MAN, THE, 1919
TONGUES OF FLAME, 1919
TONGUES OF FLAME, 1924
TONGUES OF MEN, THE, 1916, A
TONGUES OF SCANDAL, 1927
TONI, 1928
TONI, 1968, C
TONIGHT A TOWN DIES, 1961, C
TONIGHT AND EVERY NIGHT, 1945, A
TONIGHT AT 8:30, 1953, A
TONIGHT AT TWELVE, 1929, A
TONIGHT FOR SURE, 1962, O
TONIGHT IS OURS, 1933, A
TONIGHT OR NEVER, 1931, A-C
TONIGHT THE SKIRTS FLY, 1956, C
TONIGHT WE RAID CALAIS, 1943, A
TONIGHT WE SING, 1953, A
TONIGHT'S THE NIGHT, 1932, A
TONIGHT'S THE NIGHT, 1954, A
TONIO KROGER, 1968, C
TONIO, SON OF THE SIERRAS, 1925
TONKA, 1958, AAA
TONS OF MONEY, 1924
TONS OF MONEY, 1931, A
TONS OF TROUBLE, 1956, AA
TONTO BASIN OUTLAWS, 1941, A
TONTO KID, THE, 1935
TONY AMERICA, 1918
TONY DRAWS A HORSE, 1951, A-C
TONY ROME, 1967, C
TONY RUNS WILD, 1926, A
TOO BAD SHE'S BAD, 1954, C
TOO BUSY TO WORK, 1932, A
TOO BUSY TO WORK, 1939, A
TOO DANGEROUS TO LIVE, 1939, A
TOO DANGEROUS TO LOVE
TOO FAT TO FIGHT, 1918
TOO HOT TO HANDLE, 1938, A-C
TOO HOT TO HANDLE, 1961, C
TOO HOT TO HANDLE, 1976
TOO LATE BLUES, 1962, C
TOO LATE FOR TEARS, 1949, O
TOO LATE THE HERO, 1970, C
TOO MANY BLONDES, 1941, A
TOO MANY CHEFS
TOO MANY COOKS, 1931, A
TOO MANY CROOKS, 1919
TOO MANY CROOKS, 1927
TOO MANY CROOKS, 1959, A
TOO MANY GIRLS, 1940, A
TOO MANY HUSBANDS, 1938, AA
TOO MANY HUSBANDS, 1940, A
TOO MANY KISSES, 1925
TOO MANY MILLIONS, 1918
TOO MANY MILLIONS, 1934, A
TOO MANY PARENTS, 1936, A
TOO MANY THIEVES, 1968, A
TOO MANY WINNERS, 1947, A
TOO MANY WIVES, 1927
TOO MANY WIVES, 1933, A
TOO MANY WIVES, 1937, A
TOO MANY WOMEN, 1942, A
TOO MANY WOMEN, 1931
TOO MUCH BEEF, 1936, A
TOO MUCH BUSINESS, 1922, A
TOO MUCH FOR ONE MAN
TOO MUCH HARMONY, 1933, A
TOO MUCH JOHNSON, 1920
TOO MUCH MARRIED, 1921
TOO MUCH MONEY, 1926
TOO MUCH SPEED, 1921, A
TOO MUCH WIFE, 1922
TOO MUCH YOUTH, 1925
TOO MUCH, TOO SOON, 1958, C
TOO SOON TO LOVE, 1960, C
TOO TOUGH TO KILL, 1935, A
TOO WISE WIVES, 1921
TOO YOUNG TO KISS, 1951, A
TOO YOUNG TO KNOW, 1945, A
TOO YOUNG TO LOVE, 1960, C
TOO YOUNG TO MARRY, 1931, A
TOO YOUNG, TOO IMMORAL!, 1962, O
TOOLBOX MURDERS, THE, 1978, O
TOOMORROW, 1970, A
TOOTSIE, 1982, C
TOP BANANA, 1954, A
TOP DOG, THE, 1918
TOP FLOOR GIRL, 1959, A
TOP GUN, 1955, A-C
TOP HAND, 1925
TOP HAT, 1935, A
TOP JOB
TOP MAN, 1943, A
TOP O' THE MORNING, 1949, A
TOP O' THE MORNING, THE, 1922
TOP OF NEW YORK, THE, 1925, A
TOP OF THE BILL
TOP OF THE FORM, 1953, A
TOP OF THE HEAP, 1972, O
TOP OF THE TOWN, 1937, A
TOP OF THE WORLD, 1955, A
TOP OF THE WORLD, THE, 1925
TOP SECRET
TOP SECRET AFFAIR, 1957, A
TOP SECRET!, 1984
TOP SENSATION
TOP SERGEANT, 1942, A
TOP SERGEANT MULLIGAN, 1928
TOP SERGEANT MULLIGAN, 1941, A
TOP SPEED, 1930, A
TOPA TOPA, 1938
TOPAZ, 1969, C
TOPAZE, 1933, C
TOPAZE, 1935, A
TOPEKA, 1953, A
TOPEKA TERROR, THE, 1945, A
TOPKAPI, 1964, A-C
TOPPER, 1937, A
TOPPER RETURNS, 1941, A
TOPPER TAKES A TRIP, 1939, A
TOPS IS THE LIMIT
TOPSY AND EVA, 1927
TOPSY-TURVY JOURNEY, 1970, A
TORA! TORA! TORA!, 1970, C
TORA-SAN PART 2, 1970, C
TORA-SAN'S CHERISHED MOTHER
TORCH BEARER, THE, 1916
TORCH SINGER, 1933, A
TORCH SONG, 1953, A
TORCH SONG, 953
TORCH, THE, 1950, A
TORCHBEARER, THE
TORCHLIGHT, 1984, O
TORCHY BLANE IN CHINATOWN, 1938, A
TORCHY BLANE IN PANAMA, 1938, A
TORCHY BLANE RUNS FOR MAYOR
TORCHY BLANE, THE ADVENTUROUS BLONDE
TORCHY GETS HER MAN, 1938, A
TORCHY PLAYS WITH DYNAMITE, 1939, A
TORCHY RUNS FOR MAYOR, 1939, A
TORMENT, 1924, A
TORMENT, 1947, A
TORMENT, 1950, Brit.
TORMENTED, 1960, C
TORMENTED, THE, 1978, O
TORN CURTAIN, 1966, C
TORN SAILS, 1920
TORNADO, 1943, A
TORNADO IN THE SADDLE, A, 1942
TORNADO RANGE, 1948, A
TORNADO, THE, 1924
TORPEDO ALLEY, 1953, A
TORPEDO BAY, 1964, C
TORPEDO BOAT, 1942, A
TORPEDO RUN, 1958, A-C
TORPEDOED, 1939, C
TORRENT, THE, 1921, A
TORRENT, THE, 1924
TORRENT, THE, 1926, A
TORRID ZONE, 1940, A

TORSO, 1974, O
TORSO MURDER MYSTERY, THE, 1940, C
TORTILLA FLAT, 1942, A
TORTURE CHAMBER OF DR. SADISM, THE
TORTURE DUNGEON, 1970, O
TORTURE GARDEN, 1968, O
TORTURE ME KISS ME, 1970, O
TORTURE SHIP, 1939, A
TORTURED HEART, A, 1916
TOTO AND THE POACHERS, 1958, AA
TOTO IN THE MOON, 1957, A
TOTO, VITTORIO E LA DOTTORESSA
TOTON, 1919
TOUCH AND GO, 1955, C
TOUCH ME NOT, 1974, C
TOUCH OF A CHILD, THE, 1918
TOUCH OF CLASS, A, 1973, C
TOUCH OF DEATH, 1962, A
TOUCH OF EVIL, 1958, C
TOUCH OF FLESH, THE, 1960, C
TOUCH OF HELL, A
TOUCH OF HER FLESH, THE, 1967, O
TOUCH OF HER LIFE, THE
TOUCH OF LARCENY, A, 1960, A
TOUCH OF LOVE, A
TOUCH OF SATAN, THE, 1971, O
TOUCH OF SATAN, THE, 1974
TOUCH OF THE MOON, A, 1936, A
TOUCH OF THE OTHER, A, 1970, O
TOUCH OF THE SUN, A, 1956, A
TOUCH WHITE, TOUCH BLACK
TOUCH, THE, 1971, O
TOUCHABLES, THE, 1968
TOUCHDOWN, 1931, A
TOUCHDOWN, ARMY, 1938, A
TOUCHE PAS A LA FEMME BLANCHE
TOUCHED, 1983, C
TOUCHED BY LOVE, 1980, A
TOUGH, 1974
TOUGH AS THEY COME, 1942, A
TOUGH ASSIGNMENT, 1949, A
TOUGH ENOUGH, 1983, C
TOUGH GUY, 1936, A
TOUGH GUY, THE, 1926
TOUGH KID, 1939, A
TOUGH TO HANDLE, 1937, A
TOUGHER THEY COME, THE, 1950, A
TOUGHEST GUN IN TOMBSTONE, 1958, A
TOUGHEST MAN ALIVE, 1955, A
TOUGHEST MAN IN ARIZONA, 1952, A
TOURIST TRAP, THE, 1979, C
TOUT VA BIEN, 1973, C
TOVARICH, 1937, AA
TOWARD THE UNKNOWN, 1956, A
TOWARDS THE LIGHT, 1918
TOWER OF EVIL, 1972
TOWER OF EVIL, 1981
TOWER OF IVORY
TOWER OF JEWELS, THE, 1920
TOWER OF LIES, THE, 1925, C
TOWER OF LONDON, 1939, A
TOWER OF LONDON, 1962, A
TOWER OF STRENGTH
TOWER OF TERROR, 1971
TOWER OF TERROR, THE, 1942, A
TOWERING INFERNO, THE, 1974, C
TOWING, 1978, C
TOWN CALLED BASTARD, A
TOWN CALLED HELL, A, 1971, O
TOWN LIKE ALICE, A, 1958, A
TOWN OF CROOKED WAYS, THE, 1920
TOWN ON TRIAL, 1957, C
TOWN SCANDAL, THE, 1923, A
TOWN TAMER, 1965, A
TOWN THAT CRIED TERROR, THE
TOWN THAT DREADED SUNDOWN, THE, 1977, O
TOWN THAT FORGOT GOD, THE, 1922
TOWN WENT WILD, THE, 1945, A
TOWN WITHOUT PITY, 1961, C-O
TOXI, 1952, A
TOY BOX, THE, 1971
TOY SOLDIERS, 1983
TOY SOLDIERS, 1984, O
TOY TIGER, 1956, AA
TOY WIFE, THE, 1938, A-C
TOY, THE, 1982, C
TOYGRABBERS, THE
TOYS ARE NOT FOR CHILDREN, 1972, O
TOYS IN THE ATTIC, 1963, C
TOYS OF FATE, 1918
TRACK OF THE CAT, 1954, C
TRACK OF THE MOONBEAST, 1976, C-O
TRACK OF THE VAMPIRE,
TRACK OF THUNDER, 1967, A
TRACK THE MAN DOWN, 1956, A
TRACKDOWN, 1976, O
TRACKED, 1928
TRACKED BY THE POLICE, 1927
TRACKED IN THE SNOW COUNTRY, 1925
TRACKED TO EARTH, 1922, A
TRACKING THE ZEPPELIN RAIDERS, 1916
TRACKS, 1922
TRACKS, 1977, O
TRACY RIDES, 1935
TRACY THE OUTLAW, 1928
TRADE WINDS, 1938, A
TRADER HORN, 1931, C
TRADER HORN, 1973, A
TRADER HORNEE, 1970, O
TRADING PLACES, 1983, C-O
TRAFFIC, 1915
TRAFFIC, 1972, AAA
TRAFFIC COP, THE, 1916, A
TRAFFIC COP, THE, 1926
TRAFFIC IN CRIME, 1946, A
TRAFFIC IN HEARTS, 1924
TRAFFIC IN SOULS, 1913, A
TRAGEDIES OF THE CRYSTAL GLOBE, THE, 1915
TRAGEDY AT MIDNIGHT, A, 1942, A
TRAGEDY OF A RIDICULOUS MAN, THE, 1982, A
TRAGEDY OF BASIL GRIEVE, THE
TRAGEDY OF LOVE, 1923
TRAGEDY OF YOUTH, THE, 1928, A
TRAIL BEYOND, THE, 1934, A
TRAIL BLAZERS, 1953
TRAIL BLAZERS, THE, 1940, A
TRAIL DRIVE, THE, 1934, A
TRAIL DUST, 1924
TRAIL DUST, 1936, A
TRAIL GUIDE, 1952, A
TRAIL MARRIAGE, 1929
TRAIL OF COURAGE, THE, 1928
TRAIL OF HATE, 1922
TRAIL OF KIT CARSON, 1945, A
TRAIL OF ROBIN HOOD, 1950, A
TRAIL OF TERROR, 1935, AA
TRAIL OF TERROR, 1944, A
TRAIL OF THE ARROW, 1952
TRAIL OF THE AXE, THE, 1922, A
TRAIL OF THE CIGARETTE, THE, 1920
TRAIL OF THE HAWK, 1935
TRAIL OF THE HORSE THIEVES, THE, 1929
TRAIL OF THE LAW, 1924
TRAIL OF THE LONESOME PINE, THE, 1914
TRAIL OF THE LONESOME PINE, THE, 1916
TRAIL OF THE LONESOME PINE, THE, 1936, A-C
TRAIL OF THE LONESOME, THE, 1923
TRAIL OF THE PINK PANTHER, THE, 1982, C
TRAIL OF THE RUSTLERS, 1950
TRAIL OF THE SHADOW, THE, 1917, C
TRAIL OF THE SILVER SPURS, 1941, A
TRAIL OF THE VIGILANTES, 1940, A
TRAIL OF THE YUKON, 1949, A
TRAIL OF VENGEANCE, 1937, A
TRAIL OF VENGEANCE, THE, 1924
TRAIL OF '98, THE, 1929, A
TRAIL RIDER, THE, 1925
TRAIL RIDERS, 1928
TRAIL RIDERS, 1942, AA
TRAIL STREET, 1947, A
TRAIL TO GUNSIGHT, 1944, AA
TRAIL TO LAREDO, 1948
TRAIL TO MEXICO, 1946
TRAIL TO RED DOG, THE, 1921
TRAIL TO SAN ANTONE, 1947, A
TRAIL TO VENGEANCE, 1945, A
TRAIL TO YESTERDAY, THE, 1918
TRAIL'S END, 1922, A
TRAIL'S END, 1935
TRAIL'S END, 1949, A
TRAILIN', 1921
TRAILIN' BACK, 1928
TRAILIN' TROUBLE, 1930
TRAILIN' TROUBLE, 1937
TRAILIN' WEST, 1936, A
TRAILING DANGER, 1947
TRAILING DOUBLE TROUBLE, 1940, A
TRAILING NORTH, 1933
TRAILING THE KILLER, 1932, A
TRAILING TROUBLE, 1930, A
TRAILING TROUBLE, 1937, A
TRAILS OF ADVENTURE, 1935
TRAILS OF DANGER, 1930
TRAILS OF DESTINY, 1926
TRAILS OF PERIL
TRAILS OF THE GOLDEN WEST, 1931
TRAILS OF THE WILD, 1935, A
TRAILS OF TREACHERY, 1928
TRAIN 2419
TRAIN GOES EAST, THE, 1949, A
TRAIN GOES TO KIEV, THE, 1961, A
TRAIN OF EVENTS, 1952, A
TRAIN RIDE TO HOLLYWOOD, 1975, A
TRAIN ROBBERS, THE, 1973, A
TRAIN ROBBERY CONFIDENTIAL, 1965, A
TRAIN TO ALCATRAZ, 1948, A
TRAIN TO TOMBSTONE, 1950, A
TRAIN WRECKERS, THE, 1925
TRAIN, THE, 1965, C
TRAINED TO KILL
TRAINER AND THE TEMPTRESS, 1925
TRAITOR, 1926
TRAITOR SPY
TRAITOR WITHIN, THE, 1942, A
TRAITOR'S GATE, 1966, A
TRAITOR, THE, 1936, A
TRAITOR, THE, 1957
TRAITORS, 1957, A
TRAITORS, THE, 1963, A
TRAITORS, THE, 1958, Brit.
TRAMP, TRAMP, TRAMP, 1926, A
TRAMP, TRAMP, TRAMP, 1942, A
TRAMPLERS, THE, 1966, C
TRANS-EUROP-EXPRESS, 1968, O
TRANSATLANTIC, 1931, A
TRANSATLANTIC, 1961, A
TRANSATLANTIC MERRY-GO-ROUND, 1934, A
TRANSATLANTIC TROUBLE
TRANSATLANTIC TUNNEL, 1935, A
TRANSCONTINENT EXPRESS
TRANSCONTINENTAL LIMITED, 1926
TRANSGRESSION, 1917
TRANSGRESSION, 1931, A
TRANSGRESSOR, THE, 1918
TRANSIENT LADY, 1935, A
TRANSPORT FROM PARADISE, 1967, A
TRANSPORT OF FIRE, 1931
TRAP DOOR, THE, 1980, O
TRAP ON COUGAR MOUNTAIN, 1972
TRAP, THE, 1918
TRAP, THE, 1919
TRAP, THE, 1922, A
TRAP, THE, 1947, A
TRAP, THE, 1959, A
TRAP, THE, 1967, A
TRAPEZE, 1932, A
TRAPEZE, 1956, A-C
TRAPP FAMILY, THE, 1961, A
TRAPPED, 1925
TRAPPED, 1931, A
TRAPPED, 1937, A
TRAPPED, 1949, A
TRAPPED, 1982
TRAPPED BY BOSTON BLACKIE, 1948, A
TRAPPED BY G-MEN, 1937, A
TRAPPED BY TELEVISION, 1936, A
TRAPPED BY THE LONDON SHARKS, 1916, A
TRAPPED BY THE MORMONS, 1922, C
TRAPPED BY THE TERROR, 1949, AAA
TRAPPED BY WIRELESS
TRAPPED IN A SUBMARINE, 1931, A
TRAPPED IN TANGIERS, 1960, A
TRAPPED IN THE AIR, 1922
TRAPPED IN THE SKY, 1939, A
TRAQUENARDS
TRAUMA, 1962, C
TRAUMSTADT
TRAVAIL, 1920
TRAVELIN' FAST, 1924
TRAVELIN' ON, 1922, A
TRAVELING EXECUTIONER, THE, 1970, O
TRAVELING HUSBANDS, 1931, O
TRAVELING LADY
TRAVELING SALESLADY, THE, 1935, A
TRAVELING SALESMAN, THE, 1916
TRAVELING SALESMAN, THE, 1921
TRAVELING SALESWOMAN, 1950, A
TRAVELLER'S JOY, 1951, A
TRAVELS WITH ANITA
TRAVELS WITH MY AUNT, 1972, C
TRE NOTTI D'AMORE
TRE NOTTI VIOLENTE
TRE PASSI NEL DELIRIO
TREACHERY ON THE HIGH SEAS, 1939, A
TREACHERY RIDES THE RANGE, 1936, A
TREAD SOFTLY, 1952, A
TREAD SOFTLY STRANGER, 1959, A
TREASON, 1917
TREASON, 1918
TREASON, 1933
TREASON, 1937
TREASON, 1950
TREASURE, 1918
TREASURE AT THE MILL, 1957, AAA
TREASURE CANYON, 1924
TREASURE HUNT, 1952, A
TREASURE ISLAND, 1917
TREASURE ISLAND, 1920, A
TREASURE ISLAND, 1934, A
TREASURE ISLAND, 1950, A-C
TREASURE ISLAND, 1972, A
TREASURE OF ARNE, THE
TREASURE OF FEAR
TREASURE OF HEAVEN, THE, 1916
TREASURE OF JAMAICA REEF, THE, 1976, C
TREASURE OF KALIFA
TREASURE OF LOST CANYON, THE, 1952, A

TREASURE OF MAKUBA, THE, 1967, A
TREASURE OF MATECUMBE, 1976, AA
TREASURE OF MONTE CRISTO, 1949, A
TREASURE OF MONTE CRISTO, THE
TREASURE OF PANCHO VILLA, THE, 1955, A
TREASURE OF RUBY HILLS, 1955, A
TREASURE OF SAN GENNARO, 1968, A
TREASURE OF SAN TERESA, THE
TREASURE OF SILVER LAKE, 1965, A
TREASURE OF TAYOPA, 1974
TREASURE OF THE AMAZON, 1983
TREASURE OF THE FOUR CROWNS, 1983, A
TREASURE OF THE GOLDEN CONDOR, 1953, A
TREASURE OF THE PIRANHA
TREASURE OF THE SEA, 1918
TREASURE OF THE SIERRA MADRE, THE, 1948, C
TREASURE OF THE YANKEE ZEPHYR, 1984, A-C
TREAT 'EM ROUGH, 1919
TREAT EM' ROUGH, 1942, A
TREATMENT, THE
TREE GROWS IN BROOKLYN, A, 1945, C
TREE OF KNOWLEDGE, THE, 1920
TREE OF LIBERTY
TREE OF WOODEN CLOGS, THE, 1979, A-C
TREE, THE, 1969, O
TRELAWNEY OF THE WELLS, 1916
TREMBLING HOUR, THE, 1919
TREMENDOUSLY RICH MAN, A, 1932, A
TRENCHCOAT, 1983, A
TRENT'S LAST CASE, 1920
TRENT'S LAST CASE, 1929
TRENT'S LAST CASE, 1953, A
TRES NOCHES VIOLENTAS
TRESPASSER, THE, 1929, A
TRESPASSER, THE, 1947, A
TRESPASSER, THE, 1946
TRESPASSERS, THE, 1976, O
TRI
TRI SESTRY
TRIAL, 1955, A
TRIAL AND ERROR, 1962, A
TRIAL BY COMBAT
TRIAL MARRIAGE, 1928
TRIAL OF BILLY JACK, THE, 1974, C
TRIAL OF JOAN OF ARC, 1965, C
TRIAL OF LEE HARVEY OSWALD, THE, 1964, A
TRIAL OF MADAM X, THE, 1948, A
TRIAL OF MARY DUGAN, THE, 1929, C
TRIAL OF MARY DUGAN, THE, 1941, A
TRIAL OF PORTIA MERRIMAN, THE
TRIAL OF SERGEANT RUTLEDGE, THE
TRIAL OF THE CATONSVILLE NINE, THE, 1972, A
TRIAL OF VIVIENNE WARE, THE, 1932, A
TRIAL WITHOUT JURY, 1950, A
TRIAL, THE, 1948, A
TRIAL, THE, 1963, C
TRIALS OF OSCAR WILDE, THE
TRIANGLE, 1971
TRIBES, 1970, A
TRIBUTE, 1980, C
TRIBUTE TO A BADMAN, 1956, C
TRICET JEDNA VE STINU
TRICK BABY, 1973, O
TRICK FOR TRICK, 1933, A
TRICK OF FATE, A, 1919
TRICK OF HEARTS, A, 1928
TRICK OR TREATS, 1982, O
TRICK OR TREATS, 1983
TRICKED
TRICKS, 1925
TRIFLERS, THE, 1920
TRIFLERS, THE, 1924
TRIFLING WITH HONOR, 1923
TRIFLING WOMEN, 1922
TRIGGER FINGER, 1924
TRIGGER FINGERS, 1946
TRIGGER FINGERS, 1939, A
TRIGGER HAPPY
TRIGGER LAW, 1944
TRIGGER PALS, 1939, A
TRIGGER SMITH, 1939, A
TRIGGER TOM, 1935
TRIGGER TRAIL, 1944, A
TRIGGER TRICKS, 1930, A
TRIGGER TRIO, THE, 1937, A
TRIGGER, JR., 1950, A
TRIGGERMAN, 1948
TRILBY, 1914
TRILBY, 1915, A
TRILBY, 1923
TRILOGY
TRIMMED, 1922
TRIMMED IN SCARLET, 1923
TRINITY, 1975
TRINITY AND SARTANA, 1972
TRINITY IS STILL MY NAME, 1971, A
TRIO, 1950, A
TRIP TO AMERICA, A
TRIP TO CHINATOWN, A, 1926
TRIP TO ITALY, A
TRIP TO MARS, A, 1920
TRIP TO PARADISE, A, 1921
TRIP TO PARIS, A, 1938, A
TRIP TO TERROR
TRIP WITH ANITA, A
TRIP WITH THE TEACHER, 1975
TRIP, THE
TRIP, THE, 1967, O
TRIPLE ACTION, 1925
TRIPLE CROSS, 1967, C-O
TRIPLE CROSS, THE
TRIPLE DECEPTION, 1957, A
TRIPLE ECHO, THE, 1973, O
TRIPLE IRONS, 1973, O
TRIPLE JUSTICE, 1940, A
TRIPLE PASS, 1928
TRIPLE THREAT, 1948, A
TRIPLE TROUBLE
TRIPLE TROUBLE, 1950, A
TRIPLEPATTE, 1922
TRIPOLI, 1950, A
TRISTANA, 1970, C
TRITIY TAYM
TRIUMPH, 1917
TRIUMPH, 1924
TRIUMPH OF ROBIN HOOD, THE, 1960
TRIUMPH OF SHERLOCK HOLMES, THE, 1935, A
TRIUMPH OF THE RAT, THE, 1926
TRIUMPH OF THE SCARLET PIMPERNEL
TRIUMPH OF THE WEAK, THE, 1918
TRIUMPH OF VENUS, THE, 1918
TRIUMPHS OF A MAN CALLED HORSE, 1983, O
TRIXIE FROM BROADWAY, 1919
TROCADERO, 1944, A
TROG, 1970, A
TROIKA, 1969, O
TROIS HOMMES A ABATTRE
TROIS JEUNES FILLES, 1928
TROIS VERITES
TROJAN BROTHERS, THE, 1946, A
TROJAN HORSE, THE, 1962, AA
TROJAN WAR, THE
TROJAN WOMEN, THE, 1971, C
TROLLENBERG TERROR, THE
TROMBA, THE TIGER MAN, 1952, C
TRON, 1982, A
TROOP TRAIN, THE
TROOPER 44, 1917
TROOPER HOOK, 1957, C
TROOPER O'NEIL, 1922
TROOPER, THE
TROOPERS THREE, 1930, AA
TROOPSHIP, 1938, C
TROPIC FURY, 1939, A
TROPIC HOLIDAY, 1938, A
TROPIC MADNESS, 1928
TROPIC ZONE, 1953, A
TROPICAL HEAT WAVE, 1952, A
TROPICAL LOVE, 1921
TROPICAL NIGHTS, 1928
TROPICAL TROUBLE, 1936, A
TROPICANA
TROPICS, 1969, O
TROTTIE TRUE
TROUBLE, 1922, A
TROUBLE, 1933, A
TROUBLE AHEAD, 1936, A
TROUBLE ALONG THE WAY, 1953, O
TROUBLE AT 16
TROUBLE AT MELODY MESA, 1949
TROUBLE AT MIDNIGHT, 1937, A
TROUBLE BREWING, 1939, A
TROUBLE BUSTER, THE, 1917
TROUBLE BUSTER, THE, 1925
TROUBLE BUSTERS, 1933
TROUBLE CHASER
TROUBLE CHASER, 1926
TROUBLE CHASERS, 1945
TROUBLE FOR EDGAR, 1915
TROUBLE FOR TWO, 1936, A
TROUBLE IN MOROCCO, 1937, A
TROUBLE IN PANAMA
TROUBLE IN PARADISE, 1932, C
TROUBLE IN STORE, 1955, A
TROUBLE IN SUNDOWN, 1939, A
TROUBLE IN TEXAS, 1937, A
TROUBLE IN THE AIR, 1948, A
TROUBLE IN THE GLEN, 1954, A
TROUBLE IN THE SKY, 1961, C
TROUBLE MAKERS, 1948
TROUBLE MAN, 1972, O
TROUBLE ON THE TRAIL, 1954
TROUBLE PREFERRED, 1949, A
TROUBLE SHOOTER, THE, 1924
TROUBLE TRAIL, 1924
TROUBLE WITH ANGELS, THE, 1966, AA
TROUBLE WITH EVE
TROUBLE WITH GIRLS (AND HOW TO GET INTO IT), THE, 1969, A
TROUBLE WITH HARRY, THE, 1955, A-C
TROUBLE WITH WIVES, THE, 1925
TROUBLE WITH WOMEN, THE, 1947, A
TROUBLE-FETE, 1964, O
TROUBLED WATERS, 1936, A
TROUBLED WATERS, 1964
TROUBLEMAKER, THE, 1964, O
TROUBLEMAKERS, 1917
TROUBLES OF A BRIDE, 1924
TROUBLES THROUGH BILLETS
TROUBLESOME DOUBLE, THE, 1971, AA
TROUBLESOME WIVES, 1928
TROUPER, THE, 1922
TROUPING WITH ELLEN, 1924
TROUSERS, 1920
TROUT, THE, 1982, O
TRUANT HUSBAND, THE, 1921
TRUANT SOUL, THE, 1917
TRUANT, THE
TRUANTS, THE, 1922
TRUCK BUSTERS, 1943, A
TRUCK STOP WOMEN, 1974, O
TRUCK TURNER, 1974, O
TRUCKER'S TOP HAND, 1924
TRUCKIN', 1975
TRUCKIN' BUDDY McCOY, 1983
TRUCKIN' MAN, 1975
TRUE AND THE FALSE, THE, 1955, O
TRUE AS A TURTLE, 1957, A
TRUE AS STEEL, 1924
TRUE BLUE, 1918
TRUE CONFESSION, 1937, A
TRUE CONFESSIONS, 1981, O
TRUE DIARY OF A WAHINE
TRUE GRIT, 1969, A
TRUE HEART SUSIE, 1919, A
TRUE HEAVEN, 1929
TRUE NOBILITY, 1916
TRUE STORY OF A WAHINE
TRUE STORY OF ESKIMO NELL, THE, 1975, O
TRUE STORY OF JESSE JAMES, THE, 1957, A
TRUE STORY OF LYNN STUART, THE, 1958, A
TRUE TILDA, 1920, A
TRUE TO LIFE, 1943, A
TRUE TO THE ARMY, 1942, AAA
TRUE TO THE NAVY, 1930, A
TRUFFLERS, THE, 1917
TRUMAN CAPOTE'S TRILOGY, 1969, A
TRUMPET BLOWS, THE, 1934, A
TRUMPET CALL, THE, 1915
TRUMPET ISLAND, 1920
TRUMPIN' TROUBLE, 1926
TRUNK CRIME
TRUNK MYSTERY, THE
TRUNK MYSTERY, THE, 1927
TRUNK TO CAIRO, 1966, C
TRUNK, THE, 1961, C
TRUNKS OF MR. O.F., THE, 1932, A
TRUST THE NAVY, 1935, A
TRUST YOUR WIFE
TRUST YOUR WIFE, 1921
TRUST, THE
TRUSTED OUTLAW, THE, 1937, A
TRUTH ABOUT HELEN, THE, 1915
TRUTH ABOUT HUSBANDS, THE, 1920
TRUTH ABOUT MEN, 1926
TRUTH ABOUT MURDER, THE, 1946, A
TRUTH ABOUT SPRING, THE, 1965, AA
TRUTH ABOUT WIVES, THE, 1923
TRUTH ABOUT WOMEN, THE, 1924
TRUTH ABOUT WOMEN, THE, 1958, A
TRUTH ABOUT YOUTH, THE, 1930, A
TRUTH AND JUSTICE, 1916
TRUTH IS STRANGER
TRUTH WAGON, THE, 1914, A
TRUTH, THE, 1920, A
TRUTH, THE, 1961, O
TRUTHFUL LIAR, THE, 1922
TRUTHFUL SEX, THE, 1926
TRUTHFUL TULLIVER, 1917
TRUTHFUL TULLIVER, 1917, A
TRUXTON KING, 1923
TRY AND FIND IT
TRY AND GET IT, 1924
TRY AND GET ME
TRYGON FACTOR, THE, 1969, C
TRYING, 1967, A
TSAR IVAN VASILYEVICH GROZNY, 1915
TSAR NIKOLAI II, 1917
TSAR'S BRIDE, THE, 1966, C
TSARSKAYA NEVESTA
TSUBAKI SANJURO
TU M'APPARTIENS, 1929
TU PERDONAS..YO NO
TU SERAS TERRIBLEMENT GENTILLE
TUCK EVERLASTING, 1981
TUCSON, 1949, A

TUCSON RAIDERS, 1944, A
TUDOR ROSE
TUGBOAT ANNIE, 1933, A
TUGBOAT ANNIE SAILS AGAIN, 1940, AA
TUGBOAT PRINCESS, 1936
TULIPS, 1981, C
TULSA, 1949, A
TULSA KID, THE, 1940, A
TUMBLEDOWN RANCH IN ARIZONA, 1941, A
TUMBLEWEED, 1953, A
TUMBLEWEED TRAIL, 1942
TUMBLEWEED TRAIL, 1946, A
TUMBLEWEEDS, 1925, A
TUMBLING RIVER, 1927, A
TUMBLING TUMBLEWEEDS, 1935, AA
TUNA CLIPPER, 1949, A
TUNDRA, 1936, A
TUNES OF GLORY, 1960, C
TUNNEL 28
TUNNEL OF LOVE, THE, 1958, C
TUNNEL TO THE SUN, 1968, C
TUNNEL, THE
TUNNELVISION, 1976, O
TURF CONSPIRACY, A, 1918
TURKEY SHOOT
TURKEY TIME, 1933, A
TURKISH CUCUMBER, THE, 1963, C
TURKISH DELIGHT, 1927
TURKSIB, 1930
TURLIS ABENTEUER
TURMOIL, THE, 1916
TURMOIL, THE, 1924
TURN BACK THE CLOCK, 1933, A
TURN BACK THE HOURS, 1928
TURN IN THE ROAD, THE, 1919
TURN OF THE CARD, THE, 1918
TURN OF THE ROAD, THE, 1915
TURN OF THE TIDE, 1935, A
TURN OF THE WHEEL, THE, 1918
TURN OFF THE MOON, 1937, A
TURN ON TO LOVE, 1969, O
TURN THE KEY SOFTLY, 1954, C
TURN TO THE RIGHT, 1922
TURNABOUT, 1940, A
TURNED OUT NICE AGAIN, 1941, A
TURNED UP, 1924
TURNERS OF PROSPECT ROAD, THE, 1947, A
TURNING POINT, THE, 1920
TURNING POINT, THE, 1952, C-O
TURNING POINT, THE, 1977, C
TURNING THE TABLES, 1919
TUSK, 1980
TUTTE LE ALTRE RAGAZZE LO FANNO
TUTTI A CASA
TUTTI FRUTTI
TUTTI PAZZI MENO IO
TUTTLES OF TAHITI, 1942, A
TUXEDO JUNCTION, 1941, A
TUXEDO WARRIOR, 1982
TVA LEVANDE OCH EN DOD
TWAS EVER THUS, 1915
TWELFTH NIGHT, 1956, A
12 ANGRY MEN, 1957, A
TWELVE CHAIRS, THE, 1970, A-C
TWELVE CROWDED HOURS, 1939, A
TWELVE GOOD MEN, 1936, A
TWELVE HOURS TO KILL, 1960, A
TWELVE MILES OUT, 1927, A
TWELVE O'CLOCK HIGH, 1949, C
TWELVE PLUS ONE, 1970, A
TWELVE POUND LOOK, THE, 1920
TWELVE TO THE MOON, 1960, A
TWELVE-HANDED MEN OF MARS, THE, 1964, A
TWENTIETH CENTURY, 1934, A
20TH CENTURY OZ, 1934, A
25TH HOUR, THE, 1967, C
24 HOURS, 1931, A
24 HOURS IN A WOMAN'S LIFE, 1968, C
24 HOURS TO KILL, 1966, C
24-HOUR LOVER, 1970, O
20 MILLION MILES TO EARTH, 1957, A
TWENTY MILLION SWEETHEARTS, 1934, A
TWENTY MULE TEAM, 1940, A
TWENTY PLUS TWO, 1961, C-O
TWENTY QUESTIONS MURDER MYSTERY, THE, 1950, A
27A, 1974, O
27TH DAY, THE, 1957, A-C
20,000 EYES, 1961, C
20,000 LEAGUES UNDER THE SEA, 1954, A
20,000 MEN A YEAR, 1939, A
20,000 POUNDS KISS, THE, 1964, C
20,000 YEARS IN SING-SING, 1933, A
23 1/2 HOURS LEAVE, 1937, A
23 PACES TO BAKER STREET, 1956, C
TWENTY-ONE, 1918
TWENTY-ONE, 1923
TWENTY-ONE DAYS
TWENTY-ONE DAYS TOGETHER, 1940, A

TWICE A MAN, 1964, O
TWICE AROUND THE DAFFODILS, 1962, A
TWICE BLESSED, 1945, A
TWICE BRANDED, 1936, A
TWICE TOLD TALES, 1963, C
TWICE UPON A TIME, 1953, A
TWICE UPON A TIME, 1983, A
TWILIGHT, 1919
TWILIGHT FOR THE GODS, 1958, A
TWILIGHT HOUR, 1944, A
TWILIGHT IN THE SIERRAS, 1950, A
TWILIGHT OF HONOR, 1963, C
TWILIGHT OF THE DEAD
TWILIGHT ON THE PRAIRIE, 1944, A
TWILIGHT ON THE RIO GRANDE, 1947, A
TWILIGHT ON THE TRAIL, 1941, A
TWILIGHT PATH, 1965, C
TWILIGHT PEOPLE, 1972, O
TWILIGHT STORY, THE, 1962, O
TWILIGHT TIME, 1983, C
TWILIGHT WOMEN, 1953, C
TWILIGHT ZONE—THE MOVIE, 1983, C-O
TWILIGHT'S LAST GLEAMING, 1977, O
TWIN BEDS, 1920, A
TWIN BEDS, 1929, A
TWIN BEDS, 1942, A
TWIN FACES, 1937, A
TWIN FLAPPERS, 1927
TWIN HUSBANDS, 1934, A
TWIN KIDDIES, 1917
TWIN PAWNS, THE, 1919
TWIN SISTERS OF KYOTO, 1964, C
TWIN SIX O'BRIEN, 1926
TWIN TRIANGLE, THE, 1916
TWIN TRIGGERS, 1926
TWINKLE AND SHINE
TWINKLE IN GOD'S EYE, THE, 1955, A
TWINKLE, TWINKLE, KILLER KANE
TWINKLER, THE, 1916
TWINKLETOES, 1926, A
TWINKY
TWINS OF EVIL, 1971, O
TWINS OF SUFFERING CREEK, 1920
TWIST ALL NIGHT, 1961, A
TWIST AROUND THE CLOCK, 1961, A
TWIST OF FATE
TWIST OF SAND, A, 1968, A
TWIST, THE, 1976, C-O
TWISTED BRAIN
TWISTED LIVES
TWISTED NERVE, 1969, O
TWISTED RAILS, 1935
TWISTED ROAD, THE
TWISTED TRIGGERS, 1926
TWITCH OF THE DEATH NERVE, 1973, O
TWO, 1975, O
TWO A PENNY, 1968, A
TWO AGAINST THE WORLD, 1932, A
TWO AGAINST THE WORLD, 1936, A
TWO ALONE, 1934, A
TWO AND ONE TWO, 1934, A
TWO AND TWO MAKE SIX, 1962, C
TWO ARABIAN KNIGHTS, 1927
TWO ARE GUILTY, 1964, C
TWO BLACK SHEEP
TWO BLONDES AND A REDHEAD, 1947, A
TWO BRIDES, THE, 1919
TWO BRIGHT BOYS, 1939, A
TWO CAN PLAY, 1926
TWO CATCH TWO, 1979
TWO COLONELS, THE, 1963, A
TWO DAUGHTERS, 1963, A
TWO DAYS, 1929
TWO DOLLAR BETTOR, 1951, A
TWO ENEMIES
TWO ENGLISH GIRLS, 1972, O
TWO EYES, TWELVE HANDS, 1958, C
TWO FACES OF DR. JEKYLL
TWO FACES OF EVIL, THE, 1981
TWO FISTED, 1935, A
TWO FISTED AGENT
TWO FISTED BUCKAROO, 1926
TWO FISTED JUSTICE, 1924
TWO FISTED JUSTICE, 1943, A
TWO FISTED TENDERFOOT, A, 1924
TWO FISTED THOMPSON, 1925
TWO FLAGS WEST, 1950, A
TWO FLAMING YOUTHS, 1927, A
TWO FOR DANGER, 1940, A
TWO FOR THE ROAD, 1967, C
TWO FOR THE SEESAW, 1962, C
TWO FOR TONIGHT, 1935, A
TWO GALS AND A GUY, 1951, A
TWO GENTLEMEN SHARING, 1969, O
TWO GIRLS AND A SAILOR, 1944, A
TWO GIRLS ON BROADWAY, 1940, A
TWO GROOMS FOR A BRIDE, 1957, A
TWO GUN CABALLERO, 1931
TWO GUN LAW, 1937, A

TWO GUN MAN, THE, 1931, A
TWO GUN MURPHY, 1928
TWO GUN O'BRIEN, 1928
TWO GUN SAP, 1925
TWO GUN SHERIFF, 1941, A
TWO GUNS AND A BADGE, 1954, A
TWO GUYS FROM TEXAS, 1948, A
TWO HEADS ON A PILLOW, 1934, A
TWO HEARTS IN HARMONY, 1935, A
TWO HEARTS IN WALTZ TIME, 1934, A
TWO HUNDRED MOTELS, 1971, O
TWO IN A CROWD, 1936, A
TWO IN A MILLION
TWO IN A SLEEPING BAG, 1964, C
TWO IN A TAXI, 1941, A
TWO IN REVOLT, 1936, AAA
TWO IN THE DARK, 1936, A
TWO IN THE SHADOW, 1968, C
TWO IS A HAPPY NUMBER
TWO KINDS OF LOVE, 1920
TWO KINDS OF WOMEN, 1922
TWO KINDS OF WOMEN, 1932, C
TWO KOUNEY LEMELS, 1966, A
TWO LANCASHIRE LASSES IN LONDON, 1916
TWO LATINS FROM MANHATTAN, 1941, A
TWO LEFT FEET, 1965, O
TWO LETTER ALIBI, 1962, A
TWO LITTLE BEARS, THE, 1961
TWO LITTLE DRUMMER BOYS, 1928
TWO LITTLE IMPS, 1917
TWO LITTLE WOODEN SHOES, 1920
TWO LIVING, ONE DEAD, 1964, C
TWO LOST WORLDS, 1950, A
TWO LOVERS, 1928, A
TWO LOVES, 1961, C
TWO MEN AND A GIRL
TWO MEN AND A MAID, 1929, A
TWO MEN AND A WOMAN, 1917
TWO MEN IN TOWN, 1973, O
TWO MEN OF SANDY BAR, 1916
TWO MINUTES TO GO, 1921, A
TWO MINUTES TO PLAY, 1937, A
TWO MINUTES' SILENCE, 1934, A
TWO MOONS, 1920
TWO MRS. CARROLLS, THE, 1947, A-C
TWO MUGS FROM BROOKLYN, 1942
TWO MULES FOR SISTER SARA, 1970, C
TWO NIGHTS WITH CLEOPATRA, 1953, C
TWO O'CLOCK COURAGE, 1945, C
TWO OF A KIND, 1951, C
TWO OF A KIND, 1983, C
TWO OF US, THE, 1938, A
TWO OF US, THE, 1968, A
TWO ON A DOORSTEP, 1936, A
TWO ON A GUILLOTINE, 1965, C
TWO ON THE TILES
TWO OR THREE THINGS I KNOW ABOUT HER, 1970, O
TWO ORPHANS, THE, 1915
TWO OUTLAWS, THE, 1928
TWO PEOPLE, 1973, O
TWO ROADS
TWO RODE TOGETHER, 1961, C
TWO SECONDS, 1932, C
TWO SENORITAS
TWO SENORITAS FROM CHICAGO, 1943, A
TWO SHALL BE BORN, 1924
TWO SINNERS, 1935, A
TWO SISTERS, 1929
TWO SISTERS, 1938, A
TWO SISTERS FROM BOSTON, 1946, A
TWO SMART MEN, 1940, A
TWO SMART PEOPLE, 1946, A
TWO SOLITUDES, 1978, A
TWO SOULED WOMAN, THE
TWO SUPER COPS, 1978, C
TWO TEXAS KNIGHTS
TWO THOROUGHBREDS, 1939, A
TWO THOUSAND MANIACS, 1964, O
2,000 WEEKS, 1970, C
2,000 WOMEN, 1944, A
2000 YEARS LATER, 1969, O
2001: A SPACE ODYSSEY, 1968, A
TWO THOUSAND YEARS LATER, 1969
TWO TICKETS TO BROADWAY, 1951, A
TWO TICKETS TO LONDON, 1943, A
TWO TICKETS TO PARIS, 1962, A
TWO TIMES TWO
TWO TONS OF TURQUOISE TO TAOS, 1967
TWO VIOLENT MEN, 1964
TWO VOICES, 1966, C
TWO WEEKS, 1920
TWO WEEKS IN ANOTHER TOWN, 1962, O
TWO WEEKS IN SEPTEMBER, 1967, O
TWO WEEKS OFF, 1929, A
TWO WEEKS TO LIVE, 1943, A
TWO WEEKS WITH LOVE, 1950, A
TWO WEEKS WITH PAY, 1921
TWO WHITE ARMS

TWO WHO DARED, 1937, A
TWO WISE MAIDS, 1937, A
TWO WIVES AT ONE WEDDING, 1961, A
TWO WOMEN, 1919
TWO WOMEN, 1940, A
TWO WOMEN, 1961, C-O
TWO WORLD, 1930, A
TWO WORLDS OF ANGELITA, THE, 1982
TWO WORLDS OF CHARLY GORDON, THE
TWO YANKS IN TRINIDAD, 1942, A
TWO YEARS BEFORE THE MAST, 1946, C
TWO YEARS HOLIDAY
TWO'S COMPANY, 1939, A
TWO-BITS SEATS, 1917
TWO-EDGED SWORD, THE, 1916, A
TWO-FACED WOMAN, 1941, A
TWO-FISTED GENTLEMAN, 1936, A
TWO-FISTED JEFFERSON, 1922
TWO-FISTED JONES, 1925
TWO-FISTED JUSTICE, 1931, A
TWO-FISTED LAW, 1932, AA
TWO-FISTED RANGERS, 1940, A
TWO-FISTED SHERIFF, 1937, A
TWO-FISTED SHERIFF, A, 1925
TWO-FISTED STRANGER, 1946
TWO-GUN BETTY, 1918
TWO-GUN CUPID
TWO-GUN JUSTICE, 1938, A
TWO-GUN LADY, 1956, A
TWO-GUN MAN FROM HARLEM, 1938
TWO-GUN MAN, THE, 1926
TWO-GUN OF THE TUMBLEWEED, 1927
TWO-GUN TROUBADOR, 1939, A
TWO-HEADED SPY, THE, 1959, C
TWO-LANE BLACKTOP, 1971, O
TWO-MAN SUBMARINE, 1944, A
TWO-MINUTE WARNING, 1976, O
TWO-SOUL WOMAN, THE, 1918
TWO-WAY STRETCH, 1961, A-C
TWONKY, THE, 1953, A
TYCOON, 1947, A
TYPHOON, 1940, A
TYPHOON LOVE, 1926
TYPHOON TREASURE, 1939, A
TYPHOON, THE, 1914, A
TYRANT FEAR, 1918
TYRANT OF RED GULCH, 1928
TYRANT OF SYRACUSE, THE
TYRANT OF THE SEA, 1950, A
TYRANT, THE, 1972
TYSTNADEN

-U-

U KRUTOGO YARA
U-47 LT. COMMANDER PRIEN, 1967, A
U-BOAT 29, 1939, A
U-BOAT PRISONER, 1944, A
U-TURN, 1973, C
U.P. TRAIL, THE, 1920
U.S.S. TEAKETTLE
UCCELLACCI E UCCELLINI
UCCIDERO UN UOMO
UCHUJIN TOKYO NI ARAWARU
UFO
UFO: TARGET EARTH, 1974, A
UGETSU, 1954, A
UGLY AMERICAN, THE, 1963, A-C
UGLY DACHSHUND, THE, 1966, AAA
UGLY DUCKLING, THE, 1920
UGLY DUCKLING, THE, 1959, A
UGLY ONES, THE, 1968, O
UKIGUSA
ULTIMATE CHASE, THE
ULTIMATE SOLUTION OF GRACE QUIGLEY, THE, 1984, C
ULTIMATE THRILL, THE, 1974, A-C
ULTIMATE WARRIOR, THE, 1975, O
ULTIMATUM, 1940, A
ULTUS, THE MAN FROM THE DEAD, 1916
ULYSSES, 1955, C
ULYSSES, 1967, C
ULZANA'S RAID, 1972, O
UMBERTO D, 1955, C
UMBRELLA, THE, 1933, A
UMBRELLAS OF CHERBOURG, THE, 1964, A-C
UN AMOUR DE POCHE, 1957
UN AMOUR DE SWANN
UN AMOUR EN ALLEMAGNE
UN AVENTUERIER, 1921
UN BON PETIT DIABLE, 1923
UN CARNET DE BAL, 1938, A
UN CHATEAU DE LA MORT LENTE, 1925
UN CRIME A ETE COMMIS, 1919
UN DIMANCHE A LA CAMPAGNE
UN DRAME SOUS NAPOLEON, 1921
UN FIL A LA PATTE, 1924
UN FILE
UN FILS D'AMERIQUE, 1925
UN HOMME ET UNE FEMME
UN HOMME PASSA, 1917
UN MARIAGE DE RAISON, 1916
UN OURS, 1921
UN ROMAN D'AMOUR ET D'AVENTURES, 1918
UN SEUL AMOUR
UN SOIR, 1919
UN TAXI MAUVE
UN UOMO, UN CAVALLO, UNA PISTOLA
UN, DEUX, TROIS, QUATRE?
UNA MOGLIE AMERICANA
UNA SIGNORA DELL'OVEST, 1942, A
UNAFRAID, THE, 1915
UNAKRSNA VATRA
UNASHAMED, 1932, A
UNASHAMED, 1938, O
UNATTAINABLE, THE, 1916
UNBEATABLE GAME, THE, 1925
UNBELIEVER, THE, 1918
UNBLAZED TRAIL, 1923
UNBROKEN PROMISE, THE, 1919
UNBROKEN ROAD, THE, 1915
UNCANNY ROOM, THE, 1915
UNCANNY, THE, 1977, C
UNCENSORED, 1944, A
UNCERTAIN GLORY, 1944, A
UNCERTAIN LADY, 1934, A
UNCHAINED
UNCHAINED, 1955, A
UNCHARTED CHANNELS, 1920
UNCHARTED SEAS, 1921
UNCHASTENED WOMAN, 1925, A
UNCIVILISED, 1937, A
UNCLAIMED GOODS, 1918
UNCLE DICK'S DARLING, 1920
UNCLE HARRY, 1945, C
UNCLE JASPAR'S WILL, 1922
UNCLE JOE SHANNON, 1978, C
UNCLE MOSES, 1932
UNCLE NICK, 1938
UNCLE SAM AWAKE, 1916
UNCLE SCAM, 1981, O
UNCLE SILAS
UNCLE TOM'S CABIN, 1914, A
UNCLE TOM'S CABIN, 1918
UNCLE TOM'S CABIN, 1927
UNCLE TOM'S CABIN, 1969, C
UNCLE VANYA, 1958, A
UNCLE VANYA, 1972, A
UNCLE VANYA, 1977, A
UNCLE, THE, 1966, A
UNCOMMON THIEF, AN, 1967, A
UNCOMMON VALOR, 1983, O
UNCONQUERED, 1917
UNCONQUERED, 1947, A
UNCONQUERED BANDIT, 1935
UNCONQUERED WOMAN, 1922
UND IMMER RUFT DAS HERZ
...UND MORGEN FAHRT IHR ZUR HOLIE
UNDEAD, THE, 1957, A
UNDEFEATED, THE, 1951
UNDEFEATED, THE, 1969, A
UNDER A CLOUD, 1937, A
UNDER A TEXAS MOON, 1930, A
UNDER AGE, 1941, A-C
UNDER AGE, 1964, O
UNDER ARIZONA SKIES, 1946, A
UNDER CALIFORNIA SKIES
UNDER CALIFORNIA STARS, 1948, A
UNDER CAPRICORN, 1949, C
UNDER COLORADO SKIES, 1947, A
UNDER COVER, 1916
UNDER COVER OF NIGHT, 1937, A
UNDER COVER ROGUE
UNDER CRIMSON SKIES, 1920
UNDER EIGHTEEN, 1932, A
UNDER FALSE COLORS, 1917
UNDER FIESTA STARS, 1941, A
UNDER FIRE, 1926, A
UNDER FIRE, 1957, A
UNDER FIRE, 1983, O
UNDER HANDICAP, 1917
UNDER MEXICALI SKIES
UNDER MEXICALI STARS, 1950, A
UNDER MILK WOOD, 1973, C
UNDER MONTANA SKIES, 1930, A
UNDER MY SKIN, 1950, A
UNDER NEVADA SKIES, 1946, A
UNDER NEW MANAGEMENT
UNDER NORTHERN LIGHTS, 1920
UNDER OATH, 1922
UNDER PRESSURE, 1935, A
UNDER PROOF, 1936, A
UNDER SECRET ORDERS, 1933, A
UNDER SECRET ORDERS, 1943, A-C
UNDER SOUTHERN SKIES, 1915
UNDER STRANGE FLAGS, 1937, A
UNDER SUSPICION, 1916
UNDER SUSPICION, 1918
UNDER SUSPICION, 1919
UNDER SUSPICION, 1919, A
UNDER SUSPICION, 1931, A
UNDER SUSPICION, 1937, A
UNDER TEN FLAGS, 1960, C
UNDER TEXAS SKIES, 1931, A
UNDER TEXAS SKIES, 1940, A
UNDER THE BANNER OF SAMURAI, 1969, C
UNDER THE BIG TOP, 1938, A
UNDER THE BLACK EAGLE, 1928
UNDER THE CLOCK
UNDER THE DOCTOR, 1976
UNDER THE GASLIGHT, 1914
UNDER THE GREENWOOD TREE, 1918
UNDER THE GREENWOOD TREE, 1930, A
UNDER THE GUN, 1951, A
UNDER THE LASH, 1921
UNDER THE PAMPAS MOON, 1935, A
UNDER THE RAINBOW, 1981, C
UNDER THE RED ROBE, 1915
UNDER THE RED ROBE, 1923, A
UNDER THE RED ROBE, 1937, A
UNDER THE ROOFS OF PARIS, 1930, A
UNDER THE ROUGE, 1925
UNDER THE SIGN OF CAPRICORN, 1971
UNDER THE SOUTHERN CROSS
UNDER THE SUN OF ROME, 1949, A
UNDER THE TABLE YOU MUST GO, 1969
UNDER THE TONTO RIM, 1928
UNDER THE TONTO RIM, 1933, A
UNDER THE TONTO RIM, 1947, A
UNDER THE TOP, 1919
UNDER THE VOLCANO, 1984, O
UNDER THE WESTERN SKIES, 1921
UNDER THE YOKE, 1918
UNDER THE YUM-YUM TREE, 1963, C-O
UNDER TWO FLAGS, 1916
UNDER TWO FLAGS, 1922
UNDER TWO FLAGS, 1936, A-C
UNDER WESTERN SKIES, 1926
UNDER WESTERN SKIES, 1945, A
UNDER WESTERN STARS, 1938, A
UNDER YOUR HAT, 1940, A
UNDER YOUR SPELL, 1936, A
UNDER-COVER MAN, 1932, A
UNDER-PUP, THE, 1939, A
UNDERCOVER
UNDERCOVER AGENT, 1935, A
UNDERCOVER AGENT, 1939, A
UNDERCOVER DOCTOR, 1939, A
UNDERCOVER GIRL
UNDERCOVER GIRL, 1950, A
UNDERCOVER GIRL, 1957, A
UNDERCOVER MAISIE, 1947, A
UNDERCOVER MAN, 1936, A
UNDERCOVER MAN, 1942, A
UNDERCOVER MAN, THE, 1949, C
UNDERCOVER MEN, 1935
UNDERCOVER WOMAN, THE, 1946, A
UNDERCOVERS HERO, 1975, O
UNDERCURRENT, 1946, A-C
UNDERCURRENT, THE, 1919
UNDERDOG, THE, 1943, A
UNDERGROUND, 1928
UNDERGROUND, 1941, A
UNDERGROUND, 1970, C
UNDERGROUND ACES, 1981
UNDERGROUND AGENT, 1942, A
UNDERGROUND GUERRILLAS, 1944, A
UNDERGROUND RUSTLERS, 1941, A
UNDERGROUND U.S.A., 1980, O
UNDERNEATH THE ARCHES, 1937, A
UNDERSEA GIRL, 1957, A
UNDERSEA ODYSSEY, AN
UNDERSTANDING HEART, THE, 1927
UNDERSTUDY, THE, 1917
UNDERSTUDY, THE, 1922
UNDERTAKER AND HIS PALS, THE, 1966, O
UNDERTOW, 1930, A
UNDERTOW, 1949, A
UNDERTOW, THE, 1916
UNDERWATER CITY, THE, 1962, A
UNDERWATER ODYSSEY, AN
UNDERWATER WARRIOR, 1958, A
UNDERWATER!, 1955, C-O
UNDERWORLD, 1927, A
UNDERWORLD, 1937, A-C
UNDERWORLD AFTER DARK
UNDERWORLD INFORMERS, 1965, A
UNDERWORLD OF LONDON, THE, 1915
UNDERWORLD STORY, THE
UNDERWORLD TERROR, 1936
UNDERWORLD U.S.A., 1961, C
UNDINE, 1916
UNDISPUTED EVIDENCE, 1922
UNDRESSED, 1928
UNDYING FLAME, THE, 1917
UNDYING MONSTER, THE, 1942, A
UNE AVENTURE, 1922
UNE ETRANGERE, 1924

UNE FEMME DEUCE
UNE FEMME EST UNE FEMME
UNE FEMME INCONNUE, 1918
UNE FLEUR DANS LES RONCES, 1921
UNE HISTOIRE DE BRIGANDS, 1920
UNE HISTOIRE IMMORTELLE
UNE JEUNE FILLE
UNE MERE, UNE FILLE
UNE NUIT AGITEE, 1920
UNE PARISIENNE
UNE VIE SANS JOIE
UNEARTHLY STRANGER, THE, 1964, A
UNEARTHLY, THE, 1957, O
UNEASY MONEY, 1918
UNEASY PAYMENTS, 1927
UNEASY TERMS, 1948
UNEASY VIRTUE, 1931, A
UNEXPECTED FATHER, 1932, A
UNEXPECTED FATHER, 1939, A
UNEXPECTED GUEST, 1946, A
UNEXPECTED PLACES, 1918
UNEXPECTED UNCLE, 1941, A
UNFAIR SEX, THE, 1926
UNFAITHFUL, 1931, A
UNFAITHFUL WIFE, THE
UNFAITHFUL WIFE, THE, 1915
UNFAITHFUL, THE, 1947, A
UNFAITHFULLY YOURS, 1948, A-C
UNFAITHFULLY YOURS, 1984, C
UNFAITHFULS, THE, 1960, A
UNFINISHED BUSINESS, 1941, A
UNFINISHED DANCE, THE, 1947, A
UNFINISHED SYMPHONY, THE, 1953, A
UNFOLDMENT, THE, 1922
UNFORGIVEN, THE, 1960, C
UNFORSEEN, THE, 1917
UNFORTUNATE SEX, THE, 1920
UNGUARDED GIRLS, 1929
UNGUARDED HOUR, THE, 1925, A
UNGUARDED HOUR, THE, 1936, A
UNGUARDED MOMENT, THE, 1956, A
UNGUARDED WOMEN, 1924
UNHINGED, 1982, O
UNHOLY DESIRE, 1964, O
UNHOLY FOUR, THE, 1954, A
UNHOLY FOUR, THE, 1969, C
UNHOLY GARDEN, THE, 1931, A
UNHOLY LOVE, 1932, A
UNHOLY NIGHT, THE, 1929, A
UNHOLY PARTNERS, 1941, A
UNHOLY QUEST, THE, 1934, A
UNHOLY ROLLERS, 1972, O
UNHOLY THREE, THE, 1925, A
UNHOLY THREE, THE, 1930, C
UNHOLY WIFE, THE, 1957, A
UNIDENTIFIED FLYING ODDBALL, THE, 1979, A
UNIFORM LOVERS
UNINHIBITED, THE, 1968, C
UNINVITED GUEST, THE, 1923, A
UNINVITED GUEST, THE, 1924
UNINVITED, THE, 1944, C
UNION CITY, 1980, A
UNION DEPOT, 1932, A
UNION PACIFIC, 1939, A
UNION STATION, 1950, C
UNITED STATES SMITH, 1928
UNIVERSAL SOLDIER, 1971, C
UNIVERSITY OF LIFE, 1941, C
UNJUSTLY ACCUSED, 1913
UNKILLABLES, THE
UNKISSED BRIDE, 1966
UNKISSED BRIDE, THE
UNKNOWN 274, 1917
UNKNOWN BATTLE, THE
UNKNOWN BLONDE, 1934, A
UNKNOWN CAVALIER, THE, 1926, A
UNKNOWN DANGERS, 1926
UNKNOWN GUEST, THE, 1943, A
UNKNOWN ISLAND, 1948, A
UNKNOWN LOVE, THE, 1919
UNKNOWN LOVER, THE, 1925
UNKNOWN MAN OF SHANDIGOR, THE, 1967, A
UNKNOWN MAN, THE, 1951, C
UNKNOWN POWERS, 1979
UNKNOWN PURPLE, THE, 1923
UNKNOWN QUANTITY, THE, 1919
UNKNOWN RANGER, THE, 1936, A
UNKNOWN RIDER, THE, 1929
UNKNOWN SATELLITE OVER TOKYO
UNKNOWN SOLDIER, THE, 1926
UNKNOWN TERROR, THE, 1957, A
UNKNOWN TREASURES, 1926
UNKNOWN VALLEY, 1933, A
UNKNOWN WIFE, THE, 1921
UNKNOWN WOMAN, 1935, A
UNKNOWN WORLD, 1951, A
UNKNOWN, THE, 1915
UNKNOWN, THE, 1921, A
UNKNOWN, THE, 1927, C
UNKNOWN, THE, 1946, A
UNMAN, WITTERING AND ZIGO, 1971, C
UNMARRIED, 1920
UNMARRIED, 1939, A
UNMARRIED WIVES, 1924
UNMARRIED WOMAN, AN, 1978, C-O
UNMASKED, 1929
UNMASKED, 1929, A
UNMASKED, 1950, A
UNNAMED WOMAN, THE, 1925
UNO DEI TRE
UNPAINTED WOMAN, THE, 1919
UNPARDONABLE SIN, THE, 1916
UNPARDONABLE SIN, THE, 1919
UNPROTECTED, 1916
UNPUBLISHED STORY, 1942, A
UNRECONCILED
UNREST, 1920, A
UNRESTRAINED YOUTH, 1925
UNRUHIGE NACHT
UNSATISFIED, THE, 1964, A
UNSEEING EYES, 1923
UNSEEN ENEMIES, 1926
UNSEEN ENEMY, 1942, A
UNSEEN FORCES, 1920
UNSEEN HANDS, 1924
UNSEEN HEROES
UNSEEN, THE, 1945, A
UNSEEN, THE, 1981, O
UNSENT LETTER, THE
UNSER BOSS IST EINE DAME
UNSINKABLE MOLLY BROWN, THE, 1964, A
UNSTOPPABLE MAN, THE, 1961, A
UNSTRAP ME, 1968, O
UNSUITABLE JOB FOR A WOMAN, AN, 1982, C-O
UNSUSPECTED, THE, 1947, A
UNTAMEABLE, THE, 1923
UNTAMED, 1918
UNTAMED, 1929, A-C
UNTAMED, 1940, A
UNTAMED, 1955, C-O
UNTAMED BREED, THE, 1948, A
UNTAMED FRONTIER, 1952, A
UNTAMED FURY, 1947, A
UNTAMED HEIRESS, 1954, A
UNTAMED JUSTICE, 1929
UNTAMED LADY, THE, 1926, A
UNTAMED MISTRESS, 1960, O
UNTAMED WEST, THE
UNTAMED WOMEN, 1952, A
UNTAMED YOUTH, 1924
UNTAMED YOUTH, 1957, A
UNTAMED, THE, 1920
UNTER GEIERN
UNTIL SEPTEMBER, 1984, O
UNTIL THE DAY WE MEET AGAIN, 1932
UNTIL THEY GET ME, 1918
UNTIL THEY SAIL, 1957, C
UNTITLED
UNTO EACH OTHER, 1929
UNTO THOSE WHO SIN, 1916
UNTOUCHABLES, THE
UNTOUCHED, 1956, A
UNVANQUISHED, THE
UNVEILING HAND, THE, 1919
UNWANTED, THE, 1924, A
UNWED MOTHER, 1958, C-O
UNWELCOME MOTHER, THE, 1916
UNWELCOME MRS. HATCH, THE, 1914
UNWELCOME STRANGER, 1935, A
UNWELCOME VISITORS
UNWELCOME WIFE, THE, 1915
UNWILLING AGENT, 1968, A
UNWILLING HERO, AN, 1921
UNWRITTEN CODE, THE, 1919
UNWRITTEN CODE, THE, 1944, A
UNWRITTEN LAW, THE, 1916
UNWRITTEN LAW, THE, 1925
UNWRITTEN LAW, THE, 1932, A
UP AND AT 'EM, 1922
UP AND GOING, 1922
UP FOR MURDER, 1931, A
UP FOR THE CUP, 1931, A
UP FOR THE CUP, 1950, A
UP FOR THE DERBY, 1933, A
UP FROM THE BEACH, 1965, A
UP FROM THE DEPTHS, 1915
UP FROM THE DEPTHS, 1979, O
UP FRONT, 1951, A
UP GOES MAISIE, 1946, A
UP IN ARMS, 1944, AA
UP IN CENTRAL PARK, 1948, A
UP IN MABEL'S ROOM, 1926
UP IN MABEL'S ROOM, 1944, A
UP IN MARY'S ATTICK, 1920
UP IN SMOKE, 1957, A
UP IN SMOKE, 1978, O
UP IN THE AIR, 1940, A
UP IN THE AIR, 1969, AA
UP IN THE AIR ABOUT MARY, 1922
UP IN THE CELLAR, 1970, C
UP IN THE WORLD, 1957, A
UP JUMPED A SWAGMAN, 1965, A
UP JUMPED THE DEVIL, 1941
UP OR DOWN, 1917
UP PERISCOPE, 1959, A
UP POMPEII, 1971, O
UP POPS THE DEVIL, 1931, A
UP RIVER, 1979
UP ROMANCE ROAD, 1918
UP SHE GOES
UP THE ACADEMY, 1980, O
UP THE CHASTITY BELT, 1971, O
UP THE CREEK, 1958, A
UP THE CREEK, 1984, O
UP THE DOWN STAIRCASE, 1967, A-C
UP THE FRONT, 1972, C
UP THE JUNCTION, 1968, O
UP THE LADDER, 1925
UP THE MACGREGORS, 1967, A
UP THE RIVER, 1930, A
UP THE RIVER, 1938, A
UP THE ROAD WITH SALLIE, 1918
UP THE SANDBOX, 1972, C-O
UP TIGHT
UP TO HIS EARS, 1966, C
UP TO HIS NECK, 1954, A
UP TO THE NECK, 1933, A
UP WITH THE LARK, 1943, A
UP YOUR ALLEY, 1975
UP YOUR TEDDY BEAR, 1970, O
UPHEAVAL, THE, 1916
UPLAND RIDER, THE, 1928
UPLIFTERS, THE, 1919
UPPER CRUST, THE, 1917
UPPER HAND, THE, 1967, C
UPPER UNDERWORLD
UPPER WORLD, 1934, A
UPPERCRUST, THE, 1982
UPRISING, 1918
UPS AND DOWNS, 1981
UPSIDE DOWN, 1919
UPSTAGE, 1926
UPSTAIRS, 1919
UPSTAIRS AND DOWN, 1919
UPSTAIRS AND DOWNSTAIRS, 1961, A
UPSTART, THE, 1916
UPSTATE MURDERS, THE
UPSTREAM, 1927
UPTIGHT, 1968, O
UPTOWN NEW YORK, 1932, A
UPTOWN SATURDAY NIGHT, 1974, C
UPTURNED GLASS, THE, 1947, A-C
URANIUM BOOM, 1956, A
URBAN COWBOY, 1980, C
URGE TO KILL, 1960, C
URGENT CALL
URSUS
URSUS, IL GLADIATORE RIBELLE
URUBU, 1948
USCHI DAI SENSO
USED CARS, 1980, O
USURPER, THE, 1919
UTAH, 1945, A
UTAH BLAINE, 1957, A
UTAH KID, THE, 1930, A
UTAH KID, THE, 1944
UTAH TRAIL, 1938, A
UTAH WAGON TRAIN, 1951, A
UTILITIES, 1983, C-O
UTOPIA, 1952, A
UTU, 1984, O

-V-

V.D., 1961, O
V.I.P.s, THE, 1963, A
V1
VACATION DAYS, 1947, A
VACATION FROM LOVE, 1938, A
VACATION FROM MARRIAGE, 1945, A
VACATION IN RENO, 1946, A
VACATION, THE, 1971, C
VADO...L'AMMAZZO E TORNO
VAGABOND CUB, THE, 1929
VAGABOND KING, THE, 1930, A
VAGABOND KING, THE, 1956, A
VAGABOND LADY, 1935, A
VAGABOND LOVER, 1929, A
VAGABOND LUCK, 1919
VAGABOND PRINCE, THE, 1916
VAGABOND QUEEN, THE, 1931, A
VAGABOND TRAIL, THE, 1924
VAGABOND VIOLINIST
VAGABOND'S REVENGE, A, 1915
VAGHE STELLE DELL'ORSA
VALACHI PAPERS, THE, 1972, O
VALDEZ IS COMING, 1971, O
VALENCIA, 1926

VALENTINE GIRL, THE, 1917
VALENTINO, 1951, C
VALENTINO, 1977, C-O
VALERIE, 1957, C
VALIANT HOMBRE THE, 1948, A
VALIANT IS THE WORD FOR CARRIE, 1936, A-C
VALIANT, THE, 1929, A-C
VALIANT, THE, 1962, A
VALIANTS OF VIRGINIA, THE, 1916
VALLEY GIRL, 1983, C
VALLEY OF BLOOD, 1973
VALLEY OF BRAVERY, THE, 1926, A
VALLEY OF DEATH, THE
VALLEY OF DECISION, THE, 1916
VALLEY OF DECISION, THE, 1945, A
VALLEY OF DOUBT, THE, 1920
VALLEY OF EAGLES, 1952, A
VALLEY OF FEAR
VALLEY OF FEAR, 1947
VALLEY OF FEAR, THE, 1916
VALLEY OF FEAR, THE, 1917
VALLEY OF FIRE, 1951, A
VALLEY OF FURY
VALLEY OF GWANGI, THE, 1969, A
VALLEY OF HATE, THE, 1924
VALLEY OF HELL, THE, 1927
VALLEY OF HUNTED MEN, 1942, A
VALLEY OF HUNTED MEN, THE, 1928
VALLEY OF LOST HOPE, THE, 1915
VALLEY OF LOST SOULS, THE, 1923
VALLEY OF MYSTERY, 1967, A
VALLEY OF SILENT MEN, THE, 1922, A
VALLEY OF SONG
VALLEY OF TERROR, 1937
VALLEY OF THE DOLLS, 1967, O
VALLEY OF THE DRAGONS, 1961, A
VALLEY OF THE GHOSTS, 1928
VALLEY OF THE GIANTS, 1938, A
VALLEY OF THE GIANTS, THE, 1919
VALLEY OF THE GIANTS, THE, 1927
VALLEY OF THE HEADHUNTERS, 1953, A
VALLEY OF THE KINGS, 1954, A-C
VALLEY OF THE LAWLESS, 1936, A
VALLEY OF THE MOON, THE, 1914
VALLEY OF THE REDWOODS, 1960, A
VALLEY OF THE SUN, 1942, A
VALLEY OF THE SWORDS
VALLEY OF THE WHITE WOLVES
VALLEY OF THE ZOMBIES, 1946, C
VALLEY OF TOMORROW, THE, 1920
VALLEY OF VANISHING MEN, THE, 1924
VALLEY OF VENGEANCE, 1944, A
VALLEY OF WANTED MEN, 1935
VALUE FOR MONEY, 1957, A
VAMP, THE, 1918
VAMPING, 1984, O
VAMPING VENUS, 1928, A
VAMPIRA
VAMPIRE AND THE BALLERINA, THE, 1962, C
VAMPIRE AND THE ROBOT, THE
VAMPIRE BAT, THE, 1933, C
VAMPIRE BEAST CRAVES BLOOD, THE
VAMPIRE CIRCUS, 1972, C-O
VAMPIRE GIRLS, THE
VAMPIRE HOOKERS, THE, 1979, O
VAMPIRE LOVERS, THE, 1970, O
VAMPIRE MEN OF THE LOST PLANET
VAMPIRE OVER LONDON
VAMPIRE PEOPLE, THE
VAMPIRE'S COFFIN, THE, 1958, O
VAMPIRE'S GHOST, THE, 1945, C
VAMPIRE'S NIGHT ORGY, THE, 1973, O
VAMPIRE, THE
VAMPIRE, THE, 1915
VAMPIRE, THE, 1957, C
VAMPIRE, THE, 1968, C
VAMPIRES
VAMPIRES, THE, 1969, O
VAMPYR, 1932, O
VAMPYRES, DAUGHTERS OF DRACULA, 1977, O
VAN NUYS BLVD., 1979, O
VAN, THE, 1977, O
VANDERGILT DIAMOND MYSTERY, THE, 1936, A
VANDERHOFF AFFAIR, THE, 1915
VANESSA, HER LOVE STORY, 1935, A
VANINA, 1922
VANISHING AMERICAN, THE, 1925
VANISHING AMERICAN, THE, 1955, A
VANISHING FRONTIER, 1962
VANISHING FRONTIER, THE, 1932, A
VANISHING HOOFS, 1926, A
VANISHING MEN, 1932
VANISHING OUTPOST, THE, 1951, A
VANISHING PIONEER, THE, 1928
VANISHING POINT, 1971, C
VANISHING RIDERS, 1935
VANISHING VIRGINIAN, THE, 1941, A
VANISHING WESTERNER, THE, 1950, A
VANITY, 1917
VANITY, 1927, A
VANITY, 1935, A
VANITY FAIR, 1915
VANITY FAIR, 1923
VANITY FAIR, 1932, C
VANITY POOL, THE, 1918
VANITY STREET, 1932, A
VANITY'S PRICE, 1924
VANQUISHED, THE, 1953, A
VARAN THE UNBELIEVABLE, 1962, A
VARELSERNA
VARIETY, 1925, C
VARIETY, 1935, A
VARIETY, 1984, O
VARIETY GIRL, 1947, AA
VARIETY HOUR, 1937, A
VARIETY JUBILEE, 1945, A
VARIETY LIGHTS, 1965, A
VARIETY PARADE, 1936, A
VARMINT, THE, 1917
VARSITY, 1928
VARSITY, 1928, A
VARSITY, 1930
VARSITY SHOW, 1937, A
VAULT OF HORROR, THE, 1973, C-O
VAXDOCKAN
VECHERA NA KHUTORE BLIZ DIKANKI
VEIL, THE
VEILED ADVENTURE, THE, 1919
VEILED ARISTOCRATS, 1932
VEILED MARRIAGE, THE, 1920
VEILED WOMAN, THE, 1917, A
VEILED WOMAN, THE, 1922
VEILED WOMAN, THE, 1929
VEILLE D'ARMES, 1925
VEILS OF BAGDAD, THE, 1953, A
VELVET HAND, THE, 1918
VELVET HOUSE
VELVET PAW, THE, 1916
VELVET TOUCH, THE, 1948, A
VELVET TRAP, THE, 1966, O
VELVET VAMPIRE, THE, 1971, O
VENDEMIAIRE, 1919
VENDETTA, 1914
VENDETTA, 1921
VENDETTA, 1950, A
VENDETTA DELLA MASCHERA DI FERRO
VENDETTA, 1965
VENDREDI 13 HEURES
VENETIAN AFFAIR, THE, 1967, C
VENETIAN BIRD
VENETIAN LOVERS, 1925
VENETIAN NIGHTS
VENGEANCE, 1918
VENGEANCE, 1930, A
VENGEANCE, 1964, A
VENGEANCE, 1968, C
VENGEANCE IS MINE, 1916
VENGEANCE IS MINE, 1918
VENGEANCE IS MINE, 1948, A
VENGEANCE IS MINE, 1969, A
VENGEANCE IS MINE, 1980, O
VENGEANCE OF DURAND, THE, 1919
VENGEANCE OF FU MANCHU, THE, 1968, A
VENGEANCE OF GREGORY
VENGEANCE OF NANA, 1915
VENGEANCE OF PIERRE, THE, 1923
VENGEANCE OF RANNAH, 1936
VENGEANCE OF SHE, THE, 1968, A
VENGEANCE OF THE DEAD, 1917
VENGEANCE OF THE DEEP, 1923
VENGEANCE OF THE DEEP, 1940, A
VENGEANCE OF THE VAMPIRE WOMEN, THE, 1969, O
VENGEANCE OF THE WEST
VENGEANCE OF THE WEST, 1942
VENGEANCE OF VIRGO, 1972
VENGEANCE TRAIL, THE, 1921
VENGEANCE VALLEY, 1951, A
VENGEANCE, 1944
VENGEANCE, 1945
VENGEANCE, 1965
VENOM, 1968, O
VENOM, 1982, O
VENOM, 1976
VENT DEBOUT, 1923
VENTO DELL'EST
VENUS, 1929
VENUS DER PIRATEN
VENUS IN FURS, 1970, O
VENUS IN THE EAST, 1919
VENUS MAKES TROUBLE, 1937, A
VENUS MODEL, THE, 1918
VENUS OF THE SOUTH SEAS, 1924
VENUS OF VENICE, 1927
VENUS VICTRIX, 1917
VENUSIAN, THE
VERA CRUZ, 1954, C-O
VERA, THE MEDIUM, 1916
VERBOTEN?, 1959, C
VERBRECHEN NACH SCHULSCHLUSS
VERDICT, 1975, C
VERDICT OF THE DESERT, THE, 1925
VERDICT OF THE HEART, THE, 1915
VERDICT OF THE SEA, 1932, A
VERDICT, THE, 1925
VERDICT, THE, 1946, C
VERDICT, THE, 1964, A
VERDICT, THE, 1982, C-O
VERDUN, VISIONS D'HISTOIRE, 1929
VERFUHRUNG AM MEER
VERGELTUNG IN CATANO
VERGINITA, 1953, A-C
VERKLUGENE MELODIE
VERMILION DOOR, 1969, A
VERMILION PENCIL, THE, 1922
VERNON, FLORIDA, 1982
VERONA TRIAL, THE, 1963, A
VERONIKA VOSS, 1982, O
VERS ABECHER LA MYSTERIEUSE, 1924
VERSPATUNG IN MARIENBORN
VERTIGO, 1958, C
VERY BIG WITHDRAWAL, A
VERY CONFIDENTIAL, 1927
VERY CURIOUS GIRL, A, 1970, O
VERY EDGE, THE, 1963, C
VERY GOOD YOUNG MAN, A, 1919
VERY HANDY MAN, A, 1966, C
VERY HAPPY ALEXANDER, 1969, A
VERY HONORABLE GUY, A, 1934, A
VERY IDEA, THE, 1920
VERY IDEA, THE, 1929, A
VERY IMPORTANT PERSON, A
VERY NATURAL THING, A, 1974, O
VERY PRIVATE AFFAIR, A, 1962, C
VERY SPECIAL FAVOR, A, 1965, A
VERY THOUGHT OF YOU, THE, 1944, A
VERY TRULY YOURS, 1922
VERY YOUNG LADY, A, 1941, A
VESSEL OF WRATH
VET IN THE DOGHOUSE
VETERAN, THE
VI OF SMITH'S ALLEY, 1921
VIA MARGUTTA
VIA PONY EXPRESS, 1933, A
VIA WIRELESS, 1915
VIAGGIO IN ITALIA
VIBRATION, 1969, O
VIC DYSON PAYS, 1925
VICAR OF BRAY, THE, 1937, A
VICAR OF WAKEFIELD, THE, 1913
VICAR OF WAKEFIELD, THE, 1916
VICAR OF WAKEFIELD, THE, 1917
VICE AND VIRTUE, 1965, O
VICE AND VIRTUE; OR, THE TEMPTERS OF LONDON (1915, Brit.)
VICE DOLLS, 1961, C
VICE GIRLS, LTD., 1964, O
VICE OF FOOLS, THE, 1920
VICE RACKET, 1937, A
VICE RAID, 1959, C
VICE SQUAD, 1953, A
VICE SQUAD, 1982, O
VICE SQUAD, THE, 1931, A
VICE VERSA, 1948, A
VICIOUS CIRCLE, THE, 1948, A
VICIOUS CIRCLE, THE, 1959
VICIOUS YEARS, THE, 1950, A
VICKI, 1953, C
VICKY VAN, 1919
VICTIM, 1961, C-O
VICTIM FIVE
VICTIM, THE, 1914
VICTIM, THE, 1916
VICTIM, THE, 1917
VICTIM, THE, 1921
VICTIMS OF PERSECUTION, 1933, A
VICTIMS OF THE BEYOND
VICTOR FRANKENSTEIN, 1975, C
VICTOR, THE, 1923
VICTOR/VICTORIA, 1982, O
VICTORIA CROSS, THE, 1916
VICTORIA THE GREAT, 1937, A
VICTORS, THE, 1963, O
VICTORY, 1913
VICTORY, 1919
VICTORY, 1928
VICTORY, 1940, A-C
VICTORY, 1981, A-C
VICTORY AND PEACE, 1918
VICTORY OF CONSCIENCE, THE, 1916
VICTORY OF VIRTUE, THE, 1915
VIDEO MADNESS
VIDEODROME, 1983, O
VIENNA WALTZES, 1961, A
VIENNA, CITY OF SONGS, 1931, A
VIENNESE NIGHTS, 1930, A
VIEW FROM POMPEY'S HEAD, THE, 1955, C-O

VIEW FROM THE BRIDGE, A, 1962, C
VIGIL, 1984, C
VIGIL IN THE NIGHT, 1940, C
VIGILANTE, 1983, O
VIGILANTE FORCE, 1976, C
VIGILANTE HIDEOUT, 1950, A
VIGILANTE TERROR, 1953, A
VIGILANTES, 1920
VIGILANTES OF BOOMTOWN, 1947, A
VIGILANTES OF DODGE CITY, 1944, AA
VIGILANTES RETURN, THE, 1947, A
VIGILANTES RIDE, THE, 1944
VIGOUR OF YOUTH
VIKING QUEEN, THE, 1967, A
VIKING WOMEN AND THE SEA SERPENT
VIKING, THE, 1929
VIKING, THE, 1931, A
VIKINGS, THE, 1958, C
VILLA DESTIN, 1921
VILLA RIDES, 1968, O
VILLA?, 1958, A
VILLAGE BARN DANCE, 1940, A
VILLAGE BLACKSMITH, THE, 1922
VILLAGE HOMESTEAD, THE, 1915
VILLAGE IN CRISIS, 1920
VILLAGE OF DAUGHTERS, 1962, A
VILLAGE OF THE DAMNED, 1960, C
VILLAGE OF THE GIANTS, 1965, A
VILLAGE SLEUTH, A, 1920
VILLAGE SQUIRE, THE, 1935, A
VILLAGE TALE, 1935, A
VILLAGE, THE, 1953, A
VILLAIN, 1971, O
VILLAIN STILL PURSUED HER, THE, 1940, A
VILLAIN, THE, 1979, A
VILLE SANS PITTE
VILLIERS DIAMOND, THE, 1938, A
VILNA LEGEND, A, 1949, A
VINETU
VINETU II
VINETU III
VINGT ANS APRES
VINTAGE WINE, 1935, A
VINTAGE, THE, 1957, A
VIOLATED, 1953, C
VIOLATED LOVE, 1966, C
VIOLATED PARADISE, 1963, O
VIOLATORS, THE, 1957, A
VIOLENCE, 1947, A
VIOLENT AND THE DAMNED, THE, 1962, C
VIOLENT ANGELS, THE
VIOLENT CITY
VIOLENT ENEMY, THE, 1969, A
VIOLENT FOUR, THE, 1968, A
VIOLENT HOUR, THE
VIOLENT JOURNEY
VIOLENT LOVE
VIOLENT MEN, THE, 1955, A
VIOLENT MIDNIGHT
VIOLENT MOMENT, 1966, C
VIOLENT ONES, THE, 1967, C
VIOLENT PLAYGROUND, 1958, A
VIOLENT ROAD, 1958, A
VIOLENT SATURDAY, 1955, O
VIOLENT STRANGER, 1957, A
VIOLENT STREETS
VIOLENT SUMMER, 1961, C
VIOLENT WOMEN, 1960, O
VIOLENT YEARS, THE, 1956, C-O
VIOLENZA PER UNA MONACA
VIOLETTE, 1978, O
VIOLETTES IMPERIALES, 1924
VIOLIN AND ROLLER, 1962, A
VIPER, THE, 1938, A
VIRGIN AND THE GYPSY, THE, 1970, O
VIRGIN AQUA SEX, THE
VIRGIN COCOTTE, THE
VIRGIN FOR THE PRINCE, A
VIRGIN ISLAND, 1960, C
VIRGIN LIPS, 1928
VIRGIN OF NUREMBURG, THE
VIRGIN OF SEMINOLE, THE, 1923
VIRGIN OF STAMBOUL, THE, 1920
VIRGIN PARADISE, A, 1921
VIRGIN PRESIDENT, THE, 1968, A
VIRGIN QUEEN, THE, 1923
VIRGIN QUEEN, THE, 1955, A-C
VIRGIN SACRIFICE, 1959, C
VIRGIN SOLDIERS, THE, 1970, O
VIRGIN SPRING, THE, 1960, C
VIRGIN WIFE, THE, 1926
VIRGIN WITCH, THE, 1973, O
VIRGIN'S SACRIFICE, A, 1922
VIRGIN, THE, 1924
VIRGINIA, 1941, A
VIRGINIA CITY, 1940, A
VIRGINIA COURTSHIP, A, 1921
VIRGINIA JUDGE, THE, 1935, A
VIRGINIA'S HUSBAND, 1928, A
VIRGINIA'S HUSBAND, 1934, AAA
VIRGINIAN OUTCAST, 1924
VIRGINIAN, THE, 1914, A
VIRGINIAN, THE, 1923, A
VIRGINIAN, THE, 1929, A
VIRGINIAN, THE, 1946, A-C
VIRIDIANA, 1962, C-O
VIRTOUS SINNERS, 1919
VIRTUE, 1932, C
VIRTUE'S REVOLT, 1924
VIRTUOUS HUSBAND, 1931, A
VIRTUOUS LIARS, 1924
VIRTUOUS MEN, 1919
VIRTUOUS MODEL, THE, 1919
VIRTUOUS OUTCAST, THE
VIRTUOUS SIN, THE, 1930, A
VIRTUOUS THIEF, THE, 1919
VIRTUOUS TRAMPS, THE
VIRTUOUS VAMP, A, 1919
VIRTUOUS WIFE, THE
VIRTUOUS WIVES, 1919
VIRUS, 1980, C
VISA TO CANTON
VISAGE D'ENFANTS, 1926
VISAGES VIOLES...AMES CLOSES, 1921
VISCOUNT, THE, 1967, C
VISIT TO A CHIEF'S SON, 1974, AA
VISIT TO A SMALL PLANET, 1960, A
VISIT, THE, 1964, C
VISITING HOURS, 1982, O
VISITOR, THE, 1973, C-O
VISITOR, THE, 1980, O
VISITORS FROM THE GALAXY, 1981, AA
VISITORS, THE, 1972, O
VISKINGAR OCH ROP
VITA PRIVATA
VITAL QUESTION, THE, 1916
VITE PERDUTE
VITELLONI, 1956, C
VIVA CISCO KID, 1940, A
VIVA ITALIA, 1978, O
VIVA KNIEVEL?, 1977, A
VIVA LAS VEGAS
VIVA LAS VEGAS, 1964, A
VIVA MARIA, 1965, C
VIVA MAX?, 1969, A
VIVA VILLA!, 1934, A-C
VIVA ZAPATA!, 1952, C
VIVACIOUS LADY, 1938, A
VIVE LA FRANCE, 1918
VIVEMENT DIAMANCHE?
VIVERE PER VIVERE
VIVIAMO OGGI
VIVIETTE, 1918
VIVIR DESVIVIENDOSE
VIVO PER LA TUA MORTE
VIVRE, 1928
VIVRE POUR VIVRE
VIVRE SA VIE
VIXEN, 1970, O
VIXEN, THE, 1916
VIXENS, THE, 1969, O
VOGUES
VOGUES OF 1938, 1937, A
VOICE FROM THE MINARET, THE, 1923
VOICE IN THE DARK, 1921, A
VOICE IN THE MIRROR, 1958, A
VOICE IN THE NIGHT
VOICE IN THE NIGHT, 1934, A
VOICE IN THE NIGHT, A, 1941, A
VOICE IN THE WIND, 1944, A
VOICE IN YOUR HEART, A, 1952, C
VOICE OF BUGLE ANN, 1936, A
VOICE OF CONSCIENCE, THE, 1917
VOICE OF DESTINY, THE, 1918
VOICE OF LOVE, THE, 1916
VOICE OF MERRILL, THE
VOICE OF TERROR
VOICE OF THE CITY, 1929, A
VOICE OF THE HURRICANE, 1964, A
VOICE OF THE STORM, THE, 1929
VOICE OF THE TURTLE, THE, 1947, A
VOICE OF THE WHISTLER, 1945, C
VOICE OVER, 1983
VOICE WITHIN, THE, 1929
VOICE WITHIN, THE, 1945, A
VOICES, 1920
VOICES, 1973, O
VOICES, 1979, C
VOICES FROM THE PAST, 1915
VOLCANO, 1926, A
VOLCANO, 1953, A
VOLCANO, 1969
VOLCANO, THE, 1919
VOLGA AND SIBERIA, 1914
VOLGA BOATMAN, THE, 1926, A
VOLONTE, 1917
VOLPONE, 1947, A
VOLTAIRE, 1933, A
VOLUNTEER ORGANIST, THE, 1914
VOLUNTEER, THE, 1918
VON RICHTHOFEN AND BROWN, 1970, C
VON RYAN'S EXPRESS, 1965
VOODOO BLOOD BATH
VOODOO GIRL
VOODOO HEARTBEAT, 1972, O
VOODOO ISLAND, 1957, A
VOODOO MAN, 1944, A
VOODOO TIGER, 1952, A
VOODOO WOMAN, 1957, A
VOR SONNENUNTERGANG, 1961, A
VORTEX
VORTEX, 1982, O
VORTEX OF FATE, THE, 1913
VORTEX, THE, 1918
VORTEX, THE, 1927, A
VOSKRESENIYE
VOTE FOR HUGGETT, 1948, A
VOULEZ-VOUS DANSER AVEC MOI
VOW OF VENGEANCE, THE, 1923
VOW, THE, 1915
VOW, THE, 1947, A
VOYAGE BEYOND THE SUN
VOYAGE IN A BALLOON
VOYAGE OF SILENCE, 1968, A
VOYAGE OF THE DAMNED, 1976, A-C
VOYAGE TO AMERICA, 1952, A
VOYAGE TO PREHISTORY
VOYAGE TO THE BOTTOM OF THE SEA, 1961, A
VOYAGE TO THE END OF THE UNIVERSE, 1963, A
VOYAGE TO THE PLANET OF PREHISTORIC WOMEN, 1966, A
VOYAGE TO THE PREHISTORIC PLANET, 1965, A
VOYAGE, THE, 1974, 0
VOYNA I MIR
VRAZDA PO CESKU
VRAZDA PO NASEM
VREDENS DAG
VROODER'S HOOCH
VU DU PONT
VULCAN AFFAIR, THE
VULCANO
VULGAR YACHTSMEN, THE, 1926
VULTURE OF GOLD, THE, 1914
VULTURE, THE, 1937, A
VULTURE, THE, 1967, C
VULTURES IN PARADISE, 1984
VULTURES OF SOCIETY, 1916
VULTURES OF THE LAW
VYNALEZ ZKAZY
VZROSLYYE DETI

-W-

W, 1974, C
W. W. AND THE DIXIE DANCEKINGS, 1975, A
W.C. FIELDS AND ME, 1976, C
W.I.A. (WOUNDED IN ACTION), 1966, A
"W" PLAN, THE, 1931, A
WABASH AVENUE, 1950, A
WAC FROM WALLA WALLA, THE, 1952, A
WACKIEST SHIP IN THE ARMY, THE, 1961, A
WACKIEST WAGON TRAIN IN THE WEST, THE, 1976, A
WACKO, 1983, C
WACKY WORLD OF DR. MORGUS, THE, 1962, A
WACKY WORLD OF MOTHER GOOSE, THE,, 1967, AAA
WACO, 1952, A
WACO, 1966, C
WAGA KOI WAGA UTA
WAGER, THE, 1916
WAGES FOR WIVES, 1925, A
WAGES OF CONSCIENCE, 1927
WAGES OF FEAR, 1977
WAGES OF FEAR, THE, 1955, O
WAGES OF SIN, THE, 1918
WAGES OF SIN, THE, 1922
WAGES OF SIN, THE, 1929
WAGES OF VIRTUE, 1924
WAGNER, 1983, C-O
WAGON MASTER, THE, 1929, A
WAGON SHOW, THE, 1928
WAGON TEAM, 1952, A
WAGON TRACKS, 1919
WAGON TRACKS WEST, 1943, A
WAGON TRAIL, 1935, A
WAGON TRAIN, 1940, A
WAGON TRAIN, 1952
WAGON WHEELS, 1934, A
WAGON WHEELS WESTWARD, 1956, AA
WAGONMASTER, 1950, A
WAGONS ROLL AT NIGHT, THE, 1941, A
WAGONS WEST, 1952, A
WAGONS WESTWARD, 1940, A
WAHINE
WAIF, THE, 1915
WAIFS, 1918
WAIFS, THE, 1916

WAIKIKI WEDDING, 1937, A
WAIT 'TIL THE SUN SHINES, NELLIE, 1952, A
WAIT AND SEE, 1928
WAIT UNTIL DARK, 1967, O
WAITING AT THE CHURCH
WAITING FOR CAROLINE, 1969, C
WAITING FOR THE BRIDE
WAITING SOUL, THE, 1917
WAITING WOMEN
WAITRESS, 1982, O
WAJAN, 1938, A
WAKAMBA?, 1955, AA
WAKAMONO TACHI
WAKARE
WAKARETE IKURU TOKI MO
WAKE ISLAND, 1942, A
WAKE ME WHEN IT'S OVER, 1960, A
WAKE OF THE RED WITCH, 1949, A-C
WAKE UP AND DIE, 1967, C
WAKE UP AND DREAM, 1934, A
WAKE UP AND DREAM, 1946, A
WAKE UP AND DREAM, 1942
WAKE UP AND LIVE, 1937, AA
WAKE UP FAMOUS, 1937, A
WAKEFIELD CASE, THE, 1921
WAKING UP THE TOWN, 1925
WALK A CROOKED MILE, 1948, A
WALK A CROOKED PATH, 1969, O
WALK A TIGHTROPE, 1964, A-C
WALK CHEERFULLY, 1930
WALK EAST ON BEACON, 1952, A
WALK IN THE SHADOW, 1966, A
WALK IN THE SPRING RAIN, A, 1970, C
WALK IN THE SUN, A, 1945, C
WALK INTO HELL, 1957, A
WALK LIKE A DRAGON, 1960, O
WALK ON THE WILD SIDE, 1962, O
WALK PROUD, 1979, C
WALK SOFTLY, STRANGER, 1950, C
WALK TALL, 1960, A
WALK THE ANGRY BEACH, 1961, C
WALK THE DARK STREET, 1956, C
WALK THE PROUD LAND, 1956, A
WALK THE WALK, 1970, O
WALK WITH LOVE AND DEATH, A, 1969, C
WALK, DON'T RUN, 1966, A
WALK-OFFS, THE, 1920
WALKABOUT, 1971, C
WALKING BACK, 1928, A
WALKING DEAD, THE, 1936, A
WALKING DOWN BROADWAY, 1938, A
WALKING DOWN BROADWAY, 1935
WALKING HILLS, THE, 1949, A
WALKING MY BABY BACK HOME, 1953, A
WALKING ON AIR, 1936, A
WALKING ON AIR, 1946, AAA
WALKING STICK, THE, 1970, C
WALKING TALL, 1973, O
WALKING TALL, PART II, 1975, O
WALKING TARGET, THE, 1960, C
WALKOVER, 1969, C
WALKOWER
WALL BETWEEN, THE, 1916
WALL FLOWER, THE, 1922, A
WALL FOR SAN SEBASTIAN
WALL OF NOISE, 1963, A
WALL STREET, 1929, A
WALL STREET COWBOY, 1939, A
WALL STREET MYSTERY, THE, 1920
WALL STREET TRAGEDY, A, 1916
WALL STREET WHIZ, THE, 1925
WALL, THE
WALL-EYED NIPPON, 1963, A
WALLABY JIM OF THE ISLANDS, 1937, A
WALLET, THE, 1952, A
WALLFLOWER, 1948, A
WALLFLOWER, THE
WALLFLOWERS, 1928
WALLOP, THE, 1921, A
WALLOPING KID, 1926
WALLOPING WALLACE, 1924, A
WALLS CAME TUMBLING DOWN, THE, 1946, A
WALLS OF GOLD, 1933, C
WALLS OF HELL, THE, 1964, A
WALLS OF JERICHO, 1948, C
WALLS OF JERICHO, THE, 1914
WALLS OF MALAPAGA, THE, 1950, A
WALLS OF PREJUDICE, 1920, A
WALPURGIS NIGHT, 1941, A-C
WALTZ ACROSS TEXAS, 1982, A-C
WALTZ DREAM, A, 1926
WALTZ OF THE TOREADORS, 1962, A-C
WALTZ TIME, 1933, A
WALTZ TIME, 1946, A
WALTZES FROM VIENNA
WANDA, 1971, C
WANDA NEVADA, 1979, A-C
WANDER LOVE STORY
WANDERER BEYOND THE GRAVE, 1915
WANDERER OF THE WASTELAND, 1924
WANDERER OF THE WASTELAND, 1935, A
WANDERER OF THE WASTELAND, 1945, A
WANDERER OF THE WEST, 1927
WANDERER, THE, 1926
WANDERER, THE, 1969, A
WANDERERS OF THE WEST, 1941, A
WANDERERS, THE, 1979, O
WANDERING DAUGHTERS, 1923
WANDERING FIRES, 1925
WANDERING FOOTSTEPS, 1925
WANDERING GIRLS, 1927, A
WANDERING HUSBANDS, 1924
WANDERING JEW, THE, 1913
WANDERING JEW, THE, 1923
WANDERING JEW, THE, 1933, A
WANDERING JEW, THE, 1935, A
WANDERING JEW, THE, 1948, O
WANDERING STARS, 1927
WANDERLOVE, 1970, O
WANDERLUST
WANING SEX, THE, 1926, A
WANT A RIDE LITTLE GIRL?
WANTED, 1937, A
WANTED—A BROTHER, 1918
WANTED—A HOME, 1916
WANTED—A HUSBAND, 1919
WANTED—A MOTHER, 1918
WANTED—A WIDOW, 1916
WANTED—A WIFE, 1918
WANTED AT HEADQUARTERS, 1920
WANTED BY SCOTLAND YARD, 1939, A
WANTED BY THE LAW, 1924
WANTED BY THE POLICE, 1938, A
WANTED DEAD OR ALIVE, 1951
WANTED FOR MURDER, 1919, A
WANTED FOR MURDER, 1946, C
WANTED FOR MURDER, OR BRIDE OF HATE
WANTED MEN, 1931
WANTED MEN, 1936
WANTED WOMEN
WANTED, 1929
WANTED, 1933
WANTED—A COWARD, 1927, A
WANTED: JANE TURNER, 1936, A
WANTERS, THE, 1923, A
WANTON CONTESSA, THE
WAR
WAR AGAINST MRS. HADLEY, THE, 1942, A
WAR AND PEACE, 1915
WAR AND PEACE, 1956, A-C
WAR AND PEACE, 1968, A-C
WAR AND PEACE, 1983, C
WAR AND PIECE
WAR AND THE WOMAN, 1917
WAR ARROW, 1953, A
WAR BETWEEN MEN AND WOMEN, THE, 1972, A-C
WAR BETWEEN THE PLANETS, 1971, A
WAR BRIDE'S SECRET, THE, 1916
WAR BRIDES, 1916
WAR CORRESPONDENT, 1932, A
WAR DOGS, 1942, A
WAR DRUMS, 1957, A
WAR EXTRA, THE, 1914
WAR GAMES, 1970
WAR GAMES, 1983
WAR GODS OF THE DEEP
WAR HEAD
WAR HERO, WAR MADNESS
WAR HORSE, THE, 1927, A
WAR HUNT, 1962, C
WAR IS A RACKET, 1934, A-C
WAR IS HELL, 1964, A-C
WAR IS OVER, THE
WAR ITALIAN STYLE, 1967, A
WAR LORD, THE, 1965, O
WAR LORD, THE, 1937
WAR LOVER, THE, 1962, C-O
WAR MADNESS
WAR NURSE, 1930, A
WAR OF THE ALIENS
WAR OF THE BUTTONS, 1963, A
WAR OF THE COLOSSAL BEAST, 1958, A
WAR OF THE GARGANTUAS, THE, 1970, A
WAR OF THE MONSTERS, 1972, A
WAR OF THE PLANETS, 1977, A
WAR OF THE RANGE, 1933, A
WAR OF THE SATELLITES, 1958, A
WAR OF THE TONGS, THE, 1917
WAR OF THE WILDCATS
WAR OF THE WIZARDS, 1983, C
WAR OF THE WORLDS, THE, 1953, C
WAR OF THE WORLDS—NEXT CENTURY, THE, 1981, C
WAR OF THE ZOMBIES, THE, 1965, C-O
WAR PAINT, 1926, A
WAR PAINT, 1953, A
WAR PARTY, 1965, A
WAR SHOCK
WAR WAGON, THE, 1967, A
WAR'S WOMEN, 1916
WAR'S WOMEN, 1923
WARD 13
WARE CASE, THE, 1917, A
WARE CASE, THE, 1928
WARE CASE, THE, 1939, A
WARFARE OF THE FLESH, THE, 1917
WARGAMES, 1983, A
WARHEAD, 1974
WARKILL, 1968, O
WARLOCK, 1959, C
WARLOCK MOON, 1973
WARLORD OF CRETE, THE
WARLORDS OF ATLANTIS, 1978, AA
WARLORDS OF THE 21ST CENTURY
WARLORDS OF THE DEEP
WARM BODY, THE
WARM CORNER,A, 1930, AA
WARM DECEMBER, A, 1973, C
WARM IN THE BUD, 1970, A
WARMING UP, 1928, A
WARN LONDON?, 1934, A
WARN THAT MAN, 1943, A
WARNED OFF, 1928
WARNING FORM SPACE
WARNING SHADOWS, 1924
WARNING SHOT, 1967, A-C
WARNING SIGNAL, THE, 1926
WARNING TO WANTONS, A, 1949, A
WARNING, THE, 1915
WARNING, THE, 1927, A
WARNING, THE, 1928
WARPATH, 1951, A
WARREN CASE, THE, 1934, A
WARRENS OF VIRGINIA, THE, 1915, A
WARRENS OF VIRGINIA, THE, 1924, A
WARRING CLANS, 1963, C
WARRING MILLIONS, THE, 1915
WARRIOR AND THE SLAVE GIRL, THE, 1959, A
WARRIOR AND THE SORCERESS, THE, 1984, O
WARRIOR EMPRESS, THE, 1961, O
WARRIOR GAP, 1925
WARRIOR STRAIN, THE, 1919
WARRIOR'S HUSBAND THE, 1933, C
WARRIORS FIVE, 1962, A
WARRIORS OF THE WASTELAND, 1984, O
WARRIORS OF THE WIND, 1984, C
WARRIORS, THE, 1955, A-C
WARRIORS, THE, 1979, O
WARRIORS, THE, 1970
WAS HE GUILTY?, 1927
WAS IT BIGAMY?, 1925, A
WAS SHE GUILTY?, 1922
WAS SHE JUSTIFIED?, 1922
WAS SHE TO BLAME?, 1915
WASHINGTON AFFAIR, THE, 1978
WASHINGTON AT VALLEY FORGE, 1914, A
WASHINGTON B.C.
WASHINGTON COWBOY
WASHINGTON MASQUERADE, 1932, A
WASHINGTON MELODRAMA, 1941, A
WASHINGTON MERRY-GO-ROUND, 1932, A
WASHINGTON STORY, 1952, A
WASP WOMAN, THE, 1959, A
WASP, THE, 1918
WASTED LIVES, 1923
WASTED LIVES, 1925, A
WASTED LOVE, 1930
WASTED YEARS, THE, 1916
WASTER, THE, 1926
WASTREL, THE, 1963, C
WASTRELS, THE
WATASHI GA SUTETA ONNA
WATCH BEVERLY, 1932, A
WATCH HIM STEP, 1922, A
WATCH IT, SAILOR?, 1961, A
WATCH ON THE RHINE, 1943, A
WATCH THE BIRDIE, 1950, A
WATCH YOUR STEP, 1922, A
WATCH YOUR STERN, 1961, A
WATCH YOUR WIFE, 1926, A
WATCHED, 1974, O
WATCHER IN THE WOODS, THE, 1980, C
WATCHING EYES, 1921, A
WATER BABIES, THE, 1979, AAA
WATER CYBORGS
WATER FOR CANITOGA, 1939, A
WATER GIPSIES, THE
WATER GYPSIES, THE, 1932, A
WATER HOLE, THE, 1928
WATER LILY, THE, 1919
WATER RUSTLERS, 1939, A
WATER, WATER, EVERYWHERE, 1920
WATERFRONT, 1928
WATERFRONT, 1939, A
WATERFRONT, 1944, A
WATERFRONT AT MIDNIGHT, 1948, A
WATERFRONT LADY, 1935, A

WATERFRONT WOLVES, 1924
WATERFRONT WOMEN, 1952, A
WATERFRONT, 1952
WATERHOLE NO. 3, 1967, C
WATERLOO, 1970, C
WATERLOO BRIDGE, 1940
WATERLOO BRIDGE, 1931, C
WATERLOO ROAD, 1949, A
WATERMELON MAN, 1970, C
WATERSHIP DOWN, 1978, C-O
WATTS MONSTER, THE
WATUSI, 1959, A
WATUSI A GO-GO
WAVE, A WAC AND A MARINE, A, 1944, A
WAVELENGTH, 1983, C
WAX MODEL, THE, 1917
WAXWORKS, 1924
WAY AHEAD, THE, 1945, A
WAY BACK HOME, 1932, A
WAY BACK, THE, 1915
WAY DOWN EAST, 1920, A
WAY DOWN EAST, 1935, A
WAY DOWN SOUTH, 1939, A
WAY FOR A SAILOR, 1930, A
WAY MEN LOVE, THE
WAY OF A GAUCHO, 1952, A
WAY OF A GIRL, THE, 1925
WAY OF A MAID, THE, 1921, A
WAY OF A MAN WITH A MAID, THE, 1918
WAY OF A MAN, THE, 1921
WAY OF A WOMAN, 1919, A
WAY OF A WOMAN, THE, 1925
WAY OF ALL FLESH, THE, 1927, A
WAY OF ALL FLESH, THE, 1940, A
WAY OF ALL MEN, THE, 1930, A
WAY OF AN EAGLE, THE, 1918, A
WAY OF LIFE, THE
WAY OF LOST SOULS, THE, 1929, C
WAY OF THE STRONG, THE, 1919
WAY OF THE STRONG, THE, 1928, A
WAY OF THE TRANSGRESSOR, THE, 1923
WAY OF THE WEST, THE, 1934, A
WAY OF THE WORLD, THE, 1916
WAY OF THE WORLD, THE, 1920
WAY OF YOUTH, THE, 1934, A
WAY OUT, 1966, O
WAY OUT LOVE
WAY OUT WEST, 1930, A
WAY OUT WEST, 1937, AAA
WAY OUT, THE, 1918
WAY OUT, THE, 1956, A
WAY OUT, WAY IN, 1970, O
WAY TO LOVE, THE, 1933, A
WAY TO THE GOLD, THE, 1957, A
WAY TO THE STARS, THE
WAY WE LIVE NOW, THE, 1970, O
WAY WE LIVE, THE, 1946, A
WAY WE WERE, THE, 1973, C
WAY WEST, THE, 1967, A
WAY WOMEN LOVE, THE, 1920
WAY...WAY OUT, 1966, C-O
WAYLAID WOMEN
WAYS OF LOVE, 1950, C-O
WAYS OF THE WORLD, THE, 1915
WAYSIDE PEBBLE, THE, 1962, A
WAYWARD, 1932, A
WAYWARD BUS, THE, 1957, C
WAYWARD GIRL, THE, 1957, A
WE ACCUSE
WE AMERICANS, 1928
WE ARE ALL MURDERERS, 1957, C
WE ARE ALL NAKED, 1970, O
WE ARE IN THE NAVY NOW
WE ARE NOT ALONE, 1939, A-C
WE CAN'T HAVE EVERYTHING, 1918
WE DIVE AT DAWN, 1943, A
WE GO FAST, 1941, A
WE HAVE ONLY ONE LIFE, 1963, A
WE HAVE OUR MOMENTS, 1937, A
WE HUMANS
WE JOINED THE NAVY, 1962, A
WE LIVE AGAIN, 1934, C
WE MODERNS, 1925
WE OF THE NEVER NEVER, 1983, C
WE SHALL RETURN, 1963, A
WE SHALL SEE, 1964, C
WE SHOULD WORRY, 1918
WE STILL KILL THE OLD WAY, 1967, C
WE THREE
WE WANT TO LIVE ALONE
WE WENT TO COLLEGE, 1936, A
WE WERE DANCING, 1942, A
WE WERE STRANGERS, 1949, C
WE WHO ARE ABOUT TO DIE, 1937, A
WE WHO ARE YOUNG, 1940, A-C
WE WILL REMEMBER, 1966, C-O
WE WOMEN, 1925
WE'LL GROW THIN TOGETHER, 1979, C
WE'LL MEET AGAIN, 1942
WE'LL SMILE AGAIN, 1942, A
WE'RE ALL GAMBLERS, 1927, A
WE'RE GOING TO BE RICH, 1938, A
WE'RE IN THE ARMY NOW
WE'RE IN THE LEGION NOW, 1937, A
WE'RE IN THE MONEY, 1935, A
WE'RE IN THE NAVY NOW, 1926
WE'RE NO ANGELS, 1955, A-C
WE'RE NOT DRESSING, 1934, A
WE'RE NOT MARRIED, 1952, A
WE'RE ON THE JURY, 1937, A
WE'RE ONLY HUMAN, 1936, A
WE'RE RICH AGAIN, 1934, A
WE'VE GOT THE DEVIL ON THE RUN, 1934
WE'VE NEVER BEEN LICKED, 1943, A
WEAK AND THE WICKED, THE, 1954, A
WEAKER SEX, THE, 1917
WEAKER SEX, THE, 1949, A
WEAKER VESSEL, THE, 1919
WEAKNESS OF MAN, THE, 1916
WEAKNESS OF STRENGTH, THE, 1916
WEALTH, 1921, A
WEAPON, THE, 1957, C
WEAPONS OF DEATH, 1982
WEARY DEATH, THE
WEARY RIVER, 1929, A
WEATHER IN THE STREETS, THE, 1983, C
WEAVER OF DREAMS, 1918
WEAVERS OF FORTUNE, 1922, A
WEAVERS OF LIFE, 1917
WEB OF CHANCE, THE, 1919
WEB OF DANGER, THE, 1947, A
WEB OF DECEIT, THE, 1920
WEB OF DESIRE, THE, 1917
WEB OF EVIDENCE
WEB OF FATE, 1927, A
WEB OF FEAR, 1966, C
WEB OF LIFE, THE, 1917
WEB OF PASSION, 1961, C
WEB OF SUSPICION, 1959, A
WEB OF THE LAW, THE, 1923, A
WEB OF THE SPIDER, 1972, O
WEB OF VIOLENCE, 1966, C
WEB, THE, 1947, A
WEBS OF STEEL, 1925
WEBSTER BOY, THE, 1962, A
WEDDING BELLS
WEDDING BELLS, 1921
WEDDING BILL, 1927, A
WEDDING BREAKFAST
WEDDING GROUP
WEDDING IN WHITE, 1972, O
WEDDING MARCH, THE, 1927, A
WEDDING NIGHT, 1970, O
WEDDING NIGHT, THE, 1935, A
WEDDING OF LILLI MARLENE, THE, 1953, A
WEDDING ON THE VOLGA, THE, 1929
WEDDING PARTY, THE, 1969, O
WEDDING PRESENT, 1936, A
WEDDING PRESENT, 1963
WEDDING REHEARSAL, 1932, A
WEDDING RINGS, 1930, A
WEDDING SONG, THE, 1925, A
WEDDING, A, 1978, C
WEDDINGS AND BABIES, 1960, A
WEDDINGS ARE WONDERFUL, 1938, A
WEDLOCK, 1918
WEDNESDAY CHILDREN, THE, 1973, C
WEDNESDAY'S CHILD
WEDNESDAY'S CHILD, 1934, A
WEDNESDAY'S LUCK, 1936, A
WEE GEORDIE, 1956, A
WEE LADY BETTY, 1917
WEE MACGREGOR'S SWEETHEART, THE, 1922
WEE WILLIE WINKIE, 1937, AA
WEEK END HUSBANDS, 1924
WEEK-END MADNESS
WEEK-END MARRIAGE, 1932, A
WEEK-END, THE, 1920
WEEK-ENDS ONLY, 1932, A
WEEKEND, 1964, C
WEEKEND, 1968, O
WEEKEND A ZUYDCOOTE
WEEKEND AT DUNKIRK, 1966, A
WEEKEND AT THE WALDORF, 1945, A
WEEKEND BABYSITTER
WEEKEND FOR THREE, 1941, A
WEEKEND IN HAVANA, 1941, A
WEEKEND LOVER, 1969
WEEKEND MILLIONAIRE, 1937, A
WEEKEND MURDERS, THE, 1972, O
WEEKEND OF FEAR, 1966, C
WEEKEND OF SHADOWS, 1978, C
WEEKEND PASS, 1944, A
WEEKEND PASS, 1984, O
WEEKEND WITH FATHER, 1951, A
WEEKEND WITH LULU, A, 1961, A
WEEKEND WITH THE BABYSITTER, 1970, O
WEEKEND WIVES
WEEKEND WIVES, 1928, A
WEEKEND, ITALIAN STYLE, 1967, A
WEIRD LOVE MAKERS, THE, 1963, O
WEIRD ONES, THE, 1962, C
WEIRD WOMAN, 1944, A
WELCOME CHILDREN, 1921, A
WELCOME DANGER, 1929, A
WELCOME HOME
WELCOME HOME, 1925
WELCOME HOME, 1935, A
WELCOME HOME, BROTHER CHARLES, 1975
WELCOME HOME, SOLDIER BOYS, 1972, O
WELCOME KOSTYA?, 1965, AA
WELCOME STRANGER, 1924, A
WELCOME STRANGER, 1947, A
WELCOME STRANGER, 1941
WELCOME TO ARROW BEACH
WELCOME TO BLOOD CITY, 1977, O
WELCOME TO HARD TIMES, 1967, O
WELCOME TO L.A., 1976, O
WELCOME TO OUR CITY, 1922
WELCOME TO THE CLUB, 1971, O
WELCOME, MR. BEDDOES
WELCOME, MR. WASHINGTON, 1944, A
WELL DONE, HENRY, 1936, A
WELL, THE, 1951, A
WELL-DIGGER'S DAUGHTER, THE, 1946, C
WELL-GROOMED BRIDE, THE, 1946, A
WELLS FARGO, 1937, A
WELLS FARGO GUNMASTER, 1951, A
WELSH SINGER, A, 1915, A
WENT THE DAY WELL?
WEREWOLF IN A GIRL'S DORMITORY, 1961, C-O
WEREWOLF OF LONDON, THE, 1935, C
WEREWOLF OF WASHINGTON, 1973, C
WEREWOLF VS. THE VAMPIRE WOMAN, THE, 1970, O
WEREWOLF, THE, 1956, C-O
WEREWOLVES ON WHEELS, 1971, O
WEST 11, 1963, C
WEST IS EAST
WEST IS STILL WILD, THE, 1977
WEST IS WEST, 1920
WEST OF ABILENE, 1940, A
WEST OF ARIZONA, 1925
WEST OF BROADWAY, 1926
WEST OF BROADWAY, 1931, A
WEST OF CARSON CITY, 1940, A
WEST OF CHEYENNE, 1931, A
WEST OF CHEYENNE, 1938, A
WEST OF CHICAGO, 1922, A
WEST OF CHICAGO, 1922, A
WEST OF CIMARRON, 1941, A
WEST OF DODGE CITY, 1947
WEST OF EL DORADO, 1949, A
WEST OF MONTANA
WEST OF NEVADA, 1936, A
WEST OF PARADISE, 1928
WEST OF PINTO BASIN, 1940, A
WEST OF RAINBOW'S END, 1938, A
WEST OF SANTA FE, 1928, A
WEST OF SANTA FE, 1938, A
WEST OF SHANGHAI, 1937, A
WEST OF SINGAPORE, 1933, A
WEST OF SONORA, 1948, A
WEST OF SUEZ
WEST OF TEXAS, 1943, A
WEST OF THE ALAMO, 1946, A
WEST OF THE BRAZOS, 1950, A
WEST OF THE DIVIDE, 1934, A
WEST OF THE GREAT DIVIDE
WEST OF THE LAW, 1926, A
WEST OF THE LAW, 1942, A
WEST OF THE MOJAVE, 1925
WEST OF THE PECOS, 1922
WEST OF THE PECOS, 1935, A-C
WEST OF THE PECOS, 1945, A
WEST OF THE RAINBOW'S END, 1926, A
WEST OF THE RIO GRANDE, 1921
WEST OF THE RIO GRANDE, 1944
WEST OF THE ROCKIES, 1929, A
WEST OF THE ROCKIES, 1931, A
WEST OF THE SACRED GEM, THE, 1914
WEST OF THE SUEZ
WEST OF THE WATER TOWER, 1924
WEST OF TOMBSTONE, 1942, A
WEST OF WYOMING, 1950, A
WEST OF ZANZIBAR, 1928, A
WEST OF ZANZIBAR, 1954, A
WEST ON PARADE, 1934
WEST POINT, 1928, A
WEST POINT OF THE AIR, 1935, A
WEST POINT STORY, THE, 1950, A
WEST POINT WIDOW, 1941, A
WEST SIDE KID, 1943, A
WEST SIDE STORY, 1961, A-C
WEST TO GLORY, 1947, A
WEST VS. EAST, 1922
WESTBOUND, 1924, A

WESTBOUND, 1959, A
WESTBOUND LIMITED, 1937, A
WESTBOUND LIMITED, THE, 1923
WESTBOUND MAIL, 1937, A
WESTBOUND STAGE, 1940, A
WESTERN ADVENTURER, A, 1921
WESTERN BLOOD, 1918
WESTERN BLOOD, 1923
WESTERN CARAVANS, 1939, A
WESTERN CODE, 1932
WESTERN COURAGE, 1927, A
WESTERN COURAGE, 1935, A
WESTERN CYCLONE, 1943, A
WESTERN DEMON, A, 1922, A
WESTERN ENGAGEMENT, A, 1925
WESTERN FATE, 1924, A
WESTERN FEUDS, 1924
WESTERN FIREBRANDS, 1921, A
WESTERN FRONTIER, 1935, A
WESTERN GOLD, 1937, A
WESTERN GOVERNOR'S HUMANITY, A, 1915
WESTERN GRIT, 1924
WESTERN HEARTS, 1921, A
WESTERN HERITAGE, 1948, A
WESTERN HONOR
WESTERN JAMBOREE, 1938, A
WESTERN JUSTICE, 1923
WESTERN JUSTICE, 1935, A
WESTERN LIMITED, 1932, A
WESTERN LUCK, 1924, A
WESTERN MAIL, 1942, A
WESTERN METHODS, 1929
WESTERN MUSKETEER, THE, 1922, A
WESTERN PACIFIC AGENT, 1950, A
WESTERN PLUCK, 1926
WESTERN PROMISE, 1925
WESTERN RACKETEERS, 1935
WESTERN RENEGADES, 1949, A
WESTERN ROVER, THE, 1927, A
WESTERN SPEED, 1922
WESTERN THOROUGHBRED, A, 1922
WESTERN TRAILS, 1926
WESTERN TRAILS, 1938, A
WESTERN UNION, 1941, A
WESTERN VENGEANCE, 1924, A
WESTERN WALLOP, THE, 1924
WESTERN WHIRLWIND, THE, 1927, A
WESTERN YESTERDAYS, 1924
WESTERNER, THE, 1936, A
WESTERNER, THE, 1940, A
WESTERNERS, THE, 1919
WESTLAND CASE, THE, 1937, A
WESTMINSTER PASSION PLAY—BEHOLD THE MAN, THE, 1951, A
WESTWARD BOUND, 1931, A
WESTWARD BOUND, 1944, A
WESTWARD DESPERADO, 1961, C
WESTWARD HO, 1919
WESTWARD HO, 1936, A
WESTWARD HO, 1942, A
WESTWARD HO THE WAGONS?, 1956, A
WESTWARD PASSAGE, 1932, A
WESTWARD THE WOMEN, 1951, A
WESTWARD TRAIL, THE, 1948, A
WESTWORLD, 1973, C
WET GOLD, 1921, A
WET PAINT, 1926, A
WET PARADE, THE, 1932, C
WETBACKS, 1956, A
WHALE OF A TALE, A, 1977, AAA
WHALERS, THE, 1942, A
WHARF ANGEL, 1934, A
WHARF RAT, THE, 1916
WHAT A BLONDE, 1945, A
WHAT A CARRY ON?, 1949, A
WHAT A CARVE UP?, 1962, A
WHAT A CHASSIS?
WHAT A CRAZY WORLD, 1963, A
WHAT A LIFE, 1939, A
WHAT A MAN, 1930, A
WHAT A MAN, 1941
WHAT A MAN?, 1937, A
WHAT A MAN?, 1944, A
WHAT A NIGHT, 1928, A
WHAT A NIGHT?, 1931, A
WHAT A WAY TO GO, 1964, A-C
WHAT A WHOPPER, 1961, A
WHAT A WIDOW, 1930, A
WHAT A WIFE LEARNED, 1923
WHAT A WOMAN
WHAT A WOMAN?
WHAT A WOMAN?, 1943, A
WHAT AM I BID?, 1919
WHAT AM I BID?, 1967, A
WHAT BECAME OF JACK AND JILL?, 1972, C-O
WHAT BECOMES OF THE CHILDREN?, 1918
WHAT CHANGED CHARLEY FARTHING?, 1976, C
WHAT DID YOU DO IN THE WAR, DADDY?, 1966, A-C
WHAT DO I TELL THE BOYS AT THE STATION, 1972
WHAT DO MEN WANT?, 1921, A
WHAT DO WE DO NOW?, 1945, A
WHAT DOES A WOMAN NEED MOST, 1918
WHAT EIGHTY MILLION WOMEN WANT, 1913
WHAT EVER HAPPENED TO AUNT ALICE?, 1969, C
WHAT EVERY GIRL SHOULD KNOW, 1927, A
WHAT EVERY WOMAN KNOWS, 1917, A
WHAT EVERY WOMAN KNOWS, 1921, A
WHAT EVERY WOMAN KNOWS, 1934, A
WHAT EVERY WOMAN LEARNS, 1919
WHAT EVERY WOMAN WANTS, 1954, A
WHAT EVERY WOMAN WANTS, 1962, A
WHAT FOOLS MEN, 1925, A
WHAT FOOLS MEN ARE, 1922, A
WHAT GOES UP, 1939
WHAT HAPPENED AT 22, 1916
WHAT HAPPENED THEN?, 1934, A
WHAT HAPPENED TO FATHER, 1915
WHAT HAPPENED TO FATHER, 1927, A
WHAT HAPPENED TO HARKNESS, 1934, AAA
WHAT HAPPENED TO JONES, 1915
WHAT HAPPENED TO JONES, 1920
WHAT HAPPENED TO JONES, 1926, A
WHAT HAPPENED TO ROSA?, 1921, A
WHAT LOLA WANTS
WHAT LOVE CAN DO, 1916
WHAT LOVE FORGIVES, 1919
WHAT LOVE WILL DO, 1921
WHAT LOVE WILL DO, 1923
WHAT MAISIE KNEW, 1976
WHAT MEN WANT, 1930, A
WHAT MONEY CAN BUY, 1928
WHAT MONEY CAN'T BUY, 1917
WHAT NEXT, CORPORAL HARGROVE?, 1945, A
WHAT NEXT?, 1928
WHAT NO MAN KNOWS, 1921, A
WHAT PRICE BEAUTY, 1928
WHAT PRICE BEAUTY?
WHAT PRICE CRIME?, 1935, A
WHAT PRICE DECENCY?, 1933, O
WHAT PRICE FAME, 1928
WHAT PRICE GLORY, 1926, A
WHAT PRICE GLORY?, 1952, C
WHAT PRICE HOLLYWOOD?, 1932, C
WHAT PRICE INNOCENCE?, 1933, A
WHAT PRICE LOVE, 1927
WHAT PRICE LOVING CUP?, 1923
WHAT PRICE MELODY?
WHAT PRICE VENGEANCE?, 1937, A
WHAT SHALL I DO?, 1924
WHAT SHALL IT PROFIT
WHAT SHALL WE DO WITH HIM?, 1919
WHAT THE BUTLER SAW, 1924
WHAT THE BUTLER SAW, 1950, A
WHAT THE PEEPER SAW
WHAT THREE MEN WANTED, 1924
WHAT WILL PEOPLE SAY, 1915
WHAT WIVES DON'T WANT
WHAT WIVES WANT, 1923, A
WHAT WOMEN DREAM, 1933, A
WHAT WOMEN LOVE, 1920
WHAT WOMEN WANT, 1920
WHAT WOMEN WILL DO, 1921, A
WHAT WOULD A GENTLEMAN DO?, 1918
WHAT WOULD YOU DO, CHUMS?, 1939, A
WHAT WOULD YOU DO?, 1920
WHAT WOULD YOU SAY TO SOME SPINACH, 1976, A
WHAT YOU TAKE FOR GRANTED, 1984, O
WHAT'S A WIFE WORTH?, 1921, A
WHAT'S BRED...COMES OUT IN THE FLESH, 1916
WHAT'S BUZZIN COUSIN?, 1943, A
WHAT'S COOKIN'?, 1942, A
WHAT'S GOOD FOR THE GANDER
WHAT'S GOOD FOR THE GOOSE, 1969, O
WHAT'S HIS NAME?, 1914
WHAT'S IN IT FOR HARRY?
WHAT'S NEW, PUSSYCAT?, 1965, C
WHAT'S NEXT?, 1975, AAA
WHAT'S SO BAD ABOUT FEELING GOOD?, 1968, A
WHAT'S THE MATTER WITH HELEN?, 1971, O
WHAT'S UP FRONT, 1964, C
WHAT'S UP, DOC?, 1972, AA
WHAT'S UP, TIGER LILY?, 1966, C
WHAT'S WORTH WILLIE?, 1921
WHAT'S WRONG WITH THE WOMEN?, 1922
WHAT'S YOUR HURRY?, 1920, A
WHAT'S YOUR HUSBAND DOING?, 1919
WHAT'S YOUR RACKET?, 1934, A
WHAT'S YOUR REPUTATION WORTH?, 1921
WHAT?
WHAT?, 1965, O
WHAT? NO BEER?, 1933, A
WHATEVER HAPPENED TO BABY JANE?, 1962, C
WHATEVER SHE WANTS, 1921, A
WHATEVER THE COST, 1918
WHEATS AND TARES, 1915
WHEEL OF ASHES, 1970, C
WHEEL OF CHANCE, 1928
WHEEL OF DEATH, THE, 1916
WHEEL OF DESTINY, THE, 1927, A
WHEEL OF FATE, 1953, A
WHEEL OF FORTUNE
WHEEL OF LIFE, THE, 1929, A
WHEEL OF THE LAW, THE, 1916
WHEEL, THE, 1925
WHEELER DEALERS, THE, 1963, A
WHEELS OF CHANCE, THE, 1922
WHEELS OF DESTINY, 1934, A
WHEELS OF JUSTICE, 1915, A
WHEN A DOG LOVES, 1927
WHEN A FELLER NEEDS A FRIEND
WHEN A GIRL LOVES, 1919
WHEN A GIRL LOVES, 1924
WHEN A GIRL'S BEAUTIFUL, 1947, A
WHEN A MAN LOVES, 1920
WHEN A MAN LOVES, 1927
WHEN A MAN RIDES ALONE, 1919
WHEN A MAN RIDES ALONE, 1933, A
WHEN A MAN SEES RED, 1917
WHEN A MAN SEES RED, 1934, A
WHEN A MAN'S A MAN, 1924
WHEN A MAN'S A MAN, 1935, A
WHEN A STRANGER CALLS, 1979, O
WHEN A WOMAN ASCENDS THE STAIRS, 1963, C
WHEN A WOMAN LOVES, 1915
WHEN A WOMAN SINS, 1918, A
WHEN A WOMAN STRIKES, 1919
WHEN ANGELS DON'T FLY
WHEN ARIZONA WON, 1919
WHEN BABY FORGOT, 1917
WHEN BEARCAT WENT DRY, 1919
WHEN BLONDE MEETS BLONDE
WHEN BOYS LEAVE HOME, 1928, A
WHEN BROADWAY WAS A TRAIL, 1914, A
WHEN DANGER CALLS, 1927
WHEN DANGER SMILES, 1922
WHEN DAWN CAME, 1920
WHEN DESTINY WILLS, 1921
WHEN DINOSAURS RULED THE EARTH, 1971, A
WHEN DO WE EAT?, 1918, A
WHEN DOCTORS DISAGREE, 1919
WHEN DREAMS COME TRUE, 1929
WHEN EAST COMES WEST, 1922, A
WHEN EAST COMES WEST, 1915
WHEN EIGHT BELLS TOLL, 1971, C
WHEN FALSE TONGUES SPEAK, 1917
WHEN FATE DECIDES, 1919
WHEN FATE LEADS TRUMP, 1914
WHEN G-MEN STEP IN, 1938, A
WHEN GANGLAND STRIKES, 1956, A
WHEN GIRLS LEAVE HOME
WHEN GREEK MEETS GREEK, 1922, A
WHEN HELL BROKE LOOSE, 1958, A
WHEN HUSBANDS DECEIVE, 1922
WHEN HUSBANDS FLIRT, 1925
WHEN I GROW UP, 1951
WHEN IN ROME, 1952, A
WHEN IT STRIKES HOME, 1915
WHEN IT WAS DARK, 1919
WHEN JOHNNY COMES MARCHING HOME, 1943, A
WHEN KNIGHTHOOD WAS IN FLOWER
WHEN KNIGHTHOOD WAS IN FLOWER, 1922, A
WHEN KNIGHTS WERE BOLD, 1916
WHEN KNIGHTS WERE BOLD, 1929
WHEN KNIGHTS WERE BOLD, 1942, A
WHEN LADIES MEET, 1933, A
WHEN LADIES MEET, 1941, A-C
WHEN LAW COMES TO HADES, 1923
WHEN LIGHTS ARE LOW
WHEN LONDON BURNED, 1915
WHEN LONDON SLEEPS, 1914
WHEN LONDON SLEEPS, 1932, A
WHEN LONDON SLEEPS, 1934, A
WHEN LOVE CAME TO GAVIN BURKE, 1918
WHEN LOVE COMES, 1922
WHEN LOVE GROWS COLD, 1925
WHEN LOVE IS KING, 1916
WHEN LOVE IS YOUNG, 1922
WHEN LOVE IS YOUNG, 1937, A
WHEN LOVE WAS BLIND, 1917
WHEN LOVERS MEET
WHEN MEN ARE BEASTS
WHEN MEN ARE TEMPTED, 1918
WHEN MEN DESIRE, 1919
WHEN MY BABY SMILES AT ME, 1948, A-C
WHEN MY SHIP COMES IN, 1919
WHEN ODDS ARE EVEN, 1923, A
WHEN PARIS SLEEPS, 1917
WHEN QUACKEL DID HYDE, 1920
WHEN ROMANCE RIDES, 1922
WHEN ROME RULED, 1914, A
WHEN SCOUTING WON, 1930, A
WHEN SECONDS COUNT, 1927, A
WHEN STRANGERS MARRY, 1933, A
WHEN STRANGERS MARRY, 1944, C
WHEN STRANGERS MEET, 1934, A
WHEN THE BOUGH BREAKS, 1947, A

WHEN THE BOYS MEET THE GIRLS, 1965, A
WHEN THE CLOCK STRIKES, 1961, A
WHEN THE CLOCK STRUCK NINE, 1921
WHEN THE CLOUDS ROLL BY, 1920, A
WHEN THE DALTONS RODE, 1940, A
WHEN THE DESERT CALLS, 1922
WHEN THE DESERT SMILES, 1919
WHEN THE DEVIL DRIVES, 1922, A
WHEN THE DEVIL WAS WELL, 1937, A
WHEN THE DOOR OPENED
WHEN THE DOOR OPENED, 1925
WHEN THE GIRLS MEET THE BOYS
WHEN THE GIRLS TAKE OVER, 1962, C
WHEN THE LAD CAME HOME, 1922
WHEN THE LAW RIDES, 1928
WHEN THE LEGENDS DIE, 1972, C
WHEN THE LIGHTS GO ON AGAIN, 1944, A
WHEN THE NORTH WIND BLOWS, 1974
WHEN THE REDSKINS RODE, 1951, A
WHEN THE STRINGS OF THE HEART SOUND, 1914
WHEN THE TREES WERE TALL, 1965, A
WHEN THE WIFE'S AWAY, 1926, A
WHEN THIEF MEETS THIEF, 1937, A
WHEN TIME RAN OUT, 1980, C
WHEN TOMORROW COMES, 1939, A
WHEN TOMORROW DIES, 1966, C
WHEN WE ARE MARRIED, 1943, A
WHEN WE LOOK BACK
WHEN WE WERE TWENTY-ONE, 1915
WHEN WE WERE TWENTY-ONE, 1921
WHEN WERE YOU BORN?, 1938, A
WHEN WILL WE DEAD AWAKEN?, 1918
WHEN WILLIE COMES MARCHING HOME, 1950, A
WHEN WINTER WENT, 1925
WHEN WOMAN HATES, 1916
WHEN WOMEN HAD TAILS, 1970, O
WHEN WORLDS COLLIDE, 1951, A
WHEN YOU AND I WERE YOUNG, 1918
WHEN YOU COME HOME, 1947, A
WHEN YOU COMIN' BACK, RED RYDER?, 1979, O
WHEN YOU'RE IN LOVE, 1937, A
WHEN YOU'RE SMILING, 1950, A
WHEN YOUTH CONSPIRES
WHEN'S YOUR BIRTHDAY?, 1937, AA
WHERE AMBITION LEADS, 1919
WHERE ANGELS GO...TROUBLE FOLLOWS, 1968, C
WHERE ARE MY CHILDREN?, 1916
WHERE ARE THE DREAMS OF YOUTH?, 1932
WHERE ARE YOUR CHILDREN?, 1943, A
WHERE BONDS ARE LOOSED, 1919
WHERE D'YE GET THAT STUFF?, 1916
WHERE DANGER LIVES, 1950, A
WHERE DID YOU GET THAT GIRL?, 1941, A
WHERE DO WE GO FROM HERE?, 1945, AA
WHERE DOES IT HURT?, 1972, C-O
WHERE EAGLES DARE, 1968, C
WHERE EAST IS EAST, 1929, A
WHERE HAS POOR MICKEY GONE?, 1964, A
WHERE IS MY CHILD?, 1937, A
WHERE IS MY FATHER?, 1916
WHERE IS MY WANDERING BOY TONIGHT?, 1922
WHERE IS PARSIFAL?, 1984, C
WHERE IS THIS LADY?, 1932, A
WHERE IS THIS WEST?, 1923
WHERE IT'S AT, 1969, O
WHERE LIGHTS ARE LOW, 1921, A
WHERE LOVE HAS GONE, 1964, C
WHERE LOVE IS, 1917
WHERE LOVE LEADS, 1916
WHERE MEN ARE MEN, 1921, A
WHERE NO VULTURES FLY
WHERE ROMANCE RIDES, 1925
WHERE SINNERS MEET, 1934, A
WHERE THE BLOOD FLOWS
WHERE THE BOYS ARE, 1960, A-C
WHERE THE BOYS ARE '84, 1984, O
WHERE THE BUFFALO ROAM, 1938, A
WHERE THE BUFFALO ROAM, 1980, O
WHERE THE BULLETS FLY, 1966, A
WHERE THE HOT WIND BLOWS, 1960, O
WHERE THE LILIES BLOOM, 1974, A
WHERE THE NORTH BEGINS, 1923
WHERE THE NORTH HOLDS SWAY, 1927
WHERE THE PAVEMENT ENDS, 1923
WHERE THE RAINBOW ENDS, 1921
WHERE THE RED FERN GROWS, 1974, A
WHERE THE RIVER BENDS
WHERE THE SIDEWALK ENDS, 1950, C
WHERE THE SPIES ARE, 1965, A
WHERE THE TRAIL DIVIDES, 1914, A
WHERE THE TRUTH LIES, 1962, A-C
WHERE THE WEST BEGINS, 1919
WHERE THE WEST BEGINS, 1928
WHERE THE WEST BEGINS, 1938, A
WHERE THE WORST BEGINS, 1925
WHERE THERE'S A WILL, 1936, A
WHERE THERE'S A WILL, 1937, A
WHERE THERE'S A WILL, 1955, A
WHERE THERE'S LIFE, 1947, A
WHERE TRAILS BEGIN, 1927
WHERE TRAILS DIVIDE, 1937, A
WHERE TRAILS END, 1942
WHERE WAS I?, 1925
WHERE WERE YOU WHEN THE LIGHTS WENT OUT?, 1968, A-C
WHERE'S CHARLEY?, 1952, AA
WHERE'S GEORGE?
WHERE'S JACK?, 1969, A
WHERE'S POPPA?, 1970, C-O
WHERE'S SALLY?, 1936, A
WHERE'S THAT FIRE?, 1939, A
WHERE'S WILLIE?, 1978
WHEREVER SHE GOES, 1953, A
WHICH SHALL IT BE?, 1924
WHICH WAY IS UP?, 1977, O
WHICH WAY TO THE FRONT?, 1970, A
WHICH WILL YOU HAVE?
WHICH WOMAN?, 1918
WHIFFS, 1975, A
WHILE FIRE RAGED, 1914
WHILE I LIVE, 1947, A
WHILE JUSTICE WAITS, 1922
WHILE LONDON SLEEPS
WHILE LONDON SLEEPS, 1922
WHILE LONDON SLEEPS, 1926
WHILE NEW YORK SLEEPS, 1920, A
WHILE NEW YORK SLEEPS, 1938, A
WHILE NEW YORK SLEEPS, 1934
WHILE PARENTS SLEEP, 1935, A
WHILE PARIS SLEEPS, 1923
WHILE PARIS SLEEPS, 1932, A
WHILE PLUCKING THE DAISIES
WHILE SATAN SLEEPS, 1922, A
WHILE THE ATTORNEY IS ASLEEP, 1945, A
WHILE THE CITY SLEEPS, 1928, A
WHILE THE CITY SLEEPS, 1956, C
WHILE THE DEVIL LAUGHS, 1921
WHILE THE PATIENT SLEPT, 1935, A
WHILE THE SUN SHINES, 1950, A
WHILE THOUSANDS CHEER, 1940
WHIMS OF SOCIETY, THE, 1918
WHIP HAND, THE, 1951, A
WHIP WOMAN, THE, 1928, A
WHIP'S WOMEN, 1968, O
WHIP, THE, 1917
WHIP, THE, 1928
WHIPLASH, 1948, A
WHIPPED, THE, 1950, A
WHIPPING BOSS, THE, 1924
WHIPSAW, 1936, A
WHIRL OF LIFE, THE, 1915
WHIRLPOOL, 1934, A
WHIRLPOOL, 1949, A
WHIRLPOOL, 1959, A
WHIRLPOOL OF DESTINY, THE, 1916
WHIRLPOOL OF FLESH
WHIRLPOOL OF WOMAN, 1966, O
WHIRLPOOL OF YOUTH, THE, 1927
WHIRLPOOL, THE, 1918
WHIRLWIND, 1951, A
WHIRLWIND, 1968, C
WHIRLWIND HORSEMAN, 1938, A
WHIRLWIND OF PARIS, 1946, A
WHIRLWIND RAIDERS, 1948, A
WHIRLWIND RANGER, THE, 1924
WHIRLWIND RIDER, THE, 1935
WHIRLWIND, THE, 1933
WHISKEY MOUNTAIN, 1977
WHISKY GALORE
WHISPER MARKET, THE, 1920
WHISPERED NAME, THE, 1924
WHISPERERS, THE, 1967, C
WHISPERING CANYON, 1926
WHISPERING CHORUS, THE, 1918
WHISPERING CITY, 1947, A
WHISPERING DEATH
WHISPERING DEVILS, 1920
WHISPERING ENEMIES, 1939, A
WHISPERING FOOTSTEPS, 1943, A
WHISPERING GHOSTS, 1942, A
WHISPERING JOE, 1969, O
WHISPERING PALMS, 1923
WHISPERING SAGE, 1927
WHISPERING SHADOWS, 1922
WHISPERING SKULL, THE, 1944, A
WHISPERING SMITH, 1916
WHISPERING SMITH, 1926, A
WHISPERING SMITH, 1948, A
WHISPERING SMITH HITS LONDON
WHISPERING SMITH SPEAKS, 1935, A
WHISPERING SMITH VERSUS SCOTLAND YARD, 1952, A
WHISPERING TONGUES, 1934, A
WHISPERING WINDS, 1929, A
WHISPERING WIRES, 1926
WHISPERING WOMEN, 1921
WHISPERS, 1920, A
WHISPERS, 1920, A
WHISTLE AT EATON FALLS, 1951, A
WHISTLE DOWN THE WIND, 1961, A
WHISTLE STOP, 1946, A-C
WHISTLE, THE, 1921
WHISTLER, THE, 1944, A
WHISTLIN' DAN, 1932, A
WHISTLING BULLETS, 1937, A
WHISTLING HILLS, 1951, A
WHISTLING IN BROOKLYN, 1943, A
WHISTLING IN DIXIE, 1942, A
WHISTLING IN THE DARK, 1933, A
WHISTLING IN THE DARK, 1941, A
WHISTLING JIM, 1925
WHITE AND UNMARRIED, 1921, A
WHITE ANGEL, THE, 1936, A
WHITE BANNERS, 1938, A
WHITE BLACK SHEEP, THE, 1926, A
WHITE BONDAGE, 1937, A
WHITE BUFFALO, THE, 1977, C-O
WHITE CAPTIVE
WHITE CARGO, 1929
WHITE CARGO, 1930, C
WHITE CARGO, 1942, C
WHITE CAT, THE
WHITE CHRISTMAS, 1954, AA
WHITE CIRCLE, THE, 1920
WHITE CLIFFS OF DOVER, THE, 1944, A-C
WHITE COCKATOO, 1935, A
WHITE COMANCHE, 1967
WHITE CORRIDORS, 1952, A
WHITE CRADLE INN
WHITE DAWN, THE, 1974, O
WHITE DEATH, 1936, A
WHITE DEMON, THE, 1932, C
WHITE DESERT, THE, 1925
WHITE DEVIL, THE, 1948, C
WHITE DOG, 1982, O
WHITE DOVE, THE, 1920
WHITE EAGLE, 1932, A
WHITE EAGLE, THE, 1928
WHITE ELEPHANT, 1984, C
WHITE ENSIGN, 1934, A
WHITE FACE, 1933, A
WHITE FANG, 1925
WHITE FANG, 1936, A
WHITE FEATHER, 1955, A
WHITE FIRE, 1953, A
WHITE FLAME, 1928
WHITE FLANNELS, 1927, A
WHITE FLOWER, THE, 1923, A
WHITE GODDESS, 1953, A
WHITE GOLD, 1927, A
WHITE GORILLA, 1947, A
WHITE HANDS, 1922, A
WHITE HEAT, 1926
WHITE HEAT, 1934, O
WHITE HEAT, 1949, C
WHITE HEATHER, THE, 1919
WHITE HELL, 1922
WHITE HEN, THE, 1921
WHITE HOPE, THE, 1915
WHITE HOPE, THE, 1922
WHITE HORSE INN, THE, 1959, A
WHITE HUNTER, 1936, A
WHITE HUNTER, 1965, A
WHITE HUNTRESS, 1957, A
WHITE LEGION, THE, 1936, A
WHITE LIES, 1920
WHITE LIES, 1935, A
WHITE LIGHTING, 1953, A
WHITE LIGHTNIN' ROAD, 1967, A
WHITE LIGHTNING, 1973, C
WHITE LILAC, 1935, A
WHITE LINE FEVER, 1975, C
WHITE LINE, THE, 1952, C
WHITE LIONS, 1981
WHITE MAN, 1924
WHITE MAN'S LAW, THE, 1918
WHITE MAN, THE
WHITE MASKS, THE, 1921
WHITE MICE, 1926
WHITE MOLL, THE, 1920
WHITE MONKEY, THE, 1925
WHITE MOTH, THE, 1924
WHITE NIGHTS, 1961, O
WHITE OAK, 1921, A
WHITE ORCHID, THE, 1954, A
WHITE OUTLAW, THE, 1925, A
WHITE OUTLAW, THE, 1929
WHITE PANTHER, THE, 1924
WHITE PANTS WILLIE, 1927, A
WHITE PARADE, THE, 1934, A
WHITE PEBBLES, 1927
WHITE PONGO, 1945, AA
WHITE RAT, 1972, O
WHITE RAVEN, THE, 1917
WHITE RENEGADE, 1931
WHITE RIDER, THE, 1920
WHITE ROSE OF HONG KONG, 1965, O

WHITE ROSE, THE, 1923, A
WHITE ROSETTE, THE, 1916
WHITE SAVAGE, 1943, A
WHITE SAVAGE, 1941
WHITE SCAR, THE, 1915
WHITE SHADOW, THE
WHITE SHADOWS, 1924
WHITE SHADOWS IN THE SOUTH SEAS, 1928, A
WHITE SHEEP, THE, 1924
WHITE SHEIK, THE, 1928
WHITE SHEIK, THE, 1956, C
WHITE SHOULDERS, 1922
WHITE SHOULDERS, 1931, A
WHITE SIN, THE, 1924
WHITE SISTER, 1973, O
WHITE SISTER, THE, 1915
WHITE SISTER, THE, 1923, A
WHITE SISTER, THE, 1933, A
WHITE SLAVE SHIP, 1962, C
WHITE SLAVE, THE, 1929
WHITE SLIPPERS
WHITE SQUAW, THE, 1956, A
WHITE STALLION, 1947, A
WHITE STAR, THE, 1915
WHITE TERROR, THE, 1915
WHITE THUNDER, 1925
WHITE TIE AND TAILS, 1946, A
WHITE TIGER, 1923
WHITE TOWER, THE, 1950, A
WHITE TRAP, THE, 1959, C
WHITE TRASH ON MOONSHINE MOUNTAIN
WHITE UNICORN, THE
WHITE VOICES, 1965, O
WHITE WARRIOR, THE, 1961, C
WHITE WITCH DOCTOR, 1953, A
WHITE WOMAN, 1933, C
WHITE YOUTH, 1920, A
WHITE ZOMBIE, 1932, O
WHITE, RED, YELLOW, PINK, 1966, O
WHITEFACE
WHITHER THOU GOEST, 1917
WHO AM I?, 1921
WHO ARE MY PARENTS?, 1922
WHO CAN KILL A CHILD
WHO CARES, 1925
WHO CARES?, 1919
WHO DARES WIN
WHO DONE IT?, 1942, A
WHO DONE IT?, 1956, C
WHO FEARS THE DEVIL, 1972, A
WHO GOES NEXT?, 1938, C
WHO GOES THERE?
WHO GOES THERE?, 1917
WHO HAS SEEN THE WIND, 1980, A
WHO IS GUILTY?, 1940, A
WHO IS HARRY KELLERMAN AND WHY IS HE SAYING THOSE TERRIBLE THINGS ABOUT ME?, 1971, C
WHO IS HOPE SCHUYLER?, 1942, A
WHO IS KILLING THE GREAT CHEFS OF EUROPE?, 1978, C
WHO IS KILLING THE STUNTMEN?
WHO IS THE MAN?, 1924
WHO IS TO BLAME?, 1918
WHO KILLED "DOC" ROBBIN?, 1948, AAA
WHO KILLED AUNT MAGGIE?, 1940, A
WHO KILLED FEN MARKHAM?, 1937, A
WHO KILLED GAIL PRESTON?, 1938, A
WHO KILLED JESSIE?, 1965, C
WHO KILLED JOE MERRION?, 1915
WHO KILLED JOHN SAVAGE?, 1937, A
WHO KILLED MARY WHAT'SER NAME?, 1971, O
WHO KILLED TEDDY BEAR?, 1965, O
WHO KILLED THE CAT?, 1966, A-C
WHO KILLED VAN LOON?, 1984, A
WHO KILLED WALTON?, 1918
WHO KNOWS?, 1918
WHO LOVED HIM BEST?, 1918
WHO RIDES WITH KANE?
WHO SAYS I CAN'T RIDE A RAINBOW?, 1971, AAA
WHO SHALL TAKE MY LIFE?, 1918
WHO SLEW AUNTIE ROO?, 1971, O
WHO VIOLATES THE LAW, 1915
WHO WANTS TO KILL JESSIE?
WHO WAS MADDOX?, 1964, A
WHO WAS THAT LADY?, 1960, A
WHO WAS THE OTHER MAN?, 1917
WHO WILL MARRY ME?, 1919
WHO WOULD KILL A CHILD
WHO'LL STOP THE RAIN?, 1978, C
WHO'S AFRAID OF VIRGINIA WOOLF?, 1966, O
WHO'S BEEN SLEEPING IN MY BED?, 1963, C
WHO'S CHEATING?, 1924
WHO'S CRAZY, 1965
WHO'S GOT THE ACTION?, 1962, A
WHO'S GOT THE BLACK BOX?, 1970, O
WHO'S MIDING THE MINT?, 1967, A
WHO'S MINDING THE STORE?, 1963, A
WHO'S THAT KNOCKING AT MY DOOR?, 1968, O
WHO'S WHO IN SOCIETY, 1915
WHO'S YOUR BROTHER?, 1919
WHO'S YOUR FATHER?, 1935, A
WHO'S YOUR FRIEND, 1925
WHO'S YOUR LADY FRIEND?, 1937, A
WHO'S YOUR NEIGHBOR?, 1917
WHO'S YOUR SERVANT?, 1920
WHO?, 1975, C
WHOEVER SLEW AUNTIE ROO?
WHOLE DAMN WAR, THE
WHOLE DARN WAR, THE, 1928
WHOLE SHOOTIN' MATCH, THE, 1979, C
WHOLE TOWN'S TALKING, THE, 1926
WHOLE TOWN'S TALKING, THE, 1935, A
WHOLE TRUTH, THE, 1958, A
WHOLLY MOSES, 1980, C
WHOM GOD HATH JOINED, 1919
WHOM SHALL I MARRY, 1926
WHOM THE GODS DESTROY, 1916
WHOM THE GODS DESTROY, 1934, A
WHOM THE GODS LOVE
WHOM THE GODS WOULD DESTROY, 1915
WHOM THE GODS WOULD DESTROY, 1919
WHOOPEE, 1930, AA
WHOSE CHILD AM I?, 1976
WHOSE LIFE IS IT ANYWAY?, 1981, C-O
WHOSE WIFE?, 1917
WHOSO DIGGETH A PIT, 1915
WHOSO FINDETH A WIFE
WHOSO IS WITHOUT SIN, 1916
WHOSO TAKETH A WIFE, 1916
WHOSOEVER SHALL OFFEND, 1919
WHY AMERICA WILL WIN, 1918
WHY ANNA?
WHY ANNOUNCE YOUR MARRIAGE?, 1922
WHY BE GOOD?, 1929, A
WHY BLAME ME?
WHY BOTHER TO KNOCK, 1964
WHY BRING THAT UP?, 1929, A
WHY CHANGE YOUR HUSBAND?
WHY CHANGE YOUR WIFE?, 1920
WHY DOES HERR R. RUN AMOK?, 1977, O
WHY GERMANY MUST PAY, 1919
WHY GIRLS GO BACK HOME, 1926
WHY GIRLS LEAVE HOME, 1921
WHY GIRLS LEAVE HOME, 1945, C
WHY I WOULD NOT MARRY, 1918
WHY KILL AGAIN?, 1965
WHY LEAVE HOME?, 1929, A
WHY MEN FORGET, 1921
WHY MEN LEAVE HOME, 1924
WHY MUST I DIE?, 1960, C
WHY NOT MARRY?, 1922
WHY NOT?
WHY PICK ON ME?, 1937, A
WHY ROCK THE BOAT?, 1974, O
WHY RUSSIANS ARE REVOLTING, 1970, O
WHY SAILORS GO WRONG, 1928
WHY SAILORS LEAVE HOME, 1930, A
WHY SAPS LEAVE HOME, 1932, A
WHY SHOOT THE TEACHER, 1977, C
WHY SMITH LEFT HOME, 1919
WHY SPY
WHY TRUST YOUR HUSBAND?, 1921
WHY WOMEN LOVE, 1925
WHY WOMEN REMARRY, 1923
WHY WORRY, 1923, A
WHY WOULD ANYONE WANT TO KILL A NICE GIRL LIKE YOU?
WHY WOULD I LIE, 1980, C
WICHITA, 1955, A
WICKED, 1931, A
WICKED AS THEY COME
WICKED DARLING, THE, 1919
WICKED DIE SLOW, THE, 1968, O
WICKED DREAMS OF PAULA SCHULTZ, THE, 1968, C
WICKED GO TO HELL, THE, 1961, O
WICKED LADY, THE, 1946, A
WICKED LADY, THE, 1983, O
WICKED WIFE, 1955, O
WICKED WOMAN, 1953, O
WICKED WOMAN, A, 1934, C
WICKED, WICKED, 1973, O
WICKEDNESS PREFERRED, 1928
WICKER MAN, THE, 1974, O
WICKHAM MYSTERY, THE, 1931, A
WIDE BOY, 1952, A
WIDE OPEN, 1927
WIDE OPEN, 1930, A
WIDE OPEN FACES, 1938, A
WIDE OPEN TOWN, 1941, A
WIDE-OPEN TOWN, A, 1922, A
WIDECOMBE FAIR, 1928
WIDOW AND THE GIGOLO, THE
WIDOW BY PROXY, 1919
WIDOW FROM CHICAGO, THE, 1930, A-C
WIDOW FROM MONTE CARLO, THE, 1936, A
WIDOW IN SCARLET, 1932, A
WIDOW IN SCARLET, 1932
WIDOW IS WILLING, THE
WIDOW TWAN-KEE
WIDOW'S MIGHT, 1934, A
WIDOW'S MIGHT, THE, 1918
WIDOWS' NEST, 1977, O
WIE ER IN DE WELT
WIE ER IN DE WELT
WIEN TANZT
WIEN, DU STADT DER LIEDER
WIFE AGAINST WIFE, 1921, A
WIFE BY PROXY, A, 1917
WIFE HE BOUGHT, THE, 1918
WIFE HUNTERS, THE, 1922
WIFE IN NAME ONLY, 1923
WIFE LOST, 1928
WIFE NUMBER TWO, 1917
WIFE OF GENERAL LING, THE, 1938, A
WIFE OF MONTE CRISTO, THE, 1946, A
WIFE OF THE CENTAUR, 1924
WIFE OF THE PHARAOH, THE, 1922
WIFE ON TRAIL, A, 1917
WIFE OR COUNTRY, 1919
WIFE OR TWO, A, 1935, A
WIFE SAVERS, 1928, A
WIFE SWAPPERS, THE
WIFE TAKES A FLYER, THE, 1942, A
WIFE TRAP, THE, 1922
WIFE VERSUS SECRETARY, 1936, A
WIFE WANTED, 1946, A
WIFE WHO WASN'T WANTED, THE, 1925
WIFE'S AWAKENING, A, 1921, A
WIFE'S FAMILY, THE
WIFE'S RELATIONS, THE, 1928
WIFE'S ROMANCE, A, 1923
WIFE'S SACRIFICE, A, 1916
WIFE, DOCTOR AND NURSE, 1937, A
WIFE, HUSBAND AND FRIEND, 1939, A
WIFEMISTRESS, 1979, O
WILBY CONSPIRACY, THE, 1975, C
WILD 90, 1968, O
WILD AFFAIR, THE, 1966, O
WILD AND THE INNOCENT, THE, 1959, C
WILD AND THE SWEET, THE
WILD AND THE WILLING, THE
WILD AND WILLING
WILD AND WONDERFUL, 1964, A
WILD AND WOOLLY, 1917, A
WILD AND WOOLLY, 1937
WILD ANGELS, THE, 1966
WILD ARCTIC
WILD BEAUTY, 1927
WILD BEAUTY, 1946, A
WILD BILL HICKOK, 1923
WILD BLOOD, 1929, A
WILD BLUE YONDER, THE, 1952, A
WILD BORN, 1927
WILD BOY, 1934, A
WILD BOYS OF THE ROAD, 1933, A-C
WILD BRIAN KENT, 1936, A
WILD BULL'S LAIR, THE, 1925
WILD BUNCH, THE, 1969, O
WILD CARGO
WILD CAT OF PARIS, THE, 1919
WILD CHILD, THE, 1970, C-O
WILD COMPANY, 1930, A
WILD COUNTRY, 1947, A
WILD COUNTRY, THE, 1971, AA
WILD DAKOTAS, THE, 1956, A
WILD DRIFTER
WILD DUCK, THE, 1977, A
WILD DUCK, THE, 1983, C
WILD EYE, THE, 1968, O
WILD FOR KICKS
WILD FRONTIER, THE, 1947, A
WILD GAME
WILD GEESE, 1927
WILD GEESE CALLING, 1941, A-C
WILD GEESE, THE, 1978, O
WILD GIRL, 1932, A
WILD GIRL OF THE SIERRAS, A, 1916
WILD GIRL, THE, 1917
WILD GIRL, THE, 1925, A
WILD GOLD, 1934, A
WILD GOOSE CHASE, 1919
WILD GOOSE CHASE, THE, 1915, A
WILD GOOSE, THE, 1921, A
WILD GUITAR, 1962, A
WILD GYPSIES, 1969, O
WILD HARVEST, 1947, A
WILD HARVEST, 1962, O
WILD HEART, THE, 1952, C
WILD HEATHER, 1921
WILD HERITAGE, 1958, A
WILD HONEY, 1919, A
WILD HONEY, 1922, A
WILD HORSE, 1931, A
WILD HORSE AMBUSH, 1952, A
WILD HORSE CANYON, 1939, A

WILD HORSE HANK, 1979, A
WILD HORSE MESA, 1925
WILD HORSE MESA, 1932, A
WILD HORSE MESA, 1947, A
WILD HORSE PHANTOM, 1944, A
WILD HORSE RANGE, 1940
WILD HORSE RODEO, 1938, A
WILD HORSE ROUND-UP, 1937, A
WILD HORSE RUSTLERS, 1943, A
WILD HORSE STAMPEDE, 1943, A
WILD HORSE STAMPEDE, THE, 1926
WILD HORSE VALLEY, 1940, A
WILD HORSES, 1984, C
WILD IN THE COUNTRY, 1961, A
WILD IN THE SKY
WILD IN THE STREETS, 1968, C
WILD INNOCENCE, 1937, A
WILD IS MY LOVE, 1963, O
WILD IS THE WIND, 1957, A
WILD JUNGLE CAPTIVE
WILD JUSTICE, 1925
WILD LIFE, 1918
WILD LIFE, THE, 1984, C-O
WILD LOVE-MAKERS
WILD MAN OF BORNEO, THE, 1941, A
WILD MONEY, 1937, A
WILD MUSTANG, 1935, A
WILD McCULLOCHS, THE, 1975, O
WILD NORTH, THE, 1952, A
WILD OATS, 1915
WILD OATS, 1916
WILD OATS, 1919
WILD OATS LANE, 1926, A
WILD ON THE BEACH, 1965, A
WILD ONE, THE, 1953, C
WILD ONES ON WHEELS, 1967, C-O
WILD ORANGES, 1924
WILD ORCHIDS, 1929, A
WILD PACK, THE, 1972, O
WILD PARTY, THE, 1923
WILD PARTY, THE, 1956, C-O
WILD PARTY, THE, 1975, O
WILD PARTY, THE, 1929, A
WILD PRIMROSE, 1918
WILD RACERS, THE, 1968, A-C
WILD REBELS, THE, 1967, O
WILD RIDE, THE, 1960, C
WILD RIDERS, 1971, O
WILD RIVER, 1960, A-C
WILD ROVERS, 1971, C-O
WILD SCENE, THE, 1970, O
WILD SEASON, 1968, A
WILD SEED, 1965, A
WILD SIDE, THE
WILD STALLION, 1952, A
WILD STRAIN, THE, 1918
WILD STRAWBERRIES, 1959, O
WILD SUMAC, 1917
WILD TO GO, 1926
WILD WEED, 1949, A-C
WILD WEST, 1946, A
WILD WEST ROMANCE, 1928
WILD WEST SHOW, THE, 1928
WILD WEST WHOOPEE, 1931, A
WILD WESTERNERS, THE, 1962, A
WILD WHEELS, 1969, O
WILD WINSHIP'S WIDOW, 1917
WILD WOMEN, 1918
WILD WOMEN OF WONGO, THE, 1959, C
WILD WORLD OF BATWOMAN, THE, 1966, C
WILD YOUTH, 1918
WILD YOUTH, 1961, C
WILD, FREE AND HUNGRY, 1970, C
WILD, WILD PLANET, THE, 1967, A-C
WILD, WILD SUSAN, 1925
WILD, WILD WINTER, 1966, A
WILD, WILD WOMEN, THE
WILDCAT
WILDCAT, 1942, A
WILDCAT BUS, 1940, A
WILDCAT JORDAN, 1922
WILDCAT OF TUCSON, 1941, A
WILDCAT SAUNDERS, 1936
WILDCAT TROOPER, 1936, A
WILDCAT, THE, 1917
WILDCAT, THE, 1924
WILDCAT, THE, 1926
WILDCATS OF ST. TRINIAN'S, THE, 1980, A
WILDCATTER, THE, 1937, A
WILDE SEISON
WILDERNESS FAMILY PART 2
WILDERNESS MAIL, 1935, A
WILDERNESS TRAIL, THE
WILDERNESS TRAIL, THE, 1919
WILDERNESS WOMAN, THE, 1926, A
WILDFIRE, 1915
WILDFIRE, 1925
WILDFIRE, 1945, A
WILDFIRE; THE STORY OF A HORSE
WILDFLOWER, 1914
WILDNESS OF YOUTH, 1922
WILDWECHSEL
WILFUL YOUTH, 1927
WILL AND A WAY, A, 1922
WILL ANY GENTLEMAN?, 1955, A
WILL BILL HICKOK RIDES, 1942, A
WILL JAMES' SAND
WILL O' THE WISP, THE, 1914
WILL OF HER OWN, A, 1915
WILL OF THE PEOPLE, THE
WILL PENNY, 1968, A-C
WILL SUCCESS SPOIL ROCK HUNTER?, 1957, A-C
WILL TOMORROW EVER COME
WILL YOU BE STAYING FOR SUPPER?, 1919
WILL, THE, 1921
WILLARD, 1971, O
WILLIAM COMES TO TOWN, 1948, A
WILLIAM FOX MOVIETONE FOLLIES OF 1929
WILLIAM TELL, 1925
WILLIE AND JOE BACK AT THE FRONT
WILLIE AND PHIL, 1980, O
WILLIE AND SCRATCH, 1975
WILLIE DYNAMITE, 1973, O
WILLIE MCBEAN AND HIS MAGIC MACHINE, 1965, AAA
WILLOW TREE, THE, 1920
WILLY, 1963, A
WILLY DYNAMITE
WILLY REILLY AND HIS COLLEEN BAWN, 1918
WILLY WONKA AND THE CHOCOLATE FACTORY, 1971, A
WILSON, 1944, A
WILSON OR THE KAISER?
WIN THAT GIRL, 1928
WIN(K)SOME WIDOW, THE, 1914
WIN, LOSE OR DRAW, 1925
WIN, PLACE AND SHOW
WIN, PLACE, OR STEAL, 1975, A
WINCHESTER WOMAN, THE, 1919
WINCHESTER '73, 1950, C
WIND ACROSS THE EVERGLADES, 1958, C
WIND AND THE LION, THE, 1975, C
WIND BLOWETH WHERE IT LISTETH, THE
WIND CANNOT READ, THE, 1958, A
WIND FROM THE EAST, 1970, C
WIND OF CHANGE, THE, 1961, A
WIND, THE, 1928, C
WINDBAG THE SAILOR, 1937, A
WINDFALL, 1935, A
WINDFALL, 1955, A
WINDFLOWERS, 1968, C
WINDING ROAD, THE, 1920
WINDING STAIR, THE, 1925, A
WINDING TRAIL, THE, 1918
WINDING TRAIL, THE, 1921
WINDJAMMER, 1937, A
WINDJAMMER, THE, 1926
WINDJAMMER, THE, 1931, A
WINDMILL, THE, 1937, A
WINDOM'S WAY, 1958, A-C
WINDOW IN LONDON, A
WINDOW IN PICCADILLY, A, 1928
WINDOW TO THE SKY, A
WINDOW, THE, 1949, C
WINDOWS, 1980, O
WINDOWS OF TIME, THE, 1969, A
WINDS OF AUTUMN, THE, 1976
WINDS OF CHANCE, 1925
WINDS OF THE PAMPAS, 1927
WINDS OF THE WASTELAND, 1936, A
WINDSPLITTER, THE, 1971, C
WINDWALKER, 1980, C
WINDY CITY, 1984, C
WINE, 1924
WINE AND THE MUSIC, THE
WINE GIRL, THE, 1918
WINE OF LIFE, THE, 1924
WINE OF YOUTH, 1924
WINE, WOMEN AND HORSES, 1937, A
WINE, WOMEN, AND SONG, 1934, A
WING AND A PRAYER, 1944, A
WING TOY, 1921, A
WINGED DEVILS
WINGED HORSEMAN, THE, 1929
WINGED IDOL, THE, 1915
WINGED MYSTERY, THE, 1917
WINGED SERPENT
WINGED SERPENT, THE
WINGED VICTORY, 1944, A
WINGS, 1927, A
WINGS AND THE WOMAN, 1942, A
WINGS FOR THE EAGLE, 1942, A
WINGS IN THE DARK, 1935, A
WINGS OF A SERF, 1926
WINGS OF ADVENTURE, 1930, A
WINGS OF CHANCE, 1961, A
WINGS OF DANGER
WINGS OF EAGLES, THE, 1957, A
WINGS OF MYSTERY, 1963, AAA
WINGS OF THE HAWK, 1953, A
WINGS OF THE MORNING, 1937, A
WINGS OF THE MORNING, THE, 1919
WINGS OF THE NAVY, 1939, A
WINGS OF THE STORM, 1926, A
WINGS OF VICTORY, 1941, A
WINGS OF YOUTH, 1925
WINGS OVER AFRICA, 1939, A
WINGS OVER HONOLULU, 1937, A
WINGS OVER THE PACIFIC, 1943, A
WINGS OVER WYOMING
WINIFRED THE SHOP GIRL, 1916
WINK OF AN EYE, 1958, A
WINNER TAKE ALL, 1924
WINNER TAKE ALL, 1932, A
WINNER TAKE ALL, 1939, A
WINNER TAKE ALL, 1948
WINNER TAKES ALL, 1918
WINNER'S CIRCLE, THE, 1948, A
WINNER, THE
WINNER, THE, 1926
WINNERS OF THE WILDERNESS, 1927
WINNERS, THE
WINNETOU, PART I
WINNETOU, PART II
WINNETOU, PART III
WINNING, 1969, A-C
WINNING A CONTINENT, 1924
WINNING A WOMAN, 1925
WINNING GIRL, THE, 1919
WINNING GOAL, THE, 1929, A
WINNING GRANDMA, 1918
WINNING HIS FIRST CASE, 1914
WINNING OAR, THE, 1927
WINNING OF BARBARA WORTH, THE, 1926, A
WINNING OF BEATRICE, THE, 1918
WINNING OF SALLY TEMPLE, THE, 1917
WINNING OF THE WEST, 1922
WINNING OF THE WEST, 1953, A
WINNING POSITION
WINNING STROKE, THE, 1919, A
WINNING TEAM, THE, 1952, A
WINNING THE FUTURITY, 1926
WINNING TICKET, THE, 1935, A
WINNING WALLOP, THE, 1926
WINNING WAY, THE
WINNING WITH WITS, 1922
WINSLOW BOY, THE, 1950, A
WINSTANLEY, 1979, C
WINSTON AFFAIR, THE
WINTER A GO-GO, 1965, A
WINTER CARNIVAL, 1939, A
WINTER COMES EARLY, 1972
WINTER FLIGHT, 1984, C
WINTER KEPT US WARM, 1968, C
WINTER KILLS, 1979, O
WINTER LIGHT, THE, 1963, C
WINTER MEETING, 1948, A
WINTER OF OUR DREAMS, 1982, O
WINTER RATES
WINTER WIND, 1970, C
WINTER WONDERLAND, 1947, A
WINTER'S TALE, THE, 1968, A
WINTERHAWK, 1976, C
WINTERSET, 1936, A-C
WINTERTIME, 1943, A
WIRE SERVICE, 1942, A
WIRELESS, 1915
WIRETAPPERS, 1956, A
WISE BLOOD, 1979, O
WISE FOOL, A, 1921, A
WISE GIRL, 1937, A
WISE GIRLS, 1930, A
WISE GUY, THE, 1926
WISE GUYS, 1937, A
WISE GUYS, 1969, A
WISE HUSBANDS, 1920, A
WISE KID, THE, 1922
WISE VIRGIN, THE, 1924
WISE WIFE, THE, 1927
WISER AGE, 1962, C
WISER SEX, THE, 1932, A
WISHBONE CUTTER, 1978, C
WISHBONE, THE, 1933, A
WISHING MACHINE, 1971, AAA
WISHING RING MAN, THE, 1919
WISHING RING, THE, 1914, A
WISP O' THE WOODS, 1919
WISTFUL WIDOW OF WAGON GAP, THE, 1947, A
WISTFUL WIDOW, THE
WIT WINS, 1920
WITCH BENEATH THE SEA, THE
WITCH DOCTOR
WITCH WHO CAME FROM THE SEA, THE, 1976
WITCH WITHOUT A BROOM, A, 1967, C
WITCH WOMAN, THE, 1918
WITCH'S CURSE, THE, 1963, A
WITCH'S LURE, THE, 1921

WITCH'S MIRROR, THE, 1960, C
WITCH, THE, 1916
WITCH, THE, 1969, C
WITCHCRAFT, 1916
WITCHCRAFT, 1964, A
WITCHCRAFT THROUGH THE AGES, 1921
WITCHES CURSE, THE
WITCHES' BREW, 1980
WITCHES, THE
WITCHES, THE, 1969, C
WITCHES—VIOLATED AND TORTURED TO DEATH
WITCHFINDER GENERAL
WITCHING EYES, THE, 1929
WITCHING HOUR, THE, 1916
WITCHING HOUR, THE, 1921, A
WITCHING HOUR, THE, 1934, A
WITCHING, THE
WITCHMAKER, THE, 1969, C
WITH A SMILE, 1939, A
WITH A SONG IN MY HEART, 1952, A
WITH ALL HER HEART, 1920
WITH BRIDGES BURNED, 1915
WITH DAVY CROCKETT AT THE FALL OF THE ALAMO
WITH FIRE AND SWORD
WITH GENERAL CUSTER AT LITTLE BIG HORN
WITH GUNILLA MONDAY EVENING AND TUESDAY
WITH HOOPS OF STEEL, 1918
WITH JOYOUS HEART
WITH KIT CARSON OVER THE GREAT DIVIDE
WITH LOVE AND KISSES, 1937, A
WITH LOVE AND TENDERNESS, 1978, A
WITH NAKED FISTS, 1923
WITH NEATNESS AND DISPATCH, 1918
WITH SITTING BULL AT THE SPIRIT LAKE MASSACRE
WITH SIX YOU GET EGGROLL, 1968, A
WITH THIS RING, 1925
WITH WINGS OUTSPREAD, 1922
WITHIN PRISON WALLS
WITHIN THE CUP, 1918
WITHIN THE LAW
WITHIN THE LAW, 1917
WITHIN THE LAW, 1923
WITHIN THE LAW, 1939, A
WITHIN THESE WALLS, 1945, A
WITHOUT A HOME, 1939, A
WITHOUT A SOUL
WITHOUT A SOUL, 1916
WITHOUT A TRACE, 1983, A
WITHOUT APPARENT MOTIVE, 1972, O
WITHOUT BENEFIT OF CLERGY, 1921
WITHOUT CHILDREN
WITHOUT COMPROMISE, 1922
WITHOUT EACH OTHER, 1962, A
WITHOUT FEAR, 1922, A
WITHOUT HONOR, 1918
WITHOUT HONOR, 1949, A
WITHOUT HONORS, 1932, A
WITHOUT HOPE, 1914, A
WITHOUT LIMIT, 1921, A
WITHOUT LOVE, 1945, A
WITHOUT MERCY, 1925
WITHOUT ORDERS, 1926
WITHOUT ORDERS, 1936, A
WITHOUT PITY, 1949, C
WITHOUT REGRET, 1935, A
WITHOUT RESERVATIONS, 1946, A
WITHOUT RISK
WITHOUT WARNING
WITHOUT WARNING, 1952, C
WITHOUT WARNING, 1980, O
WITHOUT YOU, 1934, A
WITNESS CHAIR, THE, 1936, A
WITNESS FOR THE DEFENSE, THE, 1919
WITNESS FOR THE PROSECUTION, 1957, A
WITNESS IN THE DARK, 1959, A
WITNESS OUT OF HELL, 1967
WITNESS TO MURDER, 1954, C
WITNESS VANISHES, THE, 1939, A
WITNESS, THE, 1959
WITNESS, THE, 1982, C
WITS VS. WITS, 1920
WIVES AND LOVERS, 1963, A
WIVES AND OTHER WIVES, 1919
WIVES AT AUCTION, 1926
WIVES BEWARE, 1933, A
WIVES NEVER KNOW, 1936, A
WIVES OF MEN, 1918
WIVES OF THE PROPHET, THE, 1926
WIVES UNDER SUSPICION, 1938, A
WIZ, THE, 1978, C
WIZARD OF BAGHDAD, THE, 1960, A
WIZARD OF GORE, THE, 1970, O
WIZARD OF MARS, 1964, A
WIZARD OF OZ, THE, 1925, A
WIZARD OF OZ, THE, 1939, AAA
WIZARD OF THE SADDLE, 1928
WIZARD, THE, 1927
WIZARDS, 1977, C
WOLF AND HIS MATE, THE, 1918
WOLF BLOOD, 1925
WOLF CALL, 1939, A
WOLF DOG, 1958, AA
WOLF FANGS, 1927
WOLF HUNTERS, THE, 1926
WOLF HUNTERS, THE, 1949, A
WOLF LAKE, 1979
WOLF LARSEN, 1958, A
WOLF LARSEN, 1978, A
WOLF LAW, 1922, A
WOLF LOWRY, 1917
WOLF MAN, 1924
WOLF MAN, THE, 1924
WOLF MAN, THE, 1941, C
WOLF OF DEBT, THE, 1915
WOLF OF NEW YORK, 1940, A
WOLF OF WALL STREET THE, 1929, C
WOLF PACK, 1922, A
WOLF RIDERS, 1935
WOLF SONG, 1929, A-C
WOLF WOMAN, THE, 1916
WOLF'S CLOTHING, 1927, A
WOLF'S CLOTHING, 1936, A
WOLF'S FANGS, THE, 1922
WOLF'S TRACKS, 1923
WOLF'S TRAIL, 1927
WOLF, THE, 1914
WOLF, THE, 1919
WOLF-MAN, THE, 1915
WOLFE OR THE CONQUEST OF QUEBEC, 1914
WOLFEN, 1981, O
WOLFHEART'S REVENGE, 1925
WOLFMAN, 1979, O
WOLFPACK
WOLFPEN PRINCIPLE, THE, 1974, AA
WOLVERINE, THE, 1921, A
WOLVES, 1930, A
WOLVES OF THE AIR, 1927
WOLVES OF THE BORDER, 1918
WOLVES OF THE BORDER, 1923
WOLVES OF THE CITY, 1929
WOLVES OF THE DESERT, 1926
WOLVES OF THE NIGHT, 1919
WOLVES OF THE NORTH, 1921
WOLVES OF THE RAIL, 1918
WOLVES OF THE RANGE, 1921
WOLVES OF THE RANGE, 1943, A
WOLVES OF THE ROAD, 1925
WOLVES OF THE SEA, 1938, A
WOLVES OF THE STREET, 1920
WOLVES OF THE UNDERWORLD, 1935, A
WOMAN, 1919
WOMAN ABOVE REPROACH, THE, 1920
WOMAN ACCUSED, 1933, A-C
WOMAN AGAINST THE WORLD, 1938, A
WOMAN AGAINST THE WORLD, A, 1928
WOMAN AGAINST WOMAN, 1938, A
WOMAN ALONE, A
WOMAN ALONE, A, 1917
WOMAN ALONE, THE
WOMAN AND OFFICER 26, THE, 1920
WOMAN AND THE BEAST, THE, 1917
WOMAN AND THE HUNTER, THE, 1957, A
WOMAN AND THE LAW, 1918
WOMAN AND THE PUPPET, THE, 1920
WOMAN AND WIFE, 1918
WOMAN AND WINE, 1915, A
WOMAN AT HER WINDOW, A, 1978, O
WOMAN BENEATH, THE, 1917
WOMAN BETWEEN, 1931, C
WOMAN BETWEEN FRIENDS, THE, 1918
WOMAN BETWEEN, THE, 1931
WOMAN BETWEEN, THE, 1937
WOMAN BREED, THE, 1922
WOMAN CHASES MAN, 1937, A
WOMAN COMMANDS, A, 1932, A
WOMAN CONDEMNED, 1934
WOMAN CONQUERS, THE, 1922
WOMAN DECIDES, THE, 1932, A
WOMAN DESTROYED, A
WOMAN DISPUTED, THE, 1928
WOMAN DOCTOR, 1939, A
WOMAN EATER, THE, 1959, C
WOMAN ETERNAL, THE, 1918
WOMAN FLAMBEE, A
WOMAN FOR ALL MEN, A, 1975
WOMAN FOR CHARLEY, A
WOMAN FOR JOE, THE, 1955, A
WOMAN FROM CHINA, THE, 1930
WOMAN FROM HEADQUARTERS, 1950, A
WOMAN FROM HELL, THE, 1929
WOMAN FROM MONTE CARLO, THE, 1932, A
WOMAN FROM MOSCOW, THE, 1928
WOMAN FROM TANGIER, THE, 1948, A
WOMAN GAME, THE, 1920
WOMAN GIVES, THE, 1920
WOMAN GOD CHANGED, THE, 1921, A
WOMAN GOD FORGOT, THE, 1917
WOMAN GOD SENT, THE, 1920
WOMAN HATER, 1949, A
WOMAN HATER, THE, 1925
WOMAN HE LOVED, THE, 1922
WOMAN HE MARRIED, THE, 1922
WOMAN HE SCORNED, THE, 1930, A
WOMAN HUNGRY, 1931, C
WOMAN HUNT, 1962, C
WOMAN HUNT, THE, 1975, O
WOMAN I LOVE, THE, 1929
WOMAN I LOVE, THE, 1937, A
WOMAN I STOLE, THE, 1933, A
WOMAN IN 47, THE, 1916
WOMAN IN BLACK, THE, 1914
WOMAN IN BONDAGE, 1932
WOMAN IN BONDAGE, 1943
WOMAN IN BROWN
WOMAN IN CHAINS, 1932, A
WOMAN IN CHAINS, THE, 1923
WOMAN IN COMMAND, THE, 1934, A
WOMAN IN DISTRESS, 1937, A
WOMAN IN FLAMES, A, 1984, O
WOMAN IN GREEN, THE, 1945, A
WOMAN IN HER THIRTIES, A
WOMAN IN HIDING, 1949, A-C
WOMAN IN HIDING, 1953, A
WOMAN IN HIS HOUSE, THE
WOMAN IN HIS HOUSE, THE, 1920
WOMAN IN PAWN, A, 1927
WOMAN IN POLITICS, THE, 1916
WOMAN IN QUESTION, THE
WOMAN IN RED, THE, 1935, A
WOMAN IN RED, THE, 1984, C
WOMAN IN ROOM 13, THE, 1920
WOMAN IN ROOM 13, THE, 1932, A
WOMAN IN THE CASE, 1935
WOMAN IN THE CASE, A, 1916
WOMAN IN THE CASE, THE, 1945
WOMAN IN THE DARK, 1934, A
WOMAN IN THE DARK, 1952, A
WOMAN IN THE DUNES, 1964, O
WOMAN IN THE HALL, THE, 1949, A
WOMAN IN THE NIGHT, A, 1929
WOMAN IN THE RAIN, 1976
WOMAN IN THE SUITCASE, THE, 1920
WOMAN IN THE WINDOW, THE, 1945, C
WOMAN IN WHITE, THE, 1917
WOMAN IN WHITE, THE, 1929
WOMAN IN WHITE, THE, 1948, C
WOMAN INSIDE, THE, 1981, O
WOMAN IS A WOMAN, A, 1961, A
WOMAN IS THE JUDGE, A, 1939, A
WOMAN MICHAEL MARRIED, THE, 1919
WOMAN NEXT DOOR, THE
WOMAN NEXT DOOR, THE, 1915
WOMAN NEXT DOOR, THE, 1981, O
WOMAN OBSESSED, 1959, A-C
WOMAN OF AFFAIRS, A, 1928, A
WOMAN OF ANTWERP
WOMAN OF BRONZE, THE, 1923
WOMAN OF DARKNESS, 1968, O
WOMAN OF DISTINCTION, A, 1950, A
WOMAN OF DOLWYN
WOMAN OF EXPERIENCE, A, 1931, A
WOMAN OF FLESH, A, 1927
WOMAN OF HIS DREAM, THE, 1921
WOMAN OF IMPULSE, A, 1918
WOMAN OF LIES, 1919
WOMAN OF MYSTERY, A, 1957, A
WOMAN OF MYSTERY, THE, 1914, A
WOMAN OF NO IMPORTANCE, A, 1921
WOMAN OF PARIS, A, 1923, C
WOMAN OF PLEASURE, 1924
WOMAN OF PLEASURE, A, 1919
WOMAN OF REDEMPTION, A, 1918
WOMAN OF ROME, 1956, O
WOMAN OF SIN, 1961, A
WOMAN OF STRAW, 1964, C
WOMAN OF THE DUNES
WOMAN OF THE IRON BRACELETS, THE, 1920
WOMAN OF THE NORTH COUNTRY, 1952, A
WOMAN OF THE RIVER, 1954, O
WOMAN OF THE SEA, A, 1926
WOMAN OF THE TOWN, THE, 1943, A
WOMAN OF THE WORLD, A
WOMAN OF THE WORLD, A, 1925
WOMAN OF THE YEAR, 1942, AA
WOMAN OF TOKYO, 1933
WOMAN OF TOMORROW, 1914
WOMAN ON FIRE, A, 1970, O
WOMAN ON PIER 13, THE, 1950, A
WOMAN ON THE BEACH, THE, 1947, A
WOMAN ON THE INDEX, THE, 1919
WOMAN ON THE JURY, THE, 1924
WOMAN ON THE MOON, THE, 1929, A
WOMAN ON THE RUN, 1950, A
WOMAN ON TRIAL, THE, 1927, A
WOMAN PAYS, THE, 1915

WOMAN POSSESSED,A, 1958, A
WOMAN PURSUED, 1931
WOMAN RACKET, THE, 1930, A
WOMAN REBELS , A, 1936, A-C
WOMAN REDEEMED, A, 1927
WOMAN TAMER
WOMAN TEMPTED, THE, 1928, A
WOMAN THE GERMANS SHOT, 1918
WOMAN THERE WAS, A, 1919
WOMAN THEY ALMOST LYNCHED, THE, 1953, A
WOMAN THOU GAVEST ME, THE, 1919
WOMAN TIMES SEVEN, 1967, C-O
WOMAN TO WOMAN, 1923
WOMAN TO WOMAN, 1929, A
WOMAN TO WOMAN, 1946, A
WOMAN TRAP, 1929, A
WOMAN TRAP, 1936, A
WOMAN UNAFRAID, 1934, A
WOMAN UNDER COVER, THE, 1919
WOMAN UNDER OATH, THE, 1919
WOMAN UNDER THE INFLUENCE, A, 1974, C
WOMAN UNTAMED, THE, 1920
WOMAN WANTED, 1935, A
WOMAN WHO BELIEVED, THE, 1922
WOMAN WHO CAME BACK, 1945, A
WOMAN WHO DARED, 1949, A
WOMAN WHO DARED, THE
WOMAN WHO DARED, THE, 1916
WOMAN WHO DID NOT CARE, THE, 1927, A
WOMAN WHO DID, A, 1914
WOMAN WHO DID, THE, 1915
WOMAN WHO FOOLED HERSELF, THE, 1922, A
WOMAN WHO GAVE, THE, 1918
WOMAN WHO INVENTED LOVE, THE, 1918
WOMAN WHO LIED, THE, 1915
WOMAN WHO OBEYED, THE, 1923
WOMAN WHO SINNED, A, 1925, A
WOMAN WHO TOUCHED THE LEGS, THE, 1926
WOMAN WHO UNDERSTOOD, A, 1920
WOMAN WHO WALKED ALONE, THE, 1922, A
WOMAN WHO WAS FORGOTTEN, THE, 1930
WOMAN WHO WAS NOTHING, THE, 1917
WOMAN WHO WOULDN'T DIE, THE, 1965, A
WOMAN WISE, 1928, A
WOMAN WITH A DAGGER, 1916
WOMAN WITH FOUR FACES, THE, 1923
WOMAN WITH NO NAME, THE
WOMAN WITH RED BOOTS, THE, 1977, O
WOMAN WITH THE FAN, THE, 1921
WOMAN WITHOUT A FACE
WOMAN WITHOUT CAMELLIAS, THE
WOMAN WOMAN, 1919
WOMAN'S ANGLE, THE, 1954, A
WOMAN'S AWAKENING, A, 1917
WOMAN'S BUSINESS, A, 1920, A
WOMAN'S DARING, A, 1916
WOMAN'S DEVOTION, A, 1956, A
WOMAN'S EXPERIENCE, A, 1918
WOMAN'S FACE, A, 1939, A
WOMAN'S FACE, A, 1941, A-C
WOMAN'S FAITH, A, 1925
WOMAN'S FIGHT, A, 1916
WOMAN'S FOOL, A, 1918
WOMAN'S HEART, A, 1926
WOMAN'S HONOR, A, 1916
WOMAN'S LAW, 1927
WOMAN'S LAW, THE, 1916
WOMAN'S LIFE, A, 1964, A
WOMAN'S MAN, 1920, A
WOMAN'S MAN, A, 1934
WOMAN'S PAST, A, 1915
WOMAN'S PLACE, 1921, A
WOMAN'S PLACE, A
WOMAN'S POWER, A, 1916
WOMAN'S RESURRECTION, A, 1915
WOMAN'S REVENGE, A
WOMAN'S SACRIFICE, A
WOMAN'S SECRET, A, 1924, A
WOMAN'S SECRET, A, 1949, A
WOMAN'S SIDE, THE, 1922
WOMAN'S TEMPTATION, A, 1959, A
WOMAN'S TRIUMPH, A, 1914
WOMAN'S URGE, A, 1966
WOMAN'S VENGEANCE, A, 1947, A
WOMAN'S VENGEANCE, A, 1939
WOMAN'S WAY, A, 1916
WOMAN'S WAY, A, 1928
WOMAN'S WEAPONS, 1918
WOMAN'S WOMAN, A, 1922
WOMAN'S WORLD, 1954, A-C
WOMAN, THE, 1915, A
WOMAN, WAKE UP, 1922
WOMAN-PROOF, 1923
WOMAN-WISE, 1937, A
WOMANEATER
WOMANHANDLED, 1925, A
WOMANHOOD, 1917
WOMANHOOD, 1934, A
WOMANLIGHT, 1979, C
WOMANPOWER, 1926, A
WOMBLING FREE, 1977, AAA
WOMEN AND BLOODY TERROR, 1970, O
WOMEN AND DIAMONDS, 1924
WOMEN AND GOLD, 1925
WOMEN AND WAR, 1965, C
WOMEN ARE LIKE THAT, 1938, A
WOMEN ARE STRONG, 1924
WOMEN ARE TROUBLE, 1936, A
WOMEN AREN'T ANGELS, 1942, A
WOMEN EVERYWHERE, 1930, A
WOMEN FIRST, 1924
WOMEN FOR SALE, 1975
WOMEN FROM HEADQUARTERS
WOMEN GO ON FOREVER, 1931, A
WOMEN IN A DRESSING GOWN, 1957, A
WOMEN IN BONDAGE, 1943, A
WOMEN IN CAGES, 1972
WOMEN IN CELL BLOCK 7, 1977, O
WOMEN IN CHAINS, THE
WOMEN IN HIS LIFE, THE, 1934, A
WOMEN IN LIMBO
WOMEN IN LOVE, 1969, O
WOMEN IN PRISON
WOMEN IN PRISON, 1938, A
WOMEN IN PRISON, 1957, O
WOMEN IN THE NIGHT, 1948, A
WOMEN IN THE WIND, 1939, A
WOMEN IN WAR, 1940, A
WOMEN IN WAR, 1965
WOMEN LOVE DIAMONDS, 1927
WOMEN LOVE ONCE, 1931, A
WOMEN MEN FORGET, 1920
WOMEN MEN LIKE, 1928
WOMEN MEN LOVE, 1921
WOMEN MEN MARRY, 1922
WOMEN MEN MARRY, 1931, A
WOMEN MEN MARRY, THE, 1937, A
WOMEN MUST DRESS, 1935, A
WOMEN OF ALL NATIONS, 1931, A-C
WOMEN OF DESIRE, 1968, O
WOMEN OF GLAMOUR, 1937, A
WOMEN OF NAZI GERMANY
WOMEN OF PITCAIRN ISLAND, THE, 1957, A
WOMEN OF RYAZAN, 1927
WOMEN OF THE NORTH COUNTRY
WOMEN OF THE PREHISTORIC PLANET, 1966, A
WOMEN OF TWILIGHT
WOMEN ON THE FIRING LINE, 1933
WOMEN THEY TALK ABOUT, 1928, A
WOMEN WHO DARE, 1928
WOMEN WHO GIVE, 1924
WOMEN WHO PLAY, 1932, A
WOMEN WHO WAIT
WOMEN WHO WIN, 1919
WOMEN WITHOUT MEN
WOMEN WITHOUT NAMES, 1940, A
WOMEN WON'T TELL, 1933, A
WOMEN'S PRISON, 1955, A-C
WOMEN'S WARES, 1927
WOMEN'S WEAPONS
WOMEN, THE, 1939, C
WOMEN, THE, 1969
WON BY A HEAD, 1920, A
WON IN THE CLOUDS, 1928
WON TON TON, THE DOG WHO SAVED HOLLYWOOD, 1976, A
WON'T WRITE HOME, MOM—I'M DEAD, 1975
WONDER BAR, 1934, A
WONDER BOY, 1951, A
WONDER CHILD
WONDER KID
WONDER MAN, 1945, AA
WONDER MAN, THE, 1920
WONDER OF WOMEN, 1929, A
WONDER PLANE
WONDER WOMEN, 1973, C
WONDERFUL ADVENTURE, THE, 1915
WONDERFUL CHANCE, THE, 1920
WONDERFUL COUNTRY, THE, 1959, A
WONDERFUL DAY
WONDERFUL LAND OF OZ, THE, 1969, AAA
WONDERFUL LIFE
WONDERFUL STORY, THE, 1932, A
WONDERFUL THING, THE, 1921
WONDERFUL THINGS?, 1958, A
WONDERFUL TO BE YOUNG?, 1962, A
WONDERFUL WIFE, A, 1922, A
WONDERFUL WOOING, THE
WONDERFUL WORLD OF THE BROTHERS GRIMM, THE, 1962, A-C
WONDERFUL YEAR, THE, 1921
WONDERFUL YEARS, THE
WONDERS OF ALADDIN, THE, 1961, AA
WONDERS OF THE SEA, 1922
WONDERWALL, 1969, O
WOOD NYMPH, THE, 1916
WOODEN HORSE, THE, 1951, A
WOODEN SHOES, 1917, A
WOODPIGEON PATROL, THE, 1930
WOOING OF PRINCESS PAT, THE, 1918
WOORUZHYON I OCHEN OPASEN
WORD, THE
WORDS AND MUSIC, 1929, A
WORDS AND MUSIC, 1948, A
WORDS AND MUSIC BY..., 1919
WORK IS A FOUR LETTER WORD, 1968, C
WORKING GIRLS, 1931, A
WORKING GIRLS, THE, 1973, O
WORKING MAN, THE, 1933, A
WORKING OF A MIRACLE, THE, 1915
WORKING WIVES
WORLD ACCORDING TO GARP, THE, 1982, C-O
WORLD ACCUSES, THE, 1935, A
WORLD AFLAME, THE, 1919
WORLD AGAINST HIM, THE, 1916
WORLD AND HIS WIFE, THE
WORLD AND HIS WIFE, THE, 1920
WORLD AND ITS WOMAN, THE, 1919
WORLD AND THE FLESH, THE, 1932, A
WORLD AND THE WOMAN, THE, 1916
WORLD APART, THE, 1917
WORLD AT HER FEET, THE, 1927
WORLD CHANGES, THE, 1933, A
WORLD FOR RANSOM, 1954, C-O
WORLD FOR SALE, THE, 1918
WORLD GONE MAD, THE, 1933, A
WORLD IN HIS ARMS, THE, 1952, A-C
WORLD IN MY CORNER, 1956, A
WORLD IN MY POCKET, THE, 1962, A
WORLD IS FULL OF MARRIED MEN, THE, 1980, O
WORLD IS JUST A 'B' MOVIE, THE, 1971, O
WORLD MOVES ON, THE, 1934, A
WORLD OF APU, THE, 1960, A
WORLD OF FOLLY, A, 1920
WORLD OF HANS CHRISTIAN ANDERSEN, THE, 1971, AAA
WORLD OF HENRY ORIENT, THE, 1964, C
WORLD OF SPACE, THE
WORLD OF SUZIE WONG, THE, 1960, O
WORLD OF TODAY, THE, 1915
WORLD OWES ME A LIVING, THE, 1944, A
WORLD PREMIERE, 1941, A
WORLD TEN TIMES OVER, THE
WORLD TO LIVE IN, THE, 1919
WORLD WAR III BREAKS OUT
WORLD WAS HIS JURY, THE, 1958, A
WORLD WITHOUT A MASK, THE, 1934, A
WORLD WITHOUT END, 1956, A
WORLD'S A STAGE, THE, 1922
WORLD'S APPLAUSE, THE, 1923
WORLD'S CHAMPION, THE, 1922, A
WORLD'S DESIRE, THE, 1915
WORLD'S GREAT SNARE, THE, 1916
WORLD'S GREATEST ATHLETE, THE, 1973, AAA
WORLD'S GREATEST LOVER, THE, 1977, A-C
WORLD'S GREATEST SINNER, THE, 1962, O
WORLD'S GREATEST SWINDLES
WORLD, THE FLESH AND THE DEVIL, THE, 1914
WORLD, THE FLESH, AND THE DEVIL, THE, 1932, A
WORLD, THE FLESH, AND THE DEVIL, THE, 1959, A
WORLDLINGS, THE, 1920, A
WORLDLY GOODS, 1924
WORLDLY GOODS, 1930, A
WORLDLY MADONNA, THE, 1922
WORLDS APART, 1921
WORLDS APART, 1980, C
WORLDS OF GULLIVER, THE
WORM'S EYE VIEW, 1951, A
WORMWOOD, 1915
WORRYING AND LOVE THE BOMB, 1964, C
WORST SECRET AGENTS
WORST WOMAN IN PARIS, 1933, A
WORTHY DECEIVER
WOULD YOU BELIEVE IT, 1929
WOULD YOU BELIEVE IT?, 1930, AAA
WOULD YOU FORGIVE?, 1920
WOULD-BE GENTLEMAN, THE, 1960, A
WOZZECK, 1962, A
WRAITH OF THE TOMB, THE
WRANGLER'S ROOST, 1941, A
WRATH, 1917
WRATH OF GOD, THE, 1972, C-O
WRATH OF JEALOUSY, 1936, A
WRATH OF LOVE, 1917
WRATH OF THE GODS, THE or THE DESTRUCTION OF SAKURA JIMA, 1914, A
WRECK OF THE HESPERUS, 1948
WRECK OF THE HESPERUS, THE, 1927
WRECK OF THE MARY DEARE, THE, 1959, A
WRECK, THE, 1919
WRECK, THE, 1927
WRECKAGE, 1925
WRECKER OF LIVES, THE, 1914
WRECKER, THE, 1928
WRECKER, THE, 1933, A
WRECKERS, THE
WRECKING CREW, 1942, A

WRECKING CREW, THE, 1968, C
WRECKING YARD, THE
WRESTLER, THE, 1974, C
WRESTLING QUEEN, THE, 1975
WRIGHT IDEA, THE, 1928
WRITING ON THE WALL, THE, 1916
WRITTEN LAW, THE, 1931, A
WRITTEN ON THE SAND
WRITTEN ON THE WIND, 1956, C
WRONG ARM OF THE LAW, THE, 1963, A
WRONG BOX, THE, 1966, A
WRONG DAMN FILM, THE, 1975, C-O
WRONG DOERS, THE, 1925
WRONG DOOR, THE, 1916
WRONG IS RIGHT, 1982, O
WRONG KIND OF GIRL, THE
WRONG MAN, THE, 1956, A
WRONG MR. RIGHT, THE, 1939
WRONG MR. WRIGHT, THE, 1927
WRONG NUMBER, 1959, A
WRONG ROAD, THE, 1937, A
WRONG WOMAN, THE, 1915
WRONG WOMAN, THE, 1920
WRONGLY ACCUSED
WRONGS RIGHTED, 1924
WU-HOU
WUSA, 1970, C
WUTHERING HEIGHTS, 1920
WUTHERING HEIGHTS, 1939, C
WUTHERING HEIGHTS, 1970, A
WYLIE
WYOMING, 1928
WYOMING, 1940, A
WYOMING, 1947, A
WYOMING BANDIT, THE, 1949, A
WYOMING HURRICANE, 1944
WYOMING KID, THE
WYOMING MAIL, 1950, A
WYOMING OUTLAW, 1939, A
WYOMING RENEGADES, 1955, A
WYOMING ROUNDUP, 1952
WYOMING TORNADO, 1929
WYOMING WHIRLWIND, 1932
WYOMING WILDCAT, 1941, A
WYOMING WILDCAT, THE, 1925

-X-

X
X MARKS THE SPOT, 1931, A
X MARKS THE SPOT, 1942, A
"X"—THE MAN WITH THE X-RAY EYES, 1963, C
X THE UNKNOWN, 1957, A-C
X Y & ZEE, 1972, O
X-15, 1961, A
X-RAY
XANADU, 1980, C
XICA, 1982, O
XICA DA SILVA
XOCHIMILCO
XTRO, 1983, O

-Y-

...Y EL DEMONIO CREO A LOS HOMBRES
YA KUPIL PAPU
YA SHAGAYU PO MOSKVE
YABU NO NAKA NO KURONEKO
YABUNIRAMI NIPPON
YAGYU BUGEICHO
YAGYU SECRET SCROLLS
YAKUZA, THE, 1975, O
YAMANEKO SAKUSEN
YAMBAO
YANCO, 1964, A
YANG KWEI FEI
YANGTSE INCIDENT
YANK AT ETON, A, 1942, A
YANK AT OXFORD, A, 1938, A
YANK IN DUTCH, A
YANK IN ERMINE, A, 1955, A
YANK IN INDO-CHINA, A, 1952, A
YANK IN KOREA, A, 1951, A
YANK IN LIBYA, A, 1942, A
YANK IN LONDON, A, 1946, A
YANK IN THE R.A.F., A, 1941, A
YANK IN VIET-NAM, A, 1964, A
YANK ON THE BURMA ROAD, A, 1942, A
YANKEE AT KING ARTHUR'S COURT, THE
YANKEE BUCCANEER, 1952, A
YANKEE CLIPPER, THE, 1927, A
YANKEE CONSUL, THE, 1924
YANKEE DON, 1931, A
YANKEE DOODLE DANDY, 1942, AAA
YANKEE DOODLE, JR., 1922
YANKEE FAKIR, 1947, A
YANKEE FROM THE WEST, A, 1915
YANKEE GIRL, THE, 1915
YANKEE GO-GETTER, A, 1921
YANKEE IN KING ARTHUR'S COURT, A
YANKEE MADNESS, 1924
YANKEE PASHA, 1954, A
YANKEE PLUCK, 1917
YANKEE PRINCESS, A, 1919
YANKEE SENOR, THE, 1926, A
YANKEE SPEED, 1924
YANKEE WAY, THE, 1917
YANKS, 1979, C-O
YANKS AHOY, 1943, A
YANKS ARE COMING, THE, 1942, A
YAQUI DRUMS, 1956, AA
YAQUI, THE, 1916
YASMINA, 1926
YATO KAZE NO NAKA O HASHIRU
YAWARA SEMPU DOTO NO TAIKETSU
YE BANKS AND BRAES, 1919, A
YEAR 2889
YEAR OF LIVING DANGEROUSLY, THE, 1982, C
YEAR OF THE CRICKET
YEAR OF THE HORSE
YEAR OF THE HORSE, THE, 1966, AA
YEAR OF THE TIGER, THE
YEAR OF THE YAHOO, 1971, O
YEAR ONE, 1974, A
YEARLING, THE, 1946, AA
YEARNING, 1964, C
YEARS BETWEEN, THE, 1947, A
YEARS OF THE LOCUST, THE, 1916
YEARS WITHOUT DAYS
YEKATERINA IVANOVNA, 1915
YELLOW BACK, THE, 1926, A
YELLOW BALLOON, THE, 1953, A
YELLOW BULLET, THE, 1917
YELLOW CAB MAN, THE, 1950, A
YELLOW CANARY, THE, 1944, A
YELLOW CANARY, THE, 1963, A
YELLOW CARGO, 1936, A
YELLOW CLAW, THE, 1920
YELLOW CONTRABAND, 1928
YELLOW DOG, 1973, A-C
YELLOW DOG, THE, 1918
YELLOW DUST, 1936, A
YELLOW FIN, 1951, A
YELLOW FINGERS, 1926, A
YELLOW GOLLIWOG, THE
YELLOW HAIR AND THE FORTRESS OF GOLD, 1984, O
YELLOW HAIRED KID, THE, 1952
YELLOW HAT, THE, 1966, A
YELLOW JACK, 1938, A
YELLOW LILY, THE, 1928
YELLOW MASK, THE, 1930, A
YELLOW MEN AND GOLD, 1922
YELLOW MOUNTAIN, THE, 1954, A
YELLOW PASSPORT, THE
YELLOW PASSPORT, THE, 1916
YELLOW PAWN, THE, 1916
YELLOW ROBE, THE, 1954, A
YELLOW ROLLS-ROYCE, THE, 1965, C
YELLOW ROSE OF TEXAS, THE, 1944, A
YELLOW SANDS, 1938, A
YELLOW SKY, 1948, A
YELLOW SLIPPERS, THE, 1965, A
YELLOW STAIN, THE, 1922, A
YELLOW STOCKINGS, 1928
YELLOW STOCKINGS, 1930, AA
YELLOW STREAK, A, 1915
YELLOW STREAK, A, 1927
YELLOW SUBMARINE, 1958, A
YELLOW TAIFUN, THE, 1920
YELLOW TEDDYBEARS, THE
YELLOW TICKET, THE, 1918
YELLOW TICKET, THE, 1931, A
YELLOW TOMAHAWK, THE, 1954, A
YELLOW TRAFFIC, THE, 1914
YELLOW TYPHOON, THE, 1920
YELLOWBACK, THE, 1929
YELLOWBEARD, 1983, C-O
YELLOWNECK, 1955, A
YELLOWSTONE, 1936, A
YELLOWSTONE KELLY, 1959, A
YENTL, 1983, C
YES OR NO?, 1920
YES SIR, MR. BONES, 1951, A
YES SIR, THAT'S MY BABY, 1949, A
YES, GIORGIO, 1982, C
YES, MADAM?, 1938, A
YES, MR. BROWN, 1933, A
YES, MY DARLING DAUGHTER, 1939, A
YESTERDAY, 1980, C
YESTERDAY'S ENEMY, 1959, O
YESTERDAY'S HERO, 1979, C-O
YESTERDAY'S HERO, 1937
YESTERDAY'S HEROES, 1940, A
YESTERDAY'S WIFE, 1923, A
YESTERDAY, TODAY, AND TOMORROW, 1964, O
YETI, 1977, A
YIDDLE WITH HIS FIDDLE, 1937, A
YIELD TO THE NIGHT
YIN AND YANG OF DR. GO, THE, 1972
YNGSJOMORDET
YO YO, 1967, A
YODELIN' KID FROM PINE RIDGE, 1937, A
YOG-MONSTER FROM SPACE, 1970, A
YOICKS!, 1932, AA
YOJIMBO, 1961, O
YOKE OF GOLD, A, 1916
YOKEL BOY, 1942, A
YOL, 1982, O
YOLANDA, 1924
YOLANDA AND THE THIEF, 1945, A
YOLANTA, 1964, A
YONGKARI MONSTER FROM THE DEEP, 1967, A
YOR, THE HUNTER FROM THE FUTURE, 1983, A
YORK STATE FOLKS, 1915
YOSAKOI JOURNEY, 1970, C
YOSAKOI RYOKO
YOSEI GORASU
YOSEMITE TRAIL, THE, 1922
YOSIE GORATH
YOTSUYA KAIDAN
YOU AND I
YOU AND ME, 1938, A-C
YOU AND ME, 1975
YOU ARE GUILTY, 1923
YOU ARE IN DANGER
YOU ARE THE WORLD FOR ME, 1964, A
YOU BELONG TO ME, 1934, A
YOU BELONG TO ME, 1941, A
YOU BELONG TO MY HEART
YOU BETTER WATCH OUT, 1980, O
YOU CAME ALONG, 1945, A
YOU CAME TOO LATE, 1962, A
YOU CAN'T BEAT LOVE, 1937, A
YOU CAN'T BEAT THE IRISH, 1952, A
YOU CAN'T BEAT THE LAW
YOU CAN'T BEAT THE LAW, 1928
YOU CAN'T BELIEVE EVERYTHING, 1918
YOU CAN'T BUY EVERYTHING, 1934, A
YOU CAN'T BUY LUCK, 1937, A
YOU CAN'T CHEAT AN HONEST MAN, 1939, A
YOU CAN'T DO THAT TO ME
YOU CAN'T DO WITHOUT LOVE, 1946, A
YOU CAN'T ESCAPE, 1955, A
YOU CAN'T ESCAPE FOREVER, 1942, A
YOU CAN'T FOOL AN IRISHMAN, 1950, A
YOU CAN'T FOOL YOUR WIFE, 1923
YOU CAN'T FOOL YOUR WIFE, 1940, A
YOU CAN'T GET AWAY WITH IT, 1923
YOU CAN'T GET AWAY WITH MURDER, 1939, A-C
YOU CAN'T HAVE EVERYTHING, 1937, A
YOU CAN'T HAVE EVERYTHING, 1972
YOU CAN'T KEEP A GOOD MAN DOWN, 1922
YOU CAN'T RATION LOVE, 1944, A
YOU CAN'T RUN AWAY FROM IT, 1956, A
YOU CAN'T RUN FAR
YOU CAN'T SEE 'ROUND CORNERS, 1969, A
YOU CAN'T SLEEP HERE
YOU CAN'T STEAL LOVE
YOU CAN'T TAKE IT WITH YOU, 1938, A
YOU CAN'T TAKE MONEY
YOU CAN'T WIN 'EM ALL
YOU CAN'T WIN 'EM ALL, 1970, C
YOU DON'T NEED PAJAMAS AT ROSIE'S
YOU FIND IT EVERYWHERE, 1921
YOU FOR ME, 1952, A
YOU GOTTA STAY HAPPY, 1948, A
YOU HAVE TO RUN FAST, 1961, A
YOU JUST KILL ME
YOU KNOW WHAT SAILORS ARE, 1928
YOU KNOW WHAT SAILORS ARE, 1954, A
YOU LIGHT UP MY LIFE, 1977, C
YOU LIVE AND LEARN, 1937, A
YOU LUCKY PEOPLE, 1955, A
YOU MADE ME LOVE YOU, 1934, A
YOU MAY BE NEXT, 1936, A
YOU MUST BE JOKING?, 1965, A
YOU MUST GET MARRIED, 1936, A
YOU NEVER CAN TELL, 1920
YOU NEVER CAN TELL, 1951, A
YOU NEVER KNOW
YOU NEVER KNOW, 1922
YOU NEVER KNOW WOMEN, 1926
YOU NEVER KNOW YOUR LUCK, 1919
YOU NEVER SAID SUCH A GIRL, 1919
YOU ONLY LIVE ONCE, 1937, C
YOU ONLY LIVE ONCE, 1969, A
YOU ONLY LIVE TWICE, 1967, C
YOU PAY YOUR MONEY, 1957, A
YOU SAID A MOUTHFUL, 1932, A
YOU WERE MEANT FOR ME, 1948, A
YOU WERE NEVER LOVELIER, 1942, A
YOU WILL REMEMBER, 1941, A
YOU'D BE SURPRISED, 1926
YOU'D BE SURPRISED?, 1930, A
YOU'LL FIND OUT, 1940, A
YOU'LL LIKE MY MOTHER, 1972, C
YOU'LL NEVER GET RICH, 1941, A
YOU'RE A BIG BOY NOW, 1966, C

YOU'RE A LUCKY FELLOW, MR. SMITH, 1943, A
YOU'RE A SWEETHEART, 1937, A
YOU'RE DEAD RIGHT
YOU'RE FIRED, 1919
YOU'RE FIRED, 1925
YOU'RE IN THE ARMY NOW, 1937, A
YOU'RE IN THE ARMY NOW, 1941, A
YOU'RE IN THE NAVY NOW, 1951, A
YOU'RE MY EVERYTHING, 1949, A
YOU'RE NEVER TOO YOUNG, 1955, A
YOU'RE NOT SO TOUGH, 1940, A
YOU'RE ONLY YOUNG ONCE, 1938, A
YOU'RE ONLY YOUNG TWICE, 1952, A
YOU'RE OUT OF LUCK, 1941, A
YOU'RE TELLING ME, 1934, A
YOU'RE TELLING ME, 1942, A
YOU'RE THE DOCTOR, 1938, A
YOU'RE THE ONE, 1941, A
YOU'VE GOT TO BE SMART, 1967, A
YOU'VE GOT TO WALK IT LIKE YOU TALK IT OR YOU'LL LOSE THAT BEAT, 1971, O
YOUND AND WILD, 1958, A
YOUNG AMERICA, 1918
YOUNG AMERICA, 1932, AA
YOUNG AMERICA, 1942, AA
YOUNG AND BEAUTIFUL, 1934, A
YOUNG AND DANGEROUS, 1957, A
YOUNG AND EAGER
YOUNG AND EVIL, 1962, C
YOUNG AND IMMORAL, THE
YOUNG AND INNOCENT, 1938, A
YOUNG AND THE BRAVE, THE, 1963, A
YOUNG AND THE COOL, THE
YOUNG AND THE DAMNED, THE
YOUNG AND THE GUILTY, THE, 1958, A
YOUNG AND THE IMMORAL, THE
YOUNG AND THE PASSIONATE, THE
YOUNG AND WILD, 1975
YOUNG AND WILLING, 1943, A
YOUNG AND WILLING, 1964, C
YOUNG ANIMALS, THE
YOUNG APHRODITES, 1966, C
YOUNG APRIL, 1926
YOUNG AS YOU FEEL, 1931, AAA
YOUNG AS YOU FEEL, 1940, AAA
YOUNG AT HEART, 1955, A
YOUNG BESS, 1953, A
YOUNG BILL HICKOK, 1940, A
YOUNG BILLY YOUNG, 1969, A
YOUNG BLOOD, 1932, A
YOUNG BRIDE, 1932, C
YOUNG BUFFALO BILL, 1940, AAA
YOUNG CAPTIVES, THE, 1959, O
YOUNG CASSIDY, 1965, C
YOUNG CYCLE GIRLS, THE, 1979, O
YOUNG DANIEL BOONE, 1950, AAA
YOUNG DESIRE, 1930, C
YOUNG DETECTIVE, THE, 1964
YOUNG DIANA, THE, 1922
YOUNG DILLINGER, 1965, O
YOUNG DOCTORS IN LOVE, 1982, O
YOUNG DOCTORS, THE, 1961, A-C
YOUNG DON'T CRY, THE, 1957, C
YOUNG DONOVAN'S KID, 1931, A
YOUNG DR. KILDARE, 1938, A
YOUNG DRACULA
YOUNG DYNAMITE, 1937, A
YOUNG EAGLES, 1930, AA
YOUNG FRANKENSTEIN, 1974, C
YOUNG FUGITIVES, 1938, A
YOUNG FURY, 1965, C
YOUNG GIANTS, 1983, A
YOUNG GIRLS OF ROCHEFORT, THE, 1968, A
YOUNG GIRLS OF WILKO, THE, 1979, C
YOUNG GO WILD, THE, 1962, C
YOUNG GRADUATES, THE, 1971, O
YOUNG GUNS OF TEXAS, 1963, C
YOUNG GUNS, THE, 1956, A-C
YOUNG GUY GRADUATES, 1969, C
YOUNG GUY ON MT. COOK, 1969, A
YOUNG HELLIONS
YOUNG HUSBANDS, 1958, A
YOUNG IDEAS, 1924
YOUNG IDEAS, 1943, A
YOUNG IN HEART, THE, 1938, A
YOUNG INVADERS
YOUNG JACOBITES, 1959
YOUNG JESSE JAMES, 1960, C
YOUNG LAND, THE, 1959, A
YOUNG LIONS, THE, 1958, C-O
YOUNG LOCHINVAR, 1923
YOUNG LORD, THE, 1970, A
YOUNG LOVERS, THE, 1964, C-O
YOUNG LOVERS, THE, 1950
YOUNG LOVERS, THE, 1954
YOUNG MAN OF MANHATTAN, 1930, A
YOUNG MAN OF MUSIC
YOUNG MAN WITH A HORN, 1950, C
YOUNG MAN WITH IDEAS, 1952, A
YOUNG MAN'S BRIDE, THE, 1968
YOUNG MAN'S FANCY, 1943, A
YOUNG MISS, 1930
YOUNG MONK, THE, 1978, O
YOUNG MOTHER HUBBARD, 1917
YOUNG MR. LINCOLN, 1939, A
YOUNG MR. PITT, THE, 1942, A
YOUNG MRS. WINTHROP, 1920
YOUNG NOWHERES, 1929, A
YOUNG NURSES, THE, 1973, O
YOUNG ONE, THE, 1961, O
YOUNG ONES, THE
YOUNG PAUL BARONI
YOUNG PEOPLE, 1940, AAA
YOUNG PHILADELPHIANS, THE, 1959, C
YOUNG RACERS, THE, 1963, C
YOUNG RAHAH, THE, 1922
YOUNG REBEL, THE, 1969, C
YOUNG REBELS, THE
YOUNG ROMANCE, 1915
YOUNG RUNAWAYS, THE, 1968, O
YOUNG SAVAGES, THE, 1961, C
YOUNG SCARFACE
YOUNG SEDUCERS, THE, 1974
YOUNG SINNER, THE, 1965, C
YOUNG SINNERS, 1931, A
YOUNG STRANGER, THE, 1957, C
YOUNG SWINGERS, THE, 1963, AA
YOUNG SWORDSMAN, 1964, C
YOUNG TOM EDISON, 1940, AAA
YOUNG TORLESS, 1968, C
YOUNG WARRIORS, 1983, O
YOUNG WARRIORS, THE, 1967, C
YOUNG WHIRLWIND, 1928, A
YOUNG WIDOW, 1946, A
YOUNG WINSTON, 1972, A-C
YOUNG WIVES' TALE, 1954, A
YOUNG WOODLEY, 1929
YOUNG WOODLEY, 1930, C
YOUNG WORLD, A, 1966, C
YOUNG, THE EVIL AND THE SAVAGE, THE, 1968, O
YOUNG, WILLING AND EAGER, 1962, C
YOUNGBLOOD, 1978, O
YOUNGBLOOD HAWKE, 1964, O
YOUNGER BROTHERS, THE, 1949, A
YOUNGER GENERATION, 1929, A
YOUNGEST PROFESSION, THE, 1943, A
YOUNGEST SPY, THE
YOUR ACQUAINTANCE, 1927
YOUR BEST FRIEND, 1922
YOUR CHEATIN' HEART, 1964, A
YOUR FRIEND AND MINE, 1923
YOUR GIRL AND MINE, 1914
YOUR MONEY OR YOUR WIFE, 1965, A
YOUR NUMBER'S UP, 1931, C
YOUR OBEDIENT SERVANT, 1917
YOUR PAST IS SHOWING, 1958, A
YOUR SHADOW IS MINE, 1963, O
YOUR TEETH IN MY NECK
YOUR THREE MINUTES ARE UP, 1973, O
YOUR TURN, DARLING, 1963, C
YOUR UNCLE DUDLEY, 1935, A
YOUR WIFE AND MINE, 1919
YOUR WIFE AND MINE, 1927, A
YOUR WITNESS
YOURS FOR THE ASKING, 1936, A
YOURS TO COMMAND, 1927
YOURS, MINE AND OURS, 1968, AAA
YOUTH, 1917
YOUTH AFLAME, 1945, A
YOUTH AND ADVENTURE, 1925
YOUTH AND HIS AMULET, THE, 1963, C
YOUTH FOR SALE, 1924, A
YOUTH IN FURY, 1961, O
YOUTH MUST HAVE LOVE, 1922
YOUTH OF FORTUNE, A, 1916
YOUTH ON PARADE, 1943, AAA
YOUTH ON PAROLE, 1937, A
YOUTH ON TRIAL, 1945, A
YOUTH RUNS WILD, 1944, C
YOUTH TAKES A FLING, 1938, AA
YOUTH TAKES A HAND
YOUTH TO YOUTH, 1922, A
YOUTH WILL BE SERVED, 1940, A
YOUTH'S DESIRE, 1920
YOUTH'S ENDEARING CHARM, 1916
YOUTH'S GAMBLE, 1925
YOUTHFUL CHEATERS, 1923
YOUTHFUL FOLLY, 1920
YOUTHFUL FOLLY, 1934, A
YOYO
YR ALCOHOLIG LION, 1984, C
YUKIGUMI
YUKON FLIGHT, 1940, A
YUKON GOLD, 1952, A
YUKON MANHUNT, 1951, A
YUKON VENGEANCE, 1954, A
YUM-YUM GIRLS, 1976
YUSHA NOMI
YUSHU HEIYA
YVETTE, 1928
YVONNE FROM PARIS, 1919

-Z-

Z, 1969, C-O
Z.P.G., 1972, C
ZA DVUNMYA ZAYTSAMI
ZABRISKIE POINT, 1970, O
ZACHARIAH, 1971, C
ZAMBA, 1949, A
ZAMBA THE GORILLA
ZANDER THE GREAT, 1925, A
ZANDY'S BRIDE, 1974, A
ZANZIBAR, 1940, A
ZAPPA, 1984, O
ZAPPED, 1982, O
ZARAK, 1956, C
ZARDOZ, 1974, O
ZARTE HAUT IN SCHWARZER SEIDE
ZATO ICHI CHIKEMURI KAIDO
ZATO ICHI KENKATABI
ZATO ICHI TO YONJINBO
ZATOICHI, 1968, A
ZATOICHI CHALLENGED, 1970, A
ZATOICHI JOGKUTABI
ZATOICHI MEETS YOJIMBO, 1970, C
ZATOICHI'S CONSPIRACY, 1974, A
ZAZA, 1923
ZAZA, 1939, C
ZAZIE, 1961, A
ZAZIE DANS LE METRO
ZBEHOVIA A PUTNICI
ZEBRA FORCE, 1977
ZEBRA IN THE KITCHEN, 1965, AAA
ZEBRA KILLER, THE, 1974
ZEE & CO.
ZEEBRUGGE, 1924
ZELIG, 1983, A
ZEMLYA
ZENOBIA, 1939, A
ZEPPELIN, 1971, A
ZEPPELIN'S LAST RAID, THE, 1918
ZERO, 1928, C
ZERO HOUR, 1957, A
ZERO HOUR, THE, 1918
ZERO HOUR, THE, 1923
ZERO HOUR, THE, 1939, C
ZERO IN THE UNIVERSE, 1966, O
ZERO POPULATION GROWTH
ZERO TO SIXTY, 1978, C
ZETA ONE, 1969
ZHENITBA BALZAMINOVA
ZHILI-BYLI STARIK SO STARUKHOY
ZIEGFELD FOLLIES, 1945, AA
ZIEGFELD GIRL, 1941, A
ZIG-ZAG, 1975, O
ZIGZAG, 1970, C
ZIS BOOM BAH, 1941, A
ZISKA LA DANSEUSE ESPIONNE, 1922
ZITA, 1968, O
ZOKU MIYAMOTO MUSHASHI
ZOKU NINGEN NO JOKEN
ZOLLENSTEIN, 1917
ZOLTAN, HOUND OF DRACULA
ZOMBIE, 1980, O
ZOMBIE CREEPING FLESH, 1981, O
ZOMBIE ISLAND MASSACRE, 1984
ZOMBIE, 1971
ZOMBIES OF MORA TAU, 1957, O
ZOMBIES OF SUGAR HILL
ZOMBIES OF THE STRATOSPHERE
ZOMBIES ON BROADWAY, 1945, A
ZON, 1920
ZONGAR, 1918
ZONTAR, THE THING FROM VENUS, 1966, A
ZOO BABY, 1957, AAA
ZOO IN BUDAPEST, 1933, A
ZOOT SUIT, 1981, O
ZORBA THE GREEK, 1964, A
ZORRO CONTRO MACISTE
ZORRO, THE GAY BLADE, 1981, A-C
ZOTZ, 1962, A
ZULU, 1964, C
ZULU DAWN, 1980, C-O
ZVENIGORA, 1928
ZVEROLOVY
ZVONYAT, OTKROYTE DVER
ZVYODY I SOLDATY
ZWEI SARGE AUF BESTELLUNG

-1985 Films-

-A-

A ME MI PIACE, 1985, O
A MOURA ENCANTADA, 1985, A
A NOUS LES GARCONS, 1985, A
A REJTOZKODO, 1985, O
A TANITVANYOK, 1985, A

ABEL, 1985, O
ABIGEL, 1985, A
ACQUA E SAPONE, 1985, C
ACTAS DE MARUSIA
ADIEU BLAIREAU, 1985, O
ADIEU, BONAPARTE, 1985, O
ADVENTURES OF HERCULES
ADVENTURES OF MARK TWAIN, THE, 1985, AAA
AFTER DARKNESS, 1985, O
AFTER HOURS, 1985, O
AGADA, 1985, O
AGNES OF GOD, 1985, C
AIDS—GEFAHR FUR DIE LIEBE, 1985, O
AKE AND HIS WORLD, 1985, O
AL LIMITE, CIOE, NON GLIELO DICO, 1985, C-O
ALAMO BAY, 1985, O
ALLONSANFAN, 1985, C
ALWAYS, 1985, O
AMATEUR HOUR, 1985, O
AMERICAN FLYERS, 1985, C
AMERICAN NINJA, 1985, O
AMICI MIEI ATTO III, 1985, C-O
AMONG THE CINDERS, 1985, O
ANA, 1985, C
ANNIE'S COMING OUT, 1985, C
ANNIHILATORS, THE, 1985, O
APPOINTMENT WITH FEAR, 1985, O
ASSAM GARDEN, THE, 1985, A-C
ASSISI UNDERGROUND, THE, 1985, C
ASTERIX VS. CESAR, 1985, AA
AT MIDDLE AGE, 1985, C
ATALIA, 1985, C
ATTENTION! UNE FEMME PEUT EN CACHER UNE AUTR
AURORA
AURORA ENCOUNTER, THE, 1985, C
AVENGING ANGEL, 1985, O
AVIATOR, THE, 1985, A-C
AZ ELVARAZSOLT DOLLAR, 1985, C

-B-

BABY: SECRET OF A LOST LEGEND, 1985, C
BACK TO THE FUTURE, 1985, C
BAD MEDICINE, 1985, C
BAR ESPERANZA, 1985, O
BARBARIAN QUEEN, 1985, O
BASIC TRAINING, 1985, O
BASTILLE, 1985, C-O
BATON ROUGE, 1985, C
BAYAN KO, 1985, O
BEETHOVEN'S NEPHEW, 1985, O
BEFORE AND AFTER, 1985, C
BEKCI, 1985, C
BERLIN AFFAIR, THE, 1985, O
BETROGEN, 1985, O
BETTER OFF DEAD, 1985, C
BEYOND THE WALLS, 1985, O
BILLY ZE KICK, 1985, C
BLACK CAULDRON, THE, 1985, A-C
BLANCHE ET MARIE, 1985, O
BLASTFIGHTER, 1985, O
BLESSURE, 1985, C
BLISS, 1985, O
BLUE HEAVEN, 1985, O
BLUES METROPOLITANO, 1985, O
BOGGY CREEK II, 1985, C
BOJ OM MOSKVU, 1985, A
BORDELLO, 1985, O
BOY MEETS GIRL, 1985, O
BOYS NEXT DOOR, THE, 1985, O
BRAS DE FER, 1985, C
BRAZIL, 1985, O
BREAKFAST CLUB, THE, 1985, O
BREAKING ALL THE RULES, 1985, O
BREWSTER'S MILLIONS, 1985, O
BRIDE, THE, 1985, C
BRIGADE DES MOEURS, 1985, O
BROKEN MIRRORS, 1985, O
BUDDIES, 1985, O
BURKE & WILLS, 1985, A-C
BURMESE HARP, THE, 1985, O

-C-

CA N'ARRIVE QU'A MOI, 1985, C
CAFFE ITALIA, 1985, C-O
CALAMARI UNION, 1985, C
CAME A HOT FRIDAY, 1985, C
CAMILA, 1985, O
CARABINIERI SI NASCE, 1985, C
CARE BEARS MOVIE, THE, 1985, AAA
CAROVNE DEDICTVI, 1985, AA
CARRE BLANC, 1985, C
CARRY ON DOCTORS AND NURSES, 1985, O
CASABLANCA CASABLANCA, 1985, C
CASAS VIEJAS, 1985, O
CASO CERRADO, 1985, C
CAT'S EYE, 1985, C
CAVE GIRL, 1985, O
CAVIAR ROUGE, 1985, C
CEASE FIRE, 1985, O
CEMENTERIO DEL TERROR, 1985, O
CENT FRANCS L'AMOUR, 1985, O
CERTAIN FURY, 1985, O
CHAIN GANG, 1985, O
CHAIN LETTERS, 1985, O
CHAIN, THE, 1985, C
CHAOS-KAOS
CHICK FOR CAIRO, A, 1985, AAA
CHILLY NIGHTS, 1985, A
CHORUS LINE, A, 1985, C
CHRONIC INNOCENCE, 1985, C
CIEN JUZ NIEDALEKO, 1985, A
CITY HERO, 1985, C
CITY LIMITS, 1985, C
CLIN D'OEIL, 1985, C
CLUE, 1985, O
COCA-COLA KID, THE, 1985, O
COCOON, 1985, C
CODE NAME: EMERALD, 1985, C
CODE OF SILENCE, 1985, O
CODENAME WILDGEESE, 1985, O
COLONEL REDL, 1985, O
COLOR PURPLE, THE, 1985, A-C
COLPI DI LUCE, 1985, O
COLPO DI FULMINE, 1985, C-O
COMMANDO, 1985, O
COMME LA NUIT, 1985, O
COMMITTED, 1985, O
COMPANY OF WOLVES, THE, 1985, O
COMPROMISING POSITIONS, 1985, C-O
COUNTDOWN, 1985, C
COURT OF THE PHARAOH, THE, 1985, C
CREATOR, 1985, O
CREATURE, 1985, O
CREEPERS, 1985, O
CRIMEWAVE, 1985, C
CROSSOVER DREAMS, 1985, C-O
CSAK EGY MOZI, 1985, C

-D-

D.A.R.Y.L., 1985, AA
DA CAPO, 1985, C
DANCE WITH A STRANGER, 1985, C-O
DANGEROUS MOVES, 1985, C
DARK OF THE NIGHT
DARSE CUENTA, 1985, C-O
DAWANDEH, 1985, A-C
DAY OF THE COBRA, THE, 1985, O
DAY OF THE DEAD, 1985, O
DAYS OF JUNE, THE, 1985, O
DE DEUR VAN HET HUIS, 1985, C
DE DROOM, 1985, C-O
DE L'AUTRE COTE DE L'IMAGE, 1985, C
DEADLY PASSION, 1985, O
DEATH OF AN ANGEL, 1985, C
DEATH OF MARIO RICCI, THE, 1985, C
DEATH WISH 3, 1985, O
DEF-CON 4, 1985, O
DEFENCE OF THE REALM, 1985, C-O
DEJA VU, 1985, O
DEMONS, 1985, O
DEN KRONISKE USKYLD
DER ANGRIFF DER GEGENWART AUF DIE UBRIGE ZEIT, 1985, C
DER UNBESIEGEBARE, 1985, O
DERBORENCE, 1985, C
DESERT HEARTS, 1985, O
DESERT WARRIOR, 1985, O
DESPERATELY SEEKING SUSAN, 1985, O
DETECTIVE, 1985, O
DIESEL, 1985, O
DILES QUE NO ME MATEN, 1985, C
DIM SUM: A LITTLE BIT OF HEART, 1985, A
DLUZNICY SMIERCI, 1985, C
DO OUTRO LADO DO ESPELHO ATLANTIDA, 1985, C
DO ZUBU A DO SRDICKA, 1985, AA
DOCTOR AND THE DEVILS, THE, 1985, O
DODSPOLARE, 1985, C
DOIN' TIME, 1985, O
DOOMED TO DIE, 1985, O
DORMIRE, 1985, C
DOT AND THE KOALA, 1985, AAA
DR. JEKYLL, 1985, O
DREAMCHILD, 1985, A
DREI GEGEN DREI, 1985, C
DRESSAGE, 1985, O
DROLE DE SAMEDI, 1985, C
DRUHY TAH PESCE, 1985, A
DUMA VEZ POR TODAS, 1985, O
DUNGEONMASTER, 1985, C-O
DUST, 1985, O
DUVAR

-E-

E ARRIVATO MIO FRATELLO, 1985, O
EGESZSEGES EROTIKA, 1985, O
833-85VESNICKO MA STREDISKOV
EIN MANN WIE EVA
EL DIPUTADO, 1985, O
EL JARDIN SECRETO, 1985, O
ELENI, 1985, A-C
ELSO KETSZAZ EVEM, 1985, C
EMBRYOS, 1985, O
EMERALD FOREST, THE, 1985, C-O
EMPTY BEACH, THE, 1985, O
EMPTY QUARTER, 1985, O
EN PLO, 1985, C
END OF THE WORLD MAN, THE, 1985, AAA
ENEMY MINE, 1985, A-C
ENORMOUS CHANGES AT THE LAST MINUTE, 1985, A
ERA UNA NOTTE BUIA E TEMPESTOSA, 1985, O
ESCALIER C, 1985, C
ESCAPE FROM THE BRONX, 1985, O
ETE UND ALI, 1985, C
EVILS OF THE NIGHT, 1985, O
EXPERIMENT EVA, 1985, C
EXPLORERS, 1985, C
EXTERMINATORS OF THE YEAR 3000, THE, 1985, O
EXTRAMUROS, 1985, O

-F-

FAIR GAME, 1985, O
FALCON AND THE SNOWMAN, THE, 1985, O
FALFURO, 1985, O
FALL GUY, 1985, C
FALSK SOM VATTEN, 1985, O
FANDANGO, 1985, C
FAST FORWARD, 1985, A-C
FAST TALKING, 1985, C-O
FATTO SU MISURA, 1985, O
FAVORITES OF THE MOON, 1985, C
FESTA DI LAUREA, 1985, A-C
FEVER PITCH, 1985, C-O
FIEBRE DE AMOR, 1985, AA
FIGLIO MIO INFINITAMENTE CARO, 1985, O
FINAL JUSTICE, 1985, O
FIRE FESTIVAL
FIX, THE, 1985, C-O
FLANAGAN, 1985, O
FLAXFIELD, THE, 1985, O
FLESH AND BLOOD, 1985, O
FONTANA PRE ZUZANU, 1985, A
FOOL FOR LOVE, 1985, O
FOR YOUR HEART ONLY, 1985, O
FORGET MOZART!, 1985, A
FRACCHIA CONTRO DRACULA, 1985, A
FRAN, 1985, O
FRATERNITY VACATION, 1985, C
FRIDAY THE 13TH, PART V—A NEW BEGINNING, 1985, O
FRIGHT NIGHT, 1985, O
FROG PRINCE, THE, 1985, O
FUNNY, DIRTY LITTLE WAR, A, 1985, O
FUTURE-KILL, 1985, O

-G-

G.I. EXECUTIONER, THE, 1985, O
GARCON!, 1985, C
GEBROKEN SPIEGELS
GHOULIES, 1985, O
GIG, THE, 1985, A-C
GIOCHI D'ESTATE, 1985, C
GIRL IN THE PICTURE, THE, 1985, C
GIRLS JUST WANT TO HAVE FUN, 1985, C
GLAMOUR, 1985, O
GO MASTERS, THE, 1985, C
GODNOSC, 1985, A-C
GODZILLA 1985, 1985, C
GOING AND COMING BACK, 1985, O
GOLFO DE VIZCAYA, 1985, O
GOODBYE NEW YORK, 1985, O
GOONIES, THE, 1985, C
GOSPODIN ZA EDIN DEN, 1985, A
GOTCHA!, 1985, O
GREGORIO, 1985, C-O
GRUNT! THE WRESTLING MOVIE, 1985, O
GUARDIAN OF HELL, 1985, O
GUNEY'S: THE WALL
GYEREKRABLAS A PALANK UTCABAN, 1985, A
GYMKATA, 1985, O

-H-

HAIL, MARY, 1985, O
HANNA D., LA RAGAZZA DEL VONDEL PARK, 1985, O
HANY AZ ORA, VEKKER UR?
HARD TRAVELING, 1985, C
HAREM, 1985, O
HASTA CIERTO PUNTO
HAVARIE, 1985, A
HAY UNOS TIPOS ABAJO, 1985, O
HE DIED WITH HIS EYES OPEN, 1985, O
HEART OF THE DRAGON, 1985, C
HEAVEN HELP US, 1985, 0
HEAVENLY BODIES, 1985, O
HEAVENLY KID, THE, 1985, O

HECHOS CONSUMADOS, 1985, A
HEIMAT, 1985, C-O
HELLHOLE, 1985, O
HENRY IV, 1985, O
HERCULES II, 1985, C
HERE COME THE LITTLES, 1985, AAA
HILLS HAVE EYES II, THE, 1985, O
HIMATSURI, 1985, O
HIT, THE, 1985, O
HLEDAM DUM HOLUBI, 1985, A
HODJA FRA PJORT, 1985, AAA
HOLCROFT COVENANT, THE, 1985, O
HOLD-UP, 1985, C
HOLLYWOOD HARRY, 1985, O
HOMELAND
HONEST, DECENT AND TRUE, 1985, O
HONG KONG GRAFFITI, 1985, O
HORS LA LOI, 1985, O
HOT RESORT, 1985, O
HOT TARGET, 1985, C-O
HOTEL NEW YORK, 1985, O
HOUSE ON THE EDGE OF THE PARK, 1985, O
HOWLING II...YOUR SISTER IS A WEREWOLF, 1985, O
HULYESEG NEM AKADALY, 1985, A
HURLEVENT, 1985, O
HUSTRUER, 2—TI AR ETTER

-I-

I MERCENARI RACCONTANO, 1985, O
I POMPIERI, 1985, A
I SKIACHTRA, 1985, AAA
I SOLITI IGNOTI VENT'ANNI DOPO, 1985, C
IDO VAN, 1985, O
IL CANTANTE E IL CAMPIONE, 1985, C-O
IL CAVALIERE, LA MORTE E IL DIAVOLO, 1985, O
IL MISTERO DI BELLAVISTA, 1985, C
IL PENTITO, 1985, C
ILLUSIONIST, THE, 1985, C
ILLUSTRES INCONNUS, 1985, O
IMPERATIVE, 1985, C
IMPIEGATI, 1985, C
IN DE SCHADUW VAN DE OVERWINNING
INA LASKA, 1985, C
INDECENT OBSESSION, AN, 1985, C-O
INFATUATION, 1985, A
INFERNO IN DIRETTA, 1985, O
INGANNI, 1985, C
INHERITORS, THE, 1985, O
INNOCENT, THE, 1985, A
INSIGNIFICANCE, 1985, O
INTERNO BERLINESE
INTO THE NIGHT, 1985, O
INVASION U.S.A., 1985, O
INVITATION TO THE WEDDING, 1985, A
IRITH, IRITH, 1985, C
ISLAND (LIFE AND DEATH), THE, 1985, O
IT DON'T PAY TO BE AN HONEST CITIZEN, 1985, O

-J-

JA NEJSEM JA, 1985, A-C
JACK KEROUAC'S AMERICA
JACQUES AND NOVEMBER, 1985, C
JAGGED EDGE, THE, 1985, O
JAKO JED, 1985, C
JAMES JOYCE'S WOMEN, 1985, O
JANGNAM, 1985, A
JANYO-NOK, 1985, C
JATSZANI KELL
JE VOUS SALUE, MARIE
JENNY KISSED ME, 1985, C
JEWEL OF THE NILE, THE, 1985, C
JOAN LUI: MA UN GIORNO NEL PAESE ARRIVO IO DI LUNEDI, 1985, O
JOEY, 1985, A
JOHANNES' HEMMELIGHED, 1985, A
JONNY ROOVA, 1985, A
JOSHUA THEN AND NOW, 1985, O
JOURNEY OF NATTY GANN, THE, 1985, C
JOY AND JOAN, 1985, O
JUST ONE OF THE GUYS, 1985, C

-K-

KALT IN KOLUMBIEN, 1985, O
KAMATA KOSHINKYOKU
KAOS, 1985, O
KARA PLNA BOLESTI, 1985, O
KEPVADASZOK, 1985, C
KEROUAC, 1985, O
KEY EXCHANGE, 1985, O
KEY, THE, 1985, O
KILL ZONE, 1985, O
KIM JEST TEN CZLOWIEK, 1985, C
KING DAVID, 1985, C
KING SOLOMON'S MINES, 1985, C
KISS OF THE SPIDER WOMAN, 1985, O
KNIGHTS OF THE CITY, 1985, O
KOBIETA Z PROWINCJI, 1985, A-C
KOMBA, DIEU DES PYGMEES, 1985, C
KRUSH GROOVE, 1985, O
KRYSAR, 1985, AAA
KUCKEN FUR KAIRO

-L-

L'ADDITION, 1985, O
L'ALCOVA, 1985, O
L'AMOUR BRAQUE, 1985, O
L'AMOUR EN DOUCE, 1985, C
L'AMOUR PROPRE...NE LE RESTE JAMAIS TRES LONGTEMPS, 1985, O
L'ATTENZIONE, 1985, O
L'EFFRONTEE, 1985, A
L'EVEILLE DU PONT D'ALMA, 1985, O
L'HOMME AUX YEUX D'ARGENT, 1985, C-O
L'HOMME BLESSE, 1985, O
L'INTRUSE, 1985, C-O
LA BASTON, 1985, O
LA CAGE AUX FOLLES 3: THE WEDDING, 1985, C
LA CASA NEL PARC
LA CHEVRE, 1985, A-C
LA CORTE DE FARAON
LA DIAGONALE DU FOU
LA DONNA DELLE MERAVIGLIE, 1985, O
LA GABBIA, 1985, O
LA HISTORIA OFICIAL
LA HORA BRUJA, 1985, C
LA HORA TEXACO, 1985, C
LA JEUNE FILLE ET LES LECONS DE L'ENFER, 1985, O
LA MESSA E'FINIT
LA NUIT PORTE JARRETELLES, 1985, O
LA SCARLATINE, 1985, C
LA SEGUA, 1985, O
LA TENTATION D'ISABELLE, 1985, O
LA TUA PRIMA VOLTA, 1985, C
LA VAQUILLA, 1985, A-C
LA VIE DE FAMILLE, 1985, O
LA VIEJA MUSICA, 1985, A
LADIES ON THE ROCKS, 1985, C-O
LADYHAWKE, 1985, C
LAMB, 1985, A
LAS VEGAS WEEKEND, 1985, O
LAST DRAGON, THE, 1985, C
LATINO, 1985, C-O
LE 4E POUVOIR, 1985, O
LE DECLIC, 1985, O
LE DUE VITE DI MATTIA PASCAL
LE FACTEUR DE SAINT-TROPEZ, 1985, C
LE FEU SOUS LA PEAU, 1985, O
LE FOU DE GUERRE, 1985, O
LE GAFFEUR, 1985, C
LE JEUNE MARIE, 1985, C
LE LEOPARD, 1985, O
LE MARIAGE DU SIECLE, 1985, O
LE MEILLEUR DE LA VIE, 1985, O
LE MUR
LE NEVEU DE BEETHOVE
LE PACTOLE, 1985, O
LE POUVOIR DU MAL
LE ROI DE LA CHINE, 1985, O
LE SOULIER DE SATIN
LE TABLIER BRODE DE MA MERE S'ETALE DANS MA VIE, 1985, C
LE TELEPHONE SONNE TOUJOURS DEUX FOIS, 1985, C-O
LE TEMPS D'UN INSTANT, 1985, A
LE THE AU HAREM D'ARCHIMEDES
LE TRANSFUGE, 1985, O
LE VOYAGE A PAIMPOL, 1985, C-O
LE "COWBOY", 1985, O
LEGEND, 1985, A
LEGEND OF BILLIE JEAN, THE, 1985, O
LEGEND OF SURAM FORTRESS, 1985, C
LEILA AND THE WOLVES, 1985, A
LEOPARD, THE
LES BALISEURS DU DESERT, 1985, C
LES ENRAGES, 1985, O
LES FAVORIS DE LA LUNE
LES LOUPS ENTRE EUX, 1985, O
LES LOUVES
LES MOTS POUR LE DIRE, 1985, C
LES NANAS, 1985, C
LES PLOUFFE, 1985, C
LES POINGS FERMES, 1985, C
LES ROIS DU GAG, 1985, C
LES SPECIALISTES, 1985, O
LES TROTTOIRS DE SATURNE, 1985, C
LETTERS FROM MARUSIA, 1985, C
LETTERS TO AN UNKNOWN LOVER, 1985, C
LIBERTE, EGALITE, CHOUCROUTE, 1985, O
LIFEFORCE, 1985, O
LIGHTSHIP, THE, 1985, O
LILY IN LOVE, 1985, C
LITTLE FLAMES, 1985, O
LITTLE SISTER, THE, 1985, O
LITTLE TREASURE, 1985, O
LOOSE SCREWS, 1985, O
LOS DIAS DE JUNIO
LOS MOTIVOS DE LUZ, 1985, C
LOSER, THE HERO, THE, 1985, A
LOST EMPIRE, THE, 1985, O
LOST IN AMERICA, 1985, O
LOVE TILL FIRST BLOOD, 1985, C-O
LUI E PEGGIO DI ME, 1985, C-O
LUNE DE MIEL, 1985, O
LUNE DE NOVEMBRE, 1985, O
LUST IN THE DUST, 1985, O

-M-

MACARONI, 1985, C
MACARTHUR'S CHILDREN, 1985, C
MACH A SEBESTOVA, K TABULI!, 1985, AA
MACHO Y HEMBRA, 1985, C
MAD MAX BEYOND THUNDERDOME, 1985, C-O
MAI CON LE DONNE, 1985, C-O
MAKIOKA SISTERS, THE, 1985, C-O
MAMMA EBE, 1985, O
MAN LIKE EVA, A, 1985, O
MAN UNDER SUSPICION, 1985, C
MAN WHO ENVIED WOMEN, THE, 1985, C
MAN WITH ONE RED SHOE, THE, 1985, C
MANCHURIAN AVENGER, 1985, O
MANGIATI VIVI
MANIA, 1985, O
MANNER
MARIA'S LOVERS, 1985, O
MARIE, 1985, C
MARK TWAIN
MARTIN'S DAY, 1985, C
MASK, 1985, C
MASS IS ENDED, THE, 1985, C
MASSIMAMENTE FOLLE, 1985, O
MATA HARI, 1985, O
MAXIE, 1985, C
MEAN SEASON, THE, 1985, O
MEDIUM, 1985, C
MEGFELELO EMBER KENYES FELADATRA, 1985, C
MEIN LIEBER SCHATZ, 1985, C
MEN, 1985, O
METEORO KAI SKIA, 1985, C
MEZEK, 1985, C
MEZZO DESTRO, MEZZO SINISTRO, 1985, C-O
MI FACCIA CAUSA, 1985, O
MIA TOSO MAKRINI APOUSSIA, 1985, O
MIRANDA, 1985, O
MISCHIEF, 1985, O
MISHIMA, 1985, O
MISSING IN ACTION 2—THE BEGINNING, 1985, O
MITT LIV SOM HUND, 1985, C
MITTEN INS HERZ
MOI VOULOIR TOI, 1985, O
MONSIEUR DE POURCEAUGNAC, 1985, O
MORONS FROM OUTER SPACE, 1985, C
MOVERS AND SHAKERS, 1985, C
MOVING VIOLATIONS, 1985, O
MR. SKEETER, 1985, AAA
MR. WRONG, 1985, O
MRAVENCI NESOU SMRT, 1985, C
MURPHY'S ROMANCE, 1985, C-O
MUTILATOR, THE, 1985, O
MUZ NA DRATE, 1985, C
MY AMERICAN COUSIN, 1985, A-C
MY FIRST WIFE, 1985, O
MY OTHER HUSBAND, 1985, C
MY OWN COUNTRY
MY SCIENCE PROJECT, 1985, C-O
MY SWEET LITTLE VILLAGE, 1985, A
MYSTERY OF ALEXINA, THE, 1985, O
McGUFFIN, THE, 1985, A-C

-N-

NAAR ENGLE ELSKER, 1985, C
NADZOR, 1985, C
NASDINE HODJA AU PAYS DU BUSINESS, 1985, C-O
NATIONAL LAMPOON'S EUROPEAN VACATION, 1985, C
...NEBO BYT ZABIT, 1985, C
NE PRENDS PAS LES POULETS POUR DES PIGEONS, 1985, O
NEW KIDS, THE, 1985, O
NI AVEC TOI, NI SANS TOI, 1985, O
NICKEL MOUNTAIN, 1985, C
NIGHT MAGIC, 1985, C
NIGHT TRAIN TO TERROR, 1985, O
NIGHTMARE ON ELM STREET PART 2: FREDDY'S REVENGE, A, 1985, O
9 DEATHS OF THE NINJA, 1985, O
NO MAN'S LAND, 1985, O
NOI TRE
NOMADS, 1985, O
NOT QUITE JERUSALEM, 1985, O

-O-

O BARAO DE ALTAMIRA, 1985, C-O
O LUGAR DO MORTO, 1985, C
O SAPATO DE CETIM, 1985, A
O TEMPO DOS LEOPARDOS, 1985, A

O VIASMOS TIS APHRODITES, 1985, A
OBJECTION, 1985, C
ODD BIRDS, 1985, A
ODYSSEA, 1985, A
OFELIA KOMMER TIL BYEN, 1985, O
OFFICIAL STORY, THE, 1985, O
OLD FOREST, THE, 1985, C
ON NE MEURT QUE 2 FOIS
ON THE EDGE, 1985, O
ONCE BITTEN, 1985, O
1918, 1985, C
ONE MAGIC CHRISTMAS, 1985, AA
ONE WOMAN OR TWO
ORFEUSZ ES EURYDIKE, 1985, A
ORIANE, 1985, O
OSA, 1985, O
OSNISTY ANIOL, 1985, C
OTHER HALVES, 1985, C
OTRA VUELTA DE TUERCA
OTRYAD, 1985, A
OUR FATHER, 1985, O
OUT OF AFRICA, 1985, C
OUT OF CONTROL, 1985, O
OUT OF ORDER, 1985, C
OUT OF THE DARKNESS, 1985, A

-P-

P'TIT CON
P.R.O.F.S., 1985, O
PACIFIC INFERNO, 1985, C
PADRE NUESTRO
PALACE, 1985, C
PALE RIDER, 1985, O
PARADISE MOTEL, 1985, O
PARKER, 1985, C
PARKING, 1985, C
PAROLE DE FLIC, 1985, O
PARTIR REVENIR
PASSAGE SECRET, 1985, O
PATAKIN, 1985, A
PAUL CHEVROLET AND THE ULTIMATE HALLUCINATION, 1985, O
PAVLOVA—A WOMAN FOR ALL TIME, 1985, A-C
PEANUT BUTTER SOLUTION, THE, 1985, AA
PEE-WEE'S BIG ADVENTURE, 1985, A
PELLE SVANSLOS I AMERIKATT, 1985, AAA
PERFECT, 1985, O
PERIL, 1985, O
PERINBABA, 1985, AAA
PETIT CON, 1985, C-O
PETKA S HVEZDICKOV, 1985, A
PETRINA CHRONIA, 1985, C
PHARAOH'S COURT
PHENOMENA
PHILADELPHIA ATTRACTION, THE, 1985, A
PICCOLI FUOCHI
PINK NIGHTS, 1985, A
PISMAK, 1985, A
PIZZA CONNECTION
PIZZAIOLO ET MOZZAREL, 1985, O
PLAYING FOR KEEPS
PLENTY, 1985, O
POBOJOWISKO, 1985, A
PODFUK, 1985, A
PODIVNA PRATELSTVI HERCE JESINIA, 1985, A
POHADKA O MALICKOVI, 1985, AAA
POHADKY POD SNEHEM, 1985, AAA
POHLAD KOCCE USI, 1985, A
POLICE, 1985, O
POLICE ACADEMY 2: THEIR FIRST ASSIGNMENT, 1985, O
POP CORN E PATATINE, 1985, C-O
PORKY'S REVENGE, 1985, O
POULET AU VINAIGRE, 1985, O
POWER OF EVIL, THE, 1985, O
PRIME RISK, 1985, C
PRINCE JACK, 1985, A
PRIVATE CONVERSATION, A, 1985, A
PRIVATE FUNCTION, A, 1985, O
PRIVATE RESORT, 1985, O
PRIVATE SHOW, 1985, O
PRIZZI'S HONOR, 1985, O
PROSTI MENYA, ALYOSHA, 1985, A
PROTECTOR, THE, 1985, O
PURPLE ROSE OF CAIRO, THE, 1985, C

-Q-

QUALCOSA DI BIONDO, 1985, O
QUI JIN, 1985, A
QUIET EARTH, THE, 1985, O

-R-

RAINBOW BRITE AND THE STAR STEALER, 1985, AA
RAMBO: FIRST BLOOD, PART II, 1985, O
RAN, 1985, O
RANJAU SEPANJANG JALAN, 1985, A
RAPPIN', 1985, O
RASPUTIN, 1985, O
RE-ANIMATOR, 1985, O
REAL GENIUS, 1985, C
REBEL, 1985, O
RED KISS, 1985, O
RED SONJA, 1985, C-O
REDL EZREDES
REMBETIKO, 1985, C
REMO WILLIAMS: THE ADVENTURE BEGINS, 1985, C
RENDEZVOUS, 1985, O
RENSHENG, 1985, A
RESTLESS NATIVES, 1985, C
RETURN OF THE LIVING DEAD, 1985, O
RETURN TO OZ, 1985, C
RETURN TO WATERLOO, 1985, C
REVOLUTION, 1985, C
RIGGED, 1985, C
RIVER WITHOUT BUOYS, 1985, A
ROBBERY UNDER ARMS, 1985, C
ROCKY IV, 1985, C
ROMAN BEHEMSHECHIM, 1985, C
ROSA LA ROSE, FILLE PUBLIQUE, 1985, O
ROSSO, 1985, C-O
ROUGE BAISER
ROUGE GORGE, 1985, C-O
RUNAWAY TRAIN, 1985, O
RUSTLER'S RHAPSODY, 1985, C
RUTHLESS ROMANCE, 1985, C

-S-

SMOOTH TALK, 1985, C-O
SMUGGLARKUNGEN, 1985, C-O
SOFTLY, SOFTLY
SONO UN FENOMENO PARANORMALE, 1985, O
SORTUZ EGY FEKETE BIVALYERT, 1985, C
SOTTO IL VESTITO NIENTE, 1985, O
SOTTO...SOTTO, 1985, O
SOUTH BRONX HEROES, 1985, O
SPECIAL POLICE, 1985, O
SPIES LIKE US, 1985, C
STAND ALONE, 1985, O
STAND-IN, THE, 1985, C-O
STARCHASER: THE LEGEND OF ORIN, 1985, C
STATIC, 1985, C-O
STEAMING, 1985, O
STEPHEN KING'S SILVER BULLET, 1985, O
STICK, 1985, O
STILLEBEN, 1985, C
STIN KAPRADINY, 1985, C
STITCHES, 1985, O
STRAIGHT THROUGH THE HEART, 1985, O
STREET TO DIE, A, 1985, O
STREETWALKIN', 1985, O
STRONGHOLD
STUFF, THE, 1985, C
SUBWAY, 1985, C-O
SUDDEN DEATH, 1985, O
SUGARBABY, 1985, C-O
SUMMER RENTAL, 1985, C
SUMMERTIME, 1985, C
SUPERGRASS, THE, 1985, C-O
SUPERSTITION, 1985, O
SURE THING, THE, 1985, C
SURPRISE PARTY, 1985, C
SVINDLANDE AFFARER, 1985, C
SWEET DREAMS, 1985, C-O
SWORD OF HEAVEN, 1985, O
SYLVESTER, 1985, A
SYLVIA, 1985, A-C
SZERELEM ELSO VERIG

-T-

TA PAIDIA TOU KRONOU, 1985, O
TACOS ALTOS, 1985, O
TALES OF THE THIRD DIMENSION, 1985, O
TANGOS, 1985, O
TARGET, 1985, O
TEA IN THE HAREM OF ARCHIMEDE, 1985, C-O
TEEN WOLF, 1985, A-C
TENKOSAI, 1985, C
TERMINAL CHOICE, 1985, O
TEST OF LOVE
TEX E IL SIGNORE DEGLI ABISSI, 1985, A
THAT WAS THEN...THIS IS NOW, 1985, O
THAT'S MY BABY, 1985, O
THREE MEN AND A CRADLE, 1985, C
THUNDER ALLEY, 1985, O
TICHA RADOST, 1985, C
TIEMPO DE MORIR
TIGIPIO, 1985, O
TIME AFTER TIME, 1985, A-C
TIME TO DIE, A, 1985, C
TISNOVE VOLANI, 1985, A
TO AROMA TIS VIOLETTAS, 1985, C
TO KILL A STRANGER, 1985, O
TO KOLLIE, 1985, C
TO LIVE AND DIE IN L.A., 1985, O
TO THERMOKIPIO, 1985, O
TOMBOY, 1985, O
TOO SCARED TO SCREAM, 1985, O
TOPOS, 1985, C
TORNADO, 1985, C
TOXIC AVENGER, THE, 1985, O
TRANCERS, 1985, O
TRANSYLVANIA 6-5000, 1985, C
TREASURE OF THE AMAZON, THE, 1985, O
TREFFPUNKT LEIPZIG, 1985, O
TRETI SARKAN, 1985, A
TRIP TO BOUNTIFUL, THE, 1985, C
TRISTESSE ET BEAUTE, 1985, O
TROIS HOMMES ET UN COUFFIN
TROUBLE IN MIND, 1985, O
TRZY STOPY NAD ZIEMIA, 1985, O
TUFF TURF, 1985, O
TURK 182!, 1985, C
TURN OF THE SCREW, 1985, O
TURTLE DIARY, 1985, C
TUTTA COLPA DEL PARADISO, 1985, C
TVATTEN, 1985, AA
TWICE IN A LIFETIME, 1985, O
TWISTED PASSION, 1985, O
2020 TEXAS GLADIATORS, 1985, O
TWO LIVES OF MATTIA PASCAL, THE, 1985, O

-U-

UCCELLI D'ITALIA, 1985, O
UFORIA, 1985, C
UM ADEUS PORTUGUES, 1985, A
UNA NOVIA PARA DAVID, 1985, A
UNDERWORLD, 1985, C
UNE FEMME OU DEUX, 1985, C
UNFINISHED BUSINESS, 1985, O
UNSUITABLE JOB FOR A WOMAN, AN, 1985, C
UNWRITTEN LAW, THE, 1985, A
UP TO A CERTAIN POINT, 1985, C
URAMISTEN
URGENCE, 1985, O

-V-

VACANZE D'ESTATE, 1985, C
VAGABOND, 1985, O
VALS, THE, 1985, O
VARIETES, 1985, C
VAROSBUJOCSKA, 1985, C
VAUDEVILLE, 1985, C-O
VERGESST MOZART
VERONIKA, 1985, C
VERTIGES, 1985, C
VERY MORAL NIGHT, A, 1985, O
VIEW TO A KILL, A, 1985, C
VISION QUEST, 1985, O
VISSZASZAMLALAS
VOLUNTEERS, 1985, O
VYJIMECNA SITUALE, 1985, A

-W-

WALKING THE EDGE, 1985, O
WALL, THE, 1985, O
WALTER & CARLO: OP PA FARS HAT, 1985, C
WAR AND LOVE, 1985, O
WARNING SIGN, 1985, O
WATER, 1985, C-O
WE THREE, 1985, C
WEIRD SCIENCE, 1985, O
WEST INDIES, 1985, A
WETHERBY, 1985, O
WHAT'S THE TIME, MR. CLOCK?, 1985, A
WHEN FATHER WAS AWAY ON BUSINESS, 1985, O
WHEN NATURE CALLS, 1985, O
WHEN THE RAVEN FLIES, 1985, O
WHERE THE GREEN ANTS DREAM, 1985, O
WHERE'S PICONE?, 1985, O
WHITE NIGHTS, 1985, C
WILD GEESE II, 1985, O
WILDROSE, 1985, C
WILDSCHUT, 1985, O
WILLS AND BURKE, 1985, C
WITNESS, 1985, C-O
WIVES—TEN YEARS AFTER, 1985, O
WIZARDS OF THE LOST KINGDOM, 1985, A
WORKING CLASS, 1985, C

-Y-

Y'A PAS LE FEU, 1985, C
YASHA, 1985, O
YEAR OF THE DRAGON, 1985, O
YOUNG SHERLOCK HOLMES, 1985, C
YUMECHIYO NITSUKI, 1985, O

-Z-

ZABICIE CIOTKI, 1985, C
ZABUDNITE NA MOZARTA
ZAHN UM ZAHN, 1985, C
ZASTIHLA ME NOC, 1985, A
ZATAH, 1985, C
ZED & TWO NOUGHTS, A, 1985, O
ZELENA LETA, 1985, A
ZINA, 1985, C
ZIVILE KNETE, 1985, A

ZOO GANG, THE, 1985, C

-1986 Films-

-A-

A BALADA DA PRAIA DOS CAES, 1986, NR
A FLOR DO MAR, 1986, NR
A LA PALIDA LUZ DE LA LUNA, 1986, NR
A LA SALIDA NOS VEMOS, 1986, NR
AAH . . . BELINDA, 1986, NR
AB HEUTE ERWACHSEN, 1986, C
ABDUCTED, 1986, O
ABOUT LAST NIGHT, 1986, O
ABSOLUTE BEGINNERS, 1986, C
ACES GO PLACES IV, 1986, NR
ADA, 1986, NR
ADI VASFIYE, 1986, NR
ADIOS PEQUENA, 1986, NR
ADVENTURE OF FAUSTUS BIDGOOD, THE, 1986, V
ADVENTURES OF THE AMERICAN RABBIT, 1986, AAA
AFZIEN, 1986, O
AGENT ON ICE, 1986, O
AGHAAT, 1986, C
AKLI MIKLOS, 1986, NR
AL ASHEKE, 1986, O
AL BEDAYA, 1986, O
AL DAHIYA, 1986, O
AL KETTAR, 1986, C-O
AL-KAS, 1986, NR
ALCESTES, 1986, O
ALEX KHOLE AHAVA, 1986, C-O
ALIENS, 1986, O
ALLA VI BARN I BULLERBY, 1986, AA
ALLIGORIA, 1986, NR
ALMACITA DI DESOLATA, 1986, C
AM NACHESTEN MORGAN KEHRTE DER MINISTER NICHT AN SEINEN, 1986, O
AMANSIZ UOL, 1986, A-C
AMERICA, 1986, O
AMERICA 3000, 1986, C
AMERICAN ANTHEM, 1986, C
AMERICAN COMMANDOS, 1986, O
AMERICAN JUSTICE, 1986, O
AMERICAN TAIL, AN, 1986, AAA
AMIGOS, 1986, C
AMMA ARIYAN, 1986, O
AMOR A LA VUELTA DE LA ESQUINA, 1986, O
AMORE INQUIETO DI MARIA, 1986, C-O
AMOROSA, 1986, O
ANAADI ANANT, 1986, NR
ANANTARAM, 1986, C
ANCHE LEI FUMAVA IL SIGARO, 1986, O
ANEMIA, 1986, O
ANGEL RIVER, 1986, O
ANGKOR—CAMBODIA EXPRESS, 1986, O
ANGRY HARVEST, 1986, C
ANNE TRISTER, 1986, O
ANOTHER LOVE STORY, 1986, O
ANTICASANOVA, 1986, NR
APRIL FOOL'S DAY, 1986, O
ARBEITSPLATZ ZURUCK, 1986, O
ARMED AND DANGEROUS, 1986, C
ARMED RESPONSE, 1986, O
ARMOUR OF GOD, THE, 1986, O
AROUND THE WORLD IN EIGHTY WAYS, 1986, C-O
ARRIVING TUESDAY, 1986, O
ARTHUR'S HALLOWED GROUND, 1986, C
ARUNATA PERA, 1986, A-C
AS SETE VAMPIRAS, 1986, O
ASILACAK KADIN, 1986, NR
ASSAULT, THE, 1986, C
ASTERIX CHEZ LES BRETONS, 1986, AA
AT CLOSE RANGE, 1986, O
ATOMOVA KATEDRALA, 1986, NR
AUF IMMER UND EWIG, 1986, O
AURELIA, 1986, O
AUSTRALIAN DREAM, 1986, O
AVAETE, A SEMENTE DA VINGANCA, 1986, C
AVANTI POPOLO, 1986, O
AVENGING FORCE, 1986, O
AWAITING THE PALLBEARERS, 1986, C-O
AWDAT MOWATIN, 1986, C
AZ DO KONCE, 1986, NR
AZ UTOLSO KEZIRAT, 1986, NR

-B-

BABEL OPERA, OU LA REPETITION DE DON JUAN, 1986, C
BACK TO SCHOOL, 1986, C
BACKLASH, 1986, O
BACKSTAGE, 1986, O
BAD COMPANY, 1986, O
BAD GUYS, 1986, C-O
BAIROLETTO, 1986, NR
BAL NA VODI, 1986, C
BALBOA, 1986, O
BALLERUP BOULEVARD, 1986, AA
BANANHEJKERINGO, 1986, NR
BAND OF THE HAND, 1986, O
BANDERA NEGRA, 1986, O
BAR 51, 1986, O
BARNDOMMENS GADE, 1986, C
BBONG, 1986, O
BEAU TEMPS, MAIS ORAGEUX EN FIN DE JOURNEE, 1986, C
BEER, 1986, O
BEGINNER'S LUCK, 1986, O
BEI AIQING YIWANG DI JIAOLUO, 1986, A-C
BELIZAIRE THE CAJUN, 1986, C
BEST MAN, THE, 1986, A-C
BEST OF TIMES, THE, 1986, O
BETTER TOMORROW, A, 1986, O
BETTY BLUE, 1986, O
BEYOND THE MIST, 1986, O
BI CHAMD KHAYRTAY, 1986, A
BIBBI, ELIN AND CHRISTINA, 1986, NR
BIG BET, THE, 1986, NR
BIG HURT, THE, 1986, O
BIG TROUBLE, 1986, C
BIG TROUBLE IN LITTLE CHINA, 1986, C-O
BIGGLES, 1986, C
BILLY GALVIN, 1986, A-C
BIR AVUC CENNET, 1986, C-O
BLACK AND WHITE, 1986, O
BLACK JOY, 1986, O
BLACK MIC-MAC, 1986, C
BLACK MOON RISING, 1986, O
BLACK TUNNEL, 1986, O
BLACKOUT, 1986, O
BLADE IN THE DARK, 1986, O
BLEU COMME L'ENFER, 1986, O
BLIND DIRECTOR, 1986, O
BLOOD RED ROSES, 1986, A-C
BLOODY BIRTHDAY, 1986, O
BLOUDENI ORIENTACNIHO BEZCE, 1986, NR
BLUE CITY, 1986, O
BLUE MAN, 1986, O
BLUE VELVET, 1986, O
BORIS GUDUNOV, 1986, O
BORN AMERICAN, 1986, O
BOSS' WIFE, THE, 1986, C-O
BOY IN BLUE, THE, 1986, C-O
BOY WHO COULD FLY, THE, 1986, A
BOYCOTT, 1986, NR
BRAS CUBAS, 1986, A-C
BREEDERS, 1986, O
BRENNENDE BLOMSTER, 1986, NR
BRIDGE TO NOWHERE, 1986, O
BRIGHTON BEACH MEMOIRS, 1986, C
BRODERNA MOZART, 1986, C
BULLIES, 1986, O
BULLSEYE, 1986, C-O
BUS, THE, 1986, NR
BUSTED UP, 1986, O
BUTNSKALA, 1986, NR

-C-

CABARET, 1986, O
CACTUS, 1986, C
CAGED GLASS, 1986, O
CALACAN, 1986, A
CAMORRA, 1986, O
CAN YUE, 1986, A
CAPABLANCA, 1986, O
CAPTIVE, 1986, O
CAR TROUBLE, 1986, C-O
CARAVAGGIO, 1986, O
CARAVAN SARAI, 1986, C-O
CARE BEARS MOVIE II: A NEW GENERATION, 1986, AAA
CARNAGE, 1986, C
CARNE CHE CRESCE, 1986, C
CASTAWAY, 1986, O
CASTIGHI, 1986, NR
CATTIVI PIERROT, 1986, O
CHAMS, 1986, O
CHARLEY, 1986, O
CHARLOTTE FOR EVER, 1986, O
CHECK IS IN THE MAIL, THE, 1986, O
CHICHERIN, 1986, A
CHICO REI, 1986, O
CHIDAMBARAM, 1986, O
CHILDREN OF A LESSER GOD, 1986, C-O
CHOKE CANYONyrate1986A
CHOPPER, 1986, NR
CHOPPING MALL, 1986, O
CHREZSNISAK, 1986, A-C
CHRISTOPHORUS, 1986, O
CHTO U SENJKI BYIO, 1986, AAA
CHUZHAJA, BELAJA I RJABAJ, 1986, A
CINEMA FALADO, 1986, A
CIPLAK VATANDAS, 1986, NR
CITY OF MICE, THE, 1986, NR
CLAN OF THE CAVE BEAR, THE, 1986, O
CLASS OF NUKE' EM HIGH, 1986, O
CLASS RELATIONS, 1986, A-C
CLOCKWISE, 1986, A
CLOSE TO HOME, 1986, O
CLOSED CIRCUIT, 1986, A
CLUB PARADISE, 1986, C
COBRA, 1986, O
COBRA MISSION, 1986, O
COCAINE WARS, 1986, O
COLOR OF MONEY, THE, 1986, C-O
COM LIENCA, EU VOU A LUTA, 1986, O
COMBAT SHOCK, 1986, O
COME AND SEE, 1986, O
COME LA VIDA MISMA, 1986, C
COMIC MAGAZINE, 1986, O
COMING UP ROSES, 1986, A
COMRADES, 1986, C
CONFIDENTIAL, 1986, OC-O
CONGO EXPRESS, 1986, O
CONSEIL DE FAMILLE, 1986, NR
CONTACTO CHICANO, 1986, O
CONTAR HASTA 10, 1986, O
COOL CHANGE, 1986, C
COPABLANCA, 1986, C
CORPS ET BIEN, 1986, C
COSMIC EYE, THE, 1986, AA
COURS PRIVE, 1986, O
CRAWLSPACE, 1986, O
CRAZY BUNCH, THEyrate1986C
CRAZY FAMILY, THE, 1986, O
CRAZY MOON, 1986, O
CRIMES OF THE HEART, 1986, C-O
CRITTERS, 1986, C-O
CROCODILE DUNDEE, 1986, A-C
CRONICA DE FAMILIA, 1986, O
CROSSROADS, 1986, C-O
CRVENI I CRNI, 1986, NR
CRY FROM THE MOUNTAIN, 1986, A
CUODIAN YUANYANG, 1986, C
CUT AND RUN, 1986, O
CYOEI NO MURE, 1986, C

-D-

DA EBICHASH NA INAT, 1986, C
DAHALO DAHALO, 1986, C
DAHAN, 1986, C-A
DANCING IN THE DARK, 1986, C
DANGEROUS ORPHANS, 1986, O
DANGEROUSLY CLOSE, 1986, O
DANILO TRELES, O FIMISMENOS ANDALOUISIANOS MOUSIKOS, 1986, C
DANS UN MIROIR, 1986, O
DARK AGE, 1986, O
DARK NIGHT, 1986, O
DAS HAUS AM FLUSS, 1986, O
DAS SCHWEIGEN DES DICHTERS, 1986, C
DAYS OF HELL, 1986, O
DE L'ARGENTINE, 1986, O
DE VAL VAN PATRICIA HIGHSMITH, 1986, C-O
DE WISSELWACHTER, 1986, O
DEAD END DRIVE-IN, 1986, O
DEAD END KIDS, 1986, C-O
DEADLY FRIEND, 1986, O
DEATH OF A SOLDIER, 1986, O
DEATH OF THE HEART, THE, 1986, C-O
DEATH SENTENCE, 1986, O
DEATHMASK, 1986, O
DEBAJO DEL MUNDO, 1986, NR
DEBELI I MRSAVI, 1986, NR
DEBSHISHU, 1986, C
DECLARATIE DE DRAGOSTEyrate1986O
DECLINE OF THE AMERICAN EMPIRE, 1986, O
DELITTI, 1986, O
DELTA FORCE, THE, 1986, O
DEMONER, 1986, O
DEMONS II—THE NIGHTMARE IS BACK, 1986, O
DEN FRUSNA LEOPARDEN, 1986, O
DEN GNEVA, 1986, O
DEPARTURE, 1986, O
DER PENDLER, 1986, O
DER POLENWEIHER, 1986, O
DER ROSENKONIG, 1986, O
DER SCHWARZE TANNER, 1986, O
DER SEXTE SINN, 1986, O
DER SOMMER DES SAMURAI, 1986, O
DER WILDE CLOWN, 1986, O
DERNIER CRI, 1986, O
DESCENDENT OF THE SNOW LEOPARD, 1986, AA
DESCENTE AUX ENFERS, 1986, O
DESERT BLOOM, 1986, A-C
DESIDERANDO GIULIA, 1986, O
DESORDE, 1986, O
DESPERATE MOVES, 1986, C-O
DETECTIVE SCHOOL DROPOUTS, 1986, A-C
DEVASTATOR, THE, 1986, O
DEVIL IN THE FLESH, 1986, C
DIAPASON, 1986, O
DIE LIEBESWUSTE, 1986, O
DIE NACHTMEERFAHRT, 1986, C-O
DIE WALSCHE, 1986, C
DIE ZWEI GEISCHTER DES JANUAR, 1986, O
DIRT BIKE KID, THE, 1986, A

DIRTY GAMES, 1986, O
DO YOU REMEMBER DOLLY BELL?, 1986, O
DOBRE SVETIO, 1986, NR
DOBROVOLJCI, 1986, O
DOCTOR OTTO & THE RIDDLE OF THE GLOOM BEAM, 1986, A
DOEA TANDA MATA, 1986, C
DOGS IN SPACE, 1986, C-O
DOKTOR, 1986, O
DONA HERLINDA AND HER SON, 1986, O
DONNA ROSEBUD, 1986, C
DOT AND KEETO, 1986, AAA
DOT AND THE WHALE, 1986, O
DOUBLE MESSIEURS, 1986, C
DOUCE FRANCE, 1986, O
DOWN AND OUT IN BEVERLY HILLS, 1986, C-O
DOWN BY LAW, 1986, O
DRAGON RAPIDE, 1986, C
DREAM LOVER, 1986, C
DREAM LOVERS, 1986, C
DREAM OF NORTHERN LIGHTS, 1986, NR
DREPTATE IN LANTURI, 1986, C
DROMMESLOTTER, 1986, O
DRZANJE ZA VAZDUH, 1986, NR
DUAN QING, 1986, O
DUET FOR ONE, 1986, O
DUNKI-SCHOTT, 1986, C

-E-

EAST OF THE WALL, 1986, C
EAT AND RUN, 1986, O
EAT THE PEACH, 1986, C
ECHO PARK, 1986, O
EHRENGARD, 1986, C
8 MILLION WAYS TO DIE, 1986, O
EIN BLICK UNE DIE LIEBE BRICT AUS, 1986, O
EIN FLIEHENDES PFERD, 1986, O
EINS OG SKEPNAN DEYR, 1986, O
EL AMOR BRUJO, 1986, A
EL ANO DE LAS LUCES, 1986, O
EL BRONCO, 1986, O
EL CABALLERO DEL DRAGON, 1986, O
EL CORAZON SOBRE LA TIERRA, 1986, O
EL DIA DE LOS ALBANILES II, 1986, O
EL DIA QUE ME QUIRAS, 1986, O
EL DISPUTADO VOTO DEL SR. CAYO, 1986, O
EL ESTRANGER—OH! DE LA CALLE CRUZ DEL SUR, 1986, O
EL EXTRANO HIJO DEL SHERIFF, 1986, O
EL HERMANO BASTARDO DE DIOS, 1986, C
EL HOMBRE QUE GANO LE RAZON, 1986, O
EL IMPERIO DE LA FORTUNA, 1986, O
EL JUEGO DE LA MUERTE, 1986, O
EL MALEFICIO II, 1986, O
EL MERCADO DE HUMILDES, 1986, O
EL NARCO—DUELO ROJO, 1986, O
EL OMBLIGO DE LA LUNA, 1986, NR
EL PUENTE, 1986, O
EL RIGOR DEL DESTINO, 1986, NR
EL RIO DE ORO, 1986, C-O
EL SECUESTRO DE CAMARENA, 1986, O
EL SEQUESTRO DE LOLA—LOLA LA TRAILERA II, 1986, O
EL SOL EN BOTELLITAS, 1986, NR
EL SUIZO—UN AMOUR EN ESPAGNE, 1986, O
EL TREN DE LOS PIONEROS, 1986, O
EL VECINDARIO—LOS MEXICANOS CALIENTES, 1986, O
EL-GOOA, 1986, O
EL-SADA EL RIGAL, 1986, O
EL-TOUK WA EL-ESSWERA, 1986, O
EL-YOM EL SADES, 1986, O
ELIMINATORS, 1986, AC-O
ELOGIO DELLA PAZZIA, 1986, O
ELVIS GRETTON LE KING DES KINGS, 1986, NR
ELYSIUM, 1986, O
EMMA'S WAR, 1986, C
EN PENUMBRA, 1986, O
ENAS ISICHOS THANATOS, 1986, O
END, THE, 1986, NR
EQUINOXE, 1986, C
ER WOO DONG, 1986, O
ERDSEGEN, 1986, NR
ERZEKENY BUCSU A FEJEDELEMTOL, 1986, NR
ES MI VIDA—EL NOA NOA 2, 1986, NR
ESE LOCO LOCO HOSPITAL, 1986, O
ESQUADRON DE LA MUERTE, 1986, NR
ESTHER, 1986, O
ET SKUD FRA HJERTET, 1986, O
ETATS D'AME, 1986, O
EU SEI QUE VOI TE AMAR, 1986, O
EVERY TIME WE SAY GOODBYE, 1986, C
EVIXION, 1986, O
EXIT—EXILE, 1986, O
EXTREMITIES, 1986, O
EYE OF THE TIGER, 1986, O

-F-

F/X, 1986, C-O
FAILURE, THE, 1986, O
FAIR GAME, 1986, O
FALOSNY PRINC, 1986, NR
FAMILY, THE, 1986, A
FAREWELL, ILLUSIONS, 1986, O
FAT GUY GOES NUTZOID, 1986, O
FATHERLAND, 1986, C
FAUBOURG SAINT-MARTIN, 1986, O
FEAR, 1986, O
FEIFA YIMIN, 1986, A
FEMMES DE PERSONNE, 1986, O
FERRIS BUELLER'S DAY OFF, 1986, OC
FIELD OF HONOR, 1986, O
50/50, 1986, O
52 PICK-UP, 1986, O
FILME DIMENCIA, 1986, O
FINAL EXECUTIONER, THE, 1986, O
FINAL MISSION, 1986, O
FINE MESS, A, 1986, A-C
FIRE IN THE NIGHT, 1986, O
FIRE WITH FIRE, 1986, O
FIREWALKER, 1986, A
FLAGRANT DESIR, 1986, O
FLAMBEREDE HJERTER, 1986, C
FLAMING BORDERS, 1986, C
FLASH, 1986, C
FLIGHT NORTH, 1986, O
FLIGHT OF RAINBIRDS, A, 1986, O
FLIGHT OF THE NAVIGATOR, 1986, A
FLIGHT OF THE SPRUCE GOOSE, 1986, C
FLODDER, 1986, C
FLOODSTAGE, 1986, C-O
FLY, THE, 1986, O
FLYING, 1986, C
FOLLOWING THE FUHRER, 1986, C
FOOTROT FLATS, 1986, A
FOR LOVE ALONE, 1986, O
FOREIGN BODY, 1986, O
FORMULA FOR MURDER, 1986, O
40 SQUARE METERS OF GERMANY, 1986, A
45 MO PARALLELO, 1986, O
FOTOROMANZO, 1986, C
FOUETTE, 1986, O
14 NUMARA, 1986, O
FOXTRAP, 1986, O
FRANCESCA E MIA, 1986, O
FRANZA, 1986, O
FREE ENTERPRISE, 1986, NR
FREE RIDE, 1986, O
FRENCH LESSON, 1986, C
FRIDAY THE 13TH PART VI: JASON LIVES, 1986, O
FRINGE DWELLERS, THE, 1986, A-C
FROM BEYOND, 1986, O
FROSTY ROADS, 1986, A
FULANINHA, 1986, C-O
FUTURE OF EMILY, THE, 1986, C-O

-G-

GALOSE STASTIA, 1986, NR
GARDIEN DE LA NUIT, 1986, O
GAVILAN O PALOMA, 1986, C
GENESIS, 1986, C
GENKAI TSUREZURE BUSHI, 1986, NR
GERONIMA, 1986, A
GETTING EVEN, 1986, O
GHAME AFGHAN, 1986, A-C
GILSODOM, 1986, O
GINGA-TETSUDO NO YORU, 1986, NR
GINGER AND FRED, 1986, A-C
GIOVANNI SENZA PENSIERI, 1986, O
GIRL FROM MANI, THE, 1986, O
GIRLS SCHOOL SCREAMERS, 1986, O
GIURO CHE TI AMO, 1986, O
GOBOTS: BATTLE OF THE ROCK LORDS, 1986, AAA
GOING SANE, 1986, O
GOLDEN CHILD, THE, 1986, C
GOLDEN EIGHTIES, 1986, A
GOOD FATHER, THE, 1986, O
GOOD TO GO, 1986, O
GOSPEL ACCORDING TO VIC, 1986, C
GRANDEUR ET DECADENCE D'UN PETIT COMMERCE DE CINEMA, 1986, O
GRANDFATHER, 1986, NR
GRANDI MAGAZZINI, 1986, C
GRANNY GENERAL, 1986, C
GREAT EXPECTATIONS—THE AUSTRALIAN STORY, 1986, NR
GREAT GENERATION, THE, 1986, O
GREAT MOUSE DETECTIVE, THE, 1986, AAA
GREAT WALL, A, 1986, A
GRITTA VOM RATTENSCHLOSS, 1986, A-C
GRONA GUBBER FRAN Y.R., 1986, AA
GULSUSAN, 1986, NR
GUNESE KOPRU, 1986, NR
GUNG HO, 1986, C
GURU DAKSHINA, 1986, NR

-H-

HADDA, 1986, C-O
HAJNALI HAZTETOK, 1986, NR
HAKRAV AL HAVAAD, 1986, C
HALF MOON STREET, 1986, C
HAMBURGER—THE MOTION PICTURE, 1986, O
HAME'AHEV, 1986, O
HANA ICHIMOMME, 1986, O
HANDS OF STEEL, 1986, O
HANNAH AND HER SISTERS, 1986, C
HAPPILY EVER AFTER, 1986, O
HAPPY DIN DON, 1986, O
HARD ASFALT, 1986, O
HARDBODIES 2, 1986, O
HARU NO KANE, 1986, NR
HARUKOMA NO UTA, 1986, NR
HASHIGAON HAGADOL, 1986, C
HAUNTED HONEYMOON, 1986, A
HEAD OFFICE, 1986, C
HEARTBREAK RIDGE, 1986, O
HEARTBURN, 1986, C-O
HEATHCLIFF: THE MOVIE, 1986, AAA
HEIDENLOCHER, 1986, C
HEILT HITLER, 1986, O
HELL SQUAD, 1986, O
HELLFIRE, 1986, O
HENRI, 1986, A
HIGH SPEED, 1986, O
HIGHLANDER, 1986, O
HIJO DEL PALENQUE, 1986, O
HITCHER, THE, 1986, O
HITOHIRA NO YUKI, 1986, NR
HOB FEE BAGHDAD, 1986, A
HOLLYWOOD VICE SQUAD, 1986, O
HOLLYWOOD ZAP, 1986, O
HONG KONG, 1986, O
HOOSIERS, 1986, A-C
HORVATOV IZBOR, 1986, NR
HOT CHILI, 1986, O
HOTEL DU PARADIS, 1986, O
HOUR OF THE STAR, 1986, O
HOUSE, 1986, C-O
HOWARD THE DUCK, 1986, A-C
HRY PRO MIRNE POKROCILE, 1986, NR
HUAJI SHIDAI, 1986, O
HUD, 1986, O
HUNGARY, 1986, O
HUOMENNA, 1986, C
HYPER SAPIEN: PEOPLE FROM ANOTHER STAR, 1986, A

-I-

I LAGENS NAMN, 1986, C
I LOVE YOU, 1986, O
I NICHTA ME TI SILENA, 1986, O
I PHOTOGRAPHIA, 1986, C-O
I TO CE PROCI, 1986, NR
IDEAALMAASTIK, 1986, A
IL BI E IL BA, 1986, O
IL CAMMISSARIO LO GATTO, 1986, A
IL CAMORRISTA, 1986, C
IL CASO MORO, 1986, C
IL DIAVOLO IN CORPO, 1986, O
IL GIARDINO DEGLI INGANNI, 1986, O
IL MIELE DEL DIAVOLO, 1986, O
IL MOSTRO DE FIRENZE, 1986, O
IL RAGAZZO DEL PONY EXPRESS, 1986, O
IL TENENTE DEI CARABINIERI, 1986, O
ILLUSION, THE, 1986, NR
IMAGEMAKER, THE, 1986, C-OO
IMPURE THOUGHTS, 1986, A-C
IN 'N' OUT, 1986, C
IN THE RAIN, 1986, NR
IN THE SHADOW OF KILIMANJARO, 1986, O
IN THE WILD MOUNTAINS, 1986, C
INDONESIA, 1986, O
INNOCENZA, 1986, O
INSIDE OUT, 1986, O
INSOMNIACS, 1986, O
INSPECTEUR LAVARDIN, 1986, O
INSTANT JUSTICE, 1986, O
INTIMATE POWER, 1986, O
INTRUDER, THE, 1986, O
INVADERS FROM MARS, 1986, C
IRAN, 1986, O
IRON EAGLE, 1986, C
ISLE OF FANTASY, 1986, C
ITALIAN FAST FOOD, 1986, C

-J-

JAILBREAK . . . 1958, 1986, C
JAKE SPEED, 1986, A-C
JAZOL, 1986, NR
JE HAIS LES ACTEURS, 1986, C
JEAN DE FLORETTE, 1986, C
JEZIORO BODENSKIE, 1986, C
JIBARO, 1986, A-C
JO JO DANCER, YOUR LIFE IS CALLING, 1986, C-O
JOGO DURO, 1986, C

JONAS, DEJME TOMU VE STREDU, 1986, C
JONSSONLIGAN DYKER UPP IGEN, 1986, A
JOUR ET NUIT, 1986, O
JOURNEY, THE, 1986, O
JRI FALESNY HRAC, 1986, NR
JUBIABA, 1986, O
JUDGEMENT IN STONE, A, 1986, C
JUE XIANG, 1986, C
JUMPIN' JACK FLASH, 1986, O
JUNGLE RAIDERS, 1986, A-C
JUST BETWEEN FRIENDS, 1986, O
JUST LIKE THE WEATHER, 1986, C

-K-

KAHAN KAHAN SE GUZAR GAYA, 1986, O
KAHIR ELZAMAN, 1986, A
KAK MOLODY MY BYLI, 1986, A
KALI PATRITHA SYNTROPHE, 1986, A
KAM DOSKACE RANNI PTACE, 1986, NR
KAMIKAZE, 1986, O
KAMIKAZE HEARTS, 1986, O
KANGAROO, 1986, C
KAPAX DEL AMAZONS, 1986, C
KARATE KID PART II, THE, 1986, A-C
KARMA, 1986, O
KATAKU NO HITO, 1986, NR
KATAYOKU DAKE NO TENSHI, 1986, NR
KDO SE BOJI, UTIKA, 1986, NR
KESERU IGAZSAG, 1986, A
KGB—THE SECRET WAR, 1986, O
KHOZIAIN, 1986, A
KHRANI MENIO, MOI TALISMAN, 1986, A
KILLER PARTY, 1986, O
KILLING CARS, 1986, O
KILLING MACHINE, 1986, O
KILLING OF SATANyrate1986O
KIMI GA KAGAYAKU TOKI, 1986, NR
KIMI WA HADASHI NO KAMI O MITAKA, 1986, NR
KIND OF ENGLISH, A, 1986, A-C
KINEMA NO TENCHI, 1986, C
KING AND HIS MOVIE, A, 1986, C
KING KONG LIVES, 1986, C
KING OF THE STREETS, 1986, O
KIRPLANGIC FIRTINASI, 1986, A
KISMASZAT ES A GEZENGUZOK, 1986, A
KNIGHTS AND EMERALDS, 1986, C
KNOCK OUT, 1986, C
KOHUT NEZASPIEVA, 1986, NR
KOJACK BUDAPESTEN, 1986, A
KOL AHAVO-TAI, 1986, O
KONEKO MONOGATARI, 1986, AA
KONZERT FUR ALICE, 1986, C
KORMORAN, 1986, O
KOUZELNIKUV NAVRAT, 1986, NR
KRAJ RATA, 1986, NR
KRAJINA S NABYTKEM, 1986, NR
KRONICA WY PADKOW MYLO SINYCH, 1986, O
KUEI-MEI, A WOMAN, 1986, A-C
KUKACKA V TEMNEM LESE, 1986, NR
KUNINGAS LAHTEE RANSKAAN, 1986, A
KURBAGALAR, 1986, A
KURSUN ATA ATA BITER, 1986, NR
KUYUCAKLI YUSUF, 1986, A

-L-

L'AMANT MAGNIFIQUE, 1986, O
L'APACHE BIANCO, 1986, O
L'AUBE, 1986, O
L'ETAT DE GRACE, 1986, O
L'EXECUTRICE, 1986, O
L'INCHIESTA, 1986, A-C
L'ISOLA, 1986, O
L'ULTIMA MAZURKA, 1986, C-O
L'ULTIMO GIORNO, 1986, C
L'UNIQUE, 1986, O
LA ALACRANA, 1986, O
LA BALLATA DI EVA, 1986, O
LA BANDA DE LOS PANCHITOS, 1986, O
LA BODA DEL ACORDEONISTA, 1986, O
LA BONNE, 1986, O
LA CASA DEL BUON RITORNO, 1986, O
LA CROCE DALLE 7 PIETRE, 1986, O
LA FEMME DE MA VIE, 1986, O
LA FEMME SECRETE, 1986, O
LA GALETTE DU ROI, 1986, C
LA GITANE, 1986, O
LA GUEPE, 1986, O
LA MACHINE A DECOUDRE, 1986, O
LA MANSION DE ARAUCAIMA, 1986, O
LA MITAD DEL CIELO, 1986, O
LA MOITIE D L'AMOUR, 1986, O
LA MONACA NEL PECCATO, 1986, O
LA MUERTE CRUZO EL RIO BRAVO, 1986, O
LA NOCHE DE LOS LAPICES, 1986, O
LA PURITAINE, 1986, O
LA RADIO FOLLA, 1986, NR
LA RAGAZZA DEI LILLA, 1986, O
LA ROSSA DEL BAR, 1986, NR
LA SECONDA NOTTE, 1986, C
LA SIGNORA DELLA NOTTE, 1986, O
LA SPOSA AMERICANA, 1986, O
LA SPOSA ERA BELLISSIMA, 1986, O
LA STORIA, 1986, C
LA TERRA PROMETIDA, 1986, C
LA VENEXIANA, 1986, O
LA VITA DI SCORTA, 1986, O
LABYRINTH, 1986, AAA
LADIES CLUB, THE, 1986, O
LADY JANE, 1986, C
LAND OF DOOM, 1986, C
LANDSCAPE SUICIDE, 1986, O
LAONIANG GOUSAO, 1986, NR
LAPUTA, 1986, O
LAS NOCHES DEL CALIFAS, 1986, O
LAST EMPEROR, THE, 1986, O
LAST IMAGE, THE, 1986, C
LAST OF PHILIP BANTER, THE, 1986, O
LAST RESORT, 1986, O
LAST SONG, 1986, O
LAST SONG IN PARIS, 1986, O
LE BONHEUR A ENCORE FRAPPE, 1986, O
LE COMPLEXE DU KANGOUROU, 1986, O
LE DEBUTANT, 1986, O
LE MAL D'AIMER, 1986, O
LE MATOU, 1986, O
LE MINIERE DEL KILIMANGIARO, 1986, O
LE PALTOQUET, 1986, C
LE PASSAGE, 1986, C
LEGAL EAGLES, 1986, C
LEJANIA, 1986, A
LEL HAB KESSA AKHIRA, 1986, A
LEPOTA POROKA, 1986, O
LES CLOWNS DE DIEU, 1986, O
LES FRERES PETARD, 1986, C
LES FUGITIFS, 1986, O
LES LONGS MANTEAUX, 1986, C
LET'S HOPE IT'S A GIRL, 1986, O
LETTER TO BREZHNEV, 1986, C-O
LEV S BILOU HRIVOU, 1986, NR
LIANGJIA FUNU, 1986, A
LICEENII, 1986, C
LIGHTNING—THE WHITE STALLION, 1986, A
LIGHTSHIP, THE, 1986, C
LIJEPE ZENE PROLAZE KROZ GRAD, 1986, O
LINK, 1986, O
LINNA, 1986, O
LISI UND DER GENERAL, 1986, O
LITTLE SHOP OF HORRORS, 1986, C
LJUBAVNA, 1986, NR
LJUBEZEN, 1986, NR
LOI RE TRAI TREN DUONG MON, 1986, A
LOLA, 1986, O
LONGSHOT, THE, 1986, O
LOS ASES DE CONTRABANDO, 1986, O
LOS HIJOS DE LA GUERRA FRIA, 1986, NR
LOS PARAISOS PERDIDOS, 1986, C
LOST, 1986, A-C
LOVE LETTER, 1986, A-C
LOVE ME!, 1986, O
LOVE SONGS, 1986, C
LOW BLOW, 1986, O
LOYALTIES, 1986, O
LUCAS, 1986, A
LULU DE NOCHE, 1986, O
LUNATICS, 1986, O
LUSSURIA, 1986, O

-M-

MACARONI BLUES, 1986, C
MAHULIENA ZLATA PANNA, 1986, NR
MAINE-OCEAN, 1986, C
MALA NOCHE, 1986, O
MALABRIGO, 1986, O
MALACCA, 1986, O
MALANDRO, 1986, O
MALCOLM, 1986, C
MALKAT HAKITA, 1986, C
MAMA IS MAD!, 1986, C-OO
MAMBRU SE FEU A LA GUERRA, 1986, C
MAMMAME, 1986, NR
MAN AND A WOMAN: 20 YEARS LATER, Ayrate1986C
MAN FACING SOUTHEAST, 1986, O
MAN OF ASHES, 1986, O
MANANA DE COBREyrate1986NR
MANDEN I MAANEN, 1986, C-O
MANHATTAN BABY, 1986, O
MANHATTAN PROJECT, THE, 1986, A
MANHUNT, THE, 1986, O
MANHUNTER, 1986, O
MANON, 1986, O
MANON DES SOURCES, 1986, C
MARE, 1986, A
MARIA, 1986, O
MARTIAL ARTS OF SHAOLIN, 1986, A-C
MARVADA CARNE, 1986, NR
MASSEY SAHIB, 1986, A
MATADOR, 1986, O
MATANZA EN MATAMOROS, 1986, O
MAUVAIS SANG, 1986, O
MAX MON AMOUR, 1986, O
MAXIMUM OVERDRIVE, 1986, O
ME HACE FALTA UN BIGOTE, 1986, A
MEGLIO BACIARE UN COBRA, 1986, O
MEIER, 1986, C
MELO, 1986, C
MEMOIRES D'UN JUIF TROPICAL, 1986, O
MEN'S CLUB, THE, 1986, C-O
MENAGE, 1986, O
MERCI MONSIEUR ROBERTSON, 1986, NR
MES ENLLA DE LA PASSIO, 1986, NR
MESHWAR OMAR, 1986, C
MIAMI GOLEM, 1986, O
MILLIONAIRE'S EXPRESS, THE, 1986, O
MILWYR BYCHAN, 1986, O
MIN PAPA AR TARZAN, 1986, AA
MIRCH MASALA, 1986, O
MIRZA NOWROUZ' SHOES, 1986, AA
MISS MARY, 1986, O
MISSION, THE, 1986, C
MISTER LOVE, 1986, A
MISTER VAMPIRE, 1986, C
MLADE VINO, 1986, NR
MOA, 1986, C
MODERN GIRLS, 1986, O
MOI DRUG IVAN LAPSHIN, 1986, C
MOMO, 1986, A
MON BEAU-FRERE A TUE MA SOEUR, 1986, NR
MON CAS, 1986, NR
MONA LISA, 1986, O
MONEY PIT, THE, 1986, A-C
MONITORS, 1986, O
MONSTER DOG, 1986, O
MONSTER SHARK, 1986, O
MONSTER, THE, 1986, C-O
MORD I MORKET, 1986, O
MORE THINGS CHANGE, THE, 1986, C-O
MORENA, 1986, O
MORIRAI A MEZZANOTTE, 1986, O
MORNING AFTER, THE, 1986, C-O
MORRHAR OCH ARTOR, 1986, O
MORT UN DIMANCHE DE PLUIE, 1986, O
MOSQUITO COAST, THE, 1986, O
MOTTEN IM LICHT, 1986, O
MOUNTAINTOP MOTEL MASSACRE, 1986, O
MOVIE HOUSE MASSACRE, 1986, O
MUJ HRISNY MUZ, 1986, NR
MUKHAMUKHAM, 1986, O
MULLERS BURO, 1986, O
MURPHY'S LAW, 1986, O
MUTCHAN NO UTA, 1986, NR
MUZ NA DRATE, 1986, NR
MUZSKOE VOSPITANIE, 1986, AA
MY BEAUTIFUL LAUNDRETTE, 1986, O
MY CHAUFFEUR, 1986, O
MY LITTLE PONY, 1986, AAA
MY MAN ADAM, 1986, O

-N-

NADIA, 1986, A
NAERTA OMETI, 1986, C
NAKED CAGE, THE, 1986, O
NAKED VENGEANCE, 1986, O
NAME OF THE ROSE, THE, 1986, C-O
NANOUyrate1986NR
NAS CLOVEK, 1986, NR
NATIVE SON, 1986, C
NATTSEILERE, 1986, NR
NAVRAT JANA PETRU, 1986, NR
NEBYVALSHINA, 1986, A
NEM TUDO E VERDADE, 1986, NR
NEMESIO, 1986, NR
NENI SIROTEK JAKO SIROTEK, 1986, NR
NEON MANIACS, 1986, O
NEVER TOO YOUNG TO DIE, 1986, O
NEW DELHI TIMES, 1986, C
NEW MORNING OF BILLY THE KID, THE, 1986, NR
NEXT SUMMER, 1986, O
'NIGHT, MOTHER, 1986, C
NIGHT OF THE CREEPS, 1986, O
NIGHTMARE WEEKEND, 1986, O
NIGHTMARE'S PASSENGERS, 1986, NR
NIJE LAKO S MUSKARCIMA, 1986, O
9 1/2 WEEKS, 1986, O
NINETY DAYS, 1986, O
NINGUEN NO YAKUSOKU, 1986, O
NINI TERNOSECCO, 1986, O
NINJA TURF, 1986, O
NJERIU PREJ DHEU, 1986, NR
NO MERCY, 1986, O
NO RETREAT, NO SURRENDER, 1986, C
NO SURRENDER, 1986, O
NO TIME TO DIE, 1986, O
NOAH UND DER COWBOY, 1986, C
NOBODY'S FOOL, 1986, C
NOCHE DE JUERGA, 1986, O
NOE HEIT ANNET, 1986, A-C
NOI CEI DIN LINIA INTII, 1986, C

NOTHING IN COMMON, 1986, A-C
NOVEMBERKATZEN, 1986, A
NTTURUDA, 1986, AA
NUIT D'IVRESSE, 1986, NR
NUREN XIN, 1986, NR
NUTCRACKER, THE: THE MOTION PICTURE, 1986, AAA
NYAMANTON, 1986, C

-O-

O HOMEM DA CAPA PRETA, 1986, C
O JE, 1986, NR
O MELISSOKOMOS, 1986, O
O MEU CASO—REPETICOES, 1986, A
O SLAVE A TRAVE, 1986, NR
O VESTIDO COR DE FOGO, 1986, C
OBDULIA, 1986, A-C
OBECANA ZEMLJA, 1986, O
OCEAN DRIVE WEEKEND, 1986, C
OD PETKA DO PETKA, 1986, NR
ODA NA RADOST, 1986, NR
ODD JOBS, 1986, C-O
ODINOTCHNOYE PLAVANIYE, 1986, C
OFELIA KOMMER TIL BYEN, 1986, C
OFF BEAT, 1986, NR
OLDRICH A BOZENA, 1986, NR
OLMEZ AGACI, 1986, O
ON A VOLE CHARLIE SPENCER!, 1986, O
ON VALENTINE'S DAY, 1986, A-C
ONE CRAZY SUMMER, 1986, C
ONE MORE SATURDAY NIGHT, 1986, C-O
ONE NIGHT ONLY, 1986, O
OP HOOP VAN ZEGEN, 1986, C
OPERACE ME DCERY, 1986, NR
ORA TOKYO SA YUKUDA, 1986, C
ORDOGI KISERTETEK, 1986, C
ORIDATH, 1986, C
ORKESTAR JEDNE MLADOSTI, 1986, NR
ORMENS VAG PA HALLEBERGET, 1986, O
OSOBISTY PAMIETNIK GRZESNIKA PRZEZ . . . , 1986, C
OTELLO, 1986, OA-C
OTOKO WA TSURAIYO, SHIBAMATA YORI AI O KOMETE, 1986, NR
OUR EXPLOITS AT WEST POLEY, 1986, NR
OUT OF BOUNDS, 1986, O
OUTSIDER, 1986, NR
OVER THE SUMMER, 1986, O
OVERNIGHT, 1986, O
OVNI IN MAMUTI, 1986, O

-P-

P.O.W. THE ESCAPE, 1986, O
PA LIV OCH DOD, 1986, O
PANTHER SQUAD, 1986, A
PAPILIO, 1986, NR
PARADIES, 1986, O
PARENTAL CLAIM, 1986, O
PARIS MINUIT, 1986, NR
PARTING GLANCES, 1986, O
PASO DOBLE, 1986, C
PASODOBLE PRE TROCH, 1986, NR
PASSION, 1986, A
PASSION OF REMEMBRANCE, THE, 1986, O
PATRIOT, THE, 1986, O
PAULETTE, 1986, O
PAVUCINA, 1986, O
PEAU D'ANGE, 1986, O
PEESUA LAE DOKMAI, 1986, A
PEGGY SUE GOT MARRIED, 1986, C
PEKIN CENTRAL, 1986, C
PEKING OPERA BLUES, 1986, C
PEQUENA REVANCHA, 1986, C
PERDOA ME POR ME TRAIRES, 1986, NR
PERILS OF P.K., THE, 1986, O
PERROS DE LA NOCHE, 1986, O
PERVOLA: TRACKS IN THE SNOW, 1986, C
PESTI VE TME, 1986, NR
PIAOBO QIYU, 1986, A
PICARDIA MEXICANA NUMERO DOS, 1986, C
PIMEYS ODOTTA, 1986, C
PING PONG, 1986, C
PINK CHIQUITAS, THE, 1986, C-O
PIRATES, 1986, C
PISINGANA, 1986, NR
PISMA MERTVOGO CHELOVEKA, 1986, C
PLACE OF WEEPING, 1986, C-O
PLACIDO, 1986, C
PLASTIKKPOSEN, 1986, NR
PLATOON, 1986, O
PLAY DEAD, 1986, O
PLAYING AWAY, 1986, A-C
PLAYING BEATIE BOW, 1986, A-C
PLAYING FOR KEEPS, 1986, C
POBRE MARIPOSA, 1986, C-O
POLICE, 1986, O
POLICE ACADEMY 3: BACK IN TRAINING, 1986, C-O
POLTERGEIST II, 1986, O
POMNALUI NUNSOGI, 1986, A
POPULATION: ONE, 1986, O
POR UN VESTIDO DE NOVIA, 1986, O
POSITIVE I.D., 1986, O
POTERYALSYA SLON, 1986, AA
POWER, 1986, O
PPPERFORMER, THE, 1986, A
PRAY FOR DEATH, 1986, O
PRENSES, 1986, 0
PRETTY IN PINK, 1986, C
PROKA, 1986, NR
PROMISES TO KEEP, 1986, NR
PRUNELLE BLUES, 1986, O
PSYCHO III, 1986, O
PULSEBEAT, 1986, O

-Q-

QINGCHUN JI, 1986, A-C
QINGCHUN NUCHAO, 1986, NR
QUE ME MATEN DE UNA VEZ, 1986, NR
QUEEN CITY ROCKER, 1986, O
QUI A TIRE SUR NOS HISTOIRES D'AMOUR, 1986, NR
QUI TROP EMBRASSE, 1986, O
QUICKSILVER, 1986, A-C
QUIET COOL, 1986, O
QUILOMBO, 1986, O

-R-

RAD, 1986, A-C
RADIOCATIVE DREAMS, 1986, O
RAFAGA DE PLOMO, 1986, O
RAGE, 1986, O
RAGING VENDETTA, 1986, O
RAI, 1986, C
RAO SAHEB, 1986, A
RATBOY, 1986, C
RATTIS, 1986, A
RAVEN, 1986, O
RAW DEAL, 1986, O
RAW TUNES, 1986, C-O
REBEL LOVE, 1986, C-O
RECRUITS, 1986, O
REDONDO, 1986, C
REFORM SCHOOL GIRLS, 1986, O
REGALO DI NATALE, 1986, C
REI DO RIO, 1986, C-O
REIS 222, 1986, A
REPORTER X, 1986, O
REQUIEM POR UN CAMPESINO ESPANOL, 1986, NR
RETURN, 1986, O
REVENGE, 1986, O
REVENGE FOR JUSTICEyrate1986O
REVENGE OF THE TEENAGE VIXENS FROM OUTER SPACE, 1986, C
REZHOU, 1986, NR
RIISUMINEN, 1986, O
RIVERBED, 1986, C
ROBINSONIADA ANU CHEMI INGLISELI PAPA, 1986, C
ROCINANTE, 1986, A-C
ROCKIN' ROAD TRIP, 1986, C-O
ROKUMEIKAN, 1986, NR
ROLLER BLADE, 1986, O
ROMANCE, 1986, O
ROMANTICHNA-ISTORIJA, 1986, O
ROOM WITH A VIEW, A, 1986, C
ROSA LUXEMBURG, 1986, O
ROSE, 1986, C
ROUND MIDNIGHT, 1986, C
ROYAL WARRIORS, 1986, C-O
RUE DU DEPART, 1986, O
RUNNING OUT OF LUCK, 1986, O
RUNNING SCARED, 1986, C-O
RUTHLESS PEOPLE, 1986, C-O
RYDER, P.I., 1986, C-O

-S-

SACRIFICE, THE, 1986, C
SALOME, 1986, O
SALVADOR, 1986, O
SAMUEL LOUNT, 1986, A-C
SAN ANTONITO, 1986, C
SAN O RUZI, 1986, C
SAPIRHURIN, 1986, C
SAPORE DEL GRANO, 1986, O
SARRAOUNIA, 1986, O
SAUVE-TOI, LOLA, 1986, O
SAVING GRACE, 1986, A
SAY YES, 1986, O
SCALPS, 1986, O
SCENE OF THE CRIME, 1986, O
SCENY DZIECIECE Z ZYCIA PROWINCJI, 1986, O
SCHETIKA ME TON VASSILI, 1986, C
SCHLEUSE 17, 1986, O
SCHMUTZ, 1986, O
SCHOOL FOR VANDALS, 1986, AAA
SCHWARZ UND OHNE ZUCKER, 1986, C
SCORPION, 1986, O
SCREAMPLAY, 1986, O
SCREAMTIME, 1986, O
SCREEN TEST, 1986, O
SCUOLA DI LADRI, 1986, A-C
SE SUFRA PERON SE GOZA, 1986, O
SEA SERPENT, THE, 1986, A
SECANGKIR KOPI PAHIT, 1986, C
SECOND VICTORY, THE, 1986, C
SECVENTE, 1986, C
SEMBRA MORTO . . . MA E SOLO SVENUTO, 1986, C-O
SEN TURKULERINI SOYLE, 1986, O
SENSI, 1986, O
SENZA SCRUPOLI, 1986, O
SEPARATE VACATIONS, 1986, O
SEPARATI IN CASA, 1986, C
SERE CUALQUIER COSA PERO TE QUIERO, 1986, C-O
SEVEN MINUTES IN HEAVEN, 1986, C
SEX APPEAL, 1986, O
SEX O'CLOCK NEWS, THE, 1986, O
SEY SARSILIYOR, 1986, O
SHADOW OF VICTORY, 1986, O
SHADOW PLAY, 1986, O
SHADOWS RUN BLACK, 1986, O
SHANGHAI SURPRISE, 1986, C
SHE'S GOTTA HAVE IT, 1986, O
SHIN YOROKOBIMO KANASHIMIMO IKUTOSHITSUKI, 1986, A
SHOKUTAKU NO NAI IE, 1986, NR
SHOOT FOR THE SUNyrate1986C-O
SHORT CHANGED, 1986, C
SHORT CIRCUIT, 1986, A-C
SHTAY ETZBA'OT M'TZIDON, 1986, C
SHUKUJI, 1986, NR
SID AND NANCY, 1986, O
SIESTA VETA, 1986, O
SIKAT SAFAR, 1986, NR
SILENT LOVE, 1986, A
SILK, 1986, O
SINCERELY CHARLOTTE, 1986, C-O
SININEN IMETAJA, 1986, A
SIZZLE BEACH, U.S.A., 1986, O
SKUPA MOYA, SKUPI MOY, 1986, C
SKY BANDITS, 1986, A-C
SKY PIRATES, 1986, C
SLADKE STAROSTI, 1986, NR
SLEEPWALK, 1986, NR
SLOANE, 1986, O
SMART ALEC, 1986, O
SMICH SE LEPI NA PATY, 1986, NR
SMILE OF THE LAMB, THE, 1986, O
SMRT KRASNYCH SRNCU, 1986, NR
SNO-LINE, 1986, O
SOBREDOSIS, 1986, O
SOLARBABIES, 1986, A-C
SOLDIER'S REVENGE, 1986, C
SOMETHING WILD, 1986, O
SOREKARA, 1986, C
SOROROTY HOUSE MASSACRE, 1986, O
SOUL MAN, 1986, C
SPACECAMP, 1986, A
SPIRITS OF THE AIR, 1986, NR
SPOSERO SIMON LE BON, 1986, C
SPRING SYMPHONY, 1986, A-C
SPRINGEN, 1986, O
SQUADRA SELVAGGIA, 1986, O
SRECNA NOVA '49, 1986, O
STAMMHEIM, 1986, C
STAND BY ME, 1986, C
STAR CRYSTAL, 1986, O
STAR TREK IV: THE VOYAGE HOME, 1986, A-C
STEWARDESS SCHOOL, 1986, O
STILL POINT, THE, 1986, O
STONE BOY, THE, 1986, C
STOOGEMANIA, 1986, A
STORIA D'AMORE, 1986, O
STREETS OF GOLD, 1986, C
STRIPPER, 1986, O
SUIVEZ MON REGARD, 1986, NR
SUMMER, 1986, O
SUMMER AT GRANDPA'S, 1986, A
SUMMER NIGHT WITH GREEK PROFILE, ALMOND EYES, AND SCENT OFBASIL , 1986, O
SUN ON A HAZY DAY, 1986, O
SUNSET STRIP, 1986, O
SUNUS PALAIDUNAS, 1986, C
SUPER CITIZEN, 1986, O
SUSMAN, 1986, O
SUURI ILLUSIONI, 1986, O
SVESAS KAISLIBAS, 1986, O
SWEET LIBERTY, 1986, A-C

-T-

TABARANAKATHE, 1986, C-O
TAGEDIEBE, 1986, O
TAHOUNET AL SAYED FABRE, 1986, C
TAI-PAN, 1986, O
TAKE IT EASY, 1986, O
TAMPOPO, 1986, C-O
TAROT, 1986, A
TAXI BOY, 1986, NR

TE AMO, 1986, NR
TELEPHONE CALLS, THE, 1986, NR
TENEMENT, 1986, O
TEO EL PELIRROJO, 1986, C
TERROR Y ENCAJES NEGROS, 1986, O
TERRORVISION, 1986, O
TERRY ON THE FENCE, 1986, A
TEXAS CHAINSAW MASSACRE PART II, THE, 1986, O
TEYZEM, 1986, NR
THANATOS, 1986, O
THAT'S LIFE, 1986, C
THERESE, 1986, C
'38, 1986, O
THOMAS EN SENIOR OP HET SPOOR VAN BRUTE BAREND, 1986, AA
THRASHIN', 1986, A-C
THREE AMIGOS, 1986, C
3:15—THE MOMENT OF TRUTH, 1986, O
THRONE OF FIRE, THE, 1986, O
THUNDER RUN, 1986, C
THUNDER WARRIOR, 1986, O
TIEMPO DE SILENCIO, 1986, C
TIME TO LIVE AND A TIME TO DIE, 1986, C
TIMING, 1986, NR
TITAN SERAMBUT DIBELAH, 1986, C
TO DENDRO POUU PLIGONAME, 1986, A
TO SLEEP SO AS TO DREAM, 1986, A
TOBY MCTEAGUE, 1986, A
TOKIMEDI NI SHISU, 1986, O
TOMB, THE, 1986, O
TOMMASO BLU, 1986, O
TONGS—A CHINATOWN STORY, 1986, O
TOP GUN, 1986, A-C
TOP OF THE WHALE, 1986, NR
TORMENT, 1986, O
TORPIDONOSTCI, 1986, A
TOUCH AND GO, 1986, C-O
TOUGH GUYS, 1986, C
TRAMP AT THE DOOR, 1986, A-C
TRANSFORMERS, THE, 1986, A-C
TRAVELLING NORTH, 1986, C-O
TRE SUPERMAN A SANTO DOMINGO, 1986, C
TRICK OR TREAT, 1986, O
TRIKAL, 1986, C
TROLL, 1986, C
TROPPO FORTE, 1986, NR
TRUE STORIES, 1986, A
TUNTEMATON SOTILAS, 1986, C
TWELFTH NIGHT, 1986, A
27 HORAS, 1986, C
TWIST AGAIN IN MOSCOU, 1986, C
TWIST AND SHOUT, 1986, O
TWO FRIENDS, 1986, C
TYPHOON CLUB, 1986, C-O

-U-

UC HALKA YIRMIBES, 1986, NR
UMA RAPARIGA NO VERAO, 1986, A
UMUT SOKAGI, 1986, NR
UMUTLU SAFAKLLAR, 1986, NR
UN HOMBRE DE EXITO, 1986, C
UN HOMBRE VIOLENTE, 1986, O
UN OASPETE LA CINA, 1986, A-C
UN RAGAZZO COME TANTI, 1986, O
UNA CASA IN BILICO, 1986, C
UNA DOMENICA SI, 1986, C
UNA DONNA SENZA NOME, 1986, O
UNA NOTTE DI PIOGGIA, 1986, O
UNA SPINA NEL CUORE, 1986, O
UNA STORIA AMBIGUA, 1986, O
UNA TENERA FOLLIA, 1986, O
UNDER THE CHERRY MOON, 1986, O
UNTERMEHMEN GEIGENKASTEN, 1986, A-C
UPHILL ALL THE WAY, 1986, C
USUGESHO, 1986, NR
UTEKAME, UZ IDEI, 1986, NR

-V-

VA BANQUE, 1986, C
VAKVILAGBAN, 1986, C
VALHALLA, 1986, A
VALKOINEN KAAPIO, 1986, C
VAMP, 1986, O
VAROSBUJOCSKA, 1986, O
VASECTOMY: A DELICATE MATTER, 1986, O
VECERNJA ZVONA, 1986, O
VELKA FILMOVA LOUPEZ, 1986, O
VENDETTA, 1986, O
VENENO PARA LAS HADAS, 1986, O
VERY CLOSE QUARTERS, 1986, O
VESELE VANOCE PREJI CHOBOTNICE, 1986, O
VIAJE A NINGUNA PARTE, 1986, O
VIOLATED, 1986, O
VIOLENT BREED, 1986, O
VIOLETS ARE BLUE, 1986, C-O
VIRUS HAS NO MORALS, A, 1986, O
VISA U.S.A., 1986, O
VISAGE PALE, 1986, O
VLCI BOUDA, 1986, O
VOGLIA DIGUARDARE, 1986, O
VYHRAVAT POTICHU, 1986, O
VYITI ZAMUZH ZA KAPITANA, 1986, C

-W-

WAEBULLEO, 1986, NR
WALKMAN BLUES, 1986, A
WAY IT IS?, THE, 1986, NR
WEEKEND WARRIORS, 1986, O
WELCOME IN VIENNA, 1986, O
WELCOME TO 18, 1986, O
WELCOME TO THE PARADE, 1986, O
WERTHER, 1986, O
WHAT COMES AROUND, 1986, C
WHAT HAPPENED NEXT YEAR, 1986, O
WHAT WAITS BELOW, 1986, O
WHATEVER IT TAKES, 1986, O
WHEN THE WIND BLOWS, 1986, O
WHERE ARE THE CHILDREN?, 1986, O
WHERE THE RIVER RUNS BLACK, 1986, A
WHITE SLAVE, 1986, O
WHOOPEE BOYS, THE, 1986, O
WILD BEASTS, 1986, O
WILD WIND, THE, 1986, A-C
WILDCATS, 1986, C-O
WINDRIDER, 1986, C
WINDSCHADUW, 1986, C
WIRED TO KILL, 1986, O
WISDOM, 1986, O
WISE GUYS, 1986, C-O
WITCHFIRE, 1986, O
WO ERH HAN-SHENG, 1986, NR
WOHIN MIT WILLFRIED, 1986, AA
WOLF AT THE DOOR, THE, 1986, O
WOMEN'S PRISON MASSACRE, 1986, O
WORKING GIRLS, 1986, O
WRAITH, THE, 1986, C
WRONG WORLD, 1986, O

-XYZ-

X, 1986, O
XIANGNU XIAOXIAO, 1986, NR
YAKO—CAZADOR DE MALDITOS, 1986, O
YAMASHITA SHONEN MONOGATARI, 1986, NR
YARI NO GONZA, 1986, C-O
YELLOW EARTH, 1986, A
YEOJAEUI BANRAN, 1986, NR
YES, DET ER FAR!, 1986, A
YIDDISH CONNECTION, 1986, C-O
YILANLARIN, 1986, NR
YOUNG COMPOSER'S ODYSSEY, Ayrate1986O
YOUNG EINSTEIN, 1986, NR
YOUNGBLOOD, 1986, O
YU QING SAO, 1986, O
YUPPIES, I GIOVANI DI SUCCESSO, 1986, O
ZA KUDE PUTOVATE, 1986, C
ZA SRECU JE POTREBNO TROJE, 1986, C
ZABRAVOTE TOZI SLOCHAI, 1986, C
ZABY A INE RYBY, 1986, NR
ZAKAZANE UVOLNEI, 1986, NR
ZAKONNY BRAK, 1986, C
ZANGIR, 1986, C
ZAZZENNYJ FONAR, 1986, A
ZELENA LETA, 1986, NR
ZIMNI VECHER V GAGRAKH, 1986, A
ZKROCENI ZLEHO MUZE, 1986, NR
ZONE ROUGE, 1986, NR
ZONE TROOPERS, 1986, A
ZONING, 1986, C
ZUGURT, 1986, NR

Index

Films by Country of Origin

Below is a listing of films in the 1988 annual arranged by the country which produced the film. Where more than one country was involved with the production, the film is listed under each of the producing countries, and a co-production notation (co:) included with the title. The films are all listed by the titles under which they appear in this annual. Where necessary, foreign and alternate release titles have been added parenthetically.

AFGHANISTAN
Perlyotniye Ptit

ARGENTINA
A Dos Aguas
Chechechela—Una Chica Del Barrio
Chorros
El Amor Es Una Mujer Gorda
El Ano Del Conejo
El Dueno Del Sol
El Hombre De La Deuda Externa
En El Nombre Del Hijo
En Retarada
La Busqueda
Los Duenos Del Silencio (co: Swed.)
Made in Argentina
Miss Mary
Sentimientos: Mirta De Liniers A Estambul
Sinfin, La Muerte No Es Ninguna Solucion
Sledy Obortnya (co: USSR)
Sofia
Stranger, The (co: US)
Svart Gryning (co: Swed.)

AUSTRALIA
Around the World in 80 Ways
As Time Goes By
Bachelor Girl, Australia
Belinda
Bit Part, The
Bushfire Moon (Christmas Visitor)
Cassandra
Coda
Custody
Dear Cardholder
Dot Goes To Hollywood
Frenchman's Farm
Good Wife, The
Ground Zero
High Tide
Howling III: The Marsupials
Initiation
Jilted
Landslides
Les Patterson Saves The World
Lighthorseman, The
Pursuit of Happiness, The
Right Hand Man, The
Running From The Guns
Shadows of the Peacock
Slate, Wyn and Me
Surfer, The
Tale of Ruby Rose, The
Those Dear Departed
Time Guardian, The
To Market, To Market
Vincent—The Life and Death of Vincent Van Gogh (co: Neth.)
Warm Nights On A Slow Moving Train
Witch Hunt
With Love To The Person Next To Me
Year My Voice Broke, The

AUSTRIA
Die Dreckschlauder
Magic Sticks (co: Ger.)
Wannsee Conference, The (Die Wannseekonferenz; co: Ger.)

BELGIUM
Big Bang, The (co: Fr.)
Boran—Zeit Zum Zielen (co: Ger.)
Diary of a Mad Old Man (co: Neth.)
Falsch (co: Fr.)
Hector (co: Neth.)
La Vie Est Belle (co: Fr./Zaire)
Les Noces Barbares (The Cruel Embrace; co: Fr.)
Love is a Dog from Hell (Crazy Love)
Mascara (co: Fr./Neth./US)
Noce En Galilee (co: Fr.)
Van Paemel Family, The (Het Gezin Van Paemel)

BRAZIL
A Danca Dos Bonecos
Anjos Do Arrabalde
Areias Escaldantes
Baixo Gavea
Beijo Na Boca
Besame Mucho
Cidade Oculta
Color of Destiny (A Cor Do Seu Destino)
Ele, O Boto
Eu
Fonte Da Saudade
Leila Diniz
Night Angels (Anjos Da Noite)
Um Trem Para As Estrelas
Um Film 100% Brazileiro
Vera

BULGARIA
Cernite Lebedi
Prizemyavane
Trinajstata Godenica Na Princa
Zlota Mahmudia (co: Pol.)

BURKINA FASO
Yam Daabo

CANADA
Bach and Broccoli
Birds of Prey
Cat City (Macskafogo; co: Hung./Ger.)
Climb, The
Concrete Angels
Eva Guerrillera
Family Viewing
Great Land of Small, The
Hello Mary Lou: Prom Night 2 (The Haunting of Hamilton High)
High Stakes
Higher Education
Home is Where the Hart Is
Housekeeper, The (Judgement in Stone)
Il Giorno Prima (co: It.)
I've Heard The Mermaids Singing
John and the Missus
Keeping Track
Kid Brother, The (co: Jap./US)
La Couleur Encerclee
Ladies of the Lotus
Last Straw, The
Le Jeune Magicien (Cudowne Dziecko; co: Pol.)
Le Sourd Dans La Ville
Les Fous De Bassan (co: Fr.)
Life Classes
Morning Man, The
Night Zoo (Un Zoo, La Nuit)
Psycho Girls
Remembering Mel
Rock 'n' Roll Nightmare (Edge of Hell)
Shelley
Sitting in Limbo
Too Outrageous
Train Of Dreams
Tuesday Wednesday
Winter Tan, A

CHILE
La Estacion Del Regreso

CHINA
Big Parade, The (Da Yue Bing)
Black Cannon Incident, The (Hei Pao Shi Jian)
Cuo Wei
Dao Mazei (Horse Thief)
Dr. Sun Yatsen
Last Empress, The
Mirage (co: Hong Kong)
Old Well (Lao Jing)
Romance of Book and Sword (co: Hong Kong)

COLOMBIA
De Mujer A Mujer (co: Ven.)
Visa U.S.A. (co: Cuba)

COSTA RICA
Eulalia

CUBA
Amor en Campo Minado
De Tal Pedro, Tal Estilla
El Socio De Dios (co: Peru)
Mujeres De La Frontera (co: Nicaragua)
Successful Man, A (Un Hombre De Exito)
Visa U.S.A. (co: Col.)

CZECHOSLOVAKIA
Cena Medu
Cena Odvahy
Chobotnice Z (II. Patra)
Cizim Vstup Povolen (co: USSR)
Discopribeh
Pohadka O Malickovi (Malchik S Palchik; co: USSR)
Pratele Bermudskeho Trojuhelniku
Proc?
Wolf's Hole (Vlci Bouda)

DENMARK
Babette's Gastebud
Elise
Epidemic
Hip, Hip, Hurra! (co: Nor./Swed.)
Jag Elsker Dig
Kampen Om Den Rode Ko
Negerkys & Labre Larver
Peter Von Scholten
Sidste Akt
Strit Og Stumme
Venner For Altid (Friends Forever)
Valhalla

EGYPT
Al-Touq Wal-Iswira
Zawgat Ragol Mohim

FINLAND
Akallinen Mies
Ala Itke, Iines
Elaman Vonkamies
Elvis—Kissan Jaljilla
Hamlet
Helsinki Napoli—All Night Long
Inuksuk
Jaahyvaiset Presidentille
Jaan Kaantopiiri
Kill City
Kuningas Lear
Lain Ulkopuolella
Liian Iso Keikka
Macbeth
Nakeminn, Hyvasti
Pekka Puupaa Poliisina
Pikkupojat
Snow Queen, The (Lumikuningatar)
Tilinteko
Ursula
Uuno Turhapuro Muuttaa Maalle
V.Y. Vihdoinkin Yhdessa
Varjoja Paratiisissa

FRANCE
Accroche-Coeur
Agent Trouble
Attention Bandits
Au Revoir Les Enfants (co: Ger.)

Avril Brise
Bad Blood (Mauvais Sang; The Night is Young)
Big Bang, The (co: Bel.)
Buisson Ardent
Champ d'Honneur
Charlie Dingo
Chronicle Of A Death Foretold (Cronaca Di Une Morte Annunciata; co: It.)
Club De Rencontres
Coeurs Croises
Comedie!
Cross
Der Himmer Uber Berlin (co: Ger.)
Der Todd Des Empedokles (co: Ger.)
Diary Of A Mad Old Man (co: Bel./Neth.)
Dreamers (co: Neth.; Once We Were Dreamers)
Emmanuelle 5
Ennemis Intimes
F . . . ing Ferdinand (co: Ger.)
Falsch (co: Bel.)
Family, The (co: It., La Famiglia)
Fuegos
Gandahar
Gli Occhiali d'Oro (co: It./Yugo.)
Good Morning, Babylon (co: It.)
Grand Guignol
Hotel De France
Il Est Genial Papy!
Jean De Florette
Jenatsch (co: Switz.)
Jeux D'Artifices
Johnny Monroe
La Brute
La Moine Et La Sorciere (co: US; Sorceress)
La Passion Beatrice (co: It.)
La Rumba
La Vallee Fantome (co: Switz.)
La Vie Dissolue De Gerard Floque
La Vie Est Belle (co: Bel./Zaire)
La Vie Platinee (co: Ivory Coast)
L'Ami De Mon Amie
L'Annee Des Medusas
L'Association Des Malfaiteurs
Le Beauf
Le Cri Di Hibou (co: It.)
Le Grand Chemin
Le Journal D'un Fou
Le Miracule
Le Moustachu
Le Solitaire
Les Deux Crocodiles
Les Exploits D'un Jeune Don Juan (co: It.)
Les Fois De Bassan (co: Can.)
Les Mendiants (co: Switz.)
Les Mois D'Avril Sont Meurtriers
Les Noces Barbares (co: Bel.; The Cruel Embrace)
Les Oreilles Entre Les Dents
L'Ete Dernier A Tanger
L'Ete En Pente Douce
Levy et Goliath
L'Homme Voile (co: Lebanon)
L'Oeil Au Beurre Noir
Lucky Ravi
Macbeth
Maladie D'Amour
Man on Fire (co: It.)
Manon of the Spring (Manon Des Sources)
Manuela's Loves (Le Jupon Rouge)
Mascara (co: Bel./Neth./US)
Masques
Melo
Memoire Des Apparences: La Vie Est Un Songe
Miss Mona
Mon Bel Amour, Ma Dechirure
Noce En Galilee (co: Bel.)
Noyade Interdite (co: It.)
Nuit Docile
O Desejado—Les Montagnes De La Lune (co: Port.)
Pierre et Djemila
Poisons (co: Switz.)
Poule Et Frites
Poussiere D'Ange
Quatre Aventures De Reinette et Mirabelle
Sale Destin!
Si Le Soleil Ne Revenait Pas (co: Switz.)
Soigne Ta Droite (co: Switz.)
Sous Le Soleil De Satan
Spirale
Tandem
Tant Qu'il Aura Des Femmes
Terminus (co: Ger.)
Testament d'un Poete Juif Assassine
Travelling Avant
Un Amour A Paris
Un Homme Amoureux
Un Ragazzo Di Calabria (co: It.)
Une Flamme Dans Mon Coeur (co: Switz.)

EAST GERMANY
Der Barenhauter
Der Junge Mit Dem Grosse Schwarze Hund
Der Traum Vom Elch
Jesus: Der Film (co: Ger.)
So Viele Traume
Vernehmung Der Zeugen

GREAT BRITAIN
Aria (co: US)
Bellman and True
Belly of an Architect (co: It.)
Bloody New Year (Time Warp Terror)
Born of Fire
Business As Usual
Comrades
Deadline (co: Ger.; War Zone)
Dogs In Space
Eat The Peach
Eat The Rich
Empire State
Fourth Protocol, The
Friendship's Death
Girl, The
Gothic
Gunpowder
Hellraiser
Hidden City
High Season
Hope and Glory
Hotel Du Paradis
Indian Summer
Jane and the Lost City
Kitchen Toto, The
Last Emperor, The
Last of England, The
Little Dorrit
Living Daylights, The
Lonely Passion of Judith Hearne, The
Love Child, The
Maschenka (co: Ger.)
Maurice
Month in the Country, A
More Bad News
Out Of Order
Personal Services
Prick Up Your Ears
Rawhead Rex
Rita, Sue and Bob Too!
Sammy and Rosie Get Laid
Shadey
Silent Heroes
Slam Dance (co: US)
Sleep Well, My Love (co: Swed.)
Straight To Hell
T. Dan Smith
Wheels Of Terror (co: US)
When the Wind Blows
Whistle Blower
White Mischief
White Of The Eye
Whoops Apocalypse
Wish You Were Here
Withnail and I

GREECE
Angelos
Apousies
Archangelos Tou Pathous
Doxobus
Fakelos Polk Ston Aera
I Kekarmeni
Ikona Enos Mythikou Prosopou (Kapetan Meitanos)
Ke Dyo Avga Tourkias
Klios
O Paradissos Anigi Me Antiklidi
Oh, Babylon
120 Decibels
Oniro Aristeris Nichtas
Photograph, The (I Photographia)
Proini Peripolos
Ta Paidia Tis Chelidonas
Teleftaio Stichima
Terirem
Theofilos
Tree We Hurt, The (To Dendro Pou Pligoname)
Vios Ke Politia
Yenethlia Poli

HONG KONG
Autumn's Tale, An
Better Tomorrow, A (Yingxiong Bense)
Black Dragon, The
Brotherhood
Buddha's Lock
Chinese Ghost Story, A
Chocolate Inspector
City on Fire
Dixia Qing
Eastern Condors
Final Test
Happy Bigamist
Heartbeat 100
Killer's Nocturne
Laoniang Gou Sao
Legacy of Rage
Legend of Wisely, The
Magnificent Warriors
Midnight
Mirage (co: China)
My Will, I Will
Ninja Thunderbolt
Peking Opera Blues (Dao Ma Dan)
Prison on Fire
Project A—Part II
Rich And Famous
Romance of Book and Sword (co: Chi.)
Sapporo Story
Seven Years Itch
Story of Dr. Sun Yat-sen, The (co: Taiwan)
Sworn Brothers
Thirty Million Rush, The
True Colors
Wonder Women
Wrong Couples, The
Yi Lou Yi

HUNGARY
A Javor
A Santa Dervis
Az Erdo Kapitanya
Az Utolso Kezirat
C.K. Dezerterzy (co: Pol.)
Cat City (Macskafogo, co: Can, W.Ger.)
Csok, Anyu
Diary For My Loved Ones (Naplo Szerelmeimnek)
Doktor Minorka Vidor Nagy Napja
Gondoviseles
Hol Volt, Hol Nem Volt
Hotreal
Isten Veletek, Barataim
Ket Valasztas Magyarorszagon
Laura
Lenz
Lutra
Malom A Pokolban
Szornyek Evadja
Tiszta Amerika (co: Jap.)
Utolso Kezirat
Whooping Cough (Szamarkohoges)
Zuhanas Kozben

ICELAND
Skytturnar (White Whales)

INDIA
Aaj Ka Robin Hood
Allari Krishnayya
Amar Bandhan
Amar Kantak

Amar Sangi
America Abbal
Amritamgamaya
Anjaam
Anjuman
Apan Gharey
Arpan
Babula
Bhargava Ramudu
Bidrohi
Chinnathambi Periyathambi
Dacaite
Dadagiri
Daku Hasina
Dongamogudu
Dongoduchhadu
Gadbad Ghotala
Ghulami Ki Zanjeer
Hamari Jung
Inaam Dus Hazaar
Insaniyat Ke Dushman
Jaidev
Jalwa
January Ororma
Jawab Hum Denge
Jhanjhaar
Jhooti
Kalyana Thambulam
Kathakku Pinnil
Kaun Kitney Paani Mein
Lalan Fakir
Lawyer Suhasini
Loha
Maa Beti
Maashuka
Madhvacharya
Majnu
Mandaladheesudu
Mera Lahoo
Mirch Masala
Mr. India
Nazrana
Nilakurinhi Poothapool
Panchagni
Panchvati (co: Nepal)
Pandavapuram
Phera
Poovizhi Vasalile
Pratighaat
Pudhche Paol
Pyar Karke Dekho
Rowdy Police
Rudrabeena
Samsaram Oka Chadarangam
Sheela
Sutradhar
Tamas
Thirtham
Thirumathi Oru Vegumathi
This Is Not Our Destination
Tunda Baida
Ummadi Mogudu
Uppu
Vilambaram

INDONESIA
Ibunda
Stabilizer, The

IRAN
Captain Korshid
Djadde Haye Sard
Gozaresh-E Yek Ghatl
Lodgers
Manuscripts
Peddler, The
Sheere Sanggy

IRELAND
Budawanny

ISRAEL
Bouba
Choze Ahava
Ha'Instalator
Himmo Melech Yerushalaim
Kfafot
Kol Ahavotai
Late Summer Blues (Blues Ha-chofesh Ha-gadol)
Lo Sam Zayin
Tel Aviv—Berlin
Yaldei Stalin
Yehoshua-Yehoshua

ITALY
A Fior Di Pelle
Adelmo
Aladdin (Superfantagenio)
Angelus Novus
Aurelia
Barbarians (co: US)
Bellifreschi
Belly of an Architect (co: Brit.)
Camping Del Terrore
Capriccio
Caramelle Da Uno Sconosciuto
Cartoline Italiane
Chi C'e C'e
Chronicle Of A Death Foretold (co: Fr.; Cronaca Di Una Morte Annunciata)
Dark Eyes (Oci Ciornie)
D'Annunzio
Deliria
Delitti
Delizia
Devil in the Flesh (Diavlo In Corpo)
Distant Lights
Dolce Assenza
Dolce Pelle Diangela
Family, The (co: Fr., La Famiglia)
Gli Occhiali D'Oro (co: Fr./Yugo.)
Good Morning, Babylon (co: Fr.)
Hotel Colonial (co: US)
I Miei Primi Quarant'Anni
I Picari (co: Sp.)
Il Burbero
Il Coraggio Di Parlare
Il Fascino Sottile Del Paccato
Il Giorno Prima (co: Can.)
Il Grande Blek
Il Lupo Di Marie
Il Ragazzo Di Ebalus
Illuminazioni
Intervista (Federico Fellini's Intervista)
Io E Mia Sorella
Iron Warrior
Italiani a Rio
La Coda Del Diavolo
La Croce Dalle Sette Pietre
La Donna Del Traghetto
La Monaca Di Monza
La Passion Beatrice (co: Fr.)
La Trasgressione
Le Cri Du Hibou (co: Fr.)
Le Foto Di Gioia
Le Vie Del Signore Sono Finite
Les Exploits D'un Jeune Don Juan (co: It.)
Les Fois De Bassan (co: Can.)
L'Estate Sta Finendo
Lunga Vita Alla Signora!
Man on Fire (co: Fr.)
Massacre in Dinosaur Valley
Mefisto Funk
Messenger, The (co: US)
Missione Eroica
Montecarlo Gran Casino
Moro Affair, The (Il Caso Moro)
Mosca Addio
Noi Uomini Duri
Notte Italiana
Noyade Interdite (co: Fr.)
Opera
Profumo
Quartiere
Quel Ragazzo Della Curva "B"
Regina
Renegade, Un Osso Troppo Duro
Rimini, Rimini
Roba Da Ricchi
Scuola Di Ladri 2
Sembra Morto . . . Ma E Solo Svenuto
Soldati: 365 Giorni All'Alba
Sotto il Ristorante Cinese
Sottozero
Specters (Spettri)
Stregati
Strike Commando
Superfantozzi
Tenerezza
Tentazione
Teresa
Ternosecco
Thunder Warrior II
Ultimo Minuto
Un Ragazzo Di Calabria (co: Fr.)
Un Tassinaro A New York
Una Casa In Bilico
Una Donna Da Scoprire
11 Giorni, 11 Notte
Via Montenapoleone

IVORY COAST
Faces Of Women
La Vie Platinee (co: Fr.)

JAPAN
Bus
Death Shadows (Jittemai)
Dixieland Daimyo
Eiga Joyu
Final Take: The Golden Days of Movies (Kinema No Tenchi)
Gondola
Hikaru Anna
Hotarugawa
Itazu
Kataku No Hito
Kid Brother, The (co: Can./US)
Laputa: The Castle in the Sky (Tenku No Shiru Laputa)
Love Letter
Magino—Mura Monogatari
Princess from the Moon (Taketori Monogatari)
Robinson No Niwa
Ryoma O Kitta Otoko
Saraba Itoshiki Hito Yo
Sea and Poison, The (Uni To Dokuyaku)
Shinran: Shiroi Michi
Sorobanzuku (The Mercenaries)
Star Quest
Sure Death 4
Taxing Woman, A (Marusa No Onna)
Tiszta Amerika (co: Hung.)
Tokyo Blackout (Shuto Shoshitu)
Tora-San's Bluebird Fantasy (Otokowa Tsuraiyo Shiawase No Aoi Tori)
Uhoho Tankentai
Watashi O Ski Ni Tsuretette
Yoshiwara Enjo
Zegen

KENYA
Kolormask

LEBANON
L'Homme Voile (co: Fr.)

MALAYSIA
Bejalai

MALI
Yeelen

MEXICO
Albures Mexicanos
Arquiesta Emilio Varela
Beaks
Cartuche Cortada
5 Nacos Asaltan A Las Vegas
Corrupcion
Delincuente
El Ansia De Matar
El Diablo, El Santo e El Tonto
El Hijo De Pedro Navajas
El Hombre Desnudo
El Mofles Y Los Mecanicos
El Muerto Del Palomo
El Placer De La Venganza
Entre Ficheras Anda El Diablo
Esta Noche Cena Pancho (Despedida De Soltero)
Fieras En Brama

Forajidos En El Mira
Frida
Herencia De Vilientes
Juana La Cantinera
Juntos
La Fuga De Carrasco
La Raza Nunca Pierde—Huele A Gas, Mexico
La Ruletera
Las Movidas Del Mofles
Las Traigo . . . Muertas
Lo Del Cesar
Lo Negro Del Negro
Macho Que Ladra No Muerde II
Mas Buenas Que El Pan
Mas Vale Pajaro En Mano . . .
Matar O Morir
Mi Nombre Es Gatillo
Mujeres Salvajes
Murieron A Mitad Del Rio
Narco Terror
Ni De Aqui, Ni De Alla
Nocturno Amor Que Te Vas
Nos Reimos De La Migra
Olor A Muerte
Operacion Marijuana
Policias De Narcoticos
Ratas De La Ciudad
Realm of Fortune, The (El Imperio De La Fortuna)
Reto A La Vida
Robachicos
Rosa De La Frontera
Sinverguenza . . . Pero Honrado
Tierra De Valientes
Toda La Vida
Tragico Terremoto En Mexico
Un Sabado Mas
Una Pura Y Dos Con Sal
Va De Nuez
Viaje Al Paraiso
Welcome Maria
Yerba Sangriente
Yo, El Ejecutor

MOROCCO
Abbes
La Compromission
La Vengeance Du Protecteur

NEPAL
Panchvati (co: India)

NETHERLANDS
Als In Een Roes
Blond Dolly
De Orionnevel
De Ratelrat
Diary of A Mad Old Man (co: Bel./Fr.; Dagboek Ban Een Oude Dwaas)
Dreamers (co: Fr./US; Once We Were Dreamers)
Een Maand Later
Havinck
Hector (co: Bel.)
Iris
Julia's Geheim
Looking for Eileen (Zoeken Naar Eileen)
Mascara (co: Bel./Fr./US)
Nitwits
Odyssee D'Amour
Quatre Mains (co: Ger.)
Red Desert Penitentiary
Terug Naar Oegstgeest
Van Geluk Gesproken
Vincent—Life and Death of Vincent Van Gogh (co: Aust.)
Vroeger Is Dood
Zjoek

NEW ZEALAND
Leading Edge, The
Ngati
Starlight Hotel

NICARAGUA
Mujeres De La Frontera (co: Cuba)
Okhota Na Drakona (co: USSR)

NORTH KOREA
Sekunda Na Podvig (co: USSR)
Talmae Wa Pomdari

NORWAY
Etter Rubicon
Feldmann Case, The (Over Grensen)
Hip, Hip, Hurra! (co: Den./Swed.)
Is-Slottet
Jor
Kamilla Og Tyven
Mio, Moy Mio (co: Swed./USSR; Mio In The Land Of Faraway)
Ofelas (Veiviseren)
Pa Stigende Kurs
Plastposen
Prinsen Fra Fogo
Resan Till Melonia (co: Swed.; Reisen Til Melonia)
Turnaround

PERU
City and the Dogs, The (La Ciudad Y Los Perros)
El Socio De Dios (co: Cuba)

PHILIPPINES
Alapaap
Damortis
Daughters Of Eve
Day They Robbed America, The
Deadly Justice
Deadly Target
Eye of the Eagle
Get the Terrorists
Heated Fists
Hill 171
Hostage Syndrome
Hunted, The
Igorota
Mad Killer
Manila, Open City
Missing in Action
No Blood No Surrender
On the Edge of Hell
Operation: Get Victor Corpus The Rebel Soldier
Reign of the Rascals, The
Time for Dying, A
Tough Cop
Ultimax Force
Vengeance is Mine
Wild Force
Zimatar

POLAND
Blind Chance (Przypadek)
Bohater Roku
C.K. Dezerterzy (co: Hung.)
Cubzoziemka
Czas Nadziei
ESD
Inna Wyspa
Komedianci Z Wczorajszej Ulicy
Komediantka
Le Jeune Magicien (co: Can.; Cudowne Dziecko)
Magnat
Maskarada
Matka Krolow
Miedzy Ustami A Brzegiem Pucharu
Nad Niemnem
Pan Samochodzik I Niesamowity Dwor
Pierscien I Roza
Pociag Do Hollywood
Prywatne Sledztwo
Przyjaciel Wesolego Diabla
Rykowisko
Siekierezada
Stanislaw I Anna
W Starym Dworku
W Zawieszeniu
Wryfikacja
Wierna Rzeka
Zlota Mahmudia (co: Bul.)
Zloty Pociag (co: Rum.)
Zycie Wewnetrzne
Zygfryd

PORTUGAL
Balada Da Praia Dos Caes (co: Sp.)
Duma Vez Por Todas
Jester (O Bobo)
O Desejado—Les Montagnes De La Lune (co: Fr.)
Relacao Fiel E Verdadeira

PUERTO RICO
La Gran Fiesta

RUMANIA
Padureanca
Zloty Pociag (co: Pol.)

SOUTH AFRICA
City of Blood
Saturday Night At The Palace

SOUTH KOREA
Kyeoul Nagune
Man With Three Coffins, The
Nae-shi
Sibaji
Ticket

SPAIN
A Los Cuatro Vienos
Angustia
Asi Como Habian Sido
Asignatura Aprobada
Balada Da Praia Dos Caes (co: Port.)
Barcelona
Cale
Cara De Acelga
Divinas Palabras
El Amor De Ahora
El Bosque Animados
El Gran Serafin
El Lute—Camina O Revienta
Hay Que Deshacer La Casa
I Picari (co: It.)
La Casa De Bernarda Alba
La Estanquera De Vallecas
La Guerra De Los Locos
La Rubia Del Bar
La Rusa
La Senyora
La Vida Alegre
Las Dos Orillas
Law of Desire, The (La Lei Del Deseo)
L'Escot
Long Strider (Pasos Largos)
Los Invitados
Madrid
Mientras Haya Luz
Moros Y Cristianos
My General (Mi General)
Policia
Redondela
Romanca Final
Sufre Mamon
Year of Awakening, The (El Ano De Las Luces)

SRI LANKA
Maldeniye Simion
Viragaya (The Way Of The Lotus)
Witness To A Killing

SWEDEN
Blood Tracks
De Flygande Djavlarna
Demons (Demoner)
Det Stora Loftet
Fadern, Sonen Och Den Helige Ande
Hip, Hip, Hurra! (co: Den./Nor.)
Jim Och Piraterna Blom
Leif
Los Duenos Del Silencio (co: Arg.)
Malacca
Malarpirater
Mannen Fran Mallorca
Mio, Moy Mio (co: Nor./USSR; Mio In The Land Of Faraway)
Mitt Hjarta Har Tva Tungor
More About The Children Of Bullerby Village (Mer Om Oss Barn I Bullerby)

My Life As A Dog (Mitt Liv Som Hund)
Nagra Sommarkvallar Pa Jorden
Nionde Kompaniet
Om Karlek
Pelle Erovraren
Res Aldrig Pa Enkel Biljett
Resan Till Melonia (co: Nor.; Reisen Til Me lonia)
Seppan
Serpent's Way (Ormens Vag Pa Halleberget)
Sleep Well, My Love (co: Brit.)
Sparvagn Till Havet
Svart Gryning (co: Arg.)
Testet
Victoria

SWITZERLAND
Alpine Fire (Hohenfeuer)
Der Nachbar (co: Ger.)
Dilan (co: Turk./Ger.)
Dragon's Food (Drachenfutter, co: Ger.)
Jenatsch (co: Fr.)
La Vallee Fantome (co: Fr.)
Les Mendiants (co: Fr.)
Personaggi & Interpreti
Poisons (co: Fr.)
Same To You (Du Mich Auch, co: Ger.)
Si Le Soleil Ne Revenait Pas (co: Fr.)
Soigne Ta Droite (co: Fr.)
Une Flamme Dans Mon Coeur (co: Fr.)

SYRIA
Mirazhi Lyubri (co: USSR)
Novye Skazki Shakherezady (co: USSR)

TAIWAN
Heroic Pioneers
Lien Lien Fung Chen
Outsiders, The (Yu K'an-P'ing)
Sakura Killers (co: US)
Story of Dr. Sun Yat-sen, The (co: Hong Kong)
Terrorizers, The (Konbu Finze)

THAILAND
Cobra Thunderbolt
Commander Lamine
House
Last Song, The

TURKEY
Anayurt Oteli
Degirmen
Dilan (co: Ger./Switz.)
Son Urfali
Water Also Burns
Yer Demir, Gok Bakir (co: Ger.)

UNITED STATES
Adventure of the Action Hunters
Adventures in Babysitting
Alien Predator
Allan Quartermain in the Lost City of Gold
Allnighter, The
Amazing Grace and Chuck
Amazon Women of The Moon
Amazons
American Drive-In
American Ninja II: The Confrontation
Angel Heart
Anna
Aria (co: Brit.)
Assassination
Baby Boom
Back to the Beach
Banzai Runner
Barbarians, The (co: It.)
Barfly
Batteries Not Included
Beat, The
Beauty and the Beast
Bedroom Window
Believers, The
Bell Diamond
Benji the Hunted
Best Seller
Beverly Hills Cop II
Beyond Therapy
Big Bad Mama II
Big Easy, The
Big Shots
Big Town
Black Widow
Blind Date
Blood Diner
Blood Hook
Blood Sisters
Bloodsuckers From Outer Space
Bloody Wednesday
Blue Monkey (Green Monkey)
Border Radio
Born in East L.A.
Brave Little Toaster
Broadcast News
Bullet Proof
Burglar
Campus Man
Can't Buy Me Love (Boy Rents Girl)
Captive Hearts
Care Bears Adventure in Wonderland, The
Catch the Heat (Feel the Heat)
Caught
Checkpoint
China Girl
Chipmunk Adventure, The
Club Life
Code Name: Zebra
Cold Steel
Commando Squad
Creepozoids
Creepshow 2
Crime Killer, The (co: Gr.)
Critical Condition
Cross My Heart
Cry Wilderness
Crystal Heart
Curse, The
Cyclone
Dancers
Danger Zone
Date With an Angel
Dead, The
Dead Of Winter
Deadly Illusion
Deadly Prey
Deadtime Stories
Death Before Dishonor
Death Wish 4
Deathrow Gameshow
Delos Adventure, The
Deranged
Dirty Dancing
Dirty Laundry
Dirty Rebel (co: Yugo.)
Disorderlies
Dolls
Down Twisted
Dragnet
Dreamaniac
Dudes
Dutch Treat
84 Charing Cross Road
Emanon
Emperor's New Clothes
Empire of the Sun
Enemy Territory
Equalizer 2000
Ernest Goes to Camp
Escapes
Evil Dead 2
Evil Spawn (Deadly Sting)
Evil Town
Extreme Prejudice
Fatal Attraction
Fatal Beauty
Fire and Ice
Firehouse
Flicks
Flowers in the Attic
Forever, Lulu
Forty Days of Musa Dagh
From The Hip
Full Metal Jacket
Gaby—A True Story
Garbage Pail Kids, The
Gardens of Stone
Gate, The
Ghost Fever
Glass Menagerie, The
Good Morning, Vietnam
Goofballs
Graveyard Shift
Hamburger Hill
Hanoi Hilton
Hansel and Gretel
Happy Hour
Happy New Year
Hard Ticket To Hawaii
Harry and the Hendersons
Heart
Hearts of Fire
Heat
Hello Again
He's My Girl
Hidden, The
Hiding Out (Adult Education)
Hollywood Shuffle
Hostage
Hot Child in the City
Hot Pursuit
Hotel Colonial (co: It.)
Hotshot
Hour of the Assassin
House of Games
House II: The Second Story
Housekeeping
Hunk
Hunter's Blood
I Love N.Y.
I Was A Teenage T.V. Terrorist
I Was A Teenage Zombie
If Looks Could Kill
In the Mood
Innerspace
Ironweed
Ishtar
Jaws IV: The Revenge
Jocks
Kid Brother, The (co: Can./Jap.)
Killer Workout
Killing Time
Kindred
Kiss Daddy Good Night
La Bamba
La Moine Et La Sorciere (co: Fr.; Sorcerer)
Lady Beware
Leonard, Part 6
Less Than Zero
Lethal Weapon
Let's Get Harry
Light of Day
Like Father, Like Son
Lionheart
Living On Tokyo Time
Lost Boys, The
Made in Heaven
Magdalena Viraga
Magic Snowman (co: Yugo.; A Winter Tale)
Maid to Order
Making Mr. Right
Malibu Bikini Shop (Bikini Shop)
Malone
Man Outside
Mankillers
Mannequin
Mascara (co: Bel./Fr./Neth.)
Masterblaster
Masters of the Universe
Matewan
Meatballs III
Messenger, The (co: It.)
Million Dollar Mystery
Mind Killer
Miracles
Mission Kill
Monster in the Closet
Monster Squad
Moon in Scorpio
Moonstruck
Morgan Stewart's Coming Home
Moving Targets
Munchies

Murder Lust
Mutant Hunt
My Dark Lady
My Demon Lover
My Little Girl
Nadine
Nail Gun Massacre
Near Dark
Necropolis
Nice Girls Don't Explode
Night Stalker, The
Nightfliers
Nightforce
Nightmare at Shadow Woods
Nightmare on Elm Street III: Dream Warriors
No Dead Heroes
No Man's Land
No Way Out
North Shore
Nowhere To Hide
Number One With A Bullet
Nuts
O.C. and Stiggs
Off The Mark
Offspring (From A Whisper To A Scream)
Omega Syndrome
Open House
Opposing Force
Oracle, The
Orphans
Outing, The (The Lamp)
Outrageous Fortune
Outtakes
Over the Top
Overboard
Overkill
P.I. Private Investigations (Private Investigations)
P.K. and the Kid
Party Camp
Penitentiary III
Perfect Match, The
Personal Foul
Pick-up Artist, The
Pinocchio and the Emperor of the Night
Planes, Trains and Automobiles
Police Academy 4: Citizens on Patrol
Prayer for the Dying, A
Predator
Pretty Smart
Prettykill
Prince of Darkness
Princess Academy
Princess Bride, The
Principal, The
Programmed to Kill
Project X
Promised Land
Psychos in Love
Radio Days
Rage of Honor
Raising Arizona
Real Men
Red Riding Hood
Red-Headed Stranger
Return of Josey Wales, The
Return to Horror High
Revenge of the Nerds 2: Nerds in Paradise
River's Edge
Robocop
Robot Holocaust
Rosary Murders, The
Roxanne
Rumpelstiltsken
Running Man, The
Russkies
Sakura Killers (co: Taiw.)
Salvation!
Secret of My Success, The
September
She Must Be Seeing Things
Shy People
Sicilian, The
Siesta
Silent Night, Deadly Night Part II
Slam Dance (co: Brit.)
Slammer Girls
Slaughter High
Slave Girls From Beyond Infinity
Sleeping Beauty
Slumber Party Massacre 2
Snow White
Some Kind of Wonderful
Someone to Watch Over Me
Someone to Love
Something Special
South of Reno
Space Rage
Spaceballs
Square Dance
Squeeze, The
Stacking (Season of Dreams)
Stakeout
Steel Dawn
Steele Justice
Stepfather, The
Stranded
Stranger, The (co: Arg.)
Street Smart
Street Trash
Stripped to Kill
Student Confidential
Suicide Club, The
Sullivan's Pavilion
Summer Camp Nightmare (Butterfly Revolution)
Summer Heat
Summer School
Superman IV: The Quest For Peace
Supernaturals, The
Surf Nazis Must Die
Surrender
Survival Game
Suspect
Sweet Country
Sweet Lorraine
Sweet Revenge
Talking Walls
Teen Wolf II
Terminal Exposure
They Still Call Me Bruce
Thin Line, The
Thou Shalt Not Kill . . . Except
Three Bewildered People in the Night
Three For the Road
Three Kinds of Heat
Three Men and a Baby
Three O'Clock High
Throw Momma From the Train
Tin Men
Too Much
Tough Guys Don't Dance
Tresspasses
Trouble with Dick, The
Trouble with Spies
Under Cover
Unfinished Business
Untouchables, The
Valet Girls
Vicious Lips
Video Dead, The
Violins Came With The Americans, The
Waiting For The Moon
Walk Like A Man
Walk on the Moon, A
Walker
Wall Street
Wanted: Dead or Alive
War Dogs
Warrior Queen
Warriors of the Apocalypse
Weeds
Whales of August, The
Wheels of Terror (co: Brit.)
White Phantom
White Water Summer
Who's That Girl?
Wild Pair, The (Devil's Odds)
Wild Thing
Wimps
Wind, The
Winners Take All
Witchboard
Witches of Eastwick, The
You Talkin' To Me?
Zero Boys, The
Zombie High
Zombie Nightmare

USSR
Aktsia
Bludnyy Syn
Chegemskiy Detektiv
Chelovek C Akkordeonom
Cherez Sto Let V Mae
Chkatulka Iz Kreposti
Chuzhie Zdes Ne Khodyat
Chyornaya Strela
Cizim Vstup Povolen (co: Czech.)
Dikiy Khmel
Dolghyie Provod
Dublyor Nachinaet Deystvovat
Dvadstat Dnei Bez
Dvoe Pod Odnim Zontom
Farewell (Proshchanie)
Geroy Yeyo Romana
Gospoda Avanyuristy
Govorit Moskva
Grubaya Posadka
Gruz Bez Markirovki
I Nikto Na Svete
Interventsia
Irgy Dlja Detej Skol'Nogo Vozrasta
Iskrenne Vash . . .
Iskushenie Don Zhuana
Iz Zhizni Nachalnika Ugolovnogo Rozyska
Iz Zhizni Potapova
Izvinite Pozhaluysta
Kak Stat Schastlivym
Kapitan "Piligrima"
Kapkan Dlya Shakalov
Karusel Na Bazarnoy Ploshchadi
Kazhdyy Okhotnik Zhelaet Znat
Kin-Dza-Dza
Komissar
Konets Operatsii "Rezident"
Kontrudar
Koordinaty Smerti (co: Vietnam)
Korabl Prisheltsev
Korotkie Vstrechi (Brief Encounters)
Krasnaya Strela
Kreutzerova Sonata
Krugovorot
Kurier
Legenda Serebryanogo Ozera
Lermontov
Levsha
Lichnoe Delo Sudyi Ivanovoy
Lyubovyu Za Lyubov
Magia Chyornaya I Belaya
Million V Brachnoy Korzine
Mio, Moy Mio (co: Nor./Swed.; Mio In The Land Of Faraway)
Mirazhi Lyubri (co: Syria)
Moy Lyubimyy Kloun
Moya Malenkaya Zhena
My Obvinyaem
Nabat Na Rassvete
Neylonovaya Yolka
Novye Skazki Shakherezady (co: Syria)
O Rozvrashchenii Zabyt
Obeshchayu Byt
Oboroten Tom
Obryv
Obvinyaetsya Svadba
Ochnaya Stavka
Odinokaya Oreshina
Odinokaya Zhenchina Zhelaet Poznakomitaya
Odinokij Golos Celoveka
Ogni
Okhota Na Drakona (co: Nicaragua)
Pesn Proshedshikh Dney
Pliumbum, Ili Opasnaia Igia
Ploshchad Vosstania
Po Glavnoy Ulitse S Orkestrom
Po Zakonu Voennogo Vremeni
Podsudimyy
Poezd Vne Raspisania
Poezdki Na Starom Avtomoblie
Pohadka O Malickovi (co: Czech.; Malchik S Palchik)
Poklonis Do Zemli
Polevaya Gvardia Mozzhukhina

Poslednyaya Doroga
Priklyuchenia Na Malenkikh Ostrovakh
Prodelki V Starinnom Dukhe
Proryv
Proshal Zelen Leta
Prosti
Pyat Nevest Do Lyubimoy
Razmakh Kryliev
Repentance (Pokayaniye)
Requiem
Rodnik Dlia Zhazhdushchikh
Rus Iznachalna
Samaya Obayatelnaya I Privlekatelnaya
Sashshennyi Fonar
Sdelka
Sekunda Na Podvig (co: No. Korea)
Sentimentalnoe Puteshestvie Na Kartoshku
Serebryanaya Pryazha Karoliny
Severny Anekdot
Sezon Chudes
Skazka O PrekRasnoy Aysulu
Skorbnoe Beschuvstvie
Sledy Oborotnya (co: Arg.)
Sluchaynye Passazhiry
Snaypery
Son V Ruku, Ili Chemodon
Sopernitsy
Souchastniki
Sportloto-82
Staraya Azbuka
Strakh
Strannayar Istoriyar Doktora Dzhekila I Mistera Khaida
Stupen
Svidanie Na Mlechnom Puti
Takaya Zhestokaya Igra—Khokkey
Tantsploshchadka
Taynaya Progulka
Taynoe Puteshestvie Emira
Tayny Madam Vong
Tema
Tvoyo Mirnoe Nebo
Uchenik Lekaria
Utro Obrechennogo Priiska
V Strelyayushchey Glushi
V Talom Snege Zvon Ruchia
Valentin I Valentina
Veliky Pokhod Za Nevestoy
Vina Leytenanta Nekrasova
Vo Vremena Volchyikh Zakanov
Voenno-Polevoi Roman
Volny Umirayut Na Beregu
Vot Moya Derevnya
Vremya Zhelaniy
Vykup
Vzlomshchik
Weekend
Ya Lyubil Vac Bolshe Zhizni
Ya Tebya Pomnyu
Ya Yey Nravlyus
Yaguar
Zavtra Bila Voina
Zemlya I Zoloto
Zheleznoe Pole
Zina-Zinulya
Znak Bedy
Znay Nashikh
Zolotaya Baba
Zontik Dlya Novobrachnykh

VENEZUELA
De Mujer A Mujer (co: Col.)
La Oveja Negra
Macu: La Mujer Del Policia
Manon
Mas Alla Del Silencio
Por Los Caminos Verdes

VIETNAM
Koordinaty Smerti (co: USSR)

YUGOSLAVIA
Andjeo Cuvar
Die Verliebten (co: Ger.)
Dirty Rebel (co: US)
Gli Occhiali D'Oro (co: Fr./It.)
Hey Babu Riba (Bal Na Vodi)
Kraljeva Zavrsnica
Magic Snowman, The (co: US; A Winter Tale)
Na Puta Za Katangu
Oficir S Ruzon
Oktoberfest
Strategija Svrake
U Ime Naroda
Usodni Telefon
Uvek Spremne Zene
Vec Vidjeno
Zivot Radnika

WALES
Boy Soldier (Milwr Bychan)

WEST GERMANY
Anita—Dances of Vice (Anita—Tanze des Lasters)
Au Revoir, Les Enfants (co: Fr.)
Boran—Zeit Zum Zielen (co: Bel.)
Caspar David Friedrich
Cat City (Macskafogo, co: Hung., Can.)
Cemil
Chinese Are Coming, The (Die Chinesen Kommen)
Cobra Verde
Crazy Boys
Crime of Honor
Dann Ist Nichts Mehr Wie Vorher
Das Treibhaus
Deadline (co: Brit.; War Zone)
Death Stone
Der Himmel Uber Berlin (co: Fr.)
Der Nachbar (co: Switz.)
Der Todd Des Empedokles (co: Fr.)
Der Unsichtbare
Devil's Paradise
Die Verliebten (co: Yugo.)
Dilan (co: Switz./Turk.)
Dragon's Food (Drachenfutter, co: Switz.)
Ein Blick—Und Liebe Bricht Aus
F . . . ing Ferdinand (co: Fr.)
Flyer, The (Der Flieger)
Francesca
In Der Wuste
Jesus: Der Film (co: E. Ger.)
Konzert Fur Die Rechte Hand
Lady of the Camelias (Die Kameliendame)
Little Prosecutor, The (Der Kleine Staatsanwalt)
Magic Sticks (co: Aust.)
Maschenka (co: Brit.)
Meier
Otto—Der Neue Film
Out of Rosenheim
Peng! Du Bist Tot!
Poet's Silence, The (Das Schweigen Des Dichters)
Quatre Mains (co: Neth.)
Same To You (Du Mich Auch, co: Switz.)
Schloss und Siegel
Sierra Leone
Sommer
Stadtrand
Tarot
Taxi Nach Kairo
Terminus (co: Fr.)
Triumph de Gerechten
Vermischte Nachrichten
Versteckte Liebe
Wannsee Conference, The (Die Wannseekonferenz, co: Aust.)
Yer Demir, Gok Bakir (co: Turk.)
Zabou
Zartliche Chaoten
Zischke

ZAIRE
La Vie Est Belle (co: Fr.)

NAME INDEX

This index comprises a filmography of all the people listed in the cast and production credits sections of the movie reviews in this volume. The names are arranged by functions as follows:

Actors/Actresses
Animation
Art Directors
Choreographers
Cinematographers
Composers of Musical Scores
Costumes
Directors
Editors
Makeup
Music & Lyric Composers
Musical Directors
Producers
Production Designers
Set Designers
Special Effects
Stunts
Technical Advisers
Writers (both screenplay and source material)

This index lists names, aliases, and sobriquets of both players and technical staff as given in the credits for a particular picture. Thus, the same person may be listed more than once—as Robert, for example, then again as Bob.

ACTOR/ACTRESS

Aalto, Petri
URSULA
Aaron, Caroline
O. C. AND STIGGS
Aaron, Michael
CLUB LIFE
Aaving, Kerttu
IGRY DLJA DETEJ SKO'NOGO VOZRASTA
Abakaz, Suvit
GOOD MORNING, VIETNAM
Abalyan, Evard
ZEMLYA I ZOLOTO
Abashidze, Leila
KRUGOVOROT
Abatatuono, Diego
UN RAGAZZO DI CALABRIA
Abaunza, Jorge
JUNTOS
Abbasov, R.
VZLOMSHCHIK
Abbate, Marisa
LUNGA VITA ALLA SIGNORA!
Abbati, Stefano
DEVIL IN THE FLESH
MORO AFFAIR, THE
Abbato, John
NECROPOLIS
Abbott, Bruce
SUMMER HEAT
Abdel-Azuz, Ahmed
AL-TAUQ WAL-ISWIRA
Abdel-Hamid, Fardos
AL-TAUQ WAL-ISWIRA
Abdelkader
PIERRE ET DJEMILA
Abdi, Akbar
LODGERS
Abdul-Samad, Hakeem
ERNEST GOES TO CAMP
Abdulaikhasov, Sher
V TALOM SNEGE ZVON RUCHIA
Abdullayev, Nurillo
KAPKAN DLYA SHAKALOV
Abdulov, Alexandr
SAMAYA OBAYATELNAYA I PRIVLEKATELNAYA
Abdurakhmanova, Gulnara
TAYNOE PUTESHESTVIE EMIRA
Abdurazakov, Abib
A SANTA DERVIS
Abe, Mitzie
LIVING ON TOKYO TIME
Abel, Antwanette
BELIEVERS, THE
Abel, Liane
ROCK 'N' ROLL NIGHTMARE
Abel, Mohammad
NINJA THUNDERBOLT
Abele, Jim
WIMPS
Abelson, Arthur
WINNERS TAKE ALL
Abernathy, Ric
SQUEEZE, THE
Abeywicrema, Joe
MALDENIYESIMION
Abner, Teddy
WILD THING
Aboutboul, Alon
KOL AHAVOTAI
Abraham, Dawn
DEADLY PREY
Abraham, Josef
C. K. DEZERTERZY
Abraham, Ken
CREEPOZOIDS
Abramowitz, Elkan
HELLO AGAIN
Abrams, Herb
CLUB LIFE
Abrams, Marilyn
OUTTAKES
Abramson, Stuart
ISHTAR
Abrego, Fidel
FORAJIDOS EN LA MIRA
LETS GET HARRY
Abril, Victoria
EL LUTE—CAMINA O REVIENTA
TERNOSECCO
Abston, Dean
BEST SELLER
OVER THE TOP
Abuba, Earnest
FOREVER, LULU
Abujamra, Adriana
VERA
Abujamra, Clarisse
ANJOS DO ARRABALDE
Abuladze, Ketevan
REPENTANCE
Accolas, Raymond
TOO OUTRAGEOUS
Acevedo, Alberto
POR LOS CAMINOS VERDES
Acevedo, Maria Angeles
LA VIDA ALEGRE
Achdian, Anna
NOCE EN GALILEE
Ache, Christina
AREIAS ESCALADANTES
Acheson, James
ASSASSINATION
DAY THEY ROBBED AMERICA, THE
Acheson, Mark
HOME IS WHERE THE HART IS
Acker, Iris
WHOOPS APOCALYPSE
Ackerman, Forrest J.
EVIL SPAWN
Ackerman, Vickie
SOMETHING SPECIAL!
Ackland, Joss
SICILIAN, THE
WHITE MISCHIEF
Ackridge, Bill
P.K. & THE KID
Acosta, T.J.
NIGHTFORCE
Acovone, Jay
COLD STEEL
Acree, Dennis
BEST SELLER
Adabashyan, Alexander
OBVINYAETSYA SVADBA
Adair, Alice
BEVERLY HILLS COP II
Adair, Anna
PETER VON SCHOLTEN
Adair, Barbara
EAT THE PEACH
Adam, Joel
ANGEL HEART
Adambo, Greg
KOLORMASK
Adams, Brian
HOWLING III, THE
Adams, Brooke
MAN ON FIRE
Adams, Cedric
LETHAL WEAPON
Adams, Christopher R.
BEVERLY HILLS COP II
Adams, Dave
BIG SHOTS
Adams, Don
BACK TO THE BEACH
Adams, Edwin M.
SUSPECT
Adams, Jeb Stuart
FLOWERS IN THE ATTIC
Adams, Lillian
SUMMER SCHOOL
Adams, Lynne
NIGHT ZOO
STREET SMART
WILD THING
Adams, Martin
FULL METAL JACKET
Adams, Mary
CRYSTAL HEART
Adams, Maude
JANE AND THE LOST CITY
Adams, Mike
P.K. & THE KID
Adams, Simon
PRICK UP YOUR EARS
Adams, Stacey
OPEN HOUSE
SWEET REVENGE
Adams, Tony
ALADDIN
Adamson, Nathan
BLUE MONKEY

Adedunyo, Obaka
BEST SELLER

Adele, Jan
HIGH TIDE

Adelin, Jean-Claude
BUISSON ARDENT
LA PASSION BEATRICE

Adhiambo, Moniccah
KOLORMASK

Adi, Dorit
KOL AHAVOTAI
SNOW WHITE

Adim, Odella
PERLYOTNIYE PTIT

Adjani, Isabelle
ISHTAR

Adjavon, Raymond
PETER VON SCHOLTEN

Adkins, Tracey D.
SQUARE DANCE

Adler, Charles
CHIPMUNK ADVENTURE, THE

Adler, Matt
AMAZON WOMEN ON THE MOON
NORTH SHORE
WHITE WATER SUMMER

Adler, Rudi
STREET SMART

Adomaitis, Regimantas
KARUSEL NA BAZARNOY PLOSHCHADI

Adomaytis, Regimantas
IZVINITEPOZHALUYSTA

Adorf, Mario
DEVILS PARADISE, THE
NOTTE ITALIANA

Adoskin, Anatoly
STRANNAYAR ISTORIYAR DOKTORA DZHEKILA I MISTERA KHAIDA

Adrianson, Stephen
HOLLYWOOD SHUFFLE

Adrianzen, Eduardo
CITY AND THE DOGS, THE

Adrienne, Sigrid
EEN MAAND LATER

Adu, Robinson Frank
HEART

Aedma, Alar
BIG TOWN, THE

Aegidius, Hans Christian
PETER VON SCHOLTEN

Aendenboom, Frank
HECTOR

Affleck, Neil
WILD THING

Afonso, Yves
O DESEJADO—LES MONTAGNES DE LA LUNE

Afthinos, Christos
O PARADISSOS ANIGI ME ANTIKLIDI

Afzali, Mahnaz
GOZARESH-E YEK GHATL

Agafonov, Ivan
TAYNOE PUTESHESTVIE EMIRA
V STRELYAYUSHCHEY GLUSHI

Agafonova, Tatiana
ZINA-ZINULYA

Agay, Iren
A JAVOR

Agenin, Beatrice
LANNEE DES MEDUSES

Ageyeva, Olga
PO ZAKONU VOENNOGO VREMENI

Agnred, Knut
LEIF

Agoris, Takis
TREE WE HURT, THE

Agosti, Carlos
EL MUERTO DEL PALOMO

Agosti, Paola
QUARTIERE

Agren, Janet
ALADDIN

Agudelo, Marcela
VISA U.S.A.

Aguero, Juan Manuel
BELIEVERS, THE

Aguilar, Claire
MAGDALENA VIRAGA

Aguilar, Orietta
LA RULETERA

Aguilar F, Juliana
LA RULETERA

Aguirre, Ramon
A LOS CUATRO VIENTOS

Ahonen, Olavi
JAAHYVAISET PRESIDENTILLE

Ahrle, Leif
NAGRA SOMMARKVALLAR PA JORDEN

Ahuet, Clarissa
HERENCIA DE VALIENTES

Ahuet, Julio
MI NOMBRE ES GATILLO

Ahumada, Regulo
CHRONICLE OF A DEATH FORETOLD

Aiello, Danny
MAN ON FIRE
MOONSTRUCK
PICK-UP ARTIST, THE
RADIO DAYS
SQUEEZE, THE

Aiello III, Danny
GOOD MORNING, VIETNAM

Aihaud, Yveline
POUSSIERE D'ANGE

Aim, Carl Olof
MALARPIRATER

Ainsley, Trevor
COMRADES

Ait-Hamouda, Djedjigue
PIERRE ET DJEMILA

Aitchison, Suzy
BLOODY NEW YEAR

Aitken, Tony
HEARTS OF FIRE

Aitkens, Michael
MOVING TARGETS

Aizaz
PRATIGHAAT

Ajaye, Franklyn
HOLLYWOOD SHUFFLE

Akahoshi, Steve
FATAL BEAUTY

Akan, Tarik
WATER ALSO BURNS

Akca, Tuncay
YER DEMIR, GOK BAKIR

Akerblom, Johan
JIM OCH PIRATERNA BLOM

Akhavan, Frazaneh Neshat
DJADDE HAYE SARD

Akifyeva, Yelena
ZNAY NASHIKH

Akili, Ali Mohammed
NOCE EN GALILEE

Akimova, Natalia
V STRELYAYUSHCHEY GLUSHI

Akin, Philip
PRETTYKILL

Akin, Phillip
BLUE MONKEY

Akina, Henry
KONZERT FUR DIE RECHTE HAND

Akins, Claude
CURSE, THE
MONSTER IN THE CLOSET

Akiyoshi, Michiru
HIKARU ANNA

Akly, Nazih
NOCE EN GALILEE

Ako
SHINRAN: SHIRO MICHI

Akramov, Bakhrom
YA YEY NRAVLYUS

Aksoy, Serap
DEGIRMEN
YER DEMIR, GOK BAKIR

Aksyuta, Titiana
POLEVAYA GVARDIA MOZZHUKHINA

Akulova, Tamara
IZ ZHIZNI POTAPOVA

Alafouzos, Socrates
KLIOS

Alahani, Sheeba
BARBARIANS, THE

Alan, Craig
GET THE TERRORISTS
MANKILLERS

Alano, Nell
CLUB LIFE

Alarcon, Luis
LA ESTACION DEL REGRESO

Alaverdian, Genrich
SASHSHENNYI FONAR

Albee, Mary
MONSTER SQUAD, THE

Albert, Eddie
TURNAROUND

Albert, Wil
BARFLY

Albertia, Robert
SUMMER HEAT

Albertini, Michal
LHOMME VOILE

Alberto
ESTA NOCHE CENA PANCHO (DESPEDIDA DE SOLTERO)

Albiston, Mark
FRENCHMAN'S FARM

Alcaide, Chris
ASSASSINATION

Alcalay, Moscu
TESTAMENT D'UN POETE JUIF ASSASSINE

Alcaniz, Muntsa
LA RUSA

Alcocer, Victor
TIERRA DE VALIENTES

Alcon, Alfredo
EL DUENO DEL SOL

Alcon, Pilar
POLICIA

Alcroft, Jamie
MILLION DOLLAR MYSTERY

Alda, Antony
HOT CHILD IN THE CITY

Alda, Rutanya
BLACK WIDOW
HOT SHOT

Alden, Cary
BIG EASY, THE

Alden, Norman
OFF THE MARK

Alden, Stacey
NIGHTMARE ON ELM STREET 3: DREAM WARRIORS, A

Aldon, Lynda
MANKILLERS

Aldredge, Tom
BATTERIES NOT INCLUDED

Aldridge, Kevin
FULL METAL JACKET

Aldridge, Kitty
MAURICE

Aleandro, Norma
GABY—A TRUE STORY

Alegro, Arturo
MURIERON A MITAD DEL RIO
POLICIAS DE NARCOTICOS

Aleinikova, Arina
CHELOVEK C AKKORDEONOM

Alejandra, Mayra
MANON

Aleman, Julio
POLICIAS DE NARCOTICOS

Aleman, Selva
LOS DUENOS DEL SILENCIO

Alemann, Katja
EL ANO DEL CONEJO

Alentova, Vera
VREMYA ZHELANIY

Aleong, Aki
HANOI HILTON, THE

Alessandri, Lorenzo
CHI C'E C'E

Alex, Lalu
JANUARY ORORMA

Alexander, Dean
AMAZING GRACE AND CHUCK

Alexander, Dick
CAMPUS MAN
RAISING ARIZONA

Alexander, Erika
MY LITTLE GIRL

Alexander, Gregory "Popeye"
HOLLYWOOD SHUFFLE

Alexander, Jace
MATEWAN

Alexander, Jane
SQUARE DANCE
SWEET COUNTRY

Alexander, Jon
TUESDAY WEDNESDAY

Alexander, Max
ROXANNE

Alexander, Natalie
ASSASSINATION

Alexander, O'Clair
DATE WITH AN ANGEL

Alexander, Rene
NIGHTFORCE

Alexander, Susana
GABY—A TRUE STORY

Alexandra, Tiana
CATCH THE HEAT

Alexandrakis, Alekos
TA PAIDIA TIS CHELIDONAS

Alexandre, Henri-Charles
MAN ON FIRE

Alexandre, Manuel
YEAR OF AWAKENING, THE

Alexandrov, Constantin
MAN IN LOVE, A

Alexeyev, Pavel
PLOSHCHAD VOSSTANIA

Alexi-Meskhishvili, Salome
KRUGOVOROT

Alfaro, Marcelo
SENTIMIENTOS: MIRTA DE LINIERS A ESTAMBUL

Alferova, Irina
CHELOVEK C AKKORDEONOM
GRUBAYA POSADKA

Alfredo
EULALIA
ESTA NOCHE CENA PANCHO (DESPEDIDA DE SOLTERO)
LA RAZA NUNCA PIERDE—HUELE A GAS
LAPUTA: THE CASTLE IN THE SKY

Alfredson, Hans
JIM OCH PIRATERNA BLOM

Alfredsson, Arnold
MY LIFE AS A DOG

Algelear, Pia
PRETTY SMART

Algora, Francisco
LA GUERRA DE LOS LOCOS

Algora, Paco
LA GUERRA DE LOS LOCOS

Alianak, Hrant
FAMILY VIEWING

Alice's Boyfriend
MY LITTLE GIRL

Alicia, The
VZLOMSHCHIK

Alina
NAKEMIIN, HYVASTI

Aliquo, Manfredi
MAN ON FIRE

Aliresi, Ali
ALSHAZIA

Alisova
RODNIK DLIA ZHAZHDUSHCHIKH

Aliyev, Ibragim
CHKATULKA IZ KREPOSTI

Alkeou, Maria
ANGELOS

Alkins, April
LADIES OF THE LOTUS

Allain, Valerie
ARIA
CLUB DE RENCONTRES

Allan, Denisa
WINNERS TAKE ALL

Allan, Jack
AROUND THE WORLD IN EIGHTY WAYS

Allan, Johnny
FOURTH PROTOCOL, THE

Allaoui, Karim
LA RUMBA
UN AMOUR A PARIS

Allary, Firmin
MASCARA

Allen, Antony
HELLRAISER

Allen, Barry
NGATI

Allen, Carolyn
PERSONAL SERVICES

Allen, Domenick
CLUB LIFE

Allen, Frederick
NO WAY OUT

Allen, Hilda
EMANON

Allen, Howard
HOLLYWOOD SHUFFLE

Allen, Jim
AMAZING GRACE AND CHUCK

Allen, Julie
REMEMBERING MEL

Allen, Karen
GLASS MENAGERIE, THE
TERMINUS

Allen, Keith
COMRADES

Allen, Kevin
EAT THE RICH
LOVECHILD, THE

Allen, Nancy
ROBOCOP
SWEET REVENGE

Allen, Penelope
BEDROOM WINDOW, THE

Allen, Ronald
EAT THE RICH

Allen, Sarita
ANGEL HEART

Allen, Steve
AMAZON WOMEN ON THE MOON

Allen, Teresa Mae
BLOODY WEDNESDAY

Allen, Todd
WITCHBOARD

Allen, Woody
RADIO DAYS

Alley, Kirstie
SUMMER SCHOOL

Alley's Manager
CRYSTAL HEART

Allison, Don
PURSUIT OF HAPPINESS, THE

Allocca, Antonio
QUEL RAGAZZO DELLA CURVA "B"

Almada, Fernando
CARTUCHA CORTADA
HERENCIA DE VALIENTES

Almada, Mario
ARQUIESTA EMILIO VARELA
CARTUCHA CORTADA
EL ANSIA DE MATAR
EL MUERTO DEL PALOMO
OPERACION MARIJUANA
TRAGICO TERREMOTO EN MEXICO
YO, EL EJECUTOR

Almeida, Cida
VERA

Almgren, Kristian
MALARPIRATER

Almodovar, Tinin
LAW OF DESIRE

Almond, Matt
SUMMER HEAT

Almos, Eva
CARE BEARS ADVENTURE IN WONDERLAND, THE

Almquist, Gregg
RADIO DAYS

Alon, Roy
FOURTH PROTOCOL, THE

Alonso, Alberto
LA GUERRA DE LOS LOCOS

Alonso, Aurora
SINVERGUENZA . . . PERO HONRADO

Alonso, Jose
EL HOMBRE DESNUDO
LA FUGA DE CARRASCO

Alonso, Maria Conchita
EXTREME PREJUDICE
RUNNING MAN, THE

Alonso, Rafael
MY GENERAL

Alonzo, Anthony
MAD KILLER

Alpi, Roberto
DA NNUNZIO

Alpiner, Saul
I WAS A TEENAGE T.V. TERRORIST

Alquabaili, Altaher
ALSHAZIA

Alt, Carol
I MIEI PRIMI QUARANT'ANNI
VIA MONTENAPOLEONE

Altaras, Adriana
IN DER WUSTE

Altbach, Susann
HOT CHILD IN THE CITY

Alterio, Hector
EL HOMBRE DE LA DEUDA EXTERNA
MY GENERAL
SOFIA

Altmann, Michael
ZISCHKE

Aluzas, Jonathan
MONSTER IN THE CLOSET

Alvarado, Daniel
DE MUJER A MUJER

Alvarado, Julio
MAS VALE PAJARO EN MANO . . .
RETO A LA VIDA

Alvarado, Max
NO BLOOD NO SURRENDER

Alvarado, Trini
SWEET LORRAINE

Alvarez, Al
CINCO NACOS ASALTAN A LAS VEGAS

Alvarez, Connie
LA BAMBA

Alvarez, Diego
VISA U.S.A.

Alvarez, Itziar
LA VIDA ALEGRE

Alvarez, Luis
CITY AND THE DOGS, THE

Alvarez, Manny
BROADCAST NEWS

Alvarez, Ramon
WALKER

Alvarez-Osorio, Pedro
LAS DOS ORILLAS

Alves, Vanessa
ANJOS DO ARRABALDE

Alvin, Dave
BORDER RADIO

Alzado, Lyle
ERNEST GOES TO CAMP

Amadis, Said
LETE DERNIER A TANGER

Amador, Rafael
JUNTOS

Amall, Yaskov
DREAMERS

Aman, Zeenat
DAKU HASINA

Amanova, Svetlana
SPORTLOTO—82

Amar, Sonia
NOCE EN GALILEE

Amaral, Yara
LEILA DINIZ

Amarasena, Sriyani
VIRAGAYA

Amateau, Chloe
GARBAGE PAIL KIDS MOVIE, THE

Amateau, J.P.
GARBAGE PAIL KIDS MOVIE, THE

Amato, Gerardo
CARAMELLE DA UNO SCONOSCIUTO

Amato, Leandro
DANCERS

Ambabo, Donald
OUTRAGEOUS FORTUNE

Amberla, Tuula
KILL CITY

Ambika
VILAMBARAM

Ameche, Don
HARRY AND THE HENDERSONS

Ameijeiras, Antonio
COLOR OF DESTINY, THE

Ameli and his Orchestra
A LOS CUATRO VIENTOS

Amendola, Claudio
SOLDATI: 365 GIORNI ALL' ALBA

Amendolia, Don
SECRET OF MY SUCCESS, THE

American Ballet Theater Dancer
DANCERS

American Intelligence
WHOOPS APOCALYPSE

Amerson, Tammy
MORGAN STEWART'S COMING HOME

Ames, Trudy
ZERO BOYS, THE
Amidou, Saouad
LEVY ET GOLIATH
Amidou, Souad
LA COMPROMISSION
MALADIE D'AMOUR
Amiel, Alan
RAGE OF HONOR
Amigo, Hank
OUTING, THE
Amin, Mervet
ZAWGAT RAGOL MOHIM
Amini, Alexandra
THREE MEN AND A BABY
Amis, Suzy
BIG TOWN, THE
Amitova, Viktorija
SKORBNOE BESCHUVSTVIE
Ammons, Marilyn
WHO'S THAT GIRL
Amon, Santiago
ASIGNATURA APROBADA
Amoruso, Paolo
IL RAGAZZO DI EBALUS
Amzic, Jakup
ANDJEO CUVAR
An, L.
SKORBNOE BESCHUVSTVIE
An, Wang
TERRORIZERS, THE
An So-Young
TICKET
Anastasiades, Dimitri
MASCARA
Anaya, Manuel
FORAJIDOS EN LA MIRA
Anconina, Richard
LEVY ET GOLIATH
Anders, Devon
BORDER RADIO
Anders, Karen
MALIBU BIKINI SHOP, THE
Anders, Luana
BORDER RADIO
Andersen, Asta Esper
BABETTE'S GASTEBUD
Andersen, Bibi
LAW OF DESIRE
Andersen, Bridgette
TOO MUCH
Andersen, Dana
O. C. AND STIGGS
Andersen, Iva
REAL MEN
Andersen, Scott
BELL DIAMOND
STAKEOUT
Anderson, Charmaine
PRINCIPAL, THE
Anderson, Daryl
MONSTER SQUAD, THE
Anderson, Dave
NO DEAD HEROES
Anderson, Del
FULL METAL JACKET
Anderson, Duncan
STARLIGHT HOTEL
Anderson, Kevin
ORPHANS
WALK ON THE MOON, A
Anderson, Kurt
DIRTY LAUNDRY
Anderson, Lyda
DEAD, THE
Anderson, Martha
MASSACRE IN DINOSAUR VALLEY
Anderson, Michael J.
GREAT LAND OF SMALL, THE
Anderson, Miles
CRY FREEDOM
Anderson, Mitchell
JAWS: THE REVENGE
Andersson, Bibi
BABETTE'S GASTEBUD
LOS DUENOS DEL SILENCIO
SVART GRYNING
Andersson, Harriet
NAGRA SOMMARKVALLAR PA JORDEN
Andersson, Inga-Lill
NAGRA SOMMARKVALLAR PA JORDEN
Andiyev, Soslan
ZNAY NASHIKH
Ando, Kyoichi
BUS
Andolfi, Eddy
LA CROCE DALLE SETTE PIETRE
Andolong, Sandy
OPERATION: GET VICTOR CORPUS THE REBEL SOLDIER
Andorai, Peter
CSOK, ANYU
Andrade, Miguel
GABY—A TRUE STORY
Andre, E.J.
EVIL TOWN
Andre, Jean-Pierre
PIERRE ET DJEMILA
Andre the Giant
PRINCESS BRIDE, THE
Andrei, Damir
MORNING MAN, THE
Andrei, Valerio
NOI UOMINI DURI
Andreichenko, Natalia
PROSTI
VOENNO-POLEVOI ROMAN
Andreini, Flavio
CHI C'E C'E
Andreitchenko, Natalia
DVOE POD ODNIM ZONTOM
Andreoli, Elvia
SENTIMIENTOS: MIRTA DE LINIERS A ESTAMBUL
Andreou, Lazaros
DOXOBUS
Andres, Bill
RAISING ARIZONA
Andreu, Simon
CRYSTAL HEART
LA ESTANQUERA DE VALLECAS
Andrews, Anthony
LIGHTHORSEMEN, THE
Andrews, Garfield
FAMILY VIEWING
Andrews, Jodie
HOPE AND GLORY
Andrews, Michael
HARD TICKET TO HAWAII
TALKING WALLS
Andrews, Nathan
LADIES OF THE LOTUS
Andrews, Real
WILD THING
Andrich, Steve
HAPPY HOUR
Androfsky, Carol
BIG BANG, THE
Androsov, Anton
PLIUMBUM, ILI OPASNAIA IGIA
Andueza, Juana
LA VIDA ALEGRE
Anemone
LE GRAND CHEMIN
POULE ET FRITES
Angela, Rita
VENNER FOR ALTID
Angelidou, Nellie
ONE HUNDRED AND TWENTY DECIBELS
Angeliglesias, Miguel
EL AMOR DE AHORA
Anger, Mark
PRINCIPAL, THE
Anglade, Jean-Hugues
MALADIE D'AMOUR
Anglim, Jennifer
UNTOUCHABLES, THE
Anglim, Philip
MALONE
Angrisano, Franco
TERNOSECCO
Angulo, Alex
EL AMOR DE AHORA
Ankri, Ette
DEADLINE
Annacker, Markus
LADY OF THE CAMELIAS
Anne Redfern
DEADTIME STORIES
Annesley, Imogen
HOWLING III, THE
Anno, Kelby
FIRE AND ICE
Anofriyev, Oleg
SEKUNDA NA PODVIG
Anorve, Edith Olivia
NOS REIMOS DE LA MIGRA
Ansara, Michael
ASSASSINATION
Anschutz, Niels
DER JUNGE MIT DEM GROSSEN SCHWARZEN HUND
Anspach, Susan
BLUE MONKEY
Ant, Adam
COLD STEEL
SLAMDANCE
Anthony, Corwyn
STUDENT CONFIDENTIAL
Anthony, David
MONSTER IN THE CLOSET
Anthony, Lysette
EMPEROR'S NEW CLOTHES, THE
LOOKING FOR EILEEN
Anthony, Mark
EVIL SPAWN
Anthony, Shirley
BELIEVERS, THE
Antin, Steve
PENITENTIARY III
Antique Dealer
HAPPY NEW YEAR
Antonelli, Laura
RIMINI RIMINI
ROBA DA RICCHI
Antoni, Thomas
WOLF AT THE DOOR, THE
Antonik, Vladimir
RUS IZNACHALNA
Antonio, Jim
AMAZING GRACE AND CHUCK
BIG SHOTS
Antonov, Georgy
OBRYV
Antonutti, Omero
GOOD MORNING BABYLON
Anwer, Razi
WITNESS TO A KILLING
Anzell, Hy
IRONWEED
RADIO DAYS
Aoki, Brenda
LIVING ON TOKYO TIME
Apaolaza, Joseba
A LOS CUATRO VIENTOS
Aparajita
TUNDA BAIDA
Aparicio, Rafaela
CARA DE ACELGA
LA VIDA ALEGRE
YEAR OF AWAKENING, THE
Aparicio, Yirah
LAPUTA: THE CASTLE IN THE SKY
TODA LA VIDA
Apfelberg, Ran
KOL AHAVOTAI
Apick, Mary
CHECKPOINT
Applebaum, Bill
OVERBOARD
Applegate, Royce D.
MILLION DOLLAR MYSTERY
Appu
PANDAVAPURAM
Apsega, Alejo
RAGE OF HONOR
Aquila, Diane
WINTER TAN, A
Aquilar, George
OUT OF ROSENHEIM
Aquino, Michelle
NO BLOOD NO SURRENDER
Ara, Roshan
INDIAN SUMMER
Aragon, Alejandro
LO DEL CESAR
Aragon, Angelica
LO DEL CESAR
Aragon, Emilio
POLICIA

Aragon, Jesse
HOLLYWOOD SHUFFLE
WANTED: DEAD OR ALIVE

Aragon, John
MANKILLERS

Arai, Hiro
EMPIRE OF THE SUN

Araiza, Raul
EL PLACER DE LA VENGANZA
SINVERGUENZA . . . PERO HONRADO

Arakawa, Jane
STREET TRASH

Aram, Asadullah
PERLYOTNIYE PTIT

Arana, Hugo
CHORROS
MADE IN ARGENTINA

Aranda, Juan Ignacio
MISSION KILL

Aranda, Michael
CREEPOZOIDS

Arantes, Romulo
LEILA DINIZ

Aranza, Fabian
NARCOTERROR

Araoz, Elida
EIN BLICK-UND DIE LIEBE BRICHT AUS

Arashi, Clifford
FOREVER, LULU

Arau, Alfonso
WALKER

Arau I., Ademar
RETO A LA VIDA

Araya, Zeudi
IL GIORNO PRIMA

Arbas, Derya
DILAN

Arbatt, Alexandre
AVRIL BRISE

Arbour, France
BACH AND BROCCOLI

Arbus, Allan
FROM THE HIP

Archer, Anne
FATAL ATTRACTION

Archer, Melba
STREET SMART

Archer, Steve
CAMPUS MAN

Archerd, Selma
LETHAL WEAPON

Archie, John
WHOOPS APOCALYPSE

Ardant, Fanny
FAMILY BUSINESS
FAMILY, THE
MELO

Arden, Robert
WHOOPS APOCALYPSE

Ardisson, Giorgio
DELITTI
LA TRASGRESSIONE

Arditi, Catherine
MELO

Arditi, Pierre
AGENT TROUBLE
MELO

Aren, Reine
SEREBRYANAYA PRYAZHA KAROLINY

Arenas, Reynaldo
HOUR OF THE ASSASSIN

Arenberg, Lee
CROSS MY HEART

Arendt, Jeremy
RAISING ARIZONA

Arentzen, Jens
HIP, HIP, HURRA!

Arestrup, Niels
CHARLIE DINGO
LA RUMBA

Arevalo, Mario
MIRACLES

Argand, Robert
DANCERS

Argenziano, Carmen
UNDER COVER

Argiro, Vinny
DATE WITH AN ANGEL

Argula, Teri
MALIBU BIKINI SHOP, THE

Ari, Bob
BLIND DATE

Arias, Imanol
DIVINAS PALABRAS
EL LUTE—CAMINA O REVIENTA

Ariel, Blanche
MASQUES

Arimori, Narimi
FINAL TAKE: THE GOLDEN AGE OF MOVIES

Arinaga, Alberto Martin
A LOS CUATRO VIENTOS

Arinbasarova, Natalia
SEKUNDA NA PODVIG

Aris, Ann
BUSINESS AS USUAL

Arjmand, Darioush
CAPTAIN KHORSHID

Arjonce, Ana
NI DE AQUI, NI DE ALLA

Arkin, Adam
PERSONAL FOUL

Arlauskas, Alghis
SPORTLOTO—82

Armel, Francoise
BEYOND THERAPY

Armendariz, Pedro
EL PLACER DE LA VENGANZA
MATAR O MORIR
WALK ON THE MOON, A
WALKER

Armour, Ann
PRINCIPAL, THE

Arms Dealer
EAT THE RICH

Armstrong, Buki
BUSINESS AS USUAL

Armstrong, Curtis
REVENGE OF THE NERDS II: NERDS IN PARADISE

Armstrong, Mary
HELLO AGAIN

Armstrong, R.G.
BULLETPROOF
JOCKS
PREDATOR
RED HEADED STRANGER

Armstrong, Victoria
EAT THE PEACH

Armstrong, William
HOPE AND GLORY

Armus, Sidney
MAKING MR.RIGHT

Arndt, Jacques
AMAZONS

Arndt, Stefanie
LADY OF THE CAMELIAS

Arneric, Neda
ANDJEO CUVAR

Arneson, Erni
SIDSTE AKT

Arnold, Evan
MONSTER IN THE CLOSET

Arnold, Richard E.
BLACK WIDOW

Arnott, David
HOUSE TWO: THE SECOND STORY

Arnoul, Francoise
NUIT DOCILE

Arone, James
MONSTER IN THE CLOSET

Arons, Nancy
MUTANT HUNT

Aronson, Jack
MAGIC SNOWMAN, THE

Arquette, Patricia
NIGHTMARE ON ELM STREET 3: DREAM WARRIORS, A
PRETTY SMART

Arquette, Rosanna
AMAZON WOMEN ON THE MOON

Arrazola, Agustin
A LOS CUATRO VIENTOS

Arriaga, Felipe
EL DIABLO, EL SANTO Y EL TONTO
MAS BUENAS QUE EL PAN

Arrick, Rose
ISHTAR

Artesi, Benito
QUEL RAGAZZO DELLA CURVA "B"

Arthur, Alain
SOUS LE SOLEIL DE SATAN

Artzorn, Robert
WANNSEE CONFERENCE, THE

Arundale, Vicky
MONTH IN THE COUNTRY, A

Arup
HAMARI JUNG

Arutyunyan, Aneta
ODINOKAYA ORESHINA

Arvelo, Ritva
NAKEMIIN, HYVASTI

Arvizu, Alberto
EL ANSIA DE MATAR

Ary, Zander
REMEMBERING MEL

Arzatz, Arminus
MISSION KILL

Asada, Masayo
SHINRAN: SHIRO MICHI

Asbil, Neil
REMEMBERING MEL

Ascensao, Jose Manuel
LA OVEJA NEGRA

Ash, Albert
DATE WITH AN ANGEL

Ash, Leslie
SHADEY

Asha
INDIAN SUMMER

Ashani, Stafford
TISZTA AMERIKA

Ashcroft, Peggy
WHEN THE WIND BLOWS

Ashdot, Yossi
DEATH BEFORE DISHONOR

Ashida, Shinsuke
TAXING WOMAN, A

Ashimov, Sagui
SKAZKA O PREKRASNOY AYSULU

Ashley, Elizabeth
DRAGNET

Ashmore, Frank
MONSTER IN THE CLOSET

Ashokan
VILAMBARAM

Ashton, John
BEVERLY HILLS COP II
SOME KIND OF WONDERFUL

Ashton, Queenie
YEAR MY VOICE BROKE, THE

Ashworth, Tom
IN THE MOOD

Asinas, Stephen R.
NO WAY OUT

Askew, Nicholas
HOPE AND GLORY

Asmussen, Troels
PELLE EROVRAREN

Asner, Edward
PINOCCHIO AND THE EMPEROR OF THE NIGHT

Asoh, Hajimeh
TAXING WOMAN, A

Asparagus, Fred
FATAL BEAUTY

Aspesanshkwat
OUT OF ROSENHEIM

Assa, Rene
WALKER

Assenza, Betty
LANNEE DES MEDUSES

Asseo, Avraham
HA INSTALATOR

Assistant Director
HOWLING III, THE

Ast, Pat
CLUB LIFE

Astarloa, Esteban
EL AMOR DE AHORA

Astin, John
TEEN WOLF TOO

Astin, Mackenzie
GARBAGE PAIL KIDS MOVIE, THE

Astin, Sean
LIKE FATHER, LIKE SON
WHITE WATER SUMMER

Astor, Patti
FOREVER, LULU

Astrid Plane
STEELE JUSTICE

Aswini
AMERICA ABBAI

Athie, Oscar
JUNTOS

Athie's Manager
JUNTOS

Atias, Karmen
DE FLYGANDE DJAVLARNA

Atkin, Mike
I WAS A TEENAGE T.V. TERRORIST

Atkine, Feodor
LA MOINE ET LA SORCIERE
LES OREILLES ENTRE LES DENTS

Atkins, Christopher
BEAKS

Atkins, Dave
COMRADES
HELLRAISER
PERSONAL SERVICES
PRICK UP YOUR EARS

Atkins, Tom
LETHAL WEAPON

Atsumi, Kiyoshi
FINAL TAKE: THE GOLDEN AGE OF MOVIES
TORA-SAN'S BLUEBIRD FANTASY

Attal, Henri
MASQUES

Attorney
SURRENDER

Atzmon, Anat
CHOZE AHAVA

Atzmon, Shmuel
CHOZE AHAVA

Auberjonois, Rene
WALKER

Aubrey, James
CRY FREEDOM

Auction
VZLOMSHCHIK

Audelin, Jean-Claude
AVRIL BRISE

Auder, Alexandra
HIDING OUT

Audier, Marion
CHAMP D'HONNEUR

Audley, Michael
SHY PEOPLE

Audran, Stephane
BABETTE'S GASTEBUD

Audray, Elvire
RIMINI RIMINI

Auerbach, Red
AMAZING GRACE AND CHUCK

Auffray, Jacques
QUATRE AVENTURES DE REINETTE ET MIRABELLE

Aufiery, Joe
ANNA

Augenstein, Helen
MANKILLERS

Augenstein, Jeff
MANKILLERS

Auger, Claudine
LES EXPLOITS DUN JEUNE DON JUAN

Augeson, Roxanna
VIDEO DEAD, THE

August, Lance
PROJECT X

Augusta, Karel
PRATELE BERMUDSKEHO TROJUHELNIKU

Augustin, Christina
ALIEN PREDATOR

Augusto, Otavio
LEILA DINIZ

Ault, David
SUPERNATURALS, THE

Aumont, Jean-Pierre
JOHNNY MONROE
SWEET COUNTRY

Aumont, Michel
POUSSIERE D'ANGE
SALE DESTIN!

Ausden, Steve
EMPIRE STATE

Ausenda, Dorotea
GOOD MORNING BABYLON

Ausland, John
ETTER RUBICON

Austern, Robert
WILD THING

Austin, Joe
HOME IS WHERE THE HART IS

Auteuil, Daniel
JEAN DE FLORETTE
MANON OF THE SPRING

Autry, Alan
AMAZING GRACE AND CHUCK
O. C. AND STIGGS

Avaki, Paul
OVERKILL

Avalon, Frankie
BACK TO THE BEACH

Avalos, Luis
GHOST FEVER

Avdeliodis, Demos
TREE WE HURT, THE

Avdeliodis, Yannis
TREE WE HURT, THE

Avellone, Gregory
NO WAY OUT

Avendano, Jose Luis
FORAJIDOS EN LA MIRA

Averett, Mary Ellen
RETURN OF JOSEY WALES, THE

Avery, James
NIGHTFLYERS
THREE FOR THE ROAD

Avery, Val
MESSENGER, THE

Avia
VZLOMSHCHIK

Aviles, Rick
SECRET OF MY SUCCESS, THE
STREET SMART

Avlianou, Christina
ONIRO ARISTERIS NICHTAS

Axelrod, Robert
ASSASSINATION

Ayala, Brandy
NO BLOOD NO SURRENDER

Ayala, Joe
MANKILLERS

Ayarza, Emilia
FATAL BEAUTY

Aykroyd, Dan
DRAGNET

Aylett, Martin
WALKER

Ayllet, Martin
NI DE AQUI, NI DE ALLA

Aylward, Peter
UNTOUCHABLES, THE

Azema, Sabine
MELO

Azer, Irina
KONETS OPERATSII "REZIDENT"

Azhibekova, Gulsara
VOLNY UMIRAYUT NA BEREGU

Aziz, Nasser
PERLYOTNIYE PTIT

Aziz, Rutkay
YER DEMIR, GOK BAKIR

Azmi, Shabana
ANJUMAN

Azzolina, Michael
ROBOT HOLOCAUST

B. Jr., Jimi
TOUGH COP

Baal, Karin
DANN IST NICHTS MEHR WIE VORHER

Babbar, Raj
INSANIYAT KE DUSHMAN
JHOOTHI

Babe, Fabienne
DOLCE ASSENZA

Babendure, Jeremy
RAISING ARIZONA

Babu, Sarat
SAMSARAM OKA CHADARANGAM

Babu, Sobhan
KALYANA THAMBULAM
UMMADI MOGUDU

Bacarella, Mike
UNTOUCHABLES, THE

Bache, Elizabeth A.
HIDING OUT

Bachelder, John
DEADTIME STORIES

Bacher, Rick
TIME FOR DYING, A

Backer, Brian
POLICE ACADEMY 4: CITIZENS ON PATROL

Bacon, Kevin
PLANES, TRAINS AND AUTOMOBILES
WHITE WATER SUMMER

Bacquier, Gabriel
MANON OF THE SPRING

Bacri, Jean-Pierre
LETE EN PENTE DOUCE

Badalato, Billy
WEEDS

Bade, Colleen
UNTOUCHABLES, THE

Bademsoy, Mehmet
SIERRA LEONE

Bader, Bill
GOOD WIFE, THE

Badila, John
BROADCAST NEWS

Badiola, Klara
EL AMOR DE AHORA

Badreddine, Majda
ABBES

Baena, Begona
A LOS CUATRO VIENTOS

Baes, Steve
LES MENDIANTS

Baez, Claudio
HOTEL COLONIAL
NARCOTERROR

Bagala, Katrin
SEREBRYANAYA PRYAZHA KAROLINY

Bagdasarian, Ross
CHIPMUNK ADVENTURE, THE

Bagdasaryan, Narine
PESN PROSHEDSHIKH DNEY

Bagdonas, Vladas
O ROZVRASHCHENII ZABYT

Baggett, Ken
I WAS A TEENAGE ZOMBIE

Baghboudarian, Vasag
FAMILY VIEWING

Baigent, Harold
SLATE, WYN & ME

Bailey, Bill
ISHTAR

Bailey, Bunty
DOLLS

Bailey, David
WINNERS TAKE ALL

Bailey, Donna
STREET SMART

Bailey, Frederick
EQUALIZER 2000

Bailey, G.W.
BURGLAR
MANNEQUIN
POLICE ACADEMY 4: CITIZENS ON PATROL

Bailey, Jim
PENITENTIARY III

Bailey, John
PERSONAL SERVICES

Bailey, Philip
FULL METAL JACKET

Bailey, Robin
JANE AND THE LOST CITY

Bailey, Rosalind
INDIAN SUMMER

Bailey, Sharon
STRAIGHT TO HELL

Baillargeon, Paule
IVE HEARD THE MERMAIDS SINGING

Baio, Scott
I LOVE NEW YORK

Baird, Amanda
DEAD, THE

Baird, Jeanne
NIGHTFORCE

Baird, Roxanne
OPEN HOUSE

Baisho, Chieko
FINAL TAKE: THE GOLDEN AGE OF MOVIES
TORA-SAN'S BLUEBIRD FANTASY

Baisho, Mitsuko
ZEGEN

Baisyo, Mitsuko
SURE DEATH 4

Bajic, Rados
NA PUTA ZA KATANGU

Bajramovic, Saban
ANDJEO CUVAR

Bakaba, Sidiki
FACES OF WOMEN

Baker, Benny
MONSTER IN THE CLOSET

Baker, Carroll
IRONWEED

Baker, Cheryl
LETHAL WEAPON

Baker, Dylan
PLANES, TRAINS AND AUTOMOBILES

Baker, Frank
ARIA
HELLRAISER

Baker, George
OUT OF ORDER

Baker, Jamie
MALIBU BIKINI SHOP, THE

Baker, Jill
HOPE AND GLORY

Baker, Joe Don
KILLING TIME, THE
LEONARD PART 6
LIVING DAYLIGHTS, THE

Baker, Justice Eric
CUSTODY

Baker, Kathy
STREET SMART

Baker, Kelly
SLAUGHTER HIGH

Baker, Kenny
SLEEPING BEAUTY

Baker, Kirsten
WEEDS

Baker, Lee Ann
PSYCHOS IN LOVE
NECROPOLIS
MUTANT HUNT

Baker, Lesley
SLATE, WYN & ME

Baker, Nat
ANGUSTIA

Baker, Pamela
BLOODY WEDNESDAY

Baker, Penny
MILLION DOLLAR MYSTERY

Baker, Ray
STACKING

Baker, Ruby
FRIENDSHIP'S DEATH
HIGH SEASON

Baker, Scott Thompson
OPEN HOUSE

Bakhshai, Shapoor
MANUSCRIPTS

Bakocevic, Nebojsa
HEY BABU RIBA

Bakri, Muhamad
DEATH BEFORE DISHONOR

Balabanov, Sergey
O ROZVRASHCHENII ZABYT

Balacek, Dana
NECROPOLIS

Balague, Carmen
CALE

Balaguer, Asuncion
EL AMOR DE AHORA

Balaj, Savita
PRATIGHAAT

Balakrishna
ALLARI KRISHNAYA
BHARGAVA RAMUDU

Balamir, Hakan
DILAN

Balandis, Saulus
MOYA MALENKAYA ZHENA

Balasis, Jorgos
VERSTECKTE LIEBE

Balaski, Belinda
AMAZON WOMEN ON THE MOON

Balaw, Sebastiano
IO E MIA SORELLA

Balazsovits, Lajos
SZORNYEK EVADJA

Balbuena, Jose
A LOS CUATRO VIENTOS

Balderson, Robert
LIKE FATHER, LIKE SON

Baldinova, Elvira
POHADKA O MALICKOVI

Baldoni, Samuel V.
BEST SELLER

Balducci, Alessandro
DOLCE ASSENZA

Baldwin, Adam
FULL METAL JACKET

Baldwin, Alec
FOREVER, LULU

Baldwin, Judy
TALKING WALLS

Baldwin, Karen
WHO'S THAT GIRL

Bale, Christian
EMPIRE OF THE SUN
MIO, MOY MIO

Balfa, Dewey
BIG EASY, THE

Balfour, Noelle
AMAZONS

Balgobin, Jennifer
STRAIGHT TO HELL

Baliani, Mark
NIGHTFORCE

Balint, Andras
SZORNYEK EVADJA

Balkay, Geza
HOL VOLT, HOL NEM VOLT
ZUHANAS KOZBEN

Ball, Charlotte
WISH YOU WERE HERE

Ball, Vincent
YEAR MY VOICE BROKE, THE

Ballard, J.G.
EMPIRE OF THE SUN

Ballerio, Antonio
VIA MONTENAPOLEONE

Ballesteros, Sandra
MISS MARY

Balsam, Martin
P.I. PRIVATE INVESTIGATIONS

Balsam, Talia
IN THE MOOD
KINDRED, THE
P.I. PRIVATE INVESTIGATIONS
SUPERNATURALS, THE

Balson, Allison
BEST SELLER

Balzaretti, Jorge
VIAJE AL PARAISO

Balzer, Ursula
BLUE MONKEY

Bamford, Simon
HELLRAISER

Bamman, Gerry
HIDING OUT
SECRET OF MY SUCCESS, THE

Banck, Christer
GIRL, THE

Bancroft, Anne
EIGHTY FOUR CHARING CROSS ROAD

Bancroft, Bradford
ALLNIGHTER, THE
SUPERNATURALS, THE

Bandel, Murray
ANGEL HEART

Banderas, Antonio
ASI COMO HABIAN SIDO
LAW OF DESIRE

Bandini, Armando
UNA CASA IN BILICO

Bandoni, Michael
IN THE MOOD

Banegas, Cristina
SENTIMIENTOS: MIRTA DE LINIERS A ESTAMBUL
SINFIN, LA MUERTA NO ES NINGUNA SOLUCION

Banfi, Lino
BELLIFRESCHI
MISSIONE EROICA
ROBA DA RICCHI

Banfi, Rosanna
BELLIFRESCHI
LA TRASGRESSIONE

Banier, Francois-Marie
QUATRE AVENTURES DE REINETTE ET MIRABELLE

Banjac, Mira
ZIVOT RADNIKA

Bank, Ashley
MONSTER SQUAD, THE

Bank-Mikkelsen, Nis
PELLE EROVRAREN

Banks, Jonathan
COLD STEEL

Banks, Marilyn
ANGEL HEART

Banks, Randy
OVERKILL

Banks, Steven
DATE WITH AN ANGEL

Bankston, Scott
OUTING, THE

Bannen, Ian
HOPE AND GLORY

Banner, Steve
LES FOUS DE BASSAN

Bannister, Shulie
PERSONAL SERVICES

Banquells, Don Rafael
NI DE AQUI, NI DE ALLA

Bansagi, Ildiko
CSOK, ANYU

Bansal, Balwant
PRATIGHAAT

Banupriya.
ALLARI KRISHNAYA

Bao, Viet
KOORDINATY SMERTI

Baokar, Uttara
TAMAS

Baozong, Yang
LAST EMPEROR, THE

Baptist, Stacy
PARTY CAMP

Baptista, Cyro
WEEDS

Bar-Aba, Sholomo
DEADLINE

Bar-Ziv, Sharon
LATE SUMMER BLUES

Baracchi, Raffaella
BARBARIANS, THE

Baranov, Vyacheslav
RAZMAKH KRYLIEV
STARAYA AZBUKA

Baranski, Christine
PICK-UP ARTIST, THE

Baratta, Giorgio
DER TOD DES EMPEDOKLES

Baratta, Martina
DER TOD DES EMPEDOKLES

Baratta, Vladimir
DER TOD DES EMPEDOKLES

Barba, Vana
VIOS KE POLITIA

Barbareschi, Luca
TERESA
VIA MONTENAPOLEONE

Barbeau, Adrienne
OPEN HOUSE

Barbee, Victor
DANCERS

Barbelivien, Christine
ATTENTION BANDITS

Barber, Frances
PRICK UP YOUR EARS
SAMMY AND ROSIE GET LAID

Barber, Gillian
STEPFATHER, THE

Barber, Nigel
HAPPY HOUR

Barberi, Katie
GARBAGE PAIL KIDS MOVIE, THE

Barberini, Urbano
OPERA

Barbero, Aldo
SINFIN, LA MUERTA NO ES NINGUNA SOLUCION

Barberto, Luis
CARA DE ACELGA

Barbetti, Cesare
DA NNUNZIO

Barbieri, Andrea
EL ANO DEL CONEJO

Barbini, Alexander
UTOLSO KEZIRAT

Barbour, Thomas
SUSPECT

Barbuk, Gennady
ZNAK BEDY

Barcanic, Steve
GARDENS OF STONE

Barchuk, Sergei
TAYNAYA PROGULKA

Barclay, Caroline
ROXANNE

Barclay, Clare
CONCRETE ANGELS

Barco, Patxi
A LOS CUATRO VIENTOS

Bardhal, Maria
LA RULETERA

Bardini, Alexander
AZ UTOLSOKEZIRAT

Bardon, John
EIGHTY FOUR CHARING CROSS ROAD

Barea, Ramon
A LOS CUATRO VIENTOS

Baret, Dora
SOFIA

Barjac, Sophie
LEVY ET GOLIATH

Barker, Charlotte
WISH YOU WERE HERE

Barker, Collette
COMRADES

Barker, Rick
WALKER

Barkin, Ellen
BIG EASY, THE
MADE IN HEAVEN
SIESTA

Barle, Gail
SPACEBALLS

Barling, Susan
CASSANDRA

Barlotti, Louis
FULL METAL JACKET

Barnabe, Arrigo
CIDADE OCULTA

Barnes, Carver
RAISING ARIZONA

Barnes, Gay
HELLRAISER

Barnes, Jonathan
DIRTY DANCING

Barnes, Sean Allen
PRINCIPAL, THE

Barnes, Susan
STRANDED

Barnes, Suzanne
HELLO AGAIN

Barnes-Hopkins, Barbara
HEARTS OF FIRE

Barnett, Eileen
TALKING WALLS

Baro, Amparo
CARA DE ACELGA

Baron, Bruce
LEGEND OF WISELY, THE

Baron, Geraldine
SOMEONE TO LOVE

Baron, Joan-Carroll
MONSTER SQUAD, THE

Baron, Joanne
SOMEONE TO WATCH OVER ME

Baron, Sandy
MISSION KILL

Barone, Anita
ROSARY MURDERS, THE

Baroni, Paolo
DARK EYES

Barr, Glen
THOU SHALT NOT KILL . . . EXCEPT

Barr, Jean-Marc
HOPE AND GLORY

Barr, Sharon
WALKER

Barra, Gianfranco
LA CODA DEL DIAVOLO

Barrado, Lupe
LAW OF DESIRE

Barragan, Ramon
GABY—A TRUE STORY

Barranto, Olga Marta
EULALIA

Barrault, Marie-Christine
MANUELA'S LOVES

Barrault, Veronique
MON BEL AMOUR, MA DECHIRURE

Barrera, Rene
MISSION KILL

Barret, Kate
WITCHES OF EASTWICK, THE

Barrett, Jamie
CLUB LIFE

Barrett, Ray
AS TIME GOES BY
FRENCHMAN'S FARM

Barrett, Robert
GOOD WIFE, THE

Barrett, Simon
BUSINESS AS USUAL

Barrett, Victoria
THREE KINDS OF HEAT

Barrette, Jacqueline
BACH AND BROCCOLI

Barrie, Barbara
REAL MEN

Barrientos, Marie
STREET SMART

Barrier, Maurice
CHARLIE DINGO

Barrile, Anthony
HAMBURGER HILL

Barringer, Lee
VIRGIN QUEEN OF ST. FRANCIS HIGH, THE

Barringer, Paul
MONSTER SQUAD, THE

Barron, Dana
DEATH WISH 4: THE CRACKDOWN

Barron, Robert
SUPERNATURALS, THE

Barry, B. Constance
ORPHANS

Barry, Bruce
GOOD WIFE, THE

Barry, Katie
MISSION KILL

Barry, Matthew
NO WAY OUT

Barry, Neill
FATAL BEAUTY
HEAT
O. C. AND STIGGS

Barry, Prudence
SUSPECT

Barry, Raymond J.
THREE FOR THE ROAD

Barry, Tony
INITIATION
SURFER, THE

Barrymore, Deborah
LIONHEART

Barsack, Yves
WOLF AT THE DOOR, THE

Barsi, Judith
JAWS: THE REVENGE
SLAMDANCE

Bartel, Joanna
KOMEDIANCI Z WCZORAJSZEJ ULICY

Bartel, Paul
AMAZON WOMEN ON THE MOON
MUNCHIES

Bartell, J.
STRIPPED TO KILL

Barth, Isolde
CRAZY BOYS

Barth, Karen
TIN MEN

Bartholomew, Ian
PRAYER FOR THE DYING, A

Bartis, Ricardo
SENTIMIENTOS: MIRTA DE LINIERS A ESTAMBUL

Bartlett, Calvin
DUDES

Bartlett, Devin
BEVERLY HILLS COP II

Bartlett, Lisbeth
SUSPECT

Bartoli, Luciano
MORO AFFAIR, THE
PROFUMO

Bartolo, Bart
TALKING WALLS

Barty, Billy
MASTERS OF THE UNIVERSE
OFF THE MARK
RUMPELSTILTSKIN
SNOW WHITE

Baruch, Rami
HA INSTALATOR

Baryshnikov, Mikhail
DANCERS

Barzaghi, Rashad
PARTY CAMP

Basaraba, Gary
WHO'S THAT GIRL

Basic, Relja
HEY BABU RIBA

Basilashvili, Oleg
KURIER

Basinger, Kim
BLIND DATE
NADINE

Basler, Marianne
LE BEAUF
LES NOCES BARBARES
TANT QU'IL AURA DES FEMMES

Basouri, Tavyeti
ONIRO ARISTERIS NICHTAS

Basov, Vladimir
CHUZHIE ZDES NE KHODYAT
SON V RUKU, ILI CHEMODON

Basque Province
A LOS CUATRO VIENTOS

Bass, Amy C.
WEEDS

Bass, Bobby
SQUEEZE, THE

Bassett, Linda
WAITING FOR THE MOON

Bassili, Father
HIGH SEASON

Bassin, Roberta
BARFLY

Basson, Limpie
HOSTAGE

Bastel, Vickie
VIDEO DEAD, THE

Basti, Juli
LAURA

Bastianelli, Laura
IN THE MOOD

Bastiani, Billy
SALVATION!

Bastianoni, Giancarlo
ALADDIN

Bastien, Fanny
POUSSIERE D'ANGE
WOLF AT THE DOOR, THE

Batalov, Alexey
WEEKEND

Batalov, Alexi
ZONTIK DLYA NOVOBRACHNYKH

Batanides, Arthur
POLICE ACADEMY 4: CITIZENS ON PATROL

Bate, Natalie
GROUND ZERO

Bateman, Jason
TEEN WOLF TOO

Bateman, Stephen
COMRADES

Bates, Alan
PRAYER FOR THE DYING, A

Bates, Big Bull
STEELE JUSTICE

Bates, Jo Anne
BLUE MONKEY

Bates, Kathy
SUMMER HEAT

Bates, Paul
HOT PURSUIT

Bathurst, Robert
WHOOPS APOCALYPSE

Batiwala, Roy
OPPOSING FORCE

Battaglia, Guillermo
MISS MARY
SENTIMIENTOS: MIRTA DE LINIERS A ESTAMBUL

Batten, Paul
STEPFATHER, THE

Battersby, Julian
WHISTLE BLOWER, THE

Bauchau, Patrick
ACCROCHE-COEUR
ARCHANGELOS TOU PATHOUS
BALADA DA PRAIA DOS CAES

CROSS
FAMILY BUSINESS
FRIENDSHIP'S DEATH
LA PLAYA DE LOS PERROS
Bauer, Belinda
ROSARY MURDERS, THE
Bauer, Michelle
OVERKILL
Bauer, Richard
SICILIAN, THE
Baugham, Jonas
NICE GIRLS DON'T EXPLODE
Baumann, Brent
BIRDS OF PREY
Baumgartner, Monika
CHINESE ARE COMING, THE
Bausili, Andrew
NECROPOLIS
Bautista, Aurora
DIVINAS PALABRAS
Baxter, Charlie
SUMMER HEAT
Baxter, Trevor
INDIAN SUMMER
Bayer, Leonid
MASSACRE IN DINOSAUR VALLEY
Bazaka, Themis
APOUSIES
Bazilskaia, L.
KOROTKIE VSTRECHI
Bea
CAPRICCIO
Beach, Michael
SUSPECT
Beach, Reb
HEARTS OF FIRE
Beal, Cindy
SLAVE GIRLS FROM BEYOND INFINITY
Bean, Orson
INNERSPACE
Beano
DEATHROW GAMESHOW
Beanz, Gillie
STABILIZER, THE
Beard, David
EAT THE RICH
Beart, Emmanuelle
DATE WITH AN ANGEL
MANON OF THE SPRING
Beasley, Darrel
ANGEL HEART
Beasley, Mitch
BIG SHOTS
Beasley, Stephen
ANGEL HEART
Beasor, Terrence
MONSTER IN THE CLOSET
Beata Tyszkiewicz
W STARYM DWORKU
Beatheala, Robert
MANKILLERS
Beato, Eloy
A LOS CUATRO VIENTOS
Beaton, Ian
STREET SMART
Beattie, Bob
OVER THE TOP
Beatty, Ned
BIG EASY, THE
FOURTH PROTOCOL, THE
TROUBLE WITH SPIES, THE
Beatty, Warren
ISHTAR
Beauchamp, Steve
ADVENTURE OF THE ACTION HUNTERS
Beaumont, Debra
SLEEP WELL, MY LOVE
Beaune, Michel
LE SOLITAIRE
Bebel, Andrea
BIG SHOTS
Beck, Alan
MORGAN STEWART'S COMING HOME
Beck, Billy
NEAR DARK
Beck, Bonnie
WILD THING
Beck, Jackson
RADIO DAYS
Beck, Michael
KILLER WORKOUT
Becker, Desiree
GOOD MORNING BABYLON
Beckford, Ruth
PRINCIPAL, THE
Beckhaus, Friedrich
WANNSEE CONFERENCE, THE
Beckmann, Bettina
LADY OF THE CAMELIAS
Beddows, John
FULL METAL JACKET
Bedeir, Ahmed
AL-TAUQ WAL-ISWIRA
Bedelia, Bonnie
STRANGER, THE
Bedi, Kabir
FORTY DAYS OF MUSA DAGH
Bednarski, Robert
WILD THING
Bedos, Guy
IL EST GENIAL PAPY!
Bee, Joseph
BEAUTY AND THE BEAST
Bee, Kenny
HAPPY BIGAMIST
Beech, Paul
WHOOPS APOCALYPSE
Beecroft, David
CREEPSHOW 2
Beer, Daniel
CREEPSHOW 2
Beers, Francine
THREE MEN AND A BABY
Beeson, Lana
PINOCCHIO AND THE EMPEROR OF THE NIGHT
Begalishvili, Baadur
CHEGEMSKIY DETEKTIV
Beggs, Hagan
HOME IS WHERE THE HART IS
Begley, Ed
AMAZON WOMEN ON THE MOON
Begoli, Istref
ZIVOT RADNIKA
Begovic, Ena
KRALJEVA ZAVRSNICA
Behar, Joy
HIDING OUT
Behean, Katy
COMRADES
Behets, Briony
CASSANDRA
Behzadpour, Behzad
PEDDLER, THE
Bekbulatov, Aleukhan
ZNAY NASHIKH
Bekker, Allard
EEN MAAND LATER
Belanger, George
GABY—A TRUE STORY
WALKER
Belanger, Guy
MORNING MAN, THE
Belatti, Gustavo
EL DUENO DEL SOL
Belen, Ana
DIVINAS PALABRAS
LA CASA DE BERNARDA ALBA
Belginer, Haluk
ISHTAR
Beliard, Florence
LOVE IS A DOG FROM HELL
Belisle, Raymond
KEEPING TRACK
Bell, Danny
NO DEAD HEROES
Bell, Douglas
VIDEO DEAD, THE
Bell, Francis
BUSHFIRE MOON
Bell, Marshall
NO WAY OUT
Bell, Peter
NO WAY OUT
Bell, Robert
GARBAGE PAIL KIDS MOVIE, THE
Bell, Tom
WISH YOU WERE HERE
Bell, Vicki
NECROPOLIS
Bellamy, Diana
BLIND DATE
OUTRAGEOUS FORTUNE
STRIPPED TO KILL
Bellamy, Ralph
AMAZON WOMEN ON THE MOON
DISORDERLIES
Bellazecca, Pasquale
BARBARIANS, THE
Belle, Annie
LA CROCE DALLE SETTE PIETRE
Belli, Agostina
SOLDATI: 365 GIORNI ALL' ALBA
UNA DONNA DA SCOPRIRE
Belliawski, A.
SASHSHENNYI FONAR
Belliveau, Cynthia
GOOFBALLS
Belliveau Sf2, Cynthia
BLUE MONKEY
Bellman, Joe
P.K. & THE KID
Bello, Jose Manuel
LAW OF DESIRE
Belmondo, Jean-Paul
LE SOLITAIRE
Belmont, Penny
TUESDAY WEDNESDAY
Belmonte, Lara
CRYSTAL HEART
Belogurova, Larisa
PROSHAL ZELEN LETA
Beltran, Robert
GABY—A TRUE STORY
SLAMDANCE
Beltrao, Andrea
COLOR OF DESTINY, THE
Belushi, James
PRINCIPAL, THE
REAL MEN
Belyaeva, Galina
CHYORNAYA STRELA
GEROY YEYOROMANA
Belyayev, Yury
CHUZHIE ZDES NE KHODYAT
Belyayeva, Galina
LERMONTOV
Belzer, Richard
FLICKS
Ben Badis, Zaira
UN AMOUR A PARIS
Ben Ze'ev, Dudu
LO SAM ZAYIN
Ben-Sira, Jacob
POET'S SILENCE, THE
Benair, Jonathon
BRAVE LITTLE TOASTER, THE
Benaron, Teri
GARBAGE PAIL KIDS MOVIE, THE
Benchley, Nathan
BROADCAST NEWS
Bencini, Ugo
GOOD MORNING BABYLON
Bendel, John
BELIEVERS, THE
Bendich, Nora
MAGDALENA VIRAGA
Benedek, Gyula
A SANTA DERVIS
Benedek, Peter
RAISING ARIZONA
Benedetto, Bertino
JEAN DE FLORETTE
Benfield, Derek
GIRL, THE
Benfield, John
WHOOPS APOCALYPSE
Bengel, Norma
COLOR OF DESTINY, THE
Bengell, Norma
FONTE DA SAUDADE
Benguigui, Jean
IL GIORNO PRIMA
Benitez, Manuel
MI NOMBRE ES GATILLO
Benjamin, Paul
NUTS

Benji
BENJI THE HUNTED
Benn, Patrick
FULL METAL JACKET
Benn, Susann
MILLION DOLLAR MYSTERY
Bennato, Serena
IL LUPO DI MARE
Bennet, Walter Allen
STREET SMART
Bennett, Alan
LITTLE DORRIT
Bennett, Charles
MORGAN STEWART'S COMING HOME
Bennett, Chuck
PROJECT X
Bennett, Elizabeth
BABY BOOM
Bennett, Hywel
DEADLINE
Bennett, Joel
AMERICAN DRIVE-IN
Bennett, Mac
ERNEST GOES TO CAMP
Bennett, Michelle
DOGS IN SPACE
Bennett, Norman
NADINE
Bennett, Perk
MORGAN STEWART'S COMING HOME
Bennett, Reggie
OVER THE TOP
Bennett, Roberta
RADIO DAYS
Benoit, Ludwik
PAN SAMOCHODZIK I NIESAMOWITY DWOR
Benoit, Mariusz
LE JEUNE MAGICIEN
Bensen, Carl
THEY STILL CALL ME BRUCE
Benskin, Tyrone
WILD THING
Benson, Chris
BIG TOWN, THE
Benson, Dale
OVER THE TOP
Benson, David
NECROPOLIS
Benson, Deborah
GHOST FEVER
Benson, Gordon
HAPPY HOUR
Benson, Laura
HOTEL DE FRANCE
Benson, Lynnea
BLOOD SISTERS
I WAS A TEENAGE ZOMBIE
Benson, Mark
CONCRETE ANGELS
Benson III, Robert G.
ERNEST GOES TO CAMP
Bentivoglio, Fabrizio
REGINA
VIA MONTENAPOLEONE
Bentley, Gary
SUPERNATURALS, THE
Bentley, Jim
FATAL BEAUTY
SPACE RACE
Bently, Rowena
EAT THE RICH
Bentzen, Jayne
NIGHTMARE AT SHADOW WOODS
Benvenuti, Alessandro
SOLDATI: 365 GIORNI ALL' ALBA
Benya, Jonathan
BROADCAST NEWS
Benz, Donna Kei
MOON IN SCORPIO
Benzali, Daniel
WHOOPS APOCALYPSE
Beramen, Ramon
GHOST FEVER
Berardi, Joe
VALET GIRLS
Beraza, Enrique
WALKER
Berbert, Marcel
JEAN DE FLORETTE
Berden, Charlotte
MASCARA
Berencsi, Attila
HOTREAL
Berenett, Lars-Erik
MALARPIRATER
Berenger, Tom
SOMEONE TO WATCH OVER ME
Berenguer, Ana Helena
IN THE MOOD
Berenson, Marisa
VIA MONTENAPOLEONE
Berg, Birte
DEATH STONE
Berg, Eva Jean
TIN MEN
Berg, Matraca
MADE IN HEAVEN
Bergen, Polly
MAKING MR.RIGHT
Berger, Belle
RADIO DAYS
Berger, Jacob
LA VALLEE FANTOME
Berger, Senta
DE FLYGANDE DJAVLARNA
Berger, William
DISTANT LIGHTS
IL GIORNO PRIMA
TAROT
Berger, Wolfram
ZABOU
Bergeron, Loys T.
ANGEL HEART
Berggren, Arthur
MONSTER IN THE CLOSET
Berglass, Ron
ISHTAR
Berglund, Joanie
PRETTY SMART
Bergman, Boris
LE BEAUF
Bergman, Harold
WHOOPS APOCALYPSE
Bergman, Mats
JIM OCH PIRATERNA BLOM
Bergman, Sandahl
PROGRAMMED TO KILL
Bergman, Sunny
EEN MAAND LATER
Bergman, Tijmen
EEN MAAND LATER
Bergner, Marcus
DOGS IN SPACE
Bergner, Patrik
NIONDE KOMPANIET
Bergonzi, Carlo
ARIA
Bergstrom, Jonas
FADERN, SONEN OCH DEN HELIGE ANDE
Bergstrom, Linda
MORE ABOUT THE CHILDREN OF BULLERBY VILLAGE
Bergstrom, Pirjo
SNOW QUEEN, THE
Beri, Shandra
ROXANNE
Berkeley, Xander
STRAIGHT TO HELL
WALKER
Berkeley, Xander R.
OMEGA SYNDROME
Berlanger, Marilyn
LADY OF THE CAMELIAS
Berle, Gail
REAL MEN
Berleand, Francois
AU REVOIR, LES ENFANTS
LES MOIS D'AVRIL SONT MEURTRIERS
Berlin-Irving, Susan
EMPEROR'S NEW CLOTHES, THE
Berlinger, Michael
DEADTIME STORIES
Berman, Caroline
KOLORMASK
Berman, David
SOMEONE TO WATCH OVER ME
Berman, Paul
RADIO DAYS
Berman, Susan
MAKING MR.RIGHT
Bermel, Patrick
LADIES OF THE LOTUS
Bermont, Pascal
ARIA
Bern, Thomas
DREAMANIAC
Bernadet, Renaud
LES MENDIANTS
Bernal, Agustin
EL ANSIA DE MATAR
Bernal, Rosenda
YERBA SANGRIENTE
Bernard, Crystal
SLUMBER PARTY MASSACRE II
Bernard, Ed
SURVIVAL GAME
Bernard, Jason
NO WAY OUT
Bernard, Philippe
FIRE AND ICE
Bernardo, Al
PRETTYKILL
Berne, Allan
O. C. AND STIGGS
Bernhardsson, Lena Pia
PELLE EROVRAREN
Bernini, Nanni
BARBARIANS, THE
Bernsen, Corbin
HELLO AGAIN
Bernstein, Steven
MUNCHIES
Bernusova, Lucia
CENA ODVAHY
Berry, Iris
BORDER RADIO
Berry, John
MAN IN LOVE, A
Berry, Richard
SPIRALE
Berry, Ron
EMPIRE STATE
Berry, Sarah
EVIL DEAD 2: DEAD BY DAWN
Berryman, Joe
NADINE
Berryman, Michael
BARBARIANS, THE
Berteloot, Jean Yves
EEN MAAND LATER
Bertenshaw, Michael
BELLMAN AND TRUE
Bertheau, Julien
FAMILY BUSINESS
Berthelot, Jean-Yves
UNE FLAMME DANS MON COEUR
Berthet, Francois
POISONS
Bertin, Roland
JENATSCH
Bertinelli, Valerie
NUMBER ONE WITH A BULLET
Bertini, Edouardo
LADY OF THE CAMELIAS
Bertish, Suzanne
HEARTS OF FIRE
Berto, Juliet
UN AMOUR A PARIS
Berton, Leon
LOVECHILD, THE
Bertrand, Jo
MASCARA
Berube, Jocelyn
LES FOUS DE BASSAN
Berumen, Ana
LA RAZA NUNCA PIERDE—HUELE A GAS
NOS REIMOS DE LA MIGRA
Berven, Oivind
FELDMANN CASE, THE
Berven, Oyvin
JOR
Bervoerts, Gene
LOVE IS A DOG FROM HELL
Berwick, Brad David
STRIPPED TO KILL
Besch, Bibi
DATE WITH AN ANGEL

WHO'S THAT GIRL

Besnehard, Dominique
LA VIE DISSOLUE DE GERARD FLOQUE
LETE EN PENTE DOUCE

Best, Kevin
MANKILLERS

Best, Oscar
ANGEL HEART

Best, Sheila
MANKILLERS

Bestvater, Thomas
MEIER

Beswicke, Martine
CYCLONE
OFFSPRING, THE

Bette, Francoise
FAMILY BUSINESS

Better, Debbie
MADE IN ARGENTINA

Betti, Laura
CARAMELLE DA UNO SCONOSCIUTO
JENATSCH
NOYADE INTERDITE

Betti, Paulo
BESAME MUCHO
FONTE DA SAUDADE

Bettman, Gil
CRYSTAL HEART

Bettmann, Gary
CYCLONE

Betton, Marc
JEAN DE FLORETTE
MANON OF THE SPRING

Bevis, Leslie
SPACEBALLS
SQUEEZE, THE

Beyer, Lene
SOMMER

Beyer, Troy
DISORDERLIES

Bezeredy, Zoltan
C. K. DEZERTERZY

Bhandari, Mohan
PRATIGHAAT

Bhang, Yong
OVERKILL

Bhanuchander
LAWYER SUHASINI
ROWDY POLICE

Bhanumathi, P.
MANDALADHEESUDU

Bhanupriya
BHARGAVA RAMUDU

Bharati, Raj
PRATIGHAAT

Bhasker
DRAGON'S FOOD

Bhimraj
PRATIGHAAT

Bi De, Yan
BUDDHA'S LOCK

Biagini, Isabella
CAPRICCIO

Biagioni, Dante
MORO AFFAIR, THE

Biana
UNE FLAMME DANS MON COEUR

Bianca, Dominic
MOVING TARGETS

Bianchi, Marta
MADE IN ARGENTINA

Bianchi, Stephen
VIDEO DEAD, THE

Bianco, Tommaso
QUEL RAGAZZO DELLA CURVA "B"

Biao, Wang
LAST EMPEROR, THE

Biao, Yuen
EASTERN CONDORS

Bibi, Krubwa
LA VIE EST BELLE

Bichir, Demian
VIAJE AL PARAISO

Bickerstaff, David
RUNNING FROM THE GUNS

Bicknell, Andrew
HOPE AND GLORY

Bideau, Jean-Luc
LES OREILLES ENTRE LES DENTS

Bidlas, Jan
WOLF'S HOLE

Biel, Dick
FIREHOUSE

Bierbichler, Josef
TRIUMPH DE GERECHTEN

Bieri, Ramon
SICILIAN, THE

Biert, Otto
JENATSCH

Bifano, Stefania
LA MONACA DIMONZA

Big Vanity Sisters
FRANCESCA

Big Yank
P.I. PRIVATE INVESTIGATIONS

Biggins, Jonathon
THOSE DEAR DEPARTED

Bijnori, Anand
PRATIGHAAT

Bijou, Marcel
CRAZY BOYS

Biker Team Manager
WINNERS TAKE ALL

Bikr, Noureddine
ABBES

Bill, Stephen
PRICK UP YOUR EARS

Bill, Tony
LESS THAN ZERO

Billery, Raoul
LA MOINE ET LA SORCIERE
LE GRAND CHEMIN
SI LE SOLEIL NE REVENAIT PAS

Billings, Earl
STAKEOUT

Billings, Josh
BROADCAST NEWS
TIN MEN

Billingsley, Pat
UNTOUCHABLES, THE

Billingsley, Peter
RUSSKIES

Billotto, Edna
JAWS: THE REVENGE

Billquist, Carl
JIM OCH PIRATERNA BLOM

Billy Crystal
PRINCESS BRIDE, THE

Bilson, David L.
ASSASSINATION

Bilton, Michael
FOURTH PROTOCOL, THE

Binder, Aaron
EMANON

Binford, Stephanie
SQUARE DANCE

Bing, Jorgen
JAG ELSKER DIG

Bingham, Bill
SHADEY

Bini, Sergio
QUARTIERE

Binoche, Juliette
BAD BLOOD

Biolos, Leigh
HOWLING III, THE

Birch, Peter
ARIA

Bird, Billie
POLICE ACADEMY 4: CITIZENS ON PATROL

Birdsall, Jesse
WISH YOU WERE HERE

Birdsall, Jessie
SHADEY

Birdsong, Lori
MUNCHIES

Birgan, Louise
YEAR MY VOICE BROKE, THE

Birger, Steve W.
PRINCIPAL, THE

Birk, Raye
BURGLAR
THROW MOMMA FROM THE TRAIN

Birkin, Jane
COMEDY!
SOIGNE TA DROITE

Birmingham, Gil
HOUSE TWO: THE SECOND STORY

Birney, David
PRETTYKILL

Biscione, Thomas
BLOOD SISTERS

Bishoff, Katya
DEATH BEFORE DISHONOR

Bishop, Anthony
SOMEONE TO WATCH OVER ME

Bishop, Ed
TURNAROUND
WHOOPS APOCALYPSE

Bishop, Kelly
DIRTY DANCING

Bishop, Kirsten
BIG TOWN, THE

Bishop, Rummy
POLICE ACADEMY 4: CITIZENS ON PATROL

Bishop, Stephen
SOMEONE TO LOVE

Bisio, Claudio
A FIOR DI PELLE

Bisquert, Patxi
EL AMOR DE AHORA

Bissell, Cathryn
RED DESERT PENITENTIARY

Bisset, Jacqueline
HIGH SEASON

Bisson, Jean-Pierre
LASSOCIATION DES MALFAITEURS
LES MOIS D'AVRIL SONT MEURTRIERS

Bista, Henryk
MIEDZY USTAMI A BRZEGIEM PUCHARU
WIERNA RZEKA
ZYCIE WEWNETRZNE

Bityukova, Olga
GRUBAYA POSADKA

Biu, Tung
SWORN BROTHERS

Bixler, Denise
EVIL DEAD 2: DEAD BY DAWN

Bjelac, Pedrag
SLEEP WELL, MY LOVE
SLEEP WELL, MY LOVE

Bjelogrlic, Dragan
HEY BABU RIBA

Bjerrum, Anne Lise Hirsch
PELLE EROVRAREN

Bjoerling, Jussi
ARIA

Bjorling, Olle
GIRL, THE

Bjornsson, Helgi
SKYTTURNAR

Black, Alexandra
FRENCHMAN'S FARM

Black, Brent
DREAMANIAC

Black, Karen
HOSTAGE

Black, Larry
ERNEST GOES TO CAMP

Black, Laura
PURSUIT OF HAPPINESS, THE

Black, Sena Ayn
HOLLYWOOD SHUFFLE

Black, Shane
PREDATOR

Black, Stephen
HIGHER EDUCATION

Blackaman
NI DE AQUI, NI DE ALLA

Blackburn, Jane
PRICK UP YOUR EARS

Blacker, David
HEARTS OF FIRE

Blackie, Sandra
WILD THING

Blackman, Andrew
FRENCHMAN'S FARM

Blackoff, Edward
BEST SELLER

Blackschmidt, Jake
HOLLYWOOD SHUFFLE

Blackwell, Rex
THUNDER WARRIOR II

Blackwood, David
BEST SELLER

Blade, Richard
CRYSTAL HEART

Blades, Ruben
CRITICAL CONDITION
FATAL BEAUTY
Blaha, Josef
CHOBOTNICE Z II. PATRA
Blahova, Dasha
HOWLING III, THE
Blain, Gerard
POUSSIERE D'ANGE
Blair, Linda
NIGHTFORCE
Blair, Lisa
THREE MEN AND A BABY
Blair, Michelle
THREE MEN AND A BABY
Blair, Nicky
SUPERNATURALS, THE
Blais, Jaqueline
MORNING MAN, THE
Blaisdell, Deborah
WIMPS
Blaisdell, Nesbitt
SUMMER HEAT
Blaise, Louis
DRAGON'S FOOD
Blake, Darry Edward
MORNING MAN, THE
Blake, Jeanette
P.K. & THE KID
Blake, Jon
LIGHTHORSEMEN, THE
RUNNING FROM THE GUNS
Blake, Richard
RAISING ARIZONA
Blake, Sydney A.
RADIO DAYS
Blakely, D.L.
WHOOPS APOCALYPSE
Blakely, Susan
OVER THE TOP
Blakeman, Ben
HOUSE OF GAMES
Blakiston, Caroline
FOURTH PROTOCOL, THE
Blakley, Ronee
SOMEONE TO LOVE
STUDENT CONFIDENTIAL
Blalock, Vaune
BELIEVERS, THE
Blanc, Anne-Marie
CRIME OF HONOR
Blanc, Felicidad
CALE
Blanchard, Susan
PRINCE OF DARKNESS
Blanche, Roland
LE MIRACULE
Blanchet, Nicholas D.
BROADCAST NEWS
Blanco, Carlos
CRYSTAL HEART
Blanco, Eva
LA OVEJA NEGRA
Blanco, Mentxu
A LOS CUATRO VIENTOS
Blanco, Ramon
LO NEGRO DEL NEGRO
Blasco, Maite
LA GUERRA DE LOS LOCOS
Blasi, Silverio
CHRONICLE OF A DEATH FORETOLD
MORO AFFAIR, THE
Blat, Ricardo
ANJOS DO ARRABALDE
Blaylock, John
ROBOT HOLOCAUST
Blazquez, Luis
A LOS CUATRO VIENTOS
Blears, Lord James
NORTH SHORE
Blech, Hans-Christian
VICTORIA
Bledsoe, Doug
RETURN OF JOSEY WALES, THE
Bledsoe, Jerry
BIG BANG, THE
Bledsoe, Mike
RETURN OF JOSEY WALES, THE
Bledsoe, Ron
RETURN OF JOSEY WALES, THE
Bledsoe, Will
HOT CHILD IN THE CITY
Blee, Debra
MALIBU BIKINI SHOP, THE
Blefari, Rosario
EIN BLICK-UND DIE LIEBE BRICHT AUS
Blier, Bernard
I PICARI
SOTTO IL RISTORANTE CINESE
Blin, Gilbert
BEYOND THERAPY
Blind, Anne-Marja
OFELAS
Bliss, Caroline
LIVING DAYLIGHTS, THE
Bliss, Lucille
ASSASSINATION
Block, Andrew
TALKING WALLS
Block, Bill
HEARTS OF FIRE
Block, Oliver
RADIO DAYS
Blocker, Dirk
PRINCE OF DARKNESS
Bloem, Marion
EEN MAAND LATER
Blok, Peter
CAUGHT
Blommaert, Susan
FOREVER, LULU
Blood, John
WITCHES OF EASTWICK, THE
Bloom, Anne
TALKING WALLS
Bloom, Bernie
BIRDS OF PREY
Bloom, Claire
SAMMY AND ROSIE GET LAID
Bloom, Thomas
MOON IN SCORPIO
Bloomfield, Evan
LEADING EDGE, THE
Blore, Catherine
FATAL BEAUTY
Blosser, Dale R.
MORGAN STEWART'S COMING HOME
Blouin, Michael
GREAT LAND OF SMALL, THE
Blount, Lisa
NIGHTFLYERS
PRINCE OF DARKNESS
Blue, Sugar
ANGEL HEART
Blum, Ina
ANITA—DANCES OF VICE
Blum, Mark
BLIND DATE
Blum, Norma
VERA
Blum, Tina
SUMMER CAMP NIGHTMARE
Blumenfeld, Alan
TIN MEN
Blumhagen, Lothar
CASPAR DAVID FRIEDRICH
Blundell, Graeme
THOSE DEAR DEPARTED
YEAR MY VOICE BROKE, THE
Blundell, John
WHOOPS APOCALYPSE
Bluteau, Lothaire
LES FOUS DE BASSAN
Blutman, Marc
MORNING MAN, THE
Blythe, Robert
LOVECHILD, THE
WHOOPS APOCALYPSE
Blythe, Robin
DEATHROW GAMESHOW
Bo
SUMMER SCHOOL
Bo, Bo
YI LOU YI
Bo, Hu
CHINESE ARE COMING, THE
Boa, Bruce
FULL METAL JACKET
Boatman, Michael Patrick
HAMBURGER HILL
Bobkova, Jaroslava
DISCOPRIBEH
Bocharov, Eduard
POLEVAYA GVARDIA MOZZHUKHINA
Bochkarev, Vasily
POLEVAYA GVARDIA MOZZHUKHINA
Bochner, Hart
MAKING MR.RIGHT
Bochner, Lloyd
CRYSTAL HEART
Bock, Mitchell
SPACEBALLS
Bockmann, Gerd
WANNSEE CONFERENCE, THE
Bockner, Michael
PSYCHO GIRLS
Bodanza, Jim
OVERKILL
Boden, Leon
STADTRAND
Bodin III, E.J.
SQUARE DANCE
Bodker, Henrik
PELLE EROVRAREN
Bodnar, Erika
CSOK, ANYU
TISZTA AMERIKA
Boeke, James
KINDRED, THE
Boelsen, Jim
MALIBU BIKINI SHOP, THE
Boelsgaard, Berthe
STRIT OG STUMME
Boepple, Beatrice
STAKEOUT
Boer, Joost
EEN MAAND LATER
Boersma, Femke
DE RATELRAT
Boets, Patrick
MASCARA
Bogachev, Vyacheslav
YA TEBYA POMNYU
Bogadtke, Jen-Uwe
DER BARENHAUTER
Bogan, Sandra
FATAL BEAUTY
Bogatiriov, Yuri
DARK EYES
Bogdanski, Zbigniew
NAD NIEMNEM
Bogiaridis, Michalis
O PARADISSOS ANIGI ME ANTIKLIDI
Bogino, Diane
SOMETHING SPECIAL!
Bohan, Amber
HAPPY HOUR
Bohdalova, Jirina
CHOBOTNICE Z II. PATRA
Bohdan
DOGS IN SPACE
Bohm, Hark
F . . . ING FERNAND
LITTLE PROSECUTOR, THE
Bohm, Katharina
TAROT
Bohm, Marquard
LITTLE PROSECUTOR, THE
Bohrer, Corinne
CROSS MY HEART
POLICE ACADEMY 4: CITIZENS ON PATROL
Bohringer, Richard
AGENT TROUBLE
LE GRAND CHEMIN
Bois, Curt
DER HIMMEL UBER BERLIN
Boismery, Alain
LES OREILLES ENTRE LES DENTS
Boisson, Christine
DREAMERS
JENATSCH
LA MOINE ET LA SORCIERE
Bokar, Hal
LEONARD PART 6
Bokhari, Yousaf
ALIEN PREDATOR
Boland, Eamon
BUSINESS AS USUAL
Boldi, Massimo
MISSIONE EROICA

MONTECARLO GRAN CASINO
SCUOLA DI LADRI 2

Boldoghy, Borbala
DOKTOR MINORKA VIDOR NAGY NAPJA

Boldrin, Rolando
ELE, O BOTO

Boles, Eugene
WITCHES OF EASTWICK, THE

Bolkan, Edna
POLICIAS DE NARCOTICOS

Bolkvadze, Rusudan
PYAT NEVEST DO LYUBIMOY

Bollain, Felipe
LAS DOS ORILLAS

Bollain, Iciar
LAS DOS ORILLAS
MIENTRAS HAYA LUZ

Bollain, Marina
LAS DOS ORILLAS

Bollen, Jacqueline
FALSCH

Bolling, Tiffany
OPEN HOUSE

Bolt, Alan
WALKER

Bolt, Jenny
EMPIRE STATE

Boltnev, Andrei
I NIKTO NA SVETE
POEZDKI NA STAROM AVTOMOBILE

Bolton, Barbara
EMPIRE OF THE SUN

Bolton, Emily
EMPIRE STATE

Bolton, Steve
HEARTS OF FIRE

Bombaywalla, Rajesh
PRATIGHAAT

Bon, Noam
OVERKILL

Bonacci, Flavio
MEFISTO FUNK

Bonacelli, Paolo
DA NNUNZIO
RIMINI RIMINI

Bonacorsa, Francesca
ZOMBIE NIGHTMARE

Bonanno, Louis
SLAMMER GIRLS
WIMPS

Bonarota, Alessandra
CARAMELLE DA UNO SCONOSCIUTO

Bonchot, Rosita
CORRUPCION

Boncza, Tony
EMPIRE OF THE SUN

Bonczak, Jerzy
W STARYM DWORKU

Bond, Deanna
DOGS IN SPACE

Bond, Margery
O. C. AND STIGGS

Bond, Michael
AMAZING GRACE AND CHUCK

Bond, Raleigh
BLACK WIDOW

Bondarchuk, Natalia
LERMONTOV

Bondarchuk, Yelena
KARUSEL NA BAZARNOY PLOSHCHADI

Bones, Ken
BELLMAN AND TRUE

Bonet, Lisa
ANGEL HEART

Bonfanti, Marie-Luce
MASCARA

Bonham, Bill
LIVING ON TOKYO TIME

Bonham Carter, Helena
MAURICE

Boni, Chris
VAN PAEMEL FAMILY, THE

Bonilla, Socorro
EL HIJO DE PEDRO NAVAJAS

Bonin, Arturo
LOS DUENOS DEL SILENCIO
SENTIMIENTOS: MIRTA DE LINIERS A ESTAMBUL
SVART GRYNING

Bonitz, John
WEEDS

Bonke, Peter
JENATSCH

Bonnaffe, Jacques
O DESEJADO—LES MONTAGNES DE LA LUNE

Bonnaire, Sandrine
SOUS LE SOLEIL DE SATAN

Bonnel, Patrick
POUSSIERE D'ANGE

Bonner, Tony
LIGHTHORSEMEN, THE

Bonney, Teresa
STARLIGHT HOTEL

Bonnin, Hermann
LA SENYORA

Bonnin, J.C.
ZIMATAR

Bono, Cesar
LAS TRAIGO . . . MUERTAS
MAS VALE PAJARO EN MANO . . .

Bono, Sonny
DIRTY LAUNDRY

Bonomi, Ariel
EN EL NOMBRE DEL HIJO

Bonos, Gigi
RENEGADE, UN OSSO TROPPO DURO

Bontempo, Pietro
ADELMO

Bonvoisin, Berangere
GOOD MORNING BABYLON
LES EXPLOITS DUN JEUNE DON JUAN

Bonvoisin, Berengere
HOTEL DU PARADIS

Bonvoisin, Bertrand
BEYOND THERAPY

Booher, Deanna
DIRTY LAUNDRY
SPACEBALLS

Booker, Harry
BLUE MONKEY

Booker, Sephus
BIG SHOTS

Boom, Peter
DER TOD DES EMPEDOKLES

Boone, Randy
WILD PAIR, THE

Boone, Walker
BLUE MONKEY
NIGHTSTICK

Boorman, Charley
HOPE AND GLORY

Boorman, John
HOPE AND GLORY

Boorman, Katrine
HOPE AND GLORY

Booth, Connie
EIGHTY FOUR CHARING CROSS ROAD

Booth, James
MOON IN SCORPIO
PROGRAMMED TO KILL

Booth, Janie
PERSONAL SERVICES

Boothe, Powers
EXTREME PREJUDICE

Borchaca, Josephine
ANGUSTIA

Borchsenius, Hanne
KAMPEN OM DEN RODE KO

Borden, Lizzie
MANKILLERS

Bordighi, Al
EMANON

Boreham, Jan
SHADOWS OF THE PEACOCK

Borelli, Carla
O. C. AND STIGGS

Borghi, Cristiana
CARTOLINE ITALIANE

Borgia, Tony
ASSASSINATION

Boris Zaidenberg
OKHOTA NA DRAKONA

Borisov, Oleg
PO GLAVNOY ULITSE S ORKESTROM
PRORYV

Borkum, Shelley
CRY FREEDOM

Borowski, Jacek
BLIND CHANCE

Borras, Joan
MY GENERAL

Borrell, Paula
LA CASA DE BERNARDA ALBA

Borruel, Maria Luisa
LOS INVITADOS

Borst, Daniele
ARIA

Bosacki, Dean
CONCRETE ANGELS

Bosch, Daniel
GOOD MORNING BABYLON

Boschetti, Desiree
P.I. PRIVATE INVESTIGATIONS

Boschi, Giulia
NOTTE ITALIANA
SICILIAN, THE

Bosco, Philip
SUSPECT
THREE MEN AND A BABY

Boscoli, Tania
UM TREM PARA AS ESTRELAS

Bose, Lucia
CHRONICLE OF A DEATH FORETOLD

Bosisio, Liu
SUPERFANTOZZI

Boskovic, Tanja
UVEK SPREMNE ZENE

Bosley, Tom
MILLION DOLLAR MYSTERY
PINOCCHIO AND THE EMPEROR OF THE NIGHT

Bosschaert, Alisa
BELLMAN AND TRUE

Bosso, J.O.
ALIEN PREDATOR

Bossyvine, Stephan
LADY OF THE CAMELIAS

Bostwick, Joan
I WAS A TEENAGE ZOMBIE

Boswell, Glen
MOVING TARGETS

Botelli, Melina
ONIRO ARISTERIS NICHTAS

Botero, Lina
CHRONICLE OF A DEATH FORETOLD

Botes, Michelle
AMERICAN NINJA 2: THE CONFRONTATION

Both, Bela
AZ UTOLSOKEZIRAT

Botha, At
HOSTAGE

Bothun, Steven
AMAZING GRACE AND CHUCK

Botinis, Panos
IKONA ENOS MYTHIKOU PROSOPOU

Botosso, Claudio
DEVIL IN THE FLESH
SOLDATI: 365 GIORNI ALL' ALBA
SOTTO IL RISTORANTE CINESE

Botsvadze, Zejnab
REPENTANCE

Bottcher, Mette
LADY OF THE CAMELIAS

Botti, Chris
HEARTS OF FIRE

Bottoms, Joseph
OPEN HOUSE

Bottoms, Sam
GARDENS OF STONE
HUNTER'S BLOOD

Bottoms, Timothy
MIO, MOY MIO

Bouchard, Jean
MANON OF THE SPRING

Boucher, Brigitte
MORNING MAN, THE

Boucher, Philip
ALLAN QUATERMAIN AND THE LOST CITY OF GOLD

Boucher, Steve
FULL METAL JACKET

Boudet, Jacques
BUISSON ARDENT
WAITING FOR THE MOON

Boudov, Jeff
ESCAPES

Bouillaud, Jean Claude
A LOS CUATRO VIENTOS

Bouillon, Didier
MASCARA

Bouise, Jean
JENATSCH

LETE DERNIER A TANGER
LETE EN PENTE DOUCE
SPIRALE

Boujenah, Michel
LEVY ET GOLIATH

Boukhanef, Kader
MISS MONA

Bouquet, Carole
JENATSCH

Bouquet, Michel
BABETTE'S GASTEBUD

Bourgine, Elizabeth
NOYADE INTERDITE

Bouriguine, Y.
INTERVENTSIA

Bourliat, Jean-Claude
SOUS LE SOLEIL DE SATAN

Bourne, Lindsay
STEPFATHER, THE

Bourrel, Marc
HOME IS WHERE THE HART IS

Boushel, Joy
KEEPING TRACK

Bouteloup, Marie
QUATRE AVENTURES DE REINETTE ET MIRABELLE

Boutsikaris, Dennis
BATTERIES NOT INCLUDED

Boutte, Lillian
ANGEL HEART

Bouvet, Jean-Christophe
SOUS LE SOLEIL DE SATAN

Bova, Joseph
MORGAN STEWART'S COMING HOME

Bovasso, Julie
MOONSTRUCK

Bovtun, Sasha
KAZHDYY OKHOTNIK ZHELAET ZNAT

Bow, Tui
FRENCHMAN'S FARM

Bowden, Erin
EXTREME PREJUDICE

Bowe, David
BACK TO THE BEACH

Bowe, John
LIVING DAYLIGHTS, THE

Bowe, Kurt
DER JUNGE MIT DEM GROSSEN SCHWARZEN HUND

Bowen, Michael
AMAZING GRACE AND CHUCK
LESS THAN ZERO

Bowen, Roger
MORGAN STEWART'S COMING HOME

Bowen, Victor
STREET SMART

Bowens, Malick
BELIEVERS, THE

Bower, Ingrid
CONCRETE ANGELS

Bower, Mike
THUNDER WARRIOR II

Bower, Sharon
HELLRAISER

Bower, Tom
BEVERLY HILLS COP II
RIVER'S EDGE

Bowers, Randall
BLIND DATE

Bowie, Angie
EAT THE RICH

Bowie, Sandra
SUSPECT

Bowleg, Charles
JAWS: THE REVENGE

Bowler, Norman
RENEGADE, UN OSSO TROPPO DURO
SLEEP WELL, MY LOVE

Bowman, Gail
LETHAL WEAPON

Bowman, Jamie
HOPE AND GLORY

Bowman, John
SECRET OF MY SUCCESS, THE

Bowman, Teresa
LIKE FATHER, LIKE SON

Bowyer, Alan
PERSONAL SERVICES

Boyar, Sully
BEST SELLER

Boyarsky, Mikhail
SEZON CHUDES

Boyce, James
MALIBU BIKINI SHOP, THE

Boyce, Sharon
WHOOPS APOCALYPSE

Boyd, Jan Gan
ASSASSINATION
STEELE JUSTICE

Boyd, Niven
CRY FREEDOM

Boyett, William
HIDDEN, THE

Boykin, Horace
MORGAN STEWART'S COMING HOME

Boylan, John
KEEPING TRACK

Boyle, David E.
WANTED: DEAD OR ALIVE

Boyle, James T.
WITCHES OF EASTWICK, THE

Boyle, Peter
SURRENDER
WALKER

Boyles, David
MALIBU BIKINI SHOP, THE

Bozovic, Petar
U IME NARODA
VEC VIDJENO

Bracci, John
UNTOUCHABLES, THE

Bracco, Lorraine
PICK-UP ARTIST, THE
SOMEONE TO WATCH OVER ME

Brace, Nebraska
IRONWEED

Brachlemanns M.D., Walter
ALLNIGHTER, THE

Bracho, Alejandro
MIRACLES

Brackett, Sarah
ODYSSEE D'AMOUR

Bradeen, Robert
BLOODSUCKERS FROM OUTER SPACE

Bradell, James
MAN ON FIRE

Braden, John
OVER THE TOP

Bradford, Andrew
WHISTLE BLOWER, THE

Bradford, Richard
UNTOUCHABLES, THE

Bradigan, Bond
STEELE JUSTICE

Bradley, Anne H.
P.K. & THE KID

Bradley, David
PRICK UP YOUR EARS

Bradley, Doug
HELLRAISER

Bradley, Jim
P.K. & THE KID

Bradley, Rebecca
EIGHTY FOUR CHARING CROSS ROAD

Bradley, Ron
RETURN OF JOSEY WALES, THE

Bradley, Scott
LIGHTHORSEMEN, THE

Bradley, Wilbert
BIG SHOTS

Brady, Bill
WITCH HUNT

Brady, Janet
OMEGA SYNDROME

Brady, Joseph
FOURTH PROTOCOL, THE

Brady, Mike
PSYCHOS IN LOVE

Braendel, Gregory
OVER THE TOP

Braerne, Trond
FELDMANN CASE, THE

Braga, Aldo
A DOS AGUAS

Bragg, Bob
CYCLONE

Bragoli, Carla
PSYCHOS IN LOVE

Brahma, Debu
BABULA

Brailsford, Pauline
BIG SHOTS

Brainin, Danny
STREET SMART

Brambila, Rasalba
EL MOFLES Y LOS MECANICOS

Brambile, Rosalba
ESTA NOCHE CENA PANCHO (DESPEDIDA DE SOLTERO)

Brambilla, Massimiliano
SOTTO IL RISTORANTE CINESE

Brammer, Shelby
NADINE

Brammer, Sidney
NADINE

Branagh, Kenneth
HIGH SEASON
MONTH IN THE COUNTRY, A

Branaman, Rustam
HARD TICKET TO HAWAII

Branche, Derrick
SICILIAN, THE

Brancia, Armando
TERNOSECCO

Brand, Gibby
ANNA

Brand, Maurice
BIRDS OF PREY

Brandalise, Simona
LUNGA VITA ALLA SIGNORA!

Brandao, Chiquinho
NIGHT ANGELS

Brandao, Divana
A DANCA DOS BONECOS

Branderburg, Larry
UNTOUCHABLES, THE

Brandi-Hansen, Sissel
JAG ELSKER DIG

Brandinelli, Francesco
NOI UOMINI DURI

Brando, David
LE FOTO DI GIOIA

Brando, Luisina
EL ANO DEL CONEJO
EL HOMBRE DE LA DEUDA EXTERNA
LA BUSQUEDA
MISS MARY

Brandon, David
CARTOLINE ITALIANE
DELIRIA
GOOD MORNING BABYLON

Brandon-Jones, Una
WITHNAIL AND I

Brandoni, Luis
MADE IN ARGENTINA

Brandt, Joseph L.
P.K. & THE KID

Brandt, Nils
SERPENT'S WAY, THE

Brandt, Percy
HIP, HIP, HURRA!

Brandy, Eden
CAMPUS MAN

Brantley, Betsy
FOURTH PROTOCOL, THE

Brard, Patty
ODYSSEE D'AMOUR

Braskite, Brone
BLUDNYY SYN

Brass, David
HOSTAGE SYNDROME
WARRIORS OF THE APOCALYPSE

Brass, Lorne
NIGHT ZOO

Braszka, Jerzy A.
CZAS NADZIEI

Bratton, Creed
WILD PAIR, THE

Braun, Charley
WALKER

Braun, Charlie
STRAIGHT TO HELL

Brauner, Asher
STEELE JUSTICE

Brauss, Arthur
ISHTAR

Braverman, Marvin
OVERBOARD

Bravo, Carlos
LA RAZA NUNCA PIERDE—HUELE A GAS

Bravo, Richard
KILLER WORKOUT

Bravo, Tony
MURIERON A MITAD DEL RIO

Braxton, Kris
DANGER ZONE, THE

Bray, Thom
BURGLAR

Brazelton, Conni Marie
HOLLYWOOD SHUFFLE

Brecht, Edwin
LIKE FATHER, LIKE SON

Brecht, Johnathan
LIKE FATHER, LIKE SON

Brecke, Sharon
SOMEONE TO WATCH OVER ME

Brecke, Sharon K.
LETHAL WEAPON

Breed, Helen Lloyd
FOREVER, LULU
WHO'S THAT GIRL
WITCHES OF EASTWICK, THE

Breidenbach, Tilli
ALPINE FIRE

Breitfuss, Gotfried
SIERRA LEONE

Brendan O'Meara
MORGAN STEWART'S COMING HOME

Brenhouse, Bob
REMEMBERING MEL

Brennan, Frank
GIRL, THE

Brennan, Kerry
PARTY CAMP
RUNNING MAN, THE

Brennan, Melissa
SUMMER CAMP NIGHTMARE

Brennan, Stephen
EAT THE PEACH

Brennan, Tom
FATAL ATTRACTION

Brennan, William Martin
FATAL BEAUTY

Brenner, Barry
SURF NAZIS MUST DIE

Brenner, Hans
CHINESE ARE COMING, THE

Brent, Eve
DATE WITH AN ANGEL

Brentano, Amy
BLOOD SISTERS
ROBOT HOLOCAUST

Brenton Whittle
LIGHTHORSEMEN, THE

Bresee, Bobbie
EVIL SPAWN
SURF NAZIS MUST DIE

Brestoff, Richard
RETURN TO HORROR HIGH

Bretherton, Philip
CRY FREEDOM

Brett, John
DERANGED

Breuer, Marita
VERMISCHTE NACHRICHTEN

Breuning, Jytte
SIDSTE AKT

Brewer, Griffith
MORNING MAN, THE
WILD THING

Brewer, Matt
ISHTAR

Brewster, Niles
IN THE MOOD

Brewster, Tony
CYCLONE

Brewton, Maia
ADVENTURES IN BABYSITTING

Brezezinski, Dawn
I WAS A TEENAGE T.V. TERRORIST

Breznahan, Tom
IN THE MOOD

Brialy, Jean-Claude
GRAND GUIGNOL
LE MOUSTACHU
LEVY ET GOLIATH
MALADIE D'AMOUR
MASCHENKA

Brian DePersia
DEADTIME STORIES

Briant, Shane
CASSANDRA

LIGHTHORSEMEN, THE
MOVING TARGETS

Bridges, Beau
KILLING TIME, THE
WILD PAIR, THE

Bridges, Don
AS TIME GOES BY

Bridges, Jeff
NADINE

Bridges, Lloyd
WILD PAIR, THE

Bridges, Verda
HOLLYWOOD SHUFFLE

Bridgesmith, Lance
ERNEST GOES TO CAMP

Brierley, Tim
EMPIRE STATE

Briggs, Vera
ESCAPES

Brigham, Big John
BLOODSUCKERS FROM OUTER SPACE

Bright, Dick
P.K. & THE KID

Brightwell, Paul
ARIA

Brigliadori, Eleonora
RIMINI RIMINI

Brill, Charles
MALIBU BIKINI SHOP, THE

Brill, Marty
TALKING WALLS

Brilli, Nancy
CAMPING DEL TERRORE
SOTTO IL RISTORANTE CINESE

Brimhall, Cynthia
HARD TICKET TO HAWAII

Brind'Amour, Yvette
MORNING MAN, THE

Brine, Adrian
BLOND DOLLY

Bringas, Carl
BEVERLY HILLS COP II

Brint, Simon
EAT THE RICH

Brisbin, David
KISS DADDY GOOD NIGHT

Brisbon, Lee Anthony
HIDING OUT

Briscomb, Adam
DOGS IN SPACE

Brisebois, Danielle
BIG BAD MAMA II

Brisseau, Jean-Claude
QUATRE AVENTURES DE REINETTE ET MIRABELLE

Bristol, Clare
WITCHBOARD

Britneva, Maria
MAURICE

Britt, Barbara
SQUARE DANCE

Britt, Ruth
STEELE JUSTICE

Brittan, Judea
MANKILLERS

Brittany, Tally
SLAMMER GIRLS

Brjancev, Dimitrij
SKORBNOE BESCHUVSTVIE

Broaderup, Bernd
TAXI NACH KAIRO

Broberg, Lily
SIDSTE AKT

Broccolino, Lidia
DEVIL IN THE FLESH

Brochet, Anne
BUISSON ARDENT
MASQUES

Brock, Phil
ALLNIGHTER, THE
DATE WITH AN ANGEL
FRENCHMAN'S FARM
RIVER'S EDGE

Brock, Stanley
AMAZON WOMEN ON THE MOON
TIN MEN

Brockman, Daniel
MANKILLERS

Brocksmith, Roy
WHO'S THAT GIRL

Broderick, Beth
SLAMMER GIRLS

Broderick, Matthew
PROJECT X

Brodow, Ed
WANTED: DEAD OR ALIVE

Brodsky, Jack
DANCERS

Brodsky, Marek
PRATELE BERMUDSKEHO TROJUHELNIKU

Brodsky, Vlastimil
CHOBOTNICE Z II. PATRA

Brogi, Julio
IKONA ENOS MYTHIKOU PROSOPOU

Brogren, Hanna
GIRL, THE

Bromfield, Valri
HOME IS WHERE THE HART IS

Bromilow, Peter
HARD TICKET TO HAWAII
PROGRAMMED TO KILL

Bron, Eleanor
LITTLE DORRIT

Bronder, William
BEST SELLER

Brondukov, Borislav
PROSHAL ZELEN LETA

Brondum, Lene
HIP, HIP, HURRA!

Bronevoi, Leonid
KONETS OPERATSII "REZIDENT"

Bronson, Charles
ASSASSINATION
DEATH WISH 4: THE CRACKDOWN

Brood, Herman
STADTRAND

Brook, Claudio
FRIDA

Brook, Irina
MASCHENKA

Brooke, Ron
OFFSPRING, THE

Brookes, Diana
GHOST FEVER

Brookes, Jacqueline
STACKING

Brooks, Albert
BROADCAST NEWS

Brooks, Amy
BROADCAST NEWS

Brooks, Annabel
NIGHTFLYERS

Brooks, Carroll
BAD BLOOD

Brooks, Claude
HIDING OUT

Brooks, David Allen
KINDRED, THE

Brooks, Jeff
SECRET OF MY SUCCESS, THE

Brooks, Julian
PRINCIPAL, THE

Brooks, Matt
PSYCHOS IN LOVE

Brooks, Matthew
REAL MEN

Brooks, Mel
SPACEBALLS

Brooks, Nikki
BLOODY NEW YEAR

Brooks, Paul
OUTRAGEOUS FORTUNE

Brooks, Randy
ASSASSINATION

Brooks, Richard
HIDDEN, THE

Brooks, Van
TRESPASSES

Brophy, Kevin
DELOS ADVENTURE, THE

Brosnan, Pierce
FOURTH PROTOCOL, THE

Brosse, Frederick
ARIA

Brossier, Anne
LADY OF THE CAMELIAS

Brost, Johannes
FADERN, SONEN OCH DEN HELIGE ANDE

Brou, Kouadio
FACES OF WOMEN

Broussard, Steve
BIG EASY, THE

Brousse, Michele
LES OREILLES ENTRE LES DENTS

Brown, Amelda
HOPE AND GLORY
LITTLE DORRIT

Brown, Andre Rosey
STUDENT CONFIDENTIAL
WHO'S THAT GIRL

Brown, Arnold
PERSONAL SERVICES

Brown, Bernard
PERSONAL SERVICES

Brown, Beverly
HOLLYWOOD SHUFFLE

Brown, Billy Joe
CYCLONE

Brown, Bryan
GOOD WIFE, THE

Brown, Christopher
BELIEVERS, THE

Brown, Clancy
EXTREME PREJUDICE

Brown, Dennis
WHO'S THAT GIRL

Brown, Dwier
HOUSE TWO: THE SECOND STORY

Brown, Ernie
IN THE MOOD
MONSTER SQUAD, THE

Brown, Henry
LETHAL WEAPON

Brown, Jeannie
THREE KINDS OF HEAT

Brown, Jim
RUNNING MAN, THE

Brown, John
ERNEST GOES TO CAMP
TALKING WALLS

Brown, Jophrey
SQUEEZE, THE

Brown, Kate Napier
EIGHTY FOUR CHARING CROSS ROAD

Brown, Keith
REMEMBERING MEL

Brown, Kimberlin
WHO'S THAT GIRL

Brown, Paula
RUNNING MAN, THE

Brown, Quentin
ARIA

Brown, Ralph
BAD BLOOD
WITHNAIL AND I

Brown, Reb
STRIKE COMMANDO

Brown, Robert
LIVING DAYLIGHTS, THE

Brown, Robert K.
HOSTAGE

Brown, Roger Aaron
NEAR DARK

Brown, Sally Kay
HOT CHILD IN THE CITY

Brown, Sally R.
OUTRAGEOUS FORTUNE

Brown, Sullivan
SUICIDE CLUB, THE

Brown, Susan
HOPE AND GLORY

Brown, Timmy
CODE NAME ZEBRA

Brown, Wren T.
HOLLYWOOD SHUFFLE

Browne, Eithne
BUSINESS AS USUAL

Browne, Leslie
DANCERS

Browne, Peter
CUSTODY
LIGHTHORSEMEN, THE

Brubaker, Anthony
RUNNING MAN, THE

Bruce, Carol
PLANES, TRAINS AND AUTOMOBILES

Bruchet, Rene
EAT THE RICH

Brucker, Jane
DIRTY DANCING

Bruel, Patrick
ATTENTION BANDITS

Brugger, Jurgen
CRIME OF HONOR

Brumfield, Terry
THOU SHALT NOT KILL . . . EXCEPT

Brunaux, Olivia
GRAND GUIGNOL

Brunet, Jacques
PIERRE ET DJEMILA

Bruni-Tedeschi, Valeria
HOTEL DE FRANCE

Brunini, Achille
DA NNUNZIO
DER TOD DES EMPEDOKLES

Brunner, Michael
HOSTAGE

Brunning, Lorraine
PERSONAL SERVICES

Bruno, Paul
MANKILLERS

Bruno, Tamara
PICK-UP ARTIST, THE

Brunskill, Robin
HEARTS OF FIRE

Bruscolotti, Giuseppe
QUEL RAGAZZO DELLA CURVA "B"

Bruskotter, Eric
CANT BUY ME LOVE

Bryan, Dwyght
DIRTY DANCING

Bryant, Emma
WHOOPS APOCALYPSE

Bryant, Tom
PRINCIPAL, THE

Bryant, Ursaline
HOT PURSUIT

Bryant, Virginia
BARBARIANS, THE

Bryll, Ernest
STANISLAW I ANNA

Brynntrup, Michael
JESUS: DER FILM

Brynolfsson, Reine
SERPENT'S WAY, THE

Bryson, Chere
CREEPSHOW 2

Bubb, Lez
EAT THE RICH

Bucci, Flavio
IL GIORNO PRIMA

Buchanan, Ester
ARIA

Buchanan, Simone
MOVING TARGETS

Buchanan, Valerie
LOVECHILD, THE

Bucher, Jan
FIRE AND ICE

Buck, Bill
MALONE

Buck, Fred
ALADDIN

Buck, George
ANGEL HEART

Buck, O.A.
DAS TREIBHAUS

Buck, William Nichols
OVER THE TOP

Buckard, Olof
FADERN, SONEN OCH DEN HELIGE ANDE

Buckley, Betty
WILD THING

Buckman, Tara
TERMINAL EXPOSURE

Buczkowski, Zbigniew
RYKOWISKO

Budd, Barbara
THREE MEN AND A BABY

Budnitskaya, Alla
STRANNAYAR ISTORIYAR DOKTORA DZHEKILA I MISTERA KHAIDA

Budzisz-Krzyzanowska, Teresa
MASKARADA

Buendia, Rafael
LO NEGRO DEL NEGRO

Bueno, Aldo
NIGHT ANGELS

Bueno, Gustavo
CITY AND THE DOGS, THE

Bufalini, Albano
NOI UOMINI DURI

Bugg, Susan
WHO'S THAT GIRL

Buggy, Niall
HELLRAISER

Bukovec, Vladimir
LADY OF THE CAMELIAS

Bukowski, Janusz
PRYWATNE SLEDZTWO

Buldakov, Alexei
VOT MOYA DEREVNYA

Bulgakova, Maya
FAREWELL

Bulinenkova, S.
VZLOMSHCHIK

Buljo, Ellen Anne
OFELAS

Buljo, Henrik H.
OFELAS

Bullard, Franklyn L.
BROADCAST NEWS

Bullen, Sarah
FOURTH PROTOCOL, THE

Bullock, Jm J.
SPACEBALLS

Bulut, Talat
SON URFALI

Bumpass, Roger
RUNNING MAN, THE

Bundgaard, Poul
KAMPEN OM DEN RODE KO

Bundy, Brooke
MISSION KILL
NIGHTMARE ON ELM STREET 3: DREAM WARRIORS, A

Bunetta, Peter
BLIND DATE

Bunge, Barbara
MISS MARY

Bunker, Eddie
RUNNING MAN, THE

Bunnag, Vithawat
SHADOWS OF THE PEACOCK

Bunser, Chris
MANKILLERS

Burbank the Cat
LETHAL WEAPON

Burchill, Andrea
HOUSEKEEPING

Burd, Tim
PRETTYKILL

Burdette, Nicole
ANGEL HEART

Burduli, Elgudzba
SDELKA

Burford, Phyllis
MOVING TARGETS

Burgess, Michael
THREE MEN AND A BABY

Burgess, Michael Lynn
BEDROOM WINDOW, THE

Burgos, Devin
LES OREILLES ENTRE LES DENTS

Burgs, Ron
MASTERBLASTER

Burk, Lisanne
LADIES OF THE LOTUS

Burke, Aloyius R.
NECROPOLIS

Burke, Kathy
EAT THE RICH
STRAIGHT TO HELL
WALKER

Burke, Simon
SLATE, WYN & ME

Burke, Solomon
BIG EASY, THE

Burket, Craig
WITCHES OF EASTWICK, THE

Burkett, Laura
OVERKILL

Burkhead, John
RETURN OF JOSEY WALES, THE

Burkley, Dennis
MALONE
NO WAY OUT
WANTED: DEAD OR ALIVE
WHO'S THAT GIRL

Burks, Rick
BLOOD DINER

Burliayev, Nikolai
VOENNO-POLEVOI ROMAN

Burlingame, Chad
HAPPY HOUR

Burlinson, Tom
TIME GUARDIAN, THE

Burlyayev, Nikolai
LERMONTOV

Burlyayev, Vanya
LERMONTOV

Burmeister, Leo
BROADCAST NEWS

Burnett, Cliff
PRAYER FOR THE DYING, A

Burnette, Mila
VIOLINS CAME WITH THE AMERICANS, THE

Burnette, Olivia
PLANES, TRAINS AND AUTOMOBILES

Burnham, Burnham
HOWLING III, THE

Burnham, Edward
LITTLE DORRIT

Burns, Danielle
EIGHTY FOUR CHARING CROSS ROAD

Burns, Jere
LETS GET HARRY

Burns, Lee
EIGHTY FOUR CHARING CROSS ROAD

Burns, Mark
KEEPING TRACK
SLEEP WELL, MY LOVE

Burns, Stan
RADIO DAYS

Burns, Terry
OVER THE TOP

Burns, Tim
BELINDA
CASSANDRA

Burr, Wally
BEST SELLER

Burrill, Rebecca
FOURTH PROTOCOL, THE

Burroughs, Jackie
HOUSEKEEPER, THE
JOHN AND THE MISSUS
WINTER TAN, A

Bursill, Tina
JILTED

Burt, Denny
WEEDS

Burton, Debra
GUNPOWDER

Burton, Elizabeth
AROUND THE WORLD IN EIGHTY WAYS

Burton, Joan L.
GARBAGE PAIL KIDS MOVIE, THE

Burton, Laura
HOUR OF THE ASSASSIN

Burton, LeVar
SUPERNATURALS, THE

Burton, Wendell
HEAT

Burton, Willie
OVERKILL

Burza, Chica
ANJOS DO ARRABALDE

Busaid, Alberto
MADE IN ARGENTINA

Busarello, Stefania
LUNGA VITA ALLA SIGNORA!

Buscaglia, John
MY DARK LADY

Buscemi, Steve
HEART
KISS DADDY GOOD NIGHT

Busey, Gary
BULLETPROOF
LETHAL WEAPON
LETS GET HARRY

Busfield, Timothy
REVENGE OF THE NERDS II: NERDS IN PARADISE

Bush, Adrian
FULL METAL JACKET

Bush, Grand
HOLLYWOOD SHUFFLE
LETHAL WEAPON

Bush, Mike
WHALES OF AUGUST, THE

Bush, Nancy
ROCK 'N' ROLL NIGHTMARE

Bush, Peter
I WAS A TEENAGE ZOMBIE

Bush, Rebeccah
HUNK

Bush, Ron
DEADTIME STORIES

Busker, Rickie
BIG SHOTS

Buson, Tommy
CRY FREEDOM

Busquet, Narciso
LA FUGA DE CARRASCO

Busquets, Narciso
OPERACION MARIJUANA
ROBACHICOS

Busse, Jochen
WANNSEE CONFERENCE, THE

Bussinger, Hans W.
WANNSEE CONFERENCE, THE

Bussotti, Fabio
MAN ON FIRE

Bustamante, Edda
EN RETIRADA

Bustamante, Sergio
LO NEGRO DEL NEGRO
ROBACHICOS

Bustamentes, Lupita
CARTUCHA CORTADA

Butler, Artie
RADIO DAYS

Butler, Daniel
ERNEST GOES TO CAMP

Butler, Dick
OMEGA SYNDROME

Butler, Eugene
BEVERLY HILLS COP II

Butler, Marie
MIRACLES

Butler, Martha
DOGS IN SPACE

Butrick, Merritt
SHY PEOPLE

Butt, Loredana
SOTTO IL RISTORANTE CINESE

Butyrtseva, Nadezhda
KARUSEL NA BAZARNOY PLOSHCHADI

Buxton, Frank
OVERBOARD

Buxton, Sarah
LESS THAN ZERO

Buza, George
MEATBALLS III

Buzancic, Boris
OFICIR S RUZOM

Byatt, Michelle
BUSINESS AS USUAL

Bykov, Rolan
CHEGEMSKIY DETEKTIV
ISKRENNE VASH . . .
KOMISSAR
PODSUDIMYY

Bynum, Jim
SQUARE DANCE

Byomkesh
JAIDEV

Byram, Ronald C.
MORGAN STEWART'S COMING HOME

Byrd, David
BEST SELLER

Byrd, Julian
MASTERBLASTER

Byrd-Nethery, Miriam
SUMMER HEAT

Byrne, Catherine
EAT THE PEACH

Byrne, Gabriel
GOTHIC
HELLO AGAIN
LIONHEART
SIESTA

Byrne, Michael P.
UNTOUCHABLES, THE

Byrne, Robert
EAT THE PEACH
RAWHEAD REX

Byrnes, Bara
MALIBU BIKINI SHOP, THE

Byrnes, Burke
WITCHBOARD

Byrnes, Edd
MANKILLERS

Byron, Carlye
STRIPPED TO KILL

Byron, Jeanne
VALET GIRLS

Bystrom, Margaretha
NAGRA SOMMARKVALLAR PA JORDEN

Bywaters, Yvonne
ANGEL HEART

Caan, James
GARDENS OF STONE

Caba, Emilio Gutierrez
CARA DE ACELGA
LA GUERRA DE LOS LOCOS
LAS DOS ORILLAS

Caba, Irene Gutierrez
LA CASA DE BERNARDA ALBA

Caballe, Montserrat
ROMANCA FINAL

Cabrera, Susana
EL MOFLES Y LOS MECANICOS

Caceras, Joshua
SLAMDANCE

Caceres, Baldomero
HOUR OF THE ASSASSIN

Caceres, Carlos
EL HOMBRE DE LA DEUDA EXTERNA

Caddick, Edward
MOVING TARGETS

Cade, John
GARBAGE PAIL KIDS MOVIE, THE

Cadedo, Oscar
TRAGICO TERREMOTO EN MEXICO

Cadell, Selina
PRICK UP YOUR EARS

Cadman, Josh
IN THE MOOD

Cadoret, Rosine
FAMILY BUSINESS

Cady, Barbara
MY DARK LADY

Cady, Gary
SIESTA

Caesar, Harry
OFFSPRING, THE

Caesar, Sid
EMPEROR'S NEW CLOTHES, THE

Cage, Nicolas
MOONSTRUCK
RAISING ARIZONA

Caggiano, Frank
SUPERNATURALS, THE

Cagman, Orhan
ANAYURT OTELI

Caicedo, Franklin
COLOR OF DESTINY, THE

Caillot, Haydee
QUATRE AVENTURES DE REINETTE ET MIRABELLE

Cain, Charlotte
WARRIORS OF THE APOCALYPSE

Cain, Lisa
DEADTIME STORIES

Cain, Sharon
SLAMMER GIRLS

Caine, Michael
FOURTH PROTOCOL, THE
JAWS: THE REVENGE
SURRENDER
WHISTLE BLOWER, THE

Caine, Richard
BIG SHOTS

Cala, Jerry
RIMINI RIMINI
SOTTOZERO

Calabrese, Nancy
SUMMER CAMP NIGHTMARE

Calacci, Miguel
EULALIA

Calahorra, Margarita
EL LUTE—CAMINA O REVIENTA

Calaman, Stanford
EMPIRE STATE

Calandra, Giuliana
IL CORAGGIO DI PARLARE
REGINA

Calderon, Arturo
LA OVEJA NEGRA

Calderon, Maria Isabel
MAS ALLA DEL SILENCIO

Caldoro, Tom
I WAS A TEENAGE ZOMBIE

Caldwell, Janette
VALET GIRLS

Cale, David
RADIO DAYS

Calero, Gerardo
VISA U.S.A.

Calfa, Don
TALKING WALLS

Calhoun, Diana
MIND KILLER

Calhoun, Jeff
ARIA

Calhoun, Monica
OUT OF ROSENHEIM

Calik, Karol
PRATELE BERMUDSKEHO TROJUHELNIKU

Calise, Ugo
TERNOSECCO

Call, Kenny
NEAR DARK

Call, R.D.
NO MAN'S LAND

Callahan, Dick
BELIEVERS, THE

Callahan, Gene
BLACK WIDOW

Callahan, Linda
WALKER

Callahan, Michael
MALIBU BIKINI SHOP, THE

Callan, Cecile
LETS GET HARRY
WHO'S THAT GIRL

Callan, Graham
BUSINESS AS USUAL

Callas, Charlie
AMAZON WOMEN ON THE MOON

Calliris, Thanos
PRETTY SMART

Callow, Simon
MAURICE

Calvin, John
BACK TO THE BEACH

Camacho, Alejandro
FORAJIDOS EN LA MIRA

Camacho, Art
MANKILLERS

Camacho, Cecilia
SINVERGUENZA . . . PERO HONRADO

Camacho, Gonzalo J.
LA OVEJA NEGRA
MANON

Camacho, Manuela
LA GUERRA DE LOS LOCOS

Camara, Josu
A LOS CUATRO VIENTOS

Camastral, Franz
JENATSCH

Camaya, Christine
FUEGOS

Cameron, Candace
SOME KIND OF WONDERFUL

Cameron, Dean
SUMMER SCHOOL

Cameron, Etta
PETER VON SCHOLTEN

Cameron, Kirk
LIKE FATHER, LIKE SON

Cameron, Patrick
LETHAL WEAPON

Camilla Horn
DER UNSICHTBARE

Camilleri, Joe
DOGS IN SPACE

Camilleri, Terry
DUTCH TREAT
IN THE MOOD
LETS GET HARRY

Cammell, China
WHITE OF THE EYE

Camp, Colleen
POLICE ACADEMY 4: CITIZENS ON PATROL
WALK LIKE A MAN

Campanaro, Philip
SLAMMER GIRLS

Campanella, Frank
OVERBOARD

Campanella, Joseph
STEELE JUSTICE

Campanella, Pierfrancesco
LA TRASGRESSIONE

Campanero, Philip
WIMPS

Campbell, Bruce
EVIL DEAD 2: DEAD BY DAWN

Campbell, David
DEADLY PREY

Campbell, David James
KILLER WORKOUT

Campbell, Jane
ROXANNE

Campbell, Jerry
DATE WITH AN ANGEL

Campbell, Laura
SLAMDANCE

Campbell, Mae E.
MIRACLES

Campbell, Peter
BIRDS OF PREY

Campbell, Richard
WILD THING

Campbell, Ron
WITCHES OF EASTWICK, THE

Campbell, Shawn
EMANON

Campillo, Abril
CORRUPCION

Campion, Cris
ARIA
BEYOND THERAPY
CHAMP D'HONNEUR

Campos, Raphael
RETURN OF JOSEY WALES, THE

Campos, Sergio Poves
EL AMOR ES UNA MUJERGORDA

Campudoni, Madison
PENITENTIARY III

Camurat, Beatrice
SPIRALE

Camurati, Carla
CIDADE OCULTA

Camus, Frnaci
JENATSCH

Canada, Christian
WELCOME MARIA

Canada, Robert
DANGER ZONE, THE

Canadian Soldier
HOPE AND GLORY

Candal, Norma
VIOLINS CAME WITH THE AMERICANS, THE

Candler, Kingsley
CYCLONE

Candy, John
PLANES, TRAINS AND AUTOMOBILES
SPACEBALLS

Canedo, Roberto
HERENCIA DE VALIENTES
LO NEGRO DEL NEGRO
TIERRA DE VALIENTES

Canelon, Jorge
POR LOS CAMINOS VERDES

Canino, Frank
POLICE ACADEMY 4: CITIZENS ON PATROL

Cannavale, Enzo
IL CORAGGIO DI PARLARE

Cannold, Tom
DIRTY DANCING

Cannon, Catherine
HIDDEN, THE

Cannon, Wanda
HOUSEKEEPER, THE

Cannonieri, Sergio
SOTTO IL RISTORANTE CINESE

Canoletti, Jessica
ANJOS DO ARRABALDE

Canovas, Anne
ARIA

Cansino, Tini
DELIZIA

Cantini, Renzo
GOOD MORNING BABYLON

Cantor, Max
DIRTY DANCING

Capaldi, Peter
LOVECHILD, THE

Capatos, Stelio
DOXOBUS

Capella, Rocky
ESCAPES

Capello, Tim
HEARTS OF FIRE

Capers, Virginia
OFF THE MARK

Capetillo, Guillermo
EL HIJO DE PEDRO NAVAJAS

Capetillo, Manuel
SINVERGUENZA . . . PERO HONRADO

Capitano, Francesco
MORO AFFAIR, THE

Caplan, Claire
ROXANNE

Caplan, Twink
TALKING WALLS

Capo, Armand
AMAZONS

Capobianco, Carmine
PSYCHOS IN LOVE

Capodice, John C.
SECRET OF MY SUCCESS, THE

Capri, Danny
ERNEST GOES TO CAMP
OVER THE TOP

Caprio, Antonio
OVERKILL

Caprioli, Vittorio
CAPRICCIO
I PICARI
ROBA DA RICCHI

Capritti, Eolo
CAPRICCIO

Capry, Barry
STABILIZER, THE

Capucine
I MIEI PRIMI QUARANT'ANNI
LE FOTO DI GIOIA

Carafotes, Paul
BLIND DATE

Carating, Lito
DAMORTIS

Carballeira, Enriqueta
LA CASA DE BERNARDA ALBA

Carbonell, Pablo
LOS INVITADOS

Carbonell, Raul
LA GRAN FIESTA

Carbucci, Carlo
ALADDIN

Carcano, Alvaro
MIRACLES

Cardak, Melih
YER DEMIR, GOK BAKIR

Cardan, Carlos
HERENCIA DE VALIENTES

Cardan, Christina
TERMINAL EXPOSURE
ZERO BOYS, THE

Cardeans, Manolo
MATAR O MORIR

Cardenal, Maria
LAPUTA: THE CASTLE IN THE SKY

Carder, Elizabeth
TALKING WALLS

Cardianl, Claudia
KEEPING TRACK

Cardinal, Maria
LA RAZA NUNCA PIERDE—HUELE A GAS
NOS REIMOS DE LA MIGRA

Cardinale, Claudia
MAN IN LOVE, A

Cardona Sr., Rene
YO, EL EJECUTOR

Cardoso, Benny
DA NNUNZIO

Cardoso, Idilio
LAS DOS ORILLAS
LOS INVITADOS

Cardoso, Louise
BAIXO GAVEA
LEILA DINIZ

Cardy, David
PRICK UP YOUR EARS
Carett, Danny
WITCH HUNT
Carew, Peter
SOMEONE TO WATCH OVER ME
Carey, Clare
ZOMBIE HIGH
Carey, Dave
RAWHEAD REX
Carey, David
EAT THE PEACH
Carey, Earleen
MASTERBLASTER
Carey, Harry
WHALES OF AUGUST, THE
Carey, Jan
WHISTLE BLOWER, THE
Carey, Levant
JAWS: THE REVENGE
Carinci, Jean Bourne
BROADCAST NEWS
Carl, Adam
MONSTER SQUAD, THE
SUMMER CAMP NIGHTMARE
Carlano, Alvaro
MISSION KILL
Carlhillos
LA RAZA NUNCA PIERDE—HUELE A GAS
Carlile, Bob
RAWHEAD REX
Carlin, George
OUTRAGEOUS FORTUNE
Carlin, Gloria
HANOI HILTON, THE
Carlin, Leila
NIGHT STALKER, THE
Carlin, Thomas A.
MATEWAN
Carlino, Natalle
EMANON
Carlisle, Anne
SUICIDE CLUB, THE
Carlisle, Steve
CURSE, THE
Carlo, Joanne
FOREVER, LULU
Carlos y Jose
EL MUERTO DEL PALOMO
Carlson, Judith
LADY OF THE CAMELIAS
Carlson, Kimberlee
CLUB LIFE
Carlson, Les
STREET SMART
Carlson, Sara
BEDROOM WINDOW, THE
Carlsoon, Ewa
MORE ABOUT THE CHILDREN OF BULLERBY VILLAGE
Carlsson, Eva
DET STORA LOFTET
Carlsson, Ewa
ETTER RUBICON
Carlsson, Ing-Marie
MY LIFE AS A DOG
Carlsson, Ralph
MY LIFE AS A DOG
Carlton, Hope Marie
HARD TICKET TO HAWAII
Carlton, Hope-Marie
TERMINAL EXPOSURE
Carlton, Robert
YEAR MY VOICE BROKE, THE
Carlucci, Tony
HEARTS OF FIRE
Carlwind, Christina
MY LIFE AS A DOG
Carmen, Loene
YEAR MY VOICE BROKE, THE
Carmet, Jean
LA BRUTE
LA MOINE ET LA SORCIERE
LES DEUX CROCODILES
MISS MONA
Carmi, Oded
DEADTIME STORIES
DEADTIME STORIES
Carmine, Michael
BATTERIES NOT INCLUDED
Carmody, Peter
WARM NIGHTS ON A SLOW MOVING TRAIN
Carmon, Joseph
TEL AVIV—BERLIN
Carmona, Rigoberto
MISSION KILL
Carnelutti, Francesco
BELLY OF AN ARCHITECT, THE
MORO AFFAIR, THE
Carnevale, Andrea
QUEL RAGAZZO DELLA CURVA "B"
Carnie, Darcia
LADIES OF THE LOTUS
Caro, Armando
RAGE OF HONOR
Caro, Ruth
SHADOWS OF THE PEACOCK
Caroit, Philippe
JOHNNY MONROE
Carol, Madalyn
BARFLY
Carol, Ronnie
FORTY DAYS OF MUSA DAGH
Carosi, L.
BARBARIANS, THE
Carothers, Veronica
MANKILLERS
Carpenter, Jack
MILLION DOLLAR MYSTERY
Carpenter, John
KID BROTHER, THE
Carpenter
OVERBOARD
Carr, Jack
BUSINESS AS USUAL
Carr, John
NO DEAD HEROES
Carradine, David
WHEELS OF TERROR
Carradine, John
EVIL SPAWN
MONSTER IN THE CLOSET
Carradine, Robert
NUMBER ONE WITH A BULLET
REVENGE OF THE NERDS II: NERDS IN PARADISE
Carraro, Tino
NOTTE ITALIANA
Carrasco, Ada
FIERAS EN BRAMA
Carrasco, Queta
RETO A LA VIDA
Carre de Malberg, Stanislas
AU REVOIR, LES ENFANTS
Carreras, Jose
ROMANCA FINAL
Carrere, Tia
ZOMBIE NIGHTMARE
Carrey, Leah
RADIO DAYS
Carrick, Antony
PERSONAL SERVICES
PRICK UP YOUR EARS
Carrier, Corey
WITCHES OF EASTWICK, THE
Carrier, Marie-France
BACH AND BROCCOLI
Carrigan, Caroline
DEADTIME STORIES
Carrillo, Elpidia
LETS GET HARRY
PREDATOR
Carrillo, Teresa
LA VIDA ALEGRE
Carrington, Debbie Lee
GARBAGE PAIL KIDS MOVIE, THE
Carrion, Jose Pedro
LA RUSA
Carrion, Ricardo
EL PLACER DE LA VENGANZA
LA FUGA DE CARRASCO
Carroll, Anne
BELLMAN AND TRUE
Carroll, Deryl
WHO'S THAT GIRL
Carroll, Helena
DEAD, THE
Carroll, J. W.
BIG TOWN, THE
Carroll, J. Winston
PRETTYKILL
Carroll, James
NIGHTMARE ON ELM STREET 3: DREAM WARRIORS, A
POLICE ACADEMY 4: CITIZENS ON PATROL
Carroll, Janet
KILLING TIME, THE
Carroll, Larry
BEVERLY HILLS COP II
Carroll, Lou Ann
MASTERBLASTER
Carroll, Paul
DEAD, THE
Carroll, Peter
CUSTODY
Carroll, Ronn
EIGHTY FOUR CHARING CROSS ROAD
HOUSE TWO: THE SECOND STORY
Carroll, Ryan
WITCHBOARD
Carron, Victor
VALET GIRLS
Carrott, Jasper
JANE AND THE LOST CITY
Carson, Crystal
WHO'S THAT GIRL
ZERO BOYS, THE
Carson, Darwin
WHO'S THAT GIRL
Carson, Darwyn
DEATHROW GAMESHOW
Carson, William
JAAN KAANTOPIIRI
Carstens, Ingeborg
YER DEMIR, GOK BAKIR
Carter, Jack
TROUBLE WITH DICK, THE
Carter, Jason
EMPEROR'S NEW CLOTHES, THE
Carter, Jim
MONTH IN THE COUNTRY, A
Carter, Ric
AROUND THE WORLD IN EIGHTY WAYS
Carter, T.K.
AMAZON WOMEN ON THE MOON
HES MY GIRL
Cartier, Caroline
LA VALLEE FANTOME
Cartier, Jean-Pierre
LA COULEUR ENCERCLEE
Cartlidge, Katrin
EAT THE RICH
Cartwright, Jon
SHADEY
Cartwright, Lynn
GARBAGE PAIL KIDS MOVIE, THE
Cartwright, Nancy
CHIPMUNK ADVENTURE, THE
Cartwright, Parnes
FIREHOUSE
Cartwright, Peter
CRY FREEDOM
FOURTH PROTOCOL, THE
Cartwright, Veronica
WITCHES OF EASTWICK, THE
Caruana, Michael
BIG TOWN, THE
BLUE MONKEY
Caruso, David
CHINA GIRL
Caruso, voice of: Enrico
ARIA
Carvalheiro, Cucha
LA PLAYA DE LOS PERROS
Carvalho, Denis
BEIJO NA BOCA
LEILA DINIZ
Carvall, Susane
MASSACRE IN DINOSAUR VALLEY
Carvana, Hugo
LEILA DINIZ
Carvana, Nancy
WITCH HUNT
Carver, Mary
BEST SELLER
Cary, Christopher
MILLION DOLLAR MYSTERY
Cary, Peter
CRY FREEDOM
Casal, Gregorio
HERENCIA DE VALIENTES

Casanas, Aledia E.
NECROPOLIS
Casanova, Fernando
FORAJIDOS EN LA MIRA
TIERRA DE VALIENTES
Case, Regina
AREIAS ESCALADANTES
Caserta, Clem
UNTOUCHABLES, THE
Caserta, Clemenze
PICK-UP ARTIST, THE
Casey, Bernie
STEELE JUSTICE
Casey, Cara
SAKURA KILLERS
Casey, Gene Scott
CLUB LIFE
Casey, Griffin
CRY WILDERNESS
Casey, Sarah
TRAIN OF DREAMS
Cash, Rosalind
OFFSPRING, THE
Cashman, Shaun
PSYCHOS IN LOVE
Casilio, Maria Pia
NOI UOMINI DURI
Casin, Orlando
DE TAL PEDRO, TAL ASTILLA
Casini, Stefania
BELLY OF AN ARCHITECT, THE
Caspary, Tina
CANT BUY ME LOVE
Cass, Christopher
SOMEONE TO WATCH OVER ME
Cass, David
BEST SELLER
Cassel, Seymour
SURVIVAL GAME
TIN MEN
Cassell, Alan
BELINDA
Cassese, Andrew
REVENGE OF THE NERDS II: NERDS IN PARADISE
Cassidy, Joanna
FOURTH PROTOCOL, THE
Cassidy, John
WHOOPS APOCALYPSE
Cassidy, Michael
HELLRAISER
Cassola, Francesca
OPERA
Castaldi, Mario
ILLUMINAZIONI
Castaldo, Jacques
MON BEL AMOUR, MA DECHIRURE
Castel, Lou
MAN ON FIRE
Castellano, Valerio
DELIZIA
Castellito, Sergio
DOLCE ASSENZA
Castellitto, Sergio
FAMILY, THE
SEMBRA MORTO . . . ME E SOLO SVENUTO
Castello, Roberto
PERSONAGGI & INTERPRETI
Castellotti, Peter
RADIO DAYS
Castillo, Abraham Hernandez
WINTER TAN, A
Castillo, E.J.
DELOS ADVENTURE, THE
Castle, Ann
EMPIRE OF THE SUN
Castrillion, Maria Lucia
VISA U.S.A.
Castro, Angelo
SWEET REVENGE
Castro, Guero
LA RAZA NUNCA PIERDE—HUELE A GAS
NOS REIMOS DE LA MIGRA
Castro, Isabel
O DESEJADO—LES MONTAGNES DE LA LUNE
Castro, Jackeline
LA RULETERA
Castro, Jacquelin
MAS BUENAS QUE EL PAN
Castro, Jacqueline
MAS VALE PAJARO EN MANO . . .
Castro, Jose
ARQUIESTA EMILIO VARELA
Castro, Maria Elena
CHRONICLE OF A DEATH FORETOLD
Castro, Patricia
ESTA NOCHE CENA PANCHO (DESPEDIDA DE SOLTERO)
Castro, Paty
LA RAZA NUNCA PIERDE—HUELE A GAS
Castro, Victor Manuel
EL MOFLES Y LOS MECANICOS
Casuccio, John
KEEPING TRACK
Catala, Paco
LA VIDA ALEGRE
Catala, Patxi
LA GUERRA DE LOS LOCOS
Catalan, Paloma
LA VIDA ALEGRE
Catalini, Mayor John
PURSUIT OF HAPPINESS, THE
Catania, Antonio
DOLCE ASSENZA
Cates, Phoebe
DATE WITH AN ANGEL
Catlett, Loyd
NADINE
Cattand, Gabriel
LES OREILLES ENTRE LES DENTS
Cattrall, Kim
MANNEQUIN
Cau, Marco Tullio
WARRIOR QUEEN
Cauchon, Christian
ARIA
Caudle, Tim
HIDING OUT
Caulfield, Maxwell
SUPERNATURALS, THE
Cavalcanti, Claudia
IL FASCINO SOTTILE DEL PECCATO
LA TRASGRESSIONE
Cavanagh, Trudy
WISH YOU WERE HERE
Caven, Ingrid
DEVILS PARADISE, THE
Cavett, Dick
NIGHTMARE ON ELM STREET 3: DREAM WARRIORS, A
Cavicchioli, Divo
CHRONICLE OF A DEATH FORETOLD
Cavicchioli, Marco
GOOD MORNING BABYLON
Cavosi, Roberto
SOLDATI: 365 GIORNI ALL' ALBA
Cawrse, Imogen
HOPE AND GLORY
Cayenne
EAT THE RICH
Cayer, Kim
PSYCHO GIRLS
Cayton, Elizabeth
SLAVE GIRLS FROM BEYOND INFINITY
Cazalet, Joe
WILD THING
Cazuza
UM TREM PARA AS ESTRELAS
Cchikvadze, Ramaz
SKORBNOE BESCHUVSTVIE
Ce, Za Chuan
EMPIRE OF THE SUN
Cecchetto, Renato
LESTATE STA FINENDO
Cecchi, Ilaria
CARAMELLE DA UNO SCONOSCIUTO
Cecil, Jane
SEPTEMBER
SUMMER HEAT
Cedar, Larry
HIDDEN, THE
Cederberg, Kerry
CAUGHT
Cederna, Giuseppe
MAN ON FIRE
SOTTO IL RISTORANTE CINESE
Cei, Pina
DARK EYES
Cela, Violeta
YEAR OF AWAKENING, THE
Celarie, Clementine
JOHNNY MONROE
LA VIE DISSOLUE DE GERARD FLOQUE
Celario, Daniel
RUNNING MAN, THE
Celario, Mario
RUNNING MAN, THE
Celentano, Adriano
IL BURBERO
Celeste, Claudia
BEIJO NA BOCA
Celeste, Joe
WALKER
Celier, Caroline
LANNEE DES MEDUSES
Celio, Teco
JENATSCH
PERSONAGGI & INTERPRETI
Cellard, Jeanne
BEYOND THERAPY
Cellier, Caroline
CHARLIE DINGO
GRAND GUIGNOL
Cellier, Peter
PERSONAL SERVICES
Cellucci, Claire
THREE MEN AND A BABY
Cenci, Athina
A FIOR DI PELLE
CARAMELLE DA UNO SCONOSCIUTO
FAMILY, THE
Cepeda, Gerardo
OLOR A MUERTE
Cerda, Maximo
WEEDS
Ceresne, Ken
MAKING MR.RIGHT
Cerna, Emma
PROC?
Cerro, Jose
EL LUTE—CAMINA O REVIENTA
Cervantes, Carlos
BARFLY
BEVERLY HILLS COP II
EXTREME PREJUDICE
FATAL BEAUTY
Cervantes, Marta Elena
LO NEGRO DEL NEGRO
YERBA SANGRIENTE
Cervenka, Exene
SALVATION!
Cervenkova, Stepankova
WOLF'S HOLE
Cervi, G.
DANGER ZONE, THE
Cervi, Robert
MANKILLERS
Cervino, Jose Manuel
EL LUTE—CAMINA O REVIENTA
LA GUERRA DE LOS LOCOS
Cestero, Carlos Augusto
LA GRAN FIESTA
Cetinkaya, Yavuzer
YER DEMIR, GOK BAKIR
Cevrevski, Danco
HI-FI
Chaal-Gohier, Muriel
NITWITS
Chabrol, Claude
JEUX D'ARTIFICES
LETE EN PENTE DOUCE
SALE DESTIN!
Chacon, Lois
MASCARA
Chacon, Thales Pan
FONTE DA SAUDADE
Chaddha, Sahila
SHEELA
Chaffee, Suzy
FIRE AND ICE
Chagrin, Julian
SLEEPING BEAUTY
Chaikin, Milton
SOMETHING SPECIAL!
Chailleux, Jacques
GRAND GUIGNOL
Chain, Angelica
ENTRE FICHERAS ANDA EL DIABLO
POLICIAS DE NARCOTICOS
RATAS DE LA CIUDAD

Chakir, Amid
LOVE IS A DOG FROM HELL
Chakraborty, Madhabi
RUDRABEENA
Chakrapani
JAIDEV
Chakravarti, Pareg
CONCRETE ANGELS
Chalem, Brent
MONSTER SQUAD, THE
Chaliapin, Feodor
MOONSTRUCK
Chalulas, Alberta
WINTER TAN, A
Chamberlain, Richard
ALLAN QUATERMAIN AND THE LOST CITY OF GOLD
Chambers, Patti
PSYCHOS IN LOVE
Chamitoff, Kenneth H.
STEELE JUSTICE
Chamorro, Bienvenida
CHRONICLE OF A DEATH FORETOLD
Champa, Jo
DOLCE ASSENZA
FAMILY, THE
Champel, Marcel
JEAN DE FLORETTE
Champion, Michael
FATAL BEAUTY
Chan, Danny
AUTUMN'S TALE, AN
Chan, Dennis
LAONIANG GOU SAO
Chan, Dick
BLACK DRAGON, THE
Chan, Doreen
CHINA GIRL
Chan, Jackie
NINJA THUNDERBOLT
PROJECT A—PART II
Chan, Pylah
OVERKILL
Chance, Carlton
CRY FREEDOM
Chandler, Estee
TEEN WOLF TOO
Chandler, Jared
IN THE MOOD
Chandler, Jeffrey Alan
IN THE MOOD
Chandler, John
ADVENTURES IN BABYSITTING
Chandler, Joseph
KILLER WORKOUT
Chandler, June
NO WAY OUT
Chandler, Michael
ANGUSTIA
Chandler, Wayne
CANT BUY ME LOVE
Chandran, Sudha
CHINNATHAMBI PERIYATHAMBI
Chanel, Tally
NIGHT STALKER, THE
WARRIOR QUEEN
Chang, Da Shi
ROMANCE OF BOOK AND SWORD, THE
Chang, Lum Pang
PSYCHOS IN LOVE
Chang, Sari
CHINA GIRL
Chang, Sylvia
SEVEN YEARS ITCH
Chaniolleau, Caroline
O DESEJADO—LES MONTAGNES DE LA LUNE
Chankin, Sidney
RUNNING MAN, THE
Chankvetadze, Ninel
KRUGOVOROT
STUPEN
Chantrell, Shirley
EMPIRE OF THE SUN
Chanut, Oliver
LADY OF THE CAMELIAS
Chao, Harvey
BELIEVERS, THE
POLICE ACADEMY 4: CITIZENS ON PATROL
Chao, Rosalind
SLAMDANCE
Chaopramong, Wichien
GOOD MORNING, VIETNAM
Chaplin, Geraldine
WHITE MISCHIEF
Chapman, Alexander
WILD THING
Chapman, Larry
ALLNIGHTER, THE
Chapman, Sean
EAT THE RICH
FOURTH PROTOCOL, THE
HELLRAISER
Chappelear, Michael
ERNEST GOES TO CAMP
Chappell, Chris
GOTHIC
Chapple, Sarah
CONCRETE ANGELS
Charanraj
PRATIGHAAT
Charles, Craig
BUSINESS AS USUAL
Charles, Danielle Jean
ISHTAR
Charles, Lynne
LADY OF THE CAMELIAS
Charles, Marie Jean
ISHTAR
Charles, Patrice Jean
ISHTAR
Charles, Walter
WEEDS
Charleson, Ian
OPERA
Charleson, Ray
EMPIRE OF THE SUN
Charlton, Ann
CUSTODY
Charney, Jordan
MY LITTLE GIRL
Charras, Charles
LE JOURNAL D'UN FOU
Chartey, Alastair
WILD THING
Chase, Carl
CRY FREEDOM
Chase, Harry
MAKING MR.RIGHT
Chase, Nicholas
KITCHEN TOTO, THE
Chasse, Betsy
PARTY CAMP
Chatfield, Lansdale
WITCHES OF EASTWICK, THE
Chatri, Sorapong
COBRA THUNDERBOLT
Chatt, Jill
LIFE CLASSES
Chatterjee, Anil
RUDRABEENA
Chatterjee, Biplab
PHERA
Chatterjee, Subhendu
APAN GHAREY
Chatto, Daniel
LITTLE DORRIT
Chatzijanni, Dora
I KEKARMENI
Chaulet, Emmanuelle
LAMI DE MON AMIE
Chaumeau, Andre
MISS MONA
Chaumette, Monique
LA PASSION BEATRICE
MASQUES
Chavan, Ashok
PRATIGHAAT
Chaves, Richard
PREDATOR
Chavez, Ivone
NOCTURNO AMOR QUE TE VAS
Chavez, Roxanna
MI NOMBRE ES GATILLO
Chavez, Uriel
NOCTURNO AMOR QUE TE VAS
Chaykin, Maury
BEDROOM WINDOW, THE
HEARTS OF FIRE
HIGHER EDUCATION
NOWHERE TO HIDE
WILD THING
Chazel, Marie-Anne
CROSS
LA VIE DISSOLUE DE GERARD FLOQUE
Cheadle, Don
HAMBURGER HILL
Cheebo
ROBINSON NO NIWA
Cheeseman, Gary
FULL METAL JACKET
Chekijian, Souren
FAMILY VIEWING
Chelelo
HERENCIA DE VALIENTES
Chelsom, Peter
INDIAN SUMMER
Chemouny, Charly
FAMILY BUSINESS
Chen, Angie
DIXIA QING
Chen, Joan
LAST EMPEROR, THE
NIGHT STALKER, THE
Cheng, Do Do
MY WILL, I WILL
Cheng, Dodo
WONDER WOMEN
Cheng, Jacky
LAONIANG GOU SAO
Cheng, Mark
PEKING OPERA BLUES
THIRTY MILLION RUSH, THE
Cheng, Olivia
SAPPORO STORY
Cheng, Richard
NINJA THUNDERBOLT
Chenil, Roland
LES FOUS DE BASSAN
Chepil, Bill
STREET TRASH
Chepishchev, G.
VZLOMSHCHIK
Cher
MOONSTRUCK
SUSPECT
WITCHES OF EASTWICK, THE
Cheriguene, Fathia
PIERRE ET DJEMILA
Chernichenko, Irina
ZAVTRA BILA VOINA
Chernin, Cayle
CONCRETE ANGELS
Cherrington, Paki
NGATI
Cherry, James
BELIEVERS, THE
Cherry, Kathy
TALKING WALLS
Chestleigh, Bernard
BIG SHOTS
Chetverikov, Gennady
NOVYE SKAZKI SHAKHEREZADY
Chetvertkov, A.
VZLOMSHCHIK
Cheung, George Kee
OPPOSING FORCE
Cheung, Kiki
EASTERN CONDORS
Cheung, Leslie
BETTER TOMORROW, A
CHINESE GHOST STORY, A
Cheung, Maggie
PROJECT A—PART II
Cheung, Roy
PRISON ON FIRE
Cheung, Vivian
ULTIMAX FORCE
Chevron, Philip
STRAIGHT TO HELL
Cheza, Fidelis
ALLAN QUATERMAIN AND THE LOST CITY OF GOLD
Chi, Li
SEVEN YEARS ITCH
Chi, Wai Tin
FINAL TEST, THE
Chian-Ren, Miaw
TERRORIZERS, THE
Chiang, H. F.
WHITE PHANTOM

Chiang, Paul
WRONG COUPLES,THE
Chiapa, Jesus Romero
GABY—A TRUE STORY
Chiapperini, Chris
IL RAGAZZO DI EBALUS
Chiaureli, Sofico
MILLION V BRACHNOY KORZINE
Chichin, Frederic
SOIGNE TA DROITE
Chichinadze, Irina
STUPEN
Chick, Derel
BLOODSUCKERS FROM OUTER SPACE
Chico, Florinda
LA CASA DE BERNARDA ALBA
Chico Che y La Crisis
ESTA NOCHE CENA PANCHO (DESPEDIDA DE SOLTERO)
Chidyamathamba, Basil
CRY FREEDOM
Chii, Takeo
DEATH SHADOWS
Chiku, Mariko
ROBINSON NO NIWA
Child, Marjorie
SHADOWS OF THE PEACOCK
Childress, Yolanda
RADIO DAYS
Chiles, Lois
CREEPSHOW 2
Chilton, John
PROJECT X
Chilvers, Simon
GROUND ZERO
Chimene, Andre
OUTING, THE
Chimento, Jim
BIG EASY, THE
Chimona, Costas Dino
FULL METAL JACKET
Chin, Glen
WHO'S THAT GIRL
Chin, Joey
CHINA GIRL
Chin, Tsai
DIXIA QING
Chinamando, Ruth
CRY FREEDOM
Ching, Lam
EASTERN CONDORS
Ching, Wong
THIRTY MILLION RUSH, THE
Ching Hsia, Lin
THIRTY MILLION RUSH, THE
Chinh, Kieu
HAMBURGER HILL
Chiota, George
ALLAN QUATERMAIN AND THE LOST CITY OF GOLD
Chirgwin, Marion
DEAR CARDHOLDER
Chissick, Jack
COMRADES
Chlapek, Andrzej
KOMEDIANCI Z WCZORAJSZEJ ULICY
Chlupova, Marcela
CIZIM VSTUP POVOLEN
Chmielnik, Jacek
MIEDZY USTAMI A BRZEGIEM PUCHARU
NAD NIEMNEM
Choc, Jaroslav
DISCOPRIBEH
Chodan, Dah-Ve
HOT PURSUIT
Choder, Jill
TALKING WALLS
Chodos, Dan
DEATH BEFORE DISHONOR
Chokomorov, Suymenkul
VOLNY UMIRAYUT NA BEREGU
Chombart, Fabien
IL EST GENIAL PAPY!
Chong, Jeffrey
WILD THING
Chong, Phil
FATAL BEAUTY
Chong, Rae Dawn
PRINCIPAL, THE
SQUEEZE, THE

Choudhary, Rahul
PRATIGHAAT
Chow, David
WHITE OF THE EYE
Chow, Michael
CHOCOLATE INSPECTOR
Chowdhury, Mahua Roy
LALAN FAKIR
Choy, Keith
LIVING ON TOKYO TIME
Chris Hillman and the Desert R
STEELE JUSTICE
Christensen, Jesper
HIP, HIP, HURRA!
Christensen, Stacy
VIRGIN QUEEN OF ST. FRANCIS HIGH, THE
Christensen, Ute
LITTLE PROSECUTOR, THE
Christian, Claudia
HIDDEN, THE
Christian, Linda
DELITTI
Christian, Perla
MANKILLERS
Christian, Peter
BUSINESS AS USUAL
Christie, Julie
MISS MARY
Christie, Marcia
MALIBU BIKINI SHOP, THE
Christina, Dana
STABILIZER, THE
Christine Harbort
SO VIELE TRAUME
Christmas, Eric
HAPPY HOUR
HOME IS WHERE THE HART IS
Christophe
SICILIAN, THE
Christopher, Dennis
ALIEN PREDATOR
Christopher, Frank
PSYCHOS IN LOVE
Christopher, Guy
IN THE MOOD
Christopher Doyle
OMEGA SYNDROME
Chronopoulou, Mary
TA PAIDIA TIS CHELIDONAS
Chryckin, Vadim
CIZIM VSTUP POVOLEN
Chrystea, Elyzebeth
HELLO AGAIN
Chrzanowska, Katarzyna
CUDZOZIEMKA
Chu, Emily
BETTER TOMORROW, A
Chubb, Paul
WITH LOVE TO THE PERSON NEXT TO ME
Chucarro, Jose M.
ANGUSTIA
Chuen Hung, Ho
BROTHERHOOD
Chufak, Kien
GOOD MORNING, VIETNAM
Chuhlian, Lu
CHINESE ARE COMING, THE
Chun, Sun
BIG PARADE, THE
Chun Se-Young
TICKET
Chun-Hsiung, Ko
ZEGEN
Chun-man, Wong
DEVILS PARADISE, THE
Chung, Cheri
AUTUMN'S TALE, AN
Chung, Cherie
PEKING OPERA BLUES
Chung, David
WALKER
Chung, Jane
FATAL BEAUTY
Chung-chul, Kim
KYEOUL NAGUNE
Chunqing, Xu
LAST EMPEROR, THE
Churchett, Stephen
BELLMAN AND TRUE

Churikova, Inna
KURIER
TEMA
VOENNO-POLEVOI ROMAN
Chursina, Lyudmila
RUS IZNACHALNA
Ciancio, Cristiano
ALADDIN
Cianfriglia, Giovanni
BARBARIANS, THE
Ciangherotti, Alejandro
LAPUTA: THE CASTLE IN THE SKY
Ciangherotti, Fernando
MAS BUENAS QUE EL PAN
Ciangottini, Valeria
LESTATE STA FINENDO
Ciani, Yolanda
JUANA LA CANTINERA
Ciardo, Gianni
ITALIANI A RIO
Ciccoritti, Gerard
PSYCHO GIRLS
Cieslinki, Peter
VERSTECKTE LIEBE
Cifa, Eliana
ANGELUS NOVUS
Ciges, Luis
HAY QUE DESHACER LA CASA
MOROS Y CRISTIANOS
Cillik, Igor
CENA ODVAHY
Cimino, Joseph
ADVENTURE OF THE ACTION HUNTERS
Cimino, Leonardo
MONSTER SQUAD, THE
Cimo, Valentino
UNTOUCHABLES, THE
Cintra, Luis Miguel
JESTER,THE
O DESEJADO—LES MONTAGNES DE LA LUNE
Circus Acrobat
ZYGFRYD
Circus Owner
ZYGFRYD
Cirile, Jim
ROCK 'N' ROLL NIGHTMARE
Cisneros, Jesus
LA ESTANQUERA DE VALLECAS
Cisse, Youssouf Tenin
YEELEN
Citrenbaum, Myron
TIN MEN
Citriniti, Michael
PSYCHOS IN LOVE
Citti, Marc
HOTEL DE FRANCE
Citti. Erland —Josephson, Franco
LA CODA DEL DIAVOLO
Cizas, Tauras
OBVINYAETSYA SVADBA
Claes, Jappe
MASCARA
Claire, Cyrielle
IL GIORNO PRIMA
Claire, Jennifer
GOOD WIFE, THE
RIGHT HAND MAN, THE
Claisse, Georges
CRIME OF HONOR
Clapp, Gordon
MATEWAN
Clarizio, Donatella
DELIZIA
Clark, Andrew
RADIO DAYS
Clark, Barry
PSYCHOS IN LOVE
Clark, Brett
EYE OF THE EAGLE
Clark, Byron
MANKILLERS
Clark, Dorian Joe
MORNING MAN, THE
Clark, Eugene
THREE MEN AND A BABY
Clark, James
ASSASSINATION
Clark, Jill
NO WAY OUT

Clark, Joe Dorian
STREET SMART

Clark, Jon
SLAUGHTER HIGH

Clark, Justin
SICILIAN, THE

Clark, Kathleen
HOLLYWOOD SHUFFLE

Clark, Liddy
CODA

Clark, Louise Caire
PROGRAMMED TO KILL

Clark, Matt
LETS GET HARRY

Clark, Melita
EMPIRE STATE

Clark, Michael
COMRADES

Clark, Neale
MATEWAN

Clark, Philip
CHIPMUNK ADVENTURE, THE

Clark, Quentin
BELIEVERS, THE

Clark, Wayne
FULL METAL JACKET

Clarke, Andrew
LES PATTERSON SAVES THE WORLD

Clarke, Caitlin
KID BROTHER, THE

Clarke, Dara
DEAD, THE

Clarke, Hope
ANGEL HEART

Clarke, John
LES PATTERSON SAVES THE WORLD
THOSE DEAR DEPARTED

Clarke, Sylvie
SITTING IN LIMBO

Clarke, Warren
ISHTAR

Clarkson, Patricia
UNTOUCHABLES, THE

Classe, Henry
LES FOUS DE BASSAN

Clatu
PROJECT X

Claudia Knapp
JENATSCH

Clausen, Liv
RAWHEAD REX

Clavel, Camille
LES MENDIANTS

Clavier, Christian
LA VIE DISSOLUE DE GERARD FLOQUE

Clawson, Steve
WINNERS TAKE ALL

Clay, Nicholas
LIONHEART
SLEEPING BEAUTY

Clay, Thomas Albert
IN THE MOOD

Clayburgh, Jill
SHY PEOPLE

Clayton, Elizabeth
SILENT NIGHT, DEADLY NIGHT PART II

Clayton, John
HIGH TIDE
WARM NIGHTS ON A SLOW MOVING TRAIN

Clayton, Kristin
NIGHTMARE ON ELM STREET 3: DREAM WARRIORS, A

Clayton, Merry
MAID TO ORDER

Clayton, R.G.
OUTRAGEOUS FORTUNE

Clayton, Rosy
FOURTH PROTOCOL, THE

Clayton-Jones, Edward
DOGS IN SPACE

Cleator, Molly
ALLNIGHTER, THE

Clelland, Don
VIDEO DEAD, THE

Clemenson, Christian
BLACK WIDOW
MAKING MR.RIGHT

Clemenson, Christina
BROADCAST NEWS

Clement, Aurore
MOSCA ADDIO

Clement, David
BLUE MONKEY

Clencie, David
MOVING TARGETS

Clennon, David
HES MY GIRL
TROUBLE WITH DICK, THE

Clery, Corinne
VIA MONTENAPOLEONE

Cleven, Harry
MASCARA

Cleverdon, Dean
HOUSE TWO: THE SECOND STORY

Clifford, Clare
PERSONAL SERVICES
WISH YOU WERE HERE

Clifford, Coleen
YEAR MY VOICE BROKE, THE

Clift, Faith
CRY WILDERNESS

Clifton, Jane
AS TIME GOES BY

Cline, Jenni
MATEWAN

Cline, Rachel
HOUSE OF GAMES

Clohessy, Robert
BELIEVERS, THE

Clooney, George
RETURN TO HORROR HIGH

Close, Del
BIG TOWN, THE
UNTOUCHABLES, THE

Close, Glenn
FATAL ATTRACTION

Clotilde, Luiza
UM FILM 100% BRAZILEIRO

Clotworthy, Robert
WHO'S THAT GIRL

Clout, Bob
BELIEVERS, THE

Clown, Roger
KEEPING TRACK

Cluff, Jennifer
DEAR CARDHOLDER
JILTED

Cluzet, Francois
LASSOCIATION DES MALFAITEURS

Cmiral, Jaroslav
PRATELE BERMUDSKEHO TROJUHELNIKU

Cnota, Jerzy
KOMEDIANCI Z WCZORAJSZEJ ULICY

Coady, Mike
NAIL GUN MASSACRE

Coady, Simon
BOY SOLDIER

Cobb, Hutton
BIG SHOTS

Cobb, Randall "Tex"
CRITICAL CONDITION
POLICE ACADEMY 4: CITIZENS ON PATROL
RAISING ARIZONA

Cobbs, Bill
SUSPECT

Cobo, Arturo
LAPUTA: THE CASTLE IN THE SKY

Cobos, German
LAW OF DESIRE

Coburn, Charles
BLOODSUCKERS FROM OUTER SPACE

Coburn, Glen
BLOODSUCKERS FROM OUTER SPACE

Cocek, Christina
DIRTY LAUNDRY

Cochran, Chuck
UNFINISHED BUSINESS . . .

Cochrane, Andrew
HOT PURSUIT

Cochrane, Tallie
EMANON

Cockburn, Adam
RIGHT HAND MAN, THE

Coco, Bibi
QUEL RAGAZZO DELLA CURVA "B"

Coco, James
HUNK

Cocza, Frank
AMAZONS

Coduri, Camille
PRAYER FOR THE DYING, A

Cody, Iron Eyes
ERNEST GOES TO CAMP

Coe, Barry
EL HOMBRE DESNUDO

Coe, George
BEST SELLER
BLIND DATE

Coego, Manolo
WHOOPS APOCALYPSE

Coffee
VZLOMSHCHIK

Coffey, T. Scott
ZOMBIE HIGH

Coffin, Frederick
BEDROOM WINDOW, THE

Coffin, Sylvie
ENNEMIS INTIMES

Coffinet, Jean
ARIA

Coffing, Barry
OUTING, THE

Cofrin, Andrew
MONSTER IN THE CLOSET

Coggin, Linda
GOTHIC

Coggio, Roger
LE JOURNAL D'UN FOU

Coghill, Joy
BLUE MONKEY

Coghill, Nikki
RUNNING FROM THE GUNS
TIME GUARDIAN, THE

Cohen, Alejandro
LA ESTACION DEL REGRESO

Cohen, J.J.
PRINCIPAL, THE

Cohen, Jehuda
POET'S SILENCE, THE

Cohen, Judith
FOREVER, LULU

Cohen, Marilyn
IN THE MOOD

Cohen, Mike
WARRIORS OF THE APOCALYPSE

Cohen, Shahar
DEADLINE

Cohen, Silvia
MEFISTO FUNK

Cohen, Vered
LATE SUMMER BLUES

Cohn, Bill
MORGAN STEWART'S COMING HOME

Cohn, Harry
BARFLY

Cohn-Bendit, Daniel
UN AMOUR A PARIS

Coine, James
CRY FREEDOM

Colanaki, Dora
KE DYO AVGA TOURKIAS

Colbert, Curt
OUTTAKES

Colbert, Pat
LEONARD PART 6

Colbert, Robert
AMAZON WOMEN ON THE MOON

Colceri, Tim
EMANON
FULL METAL JACKET

Colchat, Nicole
FALSCH

Cole, Catrin
BEVERLY HILLS COP II

Cole, Dennis
PRETTY SMART

Cole, Ellen
KILLER WORKOUT

Cole, Jeannine Ann
O. C. AND STIGGS

Cole, Olivia
BIG SHOTS

Coleby, Anja
YEAR MY VOICE BROKE, THE

Coleman, Clark
MILLION DOLLAR MYSTERY

Coleman, Clarke
WINNERS TAKE ALL

Coleman, Dabney
DRAGNET
Coleman, Derick
ARIA
Coleman, Heather
WITCHES OF EASTWICK, THE
Coleman, Jack
PURSUIT OF HAPPINESS, THE
Coleman, Johnny
NGATI
Coleman, Layne
BIG TOWN, THE
HOUSEKEEPER, THE
Coleman, R.C.
SUSPECT
Coleman, Terry
PRINCIPAL, THE
Colen, Beatrice
WHO'S THAT GIRL
Coles, Charles Honi
DIRTY DANCING
Coles, Martii
DOGS IN SPACE
Colgate, Bill
BIG TOWN, THE
Colicos, John
NOWHERE TO HIDE
Colin, Margaret
LIKE FATHER, LIKE SON
THREE MEN AND A BABY
Colitti, Rik
BARFLY
Coll, Christopher
WHOOPS APOCALYPSE
Coll, Ivonne
LA GRAN FIESTA
Coll, Jose Luis
MOROS Y CRISTIANOS
Collard, Paul
ARIA
Collard, William F.
EMANON
Colley, Kenneth
WHISTLE BLOWER, THE
Collin, Anthony
PERSONAL SERVICES
Collin, Frederique
LA COULEUR ENCERCLEE
Collin, Philippe
JEUX D'ARTIFICES
Collinge, Eamonn
BOY SOLDIER
Collingwood, Peter
LES PATTERSON SAVES THE WORLD
Collins, Alan
STRIKE COMMANDO
Collins, Albert
ADVENTURES IN BABYSITTING
Collins, Bill
HOWLING III, THE
Collins, Brad
ULTIMAX FORCE
Collins, Everitt Wayne
LETHAL WEAPON
Collins, Gene
EMANON
Collins, Joseph
NO DEAD HEROES
Collins, Michael
BARFLY
Collins, Michelle
PERSONAL SERVICES
Collins, Olivia
RETO A LA VIDA
Collins, Pamela
WHISTLE BLOWER, THE
Collins, Robert Ramsay
BIG TOWN, THE
Collins, Ruth
BLOOD SISTERS
FIREHOUSE
PSYCHOS IN LOVE
Collins, Sean
HOUSEKEEPER, THE
Collins, Tom
WALKER
Collomb, Emmanuelle
FAMILY BUSINESS
Collomb, Florence
FAMILY BUSINESS

Colner, Marc
RADIO DAYS
Colombaioni, Arnaldo
FRANCESCA
Colquhoun, Caitlyn
LIFE CLASSES
Colson, Scott
BEDROOM WINDOW, THE
Colt, Marshall
FLOWERS IN THE ATTIC
Colton, Jacque Lynn
BIG BAD MAMA II
Coltrane, Robbie
EAT THE RICH
Columbu, Franco
RUNNING MAN, THE
Colvey, Catherine
KEEPING TRACK
Colvey, Peter
MORNING MAN, THE
PRETTYKILL
Colvig, Vance
BARFLY
DUDES
Colyar, Michael K.
HOLLYWOOD SHUFFLE
Comar, Richard
BIG TOWN, THE
HEARTS OF FIRE
Comart, Jean-Paul
CLUB DE RENCONTRES
Combeau, Muriel
UN AMOUR A PARIS
Combs, Jeffrey
CYCLONE
Combs, Ray
OVERBOARD
Conabree, Bill
REMEMBERING MEL
Cone, Nancy
P.K. & THE KID
Conesa, Cari
JUANA LA CANTINERA
Conescu, Josh
HOUSE OF GAMES
Confalone, Marina
SEMBRA MORTO . . . ME E SOLO SVENUTO
Conforti, Tony
PICK-UP ARTIST, THE
Conklin, Katherine
MANNEQUIN
Conn, Michael
HOLLYWOOD SHUFFLE
Connell, Gordon
CREEPSHOW 2
Connell, Kate
LIVING ON TOKYO TIME
Connell, Malcolm
THREE KINDS OF HEAT
Connelly, Chris
MESSENGER, THE
Connelly, Christopher
STRIKE COMMANDO
Connelly, Joanne
PRICK UP YOUR EARS
Connelly, Robert
BELIEVERS, THE
Connery, Carol
BEAKS
Connery, Sean
UNTOUCHABLES, THE
Connolly, Jim
REMEMBERING MEL
Connors, Chuck
SAKURA KILLERS
SUMMER CAMP NIGHTMARE
Conoray, Ruben
RETO A LA VIDA
Conover, Skip
HAPPY HOUR
Conrad, Sydney
BEDROOM WINDOW, THE
Conradi, Birgit
PETER VON SCHOLTEN
Conroy, Frances
AMAZING GRACE AND CHUCK
Considine, John
MADE IN HEAVEN
OPPOSING FORCE

Constantin, Mihai
PADUREANCA
Constantine, Helene
BEYOND THERAPY
Constantine, Michael
FORTY DAYS OF MUSA DAGH
IN THE MOOD
Contalapiedra, Ricardo
MADRID
Conte, Derek
BLOOD SISTERS
Conte, Julie
BIG TOWN, THE
Conte, Michael
NECROPOLIS
Conte, Steve
KINDRED, THE
Conti, Denise
EMANON
Conti, Laura
LESCOT
Conti, Peter
BARFLY
Conti, Tom
BEYOND THERAPY
MIRACLES
Conti, Ugo
SOLDATI: 365 GIORNI ALL' ALBA
Conti, Vicky
NARCOTERROR
Contreras, Luis
EXTREME PREJUDICE
MISSION KILL
STRAIGHT TO HELL
WALKER
Contreras, Patricio
MADE IN ARGENTINA
Conville, David
FOURTH PROTOCOL, THE
FOURTH PROTOCOL, THE
Conway, Bert
IN THE MOOD
Conway, Cyril
FOURTH PROTOCOL, THE
Conway, Gary
AMERICAN NINJA 2: THE CONFRONTATION
Conway, Kevin
VIOLINS CAME WITH THE AMERICANS, THE
Conway, Tim
CYCLONE
Coogan, Keith
ADVENTURES IN BABYSITTING
HIDING OUT
Cook, Bonnie
DATE WITH AN ANGEL
Cook, Doria
EVIL TOWN
Cook, Garry
GOOD WIFE, THE
Cook, Graham Fletcher
CRY FREEDOM
STRAIGHT TO HELL
Cook, Ken
STARLIGHT HOTEL
Cook, Patrick
DEAR CARDHOLDER
THOSE DEAR DEPARTED
Cook, Penny
CODA
Cook, Peter
PRINCESS BRIDE, THE
WHOOPS APOCALYPSE
Cook, Sam
GIRL, THE
Cook, Steve
EQUALIZER 2000
OPPOSING FORCE
Cooney, Estelle
REMEMBERING MEL
Cooper, Alice
PRINCE OF DARKNESS
Cooper, Ann
BANZAI RUNNER
Cooper, Cami
LIKE FATHER, LIKE SON
Cooper, Charles
VALET GIRLS
Cooper, Chevis
PROJECT X

Cooper, Chris
MATEWAN
Cooper, Garry
PRICK UP YOUR EARS
Cooper, Gary
MANKILLERS
Cooper, Jackie
SUPERMAN IV: THE QUEST FOR PEACE
SURRENDER
Cooper, John
FIRE AND ICE
Cooper, Sherril
STARLIGHT HOTEL
Cooper, Steven
MY DARK LADY
Cooper, Terrance
NO WAY OUT
Cooper, Terrence
HOT PURSUIT
Cooper, Tony
SNOW WHITE
Cooper, Trevor
WHISTLE BLOWER, THE
Copeland, Bob
WELCOME MARIA
Copeland, Diane
MANKILLERS
Copeland, Dianne
KILLER WORKOUT
Copeland, Joan
HAPPY NEW YEAR
Copeland, Miles
EAT THE RICH
Copeland, Sebastian
BORDER RADIO
Copeman, Michael
DEAD OF WINTER
Copleston, Geoffrey
BELLY OF AN ARCHITECT, THE
Copley, Peter
EMPIRE OF THE SUN
Coppenbarger, Franny
BLOODSUCKERS FROM OUTER SPACE
Coppenolle, Lisa
MISSION KILL
Copping, Nick
WHOOPS APOCALYPSE
Corazzari, Bruno
MORO AFFAIR, THE
UN TASSINARO A NEW YORK
Corbellini, Vanni
BELLY OF AN ARCHITECT, THE
LE FOTO DI GIOIA
Corber, Arthur
MORNING MAN, THE
WILD THING
Corbett, Ed
NEAR DARK
Corbin, Barry
OFF THE MARK
UNDER COVER
Corbitt, Chance Michael
LOST BOYS, THE
Cordero, Joaquin
RATAS DE LA CIUDAD
Cordero, Manuel
MUTANT HUNT
Cordua, Beatrice
LADY OF THE CAMELIAS
Corduner, Allan
HEARTS OF FIRE
VALHALLA
Corey, Philip
BELIEVERS, THE
Corey, Tom
VALET GIRLS
Coria, Martin
RAGE OF HONOR
Cormack, Lynne
TOO OUTRAGEOUS
Corman, Maddie
SOME KIND OF WONDERFUL
Cormier, Jacinta
LIFE CLASSES
Cornell, Dan
BELL DIAMOND
Cornes, Lee
LOVECHILD, THE
Cornibert, Chris
FULL METAL JACKET
Cornibert, Danny
FULL METAL JACKET
Cornthwaite, Robert
WHO'S THAT GIRL
Cornuelle, Jenny
DEADLY ILLUSION
Cornwall, Judy
CRY FREEDOM
Cornwell, Hugh
EAT THE RICH
Corona, Sergio
CINCO NACOS ASALTAN A LAS VEGAS
Corre, Cecile
COERS CROISES
Corre, Luke
ARIA
Corsair, Bill
FOREVER, LULU
Corsale, Alessandra
QUARTIERE
Cortadellas, Laurence
MEMOIRE DES APPARENCES: LA VIE EST UN SONGE
Cortese, Joe
DEADLY ILLUSION
Cortese, Maria
PSYCHO GIRLS
Cortese, Valentina
VIA MONTENAPOLEONE
Cortez, Bertie
POUSSIERE D'ANGE
Cortez, Raul
VERA
Cortinas, Larry
HOLLYWOOD SHUFFLE
Cortinez, Lidia
MISS MARY
Cosby, Bill
LEONARD PART 6
Cosgrove, Don
BLOOD HOOK
Cosham, Ralph
SUSPECT
Cosse, Villanueva
EN RETIRADA
Cosso, Pierre
I MIEI PRIMI QUARANT'ANNI
Cossu, Brigette
BLOOD SISTERS
Costa, Catarina Alves
RELACAO FIEL E VERDADEIRA
Costa, Danny
WANTED: DEAD OR ALIVE
Costantini, Brian
TIN MEN
Costello, Bill
HEART
Costello, Chris
CODE NAME ZEBRA
Costello, Elvis
STRAIGHT TO HELL
Costello, Ward
PROJECT X
Costigan, George
RITA, SUE AND BOB TOO!
Costner, Kevin
NO WAY OUT
UNTOUCHABLES, THE
Costume Designer
MASCARA
Cota, Nadia
STUDENT CONFIDENTIAL
Cote, Laurence
TRAVELLING AVANT
Cote, Lorraine
ARIA
Cotoco, Sauro
ULTIMAX FORCE
Cottencon, Fanny
LE JOURNAL D'UN FOU
POUSSIERE D'ANGE
TANT QU'IL AURA DES FEMMES
Cotterell, James
AMAZING GRACE AND CHUCK
Cotterill, Ralph
HOWLING III, THE
LIGHTHORSEMEN, THE
RIGHT HAND MAN, THE
Cotton, Oliver
HIDING OUT
SICILIAN, THE
Cotton, Yves
LES NOCES BARBARES
Coulom, Ilona
ARCHANGELOS TOU PATHOUS
Coulter, Sean
DIRTY LAUNDRY
Councilman Hylen
LEIF
Courant, Gerard
QUATRE AVENTURES DE REINETTE ET MIRABELLE
Courier, Mary Jane
LIKE FATHER, LIKE SON
Court, Alyson
CARE BEARS ADVENTURE IN WONDERLAND, THE
Courtenay, Tom
HAPPY NEW YEAR
LEONARD PART 6
Courtney, Alex
PROGRAMMED TO KILL
Courtney, Fritzi Jane
JAWS: THE REVENGE
Courts, Bob
NO WAY OUT
Coutts, Julian
HOUSEKEEPER, THE
Coutu, Angele
LE SOURD DANS LA VILLE
LES FOUS DE BASSAN
Couveau, Traci
CRYSTAL HEART
Covarrubias, Robert
PROJECT X
Cover, Frankin
WALL STREET
Covert, Todd Mason
NIGHTFORCE
Cowen, Henry
RADIO DAYS
Cowley, William
SPACE RACE
Cowper, Nicola
LIONHEART
Cox, Arthur
ARIA
HOPE AND GLORY
PERSONAL SERVICES
Cox, Courteney
MASTERS OF THE UNIVERSE
Cox, Gary
BARFLY
Cox, Michael Graham
CRY FREEDOM
Cox, Richard
ZOMBIE HIGH
Cox, Ronny
BEVERLY HILLS COP II
ROBOCOP
STEELE JUSTICE
Cox, Tony
SPACEBALLS
VALET GIRLS
Coy, Jonathan
MASCHENKA
Coyle, Bob
RAWHEAD REX
Coyote, Peter
MAN IN LOVE, A
OUTRAGEOUS FORTUNE
STACKING
Cozorici, Gheorghe
ZLOTY POCIAG
Crabtree, Michael
BEST SELLER
Craden, Omie
CONCRETE ANGELS
Crahay, Christian
FALSCH
Craig, Alan S.
OUT OF ROSENHEIM
Craig, Andrew
FOREVER, LULU
Craig, Carl
HOLLYWOOD SHUFFLE
Craig, Connie
THOU SHALT NOT KILL . . . EXCEPT
Craig, Phyllis
DEADTIME STORIES
Craig, Simon
CONCRETE ANGELS

Craig, Tony
SUSPECT
Craig, Wendell
RADIO DAYS
Craigie, Ingrid
DEAD, THE
Cramer, Dag
FADERN, SONEN OCH DEN HELIGE ANDE
Cramer, Michael
SUMMER CAMP NIGHTMARE
Cramer, Mike
CONCRETE ANGELS
Crane, Nancy
FOURTH PROTOCOL, THE
Cranfield, Lee
ESCAPES
Cranitch, Lorcan
EMPIRE STATE
Cranna, Jim
LIVING ON TOKYO TIME
Crass, Cynthia
DREAMANIAC
Crauchet, Paul
LA BRUTE
Craven, Matt
TIN MEN
Crawford, Dwight
WHO'S THAT GIRL
Crawford, Ellen
WHO'S THAT GIRL
Crawford, Ralph
MUTANT HUNT
Creco, Domenica
CRAZY BOYS
Cree, Ed
OVERBOARD
Creley, Jack
POLICE ACADEMY 4: CITIZENS ON PATROL
Cremades, Michel
FAMILY BUSINESS
Cremer, Bruno
FALSCH
Cremer, Ute
DER TOD DES EMPEDOKLES
Crenshaw, Marshall
LA BAMBA
Crespi, Pierluigi
DOLCE ASSENZA
Creton, Michel
LE SOLITAIRE
Crew, Carl
BLOOD DINER
Cribb, Kirk
PARTY CAMP
Crick, Ed
EYE OF THE EAGLE
Crickenberger, Melvin
MORGAN STEWART'S COMING HOME
Crighton, Tom
BIRDS OF PREY
Crippa, Maddalena
AURELIA
Crippa, Vittorio
AURELIA
Cripple, Jonathon
MISSION KILL
Criscione, T.J.
CONCRETE ANGELS
Criscoulo, Lou
SQUEEZE, THE
Criscuolo, Lou
HIDING OUT
Criscuolo, Louis
WEEDS
Crist, Gloria
HIDING OUT
Cristal, Gloria
MASSACRE IN DINOSAUR VALLEY
Crivello, Guerrino
DOLCE PELLE DI ANGELA
Crofoot, Sharon
TIN MEN
Crofton, Mary
BOY SOLDIER
Croiset, Max
VROEGER IS DOOD
Crombie, Jonathan
HOUSEKEEPER, THE

Cromwell, James
REVENGE OF THE NERDS II: NERDS IN PARADISE
Cronce, G. Gordon
ORACLE, THE
Cronyn, Hume
BATTERIES NOT INCLUDED
Crooke, Leland
MAID TO ORDER
Crosby, Gary
NIGHT STALKER, THE
Crosby, Lindsey
CODE NAME ZEBRA
Crosby, Lucinda
OVERBOARD
Cross, Bill
NEAR DARK
Cross, Billy
WEEDS
Cross, Harley
BELIEVERS, THE
SOMEONE TO WATCH OVER ME
Cross, Sally
SLAUGHTER HIGH
Crossman, Michael
EMPIRE OF THE SUN
Crouse, Lindsay
HOUSE OF GAMES
Crouse, Wayne
BIRDS OF PREY
Crow, Wade
SUMMER CAMP NIGHTMARE
Crowder, Tracy
STRIPPED TO KILL
Crowe, Christine
BLOODSUCKERS FROM OUTER SPACE
Crowell, Christine
MANKILLERS
Crowley, Emily
BROADCAST NEWS
Crowley, Suzan
BORN OF FIRE
Crowshaw, Christine
HOPE AND GLORY
Cruciani, Mario
WARRIOR QUEEN
Cruickshank, Su
THOSE DEAR DEPARTED
Cruz, Bob
MAKING MR.RIGHT
Cruz, Ernesto Gomez
OPERACION MARIJUANA
REALM OF FORTUNE, THE
VIAJE AL PARAISO
Cruz, Lito
SOFIA
Cruz, Rebecca
VALET GIRLS
Cryan, Carmel
WHISTLE BLOWER, THE
Cryer, Gretchen
HIDING OUT
Cryer, Jon
DUDES
HIDING OUT
MORGAN STEWART'S COMING HOME
O. C. AND STIGGS
SUPERMAN IV: THE QUEST FOR PEACE
Crystal, Billy
THROW MOMMA FROM THE TRAIN
Csakanyi, Eszter
DOKTOR MINORKA VIDOR NAGY NAPJA
HOL VOLT, HOL NEM VOLT
Cserhalmi, Erzsi
SZORNYEK EVADJA
Cserhalmi, Gyorgy
SZORNYEK EVADJA
TISZTA AMERIKA
Csortos, Gyula
A JAVOR
Cuau, Marianne
HOTEL DE FRANCE
Cucciolla, Riccardo
IL CORAGGIO DI PARLARE
IL RAGAZZO DI EBALUS
UNA CASA IN BILICO
Cucumber Sandwiches
WHOOPS APOCALYPSE
Cudlin, Michael
CUSTODY

Cudney, Roger
GHOST FEVER
MIRACLES
Cuervo, Fernando G.
LAW OF DESIRE
Cuervo, Fernando Guillen
LA SENYORA
Cuesta, Raul Eguron
VISA U.S.A.
Cueto, Juan
ASIGNATURA APROBADA
Cuff, John Haslett
PSYCHO GIRLS
Cui, Cuitlahuac
YERBA SANGRIENTE
Culf, Norris
NECROPOLIS
ROBOT HOLOCAUST
Cull, Wayne
TO MARKET, TOMARKET
Cullum, John
SWEET COUNTRY
Cullum, John David
MORGAN STEWART'S COMING HOME
SOMETHING SPECIAL!
Culotta, Phil
MONSTER SQUAD, THE
Culp, Robert
BIG BAD MAMA II
Cumbuka, Ji-Tu
OUTRAGEOUS FORTUNE
Cumer, Jill
DERANGED
THIN LINE, THE
Cummings, Bobby
NIGHTFORCE
Cummings, Jim
GARBAGE PAIL KIDS MOVIE, THE
Cummings, Michael
MUTANT HUNT
Cummings, Richard
HOLLYWOOD SHUFFLE
P.I. PRIVATE INVESTIGATIONS
PROJECT X
Cummings, Sandy
MESSENGER, THE
Cummins, Juliette
SLUMBER PARTY MASSACRE II
Cummins, Peter
GOOD WIFE, THE
GROUND ZERO
SLATE, WYN & ME
Cundieff, Rusty
HOLLYWOOD SHUFFLE
Cunha, Luis
RELACAO FIEL E VERDADEIRA
Cunningham, Anne
MORE BAD NEWS
Cunningham, David
BLOODSUCKERS FROM OUTER SPACE
Cunningham, Debra
PRETTY SMART
Cunningham, Gary Wayne
NEAR DARK
Cunningham, John
HELLO AGAIN
Cunningham, Neil
EAT THE RICH
Cuny, Alain
CHRONICLE OF A DEATH FORETOLD
Cupac, Sanders
WHO'S THAT GIRL
Cupisti, Barbara
DELIRIA
OPERA
Curley, Thom
ROXANNE
Curran, Lynette
COMRADES
YEAR MY VOICE BROKE, THE
Curren, Dennis
BIG EASY, THE
Curreri, Lee
CRYSTAL HEART
Currier, Terrence
GARDENS OF STONE
Curtin, Jane
O. C. AND STIGGS
Curtis, Jamie Lee
AMAZING GRACE AND CHUCK

MAN IN LOVE, A
Curtis, John
FULL METAL JACKET
Curtis, Kelly
MAGIC STICKS
Curtis, Liane
KID BROTHER, THE
Curtis, Scott
SUMMER CAMP NIGHTMARE
Curtis, Sonia
MONSTER SQUAD, THE
Curtis, Tony
CLUB LIFE
Curzon, Fiona
SLEEP WELL, MY LOVE
Cusack, Cyril
LITTLE DORRIT
Cusack, Joan
ALLNIGHTER, THE
BROADCAST NEWS
Cusack, John
BROADCAST NEWS
HOT PURSUIT
Cush, Tom
CYCLONE
Cutell, Lou
MALIBU BIKINI SHOP, THE
Cutillo, Al
NIGHTFORCE
Cutler, J.C.
ISHTAR
Cutler, Jon
RUNNING MAN, THE
Cutter, Rex
EQUALIZER 2000
Cvetkovic, Svetozar
NA PUTA ZA KATANGU
Cvijanovic, Zoran
OKTOBERFEST
Cvijetan, Zeljka
OKTOBERFEST
Cybelle, Roxanne
BLOOD DINER
Cygan, Katarzyna
PIERSCIEN I ROZA
Cypher, Jon
MASTERS OF THE UNIVERSE
OFF THE MARK
Cyphers, Charles
BIG BAD MAMA II
HUNTER'S BLOOD
Cyr, Myriam
GOTHIC
Cyrus, Tony
LIVING DAYLIGHTS, THE
Czako, Ildiko
HOTREAL
Czapiewski, Sandy
BIG TOWN, THE
D, Chris
NO WAY OUT
D'Abbraccio, Milly
IL LUPO DI MARE
LA TRASGRESSIONE
d'Abo, Maryam
LIVING DAYLIGHTS, THE
D'Abo, Olivia
MISSION KILL
d'Alessandro, Fiorenza
GOOD MORNING BABYLON
D'Amato, Paul
SUSPECT
D'Ambrosio, Vito
UNTOUCHABLES, THE
D'Amico, Marcus
FULL METAL JACKET
D'Andrea, Anthony
BEVERLY HILLS COP II
D'Angelo, Beverly
ARIA
IN THE MOOD
MAID TO ORDER
D'Angelo, Jesse
BLOOD SISTERS
ROCK 'N' ROLL NIGHTMARE
D'Angelo, Nino
QUEL RAGAZZO DELLA CURVA "B"
D'Aquili, Marco
NOI UOMINI DURI
D'Ark, Sasha
UN TASSINARO A NEW YORK
d'At, Catherine
GRAND GUIGNOL
D'Aulan, Sophie
MALADIE D'AMOUR
d'Avanzo, Lucila
POR LOS CAMINOS VERDES
D'Eva, Giuseppina Gaspardis
BELLIFRESCHI
D'Onofrio, Vincent
FULL METAL JACKET
D'Onofrio, Vincent Phillip
ADVENTURES IN BABYSITTING
D'Orazio, Marlo
ADELMO
D'Salva, Ramon
EQUALIZER 2000
SWEET REVENGE
D., Chris
BORDER RADIO
Da Pina, Carlos Alberto Alves De Veiga
PRINSEN FRA FOGO
Daalder, Remco
EEN MAAND LATER
Daans, Layra
ROCK 'N' ROLL NIGHTMARE
Dabney, Sheila
SHE MUST BE SEEING THINGS
Dabson, Jesse
DEATH WISH 4: THE CRACKDOWN
Dacqmine, Jacques
MELO
Daddi, Frank
IRON WARRIOR
Dafis, Elfed
BOY SOLDIER
Dagelet, Hans
ZJOEK
Dagmouni, Moktar
PRICK UP YOUR EARS
Dahan, Ruth
MORNING MAN, THE
STREET SMART
Dahl, Terje
FELDMANN CASE, THE
Dahlen, Viveca
MY LIFE AS A DOG
Dahlgren, David
BIG EASY, THE
Daho, Etienne
JEUX D'ARTIFICES
Daiba
DAO MAZEI
Daichi, Yasuo
TAXING WOMAN, A
Dailey, Irene
STACKING
Daina, Raquel
LA ESTANQUERA DE VALLECAS
Dais, Ronald
KILLER WORKOUT
Dalbecchi, Jonas
MASSACRE IN DINOSAUR VALLEY
Dale, Colin
HOPE AND GLORY
Dale, Dick
BACK TO THE BEACH
Dale, Janet
EIGHTY FOUR CHARING CROSS ROAD
PRICK UP YOUR EARS
Dale, Richard
LADIES OF THE LOTUS
Dale, Vincent
CONCRETE ANGELS
Dalianis, Costas
ONIRO ARISTERIS NICHTAS
Dalla Rosa, Simone
LUNGA VITA ALLA SIGNORA!
Dallesandro, Joe
CRITICAL CONDITION
Dalton, Oakley
ANGEL HEART
Dalton, Timothy
LIVING DAYLIGHTS, THE
Daly, Julie Ann
ESCAPES
Daly, Timothy
MADE IN HEAVEN
Damian
MUTANT HUNT
Damiani, Lucien
MANON OF THE SPRING
Damlacik, Dilek
YER DEMIR, GOK BAKIR
Dammett, Blackie
LETHAL WEAPON
Damon, Gabriel
TERMINUS
Damon's Assistant
RUNNING MAN, THE
Danaher, Tom
EMPIRE OF THE SUN
Danare, Malcolm
CURSE, THE
Dance, Charles
GOOD MORNING BABYLON
HIDDEN CITY
WHITE MISCHIEF
Danchyshyn, Basil
TRAIN OF DREAMS
Dandare, Ramon Todd
ODYSSEE D'AMOUR
Dandoulaki, Katia
SWEET COUNTRY
Danelle, John
ROSARY MURDERS, THE
Danese, Connie
HUNTER'S BLOOD
Danese, Shera
BABY BOOM
Daniel
ROBOCOP
Daniel, Don
EMANON
SLUMBER PARTY MASSACRE II
Daniel, Josh
BIG BANG, THE
Danielle, Suzanne
TROUBLE WITH SPIES, THE
Daniels, Ben
WISH YOU WERE HERE
Daniels, Danny D.
OUTING, THE
Daniels, Jeff
RADIO DAYS
Daniels, Pauline
EEN MAAND LATER
Daniels, William
BLIND DATE
Danielsson/Sten —Hellstrom, Jesper
JIM OCH PIRATERNA BLOM
Danilov, S.
VZLOMSHCHIK
Danilova, Natalya
DUBLYOR NACHINAET DEYSTVOVAT
Danker, Eli
WANTED: DEAD OR ALIVE
Dann, Hugo
BIG TOWN, THE
Danning, Sybil
AMAZON WOMEN ON THE MOON
TALKING WALLS
WARRIOR QUEEN
Danno, Jacqueline
JOHNNY MONROE
Danny
KAUN KITNEY PAANI MEIN
Dano, Royal
HOUSE TWO: THE SECOND STORY
RED HEADED STRANGER
Danoff, Bill
TIN MEN
Danson, Ted
THREE MEN AND A BABY
Dante, Michael
MESSENGER, THE
Danton, Mark
BIG TOWN, THE
Danz, Patrick
BLOOD HOOK
Dapporto, Carlo
FAMILY, THE
Dapporto, Massimo
FAMILY, THE
SOLDATI: 365 GIORNI ALL' ALBA
TENEREZZA
Darby, Kim
TEEN WOLF TOO

Darc, Mireille
LA VIE DISSOLUE DE GERARD FLOQUE
Darden, Charles
SOMETHING SPECIAL!
Dardenne, Millie
FALSCH
Dardia, John
NECROPOLIS
Darin, Ricardo
STRANGER, THE
Daring, Mason
MATEWAN
Darlan, Eva
POULE ET FRITES
Darmon, Gerard
LE BEAUF
Darras, Jean-Pierre
LE JOURNAL D'UN FOU
Darrell, John
WHOOPS APOCALYPSE
Darrell, Mike
IN THE MOOD
Darrow, Henry
MISSION KILL
Darrow, Tony
STREET TRASH
Darst, Danny
O. C. AND STIGGS
Das, Ajit
TUNDA BAIDA
Das, Anita
BABULA
Das, Sukhen
AMAR KANTAK
Dash, Stacey
ENEMY TERRITORY
Dastor, Nicholas
EMPIRE OF THE SUN
Datskaya, Oxana
LICHNOE DELO SUDYI IVANOVOY
Datz, Roy
MAKING MR.RIGHT
Dauer, Roger
BLOOD DINER
Daunton, Jeffrey
PERSONAL SERVICES
Dauphin, Jean-Claude
CHARLIE DINGO
Dauscha, Kathrina
NEGERKYS & LABRE LARVER
Dautun, Berangere
FALSCH
Davalos, Dominique
SALVATION!
Davanzati, Stefano
CARTOLINE ITALIANE
Davenport, David
EIGHTY FOUR CHARING CROSS ROAD
Davi, Robert
WILD THING
David, Eleanor
EIGHTY FOUR CHARING CROSS ROAD
David, Ernie
SWEET REVENGE
David, Joanna
COMRADES
David, Keith
HOT PURSUIT
David, Larry
RADIO DAYS
David, Lolita
BIG TOWN, THE
David, Mario
DE FLYGANDE DJAVLARNA
David, Myriam
JEUX D'ARTIFICES
David, Tami
LIKE FATHER, LIKE SON
David, Vincent
TESTAMENT D'UN POETE JUIF ASSASSINE
David, Yvan
MASCARA
David, Zdenek
CENA MEDU
David's Wife
MAN ON FIRE
Davidge, Donna
FIREHOUSE
PSYCHOS IN LOVE
THIN LINE, THE
Davidson, Diana
AROUND THE WORLD IN EIGHTY WAYS
Davidson, Jack
CYCLONE
SECRET OF MY SUCCESS, THE
Davidson, John
SQUEEZE, THE
Davidson, Mel
GET THE TERRORISTS
TOUGH COP
Davidson, Tim
NIGHTFORCE
Davies, Alison
MORGAN STEWART'S COMING HOME
Davies, Art
T. DAN SMITH
Davies, Dylan
BOY SOLDIER
Davies, Harry
FULL METAL JACKET
Davies, Jackson
HIGH STAKES
HOME IS WHERE THE HART IS
STAKEOUT
STEPFATHER,·THE
Davies, James
IF LOOKS COULD KILL
Davies, Kathryn Jake
IL LUPO DI MARE
Davies, Philippa
PRICK UP YOUR EARS
Davies, Rudi
LONELY PASSION OF JUDITH HEARNE,THE
Davies, Stephen
HANOI HILTON, THE
Davies, Troy
DOGS IN SPACE
Davila, Alfonso
EL ANSIA DE MATAR
MAS BUENAS QUE EL PAN
Davila, Raul
BELIEVERS, THE
LA GRAN FIESTA
Davion, Alex
WHOOPS APOCALYPSE
Davis, Austin
JOHN AND THE MISSUS
Davis, Bette
WHALES OF AUGUST, THE
Davis, Brad
COLD STEEL
HEART
Davis, Carole
MANNEQUIN
PRINCESS ACADEMY, THE
Davis, Chalkie
STRAIGHT TO HELL
Davis, Darlene
JAWS: THE REVENGE
Davis, Don
MALONE
TALKING WALLS
Davis, Duane
SUMMER SCHOOL
Davis, Elizabeth
PRETTY SMART
Davis, Frank
HAPPY HOUR
Davis, Jacqueline C.
KOLORMASK
Davis, John
FULL METAL JACKET
Davis, Judy
HIGH TIDE
Davis, Karen
ANGEL HEART
Davis, Kate
TOO OUTRAGEOUS
Davis, Leon
HELLRAISER
Davis, Marty
EMANON
Davis, Nancy Cheryll
HOLLYWOOD SHUFFLE
Davis, Nathan
FLOWERS IN THE ATTIC
Davis, Newt
SQUARE DANCE
Davis, Noel
PRICK UP YOUR EARS
Davis, Patrick
SUPERNATURALS, THE
Davis, Philip
COMRADES
Davis, Rae
TALKING WALLS
Davis, Robert
EAT THE RICH
Davis, Sammi
HOPE AND GLORY
PRAYER FOR THE DYING, A
Davis, Sonny
PROJECT X
Davis, Steve
CURSE, THE
Davis, Veronica
KILLER WORKOUT
Davis, Viveka
MORGAN STEWART'S COMING HOME
Davis, Warren
OUTTAKES
Davish, Glenn
MANNEQUIN
Davison, Bruce
WHEELS OF TERROR
Davronov, Shodi
V TALOM SNEGE ZVON RUCHIA
Dawlabetkian, Manvel
SASHSHENNYI FONAR
Dawson, Patrick
RAWHEAD REX
Dawson, Richard
RUNNING MAN, THE
Dawson, Sidney
RAISING ARIZONA
Day, Gary
SURFER, THE
Day, Kevin
FULL METAL JACKET
Day, Norma
T. DAN SMITH
Day, Patrick
ERNEST GOES TO CAMP
Day, Sushila
KONZERT FUR DIE RECHTE HAND
Day, Timothy E.
BRAVE LITTLE TOASTER, THE
Dayan, Reuven
DEADLINE
Dayman, Leslie
WITCH HUNT
Dayton, Danny
FLICKS
Dazai, Hisao
TORA-SAN'S BLUEBIRD FANTASY
Dazzi, Cecilia
FAMILY, THE
De, Dipankar
AMAR KANTAK
De Abreu, Jose
ANJOS DO ARRABALDE
de Aguiar, Wilma
BESAME MUCHO
de Alba, Luis
CINCO NACOS ASALTAN A LAS VEGAS
ENTRE FICHERAS ANDA EL DIABLO
De Alexandre, Rodolfo
MIRACLES
de Alexandre, Rodolfo
LETS GET HARRY
de Almeida, Duarte
O DESEJADO—LES MONTAGNES DE LA LUNE
de Almeida, Joaquim
GOOD MORNING BABYLON
VIOLINS CAME WITH THE AMERICANS, THE
de Alvarado, Memo
NI DE AQUI, NI DE ALLA
de Anda, Don Raul
FIERAS EN BRAMA
de Anda, Gilberto
EL ANSIA DE MATAR
FIERAS EN BRAMA
de Anda, Rodolfo
EL HIJO DE PEDRO NAVAJAS
LO NEGRO DEL NEGRO
POLICIAS DE NARCOTICOS
RATAS DE LA CIUDAD

De Angelis, Vincenzo
ADELMO
De Avila, Maritza
CHRONICLE OF A DEATH FORETOLD
De Baer, Jean
EIGHTY FOUR CHARING CROSS ROAD
De Bello, John
HAPPY HOUR
De Blaere, Henri
MASCARA
De Blas, Manuel
EL LUTE—CAMINA O REVIENTA
de Blas, Manuel
REDONDELA
De Breuck, Patrick
MASCARA
De Broux, Lee
ROBOCOP
de Brugada, Philippe
FAMILY BUSINESS
MISS MONA
De Busschere, Josef
MASCARA
De Camp, Marianne
MONSTER SQUAD, THE
de Capitani, Grace
LE MOUSTACHU
De Carmine, Renato
LA MONACA DIMONZA
de Castillo, Jorge
EULALIA
De Castrillon, Jose
LA VIDA ALEGRE
de Cespedes, Luis
MORNING MAN, THE
De Clario, Emma
DOGS IN SPACE
De Cordovier, Jerado
MUNCHIES
de Currea Lugo, Gellver
VISA U.S.A.
De Falco, Rubens
SUCCESSFUL MAN, A
De Filippo, Francesca
IL LUPO DI MARE
De Francesco, Mauro
ITALIANI A RIO
de Freitas, Manuela
O DESEJADO—LES MONTAGNES DE LA LUNE
De Frutos, Pedro
LA ESTANQUERA DE VALLECAS
de Gooijer, Rijk
DE RATELRAT
de Goros, Jean-Claude
MAN IN LOVE, A
De Grandy, Miguel
LA ESTANQUERA DE VALLECAS
de Grazia, Julio
EN RETIRADA
LOS DUENOS DEL SILENCIO
STRANGER, THE
De Hoyas, Joe
RETURN OF JOSEY WALES, THE
de Jong, Annie
CAUGHT
de Jong, Geert
TERUG NAAR OEGSTGEEST
de Jong, Jasperina
VROEGER IS DOOD
De Jonge, Marc
EMPIRE OF THE SUN
de Juap, Jorge
MIENTRAS HAYA LUZ
De Kins, Barbara
OUTRAGEOUS FORTUNE
de Konopka, Alix
TRAVELLING AVANT
De Kuyper, Marnix
MASCARA
de la Brosse, Simon
BUISSON ARDENT
TRAVELLING AVANT
de la Chaume, Jaqueline
HOUSE OF GAMES
de la Cruz, Rene
EL SOCIO DE DIOS
De La Paz, Danny
GABY—A TRUE STORY
WILD PAIR, THE
de la Pena, Alejandro
FORAJIDOS EN LA MIRA
de la Pena, Edwardo
CINCO NACOS ASALTAN A LAS VEGAS
de la Rosa, Paul
SUSPECT
De La Torre, Humberto
EXTREME PREJUDICE
De La Vega, Antonio
CHRONICLE OF A DEATH FORETOLD
de Laviolette, Denis
POLICE ACADEMY 4: CITIZENS ON PATROL
de Leon, Fernando Perez
WINTER TAN, A
De Leon, Isabel
CHRONICLE OF A DEATH FORETOLD
De Lint, Derek
MASCARA
de Lint, Derek
DIARY OF A MAD OLD MAN
THREE MEN AND A BABY
de Loera, Ricardo
LA RULETERA
De Long, Daniel
EQUALIZER 2000
De Luca, Rudy
MILLION DOLLAR MYSTERY
De Luise, Dom
SPACEBALLS
de Luna, Alvaro
LA GUERRA DE LOS LOCOS
MY GENERAL
de Matos, Jasmin
DUMA VEZ POR TODAS
de Medeiros, Ines
O DESEJADO—LES MONTAGNES DE LA LUNE
de Medeiros, Maria
LA MOINE ET LA SORCIERE
De Melo, Anais
GABY—A TRUE STORY
De Mesa, Michael
ZIMATAR
de Montalembert, Thibault
HOTEL DE FRANCE
de Moraes, Mariana
LEILA DINIZ
De Moss, Darcy
CANT BUY ME LOVE
De Niro, Robert
ANGEL HEART
UNTOUCHABLES, THE
De Pauw, Josse
LOVE IS A DOG FROM HELL
de Poncheville, Alice
BUISSON ARDENT
De Ponti, Cinzia
LESTATE STA FINENDO
De Prijck, Lou
MASCARA
de Quevedo, Rafael
LA RAZA NUNCA PIERDE—HUELE A GAS
de Rijiter, Leontien
CAUGHT
De Rizo, Carmencita
CHRONICLE OF A DEATH FORETOLD
De Rossi, Barbara
CARAMELLE DA UNO SCONOSCIUTO
de Rossi, Massimo
SPECTERS
de Rubi, Yair
NOCTURNO AMOR QUE TE VAS
de Saint Gall, Noele
BLIND DATE
de Santis, Monica
CONCRETE ANGELS
De Santis, Orchidea
TENEREZZA
De Santis, Silvana
NOTTE ITALIANA
De Santis, Tony
NIGHTSTICK
De Sanzio, Almina
SOTTO IL RISTORANTE CINESE
De Sica, Christian
BELLIFRESCHI
MISSIONE EROICA
MONTECARLO GRAN CASINO
De Silva, Daniela
MORO AFFAIR, THE
De Simone, Alina
LA MONACA DIMONZA
De Sio, Giuliana
I PICARI
De Soto, Rosana
LA BAMBA
de Teliga, Sarah
MOVING TARGETS
De Torrebruna, Riccardo
DEVIL IN THE FLESH
IL GRANDE BLEK
SPECTERS
de Turckheim, Charlotte
SALE DESTIN!
De Vial, Maria
PRETTY SMART
De Vos, Doug
MUTANT HUNT
De Vos, Hilt
MASCARA
de Vries, Edwin
EEN MAAND LATER
de Waal, Allan
EPIDEMIC
De Wael, Charles
MASCARA
De Windt, Angelique
WILD PAIR, THE
De Yang, Roland
BIRDS OF PREY
De'Cea, Derly
A DANCA DOS BONECOS
Deak, Michael S.
EVIL SPAWN
Dean, Ali F.
CHECKPOINT
Dean, E. Brian
BEST SELLER
Dean, Felicity
WHISTLE BLOWER, THE
Dean, Ron
BIG SHOTS
Dean, William
MATEWAN
DeAngelis, Gina
RADIO DAYS
Dearborn, Dalton
WHO'S THAT GIRL
Dearlove, Jack
EMPIRE OF THE SUN
Dearth, William
BANZAI RUNNER
Deats, Danyi
ALLNIGHTER, THE
RIVER'S EDGE
Debaisieux, Francine
PIERRE ET DJEMILA
Debell, Kristine
CLUB LIFE
DeBoy, David
TIN MEN
DeBroux, Lee
HUNTER'S BLOOD
Decade, Yvonne
MASQUES
DeCamp, Kyle
SHE MUST BE SEEING THINGS
Decco, Thean
MASCARA
Dechent, Antonio
LAS DOS ORILLAS
Decker, Fred
MATEWAN
Deckert, Blue
NADINE
Decroux, Maximilien
MISS MONA
Dedet, Yann
SOUS LE SOLEIL DE SATAN
Deering, Rochelle
BROADCAST NEWS
Dees, Rick
LA BAMBA
Deese, Frank
PRINCIPAL, THE
Deeth, James
LIKE FATHER, LIKE SON
Deezen, Eddie
HAPPY HOUR
MILLION DOLLAR MYSTERY

Defago, Jean-Jacques
LADY OF THE CAMELIAS

Defauce, Felix
MADRID

Defence Secretary and Crucifee
WHOOPS APOCALYPSE

DeForest, Calvert
MY DEMON LOVER

DeFrancesco, Roberto
IL GRANDE BLEK

DeGennaro, Maurice J.
FIREHOUSE

DeGroot, Frederik
CAUGHT

Dei, Gianni
DELITTI

Dejdar, Martin
PRATELE BERMUDSKEHO TROJUHELNIKU
PROC?

Dejmek, Piotr
PRYWATNE SLEDZTWO

DeKoron, Chris Maria
ORACLE, THE

del Castillo, Eric
FIERAS EN BRAMA
FORAJIDOS EN LA MIRA
LO NEGRO DEL NEGRO
ROSA DE LA FRONTERA

del Corral, Pedro Diez
LA GUERRA DE LOS LOCOS

Del Giudice, Giovanni
PERSONAGGI & INTERPRETI

Del Pesco, Todd
MALIBU BIKINI SHOP, THE

del Sol, Laura
EL GRAN SERAFIN

del Valle, Carmen
NOS REIMOS DE LA MIGRA

Del Valle, Maria Jose
LA VIDA ALEGRE

Delaney, Anthony
JAWS: THE REVENGE

Delaney, Kevin
FIREHOUSE

Delaney, Kim
CAMPUS MAN
HUNTER'S BLOOD

Delaney, Shelley
RADIO DAYS

Delano, Laura
LA GRAN FIESTA

Delano, Michael
SLUMBER PARTY MASSACRE II

Delany, Cathleen
DEAD, THE

Deleon, Paulo
ERNEST GOES TO CAMP

Delfin, Kimberly B.
PRETTY SMART

Delfin, Orangel
LA OVEJA NEGRA

Delfina, Alma
OLOR A MUERTE

Delgado, Lauro
MISSING IN ACTION

Delgado, Naomi
MANKILLERS

Delgado, Nena
HERENCIA DE VALIENTES

Delgado, Sasha
SLAMDANCE

Delgatto, Marc Stephan
CREEPSHOW 2

Deli Owner
EIGHTY FOUR CHARING CROSS ROAD

Delilah
RUNNING FROM THE GUNS

Deliso, Debra A.
OUTRAGEOUS FORTUNE

Delivoria, Marina
TREE WE HURT, THE

Delk, Denny
P.K. & THE KID

Dell, Chip
MORGAN STEWART'S COMING HOME

Dell'Agnese, Norma
TOO OUTRAGEOUS

Dellar, Lois
STREET SMART

Dellera, Francesca
CAPRICCIO
ROBA DA RICCHI

Delli Colli, Alessandra
IL FASCINO SOTTILE DEL PECCATO

Delli Colli, Tonino
INTERVISTA

Dells, Dorothy
SPACE RACE

Delmaine, Indrani
LADY OF THE CAMELIAS

Delman, Jeff
DEADTIME STORIES

Deloera, Ricardo
LO NEGRO DEL NEGRO

Delofski, Sevilla
ARIA
WHISTLE BLOWER, THE

Delon, Anthony
CHRONICLE OF A DEATH FORETOLD

DeLongis, Anthony
CHIPMUNK ADVENTURE, THE

Delora, Jennifer
DERANGED
ROBOT HOLOCAUST

DeLorenzo, Michael
FATAL BEAUTY

Deloriae, Cecilia
PRETTY SMART

Delpy, Albert
MISS MONA

Delpy, Julie
BAD BLOOD
LA PASSION BEATRICE

Deluc, Xavier
LA BRUTE

DeLuca, Rudy
SPACEBALLS

DeLuise, Dom
UN TASSINARO A NEW YORK

DeLuise, Peter
WINNERS TAKE ALL

Delvos, Katja
MASCARA

DeMarlo, Michael
BEVERLY HILLS COP II

Demerus, Ellen
MORE ABOUT THE CHILDREN OF BULLERBY VILLAGE

Demey, Julien
MASCARA

Demich, Yuri
SOPERNITSY

Demich, Yury
PRORYV

Demidova, Alla
KREUTZEROVA SONATA

Demifova, Alla
WEEKEND

Demon, Hide
GONDOLA

DeMornay, Rebecca
BEAUTY AND THE BEAST

DeMoss, Darcy
RETURN TO HORROR HIGH

Dempsey, Martin
EAT THE PEACH

Dempsey, Patrick
CANT BUY ME LOVE
IN THE MOOD
MEATBALLS III

Demy, John
BLIND DATE

Dench, Judi
EIGHTY FOUR CHARING CROSS ROAD

Deneuve, Catherine
AGENT TROUBLE

Dengel, Jake
IRONWEED

Denham, Maurice
EIGHTY FOUR CHARING CROSS ROAD

Dennard, Tee
BLACK WIDOW

Dennehy, Brian
BELLY OF AN ARCHITECT, THE
BEST SELLER

Dennet, Peter
STARLIGHT HOTEL

Denney, David
UNDER COVER

Dennison, Denise
BLACK WIDOW

Dennsy, Renee
MASQUES

Denting, John
VALET GIRLS

Denton, Christa
GATE, THE

Denton, Scot
GATE, THE

Denver, Bob
BACK TO THE BEACH

Denver, John
FIRE AND ICE

Deol, Sunny
DACAIT

Depardieu, Elisabeth
JEAN DE FLORETTE

Depardieu, Elizabeth
MANON OF THE SPRING

Depardieu, Gerard
SOUS LE SOLEIL DE SATAN
JEAN DE FLORETTE

Depeyrat, Patrick
JOHNNY MONROE

DePinto, Joey
THROW MOMMA FROM THE TRAIN

DePrume, Cathryn
DEADTIME STORIES

Deputy
KILLING TIME, THE

Dermer, Bob
CARE BEARS ADVENTURE IN WONDERLAND, THE

Dern, Bruce
BIG TOWN, THE

Des Barres, Michael
NIGHTFLYERS

Des Granges, Alexandre
ARIA

Des Baillets, Jacques
KEEPING TRACK

Desai, Shelly
PROJECT X

DeSalle, Stefan
RUSSKIES

DeSalvo, Anne
BURGLAR

Desantis, Tony
BELIEVERS, THE

Deschamps, Hubert
LASSOCIATION DES MALFAITEURS

DeShay, David
HARD TICKET TO HAWAII
HUNTER'S BLOOD

Deslandes, Robert
FAMILY BUSINESS

Desmarais, Lorraine
GREAT LAND OF SMALL, THE

Desny, Ivan
HOTEL DE FRANCE

Despotovic, Ivana
GLI OCCHIALI D'ORO

Despotovich, Nada
MOONSTRUCK

Desset, Frantisek
CENA ODVAHY

Destounis, Manolis
O PARADISSOS ANIGI ME ANTIKLIDI

Detmers, Maruschka
DEVIL IN THE FLESH

Deu, Amerjit
CAUGHT

Deumner, Norma Christine
MASCARA

Deuter, James
WEEDS

Devan
AMRITAMGAMAYA

Devane, Pat
IRONWEED

Devasquez, Devin
CANT BUY ME LOVE
HOUSE TWO: THE SECOND STORY

Deveaux, Ernest
STREET SMART

Devilalitha
KATHAKKU PINNIL

DeVinney, Vernon R.
MANNEQUIN

DeVito, Danny
THROW MOMMA FROM THE TRAIN
TIN MEN
Devlin, Alan
LONELY PASSION OF JUDITH HEARNE,THE
Devlin, Frank
I WAS A TEENAGE ZOMBIE
Devoti, Laura
LA MONACA DIMONZA
Dey, Susan
TROUBLE WITH DICK, THE
Deyer, Julian
SLAMDANCE
Dhal, Lisbeth
KAMPEN OM DEN RODE KO
Dharmendra
DADAGIRI
INSANIYAT KE DUSHMAN
LOHA
Dhery, Robert
LA PASSION BEATRICE
Di Benedetto, Ida
REGINA
Di Biasi, Emilio
ANJOS DO ARRABALDE
di Blasi, Josie
CONCRETE ANGELS
di Blasi, Rina
CONCRETE ANGELS
Di Cicco, Bobby
NUMBER ONE WITH A BULLET
SUPERNATURALS, THE
Di Gennaro, Luigi
BARBARIANS, THE
Di Gennaro, Tiziana
BARBARIANS, THE
Di Palma, Lila
MISS MARY
Di Pinto, Nicola
MORO AFFAIR, THE
Di Santi, John
OUTRAGEOUS FORTUNE
Di Savoia, Lionello Pio
GOOD MORNING BABYLON
Di Stafano, Fulvio
FRANCESCA
Di Stasio, Alberto
DEVIL IN THE FLESH
Diab, Emtiaz
NOCE EN GALILEE
Diab, Hassan
NOCE EN GALILEE
Diakoyorgio, George
HIGH SEASON
Diakun, Alex
HIGH STAKES
MALONE
Diamant, Catherine
DEVIL IN THE FLESH
Diamant, Kathi
HAPPY HOUR
Diamantopoulos, Vassilis
TA PAIDIA TIS CHELIDONAS
Diamond, Harold
HARD TICKET TO HAWAII
Diamont, Sherry
MAKING MR.RIGHT
Diane, Lesley
BUSINESS AS USUAL
DiAquino, John
NO WAY OUT
Dias, Mark
NIGHTFORCE
Diaz, Chico
COLOR OF DESTINY, THE
FONTE DA SAUDADE
Diaz, Jose Antonio
LA ESTANQUERA DE VALLECAS
Diaz, Norberto
CHORROS
SENTIMIENTOS: MIRTA DE LINIERS A ESTAMBUL
Diaz, Rafael
MIENTRAS HAYA LUZ
Diaz, Rick
NIGHTFORCE
Diaz, Vic
EQUALIZER 2000
EYE OF THE EAGLE
Diaz Garcia, Isela
MISSION KILL
DiBenedetto, Tony
SOMEONE TO WATCH OVER ME
Dicandia, Denise
ROCK 'N' ROLL NIGHTMARE
DiCenzo, George
OMEGA SYNDROME
Dicicco, Pier Giorgio
PSYCHO GIRLS
Dick, Nigel
P.I. PRIVATE INVESTIGATIONS
Dickens, Hazel
MATEWAN
Dickens, Joanna
FOURTH PROTOCOL, THE
PERSONAL SERVICES
Dickerson, George
DEATH WISH 4: THE CRACKDOWN
Dickin, Dudley
CRY FREEDOM
Dickins, Barry
WITH LOVE TO THE PERSON NEXT TO ME
Dickinson, Angie
BIG BAD MAMA II
Dickman, Robert
WALKER
Dickson, Laurs
BLUE MONKEY
Dickson, Neil
EAT THE RICH
LIONHEART
DiCocco, Paul A.
IRONWEED
Diego, Juan
ASI COMO HABIAN SIDO
Diehl, John
HANOI HILTON, THE
WALKER
Dierkop, Charles
BANZAI RUNNER
CODE NAME ZEBRA
Dietl, Harald
WANNSEE CONFERENCE, THE
Dietz, Frank
ROCK 'N' ROLL NIGHTMARE
ZOMBIE NIGHTMARE
Dietz, Jim
WHO'S THAT GIRL
Diez, Elvira
LA ESTANQUERA DE VALLECAS
Dignam, Arthur
COMRADES
RIGHT HAND MAN, THE
THOSE DEAR DEPARTED
Diller, Maurice
VIDEO DEAD, THE
Dillman, Bradford
MAN OUTSIDE
Dillon, Arlene M.
BROADCAST NEWS
Dillon, Brendon
DEAD, THE
Dillon, Costa
HAPPY HOUR
Dillon, Matt
BIG TOWN, THE
Dillon, Melinda
HARRY AND THE HENDERSONS
Dillon, Pat
SITTING IN LIMBO
Dillon, Paul
KISS DADDY GOOD NIGHT
Dillon, Stephen
BUSINESS AS USUAL
Dillon, Thomas
OUTRAGEOUS FORTUNE
Dimambro, Joseph
CONCRETE ANGELS
Dimas, Gus
PRINCIPAL, THE
Dimitriox, Manos
PRETTY SMART
Din, Ayub Khan
SAMMY AND ROSIE GET LAID
Dingle, Jane
BLUE MONKEY
JOHN AND THE MISSUS
Dingwall, Kelly
AROUND THE WORLD IN EIGHTY WAYS
YEAR MY VOICE BROKE, THE
Dinnion, Peter
BOY SOLDIER
Diogene, Franco
IL LUPO DI MARE
Dionne, Margot
WITCHES OF EASTWICK, THE
Dipinto, Nicola
LA DONNA DEL TRAGHETTO
DiSanti, John
BATTERIES NOT INCLUDED
Disanti, John
P.K. & THE KID
Disario, Frank
OVERKILL
Dishy, Bob
CRITICAL CONDITION
Disi, Emilio
LA BUSQUEDA
Dismukes, Deborah
LETHAL WEAPON
Ditmars, Carolyn
WITCHES OF EASTWICK, THE
Ditmars, Christine
WITCHES OF EASTWICK, THE
Ditmars, Cynthia
WITCHES OF EASTWICK, THE
Diuzheva, Marina
KAK STAT SCHASTLIVYM
Diviskova, Nina
WOLF'S HOLE
Dixon, Joyce
BLOODSUCKERS FROM OUTER SPACE
Dixon, MacIntyre
BATTERIES NOT INCLUDED
SECRET OF MY SUCCESS, THE
Dixon, Malcolm
SNOW WHITE
Dixon, Siona
SUSPECT
Djadjam, Mostefa
UN AMOUR A PARIS
Djigarkhanyan, Armen
ISKRENNE VASH . . .
ODINOKAYA ORESHINA
TAYNY MADAM VONG
Dmitrieva, Elena
PLIUMBUM, ILI OPASNAIA IGIA
Dnis, Marc
KEEPING TRACK
Do, Eric
COERS CROISES
Doazan, Aurelle
SALE DESTIN!
Dobbins, Bill
RAISING ARIZONA
Dobra, Anica
VEC VIDJENO
ZIVOT RADNIKA
Dobrei, Denes
GONDOVISELES
Dobrowolska, Gosia
AROUND THE WORLD IN EIGHTY WAYS
SURFER, THE
Dobrynine, John
FALSCH
Dobson, Rashel
YALDEI STALIN
Dobus, Bruce
NO WAY OUT
Dochtermann, Trudi
DOWN TWISTED
Docolomansky, Michal
CENA ODVAHY
Doe, John
BORDER RADIO
SLAMDANCE
Doermer, Christian
DAS TREIBHAUS
Doghileva, Tatiana
IZ ZHIZNI POTAPOVA
Dogileva, Tatyana
MOY LYUBIMYY KLOUN
OGNI
Doherty, Kate
DOGS IN SPACE
Dokic, Dara
UVEK SPREMNE ZENE
Dolan, Michael
HAMBURGER HILL
LIGHT OF DAY

Dolenz, Ami
CANT BUY ME LOVE
Doll, Dora
LES DEUX CROCODILES
Dolly Dots, The
DUTCH TREAT
Dolores, Carmen
LA PLAYA DE LOS PERROS
Dolye, Johnny
ARIA
Dombasle, Arielle
JEUX D'ARTIFICES
Domeier, Richard
EVIL DEAD 2: DEAD BY DAWN
Dominguez, Adriano
POLICIA
Dominguez, Berata
LA MONACA DIMONZA
Dominguez, Maricarmen
WINTER TAN, A
Domino, Cyndi
MANKILLERS
Dommartin, Solveig
DER HIMMEL UBER BERLIN
Donadoni, M.
I KEKARMENI
Donadoni, Maurizio
LA CODA DEL DIAVOLO
MORO AFFAIR, THE
Donahue, Troy
CYCLONE
DEADLY PREY
Donaldson, Lesleh
HEARTS OF FIRE
Donat, Peter
UNFINISHED BUSINESS . . .
Donati, Danilo
INTERVISTA
Donch, Karl
FRANCESCA
Doncheff, Len
BIG TOWN, THE
Donenfeld, Henry
ZERO BOYS, THE
Doneva, Vukosava
HI-FI
Dong, Liang
LAST EMPEROR, THE
Donikian, George
WITCH HUNT
Donlevy, Martin
CONCRETE ANGELS
Donmeyer, Steve
TERMINAL EXPOSURE
Donnadieu, Bernard-Pierre
LA PASSION BEATRICE
LES FOUS DE BASSAN
Donnelly, Donal
DEAD, THE
Donnelly, James
BOY SOLDIER
Donner, Johan
URSULA
Donner, Robert
ALLAN QUATERMAIN AND THE LOST CITY OF GOLD
Donnici, Elena
QUARTIERE
Donoghue, Edwin
PETER VON SCHOLTEN
Donohue, Thomas
KEEPING TRACK
Donovan, Art
ADVENTURE OF THE ACTION HUNTERS
Donovan, John
HOSTAGE
Donovan, Peter
RAWHEAD REX
Donovan, Terence
RUNNING FROM THE GUNS
Donte, Joe
CODE NAME ZEBRA
Donzelli, Sara
PERSONAGGI & INTERPRETI
Doody, Alison
PRAYER FOR THE DYING, A
Dooley, Brian
KEEPING TRACK
Dooley, Paul
MONSTER IN THE CLOSET
O. C. AND STIGGS
Dooley, Terry
DOGS IN SPACE
DoQui, Robert
ROBOCOP
Doran, Gwen
T. DAN SMITH
Doran, Jesse
HEART
Dorantes, Dennis
HUNTER'S BLOOD
Dore, Philip
CREEPSHOW 2
Dorevska, Elizabeta
HI-FI
Dorff, Stephen
GATE, THE
Doria, Magdalena
MISSION KILL
Dorio, Rick
SUMMER CAMP NIGHTMARE
Dormandy, Simon
WHOOPS APOCALYPSE
Dorne, Sandra
EAT THE RICH
Dornen, Ralf
LADY OF THE CAMELIAS
Dorner, Gyorgy
LAURA
Doronina, Tatyana
VALENTIN I VALENTINA
Doroshenko, Vitaly
RAZMAKH KRYLIEV
Dorval, Adrien
HOME IS WHERE THE HART IS
Dosamantes, Susana
EL PLACER DE LA VENGANZA
ROSA DE LA FRONTERA
Doskey, Janice
SLAMMER GIRLS
Doss, Terri Lynn
LETHAL WEAPON
Douberne, Nathalie
WATER ALSO BURNS
Doubleday, Frank
BROADCAST NEWS
SPACE RACE
Douglas, Diana
PLANES, TRAINS AND AUTOMOBILES
Douglas, Donald
HOLLYWOOD SHUFFLE
Douglas, Eric
STUDENT CONFIDENTIAL
Douglas, Illeana
HELLO AGAIN
Douglas, Michael
FATAL ATTRACTION
WALL STREET
Douglas, Mitchell
BIRDS OF PREY
Douglas, Ralph
FIREHOUSE
Douglas, Sam
FOURTH PROTOCOL, THE
Douglas, Sarah
STEELE JUSTICE
Douglass, Grant Lee
GARDENS OF STONE
Doumerg, Jo
JEAN DE FLORETTE
Dourif, Brad
FATAL BEAUTY
Douse, Anthony
PRICK UP YOUR EARS
Dovi, Manlio
SOLDATI: 365 GIORNI ALL' ALBA
Dovlatyan, Frunze
ODINOKAYA ORESHINA
Dovletov, At
PRIKLYUCHENIA NA MALENKIKH OSTROVEKH
Dow, Ellen Albertini
MUNCHIES
Dow, Graham
LIGHTHORSEMEN, THE
Dow, Tony
BACK TO THE BEACH
Dowd, Ned
P.K. & THE KID
Dowdall, Jim
BELLMAN AND TRUE
WISH YOU WERE HERE
Dowdell, Robert
ASSASSINATION
Dowell, Dana
DANGER ZONE, THE
Dowend, Michael
ROBOT HOLOCAUST
Dowling, Bairbre
DEAD, THE
Dowling, Mark
GIRL, THE
Dowling, Rachael
DEAD, THE
Down, Shane
COMRADES
Downer, Alan
BELLMAN AND TRUE
Downey, Brian
JOHN AND THE MISSUS
Downey, Coleen
OUTTAKES
Downey, Leo
PRINCIPAL, THE
Downey, Robert
LESS THAN ZERO
PICK-UP ARTIST, THE
Doyle, Brian
I WAS A TEENAGE ZOMBIE
Doyle, Harriet
COMRADES
Doyle, Jerry
JOHN AND THE MISSUS
Doyle, Jill
EAT THE PEACH
Doyle, Kevin Michael
UNTOUCHABLES, THE
Doyle, Lorraine
WHOOPS APOCALYPSE
Doyle, Tony
DEVILS PARADISE, THE
EAT THE PEACH
Doyon, Bruno
MORNING MAN, THE
Draber, Etienne
UN AMOUR A PARIS
Drage, Olga
OBOROTEN TOM
Drago, Billy
BANZAI RUNNER
HUNTER'S BLOOD
UNTOUCHABLES, THE
Drake, Paul
BLOOD HOOK
Drake, Judith
ANGEL HEART
Drake, Laura
WHO'S THAT GIRL
Drake, Simon
EAT THE RICH
Drake, Tom
DIRTY DANCING
Drama Coach
MY DARK LADY
Draper, Polly
MAKING MR.RIGHT
PICK-UP ARTIST, THE
Dreesen, Tom
SPACEBALLS
Dreger, Reg
BLUE MONKEY
Dresden, John
COMMANDO SQUAD
NO DEAD HEROES
Dressler, Garrett
VIDEO DEAD, THE
Drever, Andrea
KILLER WORKOUT
Drew, Linzi
ARIA
Drewniak, Josef
LES PATTERSON SAVES THE WORLD
Drexel, Ruth
FRANCESCA
Dreyfus, Jean-Claude
TANDEM
Dreyfuss, Justin
MUNCHIES

Dreyfuss, Lorin
DUTCH TREAT

Dreyfuss, Randolph
LIKE FATHER, LIKE SON

Dreyfuss, Richard
NUTS
STAKEOUT
TIN MEN

Driest, Burkhard
TAXI NACH KAIRO

Drischell, Gwyn
I WAS A TEENAGE ZOMBIE

Driss, Aziz Ben
ISHTAR

Droog, Bernard
DE RATELRAT

Drotar, Dena
OPEN HOUSE

Drovandi, Ennio
LESTATE STA FINENDO

Drove, Antonio
LA GUERRA DE LOS LOCOS

Druhan, Mikhail
BLOOD SISTERS
I WAS A TEENAGE T.V. TERRORIST

Drummond, Jenny
WHOOPS APOCALYPSE

Drury, Karen
CRY FREEDOM

Dryden, Mack
MILLION DOLLAR MYSTERY

Dryden, Victoria
ORACLE, THE

Dryer, Fred
DEATH BEFORE DISHONOR

Drysdale, Lee
EMPIRE STATE

Du Bois, Frances De L'Etanche
RIVER'S EDGE

Dual, Juan Carlos
EL ANO DEL CONEJO

Duarte, Richard
MANKILLERS

Duato, Ana
MADRID

DuBarry, Denise
MONSTER IN THE CLOSET

Dubarry, Jean-Paul
LANNEE DES MEDUSES

Dube, Cyprian R.
JAWS: THE REVENGE

Dubillard, Pierre
POISONS

Dubin, Kristina
WOLF AT THE DOOR, THE

Dubinsky, Leon
LIFE CLASSES

Dublino, Daniele
MORO AFFAIR, THE

Dubois, Gerard
FAMILY BUSINESS

Dubois, Jean-Pol
LE BEAUF

Dubois, Marie
GRAND GUIGNOL

Ducey, Chris S.
BLACK WIDOW

Duchess
SICILIAN, THE

Ducommun, Rick
SPACEBALLS

Dudgeon, Neil
PRICK UP YOUR EARS

Dudikoff, Michael
AMERICAN NINJA 2: THE CONFRONTATION

Dudusova, Rita
WOLF'S HOLE

Duell, William
IRONWEED

Duering, Carl
SLEEP WELL, MY LOVE

Dufau, Graciela
SOFIA

Duff, Howard
MONSTER IN THE CLOSET
NO WAY OUT

Duff, Susan Wheeler
MIRACLES
PERSONAL FOUL

Duffek, Patty
HARD TICKET TO HAWAII

Duffy, Natalie
BUSINESS AS USUAL

Dufresne, Liz
TUESDAY WEDNESDAY

Dugan, Dennis
CANT BUY ME LOVE

Duggan, James
PRICK UP YOUR EARS

Dugoni, Andrea
SOTTO IL RISTORANTE CINESE

Duhame, Doc
MONSTER IN THE CLOSET
OMEGA SYNDROME

Dukakis, Olympia
MOONSTRUCK

Dukas, James
IRONWEED

Duke, Bill
NO MAN'S LAND
PREDATOR

Duke, O.L.
PRETTYKILL

Duke, Patty
SOMETHING SPECIAL!

Duke, Robin
BLUE MONKEY

Dukes, David
CATCH THE HEAT
DATE WITH AN ANGEL
RAWHEAD REX

Dumas, Roger
MASQUES

Dumas, Sandrine
ACCROCHE-COEUR
ARIA
BEYOND THERAPY
LHOMME VOILE

Dumeniaud, Pierre-Francois
MASQUES

Dummont, Denise
ALLNIGHTER, THE

Dumont, Denise
RADIO DAYS

Dumont, Fernand
ARIA

Dumont, Ulises
EL ANO DEL CONEJO
RAGE OF HONOR

Dun, Dennis
LAST EMPEROR, THE
PRINCE OF DARKNESS

Dunard, David
FATAL BEAUTY

Dunard, David S.
BIG SHOTS

Dunaro, David
DIRTY LAUNDRY

Dunaway, Faye
BARFLY

Dunayevsky, Fyodor
KURIER

Dunbar, Viola
ANGEL HEART

Duncan, Andrew
MORGAN STEWART'S COMING HOME

Duncan, Arlene
HEARTS OF FIRE

Duncan, Carmen
MOVING TARGETS

Duncan, Frank
EMPIRE OF THE SUN

Duncan, Gordon
FULL METAL JACKET

Duncan, Jan
LIKE FATHER, LIKE SON

Duncan, Lindsay
PRICK UP YOUR EARS

Duncan, Pamela
PERSONAL SERVICES
WISH YOU WERE HERE

Duncan-Petley, Stella
HEARTS OF FIRE

Dundas, David
WHEN THE WIND BLOWS

Duneton, Claude
LA PASSION BEATRICE

Dunham, Dale
BLOOD HOOK

Dunlop, Joe
WHISTLE BLOWER, THE

Dunn, Bill
WOLF AT THE DOOR, THE

Dunne, Chris
EAT THE PEACH

Dunne, Griffin
AMAZON WOMEN ON THE MOON
WHO'S THAT GIRL

Dunnock, Mildred
PICK-UP ARTIST, THE

Dunoyer, Francois
LE SOLITAIRE

Dupeyron, Humberto
LA RULETERA

Dupois, Starletta
HOLLYWOOD SHUFFLE

Dupon, Andre
JEAN DE FLORETTE
MANON OF THE SPRING

DuPont, Peter
LETHAL WEAPON

Duppell, Richard
PRINCIPAL, THE

Dupuy, Michel
MASQUES

Duquet, Michele
POLICE ACADEMY 4: CITIZENS ON PATROL
THREE MEN AND A BABY

Duquette, Joe
BEVERLY HILLS COP II

Duran, Alfonso
RETO A LA VIDA

Duran, Larry
EXTREME PREJUDICE

Duran, Richard
EXTREME PREJUDICE

Durang, Christopher
SECRET OF MY SUCCESS, THE

Durda, Karen
DATE WITH AN ANGEL

Durdyev, Serdar
PRIKLYUCHENIA NA MALENKIKH OSTROVEKH

Dureau, George
BIG EASY, THE

Durham, Geoffrey
WISH YOU WERE HERE

Durkin, Barbara
WISH YOU WERE HERE

Durning, Charles
HAPPY NEW YEAR
ROSARY MURDERS, THE

Durock, Dick
BLIND DATE

Durov, Lev
FAREWELL
KAK STAT SCHASTLIVYM
KAPITAN "PILIGRIMA"

Durovova, Natalija
CIZIM VSTUP POVOLEN

Durphy, T.R.
WHOOPS APOCALYPSE

Dursey, Rose
OVER THE TOP

Dury, Ian
HEARTS OF FIRE
O PARADISSOS ANIGI ME ANTIKLIDI

Dusay, Debra
MADE IN HEAVEN

Dusay, Marj
MADE IN HEAVEN

Dusek, Zdenek
PRATELE BERMUDSKEHO TROJUHELNIKU
PROC?

Dussollier, Andre
MELO

Dutheil, Marie-Ange
LES NOCES BARBARES

Dutil, Murielle
BACH AND BROCCOLI

Dutsch, Nikolaus
SIERRA LEONE

Dutt, Chhanda
PHERA

Dutt, Sanjay
INAAM DUS HAZAAR

Dutt, Yashwant
PUDHCHE PAOL

Duttweiler, Norman
TOO OUTRAGEOUS

Duval, Liana
VERA
Duvall, John
BLOODSUCKERS FROM OUTER SPACE
Duvall, Robert
HOTEL COLONIAL
LETS GET HARRY
Duvall, Rocky
VIDEO DEAD, THE
Duvall, Shelley
ROXANNE
Duvall, Susan
TIN MEN
Dux, Frank
GET THE TERRORISTS
Dvorzhetsky, Yevgeny
TANTSPLOSHCHADKA
Dworakowski, Marian
THOSE DEAR DEPARTED
Dyatlov, Vladimir
VZLOMSHCHIK
Dye, Cameron
STRANDED
Dye, John
CAMPUS MAN
Dyer, Gwynne
LAST STRAW, THE
Dykiel, Bozena
W ZAWIESZENIU
Dylan, Bob
HEARTS OF FIRE
Dyomina, Galina
KARUSEL NA BAZARNOY PLOSHCHADI
Dysart, Richard
WALL STREET
Dyson, Anne
EIGHTY FOUR CHARING CROSS ROAD
Dziamarski, Piotr
PRZYJACIEL WESOLEGO DIABLA
Dzundza, George
NO WAY OUT
Eadie, Nicholas
MOVING TARGETS
Eagle, Jeff
SLAMMER GIRLS
Earle, Tim
GIRL, THE
WARDOGS
East, Anthony
TOUGH COP
East, Carlos
ROSA DE LA FRONTERA
Easterbrook, Leslie
POLICE ACADEMY 4: CITIZENS ON PATROL
Easterday, Jesse
KID BROTHER, THE
Easterday, Kenny
KID BROTHER, THE
Eastgate, Robert
FRENCHMAN'S FARM
Eastman, George
LE FOTO DI GIOIA
Eastman, Lynn
PROJECT X
Eastman, Rodney
NIGHTMARE ON ELM STREET 3: DREAM WARRIORS, A
Easy Action
BLOOD TRACKS
Eaton, Barry
BUSINESS AS USUAL
Eaves, John
FIRE AND ICE
Eazor, Bob
OVER THE TOP
Eberhard, Erika
DER NACHBAR
Eboni
ELVIS-KISSAN JALJILLA
Ebru
DILAN
Echanove, Juan
DIVINAS PALABRAS
Echmendia, Vergilio
KAPITAN "PILIGRIMA"
Eckart-Eckhart, Hans
SIERRA LEONE
Eckhardt, Hans-Eckart
SAME TO YOU
Eckhouse, James
EIGHTY FOUR CHARING CROSS ROAD
Ecoffey, Jean-Philippe
LES MENDIANTS
Economidis, Stavros
WITCH HUNT
Ed
LOST BOYS, THE
Ed Wheeler
BROADCAST NEWS
Edelhart, Yvette
FOREVER, LULU
Edfeldt, Catti
MORE ABOUT THE CHILDREN OF BULLERBY VILLAGE
Edfeldt, Tove
MORE ABOUT THE CHILDREN OF BULLERBY VILLAGE
Edgcomb, Jim
WANTED: DEAD OR ALIVE
Edmonds, Mitchell
NIGHTFORCE
Edmondson, Adrian
EAT THE RICH
MORE BAD NEWS
Edmund, Peter
FULL METAL JACKET
Edmunds, Mike
SNOW WHITE
Edney, Beatie
DIARY OF A MAD OLD MAN
Edson, Dan
WITCHES OF EASTWICK, THE
Edson, Richard
GOOD MORNING, VIETNAM
WALKER
Eduardo
MISS MARY
Edwall, Allan
MALARPIRATER
Edward Tudor-Pole
STRAIGHT TO HELL
Edwards, Anthony
REVENGE OF THE NERDS II: NERDS IN PARADISE
SUMMER HEAT
Edwards, Connie
BIRDS OF PREY
Edwards, Glynn
OUT OF ORDER
Edwards, Jennifer
PERFECT MATCH, THE
Edwards, Keith
THREE KINDS OF HEAT
Edwards, Kenny
FIREHOUSE
Edwards, Maureen
BIT PART, THE
TO MARKET, TOMARKET
Edwards, Percy
VALHALLA
Edwards, Tony
HOLLYWOOD SHUFFLE
Edwards, Vince
RETURN TO HORROR HIGH
Edwards, William
MORGAN STEWART'S COMING HOME
Eepeda, Jorge
MISSION KILL
Efe, Pedro
BALADA DA PRAIA DOS CAES
LA PLAYA DE LOS PERROS
Efron, Marshall
BIG BANG, THE
TALKING WALLS
Efroni, Yehuda
RUMPELSTILTSKIN
Egan, Eddie
COLD STEEL
Egan, Mary
HAPPY HOUR
Egan, Richie
MONSTER IN THE CLOSET
Egas, Ean
IRONWEED
Ege, John
JOR
Eggelhoff, Kurt
HOSTAGE
Eggenweiler, Bob
P.K. & THE KID
Eggert, Nicole
OMEGA SYNDROME
Egoreva, Tat'jana
SKORBNOE BESCHUVSTVIE
Egorova, Tatiana
VREMYA ZHELANIY
Egstrom, Stig
MIO, MOY MIO
Egypt
MANNEQUIN
Ehlers, Beth
HIDING OUT
Ehlers, Heather
BROADCAST NEWS
Eiblmaier, Kerstin
TAROT
Eichhorn, Lisa
OPPOSING FORCE
Eidelsberg, Joel
RADIO DAYS
Eilbacher, Cynthia
SLUMBER PARTY MASSACRE II
Eilers, Jim Paul
SOMEONE TO WATCH OVER ME
Eiseman, Jack
WINNERS TAKE ALL
Eisen, Johnnie
FAMILY VIEWING
Eisenberg, Ned
HIDING OUT
Eisenlohr, Fred
EXTREME PREJUDICE
Eisner, Morten
KAMPEN OM DEN RODE KO
Eje, Thomas
KAMPEN OM DEN RODE KO
VALHALLA
Ekberg, Anita
DOLCE PELLE DI ANGELA
INTERVISTA
Ekblad, Stina
SERPENT'S WAY, THE
Ekland, Britt
MOON IN SCORPIO
Ekstrom, Anita
MALARPIRATER
El Basri, Ahmed
ABBES
El Campion
LA RAZA NUNCA PIERDE—HUELE A GAS
El Glaoui, Mehdi
LA COMPROMISSION
El Gran Wyoming
LA VIDA ALEGRE
El Jheur, Ahmed
PRICK UP YOUR EARS
El Jouhari, Salwa
ABBES
el Mimo, Lalo
UNA PURA Y DOS CON SAL
El Oumari, Malika
ABBES
el-Alaili, Ezzat
AL-TAUQ WAL-ISWIRA
Elam, George W.
WANTED: DEAD OR ALIVE
Elbing, Peter
BABY BOOM
Elbir, Sissy
CEMIL
Elder, Linda
BIRDS OF PREY
Elders, Mickey
DANGER ZONE, THE
Eleazar Garcia
EL PLACER DE LA VENGANZA
Elejalde, Carlos
A LOS CUATRO VIENTOS
Elfrink, Stephanie
O. C. AND STIGGS
Elgart, Sarah
ALLNIGHTER, THE
Elholm, Thomas
VENNER FOR ALTID
Eli Dankner
BOUBA
Eli Wallach
NUTS

Elian, Yona
BOUBA
Elias, Alix
MUNCHIES
Elias, Cyros
RENEGADE, UN OSSO TROPPO DURO
Elias, Hector
TALKING WALLS
Elias, Jeannie
BLIND DATE
Elias, Luis
CARTUCHA CORTADA
Eliava, Liya
KRUGOVOROT
Eliot, Stefanos
O PARADISSOS ANIGI ME ANTIKLIDI
Eliott, Tim
RIGHT HAND MAN, THE
Elizondo, Hector
OVERBOARD
Elizondo, Humberto
EL MUERTO DEL PALOMO
LA RAZA NUNCA PIERDE—HUELE A GAS
MAS VALE PAJARO EN MANO . . .
RATAS DE LA CIUDAD
Elke Muller
KILLER WORKOUT
Elkin, Karen
GREAT LAND OF SMALL, THE
Ellarye
FATAL BEAUTY
Ellerbee, Linda
BABY BOOM
Elliot, Angela
BUSINESS AS USUAL
Elliot, Beamish
DOGS IN SPACE
Elliot, Drew
WEEDS
Elliot, Jane
SOME KIND OF WONDERFUL
Elliot, Neil
IN THE MOOD
Elliott, David
BIG TOWN, THE
Elliott, Denholm
MAURICE
SEPTEMBER
Elliott, Robert Irvin
FROM THE HIP
Elliott, Sam
FATAL BEAUTY
Elliott, Stephen
ASSASSINATION
Ellis, Bob
DEAR CARDHOLDER
Ellis, Desmond
CONCRETE ANGELS
Ellis, Katherine
TIN MEN
Ellis, Laura
BLOODSUCKERS FROM OUTER SPACE
Ellis-Brown, Jeb
SOMETHING SPECIAL!
Elmendorf, Raymond
BLOODY WEDNESDAY
PROJECT X
Elmer, Phil
FULL METAL JACKET
Elmes, John
MAURICE
Elofsson, Fritz
MY LIFE AS A DOG
Elorriaga, Xabier
A LOS CUATRO VIENTOS
Elphick, Michael
LITTLE DORRIT
VALHALLA
WITHNAIL AND I
Elson, Robert
ESCAPES
Elstela, Kristiina
PEKKA PUUPAA POLIISINA
Elvis, Colin
FULL METAL JACKET
Elwes, Cary
MASCHENKA
PRINCESS BRIDE, THE
Elykomov, Oleg
VZLOMSHCHIK
Elzy, Lula
ANGEL HEART
Emerson, Douglas
MILLION DOLLAR MYSTERY
Emery, Lisa
DREAMANIAC
Emery, Richard
SUMMER HEAT
Emigholz, Jerry
NECROPOLIS
Emil, Michael
DEADLY ILLUSION
SOMEONE TO LOVE
Emmanuelle, Sarsi
DAUGHTERS OF EVE
Emmett, Michael
CONCRETE ANGELS
SUSPECT
Emmich, Cliff
RETURN TO HORROR HIGH
Emmrich, Bobby
SOMETHING SPECIAL!
Emoto, Akira
SARABA ITOSHIKI HITO YO
Enahoro, Bella
ARIA
Encinas, Carmelina
EL HIJO DE PEDRO NAVAJAS
Encines, Alicia
SINVERGUENZA . . . PERO HONRADO
Encines, Carmelina
SINVERGUENZA . . . PERO HONRADO
Ender, Gerald
BROADCAST NEWS
Enehielm, Chris af
URSULA
Eng, Ronald
EMPIRE OF THE SUN
Eng, Sandra
OUTRAGEOUS FORTUNE
Engel, Susan
SHADEY
Engelbrecht, Constanze
SIERRA LEONE
Engelbrecht, Nadja
MEIER
Engelson, George J.
MURDER LUST
Englert, Jan
MAGNAT
WERYFIKACJA
English, Alex
AMAZING GRACE AND CHUCK
English, Brad
MALIBU BIKINI SHOP, THE
Englund, Robert
NIGHTMARE ON ELM STREET 3: DREAM WARRIORS, A
Engman, Paul
HAPPY HOUR
Engongo, Alamba
LA VIE EST BELLE
Engstrom, Roger
OUTRAGEOUS FORTUNE
Enklaar, Cas
TERUG NAAR OEGSTGEEST
Ennis, Michael
SLAMDANCE
Enriques, Louis
O. C. AND STIGGS
Enriquez, Rene
BULLETPROOF
Entezami, Ezatolah
LODGERS
Entezami, Ezzatollah
SHEERE SANGGY
Eperjes, Karoly
WHOOPING COUGH
Epper, Andy
MILLION DOLLAR MYSTERY
Epper, Richard
WINNERS TAKE ALL
Epper, Tony
OUTRAGEOUS FORTUNE
Erak, Milan
DIE VERLIEBTEN
Erazo, Arquimedes
CHRONICLE OF A DEATH FORETOLD
Erchov
RODNIK DLIA ZHAZHDUSHCHIKH
Erdman, John
SHE MUST BE SEEING THINGS
Erdman, Richard
VALET GIRLS
Erickson, Dan
BLOOD SISTERS
Ericsson, Leif
MY LIFE AS A DOG
Erikci, Mehmet
DILAN
Eriksson, Anders
LEIF
Eriksson, Claes
LEIF
Eriksson, Dan
NIONDE KOMPANIET
Eriksson, Jonas
MALARPIRATER
Erlandson, Ingrid
TOUGH COP
Ermey, Lee
FULL METAL JACKET
Ernand, Allison
WELCOME MARIA
Ernblad, Gunnar
GIRL, THE
Erne, Herbert
HIDING OUT
Erne, Mary B.
HIDING OUT
Ernhoffer, Ken
KEEPING TRACK
Ernsberger, Duke
SUMMER HEAT
Ernst, Ole
ELISE
EPIDEMIC
PETER VON SCHOLTEN
Errera, Ivano
QUARTIERE
Erskine, Madelyn
RAWHEAD REX
Erwin, Lee
RADIO DAYS
Escala, Joel
POR LOS CAMINOS VERDES
Escalero, Cesar
ENTRE FICHERAS ANDA EL DIABLO
Escamillia, Charles
RETURN OF JOSEY WALES, THE
Escobar, Elba
DE MUJER A MUJER
Escobar, Leon
NI DE AQUI, NI DE ALLA
Escobar, Luis
MOROS Y CRISTIANOS
SUFRE MAMON
Esen, Ugur
YER DEMIR, GOK BAKIR
Eshimbayeva, Asel
MIRAZHI LYUBRI
Espinosa, Leandro
ESTA NOCHE CENA PANCHO (DESPEDIDA DE SOLTERO)
Espinoza, Isaura
EL HIJO DE PEDRO NAVAJAS
HERENCIA DE VALIENTES
POLICIAS DE NARCOTICOS
RATAS DE LA CIUDAD
Espinoza, Isauro
TRAGICO TERREMOTO EN MEXICO
Espinoza, James
OUTRAGEOUS FORTUNE
Espinoza, Leandro
ENTRE FICHERAS ANDA EL DIABLO
Espinoza, Roberto Lopez
WALKER
Esposito, Giancarlo
SWEET LORRAINE
Esposito, Marco
LUNGA VITA ALLA SIGNORA!
Esposti, Piera Degli
LA CODA DEL DIAVOLO
Esser, Dorine
MASCARA
Esser, Manfred
DER TOD DES EMPEDOKLES
Estebanez, Cesareo
LA GUERRA DE LOS LOCOS

Esterman, Laura
IRONWEED

Estevez, Emilio
STAKEOUT

Estrada, Carlos
RAGE OF HONOR

Estrada, Erik
HOUR OF THE ASSASSIN

Estrada, Javier
LETS GET HARRY

Estrella, Bonafe
COMMANDER LAMIN

Estrin, Patricia
BABY BOOM

Esztergalyos, Cecilia
ISTEN VELETEK, BARATAIM

Etra, Will
RETURN TO HORROR HIGH

Ettienne, Bobby
TALKING WALLS

Eun-jin, Han
SIBAJI

Evans, Art
WHITE OF THE EYE

Evans, John
BIG TOWN, THE
IVE HEARD THE MERMAIDS SINGING

Evans, Martin
LADIES OF THE LOTUS

Evans, Matthew
NO WAY OUT

Evans, Michelle
INDIAN SUMMER

Evans, Nicole
BEYOND THERAPY

Evans, Robin
RAGE OF HONOR

Evans, Rupert Holliday
PERSONAL SERVICES

Evans, Troy
NEAR DARK

Eve, Leslie
EVIL SPAWN

Everett, Rupert
CHRONICLE OF A DEATH FORETOLD
GLI OCCHIALI D'ORO
HEARTS OF FIRE
RIGHT HAND MAN, THE

Eves, Paul
TOO OUTRAGEOUS

Evigan, Greg
STRIPPED TO KILL

Evora, Cesar
SUCCESSFUL MAN, A

Evrard, Claude
SI LE SOLEIL NE REVENAIT PAS

Ewande, Lydia
ARCHANGELOS TOU PATHOUS

Ewart, John
DEAR CARDHOLDER

Ewer, Donald
HOUSEKEEPER, THE

Exarchos, Thodoros
THEOFILOS

Eyre, Peter
MAURICE

Ezkenazi, Ezequiel
RAGE OF HONOR

Faarc, Abram
VERA

Fabares, Shelley
HOT PURSUIT

Faber, Peter
DE RATELRAT

Fabian
LO NEGRO DEL NEGRO

Fabian, Diane
HOUSEKEEPER, THE
POLICE ACADEMY 4: CITIZENS ON PATROL

Fabian, Laura
OVERBOARD

Fabrini, Paco
LA DONNA DEL TRAGHETTO

Fadeyeva, Yelena
DIKIY KHMEL

Fadiman, Ramsey
BELIEVERS, THE

Fagan, Sean
GATE, THE

Fagen, Joe
HIDING OUT

Fagerbakke, Bill
SECRET OF MY SUCCESS, THE

Fagg, Jimmy
EAT THE RICH

Faggioli, Giada
UN RAGAZZO DI CALABRIA

Fagundes, Antonio
BESAME MUCHO
LEILA DINIZ
NIGHT ANGELS

Fahey, Mary
MUTANT HUNT

Fahey, Murray
SLATE, WYN & ME

Fahlke, Ruth
SAME TO YOU

Fahrner, Ted
DOGS IN SPACE

Fai, Leung Ka
PRISON ON FIRE

Faichney, Stuart
GROUND ZERO

Faigen, Glenn
BROADCAST NEWS

Fairbairn, Bruce
CYCLONE
NIGHTSTICK

Fairbrass, Fred
HEARTS OF FIRE

Fairchild, Max
HOWLING III, THE

Fairchild, Morgan
CAMPUS MAN
DEADLY ILLUSION
RED HEADED STRANGER
SLEEPING BEAUTY

Faircloth, Mitchell
AS TIME GOES BY

Fairfax, Kaarin
AROUND THE WORLD IN EIGHTY WAYS
BELINDA

Fairman, Blain
WHOOPS APOCALYPSE

Fala, Archimede
ADELMO

Falck, Serge
DEATH STONE

Falco, Anthony
WITCHES OF EASTWICK, THE

Falco, Edith
SWEET LORRAINE

Falcone, Rita
CARTOLINE ITALIANE

Falk, Lisanne
IN THE MOOD
LESS THAN ZERO

Falk, Peder
LOS DUENOS DEL SILENCIO

Falk, Peter
DER HIMMEL UBER BERLIN
HAPPY NEW YEAR
PRINCESS BRIDE, THE

Fall, Assane
LES MENDIANTS

Fallabela, Rogerio
A DANCA DOS BONECOS

Fallah, Faridkashan
PEDDLER, THE

Fallenstein, Karina
CRAZY BOYS

Faltas, Nick
WANTED: DEAD OR ALIVE

Fang, Mei
DIXIA QING
LIEN LIEN FUNG CHEN

Fann, Al
RETURN TO HORROR HIGH

Fansila, Marketta
DET STORA LOFTET

Fantoni, Sergio
BELLY OF AN ARCHITECT, THE

Faracci, James
SPACE RACE

Faracy, Stephanie
BLIND DATE

Faraon, Erika
MIRACLES

Farbman, Paul
DEATHROW GAMESHOW

Farcy, Bernard
COERS CROISES

Fardo, Maurizio
GOOD MORNING BABYLON
NOI UOMINI DURI

Farel, Frank
STREET TRASH

Farentino, Dion
CONCRETE ANGELS

Fares, Debi
HAPPY HOUR

Faria, Betty
ANJOS DO ARRABALDE
UM TREM PARA AS ESTRELAS

Farida
INDIAN SUMMER

Faris, Anick
MORNING MAN, THE

Farjad, Jalil
MANUSCRIPTS

Farmer, Buddy
WANTED: DEAD OR ALIVE

Farmer, Derek
ARIA

Farmer, Gary
BELIEVERS, THE
BIG TOWN, THE

Farmer, John
KINDRED, THE

Farmer, Mimsy
POISONS

Farmer
EAT THE RICH

Farnsworth, Richard
SPACE RACE

Farr, Jamie
HAPPY HOUR

Farr, Judi
YEAR MY VOICE BROKE, THE

Farrell, Sharon
CANT BUY ME LOVE

Farrell, Terry
OFF THE MARK

Farrington, Romeo
JAWS: THE REVENGE

Farron, Nicola
CAMPING DEL TERRORE
GLI OCCHIALI D'ORO

Farrow, Mia
RADIO DAYS
SEPTEMBER

Fasano, John
BLOOD SISTERS
ZOMBIE NIGHTMARE

Fassari, Antonella
LESTATE STA FINENDO

Fassari, Antonello
CARTOLINE ITALIANE

Fassoulis, Stamatis
THEOFILOS

Fat, Chow Yuen
BETTER TOMORROW, A

Fat, Chow Yun
AUTUMN'S TALE, AN
CITY ON FIRE
MY WILL, I WILL
PRISON ON FIRE
RICH AND FAMOUS

Fateyeva, Natalya
SON V RUKU, ILI CHEMODON

Faulk, John Henry
TRESPASSES

Faulkner, Benita
RETURN OF JOSEY WALES, THE

Faustino, Michael
MONSTER SQUAD, THE

Favalor, John
P.K. & THE KID

Favelevic, Sacha
STRANGER, THE

Favre, Herve
ATTENTION BANDITS

Fawcett, Alan
CARE BEARS ADVENTURE IN WONDERLAND, THE
MORNING MAN, THE

Fazlollahi, Shamssi
SHEERE SANGGY

Feal, Laura
MISS MARY
Fearl, Clifford
ORPHANS
Fearnley, James
STRAIGHT TO HELL
Federico Luppi
EL ANO DEL CONEJO
Federspiel, Birgitte
BABETTE'S GASTEBUD
SIDSTE AKT
Fedoseyeva-Shukshina, Lidia
PO GLAVNOY ULITSE S ORKESTROM
Feely, Eleanor
RAWHEAD REX
Feeney, Colleen
NECROPOLIS
Fegan, Jorge
JUNTOS
LO NEGRO DEL NEGRO
Fegan, Maggie
BUDAWANNY
Fegan, Roy
HOLLYWOOD SHUFFLE
Feher, Anna
WHOOPING COUGH
Fehrmann, Helma
SAME TO YOU
Fei Hu, Suen
BUDDHA'S LOCK
Feig, Paul
ZOMBIE HIGH
Feigin, Warren M.
HANSEL AND GRETEL
Feik, Eberhard
ZABOU
Fejlkova, Katerina
PROC?
Fejto, Raphael
AU REVOIR, LES ENFANTS
Fekade-Salassie, M.
BROADCAST NEWS
Feklistov, Alexander
STRANNAYAR ISTORIYAR DOKTORA DZHEKILA I MISTERA KHAIDA
Feld, Fritz
BARFLY
Felder, Clarence
AMAZING GRACE AND CHUCK
HIDDEN, THE
Feldman, Corey
LOST BOYS, THE
Feldman, Krystyna
POCIAG DO HOLLYWOOD
Feldman, Susan Marie
BROADCAST NEWS
Feldner, Sheldon
MONSTER IN THE CLOSET
Felix, Mary
NECROPOLIS
Fell, Norman
STRIPPED TO KILL
Fellini, Federico
INTERVISTA
Felloni, Arianna
GLI OCCHIALI D'ORO
Fellows, Edith
IN THE MOOD
Felter, Lisa-Marie
GARDENS OF STONE
Felty, Beth
DEADTIME STORIES
Fenn, Sherilynn
ZOMBIE HIGH
Fenner, Barbara
CRAZY BOYS
Fentanes, Oscar
LAPUTA: THE CASTLE IN THE SKY
LAS TRAIGO . . . MUERTAS
MAS VALE PAJARO EN MANO . . .
TRAGICO TERREMOTO EN MEXICO
Fenton, Ross
CLUB LIFE
Fenu, Ignazio
ANGELUS NOVUS
Fenwick, Perry
EMPIRE STATE
Ferapontov, V.
SASHSHENNYI FONAR

Ferber, Dorin
GRAVEYARD SHIFT
PSYCHO GIRLS
Fere, Tawny
MILLION DOLLAR MYSTERY
Ferency, Adam
MATKA KROLOW
Ferenczy, Martina
FOREVER, LULU
Ferguson, Andrew
BUSHFIRE MOON
Ferguson, J. Don
DATE WITH AN ANGEL
Ferguson, Jesse Lawrence
SUPERNATURALS, THE
Ferguson, Jessie Lawrence
PRINCE OF DARKNESS
Ferguson, Stacy
MONSTER IN THE CLOSET
Ferguson, Steve
ALLNIGHTER, THE
Feri, Kali
I KEKARMENI
Ferilli, Sabrina
CARAMELLE DA UNO SCONOSCIUTO
Ferjac, Anouk
BUISSON ARDENT
Ferland, Carmen
EVA: GUERRILLERA
Ferland, Danielle
RADIO DAYS
Fernan-Gomez, Fernando
MY GENERAL
Fernandez, Alberto
POLICIA
Fernandez, Arturo
GABY—A TRUE STORY
Fernandez, Cesar
CHRONICLE OF A DEATH FORETOLD
Fernandez, Elios
VISA U.S.A.
Fernandez, Isidoro
A LOS CUATRO VIENTOS
Fernandez, Jose Luis "Pirri"
LA ESTANQUERA DE VALLECAS
Fernandez, Jose Ramon
LAW OF DESIRE
Fernandez, Maribel
LA RULETERA
EL MOFLES Y LOS MECANICOS
Fernandez, Oscar
RETO A LA VIDA
Fernandez, Oswaldo
HOUR OF THE ASSASSIN
Fernandez, Pedrito
DELINCUENTE
UN SABADO MAS
Fernandez, Rafael
FORAJIDOS EN LA MIRA
Fernandez, Rudy
DAY THEY ROBBED AMERICA, THE
OPERATION: GET VICTOR CORPUS THE REBEL SOLDIER
VENGEANCE IS MINE
Fernandez, Vicente
EL DIABLO, EL SANTO Y EL TONTO
MATAR O MORIR
SINVERGUENZA . . . PERO HONRADO
UNA PURA Y DOS CON SAL
Fernando Guillen
REDONDELA
Ferrandini, Dean
STEELE JUSTICE
Ferrante, Anthony
VIDEO DEAD, THE
Ferrantini, Leonardo
LESTATE STA FINENDO
Ferrara, Alessandro
MEFISTO FUNK
Ferrara, Consuelo
MORO AFFAIR, THE
Ferrara, Frank
ORPHANS
Ferrara, Pino
MORO AFFAIR, THE
Ferrara, Stephane
MON BEL AMOUR, MA DECHIRURE
Ferrare, Ashley
CYCLONE

Ferrario, Davide
MATEWAN
Ferratti, Rebecca
BEVERLY HILLS COP II
Ferre, Francesca
TENEREZZA
Ferreira, Jamie
DANGER ZONE, THE
Ferreira, Taumaturgo
UM TREM PARA AS ESTRELAS
Ferrell, Tyra
LADY BEWARE
Ferreol, Andrea
IL GIORNO PRIMA
NOYADE INTERDITE
Ferrer, Filipe
DUMA VEZ POR TODAS
Ferrer, Jose
VIOLINS CAME WITH THE AMERICANS, THE
Ferrer, Miguel
ROBOCOP
Ferrer, Tony
BLACK DRAGON, THE
Ferrer, Violetta
GRAND GUIGNOL
Ferrero, Martin
PLANES, TRAINS AND AUTOMOBILES
Ferreti, Diana
EL HIJO DE PEDRO NAVAJAS
ROSA DE LA FRONTERA
TODA LA VIDA
Ferri, Alessandra
DANCERS
Ferri, Marcia
LA MONACA DIMONZA
Ferri, Marika
REGINA
Ferry, David
THREE MEN AND A BABY
Fertig, Steven
HOLLYWOOD SHUFFLE
Feuer, Debra
IL BURBERO
Feuillette, Denis
LADY OF THE CAMELIAS
Feza, Lokinda Mengi
LA VIE EST BELLE
Fied, Myra
HEARTS OF FIRE
Field, Chelsea
MASTERS OF THE UNIVERSE
Field, Crystal
RADIO DAYS
Field, Patrick
COMRADES
Field, Sally
SURRENDER
Field, Todd
ALLNIGHTER, THE
RADIO DAYS
Fields, Clare
BEST SELLER
Fields, Edith
NO WAY OUT
Fields, Maurie
BIT PART, THE
Fields, Robert
ANNA
Fields, Thor
HELLO AGAIN
Fierro, Lee
JAWS: THE REVENGE
Figalan, Meilani
WHO'S THAT GIRL
Figueroa, Marc
HOLLYWOOD SHUFFLE
Figura, Katarzyna
PIERSCIEN I ROZA
POCIAG DO HOLLYWOOD
SZORNYEK EVADJA
Filatov, Leonid
IZ ZHIZNI NACHALNIKA UGOLOVNOGO ROZYSKA
SOUCHASTNIKI
Filho, Daniel
UM TREM PARA AS ESTRELAS
Filipovsky, Frantisek
CHOBOTNICE Z II. PATRA
Filippenko, Alexander
IZ ZHIZNI POTAPOVA
O ROZVRASHCHENII ZABYT

Filocamo, Sebastiano
MEFISTO FUNK

Filozov, Albert
KAPITAN "PILIGRIMA"
OKHOTA NA DRAKONA
ZOLOTAYA BABA

Filpi, Carmen
WHO'S THAT GIRL

Finch, Charles
AMAZONS

Finch, Zack
MADE IN HEAVEN

Findley, Jim
CRY FREEDOM

Finer, Jem
STRAIGHT TO HELL

Finkel, Chris
ROCK 'N' ROLL NIGHTMARE

Finkel's Henchman
TOO MUCH

Finlayson, Kate
CLUB LIFE

Finley, Greg
EVIL TOWN
WILD PAIR, THE

Finn, Earl
SPACEBALLS

Finn, Joseph Patrick
BIRDS OF PREY

Finn, Voss
I WAS A TEENAGE T.V. TERRORIST

Finneran, Patricia
BLOOD SISTERS

Finneran, Siobhan
RITA, SUE AND BOB TOO!

Finney, Albert
ORPHANS

Finocchiaro, Angela
DOLCE ASSENZA
MAN ON FIRE

Finogenova, Elena
OBRYV

Finogeyeva, Yelena
ISKUSHENIE DON ZHUANA

Fiona
HEARTS OF FIRE

Fiore, Domenico
GOOD MORNING BABYLON

Fiorino, Paolo
LA CROCE DALLE SETTE PIETRE

Firios, Yannis
ONIRO ARISTERIS NICHTAS

Firth, Colin
MONTH IN THE COUNTRY, A

Firth, Julian
HEARTS OF FIRE

Firth, Peter
BORN OF FIRE

Fischer, Helmut
ZARTLICHE CHAOTEN

Fischer, Terry
MASCARA

Fiser, Roman
WOLF'S HOLE

Fish, Nancy
HIDING OUT

Fishburne, Larry
GARDENS OF STONE
NIGHTMARE ON ELM STREET 3: DREAM WARRIORS, A

Fisher, Bruce
NIGHTFORCE

Fisher, Carrie
AMAZON WOMEN ON THE MOON
TIME GUARDIAN, THE

Fisher, Frances
TOUGH GUYS DON'T DANCE

Fisher, Francis
HEART

Fisher, Gail
MANKILLERS

Fisher, George
OMEGA SYNDROME
P.K. & THE KID
PROGRAMMED TO KILL
RETURN TO HORROR HIGH
SPACE RACE

Fisher, Joely
PRETTY SMART

Fisher, Judith
AROUND THE WORLD IN EIGHTY WAYS

Fisher, Kelliene
SOMETHING SPECIAL!

Fisher, Norman
EAT THE RICH

Fisher, Tricia Leigh
PRETTY SMART

Fisk, Barbara
EMANON

Fisler, Alan
IF LOOKS COULD KILL

Fitts, Rick
BANZAI RUNNER
HANOI HILTON, THE
SUMMER CAMP NIGHTMARE

Fitz, Jacquie
NECROPOLIS

Fitz, Peter
AU REVOIR, LES ENFANTS
WANNSEE CONFERENCE, THE

Fitz-Gerald, Lewis
WARM NIGHTS ON A SLOW MOVING TRAIN

Fitzgerald, Dan
WHOOPS APOCALYPSE

Fitzgerald, Danny
ARIA

Fitzgerald, Lynne Turner
AMAZING GRACE AND CHUCK

Fitzgerald, Rob
PROJECT X

Fitzpatrick, Michael
BLOOD TRACKS

Fitzpatrick, Neil
GROUND ZERO

Fitzpatrick, Richard
PRETTYKILL

Fitzsimmons, David
DATE WITH AN ANGEL

Fitzsimmons, Peter
PRINCIPAL, THE

Fjeldstad, Jack
ETTER RUBICON

Flack, Herbert
ALS IN EEN ROES
BLOND DOLLY
MASCARA
ODYSSEE D'AMOUR

Flag, Bob
WISH YOU WERE HERE

Flagello, Ezio
ARIA

Flagg, Bob
EAT THE RICH

Flagg, Darron
OUT OF ROSENHEIM

Flagg, Tom
O. C. AND STIGGS

Flaherty, Joe
BLUE MONKEY

Flamand, Didier
LA RUSA

Flamant, Jean-Claude
WOLF AT THE DOOR, THE

Flanagan, Fionnula
P.K. & THE KID

Flanagan, John
BUSINESS AS USUAL

Flanagan, William
RADIO DAYS

Flat, Veronica
KAMILLA OG TYVEN

Flatman, Barry
TOO OUTRAGEOUS

Flaus, John
WARM NIGHTS ON A SLOW MOVING TRAIN

Flea
STRANDED
DUDES

Fleck, John
SLAMDANCE

Fleeks, Eric
DIRTY LAUNDRY

Fleetwood, Mick
RUNNING MAN, THE

Fleetwood, Susan
WHITE MISCHIEF

Fleg, Kathy
DEADTIME STORIES

Flemming, Jo
TIME GUARDIAN, THE

Flemming, Wayne
GOOFBALLS

Fletcher, Al
MANKILLERS

Fletcher, Dexter
GOTHIC
LIONHEART

Fletcher, Louise
FLOWERS IN THE ATTIC

Fletcher, M.R.
DIRTY DANCING

Fletcher, Norman
NGATI

Fliedel, Edna
LATE SUMMER BLUES

Flink, Coen
HAVINCK

Flint, Jimmy
EMPIRE STATE

Flint, Leonard
MANKILLERS

Flitton, Sheila
RAWHEAD REX

Floderer, Christine
SPARVAGN TILL HAVET

Flon, Suzanne
DIARY OF A MAD OLD MAN
NOYADE INTERDITE

Flood, Barbara
SOMEONE TO LOVE

Flood, Joe
PRINCIPAL, THE

Floores, Brian
OUTING, THE

Florance, Sheila
TALE OF RUBY ROSE, THE

Florek, Dann
ANGEL HEART

Flores, Alejandra
GABY—A TRUE STORY

Flores, Antonio
CALE

Flores, Gabriela
MADE IN ARGENTINA

Flores, Gerardo
JUNTOS

Flores, Laura
JUNTOS

Flores, Lola
LOS INVITADOS

Flores, Maria Elena
LA VIDA ALEGRE

Flores, Osvaldo
MISS MARY

Flores, Paul
RETURN OF JOSEY WALES, THE

Flores, Rosario
CALE

Flores, Victor
MAGDALENA VIRAGA

Flower, Buck
NIGHT STALKER, THE

Flowers, Eddie
BORDER RADIO

Flowers, Jennifer
FRENCHMAN'S FARM

Floy, Gregory
WHISTLE BLOWER, THE

Floyd, Lindsey
BELIEVERS, THE

Floyd, P.B.
MAKING MR.RIGHT

Fluegel, Darlanne
BULLETPROOF

Flynn, Bill
SATURDAY NIGHT AT THE PALACE

Flynn, Eric
EMPIRE OF THE SUN

Flynn, George
MIND KILLER

Flynn, Jeremy
COMRADES

Flynn, Owen
MUTANT HUNT

Fogarty, Mary
HELLO AGAIN

Fokker, Renee
QUATRE MAINS

Foklistov, Alexander
PLIUMBUM, ILI OPASNAIA IGIA

Fol, Robert
LETHAL WEAPON

Foley, David
HIGH STAKES
THREE MEN AND A BABY

Foley, Don
EAT THE PEACH

Foley, Ellen
FATAL ATTRACTION

Foley, Gary
DOGS IN SPACE

Foley, Joe
HIDING OUT

Folk, Abel
LESCOT

Follett, Hadrian
FULL METAL JACKET

Follett, Randy
JOHN AND THE MISSUS

Follows, Megan
STACKING

Fomm, Joana
BEIJO NA BOCA

Fonda, Bridget
ARIA

Fonda, Jane
LEONARD PART 6

Fondacaro, Phil
GARBAGE PAIL KIDS MOVIE, THE
STEELE JUSTICE

Fong Fong, Josephine Siu
WRONG COUPLES,THE

Fonsou, Anna
KLIOS

Fonss, Mime
SIDSTE AKT

Fontaine, Peter
EAT THE RICH

Fontana, Char
TOO MUCH

Fontelieu, Stocker
ANGEL HEART

Fontes, Guilherme
COLOR OF DESTINY, THE
UM TREM PARA AS ESTRELAS

Fonteyn, Paul
OVERBOARD

Forbes, Melanie
LEADING EDGE, THE

Forbes, Sheridan
EMPIRE OF THE SUN

Forbes, Sonny
WILD THING

Force, Deborah
AS TIME GOES BY

Forchion, Ray
MASTERBLASTER

Ford, Buck
ERNEST GOES TO CAMP

Ford, Butch
FIREHOUSE

Ford, Faith
YOU TALKIN' TO ME?

Ford, Lisa
TIN MEN

Ford, Michael
RAWHEAD REX

Ford, Mick
FOURTH PROTOCOL, THE

Ford, Peter
GOOD WIFE, THE

Ford, Rana
EMANON

Forde, Jessica
BUISSON ARDENT
QUATRE AVENTURES DE REINETTE ET MIRABELLE

Foreign Secretary and Crucifee
WHOOPS APOCALYPSE

Foreman, David
EMPIRE STATE

Foreman, Jamie
EMPIRE STATE

Foreman, Michelle
STRIPPED TO KILL

Forest, Andy J.
CAPRICCIO

Forest Inspector
RYKOWISKO

Forget, Pierre
LES MENDIANTS

Fornari, Vito
IL FASCINO SOTTILE DEL PECCATO

Forque, Veronica
LA VIDA ALEGRE
MADRID
MOROS Y CRISTIANOS
YEAR OF AWAKENING, THE

Forrest, Frederic
STACKING

Forrest, Steve
AMAZON WOMEN ON THE MOON

Forsberg, Lori E.
KILLER WORKOUT

Forsberg, Sara
NIONDE KOMPANIET

Forsey, Norm
STARLIGHT HOTEL

Forshion, Raymond
WHOOPS APOCALYPSE

Forslund, Constance
RIVER'S EDGE

Forster, Walter
EU

Forsythe, Warren
RAISING ARIZONA

Forsythe, William
EXTREME PREJUDICE
RAISING ARIZONA
WEEDS

Fortell, Albert
DEATH STONE

Fortier, Robert
O. C. AND STIGGS

Fortuna, Perfeito
BEIJO NA BOCA

Fortune, Jack
LOVECHILD, THE

Foss, Alan
MAURICE

Foss, Wenche
PA STIGENDE KURS

Foster, Barry
MAURICE
THREE KINDS OF HEAT
WHISTLE BLOWER, THE

Foster, Beverly
PERSONAL SERVICES

Foster, Eric
CRY WILDERNESS

Foster, Frances
ENEMY TERRITORY

Foster, Gloria
LEONARD PART 6

Foster, Jodie
SIESTA

Foster, Katrina
BIT PART, THE

Foster, Meg
MASTERS OF THE UNIVERSE
WIND, THE

Foster, Philip
BUSINESS AS USUAL

Foster, Stan
PROJECT X

Foster, Terry
GARDENS OF STONE

Fountain, Donny
RETURN OF JOSEY WALES, THE

Fountain, Gideon
FIREHOUSE

Fournery, Mary
AMAZONS

Fournier, Cassandre
MORNING MAN, THE

Fowler, Stuart
CUSTODY

Fox, Colin
CARE BEARS ADVENTURE IN WONDERLAND, THE

Fox, Colin R.
HELLO AGAIN

Fox, James
COMRADES
HIGH SEASON
WHISTLE BLOWER, THE

Fox, Jerry
EVIL SPAWN

Fox, Joanne
FIREHOUSE

Fox, Kevin
BIG TOWN, THE
HEARTS OF FIRE

Fox, Michael
MALIBU BIKINI SHOP, THE
OVER THE TOP

Fox, Michael J.
LIGHT OF DAY
SECRET OF MY SUCCESS, THE

Fox, Philip
MAURICE

Fraire, Raul
EL LUTE—CAMINA O REVIENTA
LONG STRIDER
LOS INVITADOS

Franaszek, Mieczyslaw
BOHATERROKU

Frances, Leopoldo
MIRACLES

Francesco, Acquaroli
LA MONACA DIMONZA

Franchetti, Rina
ADELMO

Francione, Tan Hung
FULL METAL JACKET

Francis, Carol Ann
STREET SMART
WILD THING

Francis, Laura
SUPERNATURALS, THE

Francis, Mike
BENJI THE HUNTED

Francis, Nancy
BENJI THE HUNTED

Francks, Cree Summer
HEARTS OF FIRE
WILD THING

Francks, Don
BIG TOWN, THE

Franco, James V.
BROADCAST NEWS

Francois, Jacques
LA RUSA
LA VIE DISSOLUE DE GERARD FLOQUE

Frank, Diana
MANKILLERS

Frank, Gary
ENEMY TERRITORY

Frank, Janice
MAKING MR.RIGHT

Frank, Johnny B.
DIRTY LAUNDRY

Frank, Joshua
ANGEL HEART

Frank, Sean
FULL METAL JACKET

Frank, Tony
EXTREME PREJUDICE

Frank, Wolfram
JENATSCH

Franke, Anja
SAME TO YOU

Franke, Donald
BLOOD HOOK

Franke, Ryan
BLOOD HOOK

Frankel, Art
LIKE FATHER, LIKE SON

Franken, Steve
CANT BUY ME LOVE

Franklin, Cherie
PARTY CAMP

Fransined
JEAN DE FLORETTE
MANON OF THE SPRING

Fransman, Sanna
A LA ITKE IINES

Franz, Birgit
FLYER, THE

Franz, Elizabeth
SECRET OF MY SUCCESS, THE

Frappat, Francis
MISS MONA

Frasca, Joy Lynn
WHOOPS APOCALYPSE

Fraser, Alice
NGATI
STARLIGHT HOTEL

Fraser, Bill
LITTLE DORRIT

Fraser, Duncan
MALONE

Fraser, Ivih
THOU SHALT NOT KILL . . . EXCEPT

Fraser, Shelagh
HOPE AND GLORY

Frasher, Michael
MATEWAN

Frassinelli, Monica
BELLIFRESCHI

Fratkin, Stuart
TEEN WOLF TOO
VALET GIRLS

Fravel, Phil
STEELE JUSTICE

Frazer, Mark
GARDENS OF STONE

Frazer, Rupert
EMPIRE OF THE SUN

Frazier, Joe
GHOST FEVER

Frechette, Peter
KINDRED, THE

Freddie James
WILD THING

Frederick, Patric
BIG EASY, THE

Freels, Jon Lee
STRIPPED TO KILL

Freeman, Betty
KINDRED, THE

Freeman, Eric
SILENT NIGHT, DEADLY NIGHT PART II

Freeman, Harriet
DOGS IN SPACE

Freeman, Jonathan
FOREVER, LULU

Freeman, Kathleen
DRAGNET
IN THE MOOD
INNERSPACE
MALIBU BIKINI SHOP, THE

Freeman, Loren
PSYCHOS IN LOVE

Freeman, Morgan
STREET SMART

Freeman, Scott
NO WAY OUT

Freer, Leila-Florentine
DAS TREIBHAUS

Freilino, Brian
GOOD MORNING BABYLON

Freindlich, Alisa
PROSTI

Freinlich, Bruno
STRANNAYAR ISTORIYAR DOKTORA DZHEKILA I MISTERA KHAIDA

Freistadt, Peter
POET'S SILENCE, THE

Freitag, Benedict
DER UNSICHTBARE

Freitag, Robert
CRIME OF HONOR

Fremont, Thierry
LES NOCES BARBARES
TRAVELLING AVANT

French, Dawn
EAT THE RICH
MORE BAD NEWS

Frenkel, Noemi
EL DUENO DEL SOL

Frerichs, Robert
GARDENS OF STONE

Fretun, Philippe
BAD BLOOD

Freudenheim, John
ISHTAR

Frewer, Matt
FOURTH PROTOCOL, THE

Frey, Glenn
LETS GET HARRY

Frey, Sami
BLACK WIDOW

Friberg, My
DET STORA LOFTET

Fricsay, Andras
SIERRA LEONE

Fridell, Squire
MIRACLES

Fridley, Tom
SUMMER CAMP NIGHTMARE

Fried, Justin
MAGIC SNOWMAN, THE

Friedkin, Gary
SNOW WHITE

Friedl, Jan
BACHELOR GIRL

Friedman, Bernie
FOREVER, LULU

Friedman, Daniel
DANGER ZONE, THE

Friels, Colin
GROUND ZERO
HIGH TIDE
WARM NIGHTS ON A SLOW MOVING TRAIN

Friend, Chan
HAPPY BIGAMIST

Friesen, Wes
BIRDS OF PREY

Friis Mikkelsen, Jarl
KAMPEN OM DEN RODE KO

Frimmel, Gabriel
MANKILLERS

Frishberg, Dave
SOMEONE TO LOVE

Fritschi, Christina
LADY OF THE CAMELIAS

Fritz, Natalie
MASCARA

Fritzell, Per
LEIF

Frizzell, John
WINTER TAN, A

Frohardt, Steve
DELOS ADVENTURE, THE

Froland, Dab
PA STIGENDE KURS

Froling, Ewa
DEMONS
JIM OCH PIRATERNA BLOM

Froman, David
STEELE JUSTICE

Fronczewski, Piotr
MASKARADA

Frost, Patrick
CODA
LIGHTHORSEMEN, THE

Frost, Sadie
EMPIRE STATE

Frost, Stephen
LOVECHILD, THE

Frot, Catherine
LA MOINE ET LA SORCIERE

Fruit, Percy
MATEWAN

Frumkes, Roy
STREET TRASH

Frye, Virgil
WINNERS TAKE ALL

Fryer, Sharon
OUT OF ORDER

Fryk, Tomas
NIONDE KOMPANIET

Fu, Zhang Duo
ROMANCE OF BOOK AND SWORD, THE

Fuchsova, Zaneta
CHOBOTNICE Z II. PATRA

Fudge, Alan
MY DEMON LOVER

Fuentes, Estrella
LAPUTA: THE CASTLE IN THE SKY

Fuentes, Jesus
DIRTY DANCING

Fuentes, Miguel Angel
MIRACLES
MISSION KILL

Fuji, Mariko
UHOHO TANKENTAI
YOSHIWARA ENJO

Fujioka, John
STEEL DAWN

Fujita, Makoto
SURE DEATH 4

Fujitani, Miwako
RYOMA O KITTA OTOKO

Fukazama, Masato
TOO MUCH

Fulford, Christopher
PRAYER FOR THE DYING, A

Fullenwider, Fran
EAT THE RICH

Fuller, Craig
GOOD WIFE, THE

Fuller, Kurt
RUNNING MAN, THE

Fuller, Lisa
MONSTER SQUAD, THE

Fuller, William
NIGHTMARE AT SHADOW WOODS

Fulton, Dereck
HIDING OUT

Fulton, Todd
ESCAPES

Fumetto, Rosa
CARTOLINE ITALIANE

Funes, Dr. Francisco
MIRACLES

Funicello, Annette
BACK TO THE BEACH

Funk, Terry
OVER THE TOP

Funnell, Adrian
EAT THE RICH

Funt, Jessica
LADY OF THE CAMELIAS

Funtek, Frigyes
MALOM A POKOLBAN

Furachev, Alexander
ZNAY NASHIKH

Furgler, Brigitta
CRIME OF HONOR

Furlan, Rate
BELLY OF AN ARCHITECT, THE

Furlong, Judy
JOHN AND THE MISSUS

Furlong, Mack
JOHN AND THE MISSUS

Furlow, Trish
MANKILLERS

Furuya, Ikko
DIXIELAND DAIMYO

Fuscagni, Nino
MOSCA ADDIO

Fuse, Horishi
WATASHI O SKI NI TSURETETTE

Fusheng, Li
LAST EMPEROR, THE

Fustikan, Brian
BIRDS OF PREY

Fyodorov, L.
VZLOMSHCHIK

Gabaldon, Francisca
REDONDELA

Gabay, Sason
DEADLINE

Gabb, Peter
BIG EASY, THE

Gabor, Eva
PRINCESS ACADEMY, THE

Gabor, Zsa Zsa
NIGHTMARE ON ELM STREET 3: DREAM WARRIORS, A

Gabr, Kariman
ALSHAZIA

Gabriadze, Levan
KIN-DZA-DZA

Gabriel, Ray
SQUEEZE, THE

Gabrielle, Monique
AMAZON WOMEN ON THE MOON
EMMANUELLE 5

Gaby's Nurse
GABY—A TRUE STORY

Gadbois, Babs
MORNING MAN, THE

Gaddis, Marshall
BELL DIAMOND

Gadi
BABULA

Gaffikin, Brian
BEST SELLER

Gaft, Valentin
PO GLAVNOY ULITSE S ORKESTROM

Gage, Kevin
STEELE JUSTICE

Gage, Loutz
TALKING WALLS
Gage, Patricia
HELLO AGAIN
Gagliarde, Dodo
IL LUPO DI MARE
Gagnon, Denise
LES FOUS DE BASSAN
Gago, Jenny
BEST SELLER
Gagodorca, Maria Teresa
HOUR OF THE ASSASSIN
Gaia, Aurora
RELACAO FIEL E VERDADEIRA
Gail, Tim
IF LOOKS COULD KILL
Gaines, James
OPPOSING FORCE
Gainey, M.C.
FATAL BEAUTY
Gains, Courtney
CANT BUY ME LOVE
WINNERS TAKE ALL
Gaitan, S.
VZLOMSHCHIK
Gaja, Servando
WINTER TAN, A
Galabru, Michel
GRAND GUIGNOL
LA VIE DISSOLUE DE GERARD FLOQUE
POULE ET FRITES
SOIGNE TA DROITE
Galan, Monica
SINFIN, LA MUERTA NO ES NINGUNA SOLUCION
Galang, Fred
HUNTED, THE
IGOROTA
Galani, Arianthe
DEAR CARDHOLDER
Galarza, Daniel
EL ANO DEL CONEJO
Galcedo, Jorge
WINTER TAN, A
Gale, Ed
SPACEBALLS
Gale, Lorena
WILD THING
Gale, Peter
EMPIRE OF THE SUN
Gale, Sheila
STEELE JUSTICE
Galiardo, Juan Luis
LA GUERRA DE LOS LOCOS
POLICIA
Galibin, Alexander
KOORDINATY SMERTI
Galiena, Anna
HOTEL COLONIAL
LESTATE STA FINENDO
Galkin, Boris
AKTSIA
Gallagher, John
EAT THE PEACH
Gallagher, Kelly
DOGS IN SPACE
Gallagher, Patrick
DEAD, THE
Gallagher, Peter
MY LITTLE GIRL
Gallagher, Tracy
NECROPOLIS
Gallant, Catherine
PRETTYKILL
Gallardo, Juan
FORAJIDOS EN LA MIRA
MI NOMBRE ES GATILLO
NARCOTERROR
Gallardo, Lucy
CORRUPCION
Gallego, Gina
MY DEMON LOVER
Gallegos, Christina
OPEN HOUSE
Galley, Eagle
SEA AND POISON, THE
Galligan, John
BLOOD HOOK
Gallion, Dan
BLOODSUCKERS FROM OUTER SPACE
Gallion, Randy
VALET GIRLS
Gallivan, Megan
RUNNING MAN, THE
Gallo, Alfredo
IL FASCINO SOTTILE DEL PECCATO
Gallo, Barbara
RADIO DAYS
Gallo, Gianfranco
DELITTI
Gallo, Inigo
CRIME OF HONOR
Gallo, Richard Arthur
SECRET OF MY SUCCESS, THE
Gallup, Denise
SPACEBALLS
Gallup, Dian
SPACEBALLS
Gallus, Agi
PSYCHO GIRLS
Galt, John
NADINE
RETURN OF JOSEY WALES, THE
Galvan, Armando
MI NOMBRE ES GATILLO
Galvan III, Anthony
EXTREME PREJUDICE
Gam, Giulia
BESAME MUCHO
Gamble, Tim
UNTOUCHABLES, THE
Gamelon, Laurent
LES OREILLES ENTRE LES DENTS
Gamero, Antonio
HAY QUE DESHACER LA CASA
LA ESTANQUERA DE VALLECAS
SUFRE MAMON
Gaminara, William
COMRADES
Gammell, Robin
PROJECT X
Gammon, James
IRONWEED
MADE IN HEAVEN
STACKING
Gamy, Yvonne
MANON OF THE SPRING
Ganesh
KATHAKKU PINNIL
Ganger, Ben
FLOWERS IN THE ATTIC
Gann, Merrilyn
ROXANNE
Gannon, Dennis
MURDER LUST
Gant, Richard
SUSPECT
Ganz, Bruno
DER HIMMEL UBER BERLIN
Ganzert, R.J.
SPACE RACE
Garas, Dezso
MALOM A POKOLBAN
WHOOPING COUGH
Garbary, Evelyn
LIFE CLASSES
Garcia, Alberto
MASCARA
Garcia, Andy
UNTOUCHABLES, THE
Garcia, Antonio Martinez
OVERBOARD
Garcia, Barney
OUTRAGEOUS FORTUNE
Garcia, Bernal
EULALIA
Garcia, Christina
EXTREME PREJUDICE
Garcia, Ed
MANKILLERS
Garcia, Eddie
IGOROTA
Garcia, Eleazar
ROSA DE LA FRONTERA
MI NOMBRE ES GATILLO
Garcia, Francisco
BROADCAST NEWS
Garcia, Javier
MI NOMBRE ES GATILLO
Garcia, Joaquin
LA RULETERA
LAPUTA: THE CASTLE IN THE SKY
NOS REIMOS DE LA MIGRA
Garcia, Jose G.
OUTRAGEOUS FORTUNE
Garcia, Luis
A LOS CUATRO VIENTOS
Garcia, Nestor Mendez
WALKER
Garcia, Pablo
ALIEN PREDATOR
Garcia, Ramon
HOUR OF THE ASSASSIN
Garcia, Rick
EXTREME PREJUDICE
Garcia, Stenio
LEILA DINIZ
Garcia, Yolande
CHRONICLE OF A DEATH FORETOLD
Garcia-Ortega, Rosario
LA CASA DE BERNARDA ALBA
Garden, Graeme
WHOOPS APOCALYPSE
Gardener, Cliff
VIDEO DEAD, THE
Gardenia, Vincent
MOONSTRUCK
Gardiazabal, Adriana
EL HOMBRE DE LA DEUDA EXTERNA
Gardner, Beverley
WITH LOVE TO THE PERSON NEXT TO ME
Gardner, Brooks
MALONE
Gardner, Herb
ISHTAR
Gardner, Mario
WHO'S THAT GIRL
Gardner, Micki
AROUND THE WORLD IN EIGHTY WAYS
Gardner, Wendy
MANKILLERS
Gare, Anna
PURSUIT OF HAPPINESS, THE
Garey, Tony
FULL METAL JACKET
Garfield, Allen
BEVERLY HILLS COP II
Garfield, Julie
ISHTAR
Garfinkle, Gayle
MORNING MAN, THE
Gargani, Frank
P.I. PRIVATE INVESTIGATIONS
Gargula, Milan
PRATELE BERMUDSKEHO TROJUHELNIKU
Garland, Grace
STREET SMART
Garland, Lori
EMANON
Garlington, Lee
IN THE MOOD
Garlington, Rick
BLOODSUCKERS FROM OUTER SPACE
Garmash, Sergei
KARUSEL NA BAZARNOY PLOSHCHADI
Garmsiry, Ali Asghar
GOZARESH-E YEK GHATL
Garner, Nadine
BUSHFIRE MOON
Garofani, Alessandro
ILLUMINAZIONI
Garofano, Erminia
PROFUMO
Garr, Teri
MIRACLES
Garrani, Ivo
SOLDATI: 365 GIORNI ALL' ALBA
Garratt, Evie
LOVECHILD, THE
Garreaud, Jean-Francois
TESTET
Garrel, Maurice
POISONS
Garrett, B.J.
EMANON
Garrett, Walter
VIDEO DEAD, THE

Garrison, Honorable James
BIG EASY, THE
Garrison, Miranda
DIRTY DANCING
Garson, Edward
LE JEUNE MAGICIEN
Gary, Ann Pearl
STREET SMART
Gary, Linda
PINOCCHIO AND THE EMPEROR OF THE NIGHT
Gary, Lorraine
JAWS: THE REVENGE
Gary Kelson
MILLION DOLLAR MYSTERY
Garza, Jaime
RETO A LA VIDA
Gasan-Zade, T.
VZLOMSHCHIK
Gasjunova, Dace
POHADKA O MALICKOVI
Gaspar, Sandor
ISTEN VELETEK, BARATAIM
Gassman, Alessandro
LA MONACA DIMONZA
Gassman, Vittorio
FAMILY, THE
I PICARI
Gatayev, Valery
KORABL PRISHELTSEV
Gates, Debbie
HAPPY HOUR
Gati, Cathy
FOREVER, LULU
Gatlin, Jerry
P.K. & THE KID
Gatto, Clarita
MISSIONE EROICA
Gaubardy, Serge
LANNEE DES MEDUSES
Gaudray, Bernard
ARIA
Gauny, Sam
EXTREME PREJUDICE
Gaup, Ailu
OFELAS
Gaup, Mikkel
OFELAS
Gaup, Sara Marit
OFELAS
Gautier, Anne
ENNEMIS INTIMES
Gauvin, Regent
BACH AND BROCCOLI
Gavaza, Angela
CRY FREEDOM
Gavin, Craig
STABILIZER, THE
Gavriel, Amiram
HIMMO MELECH YERUSHALAIM
Gay, Linda
BESAME MUCHO
Gayle, Diane
TALKING WALLS
Gayle, Gary
TALKING WALLS
Gayle, Jackie
TIN MEN
Gaynes, George
POLICE ACADEMY 4: CITIZENS ON PATROL
UN TASSINARO A NEW YORK
Gaynor, Gay
LAST OF ENGLAND, THE
Gazarov, Sergei
TANTSPLOSHCHADKA
YAGUAR
Gazcon, Edgardo
FIERAS EN BRAMA
HERENCIA DE VALIENTES
POLICIAS DE NARCOTICOS
Gazelle, Wendy
HOT PURSUIT
SAMMY AND ROSIE GET LAID
Gazith, Amith
LATE SUMMER BLUES
Gaziyev, Shavkat
PLOSHCHAD VOSSTANIA
Gazley, Mike
BIRDS OF PREY
Gazzara, Ben
IL GIORNO PRIMA

Ge, Chen Kai
LAST EMPEROR, THE
Gea, Juan
LA RUSA
Gearhardt, Sassy
FOREVER, LULU
Geary, Anthony
DISORDERLIES
P.I. PRIVATE INVESTIGATIONS
PENITENTIARY III
Gebuhr, Vera
SIDSTE AKT
Gedrick, Jason
PROMISED LAND
STACKING
Gee, Paul
THREE KINDS OF HEAT
Geer, Ellen
BIG SHOTS
WILD PAIR, THE
Geeta
PANCHAGNI
Geetha
AMRITAMGAMAYA
Geier, Ruthe
MAKING MR.RIGHT
Geldhof, Ille
VAN PAEMEL FAMILY, THE
Gelin, Daniel
VIA MONTENAPOLEONE
Gelin, Fiona
TANT QU'IL AURA DES FEMMES
Gelley, Kornel
ISTEN VELETEK, BARATAIM
Gelozzi, Nicholas
PRETTY SMART
Gelting, Michael
EPIDEMIC
Gemmell, Helen
PERSONAL SERVICES
Gempart, Michael
CRIME OF HONOR
Gendron, Francois-Eric
LAMI DE MON AMIE
Gendron, Laurent
LA VIE DISSOLUE DE GERARD FLOQUE
Genelle, Kim
HOLLYWOOD SHUFFLE
Genesi, Alessandro
CARTOLINE ITALIANE
Genest, Veronique
LASSOCIATION DES MALFAITEURS
Genoud, Philippe Morier
BUISSON ARDENT
Genovese, Michael
BLIND DATE
Gensac, Claude
POULE ET FRITES
Gentica, Lani
MISSING IN ACTION
Gentica, Lanie
IGOROTA
Gentile, Cristina
I KEKARMENI
Gentiles, Avril
MORGAN STEWART'S COMING HOME
Geoffrey Staines
MIO, MOY MIO
George
WISH YOU WERE HERE
FLICKS
George, Brian
BLIND DATE
ROXANNE
George, David
FULL METAL JACKET
George, Gotz
ZABOU
George, Greg
CONCRETE ANGELS
George "Buck" Flower
CODE NAME ZEBRA
George Anthony-Bayza
NECROPOLIS
Georgulakis, Michaelis
VERSTECKTE LIEBE
Geppi, Cindy
TIN MEN
Geraffi, Haim
DEATH BEFORE DISHONOR

Geraghty, Marita
BROADCAST NEWS
HIDING OUT
Gerald McArthur
MAURICE
Gerard, Charles
ATTENTION BANDITS
Gerard, Greg
RADIO DAYS
Gerasimov, Evgeny
TAKAYA ZHESTOKAYA IGRA—KHOKKEY
Gerasimov, Jevgenij
CIZIM VSTUP POVOLEN
Gerdes, George
SQUEEZE, THE
Gerdes, Heather Lea
DIRTY DANCING
Gericke, Mario
VERNEHMUNG DER ZEUGEN
Gerlini, Piero
DOLCE PELLE DI ANGELA
Germaine, Maeve
RAWHEAD REX
Gerney, Dave
THOU SHALT NOT KILL . . . EXCEPT
Gerowitz, Ralph
EMANON
Gerrish, Flo
OVER THE TOP
Gerroll, Daniel
EIGHTY FOUR CHARING CROSS ROAD
HAPPY NEW YEAR
Gersak, Savina
IRON WARRIOR
U IME NARODA
Gershon, Gina
SWEET REVENGE
Gersten, Ellen
EMANON
Gertz, Jami
LESS THAN ZERO
LOST BOYS, THE
Geter, Leo
NEAR DARK
NO WAY OUT
Getova, Plamena
PRIZEMYAVANE
Getty, Estelle
MANNEQUIN
Getz, Karen
DIRTY DANCING
Gevai, Simon G.
CSOK, ANYU
Geworkian, Violetta
SASHSHENNYI FONAR
Ghandour, Ali
ZAWGAT RAGOL MOHIM
Ghazalla, Amira
ZISCHKE
Ghekire, Joris
MASCARA
Ghent, Bill
OVERKILL
Ghini, Massimo
ASI COMO HABIAN SIDO
Ghio, Adrian
STRANGER, THE
Ghione, Gianluigi
NOI UOMINI DURI
Ghir, Kulvinder
RITA, SUE AND BOB TOO!
Ghirardi, Dario
QUARTIERE
Ghosh, Nabendu
PANCHVATI
Giachetti, Richie
OVER THE TOP
Gian, Joey
DEATH BEFORE DISHONOR
NIGHT STALKER, THE
Gianasi, Rick
MUTANT HUNT
ROBOT HOLOCAUST
Gianevsky, Helen
DOGS IN SPACE
Giannini, Giancarlo
I PICARI
TERNOSECCO
Gianotti, Claudia
REGINA

Giardina, Marco
SEMBRA MORTO . . . ME E SOLO SVENUTO

Gibb, Cynthia
MALONE

Gibb, Don
JOCKS
THEY STILL CALL ME BRUCE

Gibb, Donald
REVENGE OF THE NERDS II: NERDS IN PARADISE

Gibb, Sybil
DOGS IN SPACE

Gibbons, Leeza
ROBOCOP

Gibbs, Angela
DIRTY LAUNDRY

Gibbs, Fabian
SITTING IN LIMBO

Gibbs, Timothy
KINDRED, THE

Gibson, Cal
CRYSTAL HEART

Gibson, Gerry
RAGE OF HONOR

Gibson, Henry
INNERSPACE
MONSTER IN THE CLOSET

Gibson, Mel
LETHAL WEAPON

Gibson, Russell
STARLIGHT HOTEL

Gideon, Ray
MADE IN HEAVEN

Gidley, Pamela
DUDES

Gielgud, John
WHISTLE BLOWER, THE

Gieske, Gilbert
BLOND DOLLY

Giffin, Vincent
ULTIMAX FORCE

Gift, Roland
OUT OF ORDER
SAMMY AND ROSIE GET LAID

Giftos, Elaine
TROUBLE WITH DICK, THE

Gigi and Andrea
RIMINI RIMINI

Gignoux, Hubert
MELO

Gil, Arturo
GARBAGE PAIL KIDS MOVIE, THE
SPACEBALLS

Gil, Cremilde
RELACAO FIEL E VERDADEIRA

Gil, Ricardo
SNOW WHITE

Gil Reade
ESCAPES

Gilad, Avri
YEHOSHUA—YEHOSHUA

Gilan, Yvonne
EMPIRE OF THE SUN

Gilbert, Pamela
EVIL SPAWN

Gilbert, Ron
CLUB LIFE

Gilberts, Richard
LIKE FATHER, LIKE SON

Gilboe, Gerda
SIDSTE AKT

Gilborn, Steven
ANNA

Gilder, Susi
SOMEONE TO WATCH OVER ME

Gilgreen, John
MILLION DOLLAR MYSTERY

Gill, George
MASTERBLASTER

Gill, Jack
ASSASSINATION

Gill, John
WHISTLE BLOWER, THE

Gill, Joumana
FRIENDSHIP'S DEATH

Gill, Sheila
PERSONAL SERVICES

Gillen, Freda
BUDAWANNY

Gillespie, Emer
BOY SOLDIER

Gillette, Anita
MOONSTRUCK

Gilliam, David
GUNPOWDER

Gilliam, Julianne
ANNA

Gillies, David
WARDOGS

Gillies, Max
AS TIME GOES BY

Gilligan, Tessie
MISS MARY

Gilligan, Vivienne
LADY OF THE CAMELIAS

Gilliland, Richard
HAPPY HOUR

Gillin, Hugh
WANTED: DEAD OR ALIVE

Gillingham, Kim
VALET GIRLS

Gillis, James
DERANGED

Gillis, Jamie
IF LOOKS COULD KILL

Gillis, Mary
CROSS MY HEART
SOMEONE TO WATCH OVER ME
WHO'S THAT GIRL

Gilpin, Jack
HIDING OUT

Gilsenan, James
O. C. AND STIGGS

Gilyard, Clarence
OFF THE MARK

Gimenez, Claudia
A DANCA DOS BONECOS

Gimenez, Raul
JENATSCH

Gimignani, Alberto
FAMILY, THE

Gimle, Ingar Helge
PLASTPOSEN

Gimmelli, Barbara
LESTATE STA FINENDO

Gimmelli, Daniela
LESTATE STA FINENDO

Gimpera, Teresa
ASIGNATURA APROBADA

Ginisty, Florent
TANT QU'IL AURA DES FEMMES

Ginty, Robert
MISSION KILL
PROGRAMMED TO KILL
THREE KINDS OF HEAT

Ginzo, Juana
LA ESTANQUERA DE VALLECAS

Gio, Frank
WEEDS

Gioia, Anthony
NECROPOLIS

Giordana, Luca
DELIZIA

Giordani, Rocky
IN THE MOOD

Giordano, Bruno
QUEL RAGAZZO DELLA CURVA "B"

Giordano, Carlos
SINFIN, LA MUERTA NO ES NINGUNA SOLUCION

Giordano, Maria Angela
NOI UOMINI DURI

Giordano, Raffaella
PERSONAGGI & INTERPRETI

Giorgobiani, Edisher
REPENTANCE

Giorgobiani, Ramaz
STUPEN

Giovannini, Lucrezia
JENATSCH

Giraldo, Francisco
HOUR OF THE ASSASSIN

Girard, Louis-George
BACH AND BROCCOLI

Girard, Renee
KEEPING TRACK

Girardin, Ray
NUMBER ONE WITH A BULLET

Girardot, Hippolyte
MANON OF THE SPRING

Giraud, Roland
CROSS
LA VIE DISSOLUE DE GERARD FLOQUE
TANT QU'IL AURA DES FEMMES

Giraudeau, Bernard
LANNEE DES MEDUSES
LHOMME VOILE
POUSSIERE D'ANGE

Girolami, Bob
ISHTAR

Girven, Ross
NGATI

Gish, Annabeth
HIDING OUT

Gish, Lillian
WHALES OF AUGUST, THE

Gits, E.
VZLOMSHCHIK

Giudotti, Laurentina
QUEL RAGAZZO DELLA CURVA "B"

Givens, Lisa
CANT BUY ME LOVE

Gladkowska, Maria
MAGNAT

Gladstone, Dana
BEVERLY HILLS COP II

Gladunko, Lyudmilla
PLOSHCHAD VOSSTANIA

Gladys, Maria
UM FILM 100% BRAZILEIRO

Glagoleva, Vera
ISKRENNE VASH . . .
SNAYPERY

Glanzelius, Anton
MY LIFE AS A DOG

Glas-Drake, Amelia
SERPENT'S WAY, THE

Glascow, Len
OMEGA SYNDROME

Glass, Ann-Gisel
SIERRA LEONE

Glass, Anne Gisel
FAMILY BUSINESS

Glass, Anne-Gisel
TRAVELLING AVANT

Glassber, Ellwood
OVERKILL

Glaude, Jean
P.I. PRIVATE INVESTIGATIONS

Glavas, Make
ROXANNE

Glazary, Helen
RED RIDING HOOD

Glazer, Eugene R.
HOLLYWOOD SHUFFLE

Glazer, Eugene Robert
NO WAY OUT

Glazer, Gene
HUNTER'S BLOOD

Glazyrin, A.
KOROTKIE VSTRECHI

Gleason, Dr. Charles H.
SUMMER HEAT

Gleason, Paul
FOREVER, LULU

Gleason, Redmond M.
DEAD, THE

Glemnitz, Reinhard
CRIME OF HONOR
WANNSEE CONFERENCE, THE

Glen, David
STREET SMART

Glendenning, David
SURFER, THE

Glenn, Jeremy
NO WAY OUT

Glenn, Julie
TERMINUS

Glenn, Mary F.
RAISING ARIZONA

Glenn, Scott
MAN ON FIRE

Glick, Stacey
THREE O'CLOCK HIGH

Glickman, Marty
EIGHTY FOUR CHARING CROSS ROAD

Gligorov, Robert
DELIRIA

Glorioso, Vincent
MORNING MAN, THE

Glover, Broc
WINNERS TAKE ALL

Glover, Bruce
BIG BAD MAMA II
HUNTER'S BLOOD

Glover, Crispin
RIVER'S EDGE

Glover, Danny
LETHAL WEAPON

Glover, John
SOMETHING SPECIAL!

Glover, Julian
CRY FREEDOM
FOURTH PROTOCOL, THE
HEARTS OF FIRE

Glover, Kara
BEAT, THE

Glowna, Vadim
DEVILS PARADISE, THE

Glue, Mervyn
STARLIGHT HOTEL

Gluski, M.
SASHSHENNYI FONAR

Gluzsky, Mikhail
DUBLYOR NACHINAET DEYSTVOVAT
IZ ZHIZNI POTAPOVA

Glynn, Annie
MONSTER IN THE CLOSET

Glynn, Carlin
GARDENS OF STONE

Gnadinger, Mathias
SAME TO YOU

Gniewkowska, Katarzyna
MIEDZY USTAMI A BRZEGIEM PUCHARU

Go, Hiromi
SARABA ITOSHIKI HITO YO

Go, Jade
LAST EMPEROR, THE

Goakes, Stuart
ALLAN QUATERMAIN AND THE LOST CITY OF GOLD

Gobbi, Giorgio
UN TASSINARO A NEW YORK

Godard, Jean-Luc
SOIGNE TA DROITE

Goddard, Alan
BELL DIAMOND

Godderis, Drew
EVIL SPAWN

Godenzi, Joyce Mina
EASTERN CONDORS

Godfrey, Patrick
MAURICE

Godinez, Salvador
LETS GET HARRY

Godreche, Judith
LES MENDIANTS

Godsey, William C.
TIN MEN

Godwin, Harvey
ERNEST GOES TO CAMP

Godzdzik, Monika
BLIND CHANCE

Goetz, Peter Michael
MY LITTLE GIRL

Goff, Greer
ANGEL HEART

Goff, John
NIGHT STALKER, THE

Gogal, Ivo
CENA ODVAHY

Gogas, Thaddeus
VIDEO DEAD, THE

Goggins, Pat
STACKING

Gogin, Michael Lee
MUNCHIES

Goins, Jesse
ROBOCOP

Gold, Eric
EMPIRE STATE

Goldberg, Noa
LATE SUMMER BLUES

Goldberg, Whoopi
BURGLAR
FATAL BEAUTY

Goldblum, Jeff
BEYOND THERAPY

Goldblum, Pamela
SOMEONE TO LOVE

Golden, Annie
FOREVER, LULU

Golden, Diana
EL ANSIA DE MATAR
TRAGICO TERREMOTO EN MEXICO

Golden, Lee
MANNEQUIN

Golden, Ronnie
FOURTH PROTOCOL, THE

Goldenberg, Harvey J.
IN THE MOOD
MALIBU BIKINI SHOP, THE

Goldhand, Judi
MANNEQUIN

Goldman, Gary
DERANGED

Goldman, Rick
WANTED: DEAD OR ALIVE

Goldman, Robert
ALLNIGHTER, THE
OVERBOARD

Goldman, Theodore
TIN MEN

Goldpaugh, Kathleen
TIN MEN

Goldshmied, Gabriela
NARCOTERROR

Goldsmied, Gabriela
EL HIJO DE PEDRO NAVAJAS

Goldsmith, Merwin
MAKING MR.RIGHT

Goldstein, Jenette
NEAR DARK

Goldstein, Judith
DIRTY LAUNDRY

Goldstein, Steve
HOUSE OF GAMES

Goldstein, Steven
UNTOUCHABLES, THE

Goldthwait, Bob
BURGLAR

Goldthwait, Bobcat
POLICE ACADEMY 4: CITIZENS ON PATROL

Goldwyn, Tony
GABY—A TRUE STORY

Golino, Valeria
GLI OCCHIALI D'ORO
LETE DERNIER A TANGER

Gollings, Marcus
TO MARKET, TOMARKET

Goloborodko, Yegor
KAZHDYY OKHOTNIK ZHELAET ZNAT

Golonka, Arlene
SURVIVAL GAME

Goman, Ray
P.K. & THE KID

Gomer, Russell
BOY SOLDIER

Gomes, Laurie
FULL METAL JACKET

Gomes, Mario
BEIJO NA BOCA

Gomez, C. Victor Alcoper
MIRACLES

Gomez, Fernando Fernan
CARA DE ACELGA
EL GRAN SERAFIN
MOROS Y CRISTIANOS

Gomez, Jose Luis
LA ESTANQUERA DE VALLECAS
LAS DOS ORILLAS

Gomez, Luma
EL BOSQUE ANIMADO

Gomez, Panchito
RETURN TO HORROR HIGH

Gomez, Paulina
GABY—A TRUE STORY

Gomez, Raymundo
FORAJIDOS EN LA MIRA

Goncalves, Enio
ANJOS DO ARRABALDE

Goncalves, Milton
ITALIANI A RIO
UM TREM PARA AS ESTRELAS

Goncic, Svetislav
OKTOBERFEST

Gonella, Franca
MISSIONE EROICA

Gonzales, Carlos
MIRACLES

Gonzales, Francisco
STREET SMART

Gonzales, German
HOUR OF THE ASSASSIN

Gonzales, Henry
MANKILLERS

Gonzales, Leonor
CHRONICLE OF A DEATH FORETOLD

Gonzalez, Agustin
HAY QUE DESHACER LA CASA
MOROS Y CRISTIANOS
POLICIA
REDONDELA

Gonzalez, Carlos
MI NOMBRE ES GATILLO
NARCOTERROR

Gonzalez, Carlos J.
POR LOS CAMINOS VERDES

Gonzalez, Carmelita
EL DIABLO, EL SANTO Y EL TONTO
SINVERGUENZA . . . PERO HONRADO

Gonzalez, Cordelia
LA GRAN FIESTA

Gonzalez, Dacia
TIERRA DE VALIENTES

Gonzalez, Erando
WINTER TAN, A

Gonzalez, Guillermo
I WAS A TEENAGE T.V. TERRORIST

Gonzalez, Jay
THIN LINE, THE

Gonzalez, Marta
LA BUSQUEDA

Gonzalez, Ricardo
LA ESTANQUERA DE VALLECAS

Gonzalez, Tony
SWEET REVENGE

Gonzalez H., Jorge
RETO A LA VIDA

Goo-soon, Lee
SIBAJI

Good, Joanne
EAT THE RICH

Gooden, Donald
LETHAL WEAPON

Gooden, James
CANT BUY ME LOVE

Goodman, Dody
CHIPMUNK ADVENTURE, THE

Goodman, Doug
HAMBURGER HILL

Goodman, Elijah
MUTANT HUNT

Goodman, John
BIG EASY, THE
BURGLAR
RAISING ARIZONA

Goodman, Robert
MASTERBLASTER
WHOOPS APOCALYPSE

Goodrich, Deborah
SURVIVAL GAME

Goodrich, Theodocia
DIRTY LAUNDRY

Goodrow, Garry
DIRTY DANCING

Goodsell, Norman
CUSTODY

Goodwin, Brian
FULL METAL JACKET

Goodwin, Kevin
WITCHES OF EASTWICK, THE

Goodwins, Norm
MALIBU BIKINI SHOP, THE

Gopis, Vassilis
DOXOBUS

Goranson, Linda
GATE, THE
TOO OUTRAGEOUS

Gorbunov, Aleksei
GRUZ BEZ MARKIROVKI

Gorcey, Elizabeth
TROUBLE WITH DICK, THE

Gordon, Ben
GOOFBALLS

Gordon, Bruce
ISHTAR

Gordon, Carrie
PSYCHOS IN LOVE

Gordon, Dan
EQUALIZER 2000

Gordon, Diane
BIG TOWN, THE
Gordon, Don
LETHAL WEAPON
Gordon, Esther
HELLO AGAIN
Gordon, Joyce
HOUSEKEEPER, THE
Gordon, Julie
NIGHTMARE AT SHADOW WOODS
Gordon, Leo V.
GARBAGE PAIL KIDS MOVIE, THE
Gordon, Melissa
MALIBU BIKINI SHOP, THE
Gordon, Richard
PERSONAGGI & INTERPRETI
Gordon, Ruth
TROUBLE WITH SPIES, THE
Gordon, Staci
NAIL GUN MASSACRE
Gordon, Tony
MOVING TARGETS
Gordon-Gorecka, Antonina
ZYCIE WEWNETRZNE
Gordone, Charles
ANGEL HEART
Gorenstein, Eli
EMPEROR'S NEW CLOTHES, THE
Gorg, Galyn
MALIBU BIKINI SHOP, THE
Gorg, Gaylyn
DOWN TWISTED
Goriatcheva, Tatiana
ODINOKIJ GOLOS CELOVEKA
Gorman, Arthur V.
GARDENS OF STONE
Gorman, Brad
TALKING WALLS
Gorman, Patrick
WANTED: DEAD OR ALIVE
Gorman, Reg
SLATE, WYN & ME
Gormley, Tom
REMEMBERING MEL
Gorospe, Jose Manuel
A LOS CUATRO VIENTOS
Gosch, Christopher
SUMMER CAMP NIGHTMARE
Gosselin, Guy Simon
BIRDS OF PREY
Gossett, Louis
PRINCIPAL, THE
Gostyukhin, Vladimir
LEVSHA
SLUCHAYNYE PASSAZHIRY
TAKAYA ZHESTOKAYA IGRA—KHOKKEY
ZINA-ZINULYA
ZNAK BEDY
Goswami, Alpana
BIDROHI
Gota, Armando
LA OVEJA NEGRA
Gotell, Walter
LIVING DAYLIGHTS, THE
Gothard, Michael
SLEEP WELL, MY LOVE
Gottfried, Gilbert
BEVERLY HILLS COP II
Gottschalk, Thomas
ZARTLICHE CHAOTEN
Gottung, Phyllis
IRONWEED
Gotz, John
DIRTY DANCING
Gough, Jerry
BROADCAST NEWS
Gough, Michael
FOURTH PROTOCOL, THE
MASCHENKA
Gould, Dominic
JEUX D'ARTIFICES
Gould, Elliott
I MIEI PRIMI QUARANT'ANNI
Gould, Graydon
MALONE
Gould, Robert
IN THE MOOD
MADE IN HEAVEN
Gould, Sid
POLICE ACADEMY 4: CITIZENS ON PATROL

Goulding, Nigel
FULL METAL JACKET
Goutis, Stelios
DOXOBUS
Govea, Ivon
LO NEGRO DEL NEGRO
Govea, Ivonne
JUANA LA CANTINERA
Govinda
DADAGIRI
MERA LAHOO
PYAR KARKE DEKHO
Gowan, Peter
EAT THE PEACH
Gower, Andre
MONSTER SQUAD, THE
Goy, Luba
CARE BEARS ADVENTURE IN WONDERLAND, THE
Goyer, John
GOOD MORNING, VIETNAM
Goyri, Sergio
FORAJIDOS EN LA MIRA
HERENCIA DE VALIENTES
POLICIAS DE NARCOTICOS
Gozlino, Paolo
LA TRASGRESSIONE
Grabbe, J.
SASHSHENNYI FONAR
Graber, Yossi
BEAUTY AND THE BEAST
BOUBA
HIMMO MELECH YERUSHALAIM
Grabka, Anna
LADY OF THE CAMELIAS
Graboel, Sofie
WOLF AT THE DOOR, THE
Grabol, Sofie
PELLE EROVRAREN
Grabski, Zbigniew
PRZYJACIEL WESOLEGO DIABLA
Grace, Wayne
IN THE MOOD
RUNNING MAN, THE
Gradov, Andrei
ODINOKIJ GOLOS CELOVEKA
Graf, Alan
OVER THE TOP
SPACE RACE
Graf, David
POLICE ACADEMY 4: CITIZENS ON PATROL
Graff, Todd
SWEET LORRAINE
Gragnani, Stefano
BELLY OF AN ARCHITECT, THE
LESTATE STA FINENDO
Graham, Bill
GARDENS OF STONE
Graham, Billy
CAUGHT
Graham, Gerrit
WALKER
Graham, Hepburn
CRY FREEDOM
Graham, Raymond
BELIEVERS, THE
Graham, Ron
BIRDS OF PREY
Graham, Ronny
SPACEBALLS
Graham, Rose
PSYCHO GIRLS
Graham, Stefan
SUSPECT
Graia, Hammou
COERS CROISES
Grammenos, Thanos
O PARADISSOS ANIGI ME ANTIKLIDI
Grams, Rene
MEIER
Granados, Charito
CORRUPCION
TRAGICO TERREMOTO EN MEXICO
Granados, Daisy
AMOR EN CAMPO MINADO
SUCCESSFUL MAN, A
Granat, Anton
MAGIA CHYORNAYA I BELAYA
Granath, Bjorn
DEMONS
MALARPIRATER
PELLE EROVRAREN

Grand, Isaac
LOVECHILD, THE
Grande, Paulo Cesar
LEILA DINIZ
Grandi, Serena
LE FOTO DI GIOIA
LES EXPLOITS DUN JEUNE DON JUAN
RIMINI RIMINI
ROBA DA RICCHI
TERESA
Grandin, Isabel
WINNERS TAKE ALL
Grandmaison, Maurice
CRY WILDERNESS
Granger, Philip
SLAMDANCE
Granik, Jon
KEEPING TRACK
SULLIVAN'S PAVILION
Granja, Jose A.
LAW OF DESIRE
Granlund, Kerstin
LEIF
Granotier, Sylvie
TANDEM
Grant, Audie
WILD THING
Grant, Bruce
LEADING EDGE, THE
Grant, Christine
LEADING EDGE, THE
Grant, David Marshall
BIG TOWN, THE
Grant, Debbie
SITTING IN LIMBO
Grant, Denise
DOGS IN SPACE
Grant, Donald
MONSTER IN THE CLOSET
Grant, Erin
OVERBOARD
Grant, Gillian
IN THE MOOD
Grant, Hugh
MAURICE
Grant, James
PRICK UP YOUR EARS
Grant, Lee
BIG TOWN, THE
Grant, Micah
LIKE FATHER, LIKE SON
Grant, Paul
DEAD, THE
Grant, Richard E.
HIDDEN CITY
WITHNAIL AND I
Grant, Russell Keith
CRY FREEDOM
Grant, Sarina
STUDENT CONFIDENTIAL
Grant, Stuart
DOGS IN SPACE
Grape, Per-Olof
INUKSUK
Grassi, Antonio
COLOR OF DESTINY, THE
Grassi, Rick
SURVIVAL GAME
Graton, Francoise
GREAT LAND OF SMALL, THE
Graue, Marjory
GARBAGE PAIL KIDS MOVIE, THE
Graves, Kirk
SLAVE GIRLS FROM BEYOND INFINITY
Graves, Peter
NUMBER ONE WITH A BULLET
Graves, Rupert
MAURICE
Graves, Stacey
ORACLE, THE
Graves, Vivienne
CODA
Gray, Angie
LAW OF DESIRE
Gray, Bruce
DRAGNET
LETS GET HARRY
Gray, Callie
BUSHFIRE MOON

Gray, Cynthia
DANGER ZONE, THE
Gray, George
CANT BUY ME LOVE
ROBOT HOLOCAUST
Gray, Ian
ISHTAR
Gray, Margot
NICE GIRLS DON'T EXPLODE
Gray, Robert
OMEGA SYNDROME
RAISING ARIZONA
Gray, Sam
HEART
SUSPECT
Gray, Ty
CANT BUY ME LOVE
Gray, Willoughby
PRINCESS BRIDE, THE
Gray, Zoltan
PRINCIPAL, THE
Grazer, Corki
LIKE FATHER, LIKE SON
Graziosi, Stefania
UNA CASA IN BILICO
Grebenschikova, Larisa
SLUCHAYNYE PASSAZHIRY
VOT MOYA DEREVNYA
Grebeshkova, Nina
SPORTLOTO—82
Greca, Paul La
STUDENT CONFIDENTIAL
Greco, Joe
UNTOUCHABLES, THE
Greco, Muffie
VIDEO DEAD, THE
Green, Babbie
WITCHES OF EASTWICK, THE
Green, Dennis
FOREVER, LULU
Green, Gilbert
FORTY DAYS OF MUSA DAGH
Green, Ivan
ERNEST GOES TO CAMP
Green, Janet-Laine
BELIEVERS, THE
Green, Jeremy
CREEPSHOW 2
Green, Jimmy Mel
BROADCAST NEWS
Green, Judy
GET THE TERRORISTS
Green, Kate
I WAS A TEENAGE T.V. TERRORIST
Green, Kerri
THREE FOR THE ROAD
Green, Larry
GARBAGE PAIL KIDS MOVIE, THE
Green, Lars
DEMONS
Green, Lory
HARD TICKET TO HAWAII
Green, Maureen
GOOD WIFE, THE
Green, Mi Mi
DATE WITH AN ANGEL
Green, Pia
OM KARLEK
Green, Sandy
NECROPOLIS
Green, Seth
CANT BUY ME LOVE
RADIO DAYS
SOMETHING SPECIAL!
Green, Turnham
STRAIGHT TO HELL
Green On Red
BORDER RADIO
Greenbaum, Jacob
REMEMBERING MEL
Greene, Barry
JOHN AND THE MISSUS
Greene, Bill
MANNEQUIN
Greene, James
EMPIRE OF THE SUN
Greene, Jon
EMANON
Greene, Michael
BATTERIES NOT INCLUDED
LESS THAN ZERO
WHITE OF THE EYE
Greenhalgh, Jill
BOY SOLDIER
Greenhouse Owner
BLUE MONKEY
Greenquist, Brad
BEDROOM WINDOW, THE
Greenwood, Bobbie
EQUALIZER 2000
Greenwood, Bruce
CLIMB, THE
MALIBU BIKINI SHOP, THE
Greenwood, Joan
LITTLE DORRIT
Greenwood, Rochelle
STEPFATHER, THE
Greer, Dabbs
EVIL TOWN
Greer, Joyce
BEDROOM WINDOW, THE
Gregg, Bradley
NIGHTMARE ON ELM STREET 3: DREAM WARRIORS, A
Greggio, Ezio
MONTECARLO GRAN CASINO
Gregh, Vera
MON BEL AMOUR, MA DECHIRURE
Gregorio, Carlos
BAIXO GAVEA
Gregorio, Silas
ANJOS DO ARRABALDE
Gregory, Andre
STREET SMART
Gregory, Constantine
LAST EMPEROR, THE
Gregory, Kathleen Jordan
CURSE, THE
Gregory, Mark
THUNDER WARRIOR II
Gregory, Norman
HEARTS OF FIRE
Grehan, Dani
BOY SOLDIER
Greist, Kim
THROW MOMMA FROM THE TRAIN
Grenier, Zack
KID BROTHER, THE
Grenkowitz, Rainer
MEIER
Grennan, Sean
UNTOUCHABLES, THE
Grenzier, Charlot-Michele
PRETTY SMART
Grepi, Alejandra
EL BOSQUE ANIMADO
Gress, Googy
PROMISED LAND
Grevemberg, Robert
BROADCAST NEWS
Grevil, Laurent
HOTEL DE FRANCE
Grey, Jaimie
SWEET REVENGE
Grey, Jennifer
DIRTY DANCING
Grey, John
EL GRAN SERAFIN
Grey, Morris
ESTA NOCHE CENA PANCHO (DESPEDIDA DE SOLTERO)
Grey, Wilson
A DANCA DOS BONECOS
UM FILM 100% BRAZILEIRO
Gribauskas, Peach
PSYCHOS IN LOVE
Gribauskas, Wally
PSYCHOS IN LOVE
Griem, Helmut
CASPAR DAVID FRIEDRICH
Grier, David Alan
AMAZON WOMEN ON THE MOON
FROM THE HIP
Grier, Pam
ALLNIGHTER, THE
Gries, Jonathan
MONSTER SQUAD, THE
Grifasi, Joe
IRONWEED
MATEWAN
Griffin, James Edward
PRINCIPAL, THE
Griffin, John
JAWS: THE REVENGE
Griffin, Nonnie
BELIEVERS, THE
Griffin, Peter
NIGHTFORCE
Griffin, S.A.
IN THE MOOD
NEAR DARK
Griffin, Tony
SPACEBALLS
Griffith, Jeff
GET THE TERRORISTS
Griffith, Michael
I WAS A TEENAGE T.V. TERRORIST
Griffiths, Olwen
MAURICE
Griffiths, Richard
WITHNAIL AND I
Griffiths, Roger Ashton
EMPIRE STATE
Grigoriev, Yury
GRUZ BEZ MARKIROVKI
Grimaldi, Eva
DA NNUNZIO
Grimes, Chester
GARBAGE PAIL KIDS MOVIE, THE
Grimes, Frank
WHALES OF AUGUST, THE
Grimes, Gary
CONCRETE ANGELS
Grimes, Scott
PINOCCHIO AND THE EMPEROR OF THE NIGHT
Grimes, Taryn
SOMETHING SPECIAL!
Grinko, N.
DVADTSTAT DNEI BEZ
Grinko, Nikolai
SLUCHAYNYE PASSAZHIRY
Grisaffe, Steven
SQUARE DANCE
Grisales, Amparo
DE MUJER A MUJER
Grishaw, Jerry
ESCAPES
Grist, Reri
ARIA
Gritsenko, Lilia
LICHNOE DELO SUDYI IVANOVOY
YA TEBYA POMNYU
Grizi, Lavinia
SPECTERS
Grobon, Guillemette
MANUELA'S LOVES
Grocholski, Czeslaw
WHOOPS APOCALYPSE
Grodin, Charles
ISHTAR
Groenestege, Titus Tiel
IRIS
Groest, Dieter
WANNSEE CONFERENCE, THE
Groh, David
HOT SHOT
Gronich, Amanda
WEEDS
Gronwall, Irene
WARDOGS
Gross, Arye
HOUSE TWO: THE SECOND STORY
Gross, Mary
BABY BOOM
Grossman, Liora
LO SAM ZAYIN
Grover, Deborah
GATE, THE
Grover, Gulshan
MERA LAHOO
Grubbs, Gary
NADINE
Gruber, Marie
DER TRAUM VOM ELCH
Grueber, Charles
KINDRED, THE
Gruen, Jeff
BIRDS OF PREY

Grumberg, Ariel
REMEMBERING MEL

Grunberg, Sven
REQUIEM

Grunenwald, Peter
MASCARA

Grunwald, Morten
HIP, HIP, HURRA!
WOLF AT THE DOOR, THE

Grupo Eslabon
RETO A LA VIDA

Gryff, Stefan
ISHTAR

Grythe, Hilde
PLASTPOSEN

Guang, Fan
LAST EMPEROR, THE

Guang, Ma
LAST EMPEROR, THE

Guangli, Li
LAST EMPEROR, THE

Guardia, Maribel
LAS TRAIGO . . . MUERTAS

Guardiola, Jose
POLICIA

Gudmundsson, Eggert
SKYTTURNAR

Guedes, Joao
JESTER,THE

Guedes, Paula
JESTER,THE

Guedj, Attica
UN AMOUR A PARIS

Guedj, Didier
FUEGOS

Guedj, Vanessa
LE GRAND CHEMIN

Guelb, Jody
ARIA

Guerin, Florence
DA NNUNZIO
MONTECARLO GRAN CASINO
PROFUMO
SCUOLA DI LADRI 2

Guerra, Blanca
LA FUGA DE CARRASCO
REALM OF FORTUNE, THE
SINVERGUENZA . . . PERO HONRADO
UNA PURA Y DOS CON SAL
WALKER

Guerra, Jorge
MI NOMBRE ES GATILLO

Guerra, Kiko
ANJOS DO ARRABALDE

Guerrero, Franco
WARRIORS OF THE APOCALYPSE

Guerrero, Raul
MATAR O MORIR

Guerrieri, Anna
MAN ON FIRE

Guest, Christopher
BEYOND THERAPY
PRINCESS BRIDE, THE

Guest, Lance
JAWS: THE REVENGE

Guest, Nicholas
DOWN TWISTED

Guevara, Luis
EL ANSIA DE MATAR

Guevara, Nacha
MISS MARY

Guevera, Agustin
LA ESTANQUERA DE VALLECAS

Guggenheim, Lisa
BLOOD DINER

Guiar, Herriett
UNFINISHED BUSINESS . . .

Guidelli, Mirio
GOOD MORNING BABYLON

Guidotti, Laurentina
SPECTERS

Guijar, Covadonqa
LONG STRIDER

Guijar, Francisco
LONG STRIDER

Guilfoyle, Paul
BEVERLY HILLS COP II
THREE MEN AND A BABY

Guilhe, Albane
LA PASSION BEATRICE

Guillard, Jean-Bernard
MEMOIRE DES APPARENCES: LA VIE EST UN SONGE

Guillaumat, Gerard
JOHNNY MONROE

Guillaume, Robert
THEY STILL CALL ME BRUCE
WANTED: DEAD OR ALIVE

Guillen, Fernando
EL GRAN SERAFIN
LA ESTANQUERA DE VALLECAS
LA RUSA
LAW OF DESIRE

Guillen, Tito
MATAR O MORIR
SINVERGUENZA . . . PERO HONRADO

Guillen, Victor
ANGUSTIA

Guillory, Bennet
KINDRED, THE
WALKER

Guimaraes, Sonia
RELACAO FIEL E VERDADEIRA

Guinan, Francis V.
BEDROOM WINDOW, THE

Guinee, Christopher
PRICK UP YOUR EARS

Guinness, Alec
LITTLE DORRIT

Guiomar, Julien
LES DEUX CROCODILES
LETE DERNIER A TANGER

Guirao, Alfonso
LA SENYORA

Guiraud, Aoua
YAM DAABO

Gukasyan, Anaid
ZEMLYA I ZOLOTO

Gulager, Clu
HIDDEN, THE
HUNTER'S BLOOD
OFFSPRING, THE
SUMMER HEAT

Guldbrandsen, Kristian
PA STIGENDE KURS

Guler, Hulya
YER DEMIR, GOK BAKIR

Gulyarenko, Anna
RAZMAKH KRYLIEV

Gumede, Patricia
CRY FREEDOM

Gunatilaka, Sanath
VIRAGAYA

Gundareva, Natalia
LICHNOE DELO SUDYI IVANOVOY

Gunderman, Ralph
MAKING MR.RIGHT

Gunn, Andrew
GATE, THE

Gunn, Moses
LEONARD PART 6

Gunsberg, Roy
O. C. AND STIGGS

Gunthard, Gabrielle
LADY OF THE CAMELIAS

Gunther, Ernst
MANNEN FRAN MALLORCA
SERPENT'S WAY, THE

Gunton, Bob
MATEWAN
PICK-UP ARTIST, THE

Guram Petriashvili
NEYLONOVAYA YOLKA

Gurchenko, Liudmila
DVADTSTAT DNEI BEZ

Gurion, Israel
EMPEROR'S NEW CLOTHES, THE

Gurley, Michael
ALLNIGHTER, THE

Gurovich, Danko
WHITE OF THE EYE

Gurrola, Juan Jose
FRIDA

Gurruchaga, Javier
LA VIDA ALEGRE

Gurry, Eric
SOMETHING SPECIAL!

Gurwitch, Annabelle
KISS DADDY GOOD NIGHT

Gusani, Sukrana
STRATEGIJA SVRAKE

Gusberti, Sharon
VIA MONTENAPOLEONE

Guskin, Harold
FOREVER, LULU

Guss, Louis
MOONSTRUCK

Gustafson, Bjorn
MALARPIRATER

Gustavsson, Didrik
MY LIFE AS A DOG

Guthrie, James
UNTOUCHABLES, THE

Gutierrez, Alfredo
NARCOTERROR
TIERRA DE VALIENTES

Gutierrez, Armando
VISA U.S.A.

Gutierrez, Jose Maria
SINFIN, LA MUERTA NO ES NINGUNA SOLUCION

Gutierrez, Louis
ALLNIGHTER, THE

Gutierrez, Peio
A LOS CUATRO VIENTOS

Gutierrez, Rafael
SUFRE MAMON

Gutierrez, Zaide Silvia
MIRACLES
REALM OF FORTUNE, THE

Guttenberg, Steve
AMAZON WOMEN ON THE MOON
BEDROOM WINDOW, THE
POLICE ACADEMY 4: CITIZENS ON PATROL
SURRENDER
THREE MEN AND A BABY

Gutteridge, Lucy
TROUBLE WITH SPIES, THE

Guttman, Ronald
SQUEEZE, THE

Guttorm, Ingvald
OFELAS

Guvendi, Nahit
JULIA'S GEHEIM

Guwaza, David
CRY FREEDOM

Guybet, Henri
CLUB DE RENCONTRES

Guzeeva, Larisa
SOPERNITSY

Guzman, Baltazar
MI NOMBRE ES GATILLO

Guzman, Enrique "Flaco"
RATAS DE LA CIUDAD

Guzman, Linda
AMAZONS

Gwillim, Jack
BLIND DATE
MONSTER SQUAD, THE

Gwisdek, Michael
LITTLE PROSECUTOR, THE

Gwynne, Fred
FATAL ATTRACTION
IRONWEED
SECRET OF MY SUCCESS, THE

Gyenes, Billy
SWEET REVENGE

Gyllenhammer, Charlotte
FADERN, SONEN OCH DEN HELIGE ANDE

Gyngell, Kim
BACHELOR GIRL
BUSHFIRE MOON
WITH LOVE TO THE PERSON NEXT TO ME

Gyoriwanyi, Gyorgy
OPERA

Ha, Patricia
HAPPY BIGAMIST
KILLER'S NOCTURNE

Haag, Romy
MASCARA

Haaland, Agnete G.
KAMILLA OG TYVEN

Haas, Christian
ERNEST GOES TO CAMP

Haas, Humberto Tito
EL AMOR ES UNA MUJERGORDA

Haas, Kirk
THOU SHALT NOT KILL . . . EXCEPT

Haavisto, Elisabeth
AKALLINEN MIES

Haber, Alessandro
LA DONNA DEL TRAGHETTO

Haber, Allesandro
MAN ON FIRE

Haber, Robert
HOSTAGE

Habraken, Marja
IRIS

Hack, Shelley
STEPFATHER, THE

Hackes, Peter
BROADCAST NEWS

Hackett, Joan
FLICKS

Hackman, Gene
NO WAY OUT
SUPERMAN IV: THE QUEST FOR PEACE

Hackman, Robert
EMANON

Hacohen, Sharon
KFAFOT

Haddad, Paul
PRETTYKILL

Hadden, Siobhan
BOY SOLDIER

Haddon, John
BELINDA

Hadley, Diane
VIDEO DEAD, THE

Hadziconstanti, Irene
THEOFILOS

Hadzihafizbegovic, Emir
ZIVOT RADNIKA

Hadzikoutselis, Panos
FAKELOS POLK STON AERA

Hadzoudis, Costas
FAKELOS POLK STON AERA

Hagan, Anna
STEPFATHER, THE

Hagan, Molly
SOME KIND OF WONDERFUL

Hageb, Fijad
ISHTAR

Hagen, Ross
COMMANDO SQUAD

Hager, Brian R.
AMAZING GRACE AND CHUCK

Hager, Kristi Jean
BELL DIAMOND

Hagerty, Julie
ARIA
BEYOND THERAPY

Hagerty, Kris
KILLER WORKOUT

Hagerty, Michael
OVERBOARD

Haggerty, H.B.
MILLION DOLLAR MYSTERY

Hagiwara, Kenichi
RYOMA O KITTA OTOKO

Hagler, Nick
BIG EASY, THE

Hagon, Garrick
CRY FREEDOM
PRETTYKILL

Hagopean, Dean
MORNING MAN, THE

Hague, Tony
FULL METAL JACKET

Hahn, Archie
AMAZON WOMEN ON THE MOON
INNERSPACE

Hahn, Eric
NO DEAD HEROES

Hahn, Neal
ESCAPES

Hahn, Susie
MASSACRE IN DINOSAUR VALLEY

Hahns, Eric
ULTIMAX FORCE

Hai, Wu
LAST EMPEROR, THE

Haider, Salim
EAT THE RICH

Haig, Iranui
NGATI

Haig, Sid
COMMANDO SQUAD
FORTY DAYS OF MUSA DAGH

Haig, Terry
KEEPING TRACK
STREET SMART

Haight, Gordon
NEAR DARK

Haim, Corey
LOST BOYS, THE

Halbritch, Hugo
RAGE OF HONOR

Hale, Alan
BACK TO THE BEACH

Halfpenny, Tara
WITCHES OF EASTWICK, THE

Halkett, Craig
STARLIGHT HOTEL

Hall, Arsenio
AMAZON WOMEN ON THE MOON

Hall, Dorothy
BABY BOOM

Hall, E. Pat
SUMMER HEAT

Hall, Frederick
WISH YOU WERE HERE

Hall, Huntz
CYCLONE

Hall, Irma P.
SQUARE DANCE

Hall, Jack
BABY BOOM

Hall, Kate
BLACK WIDOW

Hall, Kevin Peter
HARRY AND THE HENDERSONS
MONSTER IN THE CLOSET
PREDATOR

Hall, Lori
CROSS MY HEART

Hall, Oliver
GOOD WIFE, THE

Hall, Philip Baker
THREE O'CLOCK HIGH

Hall, Rich
MILLION DOLLAR MYSTERY

Hall, Sands
BEST SELLER
DELOS ADVENTURE, THE

Hall, Stephen C.
MATEWAN

Hall, William
LEONARD PART 6

Hallahan, Charles
FATAL BEAUTY
P.K. & THE KID

Hallahan, Dennis
DEADLY ILLUSION

Hallak, Robert
SOMEONE TO LOVE

Halldorsson, Balduin
SKYTTURNAR

Halle-Halle, Alain
MEMOIRE DES APPARENCES: LA VIE EST UN SONGE

Halliday, Ruth
ARIA

Hallier, Lori
HIGHER EDUCATION

Halligan, Derek
RAWHEAD REX

Halligan, Tim
BIG SHOTS

Halliwell, Steve
FOURTH PROTOCOL, THE

Hallwachs, Hans Peter
CASPAR DAVID FRIEDRICH

Hallyday, David
HES MY GIRL

Hallyday, Johnny
FAMILY BUSINESS
MOVING TARGETS
TERMINUS

Halonen, Liisa
NAKEMIIN, HYVASTI

Halton, Michael
SURVIVAL GAME

Halty, Jim
NIGHTFORCE

Hamalainen, Tapio
UUNO TURHAPURO MUUTTAA MAALLE

Hamamura, Jun
PRINCESS FROM THE MOON

Hamann, Svend Ali
EPIDEMIC

Hamblin, John
MOVING TARGETS

Hambrick, John
MAKING MR.RIGHT

Hametner, Gerhard
HOSTAGE

Hamidou
LA VENGEANCE DU PROTECTEUR

Hamill, Brian
PICK-UP ARTIST, THE

Hamilton, Alexa
THREE FOR THE ROAD

Hamilton, Chico
MAGIC STICKS

Hamilton, Dan
OPPOSING FORCE

Hamilton, Jane
IF LOOKS COULD KILL
SLAMMER GIRLS
DERANGED
WIMPS

Hamilton, Julie
RAWHEAD REX

Hamilton, Laird
NORTH SHORE

Hamilton, Leigh
P.K. & THE KID

Hamilton, Murray
WHOOPS APOCALYPSE

Hamilton, Paula
EMPIRE OF THE SUN

Hamilton, Richard
IRONWEED

Hamilton, Rick
PRINCIPAL, THE

Hamilton, Rusty
ROCK 'N' ROLL NIGHTMARE

Hamilton, Suzanna
DEVILS PARADISE, THE

Hamisi, Raymond B.
KOLORMASK

Hamiton, Trip
MAKING MR.RIGHT

Hamlett, Dexter
RETURN TO HORROR HIGH

Hammack, Jack
BLOODSUCKERS FROM OUTER SPACE

Hammer, Alvin
WHO'S THAT GIRL

Hammer, Ben
MANNEQUIN

Hammer, Roger
RADIO DAYS

Hammer, Sam
OVERKILL

Hammerhead, Nicky
HIDING OUT

Hammerli, Aurea
LADY OF THE CAMELIAS

Hammett, Jeffrey
SWEET REVENGE

Hammil, John
MILLION DOLLAR MYSTERY

Hammon, Ashley
RAISING ARIZONA

Hammond, Roger
LITTLE DORRIT

Hamner, Fritz
CRIME OF HONOR

Hamnett, Olivia
CODA

Hampshire, Keith
CARE BEARS ADVENTURE IN WONDERLAND, THE

Hampton, James
TEEN WOLF TOO

Hampton, Paul
WINNERS TAKE ALL

Hampton, Roger
WINNERS TAKE ALL

Hamrell, Harald
NIONDE KOMPANIET

Han, Maggie
LAST EMPEROR, THE

Hancock, John
CATCH THE HEAT

Hancock, Lou
EVIL DEAD 2: DEAD BY DAWN

Hancock, Sheila
LOVECHILD, THE

Handan
DILAN

Handford, Paul
BAD BLOOD

Handler, Evan
SWEET LORRAINE

Hands, Steve
FULL METAL JACKET

Handy, James
BURGLAR

Hanegbi, Assi
HA INSTALATOR

Hanekan, Ron
BELL DIAMOND

Hanekom, Kalie
CRY FREEDOM

Haney, Anne
COLD STEEL

Haney, Tony
PRINCIPAL, THE

Hangal, A.K.
TAMAS

Hanganu, Patricia
WILD THING

Hanin, Roger
LA RUMBA
LETE DERNIER A TANGER

Hankin, Larry
FATAL BEAUTY
PLANES, TRAINS AND AUTOMOBILES

Hanks, Tom
DRAGNET

Hanlon, Julie
I WAS A TEENAGE T.V. TERRORIST

Hanly, Mike
MAKING MR.RIGHT

Hanna, Arnie
DOGS IN SPACE

Hanna, Elizabeth
BELIEVERS, THE
CARE BEARS ADVENTURE IN WONDERLAND, THE

Hannah
MALIBU BIKINI SHOP, THE

Hannah, Daryl
ROXANNE
WALL STREET

Hannah, Page
CREEPSHOW 2
MY LITTLE GIRL

Hannah, Will
CANT BUY ME LOVE

Hanninen, Mikko
NAKEMIIN, HYVASTI

Hannon, Kevin
DEADTIME STORIES

Hannon, Shawn
ESCAPES

Hansel, Arthur
ASSASSINATION

Hansen, Ann-Mari Max
ELISE

Hansen, Arne
PETER VON SCHOLTEN

Hansen, Benny
VALHALLA

Hansen, Claes Kastholm
EPIDEMIC

Hansen, Holger Juul
SIDSTE AKT

Hansen, Ib
EPIDEMIC

Hansen, Nina
MORGAN STEWART'S COMING HOME

Hansen, Pernille
JAG ELSKER DIG

Hansen, Thomas
NEGERKYS & LABRE LARVER

Hanson, Cheryl
THOU SHALT NOT KILL . . . EXCEPT

Hanson, Sue
OUT OF ORDER

Hansson, Knut M.
PA STIGENDE KURS

Hansson, Lena T.
JIM OCH PIRATERNA BLOM

Hanzon, Thomas
NIONDE KOMPANIET

Hara, Izumi
SHINRAN: SHIRO MICHI

Harabor, Manuela
PADUREANCA

Harada, Ernest
BLIND DATE
DIRTY LAUNDRY

Harada, Mieko
KATAKU NO HITO

Harada, Tomoyo
WATASHI O SKI NI TSURETETTE

Haraldsson, Harald G.
SKYTTURNAR

Hardcastle, Victoria
PERSONAL SERVICES

Harden, Mark
PROJECT X

Harden, Robert
OVERKILL
SURF NAZIS MUST DIE

Hardester, Crofton
EMMANUELLE 5

Hardie, Kate
CRY FREEDOM

Hardin, Jerry
LETS GET HARRY
WANTED: DEAD OR ALIVE

Harding, Jeff
BLOOD TRACKS

Harding, Robert
CUSTODY

Hardt, Arnie
POLICE ACADEMY 4: CITIZENS ON PATROL

Hardy, Dona
RUNNING MAN, THE

Hardy, Gerard
LA CODA DEL DIAVOLO

Hardy, Mark
PERSONAL SERVICES

Hardy, Peter
PURSUIT OF HAPPINESS, THE

Hardy, Suzie
RUNNING MAN, THE

Harewood, Dorian
FULL METAL JACKET

Harfouch, Corinna
LITTLE PROSECUTOR, THE

Hargitay, Mariska
JOCKS

Hargreaves, John
COMRADES
CRY FREEDOM

Harkins, Paul J.
LIGHT OF DAY

Harlap, Ruth
BEAUTY AND THE BEAST

Harleston, Hugh
GABY—A TRUE STORY

Harling, Noelle
EVIL TOWN

Harmon, Mark
LETS GET HARRY
SUMMER SCHOOL

Harms, Scott
WHO'S THAT GIRL

Harmstorf, Raimund
THUNDER WARRIOR II

Harpazy, Anat
TEL AVIV—BERLIN

Harper, Buddy
RETURN OF JOSEY WALES, THE

Harper, Robert
AMAZING GRACE AND CHUCK
WANTED: DEAD OR ALIVE

Harper, Tess
ISHTAR

Harrell, James
NADINE

Harrell, Roland
MANKILLERS

Harries, Ivor
EL HOMBRE DESNUDO

Harrington, Randy
KINDRED, THE

Harris, Albert H.
ESCAPES

Harris, Anna
REMEMBERING MEL

Harris, Barbara
NICE GIRLS DON'T EXPLODE

Harris, Betty
HOUSEKEEPER, THE

Harris, Brad
DEATH STONE

Harris, Chris
FULL METAL JACKET

Harris, Cynthia
THREE MEN AND A BABY

Harris, David
FATAL BEAUTY
UNDER COVER

Harris, Debby
RUNNING MAN, THE

Harris, Ed
WALKER

Harris, Fox
STRAIGHT TO HELL
WALKER

Harris, Gift
WEEDS

Harris, Jack
BIG EASY, THE

Harris, Jeffrey
BIG SHOTS

Harris, Jonathan
PINOCCHIO AND THE EMPEROR OF THE NIGHT

Harris, Karmen
ANGEL HEART

Harris, Lara
MANNEQUIN
NO MAN'S LAND

Harris, Mel
WANTED: DEAD OR ALIVE

Harris, Rupert
DIRTY LAUNDRY

Harrison, Cathryn
EAT THE RICH
EMPIRE STATE

Harrison, Gregory
NORTH SHORE

Harrison, Ngawai
NGATI

Harrison, Richard
NINJA THUNDERBOLT

Harrison, Richmond
BEVERLY HILLS COP II

Harrison, Simon
EMPIRE OF THE SUN

Harrison, Wendy
NIGHTFORCE

Harrold, Kathryn
SOMEONE TO LOVE

Harry
PROJECT X

Harry, Deborah
FOREVER, LULU

Harsing, Hilda
ZUHANAS KOZBEN

Harstad, Jan
ETTER RUBICON

Harstadt, Jan
PLASTPOSEN

Hart, Bill
OUTRAGEOUS FORTUNE

Hart, Bob
FULL METAL JACKET

Hart, Derek
FULL METAL JACKET

Hart, Kevin
MIND KILLER

Hart, Kitty Carlisle
RADIO DAYS

Hart, LaGena
MILLION DOLLAR MYSTERY

Hart, Nadine
ROBOT HOLOCAUST

Hart, Nora
NECROPOLIS

Harte, Jerry
FOURTH PROTOCOL, THE

Hartley, John
CRY FREEDOM

Hartline, Gene
SPACE RACE

Hartman, Gary
SLAUGHTER HIGH

Hartman, Milton
TRAIN OF DREAMS

Hartman, Phil
BLIND DATE
BRAVE LITTLE TOASTER, THE

Hartmann, Ursina
JENATSCH

Hartrey, Kay
POLICE ACADEMY 4: CITIZENS ON PATROL

Hartstein, Nadine
NECROPOLIS

Hartt, Cathryn
OPEN HOUSE

Hartwell, Greg Nave
HOLLYWOOD SHUFFLE

Hartwig, Janina
DER BARENHAUTER

Harvey, Don
CREEPSHOW 2
UNTOUCHABLES, THE

Harvey, Max
EIGHTY FOUR CHARING CROSS ROAD

Harvey, Rodney
INITIATION

Harwood, Linda
ASSASSINATION

Hasek, Vlastimil
CENA MEDU

Hashemi, Nasser
GOZARESH-E YEK GHATL

Haskell, Peter
FORTY DAYS OF MUSA DAGH

Hassan, Charu
INDIAN SUMMER

Hassan-Rad, Akbar
LODGERS

Haster, Jean
MASCARA

Hastrup, Vibeke
BABETTE'S GASTEBUD

Hatch, Eddie Earl
STREET SMART

Hatfield, Mert
SUMMER HEAT

Hatlo, Anders
PA STIGENDE KURS

Hattangady, Rahini
ANJUMAN

Hattangady, Rohini
PRATIGHAAT

Hatton, David
WISH YOU WERE HERE

Hauer, Rutger
WANTED: DEAD OR ALIVE

Hauff, Alexander
MEIER

Haugaard, Jacob
KAMPEN OM DEN RODE KO

Haughton, David Cain
WARRIOR QUEEN

Haugland, Bill
KEEPING TRACK

Haury, Yasmine
QUATRE AVENTURES DE REINETTE ET MIRABELLE

Hauser, Sara
BLOOD HOOK

Hauser, Wings
HOSTAGE
TOUGH GUYS DON'T DANCE
WIND, THE

Hausman, Willo
HOUSE OF GAMES

Hausserman, Mischa
ASSASSINATION

Havatzeleth, Moshe
LATE SUMMER BLUES

Havelka, Ondrej
CHOBOTNICE Z II. PATRA

Havens, Richie
HEARTS OF FIRE

Havers, Nigel
EMPIRE OF THE SUN
WHISTLE BLOWER, THE

Havilio, Harry
EL AMOR ES UNA MUJERGORDA

Hawker, John
ASSASSINATION
DIRTY LAUNDRY

Hawkins, Andrew
WHISTLE BLOWER, THE

Hawkins, Anthony
LIGHTHORSEMEN, THE

Hawkins, Matthew
LAST OF ENGLAND, THE

Hawkins, Richard
CREEPOZOIDS

Hawkins, Ronnie
MEATBALLS III

Hawn, Goldie
OVERBOARD

Hawthorne, Denise
BELIEVERS, THE

Hayashi, Mark
WHITE OF THE EYE

Haydee, Marcia
LADY OF THE CAMELIAS

Hayden, Dennis
SLAMDANCE

Hayden, John Kennedy
SPACEBALLS

Hayden, Maria
DEAD, THE

Hayden, Ted
WHO'S THAT GIRL

Hayes, Barry
FULL METAL JACKET

Hayes, Chad
LETHAL WEAPON

Hayes, Cynthia B.
BROADCAST NEWS

Hayes, Gloria
WITCHBOARD

Hayes, Randy
NAIL GUN MASSACRE

Hayes, Tony
FULL METAL JACKET

Hayes, William
ASSASSINATION

Haygarth, Tony
MONTH IN THE COUNTRY, A

Hayman, David
HOPE AND GLORY
WALKER

Haymer, Johnny
OPEN HOUSE

Haynes, Brenda
ERNEST GOES TO CAMP

Haynes, Margarita
GOOD WIFE, THE

Haynes, Peter
BIRDS OF PREY

Haynes, Tiger
ENEMY TERRITORY

Hayward, Nicola
COMRADES

Haywood, Charles
MATEWAN

Haywood, Chris
BIT PART, THE
DOGS IN SPACE
TALE OF RUBY ROSE, THE
WARM NIGHTS ON A SLOW MOVING TRAIN

Hazel, David
WITCHES OF EASTWICK, THE

Hazel, Deryck
BIRDS OF PREY

Hazel, Honey
HEARTS OF FIRE

Hazelbarth, Joanne
NAIL GUN MASSACRE

Hazeldine, James
BUSINESS AS USUAL

Head, Anthony
MORE BAD NEWS
PRAYER FOR THE DYING, A

Head, Kenneth
FULL METAL JACKET

Head, Murray
WHITE MISCHIEF

Head, Sandra
STEPFATHER, THE

Headly, Glenne
MAKING MR.RIGHT
NADINE

Heald, Anthony
HAPPY NEW YEAR
ORPHANS
OUTRAGEOUS FORTUNE

Healey, John J.
HELLO AGAIN

Healey, Myron
GHOST FEVER

Healey, Patricia
COMRADES

Healy, Christine
LIKE FATHER, LIKE SON

Heart, John X.
BUDDHA'S LOCK

Heath, Allison
AMERICAN DRIVE-IN

Heather L. Bailey
DEADTIME STORIES

Heatherly, May
BEAKS
CRYSTAL HEART

Hebert, Paul
LES FOUS DE BASSAN

Hecht, Gina
UNFINISHED BUSINESS . . .

Hecker, Federico
DER TOD DES EMPEDOKLES

Heckman, Paul
BLOOD HOOK

Hedden, Cindy
DIRTY LAUNDRY

Hedemann, Fritze
PETER VON SCHOLTEN

Hedgeland, Robin
FULL METAL JACKET

Hedley, Jack
THREE KINDS OF HEAT

Hedman, Sten Johan
NIONDE KOMPANIET

Hee, Bang
SIBAJI

Hee-bong, Pyon
NAE-SHI

Hee-sung, Lee
KYEOUL NAGUNE

Heeley, Bryan
RITA, SUE AND BOB TOO!

Heffley, Wayne
BLACK WIDOW

Hefner, Hugh
BEVERLY HILLS COP II

Hefner, Keith
EVIL TOWN

Heh-young, Lee
KYEOUL NAGUNE

Hehlman, Hieko
SO VIELE TRAUME

Hehr, Michael
BEVERLY HILLS COP II

Heiden, Ira
NIGHTMARE ON ELM STREET 3: DREAM WARRIORS, A

Heincke, Bruni
CAUGHT

Heine, Manfred
DER BARENHAUTER

Heins, Albert
CRAZY BOYS

Heintze, Detlef
DER TRAUM VOM ELCH

Heintzman, Michael
WIMPS

Heiskanen, Kari
A LA ITKE IINES
LAIN ULKOPUOLELLA

Heit, Sally Jane
FOREVER, LULU

Heit, Sally-Jane
SECRET OF MY SUCCESS, THE

Heitor, Fernando
JESTER,THE

Helberg, Sandy
SPACEBALLS

Helberg, Thomas
LOS DUENOS DEL SILENCIO

Held, Ingrid
ENNEMIS INTIMES

Heldman, Chris
BLOODSUCKERS FROM OUTER SPACE

Helekal, Jiri
PRATELE BERMUDSKEHO TROJUHELNIKU

Helen Hughes
BLUE MONKEY

Helfer, Britt
PRINCESS ACADEMY, THE

Helger, Anne Marie
SIDSTE AKT

Helger, Annemarie
STRIT OG STUMME

Hellberg, Thomas
SVART GRYNING
Heller, Chip
MUNCHIES
Hellman, Monte
SOMEONE TO LOVE
Hellstrom, Anders
LADY OF THE CAMELIAS
Helm, Levon
MAN OUTSIDE
Helm, Tiffany
O. C. AND STIGGS
Helman, Elzbieta
E S D
Helmi, Katerina
ANGELOS
Helmond, Katherine
OVERBOARD
SHADEY
Helmuth, Frits
ELISE
Helou, Tony
DOGS IN SPACE
Helovirta, Kauko
AKALLINEN MIES
Helsus, Vaclav
CENA MEDU
Hemblen, David
FAMILY VIEWING
Hembrow, Mark
HIGH TIDE
RUNNING FROM THE GUNS
Hemingway, Mariel
SUICIDE CLUB, THE
SUPERMAN IV: THE QUEST FOR PEACE
Hemingway, Winston
BEDROOM WINDOW, THE
Hemphill, John
GOOFBALLS
Hemsley, Sherman
GHOST FEVER
Henchoz, Jean-Marc
JENATSCH
Henderson, Albert
BARFLY
Henderson, Jo
MATEWAN
Henderson, Michael Scott
WHO'S THAT GIRL
Henderson, Ty
HAPPY HOUR
Hendricks, Eric
STACKING
Hendrie, Chris
MIRACLES
Hendrix, Leah Ayres
HOT CHILD IN THE CITY
Heney, Joan
MORNING MAN, THE
Heney, Robert
MORNING MAN, THE
Hennessey, Dan
CARE BEARS ADVENTURE IN WONDERLAND, THE
Hennessy, Mark
TERMINAL EXPOSURE
Henningsen, Ulla
JAG ELSKER DIG
NEGERKYS & LABRE LARVER
Henricksen, Benjamin Holck
PELLE EROVRAREN
Henriet, Arnaud
AU REVOIR, LES ENFANTS
Henriet, Benoit
AU REVOIR, LES ENFANTS
Henriksen, Lance
NEAR DARK
Henrikson, Mathias
MALARPIRATER
Henriksson, Krister
NIONDE KOMPANIET
Henriques, Darryl
BEVERLY HILLS COP II
NO WAY OUT
Henry, Anne
MISS MARY
Henry, Buck
ARIA
Henry, David
CRY FREEDOM

Henry, Deanne
HOME IS WHERE THE HART IS
Henry, Duncan
FULL METAL JACKET
Henry, Lenny
SUICIDE CLUB, THE
Henry, Ludovic
JEUX D'ARTIFICES
Henry, Mike
OUTRAGEOUS FORTUNE
Henry, Tom
MIND KILLER
Henshaw, Jim
CARE BEARS ADVENTURE IN WONDERLAND, THE
Hensley, Lisa
GOOD WIFE, THE
Henson, Basil
SHADEY
Henson, Debbie
ULTIMAX FORCE
Henszelman, Stefan
VENNER FOR ALTID
Hentzman, Michael
SLAMMER GIRLS
Hepton, Bernard
SHADEY
Herala, Helge
UUNO TURHAPURO MUUTTAA MAALLE
Herbert, Eric
CONCRETE ANGELS
Herbert, Percy
LOVECHILD, THE
Herczeg, Csilla
LUTRA
Herd, Richard
PLANES, TRAINS AND AUTOMOBILES
Herdigein, Kenneth
HAVINCK
LOOKING FOR EILEEN
Herdorff, Anne Cathrine
KAMPEN OM DEN RODE KO
Herkert, Richard
P.I. PRIVATE INVESTIGATIONS
Herlitzka, Roberto
DARK EYES
GLI OCCHIALI D'ORO
Hermakul, Evald
CHEREZ STO LET V MAE
Herman, Paul
RADIO DAYS
SQUEEZE, THE
WEEDS
Herman, Pee Wee
BACK TO THE BEACH
Hermanek, Karel
DEATH OF A BEAUTIFUL DREAM
Hermanin, Paolo
REGINA
Hermanjuns, Evald
IGRY DLJA DETEJ SKO'NOGO VOZRASTA
Hern, Bernie
FATAL BEAUTY
Hern, David
SUMMER CAMP NIGHTMARE
Hernadi, Judit
WHOOPING COUGH
Hernandez, Azucena
LA ESTANQUERA DE VALLECAS
Hernandez, Rafael
EL LUTE—CAMINA O REVIENTA
Hernandez, Ruben Dario
WINTER TAN, A
Hernandez, Vicky
CHRONICLE OF A DEATH FORETOLD
VISA U.S.A.
Hernvall, Bengt
LEIF
Herold, Joe
DATE WITH AN ANGEL
Herr, Marcia
TIN MEN
Herran, Luis Angel
A LOS CUATRO VIENTOS
Herrault, Fabrice
LADY OF THE CAMELIAS
Herrera, Barbara
FRANCESCA
Herrera, Guillermo
LA FUGA DE CARRASCO

Herrera, Humberto
CARTUCHA CORTADA
MATAR O MORIR
ROSA DE LA FRONTERA
Herrera, Luis
EULALIA
Herrera, Regino
FORAJIDOS EN LA MIRA
MIRACLES
Herrier, Mark
REAL MEN
Herrin, Kymberly
BEVERLY HILLS COP II
Herring, Harry
T. DAN SMITH
Herrmann, Edward
OVERBOARD
Herrmann, Sonja
LADY OF THE CAMELIAS
Herschlag, Alex
LIVING ON TOKYO TIME
Hershey, Barbara
SHY PEOPLE
TIN MEN
Hershey, Stephanie
WINNERS TAKE ALL
Herton, Tom
MALONE
Hertzberg, Jordan
CYCLONE
Hertzberg, Lauren
CYCLONE
Hervey, Jason
MONSTER SQUAD, THE
Herviale, Jeanne
LES OREILLES ENTRE LES DENTS
Herzberg, Paul
CRY FREEDOM
Herzog, Andrew S.
HIDING OUT
Heslop, Paul
T. DAN SMITH
Hess, David
CAMPING DEL TERRORE
LETS GET HARRY
Hess, Doris
OVERBOARD
Hess, Joe
MASTERBLASTER
Hesseman, Howard
AMAZON WOMEN ON THE MOON
HEAT
Heston, Joy
RETURN TO HORROR HIGH
Hetfield, Diane
JAWS: THE REVENGE
Hetherington, Gary
STEPFATHER, THE
Hevenor, George
CONCRETE ANGELS
TOO OUTRAGEOUS
Hewgill, Roland
JOHN AND THE MISSUS
Hewitt, Martin
ALIEN PREDATOR
Hewitt, Melanie
WITCHES OF EASTWICK, THE
Hewitt, Sean
WILD THING
Hewlett, Arthur
LOVECHILD, THE
PERSONAL SERVICES
Heyman, Barton
SECRET OF MY SUCCESS, THE
WEEDS
Heyns, Alex
ALLAN QUATERMAIN AND THE LOST CITY OF GOLD
Heyser, Audrey
ESCAPES
Heyward, Leona
BELIEVERS, THE
Heywood, Colin
BLOODY NEW YEAR
Heywood, John
LIGHTHORSEMEN, THE
Heywood, Pat
WISH YOU WERE HERE
Hickey, Tom
GOTHIC

Hickling, Elizabeth
EMPIRE STATE

Hicks, Catherine
LIKE FATHER, LIKE SON

Hicks, Dan
EVIL DEAD 2: DEAD BY DAWN

Hicks, Kevin
HIGHER EDUCATION

Hiemer, Hort
DER JUNGE MIT DEM GROSSEN SCHWARZEN HUND

Hieu, Joseph
HARD TICKET TO HAWAII

Hiev, Joseph
STEELE JUSTICE

Higgins, Clare
HELLRAISER

Higgins, Colin
HOPE AND GLORY

Higgins, David
HIDING OUT

Higgins, James
DELOS ADVENTURE, THE

Higgins, Michael
ANGEL HEART

Higgs, William
MUTANT HUNT

High, Angelia
ZERO BOYS, THE

Hijikata, Tatsumi
MAGINA—MURA MONOGATARI

Hildebrandt, Dieter
MEIER

Hile, Joel
SURF NAZIS MUST DIE

Hilel, Osi
YEHOSHUA—YEHOSHUA

Hill, Allanah
DOGS IN SPACE

Hill, Barry
GOOD WIFE, THE
RUNNING FROM THE GUNS

Hill, Bernard
BELLMAN AND TRUE
BOY SOLDIER

Hill, Dave
T. DAN SMITH

Hill, Georgia
PRETTY SMART

Hill, Gil
BEVERLY HILLS COP II

Hill, Lorna
LIKE FATHER, LIKE SON
MY DARK LADY

Hill, Richard
WARRIOR QUEEN

Hill, Ron
MUTANT HUNT

Hill, Ross
RENEGADE, UN OSSO TROPPO DURO

Hill, Terence
RENEGADE, UN OSSO TROPPO DURO

Hill, Thomas
BLACK WIDOW

Hiller, Crystal
RAISING ARIZONA

Hiller, Wendy
LONELY PASSION OF JUDITH HEARNE,THE

Hillman, Christianna
SUMMER CAMP NIGHTMARE

Hilton, Shari
STREET SMART

Himas, Abkas
NOCE EN GALILEE

Hin-shui, Yiu
YI LOU YI

Hind, Keith
MOVING TARGETS

Hindle, Art
FROM THE HIP

Hindman, Earl
THREE MEN AND A BABY

Hines, Damon
LETHAL WEAPON

Hines, Damons
BARFLY

Hines, Robert
HELLRAISER

Hingle, Pat
BABY BOOM

Hinkley, Tommy
BACK TO THE BEACH

Hinojosa, Joaquin
MIENTRAS HAYA LUZ

Hinrich, Thomas
SO VIELE TRAUME

Hinz, Terry
GARDENS OF STONE

Hiona, Sam
CYCLONE

Hipp, Paul
CHINA GIRL

Hirabayashi, Norihiko
ROBINSON NO NIWA

Hiroshige, Kimiko
STEELE JUSTICE

Hirsch, Daniel
ZERO BOYS, THE

Hirsch, Patrick
ZERO BOYS, THE

Hirsch, Ricky
BLIND DATE

Hirson, Alice
BLIND DATE

Hirt, Christianne
MALONE
SHELLEY

Hirvikangas, Juuso
NAKEMIIN, HYVASTI

Hitas, Nikos
FAKELOS POLK STON AERA

Hixon, Ken
MIRACLES

Hizkiahu, Avner
HA INSTALATOR

Hjelmervik, Paul
SUSPECT

Hjulstrom, Lennart
MY LIFE AS A DOG
NIONDE KOMPANIET

Ho, Chin Siu
FINAL TEST, THE

Ho, Lee Tse
BETTER TOMORROW, A

Ho, Victor
O. C. AND STIGGS

Ho-jen, Chiang
OUTSIDERS, THE

Hoare, Kelly
DOGS IN SPACE

Hoashi, Akiko
EAT THE PEACH

Hobbs, Connie
LES PATTERSON SAVES THE WORLD

Hobbs, Peter
IN THE MOOD

Hobson, I.M.
HELLO AGAIN

Hochberg, Richard
TALKING WALLS

Hodder, Kane
HOUSE TWO: THE SECOND STORY

Hode, Roger
LADY OF THE CAMELIAS

Hodge, Laurence
FRENCHMAN'S FARM

Hodge, Mike
FOREVER, LULU
MAGIC STICKS

Hodges, Tom
REVENGE OF THE NERDS II: NERDS IN PARADISE

Hodges, Zoe
EIGHTY FOUR CHARING CROSS ROAD

Hodiak, Keith
FULL METAL JACKET

Hodson, Donald
RENEGADE, UN OSSO TROPPO DURO

Hoechst, Wolfram
AMAZONS

Hoekstra, Jan Jaap
EEN MAAND LATER

Hoffman, Dustin
ISHTAR

Hoffman, Jane
BATTERIES NOT INCLUDED

Hoffman, Joel
KILLER WORKOUT
SLUMBER PARTY MASSACRE II

Hoffman, Thom
ALS IN EEN ROES
LOOKING FOR EILEEN
VAN PAEMEL FAMILY, THE

Hoffman, Todd
EMANON

Hoffmann, Susannah
HEARTS OF FIRE

Hoffs, Susanna
ALLNIGHTER, THE

Hofstede, Henk
ZJOEK

Hogan, Liam
FULL METAL JACKET

Hogan, Percy
IL BURBERO

Hogan, Trevor
FULL METAL JACKET

Hoganson, Jason
EMPIRE STATE

Hogarth, Meg
BIG TOWN, THE

Hogdal, Luke
FULL METAL JACKET

Hogg, Brian
T. DAN SMITH

Hogg, Brian J.
EAT THE PEACH

Hogue, Bert
DATE WITH AN ANGEL

Hogue, James R.
SULLIVAN'S PAVILION

Hoi, Ling Pak
PEKING OPERA BLUES

Hoi, Mang
LEGACY OF RAGE

Hojfeldt, Solbjorg
WOLF AT THE DOOR, THE

Hojgaard, Therese
BABETTE'S GASTEBUD

Holbek, Caecilia
EPIDEMIC

Holbek, Gert
EPIDEMIC

Holbrook, David
CREEPSHOW 2

Holbrook, Hal
WALL STREET

Holden, Arthur
REMEMBERING MEL
WILD THING

Holden, Frank
JOHN AND THE MISSUS

Holden, Frankie J.
HIGH TIDE

Holden, Nicholas Earl
TALKING WALLS

Holder, Raymond
MY DARK LADY

Holicker, Heidi
MALIBU BIKINI SHOP, THE

Holland, Anthony
HIGH STAKES

Holland, Chera
LIKE FATHER, LIKE SON

Holland, Erik
GARDENS OF STONE

Holland, Joe
BACK TO THE BEACH

Holland, Jools
EAT THE RICH

Holland, June
RETURN OF JOSEY WALES, THE

Hollett, Rick
JOHN AND THE MISSUS

Holliday, Charlie
IN THE MOOD

Holliday, David
SLEEPING BEAUTY

Holliday-Evans, Rupert
EIGHTY FOUR CHARING CROSS ROAD

Hollis, Jeff
BIG EASY, THE

Hollis, John
VALHALLA

Holloman, Melissa Lee
PRINCIPAL, THE

Hollstrom, Jan-Philip
MY LIFE AS A DOG

Holly Hunter
BROADCAST NEWS

Hollyfield, Gladys
SOMETHING SPECIAL!
Holm, Celeste
THREE MEN AND A BABY
Holman, Jan
COMRADES
Holman, John
COMRADES
Holme, Paul
SWEET REVENGE
Holmen, Kjersti
PA STIGENDE KURS
Holmes, Dennis
ARIA
Holmes, Michelle
RITA, SUE AND BOB TOO!
Holoubek, Gustaw
ZYGFRYD
Holt, David S.
NIGHTFORCE
Holt, Jim
TIME GUARDIAN, THE
Holt, Larry
BEST SELLER
Holt, Patrick
WHISTLE BLOWER, THE
Holt, Sondra
RUNNING MAN, THE
Holton, Mark
TEEN WOLF TOO
UNDER COVER
Holub, Hugh B.
MALIBU BIKINI SHOP, THE
Holubek, Gustaw
W STARYM DWORKU
Holzer, Jane
LA VALLEE FANTOME
Homerska, Maria
WIERNA RZEKA
Hon-ki, Cheng
YI LOU YI
Honda, Hirotaro
DIXIELAND DAIMYO
Honer, David
DER NACHBAR
Honesseau, Mikael
ANITA—DANCES OF VICE
Honeycombe, Gordon
FOURTH PROTOCOL, THE
Hong, James
BLACK WIDOW
CHINA GIRL
REVENGE OF THE NERDS II: NERDS IN PARADISE
Hong, Leanna
FULL METAL JACKET
Hong, Mou
CUO WEI
Hong, Pan
LAST EMPRESS, THE
Hongchang, Yang
LAST EMPEROR, THE
Hongnian, Luo
LAST EMPEROR, THE
Hongxiang, Cai
LAST EMPEROR, THE
Honig, Heinz
DANN IST NICHTS MEHR WIE VORHER
Honorato, Marzio
TENTAZIONE
Hood, Chet
MANKILLERS
Hood, Louis
GOOD MORNING, VIETNAM
Hooks, Kevin
INNERSPACE
Hool, Brett
STEEL DAWN
Hoole, Michael
PSYCHO GIRLS
Hoomans, Elise
TERUG NAAR OEGSTGEEST
VROEGER IS DOOD
Hooper, Elrich
STARLIGHT HOTEL
Hooper, Ewan
PERSONAL SERVICES
Hooper, Robin
PRICK UP YOUR EARS
Hoosier, Trula
TISZTA AMERIKA
Hoover, Phil
BEST SELLER
Hope, Barry
OPEN HOUSE
Hope, Richard
BELLMAN AND TRUE
Hopf, Heinz
FADERN, SONEN OCH DEN HELIGE ANDE
GIRL, THE
Hopkins, Anthony
EIGHTY FOUR CHARING CROSS ROAD
Hopkins, Harold
YEAR MY VOICE BROKE, THE
Hopkins, Karen Lee
TALKING WALLS
Hopkins, Karen Leigh
RUNNING MAN, THE
Hoppe, Marianne
FRANCESCA
Hoppe, Rolf
DER NACHBAR
Hopper, Dennis
BLACK WIDOW
O. C. AND STIGGS
PICK-UP ARTIST, THE
RIVER'S EDGE
STRAIGHT TO HELL
Hora, John
INNERSPACE
Horacek, Miroslav
POHADKA O MALICKOVI
Horacek, Petr
WOLF'S HOLE
Horan, Barbra
MALIBU BIKINI SHOP, THE
Horbiger, Christiane
VICTORIA
Hordern, Michael
COMRADES
TROUBLE WITH SPIES, THE
Horian, Richard
STUDENT CONFIDENTIAL
Horn, Ellen
ETTER RUBICON
Horne, J.R.
RADIO DAYS
Horner, Carl
SLAVE GIRLS FROM BEYOND INFINITY
Horowitz, Jeffrey
BEAT, THE
Horowitz, Merrily
WITCHES OF EASTWICK, THE
Horowitz, Steve
BUDDHA'S LOCK
Horsford, Anna Maria
STREET SMART
Horsley, John
FOURTH PROTOCOL, THE
Horton, Alex
HIDDEN CITY
Horton, Michael
LIKE FATHER, LIKE SON
Horton, Peter
AMAZON WOMEN ON THE MOON
Horvitz, Richard
SUMMER SCHOOL
Hoskins, Bob
LONELY PASSION OF JUDITH HEARNE,THE
PRAYER FOR THE DYING, A
Hossein, Robert
LEVY ET GOLIATH
Hosta, Nuria
LA RUBIA DEL BAR
Hostalot, Luis
LA RUSA
Hostetter, John
ARIA
BEVERLY HILLS COP II
LEONARD PART 6
NO WAY OUT
Houck, Joy N.
BIG EASY, THE
Houde, Germain
NIGHT ZOO
Houde, Germaine
PRETTYKILL
Houdy, Pierick
BACH AND BROCCOLI
Houghton, Barrie
EMPIRE OF THE SUN
WISH YOU WERE HERE
Houseknecht, Joyce
AUTUMN'S TALE, AN
Houser, Christie
EVIL TOWN
Housseau Family, The
QUATRE AVENTURES DE REINETTE ET MIRABELLE
Houssny, Hassan
ZAWGAT RAGOL MOHIM
Houston, Robin
WHEN THE WIND BLOWS
Hovell, Erica
NGATI
Hovell, Priscilla
NGATI
Howar, Badar
PRINCESS ACADEMY, THE
Howard, Angela
DOGS IN SPACE
Howard, Anne
PRINCE OF DARKNESS
Howard, Arliss
FULL METAL JACKET
Howard, John
AROUND THE WORLD IN EIGHTY WAYS
Howard, Kevyn Major
FULL METAL JACKET
Howard, Sheila
KILLER WORKOUT
Howard, Tony
FULL METAL JACKET
Howard, Trevor
WHITE MISCHIEF
Howarth, Andrew
NECROPOLIS
ROBOT HOLOCAUST
Howell, Bob
P.K. & THE KID
Howell, Mark
THREE BEWILDERED PEOPLE IN THE NIGHT
Howell, Norman
OVER THE TOP
Howell, Peter
BELLMAN AND TRUE
Howell, Roger L.
MOVING TARGETS
Howell, Russell
HARD TICKET TO HAWAII
Howerton, Charles
ASSASSINATION
Howlett, May
GOOD WIFE, THE
Hoy, David
DOGS IN SPACE
Hoy, Marie
DOGS IN SPACE
Hoynes, Richard
LADY OF THE CAMELIAS
Hoyo, Eduardo
ASIGNATURA APROBADA
Hoyo, Pablo
ASIGNATURA APROBADA
Hoyos, Antonio
SPACEBALLS
Hoyt, John
FORTY DAYS OF MUSA DAGH
Hrabanek, Vladimir
PRATELE BERMUDSKEHO TROJUHELNIKU
Hrachovinova, Marta
CENA MEDU
Hrusinsky, Rudolf
DISCOPRIBEH
Hryc, Andrej
CENA ODVAHY
Hsia, Lin Ching
PEKING OPERA BLUES
TRUE COLORS
Hsien, Hou Hsiao
LAONIANG GOU SAO
Hsien, Wong Tsu
CHINESE GHOST STORY, A
Hsin, Sheo
OUTSIDERS, THE
Hsu, Sam
OVERKILL
Hua, Su Zeng
DRAGON'S FOOD
Huai, Ge
BLACK CANNON INCIDENT, THE

Huaikuei, Soong
LAST EMPEROR, THE
Hubbard, Kerry
IL LUPO DI MARE
Hubbell, Chris
SUMMER CAMP NIGHTMARE
Hubbert, Cork
NIGHTFORCE
Hube, Jorg
CHINESE ARE COMING, THE
DAS TREIBHAUS
Huber, Lotti
ANITA—DANCES OF VICE
Hubert, Antoine
LE GRAND CHEMIN
Hubley, Season
PRETTYKILL
Hubley, Whip
CLUB LIFE
RUSSKIES
Hubner, Zygmunt
BLIND CHANCE
Huckabee, Cooper
CURSE, THE
Huddleson, Lindy
GARBAGE PAIL KIDS MOVIE, THE
Huddleston, Holly
MANKILLERS
Hudson, Bill
BIG SHOTS
Hudson, Caroline
HOSTAGE SYNDROME
Hudson, Ernie
WEEDS
Hudson, Peter
SPIRALE
Hudson, Rick
THOU SHALT NOT KILL . . . EXCEPT
Hudson, Steve
FULL METAL JACKET
Hudziec, Tomasz
ZYGFRYD
Huerta, Robert
EMANON
Huff, Tommy
NIGHTFORCE
Huffman, Larry
WINNERS TAKE ALL
Hugh Keays-Byrne
LES PATTERSON SAVES THE WORLD
Hughes, Barnard
LOST BOYS, THE
Hughes, Brendan
RETURN TO HORROR HIGH
STRANDED
Hughes, Jim
JIM OCH PIRATERNA BLOM
Hughes, Kirsten
JANE AND THE LOST CITY
KITCHEN TOTO, THE
Hughes, Maurice
FRENCHMAN'S FARM
GOOD WIFE, THE
Hughes, Olivia
RAISING ARIZONA
Hughes, Peter
HOPE AND GLORY
Hughes, Prince
FATAL BEAUTY
Hughes, Victor
LADY OF THE CAMELIAS
Hughes, Wendy
HAPPY NEW YEAR
SHADOWS OF THE PEACOCK
WARM NIGHTS ON A SLOW MOVING TRAIN
Huhn, Richard E.
SQUEEZE, THE
Huhtamo, Markko
SNOW QUEEN, THE
Huhtamo, Markku
JAAHYVAISET PRESIDENTILLE
Hui, Michael
CHOCOLATE INSPECTOR
Hui, Ricky
CHOCOLATE INSPECTOR
Hui, Sam
LEGEND OF WISELY, THE
Hukkanen, Esko
SNOW QUEEN, THE

Hulce, Tom
SLAMDANCE
Humphreys, Suzie
RETURN OF JOSEY WALES, THE
Humphries, Barry
HOWLING III, THE
LES PATTERSON SAVES THE WORLD
Humphries, Tessa
CASSANDRA
Hunaerts, Geert
LOVE IS A DOG FROM HELL
Hung, Samo
EASTERN CONDORS
Hungerford, Michael
NO WAY OUT
Hungerford, Mike
RIVER'S EDGE
Hunnicutt, Gayle
TURNAROUND
Hunold, Rainer
LITTLE PROSECUTOR, THE
Hunt, Helen
PROJECT X
Hunt, Linda
WAITING FOR THE MOON
Hunt, Neil
OUTRAGEOUS FORTUNE
Hunter, Chris
ARIA
MAURICE
Hunter, Holly
RAISING ARIZONA
Hunter, J. Michael
BEDROOM WINDOW, THE
Hunter, Kim
KINDRED, THE
Hunter, Lisa
OVERBOARD
Hunter, Michael
WILD THING
Hunter, Neith
BORN IN EAST L.A.
NEAR DARK
Hunter, Ronald
ADVENTURE OF THE ACTION HUNTERS
Hunter, Scott
EVIL TOWN
Hunter, Shaun
LETHAL WEAPON
Hunter, Siobhan
WIMPS
Huntsberry, Howard
LA BAMBA
Huppert, Isabelle
BEDROOM WINDOW, THE
Hurder, Lynne Anchors
SUMMER HEAT
Hurdle, James
CLIMB, THE
Hurley, Armando
BELINDA
Hurley, Elizabeth
ARIA
Hurley, Melissa
RUNNING MAN, THE
Hurst, Christopher
CRY FREEDOM
Hurt, John
ARIA
FROM THE HIP
SPACEBALLS
WHITE MISCHIEF
Hurt, Raven
OVERKILL
Hurt, Voice of Vincent: John
VINCENT—THE LIFE AND DEATH OF VINCENT VAN GOGH
Hurt, William
BROADCAST NEWS
Husak, Frantisek
HOL VOLT, HOL NEM VOLT
PRATELE BERMUDSKEHO TROJUHELNIKU
Huseman, Perry
P.K. & THE KID
Husin, Galeb
IBUNDA
Hussein, Adam
ISHTAR
Huston, Anjelica
DEAD, THE

GARDENS OF STONE
Huston, James
OUTING, THE
Hutchence, Michael
DOGS IN SPACE
Hutchings, Geoffrey
WISH YOU WERE HERE
Hutchinson, Jeff
COMMANDO SQUAD
Hutchinson, Peter
WHISTLE BLOWER, THE
Hutchinson, Tracy
MASTERBLASTER
Hutton, Lauren
MALONE
Hutton, Rif
WANTED: DEAD OR ALIVE
Hutton, Timothy
MADE IN HEAVEN
Huun, Sigrid
IS-SLOTTET
Hvenegaard, Pelle
PELLE EROVRAREN
Hwa, Wang
MIRAGE
Hwong, Lucia
LAST EMPEROR, THE
Hyatt, Gigi
LADY OF THE CAMELIAS
Hyatt, Roy
ARIA
Hyde-White, Alex
ISHTAR
Hyler, Tamara
PRETTY SMART
Hymel, Zepherin
BIG EASY, THE
Hynam, Laurence
BOY SOLDIER
Hyon-sil, Tae
NAE-SHI
Hywel, Dafydd
BOY SOLDIER
I, Young Pao
BETTER TOMORROW, A
I-Chen, Ko
LAONIANG GOU SAO
Iannaccone, Carmine
SLAUGHTER HIGH
Iapaolo, Anna-Lisa
VIRGIN QUEEN OF ST. FRANCIS HIGH, THE
Ibanez, Manuel "Flaco"
LA RULETERA
Ibu, Masato
EMPIRE OF THE SUN
Ichikawa, Glen
OVERKILL
Ichti, Sonia
LHOMME VOILE
Idemitsu, Gen
PRINCESS FROM THE MOON
Ifantis, Tassos
DOXOBUS
ONE HUNDRED AND TWENTY DECIBELS
Igarashi, Masuo
MAGINA—MURA MONOGATARI
Iglesi, Mary
TELEFTAIO STICHIMA
Iglesias, Lander
A LOS CUATRO VIENTOS
Iineos, Stephanos
TA PAIDIA TIS CHELIDONAS
Ikeda, Fumihiko
LAST EMPEROR, THE
Ikuta, Akira
LAST EMPEROR, THE
Il, Tae
NAE-SHI
Ilagan, Jay
OPERATION: GET VICTOR CORPUS THE REBEL SOLDIER
Ilial, Leo
KEEPING TRACK
Ilitch, Atanas
SLUMBER PARTY MASSACRE II
Illig, Rolf
ALPINE FIRE
Ilyichev, Viktor
ISKRENNE VASH . . .

Ilyin, Vladimir
MOY LYUBIMYY KLOUN
Ilyina, Nina
SVIDANIE NA MLECHNOM PUTI
Imada, Jeff
WINNERS TAKE ALL
Iman
NO WAY OUT
SURRENDER
Imbuga, Francis
KOLORMASK
Imbusch, Paul
PERSONAL SERVICES
Imperial, Carlos
MASSACRE IN DINOSAUR VALLEY
Inabanza, Mujinga Mbuji
LA VIE EST BELLE
Inamdar, Shafi
ANJAAM
DACAIT
Inclan, Gloria Alicia
LA RAZA NUNCA PIERDE—HUELE A GAS
Inclan, Rafael
EL MOFLES Y LOS MECANICOS
ENTRE FICHERAS ANDA EL DIABLO
LA RAZA NUNCA PIERDE—HUELE A GAS
LA RULETERA
LAPUTA: THE CASTLE IN THE SKY
NOS REIMOS DE LA MIGRA
Inclan, Rafeal
CORRUPCION
Indri, Rose
HELLO AGAIN
Inear, Doug
TOO OUTRAGEOUS
Infante, Cruz
NI DE AQUI, NI DE ALLA
Infante, Irma
SINVERGUENZA . . . PERO HONRADO
Infante, Pedro
EL MUERTO DEL PALOMO
Infante, Sonia
BEAKS
Infante Jr., Pedro
TIERRA DE VALIENTES
CORRUPCION
Infanti, Angelo
LESTATE STA FINENDO
SOTTOZERO
Ingerslev, Jess
STRIT OG STUMME
Ingle, John
AMAZON WOMEN ON THE MOON
Ingleton, Sue
GOOD WIFE, THE
Ingram, Jay
BEST SELLER
Inn, Frank
BENJI THE HUNTED
Inoue, Hirokazu
PRINCESS FROM THE MOON
Inoue, Kichiemon
MAGINA—MURA MONOGATARI
Inscoe, Joe
SUMMER HEAT
Interlenghi, Antonella
SOTTOZERO
Ioannou, Spiros
I KEKARMENI
Ionesco, Eva
JEUX D'ARTIFICES
Ionescu, Serban
PADUREANCA
Iozzino, Michael "Spike"
MUTANT HUNT
Ip, Deanie
LAONIANG GOU SAO
Ipale, Aharon
ISHTAR
Ir, Li Yen
SEKUNDA NA PODVIG
Iranzo, Antonio
LA ESTANQUERA DE VALLECAS
Irawan, Ria
IBUNDA
Ireland, Jill
ASSASSINATION
CAUGHT
Ireson, Richard
PRICK UP YOUR EARS
Irgachev, Sukhrat
A SANTA DERVIS
Irgashev, Shukhrat
TAYNOE PUTESHESTVIE EMIRA
Irizarry, Gloria
SECRET OF MY SUCCESS, THE
Ironside, Michael
EXTREME PREJUDICE
HELLO MARY LOU, PROM NIGHT II
NOWHERE TO HIDE
Irrera, Dom Jack
HOLLYWOOD SHUFFLE
Irvine, Paula
PARTY CAMP
Irving, Amy
RUMPELSTILTSKIN
Irving, Matt
WHEN THE WIND BLOWS
Irving, Michael
PERSONAL SERVICES
Irwin, Cori
IRONWEED
Irwin, Jennifer
GATE, THE
Isaac, Dickie
BEJALAI
Isaac, Susan
HOUSE TWO: THE SECOND STORY
Isaacs, Susan
HELLO AGAIN
Isakov, V.
KOROTKIE VSTRECHI
Isarov, Boris
FOURTH PROTOCOL, THE
Isbell, Tom
EIGHTY FOUR CHARING CROSS ROAD
Isbert, Maria
CARA DE ACELGA
EL BOSQUE ANIMADO
Isbert, Tony
LONG STRIDER
Isham, Steven
LIKE FATHER, LIKE SON
Ishibashi, Renji
MAGINA—MURA MONOGATARI
Ishibashi, Takaashi
SOROBANZUKU
Ishida, Ayumi
KATAKU NO HITO
Ishihara, Mariko
DEATH SHADOWS
SARABA ITOSHIKI HITO YO
Ishimatsu, Guto
SHINRAN: SHIRO MICHI
Ishimatsu, Guts
EMPIRE OF THE SUN
Ishino, Yoko
TOKYO BLACKOUT
Ishizaka, Koji
EIGA JOYU
PRINCESS FROM THE MOON
Islamaj, Hajredim
AVRIL BRISE
Islas, Benjamin
FORAJIDOS EN LA MIRA
Isler, Seth
BLIND DATE
Ito, Hiroyasu
BUS
Ito, Robert
P.I. PRIVATE INVESTIGATIONS
Ito, Shiro
TAXING WOMAN, A
Itoh, Shiro
PRINCESS FROM THE MOON
Ivanov, V.
VZLOMSHCHIK
Ivanova, Margarita
MAGIA CHYORNAYA I BELAYA
Ivey, Judith
HELLO AGAIN
Ivgi, Moshe
DEADLINE
Iza, Miguel
CITY AND THE DOGS, THE
Izaba
ROBINSON NO NIWA
Izotov, Eduard
VREMYA ZHELANIY
Izquierdo, Dora
CHRONICLE OF A DEATH FORETOLD
Izumiya, Shigeru
SHINRAN: SHIRO MICHI
Izzard, Mary
LIFE CLASSES
Izzo, Alessandra
DELITTI
J., Myra
HOLLYWOOD SHUFFLE
J.J.
GOOD MORNING, VIETNAM
J.P. Bumstead
BEST SELLER
Jabeli, Hamid
SHEERE SANGGY
Jackman, Jim
SPACEBALLS
Jackman, Mark
NEGERKYS & LABRE LARVER
Jacks, Helena
BLOOD TRACKS
Jackson, Carl
SUSPECT
Jackson, Christopher
HOLLYWOOD SHUFFLE
Jackson, Crane
IN THE MOOD
Jackson, David
CYCLONE
Jackson, Glenda
BEYOND THERAPY
BUSINESS AS USUAL
Jackson, Gordon
GUNPOWDER
WHISTLE BLOWER, THE
Jackson, Joanne
EMANON
Jackson, Marlon
STUDENT CONFIDENTIAL
Jackson, Michael J.
FOURTH PROTOCOL, THE
Jackson, Philip
FOURTH PROTOCOL, THE
Jackson, Robin
SOMETHING SPECIAL!
Jackson, Stoney
JOCKS
Jackson, Terry
BOY SOLDIER
Jackson, Todd
TIN MEN
Jackson, Valerie
ANGEL HEART
Jackson, Victoria
BABY BOOM
PICK-UP ARTIST, THE
Jackunas, Sayle
THOU SHALT NOT KILL . . . EXCEPT
Jacob, Elias
MALIBU BIKINI SHOP, THE
Jacobi, Derek
LITTLE DORRIT
Jacobi, Lou
AMAZON WOMEN ON THE MOON
Jacobs, Irene
WINNERS TAKE ALL
Jacobs, Mark
BLOOD HOOK
Jacobs, Shirley Spiegler
BIG SHOTS
Jacobs, Steve
JILTED
Jacobs, Steven
SHADOWS OF THE PEACOCK
Jacobson, David
BEAT, THE
Jacobson, Julian
FOURTH PROTOCOL, THE
Jacoby, Billy
PARTY CAMP
Jacoby, Scott
RETURN TO HORROR HIGH
SUPERNATURALS, THE
Jacquin, Caroline
CLUB DE RENCONTRES
Jacquinot, Carole
POULE ET FRITES
Jaenicke, Anja
OTTO—DER NEUE FILM

Jaenicke, Hannes
ZABOU

Jaffrey, Saeed
JALWA
TAMAS

Jafung, Ma
HEROIC PIONEERS

Jagathi
JANUARY ORORMA

Jagathy
KATHAKKU PINNIL

Jager, Angelika
ROBOT HOLOCAUST

Jagger, Dean
EVIL TOWN

Jaglom, Henry
SOMEONE TO LOVE

Jahelka, Craig
BEDROOM WINDOW, THE

Jakim, Ladislav
PROC?

Jakoubkova, Eva
CIZIM VSTUP POVOLEN

Jakowpck, Christie
MALIBU BIKINI SHOP, THE

Jakraworawut, Boonchai
GOOD MORNING, VIETNAM

Jalaja
VILAMBARAM

Jalenak, Jan
SULLIVAN'S PAVILION

Jalil, David
TERMINUS

James
PANDAVAPURAM

James, Bevan
COMRADES

James, Billie
EMANON

James, Billy T.
LEADING EDGE, THE

James, Brion
STEEL DAWN

James, Carol
BEAKS

James, Christian
MAGIC SNOWMAN, THE

James, Clifton
WHOOPS APOCALYPSE

James, Don
HAMBURGER HILL

James, Gennie
BROADCAST NEWS

James, Gerald
HOPE AND GLORY

James, Jessie
BESAME MUCHO

James, Jimmy
TOO OUTRAGEOUS

James, John William
RUNNING MAN, THE

James, Lee
CASSANDRA

James, Michael
MANKILLERS
OPPOSING FORCE
WARRIORS OF THE APOCALYPSE

James, Ron
GOOFBALLS

James, Steve
AMERICAN NINJA 2: THE CONFRONTATION

James, Steve W.
HOLLYWOOD SHUFFLE

James, Tania Perez
DE TAL PEDRO, TAL ASTILLA

James Yeater
RAISING ARIZONA

Jamet, Nicole
TANT QU'IL AURA DES FEMMES

Jamieson, Kathy
BUSINESS AS USUAL

Jamieson, Steve
BANZAI RUNNER

Jamila
PANDAVAPURAM

Jamison, Janis
EMANON

Jammal, George
EMANON

Jan, Chau
OUTSIDERS, THE

Janda, Krystyna
W ZAWIESZENIU

Jandacek, Keith
RAISING ARIZONA

Janett, Georg
JENATSCH

Janikowa, Eva
INUKSUK

Jankowska-Cieslak, Jadwiga
INNA WYSPA
MASKARADA

Jankowski, Jan
PRYWATNE SLEDZTWO

Jano, Neal
IN THE MOOD

Janra, Iara
BESAME MUCHO

Jansen, Laura
CRIME OF HONOR

Jansen, Maaike
LA VIE DISSOLUE DE GERARD FLOQUE

Jansen, Tom
TERUG NAAR OEGSTGEEST

Jansevskaya, Zane
STRAKH

Janssens, Mark
MASCARA

Jarchow, Bruce
RADIO DAYS

Jardins, Chris D.
LETHAL WEAPON

Jaregard, Ernst-Hugo
FADERN, SONEN OCH DEN HELIGE ANDE

Jarmon, Clarenze
STREET TRASH

Jarmusch, Jim
STRAIGHT TO HELL

Jarratt, John
BELINDA

Jarv, Monika
IGRY DLJA DETEJ SKO'NOGO VOZRASTA

Jarventie, Pentti
JAAHYVAISET PRESIDENTILLE

Jarvinen, Martti
AKALLINEN MIES

Jarvis, Jane
RADIO DAYS

Jarvis, Joanne
VIDEO DEAD, THE

Jason, Peter
PARTY CAMP
PRINCE OF DARKNESS

Jatin
PANCHVATI

Jauckens, Rosie
GIRL, THE

Javid, Krysia
KILLER WORKOUT

Javor, Pal
A JAVOR

Jawdocimov, Alexei
ISHTAR

Jawdokimov, Alexei
FOURTH PROTOCOL, THE

Jawkins, Judy
MORE BAD NEWS

Jay, Ricky
HOUSE OF GAMES

Jayabharathi
JANUARY ORORMA

Jayalalitha
UPPU

Jayashree
THIRUMATHI ORU VEGUMATHI

Jayawardene, Dayaratne
MALDENIYESIMION

Jayi
JAIDEV

Jean-Louis, Pascale
MASCARA
PENG! DU BIST TOT!

Jebeli, Hamid
DJADDE HAYE SARD

Jecchinis, Keiron
FULL METAL JACKET

Jecchinis, Kieron
EMPIRE OF THE SUN

Jedwab, Rusty
LE JEUNE MAGICIEN

Jeffares, Patricia
EAT THE PEACH

Jeffs, Deanne
BELINDA

Jelenska, Jirina
DISCOPRIBEH

Jellinek, Tristram
WHOOPS APOCALYPSE

Jenkin, Devon
SLAMMER GIRLS

Jenkins, Daniel H.
O. C. AND STIGGS

Jenkins, Julian
BELLY OF AN ARCHITECT, THE

Jenkins, Ken
MATEWAN

Jenkins, Mark
STACKING

Jenkins, Richard
WITCHES OF EASTWICK, THE

Jenkins, Shirley Ann
HOLLYWOOD SHUFFLE

Jenkins, Terry
EMANON

Jenkins, Timothy
TOO OUTRAGEOUS

Jenko, Lidija
SLEEP WELL, MY LOVE

Jenn, Michael
MAURICE

Jenn, Myvanwy
BEDROOM WINDOW, THE

Jennings, Julia
BLIND DATE
DRAGNET

Jennings, Paul
LES PATTERSON SAVES THE WORLD

Jenrette, Rita
MALIBU BIKINI SHOP, THE

Jensen, Christine
FOREVER, LULU

Jensen, Helle Merete
SIDSTE AKT

Jensen, Henning
ELISE
HIP, HIP, HURRA!
PETER VON SCHOLTEN

Jensen, Torben
PETER VON SCHOLTEN

Jensen, Vincent
CRIME OF HONOR

Jenson, Roy
NIGHT STALKER, THE

Jeppson, Catherine
WARDOGS

Jepson, Marlee
RAGE OF HONOR

Jermank, Vida
OFICIR S RUZOM

Jerricho, Paul
CRY FREEDOM

Jespersen, Mari-Anne
KAMPEN OM DEN RODE KO

Jess Fontana
MISSION KILL

Jessome, Leo
LIFE CLASSES

Jessop, Jack
SUSPECT

Jessop, Sharon
DOGS IN SPACE

Jetsmark, Torben
PETER VON SCHOLTEN

Jett, Joan
LIGHT OF DAY

Jezequel, Julie
COERS CROISES
TANDEM

Jia, Liu
ROMANCE OF BOOK AND SWORD, THE

Jiechen, Dong
LAST EMPEROR, THE

Jillette, Penn
TOUGH GUYS DON'T DANCE

Jim Colandrelli
OVERKILL

Jimenez, Lena
MATAR O MORIR

Jimenez, Luisa
MUJERES DE LA FRONTERA

Jimenez, Maureen
EULALIA

Jimenez, Roberto A.
MUNCHIES

Jiminez, Librado
WINTER TAN, A

Jin, Elaine
DIXIA QING
LAONIANG GOU SAO

Jin-ah, Kim
NAE-SHI

Jinaki
WHO'S THAT GIRL

Jingping, Cui
LAST EMPEROR, THE

Jinnette, Betty
IN THE MOOD

Jiranek, Jan
DEATH OF A BEAUTIFUL DREAM

Job, William
PRICK UP YOUR EARS

Jobert, Stephane
CROSS
LA RUMBA

Jobes, Heath
IN THE MOOD

Jochim, Keith
WITCHES OF EASTWICK, THE

Jochimsen, Gary
ZERO BOYS, THE

Joe-Yin, Wong
LEGEND OF WISELY, THE

Johanson, Ulf
NAGRA SOMMARKVALLAR PA JORDEN

Johansson, Lena Marie
AMAZONS

Johansson, Vivi
MY LIFE AS A DOG

John, Domenick
CREEPSHOW 2

John, Radek
PROC?

Johnmoore, Deacon
ANGEL HEART

Johnson, Al
THOU SHALT NOT KILL . . . EXCEPT

Johnson, Alan
STEELE JUSTICE

Johnson, Amy
ARIA

Johnson, Anne-Marie
HOLLYWOOD SHUFFLE

Johnson, Arleta
ESCAPES

Johnson, Arnold
MY DEMON LOVER
WEEDS

Johnson, Ben
LETS GET HARRY
TRESPASSES

Johnson, Clark
WILD THING

Johnson, Craigus R.
HOLLYWOOD SHUFFLE

Johnson, Daren Craig
DAUGHTERS OF EVE

Johnson, Delbert
ESCAPES

Johnson, Georgann
BLIND DATE

Johnson, J.J.
PRINCIPAL, THE
WEEDS

Johnson, Justine
FOREVER, LULU

Johnson, Karl
PRICK UP YOUR EARS

Johnson, Leonard
WEEDS

Johnson, Lynn-Holly
ALIEN PREDATOR

Johnson, Matt
NIGHTFORCE

Johnson, Michelle
BEAKS

Johnson, Noel
WITHNAIL AND I

Johnson, Reggie
PRINCIPAL, THE

Johnson, Reginald Vel
MAGIC STICKS

Johnson, Rick
WINNERS TAKE ALL

Johnson, Stephanie
DOGS IN SPACE

Johnson, Swede
PROJECT X

Johnson, Taborah
HEARTS OF FIRE

Johnston, Andrew
FRENCHMAN'S FARM
MORNING MAN, THE

Johnston, J.J.
FATAL ATTRACTION

Johnston, Jack
T. DAN SMITH

Johnston, Jane A.
WITCHES OF EASTWICK, THE

Johnston, John Dennis
EXTREME PREJUDICE
SQUEEZE, THE

Johnston, Kenneth
GHOST FEVER

Johnston, Rosemary
MILLION DOLLAR MYSTERY

Johny
AMRITAMGAMAYA

Jolin, Micaela
VICTORIA

Jolivet, Marc
POULE ET FRITES

Jolly, Mike
FATAL BEAUTY

Joly, Sylvie
AGENT TROUBLE
LE MIRACULE

Jonas, Mickey
TALKING WALLS

Jonasz, Michel
TESTAMENT D'UN POETE JUIF ASSASSINE

Jonathan Caplan
MORE BAD NEWS

Jones, Alexander
VALHALLA

Jones, Annie
MOVING TARGETS

Jones, Arden M.
BIG EASY, THE

Jones, Cherry
BIG TOWN, THE
LIGHT OF DAY

Jones, Christine
WILD THING

Jones, Derrick
CONCRETE ANGELS

Jones, Don
GRAVEYARD SHIFT

Jones, Eddie
BELIEVERS, THE

Jones, Freddie
COMRADES
MASCHENKA

Jones, George Ellis
ARIA

Jones, Gillian
SHADOWS OF THE PEACOCK

Jones, Grace
SIESTA
STRAIGHT TO HELL

Jones, Helen
GOOD WIFE, THE

Jones, Ignatius
THOSE DEAR DEPARTED

Jones, James Earl
ALLAN QUATERMAIN AND THE LOST CITY OF GOLD
GARDENS OF STONE
MATEWAN
MY LITTLE GIRL
PINOCCHIO AND THE EMPEROR OF THE NIGHT

Jones, Jay Arlen
CLUB LIFE
NO WAY OUT

Jones, Jeffrey
HANOI HILTON, THE

Jones, Jo
HELLO AGAIN

Jones, John Randolph
PLANES, TRAINS AND AUTOMOBILES

Jones, Josephine Jaqueline
WARRIOR QUEEN

Jones, Kathy
TIN MEN

Jones, Ken
WHOOPS APOCALYPSE

Jones, L.Q.
BULLETPROOF

Jones, Leslie
HOME IS WHERE THE HART IS

Jones, Mark
VALHALLA

Jones, Marshall
PRINCIPAL, THE

Jones, Mickey
EXTREME PREJUDICE
HUNTER'S BLOOD
NADINE

Jones, Neal
DIRTY DANCING

Jones, Noel
ANGEL HEART

Jones, Oliver
NGATI

Jones, Penny
FRENCHMAN'S FARM

Jones, Rickie Lee
PINOCCHIO AND THE EMPEROR OF THE NIGHT

Jones, Sam
JANE AND THE LOST CITY

Jones, Shirleta
ANGEL HEART

Jones, Sue
BACHELOR GIRL

Jones, Suzanne
VALHALLA

Jones, Texacala
BORDER RADIO

Jones, Tommy Lee
BIG TOWN, THE

Jonfield, Peter
BELLMAN AND TRUE

Jongen, Vincent
MASCARA

Jongewaard, Leen
NITWITS
TERUG NAAR OEGSTGEEST

Jonsson, Bill
MORE ABOUT THE CHILDREN OF BULLERBY VILLAGE

Jonsson, Pierre
LEIF

Jordal, Helge
HIP, HIP, HURRA!

Jordan, Harlan
NADINE
SQUARE DANCE

Jordan, Monty
HAPPY HOUR

Jordan, Oscar
BIG SHOTS

Jordan, Richard
SECRET OF MY SUCCESS, THE

Jordan, Stanley
BLIND DATE

Jose, Natalina
DUMA VEZ POR TODAS

Jose-Garrido, Maria
OLOR A MUERTE

Joseph, Jackie
POLICE ACADEMY 4: CITIZENS ON PATROL

Joseph, Jeffrey
ROXANNE

Joseph, Mark
DAUGHTERS OF EVE

Joseph, Ron
BARFLY

Josephson, Cheryl
I WAS A TEENAGE T.V. TERRORIST

Josephson, Erland
DE FLYGANDE DJAVLARNA
IL GIORNO PRIMA
TESTAMENT D'UN POETE JUIF ASSASSINE

Josephson, Jeffrey
BEST SELLER
SQUEEZE, THE
WANTED: DEAD OR ALIVE

Joshi, Dilip
PRATIGHAAT

Joshi, Pallavi
THIRTHAM

Josso, Fabrice
LES EXPLOITS DUN JEUNE DON JUAN

Jotie, Hay Hay
LADIES OF THE LOTUS

Jouane, Patrick
NUIT DOCILE

Jouzier, Annie
CLUB DE RENCONTRES

Jovanovski, Aco
HI-FI

Jovanovski, Meto
HI-FI

Jove, Angel
ANGUSTIA

Joy, Robert
BIG SHOTS
RADIO DAYS
SUICIDE CLUB, THE

Joy-Chagrin, Julian
EMPEROR'S NEW CLOTHES, THE
RED RIDING HOOD

Joyner, Lorain
KILLER WORKOUT

Joyner, Mario
THREE MEN AND A BABY

Joyner, Rachel M.
SUMMER HEAT

Joynt, Paul
OPPOSING FORCE

Juarbe, Israel
OVERBOARD

Juarez, Ernesto
JUNTOS

Judd, Edward
KITCHEN TOTO, THE

Jude Ciccolella
MORGAN STEWART'S COMING HOME

Jugnot, Gerard
LE BEAUF
TANDEM

Julee, Jace
STUDENT CONFIDENTIAL

Julia, Raul
LA GRAN FIESTA

Julian, Arlene
MANKILLERS

Julian, Jett
NECROPOLIS

Juliano, Lenny
LETHAL WEAPON

Julien, Jason
REVENGE OF THE NERDS II: NERDS IN PARADISE

Julio, Denis
CHRONICLE OF A DEATH FORETOLD

Julius, Ami
MALIBU BIKINI SHOP, THE

Jun, Wu
LAST EMPEROR, THE

Jun, Yu Wom
TALMAE WA POMDARI

Junco, Victor
CARTUCHA CORTADA
LAPUTA: THE CASTLE IN THE SKY

Jundeff, Jake
MANNEQUIN

Jung, Andre
VERMISCHTE NACHRICHTEN

Jung, Calvin
ROBOCOP

Junguo, Gu
LAST EMPEROR, THE

Jungwirth, Barbara
DOGS IN SPACE

Jurado, Janice
NO BLOOD NO SURRENDER

Jurgens, Deanna
CODE NAME ZEBRA

Jurisic, Melita
TALE OF RUBY ROSE, THE

Justice Minister
WANNSEE CONFERENCE, THE

Juszczakiewicz, Michael
MATKA KROLOW

Ka-yen, Leung
STORY OF DR. SUN YAT-SEN, THE

Kaa, Wi Kuki
NGATI

Kaatrasalo, Sebastian
SNOW QUEEN, THE

Kaberidis, Dimitris
THEOFILOS

Kabo, Olga
MILLION V BRACHNOY KORZINE

Kabos, Gyula
A JAVOR

Kabouche, Aziz
UNE FLAMME DANS MON COEUR

Kacer, Jan
WOLF'S HOLE

Kadi, Charlotte
LANNEE DES MEDUSES

Kadochnikova
RODNIK DLIA ZHAZHDUSHCHIKH

Kadotani, Teresa
LETHAL WEAPON

Kafetzopoulos, Antonis
ARCHANGELOS TOU PATHOUS
KE DYO AVGA TOURKIAS

Kafkaloff, Kim
SLAMMER GIRLS

Kafri, Ezra
BOUBA
KFAFOT

Kaga, Mariko
LOVE LETTER

Kagan, Jeremy Paul
SOMEONE TO LOVE

Kahan, Enrique
GABY—A TRUE STORY

Kahan, Steve
LETHAL WEAPON

Kahra, Kalevi
KUNINGAS LEAR

Kai, Kenta
GONDOLA

Kaifi, Shankat
ANJUMAN

Kaikure, Morikan
OVERKILL

Kairu, Wallace
KOLORMASK

Kaiser, Henry
SPACEBALLS

Kaiser, Ron
BLOOD HOOK

Kaitz, Tammy
HOLLYWOOD SHUFFLE

Kajrisova, Astrida
POHADKA O MALICKOVI

Kakavaze, Badri
PYAT NEVEST DO LYUBIMOY

Kalavrouzos, Christos
KLIOS

Kaldis, Panayotis
IKONA ENOS MYTHIKOU PROSOPOU

Kalfon, Jean-Pierre
LE CRI DU HIBOU

Kaliban, Bob
BIG BANG, THE

Kalimazi
LA VIE EST BELLE

Kalinovskaya, Irina
NEYLONOVAYA YOLKA

Kalipha, Stefan
BORN OF FIRE

Kalisz, Waldemar
PRZYJACIEL WESOLEGO DIABLA

Kalivocas, Dimitris
VIOS KE POLITIA

Kallai, Ferenc
SZORNYEK EVADJA

Kallan, A.J.
AMAZING GRACE AND CHUCK

Kalle, Pepe
LA VIE EST BELLE

Kalleus, Jaanika
IGRY DLJA DETEJ SKO'NOGO VOZRASTA

Kalliala, Aake
JAAHYVAISET PRESIDENTILLE
LIIAN ISO KEIKKA

Kallio, Ismo
AKALLINEN MIES

Kallio, Jaakko
PEKKA PUUPAA POLIISINA

Kalmenson, Bill
LETHAL WEAPON

Kalnyn, Ivar
DVOE POD ODNIM ZONTOM

Kalnyns, Ivar
ISKUSHENIE DON ZHUANA

Kalnynsh, Helmuts
OBOROTEN TOM

Kaloyeropoulos, Nikos
ONIRO ARISTERIS NICHTAS

Kalpana
THIRUMATHI ORU VEGUMATHI

Kalyagin, Alexander
KREUTZEROVA SONATA
POSLEDNYAYA DOROGA

Kam, Miki
LATE SUMMER BLUES

Kamakahi, Pia
STRIPPED TO KILL

Kamal, Jon Rashad
MALIBU BIKINI SHOP, THE

Kamarr
ISHTAR

Kamas, Jerzy
CUDZOZIEMKA

Kamekona, Danny
BLACK WIDOW

Kamenkova, Anna
POSLEDNYAYA DOROGA

Kamerman, Piet
BLOND DOLLY

Kamienski, Christian
VENNER FOR ALTID

Kamin, Dan
CREEPSHOW 2

Kaminer, Manuel
GABY—A TRUE STORY

Kamino, Brenda
IVE HEARD THE MERMAIDS SINGING

Kaminsky, Artem
YAGUAR

Kaminsky, Artyom
AKTSIA

Kamiyama, Shigeru
SEA AND POISON, THE

Kamkia, Kurbei
CHEGEMSKIY DETEKTIV

Kamma, Loes
STRIKE COMMANDO

Kammerer, Peter
DER TOD DES EMPEDOKLES

Kanakbayev, Serik
TAYNY MADAM VONG

Kanaventi, Dominic
CRY FREEDOM

Kanaventi, Munyaradzi
CRY FREEDOM

Kanazawa, Mitsugu
ROBINSON NO NIWA

Kandidah, Winnie
KOLORMASK

Kane, Billy
SOMEONE TO WATCH OVER ME

Kane, Carol
ISHTAR
PRINCESS BRIDE, THE

Kane, Fernn
PSYCHO GIRLS

Kane, Gordan
MORE BAD NEWS

Kane, Issiaka
YEELEN

Kane, John
PRICK UP YOUR EARS

Kane, Matt
WITCHES OF EASTWICK, THE

Kaneda, Naomi
BLOOD TRACKS

Kang, Yu Yung
MIRAGE

Kani, John
SATURDAY NIGHT AT THE PALACE

Kano, Jonathan
LETS GET HARRY

Kanter, Marianne
NIGHTMARE AT SHADOW WOODS

Kanz, Yosi
YALDEI STALIN

Kanzaki, Ai
DIXIELAND DAIMYO
Kapadia, Dimple
INSANIYAT KE DUSHMAN
Kapaulos, Michael
PRETTY SMART
Kapelos, John
ROXANNE
Kaplan, Mady
PROJECT X
Kapoor, Anil
MISTER INDIA
Kapoor, Karan
LOHA
Kapoor, Shashi
ANJAAM
SAMMY AND ROSIE GET LAID
Kappers, Marnix
CAUGHT
Kaprisky, Valerie
LANNEE DES MEDUSES
Kapture, Mitzi
HOUSE TWO: THE SECOND STORY
Kar Leung, Lau
THIRTY MILLION RUSH, THE
Kara, Juro
DIXIELAND DAIMYO
Karabatsos, Ron
COLD STEEL
Karabeti, Kariofilia
ONE HUNDRED AND TWENTY DECIBELS
Karabetsis, Dimitris
KLIOS
Karachentsov, Nikolai
OCHNAYA STAVKA
Karachentzev, Nikolai
KAK STAT SCHASTLIVYM
Karadjova, Yelena
POSLEDNYAYA DOROGA
Karady, Katalin
A JAVOR
Karaivanova, Zhana
PRIZEMYAVANE
Karamana
JANUARY ORORMA
Karanja
PROJECT X
Karanovic, Mirjana
NA PUTA ZA KATANGU
UVEK SPREMNE ZENE
Karapetyan, Artem
KRASNAYA STRELA
Karasz, Eszter
WHOOPING COUGH
Karata, Y.
EASTERN CONDORS
Karayanni, Katerina
FAKELOS POLK STON AERA
Karelskikh, Yevgeny
RAZMAKH KRYLIEV
Karen, James
WALL STREET
Kari, Gyorgyi
ISTEN VELETEK, BARATAIM
Kariara, Jonathan
KOLORMASK
Karina, Anna
LETE DERNIER A TANGER
Karis, Vassili
PRETTY SMART
Kark, Tiinu
GRUZ BEZ MARKIROVKI
Karlson, Monica
KILLER WORKOUT
Karm, Michael
VALET GIRLS
Karman, Janice
CHIPMUNK ADVENTURE, THE
Karman, Michael
PRETTY SMART
Karnad, Girish
NILAKURINHI POOTHAPPOL
SUTRADHAR
Karr, Marcia
KILLER WORKOUT
Kartalian, Buck
CHECKPOINT
Karthika
JANUARY ORORMA
NILAKURINHI POOTHAPPOL
POOVIZHI VASALILE
Karvan, Claudia
HIGH TIDE
SHADOWS OF THE PEACOCK
Karvoski, Ed
STUDENT CONFIDENTIAL
Karyo, Tcheky
LA MOINE ET LA SORCIERE
SPIRALE
Kasaki, Ben
OVERKILL
Kasongo, Kanku
LA VIE EST BELLE
Kasparian, David
BLACK WIDOW
Kasper, Gary
ARIA
Kasprzik, Anne
VERNEHMUNG DER ZEUGEN
Kasri, Lakhdar
PIERRE ET DJEMILA
Kassar, Kamal
LHOMME VOILE
Kassel, Coral
OUTRAGEOUS FORTUNE
Kaszas, Atilla
ZUHANAS KOZBEN
Katalifos, Dimitris
THEOFILOS
Kataoka, Takatoro
EMPIRE OF THE SUN
Kater, John
SWEET REVENGE
Kath, Camelia
KILLING TIME, THE
Katia
MASCARA
Katkar, Kimi
MERA LAHOO
Kato, Takeshi
PRINCESS FROM THE MOON
Katsaris, Antonis
KLIOS
Katsimanis, Dimitris
ONIRO ARISTERIS NICHTAS
Katsuk, Yu.
VZLOMSHCHIK
Katsulas, Andreas
SICILIAN, THE
SOMEONE TO WATCH OVER ME
Katz, Elia
MAN IN LOVE, A
Katz, Joycee
IN THE MOOD
Kaufman, David
MISSION KILL
Kaufman, Jill
NIGHTFORCE
Kaufmann, Christine
OUT OF ROSENHEIM
Kavanagh, John
BELLMAN AND TRUE
Kaviani, Ferdos
LODGERS
Kavner, Julie
RADIO DAYS
SURRENDER
Kavsadze, Kahki
REPENTANCE
Kavsadze, Kakha
GOSPODA AVANTYURISTY
Kawahara, Takashi
EAT THE PEACH
Kawarazaki, Choichiro
MAGINA—MURA MONOGATARI
Kawatani, Takuzo
DEATH SHADOWS
Kay, Sara
LOS DUENOS DEL SILENCIO
Kay, Stephen
ZERO BOYS, THE
Kaydanovsky, Alexander
IZVINITEPOZHALUYSTA
Kaye, Joan
BELIEVERS, THE
Kaye, Linda
RED RIDING HOOD
Kaye, Michael
SOMEONE TO LOVE
Kaye, Norman
FRENCHMAN'S FARM
WARM NIGHTS ON A SLOW MOVING TRAIN
Kaye-Mason, Clarissa
GOOD WIFE, THE
Kaysoe, Dick
PETER VON SCHOLTEN
Kayurov, Leonid
NABAT NA RASSVETE
Kaza, Elisabeth
ACCROCHE-COEUR
IRON WARRIOR
Kazan
IN THE MOOD
Kazan, Lainie
HARRY AND THE HENDERSONS
Kazan, Vangelis
FAKELOS POLK STON AERA
Kazarinova, Yelena
SVIDANIE NA MLECHNOM PUTI
Kazaryan, Shaum
PESN PROSHEDSHIKH DNEY
Kazmierczak, Anna
STANISLAW I ANNA
Kazragite, Doloresa
BLUDNYY SYN
Kazurinsky, Tim
POLICE ACADEMY 4: CITIZENS ON PATROL
Kazuro, Stefan
PIERSCIEN I ROZA
Keach, James
EVIL TOWN
Kean, Carole
MONSTER IN THE CLOSET
Kean, Marie
DEAD, THE
LONELY PASSION OF JUDITH HEARNE,THE
Keane, James
LETS GET HARRY
Keane, Kerrie
MORNING MAN, THE
NIGHTSTICK
Kearney, Mac
OVERKILL
Kearney, Robert
BIG EASY, THE
Kearns, P.K.
ESCAPES
Kearns, Sandra
FLICKS
Keating, Dick
EAT THE PEACH
Keating, Lulu
JOHN AND THE MISSUS
Keaton, Diane
BABY BOOM
RADIO DAYS
Keaton, Michael
SQUEEZE, THE
Kedem, Daniel
POET'S SILENCE, THE
Kee, Chan Pui
MIDNIGHT
Keech, Bill
BIRDS OF PREY
Keegan, Jimmy
OVER THE TOP
Keegan, Rita
SHADEY
Keegan, Robert
BUSINESS AS USUAL
Keeme, Elizabeth
KILLER WORKOUT
Keen, Geoffrey
LIVING DAYLIGHTS, THE
Keene, Christopher
SLAMDANCE
Keene, Jennifer
BIRDS OF PREY
Keener, Eliott
ANGEL HEART
BIG EASY, THE
Keerthi
UMMADI MOGUDU
Kehoe, Jack
UNTOUCHABLES, THE
Kei, Suma
HIKARU ANNA
Keita, Balla Moussa
YEELEN

Keitel, Harvey
PICK-UP ARTIST, THE
Keiter, Cindy
I WAS A TEENAGE ZOMBIE
Keith, Brian
DEATH BEFORE DISHONOR
Keith, David
WHITE OF THE EYE
Keith, Paul
IN THE MOOD
SPACE RACE
Keith, Warren
HIDING OUT
RAISING ARIZONA
Keklikian, Selma
FAMILY VIEWING
Kelaf, Pascal
NUIT DOCILE
Kelbaugh, Geri Lynn
TIN MEN
Keller, Billie
BLOODSUCKERS FROM OUTER SPACE
Keller, Fred A.
MY DARK LADY
Keller, Henry David
FIREHOUSE
Keller, Marthe
DARK EYES
Keller, Terry
BIRDS OF PREY
Kellerman, Sally
MEATBALLS III
SOMEONE TO LOVE
THREE FOR THE ROAD
Kellerman, Susan
PLANES, TRAINS AND AUTOMOBILES
SECRET OF MY SUCCESS, THE
Kelley, Sheila
WISH YOU WERE HERE
Kellogg, John
ORPHANS
Kelly, Austin
NO WAY OUT
Kelly, Barry
EAT THE PEACH
Kelly, Clare
FOURTH PROTOCOL, THE
Kelly, Daniel Hugh
NOWHERE TO HIDE
SOMEONE TO WATCH OVER ME
Kelly, David
BIRDS OF PREY
Kelly, David Patrick
WHEELS OF TERROR
Kelly, Desmond
DANCERS
Kelly, Frances
BLOOD TRACKS
Kelly, Gerard
MORE BAD NEWS
Kelly, John
MANKILLERS
Kelly, Karen
WHOOPS APOCALYPSE
Kelly, Michael F.
BEVERLY HILLS COP II
Kelly, Mike
SAKURA KILLERS
Kelly, Sharon
SLAMMER GIRLS
Kelly, Shirley
STARLIGHT HOTEL
Kelly, Simon
RAWHEAD REX
Kelly, Stephen
BOY SOLDIER
Kelly, Terry
EL HOMBRE DESNUDO
Kemble, Mark
PENITENTIARY III
Kemkhadze, Dato
REPENTANCE
Kemmer, Joachim
MEIER
OTTO—DER NEUE FILM
Kemna, Hans
LOOKING FOR EILEEN
Kemp, John
CONCRETE ANGELS
Kemp, Lindsay
CARTOLINE ITALIANE
Kempf, Angie
PICK-UP ARTIST, THE
Kendall, Tony
DEATH STONE
Kendros, Giorgos
ONIRO ARISTERIS NICHTAS
Kenna, Hans
CAUGHT
Kennedy, Betty
FLICKS
Kennedy, Frank
OVERKILL
Kennedy, George
CREEPSHOW 2
Kennedy, Gerard
LIGHTHORSEMEN, THE
RUNNING FROM THE GUNS
Kennedy, Graham
LES PATTERSON SAVES THE WORLD
Kennedy, Heather
MANKILLERS
Kennedy, Helen
WHOOPS APOCALYPSE
Kennedy, Kristina
BABY BOOM
Kennedy, Leon Isaac
PENITENTIARY III
Kennedy, Michelle
BABY BOOM
Kenney, Joel
MALIBU BIKINI SHOP, THE
Kenny, Pat
EAT THE PEACH
Kent, Daniel
WEEDS
Kent, Eric
LOVECHILD, THE
Kent, Jessie
SUMMER HEAT
Kent, Julie
DANCERS
Kent, Regina
LEGACY OF RAGE
Kenworthy, Alexandra
LIKE FATHER, LIKE SON
Kenworthy, Marylou
BANZAI RUNNER
Keogh, Barbara
WHOOPS APOCALYPSE
Keogh, Christine
AS TIME GOES BY
BUSHFIRE MOON
Kepros, Nicholas
SICILIAN, THE
Keramidas, Ghrisa
DANCERS
Kerbrat, Patrice
LE CRI DU HIBOU
Kerckhoffs, Han
DE ORIONNEVEL
Kerimov, Mikahil
CHKATULKA IZ KREPOSTI
Kerlow, Max
FRIDA
Kerlowe, Max
MURIERON A MITAD DEL RIO
Kerman, Robert
NO WAY OUT
Kern, Pouel
BABETTE'S GASTEBUD
Kern, Roger
DELOS ADVENTURE, THE
RUNNING MAN, THE
Kernan, George
VIDEO DEAD, THE
Kernen, Siegfried
CRIME OF HONOR
Kerns, Hubie
WANTED: DEAD OR ALIVE
Kerns, Joanna
CROSS MY HEART
Kerns, Matt
AMAZING GRACE AND CHUCK
Kerr, Bill
BUSHFIRE MOON
LIGHTHORSEMEN, THE
RUNNING FROM THE GUNS
Kerr, E. Katherine
SUSPECT
Kerr, Judy
WHO'S THAT GIRL
Kerr, Stu
MORGAN STEWART'S COMING HOME
Kerridge, Linda
DOWN TWISTED
Kesner, Jillian
EVIL TOWN
MOON IN SCORPIO
Kester, Brad
MONSTER IN THE CLOSET
Kestin, Brad
SUMMER CAMP NIGHTMARE
Kesting, Michael
SAME TO YOU
Kestner, Boyd R.
RUNNING MAN, THE
Kestner, Brian
MONSTER SQUAD, THE
Kestner, Bryan
RUNNING MAN, THE
Kettles, Raymond
NI DE AQUI, NI DE ALLA
Kettless, Raymund
WALKER
Keung, Cheung Kowk
SWORN BROTHERS
Keung, Cindy
NO WAY OUT
Keung, Steve
NO WAY OUT
Key, Lotis
SWEET REVENGE
Key, Sara
GIRL, THE
Keyes, Irwin
NICE GIRLS DON'T EXPLODE
Keyi, Khali
BELIEVERS, THE
Khachaturova, Yanina
YAGUAR
Khan, Amjad
KAUN KITNEY PAANI MEIN
Khan, Bridget
THREE KINDS OF HEAT
Khan, Connie
MIRAGE
Khan, Kader
GHULAMI KI ZANJEER
LOHA
PYAR KARKE DEKHO
Khan, Michelle
MAGNIFICENT WARRIORS
Khan, Mushtaq
ANJUMAN
Khan, Sumar
ISHTAR
Khan, Yaseen
EMMANUELLE 5
Khanjian, Arsinee
FAMILY VIEWING
Khanna, Rajesh
NAZRANA
Kharitonov, Leonid
IZ ZHIZNI NACHALNIKA UGOLOVNOGO ROZYSKA
Kheir-Abadi, Hamideh
LODGERS
Kher, Anupam
KAUN KITNEY PAANI MEIN
Kherkhedlidze, Mikhail
VELIKIY POKHOD ZA NEVESTOY
Khimichev, Boris
CHYORNAYA STRELA
PLOSHCHAD VOSSTANIA
Khleifi, Georges
NOCE EN GALILEE
Khodchenko, Vyacheslav
KAPITAN "PILIGRIMA"
Kholer, Gilles
LETHAL WEAPON
Khorsand, Philippe
LES OREILLES ENTRE LES DENTS
Khouri, Mabram
NOCE EN GALILEE
Kiberg, Tina
BABETTE'S GASTEBUD
Kichian, Manuel
FORTY DAYS OF MUSA DAGH

Kid, Asie
MUTANT HUNT

Kidder, Margot
KEEPING TRACK
SUPERMAN IV: THE QUEST FOR PEACE

Kidman, Nicole
BIT PART, THE

Kiel, Joe
OVER THE TOP

Kiel, Sue
STRAIGHT TO HELL

Kiely, Chris
AS TIME GOES BY

Kier, Udo
EPIDEMIC

Kieselstein, Susanne
STADTRAND

Kiev, Hector
JUNTOS

Kiger, Robby
MONSTER SQUAD, THE

Kihu, Sun
CUO WEI

Kikaleishvili, Mamuka
GOSPODA AVANTYURISTY

Kikuchi, Masao
MAGINA—MURA MONOGATARI

Kilalea, Rory
ALLAN QUATERMAIN AND THE LOST CITY OF GOLD

Killing, Laure
BEYOND THERAPY

Killingback, Debbie
EMPIRE STATE

Kilner, Gordon
HOUSEKEEPER, THE

Kilpatrick, Bruce
BUSHFIRE MOON

Kilpatrick, Lincoln
FLICKS

Kilpelainen, Heidi
URSULA

Kiltakov, Sergei
SOUCHASTNIKI

Kim, Myung-kon
MAN WITH THREE COFFINS, THE

Kim, Robert
OMEGA SYNDROME
STEELE JUSTICE

Kim, Wah Toe
OVERKILL

Kim Ji-Mi
TICKET

Kimbrough, Harry
BELIEVERS, THE

Kimchi, Alona
HIMMO MELECH YERUSHALAIM

Kimoulis, Giorgos
VIOS KE POLITIA

Kimsanov, Mashrabdjan
TAYNOE PUTESHESTVIE EMIRA

Kimura, Cho
MAGINA—MURA MONOGATARI

Kimura, Kazuya
SARABA ITOSHIKI HITO YO

Kimura, Masaki
MAGINA—MURA MONOGATARI

Kimwele, Anne
KOLORMASK

Kinashi, Noritake
SOROBANZUKU

Kinchev, Konstantin
VZLOMSHCHIK

King, Alan
YOU TALKIN' TO ME?

King, B.B.
AMAZON WOMEN ON THE MOON

King, Carole
RUSSKIES

King, Casey
NIGHTFORCE

King, Erik
PRETTYKILL
STREET SMART

King, Jan
NEAR DARK

King, Kip
STUDENT CONFIDENTIAL

King, Pascal
GOTHIC

King, Paul
FORTY DAYS OF MUSA DAGH

King, Richard
SWEET REVENGE

King, Scott
TERMINAL EXPOSURE

King, Stephen
CREEPSHOW 2

King Sunny Ade
O. C. AND STIGGS

Kinghorn, Sally
FOURTH PROTOCOL, THE

Kingsland, Marlenne
BEVERLY HILLS COP II

Kingsley, Ben
MAURICE

Kingsley, Danitza
AMAZONS

Kingsley, Gretchen
BLOOD SISTERS
WIMPS

Kingsley, Ray
LOVECHILD, THE

Kinmont, Kathleen
NIGHTFORCE
WINNERS TAKE ALL

Kinnaman, Melinda
MY LIFE AS A DOG
SERPENT'S WAY, THE

Kinner, Jackie
PROJECT X

Kinney, Terry
WALK ON THE MOON, A

Kino, Lloyd
WHO'S THAT GIRL

Kino
ZEGEN

Kinsey, Lance
POLICE ACADEMY 4: CITIZENS ON PATROL

Kinski, Nastassja
MALADIE D'AMOUR

Kio
KONZERT FUR DIE RECHTE HAND

Kipp, Bill
EQUALIZER 2000
OPPOSING FORCE

Kipshidze, Zurab
NEYLONOVAYA YOLKA

Kiran, Raj
MERA LAHOO

Kirby, Bruce
THROW MOMMA FROM THE TRAIN

Kirby, Bruno
GOOD MORNING, VIETNAM
TIN MEN

Kirby, George
LEONARD PART 6

Kirby, Grace
HELLRAISER

Kirk, Gary
BEST SELLER

Kirk, Jeffrey
LADY OF THE CAMELIAS

Kirk, Stanley
MAKING MR.RIGHT

Kirkland, Sally
ANNA
TALKING WALLS

Kirkland, Syndle
PRETTY SMART

Kirkwood, James
SUPERNATURALS, THE

Kirlton, Leigh
DEADTIME STORIES

Kirton, Mike
MALONE

Kirton, Pat
AMERICAN DRIVE-IN

Kiselus, Yuosas
SNAYPERY

Kiser, Terry
OFFSPRING, THE

Kishibe, Ittoku
FINAL TAKE: THE GOLDEN AGE OF MOVIES
TOKYO BLACKOUT

Kishida, Kyoko
SEA AND POISON, THE

Kishida, Kyoto
PRINCESS FROM THE MOON

Kishkilov, Georgi
PRIZEMYAVANE

Kiss, Cassia
ELE, O BOTO

Kissin, Harold
GOOD WIFE, THE

Kitaen, Tawny
CRYSTAL HEART
HAPPY HOUR
WITCHBOARD

Kitei, Lynne Dumin
RAISING ARIZONA

Kitten, Jesse
HOLLYWOOD SHUFFLE

Kiuchi, Midori
GONDOLA

Kivinen, Mikko
VY VIHDOINKIN YHDESSA

Kiviniemi, Erik
DET STORA LOFTET

Kiyohara, Bea
BLACK WIDOW

Kiyokawa, Nijiko
ITAZU

Kizer, James
MATEWAN

Kjellgren, Johan Hison
HIP, HIP, HURRA!

Kjellmann, Bjorn
HIP, HIP, HURRA!

Kjer, Bodil
BABETTE'S GASTEBUD

Klanfer, Francois
POLICE ACADEMY 4: CITIZENS ON PATROL

Klar, Gary
THREE MEN AND A BABY

Klar, Norman
TALKING WALLS

Klaus, Francois
LADY OF THE CAMELIAS

Klauss, Jurgen
MEIER

Kleen, Gustaf
VICTORIA

Klein, Albert
MISS MONA

Klein, Jesper
VALHALLA

Klein-Essink, Marc
MALACCA

Kleiner, Sergio
NI DE AQUI, NI DE ALLA

Kleiner, Towje
POET'S SILENCE, THE

Kleinig, Faith
MOVING TARGETS

Klement, Susanne
LADY OF THE CAMELIAS

Klenskaya, Maria
CHEREZ STO LET V MAE

Kletniecova, Dzintra
POHADKA O MALICKOVI

Klijn, Rene
CAUGHT

Klimasiewicz, Tomasz
LE JEUNE MAGICIEN

Klimpen
MY LIFE AS A DOG

Kline, Eugene
HANSEL AND GRETEL

Kline, Kevin
CRY FREEDOM

Klinger, Herb
PSYCHOS IN LOVE

Kliszczewski, Norbert
ZLOTA MAHMUDIA

Klos, Vladimir
LADY OF THE CAMELIAS

Klumpp, Donna Rey
KOLORMASK

Klyuchnikov, A.
VZLOMSHCHIK

Knabe, Miriam
DER JUNGE MIT DEM GROSSEN SCHWARZEN HUND

Knape, Ann-Sofie
MORE ABOUT THE CHILDREN OF BULLERBY VILLAGE

Kneebone, Tom
HOUSEKEEPER, THE

Kneeper, Rob
MADE IN HEAVEN

Knepper, Rob
WILD THING

Knickle, Francis
LIFE CLASSES

Kniest, Frank
RETURN TO HORROR HIGH

Knight, Gregg T.
GOOD MORNING, VIETNAM

Knight, Keith
CARE BEARS ADVENTURE IN WONDERLAND, THE

Knight, Michael E.
DATE WITH AN ANGEL

Knight, Rosalind
PRICK UP YOUR EARS

Knight, Sally
BROADCAST NEWS

Knight, Wayne
DIRTY DANCING

Knode, Kim
BANZAI RUNNER

Knott, Andy
HOUSEKEEPER, THE

Knotts, Don
PINOCCHIO AND THE EMPEROR OF THE NIGHT

Knotts, Kathryn
PRINCIPAL, THE

Knower, Rosemary
SUSPECT

Ko-Chin-hsiung
HEROIC PIONEERS

Koba, Alex
FLOWERS IN THE ATTIC

Kobayashi
EAT THE PEACH

Kobayashi, Kaoru
SOROBANZUKU

Kobayashi, Keiju
TAXING WOMAN, A

Kobin, Chris
EVIL SPAWN

Koblanck, Maria
OM KARLEK

Koch, Andrew Charles
DIRTY DANCING

Kochegarov, Nikolay
OBRYV

Koci, Premsyl
CHOBOTNICE Z II. PATRA

Kodar, Oja
SOMEONE TO LOVE

Koehler, Frederick
PICK-UP ARTIST, THE

Koen, Duvi
YEHOSHUA—YEHOSHUA

Kohl, Aditra
UNTOUCHABLES, THE

Kohl, Pier
KEEPING TRACK

Kohlhaas, Karen
HOUSE OF GAMES

Kohlman, Louis Freddie
ANGEL HEART

Kohnert, Mary
VALET GIRLS

Kohuth, Adolf
PROC?

Kokila
THIRUMATHI ORU VEGUMATHI

Kokonos, Andrea
PRETTY SMART

Kokshenov, Mikhail
SPORTLOTO—82

Koksui, Marie
OVERKILL

Kolderwijn, Edward
CAUGHT

Kolebanov, A.
VZLOMSHCHIK

Kolesar, Anne
BELL DIAMOND

Kolev, Todor
CERNITE LEBEDI

Kolhapure, Padmini
DADAGIRI
JHANJHAAR

Kollek, Amos
FOREVER, LULU

Kollo, Rene
ARIA

Kolomeir, Robert
REMEMBERING MEL

Kolousek, Karel
CENA MEDU

Koltai, Robert
C. K. DEZERTERZY
CSOK, ANYU

Koltakov, Sergei
V STRELYAYUSHCHEY GLUSHI

Koly, Souleymane
LA VIE PLATINEE

Komang, Alex
IBUNDA

Komatau, Hosei
SHINRAN: SHIRO MICHI

Komatsu, Hidehiko
BUS

Komnenic, Boris
WHEELS OF TERROR

Kondrat, Marek
C. K. DEZERTERZY
WERYFIKACJA

Kondulainen, Yelena
RUS IZNACHALNA

Kong, Venice
BEVERLY HILLS COP II

Kong-Guo-Jun
EMPIRE OF THE SUN

Kongas, Kylli
VARJOJA PARATIISISSA

Koniger, Miklos
KONZERT FUR DIE RECHTE HAND

Kono, Garitt
MAKING MR.RIGHT

Kononov, Mikhail
PRODELKI V STARINNOM DUKHE

Konstadakou, Maria
APOUSIES

Kontic, Ljiljana
DIE VERLIEBTEN

Kontoyannidis, Pavlos
FAKELOS POLK STON AERA
VIOS KE POLITIA

Koock, Guich
SQUARE DANCE

Koong-won, Nam
NAE-SHI

Kopecky, Eleanore C.
BROADCAST NEWS

Kopel, Danny
NEAR DARK

Kopel, Gil
FULL METAL JACKET

Koper, Macid
ANAYURT OTELI

Koppa, Carlos
ANJOS DO ARRABALDE

Korder, Howard
I WAS A TEENAGE T.V. TERRORIST

Korhonen, Marja
UUNO TURHAPURO MUUTTAA MAALLE

Korman, Harvey
MUNCHIES

Korman, Irene
KILLER WORKOUT

Kormunin, Pavel
POKLONIS DO ZEMLI

Korn, Renee
ARIA

Kornsakul, Rapeepan
COBRA THUNDERBOLT

Korolkov, Gennady
KONTRUDAR

Korostilyova, Rimma
DUBLYOR NACHINAET DEYSTVOVAT

Korporaal, Giovanni
RED DESERT PENITENTIARY

Korpunaite, Eleonora
MOYA MALENKAYA ZHENA

Korzen, Annie
WHEELS OF TERROR

Koscina, Sylva
RIMINI RIMINI

Kosik, Kelly
P.K. & THE KID

Kosmidis, Michalis
FAKELOS POLK STON AERA

Kossak, Christine
THREE MEN AND A BABY

Kossobudzka, Halina
CZAS NADZIEI

Kostelka, Lubomir
PRATELE BERMUDSKEHO TROJUHELNIKU

Koster, Abe
EMANON

Kostolevsky, Igor
PO GLAVNOY ULITSE S ORKESTROM
PROSTI

Kostovski, Dusko
HI-FI

Kosugi, Sho
RAGE OF HONOR

Kotamanidou, Eva
TELEFTAIO STICHIMA

Kotandis, George
PRETTY SMART

Kotanidis, Giorgos
VIOS KE POLITIA

Koteas, Elias
GARDENS OF STONE
SOME KIND OF WONDERFUL

Kotkin, Edward S.
RADIO DAYS

Kotscharian, Vladimir
SASHSHENNYI FONAR

Kottarathil, Vijayan
UPPU

Kotto, Yaphet
PRETTYKILL
RUNNING MAN, THE

Kouberskaya, Irina
DIARY FOR MY LOVED ONES

Kovacs, Danny
PRINCIPAL, THE

Kovas, Ned
RAGE OF HONOR

Kovats, Adel
DIARY FOR MY LOVED ONES
ZUHANAS KOZBEN

Kove, Martin
STEELE JUSTICE

Kovruzov, Ramiz
YA LYUBIL VAC BOLSHE ZHIZNI

Kowalewski, Krzysztof
KOMEDIANTKA

Kowanko, Pete
DATE WITH AN ANGEL

Kownacki, Waldemar
STANISLAW I ANNA

Kozak, Andras
SZORNYEK EVADJA

Kozak, Heidi
SLUMBER PARTY MASSACRE II

Kozak, John
GOOFBALLS

Kozak-Paszkowska, Katarzyna
BOHATERROKU

Kozakov, Mikhail
GEROY YEYOROMANA

Kozien, Zdzislaw
ZLOTA MAHMUDIA

Kozyrev, Sergei
CHUZHIE ZDES NE KHODYAT

Kraaykamp, John
IRIS

Krabbe, Jeroen
LIVING DAYLIGHTS, THE

Kraines, Carl
GATE, THE

Kramer, Joel
RUNNING MAN, THE

Kramer, Michael Eric
PROJECT X
RETURN TO HORROR HIGH

Kramorov, Savely
MORGAN STEWART'S COMING HOME

Krampol, Jiri
WOLF'S HOLE

Krantz, Robert
WINNERS TAKE ALL

Kranz, George
MAGIC STICKS

Krasko, Ivan
DUBLYOR NACHINAET DEYSTVOVAT

Kraus, Alfredo
ARIA

Kraus, Andrej
DISCOPRIBEH
Kraus, Jan
CENA MEDU
Krause, Hans Henrik
PETER VON SCHOLTEN
Krausova, Jana
DISCOPRIBEH
Krawford, Gary
HOUSEKEEPER, THE
Krawic, Michael
BIG SHOTS
Kray, Marilyn
I WAS A TEENAGE T.V. TERRORIST
Kreft, Annette
ZABOU
Kreger, Kelly
HAPPY HOUR
Kreisel, Jane
SLAMMER GIRLS
Kremel, Joaquin
HAY QUE DESHACER LA CASA
MY GENERAL
Krempasky, Amy
STACKING
Kretschmerova, Jaroslava
CHOBOTNICE Z II. PATRA
Kreuger, Miles
SOMEONE TO LOVE
Krevoy, Cecile G.
SWEET REVENGE
Kriener, Ulrike
FLYER, THE
Krige, Alice
BARFLY
Krinke, August
BIG EASY, THE
Krishna
DONGODUCHHADU
MANDALADHEESUDU
Kriss, Katherine
STUDENT CONFIDENTIAL
Kristensen, Morten Stig
VENNER FOR ALTID
Kristensen, Preben
KAMPEN OM DEN RODE KO
PETER VON SCHOLTEN
Kristoff, Rom
TOUGH COP
Kritzinger, Johannes
LADY OF THE CAMELIAS
Krivokapic, Miodrag
U IME NARODA
Kriz, Antonin
DISCOPRIBEH
Kroeber, Carlos
VERA
Kroetsch, Neil
WILD THING
Krogh, Malene
JAG ELSKER DIG
Kroll, Abe
ISHTAR
Kroll, Hannah
ISHTAR
Kronenfeld, Ivan
RADIO DAYS
Kroner, Jozef
AZ UTOLSOKEZIRAT
UTOLSO KEZIRAT
Kronsberg, Herb
HAPPY HOUR
Kroth, Gene
ROCK 'N' ROLL NIGHTMARE
Kruff, Jorgen Christian
EPIDEMIC
Krug, Peter
HOLLYWOOD SHUFFLE
Kruger, Johann
HOSTAGE
Kruger, Sven
LESTATE STA FINENDO
Kruk, Grazyna
POCIAG DO HOLLYWOOD
Kruk, Tony
I WAS A TEENAGE T.V. TERRORIST
Krukov, Juri
CHEREZ STO LET V MAE
Krukowski, Piotr
PAN SAMOCHODZIK I NIESAMOWITY DWOR
Krunch, M. D'Jango
STREET TRASH
Krupinski, Renny
WHISTLE BLOWER, THE
Kryuchkova, Svetlana
KURIER
Kryukov, Yuri
VO VREMENA VOLCHYIKA ZAKONOV
Ku, Sze
YI LOU YI
Kuang-Kuang
OUTSIDERS, THE
Kuay, Uikey
GOOD MORNING, VIETNAM
Kubota, Tak
STEELE JUSTICE
Kuen-Chi, Yip
DIXIA QING
Kuhlke, William
NICE GIRLS DON'T EXPLODE
Kuhlman, Ron
CLUB LIFE
OMEGA SYNDROME
Kuhn, Robert
TRESPASSES
Kuhn, T.J.
RAISING ARIZONA
Kuizenga, Bert
DE ORIONNEVEL
Kuki, Aashish
PRATIGHAAT
Kuklinska, Ewa
ZLOTY POCIAG
Kukumiagi, Arvo
CHEREZ STO LET V MAE
Kukumyagi, Arvo
VO VREMENA VOLCHYIKA ZAKONOV
Kulagin, Leonid
CHYORNAYA STRELA
Kuliskova, Tatiana
DISCOPRIBEH
Kuljis, Jan
MUNCHIES
Kulka, Janos
TERMINUS
Kulle, Jarl
BABETTE'S GASTEBUD
Kumagaya, Mami
ZEGEN
Kumalo, Alton
CRY FREEDOM
Kumar, Ajay
LOVECHILD, THE
Kumar, Arvind
PRATIGHAAT
Kumar, Ashim
LALAN FAKIR
Kumar, Ashok
MISTER INDIA
Kumar, Jagdish
PERSONAL SERVICES
Kumar, Mahesh
PRATIGHAAT
Kumpeing, Saloma
BEJALAI
Kun, Yang
CUO WEI
Kunavicus, Eduardas
BLUDNYY SYN
Kung, Cecile
JENATSCH
Kunhegyi, Ron
CONCRETE ANGELS
Kuningas, Helle
IGRY DLJA DETEJ SKO'NOGO VOZRASTA
Kuntzel, Alexandra
CEMIL
Kuoppala, Ahti
AKALLINEN MIES
Kuosmanen, Sakari
VARJOJA PARATIISISSA
Kupchenko, Irina
ODINOKAYA ZHENCHINA ZHELAET
POZNAKOMITAYA
POSLEDNYAYA DOROGA
Kupper, Yvonne
JENATSCH
Kuravlyov, Leonid
LEVSHA
SAMAYA OBAYATELNAYA I PRIVLEKATELNAYA
Kuri, Dulce
WINTER TAN, A
Kuri, Villasenor
CARTUCHA CORTADA
Kuriakidis, Vladimiros
TA PAIDIA TIS CHELIDONAS
Kurihara, Daysuke
LESTATE STA FINENDO
Kurnitz, Julie
RADIO DAYS
Kuroiwa, Tomoko
BUS
Kuroki, Yuimi
SEA AND POISON, THE
Kurtzo, Joe
RETURN OF JOSEY WALES, THE
Kusano, Hiroshi
SEA AND POISON, THE
Kushnir, Avi
HA INSTALATOR
Kussner, Evelyn
REMEMBERING MEL
Kuter, Kay
ZOMBIE HIGH
Kutner, Cortney
AMAZING GRACE AND CHUCK
Kutvolgyi, Erzsebet
DIARY FOR MY LOVED ONES
Kuusk, Edit-Hellen
IGRY DLJA DETEJ SKO'NOGO VOZRASTA
Kuypers, Felix-Jan
ZJOEK
Kuzin, Aleksandr
VINA LEYTENANTA NEKRASOVA
Kuznetsov, Yury
PODSUDIMYY
PRORYV
Kuznetsova, Olga
POEZD VNE RASPISANIA
Kvalem, Finn
FELDMANN CASE, THE
Kvasha, Igor
UTRO OBRECHENNOGO PRIISKA
Kviring, Ivo
KONZERT FUR DIE RECHTE HAND
Kwan, Pauline
WRONG COUPLES,THE
Kwan, Rosamund
PROJECT A—PART II
Kwan, Steve
NINJA THUNDERBOLT
Kwasniewska, Slawa
W ZAWIESZENIU
Kwong, Lee Wan
MIDNIGHT
Kwong, Peter
STEELE JUSTICE
Kwouk, Burt
EMPIRE OF THE SUN
Kyhan, Yusuf
MORE BAD NEWS
Kyi, Henry
LAST EMPEROR, THE
Kyle, George
FOREVER, LULU
Kyle, Jack
ARIA
Kyriakidis, Stefanos
DOXOBUS
Kyriakidis, Vladimiros
KLIOS
L'Ensemble Koteba d'Abidjan
LA VIE PLATINEE
L., Marie-Sophie
ATTENTION BANDITS
La Bourdette, Katie
MILLION DOLLAR MYSTERY
La Fortezza, Tony
WHO'S THAT GIRL
La France, LaNette
BLOOD DINER
La Freniere, Celene
EL HOMBRE DESNUDO
La Plante, Marshall
SLUMBER PARTY MASSACRE II
La Rue, Eva
BARBARIANS, THE
La Testa, Pam
BLOOD SISTERS

Laban, Jean
LADY OF THE CAMELIAS
LaBelle, Kimberly
WINNERS TAKE ALL
Labian, Piet
MASCARA
Laborde, Michel
MASCARA
Laborteaux, Patrick
SUMMER SCHOOL
LaCava, Karen
NIGHTFORCE
Lachens, Catherine
LA VIE DISSOLUE DE GERARD FLOQUE
LES DEUX CROCODILES
Lachini, Azita
SHEERE SANGGY
Lackey, Mike
STREET TRASH
Lacoste, Monica
A DOS AGUAS
Lacques, John
THREE BEWILDERED PEOPLE IN THE NIGHT
Ladalski, John
NINJA THUNDERBOLT
SAKURA KILLERS
Ladan, Katya
CONCRETE ANGELS
Ladd, Diane
BLACK WIDOW
Ladd, Jeremy
ULTIMAX FORCE
Ladd, Margaret
WHALES OF AUGUST, THE
Laezza, Luigi
CAPRICCIO
Lafond, Monique
EU
Lafont, Bernadette
MASQUES
WAITING FOR THE MOON
Lafont, Francois
MASQUES
Lafont, Jean-Philippe
BABETTE'S GASTEBUD
Lafont, Pauline
LETE EN PENTE DOUCE
SALE DESTIN!
SOIGNE TA DROITE
Laforet, Marie
F . . . ING FERNAND
IL EST GENIAL PAPY!
SALE DESTIN!
Lafortune, Roch
MORNING MAN, THE
Lage, Klaus
ZABOU
Lager, Jesper
SEPPAN
Lager, Nina
SEPPAN
Lago, Christopher
LA RAZA NUNCA PIERDE—HUELE A GAS
MI NOMBRE ES GATILLO
Lagos, Viky
POLICIA
Lagunes, Guillermo
HERENCIA DE VALIENTES
LETS GET HARRY
Lahaie, Brigitte
JOHNNY MONROE
Lahti, Christine
HOUSEKEEPING
STACKING
Lai, Chan Yuen
MIDNIGHT
Lai, Joanna
YI LOU YI
Lai, Tuan
GOOD MORNING, VIETNAM
Laide, Michael T.
WINNERS TAKE ALL
Laiho, Pekka
VARJOJA PARATIISISSA
Lain, Emilio
LA GUERRA DE LOS LOCOS
Lajtai, Kati
CSOK, ANYU
Lake, Bill
BLUE MONKEY
Lake, Don
BIG TOWN, THE
BLUE MONKEY
Lakovic, Predrag-Pepi
STRATEGIJA SVRAKE
Lalitha
NILAKURINHI POOTHAPPOL
Lallan
PRATIGHAAT
Lallouz, Allan
REMEMBERING MEL
Lalo
ENTRE FICHERAS ANDA EL DIABLO
LAS TRAIGO . . . MUERTAS
Lalo el Mimo
MAS BUENAS QUE EL PAN
MAS VALE PAJARO EN MANO . . .
Laloux, Daniel
POUSSIERE D'ANGE
Lam, Augustine
MILLION DOLLAR MYSTERY
Lam, Regina
MISS MARY
Lam, Vincent
BROTHERHOOD
Lama, Ernesto
SOLDATI: 365 GIORNI ALL' ALBA
Lamaison, Lidia
EN RETIRADA
Lamar, William
BEVERLY HILLS COP II
Lamb, Debra
DEATHROW GAMESHOW
STRIPPED TO KILL
Lamb, Larry
HEARTS OF FIRE
SHADEY
Lamb, Peadar
BUDAWANNY
Lamb, Sandy
LAONIANG GOU SAO
Lambert, Alexa
OVER THE TOP
Lambert, Anne Louise
A LOS CUATRO VIENTOS
Lambert, Kim
IF LOOKS COULD KILL
Lambert, Mark
PRAYER FOR THE DYING, A
Lambert, Ryan
MONSTER SQUAD, THE
Lambert, Serge "Lydie"
MASCARA
Lambert, Ted
MAGIC STICKS
Lamberts, Aart
VAN GELUK GESPROKEN
Lambrecht, Yves
LES EXPLOITS DUN JEUNE DON JUAN
Lambros, Helen
SOMEONE TO WATCH OVER ME
Lamers, Elizabeth
CLUB LIFE
VALET GIRLS
Lamm, Ellen
SPARVAGN TILL HAVET
Lamm, Lovisa
SPARVAGN TILL HAVET
Lamm, Regina
EIN BLICK-UND DIE LIEBE BRICHT AUS
Lamming, Sean
FULL METAL JACKET
Lammot, Anne
BEVERLY HILLS COP II
Lamond, Toni
RUNNING FROM THE GUNS
Lamoreux, Donald
WILD THING
Lamotte, Martin
F . . . ING FERNAND
SALE DESTIN!
TANT QU'IL AURA DES FEMMES
Lamour, Dorothy
CREEPSHOW 2
Lamoureux, Donald
MORNING MAN, THE
STREET SMART
Lampert, Jeffrey
MANNEQUIN
Lampreave, Chus
LA VIDA ALEGRE
MOROS Y CRISTIANOS
YEAR OF AWAKENING, THE
Lancaster, Burt
IL GIORNO PRIMA
Lancellotti, Annamaria
ILLUMINAZIONI
Lanciloti, Louis
UNTOUCHABLES, THE
Landa, Alfredo
EL BOSQUE ANIMADO
Landa, Daniel
PROC?
Landa, Miguelangel
MANON
Landau, Martin
CYCLONE
EMPIRE STATE
SWEET REVENGE
Lander, David
BIG BANG, THE
STEELE JUSTICE
Landerer, Greg
SUPERNATURALS, THE
Landers, Matt
VALET GIRLS
Landey, Clayton
FATAL BEAUTY
NIGHTMARE ON ELM STREET 3: DREAM WARRIORS, A
Landham, Sonny
PREDATOR
Landi, Sal
CLUB LIFE
SWEET REVENGE
Landin, Dan
FULL METAL JACKET
Landon-Smith, Kristine
GOTHIC
Landry, Paul
SHY PEOPLE
Landsberg, David
DUTCH TREAT
Landtroop, John
BLOODY WEDNESDAY
Lane, Campbell
MALONE
Lane, Charles
DATE WITH AN ANGEL
Lane, Christine
ALLNIGHTER, THE
Lane, Dave
ROCK 'N' ROLL NIGHTMARE
Lane, David
ROCK 'N' ROLL NIGHTMARE
Lane, Diane
BIG TOWN, THE
LADY BEWARE
Lane, James
MURDER LUST
Lane, John Francis
GOOD MORNING BABYLON
LA MONACA DIMONZA
Lane, Marcea D.
CRYSTAL HEART
Lane, Mark Stuart
EMANON
Lane, Mike
CODE NAME ZEBRA
Lane, Nathan
IRONWEED
Lane, Paul Michael
NEAR DARK
Lane, Stephanie
ARIA
Lane, Tim
IRON WARRIOR
Lane, William T.
NEAR DARK
Lane, Yuri
PRINCIPAL, THE
Lang, Archie
MONSTER IN THE CLOSET
Lang, Caroline
CHRONICLE OF A DEATH FORETOLD
Lang, Katherine Kelly
JOCKS
NIGHT STALKER, THE

Lang, Kerry
BEDROOM WINDOW, THE

Lang, Peggy
OVERKILL

Lang, Perry
JOCKS

Lang, Stephen
PROJECT X

Langan, Elise
BIG SHOTS

Langberg, Jesper
PETER VON SCHOLTEN

Lange, Marlene
RUNNING MAN, THE

Lange, Ted
TERMINAL EXPOSURE

Langella, Frank
MASTERS OF THE UNIVERSE

Langenkamp, Heather
NIGHTMARE ON ELM STREET 3: DREAM WARRIORS, A

Langland, Liane
SQUEEZE, THE

Langmack, Barbie
WINNERS TAKE ALL

Langmack, Bevie
WINNERS TAKE ALL

Langmajer, Jiri
PROC?

Langmiler, Josef
PRATELE BERMUDSKEHO TROJUHELNIKU

Langrall, James
FOREVER, LULU

Langrick, Margaret
HARRY AND THE HENDERSONS

Langridge, Philip
ARIA

Langton, David
WHISTLE BLOWER, THE

Langton, Sara
HOPE AND GLORY

Language Expert
PRINCE OF DARKNESS

Lanier, Didi
OFFSPRING, THE

Lankreyer, Anke
ZJOEK

Lanktree, David
BIRDS OF PREY

Lannom, Les
LIKE FATHER, LIKE SON

Lannon, Robert
HEARTS OF FIRE

Lanoux, Victor
SALE DESTIN!

Lanyer, Charles
DELOS ADVENTURE, THE
STEPFATHER, THE

Lanzen, Anita
PRETTY SMART

Lanzetta, Peppe
IL BURBERO

Lapalus, Jean-Francoise
MEMOIRE DES APPARENCES: LA VIE EST UN SONGE

Lapena, Antonio Andres
LAS DOS ORILLAS

LaPere, Ron
HUNTER'S BLOOD

Lapicki, Andrzej
W ZAWIESZENIU

Lapid, Lito
REIGN OF THE RASCALS, THE

Lapikiv, Ivan
UTRO OBRECHENNOGO PRIISKA

Lapin, Isadore
REMEMBERING MEL

Laplace, Victor
CHECHECHELA—UNA CHICA DEL BARRIO
CHORROS
LOS DUENOS DEL SILENCIO
SENTIMIENTOS: MIRTA DE LINIERS A ESTAMBUL

Laprade, Guy
REMEMBERING MEL

Lara, Odete
UM FILM 100% BRAZILEIRO

Larbi, Bouhaddane
ISHTAR

Larbi, Doghmi
ALLAN QUATERMAIN AND THE LOST CITY OF GOLD

Large, Ian
CONCRETE ANGELS

Larick, Dwight
MALIBU BIKINI SHOP, THE

Larionov, Vsevolod
DARK EYES

LaRocque, Paul
BLOODSUCKERS FROM OUTER SPACE

Larranaga, Carlos
REDONDELA

Larrese, Ernesto
STRANGER, THE

Larrion, Roberto
A LOS CUATRO VIENTOS

Larronde, Anita
MISS MARY

Larronde, Annie
AMAZONS

Larroquette, John
BLIND DATE

Larsen, Buster
PELLE EROVRAREN

Larsen, Christine
PA STIGENDE KURS

Larsen, Henrik
WOLF AT THE DOOR, THE

Larsen, Jan Kornum
EPIDEMIC

Larsen, John
PETER VON SCHOLTEN

Larson, Gary
MADE IN HEAVEN

Larson, Wolf
HARD TICKET TO HAWAII

Larsson, Charlotta
MALACCA

Larsson, Henrik
MORE ABOUT THE CHILDREN OF BULLERBY VILLAGE

LaSalle, Emmanuelle
STREET SMART

Lashaway, Lea
WHO'S THAT GIRL

Lashly, James
EXTREME PREJUDICE
LIKE FATHER, LIKE SON

Lasky, Mark
DEATHROW GAMESHOW

Laso, Gloria
LA ESTACION DEL REGRESO

Lass, Barbara
POET'S SILENCE, THE

Lassander, Dagmar
FAMILY, THE
INTERVISTA

Lassen, Bodil
PETER VON SCHOLTEN

Lasser, Louise
NIGHTMARE AT SHADOW WOODS
SURRENDER

Lassick, Sydney
FORTY DAYS OF MUSA DAGH

Lassman, Andrew
MORGAN STEWART'S COMING HOME

Latchaw, Paul
MONSTER IN THE CLOSET

Late, Jason
CREEPSHOW 2

LaTesta, Pam
ORACLE, THE

Latham, Bernard
BOY SOLDIER

Latham, Fiona
DOGS IN SPACE

Latham, Garl
BLOODSUCKERS FROM OUTER SPACE

Latham, John
BLOODSUCKERS FROM OUTER SPACE

Lathouris, Nicos
BELINDA

Latorraca, Ney
ELE, O BOTO

Lattanzi, Matt
ROXANNE

Lattanzio, Anthony
EXTREME PREJUDICE

Latzen, Ellen Hamilton
FATAL ATTRACTION

Lau, Andy
RICH AND FAMOUS

Lau, Carina
PROJECT A—PART II

Laudenbach, Philippe
QUATRE AVENTURES DE REINETTE ET MIRABELLE

Laughlin, Brad
DREAMANIAC

Laughlin, John
SPACE RACE

Laughlin, Ronnie
FOURTH PROTOCOL, THE

Laure, Carole
SWEET COUNTRY

Lauren, Elizabeth
ASSASSINATION

Laurence, Ashley
HELLRAISER

Laurence, Ashley J.
SECRET OF MY SUCCESS, THE

Laurence, Rachael
BUSINESS AS USUAL

Laurence, Rachel
GUNPOWDER

Laurence, Shawn
STREET SMART

Laurenti, Shelly
HIGH SEASON

Laurenzi, Anita
DEVIL IN THE FLESH
REGINA

Lauri, Hannele
LIIAN ISO KEIKKA

Lauri, Hanny
JAAHYVAISET PRESIDENTILLE

Lauria, Dan
STAKEOUT

Laurin, Marie
TALKING WALLS

Lause, Hermann
PENG! DU BIST TOT!

Lausevic, Zarko
OFICIR S RUZOM
OKTOBERFEST

Lausman, Harry
NO DEAD HEROES

Laustela, Matti
A LA ITKE IINES

Lauter, Ed
REVENGE OF THE NERDS II: NERDS IN PARADISE

Lavado, Jose Gregorio
MAS ALLA DEL SILENCIO

Lavalie, Liliana
SLEDY OBOROTNYA

Lavalle-Menard, Robert
MORNING MAN, THE

Lavanant, Dominique
AGENT TROUBLE
SOIGNE TA DROITE

Lavandier, Luc
POUSSIERE D'ANGE
TRAVELLING AVANT

Lavant, Denis
BAD BLOOD

Laven, Brad
HOLLYWOOD SHUFFLE

Lavendre, Lisa
BELLIFRESCHI

Lavi, Amos
HIMMO MELECH YERUSHALAIM

Lavie, Amos
DEADLINE

Lavie, Efrat
WHO'S THAT GIRL

Lavil, Philippe
TANT QU'IL AURA DES FEMMES

LaViolette, Michael
HOLLYWOOD SHUFFLE

Lavrov, Kirill
IZ ZHIZNI NACHALNIKA UGOLOVNOGO ROZYSKA
KRASNAYA STRELA

Law, John Phillip
MOON IN SCORPIO

Lawford, William
WISH YOU WERE HERE

Lawhorn, Delmas
MATEWAN

Lawless, Monica
NAIL GUN MASSACRE

Lawless, Sebrina
NAIL GUN MASSACRE

Lawley, Morgan
RUNNING MAN, THE

Lawlor, Tom
RAWHEAD REX

Lawrence, Bruno
AS TIME GOES BY
INITIATION

Lawrence, Claudia
SOTTO IL RISTORANTE CINESE

Lawrence, Kelly
TALKING WALLS

Lawrence, Marc
BIG EASY, THE

Lawrence, Matthew
PLANES, TRAINS AND AUTOMOBILES

Lawrence, Nicola
LOVECHILD, THE

Lawrence, Samantha
OUT OF ORDER

Lawrence, Sandra
OUT OF ORDER

Lawrence, Shawn
KEEPING TRACK

Lawrence, Toby
BIRDS OF PREY

Laws, Sam
PROJECT X

Lawton, Shaun
DANN IST NICHTS MEHR WIE VORHER

Layada, Hocine
LADY OF THE CAMELIAS

Layna, Jonathan
LHOMME VOILE

Lazaga, Pedro
ASIGNATURA APROBADA

Lazareff, Serge
LIGHTHORSEMEN, THE

Lazaridou, Olia
ARCHANGELOS TOU PATHOUS

Lazaro, Eusebio
LA RUSA
LONG STRIDER

Lazaro, Ronnie
SWEET REVENGE

Lazarova, Detelina
PRIZEMYAVANE

Lazure, Gabrielle
NOYADE INTERDITE

Le, Ngoc
FULL METAL JACKET

Le Bel, Roger
NIGHT ZOO

Le Bell, Gene
P.K. & THE KID

Le Duc, Tito
FRANCESCA

Le Flore, Julius
MONSTER SQUAD, THE

Le Gros, James
FATAL BEAUTY

Le Mat, Paul
HANOI HILTON, THE

Le Noel, Gregory
NO WAY OUT

Le Vaillant, Nigel
PERSONAL SERVICES

Lea, Ron
WILD THING

Leach, Britt
BABY BOOM

Leach, Nigel
EMPIRE OF THE SUN

Leachman, Cloris
HANSEL AND GRETEL
WALK LIKE A MAN

Leahy, Joe
RUNNING MAN, THE

Leal, Alfredo
NARCOTERROR

Leal, Amparo Soler
HAY QUE DESHACER LA CASA

Leal, Ginal
LAPUTA: THE CASTLE IN THE SKY

Leal, Tomas
MUJERES SALVAJES

Leary, H. Burton
MURDER LUST

Leaud, Jean-Pierre
BORAN—ZEIT ZUM ZIELEN

Lebb, Maria
BELIEVERS, THE

Lebedeva, Tatyana
KOORDINATY SMERTI

LeBell, David
NIGHTFORCE

Leboeuf, Marcel
BACH AND BROCCOLI

Leboeuf, Richard
AU REVOIR, LES ENFANTS

Lebor, Stanley
PERSONAL SERVICES

Lebovic, Michael
CONCRETE ANGELS

LeBow, Guy
RADIO DAYS

Lecaillon, Gerard
LASSOCIATION DES MALFAITEURS

Lecchiova, Eva
PROC?

Lech-Maczka, Krystyna
PRZYJACIEL WESOLEGO DIABLA

LeCover, Lisa
CLUB LIFE

Ledden, Edward
ANGUSTIA

Lederer, Andrew
CAMPING DEL TERRORE

Lederman, Caz
BELINDA

Ledford, Robert
O. C. AND STIGGS

Ledoyen, Virginie
LES EXPLOITS DUN JEUNE DON JUAN

Leduc, Valentina
FRIDA

Lee, Adriane
MUTANT HUNT
NECROPOLIS

Lee, Bo-hee
MAN WITH THREE COFFINS, THE

Lee, Bonnie
BLOOD HOOK

Lee, Brandon
LEGACY OF RAGE

Lee, Caroline
DOGS IN SPACE

Lee, Christopher
GIRL, THE
JOCKS
MIO, MOY MIO

Lee, Danny
BROTHERHOOD

Lee, Eric
STEELE JUSTICE

Lee, Jennifer
BELIEVERS, THE

Lee, Jimmy
BLACK DRAGON, THE
WHITE PHANTOM

Lee, John
COMRADES

Lee, Jonna
MONSTER IN THE CLOSET
TURNAROUND

Lee, Juliet D.
STRIKE COMMANDO

Lee, Kaiulani
HELLO AGAIN
STACKING

Lee, Karina
BLOOD TRACKS

Lee, Leo
OVERKILL

Lee, Lorena
PERSONAL SERVICES

Lee, Luann
BEVERLY HILLS COP II

Lee, Norma
LO NEGRO DEL NEGRO

Lee, Rollanda
BIRDS OF PREY

Lee, Rusty
RAISING ARIZONA

Lee, Stephen
DOLLS

Lee, Sunny
OVERKILL

Lee, Timothy
STARLIGHT HOTEL

Lee Heh-Young
TICKET

Lee-Furness, Deborra
BIT PART, THE

Lee-Wilson, Pete
OUT OF ORDER

Leeder, Stephen
SURFER, THE

Leeds, Marcie
NEAR DARK

Leek, Tiiu
WANTED: DEAD OR ALIVE

Leeper, Peter
A LOS CUATRO VIENTOS

Leete, Tony
FULL METAL JACKET

Lefebvre, Jim
P.K. & THE KID

Legan, Mark
MUTANT HUNT

Legault, Raymond
BACH AND BROCCOLI

Legendre, Brigitte
SOUS LE SOLEIL DE SATAN

Leger, Marc
POLICE ACADEMY 4: CITIZENS ON PATROL

Leger, Sophie
LE SOURD DANS LA VILLE

LeGon, Jeni
HOME IS WHERE THE HART IS

Legrand, Julie
PRICK UP YOUR EARS

Legrand, Xavier
AU REVOIR, LES ENFANTS

LeGros, James
NEAR DARK

Leguay, Jean-Claude
LASSOCIATION DES MALFAITEURS
LE MOUSTACHU

Lehart, Frank
CRIME OF HONOR

Lehman, Joanna
BIG BANG, THE

Lehrfeldt, Hans Henrik
WOLF AT THE DOOR, THE

Lei, Lu
BIG PARADE, THE

Leiberman, Rick
VALET GIRLS

Leibovici, Roch
ENNEMIS INTIMES
MEMOIRE DES APPARENCES: LA VIE EST UN SONGE

Leigh, Carrie
BEVERLY HILLS COP II

Leigh, Jennifer Jason
UNDER COVER

Leigh, Spencer
ARIA
LAST OF ENGLAND, THE
PRICK UP YOUR EARS

Leigh-Cooper, Ian
FRENCHMAN'S FARM

Leiner, Aida
VERA

Leitch, Ione Skye
RIVER'S EDGE

Leland, Abigail
WISH YOU WERE HERE

Leland, Beau
NAIL GUN MASSACRE

Leland, Brad
SHY PEOPLE
SQUARE DANCE
UNDER COVER
WINNERS TAKE ALL

Leland, Chloe
WISH YOU WERE HERE

Leland, David
PERSONAL SERVICES

Lelouch, Claude
HAPPY NEW YEAR

Lem, Bob
POLICE ACADEMY 4: CITIZENS ON PATROL

Lemaire, Philippe
LANNEE DES MEDUSES

Lemarquand, Sam
MORNING MAN, THE

LeMat, Paul
P.I. PRIVATE INVESTIGATIONS
P.K. & THE KID

Lemay-Thivierge, Guillaume
LE SOURD DANS LA VILLE
WILD THING

Leme, Guilherme
NIGHT ANGELS

Lemmertz, Julia
COLOR OF DESTINY, THE

Lemmy
EAT THE RICH

Lemoine, Jean-Rene
CAPRICCIO

Lemos, Jose Luis
LA ESTANQUERA DE VALLECAS

Lempert, Robert
HELLO AGAIN

Lena, Eva
SUPERFANTOZZI

Lenaerts, Andre
FALSCH

Lenehan, Nancy
LIKE FATHER, LIKE SON

Lenkov, Alexander
MAGIA CHYORNAYA I BELAYA

Lenoir, Sylvie
BEYOND THERAPY

Lenossi, Lydia
O PARADISSOS ANIGI ME ANTIKLIDI

Lenox, Adriane
FOREVER, LULU

Lentini, Susan
BEVERLY HILLS COP II
BLIND DATE

Lenz, Kay
DEATH WISH 4: THE CRACKDOWN
STRIPPED TO KILL

Lenzi, Giovanna
DELITTI

Leo, Melissa
DEADTIME STORIES

Leo Villanueva
NARCOTERROR

Leon, Annie
HOPE AND GLORY

Leon, Gabriela
MATAR O MORIR

Leon, Maruchi
LAW OF DESIRE

Leonard, Darrell
BLIND DATE

Leonard, J. Richard
BEDROOM WINDOW, THE

Leonard, Lu
PRINCESS ACADEMY, THE

Leonardi, Lisa
MANKILLERS

Leonardou, Sotiria
OH BABYLON

Leong, Al
LETHAL WEAPON
STEELE JUSTICE

Leong, Page
WHITE PHANTOM

Leong, Susan
EMPIRE OF THE SUN

Leonov, Yevgeny
KIN-DZA-DZA

Leonov-Gladyshev, Evgeny
OGNI

Leopold, Douglas
WILD THING

Leotard, Philippe
SI LE SOLEIL NE REVENAIT PAS
TESTAMENT D'UN POETE JUIF ASSASSINE

Lepage, Danielle
KEEPING TRACK

Lepetic, Zvonko
STRATEGIJA SVRAKE
ZIVOT RADNIKA

Lepsa, Petr
CENA MEDU

Lerer, Sergio
EL AMOR ES UNA MUJERGORDA

Lerner, Aida
NIGHT ANGELS

Lerner, Allen
HUNTER'S BLOOD

Lerner, Fred
P.K. & THE KID

Lerner, Ken
MIRACLES
PROJECT X

Lerner, Kenneth
RUNNING MAN, THE

Lerner, Michael
ANGUSTIA

Leroux, Maxime
CROSS
LA PASSION BEATRICE
LE MOUSTACHU
LEVY ET GOLIATH

LeRoy, Gloria
BARFLY

Leroy, Philippe
LA DONNA DEL TRAGHETTO
MONTECARLO GRAN CASINO

Leroy-Beaulieu, Philipine
ARIA

Les, Gordana
WHEELS OF TERROR

Lesley, Nic
ALLAN QUATERMAIN AND THE LOST CITY OF GOLD

Leslie, Bethel
IRONWEED

Lesniak, Matthew
BEYOND THERAPY

Lesnoy, Sergei
V TALOM SNEGE ZVON RUCHIA

Lesser, Bob
SPACE RACE

Lesser, Jamie
FIREHOUSE

Lesser, Robert
MONSTER SQUAD, THE

Lessor, Robert
BIG EASY, THE

Lester, Debi
ALLNIGHTER, THE

Letain, Ed
BIRDS OF PREY

Letelier, Christian
WHO'S THAT GIRL

Lethbridge, Robert
CUSTODY

Lethin, Lori
RETURN TO HORROR HIGH

Lett, Dan
BLUE MONKEY

Letts, Dennis
BLOODSUCKERS FROM OUTER SPACE
SQUARE DANCE

Leung, Man Chi
RICH AND FAMOUS

Leung, Tony
DIXIA QING

Levels, Calvin
ADVENTURES IN BABYSITTING

Leverington, Shelby
MIRACLES

Levin, G. Roy
HOUSE OF GAMES

Levin, Rachel
GABY—A TRUE STORY

Levina, Galina
UTRO OBRECHENNOGO PRIISKA

Levine, Anna
LEONARD PART 6

Levine, Harvey
MANNEQUIN

Levine, Ted
IRONWEED

Levinsky, Ken
RADIO DAYS

Levinsky, Sheri
BEVERLY HILLS COP II

Levinson, Gary J.
EVIL SPAWN

Levitt, Ed
ASSASSINATION
OVER THE TOP

Levitt, Joe
DIRTY LAUNDRY

Levitt, John
EMPIRE STATE

Levitt, Steve
HUNK

Levtova, Maria
NABAT NA RASSVETE

Levtova, Marina
SEKUNDA NA PODVIG

Levy, Dani
SAME TO YOU

Levy, Marty
SLAMDANCE

Levy, Mindy
STUDENT CONFIDENTIAL

Levy, Philippe
LES MENDIANTS

Levy, Shawn
WILD THING

Lew, Joyce
OVERKILL

Lew, Joycelyne
FATAL BEAUTY

Lewis, Anna
NINJA THUNDERBOLT

Lewis, Barbara C.
MORGAN STEWART'S COMING HOME

Lewis, Carl
DIRTY LAUNDRY

Lewis, Charles
EXTREME PREJUDICE

Lewis, Diana
MONSTER SQUAD, THE
SQUEEZE, THE

Lewis, Elbert
SQUARE DANCE

Lewis, Fiona
INNERSPACE

Lewis, Greg
RUNNING MAN, THE

Lewis, Gregory Mark
FLICKS

Lewis, Jeanette
HOME IS WHERE THE HART IS

Lewis, Raan
OUTING, THE

Lewis, Robert
HELLO AGAIN

Lewis, Stephen
OUT OF ORDER
PERSONAL SERVICES

Lewis, Tommy
SLATE, WYN & ME

Lewsen, Charles
EIGHTY FOUR CHARING CROSS ROAD

Lexington, Lucia
FATAL BEAUTY

Lexington, Lucia Nagy
STRIPPED TO KILL

Leysen, Johan
MACBETH

Leza, Concha
EL AMOR DE AHORA

Leza, Conchita
A LOS CUATRO VIENTOS

Lezhava, Giya
SDELKA

Lezzi, Inigo
MAN ON FIRE

Lhermitte, Thierry
F . . . ING FERNAND
LETE DERNIER A TANGER

Lhoste, Vanessa
SPIRALE

Li, Chen Li
HEROIC PIONEERS

Li, Dennis
WRONG COUPLES,THE

Li, Maggie
WRONG COUPLES,THE

Liang, Guo Xue
EMPIRE OF THE SUN

Liapus, Peter
TALKING WALLS

Libby, Brian
CATCH THE HEAT
WINNERS TAKE ALL

Lichtman, Susan
MAKING MR.RIGHT

Liden, Anki
MY LIFE AS A DOG

Lidia, Blanca
TRAGICO TERREMOTO EN MEXICO

Lieber, Shawn
STUDENT CONFIDENTIAL

Lieberman, Bradley
SUMMER CAMP NIGHTMARE

Lieberman, Ken
FIREHOUSE

Liecier, Dulice
LIVING DAYLIGHTS, THE

Liedskalnynova, Antra
POHADKA O MALICKOVI

Liegl, Edgar
TRIUMPH DE GERECHTEN

Liennel, Chantal
JEAN DE FLORETTE
MANON OF THE SPRING

Liepa, Maris
LERMONTOV

Liepinsh, Harry
KONTRUDAR

Lier, Johanna
ALPINE FIRE

Lietha, Walter
JENATSCH

Ligardi, Sebastian
MISSION KILL

Light, David
DOGS IN SPACE
EYE OF THE EAGLE
OPPOSING FORCE
WARRIORS OF THE APOCALYPSE

Light, Shawn
PSYCHOS IN LOVE

Light, Steven
REMEMBERING MEL

Lightfoot, Leonard
OPEN HOUSE

Liguori, Paola
INTERVISTA

Lih-Chyun, Lil
TERRORIZERS, THE

Lilienfeld, Jean-Paul
LETE EN PENTE DOUCE

Lillard, Tom
OUTRAGEOUS FORTUNE

Lillienfeld, Jean-Paul
SALE DESTIN!

Lim, Gary
TRUE COLORS

Lim, Kwan Hi
HARD TICKET TO HAWAII

Lima, Jim Adhi
UN AMOUR A PARIS

Lima, Tony
MANKILLERS

Lin, Ben
SWEET LORRAINE

Lin, Traci
MY LITTLE GIRL

Lincoln, Lar Park
HOUSE TWO: THE SECOND STORY
PRINCESS ACADEMY, THE

Lincovsky, Cipe
A DOS AGUAS

Lind, Gitte
EPIDEMIC

Lind, Jacov
POET'S SILENCE, THE

Lind, Stephen
LOVECHILD, THE

Linda, Boguslaw
BLIND CHANCE
MAGNAT
MASKARADA
MATKA KROLOW
W ZAWIESZENIU

Linda the Dog
STRAIGHT TO HELL

Lindberg, Lorri
HIDING OUT

Lindeberg, Sabine
NEGERKYS & LABRE LARVER

Linden, Ilana
GOOFBALLS

Lindfors, Lill
VENNER FOR ALTID

Lindfors, Viveca
UNFINISHED BUSINESS . . .

Lindgren, Anne
WITCHES OF EASTWICK, THE

Lindhardt, Thure
PELLE EROVRAREN

Lindley, Daryle Ann
MONSTER IN THE CLOSET

Lindley Hathaway, James
AMAZING GRACE AND CHUCK

Lindon, Debbie
EAT THE RICH

Lindon, Vincent
LETE DERNIER A TANGER
MAN IN LOVE, A

Lindquist, Kima
KILLER WORKOUT

Lindstedt, Carl Gustaf
MALACCA

Lindstrom, Marika
NIONDE KOMPANIET

Lindstrom, Mats
LADY OF THE CAMELIAS

Line, Helga
LAW OF DESIRE

Linesky, David
TRAIN OF DREAMS

Ling, Lee Tai
OUTSIDERS, THE

Lingmu, Zhang
LAST EMPEROR, THE

Linguet, Patrice
ARIA

Link, Olivia
TENTAZIONE

Link, Steve
FIRE AND ICE

Linke, Paul
SPACE RACE

Linn, Ivo
REQUIEM

Lionakis, Stelios
TA PAIDIA TIS CHELIDONAS

Liondaris, Renos
FOURTH PROTOCOL, THE

Lionhart, Roselyn
ANGEL HEART

Liotard, Theresa
UN RAGAZZO DI CALABRIA

Lipham, Kent
EXTREME PREJUDICE

Liping, Lu
OLD WELL

Lipinska, Marta
NAD NIEMNEM

Lipkin, Shelly
WHO'S THAT GIRL

Lippe, Steve
MANNEQUIN

Lippin, Renee
RADIO DAYS

Lippman, Chuck
BROADCAST NEWS

Lipscomb, Dennis
AMAZING GRACE AND CHUCK

Lipsky, Lubomir
CIZIM VSTUP POVOLEN

Lirova, Soia
PLIUMBUM, ILI OPASNAIA IGIA

Liserio, Joe
RETURN OF JOSEY WALES, THE

Lish, Becca
WITCHES OF EASTWICK, THE

Lisi, Virna
I LOVE NEW YORK

Liska, Ivan
LADY OF THE CAMELIAS

Liska, Stephen
BEVERLY HILLS COP II

Lissa, Eva
FRANCESCA

Lissek, Leon
PERSONAL SERVICES
WHOOPS APOCALYPSE

Lissi, Joe
FOREVER, LULU

Lister, Renny
PERSONAL SERVICES

Lister, Tom "Tiny"
BEVERLY HILLS COP II
EXTREME PREJUDICE

Litchfield, Matthew
GARDENS OF STONE

Lithgow, John
HARRY AND THE HENDERSONS

Litja, Antti
JAAHYVAISET PRESIDENTILLE
SNOW QUEEN, THE

Little, Eliza
MUTANT HUNT

Little, Gwen
SQUARE DANCE

Little, Michele
SWEET REVENGE

Little, Michelle
MY DEMON LOVER

Little, Rich
HAPPY HOUR

Littlejohn, Gary
NEAR DARK

Liu, Carina
RICH AND FAMOUS

Livanov, Aristarkh
LYUBOVYU ZA LYUBOV

Livingston, Tony
HOLLYWOOD SHUFFLE

Livingstone, Sidney
HEARTS OF FIRE
WARDOGS

Livingstone, Tony
OVERKILL

Lizzani, Flaminia
LA MONACA DIMONZA

Ljungberg, Gustav
MALARPIRATER

Llaneras, Joan
A LOS CUATRO VIENTOS

Llanita, Eddie
NO BLOOD NO SURRENDER

Llansas, Leonor
NOCTURNO AMOR QUE TE VAS

Llaurado, Adolfo
AMOR EN CAMPO MINADO
EL SOCIO DE DIOS

Llewellyn, Suzette
PERSONAL SERVICES
SAMMY AND ROSIE GET LAID

Llewellyn-Jones, Tony
TO MARKET, TOMARKET

Llewelyn, Desmond
LIVING DAYLIGHTS, THE

Llopis, Antonio
CALE

Llorca, Magali
LA BRUTE

Lloyd, Christopher
MIRACLES
WALK LIKE A MAN

Lloyd, Emily
WISH YOU WERE HERE

Lloyd, Frank
AROUND THE WORLD IN EIGHTY WAYS

Lloyd, John Bedford
SWEET LORRAINE
TOUGH GUYS DON'T DANCE

Lloyd, Kathleen
BEST SELLER

Lloyd, Kenneth
MANNEQUIN

Lloyd, Patty
GARBAGE PAIL KIDS MOVIE, THE

Lloyd, Sue
EAT THE RICH

Lo, Brenda
AUTUMN'S TALE, AN

Lo, Lowell
MAGNIFICENT WARRIORS

Lobato, Luis
WINTER TAN, A

Lobo
O. C. AND STIGGS

Lobo, Lida
MASCARA

Locantore, Carmela
LOVE IS A DOG FROM HELL
MASCARA

Locke, Nancy
HOSTAGE

Lockwood, Gary
WILD PAIR, THE

Lodi, Elvira
JUNTOS

Loeb, Caroline
COERS CROISES

Logan, Dan
EL HOMBRE DESNUDO

Logan, Phyllis
KITCHEN TOTO, THE

Logan, Robert
MAN OUTSIDE

Logeais, Franck
LADY OF THE CAMELIAS

Loggia, Robert
BELIEVERS, THE
GABY—A TRUE STORY
HOT PURSUIT
OVER THE TOP

Logothetis, Ilias
TA PAIDIA TIS CHELIDONAS

Lohfert, Carolina
LADY OF THE CAMELIAS

Lohman and Barkley
AMAZON WOMEN ON THE MOON

Lohmann, Lars
BABETTE'S GASTEBUD

Loiri, Vesa-Matti
A LA ITKE IINES
LIIAN ISO KEIKKA
PIKKUPOJAT
UUNO TURHAPURO MUUTTAA MAALLE

Lois Chiles
BROADCAST NEWS

Loisel, Anne
FAMILY BUSINESS

Loisel, Emmanuelle
FAMILY BUSINESS

Loki
DOGS IN SPACE

Lolova, Tatyana
TRINAJSTATA GODENICA NA PRINCA

Lom, Herbert
WHOOPS APOCALYPSE

Lomas, Helen
YEAR MY VOICE BROKE, THE

Lombard, Peter
RADIO DAYS

Lombardo, Gina
P.K. & THE KID

Lombardo, Lynn
P.K. & THE KID

Lomnicki, Tadeusz
BLIND CHANCE

Lone, John
LAST EMPEROR, THE
SHADOWS OF THE PEACOCK

Long, David
BROADCAST NEWS

Long, Jesse
CYCLONE

Long, Jodi
BEDROOM WINDOW, THE

Long, Shelley
HELLO AGAIN
OUTRAGEOUS FORTUNE

Longhi, Anna
UN TASSINARO A NEW YORK

Longo, Tony
IN THE MOOD
WINNERS TAKE ALL

Longrigg, Francesca
EMPIRE OF THE SUN

Longstreth, Emily
AMERICAN DRIVE-IN

Longuemare, Vincent
BEYOND THERAPY

Lonnbro, Harald
MORE ABOUT THE CHILDREN OF BULLERBY VILLAGE

Lookabill, LaGena
CRYSTAL HEART

Lopate, Fran
DEADTIME STORIES

Lopes, Xuxa
FONTE DA SAUDADE

Lopez, Alexandre
MAN ON FIRE

Lopez, Antonio
MI NOMBRE ES GATILLO

Lopez, Chenco
RETURN OF JOSEY WALES, THE

Lopez, Gerry
NORTH SHORE

Lopez, Isabel
DAUGHTERS OF EVE

Lopez, Jennifer
MY LITTLE GIRL

Lopez, Julio
CHECHECHELA—UNA CHICA DEL BARRIO

Lopez, Kamala
BORN IN EAST L.A.

Lopez, Karen
STRIKE COMMANDO

Lopez, Oscar
MISS MARY

Lopez, Patricia
REVENGE OF THE NERDS II: NERDS IN PARADISE

Lopez, Perry
DEATH WISH 4: THE CRACKDOWN

Lopez, Sal
FULL METAL JACKET
MILLION DOLLAR MYSTERY

Lopez Rojas, Eduardo
MISSION KILL

Lopez Vazquez, Jose Luis
HAY QUE DESHACER LA CASA
MY GENERAL

Lora, Gonzalo
MUJERES SALVAJES

Lorca, Isabel Garcia
ANGUSTIA

Lord, Charles N.
MANNEQUIN

Lord, Elizabeth
BELINDA

Lord, Justin
P.I. PRIVATE INVESTIGATIONS

Lorentowicz, Malgotzata
CUDZOZIEMKA

Lorenzo, Manuel
ASIGNATURA APROBADA

Loria, Absalom
SASHSHENNYI FONAR

Lorient, Lisa
PRETTY SMART

Loring, Jeanna
MALIBU BIKINI SHOP, THE

Lorinz, James
STREET TRASH

Lorraine, Carrie
DOLLS

Lorre, Arlene
BLIND DATE

Los Caminantes
RATAS DE LA CIUDAD

Los Galleros
RETO A LA VIDA

Los Tremendos Sepultureros
LA RULETERA

Louca, Samantha
FOREVER, LULU

Loucka, Andreas O.
THIN LINE, THE

Louden, Jay
OPPOSING FORCE

Louganis, Greg
DIRTY LAUNDRY

Lough, Nigel
FULL METAL JACKET

Loughlin, Edmund
I WAS A TEENAGE T.V. TERRORIST

Loughlin, Lori
BACK TO THE BEACH

Louis, John
SUMMER CAMP NIGHTMARE

Louis, Justin
HELLO MARY LOU, PROM NIGHT II

Louis A. Peretz
PROJECT X

Louise, Tina
O. C. AND STIGGS

Lounsberry, Dan
MANNEQUIN

Loureiro, Oswaldo
LEILA DINIZ

Lousberg, Anne Martien
HAVINCK

Love, Courtney
STRAIGHT TO HELL

Love, Darlene
LETHAL WEAPON

Love, Jewel
BELIEVERS, THE

Love, Mark
MANKILLERS

Lovell, George
CRY FREEDOM

Lovitz, Jon
BRAVE LITTLE TOASTER, THE

Low, Betty
EIGHTY FOUR CHARING CROSS ROAD

Lowe, Patrick
SLUMBER PARTY MASSACRE II

Lowe, Rob
SQUARE DANCE

Lowe, Terry
FULL METAL JACKET

Lowell, Carey
DOWN TWISTED

Lowenstein, Robyn
DOGS IN SPACE

Lowrie, Bill
BLOOD HOOK

Loyd, Todd
ERNEST GOES TO CAMP

Loyola, Javier
EL AMOR DE AHORA

Loys, Eduardo
CORRUPCION

Loza, Felipe
A LOS CUATRO VIENTOS

Loza, Fernando
JUANA LA CANTINERA

Loza, Victor
OPERACION MARIJUANA

Lozano, Irma
EL HOMBRE DESNUDO

Lozano, Margarita
GOOD MORNING BABYLON
JEAN DE FLORETTE
MORO AFFAIR, THE

Lozaya, Victor
TRAGICO TERREMOTO EN MEXICO

Lozinska, Slawomira
PAN SAMOCHODZIK I NIESAMOWITY DWOR
RYKOWISKO

Lozoya, Victor
OLOR A MUERTE

Lu, Lisa
LAST EMPEROR, THE

Lu-tong, Zhang
BUDDHA'S LOCK

Lubaszenko, Edward
INNA WYSPA

Lucas, Billy
NIGHTFORCE
RUNNING MAN, THE

Lucas, Carlos
A LOS CUATRO VIENTOS

Lucas, Gail
I WAS A TEENAGE ZOMBIE

Lucas, Luis
JESTER,THE

Lucas, William
WEEDS

Lucchetti, Veriano
MACBETH

Lucerito
DELINCUENTE

Lucero, Enrique
GABY—A TRUE STORY

Lucero, Urbanie
BORN IN EAST L.A.

Luchetti, Alfred
BAR-CEL-ONA
LA SENYORA
MY GENERAL

Luchini, Fabrice
FAMILY BUSINESS
HOTEL DU PARADIS
LES OREILLES ENTRE LES DENTS
QUATRE AVENTURES DE REINETTE ET MIRABELLE

Lucia, Chip
RAGE OF HONOR

Lucia, Ricardo
REDONDELA

Luciani, Mario
MADE IN ARGENTINA

Luciano, Michael
WEEDS

Lucieer, Rudolf
ZJOEK

Luck, Ingolf
PENG! DU BIST TOT!

Lucy
PROJECT X

Ludicke, Peter Rene
SO VIELE TRAUME

Ludlam, Charles
BIG EASY, THE
FOREVER, LULU

Ludovitch, Clayton
MAKING MR.RIGHT

Ludwig, Pamela
PROJECT X

Ludwizanka, Barbara
INNA WYSPA

Luebsen, J.P.
WITCHBOARD

Lugo, Daniel
LA GRAN FIESTA

Lugo, Eduardo
MIRACLES

Lugo, Frank
EXTREME PREJUDICE
SQUEEZE, THE

Lugovoy, V.
VZLOMSHCHIK

Luik, Sulev
REQUIEM

Luis, Jean Emile
NOI UOMINI DURI

Luis, Jose Miguel
WILD THING

Luis —Zuno
PRINCIPAL, THE

Lukaszewicz, Olgierd
MAGNAT
WIERNA RZEKA

Lukats, Andor
TISZTA AMERIKA

Luke
PROJECT X

Luke, Jorge
EL ANSIA DE MATAR
EL HIJO DE PEDRO NAVAJAS
MURIERON A MITAD DEL RIO
RETO A LA VIDA
TODA LA VIDA

Lukofsky, Marla
CARE BEARS ADVENTURE IN WONDERLAND, THE

Lulu
CAPRICCIO
PROJECT X

Lumbly, Carl
BEDROOM WINDOW, THE

Lumbra, Bob
HOUSE OF GAMES

Lumetta, Sal
I WAS A TEENAGE ZOMBIE

Lumsden, David
PRAYER FOR THE DYING, A

Lundblad, Peter
MASTERBLASTER

Lunde, Christine
MANKILLERS

Lundeen, Karen
HOSTAGE SYNDROME

Lundell, Neil
CYCLONE

Lundgren, Dolph
MASTERS OF THE UNIVERSE

Lung, Thomas
SAKURA KILLERS

Lung, Ti
BETTER TOMORROW, A
LEGEND OF WISELY, THE
TRUE COLORS

Lunny, Cora
RAWHEAD REX

Lunoe, Lars
PETER VON SCHOLTEN

Lunson, Lian
DOGS IN SPACE

Lupe, Kendell
ANGEL HEART

Luppi, Federico
STRANGER, THE

Lupus, Peter
ASSASSINATION

Luque, Luis
EL DUENO DEL SOL

Lutes, Eric
PSYCHOS IN LOVE

Luttge, Martin
LITTLE PROSECUTOR, THE
WANNSEE CONFERENCE, THE

Lutz, Joleen
OUTTAKES

Lutz, Linda
DUTCH TREAT
HAPPY HOUR

Lutz, Regine
SAME TO YOU

Lutzky, Dan
ORACLE, THE

Lux, Barbara
RUNNING MAN, THE

Lyden, Mona
MILLION DOLLAR MYSTERY
OVERBOARD

Lykomitros, Nikos
TELEFTAIO STICHIMA

Lyle, David
SUSPECT

Lyle, Emma
YEAR MY VOICE BROKE, THE

Lyn, Timothy
BOY SOLDIER

Lynch, Barry
NIGHTFORCE
RAWHEAD REX

Lynch, Edmund
EAT THE PEACH

Lynch, Jack
EAT THE PEACH

Lynch, Joe
EAT THE PEACH

Lynch, Kym
FRENCHMAN'S FARM

Lynch, Richard
BARBARIANS, THE
BOY SOLDIER
NIGHTFORCE

Lynch, Steve
LIKE FATHER, LIKE SON

Lyne, Allen
MOVING TARGETS

Lynn, Cheryl M.
EMANON

Lynn, Joe
THREE MEN AND A BABY

Lyon, David
EMPIRE STATE

Lyon, Steve
CAMPUS MAN
VALET GIRLS

Lyon, Wendy
HELLO MARY LOU, PROM NIGHT II

Lyons, Katherine
MONSTER IN THE CLOSET

Lyons, Stephen
BOY SOLDIER

Lyons, Susan
GOOD WIFE, THE

Lyras, Dinos
KLIOS

Lyssy, Rolf
JENATSCH

Lysted, Elsa
PLASTPOSEN

Lytton, Debbie
GARBAGE PAIL KIDS MOVIE, THE

Lyubshin, Stanislav
KIN-DZA-DZA
TEMA

Ma, Wo
CHINESE GHOST STORY, A

Maan, Alfred
PRATIGHAAT

Maas, Hidde
DE RATELRAT

Maas, Sybil
EMPIRE OF THE SUN

Mac's Wife
HOPE AND GLORY

Maccarone, Tom
CONCRETE ANGELS

Macchia, John
MIRACLES

Macdonald, Jessica
WITCHES OF EASTWICK, THE

MacDonald, William Forrest
BIG TOWN, THE

MacDougall, Julia
SLATE, WYN & ME

Mace, Greg
OUTRAGEOUS FORTUNE

MacEachern, Robin
NOWHERE TO HIDE

MacGowan, Shane
STRAIGHT TO HELL

MacGregor, Eduardo
CALE

MacGregor, Jeff
SPACEBALLS
WINNERS TAKE ALL

MacGuire, Gerard
SURFER, THE

Machacek, Miroslav
CHOBOTNICE Z II. PATRA
WOLF'S HOLE

Machackova, Vladislava
PROC?

Machado, Mario
ROBOCOP

Machalica, Henry
WIERNA RZEKA

Machalica, Piotr
BOHATERROKU

Machart, Maria
BLOOD SISTERS

Macherelli, Luciano
GOOD MORNING BABYLON

Machida, Machizo
ROBINSON NO NIWA

Macht, Stephen
MONSTER SQUAD, THE

MacHugh, Doug
HOUSE TWO: THE SECOND STORY

Macias, David
MANKILLERS
NIGHTFORCE

Macina, Anne
FAMILY BUSINESS

Mack, Gene
SUSPECT

Mackay, Angus
PRICK UP YOUR EARS

Mackay, Danette
MORNING MAN, THE

Mackay, David
FAMILY VIEWING

MacKay, Don
STEPFATHER, THE

Mackay, Don
MALONE

Mackay, John
I WAS A TEENAGE T.V. TERRORIST

MacKay, Michael
MONSTER SQUAD, THE

MacKenzie, Peter
FIREHOUSE

Mackenzie, Peter
GOOD MORNING, VIETNAM

Mackerron, Calvin
KONZERT FUR DIE RECHTE HAND

Mackintosh, Steven
PRICK UP YOUR EARS

Macklin, Albert
DATE WITH AN ANGEL

Mackriel, Peter
WHISTLE BLOWER, THE

MacLachlan, Andrew
PERSONAL SERVICES

MacLachlan, Janet
BIG SHOTS

MacLachlan, Kyle
HIDDEN, THE

MacLachlan, Ron
GARBAGE PAIL KIDS MOVIE, THE

MacLean, Warren
OPPOSING FORCE

MacLeod, Jonathan
GOOD MORNING, VIETNAM

MacNamara, Pat
SQUEEZE, THE

Macnee, Patrick
SHADEY

MacNeill, Peter
HOUSEKEEPER, THE
MacNicol, Peter
HEAT
MacPhan, Eric
SLATE, WYN & ME
MacPherson, Walt
TIN MEN
Macy, W.H.
HOUSE OF GAMES
RADIO DAYS
Madanes, Fernando
EN EL NOMBRE DEL HIJO
Madaras, Jozsef
SZORNYEK EVADJA
Madaula, Ramon
EL GRAN SERAFIN
Madden, Cassie
I WAS A TEENAGE ZOMBIE
Madden, John
P.K. & THE KID
Madhavan
UPPU
Madhavi
LOHA
Madia, Stefano
CAMPING DEL TERRORE
Madigan, Amy
NOWHERE TO HIDE
Madigan, Sean
STRAIGHT TO HELL
Madigan, Susan
SPACE RACE
Madonna
WHO'S THAT GIRL
Madruga, Marta
SUFRE MAMON
Madruga, Teresa
MIENTRAS HAYA LUZ
Madsen, Michael
KILLING TIME, THE
Madsen, Virginia
SLAMDANCE
ZOMBIE HIGH
Maeda, Gin
TORA-SAN'S BLUEBIRD FANTASY
Maes, Alfons
MASCARA
Maes, Tove
HIP, HIP, HURRA!
SIDSTE AKT
Magalashvili, Edisher
NEYLONOVAYA YOLKA
Magalhaes, Pedro Ayres
DUMA VEZ POR TODAS
Magali, Marina
STRANGER, THE
Magana, Jose
LA RULETERA
TODA LA VIDA
Magarian, Andrew
SQUEEZE, THE
Magdaleno, Maria
BELIEVERS, THE
Magdalone, Giuseppe
DA NNUNZIO
Magerman, William
RADIO DAYS
Maginnis, Chris
BIRDS OF PREY
Magli, Valeria
LA CODA DEL DIAVOLO
Magnuson, Ann
MAKING MR.RIGHT
Magnusson, Leif
EPIDEMIC
Magnusson, Robert
MANKILLERS
Magoia, Elena
LA CODA DEL DIAVOLO
Magre, Judith
SPIRALE
Magruder, Bob
RETURN OF JOSEY WALES, THE
Maguire, George
LEONARD PART 6
Maguire, Roberta
HOUSE OF GAMES
Maher, Bill
HOUSE TWO: THE SECOND STORY
Maher, Christopher
MANNEQUIN
Maheu, Gilles
NIGHT ZOO
Mahinda, Edwin
KITCHEN TOTO, THE
Mahler, Norbert
FLYER, THE
Mahoney, John
MOONSTRUCK
SUSPECT
TIN MEN
Mahoney, Louis
CRY FREEDOM
Maier, David
LEONARD PART 6
Maier, Tom
IN THE MOOD
Maija-Liisa Peuhu.
AKALLINEN MIES
Maiker, Cheryl
OUT OF ORDER
Maillan, Jacqueline
LA VIE DISSOLUE DE GERARD FLOQUE
Maillet, Christian
FALSCH
Mainardi, Giovanna
DA NNUNZIO
Maitland, Marne
BELLY OF AN ARCHITECT, THE
Majchrizak, Gary
PRETTYKILL
Majo, Enric
LA RUBIA DEL BAR
Majouga
RODNIK DLIA ZHAZHDUSHCHIKH
Majovsek, Damir
GIRL, THE
Majsaks, Egon
POHADKA O MALICKOVI
Maka, Karl
THIRTY MILLION RUSH, THE
Maka, Tomas
DISCOPRIBEH
Makaro, J.J.
STAKEOUT
Makarova, Inna
LERMONTOV
Makela, Taneli
LAIN ULKOPUOLELLA
Makhamatdinov, Fakhridin
MIRAZHI LYUBRI
Makharadze, Avtandil
REPENTANCE
Maki, Seppo
TILINTEKO
Makondo, Mawa
CRY FREEDOM
Maksimovic, Dragan
ZIVOT RADNIKA
Malahide, Patrick
MONTH IN THE COUNTRY, A
Malamed, Fred
ISHTAR
Malaon, Tuti Indra
IBUNDA
Malavoy, Christophe
LASSOCIATION DES MALFAITEURS
LE CRI DU HIBOU
Malcolm, Christopher
EAT THE RICH
WHOOPS APOCALYPSE
Malden, Karl
NUTS
Maldonado, Javier
LA ESTACION DEL REGRESO
Maleckas, George
DOGS IN SPACE
Maleczech, Ruth
ANNA
Malet, Laurent
CHARLIE DINGO
Malhotra, Deo
PRATIGHAAT
Malik, Art
LIVING DAYLIGHTS, THE
Malin, Emily
RAISING ARIZONA
Malin, Melanie
RAISING ARIZONA
Malina, Judith
CHINA GIRL
RADIO DAYS
SECRET OF MY SUCCESS, THE
Malini, Hema
ANJAAM
Malka, Dalia
KOL AHAVOTAI
Malkin, Sam
BIG TOWN, THE
DEAD OF WINTER
Malkovich, John
EMPIRE OF THE SUN
GLASS MENAGERIE, THE
MAKING MR.RIGHT
Mallamaci, Jean
FALSCH
Malland, Alf
ETTER RUBICON
Mallard, Matt
NECROPOLIS
Mallarino, Victor
MANON
Mallawarachchi, Swarna
MALDENIYESIMION
Malle, Jade
MAN ON FIRE
Malle, Martine
MAN ON FIRE
Mallette, Perry
THOU SHALT NOT KILL . . . EXCEPT
Mallia, Ed
MUTANT HUNT
Mallia, Eddie
NECROPOLIS
Mallia, Edward
ROBOT HOLOCAUST
Mallinen, Sari
A LA ITKE IINES
Mallo, Santiago
AMAZONS
Mallorie, Jill
MAKING MR.RIGHT
Mallstrom, Sofie
SEPPAN
Mally, Anita
WANNSEE CONFERENCE, THE
Malm, Mona
NAGRA SOMMARKVALLAR PA JORDEN
Malmsjo, Jan
JIM OCH PIRATERNA BLOM
Malmuth, Bruce
HAPPY NEW YEAR
Malo, Jean-Pierre
LE SOLITAIRE
Malone, Leonard
PETER VON SCHOLTEN
Malone, Mark
DEAD OF WINTER
Maloney, John Patrick
BEDROOM WINDOW, THE
Malonzo, Rey
EYE OF THE EAGLE
Malphus, Dwayne
DIRTY DANCING
Malvoisin, Patricia
LE SOLITAIRE
Maly, Arturo
STRANGER, THE
Maly, Xavier
UN AMOUR A PARIS
Malysheva, Irina
SON V RUKU, ILI CHEMODON
Mamalev, Georgi
PRIZEMYAVANE
TRINAJSTATA GODENICA NA PRINCA
Mamberti, Claudio
CIDADE OCULTA
NIGHT ANGELS
Mamet, David
BLACK WIDOW
Mammooty
KATHAKKU PINNIL
Man, Alex
BROTHERHOOD
KILLER'S NOCTURNE
RICH AND FAMOUS
STORY OF DR. SUN YAT-SEN, THE
Man, Wong
AUTUMN'S TALE, AN

Manafarov, Fakhretdin
PROSHAL ZELEN LETA

Manas, Achero
LA GUERRA DE LOS LOCOS

Manasi
PUDHCHE PAOL

Manbetov, Murat
TAYNAYA PROGULKA

Manchan, Noel
NO WAY OUT

Mancil, Charmaine
SUMMER HEAT

Mancini, Al
DELOS ADVENTURE, THE

Mancini, Ric
PENITENTIARY III

Mandakini
BHARGAVA RAMUDU
LOHA
PYAR KARKE DEKHO

Mandel, Howie
WALK LIKE A MAN

Mandel, Jonathan
FIREHOUSE

Mandelik, Gil
PROJECT X

Mandic, Miroslav
VEC VIDJENO

Mandic, Veljko
DIE VERLIEBTEN

Mandoki, Dr. Juan
GABY—A TRUE STORY

Maneri, Luisa
CAMPING DEL TERRORE
CHI C'E C'E
RENEGADE, UN OSSO TROPPO DURO

Manesh, Masha
CHECKPOINT

Manesse, Gaspard
AU REVOIR, LES ENFANTS

Manesse, Philippe
MON BEL AMOUR, MA DECHIRURE

Manferdini, Gabriel
LADY OF THE CAMELIAS

Manfredi, John
THOU SHALT NOT KILL . . . EXCEPT

Manfredi, Nino
I PICARI

Manfredi, Roberta
HELSINKI NAPOLI—ALL NIGHT LONG

Mangan, Christopher
GOOD MORNING, VIETNAM

Mangano, Silvana
DARK EYES

Mangler, Greg
O. C. AND STIGGS

Mango, Alec
GOTHIC

Maniati, Eleni
IKONA ENOS MYTHIKOU PROSOPOU

Maniatis, Michael
ANGELOS

Manibog, Myra
DAUGHTERS OF EVE

Manion, Robert
IRONWEED

Mankuma, Blu
MALONE
STEPFATHER, THE

Mann, Jessica Leigh
SUMMER HEAT

Mann, Nathalie
TRAVELLING AVANT

Mannain, Brian
RADIO DAYS

Manners, Zeek
BARFLY

Mannger, John
SUMMER CAMP NIGHTMARE

Manni, Tarmo
JAAHYVAISET PRESIDENTILLE

Manni, Vic
BEVERLY HILLS COP II

Manning, Daniel J.
JAWS: THE REVENGE

Manning, Jeffrey
HIDING OUT

Manning, Peter
FOURTH PROTOCOL, THE

Mano, Dominique
ARIA

Manoura, Agape
FAKELOS POLK STON AERA

Manriquez, Silvia
ARQUIESTA EMILIO VARELA
FORAJIDOS EN LA MIRA

Manroe, Darlene
MANKILLERS

Manser, Kevin
YEAR MY VOICE BROKE, THE

Mansfield, Elizabeth
T. DAN SMITH

Manso, Kwabena
ARIA

Manso, Leonor
MADE IN ARGENTINA

Manson, Helena
AGENT TROUBLE

Manson, Herve
AGENT TROUBLE

Mansour, Muneer
MANKILLERS

Mantegna, Joe
CRITICAL CONDITION
HOUSE OF GAMES
SUSPECT
WEEDS

Mantel, Michael A.
MATEWAN

Manthopoulos, Aias
KLIOS

Manuel
EL MOFLES Y LOS MECANICOS
LAPUTA: THE CASTLE IN THE SKY
TODA LA VIDA
ENTRE FICHERAS ANDA EL DIABLO

Manuel, Denis
GRAND GUIGNOL

Manuel, Luis
P.I. PRIVATE INVESTIGATIONS

Manukyan, Guzh
PESN PROSHEDSHIKH DNEY

Manville, Lesley
HIGH SEASON

Manville, Tammy
OUTRAGEOUS FORTUNE

Manzano, Don Miguel
LA RULETERA

Manzano, Jose Luis
LA ESTANQUERA DE VALLECAS

Manzano, Miguel
OLOR A MUERTE

Manzel, Dagmar
DER JUNGE MIT DEM GROSSEN SCHWARZEN HUND
SO VIELE TRAUME

Manzetti, Gerard
LES OREILLES ENTRE LES DENTS

Manzone, Nino
QUARTIERE

Marando, Tony
SUMMER HEAT

Maraszek, Natasza
LE JEUNE MAGICIEN

Marcel, James
NIGHTFORCE

Marcell, Joseph
CRY FREEDOM

Marchand, Corinne
ATTENTION BANDITS

Marchand, Guy
CHARLIE DINGO
FAMILY BUSINESS
GRAND GUIGNOL
LA RUMBA
LETE EN PENTE DOUCE
NOYADE INTERDITE

Marchand, Nancy
FROM THE HIP

Marchegiani, Fiorenza
DA NNUNZIO

Marcheluk, Miroslawa
INNA WYSPA
PRYWATNE SLEDZTWO

Marchena, Eddy
ODYSSEE D'AMOUR

Marchesi, Franca
DOLCE ASSENZA

Marchetti, Alessandro
DOLCE ASSENZA

Marchi, Elio
EL AMOR ES UNA MUJERGORDA

Marchica, Ray
RADIO DAYS

Marchisio, Maurizio
DELIZIA

Marciano, Harry
BACH AND BROCCOLI

Marcilisova, Milena
CIZIM VSTUP POVOLEN

Marconato, Elio
GOOD MORNING BABYLON

Marcondes, Elaine
ANJOS DO ARRABALDE

Marconi, Saverio
IL RAGAZZO DI EBALUS

Marcotulli, Bruno
MOON IN SCORPIO

Marcovicci, Andrea
SOMEONE TO LOVE

Marcucci, Ornella
LESTATE STA FINENDO

Marcucci, Roberta
IL LUPO DI MARE

Marcus, Bill
BLIND DATE
OUTRAGEOUS FORTUNE

Mardirosian, Tom
ROSARY MURDERS, THE

Mardis, Bobby
HOLLYWOOD SHUFFLE

Maredza, Claude
CRY FREEDOM

Marelli, Marco
SOTTO IL RISTORANTE CINESE

Mares, Vaclav
PRATELE BERMUDSKEHO TROJUHELNIKU

Marga, Iris
MISS MARY

Margittai, Agi
DOKTOR MINORKA VIDOR NAGY NAPJA

Margo, Larry
MALIBU BIKINI SHOP, THE

Margolin, Bill
RUNNING MAN, THE

Margolis, Mark
BEDROOM WINDOW, THE
SECRET OF MY SUCCESS, THE

Margolyes, Miriam
LITTLE DORRIT

Margulies, David
ISHTAR
MAGIC STICKS

Mari, Sheella
NO BLOOD NO SURRENDER

Mari's Husband
DIVINAS PALABRAS

Maria, Patricia
YO, EL EJECUTOR

Marichal, Poly
NI DE AQUI, NI DE ALLA

Mariche, Reyna Lobato
WINTER TAN, A

Maricic, Andrija
WHEELS OF TERROR

Marie, Jeanne
IF LOOKS COULD KILL
WIMPS

Marie, Kathleena
OVERKILL

Marie, Rose
WITCHBOARD

Marielle, Jean-Pierre
LES DEUX CROCODILES
LES MOIS D'AVRIL SONT MEURTRIERS

Marin, Cheech
BORN IN EAST L.A.
FATAL BEAUTY

Marin, Luis
EL LUTE—CAMINA O REVIENTA
LA GUERRA DE LOS LOCOS

Marinchenko, K.
KOROTKIE VSTRECHI

Marine, Jeanne
LES OREILLES ENTRE LES DENTS

Marini, Marilu
FUEGOS

Marino, Benny
P.K. & THE KID

Marino, Kenny
FOREVER, LULU
Marion, Jean Marie
UNA DONNA DA SCOPRIRE
Marius, Robert
GET THE TERRORISTS
HOSTAGE SYNDROME
WARRIORS OF THE APOCALYPSE
Marjac, Rene
MASQUES
Marjanovic, Dragana
MAGIC SNOWMAN, THE
Marjanski, Adam
NAD NIEMNEM
Mark, Chui-Lin
STREET SMART
Mark Brignal
PRICK UP YOUR EARS
Mark Brown
COMRADES
Mark Payton
MAURICE
Markee, Dwayne
BROADCAST NEWS
Markey, Jane
AROUND THE WORLD IN EIGHTY WAYS
Markham, Monte
HOT PURSUIT
Markland, Ted
BEST SELLER
Markopoulos, K.
I KEKARMENI
Markos, Andreas
PERSONAL SERVICES
Markova, Rimma
KAZHDYY OKHOTNIK ZHELAET ZNAT
OBRYV
Markovic, Rade
GLI OCCHIALI D'ORO
Marks, William E.
JAWS: THE REVENGE
Marloe, Nikki Murdock
LADIES OF THE LOTUS
Marlow, Lorrie
HOLLYWOOD SHUFFLE
Marlowe, William
CRY FREEDOM
Marner, Carmela
BEAUTY AND THE BEAST
Marnitz, Rudolf W.
STADTRAND
Maroney, Kelli
BIG BAD MAMA II
ZERO BOYS, THE
Marot, Irene
LOVECHILD, THE
Marquand, Serge
GRAND GUIGNOL
Marquand, Yann
LES MENDIANTS
Marques, Ezequias
A DANCA DOS BONECOS
Marques, Luisa
JESTER,THE
Marquez, Alfredo Garcia
UN SABADO MAS
Marquez, Ireida
JUANA LA CANTINERA
Marquez, Pablo
RETO A LA VIDA
Marquis, Phil
WHOOPS APOCALYPSE
Marra, Armando
CAPRICCIO
Marrale, Jorge
SINFIN, LA MUERTA NO ES NINGUNA SOLUCION
Marrian, Libra
BEDROOM WINDOW, THE
Marriott, Sylvia
EMPIRE OF THE SUN
Mars, Kenneth
RADIO DAYS
Mars, Michele
DEADTIME STORIES
Marsac, Laure
LES FOUS DE BASSAN
LHOMME VOILE
Marsalis, Branford
THROW MOMMA FROM THE TRAIN
Marschall, Marita
DEADLINE
Marsh, Lenny
DIXIELAND DAIMYO
Marsh, Matthew
FOURTH PROTOCOL, THE
Marsh, Michele
EVIL TOWN
Marsh, Peggy
CRY FREEDOM
Marsh, Tobi
BEDROOM WINDOW, THE
Marsh, Walter
MALONE
Marshal, Jennifer
MANKILLERS
Marshall, Claire
HOSTAGE
Marshall, Don
BIRDS OF PREY
Marshall, E.G.
LA GRAN FIESTA
Marshall, Meri D.
VALET GIRLS
Marshall, Mike
CLUB DE RENCONTRES
Marshall, Scott
OVERBOARD
Marshall, Tonie
COERS CROISES
Marshall, William
AMAZON WOMEN ON THE MOON
Marsillach, Cristina
OPERA
Marsina, Antonio
TENTAZIONE
UNA DONNA DA SCOPRIRE
Marson, Aileen
ALLAN QUATERMAIN AND THE LOST CITY OF GOLD
Marston, Jack
EMANON
Marta, Darcy
THREE BEWILDERED PEOPLE IN THE NIGHT
Martana, Bob
UNTOUCHABLES, THE
Marteau, Henri
POUSSIERE D'ANGE
Martel, K.C.
WHITE WATER SUMMER
Martell, Alan
HUNTED, THE
Martell, Denise
KILLER WORKOUT
Martell, Leon
MADE IN HEAVEN
Martelli, Bruna
DA NNUNZIO
Martelli, Isabella
CARTOLINE ITALIANE
Martica, Maria
TA PAIDIA TIS CHELIDONAS
Martin, Billy
SLAUGHTER HIGH
Martin, Dave
ROBOT HOLOCAUST
Martin, Garry
WHOOPS APOCALYPSE
Martin, Harvey
AMAZING GRACE AND CHUCK
Martin, Helen
HOLLYWOOD SHUFFLE
Martin, James
JAWS: THE REVENGE
Martin, Jim
I WAS A TEENAGE ZOMBIE
Martin, John Ara
HAPPY HOUR
Martin, Lucas
YEAR OF AWAKENING, THE
Martin, Mayeva
CHECKPOINT
Martin, Mel
BUSINESS AS USUAL
Martin, Melissa
VIDEO DEAD, THE
Martin, Michael
NIGHTFORCE
Martin, Mike
NIGHTFORCE
Martin, Monique
BELIEVERS, THE
Martin, Murray
T. DAN SMITH
Martin, Nan
NIGHTMARE ON ELM STREET 3: DREAM WARRIORS, A
Martin, Nick
ESCAPES
Martin, Pamela Sue
FLICKS
Martin, Pepe
LA RUBIA DEL BAR
Martin, Pepper
GHOST FEVER
RETURN TO HORROR HIGH
Martin, Percy
ANGEL HEART
Martin, Remi
FAMILY BUSINESS
MISS MONA
Martin, Sandy
BARFLY
Martin, Steve
PLANES, TRAINS AND AUTOMOBILES
ROXANNE
Martin, Trevor
THREE KINDS OF HEAT
Martin, Vincent
CHAMP D'HONNEUR
FAMILY BUSINESS
Martin, Wally
LAST STRAW, THE
STREET SMART
WILD THING
Martinez, Adalberto
EL HIJO DE PEDRO NAVAJAS
Martinez, Alma
BORN IN EAST L.A.
Martinez, Arturo
EL ANSIA DE MATAR
LO NEGRO DEL NEGRO
YERBA SANGRIENTE
Martinez, Benita
COMMANDO SQUAD
Martinez, Don Arturo
LO NEGRO DEL NEGRO
Martinez, Jorge
CATCH THE HEAT
Martinez, Leo
SWEET REVENGE
Martinez, Lucy
CHRONICLE OF A DEATH FORETOLD
Martinez, Mike
ESCAPES
Martinez, Mikel
A LOS CUATRO VIENTOS
Martinez, Nacho
LAW OF DESIRE
Martinez, Oscar
LOS DUENOS DEL SILENCIO
Martinez, Patrice
WALK ON THE MOON, A
Martinez, Reynaldo
MI NOMBRE ES GATILLO
Martinez, Sonia
LOS INVITADOS
Martinez, Veronica Hortensia
LA RULETERA
Martinez "Resortes", Adalberto
MIRACLES
Martinez G., Efren
RETO A LA VIDA
Martins, Josmar
ANJOS DO ARRABALDE
Martinsen, Dick
BELIEVERS, THE
Martinsen, Hilde Nyeggen
IS-SLOTTET
Martinson, Mirdza
TAYNAYA PROGULKA
Martinsone, Mirdza
MY OBVINYAEM
MY OBVINYAEM
OKHOTA NA DRAKONA
Martinsonova, Mirdza
POHADKA O MALICKOVI

Martirosian, Karlos
SASHSHENNYI FONAR

Marton Jr., Antal
TISZTA AMERIKA

Martucci, Ovidio
NOI UOMINI DURI

Marty, Albert
AMAZONS

Marty, Alberto
MISS MARY

Martyn, Lorna
NO WAY OUT

Martynov, Alexander
DIKIY KHMEL

Martynov, Andrei
SEKUNDA NA PODVIG

Martynov, Sergey
LYUBOVYU ZA LYUBOV

Marx, Horst-Gunter
DIE VERLIEBTEN

Mary Pillot
TRESPASSES

Marzo, Claudio
FONTE DA SAUDADE

Marzo, Pedro
LA VIDA ALEGRE

Masabet, Pablo
POR LOS CAMINOS VERDES

Mascarino, Pierrino
LETS GET HARRY

Masci, Robert P.
BLOOD SISTERS

Masciari, Eugenio
LA DONNA DEL TRAGHETTO

Mascolo, Joe
HEAT

Mase, Marino
BELLY OF AN ARCHITECT, THE

Mashaw, Sue
EVIL SPAWN

Masi, Mike
MANKILLERS

Masliah, Laurence
SOIGNE TA DROITE

Mason, Cilla
T. DAN SMITH

Mason, Eric
BANZAI RUNNER

Mason, Hilary
DOLLS

Mason, Raymond
HEARTS OF FIRE

Masraawi, Nader
DEADLINE

Masrevery, Jean
UN RAGAZZO DI CALABRIA

Masri, George
ISHTAR

Massey, Walter
MORNING MAN, THE

Massiel
LA VIDA ALEGRE

Masson, Han
LE SOURD DANS LA VILLE

Massoumi, Parvaneh
CAPTAIN KHORSHID

Master Deepak
PANDAVAPURAM

Masters, Ben
MAKING MR.RIGHT

Masters, Bill
FOREVER, LULU

Masters, Chris
WARDOGS

Masterson, Mary Stuart
GARDENS OF STONE
MY LITTLE GIRL
SOME KIND OF WONDERFUL

Masterson, Peter
GARDENS OF STONE

Masterson, Roxanne
HAPPY HOUR

Masterton, Susie
RUNNING FROM THE GUNS

Mastrantonio, Mary Elizabeth
SLAMDANCE

Mastroianni, Federica
IL GRANDE BLEK

Mastroianni, Marcello
DARK EYES
INTERVISTA

Masur, Richard
BELIEVERS, THE
WALKER

Masyulis, Algimantas
CHYORNAYA STRELA

Matalon, Motz
LO SAM ZAYIN

Matalova, Eva
CIZIM VSTUP POVOLEN

Matamoros, Diego
BIG TOWN, THE

Matchanov, Bakhram
GRUBAYA POSADKA

Matemavi, Walter
CRY FREEDOM

Mateshko, Olga
OBVINYAETSYA SVADBA

Mateu, Sergei
BALADA DA PRAIA DOS CAES

Mateu, Sergi
CHRONICLE OF A DEATH FORETOLD
LA PLAYA DE LOS PERROS

Mathambo, Sam
CRY FREEDOM

Mather, Dibbs
SHADOWS OF THE PEACOCK

Matheron, Marie
LE GRAND CHEMIN

Mathers, James
ARIA

Mathers, Jerry
BACK TO THE BEACH

Matheson, Lex
STARLIGHT HOTEL

Mathews, Alex
BROADCAST NEWS

Mathews, Louis
WALKER

Mathews, Thom
DOWN TWISTED

Mathews, Walter
MISSION KILL

Mathias, Bunty
ARIA

Mathias, Marthus
BESAME MUCHO

Mathou, Jacques
LE MOUSTACHU
LETE EN PENTE DOUCE

Mathus, Paul
PRETTY SMART

Mathwick, Nick
GARDENS OF STONE

Mativenga, Kimpton
CRY FREEDOM

Matlin, Marlee
WALKER

Matshikiza, John
CRY FREEDOM

Matsui, Kazuyo
TAXING WOMAN, A

Matsumoto, Koshiro
FINAL TAKE: THE GOLDEN AGE OF MOVIES

Matsumura, Fuyukaze
TOKYO BLACKOUT

Matsuzaka, Keiko
FINAL TAKE: THE GOLDEN AGE OF MOVIES
KATAKU NO HITO

Mattarella, Lea
ILLUMINAZIONI

Mattausch, Dietrich
WANNSEE CONFERENCE, THE

Mattei, Danilo
MORO AFFAIR, THE

Matteo
CAPRICCIO

Matteson, Pam
MILLION DOLLAR MYSTERY

Matthews, Dakin
LIKE FATHER, LIKE SON
NUTS

Matthews, Fritz
DEADLY PREY
KILLER WORKOUT

Matthews, Lorraine
BIG SHOTS

Matthews, Sue
LIVING ON TOKYO TIME

Matthews, Viki
BIG TOWN, THE

Mattick, Michael
SUMMER HEAT

Mattingly, Caleb
ESCAPES

Mattingly, Matthew
ESCAPES

Mattson, Denver
MONSTER SQUAD, THE

Mattsson, Per
NAGRA SOMMARKVALLAR PA JORDEN

Matuszak, John
P.K. & THE KID

Maughan, Monica
BACHELOR GIRL

Maura, Carmen
LAW OF DESIRE

Maureen O'Sullivan
STRANDED

Maurel, Jean
JEAN DE FLORETTE
MANON OF THE SPRING

Maurer, Howie
ARIA

Mauri, Paco
MISSION KILL

Mauriello, Giovani
MAN ON FIRE

Mauro, David
FORTY DAYS OF MUSA DAGH

Maurstad, Mari
PA STIGENDE KURS

Maurstad, Toralv
ETTER RUBICON

Maury, Marc
LE MIRACULE

Mavromati, Barbara
DOXOBUS

Maxakova, Lyudmila
POEZDKI NA STAROM AVTOMOBILE

Maxwell, Carol
KILLER WORKOUT

May, Dick
GOOD WIFE, THE

May, Donald
DIRTY LAUNDRY
O. C. AND STIGGS

May, Lenora
HOUSE TWO: THE SECOND STORY

May, Martin
FLYER, THE

May, Mathilda
LA VIE DISSOLUE DE GERARD FLOQUE
LE CRI DU HIBOU

Maya, Elsa
ROBACHICOS

Mayall, Rik
EAT THE RICH
MORE BAD NEWS
WHOOPS APOCALYPSE

Mayer, Frederic
CHAMP D'HONNEUR

Mayers, Patricia
MUJERES SALVAJES

Mayes, Judith
SULLIVAN'S PAVILION

Maylin, Caroline
LADY OF THE CAMELIAS

Maynard, Isaac
BOY SOLDIER

Maynard, Julian
DUMA VEZ POR TODAS

Maynard, Mimi
TALKING WALLS

Maynard, Ruth
WITCHES OF EASTWICK, THE

Mayne, Belinda
FATAL BEAUTY

Mayorano, Jorge
EL HOMBRE DE LA DEUDA EXTERNA

Mayorova, Yelena
ZINA-ZINULYA

Maza, Bob
GROUND ZERO

Mazer, Emilia
SENTIMIENTOS: MIRTA DE LINIERS A ESTAMBUL

Mazhindu, Tichatonga
CRY FREEDOM

Mazilli, Wilma
BARBARIANS, THE

Mazin, Stan
ARIA

Mazo, Aitor
A LOS CUATRO VIENTOS

Mazon, Janusz
LADY OF THE CAMELIAS

Mazurowna, Ernestine
JEAN DE FLORETTE

Mazzucca, Sylvio
BESAME MUCHO

McAlinden, Thomas
NECROPOLIS

McAlinden, Timothy
NECROPOLIS

McAnally, Ray
EMPIRE STATE
FOURTH PROTOCOL, THE
SICILIAN, THE
WHITE MISCHIEF

McArthur, Kimberly
SLUMBER PARTY MASSACRE II

McBeath, Tom
MALONE

McCabe, Michael
BANZAI RUNNER

McCafferty, John
DEATHROW GAMESHOW

McCallany, Holt
CREEPSHOW 2

McCallum, David
WIND, THE

McCallum, Paul
ASSASSINATION

McCamy, Kate
PSYCHOS IN LOVE

McCann, Donal
BUDAWANNY
DEAD, THE
RAWHEAD REX

McCann, John
HIDDEN, THE

McCann, Sean
BIG TOWN, THE

McCannon, Mark
LIKE FATHER, LIKE SON

McCants, Reed R.
PROJECT X

McCardle, Frank
FULL METAL JACKET

McCarter, Brooke
LOST BOYS, THE

McCarthur, Gerrard
LAST OF ENGLAND, THE

McCarthy, Andrew
LESS THAN ZERO
MANNEQUIN
WAITING FOR THE MOON

McCarthy, Frank
SUMMER SCHOOL

McCarthy, Kevin
HOSTAGE
INNERSPACE

McCarthy, Sheila
IVE HEARD THE MERMAIDS SINGING

McCarthy, Thomas J.
MANNEQUIN

McCartney, Paul
EAT THE RICH

McCarty, Chris
OVER THE TOP

McCarty, Leta
SUICIDE CLUB, THE

McCauley, Barbara
SQUARE DANCE

McCauley, Paul
EVIL TOWN

McCauley, Sheila
TIN MEN

McCharen, David
MONSTER IN THE CLOSET

McClarnon, Kevin
EIGHTY FOUR CHARING CROSS ROAD

McClarty, Edward
TURNAROUND

McCleery, Gary
MATEWAN

McClelland, Marsha
PARTY CAMP

McClelland, Sam David
VIDEO DEAD, THE

McClements, Catherine
RIGHT HAND MAN, THE

McClory, Sean
DEAD, THE

McCloskey, Leigh
DIRTY LAUNDRY

McClure, Doug
OMEGA SYNDROME

McClure, Kathy
WHITE PHANTOM

McClure, Marc
AMAZON WOMEN ON THE MOON
PERFECT MATCH, THE
SUPERMAN IV: THE QUEST FOR PEACE

McClure, Tang
COMMANDO SQUAD

McClurg, Edie
PLANES, TRAINS AND AUTOMOBILES

McCoin, Roger
EVIL SPAWN

McConnell, Bridget
INDIAN SUMMER

McCord, Pat
DEADTIME STORIES

McCord, Patrick
WHO'S THAT GIRL

McCorkindale, Kiri
NGATI

McCormack, Margaret H.
RAISING ARIZONA

McCormick, Gary
STARLIGHT HOTEL

McCormick, John
LIVING ON TOKYO TIME

McCormick, Maureen
RETURN TO HORROR HIGH

McCowen, Alec
CRY FREEDOM
PERSONAL SERVICES

McCown, Cort
CANT BUY ME LOVE

McCoy, Charlie
RETURN OF JOSEY WALES, THE

McCoy, Steve
I WAS A TEENAGE ZOMBIE

McCoy, Sylvester
THREE KINDS OF HEAT

McCracken, Bob
NIGHTFORCE

McCracken, Michael Shawn
KINDRED, THE

McCrane, Paul
ROBOCOP

McCrary, Darius
BIG SHOTS

McCrary, Maria
BIG SHOTS

McCrindle, Alex
COMRADES

McCulloch, Andrew
CRY FREEDOM

McCullogh, Julie
BIG BAD MAMA II

McCurrach, Ian
EMPIRE STATE

McDermotroe, Conor
MOVING TARGETS

McDermott, Dylan
HAMBURGER HILL

McDermott, Kim
WISH YOU WERE HERE

McDernottroe, Maria
DEAD, THE

McDonald, Ann Marie
IVE HEARD THE MERMAIDS SINGING

McDonald, Arona
NO WAY OUT

McDonald, Chris
OUTRAGEOUS FORTUNE

McDonald, Daniel
MILLION DOLLAR MYSTERY

McDonald, Garry
THOSE DEAR DEPARTED

McDonald, Ian
MORNING MAN, THE

McDonald, Joe
MIND KILLER

McDonald, Joshua
UNDICI GIORNI, UNDICI NOTTE

McDonald, Lana
RAWHEAD REX

McDonald, Susan
WANTED: DEAD OR ALIVE

McDonnell, Mary
MATEWAN

McDonnell, Tim
EAT THE PEACH

McDonough, Kevin
I WAS A TEENAGE T.V. TERRORIST

McDormand, Frances
RAISING ARIZONA

McDowall, Roddy
DEAD OF WINTER
OVERBOARD

McDowell, John
OVERBOARD

McEnery, Kate
BELLMAN AND TRUE

McEnnan, Mindy
SUMMER CAMP NIGHTMARE

McEnroe, Annie
WALL STREET

McEwan, Hamish
MORNING MAN, THE

McFarland, Stephen
MAKING MR.RIGHT

McFee, Dwight
MALONE

McFeeley, Daniel
HUNTER'S BLOOD

McGann, Mark
BUSINESS AS USUAL

McGann, Michael John
EIGHTY FOUR CHARING CROSS ROAD

McGann, Paul
EMPIRE OF THE SUN
WITHNAIL AND I

McGann, Stephen
BUSINESS AS USUAL

McGavin, Darren
FROM THE HIP

McGee, Bobby
HOLLYWOOD SHUFFLE

McGee, Jack
MAGIC STICKS
SOMEONE TO WATCH OVER ME

McGehee, Mike
SOMETHING SPECIAL!

McGhee, Brownie
ANGEL HEART

McGhee, Johnny Ray
PROJECT X

McGill, Bruce
WAITING FOR THE MOON

McGillis, Kelly
DREAMERS
MADE IN HEAVEN

McGinley, John
WALL STREET

McGiver, Boris
IRONWEED

McGiver, Marney
LADIES OF THE LOTUS

McGough, Joan
STUDENT CONFIDENTIAL

McGough, Richard
BEDROOM WINDOW, THE

McGovern, Elizabeth
BEDROOM WINDOW, THE

McGovern, Terence
AMAZON WOMEN ON THE MOON

McGovern, Tom
HIDING OUT

McGowan, Shane
EAT THE RICH

McGrady, Michael
PROJECT X

McGrath, Derek
POLICE ACADEMY 4: CITIZENS ON PATROL

McGrath, Jennifer
SUMMER CAMP NIGHTMARE

McGrath, Matt
IRONWEED

McGraw, Sean
WINNERS TAKE ALL

McGregor, Ken
BIG TOWN, THE
McGregor, Richard "Romeo"
HOLLYWOOD SHUFFLE
McGregor-Stewart, Kate
BEDROOM WINDOW, THE
HELLO AGAIN
McGroarty, Cherie
BIG TOWN, THE
McGroarty, Pat
MILLION DOLLAR MYSTERY
McGuire, Dorothy
SUMMER HEAT
McHallem, Christopher
LOVECHILD, THE
McHattie, Stephen
SALVATION!
McIlwraith, David
TOO OUTRAGEOUS
McInerney, Bernie
SUSPECT
McIntire, Donald
MISS MARY
McIntire, James
GOOD MORNING, VIETNAM
OUTRAGEOUS FORTUNE
McIntosh, Judy
NGATI
McIntyre, Ciaren
BOY SOLDIER
McIntyre, Clare
EMPIRE STATE
McIntyre, Marvin
RETURN TO HORROR HIGH
McIntyre, Marvin J.
PROJECT X
RUNNING MAN, THE
McIntyre, Thomas L.
DATE WITH AN ANGEL
McK, Misha
HES MY GIRL
McKamy, Kim
CREEPOZOIDS
DREAMANIAC
McKay, Danette
KEEPING TRACK
McKean, Michael
PLANES, TRAINS AND AUTOMOBILES
McKee, Lonette
GARDENS OF STONE
McKee, Robin
EMANON
McKeehan, Luke
CONCRETE ANGELS
McKenna, Breffni
MAURICE
McKenzie, Bleu
CLUB LIFE
McKenzie, Sally
WITH LOVE TO THE PERSON NEXT TO ME
McKenzie, Tim
LIGHTHORSEMEN, THE
McKeon, Doug
TURNAROUND
McKeon, Kristine
GARBAGE PAIL KIDS MOVIE, THE
McKeon, Philip
RETURN TO HORROR HIGH
McKeown, Finian
EAT THE PEACH
McKern, Roger
BELLMAN AND TRUE
McKerrow, Amanda
DANCERS
McKinney, Greg
SUSPECT
McKinstry, Deanna
EMANON
McKnight, David
HOLLYWOOD SHUFFLE
McKowen, Charles
PRICK UP YOUR EARS
McLane, Val
WISH YOU WERE HERE
McLaren, Conrad
SUMMER HEAT
McLaren, Hollis
TOO OUTRAGEOUS
McLaren, Ian
BOY SOLDIER
McLarty, Gary
NIGHTFORCE
McLaughlan, Tim
DOGS IN SPACE
McLaughlin, Craig
RAISING ARIZONA
McLean, Sharonlee
P.I. PRIVATE INVESTIGATIONS
McLean, Stephanie
MALIBU BIKINI SHOP, THE
McLean, Warren
EQUALIZER 2000
NO DEAD HEROES
TOUGH COP
McLellan, Amy
I WAS A TEENAGE T.V. TERRORIST
McLellan, Robyn
DOGS IN SPACE
McLemore, Shawn
SUMMER CAMP NIGHTMARE
McLennan, Gustavo
HOUR OF THE ASSASSIN
McLeod, Shelagh
INDIAN SUMMER
McLoughlen, Marion
BOY SOLDIER
McLoughlin, Marianne
ARIA
McLoughlin, Nancy
DATE WITH AN ANGEL
McLoughlin, Tom
DATE WITH AN ANGEL
McMahon, Shannon
BLOOD SISTERS
McManus, Don
CARE BEARS ADVENTURE IN WONDERLAND, THE
McManus, Michael
POLICE ACADEMY 4: CITIZENS ON PATROL
McMartin, John
WHO'S THAT GIRL
McMillan, Kenneth
MALONE
McMullan, Jim
ASSASSINATION
McMurray, Sam
RAISING ARIZONA
McMurtrey, Joan
NO WAY OUT
OUTRAGEOUS FORTUNE
McNabney, Ted
RAGE OF HONOR
McNally, Kevin
CRY FREEDOM
McNamara, Brian
IN THE MOOD
McNamara, Robert
CRY FREEDOM
McNamara, William
BEAT, THE
OPERA
McNamee, Chris
MUTANT HUNT
McNeice, Ian
EIGHTY FOUR CHARING CROSS ROAD
PERSONAL SERVICES
WHOOPS APOCALYPSE
McNeil, Roy
DIRTY REBEL
McNeill, Robert Duncan
MASTERS OF THE UNIVERSE
McNiece, Ian
LONELY PASSION OF JUDITH HEARNE,THE
McPherson, Neil
CRY FREEDOM
McQuade, Kris
SURFER, THE
McQueen, Chad
NIGHTFORCE
McRae, Frank
BATTERIES NOT INCLUDED
McWilliams, Caroline
WHITE WATER SUMMER
Mdledle, Nathan Dambuza
KITCHEN TOTO, THE
Mead, Phil
OUTRAGEOUS FORTUNE
Meade, Garth
LES PATTERSON SAVES THE WORLD
Meadows, Robert
OVERBOARD
Meaini, Amado
ZISCHKE
Meaney, Colm
OMEGA SYNDROME
Meany, Colm
DEAD, THE
Meara, Anne
MY LITTLE GIRL
Meat Loaf
SQUEEZE, THE
Medin, Harriet
WITCHES OF EASTWICK, THE
Medina, Crispin
SWEET REVENGE
Medina, Hugo
LA ESTACION DEL REGRESO
Medina, Ofelia
FRIDA
Medlock, Ken
EXTREME PREJUDICE
Meduwar, Joseph
PRETTY SMART
Medvedev, Vadim
POSLEDNYAYA DOROGA
Medvedyev, K.
VZLOMSHCHIK
Mee-sok, Lee
NAE-SHI
Mee-sook, Lee
KYEOUL NAGUNE
Meeley, Darrah
BLACK WIDOW
Meffre, Armand
JEAN DE FLORETTE
MANON OF THE SPRING
Megvinetukhutsesi, Otar
KRUGOVOROT
Mehlman, Romy
MALIBU BIKINI SHOP, THE
Mehta, Sujata
PRATIGHAAT
Mei, Wu Jun
LAST EMPEROR, THE
Meighan, Lynn
KILLER WORKOUT
Meijer, Erik J.
CAUGHT
Meillon, John
FRENCHMAN'S FARM
Mein, Maurizio
INTERVISTA
Meira, Tarcisio
EU
Mejia, Gerardo
CANT BUY ME LOVE
WINNERS TAKE ALL
Mejia, Griselda
EL HIJO DE PEDRO NAVAJAS
LA RAZA NUNCA PIERDE—HUELE A GAS
LA RULETERA
NOS REIMOS DE LA MIGRA
Mejias, Isabelle
HIGHER EDUCATION
MEATBALLS III
Mejzlik, Miroslav
CIZIM VSTUP POVOLEN
Melamed, Fred
SUSPECT
Melato, Mariangela
DANCERS
Melazzi, Giorgio
DOLCE ASSENZA
Melchier, John
OPPOSING FORCE
Melega, Michele
GOOD MORNING BABYLON
MAN IN LOVE, A
Melero, Victor
LA ESTANQUERA DE VALLECAS
Melia, Frank
EAT THE PEACH
RAWHEAD REX
Melki, Claude
LES OREILLES ENTRE LES DENTS
Mellegni, Sandro
GOOD MORNING BABYLON
Melles, Sunnyi
MASCHENKA
Mello, Jay
JAWS: THE REVENGE

Melton, Larry
RETURN OF JOSEY WALES, THE
Melville, Josephine
EMPIRE STATE
Melvin, Michael
DUDES
Melvin, Murray
COMRADES
Melvor, Elizabeth
LES PATTERSON SAVES THE WORLD
Menachem, David
DEADLINE
Menchov, Vladimir
KURIER
Mende, Lisa
HOLLYWOOD SHUFFLE
Mendelsohn, Ben
YEAR MY VOICE BROKE, THE
Mendenhall, David
OVER THE TOP
THEY STILL CALL ME BRUCE
Mendenhall, James
OVER THE TOP
Mendenhall, Julie
HOUSE OF GAMES
Mendez, Silvestre
NI DE AQUI, NI DE ALLA
Mendiaraz, Juan Luis
A LOS CUATRO VIENTOS
Mendillo, Stephen
BROADCAST NEWS
Mendoza, Rossy
JUANA LA CANTINERA
Mendoza, Tito
STRANGER, THE
Menegazzi, Rio
MASCARA
Menendez, Ramon
FORAJIDOS EN LA MIRA
Menkes, Trinka
MAGDALENA VIRAGA
Menon, Balachandra
VILAMBARAM
Menshikov, Oleg
MOY LYUBIMYY KLOUN
Menshov, Vladimir
PROSTI
Mensur, Irfan
KRALJEVA ZAVRSNICA
Menville, Scott
ERNEST GOES TO CAMP
Meo, Chuck
DOGS IN SPACE
DOGS IN SPACE
Meran, Joey
HARD TICKET TO HAWAII
Meraz, Raul
NARCOTERROR
Mercado, Felicia
NARCOTERROR
Mercurio, Gus
RUNNING FROM THE GUNS
Merenda, Luc
MISSIONE EROICA
SUPERFANTOZZI
Merezhko, Viktor
PROSTI
Mergault, Isabelle
CLUB DE RENCONTRES
IL EST GENIAL PAPY!
Merino, Francisco
REDONDELA
Merlo, Luis
HAY QUE DESHACER LA CASA
LA SENYORA
Merr, Jullianno
DEATH BEFORE DISHONOR
Merrill, Damon
OUTING, THE
Merrill, Peter
BLOOD TRACKS
FULL METAL JACKET
LIGHTHORSEMEN, THE
Merrill, Robert
ARIA
Meryl, Riba
BANZAI RUNNER
Mesic, Cvijeta
UVEK SPREMNE ZENE
Meskin, Amnon
SOMEONE TO LOVE
Meskin, Annon
SNOW WHITE
Mesmer, Michael
DEADTIME STORIES
Mesner, Anat
POET'S SILENCE, THE
Messelli, Johann
ROBINSON NO NIWA
Messenger, Jack
RUMPELSTILTSKIN
Messeri, Marco
NOTTE ITALIANA
Messner, Claudia
ZABOU
Mestre, Jeannine
LA SENYORA
Metcalf, Laurie
MAKING MR.RIGHT
Metcalfe, Gordon
MONSTER IN THE CLOSET
Metcalfe, Ken
WARRIORS OF THE APOCALYPSE
Metlitskaya, Irina
VYKUP
Mette, Nancy
MATEWAN
Metz, Belinda
PRETTYKILL
Metzler, Jim
RIVER'S EDGE
Meury, Anne-Laure
LAMI DE MON AMIE
Meuwissen, Sandra
BLOOD HOOK
Meyer, Alejandra
TRAGICO TERREMOTO EN MEXICO
Meyer, Bess
IN THE MOOD
Meyer, Gary
FULL METAL JACKET
Meyer, Hans
BAD BLOOD
Meyer, Jeff
NECROPOLIS
Meyer, Michelle
NAIL GUN MASSACRE
Meyer, Russ
AMAZON WOMEN ON THE MOON
Meyer, Sunny
SOMEONE TO LOVE
Meyer, Thom
TRESPASSES
Meyers, Liz
DOGS IN SPACE
Meyers, Thom
BLOODSUCKERS FROM OUTER SPACE
Meyrink, Michelle
NICE GIRLS DON'T EXPLODE
Mezieres, Myriam
UNE FLAMME DANS MON COEUR
Mezquiriz, Javier
A LOS CUATRO VIENTOS
Mezquita, Daniel
SUFRE MAMON
Mezzogiorno, Vittorio
FUEGOS
JENATSCH
Mgaloblishvili, Nodar
KAPITAN "PILIGRIMA"
Mgcina, Sophie
CRY FREEDOM
Mhuri, Aine Ni
LONELY PASSION OF JUDITH HEARNE,THE
Miano, Robert
CHINA GIRL
CLUB LIFE
OPEN HOUSE
WEEDS
Michael, Anthony
WOLF AT THE DOOR, THE
Michael, Ben
RUNNING FROM THE GUNS
Michael, Ralph
DIARY OF A MAD OLD MAN
EMPIRE OF THE SUN
Michael Green
STRANDED
Michael O'Gorman
IRONWEED
Michael O'Keefe
IRONWEED
Michaels, John
WIND, THE
ZERO BOYS, THE
Michaels, Julien
MANKILLERS
Michaels, Lorraine
BUSINESS AS USUAL
Michaels, Steve
STREET SMART
Michailidis, Peris
TA PAIDIA TIS CHELIDONAS
Michalak, Cathren
AROUND THE WORLD IN EIGHTY WAYS
Michalakopoulos, Giorgos
IKONA ENOS MYTHIKOU PROSOPOU
KLIOS
Michaud, Francoise
FAMILY BUSINESS
LA VALLEE FANTOME
Michaud, Marie
BACH AND BROCCOLI
Michaud, Sophie
LA RUMBA
Michel, Patricia Scott
VALET GIRLS
Micheli, Maurizio
RIMINI RIMINI
ROBA DA RICCHI
Michelin, Rosemary
CUSTODY
Michell, Helena
PRICK UP YOUR EARS
Michelsen, Katrine
LE FOTO DI GIOIA
SPECTERS
TENTAZIONE
Mickens II, Marion
OVER THE TOP
Micula, Stasia
SLAMMER GIRLS
WARRIOR QUEEN
Middleton, Brett
FULL METAL JACKET
Middleton, Burr
HUNTER'S BLOOD
IN THE MOOD
Middleton, Charles
NO WAY OUT
Mideri, Mako
SHINRAN: SHIRO MICHI
Midler, Bette
OUTRAGEOUS FORTUNE
Midnaia, T.
KOROTKIE VSTRECHI
Midwood, Kenneth
FOURTH PROTOCOL, THE
Miehe-Renard, Tine
BABETTE'S GASTEBUD
Miele, Giuseppe
ILLUMINAZIONI
Mifune, Toshiro
PRINCESS FROM THE MOON
Migas, Alexis
DOXOBUS
Migliarisi, Anna
CONCRETE ANGELS
Mignacco, Darlene
PSYCHO GIRLS
Miguel, Antonio
SINVERGUENZA . . . PERO HONRADO
Mihailoff, R.A.
DANGER ZONE, THE
Mihailov, Vassil
PRIZEMYAVANE
Mika
AMERICAN DRIVE-IN
Mikaberidze, Ruslan
CHEGEMSKIY DETEKTIV
NEYLONOVAYA YOLKA
Mikami, Hiroshi
WATASHI O SKI NI TSURETETTE
Mike, Mr.
MAKING MR.RIGHT
Mikhailova, Darya
PRODELKI V STARINNOM DUKHE

Mikhailova, Tatiana
PROSTI
Mikhailovsky, Nikita
ZONTIK DLYA NOVOBRACHNYKH
Mikhaylova, Darya
WEEKEND
Mikheyenko, Vadim
KAPKAN DLYA SHAKALOV
Miki, Norihei
TOKYO BLACKOUT
ZEGEN
Mikune, Rentaro
HOTARUGAWA
Milani, Kathy
PSYCHOS IN LOVE
Milas, Nikos
O PARADISSOS ANIGI ME ANTIKLIDI
Miles, Peter
WHISTLE BLOWER, THE
Miles, Sarah
HOPE AND GLORY
WHITE MISCHIEF
Miles, Sylvia
SLEEPING BEAUTY
Miles, Sylvia
CRITICAL CONDITION
WALL STREET
Miles O'Keeffe
CAMPUS MAN
Milewska, Anna
STANISLAW I ANNA
Milford, John
STUDENT CONFIDENTIAL
Milgroom, Michael
PROJECT X
Milholland, Richard
FATAL BEAUTY
Milian, Tomas
DISTANT LIGHTS
Miliutenko
RODNIK DLIA ZHAZHDUSHCHIKH
Miliutin, O.
VZLOMSHCHIK
Millan, Al
VIDEO DEAD, THE
Millar, Doug
TOO OUTRAGEOUS
Millar, Maggie
BUSHFIRE MOON
Millar, Marsha
LOVECHILD, THE
Milldorf, Kenneth
JIM OCH PIRATERNA BLOM
Millecam, Sylvia
HECTOR
Miller, Arlin
BEST SELLER
Miller, Arnie
HAPPY HOUR
Miller, Audrey
ULTIMAX FORCE
Miller, Barry
SICILIAN, THE
Miller, Beth Ann
TEEN WOLF TOO
Miller, Bob
CONCRETE ANGELS
Miller, Corissa
CANT BUY ME LOVE
Miller, Davey
ALLNIGHTER, THE
Miller, David
GUNPOWDER
Miller, Dean R.
NIGHTFORCE
PARTY CAMP
Miller, Dick
INNERSPACE
PROJECT X
Miller, Harvey Alan
OVERBOARD
Miller, Helen
RADIO DAYS
Miller, Ira
SPACEBALLS
Miller, J. Clell
OUTRAGEOUS FORTUNE
Miller, Jason
LIGHT OF DAY
Miller, Jean
SILENT NIGHT, DEADLY NIGHT PART II
Miller, Jeremy
EMANON
Miller, Joshua
NEAR DARK
RIVER'S EDGE
Miller, Kathi
KILLER WORKOUT
Miller, Maggie
BIT PART, THE
Miller, Mindy
PRETTY SMART
Miller, Nitche Vo
IN THE MOOD
Miller, Pat
SUMMER HEAT
Miller, Penelope Ann
ADVENTURES IN BABYSITTING
Miller, R.J.
WANTED: DEAD OR ALIVE
Miller, Robert
HILL 171
Miller, Stephen E.
HOME IS WHERE THE HART IS
MALONE
STEPFATHER, THE
Miller, Vera
STREET SMART
Miller, Kevin
AMERICAN DRIVE-IN
Millette, Jean-Louis
LES FOUS DE BASSAN
Millican, Cindy
RUNNING MAN, THE
Millikan, Tim
DOGS IN SPACE
DOGS IN SPACE
Million, Billy
HUNTER'S BLOOD
Millman, Ralph
MORNING MAN, THE
Mills, Adam
JOCKS
Mills, Gary Landon
FULL METAL JACKET
Mills, Joel
STUDENT CONFIDENTIAL
Mills, John
WHEN THE WIND BLOWS
WHO'S THAT GIRL
Mills, Kenneth R.
P.K. & THE KID
Millward, Wendy
WHOOPS APOCALYPSE
Milner, David
FULL METAL JACKET
Milnes, Gerald
MATEWAN
Milosavljevic, Vladica
KRALJEVA ZAVRSNICA
OKTOBERFEST
Milrud, Alejandro
SOFIA
Mimsy
CAMPING DEL TERRORE
Minard, Kim
SOMETHING SPECIAL!
Minasian, Eddie
UNTOUCHABLES, THE
Minchinton, Mark
BACHELOR GIRL
Minehart, Kitty
MANNEQUIN
Miner, David
BLIND DATE
Minet, Sophie
TRAVELLING AVANT
Minetti, Bernhard
FRANCESCA
Ming, Gao
BLACK CANNON INCIDENT, THE
Ming, Su Ming
OUTSIDERS, THE
SAPPORO STORY
Minister, Hilary
CRY FREEDOM
Miniucci, Stefania
DELIZIA
Minkus, Barbara
MALIBU BIKINI SHOP, THE
Minmagh, Sean
FULL METAL JACKET
Minmagh, Tony
FULL METAL JACKET
Minnar, Corinna
WITCHES OF EASTWICK, THE
Minor, Alan B.
MAKING MR.RIGHT
Minor, Bob
PROJECT X
Minter, Kelly
PRINCIPAL, THE
SUMMER SCHOOL
Minton, Faith
WHO'S THAT GIRL
Mintz, Felix
FOREVER, LULU
Mintz, Larry
BURGLAR
Mintz, Lazar
FOREVER, LULU
Minuzzi, Michel
MASCARA
Miot, Eric
LADY OF THE CAMELIAS
Mioteris, Nikos
TREE WE HURT, THE
Miquel, Joelle
QUATRE AVENTURES DE REINETTE ET MIRABELLE
Miralles, Joan
CALE
Miranda, Carlos
CHRONICLE OF A DEATH FORETOLD
Miranda, John
EMANON
Miranda, Robert
UNTOUCHABLES, THE
Miranda, Rogerio
CHRONICLE OF A DEATH FORETOLD
Mirano, Gy
NECROPOLIS
Miravilles, Reynaldo
DE TAL PEDRO, TAL ASTILLA
Miridjanyan, Verchaluis
PESN PROSHEDSHIKH DNEY
Mirmont, Roger
COERS CROISES
Miro, Jennifer
VIDEO DEAD, THE
Miroshnichenko, Irina
TAYNY MADAM VONG
Mirzoyev, Farhad
MIRAZHI LYUBRI
Misagawa, Ben
OVERKILL
Misaki, Chieko
TORA-SAN'S BLUEBIRD FANTASY
Mishkind, Abraham
WITCHES OF EASTWICK, THE
Mishra, Pira
JAIDEV
Misra, Prabha
PRATIGHAAT
Misset, Iris
CAUGHT
Mitchell, Bill
BEST SELLER
Mitchell, Cameron
DEADLY PREY
MESSENGER, THE
MISSION KILL
NIGHTFORCE
OFFSPRING, THE
Mitchell, Delores
PRINCIPAL, THE
Mitchell, Donna
LESS THAN ZERO
Mitchell, Gene
SURF NAZIS MUST DIE
Mitchell, Gordon
LA CROCE DALLE SETTE PIETRE
Mitchell, Hamilton
SLUMBER PARTY MASSACRE II
Mitchell, Helena
MAURICE
Mitchell, Jimmie Lee
CANT BUY ME LOVE

Mitchell, Kit
NAIL GUN MASSACRE
Mitchell, Mark
OUTING, THE
Mitchell, Roelle
ESCAPES
Mitchell, Sasha
DEATH BEFORE DISHONOR
Mitchell, Scott
THOU SHALT NOT KILL . . . EXCEPT
Mitchell, Seth
OVER THE TOP
Mitchell, Shirley
SUMMER CAMP NIGHTMARE
Mitchum, Jim
CODE NAME ZEBRA
Mitchum, John
ESCAPES
Miti, Michela
DELITTI
DOLCE PELLE DI ANGELA
Mitler, Matt
DEADTIME STORIES
THIN LINE, THE
Mitra, Devika
APAN GHAREY
Mitsouko, les Rita
SOIGNE TA DROITE
Mittleman, Ben
DIRTY LAUNDRY
Mittleman, Steve
ROXANNE
Mitzi, Suzanne
WHOOPS APOCALYPSE
Miu, Anita
CHOCOLATE INSPECTOR
HAPPY BIGAMIST
Miyahara, Nami
ROBINSON NO NIWA
Miyamoto, Nobuko
TAXING WOMAN, A
Miyashita, Junko
MAGINA—MURA MONOGATARI
Miyata, Hiroshi
ITAZU
Mizoguchi, Yo
ROBINSON NO NIWA
Mkrtchyan, Frunze
PESN PROSHEDSHIKH DNEY
Mladenova, Zornitsa
CERNITE LEBEDI
Mlambo, Nocebo
CRY FREEDOM
Mnouchkine, Alexandre
SPIRALE
Mock, Laurel
KILLER WORKOUT
Mockus, Tony
UNTOUCHABLES, THE
Mocky, Jean-Pierre
AGENT TROUBLE
Modean, Jayne
HOUSE TWO: THE SECOND STORY
Modine, Matthew
FULL METAL JACKET
ORPHANS
Modugno, Enrica Maria
MORO AFFAIR, THE
Moeller, J. David
SQUARE DANCE
Moen, Andrea
RUNNING MAN, THE
Moen, Merete
IS-SLOTTET
Moffat, Donald
MONSTER IN THE CLOSET
Moffatt, John
PRICK UP YOUR EARS
Moffett, D.W.
BLACK WIDOW
Moffett, Don W.
WHEELS OF TERROR
Moffo, Anna
ARIA
Mohamed, Atik
LIVING DAYLIGHTS, THE
Mohammad
UPPU
Mohammadi, Esmaeil
DJADDE HAYE SARD
Mohanlal
AMRITAMGAMAYA
JANUARY ORORMA
PANCHAGNI
Mohanty, Uttam
JAIDEV
Moidu, Nadia
PANCHAGNI
Moir, Richard
JILTED
Mojack, Tom
UNDICI GIORNI, UNDICI NOTTE
Mokae, Zakes
CRY FREEDOM
Moland, Peter
TAROT
Moldava, Jeff
OPPOSING FORCE
Moldovan, Jeff
MASTERBLASTER
Molga, Jerzi
ZLOTY POCIAG
Molgat, Mathurin
LEADING EDGE, THE
Molina, Alfred
PRICK UP YOUR EARS
Molina, Angela
FUEGOS
Molina, Claudio Caceres
IN DER WUSTE
Molina, Cristina
ENTRE FICHERAS ANDA EL DIABLO
LA FUGA DE CARRASCO
Molina, Javier
SUFRE MAMON
Molina, Miguel
LAW OF DESIRE
Molind, Louis
VALET GIRLS
Mollison, Max
MUTANT HUNT
Mollvig-Lewenhaupt, Grynet
SVART GRYNING
Molnar, Stanko
SICILIAN, THE
Molona, Judy
OVERKILL
Moloney, Gavin
GARBAGE PAIL KIDS MOVIE, THE
Molteni, Luis
MEFISTO FUNK
Molveig, Grynet
LOS DUENOS DEL SILENCIO
Monaco, Tony
IN THE MOOD
Monahan, Dan
FROM THE HIP
Moncayo, Bertha
LA OVEJA NEGRA
Monedero, Jose Pomedio
STRAIGHT TO HELL
Moneta, Tulio
HOSTAGE
Monette, Richard
HELLO MARY LOU, PROM NIGHT II
HIGHER EDUCATION
IVE HEARD THE MERMAIDS SINGING
Monica, Teresa
LA PLAYA DE LOS PERROS
Monie, Rickie
ANGEL HEART
Monnet, Gabriel
FUEGOS
Monni, Carlo
AURELIA
Monni, Mauro
GOOD MORNING BABYLON
Monnier, Annie
BEYOND THERAPY
Monoson, Lawrence
GABY—A TRUE STORY
Monreale, Cinzia
SOTTO IL RISTORANTE CINESE
Montagne, Guy
LES OREILLES ENTRE LES DENTS
Montalva, Alberto
HOUR OF THE ASSASSIN
Montama, Jean-Luc
TERMINUS
Montand, Yves
JEAN DE FLORETTE
MANON OF THE SPRING
Montanen, Anne-May
IL LUPO DI MARE
Montano, Maria
MATAR O MORIR
Monte, Mario
HUNTED, THE
IGOROTA
MANILA, OPEN CITY
Monteiro, Duda
COLOR OF DESTINY, THE
Montejo, Carmen
EL MUERTO DEL PALOMO
Montenegro, Sasha
EL DIABLO, EL SANTO Y EL TONTO
EL HIJO DE PEDRO NAVAJAS
ENTRE FICHERAS ANDA EL DIABLO
FIERAS EN BRAMA
LA RAZA NUNCA PIERDE—HUELE A GAS
LAS TRAIGO . . . MUERTAS
Montes, Elsa
LA RAZA NUNCA PIERDE—HUELE A GAS
Montesano, Enrico
I PICARI
NOI UOMINI DURI
Montesi, Jorge
BIRDS OF PREY
Montesinos, Guillermo
HAY QUE DESHACER LA CASA
LA VIDA ALEGRE
Montgomery, Julia
KINDRED, THE
Montgomery, Kaitlin
UNTOUCHABLES, THE
Montgomery, Reggie
WEEDS
Montgomery, Ritchie
MONSTER IN THE CLOSET
Montgomery, Wes
KILLER WORKOUT
Montiel, Mary
ENTRE FICHERAS ANDA EL DIABLO
Montiel, Roberto
NARCOTERROR
Montilla, Carlos
LA OVEJA NEGRA
Montllor, Ovidi
BAR-CEL-ONA
Montrose, Lonna
OUTRAGEOUS FORTUNE
Monty, Michael
TOUGH COP
Monty, Mike
EYE OF THE EAGLE
NO DEAD HEROES
Moody, Florence
TIN MEN
Mooney, Paul
HOLLYWOOD SHUFFLE
Moor, Bill
ISHTAR
Moor, Marianna
MALOM A POKOLBAN
Moore, Ben
NIGHTFORCE
Moore, Bill
CHRONICLE OF A DEATH FORETOLD
Moore, Bonnie
DANCERS
Moore, Christine
BUSINESS AS USUAL
Moore, Debrah
WARRIORS OF THE APOCALYPSE
Moore, Denis
BACHELOR GIRL
Moore, Dudley
LIKE FATHER, LIKE SON
Moore, Jane
MANNEQUIN
Moore, Jessica
UNDICI GIORNI, UNDICI NOTTE
Moore, Joanna
MOVING TARGETS
Moore, John
EMPIRE OF THE SUN
Moore, Laurens
SUMMER HEAT

Moore, Lee
OPEN HOUSE
Moore, Mavor
MALONE
Moore, Micki
BELIEVERS, THE
Moore, Robyn
DOT GOES TO HOLLYWOOD
Moore, Roger
MAGIC SNOWMAN, THE
Moore, Sebastian
OVERKILL
Moore, Tracey
CARE BEARS ADVENTURE IN WONDERLAND, THE
Morado, Renato
OPPOSING FORCE
Moraes, Milton
BEIJO NA BOCA
Morales, Bob
LA BAMBA
Morales, Enrique
EL AMOR ES UNA MUJERGORDA
Morales, Esai
LA BAMBA
PRINCIPAL, THE
Morales, Hector
MUTANT HUNT
Morales, Mark
DISORDERLIES
Moranis, Rick
SPACEBALLS
Moranta, Paco
MIRACLES
Morante, Jose
RETURN OF JOSEY WALES, THE
Morante, Laura
DISTANT LIGHTS
LA VALLEE FANTOME
MAN ON FIRE
Moratalla, Jose M.
MY GENERAL
Moravec, Miroslav
POHADKA O MALICKOVI
Morch, Carsten
VENNER FOR ALTID
Mordukova, Nonna
KOMISSAR
Morea, Valerie
WOLF AT THE DOOR, THE
Moreau, Jeanne
LE MIRACULE
Moreau, Marsha
BLUE MONKEY
PRETTYKILL
Moreland, Ulla
STREET SMART
Morell, Wallace R.
KOLORMASK
Morelli, Marco
DER NACHBAR
Morelli, Noemi
CHECHECHELA—UNA CHICA DEL BARRIO
Morelli, Paola
MURIERON A MITAD DEL RIO
Morelli, Robert
BIG TOWN, THE
STREET SMART
Moreno, Chari
LA ESTANQUERA DE VALLECAS
Moreno, Eva
MANON
Moreno, Fernando
GABY—A TRUE STORY
Moreno, Gerardo
MIRACLES
Moreno, Jaime
ENTRE FICHERAS ANDA EL DIABLO
Moreno, Jose Elias
DELINCUENTE
UN SABADO MAS
Moreno, Juan
LA ESTANQUERA DE VALLECAS
Morett, Gina
VIAJE AL PARAISO
Moretus, Doriane
LOVE IS A DOG FROM HELL
Morey, Bill
OMEGA SYNDROME
REAL MEN

Moreyra, Margotita
EN EL NOMBRE DEL HIJO
Morgan, Charly
MONSTER SQUAD, THE
Morgan, Gary
OUTRAGEOUS FORTUNE
Morgan, Harry
DRAGNET
Morgan, Joe
DIRTY LAUNDRY
Morgan, Jon Paul
ISHTAR
Morgan, Mary
TIN MEN
Morgan, Read
FATAL BEAUTY
Morgan, Shelley Taylor
CROSS MY HEART
Morgan, Tom
HIDING OUT
Morgan, Wendy
EIGHTY FOUR CHARING CROSS ROAD
Morgenstern, Mindy
I WAS A TEENAGE T.V. TERRORIST
RADIO DAYS
Morgenstern, Ross
RADIO DAYS
Morgenstern, Stephanie
MORNING MAN, THE
Mori, Mitsuko
EIGA JOYU
Mori, Yoshinori
TIME FOR DYING, A
Moriarty, Cathy
WHITE OF THE EYE
Moriarty, James
SOMEONE TO WATCH OVER ME
Moriarty, Michael
HANOI HILTON, THE
Morier-Genoud, Philippe
AU REVOIR, LES ENFANTS
Moritz, Dorothea
ALPINE FIRE
Moritzen, Henning
PETER VON SCHOLTEN
Moriyama, Junkyu
SHINRAN: SHIRO MICHI
Morkunas, Rimas
BLUDNYY SYN
Morley, Robert
LITTLE DORRIT
TROUBLE WITH SPIES, THE
WIND, THE
Morong, Daniel
STUDENT CONFIDENTIAL
Morono, Professor
PSYCHOS IN LOVE
Morrell, Chuck
CODE NAME ZEBRA
Morris, Anita
ARIA
Morris, Bill
MATEWAN
Morris, Garrett
CRITICAL CONDITION
Morris, Haviland
WHO'S THAT GIRL
Morris, James D.
KEEPING TRACK
Morris, Jeff
IRONWEED
Morris, Kyle
MAGIC SNOWMAN, THE
Morris, Max
BLOOD DINER
Morris, Milton
MASSACRE IN DINOSAUR VALLEY
Morris, Phil
P.I. PRIVATE INVESTIGATIONS
Morris, Wayne
PERSONAL SERVICES
Morrison, Bill
LIKE FATHER, LIKE SON
Morrison, James
UNFINISHED BUSINESS . . .
Morrison, John
FULL METAL JACKET
Morrison, P.J.
CREEPSHOW 2

Morrissey, Eamon
EAT THE PEACH
Morrow, "Cousin Brucie"
DIRTY DANCING
Morrow, Bruce
MORGAN STEWART'S COMING HOME
Morrow, Cloyce
CANT BUY ME LOVE
Morrow, Liza
THREE O'CLOCK HIGH
Morrow, Stephen
TOUGH GUYS DON'T DANCE
Morse, Clay
TALKING WALLS
Morse, David
PERSONAL FOUL
Morse, Robert
EMPEROR'S NEW CLOTHES, THE
HUNK
Mortelliti, Rocco
ADELMO
Mortelliti, Stefania
ADELMO
Mortensen, Claus Bender
VENNER FOR ALTID
Mortensen, Viggo
SALVATION!
Mortil, Janne
MALONE
Morton, Joe
STRANDED
Mosberg, David
RADIO DAYS
Mosca, Paulinho
COLOR OF DESTINY, THE
Moscati, Dodi
CAPRICCIO
Moschidis, Giorgos
KLIOS
OH BABYLON
Moschin., Gastone
AURELIA
Moschitta, John
DIRTY LAUNDRY
TALKING WALLS
Moschos, Takis
VIOS KE POLITIA
YENETHLIA POLI
Moscoso, Xerardo
SINVERGUENZA . . . PERO HONRADO
Moseley, Page
HUNK
OPEN HOUSE
Moser, Jeffrey
TIN MEN
Moses, Jared
ZERO BOYS, THE
Moses, Mark
SOMEONE TO WATCH OVER ME
Moss, Ginsey
OVERKILL
Moss, Hajna O.
GARDENS OF STONE
Moss, Ronn
HARD TICKET TO HAWAII
HOT CHILD IN THE CITY
Most, Johnny
AMAZING GRACE AND CHUCK
Mostel, Josh
MATEWAN
RADIO DAYS
WALL STREET
Motherwell, Phil
WITH LOVE TO THE PERSON NEXT TO ME
Mott, Russell
FULL METAL JACKET
Motta, Bess
YOU TALKIN' TO ME?
Motta, Maria Amelia
JESTER,THE
Motta, Zeze
NIGHT ANGELS
Mottrich, Sam
BIRDS OF PREY
Mouchet, Catherine
SI LE SOLEIL NE REVENAIT PAS
Moucka, Jaroslav
CHOBOTNICE Z II. PATRA
Mouhoub, Aziz
ABBES

Moulder-Brown, John
RUMPELSTILTSKIN
Mounir, Mohammed
AL-TAUQ WAL-ISWIRA
Mounts, Eugene
BEVERLY HILLS COP II
Mourkova, Pavlina
PROC?
Mouse, Moira
BOY SOLDIER
Mousie
PROJECT X
Mouss
FAMILY BUSINESS
MON BEL AMOUR, MA DECHIRURE
Moussa, Bologo
YAM DAABO
Mouton, Kufaru Aaron
ANGEL HEART
Mouzon, Alphonse Philippe
LETHAL WEAPON
Movin, Lisbeth
BABETTE'S GASTEBUD
SIDSTE AKT
Moynihan, Maura
BROADCAST NEWS
Moyse, Sophie
AGENT TROUBLE
LE MIRACULE
Mphatsee, Tom
HOSTAGE
Mrkic, Dragana
OFICIR S RUZOM
Mrozkovy, Hana
WOLF'S HOLE
Mrozkovy, Ivana
WOLF'S HOLE
Mucari, Carlo
DOLCE PELLE DI ANGELA
Mucci, David
NIGHTSTICK
Muchachi, Clement
CRY FREEDOM
Muel, Jean-Paul
JENATSCH
Mueller, John
RETURN TO HORROR HIGH
Mueller, Michael
EMPIRE STATE
PRICK UP YOUR EARS
Muellerleile, Marianne
TROUBLE WITH DICK, THE
Muggia, Danny
KFAFOT
Mugica, Barbara
A DOS AGUAS
Muhich, Donald
AMAZON WOMEN ON THE MOON
Muir, Geraldine
HOPE AND GLORY
Mujde, Funda
JULIA'S GEHEIM
Mukhamedjanov, Ato
A SANTA DERVIS
Mukhamedjarova, Raisa
SKAZKA O PREKRASNOY AYSULU
Mukherjee, Kamu
PHERA
Mukherjee, Santu
BIDROHI
Mukherjee, Soma
AMAR KANTAK
Mukherjee, Sunil
PHERA
Mukoko, Mazaza
LA VIE EST BELLE
Mulder, Eddie
NEAR DARK
Muldoon, Mick
BLACK WIDOW
SQUEEZE, THE
Mulgrew, Kate
THROW MOMMA FROM THE TRAIN
Mulhern, Matt
EXTREME PREJUDICE
Mulkey, Chris
HIDDEN, THE
Mull, Martin
FLICKS
HOME IS WHERE THE HART IS
O. C. AND STIGGS
Mullaly, Richard
STREET SMART
Mullen, Ruth
MAKING MR.RIGHT
Muller, Anderson
COLOR OF DESTINY, THE
Muller, Marti
CROSS MY HEART
Muller, Paco
MAS BUENAS QUE EL PAN
Muller, Pancho
CARTUCHA CORTADA
LA RAZA NUNCA PIERDE—HUELE A GAS
LA RULETERA
MAS VALE PAJARO EN MANO . . .
Mullick, Ranji
RUDRABEENA
Mullick, Ranjit
BIDROHI
Mullinar, Rod
SHADOWS OF THE PEACOCK
SURFER, THE
Mummey, Christine
MANKILLERS
Munafo, Tony
OVER THE TOP
Munarriz, Miguel
A LOS CUATRO VIENTOS
Munchel, Lois Raymond
TIN MEN
Muncker, Christopher
WHOOPS APOCALYPSE
Mundi, Coati
WHO'S THAT GIRL
Mundy, Meg
FATAL ATTRACTION
SOMEONE TO WATCH OVER ME
Munguia
RATAS DE LA CIUDAD
Munguia, Lourdes
EL MUERTO DEL PALOMO
Munkholm-Jensen, Rolf
JAG ELSKER DIG
Munne, Pep
LA GUERRA DE LOS LOCOS
Munoz, Amparo
LAS DOS ORILLAS
LOS INVITADOS
Munoz, Eduardo
RETO A LA VIDA
Munoz, Gloria
LA VIDA ALEGRE
Munoz, Jorge
EL ANSIA DE MATAR
Munoz, Margarita
EIN BLICK-UND DIE LIEBE BRICHT AUS
Munoz, Monica
RETO A LA VIDA
Munro, Caroline
SLAUGHTER HIGH
Munro, Neil
JOHN AND THE MISSUS
Munsey, P. Michael
MATEWAN
Munther, Ewa
MALARPIRATER
Muparutsa, Walter
CRY FREEDOM
Murad, Raza
DACAIT
Murali
THIRTHAM
Murati, Lili
A JAVOR
Muratova, Kira
KOROTKIE VSTRECHI
Muravyova, Irina
SAMAYA OBAYATELNAYA I PRIVLEKATELNAYA
Murayama, Noe
ROBACHICOS
TIERRA DE VALIENTES
YERBA SANGRIENTE
Murdoch, Richard
WHOOPS APOCALYPSE
Murdock, Cliff
FATAL BEAUTY
Mure, Stefano
LA CROCE DALLE SETTE PIETRE
Murer, Fredi M.
JENATSCH
Murgia, Antonella
ANGUSTIA
Murguia, Ana Ofelia
GABY—A TRUE STORY
Muriel, Alma
ROBACHICOS
Murillo, Ines
FORAJIDOS EN LA MIRA
Murillo, Maria A.
TRAGICO TERREMOTO EN MEXICO
Murney, Christopher
SECRET OF MY SUCCESS, THE
Muro, Marta Fernandez
LAW OF DESIRE
LAW OF DESIRE
Murota, Hideo
TAXING WOMAN, A
Murphy, Albert
BROADCAST NEWS
Murphy, Antonia
THOSE DEAR DEPARTED
Murphy, Cathy
LOVECHILD, THE
Murphy, Christopher
JOCKS
Murphy, Eddie
BEVERLY HILLS COP II
Murphy, Edward D.
THREE MEN AND A BABY
Murphy, Glen
CRY FREEDOM
EMPIRE STATE
Murphy, Jaqueline
THREE MEN AND A BABY
Murphy, Joe
PSYCHOS IN LOVE
Murphy, John
A FIOR DI PELLE
DOGS IN SPACE
Murphy, Maureen
ROXANNE
Murphy, Mike
BLIND DATE
Murphy, Ray
BEVERLY HILLS COP II
Murphy, Rosemary
SEPTEMBER
Murphy, Sean
ADVENTURE OF THE ACTION HUNTERS
Murphy, Sheridan
CUSTODY
Murphy, Sue
P.K. & THE KID
Murray
WHO'S THAT GIRL
Murray, Beverley
LAST STRAW, THE
Murray, Don
MADE IN HEAVEN
Murray, E.J.
HOLLYWOOD SHUFFLE
Murray, Frank
EAT THE RICH
STRAIGHT TO HELL
Murray, Guillermo
SINVERGUENZA . . . PERO HONRADO
Murray, Jack
SQUEEZE, THE
Murray, Juleen
BLACK WIDOW
Murray, Michael
RADIO DAYS
Murtagh, John
FOURTH PROTOCOL, THE
Murtaugh, James
ROSARY MURDERS, THE
Murtaugh, James F.
MAKING MR.RIGHT
Muscat, Michael
HUNTER'S BLOOD
Muschietti, Paula Maria
MISS MARY
Musgrave, June
CUSTODY
Mushonov, Moni
DEADLINE
Mushore, Marcy
CRY FREEDOM

Musi, Macha
AURELIA
Musician
LAURA
Musoyev, Niyezakhmad
YA YEY NRAVLYUS
Mussolini, Alessandra
NOI UOMINI DURI
Mustafa, Zizi
ZAWGAT RAGOL MOHIM
Muters, Melanie G.
PRINCIPAL, THE
Muti, Ornella
CHRONICLE OF A DEATH FORETOLD
IO E MIA SORELLA
STREGATI
Mutkins, Helen
JILTED
Mutoh, Keiji
HIKARU ANNA
Muzaffarov, Ulugbek
NOVYE SKAZKI SHAKHEREZADY
Mwangemi, Constance
KOLORMASK
Mybrand, Jan
NIONDE KOMPANIET
Myerovich, Alvin
DIRTY DANCING
Myers, Brent
POLICE ACADEMY 4: CITIZENS ON PATROL
Myers, Jordan
IN THE MOOD
Myers, Kim
IN THE MOOD
Myerson, Jane
SHADEY
Mykytiuk, Lubomir
BIG TOWN, THE
Mynster, Karen Lise
HIP, HIP, HURRA!
PETER VON SCHOLTEN
Myrberg, Per
LOS DUENOS DEL SILENCIO
Mystery Novelist
SURRENDER
N'Guessan, Albertine
FACES OF WOMEN
Nabors, Troy
RAISING ARIZONA
Nadarevic, Mustafa
VEC VIDJENO
Nadeau, Claire
GRAND GUIGNOL
POULE ET FRITES
Nadia
CHINNATHAMBI PERIYATHAMBI
Nadkarni, Usha
PRATIGHAAT
Naff, Lycia
LETHAL WEAPON
Nagabuchi, Tsuyoshi
TORA-SAN'S BLUEBIRD FANTASY
Nagayama, Ken
OVERKILL
Naggar, Tamra
HOLLYWOOD SHUFFLE
Nagle, Kevin
I WAS A TEENAGE ZOMBIE
Nagy, Anna
LUTRA
Nagy-Kalozy, Eszter
AZ UTOLSOKEZIRAT
Nahum, Ada Ben
LATE SUMMER BLUES
Nail, David
CROSS MY HEART
Naim, Fouad
LHOMME VOILE
Naito, Chin
SARABA ITOSHIKI HITO YO
Nakagawa, Ken
LIVING ON TOKYO TIME
Nakahara, Senas
SHINRAN: SHIRO MICHI
Nakai, Kiichi
FINAL TAKE: THE GOLDEN AGE OF MOVIES
PRINCESS FROM THE MOON
Nakamura, Katsuo
LOVE LETTER
PRINCESS FROM THE MOON
Nakamura, Reiko
RYOMA O KITTA OTOKO
Nakano, Miho
PRINCESS FROM THE MOON
Nakaya, Noboru
LOVE LETTER
Nalrach, Daniel
STREET SMART
Namkiri, Lerdcharn
GOOD MORNING, VIETNAM
Nana
PRETTY SMART
Nance, Jack
BARFLY
Nandy, Subrata
PHERA
Nanini, Marco
NIGHT ANGELS
Nanjo, Reiko
SARABA ITOSHIKI HITO YO
Nanvag, Raj
DACAIT
Naor, Igal
DEADLINE
Napier, Charles
CAMPING DEL TERRORE
NIGHT STALKER, THE
Napier, Eve
STREET SMART
Napier, Marshall
STARLIGHT HOTEL
Napoleon, Maltby
CREEPSHOW 2
Naraoka, Tomoko
HOTARUGAWA
Narcisse, Jarrett
ANGEL HEART
Nardi, Tony
CONCRETE ANGELS
Nardini, James
NICE GIRLS DON'T EXPLODE
Narens, Sherry
BIG SHOTS
Narita, Mikio
SEA AND POISON, THE
Nash, Brian
BOY SOLDIER
Nash, Camilla
BELLMAN AND TRUE
Nasiri, Majid
DJADDE HAYE SARD
Nassar, Debbie
STRIPPED TO KILL
Nasser, Joe
WANTED: DEAD OR ALIVE
Nassirian, Ali
CAPTAIN KHORSHID
DJADDE HAYE SARD
SHEERE SANGGY
Nasuda, Narumi
HIKARU ANNA
Natan, Danny
HOT CHILD IN THE CITY
Natan, Mischa
POET'S SILENCE, THE
Nathan, Adam
I WAS A TEENAGE T.V. TERRORIST
Nathanail, Elena
APOUSIES
Nathenson, Zoe
HEARTS OF FIRE
Nathuram
BABULA
Natoli, Piero
CHI C'E C'E
Natori, Yuko
TOKYO BLACKOUT
YOSHIWARA ENJO
Natsuki, Mari
DEATH SHADOWS
Natsuyagi, Isao
TOKYO BLACKOUT
Naughton, James
GLASS MENAGERIE, THE
Naumann, Jens
SAME TO YOU
Naumovsia, Dushan
NIGHTFORCE
Nause, Allen
BLACK WIDOW
Naval, Deepti
MIRCH MASALA
Naval, Dipti
PANCHVATI
Navarro, Edison
STRIKE COMMANDO
Navarro, Jose A.
LA VIDA ALEGRE
Navarro, Liliana
CITY AND THE DOGS, THE
Navarro, Lolo
VIAJE AL PARAISO
Navarro, Monica Sanchez
FIERAS EN BRAMA
Navarro, Phillip
NIGHTFORCE
Navarro, Rafael Sanchez
VA DE NUEZ
Navasero, Ding
OPPOSING FORCE
Navon, Dov
HIMMO MELECH YERUSHALAIM
KOL AHAVOTAI
Nayyar, Harsh
MAKING MR.RIGHT
Nazarov, Yury
KOORDINATY SMERTI
Nazaryeva, Anna
TANTSPLOSHCHADKA
Nazzaro, Paola
CHI C'E C'E
Ncube, Star
CRY FREEDOM
Ndinda, Albert
CRY FREEDOM
Neal, Jeffrey
HOUSEKEEPER, THE
Nealon, Kevin
ROXANNE
Neame, Christopher
STEEL DAWN
Neary, Robert
TEEN WOLF TOO
Neatrour, Joseph
T. DAN SMITH
Neblett, Carol
ARIA
Nebout, Claire
LASSOCIATION DES MALFAITEURS
NUIT DOCILE
SPIRALE
Nechaeva, Yevgeniya
TEMA
Nedari, Eddy
ISHTAR
Needham, Gordon
NO WAY OUT
Needles, Nique
AS TIME GOES BY
DOGS IN SPACE
Neely, Gail
MILLION DOLLAR MYSTERY
SURF NAZIS MUST DIE
Neely, Mark
OFF THE MARK
Neergaard, Preben
PETER VON SCHOLTEN
Neeson, Liam
PRAYER FOR THE DYING, A
SUSPECT
Neff, Dorothea
FRANCESCA
Neganov, Mikhail
WEEKEND
Negin, Louis
KEEPING TRACK
Negoda, Natalia
ZAVTRA BILA VOINA
Negret, Francois
AU REVOIR, LES ENFANTS
BAD BLOOD
Negri, Lorenzo
QUARTIERE
Negro, Roberto
A LOS CUATRO VIENTOS
Negron, Taylor
RIVER'S EDGE
Neidorf, David
EMPIRE OF THE SUN
UNDER COVER

Neil, Christopher
TRAIN OF DREAMS

Neil, Roger
ORACLE, THE

Neill, Sam
GOOD WIFE, THE

Neilson, Catherine
WHITE MISCHIEF

Nejland, Roland
POHADKA O MALICKOVI

Nekoui, Keyvan
CHECKPOINT

Nekrasov, N.
VZLOMSHCHIK

Nelevic, Mladen
ZIVOT RADNIKA

Nelias, Francois
LES MENDIANTS

Nelligan, Kate
IL GIORNO PRIMA

Nelson, Bob
MIRACLES

Nelson, Craig T.
RED RIDING HOOD

Nelson, Frank
MALIBU BIKINI SHOP, THE

Nelson, Gwen
EIGHTY FOUR CHARING CROSS ROAD

Nelson, Holly
PRETTY SMART

Nelson, Jennifer
CANT BUY ME LOVE

Nelson, Jerry
WINNERS TAKE ALL

Nelson, John Allen
HUNK

Nelson, Judd
FROM THE HIP

Nelson, Kenneth
HELLRAISER

Nelson, Lloyd
LIKE FATHER, LIKE SON

Nelson, Novella
ORPHANS

Nelson, Ron
DIXIELAND DAIMYO

Nelson, Willie
RED HEADED STRANGER

Nemeth, Stephen
OPEN HOUSE

Nemolyaeva, Anastasia
STARAYA AZBUKA

Nemolyayeva, Anastasia
KURIER

Nena
DER UNSICHTBARE

Nenadovic, Djordje
HEY BABU RIBA

Nercessian, Stepan
BEIJO NA BOCA

Nero, Danny
BEVERLY HILLS COP II

Nero, Franco
GIRL, THE
SWEET COUNTRY

Nero, Toni
COMMANDO SQUAD
NO DEAD HEROES

Nesbitt, Derren
EAT THE RICH

Ness, John
FULL METAL JACKET

Nesterenko, Alexei
PRODELKI V STARINNOM DUKHE

Neubauer, Christine
TAXI NACH KAIRO

Neumann, Deborah
TRESPASSES

Neumann, Frederick
WALKER

Neumann, Jenny
DELOS ADVENTURE, THE

Neuville, Jacques
ARIA

Nevargic, Peter
LADY BEWARE

Nevolina, Angelica
SENTIMENTALNOE PUTESHESTVIE NA KARTOSHKU

Nevzorov, Boris
GOVORIT MOSKVA
RUS IZNACHALNA

Newark, Derek
BELLMAN AND TRUE

Newark, Samantha
SUMMER CAMP NIGHTMARE

Newberth, George
MY LITTLE GIRL

Newburn, George
ADVENTURES IN BABYSITTING

Newby, Christine
GOTHIC

Newell, Jim
HAPPY HOUR

Newell, Patrick
REDONDELA

Newham, David
ESCAPES

Newlander, Jamison
LOST BOYS, THE

Newley, Anthony
GARBAGE PAIL KIDS MOVIE, THE

Newlon, Neil
ANGEL HEART

Newman, Andrew Hill
MANNEQUIN

Newman, Fred
MUNCHIES
O. C. AND STIGGS

Newman, James L.
SILENT NIGHT, DEADLY NIGHT PART II

Newman, Joy
RADIO DAYS

Newman, Phyllis
MANNEQUIN

Newman, Russell
DEAR CARDHOLDER

Newney, Raul
HELLRAISER

News Anchor
BROADCAST NEWS

Newsome, Sarah
DOGS IN SPACE

Newspaper Critic
WEEDS

Nezer, Christoforos
YENETHLIA POLI

Nezu, Jinpachi
RYOMA O KITTA OTOKO
YOSHIWARA ENJO

Ng, Richard
MAGNIFICENT WARRIORS
WRONG COUPLES,THE

Ngimbi, Bwanando
LA VIE EST BELLE

Ngoc, Tran
OVERKILL

Ngor, Dr. Haing S.
EASTERN CONDORS

Ngugi, John T.
KOLORMASK

Nguyen, Cu Ba
GOOD MORNING, VIETNAM

Nguyen, Hanh Hi
GOOD MORNING, VIETNAM

Nguyen, Hoa
GOOD MORNING, VIETNAM

Nguyen, Tu Ban
WANTED: DEAD OR ALIVE

Ni Chaoimh, Bairbee
RAWHEAD REX

Nicheli, Guido
MONTECARLO GRAN CASINO

Nicholas, Angela
PSYCHOS IN LOVE

Nicholas, Arnold
ULTIMAX FORCE

Nicholas, George
GET THE TERRORISTS

Nicholas, Larry
MUNCHIES

Nichole, Lydia
HOLLYWOOD SHUFFLE

Nicholls, Patti
RITA, SUE AND BOB TOO!

Nicholls, Phoebe
MAURICE

Nichols, George
SAKURA KILLERS

Nichols, Lance
PROJECT X

Nichols, Linda
SUMMER CAMP NIGHTMARE

Nichols, Lisa
MURDER LUST

Nichols, Mark
CHECKPOINT

Nichols, Nichelle
SUPERNATURALS, THE

Nichols, Penny
TIN MEN

Nichols, Robert
FULL METAL JACKET

Nichols, Steven
WITCHBOARD

Nicholsen, Gerda
BELINDA

Nicholson, Jack
BROADCAST NEWS
IRONWEED
WITCHES OF EASTWICK, THE

Nicholson, Nick
GET THE TERRORISTS
NO DEAD HEROES

Nick Waters
RUNNING FROM THE GUNS

Nickels, Rebecca
RADIO DAYS

Nickerson, Scott
WITCHES OF EASTWICK, THE

Nickerson, Susan
WITCHBOARD

Nickles, M.A.
HAMBURGER HILL

Nicoglou, Anton
COERS CROISES

Nicolas, Madeleine
DAMORTIS

Nicolau Sharpley, Kris
BLOODSUCKERS FROM OUTER SPACE

Nicole, O.W.
BUS

Nicolodi, Daria
LE FOTO DI GIOIA
OPERA

Niedashkovskaya, Raisa
KOMISSAR

Niehoff, Domenica
TAXI NACH KAIRO

Nielsen, Barbara
LANNEE DES MEDUSES

Nielsen, Brigitte
BEVERLY HILLS COP II

Nielsen, Claus Steenstrup
VENNER FOR ALTID

Nielsen, Finn
BABETTE'S GASTEBUD

Nielsen, Jeff
SOMEONE TO WATCH OVER ME

Nielsen, Leslie
HOME IS WHERE THE HART IS
NIGHTSTICK
NUTS

Nielsen, Ulla
VENNER FOR ALTID

Niemczyk, Leon
ZLOTA MAHMUDIA

Niemela, Juhani
TILINTEKO

Niemi, Lisa
SLAMDANCE
STEEL DAWN

Niemimaa, Jani
SEPPAN

Nieminen, Markko
JAAHYVAISET PRESIDENTILLE

Nienas, Greg
BLOOD HOOK

Nightingale, Rick
DANGER ZONE, THE

Nigishi, Kie
SEA AND POISON, THE

Nihei, Judi
LIVING ON TOKYO TIME

Nijhoff, Loudi
VAN GELUK GESPROKEN

Nijholt, Willem
HAVINCK

Nikkari, Esko
TILINTEKO
VARJOJA PARATIISISSA

Nikkonen, Harri
NAKEMIIN, HYVASTI

Nikolakakis, Nektaria
VERSTECKTE LIEBE

Nikolayeva, Lyudmila
ZOLOTAYA BABA

Nikonenko, Sergei
KORABL PRISHELTSEV
ZAVTRA BILA VOINA

Nikulin, Yuri
DVADTSTAT DNEI BEZ

Nincheri, Roland
KEEPING TRACK

Nincic, Zeljko
ZIVOT RADNIKA

Ninidze, Ija
REPENTANCE

Ninidze, Iya
PYAT NEVEST DO LYUBIMOY

Ninidze, Merab
REPENTANCE
STUPEN

Ninomiya, Sayoko
YOSHIWARA ENJO

Nirvana, Yana
CLUB LIFE

Nishida, Ken
SEA AND POISON, THE

Nishihara, Yuzo
RIVER'S EDGE

Nishikawa, Lane
LIVING ON TOKYO TIME

Nishikawa, Mineko
YOSHIWARA ENJO

Nishio, John
OVERKILL

Nisille, Bernard
HOTEL DE FRANCE

Nisonen, Ville
KILL CITY

Nissen, Claus
KAMPEN OM DEN RODE KO

Nitz, Dean
BROADCAST NEWS

Nixon, Cynthia
O. C. AND STIGGS

Njenga, Waweru
MORGAN STEWART'S COMING HOME

Njiru, Ester
KOLORMASK

Noble, Alison
RETURN TO HORROR HIGH

Noble, James
YOU TALKIN' TO ME?

Noble, Jorge
HERENCIA DE VALIENTES

Noble, Kathryn
DELOS ADVENTURE, THE

Noble, Kevin
JOHN AND THE MISSUS

Noble, Xorge
EL ANSIA DE MATAR
LA RAZA NUNCA PIERDE—HUELE A GAS
NOS REIMOS DE LA MIGRA

Nocell, Jim
DEADTIME STORIES

Nock, Thomas
ALPINE FIRE

Nocquet, Andre
TERMINUS

Noga, Tom
LETHAL WEAPON

Nogaibaev, Idris
VOLNY UMIRAYUT NA BEREGU

Nogueira, Ana Beatriz
VERA

Noiman, Rivka
TEL AVIV—BERLIN

Noiret, Philippe
FAMILY, THE
GLI OCCHIALI D'ORO
MASQUES
NOYADE INTERDITE

Nolan, David
EAT THE PEACH
RAWHEAD REX

Nolte, Nick
EXTREME PREJUDICE
WEEDS

Nomura, Ryoji
ROBINSON NO NIWA

Nono, Claire
MONSTER IN THE CLOSET

Nono, Maitre
LA VIE EST BELLE

Noodt, Brian
CREEPSHOW 2

Noonan, Greg
UNTOUCHABLES, THE

Noonan, John Ford
ADVENTURES IN BABYSITTING

Noonan, Tom
MONSTER SQUAD, THE

Noori, Al R. Shoja
MANUSCRIPTS

Noose, Ted
IN THE MOOD

Nora, Byron
BIG EASY, THE

Norby, Ghita
HIP, HIP, HURRA!
WOLF AT THE DOOR, THE

Nordberg, Marita
UUNO TURHAPURO MUUTTAA MAALLE

Norden, Donald L.
BARFLY

Nordmann, Jean-Gabriel
UNE FLAMME DANS MON COEUR

Noriega, Adela
UN SABADO MAS

Noriega, Eduardo
GABY—A TRUE STORY
JUNTOS

Norman, Joanne
OPEN HOUSE

Norman, Maria
VIOLINS CAME WITH THE AMERICANS, THE

Norris, Buckley
SLAMDANCE

Norris, Deborah
KILLER WORKOUT

Norris, Leslie
DATE WITH AN ANGEL

Norris, Mike
SURVIVAL GAME

Norrman, Borje
JIM OCH PIRATERNA BLOM

Norte, Vitor
DUMA VEZ POR TODAS

North, Alan
FOURTH PROTOCOL, THE

North, Hope
CURSE, THE
DIRTY LAUNDRY

Northey, Christopher
T. DAN SMITH

Northrup, Harry E.
PROJECT X

Norton, Alex
COMRADES

Norton, Ralph
RAISING ARIZONA

Norton, Richard
EQUALIZER 2000

Norville, Herbert
FULL METAL JACKET

Norvind, Nailea
GABY—A TRUE STORY

Nosik, Vladimir
OBESHCHAYU BYT

Nossek, Ralph
T. DAN SMITH
WHISTLE BLOWER, THE

Notario, Joaquin
LA VIDA ALEGRE

Noto, Vic
STREET TRASH

Nott, Roger
BOY SOLDIER

Notte, Luigi Mezza
MAN ON FIRE

Nouasser, Lutuf
HANSEL AND GRETEL

Nougaro, Pierre
JEAN DE FLORETTE
MANON OF THE SPRING

MASQUES

Nouri, Michael
HIDDEN, THE

Nourmand, Nicole
SUMMER CAMP NIGHTMARE

Noutsou, Phaedra
TA PAIDIA TIS CHELIDONAS

Novak, John
MORNING MAN, THE

Noveck, Fima
TROUBLE WITH SPIES, THE

Novelist
LA RUBIA DEL BAR

Novelli, Novello
NOI UOMINI DURI
STREGATI

Novembre, Tom
AGENT TROUBLE

Novikov, Alexander
AKTSIA

Novoa, J. Luis
LA VIDA ALEGRE

Novy, Pavel
DISCOPRIBEH
PRATELE BERMUDSKEHO TROJUHELNIKU

Nowak, Jolanta
ZYCIE WEWNETRZNE

Nowicki, Jan
DIARY FOR MY LOVED ONES
MAGNAT
ZYGFRYD

Noyes, Danny
PSYCHOS IN LOVE

Nucci, Leo
MACBETH

Nufaar, Celia
BLOND DOLLY

Nunez, Eslinda
EL SOCIO DE DIOS

Nunn, Alice
WHO'S THAT GIRL

Nuo, Ai
ROMANCE OF BOOK AND SWORD, THE

Nuora, Kaj
FADERN, SONEN OCH DEN HELIGE ANDE

Nurlanov, Kenes
SKAZKA O PREKRASNOY AYSULU

Nurse
W ZAWIESZENIU

Nuryagdyeva, Maya
PRIKLYUCHENIA NA MALENKIKH OSTROVEKH

Nussbaum, Mike
FATAL ATTRACTION
HOUSE OF GAMES

Nuter, Egon
VO VREMENA VOLCHYIKA ZAKONOV

Nuti, Francesco
STREGATI

Nutter, Mayf
HUNTER'S BLOOD

Nuys, Ed Van
STREET SMART

Nyako, Juli
SZORNYEK EVADJA

Nyanggai, Chiling
BEJALAI

Nycander, Maud
MITT HJARTA HAR TVA TUNGOR

Nychols, Darcy
SLAMMER GIRLS

Nye, Carrie
HELLO AGAIN

Nye, Linda
SQUARE DANCE

Nye, Louis
O. C. AND STIGGS

Nye, Will
TALKING WALLS

Nygaard, Helge
KAMILLA OG TYVEN

Nygaard, Ragnhild
PLASTPOSEN

Nyman, Tuula
SNOW QUEEN, THE

Nyrood, Gunilla
NIONDE KOMPANIET

Nystrom, Tiina
NAKEMIIN, HYVASTI

Nzunzimbu, Landu
LA VIE EST BELLE

O'Brian, Donal
LA CODA DEL DIAVOLO

O'Brian, Peter
STABILIZER, THE

O'Brien, Dayna
BEVERLY HILLS COP II

O'Brien, Frank
RADIO DAYS

O'Brien, Jeanne
DIRTY LAUNDRY

O'Brien, Kieran
BELLMAN AND TRUE

O'Brien, Niall
RAWHEAD REX

O'Brien, Thomas
BIG EASY, THE

O'Byrne, Bryan
SPACEBALLS

O'Colsdealbha, Sean
BUDAWANNY

O'Connell, Bill
MY LITTLE GIRL

O'Connell, Bob
OUTRAGEOUS FORTUNE

O'Connell, Deirdre
TIN MEN

O'Connell, Natalie
I WAS A TEENAGE T.V. TERRORIST

O'Conner, Brian
MANKILLERS

O'Conner, Gary
THOU SHALT NOT KILL . . . EXCEPT

O'Connor, Brian
BEVERLY HILLS COP II

O'Connor, Derrick
HOPE AND GLORY

O'Connor, Di
LIGHTHORSEMEN, THE

O'Connor, Pat
BELL DIAMOND

O'Conor, Hugh
RAWHEAD REX

O'Dair, Margie
BIG EASY, THE

O'Donaghue, Michael
SUICIDE CLUB, THE

O'Donnal, John
RAISING ARIZONA

O'Donnell, Steven
LOVECHILD, THE

O'Donoughue, Micky
WHOOPS APOCALYPSE

O'Donovan, Noel
EAT THE PEACH
RAWHEAD REX

O'Farrell, Tralle
ROCK 'N' ROLL NIGHTMARE

O'Flaherty, Erin
CANT BUY ME LOVE

O'Flatharta, Tomas
BUDAWANNY

O'Haco, Jeff
BLOODY WEDNESDAY

O'Halloran, Jack
DRAGNET

O'Hare, Katie
SUSPECT

O'Hare, Tim
GOOD MORNING, VIETNAM

O'Herlihy, Cormac
DEAD, THE

O'Herlihy, Dan
DEAD, THE

O'Keeffe, Miles
IRON WARRIOR

O'Key, Shirley
ESCAPES

O'Leary, William
NICE GIRLS DON'T EXPLODE
WALKER

O'Mallery, Daragh
WITHNAIL AND I

O'Mara, George
EMANON

O'Neal, Patrick
LIKE FATHER, LIKE SON

O'Neal, Ryan
TOUGH GUYS DON'T DANCE

O'Neil, Johnny
WILD THING

O'Neill, Bernadette
EAT THE PEACH

O'Neill, Errol
FRENCHMAN'S FARM

O'Neill, Jennifer
I LOVE NEW YORK

O'Neill, John
LETHAL WEAPON

O'Neill, Mark
NECROPOLIS

O'Neill, Remy
RETURN TO HORROR HIGH

O'Quinn, Terry
BLACK WIDOW
STEPFATHER, THE

O'Reilly, Dennis
THUNDER WARRIOR II

O'Reilly, Harry
HAMBURGER HILL

O'Riordan, Cait
STRAIGHT TO HELL

O'Ross, Ed
FULL METAL JACKET
HIDDEN, THE
LETHAL WEAPON

O'Rourke, Kevin
BEDROOM WINDOW, THE

O'Shaughnessy, Maureen
THOSE DEAR DEPARTED

O'Shea, Daniel
HAMBURGER HILL

O'Sullivan, Barney
EL HOMBRE DESNUDO

O'Toole, Annette
CROSS MY HEART

O'Toole, Elsa
JANE AND THE LOST CITY

O'Toole, Kate
DEAD, THE

O'Toole, Peter
LAST EMPEROR, THE

Oakes, Stephen
WITCHES OF EASTWICK, THE

Obach, Conchita
LA OVEJA NEGRA

Oberoi, Suresh
DACAIT
MIRCH MASALA
PANCHVATI

Obregon, Ana
EL GRAN SERAFIN
LA VIDA ALEGRE
POLICIA

Obregon, Rodrigo
HARD TICKET TO HAWAII

Obrist, Bethli
JENATSCH

Ocasek, Ric
MADE IN HEAVEN

Occhilupo, Mark
NORTH SHORE

Occhipinti, Andrea
FAMILY, THE
IL GIORNO PRIMA

Ochoa, Juan Manuel
CITY AND THE DOGS, THE

Odagiri, Miki
SHINRAN: SHIRO MICHI

Odaka, Megumi
PRINCESS FROM THE MOON

Odermatt, Joerg
ALPINE FIRE

Odum, Maeve
RIVER'S EDGE

Oedy, Mary Ann
RUNNING MAN, THE

Oesterberg, Birger
NIONDE KOMPANIET

Offner, Deborah
PROJECT X

Ogata, Ken
KATAKU NO HITO
ZEGEN

Ogawa, James
OVERKILL

Ogusu, Michio
SHINRAN: SHIRO MICHI

Oh, Soon-Teck
STEELE JUSTICE

Oh-Tee
BORN OF FIRE

Ohana, Claudia
BEIJO NA BOCA

Ohashi, Minako
LIVING ON TOKYO TIME

Ohta, Kumiko
ROBINSON NO NIWA

Ohtaki, Shuji
TOKYO BLACKOUT

Oishi, Mariko
SEA AND POISON, THE

Ojala, Jaska
KILL CITY

Ojeda, Manuel
LO DEL CESAR
RETO A LA VIDA

Okada, Mariko
TAXING WOMAN, A

Okada, Masumi
SEA AND POISON, THE

Okamoto, Mami
DIXIELAND DAIMYO

Okite, John
KOLORMASK

Okking, Jens
KAMPEN OM DEN RODE KO

Okko
PROJECT X

Okras, Gudron
SO VIELE TRAUME

Okten, Guler
DILAN

Okuda, Eiji
SEA AND POISON, THE

Okumura, Kinji
ROBINSON NO NIWA

Oladeinde, Frank
DRAGON'S FOOD

Olandt, Ken
SUMMER SCHOOL

Olanick, Anita
WINTER TAN, A

Olasagasti, Eneko
A LOS CUATRO VIENTOS

Olbrychski, Daniel
MOSCA ADDIO
SIEKIEREZADA
TELEFTAIO STICHIMA

Older, James
FOURTH PROTOCOL, THE

Oldham, Paul
RITA, SUE AND BOB TOO!

Oldham, Will
MATEWAN

Oldman, Gary
PRICK UP YOUR EARS

Olemans, Michel
MASCARA

Olexenko, Stepan
MY OBVINYAEM
MY OBVINYAEM

Olfson, Ken
SPACEBALLS

Olgado, Tiki
MANON OF THE SPRING

Olifson, Mark
BIRDS OF PREY

Olin, Stig
JIM OCH PIRATERNA BLOM

Olita, Joseph
KOLORMASK

Oliver, Dan
NO DEAD HEROES

Oliver, Deanna
BRAVE LITTLE TOASTER, THE

Oliver, Henry
MUTANT HUNT

Oliver, Lucy
ARIA

Oliver, Natalie
AMAZING GRACE AND CHUCK

Oliver, Roland
BUSINESS AS USUAL

Oliver-Touchstone, Julie P.
BLOODSUCKERS FROM OUTER SPACE

Oliviero, Silvio
GRAVEYARD SHIFT

PSYCHO GIRLS
Olmi, Corrado
MISSIONE EROICA
Olohan, John
RAWHEAD REX
Olschewsky, Gerhard
BLACK CANNON INCIDENT, THE
Olsen, Dick
HIDING OUT
Olsen, Ollie
DOGS IN SPACE
Olsen, Richard
BEDROOM WINDOW, THE
WEEDS
Olsen, Svein Birger
OFELAS
Olsson, Claes
ELVIS-KISSAN JALJILLA
Olsson, Gunilla
MALACCA
Olsson, Kurt
AMAZING GRACE AND CHUCK
Olsson, Vera
ELVIS-KISSAN JALJILLA
Omarova, Gamida
YA YEY NRAVLYUS
Omerek, Joseph
ISHTAR
Oms, Alba
VIOLINS CAME WITH THE AMERICANS, THE
Oms, Amanda Francisca
JOR
Onaitite, Jurate
SLEDY OBOROTNYA
Onorati, Carmen
DA NNUNZIO
Onorati, Peter
FIREHOUSE
Ontiveros, Lupe
BORN IN EAST L.A.
Ontiverous, Bill
HARRY AND THE HENDERSONS
Ontkean, Michael
ALLNIGHTER, THE
MAID TO ORDER
Oostenbrink, Jeroen
EEN MAAND LATER
Opania, Marian
BOHATERROKU
Opatoshu, David
FORTY DAYS OF MUSA DAGH
Oppenhage, Sonja
JAG ELSKER DIG
Opper, Don
SLAMDANCE
Opsahl, Arve
PA STIGENDE KURS
Orange, Gerald
WEEDS
WHO'S THAT GIRL
Orange, Gerald L.
ANGEL HEART
Orbach, Jerry
DIRTY DANCING
I LOVE NEW YORK
SOMEONE TO WATCH OVER ME
Ordonez, Mabel
LA ESTANQUERA DE VALLECAS
Ordonez, Victor
OPPOSING FORCE
Orend, Jack R.
BIG SHOTS
Orfei, Lara
DELITTI
Ori, Dr. Avraham
LO SAM ZAYIN
Orlandini, Lucas
MAN ON FIRE
Orlando, Joseph
THIN LINE, THE
Orlando, Silvio
PERSONAGGI & INTERPRETI
Ormaeche, Josu
LA VIDA ALEGRE
Ormrod, Francine
BUSHFIRE MOON
Orofino, Jean-Luc
JOHNNY MONROE
Orozco, Maurice
O. C. AND STIGGS
Orsatti, Noon
WINNERS TAKE ALL
Orso, Anna
DEVIL IN THE FLESH
Ortega, Ernie
NO BLOOD NO SURRENDER
Ortega, Gerardo
SUFRE MAMON
Ortega, Jim
NIGHTFORCE
Ortega, Jimmy
EXTREME PREJUDICE
Ortega, Rudy
P.K. & THE KID
Ortin, Polo
EL MOFLES Y LOS MECANICOS
LA RULETERA
LAPUTA: THE CASTLE IN THE SKY
LAS TRAIGO . . . MUERTAS
NOS REIMOS DE LA MIGRA
Ortiz, Marta
CARTUCHA CORTADA
Ortiz, Martha
EL DIABLO, EL SANTO Y EL TONTO
Osborne, Glenys
DOGS IN SPACE
DOGS IN SPACE
Osborne, Jean
DOGS IN SPACE
Oscarsson, Pia
DEMONS
Osipenko, Alla
SKORBNOE BESCHUVSTVIE
Ostara, Kylie
YEAR MY VOICE BROKE, THE
Ostergren, Pernilla W.
SERPENT'S WAY, THE
Osterman, George
BIG BANG, THE
Ostime, Roger
EIGHTY FOUR CHARING CROSS ROAD
Osuga, Kaneo
BUS
Otaki, Shuji
TAXING WOMAN, A
Otero, Isabel
ARCHANGELOS TOU PATHOUS
Otiijgava, Nato
REPENTANCE
Oto
ROBINSON NO NIWA
Otsuki, Manji
SAKURA KILLERS
Ott, Dennis
ZERO BOYS, THE
Ottaviani, Nadia
INTERVISTA
Ottersen, Anne-Marie
PLASTPOSEN
Ottesen, Gunner
EPIDEMIC
Ottesen, Susanne
EPIDEMIC
Otto, Barry
HOWLING III, THE
Otto, Miranda
INITIATION
Ottosson, Per
MY LIFE AS A DOG
Ou, Cindy
AUTUMN'S TALE, AN
Oudart, Gisele
FALSCH
Ousdal, Sverre Anker
ETTER RUBICON
FELDMANN CASE, THE
MIO, MOY MIO
OM KARLEK
PLASTPOSEN
Outinen, Kati
HAMLET
VARJOJA PARATIISISSA
Outlaw, Frank
RAISING ARIZONA
Ovchinnikova, P.
DVADTSTAT DNEI BEZ
Overgaard, Peter Hesse
JAG ELSKER DIG
NEGERKYS & LABRE LARVER
Oversteegen, Martin
NITWITS
Overton, Rick
MILLION DOLLAR MYSTERY
Owczarek, Danuta
KOMEDIANCI Z WCZORAJSZEJ ULICY
Owens, Chris
BIG TOWN, THE
Owens, Gerald
MAKING MR.RIGHT
Owens, Karen
RUNNING MAN, THE
Owens, Ray
BIG BANG, THE
Owens, Sharon
RUNNING MAN, THE
Owens, Warren
SLATE, WYN & ME
Ozawa, Eitaro
DEATH SHADOWS
TAXING WOMAN, A
Ozbal, Eray
YER DEMIR, GOK BAKIR
Ozelite, Nijole
ZONTIK DLYA NOVOBRACHNYKH
Ozhelite, Niyole
IZVINITEPOZHALUYSTA
Ozores, Robert
WILD THING
Ozsda, Erika
GONDOVISELES
Paaske, Erik
HIP, HIP, HURRA!
PELLE EROVRAREN
Pabsy, Mike
MANKILLERS
Pacheco, Arlette
MAS BUENAS QUE EL PAN
Pachorek, Richard
SUPERNATURALS, THE
Pacifico III, Joseph
THIN LINE, THE
Pack, Roger Lloyd
PRICK UP YOUR EARS
Packer, Michael
PERSONAL SERVICES
Pacula, Joanna
DEATH BEFORE DISHONOR
Padilla, Raul
ENTRE FICHERAS ANDA EL DIABLO
Padilla, Raul "Chato"
LA RULETERA
Paes, Dira
ELE, O BOTO
Paevatalu, Guido
PETER VON SCHOLTEN
Pagan, Antone
DIRTY DANCING
Pagano, Mark
NECROPOLIS
Page, Genevieve
ARIA
BEYOND THERAPY
CARTOLINE ITALIANE
Page, Geraldine
MY LITTLE GIRL
Page, Heather
COMRADES
Page, Ken
ROBOCOP
Page, Robbie
NORTH SHORE
Pagni, Eros
TERESA
Pagura, Ruben
EULALIA
Paiement, Mahee
BACH AND BROCCOLI
Paige, Kymberly
BEVERLY HILLS COP II
Pain, Didier
JEAN DE FLORETTE
MANON OF THE SPRING
Pais, Jorge
UN SABADO MAS
Paisley, Ray
BELIEVERS, THE
TOO OUTRAGEOUS
Pajares, Andres
MOROS Y CRISTIANOS

Pajic, Ksenija
OFICIR S RUZOM
UVEK SPREMNE ZENE

Pak, Christine
BELIEVERS, THE
LAST STRAW, THE

Pak, Ludwig
SIEKIEREZADA

Pakarinen, Kaija
TILINTEKO

Pakulnis, Maria
ZYGFRYD

Pal, Amrit
SHEELA

Palacio, Raul Antonio
RETO A LA VIDA

Palaitzidis, Tassos
DOXOBUS

Palance, Jack
OUT OF ROSENHEIM

Palaty, Tomas
WOLF'S HOLE

Palekar, Amol
JHOOTHI

Palenickova, Jana
CIZIM VSTUP POVOLEN

Palfrey, Yolande
PRINCESS ACADEMY, THE

Paliatsaras, Constantinos
OH BABYLON

Pallarp, Ake
FADERN, SONEN OCH DEN HELIGE ANDE

Pallas, Lupe
MAS BUENAS QUE EL PAN

Pallesen, Per
STRIT OG STUMME

Pallut, Philippe
SOUS LE SOLEIL DE SATAN

Palma, Loretta
DERANGED

Palme, Beatrice
RENEGADE, UN OSSO TROPPO DURO

Palmeira, Marcos
COLOR OF DESTINY, THE

Palmer
EL HOMBRE DE LA DEUDA EXTERNA

Palmer, Darryl
SUSPECT

Palmer, Debbie
CRYSTAL HEART

Palmer, Gretchen
MALIBU BIKINI SHOP, THE

Palmer, Renzo
FAMILY, THE

Palmer, Toni
PERSONAL SERVICES

Palmiero, George
GHOST FEVER

Palmisano, Esther
SPACE RACE

Palmisano, Nick
SPACE RACE

Palmisano, Victory
SPACE RACE

Palmore, J.C.
HAMBURGER HILL

Palo, Jukka-Pekka
VARJOJA PARATIISISSA

Palomina, Juan
MISS MARY

Palomo, Yolanda
ALIEN PREDATOR

Palshikar, Suhas
PRATIGHAAT

Palummella, Gennaro
QUEL RAGAZZO DELLA CURVA "B"

Panayotidis, Alkis
FAKELOS POLK STON AERA
OH BABYLON
ONE HUNDRED AND TWENTY DECIBELS
VIOS KE POLITIA

Panchito, Palito
NO BLOOD NO SURRENDER

Pancrazi, Jean-Claude
LANNEE DES MEDUSES

Pandit, Vijayeta
AMAR SANGI

Pandya
THIRUMATHI ORU VEGUMATHI

Pane, Caren
I WAS A TEENAGE ZOMBIE

Panebianco, Richard
CHINA GIRL

Panelli, Alessandra
FAMILY, THE

Pang, Ed
BLACK WIDOW

Pang, Sidney
NINJA THUNDERBOLT

Pankin, Stuart
FATAL ATTRACTION

Pankow, John
BATTERIES NOT INCLUDED
SECRET OF MY SUCCESS, THE

Panov, A.
VZLOMSHCHIK

Pansullo, Ed
BEVERLY HILLS COP II
STRAIGHT TO HELL
WALKER

Pansullo, Eddy
SPACE RACE

Pantages, Tony
STAKEOUT

Pantik, Julius
CENA ODVAHY

Pantoliano, Joe
AMAZON WOMEN ON THE MOON
EMPIRE OF THE SUN
LA BAMBA
SQUEEZE, THE

Pao, Basil
LAST EMPEROR, THE

Paolini, Lorenzo
LUNGA VITA ALLA SIGNORA!

Paolone, Catherine
PROJECT X

Pap, Vera
ISTEN VELETEK, BARATAIM

Papa, Annie
CARAMELLE DA UNO SCONOSCIUTO
SOTTOZERO

Papa, Athena
KE DYO AVGA TOURKIAS

Papa, Enrico
MAN ON FIRE

Papaconstantinou, Nikos
TELEFTAIO STICHIMA

Papadodima, Fenya
ARCHANGELOS TOU PATHOUS

Papadopoulou, Aneza
ONE HUNDRED AND TWENTY DECIBELS

Papageorgiou, Thanassis
VIOS KE POLITIA

Papamoschou, Tatiana
YENETHLIA POLI

Papanov, Anatoli
VREMYA ZHELANIY

Papas, Helen
GRAVEYARD SHIFT

Papas, Irene
CHRONICLE OF A DEATH FORETOLD
HIGH SEASON
SWEET COUNTRY

Papasian, Gerald
WANTED: DEAD OR ALIVE

Pappu
AMRITAMGAMAYA

Paquette, Pier Kohl
MORNING MAN, THE

Pardo, Don
RADIO DAYS

Pardo, M. Carmen
A LOS CUATRO VIENTOS

Pardo, Mario
BALADA DA PRAIA DOS CAES
LA PLAYA DE LOS PERROS

Pare, Michael
SPACE RACE

Paredes, Estela
HOUR OF THE ASSASSIN

Paredes, Marisa
CARA DE ACELGA
MIENTRAS HAYA LUZ

Parez, Louis
MASCARA

Parfenov, Sergei
ZOLOTAYA BABA

Parfitt, Judy
MAURICE

Parfyonov, Mikahil
VZLOMSHCHIK

Paris, Andrew
POLICE ACADEMY 4: CITIZENS ON PATROL

Paris, Julie
OVERBOARD

Parisi, Maria Pia
DOLCE PELLE DI ANGELA

Parisini, Dario
IL GRANDE BLEK

Parjiat
ANJAAM

Parke, Dorothy
NO WAY OUT

Parker, Carl
IN THE MOOD

Parker, Corey
SOMETHING SPECIAL!

Parker, Erwin
DER NACHBAR

Parker, F. William
PERSONAL FOUL

Parker, Gary
EMPIRE OF THE SUN

Parker, Jameson
PRINCE OF DARKNESS

Parker, Lindsay
FLOWERS IN THE ATTIC

Parker, Monica
HES MY GIRL

Parker, Oliver
HELLRAISER

Parker, Ray
ENEMY TERRITORY

Parker, Rocky
IN THE MOOD

Parker, William
FOURTH PROTOCOL, THE

Parkin, David
HOPE AND GLORY

Parkina, Tatiana
KAPITAN "PILIGRIMA"

Parking Valet
CLUB LIFE

Parks, Andrew
WILD PAIR, THE

Parks, Michael
CLUB LIFE
RETURN OF JOSEY WALES, THE

Parks, Richard
CREEPSHOW 2

Parnaby, Bert
PRICK UP YOUR EARS

Parnes, Richard
OPEN HOUSE

Parodi, Alejandro
REALM OF FORTUNE, THE
VA DE NUEZ
VIAJE AL PARAISO

Parola, Nieva
LA ESTANQUERA DE VALLECAS

Parr, Bob
VALET GIRLS

Parr, John
VALET GIRLS

Parragon, John
NORTH SHORE

Parrella, Loredana
DELIRIA

Parrish, Elizabeth
ORPHANS

Parros, Peter
DEATH BEFORE DISHONOR

Parrott, Jim
HAPPY HOUR

Parsekian, Tom
CLUB LIFE

Parson, Robert
MORNING MAN, THE

Parsonage, Simon
COMRADES

Parsons, Robert
KEEPING TRACK

Partanen, Elisa
NAKEMIIN, HYVASTI

Partanen, Heikki T.
ELVIS-KISSAN JALJILLA

Partexano, Alex
STREGATI
Partlow, Richard
TALKING WALLS
WANTED: DEAD OR ALIVE
Parton, William
LADY OF THE CAMELIAS
Partridge, Sarah
IN THE MOOD
Partsalakis, Giorgos
O PARADISSOS ANIGI ME ANTIKLIDI
Partsalev, Georgi
TRINAJSTATA GODENICA NA PRINCA
Parvathy
AMRITAMGAMAYA
Pas, Michael
LOVE IS A DOG FROM HELL
Pasanen, Spede
PIKKUPOJAT
UUNO TURHAPURO MUUTTAA MAALLE
Pasborg, Lennart
EPIDEMIC
Pascal, Christine
LE GRAND CHEMIN
Pasco, Isabelle
LA CODA DEL DIAVOLO
Pascoe, Don
SHADOWS OF THE PEACOCK
Pascual, Consuelo
LA ESTANQUERA DE VALLECAS
Pasdar, Adrian
NEAR DARK
Pashalinksi, Lola
ANNA
Pashalinski, Lola
IRONWEED
Pashin, Yevgeny
KAZHDYY OKHOTNIK ZHELAET ZNAT
Pashu's Wife
PHERA
Pashutin, Alexander
PLIUMBUM, ILI OPASNAIA IGIA
Paskene, Eva
BLUDNYY SYN
Paso, Encarna
EL BOSQUE ANIMADO
Pasquier, Michel
KEEPING TRACK
Passeltiner, Bernie
EIGHTY FOUR CHARING CROSS ROAD
Passy, Antonio
A LOS CUATRO VIENTOS
Pastor, Aurora
LA CASA DE BERNARDA ALBA
Pastor, Clara
ANGUSTIA
Pastor, Julian
LA GRAN FIESTA
Pastorelli, Robert
BEVERLY HILLS COP II
OUTRAGEOUS FORTUNE
Patachou
LA RUMBA
Patatin, Pepe
LAW OF DESIRE
Pate, Christopher
HOWLING III, THE
Pate, Michael
HOWLING III, THE
Patekar, Nana
PRATIGHAAT
SHEELA
SUTRADHAR
Patel, Anuradha
KAUN KITNEY PAANI MEIN
Pater, Clara
ROCK 'N' ROLL NIGHTMARE
Paterson, Bill
FRIENDSHIP'S DEATH
HIDDEN CITY
Paterson, Ronnie
GET THE TERRORISTS
Paterson, Sheila
STEPFATHER, THE
Pathak, Dina
TAMAS
Patil, Smita
MIRCH MASALA
NAZRANA
SUTRADHAR
Patinkin, Mandy
PRINCESS BRIDE, THE
Patino, Lydia
CRYSTAL HEART
Patric, Jason
LOST BOYS, THE
Patrick, Randal
PROJECT X
Patrick, Robert
EQUALIZER 2000
EYE OF THE EAGLE
Patrick Ward
RUNNING FROM THE GUNS
Patsy
EL DIABLO, EL SANTO Y EL TONTO
HERENCIA DE VALIENTES
Patten, Tom
IN THE MOOD
Patterson, Frank
DEAD, THE
Patterson, J. Michael
ASSASSINATION
Patterson, Jay
NADINE
STREET SMART
Patterson, Martin
IRONWEED
Patterson, Reese
ALLNIGHTER, THE
Patterson, Rocky
NAIL GUN MASSACRE
Patterson, Ronny
NO DEAD HEROES
Patterson, Sarah
SNOW WHITE
Patterson, Terri
PRETTY SMART
Patti, Antonella
QUEL RAGAZZO DELLA CURVA "B"
Patton, Dave
OVER THE TOP
Patton, Joshua Lee
OVER THE TOP
Patton, Will
NO WAY OUT
Patton-Hall, Michael
ESCAPES
Patwardhan, Ravi
PRATIGHAAT
Paul, Alexandra
DRAGNET
Paul, Andrew
BELLMAN AND TRUE
Paul, Bonnie
EMANON
Paul, David
BARBARIANS, THE
Paul, Don Michael
WINNERS TAKE ALL
Paul, Jaye
WITCH HUNT
Paul, John
CRY FREEDOM
Paul, Peter
BARBARIANS, THE
Paul, Randy
TALKING WALLS
Paul, Richard
PRINCESS ACADEMY, THE
Paul, Richard Joseph
REVENGE OF THE NERDS II: NERDS IN PARADISE
Paul, Steven
EMANON
Paul, Stuart
EMANON
Paul, Talia
ANGUSTIA
Paul, Tapas
AMAR BANDHAN
ARPAN
RUDRABEENA
Paul Gleason
MORGAN STEWART'S COMING HOME
Paule, Irma St.
PSYCHOS IN LOVE
Pauley, D.A.
DIRTY DANCING
Paulsen, Pat
BLOODSUCKERS FROM OUTER SPACE
THEY STILL CALL ME BRUCE
Paulsen, Rob
PERFECT MATCH, THE
Paulson, Doug
TOO OUTRAGEOUS
Pauly, Rebecca
PENG! DU BIST TOT!
Pavan, Marisa
JOHNNY MONROE
Pavis, Bobbi
MALIBU BIKINI SHOP, THE
Pavlou, Stelios
KLIOS
Pavlov, Victor
GEROY YEYOROMANA
KONTRUDAR
Pavlov, Viktor
DIKIY KHMEL
ZINA-ZINULYA
Pavuls, Eduard
STRAKH
Pawelec, Boguslawa
BLIND CHANCE
Pawlak, Iwona
NAD NIEMNEM
Pawlicki, Michal
NAD NIEMNEM
Pawlik, Kim
RUNNING MAN, THE
Pawnbroker
BIG SHOTS
Paxton, Art
EMANON
Paxton, Bill
NEAR DARK
Paymer, David
NO WAY OUT
Payne, Frank
MATEWAN
Payne, James
P.K. & THE KID
Payne, Jimmy
P.K. & THE KID
Payne, Mark
P.K. & THE KID
Payne, Richard
ANGEL HEART
Payne, Roger
NAIL GUN MASSACRE
Payne, Ruby
RADIO DAYS
Paynter, David
HAPPY HOUR
Pays, Amanda
KINDRED, THE
Payton-Wright, Pamela
IRONWEED
MY LITTLE GIRL
Pazos, Gabriel
CHRONICLE OF A DEATH FORETOLD
Pea, Alfredo
IL GIORNO PRIMA
Peace, Steve
HAPPY HOUR
Peacock, Daniel
EAT THE RICH
WHOOPS APOCALYPSE
Peak, Christine
WHOOPS APOCALYPSE
Peaks, John
EVIL DEAD 2: DEAD BY DAWN
Pean, Guylaine
LES MOIS D'AVRIL SONT MEURTRIERS
Pearce, Jacqueline
WHITE MISCHIEF
Pearce, Joanne
WHOOPS APOCALYPSE
Pearl, Barry
FLICKS
Pearl, Hazel
MATEWAN
Pearson, Burke
SECRET OF MY SUCCESS, THE
Pearson, Gerry
BIG TOWN, THE
Pearson, Jacqueline
NECROPOLIS
Pearson, Julie "Sunny"
BARFLY
Pearson, Richard
WHOOPS APOCALYPSE

Pecanac, Vesna
U IME NARODA

Pechacek, Zdenek
PROC?

Pechernikova, Irina
NABAT NA RASSVETE

Peck, Bob
KITCHEN TOTO, THE

Peck, Brian
LIKE FATHER, LIKE SON

Peck, Gregory
AMAZING GRACE AND CHUCK

Pederson, Bent
OPPOSING FORCE

Pedrin
LA RAZA NUNCA PIERDE—HUELE A GAS

Peeler, Bob
ESCAPES

Peeples, Nia
NORTH SHORE

Peerless, Kenneth
TOUGH COP

Peeters, Carine
MASCARA

Pehkonen, Jari
VY VIHDOINKIN YHDESSA

Pehle, Richard
BROADCAST NEWS

Peiris, Asoka
VIRAGAYA

Pekidou, Nikos
VERSTECKTE LIEBE

Pekny, Milan
DISCOPRIBEH

Pelaez, Juan
LO NEGRO DEL NEGRO
OPERACION MARIJUANA
VIAJE AL PARAISO

Pelayo, Luis Manuel
NOS REIMOS DE LA MIGRA
RETO A LA VIDA

Pele
HOT SHOT

Pelham, Bob
DREAMANIAC

Pelissier, Carmen
LA ESTACION DEL REGRESO

Pellant, Philippe
ARIA

Pellatt, John
FAMILY VIEWING

Pellay, Lanah
EAT THE RICH

Pellegrino, Frank
TOO OUTRAGEOUS

Pellegrino, Mark
FATAL BEAUTY

Pelletier, Andree
BACH AND BROCCOLI

Pellgrini, Elisabetta
QUARTIERE

Pellicer, Coral
LA ESTANQUERA DE VALLECAS

Pellonpaa, Matti
HAMLET
KUNINGAS LEAR
VARJOJA PARATIISISSA

Peloso, Laila
CAPRICCIO

Peluffo, Ana Luisa
CORRUPCION
EL HIJO DE PEDRO NAVAJAS
ENTRE FICHERAS ANDA EL DIABLO
JUANA LA CANTINERA
MI NOMBRE ES GATILLO

Pember, Ron
PERSONAL SERVICES

Pen, Ney
MASSACRE IN DINOSAUR VALLEY

Pena, Elizabeth
BATTERIES NOT INCLUDED
LA BAMBA

Pena, Hilario
DE TAL PEDRO, TAL ASTILLA

Pena, Vicky
LA CASA DE BERNARDA ALBA

Penalver, Diana
EL LUTE—CAMINA O REVIENTA

Pender, D. Anthony
DATE WITH AN ANGEL

Pendleton, Austin
HELLO AGAIN

Penella, Emma
LA ESTANQUERA DE VALLECAS

Penghlis, Thaao
LES PATTERSON SAVES THE WORLD

Penhall, Bruce
CAMPING DEL TERRORE

Peniche, Alejandro
TODA LA VIDA

Penkov, Nikolai
IZ ZHIZNI POTAPOVA

Penn, Edward
LADY BEWARE

Penney, Alan
HOWLING III, THE

Penney, Allan
AROUND THE WORLD IN EIGHTY WAYS
YEAR MY VOICE BROKE, THE

Pennington, Noel
DOGS IN SPACE

Pennington, Russ
I WAS A TEENAGE T.V. TERRORIST

Penny
MAKING MR.RIGHT

Penot, Jacques
LE CRI DU HIBOU
SALE DESTIN!

Pentangleo, Joseph
BELIEVERS, THE

Penvern, Andre
LES NOCES BARBARES

Penya, Anthony
RUNNING MAN, THE

Pepper, John
SPECTERS

Pepper, Tom
BUSINESS AS USUAL

Pera, Marilia
NIGHT ANGELS

Perdigon, Leticia
MAS VALE PAJARO EN MANO . . .

Peredes, Chris
OVERKILL

Perego, Didi
LA TRASGRESSIONE

Pereira, Freddy
LA OVEJA NEGRA

Pereiro, Paulo Cesar
UM FILM 100% BRAZILEIRO

Perera, Sabita
VIRAGAYA

Pereura, Rene
MIRACLES

Perez, Ben
IGOROTA

Perez, Vincent
HOTEL DE FRANCE

Perfort, Holger
BABETTE'S GASTEBUD

Peri, Jillian
ROCK 'N' ROLL NIGHTMARE

Periard, Jayme
LEILA DINIZ

Perier, Francois
SOIGNE TA DROITE

Perkins, Elizabeth
FROM THE HIP

Perkins, Millie
SLAMDANCE
WALL STREET

Perkins, Pinetop
ANGEL HEART

Perlegas, Timos
KLIOS

Perlengas, Timos
KE DYO AVGA TOURKIAS

Perlich, Max
ALLNIGHTER, THE
CANT BUY ME LOVE
IN THE MOOD

Perlini, Meme
FAMILY, THE
NOTTE ITALIANA

Perlman, Bernard
STREET TRASH

Perrier, Mireille
BAD BLOOD

Perrin, Francis
CLUB DE RENCONTRES

Perrin, Jacques
LANNEE DES MEDUSES

Perrine, Valerie
MAID TO ORDER

Perriraz, Nathalie
LADY OF THE CAMELIAS

Perrot, Francois
LES EXPLOITS DUN JEUNE DON JUAN

Perroti, Riccardo Parisio
SPECTERS

Perry, Ben
KINDRED, THE

Perry, David
FULL METAL JACKET

Perry, Evan
MY DARK LADY

Perry, Felton
ROBOCOP
WEEDS

Perry, Jack
BACHELOR GIRL

Perry, Lou
TRESPASSES

Perry, Navarre
BLOODY WEDNESDAY

Perry, Pamela
HOSTAGE

Perry, Wolfe
SPACE RACE

Perryman, John
P.K. & THE KID

Persaud, Stephen
FOURTH PROTOCOL, THE
SHADEY

Persky, Lisa Jane
BIG EASY, THE

Pertilis, Vassilis
PRETTY SMART

Pertwee, Sean
PRICK UP YOUR EARS

Pesaola, Bruno
QUEL RAGAZZO DELLA CURVA "B"

Pesce, Domenico
ANGELUS NOVUS

Pesce, Frank J.
BEVERLY HILLS COP II

Pesci, Joe
MAN ON FIRE

Pestana, Francisco
LA PLAYA DE LOS PERROS

Pesutic, Mauricio
LA ESTACION DEL REGRESO

Peszek, Jan
PRYWATNE SLEDZTWO

Petelius, Pirkka-Pekka
A LA ITKE IINES
HAMLET
VY VIHDOINKIN YHDESSA

Peter, Sinai
DREAMERS

Peters, Bruno
STADTRAND

Peters, Chris
RIVER'S EDGE

Peters, Jace
TALKING WALLS

Peters, Laurent
FAMILY BUSINESS

Peters, Randy
IN THE MOOD

Peters, Robert J.
BLACK WIDOW

Petersen, Diane
LETS GET HARRY

Petersen, Else
BABETTE'S GASTEBUD
SIDSTE AKT

Petersen, Erik
BABETTE'S GASTEBUD

Petersen, Gwen
AMAZING GRACE AND CHUCK

Petersen, Maite
AMAZING GRACE AND CHUCK

Petersen, William L.
AMAZING GRACE AND CHUCK

Peterson, Amanda
CANT BUY ME LOVE

Peterson, Bill
MUTANT HUNT

Peterson, Cassandra
ALLAN QUATERMAIN AND THE LOST CITY OF GOLD

Peterson, Jerry
BLIND DATE

Peterson, Jo Ann
VIDEO DEAD, THE

Peterson, Lauren
DREAMANIAC

Peterson, Lenka
DRAGNET

Peterson, Marion
ARIA
LES EXPLOITS DUN JEUNE DON JUAN

Peterson, Martha
FIREHOUSE

Peterson, Shelley
HOUSEKEEPER, THE

Petherbridge, Louise
STARLIGHT HOTEL

Petit, Yvette
MISS MONA

Petitjean, David
ANGEL HEART
BIG EASY, THE

Petits Fours
WHOOPS APOCALYPSE

Petrecca, Lamberto
GOOD MORNING BABYLON

Petrenko, A.
DVADTSTAT DNEI BEZ

Petrenko, Alexei
FAREWELL

Petrenko, P.
VZLOMSHCHIK

Petrie, Doris
MORNING MAN, THE

Petrie, George O.
PLANES, TRAINS AND AUTOMOBILES

Petrie, Mary
ALLNIGHTER, THE

Petrillo, Leonardo
MAN ON FIRE

Petrocelli, Antonio
MAN ON FIRE
NOTTE ITALIANA

Petrovna, Sonia
DA NNUNZIO

Pettersson, Soren
MORE ABOUT THE CHILDREN OF BULLERBY VILLAGE

Pettet, Joanna
SWEET COUNTRY

Pettinger, Gary
P.K. & THE KID

Petty, Ross
HOUSEKEEPER, THE

Petty, Tom
MADE IN HEAVEN

Pevarello, Osiride
CAPRICCIO

Pevarello, Renzo
BARBARIANS, THE

Pewhairangi, Connie
NGATI

Peyleron, Michel
MISS MONA

Peynado, Iris
IRON WARRIOR

Pezaro, Nikki
PSYCHO GIRLS

Pezzani, Denise
MASQUES

Pfaff, Dieter
ZABOU

Pfeiffer, Dedee
ALLNIGHTER, THE

Pfeiffer, Michelle
AMAZON WOMEN ON THE MOON
WITCHES OF EASTWICK, THE

Pharrez, Paco
MIRACLES

Phelan, Joe
TERMINAL EXPOSURE
ZERO BOYS, THE

Phelps, Danielle
WISH YOU WERE HERE

Phelps, Matthew
DREAMANIAC

Phelps, Peter
LIGHTHORSEMEN, THE
STARLIGHT HOTEL

Philbin, John
NORTH SHORE
SHY PEOPLE

Philip, Martin
DELIRIA

Philip, Tania
LADY OF THE CAMELIAS

Philips, Chynna
SOME KIND OF WONDERFUL

Phillips, Bruce
STARLIGHT HOTEL

Phillips, Charlie
MUNCHIES
RUNNING MAN, THE

Phillips, Dower
FATAL BEAUTY

Phillips, George
FOURTH PROTOCOL, THE

Phillips, Hal
MATEWAN

Phillips, Hazel
BELINDA

Phillips, Helen
DOGS IN SPACE

Phillips, John
LAST OF ENGLAND, THE

Phillips, Johnny
RUMPELSTILTSKIN

Phillips, Jonathan
PRICK UP YOUR EARS

Phillips, Leslie
EMPIRE OF THE SUN

Phillips, Lou Diamond
LA BAMBA
TRESPASSES

Phillips, Louise
IRONWEED

Phillips, Neville
FOURTH PROTOCOL, THE
PRICK UP YOUR EARS

Phillips, Patricia
KEEPING TRACK

Phillips, Robert
CRY FREEDOM

Phillips, Thomas Hal
O. C. AND STIGGS

Phillips, W.J.
BOY SOLDIER

Phoenix, Leaf
RUSSKIES

Phoenix, Rainbow
MAID TO ORDER

Phong, Nguyen Hue
FULL METAL JACKET

Phule, Nilu
SUTRADHAR

Phung, Dennis
P.I. PRIVATE INVESTIGATIONS

Pialat, Maurice
SOUS LE SOLEIL DE SATAN

Piani, Lorenzo
MAN ON FIRE

Piassarelli, Joseph
WHITE WATER SUMMER

Piatas, Dimitris
KE DYO AVGA TOURKIAS

Picard, Beatrice
LE SOURD DANS LA VILLE

Picard, Nicole
DEADTIME STORIES

Picardo, Robert
INNERSPACE
MUNCHIES

Piccard, Nicholas
MIO, MOY MIO

Picchio, Ana Marie
CHECHECHELA—UNA CHICA DEL BARRIO

Piccio, Betty Mae
SWEET REVENGE

Picciolo, James E.
STEELE JUSTICE

Piccoli, Michel
BAD BLOOD
LA RUMBA
LHOMME VOILE
MALADIE D'AMOUR

Piccolo, Ottavia
FAMILY, THE

Pickard, Josh
FATAL BEAUTY

Pickard, Mark
GOTHIC

Pickering, Sarah
LITTLE DORRIT

Pickern, Stacey
BARFLY

Picketts, Jason
ZERO BOYS, THE

Pickles, Christina
MASTERS OF THE UNIVERSE

Pickrell, Jim
MANKILLERS

Pickup, Ronald
FOURTH PROTOCOL, THE

Picot, Genevieve
TO MARKET, TOMARKET

Pieczka, Franciszek
MATKA KROLOW
PRZYJACIEL WESOLEGO DIABLA
RYKOWISKO
WIERNA RZEKA

Pieczynska, Malgorzata
KOMEDIANTKA
WIERNA RZEKA

Pieczynski, Andrzej
PRYWATNE SLEDZTWO

Pienaar, Jonathan
AMERICAN NINJA 2: THE CONFRONTATION

Pier, Stephen
LADY OF THE CAMELIAS

Pierce, Harvey
DEADTIME STORIES

Pierce, Tony
NEAR DARK

Pierloot, Dirk
MASCARA

Pierre, Curtis
ANGEL HEART

Pierre, Oliver
SHADEY

Pierre, Rickey
BIG EASY, THE

Pierse, Lyn
BACHELOR GIRL

Pierson, Barbara
HOPE AND GLORY

Pierson, Rex
OVER THE TOP

Pietrangeli, Giorgio
DELIZIA

Pigeon, Corky
MONSTER IN THE CLOSET
PARTY CAMP

Pigozzi, Jean
MAN IN LOVE, A

Piki, Roman
DISCOPRIBEH

Pilgaard, Ulf
KAMPEN OM DEN RODE KO

Piller, Michael
PRETTY SMART

Pillow, Mark
SUPERMAN IV: THE QUEST FOR PEACE

Pillsbury, Drew
WHO'S THAT GIRL

Pilmark, Soren
PETER VON SCHOLTEN

Pilon, Dominique
DEVILS PARADISE, THE

Pilon, Donald
KEEPING TRACK

Pimprikar, Vijay
PRATIGHAAT

Pina, Sonia
LA RULETERA
LAPUTA: THE CASTLE IN THE SKY

Pine, Jon
PARTY CAMP

Pine, Larry
ANNA

Pineda, Salvador
BEAKS

Pineres, Nelson
CHRONICLE OF A DEATH FORETOLD

Pingo, Jesus
UM FILM 100% BRAZILEIRO

Pinheiro, Richard
FIRE AND ICE
Pinkley, George
ANGUSTIA
Pinky
VALET GIRLS
Pinney, Pat
CHIPMUNK ADVENTURE, THE
Pinnock, Thomas
WHO'S THAT GIRL
Pinocchio
VZLOMSHCHIK
Pinoy, Marijke
VAN PAEMEL FAMILY, THE
Pinsent, Gordon
JOHN AND THE MISSUS
Pintea, Adrian
PADUREANCA
Pinto, Giovanni
IL RAGAZZO DI EBALUS
Pintos, Alejo Garcia
MADE IN ARGENTINA
Pinvidic, Margot
HOUSEKEEPING
Pinza, Carla
BELIEVERS, THE
Piper, Emma
EMPIRE OF THE SUN
Piper, Kelly
RAWHEAD REX
Piper, Sally
NIGHTMARE ON ELM STREET 3: DREAM WARRIORS, A
SUMMER CAMP NIGHTMARE
Piperno, Giacomo
DISTANT LIGHTS
Pipino, Roberto
DOLCE PELLE DI ANGELA
Pires, Gloria
BESAME MUCHO
Pires, Miriam
UM TREM PARA AS ESTRELAS
Pirie, Ronald
KITCHEN TOTO, THE
Pirjo
ELVIS-KISSAN JALJILLA
Pirmukhamedov, Alisher
OKHOTA NA DRAKONA
Piro, Grant
BUSHFIRE MOON
LIGHTHORSEMEN, THE
Pirskanen, Aino
FAMILY VIEWING
Pirtskhalava, Guram
GOSPODA AVANTYURISTY
KRUGOVOROT
VELIKIY POKHOD ZA NEVESTOY
Pistilli, Luigi
UNA CASA IN BILICO
Pistoia, Nicola
AURELIA
CHI C'E C'E
Pistone, Martin
PRINCIPAL, THE
Pistoni, Franco
BARBARIANS, THE
Pitkin, Frank
WHALES OF AUGUST, THE
Pitochelli, Kenneth
GOOD MORNING, VIETNAM
Pitofsky, Peter
MILLION DOLLAR MYSTERY
Pitoniak, Anne
BEST SELLER
HIDING OUT
HOUSEKEEPING
Pitt, Chris
LIONHEART
Pittinger, Bob
ESCAPES
Pitzalis, Federico
DEVIL IN THE FLESH
Pitzer, Marilyn
KILLER WORKOUT
Pizano, Jaime
FORAJIDOS EN LA MIRA
Plana, Tony
BORN IN EAST L.A.
DISORDERLIES

Planer, Nigel
EAT THE RICH
MORE BAD NEWS
Planting, Tor
JAAN KAANTOPIIRI
Platin, Pontus
GIRL, THE
Platten, Edith
EMPIRE OF THE SUN
Plaxton, Gary
KEEPING TRACK
Playten, Alice
BIG BANG, THE
Plaza, Begona
MAID TO ORDER
Pleasence, Donald
GROUND ZERO
PRINCE OF DARKNESS
SPECTERS
WARRIOR QUEEN
Pleshkite, Eugeniya
VOLNY UMIRAYUT NA BEREGU
Pletl, Lidija
WHEELS OF TERROR
Pletneva, Yelena
CHELOVEK C AKKORDEONOM
Plimpton, Martha
SHY PEOPLE
Plinio, Fernando
SUPERFANTOZZI
Plisov, Pavel
MAGIA CHYORNAYA I BELAYA
Plotnikov, Boris
DUBLYOR NACHINAET DEYSTVOVAT
LERMONTOV
SDELKA
Plummer, Amanda
MADE IN HEAVEN
Plummer, Christopher
DRAGNET
I LOVE NEW YORK
Plummer, Glen
WHO'S THAT GIRL
Plummer, Terry
EMPIRE STATE
Plunkett, Steve
LIKE FATHER, LIKE SON
Pniewski, Michael
SPACEBALLS
Poblete, Roberto
LA ESTACION DEL REGRESO
Pochon, Caroline
FAMILY BUSINESS
Pocino, Benito
ANGUSTIA
Podbrey, Maurice
LAST STRAW, THE
Poddighe, Giampaolo
DA NNUNZIO
Podoshyan, Andrei
KAPKAN DLYA SHAKALOV
Poe, Harlan Cary
SOMEONE TO WATCH OVER ME
Pogany, Judit
HOL VOLT, HOL NEM VOLT
ZUHANAS KOZBEN
Poggiani, Claudia
CHI C'E C'E
Pogue, Ken
CLIMB, THE
DEAD OF WINTER
KEEPING TRACK
Pogues, The
STRAIGHT TO HELL
Pohl, Klaus
LITTLE PROSECUTOR, THE
Pohlman, Patricia
TIN MEN
Poindexter, Jerris L.
SLAMDANCE
Poindexter, Larry
AMERICAN NINJA 2: THE CONFRONTATION
Pointer, Patrick
STARLIGHT HOTEL
Pointer, Priscilla
FROM THE HIP
NIGHTMARE ON ELM STREET 3: DREAM WARRIORS, A
RUMPELSTILTSKIN
Poiret, Jean
LE MIRACULE

Polac, Roberto
POET'S SILENCE, THE
Polanah, Ruy
ELE, O BOTO
Polding, Mike
FIREHOUSE
Pole, Edward Tudor
WALKER
Poli, Gina
DELIZIA
Polimeno, Santo
UN RAGAZZO DI CALABRIA
Polites, Ted
I WAS A TEENAGE ZOMBIE
Pollak, Cheryl A.
DATE WITH AN ANGEL
Pollak, Kevin
MILLION DOLLAR MYSTERY
Pollak, Robert
DREAMERS
Pollan, Tracy
PROMISED LAND
Pollanah, Rui
A DANCA DOS BONECOS
Pollard, Hugh
HANSEL AND GRETEL
Pollard, Michael J.
ROXANNE
Polley, Sarah
BIG TOWN, THE
BLUE MONKEY
PRETTYKILL
Polony, Anna
DIARY FOR MY LOVED ONES
Polyakova, Lyudmila
OCHNAYA STAVKA
Polychronopoulos, Tassos
FAKELOS POLK STON AERA
Pomanti, Joey
POLICE ACADEMY 4: CITIZENS ON PATROL
Pompei, Elena
CAMPING DEL TERRORE
Poncela, Eusebio
LAW OF DESIRE
Ponich, Pat
STACKING
Pons, Beatrice
FOREVER, LULU
Ponte, Maria Luisa
MADRID
MOROS Y CRISTIANOS
Ponterotto, Donna
TALKING WALLS
Ponziani, Antonella
CARAMELLE DA UNO SCONOSCIUTO
INTERVISTA
SOLDATI: 365 GIORNI ALL' ALBA
Poole, Marilyn
CRY FREEDOM
Poole, Michael
WHOOPS APOCALYPSE
Poon, Anna Maria
DATE WITH AN ANGEL
Poore, Thomas
MATEWAN
Pope, Robert Benjamin
WHO'S THAT GIRL
Popescu, Matica
ZLOTY POCIAG
Popov, Oleg
CIZIM VSTUP POVOLEN
Popova, Yelena
OCHNAYA STAVKA
Popovich, George
WILD THING
Poppa, Philip
HEARTS OF FIRE
Poppick, Eric
CROSS MY HEART
Popwell, Albert
WHO'S THAT GIRL
Porizkova, Paulina
ANNA
Porraz, Jean-Luc
MALADIE D'AMOUR
Porrett, Susan
WHISTLE BLOWER, THE
Porsanger, Sverre
OFELAS

Portales, Javier
CHORROS
Porter, Irma
UNA PURA Y DOS CON SAL
Portnow, Richard
GOOD MORNING, VIETNAM
HIDING OUT
RADIO DAYS
SQUEEZE, THE
TIN MEN
WEEDS
Porto, Paolo
SEMBRA MORTO . . . ME E SOLO SVENUTO
Poslof, James
LETHAL WEAPON
Posner, Norma
TIN MEN
Pospichal, Petr
CENA MEDU
Pospisil, Karel
PROC?
Pospisil, Radek
DISCOPRIBEH
Post, Saskia
DOGS IN SPACE
Pot, Bob
KEEPING TRACK
Potau, Joan
LA GUERRA DE LOS LOCOS
Potmesil, Jan
PROC?
Potmesil, Ladislav
DISCOPRIBEH
Potok, Andy
HOUSE OF GAMES
Potter, Madeleine
HELLO AGAIN
SUICIDE CLUB, THE
Potter, Martin
GUNPOWDER
Potter, Nicole
STREET TRASH
Pou, Jose Maria
HAY QUE DESHACER LA CASA
Poulicacos, Dimitris
KE DYO AVGA TOURKIAS
Poulikakos, Dimitris
FAKELOS POLK STON AERA
VIOS KE POLITIA
Poulos, George
CHIPMUNK ADVENTURE, THE
Poulsen, Benny
HIP, HIP, HURRA!
Poutash, Ali
CHECKPOINT
Powell, Addison
ROSARY MURDERS, THE
Powell, Brad
BLOOD TRACKS
Powell, Greg
BELLMAN AND TRUE
Powell, Nosher
EAT THE RICH
Powell, Robert
DA NNUNZIO
Power, Derry
RAWHEAD REX
Power, Sharon
BUSINESS AS USUAL
Powers, Anthony
FOREVER, LULU
Powers, Barbara
CLUB LIFE
Powers, Caroline Capers
ORACLE, THE
Powers, Ed
PSYCHOS IN LOVE
Powers, Pierre
LES FOUS DE BASSAN
Powley, Mark
BLOODY NEW YEAR
Powney, Clare
GIRL, THE
Poysti, Lasse
NAKEMIIN, HYVASTI
Pozzetto, Renato
NOI UOMINI DURI
ROBA DA RICCHI
Prabhu
CHINNATHAMBI PERIYATHAMBI

Prado, Lilia
MAS BUENAS QUE EL PAN
Praed, Michael
NIGHTFLYERS
Prasanjit
APAN GHAREY
ARPAN
Prasert
SHADOWS OF THE PEACOCK
Prashant
PUDHCHE PAOL
Prat, Jose
MADRID
Prati, Giancarlo
MAN ON FIRE
Pratt, Hugo
BAD BLOOD
Prayer, Yvette
BEYOND THERAPY
Prebble, Simon
SHADEY
Precigs, Andrzej
CUDZOZIEMKA
Preen, Zacharias
CRAZY BOYS
DANN IST NICHTS MEHR WIE VORHER
Prendes, Luis
ALIEN PREDATOR
LA GRAN FIESTA
Prescott, Robert
SPACEBALLS
Presence
VZLOMSHCHIK
Pressman, Lawrence
HANOI HILTON, THE
Presti, Ubaldo Lo
GOOD MORNING BABYLON
Preston, Glenn
POLICE ACADEMY 4: CITIZENS ON PATROL
Preston, Kelly
AMAZON WOMEN ON THE MOON
Preston, Michael
MATEWAN
Pretten, Phil
KEEPING TRACK
Previn, Fletcher Farrow
RADIO DAYS
Prevost, Dan
REMEMBERING MEL
Prevot, Eddie
WIMPS
Pribytko, P.
SKORBNOE BESCHUVSTVIE
Price, Brian
OVERBOARD
Price, Doug
WILD THING
Price, Leontyne
ARIA
Price, Lon
BLIND DATE
Price, Lonny
DIRTY DANCING
Price, Steve
EMANON
Price, Vincent
ESCAPES
OFFSPRING, THE
WHALES OF AUGUST, THE
Pridemore, Peggy
BROADCAST NEWS
Priest, Maxi
OH BABYLON
Primus, Barry
STRANGER, THE
TALKING WALLS
Prince, Marc
JEUX D'ARTIFICES
Prince, William
ASSASSINATION
Princess Kaguya
PRINCESS FROM THE MOON
Prinz, Terri
THIN LINE, THE
Prior, Charles
CLUB LIFE
FOREVER, LULU
Prior, Ted
DEADLY PREY
KILLER WORKOUT

Priscila
FORAJIDOS EN LA MIRA
Priselkov, Sergei
VYKUP
Prison Matron
SLAMMER GIRLS
Pritchett, John
HOUSE OF GAMES
Priwiezncew, Eugeniusz
POCIAG DO HOLLYWOOD
Probosz, Maria
ZYCIE WEWNETRZNE
Proboszova, Maria
CENA ODVAHY
Prochnow, Jurgen
BEVERLY HILLS COP II
DEVILS PARADISE, THE
TERMINUS
Procopio, Frank
PSYCHO GIRLS
Prodan, Andrea
BELLY OF AN ARCHITECT, THE
GOOD MORNING BABYLON
Professor of Political Law
LA RUSA
Proklova, Elena
IZ ZHIZNI NACHALNIKA UGOLOVNOGO ROZYSKA
Prosen, Irena
WHEELS OF TERROR
Proskurin, Victor
OBESHCHAYU BYT
VOENNO-POLEVOI ROMAN
Prosky, Robert
BIG SHOTS
OUTRAGEOUS FORTUNE
Prosperi, Mario
SEMBRA MORTO . . . ME E SOLO SVENUTO
Proud, Elizabeth
WHOOPS APOCALYPSE
Proussalis, Athinodoros
ONE HUNDRED AND TWENTY DECIBELS
Proval, David
MONSTER SQUAD, THE
Pruckner, Tilo
LITTLE PROSECUTOR, THE
Prudence's Therapist
BEYOND THERAPY
Pruett, Harold B.
SUMMER CAMP NIGHTMARE
Pryce, Jonathan
MAN ON FIRE
Pryor, Nicholas
LESS THAN ZERO
MORGAN STEWART'S COMING HOME
Pryor, Peter
IRONWEED
Pryor, Richard
CRITICAL CONDITION
Prysirr, Geof
HOT CHILD IN THE CITY
Psota, Iren
AZ UTOLSOKEZIRAT
Pszoniak, Wojtek
TESTAMENT D'UN POETE JUIF ASSASSINE
Puccinelli, Patrick
WANTED: DEAD OR ALIVE
Puchol, Pilar
LA CASA DE BERNARDA ALBA
Puebla, Rodrigo
MURIERON A MITAD DEL RIO
VIAJE AL PARAISO
Puente, Jesus
ASIGNATURA APROBADA
LA ESTANQUERA DE VALLECAS
Puente, Tito
RADIO DAYS
Pugacheva, Alla
SEZON CHUDES
Pugh, Carmel
WIMPS
Pugh, Robert
BOY SOLDIER
Pugh, Willard
MADE IN HEAVEN
Pugovkin, Mikhail
CHELOVEK C AKKORDEONOM
SPORTLOTO—82
Pugsley, Don
NEAR DARK

Puigcorbe, Juanjo
MY GENERAL

Pujari, Sarat
BABULA

Pujin, Tatjana
OKTOBERFEST

Puleston-Davies, Ian
BUSINESS AS USUAL

Pullman, Bill
SPACEBALLS

Punzone, Pietro
QUEL RAGAZZO DELLA CURVA "B"

Purcell, Lee
SPACE RACE

Purchase, Bruce
LIONHEART

Purdy-Gordon, Carolyn
DOLLS

Puri, Amrish
DADAGIRI
INAAM DUS HAZAAR
LOHA
MISTER INDIA
TAMAS

Puri, Om
MIRCH MASALA
TAMAS

Puscas, Jessica
CROSS MY HEART

Pushkin, Kelly Lynn
ALLNIGHTER, THE

Puskas, Tamas
LAURA

Putman, Andree
JEUX D'ARTIFICES

Puzzi, Nicole
ANJOS DO ARRABALDE

Pycha, Norbert
WOLF'S HOLE

Pyland, Dee
SQUARE DANCE

Pyritz, Gaye
RETURN OF JOSEY WALES, THE

Q.C.
WITCH HUNT

Qing, Shi Rui
EMPIRE OF THE SUN

Quaid, Dennis
BIG EASY, THE
INNERSPACE
SUSPECT

Quaid, Little Buddy
BIG EASY, THE

Quaid, Randy
NO MAN'S LAND
SWEET COUNTRY

Quarry, Robert
COMMANDO SQUAD
CYCLONE
MOON IN SCORPIO

Quartim, Glicinia
JESTER,THE

Quast, Philip
AROUND THE WORLD IN EIGHTY WAYS
TO MARKET, TOMARKET

Quattrini, Paola
I MIEI PRIMI QUARANT'ANNI

Quedraogo, Assita
YAM DAABO

Quedraogo, Fatimata
YAM DAABO

Quedraogo, Oumarou
YAM DAABO

Quedraogo, Rasmane
YAM DAABO

Quedraogo, Salif
YAM DAABO

Queen, Ron
NAIL GUN MASSACRE

Queensberry, Ann
EMPIRE OF THE SUN

Queija, Fernando
BELIEVERS, THE

Quero, Pepe
LAS DOS ORILLAS

Quesada, Alfredo
MISS MARY

Quest, Hans
CASPAR DAVID FRIEDRICH

Quick, Sarah
BEVERLY HILLS COP II

Quigley, Linnea
CREEPOZOIDS

Quill, Tim
HAMBURGER HILL
HIDING OUT
THOU SHALT NOT KILL . . . EXCEPT

Quimby, Gerald J.
SQUEEZE, THE

Quinlan, Frank
EAT THE PEACH

Quinlan, Kathleen
MAN OUTSIDE
WILD THING

Quinn, Aidan
STAKEOUT

Quinn, Colin
THREE MEN AND A BABY

Quinn, Dayna
MURDER LUST

Quinn, J.C.
BARFLY

Quinn, James W.
WITCHBOARD

Quinn, Ken
BLUE MONKEY

Quinn, Peter
NECROPOLIS

Quinn, Thomas
THREE MEN AND A BABY

Quintana, Ana Maria
BELIEVERS, THE

Quintana, Martin
MI NOMBRE ES GATILLO

Quintana, Roberto
LAS DOS ORILLAS

Quintanar, Isabel
MUJERES SALVAJES

Quinteros, Lorenzo
SINFIN, LA MUERTA NO ES NINGUNA SOLUCION

Quinton, Everett
FOREVER, LULU
HELLO AGAIN

Quiroga, Alvaro
LA CASA DE BERNARDA ALBA

Quistgaard, Berthe
SIDSTE AKT

Qvistgaard, Berthe
STRIT OG STUMME

Raaj, Anita
INSANIYAT KE DUSHMAN

Raakee
DACAIT

Rabal, Francisco
DIVINAS PALABRAS

Rabasa, Ruben
WHOOPS APOCALYPSE

Rabbett, Martin
ALLAN QUATERMAIN AND THE LOST CITY OF GOLD

Rabett, Catherine
LIVING DAYLIGHTS, THE
MAURICE

Rabinowitz, Hannah
RADIO DAYS

Race, Hugo
DOGS IN SPACE

Racette, Francine
AU REVOIR, LES ENFANTS

Rachinsky, Nikolai
NABAT NA RASSVETE

Racimo, Victoria
ERNEST GOES TO CAMP

Racine, Roger
REMEMBERING MEL

Rack, Tom
WILD THING

Rackevei, Anna
MALOM A POKOLBAN

Rackova, Simona
WOLF'S HOLE

Rad, Sudhir
MORGAN STEWART'S COMING HOME

Radakovic, Goran
HEY BABU RIBA

Radcliffe, Leroy
BELIEVERS, THE

Rader, Jack
PENITENTIARY III

Radha
DONGODUCHHADU

Radhika
AMERICA ABBAI
ROWDY POLICE
UMMADI MOGUDU

Radice, Giovanni Lombardi
DELIRIA

Radjabov, Burkhon
NOVYE SKAZKI SHAKHEREZADY

Radley, Ken
JILTED

Radovitch, Sebastien
MASCARA

Radszun, Alexander
LITTLE PROSECUTOR, THE

Radzinova, Elza
POHADKA O MALICKOVI

Radziwilowicz, Jerzy
W ZAWIESZENIU

Rae, Danette
DIRTY LAUNDRY

Rae, James
KEEPING TRACK

Rae, Melody
UNTOUCHABLES, THE

Raeder, Louise
MORE ABOUT THE CHILDREN OF BULLERBY VILLAGE

Rafal's Friend
PRYWATNE SLEDZTWO

Rafelson, Peter
SOMEONE TO LOVE

Rafferty, George
IRONWEED

Raghuvaran
POOVIZHI VASALILE

Ragno, Joseph
SECRET OF MY SUCCESS, THE

Ragusa, Angelo
BARBARIANS, THE

Rahmani, Sogand
SHEERE SANGGY

Raho, Umberto
ALADDIN
MORO AFFAIR, THE

Raiford, Renee
FIREHOUSE

Raikka, Laila
JAAHYVAISET PRESIDENTILLE

Railsback, Steve
BLUE MONKEY
WIND, THE

Raimi, Sam
THOU SHALT NOT KILL . . . EXCEPT

Raimi, Ted
THOU SHALT NOT KILL . . . EXCEPT

Raimi, Theodore
EVIL DEAD 2: DEAD BY DAWN

Rainbow, J. Zachariah
P.K. & THE KID

Rainer, Josef
CAMPUS MAN

Raines, Cristina
NORTH SHORE

Rainey, Jamie
HOUSEKEEPER, THE

Rainieri, Riccardo
ALADDIN

Rains, Gianna
FIREHOUSE

Rainville, Jacques
LA COULEUR ENCERCLEE

Raita, Marjatta
UUNO TURHAPURO MUUTTAA MAALLE

Raj, Ashok
PRATIGHAAT

Raj, Charan
SHEELA

Rajala, Kimmo
LEIF

Rajasekhar
AMERICA ABBAI

Rajnikant
DAKU HASINA

Rajput, Anil
PRATIGHAAT

Raju, Captain
AMRITAMGAMAYA

Rakhov, A.
VZLOMSHCHIK

Rakow, Jerry
PSYCHOS IN LOVE

Rall, Thomas
DANCERS

Rally, Steve
OVERKILL

Ramalho, Ana
NIGHT ANGELS

Raman, Sree
UPPU

Ramarao, A.
PRATIGHAAT

Rameriez, Ron
MANKILLERS

Ramey, Samuel
MACBETH

Ramirez, Alfredo
LETS GET HARRY
MISSION KILL

Ramirez, Carlos
ALIEN PREDATOR

Ramirez, Carlos Julio
POR LOS CAMINOS VERDES

Ramirez, Joe
CYCLONE

Ramirez, Jose
MAKING MR.RIGHT

Ramirez, Ray
SECRET OF MY SUCCESS, THE

Ramis, Harold
BABY BOOM

Ramon, Jose Luis
A LOS CUATRO VIENTOS

Ramoncin
LA RUBIA DEL BAR

Ramos, Larry
BELIEVERS, THE

Ramos, Loyda
BEST SELLER

Ramos, Luis
SECRET OF MY SUCCESS, THE

Ramos, Maria Erica
LA ESTACION DEL REGRESO

Ramos, Ruben
NO BLOOD NO SURRENDER

Ramos, Rudy
BEVERLY HILLS COP II
OPEN HOUSE

Ramos, Santiago
YEAR OF AWAKENING, THE

Ramos, Sergio
ALBURES MEXICANOS
CINCO NACOS ASALTAN A LAS VEGAS
NOCTURNO AMOR QUE TE VAS
TRAGICO TERREMOTO EN MEXICO
MAS VALE PAJARO EN MANO . . .

Ramos, Tony
LEILA DINIZ

Ramos, Victor
JESTER,THE

Rampling, Charlotte
ANGEL HEART
MASCARA

Ramras, Len
POET'S SILENCE, THE

Ramsay, Robin
DEAR CARDHOLDER

Ramsay, Sisko
ELVIS-KISSAN JALJILLA

Ramsey, Anne
THROW MOMMA FROM THE TRAIN
WEEDS

Ramsey, Jeff
BEST SELLER

Ramsey, Marion
POLICE ACADEMY 4: CITIZENS ON PATROL

Ramsey, Zohreh
CHECKPOINT

Ramsoondar, Leon Darnell
WILD THING

Ranasinghe, Douglas
VIRAGAYA

Ranasinghe, Tony
WITNESS TO A KILLING

Rand, Gerry
STEELE JUSTICE

Rand, Randy
LIKE FATHER, LIKE SON

Randall, Charles
ANNA
ENEMY TERRITORY

Randall, Dick
SLAUGHTER HIGH

Randall, Monica
CALE
MY GENERAL

Randall, Sophie
COMRADES

Randeniya, Ravindra
MALDENIYESIMION
WITNESS TO A KILLING

Randle, Theresa
NEAR DARK

Randolph, Chris Bass
SUMMER HEAT

Randolph, Windsor Taylor
PENITENTIARY III

Randolph, Windsor Taylor
AMAZONS

Rane, Ferran
LESCOT

Raney, Randy
OVER THE TOP

Ranft, Joe
BRAVE LITTLE TOASTER, THE

Ranft, Thea
EMPIRE OF THE SUN

Rangel, Antonio
MISSION KILL

Rangel, Louis
GARDENS OF STONE

Rangel, Martin
DELINCUENTE

Ranger, Cody
RAISING ARIZONA

Rangmar, Peter
LEIF

Ranjana
JHANJHAAR

Rankin, Andrew
EAT THE RICH
STRAIGHT TO HELL

Rankin, Avril
EAT THE RICH

Rankl, Philipp
SOMMER

Ranney, Juanita
DANGER ZONE, THE

Ranni, Rodolfo
EN RETIRADA
LA BUSQUEDA

Ranucci, Giorgetta
QUARTIERE

Rao, K. Sriniwas
PRATIGHAAT

Rao, Kota Srinivasa
MANDALADHEESUDU

Rapley, John
JANE AND THE LOST CITY

Rapp, Anthony
ADVENTURES IN BABYSITTING

Rappaport, Barbara
TIN MEN

Rasch, Robert
BROADCAST NEWS

Rasche, David
MADE IN HEAVEN

Rask, Magnus
MY LIFE AS A DOG

Raskin, Essar
REMEMBERING MEL

Rasmus, Rhondell
P.K. & THE KID

Rasmussen, Bryan
HUNTER'S BLOOD

Rasmussen, Jesper Bruun
WOLF AT THE DOOR, THE

Rastgar, Fahimeh
SHEERE SANGGY

Rasulala, Thalmus
BULLETPROOF

Rasulov, Eldanis
LEGENDA SEREBRYANOGO OZERA

Rasuma, Reghina
REQUIEM

Ratay, Jerry
HUNTER'S BLOOD

Ratchford, George
I WAS A TEENAGE T.V. TERRORIST

Ratchford, Jeremy
HEARTS OF FIRE

Ratti, Robert
DOGS IN SPACE

Ratzenberger, John
HOUSE TWO: THE SECOND STORY

Rauch, Siegfried
DEATH STONE

Raul
LAPUTA: THE CASTLE IN THE SKY

Raunio, Johanna
JAAN KAANTOPIIRI

Ravalec, Blanche
CLUB DE RENCONTRES

Ravel, Thierry
HOTEL DE FRANCE

Ravencroft, Thurl
BRAVE LITTLE TOASTER, THE

Ravenswood, David
BUSHFIRE MOON

Ravindra
DEATH STONE

Ravn, Jens
VENNER FOR ALTID

Rawls, Hardy
MUNCHIES

Raxel, Antonio
FORAJIDOS EN LA MIRA

Ray, Aldo
SICILIAN, THE

Ray, Ola
BEVERLY HILLS COP II
NIGHT STALKER, THE

Ray, Robyn
STEELE JUSTICE

Ray, Sushant
JHANJHAAR

Ray, Tandra
JAIDEV

Ray, Trevor
SICILIAN, THE

Raybourne, Richard
WILD THING

Rayhall, Tom
RETURN OF JOSEY WALES, THE
SUMMER CAMP NIGHTMARE

Raymond, Camille
TANT QU'IL AURA DES FEMMES

Raymond, Jon
LOVECHILD, THE

Raymond, Kessler
PENITENTIARY III

Raymond, Ricky
JOHN AND THE MISSUS

Raymond, Sid
MAKING MR.RIGHT

Raynor, Paul
EAT THE PEACH

Raynova, Diana
CERNITE LEBEDI

Raynr, David
PROJECT X

Raz, Rinat
DEATH BEFORE DISHONOR

Razatos, Spiro
OMEGA SYNDROME

Razelou, Katerina
TELEFTAIO STICHIMA

Razuma, Regina
VO VREMENA VOLCHYIKA ZAKONOV

Re, Rubi
LO NEGRO DEL NEGRO

Read, Angela
LADIES OF THE LOTUS

Read, Michelle
ARIA

Reader, Mark
BUSINESS AS USUAL

Reagan, Michael
CYCLONE

Reale, Basil
UNTOUCHABLES, THE

Rearden, Brad
WHO'S THAT GIRL

Reb, Antoine
MAN ON FIRE

Rebengiuc, Victor
PADUREANCA
Rebstock, Gary
MONSTER SQUAD, THE
Recoing, Aurelien
LES EXPLOITS DUN JEUNE DON JUAN
Reddemann, Manfred
CRIME OF HONOR
Redder, Jan
PSYCHOS IN LOVE
Reddick, Jerome
ANGEL HEART
Reddy, Tom
KID BROTHER, THE
Redfield, Dennis
SPACE RACE
Redglare, Rockets
SALVATION!
Redgrave, Lynn
MORGAN STEWART'S COMING HOME
Redgrave, Vanessa
COMRADES
PRICK UP YOUR EARS
Redl, Christian
SIERRA LEONE
Redmond, Nicola
BOY SOLDIER
Redondo, Emiliano
CRYSTAL HEART
Redpath, Martin
BUSHFIRE MOON
Redvers, Bill
WARDOGS
Reed, Arlee
MONSTER IN THE CLOSET
Reed, Bruce
CLUB LIFE
Reed, Don
HOLLYWOOD SHUFFLE
Reed, KaRan
TRESPASSES
Reed, Oliver
WHEELS OF TERROR
Reed, Penelope
AMAZONS
Reed, Sarah
COMRADES
Reed, Vivian
LA RUMBA
Reed, William K.
NECROPOLIS
Reel, Karen
THUNDER WARRIOR II
Reenberg, Jorgen
WOLF AT THE DOOR, THE
Rees, Donogh
STARLIGHT HOTEL
Rees, Suzanne
I WAS A TEENAGE T.V. TERRORIST
Reese, Axxel G.
DUDES
Reese, Barbara
HOUSEKEEPING
Reese, Michelle
NIGHT STALKER, THE
Reeve, Christopher
STREET SMART
SUPERMAN IV: THE QUEST FOR PEACE
Reeve, Katherine
WHISTLE BLOWER, THE
Reeves, Keanu
RIVER'S EDGE
Regalbuto, Joe
SICILIAN, THE
Regan, Jack
HAPPY HOUR
Regan, Mark
MILLION DOLLAR MYSTERY
Regan, Mary
BELINDA
YEAR MY VOICE BROKE, THE
Regan, Patty
CROSS MY HEART
Regehr, Duncan
MONSTER SQUAD, THE
Regent, Benoit
UNE FLAMME DANS MON COEUR
Reggiani, Serge
BAD BLOOD
Regillo, Mariano
REGINA
Regina, Marcia
ANJOS DO ARRABALDE
Rego, Luis
POULE ET FRITES
Rehor, Zdenek
POHADKA O MALICKOVI
Reichenbach, Lygia
ANJOS DO ARRABALDE
Reid, Jim
EAT THE PEACH
Reid, Kate
IL GIORNO PRIMA
TO MARKET, TOMARKET
Reid, Sheila
LONELY PASSION OF JUDITH HEARNE,THE
Reid, Steve
OVERKILL
Reid, Thomas
BELIEVERS, THE
Reidy, Steve
I WAS A TEENAGE ZOMBIE
Reifova, Magda
PRATELE BERMUDSKEHO TROJUHELNIKU
Reilly, Bob
O. C. AND STIGGS
Reilly, Francis
THIN LINE, THE
Reimer, Elin
SIDSTE AKT
Reiner, Carl
SUMMER SCHOOL
Reiner, Nicholas
ROBOT HOLOCAUST
Reiner, Rob
THROW MOMMA FROM THE TRAIN
Reinhard, Frank
LETHAL WEAPON
Reinhardt, Ray
WEEDS
Reinhold, Judge
BEVERLY HILLS COP II
Reis, Imara
VERA
Reis, Marie
MASSACRE IN DINOSAUR VALLEY
Reiser, Paul
BEVERLY HILLS COP II
CROSS MY HEART
Reitano, Tony
DATE WITH AN ANGEL
Rekert, Winston
HIGH STAKES
Rekha
JHOOTHI
Rekkor, Jaan
CHEREZ STO LET V MAE
Rellan, Miguel
EL BOSQUE ANIMADO
Rellan, Miguel A.
LA VIDA ALEGRE
Rellan, Miguel Angel
YEAR OF AWAKENING, THE
Remaeus, Eva
DET STORA LOFTET
Remker, Dana
BLOOD HOOK
Remotti, Remo
HELSINKI NAPOLI—ALL NIGHT LONG
NOTTE ITALIANA
Remsen, Bert
P.K. & THE KID
THREE FOR THE ROAD
Renart, Claude
LE SOURD DANS LA VILLE
Renata, Luckie
NGATI
Renate, Grace
ALBURES MEXICANOS
Renaud, Isabelle
HOTEL DE FRANCE
Rennes, Juliette
FAMILY BUSINESS
Renoir, Sophie
LAMI DE MON AMIE
Renteria, Ana Lillian
AMOR EN CAMPO MINADO
Renucci, Robin
LA CODA DEL DIAVOLO
MASQUES
Renzi, Maggie
MATEWAN
Renzyayeva, Alla
KAPKAN DLYA SHAKALOV
Rescher, Deedee
WANTED: DEAD OR ALIVE
Resendes, Mari Carmen
EL HIJO DE PEDRO NAVAJAS
Resendess, Maricarmen
TODA LA VIDA
Resendez, Maricarmen
MAS VALE PAJARO EN MANO . . .
Resetin, Andrej
SKORBNOE BESCHUVSTVIE
Resines, Antonio
LA VIDA ALEGRE
MOROS Y CRISTIANOS
Reski, Nadja
PIERRE ET DJEMILA
Resther, Jodie
WILD THING
Restifo, Julie
MAS ALLA DEL SILENCIO
Reta, William
AMAZONS
Rethwisch, Gus
HOUSE TWO: THE SECOND STORY
RUNNING MAN, THE
Retsos, Aris
PHOTOGRAPH, THE
Revah, Zeev
BOUBA
Reviczky, Gabor
HOL VOLT, HOL NEM VOLT
LAURA
Revill, Clive
EMPEROR'S NEW CLOTHES, THE
RUMPELSTILTSKIN
Revuelta, Raquel
SUCCESSFUL MAN, A
Rexhepi, Ted
MANKILLERS
Rey, Antonia
FOREVER, LULU
Rey, Bruno
JUNTOS
LO NEGRO DEL NEGRO
POLICIAS DE NARCOTICOS
Rey, Fernando
EL BOSQUE ANIMADO
HOTEL DU PARADIS
MY GENERAL
Rey, Leal
SINFIN, LA MUERTA NO ES NINGUNA SOLUCION
Rey, Thierry
ENNEMIS INTIMES
Reyes, Gil
EXTREME PREJUDICE
Reyes, Gilberto
DE TAL PEDRO, TAL ASTILLA
Reyes, Jaime
JUANA LA CANTINERA
MAS BUENAS QUE EL PAN
Reyes, Pedro
LOS INVITADOS
YEAR OF AWAKENING, THE
Reyna, Carola
EL HOMBRE DE LA DEUDA EXTERNA
Reynaldi, Ron
MANKILLERS
MUTANT HUNT
Reyne, David
FRENCHMAN'S FARM
Reynolds, Burt
HEAT
MALONE
Reynolds, Jim
MASTERBLASTER
Reynolds, Larry
KILLER WORKOUT
Reynolds, Martin
LAST EMPEROR, THE
Reynolds, Michael J.
BLUE MONKEY
STREET SMART
TOO OUTRAGEOUS
Reynolds, Valerie
IN THE MOOD
Reynoso, Jorge
MIRACLES

MISSION KILL
Rezza, Vito
PRETTYKILL
Rhoades, Michael
POLICE ACADEMY 4: CITIZENS ON PATROL
Rhodes, Andrew
OVER THE TOP
Rhodes, Cynthia
DIRTY DANCING
Rhodes, Jennifer
GHOST FEVER
SLUMBER PARTY MASSACRE II
Rhodes, Kenny
WITCHBOARD
Rhule, David
EMPIRE STATE
Rhys-Davies, John
LIVING DAYLIGHTS, THE
Riaboukine, Serge
BUISSON ARDENT
Rialet, Daniel
LE GRAND CHEMIN
Ribeiro, Isabel
BESAME MUCHO
Ribeyro, Ramon Garcia
HOUR OF THE ASSASSIN
Ribon, Diego
GOOD MORNING BABYLON
Ricard, Kelly
STREET SMART
Riccelli, Carlos Alberto
ELE, O BOTO
LEILA DINIZ
Ricci, Elena Sofia
IO E MIA SORELLA
Rice, Frank
BIG SHOTS
Rice, Joe
BARFLY
Rice, John
AMERICAN DRIVE-IN
Rice, Marina
TRESPASSES
Rice, William
THUNDER WARRIOR II
Rice-Edwards, Sebastian
HOPE AND GLORY
Rich, Charlie
WEEDS
Rich, Delphine
ARIA
Rich, Eli
MURDER LUST
Rich, Royce
HELLO AGAIN
Rich, Shirley
HELLO AGAIN
Richard, Emily
EMPIRE OF THE SUN
HANSEL AND GRETEL
Richard, Eric
PRICK UP YOUR EARS
Richard, Jean-Louis
HOTEL DE FRANCE
Richarde, Patricia
MONSTER IN THE CLOSET
Richards, Beah
BIG SHOTS
Richards, Elsie
VALET GIRLS
Richards, Gavin
WHOOPS APOCALYPSE
Richards, Gwill
MONSTER SQUAD, THE
Richards, Keni E.
LIKE FATHER, LIKE SON
Richards, Michael
WHOOPS APOCALYPSE
Richards, Paul
KISS DADDY GOOD NIGHT
Richards, Valerie
VALET GIRLS
Richardson, Anna Louise
PRETTYKILL
Richardson, Elizabeth
FIREHOUSE
Richardson, Ian
CRY FREEDOM
FOURTH PROTOCOL, THE
WHOOPS APOCALYPSE

Richardson, Jackie
THREE MEN AND A BABY
Richardson, Lee
AMAZING GRACE AND CHUCK
BELIEVERS, THE
SWEET LORRAINE
Richardson, Miles
MAURICE
Richardson, Miranda
EAT THE RICH
EMPIRE OF THE SUN
Richardson, Natasha
GOTHIC
MONTH IN THE COUNTRY, A
Richardson, Peter
MORE BAD NEWS
Richardson, Sy
COLD STEEL
STRAIGHT TO HELL
WALKER
Richardt, David
HARRY AND THE HENDERSONS
Richcreek, Richard
RIVER'S EDGE
Richelmy, Prospero
SEMBRA MORTO . . . ME E SOLO SVENUTO
Richman, Josh
ALLNIGHTER, THE
RIVER'S EDGE
Richman, Stella
PRICK UP YOUR EARS
Richmond, Branscombe
BEST SELLER
Richmond, Deon
ENEMY TERRITORY
Richmond, Doyle
WHISTLE BLOWER, THE
Richmond, Fiona
EAT THE RICH
Richter, Deborah
PROMISED LAND
SQUARE DANCE
WINNERS TAKE ALL
Rick's Boss
HIGH SEASON
Rickert, Nanette
BROADCAST NEWS
Rickert, Thomas
CONCRETE ANGELS
Rickman, Allen L.
I WAS A TEENAGE ZOMBIE
Rickman, Robert
THOU SHALT NOT KILL . . . EXCEPT
Rico, Cameron
MANKILLERS
Ricord, George
BLACK WIDOW
Ricordy, Tomaso
ANGELUS NOVUS
Ridge, Francesca J.
ANGEL HEART
Ridgley, Robert
BEVERLY HILLS COP II
Ridings, Richard
FOURTH PROTOCOL, THE
Riegert, Peter
MAN IN LOVE, A
STRANGER, THE
Rigaud, Manuska
ZOMBIE NIGHTMARE
Rigaud's Henchman
SQUEEZE, THE
Rigauer, Gerd
WANNSEE CONFERENCE, THE
Rigby, Dave
KEEPING TRACK
Rigg, Carl
LIVING DAYLIGHTS, THE
Rigg, Diana
SNOW WHITE
Rigzin, Cexiang
DAO MAZEI
Rijo-Vicente, Escarla
JENATSCH
Riley, Gary
PLANES, TRAINS AND AUTOMOBILES
SUMMER SCHOOL
Riley, Jack
SPACEBALLS

Riley III, Alvin
LAST EMPEROR, THE
Rilke, Rocio
NOS REIMOS DE LA MIGRA
Rimkus, Stevan
PRICK UP YOUR EARS
Rimmer, Shane
WHOOPS APOCALYPSE
Rimoux, Alain
MEMOIRE DES APPARENCES: LA VIE EST UN SONGE
Rinaldi, Gerard
LA VIE DISSOLUE DE GERARD FLOQUE
Rinar, Lilian
RAGE OF HONOR
Ring, John
WEEDS
Ringer, Catherine
SOIGNE TA DROITE
Ringuette, Lory
VIDEO DEAD, THE
Ringwald, Molly
P.K. & THE KID
PICK-UP ARTIST, THE
Rio, Nicole
ZERO BOYS, THE
Rios, Guillermo
LETS GET HARRY
MIRACLES
Rioux, Danielle
SUMMER CAMP NIGHTMARE
Rippe, Jan
LEIF
Rippert, Pierre Jean
JEAN DE FLORETTE
MANON OF THE SPRING
Ripploh, Frank
TAXI NACH KAIRO
Rippy, Leon
BEDROOM WINDOW, THE
Riquelme, Carlos
DELINCUENTE
Risch, Pierre
MASQUES
Rishi, Prem
PRATIGHAAT
Risi, Paolo
BARBARIANS, THE
Rist, Robbie
DIRTY LAUNDRY
Ristie, Yvonne
EEN MAAND LATER
Rita's Partner
FATAL BEAUTY
Ritchie, Don
BLUE MONKEY
POLICE ACADEMY 4: CITIZENS ON PATROL
Ritter, John
REAL MEN
Ritz, Peter
QUATRE MAINS
Rivamonte, Ray
RUNNING FROM THE GUNS
Rivas, Guillermo
CINCO NACOS ASALTAN A LAS VEGAS
MAS VALE PAJARO EN MANO . . .
Rivas, Luis
MAS ALLA DEL SILENCIO
Rivas, Mariela
CHRONICLE OF A DEATH FORETOLD
Rivelles, Amparo
HAY QUE DESHACER LA CASA
Rivera, Chana
MUJERES DE LA FRONTERA
Rivera, Giuliana
DOLCE ASSENZA
Rivera, Maria Elena
EIN BLICK-UND DIE LIEBE BRICHT AUS
Rivera, Marika
EAT THE RICH
Rivera, Mario Sanchez
A DOS AGUAS
Rivera, Patricia
TIERRA DE VALIENTES
Rivera, Raymond
WEEDS
Rivero, Jorge
ENTRE FICHERAS ANDA EL DIABLO
Rivero, Nestor
DE TAL PEDRO, TAL ASTILLA

Rivers, Frank
BELIEVERS, THE

Rivers, Joan
LES PATTERSON SAVES THE WORLD
SPACEBALLS

Rivet, Pascal
AU REVOIR, LES ENFANTS

Riviere, Marie
QUATRE AVENTURES DE REINETTE ET MIRABELLE

Rivin, Il'ja
SKORBNOE BESCHUVSTVIE

Rivron, Roland
EAT THE RICH

Rix, Tony
MY LIFE AS A DOG

Riza, Ahmed
URSULA

Rizacos, Angelo
BIG TOWN, THE

Rizik, Raoul N.
BROADCAST NEWS

Rizzo, Jilly
PICK-UP ARTIST, THE

Rjazanovova, Raisa
CIZIM VSTUP POVOLEN

Roa, Angelo
EVA: GUERRILLERA

Roach, Claudette
STREET SMART

Roarke, Adam
TRESPASSES

Robards, Jason
SQUARE DANCE

Robb, John
KILLER WORKOUT

Robbins, Eva
MASCARA

Robbins, Rex
SECRET OF MY SUCCESS, THE

Robbins, Tom
MADE IN HEAVEN

Roberson, Philip A.
PROJECT X

Robert Katims
BROADCAST NEWS

Robert Prosky
BROADCAST NEWS

Roberto
LA RAZA NUNCA PIERDE—HUELE A GAS
NOS REIMOS DE LA MIGRA
TODA LA VIDA

Roberts, Axel
DANGER ZONE, THE

Roberts, David Wyn
BOY SOLDIER

Roberts, Derrick R.
WIMPS

Roberts, Doris
NUMBER ONE WITH A BULLET

Roberts, Ian
JANE AND THE LOST CITY

Roberts, Ivor
PERSONAL SERVICES

Roberts, Jay
WHITE PHANTOM

Roberts, Ken
GREAT LAND OF SMALL, THE
MORNING MAN, THE
RADIO DAYS
WILD THING

Roberts, Max
T. DAN SMITH

Roberts, Pascale
LE GRAND CHEMIN

Roberts, Teal
BEVERLY HILLS COP II

Roberts, Tony
RADIO DAYS

Robertson, Ben
WHOOPS APOCALYPSE

Robertson, Cliff
MALONE

Robertson, George R.
POLICE ACADEMY 4: CITIZENS ON PATROL

Robertson, Keith
BLIND DATE

Robertson, Malcolm
YEAR MY VOICE BROKE, THE

Robertson, Owen
DOGS IN SPACE

Robertson, Robin Dale
SUMMER HEAT

Robertson, Tim
BACHELOR GIRL
TIME GUARDIAN, THE
YEAR MY VOICE BROKE, THE

Robillard, Kim
PROJECT X

Robin, Teddy
LEGEND OF WISELY, THE

Robins, Laila
PLANES, TRAINS AND AUTOMOBILES
WALK ON THE MOON, A

Robins, Lisa
LIKE FATHER, LIKE SON

Robinson, Andrew
HELLRAISER

Robinson, Dar
CYCLONE

Robinson, Darren
DISORDERLIES

Robinson, David L.
HIDING OUT

Robinson, Harriet
BLOOD TRACKS

Robinson, Jay
MALIBU BIKINI SHOP, THE

Robinson, Julia
FOREVER, LULU

Robinson, Laura
GOOFBALLS

Robinson, Mark
GIRL, THE

Robinson, Rena
LADY OF THE CAMELIAS

Robitaille, Jack
BACH AND BROCCOLI

Robitaille, Pierrette
BACH AND BROCCOLI

Robles, Walter
FATAL BEAUTY

Robson, Greer
STARLIGHT HOTEL

Robson, Wayne
DEAD OF WINTER
GOOFBALLS
HOUSEKEEPING

Rocard, Pascale
CHAMP D'HONNEUR

Rocco, Alex
P.K. & THE KID
RETURN TO HORROR HIGH

Roche, Mabel
SUCCESSFUL MAN, A

Rochefort, Jean
I MIEI PRIMI QUARANT'ANNI
LE MOUSTACHU
TANDEM

Rochon, Lela
WILD PAIR, THE

Rock, Chris
BEVERLY HILLS COP II

Rockafellow, Marilyn
SOMEONE TO WATCH OVER ME

Rocket, Charles
DOWN TWISTED
MIRACLES

Rocksavage, David
QUATRE AVENTURES DE REINETTE ET MIRABELLE

Rocz, Bill
RAISING ARIZONA

Rodde, Anne-Marie
ARIA

Rode, Ebbe
BABETTE'S GASTEBUD
SIDSTE AKT

Rodefeldt, Vanja
JIM OCH PIRATERNA BLOM

Rodero, Manuel
MI NOMBRE ES GATILLO

Rodger, Claire
WILD THING

Rodgers, Anton
FOURTH PROTOCOL, THE

Rodgers, Tee
PROJECT X

Rodrigo, Ric
IGOROTA
MANILA, OPEN CITY

Rodrigues, Guara
UM FILM 100% BRAZILEIRO

Rodriguez, Bridgette
PRINCIPAL, THE

Rodriguez, Carla
JUNTOS

Rodriguez, Luisa
MAKING MR.RIGHT

Rodriguez, Marco
DISORDERLIES
EXTREME PREJUDICE

Rodriguez, Miguel Angel
LA RAZA NUNCA PIERDE—HUELE A GAS
TRAGICO TERREMOTO EN MEXICO

Rodriguez, Milton
LA FUGA DE CARRASCO

Rodriguez, Paul
BORN IN EAST L.A.
MIRACLES

Rodriguez, Paulino
WALKER

Rodriguez, Pedro
JUANA LA CANTINERA

Rodriguez, Ralph A.
NIGHTFORCE

Roebuck, Daniel
DUDES
PROJECT X
RIVER'S EDGE

Roeg, Maximillian
ARIA

Roehbling, Randolph
SLAVE GIRLS FROM BEYOND INFINITY

Roels, Tony
MASCARA

Roffe, Carlos
EL AMOR ES UNA MUJERGORDA

Roffiel, Laly
MISSION KILL

Rogalska, Bozena
NAD NIEMNEM

Rogers, Bob
OVER THE TOP

Rogers, Danny
TALKING WALLS

Rogers, Freda
EIGHTY FOUR CHARING CROSS ROAD

Rogers, James
DOGS IN SPACE

Rogers, Mimi
SOMEONE TO WATCH OVER ME
STREET SMART

Rogers, Sheila
IN THE MOOD

Rogers, Steve
NO DEAD HEROES

Rogers, Steven
OPPOSING FORCE
WARRIORS OF THE APOCALYPSE

Rogers, Stuart
SUMMER CAMP NIGHTMARE

Rogers, Todd Michael
RAISING ARIZONA

Rogers, Wayne
KILLING TIME, THE

Rogozhin, S.
VZLOMSHCHIK

Rohini
JANUARY ORORMA

Rohner, Clayton
P.I. PRIVATE INVESTIGATIONS

Rohner, Daniel
JENATSCH

Roine, Esko
PEKKA PUUPAA POLIISINA

Rojas, Eduardo Lopez
GABY—A TRUE STORY

Rojo, Danny
COMMANDER LAMIN

Rojo, Gustavo
CORRUPCION

Rojo, Helena
RETO A LA VIDA

Rojo, Maria
ROBACHICOS

Rojo, Maria
VIAJE AL PARAISO

Rojo, Ruben
YERBA SANGRIENTE

Rola, Jorge
RELACAO FIEL E VERDADEIRA
Roland
HOUR OF THE ASSASSIN
Roland, Eugenie Cisse
FACES OF WOMEN
Roland, Marie-Rose
FALSCH
Rolant, Arlena
ANGEL HEART
Rolf, Frederick
STREET SMART
Rolfe, Guy
DOLLS
Rolffes, Kirsten
SIDSTE AKT
Rolle, Esther
P.K. & THE KID
Rolot, Francis
MASCARA
Rolston, Mark
FOURTH PROTOCOL, THE
WEEDS
Roman, Catherine
BLOODY NEW YEAR
Roman, Edgardo
CHRONICLE OF A DEATH FORETOLD
Roman, Freddie
SWEET LORRAINE
Romand, Beatrice
QUATRE AVENTURES DE REINETTE ET MIRABELLE
Romani, Pasha
MIRAGE
Romano, Andy
P.I. PRIVATE INVESTIGATIONS
RETURN TO HORROR HIGH
Romano, Carlos
GABY—A TRUE STORY
MISSION KILL
Romano, Francesco
QUEL RAGAZZO DELLA CURVA "B"
Romano, Gerardo
EL ANO DEL CONEJO
MISS MARY
Romano, Pat
WHO'S THAT GIRL
Romano, Phil
WHO'S THAT GIRL
Romanov, Earnest
SON V RUKU, ILI CHEMODON
Romashin, Anatoly
GEROY YEYOROMANA
GRUBAYA POSADKA
Romay, Pepe
NI DE AQUI, NI DE ALLA
OLOR A MUERTE
Rome, Cindy
BANZAI RUNNER
Rome, Sydne
ROMANCA FINAL
Romer, Bart
CAUGHT
Romero, Tina
MIRACLES
MUJERES SALVAJES
Romey, Pepe
EL HIJO DE PEDRO NAVAJAS
Romeyn, Michiel
DE ORIONNEVEL
VAN GELUK GESPROKEN
Rommely, Peter
FULL METAL JACKET
Romor, Laurent
FAMILY BUSINESS
POULE ET FRITES
Ron, Clara
HA INSTALATOR
Rona, Nadia
STREET SMART
Ronane, Tricia
EAT THE RICH
Ronard, Jason
LETHAL WEAPON
Roncato, Andrea
IL LUPO DI MARE
Rondell, Ronnie
OVER THE TOP
Rondinaro, Steve
MAKING MR.RIGHT
Rondinella, Clelia
ITALIANI A RIO
Roney, Robert
MASSACRE IN DINOSAUR VALLEY
Ronne, Teresia Madeleine
NEGERKYS & LABRE LARVER
Ronnie, Julian
BLOODY NEW YEAR
Roo-mee, Cho
KYEOUL NAGUNE
Rooney, Jan
CANT BUY ME LOVE
Rooney, Michael
CLUB LIFE
Roos, Casper
DEADTIME STORIES
Roos, Gordon
ALLNIGHTER, THE
Roperto, Andrew
IN THE MOOD
Rosa, Pedro
MUTANT HUNT
Rosado, Ronnie
MAKING MR.RIGHT
Rosae, Donna
MAKING MR.RIGHT
MASTERBLASTER
REVENGE OF THE NERDS II: NERDS IN PARADISE
Rosales, Thomas
OMEGA SYNDROME
Rosales, Tom
RUNNING MAN, THE
SPACE RACE
Rosario, Bert
WHO'S THAT GIRL
Rosato, Lucio
BARBARIANS, THE
Rosato, Tony
HEARTS OF FIRE
Rose, Bill
RED DESERT PENITENTIARY
Rose, Christine
ISHTAR
Rose, Clifford
GIRL, THE
Rose, Dan
GRAVEYARD SHIFT
PSYCHO GIRLS
Rose, Elizabeth
BLOOD SISTERS
Rose, Gabrielle
FAMILY VIEWING
STEPFATHER, THE
Rose, Geoffrey
HIGH SEASON
Rose, Jessica
DERANGED
Rose, Norman
RADIO DAYS
Rose, Sandy
BARFLY
Rosen, Aliza
HIMMO MELECH YERUSHALAIM
Rosen, Julieta
MATAR O MORIR
Rosen, Michelle Lynn
EXTREME PREJUDICE
Rosen, Rosa
EL HOMBRE DE LA DEUDA EXTERNA
Rosenberg, Alan
WHITE OF THE EYE
Rosenblatt, Marcell
HELLO AGAIN
Rosenblatt, Martin
RADIO DAYS
Rosenfeld, Ree
KOL AHAVOTAI
Rosenfeld, Scott
STRANDED
Rosengard, Peter
EAT THE RICH
Rosengren, Clive
WHO'S THAT GIRL
Rosenka, Evelyn
ANGUSTIA
Rosenthal, Allan
BLUE MONKEY
Rosette
LA BRUTE
LES EXPLOITS DUN JEUNE DON JUAN
LES OREILLES ENTRE LES DENTS
Roshan, Raakesh
DAKU HASINA
Roshell, Antoine
BIG SHOTS
Rosi, Carolina
CHRONICLE OF A DEATH FORETOLD
Rosier, Monique
NITWITS
Ross, Andrew
PARTY CAMP
Ross, Annie
THROW MOMMA FROM THE TRAIN
Ross, Chelcie
UNTOUCHABLES, THE
Ross, David
ARIA
Ross, Debbie Lynn
BARFLY
Ross, Greg
RUNNING FROM THE GUNS
Ross, Jeffrey
LADY OF THE CAMELIAS
Ross, Joseph A.
GARDENS OF STONE
Ross, Katharine
RED HEADED STRANGER
Ross, Lee
T. DAN SMITH
Ross, Lisa Beth
OVERBOARD
Ross, Matthew
YEAR MY VOICE BROKE, THE
Ross, Ron
EMANON
Ross, Sandi
SUSPECT
Ross, Shirley
MIND KILLER
Ross, Willie
RITA, SUE AND BOB TOO!
Rosseau, Mark
VIDEO DEAD, THE
Rossellini, Isabella
RED RIDING HOOD
SIESTA
TOUGH GUYS DON'T DANCE
Rossi, Giorgio
PERSONAGGI & INTERPRETI
Rossi, Leo
BLACK WIDOW
RIVER'S EDGE
Rossi, Pamela
RUNNING MAN, THE
Rossi, Paolo
LA CODA DEL DIAVOLO
LA DONNA DEL TRAGHETTO
MONTECARLO GRAN CASINO
VIA MONTENAPOLEONE
Rossitto, Angelo
OFFSPRING, THE
Rossitto, Sue
GARBAGE PAIL KIDS MOVIE, THE
Rossner, Renate
HELSINKI NAPOLI—ALL NIGHT LONG
Rosso, Enrica
MAN ON FIRE
MORO AFFAIR, THE
Rossovich, Rick
LETS GET HARRY
ROXANNE
Rostotsky, Andrei
PRORYV
Rotaeta, Felix
HAY QUE DESHACER LA CASA
Rotblatt, Janet
IN THE MOOD
PENITENTIARY III
Rotblatt, Steven
OUTRAGEOUS FORTUNE
Roth, Cecilia
STRANGER, THE
Roth, Ivan E.
BLUE MONKEY
Roth, Ray
WILD THING
Roth, Stuart
MY DARK LADY
Rothchild, Bruce
MISSION KILL

Rothe, Bendt
BABETTE'S GASTEBUD
Rothlein, William
WALKER
Rothman, John
HELLO AGAIN
Rotzinga, Carlos
FORAJIDOS EN LA MIRA
Rouan, Brigitte
CHARLIE DINGO
LES MOIS D'AVRIL SONT MEURTRIERS
Roudebush, Kristin
FIREHOUSE
Rouffaer, Senne
VAN PAEMEL FAMILY, THE
Rougas, Michael
NIGHTMARE ON ELM STREET 3: DREAM WARRIORS, A
Rougerie, Jean
LE MIRACULE
Roundtree, Richard
JOCKS
OPPOSING FORCE
Rourke, Mickey
ANGEL HEART
BARFLY
PRAYER FOR THE DYING, A
Roussel, Anne
LES MENDIANTS
NOYADE INTERDITE
Roussel, Myriem
LA MONACA DIMONZA
Roussillon, Jean-Paul
MALADIE D'AMOUR
Rousta, Homa
GOZARESH-E YEK GHATL
Rouvel, Catherine
FUEGOS
LE SOLITAIRE
Roven, Glen
BROADCAST NEWS
Rovere, Gina
FRANCESCA
Rovito, Gabriel
LOS DUENOS DEL SILENCIO
Rovsek, Barbara
PRINCESS ACADEMY, THE
Rowan, Kelly
GATE, THE
Rowe, Douglas
IN THE MOOD
Rowe, Prentiss
MORGAN STEWART'S COMING HOME
Rowe, Tracy
KILLER WORKOUT
Rowell, Victoria
LEONARD PART 6
Rowland, Oscar
PROMISED LAND
Rowlands, Gena
LIGHT OF DAY
Rowlands, Ian
BOY SOLDIER
Roxana, Renee
CHECHECHELA—UNA CHICA DEL BARRIO
Roy, Debasree
ARPAN
Roy, Esperanza
DIVINAS PALABRAS
Roy, Rob
KEEPING TRACK
MORNING MAN, THE
Roy, Sandhya
LALAN FAKIR
Roy, Satabdi
AMAR BANDHAN
Roy-Dutta, Alakananda
PHERA
Royal, Allan
PRETTYKILL
Royal, Daniel
PRINCIPAL, THE
Royce, Paul
HELLO AGAIN
Roych, Vic
THUNDER WARRIOR II
Roza's Daughter
CUDZOZIEMKA
Roza's Husband
CUDZOZIEMKA
Rozycki, Christopher
WHOOPS APOCALYPSE
Ruben, Andy
STRIPPED TO KILL
Ruben, Paul
NECROPOLIS
Ruben, Tom
STRIPPED TO KILL
Rubens, Ora
SOMEONE TO LOVE
Rubenstein, Phil
MANNEQUIN
Rubes, Jan
DEAD OF WINTER
Rubie, Les
BLUE MONKEY
Rubin, Blanche
ROXANNE
Rubin, Jennifer
NIGHTMARE ON ELM STREET 3: DREAM WARRIORS, A
Rubin, John Gould
THREE MEN AND A BABY
Rubin, Michael
I WAS A TEENAGE ZOMBIE
Rubinek, Saul
WALL STREET
Rubini, Sergio
IL GRANDE BLEK
INTERVISTA
MORO AFFAIR, THE
Rubinstein, John
SOMEONE TO WATCH OVER ME
Rubinstein, Zelda
ANGUSTIA
Rubirosa, Rita
DA NNUNZIO
Ruck, Alan
THREE FOR THE ROAD
Rud, Bernard
BORAN—ZEIT ZUM ZIELEN
Ruddock, Anne-Marie
STRAIGHT TO HELL
Rude, Dick
STRAIGHT TO HELL
WALKER
Rude, Marc
DUDES
Rudnick, Franz
WANNSEE CONFERENCE, THE
Rudnik, Barbara
DANN IST NICHTS MEHR WIE VORHER
DER UNSICHTBARE
Rudolf, Peter
ZUHANAS KOZBEN
Rudoy, Joshua
HARRY AND THE HENDERSONS
Ruehl, Mercedes
EIGHTY FOUR CHARING CROSS ROAD
RADIO DAYS
SECRET OF MY SUCCESS, THE
Ruf, Rudolf
CRIME OF HONOR
Ruff, Adam
ERNEST GOES TO CAMP
Ruffo, Gabriela
EL ANSIA DE MATAR
YO, EL EJECUTOR
Ruffo, Victoria
YO, EL EJECUTOR
Rufus
LES EXPLOITS DUN JEUNE DON JUAN
POISONS
Rufus, Jacques
SOIGNE TA DROITE
Ruge, George Marshall
BARFLY
Ruggeri Brothers
NOTTE ITALIANA
Ruginis, Vyto
BURGLAR
MADE IN HEAVEN
Ruic, Vicko
OFICIR S RUZOM
Ruigang, Zu
LAST EMPEROR, THE
Ruis, Jose Carlos
RETO A LA VIDA
Ruiz, Angelica
NOS REIMOS DE LA MIGRA
Ruiz, Jose Carlos
LO DEL CESAR
OLOR A MUERTE
OPERACION MARIJUANA
ROBACHICOS
VIAJE AL PARAISO
Ruiz, Pedro
MOROS Y CRISTIANOS
Rule, Timothy
DEADTIME STORIES
Ruler of Druidia
SPACEBALLS
Runciman, Gaylie
LOVECHILD, THE
Rundgren, Kicki
MY LIFE AS A DOG
Rundman, Cal-Kristian
KILL CITY
Rundolf, Chase
UN TASSINARO A NEW YORK
Ruocheng, Ying
LAST EMPEROR, THE
Ruofu, Wu
BIG PARADE, THE
Ruoti, Enzo
UN RAGAZZO DI CALABRIA
Ruperez, Antonio
A LOS CUATRO VIENTOS
Ruprecht, David
TALKING WALLS
Ruscio, Elizabeth
BURGLAR
Rusek, Martin
PRATELE BERMUDSKEHO TROJUHELNIKU
Rush, Deborah
HEAT
Rush, Robert Lee
ENEMY TERRITORY
Rushton, Jared
OVERBOARD
Rushton, John S.
SQUEEZE, THE
Ruslanova, Nina
KOROTKIE VSTRECHI
VALENTIN I VALENTINA
ZAVTRA BILA VOINA
ZNAK BEDY
Rusnak, Stephen
CONCRETE ANGELS
Ruspoli, Esmeralda
GLI OCCHIALI D'ORO
Russ, Tim
SPACEBALLS
Russ, William
DEAD OF WINTER
WANTED: DEAD OR ALIVE
Russek, Jorge
ARQUIESTA EMILIO VARELA
MIRACLES
Russek, Rita
SIERRA LEONE
Russel, Andaluz
MIRACLES
Russell, Andaluz
HOT PURSUIT
Russell, Bing
OVERBOARD
Russell, Craig
TOO OUTRAGEOUS
Russell, Derek
RAISING ARIZONA
Russell, James
WHEN THE WIND BLOWS
Russell, John
AMAZING GRACE AND CHUCK
Russell, Kurt
OVERBOARD
Russell, Nicole
RAISING ARIZONA
Russell, Roy
BLOODSUCKERS FROM OUTER SPACE
Russell, Theresa
ARIA
BLACK WIDOW
Russinova, Isabel
I MIEI PRIMI QUARANT'ANNI
NOI UOMINI DURI
Russler, Libby
VIDEO DEAD, THE

Russo, Adriana
DELIZIA

Russo, Antonio
GOOD MORNING BABYLON

Russo, Daniel
POUSSIERE D'ANGE

Russo, James
CHINA GIRL

Russo, Michael
HANOI HILTON, THE

Russom, Leon
HOT SHOT
NO WAY OUT

Ruth, Isabel
JESTER,THE
O DESEJADO—LES MONTAGNES DE LA LUNE

Ruth, Robert
WINNERS TAKE ALL

Rutherford, Karleen
SAME TO YOU

Rutherford, Susan
GUNPOWDER

Ruud, Sif
NAGRA SOMMARKVALLAR PA JORDEN

Ruvinskis, Wolf
LA FUGA DE CARRASCO

Ruzhen, Shao
LAST EMPEROR, THE

Ryabova, Svetlana
DIKIY KHMEL

Ryan, Andy
FIREHOUSE

Ryan, Anne
THREE O'CLOCK HIGH

Ryan, John Michael
STEELE JUSTICE

Ryan, John P.
DEATH WISH 4: THE CRACKDOWN
FATAL BEAUTY
THREE O'CLOCK HIGH

Ryan, Mark
ISHTAR

Ryan, Mary
RAWHEAD REX

Ryan, Meg
INNERSPACE
PROMISED LAND

Ryan, Mitchell
LETHAL WEAPON

Ryan, R.L.
FOREVER, LULU
MANNEQUIN
STREET TRASH

Ryan, Ron
FOREVER, LULU

Ryan, Rusty
TOO OUTRAGEOUS

Ryan, Sheila
OPEN HOUSE

Ryan, Stephan
EAT THE PEACH

Ryan, Thomas
IN THE MOOD
PRINCIPAL, THE

Rydberg, Inga-Lil
MALARPIRATER

Ryder, Winona
SQUARE DANCE

Rye, Prebe Lerdorff
BABETTE'S GASTEBUD

Rye, Preben Lerdorff
HIP, HIP, HURRA!

Rylance, Mark
HEARTS OF FIRE

Ryon, Rex
P.I. PRIVATE INVESTIGATIONS
YOU TALKIN' TO ME?

Rypdal, Inger Lise
FELDMANN CASE, THE

Ryskjar, Claus
KAMPEN OM DEN RODE KO
STRIT OG STUMME

Ryslinge, Helle
NEGERKYS & LABRE LARVER

Ryu, Chishu
FINAL TAKE: THE GOLDEN AGE OF MOVIES
TORA-SAN'S BLUEBIRD FANTASY

Ryu, Raita
TOKYO BLACKOUT

Saarinen, Eero
NAKEMIIN, HYVASTI

Saario, Esa
AKALLINEN MIES
JAAHYVAISET PRESIDENTILLE

Saaveda, Myrra
LAPUTA: THE CASTLE IN THE SKY

Sabatasso, Kellyann
KILLER WORKOUT

Sabate, Jorge
EN EL NOMBRE DEL HIJO

Sabath, Bernadette
ROXANNE

Sabatini, Joe
AMAZING GRACE AND CHUCK

Sabatino, Joe
DANGER ZONE, THE

Sabel, Valeria
RENEGADE, UN OSSO TROPPO DURO

Sabin, Robert C.
I WAS A TEENAGE ZOMBIE

Sable, Valeria
QUARTIERE

Sabo, Roger
MASCARA

Sabourin, Jeanne
FAMILY VIEWING

Sabrina
MASCARA

Sabulis, Remigius
MY OBVINYAEM
MY OBVINYAEM

Sabusawa, Randy
CHINA GIRL

Sacco, Antonio
ILLUMINAZIONI

Sachdev, Ranjana
PRATIGHAAT

Sachia, Kenny
VALET GIRLS

Sacks, Martin
SLATE, WYN & ME

Sacremento, Nadia Do
LA VIE PLATINEE

Sacristan, Jose
CARA DE ACELGA

Sadaba, Sergio
A LOS CUATRO VIENTOS

Sadalsky, Stanislav
ISKUSHENIE DON ZHUANA

Sadeghi, Ghotoboddin
GOZARESH-E YEK GHATL

Sadler, Bill
PROJECT X

Sadoyan, Isabelle
SOIGNE TA DROITE

Sadykov, R.
DVADTSTAT DNEI BEZ

Saez, Hector
LA FUGA DE CARRASCO

Saffran, Michael
SLAUGHTER HIGH

Safonova, Helena
DVOE POD ODNIM ZONTOM

Safonova, Yelena
OCHNAYA STAVKA

Safra, Jackie
RADIO DAYS

Sagar
PUDHCHE PAOL

Sagdullaev, Rustam
PROSHAL ZELEN LETA

Sagebrecht, Marianne
CRAZY BOYS
OUT OF ROSENHEIM

Saget, Bob
CRITICAL CONDITION

Sagoes, Ken
NIGHTMARE ON ELM STREET 3: DREAM WARRIORS, A

Sagoes, Kenneth
PROJECT X

Sahi, Deepa
TAMAS

Sahlin, Anna
MORE ABOUT THE CHILDREN OF BULLERBY VILLAGE

Saiki, Celso
CIDADE OCULTA

Saiko, Natalia
MOY LYUBIMYY KLOUN

Saint-Pere, Helene
HOTEL DE FRANCE

Sainz, Tina
LA ESTANQUERA DE VALLECAS

Saitsev, Alexeit
PLIUMBUM, ILI OPASNAIA IGIA

Saitta, Gabriella
LA DONNA DEL TRAGHETTO

Sakamoto, Mitsuwa
ROBINSON NO NIWA

Sakamoto, Ryuichi
LAST EMPEROR, THE

Sakanashi, Masfumi
RAGE OF HONOR

Sakazume, Takayuki
HOTARUGAWA

Sako, Sam
BEVERLY HILLS COP II

Sakura, Kinzo
TAXING WOMAN, A

Sakurada, Junko
ITAZU

Sala, Joe
HOME IS WHERE THE HART IS

Sala, Xavier
EL GRAN SERAFIN

Salassi, Rick
IN THE MOOD

Salazar, Ricardo
POR LOS CAMINOS VERDES

Saldivar, Dunia
NOCTURNO AMOR QUE TE VAS

Salemme, Lino
LE FOTO DI GIOIA
QUARTIERE

Salengro, Christophe
LES OREILLES ENTRE LES DENTS

Salerno, Enrico Maria
SCUOLA DI LADRI 2

Salerno, Sabrina
LE FOTO DI GIOIA

Salgado, Jose Luis
FORAJIDOS EN LA MIRA

Salim, Yusuf
HILL 171
WILD FORCE

Salimas, David
ALLNIGHTER, THE

Salinas, Carmen
ALBURES MEXICANOS
CORRUPCION
ENTRE FICHERAS ANDA EL DIABLO
ESTA NOCHE CENA PANCHO (DESPEDIDA DE SOLTERO)
LA RAZA NUNCA PIERDE—HUELE A GAS
NOS REIMOS DE LA MIGRA
OLOR A MUERTE

Salinero, Dominic
ARIA

Salmela, Tomi
URSULA

Salminen, Petteri
KILL CITY

Salminen, Sarianna
VY VIHDOINKIN YHDESSA

Salminen, Simo
PIKKUPOJAT
UUNO TURHAPURO MUUTTAA MAALLE

Salminen, Ville-Veikko
LIIAN ISO KEIKKA

Salo, Raine
URSULA

Salo. Marja —Pyykko, Elina
SNOW QUEEN, THE

Salokhov, Mukhitdin
V TALOM SNEGE ZVON RUCHIA

Salomea's Servant
WIERNA RZEKA

Saloon Owner
GOOD MORNING, VIETNAM

Salsedo, Frank S.
CREEPSHOW 2

Salter, Emma
MOVING TARGETS

Salter, Henry
TIME GUARDIAN, THE

Salthouse, John
PRICK UP YOUR EARS

Salto's Henchman
BELLMAN AND TRUE

Saluzzi, Dino
PERSONAGGI & INTERPRETI

Salverio
LAST STRAW, THE

Salvi, John
ASSASSINATION

Sam the Dog
LETHAL WEAPON

Samal, Basant
BABULA

Samardzic, Ljubisa
ANDJEO CUVAR

Sambrel, Aldo
BEAKS

Samel, Udo
CASPAR DAVID FRIEDRICH

Samir, Nahid
ZAWGAT RAGOL MOHIM

Sammarchi, Pierluigi
IL LUPO DI MARE

Samoilov, P.
VZLOMSHCHIK

Samoilov, Vladimir
PRODELKI V STARINNOM DUKHE

Samolin, Gary
BACHELOR GIRL

Samoylov, Vladimir
TAKAYA ZHESTOKAYA IGRA—KHOKKEY

Samples, Siobhan
MANKILLERS

Samsom, Ken
CHIPMUNK ADVENTURE, THE

Samsom, Noel
EL GRAN SERAFIN

Samsonadze, Mikhail
PYAT NEVEST DO LYUBIMOY

Samuca
MASSACRE IN DINOSAUR VALLEY

Samuels, Don
SULLIVAN'S PAVILION

Samuels, Sam
BROADCAST NEWS

Samuelson, Emma
OM KARLEK

Samuelson, Mikael
RES ALDRIG PA ENKEL BILJETT

Samuelsson, Mikael
SPARVAGN TILL HAVET

Samulejev, Anton
CIZIM VSTUP POVOLEN

San Juan, Christina
ALIEN PREDATOR

San Martin, Conrado
REDONDELA

Sanada, Hiroyuki
SURE DEATH 4

Sanchez, Al
NIGHTFORCE

Sanchez, Alicia
LA GUERRA DE LOS LOCOS
LA VIDA ALEGRE

Sanchez, Dorian
DIRTY DANCING

Sanchez, Eduardo
LA ESTANQUERA DE VALLECAS

Sanchez, Johnny
OUTRAGEOUS FORTUNE

Sanchez, Pedro Maria
CALE

Sanchez, Salvador
FRIDA
VIAJE AL PARAISO

Sanchez, Sergio
HERENCIA DE VALIENTES

Sanchez, Ursula
LA VIDA ALEGRE

Sanchez, Violeta
AVRIL BRISE

Sanchez, Yulay
POR LOS CAMINOS VERDES

Sanchita
HAMARI JUNG

Sancho, Fernando
POLICIA

Sand, Paul
TEEN WOLF TOO

Sanda, Dominique
LES MENDIANTS

Sander, Otto
DER HIMMEL UBER BERLIN

Sander, Ute
OTTO—DER NEUE FILM

Sanders, Beverly
MALIBU BIKINI SHOP, THE

Sanders, Brad
HOLLYWOOD SHUFFLE

Sanders, Chris
BELLMAN AND TRUE

Sanders, Dan
COMMANDO SQUAD

Sanders, Jay O.
WHEELS OF TERROR

Sanders, Michael
EEN MAAND LATER

Sanders, Noell
RAISING ARIZONA

Sanders, Scott
OPPOSING FORCE

Sanders, Zachary
RAISING ARIZONA

Sanderson, Joan
PRICK UP YOUR EARS

Sanderson, Martyn
TALE OF RUBY ROSE, THE

Sandhu, Mahendra
KAUN KITNEY PAANI MEIN

Sandlund, Debra
TOUGH GUYS DON'T DANCE

Sandoval, Douglas
MIRACLES

Sandoval, Miguel
STRAIGHT TO HELL
WALKER

Sandrelli, Amanda
SOTTO IL RISTORANTE CINESE

Sandrelli, Stefania
DA NNUNZIO
FAMILY, THE
GLI OCCHIALI D'ORO
NOYADE INTERDITE

Sands, Julian
GOTHIC
SIESTA

Sands, Pat
FULL METAL JACKET

Sands, Peggy
BEVERLY HILLS COP II

Sandy
RENEGADE, UN OSSO TROPPO DURO

Sangare, Aoua
YEELEN

Sanghamitra
BABULA

Sangineto, Frank
MAKING MR.RIGHT

Sangkao, Sangad
GOOD MORNING, VIETNAM

Sangkao, Vanlap
GOOD MORNING, VIETNAM

Sanguinetti, Maria
EN EL NOMBRE DEL HIJO

Sanjivani
PRATIGHAAT

Sank, Lesley
DEADTIME STORIES

Sanogo, Niamanto
YEELEN

Sansa, Carme
LA RUBIA DEL BAR

Santa Maria, Marcella
TRAIN OF DREAMS

Santa Maria, Raul
MISSION KILL

Santalla, Perla
EL HOMBRE DE LA DEUDA EXTERNA

Santamaria, M. Ferrara
MORO AFFAIR, THE

Santas, Costas
DOXOBUS

Santini, Pamela
BEVERLY HILLS COP II

Santino, Pat
OUTRAGEOUS FORTUNE

Santoni, Reni
PICK-UP ARTIST, THE

Santoni, Vasco
PROFUMO

Santorelli, Robert
NECROPOLIS

Santoro, Nicoletta
LADY OF THE CAMELIAS

Santos, Jaime
DELINCUENTE
UN SABADO MAS

Santos, Lucelia
BAIXO GAVEA
FONTE DA SAUDADE

Santos, Luis
LA PLAYA DE LOS PERROS

Santoyo, Jorge
MUJERES SALVAJES

Sanudo, Paco
EL HIJO DE PEDRO NAVAJAS

Sanz, Jorge
YEAR OF AWAKENING, THE

Sanz, Margarita
MIRACLES
REALM OF FORTUNE, THE

Sapru, Preeti
NAZRANA

Sarachchandra, Sunethra
VIRAGAYA

Saraf, Ashok
PRATIGHAAT

Saralidze, Tristan
GOSPODA AVANTYURISTY
VELIKIY POKHOD ZA NEVESTOY

Saramadi, Zohreh
PEDDLER, THE

Sarandon, Chris
PRINCESS BRIDE, THE

Sarandon, Susan
WITCHES OF EASTWICK, THE

Sarda, Rosa Maria
MOROS Y CRISTIANOS

Sardou, Michel
CROSS

Sargent, Richard
STEPFATHER, THE

Sari
THIRTHAM
VILAMBARAM

Saritha
VILAMBARAM

Sarkisov, Leonid
SASHSHENNYI FONAR

Sarkisyan, Rose
FAMILY VIEWING

Sarmadian, Esmail
PEDDLER, THE

Sarr, Ismaila
YEELEN

Sarrazin, Michael
KEEPING TRACK
MASCARA

Sarri, Caterina
APOUSIES

Sarri, George
YENETHLIA POLI

Sarshar, Hossein
LODGERS

Sartain, Gailard
BIG EASY, THE
ERNEST GOES TO CAMP
MADE IN HEAVEN

Sartor, Fabio
AURELIA
BELLY OF AN ARCHITECT, THE

Sarup, Jim
FULL METAL JACKET

Sas-Uhrynowski, Jacek
C. K. DEZERTERZY

Sasaki, Sumie
GONDOLA

Sasha
FIREHOUSE

Sassi, Jorge
A DOS AGUAS
EN RETIRADA

Sathyaraj
CHINNATHAMBI PERIYATHAMBI
POOVIZHI VASALILE

Sato, B-Sako
ITAZU

Sato, Koichi
SARABA ITOSHIKI HITO YO

Satoh, Hideo
GONDOLA

Sattels, Barry
NUMBER ONE WITH A BULLET

Satterfield, Paul
CREEPSHOW 2

Sattles, Barry
BANZAI RUNNER

Satz, Katrin
DER TRAUM VOM ELCH

Sauk, Stefan
HIP, HIP, HURRA!

Saunders, Enid
HOME IS WHERE THE HART IS

Saunders, Jennifer
EAT THE RICH
MORE BAD NEWS

Saunders, Stuart
WHOOPS APOCALYPSE

Saura, Marina
CRYSTAL HEART
LONG STRIDER
REDONDELA

Saurit, Hector
LAW OF DESIRE

Sauvegrain, Didier
LE BEAUF

Savadier, Russell
STEEL DAWN

Savage, Dewi
BOY SOLDIER

Savage, Fred
PRINCESS BRIDE, THE

Savage, John
BEAT, THE
BEAUTY AND THE BEAST
HOTEL COLONIAL

Savageau, Adam
RAISING ARIZONA

Savageau, Benjamin
RAISING ARIZONA

Savant, Doug
HANOI HILTON, THE

Savident, John
LITTLE DORRIT

Savini, Tom
CREEPSHOW 2

Savoy, Teresa Ann
DA NNUNZIO
IL RAGAZZO DI EBALUS

Savoy, Terese Ann
LA DONNA DEL TRAGHETTO

Sawada, Tamae
HOTARUGAWA

Sawaguchi, Yasuko
EIGA JOYU
PRINCESS FROM THE MOON

Sawalha, Nadim
ISHTAR
LIVING DAYLIGHTS, THE

Sawant, Anuradha
PRATIGHAAT

Sawicka, Teresa
INNA WYSPA

Saxon, John
NIGHTMARE ON ELM STREET 3: DREAM WARRIORS, A

Saygili, Mustafa
IN DER WUSTE

Sayle, Alexei
LOVECHILD, THE
WHOOPS APOCALYPSE

Sayle, Alexi
SIESTA

Sayles, John
MATEWAN

Saynor, Ian
BOY SOLDIER

Sayyad, Parviz
CHECKPOINT

Sazatornil, Jose
YEAR OF AWAKENING, THE

Sazontyev, Sergei
RAZMAKH KRYLIEV

Sbragia, Mattia
IL BURBERO
MORO AFFAIR, THE
TENEREZZA

Scacchi, Greta
GOOD MORNING BABYLON
MAN IN LOVE, A
WHITE MISCHIEF

Scales, Prunella
LONELY PASSION OF JUDITH HEARNE,THE

Scalondro, Paolo M.
MORO AFFAIR, THE

Scandi, Josephine
SLAUGHTER HIGH

Scanlan, Karen
BLUE MONKEY

Scarber, Sam
OVER THE TOP

Scarcella, Giuseppe
GOOD MORNING BABYLON

Scarfe, Alan
KEEPING TRACK

Scarpa, Renato
LESTATE STA FINENDO

Scarpitta, Carmen
MOSCA ADDIO

Scarwid, Diana
HEAT

Scattini, Monica
FAMILY, THE

Schaal, Wendy
INNERSPACE
MUNCHIES

Schaanning, Per
PLASTPOSEN

Schad, Daniel
MISS MONA

Schaeffer, Anthony
GUNPOWDER

Schaeffer, Rebecca
RADIO DAYS

Schahar, Chad
DREAMERS

Schall, Johanna
VERNEHMUNG DER ZEUGEN

Schallert, William
INNERSPACE

Scharffenberg, Svein
OFELAS

Schaufus, Puk
NEGERKYS & LABRE LARVER

Schech, Michael
SOMMER

Scheele, Henrik
FELDMANN CASE, THE

Schenk, Udo
CRAZY BOYS
TAXI NACH KAIRO

Schenkkan, Robert
AMAZING GRACE AND CHUCK

Scherbakov, Boris
VYKUP

Scherbakov, Dalvin
UTRO OBRECHENNOGO PRIISKA

Schereiber, Anderson
COLOR OF DESTINY, THE

Scherjon, Elsje
IRIS

Schermerhorn, David
CANT BUY ME LOVE
IN THE MOOD

Schettino, Kimura
A DANCA DOS BONECOS
UM FILM 100% BRAZILEIRO

Scheurer, Eva
DER NACHBAR

Schevelkov, Vladimir
GEROY YEYOROMANA

Schiavone, Annabella
DA NNUNZIO

Schiavoni, Gianluca
IL CORAGGIO DI PARLARE

Schidor, Dieter
TERMINUS

Schier, Nancy
HOLLYWOOD SHUFFLE

Schiffler, Carrie
ROCK 'N' ROLL NIGHTMARE

Schiller, Danny
PERSONAL SERVICES

Schilling, William
WHITE OF THE EYE

Schlief, Robert
PRETTY SMART

Schloss, Zander
STRAIGHT TO HELL
WALKER

Schluter, John
BIG EASY, THE

Schmaltz, Robert
MANKILLERS

Schmidinger, Walter
CASPAR DAVID FRIEDRICH

Schmidt, Christian
DIE DRECKSCHLEUDER

Schmidt, Gian-Reto
JENATSCH

Schmidt-Maybach, Chris
FULL METAL JACKET

Schmitt, Charles
BAD BLOOD

Schmitz, Marcelle
AS TIME GOES BY

Schnabel, Stefan
ANNA

Schneider, Bonnie
MURDER LUST

Schneider, David
RAISING ARIZONA

Schneider, Dawn
BANZAI RUNNER

Schneider, John
CURSE, THE

Schneider, Maria
CRIME OF HONOR

Schneider, Mark
SUPERNATURALS, THE

Schneider, Michael
BEAUTY AND THE BEAST
RUMPELSTILTSKIN

Schneider, Mother Superior Roswitha
FRANCESCA

Schoeffling, Michael
LETS GET HARRY

Schoelen, Jill
STEPFATHER, THE

Schoenaerts, Julien
BORAN—ZEIT ZUM ZIELEN

Schoenfelder, Friedrich
OTTO—DER NEUE FILM

Schoff, Margie
NECROPOLIS

Schofield, Lynne
FRENCHMAN'S FARM

Schofield, Nell
AROUND THE WORLD IN EIGHTY WAYS

Scholz, Duane
IRONWEED

Schonfelder, Friedrich
CASPAR DAVID FRIEDRICH

Schonherr, Deitmar
CRIME OF HONOR

School Custodian
HIDING OUT

Schopper, Phillip
ISHTAR

Schorber, Willie
EQUALIZER 2000

Schorn, Christine
VERNEHMUNG DER ZEUGEN

Schott, Bob
MILLION DOLLAR MYSTERY

Schou, Jesper "Gokke"
STRIT OG STUMME

Schouten, Joshua
HIDING OUT

Schrage, Lisa
HELLO MARY LOU, PROM NIGHT II

Schreder, Darrin
STACKING

Schreiber, Avery
HUNK

Schroder, Ernst
CRIME OF HONOR

Schroder, Sebastian C.
CRIME OF HONOR

Schroeder, Peter Henry
HOT SHOT

Schuck, John
OUTRAGEOUS FORTUNE

Schuehly, Nina
TAXI NACH KAIRO

Schuer, Helge
PETER VON SCHOLTEN

Schultz, Dennis
PURSUIT OF HAPPINESS, THE

Schultz, Jeff
STEPFATHER, THE

Schultz, Jessica
CATCH THE HEAT

Schulz, Brian
THOU SHALT NOT KILL . . . EXCEPT

Schumacher, Eddy
ERNEST GOES TO CAMP

Schutte, Mike
HIDING OUT

Schwabinger, Keith
ROBOT HOLOCAUST

Schwartz, Aaron
SUSPECT

Schwartz, Beverly E.
HUNTER'S BLOOD

Schwartz, Judith
NIGHTFORCE

Schwartz, Larry
POLICE ACADEMY 4: CITIZENS ON PATROL

Schwartz, Stephan
VICTORIA

Schwartz, Tom
MAKING MR.RIGHT

Schwarz, Magic
OVER THE TOP
PENITENTIARY III

Schwarzenegger, Arnold
PREDATOR
RUNNING MAN, THE

Schwebel, Bruno
NI DE AQUI, NI DE ALLA

Schwebel, Roberta
SULLIVAN'S PAVILION

Schweiger, Vera
DER NACHBAR

Schweitzer, Matt
FIRE AND ICE

Schwerk, Ulrike
DELIRIA

Schwidde, Jess
STACKING

Schygulla, Hanna
FOREVER, LULU

Scianablo, Joseph
UNTOUCHABLES, THE

Scoop's Girl
MONSTER IN THE CLOSET

Scorpio, Jay
EMANON

Scott, Albert
P.K. & THE KID

Scott, Bainbridge
MANKILLERS

Scott, Ben R.
WANTED: DEAD OR ALIVE

Scott, Camilla
THREE MEN AND A BABY

Scott, Carolyn
POLICE ACADEMY 4: CITIZENS ON PATROL

Scott, Cedric
JAWS: THE REVENGE

Scott, Colleen
LADY OF THE CAMELIAS

Scott, Daniele
THREE MEN AND A BABY

Scott, Garry
WANTED: DEAD OR ALIVE

Scott, Harvey
OVERKILL

Scott, John
EL HOMBRE DESNUDO

Scott, Kathryn Leigh
ASSASSINATION

Scott, Keith
DOT GOES TO HOLLYWOOD

Scott, Larry B.
EXTREME PREJUDICE
REVENGE OF THE NERDS II: NERDS IN PARADISE

Scott, Mitch
MATEWAN

Scott, Patrick
ULTIMAX FORCE

Scott, Sandra
HOUSEKEEPER, THE

Scott, Susan
STUDENT CONFIDENTIAL

Scott, Timothy
BIG SHOTS
BOY SOLDIER

Scott-Pendlebury, Anne
LIGHTHORSEMEN, THE

Scranton, Peter
STRIPPED TO KILL

Scribner, Don
MOON IN SCORPIO
SLAVE GIRLS FROM BEYOND INFINITY

Scrivano, Enrica Maria
BELLY OF AN ARCHITECT, THE

Scuddamore, Simon
SLAUGHTER HIGH

Scura, Jason
ASSASSINATION

Seacat, Sondra
PROMISED LAND

Sears, Djanet
SUSPECT

Sears, Ian
EMPIRE STATE

Sears, Scott
PSYCHOS IN LOVE

Sebastian, Kim
BABY BOOM

Second, Billy
HOSTAGE

Seda, Job
KITCHEN TOTO, THE

Sedgwick, Robert
MORGAN STEWART'S COMING HOME

Seear, Andrew
LOVECHILD, THE

Seeberg, Thore
QUATRE MAINS

Seedorf, Christine
VENNER FOR ALTID

Seely, Charlotte
PERSONAL SERVICES

Seezen, Michael
FOURTH PROTOCOL, THE

Seftel, Molly
HOSTAGE

Segal, John
SLAUGHTER HIGH

Segal, Ruth
BOUBA

Segal, Sahar
LATE SUMMER BLUES

Segal, Zohra
SHADEY

Segall, Ken
DIRTY LAUNDRY

Segall, Pamela
SOMETHING SPECIAL!

Segovia, James
TALKING WALLS

Seguin, Gael
JEUX D'ARTIFICES

Segura, Zamira
LA OVEJA NEGRA

Segura Garcia, Jose
MIENTRAS HAYA LUZ

Seibel, Mary
RAISING ARIZONA

Seidelman, Michael
MAKING MR.RIGHT

Seidl, Bia
EU

Seipp, Michelle
P.I. PRIVATE INVESTIGATIONS

Seitz, Nan J.
HUNTER'S BLOOD

Sekhar, S.V.
THIRUMATHI ORU VEGUMATHI

Sekine, Keiko
LOVE LETTER

Selby, Todd
LIKE FATHER, LIKE SON

Seldon, Barbara
DEADTIME STORIES

Selezneva, Irina
KREUTZEROVA SONATA

Selezyova, Natalya
TEMA

Sell, Jack M.
OUTTAKES

Sella, Robbie
DUTCH TREAT

Sellars, Peter
HAPPY NEW YEAR

Selleck, Tom
THREE MEN AND A BABY

Sellers, Larry
ASSASSINATION
LIKE FATHER, LIKE SON

Sellers, Marie
MAN ON FIRE

Sellers, Mary
DELIRIA

Seltzer, Will
ALLNIGHTER, THE

Selzer, Milton
WALKER

Selznick, Albie
ARIA

Semak, Pyotr
SENTIMENTALNOE PUTESHESTVIE NA KARTOSHKU
VZLOMSHCHIK

Seminara, George
I WAS A TEENAGE ZOMBIE

Sen, Moon Moon
AMAR KANTAK
APAN GHAREY

Sen, Sener
DEGIRMEN

Sender, Raul
CARA DE ACELGA

Sendino, Blanca
REDONDELA

Seneca, Joe
BIG SHOTS

Senechal, Ann
WITCHES OF EASTWICK, THE

Sengupta, Aniket
PHERA

Sentier, Jean-Pierre
POUSSIERE D'ANGE

Seppo, Aino
NAKEMIIN, HYVASTI

Septier, Patrice
MASCARA

Sequeira, Antonio Manuel
RELACAO FIEL E VERDADEIRA

Sera, Masanori
DEATH SHADOWS

Serapio
LA RAZA NUNCA PIERDE—HUELE A GAS

Serbedzija, Rade
DIE VERLIEBTEN

Serdyuk, Les
POKLONIS DO ZEMLI

Serebryakov, Alexei
OBVINYAETSYA SVADBA

Sergachev, Evstigneev
SEVERNY ANEKDOT

Seri, Mati
YEHOSHUA—YEHOSHUA

Seriese, Astrid
BLOND DOLLY

Serna, Assumpta
BALADA DA PRAIA DOS CAES
LA BRUTE
LA PLAYA DE LOS PERROS
LO DEL CESAR

Serner, Hakan
MANNEN FRAN MALLORCA

Serner, Manfred
MY LIFE AS A DOG

Seropova, Yelena
LEGENDA SEREBRYANOGO OZERA

Serra, Gino
LA CROCE DALLE SETTE PIETRE

Serra, Norberto
EIN BLICK-UND DIE LIEBE BRICHT AUS

Serra, Pablo
CITY AND THE DOGS, THE

Serra, Ray
LA VALLEE FANTOME

Serra, Raymond
FOREVER, LULU

Serrador, Pastor
ASIGNATURA APROBADA

Serrana, Tina
CHECHECHELA—UNA CHICA DEL BARRIO

Serrault, Michel
ENNEMIS INTIMES
LE MIRACULE

Serre, Jacques
TRAVELLING AVANT

Seshadri, Meenakshi
DACAIT
INAAM DUS HAZAAR

Sessa, Alida
IL RAGAZZO DI EBALUS

Sessions, John
WHOOPS APOCALYPSE

Sestili, Giuliano
PROFUMO

Seth, Roshan
LITTLE DORRIT

Sette, Brooke
MANKILLERS

Setzer, Brian
LA BAMBA

Severe, Peggy
ANGEL HEART

Severo, Marieta
LEILA DINIZ

Sevilla, Alfredo
LO DEL CESAR

Seward, Eric
RAGE OF HONOR

Seward, Roger
MALIBU BIKINI SHOP, THE

Sewell, Phillada
MAURICE

Seweryn, Andrzej
LA CODA DEL DIAVOLO

Sewrattan, Kietje
EEN MAAND LATER

Seybert, Charlie
BLOODSUCKERS FROM OUTER SPACE

Seymour, Doug
JOHN AND THE MISSUS

Seymour, Lynn
DANCERS

Seymour, Ralph
EMPIRE OF THE SUN

Seymour, Susan
WILD THING

Sferrazza, Mark
STREET TRASH

Shaban, Nabil
BORN OF FIRE

Shackelford, Ted
SWEET REVENGE

Shadowplay
KILL CITY

Shadrin, M.
VZLOMSHCHIK

Shadyac, Tom
JOCKS

Shael, Lee
NO WAY OUT

Shafer, Hal
BARFLY

Shafer, John
FAMILY VIEWING

Shafer, Robert
HOLLYWOOD SHUFFLE

Shaffy, Ramses
NITWITS

Shafi'ie, Behnam
MANUSCRIPTS

Shafie, Hammam
WANTED: DEAD OR ALIVE

Shah, B.M.
THIS IS NOT OUR DESTINATION

Shah, Khalid
PRATIGHAAT

Shah, Kiran
GOTHIC

Shah, Naseeruddin
JALWA
MIRCH MASALA

Shahan, Happy
RETURN OF JOSEY WALES, THE

Shaikh, Farouque
ANJUMAN

Shaiman, Marc
BROADCAST NEWS

Shakhmerdanov, Kyamran
CHKATULKA IZ KREPOSTI

Shakti
THREE KINDS OF HEAT

Shakurov, Sergei
LICHNOE DELO SUDYI IVANOVOY
PLOSHCHAD VOSSTANIA
SLEDY OBOROTNYA

Shaldene, Valerie
CLUB LIFE

Shallo, Karen
HELLO AGAIN

Shana, James H.
OVER THE TOP

Shaner, John Herman
GARBAGE PAIL KIDS MOVIE, THE

Shaner, Michael
LETHAL WEAPON

Shankley, Amelia
RED RIDING HOOD

Shanklin, Doug
HUNK

Shannon, Don
OVERKILL

Shannon, George
WANTED: DEAD OR ALIVE

Shanta, James Anthony
ALLNIGHTER, THE

Shanti
KALYANA THAMBULAM

Shapiro, Charles
WANTED: DEAD OR ALIVE

Shapiro, Warren
I WAS A TEENAGE T.V. TERRORIST

Sharad, Alok
PRATIGHAAT

Sharkey, Billy Ray
DUDES

Sharkey, Ray
P.I. PRIVATE INVESTIGATIONS

Sharko, Zenaida
DOLGHYIE PROVOD

Sharko, Zinaida
SLUCHAYNYE PASSAZHIRY

Sharkova, T.
VZLOMSHCHIK

Sharma, Chander
GHULAMI KI ZANJEER

Sharma, Madhav
SHADEY

Sharma, Nandlal
PRATIGHAAT

Sharp, Barney
EAT THE RICH

Sharp, Jon
SURVIVAL GAME
VALET GIRLS

Sharp, Lesley
LOVECHILD, THE
RITA, SUE AND BOB TOO!

Sharp, Rachel
TEEN WOLF TOO

Sharpe, Ascanio
SECRET OF MY SUCCESS, THE

Shattuck, Shari
HOT CHILD IN THE CITY

Shaughnessey, David
WHISTLE BLOWER, THE

Shaver, Helen
BELIEVERS, THE

Shavlak, Igor
CHYORNAYA STRELA
POEZD VNE RASPISANIA

Shaw, Michael
BELLMAN AND TRUE

Shaw, Sandy
EAT THE RICH

Shaw, Sebastian
HIGH SEASON

Shaw, Stan
MONSTER SQUAD, THE

Shaw, Steve
ZERO BOYS, THE

Shaw, Tina
BLOOD TRACKS

Shawn, Dick
MAID TO ORDER

Shawn, Wallace
BEDROOM WINDOW, THE
NICE GIRLS DON'T EXPLODE
PRICK UP YOUR EARS
PRINCESS BRIDE, THE
RADIO DAYS

Shaye, Lin
EXTREME PREJUDICE
RUNNING MAN, THE
SLAMDANCE

Shayne, Linda
BIG BAD MAMA II

She, Zhai Nai
EMPIRE OF THE SUN

Shea, Jack
NIGHTMARE ON ELM STREET 3: DREAM WARRIORS, A

Shea, John
DREAMERS

Shear, Pearl
BARFLY

Shear, Rhonda
SPACEBALLS

Shearer, Chris
BORDER RADIO

Shearer, Harry
FLICKS

Shearer, Jack
MONSTER IN THE CLOSET

Sheedy, Ally
MAID TO ORDER

Sheehan, Gladys
RAWHEAD REX

Sheen, Charlie
NO MAN'S LAND
THREE FOR THE ROAD
WALL STREET

Sheen, Lucy
BUSINESS AS USUAL

Sheen, Martin
BELIEVERS, THE
SIESTA
WALL STREET

Sheen, Ramon
TURNAROUND

Sheenan, James
I WAS A TEENAGE T.V. TERRORIST

Sheets, Chad
SUPERNATURALS, THE

Sheffer, Craig
SOME KIND OF WONDERFUL

Sheldon, Douglas
SNOW WHITE

Shell, Tom
SURF NAZIS MUST DIE
ZERO BOYS, THE

Shellen, Stephen
STEPFATHER, THE
TALKING WALLS

Shelley, Mark
EAT THE PEACH

Shelton, Darrell
BLOODSUCKERS FROM OUTER SPACE

Shelton, Deborah
HUNK

Shenar, Paul
BEDROOM WINDOW, THE
BEST SELLER
MAN ON FIRE

Shendal, Margaret
SUPERNATURALS, THE

Shenkkan, Robert
BEDROOM WINDOW, THE

Shepard, Chuck
BORDER RADIO

Shepard, Hilary
HUNK

Shepard, Jewel
PARTY CAMP

Shepard, Sam
BABY BOOM

Shepard, Susan
HAPPY HOUR

Shepherd, John
BANZAI RUNNER
CAUGHT

Sheppard, Morgan
CRY FREEDOM

Sher, Antony
SHADEY

Sherbanee, Maurice
FORTY DAYS OF MUSA DAGH

Sherentz, Azat
ZEMLYA I ZOLOTO

Sheridan, Beatriz
GABY—A TRUE STORY

Sheridan, Liz
WHO'S THAT GIRL

Sheridan, Rondell
DEADTIME STORIES

Sheridan, Traci Huber
MUNCHIES

Sheriff, Sydney D.
FOREVER, LULU

Sherihan
AL-TAUQ WAL-ISWIRA

Sherk, Scott
MUNCHIES

Sherman, Arthur
LES PATTERSON SAVES THE WORLD

Sherman, Dolly
HIDING OUT

Sherman, Everett
BEVERLY HILLS COP II

Sherman, Martin
RADIO DAYS

Sherman, Muriel "Dolly"
DATE WITH AN ANGEL

Sherman, Wendy
MILLION DOLLAR MYSTERY

Sherrard, Tudor
CANT BUY ME LOVE

Sherrod, Paul
WINNERS TAKE ALL

Sherwood, Anthony
MORNING MAN, THE
WILD THING

Shestakova, Tatiana
PODSUDIMYY

Sheta, Sadri
AVRIL BRISE

Shevchuk, Irina
SEKUNDA NA PODVIG

Shevel, Lyudmila
TANTSPLOSHCHADKA

Shevelkov, Vladimir
POEZD VNE RASPISANIA

Shields, Sonny
MISSION KILL

Shigang, Luo
LAST EMPEROR, THE

Shihong, Yu
LAST EMPEROR, THE

Shikhov, Vladimir
TAYNAYA PROGULKA

Shilkina, Elena
KONTRUDAR

Shilkina, Yelena
OBVINYAETSYA SVADBA

Shillo, Michael
NO WAY OUT

Shilo, Shmuel
LO SAM ZAYIN
YALDEI STALIN

Shilovsky, Vsevolod
KAK STAT SCHASTLIVYM

Shilton, Peter
EQUALIZER 2000

Shima, Daisuke
SARABA ITOSHIKI HITO YO

Shimada, Shogo
MAGINA—MURA MONOGATARI

Shimerman, Armin
BLIND DATE
IN THE MOOD
LIKE FATHER, LIKE SON

Shimizu, Ken
OVERKILL

Shimizu, Kiriko
TAXING WOMAN, A

Shimojo, Masami
TORA-SAN'S BLUEBIRD FANTASY

Shimono, Sab
BLIND DATE

Shimoyama, Kiyatsu
RAGE OF HONOR

Shimshoni, Beatrice
HANSEL AND GRETEL

Shine, Lexie
WHO'S THAT GIRL

Shine, Tony
EPIDEMIC

Shinew, Leonard O.
SOMETHING SPECIAL!

Shing, Yee Tung
MAGNIFICENT WARRIORS

Shinomi, Chieko
TORA-SAN'S BLUEBIRD FANTASY

Shiomi, Eysuko
TORA-SAN'S BLUEBIRD FANTASY

Shirandami, Valiollah
SHEERE SANGGY

Shire, Troy
PARTY CAMP

Shirley, Peg
SQUEEZE, THE

Shirokov, Vladimir
PO ZAKONU VOENNOGO VREMENI

Shiroto, Tish
OVERKILL

Shirvindt, Alexander
MILLION V BRACHNOY KORZINE

Shiva
HAMARI JUNG

Shivpuri, Gyan
PRATIGHAAT

Shock, Donna
EVIL SPAWN

Shoja Noori, Ali Reza
SHEERE SANGGY

Sholto, Pamela
HELLRAISER

Shoop, Kimber
BROADCAST NEWS

Short, Dana
IN THE MOOD

Short, Martin
CROSS MY HEART
INNERSPACE

Short, Paul
CYCLONE
DIRTY LAUNDRY
MUNCHIES

Shorte, Dino
PROJECT X

Shoshan, Gaby
DEADLINE

Shotadze, Leila
VELIKIY POKHOD ZA NEVESTOY

Shower, Kathy
COMMANDO SQUAD

Shrapnel, John
PERSONAL SERVICES

Shrives, Ian
AS TIME GOES BY

Shroff, Jackie
JAWAB HUM DENGE

Shrog, Maurice
RADIO DAYS

Shtefanko, Oleg
SOPERNITSY

Shu, Chen
LAST EMPEROR, THE

Shu-Fen, Sin
LIEN LIEN FUNG CHEN

Shue, Elisabeth
ADVENTURES IN BABYSITTING

Shukshin, Vasili
KOMISSAR

Shuler, Paul
MAGDALENA VIRAGA

Shulgayte, Evgeniya
IZVINITEPOZHALUYSTA

Shultz, Philip
RADIO DAYS

Shulz, Rafael
OPPOSING FORCE

Shuma, Shuma Ginny
KOLORMASK

Shumba, Simon
CRY FREEDOM

Shumputei, Koasa
PRINCESS FROM THE MOON

Shuyan, Cheng
LAST EMPEROR, THE

Shydner, Ritch
BEVERLY HILLS COP II
ROXANNE

Shyer, Annie
BABY BOOM

Shyh-Jye, Jin
TERRORIZERS, THE

Si, Mauricio
MANKILLERS

Sibley, Bill
ESCAPES

Sidaris, Andy
HARD TICKET TO HAWAII

Sideshow Owner
OFFSPRING, THE

Sidney, Jon
LIGHTHORSEMEN, THE

Siebert, Charles
WHITE WATER SUMMER

Siebert, Marie
BIG TOWN, THE

Siederman, Paul
DERANGED

Sieklov, Vladimir
PLIUMBUM, ILI OPASNAIA IGIA

Siemaszko, Casey
GARDENS OF STONE
THREE O'CLOCK HIGH

Sienkiewicz, Joanna
ZYCIE WEWNETRZNE

Sienna, Bridget
VALET GIRLS

Sierra, Gregory
LETS GET HARRY
TROUBLE WITH SPIES, THE

Siewiez, Zbigniew Zapa
BLIND CHANCE

Sifuentes, Everett
RETURN OF JOSEY WALES, THE

Sigalla, Rudy
NIGHTFORCE

Sigaux, Jacky
MON BEL AMOUR, MA DECHIRURE

Signorelli, Tom
PICK-UP ARTIST, THE
SICILIAN, THE

Sigsgaard, Thomas
VENNER FOR ALTID

Siimes, Pentti
LIIAN ISO KEIKKA

Siimes, Tarja
JAAHYVAISET PRESIDENTILLE

Siirtola, Marita
ELVIS-KISSAN JALJILLA

Sikhri, Surekha
TAMAS

Sikivie, Francois
FALSCH

Silas, Andy
MASSACRE IN DINOSAUR VALLEY

Silberg, Tusse
HIDDEN CITY

Silbersher, Marvin
BIG BANG, THE

Sileri, Silvana
CHECHECHELA—UNA CHICA DEL BARRIO

Siljander, Heidi
ELVIS-KISSAN JALJILLA

Silla, Felix
SPACEBALLS

Sillers, Mary
UNDICI GIORNI, UNDICI NOTTE

Sills, Ellen
TIN MEN

Silva, Albert
MASSACRE IN DINOSAUR VALLEY

Silva, Henry
ALLAN QUATERMAIN AND THE LOST CITY OF GOLD
AMAZON WOMEN ON THE MOON
BULLETPROOF

Silva, Rebeca
ESTA NOCHE CENA PANCHO (DESPEDIDA DE SOLTERO)
NOS REIMOS DE LA MIGRA
TODA LA VIDA

Silva, Rita
PERSONAGGI & INTERPRETI

Silva, Roland
REMEMBERING MEL

Silva, Terry E.
P.K. & THE KID

Silva, Trinidad
JOCKS

Silva, Zaide
GABY—A TRUE STORY

Silver, Joe
CREEPSHOW 2
MAGIC STICKS

Silver, Johnny
SPACEBALLS
Silver, Veronique
POUSSIERE D'ANGE
Silvester, J.D.
WALKER
Silvestre, Armando
ESTA NOCHE CENA PANCHO (DESPEDIDA DE SOLTERO)
Silveyra, Soledad
LOS DUENOS DEL SILENCIO
Silvia, Maria
ELE, O BOTO
Silvo, Satu
ELVIS-KISSAN JALJILLA
SNOW QUEEN, THE
Sim, Debra
FINAL TEST, THE
Sim, Gerald
CRY FREEDOM
Sim, Mathew
MAURICE
Simacek, Milan
CHOBOTNICE Z II. PATRA
Simancas, Jean Carlos
MAS ALLA DEL SILENCIO
Simanek, Otto
CHOBOTNICE Z II. PATRA
Simbrashe, Lawrence
CRY FREEDOM
Simek, Vasek C.
AMAZING GRACE AND CHUCK
Simmonds, Stuart
REMEMBERING MEL
Simmons, Allene
MALIBU BIKINI SHOP, THE
Simmons, Gene
WANTED: DEAD OR ALIVE
Simmons, James
EMPIRE STATE
WHISTLE BLOWER, THE
Simms, Jane Carol
MANNEQUIN
Simms, Kimberly
CAUGHT
Simms, Michael D.
CROSS MY HEART
Simms, Phil
CANT BUY ME LOVE
Simon, Eric
EMANON
Simon, Helen
AROUND THE WORLD IN EIGHTY WAYS
Simon, Jami
I WAS A TEENAGE T.V. TERRORIST
Simon, Josette
CRY FREEDOM
Simon, Stephen Kenyatta
ANGEL HEART
Simonelli, Benedetto
QUARTIERE
Simonett, Ted
POLICE ACADEMY 4: CITIZENS ON PATROL
Simonov, J.
SKORBNOE BESCHUVSTVIE
Simonov, Konstantin
DVADTSTAT DNEI BEZ
Simonov, Vladimir
PLOSHCHAD VOSSTANIA
Simonsen, Lars
PELLE EROVRAREN
Simonsen, Renee
VIA MONTENAPOLEONE
Simpers, Desiree
SUMMER CAMP NIGHTMARE
Simpron, Al
FULL METAL JACKET
Simpson, Jay
EMPIRE STATE
Simpson, Michael
EPIDEMIC
Simpson, Teresa
ROCK 'N' ROLL NIGHTMARE
Sims, Tom
FIRE AND ICE
Sims, Warwick
HES MY GIRL
RUNNING FROM THE GUNS
Sinatra, Frank
CODE NAME ZEBRA

Sincavage, Michele
WITCHES OF EASTWICK, THE
Sincavage, Nicol
WITCHES OF EASTWICK, THE
Sincere, Jean
ROXANNE
Sinclair, Hugh
ERNEST GOES TO CAMP
Singer, A. Gerald
OPEN HOUSE
Singer, Elizabeth
STUDENT CONFIDENTIAL
Singer, Linda
ZOMBIE NIGHTMARE
Singer, Lori
SUMMER HEAT
Singer, Robert
LETS GET HARRY
Singerman, Joe
MORNING MAN, THE
Singh, Archana Puran
JALWA
Singh, Harry
DIRTY LAUNDRY
Singh, Manohar
THIS IS NOT OUR DESTINATION
Singh, Tejeshwar
JALWA
Sinha, Shatrughan
INSANIYAT KE DUSHMAN
JAWAB HUM DENGE
LOHA
Sinisalo-Lahtinen, Kaija
AKALLINEN MIES
Sinjen, Sabine
CASPAR DAVID FRIEDRICH
Sinko, Laszlo
ISTEN VELETEK, BARATAIM
Sire, Benedicte
MEMOIRE DES APPARENCES: LA VIE EST UN SONGE
Sirgo, Otto
LAS TRAIGO . . . MUERTAS
Sisask, Sijri
IGRY DLJA DETEJ SKO'NOGO VOZRASTA
Sisinini, Christina
MUTANT HUNT
Sisinni, Christina
NECROPOLIS
Sisters of St. Mary's Convent
FRANCESCA
Sisto, Rocco
RED RIDING HOOD
Sithole, Evelyn
CRY FREEDOM
Sithole, Xoliswa
CRY FREEDOM
Sittig, Hans
CRY FREEDOM
Siu, Vivien
SWORN BROTHERS
Siu-ho, Chin
KILLER'S NOCTURNE
Siverio, Manuel
MUTANT HUNT
Siwkiewicz, Piotr
POCIAG DO HOLLYWOOD
Siyolwe, Wabei
CRY FREEDOM
Sizemore, Marshall
GARDENS OF STONE
Sjoblom, Robert
NIONDE KOMPANIET
Sjogren, Olof
MORE ABOUT THE CHILDREN OF BULLERBY VILLAGE
Skaggs, Jimmie F.
LETHAL WEAPON
Skala, Lilia
HOUSE OF GAMES
Skarsgard, My
JIM OCH PIRATERNA BLOM
Skarsgard, Sam
JIM OCH PIRATERNA BLOM
Skarsgard, Stellan
HIP, HIP, HURRA!
JIM OCH PIRATERNA BLOM
SERPENT'S WAY, THE
Skattum, Stein Erik
ETTER RUBICON

Skehan, Mike
BROADCAST NEWS
Skerritt, Tom
BIG TOWN, THE
MAID TO ORDER
OPPOSING FORCE
Sketheway, Ken
T. DAN SMITH
Skhirtladze, Tamara
VELIKIY POKHOD ZA NEVESTOY
Skiadaressis, Yerassimos
KLIOS
Skinner, Carole
GOOD WIFE, THE
HOWLING III, THE
Skinner, Dennis
T. DAN SMITH
Skinner, Michael
HEARTS OF FIRE
Skippr, Susan
WISH YOU WERE HERE
Skoglund, Rolf
FADERN, SONEN OCH DEN HELIGE ANDE
Skolimowski, Jerzy
BIG SHOTS
Skolmen, Jon
PLASTPOSEN
Skopecek, Jan
POHADKA O MALICKOVI
Skorokhodova, Yelena
SVIDANIE NA MLECHNOM PUTI
Skou, Christine
VENNER FOR ALTID
Skulason, Helgi
OFELAS
Sky, Paul
MASSACRE IN DINOSAUR VALLEY
Skye, Ione
STRANDED
Slabolepszy, Paul
SATURDAY NIGHT AT THE PALACE
Slade, Demian
BACK TO THE BEACH
Slade, Jon C.
SLAMDANCE
Slate, Hugh
P.I. PRIVATE INVESTIGATIONS
Slater, Helen
SECRET OF MY SUCCESS, THE
Slater, Jack
WALKER
Slater, Russell
FULL METAL JACKET
Slaughter, Lance
WHO'S THAT GIRL
Slavikova, Radka
WOLF'S HOLE
Sledge, George
TRESPASSES
Sledge, Tommy
MILLION DOLLAR MYSTERY
Sleet, Jackson
PROJECT X
Sleigh, William
BELLMAN AND TRUE
Sligter, Marjolein
EEN MAAND LATER
Slimani, Mourad
VENNER FOR ALTID
Sloan, Ron
BANZAI RUNNER
Slocum, Marjorie
IRONWEED
Sloup, Vaclav
CENA MEDU
Slovakova, Mariana
DISCOPRIBEH
Slue, Errol
BIG TOWN, THE
Slutskaya, Inara
SVIDANIE NA MLECHNOM PUTI
Smacchi, Sergio
ALADDIN
Smail, Ben
MISS MONA
Small, Ade
OUTRAGEOUS FORTUNE
Small, Edgar
KINDRED, THE

Small, Ralph
BLUE MONKEY

Small, Steven
HIDING OUT

Smart, Jason
PERSONAL SERVICES

Smart, Jean
PROJECT X

Smart, Patsy
FOURTH PROTOCOL, THE

Smart, Rebecca
SHADOWS OF THE PEACOCK

Smeeton, Phil
FOURTH PROTOCOL, THE

Smet, Jon
BLIND DATE

Smiley, Sam
UNTOUCHABLES, THE

Smillie, Bill
HOUSEKEEPING

Smirnitsky, Valentin
STARAYA AZBUKA

Smirnov, Andrey
KRASNAYA STRELA

Smirnov, Viktor
V STRELYAYUSHCHEY GLUSHI

Smirnova, Yelena
KRASNAYA STRELA

Smith, Alec
PURSUIT OF HAPPINESS, THE

Smith, Anna Devere
UNFINISHED BUSINESS . . .

Smith, Bill
BULLETPROOF
WANTED: DEAD OR ALIVE

Smith, Bobby
INITIATION

Smith, Bubba
POLICE ACADEMY 4: CITIZENS ON PATROL
WILD PAIR, THE

Smith, Bud
P.K. & THE KID

Smith, Charles "Lew"
RAISING ARIZONA

Smith, Charles Martin
UNTOUCHABLES, THE

Smith, Christina
TALKING WALLS

Smith, Cotter
LADY BEWARE

Smith, Dale
PETER VON SCHOLTEN

Smith, Danielle
WHITE OF THE EYE

Smith, Daryl
HIDING OUT

Smith, David Anthony
HANOI HILTON, THE

Smith, Deane
CREEPSHOW 2

Smith, Donegan
BLACK WIDOW

Smith, Ebbe Roe
BIG BAD MAMA II
BIG EASY, THE
FATAL BEAUTY
OUTRAGEOUS FORTUNE

Smith, Ebonie
LETHAL WEAPON

Smith, Edgar
ISHTAR

Smith, Erik
PARTY CAMP

Smith, Essex
WEEDS

Smith, Fabiana
AMAZONS

Smith, Frazer
SLAMDANCE

Smith, Gary
FULL METAL JACKET

Smith, George Sparky
DIXIELAND DAIMYO

Smith, Heather
PRETTYKILL

Smith, J.W.
LETS GET HARRY
OUTRAGEOUS FORTUNE

Smith, James
FATAL BEAUTY

Smith, Jennifer
ARIA

Smith, Julie
MANKILLERS

Smith, Julie Kirstin
PRETTY SMART

Smith, Juney
GOOD MORNING, VIETNAM

Smith, Kurtwood
DELOS ADVENTURE, THE
ROBOCOP

Smith, Lane
WEEDS

Smith, Linda
KEEPING TRACK
MORNING MAN, THE
ZOMBIE NIGHTMARE

Smith, Lois
BLACK WIDOW
FATAL ATTRACTION

Smith, Maggie
LONELY PASSION OF JUDITH HEARNE,THE

Smith, Marc
SLAUGHTER HIGH
WHOOPS APOCALYPSE

Smith, Martha L.
BROADCAST NEWS

Smith, Mary
JAWS: THE REVENGE

Smith, Megan
POLICE ACADEMY 4: CITIZENS ON PATROL

Smith, Mel
PRINCESS BRIDE, THE

Smith, Michael T.
HOLLYWOOD SHUFFLE

Smith, Miriam
DOGS IN SPACE

Smith, Natalie
BEVERLY HILLS COP II

Smith, Neville
PRICK UP YOUR EARS
WISH YOU WERE HERE

Smith, Oliver
HELLRAISER

Smith, Paul
LA VENGEANCE DU PROTECTEUR

Smith, Priscilla
IRONWEED

Smith, Putter
IN THE MOOD

Smith, Rex
NO DEAD HEROES

Smith, Roger
FULL METAL JACKET

Smith, Sanette
HOSTAGE

Smith, Shawnee
SUMMER SCHOOL

Smith, Sly Ali
OVER THE TOP

Smith, Steve
BROADCAST NEWS

Smith, Suzanna
WARRIOR QUEEN

Smith, T. Dan
T. DAN SMITH

Smith, Tammy
RIVER'S EDGE

Smith, Tony
FULL METAL JACKET

Smith, Tracy
WHOOPS APOCALYPSE

Smith, Vincent
RAWHEAD REX

Smith, William
COMMANDO SQUAD
MOON IN SCORPIO

Smith, Yayonne
CLUB LIFE

Smith-Cameron, J.
EIGHTY FOUR CHARING CROSS ROAD

Smithe, Harris
AMAZING GRACE AND CHUCK

Smithers, Joy
BELINDA

Smits, Jimmy
BELIEVERS, THE

Smoktounovski, Innokenti
DVOE POD ODNIM ZONTOM

Smoktunovsky, Innokenti
DARK EYES
STRANNAYAR ISTORIYAR DOKTORA DZHEKILA I MISTERA KHAIDA

Smoktunovsky, Innokenty
POSLEDNYAYA DOROGA
RUS IZNACHALNA

Smolek, Jeff
DIRTY LAUNDRY

Smolka, Ken
MOON IN SCORPIO

Smorchkov, Boris
PO ZAKONU VOENNOGO VREMENI

Smyczek, Karel
PROC?

Smyth, Deborah
CAUGHT

Smyth, Ethel
CAUGHT

Smyth, Patrick
STARLIGHT HOTEL

Snel, Leontine
GOOD MORNING BABYLON

Snell, Jerry
NIGHT ZOO

Snider, Andrew
STEPFATHER, THE

Snider, William
PROJECT X

Snipelli, Philip
RELACAO FIEL E VERDADEIRA

Snodgrass, Ken
RUNNING FROM THE GUNS

Snow, Rhonda
AMERICAN DRIVE-IN

Snoyink, Liz
ALS IN EEN ROES
ODYSSEE D'AMOUR

Snyder, Arlen Dean
NO MAN'S LAND

Snyder, Drew
SECRET OF MY SUCCESS, THE

Snyder, John
TOUGH GUYS DON'T DANCE

Snyder, Suzanne
PRETTYKILL

Soans, Robin
COMRADES

Soares, Alana
BEVERLY HILLS COP II

Soares, Joffrey
MASSACRE IN DINOSAUR VALLEY

Soares, Leilani
BEVERLY HILLS COP II

Sobczuk, Boguslaw
BOHATERROKU

Sobel, Barry
BLIND DATE
REVENGE OF THE NERDS II: NERDS IN PARADISE

Sobotka, Martin
PROC?

Sobrevals, Cesar
LETS GET HARRY
LO NEGRO DEL NEGRO

Soder, Rolf
PA STIGENDE KURS

Soetens, Jean-Claude
MASCARA

Sofonova, Elena
DARK EYES

Sofovich, Gerardo
EN RETIRADA

Soinee, Maija-Leena
AKALLINEN MIES

Sokolova, Galina
MILLION V BRACHNOY KORZINE

Sokolova, Irina
SKORBNOE BESCHUVSTVIE

Sola, Miguel Angel
A DOS AGUAS

Solares, Alfredo
EL MOFLES Y LOS MECANICOS

Solares, Alfredo "Pelon"
LA RULETERA

Solbach, Sigmar
VICTORIA

Solda, Maurizio
SOTTO IL RISTORANTE CINESE

Soler, Pablo
CHRONICLE OF A DEATH FORETOLD

Solin, Carlo
NOI UOMINI DURI
Solis, Charito
HUNTED, THE
IGOROTA
MANILA, OPEN CITY
MISSING IN ACTION
TIME FOR DYING, A
Solis, Javier
HOUR OF THE ASSASSIN
Sollenberger, Dick
BIG SHOTS
Solli, Sergio
STREGATI
Solnado, Raul
BALADA DA PRAIA DOS CAES
JESTER,THE
LA PLAYA DE LOS PERROS
Solomin, Vitaly
ISKRENNE VASH . . .
Solomon, Carl
VIDEO DEAD, THE
Solomon, Ken
PRETTY SMART
Solovey, Elena
IZVINITEPOZHALUYSTA
OBRYV
Solovey, Yelena
ODINOKAYA ZHENCHINA ZHELAET POZNAKOMITAYA
Solviati, Sandro
ELE, O BOTO
Soman
JANUARY ORORMA
VILAMBARAM
Soman, M.G.
KATHAKKU PINNIL
Sombra, Mercedes
EL GRAN SERAFIN
Somers, Kristi
RETURN TO HORROR HIGH
Somma, Sebastiano
I MIEI PRIMI QUARANT'ANNI
Sommer, Elke
DEATH STONE
Sommer, Josef
ROSARY MURDERS, THE
Sommerfield, Diane
NIGHT STALKER, THE
Sommers, Neil
WANTED: DEAD OR ALIVE
Somoza, Antonio
LOS INVITADOS
Son, Gho Myong
TALMAE WA POMDARI
Sona
GHULAMI KI ZANJEER
Sonderegger, Shirley
CREEPSHOW 2
Song, Magie
VALET GIRLS
Song, Young Me
DRAGON'S FOOD
Song-ki, Ahn
NAE-SHI
Sonnier, Benny
SQUARE DANCE
Sonnier, Kip
SQUARE DANCE
Sonora Santanera
NOS REIMOS DE LA MIGRA
Sonye, Michael
CYCLONE
SURF NAZIS MUST DIE
Soo Soo, Papillon
FULL METAL JACKET
Soo-yeon, Kang
SIBAJI
Sookedeo, Diana
WILD THING
Soon-Teck Oh
DEATH WISH 4: THE CRACKDOWN
Sooster, E.
VZLOMSHCHIK
Soper, Mark
NIGHTMARE AT SHADOW WOODS
Soper, Tony
HIDING OUT
Sopkiw, Michael
MASSACRE IN DINOSAUR VALLEY
Sordi, Alberto
UN TASSINARO A NEW YORK
Sorel, Frederic
LES NOCES BARBARES
Sorel, Jean
IL BURBERO
Sorensen, Heidi
ROXANNE
Sorensen, Reidar
PLASTPOSEN
Sorenson, Paula
STUDENT CONFIDENTIAL
Sorin, Lionel
ARIA
Sorrell, Rozlyn
NIGHTMARE ON ELM STREET 3: DREAM WARRIORS, A
Sorrentino, Spike
HAPPY HOUR
Sosa, Roberto
MIRACLES
WALK ON THE MOON, A
Soshalsky, Vladimir
CHELOVEK C AKKORDEONOM
SDELKA
Sosna, Edward
CZAS NADZIEI
Sothern, Ann
WHALES OF AUGUST, THE
Sotiropulos, Kopi
BEVERLY HILLS COP II
Soto, Lilly
NOS REIMOS DE LA MIGRA
Soto, Raymond
NIGHTFORCE
Sotoconil, Ruben
LA ESTACION DEL REGRESO
Souchon, Alain
COMEDY!
Souckova, Miroslava
POHADKA O MALICKOVI
Souda, Said Ali
LA VENGEANCE DU PROTECTEUR
Souille, Jean-Paul
MASCARA
Soul, David
HANOI HILTON, THE
Soule, Allen
HOUSE OF GAMES
Soulier, Yannick
ENNEMIS INTIMES
Sousa, Alexandre
LA BRUTE
Soutendijk, Renee
BORAN—ZEIT ZUM ZIELEN
EEN MAAND LATER
Souza, Roger
JEAN DE FLORETTE
MANON OF THE SPRING
Sovagovic, Fabijan
HI-FI
Soveral, Laura
RELACAO FIEL E VERDADEIRA
Soviatti, Sandro
BEIJO NA BOCA
Soza, Jose
LA ESTACION DEL REGRESO
Sozos, Haris
ONE HUNDRED AND TWENTY DECIBELS
Spaccesi, Silvio
ITALIANI A RIO
Space Bum
SPACEBALLS
Spadaro, Claudio
BELLY OF AN ARCHITECT, THE
SEMBRA MORTO . . . ME E SOLO SVENUTO
Spade, David
POLICE ACADEMY 4: CITIZENS ON PATROL
Spader, James
BABY BOOM
LESS THAN ZERO
MANNEQUIN
WALL STREET
Spadorcia, Allesandro
MAN ON FIRE
Spainhour, Lamon
HIDING OUT
Spall, Timothy
GOTHIC
Spangler, Tess
MY DARK LADY
Spaniel, Spunky
WHOOPS APOCALYPSE
Spano, Francesco
PERSONAGGI & INTERPRETI
Spano, Vincent
GOOD MORNING BABYLON
Spanou, Dimitra
VERSTECKTE LIEBE
Spantidaki, Maria
TELEFTAIO STICHIMA
Sparer, Paul
HIDING OUT
Sparks, Don
BLIND DATE
Sparrow, Sharolyn
THREE MEN AND A BABY
Sparrowhawk, Len
AMERICAN NINJA 2: THE CONFRONTATION
Spataro, George
UNTOUCHABLES, THE
Spears, Steve J.
WARM NIGHTS ON A SLOW MOVING TRAIN
Spechtenhauser, Robert Egon
PROFUMO
Speciale, Joe
CONCRETE ANGELS
Speight, Richard
ERNEST GOES TO CAMP
Speir, Dona
HARD TICKET TO HAWAII
Spence, Bruce
BACHELOR GIRL
YEAR MY VOICE BROKE, THE
Spencer, Bud
ALADDIN
Spencer, John
HIDING OUT
Spencer, Lena
IRONWEED
Spencer., Daimy
ALADDIN
Spender, Matthew
LAST EMPEROR, THE
Spengler, Volker
PENG! DU BIST TOT!
Sperr, Martin
CHINESE ARE COMING, THE
Sperry, Cory Paul
HOSTAGE SYNDROME
Spicnerova, Vlasta
PRATELE BERMUDSKEHO TROJUHELNIKU
Spiegel, Howard
WEEDS
Spiegelman, Leon
CLUB DE RENCONTRES
Spiegelman, Richard
BELIEVERS, THE
Spielberg, David
STRANGER, THE
Spielvogel, Laurent
LES EXPLOITS DUN JEUNE DON JUAN
Spill, Stormy
MUTANT HUNT
Spinak, Larry
RETURN TO HORROR HIGH
Spindola, Patricia Reyes
NOCTURNO AMOR QUE TE VAS
VA DE NUEZ
Spinell, Joe
DEADLY ILLUSION
MESSENGER, THE
PICK-UP ARTIST, THE
Spinks, James
BIG SHOTS
Spira, Serge
LA CODA DEL DIAVOLO
Spiroff, Tom
FATAL BEAUTY
Sponholz, Kuno
RADIO DAYS
Spoor, Berto
OPPOSING FORCE
Sporrle, Gunter
WANNSEE CONFERENCE, THE
Spottiswood, Greg
CONCRETE ANGELS
Sprague, Frank
O. C. AND STIGGS

Spreague, Peter
CHECKPOINT

Sprenger, Wolf-Dieter
DRAGON'S FOOD

Spring
LAST OF ENGLAND, THE

Sprinkle, Annie
WIMPS

Sprogoe, Ove
HIP, HIP, HURRA!

Spurrier, Linda
PRICK UP YOUR EARS

Spyridakis, Takis
PROINI PERIPOLOS

Srajerova, Daniela
CENA MEDU

Sridevi
JAWAB HUM DENGE
MISTER INDIA
NAZRANA

Srinivasan
NILAKURINHI POOTHAPPOL

Srur, Julio Cesar
MISS MARY

Sschauffler, Florence
STRANDED

St. Amour, Jason
TRAIN OF DREAMS

St. Clair, Andrew
MAURICE

St. Elwood, Jon
P.I. PRIVATE INVESTIGATIONS

St. Esprit, Patrick
TERMINAL EXPOSURE

St. George, Clement
MISSION KILL

St. George, Richard
MASTERBLASTER

St. Heaps, Dorothy
YEAR MY VOICE BROKE, THE

St. Ivanyi, Andra
OUTING, THE

St. Jacques, Raymond
WILD PAIR, THE

St. Louis, Louis
IRONWEED

St. Michaels, Michael
VIDEO DEAD, THE

St. Pe, Edward
BIG EASY, THE

St. Phillip, Ross
OVER THE TOP

St. Pierre, Patrick
BACH AND BROCCOLI

St.-Alix, Alain
KID BROTHER, THE

St.-Denis, John
MORNING MAN, THE

Stabb, Dinah
WHISTLE BLOWER, THE

Stacey, Peter
EAT THE RICH

Stacey, Spider
WALKER

Stach, Jiri
DEATH OF A BEAUTIFUL DREAM

Stack, Tim
BRAVE LITTLE TOASTER, THE

Stack, Timothy
BLIND DATE

Stacy, Candice
MANKILLERS

Stacy, Spider
STRAIGHT TO HELL

Stader, Paul
MILLION DOLLAR MYSTERY

Stader, Peter
BEST SELLER

Stafford, Jim
BLOODSUCKERS FROM OUTER SPACE

Stafford, John
FULL METAL JACKET

Stafford, Jon
MUNCHIES

Stafford, Maeliosa
EAT THE PEACH

Stafford, Marilyn
MANKILLERS

Stafford-Clark, Max
PRICK UP YOUR EARS

Stagnaro, Carola
DARK EYES

Stahl, Jennifer
DIRTY DANCING
FIREHOUSE
NECROPOLIS

Stahl, Richard
OVERBOARD

Stahlbrand, Sandy
MORNING MAN, THE

Staic, Liam
PRICK UP YOUR EARS

Staines, Kent
TOO OUTRAGEOUS

Stakis, Anastassia
SIESTA

Staley, James
ASSASSINATION

Stalker, Gary
LIGHTHORSEMEN, THE

Stallakis, Manos
THEOFILOS

Stallone, Frank
BARFLY

Stallone, Sylvester
OVER THE TOP

Stamp, Terence
SICILIAN, THE
WALL STREET

Stanczak, Wadeck
ENNEMIS INTIMES

Stander, Lionel
BELLIFRESCHI

Standig, Paul
ISHTAR

Standing, John
NIGHTFLYERS

Standing Bear, Jeff
ERNEST GOES TO CAMP

Standish, Miles
DOGS IN SPACE

Stanek, Frantisek
WOLF'S HOLE

Stanfield, David
WINNERS TAKE ALL

Stanger, Nigel
T. DAN SMITH

Stanislav, Jiri
FOURTH PROTOCOL, THE

Staniuta, Stefaniya
FAREWELL

Stanjofski, Harry
WILD THING

Stanley, Florence
OUTRAGEOUS FORTUNE

Stanley, Laura
LA VENGEANCE DU PROTECTEUR

Stanley, Margot
BUSINESS AS USUAL

Stanton, Charlotte
SQUARE DANCE

Stanton, Dan R.
GOOD MORNING, VIETNAM

Stanton, Don E.
GOOD MORNING, VIETNAM

Stanton, Harry Dean
SLAMDANCE

Stanton, Jim
BIRDS OF PREY

Stanyuta, Stefania
POKLONIS DO ZEMLI

Staples, Kevin
BOY SOLDIER

Stapleton, Maureen
MADE IN HEAVEN
NUTS
SWEET LORRAINE

Stapleton, Nicola
HANSEL AND GRETEL
SNOW WHITE

Stapleton, Ronnie
MATEWAN

Star, Amber
MANKILLERS

Stara, Lucia
MONTECARLO GRAN CASINO

Starcova, Svetlana
DOLCE PELLE DI ANGELA

Stardust, Angie
CRAZY BOYS

Starger, Burt
DIRTY REBEL

Stark, Craig
BORDER RADIO

Stark, Graham
BLIND DATE
JANE AND THE LOST CITY

Stark, Jonathan
HOUSE TWO: THE SECOND STORY
PROJECT X

Stark, Koo
EAT THE RICH

Starr, Mike
RADIO DAYS
WHO'S THAT GIRL

Stasio, Annadi
ARIA

Statham, Pat
KILLER WORKOUT

Staunton, Imelda
COMRADES

Staunton, James
WITCHES OF EASTWICK, THE

Stavin, Mary
OPEN HOUSE

Steadman, Ian
HOSTAGE

Steagall, Red
BENJI THE HUNTED

Steel, Amy
WALK LIKE A MAN

Steele, James
KILLER WORKOUT

Steele, Rob
AROUND THE WORLD IN EIGHTY WAYS

Steele, Terry
CONCRETE ANGELS

Steele, Tracey
P.K. & THE KID

Steen, Heather
MOVING TARGETS

Steen, Jessica
HOUSEKEEPER, THE
JOHN AND THE MISSUS

Steenburgen, Mary
DEAD OF WINTER
WHALES OF AUGUST, THE

Steensland, Mark
ESCAPES

Stefanelli, Benito
BARBARIANS, THE

Stefania, Irene
ANJOS DO ARRABALDE

Steffen, Rainer
WANNSEE CONFERENCE, THE

Steffensen, Lise S.
NEGERKYS & LABRE LARVER

Steffler, Paul
JOHN AND THE MISSUS

Stegers, Bernice
GIRL, THE

Steiger, Rod
CATCH THE HEAT
KINDRED, THE

Stein, Ben
PLANES, TRAINS AND AUTOMOBILES

Steindler, Milan
PRATELE BERMUDSKEHO TROJUHELNIKU

Steiner, John
CAMPING DEL TERRORE

Steingrimsdottir, Hronn
SKYTTURNAR

Steinhardt, Michael
FOREVER, LULU

Steinke, Rene
VERNEHMUNG DER ZEUGEN

Steinmasslova, Milena
POHADKA O MALICKOVI

Steinmetz-Nahmias, Hanny
BOUBA

Steis, William
EQUALIZER 2000
EYE OF THE EAGLE

Stelfox, Shirley
PERSONAL SERVICES

Stelios, Capt.
HIGH SEASON

Stellman, Jack
VIDEO DEAD, THE

Stenke, Claudia
BEST SELLER

Stensgaard, Hanne
BABETTE'S GASTEBUD

Stenstrom, David
PROJECT X

Stephen, Jim
MONSTER SQUAD, THE

Stephens, Lori
ASSASSINATION

Stephens, Robert
COMRADES
EMPIRE OF THE SUN
HIGH SEASON

Stephensen, Ole
KAMPEN OM DEN RODE KO

Stephenson, Edwin
FAMILY VIEWING

Stephenson, Karen
LADY OF THE CAMELIAS

Stephenson, Pamela
LES PATTERSON SAVES THE WORLD
THOSE DEAR DEPARTED

Sterling, Tisha
WHALES OF AUGUST, THE

Stern, Daniel
BORN IN EAST L.A.

Stern, Erik
ASSASSINATION

Stern, Sid
OVERKILL

Sternheim, Mirjam
VAN GELUK GESPROKEN

Sterninski, Janusz
PRZYJACIEL WESOLEGO DIABLA

Stetsky, Nikolai
VALENTIN I VALENTINA

Stevan, Diana
SHELLEY

Stevan, Robyn
SHELLEY
STEPFATHER, THE

Steve the Rabbit
IN THE MOOD

Stevenin, Jean-Francois
SALE DESTIN!

Stevens, Brinke
SLAVE GIRLS FROM BEYOND INFINITY

Stevens, Connie
BACK TO THE BEACH

Stevens, Freddie
TIN MEN

Stevens, Ruth
OM KARLEK

Stevens, Stella
MONSTER IN THE CLOSET

Stevenson, Bill
LIKE FATHER, LIKE SON

Stevenson, Charles
IN THE MOOD

Stevenson, Christopher
BUSHFIRE MOON

Stewart, April
VALET GIRLS

Stewart, Catherine Mary
DUDES
NIGHTFLYERS

Stewart, Craig
STARLIGHT HOTEL

Stewart, Debra D.
HELLO AGAIN

Stewart, Denis
P.K. & THE KID

Stewart, Frank
PSYCHOS IN LOVE

Stewart, Jaye Tyrone
SUSPECT

Stewart, John
CYCLONE

Stewart, Liz
OVERBOARD

Stewart, Lori
WIMPS

Stewart, Lynne
RUNNING MAN, THE

Stewart, Michael
RAISING ARIZONA

Stewart, Nick
HOLLYWOOD SHUFFLE

Stewart, W. Alonzo
ANGEL HEART

Steyer, Christian
DER TRAUM VOM ELCH

Stidder, Ted
HOME IS WHERE THE HART IS

Stiglitz, Hugo
EL PLACER DE LA VENGANZA
ROSA DE LA FRONTERA

Still, Dana
HOME IS WHERE THE HART IS

Stille, Robin
WINNERS TAKE ALL

Stiller, Ben
EMPIRE OF THE SUN
HOT PURSUIT

Stiller, Jerry
HOT PURSUIT
NADINE

Stilley, Lois Barden
IRONWEED

Stillin, Marie
STEPFATHER, THE

Stilwell, Diane
PERFECT MATCH, THE

Stimac, Slavko
WHEELS OF TERROR

Stine, Brett William
P.K. & THE KID

Stinson, John
LIKE FATHER, LIKE SON

Stirland, Allan
PERSONAL SERVICES

Stirpe, Danila
DOGS IN SPACE

Stjepanovic, Boro
STRATEGIJA SVRAKE
ZIVOT RADNIKA

Stock, Amy
SUMMER SCHOOL

Stocker, John
CARE BEARS ADVENTURE IN WONDERLAND, THE
CONCRETE ANGELS

Stocker, Margarita
STREET SMART

Stockinger, Richard
TALKING WALLS

Stockwell, Dean
BANZAI RUNNER
BEVERLY HILLS COP II
GARDENS OF STONE
TIME GUARDIAN, THE

Stockwell, Guy
FORTY DAYS OF MUSA DAGH

Stoeber, Orville
WEEDS

Stoker, Cliff
GRAVEYARD SHIFT

Stokke, Linn
HIP, HIP, HURRA!
OM KARLEK

Stokke, Linne
MIO, MOY MIO

Stokke, Tor
HIP, HIP, HURRA!

Stoldt, Egon
JAG ELSKER DIG

Stoltz, Eric
LIONHEART
SOME KIND OF WONDERFUL

Stolz, Trudy
MALIBU BIKINI SHOP, THE

Stolze, Lena
MASCHENKA

Stone, Dee Wallace
BUSHFIRE MOON

Stone, Michael
AMERICAN NINJA 2: THE CONFRONTATION

Stone, Rhesa
WEEDS

Stone, Sharon
ALLAN QUATERMAIN AND THE LOST CITY OF GOLD
COLD STEEL
POLICE ACADEMY 4: CITIZENS ON PATROL

Stone, Steve
GHOST FEVER

Stone, Stuart
BLUE MONKEY

Stoneburner, Sam
EIGHTY FOUR CHARING CROSS ROAD
WEEDS

Stoner, Lynda
SHADOWS OF THE PEACOCK

Storesund, Line
IS-SLOTTET

Storhoi, Dennis
KAMILLA OG TYVEN

Storm, Esben
LES PATTERSON SAVES THE WORLD

Storm, Morty
STREET TRASH

Stormare, Peter
MALARPIRATER

Storpirstis, Arunas
SEZON CHUDES

Storry, Malcolm
PRINCESS BRIDE, THE

Stothard, Lisa
MONTECARLO GRAN CASINO

Stotsky, Nikolai
LEVSHA

Stough, Ray
I WAS A TEENAGE ZOMBIE

Stowe, Madeleine
STAKEOUT

Stoyanov, Michael
BIG SHOTS

Stoyanova, Irina
CERNITE LEBEDI

Straat, Hans
NIONDE KOMPANIET

Strader, Scott
JOCKS

Straface, Joseph R.
VIRGIN QUEEN OF ST. FRANCIS HIGH, THE

Strahl, Ophelia
HA INSTALATOR

Strange, Marc
BIG TOWN, THE
MORNING MAN, THE

Strange, Richard
BELLMAN AND TRUE

Strano, Carl
SPACE RACE

Stratford, Judith
CUSTODY

Stratford, Peter
MOVING TARGETS

Strathairn, David
MATEWAN

Straton, Taya
SLATE, WYN & ME

Stratt, Jonathan
EAT THE RICH
MORE BAD NEWS

Stratton, Charles
MUNCHIES
SUMMER CAMP NIGHTMARE

Strauss, Stacy
EMANON

Streblova, Alena
PROC?

Streda, Miroslav
CENA MEDU

Streep, Meryl
IRONWEED

Streisand, Barbra
NUTS

Strempel, David
ZISCHKE

Strenga, Juris
POHADKA O MALICKOVI

Stringer, Nick
PERSONAL SERVICES

Stritch, Elaine
SEPTEMBER

Strizhenov, Oleg
AKTSIA
MOY LYUBIMYY KLOUN

Strljic, Milan
HEY BABU RIBA
KRALJEVA ZAVRSNICA

Strobye, Axel
BABETTE'S GASTEBUD
KAMPEN OM DEN RODE KO
PELLE EROVRAREN
SIDSTE AKT

Strong, Brenda
SPACEBALLS

Strong, Gwyneth
CRY FREEDOM

Strong, Lewis
MANKILLERS

Strooker, Devika
ALS IN EEN ROES
ODYSSEE D'AMOUR

Strother, Fred
SUSPECT

Strouth, Linda
PSYCHOS IN LOVE

Strummer, Joe
WALKER

Strummer, Joe
STRAIGHT TO HELL

Strumpel, Uwe
CRAZY BOYS

Struycken, Carel
WITCHES OF EASTWICK, THE

Struzik, Caroline
WITCHES OF EASTWICK, THE

Stryker's Girl
THOU SHALT NOT KILL . . . EXCEPT

Strzalkowski, Henry
EQUALIZER 2000
EYE OF THE EAGLE

Strzhelchik, Vladislav
OGNI
VREMYA ZHELANIY
WEEKEND

Stuart, Cassie
DOLLS
HIDDEN CITY

Stuart, Jason
CROSS MY HEART
EMANON

Stuart, Maxine
LIKE FATHER, LIKE SON

Stuart, Paul
CYCLONE

Stuart Walker, Adam
CRY FREEDOM

Stuart Walker, Hamish
CRY FREEDOM

Stuart Walker, Spring
CRY FREEDOM

Stubbs, Ray
T. DAN SMITH

Stuhr, Jerzy
BOHATERROKU
POCIAG DO HOLLYWOOD

Stunnenburg, Coby
ZJOEK

Sturgess, Rosie
BUSHFIRE MOON

Sturgis, Gary
BIG EASY, THE

Styles, Amber
T. DAN SMITH

Styliano, Anthony
FULL METAL JACKET

Su, Chkhve Chkhan
SEKUNDA NA PODVIG

Su, Choe Chang
TALMAE WA POMDARI

Su-yi, Chiu
HEROIC PIONEERS

Suarez, Carlos
LA RAZA NUNCA PIERDE—HUELE A GAS

Suarez, Hector
ENTRE FICHERAS ANDA EL DIABLO
MURIERON A MITAD DEL RIO

Suarez, Miguelangel
LA GRAN FIESTA

Suarez, Phillip
HIDING OUT

Subasingha, Somalatha
VIRAGAYA

Subbiraj
PRATIGHAAT

Such, Michel
UN AMOUR A PARIS

Sucharipa, Leos
PRATELE BERMUDSKEHO TROJUHELNIKU
PROC?

Suchet, David
CRIME OF HONOR
HARRY AND THE HENDERSONS

Sudell, Marjorie
WISH YOU WERE HERE

Sudrow, Penelope
NIGHTMARE ON ELM STREET 3: DREAM WARRIORS, A

Sudzin, Jeffrey
NO WAY OUT

Suescun, Matilde
CHRONICLE OF A DEATH FORETOLD

Suga, Kantaro
SHINRAN: SHIRO MICHI

Sugai, Kin
SURE DEATH 4

Sugar
CRAZY BOYS

Sugarman, Sara
STRAIGHT TO HELL

Sugawara, Bunta
EIGA JOYU

Sugden, Peter
HEARTS OF FIRE

Suhasini
LAWYER SUHASINI
SAMSARAM OKA CHADARANGAM

Sujatha
POOVIZHI VASALILE

Suk, Kim Yong
TALMAE WA POMDARI

Suk-woo, Kang
KYEOUL NAGUNE

Sukapatana, Chintara
GOOD MORNING, VIETNAM

Sukhov, Fedor
ZNAY NASHIKH

Sukowa, Barbara
DIE VERLIEBTEN
SICILIAN, THE

Sullivan, Billy
LIGHT OF DAY

Sullivan, Brad
TIN MEN
UNTOUCHABLES, THE

Sullivan, D.J.
HAPPY HOUR

Sullivan, Dennis
RAISING ARIZONA

Sullivan, Fred G.
SULLIVAN'S PAVILION

Sullivan, Katie
SULLIVAN'S PAVILION

Sullivan, Kirk
SULLIVAN'S PAVILION

Sullivan, Paul
OVER THE TOP

Sullivan, Polly
SULLIVAN'S PAVILION

Sullivan, R. Patrick
TOUGH GUYS DON'T DANCE

Sullivan, Ricky
SULLIVAN'S PAVILION

Sullivan, Rob
NO WAY OUT

Sullivan, Ron
SLAMMER GIRLS

Sullivan, Sean
WHO'S THAT GIRL

Sullivan, Tate
SULLIVAN'S PAVILION

Sullivant, Richard
CLUB LIFE

Suma, Kei
FINAL TAKE: THE GOLDEN AGE OF MOVIES

Suma, Marina
CARAMELLE DA UNO SCONOSCIUTO
UNA DONNA DA SCOPRIRE

Summers, Bunny
OUTRAGEOUS FORTUNE

Summers, Curro M.
SUFRE MAMON

Summers, David
SUFRE MAMON

Summers, Shari
WHO'S THAT GIRL

Summers, Sylvia
DREAMANIAC

Summersett, Roy
OVERKILL

Sundby, Karl
PA STIGENDE KURS

Sundown, Jim
ESCAPES

Sundquist, Bjorn
FELDMANN CASE, THE

Sung-ki, Ahn
KYEOUL NAGUNE

Supiran, Ricky
SPACE RACE

Suranyi, Imre
LUTRA

Surasu
THIRTHAM

Surer, Nur
SON URFALI

Suresh
JANUARY ORORMA
PRATIGHAAT

Surgere, Helene
ATTENTION BANDITS

Surya
KATHAKKU PINNIL

Susi, Carol Ann
OUTRAGEOUS FORTUNE

Susi, Carol-Ann
SECRET OF MY SUCCESS, THE

Susman, Todd
BEVERLY HILLS COP II

Susnin, Alexander
PRORYV

Sustersic, Miran
USODNI TELEFON

Sutcliffe, Irene
WITHNAIL AND I

Sutherland, Donald
ROSARY MURDERS, THE
TROUBLE WITH SPIES, THE
WOLF AT THE DOOR, THE

Sutherland, Kiefer
KILLING TIME, THE
LOST BOYS, THE
PROMISED LAND

Suttile, Robert
PSYCHOS IN LOVE

Sutton, Andy
LOVECHILD, THE

Sutton, Carole
BIG EASY, THE

Sutton, Henry
ZOMBIE HIGH

Suzuki, Takehiko
BUS

Svehla, Rudolf
AMAZING GRACE AND CHUCK

Sveholm, Pertti
A LA ITKE IINES

Svenson, Bo
THUNDER WARRIOR II
WHITE PHANTOM

Svetlana
WHEELS OF TERROR

Swain, John Howard
BEST SELLER

Swain, Nicola
ARIA

Swalve, Darwin
IN THE MOOD

Swalve, Darwyn
OPEN HOUSE

Swami, Jaya
JAIDEV

Swan, Robert
UNTOUCHABLES, THE
WHO'S THAT GIRL

Swann, Monet
BEVERLY HILLS COP II

Swanson, Gary
STRANDED

Swanson, Jackie
LETHAL WEAPON

Swanson, Kristy
FLOWERS IN THE ATTIC

Swanson, Laura
DOGS IN SPACE

Swarbrick, Carol
LIKE FATHER, LIKE SON

Swartout, Jared
IRONWEED

Swarts, Terry Lee
RADIO DAYS

Swartz, Aaron
FOURTH PROTOCOL, THE
Swartz, Andrea
CONCRETE ANGELS
Swastik
BABULA
Swayze, Don
SHY PEOPLE
Swayze, Patrick
DIRTY DANCING
STEEL DAWN
Sweeney, D.B.
GARDENS OF STONE
NO MAN'S LAND
Sweeney, Liam
EAT THE PEACH
Sweet, Gary
LIGHTHORSEMEN, THE
Swerdlow, Tommy
HAMBURGER HILL
SPACEBALLS
Swilling, Eddie
KILLER WORKOUT
Swink, Kitty
IN THE MOOD
LIKE FATHER, LIKE SON
Swinton, Tilda
ARIA
FRIENDSHIP'S DEATH
LAST OF ENGLAND, THE
Swit, Loretta
WHOOPS APOCALYPSE
Swofford, Ken
HUNTER'S BLOOD
Swope, Tracy Brooks
HAPPY NEW YEAR
Swords, Travis
PROJECT X
Syal, Meera
SAMMY AND ROSIE GET LAID
Syare, Richard
PRETTY SMART
Sylvester, Harold
INNERSPACE
SPACE RACE
Sylvester, Julian
PROJECT X
Sylvestre, Cleo
LOVECHILD, THE
Symo, Margit
CRAZY BOYS
Symonds, Robert
RUMPELSTILTSKIN
Symons, Redmond
MOVING TARGETS
Syphers, Keith
OVERBOARD
Sypold, Manfred
AMAZING GRACE AND CHUCK
Syriotis, Theodoros
O PARADISSOS ANIGI ME ANTIKLIDI
Szabo, Laslo
ACCROCHE-COEUR
Szabo, Laszlo
TESTAMENT D'UN POETE JUIF ASSASSINE
Szapolowska, Grazyna
MAGNAT
Szapotowska, Grazyna
W STARYM DWORKU
Szarabajka, Keith
WALKER
WHEELS OF TERROR
Szczepkowska, Joanna
CUDZOZIEMKA
Szekely, Miklos B.
SZORNYEK EVADJA
Szemes, Mari
DIARY FOR MY LOVED ONES
Szeps, Henri
LES PATTERSON SAVES THE WORLD
Szigeti, Cynthia
HUNK
Szirtes, Adam
TISZTA AMERIKA
Szirtes, Andras
LENZ
Ta, Du Hu
FULL METAL JACKET
Tabakin, Ralph
GOOD MORNING, VIETNAM
TIN MEN
Tabakov, Oleg
DARK EYES
KORABL PRISHELTSEV
Tabassum, Baby Mini
PRATIGHAAT
Tabori, George
TAROT
Tabori, Nora
DOKTOR MINORKA VIDOR NAGY NAPJA
Tachibana, Hajime
LAST EMPEROR, THE
Tacon, Gary
WHO'S THAT GIRL
Tagawa, Cary Hiroyuki
LAST EMPEROR, THE
Taggart, Rita
WEEDS
Tahiri, Larbi
DER NACHBAR
Tahmoors, Hassan
LODGERS
Taillefer, Louis-Marie
ARIA
BEYOND THERAPY
Tainsh, Tracey
FRENCHMAN'S FARM
Tak, Lui
YI LOU YI
Takahashi, Hitomi
WATASHI O SKI NI TSURETETTE
Takahashi, Mitsumi
WILD THING
Takahashi, Toshiro
MAGINA—MURA MONOGATARI
Takamatsu, Hideo
LAST EMPEROR, THE
Takashina, Kaku
SARABA ITOSHIKI HITO YO
Takeda, Takatoshi
PRINCESS FROM THE MOON
Takemura, Toshio
MAGINA—MURA MONOGATARI
Takenaka, Naoto
DEATH SHADOWS
Takeshita, Wat
PRINCIPAL, THE
Talbot, Alan
EMPIRE STATE
LIVING DAYLIGHTS, THE
Talby, Robert
WILD FORCE
Talent Agent
ISHTAR
Tallman, John
CRY WILDERNESS
Tam, Alan
RICH AND FAMOUS
Tamara
KILLER WORKOUT
Tamati, Tuta Ngarimu
NGATI
Tamayo, Alejandro
MUJERES SALVAJES
Tamba, Tetsuro
SHINRAN: SHIRO MICHI
Tamba, Tetsuroh
TOKYO BLACKOUT
Tamberi, Giovanni
SPECTERS
Tambini, Catherine
HELLO AGAIN
Tamblyn, Russ
COMMANDO SQUAD
CYCLONE
Tambor, Jeffrey
THREE O'CLOCK HIGH
Tamez, Arturo R.
RETURN OF JOSEY WALES, THE
Tamisier, Christian
JEAN DE FLORETTE
Tamm, Mary
THREE KINDS OF HEAT
Tamura, Takahiro
ITAZU
MAGINA—MURA MONOGATARI
SEA AND POISON, THE
Tanaka, Kunie
UHOHO TANKENTAI
Tanaka, Prof. Toru
CATCH THE HEAT
Tanaka, Professor Toru
RUNNING MAN, THE
Tanaka, Tomoko
CARTOLINE ITALIANE
Tanaki, Diana
OVERKILL
Tanco, Susana
SINFIN, LA MUERTA NO ES NINGUNA SOLUCION
Tandefelt, Liisi
INUKSUK
Tandy, Jessica
BATTERIES NOT INCLUDED
Tandy, Mark
MAURICE
Tangpantarat, Prasert
GOOD MORNING, VIETNAM
Tanir, Macide
YER DEMIR, GOK BAKIR
Tank, Henry
RAISING ARIZONA
Tank, Mette
PLASTPOSEN
Tanner, Mary
SOMETHING SPECIAL!
Tanney, Sacerdo
BLIND DATE
Tantay, Al
ZIMATAR
Tanus, Rassan
DEATH BEFORE DISHONOR
Tanvir, Habib
THIS IS NOT OUR DESTINATION
Tao, Wang
NINJA THUNDERBOLT
Tao, Wu
LAST EMPEROR, THE
Taplin, Terry
WHOOPS APOCALYPSE
Tara, Suzanne
DANGER ZONE, THE
Tara, Suzzane
DEADLY PREY
Tarabkova, Adriana
CENA ODVAHY
Tarafdar, Anuradha
PANCHVATI
Tarantino, Aldo
QUEL RAGAZZO DELLA CURVA "B"
Taratorkin, Georgy
NABAT NA RASSVETE
Tari, Le
HOLLYWOOD SHUFFLE
Tarkhan-Mouravi, Nana
STUPEN
Tarkington, Rockne
DEATH BEFORE DISHONOR
Tarkowski, Michal
BOHATERROKU
Tarpey, Tom
IN THE MOOD
Tarr, Bela
SZORNYEK EVADJA
Tarr, Ron
EAT THE RICH
Tarrant, Newell
HAPPY HOUR
Tarshish, Shlomo
BOUBA
DEADLINE
LO SAM ZAYIN
Tasca, Alessandro
MISSION KILL
Taschini, Emanuela
MORO AFFAIR, THE
Tashbayeva, Guli
YA TEBYA POMNYU
Tashima, Chris
OVERKILL
Tashkov, Andrei
POLEVAYA GVARDIA MOZZHUKHINA
Tashkova, Tatyana
TAKAYA ZHESTOKAYA IGRA—KHOKKEY
Tasseva, Leda
CERNITE LEBEDI
Tassoni, Coralina Cataldi
OPERA

Tate, Claudio
NOS REIMOS DE LA MIGRA

Tate, Jack
MONSTER IN THE CLOSET

Tate, Leonard J.
BARFLY

Tate, Nick
CRY FREEDOM
YEAR MY VOICE BROKE, THE

Tatiana
UN SABADO MAS

Tatsumi, Ryutaro
ITAZU

Tatulli, Frederica
MAN ON FIRE

Tatum, Judy
WITCHBOARD

Tausek, Bryant
DEADTIME STORIES

Tavares, Fernanda
LAST STRAW, THE

Tavernier, Nils
LA PASSION BEATRICE

Tavi, Tuvia
DEATH BEFORE DISHONOR

Taxi, Richard
LA VIE DISSOLUE DE GERARD FLOQUE

Taxier, Arthur
MONSTER IN THE CLOSET

Tayler, Sally
LES PATTERSON SAVES THE WORLD

Taylor, Carlton
HOPE AND GLORY

Taylor, Deborah
BIG BANG, THE

Taylor, Dexter
WALKER

Taylor, Diana
BELIEVERS, THE

Taylor, Dixie
SQUARE DANCE

Taylor, Doreen
EMPIRE STATE

Taylor, Graeme
CRY FREEDOM

Taylor, Jack
CRYSTAL HEART
POLICIA

Taylor, James Michael
RED DESERT PENITENTIARY

Taylor, Jan
MEATBALLS III

Taylor, John
MANKILLERS

Taylor, Jules
DOGS IN SPACE

Taylor, Kirk
FULL METAL JACKET

Taylor, Mark
ANGEL HEART

Taylor, Mark L.
INNERSPACE

Taylor, Matthew
SHADOWS OF THE PEACOCK

Taylor, Meshach
ALLNIGHTER, THE
FROM THE HIP
HOUSE OF GAMES
MANNEQUIN

Taylor, Mike
CONCRETE ANGELS

Taylor, Myra
SUSPECT

Taylor, Nicky
HOPE AND GLORY

Taylor, Noah
DOGS IN SPACE
YEAR MY VOICE BROKE, THE

Taylor, Rip
AMAZON WOMEN ON THE MOON

Taylor, Rochelle
MURDER LUST

Taylor, Ron
RETURN OF JOSEY WALES, THE
WHO'S THAT GIRL

Taylor, Russ
RETURN OF JOSEY WALES, THE

Taylor, Wendy E.
SUSPECT

Taylor, Wilhelmina
BELIEVERS, THE

Taylor-Block, Haley
UNFINISHED BUSINESS . . .

Tchenko, Katia
CLUB DE RENCONTRES

Teapnik, Y.
VZLOMSHCHIK

Tedde, Massimo
MORO AFFAIR, THE

Tedeschi, Simona
CAPRICCIO

Teek, Angela
HOLLYWOOD SHUFFLE

Tefkin, Blair
THREE FOR THE ROAD

Tegman, Susanne
MANKILLERS

Teir, Bjorn
KILL CITY

Teixeira, Adelaide
RELACAO FIEL E VERDADEIRA

Teixeira, Melim
LA PLAYA DE LOS PERROS

Tekand, Sahika
WATER ALSO BURNS

Telfer, David
WHISTLE BLOWER, THE

Telford, David
STARLIGHT HOTEL

Telleria, Patxo
A LOS CUATRO VIENTOS

Tellermaa, Tauri
IGRY DLJA DETEJ SKO'NOGO VOZRASTA

Telles, Kevin
PARTY CAMP

Telles, Rick
FATAL BEAUTY

Tello, Lucy Martinez
VISA U.S.A.

Tembo, Fishoo
CRY FREEDOM

Temessy, Hedy
LAURA

Temirova, Aiturgan
SNAYPERY

Temptations, The
HAPPY NEW YEAR

Temucin, Meric
IN DER WUSTE

Tennant, Victoria
BEST SELLER
FLOWERS IN THE ATTIC

Tenuta, Andrea
LA BUSQUEDA

Teocoli, Teo
I MIEI PRIMI QUARANT'ANNI
MISSIONE EROICA

Terashita, Jill
DIRTY LAUNDRY

Terekhova, Margarita
RUS IZNACHALNA

Terenghi, Desire
DOLCE ASSENZA

Terenghi, Sergio
DOLCE ASSENZA

Terhune, Bob
NEAR DARK

Terlesky, John
ALLNIGHTER, THE
VALET GIRLS

Termine, Egidio
GOOD MORNING BABYLON
LESTATE STA FINENDO

Termo, Lenny
PRAYER FOR THE DYING, A

Termo, Leonard
BARFLY

Terranova, Osvaldo
EN RETIRADA

Terrell, Anthony
DIRTY LAUNDRY

Terrence, John
EVIL SPAWN

Terris, Malcolm
COMRADES

Terry, James
RIVER'S EDGE

Terry, John
FULL METAL JACKET
LIVING DAYLIGHTS, THE

Terry O'Reilly
IRONWEED

Terzieff, Laurent
DA NNUNZIO

Teskouk, Salah
PIERRE ET DJEMILA

Tessari, Fiorenza
LESTATE STA FINENDO

Tessarin, T.
I KEKARMENI

Tesser, Osvaldo
A DOS AGUAS
EN RETIRADA

Tessier, Suzanne
BIRDS OF PREY

Tetamontie, Angie
ARIA

Tetsuya, Matsui
MAGNIFICENT WARRIORS

Tetteh-Lartey, Alex
CAUGHT

Tevis, Clayton
THUNDER WARRIOR II

Texas Ranger
EXTREME PREJUDICE

Texeira, Denise
I WAS A TEENAGE ZOMBIE

Thacker, Tab
POLICE ACADEMY 4: CITIZENS ON PATROL

Thakar, Baby Pooja
PRATIGHAAT

Thauvette, Guy
LES FOUS DE BASSAN

Thaw, John
BUSINESS AS USUAL
CRY FREEDOM

Thayer, Brynn
BIG SHOTS

Thayer, Max
NO DEAD HEROES

Thea
DEADTIME STORIES

Thelma, Alma
LA RAZA NUNCA PIERDE—HUELE A GAS
MATAR O MORIR

Theodoridis, Panos
DOXOBUS

Theodosopoulos, Costa
HOSTAGE SYNDROME

Theriaut, Pierre
LE SOURD DANS LA VILLE

Therrien, Michel
MORNING MAN, THE

Theune, Detlef
CRAZY BOYS

Thevenet, Friquette
JEUX D'ARTIFICES

Thevenet, Virginie
LE CRI DU HIBOU

Thibaudin, Beatriz
MISS MARY

Thibault, Carl
MONSTER SQUAD, THE

Thibeau, Jack
LETHAL WEAPON

Thibeault, Debi
PSYCHOS IN LOVE

Thibuis, Hedwige
LANNEE DES MEDUSES

Thigpen, Lynne
HELLO AGAIN

Thilakan
KATHAKKU PINNIL
THIRTHAM
VILAMBARAM

Thirolle, Sylvain
MEMOIRE DES APPARENCES: LA VIE EST UN SONGE

Thomas, Billy Jean
STUDENT CONFIDENTIAL

Thomas, Colin
EAT THE RICH

Thomas, Dog
FIREHOUSE

Thomas, Edward
BOY SOLDIER

Thomas, Heather
CYCLONE
DEATH STONE

Thomas, Irma
BIG EASY, THE
Thomas, Jeffrey Alan
BROADCAST NEWS
Thomas, Kristin Scott
AGENT TROUBLE
Thomas, Robin
SUMMER SCHOOL
Thomas, Sharon
PRINCIPAL, THE
Thomas, Sian
PRICK UP YOUR EARS
Thomas, Summer
WIND, THE
Thomas, Trevor
GOOD WIFE, THE
Thomerson, Tim
NEAR DARK
Thompson, Beverly
ASSASSINATION
Thompson, Bill
FULL METAL JACKET
Thompson, Brian
CATCH THE HEAT
COMMANDO SQUAD
YOU TALKIN' TO ME?
Thompson, Bryan J.
WINNERS TAKE ALL
Thompson, Don
OVERBOARD
Thompson, Fred Dalton
NO WAY OUT
Thompson, Heather
JAWS: THE REVENGE
Thompson, Jack
GROUND ZERO
Thompson, Kevin
GARBAGE PAIL KIDS MOVIE, THE
MUNCHIES
Thompson, Lea
SOME KIND OF WONDERFUL
Thompson, Marc Anthony
SLAMDANCE
Thompson, Susan J.
ASSASSINATION
Thompson, Weyman
HOT SHOT
Thompson-Austen, Lillian
CUSTODY
Thomsen, Richard
BROADCAST NEWS
Thomson, Margaret
RADIO DAYS
Thomson, Scott
POLICE ACADEMY 4: CITIZENS ON PATROL
Thoolen, Gerard
VAN GELUK GESPROKEN
Thor, Cjerste
BLOOD SISTERS
Thor, Jon-Mikl
ROCK 'N' ROLL NIGHTMARE
ZOMBIE NIGHTMARE
Thorarinsson, Thorarinn
SKYTTURNAR
Thorley, Ken
ESCAPES
Thorn, Barbara
EIGHTY FOUR CHARING CROSS ROAD
Thornburg, Maureen M.
P.K. & THE KID
Thornburg, Robert N.
P.K. & THE KID
Thorne, Diane
ARIA
Thorne, Stephen
VALHALLA
Thorne-Smith, Courtney
REVENGE OF THE NERDS II: NERDS IN PARADISE
SUMMER SCHOOL
Thornton, Ann
HOPE AND GLORY
Thornton, Billy Bob
HUNTER'S BLOOD
Thornton, Sigrid
LIGHTHORSEMEN, THE
SLATE, WYN & ME
Thoroddsen, Guddbjorg
SKYTTURNAR
Thorpe, Harriet
MAURICE

Thorsen, Sven
LETHAL WEAPON
RUNNING MAN, THE
Thrasher, Katie
RAISING ARIZONA
Thring, Frank
HOWLING III, THE
Thulin, Ingrid
IL GIORNO PRIMA
Thurman, Uma
KISS DADDY GOOD NIGHT
Thurnheer, Chris
REMEMBERING MEL
Thurnheer, Simona
REMEMBERING MEL
Thuy, Tu
WANTED: DEAD OR ALIVE
Thygesen, Rasmus
INUKSUK
Tianmin, Zhang
LAST EMPEROR, THE
Tianming, Wu
OLD WELL
Tibble, Michael
NGATI
Tichankova, Vera
PRATELE BERMUDSKEHO TROJUHELNIKU
Ticotin, Rachel
CRITICAL CONDITION
Tiemroth, Lene
HIP, HIP, HURRA!
Tien-Mu, Lee
LIEN LIEN FUNG CHEN
Tienkin, Richard
BEVERLY HILLS COP II
Tiensuu, Raili
AKALLINEN MIES
Tierney, Aidan
FAMILY VIEWING
Tierney, Lawrence
OFFSPRING, THE
TOUGH GUYS DON'T DANCE
Tifo, Marie
LES FOUS DE BASSAN
Tighe, Charles
FIREHOUSE
Tighe, Kevin
MATEWAN
Tijerina, Cecilia
GABY—A TRUE STORY
Tilakan
PANCHAGNI
Tillesley, Kim
GOTHIC
Tilley's Partner
TIN MEN
Tillinger, John
HELLO AGAIN
Tillotson, John Robert
ANNA
Tilly, Grant
WARM NIGHTS ON A SLOW MOVING TRAIN
Tilly, Jennifer
HES MY GIRL
Tilson, Robert
AMAZING GRACE AND CHUCK
Tilton, Michael
BLOOD SISTERS
Times, Themsi
ALLAN QUATERMAIN AND THE LOST CITY OF GOLD
Timoschuk, Natalie
REMEMBERING MEL
Tinder, Paul
OVERBOARD
Tingwell, Charles
BUSHFIRE MOON
Tinn, Eduard
IGRY DLJA DETEJ SKO'NOGO VOZRASTA
Tinti, Gabriele
BEAKS
Tipo, Patti
OMEGA SYNDROME
Titova, Valentin
ZHELEZNOE POLE
To, Randy
NINJA THUNDERBOLT
Toake, Yukiyo
HOTARUGAWA
UHOHO TANKENTAI

Tobey, Kenneth
INNERSPACE
Tobi, Lemy
MUTANT HUNT
Tobilevich, Nina
POKLONIS DO ZEMLI
Tobolowsky, Stephen
SPACEBALLS
Toby, Doug
SUMMER CAMP NIGHTMARE
Tochi, Brian
POLICE ACADEMY 4: CITIZENS ON PATROL
Tochinsky, Leslie
REMEMBERING MEL
Todd, Beverly
HAPPY HOUR
Todd, Lisa
BLOOD HOOK
Todd, Tony
EIGHTY FOUR CHARING CROSS ROAD
ENEMY TERRITORY
Todorovic, Marko
HEY BABU RIBA
Todorovic, Srdjan
HEY BABU RIBA
Togawa, Akiko
SEA AND POISON, THE
Tognazzi, Gianmarco
DANCERS
Tognazzi, Ricky
FAMILY, THE
Togni, Olga von
FRANCESCA
Togo, Mia
RUNNING MAN, THE
Toibin, Niall
EAT THE PEACH
RAWHEAD REX
Tokatlian, John
LIKE FATHER, LIKE SON
Tokita, Fujio
PRINCESS FROM THE MOON
Tokoro, Mihoko
ASSASSINATION
Tola, Francesco
GOOD MORNING BABYLON
Tolan, Kathleen
ROSARY MURDERS, THE
Toles-Bey, John
WEEDS
Tolkan, James
MADE IN HEAVEN
MASTERS OF THE UNIVERSE
Tolnay, Klari
A JAVOR
Tolubeev, Andrei
VINA LEYTENANTA NEKRASOVA
Tom, Tom
PRATIGHAAT
Toma, Nicolae
PADUREANCA
Tomajczyk, Diane Marie L.
SUSPECT
Tomazani, Despina
PHOTOGRAPH, THE
Tomelty, Frances
BELLMAN AND TRUE
Tomita, Shiro
OVERKILL
Tompkins, Angel
AMAZON WOMEN ON THE MOON
Tongrui, Xu
LAST EMPEROR, THE
Tonnerfors, Emma
SERPENT'S WAY, THE
Tonnerfors, Lisa
SERPENT'S WAY, THE
Tonoyama, Shinji
DIXIELAND DAIMYO
Tonoyama, Taiji
HOTARUGAWA
ZEGEN
Tontcheva, Dorothea
CERNITE LEBEDI
Tonto, Tyrone
CREEPSHOW 2
Tonunts, Yelena
ISKUSHENIE DON ZHUANA
NOVYE SKAZKI SHAKHEREZADY

Toomey, Regis
EVIL TOWN

Toompere, Hendrik
IGRY DLJA DETEJ SKO'NOGO VOZRASTA

Toorgeman, Boas
MASCARA

Topi, Francesca
ADELMO

Toppano, Peta
SHADOWS OF THE PEACOCK

Torchia, Rod
WILD THING

Tordi, Pietro
FRANCESCA

Toreky, Zsuzsa
CSOK, ANYU

Torijanac, Zvonko
OFICIR S RUZOM

Torikka, Timo
A LA ITKE IINES

Torloni, Christiane
BESAME MUCHO
EU

Tormakhova, Svetlana
STARAYA AZBUKA
ZINA-ZINULYA

Torn, Rip
EXTREME PREJUDICE
NADINE

Tornatore, Donald
NIGHTFORCE

Tornes, Stavros
DOLCE ASSENZA

Tornlund, Ylva
RES ALDRIG PA ENKEL BILJETT

Tornquist, Kristina
PELLE EROVRAREN

Torocsik, Mari
WHOOPING COUGH

Torossi, Stefano
DA NNUNZIO

Torre, Bill
STREET SMART

Torremocha, Manuel
MY GENERAL

Torres, Javier
WINTER TAN, A

Torres, Juan
STRAIGHT TO HELL

Torres, Michelle
SLATE, WYN & ME

Torti, Robert
P.I. PRIVATE INVESTIGATIONS

Tortosa, Silvia
LA SENYORA

Tosco, Geraldo
NO DEAD HEROES

Tosco, Ricardo
EL SOCIO DE DIOS

Tosi, Tarcisio
LUNGA VITA ALLA SIGNORA!

Toska, Pinon
GOOD MORNING BABYLON

Tostado, Frank
EL DIABLO, EL SANTO Y EL TONTO

Toth, Marcell
WHOOPING COUGH

Toth, Szilvia
HOL VOLT, HOL NEM VOLT

Toueg, Maurice
RADIO DAYS

Toussaint, Cecilia
FRIDA

Touzet, Corinne
LA RUMBA

Touzie, Houshang
CHECKPOINT

Towne, Robert
PICK-UP ARTIST, THE

Townsend, Barbara
TALKING WALLS

Townsend, Robert
HOLLYWOOD SHUFFLE

Tozzi, Giorgio
ARIA

Tracey, Ian
HOME IS WHERE THE HART IS
SHELLEY
STAKEOUT

Tracey Jibara
I WAS A TEENAGE T.V. TERRORIST

Tracy, Will
BUSINESS AS USUAL

Trafankowska, Daria
INNA WYSPA
LE JEUNE MAGICIEN

Trafford, Steve
T. DAN SMITH

Train, Sally
P.K. & THE KID

Train Latino
EULALIA

Trainor, Mary Ellen
LETHAL WEAPON
MONSTER SQUAD, THE

Trajanovsky, Daniela
EIN BLICK-UND DIE LIEBE BRICHT AUS

Tran, April
STEELE JUSTICE

Tran, Helen
SOMEONE TO WATCH OVER ME

Tran, Laure
COERS CROISES

Tran, No
GOOD MORNING, VIETNAM

Tran, Tung Thanh
GOOD MORNING, VIETNAM

Traore, Soumba
YEELEN

Trapaga, Monica
HIGH TIDE

Trass, Raivo
KORABL PRISHELTSEV

Traven, Oscar
UNA PURA Y DOS CON SAL

Travis, Greg
MILLION DOLLAR MYSTERY

Travis, Nancy
THREE MEN AND A BABY

Travolta, Joey
AMAZON WOMEN ON THE MOON
HUNTER'S BLOOD
THEY STILL CALL ME BRUCE

Treadway, Patrick
VIDEO DEAD, THE

Trebbi, Danila
IL FASCINO SOTTILE DEL PECCATO

Trebor, Robert
MAKING MR.RIGHT
MY DEMON LOVER

Trela, Jerzy
PRYWATNE SLEDZTWO

Tremlett, Doug
BACHELOR GIRL

Trent, Daniel
BEST SELLER

Tress, Jessica
ZERO BOYS, THE

Trevarthan, Noel
TO MARKET, TOMARKET

Trevena, David
CRY FREEDOM

Trevisannelo, Francesca
QUARTIERE

Trevisi, Franco
MAN ON FIRE
MORO AFFAIR, THE

Tridian, Patrice
ARIA

Trieste, Leopoldo
IL CORAGGIO DI PARLARE
INTERVISTA

Trim, David
MILLION DOLLAR MYSTERY

Trimboli, Robert
DEADTIME STORIES

Trinchet, Jorge
SUCCESSFUL MAN, A

Trindade, Ze
UM TREM PARA AS ESTRELAS

Trinidad, Arnsenio "Sonny"
BLACK WIDOW

Trintignant, Jean-Louis
LA VALLEE FANTOME
LE MOUSTACHU

Trintignant, Marie
NOYADE INTERDITE

Tripp, Louis
GATE, THE

Trippe, Lane
BIG EASY, THE

Tristancho, Carlos
EL LUTE—CAMINA O REVIENTA

Trivalic, Vesna
OKTOBERFEST

Trofimov, Alexander
KREUTZEROVA SONATA

Trofimov, Nikolai
PRODELKI V STARINNOM DUKHE

Troisi, Lino
TERNOSECCO

Troisi, Massimo
HOTEL COLONIAL

Troitsky, Andrei
TAYNAYA PROGULKA

Trojan, Ladislav
CENA MEDU
PRATELE BERMUDSKEHO TROJUHELNIKU

Trompette, Francoise
MANON OF THE SPRING

Trooger, Sabina
VERMISCHTE NACHRICHTEN

Trousdale, Theresa
DANGER ZONE, THE

Trowbridge, Linda
PRINCIPAL, THE

Trowe, Jose Chavez
MIRACLES

Trueman, Jeff
CASSANDRA

Trueman, Paula
DIRTY DANCING

Truesdale, Teresa
KILLER WORKOUT

Trujillo, Gilberto
EL ANSIA DE MATAR
FIERAS EN BRAMA
OLOR A MUERTE
UN SABADO MAS

Trujillo, Raul
EL ANSIA DE MATAR
OLOR A MUERTE

Trujillo, Valentin
EL ANSIA DE MATAR
EL MUERTO DEL PALOMO
FIERAS EN BRAMA
OLOR A MUERTE
POLICIAS DE NARCOTICOS
RATAS DE LA CIUDAD
YO, EL EJECUTOR

Trulsson, Lil
SEPPAN

Trumpbour, John
ISHTAR

Trussler, Menna
BOY SOLDIER

Trusty, Guy
MAKING MR.RIGHT

Trybala, Marzena
BLIND CHANCE
KOMEDIANTKA

Tsakiridis, N.
I KEKARMENI

Tsakiroglou, Nikitas
APOUSIES

Tsang, Eric
SEVEN YEARS ITCH
THIRTY MILLION RUSH, THE

Tsangas, Christos
FAKELOS POLK STON AERA
PHOTOGRAPH, THE
TELEFTAIO STICHIMA

Tsankov, Nickolai
TRINAJSTATA GODENICA NA PRINCA

Tsapekos, Costas
YENETHLIA POLI

Tschechowa, Vera
TAROT

Tselios, Paris
HIGH SEASON

Tsibidis, Vassilis
ONIRO ARISTERIS NICHTAS

Tsilyra, Athena
ONE HUNDRED AND TWENTY DECIBELS

Tsin-Wen, Wang
LIEN LIEN FUNG CHEN

Tsokkinen, Martti
VY VIHDOINKIN YHDESSA

Tsou, Tijger
LAST EMPEROR, THE

Tsu, Irene
STEELE JUSTICE

Tsugayama, Masatane
SEA AND POISON, THE

Tsui, Paula
THIRTY MILLION RUSH, THE

Tsui, Siu-Ming
MIRAGE

Tsuji, Rancho
SEA AND POISON, THE

Tsylinsky, Gunnar
OBOROTEN TOM

Tubert, Marc
STEELE JUSTICE

Tucci, Stanley
WHO'S THAT GIRL

Tuck, Emma
COMRADES

Tucker, Forrest
OUTTAKES

Tucker, Michael
RADIO DAYS
TIN MEN

Tucker-Smith, Linda
MURDER LUST

Tudorpole, Edward
STRAIGHT TO HELL

Tudsen, Axel
CRAZY BOYS

Tuerpe, Paul
LETHAL WEAPON

Tuinman, Peter
BLOND DOLLY
VAN GELUK GESPROKEN

Tullin, Michael
BANZAI RUNNER

Tullis, Dan
EXTREME PREJUDICE

Tumba
LA VIE EST BELLE

Tuminello, Sal
RADIO DAYS

Tunie, Tamara
SWEET LORRAINE

Tuomey, James
AMAZING GRACE AND CHUCK

Turabov, Gasan
CHKATULKA IZ KREPOSTI

Turbide, Elizabeth
WILD THING

Turek, Jerzy
WIERNA RZEKA

Turell, Chili
WOLF AT THE DOOR, THE

Turenne, Louis
PRETTYKILL

Turjansky, Mike
FULL METAL JACKET

Turmel, Michelle Elaine
GREAT LAND OF SMALL, THE

Turner, Anna
EMPIRE OF THE SUN

Turner, Elise
ZERO BOYS, THE

Turner, Frank C.
MALONE

Turner, Jim
PROGRAMMED TO KILL

Turner, Michael
CRY FREEDOM

Turner, Peter
MESSENGER, THE

Turner, Richard
KILLER WORKOUT

Turton, Stuart
EMPIRE STATE

Turturro, John
SICILIAN, THE

Tushingham, Aisha
HOUSEKEEPER, THE

Tushingham, Rita
HOUSEKEEPER, THE

Tuttle, Lurene
EVIL TOWN

Tuula's Father
NAKEMIIN, HYVASTI

Tweed, Shannon
MEATBALLS III
STEELE JUSTICE

Twelvetree, Alan
T. DAN SMITH

Twin Brothers
CHRONICLE OF A DEATH FORETOLD

Tyhurst, Tyler
WANTED: DEAD OR ALIVE

Tyler, Ian
FULL METAL JACKET

Tyler, Kell
LIVING DAYLIGHTS, THE

Tyner, Charles
PLANES, TRAINS AND AUTOMOBILES

Tyner, Harold
BEST SELLER

Tyrrell, Joan
BEYOND THERAPY

Tyrrell, Susan
CHIPMUNK ADVENTURE, THE
OFFSPRING, THE

Tyson, Cathy
BUSINESS AS USUAL

Tyson, Richard
THREE O'CLOCK HIGH

Tyszkiewicz, Beata
KOMEDIANTKA

Tyus, Vivian
ASSASSINATION

Tyzack, Margaret
PRICK UP YOUR EARS

Tzador, Arnon
PROGRAMMED TO KILL

Tzafir, Tuvia
HA INSTALATOR

Tzarfati, Asher
BOUBA

Tzoias, Nikos
APOUSIES

Tzoumas, Constantinos
FAKELOS POLK STON AERA

Tzoumas, Konstantinos
PRETTY SMART

Tzudiker, Bob
OMEGA SYNDROME
WALKER

Tzur, Idith
LO SAM ZAYIN

Uchida, Yuya
SARABA ITOSHIKI HITO YO

Udehn, Johanna
MY LIFE AS A DOG

Udenio, Fabiana
SUMMER SCHOOL

Udovichenko, Larisa
MILLION V BRACHNOY KORZINE

Udovichenko, Larissa
LYUBOVYU ZA LYUBOV

Udsen, Bodil
PETER VON SCHOLTEN

Udvaros, Dorottya
CSOK, ANYU

Udy, Claudia
NIGHTFORCE

Udy, Helene
NIGHTFLYERS

Uemura, Keiko
GONDOLA

Ueno, Yuko
ROBINSON NO NIWA

Uganda
TOO MUCH

Ugel, Phil
BROADCAST NEWS

Ugo, Antonio
A DOS AGUAS

Uhler, Phil
SUMMER HEAT

Uitto, Pirkko
VY VIHDOINKIN YHDESSA

Ujlaky, Denes
DOKTOR MINORKA VIDOR NAGY NAPJA

Ulaner, Warren
MUTANT HUNT

Ulc, Anthony
MORNING MAN, THE

Ulewicz, Waclaw
ZLOTY POCIAG

Ulfsson, Birgitta
SERPENT'S WAY, THE

Ulfung, Ragnar
GIRL, THE

Ullmann, Liv
GABY—A TRUE STORY
MOSCA ADDIO

Ulrich, Ed
OMEGA SYNDROME

Uluocak, Vedat
CEMIL

Ulusoy, Keriman
DILAN

Ulyanov, Mikhail
TEMA

Umbach, Martin
DEADLINE

Umile, Mark
MUTANT HUNT

Underwood, Hank
BIG SHOTS

Underwood, Jay
PROMISED LAND

Unger, Joe
BARFLY

Uotila, Pekka
URSULA

Uralde, Rafael Enrique
A LOS CUATRO VIENTOS

Urbanczik, Ales
DER NACHBAR

Urbanus
HECTOR

Ure, Alberto
SINFIN, LA MUERTA NO ES NINGUNA SOLUCION

Urgay, Saim
SENTIMIENTOS: MIRTA DE LINIERS A ESTAMBUL

Uribe, Merle
LAPUTA: THE CASTLE IN THE SKY
MAS VALE PAJARO EN MANO . . .

Urquhart, Robert
KITCHEN TOTO, THE

Urreta, Julio
DELINCUENTE

Ursin, David
BEST SELLER

Urstein, Laura
O. C. AND STIGGS

Ursu, Melania
PADUREANCA

Usay, Carlos
MISS MARY

USMC
IN THE MOOD

Ussani, Riccardo
BELLY OF AN ARCHITECT, THE

Ussing, Olaf
EPIDEMIC
PETER VON SCHOLTEN

Ustvedt, Marianne
PLASTPOSEN

Usztics, Matyas
LUTRA

Utay, William
WALKER

Utman, Bryan
OPEN HOUSE

Utsi, Inger
OFELAS

Utsi, Nils
OFELAS

Uttam
TUNDA BAIDA

Utterback, Clark
CREEPSHOW 2

Uziely, Yael
RUMPELSTILTSKIN

Uzzaman, Badi
BELLMAN AND TRUE
CRY FREEDOM
PERSONAL SERVICES
SAMMY AND ROSIE GET LAID

Uzzaman, Buddy
DRAGON'S FOOD

Vaananen, Kari
A LA ITKE IINES
HAMLET
HELSINKI NAPOLI—ALL NIGHT LONG

Vaassen, Fred
BLOND DOLLY

Vail, Kary Lynn
HAPPY HOUR

Vaimo
ELVIS-KISSAN JALJILLA
Vainionkulma, Outi
SNOW QUEEN, THE
Valandrey, Charlotte
F . . . ING FERNAND
LES FOUS DE BASSAN
Valavanidis, Christos
PHOTOGRAPH, THE
Valcke, Serge-Henri
MASCARA
Valcorta, Irma
LA BAMBA
Valderrama, Elliott S.
PRINCIPAL, THE
Valderrama, Joan
PRINCIPAL, THE
Valderrama, Luis
BROADCAST NEWS
Valdes, Omar
AMOR EN CAMPO MINADO
Valdes, Thais
DE TAL PEDRO, TAL ASTILLA
Valdez, Chayito
TIERRA DE VALIENTES
Valdez, Daniel
LA BAMBA
Valdez, Manuel
RETURN OF JOSEY WALES, THE
Valdina, Jordan
IRONWEED
Vale, Raul
OPERACION MARIJUANA
Valentin, Joel
PRINCIPAL, THE
Valentin, Juan
TIERRA DE VALIENTES
YERBA SANGRIENTE
Valentine, Scott
DEADTIME STORIES
MY DEMON LOVER
Valentini, Emi
DELITTI
Valentini, Mariella
A FIOR DI PELLE
Valentino
RETURN OF JOSEY WALES, THE
Valentino, Charlie
MAS BUENAS QUE EL PAN
TODA LA VIDA
Valentino, Charly
LAPUTA: THE CASTLE IN THE SKY
Valento, Tony
LA ESTANQUERA DE VALLECAS
Valenzuela, Maria
LOS DUENOS DEL SILENCIO
Valenzuela, Mrs. Connie
LA BAMBA
Valera, Dominique
TERMINUS
Valerio, Be
NIGHT ANGELS
Valero, Antonio
EL AMOR DE AHORA
EL LUTE—CAMINA O REVIENTA
Valero, Carolyn
GABY—A TRUE STORY
Valier, Francois
QUATRE AVENTURES DE REINETTE ET MIRABELLE
Valkama, Ritva
LIIAN ISO KEIKKA
Vallalpando, David
DELOS ADVENTURE, THE
Vallance, Louise
THREE MEN AND A BABY
Vallecillo, Rafael
LA ESTANQUERA DE VALLECAS
Vallee, Manon
STREET SMART
Vallentine, Senator Jo
PURSUIT OF HAPPINESS, THE
Valley, Michelle
PRETTY SMART
PROINI PERIPOLOS
YENETHLIA POLI
Valli, Alida
MANUELA'S LOVES
Valli, Frankie
DIRTY LAUNDRY
Vallone, Saverio
DELITTI
IL FASCINO SOTTILE DEL PECCATO
MOSCA ADDIO
Valls, Jaume
LESCOT
Vally, Paul
MASQUES
Valoppi, Stefano
ANGELUS NOVUS
Valota, Patrice
F . . . ING FERNAND
Valter, Marek
DEATH OF A BEAUTIFUL DREAM
Valverde, Fernando
EL BOSQUE ANIMADO
Van, Le
KOORDINATY SMERTI
Van Avermaet, Annick
MASCARA
Van Bergen, Lewis
RAGE OF HONOR
SPACE RACE
Van Bergen, Louis
MOON IN SCORPIO
Van Cleemput, Robert
MASCARA
Van Crombrugge, Marc
MASCARA
van de Ven, Monique
EEN MAAND LATER
IRIS
van den Berg, Carolien
HAVINCK
Van Den Berghe, Hugo
MASCARA
van der Groen, Dora
DIARY OF A MAD OLD MAN
HAVINCK
van der Meulen, Marjo
EEN MAAND LATER
van der Molen, Ina
DIARY OF A MAD OLD MAN
Van Der Noot, Alexandra
MASCARA
van der Pol, Marieke
BLOND DOLLY
Van Der Velde, Nadine
MUNCHIES
Van Der Velden, Kelly
I LOVE NEW YORK
van der Zee, Mr.
EEN MAAND LATER
Van Deven, Susan
FIREHOUSE
van Doesburgh, Coot
EEN MAAND LATER
Van Dreelen, John
MASCARA
van Dreelen, John
LOOKING FOR EILEEN
ODYSSEE D'AMOUR
van Eeghem, Marc
HECTOR
van Eimeren, Mr.
EEN MAAND LATER
Van Essche, An
LOVE IS A DOG FROM HELL
Van Evera, Warren
CONCRETE ANGELS
Van Gelderen, Mercedes
MISS MARY
Van Gorder, David
OVER THE TOP
Van Gyen, Hans
MOVING TARGETS
Van Heerden, Marcel
STEEL DAWN
van Heerden, Marcel
HOSTAGE
Van Hoof, Tom
MANKILLERS
van Hool, Roger
IRIS
van Hoven, Femke
EEN MAAND LATER
Van Kamp, Merete
MISSION KILL
van Kampen, Sep
EEN MAAND LATER
van Kralingen, Will
HAVINCK
Van Laere, Gaston
MASCARA
Van Lidth, Erland
RUNNING MAN, THE
Van Malder, Frank
MASCARA
van Mieghem, Hilde
BLOND DOLLY
Van Ness, Jon
LETS GET HARRY
Van Orsteiner, Joel
MUTANT HUNT
Van Os, Angeli
LA RUSA
Van Pallandt, Nina
ASI COMO HABIAN SIDO
O. C. AND STIGGS
Van Patten, Dick
SPACEBALLS
Van Patten, James
NIGHTFORCE
Van Patten, Joyce
BLIND DATE
Van Peebles, Mario
HOT SHOT
JAWS: THE REVENGE
Van Peebles, Melvin
JAWS: THE REVENGE
O. C. AND STIGGS
Van Sickle, J.D.
HAMBURGER HILL
Van Stuen, Hegle
IL LUPO DI MARE
van Tilborgh, Guusje
ZJOEK
van Vooren, Monique
WALL STREET
van Voss, Arend Jan Heerma
VAN GELUK GESPROKEN
Van Wart, Peter
BLUE MONKEY
Vance, Courtney
HAMBURGER HILL
Vance, Tommy
MORE BAD NEWS
Vancururova, Marta
DEATH OF A BEAUTIFUL DREAM
Vander Woude, Teresa
KILLER WORKOUT
Vander Woude, Vikki Lynn
KILLER WORKOUT
Vanderborght, Jan
MASCARA
Vandermeulen, Johan
MASCARA
Vandernoot, Alexandra
LES EXPLOITS DUN JEUNE DON JUAN
Vandersteene, Zeger
ARIA
Vanderstraete, Mike
MASCARA
Vanderwyth, Richard
ALLNIGHTER, THE
Vanech, Susan
REVENGE OF THE NERDS II: NERDS IN PARADISE
Vaneck, Pierre
LANNEE DES MEDUSES
SWEET COUNTRY
Vanel, Charles
SI LE SOLEIL NE REVENAIT PAS
Vaner, Maria
EN RETIRADA
LOS DUENOS DEL SILENCIO
Vaner, Marla
SENTIMIENTOS: MIRTA DE LINIERS A ESTAMBUL
Vanity
DEADLY ILLUSION
Vanparys, Karen
LOVE IS A DOG FROM HELL
Vansittart, Rupert
EAT THE RICH
Vaquier, Pedro
JUNTOS
Varadi, Hedi
AZ UTOLSOKEZIRAT
Vardund, Ingerid
FELDMANN CASE, THE

Varela, Carlos
CHRONICLE OF A DEATH FORETOLD
Varela, Gina
KILLER WORKOUT
Varela, Jay
IN THE MOOD
Varelli, Alfredo
BELLY OF AN ARCHITECT, THE
Varga, Maria
HOL VOLT, HOL NEM VOLT
Vargas, Jacob
ERNEST GOES TO CAMP
PRINCIPAL, THE
Vargas, John
HANOI HILTON, THE
Vargas, Jorge
ROSA DE LA FRONTERA
Vargas, Paulino
ROSA DE LA FRONTERA
Vargas, Valentina
FUEGOS
Varik, Andrus
REQUIEM
Varlejova, Natalija
CIZIM VSTUP POVOLEN
Varnese, Rosemary
CONCRETE ANGELS
Varney, Jim
ERNEST GOES TO CAMP
Varney, Robert
STUDENT CONFIDENTIAL
Varona, Dante
COMMANDER LAMIN
ON THE EDGE OF HELL
Varouchas, Andreas
ONIRO ARISTERIS NICHTAS
Vasilyeva, E.
DVADTSTAT DNEI BEZ
Vasilyeva, Tatyana
SAMAYA OBAYATELNAYA I PRIVLEKATELNAYA
Vasilyeva, Yekaterina
AKTSIA
Vasoni, Ana
ASI COMO HABIAN SIDO
Vassilakopoulou, Rubini
ONE HUNDRED AND TWENTY DECIBELS
Vassilopoulos, Dimitri
RADIO DAYS
Vassilyev, Anatoly
GRUBAYA POSADKA
Vatanzad, Amir
MANUSCRIPTS
Vaucher, Suzanna
DEADTIME STORIES
Vaughan, Paris
PRETTY SMART
Vaughan, Skeeter
LIKE FATHER, LIKE SON
Vaughan, Stevie Ray
BACK TO THE BEACH
Vaughn, Robert
HOUR OF THE ASSASSIN
NIGHTSTICK
RENEGADE, UN OSSO TROPPO DURO
Vavilova, Natalia
POEZD VNE RASPISANIA
Vavra, Bohumil
DISCOPRIBEH
Vavrova, Hana
CENA MEDU
Vayani, Rika
ONIRO ARISTERIS NICHTAS
Vazdiks, Uldis
BLUDNYY SYN
OBOROTEN TOM
Vazquez, Arturo
OLOR A MUERTE
Vazquez, Jose Luis Lopez
MOROS Y CRISTIANOS
Vazquez, Vicky
MUJERES SALVAJES
Vazzoler, Alessandra
FRANCESCA
Vecker, Bob
O. C. AND STIGGS
Vega, Henry
MANKILLERS
Vega, Isela
NOS REIMOS DE LA MIGRA
Vegvari, Tamas
ZUHANAS KOZBEN
Veillard, Eric
LAMI DE MON AMIE
Veksler, Sergei
YAGUAR
Vela, Paco
RETURN OF JOSEY WALES, THE
Velasco, Esther
A LOS CUATRO VIENTOS
Velasco, Manuela
LAW OF DESIRE
Velasco, Maria Elena
NI DE AQUI, NI DE ALLA
Velat, Carlos
REDONDELA
Velazquez, Esther
AMAZONS
Velazquez, Tere
EL ANSIA DE MATAR
Velez, Felipe
LONG STRIDER
Vella, Bruno
POLICIA
Velyaminov, Pyotr
KONETS OPERATSII "REZIDENT"
ZHELEZNOE POLE
Venantini, Luca
ALADDIN
Venantini, Venantino
CAPRICCIO
Vendrell, Carlos
MIRACLES
Venegas, Arturo
WHISTLE BLOWER, THE
Venier, Mara
CARAMELLE DA UNO SCONOSCIUTO
Veninger, Ingrid
GATE, THE
Venniro, Charles
KILLER WORKOUT
Venora, Diane
IRONWEED
Ventura, Ana Maria
LA CASA DE BERNARDA ALBA
Ventura, Jesse
PREDATOR
RUNNING MAN, THE
Ventura, Lino
LA RUMBA
Venture, Richard
SICILIAN, THE
Venturiello, Massimo
GOOD MORNING BABYLON
Venturini, Mark
BEST SELLER
Venu, Nedumudi
KATHAKKU PINNIL
NILAKURINHI POOTHAPPOL
THIRTHAM
Veokeki, Joe B.
GOOD MORNING, VIETNAM
Vera, Billy
BLIND DATE
Vera, Victoria
ASIGNATURA APROBADA
Verdin, Octavia
FOURTH PROTOCOL, THE
Verdon, Gwen
NADINE
Verdone, Carlo
IO E MIA SORELLA
Verdoorn, Annemieke
DE RATELRAT
Verdu, Maribel
LA ESTANQUERA DE VALLECAS
YEAR OF AWAKENING, THE
Verduzco, Juan
NARCOTERROR
Vergel, Ace
ZIMATAR
Vermaaten, Michael
LAST EMPEROR, THE
Vermandere, Christ
MASCARA
Vermes, Arpad
HOL VOLT, HOL NEM VOLT
Vernan, Ron
BIG BANG, THE
Vernier, Pierre
LE SOLITAIRE
Vernon, Harvey
SOMEONE TO WATCH OVER ME
Vernon, Howard
DER TOD DES EMPEDOKLES
Vernon, John
BLUE MONKEY
ERNEST GOES TO CAMP
NIGHTSTICK
Vernon, Richard
MONTH IN THE COUNTRY, A
Vero, Dennis
STRANDED
Veron, Susana
MISS MARY
Veronica, Consuelo
LO NEGRO DEL NEGRO
Veronique, Mahile
FACES OF WOMEN
Veronis, Alexandros
IKONA ENOS MYTHIKOU PROSOPOU
Verrell, Cec
EYE OF THE EAGLE
Verrett, Shirley
ARIA
MACBETH
Verrette, Christopher
WITCHES OF EASTWICK, THE
Verroca, Joe
HUNTER'S BLOOD
Versluys, Martin
CAUGHT
Verstraete, Mark
MASCARA
Vertanian, Zareh
DREAMERS
Vertinskaya, Marianna
ODINOKAYA ZHENCHINA ZHELAET
POZNAKOMITAYA
Vesely, Lubos
CENA MEDU
Veskrnova, Dagmar
CHOBOTNICE Z II. PATRA
PRATELE BERMUDSKEHO TROJUHELNIKU
Vesnik, Yevgeni
TEMA
Vetchy, Ondrej
PRATELE BERMUDSKEHO TROJUHELNIKU
Veterinarian
BABY BOOM
Vetrovsky, Daniel
PROC?
Vettorazzo, Giovanni
CRIME OF HONOR
LA DONNA DEL TRAGHETTO
Veugelers, Marijke
VAN GELUK GESPROKEN
Vhen, Rey
ULTIMAX FORCE
Viana, Henrique
BALADA DA PRAIA DOS CAES
DUMA VEZ POR TODAS
LA PLAYA DE LOS PERROS
Vibert, Ronan
EMPIRE STATE
Vick, John Allen
PRINCIPAL, THE
Vickers, George
T. DAN SMITH
Vicky
DUMA VEZ POR TODAS
Victor, Paula
FLICKS
Victoria, Jorge
HERENCIA DE VALIENTES
OPERACION MARIJUANA
Victoria, Maria
WELCOME MARIA
Vicz, Melanie
HUNK
Vida, Piero
MAN ON FIRE
MORO AFFAIR, THE
Vidakovic, Bane
WHEELS OF TERROR
Vidal, Alexandra
FAMILY BUSINESS
Vidal, Javier
MAS ALLA DEL SILENCIO

Vidal, Stephanie
FAMILY BUSINESS
Vidale, Fabrizio
LESTATE STA FINENDO
Vidarte, Walter
EL AMOR DE AHORA
Videnieks, Alfreds
POHADKA O MALICKOVI
Videnovic, Gala
HEY BABU RIBA
Vidler, Steven
GOOD WIFE, THE
Vidor, John
CLUB LIFE
Viebrock, Kierstin
PRETTY SMART
Vieira, Cinthia
A DANCA DOS BONECOS
Vierikko, Vesa
A LA ITKE IINES
Vigil, Gerado
ROBACHICOS
Vignali, Giorgio
LESTATE STA FINENDO
Vigneaud, Sophie
UN AMOUR A PARIS
Viharo, Robert
NIGHT STALKER, THE
Vijayalakshmi
KATHAKKU PINNIL
Vijayashanti
BHARGAVA RAMUDU
Vikland, O.
KOROTKIE VSTRECHI
Vilela, Diogo
AREIAS ESCALADANTES
LEILA DINIZ
Vilims, Aigar
STRAKH
Vilkina, Natalia
SOUCHASTNIKI
Villa, Federico
JUANA LA CANTINERA
Villa, Gabriele
MORO AFFAIR, THE
Villa, Monica
SOFIA
Villa, Nova
MISSING IN ACTION
Villaggio, Paolo
MISSIONE EROICA
RIMINI RIMINI
ROBA DA RICCHI
SCUOLA DI LADRI 2
SUPERFANTOZZI
Villani, John
KILLER WORKOUT
Villanueva, Leo
LA RULETERA
LAPUTA: THE CASTLE IN THE SKY
Villanueva, Roberto
DAMORTIS
Villard, Tom
TROUBLE WITH DICK, THE
Villaume, Astrid
PELLE EROVRAREN
Villeret, Jacques
LETE DERNIER A TANGER
LETE EN PENTE DOUCE
SOIGNE TA DROITE
Vilojni, Shmuel
LO SAM ZAYIN
Vilozny, Shmuel
TEL AVIV—BERLIN
Vilpas, Eija
A LA ITKE IINES
URSULA
Vince, Nicholas
HELLRAISER
Vince, Pruitt Taylor
ANGEL HEART
BARFLY
SHY PEOPLE
Vincent, Frank
MADE IN ARGENTINA
Vincent, Jan-Michael
BORN IN EAST L.A.
ENEMY TERRITORY
Vincent, Louise
TERMINUS

Vincze, Geza
HOTREAL
Ving, Lee
DUDES
Vinicius, Paulo
ELE, O BOTO
Vinnichenko, Letza
MORGAN STEWART'S COMING HOME
Vinogradova, Maria
OBESHCHAYU BYT
Vinovich, Stephen
MANNEQUIN
Vintas, Gustav
LETHAL WEAPON
Viola, Ron
BLIND DATE
Virden, Marshall
DIRTY LAUNDRY
Viro, Marina
BELLIFRESCHI
Virtanen, Ville
URSULA
Viruboff, Sofia
MISS MARY
Virzansky, Yossi
DEATH BEFORE DISHONOR
Visan, Dorel
PADUREANCA
Viscakova, Jana
POHADKA O MALICKOVI
Viscardi, Francesca
IL LUPO DI MARE
Visconti, Valentina
IL LUPO DI MARE
Viscuso, Sal
SPACEBALLS
Visentin, Giovanni
MAN ON FIRE
Visotski, Vladimir
KOROTKIE VSTRECHI
Vitale, Alex
STRIKE COMMANDO
Vitale, Antonella
NOI UOMINI DURI
OPERA
Vitali, Elisabeth
IL EST GENIAL PAPY!
Vitasek, Andreas
DIE DRECKSCHLEUDER
Vitorgan, Emmanuel
TVOYO MIRNOE NEBO
Vitorgan, Emmanuil
VYKUP
Vitzin, Georgy
SOPERNITSY
Vivaldi, Piero
LA CROCE DALLE SETTE PIETRE
Viverito, Vince
UNTOUCHABLES, THE
Vives, Gerrard
ARIA
Viviani, Joe
FIREHOUSE
Vivino, Floyd
GOOD MORNING, VIETNAM
Vivo, Jose
LA GUERRA DE LOS LOCOS
Vlach, Oldrich
CENA MEDU
Vlachovsky, Milan
DISCOPRIBEH
Vladimirski, Oleg
DOLGHYIE PROVOD
Vlady, Marina
LES EXPLOITS DUN JEUNE DON JUAN
UNA CASA IN BILICO
Vlahovics, Edit
MALOM A POKOLBAN
Vlasak, Jan
PROC?
Vlissidis, Antonis
TELEFTAIO STICHIMA
Vocca, Ginella
MORO AFFAIR, THE
Vochecowizc, Liz
RADIO DAYS
Vochoc, Karel
DISCOPRIBEH

Voe, Sandra
COMRADES
Voets, Bas
EEN MAAND LATER
Vogel, Ellen
ALS IN EEN ROES
Vogel, Tony
CRY FREEDOM
Vogler, Rudiger
MADRID
TAROT
Vogue-Anzlovar, Vinoi
USODNI TELEFON
Voit, Mieczyslaw
STANISLAW I ANNA
Voita, Michel
JENATSCH
Vol-au-vents
WHOOPS APOCALYPSE
Volanaki, Dora
ONE HUNDRED AND TWENTY DECIBELS
Voland, Mark
SOMEONE TO WATCH OVER ME
Voldstedlund, Merete
WOLF AT THE DOOR, THE
Volkov, Vladimir
I NIKTO NA SVETE
Volkova, Olga
SON V RUKU, ILI CHEMODON
Volonte, Gian Maria
CHRONICLE OF A DEATH FORETOLD
MORO AFFAIR, THE
UN RAGAZZO DI CALABRIA
Volontir, Mihai
SLEDY OBOROTNYA
Volosach, Liudmila
VINA LEYTENANTA NEKRASOVA
Voloshin, Julian
ALADDIN
Volter, Philippe
MACBETH
vom Baur, Barbara
SOMMER
von Bauer, Reinhard
QUATRE MAINS
Von Bromssen, Thomas
MANNEN FRAN MALLORCA
von Bromssen, Tomas
SERPENT'S WAY, THE
von Dobschutz, Ulrich
LITTLE PROSECUTOR, THE
Von Donna, Roxy
LAW OF DESIRE
Von Leer, Hunter
TALKING WALLS
von Manteuffel, Felix
TRIUMPH DE GERECHTEN
Von Ornsteiner, Joel
NECROPOLIS
ROBOT HOLOCAUST
von Orsteiner, Joel
I WAS A TEENAGE T.V. TERRORIST
von Rauch, Andreas
DER TOD DES EMPEDOKLES
Von Schellendorf, Heinrich
RAWHEAD REX
von Schneider, Kurt
SLATE, WYN & ME
von Sydow, Max
PELLE EROVRAREN
WOLF AT THE DOOR, THE
von Trier, Lars
EPIDEMIC
von Tscharner, Gian-Battista
JENATSCH
von von Bromssen, Tomas
MY LIFE AS A DOG
von Witte, Vladimir
JAAN KAANTOPIIRI
von Zerneck, Danielle
LA BAMBA
Vondracek, Jiri
CENA MEDU
Voronina, Yekaterina
KORABL PRISHELTSEV
Vorsel, Niels
EPIDEMIC
Vortanz, Julie
BLOOD HOOK

Vos, Herma
CLUB DE RENCONTRES
Vosmaer, Pim
CAUGHT
Voulpe, Bogdana
PRIZEMYAVANE
Voutsas, Costas
ONE HUNDRED AND TWENTY DECIBELS
Voyatzis, Lefteris
TA PAIDIA TIS CHELIDONAS
Voyiatzi, Cassandra
O PARADISSOS ANIGI ME ANTIKLIDI
Vrablik, Antonin
WOLF'S HOLE
Vrana, Vlasta
KEEPING TRACK
MORNING MAN, THE
Vraniqi, Xhemil
AVRIL BRISE
Vrchota, Robert
PRATELE BERMUDSKEHO TROJUHELNIKU
Vrenon, Taunie
MUTANT HUNT
Vrettos, Nicos
DOXOBUS
Vukotic, Milena
ROBA DA RICCHI
Vuletic, Jenny
HOWLING III, THE
Vultchanov, Yassen
CERNITE LEBEDI
Vundla, Ka
KOLORMASK
Vuu, Richard
LAST EMPEROR, THE
Vysotsky, Vladimir
INTERVENTSIA
Waalkes, Otto
OTTO—DER NEUE FILM
Wabgaonkar, Ashalata
PUDHCHE PAOL
Wachowiak, Jutta
SO VIELE TRAUME
Wade, Christopher
MIND KILLER
Wade, Michael
JOHN AND THE MISSUS
Wade, Nemon
PRINCIPAL, THE
Wade, Tara
STUDENT CONFIDENTIAL
Wadham, Julian
MAURICE
Wagelie, Meredith
CANT BUY ME LOVE
Wagenar, Hillary
MASCARA
Wagner, Alessandro
DOLCE ASSENZA
Wagner, Thomas
NEAR DARK
Wah, Lau Tak
SWORN BROTHERS
Wahl, Corinne
EQUALIZER 2000
Wahl, Ken
OMEGA SYNDROME
Wahlgren, Pernilla
SERPENT'S WAY, THE
Wai, Lam
BROTHERHOOD
Wai-leung, Pau
YI LOU YI
Wai-man, Chan
LEGACY OF RAGE
Wain, Lance
BROADCAST NEWS
Wainscott, Richard
BLOODSUCKERS FROM OUTER SPACE
Waite, John
STARLIGHT HOTEL
Waites, Thomas G.
LIGHT OF DAY
Waits, Tom
IRONWEED
Wakao, Ayako
PRINCESS FROM THE MOON
Walcott, Gregory
HOUSE TWO: THE SECOND STORY
Walden, Randall
BLOOD SISTERS
Waldman, Grant
CYCLONE
Waldo's Wife
ZYGFRYD
Waldon, Louis
MISSION KILL
Waldron, Patrick
BOY SOLDIER
Waldrup, Hal
BELL DIAMOND
Walken, Christopher
DEADLINE
Walker, Angela
ARIA
Walker, Bill
STARLIGHT HOTEL
Walker, Charles
NO WAY OUT
Walker, Christopher
FOURTH PROTOCOL, THE
Walker, Harry
EMPIRE STATE
Walker, James
EMPIRE OF THE SUN
Walker, John
HIDING OUT
WINTER TAN, A
Walker, Kasey
DEATH BEFORE DISHONOR
Walker, Lou
HIDING OUT
Walker, Mark
KEEPING TRACK
Walker, Paul
MONSTER IN THE CLOSET
Walker, Paul W.
PROGRAMMED TO KILL
Walker, Peter
ADVENTURE OF THE ACTION HUNTERS
Walker, Ray
NADINE
Walker, Robert
EVIL TOWN
Walker, Samantha
BLOODSUCKERS FROM OUTER SPACE
Walker, Sara
HOUSEKEEPING
Walker, Steven
OVERBOARD
Walker, Tracye
OUTING, THE
Walker III, Linwood P.
NADINE
Wall, Anita
MALARPIRATER
Wall, Max
LITTLE DORRIT
Wallace, Dee
CLUB LIFE
Wallace, Jack
HOUSE OF GAMES
Wallace, Julie T.
LIVING DAYLIGHTS, THE
Wallace, Wayne
O. C. AND STIGGS
Wallach, Ketherine
SOMEONE TO LOVE
Wallach, Roberta
BIG BANG, THE
Walle, Knut
OFELAS
Wallenson, Wanda
EL HOMBRE DESNUDO
Wallis, Bill
WHISTLE BLOWER, THE
Walsh, Bill
MURDER LUST
Walsh, Gerry
RAWHEAD REX
Walsh, Gwynyth
BLUE MONKEY
Walsh, J.T.
GOOD MORNING, VIETNAM
HOUSE OF GAMES
TIN MEN
Walsh, John
KEEPING TRACK
MONSTER IN THE CLOSET
Walsh, John J.
UNTOUCHABLES, THE
Walsh, Kenneth
CLIMB, THE
Walsh, M. Emmet
HARRY AND THE HENDERSONS
NO MAN'S LAND
RAISING ARIZONA
Walsh, Paul
HOUSE OF GAMES
Walsh, Peter
DOGS IN SPACE
Walsh, Richard
BELLMAN AND TRUE
Walsh, Robert
BROADCAST NEWS
SUSPECT
Walsh, Steve
EAT THE RICH
MORE BAD NEWS
Walsh, Sydney
P.I. PRIVATE INVESTIGATIONS
Walsh, Thyais
MANKILLERS
Walsh, Todd
CANT BUY ME LOVE
Walston, Ray
FROM THE HIP
O. C. AND STIGGS
Walter, Luke
MISSION KILL
Walter, Perla
OMEGA SYNDROME
Walter, Tracey
MALONE
Walters, Julie
PERSONAL SERVICES
PRICK UP YOUR EARS
Walton, Emma
BLIND DATE
Walton, Jim
SUSPECT
Walton, John
LIGHTHORSEMEN, THE
Waltrip, Kim
PRETTY SMART
Waltze, Mike
FIRE AND ICE
Wan, Irene
DIXIA QING
Wanamaker, Sam
BABY BOOM
SUPERMAN IV: THE QUEST FOR PEACE
Wang, Joe
OVERKILL
Wanjugu, Ann
KITCHEN TOTO, THE
Wansdronk, Maarten
EEN MAAND LATER
Wansink, Maarten
ZJOEK
Wapler, Eric
CHAMP D'HONNEUR
Ward, Fred
TRAIN OF DREAMS
Ward, Geoff
LOVECHILD, THE
Ward, James
UNFINISHED BUSINESS . . .
Ward, John
HIDING OUT
Ward, Jonathan
WHITE WATER SUMMER
Ward, Lyman
PLANES, TRAINS AND AUTOMOBILES
Ward, Rachel
GOOD WIFE, THE
HOTEL COLONIAL
Ward, Sela
HELLO AGAIN
STEELE JUSTICE
Ward, Sophie
ARIA
LITTLE DORRIT
Warden, Jack
SEPTEMBER
Warden, Samantha
EMPIRE OF THE SUN
Wardle, Michael
WITHNAIL AND I

Ware, Herta
DIRTY LAUNDRY
PROMISED LAND
SLAMDANCE

Waring, Derek
INDIAN SUMMER

Warlock, Billy
HOT SHOT

Warlock, Dick
OMEGA SYNDROME

Warner, Amy
WITCHES OF EASTWICK, THE

Warner, David
HANSEL AND GRETEL

Warner, Richard
MAURICE

Warner, Rick
HIDING OUT

Warren, D.C.
O. C. AND STIGGS

Warren, Jennifer
FATAL BEAUTY

Warren, Jennifer Leigh
FOREVER, LULU

Warren, Lesley Ann
BURGLAR

Warren, Michael
DREAMANIAC

Warren, Nicola
CAPRICCIO

Warren, Ted
BANZAI RUNNER

Warrilow, David
RADIO DAYS

Warrington, Seraphine
BLOOD SISTERS

Washburn, Rick
ANGEL HEART

Washington, Denzel
CRY FREEDOM

Washington, Ludie
HOLLYWOOD SHUFFLE

Wass, Vincent
MALDENIYESIMION

Wassard, Lone
VENNER FOR ALTID

Wasserman, Renessa
KILLER WORKOUT

Wasson, Craig
NIGHTMARE ON ELM STREET 3: DREAM WARRIORS, A

Watanabe, Craig
OVERKILL

Watanabe, Hiroyuki
TOO MUCH

Watanabe, Ken
SEA AND POISON, THE

Watanabe, Maria
SEA AND POISON, THE

Watase, Tsunehiko
TOKYO BLACKOUT

Waterman, Juanita
CRY FREEDOM
FOURTH PROTOCOL, THE

Waters, John
BUSHFIRE MOON

Waterston, Sam
DEVILS PARADISE, THE
SEPTEMBER

Watford, Gwen
CRY FREEDOM

Watkins, Dr. Clifford
DIRTY DANCING

Watkins, James Louis
NIGHT STALKER, THE

Watkins, Michael
BELLMAN AND TRUE

Watkins, Michelle
OUTING, THE

Watkins, Susy Anne
MORE BAD NEWS

Watson, Alberta
WHITE OF THE EYE

Watson, Billy
FRENCHMAN'S FARM

Watson, Charles Keller
UNTOUCHABLES, THE

Watson, Ernest
ANGEL HEART

Watson, John
STARLIGHT HOTEL

Watson, Nigel
BOY SOLDIER

Watts, Cheryl
P.K. & THE KID

Watts, Cliff
VIDEO DEAD, THE

Watts, Linda
DREAMANIAC

Waugh, Claire
PERSONAL SERVICES

Wax, Ruby
EAT THE RICH

Waxman, Al
MEATBALLS III

Waxman, Anath
LO SAM ZAYIN

Way, Bruce
OVER THE TOP

Wayans, Damon
HOLLYWOOD SHUFFLE
ROXANNE

Wayans, Keenen Ivory
HOLLYWOOD SHUFFLE

Wayans, Kim
HOLLYWOOD SHUFFLE

Waymire, Rhonda
REVENGE OF THE NERDS II: NERDS IN PARADISE

Waymon, Sam L.
WEEDS

Wayne, April
MOON IN SCORPIO
PARTY CAMP

Wayne, Michael
DANGER ZONE, THE

Wayne Knight
FOREVER, LULU

Wearing, Geoffrey
STARLIGHT HOTEL

Weathers, Carl
PREDATOR

Weaver, Lois
SHE MUST BE SEEING THINGS

Weaving, Hugo
RIGHT HAND MAN, THE

Webb, Chloe
BELLY OF AN ARCHITECT, THE

Webb, Christy
MALIBU BIKINI SHOP, THE

Webb, John
BLOODSUCKERS FROM OUTER SPACE

Webb, Rod
TIME FOR DYING, A

Webb, Simon
HOME IS WHERE THE HART IS

Webb, T.K.
ZERO BOYS, THE

Webber, Robert
NUTS

Webber, Timothy
JOHN AND THE MISSUS

Weber, Pedro
EL DIABLO, EL SANTO Y EL TONTO
EL MOFLES Y LOS MECANICOS
SINVERGUENZA . . . PERO HONRADO
TRAGICO TERREMOTO EN MEXICO
MAS BUENAS QUE EL PAN
YO, EL EJECUTOR

Weber, Rick
SPACE RACE

Weber, Steven
HAMBURGER HILL

Webster, Gary
EMPIRE STATE
OUT OF ORDER

Webster, Jack
HIGH STAKES

Webster, Ron
WHOOPS APOCALYPSE

Webster, Sandy
BLUE MONKEY

Webster, Tony
NO WAY OUT

Weckstrom, Markus
ELVIS-KISSAN JALJILLA

Wedell, Mimi
ANNA

Weden, Nicole
IRONWEED

Wedgeworth, Ann
MADE IN HEAVEN

Weeden, Paul
WEEDS

Weeks, Christopher
VALET GIRLS

Weenick, Annabelle
SQUARE DANCE

Weenink, Els
EEN MAAND LATER

Weerasinghe, Anoja
MALDENIYESIMION
WITNESS TO A KILLING

Weerasinghe, Swineetha
WITNESS TO A KILLING

Wegner, Sabine
VERMISCHTE NACHRICHTEN

Wegrzyniak, Rafal
POCIAG DO HOLLYWOOD
ZLOTA MAHMUDIA

Wei, Yu Chi
MIDNIGHT

Wei-sung, Lam
STORY OF DR. SUN YAT-SEN, THE

Wei-wei, Tien
OUTSIDERS, THE

Weichenhanh, Gudrun
POET'S SILENCE, THE

Weidlin, Jane
SLEEPING BEAUTY

Weidner, Rebecca Lucia
TIN MEN

Weigl, Vladimir
POET'S SILENCE, THE

Weil, Robert E.
WHO'S THAT GIRL

Weinberg, Guri
DEATH BEFORE DISHONOR

Weinberg, Joanna
SATURDAY NIGHT AT THE PALACE

Weingarten, Isabelle
UN AMOUR A PARIS

Weinmann, Martin
SEREBRYANAYA PRYAZHA KAROLINY

Weinstock, Jerry
DEADLINE

Weiss, Bertha
ARIA

Weiss, Neil
ZERO BOYS, THE

Weiss, Roberta
HIGH STAKES

Weisser, Norbert
DOWN TWISTED
WALKER

Weist, Dwight
RADIO DAYS

Weivers, Margreth
NIONDE KOMPANIET

Welch, Jane
BROADCAST NEWS

Welch, Laura
HIDDEN CITY

Welch, Patrick
GHOST FEVER

Welch, Steve
HAPPY HOUR

Welch, Tahnee
SLEEPING BEAUTY

Welden, Michael
ASSASSINATION

Weldon, Dan
FULL METAL JACKET

Welker, Frank
CHIPMUNK ADVENTURE, THE
MUNCHIES
PINOCCHIO AND THE EMPEROR OF THE NIGHT

Wellamette, John
NIGHTFORCE

Weller, Peter
ROBOCOP

Welles, Mel
COMMANDO SQUAD

Welles, Orson
SOMEONE TO LOVE

Wellington, Don
WHOOPS APOCALYPSE

Wells, Belinda
NICE GIRLS DON'T EXPLODE

Wells, Dennis
FULL METAL JACKET

Wells, Doris
MAS ALLA DEL SILENCIO

Wells, Orlando
MAURICE

Wells, Vernon
INNERSPACE
P.I. PRIVATE INVESTIGATIONS

Wells, Veronica
DA NNUNZIO

Welsh, John
CAMPUS MAN

Welsh, Kenneth
RADIO DAYS

Welter, Ariadne
MAS VALE PAJARO EN MANO . . .

Wemba, Papa
LA VIE EST BELLE

Wen, Jian
LAST EMPRESS, THE

Wendel, David
MONSTER SQUAD, THE

Wendel, Lara
INTERVISTA

Wendenius, Crispin Dickson
MORE ABOUT THE CHILDREN OF BULLERBY VILLAGE

Wendl, Joyce Flick
BEDROOM WINDOW, THE

Wendt, Pierre
CRAZY BOYS

Wenjie, Huang
LAST EMPEROR, THE

Wennemann, Klaus
DER UNSICHTBARE

Wennerstrom, Leif
DEADTIME STORIES

Wentz, Robert
P.K. & THE KID

Wenzhi, Liu
DOCTOR SUN YATSEN

Werba, Amy
DANCERS

Werner, Lori
SOMETHING SPECIAL!

Werner, Rita
CRAZY BOYS

Werntz, Gary
WANTED: DEAD OR ALIVE

Wertheim, Ronald
NECROPOLIS

Wesley, Kassie
EVIL DEAD 2: DEAD BY DAWN

West, Adam
ZOMBIE NIGHTMARE

West, Johnson
ERNEST GOES TO CAMP

West, Martin
BEST SELLER

West, Tegan
HAMBURGER HILL

West, Timothy
CRY FREEDOM

Westaway, Simon
SLATE, WYN & ME

Westberg, Dana Burns
EMMANUELLE 5

Westersund, Laila
LEIF

Westheimer, Dr. Ruth
FOREVER, LULU

Westman, Per
LEIF

Westmore, Joy
LES PATTERSON SAVES THE WORLD

Weston, Jack
DIRTY DANCING
ISHTAR

Weston, Jeff
AMERICAN NINJA 2: THE CONFRONTATION

Westover, Mark
HOLLYWOOD SHUFFLE

Wetterholm, Susanna
MY LIFE AS A DOG

Wexler, Bobbi
OUTTAKES

Whaley, Andrew
CRY FREEDOM

Whaley, Frank
IRONWEED

Wheat, Ricco
BIG EASY, THE

Wheatley, Thomas
LIVING DAYLIGHTS, THE

Wheaton, Amy
CURSE, THE

Wheaton, Wil
CURSE, THE

Wheeler, Gary
MORGAN STEWART'S COMING HOME

Wheeler, Ira
RADIO DAYS
SEPTEMBER

Wheeler, Ira B.
SECRET OF MY SUCCESS, THE

Wheeler, John
BANZAI RUNNER

Whelan, Gary
CRY FREEDOM

Whelan, Jeremy
TALKING WALLS

Whetu, Mark
LEADING EDGE, THE

Whinnery, Barbara
MIRACLES

Whip, Joseph
MIRACLES

Whipp, Joseph
AMAZONS

Whitaker, Forest
GOOD MORNING, VIETNAM
STAKEOUT

Whitaker, Jonathan
THREE MEN AND A BABY

Whitaker, Richard B.
LETHAL WEAPON

Whitcraft, Elizabeth
ANGEL HEART

White, Al
OMEGA SYNDROME

White, Bob
T. DAN SMITH

White, Carole Ita
TALKING WALLS
WITCHES OF EASTWICK, THE

White, Donna
MALONE

White, Doug
PRINCIPAL, THE

White, Florence
O. C. AND STIGGS

White, Jesse
MONSTER IN THE CLOSET

White, Ken
BIG SHOTS

White, Kerryann
LOVECHILD, THE

White, Lloyd
SUSPECT

White, Michael
BEST SELLER

White, Robin
LADY OF THE CAMELIAS

White, Ron
PRETTYKILL
TOO OUTRAGEOUS

White, Sailor
REMEMBERING MEL

White, Stephanie
MONSTER IN THE CLOSET

White, Ted
HOT PURSUIT
WANTED: DEAD OR ALIVE

White, Tim
BROADCAST NEWS

White, Willie
BELIEVERS, THE

Whitehead, Robert
HOSTAGE

Whitelaw, Billie
MAURICE
SHADEY

Whitfield, Lynn
JAWS: THE REVENGE

Whitford, Bradley
ADVENTURES IN BABYSITTING
REVENGE OF THE NERDS II: NERDS IN PARADISE

Whitford, Peter
RUNNING FROM THE GUNS
WARM NIGHTS ON A SLOW MOVING TRAIN

Whiting, Christopher
BLOOD HOOK

Whitley, George
HIDING OUT

Whitlock, Lee
WISH YOU WERE HERE

Whitman, Kari
BEVERLY HILLS COP II
MASTERBLASTER

Whitman, Parker
FATAL BEAUTY

Whitmore, James
NUTS

Whitney, Carl
BEDROOM WINDOW, THE

Whitney, David
LES PATTERSON SAVES THE WORLD

Whitrow, Benjamin
PERSONAL SERVICES

Whittaker, Maria
WHOOPS APOCALYPSE

Whittaker, Steve
IN THE MOOD

Whitted, Pharez
DIXIELAND DAIMYO

Whittingham, Christopher
LOVECHILD, THE

Whittington, Valerie
COMRADES

Whitton, Margaret
IRONWEED
SECRET OF MY SUCCESS, THE

Whorman, Bill
MASTERBLASTER

Whybrow, Alan
MAURICE

Whybrow, Arthur
BELLMAN AND TRUE
PERSONAL SERVICES

Whyle, James
STEEL DAWN

Wiazemsky, Anne
TESTAMENT D'UN POETE JUIF ASSASSINE

Wickliff, Mimi
P.K. & THE KID

Wickstrom, Sven
PA STIGENDE KURS

Widem, Susan
OPEN HOUSE

Widerberg, Johan
SERPENT'S WAY, THE

Widerholt, Wesley
ESCAPES

Wieder, Anna Marie
HELLO AGAIN
OUTRAGEOUS FORTUNE

Wiesmeier, Lynda
EVIL TOWN

Wiest, Dianne
LOST BOYS, THE
RADIO DAYS
SEPTEMBER

Wieth, Pia
HIP, HIP, HURRA!

Wight, Kay
T. DAN SMITH

Wight, Peter
PERSONAL SERVICES

Wightman, Robert
OPPOSING FORCE

Wilbur, George P.
RUNNING MAN, THE

Wilby, James
MAURICE

Wild, Jamie
OVERBOARD

Wilde, Cecilia
PSYCHOS IN LOVE

Wilde, Wilbur
BIT PART, THE

Wilder, Cara
AMAZING GRACE AND CHUCK

Wilder, Glenn
MORGAN STEWART'S COMING HOME

Wilder, James
ZOMBIE HIGH

Wildgruber, Ulrich
DRAGON'S FOOD

Wilding, Michael
DEADLY ILLUSION

Wildman, Valerie
BEVERLY HILLS COP II

Wildsmith, Dawn
COMMANDO SQUAD
CYCLONE
SURF NAZIS MUST DIE

Wilduruber, Ulrich
PENG! DU BIST TOT!

Wiles, Mike
DANGER ZONE, THE

Wiley, Richard
RAGE OF HONOR

Wilhelmi, Roman
PRYWATNE SLEDZTWO
RYKOWISKO

Wilhemova, Gabriela
PROC?

Wilhoite, Kathleen
ANGEL HEART
CAMPUS MAN
UNDER COVER
WITCHBOARD

Wilkening, Catherine
MON BEL AMOUR, MA DECHIRURE
UN AMOUR A PARIS

Wilkens, Joseph
BELIEVERS, THE

Wilker, Jose
BAIXO GAVEA
BESAME MUCHO
FONTE DA SAUDADE
LEILA DINIZ
UM TREM PARA AS ESTRELAS

Wilkerson, June
TALKING WALLS

Wilkes, Elaine
BLIND DATE
WHO'S THAT GIRL

Wilkinson, Amber
COMRADES

Wilkinson, Gina
BLUE MONKEY

Wilkinson, Jack
BLOODSUCKERS FROM OUTER SPACE

Willard, Fred
ROXANNE

Willard, Tony
SUMMER CAMP NIGHTMARE

Willcox, Pete
DUDES

Willey, Walt
I WAS A TEENAGE T.V. TERRORIST

William Prince
NUTS

Williamette, John
STUDENT CONFIDENTIAL

Williams, Alon
WHO'S THAT GIRL

Williams, Bert
PENITENTIARY III

Williams, Billy
SUSPECT

Williams, Billy Dee
DEADLY ILLUSION
NUMBER ONE WITH A BULLET

Williams, Cathy
BUSINESS AS USUAL

Williams, Danny
PRINCIPAL, THE

Williams, David
PRINCIPAL, THE

Williams, Dean
BUSINESS AS USUAL

Williams, Dick Anthony
GARDENS OF STONE

Williams, Don S.
STEPFATHER, THE

Williams, Edy
DIRTY LAUNDRY
MANKILLERS

Williams, Eileen
HOUSEKEEPER, THE

Williams, Ewart Everard
SUSPECT

Williams, Eyan
OUTRAGEOUS FORTUNE

Williams, Heathcote
WISH YOU WERE HERE

Williams, Ian Patrick
DOLLS

Williams, Ida
MATEWAN

Williams, Jason
DANGER ZONE, THE

Williams, Jerald
OPPOSING FORCE

Williams, Jerry
NIONDE KOMPANIET

Williams, Julia Beals
SUMMER HEAT

Williams, Kevin
MAKING MR.RIGHT

Williams, Liz
SQUARE DANCE

Williams, Mae
IN THE MOOD

Williams, Mark
HIGH SEASON

Williams, Michael
FULL METAL JACKET

Williams, Natasha
OUT OF ORDER

Williams, Olivia Frances
MANNEQUIN

Williams, Paul
ZOMBIE HIGH

Williams, Robin
GOOD MORNING, VIETNAM

Williams, Ryk
HAPPY HOUR

Williams, Spice
STRANDED

Williams, Tara
MATEWAN

Williams, Terrilyn
BELL DIAMOND

Williams, Tony
OPPOSING FORCE

Williams, Vanessa
PICK-UP ARTIST, THE

Williams III, Clarence
TOUGH GUYS DON'T DANCE

Williamson, Fred
MESSENGER, THE

Williamson, Mykel T.
NUMBER ONE WITH A BULLET
YOU TALKIN' TO ME?

Williamson, Nicol
BLACK WIDOW

Williamson, Phillip
BELIEVERS, THE

Williamson, William
GARDENS OF STONE

Williard, Carol
OVERBOARD

Willie
PROJECT X

Willingham, Noble
GOOD MORNING, VIETNAM
SUMMER HEAT

Willis, Bruce
BLIND DATE

Willis, Johnny "Sugarbear"
BLACK WIDOW

Willis, Michael S.
TIN MEN

Willis, Sugarbear
HOUSE OF GAMES

Willowbrook
IN THE MOOD

Wills, Eural
PRINCIPAL, THE

Wilmore, Duncan
PROJECT X

Wilmore, Naeemah
MY LITTLE GIRL

Wilmot, Ronan
EAT THE PEACH
RAWHEAD REX

Wilms, Andre
CHAMP D'HONNEUR

Wilson, Dale
STEPFATHER, THE

Wilson, David
JAWS: THE REVENGE

Wilson, Elizabeth
BELIEVERS, THE

Wilson, Elvira
CAUGHT

Wilson, Jean
ERNEST GOES TO CAMP

Wilson, Jessica
PRINCIPAL, THE

Wilson, John
EAT THE RICH
FULL METAL JACKET

Wilson, Joi
CREEPOZOIDS

Wilson, Kaprice
PRINCIPAL, THE

Wilson, Lambert
BELLY OF AN ARCHITECT, THE

Wilson, Lillian
DOGS IN SPACE

Wilson, Peter Lee
DE FLYGANDE DJAVLARNA

Wilson, Richard
PRICK UP YOUR EARS
WHOOPS APOCALYPSE

Wilson, Scott
MALONE

Wilson, Shirley Ann
TIN MEN

Wilson, Tom
LETS GET HARRY

Wilson, Trey
RAISING ARIZONA

Wilson, Wayne
SPACEBALLS

Wiltgen, Ana Beatriz
UM TREM PARA AS ESTRELAS

Wilton, Penelope
CRY FREEDOM

Wilton, Philip
GOOD WIFE, THE

Wilton, Robert
BLUE MONKEY

Wimbley, Damon
DISORDERLIES

Winburn, James
BEST SELLER

Winbush, Troy
PRINCIPAL, THE

Winchester, Arna-Maria
CODA
INITIATION

Wincott, Michael
SICILIAN, THE

Winde, Beatrice
FROM THE HIP

Windom, William
PINOCCHIO AND THE EMPEROR OF THE NIGHT
PLANES, TRAINS AND AUTOMOBILES
SPACE RACE

Windsor, Barbara
COMRADES

Windsor, Marie
COMMANDO SQUAD

Winfield, Paul
BIG SHOTS
DEATH BEFORE DISHONOR

Winfrey, Oprah
THROW MOMMA FROM THE TRAIN

Winger, Debra
BLACK WIDOW

Winley, Robert
NEAR DARK

Winningham, Mare
MADE IN HEAVEN
SHY PEOPLE

Winslow, Michael
POLICE ACADEMY 4: CITIZENS ON PATROL
SPACEBALLS
ZARTLICHE CHAOTEN

Winstanely, Michele
WALKER

Winstanley, Michele
STRAIGHT TO HELL

Winston, Jean
DIRTY REBEL

Winston, Tom
PRINCIPAL, THE

Wint, Barbara
IN THE MOOD

Winter, Alexander
LOST BOYS, THE
Winter, Charles
EAT THE PEACH
Winter, Edward
FROM THE HIP
Winter, Gordon
ARIA
Winter, Iain
HOSTAGE
Winters, Deborah
OUTING, THE
Winters, Don
BLOOD HOOK
Winther-Lembourn, Ellen
KAMPEN OM DEN RODE KO
Wirth, Billy
LOST BOYS, THE
Wisch, Allen
OVERKILL
Wise, Alfie
HEAT
Wise, Jonathan
THREE O'CLOCK HIGH
Wise, Peter
ENEMY TERRITORY
Wise, Ray
ROBOCOP
Wise, Tim
EMANON
Wisecarver, Ellsworth "Sonny"
IN THE MOOD
Wiseman, Jeffrey
OVERBOARD
Wishinsky, Shlomo
BOUBA
Wisniewska, Ewa
CUDZOZIEMKA
Wisniewski, Andreas
ARIA
GOTHIC
LIVING DAYLIGHTS, THE
Witcher, Geoff
WINNERS TAKE ALL
With, Ebba
BABETTE'S GASTEBUD
Witherspoon, John
HOLLYWOOD SHUFFLE
Withrow, Glenn
BEVERLY HILLS COP II
DUDES
NIGHTFLYERS
Witkin, Francine
NIGHTFORCE
Wittig, John
PELLE EROVRAREN
Wivesson, Gudmar
BABETTE'S GASTEBUD
Wiwatpanachat, Panas
GOOD MORNING, VIETNAM
Wizard, The
STARLIGHT HOTEL
Wodehouse, Charlotte
PRICK UP YOUR EARS
Wodoslawsky, Stefan
LAST STRAW, THE
Woessner, Hank
BEST SELLER
Wohl, David
LIKE FATHER, LIKE SON
Woinski, Marcos
STRANGER, THE
Woinsky, Marc
AMAZONS
Wojcik, Magda Teresa
MATKA KROLOW
Wojcik, Wieslaw
PAN SAMOCHODZIK I NIESAMOWITY DWOR
Wojtkowiak, Alicja
E S D
Wolf, Susan
TALKING WALLS
Wolfe, Kedric
LIKE FATHER, LIKE SON
Wolfe, Traci
LETHAL WEAPON
Wolff, Patricia
HOUSE OF GAMES
Wollter, Kalle
OM KARLEK
Wollter, Sven
MANNEN FRAN MALLORCA
OM KARLEK
Woloshen, Sharon
REMEMBERING MEL
Womble, Wendy
BEDROOM WINDOW, THE
Wonderling., John
FULL METAL JACKET
Wong, Andy
OVERKILL
Wong, Brian
SAKURA KILLERS
Wong, Eddie
OPEN HOUSE
Wong, Gigi
AUTUMN'S TALE, AN
Wong, Jonathan
FATAL BEAUTY
Wong, Michael
LEGACY OF RAGE
WONDER WOMEN
Wong, Raymond
SEVEN YEARS ITCH
TRUE COLORS
Wong, Russell
CHINA GIRL
Wong, Victor
LAST EMPEROR, THE
PRINCE OF DARKNESS
Wong, Willie
STEELE JUSTICE
Wood, Gavin
DOGS IN SPACE
Wood, John
BIT PART, THE
Wood, John Lisbon
BEVERLY HILLS COP II
OMEGA SYNDROME
Wood, Josh
PRINCIPAL, THE
Wood, Paul
BIRDS OF PREY
STRAIGHT TO HELL
Wood, Robert
FORTY DAYS OF MUSA DAGH
Wood, Terence
EAT THE RICH
Wood-Chappelle, Robin
IRONWEED
Woodbeck, Victoria
FORTY DAYS OF MUSA DAGH
Woodruff, Tom
MONSTER SQUAD, THE
Woods, Glennis
STARLIGHT HOTEL
Woods, James
BEST SELLER
Woods, Leon
MUTANT HUNT
Woods, Michael
LADY BEWARE
Woods, Nan
IN THE MOOD
Woods, Ren
WALKER
Woods, Terry
STRAIGHT TO HELL
Woodward, Allison
DEADLY ILLUSION
Woodward, Jimmy
HOLLYWOOD SHUFFLE
Woodward, Joanne
GLASS MENAGERIE, THE
Woodward, Lenore
IN THE MOOD
Woodward, Tim
PERSONAL SERVICES
Woodworth, Andy
ERNEST GOES TO CAMP
Wooldridge, Susan
HOPE AND GLORY
Woolf, Harry
DIRTY LAUNDRY
Woolrich, Abel
MUJERES SALVAJES
Worden, Hank
SPACE RACE
Workman, David
BANZAI RUNNER
Woronov, Mary
BLACK WIDOW
Woronowicz, Dorota
E S D
Worth, Nicholas
DIRTY LAUNDRY
NO WAY OUT
Wortham, Jim
RED DESERT PENITENTIARY
Wortham, Trudy
RED DESERT PENITENTIARY
Worthey, Athena
STRIPPED TO KILL
Worzbach, Dolly
FRANCESCA
Wosien, Bernhard
FRANCESCA
Wostrikoff, Nicolas
LE BEAUF
Wotton, Bev
VIRGIN QUEEN OF ST. FRANCIS HIGH, THE
Wotton, J.T.
VIRGIN QUEEN OF ST. FRANCIS HIGH, THE
Wouk, Suzanne
WANTED: DEAD OR ALIVE
Wouters, Willy
MASCARA
Wright, Adrian
LIGHTHORSEMEN, THE
Wright, Bethany
THEY STILL CALL ME BRUCE
Wright, Bruce
WALKER
Wright, Ian James
SNOW WHITE
Wright, Jack
OVER THE TOP
Wright, James
LIGHTHORSEMEN, THE
RUNNING FROM THE GUNS
Wright, James C.
EMANON
Wright, Janet
HOME IS WHERE THE HART IS
Wright, Jenny
NEAR DARK
Wright, John
IRONWEED
Wright, Ken
HANOI HILTON, THE
OPPOSING FORCE
PRINCE OF DARKNESS
Wright, Kevin
FIRE AND ICE
Wright, Mary Catherine
SECRET OF MY SUCCESS, THE
Wright, Michael
PRINCIPAL, THE
Wright, Michael David
MALIBU BIKINI SHOP, THE
Wright, Patrick
EMANON
Wright, Robin
PRINCESS BRIDE, THE
Wright, Tim
OVERBOARD
Wright, Tom
CREEPSHOW 2
MATEWAN
OVERBOARD
Wringer, Leo
KITCHEN TOTO, THE
Wrye, Brian Charlton
BLOOD SISTERS
Wu, Ping
STEELE JUSTICE
Wuhl, Robert
GOOD MORNING, VIETNAM
Wurlitzer, Rudy
WALKER
Wust, Hannelore
CRAZY BOYS
Wyman, Bill
EAT THE RICH
Wyman, Nicholas
PLANES, TRAINS AND AUTOMOBILES
WEEDS
Wymark, Tristram
EMPIRE STATE

Wyn, Eric
BOY SOLDIER

Wyn, Marco
MASCARA

Wyner, George
SPACEBALLS

Wynne, Laura
WHOOPS APOCALYPSE

Wysocki, Wojciech
WIERNA RZEKA
ZYCIE WEWNETRZNE

Wyss, Sarah
BELL DIAMOND

Xanthos, Dionyssis
ANGELOS

Xin, Indio
MASSACRE IN DINOSAUR VALLEY

Xinmin, Cui
LAST EMPEROR, THE

Xireng, Jian
LAST EMPEROR, THE

Xueqi, Huang
BIG PARADE, THE

Yaeger, Bill
STRAIGHT TO HELL

Yaeger, Donna
SLAUGHTER HIGH

Yaffe, Ruth
BACHELOR GIRL

Yahger, Jeff
BIG BAD MAMA II

Yahn, Erica
AMAZON WOMEN ON THE MOON

Yakar, Rachel
ARIA

Yakovenko, Vadim
FAREWELL

Yakovlev, Sergei
MY OBVINYAEM

Yakovlev, Yuri
PRIZEMYAVANE

Yakovlev, Yury
KIN-DZA-DZA
LEVSHA

Yakovleva, Alexandra
PROSTI
TANTSPLOSHCHADKA

Yakovleva, Elena
PLIUMBUM, ILI OPASNAIA IGIA

Yakovleva, Marina
SNAYPERY

Yale, Stan
P.I. PRIVATE INVESTIGATIONS

Yama, Michael
WINNERS TAKE ALL

Yamada, Takao
EMPIRE OF THE SUN

Yamaguchi, Hirokazu
PRINCESS FROM THE MOON

Yamanoi, Katsumi
BUS

Yamanouchi, Haruhiko
SOTTO IL RISTORANTE CINESE

Yamashita, Daisuke
TAXING WOMAN, A

Yamashita, Shinji
TOKYO BLACKOUT

Yamazaki, Tsutomu
TAXING WOMAN, A

Yamone, Bruce
OVERKILL

Yandirer, Mehmed
CRAZY BOYS

Yandiyeva, Tamara
NOVYE SKAZKI SHAKHEREZADY

Yanez, David
MALIBU BIKINI SHOP, THE

Yanez, Eduardo
NARCOTERROR

Yanez, Ernesto
REALM OF FORTUNE, THE

Yang-Ha, Yoon
SIBAJI

Yankovsky, Filipp
SENTIMENTALNOE PUTESHESTVIE NA KARTOSHKU

Yankovsky, Oleg
KREUTZEROVA SONATA

Yannakopoulos, Dimitris
ONIRO ARISTERIS NICHTAS

Yannatos, Michael
PRETTY SMART
WIND, THE

Yanne, Jean
ATTENTION BANDITS
F . . . ING FERNAND
WOLF AT THE DOOR, THE

Yannou, Dina
WIND, THE

Yarbrough, Bill
PRINCIPAL, THE

Yarden, Hugu
YALDEI STALIN

Yarmolnik, Leonid
KONETS OPERATSII "REZIDENT"
LYUBOVYU ZA LYUBOV

Yarnall, Celeste
FATAL BEAUTY

Yarnell, Lorene
SPACEBALLS

Yaroshenko, Lyudmilla
TVOYO MIRNOE NEBO

Yarvet, Yuri
VO VREMENA VOLCHYIKA ZAKONOV

Yasbeck, Amy
HOUSE TWO: THE SECOND STORY

Yashima, Momo
BLIND DATE

Yasuaki, Kulada
NINJA THUNDERBOLT

Yasuda, Narumi
SOROBANZUKU

Yasulovich, Igor
MIO, MOY MIO
PO ZAKONU VOENNOGO VREMENI

Yates, Jim
MORGAN STEWART'S COMING HOME

Yatskina, Galina
TAYNOE PUTESHESTVIE EMIRA

Yazhou, Yang
BLACK CANNON INCIDENT, THE

Ybanez, Boy
OPPOSING FORCE

Ye, Lu
EMPIRE OF THE SUN

Yeager, Biff
WALKER

Yeager, Bill
BANZAI RUNNER

Yee, Chan Shuk
MIDNIGHT

Yegorova, Natalia
VOT MOYA DEREVNYA

Yeh, Sally
PEKING OPERA BLUES

Yeh, Tracey
NINJA THUNDERBOLT

Yekim, Letnam
NECROPOLIS

Yen, Ann
PRINCE OF DARKNESS

Yeoh, Eddie
EAT THE RICH

Yeremin, Vladimir
KRASNAYA STRELA

Yevgenyev, A.
VZLOMSHCHIK

Yi, Wang
BLACK CANNON INCIDENT, THE

Yilmaz, Levent
DEGIRMEN

Yilmaz, Sera
ANAYURT OTELI

Yimou, Zhang
OLD WELL

Yin, Lee Sau
CITY ON FIRE

Yin, Li Sau
RICH AND FAMOUS

Yin, Tsen
KILLER'S NOCTURNE

Ying
EASTERN CONDORS

Ying-Hung, Hui
STORY OF DR. SUN YAT-SEN, THE

Yip, Cecilia
WONDER WOMEN

Yip, David
OUT OF ORDER

Yiwei, Fu
LAST EMPRESS, THE

Ylitapio, Anne-Maria
KILL CITY

Yoham, James
IRONWEED

Yokoyama, Michiyo
PRINCESS FROM THE MOON

Yokoyama, Sakevi
ROBINSON NO NIWA

Yong-woo, Kil
NAE-SHI

York, Gerald
MALIBU BIKINI SHOP, THE

York, Kathleen
WINNERS TAKE ALL

York, Susannah
MIO, MOY MIO
PRETTYKILL

Yorke, Steve
BIG TOWN, THE

Yoshida, Hideaki
MAGINA—MURA MONOGATARI

Yoshinaga, Sayuri
EIGA JOYU

Youmans, William
NADINE

Young, Cedric
BIG SHOTS

Young, Cletus
IN THE MOOD

Young, Dey
RUNNING MAN, THE
SPACEBALLS

Young, Karen
HEAT
JAWS: THE REVENGE

Young, Kathi Sawyer
TALKING WALLS

Young, Neil
MADE IN HEAVEN

Young, Ray
HUNTER'S BLOOD

Young, Ric
DRAGON'S FOOD
LAST EMPEROR, THE

Young, Ruben
RAISING ARIZONA

Young, Sean
NO WAY OUT
WALL STREET

Young, Sharon
KILLER WORKOUT

Young, Tracy
WIND, THE

Young, Wycliffe
MONSTER IN THE CLOSET

Youngman, Henny
AMAZON WOMEN ON THE MOON

Youngs, Jim
HOT SHOT
YOU TALKIN' TO ME?

Yu, Fang Dong
MIRAGE

Yu, Li
LAST EMPEROR, THE

Yu, Ngan Lai
MIDNIGHT

Yuan, Jin
LAST EMPEROR, THE

Yuan-ting, Chang
HEROIC PIONEERS

Yuanik, Dilaver
DILAN

Yucekaya, Halil
CEMIL

Yueh, Suen
OUTSIDERS, THE

Yueh, Sun
CITY ON FIRE

Yuen, Barbara
NINJA THUNDERBOLT

Yujin, Liang
OLD WELL

Yuk, Henry
RADIO DAYS

Yukskyula, Aarne
REQUIEM

Yulin, Harris
BELIEVERS, THE

FATAL BEAUTY
Yumatov, Georgy
AKTSIA
Yun-fat, Chow
DIXIA QING
Yune, Johnny
THEY STILL CALL ME BRUCE
Yung, Galen
OVERKILL
Yunus, Tariq
FOURTH PROTOCOL, THE
Yurchenko, Valery
I NIKTO NA SVETE
Yurdashev, Bokhodyr
OKHOTA NA DRAKONA
Yuri, Toru
ITAZU
Yurttas, Savas
SON URFALI
Yustis, Carlos
TODA LA VIDA
Yusuf
DILAN
Yusupov, Yunus
KAPKAN DLYA SHAKALOV
Yusupova, Shukufa
LEGENDA SEREBRYANOGO OZERA
Z, Bunki
KINDRED, THE
Zaari, Maati
ISHTAR
Zabou
LE BEAUF
Zabriski, Grace
BIG EASY, THE
Zabriskie, Grace
LEONARD PART 6
Zabu
SHADEY
Zaccheddu, Zaira
LA CROCE DALLE SETTE PIETRE
Zacha, W.T.
IN THE MOOD
Zachar, Jan
PRATELE BERMUDSKEHO TROJUHELNIKU
Zacharakis, Costas
DOXOBUS
Zacharias, Ann
TESTET
Zacharias, Anne
TESTAMENT D'UN POETE JUIF ASSASSINE
Zacher, Rolf
CHINESE ARE COMING, THE
PENG! DU BIST TOT!
Zadok, Arnon
DEADLINE
DREAMERS
Zafer, Yilmaz
DILAN
Zafir, Yoav
LATE SUMMER BLUES
Zagaria, Anita
CHI C'E C'E
MAN ON FIRE
SEMBRA MORTO . . . ME E SOLO SVENUTO
Zagarino, Frank
ASSASSINATION
Zagoni, Zsolt
LUTRA
Zaharian, Ruth
ALLNIGHTER, THE
Zahed, Ataollah
SHEERE SANGGY
Zahrn, Will
IRONWEED
UNTOUCHABLES, THE
Zaitseva, Lyudmila
GOVORIT MOSKVA
Zaitsu, Ichiro
DIXIELAND DAIMYO
TOKYO BLACKOUT
Zajcova, Anda
POHADKA O MALICKOVI
Zakariadze, Nino
REPENTANCE
Zaki, Ahmed
ZAWGAT RAGOL MOHIM
Zakrzenski, Janusz
NAD NIEMNEM
Zaks, Jerry
OUTRAGEOUS FORTUNE
Zal, Roxana
RIVER'S EDGE
Zalazar, Delicia
EL SOCIO DE DIOS
Zaleski, Krzysztof
MATKA KROLOW
Zalewski, Igor
NOI UOMINI DURI
Zaliwski, Tomasz
ZLOTY POCIAG
Zamachowski, Zbigniew
PIERSCIEN I ROZA
Zamanskij, Vladimor
SKORBNOE BESCHUVSTVIE
Zamansky, Vladimir
RAZMAKH KRYLIEV
ZAVTRA BILA VOINA
Zambrano, Jose
MAS VALE PAJARO EN MANO . . .
RETO A LA VIDA
Zamora, Del
P.I. PRIVATE INVESTIGATIONS
ROBOCOP
STRAIGHT TO HELL
WALKER
Zand, Michael
CHECKPOINT
Zanelli, Eugenia
LA MONACA DIMONZA
Zaniboni, Giovanni
ADELMO
Zanin, Bruno
MORO AFFAIR, THE
Zanjanpour, Akbar
GOZARESH-E YEK GHATL
Zann, Lenore
GIRL, THE
PRETTYKILL
Zannino, Tressa
PSYCHOS IN LOVE
Zaorski, Andrzej
MASKARADA
Zapasiewicz, Zbigniew
BLIND CHANCE
C. K. DEZERTERZY
LAURA
MASKARADA
MATKA KROLOW
ZUHANAS KOZBEN
Zapata, Javier
LA OVEJA NEGRA
Zappa, Dweezil
RUNNING MAN, THE
Zaragoza, Greg
THIN LINE, THE
Zarchen, John
IN THE MOOD
SUPERNATURALS, THE
Zardi, Dominique
MASQUES
Zaremba, Justyna
E S D
Zarkadas, Christos
I KEKARMENI
Zarkov, Alexi
PROSTI
Zarpa, Zozo
PHOTOGRAPH, THE
Zarrabi, Morteza
PEDDLER, THE
Zarubica, Shawne
HARD TICKET TO HAWAII
Zarzo, Manolo
EL LUTE—CAMINA O REVIENTA
Zayas, Alfonso
ALBURES MEXICANOS
ENTRE FICHERAS ANDA EL DIABLO
ESTA NOCHE CENA PANCHO (DESPEDIDA DE SOLTERO)
Zborowski, Wiktor
C. K. DEZERTERZY
Zbruyev, Alexander
ODINOKAYA ZHENCHINA ZHELAET POZNAKOMITAYA
ZINA-ZINULYA
Zdar, Robert
NIGHT STALKER, THE
Zdenek, Jakub
CENA MEDU
Zdenicki, Marcin
PRZYJACIEL WESOLEGO DIABLA
Zech, Rosel
VERMISCHTE NACHRICHTEN
Zednicek, Pavel
CHOBOTNICE Z II. PATRA
Zehrova, Vlasta
POHADKA O MALICKOVI
Zelenkova, Jitka
WOLF'S HOLE
Zelles, Carole
STREET SMART
Zenios, George
FOURTH PROTOCOL, THE
Zentara, Edward
SIEKIEREZADA
Zepeda, Jorge
LETS GET HARRY
VA DE NUEZ
VIAJE AL PARAISO
Zeppari, Bernardo
ADELMO
Zerar, Alain
MASCARA
Zerbe, Anthony
OPPOSING FORCE
P.I. PRIVATE INVESTIGATIONS
STEEL DAWN
Zeri, Walter G.
IN THE MOOD
Zermeno, Alvaro
JUANA LA CANTINERA
YERBA SANGRIENTE
MI NOMBRE ES GATILLO
Zevnick, Neil
ISHTAR
Zewe, Jim
P.K. & THE KID
Zeza, Dimitra
ONIRO ARISTERIS NICHTAS
Zezima, Michael
NECROPOLIS
ROBOT HOLOCAUST
Zhang Daxing
LAST EMPEROR, THE
Zhang —Liangbin
LAST EMPEROR, THE
Zhao, Ge Yan
EMPIRE OF THE SUN
Zharkov, Aleksei
VINA LEYTENANTA NEKRASOVA
Zhendong, Dong
LAST EMPEROR, THE
Zhenduo, Li
LAST EMPEROR, THE
Zhigalov, Mikhail
PODSUDIMYY
Zhiji, Dan
DAO MAZEI
Zhubi, Hasan
AVRIL BRISE
Zhumartova, Saule
SKAZKA O PREKRASNOY AYSULU
Zhuravlyova, V.
VZLOMSHCHIK
Zhzhenov, Georgy
KONETS OPERATSII "REZIDENT"
Zien, Chip
HELLO AGAIN
Zifeng, Liu
BLACK CANNON INCIDENT, THE
CUO WEI
Zigler, Scott
HOUSE OF GAMES
Ziman, Sharon
TIN MEN
Zimkova, Emilia
PROC?
Zimmer, Pierre
KEEPING TRACK
Zimmerman, Natalie
LETHAL WEAPON
Zimmermann, Vera
BESAME MUCHO
Zingaretti, Luca
GLI OCCHIALI D'ORO
Zinny, Karl
LE FOTO DI GIOIA
Zinny, Vittoria
QUARTIERE

Zinsky, Nora
MISS MARY

Zipp, Debbie
LIKE FATHER, LIKE SON

Zipp, William
DEADLY PREY
MANKILLERS

Zischler, Hanns
DAS TREIBHAUS
TAROT

Ziskie, Dan
O. C. AND STIGGS

Zivkovic, Radmila
STRATEGIJA SVRAKE
UVEK SPREMNE ZENE

Zivojinovic, Bata
DIE VERLIEBTEN

Zivojinovic, Velimir-Bata
OKTOBERFEST

Zmozkova, Marketa
PROC?

Zobel, Richard
FROM THE HIP
WALKER

Zogbo Junior, Yves
LA VIE PLATINEE

Zogg, Andrea
JENATSCH

Zohar, Ika
CHOZE AHAVA
KFAFOT

Zohar, Ikka
LO SAM ZAYIN

Zohar, Ravit
CHOZE AHAVA

Zolnay, Pal
DIARY FOR MY LOVED ONES

Zolothukin, Dimitri
DARK EYES

Zolotukhin, Dimitry
ZNAY NASHIKH

Zolotukhin, Valery
CHELOVEK C AKKORDEONOM

Zong Wan, Wei
BUDDHA'S LOCK

Zoroiz, Jose Ramon
A LOS CUATRO VIENTOS

Zounar, Miroslav
CENA MEDU

Zouni, Pemy
APOUSIES

Zsoter, Sandor
HOTREAL
ISTEN VELETEK, BARATAIM

Zsuzsa Zczinkoczi
DIARY FOR MY LOVED ONES

Zuanic, Rod
TALE OF RUBY ROSE, THE
WARM NIGHTS ON A SLOW MOVING TRAIN

Zubiaga, Antonio
HERENCIA DE VALIENTES

Zucca, Jerome
BAD BLOOD

Zucchi, Augusto
LA MONACA DIMONZA
MORO AFFAIR, THE

Zucker, Miriam
STREET TRASH

Zudina, Marina
LICHNOE DELO SUDYI IVANOVOY
PO GLAVNOY ULITSE S ORKESTROM
VALENTIN I VALENTINA

Zuehlke, Joshua
AMAZING GRACE AND CHUCK

Zuiderhoek, Olga
VAN GELUK GESPROKEN

Zuk, Vadim
SKORBNOE BESCHUVSTVIE

Zumwalt, Rick
OVER THE TOP
PENITENTIARY III

Zuniga, Daphne
SPACEBALLS

Zuniga, Rosita
EULALIA

Zurita, Humberto
DE MUJER A MUJER
LO DEL CESAR

Zutant, Brad
PRETTY SMART

Zutaut, Brad
HOSTAGE SYNDROME
PRETTY SMART

Zutic, Milos
HEY BABU RIBA

Zuviria, Facundo
MISS MARY

Zvaric, Pavel
PROC?

Zweigenbom, Dor
LATE SUMMER BLUES

ANIMATION

Armstrong, John
WITCHES OF EASTWICK, THE

Bristow, Becky
CHIPMUNK ADVENTURE, THE

Catizone, Rick
CREEPSHOW 2

Caza, Philippe
GANDAHAR

Celestri, John
PINOCCHIO AND THE EMPEROR OF THE NIGHT

Chevallier, Wolfgang
DER BARENHAUTER

Collins, John Laurence
CARE BEARS ADVENTURE IN WONDERLAND, THE

Ebert, Heiko
DER BARENHAUTER

Gaskill, Andrew
CHIPMUNK ADVENTURE, THE

Gemes, Jozsef
CAT CITY

Green, Chris
WITCHES OF EASTWICK, THE

Gunther, Erich
DER BARENHAUTER

Harvey, Chuck
PINOCCHIO AND THE EMPEROR OF THE NIGHT

Henderson, Kirk
FLICKS

Henry, Athol
DOT GOES TO HOLLYWOOD

Jones, Skip
CHIPMUNK ADVENTURE, THE

Katto, Seishi
CHOBOTNICE Z II. PATRA

Lichtwardt, Ellen
WITCHES OF EASTWICK, THE

Loeser, Tony
DER BARENHAUTER

Maros, Zoltan
CAT CITY

Rochon, Mitch
CHIPMUNK ADVENTURE, THE

Song, Kamoon
PINOCCHIO AND THE EMPEROR OF THE NIGHT

Spencer, Don
CHIPMUNK ADVENTURE, THE

Stout Studio
BIG BANG, THE

Vojta, J.
CHOBOTNICE Z II. PATRA

Wittstock, Frank
DER BARENHAUTER

ART DIRECTORS

Abdullayev, Abdulsalom
KAPKAN DLYA SHAKALOV

Abdurakhmanov, Arif
CHKATULKA IZ KREPOSTI

Abed, Hisham
ZOMBIE HIGH

Abreu, Ana Maria
CIDADE OCULTA

Abuseif, Onsy
ZAWGAT RAGOL MOHIM

Acin, Sava
HEY BABU RIBA

Ackland-Snow, Terry
LIVING DAYLIGHTS, THE

Adabachian, Alexander
DARK EYES

Adipietro, Phil
BLOODY WEDNESDAY

Agabekov, Mais
LEGENDA SEREBRYANOGO OZERA

Agate, Carmelo
SPECTERS

Agliotti, Antonello
CARTOLINE ITALIANE

Agoyan, Sovet
ZINA-ZINULYA

Agranov, Vladimir
I NIKTO NA SVETE

Ahmad, Maher
BIG TOWN, THE

Allen, James
REAL MEN

Almonacid, Esmeralda
MISS MARY

Amaral, Cristiano
NIGHT ANGELS

Amelchenko, Viktor
SON V RUKU, ILI CHEMODON

Amelnikov, Viktor
VOT MOYA DEREVNYA

Amend, Richard
MANNEQUIN

Amies, Caroline
EAT THE RICH

Ammerlaan, Harry
TERUG NAAR OEGSTGEEST

Andranikyan, Stepan
ZEMLYA I ZOLOTO

Andre, Dominique
NOYADE INTERDITE
SPIRALE

Andres, Gomer
ALIEN PREDATOR

Anfilov, Anatoly
SDELKA

Anfilova, Galina
GOVORIT MOSKVA

Antone, Icar
STRAKH

Aranburuzabala, Mikel
EL AMOR DE AHORA

Aravadinou, Marilena
APOUSIES

Ardjevanidze, Temur
NEYLONOVAYA YOLKA

Arganov, Vladimir
MY OBVINYAEM
MY OBVINYAEM

Arnold, Nancy
OMEGA SYNDROME

Aronshon, Sergio
HA INSTALATOR

Arseny Klopotovsky
OBESHCHAYU BYT

Astich-Barre, Frederic
LA BRUTE

Atayeva, Viktoria
PRIKLYUCHENIA NA MALENKIKH OSTROVEKH

Attrill, Sandy
SATURDAY NIGHT AT THE PALACE

Attrill, Wayne
SATURDAY NIGHT AT THE PALACE

Au, Tony
LAONIANG GOU SAO
SWORN BROTHERS

Avakov, Konstantin
NOVYE SKAZKI SHAKHEREZADY

Avanesov, Eduard
VINA LEYTENANTA NEKRASOVA

Avivi, Avi
EMPEROR'S NEW CLOTHES, THE

Azyzyan, Marina
OBRYV

Babayan, Rafael
ODINOKAYA ORESHINA

Babayan, Raphael
PESN PROSHEDSHIKH DNEY

Badurashvili, Nodar
PYAT NEVEST DO LYUBIMOY

Bahovec, Roman
USODNI TELEFON

Ballowe, John
MUNCHIES

Banovich, Tamas
SZORNYEK EVADJA

Barbasso, Maria Teresa
LAST EMPEROR, THE

Barclay, William
HELLO AGAIN

Barda, Suzy
HIMMO MELECH YERUSHALAIM

Barrett, Keith
BLOOD DINER

Barreus, Anders
GIRL, THE

Bartholomew, Marie Louise
PROINI PERIPOLOS

Baruti, Barly
LA VIE EST BELLE

Barzily, Yoram
DEADLINE

Basili, Giancarlo
NOTTE ITALIANA

Bassan, Davide
OPERA

Bauer, Franz
POET'S SILENCE, THE

Bauer, Jean
LE BEAUF

Bazerolle, Jean-Pierre
CLUB DE RENCONTRES
IL EST GENIAL PAPY!

Bennett, Randy
EVIL DEAD 2: DEAD BY DAWN

Benoit-Frecso, Francoise
MASQUES

Bertotto, Julie
AMAZONS

Besinger, Joanne
ENEMY TERRITORY

Biagetti, Paolo
CAPRICCIO

Biesiot, Freek
VROEGER IS DOOD

Biessiot, Freek
NITWITS

Billerman, Mark
PRINCIPAL, THE

Bingham, Mike
NIGHTFLYERS

Bishop, Charles
EMPIRE OF THE SUN

Bishop, Dan
MATEWAN

Blackman, Jack
FATAL ATTRACTION
MAKING MR.RIGHT
WHO'S THAT GIRL

Blanchard, David
ZOMBIE NIGHTMARE

Block, Becky
KINDRED, THE
TRESPASSES

Bogorodsky, Dmitry
NABAT NA RASSVETE

Boim, Alexander
CHELOVEK C AKKORDEONOM

Borecki, Andrzej
CUDZOZIEMKA

Borisov, Alexander
IZ ZHIZNI POTAPOVA

Borland, Jody
DOGS IN SPACE

Bosselman, Carol
HANOI HILTON, THE

Bozhkova, Yuliana
PRIZEMYAVANE

Bradford, Dennis
FROM THE HIP

Brinkers, Gert
DE ORIONNEVEL

Brockliss, Anthony
NO WAY OUT

Brover, Yves
NOCE EN GALILEE
TESTAMENT D'UN POETE JUIF ASSASSINE

Brown, Ray
BENJI THE HUNTED

Bruley, Laurence
POISONS

Bryl, Igor
DVOE POD ODNIM ZONTOM
SEZON CHUDES

Buchanan, Michael
GOTHIC

Buck, William
THREE FOR THE ROAD

Bufnoir, Jacques
ATTENTION BANDITS
F . . . ING FERNAND

Burbank, Lynda
BORN IN EAST L.A.

Burchiellaro, Giantito
MAN ON FIRE

Burchilliaro, Giantito
HOTEL COLONIAL

Burdick, Sarah
WITCHBOARD

Burian-Mohr, Chris
SOMEONE TO WATCH OVER ME

Burke, Chris
WHISTLE BLOWER, THE

Burmistrov, Boris
SENTIMENTALNOE PUTESHESTVIE NA KARTOSHKU
SLUCHAYNYE PASSAZHIRY
SOPERNITSY

Capetanos, Leon
INTERVISTA

Capra, Bernt Amadeus
OUT OF ROSENHEIM

Capuano, Mario-Angela
FRANCESCA

Carinhas, Nuno
DUMA VEZ POR TODAS

Carlos Prieto
FONTE DA SAUDADE

Carmona, Luis Manuel
LAS DOS ORILLAS

Caro, Rafael
BEDROOM WINDOW, THE

Carter, Rick
TALKING WALLS

Cassidy, William J.
REAL MEN

Castillo, Toto
HAMBURGER HILL

Caziot, Jean-Jacques
LANNEE DES MEDUSES

Cervinka, Milos
POHADKA O MALICKOVI

Challier, Alain
TERMINUS

Chan, David
CHOCOLATE INSPECTOR

Chan, Raymond
SEVEN YEARS ITCH

Chang, William
DIXIA QING

Charette, Cyntha Kay
HES MY GIRL

Chernyayev, Evgeny
LYUBOVYU ZA LYUBOV

Cherry, Kathy Emily
ERNEST GOES TO CAMP

Chertovich, Alexander
SNAYPERY

Chetwyn, Derrick
COMRADES

Chiari, Mario
I MIEI PRIMI QUARANT'ANNI
VIA MONTENAPOLEONE

Childs, Peter
ISHTAR

Chiti, Ugo
STREGATI

Choi, Hua Wing
MIDNIGHT

Chorney, Jo Ann
SUPERNATURALS, THE

Cielewicz, Tadeusz
PAN SAMOCHODZIK I NIESAMOWITY DWOR

Clement, Jerome
GRAND GUIGNOL

Cochetti, Ranieri
UN RAGAZZO DI CALABRIA

Colby, Alexander M.
THUNDER WARRIOR II

Coleman, Jane
PERSONAL SERVICES

Conrad, Albrect
MASCHENKA

Corenblith, Michael
BURGLAR

Corevi, Massimo
IL BURBERO

Cornford, Bill
P.K. & THE KID

Costello, George
DISORDERLIES

Craig, Alan Hunter
THREE KINDS OF HEAT

Crisanti, Andrea
CHRONICLE OF A DEATH FORETOLD
DEVIL IN THE FLESH

Cruz, Ronnie
EQUALIZER 2000

Culp, Joshua S.
ASSASSINATION

Cunningham, Cliff
SPACE RACE

Cusack, Marty
DANGER ZONE, THE

Czettel, Rudolf
DIE DRECKSCHLEUDER

Dagort, Phil
DUTCH TREAT

Daneau, Violette
BACH AND BROCCOLI
GREAT LAND OF SMALL, THE

Danielsen, Dins
VALET GIRLS

Danielson, Dins
IN THE MOOD

Dasgupta, Bijon
PRATIGHAAT

de Andrade, Francisco
NIGHT ANGELS

de Paco, Felipe
ANGUSTIA

de Souza, Sebastiao
ANJOS DO ARRABALDE

Debou, Dirk
MASCARA

Dein, Robert
GROUND ZERO

Dekawa, Mitsuo
FINAL TAKE: THE GOLDEN AGE OF MOVIES
TORA-SAN'S BLUEBIRD FANTASY

Del Rosario, Linda
FAMILY VIEWING

Deleu, Francoise
LASSOCIATION DES MALFAITEURS

Dementyev, Vladimir
ZNAK BEDY

Demusiak, Kirk
RAGE OF HONOR

Dentici, Marco
RIMINI RIMINI

Deskin, Andrew
HIGHER EDUCATION

Despotovic, Veljko
DIE VERLIEBTEN

Di Salvor, Anibal
EL DUENO DEL SOL

di Santo, Byrnadette
OUT OF ROSENHEIM

Dick, Douglas
MY DEMON LOVER

Diers, Don
HOUSE TWO: THE SECOND STORY

diSanto, Byrnadette
SURF NAZIS MUST DIE

Dobrina, Stanko
OFICIR S RUZOM

Dobrowolska, Halina
MASKARADA

Doherty, Tom
CONCRETE ANGELS

Dominquez, Enrique
ROBACHICOS

Donati, Danilo
INTERVISTA

Dorme, Norman
CRY FREEDOM
EMPIRE OF THE SUN

Dorrington, Chris
HOT PURSUIT

Dossett, Don
HOPE AND GLORY

Dostal, Martin
MEIER

Dubois, Paulo
BAIXO GAVEA

Dubus, Jack
BAD BLOOD

Duffield, Tom
LOST BOYS, THE

Duffin, Philip
CLUB LIFE
EVIL DEAD 2: DEAD BY DAWN
Dugied, Jacques
CHARLIE DINGO
LETE EN PENTE DOUCE
Dultz, Jim
OVERBOARD
Dumala, Piotr
PRZYJACIEL WESOLEGO DIABLA
Dunlop, Charles
MORNING MAN, THE
Dunphy, Barbara
HEARTS OF FIRE
Dyk, Dao
KOORDINATY SMERTI
Edgar, Craig
MIRACLES
Elliot, Bill
CROSS MY HEART
Elliott, William
THROW MOMMA FROM THE TRAIN
Elliott, William A.
UNTOUCHABLES, THE
Elton, Philip
PRICK UP YOUR EARS
Elton, Richard
MONTH IN THE COUNTRY, A
Engfeld, Dotty
WIND, THE
Ereth, Renate
DER UNSICHTBARE
Ershov, Vyacheslav
GRUZ BEZ MARKIROVKI
Esteban, Julio
LA ESTANQUERA DE VALLECAS
Eue, Ralph
STADTRAND
Facello, Abel
RAGE OF HONOR
Farbikov, Vladimir
KREUTZEROVA SONATA
Farchi, Tali
YEHOSHUA—YEHOSHUA
Farquhar, Melba Katzman
HOLLYWOOD SHUFFLE
Faure, Alain
EMMANUELLE 5
Fawdry, Richard
WHEN THE WIND BLOWS
Filippov, Valery
WEEKEND
Fiorentini, Enrico
I PICARI
Fischer, David
ROXANNE
Flaksman, Paulo
ELE, O BOTO
Flamand, Thierry
LE GRAND CHEMIN
Flating, Janice
OPPOSING FORCE
Fomina, Elena
DUBLYOR NACHINAET DEYSTVOVAT
Fomina, Yelena
PODSUDIMYY
Foreman, Philip Dean
SLAMDANCE
Forestenko, Konstantin
SEKUNDA NA PODVIG
Forostenko, Konstantin
KURIER
Forsmith, Douglas
HUNTER'S BLOOD
Fowler, Maurice
EMPIRE OF THE SUN
Fox, Bob
WHALES OF AUGUST, THE
Fox, J. Rae
BORN IN EAST L.A.
Fox, K.C.
WHALES OF AUGUST, THE
Franenberg, Barry
SUMMER CAMP NIGHTMARE
Freed, Reuben
BLUE MONKEY
HOUSEKEEPER, THE
NIGHTSTICK
Freitag, Craig
PENITENTIARY III

Frigeri, Francesco
MORO AFFAIR, THE
Fuller, Rhiley
POLICE ACADEMY 4: CITIZENS ON PATROL
Fulton, Larry
HOUSE TWO: THE SECOND STORY
Fung, Luk Tze
CITY ON FIRE
PRISON ON FIRE
Gailling, Hans
DER UNSICHTBARE
Galloin, Jean-Claude
LE SOLITAIRE
Gallouin, Jean-Claude
MALADIE D'AMOUR
Gang, Yang
OLD WELL
Ganz, Armin
ANGEL HEART
Garakanidze, Mikhail
TAYNY MADAM VONG
Garbuglia, Mario
DARK EYES
Garlington, Rick
BLOODSUCKERS FROM OUTER SPACE
Gattoni, Pierre
PIERRE ET DJEMILA
Gaudry, Alain
LA VIE DISSOLUE DE GERARD FLOQUE
Gaukhman-Sverdlov, Marksen
POSLEDNYAYA DOROGA
Gaukman-Sverdlov, Marksen
TEMA
Geskus, Rebecca
ALS IN EEN ROES
Gillis, Richard
EVIL TOWN
Gimenez, Raul
JENATSCH
Ginn, Jeffrey S.
DATE WITH AN ANGEL
Giovagnoni, Gianni
LAST EMPEROR, THE
Gloor, Hans
DER NACHBAR
Goetz, Jindrich
CHOBOTNICE Z II. PATRA
Goldstein, Jeffrey L.
WHITE WATER SUMMER
Golikov, Vassily
PO ZAKONU VOENNOGO VREMENI
Gonzalez, Donnie
NO DEAD HEROES
Gorelik, Marc
TAYNAYA PROGULKA
Gorelik, Mark
KONETS OPERATSII "REZIDENT"
Goulder, Susan
I WAS A TEENAGE T.V. TERRORIST
Graham, Angelo
BATTERIES NOT INCLUDED
Grall, Valerie
LES MOIS D'AVRIL SONT MEURTRIERS
Greenbaum, Billie
BIG BAD MAMA II
Groom, Bill
ISHTAR
PICK-UP ARTIST, THE
Gropman, David
O. C. AND STIGGS
Grusd, John
PINOCCHIO AND THE EMPEROR OF THE NIGHT
Guerin, Andre
WOLF AT THE DOOR, THE
Guerra, Robert
IRONWEED
Gui, Huang Qia
EMPIRE OF THE SUN
Guise, Roger
STARLIGHT HOTEL
Gukov, Yevgeny
KRASNAYA STRELA
Gulbin, Mike
NIGHTFORCE
Gulenko, Igor
PROSHAL ZELEN LETA
TAYNOE PUTESHESTVIE EMIRA
Haack, Mark
DIRTY DANCING

Haber, David M.
MONSTER SQUAD, THE
Hajdu, Alex
AMAZON WOMEN ON THE MOON
Hall, Tony
SUSPECT
Halmi, Boris
PRATELE BERMUDSKEHO TROJUHELNIKU
PROC?
Hanania, Caroline
STRAIGHT TO HELL
Haninia, Caroline
HIGH SEASON
Hardwicke, Catherine
HUNK
Harris, Henry
COMRADES
LONELY PASSION OF JUDITH HEARNE,THE
WITHNAIL AND I
Hausmanis, Andris
PRETTYKILL
TOO OUTRAGEOUS
Hayashida, Yuji
ROBINSON NO NIWA
Hedal, Karl-Otto
WOLF AT THE DOOR, THE
Heidecke, Marianne
OUTTAKES
Held, Bruno
UN AMOUR A PARIS
Hershkowitz, Zmira
LATE SUMMER BLUES
Hill, Geoff
HOSTAGE
Hing, Leung Chi
PEKING OPERA BLUES
Hofer-Ach, Robert
WANNSEE CONFERENCE, THE
Hole, Frederick
EMPIRE OF THE SUN
Holland, Richard
PRINCESS BRIDE, THE
Holt, Willy
AU REVOIR, LES ENFANTS
Hopkins, Speed
RADIO DAYS
SEPTEMBER
Howland, Robert
BEST SELLER
MASTERS OF THE UNIVERSE
Hudolin, Richard
STAKEOUT
Hummell, Richard
DOWN TWISTED
Huntingford, Len
RAWHEAD REX
RITA, SUE AND BOB TOO!
WHITE MISCHIEF
Hutchinson, Tim
FOURTH PROTOCOL, THE
Hutman, Jon
SIESTA
SURRENDER
WANTED: DEAD OR ALIVE
Hwa, Liu Ji
LIEN LIEN FUNG CHEN
Hyrak, Toomas
CHEREZ STO LET V MAE
Iglesias, Alfredo
CHECHECHELA—UNA CHICA DEL BARRIO
Ikuno, Juichi
TOKYO BLACKOUT
Ilander, Kicki
SERPENT'S WAY, THE
Irwin, Colin
NIGHTFORCE
Ishige, Akira
ROBINSON NO NIWA
Istikopoulou, Thalia
TA PAIDIA TIS CHELIDONAS
Istratov, Yury
ZHELEZNOE POLE
Ituarte, Agustin
LETS GET HARRY
Ivanov, Oleg
RAZMAKH KRYLIEV
Ivanov, Vladlen
O ROZVRASHCHENII ZABYT
Ivars, Ramon B.
LESCOT

Ivezic, Mario
KRALJEVA ZAVRSNICA

Iyevleva, Natalia
MILLION V BRACHNOY KORZINE

Jacques, Serge
STREET SMART

James, Jocelyn
HELLRAISER

James, Peter
MAURICE

Jasmin
JESTER,THE

Javonillo, John
DIRTY LAUNDRY

Jenkinson, Robert
AMERICAN NINJA 2: THE CONFRONTATION

Johansson, Pelle
SERPENT'S WAY, THE

Johnson, Bo
SUMMER HEAT

Joyce, Robert
STUDENT CONFIDENTIAL

Junqueira, Juliana
A DANCA DOS BONECOS

Kalganov, Georgy
VYKUP

Kalinauskas, Vitautas
IZVINITEPOZHALUYSTA

Kamaya, Benjie
ULTIMAX FORCE

Kanardova, Alexandra
KOROTKIE VSTRECHI

Kann, Hadassah
EEN MAAND LATER

Kantake, Tsuneo
TOO MUCH

Kaplan, Corey
COMMANDO SQUAD

Kapouralis, Petros
HIGH SEASON

Karafilis, Simos
YENETHLIA POLI

Karapiperis, Mikes
DOXOBUS

Kasarda, John
BELIEVERS, THE
GLASS MENAGERIE, THE

Kasymaliev, Zholtzotbek
VOLNY UMIRAYUT NA BEREGU

Katsoulogiannakis, Dora
I WAS A TEENAGE ZOMBIE

Katz, Mikhail
POEZD VNE RASPISANIA

Kazorezenko, Pyotr
DIKIY KHMEL

Kedmi, Ron
HIMMO MELECH YERUSHALAIM

Keen, Gregory
ADVENTURES IN BABYSITTING

Keita, Kossa Mody
YEELEN

Kelly, Errol
WITNESS TO A KILLING

Khamdamov, Rustam
YA TEBYA POMNYU

Khon, Kim Chkhol
SEKUNDA NA PODVIG

Khrac, Tomas
REQUIEM

Kight, Lisa
TRESPASSES

Kimura, Takee
SHINRAN: SHIRO MICHI

King, John
CRY FREEDOM

Kladiyenko, Yury
ZONTIK DLYA NOVOBRACHNYKH

Klicus, Galgos
MOYA MALENKAYA ZHENA

Kochurov, Anatoli
ZAVTRA BILA VOINA

Kolganov, Georgy
VALENTIN I VALENTINA

Koliopandos, G.
WIND, THE

Kolman, Ronald
SEREBRYANAYA PRYAZHA KAROLINY

Konik, Marc
DVOE POD ODNIM ZONTOM

Konovalov, Valentin
PO GLAVNOY ULITSE S ORKESTROM
VOENNO-POLEVOI ROMAN

Kosarewicz, Tadeusz
W ZAWIESZENIU

Kostin, Vladimir
CHUZHIE ZDES NE KHODYAT

Kott, Jan
ZABOU

Kotzia, Aphrodite
VIOS KE POLITIA

Krakovsky, M.
DVADTSTAT DNEI BEZ

Kravchenya, Olga
LICHNOE DELO SUDYI IVANOVOY

Kropachyov, Georgy
OGNI

Krumpeter, Jochen
LITTLE PROSECUTOR, THE

Kuitka, Guillermo
EIN BLICK-UND DIE LIEBE BRICHT AUS

Kukenkov, Valery
ZOLOTAYA BABA

Kusakova, Lyudmila
PLOSHCHAD VOSSTANIA

Kuznetsov, Alexander
CHYORNAYA STRELA

Kyle, Leigh
SHE MUST BE SEEING THINGS

Labarthe, Francois-Renaud
BUISSON ARDENT

Labelle, Denise
STREET TRASH

Landau, Eli
TEL AVIV—BERLIN

Lanier, Jessica
SALVATION!

Laperadze, Guiya
STUPEN

Lapshina, Tatiana
VREMYA ZHELANIY

Lasic, Vladislav
OKTOBERFEST

Lavallen, Julio
A DOS AGUAS

Lazarevski, Nikola
HI-FI

Lebedev, Vladimir
ODINOKIJ GOLOS CELOVEKA

Lednev, Viktor
ZNAY NASHIKH

Lee, Jennifer
TOUGH COP

Legler, Steve
MADE IN HEAVEN

Leguillon, Jacques
LE CRI DU HIBOU

Lehmann, Paul
DER BARENHAUTER

Lelouda, Dora
FAKELOS POLK STON AERA

Lemeshev, Igor
KREUTZEROVA SONATA

Lenpold, Harri
VERNEHMUNG DER ZEUGEN

Leon, Charlie
POET'S SILENCE, THE

Leonard, Douglas H.
DOWN TWISTED

Lepp, Karine
EVA: GUERRILLERA

Leung, Eagle
NINJA THUNDERBOLT

Levchenko, Alexei
ODINOKAYA ZHENCHINA ZHELAET
POZNAKOMITAYA

Levy, Eitan
BOUBA

Levy, Etan
SNOW WHITE

Levy, Georges
TRAVELLING AVANT

Li, Andy
TRUE COLORS

Licheri, Giovanni
ROBA DA RICCHI

Liebetanz, Joe
STADTRAND

Lier, Karel
DEATH OF A BEAUTIFUL DREAM

Lineweaver, Stephen
DIRTY DANCING

Liu, Bennie
BETTER TOMORROW, A

Lopate, Joan
DEADTIME STORIES

Lounsbury, Ruth
DEADLY ILLUSION
NECROPOLIS
ROBOT HOLOCAUST

Lukovac, Predrag
STRATEGIJA SVRAKE

Luna, Alejandro
GABY—A TRUE STORY

Lundberg, Karin
WARDOGS

Luppi, Giorgio
DA NNUNZIO

Madsen, Peter
VALHALLA

Magallon, Francisco
MISSION KILL

Majlitis, Ivar
POHADKA O MALICKOVI

Makarov, Alexander
CHELOVEK C AKKORDEONOM

Makris, Miltiadis
O PARADISSOS ANIGI ME ANTIKLIDI

Maleret, Dominique
POUSSIERE D'ANGE

Malkov, Mikhail
SLEDY OBOROTNYA

Man, Kenneth Yee Chung
LEGEND OF WISELY, THE

Man, Lee King
EASTERN CONDORS

Mansbridge, Mark
WITCHES OF EASTWICK, THE

Marchione, Luigi
DANCERS

Markovich, Yevgeny
TANTSPLOSHCHADKA

Martinez, Ana Maria
RETO A LA VIDA

Maruyama, Yuji
SARABA ITOSHIKI HITO YO

Matolin, Jiri
DISCOPRIBEH

Matos, Jose
O DESEJADO—LES MONTAGNES DE LA LUNE

Matthews, William
INNERSPACE

Matthews, William F.
HAPPY NEW YEAR

Matthies, Mathias
CRIME OF HONOR

Maussion, Ivan
TANDEM

Mayer-Woppermann, Katharina
DRAGON'S FOOD

Mazursky, Paul
INTERVISTA

McClellan, Peg
TEEN WOLF TOO

McCoin, Roger
EVIL SPAWN

McDonald, Leslie
SHY PEOPLE

McEntee, Brian
BRAVE LITTLE TOASTER, THE

McGuire, Richard
MISSION KILL

McManus, Jeff
THEY STILL CALL ME BRUCE

Medeiros, Anisio
A DANCA DOS BONECOS

Melery, Veronique
LES NOCES BARBARES

Melton, Gregory
ZERO BOYS, THE

Melton, Larry
RETURN OF JOSEY WALES, THE

Mendez, Martha
HOUR OF THE ASSASSIN

Merkmanis, Andris
OBOROTEN TOM

Mery, Etienne
LE MIRACULE
Meurisse, Theo
LEVY ET GOLIATH
MON BEL AMOUR, MA DECHIRURE
Michelson, Harold
PLANES, TRAINS AND AUTOMOBILES
SPACEBALLS
Michnevich, Anamarie
TAROT
Migulko, Victor
KONTRUDAR
Mikeladze, Georgy
KRUGOVOROT
Ming-Tang, Lai
TERRORIZERS, THE
Miric, Miodrag
NA PUTA ZA KATANGU
Mirzashvili, Revaz
VELIKIY POKHOD ZA NEVESTOY
Mladenova, Valentin
TRINAJSTATA GODENICA NA PRINCA
Modai, Michel
LES OREILLES ENTRE LES DENTS
Molinelli, Tom
STREET TRASH
Monteiro, Mauro
MASSACRE IN DINOSAUR VALLEY
Montero, Luis
O DESEJADO—LES MONTAGNES DE LA LUNE
Montesi, Jorge
BIRDS OF PREY
Montiel, Cecilia
WALKER
Moore, Jay
SOMEONE TO WATCH OVER ME
Moore, John Jay
ORPHANS
WALL STREET
Mordfin, Susan
OPEN HOUSE
Morin, Loula
TANT QU'IL AURA DES FEMMES
Mputu, Mutoke Wa
LA VIE EST BELLE
Muhlfriedel, Mick
RIVER'S EDGE
Murakami, James J.
BEVERLY HILLS COP II
Murakoshi, Souki
BUS
Murphy, Matthew
NGATI
Myhre, John
AMAZING GRACE AND CHUCK
Naert, Didier
LE MOUSTACHU
Nagayev, Rais
KARUSEL NA BAZARNOY PLOSHCHADI
PRODELKI V STARINNOM DUKHE
Nakamura, Shuji
TAXING WOMAN, A
Nardone, Robert
SALE DESTIN!
Neal, Susan
SULLIVAN'S PAVILION
Neel, Beala
BABY BOOM
Nemec, Joseph C.
EXTREME PREJUDICE
Nemechek, Eleonora
POLEVAYA GVARDIA MOZZHUKHINA
Nicdao, Ramon
NO DEAD HEROES
Nikoladze, Noshrevan
STUPEN
Nikolayeva, E.
VZLOMSHCHIK
Nishioka, Yoshinobu
DEATH SHADOWS
Norton, Escott
SLAVE GIRLS FROM BEYOND INFINITY
Novak, Frank
SLUMBER PARTY MASSACRE II
Nowak, Christopher
SQUEEZE, THE
O'Connor, A. Kendall
BRAVE LITTLE TOASTER, THE
Odalovic, Bosko
U IME NARODA
Odinayev, Rustam
MIRAZHI LYUBRI
Ohrbach, Yosi
HA INSTALATOR
Olivo, Pablo
EN RETIRADA
Olmo, Arturo
EL GRAN SERAFIN
Oludhe, Winnie
KOLORMASK
Orbom, Eric
NUTS
Ortolani, Stefano
SICILIAN, THE
Osawa, Minoru
ROBINSON NO NIWA
Pain, Keith
FULL METAL JACKET
PRINCESS BRIDE, THE
Palmero, Rafael
LA RUSA
Panosian, W.
SASHSHENNYI FONAR
Pantages, George
LADIES OF THE LOTUS
Pashkevich, Pyotr
KOORDINATY SMERTI
Paton, Alastair
HIDDEN CITY
Patrono, Carmelo
SOTTO IL RISTORANTE CINESE
Paul, Vicki
ISHTAR
Paultre, Olivier
POULE ET FRITES
Pavel Pitner
SOMMER
Peckre, Thomas
BAD BLOOD
Pedreira, Luis
MADE IN ARGENTINA
Peduzzi, Richard
LHOMME VOILE
Perederi, Oleg
KOROTKIE VSTRECHI
Perera, K.A. Milton
VIRAGAYA
Perranso, Vincent
ADVENTURE OF THE ACTION HUNTERS
Perrin, Bryce
TALE OF RUBY ROSE, THE
Perryman, Dian
MALIBU BIKINI SHOP, THE
NEAR DARK
Pessoa, Paulo Henrique
A DANCA DOS BONECOS
Petrov, Boris
LERMONTOV
Petrovic, Nemanja
UVEK SPREMNE ZENE
Pezanou, Lili
ARCHANGELOS TOU PATHOUS
Phelps, D. Gary
IF LOOKS COULD KILL
WIMPS
Phelps, Nigel
WISH YOU WERE HERE
Pickrell, Greg
SOME KIND OF WONDERFUL
Pinter, Herbert
MOVING TARGETS
Plakhov, Leonid
OCHNAYA STAVKA
Plastinkin, Ivan
UTRO OBRECHENNOGO PRIISKA
Plate, Roberto
FUEGOS
Platov, Leonid
DIKIY KHMEL
Pomeroy, William
SPACE RACE
Pouille, Hubert
LOVE IS A DOG FROM HELL
Poveda, Jean-Louis
LETE DERNIER A TANGER
Preston, Earl
JOHN AND THE MISSUS
Prokopets, Georgy
TVOYO MIRNOE NEBO
Proulx, Michel
LES FOUS DE BASSAN
Pruess, Mark
DEADTIME STORIES
Putowski, Maciej
SIEKIEREZADA
Rabinowicz, Mort
LETS GET HARRY
Rafter, Nick
P.I. PRIVATE INVESTIGATIONS
Ralph, John
BELLMAN AND TRUE
Ramirez, Fernando
HOT PURSUIT
Ramirez "El Polo, Fernando
MIRACLES
Ramonkulov, Sergei
V TALOM SNEGE ZVON RUCHIA
YA YEY NRAVLYUS
Raney, Susan
HEART
Raubertas, Paul
STRIPPED TO KILL
Reading, Tony
ISHTAR
Reinhart, John K.
PREDATOR
Renault, Patrice
LE MIRACULE
Renha, Lia
UM TREM PARA AS ESTRELAS
Ricceri, Luciano
FAMILY, THE
GLI OCCHIALI D'ORO
Rice, Stephen
LESS THAN ZERO
Richards, Craig
PSYCHO GIRLS
Richardson, " George
MIRACLES
Richardson, George
CRY FREEDOM
Richwood, Frank
DRAGNET
PREDATOR
Riggs, Bob
BENJI THE HUNTED
Ritter, Michael
STAKEOUT
Rjachovsky, Roman
CENA ODVAHY
Rochline, David
JEUX D'ARTIFICES
Rodrigues, E.
DOLGHYIE PROVOD
Rodriguez, Hector
BORN IN EAST L.A.
Roelfs, Jan
HAVINCK
Roelofs, Jan
BLOND DOLLY
Rollison, Richard
SPACE RACE
Romankulov, Sergey
MIRAZHI LYUBRI
Romanovsky, Stanislav
PROSTI
Rooker, Richard
FRENCHMAN'S FARM
Rosenstein, Mikhail
V STRELYAYUSHCHEY GLUSHI
Rouse, Virginia
TO MARKET, TOMARKET
Roy, Nitish
TAMAS
Rozewicz, Zenon
NAD NIEMNEM
Ruben, Denise
MORE BAD NEWS
Rubino, Beth
FIREHOUSE
Russell, Blake
LEONARD PART 6
Saenz, Jorge
PREDATOR
Safronov, Viktor
KORABL PRISHELTSEV
Sainz, Jorge
WALKER

Sajko, Jerzy
ZYGFRYD
Sakagu, Ela
YALDEI STALIN
Samulekin, Alexander
KIN-DZA-DZA
Sancha, Jun
GET THE TERRORISTS
HOSTAGE SYNDROME
Sanchez, Anna
REALM OF FORTUNE, THE
Sanktjohanser, Josef
ZARTLICHE CHAOTEN
Sardanis, Steve
SUSPECT
Saulnier, Jacques
LES EXPLOITS DUN JEUNE DON JUAN
Sauriol, Gaudeline
LE SOURD DANS LA VILLE
Saushin, Nikolai
PRODELKI V STARINNOM DUKHE
Saushkin, Nikolai
KARUSEL NA BAZARNOY PLOSHCHADI
Sbarra, Gianni
GOOD MORNING BABYLON
Scarpa, Leonardo
NOTTE ITALIANA
Scavya, Bart
STRIKE COMMANDO
Schell, Jurgen
VERMISCHTE NACHRICHTEN
Schillemans, Dick
QUATRE MAINS
Schultz, Lenny
WIND, THE
Schulz, Karen
CAMPUS MAN
SWEET LORRAINE
Scott, Jill
HOME IS WHERE THE HART IS
Seguin, Francois
MORNING MAN, THE
Semenowicz, Danka
MANUELA'S LOVES
Senechal, Annie
BEYOND THERAPY
Senechel, Annie
LES DEUX CROCODILES
Senecic, Zeljko
GIRL, THE
Ser, Randy
FORTY DAYS OF MUSA DAGH
JOCKS
Serganov, Yevgeny
AKTSIA
Sevenet, Jean-Claude
LE MIRACULE
Seymour, Sharon
STACKING
Shanahan, James
OVERBOARD
Sheir, Yoram
KFAFOT
Shepard, Maxine
COLD STEEL
CYCLONE
Sheremet, Alexander
KAZHDYY OKHOTNIK ZHELAET ZNAT
Sheykin, Eduard
OBVINYAETSYA SVADBA
Shibayev, Anatoly
GRUBAYA POSADKA
Shildknecht, Viktor
SVIDANIE NA MLECHNOM PUTI
Shinkevich, Vladimir
RAZMAKH KRYLIEV
Shponko, Leonid
NOVYE SKAZKI SHAKHEREZADY
Shreter, Irina
ISKRENNE VASH . . .
POEZDKI NA STAROM AVTOMOBILE
YAGUAR
Siebert, Wolfgang
ROCK 'N' ROLL NIGHTMARE
Siebner, Barbara
WANNSEE CONFERENCE, THE
Silvestri, Gianni
LAST EMPEROR, THE
Simon, Eric
FAMILY BUSINESS
Simon, Gayle
ROBOCOP
Sing, Ho Kim
PEKING OPERA BLUES
Siroky, Ludvik
CENA MEDU
WOLF'S HOLE
Skinner, William
OVER THE TOP
Slabinsky, Pyotr
POKLONIS DO ZEMLI
Smith, Peter Lansdown
BLIND DATE
NADINE
Smola, Petr
CIZIM VSTUP POVOLEN
Smolders, Liesje
ALS IN EEN ROES
Snyder, Dawn
MILLION DOLLAR MYSTERY
Sofronov, Viktor
SOUCHASTNIKI
Solle, Bogdan
WIERNA RZEKA
Sorensen, Soren Krag
PETER VON SCHOLTEN
Sotullo, Juan
RELACAO FIEL E VERDADEIRA
Sowder, Cynthia
AMERICAN DRIVE-IN
CLUB LIFE
Spence, Steve
GOOD MORNING, VIETNAM
Spier, Carol
BELIEVERS, THE
Spoon, Zachary
OPEN HOUSE
Stabley, Tony
DELOS ADVENTURE, THE
Stampa, Tom
I WAS A TEENAGE ZOMBIE
Stamps, Donna
EMANON
Stark, Hilda
WALL STREET
Stavridou, Julia
THEOFILOS
Steckle, Mary
LIFE CLASSES
Stein, Dave Howard
WITCHES OF EASTWICK, THE
Stein, Yaakov
KOL AHAVOTAI
Stratford, Rod
FULL METAL JACKET
Strawn, C.J.
NIGHTMARE ON ELM STREET 3: DREAM WARRIORS, A
Strawn, Mick
NIGHTMARE ON ELM STREET 3: DREAM WARRIORS, A
Stubenrauch, Max
CRIME OF HONOR
Sugzda, Algimantas
BLUDNYY SYN
Surrey, Kit
HEARTS OF FIRE
Suzdalev, Mikhail
PRORYV
Switoniak, Jaroslaw
ZLOTY POCIAG
Tagliaferro, Pat
WEEDS
Takenaka, Kazuo
DIXIELAND DAIMYO
Talantsev, Alfred
RUS IZNACHALNA
Talpers, Danny
ANNA
Tapiador, Jose Marie
SIESTA
Tapu, Victor
ZLOTY POCIAG
Tard, Jean-Baptists
NIGHT ZOO
Tavoularis, Alex
GARDENS OF STONE
Tavoularis, Dean
MAN IN LOVE, A
Taylor, Greg
LEADING EDGE, THE
Terechov, Nikolaj
CIZIM VSTUP POVOLEN
Tezhik, Teodor
KIN-DZA-DZA
Theune, Detlef
CRAZY BOYS
Thiemann, Hans
FRANCESCA
Thomas, Philip
FLICKS
Thrasher, Harold
RAISING ARIZONA
Togel, Ingo
CRIME OF HONOR
Tokarev, Alexander
ISKUSHENIE DON ZHUANA
Tolkachev, Alexander
PLIUMBUM, ILI OPASNAIA IGIA
Tomkins, Les
FULL METAL JACKET
Tomkins, Leslie
SUPERMAN IV: THE QUEST FOR PEACE
Toro, Jorge
DEADTIME STORIES
Torosian, Grigor
SASHSHENNYI FONAR
Torras, Isabel
LA RUBIA DEL BAR
Trauner, Alexandre
LE MOUSTACHU
Ubell, Marc
DERANGED
Ulitko, Vsevolod
MAGIA CHYORNAYA I BELAYA
Usachev, Nikolay
TAKAYA ZHESTOKAYA IGRA—KHOKKEY
Vagichev, Alexander
IZ ZHIZNI NACHALNIKA UGOLOVNOGO ROZYSKA
Vakher, Pryit
VO VREMENA VOLCHYIKA ZAKONOV
Valles, Luis
A LOS CUATRO VIENTOS
Van Belleghem, Erik
LOVE IS A DOG FROM HELL
van Beverwijk, Anne Marie
JULIA'S GEHEIM
Van Den Zanden, Hans
STEEL DAWN
van der Linden, Dorus
DE RATELRAT
IRIS
VAN GELUK GESPROKEN
Van Os, Ben
BLOND DOLLY
van Os, Ben
HAVINCK
Vandestien, Michel
BAD BLOOD
PIERRE ET DJEMILA
Vasilyeva, Natalia
LEVSHA
Vayer, Tamas
AZ UTOLSOKEZIRAT
Vedonilli-Levi, Luciano
REGINA
Vedovelli, Luciana
BELLY OF AN ARCHITECT, THE
Veneziano, Sandy
OUTRAGEOUS FORTUNE
Vera, Gerardo
DIVINAS PALABRAS
Vermeiren, Misjel
MASCARA
Vermeylen, Wim
FALSCH
Vezat, Bernard
LA MOINE ET LA SORCIERE
Vinnitsky, Yevgeny
CHEGEMSKIY DETEKTIV
Vinnitzky, Evgeny
SAMAYA OBAYATELNAYA I PRIVLEKATELNAYA
Vitale, Fabio
TERESA
Vladimir Fabrikov
LYUBOVYU ZA LYUBOV
Vonnanadu, S.
PANCHAGNI

Vyrvich, Valentina
GEROY YEYOROMANA

Wada, Hiroshi
WATASHI O SKI NI TSURETETTE

Wai, Vicent
PEKING OPERA BLUES

Wai, Vincent
THIRTY MILLION RUSH, THE

Wai-hong, Szeto
HAPPY BIGAMIST

Wallach, Jeffrey
BLOOD SISTERS

Weinstock, Marcos
BESAME MUCHO

Westfelt, Lasse
MY LIFE AS A DOG

Wheeler, Whitney Brooke
DEATH WISH 4: THE CRACKDOWN

White, Cary
NADINE

Wichman, Sven
BABETTE'S GASTEBUD

Wilheim, Ladislav
DEATH BEFORE DISHONOR

Williams, Ann
I WAS A TEENAGE T.V. TERRORIST

Williams, Jimmy
PRETTYKILL

Willson, David
STEPFATHER, THE

Wloch, Malgorzata
PRYWATNE SLEDZTWO

Wolstenholme, Val
EMPIRE STATE

Wong, Oliver
MAGNIFICENT WARRIORS

Wood, Carol
HIDING OUT

Wood, Joe
SUMMER SCHOOL

Woodruff, Don
HARRY AND THE HENDERSONS
JAWS: THE REVENGE
WHO'S THAT GIRL

Wozniak, Bohdan
DAS TREIBHAUS

Wunderlich, Jerry
HEAT

Wynack, Bernadette
BUSHFIRE MOON

Yamasaki, Yurika
LEILA DINIZ

Yarhi, Dan
BIG TOWN, THE
THREE MEN AND A BABY

Ying, Fong
WRONG COUPLES,THE

Yokeo, Yoshimaga
ZEGEN

Zaleska, Malgorzata
W STARYM DWORKU

Zarifis, Damianos
ONE HUNDRED AND TWENTY DECIBELS

Zea, Kristi
ANGEL HEART
BROADCAST NEWS

Zeinalov, Nadir
YA LYUBIL VAC BOLSHE ZHIZNI

Zenkov, Victor
TAKAYA ZHESTOKAYA IGRA—KHOKKEY

Zenkov, Viktor
MOY LYUBIMYY KLOUN

Zillmann, Hans
TAXI NACH KAIRO

Ziyamukhamedov, Sadritdin
OKHOTA NA DRAKONA

Zografos, Tassos
OH BABYLON
TELEFTAIO STICHIMA

Zurkow, Marina
DEADLY ILLUSION
NECROPOLIS
ROBOT HOLOCAUST

CHOREOGRAPHERS

Abdul, Paula
CANT BUY ME LOVE
RUNNING MAN, THE

Alonso, Juan
ENTRE FICHERAS ANDA EL DIABLO

Barkley, Lynnette
ORPHANS

Baryshnikov, Mikhail
DANCERS

Brown, Andrea
EVIL DEAD 2: DEAD BY DAWN

Burgos, Christine
BAD BLOOD

Copeland, Dianne
KILLER WORKOUT

Delgado, Miguel
IN THE MOOD

Desio, Alfredo
PINOCCHIO AND THE EMPEROR OF THE NIGHT

Douglass, Donald
HOLLYWOOD SHUFFLE

Evans, Jerry
WEEDS

Falco, Louis
ANGEL HEART
LEONARD PART 6

Forrest, David
DIRTY DANCING

Freeman, Damita Jo
VALET GIRLS

Gilbert, Terry
ARIA

Gorg, Gentry
MALIBU BIKINI SHOP, THE

Grusman, Doraine
MALIBU BIKINI SHOP, THE

Guerrero, Franco
WARRIORS OF THE APOCALYPSE

Howard, Sheila
KILLER WORKOUT

Johnson, Carleton
GHOST FEVER

Kelly Robinson
BIG TOWN, THE

Khan, Saroj
MISTER INDIA

Kosugi, Sho
RAGE OF HONOR

Kutash, Jeff
STEELE JUSTICE

La Chapelle, Gilbert
DIRTY DANCING

Labatt, Susan
EVIL DEAD 2: DEAD BY DAWN

Landi, Gino
GOOD MORNING BABYLON

Lane, Marcea D.
CRYSTAL HEART

Lee, Jimmy
WHITE PHANTOM

Leong, Page
WHITE PHANTOM

Lin, Ted
STRIPPED TO KILL

Michael Stone
AMERICAN NINJA 2: THE CONFRONTATION

Mjacin, J.
SKORBNOE BESCHUVSTVIE

Moase, Robyn
BELINDA

Neumeier, John
LADY OF THE CAMELIAS

Ortega, Kenny
DIRTY DANCING

Owens, Michael
BEDROOM WINDOW, THE

Paterson, Vincent
MANNEQUIN

Pokorny, Frantisek
POHADKA O MALICKOVI

Rawles, Denmon
CLUB LIFE

Rebec, Jiri
DISCOPRIBEH

Reynaldi, Ron
MUTANT HUNT

Sanchez, Enrique
ENTRE FICHERAS ANDA EL DIABLO

Sarkar, Subal
PRATIGHAAT

Stardust, Angie
CRAZY BOYS

Taylor, Wilhelmina
BELIEVERS, THE

Titchnell, David
SLAMDANCE

Travolta, Lofti
MOONSTRUCK

Tung, Ching Sui
PEKING OPERA BLUES

Van Laast, Anthony
HOPE AND GLORY

Vrenon, Taunie
NECROPOLIS

Warner, Tam G.
EVIL DEAD 2: DEAD BY DAWN

CINEMATOGRAPHERS

Abderrahmane Tazi, Mohamed
LA COMPROMISSION

Abramov, Avraam
KAPKAN DLYA SHAKALOV

Abramov, Vitaly
SPORTLOTO—82

Abramyan, Henry
GEROY YEYOROMANA

Adamek, Witold
BOHATERROKU
C. K. DEZERTERZY
MATKA KROLOW
POCIAG DO HOLLYWOOD
W STARYM DWORKU

Agosti, Silvano
QUARTIERE

Agostini, Claude
LE MOUSTACHU

Agranovich, Mikhail
KREUTZEROVA SONATA
REPENTANCE

Aguirresarobe, Javier
LA OVEJA NEGRA
MANON

Aguirresarobe, Xavier
EL BOSQUE ANIMADO

Ahlberg, Mac
DOLLS
HOUSE TWO: THE SECOND STORY

Ahmed, Moheen
ZAWGAT RAGOL MOHIM

Ahrweiler, Arthur
STADTRAND

Aidaraliev, Bekbolot
VOLNY UMIRAYUT NA BEREGU

Aladpoush, Mohammed
GOZARESH-E YEK GHATL

Alazraki, Robert
FAMILY BUSINESS
LETE DERNIER A TANGER

Albani, Romano
DA NNUNZIO
LA MONACA DIMONZA

Albert, Arthur
PRINCIPAL, THE
SQUEEZE, THE

Alcaine, Jose Luis
EL LUTE—CAMINA O REVIENTA
HAY QUE DESHACER LA CASA

Alcalde, Jose
DE MUJER A MUJER

Alcott, John
MIRACLES
NO WAY OUT
WHITE WATER SUMMER

Alekan, Henri
DER HIMMEL UBER BERLIN

Alexakis, Tassos
APOUSIES
TELEFTAIO STICHIMA

Alexander
CRYSTAL HEART

Alexander, Kevin
VIRGIN QUEEN OF ST. FRANCIS HIGH, THE

Alisov, Vadim
IZ ZHIZNI POTAPOVA

Aliyev, Murat
SNAYPERY

Almendros, Nestor
NADINE

Alonzo, John A.
OVERBOARD
REAL MEN

Alvarado, Agustin Lara
TRAGICO TERREMOTO EN MEXICO
Alvaro, Arnold
HOSTAGE SYNDROME
Amasiysky, Igor
VELIKIY POKHOD ZA NEVESTOY
Ambat, Madhu
UPPU
Amoros, Juan
REDONDELA
YEAR OF AWAKENING, THE
Anchia, Juan Ruiz
HOUSE OF GAMES
SURRENDER
Andor, Tamas
ISTEN VELETEK, BARATAIM
Andracke, Greg
HOT SHOT
Andry, Richard
MON BEL AMOUR, MA DECHIRURE
Andrzej Bartkowiak
NUTS
Anisimov, Valery
GRUZ BEZ MARKIROVKI
Antipenko, Alexander
MIO, MOY MIO
Arana, Miguel
MI NOMBRE ES GATILLO
Araojo, Johnny
EQUALIZER 2000
Arbogast, Thierry
LE BEAUF
Ardabak, Umit
SON URFALI
Ardabyevsky, Mikhail
CHYORNAYA STRELA
Arellanos, Alberto
NI DE AQUI, NI DE ALLA
Arellanos Bustamante, Armando
OPERACION MARIJUANA
Argall, Ray
WITH LOVE TO THE PERSON NEXT TO ME
Armenaki, Arledge
OFF THE MARK
Armstrong, Gary
BIRDS OF PREY
Aronovich, Ricardo
FAMILY, THE
Arribas, Fernando
DIVINAS PALABRAS
LA CASA DE BERNARDA ALBA
Arutyunov, Konstantin
OBESHCHAYU BYT
Arvanitis, Giorgos
DOXOBUS
Arya, Ishan
ANJUMAN
Ashley-Blake, Stephen
KILLER WORKOUT
Assuerus, Jacques
LES OREILLES ENTRE LES DENTS
TRAVELLING AVANT
Astakhov, Sergey
PRORYV
Atherton, Howard
FATAL ATTRACTION
Atoyanz, Levon
SASHSHENNYI FONAR
Attewell, Warrick
STARLIGHT HOTEL
Avloshenko, Vadim
MILLION V BRACHNOY KORZINE
Azevedo, Gilberto
ACCROCHE-COEUR
MASCARA
Azmi, Baba
MISTER INDIA
Baer, Hanania
ASSASSINATION
MASTERS OF THE UNIVERSE
SOMEONE TO LOVE
Bagayev, Ivan
PROSTI
Bailey, John
LIGHT OF DAY
TOUGH GUYS DON'T DANCE
Baker, Ian
ROXANNE
Ballhaus, Michael
BROADCAST NEWS
GLASS MENAGERIE, THE
Bao, Peter
LEGEND OF WISELY, THE
Baranyai, Laszlo
A SANTA DERVIS
Barrio, Cusi
HOUR OF THE ASSASSIN
Bartle, James
GOOD WIFE, THE
Bassuk, Craig
DEATHROW GAMESHOW
Batista, Edison
MASSACRE IN DINOSAUR VALLEY
Battaglia, Gianlorenzo
BARBARIANS, THE
LE FOTO DI GIOIA
Battaglia, Lorenzo
WARRIOR QUEEN
Baudour, Michel
LA VIE EST BELLE
Bazelli, Bojan
CHINA GIRL
Bazzoni, Camillo
MORO AFFAIR, THE
Beato, Affonso
BIG EASY, THE
Bechard, Gorman
PSYCHOS IN LOVE
Becker, Greg
VIDEO DEAD, THE
Beeson, Paul
JANE AND THE LOST CITY
Bek, Igor
MOY LYUBIMYY KLOUN
Belenky, Grigory
PRODELKI V STARINNOM DUKHE
Bell, Ron
OUTTAKES
Bellis, Andreas
ARCHANGELOS TOU PATHOUS
SWEET COUNTRY
Bellis, Andrew
WIND, THE
Bendtsen, Henning
EPIDEMIC
Benison, Peter
MEATBALLS III
Benoni, Martin
CENA MEDU
Berardini, Giuseppe
CARAMELLE DA UNO SCONOSCIUTO
SOLDATI: 365 GIORNI ALL' ALBA
Berga, Marcel
VENNER FOR ALTID
Bergman, Robert
GRAVEYARD SHIFT
PSYCHO GIRLS
Beristain, Gabriel
ARIA
ARIA
Berkovich, Alexei
SKAZKA O PREKRASNOY AYSULU
Berta, Renato
AU REVOIR, LES ENFANTS
DER TOD DES EMPEDOKLES
JENATSCH
LANNEE DES MEDUSES
Biddle, Adrian
PRINCESS BRIDE, THE
Bierkens, Theo
BLOND DOLLY
Bin, Lee Ping
LIEN LIEN FUNG CHEN
Bisignani, Elio
IL CORAGGIO DI PARLARE
Bitonti, Joseph
VIRGIN QUEEN OF ST. FRANCIS HIGH, THE
Bjorne, Lasse
NAGRA SOMMARKVALLAR PA JORDEN
Blake, Stephen A.
DEADLY PREY
Blawut, Jacek
ZYCIE WEWNETRZNE
Blinov, Valery
PODSUDIMYY
VOENNO-POLEVOI ROMAN
Block, Axel
ZABOU
Blossier, Patric
LHOMME VOILE
Blossier, Patrick
AVRIL BRISE
LA MOINE ET LA SORCIERE
LA VALLEE FANTOME
MISS MONA
SALE DESTIN!
TESTAMENT D'UN POETE JUIF ASSASSINE
Bode, Ralf D.
BIG TOWN, THE
CRITICAL CONDITION
Bogner, Willy
FIRE AND ICE
Bonacinn, Diego
SENTIMIENTOS: MIRTA DE LINIERS A ESTAMBUL
Bondarenko, Boris
KARUSEL NA BAZARNOY PLOSHCHADI
Bonilla, Peter
KILLER WORKOUT
Borbely, Janos
LUTRA
Borbiyev, Nurtai
MIRAZHI LYUBRI
Bose, Devlin
THIS IS NOT OUR DESTINATION
Bose, Dhrubajyoti
PHERA
Boumendil, Jacques
NUIT DOCILE
Bouquin, Jacques
MEMOIRE DES APPARENCES: LA VIE EST UN SONGE
Bourykine, Vladimir
INTERVENTSIA
Bowen, Richard
STACKING
Boyd, Russell
HIGH TIDE
Brabec, Jaroslav
PROC?
Bragado, Julio
RAGE OF HONOR
Brand, Peter
DER TRAUM VOM ELCH
Brault, Michel
GREAT LAND OF SMALL, THE
Brennecke, Alan
SAKURA KILLERS
WHITE PHANTOM
Brenner, Jules
TEEN WOLF TOO
Bridges, David
P.I. PRIVATE INVESTIGATIONS
WALKER
Brix, Klaus
LITTLE PROSECUTOR, THE
Bromet, Frans
ALS IN EEN ROES
DE RATELRAT
IRIS
ODYSSEE D'AMOUR
Brooks, Richard
MORGAN STEWART'S COMING HOME
Brooks, Richard E.
NIGHTMARE AT SHADOW WOODS
Brozhovsky, Boris
TAKAYA ZHESTOKAYA IGRA—KHOKKEY
Bukowski, Bobby
ANNA
KISS DADDY GOOD NIGHT
Burgess, Don
DEATH BEFORE DISHONOR
NIGHT STALKER, THE
SUMMER CAMP NIGHTMARE
Burk, Tim
LAST OF ENGLAND, THE
Burmann, Hans
EL GRAN SERAFIN
LA RUSA
Burr, David
THOSE DEAR DEPARTED
Burton, Geoff
TIME GUARDIAN, THE
YEAR MY VOICE BROKE, THE
Burum, Stephen H.
UNTOUCHABLES, THE
Burykin, Vladimir
DUBLYOR NACHINAET DEYSTVOVAT
KRASNAYA STRELA
SLUCHAYNYE PASSAZHIRY
SON V RUKU, ILI CHEMODON
VOT MOYA DEREVNYA

Bustamante, Alberto Arellanos
MAS VALE PAJARO EN MANO . . .

Bustamantes, Alberto Arellanos
LAS TRAIGO . . . MUERTAS

Bustamente, Alberto Arellanos
RETO A LA VIDA

Byers, Frank
FLOWERS IN THE ATTIC

Cabatuan, Joseph
DOT GOES TO HOLLYWOOD

Callaway, Thomas
SLAVE GIRLS FROM BEYOND INFINITY
SLUMBER PARTY MASSACRE II

Calloway, Thomas
CREEPOZOIDS

Cameron, Alistair
GUNPOWDER

Camorino, Marcelo
EIN BLICK-UND DIE LIEBE BRICHT AUS

Campanelli, Steve
REMEMBERING MEL

Canfarelli, Giovanni
DER TOD DES EMPEDOKLES

Canton, Daniel B.
DEADTIME STORIES

Cardiff, Jack
MILLION DOLLAR MYSTERY

Carlini, Carlo
CARTOLINE ITALIANE

Carmillio Barzoni
TENEREZZA

Caron, Michel
LE SOURD DANS LA VILLE

Carpenter, Stephen
KINDRED, THE

Castiglioni, Agostino
NOTTE ITALIANA
SOTTO IL RISTORANTE CINESE

Catonne, Francois
CHAMP D'HONNEUR

Cenek, Michel
LETE EN PENTE DOUCE

Cerchio, Carlo
CHI C'E C'E

Champetier, Caroline
SOIGNE TA DROITE

Champetier, Carolyn
ARIA

Chan, Chang
TERRORIZERS, THE

Chan, Henry
TRUE COLORS

Chan, Paul
SEVEN YEARS ITCH

Chapman, Michael
LOST BOYS, THE

Chapuis, Dominique
SOMETHING SPECIAL!

Chechulin, Alexander
CHUZHIE ZDES NE KHODYAT

Chelidze, Georgy
GOSPODA AVANTYURISTY

Cheung, Ma Kam
MIDNIGHT

Cheung, Raymond
NINJA THUNDERBOLT

Choi, Nam Nai
KILLER'S NOCTURNE

Choudhury, Jahangir
MIRCH MASALA

Chyorny, Aleksandr
KONTRUDAR

Chyorny, Mikhail
KONTRUDAR

Cianchetti, Fabio
A FIOR DI PELLE

Ciccarese, Luigi
IL FASCINO SOTTILE DEL PECCATO

Cirillo, Claudio
IL LUPO DI MARE

Civit, Jose M.
POLICIA

Civit, Josep Maria
ANGUSTIA

Clark, Ernest
MOVING TARGETS

Clement, John
TUESDAY WEDNESDAY

Clerval, Denys
LA BRUTE

Colace, Hugo
MADE IN ARGENTINA
SINFIN, LA MUERTA NO ES NINGUNA SOLUCION

Colin, Fernando
CORRUPCION
ENTRE FICHERAS ANDA EL DIABLO

Colin, Fernando Alvarez
LO NEGRO DEL NEGRO
YERBA SANGRIENTE

Colin, Francisco
EL HOMBRE DESNUDO

Colli, Tonino Delli
INTERVISTA

Collister, Peter
SUPERNATURALS, THE

Collister, Peter Lyons
CANT BUY ME LOVE
HES MY GIRL

Cologne, Patrice
POISONS

Colon, Francisco
OLOR A MUERTE

Combes, Marcel
LE MIRACULE

Condon, Christopher
EVIL SPAWN

Connell, David
LES PATTERSON SAVES THE WORLD
SLATE, WYN & ME

Contini, Alfio
IL BURBERO
RENEGADE, UN OSSO TROPPO DURO

Contner, James
HEAT

Contner, James A.
LETS GET HARRY

Corradi, Pio
ALPINE FIRE

Correll, Charles
REVENGE OF THE NERDS II: NERDS IN PARADISE

Costa e Silva, Manuel
RELACAO FIEL E VERDADEIRA

Coulter, Michael
HOUSEKEEPING

Coutalon, Esteban
EN EL NOMBRE DEL HIJO

Coutard, Raoul
FUEGOS

Cox, Paul
VINCENT—THE LIFE AND DEATH OF VINCENT VAN GOGH

Coyne, Brian
ZOMBIE HIGH

Crabe, James
HAPPY NEW YEAR

Cronenweth, Jordan
GARDENS OF STONE

Cruz, Javier
MATAR O MORIR
SINVERGUENZA . . . PERO HONRADO
UNA PURA Y DOS CON SAL

Cruz, Xavier
EL PLACER DE LA VENGANZA
ROSA DE LA FRONTERA

Cundey, Dean
PROJECT X

Curiel, Miquel
POR LOS CAMINOS VERDES

Curry, Phil
TRESPASSES

D'Almeida, Acaccio
LA PLAYA DE LOS PERROS

D'Eva, Alessandro
NOI UOMINI DURI

d'Eva, Alessandro
SCUOLA DI LADRI 2

D'Eva, Sandro
MISSIONE EROICA

D'Offizi, Sergio
ROBA DA RICCHI
THUNDER WARRIOR II

D'Ottavi, Paolo
IL RAGAZZO DI EBALUS

Dabal, Wit
LE JEUNE MAGICIEN

Dafnos, Prokopis
FAKELOS POLK STON AERA

Daniels, Mark
SHE MUST BE SEEING THINGS

Danzig, Gad
HA INSTALATOR
KOL AHAVOTAI

Danzig, Gadi
TEL AVIV—BERLIN
YALDEI STALIN

Davanzati, Roberto Forges
SOTTOZERO

Daviau, Allen
EMPIRE OF THE SUN
HARRY AND THE HENDERSONS

David, Andras
LENZ

David, Zoltan
HOTREAL
TISZTA AMERIKA

Davies, Robert
SATURDAY NIGHT AT THE PALACE

Davis, Benjamin
VIOLINS CAME WITH THE AMERICANS, THE

Davis, Elliot
SUMMER HEAT

Davis, Michael
CHECKPOINT

Day, Ernest
SUPERMAN IV: THE QUEST FOR PEACE

de Almeida, Acacio
BALADA DA PRAIA DOS CAES
LES MENDIANTS
UNE FLAMME DANS MON COEUR

de Anda, Antonio
ALBURES MEXICANOS
EL ANSIA DE MATAR
EL HIJO DE PEDRO NAVAJAS
FIERAS EN BRAMA
NARCOTERROR
POLICIAS DE NARCOTICOS
RATAS DE LA CIUDAD
YO, EL EJECUTOR

de Barros, Jose
UM FILM 100% BRAZILEIRO

de Battista, Gerard
ENNEMIS INTIMES
HOTEL DU PARADIS
POULE ET FRITES

de Bont, Peter
EEN MAAND LATER
NITWITS

de Carvalho, Mario
JESTER,THE

De Groot, Andrew
DOGS IN SPACE

de Keyzer, Bruno
LA PASSION BEATRICE
LITTLE DORRIT

de la Rosa, Arturo
NOCTURNO AMOR QUE TE VAS

De Luca, Riccardo
ILLUMINAZIONI

De Maria, Felice
ADELMO

de Santis, Pasqualino
CHRONICLE OF A DEATH FORETOLD

de Volpi, David
TRAIN OF DREAMS

Deakins, Robert
WHITE MISCHIEF

Deakins, Roger
KITCHEN TOTO, THE
PERSONAL SERVICES
SHADEY

Deasy, Seamus
BUDAWANNY

DeBont, Jan
LEONARD PART 6
WHO'S THAT GIRL

Del Negro, Daniel
DUMA VEZ POR TODAS

Del Ruth, Thomas
CROSS MY HEART
RUNNING MAN, THE

Delahoussaye, R. Michael
THEY STILL CALL ME BRUCE

Delgado, Livio
SUCCESSFUL MAN, A

Deming, Peter
EVIL DEAD 2: DEAD BY DAWN
HOLLYWOOD SHUFFLE

Denevi, Rodolfo
A DOS AGUAS

CHECHECHELA—UNA CHICA DEL BARRIO

DeNobe, Tom
HUNTER'S BLOOD

Denove, Tom
CODE NAME ZEBRA
COLD STEEL
MISSION KILL

Desideri, Danilo
IO E MIA SORELLA
RIMINI RIMINI

Desplechin, Arnaud
PHOTOGRAPH, THE

Deubel, Claus
ZISCHKE

Dhooge, Monte
TRESPASSES

Di Battista, Giorgio
PROFUMO

di Battista, Giorgio
BELLIFRESCHI

Di Giacomo, Franco
UN RAGAZZO DI CALABRIA

di Giacomo, Franco
DARK EYES

di Marcantonio, Aldo
LA DONNA DEL TRAGHETTO

Di Palma, Carlo
RADIO DAYS
SECRET OF MY SUCCESS, THE
SEPTEMBER

Di Salvor, Anibal
EL DUENO DEL SOL

Di Virgillo, Bruno
ANGELUS NOVUS

DiCillo, Tom
BEAT, THE

Dicillo, Tom
ROBINSON NO NIWA

Dickerson, Ernest
ENEMY TERRITORY

Dickson, Bill
CODE NAME ZEBRA

Dickson, Billy
NIGHTFORCE

Dickson, James
STUDENT CONFIDENTIAL

Dobson, Steve
GROUND ZERO

Dolinin, Dmitry
OGNI

Dominguez, Raul
ESTA NOCHE CENA PANCHO (DESPEDIDA DE SOLTERO)
LA RAZA NUNCA PIERDE—HUELE A GAS
NOS REIMOS DE LA MIGRA
TODA LA VIDA

Dostie, Alain
LES FOUS DE BASSAN

Doyle, Cristopher
LAONIANG GOU SAO

Dryburgh, Stuart
LEADING EDGE, THE

Duarte, Fernando
A DANCA DOS BONECOS

Dufaux, Guy
BACH AND BROCCOLI
NIGHT ZOO

Duganov, Marat
SNAYPERY

Duggan, Bryan
P.I. PRIVATE INVESTIGATIONS

Dupouey, Pierre
MACBETH

Edols, Michael
PURSUIT OF HAPPINESS, THE
SURFER, THE

Eglitis, Valdis
SVIDANIE NA MLECHNOM PUTI

Eichhammer, Klaus
MEIER

el-Telmessani, Tarek
AL-TAUQ WAL-ISWIRA

Eliezar, Jose Roberto
CIDADE OCULTA

Eliezer, Jose Roberto
NIGHT ANGELS

Elliot, Paul
CYCLONE

Elmes, Frederick
ALLAN QUATERMAIN AND THE LOST CITY OF GOLD
ARIA
RIVER'S EDGE

Elswit, Robert
AMAZING GRACE AND CHUCK

England, Bryan
HUNK

Ennis, Robert
HOME IS WHERE THE HART IS

Ericson, Rune
MALARPIRATER

Erkomaishvili, Nugzar
KRUGOVOROT

Erkomanishvili, Nugzar
GOSPODA AVANTYURISTY

Escamilla, Teo
MY GENERAL

Escoffier, Jean-Yves
BAD BLOOD

Escorel, Lauro
IRONWEED

Estevao, Vitor
LAS DOS ORILLAS

Estrela, Nonato
LEILA DINIZ

Evans, Cerith Wyn
LAST OF ENGLAND, THE

Evans, Roger Pugh
BOY SOLDIER

Evers, Ralph
JIM OCH PIRATERNA BLOM

Fakhimi, Mehrdad
CAPTAIN KHORSHID
PEDDLER, THE

Fandli, Juraj
CIZIM VSTUP POVOLEN

Fanetti, Pasqualino
DOLCE PELLE DI ANGELA

Farkas, Pedro
ELE, O BOTO
FONTE DA SAUDADE

Fash, Mike
WHALES OF AUGUST, THE

Fatori, Jean
LA VENGEANCE DU PROTECTEUR

Fauer, John
LA VENGEANCE DU PROTECTEUR

Fedosov, Valery
DVADTSTAT DNEI BEZ
LEVSHA

Fei, Zhao
DAO MAZEI

Felperlaan, Marc
TERUG NAAR OEGSTGEEST

Fernandes, Joao
PRETTYKILL

Fernandez, Angel Luis
LAW OF DESIRE

Fernandez Balbuena, Augusto G.
MADRID

Ferragut, Jean-Noel
YEELEN

Ferrando, Giancarlo
MESSENGER, THE

Filac, Vilko
ZIVOT RADNIKA

Filipashvili, Archil
STUPEN

Filippov, Sergei
KOORDINATY SMERTI

Findlay, Roberta
BLOOD SISTERS
ORACLE, THE

Firth, Mike
LEADING EDGE, THE

Fischer, Jens
MORE ABOUT THE CHILDREN OF BULLERBY VILLAGE
NIONDE KOMPANIET

Fisher, Gerry
MAN ON FIRE

Flaxton, Terry
OUT OF ORDER

Flynn, Frank Pershing
MASTERBLASTER

Foreman, David
CODA

Forges, Robert D.
CURSE, THE

Fraisse, Robert
SPIRALE

Fraker, William A.
BABY BOOM
BURGLAR

Franco, David
REMEMBERING MEL

Fraschetti, Silvio
QUEL RAGAZZO DELLA CURVA "B"

Fresco, Robert
NIGHTSTICK

Frez, Ilya
LICHNOE DELO SUDYI IVANOVOY

Friedrich, Gerhard
KONZERT FUR DIE RECHTE HAND

Fujii, Yoshihisa
BUS

Fujisawa, Junichi
SARABA ITOSHIKI HITO YO

Galisteo, Jose G.
LA SENYORA
LOS INVITADOS

Galisteo, Jose Garcia
A LOS CUATRO VIENTOS

Ganeea, Svetla
PRIZEMYAVANE

Gantman, Yuri
UTRO OBRECHENNOGO PRIISKA

Garcia, Beltran
LA ESTACION DEL REGRESO

Garcia, Guadalupe
ROBACHICOS
VIAJE AL PARAISO

Garcia Galisteo, Jose
LONG STRIDER

Garfath, Mike
PRAYER FOR THE DYING, A

Garibyan, Alexander
RUS IZNACHALNA

Garzon, Miguel
VA DE NUEZ

Gatti, Marcello
TERNOSECCO

Gaudry, Daniel
CLUB DE RENCONTRES

Gavrjusjov, Mischa
OM KARLEK

Gee, Zand
LIVING ON TOKYO TIME

Geick, Eberhard
CRAZY BOYS
FRANCESCA

Gelein, Igor
LYUBOVYU ZA LYUBOV

Gelsini, Alessio
IL GRANDE BLEK

Genkins, Harvey
GARBAGE PAIL KIDS MOVIE, THE
OMEGA SYNDROME
SILENT NIGHT, DEADLY NIGHT PART II

Gentil, Dominique
FACES OF WOMEN

Gentleman, Wally
IRON WARRIOR

Gholizadeh, Hassan
LODGERS

Giltay, Geert
VROEGER IS DOOD

Giltay, Goert
DE ORIONNEVEL

Ginzberg, Valeri
KOMISSAR

Ginzburg, Valery
SOUCHASTNIKI

Girardi, Nicolae
ZLOTY POCIAG

Girometti, Roberto
TENTAZIONE

Gitau, Njuguna
KOLORMASK

Giurato, Blasco
LESTATE STA FINENDO
TERESA

Giuseppe Rotunno
HOTEL COLONIAL

Glouner, Richard C.
HOT CHILD IN THE CITY

Goded, Angel
FRIDA
LO DEL CESAR
REALM OF FORTUNE, THE

Godina, Karpo
MAGIC SNOWMAN, THE

Goldblatt, Stephen
LETHAL WEAPON

Goldsmith, Paul H.
KILLING TIME, THE

Golia, David
ROSARY MURDERS, THE

Gondre, Jean-Francis
LES MOIS D'AVRIL SONT MEURTRIERS

Gothe, Michael
DER JUNGE MIT DEM GROSSEN SCHWARZEN HUND

Grant, Freddie C.
NO DEAD HEROES

Grant, Jaems
TO MARKET, TOMARKET

Gras, Richard
STRIKE COMMANDO

Graver, Gary
COMMANDO SQUAD
MOON IN SCORPIO
PARTY CAMP

Green, Jack N.
LIKE FATHER, LIKE SON

Greenberg, Adam
JOCKS
LA BAMBA
NEAR DARK
THREE MEN AND A BABY
WALK ON THE MOON, A

Greene, Craig
MESSENGER, THE
OFFSPRING, THE

Gressmann, Martin
DILAN

Grumman, Francis
BULLETPROOF

Gruszynski, Alexander
PROMISED LAND
UNDER COVER

Gu Jung-mo
TICKET

Guarnieri, Ennio
DANCERS
MOSCA ADDIO

Guerra, Pili Flores
CITY AND THE DOGS, THE

Gurevitz, Jorge
HIMMO MELECH YERUSHALAIM

Gurfinkel, David
EMPEROR'S NEW CLOTHES, THE
OVER THE TOP
RUMPELSTILTSKIN
SLEEPING BEAUTY

Gusi, Carlos
EL AMOR DE AHORA

Guslinsky, Evgeny
KAK STAT SCHASTLIVYM

Guthe, Fred
TOO OUTRAGEOUS

Haan, Rolv
FELDMANN CASE, THE

Haitkin, Jacques
HIDDEN, THE
MY DEMON LOVER

Hall, Conrad L.
BLACK WIDOW

Hamer, Ingo
LADY OF THE CAMELIAS

Hannan, Peter
LONELY PASSION OF JUDITH HEARNE,THE
WITHNAIL AND I

Harris, Eitan
LATE SUMMER BLUES

Harris, Frank
CATCH THE HEAT

Harris, John
HOPE AND GLORY

Harrison, Harvey
ARIA

Hart, Dick
CREEPSHOW 2

Hasegawa, Genkichi
WATASHI O SKI NI TSURETETTE

Hassapis, Stavros
O PARADISSOS ANIGI ME ANTIKLIDI

Haydu, Jorge
DE TAL PEDRO, TAL ASTILLA

Hayes, Robert
OPEN HOUSE

Heimann, Gunter
DER BARENHAUTER

Heinl, Bernd
OUT OF ROSENHEIM

Hengli, Wang
DOCTOR SUN YATSEN

Herrera, Juan
CINCO NACOS ASALTAN A LAS VEGAS

Herrera, Juan Manuel
MAS BUENAS QUE EL PAN

Herrington, David
HOUSEKEEPER, THE

Herzog, John
HELLO MARY LOU, PROM NIGHT II

Heslop, Richard
LAST OF ENGLAND, THE

Himeda, Masahisa
HOTARUGAWA

Hirschfeld, Gerald
MALONE

Hirvonen, Tahvo
A LA ITKE IINES

Holender, Adam
STREET SMART

Holland, Keith
MANKILLERS

Holmberg, Sten
HIP, HIP, HURRA!

Holub, Antonin
PRATELE BERMUDSKEHO TROJUHELNIKU

Holzman, Ernest
PROGRAMMED TO KILL

Howard A. Wexler
BANZAI RUNNER

Hubbs, Gil
FLOWERS IN THE ATTIC

Hughes, Brant A.
RETURN OF JOSEY WALES, THE

Hughes, Christopher
LAST OF ENGLAND, THE

Hume, Alan
HEARTS OF FIRE

Humeau, Jean-Michel
YEELEN

Huneck, John
DIRTY LAUNDRY

Hurtado, Genaro
MUJERES SALVAJES

Hurwitz, Tom
CREEPSHOW 2

Hyon-chae, Sohn
NAE-SHI

Ibragimov, Rifkat
YA TEBYA POMNYU

Icho, Arvo
IGRY DLJA DETEJ SKO'NOGO VOZRASTA

Iimura, Masahiko
TOKYO BLACKOUT

Ike, Karol
CONCRETE ANGELS

Imi, Tony
EMPIRE STATE

Insley, David
ADVENTURE OF THE ACTION HUNTERS

Ioniccio, Bob
EVIL TOWN

Ippoliti, Silvano
ALADDIN
CAPRICCIO
SPECTERS

Irola, Judy
JAG ELSKER DIG

Irving, Louis
AROUND THE WORLD IN EIGHTY WAYS
HOWLING III, THE

Irwin, Mark
HANOI HILTON, THE

Ishihara, Koh
SURE DEATH 4

Isohata, Yukio
EIGA JOYU

Ivanov, Anatoly
YAGUAR

Ivanov, Nikolai
MILLION V BRACHNOY KORZINE

Ivanov, Vladimir
SENTIMENTALNOE PUTESHESTVIE NA KARTOSHKU

Ivanov, Wladimir
LEVY ET GOLIATH

Jaakkola, Eero
PIKKUPOJAT

Jalasti, Juha
LIIAN ISO KEIKKA
UUNO TURHAPURO MUUTTAA MAALLE

Jalasti, Jussi
PIKKUPOJAT

Jalasti, Timo
PIKKUPOJAT

James, Peter
RIGHT HAND MAN, THE
SHADOWS OF THE PEACOCK

Janas, Henryk
KOMEDIANCI Z WCZORAJSZEJ ULICY
PAN SAMOCHODZIK I NIESAMOWITY DWOR

Jancso, Miklos
DIARY FOR MY LOVED ONES

Jarman, Derek
LAST OF ENGLAND, THE

Jeng, Heh Yong
OUTSIDERS, THE

Jie, Li Wan
MIRAGE

Johnson, Shelly
MAID TO ORDER
NIGHTFLYERS

Johnsson, Olof
SERPENT'S WAY, THE

Jones, Alan
WHITE OF THE EYE

Jones, Michael A.
OPPOSING FORCE

Joshi, Rajsh
PANCHVATI

Jost, Jon
BELL DIAMOND

Jovanovic, Savo
U IME NARODA

Jur, Jeff
DIRTY DANCING
STRANDED

Jurges, Jurgen
DANN IST NICHTS MEHR WIE VORHER
FLYER, THE
YER DEMIR, GOK BAKIR

Jurizdickkij, Sergej
SKORBNOE BESCHUVSTVIE

Jutzeler, Denis
LES MENDIANTS

Kabachenko, Viktor
POEZD VNE RASPISANIA

Kaczmarek, Zdzislaw
ZLOTA MAHMUDIA

Kahm, Marsha
BLOOD HOOK

Kalari, Mahmoud
SHEERE SANGGY

Kalashnikov, Leonid
TEMA

Kaman, Steven
FIREHOUSE

Kamarullah, George
IBUNDA

Kambarov, Rafik
LEGENDA SEREBRYANOGO OZERA

Kaplan, Ervin L.
PINOCCHIO AND THE EMPEROR OF THE NIGHT

Karasev, Victor
SOPERNITSY

Karavayev, Elizbar
SEKUNDA NA PODVIG

Kariuk, Gennadi
KOROTKIE VSTRECHI

Kariuk, Ghenadi
DOLGHYIE PROVOD

Karpick, Avi
BEAUTY AND THE BEAST

Karpick, Avraham
SURVIVAL GAME

Karyuk, Gennady
SEZON CHUDES

Kasteyev, Abiltai
TAYNY MADAM VONG

Katajisto, Heikki
KUNINGAS LEAR
NAKEMIIN, HYVASTI

Kato, Yudai
DIXIELAND DAIMYO
KID BROTHER, THE

Katsouridis, Dinos
ONE HUNDRED AND TWENTY DECIBELS
ONIRO ARISTERIS NICHTAS
PROINI PERIPOLOS

Katz, Steven
NICE GIRLS DON'T EXPLODE

Kawakami, Koichi
LOVE LETTER

Kedzierski, Grzegorz
ZYGFRYD

Kelley, Jim
MIND KILLER

Kelly, Shane
SWEET REVENGE

Kemper, Victor J.
WALK LIKE A MAN

Kende, Janos
SZORNYEK EVADJA

Kenny, Francis
CAMPUS MAN
SALVATION!

Kerimov, Valery
CHKATULKA IZ KREPOSTI
YA LYUBIL VAC BOLSHE ZHIZNI

Kesterman, Rolf
DISORDERLIES
SURF NAZIS MUST DIE

Khamidov, Okil
KAPKAN DLYA SHAKALOV

Khan, Chon Ik
SEKUNDA NA PODVIG

Kibbe, Gary B.
PRINCE OF DARKNESS

Kiesser, Jan
MADE IN HEAVEN
SOME KIND OF WONDERFUL

Kikabidze, Yury
PYAT NEVEST DO LYUBIMOY

Kimball, Jeffrey L.
BEVERLY HILLS COP II

Kimura, Daisaku
KATAKU NO HITO
TOO MUCH

King, Joel
CLUB LIFE

Kirillov, Andrei
KORABL PRISHELTSEV

Kitzanuk, Andrew
LAST STRAW, THE

Klejns, Martins
POHADKA O MALICKOVI

Klitgaard, Peter
KAMPEN OM DEN RODE KO

Klosinski, Edward
MAGIC STICKS
MATKA KROLOW

Kobayashi, Setsuo
PRINCESS FROM THE MOON

Koch, Douglas
IVE HEARD THE MERMAIDS SINGING

Koch, Jakob
STRIT OG STUMME

Koltai, Lajos
GABY—A TRUE STORY

Konermann, Lutz
DRAGON'S FOOD

Koo, Johnny
DIXIA QING

Koons, Ed
P.K. & THE KID

Korcelli, Jacek
E S D
PIERSCIEN I ROZA

Kornilyev, Vadim
KONETS OPERATSII "REZIDENT"

Koschnick, Carl Friedrich
SAME TO YOU

Kosh, Yoav
YEHOSHUA—YEHOSHUA

Kothari, Rajan
DACAIT

Koutsaftis, Philippos
TREE WE HURT, THE

Kovalchuk, Alexander
IZ ZHIZNI NACHALNIKA UGOLOVNOGO ROZYSKA

Kovzel, Vladimir
POSLEDNYAYA DOROGA

Kramm, Peter
KONZERT FUR DIE RECHTE HAND

Krieger, Klaus
KONZERT FUR DIE RECHTE HAND

Kristiansen, Henning
BABETTE'S GASTEBUD

Kristinsson, Ari
SKYTTURNAR

Krovel, Svein
PA STIGENDE KURS
PRINSEN FRA FOGO

Kubiza, Ernst
SOMMER

Kuc, Dariusz
W ZAWIESZENIU

Kuhn, Toni
RED DESERT PENITENTIARY

Kuhn, Tony
QUATRE MAINS

Kuhrober, Norbert
DER JUNGE MIT DEM GROSSEN SCHWARZEN HUND

Kurant, Willy
SOUS LE SOLEIL DE SATAN

Kuveiller, Luigi
I MIEI PRIMI QUARANT'ANNI
MONTECARLO GRAN CASINO
VIA MONTENAPOLEONE

Kuznetsov, Anatoli
SEVERNY ANEKDOT

Kvas, Valery
POKLONIS DO ZEMLI

Kwang-suk, Chung
KYEOUL NAGUNE

Lachman, Edward
LESS THAN ZERO
MAKING MR.RIGHT

Lam, Andrew
CITY ON FIRE

Lambert, John
EMANON

Lanci, Giuseppe
DEVIL IN THE FLESH
GOOD MORNING BABYLON
HAVINCK

Landen, Hal
SULLIVAN'S PAVILION

Lara, Agustin
EL DIABLO, EL SANTO Y EL TONTO
HERENCIA DE VALIENTES

Larrieu, Jean-Claude
UN AMOUR A PARIS

Laskus, Jacek
HEART
SQUARE DANCE

Lassally, Walter
INDIAN SUMMER

Laszlo, Andrew
INNERSPACE

Lau, Andrew
THIRTY MILLION RUSH, THE

Le Mener, Jean-Yves
ATTENTION BANDITS
LES DEUX CROCODILES

Le Rigoleur, Dominique
BUISSON ARDENT

Lebeshev, Pavel
KIN-DZA-DZA

Leblanc, J.
PERSONAL FOUL

Leblanc, John
STRIPPED TO KILL

Leclerc, Martin
LA COULEUR ENCERCLEE

Lecomte, Claude
LE GRAND CHEMIN
LE JOURNAL D'UN FOU

Lenardi, John C.
LA BUSQUEDA

Lenardi, Juan Carlos
EL HOMBRE DE LA DEUDA EXTERNA
EN RETIRADA
LOS DUENOS DEL SILENCIO

Lenoir, Denis
TANDEM

Lent, Dean
BORDER RADIO

Lentchevski, Richard
CERNITE LEBEDI

Leonetti, Matthew F.
DRAGNET
EXTREME PREJUDICE

Leslie, Bill
NAIL GUN MASSACRE

Letterman, Richard
CLIMB, THE

Lewnes, Peter
I WAS A TEENAGE ZOMBIE

Lhomme, Pierre
CHARLIE DINGO
MAURICE
MY LITTLE GIRL

Ligon, Ricky
DAMORTIS

Lindley, John
IN THE MOOD

Lindley, John W.
STEPFATHER, THE

Lindstrom, Rolf
MY LIFE AS A DOG
SERPENT'S WAY, THE

Liubshin, Yury
PROSHAL ZELEN LETA

Lloyd, Walt
DOWN TWISTED

Loffredo, Emilio
CAMPING DEL TERRORE

Loftus, Bryan
SIESTA

Loginova, Tatiana
ZNAK BEDY

Lommi, Mario
ITALIANI A RIO

Loof, Claus
SIDSTE AKT

Lopez, Rodolfo
EL SOCIO DE DIOS

Lopez Linares, Jose Luis
MIENTRAS HAYA LUZ

Loureiro, Jose Antonio
LES MENDIANTS

Louvart, Helene
COERS CROISES

Louzon, Gary
OPEN HOUSE

Lubtchansky, William
AGENT TROUBLE
COMEDY!

Lukaszewicz, Jerzy
PRZYJACIEL WESOLEGO DIABLA
SIEKIEREZADA

Lukshin, Igor
ZHELEZNOE POLE

Lund, Michael
SIESTA

Lung, Yee Tung
WRONG COUPLES,THE

Lupinc, Andrej
USODNI TELEFON

Luring, Werner
VERMISCHTE NACHRICHTEN

Lutic, Bernard
LAMI DE MON AMIE
POUSSIERE D'ANGE

Lux, David
ZOMBIE HIGH

Lyubimov, Yury
TAYNOE PUTESHESTVIE EMIRA

MacDonald, Peter
HAMBURGER HILL

Macdonald, Robert
FAMILY VIEWING

Machuel, Emmanuel
PIERRE ET DJEMILA

MacKay, Mark
ROCK 'N' ROLL NIGHTMARE

Macmillan, Kenneth
MONTH IN THE COUNTRY, A

Maeda, Yonezo
SOROBANZUKU
TAXING WOMAN, A

Magliulo, Giorgio
UNA CASA IN BILICO

Maintigneux, Sophie
QUATRE AVENTURES DE REINETTE ET MIRABELLE

Maira, Horacio
STRANGER, THE

Makeranets, Vladimir
V STRELYAYUSHCHEY GLUSHI

Makinen, Keijo
PEKKA PUUPAA POLIISINA

Mancori, Sandro
UNA DONNA DA SCOPRIRE
Maniatis, Sakis
KE DYO AVGA TOURKIAS
Mann, Bill
EVIL TOWN
Mansoori, Toraj
DJADDE HAYE SARD
Marandjan, Genrikh
MAGIA CHYORNAYA I BELAYA
Marcheux, Serge
JOHNNY MONROE
Margas, Thodoros
THEOFILOS
Marini, Thom
MY DARK LADY
Marion, Nicolas
REMEMBERING MEL
Mark, Ivan
MALOM A POKOLBAN
Markko, Timo
TILINTEKO
Markova, Nadine
WELCOME MARIA
Marks, Arthur D.
NECROPOLIS
ROBOT HOLOCAUST
Martevo, Pekka
INUKSUK
Marti, Pascal
HOTEL DE FRANCE
JEUX D'ARTIFICES
Martynov, Oleg
LERMONTOV
STARAYA AZBUKA
Maruike, Osamu
UHOHO TANKENTAI
Mason, Steve
TALE OF RUBY ROSE, THE
Massaccesi, Aristide
DELIZIA
Mathe, Tibor
WHOOPING COUGH
Mathias, Harry
ERNEST GOES TO CAMP
Mattison, James
MURDER LUST
Mauch, Thomas
DEADLINE
VERMISCHTE NACHRICHTEN
May, Bradford
MONSTER SQUAD, THE
May, Jim
ERNEST GOES TO CAMP
Mazinani, Al Akbar
MANUSCRIPTS
McAlpine, Donald
ORPHANS
PREDATOR
McConkey, Larry
WHITE OF THE EYE
McCulloch, Malcolm
FRENCHMAN'S FARM
McCullogh, Malcolm
BELINDA
McDougall, Tom
KAMILLA OG TYVEN
McGowan, Bruce
BORN OF FIRE
McKay, Doug
HIGH STAKES
Mckenkamp, Fred
JULIA'S GEHEIM
McLean, Nick
SPACEBALLS
McLeish, Ronald W.
MONSTER IN THE CLOSET
McLin, Sean
UNFINISHED BUSINESS . . .
McPherson, John
BATTERIES NOT INCLUDED
JAWS: THE REVENGE
Medina, Luis
DELINCUENTE
EL MUERTO DEL PALOMO
UN SABADO MAS
Mednikov, Mikhail
ISKUSHENIE DON ZHUANA
Meheux, Phil
FOURTH PROTOCOL, THE
Meliande, Antonio
EU
Melita, Salvador
CHORROS
Melnikov, Igor
DIKIY KHMEL
Menges, Chris
HIGH SEASON
SHY PEOPLE
Menon, Divakara
PANDAVAPURAM
Mertes, Raffaele
AURELIA
Mertz, Lorand
DOKTOR MINORKA VIDOR NAGY NAPJA
Mesa, Luis Garcia
MUJERES DE LA FRONTERA
Mescheryagin, Rudolf
ZOLOTAYA BABA
Metcalfe, John
MORE BAD NEWS
RAWHEAD REX
Mettler, Peter
FAMILY VIEWING
Meurer, William
DELOS ADVENTURE, THE
Mezzabotta, Roberto
MEFISTO FUNK
Mieroslawski, Jacek
PRYWATNE SLEDZTWO
WERYFIKACJA
Migeat, Francois
FACES OF WOMEN
Mignot, Pierre
ARIA
BEYOND THERAPY
O. C. AND STIGGS
Mihok, Barna
LENZ
Mikesch, Elfi
ANITA—DANCES OF VICE
Mikutenas, Algimantas
MOYA MALENKAYA ZHENA
Milan Spasic
ANDJEO CUVAR
Miller, Scott
FLICKS
TALKING WALLS
Mills, Alec
LIONHEART
LIVING DAYLIGHTS, THE
Milsome, Douglas
FULL METAL JACKET
Mironov, Valery
VZLOMSHCHIK
Mitran, Doru
PADUREANCA
Mokri, Amir
SLAMDANCE
Monkonmung, Boonyong
HOUSE
Monreal, Manuel Tejeda
FORAJIDOS EN LA MIRA
Monsigny, Jean
F . . . ING FERNAND
YAM DAABO
Montheillet, Max
EMMANUELLE 5
Morita, Fujio
RYOMA O KITTA OTOKO
YOSHIWARA ENJO
Morita, Fujiro
DEATH SHADOWS
Morrisey, Kevin
HAPPY HOUR
Moura, Edgar
HOT SHOT
UM TREM PARA AS ESTRELAS
Mukhamedjanov, Rustam
NOVYE SKAZKI SHAKHEREZADY
Muller, Robby
BARFLY
BELIEVERS, THE
Muller-Laue, Klaus
SIERRA LEONE
Muradov, Alekper
CHKATULKA IZ KREPOSTI
Muratnazarov, Yakub
PRIKLYUCHENIA NA MALENKIKH OSTROVEKH
Murphy, Fred
BEST SELLER
DEAD, THE
Murphy, Thomas
MUTANT HUNT
Murphy II, Fred V.
WINNERS TAKE ALL
Murthy, V.K.
TAMAS
Mutanen, Pertti
URSULA
Myhrman, Dan
LEIF
Naess, Halvor
IS-SLOTTET
Naganuma, Mutsuo
HIKARU ANNA
Nagy, Csaba
CAT CITY
Nagy, Wladyslaw
CZAS NADZIEI
Naidenov, Alexei
AKTSIA
Nakhabtsev, Vladimir
OCHNAYA STAVKA
Nannuzzi, Armando
GLI OCCHIALI D'ORO
I LOVE NEW YORK
IL GIORNO PRIMA
Narayan, H. Laxmi
PRATIGHAAT
Nardi, Tonino
I PICARI
REGINA
Narita, Hiro
NO MAN'S LAND
Nass, Halvor
PLASTPOSEN
Neau, Andre
WAITING FOR THE MOON
Nemenyi, Maria
CAT CITY
Nemolyayev, Nikolai
KURIER
PLOSHCHAD VOSSTANIA
ZINA-ZINULYA
Nepomniaschy, Alex
WANTED: DEAD OR ALIVE
Neumann, Claus
VERNEHMUNG DER ZEUGEN
Neuwirth, Tom
LADY BEWARE
Nevsky, Yuri
CHELOVEK C AKKORDEONOM
Nevsky, Yury
POLEVAYA GVARDIA MOZZHUKHINA
New, Robert C.
BIG BAD MAMA II
Neyman, Ye'ehi
RED RIDING HOOD
Nguyen, Ngoc Minh
DOT GOES TO HOLLYWOOD
Nicolle, Victor
LADIES OF THE LOTUS
Nihalani, Govind
TAMAS
Nihalsingha, D.B.
MALDENIYESIMION
Nikolic, George
WHEELS OF TERROR
Nilov, Alexander
ZNAY NASHIKH
Nilsson, Anders
WARDOGS
Nilsson, Goran
DEMONS
Nissim
LO SAM ZAYIN
Nissim, Nitcho Lion
PROGRAMMED TO KILL
Nitcho, Nissim Leon
CATCH THE HEAT
Novak, Emil
ZUHANAS KOZBEN
Nuytten, Bruno
JEAN DE FLORETTE
MANON OF THE SPRING
Nyholm, Kristoffer
EPIDEMIC

O'Shea, Rory
NGATI
O'Sullivan, Thaddeus
LOVECHILD, THE
Ogaard, Philip
JOR
Ogden, John
AS TIME GOES BY
Oguz, Orhan
ANAYURT OTELI
DEGIRMEN
Ohashi, Rene
SWEET LORRAINE
Okada, Daryn
WITNESS TO A KILLING
Okazaki, Kozo
O DESEJADO—LES MONTAGNES DE LA LUNE
Okazaki, Steven
LIVING ON TOKYO TIME
Ollstein, Marty
PENITENTIARY III
Olmi, Ermanno
LUNGA VITA ALLA SIGNORA!
Olonovski, Nikolai
VREMYA ZHELANIY
Ondricek, Miroslav
BIG SHOTS
Ono, Antonio
BAR-CEL-ONA
Osipov, Albert
DVOE POD ODNIM ZONTOM
Ouedraogo, Sekou
YAM DAABO
Oya, Edward
VO VREMENA VOLCHYIKA ZAKONOV
Paalgard, Harald
ETTER RUBICON
Paatashvili, Levan
NEYLONOVAYA YOLKA
Paersch, Henrik
SNOW QUEEN, THE
VY VIHDOINKIN YHDESSA
Pakulski, Krzysztof
BLIND CHANCE
Pankau, Justus
POET'S SILENCE, THE
Pankov, Vladimir
POEZD VNE RASPISANIA
Pann, Aleksandr
VINA LEYTENANTA NEKRASOVA
Panoussopoulos, Giorgos
VIOS KE POLITIA
Pap, Ferenc
GONDOVISELES
LAURA
Papacostantis, Dimitri
PRETTY SMART
Pardo, Rafael Fuster
IN DER WUSTE
Park, Seung bae
MAN WITH THREE COFFINS, THE
Pavlopoulos, Lefteris
YENETHLIA POLI
Payvar, Homayun
PEDDLER, THE
Pearl, Daniel
AMAZON WOMEN ON THE MOON
DEADLY ILLUSION
HIDING OUT
Pechura, Donatas
IZVINITEPOZHALUYSTA
Pecura, Donatas
SLEDY OBOROTNYA
Penido, Antonio
BAIXO GAVEA
BEIJO NA BOCA
Penson, Miron
VINA LEYTENANTA NEKRASOVA
Penzer, Jean
LA RUMBA
Pereira, Jun
WARRIORS OF THE APOCALYPSE
Perles, Barry
SITTING IN LIMBO
Perreira, John
TOUGH COP
Perreira, Jun
GET THE TERRORISTS
Persson, Jorgen
MY LIFE AS A DOG
PELLE EROVRAREN
SERPENT'S WAY, THE
Peterman, Don
PLANES, TRAINS AND AUTOMOBILES
Peterson, Joel
CUSTODY
Petrosyan, Vrez
ZEMLYA I ZOLOTO
Phillips, Alex
ALLAN QUATERMAIN AND THE LOST CITY OF GOLD
BORN IN EAST L.A.
NUMBER ONE WITH A BULLET
TROUBLE WITH SPIES, THE
Piganov, Valentin
CHEGEMSKIY DETEKTIV
SAMAYA OBAYATELNAYA I PRIVLEKÁTELNAYA
Pinter, Tom
DIRTY REBEL
Pinter, Tomislav
GIRL, THE
HEY BABU RIBA
SLEEP WELL, MY LOVE
Pladevall, Tomas
LA RUBIA DEL BAR
Pluchik, Eduard
MY OBVINYAEM
MY OBVINYAEM
Pogany, Cristiano
SUPERFANTOZZI
Poletti, Carlo
LA CROCE DALLE SETTE PIETRE
LA TRASGRESSIONE
Poluyanov, Sergei
SPORTLOTO—82
Popovic, Predrag
DIE VERLIEBTEN
OKTOBERFEST
Porath, Gideon
AMERICAN NINJA 2: THE CONFRONTATION
DEATH WISH 4: THE CRACKDOWN
Posegga, Hans
CASPAR DAVID FRIEDRICH
Posey, Steve
AMERICAN DRIVE-IN
THREE FOR THE ROAD
Poster, Steven
SOMEONE TO WATCH OVER ME
Poulsson, Andreas
SITTING IN LIMBO
Pozdnyakov, Ivan
O ROZVRASHCHENII ZABYT
Prizzi, Frank
SUICIDE CLUB, THE
Prokopenko, Alexei
TVOYO MIRNOE NEBO
Ptak, Krzysztof
INNA WYSPA
Puchkov, Nikolai
GOVORIT MOSKVA
Pudney, Alain
SLAUGHTER HIGH
Quijano, Rudy
NO BLOOD NO SURRENDER
Rabier, Jean
LE CRI DU HIBOU
MASQUES
Racine, Robert
ZOMBIE NIGHTMARE
Raditschnig, Herbert
OUTING, THE
Ragalyi, Elemer
CSOK, ANYU
HOL VOLT, HOL NEM VOLT
Ralke, Cliff D.
TERMINAL EXPOSURE
Ramirez, Pedro
CINCO NACOS ASALTAN A LAS VEGAS
Ramlau, Andrzej
KOMEDIANTKA
Rath, Franz
DER UNSICHTBARE
Reddy, Don
BENJI THE HUNTED
Remias, Ricardo
EYE OF THE EAGLE
Rerberg, George
PLIUMBUM, ILI OPASNAIA IGIA
Rerberg, Gueorgy
WEEKEND
Revene, Larry
DERANGED
IF LOOKS COULD KILL
SLAMMER GIRLS
WIMPS
Ribeiro, Jose Tadeu
BESAME MUCHO
COLOR OF DESTINY, THE
Ribes, Federico
ASI COMO HABIAN SIDO
CALE
LA GUERRA DE LOS LOCOS
Richardson, Robert
DUDES
WALL STREET
Richmond, Tom
MALIBU BIKINI SHOP, THE
SPACE RACE
STRAIGHT TO HELL
Rimminen, Sakari
ELVIS-KISSAN JALJILLA
Rinzler, Lisa
FOREVER, LULU
I WAS A TEENAGE T.V. TERRORIST
Roach, Neil
RED HEADED STRANGER
Robin, Jean-Francois
LE SOLITAIRE
MALADIE D'AMOUR
Rodallec, Yves
LA VIE DISSOLUE DE GERARD FLOQUE
Rodionov, Alexei
FAREWELL
Rodriguez, Miguel
MISS MARY
SOFIA
Rojas, Manuel
ASIGNATURA APROBADA
LA ESTANQUERA DE VALLECAS
Rose, Charles
DOLCE ASSENZA
Rosenberg, Ilan
BOUBA
HANSEL AND GRETEL
Rosengren, Bertil
JIM OCH PIRATERNA BLOM
Rousselot, Philippe
HOPE AND GLORY
Ruiz, Antonio
JUANA LA CANTINERA
LA RULETERA
LAPUTA: THE CASTLE IN THE SKY
TIERRA DE VALIENTES
Ruiz, Jose Antonio
EL MOFLES Y LOS MECANICOS
LA FUGA DE CARRASCO
Ruiz, Rafael
MUJERES DE LA FRONTERA
Ruiz Juarez, Antonio
CARTUCHA CORTADA
Ruus, Ago
SEREBRYANAYA PRYAZHA KAROLINY
Ruvalcaba, Zavier Cruz
GHOST FEVER
Ruzzolini, Giuseppe
LA CODA DEL DIAVOLO
STREGATI
UN TASSINARO A NEW YORK
Ryan, Ellery
BIT PART, THE
Ryan, Paul
YOU TALKIN' TO ME?
Ryan, Robert
BLOODY WEDNESDAY
Saad, Robert
POLICE ACADEMY 4: CITIZENS ON PATROL
Saether, Odd Geir
TURNAROUND
Sahl, Michael
WAITING FOR THE MOON
Salminen, Timo
HAMLET
TILINTEKO
VARJOJA PARATIISISSA
Salmones, Javier G.
LA VIDA ALEGRE
Salomon, Amnon
DEADLINE
DREAMERS
Salomon, Mikael
PETER VON SCHOLTEN
WOLF AT THE DOOR, THE

Samoilovski, Miso
HI-FI

Sanchez, Conrado
ANJOS DO ARRABALDE

Sanchez, Rodolfo
VERA

Sandor, Gregory
FORTY DAYS OF MUSA DAGH

Sanz, Nestor
EL AMOR ES UNA MUJERGORDA

Sarin, Vic
NOWHERE TO HIDE

Sas, Tamas
GONDOVISELES

Schafer, Martin
DEVILS PARADISE, THE
TAROT

Schenkel, Hansueli
PERSONAGGI & INTERPRETI

Scheuren, Jose Vincente
MAS ALLA DEL SILENCIO

Schier, Horst
WANNSEE CONFERENCE, THE

Schmidt-Reitwein, Jorg
DER NACHBAR
TRIUMPH DE GERECHTEN

Schneider, Robert
CEMIL

Schott, Hans
TESTET

Schubert, Franz
CASPAR DAVID FRIEDRICH

Schwarzenberger, Xaver
OTTO—DER NEUE FILM

Seale, John
STAKEOUT

Selikovsky, Hans
DIE DRECKSCHLEUDER

Sell, Jack M.
OUTTAKES

Semenovykh, Vadim
ZAVTRA BILA VOINA

Semin, Vyacheslav
VYKUP

Semler, Dean
LIGHTHORSEMEN, THE

Seng, Poon Hung
PEKING OPERA BLUES

Senkay, Ertunc
WATER ALSO BURNS

Seredin, Boris
TAYNAYA PROGULKA

Seresin, Michael
ANGEL HEART

Sevastyanov, Valery
RAZMAKH KRYLIEV

Shabatayev, Alexander
YA YEY NRAVLYUS

Shaji
PANCHAGNI

Shann, John
BLOODY NEW YEAR

Sharpe, Graham
DOT GOES TO HOLLYWOOD

Shaw, Steve
ZERO BOYS, THE

Shestoperov, Viktor
TANTSPLOSHCHADKA

Shevtsik, Vladimir
ZONTIK DLYA NOVOBRACHNYKH

Shhirtladze, Yuri
FAREWELL

Shing, Lam Wan
MAGNIFICENT WARRIORS

Shing-tung, Cheung
HAPPY BIGAMIST

Shkolnikov, Victor
VO VREMENA VOLCHYIKA ZAKONOV

Shlugleit, Eugene
EVIL DEAD 2: DEAD BY DAWN

Shnegur, Danny
RED RIDING HOOD

Shum, Jim
BEJALAI

Shuvalov, Valery
PO GLAVNOY ULITSE S ORKESTROM
STRANNAYAR ISTORIYAR DOKTORA DZHEKILA I MISTERA KHAIDA

Sillart, Juri
CHEREZ STO LET V MAE

Sillart, Yury
REQUIEM

Simakov, Vsevolod
ISKRENNE VASH . . .
POEZDKI NA STAROM AVTOMOBILE

Simanis, Davis
OBOROTEN TOM

Simmons, Lionel
LIFE CLASSES

Simon, Gerard
GRAND GUIGNOL

Simoncic, Dodo
CENA ODVAHY
TAXI NACH KAIRO

Simpson, Geoff
JILTED

Simpson, Geoffrey
INITIATION

Sirotek, Emil
CHOBOTNICE Z II. PATRA

Skwirczynski, Przemyslaw
MASKARADA
RYKOWISKO

Slama, David
CHINESE ARE COMING, THE
DAS TREIBHAUS
PENG! DU BIST TOT!

Slonisco, Federico
UNDICI GIORNI, UNDICI NOTTE

Smaragdis, Nikos
KLIOS

Smith, Chad D.
BLOODSUCKERS FROM OUTER SPACE

Smokler, Peter
NORTH SHORE

Smoot, Reed
RUSSKIES

Smutny, Vladimir
DEATH OF A BEAUTIFUL DREAM
DISCOPRIBEH

Sobocinski, Piotr
MAGNAT
ZJOEK

Sobocinski, Witold
ZJOEK

Sofr, Jaromir
WOLF'S HOLE

Sohlberg, Kari
JAAHYVAISET PRESIDENTILLE

Sokol, Yuri
WARM NIGHTS ON A SLOW MOVING TRAIN

Solano, Domingo
MOROS Y CRISTIANOS

Solares, Adolfo Martinez
ARQUIESTA EMILIO VARELA

Solis, Leonard
AMAZONS

Solis, Leonardo Rodriguez
EL ANO DEL CONEJO

Sonnenfeld, Barry
RAISING ARIZONA
THREE O'CLOCK HIGH
THROW MOMMA FROM THE TRAIN

Southon, Mike
ARIA
GOTHIC

Sova, Peter
GOOD MORNING, VIETNAM
TIN MEN

Spencer, Brenton
BLUE MONKEY
HIGHER EDUCATION

Sperling, David
STREET TRASH

Spinotti, Dante
ARIA
FROM THE HIP

Stanciu, Marian
ZLOTY POCIAG

Stannett, Ron
KEEPING TRACK

Stapleton, Oliver
ARIA
PRICK UP YOUR EARS
SAMMY AND ROSIE GET LAID

Stassen, Willy
HECTOR
LOVE IS A DOG FROM HELL

Stavrou, Aris
PHOTOGRAPH, THE
TA PAIDIA TIS CHELIDONAS

Stawicki, Jerzy
STANISLAW I ANNA
WIERNA RZEKA

Steiger, Ueli
PROMISED LAND

Stein, Peter
WILD PAIR, THE

Stepanov, Vladimir
LYUBOVYU ZA LYUBOV

Stephens, John M.
STEELE JUSTICE

Steyn, Jacques
CROSS

Stok, Witold
EAT THE RICH
FRIENDSHIP'S DEATH
HIDDEN CITY

Storaro, Vittorio
ISHTAR
LAST EMPEROR, THE

Stowicki, Jerzy
CUDZOZIEMKA

Stradling, Harry
BLIND DATE

Strasburg, Ivan
RITA, SUE AND BOB TOO!

Studebaker, Daryl
TROUBLE WITH DICK, THE

Suarez, Carlos
CARA DE ACELGA

Suarez, Ramon
MANUELA'S LOVES

Suerra, Eduardo
TANT QU'IL AURA DES FEMMES

Suhrstedt, Tim
MANNEQUIN

Suhrstedt, Timothy
SPACE RACE

Sukalo, Danijal
STRATEGIJA SVRAKE

Surtees, Bruce
BACK TO THE BEACH

Tafuri, Renato
DELIRIA
DISTANT LIGHTS
SEMBRA MORTO . . . ME E SOLO SVENUTO

Tahiri, Kader
PERLYOTNIYE PTIT

Tai, Wong Yau
EASTERN CONDORS

Takaba, Tetsuo
FINAL TAKE: THE GOLDEN AGE OF MOVIES
TORA-SAN'S BLUEBIRD FANTASY

Takashi, James
OVERKILL

Tammes, Fred
WHISTLE BLOWER, THE

Tamura, Masaki
MAGINA—MURA MONOGATARI

Tarasin, Tomasz
MIEDZY USTAMI A BRZEGIEM PUCHARU
NAD NIEMNEM

Tarbes, Jean-Jacques
LASSOCIATION DES MALFAITEURS

Tassos Alexakis
ANGELOS

Tataskin, Sergei
FAREWELL

Tattersall, Gale
ARIA
COMRADES

Taylor, Gil
BEDROOM WINDOW, THE

Taylor, Ronald Charles
OPERA

Taylor, Ronnie
CRY FREEDOM

Techizawa, Masao
ZEGEN

Tejada, Manuel
JUNTOS

Telsavaara, Timo
KILL CITY

Temerin, Alexei
PO ZAKONU VOENNOGO VREMENI

Tenas, Tote
SUFRE MAMON

Teran, Manuel
LA VIE PLATINEE

Terry Cole
THREE KINDS OF HEAT
Thiombiano, Issaka
YAM DAABO
Thompson, Bob
THIRTY MILLION RUSH, THE
Thomson, Alex
DATE WITH AN ANGEL
SICILIAN, THE
Thu, Dan
KOORDINATY SMERTI
Thurmann-Andersen, Erling
OFELAS
Tidy, Frank
HOT PURSUIT
JOHN AND THE MISSUS
Tirl, George
STEEL DAWN
Tochizawa, Masao
SEA AND POISON, THE
Tomasiavicus, Yonas
BLUDNYY SYN
Tomsic, Gary
ESCAPES
Tonelli, Renato
THIN LINE, THE
Toraille, Jean-Paul
DER TOD DES EMPEDOKLES
Torrance, Bob
PERFECT MATCH, THE
Torruella, Magi
LESCOT
Toth, Janos
AZ UTOLSOKEZIRAT
Tovar, Carlos
POR LOS CAMINOS VERDES
Travitsky, Leonid
GRUBAYA POSADKA
OKHOTA NA DRAKONA
Trbuljak, Goran
OFICIR S RUZOM
Tremblay, Jean-Charles
EVA: GUERRILLERA
Trenas, Tote
ALIEN PREDATOR
Treu, Wolfgang
CRIME OF HONOR
Treu, Wolgang
MASCHENKA
Triandafilou, Christos
I KEKARMENI
Trier, Bodil
NEGERKYS & LABRE LARVER
Trimakno, Bambang
STABILIZER, THE
Trushkovsky, Vasily
KAPITAN "PILIGRIMA"
Trutkovsky, Vasily
ODINOKAYA ZHENCHINA ZHELAET POZNAKOMITAYA
Tunes, Joe
ULTIMAX FORCE
Tuomi, Olavie
AKALLINEN MIES
Turkovic, Boris
KRALJEVA ZAVRSNICA
Turnbull, Tom
SHELLEY
Tutunov, Gassant
IZ ZHIZNI NACHALNIKA UGOLOVNOGO ROZYSKA
Tynyshpayev, Iskander
ZNAY NASHIKH
Ulloa, Alejandro
ROMANCA FINAL
Urbanczyk, Joseph
ALLNIGHTER, THE
Urbanczyk, Joseph D.
CRY WILDERNESS
Ureta, Raul Perez
VISA U.S.A.
Uriu, Toshihiko
GONDOLA
Vacano, Jost
ROBOCOP
Vamos, Thomas
GATE, THE
Van Damme, Charles
NOYADE INTERDITE
Van Damme, Charlie
MELO
van de Sande, Theo
LOOKING FOR EILEEN
van den Bos, Paul
DIARY OF A MAD OLD MAN
VAN GELUK GESPROKEN
Van Den Ende, Walther
BORAN—ZEIT ZUM ZIELEN
van den Ende, Walther
LES NOCES BARBARES
NOCE EN GALILEE
Van Der Enden, Eddie
CAUGHT
van der Vyver, Johan
HOSTAGE
Vanden Ende, Walther
FALSCH
Vandenberg, Gerard
CASPAR DAVID FRIEDRICH
Varga, Gyorgy
CAT CITY
Varja, Olli
LAIN ULKOPUOLELLA
Varvarigos, Yannis
IKONA ENOS MYTHIKOU PROSOPOU
Vatinyan, Rudolf
PESN PROSHEDSHIKH DNEY
Vega, Victor
EULALIA
Vereschak, Vadim
I NIKTO NA SVETE
Verga, Luigi
LES EXPLOITS DUN JEUNE DON JUAN
Verzhbitsky, Bogdan
KAZHDYY OKHOTNIK ZHELAET ZNAT
Verzier, Rene
MORNING MAN, THE
WILD THING
Veseler, Roman
NABAT NA RASSVETE
Vicquery, Jean-Claude
TERMINUS
Vidgeon, Robin
HELLRAISER
Vierny, Sacha
BELLY OF AN ARCHITECT, THE
Vilensky, Valery
V TALOM SNEGE ZVON RUCHIA
Villalobos, Reynaldo
RUNNING MAN, THE
Villarias, Leoncio
MURIERON A MITAD DEL RIO
Villasenor, Leopoldo
BEAKS
Vincze, Ernie
BUSINESS AS USUAL
Vladic, Radoslav
NA PUTA ZA KATANGU
Vogel, Daniel
IL EST GENIAL PAPY!
von Dittmer, Hans
BLOOD TRACKS
Von Sternberg, Nicholas
VALET GIRLS
Vovnyanko, Igor
TAYNY MADAM VONG
Vuorinen, Esa
JAAN KAANTOPIIRI
Wages, William
MAN OUTSIDE
Wagner, Roy
NIGHTMARE ON ELM STREET 3: DREAM WARRIORS, A
RETURN TO HORROR HIGH
Wagner, Roy H.
NIGHTFORCE
WITCHBOARD
Wagstaff, Keith
RUNNING FROM THE GUNS
Wah, Ma Chun
MAGNIFICENT WARRIORS
Wahlberg, Tomas
MANNEN FRAN MALLORCA
Waite, Ric
ADVENTURES IN BABYSITTING
Wakeford, Kent
PRINCESS ACADEMY, THE
Walker, John
WINTER TAN, A
Walsh, David M.
FATAL BEAUTY
OUTRAGEOUS FORTUNE
SUMMER SCHOOL
Walther, Jurg
BLOOD DINER
Wancai, Chen
OLD WELL
Wapshott, Gary
CASSANDRA
Watkin, David
MOONSTRUCK
Wegenstein, Grisha
TRINAJSTATA GODENICA NA PRINCA
Wei, Feng
BLACK CANNON INCIDENT, THE
Wein, Yossi
CHOZE AHAVA
KFAFOT
Weincke, Jan
DEAD OF WINTER
HELLO AGAIN
WEEDS
Weindler, Helge
HELSINKI NAPOLI—ALL NIGHT LONG
Werdin, Egon
VERSTECKTE LIEBE
Werner, Klaus
ZARTLICHE CHAOTEN
Wertwyn, Lex
VAN PAEMEL FAMILY, THE
West, Brian
EIGHTY FOUR CHARING CROSS ROAD
West, Jonathan
MUNCHIES
Westbury, Ken
BELLMAN AND TRUE
Wexler, Haskell
MATEWAN
Wexler, Howard
DREAMANIAC
HARD TICKET TO HAWAII
Whitteron, John
BACHELOR GIRL
Wiatrak, Ken
SLAVE GIRLS FROM BEYOND INFINITY
Wickremarachchi, Lal
VIRAGAYA
Williams, Billy
SUSPECT
Willis, Gordon
PICK-UP ARTIST, THE
Wilson, Ian
WISH YOU WERE HERE
Wilson, Tony
DEAR CARDHOLDER
Wing-hang, Wong
BETTER TOMORROW, A
Won, Pak Gyong
TALMAE WA POMDARI
Wooster, Arthur
EAT THE PEACH
Xinsheng, Wang
BLACK CANNON INCIDENT, THE
CUO WEI
Yakovitch, Mikhail
SDELKA
Yakushev, Viktor
VALENTIN I VALENTINA
Yamazaki, Takaya
ITAZU
Yamazaki, Yoshi
SHINRAN: SHIRO MICHI
Yanovsky, Alexander
OBVINYAETSYA SVADBA
Yarussi, Daniel
DANGER ZONE, THE
Yau, Herman
YI LOU YI
Yavuryan, Albert
ODINOKAYA ORESHINA
Yimou, Zhang
BIG PARADE, THE
OLD WELL
Yong, Han
CUO WEI
Yong, Hou
DAO MAZEI
Youkana, Karim
LES MENDIANTS
Young, Hou
DOCTOR SUN YATSEN

Yourizditzky, Sergei
ODINOKIJ GOLOS CELOVEKA

Yuan-Xing, Chow
HEROIC PIONEERS

Yue, Lu
BUDDHA'S LOCK

Yuri —Ilienko
RODNIK DLIA ZHAZHDUSHCHIKH

Zabolotsky, Anatoly
OBRYV

Zaccaro, Maurizio
LUNGA VITA ALLA SIGNORA!

Zalar, Zivko
UVEK SPREMNE ZENE
VEC VIDJENO

Zanati, Ahmed
ABBES

Zarindast, Ali R.
PEDDLER, THE

Zervoulakos, Takis
OH BABYLON

Zhiguo, An
LAST EMPRESS, THE

Ziao Lie, Wang
BUDDHA'S LOCK

Ziesche, Peter
SO VIELE TRAUME

Zitzermann, Bernard
MAN IN LOVE, A
SI LE SOLEIL NE REVENAIT PAS

Zolotaryov, Alexei
KAPITAN "PILIGRIMA"

Zsigmond, Vilmos
WITCHES OF EASTWICK, THE

Zurinaga, Marcos
LA GRAN FIESTA

Zvirbulis, Mik
STRAKH

COMPOSERS OF MUSICAL SCORES

Abril, Anton Garcia
LA RUSA

Aceves, Heriberto
EL DIABLO, EL SANTO Y EL TONTO

Adam, Adolphe
DANCERS

Adonias, Nelson
SDELKA

Agmussen, Claus
JAG ELSKER DIG

Agmussen, Svend
JAG ELSKER DIG

Ahvenlahti, Olli
PIKKUPOJAT

Alarcon, Sebastian
YAGUAR

Alcaraz, Luis
CINCO NACOS ASALTAN A LAS VEGAS

Alcover, Raul
LOS INVITADOS

Alexandrov, Gennady
NOVYE SKAZKI SHAKHEREZADY
YA YEY NRAVLYUS

Aliyev, Rafik
CHKATULKA IZ KREPOSTI

Alizade, Akshin
YA LYUBIL VAC BOLSHE ZHIZNI

Allan, Cameron
GOOD WIFE, THE

Allen, Scott
POULE ET FRITES

Allessandrini, Raymond
TRAVELLING AVANT

Alonso, Miguel Angel
WELCOME MARIA

Alvarez, Lucia
REALM OF FORTUNE, THE

Alvin, Dave
BORDER RADIO

Amaldev, Jerry
NILAKURINHI POOTHAPPOL

Amaran, Ganagai
CHINNATHAMBI PERIYATHAMBI

Amivi, Banio
IL FASCINO SOTTILE DEL PECCATO

Anderson, Benny
MIO, MOY MIO

Andion, Patxi
LA ESTANQUERA DE VALLECAS

Angel "Cucco" Pena
LA GRAN FIESTA

Aragon, Emilio
POLICIA

Arancibia, Rivas
SDELKA

Arkin, Eddie
PRETTY SMART

Armando Manzanero
RETO A LA VIDA

Armstrong, Michael
SILENT NIGHT, DEADLY NIGHT PART II

Arriagada, Jorge
BUISSON ARDENT
LE MIRACULE
LES MENDIANTS
MEMOIRE DES APPARENCES: LA VIE EST UN SONGE

Arroyo, Pascal
SALE DESTIN!

Arseny Klopotovsky
OBESHCHAYU BYT

Artemyev, Eduard
KAZHDYY OKHOTNIK ZHELAET ZNAT
KORABL PRISHELTSEV
KURIER
PROSHAL ZELEN LETA
SEKUNDA NA PODVIG
STRANNAYAR ISTORIYAR DOKTORA DZHEKILA I MISTERA KHAIDA

Artyomyev, Eduard
V TALOM SNEGE ZVON RUCHIA

Aserud, Bent
ETTER RUBICON
PLASTPOSEN

Asselbergs, Lucas
BLOND DOLLY

Atkinson, Michael
DEAR CARDHOLDER

Atkinson ed, Michael
JILTED

Auberson, Antoine
SI LE SOLEIL NE REVENAIT PAS

Augusto, Servulo
NIGHT ANGELS

Azevedo, Carlos
JESTER,THE

Babayan, Rafael
ODINOKAYA ORESHINA

Babida, Chris
SWORN BROTHERS

Babushkin, Viktor
AKTSIA
YAGUAR

Bach, Johann Sebastian
EPIDEMIC
MELO
UNE FLAMME DANS MON COEUR
ZYCIE WEWNETRZNE

Bach, Peter
EPIDEMIC

Bachelet, Pierre
EMMANUELLE 5

Badalamenti, Angelo
NIGHTMARE ON ELM STREET 3: DREAM WARRIORS, A
TOUGH GUYS DON'T DANCE
WEEDS

Bahjawa
ISHTAR

Baker, Michael Conway
JOHN AND THE MISSUS
SHELLEY

Bakhor, Firus
A SANTA DERVIS

Balazs, Ferenc
GONDOVISELES
LAURA

Balsara, V.
RUDRABEENA

Bandhu, Singh
TAMAS

Banerjee, Mrinal
APAN GHAREY

Banks, Brian
NICE GIRLS DON'T EXPLODE
PINOCCHIO AND THE EMPEROR OF THE NIGHT

Bantzer, Claus
DRAGON'S FOOD

Bardanashvili, Iosif
CHEGEMSKIY DETEKTIV

Barnabe, Arrigo
CIDADE OCULTA
VERA

Barry, John
HEARTS OF FIRE
LIVING DAYLIGHTS, THE

Bashung, Alain
LE BEAUF

Basner, Veniamin
TAYNAYA PROGULKA

Bateman, Bill
BORDER RADIO

Bates, Steve
DUTCH TREAT

Bazz, John
BORDER RADIO

Bebey, Francis
YAM DAABO

Bechard, Gorman
PSYCHOS IN LOVE

Beckert, Dieter
DER JUNGE MIT DEM GROSSEN SCHWARZEN HUND

Bell, Wayne
TRESPASSES

Bellavance, Ginette
LE SOURD DANS LA VILLE

Bellini, Vincenzo
MASCARA

Bellon, Roger
PRINCESS ACADEMY, THE

Belyaiev, Alexander
VREMYA ZHELANIY

Belyayev, Alexander
DIKIY KHMEL

Bennett, Eddy
ODYSSEE D'AMOUR

Berardi, Daniel
EL HOMBRE DE LA DEUDA EXTERNA

Berenzy, John
MAGIC SNOWMAN, THE

Beresford, Steve
AVRIL BRISE

Beretta, Mario
ALPINE FIRE

Berger, Okko
BORAN—ZEIT ZUM ZIELEN

Berlin, Steve
BORDER RADIO

Berlin Game
DOWN TWISTED

Bernaola, Carmelo
A LOS CUATRO VIENTOS
MADRID

Bernheim, Francois
TANDEM

Bernstein, Charles
ALLNIGHTER, THE
DUDES

Bernstein, Elmer
AMAZING GRACE AND CHUCK
LEONARD PART 6

Bernstein, Peter
MIRACLES
MORGAN STEWART'S COMING HOME

Best, Peter
CUSTODY

Bhatia, Vanraj
TAMAS

Bibergan, Vadim
DUBLYOR NACHINAET DEYSTVOVAT
KRASNAYA STRELA
PROSTI
SON V RUKU, ILI CHEMODON
TEMA

Biglin, David
FIREHOUSE

Bijlstra, Cees
VAN GELUK GESPROKEN

Bilinski, Marek
PRZYJACIEL WESOLEGO DIABLA

Billy, Jean-Marie
FALSCH

Bisharat, John
DEATH WISH 4: THE CRACKDOWN

Bishop, Michael
THREE KINDS OF HEAT

Biswas, Hemanga
LALAN FAKIR

Bizet, G.
ISKUSHENIE DON ZHUANA
Bjerkestrand, Kjetil
OFELAS
Blades, Ruben
POR LOS CAMINOS VERDES
Blake, Howard
MONTH IN THE COUNTRY, A
Bobokhidze, Yakov
GOSPODA AVANTYURISTY
Boddicker, Michael
WHITE WATER SUMMER
Bogart Co
PEKKA PUUPAA POLIISINA
Bogdanowicz, Mariusz
MASKARADA
Bohren, Geir
ETTER RUBICON
PLASTPOSEN
Bola, Jesus
LAS DOS ORILLAS
Bolling, Claude
LA RUMBA
Bonebrake, DJ
BORDER RADIO
Bonezzi, Bernardo
MIENTRAS HAYA LUZ
Bongusto, Fred
SUPERFANTOZZI
Bos, Ruud
DE RATELRAT
Boswell, Simon
DELIRIA
LE FOTO DI GIOIA
Boulanger, Lili
LA PASSION BEATRICE
Bourland, Roger
TROUBLE WITH DICK, THE
Bouvot, Vincent-Marie
POUSSIERE D'ANGE
Box, Betty
BENJI THE HUNTED
Box, Euel
BENJI THE HUNTED
Brahms, Johannes
HIP, HIP, HURRA!
IL EST GENIAL PAPY!
MELO
TO MARKET, TOMARKET
Branca, Glenn
BELLY OF AN ARCHITECT, THE
Branduardi, Angelo
DISTANT LIGHTS
Brauns, Martina
SVIDANIE NA MLECHNOM PUTI
Bravo, Roberto
EL SOCIO DE DIOS
Bray, Stephen
WHO'S THAT GIRL
Breant, Francois
LA VIE PLATINEE
Breiner, Peter
TAXI NACH KAIRO
Brint, Simon
EAT THE RICH
Britten, Benjamin
BAD BLOOD
Brody, Janos
CSOK, ANYU
Broughton, Bruce
BIG SHOTS
CROSS MY HEART
HARRY AND THE HENDERSONS
MONSTER SQUAD, THE
SQUARE DANCE
Brouwer, Leo
VISA U.S.A.
Brown, Greg
PERSONAL FOUL
Bruel, Sanne
NEGERKYS & LABRE LARVER
Bruzdowicz, Joanna
MANUELA'S LOVES
Budd, Roy
BIG BANG, THE
Burger, Simon
VROEGER IS DOOD
Burman, R.D.
DACAIT
INAAM DUS HAZAAR
Burns, Ralph
IN THE MOOD
Burwell, Carter
BEAT, THE
RAISING ARIZONA
Butsko, Yury
NABAT NA RASSVETE
Byrne, David
LAST EMPEROR, THE
Bystryakov, Vladimir
OBVINYAETSYA SVADBA
Cabral, Pedro Caldeira
JESTER,THE
Cacciapaglia, Roberto
A FIOR DI PELLE
Calabrese, James
SULLIVAN'S PAVILION
Calayud, Juan Jose
MUJERES SALVAJES
Camp, Oscar
AMAZONS
Campannio, Franco
ITALIANI A RIO
Campos, Kiko
YO, EL EJECUTOR
Cantarelli, Beppe
NOI UOMINI DURI
VIA MONTENAPOLEONE
Capobianco, Carmine
PSYCHOS IN LOVE
Carjamming
UNA DONNA DA SCOPRIRE
Carmody, Mark
TUESDAY WEDNESDAY
Carow, Stefan
SO VIELE TRAUME
Carpenter, John
PRINCE OF DARKNESS
Carpi, Fiorenzo
NOTTE ITALIANA
Carras, Nicholas
OMEGA SYNDROME
Carreon, Gustavo C.
LAS TRAIGO . . . MUERTAS
Carrion, Gustavo C.
ENTRE FICHERAS ANDA EL DIABLO
MAS VALE PAJARO EN MANO . . .
Carrion, Gustavo Cesar
FORAJIDOS EN LA MIRA
Carrion, Rafael
ARQUIESTA EMILIO VARELA
TIERRA DE VALIENTES
Carrion, Ricardo
EL MUERTO DEL PALOMO
ROSA DE LA FRONTERA
Carter, Ron
LA PASSION BEATRICE
Casale, Gerald V.
REVENGE OF THE NERDS II: NERDS IN PARADISE
Castagnos, Miguel
POULE ET FRITES
Castineiras de Dios, Jose Louis
CHECHECHELA—UNA CHICA DEL BARRIO
Castro, Arturo
EL HIJO DE PEDRO NAVAJAS
Castro, Javier
EL HOMBRE DESNUDO
Ceccarelli, Lou
STRIKE COMMANDO
Ceccarelli, Luigi
DEATH STONE
Cengiz Yaltkaya
I WAS A TEENAGE T.V. TERRORIST
Chabrol, Mathieu
LE CRI DU HIBOU
Chabrol, Matthieu
MASQUES
Chagas, Luis
ANJOS DO ARRABALDE
Chalaris, Christodoulos
PHOTOGRAPH, THE
Chang II, Chon
TALMAE WA POMDARI
Chaplin, Charlie
BAD BLOOD
Charpentier, Gustave
ARIA
Chase, Gary
SUMMER CAMP NIGHTMARE
Chase, Thomas
CATCH THE HEAT
Chase/Rucker Productions
ALIEN PREDATOR
Chekalov, Pavel
GOVORIT MOSKVA
Chernavsky, Yury
SEZON CHUDES
Chernetsky, Vitaly
SENTIMENTALNOE PUTESHESTVIE NA KARTOSHKU
Cheshm-Azar, Nasser
LODGERS
Chevalier, Christian
CHARLIE DINGO
Chiaravalle, Franco
QUEL RAGAZZO DELLA CURVA "B"
Chihara, Paul
KILLING TIME, THE
WALK ON THE MOON, A
Chino, Shuichi
RYOMA O KITTA OTOKO
Chopin, Frederic
LADY OF THE CAMELIAS
Chouchan, Francois
IL EST GENIAL PAPY!
Chow, Johnson
TRUE COLORS
Christie, Tony
SIERRA LEONE
Chung, Danny
LAONIANG GOU SAO
TRUE COLORS
Cipriani, Stelvio
BEAKS
RAGE OF HONOR
Cirino, Chuck
BIG BAD MAMA II
Clapton, Eric
LETHAL WEAPON
Claus Bantzer
POET'S SILENCE, THE
Clausen, Alf
NUMBER ONE WITH A BULLET
Cleff, Johnny
SATURDAY NIGHT AT THE PALACE
Clinton, George S.
TOO MUCH
WILD THING
Cohen, Michael
HANSEL AND GRETEL
Coleman, Patrick
BLUE MONKEY
HOUSEKEEPER, THE
Columbier, Michel
SURRENDER
Conrad, Jack
CLUB LIFE
Conte, Paolo
AURELIA
Conti, Bill
BABY BOOM
BROADCAST NEWS
HAPPY NEW YEAR
I LOVE NEW YORK
MASTERS OF THE UNIVERSE
PRAYER FOR THE DYING, A
Continiello, Ubaldo
DOLCE PELLE DI ANGELA
Convertino, Michael
HIDDEN, THE
Cookerly, Jack
OMEGA SYNDROME
Copeland, Stewart
WALL STREET
Coppola, Carmine
GARDENS OF STONE
Corriveau, Jean
NIGHT ZOO
Cortazar, Ernesto
CORRUPCION
FIERAS EN BRAMA
OLOR A MUERTE
YERBA SANGRIENTE
Cosma, Vladimir
COERS CROISES
LE MOUSTACHU
LEVY ET GOLIATH
NITWITS
Courage, Alexander
SUPERMAN IV: THE QUEST FOR PEACE

Cox, Andy
TIN MEN

Craddock, Kenny
LOVECHILD, THE

Creatures, The
UNA DONNA DA SCOPRIRE

Crivelli, Carlo
DEVIL IN THE FLESH

Cullen, Trish
CARE BEARS ADVENTURE IN WONDERLAND, THE

Cunningham, David
TERMINUS

D'Andrea, John
HUNTER'S BLOOD

d'lla Torre, Cedrick
MUJERES DE LA FRONTERA

Dahlgren, Eva
TESTET

Daily News
LA VIE DISSOLUE DE GERARD FLOQUE

Dalla, Lucio
I PICARI

Dalvanius
NGATI

Dambis, Pauls
OBOROTEN TOM

Daniels, Rich
OUTTAKES

Danna, Michael
FAMILY VIEWING

Dante, Carl
SLAVE GIRLS FROM BEYOND INFINITY

Daring, Mason
MATEWAN

Das, Ajay
AMAR KANTAK

Das, Balakrishna
JAIDEV

Das, Robin
THIS IS NOT OUR DESTINATION

Das., Ajay
ARPAN

Dasgupta., Jyothishka
PHERA

Dashkevich, Vladimir
PLIUMBUM, ILI OPASNAIA IGIA

Dashkevitch, Vladimir
KAK STAT SCHASTLIVYM

Davis, Carl
CRIME OF HONOR

Davis, Miles
STREET SMART

De Angelis, Guido
DELITTI

De Angelis, Maurizio
DELITTI

de Boer, Lodewijk
ALS IN EEN ROES

de Diego, Emilio
LONG STRIDER

De Falla
ISKUSHENIE DON ZHUANA

de Hollanda, Chico Buarque
AMOR EN CAMPO MINADO

de Matteo, Luis
LOS DUENOS DEL SILENCIO

De Rossi, Ugo
SOTTO IL RISTORANTE CINESE

De Sica, Manuel
BELLIFRESCHI
MONTECARLO GRAN CASINO
SOLDATI: 365 GIORNI ALL' ALBA

de Wilde, Jan
HECTOR

Deak, Tamas
CAT CITY

Debney, John
WILD PAIR, THE

Debski, Krzesimir
LE JEUNE MAGICIEN

del Rio, Javier
JUANA LA CANTINERA

DeLabio, Richard
DELOS ADVENTURE, THE

Delerue, Georges
FAMILY BUSINESS
LONELY PASSION OF JUDITH HEARNE,THE
MAID TO ORDER
MAN IN LOVE, A
PICK-UP ARTIST, THE

Delia, Joe
CHINA GIRL

Demay, Andre
JEUX D'ARTIFICES

Denver, John
FIRE AND ICE

Dev, Sarang
PANCHVATI

Devrees, Frederic
LES NOCES BARBARES

Dholakia, Rajat
MIRCH MASALA

Dholakla, Rajat
THIS IS NOT OUR DESTINATION

Di Stafano, Fulvio
FRANCESCA

Diamond, Joel
SUICIDE CLUB, THE

Dikker, Loek
IRIS

Din, Hamza Bl
ROBINSON NO NIWA

Djanelidze, Nana
REPENTANCE

Dmitri Shostakovich
LAW OF DESIRE

Doble, Vainica
MY GENERAL

Doe, John
BORDER RADIO

Doga, Yevgeny
TANTSPLOSHCHADKA
VALENTIN I VALENTINA

Dolby, Thomas
GOTHIC

Dome, Zsolt
DIARY FOR MY LOVED ONES

Dompierre, Francois
KID BROTHER, THE

Donaggio, Pino
BARBARIANS, THE
DANCERS
HOTEL COLONIAL
JENATSCH
LA MONACA DIMONZA
MORO AFFAIR, THE

Donohue, Marc
OPPOSING FORCE

Dorff, Steve
BACK TO THE BEACH

Doukkali, Abdelouaheb
ABBES

Doyle, Roger
BUDAWANNY

Dreith, Dennis
PARTY CAMP

Dreoni, Elena
DELIZIA

Duchesne, Andre
LA COULEUR ENCERCLEE

Dudley, Anne
HIDING OUT

Dundas, David
WITHNAIL AND I

Duprez, John
PERSONAL SERVICES

Dutilleux, Henri
SOUS LE SOLEIL DE SATAN

Dvorak, Antonin
YALDEI STALIN

Dvorak, Milan
CENA MEDU

Dzierlatka, Arie
LA VALLEE FANTOME

Eca, Luiz
UM FILM 100% BRAZILEIRO

Edelman, Randy
CHIPMUNK ADVENTURE, THE

Einhorn, Richard
DEAD OF WINTER
NIGHTMARE AT SHADOW WOODS

Ekhala, Olva
SEREBRYANAYA PRYAZHA KAROLINY

El Ghiwane, Nass
ABBES

Elfers, Konrad
ANITA—DANCES OF VICE

Elfman, Danny
SUMMER SCHOOL

Elgar, Edward
LAST OF ENGLAND, THE

Elias, Anders
MIO, MOY MIO

Emiliano, Antonio
DUMA VEZ POR TODAS

Emmett, Richard
HOUR OF THE ASSASSIN

English, Jon
BELL DIAMOND

Entezami, Madjid
PEDDLER, THE

Epstein, Jep
TRAGICO TERREMOTO EN MEXICO

Eriksson, Claes
LEIF

Erkin, Arif
DEGIRMEN

Ersoy, Bulent
SIERRA LEONE

Esperon, Manuel
MI NOMBRE ES GATILLO

Esquivel, Alvaro
EULALIA

Etoll, Robert
DANGER ZONE, THE

Fabricius-Bjerre, Bent
PETER VON SCHOLTEN

Fakhreldini, Farhad
GOZARESH-E YEK GHATL

Falk, Charles
LEIF

Faltermeyer, Harold
BEVERLY HILLS COP II
FATAL BEAUTY
FIRE AND ICE
RUNNING MAN, THE

Fancy
CEMIL

Farrell, Mike
LEADING EDGE, THE

Fataar, Ricky
HIGH TIDE

Febre, Louis
CODE NAME ZEBRA

Feidel, Brad
BIG EASY, THE

Fenton, George
CRY FREEDOM
EIGHTY FOUR CHARING CROSS ROAD
WHITE MISCHIEF

Ferguson, Jay
BEST SELLER

Fernando, Sarath
VIRAGAYA
WITNESS TO A KILLING

Ferre, Mario
EL DUENO DEL SOL

Ferrick, Billy
SPACE RACE

Fiedel, Brad
LETS GET HARRY
NOWHERE TO HIDE

Fikejz, Daniel
PRATELE BERMUDSKEHO TROJUHELNIKU

Fikejz, Nahral D.
PRATELE BERMUDSKEHO TROJUHELNIKU

Finn, Tim
LES PATTERSON SAVES THE WORLD

Fischer, Gunther
DER BARENHAUTER

Fiser, Lubos
DEATH OF A BEAUTIFUL DREAM

Fitzgerald, Ben
TO MARKET, TOMARKET

Flebig, Frank
CEMIL

Flores, Marco
RATAS DE LA CIUDAD

Flores, Marcos
JUNTOS

Folk, Robert
CANT BUY ME LOVE
POLICE ACADEMY 4: CITIZENS ON PATROL

Foster, David
SECRET OF MY SUCCESS, THE

Fox, Neal
HAPPY HOUR

Fradkin, Carlos
EL HOMBRE DE LA DEUDA EXTERNA

Fradkin, Marc
TVOYO MIRNOE NEBO

Frank, David
OFF THE MARK

Franssen, Jan
FALSCH

Frederick, Jesse
MISSION KILL

Friis Mikkelsen, Jarl
KAMPEN OM DEN RODE KO

Friman, Leo
TILINTEKO

Frizzi, Fabio
ALADDIN
TENTAZIONE

Froom, Mitchell
SLAMDANCE

Furst, Baby Lopez
EN RETIRADA

Furts, Baby Lopez
LA BUSQUEDA

Fuzzy
HIP, HIP, HURRA!
STRIT OG STUMME

Gabrielov, Miki
HA INSTALATOR

Gabuniya, Nodar
VELIKIY POKHOD ZA NEVESTOY

Ganesh, Shanker
THIRUMATHI ORU VEGUMATHI

Geller, Herb
LITTLE PROSECUTOR, THE

Gelmetti, Vittorio
ANGELUS NOVUS

Genkov, Georgi
TRINAJSTATA GODENICA NA PRINCA

George S. Clinton
AMERICAN NINJA 2: THE CONFRONTATION

Gerard, Philippe
MELO

Gevorgyan, Andrei
IZ ZHIZNI NACHALNIKA UGOLOVNOGO ROZYSKA
TAYNY MADAM VONG

Gevorkyan, Yevgeny
SOUCHASTNIKI

Gibbs, Michael
HEAT
HOUSEKEEPING

Gibson, Colin
LOVECHILD, THE

Gibson, Don
SIERRA LEONE

Gil, Gilberto
UM TREM PARA AS ESTRELAS

Gil, Jose Alberto
RELACAO FIEL E VERDADEIRA

Gintrowski, Przemyslaw
MATKA KROLOW
WERYFIKACJA

Girre, Ronan
QUATRE AVENTURES DE REINETTE ET MIRABELLE

Gladkov, Grigory
POEZD VNE RASPISANIA

Glasel, Jan
KAMPEN OM DEN RODE KO

Glass, Philip
HAMBURGER HILL

Glasser, Richard
TALKING WALLS

Gleason, Patrick
DEADLY ILLUSION

Gleeson, Patrick
BEDROOM WINDOW, THE
STACKING

Glenmark, Andres
TESTET

Glinka, M.
ISKUSHENIE DON ZHUANA

Glowna, Nick
MASCHENKA

Gluck, Jesus
ASIGNATURA APROBADA
REDONDELA

Gock, Les
BELINDA

Goglat, Michel
CROSS

Goldberg, Barry
THREE FOR THE ROAD

Goldenberg, Mark
TEEN WOLF TOO

Goldshtein, Alexander
STARAYA AZBUKA

Goldsmith, Jerry
ALLAN QUATERMAIN AND THE LOST CITY OF GOLD
EXTREME PREJUDICE
INNERSPACE
LIONHEART

Goldsmith, Joel
BANZAI RUNNER
CRYSTAL HEART
MURIERON A MITAD DEL RIO

Goldstein, Alexander
CHELOVEK C AKKORDEONOM

Goldstein, William
HELLO AGAIN

Goodman, Miles
LA BAMBA
LIKE FATHER, LIKE SON
SQUEEZE, THE

Goodwin, Ron
VALHALLA

Goold, Barry
EVA: GUERRILLERA

Gorgoni, Al
MILLION DOLLAR MYSTERY

Gorny, Zbigniew
PRYWATNE SLEDZTWO

Gounod, Charles-Francois
CHOBOTNICE Z II. PATRA

Grabowsky, Paul
BIT PART, THE

Graham, David
COMRADES

Granier, Georges
LE GRAND CHEMIN

Great, Don
NECROPOLIS

Gregoire, Richard
LES FOUS DE BASSAN

Grieg, Edvard
SOFIA

Grigoriou, Michalis
O PARADISSOS ANIGI ME ANTIKLIDI

Griva, Alexander
RAZMAKH KRYLIEV

Gross, Gregg
DEATHROW GAMESHOW

Gross, Guy
DOT GOES TO HOLLYWOOD

Grunberg, Sven
REQUIEM
VO VREMENA VOLCHYIKA ZAKONOV

Grupo Travieso
MAGDALENA VIRAGA

Gruska, Jay
PRINCIPAL, THE

GSD'Arto
STABILIZER, THE

Guard, Barrie
INDIAN SUMMER
MONSTER IN THE CLOSET

Guba, Vladimir
POKLONIS DO ZEMLI

Gubaidulina, Sofia
KREUTZEROVA SONATA

Guerrero, Francisco
YEAR OF AWAKENING, THE

Gulgowski, Wlodek
OM KARLEK

Gwangwa, Jonas
CRY FREEDOM

Hadzinassios, Giorgios
PROINI PERIPOLOS

Hakparast, Mohamed Shah
PERLYOTNIYE PTIT

Hamlisch, Marvin
THREE MEN AND A BABY

Hannah, Jonathan
IF LOOKS COULD KILL

Hanoch, Shalom
KFAFOT

Harpaz, Udi
HOLLYWOOD SHUFFLE

Harrison, Nigel
NIGHTFORCE

Hart, James
GHOST FEVER

Hassan, Ahmend
WINTER TAN, A

Hawkes, Greg
ANNA

Hayen, Todd
KILLER WORKOUT

Hector
JAAN KAANTOPIIRI

Heede, Fritz
CRY WILDERNESS

Heintz, Tim
DEADLY PREY
MANKILLERS

Heller, Bill
DERANGED

Hendorff, Christoph Leis
OTTO—DER NEUE FILM

Hensel, Rainer
TERUG NAAR OEGSTGEEST

Henze, Hans Werner
COMRADES

Herrera, Diego
EL ANSIA DE MATAR
HERENCIA DE VALIENTES

Hersant, Philippe
O DESEJADO—LES MONTAGNES DE LA LUNE

Heyne, Chris
VERSTECKTE LIEBE

Higgins, Kenneth
SULLIVAN'S PAVILION

Hilmarsson, Hilmar Oern
SKYTTURNAR

Hiltunen, Risto
AKALLINEN MIES

Hirao, Masaaki
SURE DEATH 4

Hoenig, Michael
GATE, THE

Hofstede, Henk
ZJOEK

Holdridge, Lee
BORN IN EAST L.A.
WALK LIKE A MAN

Honda, Toshiyuki
TAXING WOMAN, A

Hopgood, Fincina
TO MARKET, TOMARKET

Horian, Richard
STUDENT CONFIDENTIAL

Horner, James
BATTERIES NOT INCLUDED
P.K. & THE KID
PROJECT X

Houdy, Pierick
BACH AND BROCCOLI

Howard, James Newton
CAMPUS MAN
PROMISED LAND

Howarth, Alan
PRINCE OF DARKNESS

Hoyer, Ole
WARRIORS OF THE APOCALYPSE
WHEELS OF TERROR

Humperdinck, Engelbert
HANSEL AND GRETEL

Hunter, Denise
JILTED

Huxley, Craig
PROGRAMMED TO KILL

Hyman, Dick
MOONSTRUCK

Hytti, Antti
URSULA

Iglesias, Alberto
BALADA DA PRAIA DOS CAES
LA PLAYA DE LOS PERROS

Igor Stravinsky
LAW OF DESIRE

Ikaba, Shinichiro
ZEGEN

Ilayaraja
POOVIZHI VASALILE

Immel, Jerry
PROGRAMMED TO KILL

Infantino, Antonio
TERNOSECCO

Inoue, Takayuki
KATAKU NO HITO

Inti-Illimani
IN DER WUSTE

Irving, Robert
STREET SMART
Isfalt, Bjorn
MY LIFE AS A DOG
Isham, Mark
MADE IN HEAVEN
Island, Brian
VIRGIN QUEEN OF ST. FRANCIS HIGH, THE
Izykowska-Mironowicz, Anna
CUDZOZIEMKA
Jackson, David A.
COLD STEEL
CYCLONE
Jagatara
ROBINSON NO NIWA
Jain, Ravindra
GHULAMI KI ZANJEER
James, Tim
DEADLY PREY
MANKILLERS
Jankel, Chaz
MAKING MR.RIGHT
Jans, Alaric
HOUSE OF GAMES
Jansen, Hans
DEADLINE
Jarre, Maurice
FATAL ATTRACTION
GABY—A TRUE STORY
NO WAY OUT
TOKYO BLACKOUT
Jermyn, Peter
CLIMB, THE
Jesus
NARCOTERROR
Ji Ping, Zhao
BUDDHA'S LOCK
Jobim, Antonio Carlos
FONTE DA SAUDADE
Joffe, Kai
SLAMMER GIRLS
WIMPS
Joffee, Kai
WARRIOR QUEEN
John, Zdenek
CIZIM VSTUP POVOLEN
Jojic, Boris
DER UNSICHTBARE
Jones, Brynmore
EIN BLICK-UND DIE LIEBE BRICHT AUS
Jones, Trevor
ANGEL HEART
Jopson, Susan
IF LOOKS COULD KILL
Jost, Jon
BELL DIAMOND
Juster, Diane
MORNING MAN, THE
Kabiljo, Alfi
GIRL, THE
SLEEP WELL, MY LOVE
Kabiljo, Ilan
GIRL, THE
Kadishzon, Rafi
LATE SUMMER BLUES
Kalnins, Imant
STRAKH
Kalnyns, Imant
POHADKA O MALICKOVI
Kalovarsky, Anatoly
GRUBAYA POSADKA
Kalyanji-Anandji
JHANJHAAR
Kamen, Michael
ADVENTURES IN BABYSITTING
LETHAL WEAPON
RITA, SUE AND BOB TOO!
SOMEONE TO WATCH OVER ME
SUSPECT
Kancheli, Gia
KIN-DZA-DZA
Kancheli, Giya
KRUGOVOROT
Kantyukov, Igor
CHYORNAYA STRELA
PO GLAVNOY ULITSE S ORKESTROM
Karabanchiuk, O.
DOLGHYIE PROVOD
Karavaichuk, Oleg
KOROTKIE VSTRECHI

Karetnikov, Nikolai
SEVERNY ANEKDOT
VINA LEYTENANTA NEKRASOVA
Karlowicz, Mieczyslaw
STANISLAW I ANNA
Katayev, Ilya
MILLION V BRACHNOY KORZINE
Kauderer, Emilio
MADE IN ARGENTINA
Kaufman, Ken
MY DARK LADY
Kaye, Norman
VINCENT—THE LIFE AND DEATH OF VINCENT VAN GOGH
Kazazian, George
ZAWGAT RAGOL MOHIM
Kazhlayev, Murad
ZNAY NASHIKH
Keane, John
KITCHEN TOTO, THE
Keister, Shane
ERNEST GOES TO CAMP
Kemadasa, Premasiri
MALDENIYESIMION
Kerber, Randy
DATE WITH AN ANGEL
Khanna, Usha
DAKU HASINA
Khayyam
ANJUMAN
Khrapachev, Vadim
ODINOKAYA ZHENCHINA ZHELAET POZNAKOMITAYA
Khrennikov, Tikhon
LYUBOVYU ZA LYUBOV
Kilar, Wojciech
BLIND CHANCE
King, Don
KISS DADDY GOOD NIGHT
King Sunny Ade
O. C. AND STIGGS
Kisin, Viktor
VZLOMSHCHIK
Kitay, David
NIGHT STALKER, THE
Kiva, Oleg
GRUZ BEZ MARKIROVKI
Klingler, Kevin
WHITE PHANTOM
Klintberg, Goran
NAGRA SOMMARKVALLAR PA JORDEN
Klocke, Piet
PENG! DU BIST TOT!
Klody
LA VIE EST BELLE
Knabl, Rudolf Gregor
TRIUMPH DE GERECHTEN
Knieper, Jurgen
DER HIMMEL UBER BERLIN
DEVILS PARADISE, THE
DIE VERLIEBTEN
RIVER'S EDGE
Knopfler, Mark
PRINCESS BRIDE, THE
Koblyakov, Alexander
PRIKLYUCHENIA NA MALENKIKH OSTROVEKH
Kocab, Michael
WOLF'S HOLE
Kohler, Lutz
DANN IST NICHTS MEHR WIE VORHER
Komarov, Vladimir
OBESHCHAYU BYT
Konicek, Stepan
CENA ODVAHY
Konstantinov, Ljupco
HI-FI
Kontyukov, Igor
VOENNO-POLEVOI ROMAN
Koo, Joseph
BETTER TOMORROW, A
MIRAGE
Kops, Pim
LOOKING FOR EILEEN
Korngold, Erich Wolfgang
ARIA
Korven, Mark
IVE HEARD THE MERMAIDS SINGING
Korzynski, Andrzej
PIERSCIEN I ROZA

Kosinaki, Richard Koz
ENEMY TERRITORY
Kostic, Voy
DIRTY REBEL
Kotwitz, Kenny
DELOS ADVENTURE, THE
Kounadis, Argyris
KLIOS
Kowalski, Olivier
PIERRE ET DJEMILA
Koz, Jeff
MISSION KILL
Krajewski, Seweryn
ZLOTA MAHMUDIA
Kranz, George
MAGIC STICKS
Kretschmer, Robert
MOVING TARGETS
Kristof, Gabor
PIERRE ET DJEMILA
Krivoshei, David
EMPEROR'S NEW CLOTHES, THE
Kruger, Jan
BORAN—ZEIT ZUM ZIELEN
Krylatov, Yevgeny
KOORDINATY SMERTI
Kukhiaindze, Vakhtang
PYAT NEVEST DO LYUBIMOY
Kukuck, Thomas
OTTO—DER NEUE FILM
Kukulski, Jaroslaw
KOMEDIANCI Z WCZORAJSZEJ ULICY
PAN SAMOCHODZIK I NIESAMOWITY DWOR
Kulenovic, Vuk
KRALJEVA ZAVRSNICA
U IME NARODA
Kurtz, David
HUNK
Kurylewicz, Andrzej
NAD NIEMNEM
RYKOWISKO
Kuusi, Kim
A LA ITKE IINES
Kvernadze, Bidzin
NEYLONOVAYA YOLKA
Kwok, Alvin
THIRTY MILLION RUSH, THE
Kyarnagis, Vitautas
IZVINITEPOZHALUYSTA
La Bionda, Carmelo
LESTATE STA FINENDO
ROBA DA RICCHI
La Bionda, Michelangelo
LESTATE STA FINENDO
ROBA DA RICCHI
Laberer, Helmut
REGINA
Lafferriere, Fernando
KONZERT FUR DIE RECHTE HAND
Lage, Klaus
ZABOU
Lahiri, Bappi
JHOOTHI
PYAR KARKE DEKHO
SHEELA
Lai, Francis
ATTENTION BANDITS
DARK EYES
LASSOCIATION DES MALFAITEURS
Lam, George
WONDER WOMEN
Lam, Violet
DIXIA QING
Lane, James
MURDER LUST
Lang, John
WINTER TAN, A
Latenas, Faustas
MOYA MALENKAYA ZHENA
Laurel, Bobby
ROSARY MURDERS, THE
Lauzon, Robert
LAST STRAW, THE
Lavrov, V.
DVADTSTAT DNEI BEZ
Lawrence, Stephen
RED RIDING HOOD
Laxman, Rax
KAUN KITNEY PAANI MEIN

Laxmikant
MISTER INDIA
Lay, Chris
OUTTAKES
Le, Jose
ALS IN EEN ROES
Le Masne, Luc
ACCROCHE-COEUR
Lebedev, Victor
GEROY YEYOROMANA
Lebedev, Viktor
ISKRENNE VASH . . .
SNAYPERY
Ledenev, Roman
IZ ZHIZNI POTAPOVA
Lee, Jong-gu
MAN WITH THREE COFFINS, THE
Legrand, Michel
CLUB DE RENCONTRES
SPIRALE
Leonard, Patrick
WHO'S THAT GIRL
Leoncavallo, Ruggero
ARIA
Leong, Chan Wing
MAGNIFICENT WARRIORS
Leroux, Les
REMEMBERING MEL
Levay, Sylvester
BURGLAR
MANNEQUIN
Levin, Geoff
HEART
Levy, Jay
PRETTY SMART
Lewis, W. Michael
HOT CHILD IN THE CITY
Liberatore, Fabio
IO E MIA SORELLA
Lieber, Ed
ANITA—DANCES OF VICE
Lifshitz, Marcos
ESTA NOCHE CENA PANCHO (DESPEDIDA DE SOLTERO)
LA RAZA NUNCA PIERDE—HUELE A GAS
NOS REIMOS DE LA MIGRA
Lindahl, Thomas
MALARPIRATER
Lindh, Bjorn
MANNEN FRAN MALLORCA
Lindsay, Duncan
KISS DADDY GOOD NIGHT
Linkola, Jukka
SNOW QUEEN, THE
Linn, Michael
ALLAN QUATERMAIN AND THE LOST CITY OF GOLD
EVIL TOWN
SURVIVAL GAME
Litovsky, Michael
BLOOD SISTERS
ORACLE, THE
Little, Russ
TOO OUTRAGEOUS
Livaneli, Omer Zulfu
YER DEMIR, GOK BAKIR
Llorca, Magali
LA BRUTE
Lloyd, Michael
GARBAGE PAIL KIDS MOVIE, THE
Lo, Lowell
AUTUMN'S TALE, AN
PRISON ON FIRE
Lo Duca, Joseph
EVIL DEAD 2: DEAD BY DAWN
THOU SHALT NOT KILL . . . EXCEPT
Loginov, Valery
O ROZVRASHCHENII ZABYT
Low, Ben
KEEPING TRACK
Lowe, Danny
VIRGIN QUEEN OF ST. FRANCIS HIGH, THE
Lubat, Bernard
MISS MONA
Lucas, Trevor
CASSANDRA
Ludovic, Vinicio
MAS ALLA DEL SILENCIO
Lully, Jean-Baptiste
ARIA
Lunny, Donal
EAT THE PEACH
Lyubenov, Raicho
PRIZEMYAVANE
Macchi, Egisto
DIARY OF A MAD OLD MAN
HAVINCK
LA CODA DEL DIAVOLO
MASCARA
Macchi, Lamberto
CHI C'E C'E
SEMBRA MORTO . . . ME E SOLO SVENUTO
Mackenzi, Malcolm
TRAIN OF DREAMS
Magnus, Nick
BLOODY NEW YEAR
Magomaev, Muslim
LEGENDA SEREBRYANOGO OZERA
Mahapatra, Guru Keluchuran
JAIDEV
Mahler, Gustav
HIP, HIP, HURRA!
INNA WYSPA
LENZ
TO MARKET, TOMARKET
Mainetti, Stefano
DELIZIA
Mainotti, Stefano
CARTOLINE ITALIANE
Maioli, Claudio
TERESA
Makarevich, Andrei
PRORYV
Malavasi, Claudio
I PICARI
Malik, Annu
DADAGIRI
INSANIYAT KE DUSHMAN
MERA LAHOO
Mamagakis, Nicos
VIOS KE POLITIA
Mamet, Bob
WHITE PHANTOM
Mancini, Henry
BLIND DATE
GLASS MENAGERIE, THE
Manfredini, Harry
SLAUGHTER HIGH
Manfredini, Henry
HOUSE TWO: THE SECOND STORY
Mankewitz, Lothar
KONZERT FUR DIE RECHTE HAND
Manoranjan
AMAR BANDHAN
Mansfield, David
SICILIAN, THE
Mansurian, Tigran
SASHSHENNYI FONAR
Mansuryan, Tigran
PESN PROSHEDSHIKH DNEY
Manuel, Marita A.
GET THE TERRORISTS
Many, Chris
HEART
Manzie, Jim
OFFSPRING, THE
Marathe, Saratchandra
UPPU
Marcel, Leonard
VIDEO DEAD, THE
Marchetti, Gianni
LA TRASGRESSIONE
Marchitelli, Lele
SPECTERS
Marczewski, Piotr
E S D
MIEDZY USTAMI A BRZEGIEM PUCHARU
Mariano, Detto
IL BURBERO
Marie, Vincent
NUIT DOCILE
Marin, Carlos Torres
EL PLACER DE LA VENGANZA
LO NEGRO DEL NEGRO
TODA LA VIDA
Marinelli, Anthony
NICE GIRLS DON'T EXPLODE
PINOCCHIO AND THE EMPEROR OF THE NIGHT
Marisco, Maurizio
MEFISTO FUNK
Marks, Alan
ANITA—DANCES OF VICE
Marquez, Juan
EL SOCIO DE DIOS
Martel, Fernand
LAST STRAW, THE
Martha, Istvan
DOKTOR MINORKA VIDOR NAGY NAPJA
Martin, Peter
HOPE AND GLORY
Masik, Janos
HOTREAL
Mason, Ian
CASSANDRA
Mason, Nick
WHITE OF THE EYE
Matsiyevsky, Igor
LEVSHA
Matsumura, Teizo
SEA AND POISON, THE
Matula, Jerzy
POCIAG DO HOLLYWOOD
Matuszkiewicz, Jerzy
WIERNA RZEKA
Mavroudis, N.
I KEKARMENI
May, Brian
DEATH BEFORE DISHONOR
STEEL DAWN
May, Daniel
ZOMBIE HIGH
McCallum, Jon
SURF NAZIS MUST DIE
McCallum, Paul
DEATH WISH 4: THE CRACKDOWN
McCallum, Valentine
ASSASSINATION
DEATH WISH 4: THE CRACKDOWN
McClintock, Steve
DEADLY PREY
MANKILLERS
McEuen, John
MAN OUTSIDE
McHugh, David
JOCKS
SOMETHING SPECIAL!
McKelvey, Lori
BEAUTY AND THE BEAST
McMahon, Kevin
VIDEO DEAD, THE
McNeely, Joel
YOU TALKIN' TO ME?
Mead, Abigail
FULL METAL JACKET
Medaglia, Juilio
EU
Mederos, Rodolfo
A DOS AGUAS
HOTEL DU PARADIS
Melia, Marco
ILLUMINAZIONI
Melvoin, Michael
BIG TOWN, THE
Mendlessohn, Felix
BEDROOM WINDOW, THE
Mendoza-Nava, Jaime
FORTY DAYS OF MUSA DAGH
Mertens, Wim
BELLY OF AN ARCHITECT, THE
Mexis, Thomas
WITCH HUNT
Micalizzi, Franco
CURSE, THE
Michajlov, Angelo
CHOBOTNICE Z II. PATRA
Milano, Tom
NECROPOLIS
Milind, Anand
JALWA
Milladoiro
DIVINAS PALABRAS
Miller, Marcus
SIESTA
Millo, Mario
LIGHTHORSEMEN, THE
Mimms and the —Enchanters, Garnet
SIERRA LEONE
Minkov, Mark
LICHNOE DELO SUDYI IVANOVOY
PRODELKI V STARINNOM DUKHE

ZINA-ZINULYA

Miralles, Ricardo
CARA DE ACELGA

Mirzamani, Mohammad
MANUSCRIPTS

Misra, Bhubaneshwar
BABULA

Mitsouko, les Rita
SOIGNE TA DROITE

Moffiatt, Mark
HIGH TIDE

Moghe, Sudheer
SUTRADHAR

Mohan
PANDAVAPURAM

Mompou, Federico
DEMONS

Moner, Beltran
CALE

Monn-Iversen, Egil
PA STIGENDE KURS

Montanari, Piero
UNDICI GIORNI, UNDICI NOTTE

Montes, Michael
FIREHOUSE

Moon, Guy
CREEPOZOIDS

Morales, Miguel
HAY QUE DESHACER LA CASA

Morales, Roland
YI LOU YI

Moran, Chilo
LA FUGA DE CARRASCO

Moraz, Patrick
STEPFATHER, THE

Morgan, John
FLICKS

Moroder, Giorgio
OVER THE TOP

Morricone, Ennio
GLI OCCHIALI D'ORO
IL GIORNO PRIMA
MOSCA ADDIO
QUARTIERE
UNTOUCHABLES, THE

Morris, John
DIRTY DANCING
IRONWEED
SPACEBALLS

Morse, Fuzzbee
DOLLS

Morthens, Bubbi
SKYTTURNAR

Mothersbaugh, Mark
REVENGE OF THE NERDS II: NERDS IN PARADISE

Motta, Pepe
EN EL NOMBRE DEL HIJO

Motzing, William
SHADOWS OF THE PEACOCK

Mozart
HOL VOLT, HOL NEM VOLT

Mozart, Wolfgang Amadeus
ROMANCA FINAL

Muana, Tshala
LA VIE EST BELLE

Muller, Marlus
OFELAS

Munoz-Alonso, Angel
EL AMOR DE AHORA

Munro, Murray
P.I. PRIVATE INVESTIGATIONS

Muntaner, Ramon
LESCOT

Murphy, Robert
HOUSEKEEPER, THE

Musser, John
SOME KIND OF WONDERFUL

Musumarra, Romano
MALADIE D'AMOUR
MON BEL AMOUR, MA DECHIRURE

Musy, Jean
JOHNNY MONROE
LE JOURNAL D'UN FOU

Myers, Stanley
PRICK UP YOUR EARS
SAMMY AND ROSIE GET LAID
WIND, THE
WISH YOU WERE HERE
ZERO BOYS, THE

Mylonas, Costas
FAKELOS POLK STON AERA

Myrow, Fred
HOUR OF THE ASSASSIN

Nagari, Benny
LO SAM ZAYIN

Nakanishi, Toshihiro
SARABA ITOSHIKI HITO YO

Nam-yoon, Kim
KYEOUL NAGUNE

Nannini, Gianna
DEMONS

Naseri, F.
CAPTAIN KHORSHID

Natzke, Paul
EVIL SPAWN

Naunas, Thomas A.
BLOOD HOOK

Nazarov, Vyacheslav
I NIKTO NA SVETE

Neal, Chris
AROUND THE WORLD IN EIGHTY WAYS
GROUND ZERO

Neeley, Ted
CAUGHT
SUMMER CAMP NIGHTMARE

Nelson, Anders G.
SEVEN YEARS ITCH

Newborn, Ira
DRAGNET
PLANES, TRAINS AND AUTOMOBILES

Newman, David
BRAVE LITTLE TOASTER, THE
KINDRED, THE
MALONE
MY DEMON LOVER
THROW MOMMA FROM THE TRAIN

Newman, Thomas
LESS THAN ZERO
LIGHT OF DAY
LOST BOYS, THE

Niehaus, Lennie
EMANON

Nieto, Jose
EL LUTE—CAMINA O REVIENTA

Nieto, Pepe
EL BOSQUE ANIMADO

Nikitin, Sergei
POEZDKI NA STAROM AVTOMOBILE

Nilsson, Stefan
JIM OCH PIRATERNA BLOM
PELLE EROVRAREN
SERPENT'S WAY, THE

Nizamettin
DILAN

Nono, Luigi
SUCCESSFUL MAN, A

Norgard, Per
BABETTE'S GASTEBUD

Norrlatar
INUKSUK

North, Alex
DEAD, THE
GOOD MORNING, VIETNAM

Novak, Janos
WHOOPING COUGH

Novotny, Paul
BLUE MONKEY

Nuti, Giovanni
STREGATI

Nyberget, Nissa
FELDMANN CASE, THE

O'Kennedy, John
STRIPPED TO KILL

Oliver, Christoph
TAROT

Omi, Sonik
HAMARI JUNG

Orbit, William
HOT SHOT

Ornelas, Nivaldo
A DANCA DOS BONECOS

Oroszlan, Gabor
LUTRA

Oroszlan, Gyorgy
LUTRA

Ortolani, Riz
CAPRICCIO

Osborn, Jason
HIGH SEASON

Ousappachan
JANUARY ORORMA

Ouseppachan
KATHAKKU PINNIL

Ozdomiroglu, Atilla
ANAYURT OTELI

Ozhan, Sarper
WATER ALSO BURNS

Ozkan, Haluk
SON URFALI

Pagan, J.M.
ANGUSTIA

Pagani, Mauro
DOLCE ASSENZA

Page, Scott
THREE KINDS OF HEAT

Paiva, Manoel
ANJOS DO ARRABALDE

Pallumbo, John
ADVENTURE OF THE ACTION HUNTERS

Palmer, Vincent
POULE ET FRITES

Panarama
FIRE AND ICE

Panayotou, Thessia
OH BABYLON

Papadakis, Giorgios
THEOFILOS

Papademetriou, Demetris
TREE WE HURT, THE

Papadimitriou, Dimitris
ARCHANGELOS TOU PATHOUS

Parr, Robert
VALET GIRLS

Parsons, Alan
FIRE AND ICE

Pasquali, Marcella
IL RAGAZZO DI EBALUS

Patterson, Rick
HAPPY HOUR

Paulavicus, Algis
ZOLOTAYA BABA

Pavlicek, Michal
PROC?

Pawluskiewicz, Jan Kanty
BOHATERROKU

Pejman, Ahmad
CHECKPOINT

Penn, Rick
WHITE OF THE EYE

Pennell, Chuck
TRESPASSES

Perez, Gato
LA RUBIA DEL BAR

Peterdi, Peter
ZUHANAS KOZBEN

Petit, Jean-Claude
F . . . ING FERNAND
JEAN DE FLORETTE
MANON OF THE SPRING
TANT QU'IL AURA DES FEMMES

Petkov, Bojidar
CERNITE LEBEDI

Petrov, Andrei
POSLEDNYAYA DOROGA

Petrov, Boris
V STRELYAYUSHCHEY GLUSHI

Petrova, Olga
MOY LYUBIMYY KLOUN

Phadke, Sudhir
PUDHCHE PAOL

Pheloung, Barrington
FRIENDSHIP'S DEATH

Pi-Rats
DER NACHBAR

Piccioni, Piero
CHRONICLE OF A DEATH FORETOLD

Piersanti, Franco
LA DONNA DEL TRAGHETTO
PROFUMO
UNA CASA IN BILICO

Pike, Nicholas
GRAVEYARD SHIFT

Pimental, Gustavo
POLICIAS DE NARCOTICOS

Pimentel, Gustavo
EL MOFLES Y LOS MECANICOS
LA RULETERA
LAPUTA: THE CASTLE IN THE SKY
MAS BUENAS QUE EL PAN

Piovani, Nicola
GOOD MORNING BABYLON
INTERVISTA
LES EXPLOITS DUN JEUNE DON JUAN

Placenicia, Pedro
ALBURES MEXICANOS

Plasa, Franz
CRAZY BOYS

Podheiz, Yefrem
CHUZHIE ZDES NE KHODYAT

Pogues, The
STRAIGHT TO HELL

Poledouris, Basil
NO MAN'S LAND
ROBOCOP

Popple, Todd
ESCAPES

Portal, Michel
CHAMP D'HONNEUR
LA MOINE ET LA SORCIERE
YEELEN

Portocaloglou, Nicos
KE DYO AVGA TOURKIAS

Posegga, Hans
CASPAR DAVID FRIEDRICH

Pray For Rain
STRAIGHT TO HELL

Prenen, Paul
QUATRE MAINS

Preston, Don
BLOOD DINER

Price, Alan
WHALES OF AUGUST, THE

Prokofiev, Serge
BAD BLOOD

Ptichkin, Yevgeny
UTRO OBRECHENNOGO PRIISKA

Puccini, Giacomo
ARIA
DEMONS
OPERA

Pyarelal
MISTER INDIA

Pyarelal, Laxmikant
JAWAB HUM DENGE
LOHA
NAZRANA

Quiping, Zhao
BIG PARADE, THE

Rabinowitsk, Stuart
VIDEO DEAD, THE

Rachmaninoff, Sergei
PODSUDIMYY

Ragland, Robert
DIRTY REBEL

Ragland, Robert O.
ASSASSINATION
MOON IN SCORPIO
NIGHTSTICK
PRETTYKILL
SUPERNATURALS, THE

Rague, Stephen
SOME KIND OF WONDERFUL

Raj, Zbigniew
W STARYM DWORKU

Raja, Ilaya
INDIAN SUMMER

Rameau, Jean-Philippe
ARIA

Raninen, Aarno
LIIAN ISO KEIKKA

Rareview
HOT PURSUIT

Ravan, Kambiz Roshan
DJADDE HAYE SARD

Ravi
PANCHAGNI

Ray, Greg
LADIES OF THE LOTUS

Rea, Daniele
SPECTERS

Rebic, Don
UNFINISHED BUSINESS . . .

Reed, Les
CREEPSHOW 2

Regan, Pat
OFFSPRING, THE

Rego, Luis
POULE ET FRITES

Reid, Kate
TO MARKET, TOMARKET

Reiser, Nicki
SAME TO YOU

Reiser, Rio
CHINESE ARE COMING, THE

Renzetti, Joseph
WANTED: DEAD OR ALIVE

Resetar, Robert J.
WHITE PHANTOM

Rettberg, Robert
GOOFBALLS

Richards, Andy
TURNAROUND

Riedel, George
MORE ABOUT THE CHILDREN OF BULLERBY VILLAGE

Rimsky-Korsakoff
ABBES

Ritz, Walter
THUNDER WARRIOR II

Rivron, Roland
EAT THE RICH

Robbins, Richard
MAURICE
MY LITTLE GIRL
SWEET LORRAINE

Robellaz, Jacques
POISONS

Robert, Max
RUMPELSTILTSKIN

Roberts, Jonathan
I WAS A TEENAGE ZOMBIE

Robertson, Eric N.
HOME IS WHERE THE HART IS

Robertson, Harry
JANE AND THE LOST CITY

Robin, Teddy
CITY ON FIRE

Robinson, J. Peter
BELIEVERS, THE
GATE, THE

Rodriguez, Caloy
NO BLOOD NO SURRENDER

Rodriguez, Carlos
ZIMATAR

Rodriguez, Francisco
EL HOMBRE DESNUDO

Rodriguez, Susy
OPERACION MARIJUANA

Roebuck, Bill
OVERKILL

Rolling Stones, The
OPERA

Rood, Jurrien
DE ORIONNEVEL

Rose, Bob
NIGHTFORCE

Rosenbaum, Joel
OUTING, THE
PSYCHO GIRLS

Rossini, Gioacchino
VINCENT—THE LIFE AND DEATH OF VINCENT VAN GOGH

Rotter, Peter
CODE NAME ZEBRA

Rowland, Bruce
BUSHFIRE MOON
RUNNING FROM THE GUNS

Rubashevsky, Vladimir
SAMAYA OBAYATELNAYA I PRIVLEKATELNAYA

Rubbert, Rainer
ANITA—DANCES OF VICE

Rubin, Amparo
LO DEL CESAR
VA DE NUEZ

Rubin, Rick
LESS THAN ZERO

Rubinstein, Arthur B.
STAKEOUT

Rucker, Steve
CATCH THE HEAT

Ruiz, Federico
LA OVEJA NEGRA
MANON

Rundgren, Todd
UNDER COVER

Rushen, Patrice
HOLLYWOOD SHUFFLE

Rustichelli, Paolo
LA CROCE DALLE SETTE PIETRE

Rybnikov, Alexei
RUS IZNACHALNA
VOT MOYA DEREVNYA

Saad, James
CYCLONE

Sabu, Paul
AMERICAN DRIVE-IN

Saegusa, Shigeaki
HIKARU ANNA

Safan, Craig
LADY BEWARE
STRANGER, THE

Sagild, Kim
VENNER FOR ALTID

Sakamoto, Ryuichi
LAST EMPEROR, THE

Salo, Jaakko
UUNO TURHAPURO MUUTTAA MAALLE

Salo, Raine
URSULA

Saluzzi, Dino
PERSONAGGI & INTERPRETI

Salvati, Alain
MASTERBLASTER

Sanay, Samime
SIERRA LEONE

Sandrelli, Sergio
DA NNUNZIO

Sanfelice, Leopoldo
FRANCESCA

Sangy
UNA DONNA DA SCOPRIRE

Santana, Carlos
LA BAMBA

Saraceni, Sergio G.
BAIXO GAVEA

Saraceni, Sergio Guilherme
BEIJO NA BOCA

Sarde, Philippe
COMEDY!
ENNEMIS INTIMES
LES DEUX CROCODILES
LES MOIS D'AVRIL SONT MEURTRIERS
LETE DERNIER A TANGER
NOYADE INTERDITE

Sardi, Idris
IBUNDA

Sarmanto, Heikki
JAAHYVAISET PRESIDENTILLE

Satanowski, Jerzy
MAGNAT
SIEKIEREZADA
W ZAWIESZENIU
ZYGFRYD

Satie, Erik
LOVECHILD, THE
MISS MARY

Sato, Masaru
DEATH SHADOWS
ITAZU
YOSHIWARA ENJO

Saulsky, Yury
OCHNAYA STAVKA

Schell, Daniel
VAN PAEMEL FAMILY, THE

Schiavoni, Marco
ILLUMINAZIONI

Schifrin, Lalo
FOURTH PROTOCOL, THE

Schloss, Zander
SPACE RACE

Schmidt, Ole
WOLF AT THE DOOR, THE

Schnitke, Alfred
KOMISSAR

Schone, Gerhard
DER JUNGE MIT DEM GROSSEN SCHWARZEN HUND

Schubert, Franz
CASPAR DAVID FRIEDRICH

Schubert, Franz Peter
MASCARA

Schulmann, Patrick
LES OREILLES ENTRE LES DENTS

Schutze, Paul
TALE OF RUBY ROSE, THE

Schwarz, Isaak
DVOE POD ODNIM ZONTOM
PLOSHCHAD VOSSTANIA
POLEVAYA GVARDIA MOZZHUKHINA
ZONTIK DLYA NOVOBRACHNYKH

Schyman, Garry
PENITENTIARY III

Scott, Andrew
BUSINESS AS USUAL

Scott, Charles
IRON WARRIOR

Scott, John
MAN ON FIRE
WHISTLE BLOWER, THE

Scott, Phil
THOSE DEAR DEPARTED

Scott, William
SAKURA KILLERS

Seal, Samir
BIDROHI

Sear, Walter E.
BLOOD SISTERS
ORACLE, THE

Sebesky, Don
ROSARY MURDERS, THE

Seeman, Craig
I WAS A TEENAGE ZOMBIE

Segal, Misha
DREAMERS
STEELE JUSTICE

Sell, Jack M.
OUTTAKES

Selmeczi, Gyorgy
LAURA
TISZTA AMERIKA

Selmeczy, Gyorgy
C. K. DEZERTERZY
ZUHANAS KOZBEN

Sendry, Al
BLOODY WEDNESDAY

Senia, Jean Marie
UN AMOUR A PARIS

Senia, Jean-Marie
FUEGOS
LA BRUTE
NOCE EN GALILEE

Senza, Leon
POUSSIERE D'ANGE

Serkebaev, Baigali
SKAZKA O PREKRASNOY AYSULU

Serra, Luis Maria
MISS MARY
SOFIA

Seuberth, Ernie
DIE DRECKSCHLEUDER

Shahbazian, Fareidoun
SHEERE SANGGY

Shainsky, Vladimir
SOPERNITSY

Shakaryan, Stepan
ZEMLYA I ZOLOTO

Shakhidi, Tolib
KAPKAN DLYA SHAKALOV

Shaw, Francis
FOURTH PROTOCOL, THE

Shaw, Ian
SLAMMER GIRLS
WARRIOR QUEEN
WIMPS

Sheykin, Eduard
OBVINYAETSYA SVADBA

Shinozaki, Masatsugu
HOTARUGAWA

Shirui, Zhu
BLACK CANNON INCIDENT, THE

Shnitke, Alfred
WEEKEND

Shore, Howard
NADINE

Shreeve, Mark
TURNAROUND

Shrieve, Michael
BEDROOM WINDOW, THE

Shvarts, Isaak
OBRYV

Sidelnikov, Nikolai
VYKUP

Silvestri, Alan
CRITICAL CONDITION
OUTRAGEOUS FORTUNE
OVERBOARD
PREDATOR

Simijanovic, Zoran
ANDJEO CUVAR

Simjanovic, Zoran
HEY BABU RIBA
UVEK SPREMNE ZENE
VEC VIDJENO
ZIVOT RADNIKA

Simon, Zoltan
SZORNYEK EVADJA

Simonec, Tom
SURVIVAL GAME

Simonetti, Claudio
CAMPING DEL TERRORE

Sirvinskas, Juozas
SLEDY OBOROTNYA

Sirvinskas, Yuosas
BLUDNYY SYN

Skeel, Christian
VENNER FOR ALTID

Slawinski, Adam
KOMEDIANTKA

Sliomis, Thomas
YENETHLIA POLI

Smaila, Umberto
CARAMELLE DA UNO SCONOSCIUTO
I MIEI PRIMI QUARANT'ANNI
SOTTOZERO

Small, Michael
BLACK WIDOW
JAWS: THE REVENGE
ORPHANS

Smeaton, Bruce
ROXANNE

Smires, Mohamed
ABBES

Smith & Band, Joycelyn Bernadette
IN DER WUSTE

Socializma, Otroci
USODNI TELEFON

Solomon, Elliot
DIRTY LAUNDRY

Sonora Santanera
NOS REIMOS DE LA MIGRA

Spanoudakis, Stamatis
ANGELOS
APOUSIES

Stankovich, Evgeny
KONTRUDAR

Steckel, Brad
VIRGIN QUEEN OF ST. FRANCIS HIGH, THE

Steele, David
TIN MEN

Stevens, Morton
THEY STILL CALL ME BRUCE

Stockdale, Gary
HARD TICKET TO HAWAII

Stoklosa, Janusz
MASKARADA

Stone, Richard
NORTH SHORE

Storey, Michael
HIDDEN CITY

Stotter, Patricia Lee
UNFINISHED BUSINESS . . .

Strangio, Frank
CODA

Strauss, Johann
ASIGNATURA APROBADA

Strauss, Richard
MASCARA

Streisand, Barbra
NUTS

Strummer, Joe
WALKER

Stubbs, Ray
T. DAN SMITH

Stuckey, William
MESSENGER, THE

Studer, Jim
OPEN HOUSE

Su, Cong
LAST EMPEROR, THE

Suburbano
LA VIDA ALEGRE

Sujatovich, Leo
CHORROS
EL ANO DEL CONEJO
SENTIMIENTOS: MIRTA DE LINIERS A ESTAMBUL

Sullivan, Matt
UNFINISHED BUSINESS . . .

Sullivan, Peter
AS TIME GOES BY
SLATE, WYN & ME
WARM NIGHTS ON A SLOW MOVING TRAIN

Sumarokov, Victor
VOLNY UMIRAYUT NA BEREGU

Sumera, Lepo
IGRY DLJA DETEJ SKO'NOGO VOZRASTA

Summers, David
SUFRE MAMON

Suzuki, Saeko
UHOHO TANKENTAI

Sverige
INUKSUK

Sykurmolarnir
SKYTTURNAR

Symons, Red
BIT PART, THE

Tabrizi, Davood
SURFER, THE

Taj
DEADTIME STORIES

Takeo, Kiyoski
BUS

Tamassy, Zdenko
ISTEN VELETEK, BARATAIM

Tanaka, Michi
LOVE LETTER

Tangerine Dream
NEAR DARK
SHY PEOPLE
THREE O'CLOCK HIGH

Tanigawa, Kensaku
EIGA JOYU

Tano, Aneiro
DE TAL PEDRO, TAL ASTILLA

Tano, Tony
DE TAL PEDRO, TAL ASTILLA

Taranu, Cornel
PADUREANCA

Tarenskeen, Boudewijn
LOOKING FOR EILEEN

Tariverdiyev, Michael
KONETS OPERATSII "REZIDENT"

Tautu, Cornelia
ZLOTY POCIAG

Taylor, James Michael
RED DESERT PENITENTIARY

Teleman, Georg Philip
LUNGA VITA ALLA SIGNORA!

Telson, Bob
OUT OF ROSENHEIM

Tenney, Dennis Michael
WITCHBOARD

Thielemans, Toots
LITTLE PROSECUTOR, THE

Thirteen Moons
NAGRA SOMMARKVALLAR PA JORDEN

Thomas, Whitey
NAIL GUN MASSACRE

Thor, Jon-Mikl
ZOMBIE NIGHTMARE

Thorne, Ken
TROUBLE WITH SPIES, THE

Thornhill, Rusty
RETURN OF JOSEY WALES, THE

Tilley, Alexandra
LIFE CLASSES

Timm, Doug
NIGHTFLYERS
WINNERS TAKE ALL

Tishenko, Boris
OGNI

Tiso, Wagner
BESAME MUCHO
ELE, O BOTO

Todorovsky, Pyotr
VOENNO-POLEVOI ROMAN

Togashi, Masahiko
MAGINA—MURA MONOGATARI

Torrance, Tim
PERFECT MATCH, THE

Torres, Carlos
CARTUCHA CORTADA
MATAR O MORIR
SINVERGUENZA . . . PERO HONRADO
UNA PURA Y DOS CON SAL

Towns, Colin
BELLMAN AND TRUE
SHADEY

Towns, Collin
RAWHEAD REX

Trepanier, Guy
GREAT LAND OF SMALL, THE

Troost, Ernest
SWEET REVENGE
Trovajoli, Armando
FAMILY, THE
Tsangaris, Giorgos
TA PAIDIA TIS CHELIDONAS
Tsutsui, Yasutaka
DIXIELAND DAIMYO
Tukhmanov, David
ZHELEZNOE POLE
Tuominen, Matti
PEKKA PUUPAA POLIISINA
Turner, Simon
LAST OF ENGLAND, THE
Tuur, Erkki-Sven
CHEREZ STO LET V MAE
Tycho, Tommy
FRENCHMAN'S FARM
Tygel, David
COLOR OF DESTINY, THE
LEILA DINIZ
Tyrell, Steve
SUMMER HEAT
Ulfik, Rick
STREET TRASH
Unenge, Dag
BLOOD TRACKS
WARDOGS
Uribe, Alejandro Blanco
DE MUJER A MUJER
Valazquez, Leonardo
ROBACHICOS
Valero, Jean-Louis
LAMI DE MON AMIE
QUATRE AVENTURES DE REINETTE ET MIRABELLE
Valkeapaa, Nils-Aslak
OFELAS
Van Brugge, Paul Michael
EL AMOR ES UNA MUJERGORDA
van Donselaar, Rob
EEN MAAND LATER
Van Het Groenewoud, Raymond
LOVE IS A DOG FROM HELL
van Noord, Adriaan
ALS IN EEN ROES
ODYSSEE D'AMOUR
Vartazaryan, Martin
ODINOKAYA ORESHINA
Vartkes, Baronijan
NA PUTA ZA KATANGU
Velazquez, Consuelo
BESAME MUCHO
Velazquez, Leonardo
VIAJE AL PARAISO
Verdi, Giuseppe
ARIA
DEMONS
LITTLE DORRIT
MACBETH
MANON OF THE SPRING
OPERA
ROMANCA FINAL
URSULA
Vidovszky, Laszlo
AZ UTOLSOKEZIRAT
Vigner, Ivar
RAZMAKH KRYLIEV
Vildanov, Rumil
MIRAZHI LYUBRI
Vincent, Roland
LETE EN PENTE DOUCE
Virtzberg, Ilan
HIMMO MELECH YERUSHALAIM
Visotski, Vladimir
KOROTKIE VSTRECHI
Vivaldi, Antonio
SIEKIEREZADA
UN RAGAZZO DI CALABRIA
VINCENT—THE LIFE AND DEATH OF VINCENT VAN GOGH
Vizki, Morti
VENNER FOR ALTID
Vomvolos, Costas
DOXOBUS
Von Dallwitz, Burkhart
BACHELOR GIRL
von Gluck, Christoph Willibald
MASCARA
Voss, Bernhard
STADTRAND
Vranesevic, Braca
STRATEGIJA SVRAKE
Vranesevic Brothers
OKTOBERFEST
Wagner, Richard
ARIA
EPIDEMIC
ROMANCA FINAL
Wahlberg, Ulf
OM KARLEK
Wakeman, Rick
CREEPSHOW 2
Waters, Roger
WHEN THE WIND BLOWS
Webb, Jimmy
HANOI HILTON, THE
Wee Papa Girl Rappers
OUT OF ORDER
Weinberg, Fred
VIOLINS CAME WITH THE AMERICANS, THE
Weinstein, Shalom
TEL AVIV—BERLIN
Weller, Paul
BUSINESS AS USUAL
Wellman, Marita M.
NO DEAD HEROES
Wemba, Papa
LA VIE EST BELLE
Wenzel, Hans Jurgen
DER TRAUM VOM ELCH
Westphal, Lonzo
BORAN—ZEIT ZUM ZIELEN
Widelitz, Stacy
RETURN TO HORROR HIGH
STRANDED
Williams, Graham
BOY SOLDIER
Williams, John
EMPIRE OF THE SUN
JAWS: THE REVENGE
SUPERMAN IV: THE QUEST FOR PEACE
WITCHES OF EASTWICK, THE
Winans, Sam
DIRTY LAUNDRY
ENEMY TERRITORY
Winston
DAMORTIS
Wisniak, Alain
LANNEE DES MEDUSES
Wissmann, Friedbert
VERNEHMUNG DER ZEUGEN
Wong, James
PEKING OPERA BLUES
Wood, Jeffrey
GUNPOWDER
MIND KILLER
Woodruff, Christine
YEAR MY VOICE BROKE, THE
Working Week
OUT OF ORDER
Wright, Gary
FIRE AND ICE
Xarhakos, Stavros
SWEET COUNTRY
Xiaosong, Qu
BIG PARADE, THE
Yamamoto, Naozumi
FINAL TAKE: THE GOLDEN AGE OF MOVIES
TORA-SAN'S BLUEBIRD FANTASY
Yamashita, Yosuke
DIXIELAND DAIMYO
Yanchenko, Oleg
KARUSEL NA BAZARNOY PLOSHCHADI
ZNAK BEDY
Yanov-Yanovsky, Felix
TAYNOE PUTESHESTVIE EMIRA
Yared, Gabriel
BEYOND THERAPY
GANDAHAR
LHOMME VOILE
TESTAMENT D'UN POETE JUIF ASSASSINE
Yared, Garbiel
AGENT TROUBLE
Yari
ELVIS-KISSAN JALJILLA
YAS-KAZ
SHINRAN: SHIRO MICHI
Yau, Herman
YI LOU YI
Yefremov, Igor
TAKAYA ZHESTOKAYA IGRA—KHOKKEY
Yen, Ko Su
SEKUNDA NA PODVIG
Yon-joo, Chong
NAE-SHI
Yong, Han
CUO WEI
Yoshida, Satoru
GONDOLA
Yoshikawa, Yoichirou
ROBINSON NO NIWA
Youfu, Xu
OLD WELL
Young, Bob
DOT GOES TO HOLLYWOOD
Young, Christopher
FLOWERS IN THE ATTIC
HELLRAISER
Young, Victor
LAS DOS ORILLAS
Zaiko Langa Langa
LA VIE EST BELLE
Zambrini, Bruno
MISSIONE EROICA
SCUOLA DI LADRI 2
Zarzosa, Chucho
NI DE AQUI, NI DE ALLA
Zarzosa, Jonathan
DELINCUENTE
Zarzosa, Jorge
UN SABADO MAS
Zavallone, Paolo
IL CORAGGIO DI PARLARE
Zavod, Allan
HOWLING III, THE
RIGHT HAND MAN, THE
TIME GUARDIAN, THE
Zaza, Paul
FROM THE HIP
HELLO MARY LOU, PROM NIGHT II
HIGH STAKES
HIGHER EDUCATION
MEATBALLS III
Zeltzer, Duby
BOUBA
Zhurbin, Alexander
MAGIA CHYORNAYA I BELAYA
Zimmer, Hans
TERMINAL EXPOSURE
WIND, THE
ZERO BOYS, THE
Zingaro, Carlos
JESTER,THE
Ziv, Mikhail
OKHOTA NA DRAKONA
Ziyamukhamedov, Sadritdin
OKHOTA NA DRAKONA
Zorn, John
SHE MUST BE SEEING THINGS
Zsa Zsa, Paul
BIRDS OF PREY
Zubkov, Valery
PO ZAKONU VOENNOGO VREMENI
Zwart, Jacques
DEADLINE

COSTUMES

A. Radgabi
GOZARESH-E YEK GHATL
Abdulayevoi, N.
VZLOMSHCHIK
Abraham, Betty
AMAZONS
Abramson, Richard
WIND, THE
ZERO BOYS, THE
Abreu, Ana Maria
CIDADE OCULTA
Achcar, Mila
BAIXO GAVEA
Acheson, James
LAST EMPEROR, THE
Agliotti, Antonello
CARTOLINE ITALIANE
Aikens, Jean
RAGE OF HONOR
Aisa, Daphne
HOSTAGE SYNDROME

Albert, Pierre
MEMOIRE DES APPARENCES: LA VIE EST UN SONGE
Alexander, Alisa
TOO OUTRAGEOUS
Alfredson, Gunilla
JIM OCH PIRATERNA BLOM
Allen, Gaelle
PRETTY SMART
Allen, Marit
WHITE MISCHIEF
Alonzo, Ramon
EQUALIZER 2000
Amos, Dorothy
CYCLONE
Amsinskaja, Elena
SKORBNOE BESCHUVSTVIE
Andersen, Lars
VENNER FOR ALTID
Andres, Gumersindo
LA GUERRA DE LOS LOCOS
LOS INVITADOS
Anni, Anna
DANCERS
Antolin, Julia
HOUR OF THE ASSASSIN
Artinano, Javier
A LOS CUATRO VIENTOS
Astrom-DeFina, Marianna
PRINCIPAL, THE
Atwood, Coleen
CRITICAL CONDITION
Atwood, Colleen
PICK-UP ARTIST, THE
SOMEONE TO WATCH OVER ME
Aulisi, Joseph G.
SECRET OF MY SUCCESS, THE
Autran, Francoise
LA MOINE ET LA SORCIERE
Avdeliodis, Maria
TREE WE HURT, THE
Babcock, Judy
OMEGA SYNDROME
Baetz, Regine
OUT OF ROSENHEIM
Bakker, Trish
PRETTYKILL
Bakker, Trysha
GATE, THE
Bales, Cynthia
MIRACLES
Ballard, Leslie Peters
OPEN HOUSE
Banovich, Tamas
SZORNYEK EVADJA
Bansmer, Audrey M.
AMERICAN NINJA 2: THE CONFRONTATION
Barda, Suzy
HIMMO MELECH YERUSHALAIM
Barin, Lennie
PROGRAMMED TO KILL
Baron, Lennie
MISSION KILL
Barsacq, Alberte
MAN ON FIRE
Bartholomew, Marie Louise
PROINI PERIPOLOS
Bass, Linda
IN THE MOOD
STACKING
Bates, Sandy
P.K. & THE KID
Batz, Regina
CRIME OF HONOR
Batz, Regine
DEVILS PARADISE, THE
Baum, Barbara
MASCHENKA
Beavan, Jenny
MAURICE
Becker, Susan
BABY BOOM
BURGLAR
LOST BOYS, THE
Beckett, Angee
DOLLS
Benedek, Maria
LAURA
Berluti, Olga
LES MOIS D'AVRIL SONT MEURTRIERS
Bernard, Delphine
MON BEL AMOUR, MA DECHIRURE
Blackburn, Ticia
HEART
Blackman, Robert
RUNNING MAN, THE
Bloomfield, John
SUPERMAN IV: THE QUEST FOR PEACE
Bogers, Linda
EEN MAAND LATER
Bottomley, Gwen
LADIES OF THE LOTUS
Bouquiere, Pascale
GRAND GUIGNOL
Boxer, John
ORPHANS
Boyd, Beverly
VINCENT—THE LIFE AND DEATH OF VINCENT VAN GOGH
Boyle, Consolata
RAWHEAD REX
Breindel, Hali
ANNA
Bright, John
MAURICE
Brignon, Laurence
LA RUMBA
Brodbeck, Kathleen
MONSTER IN THE CLOSET
Bronson, Tom
OVER THE TOP
Bronson-Howard, Aude
ANGEL HEART
Brown, Claudia
RIVER'S EDGE
Bruley, Laurence
POISONS
Bruno, Richard
BIG SHOTS
ROXANNE
Bryhni, Anne Siri
ETTER RUBICON
Buehler, Jack
AMAZING GRACE AND CHUCK
Cacavas, Lisa
MOON IN SCORPIO
Cameron, Jeanie
SLATE, WYN & ME
Campbell, Janet
LAST STRAW, THE
Cannon, Poppy
STEEL DAWN
Canonero, Milena
BARFLY
Cantlon, Catherine
MOVING TARGETS
Capone, Clifford
BEDROOM WINDOW, THE
FROM THE HIP
MILLION DOLLAR MYSTERY
Castillo, Federico
LA GRAN FIESTA
Cecchi, Nana
GLI OCCHIALI D'ORO
LIONHEART
Champion, Judie
GARBAGE PAIL KIDS MOVIE, THE
Cheminal, Mic
LETE DERNIER A TANGER
Chevalier, Susan
GHOST FEVER
Chitty, Alison
ARIA
Chong, Rose
BUSHFIRE MOON
Cibula, Nan
HOUSE OF GAMES
Cidron, Juan Antonio
ROMANCA FINAL
Clark, Kathie
VALET GIRLS
Clason, Charlotte
WOLF AT THE DOOR, THE
Clements, Candace
FOREVER, LULU
Cook, Cathy
FRIENDSHIP'S DEATH
Cooke, Catherine
RITA, SUE AND BOB TOO!
Cossio, Jose M.
LAW OF DESIRE
Csengey, Emoke
AZ UTOLSOKEZIRAT
HOTREAL
Culotta, Sandra
HELLO AGAIN
Cunliffe, Shay
BELIEVERS, THE
Dalton, Phyllis
PRINCESS BRIDE, THE
Dandanell, Lotte
NEGERKYS & LABRE LARVER
PETER VON SCHOLTEN
Daniel, Malissa
SLAMDANCE
Dare, Daphne
HIDDEN CITY
Darragh, Barbara
STARLIGHT HOTEL
Dawson, Thomas
WHITE WATER SUMMER
De Chellis, Taryn "Teri"
HOT PURSUIT
de Nesle, Yvonne Sassinot
LES EXPLOITS DUN JEUNE DON JUAN
De Santo, Susie
DISORDERLIES
de Vivaise, Caroline
HOTEL DE FRANCE
DeChellis, Taryn
AMAZON WOMEN ON THE MOON
DRAGNET
Denny, Keith
FULL METAL JACKET
GOOD MORNING, VIETNAM
Deramus, Theda
SPACE RACE
WALKER
Diappi, Carlo
DARK EYES
Dillon, Rudy
MAKING MR.RIGHT
WHALES OF AUGUST, THE
Dimitrov, Olga
JOHN AND THE MISSUS
diSanto, Byrnadette
SURF NAZIS MUST DIE
Donay, Lucile
GABY—A TRUE STORY
Donfeld
SPACEBALLS
Dorleac, Jean-Pierre
KILLING TIME, THE
Doron, Rina
POET'S SILENCE, THE
Dorso, Bianca
ERNEST GOES TO CAMP
Dorst, Christian
CASPAR DAVID FRIEDRICH
Drangsgaard, Else
PETER VON SCHOLTEN
Eaton, Jeanne Button
I WAS A TEENAGE T.V. TERRORIST
Espinoza, Charmin
P.I. PRIVATE INVESTIGATIONS
Essex, Karen
RETURN OF JOSEY WALES, THE
Fadejevova, Nadezda
CIZIM VSTUP POVOLEN
Faith, Dannah
TOUGH COP
Fakiola, Georgia
IKONA ENOS MYTHIKOU PROSOPOU
Falck, Susanne
MORE ABOUT THE CHILDREN OF BULLERBY VILLAGE
MY LIFE AS A DOG
Fanaka, Maria Burrell
PENITENTIARY III
Fang, Shirley Chan Ku
LEGEND OF WISELY, THE
Fassler, Marianne
ALLAN QUATERMAIN AND THE LOST CITY OF GOLD
Ferry, April
MADE IN HEAVEN
PLANES, TRAINS AND AUTOMOBILES
Field, Patricia
HES MY GIRL

Fields, Patricia
LADY BEWARE

Figueroa, Tolita
GABY—A TRUE STORY

Fincher, Ed
RAGE OF HONOR

Finkelman, Wayne
OVERBOARD
SICILIAN, THE

Finlayson, Bruce
COMRADES

Fionn
HARD TICKET TO HAWAII

Fischini, Domingos
BESAME MUCHO

Flesch, Andrea
HOL VOLT, HOL NEM VOLT
TISZTA AMERIKA

Flynt, Cynthia
MATEWAN
SWEET LORRAINE

Fonne, Runa
PA STIGENDE KURS

Forsen, Mona Theresia
DEMONS

Frank, Yvette
LANNEE DES MEDUSES

Froehlich, Marcy Grace
RETURN TO HORROR HIGH

Fuentes, Angelica
LOS DUENOS DEL SILENCIO

Fustier, Magali
MASQUES

Gabridge, Carol
SULLIVAN'S PAVILION

Gagne, Hugette
BACH AND BROCCOLI

Galan, Graciela
MISS MARY

Galer, Andrea
WITHNAIL AND I

Gallo, Horacio
SINFIN, LA MUERTA NO ES NINGUNA SOLUCION

Gallwey, Kay
GOTHIC

Gammie, Susan
HIDING OUT
MY LITTLE GIRL

Gautrelet, Sylvie
JEAN DE FLORETTE
MANON OF THE SPRING

Gecser, Lujza
LENZ

George, Tudor
SHADEY

Georgiadou, Rena
KLIOS

Gilda, Leslie
ARIA

Gilles, Heidi F.
HOUSE TWO: THE SECOND STORY

Gisotti, Michela
BARBARIANS, THE

Glaesner, Ole
WOLF AT THE DOOR, THE

Glasner, Ole
SIDSTE AKT

Goldman, Pamela
SALVATION!

Gord, Eva
NIGHTSTICK

Graff, Vicki
PROGRAMMED TO KILL

Greene, Merrill
WITCHBOARD

Greenwood, Jane
EIGHTY FOUR CHARING CROSS ROAD
SQUEEZE, THE

Gregogna, Dominique
BAD BLOOD

Gresham, Gloria
TIN MEN

Gresham, Gloris
OUTRAGEOUS FORTUNE

Gruse, Brigit
SIERRA LEONE

Guerin, Paul-Andre
WILD THING

Guezel, Maika
LA VIE DISSOLUE DE GERARD FLOQUE

MISS MONA

Guimaraes, Marisa
NIGHT ANGELS

Gyarmathy, Agnes
WHOOPING COUGH

Haggett, Frances
EAT THE RICH
MORE BAD NEWS

Hamel, Michele
GREAT LAND OF SMALL, THE

Hamfeldt, Elisabeth
DEMONS

Hamre, Anne
PA STIGENDE KURS

Hanninen, Johanna
ELVIS-KISSAN JALJILLA

Harrison, Evangeline
PRAYER FOR THE DYING, A

Harwood, Shuna
ARIA
PERSONAL SERVICES
WISH YOU WERE HERE

Hauberg, Annelise
BABETTE'S GASTEBUD
SIDSTE AKT
WOLF AT THE DOOR, THE

Havelkova, Hana
DISCOPRIBEH

Hay, Jay
ARIA

Hay, John
BEYOND THERAPY

Heath, Eddie
SLAMMER GIRLS

Hejnova, Sarka
CHOBOTNICE Z II. PATRA
WOLF'S HOLE

Hemming, Lindy
EIGHTY FOUR CHARING CROSS ROAD

Hendly, Dafna
TEL AVIV—BERLIN

Henkler, Gunilla
LEIF

Herbert, Patsy
BLOOD HOOK

Herrera, Shiz
BLOOD DINER

Hettmann, Rosemarie
ZABOU

Hilkamo, Tuula
VARJOJA PARATIISISSA

Hines, Celeste
ROBOT HOLOCAUST

Hoffman, Michael
MONSTER SQUAD, THE

Hogan, Maureen
KID BROTHER, THE

Holloway, Victoria
PROMISED LAND

Holmes, Lynne A.
KINDRED, THE

Holmestrand, Marit Sofie
OFELAS

Hornung, Richard
CHINA GIRL
LESS THAN ZERO
RAISING ARIZONA

Houblinne, Mouchi
LA MOINE ET LA SORCIERE

Howe, Monica
BUSINESS AS USUAL

Huete, Lala
LA VIDA ALEGRE

Hughes, Raymond
WHISTLE BLOWER, THE

Huillet, Daniele
DER TOD DES EMPEDOKLES

Hye-yoon, Lee
NAE-SHI

Iglesias, Maria Jose
ASI COMO HABIAN SIDO

Ilander, Kicki
PELLE EROVRAREN

Isho, Kyoto
ITAZU

Iso-Lotila, Airi
JAAN KAANTOPIIRI

Jacobs, Monika
DER HIMMEL UBER BERLIN

James, Kathe
NORTH SHORE

Jeakins, Dorothy
DEAD, THE

Jensen, Lisa
MAID TO ORDER
MANNEQUIN

Johnson, Jacqueline
HUNTER'S BLOOD
NIGHTFORCE

Johnston, Joanna
HELLRAISER

Johnston, Renee
DOWN TWISTED

Jud, Anne
ANITA—DANCES OF VICE

Junqueira, Juliana
A DANCA DOS BONECOS

Kaczenski, Heidi
HOUSE TWO: THE SECOND STORY

Kadrnozka, Dimitrij
CENA MEDU

Kakridas, Dimitris
IKONA ENOS MYTHIKOU PROSOPOU

Kaplan, Michael
TOUGH GUYS DON'T DANCE

Karidis, Giannis
APOUSIES

Katila, Sirkku
ELVIS-KISSAN JALJILLA

Katsoulogiannakis, Dora
I WAS A TEENAGE ZOMBIE

Katsushima, Morihiko
BUS

Keita, Kossa Mody
YEELEN

Keller, Elizabeth Haas
MY DARK LADY

Kemenes, Fanni
CSOK, ANYU
DIARY FOR MY LOVED ONES
ISTEN VELETEK, BARATAIM

Kidd, Barbara
KITCHEN TOTO, THE
SAMMY AND ROSIE GET LAID

Kiellerman, Gina
BLUE MONKEY

Kim, Willa
GARDENS OF STONE

Kjeltoft, Marcella
PETER VON SCHOLTEN

Knox, Christopher
LADIES OF THE LOTUS

Kolinsky, Petr
PROC?

Kolvig, Gitte
PELLE EROVRAREN

Komarov, Shelley
ASSASSINATION

Kotzia, Aphrodite
VIOS KE POLITIA

Kranz, Petra
MEIER

Kubo, Satoyoshi
HOTARUGAWA

Kundzinova, Ieva
POHADKA O MALICKOVI

Kurland, Jeffrey
RADIO DAYS
REVENGE OF THE NERDS II: NERDS IN PARADISE
SEPTEMBER

Kwitney, Dana
IRON WARRIOR

Kyriakidis, Pavlos
OH BABYLON

Lachaud, Claudine
FUEGOS

Lagerfeld, Karl
BABETTE'S GASTEBUD

Lagergren, Cecilia
JIM OCH PIRATERNA BLOM

Lahiani, Habiba
JENATSCH

Lakeman, Jill
BIRDS OF PREY

LaMotte, Richard
HANOI HILTON, THE

Landau, Natasha
SUICIDE CLUB, THE

Le Mol, Anne
CHAMP D'HONNEUR

Leff, Ella
CRYSTAL HEART

Leifer, Michele
STREET TRASH

Lekkos, Yannis
ONIRO ARISTERIS NICHTAS

Lelouda, Dora
FAKELOS POLK STON AERA

Leon, Debbie
RUMPELSTILTSKIN
SLEEPING BEAUTY

Leterrier, Catherine
MELO

Levin, Leslie
GHOST FEVER

Levine, Darryl
WINNERS TAKE ALL

Lindgren, Gertie
MALARPIRATER

Ling, Ng Po
PEKING OPERA BLUES

Lokrantz, Kerstin
HIP, HIP, HURRA!

Loman, Brad R.
NIGHTFLYERS

Lovatelli, Flavia
ALIEN PREDATOR

Lutz, Adelle
MAKING MR.RIGHT

Lyon, Aggie
MONSTER SQUAD, THE

MacDonald, Aleida
POLICE ACADEMY 4: CITIZENS ON PATROL

Maginnis, Molly
BROADCAST NEWS
BROADCAST NEWS

Magny, Ginette
KEEPING TRACK

Mago
GIRL, THE

Major, Ann Somers
FLOWERS IN THE ATTIC

Major, Ross
HOWLING III, THE

Makovsky, Judianna
GARDENS OF STONE

Makris, Miltiadis
O PARADISSOS ANIGI ME ANTIKLIDI

Malin, Mary
LETHAL WEAPON

Marando, Anthony
SUMMER HEAT

Marin, Maiki
ASIGNATURA APROBADA

Massaini, Marineida M.C.
EU

Massone, Nicoletta
MORNING MAN, THE

Matheson, Linda
HOUSEKEEPER, THE

Mayer, Martha
HOUR OF THE ASSASSIN

McBride, Elizabeth
SQUARE DANCE

McKinley, Tom
MY DEMON LOVER
WANTED: DEAD OR ALIVE

Medeiros, Anisio
A DANCA DOS BONECOS

Meletopoulos, Nikos
PHOTOGRAPH, THE

Mendoza, Monica
CHORROS

Menichetti, Frederique
MON BEL AMOUR, MA DECHIRURE

Metert, Martine
BAD BLOOD

Mialkovszky, Erzsebet
DOKTOR MINORKA VIDOR NAGY NAPJA

Milani, Marianne
JENATSCH

Millenotti, Maurizio
BELLY OF AN ARCHITECT, THE

Miller, Nolan
PRINCESS ACADEMY, THE

Mirojnick, Ellen
FATAL ATTRACTION
WALL STREET

Mittelman, Mina
STEPFATHER, THE

Mollo, John
CRY FREEDOM

Monaghan, Tish
ROXANNE

Moorcroft, Judy
MONTH IN THE COUNTRY, A

Moore, Dan
EXTREME PREJUDICE

Moreau, Jacqueline
LA PASSION BEATRICE
TERMINUS

Morin, Andree
NIGHT ZOO

Morley, Ruth
HELLO AGAIN

Mussenden, Isis
ALLNIGHTER, THE

Myen, Danika
GET THE TERRORISTS

Myrdal, Pia
BABETTE'S GASTEBUD
SIDSTE AKT

Nardone, Robert
BAD BLOOD

Naylor, Katharine
LOVECHILD, THE

Nel, Karlien
MON BEL AMOUR, MA DECHIRURE

Nelke, Kia
POLICIA

Nemerson, Andrea
VIDEO DEAD, THE

Newbery, Pip
HEARTS OF FIRE

Nicholls, Tiny
FOURTH PROTOCOL, THE

Nierhaus, Brigitte
MAN IN LOVE, A

Nissinen, Marjatta
JAAHYVAISET PRESIDENTILLE

Noir, Gil
SOUS LE SOLEIL DE SATAN

Norris, Patricia
BLACK WIDOW

Norris, Patrick
FORTY DAYS OF MUSA DAGH

Norton, Rosanna
INNERSPACE

Novotna, Kristyna
PRATELE BERMUDSKEHO TROJUHELNIKU

O'Brien, Bernadette
HUNK

O'Leary, Maureen
SOMETHING SPECIAL!

O'Neal, Donna
DATE WITH AN ANGEL

Okubo, Tomio
HOTARUGAWA

Olhson, Christina
MANUELA'S LOVES

Oludhe, Winnie
KOLORMASK

Oroveanu, Ileana
ZLOTY POCIAG

Ossi, Obbie
HA INSTALATOR

Palacios, Guillermo
SENTIMIENTOS: MIRTA DE LINIERS A ESTAMBUL

Palmer, Elizabeth
PERSONAL FOUL

Panicali, Francesca
BARBARIANS, THE

Papantoniou, Ioanna
DOXOBUS

Parisi, Lucio
WARRIOR QUEEN

Parry, Llinos Non
BOY SOLDIER

Partenyi, Zsuzsa
ZUHANAS KOZBEN

Partridge, Wendy
BIG TOWN, THE

Patterson, Clarissa
SHADOWS OF THE PEACOCK

Patterson, Clarrissa
AROUND THE WORLD IN EIGHTY WAYS

Pawar, Tulsi
PRATIGHAAT

Pegg, Katie
BOY SOLDIER

Pehrsson, Inger
MORE ABOUT THE CHILDREN OF BULLERBY VILLAGE
MY LIFE AS A DOG

Peirce, William
EMPIRE STATE

Pelletier, Nicole
LES FOUS DE BASSAN

Pelletier, Olga
LASSOCIATION DES MALFAITEURS
LES OREILLES ENTRE LES DENTS

Pena, Hugo
JAWS: THE REVENGE

Pernia, Patricia
EL ANO DEL CONEJO

Perry, David
BELLMAN AND TRUE

Perry, Karen
HOT SHOT

Pessoa, Paulo Henrique
A DANCA DOS BONECOS

Petersen, Wenche
ETTER RUBICON

Phillips, Erica Edell
ROBOCOP

Pierce, Karen
BLOODSUCKERS FROM OUTER SPACE

Plaza, Felix Sanchez
STRANGER, THE

Poe, Gregory
CANT BUY ME LOVE

Poppel, Ann
DER NACHBAR
TRIUMPH DE GERECHTEN

Porro, Joseph
NEAR DARK

Porteous, Emma
LIVING DAYLIGHTS, THE

Powell, Anthony
ISHTAR

Powell, Sandy
ARIA
LAST OF ENGLAND, THE

Preisler, Mariann
JAG ELSKER DIG

Price, Antony
HEARTS OF FIRE

Pruess, Angela
DEADTIME STORIES

Purcell, Graham
RIGHT HAND MAN, THE

Qualmann, Birthe
PELLE EROVRAREN

Rajk, Laszlo
LENZ

Ranning, Bente
VENNER FOR ALTID

Rasmussen, Manon
NEGERKYS & LABRE LARVER

Raspe, Gioia
TAROT

Rawsthorne, Sue
BOY SOLDIER

Read, Bobbie
BEVERLY HILLS COP II

Reimers, Nadine
SLUMBER PARTY MASSACRE II

Reindl, Vroni
TRIUMPH DE GERECHTEN

Remy, Diemut
WANNSEE CONFERENCE, THE

Renard, Renee
LES MENDIANTS

Reyes, Bong
SWEET REVENGE

Reyner, Mary-Jane
HOUSEKEEPING

Richards, Edward
VIDEO DEAD, THE

Riggs, Rita
MALIBU BIKINI SHOP, THE

Ringwood, Bob
PRICK UP YOUR EARS

Rodenbush, Marty
UNFINISHED BUSINESS . . .

Rodgers, Aggie Guerard
BATTERIES NOT INCLUDED
FATAL BEAUTY
LEONARD PART 6
WITCHES OF EASTWICK, THE

Rogiani, Elisabetta
CAMPUS MAN

Romano, Norma
EN EL NOMBRE DEL HIJO

Rosenfeld, Hilary
DIRTY DANCING

Roswell, Arthur
DEAD OF WINTER

Rowe, David
LIGHTHORSEMEN, THE

Rubio, Jose
LA CASA DE BERNARDA ALBA

Russell, Shirley
HOPE AND GLORY

Russell, Victoria
ARIA
GOTHIC

Russo, Mario
ALADDIN

Ryack, Rita
SUSPECT

S. Tonoian
SASHSHENNYI FONAR

Sabbatini, Enrico
CHRONICLE OF A DEATH FORETOLD

Saez, Gloria
LA GRAN FIESTA

Salling, Norman
HEAT
MALONE

Salvador, Lola
CALE

Sands Films
LITTLE DORRIT

Santos, Mara
LEILA DINIZ

Sartori, Francesca
LUNGA VITA ALLA SIGNORA!

Scandiuzzi, Scilla
DIRTY LAUNDRY

Schaffer, Judit
MALOM A POKOLBAN

Schlom, Marla Denise
JAWS: THE REVENGE

Scholberg, Eva
OFELAS

Schuster, Regina
DEADTIME STORIES

Schutte, Ulrike
F . . . ING FERNAND
MAGIC STICKS

Scott, Deborah Lynn
WHO'S THAT GIRL

Scott, Elisabeth
CLUB LIFE

Scott, Lee
SLAUGHTER HIGH

Seeman, Tanya
SALVATION!

Senior, Anna
LES PATTERSON SAVES THE WORLD

Serafini, Enrico
DANCERS

Sewell, Ted
TROUBLE WITH DICK, THE

Shewsbury, Judy
AVRIL BRISE

Shieff, Buki
EMPEROR'S NEW CLOTHES, THE

Shiff, Buki
BEAUTY AND THE BEAST

Sieff, Eileen
CREEPSHOW 2

Silberska, Maria
CENA ODVAHY

Silk, Ilkay
TUESDAY WEDNESDAY

Silveira, Sergio
ELE, O BOTO

Spadaro, Adriana
DANCERS

Sparks, Katie
MUNCHIES

Sperdouklis, Denis
LE SOURD DANS LA VILLE

Staszewska, Christine
INDIAN SUMMER

Stavridou, Julia
THEOFILOS

Steinmatz, Meira
HANSEL AND GRETEL

Steinmatz, Mirra
RED RIDING HOOD

Steward, Marlene
BACK TO THE BEACH

Stewart, Marlene
SIESTA

Still, Jane
HOME IS WHERE THE HART IS

Stjernsward, Louise
HIGH SEASON

Stockdale, Muriel
I WAS A TEENAGE T.V. TERRORIST

Stolz, Mary Kay
WEEDS

Stringer, Merrill
TISZTA AMERIKA

Summers, Ray
SUMMER SCHOOL

Szczek, Anna
ZLOTY POCIAG

Tait, Pam
STRAIGHT TO HELL
WALKER

Tasaki, Ana
RAGE OF HONOR

Tate, Jennie
GOOD WIFE, THE
VINCENT—THE LIFE AND DEATH OF VINCENT VAN GOGH

Tavernier, Elizabeth
WAITING FOR THE MOON

Taviani, Lina Nerli
DEVIL IN THE FLESH
GOOD MORNING BABYLON

Tax, Yan
MASCARA

Termann, Jette
HIP, HIP, HURRA!

Texter, Gilda
LETS GET HARRY

Thevenet, Friquette
JEUX D'ARTIFICES

Thibeault, Debi
PSYCHOS IN LOVE

Tillen, Jodie
LIGHT OF DAY
REAL MEN

Tomkins, Joe
NUTS

Tonnema, Pat
FLICKS

Torgeyevoi, N.
DVADTSTAT DNEI BEZ

Torok, Flora
GONDOVISELES

Tournafond, Francoise
LE JOURNAL D'UN FOU

Touzinaud, Alain
FELDMANN CASE, THE

Trandafira, Mioara
PADUREANCA

Tsouloyanni, Fani
TA PAIDIA TIS CHELIDONAS

Tsu, Irene
TALKING WALLS

Turturice, Robert
LIKE FATHER, LIKE SON

Tynan, Alexandra
WARM NIGHTS ON A SLOW MOVING TRAIN

Tynan, Tracy
BIG EASY, THE
BLIND DATE

Tyson, James W.
BEVERLY HILLS COP II

Urdiciain, Andres
LA SENYORA

Uria, Pepe
MADE IN ARGENTINA

Vaccari, Laura
MORO AFFAIR, THE

Valles, Luis
CARA DE ACELGA

Van Soest, Isabella
BORN IN EAST L.A.

Vance-Straker, Marilyn
CROSS MY HEART
SOME KIND OF WONDERFUL
THROW MOMMA FROM THE TRAIN
UNTOUCHABLES, THE

Vega-Vasquez, Sylvia
LA BAMBA

Vera, Gerardo
DIVINAS PALABRAS

Vesperini, Edith
MISS MONA

Viertel, Regina
SO VIELE TRAUME

Viola, Gale
SUPERNATURALS, THE

Vogt, Mary
PROJECT X

Voison, Cassandra
STUDENT CONFIDENTIAL

Vollmer, Britta
EIN BLICK-UND DIE LIEBE BRICHT AUS

Vollmer, Marion
EIN BLICK-UND DIE LIEBE BRICHT AUS

Von Oppen, Karen
SALVATION!

Vuarin, Danielle
GRAND GUIGNOL

Wada, Emi
PRINCESS FROM THE MOON

Wallach, Jeffrey
BLOOD SISTERS
MUTANT HUNT

Waller, Elizabeth
LONELY PASSION OF JUDITH HEARNE,THE

Walton, Tony
GLASS MENAGERIE, THE

Warcyzek, Isolde
DER JUNGE MIT DEM GROSSEN SCHWARZEN HUND

Warner, Elizabeth
OUT OF ROSENHEIM

Watkins, Katja
NIONDE KOMPANIET

Watkinson, Doreen
COMRADES

Weiss, Barbara
FOREVER, LULU

Weiss, Julie
MASTERS OF THE UNIVERSE
WHALES OF AUGUST, THE

Wells, Belinda
NICE GIRLS DON'T EXPLODE

Wells, Larry
THREE MEN AND A BABY

Wessely, Jane
VENNER FOR ALTID

Willis, Ruth
OUT OF ORDER

Wilshire, Leslie
STEELE JUSTICE

Wolker, Vickie
OVERKILL

Wolsky, Albert
NADINE

Wright, Hillary
THREE FOR THE ROAD

Ynocenio, Jo
STREET SMART

Yontan, Yudum
YER DEMIR, GOK BAKIR

Zaltzman, Rochelle
DEATH BEFORE DISHONOR

DIRECTORS

Aaltonen, Veikko
TILINTEKO

Aaron, Paul
MORGAN STEWART'S COMING HOME

AAV Creative Unit
NINJA THUNDERBOLT

Abdrashitov, Vadim
PLIUMBUM, ILI OPASNAIA IGIA

Abeysekara, Tisssa
VIRAGAYA

Abuladze, Tenghiz
REPENTANCE

Acin, Jovan
HEY BABU RIBA

Adar, Rafi
KFAFOT

Adlon, Percy
OUT OF ROSENHEIM

Aga-Mirzayev, Mukhtar
GRUBAYA POSADKA

Agosti, Silvano
QUARTIERE

Agresti, Alejandro
EL AMOR ES UNA MUJERGORDA

Ahlin, Per
RESAN TILL MELONIA

Aivasian, Agassi
SASHSHENNYI FONAR

Akhadov, Valeri
A SANTA DERVIS

Alarcon, Sebastian
YAGUAR

Alexandersson, Hakan
RES ALDRIG PA ENKEL BILJETT
SPARVAGN TILL HAVET

Alfarjani, Mohamed Ali
ALSHAZIA

Alfredson, Hans
JIM OCH PIRATERNA BLOM

Ali, Muzaffar
ANJUMAN

Allen, Woody
RADIO DAYS
SEPTEMBER

Allouache, Merzak
UN AMOUR A PARIS

Almodovar, Pedro
LAW OF DESIRE

Alov, Alexander
SEVERNY ANEKDOT

Altberg, Marcos
FONTE DA SAUDADE

Altman, Robert
ARIA
BEYOND THERAPY
O. C. AND STIGGS

Amar, Denia
ENNEMIS INTIMES

Amateau, Rod
GARBAGE PAIL KIDS MOVIE, THE

Amoureux, Yves
LE BEAUF

Anders, Allison
BORDER RADIO

Andersen, Hans Christian
SNOW QUEEN, THE

Anderson, Lindsay
WHALES OF AUGUST, THE

Andolfi, Marco Antonio
LA CROCE DALLE SETTE PIETRE

Andrews, V.C.
FLOWERS IN THE ATTIC

Ansara, Martha
PURSUIT OF HAPPINESS, THE

Apted, Michael
CRITICAL CONDITION

Araki, Gregg
THREE BEWILDERED PEOPLE IN THE NIGHT

Aranda, Vicente
EL LUTE—CAMINA O REVIENTA

Arcady, Alexandre
LETE DERNIER A TANGER

Ardolino, Emile
DIRTY DANCING

Arehn, Mats
OM KARLEK

Argento, Dario
OPERA

Arguello, Ivan
MUJERES DE LA FRONTERA

Arias, Alfredo
FUEGOS

Aristarain, Adolfo
STRANGER, THE

Arizal
STABILIZER, THE

Armstrong, Gillian
HIGH TIDE

Arnold, Newt
ALLAN QUATERMAIN AND THE LOST CITY OF GOLD

Arthur, Karen
LADY BEWARE

Askoldov, Alexander
KOMISSAR

Attenborough, Sir Richard
CRY FREEDOM

August, Bille
PELLE EROVRAREN

Aurelio Chiesa
DISTANT LIGHTS

Avallone, Marcello
SPECTERS

Avdeliodis, Demos
TREE WE HURT, THE

Avildsen, John G.
HAPPY NEW YEAR

Axel, Gabriel
BABETTE'S GASTEBUD

Ayala, Fernando
EL ANO DEL CONEJO

Azimzade, Gulbeniz
CHKATULKA IZ KREPOSTI

Azzopardi, Mario
NOWHERE TO HIDE

B., Beth
SALVATION!

Baba, Yasuo
WATASHI O SKI NI TSURETETTE

Babenco, Hector
IRONWEED

Babu, D. Rajendra
PYAR KARKE DEKHO

Badham, John
STAKEOUT

Bagdadi, Maroun
LHOMME VOILE

Bahaduri, Rajesh
HAMARI JUNG

Bajon, Filip
MAGNAT

Baledon, Rafael
LAS TRAIGO . . . MUERTAS
RETO A LA VIDA

Baletic, Branko
UVEK SPREMNE ZENE

Balraj, Deepak
SHEELA

Banionis, Raimundas
MOYA MALENKAYA ZHENA

Bapu
KALYANA THAMBULAM

Barbash, Uri
DREAMERS

Barbosa, Haroldo Marinho
BAIXO GAVEA

Barclay, Barry
NGATI

Barker, Clive
HELLRAISER

Barrera, Victor
LOS INVITADOS

Barrett, Lezli-An
BUSINESS AS USUAL

Barros, Wilson
NIGHT ANGELS

Bartelski, Leslaw
ZLOTA MAHMUDIA

Bartlett, Michael
KONZERT FUR DIE RECHTE HAND

Bassoff, Lawrence
HUNK

Batyrov, Roald
VINA LEYTENANTA NEKRASOVA

Bava, Lamberto
LE FOTO DI GIOIA

Beaumont, Gabrielle
HES MY GIRL

Bechard, Gorman
PSYCHOS IN LOVE

Beck, Walter
DER BARENHAUTER

Becker, Josh
THOU SHALT NOT KILL . . . EXCEPT

Begeja, Liria
AVRIL BRISE

Behagan, Miki
HA INSTALATOR

Behat, Gilles
CHARLIE DINGO

Bellocchio, Marco
DEVIL IN THE FLESH

Belson, Jerry
SURRENDER

Bemberg, Maria Luisa
MISS MARY

Benner, Dick
TOO OUTRAGEOUS

Bennett, Bill
DEAR CARDHOLDER
JILTED

Benton, Robert
NADINE

Ber, Ryszard
CUDZOZIEMKA

Beresford, Bruce
ARIA

Berezantseva, Tatyana
LYUBOVYU ZA LYUBOV

Berger, Helmut
SAME TO YOU

Bergonzelli, Sergio
TENTAZIONE

Bergquist, Peter L.
MONSTER IN THE CLOSET

Berlanga, Luis Garcia
MOROS Y CRISTIANOS

Bernaza, Luis Felipe
DE TAL PEDRO, TAL ASTILLA

Bernstein, Armyan
CROSS MY HEART

Bernstein, Henry
MELO

Berri, Claude
JEAN DE FLORETTE
MANON OF THE SPRING

Berry, Bill
OFF THE MARK

Bertolucci, Bernardo
LAST EMPEROR, THE

Berz, Michael
SNOW WHITE

Beshara, Khairy
AL-TAUQ WAL-ISWIRA

Bettman, Gil
CRYSTAL HEART

Bezhanov, Gerald
SAMAYA OBAYATELNAYA I PRIVLEKATELNAYA

Bharathan
NILAKURINHI POOTHAPPOL

Bhaskara Rao, B.
UMMADI MOGUDU

Bhattacharya, Basu
PANCHVATI

Bianchi, Andrea
DOLCE PELLE DI ANGELA

Bierbichler, Josef
TRIUMPH DE GERECHTEN

Bigelow, Kathryn
NEAR DARK

Birman, Naum
MAGIA CHYORNAYA I BELAYA

Bivens, Loren
TRESPASSES

Blain, Gerard
PIERRE ET DJEMILA

Blake, "T.C."
NIGHTFLYERS

Blazevski, Vladimir
HI-FI

Bleckner, Jeff
WHITE WATER SUMMER

Blixen, Karen
BABETTE'S GASTEBUD

Block, Bruce
PRINCESS ACADEMY, THE

Blom, Per
IS-SLOTTET

Bloom, Jeffrey
FLOWERS IN THE ATTIC

Bogayevicz, Yurek
ANNA

Bogner, Willy
FIRE AND ICE

Bohm, Hark
LITTLE PROSECUTOR, THE

Bojorquez, Alberto
ROBACHICOS

Bokova, Jana
HOTEL DU PARADIS

Bolivar, Cesar
MAS ALLA DEL SILENCIO

Bollain, Juan Sebastian
LAS DOS ORILLAS

Bolognini, Mauro
MOSCA ADDIO

Bolt, Ben
BIG TOWN, THE

Bonner, Lee
ADVENTURE OF THE ACTION HUNTERS

Boorman, John
HOPE AND GLORY

Borek, Jaromir
CENA MEDU

Boris, Robert
STEELE JUSTICE

Borowczyk, Walerian
EMMANUELLE 5

Bosse, Malcolm
AGENT TROUBLE

Boszormenyi, Geza
LAURA

Botelho, Chico
CIDADE OCULTA

Bozzacchi, Gianni
I LOVE NEW YORK

Bozzetto, Bruno
SOTTO IL RISTORANTE CINESE

Bradley, Al
IRON WARRIOR

Brander, Gary
HOWLING III, THE

Brandt, Carsten
DEMONS

Brandys, Kazimierz
MATKA KROLOW

Brass, Giovanni Tinto
CAPRICCIO

Bravman, Jack
ZOMBIE NIGHTMARE

Brescanu, Vasily
O ROZVRASHCHENII ZABYT

Bridges, Beau
WILD PAIR, THE

Brigadere, Anna
POHADKA O MALICKOVI

Brock, Deborah
SLUMBER PARTY MASSACRE II

Bromfield, Rex
HOME IS WHERE THE HART IS

Brooks, Adam
RED RIDING HOOD

Brooks, James L.
BROADCAST NEWS

Brooks, Mel
SPACEBALLS

Bruce, James
SUICIDE CLUB, THE

Bruckner, Jutta
EIN BLICK-UND DIE LIEBE BRICHT AUS

Bruyere, Christian
SHELLEY

Bryden, Bill
ARIA

Buduris, Vassilis
O PARADISSOS ANIGI ME ANTIKLIDI

Burlyayev, Nikolai
LERMONTOV

Burr, Jeff
OFFSPRING, THE

Burroughs, Jackie
WINTER TAN, A

Butler, Heinz
PERSONAGGI & INTERPRETI

Cacoyannis, Michael
SWEET COUNTRY

Cadena, Jordi
LA SENYORA

Cadiou, Claude
LA VIE PLATINEE

Cain, Christopher
PRINCIPAL, THE

Cameron, Ken
GOOD WIFE, THE

Cammell, Donald
WHITE OF THE EYE

Cammermans, Paul
VAN PAEMEL FAMILY, THE

Camp, Joe
BENJI THE HUNTED

Camus, Mario
LA CASA DE BERNARDA ALBA
LA RUSA

Capitani, Giorgio
MISSIONE EROICA

Carax, Leos
BAD BLOOD

Cardona Jr., Rene
BEAKS

Carlsen, Henning
WOLF AT THE DOOR, THE

Carlstroem, Bjorn
WARDOGS

Carow, Heiner
SO VIELE TRAUME

Carpenter, John
PRINCE OF DARKNESS

Carpenter, Stephen
KINDRED, THE

Carver, Steve
BULLETPROOF
JOCKS

Casden, Ron
CAMPUS MAN

Cassenti, Franck
TESTAMENT D'UN POETE JUIF ASSASSINE

Castellani, Leandro
IL CORAGGIO DI PARLARE

Castellano
IL BURBERO

Castillo, Oscar
EULALIA

Castro, Victor Manuel
EL MOFLES Y LOS MECANICOS

Cazals, Felipe
LO DEL CESAR

Chabrol, Claude
LE CRI DU HIBOU
MASQUES

Chakraborty, Srinivas
ARPAN

Chalbaud, Roman
LA OVEJA NEGRA
MANON

Chan, Jackie
PROJECT A—PART II

Chan, Philip
CHOCOLATE INSPECTOR

Chandra, N.
PRATIGHAAT

Charef, Mehdi
MISS MONA

Chatterjee, Shakti
LALAN FAKIR

Chaussois, Dominique
LE MOUSTACHU

Chereau, Patrice
HOTEL DE FRANCE

Cherry III, John R.
ERNEST GOES TO CAMP

Chetwynd, Lionel
HANOI HILTON, THE

Chi-gyoon, Kwak
KYEOUL NAGUNE

Chiang, John
WRONG COUPLES,THE

Chkheidze, Bidzina
GOSPODA AVANTYURISTY

Chmielewski, Tadeusz
WIERNA RZEKA

Chobocky, Barbara A.
WITCH HUNT

Chokheli, Goderdzi
VELIKIY POKHOD ZA NEVESTOY

Chouraqui, Elie
MAN ON FIRE

Chowdhury, Anjan
BIDROHI

Chowdhury, Pinaki
APAN GHAREY

Chueng, Yuen Ting
AUTUMN'S TALE, AN

Chugunov, Victor
SKAZKA O PREKRASNOY AYSULU

Chukhrai, Pavel
ZINA-ZINULYA

Chuliukin, Yury
KAK STAT SCHASTLIVYM

Chung, David
MAGNIFICENT WARRIORS

Chytilova, Vera
WOLF'S HOLE

Ciccoritti, Gerard
GRAVEYARD SHIFT
PSYCHO GIRLS

Cimino, Michael
SICILIAN, THE

Cinco, Manuel
DAY THEY ROBBED AMERICA, THE

Cisse, Souleymane
YEELEN

Clark, Bob
FROM THE HIP

Clark, Louise
WINTER TAN, A

Clarke, Alan
RITA, SUE AND BOB TOO!

Clayton, Jack
LONELY PASSION OF JUDITH HEARNE,THE

Clucher, E.B.
RENEGADE, UN OSSO TROPPO DURO

Coburn, Glen
BLOODSUCKERS FROM OUTER SPACE

Coen, Joel
RAISING ARIZONA

Coggio, Roger
LE JOURNAL D'UN FOU

Cohen, Avi
YEHOSHUA—YEHOSHUA

Cohen, Larry
DEADLY ILLUSION

Cokliss, Harley
MALONE

Collier, James F.
CAUGHT

Collins, Edward
EVIL TOWN

Colomo, Fernando
LA VIDA ALEGRE

Columbus, Chris
ADVENTURES IN BABYSITTING

Comencini, Luigi
UN RAGAZZO DI CALABRIA

Coninx, Stijn
HECTOR

Conrad, Patrick
MASCARA

Conway, Kevin
VIOLINS CAME WITH THE AMERICANS, THE

Coppola, Francis
GARDENS OF STONE

Corbucci, Bruno
ALADDIN

Corbucci, Sergio
RIMINI RIMINI
ROBA DA RICCHI

Cortini, Bruno
LESTATE STA FINENDO

Coscia, Jorge
CHORROS
SENTIMIENTOS: MIRTA DE LINIERS A ESTAMBUL

Costa Muste, Pedro
REDONDELA

Costa-Gavras, Constantin
FAMILY BUSINESS

Coutsomitis, Costas
KLIOS

Cox, Alex
STRAIGHT TO HELL
WALKER

Cox, Paul
VINCENT—THE LIFE AND DEATH OF VINCENT VAN GOGH

Crevenna, Alfredo B.
ALBURES MEXICANOS
CINCO NACOS ASALTAN A LAS VEGAS
LA FUGA DE CARRASCO
MAS BUENAS QUE EL PAN

Cuerda, Jose Luis
EL BOSQUE ANIMADO

D'Amato, Joe
UNDICI GIORNI, UNDICI NOTTE

d'Anna, Claude
MACBETH

Dahlin, Bob
MONSTER IN THE CLOSET

Daley, Tom
OUTING, THE

Danelia, Georgy
KIN-DZA-DZA
Daniel, Rod
LIKE FATHER, LIKE SON
Danneborn, Bengt
DET STORA LOFTET
Dansereau, Mireille
LE SOURD DANS LA VILLE
Dante, Joe
AMAZON WOMEN ON THE MOON
INNERSPACE
Dardenne, Jean-Pierre
FALSCH
Dardenne, Luc
FALSCH
Das, Sukhen
AMAR KANTAK
Dasgupta, Buddhadeb
PHERA
Dashiev, Arya
UTRO OBRECHENNOGO PRIISKA
David DeCouteau
CREEPOZOIDS
Davidson, Boaz
DUTCH TREAT
Davies, Robert
SATURDAY NIGHT AT THE PALACE
Davletshin, Farid
TAYNOE PUTESHESTVIE EMIRA
Dawn, Vincent
STRIKE COMMANDO
de Almeida, Paulo Sergio
BEIJO NA BOCA
de Anda, Gilberto
EL ANSIA DE MATAR
FIERAS EN BRAMA
FORAJIDOS EN LA MIRA
POLICIAS DE NARCOTICOS
de Arminan, Jaime
MY GENERAL
De Bello, John
HAPPY HOUR
De Geer Bergenstrahle, Marie-Louise
FADERN, SONEN OCH DEN HELIGE ANDE
De Guzman, Ruben
WILD FORCE
de Heredia, Alvaro Saenz
POLICIA
de la Barca, Pedro Calderon
MEMOIRE DES APPARENCES: LA VIE EST UN SONGE
de la Iglesia, Eloy
LA ESTANQUERA DE VALLECAS
de la Parra, Pim
ALS IN EEN ROES
ODYSSEE D'AMOUR
De Lillo, Antonietta
UNA CASA IN BILICO
de Mareuil, Stephanie
COERS CROISES
De Palma, Brian
UNTOUCHABLES, THE
de Paula, Francisco
AREIAS ESCALADANTES
de Sanzo, Juan Carlos
EN RETIRADA
EN RETIRADA
Dear, William
HARRY AND THE HENDERSONS
DeCoteau, David
DREAMANIAC
Dehlavi, Jamil
BORN OF FIRE
Deimel, Mark
PERFECT MATCH, THE
Dekker, Fred
MONSTER SQUAD, THE
Del Rio, Ernesto
EL AMOR DE AHORA
Delgado, Miguel M.
ENTRE FICHERAS ANDA EL DIABLO
Delman, Jeffrey
DEADTIME STORIES
Denis, Jean-Pierre
CHAMP D'HONNEUR
Deodato, Ruggero
BARBARIANS, THE
CAMPING DEL TERRORE
Deray, Jacques
LE SOLITAIRE
MALADIE D'AMOUR
Deruddere, Dominique
LOVE IS A DOG FROM HELL
des Cars, Guy
LA BRUTE
Deutch, Howard
SOME KIND OF WONDERFUL
DeVito, Danny
THROW MOMMA FROM THE TRAIN
Dick, Nigel
P.I. PRIVATE INVESTIGATIONS
Dickens, Charles
LITTLE DORRIT
Diegues, Carlos
UM TREM PARA AS ESTRELAS
Dixon, John
RUNNING FROM THE GUNS
Dixon, Ken
SLAVE GIRLS FROM BEYOND INFINITY
Doillon, Jacques
COMEDY!
Dolinin, Dmitry
SENTIMENTALNOE PUTESHESTVIE NA KARTOSHKU
Domalik, Andrzej
ZYGFRYD
Dominguez, Rudy
NO BLOOD NO SURRENDER
Donaldson, Roger
NO WAY OUT
Donner, Richard
LETHAL WEAPON
Doo-yong, Lee
NAE-SHI
Doria, Alejandro
SOFIA
Dorman, Veniamin
KONETS OPERATSII "REZIDENT"
Dostal, Nikolai
CHELOVEK C AKKORDEONOM
Douglas, Bill
COMRADES
Dovgan, Vladimir
I NIKTO NA SVETE
Dovlatyan, Frunze
ODINOKAYA ORESHINA
Drach, Michel
IL EST GENIAL PAPY!
Dragin, Bert L.
SUMMER CAMP NIGHTMARE
Drake, Jim
POLICE ACADEMY 4: CITIZENS ON PATROL
Drew, Di
RIGHT HAND MAN, THE
Dugdale, George
SLAUGHTER HIGH
Duigan, John
YEAR MY VOICE BROKE, THE
Duque, Lisandro
VISA U.S.A.
Duran, Fernando
HERENCIA DE VALIENTES
Duran, Javier
LAPUTA: THE CASTLE IN THE SKY
Duran, Jorge
COLOR OF DESTINY, THE
Duran, Rafael Rosales
JUNTOS
Dutt, Raj
PUDHCHE PAOL
Dziki, Waldemar
LE JEUNE MAGICIEN
Ecare, Desire
FACES OF WOMEN
Edmondson, Adrian
MORE BAD NEWS
Edwall, Allan
MALARPIRATER
Edwards, Blake
BLIND DATE
Edzard, Christine
LITTLE DORRIT
Eggleston, Colin
CASSANDRA
Egoyan, Atom
FAMILY VIEWING
Ellis, Bob
WARM NIGHTS ON A SLOW MOVING TRAIN
Endo, Shusaku
SEA AND POISON, THE
Enzo Millioni
TENEREZZA
Erdoss, Pal
GONDOVISELES
Erichsen, Bente
FELDMANN CASE, THE
Eriksson, Claes
LEIF
Esadze, Rezo
NEYLONOVAYA YOLKA
Espinosa, Benjamin Escamilla
LO NEGRO DEL NEGRO
Ezra, Mark
SLAUGHTER HIGH
Fagerstrom-Olsson, Agneta
SEPPAN
Fago, Amedeo
LA DONNA DEL TRAGHETTO
Faiziyev, Latif
OKHOTA NA DRAKONA
Falk, Feliks
BOHATERROKU
Fanaka, Jamaa
PENITENTIARY III
Farina, Felice
SEMBRA MORTO . . . ME E SOLO SVENUTO
Fasano, John
ROCK 'N' ROLL NIGHTMARE
Fazil
POOVIZHI VASALILE
Feinmann
EN RETIRADA
Feldman, Dennis
REAL MEN
Fellini, Federico
INTERVISTA
Fels, Hans
QUATRE MAINS
Ferrara, Abel
CHINA GIRL
Ferrara, Giuseppe
MORO AFFAIR, THE
Ferrini, Franco
CARAMELLE DA UNO SCONOSCIUTO
Ferris, Costas
OH BABYLON
Filan, Ludovit
CENA ODVAHY
Findlay, Roberta
BLOOD SISTERS
ORACLE, THE
Firstenberg, Sam
AMERICAN NINJA 2: THE CONFRONTATION
Firth, Mike
LEADING EDGE, THE
Fischer, Markus
DER NACHBAR
Fleischer, Richard
MILLION DOLLAR MYSTERY
Fleming, Edward
SIDSTE AKT
Florea, John
HOT CHILD IN THE CITY
Flynn, John
BEST SELLER
Foldes, Lawrence D.
NIGHTFORCE
Foley, James
WHO'S THAT GIRL
Fomenko, Pyotr
POEZDKI NA STAROM AVTOMOBILE
Fonseca E Costa, Jose
LA PLAYA DE LOS PERROS
Fonseca e Costa, Jose
BALADA DA PRAIA DOS CAES
Forder, Timothy
INDIAN SUMMER
Foriadis, Aris
KE DYO AVGA TOURKIAS
Forque, Jose Maria
ROMANCA FINAL
Forsch, Gerd Roman
DANN IST NICHTS MEHR WIE VORHER
Forsyth, Bill
HOUSEKEEPING
Francis, Karl
BOY SOLDIER
Frank, Christopher
LANNEE DES MEDUSES

SPIRALE
Frank, Melvin
WALK LIKE A MAN
Franke, Anja
SAME TO YOU
Frears, Stephen
PRICK UP YOUR EARS
SAMMY AND ROSIE GET LAID
Freed, Herb
SURVIVAL GAME
Frez, Ilya
LICHNOE DELO SUDYI IVANOVOY
Fridriksson, Fridrik Thor
SKYTTURNAR
Friend, Chan
HAPPY BIGAMIST
Friis Mikkelsen, Jarl
KAMPEN OM DEN RODE KO
Frizzell, John
WINTER TAN, A
Froehlich, Bill
RETURN TO HORROR HIGH
Fruet, William
BLUE MONKEY
Fuhrer, Volker
STADTRAND
Fukasaku, Kinji
KATAKU NO HITO
Fukasaku, Kinju
SURE DEATH 4
Fuller, Tex
STRANDED
Fumagalli, Gianluca
A FIOR DI PELLE
Furie, Sidney J.
SUPERMAN IV: THE QUEST FOR PEACE
Gagne, Jean
LA COULEUR ENCERCLEE
Gagne, Serge
LA COULEUR ENCERCLEE
Gagnon, Claude
KID BROTHER, THE
Gaidai, Leonid
SPORTLOTO—82
Galindo, Ruben
NARCOTERROR
Galindo III, Pedro
EL MUERTO DEL PALOMO
MI NOMBRE ES GATILLO
Gamba, Giuliana
PROFUMO
Gamba, Sao
KOLORMASK
Garci, Jose Luis
ASIGNATURA APROBADA
Garcia, Federico
EL SOCIO DE DIOS
Garcia Sanchez, Jose Luis
HAY QUE DESHACER LA CASA
Gardos, Peter
WHOOPING COUGH
Gasparov, Samvel
KOORDINATY SMERTI
Gaup, Nils
OFELAS
Gazdag, Gyula
HOL VOLT, HOL NEM VOLT
Gedris, Marionas
BLUDNYY SYN
George, K.G.
KATHAKKU PINNIL
George, Peter
SURF NAZIS MUST DIE
Gherman, Alexei
DVADTSTAT DNEI BEZ
Giannini, Giancarlo
TERNOSECCO
Gibbons, Pamela
BELINDA
Gies, Hajo
ZABOU
Gil, Margarida
RELACAO FIEL E VERDADEIRA
Gilhuis, Mark G.
BLOODY WEDNESDAY
Gilles, Guy
NUIT DOCILE
Gio, Lo
BLACK DRAGON, THE
Giraldi, Bob
HIDING OUT
Glagolev, Gennady
RAZMAKH KRYLIEV
Glaser, Paul Michael
RUNNING MAN, THE
Gleason, Michie
SUMMER HEAT
Glen, John
LIVING DAYLIGHTS, THE
Glenn, Pierre-William
TERMINUS
Glowna, Vadim
DEVILS PARADISE, THE
Godard, Jean-Luc
ARIA
SOIGNE TA DROITE
Goddard, Gary
MASTERS OF THE UNIVERSE
Godmilow, Jill
WAITING FOR THE MOON
Goedel, Peter
DAS TREIBHAUS
Goel, Jyotin
INAAM DUS HAZAAR
Goethe, Johann Wolfgang von
MEFISTO FUNK
Gogoberidze, Lana
KRUGOVOROT
Golan, Menahem
OVER THE TOP
Goldschmidt, John
CRIME OF HONOR
MASCHENKA
Gomer, Steve
SWEET LORRAINE
Goncharov, Ivan
OBRYV
Gonzalez, Rogelio A.
EL HOMBRE DESNUDO
Gordeladze, Leila
PYAT NEVEST DO LYUBIMOY
Gordon, Alexander
VYKUP
Gordon, Stuart
DOLLS
Gordon Pinsent
JOHN AND THE MISSUS
Goretta, Claude
SI LE SOLEIL NE REVENAIT PAS
Gorkovenko, Yuri
GEROY YEYOROMANA
Gornick, Michael
CREEPSHOW 2
Gorpenko, Vladimir
TVOYO MIRNOE NEBO
Gosha, Hideo
DEATH SHADOWS
YOSHIWARA ENJO
Gothar, Peter
TISZTA AMERIKA
Goto, Toshio
ITAZU
Gottlieb, Carl
AMAZON WOMEN ON THE MOON
Gottlieb, Franz Josef
DEATH STONE
ZARTLICHE CHAOTEN
Gottlieb, Michael
MANNEQUIN
Graf, Oskar Maria
TRIUMPH DE GERECHTEN
Grammatikov, Vladimir
MIO, MOY MIO
Granier-Deferre, Pierre
NOYADE INTERDITE
Grassia, Nini
IL FASCINO SOTTILE DEL PECCATO
Graver, Gary
MOON IN SCORPIO
PARTY CAMP
Grede, Kjell
HIP, HIP, HURRA!
Greenaway, Peter
BELLY OF AN ARCHITECT, THE
Grigoratos, Dionyssis
FAKELOS POLK STON AERA
Grigoryevs, Renita
GOVORIT MOSKVA
Grigoryevs, Yury
GOVORIT MOSKVA
Grikyavicus, Almantas
SLEDY OBOROTNYA
Grimm, the Brothers
DER BARENHAUTER
Grishin, Alexander
POEZD VNE RASPISANIA
Grissmer, John W.
NIGHTMARE AT SHADOW WOODS
Groning, Philip
SOMMER
Gronowski, Miroslaw
WERYFIKACJA
Gross, Yoram
DOT GOES TO HOLLYWOOD
Grossman, Vasily
KOMISSAR
Grosso, Alfonso
LOS INVITADOS
Grubcheva, Ivanka
TRINAJSTATA GODENICA NA PRINCA
Gruza, Jerzy
PIERSCIEN I ROZA
Guerrero, Francisco
TRAGICO TERREMOTO EN MEXICO
Guha, Sujit
AMAR SANGI
Guillemot, Claude
LA BRUTE
Gurrola, Alfredo
VA DE NUEZ
Gutman, Nathaniel
DEADLINE
Guttman, Amos
HIMMO MELECH YERUSHALAIM
Gyu, Yun Ryong
TALMAE WA POMDARI
Hall, Kenneth J.
EVIL SPAWN
Hallstrom, Lasse
MORE ABOUT THE CHILDREN OF BULLERBY VILLAGE
MY LIFE AS A DOG
Hancock, John
WEEDS
Hanin, Roger
LA RUMBA
Hannant, Brian
TIME GUARDIAN, THE
Hansel, Marion
LES NOCES BARBARES
Hanson, Curtis
BEDROOM WINDOW, THE
Harada, Masato
SARABA ITOSHIKI HITO YO
Hariharan
AMRITAMGAMAYA
ANJAAM
PANCHAGNI
Hark, Tsui
PEKING OPERA BLUES
Harris, Doug
REMEMBERING MEL
Harry, Lee
SILENT NIGHT, DEADLY NIGHT PART II
Hars, Mihaly
LUTRA
Hartman, Rivka
BACHELOR GIRL
Hartzell, Paivi
SNOW QUEEN, THE
Hastrup, Jannik
STRIT OG STUMME
Heifits, Iosif
PODSUDIMYY
Henszelman, Stefan
VENNER FOR ALTID
Herbert, Peter
BIT PART, THE
Hermansson, Bo
PA STIGENDE KURS
Hessler, Gordon
RAGE OF HONOR
WHEELS OF TERROR
Heynemann, Laurent
LES MOIS D'AVRIL SONT MEURTRIERS
Hickey, Bruce
NECROPOLIS

Higashi, Yoichi
LOVE LETTER

Hill, Walter
EXTREME PREJUDICE

Hiller, Arthur
OUTRAGEOUS FORTUNE

Hirsch, Bettina
MUNCHIES

Hjortsberg, William
ANGEL HEART

Ho, Godfrey
NINJA THUNDERBOLT

Ho, Yim
BUDDHA'S LOCK

Hobbs, Lyndall
BACK TO THE BEACH

Hodges, Mike
PRAYER FOR THE DYING, A

Hoffman, Michael
PROMISED LAND

Hoffs, Tamar Simon
ALLNIGHTER, THE

Holden, Anne
BEDROOM WINDOW, THE

Holderlin, Friedrich
DER TOD DES EMPEDOKLES

Holland, Tom
FATAL BEAUTY

Holzman, Allan
PROGRAMMED TO KILL

Hook, Harry
KITCHEN TOTO, THE

Hool, Lance
STEEL DAWN

Horian, Richard
STUDENT CONFIDENTIAL

Horton, Peter
AMAZON WOMEN ON THE MOON

Hsien, Hou Hsiao
LIEN LIEN FUNG CHEN

Hubenbecker, Daniel
WARDOGS

Hubert, Jean-Loup
LE GRAND CHEMIN

Huemer, Peter Ily
KISS DADDY GOOD NIGHT

Hughes, John
PLANES, TRAINS AND AUTOMOBILES

Hughes, Robert C.
HUNTER'S BLOOD

Hui, Ann
ROMANCE OF BOOK AND SWORD, THE

Huillet, Daniele
DER TOD DES EMPEDOKLES

Hung, Samo
EASTERN CONDORS

Hunt, Peter
ASSASSINATION

Hunter, Tim
RIVER'S EDGE

Huston, John
DEAD, THE

Hylkema, Hans
JULIA'S GEHEIM

Ichikawa, Kon
EIGA JOYU
PRINCESS FROM THE MOON

Icho, Arvo
IGRY DLJA DETEJ SKO'NOGO VOZRASTA

Ilienko, Yuri
RODNIK DLIA ZHAZHDUSHCHIKH

Ilyenko, Michail
KAZHDYY OKHOTNIK ZHELAET ZNAT

Im Kwon-t'ack
TICKET

Imamura, Shohei
ZEGEN

Imberman, Shmuel
LO SAM ZAYIN

Ingvordsen, J. Christian
FIREHOUSE

Irvin, John
HAMBURGER HILL

Irving, David
EMPEROR'S NEW CLOTHES, THE
RUMPELSTILTSKIN
SLEEPING BEAUTY

Ishmukhamedov, Elyor
PROSHAL ZELEN LETA

Itami, Juzo
TAXING WOMAN, A

Itoh, Chisho
GONDOLA

Itygilov, Alexander
OBVINYAETSYA SVADBA

Ivory, James
MAURICE

Iwaszkiewicz, J.
ZYGFRYD

Izmailov, Rasim
YA LYUBIL VAC BOLSHE ZHIZNI

Jackson, Mike
BLOOD TRACKS

Jacquot, Benoit
LES MENDIANTS

Jafelice, Raymond
CARE BEARS ADVENTURE IN WONDERLAND, THE

Jaglom, Henry
SOMEONE TO LOVE

Jancso, Miklos
SZORNYEK EVADJA

Jarman, Derek
ARIA
LAST OF ENGLAND, THE

Jasny, Vojtech
GREAT LAND OF SMALL, THE

Jassan, Ernest
PROSTI

Jewison, Norman
MOONSTRUCK

Jialin, Chen
LAST EMPRESS, THE

Jianxin, Huang
BLACK CANNON INCIDENT, THE
CUO WEI

Jo Schafer
CEMIL

Joanou, Phil
THREE O'CLOCK HIGH

John C.
LA BUSQUEDA

Jones, Amy
MAID TO ORDER

Jones, David
EIGHTY FOUR CHARING CROSS ROAD

Jones, Donald
MURDER LUST

Jones, Terry
PERSONAL SERVICES

Joshi
JANUARY ORORMA

Joshi, Chandrakant
SUTRADHAR

Jost, Jon
BELL DIAMOND

Jozani, Massood Jafari
SHEERE SANGGY

Jozani, Massoud Jafari
DJADDE HAYE SARD

Junker, Gottfried
VERSTECKTE LIEBE

Jusid, Juan Jose
MADE IN ARGENTINA

K'an-p'ing, Yu
OUTSIDERS, THE

Kachyna, Karel
DEATH OF A BEAUTIFUL DREAM

Kaczender, George
PRETTYKILL

Kaige, Chen
BIG PARADE, THE

Kaiserman, Connie
MY LITTLE GIRL

Kalisky, Rene
FALSCH

Kaloyeropoulos, N.
ONIRO ARISTERIS NICHTAS

Kamin, Bebe
CHECHECHELA—UNA CHICA DEL BARRIO

Kaminka, Didier
TANT QU'IL AURA DES FEMMES

Kanievska, Marek
LESS THAN ZERO

Kaplan, Jonathan
PROJECT X

Kapur, Shekhar
MISTER INDIA

Kara, Yuri
ZAVTRA BILA VOINA

Karman, Janice
CHIPMUNK ADVENTURE, THE

Karson, Eric
OPPOSING FORCE

Karya, Teguh
IBUNDA

Kassila, Matti
JAAHYVAISET PRESIDENTILLE

Katakouzinos, George
ANGELOS
APOUSIES

Kato, Yudai
KID BROTHER, THE

Katsouridis, Dinos
ONIRO ARISTERIS NICHTAS

Kaurismaki, Aki
HAMLET
VARJOJA PARATIISISSA

Kaurismaki, Mike
HELSINKI NAPOLI—ALL NIGHT LONG

Kavur, Omer
ANAYURT OTELI

Kay, Wong Wah
SAPPORO STORY

Kedzielawska, Grazyna
INNA WYSPA

Keglevic, Peter
MAGIC STICKS

Kei, Shu
LAONIANG GOU SAO

Keith, David
CURSE, THE

Keller, Frederick King
MY DARK LADY

Kemal, Yashmar
YER DEMIR, GOK BAKIR

Kennedy, Burt
TROUBLE WITH SPIES, THE

Kent, Larry
HIGH STAKES

Kern, Peter
CRAZY BOYS

Keusch, Erwin
FLYER, THE

Khamrayev, Ali
YA TEBYA POMNYU

Khamrayev, Iskander
KRASNAYA STRELA

Khan, Mohammed
ZAWGAT RAGOL MOHIM

Khleifi, Michel
NOCE EN GALILEE

Khodjikov, Sultan
ZNAY NASHIKH

Khotinenko, Vladimir
V STRELYAYUSHCHEY GLUSHI

Khouri, Walter Hugo
EU

Khudonazarov, Davlat
V TALOM SNEGE ZVON RUCHIA

Kidawa, Janusz
KOMEDIANCI Z WCZORAJSZEJ ULICY
PAN SAMOCHODZIK I NIESAMOWITY DWOR

Kiersch, Fritz
WINNERS TAKE ALL

Kieslowski, Krzysztof
BLIND CHANCE

Kijowski, Janusz
MASKARADA

Kin, Lo
FINAL TEST, THE

Kincaid, Tim
MUTANT HUNT
ROBOT HOLOCAUST

King, Rick
HOT SHOT
KILLING TIME, THE

Kiral, Erden
DILAN

Kis, Jozsef
A SANTA DERVIS

Kiysk, Kalie
CHEREZ STO LET V MAE

Kjarulff-Schmidt, Palle
PETER VON SCHOLTEN

Kleven, Max
NIGHT STALKER, THE

Klimov, Elem
FAREWELL
Kluge, Alexander
VERMISCHTE NACHRICHTEN
Kobzev, Viktor
ZOLOTAYA BABA
Kocking, Leonardo
LA ESTACION DEL REGRESO
Koeppen, Wolfgang
DAS TREIBHAUS
Kohli, Raj Kumar
INSANIYAT KE DUSHMAN
Kokkonen, Ere
LIIAN ISO KEIKKA
PIKKUPOJAT
UUNO TURHAPURO MUUTTAA MAALLE
Kollek, Amos
FOREVER, LULU
Koltunov, Grigory
ISKUSHENIE DON ZHUANA
Komatsu, Takashi
BUS
Konchalovsky, Andrei
SHY PEOPLE
Kong, Jackie
BLOOD DINER
Konrad, Kazimierz
STANISLAW I ANNA
Kopjitti, Chart
HOUSE
Kordon, Arkady
NABAT NA RASSVETE
Kosberg, Bob
IN THE MOOD
Koterski, Marek
ZYCIE WEWNETRZNE
Kotkowski, Andrzej
W STARYM DWORKU
Kouf, Jim
MIRACLES
Kozole, Damjan
USODNI TELEFON
Krabbe, Tim
RED DESERT PENITENTIARY
Krawczyk, Gerard
LETE EN PENTE DOUCE
Kremnev, Valery
OCHNAYA STAVKA
Kresoja, Dragan
OKTOBERFEST
Krieger, Martin Theo
ZISCHKE
Krishtofovich, Vyacheslav
ODINOKAYA ZHENCHINA ZHELAET POZNAKOMITAYA
Kristek, Vaclav
PRATELE BERMUDSKEHO TROJUHELNIKU
Krueger, Michael
MIND KILLER
Krzystek, Waldemar
W ZAWIESZENIU
Kubrick, Stanley
FULL METAL JACKET
Kuhn, Siegfried
DER TRAUM VOM ELCH
Kuliev, Eldar
LEGENDA SEREBRYANOGO OZERA
Kumai, Kei
SEA AND POISON, THE
Kuri, Rafael Vilasenor
UNA PURA Y DOS CON SAL
Kuri, Rafael Villasenor
EL DIABLO, EL SANTO Y EL TONTO
MATAR O MORIR
SINVERGUENZA . . . PERO HONRADO
Kurys, Diane
MAN IN LOVE, A
Kushnerov, Yury
MOY LYUBIMYY KLOUN
Kuusi, Janne
A LA ITKE IINES
Kuzminski, Zbigniew
MIEDZY USTAMI A BRZEGIEM PUCHARU
NAD NIEMNEM
Kwan, Stanley
DIXIA QING
Kwok-leong, Kam
WONDER WOMEN
Kyronseppa, Kari
VY VIHDOINKIN YHDESSA

Lacerda, Luiz Carlos
LEILA DINIZ
Lahiff, Craig
CODA
Lahlou, Latif
LA COMPROMISSION
Lai, David
SWORN BROTHERS
Lai-Choi, Nam
KILLER'S NOCTURNE
Laine, Edvard
AKALLINEN MIES
Lajus, Lejda
IGRY DLJA DETEJ SKO'NOGO VOZRASTA
Laloux, Rene
GANDAHAR
Lam, Ringo
CITY ON FIRE
PRISON ON FIRE
Lambert, Mary
SIESTA
Lambrinos, Fotos
DOXOBUS
Lamy, Benoit
LA VIE EST BELLE
Landis, John
AMAZON WOMEN ON THE MOON
Lang, Michel
CLUB DE RENCONTRES
Lange, Monique
ACCROCHE-COEUR
Langman, Chris
MOVING TARGETS
Langton, Simon
WHISTLE BLOWER, THE
Lapshin, Yaropolk
ZHELEZNOE POLE
Latif, Latif Abdul
PERLYOTNIYE PTIT
Latsis, Eric
OBOROTEN TOM
Lautner, Georges
LA VIE DISSOLUE DE GERARD FLOQUE
Lauzon, Jean-Claude
NIGHT ZOO
Lavanic, Zlatko
STRATEGIJA SVRAKE
Leconte, Patrice
TANDEM
Leduc, Paul
FRIDA
Lee, Chang-ho
MAN WITH THREE COFFINS, THE
Lee-Thompson, J.
DEATH WISH 4: THE CRACKDOWN
Lefebvre, Genevieve
MANUELA'S LOVES
Lehmuskallio, Markku
INUKSUK
Leitao, Joaquim
DUMA VEZ POR TODAS
Leitch, Christopher
TEEN WOLF TOO
Leland, David
WISH YOU WERE HERE
Lelouch, Claude
ATTENTION BANDITS
Lemick, Michael E.
MASSACRE IN DINOSAUR VALLEY
Lemmo, James
HEART
Lemos, Carlos
LOS DUENOS DEL SILENCIO
SVART GRYNING
Lent, Dean
BORDER RADIO
Lenzi, Giovanna
DELITTI
Leonard, Terry J.
DEATH BEFORE DISHONOR
Leslie, Bill
NAIL GUN MASSACRE
Leszczynski, Witold
SIEKIEREZADA
Levchuk, Timofei
MY OBVINYAEM
MY OBVINYAEM
Levin, Vasily
ISKUSHENIE DON ZHUANA

Levinson, Barry
GOOD MORNING, VIETNAM
TIN MEN
Levitan, Nadav
YALDEI STALIN
Levitin, Jacqueline
EVA: GUERRILLERA
Levy, Dani
SAME TO YOU
Lichtenheld, Ted
PERSONAL FOUL
Liconti, Carlo
CONCRETE ANGELS
Ligon, Stanislaw
KOMEDIANCI Z WCZORAJSZEJ ULICY
Lilienthal, Peter
POET'S SILENCE, THE
Lima, Walter
ELE, O BOTO
Linares, Andres
ASI COMO HABIAN SIDO
Lindblom, Gunnel
NAGRA SOMMARKVALLAR PA JORDEN
Lindfors, Viveca
UNFINISHED BUSINESS . . .
Lindgren, Torgny
SERPENT'S WAY, THE
Lindholm, Peter
KILL CITY
Link, Ron
ZOMBIE HIGH
Lisberger, Steven
HOT PURSUIT
List, Niki
DIE DRECKSCHLEUDER
Litten, Peter
SLAUGHTER HIGH
Livaneli, Omer Zulfu
YER DEMIR, GOK BAKIR
Llagostera i Colli, Ferran
BAR-CEL-ONA
Llosa, Luis
HOUR OF THE ASSASSIN
Lo, Wong Tai
RICH AND FAMOUS
Lofton, Terry
NAIL GUN MASSACRE
Logothetis, Dimitri
PRETTY SMART
Lombardi, Francisco J.
CITY AND THE DOGS, THE
Lombardo, Lou
P.K. & THE KID
Lommel, Ulli
OVERKILL
Loncraine, Richard
BELLMAN AND TRUE
Lonskoy, Valery
POLEVAYA GVARDIA MOZZHUKHINA
Loucka, Andreas O.
THIN LINE, THE
Louis Malle
AU REVOIR, LES ENFANTS
Lovell, Marc
TROUBLE WITH SPIES, THE
Loventhal, Charles
MY DEMON LOVER
Lowenstein, Richard
DOGS IN SPACE
Loza, Pepe
JUANA LA CANTINERA
Lucente, Francesco
VIRGIN QUEEN OF ST. FRANCIS HIGH, THE
Lucidi, Maurizio
IL LUPO DI MARE
Ludman, Larry
THUNDER WARRIOR II
Lukaszewicz, Jerzy
PRZYJACIEL WESOLEGO DIABLA
Luna, Bigas
ANGUSTIA
Lyne, Adrian
FATAL ATTRACTION
Maar, Gyula
MALOM A POKOLBAN
MacFadyen, Ian
BIT PART, THE
MacGillivray, William D.
LIFE CLASSES

Mackenzie, John
FOURTH PROTOCOL, THE
Maclean, Stephen
AROUND THE WORLD IN EIGHTY WAYS
Madigan, Sylvain
SALE DESTIN!
Madsen, Peter
VALHALLA
Magliulo, Giorgio
UNA CASA IN BILICO
Maher, Brendan
BIT PART, THE
Mahmudov, Mukadas
KAPKAN DLYA SHAKALOV
Mailer, Norman
TOUGH GUYS DON'T DANCE
Maillard, Pierre
POISONS
Majewski, Janusz
C. K. DEZERTERZY
Majumdar, Tarun
SIBAJI
Maka, Karl
THIRTY MILLION RUSH, THE
Makela, Ville
LAIN ULKOPUOLELLA
Makhmal Baf, Mohsen
PEDDLER, THE
Makinen, Visa
PEKKA PUUPAA POLIISINA
Makk, Karoly
AZ UTOLSOKEZIRAT
UTOLSO KEZIRAT
Makris, Dimitris
I KEKARMENI
Maksakov, Vyacheslav
OBESHCHAYU BYT
Mallon, James
BLOOD HOOK
Mamet, David
HOUSE OF GAMES
Manaryan, Armen
ZEMLYA I ZOLOTO
Mandel, Robert
BIG SHOTS
Mandic, Miroslav
ZIVOT RADNIKA
Mandoki, Luis
GABY—A TRUE STORY
Manduke, Joseph
OMEGA SYNDROME
Manivarnan
CHINNATHAMBI PERIYATHAMBI
Mankiewicz, Tom
DRAGNET
Manoogian, Peter
ENEMY TERRITORY
Manttari, Anssi
KUNINGAS LEAR
NAKEMIIN, HYVASTI
Marboeuf, Jean
GRAND GUIGNOL
Marcel, Terry
JANE AND THE LOST CITY
Margineanu, Nicolae
PADUREANCA
Marin, Richard
BORN IN EAST L.A.
Mariscal, Alberto
FORAJIDOS EN LA MIRA
Markaryan, Henry
ZEMLYA I ZOLOTO
Markovic, Goran
VEC VIDJENO
Marner, Eugene
BEAUTY AND THE BEAST
Marquand, Richard
HEARTS OF FIRE
Marshall, Garry
OVERBOARD
Martinez, Chuck
NICE GIRLS DON'T EXPLODE
Massaccesi, Aristide
DELIZIA
Mastorakis, Nico
TERMINAL EXPOSURE
WIND, THE
ZERO BOYS, THE
Mastroianni, Armand
SUPERNATURALS, THE
Masuda, Toshio
TOKYO BLACKOUT
Matji, Manolo
LA GUERRA DE LOS LOCOS
Mattson, Arne
GIRL, THE
SLEEP WELL, MY LOVE
May, Elaine
ISHTAR
Mazzacurati, Carlo
NOTTE ITALIANA
McBride, Jim
BIG EASY, THE
McCarthy, Peter
SPACE RACE
McKenzie, Brian
WITH LOVE TO THE PERSON NEXT TO ME
McLaughlin, Sheila
SHE MUST BE SEEING THINGS
McLennan, Don
SLATE, WYN & ME
McLoughlin, Tom
DATE WITH AN ANGEL
McTiernan, John
PREDATOR
Meerapfel, Jeanine
DIE VERLIEBTEN
Meher, Sadhu
BABULA
Mehrjui, Darioush
LODGERS
Mehta, Ketan
MIRCH MASALA
Melancon, Andre
BACH AND BROCCOLI
Menaker, Leonid
POSLEDNYAYA DOROGA
Mendeluk, George
MEATBALLS III
Mendoza, Orlando R.
FORAJIDOS EN LA MIRA
Menkes, Nina
MAGDALENA VIRAGA
Menon, Balachandra
VILAMBARAM
Merinero, Carlos P.
CARA DE ACELGA
Meszaros, Marta
DIARY FOR MY LOVED ONES
Michalakias, John Elias
I WAS A TEENAGE ZOMBIE
Miehe, Ulf
DER UNSICHTBARE
Mikhailovsky, Valery
TAYNAYA PROGULKA
Mikhalkov, Nikita
DARK EYES
Mikuni, Rentaro
SHINRAN: SHIRO MICHI
Milan, Wilfred
ULTIMAX FORCE
Milkina, Sofia
KREUTZEROVA SONATA
Miller, George
BUSHFIRE MOON
LES PATTERSON SAVES THE WORLD
WITCHES OF EASTWICK, THE
Miller, J.C.
NO DEAD HEROES
Ming, Luk Kim
MY WILL, I WILL
Mingozzi, Gianfranco
LES EXPLOITS DUN JEUNE DON JUAN
Minoui, Mehrzad
MANUSCRIPTS
Mishra, Sudhir
THIS IS NOT OUR DESTINATION
Mitra, Narendranath
PHERA
Mkrtchyan, Albert
PESN PROSHEDSHIKH DNEY
Mocky, Jean-Pierre
AGENT TROUBLE
LE MIRACULE
Moctezuma, Juan Lopez
WELCOME MARIA
Mohan
THIRTHAM
Mohr, Hanro
HOSTAGE
Molteni, Giorgio
AURELIA
Mones, Paul
BEAT, THE
Monicelli, Mario
I PICARI
Montaldo, Giuliano
GLI OCCHIALI D'ORO
IL GIORNO PRIMA
Montaya, Romeo
HILL 171
Montesi, Jorge
BIRDS OF PREY
Montoya, Jesus Fragoso
MAS VALE PAJARO EN MANO . . .
Mora, Philippe
HOWLING III, THE
Morais, Jose Alvaro
JESTER,THE
Mordillat, Gerard
F . . . ING FERNAND
Moreno Alba, Rafael
LONG STRIDER
Morita, Yoshimitsu
SOROBANZUKU
Mortelliti, Rocco
ADELMO
Mortola, Rodolfo
EL DUENO DEL SOL
Morya, Alberto
PEDDLER, THE
Mouli
ROWDY POLICE
Mouradian, Sarky
FORTY DAYS OF MUSA DAGH
Mukherjee, Hrishikesh
JHOOTHI
Mukherjee, Pinaki
RUDRABEENA
Mukherjee, Shyamal
JAIDEV
Mundhra, Jag
OPEN HOUSE
Munro, Ian
CUSTODY
Murakami, Jimmy T.
WHEN THE WIND BLOWS
Muratova, Kira
DOLGHYIE PROVOD
KOROTKIE VSTRECHI
Murdmaa, Helle
SEREBRYANAYA PRYAZHA KAROLINY
Murer, Fredi M.
ALPINE FIRE
Muro, Jim
STREET TRASH
Mutteraman., S.P.
SAMSARAM OKA CHADARANGAM
Mweze, Ngangura
LA VIE EST BELLE
Myles, Bruce
GROUND ZERO
N.S. Leskov
LEVSHA
Nadjafi, Mohammed Ali
GOZARESH-E YEK GHATL
Nagibin, Yuri
WEEKEND
Nakhapetov, Rodion
ZONTIK DLYA NOVOBRACHNYKH
Name, Hernando
EL PLACER DE LA VENGANZA
ROSA DE LA FRONTERA
Nasca, Sergio
DA NNUNZIO
Natanson, Georgy
VALENTIN I VALENTINA
Natoli, Piero
CHI C'E C'E
Naumov, Vladimir
SEVERNY ANEKDOT
Negishi, Kichitaro
UHOHO TANKENTAI
Nelson, Dusty
SAKURA KILLERS
WHITE PHANTOM
Nelson, Gary
ALLAN QUATERMAIN AND THE LOST CITY OF GOLD

Neuland, Olav
REQUIEM
VO VREMENA VOLCHYIKA ZAKONOV

Neumeier, John
LADY OF THE CAMELIAS

Newell, Mike
AMAZING GRACE AND CHUCK

Newman, Paul
GLASS MENAGERIE, THE

Nexo, Martin Andersen
PELLE EROVRAREN

Nicart, Eddie
COMMANDER LAMIN

Nicolayssen, Hans Otto
PLASTPOSEN

Nicolle, Douglas C.
LADIES OF THE LOTUS

Niermans, Edouard
POUSSIERE D'ANGE

Nieto Ramirez, Jose
MURIERON A MITAD DEL RIO

Nihalani, Govind
TAMAS

Nihalsingha, D.B.
MALDENIYESIMION

Nikolaidis, Nikos
PROINI PERIPOLOS

Nikolic, Zivko
U IME NARODA

Nikonenko, Sergei
KORABL PRISHELTSEV

Nimoy, Leonard
THREE MEN AND A BABY

Nitchev, Ivan
CERNITE LEBEDI

Noah Blogh
ALIEN PREDATOR

Noel Coward
SIDSTE AKT

Noren, Lars
DEMONS

Norton, B.W.L.
THREE FOR THE ROAD

Noyce, Phillip
SHADOWS OF THE PEACOCK

Nuti, Francesco
STREGATI

Nutley, Colin
NIONDE KOMPANIET

O'Connor, Pat
MONTH IN THE COUNTRY, A

Obrow, Jeffrey
KINDRED, THE

Odorisio, Luciano
LA MONACA DIMONZA

Ogawa, Shinsuke
MAGINA—MURA MONOGATARI

Ogorodnikov, Valery
VZLOMSHCHIK

Okamoto, Kihachi
DIXIELAND DAIMYO

Okazaki, Steven
LIVING ON TOKYO TIME

Okeyev, Tolomush
MIRAZHI LYUBRI

Oldoini, Enrico
BELLIFRESCHI

Olguin, Carlos
A DOS AGUAS

Olivo, Pablo
EL HOMBRE DE LA DEUDA EXTERNA

Olmi, Ermanno
LUNGA VITA ALLA SIGNORA!

Olsson, Claes
ELVIS-KISSAN JALJILLA

On, Yeung Ka
MIDNIGHT

Ordovsky, Mikhail
SLUCHAYNYE PASSAZHIRY

Orlov, Alexander
STRANNAYAR ISTORIYAR DOKTORA DZHEKILA I MISTERA KHAIDA

Ormrod, Peter
EAT THE PEACH

Orr, James
THEY STILL CALL ME BRUCE

Osyka, Leonid
POKLONIS DO ZEMLI

Ouedraogo, Idrissa
YAM DAABO

Oury, Gerard
LEVY ET GOLIATH

Out of Jail
SUMMER HEAT

Ovcharov, Sergei
LEVSHA

Oves
EN RETIRADA

Ozgenturk, Ali
WATER ALSO BURNS

Pakula, Alan J.
ORPHANS

Palmisano, Conrad E.
SPACE RACE

Panfilov, Gleb
TEMA

Panicker, G.S.
PANDAVAPURAM

Pankratov, Alexander
PRODELKI V STARINNOM DUKHE

Papastathis, Lakis
THEOFILOS

Papatakis, Nikos
PHOTOGRAPH, THE

Papayannidis, Takis
YENETHLIA POLI

Parashar, Punkaj
JALWA

Pardo, Rafael Fuster
IN DER WUSTE

Parenti, Neri
SCUOLA DI LADRI 2
SUPERFANTOZZI

Park-huen, Kwan
YI LOU YI

Parker, Alan
ANGEL HEART

Parks, Michael
RETURN OF JOSEY WALES, THE

Paskaljevic, Goran
ANDJEO CUVAR

Pasquale Misuraca
ANGELUS NOVUS

Patino, Basilio Martin
MADRID

Pattinson, Michael
GROUND ZERO

Paul, Stuart
EMANON

Pauls, Cristian
SINFIN, LA MUERTA NO ES NINGUNA SOLUCION

Pavithran
UPPU

Pavlou, George
RAWHEAD REX

Pavlovic, Zivojin
NA PUTA ZA KATANGU

Peak, Barry
AS TIME GOES BY

Pearce, Michael
INITIATION

Peck, Ron
EMPIRE STATE

Pedersen, John
TUESDAY WEDNESDAY

Penn, Arthur
DEAD OF WINTER

Peploe, Clare
HIGH SEASON

Perakis, Nicos
VIOS KE POLITIA

Perlini, Meme
CARTOLINE ITALIANE

Perrin, Laurent
BUISSON ARDENT

Perry, Frank
HELLO AGAIN

Petko, Alex
DIRTY REBEL

Petrie, Daniel
SQUARE DANCE

Petrocchi, Roberto
ILLUMINAZIONI

Petrova, Roumyana
PRIZEMYAVANE

Phelps, William
NORTH SHORE

Pialat, Maurice
SOUS LE SOLEIL DE SATAN

Picault, Chantal
ACCROCHE-COEUR

Piccioni, Giuseppe
IL GRANDE BLEK

Picha, Jean-Marc
BIG BANG, THE

Piesis, Gunar
POHADKA O MALICKOVI

Pillsbury, Sam
STARLIGHT HOTEL

Pinheiro, Jose
MON BEL AMOUR, MA DECHIRURE

Pinkava, Josef
CIZIM VSTUP POVOLEN

Pipolo
IL BURBERO

Pirro, Mark
DEATHROW GAMESHOW

Piscicelli, Salvatore
REGINA

Pittman, Bruce
HELLO MARY LOU, PROM NIGHT II

Piwowarski, Radislaw
POCIAG DO HOLLYWOOD

Pleijel, Agneta
NAGRA SOMMARKVALLAR PA JORDEN

Ploug, Claus
ELISE

Polaco, Jorge
EN EL NOMBRE DEL HIJO

Polak, Jindrich
CHOBOTNICE Z II. PATRA

Poliakoff, Stephen
HIDDEN CITY

Polidoro, Gianluigi
SOTTOZERO

Poloka, Gennady
INTERVENTSIA

Poma, Marco
MEFISTO FUNK

Pons, Ventura
LA RUBIA DEL BAR

Ponzi, Maurizio
NOI UOMINI DURI

Popkov, Vladimir
GRUZ BEZ MARKIROVKI

Poreba, Bohdan
ZLOTY POCIAG

Portillo, Ralph
ARQUIESTA EMILIO VARELA

Prachenko, Andrei
KAPITAN "PILIGRIMA"

Prior, David A.
DEADLY PREY
KILLER WORKOUT
MANKILLERS

Prokhorov, Victor
STARAYA AZBUKA

Prokop, Jan
PRATELE BERMUDSKEHO TROJUHELNIKU

Ptashuk, Mikhai
ZNAK BEDY

Puchinyan, Stepan
IZ ZHIZNI NACHALNIKA UGOLOVNOGO ROZYSKA
TAYNY MADAM VONG

Purcell, Joseph
DELOS ADVENTURE, THE

Puzo, Dorothy Ann
COLD STEEL

Pyhala, Jaakko
URSULA

Pyun, Albert
DOWN TWISTED

Qingguo, Sun
LAST EMPRESS, THE

Queffelec, Yann
LES NOCES BARBARES

Quinn, Bob
BUDAWANNY

R.M.
HEAT

Rademakers, Lili
DIARY OF A MAD OLD MAN

Radford, Michael
WHITE MISCHIEF

Rafelson, Bob
BLACK WIDOW

Raimi, Sam
EVIL DEAD 2: DEAD BY DAWN
Raisman, Yuli
VREMYA ZHELANIY
Ramakrishna, Kodi
DONGODUCHHADU
Ramalho, Francisco
BESAME MUCHO
Ramesh, Nandamuri
ALLARI KRISHNAYA
Rampelli, Fabrizio
LA TRASGRESSIONE
Ramuz, Charles Ferdinand
SI LE SOLEIL NE REVENAIT PAS
Rao, Singeetham Srinivas
AMERICA ABBAI
Rash, Steve
CANT BUY ME LOVE
Ratton, Helvecio
A DANCA DOS BONECOS
Rawail, Rahul
DACAIT
Rawi, Ousama
HOUSEKEEPER, THE
Ray, Fred Olen
COMMANDO SQUAD
CYCLONE
Raynov, Bogumil
CERNITE LEBEDI
Razumovsky, Andrey
TAKAYA ZHESTOKAYA IGRA—KHOKKEY
Razzakov, Tynchylyk
VOLNY UMIRAYUT NA BEREGU
Reddy, A. Kodidandarami
BHARGAVA RAMUDU
Reddy, Prabhakara
MANDALADHEESUDU
Reddy, Vijay
JAWAB HUM DENGE
Rees, Jerry
BRAVE LITTLE TOASTER, THE
Refn, Anders
DE FLYGANDE DJAVLARNA
Rego, Luis
POULE ET FRITES
Reichenbach, Carlos
ANJOS DO ARRABALDE
Reid, Max
WILD THING
Reiner, Carl
SUMMER SCHOOL
Reiner, Rob
PRINCESS BRIDE, THE
Rekhviashvili, Alexander
STUPEN
Resnais, Alain
MELO
Retes, Gabriel
MUJERES SALVAJES
Retes, Ignacio
VIAJE AL PARAISO
Revah, Zeev
BOUBA
Richards, Caroline
SWEET COUNTRY
Richardson, Peter
EAT THE RICH
Rico, Luis Quintanila
TIERRA DE VALIENTES
Ripploh, Frank
TAXI NACH KAIRO
Ripstein, Arturo
REALM OF FORTUNE, THE
Risan, Leidulv
ETTER RUBICON
Risi, Dino
TERESA
Risi, Marco
SOLDATI: 365 GIORNI ALL' ALBA
Ritt, Martin
NUTS
Roarke, Adam
TRESPASSES
Robbins, Matthew
BATTERIES NOT INCLUDED
Robin, Teddy
LEGEND OF WISELY, THE
Robinson, Bruce
WITHNAIL AND I
WITHNAIL AND I
Robinson, Marilynne
HOUSEKEEPING
Robinson, Phil Alden
IN THE MOOD
IN THE MOOD
Robinson, Ted
THOSE DEAR DEPARTED
Rocha, Paulo
O DESEJADO—LES MONTAGNES DE LA LUNE
Rochat, Eric
TOO MUCH
Roddam, Franc
ARIA
Rodriguez, Ismael
OLOR A MUERTE
YERBA SANGRIENTE
Rodriguez, Ismeal
CORRUPCION
Roeg, Nicolas
ARIA
Rohmer, Eric
LAMI DE MON AMIE
QUATRE AVENTURES DE REINETTE ET MIRABELLE
Rood, Jurrien
DE ORIONNEVEL
Rosas Priego R., Alfonso
EL HIJO DE PEDRO NAVAJAS
Rosen, Martin
STACKING
Rosenthal, Rick
RUSSKIES
Rosi, Francesco
CHRONICLE OF A DEATH FORETOLD
Ross, Herbert
DANCERS
SECRET OF MY SUCCESS, THE
Roth, Joe
REVENGE OF THE NERDS II: NERDS IN PARADISE
Rouse, Virginia
TO MARKET, TOMARKET
Roy, Ashok
DAKU HASINA
Rozema, Patricia
IVE HEARD THE MERMAIDS SINGING
Rozsa, Janos
CSOK, ANYU
Ruben, Joseph
STEPFATHER, THE
Ruben, Katt Shea
STRIPPED TO KILL
Rudolph, Alan
MADE IN HEAVEN
Rudolph, Verena
FRANCESCA
Rudolph van den Berg
LOOKING FOR EILEEN
Ruiz, Raul
MEMOIRE DES APPARENCES: LA VIE EST UN SONGE
Russell, Chuck
NIGHTMARE ON ELM STREET 3: DREAM WARRIORS, A
Russell, Ken
ARIA
GOTHIC
Rustam, Mardi
EVIL TOWN
Rutnam, Chandran
WITNESS TO A KILLING
Ryck, Francis
FAMILY BUSINESS
Sabirov, Takhir
NOVYE SKAZKI SHAKHEREZADY
Sacristan, Jose
CARA DE ACELGA
CARA DE ACELGA
Sadovsky, Victor
SOPERNITSY
Saha, Tapan
AMAR BANDHAN
Saint-Pierre, Renaud
JOHNNY MONROE
Saks, Mady
IRIS
Salomonsen, Grete
KAMILLA OG TYVEN
Samsonov, Samson
TANTSPLOSHCHADKA
Sanchez, Jose Luis Garcia
DIVINAS PALABRAS
Santiago, Cirio H.
EQUALIZER 2000
EYE OF THE EAGLE
Santiago, Pablo
OPERATION: GET VICTOR CORPUS THE REBEL SOLDIER
Santiago, Ric
ZIMATAR
Santos, Briccio
DAMORTIS
Saparov, Usman
PRIKLYUCHENIA NA MALENKIKH OSTROVEKH
Sarafian, Deran
ALIEN PREDATOR
Sargent, Joseph
JAWS: THE REVENGE
Saura, Guillermo
CHORROS
SENTIMIENTOS: MIRTA DE LINIERS A ESTAMBUL
Saville, Philip
SHADEY
Sayles, John
MATEWAN
Sayyad, Parviz
CHECKPOINT
Scandariato, Romano
QUEL RAGAZZO DELLA CURVA "B"
Scanlan, Joseph L.
NIGHTSTICK
Scarnacci and R. —Tarabusi, D.
MILLION V BRACHNOY KORZINE
Schaffner, Franklin J.
LIONHEART
Schamoni, Peter
CASPAR DAVID FRIEDRICH
Schatzberg, Jerry
STREET SMART
Schenkkan, Ine
VROEGER IS DOOD
Schepisi, Fred
ROXANNE
Schiffman, Suzanne
LA MOINE ET LA SORCIERE
Schirk, Heinz
WANNSEE CONFERENCE, THE
Schito, Giuseppe
IL RAGAZZO DI EBALUS
Schlesinger, John
BELIEVERS, THE
Schlondorff, Volker
VERMISCHTE NACHRICHTEN
Schlossberg Cohen, Jay
CRY WILDERNESS
Schmid, Daniel
JENATSCH
Schneider, Paul
SOMETHING SPECIAL!
Scholes, Roger
TALE OF RUBY ROSE, THE
Scholz, Gunther
VERNEHMUNG DER ZEUGEN
Schorr, Renen
LATE SUMMER BLUES
Schrader, Paul
LIGHT OF DAY
Schrader, Uwe
SIERRA LEONE
Schroeder, Barbet
BARFLY
Schulmann, Patrick
LES OREILLES ENTRE LES DENTS
Schultz, Michael
DISORDERLIES
Schumacher, Joel
LOST BOYS, THE
Schutte, Jan
DRAGON'S FOOD
Schwarzenberger, Xaver
OTTO—DER NEUE FILM
Schweitzer, Mikhail
KREUTZEROVA SONATA
Scola, Ettore
FAMILY, THE
Scott, Ridley
SOMEONE TO WATCH OVER ME
Scott, Robert
VIDEO DEAD, THE

Scott, Tony
BEVERLY HILLS COP II

Seidelman, Susan
MAKING MR.RIGHT

Sell, Jack M.
OUTTAKES

Sen, Om Ghil
SEKUNDA NA PODVIG

Senje, Sigurd
FELDMANN CASE, THE

Seria, Joel
LES DEUX CROCODILES

Serrano, Carlos
CALE

Sesani, Riccardo
UNA DONNA DA SCOPRIRE

Sessa, Alex
AMAZONS

Sestieri, Claudio
DOLCE ASSENZA

Setbon, Philippe
CROSS

Sette, Jose
UM FILM 100% BRAZILEIRO

Shah, Krishna
AMERICAN DRIVE-IN

Shakespeare, William
KUNINGAS LEAR

Shakhnazarov, Karen
KURIER

Shamshiyev, Bolotbek
SNAYPERY

Shamshurin, Vladimir
AKTSIA

Shang-zi, Ting
STORY OF DR. SUN YAT-SEN, THE

Shantaram, V.
JHANJHAAR

Sharma, Chander
GHULAMI KI ZANJEER

Shebib, Don
CLIMB, THE

Sheppard, John
HIGHER EDUCATION

Sherman, Gary
WANTED: DEAD OR ALIVE

Sheshukov, Igor
KRASNAYA STRELA

Shevchenko, Vladimir
KONTRUDAR

Shields, Frank
SURFER, THE

Shilovsky, Vsevolod
MILLION V BRACHNOY KORZINE

Shin, Stephen
BROTHERHOOD

Shing, Lee
HEROIC PIONEERS

Shivdasani, Deepak
DADAGIRI

Shmaruk, Isaac
TVOYO MIRNOE NEBO

Sholder, Jack
HIDDEN, THE

Short, Robert
PROGRAMMED TO KILL

Shuster, Solomon
OGNI

Shyer, Charles
BABY BOOM

Sibal, Jose F.
ZIMATAR

Sicha, Petr
PRATELE BERMUDSKEHO TROJUHELNIKU

Sidaris, Andy
HARD TICKET TO HAWAII

Silberg, Joel
CATCH THE HEAT

Silver, Raphael
WALK ON THE MOON, A

Simandl, Lloyd A.
LADIES OF THE LOTUS

Simo, Sandor
ISTEN VELETEK, BARATAIM

Simon, David
IN THE MOOD

Simoneau, Yves
LES FOUS DE BASSAN

Singer, Stanford
I WAS A TEENAGE T.V. TERRORIST

Sippy, Raj
LOHA

Siwertz, Sigfrid
MALARPIRATER

Sjoman, Vilgot
MALACCA

Skurski, Grzegorz
RYKOWISKO

Skuybin, Nikolai
IZ ZHIZNI POTAPOVA

Slabnevich, Igor
PO ZAKONU VOENNOGO VREMENI

Sluizer, George
RED DESERT PENITENTIARY

Smight, Jack
NUMBER ONE WITH A BULLET

Smith, Dominic Elmo
GET THE TERRORISTS
HOSTAGE SYNDROME
TOUGH COP

Smith, John N.
SITTING IN LIMBO
TRAIN OF DREAMS

Smith, Robert
LOVECHILD, THE

Smithee, Alan
MORGAN STEWART'S COMING HOME
GHOST FEVER
LETS GET HARRY

Smyczek, Karel
PROC?

Soavi, Michele
DELIRIA

Sobel, Mark
SWEET REVENGE

Sokolowska, Anna
E S D

Sokourov, Aleksandr
ODINOKIJ GOLOS CELOVEKA

Sokurov, Aleksandr
SKORBNOE BESCHUVSTVIE

Solas, Humberto
SUCCESSFUL MAN, A

Solum, Ola
TURNAROUND

Solyom, Andras
DOKTOR MINORKA VIDOR NAGY NAPJA

Somai, Shinji
HIKARU ANNA

Sorak, Dejan
OFICIR S RUZOM

Sordi, Alberto
UN TASSINARO A NEW YORK

Souda, Said Ali
LA VENGEANCE DU PROTECTEUR

Soukup, Jaroslav
DISCOPRIBEH

Spheeris, Penelope
DUDES

Spiegel, Larry
EVIL TOWN

Spielberg, Steven
EMPIRE OF THE SUN

Spota, Luis
MURIERON A MITAD DEL RIO

Spry, Robin
KEEPING TRACK

Srichua, Tanong
COBRA THUNDERBOLT

Stachura, Edward
SIEKIEREZADA

Stambula, Nikolai
KARUSEL NA BAZARNOY PLOSHCHADI

Stanner, C.
MAGIC SNOWMAN, THE

Steensland, David
ESCAPES

Stefaniak, Piotr
STANISLAW I ANNA

Stelzer, Manfred
CHINESE ARE COMING, THE

Stephensen, Ole
KAMPEN OM DEN RODE KO

Stevens, Leslie
THREE KINDS OF HEAT

Stevenson, Robert Louis
CHYORNAYA STRELA

Stockwell, John
UNDER COVER

Stone, Oliver
WALL STREET

Stouffer, Mark
MAN OUTSIDE

Straub, Jean-Marie
DER TOD DES EMPEDOKLES

Streich, Ian
SVIDANIE NA MLECHNOM PUTI

Sturridge, Charles
ARIA

Suarez, Bobby A.
TOUGH COP
WARRIORS OF THE APOCALYPSE

Sugawa, Eizo
HOTARUGAWA

Suissa, Daniele J.
MORNING MAN, THE

Sullivan, Fred G.
SULLIVAN'S PAVILION

Summers, Manuel
SUFRE MAMON

Surikova, Alla
ISKRENNE VASH . . .

Sutherland, Hal
PINOCCHIO AND THE EMPEROR OF THE NIGHT

Svetlov, Alexander
CHEGEMSKIY DETEKTIV

Svetozarov, Dimitry
PRORYV

Szabo, Ildiko
HOTREAL

Szirtes, Andras
LENZ

Sztwiertnia, Jerzy
KOMEDIANTKA

Tacchella, Jean-Charles
TRAVELLING AVANT

Taghvai, Nasser
CAPTAIN KHORSHID

Takacs, Tibor
GATE, THE

Talan, Len
HANSEL AND GRETEL

Talankin, Igor
WEEKEND

Tandon, Ravi
NAZRANA

Tannen, William
DEADLY ILLUSION

Tanner, Alain
LA VALLEE FANTOME
UNE FLAMME DANS MON COEUR

Tarantini, Michele Massimo
ITALIANI A RIO

Tarasov, Sergei
CHYORNAYA STRELA

Tarnas, Kazimierz
ZLOTA MAHMUDIA

Tavernier, Bertrand
LA PASSION BEATRICE

Taviani, Paolo
GOOD MORNING BABYLON

Taviani, Vittorio
GOOD MORNING BABYLON

Taylor, R.O.
RETURN OF JOSEY WALES, THE

Tazhibaev, Rustem
SKAZKA O PREKRASNOY AYSULU

Tazi, Mohamed
ABBES

Tej, Govind
TUNDA BAIDA

Temple, Julien
ARIA

Tenney, Kevin S.
WITCHBOARD

Tenvik, Inge
PRINSEN FRA FOGO

Teo, Stephen
BEJALAI

Ternovszky, Bela
CAT CITY

Thackeray, William Makepeace
PIERSCIEN I ROZA

Theos, Dimos
IKONA ENOS MYTHIKOU PROSOPOU

Thevenet, Virginie
JEUX D'ARTIFICES

Thomas, John G.
BANZAI RUNNER

Thome, Rudolph
TAROT

Tianming, Wu
OLD WELL

Timm, Peter
MEIER

To, Johnny
SEVEN YEARS ITCH

Toback, James
PICK-UP ARTIST, THE

Todorovsky, Pyotr
PO GLAVNOY ULITSE S ORKESTROM
VOENNO-POLEVOI ROMAN

Tokarev, Boris
PLOSHCHAD VOSSTANIA

Toledo, Sergio
VERA

Tolmar, Tamas
ZUHANAS KOZBEN

Tomic, Zivorad
KRALJEVA ZAVRSNICA

Torhonen, Lauri
JAAN KAANTOPIIRI

Tornatore, Joe
CODE NAME ZEBRA

Torrini, Cinzia Th
HOTEL COLONIAL

Townsend, Robert
HOLLYWOOD SHUFFLE

Traynor, Peter S.
EVIL TOWN

Tregubovich, Viktor
VOT MOYA DEREVNYA

Treves, Giorgio
LA CODA DEL DIAVOLO

Trope, Tzipi
TEL AVIV—BERLIN

Trueba, Fernando
YEAR OF AWAKENING, THE

Trujillo, Valentin
RATAS DE LA CIUDAD
YO, EL EJECUTOR

Tselinsky, Gunar
STRAKH

Tsui, Siu-Ming
MIRAGE

Tumanyan, Ina
SOUCHASTNIKI

Tung, Ching Siu
CHINESE GHOST STORY, A

Turayev, Anvar
YA YEY NRAVLYUS

Turner, Brad
GOOFBALLS

Turpie, Jonnie
OUT OF ORDER

Tyan, Nguen Shang
KOORDINATY SMERTI

Ugur, Omer
SON URFALI

Ulloque, Jose Maria
EL GRAN SERAFIN

Ungwald-Khilkevich, Georgy
SEZON CHUDES

Unterberg, Hannelore
DER JUNGE MIT DEM GROSSEN SCHWARZEN HUND

Urazbayev, Eldor
SEKUNDA NA PODVIG

Urquieta, Jose Luis
OPERACION MARIJUANA

Vafeas, Vassilis
ONE HUNDRED AND TWENTY DECIBELS

Valdez, Luis
LA BAMBA

Vamsi
LAWYER SUHASINI

van Brakel, Nouchka
EEN MAAND LATER

van der Heyde, Nikolai
NITWITS

van Dullemen, Inez
VROEGER IS DOOD

van Elst, Gerrit
BLOND DOLLY

Van Gogh, Theo
TERUG NAAR OEGSTGEEST

van Zuylen, Eric
ZJOEK

Vane, Norman Thaddeus
CLUB LIFE

Vane and Bleu —McKenzie, Norman Thaddeus
CLUB LIFE

Vanzina, Carlo
I MIEI PRIMI QUARANT'ANNI
MONTECARLO GRAN CASINO
VIA MONTENAPOLEONE

Vasilyev, Gennady
RUS IZNACHALNA

Vazquez, Angel Rodriguez
LO NEGRO DEL NEGRO

Vedyshev, Mikahil
SDELKA

Vega, Felipe
MIENTRAS HAYA LUZ

Vega, Pastor
AMOR EN CAMPO MINADO

Vejar, Sergio
DELINCUENTE
UN SABADO MAS

Velasco, Maria Elena
NI DE AQUI, NI DE ALLA

Vengerov, Vladimir
OBRYV

Vennerod, Petter
JOR

Vera, Marilda
POR LOS CAMINOS VERDES

Verdaguer, Antoni
LESCOT

Verdone, Carlo
IO E MIA SORELLA

Vergitsis, Nicos
ARCHANGELOS TOU PATHOUS

Verhoeff, Pieter
VAN GELUK GESPROKEN

Verhoeven, Paul
ROBOCOP

Vernon, Henry
DANGER ZONE, THE

Verona, Stephen
TALKING WALLS

Verstappen, Wim
DE RATELRAT

Vesaas, Tarjei
IS-SLOTTET

Victor Manue
ESTA NOCHE CENA PANCHO (DESPEDIDA DE SOLTERO)

Victor Manuel
LA RAZA NUNCA PIERDE—HUELE A GAS
LA RULETERA
NOS REIMOS DE LA MIGRA
TODA LA VIDA

Villasenor Kuri, Rafael
CARTUCHA CORTADA

Vilstrup, Li
JAG ELSKER DIG
NEGERKYS & LABRE LARVER

Vincent, Chuck
DERANGED
IF LOOKS COULD KILL
SLAMMER GIRLS
WARRIOR QUEEN
WIMPS

Violante, Marcela Fernandez
NOCTURNO AMOR QUE TE VAS

Virendra
MERA LAHOO

Visu
THIRUMATHI ORU VEGUMATHI

Vizard, Stephen
BIT PART, THE

Vokhotko, Anatoly
CHUZHIE ZDES NE KHODYAT

von Praunheim, Rosa
ANITA—DANCES OF VICE

von Trier, Lars
EPIDEMIC

Voss, Kurt
BORDER RADIO

Vrettakos, Costas
TA PAIDIA TIS CHELIDONAS

Waalkes, Otto
OTTO—DER NEUE FILM

Walerstein, Mauricio
DE MUJER A MUJER

Walker, Giles
LAST STRAW, THE

Walker, John
WINTER TAN, A

Walkow, Gary
TROUBLE WITH DICK, THE

Walton, Fred
ROSARY MURDERS, THE

Wam, Svend
JOR

Wang, Wayne
SLAMDANCE

Ward, Richard
SAKURA KILLERS

Warren, Norman J.
BLOODY NEW YEAR
GUNPOWDER

Way, Ron
FRENCHMAN'S FARM

Webb, William
DIRTY LAUNDRY

Wechter, David
MALIBU BIKINI SHOP, THE

Weckstrom, Kim
URSULA

Weiland, Paul
LEONARD PART 6

Weiss, Robert K.
AMAZON WOMEN ON THE MOON

Weissman, Aerlyn
WINTER TAN, A

Weisz, Franz
HAVINCK

Wenders, Wim
DER HIMMEL UBER BERLIN

Werner, Peter
NO MAN'S LAND

Wickramasinghe, Martin
VIRAGAYA

Widerberg, Bo
MANNEN FRAN MALLORCA
SERPENT'S WAY, THE
VICTORIA

Wilder, Glenn R.
MASTERBLASTER

Wiley, Ethan
HOUSE TWO: THE SECOND STORY

Williamson, Fred
MESSENGER, THE

Wilson, Hugh
BURGLAR

Wincer, Simon
LIGHTHORSEMEN, THE

Winkelmann, Adolf
PENG! DU BIST TOT!

Winkler, Charles
YOU TALKIN' TO ME?

Winograd, Peter
FLICKS

Winsor, Terry
MORGAN STEWART'S COMING HOME

Winters, David
MISSION KILL

Wionczek, Roman
CZAS NADZIEI

Wistrom, Mikael
MITT HJARTA HAR TVA TUNGOR

Witkiewicz, Stanislaw Ignacy
W STARYM DWORKU

Wittliff, William
RED HEADED STRANGER

Wojcik, Wojciech
PRYWATNE SLEDZTWO

Wolkers, Jan
TERUG NAAR OEGSTGEEST

Wollen, Peter
FRIENDSHIP'S DEATH

Wolman, Dan
CHOZE AHAVA

Wong, Kirk
TRUE COLORS

Wong, Manfred
SWORN BROTHERS

Woo, John
BETTER TOMORROW, A

Wynorski, Jim
BIG BAD MAMA II

Yamada, Yoji
FINAL TAKE: THE GOLDEN AGE OF MOVIES
TORA-SAN'S BLUEBIRD FANTASY
Yamamoto, Masashi
ROBINSON NO NIWA
Yamashita, Kosaku
RYOMA O KITTA OTOKO
Yang, Edward
TERRORIZERS, THE
Yasan, Earnest
SON V RUKU, ILI CHEMODON
Yasan, Ernest
DUBLYOR NACHINAET DEYSTVOVAT
Yates, Peter
SUSPECT
Yershov, Roman
CHUZHIE ZDES NE KHODYAT
Yilmaz, Atif
DEGIRMEN
Yinnan, Sing
DOCTOR SUN YATSEN
Yohanan
KOL AHAVOTAI
Yohoshua, Abraham B.
POET'S SILENCE, THE
Young, Roger
SQUEEZE, THE
Yu, Ronnie
LEGACY OF RAGE
Yune, Johnny
THEY STILL CALL ME BRUCE
Yung, Jin
ROMANCE OF BOOK AND SWORD, THE
Yungwald-Khilkevich, Georgy
DVOE POD ODNIM ZONTOM
Zacharias, Ann
TESTET
Zaorski, Janusz
MATKA KROLOW
Zhalakyavichus, Vitautas
IZVINITEPOZHALUYSTA
Zhuang-zhuang, Tian
DAO MAZEI
Zidi, Claude
LASSOCIATION DES MALFAITEURS
Zielinski, Rafal
VALET GIRLS
Zirinis, Costas
TELEFTAIO STICHIMA
Zorrilla, Jose A.
A LOS CUATRO VIENTOS
Zurinaga, Marcos
LA GRAN FIESTA
Zuta, Daniel
BORAN—ZEIT ZUM ZIELEN

EDITORS

Abrahamson, Neil
ARIA
Adam, Peter R.
TAXI NACH KAIRO
VERSTECKTE LIEBE
Agosti, Silvano
QUARTIERE
Ajoub, Uta
BORAN—ZEIT ZUM ZIELEN
Akers, George
PERSONAL SERVICES
WISH YOU WERE HERE
Alabisio, Fulvio
ITALIANI A RIO
Alabiso, Daniele
ALADDIN
Alabiso, Eugenio
BARBARIANS, THE
CAMPING DEL TERRORE
RENEGADE, UN OSSO TROPPO DURO
Albert, Ross
WANTED: DEAD OR ALIVE
Albrecht-Lovell, Ute
ZARTLICHE CHAOTEN
Alcalde, Jose
MANON
Aledo, Ivan
MIENTRAS HAYA LUZ
Alepis, Babis
OH BABYLON
Alice, Mauro
BESAME MUCHO
Allen, Stanford C.
NIGHT STALKER, THE
Alonso, Mercedes
ROMANCA FINAL
Alves, Amauri
UM FILM 100% BRAZILEIRO
Andersen, Niels Pagh
OFELAS
Anderson, Pippa
FRENCHMAN'S FARM
Anderson, William
BIG SHOTS
Andolfi, Marco Antonio
LA CROCE DALLE SETTE PIETRE
Andreadakis, Andreas
PROINI PERIPOLOS
Appleby, George
TOO OUTRAGEOUS
Arcand, Michel
NIGHT ZOO
Argall, Ray
WITH LOVE TO THE PERSON NEXT TO ME
Arissman, Henri
VAN PAEMEL FAMILY, THE
Ascher, Tova
BEAUTY AND THE BEAST
Asher, Tova
DREAMERS
Askoldov, Alexander
KOMISSAR
Asseo, Aline
LES OREILLES ENTRE LES DENTS
Audiard, Marie Josee
UN AMOUR A PARIS
Audsley, Michael
COMRADES
Audsley, Mick
PRICK UP YOUR EARS
SAMMY AND ROSIE GET LAID
Auge, Jennifer
ARIA
BEYOND THERAPY
Aupart, Ramon
NOCTURNO AMOR QUE TE VAS
Auvray, Dominique
LES MENDIANTS
Avrahamian, Zion
BOUBA
Babinet, Marielle
LES MENDIANTS
Babu, Suresh
PANDAVAPURAM
Bacyne, Sigfrido
EULALIA
Baird, Stuart
LETHAL WEAPON
Balinova, Lienite
POHADKA O MALICKOVI
Baragli, Nino
DA NNUNZIO
HOTEL COLONIAL
INTERVISTA
UN RAGAZZO DI CALABRIA
Bargero, Osvaldo
A FIOR DI PELLE
Barnier, Luc
AVRIL BRISE
LHOMME VOILE
Barrachin, Nicholas
FACES OF WOMEN
Barraque, Martine
LA MOINE ET LA SORCIERE
Bartczak, Jozef
MATKA KROLOW
PIERSCIEN I ROZA
Bartels, Gaby
KONZERT FUR DIE RECHTE HAND
Barthelmes, Raimund Maria
ZISCHKE
Bartlett, David
COLD STEEL
Bartlett, Michael
KONZERT FUR DIE RECHTE HAND
Bartolini, Gino
LESTATE STA FINENDO
Barton, Sean
HEARTS OF FIRE
Baskin, Sonny
OVERBOARD
Bauer, Mary
SUMMER HEAT
Beauman, Nicholas
HIGH TIDE
Bechard, Gorman
PSYCHOS IN LOVE
Bell, Greg
SURFER, THE
Bender, Joel
WARRIOR QUEEN
Benny, B.
IBUNDA
Berger, Peter E.
FATAL ATTRACTION
LESS THAN ZERO
Bergman, Robert
GRAVEYARD SHIFT
Bergonzelli, Sergio
TENTAZIONE
Berlanga, Juan Luis
LAS DOS ORILLAS
Berlin, Helene
NAGRA SOMMARKVALLAR PA JORDEN
Bernard, Catherine
IL EST GENIAL PAPY!
Beyda, Kent
INNERSPACE
Bianchini, Cesare
DOLCE PELLE DI ANGELA
Bidstrup, Jens
SKYTTURNAR
Bigley, Ivan L.
RETURN OF JOSEY WALES, THE
Bilcock, Jill
DOGS IN SPACE
Biurrun, Jose Maria
LA CASA DE BERNARDA ALBA
LA RUSA
Blanco, Armando
A DOS AGUAS
Blangsted, David G.
EVIL TOWN
Blin, Arnaud
YAM DAABO
Bloom, John
BLACK WIDOW
Blough, Noah
BIG BAD MAMA II
Blumenthal, Sharyn C.
UNFINISHED BUSINESS . . .
Bohler, Bettina
YER DEMIR, GOK BAKIR
Bohmann, Inge
LITTLE PROSECUTOR, THE
Boiche, Marie-Therese
ARIA
ARIA
LA VIE PLATINEE
Boischot, Dominique
UM TREM PARA AS ESTRELAS
Boisson, Noelle
JEAN DE FLORETTE
MAN ON FIRE
Boita, Peter
LEONARD PART 6
Bojanowska, Agnieszka
KOMEDIANCI Z WCZORAJSZEJ ULICY
Bolivar, Cesar
MAS ALLA DEL SILENCIO
Bonanni, Mauro
LA MONACA DIMONZA
Bonanni., Mauro
LE FOTO DI GIOIA
Bonner, Lee
ADVENTURE OF THE ACTION HUNTERS
Bonnot, Francoise
SICILIAN, THE
Bose, Amit
AMERICAN DRIVE-IN
Bottanelli, Lia
MEFISTO FUNK
Bouche, Claudine
LES DEUX CROCODILES
Bouquin, Martine
MEMOIRE DES APPARENCES: LA VIE EST UN SONGE
Bowers, George
STEPFATHER, THE

Boyle, Peter
PRAYER FOR THE DYING, A
Bradsell, Michael
ARIA
GOTHIC
Brady, Jerome F.
WELCOME MARIA
Brajsblat, Carlos
FONTE DA SAUDADE
Brandstaedter, Jutta M.
IRIS
Brass, Giovanni Tinto
CAPRICCIO
Bravo, Roberto
EL SOCIO DE DIOS
Breigutu, Bjorn
FELDMANN CASE, THE
Bressan, Arthur
SPACE RACE
Bretherton, David
LIONHEART
PICK-UP ARTIST, THE
Briemont, Wendy Greene
SURRENDER
Broglio, Carlo
QUEL RAGAZZO DELLA CURVA "B"
Brown, O. Nicholas
PROJECT X
Brown, Robert
LOST BOYS, THE
Brown, Sharon
ALS IN EEN ROES
Brozek, Jiri
DISCOPRIBEH
WOLF'S HOLE
Bruce, James
SUICIDE CLUB, THE
Bruchu, Don
LA BAMBA
Bruckner, Jutta
EIN BLICK-UND DIE LIEBE BRICHT AUS
Bruer, Jeffrey
WITCH HUNT
Brusendorff, Merete
PETER VON SCHOLTEN
Buff IV, Conrad
SPACEBALLS
Bulane, Seipati
YEELEN
Burcksen, Edgar
EEN MAAND LATER
Bustos, Jorge
ENTRE FICHERAS ANDA EL DIABLO
Butler, Bill
WALK LIKE A MAN
Butler, Steve
WALK LIKE A MAN
Cacoyannis, Michael
SWEET COUNTRY
Calmes, Lynn Leneau
NAIL GUN MASSACRE
Camacho, Angel
OLOR A MUERTE
TIERRA DE VALIENTES
Cambas, Jacqueline
LIGHT OF DAY
Cambern, Donn
HARRY AND THE HENDERSONS
Campbell, Malcolm
AMAZON WOMEN ON THE MOON
Cannon, Bruce
WIND, THE
Caron, Alain
JOHNNY MONROE
Carow, Evelyn
SO VIELE TRAUME
Carr, Adrian
LIGHTHORSEMEN, THE
Carreras, Amat
LA RUBIA DEL BAR
LA SENYORA
LESCOT
Carrere, Leon
GARBAGE PAIL KIDS MOVIE, THE
Carrier, Alan
MANKILLERS
Carrion, Gloria
CALE
Cartwright, Peter
ARIA
LAST OF ENGLAND, THE
Cary, John
WHEN THE WIND BLOWS
Casey, Richard
DIRTY LAUNDRY
Casini Morigi, Tatiana
UN TASSINARO A NEW YORK
Castanedo, Rafael
FRIDA
Castro, Emmanuelle
AU REVOIR, LES ENFANTS
Chan, Leung Wing
NINJA THUNDERBOLT
Charkova, Olga
KOROTKIE VSTRECHI
Chaskel, Pedro
LA ESTACION DEL REGRESO
Chestnut, Scott
P.I. PRIVATE INVESTIGATIONS
Cheung-Kan, Chow
DIXIA QING
Chew, Richard
REVENGE OF THE NERDS II: NERDS IN PARADISE
Chiu, Francisco
FIERAS EN BRAMA
LAS TRAIGO . . . MUERTAS
LO NEGRO DEL NEGRO
RETO A LA VIDA
Chivulescu, Nita
PADUREANCA
Chorynska, Irena
POCIAG DO HOLLYWOOD
RYKOWISKO
Chow, Johnson
TRUE COLORS
Chow, Tony
THIRTY MILLION RUSH, THE
Chukri, Nadia
ZAWGAT RAGOL MOHIM
Cinema City
PRISON ON FIRE
Ciniselli, Giulia
LUNGA VITA ALLA SIGNORA!
Cirincione, Richard
ISHTAR
Clausen, Peter
TAXI NACH KAIRO
Coates, Anne V.
MASTERS OF THE UNIVERSE
Cohen, Martin
PRINCESS ACADEMY, THE
Cohen, Steve
NO MAN'S LAND
Colangeli, Otello
IL RAGAZZO DI EBALUS
Cole, Stan
FROM THE HIP
HOUSEKEEPER, THE
Colton, Craig
PERFECT MATCH, THE
SURF NAZIS MUST DIE
Connock, Jim
SLAUGHTER HIGH
Conrad, Scott
BEDROOM WINDOW, THE
WILD PAIR, THE
Conte, Mark
OPPOSING FORCE
Cook, Angus
ARIA
LAST OF ENGLAND, THE
Cooke, Josephine
CASSANDRA
Corrao, Angelo
PICK-UP ARTIST, THE
Corriveau, Andre
KID BROTHER, THE
LE JEUNE MAGICIEN
Cote, Louise
LE SOURD DANS LA VILLE
Coulibaly, Dounamba
YEELEN
Coulson, Peter
HIDDEN CITY
Cox, Alex
WALKER
Cox, Paul
VINCENT—THE LIFE AND DEATH OF VINCENT VAN GOGH
Crafford, Ian
HOPE AND GLORY
Craven, Garth
GABY—A TRUE STORY
Cristiani, Gabriella
HIGH SEASON
LAST EMPEROR, THE
Crociani, Raimondo
BELLIFRESCHI
SOTTOZERO
Csakany, Zsuzsa
CSOK, ANYU
SZORNYEK EVADJA
Curiel, Sergio
LA OVEJA NEGRA
Cutry, Claudio
OUTING, THE
Cutry, Claudio M.
CURSE, THE
D'Angiolillo, Luis Cesar
MISS MARY
da Mota, Tercio G.
VERA
Daley, Ray
RUNNING FROM THE GUNS
Dali, Chen
OLD WELL
Dansie, Peter
HIGH SEASON
Darmois, Hugues
ATTENTION BANDITS
Davalos, James
DERANGED
IF LOOKS COULD KILL
WIMPS
Davanture, Andree
YEELEN
David, Michele
LA VIE DISSOLUE DE GERARD FLOQUE
Davidson, Bruria
DUTCH TREAT
Davies, Freeman
EXTREME PREJUDICE
Davies, John
LOVECHILD, THE
Davies, Peter
LIVING DAYLIGHTS, THE
Davis, Battle
WILD THING
Davis, Kaye
EVIL DEAD 2: DEAD BY DAWN
Dawn, Vincent
STRIKE COMMANDO
De Bello, John
HAPPY HOUR
de Chateaubriant, Frederic
ACCROCHE-COEUR
de Graaff, Ton
DIARY OF A MAD OLD MAN
NITWITS
De La Bouillerie, Hubert C.
WITCHES OF EASTWICK, THE
De Luca, Riccardo
ILLUMINAZIONI
de Luze, Herve
JEAN DE FLORETTE
MANON OF THE SPRING
de Rozas, Elena Sainz
SUFRE MAMON
De Stefano, Lorenzo
WINNERS TAKE ALL
de Stefano, Lorenzo
KILLING TIME, THE
De Zarraga, Tony
FORTY DAYS OF MUSA DAGH
Dearberg, Bob
THREE KINDS OF HEAT
Debril, Marie-Aimee
TRAVELLING AVANT
Dedet, Yann
SOUS LE SOLEIL DE SATAN
Deiller, Catherine
PIERRE ET DJEMILA
del Almo, Pablo
BALADA DA PRAIA DOS CAES
Del Amo, Pablo G.
DIVINAS PALABRAS
REDONDELA
del Amo, Pablo G.
HAY QUE DESHACER LA CASA

Del Amo, Pablo Glez.
LA PLAYA DE LOS PERROS

Del Amo, Pablo Gonzalez
A LOS CUATRO VIENTOS

del Rey, Pedro
LONG STRIDER

Delcampo, Tony
WARRIOR QUEEN

Dennis O'Connor
WEEDS

Denys, Marek
INNA WYSPA
PRYWATNE SLEDZTWO

Derocles, Thierry
TERMINUS

Deschamps, Yves
POUSSIERE D'ANGE

Desfons, Delphine
PHOTOGRAPH, THE

Di Mauro, Claudio
SOLDATI: 365 GIORNI ALL' ALBA

Dietz, Corinna
MEIER

Diniz, Ana Maria
LEILA DINIZ

Dje-dje, Mme
FACES OF WOMEN

Dodd, Patrick
STACKING

Domalik, Malgorzata
ZYGFRYD

Don Brocha
BORN IN EAST L.A.

Dop, Jan
ZJOEK

Dringenberg, Katja
CASPAR DAVID FRIEDRICH

Duffner, J. Patrick
EAT THE PEACH

Duffy, Martin
BUDAWANNY

Dumieuz, Jean
LA COULEUR ENCERCLEE

Duncan, Daniel
WITCHBOARD

Dunn, Steve
BEYOND THERAPY

Dunnewijk, Hans
QUATRE MAINS

Duthie, Michael J.
AMERICAN NINJA 2: THE CONFRONTATION
NUMBER ONE WITH A BULLET

Dyck, Doris
SHELLEY

Egoyan, Atom
FAMILY VIEWING

El Khabbaz, Lahcen
ABBES

Elgood, Rick
ARIA

Elias, Luiz
EU

Ellis, Michael
HOUSEKEEPING

Elzbieta Kurowska
BLIND CHANCE

Emami, Ruhollah
SHEERE SANGGY

Evans, Aled
BOY SOLDIER

Evans, Brian
DEADLY PREY

Fanfara, Stephan
HIGHER EDUCATION

Fardoulis, Monique
LE CRI DU HIBOU
MASQUES

Farugia, Lena
SATURDAY NIGHT AT THE PALACE

Fernando, Cladwin
WITNESS TO A KILLING

Findlay, Roberta
BLOOD SISTERS
ORACLE, THE

Finfer, David
BACK TO THE BEACH

Fischer, Jutta
VENNER FOR ALTID

Fischer, Markus
DER NACHBAR

Flicker, William
HOUR OF THE ASSASSIN

Fogle, Joe Anne
THREE O'CLOCK HIGH

Font, Teresa
EL LUTE—CAMINA O REVIENTA

Fontana, Carlo
AURELIA
CARTOLINE ITALIANE

Forner, Nancy
RETURN TO HORROR HIGH

Foundas, Costas
TREE WE HURT, THE

Francis-Bruce, Richard
WITCHES OF EASTWICK, THE

Frank, Peter
WALK ON THE MOON, A

Frank, Peter C.
DIRTY DANCING
HELLO AGAIN

Franko, David
ZOMBIE NIGHTMARE

Fraticelli, Franco
CARAMELLE DA UNO SCONOSCIUTO
OPERA
TERNOSECCO

Frattini, Roberto
SOTTO IL RISTORANTE CINESE

Freeman, Jeff
BULLETPROOF

Freeman-Fox, Lois
LIKE FATHER, LIKE SON

Freire, Vera
A DANCA DOS BONECOS

Frenck, Jenny
YEELEN

Freund, Jay
FOREVER, LULU

Frias, Carmen
YEAR OF AWAKENING, THE

Friedrich, Peter
SLATE, WYN & ME

Fruet, Michael
BLUE MONKEY

Furubrand, Christer
MY LIFE AS A DOG

Galliti, Alberto
TERESA

Galloway, Sherri
TRESPASSES

Gandara, Roberto
LA GRAN FIESTA

Garcia, Maria Luisa
LAMI DE MON AMIE

Garcia, Maria-Luisa
QUATRE AVENTURES DE REINETTE ET MIRABELLE

Garcia, Sigfredo
ROSA DE LA FRONTERA

Garcia, Sigfrido
LO DEL CESAR

Gardos, Eva
BARFLY

Garlicka, Miroslawa
PRZYJACIEL WESOLEGO DIABLA
WIERNA RZEKA
ZYCIE WEWNETRZNE

Garnier-Klippel, Nicole
BIG BANG, THE

Garrett, W.O.
HOLLYWOOD SHUFFLE
OFFSPRING, THE

Garrone, Mirco
DEVIL IN THE FLESH
NOTTE ITALIANA
UNA CASA IN BILICO

Gaster, Nicolas
WHALES OF AUGUST, THE

Gebhard, Paoloa
PERSONAGGI & INTERPRETI

Gebura, Karen
SURVIVAL GAME

Gehr, Jeffrey Patrick
PINOCCHIO AND THE EMPEROR OF THE NIGHT

George, Louis
DANGER ZONE, THE

Gerber, Helena
ALPINE FIRE

Gessat, Wolfgang
STADTRAND

Ghaffari, Earl
KINDRED, THE

Gibson, Robert
THOSE DEAR DEPARTED

Gilbert, David
BLOOD TRACKS

Giordano, Martine
LA VIE EST BELLE

Girard, Helene
GREAT LAND OF SMALL, THE

Gislason, Tomas
SKYTTURNAR

Godard, Jean-Luc
ARIA
SOIGNE TA DROITE

Goedel, Peter
DAS TREIBHAUS

Goldman, Mia
BIG EASY, THE
CROSS MY HEART

Gordean, William D.
DRAGNET

Gordon, Bob
WHEELS OF TERROR

Gordon, Robert
NORTH SHORE
RAGE OF HONOR

Gorini, Luigi
LA TRASGRESSIONE
TENTAZIONE

Gosnell, Raja
MONSTER IN THE CLOSET
TEEN WOLF TOO

Goursaud, Anne
IRONWEED

Gourson, Jeff
CANT BUY ME LOVE

Goussias, Vagelis
THEOFILOS

Green, Bruce
SQUARE DANCE

Green, Paul
BELLMAN AND TRUE

Greenberg, Jerry
UNTOUCHABLES, THE

Greenbury, Christopher
THREE FOR THE ROAD

Greig, David
WITH LOVE TO THE PERSON NEXT TO ME

Griffen, Gary
ALLAN QUATERMAIN AND THE LOST CITY OF GOLD

Grimley, Simon
HOSTAGE

Groning, Philip
SOMMER

Gross, Daniel
PRETTY SMART

Grover, John
LIVING DAYLIGHTS, THE

Grunenvaldt, Luce
LETE DERNIER A TANGER

Guandamuz, Eduardo
MUJERES DE LA FRONTERA

Guignet, Eliane
SI LE SOLEIL NE REVENAIT PAS

Guillemot, Agnes
FUEGOS
LA BRUTE

Gupta, Shutanu
TAMAS

Guru
MISTER INDIA

Guterres, Leonor
DUMA VEZ POR TODAS
RELACAO FIEL E VERDADEIRA

Guyatt, Kit
PURSUIT OF HAPPINESS, THE

Guyot, Raymonde
LE GRAND CHEMIN

Hache, Joelle
TANDEM

Hagstrom, Lars
DEMONS

Haight, Michael
HARD TICKET TO HAWAII

Haines, Richard
LIONHEART

Hall, Kiplan
ESCAPES

Hallman, Sigurd
HIP, HIP, HURRA!
Halsey, Richard
DRAGNET
JOCKS
MANNEQUIN
Hambling, Gerry
ANGEL HEART
LEONARD PART 6
Hamilton, Marcy
HOT CHILD IN THE CITY
Handman, David
YOU TALKIN' TO ME?
Handof, Heidi
DEVILS PARADISE, THE
Hansen, Ed
NIGHTFORCE
Hanson, Ed
CODE NAME ZEBRA
Hap, Magda
CAT CITY
Haratzis, Denise
INITIATION
Hardin, Shawn
ZOMBIE HIGH
Harding, John
CONCRETE ANGELS
Hardouin, Anne-Marie
COERS CROISES
Hargreaves, Robert
FRIENDSHIP'S DEATH
Harker, Ed
PENITENTIARY III
Harris, Doug
REMEMBERING MEL
Hars, Mihaly
LUTRA
Harvey, Marshall
AMAZON WOMEN ON THE MOON
DATE WITH AN ANGEL
ERNEST GOES TO CAMP
Haslem, Denise
CUSTODY
Hassan-Doost, Hassan
LODGERS
Hay, Rod
DOT GOES TO HOLLYWOOD
Hazan, Shlomo
LATE SUMMER BLUES
Heckert, James
ASSASSINATION
Hee-su, Kim
KYEOUL NAGUNE
Helfrich, Mark
PREDATOR
Henderickx, Guido
LOVE IS A DOG FROM HELL
Henriksen, Finn
BABETTE'S GASTEBUD
Henszelman, Stefan
VENNER FOR ALTID
Henze, Roswitha
DILAN
Hering, Jutta
OTTO—DER NEUE FILM
Hermansson, Bo
PA STIGENDE KURS
Herring, Pembroke
WHO'S THAT GIRL
Herzner, Norbert
OUT OF ROSENHEIM
Hill, Dennis
ALIEN PREDATOR
Hirsch, Paul
PLANES, TRAINS AND AUTOMOBILES
SECRET OF MY SUCCESS, THE
Hoenig, Dov
OVERBOARD
Hof, Ursula
EIN BLICK-UND DIE LIEBE BRICHT AUS
Hofstra, Jack
PRINCIPAL, THE
Hoggan, Joyce L.
PARTY CAMP
Hoggan, Michael B.
PARTY CAMP
Holewa, Thomas
MALARPIRATER
Hollywood, Peter
AMAZING GRACE AND CHUCK

Holmes, Christopher
CATCH THE HEAT
WILD PAIR, THE
Holmes, Darren
CATCH THE HEAT
Honess, Peter
BELIEVERS, THE
Hoogenboom, Willem
TERUG NAAR OEGSTGEEST
Hoogland, jorge
VROEGER IS DOOD
Horenstein, Atara
LO SAM ZAYIN
Horian, Richard
STUDENT CONFIDENTIAL
Horton, Mike
STARLIGHT HOTEL
Horvitch, Andy
DUDES
RAWHEAD REX
Hugget, David
BELINDA
Huillet, Daniele
DER TOD DES EMPEDOKLES
Humphreys, Ned
DISORDERLIES
MISSION KILL
Hunter, Denise
DEAR CARDHOLDER
Hunter, Martin
FULL METAL JACKET
Ichida, Isamu
YOSHIWARA ENJO
Ichihara, Keiko
LOVE LETTER
Iizuka, Toshio
MAGINA—MURA MONOGATARI
Ilnicki, Diann
KEEPING TRACK
Inoue, Osamu
SEA AND POISON, THE
SHINRAN: SHIRO MICHI
Iordanidis, K.
I KEKARMENI
Irvine, Frank
HIGH STAKES
Isaacs, Stephen A.
OMEGA SYNDROME
Ivanovic, Shezana
HEY BABU RIBA
Jaakontalo, Eva
AKALLINEN MIES
LIIAN ISO KEIKKA
UUNO TURHAPURO MUUTTAA MAALLE
Jablow, Michael
THROW MOMMA FROM THE TRAIN
Jager, Siegrun
POET'S SILENCE, THE
Jahn, Christiane
DAS TREIBHAUS
Jakubowicz, Alain
ALLAN QUATERMAIN AND THE LOST CITY OF GOLD
SHY PEOPLE
TOO MUCH
Jansen, Janus Billeskov
PELLE EROVRAREN
WOLF AT THE DOOR, THE
Jeromaa, Juha
TILINTEKO
Jiande, Zhang
BEJALAI
Jimenez, Frank
MANNEQUIN
Jones, Alan
JANE AND THE LOST CITY
Jones, Donald
MURDER LUST
Jost, Jon
BELL DIAMOND
Julius, Maxine
GUNPOWDER
Jurgenson, Albert
HOTEL DE FRANCE
LEVY ET GOLIATH
MELO
Kacirkova, Ivana
CENA MEDU
Kadish, Lina
YEHOSHUA—YEHOSHUA

Kahm, Marsha
BLOOD HOOK
Kahn, Michael
EMPIRE OF THE SUN
FATAL ATTRACTION
Kahn, Sheldon
BIG SHOTS
LA BAMBA
Kakesu, Shuichi
GONDOLA
Kaman, Steven
FIREHOUSE
Karen, Debra
MEATBALLS III
Karides-Fuchs, Aristides
TELEFTAIO STICHIMA
Karmento, Eva
DIARY FOR MY LOVED ONES
LAURA
Karydis-Fuchs, Aristide
ANGELOS
Karydis-Fuchs, Aristides
APOUSIES
Karydis-Fuchs, Aristidis
DOXOBUS
Katsourides, Dinos
SWEET COUNTRY
Katsouridis, Dinos
ONE HUNDRED AND TWENTY DECIBELS
Kawashima, Akimasa
UHOHO TANKENTAI
Kelber, Catherine
POULE ET FRITES
Kelly, Chris
SHADEY
Kelly, Christopher
EMPIRE STATE
Kelly, Michael
PROGRAMMED TO KILL
Kenneally, Carole A.
WHITE PHANTOM
Kennedy, Patrick
IN THE MOOD
Keramidas, Harry
SQUEEZE, THE
Kerlaan, Herve
EVA: GUERRILLERA
Kern, David
CLUB LIFE
Key, Richard
CRIME OF HONOR
Kezner, Tom
IRON WARRIOR
King, Dell
NGATI
King, Richard
I WAS A TEENAGE T.V. TERRORIST
Kirkpatrick, Rob
CARE BEARS ADVENTURE IN WONDERLAND, THE
Klenovsky, Eduard
CENA ODVAHY
Kling, Elizabeth
BEAT, THE
O. C. AND STIGGS
SALVATION!
Klingman, Lynzee
BABY BOOM
Kloomok, Darren
MAGIC STICKS
MY DARK LADY
Klotz, George
WAITING FOR THE MOON
Klotz, Georges
LE MOUSTACHU
Knue, Michael
HIDDEN, THE
Koch, Simon
VENNER FOR ALTID
Kogak, Mevlud
ANAYURT OTELI
Koller, Ingrid
DIE DRECKSCHLEUDER
Komatsu, Takashi
BUS
Konink, Hetty
JULIA'S GEHEIM
Kovacs, Eszter
LENZ
Krag, Thomas
EPIDEMIC

Krause, Elsa
DER JUNGE MIT DEM GROSSEN SCHWARZEN HUND
Krex, Brigitte
DER TRAUM VOM ELCH
Kuon, Chiang Kowk
MAGNIFICENT WARRIORS
Kurkowska, Elzbieta
C. K. DEZERTERZY
Kuroiwa, Yoshitami
DIXIELAND DAIMYO
Kurson, Jane
HAPPY NEW YEAR
Kuzminska-Lebiedzik, Maria
NAD NIEMNEM
Kyong-ja, Lee
NAE-SHI
Lack, Christiane
O DESEJADO—LES MONTAGNES DE LA LUNE
Lafaurie, Nathalie
LANNEE DES MEDUSES
SPIRALE
Lahaye, Susann
FRANCESCA
Lakanen, Anne
A LA ITKE IINES
SNOW QUEEN, THE
Lam, Sone Ming
CITY ON FIRE
Lambert, Robert K.
CRITICAL CONDITION
Landi, Rosanna
DELIRIA
Langlois, Yves
MORNING MAN, THE
Langmann, Arlette
JEAN DE FLORETTE
Lanoe, Henri
LE SOLITAIRE
MALADIE D'AMOUR
Lapid, Era
KOL AHAVOTAI
Latham, Karen D.
BLOODSUCKERS FROM OUTER SPACE
Lawson, Tony
ARIA
Lawton, Jonathan
TALKING WALLS
Lazeta, Vesna
OFICIR S RUZOM
USODNI TELEFON
Lebenzon, Chris
BEVERLY HILLS COP II
Lebiedzik, Maria
MIEDZY USTAMI A BRZEGIEM PUCHARU
Lebrun, Anne-France
GRAND GUIGNOL
Lee, Alan
WINTER TAN, A
Lee-Thompson, Peter
DEATH WISH 4: THE CRACKDOWN
Leighton, Robert
PRINCESS BRIDE, THE
Leighton, Warner E.
TROUBLE WITH SPIES, THE
Lemick, Michael E.
MASSACRE IN DINOSAUR VALLEY
Lepage, Jean
MORNING MAN, THE
Leppe, Angel Camacho
FORAJIDOS EN LA MIRA
Letterman, Bob
MORGAN STEWART'S COMING HOME
Levin, Sidney
NUTS
Lewis, Tim
WARM NIGHTS ON A SLOW MOVING TRAIN
Li-Ho, Jose
UN SABADO MAS
Liho, Jose
DELINCUENTE
ESTA NOCHE CENA PANCHO (DESPEDIDA DE SOLTERO)
NOS REIMOS DE LA MIGRA
Linder, Stu
GOOD MORNING, VIETNAM
TIN MEN
Link, John F.
PREDATOR
Linnman, Susanne
MY LIFE AS A DOG
Lino, Jose
LA RAZA NUNCA PIERDE—HUELE A GAS
Linthorst, Kees
HECTOR
ODYSSEE D'AMOUR
Lipsky, Dalibor
CHOBOTNICE Z II. PATRA
Lloyd, Russell
ETTER RUBICON
Loewenthal, Dan
ALLAN QUATERMAIN AND THE LOST CITY OF GOLD
Lohlein, Margot
PENG! DU BIST TOT!
Lombardo, Lou
MOONSTRUCK
Lombardo, Tony
MAN OUTSIDE
P.K. & THE KID
Longfellow, Matthew
ARIA
Lopez, Eduardo
EL ANO DEL CONEJO
STRANGER, THE
Lorente, Isabelle
LES MENDIANTS
Lores, Mirita
DE TAL PEDRO, TAL ASTILLA
Lottman, Evan
ORPHANS
Louveau, Genevieve
MANON OF THE SPRING
Louw, Ot
VAN GELUK GESPROKEN
Louwrier, Win
LOOKING FOR EILEEN
Lovejoy, Ray
SUSPECT
Lovitt, Bert
AMAZON WOMEN ON THE MOON
Lowe, Edward
AMAZONS
Lubtchansky, Nicole
CROSS
Lucente, Francesco
VIRGIN QUEEN OF ST. FRANCIS HIGH, THE
Lucidi, Allesandro
IL LUPO DI MARE
Ma, Kam
BETTER TOMORROW, A
Macdonald, Bruce
FAMILY VIEWING
MacGillivray, William D.
LIFE CLASSES
Macia, Juan Carlos
MADE IN ARGENTINA
Maclean, Fraser
LITTLE DORRIT
Mainka-Jellinghaus, Beate
VERMISCHTE NACHRICHTEN
Majoros, Klara
GONDOVISELES
Makhankovoi, E.
DVADTSTAT DNEI BEZ
Makhmal Baf, Mohsen
PEDDLER, THE
Maldonado, Guillermo S.
ASI COMO HABIAN SIDO
Malkin, Barry
GARDENS OF STONE
Malvestito, Marcello
ADELMO
Mancilla, Jess
EVIL TOWN
Mani, M.S.
PANCHAGNI
Marden, Richard
HELLRAISER
Mari, Pablo
SINFIN, LA MUERTA NO ES NINGUNA SOLUCION
Mariani, Jacqueline
JEUX D'ARTIFICES
Marie-Sophie Dubus
FAMILY BUSINESS
Marinelli, Lorenzo
HEART
Mark Conte
STEEL DAWN
Markovic, Petar
HI-FI
Marks, Richard
BROADCAST NEWS
Martin, Dave
STRAIGHT TO HELL
Martin, Dominique B.
SALE DESTIN!
Martin, Nieves
LA GUERRA DE LOS LOCOS
Martin, Susan
WINTER TAN, A
Massaccesi, Aristide
DELIZIA
Mastorakis, Nico
TERMINAL EXPOSURE
WIND, THE
Mastroianni, Ruggero
CHRONICLE OF A DEATH FORETOLD
I MIEI PRIMI QUARANT'ANNI
I PICARI
IL GIORNO PRIMA
MONTECARLO GRAN CASINO
ROBA DA RICCHI
VIA MONTENAPOLEONE
Matesanz, Jose Luis
CARA DE ACELGA
MOROS Y CRISTIANOS
MY GENERAL
Mathieu, Franck
EMMANUELLE 5
Matous, Ivan
CIZIM VSTUP POVOLEN
Maybury, John
LAST OF ENGLAND, THE
Mazini, Eder
ANJOS DO ARRABALDE
McDermott, Debra
TOUGH GUYS DON'T DANCE
McLennan, Scott
BIT PART, THE
Medaglia, Susan
DANGER ZONE, THE
Mehtonen, Tuula
JAAN KAANTOPIIRI
Meniconi, Enzo
DARK EYES
Merchant, Tom
PRETTYKILL
Mercier, Annie
TESTAMENT D'UN POETE JUIF ASSASSINE
Merck, Renate
DRAGON'S FOOD
Meshelski, Thomas
BLOOD DINER
Mesherski, Tom
NECROPOLIS
Metz, Akiko B.
VALET GIRLS
Meuller
MESSENGER, THE
Meyer, Richard
EMANON
Michalakias, John Elias
I WAS A TEENAGE ZOMBIE
Miguel A. Santamaria
MIENTRAS HAYA LUZ
Mikaelian, I.
SASHSHENNYI FONAR
Miljevic, Josie
MANUELA'S LOVES
Miller, Michael R.
NIGHTMARE AT SHADOW WOODS
RAISING ARIZONA
SOMETHING SPECIAL!
Miller, W. Peter
SPACE RACE
Ming Lam, Wong
THIRTY MILLION RUSH, THE
Minoui, Mehrzad
MANUSCRIPTS
Miqueau, Marie-Catherine
YEELEN
Mirkovich, Steve
DEADLY ILLUSION
DEATH BEFORE DISHONOR
PRINCE OF DARKNESS
Miski, Giselle
FACES OF WOMEN
Mitchell, James
MONSTER SQUAD, THE
Miziolek, Teresa
E S D

Mocky, Jean-Pierre
AGENT TROUBLE
LE MIRACULE

Moldrup, Grete
SIDSTE AKT

Molin, Bud
SUMMER SCHOOL

Mollinger, Ursula
WANNSEE CONFERENCE, THE

Monaghan, Pat
LEADING EDGE, THE

Mondshein, Andrew
MAKING MR.RIGHT

Montanari, Sergio
MISSIONE EROICA
NOI UOMINI DURI
PROFUMO
SCUOLA DI LADRI 2
STREGATI

Montesi, Jorge
BIRDS OF PREY

Moreira, Renato Neiva
NIGHT ANGELS

Morgan, Glenn A.
SIESTA

Morgan, Robert
WHISTLE BLOWER, THE

Moriani, Alberto
UNA DONNA DA SCOPRIRE

Morigi, Tatiana Casini
RIMINI RIMINI

Morrison, Jane
SHELLEY

Morse, Susan E.
MIRACLES
RADIO DAYS
SEPTEMBER

Moryalty, Albert
THUNDER WARRIOR II

Moser, Jonathan
MIND KILLER

Mounir, Adel
AL-TAUQ WAL-ISWIRA

Moussek, Nissim
HA INSTALATOR

Ms, Benny
STABILIZER, THE

Muk-leung, Chow
ROMANCE OF BOOK AND SWORD, THE

Mullenix, Steve
PERSONAL FOUL

Muller-Laue, Klaus
SIERRA LEONE

Murillo, Enrique
HERENCIA DE VALIENTES
JUANA LA CANTINERA
JUNTOS
ROSA DE LA FRONTERA

Murphy, Catherine
CODA

Murphy, Michael S.
SWEET REVENGE

Murray, Mike
INDIAN SUMMER

Muscat, Tony
KOLORMASK

Muschietti, Alfredo
GLI OCCHIALI D'ORO
LA DONNA DEL TRAGHETTO

Muschietto, Alfredo
LES EXPLOITS DUN JEUNE DON JUAN

Mutti, Luis
LOS DUENOS DEL SILENCIO

Nabeshima, Atsushi
ITAZU

Nabeshima, Jun
HOTARUGAWA

Nadal, Liliana
CHORROS

Nadal, Susana
SENTIMIENTOS: MIRTA DE LINIERS A ESTAMBUL

Nagy, Maria
TISZTA AMERIKA

Napoli, Anna
DISTANT LIGHTS

Nascimento, Jose
JESTER,THE

Nater, Thorsten
CHINESE ARE COMING, THE

Naudon, Jean-Francois
IL EST GENIAL PAPY!

Nedd, Priscilla
STREET SMART

Neeman, Tova
EMPEROR'S NEW CLOTHES, THE
RUMPELSTILTSKIN
SLEEPING BEAUTY

Nelson, Andrew
WARDOGS

Nicholson, Marty
HOUSE TWO: THE SECOND STORY

Nicolini, Angelo
IL GRANDE BLEK

Nicolle, Douglas C.
LADIES OF THE LOTUS

Nieto Ramirez
MURIERON A MITAD DEL RIO

Nikel, Hannes
ZABOU

Nino Baragli
MOSCA ADDIO

Nordquist, Margit
PLASTPOSEN

Norman, Ron
OVERKILL

Nuttall, Nancy
BIG BAD MAMA II

Nyznik, Bruce
JOHN AND THE MISSUS

O'Connor, Dennis
DOWN TWISTED

O'Connor, John
STEELE JUSTICE

O'Steen, Sam
NADINE

Obradov, Olga
ANDJEO CUVAR

Ogawa, Shinsuke
MAGINA—MURA MONOGATARI

Ojala, Jaska
KILL CITY

Okazaki, Steven
LIVING ON TOKYO TIME

Oleinik, V.
DOLGHYIE PROVOD

Oliveti, Gennaro
DOLCE ASSENZA

Olmi, Ermanno
LUNGA VITA ALLA SIGNORA!

Ortega, Carlos Puente
WALKER

Ortiz, Emilio
EL GRAN SERAFIN

Osada, Chizuko
EIGA JOYU
PRINCESS FROM THE MOON

Oshima, Tomoyo
SARABA ITOSHIKI HITO YO

Osiecki, Krzysztof
W ZAWIESZENIU

Osinski, Zbigniew
ZLOTA MAHMUDIA

Osko, Lucja
BOHATERROKU
SIEKIEREZADA

Ostanowko, Jaroslaw
PAN SAMOCHODZIK I NIESAMOWITY DWOR

Otello Colangeli
TENEREZZA

Palewski, Stephanie
MONSTER IN THE CLOSET

Pankow, Bill
UNTOUCHABLES, THE

Papakyriakopoulos, Panos
KLIOS

Pappalardo, Jorge
EL DUENO DEL SOL

Pappe, Stuart
BIG TOWN, THE

Parasheles, Peter
EVIL TOWN

Pardo, Alvaro
ELVIS-KISSAN JALJILLA

Pardo, Rafael Fuster
IN DER WUSTE

Paredes, Jesus
BEAKS
VIAJE AL PARAISO

Paris, Dominique
COLOR OF DESTINY, THE

Park-huen, Kwan
YI LOU YI

Pascual, Pablo Martin
MADRID

Paterson, Tony
TO MARKET, TOMARKET

Pavan, Edgardo
MUJERES SALVAJES

Pedersen, John
TUESDAY WEDNESDAY

Pekalski, Jerzy
ZLOTY POCIAG

Peltier, Kenout
MISS MONA

Pena, Julio
LA ESTANQUERA DE VALLECAS

Penney, John
KINDRED, THE

Percy, Lee
DOLLS
SLAMDANCE

Pergament, Robert
BLIND DATE

Perpignani, Roberto
ANGELUS NOVUS
GOOD MORNING BABYLON
MORO AFFAIR, THE

Persson, Jan
JIM OCH PIRATERNA BLOM
LEIF

Peters, Ilse
DER BARENHAUTER

Petr Sitar
PRATELE BERMUDSKEHO TROJUHELNIKU

Phifer Mate, Wende
NICE GIRLS DON'T EXPLODE

Pina, Jorge
TRAGICO TERREMOTO EN MEXICO

Pinheiro-L'Itevevder, Claire
MON BEL AMOUR, MA DECHIRURE

Piorecki, Zenon
STANISLAW I ANNA

Piscicelli, Salvatore
REGINA

Piyasena, Lal
VIRAGAYA

Plemiannikov, Helene
CLUB DE RENCONTRES

Plemmianikoff, Helene
LE JOURNAL D'UN FOU

Plotts, Gregory F.
FLOWERS IN THE ATTIC

Pokras, Barbara
FLICKS

Polivka, Steven
CAMPUS MAN
TEEN WOLF TOO

Polonsky, Sonya
MATEWAN

Portillo, Reynaldo
ROBACHICOS

Portillo, Roberto Benet
CINCO NACOS ASALTAN A LAS VEGAS

Posan, Zsuzsa
HOTREAL

Postek, Ziva
HIMMO MELECH YERUSHALAIM

Prahash, Om
PANCHVATI

Preissel, Miriam
CREEPOZOIDS

Presgodard, Peter
WATER ALSO BURNS

Priestley, Tom
KITCHEN TOTO, THE
WHITE MISCHIEF

Prim, Minique
TANT QU'IL AURA DES FEMMES

Prior, David A.
KILLER WORKOUT

Prouse, Andrew
MOVING TARGETS

Prowse, Andrew
TIME GUARDIAN, THE

Prugar-Ketling, Halina
MASKARADA
WERYFIKACJA

Przygodda, Peter
DEADLINE
DER HIMMEL UBER BERLIN

Psenny, Armand
LA PASSION BEATRICE
LES MOIS D'AVRIL SONT MEURTRIERS

Pulbrook, David
GROUND ZERO

Quesemand, Catherine
COMEDY!

Quettier, Nelly
BAD BLOOD

Quinton, Marie-Helene
NUIT DOCILE

Radford, Daniel
NIGHTSTICK

Ramirez, Antonio
POLICIA

Ramsay, Todd
MALONE

Rasche, Ina
CRAZY BOYS

Raskin, Larry
REMEMBERING MEL

Ravel, Jean
NOYADE INTERDITE

Rawlings, Terry
LONELY PASSION OF JUDITH HEARNE,THE
WHITE OF THE EYE

Rawlins, David
POLICE ACADEMY 4: CITIZENS ON PATROL

Ray, David
GLASS MENAGERIE, THE
WHITE WATER SUMMER

Raz, Irit
HANSEL AND GRETEL

Redman, Anthony
CHINA GIRL

Refseth, Yngve
ETTER RUBICON

Renault, Catherine
LE BEAUF

Rennick, Don
REMEMBERING MEL

Reynolds, William
DANCERS
ISHTAR

Rich, Dan M.
ALLNIGHTER, THE

Richardson, Henry
BUSINESS AS USUAL

Richter, Thea
VERNEHMUNG DER ZEUGEN

Ridsdale, Chris
EAT THE RICH

Rigo, Maria
ISTEN VELETEK, BARATAIM
WHOOPING COUGH

Riley, Janet
EMANON

Ripps, Michael
STAKEOUT

Rivera, Jorge
ALBURES MEXICANOS
LA FUGA DE CARRASCO
NI DE AQUI, NI DE ALLA

Robert Bergman
PSYCHO GIRLS

Roderer, Daniela
JENATSCH

Rodriguez, Nelson
SUCCESSFUL MAN, A
VISA U.S.A.

Rolf, Tom
OUTRAGEOUS FORTUNE
STAKEOUT

Roose, Ronald
MY DEMON LOVER

Rosenberg, George
ZERO BOYS, THE

Rosenbloom, David
BEST SELLER

Rosenblum, Steve
STEELE JUSTICE

Rosenblum, Steven
WILD THING

Rosenstock, Harvey
TEEN WOLF TOO

Ross, Angelo
MASTERBLASTER

Ross, Sharyn L.
UNDER COVER

Rossberg, Susana
LES NOCES BARBARES
MASCARA

Rotter, Stephen A.
ISHTAR

Rotundo, Nick
HELLO MARY LOU, PROM NIGHT II

Rouse, Keith
SUICIDE CLUB, THE

Rozema, Patricia
IVE HEARD THE MERMAIDS SINGING

Rubasinghe, Chandradasa
MALDENIYESIMION

Ruxin, James
GHOST FEVER

Ruys, Ton
BLOND DOLLY
HAVINCK

Sabin, Tom
ANGUSTIA

Sablone, Lidia
VALHALLA

Saenz, Marcela
EN EL NOMBRE DEL HIJO

Sahbi, Allal
LA COMPROMISSION

Salcedo, Jose
LAW OF DESIRE

Salfas, Stan
HOT SHOT

Samuelson, Thomas
OM KARLEK

San Mateo, Juan
EL AMOR DE AHORA

San Mateo, Juan Ignacio
EL BOSQUE ANIMADO

Sanchez, Amang
GET THE TERRORISTS
HOSTAGE SYNDROME
TOUGH COP

Sanchez, Max
CARTUCHA CORTADA
EL DIABLO, EL SANTO Y EL TONTO
MATAR O MORIR
SINVERGUENZA . . . PERO HONRADO
TODA LA VIDA
UNA PURA Y DOS CON SAL

Sanchez, Pacifico
EQUALIZER 2000

Sanders, Jim
WARRIOR QUEEN

Sandrock, Carla
SATURDAY NIGHT AT THE PALACE

Santamaria, Miguel A.
LA VIDA ALEGRE

Santeiro, Gilberto
BAIXO GAVEA
UM TREM PARA AS ESTRELAS

Santos, Gervacio
EYE OF THE EAGLE

Sarantsoglou, Christos
TA PAIDIA TIS CHELIDONAS

Sarles, Bob
VIDEO DEAD, THE

Saunders, Don
RIGHT HAND MAN, THE

Saunier, Nicole
F . . . ING FERNAND
LASSOCIATION DES MALFAITEURS

Savage, Carlos
EL HOMBRE DESNUDO
MI NOMBRE ES GATILLO
NARCOTERROR
REALM OF FORTUNE, THE

Sayyad, Parviz
CHECKPOINT

Schafer, Jo
CEMIL

Schaffer, Perry
NIONDE KOMPANIET

Scheider, Cynthia
BATTERIES NOT INCLUDED

Schiavone, Roberto
SEMBRA MORTO . . . ME E SOLO SVENUTO

Schmidbauer, Tanja
MASCHENKA

Schneider, Robert
CEMIL

Schyberg, Kasper
DEMONS
PETER VON SCHOLTEN

Scola, Ettore
FAMILY, THE

Scott, John
GOOD WIFE, THE
ROXANNE

Sear, Walter E.
BLOOD SISTERS

Secrist, Kim
TEEN WOLF TOO

Seitz, Jane
VERMISCHTE NACHRICHTEN

Selakovich, Dan
OPEN HOUSE

Sell, Jack M.
OUTTAKES

Sello, Hajnal
DOKTOR MINORKA VIDOR NAGY NAPJA

Semenova, Leda
SKORBNOE BESCHUVSTVIE

Shaffer, William
EVIL SPAWN

Shah, Sanjiv
MIRCH MASALA

Shaine, Rich
DEAD OF WINTER

Shaw, Penelope
HANOI HILTON, THE

Shengde, Shen
BEJALAI

Shephard, Mike
ANITA—DANCES OF VICE

Ship, Trudy
HELLO AGAIN
HOUSE OF GAMES

Shirashi, Yoko
MAGINA—MURA MONOGATARI

Shirley, John
SUPERMAN IV: THE QUEST FOR PEACE

Shoemaker, Tim
DEATHROW GAMESHOW

Siciliano, Antonio
IL BURBERO
IO E MIA SORELLA

Siiter, Tom
JOCKS
NIGHTFLYERS

Silliman, Drake
BANZAI RUNNER

Silvi, Roberto
DEAD, THE

Simandl, Lloyd A.
LADIES OF THE LOTUS

Simmons, Charles
SURVIVAL GAME

Simoncelli, Giancarlo
LA CODA DEL DIAVOLO

Simpson, Claire
SOMEONE TO WATCH OVER ME
WALL STREET

Sinde, Miguel Gonzalez
ASIGNATURA APROBADA

Singleton, Stephen
RITA, SUE AND BOB TOO!

Sinoway, Mitchell
HOT PURSUIT

Sivo, Gyorgy
AZ UTOLSOKEZIRAT

Sivo, Julia
HOL VOLT, HOL NEM VOLT
MALOM A POKOLBAN

Skousen, Camilla
JAG ELSKER DIG
NEGERKYS & LABRE LARVER
VENNER FOR ALTID

Skrigin, Olga
ANDJEO CUVAR

Sloane, Julie
ANNA
RED DESERT PENITENTIARY

Sluizer, George
RED DESERT PENITENTIARY

Smith, Bud
SOME KIND OF WONDERFUL

Smith, Howard
NEAR DARK
RIVER'S EDGE

Smith, John N.
TRAIN OF DREAMS
Smith, John Victor
MONTH IN THE COUNTRY, A
Smith, Lee
HOWLING III, THE
Smith, Norman
GRAVEYARD SHIFT
Smith, Scott
SOME KIND OF WONDERFUL
Soinio, Olli
SNOW QUEEN, THE
VY VIHDOINKIN YHDESSA
Solomon, Laurence
SWEET LORRAINE
Sones, Sonya
RIVER'S EDGE
Song, Laiw Ching
OUTSIDERS, THE
Soriano, Maria Luisa
LOS INVITADOS
Soto, Sergio
EL ANSIA DE MATAR
EL MOFLES Y LOS MECANICOS
LA RULETERA
LAPUTA: THE CASTLE IN THE SKY
POLICIAS DE NARCOTICOS
RATAS DE LA CIUDAD
VA DE NUEZ
YO, EL EJECUTOR
Soya, May
KAMPEN OM DEN RODE KO
Spang, Ronald
DEADLY ILLUSION
Sparr, Rick R.
LETS GET HARRY
Spence, Michael
SUMMER CAMP NIGHTMARE
Spiers, David
PROMISED LAND
Staenberg, Zach
STRIPPED TO KILL
Stafford, Keith
DIRTY REBEL
Steinkamp, Fredric
ADVENTURES IN BABYSITTING
BURGLAR
Steinkamp, William
ADVENTURES IN BABYSITTING
BURGLAR
Stephen E. Rivkin
STRANDED
Stevens, Tony
BACHELOR GIRL
Stevenson, Michael A.
THREE MEN AND A BABY
Stewart, James A.
SLAVE GIRLS FROM BEYOND INFINITY
Stieber, Dale Ann
UNFINISHED BUSINESS . . .
Stockman, Olivier
LITTLE DORRIT
Stokes, Terry
NIGHTMARE ON ELM STREET 3: DREAM WARRIORS, A
Strachan, Alan
WITHNAIL AND I
Strasser, Ralph
AS TIME GOES BY
Stratton, Kathleen
UNDICI GIORNI, UNDICI NOTTE
Straub, Jean-Marie
DER TOD DES EMPEDOKLES
Stubblefield, Bruce
SLAVE GIRLS FROM BEYOND INFINITY
Sullivan, Fred G.
SULLIVAN'S PAVILION
Sung, Liao Ching
LIEN LIEN FUNG CHEN
TERRORIZERS, THE
Suzuki, Akira
SOROBANZUKU
TAXING WOMAN, A
Svoboda, Jan
PROC?
Symons, James
OVER THE TOP
Szarka, William
DEADTIME STORIES
Tadeu, Danilo
CIDADE OCULTA
Taghvai, Nasser
CAPTAIN KHORSHID
Tagliano, Andriano
SPECTERS
Taina, Irma
JAAHYVAISET PRESIDENTILLE
Tal, Omer
MOON IN SCORPIO
Talvio, Raija
VARJOJA PARATIISISSA
Tamir, Shimon
YALDEI STALIN
Taniguchi, Toshio
TOKYO BLACKOUT
Tanner, Peter
HAMBURGER HILL
Tarnate, Marc
GET THE TERRORISTS
HOSTAGE SYNDROME
Tarnate, Mark
ULTIMAX FORCE
Tauchner, Brigitte
DIE DRECKSCHLEUDER
Tavares, Mair
ELE, O BOTO
Tavares de Barros, Jose
UM FILM 100% BRAZILEIRO
Tavazoie, Samad
GOZARESH-E YEK GHATL
Tedesco, Dario
CHORROS
SENTIMIENTOS: MIRTA DE LINIERS A ESTAMBUL
Teschner, Peter
ALIEN PREDATOR
DREAMANIAC
ENEMY TERRITORY
Theos, Dimos
IKONA ENOS MYTHIKOU PROSOPOU
Thomson, Carl
BLOODY NEW YEAR
Thorndike, Karen
BENJI THE HUNTED
Thumpston, Neil
YEAR MY VOICE BROKE, THE
Timar, Peter
ZUHANAS KOZBEN
Tintori, John
VIOLINS CAME WITH THE AMERICANS, THE
Tobni, Youcef
LA RUMBA
Todd, Michael
HOME IS WHERE THE HART IS
Tomita, Isao
WATASHI O SKI NI TSURETETTE
Tour, David
KFAFOT
RED RIDING HOOD
Travis, Neil
NO WAY OUT
Travnecek, Claudia
FIRE AND ICE
Trigg, Derek
GIRL, THE
SLEEP WELL, MY LOVE
Troch, Ludo
LOVE IS A DOG FROM HELL
Tronick, Michael
BEVERLY HILLS COP II
LESS THAN ZERO
Tsilifonis, Andreas
O PARADISSOS ANIGI ME ANTIKLIDI
Tsitsopoulos, Giannis
ARCHANGELOS TOU PATHOUS
Tsitsopoulos, Yannis
VIOS KE POLITIA
YENETHLIA POLI
Tweten, Roger
TERMINAL EXPOSURE
Ubell, Marc
IF LOOKS COULD KILL
SLAMMER GIRLS
WIMPS
Uhler, Laurent
LA VALLEE FANTOME
UNE FLAMME DANS MON COEUR
Urioste, Frank J.
ROBOCOP
Valencia, Jorge
A DOS AGUAS
Valero, Armando
POR LOS CAMINOS VERDES
Valve, Marjo
NAKEMIIN, HYVASTI
Valverde, Raphael
BEIJO NA BOCA
Van Effenterre, Joele
MAN IN LOVE, A
Van Effenterre, Joelle
LES FOUS DE BASSAN
van Steensel, Rob
DE RATELRAT
Vandenburg, Franz
SHADOWS OF THE PEACOCK
Varella, Elvira
KE DYO AVGA TOURKIAS
Varone, Domenico
CHI C'E C'E
REGINA
Vasquez, Marie Castro
NOCE EN GALILEE
Vasseur, Jean-Marc
MALIBU BIKINI SHOP, THE
Vauban, Jean-Paul
TESTET
Vaury, Genevieve
CHARLIE DINGO
Vega, Justo
MUJERES DE LA FRONTERA
Velasquez, Pedro
ARQUIESTA EMILIO VARELA
Vincent, Chuck
WARRIOR QUEEN
Vindevogel, Denise
FALSCH
Vine, Edgar
NO DEAD HEROES
Virkler, Dennis
BIG SHOTS
MIRACLES
Virmond, Christian
TRIUMPH DE GERECHTEN
Vitale, Sam
ROSARY MURDERS, THE
Volz, Dorte
TAROT
von Buuren, Marc
AROUND THE WORLD IN EIGHTY WAYS
von Dongen, Hans
DE ORIONNEVEL
Von Hasperg, Ila
SHE MUST BE SEEING THINGS
von Hasperg, Ila
KISS DADDY GOOD NIGHT
Von Oelffen, Petra
FIRE AND ICE
von Trier, Lars
EPIDEMIC
von Weitershausen, Barbara
DER UNSICHTBARE
Wagner, Zoltan
KRALJEVA ZAVRSNICA
STRATEGIJA SVRAKE
Wah, Fong Po
LAONIANG GOU SAO
Walker, Graham
FOURTH PROTOCOL, THE
Walker, Lesley
CRY FREEDOM
Walkowishky, G.A.
TROUBLE WITH DICK, THE
Waller, Stephen J.
WITCHBOARD
Wallis, Rit
GATE, THE
NOWHERE TO HIDE
Walls, Tom
MADE IN HEAVEN
Waman
MISTER INDIA
Warner, Mark Roy
RUNNING MAN, THE
Warschilka, Edward
HIDING OUT
Warschilka, Edward A.
RUNNING MAN, THE
Watts, Roy
HES MY GIRL
LADY BEWARE
THEY STILL CALL ME BRUCE

Weatherly, Peter
CREEPSHOW 2

Weaver, Kathie
COMMANDO SQUAD

Weber, Billy
BEVERLY HILLS COP II

Wedeles, Rodolfo
POISONS

Wedeles, Rodolpho
MEMOIRE DES APPARENCES: LA VIE EST UN SONGE

Weiss, Chuck
NIGHTMARE ON ELM STREET 3: DREAM WARRIORS, A

Wekstein, Reine
MACBETH

Wellburn, Tim
BUSHFIRE MOON
LES PATTERSON SAVES THE WORLD

Wells, Richard
NIGHTSTICK

Wenning, Katherine
MAURICE
MY LITTLE GIRL

Wentworth, Nicholas
CRYSTAL HEART

Werner, Dennis
STREET TRASH

West, Ursula
DIE VERLIEBTEN

Westover, Richard E.
HUNK

Westvic, Dane
ESCAPES

Wheeler, John W.
MILLION DOLLAR MYSTERY

Whitney, James
ZOMBIE HIGH

Widerberg, Bo
MANNEN FRAN MALLORCA
SERPENT'S WAY, THE

Wiegmans, Rene
EL AMOR ES UNA MUJERGORDA

Williams, Robert
ROCK 'N' ROLL NIGHTMARE

Wilska, Anna
KOMEDIANTKA

Wilson, David
LAST STRAW, THE
SITTING IN LIMBO

Wilson, John
BELLY OF AN ARCHITECT, THE

Wimble, Chris
EIGHTY FOUR CHARING CROSS ROAD

Winding, Genevieve
CHAMP D'HONNEUR

Winters, Ralph E.
LETS GET HARRY

Wisman, Ron
CLIMB, THE

Witta, Jacques
ENNEMIS INTIMES
POUSSIERE D'ANGE

Wolejko, Jaroslaw
W STARYM DWORKU

Wolf, Jeffrey
HEAT

Wolinsky, Sidney
MAID TO ORDER

Wolman, Shoshi
CHOZE AHAVA

Woodward, Phil
OUT OF ORDER

Wright, John
RUNNING MAN, THE

Wright, Rob
MORE BAD NEWS

Wu, David
PEKING OPERA BLUES
SEVEN YEARS ITCH

Xinxia, Zhou
BIG PARADE, THE

Yaguil, Rachel
TEL AVIV—BERLIN

Yeadon, Sally
LAST OF ENGLAND, THE

Yooseffian, Davood
DJADDE HAYE SARD

Yoyotte, Marie-Josephe
LETE EN PENTE DOUCE

Zafranovic, Andrija
OKTOBERFEST
ZIVOT RADNIKA

Zeman, Wanda
MAGNAT

Zervou, Despina
O PARADISSOS ANIGI ME ANTIKLIDI

Zetlin, Barry
HUNTER'S BLOOD
MUTANT HUNT
NECROPOLIS
ROBOT HOLOCAUST

Zimmerman, Don
FATAL BEAUTY
OVER THE TOP

Zotola, Sergio
EL HOMBRE DE LA DEUDA EXTERNA

Zottla, Sergio
EN RETIRADA

Zottola, Sergio
LA BUSQUEDA

Zuniga, Rogelio
EL PLACER DE LA VENGANZA
MAS VALE PAJARO EN MANO . . .
OPERACION MARIJUANA
YERBA SANGRIENTE

MAKEUP

Abrums, Steve
BEVERLY HILLS COP II

Aguinaga, Narga
HOUR OF THE ASSASSIN

Alan Weisinger
SOMEONE TO WATCH OVER ME

Alice Adamson
RAGE OF HONOR

Allsop, Christine
FULL METAL JACKET

Allwright, Eric
GOOD MORNING, VIETNAM

Altamura, Lorraine
DEADTIME STORIES

Amparo
SWEET REVENGE

Anaff, Matiki
DEADTIME STORIES

Anderson, Steve E.
PRINCIPAL, THE

Androff, Patty
MILLION DOLLAR MYSTERY

Angier, Don
DEATH BEFORE DISHONOR

Apone, Alan
MISSION KILL

Apone, Allan A.
HUNTER'S BLOOD

Aradottir, Vilborg
ARIA
P.I. PRIVATE INVESTIGATIONS

Armstrong, Del
OUTRAGEOUS FORTUNE

Arrington, Richard
IN THE MOOD
MANNEQUIN
TALKING WALLS

Baca, Theresa
PRETTY SMART

Badoux, Nancy
EEN MAAND LATER

Baker, Rick
SUMMER SCHOOL

Balazs
PRINCIPAL, THE

Bann, Cecile
NO DEAD HEROES

Baumann, Brent
BIRDS OF PREY

Baun, Cecille
HAMBURGER HILL

Baurens, Muriel
TERMINUS

Beauchesne, Robin
KILLER WORKOUT

Beaudoin, Jocelyn
I WAS A TEENAGE T.V. TERRORIST

Bell, Wendy
EVIL DEAD 2: DEAD BY DAWN

Benoit, Suzanne
HOUSEKEEPER, THE
JOHN AND THE MISSUS

Bentley, Lon
THREE MEN AND A BABY

Berger, Howard
CREEPSHOW 2

Bergmark, Suzanne
DEMONS

Berkely, Craig
SLAUGHTER HIGH

Biggs, Chris
NIGHTMARE ON ELM STREET 3: DREAM WARRIORS, A

Bihr, Kathryn
HELLO AGAIN
SQUEEZE, THE

Bingham, Chris
SALVATION!

Bisson, John
ENEMY TERRITORY

Black, Sue
BUSINESS AS USUAL

Blackman, Charles
ESCAPES

Blake, John
WITCHBOARD

Blanchard, Marc
LES EXPLOITS DUN JEUNE DON JUAN

Boost, Jennifer
FULL METAL JACKET

Booth, Tom
KEEPING TRACK

Bouquiere, Pascale
GRAND GUIGNOL

Boyle, Alan
ISHTAR

Breitner-Protat, Marie-Angele
MORNING MAN, THE
WILD THING

Brickman, June
MISSION KILL
ZERO BOYS, THE

Brooke, Ken
POLICE ACADEMY 4: CITIZENS ON PATROL

Brubaker, Gail
GARBAGE PAIL KIDS MOVIE, THE

Buchanan, Anni
ARIA

Buchman, Irving
TIN MEN

Buchner, Fern
RADIO DAYS
SECRET OF MY SUCCESS, THE

Burman Studio, The
RUNNING MAN, THE

Cannom, Greg
NIGHTMARE ON ELM STREET 3: DREAM WARRIORS, A

Carballo, Jean
ORACLE, THE

Carbolla, Jean
BLOOD SISTERS

Carew, Elaine
COMRADES
PRICK UP YOUR EARS

Casboro, Rick
ARIA

Case, E. Thomas
OVERBOARD

Case, Tom
CROSS MY HEART

Chadwick, Kristine
WINNERS TAKE ALL

Chadwick, N. Kristine
NIGHTFORCE

Choi, Jenny
NINJA THUNDERBOLT

Chomnalez, Selva
MISS MARY

Christensen, Birte
WOLF AT THE DOOR, THE

Cohen, Phylis
ARIA

Colladant, Dominique
MON BEL AMOUR, MA DECHIRURE

Corridoni, Franco
BELLY OF AN ARCHITECT, THE

Cossu, Walter
CHRONICLE OF A DEATH FORETOLD

Criado, Cristobal
LA RUSA
LOS INVITADOS

Cruz, Ed
HOSTAGE SYNDROME

Davies, Troy
DOGS IN SPACE

Dawn, Jefferson
LETS GET HARRY
RUNNING MAN, THE

Dawn, Wes
LETS GET HARRY

De Abreu, Ronaldo Ribeiro
BEYOND THERAPY

de Buck, Valerie
SI LE SOLEIL NE REVENAIT PAS

de Diego, Angel Luis
LA GUERRA DE LOS LOCOS

de Diego, Ramon
MY GENERAL

de Luca, Josee
MASQUES

De Vorges, Dominique
ARIA
BEYOND THERAPY
MELO

Dean, Richard
SUSPECT

Deborah Figuly
BEST SELLER

Del Brocco, Giancarlo
DOLLS
MIRACLES

Delamar —Shawyer, Penny
ARIA

Delany, Toni
EAT THE PEACH

Deruelle, Michele
JEAN DE FLORETTE
MANON OF THE SPRING

Dolejsi, Jana
WOLF'S HOLE

Drucker, Loraina
BLOOD DINER

Dryhurst, Anna
HOPE AND GLORY

Duncan, Karen
ERNEST GOES TO CAMP

Eagan, Lynne
MUNCHIES

Eddo, Scott
LETHAL WEAPON
WHO'S THAT GIRL

Elek, Katalin
MONSTER SQUAD, THE

Ellingwood, Tom
MALONE

Elliott, Margaret
MALIBU BIKINI SHOP, THE

Enders, Debra
HAPPY HOUR

Engelen, Paul
EMPIRE OF THE SUN

Engleman, Leonard
SUSPECT
WITCHES OF EASTWICK, THE

Estocin, Kathy
AMAZING GRACE AND CHUCK

Evans, Helen
MOVING TARGETS

Evans, Sallie
WHISTLE BLOWER, THE

Exelby, Sandra
SHADEY

Eychenne, Jean-Pierre
JEAN DE FLORETTE
MANON OF THE SPRING

Fabregat, Matilde
ANGUSTIA

Fava, Stefano
BEDROOM WINDOW, THE

Felix, Maryse
LA VIE DISSOLUE DE GERARD FLOQUE

Fifer, John R.
HUNTER'S BLOOD

Fischa, Devorah
MUNCHIES

Fleet, Janine
CONCRETE ANGELS

Flora, Janet
MAKING MR.RIGHT

Floutz, Thom
EVIL SPAWN

Flowers, Sher
CLUB LIFE

Forder, Nick
HIGH SEASON

Forrest, David
ANGEL HEART
DIRTY DANCING

Forrest, David Craig
IRONWEED
O. C. AND STIGGS

Fraker, Heather
SWEET REVENGE

Frank Carrisosa
BIG SHOTS

French, Ed
CREEPSHOW 2
MUTANT HUNT

Friedin, Robert
ESCAPES

Frier, Rocky
P.K. & THE KID

Gaffney, Magdelen
WHISTLE BLOWER, THE

Germain, Michael
EXTREME PREJUDICE

Germain, Mike
FATAL BEAUTY

Gerson, Norma
ERNEST GOES TO CAMP

Gillespie, Jim
WANTED: DEAD OR ALIVE

Gonzalez, Romi
ASIGNATURA APROBADA

Gordon, Sally
GOOD WIFE, THE

Greene, Ali
JOCKS

Guedel, Barbara
GABY—A TRUE STORY

Hall, Alison
SLAUGHTER HIGH

Hall, Cleve
EVIL SPAWN

Hancock, Michael A.
NO WAY OUT

Hannig, Marce
HAPPY HOUR

Haro, Maria
PROGRAMMED TO KILL

Hay, Pat
GOTHIC
HEARTS OF FIRE

Hayney, Kevin
BELIEVERS, THE

Hemat, Asghar
MANUSCRIPTS

Henriques, Edouard F.
WEEDS

Hernandez, Juan P.
LA CASA DE BERNARDA ALBA

Hernandez, Juan Pedro
EL LUTE—CAMINA O REVIENTA

Heron, Marysue
PRETTYKILL

Hewett, Julie
WHALES OF AUGUST, THE

Hillman, Mary
MAURICE

Houdoy, Chantal
BAD BLOOD
MANUELA'S LOVES

Hunte, Ephraim
DEADTIME STORIES

Huylebroeck, Monique
LA RUMBA

Hvasta, Nancy J.
OMEGA SYNDROME

Jalemo, Agneta
MY LIFE AS A DOG

Jallali, Saeed
GOZARESH-E YEK GHATL

James-Cosburn, Katherine
RAISING ARIZONA

Jarbyn, Siw
SERPENT'S WAY, THE

Jayanta, S.
PRATIGHAAT

Jiras, Bob
ISHTAR

Johnson, Greg
STEELE JUSTICE

Joyce, J.P.
BLOODSUCKERS FROM OUTER SPACE

Kabrizi, Carla Roseto
STEELE JUSTICE

Kato, Mako
ROBINSON NO NIWA

Katsoulogiannakis, Dora
I WAS A TEENAGE ZOMBIE

Kaufman, Susan
BEST SELLER

Kay, Gordon
EAT THE RICH

Kelly, Barbara
THREE MEN AND A BABY

Kent, Irene
SUSPECT

Kent, Nina
HOT CHILD IN THE CITY
STUDENT CONFIDENTIAL

Kernyaiszky, Gabor
RIVER'S EDGE

Kindahl, Jan
GIRL, THE

King, Peter Robb
FOURTH PROTOCOL, THE

Klaudi, Inge
TOO OUTRAGEOUS

Knight, Darcy
BLOOD HOOK

Konze, Willi P.
ANITA—DANCES OF VICE

Kouroupou, A.
WIND, THE

Kraft, Nina
MOON IN SCORPIO

Kruk, Rieko
MON BEL AMOUR, MA DECHIRURE

Kunz, Gerlinde
CRIME OF HONOR

La Chapelle, Gilbert
DIRTY DANCING

Lackey, Mike
STREET TRASH

Laden, Robert
ANGEL HEART
HAPPY NEW YEAR

Lane, Brogan
LIKE FATHER, LIKE SON

Laurenti, Federico
CHRONICLE OF A DEATH FORETOLD

Laurenti, Giuliano
CHRONICLE OF A DEATH FORETOLD

Lauten, Tom
ROBOT HOLOCAUST

Lavau, Joel
MAN IN LOVE, A

Laya Saul
DIRTY LAUNDRY

Le Marinel, Paul
LA PASSION BEATRICE

Leavitt, Norman T.
BLIND DATE

Levine, Angela
MANKILLERS

Lindberg, Helena
ELVIS-KISSAN JALJILLA

Ljunggren, Dick
BLOOD TRACKS

Lloyd, Tony
JAWS: THE REVENGE

Logan, Dathryn
SPACE RACE

Loizou, Sula
OUT OF ORDER

Lucas, Tom
OUTRAGEOUS FORTUNE

Lyngsoe, Birthe
PETER VON SCHOLTEN
WOLF AT THE DOOR, THE

Marc, Daniel
HOUSE TWO: THE SECOND STORY
SUPERNATURALS, THE

Markel, Donn
FORTY DAYS OF MUSA DAGH

Martin, Manuel
CRYSTAL HEART

Mathews, Thelma
LAST OF ENGLAND, THE

Mayo, Ann
RAGE OF HONOR

Mazur, Bernadette
GARDENS OF STONE

McDowell, Tim
BLOODSUCKERS FROM OUTER SPACE

McKay, Glynn
ARIA

McKinney, Joe
FATAL BEAUTY

Mecacci, Gianfranco
GOOD MORNING BABYLON

Menzel, Karin
DER JUNGE MIT DEM GROSSEN SCHWARZEN HUND

Menzel, Uschi
ANITA—DANCES OF VICE

Mepham, Viv
STARLIGHT HOTEL

Merceder, Teresa
EQUALIZER 2000

Mills, Bob
OUTRAGEOUS FORTUNE

Mills, Robert
NADINE

Mills, Robert J.
OVER THE TOP
OVERBOARD

Mucyn, Natalie
STACKING

Mungel, Mathew
NIGHTMARE ON ELM STREET 3: DREAM WARRIORS, A

Mungle, Matthew
KINDRED, THE

Munoz, Lucrecia
GABY—A TRUE STORY

Myers, Ken
RIVER'S EDGE

Naulin, John A.
OPEN HOUSE

Navarro, Joaquin
LESCOT

Navedi, Mahein
GOZARESH-E YEK GHATL

Nellen, Thomas
JENATSCH

Newman, Phyllis
MALONE

Nieto, Toni
EL GRAN SERAFIN

Nieto, Tony
POLICIA

Nott, Carolyn
DOGS IN SPACE

Nottestad, Linda
DREAMANIAC

Nye, Ben
SPACEBALLS

Nye III, Ben
WITCHES OF EASTWICK, THE

Offers, Elaine
WINNERS TAKE ALL

Offredo, Didier
OPEN HOUSE

Olofsson-Carmback, Helena
MY LIFE AS A DOG

Palmer, Barbara
THREE MEN AND A BABY

Palmer, Carla
SQUARE DANCE

Paolocci, Francesco
BARBARIANS, THE

Paolocci, Gaetano
BARBARIANS, THE

Parker, Connie
HOME IS WHERE THE HART IS

Pearl, Dorothy
BLACK WIDOW

Pedrianna, Lisa Ann
CRYSTAL HEART

Perez, Francis
TOUGH COP
ULTIMAX FORCE

Peyrelade, Genevieve
JEUX D'ARTIFICES

Pieteman, Pam
MISSION KILL

Placks, Viven
BELLMAN AND TRUE

Posnick, Susan
RETURN OF JOSEY WALES, THE

Preston, Linda
GATE, THE

Puigcerver, Ana
LA VIDA ALEGRE

Purcell, Julie
BIG EASY, THE

Puzon, Violy
SWEET REVENGE

Quetglas, Jose
A LOS CUATRO VIENTOS

Ragozzine, Karen
SALVATION!

Ramirez, Tony
GHOST FEVER

Ranger, Irene
BOY SOLDIER

Reardon, Craig
GATE, THE

Reece, Debra
SALVATION!

Reed, Sharon Ilsen
HIDING OUT

Reiner, Susan
SLUMBER PARTY MASSACRE II

Reisman, Martha
BANZAI RUNNER

Reusch, Christ
SUMMER CAMP NIGHTMARE

Reusch, Christa
SUMMER HEAT

Reynal, Jackie
MASQUES

Robinson, Joanna
FOREVER, LULU

Rocchetti, Manlio
MAN ON FIRE

Rohani-Moghadam, Mehran
LODGERS

Rosenthal, Lynn Barber
SOMETHING SPECIAL!

Ross, Michelle
MILLION DOLLAR MYSTERY

Ross, Morag
ARIA
FRIENDSHIP'S DEATH
STRAIGHT TO HELL
WALKER

Rossi, Glauca
ARIA

Rowbottom, Amanda
BUSHFIRE MOON

Rupe, Suzana
KILLER WORKOUT

Russell, Frank
CURSE, THE

Safdari, Iraj
SHEERE SANGGY

Sammartino, Philomene
ARIA

Sarzotti, James
MATEWAN

Schneiderman, Wally
CRY FREEDOM

Schoeffel, Felicity
SLATE, WYN & ME

Schofield, Ann
HOSTAGE

Schwartz, Tom
DREAMANIAC

Schwartz, Wally
BIG SHOTS

Scott, Mickey
HELLO AGAIN

Scott, Micky
BELIEVERS, THE

Selway, Wendy
LAST OF ENGLAND, THE

Sese, Miguel
LA PLAYA DE LOS PERROS

Sforza, Fabrizio
LAST EMPEROR, THE

Sharp, Rick
BLIND DATE
SOMEONE TO WATCH OVER ME

Shawyer, Penny Delamar
ARIA
ARIA

Shircore, Jenny
ARIA
PERSONAL SERVICES
WISH YOU WERE HERE

Shorkey, Kathy
CYCLONE

Short, Sheri
EMANON
SLAMDANCE

Shostrom, Mark
EVIL DEAD 2: DEAD BY DAWN

Shostrum, Mark
NIGHTMARE ON ELM STREET 3: DREAM WARRIORS, A

Silvi, Maurizio
CHRONICLE OF A DEATH FORETOLD

Simard, Daine
BACH AND BROCCOLI

Simon, Davida
NEAR DARK

Simpson, Sancia
PERSONAL SERVICES

Slater, Cher
CANT BUY ME LOVE

Smallwood, Neville
HAMBURGER HILL

Smith, Bob
RAGE OF HONOR

Smith, Christina
OVER THE TOP

Smith, Gordon
NEAR DARK

Solovyeva, B.
DVADTSTAT DNEI BEZ

Sorel, Ferri
SUMMER CAMP NIGHTMARE

Southern, Katherine
BIG TOWN, THE

Spatola, Mike
HUNTER'S BLOOD
RETURN TO HORROR HIGH

Spector, Ronnie
PRETTYKILL

Spiers, Ann
EMPIRE STATE

Stadlinger, Horst
SERPENT'S WAY, THE

Stanley, Penelope
MONSTER IN THE CLOSET

Stein, Michael
PARTY CAMP

Stewart, Frank
PSYCHOS IN LOVE

Streipke, Dan
WHITE WATER SUMMER

Striepeke, Dan
JAWS: THE REVENGE

Sunshine, Margaret
NICE GIRLS DON'T EXPLODE

Suthers, James
BLOOD HOOK

Sutton, Sally
HELLRAISER
MORE BAD NEWS

Talplacido, Malou
GET THE TERRORISTS

Ternes, Ed
WHO'S THAT GIRL

Thompson, Claudia
ASSASSINATION

Thryion, Claudine
MASCARA

Todero, Guerino
JENATSCH

Tomlinson, Ernie
BIRDS OF PREY

Trani, Dante
SPECTERS

Trimble, Toni
WHALES OF AUGUST, THE

Van Dyk, Cheree
BLUE MONKEY

Vuarin, Danielle
GRAND GUIGNOL

Weisinger, Allen
ORPHANS

Westmore, Michael
MASTERS OF THE UNIVERSE
ROXANNE
STRIPPED TO KILL

Westmore, Monty
GARDENS OF STONE
LIKE FATHER, LIKE SON

White, Carla
ANGEL HEART

White, Douglas J.
HUNTER'S BLOOD

Wiktorson, Eva Helene
GIRL, THE

Wilder, Brad
GARDENS OF STONE

Williams, Laurie Aiello
DEADTIME STORIES

Williamson, Lizbeth
OUT OF ROSENHEIM

Yagher, Kevin
NIGHTMARE ON ELM STREET 3: DREAM WARRIORS, A

Zavyalovoi, L.
VZLOMSHCHIK

Zelop, Laura
AMAZONS

Ziem, Oliver
ANITA—DANCES OF VICE

Zoltan
MONSTER SQUAD, THE

Zurlo, Rose Marie
DATE WITH AN ANGEL

MUSIC AND LYRICS

A'Court, Mick
HIDING OUT

Abreu, Zequinha
RADIO DAYS

Achieng, Mburak
KOLORMASK

Adams, Kaylee
WHITE WATER SUMMER

Adams, Skip
MALIBU BIKINI SHOP, THE

Adams, Stanley
IRONWEED

Adamson, Barry
LAST OF ENGLAND, THE

Adamson, Harold
MISS MARY

Adamson, S.
P.I. PRIVATE INVESTIGATIONS

Agent, David
WHO'S THAT GIRL

Ager, Milton
MISS MARY

Akhtar, Javed
MISTER INDIA

Albrecht, Elmer
MISS MARY

Alda, Antony
HOT CHILD IN THE CITY

Alexander, Gregory "Popeye"
HOLLYWOOD SHUFFLE

Allman, Greg
CAMPUS MAN

Altman, Arthur
RADIO DAYS

Alvin, Dave
SOMEONE TO WATCH OVER ME

Amphlett, C.
STEPFATHER, THE

Anderson, Maxwell
RADIO DAYS

Angelo
SALVATION!

Anka, Paul
NO WAY OUT

Aplin, David
ROCK 'N' ROLL NIGHTMARE

Arkin, Eddie
PRETTY SMART

Arlen, Harold
ISHTAR

Armstrong, Ann
BLOODSUCKERS FROM OUTER SPACE

Arnheim, Gus
ANGEL HEART

Aronson, Emilie
BLOODSUCKERS FROM OUTER SPACE

Arrington, Richard
MANNEQUIN

Ash, Daniel
ALLNIGHTER, THE

Astbury, Ian
WHITE WATER SUMMER

Atteridge, Harold
PRICK UP YOUR EARS

Aznavour, Charles
BAD BLOOD

B., Andy
SALVATION!

B., Beth
SALVATION!

Bacharach, Burt
BABY BOOM

Backstrom, David
JOCKS

Badarou, W.
P.I. PRIVATE INVESTIGATIONS

Baker, Arthur
SALVATION!

Baker, M.
DIRTY DANCING

Baker, Paul
TALKING WALLS

Baldry, Long John
HOME IS WHERE THE HART IS

Barden, Rich
MILLION DOLLAR MYSTERY

Barnes, Bill
FIREHOUSE

Barnum, H.B.
BLOOD DINER

Barry, Jeff
DIRTY DANCING
FULL METAL JACKET

Barry, John
LIVING DAYLIGHTS, THE

Bartack, Craig
CLUB LIFE

Bassman, George
RADIO DAYS

Batella, Pearl
MIRACLES

Baxter, Jeff "Skunk"
ROXANNE

Beatty, Warren
ISHTAR

Beethoven, Ludwig van
IRONWEED

Bell, William
BARFLY

Benatar, Pat
SECRET OF MY SUCCESS, THE

Benavides, Filiberto
EXTREME PREJUDICE

Bergman, Boris
MASCARA

Bergner, Marcus
DOGS IN SPACE

Berlin, Irving
ISHTAR

Bernard, M.
NECROPOLIS

Bernstein, Charles
ALLNIGHTER, THE

Berry, Chuck
CONCRETE ANGELS

Bigger Splash, A
EMPIRE STATE

Birthday Party, The
DOGS IN SPACE

Bishop, Joe
MASCARA

Black, John
JOCKS

Black, Johnny S.
RADIO DAYS

Blades, Jack
SECRET OF MY SUCCESS, THE

Blake, Eubie
IN THE MOOD

Blank, Boris
EMPIRE STATE
SECRET OF MY SUCCESS, THE

Blockheads, The
MOVING TARGETS

Blood, Mick
HIDING OUT

Blum, Michael
KILLER WORKOUT

Boals, Mark
WHITE WATER SUMMER

Boddicker, Michael
WHITE WATER SUMMER

Boehm, Frank
ROCK 'N' ROLL NIGHTMARE

Bogner, Jonathan
WILD THING

Bokowski, John
FATAL BEAUTY

Bon Jovi
P.I. PRIVATE INVESTIGATIONS

Bon Jovi, Jon
SPACEBALLS

Bond, Jim
DIRTY LAUNDRY

Bonezzi, Bernardo
LAW OF DESIRE

Bongusto, Fred
LAW OF DESIRE

Bonx, Nat
RADIO DAYS

Booberg, Stan
HIDING OUT

Boston, Rick
POLICE ACADEMY 4: CITIZENS ON PATROL
ROXANNE

Bourque, Julia
GATE, THE

Bowie, David
BAD BLOOD
WHEN THE WIND BLOWS

Bradford, J.
CONCRETE ANGELS

Brady, Paul
EAT THE PEACH
P.I. PRIVATE INVESTIGATIONS

Brahe, May
PERSONAL SERVICES

Bray, Stephen
BEVERLY HILLS COP II
WHO'S THAT GIRL

Brecht, Bertolt
BIG TOWN, THE

Brooks, Jack
ISHTAR

Brooks, Mel
SPACEBALLS

Brooks, Victor
POLICE ACADEMY 4: CITIZENS ON PATROL

Brown, L. Russell
BLIND DATE

Brown, Larry
BLIND DATE
STRIPPED TO KILL

Brown, Lew
RADIO DAYS

Brown, Sheree
HOLLYWOOD SHUFFLE

Bryan, Vincent
IRONWEED

Bryant, Sam
HEARTS OF FIRE

Bryson, Tim
JOCKS

Buchner, Fern
RADIO DAYS

Bugatti, Dominic
CLUB LIFE

Bulling, Erich
DIRTY DANCING

Bullock, Jeff
STACKING

Burns, Ralph
IN THE MOOD

Burns, Sheila
ALLNIGHTER, THE

Burston, Michael
EAT THE RICH

Burton, Nat
RADIO DAYS

Butcher, Jon
BEDROOM WINDOW, THE

Butcher, Raun
BEDROOM WINDOW, THE
Byrne, David
CROSS MY HEART
Cabaret Voltaire
SALVATION!
Cabrel, Francis
BROADCAST NEWS
Caesar, Irving
ORPHANS
Caffey, Charlotte
MANNEQUIN
Cain, Jonathan
WHITE WATER SUMMER
Caine, Andy
LE SOLITAIRE
Calhoun, Charles
BIG TOWN, THE
Callan, Kelly
SLUMBER PARTY MASSACRE II
Callan, Kristi
SLUMBER PARTY MASSACRE II
Calloway, Reggie
FATAL BEAUTY
Camp, Nicki
SALVATION!
Campbell, Phillip
EAT THE RICH
Campos, Rene
HIDING OUT
Cannon, Gus
SOMEONE TO WATCH OVER ME
Carey, Julius
MALIBU BIKINI SHOP, THE
Carlucci, Vince
GATE, THE
Carmichael, Hoagy
IRONWEED
Carr, Michael
EMPIRE OF THE SUN
Carroll, Harry
PRICK UP YOUR EARS
WAITING FOR THE MOON
Cash, Johnny
BIG TOWN, THE
Catalani, Alfredo
SOMEONE TO WATCH OVER ME
Cavaliere, Felix
HIDING OUT
Cavanaugh, Neal
DIRTY DANCING
Cecil, Bruce
HOLLYWOOD SHUFFLE
Channel, Bruce
DIRTY DANCING
Charles, D.W.
P.I. PRIVATE INVESTIGATIONS
Charmaine, Jeanice
MALIBU BIKINI SHOP, THE
Charnin, Martin
ISHTAR
Chase, Gary
SUMMER CAMP NIGHTMARE
Chase, Lincoln
BIG TOWN, THE
Chung, Wang
HEARTS OF FIRE
Clapp, Sunny
ANGEL HEART
Clapton, Eric
P.I. PRIVATE INVESTIGATIONS
Clark, W.C.
BEDROOM WINDOW, THE
Cleveland, Alfred
HAMBURGER HILL
Clinton, Larry
RADIO DAYS
Close, Jon
CLUB LIFE
Cobb, Edward C.
HEARTS OF FIRE
Cobb, M.
DIRTY DANCING
Cocker, Joe
ZABOU
Cohen, David
KILLER WORKOUT
Cohen, Janice
KILLER WORKOUT
Cohen, Jeffrey
CROSS MY HEART
Cohen, Michael
HANSEL AND GRETEL
Coinman, John
SLUMBER PARTY MASSACRE II
Coles, Richard
EMPIRE STATE
Conner, Thomas
BELLMAN AND TRUE
Conrad, Con
IRONWEED
Conrad, Jack
CLUB LIFE
Conrad, P.
MASCARA
Conti, Bill
BABY BOOM
Cooler, Whey
HIDING OUT
Cooley, Eddie
BIG TOWN, THE
NEAR DARK
Cooper, Bernadette
FATAL BEAUTY
Corbetta, Jerry
MANNEQUIN
Cornwall, Hugh
WHEN THE WIND BLOWS
Cortazar, Ernesto
EXTREME PREJUDICE
Couglan
SPACE RACE
Cousins, Richard
CAMPUS MAN
Cox, P.
HOT CHILD IN THE CITY
Cox, Terry
ROXANNE
Cray, Robert
CAMPUS MAN
Crewe, B.
DIRTY DANCING
Crewe, Bob
MANNEQUIN
Cropper, Steve
BARFLY
HAMBURGER HILL
Crunk, Stewart
BLOOD DINER
Cruz, Francisco
SECRET OF MY SUCCESS, THE
Cseh, Tamas
SZORNYEK EVADJA
Cugat, Xavier
RADIO DAYS
Cumming, David
SECRET OF MY SUCCESS, THE
Cummings, Stephen
MOVING TARGETS
Curcio, E.J.
MILLION DOLLAR MYSTERY
Curiale, Joe
ROXANNE
Cutler, Scott
FATAL BEAUTY
Cymbal, John
CONCRETE ANGELS
Cymone, Andre
BEVERLY HILLS COP II
D'Andrea, John
DIRTY DANCING
Dallin
P.I. PRIVATE INVESTIGATIONS
Damerell, Stanley J.
RADIO DAYS
Daniel, Jonathan
VIDEO DEAD, THE
Darlow, Simon
HEARTS OF FIRE
Davalos, Dominique
SALVATION!
Davenport, John
BIG TOWN, THE
NEAR DARK
Davidson, Michael
WHO'S THAT GIRL
Davies, Richard
WILD THING
Davis, Benny
IRONWEED
Davis, Jimmie
WANTED: DEAD OR ALIVE
Davis, Spencer
HAMBURGER HILL
Day, Valerie
CAMPUS MAN
de Nieve, Bola
LAW OF DESIRE
De Prijck, Lou
MASCARA
Deacon, George
COMRADES
Debussy, Claude
BEST SELLER
Deitz, Howard
RADIO DAYS
DeLange, Eddie
IN THE MOOD
Delerue, Georges
SUMMER HEAT
Delibes, Leo
SOMEONE TO WATCH OVER ME
Delman, Jeffrey
DEADTIME STORIES
Delroy
BIG BANG, THE
Deming, C.
BLOOD HOOK
DeNicola, John
DIRTY DANCING
Devo
HAPPY HOUR
Dexter, Al
RADIO DAYS
Dexter, John
HEARTS OF FIRE
Dias, Allan
HIDING OUT
Dicandia, Thomas
ROCK 'N' ROLL NIGHTMARE
Dick, Nigel
P.I. PRIVATE INVESTIGATIONS
DiMucci, D.
CONCRETE ANGELS
Dokken, Don
NIGHTMARE ON ELM STREET 3: DREAM WARRIORS, A
Dominguez, A.
RADIO DAYS
Donaldson, Walter
MISS MARY
Douglas, Glen
BIG TOWN, THE
Dozier, Lamont
BEDROOM WINDOW, THE
BEST SELLER
Dragin, Robert
SUMMER CAMP NIGHTMARE
Drake, Ervin
RADIO DAYS
Drake, Milton
RADIO DAYS
Drummie, R.
HOT CHILD IN THE CITY
Dubin, Al
RADIO DAYS
DuBois, Tim
SECRET OF MY SUCCESS, THE
Duckworth, Timothy
MORGAN STEWART'S COMING HOME
Duffy, Billy
WHITE WATER SUMMER
Dukes, Kevin
BANZAI RUNNER
CRYSTAL HEART
Duncan, Darryl
POLICE ACADEMY 4: CITIZENS ON PATROL
Dunn, Donald
BARFLY
Dylan, Bob
HAMBURGER HILL
HEARTS OF FIRE
WITHNAIL AND I
Easy Action
BLOOD TRACKS
Eaton, Jimmy
RADIO DAYS

Eaton, John
BEVERLY HILLS COP II
Eaton, Steve
MALIBU BIKINI SHOP, THE
Edmonds, Lu
HIDING OUT
Edwards, Gus
IRONWEED
Eede, Nicholas
WHITE WATER SUMMER
Eliscu, Edward
RADIO DAYS
Ellington, Duke
IN THE MOOD
MISS MARY
Elliston, Kevin
HIDING OUT
Elliston, Ron
HIDING OUT
Elman, Ziggy
BIG SHOTS
England, John
BLOODSUCKERS FROM OUTER SPACE
Eno, Brian
DOGS IN SPACE
Esperon, Manuel
EXTREME PREJUDICE
Espinoza, Jose Lopez
EXTREME PREJUDICE
Espy, Mark
P.K. & THE KID
Etheridge, Melissa
WEEDS
Evans, Anthony
ANGEL HEART
Evans, Tolchard
RADIO DAYS
Everything, Eva
GATE, THE
Eyton, Frank
RADIO DAYS
Fagg, Jimmy
EAT THE RICH
Fahey
P.I. PRIVATE INVESTIGATIONS
Fahey, Siobhan
SECRET OF MY SUCCESS, THE
Fain, Sammy
RADIO DAYS
Fake, Ken
STRIPPED TO KILL
Faltermeyer, Harold
BEVERLY HILLS COP II
FATAL BEAUTY
Farren, Chris
MALIBU BIKINI SHOP, THE
Fearnley
STRAIGHT TO HELL
Ferguson, Jay
CRYSTAL HEART
Ferguson, Steve
ALLNIGHTER, THE
Fernandez, Carlo
EL DIABLO, EL SANTO Y EL TONTO
Ferran, Charlie
SALVATION!
Fields, Dorothy
MISS MARY
Finer
STRAIGHT TO HELL
Finley, John
SOMETHING SPECIAL!
Fisher, Fred
ORPHANS
Flanagan, Fiona
HEARTS OF FIRE
Flemming, George
BIG SHOTS
SOMEONE TO WATCH OVER ME
Fogerty, John C.
HEARTS OF FIRE
Ford, Butch
FIREHOUSE
Forrest, Chet
RADIO DAYS
Forsey, Keith
BEVERLY HILLS COP II
Foster, David
SECRET OF MY SUCCESS, THE

Foster, Denzil
WHO'S THAT GIRL
Frank, David
FATAL BEAUTY
Frantz, Chris
CROSS MY HEART
Fraser, Wendy
RETURN TO HORROR HIGH
Frazier, A.
FULL METAL JACKET
Frederick, Jesse
MISSION KILL
Freed, Arthur
ANGEL HEART
Freeland, Roger
BANZAI RUNNER
CRYSTAL HEART
Freeman, Denny
BLOOD DINER
Friend, Cliff
BIG TOWN, THE
Friml, Rudolph
RADIO DAYS
Frischer, Gary
SOMETHING SPECIAL!
Fryer, Terry
DIRTY DANCING
Fulton, Jack
RADIO DAYS
Funaro, Arthur
POLICE ACADEMY 4: CITIZENS ON PATROL
Futterman, Enid
HANSEL AND GRETEL
Gabriel, Peter
PROJECT X
Galas, Diamanda
LAST OF ENGLAND, THE
Gale, Billy
BIG SHOTS
Gallup, Sammy
MISS MARY
Gamson, David
WHO'S THAT GIRL
Ganem, Claude
POLICE ACADEMY 4: CITIZENS ON PATROL
Gang of Four
DOGS IN SPACE
Garland, Joe
RADIO DAYS
Garland, Joseph
IN THE MOOD
Gartside, Green
WHO'S THAT GIRL
Gaudio, B.
DIRTY DANCING
Genesis
WHEN THE WIND BLOWS
George, Lowell
ALLNIGHTER, THE
Geraldo, N.
STEPFATHER, THE
Gershwin, George
BEYOND THERAPY
SOMEONE TO WATCH OVER ME
Gershwin, Ira
BEYOND THERAPY
SOMEONE TO WATCH OVER ME
Gertz, Ron
MIRACLES
Giardi, Jimmy
FIREHOUSE
Gibson, Debbie
FATAL BEAUTY
Gideon, Steve
MUNCHIES
Gift, Roland
SOMEONE TO WATCH OVER ME
Gil, Hermanos Martinez
EXTREME PREJUDICE
Gilder-McCulloch
HOT CHILD IN THE CITY
Gill, Andy
LAST OF ENGLAND, THE
Gill, Peter
EAT THE RICH
Glass, Preston
CROSS MY HEART
Glasser, Richard
TALKING WALLS

Glenister, P.
P.I. PRIVATE INVESTIGATIONS
Glenn, Garry
POLICE ACADEMY 4: CITIZENS ON PATROL
Glover, Henry
BIG TOWN, THE
Goffin, Gerry
CONCRETE ANGELS
DATE WITH AN ANGEL
DIRTY DANCING
Goffing, Barry
WILD THING
Golde, Franne
BEVERLY HILLS COP II
MALIBU BIKINI SHOP, THE
Goldmark, Andy
HEARTS OF FIRE
PRINCIPAL, THE
Goldsmith, Joel
BANZAI RUNNER
CRYSTAL HEART
Goldstein, Bruce
MUNCHIES
Good, Larry
VIDEO DEAD, THE
Goodman, Benny
IN THE MOOD
Gordon, Bruce
ISHTAR
Gordon, J.
P.I. PRIVATE INVESTIGATIONS
Gordon, Mack
RADIO DAYS
Gordon, Paul
PRINCIPAL, THE
Gordy, Berry
CONCRETE ANGELS
DIRTY DANCING
Gould, P.
P.I. PRIVATE INVESTIGATIONS
Gould, R.
P.I. PRIVATE INVESTIGATIONS
Graf, Tom
DIRTY DANCING
Grant, J.
P.I. PRIVATE INVESTIGATIONS
Graves, John Woodcock
BELLMAN AND TRUE
Green, Eddie
ANGEL HEART
Green, John W.
RADIO DAYS
Green, Linda "Peaches"
JOCKS
Greenwich, Ellie
DIRTY DANCING
FULL METAL JACKET
Grombacher, M.
STEPFATHER, THE
Gruska, Jay
PRINCIPAL, THE
Gurley, M. Clark
ALLNIGHTER, THE
Gutierrez, Louis
ALLNIGHTER, THE
Haag, R.
MASCARA
Hackman, Paul
HEARTS OF FIRE
Hagen, Earle
BIG TOWN, THE
Hagen, Nina
LANNEE DES MEDUSES
Hairston, Jester
PERSONAL SERVICES
Hall, Ashley
MILLION DOLLAR MYSTERY
Hall, Audrey
SOMEONE TO WATCH OVER ME
Hall, Terry
HOT CHILD IN THE CITY
Hall, Tom T.
FULL METAL JACKET
Halstead, Chip
KILLER WORKOUT
Hamlin, Rose
DATE WITH AN ANGEL
Hammer, Jimmy
MANKILLERS

Hammond, Albert
DATE WITH AN ANGEL
MANNEQUIN
Hammond, Pete
WHEN THE WIND BLOWS
Harbach, Otto
SOMEONE TO WATCH OVER ME
Hard Ons, The
ALLNIGHTER, THE
Hardcastle, Paul
WHEN THE WIND BLOWS
Hargreaves, Robert
RADIO DAYS
Harper, Victoria
BLOOD HOOK
Harpham, James
HEARTS OF FIRE
Harris, D.
BLOOD HOOK
Harris, J.
FULL METAL JACKET
Harrison, Ken
NIGHTMARE ON ELM STREET 3: DREAM WARRIORS, A
Harrison, Nigel
NIGHTFORCE
Hart, Roderick
HIDING OUT
Harvey, David
CLUB LIFE
Hawkins, Frank
KILLER WORKOUT
Hawkins, Mark
MILLION DOLLAR MYSTERY
Hawks, J.P.
MASCARA
Hayen, Todd
KILLER WORKOUT
Haynes, Tony
BEDROOM WINDOW, THE
FATAL BEAUTY
Hazlewood, Lee
FULL METAL JACKET
Heckler, Robert
ALLNIGHTER, THE
Heeremans, Victor
EEN MAAND LATER
Helga Penzabene
HAMBURGER HILL
Hellberg, Niklas
HIDING OUT
Henderson, Patrick
HEARTS OF FIRE
Herman, Woody
MASCARA
Herrmann, Bernard
MORGAN STEWART'S COMING HOME
Heyman, Edward
RADIO DAYS
Hiatt, John
HEARTS OF FIRE
Hientz, Tim
KILLER WORKOUT
Hild, Robin
HIDING OUT
Hilden, S.
NECROPOLIS
Hilden, Sunny
KILLER WORKOUT
Hill, Andy
CLUB LIFE
Hill, Beau
HEARTS OF FIRE
Hill, Dan
ALLNIGHTER, THE
Hill, Mildred J.
BEDROOM WINDOW, THE
Hill, Patty S.
BEDROOM WINDOW, THE
Hodgson, Roger
WILD THING
Hoffman, Al
RADIO DAYS
Hoffman, Dustin
ISHTAR
Holding, Mark
MALIBU BIKINI SHOP, THE
Holland, Brian
BEDROOM WINDOW, THE
Holland, Edward
BEDROOM WINDOW, THE
Holley, C.
CONCRETE ANGELS
Holly, Buddy
LA BAMBA
Hood, The
SALVATION!
Hooker, James
BIG SHOTS
SOMEONE TO WATCH OVER ME
Hopkins, James
HOLLYWOOD SHUFFLE
Hornbacher, Brad
HEARTS OF FIRE
Hornsby, Bruce
WHITE WATER SUMMER
Hornsby, John
WHITE WATER SUMMER
Howard, Roland S.
DOGS IN SPACE
Howell, Kurt
POLICE ACADEMY 4: CITIZENS ON PATROL
Hoy, Marie
DOGS IN SPACE
Hucknall, Mick
CROSS MY HEART
Hughes, Steve
BLOODSUCKERS FROM OUTER SPACE
Hunter, Ivory Joe
BIG TOWN, THE
Hyman, Dick
RADIO DAYS
Hyman, Floyd
MILLION DOLLAR MYSTERY
Hynde, Chrissie
LIVING DAYLIGHTS, THE
Idol, Billy
HOT CHILD IN THE CITY
Ingber, Ira
HOT CHILD IN THE CITY
Irving, Bob
JOCKS
Isaak, Chris
MORGAN STEWART'S COMING HOME
Iyall, Deborah
VIDEO DEAD, THE
Jackson, Al
BARFLY
Jackson, Julian
BEVERLY HILLS COP II
Jackson, Liz
CRYSTAL HEART
Jackson, Randy
CRYSTAL HEART
Jackson, William
CROSS MY HEART
Jaffe, Moe
RADIO DAYS
Jagger, Mick
FULL METAL JACKET
James, Jamie
CRYSTAL HEART
James, Jimmi
HOT CHILD IN THE CITY
James, Mark
SOMEONE TO WATCH OVER ME
James, Rick
BEDROOM WINDOW, THE
James, Tim
KILLER WORKOUT
MANKILLERS
Jazz Butcher, the
SPACE RACE
Jenkins, Gordon
RADIO DAYS
Jennings, Will
DATE WITH AN ANGEL
PINOCCHIO AND THE EMPEROR OF THE NIGHT
SUMMER HEAT
Jerome, William
RADIO DAYS
Jimenez, Jose Alfredo
EXTREME PREJUDICE
Johann Sebastian Bach
GABY—A TRUE STORY
John Hoke
KILLER WORKOUT
Johnson, Steve
FIREHOUSE
Jolley
P.I. PRIVATE INVESTIGATIONS
Jolley, Steve
HEARTS OF FIRE
Jones, Booker T.
BARFLY
Jones, David Allen
BEVERLY HILLS COP II
Jones, Michael
HIDING OUT
Jordan, Stanley
BLIND DATE
Jorgensen, Clyde
P.K. & THE KID
Julian, Don
BLOOD DINER
Jurgens, Dick
MISS MARY
Juris, Larry
DEADTIME STORIES
Kaempfert, Burt
ISHTAR
Kahn, Gus
RADIO DAYS
Kairo, Judy
KOLORMASK
Kane, Gregory
HIDING OUT
Kane, Patrick
HIDING OUT
Kay, Steven
NIGHTFORCE
Kaye, Sammy
RADIO DAYS
Keane, Tom
SECRET OF MY SUCCESS, THE
Kelly, Casey
NEAR DARK
Kelly, Paul
MOVING TARGETS
Kelly, Tom
ALLNIGHTER, THE
Kendred, Mike
BEDROOM WINDOW, THE
Kennard, Phillip
JOCKS
Kennedy, Jimmy
EMPIRE OF THE SUN
Kennedy, William
IRONWEED
Kent, Jeff
ROXANNE
Kent, Walter
RADIO DAYS
Kerber, Randy
DATE WITH AN ANGEL
Kern, Jerome
SOMEONE TO WATCH OVER ME
Kerr, Richard
CLUB LIFE
Kessler, Mary
WHO'S THAT GIRL
Kilmister, Ian
EAT THE RICH
Kimball, Stu
SALVATION!
King, Carole
CONCRETE ANGELS
DATE WITH AN ANGEL
DIRTY DANCING
King, Jay
WHO'S THAT GIRL
King, M.
P.I. PRIVATE INVESTIGATIONS
Kirby, David
WILD THING
Kirk, Alan
MIRACLES
Kizilcay, Erdal
WHEN THE WIND BLOWS
Klein, Danny
MASCARA
Knight, Holly
SECRET OF MY SUCCESS, THE
Kohlman, Churchill
SOMEONE TO WATCH OVER ME
Korie, Michael
RED RIDING HOOD

Kosinski, Richard
WILD THING
Koster, Irene
MALIBU BIKINI SHOP, THE
Kowalski, Olivier
PIERRE ET DJEMILA
Kristof, Gabor
PIERRE ET DJEMILA
Kristofferson, Kris
MASCARA
Kunin, Sam
MALIBU BIKINI SHOP, THE
TALKING WALLS
Kushel, Roy
EEN MAAND LATER
L'Neire, Keith
BLIND DATE
La Bostrie, Dorothy
BIG SHOTS
La Televison, Amy
CAMPUS MAN
LaBostrie, Dorothy
DATE WITH AN ANGEL
Lacey, Fred
BARFLY
Lage, Klaus
ZABOU
Lai, Francis
DATE WITH AN ANGEL
Lamers, Elizabeth
CLUB LIFE
Landau, Michael
SECRET OF MY SUCCESS, THE
Landy, Eugene E.
POLICE ACADEMY 4: CITIZENS ON PATROL
Lauber, Ken
VIDEO DEAD, THE
Lawrence, Jack
RADIO DAYS
Lawrence, Rhet
JOCKS
Lawrence, Stephen
RED RIDING HOOD
Lawrence, Trevor
CLUB LIFE
Lecuona, Margarita
RADIO DAYS
Lee, Dino
BLOOD DINER
Legassick, Steve
CROSS MY HEART
Leiber, Jerry
BIG TOWN, THE
STRAIGHT TO HELL
Lennon, Gail
STRIPPED TO KILL
Lennon, John
CONCRETE ANGELS
PRICK UP YOUR EARS
Leonard, Patrick
WHO'S THAT GIRL
Lerner, Samuel
ORPHANS
Levay, Sylvester
FATAL BEAUTY
Levy, Jan
MALIBU BIKINI SHOP, THE
Levy, Jay
CLUB LIFE
PRETTY SMART
Lewis, Calvin
HAMBURGER HILL
Lewis, Mike
DOGS IN SPACE
Lieberman, Clyde
SPACEBALLS
Liebermann, Clyde
STRIPPED TO KILL
Liebhart, Janice
POLICE ACADEMY 4: CITIZENS ON PATROL
Liebhart, Janis
CRYSTAL HEART
Lind, Jon
PRINCIPAL, THE
Lindup, M.
P.I. PRIVATE INVESTIGATIONS
Link, Harry
EMPIRE OF THE SUN
List and the —Spikes, Ian
SPACE RACE
Livingston, Jerry
RADIO DAYS
Lloyd, Michael
DIRTY DANCING
Locorriere, Dennis
HEARTS OF FIRE
Loesser, Frank
RADIO DAYS
Logan, John Jake
SLUMBER PARTY MASSACRE II
Loov, Peter
HIDING OUT
Los Caminantes
RATAS DE LA CIUDAD
Los Panchos
LAW OF DESIRE
Love and Rockets
ALLNIGHTER, THE
Lowe, Ruth
IN THE MOOD
Lowen, Eric
POLICE ACADEMY 4: CITIZENS ON PATROL
Lubin, Joe
BIG SHOTS
DATE WITH AN ANGEL
Luciani, Marko
DIRTY DANCING
Ludwig van Beethoven
GABY—A TRUE STORY
Lunny, Donal
EAT THE PEACH
Lurie, John
BARFLY
Lussier, Chris
WINNERS TAKE ALL
Luttrelle, Mark
WHITE WATER SUMMER
Lydon, John
HIDING OUT
Lyman, Abe
ANGEL HEART
Macaluso, Lenny
SPACEBALLS
MacDonald, Ballard
WAITING FOR THE MOON
MacFayden, Sandy
GATE, THE
MacGowan
STRAIGHT TO HELL
MacManus
STRAIGHT TO HELL
Madara, J.
DIRTY DANCING
Madonna
WHO'S THAT GIRL
Maher, Brent
STACKING
Malcaluso, Lenny
MALIBU BIKINI SHOP, THE
Mallaber, Gary
PROJECT X
Mancini, Henry
BLIND DATE
Manikoff, John
MORGAN STEWART'S COMING HOME
Manilow, Barry
IN THE MOOD
Manley, Cynthia
CLUB LIFE
Mann, Barry
HAMBURGER HILL
MILLION DOLLAR MYSTERY
PINOCCHIO AND THE EMPEROR OF THE NIGHT
SUMMER HEAT
Manning, Michael
P.K. & THE KID
Manonoff, Rok
ROCK 'N' ROLL NIGHTMARE
Mantin, Mick
ESCAPES
Manuel, Marita A.
GET THE TERRORISTS
Marascalco, John
BIG TOWN, THE
Marcel, Leonard
VIDEO DEAD, THE
Marchello, Peppi
ROCK 'N' ROLL NIGHTMARE
Marcial, Robert
SECRET OF MY SUCCESS, THE
Maresca, E.
CONCRETE ANGELS
Marinelli, Anthony
PINOCCHIO AND THE EMPEROR OF THE NIGHT
Mark
HEARTS OF FIRE
Mark, John
HEARTS OF FIRE
Markowitz, Don
DIRTY DANCING
Marks, Gerald
ORPHANS
Marland, Ollie
SECRET OF MY SUCCESS, THE
Martel, Ed
STRIPPED TO KILL
Martin, Tony
WINNERS TAKE ALL
Martini, Jean Paul
BEST SELLER
Marvell, Holt
EMPIRE OF THE SUN
Marx, Richard
NO WAY OUT
Maschwitz, Eric
EMPIRE OF THE SUN
Maslin, Harry
POLICE ACADEMY 4: CITIZENS ON PATROL
Maslon, Jimmy
BLOOD DINER
Mason, Barry
STRAIGHT TO HELL
Massey, Guy
ORPHANS
Matarazzo, Maisa
LAW OF DESIRE
May, Elaine
ISHTAR
McAlpin, Lillie
BIG TOWN, THE
McBurnie, John
STEPFATHER, THE
McCafferty, Dan
FIREHOUSE
McCartney, Paul
CONCRETE ANGELS
PRICK UP YOUR EARS
McCarty, Chris
PROJECT X
McClintock, Steve
KILLER WORKOUT
MANKILLERS
McCrary, Linda
JOCKS
McDaniel, Ellis
BIG TOWN, THE
McDaniels, Khris
SECRET OF MY SUCCESS, THE
McDonald, Joe
HAMBURGER HILL
McDonald, Michael
NO WAY OUT
McDonald, Pat
ALLNIGHTER, THE
CAMPUS MAN
McElbone
P.I. PRIVATE INVESTIGATIONS
McElroy, Thomas
WHO'S THAT GIRL
McEntee, M.
STEPFATHER, THE
McGeoch, John
HIDING OUT
McGhee, Brownie
ANGEL HEART
McGilpin, Bob
KILLER WORKOUT
McHugh, David
JOCKS
SOMETHING SPECIAL!
McHugh, Jimmy
MISS MARY
RADIO DAYS
McKinnis, Mark
STRIPPED TO KILL
McMahon, Kevin
VIDEO DEAD, THE
McNabb, Robert Ian
DATE WITH AN ANGEL

McTeague, Bert
BANZAI RUNNER

Meacham, F.W.
RADIO DAYS

Medley, P.
CONCRETE ANGELS

Meier, Dieter
EMPIRE STATE
SECRET OF MY SUCCESS, THE

Melnick, Peter R.
ROXANNE

Melson, Joe
HIDING OUT

Melton, John
KILLER WORKOUT

Men Without Hats
DATE WITH AN ANGEL

Mendosa, Lydia
EXTREME PREJUDICE

Mercer, Frederic
WHO'S THAT GIRL

Mercer, Johnny
BIG SHOTS
IN THE MOOD
ISHTAR

Merrill, George
BLIND DATE

Michael, George
BEVERLY HILLS COP II

Michaels, Robert
DIRTY LAUNDRY
KILLER WORKOUT

Midler, Bette
IN THE MOOD

Mierop, Jack
BANZAI RUNNER

Miller, Harvey
OVERBOARD

Mills, Irving
BIG TOWN, THE
IN THE MOOD

Mimms, Cornelius
FATAL BEAUTY

Mitchell, Charles
WANTED: DEAD OR ALIVE

Mitchell, Charlie
WHITE WATER SUMMER

Mitchell, Clay
JOCKS

Mitchell, Daniel
TURNAROUND

Mockler, Robert
MALIBU BIKINI SHOP, THE

Modell, John
WILD THING

Monagan, Michael
SLUMBER PARTY MASSACRE II

Monge, Jesus
EXTREME PREJUDICE

Monroe, Charlie
RAISING ARIZONA

Moon, Guy
WILD THING

Moore, Fleecie
IN THE MOOD

Moore, Lattie
BIG TOWN, THE

Moraz, Patrick
STEPFATHER, THE

More, Andd
HOT CHILD IN THE CITY

Moroder, Giorgio
OVER THE TOP

Morodor, Giorgio
BEVERLY HILLS COP II

Mosimann
SALVATION!

Moss, Neil
CROSS MY HEART

Moten, Bennie
MISS MARY

Moten, Buster
MISS MARY

Motola, George
BIG TOWN, THE

Mugrage, Michael
HIDING OUT

Mundi, Coati
WHO'S THAT GIRL

Munro, Murray
P.I. PRIVATE INVESTIGATIONS

Murphy, Kevin
BLOOD HOOK

Murphy, Mic
FATAL BEAUTY

Murray, A.
P.I. PRIVATE INVESTIGATIONS

Murray, Tony
MOVING TARGETS

Musker, Frank
CLUB LIFE

Mussorgsky
STRAIGHT TO HELL

Musumarra, Romano
MON BEL AMOUR, MA DECHIRURE

Myers, Stanley
PRICK UP YOUR EARS

Myhill, Richard
PRICK UP YOUR EARS

Naunas, Thomas A.
BLOOD HOOK

Navarro, Dan
POLICE ACADEMY 4: CITIZENS ON PATROL

Nead, Jeff
SECRET OF MY SUCCESS, THE

Neeley, Ted
SUMMER CAMP NIGHTMARE

Neil, Chris
ALLNIGHTER, THE

Neiman, Jeff
CRYSTAL HEART

Nelson, Dennis
BEDROOM WINDOW, THE

Never, Linda
FATAL BEAUTY

Nevil, Robbie
MALIBU BIKINI SHOP, THE

Neville, Art
HEARTS OF FIRE

Neville, Cyril
HEARTS OF FIRE

New Order
EMPIRE STATE
SALVATION!

Newborn, Ira
SECRET OF MY SUCCESS, THE

Nicklaus, Randy
BANZAI RUNNER

Niehaus, Lennie
EMANON

No Prisoners
DATE WITH AN ANGEL

Noble, Ray
SOMEONE TO WATCH OVER ME

Norman, Monty
LIVING DAYLIGHTS, THE

Not So Not So
ESCAPES

O'Connor, Chris
SPACE RACE

O'Connor, Morris
HOLLYWOOD SHUFFLE

O'Hagan, Sean
SPACE RACE

O'Holmes, Wayne
STABILIZER, THE

O'Kennedy, John
STRIPPED TO KILL

Ocasek, "Ric"
DATE WITH AN ANGEL

Oehlen, Albert
LAST OF ENGLAND, THE

Oliveira, Aloysio
RADIO DAYS

Oliver, Sy
RADIO DAYS

Olsen, Ollie
DOGS IN SPACE

Orbison, Roy
HIDING OUT

Orzabal, R.
P.I. PRIVATE INVESTIGATIONS

Pace, Natalie
DATE WITH AN ANGEL

Pain, Duncan
MALIBU BIKINI SHOP, THE

Palmer, Robert
BEDROOM WINDOW, THE

Pardee, Rudy
POLICE ACADEMY 4: CITIZENS ON PATROL

Parish, Mitchell
IN THE MOOD
MISS MARY

Parker, John Lewis
MILLION DOLLAR MYSTERY

Parks, Van Dyke
BRAVE LITTLE TOASTER, THE

Parr, John
NEAR DARK

Parris, F.
DIRTY DANCING

Parro, Gilberto
EXTREME PREJUDICE

Parsons, Steve
EMPIRE STATE

Paul, Dorothy
EMANON

Payne, Harold
BEVERLY HILLS COP II

Payne, Robert
CAMPUS MAN

Peck, Danny
SECRET OF MY SUCCESS, THE

Penn, Peter
WILD THING

Penniman, Richard
BIG SHOTS
DATE WITH AN ANGEL

Penzabene, Carl
HAMBURGER HILL

Penzabene, Rodger
HAMBURGER HILL

Perez, Lou
DIRTY DANCING

Perkins, Frank
MISS MARY

Perry, Steve
WHITE WATER SUMMER

Person, Michael
POLICE ACADEMY 4: CITIZENS ON PATROL

Pescetto, Jeff
SPACEBALLS

Pesco, Paul
ROXANNE

Peter H. Schless
OVER THE TOP

Peterson, Randy
WINNERS TAKE ALL

Petty, N.
CONCRETE ANGELS

Pierce, Tony
BEVERLY HILLS COP II

Pizzulo, Joe
BANZAI RUNNER

Policarpop Calle
GABY—A TRUE STORY

Pomerantz, Susan
MALIBU BIKINI SHOP, THE

Pop, Iggy
DOGS IN SPACE

Porter, Cole
RADIO DAYS

Previte, Frankie
DIRTY DANCING

Price, Steve
ROCK 'N' ROLL NIGHTMARE

Price, Tommy
ALLNIGHTER, THE

Primitive Calculators, The
DOGS IN SPACE

Puente, Tito
SECRET OF MY SUCCESS, THE

Rabinowitsk, Stuart
VIDEO DEAD, THE

Radlayer, Dan
KILLER WORKOUT

Rafelson, Peter
BLACK WIDOW
CAMPUS MAN

Ragland, Robert O.
MOON IN SCORPIO

Ramel, Povel
MY LIFE AS A DOG

Raney, Joel
MUNCHIES

Rankin
STRAIGHT TO HELL

Ray, Brian
CROSS MY HEART

Ray, Greg
LADIES OF THE LOTUS

Razaf, Andy
IN THE MOOD

Redding, Otis
ALLNIGHTER, THE
DIRTY DANCING
HAMBURGER HILL

Reed, Les
STRAIGHT TO HELL

Reed, Lou
HOT CHILD IN THE CITY

Reed, Ronnie
P.K. & THE KID

Rehak, Rambeau
CONCRETE ANGELS

Reid, Don
RADIO DAYS

Renzetti, Joseph
WANTED: DEAD OR ALIVE

Rew, Kimberley
SECRET OF MY SUCCESS, THE

Reyes, Tomas Ponce
EXTREME PREJUDICE

Rheault, Michael
LADIES OF THE LOTUS

Richards, Deke
WINNERS TAKE ALL

Richards, Keith
FULL METAL JACKET

Riddle, Ron
ALLNIGHTER, THE

Riely, Tim
MILLION DOLLAR MYSTERY

Riley, Melvin
BEVERLY HILLS COP II

Rimsky-Korsakoff, N.A.
RADIO DAYS

Rio, Chuck
DOGS IN SPACE

Riopelle, Jerry
BANZAI RUNNER

Rist, Robbie
DIRTY LAUNDRY

Rivaud, Michel
BACH AND BROCCOLI

Robert, Dr.
POLICE ACADEMY 4: CITIZENS ON PATROL

Roberts, Bruce
PRINCIPAL, THE

Robertson, B.A.
ALLNIGHTER, THE

Robertson, Baxter
CRYSTAL HEART

Robinson, J. Russel
IRONWEED

Robinson, Phil Alden
IN THE MOOD

Robinson, S.
DIRTY DANCING

Robinson, William
HAMBURGER HILL
MANNEQUIN

Rodewald, Heidi
SLUMBER PARTY MASSACRE II

Rodriguez, Matos
RADIO DAYS

Rollot, Maurice
PIERRE ET DJEMILA

Ropelle, Jerry
CRYSTAL HEART

Rose, Bob
NIGHTFORCE

Rosen, Jenni
DIRTY LAUNDRY

Roundtree, Huey
BLOOD DINER

Rubalcava, Alfred
CAMPUS MAN

Ruben, Andy
STRIPPED TO KILL

Rubenhold, Leon
WINNERS TAKE ALL

Rubicam, Shannon
BLIND DATE

Rudolph, Dick
CAMPUS MAN

Ruff, Barry
JOCKS

Ruff, Renee
JOCKS

Rushen, Patrice
HOLLYWOOD SHUFFLE

Russel, B.
CONCRETE ANGELS

Russell, B.
DIRTY DANCING

Russell, Bob
MISS MARY

Russell, Louis
MALIBU BIKINI SHOP, THE

Russell, Robert
MALIBU BIKINI SHOP, THE

Russell, S.K.
RADIO DAYS

Russio, David
STRIPPED TO KILL

Rutherford, Mike
ALLNIGHTER, THE

Sabu, Paul
MILLION DOLLAR MYSTERY

Sager, Carole Bayer
BABY BOOM

Sambora, R.
P.I. PRIVATE INVESTIGATIONS

Sambora, Richie
SPACEBALLS

Sampson, Edgar
IN THE MOOD

Samudio, Domingo
FULL METAL JACKET

Sanchez, David
HIDING OUT

Sandoval, Miguel
STRAIGHT TO HELL

Sanford, Ed
LETS GET HARRY

Santiago Jimenez
GABY—A TRUE STORY

Scher, Richard
SALVATION!

Schilling, Gregory Lee
SLUMBER PARTY MASSACRE II

Schloss, Zander
STRAIGHT TO HELL

Schmit, Timothy B.
LETS GET HARRY

Schon, Neil
WHITE WATER SUMMER

Schwartz, Arthur
RADIO DAYS

Schwartz, Jean
RADIO DAYS

Scola, Mark
DIRTY DANCING

Scott, Steven
ROCK 'N' ROLL NIGHTMARE

Sebastian, John
CARE BEARS ADVENTURE IN WONDERLAND, THE

Seeger, Pete
RAISING ARIZONA

Seger, Bob
BEVERLY HILLS COP II

Seitz, Jeff
BLOOD HOOK

Sejavka, Sam
DOGS IN SPACE

Self, Ronnie
BIG TOWN, THE

Sembello, Danny
CAMPUS MAN
FATAL BEAUTY
HIDING OUT

Sembello, Michael
CAMPUS MAN
CLUB LIFE

Sepack, David
CRYSTAL HEART

Serradell, Narciso
EXTREME PREJUDICE

Sexton, Charlie
BEVERLY HILLS COP II

Shaddick, Terry
CLUB LIFE
MALIBU BIKINI SHOP, THE
PRETTY SMART

Shand, Terry
RADIO DAYS

Sheridan Steve —Diamond, Sue
HEARTS OF FIRE

Sherman, Sandy
POLICE ACADEMY 4: CITIZENS ON PATROL

Sherwin, Manning
EMPIRE OF THE SUN

Shifrin, Sue
MALIBU BIKINI SHOP, THE

Silencers, The
MORGAN STEWART'S COMING HOME

Silva, P.
NECROPOLIS

Silverstein, Shel
HEARTS OF FIRE

Simmons, P.
NEAR DARK

Simon, Paul
ISHTAR

Simon, Zoltan
SZORNYEK EVADJA

Singer, Lou
MASCARA

Singleton, Charles
ISHTAR

Skelrou, Gloria
MALIBU BIKINI SHOP, THE

Skinner
P.I. PRIVATE INVESTIGATIONS

Sklerov, Gloria
SPACEBALLS

Slamer, Mike
WHITE WATER SUMMER

Slick, Grace
WILD THING

Slider, Dan
MIRACLES

Smeaton, Bruce
ROXANNE

Smith, Bruce
HIDING OUT

Smith, E.
DIRTY DANCING

Smith, Jimmy
BARFLY

Smith, John
CAMPUS MAN

Smith, Sterling E.
SLUMBER PARTY MASSACRE II

Snyder, Eddie
ISHTAR

Solomen, Elliot
STABILIZER, THE

Solomon, Elliot
ROCK 'N' ROLL NIGHTMARE

Solomon, Maribeth
CARE BEARS ADVENTURE IN WONDERLAND, THE

Somerville, Jimmy
EMPIRE STATE

Souchon, Alain
COMEDY!

Sour, Robert
RADIO DAYS

Spaniola, Gary
BEVERLY HILLS COP II

Spector, Phil
DIRTY DANCING
FULL METAL JACKET

Springsteen, Bruce
LIGHT OF DAY

Spykes, Ken
SPACE RACE

Squeeze
WHEN THE WIND BLOWS

St. James, John
CRYSTAL HEART

Stallone, Frank
OVER THE TOP

Stanley
P.I. PRIVATE INVESTIGATIONS

Starling, Jade
HIDING OUT

Steele, David
SOMEONE TO WATCH OVER ME

Steinberg, Billy
ALLNIGHTER, THE

Steiner, Fred
DATE WITH AN ANGEL

Steiner, Max
ORPHANS
Steinman, J.
NECROPOLIS
Steinman, Joe
KILLER WORKOUT
Stepheen, Ian
MOVING TARGETS
Stephens, Jeff
ALLNIGHTER, THE
SPACE RACE
Stevens, Steve
HOT CHILD IN THE CITY
Stillman, Al
RADIO DAYS
Stoeber, Orville
WEEDS
Stokes, Simon
WANTED: DEAD OR ALIVE
Stoller, Mike
BIG TOWN, THE
STRAIGHT TO HELL
Stone, Steve
MILLION DOLLAR MYSTERY
Stothart, Herbert
RADIO DAYS
Stowell, Jim
MIRACLES
Strachey, Jack
EMPIRE OF THE SUN
Straigis, Roy
CROSS MY HEART
Straughter, David
MALIBU BIKINI SHOP, THE
Straughter, Ernest
MALIBU BIKINI SHOP, THE
Strauss, John
ISHTAR
Strayhorn, Billy
IN THE MOOD
RADIO DAYS
Strong, Barrett
HAMBURGER HILL
Strouse, Charles
ISHTAR
Strowman, William D.
HIDING OUT
Strummer, Joe
STRAIGHT TO HELL
Stuart, Mike
POLICE ACADEMY 4: CITIZENS ON PATROL
Styne, Jule
RADIO DAYS
Sulton, Kasim
ALLNIGHTER, THE
Summers, Bob
MALIBU BIKINI SHOP, THE
Summers, Penny
MALIBU BIKINI SHOP, THE
Surfaris, The
DIRTY DANCING
MORGAN STEWART'S COMING HOME
Svensson, Benkt
HIDING OUT
Swain
P.I. PRIVATE INVESTIGATIONS
Swain, Tony
HEARTS OF FIRE
Swayze, Patrick
DIRTY DANCING
Swing, The
ISHTAR
Sykes, Steve
STRIPPED TO KILL
Szelugia, Rick
CAMPUS MAN
Tafel, Carl
GATE, THE
Tarczon, Phil
BANZAI RUNNER
Tavani, Stephen
JOCKS
Taylor, Chip
WILD THING
Taylor, Gary
POLICE ACADEMY 4: CITIZENS ON PATROL
Taylor, Helen
PERSONAL SERVICES
Terry, Mark
MIRACLES
Thibault, Fabienne
BACH AND BROCCOLI
Thompson, Mayo
LAST OF ENGLAND, THE
Thompson, Michael
KILLER WORKOUT
Thor, Jon-Mikl
ROCK 'N' ROLL NIGHTMARE
Thornton, James
IRONWEED
Throckmorten, Sonny
NEAR DARK
Thrush and the C . . . s
DOGS IN SPACE
Tilbrook, Glenn
WHEN THE WIND BLOWS
Tillis, Mel
HAMBURGER HILL
Tim, Doug
WINNERS TAKE ALL
Toby, Doug
SUMMER CAMP NIGHTMARE
Tonin, John
ROCK 'N' ROLL NIGHTMARE
Tony Romeo
GABY—A TRUE STORY
Townsend, Robert
HOLLYWOOD SHUFFLE
Travers
P.I. PRIVATE INVESTIGATIONS
Tyler, Kim
CLUB LIFE
Tyrell, Stephanie
MILLION DOLLAR MYSTERY
Tyrell, Steve
MILLION DOLLAR MYSTERY
PINOCCHIO AND THE EMPEROR OF THE NIGHT
Ure, Midge
TURNAROUND
Usher, Gary
POLICE ACADEMY 4: CITIZENS ON PATROL
Valens, Ritchie
LA BAMBA
van Donselaar, Rob
EEN MAAND LATER
Van Holme, S.
MASCARA
Van Holmen
BIG BANG, THE
Vangelis
SOMEONE TO WATCH OVER ME
Vera, Billy
BLIND DATE
Vian, Boris
BAD BLOOD
Ving, Lee
SUMMER CAMP NIGHTMARE
Vysotsky, Vladimir
INTERVENTSIA
Waaktaar, Pal
LIVING DAYLIGHTS, THE
Waits, Tom
IRONWEED
Walden, Narada Michael
CROSS MY HEART
Walker, Dennis
CAMPUS MAN
Waller, Paul
SECRET OF MY SUCCESS, THE
Walter, J.
BAD BLOOD
Ward, Roy
WHITE WATER SUMMER
Ward, Wayne
WILD THING
Warren, Diane
MANNEQUIN
Warren, Harry
ISHTAR
RADIO DAYS
Warwick, Steve
HEARTS OF FIRE
Was, David
P.I. PRIVATE INVESTIGATIONS
Was, Ron
P.I. PRIVATE INVESTIGATIONS
Washington, Ned
RADIO DAYS
Waters, Roger
WHEN THE WIND BLOWS
Weatherly, Jim
BROADCAST NEWS
Webb, Chick
IN THE MOOD
Wechter, Julius
BEVERLY HILLS COP II
Weidlin, Jane
HOT CHILD IN THE CITY
Weil, Cynthia
FATAL BEAUTY
HAMBURGER HILL
Weill, Kurt
BIG TOWN, THE
RADIO DAYS
Weinmaster, Collin
LADIES OF THE LOTUS
Weir, Larry
RETURN TO HORROR HIGH
Weller, Paul
BUSINESS AS USUAL
Wells, Jo
MILLION DOLLAR MYSTERY
White, C.
FULL METAL JACKET
White, D.
DIRTY DANCING
White, Ronald
MANNEQUIN
Whitehead, J.
BLOOD HOOK
Whitfield, Norman
HAMBURGER HILL
Whitlock, Tom
BEVERLY HILLS COP II
FATAL BEAUTY
OVER THE TOP
Whyle, Mike
CAMPUS MAN
Widelitz, Stacy
DIRTY DANCING
RETURN TO HORROR HIGH
Wilde, Danny
BEDROOM WINDOW, THE
Wilk, Scott
BEVERLY HILLS COP II
FATAL BEAUTY
Willard, Patrik
HIDING OUT
William, David
CAMPUS MAN
Williams, Clarence
ANGEL HEART
Williams, Dootsie
BLOOD DINER
Williams, George
CROSS MY HEART
Williams, John
SECRET OF MY SUCCESS, THE
Williams, Larry
HIDING OUT
Williams, Maurice
DIRTY DANCING
ISHTAR
Williams, Paul
ISHTAR
Williamson, Sonny Boy
BARFLY
Willis, Allee
BEVERLY HILLS COP II
HIDING OUT
Willis, Chuck
BIG TOWN, THE
Willson, Meredith
RADIO DAYS
Wilson, Brian
BIG BANG, THE
POLICE ACADEMY 4: CITIZENS ON PATROL
Wilson, Joey
WHO'S THAT GIRL
Wilson, T.
FULL METAL JACKET
Wilson, Terry
JOCKS
Winans, Sam
DIRTY LAUNDRY
Winn, Anona
SOMEONE TO WATCH OVER ME

Winwood, Muff
HAMBURGER HILL

Winwood, Steve
BIG SHOTS
DATE WITH AN ANGEL
HAMBURGER HILL
SOMEONE TO WATCH OVER ME

Wirrick, James
BEVERLY HILLS COP II

Wisniak, Alain
LANNEE DES MEDUSES

Wong, James
PEKING OPERA BLUES

Woods, H.
SOMEONE TO WATCH OVER ME

Woods, Marcia
MOON IN SCORPIO

Woodward
P.I. PRIVATE INVESTIGATIONS

Woody, D.
NEAR DARK

Woolley, Bruce
HEARTS OF FIRE

Wray, Brad
BLOOD HOOK

Wright, Andrew
HAMBURGER HILL

Wright, Bob
RADIO DAYS

Wul, Dan
STRAIGHT TO HELL

Wyn, Steve
SPACE RACE

Yellen, Jack
MISS MARY

Youmans, Vincent
RADIO DAYS

Young, Neil
HEARTS OF FIRE
MADE IN HEAVEN

Zappacosta, Alfie
DIRTY DANCING

Zimmerman, Charles
HIDING OUT

Zuckerman, Andy
BANZAI RUNNER

Williams, Spencer
ANGEL HEART

MUSIC DIRECTORS

Achacoso, Edward
EQUALIZER 2000

Benitez, Jellybean
PRINCIPAL, THE

Benson, Kevin
MY DEMON LOVER

Bocci, Tom
BLIND DATE

Bogner, Jonathan Scott
SLAVE GIRLS FROM BEYOND INFINITY

Brien, Jeb
SECRET OF MY SUCCESS, THE

Bunetta, Al
BLIND DATE

Burns, Ralph
IN THE MOOD

Carr, Budd
BEST SELLER

Courage, Alexander
SUPERMAN IV: THE QUEST FOR PEACE

Cruz, Willie
ULTIMAX FORCE

Davis, Carl
CRIME OF HONOR

De Melis, Enrico
CHRONICLE OF A DEATH FORETOLD

Erickson, Paula
ASSASSINATION
OVER THE TOP

Fenton, George
CRY FREEDOM
WHITE OF THE EYE

Folk, Robert
CANT BUY ME LOVE

Ganot, Michel
MASQUES

Garcia Abril, Anton
ROMANCA FINAL

Great, Don
DREAMANIAC

Harle, John
PRICK UP YOUR EARS

Henze, Hans Werner
COMRADES

Hill, Beau
HEARTS OF FIRE

Holzkamp, Jens
KONZERT FUR DIE RECHTE HAND

Hyman, Dick
RADIO DAYS

Ives, Ralph
CRY WILDERNESS

Manuel, Marita
EYE OF THE EAGLE
HOSTAGE SYNDROME

Manuel, Marita A.
GET THE TERRORISTS

Martin, Peter
HOPE AND GLORY

Massara, Natale
MORO AFFAIR, THE

Matsui, Kazu
TOKYO BLACKOUT

May, Brian
DEATH BEFORE DISHONOR

Mendez, Fernando
SINVERGUENZA . . . PERO HONRADO

Milano, Tom
DREAMANIAC
MUTANT HUNT

Moores, Philip
CLUB LIFE

Mottola, Tommy
SECRET OF MY SUCCESS, THE

Olsen, Ollie
DOGS IN SPACE

Osborn, Jason
HIGH SEASON

Perry, Don
MALIBU BIKINI SHOP, THE

Petit, Jean-Claude
JEAN DE FLORETTE

Roebuck, Bill
OVERKILL

Sanvoisin, Michel
LITTLE DORRIT

Scheimer, Erika
PINOCCHIO AND THE EMPEROR OF THE NIGHT

Schifrin, Lalo
FOURTH PROTOCOL, THE

Scott, John
MAN ON FIRE
WHISTLE BLOWER, THE

Snell, David
PERSONAL SERVICES

Tanigawa, Kensaku
PRINCESS FROM THE MOON

Thomas, Michael Tilson
DANCERS

Tyrell, Steve
NIGHT STALKER, THE

Vergara, Rogelio
RETO A LA VIDA

Wadsworth, Derek
WHALES OF AUGUST, THE

Williams, John
WITCHES OF EASTWICK, THE

Williams, Ray
LAST EMPEROR, THE
WHEN THE WIND BLOWS

Wilson, Alan
BELLMAN AND TRUE

Witt, Paul Francis
HELLRAISER

PRODUCERS

Abeille, Claude
SOUS LE SOLEIL DE SATAN
TRAVELLING AVANT

Abrams, Peter
KILLING TIME, THE

Abusaid, Juan
EL MOFLES Y LOS MECANICOS

Adams, Tony
BLIND DATE

Adarsh, B.K.
DAKU HASINA

Adelson, Gary
IN THE MOOD

Adlon, Eleonore
OUT OF ROSENHEIM

Adlon, Percy
OUT OF ROSENHEIM

Agosti, Silvano
QUARTIERE

Agrasanchez, David
ALBURES MEXICANOS
LA FUGA DE CARRASCO

Albakri, Zarul
BEJALAI

Alexakis, Costas
SWEET COUNTRY

Alexander Kluge
VERMISCHTE NACHRICHTEN

Ali, Muzaffar
ANJUMAN

Almanza, Naty A.
COMMANDER LAMIN

Alschuler, Melanie J.
PRETTY SMART

Altman, Robert
O. C. AND STIGGS

Alvarez, Carlos
MUJERES DE LA FRONTERA

Alveberg, Dag
ETTER RUBICON

Alward, Jennifer
HEARTS OF FIRE

Amateau, Rod
GARBAGE PAIL KIDS MOVIE, THE

Amiel, Alan
COMMANDO SQUAD
MOON IN SCORPIO

Amigo, Angel
A LOS CUATRO VIENTOS

Amir, Ami
KFAFOT

Amir, Gideon
SURVIVAL GAME

Anand, Gul
JALWA

Andersen, Hans Christian
SNOW QUEEN, THE

Angeletti, Pio
TERESA

Ansara, Martha
PURSUIT OF HAPPINESS, THE

Appelbaum, Lawrence
SILENT NIGHT, DEADLY NIGHT PART II

Appleby, Basil
RIGHT HAND MAN, THE

Apuzzo, Carla
REGINA

Arcady, Alexandre
LETE DERNIER A TANGER

Argento, Claudio
DISTANT LIGHTS

Arnaud, Jacques
AVRIL BRISE

Assonitis, Ovidio G.
CURSE, THE

Attenborough, Sir Richard
CRY FREEDOM

Attew, Kevin
RAWHEAD REX

Aured, Carlos
ALIEN PREDATOR

Avdeliodis, Demos
TREE WE HURT, THE

Avila, Ricardo
DE TAL PEDRO, TAL ASTILLA

Avnet, Jon
LESS THAN ZERO

Axelrod, David
FLICKS

Azriely, Smadar
TEL AVIV—BERLIN

B., Beth
SALVATION!

Babenco, Hector
BESAME MUCHO

Badalato, Bill
WEEDS

Bagdasarian, Ross
CHIPMUNK ADVENTURE, THE
Balachander, K.
THIRUMATHI ORU VEGUMATHI
Balamir, Hakan
DILAN
Balasubramaniam, M.
SAMSARAM OKA CHADARANGAM
Balian, Haig
TERUG NAAR OEGSTGEEST
Ball, David
CREEPSHOW 2
Ballantyne, Jane
INITIATION
Ballew, Jerry
CAUGHT
Balsan, Humbert
LHOMME VOILE
Barbagallo, Angelo
NOTTE ITALIANA
Barbault, Armand
MAN IN LOVE, A
Barish, Keith
IRONWEED
LIGHT OF DAY
Barragan, Miguel Angel
ARQUIESTA EMILIO VARELA
Barrajas, Salvador
CINCO NACOS ASALTAN A LAS VEGAS
Barrera, Victor
LOS INVITADOS
Barreto, L.C.
ELE, O BOTO
Barrett, Eric
SPACE RACE
Bart, Peter
REVENGE OF THE NERDS II: NERDS IN PARADISE
Bateman, Kent
TEEN WOLF TOO
Beatty, Warren
ISHTAR
Bechard, Gorman
PSYCHOS IN LOVE
Begun, Jeff
PRETTY SMART
Beilby, Peter
BUSHFIRE MOON
Bellina, Lionel
ACCROCHE-COEUR
Belmondo, Alain
LE SOLITAIRE
Belmont, Vera
F . . . ING FERNAND
Bendico, Silvia D'Amico
DARK EYES
Benn, Harry
GOOD MORNING, VIETNAM
Bennett, Bill
DEAR CARDHOLDER
JILTED
Benson, Jay
STEPFATHER, THE
Berardi, Mauro
HOTEL COLONIAL
MORO AFFAIR, THE
Bergendahl, Waldemar
LEIF
MORE ABOUT THE CHILDREN OF BULLERBY VILLAGE
MY LIFE AS A DOG
Bergendal, Waldemar
JIM OCH PIRATERNA BLOM
Berger, Pamela
LA MOINE ET LA SORCIERE
Bergmann, Michel
FLYER, THE
Bergquist, Peter L.
MONSTER IN THE CLOSET
Bergstein, Eleanor
DIRTY DANCING
Berk, Daniel Jay
OPPOSING FORCE
Berkis, Luis
MATAR O MORIR
Bernard, Yannick
MON BEL AMOUR, MA DECHIRURE
Bernart, Maurice
AGENT TROUBLE
Berner, Fred
SOMETHING SPECIAL!
Bernhard, Harvey
LOST BOYS, THE
Bertolucci, Giovanni
CAPRICCIO
Betancourt, Luis Felipe
DE MUJER A MUJER
Betzer, Just
WHEELS OF TERROR
Bevan, Tim
PERSONAL SERVICES
SAMMY AND ROSIE GET LAID
Bhaskar, S.
ALLARI KRISHNAYA
Bhatt, Bhargav
MERA LAHOO
Bhattacharya, Basu
PANCHVATI
Bivens, Loren
TRESPASSES
Blatt, Daniel H.
LETS GET HARRY
Bleiberg, Ehud
HIMMO MELECH YERUSHALAIM
Blieberg, Ehud
CHOZE AHAVA
Blocker, David
MADE IN HEAVEN
Bloomgarden, John
DEAD OF WINTER
Bockner, Michael
GRAVEYARD SHIFT
PSYCHO GIRLS
Boeken, Ludi
DREAMERS
Bogayevicz, Yurek
ANNA
Bogner, Willy
FIRE AND ICE
Bokadia, K.C.
JAWAB HUM DENGE
Bolivar, Cesar
MAS ALLA DEL SILENCIO
Bonivento, Claudio
SOLDATI: 365 GIORNI ALL' ALBA
Boorman, John
HOPE AND GLORY
Borde, Mark
PARTY CAMP
Borden, Bill
LA BAMBA
Bottcher, Jurgen
LITTLE PROSECUTOR, THE
Bowey, John R.
PRETTYKILL
Boyd, Don
ARIA
LAST OF ENGLAND, THE
Bozzacchi, Gianni
I LOVE NEW YORK
Brabourne, John
LITTLE DORRIT
Branca, Maria
DAMORTIS
Branco, Paolo
UNE FLAMME DANS MON COEUR
Bregman, Martin
REAL MEN
Bresee, Frank
EVIL SPAWN
Brewster, Anthony
EVIL SPAWN
Brezner, Larry
GOOD MORNING, VIETNAM
THROW MOMMA FROM THE TRAIN
Briley, John
CRY FREEDOM
Broccoli, Albert R.
LIVING DAYLIGHTS, THE
Brock, Deborah
SLUMBER PARTY MASSACRE II
Brodek, Thomas H.
PRINCIPAL, THE
Brooks, James L.
BROADCAST NEWS
Brooks, Mel
SPACEBALLS
Brouwer, Chris
TERUG NAAR OEGSTGEEST
Brown, Andrew
PRICK UP YOUR EARS
Brown, Chris
SIESTA
Brown, G. Mac
HELLO AGAIN
Brown, Jamie
KEEPING TRACK
Bruce, James
SUICIDE CLUB, THE
Bruckheimer, Jerry
BEVERLY HILLS COP II
Bruyere, Christian
SHELLEY
Brynntrup, Michael
JESUS: DER FILM
Buddenstedt, Fritz
MASCHENKA
Bull, Stein Roger
PA STIGENDE KURS
Burghard, Tom
JULIA'S GEHEIM
Burr, William
OFFSPRING, THE
Burrell, Peter
STACKING
Burrill, Timothy
FOURTH PROTOCOL, THE
Burrowes, Geoff
RUNNING FROM THE GUNS
Burstall, Tom
SLATE, WYN & ME
Byers, Mark
STRIPPED TO KILL
Cacoyannis, Michael
SWEET COUNTRY
Calderon, Guillermo
ESTA NOCHE CENA PANCHO (DESPEDIDA DE SOLTERO)
Calderon Stell, Guillermo
NOS REIMOS DE LA MIGRA
Callender, Colin
BELLY OF AN ARCHITECT, THE
Calligari, Guillermo
LOS DUENOS DEL SILENCIO
Calloway, David
WILD THING
Camhe, Beverly
BELIEVERS, THE
Caminito, Augusto
RIMINI RIMINI
ROBA DA RICCHI
SUPERFANTOZZI
Campos, Miguel A. Perez
LAW OF DESIRE
Canton, Neil
WITCHES OF EASTWICK, THE
Carabatsos, JIm
HAMBURGER HILL
Carcassonne, Philippe
TANDEM
Cardona Jr., Rene
BEAKS
Carelli, Joann
SICILIAN, THE
Carlsen, Henning
WOLF AT THE DOOR, THE
Carlstroem, Bjorn
WARDOGS
Carmody, Don
BIG TOWN, THE
MEATBALLS III
Carvalho, Wagner
CIDADE OCULTA
Casati, Franco
DA NNUNZIO
Castello, Al
PERSONAGGI & INTERPRETI
Castillo, Oscar
EULALIA
Castravelli, Claude
REMEMBERING MEL
Cecchi Gori, Mario
I MIEI PRIMI QUARANT'ANNI
IL BURBERO
IO E MIA SORELLA
OPERA
Cecchi Gori, Vittorio
I MIEI PRIMI QUARANT'ANNI
IL BURBERO
IO E MIA SORELLA
OPERA

Chan, Betty
NINJA THUNDERBOLT
Chaney, Warren
OUTING, THE
Chang, Catherine
PRISON ON FIRE
Chang, Chiang Hsien
NINJA THUNDERBOLT
Cheung, Claudue
CHINESE GHOST STORY, A
Chi-chung, Hu
OUTSIDERS, THE
Chi-tse, Li
HEROIC PIONEERS
Childers, Michael
BELIEVERS, THE
Chilewich, M. David
SOMETHING SPECIAL!
Chitram, Parna
AMAR KANTAK
Chobocky, Barbara A.
WITCH HUNT
Chow, Raymond
CHOCOLATE INSPECTOR
Chowdhury, Pinaki
APAN GHAREY
Christensen, Bo
BABETTE'S GASTEBUD
Chung, Claudie
PEKING OPERA BLUES
Cimino, Michael
SICILIAN, THE
Cingolani, Luigi G.
OMEGA SYNDROME
Ciriaci, Pier Luigi
MESSENGER, THE
Clark, Bob
FROM THE HIP
Clark, Louise
WINTER TAN, A
Claudon, Paul
LE MOUSTACHU
Claus, Richard
PENG! DU BIST TOT!
Clausen, Finn
JAG ELSKER DIG
Cleitman, Rene
TANDEM
Clermont, Nicolas
WILD THING
Coates, John
WHEN THE WIND BLOWS
Cobe, Sandy
OPEN HOUSE
Coe, Edward
GHOST FEVER
Coen, Ethan
RAISING ARIZONA
Coggio, Roger
LE JOURNAL D'UN FOU
Cohen, Rob
LIGHT OF DAY
Colesberry, Robert L.
HOUSEKEEPING
Colgin, Russell W.
NIGHTFORCE
Committeri, Franco
FAMILY, THE
Coppola, Francis
GARDENS OF STONE
Corke, Penny
GOTHIC
Corman, Roger
BIG BAD MAMA II
MUNCHIES
Cort, Robert
CRITICAL CONDITION
REVENGE OF THE NERDS II: NERDS IN PARADISE
Cort, Robert W.
OUTRAGEOUS FORTUNE
THREE MEN AND A BABY
Cosby, Bill
LEONARD PART 6
Costa Muste, Pedro
REDONDELA
Cousineau, Gaston
MORNING MAN, THE
Cox, Penney Finkelman
BROADCAST NEWS

Crezias, George
APOUSIES
Crisman, Steve
SUICIDE CLUB, THE
Crow, Robert T.
SUMMER CAMP NIGHTMARE
Cruthers, John
WITH LOVE TO THE PERSON NEXT TO ME
Cucchi, Carlo
DARK EYES
Cunilles, Jose Maria
EL LUTE—CAMINA O REVIENTA
Cunningham, Sean S.
HOUSE TWO: THE SECOND STORY
Curtis, Doug
NICE GIRLS DON'T EXPLODE
Curtis, John A.
LADIES OF THE LOTUS
Daniel, Don
SLUMBER PARTY MASSACRE II
Dasgupta, Buddhadeb
PHERA
Dauman, Anatole
DER HIMMEL UBER BERLIN
David, Pierre
HOT PURSUIT
Davies, Robert
SATURDAY NIGHT AT THE PALACE
Davis, John
PREDATOR
Dawson, Vivienne
T. DAN SMITH
Day, Jenny
JILTED
de Anda, Gilberto
EL ANSIA DE MATAR
YO, EL EJECUTOR
de Anda, Raul
FIERAS EN BRAMA
de Anda, Rodolfo
POLICIAS DE NARCOTICOS
De Bello, John
HAPPY HOUR
de Ganay, Thierry
SOMEONE TO WATCH OVER ME
de Goldschmidt, Gilbert
LES OREILLES ENTRE LES DENTS
De Haven, Carter
BEST SELLER
De Laurentiis, Aurelio
MONTECARLO GRAN CASINO
De Laurentiis, Luigi
MONTECARLO GRAN CASINO
De Leon, Marcus
BORDER RADIO
De Micheli, Adriano
TERESA
de Montbrial, Marie-Christine
LE MOUSTACHU
De Negri, Giuliani G.
GOOD MORNING BABYLON
de Tamez, Guadalupe Viuda
HERENCIA DE VALIENTES
de Winter, Leon
LOOKING FOR EILEEN
de —Anda, Rodolfo
RATAS DE LA CIUDAD
De-Vries, Ilan
LATE SUMMER BLUES
Dear, William
HARRY AND THE HENDERSONS
DeCoteau, David
DREAMANIAC
DeCouteau, David
CREEPOZOIDS
Deddens, Heinz
KONZERT FUR DIE RECHTE HAND
Dehlavi, Jamil
BORN OF FIRE
Deimel, Mark
PERFECT MATCH, THE
Delgado, Arnulfo
TIERRA DE VALIENTES
Delgado, Guillermo Calle
VISA U.S.A.
Demers, Rock
BACH AND BROCCOLI
GREAT LAND OF SMALL, THE
LE JEUNE MAGICIEN

den Drijver, Ruud
ALS IN EEN ROES
ODYSSEE D'AMOUR
DePaula, Cynthia
ENEMY TERRITORY
MUTANT HUNT
NECROPOLIS
ROBOT HOLOCAUST
Deshingkar, Vasudev
SUTRADHAR
Devine, Zanne
ANNA
Dhanoa, Ravindra
MERA LAHOO
Di Clemente, Giovanni
I PICARI
Diaz, Philippe
PIERRE ET DJEMILA
Diego Leers, Heinz
CRAZY BOYS
Dimitri, Michele
MANUELA'S LOVES
Dimsey, Ross
WARM NIGHTS ON A SLOW MOVING TRAIN
Dixon, Ken
SLAVE GIRLS FROM BEYOND INFINITY
Djaoui, Andre
CROSS
Doctor, Shabha
ANJUMAN
Doctor, Shobha
PANCHVATI
Donner, Richard
LETHAL WEAPON
Donohue, Walter
BELLY OF AN ARCHITECT, THE
Donovan, Arlene
NADINE
Doo-yong, Lee
NAE-SHI
Downs, Clare
HIGH SEASON
Drainville, Elaine
T. DAN SMITH
Drouot, Pierre
DIARY OF A MAD OLD MAN
MASCARA
Dryhurst, Michael
HOPE AND GLORY
Ducay, Eduardo
EL BOSQUE ANIMADO
Dunning, John
MEATBALLS III
Dupont, Rene
FROM THE HIP
Duprez, Jean-Marie
LETE EN PENTE DOUCE
SALE DESTIN!
Duran, Enrique Rosales
JUNTOS
Duran, Jorge
COLOR OF DESTINY, THE
Duran, Robert Rosales
JUNTOS
Dussart, Eric
CHAMP D'HONNEUR
Duval, Claire
LES EXPLOITS DUN JEUNE DON JUAN
Dwyer, Finola
STARLIGHT HOTEL
Eadington, Dave
T. DAN SMITH
Ecare, Desire
FACES OF WOMEN
Eckert, John M.
HOME IS WHERE THE HART IS
Edmonds, Don
NIGHT STALKER, THE
Eguiraun, Luis
EL AMOR DE AHORA
Eichinger, Sabine
DER UNSICHTBARE
Elfick, David
AROUND THE WORLD IN EIGHTY WAYS
Elkerbout, Ben
DREAMERS
Elwes, Cassian
WHITE OF THE EYE
Emanuel, Phillip
THOSE DEAR DEPARTED

Eng, John
SLAVE GIRLS FROM BEYOND INFINITY

Engelberg, Mort
MAID TO ORDER
THREE FOR THE ROAD

Eran, Doron
YALDEI STALIN
YEHOSHUA—YEHOSHUA

Ergin, Cengiz
ANAYURT OTELI

Ergun, Cengiz
DEGIRMEN

Erichsen, Bente
FELDMANN CASE, THE

Erickson, C.O.
IRONWEED

Eriksen, Jacob
EPIDEMIC

Evans, Bruce A.
MADE IN HEAVEN

Everard, Barrie
LEADING EDGE, THE

Falconer, Dale
GOOFBALLS

Fanaka, Jamaa
PENITENTIARY III

Farago, Katinka
HIP, HIP, HURRA!

Fei, Ling Deng
LIEN LIEN FUNG CHEN

Feitshans, Buzz
EXTREME PREJUDICE

Fellner, Eric
STRAIGHT TO HELL

Feng, Hsu
LAONIANG GOU SAO

Fernandez, Vicente
UNA PURA Y DOS CON SAL

Field, David
AMAZING GRACE AND CHUCK

Field, Ted
CRITICAL CONDITION
OUTRAGEOUS FORTUNE
REVENGE OF THE NERDS II: NERDS IN PARADISE
THREE MEN AND A BABY

Figg, Christopher
HELLRAISER

Finnegan, William
NORTH SHORE

Finnell, Michael
INNERSPACE

Fishburn, James
FRENCHMAN'S FARM

Fisher, Mary Ann
HOUR OF THE ASSASSIN

Foldes, Lawrence D.
NIGHTFORCE

Folino, Thomas
HELLO AGAIN

Forque, Jose Maria
ROMANCA FINAL

Fowler, Peggy
CAMPUS MAN

Fraisse, Charlotte
LE BEAUF

Francis, Karl
BOY SOLDIER

Franco, Larry
PRINCE OF DARKNESS

Francois, Anne
TERMINUS

Frank, Ilana
HIGHER EDUCATION

Frappier, Roger
NIGHT ZOO

Frey, Diana
SOFIA

Fridriksson, Fridrik Thor
SKYTTURNAR

Friedman, Stephen
BIG EASY, THE
MORGAN STEWART'S COMING HOME

Friedman, Tom
DANGER ZONE, THE

Fries, Thomas
FLOWERS IN THE ATTIC

Frumkes, Roy
STREET TRASH

Frydman, Sylvette
LES MENDIANTS
SI LE SOLEIL NE REVENAIT PAS

Fuchs, Leo L.
MALONE

Fuhrer, Volker
STADTRAND

Fujii, Hiroaki
PRINCESS FROM THE MOON

Fujimoto, Kiyoshi
HOTARUGAWA
KID BROTHER, THE
SHINRAN: SHIRO MICHI

Fung, Wellington
THIRTY MILLION RUSH, THE

Fuseya, Hiro
MAGINA—MURA MONOGATARI

Gabilan, J. Fernando Perez
LAS TRAIGO . . . MUERTAS

Galante, Antonio Polo
ANJOS DO ARRABALDE

Galindo, Daniel
DELINCUENTE
UN SABADO MAS

Galindo, Jesus
EL MUERTO DEL PALOMO

Galindo, Pedro
MI NOMBRE ES GATILLO

Gamba, Sao
KOLORMASK

Gandara, Roberto
LA GRAN FIESTA

Gannage, Antoine
CHAMP D'HONNEUR

Garci, Jose Luis
ASIGNATURA APROBADA

Garcia Gardelle, Ignacio
TRAGICO TERREMOTO EN MEXICO

Garcia Sanchez, Jose Luis
MADRID

Gardelin, Rolando
CHECHECHELA—UNA CHICA DEL BARRIO

Garland, Robert
NO WAY OUT

Garrido, Pedro Martinez
EL MOFLES Y LOS MECANICOS
LA RULETERA

Garroni, Andrew
I LOVE NEW YORK

Gasser, Yves
CHRONICLE OF A DEATH FORETOLD

Gassot, Charles
AVRIL BRISE

Gauchi, John
BIT PART, THE

Gaudenzi, Franco
STRIKE COMMANDO

Gavilan, J. Fernando
RETO A LA VIDA

Gavilan, J. Fernando Perez
MAS VALE PAJARO EN MANO . . .

Gazcon, Edgardo
FIERAS EN BRAMA

Geater, Sara
BUSINESS AS USUAL

Gelin, Evelyne
TANT QU'IL AURA DES FEMMES

Gelin, Xavier
TANT QU'IL AURA DES FEMMES

Gendron, Pierre
NIGHT ZOO

Geoffray, Gerold
WITCHBOARD

Ghazal, Aziz
ZOMBIE HIGH

Ghosh, Debesh
JHOOTHI

Gideon, Raynold
MADE IN HEAVEN

Gilhuis, Mark G.
BLOODY WEDNESDAY

Gilhuis, Susan
BLOODY WEDNESDAY

Glaser, Tamar E.
OPPOSING FORCE

Globus, Yoram
ALLAN QUATERMAIN AND THE LOST CITY OF GOLD
AMERICAN NINJA 2: THE CONFRONTATION
BEAUTY AND THE BEAST
DANCERS
DOWN TWISTED
DUTCH TREAT
EMPEROR'S NEW CLOTHES, THE
HANOI HILTON, THE
HANSEL AND GRETEL
MASTERS OF THE UNIVERSE
NUMBER ONE WITH A BULLET
OVER THE TOP
RED RIDING HOOD
RUMPELSTILTSKIN
SHY PEOPLE
SLEEPING BEAUTY
SNOW WHITE
STREET SMART
SUPERMAN IV: THE QUEST FOR PEACE
TOO MUCH
TOUGH GUYS DON'T DANCE
UNDER COVER

Gloor, Luciano
DILAN
JENATSCH

Glowna, Vadim
DEVILS PARADISE, THE

Gmelin, Albrecht
KONZERT FUR DIE RECHTE HAND

Gockel, Rosy
DER TOD DES EMPEDOKLES

Goel, Jyotin
INAAM DUS HAZAAR

Golan, Menahem
ALLAN QUATERMAIN AND THE LOST CITY OF GOLD
AMERICAN NINJA 2: THE CONFRONTATION
BEAUTY AND THE BEAST
DANCERS
DOWN TWISTED
DUTCH TREAT
EMPEROR'S NEW CLOTHES, THE
HANOI HILTON, THE
HANSEL AND GRETEL
MASTERS OF THE UNIVERSE
NUMBER ONE WITH A BULLET
OVER THE TOP
RED RIDING HOOD
RUMPELSTILTSKIN
SHY PEOPLE
SLEEPING BEAUTY
SNOW WHITE
STREET SMART
SUPERMAN IV: THE QUEST FOR PEACE
TOO MUCH
TOUGH GUYS DON'T DANCE
UNDER COVER

Golin, Steven
P.I. PRIVATE INVESTIGATIONS

Gomer, Steve
SWEET LORRAINE

Gomez, Andres Vicente
YEAR OF AWAKENING, THE

Gon, Wu
OUTSIDERS, THE

Goodwin, Richard
LITTLE DORRIT

Gopalrao, Rao
BHARGAVA RAMUDU

Gopinath, M.G.
PANCHAGNI

Gordon, Lawrence
PREDATOR

Gori, Mario
VIA MONTENAPOLEONE

Gori, Mario Cecchi
NOI UOMINI DURI

Gori, Vittorio Cecchi
NOI UOMINI DURI
VIA MONTENAPOLEONE

Gottlieb, Linda
DIRTY DANCING

Grana, Sam
TRAIN OF DREAMS

Grant, Mickey
RETURN OF JOSEY WALES, THE

Grassick, Richard
T. DAN SMITH

Grau, Louis
LES MOIS D'AVRIL SONT MEURTRIERS

Graun, Jane
PETER VON SCHOLTEN

Grazer, Brian
LIKE FATHER, LIKE SON

Greene, David
VIOLINS CAME WITH THE AMERICANS, THE

Greenhut, Robert
RADIO DAYS
SEPTEMBER

Greisman, Alan
SURRENDER

Grinter, Randy
MASTERBLASTER

Grise, Pierre
ZOMBIE NIGHTMARE

Grives, Steven
RIGHT HAND MAN, THE

Groning, Philip
SOMMER

Gross, Michael C.
BIG SHOTS

Gross, Yoram
DOT GOES TO HOLLYWOOD

Grosso, Alfonso
LOS INVITADOS

Grunstein, Pierre
JEAN DE FLORETTE
MANON OF THE SPRING

Guber, Peter
WITCHES OF EASTWICK, THE

Guhan, M.S.
SAMSARAM OKA CHADARANGAM

Guissani, Roberto
MAN IN LOVE, A

Gurrido, Pedro Martin
LAPUTA: THE CASTLE IN THE SKY

Gutierrez, Luis
MADRID

Haase, Jurgen
QUATRE MAINS

Hackford, Taylor
LA BAMBA

Haft, Steven M.
BEYOND THERAPY

Hald, Peter
NAGRA SOMMARKVALLAR PA JORDEN

Hamori, Andras
GATE, THE
NOWHERE TO HIDE

Hansel, Marion
LES NOCES BARBARES

Hansen, Lisa M.
COLD STEEL

Hansen, Max
VENNER FOR ALTID

Hardie-Brown, Laurie
INDIAN SUMMER

Hare, Ellin
T. DAN SMITH

Hark, Tsui
BETTER TOMORROW, A
CHINESE GHOST STORY, A
PEKING OPERA BLUES

Harris, Burtt
GLASS MENAGERIE, THE

Hartzell, Paivi
SNOW QUEEN, THE

Harvey, Rubert
SLAMDANCE

Hausman, Michael
HOUSE OF GAMES

Hawkins, Don
RAWHEAD REX

Hayashi, Dennis
LIVING ON TOKYO TIME

Hayes, Terry
YEAR MY VOICE BROKE, THE

Haynes, Peter
BIRDS OF PREY

Heinesen, Thomas
VENNER FOR ALTID

Heller, Paul M.
WITHNAIL AND I

Heller, Rosilyn
WHO'S THAT GIRL

Hellwig, Klaus
DER TOD DES EMPEDOKLES

Helman, Geoffrey
EIGHTY FOUR CHARING CROSS ROAD

Hemingway, Mariel
SUICIDE CLUB, THE

Henchoz, Jean-Marc
LES MENDIANTS
SI LE SOLEIL NE REVENAIT PAS

Herald, Peter V.
OUTRAGEOUS FORTUNE

Herbert, David
BLOOD HOOK

Herbert, Peter
BIT PART, THE

Hermes, Leonard
EQUALIZER 2000

Hernandez, Humberto
SUCCESSFUL MAN, A

Herold, Paula
SUICIDE CLUB, THE

Heroux, Justine
LES FOUS DE BASSAN

Herrera, Guillermo
CARTUCHA CORTADA
MAS BUENAS QUE EL PAN

Herrera, Victor
CINCO NACOS ASALTAN A LAS VEGAS

Hertzberg, Paul
BULLETPROOF
CYCLONE

Heumann, Eric
NOYADE INTERDITE

Heyman, Norma
EMPIRE STATE

Heyns, Thys
HOSTAGE

Hill, Debra
ADVENTURES IN BABYSITTING

Hinsch, Jorgen
PETER VON SCHOLTEN

Hirsh, Michael
BURGLAR
CARE BEARS ADVENTURE IN WONDERLAND, THE

Hirsh, Richard
I WAS A TEENAGE ZOMBIE

Hitzig, Rupert
SQUEEZE, THE

Ho, A. Kitman
WALL STREET

Ho, Leonard
EASTERN CONDORS
FINAL TEST, THE
PROJECT A—PART II

Hoffs, Tamar Simon
ALLNIGHTER, THE

Holland, Mary
ADVENTURE OF THE ACTION HUNTERS

Holmberg, Kaj
JAAHYVAISET PRESIDENTILLE

Holst, Per
PELLE EROVRAREN

Hommais, Pascal
LE GRAND CHEMIN
LETE EN PENTE DOUCE
SALE DESTIN!

Hooberman, Lucy
OUT OF ORDER

Hool, Conrad
STEEL DAWN

Hool, Lance
STEEL DAWN

Horian, Richard
STUDENT CONFIDENTIAL

Hosogoe, Seigo
TAXING WOMAN, A

Houtman, Chris
NITWITS

Houwer, Rob
VAN GELUK GESPROKEN

Howard, Andy
SUMMER CAMP NIGHTMARE

Hsiang, Wang Hing
SAPPORO STORY

Hubenbecker, Daniel
WARDOGS

Huete, Angel
LA ESTANQUERA DE VALLECAS

Hughes, John
PLANES, TRAINS AND AUTOMOBILES
SOME KIND OF WONDERFUL

Hui, Michael
CHOCOLATE INSPECTOR

Hunter, John
JOHN AND THE MISSUS

Hussain, Sultan
HAMARI JUNG

Hynnekleiv, Odd
KAMILLA OG TYVEN

Ichikawa, Kon
EIGA JOYU

Infante, Gonzalo
VA DE NUEZ

Ingvordsen, J. Christian
FIREHOUSE

Isaacs, Susan
HELLO AGAIN

Israel, Marjorie
MAN IN LOVE, A

Israel, Nancy
ALLNIGHTER, THE

Jackson, George
DISORDERLIES

Jacobsen, John M.
OFELAS

Jaffe, Herb
DUDES
MAID TO ORDER
THREE FOR THE ROAD

Jaffe, Michael
DISORDERLIES

Jaffe, Robert
NIGHTFLYERS

Jaffe, Stanley R.
FATAL ATTRACTION

Jaffe, Steven-Charles
NEAR DARK

Jayatilaka, Jayantha
WITNESS TO A KILLING

Jennings, Terry
CODA

Jewison, Norman
MOONSTRUCK

Jin Sung-man
TICKET

Jo Schafer
CEMIL

Johnson, Mark
GOOD MORNING, VIETNAM
TIN MEN

Johnson, Richard
LONELY PASSION OF JUDITH HEARNE,THE

Jones, Ian
LIGHTHORSEMEN, THE

Jonsson, Bo
DEMONS

Jordan, Ben
THIN LINE, THE

Jost, Jon
BELL DIAMOND

Jozani, Massood Jafari
SHEERE SANGGY

Juillet, Patric
WARM NIGHTS ON A SLOW MOVING TRAIN

Julius, Maxine
BLOODY NEW YEAR
GUNPOWDER

Junker, Gottfried
VERSTECKTE LIEBE

Jurgensen, Randy
HEART

Kabitzke, Siegfried
DER BARENHAUTER

Kabriel, Bedrich
BELINDA

Kagan, Michael J.
THREE KINDS OF HEAT

Kaiserman, Connie
MY LITTLE GIRL

Kakutani, Masaru
PRINCESS FROM THE MOON
SOROBANZUKU

Kalla, Hussein
AL-TAUQ WAL-ISWIRA
ZAWGAT RAGOL MOHIM

Kaman, Steven
FIREHOUSE

Kamerman, Bert
FLICKS

Kanter, Marianne
NIGHTMARE AT SHADOW WOODS

Kapic, Suleymane
OFICIR S RUZOM

Kaplan, Mike
WHALES OF AUGUST, THE

Kapoor, Boney
MISTER INDIA

Karmitz, Marin
MASQUES
MELO

Kasahara, Motoki
TOKYO BLACKOUT

Kasander, Kees
ZJOEK

Kasdan, Lawrence
CROSS MY HEART

Kastner, Elliott
ANGEL HEART

Katakouzinos, George
APOUSIES

Kaufman, Susan
I WAS A TEENAGE T.V. TERRORIST

Kaurismaki, Aki
TILINTEKO

Kay, Wong Wah
SAPPORO STORY

Kelleher, John
EAT THE PEACH

Kemeny, John
GATE, THE

Kennedy, Burt
TROUBLE WITH SPIES, THE

Kennedy, Kathleen
EMPIRE OF THE SUN

Kennedy, Leon Isaac
PENITENTIARY III

Kent, Suzanne
UNFINISHED BUSINESS . . .

Keren, Dov
KOL AHAVOTAI

Kerner, Jordan
LESS THAN ZERO

Kesten, Stephen F.
MILLION DOLLAR MYSTERY

Keytsman, Alain
BORAN—ZEIT ZUM ZIELEN
LOVE IS A DOG FROM HELL

Khleifi, Michel
NOCE EN GALILEE

Kiely, Chris
AS TIME GOES BY

Kieslowski, Krzysztof
BLIND CHANCE

Kincaid, Tim
ENEMY TERRITORY
NECROPOLIS

Kirkwood, Gene
IRONWEED

Klik, Jon
BEAT, THE

Kloiber, Herbert G.
MASCHENKA

Knapman, Steve
AROUND THE WORLD IN EIGHTY WAYS

Knight, Christopher W.
WINNERS TAKE ALL

Kobayasahi, Shunichi
TORA-SAN'S BLUEBIRD FANTASY

Kobayashi, Masao
DIXIELAND DAIMYO

Kohli, Raj Kumar
INSANIYAT KE DUSHMAN

Kohner, Pancho
ASSASSINATION
DEATH WISH 4: THE CRACKDOWN

Kollek, Amos
FOREVER, LULU

Koller, Sylvia
SIERRA LEONE

Kon, Kinuko
RYOMA O KITTA OTOKO

Kong, Jackie
BLOOD DINER

Konttinen, Sirkka-Liisa
T. DAN SMITH

Korytowski, Manfred
WANNSEE CONFERENCE, THE

Korzen, Benni
WHEELS OF TERROR

Koster-Paul, Dorothy
EMANON

Kouf, Jim
STAKEOUT

Koyzky, Jacob
BOUBA

Krabbe, Tim
RED DESERT PENITENTIARY

Kramreither, Anthony
CONCRETE ANGELS

Krevoy, Brad
SWEET REVENGE

Kroll, Leonard
FATAL BEAUTY
WALK LIKE A MAN

Kroopf, Scott
OUTRAGEOUS FORTUNE

Kropenin, Peter
OM KARLEK

Krost, Roy
TOO OUTRAGEOUS

Kubik, Lawrence
DEATH BEFORE DISHONOR

Kubrick, Stanley
FULL METAL JACKET

Kuk, Linda
BROTHERHOOD
MAGNIFICENT WARRIORS

Kumar, G.P. Vijay
PANCHAGNI

Kundu, Bhabesh
BIDROHI

Kuo-Liang, Hsu
TERRORIZERS, THE

Kurfirst, Gary
SIESTA

Kurkjian, John
FORTY DAYS OF MUSA DAGH

Kushner, Donald
BRAVE LITTLE TOASTER, THE

Lagettie, Robert
TIME GUARDIAN, THE

Lago, Jose Luis Rey
SENTIMIENTOS: MIRTA DE LINIERS A ESTAMBUL

Lai, Joseph
NINJA THUNDERBOLT

Lam, Ringo
CITY ON FIRE

Lamonica, Hugo
STRANGER, THE

Landa, Miguelangel
LA OVEJA NEGRA
MANON

Landau, Jon
CAMPUS MAN

Lander, Ned
BACHELOR GIRL

Lane, James
MURDER LUST

Lang, Bernard
ALPINE FIRE

Lang, Lin
OUTSIDERS, THE

Lange, Henry
DIARY OF A MAD OLD MAN
MASCARA

Lansing, Sherry
FATAL ATTRACTION

Lapaire, Chantal
EVA: GUERRILLERA

Larguier, Jean-Luc
MEMOIRE DES APPARENCES: LA VIE EST UN SONGE

Larramendi, Dario
AMOR EN CAMPO MINADO

Lasker, Lawrence
PROJECT X

Latham, Garl Boyd
BLOODSUCKERS FROM OUTER SPACE

Laurel, Robert G.
ROSARY MURDERS, THE

Le Tet, Robert
BUSHFIRE MOON

Leduc, Paul
FRIDA

Lee, Myung-won
MAN WITH THREE COFFINS, THE

Lee, Pierre C.
GET THE TERRORISTS
TOUGH COP
ULTIMAX FORCE

Leibovici, Annie
LA MOINE ET LA SORCIERE

Leichter, Leo
MALIBU BIKINI SHOP, THE

Leipzig, Matt
STRIPPED TO KILL

Lelouch, Claude
ATTENTION BANDITS

Lepetit, Jean-Francois
LE GRAND CHEMIN
LETE EN PENTE DOUCE
SALE DESTIN!

Lesniak-Crow, Emilia
SUMMER CAMP NIGHTMARE

Levin, Sy
FLOWERS IN THE ATTIC

Levinson, Art
MANNEQUIN

Levinson, Mark
RUSSKIES
STRANDED

Levitin, Jacqueline
EVA: GUERRILLERA

Levy, David
MONSTER IN THE CLOSET

Levy, Michael I.
GARDENS OF STONE

Levy, Robert L.
KILLING TIME, THE

Levy, Sandra
HIGH TIDE

Lichtenheld, Ted
PERSONAL FOUL

Liconti, Carlo
CONCRETE ANGELS

Lieberson, Sandy
RITA, SUE AND BOB TOO!

Liles, Sarah H.
MIND KILLER

Lim, K.L.
SAKURA KILLERS
WHITE PHANTOM

Limpipholpiboon, Manae
HOUSE

Linder, George
RUNNING MAN, THE

Lindstrom, Goran
LOS DUENOS DEL SILENCIO
MANNEN FRAN MALLORCA
SERPENT'S WAY, THE

Linson, Art
UNTOUCHABLES, THE

Lipkies, Ivan
NI DE AQUI, NI DE ALLA

Lisson, Mark
RETURN TO HORROR HIGH

Livaneli, Ulker
YER DEMIR, GOK BAKIR

Llewellyn-Jones, Tony
VINCENT—THE LIFE AND DEATH OF VINCENT VAN GOGH

Llosa, Luis
HOUR OF THE ASSASSIN

Lofton, Terry
NAIL GUN MASSACRE

Lombardi, Francisco J.
CITY AND THE DOGS, THE

Lommel, Ulli
OVERKILL

Long, Kathleen
PERSONAL FOUL

Lorain, Bernard
NOCE EN GALILEE

Loubert, Patrick
CARE BEARS ADVENTURE IN WONDERLAND, THE

Louis Malle
AU REVOIR, LES ENFANTS

Lovell, Marc
TROUBLE WITH SPIES, THE

Loza, Pepe
JUANA LA CANTINERA

Lucas, Trevor
CASSANDRA

Lucchese, Joseph
CODE NAME ZEBRA

Lucisano, Fulvio
UN RAGAZZO DI CALABRIA
UN TASSINARO A NEW YORK

Luddy, Tom
BARFLY

Lyons, Stuart
TURNAROUND

Macgregor-Scott, Peter
BORN IN EAST L.A.

Machlis, Neil A.
MONSTER SQUAD, THE

Mack, Karen
IN THE MOOD

Mackey, James
LAST OF ENGLAND, THE

Madhusudhana Rao, D.
AMERICA ABBAI

Maeda, Katsuhiro
LOVE LETTER

Magnusson, Tivi
NEGERKYS & LABRE LARVER
PETER VON SCHOLTEN
STRIT OG STUMME

Mak, Johnny
RICH AND FAMOUS

Makris, Dimitris
I KEKARMENI

Mancuso, Frank
BACK TO THE BEACH

Mandel, Yoram
TISZTA AMERIKA

Mandoki, Luis
GABY—A TRUE STORY

Maniatis, Sakis
KE DYO AVGA TOURKIAS

Manners, Harley
MOVING TARGETS
TIME GUARDIAN, THE

Marboeuf, Jean
GRAND GUIGNOL

Marini, Angel Flores
WALKER

Markey, Patrick
STACKING

Markovic, Jovan
MAGIC SNOWMAN, THE

Marnell, Jan
NIONDE KOMPANIET

Marquand, Richard
HEARTS OF FIRE

Marshall, Alan
ANGEL HEART

Marshall, Frank
EMPIRE OF THE SUN

Martin, Murray
T. DAN SMITH

Martinelli, Sergio
DA NNUNZIO

Masiello, Nino
QUEL RAGAZZO DELLA CURVA "B"

Maslansky, Paul
POLICE ACADEMY 4: CITIZENS ON PATROL

Maslon, Jimmy
BLOOD DINER

Masmuoto, Nobutoshi
FINAL TAKE: THE GOLDEN AGE OF MOVIES

Mason, Paul
WILD PAIR, THE

Mastorakis, Nico
TERMINAL EXPOSURE
WIND, THE
ZERO BOYS, THE

Matthews, Temple
OFF THE MARK

Mattson, Arne
GIRL, THE

McAree, Roy
SAKURA KILLERS
WHITE PHANTOM

McCarthy, Pat
T. DAN SMITH

McCormick, Kevin
BURGLAR

McLaughlin, Sheila
SHE MUST BE SEEING THINGS

McLeod, David L.
PICK-UP ARTIST, THE

Medina, Francis
BEAKS

Medjuck, Joe
BIG SHOTS

Mehlman, Gary
MALIBU BIKINI SHOP, THE

Melnick, Daniel
ROXANNE

Meltzer, Michael
HIDDEN, THE

Mendoza, Orlando R.
FORAJIDOS EN LA MIRA

Menegoz, Margaret
LAMI DE MON AMIE

Menkes, Nina
MAGDALENA VIRAGA

Menzies, Bryce
TALE OF RUBY ROSE, THE

Merchant, Ismail
MAURICE

Messere, Daniel
COERS CROISES

Meyer, Irwin
DEADLY ILLUSION

Meyerink, Victoria Paige
NIGHTFORCE

Meyers, Nancy
BABY BOOM

Miall, Tristram
CUSTODY

Michalakias, John Elias
I WAS A TEENAGE ZOMBIE

Mickelson, Martin
HELLO AGAIN
OUTRAGEOUS FORTUNE

Milchan, Arnon
MAN ON FIRE

Miller, George
YEAR MY VOICE BROKE, THE

Miller, J.C.
NO DEAD HEROES

Miller, Jennifer
HEARTS OF FIRE

Milliken, Sue
LES PATTERSON SAVES THE WORLD

Milojevic, Djordje
OFICIR S RUZOM

Minasian, Steve
SLAUGHTER HIGH

Mishra, Sudhir
THIS IS NOT OUR DESTINATION

Mitchell, Doug
YEAR MY VOICE BROKE, THE

Mitra, Narendranath
PHERA

Mitsui, Yasushi
WATASHI O SKI NI TSURETETTE

Mitterrand, Frederic
AVRIL BRISE

Miyagawa, Takayoshi
SEA AND POISON, THE

Mizoguchi, Katsumi
TOKYO BLACKOUT

Moniwa, Yoshinori
SARABA ITOSHIKI HITO YO

Montesi, Jorge
BIRDS OF PREY

Mora, Philippe
HOWLING III, THE

Moreno, Mario Arturo
WELCOME MARIA

Moretti, Nanni
NOTTE ITALIANA

Mortorff, Lawrence Taylor
HES MY GIRL
LADY BEWARE

Moses, Ben
GOOD MORNING, VIETNAM

Mount, Thom
CANT BUY ME LOVE

Moussa, Ibrahim
INTERVISTA

Mula, Isabel
EL LUTE—CAMINA O REVIENTA

Muller, Hans Willy
IN DER WUSTE

Murphey, Michael S.
SUPERNATURALS, THE

Murphy, Dennis
VALET GIRLS

Nainchrik, Jean
CHARLIE DINGO

Nasatir, Marcia
HAMBURGER HILL
IRONWEED

Neame, Christopher
BELLMAN AND TRUE

Neatrour, Jane
T. DAN SMITH

Nelson, Peter
LONELY PASSION OF JUDITH HEARNE,THE

Nelson, Willie
RED HEADED STRANGER

Nepomuceno, Luis
IGOROTA

Nesher, Doron
LATE SUMMER BLUES

Neto, Anibal Massaini
EU

Newalkar, Vinay
PUDHCHE PAOL

Newman, Peter
O. C. AND STIGGS

Nico
PETER VON SCHOLTEN

Nigro-Chacon, Giovanna
HOT CHILD IN THE CITY

Nilsson, Anders
WARDOGS

Niogret, Hubert
TESTAMENT D'UN POETE JUIF ASSASSINE

Nishioka, Yoshinobu
RYOMA O KITTA OTOKO

Noe, Francesca
ANGELUS NOVUS

Nomura, Yoshitaro
FINAL TAKE: THE GOLDEN AGE OF MOVIES

Nozik, Michael
CHINA GIRL

Nugent, Ginny
MUNCHIES

O'Brian, Peter
JOHN AND THE MISSUS

O'Brien, Lorenzo
WALKER

O'Brien, Maureen
KISS DADDY GOOD NIGHT

O'Brien, Rebecca
FRIENDSHIP'S DEATH

O'Donnell, Lynn
LIVING ON TOKYO TIME

O'Shea, John
NGATI

O'Toole, Stanley
LIONHEART

Obrow, Jeffrey
KINDRED, THE

Obst, Lynda
ADVENTURES IN BABYSITTING

Odenthal, Wolfgang
MAGIC STICKS

Okada, Shigeru
YOSHIWARA ENJO

Okada, Yutaka
UHOHO TANKENTAI

Oliver, Tom
RIGHT HAND MAN, THE

Olivera, Hector
AMAZONS
EL ANO DEL CONEJO

Olson, Gerald T.
HIDDEN, THE

Olsson, Claes
ELVIS-KISSAN JALJILLA

Ooba, Jire
ZEGEN

Opper, Barry
SLAMDANCE

Ormieres, Jean-Luc
BUISSON ARDENT

Orr, James
THEY STILL CALL ME BRUCE

Orthel, Rolf
QUATRE MAINS

Otsuka, Kanou
SEA AND POISON, THE

Pakula, Alan J.
ORPHANS

Palmer, Patrick
MOONSTRUCK

Panajotovic, Ika
DIRTY REBEL

Panicker, G.S.
PANDAVAPURAM

Papastathis, Lakis
THEOFILOS

Papayannidis, Takis
YENETHLIA POLI

Pappas, George
HEAT

Pappas, Steve
HOT SHOT

Parkes, Walter F.
PROJECT X

Parr, Larry
STARLIGHT HOTEL

Parvin, Theodore R.
HOT PURSUIT
Pasic, Mirza
ZIVOT RADNIKA
Paskaljevic, Goran
ANDJEO CUVAR
Passalia, Antonio
LE CRI DU HIBOU
Pattinson, Michael
GROUND ZERO
Paul, Bill
DEADTIME STORIES
Paul, Hank
EMANON
Paul, Kishan
PYAR KARKE DEKHO
Peace, J. Stephen
HAPPY HOUR
Pearce, Hayden
BLOODY NEW YEAR
Pedersen, John
TUESDAY WEDNESDAY
Pedersen, Vibeke
VENNER FOR ALTID
Perakis, Nicos
VIOS KE POLITIA
Perez Giner, Josep Anton
LESCOT
Permut, David
DRAGNET
Perry, Frank
HELLO AGAIN
Perry, Pinchas
GABY—A TRUE STORY
Perry, Simon
WHITE MISCHIEF
Pescarolo, Leo
DEVIL IN THE FLESH
GLI OCCHIALI D'ORO
Peters, Elke
CHINESE ARE COMING, THE
FRANCESCA
Peters, Jon
WITCHES OF EASTWICK, THE
Peters, Robert C.
WANTED: DEAD OR ALIVE
Petrie, Daniel
SQUARE DANCE
Pfeiffer, Carolyn
WHALES OF AUGUST, THE
ph & ed
MAGDALENA VIRAGA
ph&ed
T. DAN SMITH
Philadelphia, Sam
NILAKURINHI POOTHAPPOL
Philippe Diaz
BAD BLOOD
Phillips, Julia
BEAT, THE
Piccioli, Gianfranco
STREGATI
Pickard, Therese
BORN OF FIRE
Pierce, Hayden
BOY SOLDIER
Pillsbury, Sarah
RIVER'S EDGE
Planborg, Conny
SLEEP WELL, MY LOVE
Plaschkes, Otto
SHADEY
Pleutot, Denys
AVRIL BRISE
Poire, Alain
LEVY ET GOLIATH
Poiroux, Claude-Eric
JEUX D'ARTIFICES
Polaire, Michael
YOU TALKIN' TO ME?
Pollock, Patsy
RITA, SUE AND BOB TOO!
Ponce, Manuel Barbachanco
FRIDA
Poon, Dickson
BROTHERHOOD
DIXIA QING
Poor, Syamak Taghi
DJADDE HAYE SARD
Popovic, Dragoljub
HEY BABU RIBA
Popovic, Nikola
HEY BABU RIBA
Porchet, Jean-Louis
LA VALLEE FANTOME
Portet, Jacques
JOHNNY MONROE
Powell, Lorna
T. DAN SMITH
Pradelsky, Yair
LO SAM ZAYIN
Prakash, S.
THIRTHAM
Prasad, D.S.
LAWYER SUHASINI
Preisler, Ebbe
JAG ELSKER DIG
Pressman, Edward R.
WALL STREET
Prior, David A.
KILLER WORKOUT
Proevska, Pavlina
MAGIC SNOWMAN, THE
Proser, Chip
INNERSPACE
Provoost, Erwin
HECTOR
LOVE IS A DOG FROM HELL
Purcell, Joseph
DELOS ADVENTURE, THE
Puzon, Conrad C.
GET THE TERRORISTS
ULTIMAX FORCE
Queffelec, Yann
LES NOCES BARBARES
Quinn, Bob
BUDAWANNY
Rachmil, Michael
ROXANNE
Radclyffe, Sarah
SAMMY AND ROSIE GET LAID
WISH YOU WERE HERE
Rademakers, Fons
DIARY OF A MAD OLD MAN
Raffe, Alexandra
IVE HEARD THE MERMAIDS SINGING
Rahim, K.M.A.
UPPU
Rajski, Peggy
MATEWAN
Raju, D.V.N.
MANDALADHEESUDU
Raju, G.V.
ROWDY POLICE
Raleigh, Paul
HOSTAGE
Ramalho, Francisco
BESAME MUCHO
Ramanayake, Vijaya
MALDENIYESIMION
Randall, Dick
SLAUGHTER HIGH
Ransohoff, Martin
BIG TOWN, THE
Rao, Ramoji
PRATIGHAAT
Rasker, Frans
DE ORIONNEVEL
DE RATELRAT
IRIS
Rawail, Rahul
DACAIT
Rawson, Stratton
MY DARK LADY
Ray, Fred Olen
COMMANDO SQUAD
Ray-Gavras, Michele
FAMILY BUSINESS
MISS MONA
Red, Eric
NEAR DARK
Reed, Morton
SPACE RACE
Reeve, Geoffrey
WHISTLE BLOWER, THE
Reibenbach, Rafi
HA INSTALATOR
Reiner, Rob
PRINCESS BRIDE, THE
Reinhart, George
LA MOINE ET LA SORCIERE
Reitz, Edgar
POET'S SILENCE, THE
Relph, Simon
COMRADES
Renzi, Maggie
MATEWAN
Resendi, Carlos
LO DEL CESAR
Retes, Gabriel
MUJERES SALVAJES
Reynolds, Stephen
LIFE CLASSES
Reyre, Marie-Laure
FUEGOS
MALADIE D'AMOUR
Rich, Ron
GHOST FEVER
Richardson, Peter
MORE BAD NEWS
Richmond, Adrianne
OUTTAKES
Rimbach, Herbert
MEIER
Ringel, Israel
LO SAM ZAYIN
Rios, Juan Abusaid
LA RULETERA
LAPUTA: THE CASTLE IN THE SKY
Ripka, William
KISS DADDY GOOD NIGHT
Ripploh, Frank
TAXI NACH KAIRO
Risher, Sara
NIGHTMARE ON ELM STREET 3: DREAM WARRIORS, A
Roberts, Peter
T. DAN SMITH
Robertson, Harry
JANE AND THE LOST CITY
Robins, Leslie
TROUBLE WITH DICK, THE
Rocha, Paulo
O DESEJADO—LES MONTAGNES DE LA LUNE
Rodriguez, Robert
OPERACION MARIJUANA
Rodriguez, Tonatihu
OLOR A MUERTE
Rodriguez Jr., Ismael
YERBA SANGRIENTE
Rohrbach, Gunter
ZABOU
Roos, Fred
BARFLY
Roos, Gerd
VENNER FOR ALTID
Rosas Priego R., Alfonso
EL HIJO DE PEDRO NAVAJAS
Rose, Alexandra
OVERBOARD
Rosen, Martin
STACKING
Rosen, Mel
HA INSTALATOR
Rosenfelt, Scott
RUSSKIES
STRANDED
Rosetta, Richard
TRESPASSES
Ross, Herbert
SECRET OF MY SUCCESS, THE
Rotcop, J. Kenneth
MALIBU BIKINI SHOP, THE
Roth, Joe
P.K. & THE KID
Roth, Steve
MIRACLES
Rothberg, Jeff
HIDING OUT
Rotman, Keith
HEAT
Rottenberg, Enrique
HIMMO MELECH YERUSHALAIM
Rouse, Virginia
TO MARKET, TOMARKET
Routray, Sachi
JAIDEV
Rowe, Glenys
DOGS IN SPACE

Rozema, Patricia
IVE HEARD THE MERMAIDS SINGING

Ruben, Andy
STRIPPED TO KILL

Rutnam, Chandran
DEATH STONE

Ryan, Robert
BLOODY WEDNESDAY

Sadasue, Mayato
GONDOLA

Sager, Ray
HIGHER EDUCATION

Salim
LOHA

Sanchez, Victor Manuel San Jose
DIVINAS PALABRAS

Sanders, Angela
ESCAPES

Sandhu, Mahendra
KAUN KITNEY PAANI MEIN

Sandrin, Patrick
O DESEJADO—LES MONTAGNES DE LA LUNE

Sanford, Midge
RIVER'S EDGE

Sansad, Shilpi
RUDRABEENA

Santiago, Cirio H.
EYE OF THE EAGLE

Santo, Henrique Espirito
JESTER,THE

Santoni, Joel
COERS CROISES

Sanz, Luis
HAY QUE DESHACER LA CASA

Sarafian, Deran
ALIEN PREDATOR

Saravanar, M.
SAMSARAM OKA CHADARANGAM

Sarde, Alain
COMEDY!
LES DEUX CROCODILES

Sargent, Joseph
JAWS: THE REVENGE

Sastry, C.V.K.
NAZRANA

Sato, Masao
KATAKU NO HITO

Satyanarayana, Ch.
ALLARI KRISHNAYA

Satyanarayana, P.V.V.
UMMADI MOGUDU

Saura, Guillermo
CHORROS

Sayag, Pierre
POULE ET FRITES

Sayyad, Parviz
CHECKPOINT

Schamoni, Peter
CASPAR DAVID FRIEDRICH

Schapiro, Angela
HES MY GIRL

Scheimer, Lou
PINOCCHIO AND THE EMPEROR OF THE NIGHT

Scheinman, Arnold
PRINCESS BRIDE, THE

Scherer, Hugo
VA DE NUEZ

Scherer, Theres
JENATSCH

Schlesinger, John
BELIEVERS, THE

Schlossberg-Cohen, Jay
CRY WILDERNESS

Schmidt, Arne
ROBOCOP

Schneider, Harold
BLACK WIDOW
SOMEONE TO WATCH OVER ME

Schorr, Renen
LATE SUMMER BLUES

Schory, Katrial
DREAMERS

Schrader, Uwe
SIERRA LEONE

Schreiner, Dirk
QUATRE MAINS

Schriebman, Myrl A.
HUNTER'S BLOOD

Schroeder, Barbet
BARFLY

Schulberg, Sandra
WAITING FOR THE MOON

Schultz, Michael
DISORDERLIES

Schulz-Keil, Wieland
DEAD, THE

Schumacher, Martha
BEDROOM WINDOW, THE
DATE WITH AN ANGEL

Schwary, Ronald L.
BATTERIES NOT INCLUDED

Scott, Darin
OFFSPRING, THE

Scott, Jane
SHADOWS OF THE PEACOCK

Scott, Robert
VIDEO DEAD, THE

Scotti, Tony
LADY BEWARE

Sear, Walter E.
BLOOD SISTERS
ORACLE, THE

Sell, Jack M.
OUTTAKES

Serapilia, Peter
REMEMBERING MEL

Serrano, Carlos
CALE

Shah, Krishna
AMERICAN DRIVE-IN

Sham, John
AUTUMN'S TALE, AN
LAONIANG GOU SAO
MAGNIFICENT WARRIORS
SAPPORO STORY
WRONG COUPLES,THE

Shamberg, Michael H.
SALVATION!

Shannon, Roger
OUT OF ORDER

Shantaram, V.
JHANJHAAR

Shapiro, George
SUMMER SCHOOL

Sharma, Chander
GHULAMI KI ZANJEER

Sharp, Jan
GOOD WIFE, THE

Shaye, Robert
HIDDEN, THE
MY DEMON LOVER
NIGHTMARE ON ELM STREET 3: DREAM WARRIORS, A

Sherkow, Daniel A.
SUSPECT

Sherman, Harve
HOUSEKEEPER, THE

Shields, Frank
SURFER, THE

Shimazu, Kiyoshi
FINAL TAKE: THE GOLDEN AGE OF MOVIES

Shinohara, Aya
ROBINSON NO NIWA

Shinsaka, Junichi
PRINCESS FROM THE MOON

Shire, Talia
LIONHEART

Shivdasani, Deepak
DADAGIRI

Shmuger, Marc
DEAD OF WINTER

Shoja Noori, Ali Reza
SHEERE SANGGY

Showalter, John
CREEPOZOIDS

Sidaris, Arlene
HARD TICKET TO HAWAII

Siegel, William M.
HOTEL COLONIAL

Sievernich, Chris
DEAD, THE

Sighvatsson, Sigurjon
P.I. PRIVATE INVESTIGATIONS

Sill, Sam
IRON WARRIOR

Silver, Dina
WALK ON THE MOON, A

Silver, Joel
LETHAL WEAPON
PREDATOR

Silverman, Mark
RAISING ARIZONA

Simandl, Lloyd A.
LADIES OF THE LOTUS

Simon, Benjamin
JOHNNY MONROE

Simonsons, M.H.
SOMEONE TO LOVE

Simpson, Don
BEVERLY HILLS COP II

Simpson, Peter
HELLO MARY LOU, PROM NIGHT II
HIGH STAKES
HIGHER EDUCATION

Singer, Robert
LETS GET HARRY

Siritzky, Alain
EMMANUELLE 5

Sjoberg, Tom
BLOOD TRACKS

Sjoman, Vilgot
MALACCA

Skinner, Ann
KITCHEN TOTO, THE

Sklar, William D.
EVIL TOWN

Sluizer, George
RED DESERT PENITENTIARY

Smith, Brian J.
DEATHROW GAMESHOW

Smith, Clive A.
CARE BEARS ADVENTURE IN WONDERLAND, THE

Smith, Iain
HEARTS OF FIRE

Smith, John N.
SITTING IN LIMBO

Snell, Peter
PRAYER FOR THE DYING, A

Soenarso, R.
IBUNDA

Soisson, Joel
SUPERNATURALS, THE

Solleveld, Rene
MASCARA

Solomon, Ken
PRETTY SMART

Solt, Susan
ORPHANS

Solum, Wenche
PLASTPOSEN

Sorlat, Stephane
NOYADE INTERDITE

Souda, Said Ali
LA VENGEANCE DU PROTECTEUR

Sourapas, Michael
ALIEN PREDATOR

Spelling, Aaron
SURRENDER

Spencer, Norman
CRY FREEDOM

Spiegel, Scott
THOU SHALT NOT KILL . . . EXCEPT

Spiehs, Karl
ZARTLICHE CHAOTEN

Spielberg, Steven
EMPIRE OF THE SUN

Spry, Robin
KEEPING TRACK

Stabler, Steven
SWEET REVENGE

Stantic, Lita
MISS MARY

Steensland, David
ESCAPES

Stell, Guillermo Calderon
ENTRE FICHERAS ANDA EL DIABLO
LA RAZA NUNCA PIERDE—HUELE A GAS

Stern, Don
PROGRAMMED TO KILL

Stern, Joseph
NO MAN'S LAND

Stevenson, Rick
PROMISED LAND

Stieber, Dale Ann
UNFINISHED BUSINESS . . .

Stojanovic, Aleksandar
DIE VERLIEBTEN

Stouffer, Mark
MAN OUTSIDE

Streisand, Barbra
NUTS

Streit, David
RIVER'S EDGE

Strong, John
STEELE JUSTICE

Stubbs, Ray
T. DAN SMITH

Suarez, Bobby A.
WARRIORS OF THE APOCALYPSE

Sudwakitmono
IBUNDA

Sugisaki, Shigemi
FINAL TAKE: THE GOLDEN AGE OF MOVIES

Sugiyama, Yoshiniko
ZEGEN

Suissa, Daniele J.
MORNING MAN, THE

Sullivan, Fred G.
SULLIVAN'S PAVILION

Summers, Cathleen
STAKEOUT

Sundby, Jeanette
FELDMANN CASE, THE

Suzuki, Yutaka
BUS

Swindale, Mary
INDIAN SUMMER

Sylbert, Anthea
OVERBOARD

Szulzinger, Boris
BIG BANG, THE

Takawa, Tan
KATAKU NO HITO

Takkinen, Heikki
URSULA

Tamaoki, Yasushi
TAXING WOMAN, A

Tamez, Orlando
HERENCIA DE VALIENTES

Tanaka, Tomoyuki
EIGA JOYU

Tannen, Michael
SQUEEZE, THE

Tapert, Robert G.
EVIL DEAD 2: DEAD BY DAWN

Tarjanne, Petra
NAKEMIIN, HYVASTI

Tarlov, Mark
WHITE WATER SUMMER

Tatum, Tom
WINNERS TAKE ALL

Tazi, Mohamed
ABBES

Techaratanaprsert, Somsak
COBRA THUNDERBOLT

Tedesco, Maurizio
SPECTERS

Teets, Edward
THREE MEN AND A BABY

Teitelbaum, Irving
HIDDEN CITY

Tejada-Flores, Miguel
DUDES

Tennant, William
SUMMER HEAT

Tenser, Marilyn J.
HUNK

Teo, Stephen
BEJALAI

Terranova, Carole
MY DARK LADY

Terzian, Alain
CLUB DE RENCONTRES
LANNEE DES MEDUSES

Theos, Dimos
IKONA ENOS MYTHIKOU PROSOPOU

Thomas, Jeremy
LAST EMPEROR, THE

Thomas, John G.
BANZAI RUNNER

Thompson, John
BARBARIANS, THE

Thor, Jon-Mikl
ROCK 'N' ROLL NIGHTMARE

Tinnell, Robert
SURF NAZIS MUST DIE

Tiwari, Ramesh
ANJAAM

Toback, James
PICK-UP ARTIST, THE

Toberoff, Marc
ZOMBIE HIGH

Tokoshige, Kunio
ZEGEN

Toledo, Sergio
VERA

Tomlinson, Judith
T. DAN SMITH

Topping, Angela
LOVECHILD, THE

Torno, Randall
WILD PAIR, THE

Torrance, Bob
PERFECT MATCH, THE

Towers, Harry Alan
WARRIOR QUEEN

Townsend, Robert
HOLLYWOOD SHUFFLE

Trafford, Steve
T. DAN SMITH

Trattner, Ira
OFF THE MARK

Traynor, Peter S.
EVIL TOWN

Trodd, Kenith
MONTH IN THE COUNTRY, A

Tronel, Jacques
AVRIL BRISE

Tschechowa, Vera
DEVILS PARADISE, THE

Tuber, Joel
MAKING MR.RIGHT

Tucci, Ugo
ALADDIN

Tusell, Felix
MOROS Y CRISTIANOS

Ubierna, Ruben Galindo
NARCOTERROR

Valdes, David
LIKE FATHER, LIKE SON

Vamsi
LAWYER SUHASINI

Van Atta, Don
CATCH THE HEAT
RAGE OF HONOR

van der Linden, Jos
HECTOR
VROEGER IS DOOD

van Heijningen, Matthijs
EEN MAAND LATER

van Raemdorick, Jan
VAN PAEMEL FAMILY, THE

Van Rellim, Tim
EAT THE RICH

Vane, Norman Thaddeus
CLUB LIFE

Vane, Richard
HARRY AND THE HENDERSONS

Vasallo, Carlos
CRYSTAL HEART
EL PLACER DE LA VENGANZA
MURIERON A MITAD DEL RIO
ROSA DE LA FRONTERA
TODA LA VIDA

Vaughn, Ben
BENJI THE HUNTED

Vennerod, Petter
JOR

Ventura, Bella
DE MUJER A MUJER

Vera, Marilda
POR LOS CAMINOS VERDES

Verges, Chrisann
UNFINISHED BUSINESS . . .

Vergitsis, Nicos
ARCHANGELOS TOU PATHOUS

Vernon, James M.
SURFER, THE

Versluys, Gijs
BLOND DOLLY

Versluys, Gys
HAVINCK

Vidigal, Tarcisio
UM FILM 100% BRAZILEIRO

Viezzi, Adolphe
IL EST GENIAL PAPY!

Vincent, Chuck
DERANGED
IF LOOKS COULD KILL
SLAMMER GIRLS
WIMPS

Vizard, Stephen
BIT PART, THE

Vogel, David E.
THREE O'CLOCK HIGH

Volkenborn, Klaus
CHINESE ARE COMING, THE

Von Buren, Francis
CHRONICLE OF A DEATH FORETOLD

von Praunheim, Rosa
ANITA—DANCES OF VICE

von Vietinghoff, Joachim
DIE VERLIEBTEN
EIN BLICK-UND DIE LIEBE BRICHT AUS

Wacko, Wendy
CLIMB, THE

Waksal, Sam
SUICIDE CLUB, THE

Walker, Giles
LAST STRAW, THE

Walkow, Gary
TROUBLE WITH DICK, THE

Walters, Martin
BLUE MONKEY
NIGHTSTICK
PRETTYKILL

Wam, Svend
JOR

Waterstreet, Charles
HOWLING III, THE

Waxman, Philip A.
TALKING WALLS

Wearing, Michael
BELLMAN AND TRUE

Webb, Monica
DIRTY LAUNDRY

Webb, William
DIRTY LAUNDRY

Wechsler, Nick
BEAT, THE

Weiner, William S.
NIGHTFORCE

Weingartshofer, Patricia
NOCTURNO AMOR QUE TE VAS

Weintraub, Jerry
HAPPY NEW YEAR

Weintraub, Sandra
PRINCESS ACADEMY, THE

Weiss, Robert K.
AMAZON WOMEN ON THE MOON
DRAGNET

Wells, John
NICE GIRLS DON'T EXPLODE

Wenders, Wim
DER HIMMEL UBER BERLIN
YER DEMIR, GOK BAKIR

Wendlandt, Horst
OTTO—DER NEUE FILM

Werner, Theo M.
DEATH STONE

Wesemann, Alexander
PENG! DU BIST TOT!

West, Howard
SUMMER SCHOOL

Widerberg, Bo
VICTORIA

Wigman, Denis
ZJOEK

Wijngaarde, Eddy
LOOKING FOR EILEEN

Wilhite, Thomas L.
BRAVE LITTLE TOASTER, THE

Wilkinson, Norman
TIME GUARDIAN, THE

Williams, Bernard
MIRACLES
WHO'S THAT GIRL

Williams, Jason
DANGER ZONE, THE

Williams, Stacy
ERNEST GOES TO CAMP

Williamson, Fred
MESSENGER, THE

Wilson, David
LAST STRAW, THE
SITTING IN LIMBO

Wilson, Michael G.
LIVING DAYLIGHTS, THE

Wincer, Simon
LIGHTHORSEMEN, THE

Winters, David
MISSION KILL

Wise, Mike
MAKING MR.RIGHT

Wiseman, Andrew
TALE OF RUBY ROSE, THE

Wittliff, William
RED HEADED STRANGER

Wolf, Dick
NO MAN'S LAND

Wolf, Mark
SLAVE GIRLS FROM BEYOND INFINITY

Wolman, Dan
CHOZE AHAVA

Wolters-Alfs, Elisabeth
DEADLINE

Wong, Raymond
SEVEN YEARS ITCH

Wongsoredjo, Lea
ALS IN EEN ROES
ODYSSEE D'AMOUR

Woo-suk, Lee
KYEOUL NAGUNE

Worth, Marvin
LESS THAN ZERO

Wright, Simon
MORE BAD NEWS

Wu, Sally
LAONIANG GOU SAO

Wyman, Brad
WHITE OF THE EYE

Xu Ke
PEKING OPERA BLUES

Yabe, Hisashi
ITAZU

Yamamoto, Yo
DIXIELAND DAIMYO

Yasa, Ahmet
JOCKS

Yordan, Philip
BLOODY WEDNESDAY
CRY WILDERNESS

Yoss, Robert E.
MAN OUTSIDE

Yune, Johnny
THEY STILL CALL ME BRUCE

Yuval, Peter
DEADLY PREY
KILLER WORKOUT
MANKILLERS

Yuzna, Brian
DOLLS

Zacharias, Ann
TESTET

Zakani, Jose Lorenzo
EL HOMBRE DESNUDO

Zanussi, Krzysztof
LE JEUNE MAGICIEN

Zecevic, George
HEY BABU RIBA

Zenk, Peter
DER UNSICHTBARE

Zidi, Claude
LASSOCIATION DES MALFAITEURS

Zimbert, Jonathan A.
MONSTER SQUAD, THE

Zinnemann, Tim
RUNNING MAN, THE

Ziskin, Laura
NO WAY OUT

Zurinaga, Marcos
LA GRAN FIESTA

Zuta, Daniel
BORAN—ZEIT ZUM ZIELEN

PRODUCTION DESIGNERS

Ackland-Snow, Brian
MAURICE

Akune, Iwao
HOTARUGAWA

Alarcon, Jose Maria
CRYSTAL HEART

Allen, Chet
P.K. & THE KID

Allen, Linda
THREE FOR THE ROAD

Altman, Stephen
ARIA
BEYOND THERAPY
NEAR DARK

Amies, Caroline
WISH YOU WERE HERE

Ammon, Ruth
HOT SHOT

Amrohi, Manzoor
INDIAN SUMMER

Amsinskaja, Elena
SKORBNOE BESCHUVSTVIE

Angwin, Neil
RIGHT HAND MAN, THE
VINCENT—THE LIFE AND DEATH OF VINCENT VAN GOGH

Arthur —Nicdao, Ruben
WARRIORS OF THE APOCALYPSE

Artinano, Javier
LONG STRIDER

Asp, Anna
PELLE EROVRAREN

Atkinson, Adrienne
HOUSEKEEPING

Austin, Leo
MONTH IN THE COUNTRY, A

Avellana, Joe Mari
EQUALIZER 2000
EYE OF THE EAGLE

Ayabe, Toshiro
LOVE LETTER

Bahs, Hanning
SIDSTE AKT

Balet, Mark
NORTH SHORE

Banovich, Tamas
MALOM A POKOLBAN

Baron, Norm
NUMBER ONE WITH A BULLET

Barreus, Anders
GIRL, THE

Bartholomew, Sid
MAGIC STICKS

Basse, Per Flink
JAG ELSKER DIG

Bassiner, Jonni
LA SENYORA

Beacroft, Mike
STARLIGHT HOTEL

Beard, John
SIESTA

Beeton, William
GATE, THE

Bennett, Charles
MORGAN STEWART'S COMING HOME

Berger, Stephen
WILD PAIR, THE

Berman, Lester
GRAVEYARD SHIFT

Betchler, Hildegard
BUSINESS AS USUAL

Bhattacharya, Bhaswati
PANCHVATI

Bilowit, Bill
KID BROTHER, THE

Binns, Leslie
RUNNING FROM THE GUNS

Bissell, James
HARRY AND THE HENDERSONS

Bissell, Jim
SOMEONE TO WATCH OVER ME

Block, Becky
UNDER COVER

Boquist, Stig
JIM OCH PIRATERNA BLOM

Bornebusch, Cian
OM KARLEK

Bourne, Mel
FATAL ATTRACTION

Boyle, Robert F.
DRAGNET

Brenner, Albert
MONSTER SQUAD, THE

Brodie, Bill
DEAD OF WINTER

Buchanan, Mike
HELLRAISER

Bugenhaven, Tom
THREE O'CLOCK HIGH

Bunker, Jon
BELLMAN AND TRUE

Burns, Robert
OUTING, THE

Bushnell, Scott
ARIA
O. C. AND STIGGS

Callahan, Gene
BLACK WIDOW

Cameron, Allan
FOURTH PROTOCOL, THE

Cameron, Duncan
THREE KINDS OF HEAT

Campbell, Sally
GOOD WIFE, THE
HIGH TIDE

Capra, Bernt Amadeus
KILLING TIME, THE

Cassidy, William J.
HAPPY NEW YEAR

Chapman, David
DIRTY DANCING

Chauvelot, Sylvain
HOTEL DE FRANCE

Chavooshian, Nora
MATEWAN
SOMETHING SPECIAL!

Cohen, Lester
ANNA
SALVATION!

Cohen, Lynda
MONSTER IN THE CLOSET

Collis, Jack T.
RUNNING MAN, THE

Conroy, Tom
BUDAWANNY

Cooke, Ro
BACHELOR GIRL

Coote, Lissa
AROUND THE WORLD IN EIGHTY WAYS

Coromina, Andreu
ANGUSTIA

Corona, Dora
GHOST FEVER

Corso, John W.
PLANES, TRAINS AND AUTOMOBILES

Craig, Stuart
CRY FREEDOM

Creber, William J.
HOT PURSUIT

Cresciman, Vince
LA BAMBA

Cristante, Ivo
AMAZON WOMEN ON THE MOON

Cross, Ronnie
ULTIMAX FORCE

Cruse, William
ASSASSINATION

Dabao, Vic
SWEET REVENGE

Das, Robin
THIS IS NOT OUR DESTINATION

Davis, Ken
BEVERLY HILLS COP II

de Aguiar, Jose Duarte
EU

DeGovia, Jack
ROXANNE

Devilla, Debbie
FIREHOUSE

Dicdao, Art
OPPOSING FORCE

Dilley, Leslie
ALLAN QUATERMAIN AND THE LOST CITY OF GOLD

Dillon, Constantine
HAPPY HOUR

Diss, Eileen
EIGHTY FOUR CHARING CROSS ROAD

Dobrowlski, Marek
EMPEROR'S NEW CLOTHES, THE
SLEEPING BEAUTY

Dobrowolska, Halina
BOHATERROKU

Dobrowolski, Marek
BEAUTY AND THE BEAST

HANSEL AND GRETEL
RUMPELSTILTSKIN

Dowding, Jon
INITIATION

Drummond, Mario
UM FILM 100% BRAZILEIRO

Dufficey, Paul
ARIA

Dunlop, Charles
MEATBALLS III

Eads, Paul
WANTED: DEAD OR ALIVE

Evein, Bernard
LA RUMBA

Fariborzi, Vahij Ollah
DJADDE HAYE SARD

Fonseca, Gregg
HOUSE TWO: THE SECOND STORY

Ford, Roger
THOSE DEAR DEPARTED
YEAR MY VOICE BROKE, THE

Foreman, Ron
BEDROOM WINDOW, THE

Forsen, Mona Theresia
DEMONS

Francois, Guy-Claude
LA PASSION BEATRICE
LE JOURNAL D'UN FOU

Furst, Anton
FULL METAL JACKET

Gallagher, Lester
WIND, THE

Gallo, Horacio
SINFIN, LA MUERTA NO ES NINGUNA SOLUCION

Ganz, Armin
TOUGH GUYS DON'T DANCE

Gardonyi, Laszlo
ZUHANAS KOZBEN

Garwood, Norman
PRINCESS BRIDE, THE
SHADEY

Gassner, Dennis
IN THE MOOD
LIKE FATHER, LIKE SON

Geskus, Rebecca
ODYSSEE D'AMOUR

Gorton, Adrian
RAGE OF HONOR

Graff, Philippe
DIARY OF A MAD OLD MAN

Graffe, Philippe
VAN PAEMEL FAMILY, THE

Graham
LES PATTERSON SAVES THE WORLD

Grantham, Lyne J.
LADIES OF THE LOTUS

Grasso, Sal
HARD TICKET TO HAWAII

Graysmark, John
SUPERMAN IV: THE QUEST FOR PEACE

Grigorian, Greta
RETURN TO HORROR HIGH

Grimes, Stephen
DEAD, THE

Gropman, David
CAMPUS MAN
SWEET LORRAINE

Gross, Holger
AMERICAN NINJA 2: THE CONFRONTATION
WALK ON THE MOON, A

Grosvenor, Carol Holman
CHIPMUNK ADVENTURE, THE

Gukov, Yevgeny
DVADTSTAT DNEI BEZ

Haghighi, Ebrahim
GOZARESH-E YEK GHATL

Hakansson, Rolf Allan
LEIF

Halinski, Andrzej
C. K. DEZERTERZY

Hall, Patricia
TERMINAL EXPOSURE

Hall, Roger
WHITE MISCHIEF

Hallowell, Todd
ADVENTURES IN BABYSITTING
BURGLAR

Hanania, Caroline
LOVECHILD, THE

Harris, Donald L.
CANT BUY ME LOVE

Harris, William H.
HOT CHILD IN THE CITY

Harrison, Philip
STAKEOUT

Haruki, Akira
ITAZU

Harvey, Carole
BIT PART, THE

Hawkins, Kai
NO WAY OUT

Haworth, Ted
BATTERIES NOT INCLUDED

Hay, John
ARIA

Helmy, Michael
BACK TO THE BEACH

Hendrickson, Stephen
WALL STREET

Herbert, Jocelyn
WHALES OF AUGUST, THE

Hercules, Evan
PRAYER FOR THE DYING, A

Heschong, Albert
EXTREME PREJUDICE

Hidalgo, Eduardo
LONG STRIDER

Hides, Bernard
LIGHTHORSEMEN, THE

Hinds, Marsha
SUMMER HEAT

Hirvikoski, Reija
SNOW QUEEN, THE

Hobbs, Christopher
ARIA
GOTHIC
LAST OF ENGLAND, THE

Hoimark, Peter
HIP, HIP, HURRA!

Holland, Simon
BELIEVERS, THE

Holmes, Kerith
WITH LOVE TO THE PERSON NEXT TO ME

Hooser, J. Michael
CAUGHT

Hopkins, Chris
KINDRED, THE

Howard, Jeffrey
BABY BOOM

Ivanov, Viktor
VZLOMSHCHIK

Jackson, Gemma
FRIENDSHIP'S DEATH

Jacobs, Mathew
ARIA

Jaen, Manuel
LA VIDA ALEGRE

Jamison, Peter
TIN MEN

Jenkins, George
ORPHANS

Jillson, Robert I.
GARBAGE PAIL KIDS MOVIE, THE

Joaquin F. Igual
CALE

Johnson, Martin
HIDDEN CITY

Johnstone, Diana
ARIA

Joli, Jocelyn
WILD THING

Jones, Bill
PERSONAL FOUL

Jones, Eric
TROUBLE WITH DICK, THE

Joseph T. Garrity
WEEDS

Kaczenski, Chester
DOWN TWISTED

Kanate, Alma
LA VIE PLATINEE

Kasai, Takeo
BUS

Kenney, Bill
BIG TOWN, THE

Kilvert, Lilly
SURRENDER

Kimura, Takeo
SEA AND POISON, THE

Kirkland, Geoffrey
LEONARD PART 6

Kohut-Svelko, Jean-Pierre
ENNEMIS INTIMES

Konovalov, Valentin
STARAYA AZBUKA

Konrad, Albrecht
OTTO—DER NEUE FILM

Kosarewicz, Tadeusz
POCIAG DO HOLLYWOOD

Kozinets, Matthew
ZOMBIE HIGH

Kroeger, Wolf
SICILIAN, THE

Krogh, Frode
ETTER RUBICON
PLASTPOSEN

Kwan, Mango
YI LOU YI

Kybartas, Sandy
HELLO MARY LOU, PROM NIGHT II

Lagrange, Michel
AVRIL BRISE

Lamont, Peter
LIVING DAYLIGHTS, THE

Larkin, Peter
SECRET OF MY SUCCESS, THE
THREE MEN AND A BABY

Larsen, Kaj
NAGRA SOMMARKVALLAR PA JORDEN

Lasic, Vladislav
WHEELS OF TERROR

Lee, Robert
GET THE TERRORISTS
HOSTAGE SYNDROME

Leigh, Dan
CHINA GIRL
HIDING OUT
MY LITTLE GIRL
STREET SMART

Lemeshev, Igor
STRANNAYAR ISTORIYAR DOKTORA DZHEKILA I MISTERA KHAIDA

Leonard, Jamie
KITCHEN TOTO, THE

Leovey, Johanna
UNFINISHED BUSINESS . . .

Levy, Eilon
DREAMERS

Li, Pui Pui
TROUBLE WITH DICK, THE

Liddle, George
TIME GUARDIAN, THE

Ling, Barbara
LESS THAN ZERO
MAKING MR.RIGHT

Livingstone, Alistair
MOVING TARGETS

Lloyd, John
CRITICAL CONDITION

Lloyd, John J.
JAWS: THE REVENGE

Lomino, Daniel
PRINCE OF DARKNESS

Loquasto, Santo
RADIO DAYS
SEPTEMBER

Lounsbury, Ruth
MUTANT HUNT

Luczyc-Wyhowski, Hugo
PERSONAL SERVICES
PRICK UP YOUR EARS

Ludi, Heidi
DER HIMMEL UBER BERLIN

Major, Ross
HOWLING III, THE

Malley, Bill
BIG SHOTS
WALK LIKE A MAN

Mangano, Giuseppe
BARBARIANS, THE

Marasescu, Magdalena
PADUREANCA

Marchegiani, Jorge
CATCH THE HEAT
EL HOMBRE DE LA DEUDA EXTERNA

Marcucci, Robert
STREET TRASH

Marsh, Steve
SHY PEOPLE
Marsh, Terence
MIRACLES
SPACEBALLS
Martin, Eva
DIARY FOR MY LOVED ONES
Matthews, Bill
THREE O'CLOCK HIGH
Maus, Rodger
BLIND DATE
McAlpine, Andrew
ARIA
HIGH SEASON
STRAIGHT TO HELL
McAnelly, Jack
FLICKS
McCabe, Stephen
FOREVER, LULU
MAGIC STICKS
McCabe, Steven
SUICIDE CLUB, THE
McGuire, Richard
SUMMER CAMP NIGHTMARE
McGuire, Richard N.
STEELE JUSTICE
Medusa
ROBOT HOLOCAUST
Medusa Studios
ENEMY TERRITORY
Megruve, Richard
LA VENGEANCE DU PROTECTEUR
Meighen, John
WILD THING
Mercier, Patrice
WAITING FOR THE MOON
Merritt, Michael
HOUSE OF GAMES
Mikeladze, Georgy
REPENTANCE
Miller, Bruce
CREEPSHOW 2
Moretti, D.
I KEKARMENI
Morris, Brian
ANGEL HEART
Morris, Diana
SURVIVAL GAME
Munneke, Peter
HARD TICKET TO HAWAII
Muraki, Shinobu
EIGA JOYU
Murray, Graeme
MALONE
Murray-Leach, Roger
HEARTS OF FIRE
Musky, Jane
RAISING ARIZONA
Muto, John
FLOWERS IN THE ATTIC
NIGHTFLYERS
RIVER'S EDGE
Newport, James William
FATAL BEAUTY
STEPFATHER, THE
Nilsson, Lars Rune
VENNER FOR ALTID
Nishioka, Yoshinobu
RYOMA O KITTA OTOKO
YOSHIWARA ENJO
O'Neill, Martin
SURFER, THE
Olivares, Christian
MEMOIRE DES APPARENCES: LA VIE EST UN SONGE
Oppewall, Jeannine C.
IRONWEED
Oppewall, Jeannine Claudia
BIG EASY, THE
LIGHT OF DAY
Oquist, Jan
MANNEN FRAN MALLORCA
Parisi, Lucio
WARRIOR QUEEN
Parrondo, Gil
LIONHEART
Paul, Vicki
HEART
Paull, Lawrence G.
CROSS MY HEART
PROJECT X
Pearce, Hayden
BLOODY NEW YEAR
GUNPOWDER
Perakis, Nicos
DEVILS PARADISE, THE
Peters, Paul
MADE IN HEAVEN
NO MAN'S LAND
Petersen, Ron
BLOOD DINER
Peterson, Beau
PRETTY SMART
Petitjean, Marc
CHAMP D'HONNEUR
Pickwoad, Michael
COMRADES
LONELY PASSION OF JUDITH HEARNE,THE
WITHNAIL AND I
Pickwoad, Mick
JANE AND THE LOST CITY
Pierce, Hayden
BOY SOLDIER
Pinter, Herbert
BELINDA
Pinzon, John Paul
TOUGH COP
Pisoni, Edward
EIGHTY FOUR CHARING CROSS ROAD
HELLO AGAIN
SECRET OF MY SUCCESS, THE
Platt, Polly
WITCHES OF EASTWICK, THE
Plowden, Piers
P.I. PRIVATE INVESTIGATIONS
Pratt, Anthony
HOPE AND GLORY
Proulx, Michel
KEEPING TRACK
Quaranta, Gianni
DANCERS
Qun, He
BIG PARADE, THE
Random, Ida
THROW MOMMA FROM THE TRAIN
WHO'S THAT GIRL
Rawson, Stratton
MY DARK LADY
Reardon, Paddy
AS TIME GOES BY
SLATE, WYN & ME
Reynolds, Norman
EMPIRE OF THE SUN
Riva, J. Michael
LETHAL WEAPON
Riva, Manuel
OVERKILL
Rogers, Katalin
VIDEO DEAD, THE
Romvari, Jozsef
CSOK, ANYU
WHOOPING COUGH
Rosen, Charles
BROADCAST NEWS
Rosenberg, Philip
MOONSTRUCK
Roth, Dena
AMAZING GRACE AND CHUCK
Rotstein, Sarina
NICE GIRLS DON'T EXPLODE
Rubeo, Bruno
WALKER
Rudolf, Gene
BEST SELLER
Rule, Jim
NIGHTMARE AT SHADOW WOODS
Rundo, Slobodan
VEC VIDJENO
Russell, Judith
SHADOWS OF THE PEACOCK
Russo, Josan
MANNEQUIN
SOME KIND OF WONDERFUL
Sabatino, Anthony
HOT CHILD IN THE CITY
Sandell, William
ROBOCOP
Sandor, Kuli
DEATH BEFORE DISHONOR
Santana, Andres
A LOS CUATRO VIENTOS
Sardanis, Steve P.
WINNERS TAKE ALL
Saulnier, Jacques
MELO
Scarfiotti, Ferdinando
LAST EMPEROR, THE
Schaper, Rainer
DIE VERLIEBTEN
Schiller, Joel
NUTS
Schlubach, Jan
MASCHENKA
Schneider, Christopher
SO VIELE TRAUME
Schnell, Curtis A.
NIGHTFORCE
Schnell, Jurgen
BORAN—ZEIT ZUM ZIELEN
Schoppe, James
OVER THE TOP
Schroder, Ulrich
OTTO—DER NEUE FILM
Scott, Jan
SQUARE DANCE
Scott, Jock
OUT OF ORDER
Searcy, R. Clifford
HANOI HILTON, THE
Segall, Berta
HOT SHOT
Sharpe, Geoff
SLAUGHTER HIGH
Shepard, Maxine
PERFECT MATCH, THE
Shohan, Naomi
OPEN HOUSE
Silber, Rene
VERA
Silk, Ilkay
TUESDAY WEDNESDAY
Simon, Eric
MACBETH
Simon, Mark
DEATHROW GAMESHOW
Smith, Adrian
EMPIRE STATE
Smith, Morley
WHISTLE BLOWER, THE
Snyder, David L.
SUMMER SCHOOL
So, Stephen
NINJA THUNDERBOLT
Sowder, Cynthia
ALLNIGHTER, THE
Spencer, James H.
INNERSPACE
Spriggs, Austen
HAMBURGER HILL
Stearns, Craig
DATE WITH AN ANGEL
Stewart Burnside
CASSANDRA
Stolfo, Otello
BUSHFIRE MOON
Stoll, George
BEAT, THE
Stout, William
MASTERS OF THE UNIVERSE
Strawn, C.J.
HIDDEN, THE
Strawn, Mick
HIDDEN, THE
Stringer, Michael
FROM THE HIP
Strohschein, Marion
SAME TO YOU
Swift, Brent
MY DEMON LOVER
Sylbert, Paul
ISHTAR
NADINE
PICK-UP ARTIST, THE
Tapiador, Jose Maria
TROUBLE WITH SPIES, THE
Taucher, Rozanne
DREAMANIAC

Tavares, Fernando
UM FILM 100% BRAZILEIRO

Tavoularis, Alex
STEEL DAWN

Tavoularis, Dean
GARDENS OF STONE

Taylor, Jack G.
MILLION DOLLAR MYSTERY

Terry, Allen
NIGHT STALKER, THE

Thomas, Philip
WHITE OF THE EYE

Thompson, Brian
GROUND ZERO

Toomey, Marshall
PENITENTIARY III

Townsend, Jeffrey
MAID TO ORDER

Trapeznikov, Vladimir
SKAZKA O PREKRASNOY AYSULU

Vallone, John
PREDATOR

Vance, James D.
OUTRAGEOUS FORTUNE

Vanorio, Frank
CURSE, THE

Vezat, Bernard
JEAN DE FLORETTE
MANON OF THE SPRING

Vischkof, Katia
SOUS LE SOLEIL DE SATAN

Walker, Roy
GOOD MORNING, VIETNAM

Waltenberger, Rafal
BLIND CHANCE

Walton, Tony
GLASS MENAGERIE, THE

Wasco, David
STACKING
STUDENT CONFIDENTIAL

Washington, Dennis
DEAD, THE
NO WAY OUT

Wassberg, Goran
MALARPIRATER

Waters, Simon
SQUEEZE, THE

Watt, Tracy
WARM NIGHTS ON A SLOW MOVING TRAIN

Welch, Bo
LOST BOYS, THE

Westfelt, Lasse
MORE ABOUT THE CHILDREN OF BULLERBY VILLAGE
NIONDE KOMPANIET

Wickman, Sven
PA STIGENDE KURS

Williams, Trevor
ALLAN QUATERMAIN AND THE LOST CITY OF GOLD
POLICE ACADEMY 4: CITIZENS ON PATROL
REVENGE OF THE NERDS II: NERDS IN PARADISE

Wilson, David
EAT THE PEACH

Wurtzel, Stuart
SUSPECT

Wyhowski, Hugo Lyczyc
SAMMY AND ROSIE GET LAID

Yichuan, Liu
BLACK CANNON INCIDENT, THE

Yontan, Gurel
YER DEMIR, GOK BAKIR

Zacharias, Ann
TESTET

Zagorsky, Konstantin
MIO, MOY MIO

Zanetti, Eugenio
PROMISED LAND
SLAMDANCE

Zeljko Senecic
SLEEP WELL, MY LOVE

Ziembicki, Bob
BARFLY

Ziembicki, Robert
DUDES

Zurkow, Marina
ENEMY TERRITORY

SET DESIGNERS

Abou-Soufiane, Mustapha
ABBES

Abramson, Philip
TIN MEN

Aird, Gilles
MORNING MAN, THE

Alarcon, Victor
MOROS Y CRISTIANOS

Allen, Linda
NUMBER ONE WITH A BULLET
THREE FOR THE ROAD

Alonso, Juan
ENTRE FICHERAS ANDA EL DIABLO

Altamura, Ello
DANCERS

Amalfitano, Bruno
MAN ON FIRE

Ambrose, Scott
COLD STEEL

Anderson, John
BEVERLY HILLS COP II

Andres, Gumersindo
SUFRE MAMON

Andrew, Mark
DEATH WISH 4: THE CRACKDOWN

Ayres, Bruce
MILLION DOLLAR MYSTERY

Barrows, James
NIGHTMARE ON ELM STREET 3: DREAM WARRIORS, A

Barska, Teresa
MATKA KROLOW

Basaldua, Emilio
EL ANO DEL CONEJO

Baugh, Gary
BIG SHOTS

Beale, Lesley
HOME IS WHERE THE HART IS

Beale, Leslie
STAKEOUT

Beck, Bill
LEONARD PART 6

Benetazzo, Nordana
BESAME MUCHO

Berger, Richard G.
RUNNING MAN, THE

Bergstrom, Jan K.
SUMMER HEAT

Bernard, Andrew
CANT BUY ME LOVE

Biddiscombe, Carl
BLIND DATE

Block-Cummins, Becky
DOLLS

Bloom, Lee
WHO'S THAT GIRL

Bloom, Les
RADIO DAYS

Bloom, Leslie
WALL STREET

Bode, Susan
BELIEVERS, THE
GLASS MENAGERIE, THE
SECRET OF MY SUCCESS, THE
WALL STREET

Bogart, Jane
BROADCAST NEWS

Bond, Olivia
GABY—A TRUE STORY

Bordock, Elizabeth
VIDEO DEAD, THE

Bordolin, Enrique
EL DUENO DEL SOL

Boris, Richard
MILLION DOLLAR MYSTERY

Braden, Hub
GARBAGE PAIL KIDS MOVIE, THE

Brandenburg, Rosemary
LA BAMBA

Brolly, Barry
MALONE

Brown, Rick
PRINCIPAL, THE

Brull, Pieter
NITWITS

Bueno, Clovis
COLOR OF DESTINY, THE

Burbank, Linda
FLICKS

Burman, Wolfgang
ROMANCA FINAL

Butler, Chris
BEST SELLER

Calderhead, Liz
TOO OUTRAGEOUS

Call, Laura
WITCHBOARD

Camaya, Boyet
EQUALIZER 2000

Cammer, Judy
INNERSPACE
OVERBOARD

Camposano, Josie
SWEET REVENGE

Chen, E.C.
UNTOUCHABLES, THE

Chevalier, Joseph Mifsud
SICILIAN, THE

Christopher, Lynn
PROJECT X

Clay Griffith
DIRTY DANCING

Clayton, Gil
UNTOUCHABLES, THE

Cliff, T. Edward
OMEGA SYNDROME

Cloudia
WHO'S THAT GIRL

Combs, Debra
ALLNIGHTER, THE

Conrad, Albrecht
HELSINKI NAPOLI—ALL NIGHT LONG

Cooper, Dorree
HOUSE TWO: THE SECOND STORY

Cordwell, Harry
EMPIRE OF THE SUN

Cramer, Ian
HANOI HILTON, THE

Csik, Gyorgy
ISTEN VELETEK, BARATAIM

Cutler, Jeff
GATE, THE
PRETTYKILL

Davies, Tessa
GOOD MORNING, VIETNAM

de Leeus, Wilem
IRIS

De Moleron, Arnaud
ARIA

de Souza, Naum Alvez
VERA

Dean, Lisa
BARFLY

Denny, Keith
FULL METAL JACKET

Desideri, Giorgio
BELLY OF AN ARCHITECT, THE

DeTitta, George
FATAL ATTRACTION
OUTRAGEOUS FORTUNE
SEPTEMBER

Di Santo, Byrnadette
KILLING TIME, THE

Dick, Jaro
HOUSEKEEPER, THE

Diskomonous, Tajos
PRETTY SMART

Dreizen, Sherry
CLUB LIFE

Duffy, Jim
BLACK WIDOW
RUNNING MAN, THE

Duggan-Smith, Tony
NIGHTSTICK

Dwyer, John
JAWS: THE REVENGE

E.C. Chen
FATAL BEAUTY

Eagan, Beverli
EXTREME PREJUDICE

Edward
FROM THE HIP

Efrat, Doron
DEATH BEFORE DISHONOR

Elo, Kristine
UUNO TURHAPURO MUUTTAA MAALLE

Emshwiller, Susan
KINDRED, THE

Espada, J.M.
LA SENYORA

Esteban, Julio
REDONDELA

Estevez, Enrique
BORN IN EAST L.A.
LETS GET HARRY
PREDATOR

Evans, Deborah
P.I. PRIVATE INVESTIGATIONS

Fabus, Mark
LETS GET HARRY

Facello, Abel
STRANGER, THE

Fernandez, Javier
LAW OF DESIRE

Fettis, Gary
GARDENS OF STONE

Fischer, Lisa
BABY BOOM
BIG EASY, THE
LIGHT OF DAY

Fleischman, Raymond
BIG TOWN, THE

Ford, Michael
LIVING DAYLIGHTS, THE

Ford, Michael D.
EMPIRE OF THE SUN

Forest, Michele
NIGHT ZOO

Foutz, Terril
PARTY CAMP

Franco, John
SPACEBALLS

Franco, Robert J.
ANGEL HEART
HELLO AGAIN

Freeborn, Mark
BIG TOWN, THE

Freeborn, Mark S.
DEAD OF WINTER

Frischette, Suzie
WALKER

Fuenzalida, Patricia
WITCHBOARD

Fuhrman, Harold
MONSTER SQUAD, THE

Galbraith, Elinor Rose
BELIEVERS, THE

Galicia, Jose Luis
POLICIA

Gallichotte, Ross
OVER THE TOP

Gausman, Hal
JAWS: THE REVENGE

Gecser, Lujza
LENZ

Gelfield, Arthur
NO DEAD HEROES

Gelinas, Pierre
LE SOURD DANS LA VILLE

Gentz, Rick T.
OUTRAGEOUS FORTUNE

George, Tudor
SHADEY

Gervasci, Carlo
DARK EYES

Gibeson, Bruce
NO WAY OUT
WHITE WATER SUMMER

Gibra, Eva
MISSION KILL

Glass, Ted
SQUEEZE, THE

Gluck, Daniel
MASTERS OF THE UNIVERSE

Gould, Robert
ROBOCOP

Goulder, Susan
I WAS A TEENAGE T.V. TERRORIST

Graham, Marlene
GATE, THE
TOO OUTRAGEOUS

Gray, Maggie
PRINCESS BRIDE, THE
SHADEY

Green, Ron
MILLION DOLLAR MYSTERY

Gruse, Brigit
SIERRA LEONE

Gyurki, Andras
DOKTOR MINORKA VIDOR NAGY NAPJA

Hall, Patricia
ASSASSINATION
MONSTER IN THE CLOSET

Hamilton-Doney, Robyn
THREE KINDS OF HEAT

Harris, Ann
SOMEONE TO WATCH OVER ME

Hay, John
O. C. AND STIGGS

Henshaw, Buck
BLACK WIDOW

Hicks, Alan
ISHTAR

Hicks, John Alan
PICK-UP ARTIST, THE

Hidalgo, Eduardo
REDONDELA

Highfill, J. Allen
CAMPUS MAN

Hilkamo, Pertti
A LA ITKE IINES
VARJOJA PARATIISISSA

Hill, Caron
HOSTAGE

Hill, Derek
HOUSE OF GAMES

Hill, Roland
MONSTER SQUAD, THE

Hill, Roland E.
OVER THE TOP

Holzman, Cecilla
ORACLE, THE

Honda, Atsushi
BUS

Hoover, Richard
IN THE MOOD
SWEET LORRAINE

Hormel, Michelle
CLUB LIFE

Howitt, Peter
FOURTH PROTOCOL, THE

Hublitz, Sosie
WHALES OF AUGUST, THE

Huntley, Anne
RIVER'S EDGE

Huntley-Ahrens, Anne
NIGHTFLYERS

Hyo-jin, Park
NAE-SHI

I Bombin, Polo
MADRID

Iversen, Portia
ALLAN QUATERMAIN AND THE LOST CITY OF GOLD

Ivey, Don
HAPPY NEW YEAR

Jacobson, Scott
MAKING MR.RIGHT

James Teegarden, William
HARRY AND THE HENDERSONS

Jely, Ferenc
GONDOVISELES

Joffe, Carol
ORPHANS
RADIO DAYS

Johnson, Michael
MASTERS OF THE UNIVERSE

Jones, Martin
ZOMBIE HIGH

Jordan, Steve
ISHTAR

Karatzas, Steven
BORN IN EAST L.A.

Kardestuncer, Sermin
SALVATION!

Kaufman, Susan
BEST SELLER

Kayla Koeber
MALIBU BIKINI SHOP, THE

Keller, Joachim
DER JUNGE MIT DEM GROSSEN SCHWARZEN HUND

Kempster, Victor
MORGAN STEWART'S COMING HOME

Kicenik, Alexandra
SUPERNATURALS, THE

Kienlan, Joan M.
BLOODSUCKERS FROM OUTER SPACE

Klompus, Betsy
HOT SHOT

Kohlmeyer, Charly
HAPPY HOUR

Kosarewicz, Tadeusz
INNA WYSPA

Kowalczyk, Andrzej
MAGNAT

Kracik, Robert
RAISING ARIZONA

Kraus, Paul
LEONARD PART 6

Kyriakoulis, Antonis
SWEET COUNTRY

Laborczy, Nicholas
UNTOUCHABLES, THE

Langer, Renate
SIERRA LEONE

Larose, Raymond
STREET SMART

Laude, Marcel
JEAN DE FLORETTE

Lawrence, Richard J.
WALK LIKE A MAN

Lee, Sam
NINJA THUNDERBOLT

Lehtinen, Erkki
NAKEMIIN, HYVASTI

Lekkos, Yannis
ONIRO ARISTERIS NICHTAS

Lewandowski, Marek
PIERSCIEN I ROZA

Lindstrom, Kara
SIESTA

Lopate, Joan
DEADTIME STORIES

Lovas, Pal
HOTREAL

Lumaldo, Miguel Angel
EL DUENO DEL SOL
LOS DUENOS DEL SILENCIO

MacAvin, Josie
LONELY PASSION OF JUDITH HEARNE,THE

Majda, Wojciech
KOMEDIANCI Z WCZORAJSZEJ ULICY

Maltese, Dan
REAL MEN

Maltese, Daniel
OUTRAGEOUS FORTUNE

Mann, Louis
PLANES, TRAINS AND AUTOMOBILES

March, Marvin
LETHAL WEAPON

Marcus, Michael C.
SLAMDANCE

Massone, Nicoletta
MORNING MAN, THE

Mathewson, Katherine
STREET SMART

Matwijkow, Gary
MY DARK LADY

May, Dan
ADVENTURES IN BABYSITTING

May, Daniel Loren
BURGLAR

Mays, Richard
SURRENDER

McAvin, Josie
DEAD, THE
EAT THE PEACH

McCulley, Anne
NUTS

McCulley, Anne D.
THROW MOMMA FROM THE TRAIN

McElvin, Bob
OVERKILL

McSherry, Rose Marie
BIG TOWN, THE
STAKEOUT

Mejia, Esteban
HOUR OF THE ASSASSIN

Meletopoulos, Nikos
PHOTOGRAPH, THE

Mellery, Veronique
MASCARA

Melton, Gregory
JOCKS

Mercadante, Francine
WEEDS
Michnevich, Anamarie
MATEWAN
Mikado, Sadatoshi
MAGINA—MURA MONOGATARI
Mollo, Ann
BELLMAN AND TRUE
Moore, Elizabeth
EVIL DEAD 2: DEAD BY DAWN
Moore, Randy
DATE WITH AN ANGEL
Morales, Leslie
SHY PEOPLE
Morawski, Marek
E S D
Morong, David
NECROPOLIS
Mowat, Doug
NIGHTFORCE
Muraki, Shinobu
PRINCESS FROM THE MOON
Murcia, Felix
CARA DE ACELGA
EL BOSQUE ANIMADO
MY GENERAL
Navarro, Nick
CROSS MY HEART
RUNNING MAN, THE
Nelson, George R.
BATTERIES NOT INCLUDED
Nelson, George Robert
CRITICAL CONDITION
Nollman, Gene
INNERSPACE
Nowak, Barbara
WERYFIKACJA
Nye, Nancy
LESS THAN ZERO
Pacelli, Joseph
PROJECT X
Palacios, Guillermo
SENTIMIENTOS: MIRTA DE LINIERS A ESTAMBUL
Palmero, Rafael
LA CASA DE BERNARDA ALBA
Paraiso, Nene
LA PLAYA DE LOS PERROS
Parker, Arthur Jeph
DRAGNET
SUSPECT
Parker, Michael
PROGRAMMED TO KILL
Passi, Mauro
CHRONICLE OF A DEATH FORETOLD
Patton, Nancy
RUNNING MAN, THE
Pecanins, Maria Teresa
LA GRAN FIESTA
Pedigo, Tom
REAL MEN
Perrin, Bryce
WALKER
Perryman, Dian
P.K. & THE KID
Peters, Paul
MADE IN HEAVEN
Peterson, George
HOT CHILD IN THE CITY
Pierce, Chuck
BIG SHOTS
Poll, Lee
NADINE
Pope, Leslie
ANGEL HEART
IRONWEED
MATEWAN
Potter, Stephen
MILLION DOLLAR MYSTERY
Pray, Jennifer
SUMMER CAMP NIGHTMARE
Pyhala, Jaakko
URSULA
Quiros, Jesus
ASIGNATURA APROBADA
Rajk, Laszlo
LENZ
Ramirez, Cornelio
GET THE TERRORISTS
Randall, Gary D.
HES MY GIRL
Raney, Sue
VIOLINS CAME WITH THE AMERICANS, THE
Rantanen, Tapio
LIIAN ISO KEIKKA
Raskin, Simone
VERA
Rau, Gretchen
TOUGH GUYS DON'T DANCE
Reindl, Hans
TRIUMPH DE GERECHTEN
Reyeros, Rafael
LA OVEJA NEGRA
Richardson, Kimberley
STEPFATHER, THE
Richardson, Kimberly
ROXANNE
Ridgeway, Valanne
IVE HEARD THE MERMAIDS SINGING
Robinson II, Jimmy
MAKING MR.RIGHT
Rogalla, Erica
SQUARE DANCE
Rollins, Leslie
CHINA GIRL
HIDING OUT
Romano, Norma
EN EL NOMBRE DEL HIJO
Romvari, Jozsef
HOL VOLT, HOL NEM VOLT
LAURA
Rosell, Josep
EL LUTE—CAMINA O REVIENTA
YEAR OF AWAKENING, THE
Rosemarin, Hilton
BEDROOM WINDOW, THE
THREE MEN AND A BABY
Rowland, Elise "Cricket"
MANNEQUIN
Rubens, Denise
FRIENDSHIP'S DEATH
Russhon, Christian W.
CANT BUY ME LOVE
Saarainen, Erkki
JAAHYVAISET PRESIDENTILLE
Saloni-Marczewski, Wojciech
ZYCIE WEWNETRZNE
Sanchez, Enrique
ENTRE FICHERAS ANDA EL DIABLO
Sardanis, Steven P.
UNTOUCHABLES, THE
Sauter, Bernhard
ALPINE FIRE
Schlee, Ana
ELE, O BOTO
Schmidt, Phoebe
NIGHTFORCE
Schreiber, Pola
PROGRAMMED TO KILL
Schwartz, Steve
JAWS: THE REVENGE
Scolacchia, Nazzareno
FRANCESCA
Scoppa, Justin
THREE MEN AND A BABY
Scott, Laurie
RAGE OF HONOR
Seirton, Michael
CRY FREEDOM
MIRACLES
Sessa, Robert
WITCHES OF EASTWICK, THE
Shewchuk, Steve
POLICE ACADEMY 4: CITIZENS ON PATROL
SUSPECT
Shohan, Naomi
MUNCHIES
Simmonds, Stephen
FULL METAL JACKET
Simpson, C.J.
HIDING OUT
Simpson, Rick
BLACK WIDOW
Skrzepinski, Jerzy
STANISLAW I ANNA
Smith, Brendon
BLUE MONKEY
Snyder, Dawn
AMAZING GRACE AND CHUCK
Solle, Bogdan
KOMEDIANTKA
Spheeris, Linda
SOME KIND OF WONDERFUL
Staple, Jeanie M.
JOHN AND THE MISSUS
Starbuck, Michele
FLOWERS IN THE ATTIC
Steinman, Lindy
STEEL DAWN
Stevens, Todd
ZOMBIE HIGH
Stiborski, Inge
ANITA—DANCES OF VICE
Switoniak, Jaroslaw
MIEDZY USTAMI A BRZEGIEM PUCHARU
Talbert, Tom
WINNERS TAKE ALL
Tapola, Vesa
UUNO TURHAPURO MUUTTAA MAALLE
Taponen, Matti
INUKSUK
Tard, Jean-Baptiste
MORNING MAN, THE
Tatlock, John
ANNA
Tatsumi, Shiro
MAGINA—MURA MONOGATARI
Taucher, Rozanne
SLUMBER PARTY MASSACRE II
Teegarden, Jim
SOMEONE TO WATCH OVER ME
Teegarden, William James
OVERBOARD
Thomas, Lisette
STRANDED
Tichler, John Nelson
STEELE JUSTICE
Tocci, James
ROBOCOP
Toledo, Veronica
MOROS Y CRISTIANOS
Towery, Julie Kaye
AMAZON WOMEN ON THE MOON
Trinz, Bundy
BIG SHOTS
Tropp, Stan
WITCHES OF EASTWICK, THE
Trow, Bob
MILLION DOLLAR MYSTERY
Vallin, Katherine
CLUB LIFE
Vasquez, Awie
TOUGH COP
Vazquez, Luis
ASIGNATURA APROBADA
Vera, Gerardo
HAY QUE DESHACER LA CASA
Vera, Maria Adelina
POR LOS CAMINOS VERDES
Verdugo, Fernando
ASI COMO HABIAN SIDO
Virve, Tynu
IGRY DLJA DETEJ SKO'NOGO VOZRASTA
Volz, Christina
EMANON
von Schilling, Klaus
PENG! DU BIST TOT!
Walker, John T.
LIKE FATHER, LIKE SON
Warnke, John
LOST BOYS, THE
SUMMER SCHOOL
Wasco, Sandy Reynolds
STACKING
Wells, Tom
LADY BEWARE
White, Wally
NORTH SHORE
Williams, Diana Allen
SPACE RACE
Willis, Patrick
ALLAN QUATERMAIN AND THE LOST CITY OF GOLD
Wilshire, Catherine
HUNTER'S BLOOD
Wionczek-Lozinska, Joanna
CZAS NADZIEI
Wolverton, Lynn
SOMETHING SPECIAL!

Wolyniec, Roman
RYKOWISKO

Woollard, Joan
HOPE AND GLORY

Yates, Ron
OVERBOARD

Young, Peter
SUPERMAN IV: THE QUEST FOR PEACE

Zolfo, Victor
FOREVER, LULU

Zurkow, Marina
MUTANT HUNT

SPECIAL EFFECTS

A & A Special Effects
HAPPY HOUR

Abades, Reyes
LA ESTANQUERA DE VALLECAS
LA PLAYA DE LOS PERROS

Ace Effects
BELLMAN AND TRUE
EAT THE RICH
GOTHIC

Acord, Cal
WANTED: DEAD OR ALIVE

Adler, Nick
PRINCESS BRIDE, THE

Agostini, Renato
MAN ON FIRE

Albain, Dick
FLOWERS IN THE ATTIC

Albiez, Peter
SPACEBALLS

Allard, Eric
ALLAN QUATERMAIN AND THE LOST CITY OF GOLD

Allen, David
DOLLS

Anderson, Max W.
MADE IN HEAVEN

Anderson, Tom
RUSSKIES

Angress, Percy
SPACEBALLS

Any Effects
EAT THE RICH

Apelquist, Susanne
WARDOGS

Apogee
SPACEBALLS

Arthur, Colin
ALLAN QUATERMAIN AND THE LOST CITY OF GOLD

Aspinall, Jennifer
PSYCHOS IN LOVE
STREET TRASH

Bahs, Henning
BABETTE'S GASTEBUD

Balandin, John
ALIEN PREDATOR

Balandin, Pedro
LA CASA DE BERNARDA ALBA

Barefoot, Rick
WEEDS

Barton, Dave
MORE BAD NEWS

Baur, Tassilo
MALIBU BIKINI SHOP, THE
WITCHBOARD

Beauchamp, James Wayne
RETURN TO HORROR HIGH
STEELE JUSTICE

Beauchamp, Wayne
MISSION KILL

Becker, Martin
MONSTER IN THE CLOSET
OUTING, THE

Bellek, A.
WIND, THE

Bennett, Jack
SQUARE DANCE

Bessara, Margaret
ALIEN PREDATOR

Bessera, Margaret
SLUMBER PARTY MASSACRE II

Biggs, Chris
ZOMBIE HIGH

Bird, Jaime
ERNEST GOES TO CAMP

Blais, Pascal
GREAT LAND OF SMALL, THE

Bohus, Ted A.
MIND KILLER

Bordona, Dan
EVIL SPAWN

Borgli, Petter
ETTER RUBICON

Bottin, Rob
INNERSPACE
ROBOCOP
WITCHES OF EASTWICK, THE

Boyajian, Craig
SPACEBALLS

Brink, Connie
BELIEVERS, THE

Brooks, Matt
PSYCHOS IN LOVE

Brotherhood, J.C.
ANGEL HEART

Brunner, John
DOLLS

Brunner, Vivian
DOLLS

Bua, Anthony
ROCK 'N' ROLL NIGHTMARE

Buechler, John
GARBAGE PAIL KIDS MOVIE, THE
SLAVE GIRLS FROM BEYOND INFINITY

Buechler, John Carl
DOLLS

Burman, Rob
OFFSPRING, THE

Caban, Willie
FOREVER, LULU

Caglione, John
MY DEMON LOVER

Callaway, Tom
BANZAI RUNNER

Cannom, Greg
LOST BOYS, THE

Capobianco, Carmine
PSYCHOS IN LOVE

Carere, Frank
GATE, THE

Carere Special Effects
NIGHTSTICK

Carmona, Joe
TOUGH COP

Carter, John
EMANON
PROGRAMMED TO KILL

Casady, Chris
RUNNING MAN, THE

Cassar, Mario
IRON WARRIOR

Catizone, Rick
EVIL DEAD 2: DEAD BY DAWN

Cavanaugh, Larry
RUNNING MAN, THE

Chesney, Peter
NIGHTMARE ON ELM STREET 3: DREAM WARRIORS, A

Cinefex Workshop
PEKING OPERA BLUES

Cirile, Jim
ROCK 'N' ROLL NIGHTMARE

Coast to Coast Productions
SLAUGHTER HIGH

Cohen, David
SLAVE GIRLS FROM BEYOND INFINITY

Colladant, Dominique
MON BEL AMOUR, MA DECHIRURE

Collins, Michael
HOPE AND GLORY

Compton, Jill
BLUE MONKEY

Conway, Richard
SUPERMAN IV: THE QUEST FOR PEACE

Cook, Randall William
GATE, THE

Cordero, Laurencio "Choby"
PREDATOR

Cordero, Ralph
ROBOT HOLOCAUST

Cordon, Felix
A LOS CUATRO VIENTOS

Corridori, Giovanni
MAN ON FIRE

Corso, Bill
SLUMBER PARTY MASSACRE II

Cory, Phil
MONSTER SQUAD, THE

Cosgrove, Ryal
MORNING MAN, THE

Coulter, J. Scott
SLUMBER PARTY MASSACRE II

Courtley, Steve
LIGHTHORSEMEN, THE

Cox, Brian
LES PATTERSON SAVES THE WORLD

Craig, Louis
GREAT LAND OF SMALL, THE

Cramer, Fred
GOOD MORNING, VIETNAM

Criswell, John
SLUMBER PARTY MASSACRE II

Crum, Eugene
DEATH BEFORE DISHONOR

Cummins, James
ALIEN PREDATOR

Cundom, Tom
RAGE OF HONOR

Davies, Craig
ROBOCOP

de Marchis, Carlo
EL GRAN SERAFIN

De Rossi, Gino
LAST EMPEROR, THE

de Velasco, Fernando Vasquez
HOUR OF THE ASSASSIN

Del Brocco, Giancarlo
DOLLS

DeMarco, Frank
SPACE RACE

Di Sarro, Al
PREDATOR

Diaz, Hugo
RAGE OF HONOR

Dietz, Frank
ROCK 'N' ROLL NIGHTMARE

Dion, Dennis
MALONE
OUTRAGEOUS FORTUNE

Doublin, Anthony
FLICKS

Doug Beswick Productions
EVIL DEAD 2: DEAD BY DAWN

Downey, Roy
BLIND DATE
NADINE

Doyle, Jim
HELLO MARY LOU, PROM NIGHT II

Dream Quest Images
PREDATOR

Drexler, Doug
MY DEMON LOVER

Dumont, David
SALVATION!

Durey, Ken
NO WAY OUT

Edlund, Richard
DATE WITH AN ANGEL
LEONARD PART 6
MASTERS OF THE UNIVERSE
MONSTER SQUAD, THE

Eggett, John
P.I. PRIVATE INVESTIGATIONS

Ellenshaw, Harrison
SUPERMAN IV: THE QUEST FOR PEACE

Elmendorf, Gary
SQUEEZE, THE

Eng, John
SLAVE GIRLS FROM BEYOND INFINITY

Erham, Kevin
CURSE, THE

Evans, Andy
BIG SHOTS

Evans, John
FULL METAL JACKET
SUPERMAN IV: THE QUEST FOR PEACE

Farjallo, Sergio
ELE, O BOTO

Farley, Jeff
SLUMBER PARTY MASSACRE II

Fasano, John
ROCK 'N' ROLL NIGHTMARE

Ferren, Bran
MAKING MR.RIGHT
Fink, Michael
PROJECT X
Fisher, Tom
EXTREME PREJUDICE
Fite, Randy
RETURN OF JOSEY WALES, THE
Ford, Thomas
WHITE OF THE EYE
Franca, Marco Antonio
ELE, O BOTO
Frank, Jeremie
ROBOT HOLOCAUST
Frazee, Terry
NO WAY OUT
Frazier, John
GARDENS OF STONE
LIKE FATHER, LIKE SON
Fredburg, Jim
SUSPECT
Freire, Persio
ELE, O BOTO
French, Ed
NECROPOLIS
NIGHTMARE AT SHADOW WOODS
ROBOT HOLOCAUST
French, Edward
DEADTIME STORIES
Fuller, Rodney
HOPE AND GLORY
Fullerton, Carl
MY DEMON LOVER
Gagnon, Scott
FIREHOUSE
Galich, Steve
NEAR DARK
Gant, John
THREE KINDS OF HEAT
Gardner, Marvin
WEEDS
Gargiulo II, Arnold
ROCK 'N' ROLL NIGHTMARE
Gaspar, Chuck
LETHAL WEAPON
Gastineau, Frederic
TERMINUS
Gastineau, Jacques
TERMINUS
Gen, Ye Mao
EMPIRE OF THE SUN
George, Roger
MUNCHIES
SPACE RACE
STRIPPED TO KILL
Gibson, John
ROCK 'N' ROLL NIGHTMARE
Godbout, Jacques
KEEPING TRACK
WILD THING
Gray, John
SQUEEZE, THE
Grigg, Gene
POLICE ACADEMY 4: CITIZENS ON PATROL
Guastini, Vincent
DERANGED
Guastini, Vincent J.
MIND KILLER
Guzman, Marcellino Pacheco
WALKER
Hall, Allan
O. C. AND STIGGS
Hall, Allen
BLACK WIDOW
STRANDED
Hall, Dale
VIDEO DEAD, THE
Harris, David
CRY FREEDOM
Harris, Tom
ARIA
ARIA
EAT THE RICH
Hauser, Robin
GARDENS OF STONE
Henriksen, Soren Gam
EPIDEMIC
Herrmann, Karl
RUSSKIES

Hill, Tex
RETURN OF JOSEY WALES, THE
Ho, Martin
NINJA THUNDERBOLT
Horrorefx
ORACLE, THE
Hutchinson, Peter
FOURTH PROTOCOL, THE
Hyde, Vern
EVIL DEAD 2: DEAD BY DAWN
PROGRAMMED TO KILL
Hynek, Joel
PREDATOR
Industrial Light & Magic
BATTERIES NOT INCLUDED
Industrial Light and Magic
EMPIRE OF THE SUN
SPACEBALLS
Inez, Frank
OUTING, THE
Isaac, Jim
HOUSE TWO: THE SECOND STORY
Johnston, Gerry
RAWHEAD REX
Jones, Gary
THOU SHALT NOT KILL . . . EXCEPT
Joyce, J.P.
BLOODSUCKERS FROM OUTER SPACE
Kaleva, Lenna
SOMETHING SPECIAL!
Kari, Antti
SNOW QUEEN, THE
Kavanagh, Michael
THREE MEN AND A BABY
Keen, Bob
HELLRAISER
Kerrigan, Rick
AMAZING GRACE AND CHUCK
Kirshoff, Steve
IRONWEED
SQUEEZE, THE
Kitakawa, Koichi
HOTARUGAWA
Knott, Robby
IN THE MOOD
Kruk, Reiko
MON BEL AMOUR, MA DECHIRURE
Kung, Osamu
TOO MUCH
Kunz, Peter
BEST SELLER
Lacky, Mike
I WAS A TEENAGE ZOMBIE
Landerer, Gregory
SUPERNATURALS, THE
Lanteri, Mike
WITCHES OF EASTWICK, THE
Lauten, Tom
MUTANT HUNT
Lazzarini, Rick
SPACEBALLS
Les Productions
GREAT LAND OF SMALL, THE
Litten, Peter
RAWHEAD REX
SLAUGHTER HIGH
Little, Jeff
DOGS IN SPACE
Lockwood, Dean
MALONE
Lofton, Terry
NAIL GUN MASSACRE
Logan, Dan
EL HOMBRE DESNUDO
Lombardi, Joe
HAMBURGER HILL
Lorimer, Alan E.
OVERBOARD
Ludovik, L.
WIND, THE
Ludwig, Heinz
ZABOU
Malivoire, Martin
HOUSEKEEPER, THE
Martin, Dale
NEAR DARK
ROBOCOP
Martinelli, Fabrizio
LAST EMPEROR, THE

Martz, Neal
MY DEMON LOVER
Mason, Andrew
TIME GUARDIAN, THE
McCarron, Bob
HOWLING III, THE
LES PATTERSON SAVES THE WORLD
McCarthy, Kevin
COMMANDO SQUAD
CYCLONE
McCarthy, Sandy
COMMANDO SQUAD
McCracken, Michael John
KINDRED, THE
McDowell, Tim
BLOODSUCKERS FROM OUTER SPACE
McNeill, Valarie
ROBOT HOLOCAUST
Mechanical Make-up Imageries
GARBAGE PAIL KIDS MOVIE, THE
Menzel, Mike
WEEDS
Messenger, Mark
ZOMBIE HIGH
Miles, Hal
SLUMBER PARTY MASSACRE II
Millar, Henry
JAWS: THE REVENGE
Miller, Ralph
EVIL SPAWN
Modica, Vincent
ROCK 'N' ROLL NIGHTMARE
Molin, Mark
HOUSEKEEPER, THE
Molina, Antonio
CRYSTAL HEART
Molina, Juan Ramon
STRAIGHT TO HELL
Molinelli, Tom
PSYCHOS IN LOVE
Moller, Mark
CURSE, THE
Monak, Gary
DEATH BEFORE DISHONOR
Monroe, Jack
NADINE
NO WAY OUT
Muren, Dennis
INNERSPACE
Naelgas, Guy
HOSTAGE SYNDROME
Nakano, Shokei
PRINCESS FROM THE MOON
Nakano, Teruyoshi
TOKYO BLACKOUT
Neale, Tony
LAST OF ENGLAND, THE
Nielson, Jim
EL HOMBRE DESNUDO
Noelgas, Edilbert
ULTIMAX FORCE
Noelgas, Guy
GET THE TERRORISTS
Olmstead, Robert
BEST SELLER
Orr, Bill
ROXANNE
Pamplin, H. Shep
PSYCHOS IN LOVE
Parra, Antonio
EMPIRE OF THE SUN
Parra, Pepe
MI NOMBRE ES GATILLO
Pearce, Brian
MOVING TARGETS
RUNNING FROM THE GUNS
Pedis, Jan
PSYCHOS IN LOVE
Pepiot, Kenneth D.
FATAL BEAUTY
Pereira, Peter
MISTER INDIA
Pestov, L.
VZLOMSHCHIK
Peterson, Dennis
OVER THE TOP
Phoenix
MANKILLERS
Pier, David
PRINCIPAL, THE

Pierce, Brian
SLATE, WYN & ME

Pitkanen, Lauri
SNOW QUEEN, THE

Polack, Yoram
DEADLINE

Port, Nina
PSYCHOS IN LOVE

Price, Ted
TIME GUARDIAN, THE

Purcell, Bill
BIG EASY, THE

Quinlivan, Joe
STEEL DAWN

R/Greenberg
PREDATOR

Radder, Jan
PSYCHOS IN LOVE

Rambell, Jun
NO DEAD HEROES

Ramsey, Joe
SUSPECT

Ratliff, Richard
SPACEBALLS

Ray, Christopher
EVIL SPAWN

Reader, Joe
SLAVE GIRLS FROM BEYOND INFINITY

Reel EFX
OUTING, THE

Richardson, John
LIVING DAYLIGHTS, THE

Richtsfeld, Richard
FIRE AND ICE

Rick Baker
HARRY AND THE HENDERSONS

Roberts, L. Michael
BLUE MONKEY

Robertson, Stuart
PREDATOR

Ronzani, Peter
ROBOCOP

Ross, Ted
BELIEVERS, THE

Ruano, Isidro
A LOS CUATRO VIENTOS

Ruohomaki, Jukka
SNOW QUEEN, THE

Samiotis, M.
WIND, THE

Schaidt, Gunther
BORAN—ZEIT ZUM ZIELEN

Schultze-Jena, Stephan
DER UNSICHTBARE

Scoones, Ian
PRAYER FOR THE DYING, A

Shelley, Bob
BIG SHOTS
BIG SHOTS

Shepherd, Robert
SPACEBALLS

Shoftrom, Mark
ALIEN PREDATOR

Short, Robert
NIGHTFLYERS

Shostrom, Mark
SUPERNATURALS, THE

Sirius Effects
BLUE MONKEY

Smith, Willy
AMAZONS

Sorenson, Carl
I WAS A TEENAGE ZOMBIE

Speed, Ken
BEST SELLER

St. Domingo, Jess
EQUALIZER 2000

Standlee, Robert
SLUMBER PARTY MASSACRE II

Stanton, Stephen
BANZAI RUNNER

Staples, Paul
DELOS ADVENTURE, THE
NIGHTFORCE
RAGE OF HONOR

Stapley, Paul
NIGHT STALKER, THE

Stears, John
MIRACLES

Steinheimer, Bruce
RUNNING MAN, THE

Stirber, John
MILLION DOLLAR MYSTERY

Stivaletti, Sergio
SPECTERS

Stokes, Phil
HOPE AND GLORY

Stubbs, Peter
BUSHFIRE MOON
DOGS IN SPACE
SLATE, WYN & ME

Sturgeon, Bill
ALIEN PREDATOR

Sullivan, Mark
NADINE

Sullivan, Tom
EVIL DEAD 2: DEAD BY DAWN

Sundahl, Martin
WARDOGS

Tausek, Bryant
DEADTIME STORIES

Teres, Paco
ANGUSTIA

Thompson, Jamie
MOVING TARGETS

Tracy Design
CYCLONE

Trielli, Guy
BAD BLOOD

Trifunovich, Neil
BIG TOWN, THE

Trumble, Ben
GUNPOWDER

Vasquez, Miguel
GHOST FEVER

Visual Effect P/L
DOGS IN SPACE

Vogel, Matt
ENEMY TERRITORY
HIDING OUT
MUTANT HUNT

Walas, Chris
HOUSE TWO: THE SECOND STORY

Walsh, John
MORNING MAN, THE

Warren, Gene
NIGHTFLYERS

Watkins, David
EMPIRE OF THE SUN

West, Kit
EMPIRE OF THE SUN

Weston, Stephen
WHEN THE WIND BLOWS

Willard, Robert
HOUSE OF GAMES

Williams, David
BOY SOLDIER

Williams, Jerry
BLACK WIDOW
SLAMDANCE

Winston, Stan
MONSTER SQUAD, THE
PREDATOR

Wolf, Mark
SLAVE GIRLS FROM BEYOND INFINITY

Yeatman, Hoyt
NIGHTMARE ON ELM STREET 3: DREAM WARRIORS, A

Zahlava, Bruce
BLOOD DINER

Zamora, George
CROSS MY HEART

Zarlengo, James
TROUBLE WITH DICK, THE

STUNTS

Alon, Roy
EAT THE RICH

Amiel, Alan
CATCH THE HEAT

Anderson, Chris
GOOD WIFE, THE
RUNNING FROM THE GUNS

Armstrong, Peter
COMRADES

Armstrong, Vic
EMPIRE OF THE SUN

Arnold, Denny
PARTY CAMP

Barbour, Bruce Paul
SPACE RACE

Barker, Rich
NIGHTMARE ON ELM STREET 3: DREAM WARRIORS, A

Barker, Rick
SPACE RACE
WALKER

Barrett, John
STEEL DAWN

Bass, Bobby
LETHAL WEAPON
LETS GET HARRY
MANNEQUIN

Baxley, Craig
PREDATOR

Bell, Peter
NO WAY OUT

Bledsoe, Mike
RETURN OF JOSEY WALES, THE

Boswell, Glenn
DOGS IN SPACE

Boyle, Marc
EMPIRE STATE

Brace, Peter
CRY FREEDOM

Bradley, Dan
PRETTYKILL
VALET GIRLS
WHITE OF THE EYE

Branagan, John
SUMMER CAMP NIGHTMARE

Brayham, Peter
RAWHEAD REX

Browning, Ricou
OPPOSING FORCE

Burke, Michelle
STRANDED

Cardwell, Shane
BLUE MONKEY
PRETTYKILL

Cass, David
FLICKS

Cohen, Marvin
OVER THE TOP

Cooper, Greg
SLAVE GIRLS FROM BEYOND INFINITY

Cooper, Mike
SLAVE GIRLS FROM BEYOND INFINITY

Copeland, Dave
ENEMY TERRITORY

Couch, Bill
HIDING OUT

Couch, Chuck
WITCHBOARD

Cox, Peter
WILD THING

Creach, Everett
NEAR DARK
PRINCIPAL, THE

Curtis, Clive
GOOD MORNING, VIETNAM

Davis, B.J.
AMERICAN NINJA 2: THE CONFRONTATION

Davis, Bud
MALONE
MIRACLES
WHO'S THAT GIRL

Deadrick, Vince
ZERO BOYS, THE

Dell'Acqua, Aldo
DOLLS

DeLuna, Michael
POLICE ACADEMY 4: CITIZENS ON PATROL

Disanto, Frank
OVERKILL

Dobbins, Bennie
EXTREME PREJUDICE
RUNNING MAN, THE

Doge, Francois
ZABOU

Donino, Eddy
NIGHTFORCE

Dowdall, Jim
HELLRAISER
PERSONAL SERVICES
WISH YOU WERE HERE

Doyle, Christopher
ALLNIGHTER, THE

Duhame, Doc
MONSTER IN THE CLOSET

Dunne, Joe
BLIND DATE
ROXANNE
WEEDS

Ellgren, Tommy
BLOOD TRACKS

Espiana, Fred
EYE OF THE EAGLE

Falcis, Roland
GET THE TERRORISTS
HOSTAGE SYNDROME
TOUGH COP
ULTIMAX FORCE

Farnsworth, Diamond
BIG EASY, THE
NADINE

Farnsworth, Richard Diamond
NO WAY OUT

Ferrara, Frank
ORPHANS

Fife, Randy
O. C. AND STIGGS

Fisher, George
MILLION DOLLAR MYSTERY
RETURN TO HORROR HIGH

Forrestal, Terry
BELLMAN AND TRUE

Frohardt, Steve
DELOS ADVENTURE, THE

Gibbs, Alan
IRONWEED
WITCHES OF EASTWICK, THE

Gibson, Jeffrey Lee
SALVATION!

Gill, Jack
ASSASSINATION

Hal Burton
OVERBOARD

Hallard, Thierry
MASCARA

Harvey, Orwin
AMAZING GRACE AND CHUCK

Hewitt, Jery
RAISING ARIZONA

Hodder, Kane
HOUSE TWO: THE SECOND STORY

Holton, Sean
MANKILLERS

Hooker, Buddy Joe
GARDENS OF STONE

Howell, Russell
HARD TICKET TO HAWAII

Hutchinson, Rawn
HUNTER'S BLOOD

Hymes, Gary
UNTOUCHABLES, THE

James, Steve W.
HOLLYWOOD SHUFFLE

James, Terrance
NIGHTFORCE

Janes, Loren
STACKING

Jeffries, Dean
BELIEVERS, THE

Jogueta, Jolly
HOSTAGE SYNDROME

John Branagan
STRANDED

Joqueta, Jolly
GET THE TERRORISTS
TOUGH COP

Jordan, Monty
HAPPY HOUR

Julienne, Remy
LE SOLITAIRE
LIVING DAYLIGHTS, THE

Koniger, Erik
FOREVER, LULU

Kreigsman, Jan
DEMONS

Kulzer, William J.
MURDER LUST

Kurtzo, Joe
RETURN OF JOSEY WALES, THE

Lai, T.H.
WHITE PHANTOM

Lambert, Steve
BEST SELLER

Lerner, Fred
NUMBER ONE WITH A BULLET

Li, Tom
NINJA THUNDERBOLT

Lykins, Ray
OPPOSING FORCE

Madsen, Harry
ANGEL HEART

Magnotta, Vic
ORPHANS
SECRET OF MY SUCCESS, THE

Martin Grace
OFELAS

Marx, Solly
ALLAN QUATERMAIN AND THE LOST CITY OF GOLD

Matthews, Fritz
DEADLY PREY
MANKILLERS

McBride, Mark
EAT THE RICH

McDancer, Buck
WITCHBOARD

McLarty, Gary
BEVERLY HILLS COP II
OVER THE TOP

Megison, Eric
DEATHROW GAMESHOW

Milne, Gareth
HEARTS OF FIRE

Moio, John
MONSTER SQUAD, THE

Moldovan, Jeff
MAKING MR.RIGHT

Moraga, Tom
MISSION KILL

Morris, Val
NO DEAD HEROES

Norman, Michel
TERMINUS

Nuckles, Paul
MAKING MR.RIGHT

Oliney, Alan
BEVERLY HILLS COP II
P.I. PRIVATE INVESTIGATIONS

Orsatti, Ernie
DEATH WISH 4: THE CRACKDOWN

Page, Grant
LIGHTHORSEMEN, THE

Peter Diamond
THREE KINDS OF HEAT

Petit, Alain
THUNDER WARRIOR II

Pike, Don
ALLAN QUATERMAIN AND THE LOST CITY OF GOLD

Powell, Dinny
EAT THE RICH

Razatos, Spiro
OMEGA SYNDROME

Rigby, Dave
KEEPING TRACK

Robinson, Dar
LETHAL WEAPON
MILLION DOLLAR MYSTERY

Rondell, Ronnie
SOMEONE TO WATCH OVER ME

Rosaies, Thomas
BEDROOM WINDOW, THE

Rosales, Thomas
DATE WITH AN ANGEL

Rossall, Kerry
DEATH BEFORE DISHONOR

Ruffin, Don
SOMETHING SPECIAL!

Ruiters, Reo
HOSTAGE

Ryan, Jake
DREAMANIAC

Scott, T.J.
HEARTS OF FIRE

Scott, Walter
MASTERS OF THE UNIVERSE
WANTED: DEAD OR ALIVE

Shaw, Margot
GABY—A TRUE STORY

Sherrod, John
PENITENTIARY III

Shields, Sonny
MISSION KILL

Silver, Spike
BIG SHOTS

Skeaping, Colin
PRAYER FOR THE DYING, A

Smolek, Jeff
DIRTY LAUNDRY
SUSPECT

Stacey, Eddie
EAT THE RICH
FOURTH PROTOCOL, THE

Statham, Patrick
HOUR OF THE ASSASSIN

Stavrakis, Taso N.
CREEPSHOW 2

Stefanelli, Benito
BARBARIANS, THE

Stewart, John
CYCLONE
OPEN HOUSE
STRIPPED TO KILL

Street, Roy
GOTHIC

Stuart, Alan
PERSONAL SERVICES

Stuntco Intl
BIG TOWN, THE

Svenska Stuntgruppen
LEIF

Taylor, Rocky
EAT THE RICH

Teller, Keith
ERNEST GOES TO CAMP

Tipping, Tip
HAMBURGER HILL

Toren, Johan
LEIF
NIONDE KOMPANIET

Tsui, Siu-Ming
MIRAGE

Vazquez, Alberto
MI NOMBRE ES GATILLO

Verite, Daniel
ENNEMIS INTIMES

Victor Magnotta
SQUEEZE, THE

Walker, Greg
UNDER COVER

Walsh, Terry
EAT THE RICH

Walter Scott
FATAL BEAUTY

Wardlow, V. John
ROXANNE

Warlock, Richard
SPACEBALLS

Webb, Chris
EAT THE RICH

Weston, Paul
LIVING DAYLIGHTS, THE

Whinery, Webster
ORACLE, THE

Wilder, Glenn
SOMEONE TO WATCH OVER ME

Wilder, Glenn R.
OUTRAGEOUS FORTUNE

Wilder, Scott
MASTERBLASTER

Winburn, James
NIGHT STALKER, THE

Worth, B.J.
LIVING DAYLIGHTS, THE

TECHNICAL ADVISERS

Bernsen, Rod
LETHAL WEAPON

Ermey, Lee
FULL METAL JACKET

Fransen, Art
LETHAL WEAPON

Luquet, Claude
MANUELA'S LOVES

Meldrum, Bruce
ROXANNE

Whitaker, Richard
LETHAL WEAPON

Woods, Donald
CRY FREEDOM

Woods, Wendy
CRY FREEDOM

WRITERS (screenplay or source)

Aaltonen, Veikko
TILINTEKO

AAV Creative Unit
NINJA THUNDERBOLT

Abdulla, Raficq
BORN OF FIRE

Abeysekara, Tisssa
VIRAGAYA

Abramov, Sergei
DVOE POD ODNIM ZONTOM
SEZON CHUDES

Abuladze, Tenghiz
REPENTANCE

Acin, Jovan
HEY BABU RIBA

Adabachian, Alexander
DARK EYES

Adabashyan, Alexander
MOY LYUBIMYY KLOUN

Adams, Neal
LA VENGEANCE DU PROTECTEUR

Adar, Rafi
KFAFOT

Adlon, Eleonore
OUT OF ROSENHEIM

Adlon, Percy
OUT OF ROSENHEIM

Afkhami, Behrouz
MANUSCRIPTS

Agababov, Arnold
ODINOKAYA ORESHINA

Agosti, Silvano
QUARTIERE

Agresti, Alejandro
EL AMOR ES UNA MUJERGORDA

Ahlin, Per
RESAN TILL MELONIA

Aiken, Robert S.
MOON IN SCORPIO

Aivasian, Agassi
SASHSHENNYI FONAR

Akhtar, Javed
DACAIT

Akimov, Vladimir
KAPKAN DLYA SHAKALOV

Alarcon, Sebastian
YAGUAR

Albanelli, Josep
BAR-CEL-ONA

Aldridge, William
MIO, MOY MIO

Alexandrov, Alexander
STARAYA AZBUKA

Alfarjani, Mohamed Ali
ALSHAZIA

Alfredson, Hans
JIM OCH PIRATERNA BLOM

Allen, Woody
RADIO DAYS
SEPTEMBER

Allouache, Merzak
UN AMOUR A PARIS

Almadani, Abdul Salam
ALSHAZIA

Almodovar, Pedro
LAW OF DESIRE

Alov, Alexander
SEVERNY ANEKDOT

Alschuler, Melanie J.
PRETTY SMART

Alston, Emmett
HUNTER'S BLOOD

Altberg, Julia
FONTE DA SAUDADE

Altman, Robert
BEYOND THERAPY

Altman, Shelly
SWEET LORRAINE

Amar, Denis
ENNEMIS INTIMES

Amateau, Rod
GARBAGE PAIL KIDS MOVIE, THE

Amendola, Mario
ALADDIN
RIMINI RIMINI
ROBA DA RICCHI

Ames, Taylor
HES MY GIRL

Amigo, Angel
A LOS CUATRO VIENTOS

Amir, Gideon
AMERICAN NINJA 2: THE CONFRONTATION

Amoureux, Yves
LE BEAUF

Anders, Allison
BORDER RADIO

Andersen, Dortea Birkedal
NEGERKYS & LABRE LARVER

Andersen, Hans Christian
EMPEROR'S NEW CLOTHES, THE
SNOW QUEEN, THE

Anderson, Clyde
STRIKE COMMANDO
UNDICI GIORNI, UNDICI NOTTE

Anderson, Gail
BLOOD HOOK

Andolfi, Marco Antonio
LA CROCE DALLE SETTE PIETRE

Andrei, Marcello
MOSCA ADDIO

Andrevon, Jean-Pierre
GANDAHAR

Andrew Coburn
NOYADE INTERDITE

Andrews, V.C.
FLOWERS IN THE ATTIC

Angela, Piero
IL GIORNO PRIMA

Angelucci, Gianfranco
INTERVISTA

Ansal, Kusum
PANCHVATI

Ansara, Martha
PURSUIT OF HAPPINESS, THE

Antonov, Boris
MY OBVINYAEM

Anuya, Alfonso
ESTA NOCHE CENA PANCHO (DESPEDIDA DE SOLTERO)

Anwari, Sarwar
PERLYOTNIYE PTIT

Apollinaire, Guillaume
LES EXPLOITS DUN JEUNE DON JUAN

Appelbaum and a character crea, Lawrence
SILENT NIGHT, DEADLY NIGHT PART II

Applegate, Royce
EVIL TOWN

Apuzzo, Carla
REGINA

Arabov, Joury
ODINOKIJ GOLOS CELOVEKA

Arabov, Jurij
SKORBNOE BESCHUVSTVIE

Arago, Jorge
DAMORTIS

Araki, Gregg
THREE BEWILDERED PEOPLE IN THE NIGHT

Aranda, Vicente
EL LUTE—CAMINA O REVIENTA

Arcady, Alexandre
LETE DERNIER A TANGER

Archibugi, Francesca
LESTATE STA FINENDO

Arehn, Mats
OM KARLEK

Argento, Dario
OPERA

Arguello, Ivan
MUJERES DE LA FRONTERA

Arias, Alfredo
FUEGOS

Armand, Deddy
STABILIZER, THE

Arnaud, Marguerite
BUISSON ARDENT

Arnstein, Larry
FLICKS

Arsan, Emmanuelle
EMMANUELLE 5

Arsenishvili, Zaira
KRUGOVOROT

Arsenyev, Nikolai
PO ZAKONU VOENNOGO VREMENI

Arvizu, Ruben
WELCOME MARIA

Asama, Yoshitaka
FINAL TAKE: THE GOLDEN AGE OF MOVIES
TORA-SAN'S BLUEBIRD FANTASY

Askarov, S.
SNAYPERY

Askoldov, Alexander
KOMISSAR

Aspron, Sarah
UNDICI GIORNI, UNDICI NOTTE

Assayas, Olivier
AVRIL BRISE

au Petit, Hubert
CHAMP D'HONNEUR

Audiard, Jacques
POUSSIERE D'ANGE

August, Bille
PELLE EROVRAREN

Aurenche, Jean
F . . . ING FERNAND

Avallone, Marcello
SPECTERS
SPECTERS

Avalon, Joe
ULTIMAX FORCE

Avdeliodis, Demos
TREE WE HURT, THE

Avdeyenko, Yury
DIKIY KHMEL

Avellana, Joe Mari
EQUALIZER 2000

Axel, Gabriel
BABETTE'S GASTEBUD

Aykroyd, Dan
DRAGNET

Ayre, Jon
SURF NAZIS MUST DIE

Ayres, Mark
EMPIRE STATE

Azcona, Rafael
EL BOSQUE ANIMADO
HAY QUE DESHACER LA CASA
MOROS Y CRISTIANOS
YEAR OF AWAKENING, THE

Azernikov, Valentin
ISKRENNE VASH . . .

Azmi, Yehia
AL-TAUQ WAL-ISWIRA

B., Beth
SALVATION!

Bach, Danilo
BEVERLY HILLS COP II

Bachman, Richard
RUNNING MAN, THE

Badalucco, Nicola
GLI OCCHIALI D'ORO

Baere, Geoffrey
CAMPUS MAN

Bagdadi, Maroun
LHOMME VOILE

Bagdasarian, Ross
CHIPMUNK ADVENTURE, THE

Bagdasarov, Viktor
YA YEY NRAVLYUS

Bailey, Frederick
EQUALIZER 2000

Bailey, Sandra K.
PRETTYKILL
TURNAROUND

Bajic, Rados
NA PUTA ZA KATANGU

Bajon, Filip
MAGNAT

Bakhnov, Vladlen
SPORTLOTO—82

Balducci, Armenia
MORO AFFAIR, THE

Baletic, Branko
UVEK SPREMNE ZENE

Ball, David
AMERICAN DRIVE-IN

Ballard, J.G.
EMPIRE OF THE SUN

Bandiera Freire, Pedro
BALADA DA PRAIA DOS CAES

Baran, Jack
BIG EASY, THE

Barbash, Benny
DREAMERS
Barbera, Neal
P.K. & THE KID
Barboni, Marco Tullio
RENEGADE, UN OSSO TROPPO DURO
Barbosa, Haroldo Marinho
BAIXO GAVEA
Barker, Clive
HELLRAISER
RAWHEAD REX
Barmak, Ira R.
HOTEL COLONIAL
Barnabe, Arrigo
CIDADE OCULTA
Barrera, Victor
LOS INVITADOS
Barreto, Lima
ELE, O BOTO
Barrett, Lezli-An
BUSINESS AS USUAL
Barrie, Michael
AMAZON WOMEN ON THE MOON
Barros, Wilson
NIGHT ANGELS
Barski, Odile
LE CRI DU HIBOU
MASQUES
Bartelski, Leslaw
ZLOTA MAHMUDIA
Bartlett, Michael
KONZERT FUR DIE RECHTE HAND
Barton, James
INITIATION
based on
LADY OF THE CAMELIAS
Bass, Ronald
BLACK WIDOW
GARDENS OF STONE
Bassani, Giorgio
GLI OCCHIALI D'ORO
Basso, Gina
IL CORAGGIO DI PARLARE
Bassoff, Lawrence
HUNK
Baxter, John
TIME GUARDIAN, THE
Beaumont, Guy
LE BEAUF
Bechard, Gorman
PSYCHOS IN LOVE
Beck, Walter
DER BARENHAUTER
Becker, Josh
THOU SHALT NOT KILL . . . EXCEPT
Begeja, Liria
AVRIL BRISE
Begun, Jeff
PRETTY SMART
Behat, Gilles
CHARLIE DINGO
Behr, Jack
NO MAN'S LAND
Bekes, Pal
DOKTOR MINORKA VIDOR NAGY NAPJA
Bellanti, Louis
JOHNNY MONROE
Belli, Gioconda
MUJERES DE LA FRONTERA
Bellocchio, Marco
DEVIL IN THE FLESH
Belmont, Vera
F . . . ING FERNAND
Beloshnikov, Sergei
I NIKTO NA SVETE
Belson, Jerry
SURRENDER
Belushi, James
NUMBER ONE WITH A BULLET
Belyaev, Alexander
TVOYO MIRNOE NEBO
Bemberg, Maria Luisa
MISS MARY
MISS MARY
Ben Amotz, Dan
LO SAM ZAYIN
Benavides, Arnulfo
HERENCIA DE VALIENTES
Benchley, Peter
JAWS: THE REVENGE

Bencivenni, Alessandro
SUPERFANTOZZI
Benner, Dick
TOO OUTRAGEOUS
Bennett, Alan
PRICK UP YOUR EARS
Bennett, Bill
DEAR CARDHOLDER
JILTED
Bennett, Wallace
RAGE OF HONOR
Benson, Richard
EVIL TOWN
Benton, Daniel
HOSTAGE SYNDROME
Benton, Robert
NADINE
Benvenuti, Leo
I PICARI
IL GIORNO PRIMA
IO E MIA SORELLA
NOI UOMINI DURI
SUPERFANTOZZI
Bercini, Reyes
TRAGICO TERREMOTO EN MEXICO
Berckmans, Nicole
MANUELA'S LOVES
Berezantseva, Tatyana
LYUBOVYU ZA LYUBOV
Berger, Helmut
SAME TO YOU
Berger, Pamela
LA MOINE ET LA SORCIERE
Berglund, Per
MY LIFE AS A DOG
Bergman, Boris
LE BEAUF
Bergonzelli, Sergio
TENTAZIONE
Bergquist, Peter L.
MONSTER IN THE CLOSET
Bergstein, Eleanor
DIRTY DANCING
Berlanga, Luis Garcia
MOROS Y CRISTIANOS
Bernanos, Georges
SOUS LE SOLEIL DE SATAN
Bernaza, Luis Felipe
DE TAL PEDRO, TAL ASTILLA
Bernini, Franco
NOTTE ITALIANA
Bernstein, Armyan
CROSS MY HEART
Bernstein, Henry
MELO
Berri, Claude
JEAN DE FLORETTE
MANON OF THE SPRING
Berroyer, Jackie
POULE ET FRITES
Berry, Bill
OFF THE MARK
Berry, David
WHALES OF AUGUST, THE
Bertolucci, Bernardo
LAST EMPEROR, THE
Berube from a novel by Marie-C, Therese
LE SOURD DANS LA VILLE
Berz, Michael
SLEEPING BEAUTY
SNOW WHITE
Beshara, Khairy
AL-TAUQ WAL-ISWIRA
Betti, Liliana
BELLIFRESCHI
Bezhanov, Gerald
SAMAYA OBAYATELNAYA I PRIVLEKATELNAYA
Bhattacharya, Basu
PANCHVATI
Bianchi, Andrea
DOLCE PELLE DI ANGELA
Bierbichler, Josef
TRIUMPH DE GERECHTEN
Bigelow, Kathryn
NEAR DARK
Bird, Brad
BATTERIES NOT INCLUDED
Birnbaum, Stuart
SUMMER SCHOOL

Biro, Zsuzsa
ISTEN VELETEK, BARATAIM
Bivens, Loren
TRESPASSES
Black, Laura
PURSUIT OF HAPPINESS, THE
Black, Shane
LETHAL WEAPON
MONSTER SQUAD, THE
Blades, Ruben
EL HIJO DE PEDRO NAVAJAS
Blain, Gerard
PIERRE ET DJEMILA
Blanco, Jose Joaquin
FRIDA
Bleicher, Margot
DER JUNGE MIT DEM GROSSEN SCHWARZEN HUND
Blicher, Steen Steensen
ELISE
Blieberg, Ehud
CHOZE AHAVA
Blixen, Karen
BABETTE'S GASTEBUD
Block, Lawrence
BURGLAR
Blom, Per
IS-SLOTTET
Bloom, Jeffrey
FLOWERS IN THE ATTIC
Bloom, Steven L.
LIKE FATHER, LIKE SON
Boam, Jeffrey
INNERSPACE
LOST BOYS, THE
Bochner, Sally
TRAIN OF DREAMS
Bockner, Michael
PSYCHO GIRLS
Bogayevicz, Yurek
ANNA
Bogner, Willy
FIRE AND ICE
Bohl, Charles F.
HES MY GIRL
Bohlinger, Don
KILLING TIME, THE
Bohm, Hark
LITTLE PROSECUTOR, THE
Bojorquez, Alberto
ROBACHICOS
Bokova, Jana
HOTEL DU PARADIS
Bolivar, Cesar
MAS ALLA DEL SILENCIO
Bollain, Juan Sebastian
LAS DOS ORILLAS
Bond, Julian
WHISTLE BLOWER, THE
Bonitzer, Pascal
LES MENDIANTS
Bonner, Lee
ADVENTURE OF THE ACTION HUNTERS
Boorman, John
HOPE AND GLORY
Booth, James
AMERICAN NINJA 2: THE CONFRONTATION
Boris, Robert
STEELE JUSTICE
Boris Tokarev
PLOSHCHAD VOSSTANIA
Borodyansky, Alexander
CHELOVEK C AKKORDEONOM
KURIER
SEKUNDA NA PODVIG
Borowczyk, Walerian
EMMANUELLE 5
Bosse, Malcolm
AGENT TROUBLE
Boszormenyi, Geza
LAURA
Botelho, Chico
CIDADE OCULTA
Boucher, Philippe
LES MOIS D'AVRIL SONT MEURTRIERS
Bouchibi, Mohamed
PIERRE ET DJEMILA
Boudard, Alphonse
LE SOLITAIRE
Boujedria, Rachid
LA COMPROMISSION

Bouvier, Claudine
DIARY OF A MAD OLD MAN

Bozzacchi, Gianni
I LOVE NEW YORK

Bozzetto, Bruno
SOTTO IL RISTORANTE CINESE

Brach, Gerard
FUEGOS
JEAN DE FLORETTE
MANON OF THE SPRING
SHY PEOPLE

Bradley, Al
IRON WARRIOR

Braginsky, Emil
POEZDKI NA STAROM AVTOMOBILE

Bramos, Giorgos
KLIOS

Brander, Gary
HOWLING III, THE

Brandi, Carlos
EL HOMBRE DE LA DEUDA EXTERNA

Brandt, Carsten
DEMONS

Brandys, Kazimierz
MATKA KROLOW

Brannstrom, Brasse
MY LIFE AS A DOG

Brass, David
GET THE TERRORISTS
HOSTAGE SYNDROME

Brass, Giovanni Tinto
CAPRICCIO

Brigadere, Anna
POHADKA O MALICKOVI

Briggs, Raymond
WHEN THE WIND BLOWS

Briley, John
CRY FREEDOM

Brock, Deborah
SLUMBER PARTY MASSACRE II

Brodney, Oscar
GHOST FEVER

Bromfield, Rex
HOME IS WHERE THE HART IS

Brook, Gene
MY DARK LADY

Brooks, James L.
BROADCAST NEWS

Brooks, Mel
SPACEBALLS

Brooksbank, Anne
SHADOWS OF THE PEACOCK

Brouwers, Marja
HAVINCK

Brown, Jamie
KEEPING TRACK

Brown, Paul L.
PARTY CAMP

Bruckner, Jutta
EIN BLICK-UND DIE LIEBE BRICHT AUS

Bruer, Jeffrey
WITCH HUNT

Bruyere, Christian
SHELLEY

Brynntrup, Michael
JESUS: DER FILM

Buchin, Mirko
CHECHECHELA—UNA CHICA DEL BARRIO

Buduris, Vassilis
O PARADISSOS ANIGI ME ANTIKLIDI

Buford Hauser
CREEPOZOIDS

Buhai, Jeff
REVENGE OF THE NERDS II: NERDS IN PARADISE

Buki, Matyas
LENZ

Bukowski, Charles
BARFLY
LOVE IS A DOG FROM HELL

Bulganin, Alexander
VYKUP

Buravsky, Alexander
PO GLAVNOY ULITSE S ORKESTROM

Burlyayev, Nikolai
LERMONTOV

Burr, David
PERFECT MATCH, THE

Burr, Jeff
OFFSPRING, THE

Burridge, Richard
FOURTH PROTOCOL, THE

Burroughs, Jackie
WINTER TAN, A

Butler, Heinz
PERSONAGGI & INTERPRETI

Butler, William
SUMMER CAMP NIGHTMARE

Buysse, Cyriel
VAN PAEMEL FAMILY, THE

Buzura, Agustin
PADUREANCA

Byars, Floyd
MAKING MR.RIGHT

Bykhovsky, Alexander
NABAT NA RASSVETE

Bykov, Vasil
ZNAK BEDY

Cabrujas, Jose Ignacio
MAS ALLA DEL SILENCIO

Cacoyannis, Michael
SWEET COUNTRY

Cadena, Jordi
LA SENYORA

Caimi, Paul
SILENT NIGHT, DEADLY NIGHT PART II

Calaferte, Louis
MON BEL AMOUR, MA DECHIRURE

Cameron, Lorne
LIKE FATHER, LIKE SON

Camilleri, Andreina
ADELMO

Cammell, China
WHITE OF THE EYE

Cammell, Donald
WHITE OF THE EYE

Camp, Joe
BENJI THE HUNTED

Campanella, Pierfrancesco
LA TRASGRESSIONE

Campbell, Bruce
THOU SHALT NOT KILL . . . EXCEPT

Camus, Mario
LA CASA DE BERNARDA ALBA
LA RUSA

Cantrell, Donald
O. C. AND STIGGS

Capobianco, Carmine
PSYCHOS IN LOVE

Capone, Alesandro
CAMPING DEL TERRORE

Capone, Gino
LA MONACA DIMONZA

Caportoto, Carl
SUICIDE CLUB, THE

Carabatsos, Jim
HAMBURGER HILL

Carabatsos, Steven
HOT PURSUIT

Carax, Leos
BAD BLOOD

Carballido, Emilio
MANON

Carbone, Walter
SOMETHING SPECIAL!

Cardona Jr., Rene
BEAKS

Cardoso E Pires, Jose
LA PLAYA DE LOS PERROS

Carlsen, Henning
WOLF AT THE DOOR, THE

Carlstroem, Bjorn
WARDOGS

Carlton, Clark
VALET GIRLS

Carner, Charles Robert
LETS GET HARRY

Carothers, A.J.
SECRET OF MY SUCCESS, THE

Carow, Heiner
SO VIELE TRAUME

Carpenter, Stephen
KINDRED, THE

Carr, J.L.
MONTH IN THE COUNTRY, A

Carriere, Jean-Claude
LES EXPLOITS DUN JEUNE DON JUAN
WOLF AT THE DOOR, THE

Carroll, Tod
O. C. AND STIGGS

Carter, Forrest
RETURN OF JOSEY WALES, THE

Carver, Steve
BULLETPROOF

Casares, Adolfo Bioy
EL GRAN SERAFIN

Cash, Jim
SECRET OF MY SUCCESS, THE

Casile, Demetrio
UN RAGAZZO DI CALABRIA

Cassenti, Franck
TESTAMENT D'UN POETE JUIF ASSASSINE

Castellano
IL BURBERO

Castellitto, Sergio
SEMBRA MORTO . . . ME E SOLO SVENUTO

Castle, Alan
STRANDED

Castro, Jose
ARQUIESTA EMILIO VARELA

Castro, Victor Manuel
NOS REIMOS DE LA MIGRA

Cavazos, Francisco
ENTRE FICHERAS ANDA EL DIABLO
ESTA NOCHE CENA PANCHO (DESPEDIDA DE SOLTERO)
LA RAZA NUNCA PIERDE—HUELE A GAS
NOS REIMOS DE LA MIGRA

Cebrian, Juan Luis
LA RUSA

Cech, Frantisek R.
PRATELE BERMUDSKEHO TROJUHELNIKU

Cendrars, Blaise
UM FILM 100% BRAZILEIRO

Cerami, Vincenzo
LA CODA DEL DIAVOLO
STREGATI

Cerasi, Massimo Nota
PROFUMO

Cervi, Tonino
ITALIANI A RIO

Chabrol, Claude
LE CRI DU HIBOU
MASQUES

Chad, Sheldon
LES FOUS DE BASSAN

Chalbaud, Roman
LA OVEJA NEGRA
MANON

Chan, John
WRONG COUPLES,THE

Chandra, N.
PRATIGHAAT

Chaney, Warren
OUTING, THE

Chaplin, Patrice
SIESTA

Charef, Mehdi
MISS MONA

Charlton, Ann
CUSTODY

Chaskin, David
CURSE, THE

Chaussois, Dominique
LE MOUSTACHU

Chekhov, Anton
HOTEL DE FRANCE
OGNI

Cheong, Tsang Kan
MAGNIFICENT WARRIORS

Chereau, Patrice
HOTEL DE FRANCE

Chernykh, Valentin
DUBLYOR NACHINAET DEYSTVOVAT

Cherry III, John R.
ERNEST GOES TO CAMP

Chervinsky, Aleksandr
OGNI

Chervinsky, Alexander
TEMA

Chetwynd, Lionel
HANOI HILTON, THE

Chiara, Piero
DA NNUNZIO
LA MONACA DIMONZA

Chichinadze, Amiran
GOSPODA AVANTYURISTY

Chiesa, Aurelio
DISTANT LIGHTS

Ching, Wong
KILLER'S NOCTURNE

Chmielewska, Halina
WIERNA RZEKA

Chmielewski, Tadeusz
WIERNA RZEKA

Chobocky, Barbara A.
WITCH HUNT

Chokheli, Goderdzi
VELIKIY POKHOD ZA NEVESTOY

Chouraqui, Elie
MAN ON FIRE

Chowdhury, Anjan
SIBAJI

Chugunov, Victor
SKAZKA O PREKRASNOY AYSULU

Chuliukin, Yury
KAK STAT SCHASTLIVYM

Chun, Man
KILLER'S NOCTURNE

Chynowski, Pawel
STANISLAW I ANNA

Chytilova, Vera
WOLF'S HOLE

Chzhun, Pek In
SEKUNDA NA PODVIG

Ciccoritti, Gerard
GRAVEYARD SHIFT
PSYCHO GIRLS

Cisse, Souleymane
YEELEN

Clark, Bob
FROM THE HIP

Claus, Hugo
DIARY OF A MAD OLD MAN
MASCARA
VAN PAEMEL FAMILY, THE

Clavier, Christian
LA VIE DISSOLUE DE GERARD FLOQUE

Clerici, Gianfranco
LE FOTO DI GIOIA

Cluzel, Raphael
GANDAHAR

Coburn, Glen
BLOODSUCKERS FROM OUTER SPACE

Coen, Ethan
RAISING ARIZONA

Coen, Joel
RAISING ARIZONA

Coggio, Roger
LE JOURNAL D'UN FOU

Cohen, Charles Zev
LADY BEWARE

Cohen, Larry
BEST SELLER
DEADLY ILLUSION

Colgin, Russell W.
NIGHTFORCE

Collier, James F.
CAUGHT

Colomo, Fernando
LA VIDA ALEGRE

Comana, Fabio
SOTTO IL RISTORANTE CINESE

Comencini, Francesca
UN RAGAZZO DI CALABRIA

Comencini, Luigi
UN RAGAZZO DI CALABRIA

Conde, Nicholas
BELIEVERS, THE

Coninx, Stijn
HECTOR

Connell, David
BUSHFIRE MOON

Conrad, Patrick
MASCARA

Conte, Antonio
MUJERES DE LA FRONTERA

Contreras, Marco E.
EL MOFLES Y LOS MECANICOS

Contreras, Marco Eduardo
LAPUTA: THE CASTLE IN THE SKY

Conway, Gary
AMERICAN NINJA 2: THE CONFRONTATION
OVER THE TOP

Conway from characters created, Gary
AMERICAN NINJA 2: THE CONFRONTATION

Cook, Robin
LES MOIS D'AVRIL SONT MEURTRIERS

Corbucci, Bruno
ALADDIN
RIMINI RIMINI
ROBA DA RICCHI

Corbucci, Sergio
RIMINI RIMINI
ROBA DA RICCHI

Cosby, Bill
LEONARD PART 6

Coscia, Jorge
CHORROS
SENTIMIENTOS: MIRTA DE LINIERS A ESTAMBUL

Costa Muste, Pedro
REDONDELA

Costa-Gavras, Constantin
FAMILY BUSINESS

Costella, Paolo
BELLIFRESCHI

Coutsomitis, Costas
KLIOS

Cowan, Gil
OPPOSING FORCE

Cox, Alex
STRAIGHT TO HELL

Cox, Paul
VINCENT—THE LIFE AND DEATH OF VINCENT VAN GOGH

Crabbe, Kerry
PLASTPOSEN

Craven, Wes
NIGHTMARE ON ELM STREET 3: DREAM WARRIORS, A

Cristofer, Michael
WITCHES OF EASTWICK, THE

Crowther, John
WILD PAIR, THE

Cruickshank, Jim
THREE MEN AND A BABY

Cunningham, Alex
EMMANUELLE 5

Cunningham, Jere
HUNTER'S BLOOD

Curtelin, Jean
LA RUMBA

D'Agostini, Fabio
DA NNUNZIO

D'Amico, Suso Cecchi
DARK EYES
I PICARI

Dahl, John
P.I. PRIVATE INVESTIGATIONS

Dahlin, Bob
MONSTER IN THE CLOSET

Dalvi, Jaywant
PUDHCHE PAOL

Daly, Mary
MAGDALENA VIRAGA

Dan, Kazuo
KATAKU NO HITO

Danelia, Georgy
KIN-DZA-DZA

Dansereau, Mireille
LE SOURD DANS LA VILLE

Dante, Maria
MISSION KILL

Danton, Sylvie
SOUS LE SOLEIL DE SATAN

Darabont, Frank
NIGHTMARE ON ELM STREET 3: DREAM WARRIORS, A

Dardenne, Jean-Pierre
FALSCH

Dardenne, Luc
FALSCH

Dasgupta, Buddhadeb
PHERA

Dashev, David
SUMMER SCHOOL

Dashiev, Arya
UTRO OBRECHENNOGO PRIISKA

David, Marjorie
SHY PEOPLE

Davydova, Nina
SKAZKA O PREKRASNOY AYSULU

Dawn, Vincent
STRIKE COMMANDO

Dawson, Vivienne
T. DAN SMITH

de Anda, Gilberto
EL ANSIA DE MATAR
FORAJIDOS EN LA MIRA
RATAS DE LA CIUDAD

de Arminan, Jaime
MY GENERAL

De Bello, John
HAPPY HOUR

De Bernardi, Piero
I PICARI
IO E MIA SORELLA
NOI UOMINI DURI
SUPERFANTOZZI

De Concini, Ennio
DEVIL IN THE FLESH

De Geer Bergenstrahle, Marie-Louise
FADERN, SONEN OCH DEN HELIGE ANDE

de Guzman, Michael
JAWS: THE REVENGE

de Heredia, Alvaro Saenz
POLICIA

de Jong, Ate
EEN MAAND LATER

De Klein, John
CARE BEARS ADVENTURE IN WONDERLAND, THE

de la Barca, Pedro Calderon
MEMOIRE DES APPARENCES: LA VIE EST UN SONGE

de la Iglesia, Eloy
LA ESTANQUERA DE VALLECAS

de la Parra, Pim
ALS IN EEN ROES
ODYSSEE D'AMOUR

de la Pena, Eduardo
CINCO NACOS ASALTAN A LAS VEGAS
MAS VALE PAJARO EN MANO . . .

De Lillo, Antonietta
UNA CASA IN BILICO

De Luca, Rudy
MILLION DOLLAR MYSTERY

de Mareuil, Stephanie
COERS CROISES

de Nimes, Susannah
SURVIVAL GAME

de Sanzo, Juan Carlos
EN RETIRADA

de Souza, Steven E.
RUNNING MAN, THE

De Villeneuve, Madame
BEAUTY AND THE BEAST

de Vries, Marietta
ZJOEK

de Winter, Leon
LOOKING FOR EILEEN

Dead Honest Soul Searchers, The
OUT OF ORDER

Dear, William
HARRY AND THE HENDERSONS

Dearden, James
FATAL ATTRACTION

Decoin, Didier
LHOMME VOILE

DeCouteau, David
CREEPOZOIDS

Deese, Frank
PRINCIPAL, THE

Deimel, Mark
PERFECT MATCH, THE

Dekker, Fred
MONSTER SQUAD, THE

Del Rio, Ernesto
EL AMOR DE AHORA

del Valle-Inclan, Ramon
DIVINAS PALABRAS

Del Vando, Alfonso
LAS DOS ORILLAS

Delgado, Jose Luis Rauda
TIERRA DE VALIENTES

Delman, Jeffrey
DEADTIME STORIES

Denis, Jean-Pierre
CHAMP D'HONNEUR

Deray, Jacques
LE SOLITAIRE

Deruddere, Dominique
LOVE IS A DOG FROM HELL

Dery, Tibor
AZ UTOLSOKEZIRAT
UTOLSO KEZIRAT

des Cars, Guy
LA BRUTE
Des Forets, Louis-Rene
LES MENDIANTS
Dewolf, Patrick
TANDEM
Di Gregorio, Gianni
SEMBRA MORTO . . . ME E SOLO SVENUTO
di Meana, Marina Ripa
I MIEI PRIMI QUARANT'ANNI
Diana, Graziano
TERESA
Diaz, Reynaldo
JUNTOS
Dick, Nigel
P.I. PRIVATE INVESTIGATIONS
Dickens, Charles
LITTLE DORRIT
Didden, Marc
LOVE IS A DOG FROM HELL
Diegues, Carlos
UM TREM PARA AS ESTRELAS
Dionyssis Chronopoulos
TA PAIDIA TIS CHELIDONAS
Dixon, John
RUNNING FROM THE GUNS
Dixon, Ken
SLAVE GIRLS FROM BEYOND INFINITY
Dixon, Leslie
OUTRAGEOUS FORTUNE
OVERBOARD
Djanelidze, Nana
REPENTANCE
Docherty, James J.
NIGHTSTICK
Doherty, Chris
DEVILS PARADISE, THE
Doherty, Christopher
OUT OF ROSENHEIM
Doillon, Jacques
COMEDY!
Dolidze, Amiran
NEYLONOVAYA YOLKA
Dolna, Didier
LES OREILLES ENTRE LES DENTS
Domalik, Andrzej
ZYGFRYD
Donati, Sergio
MAN ON FIRE
RENEGADE, UN OSSO TROPPO DURO
Donkers, Jan
EEN MAAND LATER
Dorff, Matt
CAMPUS MAN
CAMPUS MAN
Doria, Alejandro
SOFIA
Douglas, Bill
COMRADES
Dovgan, Vladimir
I NIKTO NA SVETE
Dovlatyan, Frunze
ODINOKAYA ORESHINA
Doyle, Tim
ZOMBIE HIGH
Drach, Michel
IL EST GENIAL PAPY!
Dragin, Bert L.
SUMMER CAMP NIGHTMARE
Drainville, Elaine
T. DAN SMITH
Drakopoulou, Soula
TA PAIDIA TIS CHELIDONAS
Dratch
RODNIK DLIA ZHAZHDUSHCHIKH
Dreoni, Elena
DELIZIA
Dreyfuss, Lorin
DUTCH TREAT
Drouot, Pierre
MASCARA
Du Corail, Patrick
LA VIE PLATINEE
Dubrovsky, Edgar
KRASNAYA STRELA
Dudognong, Francoise
CHAMP D'HONNEUR
Dugdale, George
SLAUGHTER HIGH
Duigan, John
YEAR MY VOICE BROKE, THE
Dunbar, Andrea
RITA, SUE AND BOB TOO!
Duran, Jorge
COLOR OF DESTINY, THE
Duran, Rafael Rosales
JUNTOS
Durang, Christopher
BEYOND THERAPY
BEYOND THERAPY
Duretta, Nick
PERFECT MATCH, THE
Duvic, Patrice
TERMINUS
Dvortsov, Vladimir
TAKAYA ZHESTOKAYA IGRA—KHOKKEY
Dziki, Waldemar
LE JEUNE MAGICIEN
Eadington, Dave
T. DAN SMITH
Earle, Joseph H.
SILENT NIGHT, DEADLY NIGHT PART II
Ecare, Desire
FACES OF WOMEN
Edgerton, Larry
BLOOD HOOK
Edmonds, Don
NIGHT STALKER, THE
Edmondson, Adrian
MORE BAD NEWS
Edwall, Allan
MALARPIRATER
Edzard, Christine
LITTLE DORRIT
Egan, Richard
GHOST FEVER
Ege, John
JOR
Eggleston, Colin
CASSANDRA
Egoyan, Atom
FAMILY VIEWING
Eguiraun, Luis
EL AMOR DE AHORA
Ehlers, Michel
POULE ET FRITES
Eilert, Bernd
OTTO—DER NEUE FILM
Eiramdzhan, Anatoly
SAMAYA OBAYATELNAYA I PRIVLEKATELNAYA
el-Abnoudir, Abdel-Rashman
AL-TAUQ WAL-ISWIRA
Ellis, Bob
WARM NIGHTS ON A SLOW MOVING TRAIN
Ellis, Bret Easton
LESS THAN ZERO
Ellis, Kirk
TERMINAL EXPOSURE
Elorriaga, Xabier
A LOS CUATRO VIENTOS
Elsmo, Leif
ADVENTURE OF THE ACTION HUNTERS
Endo, Shusaku
SEA AND POISON, THE
Engel, Michael
NIGHTFORCE
Engelbach, David C.
OVER THE TOP
Enzensberger, Ulrich
CHINESE ARE COMING, THE
Enzo Millioni
TENEREZZA
Epps, Jack
SECRET OF MY SUCCESS, THE
Erba, Edoardo
A FIOR DI PELLE
Erichsen, Bente
FELDMANN CASE, THE
Eriksson, Claes
LEIF
Esadze, Rezo
NEYLONOVAYA YOLKA
Escalante, Dana
RETURN TO HORROR HIGH
Espinosa, Lito
LA BUSQUEDA
Esterhazy, Peter
TISZTA AMERIKA
Eszterhas, Joe
BIG SHOTS
HEARTS OF FIRE
Evans, Bruce A.
MADE IN HEAVEN
Evans, David Mickey
OPEN HOUSE
Ezhov, Valentin
SOPERNITSY
Ezra, Mark
SLAUGHTER HIGH
Fabre, Michel
LASSOCIATION DES MALFAITEURS
Fago, Amedeo
LA DONNA DEL TRAGHETTO
Falk, Feliks
BOHATERROKU
Fanaka, Jamaa
PENITENTIARY III
Farina, Felice
SEMBRA MORTO . . . ME E SOLO SVENUTO
Fataliyev, Ramiz
OBVINYAETSYA SVADBA
YA LYUBIL VAC BOLSHE ZHIZNI
Fatallyev, Ramiz
ZONTIK DLYA NOVOBRACHNYKH
Faure, Christian
CHAMP D'HONNEUR
Fay, Jim
OUTTAKES
Fearing, Kenneth
NO WAY OUT
Feijoo, Beda Docampo
MISS MARY
Feinmann
EN RETIRADA
Feitosa, Tairone
A DANCA DOS BONECOS
Feitosa, Tirone
ELE, O BOTO
Fekete, Istvan
LUTRA
Feldberg, Mark
DISORDERLIES
LETS GET HARRY
Feldman, Dennis
REAL MEN
Fellini, Federico
INTERVISTA
Ferguson, John
DEATH STONE
Ferguson, Larry
BEVERLY HILLS COP II
Fernan-Gomez, Fernando
MY GENERAL
Fernandez Baraibar, Julio
CHORROS
Ferrara, Giuseppe
MORO AFFAIR, THE
Ferraris, Denis
COMEDY!
Ferrini, Franco
CARAMELLE DA UNO SCONOSCIUTO
OPERA
Ferris, Costas
OH BABYLON
Fiastri, Jaja
VIA MONTENAPOLEONE
Field, David
AMAZING GRACE AND CHUCK
Fields, Scott
UNDER COVER
Filan, Ludovit
CENA ODVAHY
Filatov, Arkady
NABAT NA RASSVETE
Findlay, Roberta
BLOOD SISTERS
Finkleman, Ken
WHO'S THAT GIRL
Finn, Pavel
CHUZHIE ZDES NE KHODYAT
Firth, Mike
LEADING EDGE, THE
Fischer, Janice
LOST BOYS, THE
Fischer, Markus
DER NACHBAR
Fischerova, Daniela
WOLF'S HOLE

Fishburn, James
FRENCHMAN'S FARM

Fitchett, Chris
CASSANDRA

Fleischmann, Peter
LES EXPLOITS DUN JEUNE DON JUAN

Fleming, Edward
SIDSTE AKT

Fleming, Ian
LIVING DAYLIGHTS, THE

Florez, Wenceslao Fernandez
EL BOSQUE ANIMADO

Flynn, Bill
SATURDAY NIGHT AT THE PALACE

Foldes, Lawrence D.
NIGHTFORCE

Fondato, Marcello
ALADDIN

Fonseca E Costa, Jose
LA PLAYA DE LOS PERROS

Fonseca e Costa, Jose
BALADA DA PRAIA DOS CAES

Fonvielle, Lloyd
GOOD MORNING BABYLON

Forder, Timothy
INDIAN SUMMER

Foriadis, Aris
KE DYO AVGA TOURKIAS

Forlani, Remo
IL EST GENIAL PAPY!

Forque, Jose Maria
ROMANCA FINAL

Forsch, Gerd Roman
DANN IST NICHTS MEHR WIE VORHER

Forster, E.M.
MAURICE

Forsyth, Bill
HOUSEKEEPING

Forsyth, Frederick
FOURTH PROTOCOL, THE

Fox, James
WHITE MISCHIEF

Fox, Ray Errol
HOT SHOT

Franciosa, Massimo
IL LUPO DI MARE
RIMINI RIMINI
ROBA DA RICCHI

Francis, Karl
BOY SOLDIER

Francisco
LAPUTA: THE CASTLE IN THE SKY

Frank, Christopher
LANNEE DES MEDUSES
MALONE
SPIRALE

Frank, Laurie
MAKING MR.RIGHT

Franke, Anja
SAME TO YOU

Franklin, Howard
SOMEONE TO WATCH OVER ME

Franklin, Jeff
SUMMER SCHOOL

Freed, Herb
SURVIVAL GAME

Freeman, David
STREET SMART

Fridriksson, Fridrik Thor
SKYTTURNAR

Friedman, Alan
SOMETHING SPECIAL!

Friedman, Tom
DANGER ZONE, THE

Friis Mikkelsen, Jarl
KAMPEN OM DEN RODE KO

Froehlich, Bill
RETURN TO HORROR HIGH

Frost, Mark
BELIEVERS, THE

Frumkes, Roy
STREET TRASH

Fuhrer, Volker
STADTRAND

Fujita, Don
SHINRAN: SHIRO MICHI

Fukasaku, Kinji
KATAKU NO HITO
SURE DEATH 4

Fuller, Samuel
LETS GET HARRY

Fumagalli, Gianluca
A FIOR DI PELLE

Furuta, Motomu
DEATH SHADOWS

Gabriadze, Revaz
KIN-DZA-DZA

Gabrieli, Michael
KISS DADDY GOOD NIGHT

Gaddis, Matthew
SUICIDE CLUB, THE

Gagne, Jean
LA COULEUR ENCERCLEE

Gagne, Serge
LA COULEUR ENCERCLEE

Gagnon, Claude
KID BROTHER, THE

Gaidai, Leonid
SPORTLOTO—82

Galiana, Fernando
MATAR O MORIR
RETO A LA VIDA
TODA LA VIDA

Galindo, Fernando
LAS TRAIGO . . . MUERTAS

Galindo, Kiki
DELINCUENTE

Galindo, Pedro
MI NOMBRE ES GATILLO

Galindo, Ruben
NARCOTERROR

Gallagher, Chris
WHITE PHANTOM

Galligan, John
BLOOD HOOK

Gamba, Giuliana
PROFUMO

Gamba, Sao
KOLORMASK

Garci, Jose Luis
ASIGNATURA APROBADA

Garcia Gardelle, Ignacio
TRAGICO TERREMOTO EN MEXICO

Garcia Lorca, Federico
LA CASA DE BERNARDA ALBA

Garcia Marquez, Gabriel
CHRONICLE OF A DEATH FORETOLD

Garcia Sanchez, Jose Luis
HAY QUE DESHACER LA CASA

Garciadiego, Paz Alicia
REALM OF FORTUNE, THE

Gardos, Peter
WHOOPING COUGH

Garfield, Brian
DEATH WISH 4: THE CRACKDOWN
STEPFATHER, THE

Gariby, Ricardo
CORRUPCION

Garland, Robert
NO WAY OUT

Garris and an uncredited tel, Mick
BATTERIES NOT INCLUDED

Garson, Paul
CYCLONE

Gatliff, John
DEATH BEFORE DISHONOR

Gaup, Nils
OFELAS

Gavensky, Martha
A DOS AGUAS

Gazdag, Gyula
HOL VOLT, HOL NEM VOLT

Gelfield, Arthur N.
NO DEAD HEROES

Gelman, Alexander
ZINA-ZINULYA

Gems, Jonathan
WHITE MISCHIEF

George Katakouzinos
ANGELOS

Gernhardt, Robert
OTTO—DER NEUE FILM

Gfeller, Alex
DER NACHBAR

Ghaffari, Earl
KINDRED, THE

Ghazal, Aziz
ZOMBIE HIGH

Ghione, Riccardo
DELIZIA

Giannini, Giancarlo
TERNOSECCO

Gibbons, Pamela
BELINDA

Gidding, Nelson
WHEELS OF TERROR

Gideon, Raynold
MADE IN HEAVEN

Gies, Martin
ZABOU

Gil, Margarida
RELACAO FIEL E VERDADEIRA

Gilles, Guy
NUIT DOCILE

Gillot, Alain
TERMINUS

Ginsberg, Itzhak
YEHOSHUA—YEHOSHUA

Giuseppini, Andrea
CARAMELLE DA UNO SCONOSCIUTO

Glasgow, Alex
PURSUIT OF HAPPINESS, THE

Gleason, Michie
SUMMER HEAT

Glenn, Pierre-William
TERMINUS

Glowna, Vadim
DEVILS PARADISE, THE

Glueckman, Allan Jay
RUSSKIES

Godard, Jean-Luc
ARIA
SOIGNE TA DROITE

Godinho, Rafael
JESTER,THE

Godmilow, Jill
WAITING FOR THE MOON

Goedel, Peter
DAS TREIBHAUS

Goethe, Johann Wolfgang von
MEFISTO FUNK
TAROT

Goff, John
NIGHT STALKER, THE

Gogol, Nicolai
LE JOURNAL D'UN FOU

Goicoechea, Gonzalo
LA ESTANQUERA DE VALLECAS

Goldenberg, Jorge
MISS MARY

Goldman, William
HEAT
PRINCESS BRIDE, THE

Goldsmith, George
BLUE MONKEY
HOT CHILD IN THE CITY
NOWHERE TO HIDE

Goncharov, Ivan
OBRYV

Gonzalez, Jose Gonzalez
LO NEGRO DEL NEGRO

Gonzalez, Rogelio A.
EL HOMBRE DESNUDO

Gonzalez, Santiago
EL AMOR DE AHORA

Goodman, Michael Patrick
WANTED: DEAD OR ALIVE

Gordeladze, Leila
PYAT NEVEST DO LYUBIMOY

Gordon, Yakov
POSLEDNYAYA DOROGA

Gordon Pinsent
JOHN AND THE MISSUS

Goretta, Claude
SI LE SOLEIL NE REVENAIT PAS

Gorkovenko, Yuri
GEROY YEYOROMANA

Gorokhov, Aleksandr
VOLNY UMIRAYUT NA BEREGU

Gosha, Hideo
DEATH SHADOWS

Gothar, Peter
TISZTA AMERIKA

Goto, Toshi
ITAZU

Gottlieb, Michael
MANNEQUIN

Gottschalk, Thomas
ZARTLICHE CHAOTEN
Gotz, Axel
ZABOU
Goufas, Vangelis
KLIOS
Govorukhin, Stanislav
TAYNY MADAM VONG
Goyet, Jean-Francois
COMEDY!
HOTEL DE FRANCE
Gozutuk, Cemal
SON URFALI
Graf, Oskar Maria
TRIUMPH DE GERECHTEN
Graham, Ronny
SPACEBALLS
Grana, Sam
TRAIN OF DREAMS
Granier, Patrick
LE MIRACULE
Granier-Deferre, Pierre
NOYADE INTERDITE
Grassi, Antonella
GLI OCCHIALI D'ORO
Grassia, Nini
IL FASCINO SOTTILE DEL PECCATO
Grassick, Richard
T. DAN SMITH
Gray, Simon
MONTH IN THE COUNTRY, A
Grebnev, Anatoli
VREMYA ZHELANIY
Grede, Kjell
HIP, HIP, HURRA!
Greenaway, Peter
BELLY OF AN ARCHITECT, THE
Gregorio, Angelo
PERSONAGGI & INTERPRETI
Gries, Alan
DEATHROW GAMESHOW
Grieve, Anna
CUSTODY
Grigoratos, Dionyssis
FAKELOS POLK STON AERA
Grigorescu, Ioan
ZLOTY POCIAG
Grigoryev, Yevgeny
ZNAK BEDY
Grigoryeva, Rentia
GOVORIT MOSKVA
Grimm, the Brothers
DER BARENHAUTER
RED RIDING HOOD
Grimm, the brothers
HANSEL AND GRETEL
Grinter, Randy
MASTERBLASTER
Grishin, Alexander
POEZD VNE RASPISANIA
Groning, Philip
SOMMER
Gronowski, Miroslaw
WERYFIKACJA
Grossman, Vasily
KOMISSAR
Grosso, Alfonso
LOS INVITADOS
Grovas, Jorge Perez
NOCTURNO AMOR QUE TE VAS
Gruza, Jerzy
PIERSCIEN I ROZA
Grzymkowski, Jerzy
CZAS NADZIEI
Gu, Kim Sung
TALMAE WA POMDARI
Gubarev, Vladimir
KORABL PRISHELTSEV
Gubinishvili, David
STUPEN
Gudgeon, Mac
GROUND ZERO
Guerra, Tonino
CHRONICLE OF A DEATH FORETOLD
GOOD MORNING BABYLON
Guillemot, Claude
LA BRUTE
Gunn, Joseph
WILD PAIR, THE
WILD PAIR, THE
Guntzelman, Dan
REVENGE OF THE NERDS II: NERDS IN PARADISE
Gurskis, Dan
STRANGER, THE
Guselnikov, Alexander
KAPITAN "PILIGRIMA"
Guttentag, Bill
HOT SHOT
Gwo, Suen Jeung
OUTSIDERS, THE
Gyorffy, Miklos
HOL VOLT, HOL NEM VOLT
Haggard, H. Rider
ALLAN QUATERMAIN AND THE LOST CITY OF GOLD
Haisman, Mervyn
JANE AND THE LOST CITY
Hajny, Pavel
C. K. DEZERTERZY
CENA MEDU
Hakobian, Alex
FORTY DAYS OF MUSA DAGH
Hakonsson, Soren
VALHALLA
Hale, John
WHISTLE BLOWER, THE
Hall, Kenneth J.
EVIL SPAWN
Haller, Bent
STRIT OG STUMME
Hallstrom, Lasse
MY LIFE AS A DOG
Hamill, Denis
CRITICAL CONDITION
Hamill, John
CRITICAL CONDITION
Hamilton, David
WHITE PHANTOM
Hampton, Christopher
WOLF AT THE DOOR, THE
Hancock, John
WEEDS
Handke, Peter
DER HIMMEL UBER BERLIN
Hanff, Helene
EIGHTY FOUR CHARING CROSS ROAD
Hanin, Roger
LA RUMBA
Hann, Gordon
LOVECHILD, THE
Hannant, Brian
TIME GUARDIAN, THE
Hannum, Curtis
MIND KILLER
Hansel, Marion
LES NOCES BARBARES
Hansen, Lisa M.
COLD STEEL
Hanson, Curtis
BEDROOM WINDOW, THE
Harada, Masato
SARABA ITOSHIKI HITO YO
Hare, Ellin
T. DAN SMITH
Harel, Yair
CHOZE AHAVA
Harnage, Phillip L.
BANZAI RUNNER
Harris, Doug
REMEMBERING MEL
Harris, Paul
NICE GIRLS DON'T EXPLODE
Harry, Lee
SILENT NIGHT, DEADLY NIGHT PART II
Hars, Mihaly
LUTRA
Hartley, Graham
MOVING TARGETS
Hartman, Rivka
BACHELOR GIRL
Hartmann, Hasso
DER TRAUM VOM ELCH
Hartzell, Paivi
SNOW QUEEN, THE
Hasford, Gustav
FULL METAL JACKET
Hassel, Sven
WHEELS OF TERROR
Hastrup, Jannik
STRIT OG STUMME
Hausen, Jane Mengering
LADIES OF THE LOTUS
Haynes, Peter
BIRDS OF PREY
Hedayat, H.
GOZARESH-E YEK GHATL
Heifits, Iosif
PODSUDIMYY
Heker, Reuven
CHOZE AHAVA
Hembus, Joe
DEVILS PARADISE, THE
Hendra, Tony
BIG BANG, THE
Henkin, Hilary
FATAL BEAUTY
Henszelman, Stefan
VENNER FOR ALTID
Herbert, David
BLOOD HOOK
Herbert, Peter
BIT PART, THE
Herculano, Alexandre
JESTER,THE
Hermansson, Bo
PA STIGENDE KURS
Hernadi, Gyula
SZORNYEK EVADJA
Herr, Michael
FULL METAL JACKET
Hesketh-Harvey, Kit
MAURICE
Heynemann, Laurent
LES MOIS D'AVRIL SONT MEURTRIERS
Hickey, Bruce
NECROPOLIS
Hickman, Gail Morgan
DEATH WISH 4: THE CRACKDOWN
NUMBER ONE WITH A BULLET
Hidaka, Shinya
EIGA JOYU
PRINCESS FROM THE MOON
Highsmith, Patricia
LE CRI DU HIBOU
Hikari, Agata
UHOHO TANKENTAI
Hill, Terence
RENEGADE, UN OSSO TROPPO DURO
Hillel Mittelpunkt
BOUBA
Hines, Alan
SQUARE DANCE
Hing-kai, Chan
BETTER TOMORROW, A
Hixon, Ken
MORGAN STEWART'S COMING HOME
Hjortsberg, William
ANGEL HEART
Ho, Godfrey
NINJA THUNDERBOLT
Hodgman, Helen
RIGHT HAND MAN, THE
Hoffman, Ota
CHOBOTNICE Z II. PATRA
Hoffs, Tamar Simon
ALLNIGHTER, THE
Hogge, Nigel
EYE OF THE EAGLE
Holden, Anne
BEDROOM WINDOW, THE
Holder, Maryse
WINTER TAN, A
Holderlin, Friedrich
DER TOD DES EMPEDOKLES
Hole, Jeremy
IL GIORNO PRIMA
Holland, Agnieszka
ANNA
Holm, Sven
PETER VON SCHOLTEN
Holm, Sven-Gosta
NIONDE KOMPANIET
Hook, Harry
KITCHEN TOTO, THE
Horian, Richard
STUDENT CONFIDENTIAL

Horovitz, Israel
MAN IN LOVE, A

Horrall, Craig
DERANGED
IF LOOKS COULD KILL
SLAMMER GIRLS
WIMPS

Horvat, Alex
CAMPUS MAN

Hoskins, Dan
PRETTY SMART

Hotch, Ernest
GIRL, THE
SLEEP WELL, MY LOVE

Howard, Clark
BIG TOWN, THE

Howeler, Marijke
VAN GELUK GESPROKEN

Howze, Perry
MAID TO ORDER

Howze, Randy
MAID TO ORDER

Hubenbecker, Daniel
WARDOGS

Hubert, Jean-Loup
LE GRAND CHEMIN

Huemer, Peter Ily
KISS DADDY GOOD NIGHT

Hughes, John
PLANES, TRAINS AND AUTOMOBILES
SOME KIND OF WONDERFUL

Hui, Ann
ROMANCE OF BOOK AND SWORD, THE

Huillet, Daniele
DER TOD DES EMPEDOKLES

Humbert, Nicolas
SOMMER

Humphries, Barry
LES PATTERSON SAVES THE WORLD

Hunt, Bob
HIDDEN, THE

Hurwitz, David
FLICKS

Huston, Tony
DEAD, THE

Hylkema, Hans
JULIA'S GEHEIM

Hyttinen, Niilo
INUKSUK

Ibragimbekov, Rustam
YA YEY NRAVLYUS

Ichikawa, Kon
EIGA JOYU
PRINCESS FROM THE MOON

Iglesias, Juan
SUCCESSFUL MAN, A

Il-lo, Kwak
NAE-SHI

Ilyenko, Michail
KAZHDYY OKHOTNIK ZHELAET ZNAT

Imamura, Shohei
ZEGEN

In-ho, Choi
KYEOUL NAGUNE

Inda, Estela
TIERRA DE VALIENTES

Ingvordsen, J. Christian
FIREHOUSE

Inin, Arkady
TANTSPLOSHCHADKA

Inoue, Hisashi
FINAL TAKE: THE GOLDEN AGE OF MOVIES

Irving, David
EMPEROR'S NEW CLOTHES, THE
RUMPELSTILTSKIN

Isaacs, Susan
HELLO AGAIN

Ishido, Toshiro
DIXIELAND DAIMYO

Ishigami, Mitsutoshi
PRINCESS FROM THE MOON

Ishmukhamedov, Elyor
PROSHAL ZELEN LETA

Iskanderov, Fasil
CHEGEMSKIY DETEKTIV

Iskhakov, Dzhasur
PROSHAL ZELEN LETA

Islert, Jean-Claude
IL EST GENIAL PAPY!

Israel, Neal
POLICE ACADEMY 4: CITIZENS ON PATROL

Isshiki, Nobuyuki
WATASHI O SKI NI TSURETETTE

Itami, Juzo
TAXING WOMAN, A

Itoh, Chisho
GONDOLA

Ivanov, Nikolai
OKHOTA NA DRAKONA
VYKUP

Ivanov, Sergei
IZ ZHIZNI POTAPOVA

Ivory, James
MAURICE

Iwaszkiewicz, J.
ZYGFRYD

Jackson, David A.
COMMANDO SQUAD

Jackson, Mike
BLOOD TRACKS

Jacquot, Benoit
BUISSON ARDENT
LES MENDIANTS

Jaffe, Robert
NIGHTFLYERS

Jaglom, Henry
SOMEONE TO LOVE

Jancso, Miklos
SZORNYEK EVADJA

Janicek, Boris
DISCOPRIBEH

Jannuzzi, Lino
TERNOSECCO

Jarman, Derek
ARIA

Javed, Salim
MISTER INDIA

Jen, Wu Nien
LIEN LIEN FUNG CHEN

Jenkins, Victoria
STACKING

Jennings, Terry
CODA

Jeremias, James
LOST BOYS, THE

Jimenez, Neal
RIVER'S EDGE

Jo Schafer
CEMIL

Joffily, Jose
COLOR OF DESTINY, THE

Johansen, Arthur
ETTER RUBICON

John, H.W.
DEATH STONE

John, Radek
PROC?

Johnson, Brian
MESSENGER, THE

Johnson, J. Randal
DUDES

Jones, Amy
MAID TO ORDER

Jones, Ian
LIGHTHORSEMEN, THE

Jones, Laura
HIGH TIDE

Jones, Michael
SWEET REVENGE

Jonsson, Reidar
MY LIFE AS A DOG

Jorda, Joaquin
ASI COMO HABIAN SIDO
EL LUTE—CAMINA O REVIENTA

Jordan, Ben
THIN LINE, THE

Jost, Jon
BELL DIAMOND

Joyce, James
DEAD, THE

Joyner, Courtney
OFFSPRING, THE

Jozani, Massood Jafari
SHEERE SANGGY

Junker, Gottfried
VERSTECKTE LIEBE

Jurgensen, Randy
HEART

Just, Jiri
PRATELE BERMUDSKEHO TROJUHELNIKU

Kachyna, Karel
DEATH OF A BEAUTIFUL DREAM

Kadare, Ismail
AVRIL BRISE

Kafka, Tamara
TAXI NACH KAIRO

Kaiaks, Vladimir
STRAKH

Kaiserman, Connie
MY LITTLE GIRL

Kalisky, Rene
FALSCH

Kallas, Teet
REQUIEM

Kaloyeropoulos, N.
ONIRO ARISTERIS NICHTAS

Kaman, Steven
FIREHOUSE

Kamin, Bebe
CHECHECHELA—UNA CHICA DEL BARRIO

Kaminka, Didier
LASSOCIATION DES MALFAITEURS
TANT QU'IL AURA DES FEMMES

Kaminsky, Stuart M.
ENEMY TERRITORY

Kamondy, Zoltan
AZ UTOLSOKEZIRAT

Kanekoi, Mitsuharu
LOVE LETTER

Kaniuk, Yoram
HIMMO MELECH YERUSHALAIM

Kapralov, Georgy
STRANNAYAR ISTORIYAR DOKTORA DZHEKILA I MISTERA KHAIDA

Karason, Einar
SKYTTURNAR

Kardos, Istvan
GONDOVISELES

Karen, Valerij
CIZIM VSTUP POVOLEN

Karen, Valery
NOVYE SKAZKI SHAKHEREZADY

Karman, Janice
CHIPMUNK ADVENTURE, THE

Karya, Teguh
IBUNDA

Karyakin, Pyotr
DUBLYOR NACHINAET DEYSTVOVAT

Kasdaglis, N.
I KEKARMENI

Kassila, Matti
JAAHYVAISET PRESIDENTILLE

Kassila, Taavi
JAAHYVAISET PRESIDENTILLE

Katakouzinos, George
APOUSIES

Kato, Yudai
KID BROTHER, THE

Katsouridis, Dinos
ONIRO ARISTERIS NICHTAS

Katz, Robert
HOTEL COLONIAL
MORO AFFAIR, THE

Kaurismaki, Aki
HAMLET
TILINTEKO
VARJOJA PARATIISISSA

Kaurismaki, Mika
HELSINKI NAPOLI—ALL NIGHT LONG

Kavur, Omer
ANAYURT OTELI

Kazimova, Svetlana
CHKATULKA IZ KREPOSTI

Kedzielawska, Grazyna
INNA WYSPA

Keglevic, Peter
MAGIC STICKS

Kei, Shu
LAONIANG GOU SAO

Kelleher, John
EAT THE PEACH

Keller, Fred A.
MY DARK LADY

Keller, Frederick King
MY DARK LADY

Kelley, David E.
FROM THE HIP

Kemal, Yashmar
YER DEMIR, GOK BAKIR
Kempley, Walter
PENG! DU BIST TOT!
Kenna, Peter
GOOD WIFE, THE
Kennedy, Burt
TROUBLE WITH SPIES, THE
Kennedy, William
IRONWEED
Kern, Peter
CRAZY BOYS
Kern, Roger
DELOS ADVENTURE, THE
Kernochan, Sarah
DANCERS
Kesden, Bradley
MEATBALLS III
Kessler, Lyle
ORPHANS
Khamrayev, Ali
YA TEBYA POMNYU
Khleifi, Michel
NOCE EN GALILEE
Khodjikov, Rustem
ZNAY NASHIKH
Khodjikov, Sultan
ZNAY NASHIKH
Khouri, Walter Hugo
EU
Kidawa, Janusz
KOMEDIANCI Z WCZORAJSZEJ ULICY
Kienzle, William X.
ROSARY MURDERS, THE
Kieslowski, Krzysztof
BLIND CHANCE
Kijowski, Janusz
MASKARADA
Kikushima, Ryuzou
PRINCESS FROM THE MOON
Kin, Lo
FINAL TEST, THE
Kincaid, Tim
MUTANT HUNT
ROBOT HOLOCAUST
King, Rick
HOT SHOT
King, Stephen
CREEPSHOW 2
Kinoy, Ernest
WHITE WATER SUMMER
Kiosterud, Erland
JOR
Kiral, Erden
DILAN
Kirsch, Virginie
JOHNNY MONROE
Kirstilan, Pentti
JAAHYVAISET PRESIDENTILLE
Kit, Lai
DIXIA QING
Klane, Robert
WALK LIKE A MAN
Klebanoff, Mitchell
DISORDERLIES
Kleiner, Harry
EXTREME PREJUDICE
Kleiser, Randal
NORTH SHORE
Klenov, Yefim
TAYNAYA PROGULKA
Klimov, German
FAREWELL
Kluge, Alexander
VERMISCHTE NACHRICHTEN
Knight, Christopher W.
WINNERS TAKE ALL
Knop, Patricia Louisianna
SIESTA
Knorr, Peter
OTTO—DER NEUE FILM
Kocking, Leonardo
LA ESTACION DEL REGRESO
Koeppen, Wolfgang
DAS TREIBHAUS
Kokkonen, Ere
LIIAN ISO KEIKKA
UUNO TURHAPURO MUUTTAA MAALLE

Kollek, Amos
FOREVER, LULU
Koltunov, Grigory
ISKUSHENIE DON ZHUANA
Koly, Souleymane
LA VIE PLATINEE
Komack from characters created, James
BACK TO THE BEACH
Komatsu, Takashi
BUS
Konami, Fumo
KATAKU NO HITO
Konchalovsky, Andrei
SHY PEOPLE
Konner, Lawrence
SUPERMAN IV: THE QUEST FOR PEACE
Konrad, Kazimierz
STANISLAW I ANNA
Konttinen, Sirkka-Liisa
T. DAN SMITH
Kopernik, Malgorzata
W ZAWIESZENIU
Kopjitti, Chart
HOUSE
Kordon, Arkady
NABAT NA RASSVETE
Kornfield, Randy
SWEET REVENGE
Korschen, Alexander
VENNER FOR ALTID
Korzhetz, Vladislav
SEREBRYANAYA PRYAZHA KAROLINY
Kosberg, Bob
IN THE MOOD
Koshiyama, Hiroshi
HIKARU ANNA
Kostzer, Kado
FUEGOS
Koterski, Marek
ZYCIE WEWNETRZNE
Kotkowski, Andrzej
W STARYM DWORKU
Kotzky, Jacob
BOUBA
Kouf, Jim
MIRACLES
STAKEOUT
Kouguell, Suzan
SUICIDE CLUB, THE
Kozole, Damjan
USODNI TELEFON
Krabbe, Tim
RED DESERT PENITENTIARY
Kranz, George
MAGIC STICKS
Krauzer, Steven
SWEET REVENGE
Krawczyk, Gerard
LETE EN PENTE DOUCE
Kremnev, Valery
OCHNAYA STAVKA
Kresoja, Dragan
OKTOBERFEST
Krieger, Martin Theo
ZISCHKE
Krikes, Peter
BACK TO THE BEACH
Kring, R. Timothy
TEEN WOLF TOO
Krishna, T.
PRATIGHAAT
Kroes, David Scott
OVERKILL
Kroopf, Sandy
NO MAN'S LAND
Kross, Rudi F.
ODYSSEE D'AMOUR
Krueger, Michael
MIND KILLER
Krzystek, Waldemar
W ZAWIESZENIU
Kubik, Lawrence
DEATH BEFORE DISHONOR
Kubrick, Stanley
FULL METAL JACKET
Kulenovic, Haris
ZIVOT RADNIKA
Kuliev, Eldar
LEGENDA SEREBRYANOGO OZERA

Kullenberg, Anette
OM KARLEK
Kumai, Kei
SEA AND POISON, THE
Kuncewiczowa, Maria
CUDZOZIEMKA
Kure, Henning
VALHALLA
VALHALLA
Kureishi, Hanif
SAMMY AND ROSIE GET LAID
Kurtzman, Andrew
NUMBER ONE WITH A BULLET
Kurys, Diane
MAN IN LOVE, A
Kushnirenko, Georgy
KAK STAT SCHASTLIVYM
Kusturica, Emir
STRATEGIJA SVRAKE
ZIVOT RADNIKA
Kuusi, Janne
A LA ITKE IINES
Kveselava, Rezo
REPENTANCE
Kwok-leong, Kam
WONDER WOMEN
Kyronseppa, Kari
VY VIHDOINKIN YHDESSA
Lacayo, Ramiro
MUJERES DE LA FRONTERA
Lacerda, Luiz Carlos
LEILA DINIZ
Lahiff, Craig
CODA
Lahlou, Latif
LA COMPROMISSION
Lahr, John
PRICK UP YOUR EARS
Lai, Chung
HEROIC PIONEERS
Lai, David
SWORN BROTHERS
Laine, Joan
TOO MUCH
Laloux, Rene
GANDAHAR
Lambrinos, Fotos
DOXOBUS
Lamden, Richard
NIGHTMARE AT SHADOW WOODS
Lamotte, Martin
LA VIE DISSOLUE DE GERARD FLOQUE
Lamy, Benoit
LA VIE EST BELLE
Lana Gogoberidze
KRUGOVOROT
Lanahan, Michael
JOCKS
Landry, Bernard G.
LE JOURNAL D'UN FOU
Landsberg, David
DUTCH TREAT
Lane, James
MURDER LUST
Lane, Warren
HAPPY NEW YEAR
Lang, Michel
CLUB DE RENCONTRES
Lange, Monique
ACCROCHE-COEUR
Langsner, Jacobo
SOFIA
Lani, Hriday
MIRCH MASALA
Lankford, T.L.
BULLETPROOF
CYCLONE
Lappalainen, Seppo
AKALLINEN MIES
Lapshin, Alexander
KOORDINATY SMERTI
SLEDY OBOROTNYA
Larreta, Antonio
BALADA DA PRAIA DOS CAES
LA CASA DE BERNARDA ALBA
Larretta, Antonio
LA PLAYA DE LOS PERROS
Larsen, Hanne Hostrup
JAG ELSKER DIG

Latif, Latif Abdul
PERLYOTNIYE PTIT
Latsis, Eric
OBOROTEN TOM
Launer, Dale
BLIND DATE
Lautner, Georges
LA VIE DISSOLUE DE GERARD FLOQUE
Lauzon, Jean-Claude
NIGHT ZOO
Lavrov, Alexander
IZ ZHIZNI NACHALNIKA UGOLOVNOGO ROZYSKA
Lavrov, Olga
IZ ZHIZNI NACHALNIKA UGOLOVNOGO ROZYSKA
Law, Alex
AUTUMN'S TALE, AN
Lawrence, Denny
WARM NIGHTS ON A SLOW MOVING TRAIN
Le Gassick, Steve
COMMANDO SQUAD
Le Henry, Alain
LETE DERNIER A TANGER
POUSSIERE D'ANGE
Leadon, Paul
AROUND THE WORLD IN EIGHTY WAYS
Leconte, Patrice
TANDEM
Leduc, Paul
FRIDA
Lee, Conchita
MESSENGER, THE
Lee, Jacha
MAN WITH THREE COFFINS, THE
Lefcourt, Carolyn
STEPFATHER, THE
Lefebvre, Genevieve
MANUELA'S LOVES
Lefler, Doug
STEEL DAWN
Lehmuskallio, Markku
INUKSUK
Lei, Zhang
DOCTOR SUN YATSEN
Leider, R. Allen
ORACLE, THE
Leighton, Michael
HOSTAGE
Leipzig, Matt
HOUR OF THE ASSASSIN
Leitao, Joaquim
DUMA VEZ POR TODAS
Leland, David
PERSONAL SERVICES
WISH YOU WERE HERE
Lelouch, Claude
ATTENTION BANDITS
HAPPY NEW YEAR
Lemick, Michael E.
MASSACRE IN DINOSAUR VALLEY
Lemmo, James
HEART
Lemos, Carlos
LOS DUENOS DEL SILENCIO
Lenahan, Jim
SPACE RACE
Lengline, Michel
IL EST GENIAL PAPY!
Lent, Dean
BORDER RADIO
Leon, Maryse
LA VIE EST BELLE
Leonard, Elmore
ROSARY MURDERS, THE
Leone, Robert
CODE NAME ZEBRA
Leoni, Roberto
DISTANT LIGHTS
ITALIANI A RIO
UNA DONNA DA SCOPRIRE
Leontyev, Alexei
OCHNAYA STAVKA
POEZD VNE RASPISANIA
Leopold, Keith
MOVING TARGETS
Lerici, Roberto
DISTANT LIGHTS
Leszczynski, Witold
SIEKIEREZADA
Lettich, Sheldon
RUSSKIES
THOU SHALT NOT KILL . . . EXCEPT
Lev Nikolaevich Tolstoy
STARAYA AZBUKA
Levinson, Barry
TIN MEN
Levitan, Nadav
YALDEI STALIN
Levitin, Jacqueline
EVA: GUERRILLERA
Levitt, Karen
DANGER ZONE, THE
Levy, Dani
SAME TO YOU
Lewino, Walter
F . . . ING FERNAND
Liang, Kong
BUDDHA'S LOCK
Lichtenheld, Ted
PERSONAL FOUL
Liddell, Bobby
ENEMY TERRITORY
Ligon, Stanislaw
KOMEDIANCI Z WCZORAJSZEJ ULICY
Likhanov, Albert
KARUSEL NA BAZARNOY PLOSHCHADI
Lili, Gao
BIG PARADE, THE
Lilienfeld, Jean-Paul
LETE EN PENTE DOUCE
Lilienthal, Peter
POET'S SILENCE, THE
Lillienfeld, Jean-Paul
SALE DESTIN!
Lima, Walter
ELE, O BOTO
Limpach, Hannelene
ANITA—DANCES OF VICE
Linares, Andres
ASI COMO HABIAN SIDO
Lindblom, Gunnel
NAGRA SOMMARKVALLAR PA JORDEN
Lindfors, Viveca
UNFINISHED BUSINESS . . .
Lindgren, Astrid
MIO, MOY MIO
MORE ABOUT THE CHILDREN OF BULLERBY VILLAGE
Lindgren, Torgny
SERPENT'S WAY, THE
Lindholm, Peter
KILL CITY
Linnman, Susanne
MORE ABOUT THE CHILDREN OF BULLERBY VILLAGE
Lionel, Guy
CLUB DE RENCONTRES
Lipkies, Ivette
NI DE AQUI, NI DE ALLA
Lisberger, Steven
HOT PURSUIT
Lisson, Mark
RETURN TO HORROR HIGH
List, Niki
DIE DRECKSCHLEUDER
Listov, Semyon
CHKATULKA IZ KREPOSTI
Litten, Peter
SLAUGHTER HIGH
Livaneli, Omer Zulfu
YER DEMIR, GOK BAKIR
Livanov, Vasily
MOY LYUBIMYY KLOUN
Lizzani, Carlo
LA MONACA DIMONZA
Llosa, Mario Vargas
CITY AND THE DOGS, THE
Llovet, Enrique
DIVINAS PALABRAS
Lobachevskaya, Elena
LYUBOVYU ZA LYUBOV
Lobanov, Vladimir
SON V RUKU, ILI CHEMODON
Loeb III, Joseph
BURGLAR
TEEN WOLF TOO
Lofton, Terry
NAIL GUN MASSACRE
Lombardi, Carlos
UM TREM PARA AS ESTRELAS
Lommel, Ulli
OVERKILL
Loncraine, Richard
BELLMAN AND TRUE
London, Robby
PINOCCHIO AND THE EMPEROR OF THE NIGHT
Louis Malle
AU REVOIR, LES ENFANTS
Love, Michael James
GABY—A TRUE STORY
Lovell, Marc
TROUBLE WITH SPIES, THE
Lowden, Desmond
BELLMAN AND TRUE
Lowenstein, Richard
DOGS IN SPACE
Loza, Pepe
JUANA LA CANTINERA
Lucente, Francesco
VIRGIN QUEEN OF ST. FRANCIS HIGH, THE
Ludman, Larry
THUNDER WARRIOR II
Lukaszewicz, Jerzy
PRZYJACIEL WESOLEGO DIABLA
Luna, Bigas
ANGUSTIA
Luning, Imma
SO VIELE TRAUME
Luotto, Steven
IRON WARRIOR
Lynch, Martin
PRAYER FOR THE DYING, A
Lyubomudrov, Vladimir
POKLONIS DO ZEMLI
Maar, Gyula
MALOM A POKOLBAN
Maccari, Ruggero
FAMILY, THE
MacFadyen, Ian
BIT PART, THE
MacGillivray, William D.
LIFE CLASSES
MacLean, Rory H.
GUNPOWDER
Maclean, Stephen
AROUND THE WORLD IN EIGHTY WAYS
Maddock, Brent
BATTERIES NOT INCLUDED
Madigan, Sylvain
SALE DESTIN!
Madsen, Peter
VALHALLA
Magill, Mark
WAITING FOR THE MOON
Magliulo, Giorgio
UNA CASA IN BILICO
Mahkamov, Leonid
A SANTA DERVIS
Mai, William B.
WALK ON THE MOON, A
Maibaum, Richard
LIVING DAYLIGHTS, THE
Mailer, Norman
TOUGH GUYS DON'T DANCE
Mailhot, Michele
LE SOURD DANS LA VILLE
Maillard, Pierre
POISONS
Maitland, Dennis
MAGIC SNOWMAN, THE
Majewski, Janusz
C. K. DEZERTERZY
Makhmal Baf, Mohsen
PEDDLER, THE
Makk, Karoly
AZ UTOLSOKEZIRAT
Makris, Dimitris
I KEKARMENI
Maksakov, Vyacheslav
OBESHCHAYU BYT
Malatesta, Gloria
LESTATE STA FINENDO
Malishevsky, Igor
KONTRUDAR
Malko, George
SWEET LORRAINE
Mallon, James
BLOOD HOOK

Malone, Mark
DEAD OF WINTER

Mamet, David
HOUSE OF GAMES
UNTOUCHABLES, THE

Mandic, Miroslav
ZIVOT RADNIKA

Mandoki from events narrated t, Luis
GABY—A TRUE STORY

Mankiewicz, Tom
DRAGNET

Mann, Ted
O. C. AND STIGGS

Manriquez, Jorge
YERBA SANGRIENTE

Manttari, Anssi
KUNINGAS LEAR
NAKEMIIN, HYVASTI

Marboeuf, Jean
GRAND GUIGNOL

Margineanu, Nicolae
PADUREANCA

Marin, Richard
BORN IN EAST L.A.

Marinero, Manuel
REDONDELA

Marinho, Euclydes
BEIJO NA BOCA

Mariscal, Alberto
FORAJIDOS EN LA MIRA

Markovic, adapted by Jovan
MAGIC SNOWMAN, THE

Markovic, Goran
VEC VIDJENO

Markowitz, Mitch
GOOD MORNING, VIETNAM

Marks, David
SAKURA KILLERS

Markusson, Andreas
PA STIGENDE KURS

Marmin, Michel
PIERRE ET DJEMILA

Marotta, Franco
MISSIONE EROICA
SCUOLA DI LADRI 2

Marsh, David
SURFER, THE

Marshall, Steve
REVENGE OF THE NERDS II: NERDS IN PARADISE

Martin, George R.R.
NIGHTFLYERS

Martin, James
I WAS A TEENAGE ZOMBIE

Martin, Murray
T. DAN SMITH

Martin, Steve
ROXANNE

Martin, William E.
HARRY AND THE HENDERSONS

Martini, Richard
THREE FOR THE ROAD

Martino, Luciano
LE FOTO DI GIOIA

Maruike, Osamu
UHOHO TANKENTAI

Marx, Rick
FIREHOUSE
SLAMMER GIRLS
WARRIOR QUEEN

Masiello, Nino
QUEL RAGAZZO DELLA CURVA "B"

Mason, Nan
MY LITTLE GIRL

Mastorakis, Nico
TERMINAL EXPOSURE
WIND, THE
ZERO BOYS, THE

Masuda, Toshio
TOKYO BLACKOUT

Materic, Mladen
STRATEGIJA SVRAKE

Matheson, Richard Christian
THREE O'CLOCK HIGH

Mathias, Anna
EMPEROR'S NEW CLOTHES, THE

Matji, Manolo
LA GUERRA DE LOS LOCOS

Matthews, Temple
OFF THE MARK

May, Elaine
ISHTAR

Mazia, Edna
HIMMO MELECH YERUSHALAIM

Mazur, Vladimir
GRUZ BEZ MARKIROVKI

Mazzacurati, Carlo
NOTTE ITALIANA

McCanlies, Tim
NORTH SHORE

McCann, Bryan
HIGH STAKES

McCarthy, Pat
T. DAN SMITH

McCormick, John
LIVING ON TOKYO TIME

McCoy, Steve
I WAS A TEENAGE ZOMBIE

McCoy, Tim
SWEET REVENGE

McDonough, Kevin
I WAS A TEENAGE T.V. TERRORIST

McEntee from the novella by Th, Brian
BRAVE LITTLE TOASTER, THE

McGrady, Mike
TALKING WALLS

McKenzie, Brian
WITH LOVE TO THE PERSON NEXT TO ME

McLaughlin, Sheila
SHE MUST BE SEEING THINGS

McLennan, Don
SLATE, WYN & ME

McLoughlin, Tom
DATE WITH AN ANGEL

Meehan, Thomas
SPACEBALLS

Meerapfel, Jeanine
DIE VERLIEBTEN

Meerson, Steve
BACK TO THE BEACH

Meetypov, Vladimir
UTRO OBRECHENNOGO PRIISKA

Mehrjui, Darioush
LODGERS

Melancon, Andre
BACH AND BROCCOLI

Melikadze, Issi
LEGENDA SEREBRYANOGO OZERA

Melo, Jorge Silva
O DESEJADO—LES MONTAGNES DE LA LUNE

Menaker, Leonid
POSLEDNYAYA DOROGA

Mendoza, Orlando R.
FORAJIDOS EN LA MIRA

Mendzheritsky, Ivan
MY OBVINYAEM

Mengfan, He
DOCTOR SUN YATSEN

Menkes, Nina
MAGDALENA VIRAGA

Menosky, Joe
HIDING OUT

Mercier, Annie
TESTAMENT D'UN POETE JUIF ASSASSINE

Merezhko, Viktor
ODINOKAYA ZHENCHINA ZHELAET
POZNAKOMITAYA
PROSTI

Merinero, Carlos P.
CARA DE ACELGA

Mesyatsev, Tevgeny
GRUBAYA POSADKA

Meszaros, Marta
DIARY FOR MY LOVED ONES

Metalnikov, Budimir
POLEVAYA GVARDIA MOZZHUKHINA

Metcalfe, Ken
WARRIORS OF THE APOCALYPSE

Metcalfe, Tim
MILLION DOLLAR MYSTERY
REVENGE OF THE NERDS II: NERDS IN PARADISE
THREE FOR THE ROAD

Meyers, Nancy
BABY BOOM

Meyjes, Menno
EMPIRE OF THE SUN
LIONHEART

Mezieres, Myriam
UNE FLAMME DANS MON COEUR

Michael, Simon
LE SOLITAIRE

Mickael, Simon
LASSOCIATION DES MALFAITEURS

Miehe, Ulf
DER UNSICHTBARE

Mikhail Schweitzer
KREUTZEROVA SONATA

Mikhalkov, Nikita
DARK EYES
MOY LYUBIMYY KLOUN

Mikuni, Rentaro
SHINRAN: SHIRO MICHI

Milius, John
EXTREME PREJUDICE

Miller, Grant Hinden
STARLIGHT HOTEL

Miller, J.C.
NO DEAD HEROES

Miller, Susan
LADY BEWARE

Millstead, Diane
LES PATTERSON SAVES THE WORLD

Min, Zhang
CUO WEI

Mindadze, Alexander
PLIUMBUM, ILI OPASNAIA IGIA

Miner, Michael
ROBOCOP

Ming, Luk Kim
MY WILL, I WILL

Mishra, Sudhir
THIS IS NOT OUR DESTINATION

Mitra, Narendranath
PHERA

Mittelpunkt, Hillel
BOUBA

Miyamoto, Teru
HOTARUGAWA

Mkrtchyan, Albert
PESN PROSHEDSHIKH DNEY

Mocky, Jean-Pierre
AGENT TROUBLE
LE MIRACULE

Moctezuma, Juan Lopez
WELCOME MARIA

Modugno, Marco
SOLDATI: 365 GIORNI ALL' ALBA

Moldavsky, Alexander
O ROZVRASHCHENII ZABYT

Moldova, Gyorgy
MALOM A POKOLBAN

Moldovan, Jeff
MASTERBLASTER

Molteni, Giorgio
AURELIA

Mommertz, Paul
WANNSEE CONFERENCE, THE

Mones, Paul
BEAT, THE

Monicelli, Mario
I PICARI

Montagnana, Luisa
IL LUPO DI MARE

Montaldo, Giuliano
GLI OCCHIALI D'ORO
IL GIORNO PRIMA

Montefiori, Luigi
DELIRIA

Monteiro, Joao Cesar
RELACAO FIEL E VERDADEIRA

Monteleone, Enzo
HOTEL COLONIAL

Montesi, Jorge
BIRDS OF PREY

Montoya, Jesus Fragoso
MAS VALE PAJARO EN MANO . . .

Moore, Brian
IL GIORNO PRIMA
LONELY PASSION OF JUDITH HEARNE,THE

Mora, Philippe
HOWLING III, THE

Morais, Jose Alvaro
JESTER,THE

Morandini, Lia
LA DONNA DEL TRAGHETTO

Mordillat, Gerard
F . . . ING FERNAND

Moreno Alba, Rafael
LONG STRIDER

Mori, Kotaro
DEATH SHADOWS
Morita, Yoshimitsu
SOROBANZUKU
UHOHO TANKENTAI
Morkus, Pranas
BLUDNYY SYN
Mormarev Bros., the
TRINAJSTATA GODENICA NA PRINCA
Morris, Grant
LEADING EDGE, THE
Morris, Lyle
MAGIC SNOWMAN, THE
Mortelliti, Rocco
ADELMO
Mortimer, John
MASCHENKA
Mortola, Rodolfo
EL DUENO DEL SOL
Morya, Alberto
PEDDLER, THE
Mularczyk, Andrzej
RYKOWISKO
Mulholland, Jim
AMAZON WOMEN ON THE MOON
Muller, Christa
DER TRAUM VOM ELCH
Munson, Brad
DIRTY LAUNDRY
Muratova, Kira
DOLGHYIE PROVOD
KOROTKIE VSTRECHI
Murdmaa, Helle
SEREBRYANAYA PRYAZHA KAROLINY
Murer, Fredi M.
ALPINE FIRE
Murphey, Michael S.
SUPERNATURALS, THE
Murphy, Eddie
BEVERLY HILLS COP II
Mus, Antoni
LA SENYORA
Musierowicz, Malgorzata
E S D
Mweze, Ngangura
LA VIE EST BELLE
N.S. Leskov
LEVSHA
Nabokov, Vladimir
MASCHENKA
Nadjafi, Mohammed Ali
GOZARESH-E YEK GHATL
Nagibin, Yuri
WEEKEND
Naha, Ed
DOLLS
Nair, M.T. Vasudevan
PANCHAGNI
Nakahara, Akira
SURE DEATH 4
Nakajima, Sadao
YOSHIWARA ENJO
Nakamura, Tsutomu
RYOMA O KITTA OTOKO
Nakaoka, Kyohei
HOTARUGAWA
Name, Hernando
ROSA DE LA FRONTERA
Nankin, Michael
GATE, THE
RUSSKIES
Nasca, Sergio
DA NNUNZIO
Natanson, Georgy
VALENTIN I VALENTINA
Nathan, James
KILLING TIME, THE
Nathanson, Dan
HIGHER EDUCATION
Natoli, Piero
CHI C'E C'E
Natotti, Nelson
COLOR OF DESTINY, THE
Natsume, Yashi
GONDOLA
Naumov, Vladimir
SEVERNY ANEKDOT
Neatrour, Jane
T. DAN SMITH
Nelson, Dusty
SAKURA KILLERS
WHITE PHANTOM
Nelson, Peter
LONELY PASSION OF JUDITH HEARNE,THE
Nepp, Jozsef
CAT CITY
Nesher, Doron
LATE SUMMER BLUES
Neuland, Olav
REQUIEM
Neumeier, Edward
ROBOCOP
Neunzig, Hans A.
CASPAR DAVID FRIEDRICH
Nexo, Martin Andersen
PELLE EROVRAREN
Nienacki, Zbigniew
PAN SAMOCHODZIK I NIESAMOWITY DWOR
Niermans, Edouard
POUSSIERE D'ANGE
Nieto Ramirez, Jose
MURIERON A MITAD DEL RIO
Nihalani, Govind
TAMAS
Nihalsingha, D.B.
MALDENIYESIMION
Nikich, Oscar
ZNAK BEDY
Nikolaidis, Nikos
PROINI PERIPOLOS
Nikolic, Dragan
U IME NARODA
Nikolic, Zivko
U IME NARODA
Nitchev, Ivan
CERNITE LEBEDI
Noah Blogh
ALIEN PREDATOR
Noel Coward
SIDSTE AKT
Nogami, Tatsuo
SURE DEATH 4
Nollas, Dimitris
APOUSIES
Noren, Lars
DEMONS
Novotny, Petr
PRATELE BERMUDSKEHO TROJUHELNIKU
Nowicki-Nienacki, Zbigniew
PAN SAMOCHODZIK I NIESAMOWITY DWOR
Nuccetelli, Maura
IL GRANDE BLEK
Nunez, Raul
LA RUBIA DEL BAR
Nuti, Francesco
STREGATI
Nutley, Colin
NIONDE KOMPANIET
O'Brien, Barry
PINOCCHIO AND THE EMPEROR OF THE NIGHT
O'Farrell, William
LETE DERNIER A TANGER
O'Flaherty, Dennis
PINOCCHIO AND THE EMPEROR OF THE NIGHT
O'Flaherty from, Dennis
PINOCCHIO AND THE EMPEROR OF THE NIGHT
O'Melveny, Don
NIGHTFORCE
O'Neill, Gene
DOWN TWISTED
Oas, David
JOCKS
Obon, Ramon
EL HIJO DE PEDRO NAVAJAS
EL MUERTO DEL PALOMO
LA FUGA DE CARRASCO
MAS BUENAS QUE EL PAN
YO, EL EJECUTOR
Obrow, Jeffrey
KINDRED, THE
Odell, David
MASTERS OF THE UNIVERSE
Odorisio, Luciano
LA MONACA DIMONZA
Ogawa, Shinsuke
MAGINA—MURA MONOGATARI
Okabe, Kote
ZEGEN
Okamoto, Kihachi
DIXIELAND DAIMYO
Okazaki, Steven
LIVING ON TOKYO TIME
Okeyev, Tolomush
MIRAZHI LYUBRI
Oldoini, Enrico
BELLIFRESCHI
Olguin, Carlos
A DOS AGUAS
Oliver, Ron
HELLO MARY LOU, PROM NIGHT II
Olivera, Hector
EL ANO DEL CONEJO
Olivo, Pablo
EL HOMBRE DE LA DEUDA EXTERNA
Olmi, Ermanno
LUNGA VITA ALLA SIGNORA!
Olson, Doug
MIND KILLER
Olsson, Claes
ELVIS-KISSAN JALJILLA
On, Yeung Ka
MIDNIGHT
Ono, Ryunosuke
ITAZU
Opper, Don
SLAMDANCE
Orico, from an idea of Vanja
ELE, O BOTO
Oristrell, Joaquin
CALE
Orlov, Alexander
STRANNAYAR ISTORIYAR DOKTORA DZHEKILA I MISTERA KHAIDA
Ormrod, Peter
EAT THE PEACH
Orr, James
THEY STILL CALL ME BRUCE
THREE MEN AND A BABY
Ortega, Ernie
NO BLOOD NO SURRENDER
Orzeszkowa, Eliza
NAD NIEMNEM
Oslyak, Vladimir
I NIKTO NA SVETE
Osvat, Andras
WHOOPING COUGH
Osyka, Leonid
POKLONIS DO ZEMLI
Otto, Herbert
DER TRAUM VOM ELCH
Ouedraogo, Idrissa
YAM DAABO
Oury, Gerard
LEVY ET GOLIATH
Out of Jail
SUMMER HEAT
Outten, Richard
LIONHEART
Ovcharov, Sergei
LEVSHA
Oves
EN RETIRADA
Ozhegov, Alexander
KRASNAYA STRELA
Pagni, Roberto
ADELMO
Pagnol, Marcel
JEAN DE FLORETTE
MANON OF THE SPRING
Pai, Kanneth
OUTSIDERS, THE
Pajkic, Nebojsa
KRALJEVA ZAVRSNICA
Palmer, John
DOT GOES TO HOLLYWOOD
Palmer, Melinda
GARBAGE PAIL KIDS MOVIE, THE
Panfilov, Gleb
TEMA
Pang, Thomas
YI LOU YI
Panicker, G.S.
PANDAVAPURAM
Pankratov, Alexander
PRODELKI V STARINNOM DUKHE
Pap, Tamas
LENZ

Papastathis, Lakis
THEOFILOS
Papatakis, Nikos
PHOTOGRAPH, THE
Papayannidis, Takis
YENETHLIA POLI
Parent, Gail
CROSS MY HEART
Parenti, Neri
SCUOLA DI LADRI 2
Parenti, Villaggio
SUPERFANTOZZI
Park-huen, Kwan
YI LOU YI
Parker, Alan
ANGEL HEART
Parker, David
THUNDER WARRIOR II
Parviainen, Olli-Pekka
LAIN ULKOPUOLELLA
Pasanen, Spede
PIKKUPOJAT
Pascolini, Paola
CHI C'E C'E
Paseornek, Michael
MEATBALLS III
Paskaljevic, Goran
ANDJEO CUVAR
Pasquale Misuraca
ANGELUS NOVUS
Passerelli, Elizabeth
ZOMBIE HIGH
Pataki, Eva
DIARY FOR MY LOVED ONES
Paterson, Dennis
SILENT NIGHT, DEADLY NIGHT PART II
Patino, Basilio Martin
MADRID
Patino, Jorge
EL MOFLES Y LOS MECANICOS
OPERACION MARIJUANA
VA DE NUEZ
Paul, Stuart
EMANON
Pauls, Alan
SINFIN, LA MUERTA NO ES NINGUNA SOLUCION
Pauls, Cristian
SINFIN, LA MUERTA NO ES NINGUNA SOLUCION
Peak, Barry
AS TIME GOES BY
Pearce, Frazer
BLOODY NEW YEAR
Pearce, Hayden
BLOODY NEW YEAR
Peck, Ron
EMPIRE STATE
Peck, Jeff
BUSHFIRE MOON
Pedersen, John
TUESDAY WEDNESDAY
Pedley, Ethel
DOT GOES TO HOLLYWOOD
Peet, Graham
OUT OF ORDER
Peled, Hanan
DEADLINE
HA INSTALATOR
LO SAM ZAYIN
Pelot, Pierre
LETE EN PENTE DOUCE
Penney, John
KINDRED, THE
Peploe, Clare
HIGH SEASON
Peploe, Mark
HIGH SEASON
LAST EMPEROR, THE
Perakis, Nicos
VIOS KE POLITIA
Perlini, Meme
CARTOLINE ITALIANE
Perrault, Charles
SLEEPING BEAUTY
Perrin, Laurent
BUISSON ARDENT
Perry, Fred C.
WIND, THE
ZERO BOYS, THE
Petko, Alex
DIRTY REBEL
Petraglia, Sandro
DOLCE ASSENZA
Petrie, Daniel
BEVERLY HILLS COP II
BIG EASY, THE
Petrocchi, Roberto
ILLUMINAZIONI
Pett, Norman
JANE AND THE LOST CITY
Peyton, Harley
LESS THAN ZERO
Peyton, Kathleen
RIGHT HAND MAN, THE
Phelps, William
NORTH SHORE
Phillips, Lou Diamond
TRESPASSES
Pialat, Maurice
SOUS LE SOLEIL DE SATAN
Piave, Francesco Maria
MACBETH
Picault, Chantal
ACCROCHE-COEUR
Piccioni, Giuseppe
IL GRANDE BLEK
Picha, Jean-Marc
BIG BANG, THE
Pierce, Jo Carol
TRESPASSES
Piesis, Gunar
POHADKA O MALICKOVI
Pilares, Manuel
MY GENERAL
Pinheiro, Jose
MON BEL AMOUR, MA DECHIRURE
Pipolo
IL BURBERO
Pires, Jose Cardoso
BALADA DA PRAIA DOS CAES
Pirhasan, Baris
DEGIRMEN
Pirro, Mark
DEATHROW GAMESHOW
Pirro, Ugo
UN RAGAZZO DI CALABRIA
Piscicelli, Salvatore
REGINA
Piwowarski, Radisław
POCIAG DO HOLLYWOOD
Platonov, Andrei
ODINOKIJ GOLOS CELOVEKA
Pleijel, Agneta
NAGRA SOMMARKVALLAR PA JORDEN
Plekhanov, Sergei
ZOLOTAYA BABA
Poata, Tama
NGATI
Polaco, Jorge
EN EL NOMBRE DEL HIJO
Polak, Jindrich
CHOBOTNICE Z II. PATRA
Polat, Omer
DILAN
Poliakoff, Stephen
HIDDEN CITY
Poma, Marco
MEFISTO FUNK
Ponicsan, Darryl
NUTS
Pons, Ventura
LA RUBIA DEL BAR
Ponzi, Maurizio
NOI UOMINI DURI
Pool, Robert Roy
BIG TOWN, THE
Poor, Symak Taghi
DJADDE HAYE SARD
Popeyus, Alma
BLOND DOLLY
Popova, Nevelina
PRIZEMYAVANE
Portillo, Adolfo Torres
EL DIABLO, EL SANTO Y EL TONTO
EL MUERTO DEL PALOMO
SINVERGUENZA . . . PERO HONRADO
UNA PURA Y DOS CON SAL
Portillo, Ralph
ARQUIESTA EMILIO VARELA
Powell, Lorna
T. DAN SMITH
Power, Maggie
BACHELOR GIRL
Prata, Mario
BESAME MUCHO
Prevost, Abbe
MANON
Price, Myriam S.
EL HOMBRE DESNUDO
Priemykhov, Valery
MAGIA CHYORNAYA I BELAYA
Prince, Peter
CRIME OF HONOR
Prior, David A.
DEADLY PREY
KILLER WORKOUT
MANKILLERS
Priyomykhov, Valery
VZLOMSHCHIK
Proffitt, Nicholas
GARDENS OF STONE
Proft, Pat
POLICE ACADEMY 4: CITIZENS ON PATROL
Proper, Rogier
DE RATELRAT
Proser, Chip
INNERSPACE
Protsenko, Anatoly
V STRELYAYUSHCHEY GLUSHI
Prytz, Kare
PA STIGENDE KURS
Puchinyan, Stepan
TAYNY MADAM VONG
Purcell, Joseph
DELOS ADVENTURE, THE
Purdy, Jim
CONCRETE ANGELS
Purgatori, Andrea
SPECTERS
Puzo, Dorothy Ann
COLD STEEL
Puzo, Mario
SICILIAN, THE
Pyhala, Jaakko
URSULA
Pyun, Albert
DOWN TWISTED
Quatermass, Martin
PRINCE OF DARKNESS
Queffelec, Yann
LES NOCES BARBARES
Quigley, Moe
COLD STEEL
Quinn, Bob
BUDAWANNY
Quinnell, A.J.
MAN ON FIRE
Quintano, Gene
ALLAN QUATERMAIN AND THE LOST CITY OF GOLD
POLICE ACADEMY 4: CITIZENS ON PATROL
Quiros, M.
VIOLINS CAME WITH THE AMERICANS, THE
Rabitzer, Edeltraud
DANN IST NICHTS MEHR WIE VORHER
Radford, Michael
WHITE MISCHIEF
Radiguet, Raymond
DEVIL IN THE FLESH
Radovanovic, Goran
OKTOBERFEST
Radowicz, Kazimierz
MIEDZY USTAMI A BRZEGIEM PUCHARU
NAD NIEMNEM
Ragazzo, Chris
MAGIC STICKS
Rahim, K.M.A.
UPPU
Raimi, Sam
EVIL DEAD 2: DEAD BY DAWN
Rakhamamin, Boris
RAZMAKH KRYLIEV
Ramalho, Francisco
BESAME MUCHO
Ramuz, Charles Ferdinand
SI LE SOLEIL NE REVENAIT PAS
Rancke-Madsen, Hans
VALHALLA
Rand, Douglas
BLOOD HOOK

Randa, X.
POLICIAS DE NARCOTICOS
Ranft, Joe
BRAVE LITTLE TOASTER, THE
Rannamaa, S.
IGRY DLJA DETEJ SKO'NOGO VOZRASTA
Rappaport, Ezra D.
HARRY AND THE HENDERSONS
Raskin, Larry
REMEMBERING MEL
Rasmusson, Karl
RESAN TILL MELONIA
Rasputin, Valentin
FAREWELL
Ratton, Helvecio
A DANCA DOS BONECOS
Ray, Fred Olen
BULLETPROOF
CYCLONE
Ray, Leslie
MY DEMON LOVER
Rayesian, Ali Reza
GOZARESH-E YEK GHATL
Raynov, Bogumil
CERNITE LEBEDI
Rebar, Alex
NOWHERE TO HIDE
Red, Eric
NEAR DARK
Reed, Morton
SPACE RACE
Rees, Jerry
BRAVE LITTLE TOASTER, THE
Reeve, Christopher
SUPERMAN IV: THE QUEST FOR PEACE
Regnoli, Piero
QUEL RAGAZZO DELLA CURVA "B"
Rego, Luis
POULE ET FRITES
Reichenbach, Carlos
ANJOS DO ARRABALDE
Reitinger, Richard
HELSINKI NAPOLI—ALL NIGHT LONG
Rekemchuk, Alexander
ZHELEZNOE POLE
Rekhviashvili, Alexander
STUPEN
Remiz Fataliev
SDELKA
Renaud, Bernadette
BACH AND BROCCOLI
Rendell, Ruth
HOUSEKEEPER, THE
Resnais, Alain
MELO
Restrepo, Martha Elena
VISA U.S.A.
Retes, Gabriel
MUJERES SALVAJES
Retes, Ignacio
VIAJE AL PARAISO
Reuben, Carla
SOMETHING SPECIAL!
Revah, Zeev
BOUBA
Rexer, Fred
EXTREME PREJUDICE
Reymont, Wladyslaw Stanislaw
KOMEDIANTKA
Reynolds, Jonathan
LEONARD PART 6
Reynolds, Lee
ALLAN QUATERMAIN AND THE LOST CITY OF GOLD
Reza, Rahi Masoom
ANJUMAN
Rich, Ron
GHOST FEVER
Richards, Caroline
SWEET COUNTRY
Richards, David Adams
TUESDAY WEDNESDAY
Richardson, Peter
EAT THE RICH
Richardson, Scott
HEARTS OF FIRE
Richens, Peter
EAT THE RICH
Richmond, Adrianne
OUTTAKES
Richter, Erika
SO VIELE TRAUME
Richter, Klaus
DER UNSICHTBARE
Richter, Manfred
VERNEHMUNG DER ZEUGEN
Riesner, Dean
FATAL BEAUTY
Riley, Rob
NUMBER ONE WITH A BULLET
Rinaldi, Giuditta
UNA CASA IN BILICO
Riparetti, Tom
COMMANDO SQUAD
Ripoll, Kiki Galindo
UN SABADO MAS
Ripploh, Frank
TAXI NACH KAIRO
Risan, Leifulv
ETTER RUBICON
Risi, Dino
TERESA
Risi, Marco
RIMINI RIMINI
SOLDATI: 365 GIORNI ALL' ALBA
Robbins, Matthew
BATTERIES NOT INCLUDED
Robert Louis Stevenson
STRANNAYAR ISTORIYAR DOKTORA DZHEKILA I MISTERA KHAIDA
Roberts, Peter
T. DAN SMITH
Robertson, R.J.
BIG BAD MAMA II
Robinson, Bruce
WITHNAIL AND I
WITHNAIL AND I
Robinson, Helen
DREAMANIAC
Robinson, Marilynne
HOUSEKEEPING
Robinson, Phil Alden
IN THE MOOD
IN THE MOOD
Robinson, Tom
SALVATION!
Rocha, Paulo
O DESEJADO—LES MONTAGNES DE LA LUNE
Rochat, Eric
TOO MUCH
Rodriguez, Angel
LO NEGRO DEL NEGRO
Rodriguez, Ismael
OLOR A MUERTE
YERBA SANGRIENTE
Rodriguez, Ismeal
CORRUPCION
Rodriguez, J.A.
CINCO NACOS ASALTAN A LAS VEGAS
Rodriguez, Miguel
SOFIA
Rodriguez, Robert
OPERACION MARIJUANA
Rodriquez, Milagros
POR LOS CAMINOS VERDES
Rodziewiczowna, Maria
MIEDZY USTAMI A BRZEGIEM PUCHARU
Roeg, Nicolas
ARIA
Rogerio, Walter
CIDADE OCULTA
Rohmer, Eric
LAMI DE MON AMIE
QUATRE AVENTURES DE REINETTE ET MIRABELLE
Romali, Giovanni
ROBA DA RICCHI
Roman, Jose
LA ESTACION DEL REGRESO
Romer, Jean-Claude
LE MIRACULE
Romero, George A.
CREEPSHOW 2
Romoli, Gianni
CARTOLINE ITALIANE
RIMINI RIMINI
Rood, Jurrien
DE ORIONNEVEL
Rosas Priego R., Alfonso
EL HIJO DE PEDRO NAVAJAS
Roschin, Mikahil
VALENTIN I VALENTINA
Roschin, Mikhail
VALENTIN I VALENTINA
Rosenthal, Mark
SUPERMAN IV: THE QUEST FOR PEACE
Roseo, Enrico
MOSCA ADDIO
Rosi, Francesco
CHRONICLE OF A DEATH FORETOLD
Rostand, Edmond
ROXANNE
Roth, Eric
SUSPECT
Rothberg, Jeff
HIDING OUT
Roulet, Dominique
NOYADE INTERDITE
Rouse, Virginia
TO MARKET, TOMARKET
Rovinski, Samuel
EULALIA
Rozema, Patricia
IVE HEARD THE MERMAIDS SINGING
Ruane, John
CASSANDRA
Ruben, Andy
STRIPPED TO KILL
Ruben, Katt Shea
STRIPPED TO KILL
Rud, Bernard
BORAN—ZEIT ZUM ZIELEN
Rude, Dick
STRAIGHT TO HELL
Rudolph, Verena
FRANCESCA
Rugoff, Edward
MANNEQUIN
Rui, Zhang
DAO MAZEI
Ruiz, Raul
MEMOIRE DES APPARENCES: LA VIE EST UN SONGE
Rukow, Mogens
ELISE
Rulfo, Juan
REALM OF FORTUNE, THE
Ruli, Stefano
LA DONNA DEL TRAGHETTO
Rumbold, Jonathan
SLEEP WELL, MY LOVE
Russell, Chuck
NIGHTMARE ON ELM STREET 3: DREAM WARRIORS, A
Russell, Ken
ARIA
Russell, William
FRENCHMAN'S FARM
Rust, John
STABILIZER, THE
Rutnam, Chandran
WITNESS TO A KILLING
Ryck, Francis
FAMILY BUSINESS
Saad, James
COMMANDO SQUAD
Saakov, Boris
TAYNOE PUTESHESTVIE EMIRA
Sabirov, Takhir
NOVYE SKAZKI SHAKHEREZADY
Sacristan, Jose
CARA DE ACELGA
Sadovsky, Victor
SOPERNITSY
Sagambekov, Bazarkul
VOLNY UMIRAYUT NA BEREGU
Sahni, Bhisham
TAMAS
Saindrichin, Guy Patrick
BUISSON ARDENT
Saint-Hamont, Daniel
LE SOLITAIRE
Sainz, Hermongenes
ROMANCA FINAL
Saito, Shinichi
YOSHIWARA ENJO

Saks, Mady
IRIS

Sale, Richard
ASSASSINATION

Salinas, Martin
GABY—A TRUE STORY

Salomonsen, Grete
KAMILLA OG TYVEN

Sams, Coke
ERNEST GOES TO CAMP

Samsonov, Samson
TANTSPLOSHCHADKA

Samuelson, Thomas
OM KARLEK

Sanchez, Eleuterio
EL LUTE—CAMINA O REVIENTA

Sanchez, Jose Luis Garcia
DIVINAS PALABRAS

Santiago, Catherine
EYE OF THE EAGLE

Santillan, Diego
DIVINAS PALABRAS

Santoro, Angela
A DANCA DOS BONECOS

Santos, Briccio
DAMORTIS

Saotome, Mitsugu
RYOMA O KITTA OTOKO

Saparov, Usman
PRIKLYUCHENIA NA MALENKIKH OSTROVEKH

Sarafian, Deran
ALIEN PREDATOR

Sarasohn, Lane
FLICKS

Sarchetti, Dardano
SPECTERS

Sardi, Jan
GROUND ZERO

Sargent, Alvin
NUTS

Sarshar, Reza
DJADDE HAYE SARD

Satrina, Carole Lucia
BEAUTY AND THE BEAST
RED RIDING HOOD

Sauder, Peter
CARE BEARS ADVENTURE IN WONDERLAND, THE

Saunders, Charles
AMAZONS

Saura, Guillermo
CHORROS

Sauter, Joe
HOT SHOT

Savage, Georgia
SLATE, WYN & ME

Savalis, Rimantes
MOYA MALENKAYA ZHENA

Saverni, Domenico
SUPERFANTOZZI

Sayles, John
MATEWAN
WILD THING

Sayyad, Parviz
CHECKPOINT

Sbarigia, Claudia
LESTATE STA FINENDO

Sbitnev, Yuri
SLUCHAYNYE PASSAZHIRY

Scarnacci and R. —Tarabusi, D.
MILLION V BRACHNOY KORZINE

Scarpelli, Furio
FAMILY, THE
SOLDATI: 365 GIORNI ALL' ALBA

Schamoni, Peter
CASPAR DAVID FRIEDRICH

Schatzky, Olivier
MAN IN LOVE, A

Schenkkan, Ine
VROEGER IS DOOD

Scherbakova, Galina
LICHNOE DELO SUDYI IVANOVOY

Schiffman, Suzanne
LA MOINE ET LA SORCIERE

Schiraldi, Vittorio
IL CORAGGIO DI PARLARE

Schito, Giuseppe
IL RAGAZZO DI EBALUS

Schlondorff, Volker
VERMISCHTE NACHRICHTEN

Schlosser, Roberto
EL PLACER DE LA VENGANZA
ROSA DE LA FRONTERA

Schmid, Daniel
JENATSCH

Scholes, Roger
TALE OF RUBY ROSE, THE

Scholz, Gunther
VERNEHMUNG DER ZEUGEN

Schrader, Paul
LIGHT OF DAY

Schrader, Uwe
SIERRA LEONE

Schulmann, Patrick
LES OREILLES ENTRE LES DENTS

Schumacher, Hildegard
DER JUNGE MIT DEM GROSSEN SCHWARZEN HUND

Schumacher, Siegfried
DER JUNGE MIT DEM GROSSEN SCHWARZEN HUND

Schutte, Jan
DRAGON'S FOOD

Schutz, Hein
BLOND DOLLY

Scola, Ettore
FAMILY, THE

Scott, Darin
OFFSPRING, THE

Scott, Robert
VIDEO DEAD, THE

Secerovic, Milan
UVEK SPREMNE ZENE

Seelig, Mathias
PENG! DU BIST TOT!

Sejda, Kazimierz
C. K. DEZERTERZY

Selfe, Ray
TURNAROUND

Sell, Jack M.
OUTTAKES

Seminara, George
I WAS A TEENAGE ZOMBIE

Senje, Sigurd
FELDMANN CASE, THE

Septunova, Marija
IGRY DLJA DETEJ SKO'NOGO VOZRASTA

Seria, Joel
LES DEUX CROCODILES

Serranda, T.
FIERAS EN BRAMA

Serrano, Carlos
CALE

Serreau, Coline
THREE MEN AND A BABY

Sestieri, Claudio
DOLCE ASSENZA

Setbon, Philippe
CROSS

Sethu
PANDAVAPURAM

Sette, Jose
UM FILM 100% BRAZILEIRO

Sexton, Ann
MAGDALENA VIRAGA

Shagan, Steve
SICILIAN, THE

Shah, Krishna
AMERICAN DRIVE-IN

Shakespeare, William
KUNINGAS LEAR
MACBETH

Shakhnazarov, Keran
KURIER

Sham, Tommy
CITY ON FIRE

Shamshiyev, B.
SNAYPERY

Shanley, John Patrick
MOONSTRUCK

Sharkey, John
OMEGA SYNDROME

Sharma, Trijawani
MIRCH MASALA

Sharp, Jan
SHADOWS OF THE PEACOCK

Shaw, George Bernard
SKORBNOE BESCHUVSTVIE

Shayne, Linda
CRYSTAL HEART

Shebib, Don
CLIMB, THE

Shelton, Charles F.
DEADTIME STORIES

Shepitko, Larisa
FAREWELL

Sheppard, John
HIGH STAKES
HIGHER EDUCATION

Sherman, Gary
WANTED: DEAD OR ALIVE

Shikibu, Murasaki
O DESEJADO—LES MONTAGNES DE LA LUNE

Shilovsky, Vsevolod
MILLION V BRACHNOY KORZINE

Shindo, Kaneto
EIGA JOYU

Shmelev, Oleg
KONETS OPERATSII "REZIDENT"

Shmuger, Marc
DEAD OF WINTER

Short, Robert
PROGRAMMED TO KILL
RAGE OF HONOR

Shpeer, Alexander
SOUCHASTNIKI

Shulgina, Albina
PRORYV

Shyer, Charles
BABY BOOM

Sidaris, Andy
HARD TICKET TO HAWAII

Sigmund, David
GREAT LAND OF SMALL, THE

Silke, James R.
BARBARIANS, THE

Silliphant, Stirling
CATCH THE HEAT
OVER THE TOP

Silver, Stu
THROW MOMMA FROM THE TRAIN

Simashko, M.
SNAYPERY

Simek, Milan
CIZIM VSTUP POVOLEN

Simkins, David
ADVENTURES IN BABYSITTING

Simo, Sandor
ISTEN VELETEK, BARATAIM

Simon, David
IN THE MOOD

Simonov, Konstantin
DVADTSTAT DNEI BEZ

Sims, Greg H.
RETURN TO HORROR HIGH

Singer, Bruce Franklin
KILLING TIME, THE

Singer, Stanford
I WAS A TEENAGE T.V. TERRORIST

Sipos, Dave
MIND KILLER

Siwertz, Sigfrid
MALARPIRATER

Skaaren, Warren
BEVERLY HILLS COP II

Skarmeta, Antonio
IN DER WUSTE

Skarsgard, Stellan
JIM OCH PIRATERNA BLOM

Skolmen, Jon
PLASTPOSEN

Skuybin, Nikolai
IZ ZHIZNI POTAPOVA

Slabnevich, Igor
PO ZAKONU VOENNOGO VREMENI

Slabolepszy, Paul
SATURDAY NIGHT AT THE PALACE

Slavici, Ioan
PADUREANCA

Slavine, Lev
INTERVENTSIA

Sluizer, George
RED DESERT PENITENTIARY

Smirnov, Andrei
SENTIMENTALNOE PUTESHESTVIE NA KARTOSHKU

Smith, Andrew
WHO'S THAT GIRL

Smith, Dominic Elmo
GET THE TERRORISTS
HOSTAGE SYNDROME

TOUGH COP

Smith, John N.
SITTING IN LIMBO
TRAIN OF DREAMS

Smith, Lance
MUNCHIES

Smyczek, Karel
PROC?

Snooks, Susan
CARE BEARS ADVENTURE IN WONDERLAND, THE

Soisson, Joel
SUPERNATURALS, THE

Sokolova, Ingrida
SVIDANIE NA MLECHNOM PUTI

Sola-Adar, Judith
KFAFOT

Solas, Humberto
SUCCESSFUL MAN, A

Sololowska, Anna
E S D

Sonego, Rodolfo
SOTTOZERO
UN TASSINARO A NEW YORK

Song Kil-han
TICKET

Sonye, Michael
BLOOD DINER
COLD STEEL

Sorak, Dejan
OFICIR S RUZOM

Sordi, Alberto
UN TASSINARO A NEW YORK

Sotha
MON BEL AMOUR, MA DECHIRURE

Soukup, Jaroslav
DISCOPRIBEH

Spheeris, Penelope
SUMMER CAMP NIGHTMARE

Spiegel, Larry
EVIL TOWN

Spiegel, Scott
EVIL DEAD 2: DEAD BY DAWN
THOU SHALT NOT KILL . . . EXCEPT

Spota, Luis
MURIERON A MITAD DEL RIO

Spry, Robin
KEEPING TRACK

St. John, Nicholas
CHINA GIRL

Stachura, Edward
SIEKIEREZADA

Stagnaro, Juan Batista
MISS MARY

Stallone, Sylvester
OVER THE TOP

Stamper, Larry
WILD THING

Starr, Manya
WHITE WATER SUMMER

Stasiak, Horst
IN DER WUSTE

Steensland, David
ESCAPES

Stefano, Joseph
KINDRED, THE

Stefanovski, Goran
HI-FI

Stein, Gerturde
MAGDALENA VIRAGA

Stelzer, Manfred
CHINESE ARE COMING, THE

Stepanov, Anatoly
AKTSIA

Stephensen, Ole
KAMPEN OM DEN RODE KO

Stevens, Leslie
THREE KINDS OF HEAT

Stevenson, Robert Louis
CHYORNAYA STRELA
SUICIDE CLUB, THE

Stockwell, John
UNDER COVER

Stone, Oliver
WALL STREET

Stoppard, Tom
EMPIRE OF THE SUN

Stouffer, Mark
MAN OUTSIDE

Straub, Jean-Marie
DER TOD DES EMPEDOKLES

Strekov, Andrei
PRODELKI V STARINNOM DUKHE

Strittmatter, Thomas
DRAGON'S FOOD

Stroppa, Danilo
LE FOTO DI GIOIA

Stubbs, Ray
T. DAN SMITH

Stukalov-Pogodin, Oleg
NABAT NA RASSVETE

Sturridge, Charles
ARIA

Suarez, Bobby A.
TOUGH COP
WARRIORS OF THE APOCALYPSE

Suarez, David
LA OVEJA NEGRA

Sudrie, Stefano
SOLDATI: 365 GIORNI ALL' ALBA

Sugawa, Eizo
HOTARUGAWA

Suk-wah, Leung
BETTER TOMORROW, A

Sullivan, Fred G.
SULLIVAN'S PAVILION

Summers, Manuel
SUFRE MAMON

Surmanov, Gavkhar
V TALOM SNEGE ZVON RUCHIA

Suter, Martin
JENATSCH

Svanoe, Bill
FATAL BEAUTY

Swann, P.W.
SURVIVAL GAME

Swerdlick, Michael
CANT BUY ME LOVE

Swyer, Alan
CRITICAL CONDITION

Szabo, Ildiko
HOTREAL

Szemes
A SANTA DERVIS

Szemes, Zsuzsa
A SANTA DERVIS

Szirtes, Andras
LENZ

Szollosi, Thomas
THREE O'CLOCK HIGH

Tacchella, Jean-Charles
TRAVELLING AVANT

Taggert, Brian
WANTED: DEAD OR ALIVE

Taghvai, Nasser
CAPTAIN KHORSHID

Tai-An-Ping, Chiu
DIXIA QING

Talan, Len
EMPEROR'S NEW CLOTHES, THE
HANSEL AND GRETEL

Talankin, Igor
WEEKEND

Talvik, Valery
V TALOM SNEGE ZVON RUCHIA

Tanaka, Yozo
HIKARU ANNA

Tanaka, Yozoo
LOVE LETTER

Tanizaki, Junichiro
DIARY OF A MAD OLD MAN

Tanner, Alain
LA VALLEE FANTOME
UNE FLAMME DANS MON COEUR

Taplitz, Daniel
SQUEEZE, THE

Tarantini, Michele Massimo
ITALIANI A RIO

Tarasov, Sergei
CHYORNAYA STRELA

Tarbes, Jean-Jacques
LA VIE DISSOLUE DE GERARD FLOQUE

Tardon, Bruno
ENNEMIS INTIMES

Tarnas, Kazimierz
ZLOTA MAHMUDIA

Tatikyan, Shagen
ZEMLYA I ZOLOTO

Tatum, Tom
WINNERS TAKE ALL

Tavernier, Bertrand
LES MOIS D'AVRIL SONT MEURTRIERS

Tavernier O'Hagan, Colo
LA PASSION BEATRICE

Taviani, Paolo
GOOD MORNING BABYLON

Taviani, Vittorio
GOOD MORNING BABYLON

Tawfik, Raouf
ZAWGAT RAGOL MOHIM

Taylor, R.O.
RETURN OF JOSEY WALES, THE

Tazhibaev, Rustem
SKAZKA O PREKRASNOY AYSULU

Tazi, Mohamed
ABBES

Tedesco, Maurizio
SPECTERS

Tejada-Flores, Miguel
MILLION DOLLAR MYSTERY
REVENGE OF THE NERDS II: NERDS IN PARADISE
THREE FOR THE ROAD

Tenney, Kevin S.
WITCHBOARD

Tenvik, Inge
PRINSEN FRA FOGO

Teo, Stephen
BEJALAI

Tersanszky, Jozsi Jeno
ISTEN VELETEK, BARATAIM

Thackeray, William Makepeace
PIERSCIEN I ROZA

Theodoridis, Panos
DOXOBUS

Theos, Dimos
IKONA ENOS MYTHIKOU PROSOPOU

Thevenet, Virginie
JEUX D'ARTIFICES

Thijs, Ger
HAVINCK

Thijssen, Felix
IRIS

Thomas, Jim
PREDATOR

Thomas, John
PREDATOR

Thompson, Christopher
BACK TO THE BEACH

Thompson, Daniele
LEVY ET GOLIATH
MALADIE D'AMOUR

Thompson, Keith
BACHELOR GIRL

Thor, Jon-Mikl
ROCK 'N' ROLL NIGHTMARE

Tiangco, Ped
ZIMATAR

Tik Ti, Hoang
KOORDINATY SMERTI

Tikon Khrennikov
LYUBOVYU ZA LYUBOV

Timm, Peter
MEIER

Timm, Uwe
FLYER, THE

Tiscornia, Nelly Fernandez
MADE IN ARGENTINA

Titcher, David
MORGAN STEWART'S COMING HOME

Toback, James
PICK-UP ARTIST, THE

Tobin, Noreen
DOWN TWISTED

Todorovsky, Pyotr
PO GLAVNOY ULITSE S ORKESTROM
VOENNO-POLEVOI ROMAN

Toledo, Sergio
VERA

Tolmar, Tamas
ZUHANAS KOZBEN

Tolstoy, Leo
KREUTZEROVA SONATA

Tomas, Francisco
SUFRE MAMON

Tomic, Zivorad
KRALJEVA ZAVRSNICA

Tomlinson, Judith
T. DAN SMITH

Topin, Tito
LETE DERNIER A TANGER

Topor, Tom
NUTS

Torhonen, Lauri
JAAN KAANTOPIIRI

Torrini, Cinzia Th
HOTEL COLONIAL

Tortosa, Silvia
LA SENYORA

Toscano, Laura
MISSIONE EROICA
SCUOLA DI LADRI 2

Townsend, Robert
HOLLYWOOD SHUFFLE

Tracy, Margaret
WHITE OF THE EYE

Trafford, Steve
T. DAN SMITH

Traverso, Roberto
A FIOR DI PELLE

Tregubovich, Viktor
VOT MOYA DEREVNYA

Tremblay, Jean-Joseph
LE SOURD DANS LA VILLE

Treves, Giorgio
LA CODA DEL DIAVOLO

Tristan, Dorothy
WEEDS

Trond G. Lockertsen
PRINSEN FRA FOGO

Trope, Tzipi
TEL AVIV—BERLIN

Trueba, Fernando
YEAR OF AWAKENING, THE

Trujillo, Valentin
RATAS DE LA CIUDAD
YO, EL EJECUTOR

Tsarenko, Anatoly
POEZD VNE RASPISANIA

Tsui, Siu-Ming
MIRAGE

Tsutsui, Yasutaka
DIXIELAND DAIMYO

Tuck, Leonard
DEVILS PARADISE, THE

Tumanyan, Ina
SOUCHASTNIKI

Turin, Rudolf
FAREWELL

Turner, Ed
WINNERS TAKE ALL

Turpie, Jonnie
OUT OF ORDER

Turrent, Tomas Perez
LO DEL CESAR

Ugur, Omer
SON URFALI

Ukrainka, Lesya
ISKUSHENIE DON ZHUANA

Ulloque, Jose Maria
EL GRAN SERAFIN

Ungari, Enzo
LAST EMPEROR, THE

Unt, Mati
CHEREZ STO LET V MAE

Updike, John
WITCHES OF EASTWICK, THE

Urbanus
HECTOR

Urretavizcaya, Arantxa
A LOS CUATRO VIENTOS

Usubaliev, Sharshen
TAYNAYA PROGULKA

Uytterhoeven, Pierre
ATTENTION BANDITS

Vadmand, Per
VALHALLA

Vafeas, Vassilis
ONE HUNDRED AND TWENTY DECIBELS

Vakkuri, Juha
JAAN KAANTOPIIRI

Valcarcel, Horacio
ASIGNATURA APROBADA

Valdemar, Carlos
EL PLACER DE LA VENGANZA
HERENCIA DE VALIENTES
MI NOMBRE ES GATILLO
NARCOTERROR

Valdez, Luis
LA BAMBA

Valtinos, Thanassis
YENETHLIA POLI

Valutsky, Vladimir
CHUZHIE ZDES NE KHODYAT

Vamos, Miklos
CSOK, ANYU

van Brakel, Nouchka
EEN MAAND LATER

van de Velde, Jean
VAN GELUK GESPROKEN

van de Wetering, Jan Willem
DE RATELRAT

van den Berg, Rudolph
LOOKING FOR EILEEN

van den Broeck, Walter
HECTOR

van der Heyde, Nikolai
NITWITS

van Dullemen, Inez
VROEGER IS DOOD

Van Gogh, Theo
TERUG NAAR OEGSTGEEST

van Rouveroy, Dorna
ODYSSEE D'AMOUR

Vane, Norman Thaddeus
CLUB LIFE

Vane and Bleu —McKenzie, Norman Thaddeus
CLUB LIFE

Vanzina, Carlo
I MIEI PRIMI QUARANT'ANNI
MONTECARLO GRAN CASINO
VIA MONTENAPOLEONE

Vanzina, Enrico
I MIEI PRIMI QUARANT'ANNI
MONTECARLO GRAN CASINO
VIA MONTENAPOLEONE

Varga, Domokos
LUTRA

Vasiliev, Anton
STARAYA AZBUKA

Vasiliev, Boris
ZAVTRA BILA VOINA

Vasilyev, Boris
PODSUDIMYY

Vasilyev, Gennady
RUS IZNACHALNA

Vassilikos, Vassilis
AVRIL BRISE

Vautrin, Jean
CHARLIE DINGO

Vazquez-Figueroa, Alberto
CRYSTAL HEART

Vega, Ana Lydia
LA GRAN FIESTA

Vega, Felipe
MIENTRAS HAYA LUZ

Vega, Pastor
AMOR EN CAMPO MINADO

Velasco, Maria Elena
NI DE AQUI, NI DE ALLA

Vengerov, Vladimir
OBRYV

Vennerod, Petter
JOR

Vera, Marilda
POR LOS CAMINOS VERDES

Verbin, Vyacheslav
GEROY YEYOROMANA

Verdaguer, Antoni
LESCOT

Verdone, Carlo
IO E MIA SORELLA

Vergitsis, Nicos
ARCHANGELOS TOU PATHOUS

Verhoeff, Pieter
VAN GELUK GESPROKEN

Verne, Jules
KAPITAN "PILIGRIMA"

Verona, Stephen
TALKING WALLS

Veronesi, Giovanni
STREGATI

Verstappen, Wim
DE RATELRAT

Vesaas, Tarjei
IS-SLOTTET

Vesensky, Vladimir
SLEDY OBOROTNYA

Viale, Oscar
EL ANO DEL CONEJO

Victor Manuel
ENTRE FICHERAS ANDA EL DIABLO
ESTA NOCHE CENA PANCHO (DESPEDIDA DE SOLTERO)
LA RAZA NUNCA PIERDE—HUELE A GAS
LA RULETERA

Vidor, George
DELITTI

Vila, Pere
EL GRAN SERAFIN

Viljanen, Antero
PEKKA PUUPAA POLIISINA

Villatoro, Vincenc
LESCOT

Vilstrup, Li
JAG ELSKER DIG
NEGERKYS & LABRE LARVER

Vincent, Chuck
IF LOOKS COULD KILL
SLAMMER GIRLS
WIMPS

Vinokurov, Evgeny
PO ZAKONU VOENNOGO VREMENI

Vizard, Stephen
BIT PART, THE

Volk, Stephen
GOTHIC

Volodarsky, Eduard
VINA LEYTENANTA NEKRASOVA

von Praunheim, Rosa
ANITA—DANCES OF VICE

von Trier, Lars
EPIDEMIC

Vorfolomeyev, Mikhail
RUS IZNACHALNA

Vorsel, Niels
EPIDEMIC

Voss, Kurt
BORDER RADIO

Vostokov, Vladimir
KONETS OPERATSII "REZIDENT"

Vrettakos, Costas
TA PAIDIA TIS CHELIDONAS

Waalkes, Otto
OTTO—DER NEUE FILM

Wachs, Robert D.
BEVERLY HILLS COP II

Wagner, Bruce
NIGHTMARE ON ELM STREET 3: DREAM WARRIORS, A

Wagner and charaeters created, Bruce
NIGHTMARE ON ELM STREET 3: DREAM WARRIORS, A

Wai, To Kwok
PEKING OPERA BLUES

Waisglass, Elaine
HOUSEKEEPER, THE

Walker, Giles
LAST STRAW, THE

Walkow, Gary
TROUBLE WITH DICK, THE

Wallace, Clarke
MORNING MAN, THE

Walton, Arvo
VO VREMENA VOLCHYIKA ZAKONOV

Walton, Fred
ROSARY MURDERS, THE

Wam, Svend
JOR

Ward, Edmund
PRAYER FOR THE DYING, A

Warfield, David
P.I. PRIVATE INVESTIGATIONS

Warren, Norman J.
BLOODY NEW YEAR

Washburn, Deric
EXTREME PREJUDICE

Watanabe, Jose
CITY AND THE DOGS, THE

Watton, Christian
LA VIE DISSOLUE DE GERARD FLOQUE

Watts, Larue
SLAMMER GIRLS

Way, Ron
FRENCHMAN'S FARM

Wayans, Keenen Ivory
HOLLYWOOD SHUFFLE

Wearing, Michael
BELLMAN AND TRUE

Webb, William
DIRTY LAUNDRY

Wechter, David
MALIBU BIKINI SHOP, THE

Weckstrom, Kim
URSULA

Weems, Nancy
HANSEL AND GRETEL

Wei, Li
BLACK CANNON INCIDENT, THE

Weintraub, Fred
PRINCESS ACADEMY, THE

Weintraub, Sandra
PRINCESS ACADEMY, THE

Weiser, Stanley
PROJECT X
WALL STREET

Weisman, Matthew
BURGLAR
TEEN WOLF TOO

Welbeck, Peter
WARRIOR QUEEN

Wellington, David
ZOMBIE NIGHTMARE

Wen, Chu Tien
LIEN LIEN FUNG CHEN

Wenders, Wim
DER HIMMEL UBER BERLIN

Werfel, Franz
FORTY DAYS OF MUSA DAGH

West, Skip
GOOFBALLS

Westlake, Donald E.
STEPFATHER, THE

White, Matt
FRENCHMAN'S FARM

Whitemore, Hugh
EIGHTY FOUR CHARING CROSS ROAD

Wichegrod, Michel
SALE DESTIN!

Wickramasinghe, Martin
VIRAGAYA

Widerberg, Bo
MANNEN FRAN MALLORCA
SERPENT'S WAY, THE

Wiesel, Elie
TESTAMENT D'UN POETE JUIF ASSASSINE

Wilder, Glenn R.
MASTERBLASTER

Wiley, Ethan
HOUSE TWO: THE SECOND STORY

Williams, Jason
DANGER ZONE, THE

Williams, Tennessee
GLASS MENAGERIE, THE

Williamson, Fred
MESSENGER, THE

Wilson, David
LAST STRAW, THE
SITTING IN LIMBO

Wilson, Hugh
BURGLAR

Wilson, Michael G.
LIVING DAYLIGHTS, THE

Wilson, S.S.
BATTERIES NOT INCLUDED

Wilson, Snoo
SHADEY

Wingate, William
MALONE

Winkler, Charles
YOU TALKIN' TO ME?

Winograd, Peter
FLICKS

Winski, Norman
HOSTAGE

Wisdom, Anthony
MESSENGER, THE

Witkiewicz, Stanislaw Ignacy
W STARYM DWORKU

Witt, Wolfram
SO VIELE TRAUME

Wittliff, William
RED HEADED STRANGER

Wojcik, Wojciech
PRYWATNE SLEDZTWO

Wolf, Anna
BLOOD TRACKS

Wolf, Dick
NO MAN'S LAND

Wolkers, Jan
TERUG NAAR OEGSTGEEST

Wollen, Peter
FRIENDSHIP'S DEATH

Wolman, Dan
CHOZE AHAVA

Wong, Manfred
LAONIANG GOU SAO
SWORN BROTHERS

Wong, Raymond
SEVEN YEARS ITCH
TRUE COLORS

Woo, John
BETTER TOMORROW, A

Woods, Donald
CRY FREEDOM

Workman, Chuck
MEATBALLS III

Wurlitzer, Rudy
WALKER

Wynorski, Jim
BIG BAD MAMA II

Xang Xi, Huang
BLACK CANNON INCIDENT, THE

Xiaotian, Zhang
LAST EMPRESS, THE

Xin, Huang
CUO WEI

Yakovlev, Yury
PLOSHCHAD VOSSTANIA

Yakovleva, Tatyana
YAGUAR

Yamada, Taichi
FINAL TAKE: THE GOLDEN AGE OF MOVIES

Yamada, Yoji
FINAL TAKE: THE GOLDEN AGE OF MOVIES
TORA-SAN'S BLUEBIRD FANTASY

Yamamoto, Masashi
ROBINSON NO NIWA

Yamaura, Hiroyasu
TOKYO BLACKOUT

Yang, Edward
TERRORIZERS, THE

Yasan, Ernest
DUBLYOR NACHINAET DEYSTVOVAT

Yee, Sheau
TERRORIZERS, THE

Yershov, Konstantin
OBVINYAETSYA SVADBA

Yezhov, Valentin
POKLONIS DO ZEMLI

Yi, Zheng
OLD WELL

Yim, Nam
PRISON ON FIRE

Yohanan
KOL AHAVOTAI

Yohoshua, Abraham B.
POET'S SILENCE, THE

Yoon Sam-Yook
NAE-SHI

Yordan, Philip
BLOODY WEDNESDAY
CRY WILDERNESS

Yune, Johnny
THEY STILL CALL ME BRUCE

Yung, Jin
ROMANCE OF BOOK AND SWORD, THE

Yuryev, Zinovy
TAKAYA ZHESTOKAYA IGRA—KHOKKEY

Zacharias, Ann
TESTET

Zacharias, Steve
REVENGE OF THE NERDS II: NERDS IN PARADISE

Zaorski, Janusz
MATKA KROLOW

Zapponi, Bernandino
RIMINI RIMINI

Zapponi, Bernardino
ROBA DA RICCHI
TERESA

Zemer, Michel
LES OREILLES ENTRE LES DENTS

Zeromski, Stefan
WIERNA RZEKA

Zettler, Michael
SWEET LORRAINE

Zhalakyavichus, Vitautas
IZVINITEPOZHALUYSTA

Zhukovitski, Leonid
KOROTKIE VSTRECHI

Zidi, Claude
LASSOCIATION DES MALFAITEURS

Zihlmann, Hans
TAROT

Zirinis, Costas
TELEFTAIO STICHIMA

Zoller, Ralf
SOMMER

Zorrilla, Jose A.
A LOS CUATRO VIENTOS

Zucchero, Joseph
EYE OF THE EAGLE

Zulawski, Andrzej
MALADIE D'AMOUR

Zulfikarov, Timur
MIRAZHI LYUBRI

Zurinaga, Marcos
LA GRAN FIESTA

Zuta, Daniel
BORAN—ZEIT ZUM ZIELEN

Zweibel, Alan
DRAGNET

PHOTO CREDITS

ALIVE: WHALES OF AUGUST.

AMBLIN ENTERTAINMENT: BATTERIES NOT INCLUDED.

ATLANTIC: THE GARBAGE PAIL KIDS MOVIE; THE GOOD WIFE; HOME IS WHERE THE HART IS; STEELE JUSTICE; SUMMER HEAT; WILD THING; WISH YOU WERE HERE, 2.

BUENA VISTA: BENJI THE HUNTED; CAN'T BUY ME LOVE; ERNEST GOES TO CAMP; GOOD MORNING VIETNAM; STAKEOUT.

CACTUS: DIXIA QING; THE FLYER.

CANNON: ALADDIN; ALLAN QUATERMAIN AND THE LOST CITY OF GOLD; AMERICAN NINJA 2; ASSASSINATION; BARFLY, 2; DANCERS 2; DOWN TWISTED; HANOI HILTON; MASCARA; MASTERS OF THE UNIVERSE; NUMBER ONE WITH A BULLET; OVER THE TOP; RUMPLESTILTSKIN; SHY PEOPLE, 2; SUPERMAN IV: THE QUEST FOR PEACE, 2; STREET SMART; TOUGH GUYS DON'T DANCE, 2.

CINECOM: A MAN IN LOVE; MATEWAN; MAURICE.

CINEMA GROUP: WITCHBOARD.

CINETAL: COLD STEEL; CYCLONE.

CINEPLEX ODEON: THE GLASS MENAGERIE, 2; LOVE IS A DOG FROM HELL; WITHNAIL AND I.

CINEVISTA: LAW OF DESIRE, 2.

COLUMBIA: THE BIG EASY; HOPE AND GLORY; HOUSEKEEPING; ISHTAR; LA BAMBA; THE LAST EMPEROR; ROXANNE; SOMEONE TO WATCH OVER ME.

CROWN: HUNK.

DAIEI: TOKYO BLACKOUT.

DEG: THE BEDROOM WINDOW, 2; DATE WITH AN ANGEL, 2; FROM THE HIP; HIDING OUT; MILLION DOLLAR MYSTERY; NEAR DARK, 2; WEEDS, 2.

EMPIRE: DOLLS.

EXPORT FILM BISCHOFF & COMPANY: CRAZY BOYS.

F/M ENTERTAINMENT: THE KINDRED.

FARABI: GOZARESH—E YEK GHATI; LODGERS; MANUSCRIPTS; PEDDLER; SHEERE SANGGY.

FILM POLSKI: BLIND CHANCE; CZAS NADZIEI; ESD; INNA WYSPA; KOMEDIANCI Z WCZORAJSZEJ ULICY; KOMEDIANTKA; LE JEUNE MAGICIEN; MAGNAT; MASQUERADE; MATKA KROLOW; MIEDZY USTAMI A BRZEGIEM PUCHARU; NAD NIEMNEM; PAN SAMOCHODZIK I NIESAMOWITY DWOR; PIERSCIEN I ROZA; POCIAG DO HOLLYWOOD; PRYWATNE SLEDZTWO; PRZYJACIEL WESOLEGO DIABLA; RYKOWISKO; STANISLAW I ANNA; W ZAWIESZENIU; WERYFIKACJA; WIERNA RZEKA; ZLOTA MAHUDIA; ZYCIE WEWNETRZNE; ZYGFRYD.

FILM SALES INTERNATIONAL: DIRTY DANCING.

FILMINOR: URSULA.

FILMOVE: PROC?.

FINNKINO: THE SNOW QUEEN; VARJOJA PARATIISISSA.

HAMBURGER FILMBURO: DRAGON'S FOOD.

HEMDALE: THE BELLY OF AN ARCHITECT, 2; THE WHISTLEBLOWER, 2.

HOWARD INTERNATIONAL FILM GROUP: NIGHTSTICK.

ICELANDIC FILM: SKYTTURNER.

IFEX/VIDMARK: BORN OF FIRE.

IFM: WOLF AT THE DOOR, 2.

INTERNATIONAL FILM EXCHANGE: SVIDANE NA MLECHNOM PUTI.

ION FILMS: DIVINAS PALABRAS.

ISLAND: DARK EYES; RIVER'S EDGE; SLAMDANCE, 2; SQUARE DANCE, 2; STRAIGHT TO HELL, 2.

KINO INTERNATIONAL: VERA.

LORIMAR: IN THE MOOD, 2; MADE IN HEAVEN; ORPHANS; P.K. AND THE KID.

MARE NOSTRUM FILMS: EL GRAN SERAFIN.

MEDIA: A NIGHTMARE ON ELM STREET 3: ALADDIN; DREAM WARRIORS; FLICKS; PROGRAMMED TO KILL; RAGE OF HONOR.

METROPOLIS: DIE VERLIEBTEN; DILAN; JENATSCH; SAME TO YOU.

MGM: DEAD OF WINTER; FATAL BEAUTY; MOONSTRUCK; OVERBOARD; SPACEBALLS.

MULTIVIDEO: EL LUTE.

NEW CENTURY/VISTA: DUDES, 2; THE GATE, 2; HEAT; MAID TO ORDER; MORGAN STEWART'S COMING HOME; RUSSKIES; THE STEPFATHER, 2; THREE FOR THE ROAD.

NEW LINE CINEMA: THE HIDDEN; MY DEMON LOVER; STRANDED.

NEW WORLD: BEYOND THERAPY; CREEPSHOW II; CRYSTAL HEART; DEATH BEFORE DISHONOR; THE GIRL; THE GREAT LAND OF SMALL; HELLRAISER, 2; HOUSE II; MISS MARY; OMEGA SYNDROME; PRETTY SMART; RETURN TO HORROR HIGH; TALKING WALLS; WANTED DEAD OR ALIVE.

NUEVA FILMS: A LOS CUATRO VIENTOS.

NUEVO MONDO: LA VIDA ALEGRE.

ORION: THE BELIEVERS; BEST SELLER; HOUSE OF GAMES; MAKING MR. RIGHT; MALONE; NO MAN'S LAND; NO WAY OUT; RADIO DAYS; SEPTEMBER; THROW MOMMA FROM THE TRAIN.

ORION CLASSICS: JEAN DE FLORETTE; ROBOCOP.

PARAISO: LA CASA DE BERNARDA ALBA.

PARAMOUNT: BACK TO THE BEACH; BEVERLY HILLS COP II, 2; CAMPUS MAN; CRITICAL CONDITION; FATAL ATTRACTION, 2; HAMBURGER HILL, 2; HOT PURSUIT; PLANES, TRAINS AND AUTOMOBILES; SOME KIND OF WONDERFUL, 2; SUMMER SCHOOL; THE UNTOUCHABLES, 2.

PUZON: GET THE TERRORISTS; TOUGH COP; ULTIMAX FORCE.

RANK: THE BIG TOWN; THE FOURTH PROTOCOL, 2.

RASTAR: THE SECRET OF MY SUCCESS.

ROMANIAFILM: ZLOTY POCIAG.

ROSEBUD: EVIL DEAD II, 2.

SCOTTI BROTHERS: HE'S MY GIRL.

SKOURAS: DEADLINE; DIRTY LAUNDRY; DOGS IN SPACE; EAT THE PEACH; LIVING ON TOKYO TIME; MY LIFE AS A DOG; SHADEY; WAITING FOR THE MOON, 2.

SPECTRAFILM: BLUE MONKEY; PRETTYKILL; STACKING; TOO OUTRAGEOUS.

TAFT ENTERTAINMENT: LIGHT OF DAY; THE MONSTER SQUAD; THE RUNNING MAN.

THE MOVIE STORE: MEATBALLS III.

THE OTHER CINEMA: BOY SOLDIER.

TOUCHSTONE: ADVENTURES IN BABYSITTING; OUTRAGEOUS FORTUNE; STAKEOUT; THREE MEN AND A BABY; TIN MEN.

TRANS WORLD: IRON WARRIOR.

TRI-STAR: AMAZING GRACE AND CHUCK; ANGEL HEART, 2; BLIND DATE, 2; EXTREME PREJUDICE; FOREVER, LULU; GABY—A TRUE STORY; GARDENS OF STONE, 2; IRONWEED, 2; LET'S GET HARRY; LIKE FATHER, LIKE SON; MAN ON FIRE; NADINE; THE PRINCIPAL; THE SQUEEZE; SUSPECT, 2;

TROMA TEAM: BLOOD HOOK; MONSTER IN THE CLOSET; STUDENT CONFIDENTIAL; SURF NAZIS MUST DIE.

TWENTIETH CENTURY FOX: BROADCAST NEWS; WALL STREET.

UNITED ARTISTS: BABY BOOM; THE LIVING DAYLIGHTS.

UNITED INTERNATIONAL: ASIGNATURA APROBADO.

UNIVERSAL: THE ALLNIGHTER; AMAZON WOMEN OF THE MOON; BORN IN EAST L.A.; CROSS MY HEART; CRY FREEDOM, 2; DRAGNET; HARRY AND THE HENDERSONS; JAWS IV: THE REVENGE; NORTH SHORE; PRINCE OF DARKNESS; 3 O'CLOCK HIGH; WALKER, 2.

VESTRON: CHINA GIRL; THE DEAD, 2; DIRTY DANCING; GOTHIC; PERSONAL SERVICES.

WARNER BROTHERS: BURGLAR; DISORDERLIES; EEN MAAND LATER; FULL METAL JACKET, 2; INNERSPACE; LETHAL WEAPON; LOST BOYS; NUTS; POLICE ACADEMY 4: CITIZENS ON PATROL; SURRENDER, 2; THE WITCHES OF EASTWICK; WHO'S THAT GIRL.

XALOC: LA GUERRA DE LOS LOCOS.

YORAM GROSS FILM STUDIO: DOT GOES TO HOLLYWOOD.

THE WITCHES OF EASTWICK

RIVER'S EDGE

FULL METAL JACKET

EMPIRE OF THE SUN

BLACK WIDOW

BARFLY

WALL STREET

MATEWAN